willings Press Guide

VOLUME 2: EUROPE (EXCLUDING UK)

Published by: Cision UK Ltd. Cision House, 16-22 Baltic Street West, London, EC1Y 0UL
Telephone: 020 7251 7220 E-mail: info.uk@cision.com Website: www.uk.cision.com

VAT registration number: 553 8580 17
Registered Office: Cision House, 16-22 Baltic Street West, London EC1Y 0UL

Volume 1 (UK) 2012	**ISBN**	**978-1-906035-31-0**
Volume 2 (Europe) 2012	**ISBN**	**978-1-906035-32-7**
Volume 3 (World) 2012	**ISBN**	**978-1-906035-33-4**
Volume 1 (UK) and 2 (Europe) 2012	**ISBN**	**978-1-906035-34-1**
Volume 1 (UK) and 3 (World) 2012	**ISBN**	**978-1-906035-35-8**
Volume 2 (Europe) and 3 (World) 2012	**ISBN**	**978-1-906035-36-5**
Volumes 1 (UK), 2 (Europe) and 3 (World) 2012	**ISBN**	**978-1-906035-37-2**

dpa data publishers association

CISION UK LTD. IS A MEMBER OF THE DATA PUBLISHERS ASSOCIATION

SOFTWARE AND PAGE IMAGING BY DATA STANDARDS LTD, FROME.
PRINTING BY POLESTAR WHEATONS LTD, EXETER.

EUROPE

ABOUT WILLINGS

EDITORIAL POLICY

Willings Press Guide is published in three volumes. The editorial aim of Willings is to be a comprehensive, accurate and informative guide to the UK media industry (Volume 1) and to give details about the leading newspapers and periodicals in Europe (Volume 2), as well as other countries of the world (Volume 3).

For the purposes of Willings, ''media industry'' includes: newspapers, freesheets, magazines (business and consumer), journals, newsletters and any other publication appearing on a regular basis, including directories.

Willings has not set out to include manuals, maps, diaries, calendars, partworks or local periodicals with a very low circulation such as school magazines and local activity newsheets. Books not scheduled for publication at regular intervals are also excluded.

Each publication is listed free of charge with an extensive range of information about that title. ISSN numbers are included where available.

FOR SUBSCRIPTION DETAILS

Contact the Willings Sales Team
Tel: +44 (0)20 7251 7220
Email: info.uk@cision.com

TO UPDATE ENTRY DETAILS

Contact the Research team
Tel: +44 (0)20 7251 7220
Email: changes.uk@cision.com

Willings Press Guide

CONTENTS

For UK media – SEE VOLUME 1, UK EDITION.
For Worldwide media – SEE VOLUME 3, WORLD EDITION.

Willings Volume 2
Section 1

Indices - Europe

List of Countries within Europe and Continents Guide

Index references cross-refer to newspapers, magazines and other periodicals that are listed elsewhere in this volume.

List of Countries A-Z

The page numbers in this Index refer to Sections 2, 3, 4 and 6

Willings Volume 2
Section 2

Periodicals Index

Periodicals of Europe listed by country and then by classification

For easy access to a particular subject, Magazines and Periodicals within Europe are listed first by the country in which they are published or distributed and then by subject, in alphabetical order. There are two summaries of classification, in A-Z order and by grouping.

Categories A-Z B = Business Publication C = Consumer Publication

Categories by Grouping

Business

Agriculture & Farming
Agriculture & Farming - Regional
Agriculture & Farming Related
Agriculture - Machinery & Plant
Agriculture - Supplies & Services
Dairy Farming
Livestock
Milk
Poultry
Vine Growing

Antiques

Applied Science & Laboratories

Architecture & Building
Architecture
Building
Building Related
Cleaning & Maintenance
Interior Design & Flooring
Planning & Housing
Surveying

Aviation & Aeronautics
Airlines
Airports
Aviation & Aeronautics
Aviation Related
Space Research

Baking & Confectionery
Baking
Confectioners & Tobacconists
Confectionery Manufacturing

Catering
Catering, Hotels & Restaurants

Ceramics, Pottery & Glass
Ceramics & Pottery
Glass

Chemicals

Church & School Equipment & Education
Adult Education
Careers
Church & School Equipment
Education
Education Related
Education Teachers
Junior Education
Secondary Education
Special Needs Education
Teachers & Education Management

Clothing & Textiles
Knitwear
Lingerie, Hosiery/Swimwear

Co-Operatives

Commerce, Industry & Management
Commerce Related
Commercial Design
Company Secretaries
Industry & Factories
International Commerce
Purchasing
Quality Assurance
Small Business
Trade Unions
Training & Recruitment
Work Study

Communications, Advertising & Marketing
Broadcasting
Communications Related
Conferences & Exhibitions
Press
Public Relations
Selling

Computers & Automation
Automation & Instrumentation
Computers Related
Data Processing
Data Transmission
Multimedia
Personal Computers
Professional Personal Computers

Construction
Construction Related
General (Construction)
Roads
Water Engineering

Cosmetics & Hairdressing
Cosmetics
Cosmetics & Hairdressing Related
Hairdressing

Decorating & Paint
Paint - Technical Manufacture

Defence

Drinks & Licensed Trade
Brewing
Drinks, Licensed Trade, Wines & Spirits
Licensed Trade, Wines & Spirits
Off-Licence

Electrical

Electrical Retail Trade
General (Electrical Retail Trade)
Radio & Hi-Fi
TV
Video

Electronics
General (Electronics)
Telecommunications

Energy, Fuel & Nuclear

Engineering & Machinery
CAD & CIM (Computer Integrated Manufacture)
Engineering - Design
Engineering Related
Finishing
Hydraulic Power
Machinery, Machine Tools & Metalworking
Pipelines
Production & Mechanical Engineering

Environment & Pollution

Finance & Economics
Accountancy
Banking
Building Societies
Credit Trading
Film
Financial Related
Fundraising
Insurance
Investment
Pensions
Property
Rental Leasing
Taxation

Food
Cash & Carry
Fish Trade
Food Processing & Packaging
Food Related
Frozen Food
General (Food)
Health Food
Meat Trade

Footwear

Furnishings & Furniture
Furnishings & Furniture - Kitchens & Bathrooms
Furnishings, Carpets & Flooring

Garden Trade
Garden Trade Horticulture
Garden Trade Supplies
Market Garden Traders

Gas

Gift Trade
Clocks & Watches
Fancy Goods
Jewellery
Leather

Hardware

Health & Medical
Casualty & Emergency
Chiropody
Chiropractic
Dental
Disability & Rehabilitation
Family Planning
General (Health Medical)
Health Education
Health Medical Related
Hospitals
Medical Engineering Technology
Medical Equipment
Mental Health
Nursing
Optics
Radiography

Heating & Ventilation
Domestic Heating & Ventilation
Heating & Plumbing
Industrial Heating & Ventilation
Refrigeration & Ventilation

Import & Export

Laundry & Dry Cleaning

Legal

Local Government, Leisure & Recreation
Civil Service
Community Care & Social Services
Leisure, Recreation & Entertainment
Local Government
Local Government Finance
Local Government Related
Parks
Police
Public Health & Cleaning
Swimming Pools

Marine & Shipping
Boat Trade
Commercial Fishing
Marine Engineering Equipment
Marine Related
Maritime Freight

Materials Handling

Metal, Iron & Steel

Mining & Quarrying

Motor Trade
Bicycle Trade
Driving Schools
Motor Trade Accessories
Motor Trade Related
Motorcycle Trade

Music Trade

Office Equipment

Oil & Petroleum

Other Classifications
Amusement Trade
Biology
Cinema Entertainment
Clubs
Course Maintenance
Funeral Directors, Cemeteries & Crematoria
Fur Trade
Museums
Pet Trade
Taxi Trade
Veterinary
Weather

Packaging & Bottling

Paper

Pharmaceutical & Chemists

Photographic Trade

Plastics & Rubber

Printing & Stationery
Printing
Stationery

Publishing
Libraries
Newsagents
Publishing & Book Trade
Publishing Related

Regional Business

Retailing & Wholesaling

Safety & Security
Fire Fighting
Safety
Safety Related
Security

Timber, Wood & Forestry

Tobacco

Toy Trade & Sports Goods
Sports Goods
Toy Trade
Toy Trade - Baby Goods

Transport
Bus & Coach Transport
Commercial Vehicles
Electric Vehicles
Freight
General (Transport)
Railways
Transport Related

Travel & Tourism

Consumer

Adult & Gay Magazines
Adult Magazines
Gay & Lesbian Magazines
Men's Lifestyle Magazines

Angling & Fishing

Animals & Pets
Animals & Pets Protection
Bees
Birds
Cats
Dogs
Fish
Horses & Ponies

Consumer Electronics
Consumer Electronics Related
Games
Hi-Fi & Recording
Home Computing
Video & DVD

Current Affairs & Politics

Education
Adult Education
Careers
Crafts
Education Related
General (Education)
Preparatory & Junior Education

Ethnic

Gardening

Hobbies & DIY
Collectors Magazines
Fantasy Games & Science Fiction
Games & Puzzles
Military History
Models & Modelling
Numismatics
Philately
Radio Electronics
Rail Enthusiasts

Holidays & Travel
Entertainment Guides
Holidays
Hotel Magazines
In-Flight Magazines
Travel

Motoring & Cycling
Club Cars
Cycling
Motor Sports
Motorcycling
Motoring
Motoring & Cycling Related
Veteran Cars

Music & Performing Arts
Cinema
Dance
Music
Opera
Pop Music
Theatre
TV & Radio

National & International Periodicals

Other Classifications
Credit Cards
Customer Magazines
Disability
Expatriates
Historic Buildings
Job Seekers
Miscellaneous
Paranormal
Popular Science
Restaurant Guides
War Veterans

Photography & Film Making
Film Making
Photography

Recreation & Leisure
Boating & Yachting
Camping & Caravanning
Children & Youth
Hostelling
Lifestyle
Recreation & Leisure Related

Religious

Rural & Regional Interest
Regional Interest Northern Ireland
Rural Interest

Sport
Athletics
Combat Sports
Fitness/Bodybuilding
Flight
Football
General (Sport)
Golf
Horse Racing
Other Sport
Outdoor
Racquet Sports
Rugby
Shooting
Water Sports
Winter Sports

Student Publications

The Arts & Literary
Arts
Literary

Women's Interest Consumer Magazines
Brides
Child Care
Crafts
Food & Cookery
Hair & Beauty
Home & Family
Home Purchase
Lifestyle
Personal Finance
Retirement
Secretary & PA
Slimming & Health
Teenage
Women's Interest
Women's Interest - Fashion
Women's Interest Related

Albania

Consumer

Sport

Andorra

Consumer

Rural & Regional Interest

Austria

Business

Agriculture & Farming

Antiques

Architecture & Building

Baking & Confectionery

Catering

Chemicals

Church & School Equipment & Education

Clothing & Textiles

Commerce, Industry & Management

Communications, Advertising & Marketing

Computers & Automation

Construction

Electrical

Electrical Retail Trade

Electronics

Energy, Fuel & Nuclear

Engineering & Machinery

Environment & Pollution

Finance & Economics

Belarus

Business

Commerce, Industry & Management

Computers & Automation

Electronics

Motor Trade

Consumer

Consumer Electronics

Women's Interest Consumer Magazines

Belgium

Business

Belgium: Consumer

Travel & Tourism

Consumer

Adult & Gay Magazines

Gay & Lesbian Magazines

Men's Lifestyle Magazines

Current Affairs & Politics

Education

General (Education)

Gardening

Hobbies & DIY

Hobbies & DIY

Holidays & Travel

Entertainment Guides

Holidays

Travel

Motoring & Cycling

Motor Sports

Motorcycling

Motoring

Music & Performing Arts

Music

TV & Radio

National & International Periodicals

Other Classifications

Customer Magazines

Popular Science

Recreation & Leisure

Camping & Caravanning

Rural & Regional Interest

Sport

Football

General (Sport)

The Arts & Literary

Arts

Women's Interest Consumer Magazines

Brides

Food & Cookery

Hair & Beauty

Home & Family

Home Purchase

Lifestyle

Personal Finance

Retirement

Slimming & Health

Teenage

Women's Interest

Women's Interest - Fashion

Bosnia-Herzegovina

Consumer

Current Affairs & Politics

Motoring & Cycling

Motoring

Sport

General (Sport)

Women's Interest Consumer Magazines

Lifestyle
MAXISTARS *(Weekly)* 141

Bulgaria

Business

Commerce, Industry & Management

Commerce, Industry & Management
BUSINESS WEEK BULGARIA *(Weekly)* 142

Communications, Advertising & Marketing

Public Relations
REKLAMA *(Weekly)* 142

Drinks & Licensed Trade

Drinks, Licensed Trade, Wines & Spirits
BG MENU *(6 issues yearly)* 142

Motor Trade

Motor Trade Accessories
AVTOPAZAR *(Weekly)* 142

Transport

Commercial Vehicles
AUTOOKAZION *(17 issues yearly)* 142

Consumer

Other Classifications

Popular Science
NATIONAL GEOGRAPHIC BULGARIA *(Monthly)* 142

Sport

Football
MERIDIAN MATCH *(Daily)* 142

Women's Interest Consumer Magazines

Food & Cookery
CULINARY JOURNAL FOR THE WOMAN *(Monthly)* 142
Retirement
TRETA VAZRAST *(Weekly)* 142
Slimming & Health
FORUM MEDIKUS *(Weekly)* 142
Women's Interest - Fashion
JOURNAL ZA JENATA *(Weekly)* 142

Cyprus

Business

Architecture & Building

Interior Design & Flooring
MUST DECO *(8 issues yearly)* 143

Commerce, Industry & Management

Trade Unions
DIMOSSIOS YPALLILOS *(Weekly)* 143

Communications, Advertising & Marketing

Communications, Advertising & Marketing
CHRYSES EFKAIRIES *(Weekly)* 143

Finance & Economics

Investment
CHRIMATISTIRIAKA NEA *(Monthly)* 143
Property
THE BUYSELL MAGAZINE *(Monthly)* 143

Health & Medical

General (Health Medical)
KARDIOLOGIKA NEA *(6 issues yearly)* 143

Travel & Tourism

TRAVEL NEWS EUROPE *(Monthly)* 144

Consumer

Holidays & Travel

Entertainment Guides
CITY FREE PRESS *(Weekly)* 143
In-Flight Magazines
SUNJET *(Quarterly)* 144
SUNJET RUSSIAN EDITION *(Annual)* 144

Music & Performing Arts

TV & Radio
O TILETHEATIS *(56 issues yearly)* 144
TV MANIA *(Weekly)* 144

National & International Periodicals

CYPRUS TODAY *(Weekly)* 143

Czech Republic

Business

Applied Science & Laboratories

21. STOLETÍ *(Monthly)* 144
CHEMICKÉ LISTY *(Monthly)* 146

Architecture & Building

Architecture
ARCHITEKT *(Monthly)* 145
ASB (ČR) *(8 issues yearly)* 145
STAVBA *(24 issues yearly)* 156
Building Related
STAVEBNICTVÍ (PONTIUM) *(Annual)* 156
STAVOSPOJ *(Weekly)* 156
Interior Design & Flooring
BYTY, DOMY, ZAHRADY *(24 issues yearly)* 146
Planning & Housing
RODINNÉ DOMY - PROJEKTY A REALIZACE *(Half-yearly)* 155
RODINNÉ DOMY SE SNÍŽENOU SPOTŘEBOU ENERGIÍ *(Annual)* 155
RODINNÝ DŮM *(Monthly)* 155

Chemicals

CHEMAGAZÍN *(24 issues yearly)* 146

Church & School Equipment & Education

Education
FREUNDSCHAFT *(10 issues yearly)* 148
UČITELSKÝ ZPRAVODAJ 157

Commerce, Industry & Management

Commerce, Industry & Management
CIO BUSINESS WORLD *(Monthly)* 146
Quality Assurance
KVALITA PRO ŽIVOT *(Half-yearly)* 150
Training & Recruitment
HRM *(24 issues yearly)* 149

Communications, Advertising & Marketing

AGROSPOJ *(Weekly)* 144
OPAVSKÉ REKLAMNÍ NOVINY *(Monthly)* 153
VÝCHODOČESKÉ STAVEBNÍ NOVINY *(Monthly)* 158
Communications, Advertising & Marketing
SUPER INFO *(26 issues yearly)* 156

Computers & Automation

Automation & Instrumentation
COMPUTERWORLD *(26 issues yearly)* 147
Data Processing
CHIP *(Monthly)* 146
CONNECT! *(Monthly)* 147
EXTRA PC *(Monthly)* 148
JAK NA POČÍTAČ *(Monthly)* 149
MOBILITY *(Monthly)* 151
POČÍTAČ PRO KAŽDÉHO *(26 issues yearly)* 153
SECURITY WORLD *(Quarterly)* 155
Professional Personal Computers
COMPUTER *(26 issues yearly)* 147

Construction

Construction Related
SNPLUS *(Monthly)* 155
General (Construction)
CENTRAL & EASTERN EUROPEAN CIJ *(Monthly)* 146

Electrical

SVĚTLO *(24 issues yearly)* 156

Electronics

General (Electronics)
AMATÉRSKÉ RADIO *(Monthly)* 145

Czech Republic: Consumer

Denmark

Business

Agriculture & Farming

Denmark: Business

Catering

Catering, Hotels & Restaurants
DRC-BLADET / RESTAURANT & CAFÉ (*Monthly*) 162
SMAG & BEHAG (*Monthly*) 171
VISITOR (*Monthly*) 174

Church & School Equipment & Education

Adult Education
MAGISTERBLADET (*26 issues yearly*) 168
Education
SKOLEBØRN (*Monthly*) 171
STUDY ABROAD (*Quarterly*) 171
UDDANNELSESAVISEN (*6 issues yearly*) 172
Junior Education
FOLKESKOLEN (*26 issues yearly*) 164

Commerce, Industry & Management

Commerce Related
TÆNK PENGE (*Monthly*) 172
Commerce, Industry & Management
24TIMER FORBRUG (*Daily*) 158
BIOENERGI (*6 issues yearly*) 160
BRICKS (*Quarterly*) 160
C3 MAGASINET OM LEDELSE OG ØKONOMI (*6 issues yearly*) 161
CO-INDUSTRI MAGASINET (*Monthly*) 161
DAU BLADET (*Quarterly*) 162
DS-BLADET (*Monthly*) 162
DTU AVISEN (*Monthly*) 162
EUROINVESTOR.DK (*Daily*) 163
FAGLIGT FORSVAR (*Monthly*) 163
FREELANCENØGLEN (*Annual*) 164
FRIE (*Quarterly*) 164
HÅND & VÆRK (*Monthly*) 164
KRYDSFELT (*6 issues yearly*) 166
LANDBRUG NORD (*Weekly*) 167
LANDBRUG ØST (*Weekly*) 167
LEDELSE I DAG LEDELSEIDAG.DK (*Weekly*) 167
LEDERNE (*Monthly*) 167
LEDSAGER (*6 issues yearly*) 167
MAGASINET KVALITET (*Quarterly*) 168
MALEREN (*Monthly*) 168
MONITOR (*Monthly*) 169
NPINVESTOR NPINVESTOR.DK (*Daily*) 169
PROSIT (*6 issues yearly*) 170
RUCNYT (*Monthly*) 170
SCENARIO (*6 issues yearly*) 170
SCM (*Monthly*) 170
UGEBREVET MEALS (*Weekly*) 173
UNDERVISERE (*Monthly*) 173
VOGNMALEREN (*Quarterly*) 174
International Commerce
BØRSEN VÆKST DANMARK (*Weekly*) 160
FOCUS DENMARK (*Quarterly*) 164
Trade Unions
FAGBLADET FOA (*Monthly*) 163
FINANS (*Monthly*) 163
JOURNALISTEN (*26 issues yearly*) 166
Training & Recruitment
BØRSEN UDLAND (*Daily*) 160

Communications, Advertising & Marketing

Communications, Advertising & Marketing
BUREAUBIZ.DK (*Daily*) 160
GRAFISK FREMTID (*6 issues yearly*) 164
MAGASIN K (*Quarterly*) 168
MARKEDSFØRING (*26 issues yearly*) 168
MERKONOMBLADET (*6 issues yearly*) 168
Press
MEDIAWATCH MEDIAWATCH.DK (*Daily*) 168
Selling
INBUSINESS (*Monthly*) 166

Computers & Automation

Data Processing
ALT OM DATA (*Monthly*) 159
DATATID (*Monthly*) 162
DKUUG-NYT (*Monthly*) 162
PROSABLADET (*Monthly*) 170
Personal Computers
KOMPUTER FOR ALLE (*Monthly*) 166
PC PLANET (*Monthly*) 169
PC PLAYER (*Monthly*) 169
PCWORLD.DK (*Daily*) 169
Professional Personal Computers
HARDWAREONLINE.DK 165
JYLLANDS-POSTEN, MORGENAVISEN; GISMO (*Monthly*) 166
MAGASINET DIGITALT (*Monthly*) 168
NEWZ NEWZ.DK (*Daily*) 169

Construction

General (Construction)
MESTER TIDENDE (*Monthly*) 168

Defence

CS-BLADET (*Monthly*) 161

Electrical

ELEKTRIKEREN (*6 issues yearly*) 163

Electronics

General (Electronics)
ELEKTRONIK & DATA (*Monthly*) 163
Telecommunications
MOBIL (*Monthly*) 168
MOBILSIDEN.DK 169
RADIOTELEGRAFEN (*6 issues yearly*) 170
TELEKOMMUNIKATION (*Monthly*) 172

Energy, Fuel & Nuclear

WINDPOWER MONTHLY (*Monthly*) 174

Engineering & Machinery

CAD & CIM (Computer Integrated Manufacture)
AUTOMATIK (*Monthly*) 159
Engineering & Machinery
INGENIØREN (*Weekly*) 166
TEKNIKEREN (*Monthly*) 172

Environment & Pollution

CSR (*Monthly*) 161
NATUR OG MILJØ (*Quarterly*) 169

Finance & Economics

Accountancy
DANSKE REVISORER (*Quarterly*) 162
INSPI (*Monthly*) 166
REVISION & REGNSKABSVÆSEN (*Monthly*) 170
REVISORBLADET (*Quarterly*) 170
Finance & Economics
FINANSRÅDETS NYHEDSBREV (*Monthly*) 163
SAMFUNDSØKONOMEN (*6 issues yearly*) 170
SR-SKAT (*6 issues yearly*) 171
TV 2 FINANS FINANS.TV2.DK 172
Fundraising
MAGASINET (*Monthly*) 168
Insurance
ASSURANDØR KREDSEN (*Quarterly*) 159
Investment
AKTIONÆREN (*Monthly*) 159
FINANS/INVEST (*6 issues yearly*) 163
Property
EJENDOMSMÆGLEREN (*Monthly*) 162
HUSET (*Monthly*) 165
SCANDINAVIAN PROPERTY MAGAZINE (*Annual*) 170
Taxation
SKATTEREVISOREN (*6 issues yearly*) 170
TIDSSKRIFT FOR SKATTER OG AFGIFTER (*Weekly*) 172

Food

Food Processing & Packaging
NNF-ARBEJDEREN (*Daily*) 169
General (Food)
&MÆLK (*Quarterly*) 158
HELSE GOOD FOOD (*6 issues yearly*) 165
LEVNEDSMIDDEL & FØDEVARE MAGASINET (*Quarterly*) 167
MAD&VENNER (*Monthly*) 168
SCANDINAVIAN FOOD & DRINK (*Monthly*) 170
VINBLADET (*6 issues yearly*) 174

Garden Trade

Garden Trade Horticulture
HAVEBLADET (*Quarterly*) 165

Health & Medical

Disability & Rehabilitation
HANDICAP-NYT (*6 issues yearly*) 164
HØRELSEN (*Monthly*) 165
KROP & FYSIK (*6 issues yearly*) 166
General (Health Medical)
DAGENS MEDICIN (*Weekly*) 161
DIABETES (*6 issues yearly*) 162
DL MAGASINET (*Monthly*) 162
HJERTENYT (*Half-yearly*) 165
UGESKRIFT FOR LÆGER (*Weekly*) 173
Nursing
SYGEPLEJERSKEN (*26 issues yearly*) 172
Optics
VÆRN OM SYNET (*Quarterly*) 173

Legal

DJØF BLADET (*26 issues yearly*) 162

Local Government, Leisure & Recreation

Civil Service
HK/STAT MAGASINET (*Monthly*) 165
SERVICE (*Monthly*) 170
Community Care & Social Services
BØRN & UNGE (*Weekly*) 160
SOCIALPÆDAGOGEN (*26 issues yearly*) 171
Local Government
F BLADET (*Quarterly*) 163
STAT & KOMMUNE INDKØB 171
Public Health & Cleaning
WASTE MANAGEMENT WORLD (*6 times a year*) 174

Marine & Shipping

Maritime Freight
DANMARKS TRANSPORT-TIDENDE (*26 issues yearly*) 161

Metal, Iron & Steel

METALMAGASINET (*6 issues yearly*) 168

Pharmaceutical & Chemists

FAGBLADET FARMA (*26 issues yearly*) 163
FARMACI (*Monthly*) 163
SUNDHEDSGUIDEN.DK (*Daily*) 171

Photographic Trade

BILLEDKUNSTNEREN (*Quarterly*) 159

Regional Business

MÅNEDSMAGASINET ERHVERV (*Monthly*) 168
NORDEN NU (*Quarterly*) 169

Retailing & Wholesaling

FITNEWS MAGAZINE (*Monthly*) 163

MAD! (Monthly) 167
STREET BOYS (6 issues yearly) 171

Safety & Security

Safety
AKTUEL SIKKERHED (6 issues yearly) 159
ARBEJDSMILJØ (Monthly) 159

Timber, Wood & Forestry

MESTER & SVEND (Quarterly) 168

Transport

Bus & Coach Transport
CHAUFFØREN (Monthly) 161
CHAUFFØRNYT (6 issues yearly) 161
General (Transport)
TRANSPORTMAGASINET (26 issues yearly) 172

Travel & Tourism

STAND BY (Monthly) 171
TAKE OFF TAKEOFF.DK 172

Consumer

Adult & Gay Magazines

Men's Lifestyle Magazines
EUROMAN (Monthly) 163
M! (Monthly) 167

Angling & Fishing

FISK & FRI (Monthly) 163
FISKE AVISEN (Monthly) 163
SPORTSFISKEREN (Monthly) 171

Animals & Pets

Animals & Pets Protection
DYREVENNEN (6 issues yearly) 162
LEVENDE NATUR (Quarterly) 167
Dogs
HUNDEN (Monthly) 165
Horses & Ponies
HEST OG RYTTER (Monthly) 165
WENDY (26 issues yearly) 174

Consumer Electronics

Games
PLAYRIGHT PLAYRIGHT.DK (Daily) 170

Current Affairs & Politics

DR NYHEDER TV AVISEN 21.00 (Daily) 162
POLITISK HORISONT (Quarterly) 170
SOCIALDEMOKRATEN (Quarterly) 171
TV 2 / DANMARK NYHEDERNE; 18.00 (Daily) 172

Gardening

ALT OM HAVEN (Monthly) 159
BOLIG MAGASINET (Monthly) 160
HAVEN (Monthly) 165

Hobbies & DIY

Collectors Magazines
ANTIK & AUKTION (6 issues yearly) 159
Games & Puzzles
DANSK BRIDGE (Monthly) 161
Hobbies & DIY
GØR DET SELV (Monthly) 164

Holidays & Travel

Holidays
UD & SE (Monthly) 172
VAGABOND REJS (Quarterly) 173

Motoring & Cycling

Cycling
CYKLISTER (6 issues yearly) 161
Motorcycling
TOURING NYT (6 issues yearly) 172
Motoring
BILAVISEN (Weekly) 159
BILMAGASINET (Monthly) 160
BILSNAK (Quarterly) 160
MOTOR (Monthly) 169

Music & Performing Arts

Cinema
FILM GUIDE (Monthly) 163
Music
DANSK MUSIK TIDSSKRIFT (6 issues yearly) 162
MUSIKKALENDEREN (Monthly) 169
Pop Music
FRIKVARTER (Monthly) 164
GAFFA (Monthly) 164
TV & Radio
HER OG NU (Weekly) 165
SE OG HØR (Weekly) 170

National & International Periodicals

ANDERS AND & CO (Weekly) 159
ARENA (Monthly) 159
BERLINGSKE NYHEDSMAGASIN (Weekly) 159
BOLIGLIV (Monthly) 160
BYG TEK (Monthly) 160
BYGGEPLADS (6 issues yearly) 161
COSTUME (Monthly) 161
CRN (Monthly) 161
DANISH OFFSHORE INDUSTRY (Annual) 161
DI BUSINESS (Weekly) 162
DIGITAL FOTO (Monthly) 162
ERHVERVSAVISEN FOR LOLLAND, FALSTER, SYDSJÆLLAND OG MØN (Monthly) 163
FAIR NOK (Quarterly) 163
FHM (Monthly) 163
FORÆLDRE & BØRN (Monthly) 164
FRIII (Weekly) 164
GAMEREACTOR (Monthly) 164
GASTRO (Monthly) 164
HAVENYT.DK (Daily) 165
HISTORIE (Monthly) 165
HK KOMMUNALBLADET (26 issues yearly) 165
ISABELLAS (6 issues yearly) 166
KIG IND (Weekly) 166
KULØR (Monthly) 166
LEDSAGER - ALT OM GIGT OG GODE VANER (6 issues yearly) 167
LIME (Monthly) 167
LIVING DESIGN (Quarterly) 167
LUKSUS (6 issues yearly) 167
MOMENT (Quarterly) 169
PSYKOLOGI (6 issues yearly) 170
SKIPPEREN (Monthly) 170
SPIS BEDRE (Monthly) 171
SUPER AVISEN (26 issues yearly) 171
TURENGAARTIL.DK 172
VI MED HUND (Monthly) 173
WHERE2GO (Monthly) 174

Recreation & Leisure

Boating & Yachting
BÅDMAGASINET (Monthly) 159
Camping & Caravanning
CAMPING-FRITID (Monthly) 161
CAMPISTEN (Half-yearly) 161
Children & Youth
BROEN (Quarterly) 160

Religious

KATOLSK ORIENTERING (26 issues yearly) 166
MENIGHEDSRÅDENES BLAD (Monthly) 168

Rural & Regional Interest

EKSTRA-POSTEN (Weekly) 163
SORØ AVIS (Weekly) 171
TÅRNBY BLADET (Monthly) 172
VESTERBROBLADET (Weekly) 173

Sport

Football
GOAL (Monthly) 164
TIPSBLADET (104 issues yearly) 172
General (Sport)
IDRÆTSLIV (Monthly) 166
Golf
DANSK GOLF (6 issues yearly) 162
GOLFMAGASINET (6 issues yearly) 164
Horse Racing
VÆDDELØBSBLADET (Monthly) 173
Outdoor
FRITIDSLIV (6 issues yearly) 164
Shooting
JÆGER (Monthly) 166
SKYTTEBLADET (6 issues yearly) 171
SKYTTEN (6 issues yearly) 171
Water Sports
DYK (Monthly) 162

Student Publications

CHILI MAGAZINE (Monthly) 161
UNIVERSITETSAVISEN (26 issues yearly) 173

Women's Interest Consumer Magazines

Brides
BRYLLUPSMAGASINET (Half-yearly) 160
Child Care
GRAVID - ALT OM DIG (Quarterly) 164
VI FORÆLDRE (Monthly) 173
VORES BØRN (Monthly) 174
Home & Family
BEBOERBLADET (Quarterly) 159
BILLED-BLADET (Weekly) 159
BO BEDRE (Monthly) 160
FAMILIE JOURNAL (Weekly) 163
HJEMMET (Weekly) 165
HUSFLID (6 issues yearly) 165
IDÉNYT (Monthly) 166
MAD OG BOLIG (Monthly) 167
SAMVIRKE (Monthly) 170
SØNDAG (Weekly) 171
UDE OG HJEMME (Weekly) 172
Home Purchase
EJENDOMSAVISEN HORSENS POSTEN (Weekly) 162
MIT HUS (Quarterly) 168
VI LEJERE (Quarterly) 173
Lifestyle
KULTURMAGASINET SKOPET (6 issues yearly) 166
Personal Finance
PENGE & PRIVATØKONOMI (Monthly) 169
Retirement
ÆLDRE SAGEN NU (6 issues yearly) 158
Slimming & Health
HELSE (Monthly) 165
I FORM (Monthly) 166
Teenage
TJECK MAGAZINE (Monthly) 172
VI UNGE (Monthly) 173
Women's Interest
ALT FOR DAMERNE (Weekly) 159
BAZAR (Monthly) 159
FEMINA (Weekly) 163
HENDES VERDEN (Weekly) 165
SIRENE (Monthly) 170
WOMAN (Monthly) 174
Women's Interest - Fashion
EUROWOMAN (Monthly) 163
TID & TENDENSER (6 issues yearly) 172
Women's Interest Related
BUSINESS TRAVELLER DENMARK (6 issues yearly) 160

Environment & Pollution

Finance & Economics

Food

Furnishings & Furniture

Garden Trade

Health & Medical

Heating & Ventilation

Legal

Local Government, Leisure & Recreation

Marine & Shipping

Metal, Iron & Steel

Motor Trade

Music Trade

Office Equipment

Other Classifications

Paper

Pharmaceutical & Chemists

Printing & Stationery

Publishing

Regional Business

Retailing & Wholesaling

Safety & Security

Timber, Wood & Forestry

Transport

Finland: Consumer

France

Business

Agriculture & Farming

Applied Science & Laboratories

Architecture & Building

Aviation & Aeronautics

Catering

Chemicals

Church & School Equipment & Education

Clothing & Textiles

Commerce, Industry & Management

Communications, Advertising & Marketing

Computers & Automation

Construction

Cosmetics & Hairdressing

Defence

Drinks & Licensed Trade

France: Business

Electrical

Electrical Retail Trade

Electronics

Energy, Fuel & Nuclear

Engineering & Machinery

Environment & Pollution

Finance & Economics

Food

Garden Trade

Gift Trade

Health & Medical

Import & Export

Laundry & Dry Cleaning

Legal

Local Government, Leisure & Recreation

Marine & Shipping

Motor Trade

Music Trade

Oil & Petroleum

Other Classifications

Packaging & Bottling

Pharmaceutical & Chemists

Printing & Stationery

Publishing

Safety & Security

Tobacco

Transport

Travel & Tourism

Consumer

Adult & Gay Magazines

Consumer Electronics

Current Affairs & Politics

Education

Gardening

Hobbies & DIY

Holidays & Travel

Motoring & Cycling

Music & Performing Arts

National & International Periodicals

Germany: Business

Germany

Business

Agriculture & Farming

Antiques

Applied Science & Laboratories

Architecture & Building

Aviation & Aeronautics

Baking & Confectionery

Catering

Germany: Business

Ceramics, Pottery & Glass

Ceramics & Pottery

Glass

Chemicals

Church & School Equipment & Education

Careers

Education

Education Related

Education Teachers

Junior Education

Secondary Education

Special Needs Education

Teachers & Education Management

Clothing & Textiles

Clothing & Textiles

Lingerie, Hosiery/Swimwear

Co-Operatives

Commerce, Industry & Management

Commerce Related

Commerce, Industry & Management

Germany: Business

Germany: Business

Garden Trade

Gas

Gift Trade

Hardware

Health & Medical

Heating & Ventilation

Germany: Business

Laundry & Dry Cleaning

Legal

Local Government, Leisure & Recreation

Civil Service

Community Care & Social Services

Leisure, Recreation & Entertainment

Local Government

Local Government Finance

Parks

Police

Public Health & Cleaning

Swimming Pools

Marine & Shipping

Boat Trade

Marine & Shipping

Marine Engineering Equipment

Maritime Freight

Materials Handling

Metal, Iron & Steel

Mining & Quarrying

Motor Trade

Bicycle Trade

Driving Schools

Motor Trade Accessories

Motor Trade Related

Motorcycle Trade

Music Trade

Office Equipment

Oil & Petroleum

Other Classifications

Amusement Trade

Biology

Cinema Entertainment

Clubs

Course Maintenance

Funeral Directors, Cemeteries & Crematoria

Museums

Pet Trade

Taxi Trade

Veterinary

Packaging & Bottling

Paper

Pharmaceutical & Chemists

Photographic Trade

Plastics & Rubber

Printing & Stationery

Printing

Stationery

Germany: Business

Publishing

Regional Business

Retailing & Wholesaling

Safety & Security

Timber, Wood & Forestry

Tobacco

Toy Trade & Sports Goods

Transport

Germany: Consumer

Holidays & Travel

Motoring & Cycling

Music & Performing Arts

National & International Periodicals

Other Classifications

Disability

Expatriates

Historic Buildings

Job Seekers

Miscellaneous

Popular Science

Photography & Film Making

Film Making

Photography

Recreation & Leisure

Boating & Yachting

Camping & Caravanning

Children & Youth

Hostelling

Recreation & Leisure Related

Religious

Germany: Consumer

Rural & Regional Interest

Sport

Athletics

Combat Sports

Flight

Football

General (Sport)

Golf

Horse Racing

Other Sport

Outdoor

Racquet Sports

Shooting

Water Sports

Winter Sports

Student Publications

The Arts & Literary

Arts

Literary

Women's Interest Consumer Magazines

Brides

Child Care

Crafts

Food & Cookery

Hair & Beauty

Home & Family

Home Purchase

Lifestyle

Personal Finance

Retirement

Slimming & Health

Teenage

Women's Interest

Gibraltar: Consumer

Gibraltar

Consumer

Rural & Regional Interest

Greece

Business

Health & Medical

Consumer

Holidays & Travel

Hungary

Business

Agriculture & Farming

Architecture & Building

Baking & Confectionery

Catering

Chemicals

Commerce, Industry & Management

Computers & Automation

Construction

Cosmetics & Hairdressing

Defence

Drinks & Licensed Trade

Electrical

Electrical Retail Trade

Electronics

Energy, Fuel & Nuclear

Engineering & Machinery

Iceland: Business

Iceland

Business

Consumer

Irish Republic

Business

Church & School Equipment & Education

Education
COMPUSCHOOL MAGAZINE *(3 issues yearly)*.. 601
EDUCATION *(Quarterly)* 603
IRISH JOURNAL OF EDUCATION *(Annual)* 610
Junior Education
CHILDCARE.IE MAGAZINE *(6 issues yearly)* 600
CLASSMATE *(Quarterly)* 600
Secondary Education
ASTIR *(6 issues yearly)* 598
Teachers & Education Management
IN TOUCH *(6 issues yearly)* 607
SAOL *(11 issues yearly)* 619

Commerce, Industry & Management

Commerce, Industry & Management
BUSINESS & FINANCE *(Monthly)* 599
BUSINESS PLUS *(Monthly)* 600
DECISION *(6 issues yearly)* 602
IBEC AGENDA *(Monthly)* 607
INVESCO REVIEW OF PENSIONS *(Annual)* 608
IRISH DIRECTOR *(Quarterly)* 609
STUBBS GAZETTE *(Weekly)* 620
Industry & Factories
INDUSTRIAL RELATIONS NEWS *(Weekly)* 607
TECHNOLOGY IRELAND *(6 issues yearly)* 621
International Commerce
THE MARKET *(6 issues yearly)* 614
Small Business
RUNNING YOUR BUSINESS *(10 issues yearly)* 618
Trade Unions
MANDATE NEWS *(Quarterly)* 614
WORK & LIFE *(Quarterly)* 623
Training & Recruitment
HRD IRELAND *(Quarterly)* 607
PEOPLE FOCUS *(Quarterly)* 617

Communications, Advertising & Marketing

Broadcasting
TVB EUROPE *(Monthly)* 621
Communications, Advertising & Marketing
IRISH MARKETING JOURNAL *(Monthly)* 610
MARKETING *(Monthly)* 614
MARKETING AGE *(6 issues yearly)* 614

Computers & Automation

Computers Related
KNOWLEDGE IRELAND *(6 issues yearly)* 613
Data Processing
COMPUTERSCOPE *(Monthly)* 601
IRISH COMPUTER *(Monthly)* 609
Personal Computers
PC LIVE *(Monthly)* 617
SMART COMPANY *(6 issues yearly)* 619

Construction

General (Construction)
CONSTRUCTION *(Monthly)* 601
CONSTRUCTION AND PROPERTY NEWS *(Monthly)* 601
IRISH CONSTRUCTION INDUSTRY MAGAZINE *(Monthly)* 609
PROJECT MANAGEMENT *(6 issues yearly)* 618

Cosmetics & Hairdressing

Cosmetics
SALON IRELAND *(Monthly)* 619
Hairdressing
IRISH HAIRDRESSER INTERNATIONAL MAGAZINE *(6 issues yearly)* 610

Defence

CONNECT *(Monthly)* 601
AN COSANTÓIR MAGAZINE *(10 issues yearly)* 602
SIGNAL *(Half-yearly)* 619

Drinks & Licensed Trade

Drinks, Licensed Trade, Wines & Spirits
DRINKS INDUSTRY IRELAND *(6 issues yearly)* 602
LICENSING WORLD *(Monthly)* 613

Electronics

General (Electronics)
ELECTRONICS COMPONENTS WORLD *(Daily)* 603
ELECTRONICS PRODUCTION WORLD *(Daily)* 603

Energy, Fuel & Nuclear

EM *(6 issues yearly)* 603

Engineering & Machinery

Engineering & Machinery
READ-OUT *(6 issues yearly)* 618
Engineering - Design
THE ENGINEERS JOURNAL *(Monthly)* 604

Environment & Pollution

ENVIRONMENT & ENERGY MANAGEMENT *(6 issues yearly)* 604
ENVIRO-SOLUTIONS - NEWS UPDATE *(Weekly)* 604
ORGANIC MATTERS *(6 issues yearly)* 616

Finance & Economics

Accountancy
ACCOUNTANCY IRELAND *(6 issues yearly)* 598
ACCOUNTANCY PLUS *(Quarterly)* 598
Banking
BANKING IRELAND *(Half-yearly)* 599
SPECTRUM *(Quarterly)* 620
Credit Trading
CREDIT FOCUS *(Quarterly)* 602
Finance & Economics
THE ECONOMIC & SOCIAL REVIEW *(Quarterly)* 603
FINANCE MAGAZINE *(Monthly)* 604
GLOBAL COMPANY NEWS *(Daily)* 606
PRIVATE RESEARCH *(Monthly)* 617
Insurance
IRISH BROKER *(Monthly)* 609
Pensions
PENSIONS IRELAND *(Monthly)* 617
Property
COMMERCIAL PROPERTY & INTERIORS *(Quarterly)* 601
JOURNAL OF CORPORATE REAL ESTATE *(Quarterly)* 612
THE PROPERTY PROFESSIONAL *(Quarterly)* 618
THE PROPERTY VALUER *(Quarterly)* 618
Taxation
IRISH TAX REVIEW *(6 issues yearly)* 612

Food

Food Processing & Packaging
DAIRY & FOOD INDUSTRIES MAGAZINE *(6 issues yearly)* 602
FOOD IRELAND *(Annual)* 605
General (Food)
FOOD & DRINK BUSINESS EUROPE *(Monthly)* 605
IRISH FOOD *(6 issues yearly)* 609

Furnishings & Furniture

Furnishings & Furniture - Kitchens & Bathrooms
SELECT KITCHENS AND BATHROOMS *(Annual)* 619

Hardware

IRISH HARDWARE *(Monthly)* 610
IRISH HARDWARE PAINT GUIDE *(Annual)* 610
IRISH HARDWARE TOOLS GUIDE *(Annual)* 610

Health & Medical

Casualty & Emergency
EMERGENCY SERVICES IRELAND *(6 issues yearly)* 603
Dental
COMMUNITY DENTAL HEALTH *(Quarterly)* 601
JOURNAL OF THE IRISH DENTAL ASSOCIATION *(6 issues yearly)* 612
Disability & Rehabilitation
NCBI NEWS *(Quarterly)* 616
General (Health Medical)
BJUI *(26 issues yearly)* 599
FORUM *(Monthly)* 605
IRISH JOURNAL OF MEDICAL SCIENCE *(Quarterly)* 610
IRISH MEDICAL DIRECTORY *(Annual)* 610
IRISH MEDICAL JOURNAL *(Monthly)* 610
IRISH MEDICAL NEWS *(Weekly)* 610
IRISH MEDICAL TIMES *(Weekly)* 611
MIMS (IRELAND) *(Monthly)* 615
MODERN MEDICINE OF IRELAND *(6 issues yearly)* 615
Health Medical Related
IRISH RED CROSS REVIEW *(Quarterly)* 611
Mental Health
THE IRISH PSYCHOLOGIST *(Monthly)* 611
Nursing
NURSING IN THE COMMUNITY *(Quarterly)* 616
WIN - WORLD OF IRISH NURSING & MIDWIFERY *(Monthly)* 623
Optics
EUROTIMES *(Monthly)* 604

Heating & Ventilation

Industrial Heating & Ventilation
BS NEWS (BUILDING SERVICES NEWS) *(11 issues yearly)* 599

Legal

COMMERCIAL LAW PRACTITIONER *(Monthly)* 601
EMPLOYMENT LAW REPORTS *(6 issues yearly)* 604
IRISH CURRENT LAW MONTHLY DIGEST *(Monthly)* 609
IRISH JOURNAL OF FAMILY LAW *(Quarterly)* 610
IRISH JURIST *(Annual)* 610
IRISH LAW TIMES *(26 issues yearly)* 610
IRISH LAW TIMES CHARITIES DIRECTORY *(Annual)* 610
LAW SOCIETY GAZETTE *(Monthly)* 613
MEDICO - LEGAL JOURNAL OF IRELAND *(Half-yearly)* 615

Local Government, Leisure & Recreation

Community Care & Social Services
GUIDELINE *(3 issues yearly)* 606
PUBLIC SECTOR TIMES *(Monthly)* 618
Local Government
ADMINISTRATION JOURNAL *(Quarterly)* 598
EDUCATION *(Annual)* 603
LANDSCAPE AND GROUND MAINTENANCE *(Annual)* 613
Local Government Related
INSIDE GOVERNMENT *(6 issues yearly)* 607
Police
GARDA REVIEW *(Monthly)* 605

Marine & Shipping

Commercial Fishing
AQUACULTURE IRELAND *(Annual)* 598
THE IRISH SKIPPER *(Monthly)* 611
MARINE TIMES NEWSPAPER *(Monthly)* 614

Materials Handling

HANDLING NETWORK *(6 issues yearly)* 606

Italy: Business

Other Classifications

Packaging & Bottling

Pharmaceutical & Chemists

Photographic Trade

Plastics & Rubber

Printing & Stationery

Publishing

Regional Business

Retailing & Wholesaling

Safety & Security

Timber, Wood & Forestry

Tobacco

Toy Trade & Sports Goods

Transport

Travel & Tourism

Consumer

Adult & Gay Magazines

Angling & Fishing

Animals & Pets

Consumer Electronics

Current Affairs & Politics

Gardening

Hobbies & DIY

Holidays & Travel

Motoring & Cycling

Music & Performing Arts

National & International Periodicals

Other Classifications

Photography & Film Making

Recreation & Leisure

Religious

Rural & Regional Interest

Sport

Student Publications

The Arts & Literary

Women's Interest Consumer Magazines

Finance & Economics

Finance & Economics
VERSLO KLASE *(Monthly)* ... 654

Health & Medical

General (Health Medical)
DOMASNYJ DOKTOR V LITVE *(24 issues yearly)* ... 653
MEDICINA IR DAR KAI KAS VISIEMS *(24 issues yearly)* ... 654

Safety & Security

Security
AKISTATA *(104 issues yearly)* ... 653

Consumer

Music & Performing Arts

TV & Radio
SAVAITE *(Weekly)* ... 654

Women's Interest Consumer Magazines

Lifestyle
ZMONES *(Weekly)* ... 654
Women's Interest
JI *(Weekly)* ... 653
PANELE *(Monthly)* ... 654
Women's Interest - Fashion
COSMOPOLITAN *(Monthly)* ... 653

Luxembourg

Business

Agriculture & Farming

Agriculture & Farming
DE LETZEBUERGER BAUER *(Weekly)* ... 655
Livestock
DE LËTZEBUERGER ZIICHTE *(6 issues yearly)* . 655

Architecture & Building

Architecture
ARCHITECTURE & BATIMENT *(6 issues yearly)* 654
PRINT *(Half-yearly)* ... 656

Catering

Catering, Hotels & Restaurants
MAGAZINE HORESCA *(Monthly)* ... 656
LA TOQUE BLANCHE *(6 issues yearly)* ... 657

Church & School Equipment & Education

Teachers & Education Management
ECOLE & VIE *(6 issues yearly)* ... 655

Commerce, Industry & Management

Commerce, Industry & Management
CLC CONNECT *(6 issues yearly)* ... 655
DE LËTZEBUERGER MERKUR *(Monthly)* ... 655
D'HANDWIERK *(Monthly)* ... 655
ENTERPRISES MAGAZINE *(6 issues yearly)* ... 655
Industry & Factories
ECHO DES ENTREPRISES *(6 issues yearly)* ... 655
Trade Unions
AKTUELL *(Monthly)* ... 654
SEW JOURNAL *(6 issues yearly)* ... 656

Construction

General (Construction)
WUNNEN MAGAZINE *(6 issues yearly)* ... 657

Engineering & Machinery

Engineering & Machinery
REVUE TECHNIQUE LUXEMBOURGOISE *(Quarterly)* ... 656

Environment & Pollution

ECOLOGIQUE *(Quarterly)* ... 655
KEISECKER *(Quarterly)* ... 656
REGULUS *(Quarterly)* ... 656

Finance & Economics

Finance & Economics
AGEFI LUXEMBOURG *(Monthly)* ... 654
BUSINESS REVIEW *(Monthly)* ... 655
PAPERJAM *(Monthly)* ... 656

Health & Medical

General (Health Medical)
BULLETIN DE LA SOCIÉTÉ DES SCIENCES MÉDICALES DU GRAND DUCHÉ DE LUXEMBOURG *(Half-yearly)* ... 654
LE CORPS MEDICAL *(26 issues yearly)* ... 655

Local Government, Leisure & Recreation

Local Government
FONCTION COMMUNALE *(3 issues yearly)* ... 655

Motor Trade

FLEET EUROPE *(Quarterly)* ... 655

Transport

General (Transport)
LE SIGNAL *(26 issues yearly)* ... 656

Consumer

Adult & Gay Magazines

Men's Lifestyle Magazines
ANDY A LUXEMBOURG *(Half-yearly)* ... 654

Angling & Fishing

FESCHER, JEER, AN HONDSFREM *(6 issues yearly)* ... 655

Current Affairs & Politics

DE NEIE FEIERKROP *(Weekly)* ... 655
LE JEUDI *(Weekly)* ... 656
LËTZEBUERGER GEMENGEN *(Monthly)* ... 656
LUXEMBURGER MARIENKALENDER *(Annual)*. 656
REVUE *(Weekly)* ... 656

Education

General (Education)
GALERIE *(3 issues yearly)* ... 655
HEMECHT *(Quarterly)* ... 656

Gardening

GAART AN HEEM *(6 issues yearly)* ... 655

Holidays & Travel

Entertainment Guides
AGENDALUX *(Monthly)* ... 654
NIGHTLIFE *(6 issues yearly)* ... 656
Holidays
GASTROTOUR *(3 issues yearly)* ... 655
In-Flight Magazines
FLYDOSCOPE *(6 issues yearly)* ... 655
Travel
LUXEMBOURG BONJOUR *(Quarterly)* ... 656
LUXEMBOURG TOURISME *(Quarterly)* ... 656

Motoring & Cycling

Club Cars
AUTOTOURING *(Quarterly)* ... 654
Motoring
AUTO LOISIRS - LUXEMBOURG *(Quarterly)* ... 654
AUTO MOTO *(Monthly)* ... 654
AUTO REVUE *(Monthly)* ... 654

Music & Performing Arts

Cinema
GRAFFITI *(Monthly)* ... 655
Music
PIZZICATO *(Monthly)* ... 656
REVUE MUSICALE *(6 issues yearly)* ... 656
TV & Radio
TELECRAN *(Weekly)* ... 657

National & International Periodicals

WOXX *(Weekly)* ... 657

Other Classifications

Expatriates
CONTACTO *(Weekly)* ... 655
War Veterans
RAPPEL *(3 issues yearly)* ... 656

Rural & Regional Interest

CITY MAGAZINE *(Monthly)* ... 655
MISERLAND MAGAZINE *(Half-yearly)* ... 656

The Arts & Literary

Literary
NOS CAHIERS *(Quarterly)* ... 656

Women's Interest Consumer Magazines

Home & Family
ATOUT PRIX MAGAZINE *(6 issues yearly)* ... 654
Lifestyle
DESIRS *(Quarterly)* ... 655
LUXURIANT *(Monthly)* ... 656
MADE IN LUXE *(Monthly)* ... 656
NICO *(Half-yearly)* ... 656
TENDANCES *(Monthly)* ... 657
WANE - WE ARE NEXT *(6 issues yearly)* ... 657
Retirement
ELAN *(Quarterly)* ... 655
Women's Interest
CARRIÈRE *(Quarterly)* ... 655
EXCELLENTIA MAGAZINE *(Quarterly)* ... 655
FEMMES MAGAZINE *(Monthly)* ... 655
LUXEMBOURG FÉMININ *(Quarterly)* ... 656

Netherlands: Business

Electronics

Energy, Fuel & Nuclear

Engineering & Machinery

Environment & Pollution

Finance & Economics

Food

Footwear

Furnishings & Furniture

Garden Trade

Gas

Hardware

Health & Medical

Heating & Ventilation

Laundry & Dry Cleaning

Legal

Local Government, Leisure & Recreation

Marine & Shipping

Materials Handling

Metal, Iron & Steel

Motor Trade

Music Trade

Office Equipment

Oil & Petroleum

Other Classifications

PETS INTERNATIONAL MAGAZINE *(7 issues yearly)* 697

Veterinary

TIJDSCHRIFT VOOR DIERGENEESKUNDE *(24 issues yearly)* 708
VEEHOUDER & DIERENARTS, ED. RUNDVEEHOUDERIJ *(Quarterly)* 712

Weather

METEOROLOGICA *(Quarterly)* 688

Packaging & Bottling

VERPAKKEN *(Quarterly)* 713
VERPAKKINGSMANAGEMENT *(11 issues yearly)* 713

Pharmaceutical & Chemists

INTERNATIONAL PHARMACY JOURNAL *(Half-yearly)* 681
OPTIMA FARMA *(11 issues yearly)* 695
PHARMACEUTISCH WEEKBLAD *(40 issues yearly)* 697

Photographic Trade

FM FOTOMARKT *(10 issues yearly)* 675
DE FOTOGRAAF *(6 issues yearly)* 675
FOTOGRAFISCH GEHEUGEN *(Quarterly)* 675
FOTOVISIE *(10 issues yearly)* 675

Plastics & Rubber

KUNSTSTOF EN RUBBER *(9 issues yearly)* 684
KUNSTSTOF MAGAZINE *(9 issues yearly)* 684

Printing & Stationery

Printing

KVGO-KERNNIEUWS *(Monthly)* 684
MAL & MASKER *(Quarterly)* 686
PRINT BUYER *(10 issues yearly)* 698

Publishing

Libraries

ARCHIEVENBLAD *(10 issues yearly)* 661
BIBLIOTHEEKBLAD *(20 issues yearly)* 663

Publishing & Book Trade

DE BOEKENWERELD *(5 issues yearly)* 664
HANDBOEKBINDEN *(Quarterly)* 678
MEDIAFACTS *(6 issues yearly)* 687
QUAERENDO *(Quarterly)* 699
SIGNPRO BENELUX *(6 issues yearly)* 704

Publishing Related

INFORMATIE PROFESSIONAL 680

Regional Business

ACHTERHOEK MAGAZINE *(6 issues yearly)* 659
BRABANT BUSINESS MAGAZINE *(Quarterly)* 665
EIGEN BEDRIJF *(6 issues yearly)* 671
EINDHOVEN BUSINESS *(6 issues yearly)* 672
FLEVOLAND BUSINESS *(6 issues yearly)* 674
FRIENDS IN BUSINESS *(Quarterly)* 675
GOOI- EN EEMLAND BUSINESS *(6 issues yearly)* 677
KIJK OP OOST-NEDERLAND *(8 issues yearly)* 683
NIJMEGEN BUSINESS *(7 issues yearly)* 692
OF *(13 issues yearly)* 693
RIJNMOND BUSINESS *(10 issues yearly)* 701
RIJNSTREEK BUSINESS *(6 issues yearly)* 701
RIVIERENLAND BUSINESS *(6 issues yearly)* 701
UTRECHT BUSINESS *(6 issues yearly)* 711
ZAKELIJK *(6 issues yearly)* 717
ZAKENBLAD REGIO WEERT *(Quarterly)* 718
ZAKENNIEUWS VOOR HAAGLANDEN & RIJNLAND *(11 issues yearly)* 718

Retailing & Wholesaling

INSTORE *(6 issues yearly)* 680
KREAVAK *(5 issues yearly)* 683
RETAILTRENDS *(Monthly)* 701
SUPERMARKT ACTUEEL *(26 issues yearly)* 707

Safety & Security

Fire Fighting

BRANDWEER ONTSPANNINGS MAGAZINE *(Quarterly)* 665
EÉN-EÉN-TWEE *(6 issues yearly)* 671

Safety

SECURITY MANAGEMENT *(10 issues yearly)* 703
VEILIGHEIDSNIEUWS *(Quarterly)* 712

Safety Related

DE REDDINGBOOT *(Quarterly)* 700

Timber, Wood & Forestry

HET HOUTBLAD *(8 issues yearly)* 679
TIMMERFABRIKANT *(11 issues yearly)* 709
VAKBLAD NATUUR BOS LANDSCHAP *(10 issues yearly)* 712
VVA MAGAZINE *(6 issues yearly)* 715

Toy Trade & Sports Goods

Sports Goods

BODY BIZ *(11 issues yearly)* 664
SPORT PARTNER *(10 issues yearly)* 705
SPORTACCOM *(6 issues yearly)* 705
SPORTCULT *(6 issues yearly)* 705

Toy Trade

SPEELGOED EN HOBBY *(11 issues yearly)* 705

Toy Trade - Baby Goods

BABY WERELD *(Quarterly)* 662

Transport

Commercial Vehicles

ROUTIERS *(6 issues yearly)* 702
TTM (TRUCK & TRANSPORT MANAGEMENT) *(Monthly)* 710

Electric Vehicles

OP OUDE RAILS *(Quarterly)* 694

Freight

TRANSPORTVISIE *(6 issues yearly)* 709
TRUCKSTAR *(13 issues yearly)* 710

General (Transport)

D' AMSTERDAMSE TRAM *(Weekly)* 660
AUTO IN BEDRIJF *(3 issues yearly)* 662
EVO MAGAZINE *(11 issues yearly)* 673
FLEETMOTIVE *(Quarterly)* 674
NEDERLANDS VERVOER *(10 issues yearly)* 691
TON *(6 issues yearly)* 709
TOUR MAGAZINE *(Quarterly)* 709
VEILIGHEID VOOROP *(Quarterly)* 712
WEG EN WAGEN *(3 issues yearly)* 715

Railways

STIBANS BULLETIN *(Half-yearly)* 706

Transport Related

PARKEER *(6 issues yearly)* 696
VERHUIZEN *(8 issues yearly)* 712
VERKEERSKUNDE *(8 issues yearly)* 713
VERKEERSRECHT *(11 issues yearly)* 713

Travel & Tourism

ARKE MAGAZINE *(Half-yearly)* 661
RECREATIE & TOERISME *(6 issues yearly)* 700
TEXELNU *(Quarterly)* 708
VAKANTIEDELUXE *(Annual)* 711
DE VAKANTIEKRANT *(Monthly)* 712
ZAKENREIS *(10 issues yearly)* 718

Consumer

Adult & Gay Magazines

Adult Magazines

FOXY *(Monthly)* 675
PENTHOUSE *(Monthly)* 697
PLAYBOY *(Monthly)* 697

Gay & Lesbian Magazines

COC ZWOLLE MAGAZINE *(Quarterly)* 667
GAY & NIGHT *(11 issues yearly)* 676
GAY NEWS *(Monthly)* 676
PINK *(5 issues yearly)* 697

Men's Lifestyle Magazines

THE BIG BLACK BOOK *(Half-yearly)* 663
BLVD MAN *(Quarterly)* 664
DONALD *(Half-yearly)* 670
ESQUIRE *(10 issues yearly)* 673
FHM (FOR HIM MAGAZINE) *(10 issues yearly)* 674
LINDA.MAN *(Annual)* 685
MEN'S HEALTH *(10 issues yearly)* 688
PASSIE *(Monthly)* 696
RELOAD *(Quarterly)* 701

Angling & Fishing

BEET SPORTVISSERS-MAGAZINE *(Monthly)* 663
DE KARPERWERELD *(6 issues yearly)* 682
DE NEDERLANDSE VLIEGVISSER *(Quarterly)* 691
DE ROOFVIS *(6 issues yearly)* 702
DE SPORTFISKER *(Quarterly)* 705
HET VISBLAD *(Monthly)* 713
VISSEN *(6 issues yearly)* 713
WITVIS TOTAAL *(6 issues yearly)* 717

Animals & Pets

Animals & Pets

DIER & VRIEND *(Quarterly)* 670
OVER DIEREN *(Quarterly)* 695
VLINDERS *(Quarterly)* 714
ZELDZAAM HUISDIER *(Quarterly)* 718

Animals & Pets Protection

DIER *(Quarterly)* 670
DIER EN MILIEU *(6 issues yearly)* 670
DIERENPRAKTIJKEN *(Quarterly)* 670
HART VOOR DIEREN *(Monthly)* 678
KIDS FOR ANIMALS *(6 issues yearly)* 682
KUST & ZEEGIDS *(Annual)* 684
NATUURHISTORISCH MAANDBLAD *(Monthly)* 690
DE OLIFANT *(Quarterly)* 693
PANDA *(Quarterly)* 696
PROEFDIERVRIJ MAGAZINE *(Quarterly)* 699
RELATIE MENS EN DIER *(Quarterly)* 700

Birds

DUTCH BIRDING *(6 issues yearly)* 671
LIMOSA *(Quarterly)* 685
ONZE VOGELS *(Monthly)* 694
HET VOGELJAAR *(6 issues yearly)* 714
VOGELS *(5 issues yearly)* 714

Cats

FELIKAT MAGAZINE *(5 issues yearly)* 674
KATTEN KATERN *(3 issues yearly)* 682
KATTENMANIEREN *(6 issues yearly)* 682
DE POEZENKRANT 697

Dogs

HA DIE PUP! *(Annual)* 677
HONDENSPORT EN SPORTHONDEN *(6 issues yearly)* 679
ONZE BOSTONS *(Quarterly)* 694
ONZE HOND *(Monthly)* 694
DE WELSH SPRINGER *(6 issues yearly)* 716

Horses & Ponies

BIT *(8 issues yearly)* 664
HORSE INTERNATIONAL *(9 issues yearly)* 679
PENNY *(Monthly)* 696
DE SHETLAND PONY *(Monthly)* 704

Consumer Electronics

Games

GAMES GUIDE *(10 issues yearly)* 676

Hi-Fi & Recording

MUSIC EMOTION *(11 issues yearly)* 689

Home Computing

BAAZ *(Quarterly)* 662

Video & DVD

HVT *(11 issues yearly)* 679
VIDEO EMOTION *(6 issues yearly)* 713

Current Affairs & Politics

AMNESTY IN ACTIE *(10 issues yearly)* 660
AMNESTYNL *(3 issues yearly)* 660
GROEN LINKS MAGAZINE *(6 issues yearly)* 677
HANDSCHRIFT *(5 issues yearly)* 678
HELSINKI MONITOR *(Quarterly)* 678
INTERNATIONALE SAMENWERKING-IS *(10 issues yearly)* 681
MAARTEN! *(6 issues yearly)* 686
MIJN VAKBOND.NL *(Quarterly)* 688
PROVINCIE EN GEMEENTE *(9 issues yearly)* 699
ROOD *(8 issues yearly)* 701
TRIBUNE *(Monthly)* 710
UNICEF MAGAZINE *(Half-yearly)* 711

Education

Ethnic

Gardening

Hobbies & DIY

Holidays & Travel

Motoring & Cycling

Music & Performing Arts

National & International Periodicals

Other Classifications

Photography & Film Making

Recreation & Leisure

Netherlands: Consumer

Religious

Rural & Regional Interest

Sport

Student Publications

The Arts & Literary

Women's Interest Consumer Magazines

DITJES & DATJES *(Monthly)* 670
EIGEN HUIS MAGAZINE *(11 issues yearly)* 672
ENTOURAGE *(Annual)* 672
HOME & LIVING *(8 issues yearly)* 679
HUISSTIJL *(Quarterly)* 679
KEUKEN STUDIO *(Half-yearly)* 682
LIFESTYLE MAGAZINE *(Quarterly)* 685
NUMMER 1 *(10 issues yearly)* 692
OAK *(Half-yearly)* 693
OOK *(Monthly)* 694
POST VAN PORTAAL *(Quarterly)* 698
REKELS *(Quarterly)* 700
RESIDENCE *(11 issues yearly)* 701
SINT *(Annual)* 704
TSJAKKA! *(Monthly)* 710
VERBOUWBLAD *(Annual)* 712
VT WONEN *(Monthly)* 715
DE WATERKRANT *(3 issues yearly)* 715
WONENWONEN.NL *(Half-yearly)* 717
ZWANGER! *(Annual)* 719

Home Purchase
HYPOTHEEKSHOP MAGAZINE *(Half-yearly)* 679
WELKE WONEN *(Quarterly)* 716
247 WONEN *(Monthly)* 717
WOONSTIJL *(8 issues yearly)* 717

Lifestyle
AM MAGAZINE *(6 issues yearly)* 660
AMERSFOORT VOOR JOU *(Monthly)* 660
BD MAGAZINE 663
DE BIJENKORF MAGAZINE *(9 issues yearly)* 663
BRIGHT *(6 issues yearly)* 665
COSMOGIRL! *(13 issues yearly)* 668
COUNTRY LIFE MAGAZINE *(Quarterly)* 668
EIGENWIJS *(6 issues yearly)* 672
EVA *(10 issues yearly)* 673
FLOW *(8 issues yearly)* 674
HOTSPOTS *(6 issues yearly)* 679
IDEE MAGAZINE *(Half-yearly)* 680
JAN *(11 issues yearly)* 681
JANSEN *(6 issues yearly)* 681
JOIE DE VIVRE *(Quarterly)* 682
LIEF! *(Quarterly)* 685
LOS MAGAZINE *(Monthly)* 685
LE MAGAZINE *(6 issues yearly)* 686
MORE THAN CLASSIC *(6 issues yearly)* 689
NAVENANT *(6 issues yearly)* 690
100% NL MAGAZINE *(10 issues yearly)* 692
OPZIJ *(11 issues yearly)* 695
QAVIAAR *(6 issues yearly)* 699
RED *(Monthly)* 700
REGIOJOURNAAL, EDITIE BERGEN OP ZOOM/ROOSENDAAL *(6 issues yearly)* 700
REGIOJOURNAAL, EDITIE BREDA/ OOSTERHOUT *(9 issues yearly)* 700
DE SMAAK VAN ITALIË *(6 issues yearly)* 704
STARS *(10 issues yearly)* 706
THE STYLE MAGAZINE *(Half-yearly)* 706
' THUIS MAGAZINE *(Quarterly)* 708
VIVACE MAGAZINE *(Quarterly)* 713
VORSTEN ROYALE *(13 issues yearly)* 714
WOMEN'S GLOBAL NETWORK FOR REPRODUCTIVE RIGHTS NEWSLETTER *(Half-yearly)* 717
WOONWEST *(Monthly)* 717
ZIN *(Monthly)* 718

Personal Finance
CASH *(10 issues yearly)* 666
FD PERSOONLIJK *(Weekly)* 674
FISCALERT *(10 issues yearly)* 674
GELD & BELEGGEN *(Quarterly)* 676
GELDGIDS *(8 issues yearly)* 676
GENOEG *(6 issues yearly)* 676
ONS *(10 issues yearly)* 694
WEGWIJS *(Half-yearly)* 715

Retirement
ABP MAGAZINE *(Half-yearly)* 659
ANBO MAGAZINE *(6 issues yearly)* 660
KBO-WEGWIJZER *(17 issues yearly)* 682
PENSIOEN JOURNAAL *(Quarterly)* 696
PERSPECTIEF *(10 issues yearly)* 697
PLUS MAGAZINE 697

Slimming & Health
AMSTELRING PLUS *(Quarterly)* 660
APOTHEEK & GEZONDHEID *(6 issues yearly)* 661
BEM! MAGAZINE *(5 issues yearly)* 663
BLOEDSUIKER *(Quarterly)* 664
BLOEDVERWANT *(3 issues yearly)* 664
BODYMIND OPLEIDINGEN *(Half-yearly)* 664
BOODSCHAPPEN *(Monthly)* 665
BROS/OSTEOPOROSE NIEUWS *(Quarterly)* 666
CONTACT VSN *(6 issues yearly)* 668
FIT MET VOEDING *(8 issues yearly)* 674
GEZOND VGZ MAGAZINE *(3 issues yearly)* 676
GEZONDGIDS *(10 issues yearly)* 677
GEZONDHEIDPLUS *(6 issues yearly)* 677
GEZZOND *(Quarterly)* 677
HARTSLAG *(Quarterly)* 678

MAMMAZONE *(Quarterly)* 686
DE MANTELZORGER *(Annual)* 686
MENSEN *(6 issues yearly)* 688
ORTHO *(6 issues yearly)* 695
PSYCHOLOGIE MAGAZINE *(11 issues yearly)* 699
ROND REUMA *(Quarterly)* 701
SANTÉ *(Monthly)* 703
VITRAS/CMD BIJ U THUIS *(Half-yearly)* 713
WEIGHTWATCHERS MAGAZINE *(6 issues yearly)* 715
WELLNESS LIFE *(Quarterly)* 716

Teenage
CONNECT *(6 issues yearly)* 668
DOE EEN WENSKRANT *(Quarterly)* 670
FANCY *(Monthly)* 673
GIRLZ! *(13 issues yearly)* 677
INSITE *(6 issues yearly)* 680
KIJK *(13 issues yearly)* 683
KR@SH MAGAZINE *(11 issues yearly)* 683
STOER! *(Quarterly)* 706
Z@PPMAGAZINE *(6 issues yearly)* 719

Women's Interest
COSMOPOLITAN *(Monthly)* 668
ELLE *(Monthly)* 672
ESTA *(26 issues yearly)* 673
FLAIR *(Weekly)* 674
GLAMOUR *(Monthly)* 677
INTIEM *(8 issues yearly)* 681
JACKIE *(8 issues yearly)* 681
JACKIE BUSINESS *(Annual)* 681
JUMBO MAGAZINE *(13 issues yearly)* 682
LINDA *(Monthly)* 685
LINDA.WONEN. *(Annual)* 685
MARIE CLAIRE *(Monthly)* 686
NOUVEAU *(Monthly)* 692
ORANJE BOVEN *(3 issues yearly)* 695
PRIVÉ *(Weekly)* 698
STORY *(Weekly)* 706
TALKIES MAGAZINE *(6 issues yearly)* 707
VIVA *(Weekly)* 713
VROUWEN VAN NU *(6 issues yearly)* 714

Women's Interest - Fashion
AVANTGARDE *(6 issues yearly)* 662
JAMES *(Annual)* 681
WATCHING *(Quarterly)* 715

Women's Interest Related
LAWINE NIEUWSBRIEF *(Quarterly)* 684

Norway

Business

Agriculture & Farming

Agriculture & Farming
BEDRE GARDSDRIFT *(Monthly)* 722
BONDE OG SMÅBRUKER *(Monthly)* 724
BONDEBLADET *(Weekly)* 724
FAGSENTERET FOR KJØTT - ANIMALIA; ANIMALIA.NO *(Daily)* 728
GARDSPLASSEN.NO *(Daily)* 731
HERBA *(Quarterly)* 732
LANDBRUKSTIDENDE *(26 issues yearly)* 737
NATURVITEREN *(Quarterly)* 741
NORSK LANDBRUK *(Monthly)* 742
ØKOLOGISK LANDBRUK *(Quarterly)* 744
REN MAT *(6 issues yearly)* 747
SAMVIRKE *(Monthly)* 748
SVIN *(Monthly)* 750

Dairy Farming
MEIERIPOSTEN *(Monthly)* 739

Livestock
BUSKAP *(6 issues yearly)* 724
SAU OG GEIT *(6 issues yearly)* 748
TIDSSKRIFT FOR KANINAVL *(Monthly)* 751

Poultry
FJØRFE *(Monthly)* 729

Applied Science & Laboratories

BLADET FORSKNING *(Quarterly)* 723
FORSKERFORUM *(Monthly)* 729
FORSKNING.NO 729
LABYRINT *(Quarterly)* 737
MARINE BIOLOGY RESEARCH *(6 issues yearly)* 738

MATERIALISTEN *(Quarterly)* 739
NBS-NYTT *(Quarterly)* 741
UNINYTT 752

Architecture & Building

Architecture
ARKITEKTNYTT *(6 issues yearly)* 721
ARKITEKTNYTT; ARKITEKTNYTT.NO *(Daily)* 721
BO BEDRE; BOBEDRENORGE.NO *(Daily)* 723
BYGGMESTEREN; BYGGMESTEREN.AS *(Daily)* 724
MAGASINET TEKNA *(Monthly)* 738
NORSKDESIGN.NO 743

Building
ANLEGGSMASKINEN; MEF.NO *(Daily)* 721
ARKITEKTUR N *(6 issues yearly)* 721
BYGGAKTUELT *(Monthly)* 724
BYGGAKTUELT; BYGGAKTUELT.NO *(Daily)* 724
BYGGEINDUSTRIEN *(Monthly)* 724
FDV - FORVALTNING, DRIFT OG VEDLIKEHOLD *(6 issues yearly)* 728
MUR+BETONG *(Quarterly)* 740
MURMESTEREN *(6 issues yearly)* 740
USBL-NYTT *(6 issues yearly)* 752

Cleaning & Maintenance
RENHOLDSNYTT *(6 issues yearly)* 747

Interior Design & Flooring
DESIGN:INTERIØR *(6 issues yearly)* 726
INSPIRASJON *(Half-yearly)* 734

Planning & Housing
BOLIG & MILJØ *(6 issues yearly)* 724
HUSEIER *(Quarterly)* 733
HUSEIERINFO *(Quarterly)* 733
HYTTE INFORMASJON *(Annual)* 733
KART OG PLAN *(Quarterly)* 735
PLAN *(6 issues yearly)* 745
VIIVILLA.NO 754

Surveying
POSISJON *(6 issues yearly)* 745

Aviation & Aeronautics

Aviation & Aeronautics
FLYNYTT *(6 issues yearly)* 729

Baking & Confectionery

Baking
BAKER OG KONDITOR *(Monthly)* 722

Catering

Catering, Hotels & Restaurants
APÉRITIF *(Monthly)* 721
BAR APÉRITIF *(Quarterly)* 722
HORECA *(Monthly)* 733
HOTELL, RESTAURANT & REISELIV *(6 issues yearly)* 733
KJØKKENSJEFEN *(6 issues yearly)* 735
KJØKKENSKRIVEREN *(6 issues yearly)* 735

Ceramics, Pottery & Glass

Glass
GLASS & FASADE *(Quarterly)* 731

Chemicals

KJEMI *(Monthly)* 735
TU.NO *(Daily)* 752

Church & School Equipment & Education

Adult Education
KVINNFORSKS SKRIFTSERIE *(Annual)* 737
NORSK LITTERATURVITENSKAPELIG TIDSSKRIFT *(Half-yearly)* 742

Education
ARGUMENT STUDENTTIDSSKRIFT *(6 issues yearly)* 721
BARNEHAGE *(6 issues yearly)* 722
CAMPUS *(Quarterly)* 725
EUROPAVEGEN *(Annual)* 727
FAVN (EX. KPF-KONTAKTEN) *(Quarterly)* 728
FOLKEHØGSKOLEN *(Monthly)* 729

Norway: Business

Clothing & Textiles

Commerce, Industry & Management

Communications, Advertising & Marketing

Computers & Automation

Construction

Cosmetics & Hairdressing

Decorating & Paint

Defence

Electrical

Electrical Retail Trade

Electronics

Telecommunications
MOBILEN.NO 739
NETTVERK *(Monthly)* 741

Energy, Fuel & Nuclear

AMNYTT MAGAZINE; AMNYTT.NO *(Daily)* 720
EBL FORUM *(Monthly)* 726
ELMAGASINET; ELMAGASINET.NO *(Daily)* 727
ENERGI *(Monthly)* 727
ENERGI; ENERGI-NETT.NO *(Daily)* 727
ENERGI & LEDELSE *(6 issues yearly)* 727
ENERGITEKNIKK *(Monthly)* 727
ENERGITEKNIKK; ELEKTRONETT.NO *(Daily)* 727
EUROPOWER; EUROPOWER.COM *(Daily)* 727
GASSMAGASINET *(6 issues yearly)* 731
MARINTEK REVIEW 738
NORSK ENERGI *(Quarterly)* 742
NORSK SOKKEL *(Half-yearly)* 743
PEAK MAGAZINE; PEAKMAGAZINE.NO *(Daily)* 745
PETRO.NO *(Daily)* 745
POINTCARBON.COM *(Daily)* 745
RECHARGE AS *(Weekly)* 746
RECHARGE AS ~ HOUSTON *(Weekly)* 746
RECHARGE AS~ LONDON *(Weekly)* 746
RECHARGE AS~ STAVANGER *(Weekly)* 746
RECHARGE AS~RIO DE JANEIRO *(Weekly)* 746
RECHARGE AS~SINGAPORE *(Weekly)* 746
TRAIDING CARBON MAGAZINE *(Monthly)* 751
UPSTREAM ONLINE *(Daily)* 752
VOLT *(6 issues yearly)* 754

Engineering & Machinery

Engineering & Machinery
FOTOGRAFI; FOTOGRAFI.NO *(Daily)* 730
INDUSTRIEN *(Monthly)* 734
INGENIØRNYTT *(Monthly)* 734
INGENIØRNYTT; INGENIORNYTT.NO *(Daily)* 734
TEKNISK UKEBLAD *(Weekly)* 750
Engineering Related
MASKINREGISTERET *(Monthly)* 738
NITO REFLEKS *(6 issues yearly)* 741

Environment & Pollution

BELLONA.NO 722
FAUNA NORVEGICA *(Annual)* 728
FOLKEVETT *(6 issues yearly)* 729
GREVLINGEN *(Quarterly)* 731
GRØNN HVERDAG MAGASIN *(6 issues yearly)* 731
GRONNHVERDAG.NO *(Daily)* 731
KLIMAKLUBBEN.NO *(Daily)* 736
KRETSLØPET *(6 issues yearly)* 736
MILJØ & HELSE *(Quarterly)* 739
MILJØKRIM *(Quarterly)* 739
MILJØMAGASINET *(Quarterly)* 739
MILJØSTRATEGI *(Monthly)* 739
NATUR & MILJØ *(Monthly)* 741
NORSK POLARINSTITUTTS RAPPORTSERIE *(Half-yearly)* 743
POLAR RESEARCH *(Half-yearly)* 745
PUTSJ *(Quarterly)* 746
UTEMILJØ *(6 issues yearly)* 752

Finance & Economics

Accountancy
KOMMUNEREVISOREN *(6 issues yearly)* 736
REVISJON OG REGNSKAP *(6 issues yearly)* 747
Banking
SPAREBANKBLADET *(Monthly)* 749
Building Societies
BOINFORM *(Quarterly)* 723
OBOS BLADET *(6 issues yearly)* 744
Credit Trading
FAGBLADET CREDITINFORM *(Monthly)* 727
Finance & Economics
BETA - TIDSSKRIFT FOR BEDRIFTSØKONOMI *(Half-yearly)* 722
DINSIDE; ØKONOMI 726
E24 NÆRINGSLIV *(Daily)* 726
FINANSAVISEN *(Daily)* 728
FINANSFOKUS *(Monthly)* 728
HEGNAR ONLINE 732
KAPITAL *(26 issues yearly)* 735
KOMMUNAL ØKONOMI *(Monthly)* 736
MAGMA *(6 issues yearly)* 738
NA24.NO; FINANS *(Daily)* 740
NÆRINGSAVISEN 740
NORDENS NYHETER *(Monthly)* 741
OBSERVATOR *(Quarterly)* 744
ØKONOMISKE ANALYSER *(6 issues yearly)* 744
OSLO BØRS - OSLOBORS.NO *(Daily)* 744
PRAKTISK ØKONOMI & FINANS *(Quarterly)* 746
REGNSKAP & ØKONOMI *(Quarterly)* 746
SAMFUNNSØKONOMEN *(6 issues yearly)* 748
Financial Related
NORSK ØKONOMISK TIDSSKRIFT *(Half-yearly)* 742
Fundraising
BISTANDSAKTUELT *(Monthly)* 723
Investment
AKSJONÆREN *(Quarterly)* 720
DN.NO *(Daily)* 726
STOCKLINK 750
Property
ESTATE MAGASIN *(6 issues yearly)* 727
NÆRINGSEIENDOM *(Monthly)* 741
OPP *(Weekly)* 744
Taxation
SKATTEBETALEREN *(6 issues yearly)* 748
SKATTERETT *(Quarterly)* 748

Food

FASTFOOD *(6 issues yearly)* 728
Fish Trade
FISKEBÅT-MAGASINET *(6 issues yearly)* 728
INTRAFISH.NO 734
TRYGG HAVN *(Monthly)* 752
Food Processing & Packaging
KSLMATMERK.NO *(Daily)* 736
MATINDUSTRIEN *(Monthly)* 739
MATNYTTIG *(Quarterly)* 739
General (Food)
APPETITT *(6 issues yearly)* 721
DAGLIGVAREHANDELEN *(Weekly)* 725
HANDELSBLADET FK *(Weekly)* 732
MAT.NO 739
MATOPPSKRIFT.NO 739
MATPORTALEN *(Daily)* 739
MATSIDEN.NO 739
MERKBART *(Half-yearly)* 739
NOFIMA.NO *(Daily)* 741
RØDT & HVITT VINMAGASIN *(6 issues yearly)* 747
SPIS BEDRE *(Monthly)* 749
Meat Trade
GO'MØRNING *(Quarterly)* 731
KJØTTBRANSJEN *(Monthly)* 735

Footwear

SKO *(6 issues yearly)* 749

Furnishings & Furniture

Furnishings & Furniture
MAGASINET TREINDUSTRIEN *(Monthly)* 738
MØBEL & INTERIØR *(Monthly)* 739

Garden Trade

Garden Trade
BLOMSTER *(Monthly)* 723
GARTNERYRKET *(Monthly)* 731
PARK & ANLEGG *(Monthly)* 745
Garden Trade Supplies
NORSK HAGETIDEND *(Monthly)* 742

Gift Trade

Jewellery
GULL & UR *(Monthly)* 732

Health & Medical

Casualty & Emergency
AMBULANSEFORUM *(6 issues yearly)* 720
RØDE KORS MAGASINET *(Quarterly)* 747
Dental
MS-BLADET *(Quarterly)* 740
MUNNPLEIEN *(Half-yearly)* 740
DEN NORSKE TANNLEGEFOR. TIDENDE *(Monthly)* 743
TANNSTIKKA *(6 issues yearly)* 750
TENNER I FOKUS *(Quarterly)* 750
Disability & Rehabilitation
=OSLO *(Monthly)* 719
BLINDESAKEN *(Quarterly)* 723
CP-BLADET *(Quarterly)* 725
CRESCENDO *(Quarterly)* 725
DIN HØRSEL *(6 issues yearly)* 726
DØVBLINDES UKEBLAD *(Weekly)* 726
DØVES BLAD *(6 issues yearly)* 726
DYSLEKTIKEREN *(Quarterly)* 726
FYSIOTERAPI I PRIVAT PRAKSIS *(6 issues yearly)* 730
HANDIKAPNYTT *(Monthly)* 732
REVMATIKEREN *(6 issues yearly)* 747
General (Health Medical)
ÆSCULAP *(Quarterly)* 719
AKTIVITØREN *(Quarterly)* 720
AKTUELT FRA NASJONALFORENINGEN *(Quarterly)* 720
AMBULANSEFORUM; AMBULANSEFORUM.NO 720
ASTMA ALLERGI *(6 issues yearly)* 721
BEKHTEREVER'N *(Quarterly)* 722
CØLIAKI-NYTT *(Quarterly)* 725
DAGENS MEDISIN; DAGENSMEDISIN.NO *(Daily)* 725
DIABETES *(6 issues yearly)* 726
DIABETESFORUM *(Quarterly)* 726
FOTTERAPEUTEN *(Quarterly)* 730
FREDRIKKE *(Quarterly)* 730
FYSIOTERAPEUTEN *(Monthly)* 730
FYSIOTERAPEUTEN.NO *(Daily)* 730
HELSENYHETER 732
HJERTEBARNET *(Quarterly)* 733
HMT - HELSE MEDISIN TEKNIKK *(6 issues yearly)* 733
INNSIKT 734
MEDISINSK INFORMASJON *(Quarterly)* 739
NORAFORUM *(Quarterly)* 741
NORILCO-NYTT *(6 issues yearly)* 742
PSYKISK HELSE; PSYKISKHELSE.NO *(Daily)* 746
SCANDINAVIAN JOURNAL OF TRAUMA, RESUSCIATION AND EMERGENCY MEDICINE (SJTREM) *(Daily)* 748
TIDSSKRIFT FOR DEN NORSKE LEGEFORENING *(26 issues yearly)* 751
TIDSSKRIFTET SYKEPLEIEN; SYKEPLEIEN.NO *(Daily)* 751
TIDSSKRIFTET.NO *(Daily)* 751
UTPOSTEN/FOR ALLMENN- OG SAMFUNNSMEDISIN *(Monthly)* 752
VOLVAT DOKTOR *(Quarterly)* 754
YLF-FORUM *(6 issues yearly)* 754
Health Medical Related
ALLERGI I PRAKSIS *(Quarterly)* 720
BIVIRKNINGSBLADET *(Half-yearly)* 723
DOKTORONLINE.NO 726
FOKUS PÅ FAMILIEN *(Quarterly)* 729
GEMINI *(Quarterly)* 731
GEN-I-ALT *(Quarterly)* 731
HELSESEKRETÆREN *(6 issues yearly)* 732
HELSETILSYNET 732
HOMØOPATISK TIDSSKRIFT *(Quarterly)* 733
MOT RUSGIFT *(Quarterly)* 740
NORSK LUFTAMBULANSE MAGASIN *(Quarterly)* 742
DET NYTTER *(6 issues yearly)* 744
OMSORG *(Quarterly)* 744
POSITIV *(6 issues yearly)* 745
PSYKOLOGISK TIDSSKRIFT *(Half-yearly)* 746
SKOLEPSYKOLOGI *(6 issues yearly)* 749
SPOR 749
TIDSSKRIFT FOR PSYKISK HELSEARBEID *(Quarterly)* 751
Hospitals
MUSKELNYTT *(Quarterly)* 740
Medical Engineering Technology
BIOINGENIØREN *(Monthly)* 723
Mental Health
IMPULS-TIDSSKRIFT FOR PSYKOLOGI *(Half-yearly)* 734
NORDIC JOURNAL OF PSYCHIATRY *(6 issues yearly)* 741
PSYKISK HELSE *(6 issues yearly)* 746
TIDSSKRIFT FOR NORSK PSYKOLOGFORENING *(Monthly)* 751
Nursing
SYKEPLEIEN *(Monthly)* 750
TIDSSKRIFT FOR JORDMØDRE *(6 issues yearly)* 751
Optics
OPTIKEREN *(6 issues yearly)* 744
Radiography
HOLD PUSTEN *(Monthly)* 733

Heating & Ventilation

Domestic Heating & Ventilation
VARMENYTT *(Quarterly)* 753

Norway: Business

Norway: Consumer

Music & Performing Arts

National & International Periodicals

Other Classifications

Photography & Film Making

Recreation & Leisure

Religious

Rural & Regional Interest

Sport

The Arts & Literary

Women's Interest Consumer Magazines

Poland

Business

Agriculture & Farming

Applied Science & Laboratories

Architecture & Building

Poland: Business

Electronics

Energy, Fuel & Nuclear

Engineering & Machinery

Environment & Pollution

Finance & Economics

Food

Footwear

Furnishings & Furniture

Garden Trade

Gas

Gift Trade

Health & Medical

Heating & Ventilation

Legal

Poland: Consumer

Music & Performing Arts

Cinema
FILM *(Monthly)* 761
KINO *(Monthly)* 764
KINO DOMOWE *(Monthly)* 764

Music
HIP HOP ARCHIWUM *(Monthly)* 763
HIP HOP RGB *(Monthly)* 763
HIRO *(Monthly)* 763

Pop Music
LAIF *(Monthly)* 765
MACHINA *(Monthly)* 766
PERKUSISTA *(6 issues yearly)* 771
TERAZ ROCK *(Monthly)* 779

TV & Radio
IMPERIUM TV *(Weekly)* 764
KURIER TV *(Weekly)* 765
RADIO-LIDER, TV-LIDER *(6 issues yearly)* 775
SUPER TELE *(Weekly)* 778
SUPER TV *(Weekly)* 778
ŚWIAT SERIALI *(26 issues yearly)* 778
TELE MAGAZYN *(Weekly)* 779
TELE MAX *(Weekly)* 779
TELE ŚWIAT *(Weekly)* 779
TELE TYDZIEŃ *(Weekly)* 779
TELEPROGRAM *(Weekly)* 779
TO & OWO *(Weekly)* 780
TV-SAT MAGAZYN *(Monthly)* 780

Other Classifications

Customer Magazines
PRO-TEST *(Monthly)* 774

Job Seekers
PRACA I ŻYCIE ZA GRANICĄ *(26 issues yearly)* 773

Popular Science
CHARAKTERY *(Monthly)* 757
FOCUS *(Monthly)* 761
INNE OBLICZA HISTORII *(Quarterly)* 764
MŁODY TECHNIK *(Monthly)* 768
PSYCHOLOGIA W SZKOLE *(Quarterly)* 775
READER'S DIGEST EDYCJA POLSKA *(Monthly)* 775
STYLE I CHARAKTERY *(Quarterly)* 777
ŚWIAT NAUKI *(Monthly)* 778
TATRY *(Quarterly)* 779
WIEDZA I ŻYCIE *(Monthly)* 781

Photography & Film Making

Film Making
FILM & TV KAMERA *(Quarterly)* 761

Photography
DIGITAL FOTO VIDEO *(Monthly)* 759
FOTO KURIER *(Monthly)* 761
FUTU MAGAZINE 761
MIĘDZY NAMI CAFE 768

Recreation & Leisure

Boating & Yachting
JACHTING *(Monthly)* 764
ŻAGLE *(Monthly)* 782

Camping & Caravanning
POLSKI CARAVANING *(6 issues yearly)* 772

Lifestyle
GALA *(Weekly)* 762
LAIFSTYLE *(6 issues yearly)* 765
MAXMAGAZINE *(Monthly)* 767
TOP CLASS *(Quarterly)* 780

Recreation & Leisure Related
GRACZ *(Monthly)* 763

Religious

LIST *(Monthly)* 766
W DRODZE *(Monthly)* 781
WIĘŹ *(Monthly)* 781
ZNAK *(Monthly)* 783

Rural & Regional Interest

Rural Interest
NASZA MIERZEJA *(Monthly)* 769
NASZEMIASTO.PL *(Daily)* 769

Sport

Fitness/Bodybuilding
KULTURYSTYKA I FITNESS *(Monthly)* 765

Football
PIŁKA NOŻNA *(Weekly)* 771
PIŁKA NOŻNA PLUS *(Monthly)* 771

General (Sport)
BIEGANIE *(Monthly)* 756
BIKE ACTION 756
BRAVO SPORT *(26 issues yearly)* 756
GÓRY *(Monthly)* 763
MAGAZYN GÓRSKI 766
MAGAZYN ROWEROWY 766
PRZEGLĄD SPORTOWY *(Daily)* 774

Golf
GOLF & LIFE *(Monthly)* 763
GOLF VADEMECUM *(Annual)* 763

Racquet Sports
TENISKLUB *(11 issues yearly)* 779

Shooting
ARSENAŁ *(Monthly)* 755
BRAĆ ŁOWIECKA *(Monthly)* 756
ŁOWIEC POLSKI *(Monthly)* 766

Water Sports
H2O *(Monthly)* 763
NURKOWANIE *(Monthly)* 770
SURF IT! 778
WIELKI BŁĘKIT *(6 issues yearly)* 781

Winter Sports
SKI MAGAZYN *(5 issues yearly)* 777
SNOW IT! 777

Student Publications

DLACZEGO *(Monthly)* 759
DLATEGO *(Annual)* 759
GAZETA STUDENCKA *(Monthly)* 762
MAGIEL *(Monthly)* 766
STUDENT NEWS 777
STUDIOWAĆ *(Quarterly)* 777

The Arts & Literary

Arts
AKCENT *(Quarterly)* 755
ART & LIFE 755
ARTEON *(Monthly)* 755
ARTLUK *(Quarterly)* 755
BRAIN DAMAGE *(Quarterly)* 756
DEDAL 759
FLUID *(Monthly)* 761
LAMPA *(Monthly)* 765

Literary
RES PUBLICA NOWA *(Quarterly)* 776

Women's Interest Consumer Magazines

Brides
PRZEWODNIK ŚLUBNY *(Annual)* 775
ŚLUB JAK Z BAJKI *(Half-yearly)* 777

Child Care
DZIECKO *(Monthly)* 759
MAM DZIECKO *(Monthly)* 766
MAMO, TO JA *(Monthly)* 767
RODZICE *(Monthly)* 776
TWOJE DZIECKO *(Monthly)* 780

Food & Cookery
AKADEMIA KURTA SCHELLERA 755
KUCHNIA *(Monthly)* 765
LUBIĘ GOTOWAĆ *(Monthly)* 766
MOJE GOTOWANIE *(Monthly)* 768
PANI DOMU POLECA 771
SÓL I PIEPRZ *(Monthly)* 777

Home & Family
CZTERY KĄTY *(Monthly)* 758
MÓJ PIĘKNY DOM 768
NASZE INSPIRACJE *(Quarterly)* 769
PORADNIK DOMOWY *(Monthly)* 772
PRESTIGE HOUSE *(10 issues yearly)* 773

Lifestyle
CHIC LUXURY LIFESTYLE MAGAZINE *(Quarterly)* 757
EXKLUSIV XMAGAZYN *(Monthly)* 760
GENTLEMAN *(Monthly)* 762
MAGAZYN MŁODEJ KULTURY SLAJD *(Monthly)* 766
PARTY *(26 issues yearly)* 771
PRESTIGE MAGAZINE *(Quarterly)* 773
REWIA *(Weekly)* 776
SHOW *(26 issues yearly)* 777
ŚWIAT & LUDZIE *(Weekly)* 778
TWOJE IMPERIUM *(Weekly)* 780
VIVA! *(26 issues yearly)* 780
ŻYCIE NA GORĄCO *(Weekly)* 783

Personal Finance
KURIER FINANSOWY *(6 issues yearly)* 765

Slimming & Health
CABINES *(6 issues yearly)* 757
EDEN *(Monthly)* 760
MODA NA ZDROWIE *(Monthly)* 768
NA ZDROWIE. DOSTĘPNE BEZ RECEPTY *(Quarterly)* 769
PESO PERFECTO *(Quarterly)* 771
PORADNIK ZDROWIA Z KALENDARZEM *(Annual)* 773
SAMO ZDROWIE *(Monthly)* 776
SHAPE *(Monthly)* 777
SPA BUSINESS *(6 issues yearly)* 777
SUPER LINIA 777
SUPER LINIA - WYDANIE SPECJALNE 778
VITA *(Monthly)* 780
WEGETARIAŃSKI ŚWIAT *(Monthly)* 781
ZDROWIE *(Monthly)* 782
ŻYJMY DŁUŻEJ *(Monthly)* 783

Women's Interest
AVANTI *(Monthly)* 756
BURDA *(Monthly)* 757
CHWILA DLA CIEBIE *(Weekly)* 758
CIENIE I BLASKI *(Monthly)* 758
CLAUDIA *(Monthly)* 758
COSMOPOLITAN *(Monthly)* 758
DOBRE RADY *(Monthly)* 759
KALEJDOSKOP LOSÓW *(Monthly)* 764
KOBIETA I ŻYCIE *(Monthly)* 764
NA ŚCIEŻKACH ŻYCIA *(Monthly)* 769
NAJ *(Weekly)* 769
PANI *(Monthly)* 771
PANI DOMU *(Weekly)* 771
PRZYJACIÓŁKA *(26 issues yearly)* 775
SEKRETY I NAMIĘTNOŚCI *(Monthly)* 776
SUKCESY I PORAŻKI. WYDANIE SPECJALNE 777
ŚWIAT KOBIETY *(Monthly)* 778
TINA *(26 issues yearly)* 779
TO LUBIĘ! *(Monthly)* 780
URODA *(Monthly)* 780
WRÓŻKA *(Monthly)* 782
Z ŻYCIA WZIĘTE. WYDANIE SPECJALNE 782
ZWIERCIADŁO *(Monthly)* 783

Women's Interest - Fashion
BOUTIQUE *(Monthly)* 756
ELLE *(Monthly)* 760
FASHION MAGAZINE *(Quarterly)* 761
GLAMOUR *(Monthly)* 763
MODA & STYL *(Quarterly)* 768
OLIVIA *(Monthly)* 770
TWÓJ STYL *(Monthly)* 780

Women's Interest Related
BELLA RELAKS *(Weekly)* 756
TAKIE JEST ŻYCIE *(Weekly)* 779

Portugal

Business

Agriculture & Farming

Agriculture & Farming
VIDA RURAL *(Monthly)* 806

Baking & Confectionery

DIABETES 789
ESTAÇÕES 792
RECEITAS PRÁTICAS 801

Catering

Catering, Hotels & Restaurants
INTER MAGAZINE *(Monthly)* 794

Portugal: Consumer

Church & School Equipment & Education

Education Teachers
DIRIGIR *(Quarterly)* 790

Commerce, Industry & Management

Commerce, Industry & Management
1000 MAIORES EMPRESAS (E) *(Annual)* 783
DESAFIOS *(Quarterly)* 789
EXECUTIVE DIGEST *(Monthly)* 792
JORNAL DE NEGÓCIOS *(Daily)* 796
NEGÓCIOS & FRANCHISING *(6 issues yearly)* 799
Training & Recruitment
PESSOAL *(Monthly)* 800
RECURSOS HUMANOS MAGAZINE *(6 issues yearly)* 802

Communications, Advertising & Marketing

Broadcasting
TELE SATÉLITE *(Monthly)* 804
Communications, Advertising & Marketing
BRIEFING *(Monthly)* 786
MARKETEER *(Monthly)* 797
MEIOS & PUBLICIDADE *(Weekly)* 798
OCASIÃO *(Weekly)* 800
RSM - SUPER MARKET *(Monthly)* 802
Conferences & Exhibitions
AMBIENTES DE FESTA *(Half-yearly)* 784

Computers & Automation

INOVAÇÃO & TECNOLOGIA 794
Data Processing
EXAME INFORMÁTICA *(Monthly)* 792
Data Transmission
SEMANA INFORMÁTICA *(Weekly)* 803
Professional Personal Computers
BIT *(Monthly)* 786
INTER.FACE - ADMINISTRAÇÃO PÚBLICA *(6 issues yearly)* 794
INTER.FACE - BANCA & SEGUROS *(3 issues yearly)* 794
MUNDO DO DVD ROM *(Monthly)* 798
PC GUIA *(Monthly)* 800
T3 *(Monthly)* 804

Construction

General (Construction)
ARTE & CONSTRUÇÃO *(Monthly)* 785
JORNAL DA CONSTRUÇÃO *(26 issues yearly)* 795
URBANISMO & CONSTRUÇÃO *(Monthly)* 805

Cosmetics & Hairdressing

Cosmetics & Hairdressing Related
BARBEIROS & CABELEIREIROS 786
ESTÉTICA PORTUGAL *(Quarterly)* 792
TOM SOBRE TOM *(Quarterly)* 805

Decorating & Paint

LUX DECORAÇÃO 797

Electrical Retail Trade

Radio & Hi-Fi
PRODUÇÃO PROFISSIONAL *(Monthly)* 801

Electronics

General (Electronics)
ELEKTOR ELECTRÓNICA *(Monthly)* 791
Telecommunications
COMUNICAÇÕES 788

Engineering & Machinery

Engineering & Machinery
INGENIUM *(6 issues yearly)* 794

Environment & Pollution

AMBIENTE MAGAZINE *(3 issues yearly)* 784
AMBITUR *(Monthly)* 784
CÂMARAS VERDES *(Monthly)* 787

Finance & Economics

Finance & Economics
DINHEIRO & DIREITOS *(6 issues yearly)* 790
ECONOMIA *(Weekly)* 791
EXAME *(Monthly)* 792
VIDA ECONÓMICA *(Weekly)* 805
Property
IMOBILIÁRIA *(Monthly)* 794
MERCADO IMOBILIÁRIO *(Weekly)* 798

Food

General (Food)
REVISTA DE VINHOS *(Monthly)* 802

Gift Trade

Clocks & Watches
ESPIRAL DO TEMPO *(3 issues yearly)* 791
RELÓGIOS & JÓIAS *(6 issues yearly)* 802

Health & Medical

General (Health Medical)
FITO+SAÚDE *(Half-yearly)* 792
MUNDO MÉDICO *(6 issues yearly)* 799
SEMANA MÉDICA *(26 issues yearly)* 803
Health Medical Related
NOTÍCIAS MÉDICAS *(Weekly)* 800
Nursing
NURSING *(Monthly)* 800

Local Government, Leisure & Recreation

Community Care & Social Services
AMI NOTÍCIAS *(Quarterly)* 784
Leisure, Recreation & Entertainment
VISÃO 7 GUIA 806
Swimming Pools
AMBIENTE PISCINAS *(Half-yearly)* 784

Marine & Shipping

Marine & Shipping
NOTÍCIAS DO MAR *(Monthly)* 799

Materials Handling

LOGÍSTICA & TRANSPORTES HOJE *(6 issues yearly)* 797
LOGÍSTICA MODERNA *(Monthly)* 797

Motor Trade

Motor Trade Accessories
ANECRA REVISTA *(6 issues yearly)* 784
Motorcycle Trade
MOTO JORNAL *(Weekly)* 798

Pharmaceutical & Chemists

FARMÁCIA DISTRIBUIÇÃO *(Monthly)* 792
INDÚSTRIA *(6 issues yearly)* 794

Printing & Stationery

Stationery
INTERNACIONAL CANETAS 795

Retailing & Wholesaling

DISTRIBUIÇÃO HOJE *(Monthly)* 790

Transport

Freight
CARGO *(Monthly)* 787
General (Transport)
TRANSPORTES EM REVISTA *(Monthly)* 805

Travel & Tourism

EPICUR *(6 issues yearly)* 791
FÉRIAS E VIAGENS 792
PUBLITURIS *(Weekly)* 801
ROTAS & DESTINOS *(Monthly)* 802
ROTEIRO 802
TURISMO SOCIAL 805
TURISVER *(26 issues yearly)* 805

Consumer

Adult & Gay Magazines

Men's Lifestyle Magazines
GQ *(Monthly)* 793
MEN'S HEALTH *(Monthly)* 798

Consumer Electronics

Consumer Electronics Related
ZOOM I.T. *(Monthly)* 806
Games
BGAMER *(Monthly)* 786
Video & DVD
ÁUDIO & CINEMA EM CASA *(6 issues yearly)* 785
PRODUÇÃO ÁUDIO *(Monthly)* 801

Current Affairs & Politics

DESTAK *(Daily)* 789
METRO LISBOA *(Daily)* 798
METRO PORTUGAL *(Daily)* 798
NOTÍCIAS SÁBADO *(Weekly)* 800
SÁBADO *(Weekly)* 803
SEMANÁRIO TRANSMONTANO *(Weekly)* 803

Education

General (Education)
ENSINO SUPERIOR 791
ENSINO SUPERIOR 791
ESCOLHAS *(Quarterly)* 791
MEDIA XXI *(3 issues yearly)* 797
PAIS & FILHOS *(Monthly)* 800
PÓS GRADUAÇÕES, MESTRADOS, MBA 801

Holidays & Travel

Entertainment Guides
BAIRRO ALTO & PRÍNCIPE REAL *(Half-yearly)* 786
BAIXA & CHIADO *(Half-yearly)* 786
CONVIDA *(Half-yearly)* 788
ROMA & ALVALADE *(Annual)* 802
SANTOS *(Annual)* 803
Holidays
VOLTA AO MUNDO *(Monthly)* 806
Travel
EVASÕES *(Monthly)* 792
FOLLOW ME *(Monthly)* 793
POSTAL DO ALGARVE *(Weekly)* 801
TEMPO LIVRE *(Monthly)* 804
VIAJAR *(Monthly)* 805

Motoring & Cycling

Cycling
BIKE MAGAZINE *(Monthly)* 786
Motor Sports
AUTO SPORT *(Weekly)* 785
RALLY DE PORTUGAL - REIS DA CONDUÇÃO 801
TURBO *(Monthly)* 805

Russian Federation: Business

Section 2 Periodicals by Classification

Finance & Economics

Accountancy
BUHGALTER I ZAKON *(Monthly)* 810
BUHGALTERSKY UCHET W BUDZHETNYKH I NEKOMMERCHESKIKH ORGANIZATSIYAKH *(24 issues yearly)* 810
BUHGALTERSKY UCHET W IZDATELSTVE I POLIGRAFII *(Monthly)* 810
GLAVBUKH *(24 issues yearly)* 814
MEZHDUNARODNY BUHGALTERSKY UCHIOT *(Monthly)* 818
MSFO *(6 issues yearly)* 819
VSYE DLYA BUHGALTERA *(Monthly)* 828

Banking
BANKOVSKIYE TEKHNOLOGII *(Monthly)* 809

Credit Trading
TVOYA IPOTEKA *(Monthly)* 826

Finance & Economics
BIZNES ZHURNAL *(24 issues yearly)* 809
BUSINESS & FINANCIAL MARKETS *(Weekly)* 810
BUSINESS CLASS *(Weekly)* 810
BUSINESSWEEK ROSSIYA *(Monthly)* 810
CK *(Weekly)* 810
DELOVIE LYUDI *(Monthly)* 811
DENGI *(Weekly)* 811
DIGEST FINANSY *(Monthly)* 811
EKONOMIKA I VREMYA *(Weekly)* 812
EKONOMIKA I ZHIZN *(Weekly)* 812
EKONOMIKO - PRAVOVOY BULLETEN *(Monthly)* 812
EPIGRAPH *(Weekly)* 812
EXPERT *(Weekly)* 812
EXPERT SEVERO-ZAPAD *(Weekly)* 812
FINANS *(Weekly)* 813
FINANSOVAYA GAZETA *(Weekly)* 813
FINANSOVY DIREKTOR *(11 issues yearly)* 813
FINANSY I KREDIT *(Quarterly)* 813
GDE DEN'GI *(Weekly)* 813
KAPITAL WEEKLY *(Weekly)* 815
KONTINENT SIBIR *(Weekly)* 816
POPULARNYE FINANSY *(Monthly)* 822
RBC MAGAZINE *(Monthly)* 822
REGIONALNAYA EKONOMIKA: TEORIYA I PRAKTIKA *(36 issues yearly)* 823
SHEF *(Monthly)* 824
VEDOMOSTI *(Daily)* 827
VOPROSY EKONOMIKI *(Monthly)* 828
VREMYA I DEN'GI *(208 issues yearly)* 828
ZOLOTOY ROG *(104 issues yearly)* 829

Financial Related
D' *(24 issues yearly)* 811
DALNEVOSTOCHNY KAPITAL *(Monthly)* 811

Investment
KOMMERSANT *(Daily)* 816

Property
BULLETEN' NEDVIZHIMOSTI *(104 issues yearly)* 810
BULLETEN' STROYASHEYSYA NEDVIZHIMOSTI *(Monthly)* 810
COMMERCIAL REAL ESTATE *(24 issues yearly)* 810
DELOVAYA NEDVIZHIMOST' *(Monthly)* 811
KOMMERCHESKAYA NEDVIZHIMOST ROSSII *(Annual)* 815
KVARTIRA, DACHA, OFIS *(Weekly)* 816
KVARTIRNYI VOPROS - VSYO O NEDVIZHIMOSTI *(Half-yearly)* 817
REALTOR *(6 issues yearly)* 823
SALON NEDVIZHIMOSTI *(Monthly)* 824
UPRAVLENIYE NEDVIZHIMOSTYU *(Half-yearly)* 827

Taxation
AUDIT I NALOGOOBLOZHENIYE *(Monthly)* 809
UCHET. NALOGI. PRAVO *(Weekly)* 826

Food

Food Processing & Packaging
GASTRONOMIYA. BAKALEYA *(Weekly)* 813
KHRANENIJE I PERERABOTKA SEL'KHOZSYRYA *(Monthly)* 815
PISHCHEVAYA PROMYSHLENNOST *(Monthly)* 821

Food Related
MASLOZHIROVAYA PROMYSHLENNOST *(6 issues yearly)* 817

General (Food)
PISHCHEVYE INGREDIENTY: SYRIO I DOBAVKI *(Half-yearly)* 821
SAKHARNAYA SVEKLA *(10 issues yearly)* 824

Furnishings & Furniture

Furnishings & Furniture - Kitchens & Bathrooms
SANTECHNIKA *(6 issues yearly)* 824

Gas

GAZOVY BIZNES *(6 issues yearly)* 813
SCIENCE & TECHNOLOGY IN GAS INDUSTRY *(Quarterly)* 824

Health & Medical

General (Health Medical)
MEDITSINSKI VESTNIK *(Weekly)* 817

Heating & Ventilation

Domestic Heating & Ventilation
ENERGOSBEREZHENIYE *(8 issues yearly)* 812

Industrial Heating & Ventilation
ABOK JOURNAL (VENTILATION, HEATING, AIR-CONDITIONING) *(8 issues yearly)* 808

Legal

EZH-JURIST *(Weekly)* 813
YURIST KOMPANII *(Monthly)* 829

Local Government, Leisure & Recreation

Local Government
PARLAMENTSKAYA GAZETA *(Weekly)* 821
PETERBURGSKY DNEVNIK *(Weekly)* 821
TVERSKAYA 13 *(156 issues yearly)* 826

Marine & Shipping

Marine Engineering Equipment
SUDOSTROYENIE *(6 issues yearly)* 825

Marine Related
MORSKAYA BIRZHA *(Quarterly)* 818

Materials Handling

SOVREMENNY SKLAD *(6 issues yearly)* 825

Metal, Iron & Steel

METALLY I TSENY *(24 issues yearly)* 817

Mining & Quarrying

GORNYI ZHURNAL *(Monthly)* 814
OBOGASHCHENIE RUD *(6 issues yearly)* 820
UGOL' *(Monthly)* 826

Oil & Petroleum

BURENIYE I NEFT *(11 issues yearly)* 810
NEFT' I KAPITAL *(11 issues yearly)* 820
NEFT' ROSSII *(Monthly)* 820
NEFTEGAZ.RU *(Monthly)* 820
NEFTESERVIS *(Quarterly)* 820
NEFTYANAYA TORGOVLYA *(Monthly)* 820
NEFTYANYE VEDOMOSTI *(24 issues yearly)* 820
OIL & GAS JOURNAL RUSSIA *(Monthly)* 821
OIL OF RUSSIA *(Quarterly)* 821

Other Classifications

Biology
PRIKLADNAYA BIOKHIMIYA I MIKROBIOLOGIYA *(6 issues yearly)* 822

Packaging & Bottling

PACKAGING INTERNATIONAL/PACKET *(6 issues yearly)* 821

Pharmaceutical & Chemists

APTEKAR' *(Monthly)* 808
FARMATSEVTICHESKOYE OBOZRENIYE *(Monthly)* 813
FARMATSEVTICHESKY VESTNIK *(42 issues yearly)* 813
REMEDIUM *(Monthly)* 823
ROSSISKIYE APTEKI *(24 issues yearly)* 823

Plastics & Rubber

PLASTIKS: INDUSTRIYA PERERABOTKI PLASTMASS *(10 issues yearly)* 821

Printing & Stationery

Printing
COMPUART *(Monthly)* 811
MIR ETIKETKI *(6 issues yearly)* 818

Publishing

Publishing & Book Trade
KNIZHNYI BIZNES *(10 issues yearly)* 815
KURIER PECHATI *(24 issues yearly)* 816

Retailing & Wholesaling

MOYO DELO. MAGAZIN *(Monthly)* 819
ROSSIISKAYA TORGOVLYA *(104 issues yearly)* 823
TORGOVAYA GAZETA *(104 issues yearly)* 826
VITRINA. MIR SUPERMARKETA *(11 issues yearly)* 827

Safety & Security

Safety
BDI *(6 issues yearly)* 809

Tobacco

NICOTIANA ARISTOCRATICA *(Quarterly)* 820

Transport

General (Transport)
LOGISTIKA SEGODNYA *(6 issues yearly)* 817
TRANSPORT *(Monthly)* 826

Transport Related
KONTEYNERNY BIZNES *(10 issues yearly)* 816

Travel & Tourism

GEO *(Monthly)* 813
NATIONAL GEOGRAPHIC RUSSIA *(Monthly)* 819
TOURBUSINESS *(18 issues yearly)* 826
TOURINFO *(Weekly)* 826

Consumer

Adult & Gay Magazines

Men's Lifestyle Magazines
BANZAI *(11 issues yearly)* 809
FHM *(Monthly)* 813
IVAN *(Monthly)* 815
MAXIM *(Monthly)* 817
MEDVED *(Monthly)* 817
MEN'S HEALTH *(Monthly)* 817
MUZHSKOY KLUB *(Monthly)* 819
PLAYBOY *(11 issues yearly)* 822
XXL *(Monthly)* 828

Animals & Pets

Animals & Pets Protection
RUSSIAN JOURNAL OF HERPETOLOGY *(Quarterly)* 823

Consumer Electronics

Current Affairs & Politics

Education

Gardening

Holidays & Travel

Motoring & Cycling

Music & Performing Arts

National & International Periodicals

Other Classifications

Photography & Film Making

Recreation & Leisure

Sport

The Arts & Literary

Women's Interest Consumer Magazines

San Marino

Consumer

Holidays & Travel

Slovakia

Business

Clothing & Textiles

Commerce, Industry & Management

Computers & Automation

Finance & Economics

Safety & Security

Consumer

Current Affairs & Politics

Music & Performing Arts

TV & Radio
MARKÍZA *(Weekly)*.......... 830

Women's Interest Consumer Magazines

Women's Interest
ZIVOT *(Weekly)*.......... 830

Slovenia

Business

Communications, Advertising & Marketing

Communications, Advertising & Marketing
ADUT *(Monthly)*.......... 830

Finance & Economics

Finance & Economics
DRUŽINSKI DELNIČAR *(Monthly)*.......... 831
GLAS GOSPODARSTVA *(Monthly)*.......... 831
PREMOŽENJE *(Monthly)*.......... 831
Property
DENAR & SVET NEPREMIČNIN *(26 issues yearly)*.......... 831

Consumer

Education

Education Related
IDEJA *(Quarterly)*.......... 831

Motoring & Cycling

Motorcycling
MOBIL *(Monthly)*.......... 831

National & International Periodicals

NIKA *(26 issues yearly)*.......... 831

Women's Interest Consumer Magazines

Home & Family
DELO IN DOM *(Weekly)*.......... 831
MOJ DOM *(26 issues yearly)*.......... 831

Spain

Business

Agriculture & Farming

Agriculture & Farming
ACCIÓN COOPERATIVA *(11 issues yearly)*.......... 831
AGRONEGOCIOS *(42 issues yearly)*.......... 832
LA TIERRA DEL AGRICULTOR Y EL GANADERO *(6 issues yearly)*.......... 844
Agriculture & Farming - Regional
ARDATZA *(24 issues yearly)*.......... 832
CAMP VALENCIA *(Monthly)*.......... 833
Agriculture - Machinery & Plant
LABOREO *(Monthly)*.......... 838
Vine Growing
VINOS DE ESPAÑA *(6 issues yearly)*.......... 844

Architecture & Building

Architecture
AD ARCHITECTURAL DIGEST ESPAÑA *(11 issues yearly)*.......... 832
ARQUITECTOS *(Quarterly)*.......... 832
EL CROQUIS *(5 issues yearly)*.......... 834
Cleaning & Maintenance
LIMPIEZA INFORM *(6 issues yearly)*.......... 839

Aviation & Aeronautics

Aviation & Aeronautics
AVIÓN REVUE *(Monthly)*.......... 832

Church & School Equipment & Education

Church & School Equipment
PRIMERAS NOTICIAS DE COMUNICACIÓN Y PEDAGOGÍA *(8 issues yearly)*.......... 842
Education
ANPE *(Monthly)*.......... 832
Teachers & Education Management
TRABAJADORES DE LA ENSEÑANZA *(10 issues yearly)*.......... 844

Commerce, Industry & Management

Commerce, Industry & Management
DIRIGENTES *(Monthly)*.......... 836
EMPRENDEDORES *(Monthly)*.......... 836
EN FRANQUICIA *(11 issues yearly)*.......... 836
FRANQUICIAS Y NEGOCIOS *(6 issues yearly)*.......... 837
NUESTROS NEGOCIOS *(11 issues yearly)*.......... 840
Industry & Factories
EQUIPOS PRODUCTOS INDUSTRIALES (EPI) *(11 issues yearly)*.......... 836
REVISTA TOPE *(10 issues yearly)*.......... 843
SELECCIONES TO P.E. *(3 issues yearly)*.......... 843
International Commerce
EL MUNDO DIPLOMÁTICO *(Monthly)*.......... 840
Small Business
PYMES *(11 issues yearly)*.......... 842

Computers & Automation

Automation & Instrumentation
BYTE *(Monthly)*.......... 833
Computers Related
MONOGRAFICOS BYTE *(11 issues yearly)*.......... 839
QUIÉN ES QUIÉN EN INFORMÁTICA Y TELECOMUNICACIONES *(Annual)*.......... 842
Data Processing
DR DOBB'S ESPAÑA *(Monthly)*.......... 836
PC PRO *(11 issues yearly)*.......... 841
Data Transmission
ARROBA *(Monthly)*.......... 832
Personal Computers
COMPUTER MUSIC *(Monthly)*.......... 834

Construction

General (Construction)
PRODUCTOS EQUIPOS CONSTRUCCIÓN PEC *(6 issues yearly)*.......... 842

Cosmetics & Hairdressing

Hairdressing
PELUQUERIAS *(11 issues yearly)*.......... 841
TOCADO *(11 issues yearly)*.......... 844

Defence

ARMAS Y MUNICIONES *(Monthly)*.......... 832

Drinks & Licensed Trade

Licensed Trade, Wines & Spirits
EL SOMMELIER *(11 issues yearly)*.......... 843
VINO Y GASTRONOMÍA *(6 issues yearly)*.......... 844

Electrical Retail Trade

Radio & Hi-Fi
ALTA FIDELIDAD *(Monthly)*.......... 832
Video
DVD ACTUALIDAD *(11 issues yearly)*.......... 836

Electronics

Telecommunications
CONNECT *(Monthly)*.......... 834

Engineering & Machinery

Engineering & Machinery
TÉCNICA INDUSTRIAL *(Quarterly)*.......... 843

Environment & Pollution

LA TIERRA *(9 issues yearly)*.......... 844

Finance & Economics

Banking
AUSBANC *(Monthly)*.......... 832
Finance & Economics
ACTUALIDAD ECONÓMICA *(Weekly)*.......... 831
CAPITAL *(10 issues yearly)*.......... 833
DINERO *(Monthly)*.......... 836
LA ECONOMIA *(Monthly)*.......... 836
EL ECONOMISTA *(Daily)*.......... 836
EJECUTIVOS *(10 issues yearly)*.......... 836
MERCADO DE DINERO *(26 issues yearly)*.......... 839
MI CARTERA DE INVERSIÓN *(Weekly)*.......... 839
NEGOCIO & ESTILO DE VIDA *(Daily)*.......... 840
EL NUEVO LUNES DE LA ECONOMÍA Y LA SOCIEDAD *(45 issues yearly)*.......... 841
Investment
INVERSIÓN Y CAPITAL *(Annual)*.......... 838
Property
NEGOCIO INMOBILIARIO *(Weekly)*.......... 840

Food

General (Food)
FINANCIAL FOOD *(11 issues yearly)*.......... 837

Furnishings & Furniture

Furnishings & Furniture
CASA MODA *(Half-yearly)*.......... 833

Garden Trade

Garden Trade
VIDA RURAL *(21 issues yearly)*.......... 844

Gift Trade

Jewellery
DUPLEX PRESS *(6 issues yearly)*.......... 836
JOYA MODA *(Half-yearly)*.......... 838

Health & Medical

Dental
GACETA DENTAL *(Monthly)*.......... 837
General (Health Medical)
COMPARTIR *(Quarterly)*.......... 834
DIARIO MÉDICO *(260 issues yearly)*.......... 835
DINERO Y SALUD *(10 issues yearly)*.......... 836
EL GLOBAL *(Weekly)*.......... 837

Spain: Consumer

JANO MEDICINA Y HUMANIDADES *(44 issues yearly)* 838
EL MEDICO *(Weekly)* 839
NOTICIAS MÉDICAS - EL SEMANARIO DE LA MEDICINA *(42 issues yearly)* 840
SIETE DÍAS MÉDICOS *(40 issues yearly)* 843

Hospitals
ENFERMERÍA FACULTATIVA *(10 issues yearly)* 836
MUNDO SANITARIO (PERIÓDICO DE ENFERMERÍA) *(20 issues yearly)* 840
TRIBUNA SANITARIA *(Monthly)* 844
VALDECILLA NOTICIAS *(6 issues yearly)* 844

Nursing
CRÓNICA SANITARIA *(11 issues yearly)* 834
NURSING *(10 issues yearly)* 841

Laundry & Dry Cleaning

REVITEC *(6 issues yearly)* 843

Legal

ABOGACIA ESPAÑOLA *(Quarterly)* 831

Local Government, Leisure & Recreation

Civil Service
MUFACE *(Quarterly)* 839

Community Care & Social Services
CRUZ ROJA *(Quarterly)* 834

Swimming Pools
PISCINAS *(Monthly)* 841

Marine & Shipping

Maritime Freight
GUÍA DEL TRANSPORTE MARÍTIMO *(26 issues yearly)* 837

Motor Trade

Motor Trade Accessories
AUTO VÍA *(Monthly)* 832
AUTOCEA *(11 issues yearly)* 832
CESVIMAP *(Quarterly)* 833
HORAS PUNTA DEL MOTOR *(Monthly)* 838

Motorcycle Trade
SÓLO MOTO ACTUAL *(Weekly)* 843

Other Classifications

Veterinary
PORCI *(6 issues yearly)* 842

Pharmaceutical & Chemists

FARMACÉUTICOS *(11 issues yearly)* 837

Publishing

Publishing & Book Trade
PRIMERAS NOTICIAS DE LITERATURA INFANTIL Y JUVENIL *(8 issues yearly)* 842

Regional Business

BUTLLETI DE LA CAMBRA *(Quarterly)* 833
INFORMATIU COMERÇ *(11 issues yearly)* 838
MON EMPRESARIAL *(11 issues yearly)* 839

Safety & Security

Safety
SEGURITECNÍA *(11 issues yearly)* 843

Transport

Commercial Vehicles
FLOTAS DE LEASE PLAN *(Quarterly)* 837
SÓLO CAMIÓN *(Monthly)* 843

General (Transport)
PORTNEWSPAPER *(Monthly)* 842
TRANSPORTE MUNDIAL *(Monthly)* 844
TRANSPORTE PROFESIONAL *(Monthly)* 844

Railways
LINEAS DEL TREN *(26 issues yearly)* 839

Travel & Tourism

SPAIN GOURMETOUR *(3 issues yearly)* 843

Consumer

Adult & Gay Magazines

Adult Magazines
PLAYBOY *(Monthly)* 842

Men's Lifestyle Magazines
MEN'S HEALTH *(Monthly)* 839

Consumer Electronics

Games
COMPUTER HOY *(Monthly)* 834
PLAY2MANÍA *(Monthly)* 842
PLAYSTATION 2 *(Monthly)* 842

Home Computing
PC ACTUAL *(11 issues yearly)* 841

Video & DVD
CANAL OCIO *(Monthly)* 833

Current Affairs & Politics

CONTIGO *(3 issues yearly)* 834
EL SOCIALISTA *(6 issues yearly)* 843

Education

Adult Education
GACETA UNIVERSITARIA *(Weekly)* 837
GACETA UNIVERSITARIA DE BARCELONA *(Weekly)* 837

Gardening

CASA Y JARDÍN *(11 issues yearly)* 833

Hobbies & DIY

Collectors Magazines
LLADRÓ PRIVILEGE *(Half-yearly)* 839

Holidays & Travel

Entertainment Guides
BARCELONA DIVINA *(Half-yearly)* 833

In-Flight Magazines
RONDA IBÉRIA *(Monthly)* 843

Travel
AIRELIBRE *(Monthly)* 832

Motoring & Cycling

Club Cars
AUTOCLUB *(6 issues yearly)* 832
RACC CLUB - REIAL AUTOMOBIL CLUB DE CATALUNYA *(Monthly)* 842

Motor Sports
MARCA MOTOR *(Monthly)* 839

Motoring
AUTO MAX *(Monthly)* 832
FORMULA AUTOFACIL *(Monthly)* 837
REVISTA ADA *(Quarterly)* 843

Music & Performing Arts

Cinema
CINEMANÍA *(Monthly)* 833
CINERAMA *(Monthly)* 833
ESTRENOS DE VÍDEO *(11 issues yearly)* 836
FOTOGRAMAS & DVD *(Monthly)* 837

Pop Music
SUPER POP *(26 issues yearly)* 843

TV & Radio
DIGITAL PLUS *(Monthly)* 836
REVISTA TELEPROGRAMA *(Weekly)* 843
SUPERTELE *(Weekly)* 843
TELENOVELA *(Weekly)* 843

National & International Periodicals

GACETA INTERNACIONAL *(Monthly)* 837
INTERVIU *(Weekly)* 838
EL JUEVES *(Weekly)* 838
NATIONAL GEOGRAPHIC MAGAZINE ESPAÑA *(Monthly)* 840
READER'S DIGEST SELECCIONES *(Monthly)* 842
TIEMPO DE HOY *(Weekly)* 844

Other Classifications

Miscellaneous
LA AVENTURA DE LA HISTORIA *(Monthly)* 832
HISTORIA NATIONAL GEOGRAPHIC *(Monthly)* 838

Paranormal
AÑO CERO *(Monthly)* 832

Popular Science
MUY INTERESANTE *(Monthly)* 840
QUO *(Monthly)* 842

Restaurant Guides
LUGARES DIVINOS *(Annual)* 839

Photography & Film Making

Photography
FOTO SISTEMA *(Quarterly)* 837

Recreation & Leisure

Children & Youth
DIBUS *(Monthly)* 836

Lifestyle
CALLE 20 *(Monthly)* 833
EL SEMANAL *(Weekly)* 843

Religious

MUNDO NEGRO *(11 issues yearly)* 840

Sport

Athletics
ATLETISMO ESPAÑOL *(11 issues yearly)* 832
CORRICOLARI *(Monthly)* 834

General (Sport)
DXT *(Weekly)* 836

Student Publications

GENERACIÓN XXI *(24 issues yearly)* 837
PERIÓDICO ESTUDIANTES UNIVERSITARIOS *(10 issues yearly)* 841

Women's Interest Consumer Magazines

Child Care
LA GUÍA DEL EMBARAZO Y PARTO *(7 issues yearly)* 837
MI BEBÉ Y YO *(Monthly)* 839
SU PRIMER AÑO *(Half-yearly)* 843

Crafts
LABORES DEL HOGAR *(11 issues yearly)* 838

Food & Cookery
COCINA FÁCIL *(11 issues yearly)* 833
COMER BIEN *(Monthly)* 834
COSAS DE COCINA *(Quarterly)* 834
LECTURAS ESPECIAL COCINA *(3 issues yearly)* 838

Hair & Beauty
VOGUE BELLEZA *(3 issues yearly)* 844

Home & Family
CASA AL DIA *(11 issues yearly)* 833
CASA DIEZ *(Monthly)* 833

Sweden

Business

Agriculture & Farming

Antiques

Applied Science & Laboratories

Architecture & Building

Aviation & Aeronautics

Baking & Confectionery

Catering

Ceramics, Pottery & Glass

Chemicals

Church & School Equipment & Education

Sweden: Business

Clothing & Textiles

Commerce, Industry & Management

Communications, Advertising & Marketing

Computers & Automation

PC FÖR ALLA; WWW.PCFORALLA.IDG.SE (*Daily*) ... 889
PC GAMER; PCGAMER.SE (*Daily*) ... 889
PC-TIDNINGEN; PCTIDNINGEN.SE (*Daily*) ... 889
SLITZ; SLITZ.SE (*Daily*) ... 896
TECHWORLD (*Monthly*) ... 902
TECHWORLD MIKRODATORN ... 902
TECHWORLD OPEN SOURCE (*Daily*) ... 902
TECHWORLD; WEBB (*Daily*) ... 902
TELEKOM IDAG; TELEKOMIDAG.COM (*Daily*) ... 902

Multimedia
DIGITAL LIFE (*6 issues yearly*) ... 858
IT-CHEFEN (*Quarterly*) ... 872

Personal Computers
ALLT OM PC & TEKNIK (*Monthly*) ... 848

Professional Personal Computers
DATORMAGAZIN (*Monthly*) ... 858
MACWORLD (*Monthly*) ... 880
PC-TIDNINGEN ... 889

Construction

Construction Related
LYFTET (*Annual*) ... 880

General (Construction)
AKTUELL PRODUKTION ... 846
BYGGVÄRLDEN (*26 issues yearly*) ... 855
INGENJÖREN (*Monthly*) ... 871
MASKINENTREPRENÖREN / ME-TIDNINGEN (*Monthly*) ... 881
MASKINENTREPRENÖREN / ME-TIDNINGEN; WEBB (*Daily*) ... 881
PLANERA BYGGA BO (*6 issues yearly*) ... 890
REV BULLETINEN (*Quarterly*) ... 893
SAMHÄLLSBYGGAREN (*6 issues yearly*) ... 894

Roads
LEVERANSTIDNINGEN ENTREPRENAD (*26 issues yearly*) ... 877
PÅ VÄG (*6 issues yearly*) ... 889
VÄGMÄSTAREN (*Quarterly*) ... 907

Water Engineering
CIRKULATION, VA-TIDSKRIFTEN (*6 issues yearly*) ... 856
TIDNINGEN SVENSKT VATTEN (*6 issues yearly*) ... 903

Cosmetics & Hairdressing

Cosmetics
KOSMETIK (*Quarterly*) ... 875
SHR-JOURNALEN (*Quarterly*) ... 895

Hairdressing
SVENSKA FRISÖRTIDNINGEN (*6 issues yearly*) ... 901

Decorating & Paint

Decorating & Paint
MÅLARNAS FACKTIDNING (*6 issues yearly*) ... 881
VÅRT NYA HEM (*Quarterly*) ... 908

Defence

BILKÅRISTEN (*Quarterly*) ... 852
BLÅ STJÄRNAN (*Quarterly*) ... 852
CIVIL (*Quarterly*) ... 856
FÖRSVARSUTBILDAREN (*Quarterly*) ... 865
FRONYTT (*Quarterly*) ... 866
KUNGL KRIGSVETENSKAPSAKADEMIENS HANDLINGAR OCH TIDSKRIFT (*6 issues yearly*) ... 875
LOTTANYTT (*Quarterly*) ... 880
OFFICERSTIDNINGEN (*6 issues yearly*) ... 888
RESERVOFFICEREN (*Quarterly*) ... 892
SOLDAT & TEKNIK ... 897
SVENSK MÅNGKAMP (*Quarterly*) ... 900
TIDNINGEN HEMVÄRNET (*6 issues yearly*) ... 903
TIDSKRIFT I SJÖVÄSENDET (*Quarterly*) ... 904
VÅRT FÖRSVAR (*Quarterly*) ... 908

Drinks & Licensed Trade

Drinks, Licensed Trade, Wines & Spirits
APÉRITIF (*6 issues yearly*) ... 849
MUNSKÄNKEN MED VINJOURNALEN (*6 issues yearly*) ... 884

Licensed Trade, Wines & Spirits
DINA VINER (*Monthly*) ... 859

Off-Licence
BOLAGET (*Quarterly*) ... 853

Electrical

ELBRANSCHEN (*6 issues yearly*) ... 860
ELINSTALLATÖREN (*Monthly*) ... 860
LJUSKULTUR (*6 issues yearly*) ... 878
VOLTIMUM (*Weekly*) ... 910

Electrical Retail Trade

General (Electrical Retail Trade)
ELEKTRONIKBRANSCHEN (*Monthly*) ... 860

Radio & Hi-Fi
MONITOR (*Monthly*) ... 883
QTC AMATÖRRADIO (*Monthly*) ... 891

Electronics

General (Electronics)
ELECTRONIC ENVIRONMENT (*Quarterly*) ... 860
ELEKTOR (*6 issues yearly*) ... 860
ELEKTRIKERN; ELEKTRIKERN.NU (*Daily*) ... 860
ELEKTRONIK I NORDEN (*26 issues yearly*) ... 860
ELEKTRONIK I NORDEN; ELEKTRONIKINORDEN.COM (*Daily*) ... 860
ELEKTRONIKTIDNINGEN (*6 issues yearly*) ... 860
ELINSTALLATÖREN; ELINSTALLATOREN.SE (*Daily*) ... 860
ENERGIMAGASINET; ENERGIMAGASINET.COM (*Daily*) ... 861
ENERGIVÄRLDEN (*Quarterly*) ... 861
ERA (*Monthly*) ... 861
ERA; ERA.SE (*Daily*) ... 861
MODERN TEKNIK (*6 issues yearly*) ... 883
MODERN TEKNIK; MODERNTEKNIK.NU (*Daily*) ... 883
NORDISK ENERGI (*6 issues yearly*) ... 885

Telecommunications
IT-NYTT.NU (*Weekly*) ... 872
KONTAKTEN/CONTACT ... 875
MOBIL (*Monthly*) ... 883
MOORE MAGAZINE; MOORE.SE (*Daily*) ... 883
NYHETSBREVET TELEKOM ONLINE (*Daily*) ... 887
NYHETSBREVET TELEKOMNYHETERNA (*Daily*) ... 887
TELEKOM IDAG (*Monthly*) ... 902

Energy, Fuel & Nuclear

BENSIN & BUTIK (*6 issues yearly*) ... 851
BIOENERGI (*6 issues yearly*) ... 852
ENERGI & MILJÖ; SIKI.SE (*Daily*) ... 860
ENERGIMAGASINET (*6 issues yearly*) ... 861
ENERGITEKNIK (*Half-yearly*) ... 861
INBLICK ABB (*Monthly*) ... 871
KLOKA HEM (*Quarterly*) ... 874
MEDSOLS (*Quarterly*) ... 882
NYHETSBREV SLUSSEN BUILDING SERVICES (*Weekly*) ... 887
VILLATIDNINGEN; WEBB (*Daily*) ... 910

Engineering & Machinery

CAD & CIM (Computer Integrated Manufacture)
AUTOMATION (*Monthly*) ... 850
NY TEKNIK; NY TEKNIK.SE ... 886

Engineering & Machinery
CAMPUS TEKNIK (*Quarterly*) ... 855
DIREKTKONTAKT - ENTREPENAD (*Monthly*) ... 859
FORSKNING (*Quarterly*) ... 864
IVA-AKTUELLT (*6 issues yearly*) ... 872
PROFESSIONELL DEMOLERING (*Quarterly*) ... 891
UPPFINNAREN/KONSTRUKTÖREN (*6 issues yearly*) ... 906
VERKSTÄDERNA (*Monthly*) ... 909
VERKSTADSKONTAKT (*6 issues yearly*) ... 909
VERKSTADSTIDNINGEN (*Monthly*) ... 909

Engineering Related
SVENSK VERKSTAD (*6 issues yearly*) ... 900
TEKNIKFÖRETAGEN DIREKT (*6 issues yearly*) ... 902
VERKO (*Monthly*) ... 908

Finishing
YTFORUM (*6 issues yearly*) ... 911

Machinery, Machine Tools & Metalworking
BOGGI (*Monthly*) ... 853
ENTREPRENADAKTUELLT (*Monthly*) ... 861
SVETSEN (*Quarterly*) ... 901

Production & Mechanical Engineering
MEKANIK- INFORMATION MED INDUSTRINYTT (*Quarterly*) ... 882
MEKANISTEN (*Quarterly*) ... 882

Environment & Pollution

AMBIO - A JOURNAL OF THE HUMAN ENVIRONMENT (*6 issues yearly*) ... 848
EKOLOGISKT LANTBRUK (*Monthly*) ... 860
FÅGLAR I UPPLAND (*Quarterly*) ... 862
GÅRD & TORP (*6 issues yearly*) ... 866
GRUNDVATTEN (*Half-yearly*) ... 868
KLIMATMAGASINET EFFEKT (*6 issues yearly*) ... 874
MILJÖ & HÄLSA (*Monthly*) ... 882
MILJÖ & UTVECKLING (*6 issues yearly*) ... 882
MILJÖ & UTVECKLING; WEBB (*Daily*) ... 882
MILJÖAKTUELLT (*6 issues yearly*) ... 882
MILJÖLEDAREN (*Weekly*) ... 882
MILJÖRAPPORTEN (*Monthly*) ... 882
MILJÖTIDNINGEN (*Quarterly*) ... 883
OFFENTLIGA AFFÄRER (*6 issues yearly*) ... 887
RECYCLING & MILJÖTEKNIK (*Monthly*) ... 892
RIKSETTAN (*Half-yearly*) ... 893
SVENSK BOTANISK TIDSKRIFT (*Quarterly*) ... 899
SVERIGES NATUR (*Quarterly*) ... 901
TIDNINGEN ÅTER (*Quarterly*) ... 903
UTEMILJÖ (*6 issues yearly*) ... 906

Finance & Economics

Accountancy
BALANS (*Monthly*) ... 851
KONSULTEN (*6 issues yearly*) ... 875
NYTT FRÅN REVISORN (*Monthly*) ... 887

Banking
FINANSVÄRLDEN (*Monthly*) ... 863

Finance & Economics
AFFÄRSVÄRLDEN (*Weekly*) ... 846
BÖRSVECKAN (*Weekly*) ... 853
BUSINESS ... 854
CAMPUS EKONOMI (*Quarterly*) ... 855
DRIVA EGET (*Quarterly*) ... 859
EKONOMISK DEBATT (*6 issues yearly*) ... 860
EKONOMISK DEBATT; EKONOMISKDEBATT.SE (*Daily*) ... 860
INKÖPSJOURNALEN (*6 issues yearly*) ... 872
LEXAFFÄR (*Weekly*) ... 877
LINK MAGAZINE (*Quarterly*) ... 878
MORNINGSTAR (*Daily*) ... 883
NYHETSBREVET FOND & BANK (*Monthly*) ... 887
OTC - PLACERAREN (*Monthly*) ... 889
PRIVATA AFFÄRER; PRIVATAAFFARER.SE (*Daily*) ... 891

Financial Related
LOOK AT SCANDINAVIA (*Quarterly*) ... 880

Fundraising
BARNENS FRAMTID (*Quarterly*) ... 851

Insurance
NYHETSBREVET RISK & FÖRSÄKRING (*26 issues yearly*) ... 887
SCAND. ACTUARIAL JOURNAL (*Quarterly*) ... 894

Investment
AKTIESPARAREN (*Monthly*) ... 846
PRIVATA AFFÄRER (*Monthly*) ... 891

Pensions
NYHETSBREVET PENSIONER & FÖRMÅNER (*Monthly*) ... 887

Property
ALLT OM VILLOR & HUS (*Quarterly*) ... 848
ALLTOMBOSTAD.SE (*Daily*) ... 848
BOFAST (*Monthly*) ... 853
FACILITIES (*Quarterly*) ... 862
FASTIGHETSFÖRVALTAREN (*6 issues yearly*) ... 862
FASTIGHETSMÄKLAREN (*6 issues yearly*) ... 862
FASTIGHETSNYTT (*6 issues yearly*) ... 862
HEM & HYRA ... 869
HOOM; WEBB (*Daily*) ... 870
MAGASINET FASTIGHETSSVERIGE ... 880
MÄKLARVÄRLDEN (*Quarterly*) ... 880
NYHETSBREVET DAGENS FASTIGHETSAKTIE (*Daily*) ... 887
TIDNINGEN FASTIGHETSAKTIEN; WEBB (*Daily*) ... 903
VI I VILLA; WEBB (*Daily*) ... 909

Taxation
LEXSKATT (*104 times a year*) ... 877
SKATTENYTT (*Monthly*) ... 896

Food

Food Processing & Packaging
FOODWIRE.SE (*Daily*) ... 864
FRI KÖPENSKAP; WEBB (*Daily*) ... 865
LIVSMEDEL I FOKUS (*Monthly*) ... 878
LIVSMEDEL I FOKUS; LIVSMEDELIFOKUS.SE (*Daily*) ... 878
PEJLING FRÅN SVENSK MJÖLK (*Quarterly*) ... 890

Sweden: Business

SVENSKA LIVSMEDEL *(6 issues yearly)* 901

General (Food)

ALLT OM VIN *(Monthly)* 848
AMELIA - VIKT & HÄLSA *(Annual)* 849
BUFFÉ *(Monthly)* 854
FLOTTANS MÄN *(Quarterly)* 863
FRI KÖPENSKAP *(Weekly)* 865
ICANYHETER *(Weekly)* 871
LIQUID INSPIRATION *(Half-yearly)* 878
LIVSHÄLSAN *(Half-yearly)* 878
MÅL & MEDEL *(Monthly)* 880
PHILIPSON SÖDERBERG MAGAZINE *(Quarterly)* 890
SKOLMATENS VÄNNER *(Half-yearly)* 896

Meat Trade

KÖTTBRANSCHEN *(Monthly)* 875

Furnishings & Furniture

Furnishings & Furniture

FORM *(Monthly)* 864
FORUM AID *(Quarterly)* 865
MODERN INTERIÖR *(6 issues yearly)* 883

Garden Trade

Garden Trade

BLOMSTER-BRANSCHEN *(6 issues yearly)* 853
VIOLA *(26 issues yearly)* 910

Garden Trade Horticulture

DRÖMHEM & TRÄDGÅRD - TRÄDGÅRD & BLOMMOR *(Half-yearly)* 859
HEM LJUVA HEM *(Monthly)* 869
HEM LJUVA HEM TRÄDGÅRD *(Monthly)* 869
TIDNINGEN TRÄDGÅRDSLIV SVERIGE *(Quarterly)* 903

Gas

ENERGIGAS *(Quarterly)* 861

Gift Trade

Clocks & Watches

PLAZA WATCH *(Half-yearly)* 890

Health & Medical

Chiropractic

MASSAGE & KROPPSVÅRD *(Quarterly)* 881

Dental

AJOURODONT *(Quarterly)* 846
TANDHYGIENIST TIDNINGEN *(6 issues yearly)* 901
TANDLÄKARTIDNINGEN *(Monthly)* 902
TANDSKÖTERSKETIDNINGEN *(Quarterly)* 902
TANDTEKNIKERN *(6 issues yearly)* 902
TF-BLADET *(Quarterly)* 902

Disability & Rehabilitation

AFASI-NYTT *(Quarterly)* 845
ALKOHOL & NARKOTIKA *(6 issues yearly)* 847
ALLT OM HJÄLPMEDEL *(6 issues yearly)* 847
ARBETSTERAPEUTEN 850
ASSISTANS *(6 issues yearly)* 850
AURIS *(6 issues yearly)* 850
BLÅ BANDET *(6 issues yearly)* 852
DHB-DIALOG *(Quarterly)* 858
FÖRÄLDRAKRAFT *(6 issues yearly)* 864
FYSIOTERAPI *(6 issues yearly)* 866
HJÄRNKRAFT *(Quarterly)* 870
JAGAREN *(Quarterly)* 872
NARKOTIKAFRÅGAN *(6 issues yearly)* 884
OBEROENDE *(Quarterly)* 887
RÖRELSE *(6 issues yearly)* 893
SRF-PERSPEKTIV *(6 issues yearly)* 898

General (Health Medical)

ACTA DERMATO-VENEROLOGICA *(6 issues yearly)* 845
ACTA OTO-LARYNGOLOGICA *(Monthly)* 845
ALLERGI I PRAXIS *(Quarterly)* 847
ALLERGIA *(6 issues yearly)* 847
ALLMÄN MEDICIN *(6 issues yearly)* 847
AMAZONABLADET *(Quarterly)* 848
BARN & CANCER *(6 issues yearly)* 851
BLOOD PRESSURE *(6 issues yearly)* 853
BULLETINEN *(Quarterly)* 854
C, IDÉTIDSKRIFT OM CEREALIER *(Quarterly)* 855
CANCERVÅRDEN *(6 issues yearly)* 855
CF-BLADET *(Quarterly)* 855
DAGENS MEDICIN *(Weekly)* 857
DAGENS MEDICIN; DAGENSMEDICIN.SE *(Daily)* 857
DIABETES *(6 issues yearly)* 858
DIABETESVÅRD *(Quarterly)* 858
DIETISTAKTUELLT *(6 issues yearly)* 858
DISTRIKTSLÄKAREN *(6 issues yearly)* 859
FORSKNING FÖR HÄLSA *(Quarterly)* 864
FORSKNING & MEDICIN *(Quarterly)* 865
FRISKARE LIV, VISIR-AKTUELLT *(Quarterly)* 865
GASTROKURIREN *(Quarterly)* 866
GENSVAR *(Quarterly)* 866
GRANA *(Quarterly)* 868
HÄLSOTECKEN *(Half-yearly)* 868
INCITAMENT *(6 issues yearly)* 871
IT I VÅRDEN *(Quarterly)* 872
LÄKARTIDNINGEN *(Weekly)* 876
LÄKEMEDELSVÄRLDEN; LAKEMEDELSVARLDEN.SE *(Daily)* 876
LSF-MAGAZINET *(Monthly)* 880
MEDICINSK ACCESS *(6 issues yearly)* 881
MEDICINSK VETENSKAP *(Quarterly)* 881
MEDICINSK VETENSKAP & PRAXIS *(6 issues yearly)* 881
MEDICOR MAGASIN *(Quarterly)* 881
MICROBIAL ECOLOGY IN HEALTH AND DISEASE *(Quarterly)* 882
MODERNA LÄKARE *(Quarterly)* 883
NÄRINGSVÄRT - OM KOST OCH NÄRING *(6 issues yearly)* 884
NJURFUNK *(Quarterly)* 885
OMVÅRDNADSMAGASINET *(6 issues yearly)* 888
ONKOLOGI I SVERIGE *(6 issues yearly)* 888
ORTOPEDISKT MAGASIN *(Quarterly)* 888
OSTEOPOROSNYTT *(Quarterly)* 888
PARKINSONJOURNALEN *(Quarterly)* 889
PERSPEKTIV PÅ HIV *(Half-yearly)* 890
PHARMA REPORT *(Monthly)* 890
PSORIASISTIDNINGEN *(6 issues yearly)* 891
RÄDDA LIVET *(Quarterly)* 892
RYGGTIDNINGEN *(Quarterly)* 893
SCAND. CARDIOVASCULAR JOURNAL *(6 issues yearly)* 894
SCAND. JOURNAL OF INFECTIOUS DISEASES *(6 issues yearly)* 894
SCAND. JOURNAL OF PLASTIC AND RECONSTR. SURG. *(6 issues yearly)* 894
SCAND. JOURNAL OF UROLOGY AND NEPHROLOGY *(6 issues yearly)* 894
SMITTSKYDD *(6 issues yearly)* 897
SOCIALMEDICINSK TIDSKRIFT *(6 issues yearly)* 897
STATUS *(6 issues yearly)* 898
SVENSK CARDIOLOGI *(Quarterly)* 899
SVENSK IDROTTSMEDICIN *(Quarterly)* 900
SVENSK KIRURGI *(6 issues yearly)* 900
SVENSKA EPILEPSIA *(Quarterly)* 901
TANDLÄKARTIDNINGEN; TANDLAKARTIDNINGEN.SE *(Daily)* 902

Health Medical Related

2000-TALETS VETENSKAP *(Quarterly)* 845
ADVANCES IN PHYSIOTHERAPY *(Quarterly)* 845
ANHÖRIG, FMN 849
DIABETOLOGNYTT *(Quarterly)* 858
LÄS OCH SKRIV *(6 issues yearly)* 877
LOGOPEDNYTT *(6 issues yearly)* 879
MEDTECH MAGAZINE *(Quarterly)* 882
MOTORFÖRAREN; WEBB *(Daily)* 884
NÄRINGSMEDICINSK TIDSKRIFT *(6 issues yearly)* 884
SVENSK POLIS; WEBB *(Daily)* 900

Medical Equipment

AUDIONYTT *(Half-yearly)* 850

Mental Health

DEMENSFORUM *(Quarterly)* 858
DIVAN-TIDSKRIFT FÖR PSYKOANALYS OCH KULTUR *(Half-yearly)* 859
MELLANRUMMET TIDSKR. OM BARN & UNGDOMSPSYKO. *(Half-yearly)* 882
PHRENICUS *(Quarterly)* 890
PSYKISK HÄLSA *(Quarterly)* 891
PSYKOLOGTIDNINGEN *(26 issues yearly)* 891
SOCIALVETENSKAPLIG TIDSKRIFT *(Quarterly)* 897

Nursing

BARNBLADET *(6 issues yearly)* 851
BLADET *(6 issues yearly)* 853
DIALÄSEN *(6 issues yearly)* 858
GINSTEN *(6 issues yearly)* 866
HÄLSAN I CENTRUM *(Quarterly)* 868
HJÄRTEBARNET *(Quarterly)* 870
I VÅRDEN *(Monthly)* 871
ILCO-BLADET *(Quarterly)* 871
INBLICK *(Quarterly)* 871
INTERNATIONAL FORUM OF PSYCHOANALYSIS *(Quarterly)* 872
JORDEMODERN *(Monthly)* 873
LANDSTINGSTIDNINGEN *(6 issues yearly)* 876
NERVEN *(6 issues yearly)* 885
PRAKTIKAN *(6 issues yearly)* 891
PULSEN *(6 issues yearly)* 891
SKOLHÄLSAN *(Quarterly)* 896
STILETTEN *(6 issues yearly)* 898
TIDSKRIFTEN ÄLDRE I CENTRUM *(Quarterly)* 904
UPPTINGET *(6 issues yearly)* 906
VÅRDFOKUS *(Monthly)* 907
VÄSTMANNAKONTAKT *(6 issues yearly)* 908
VENTILEN *(Quarterly)* 908

Optics

OPTIK *(Monthly)* 888

Radiography

RÖRET *(Quarterly)* 893

Heating & Ventilation

Industrial Heating & Ventilation

ENERGI & MILJÖ *(Monthly)* 860
FJÄRRVÄRMETIDNINGEN 863
VVS-FORUM *(Monthly)* 910

Refrigeration & Ventilation

KYLA+VÄRMEPUMPAR *(6 issues yearly)* 876

Import & Export

SVENSK EXPORT *(6 issues yearly)* 899

Legal

ADVOKATEN *(6 issues yearly)* 845
ADVOKATEN; WEBB *(Daily)* 845
AFTONBLADET; RÄTTSREDAKTIONEN *(Daily)* 846
ANBUDSJOURNALEN *(Weekly)* 849
CAMPUS JURIST *(Quarterly)* 855
DAGENS JURIDIK 857
INFOTORG JURIDIKS *(Monthly)* 871
JURIDISK TIDSKRIFT *(Quarterly)* 873
JUSEKTIDNINGEN *(Monthly)* 873
LEGALLY YOURS *(6 issues yearly)* 877
NÄMNDEMANNEN *(Quarterly)* 884
SVENSK JURISTTIDNING *(Monthly)* 900
TIDNINGEN RUNTIKRIM 903

Local Government, Leisure & Recreation

Civil Service

OM FÖRSVARSFÖRBUNDET *(6 issues yearly)* 888
SEKOTIDNINGEN *(6 issues yearly)* 894

Community Care & Social Services

BARNBYAR *(Quarterly)* 851
DAGENS SAMHÄLLE *(Weekly)* 857
FÖRETAGSSKÖTERSKAN *(Quarterly)* 864
FRI SIKT *(Half-yearly)* 865
LOCUS - TIDSKRIFT FÖR FORSKNING OM BARN OCH UNGDOMAR *(Quarterly)* 878
REFLEX *(6 issues yearly)* 892
REVANSCH! *(6 issues yearly)* 893
RONDEN, PERSONALTIDNING FÖR AKADEMISKA SJUKHUSET *(6 issues yearly)* 893
SIGNALEN *(Quarterly)* 895
SJUKHUSLÄKAREN *(6 issues yearly)* 895
SOCIAL OMSORG *(6 issues yearly)* 897
SOCIONOMEN *(6 issues yearly)* 897
SOLLENTUNAJOURNALEN *(6 issues yearly)* 897
ST PRESS 898
TEBLADET *(Monthly)* 902
TIDNINGEN FAMILJEDAGHEM *(6 times a year)* 903
UPPHANDLING24 *(Monthly)* 906
VI LÄNKAR *(6 issues yearly)* 909

Local Government

KOMMUNAL EKONOMI *(6 issues yearly)* 874
KOMMUNALARBETAREN *(26 issues yearly)* 875
SKTF-TIDNINGEN *(26 issues yearly)* 896
STADSBYGGNAD *(6 issues yearly)* 898
UD-KURIREN *(6 issues yearly)* 906

Parks

FRILUFTSLIV - I ALLA VÄDER *(Quarterly)* 865
GRÖNYTELEVERANTÖRERNA *(Quarterly)* 868

Police

POLISTIDNINGEN *(6 issues yearly)* 891
SVENSK POLIS *(Monthly)* 900
TIDNINGEN BROTTSOFFER *(Quarterly)* 903

Swimming Pools

SIMFRÄMJAREN LIVRÄDDAREN *(Quarterly)* 895

Marine & Shipping

Boat Trade

BÅTBRANSCHEN *(6 issues yearly)* 851

Materials Handling

Metal, Iron & Steel

Mining & Quarrying

Motor Trade

Music Trade

Other Classifications

Packaging & Bottling

Paper

Pharmaceutical & Chemists

Photographic Trade

Plastics & Rubber

Printing & Stationery

Publishing

Regional Business

Retailing & Wholesaling

Safety & Security

Timber, Wood & Forestry

Toy Trade & Sports Goods

Transport

Travel & Tourism

Sweden: Consumer

Consumer

Adult & Gay Magazines

Angling & Fishing

Animals & Pets

Consumer Electronics

Current Affairs & Politics

Education

Ethnic

Gardening

Hobbies & DIY

Holidays & Travel

Motoring & Cycling

BIKE (Monthly) 852
CLASSIC BIKE (6 issues yearly) 856
MC-FOLKET (6 issues yearly) 881
MCM - MOTORCYKELMAGASINET (6 issues yearly) 881
MC-NYTT (Monthly) 881

Motoring
4 WHEEL DRIVE (Monthly) 845
AERO-MAGAZINET (Half-yearly) 845
AUTO MOTOR & SPORT; AUTOMOTORSPORT.SE (Daily) 850
AUTOMOBIL; AUTOMOBIL.SE (Daily) 850
BIGTWIN (Monthly) 852
BIKE; BIKE.SE (Daily) 852
BILSPORT BÖRSEN (Monthly) 852
BILSPORT GATBILAR.SE (6 issues yearly) 852
CLASSIC MOTOR; CLASSICMOTOR.SE (Daily) 856
GASOLINE MAGAZINE (6 issues yearly) 866
HUSBILEN TEST (Monthly) 870
MOTOR (Monthly) 883
MOTORFÖRAREN (6 issues yearly) 883
RACE MC-SPORT (Monthly) 892
WHEELS MAGAZINE (Monthly) 910

Veteran Cars
CLASSIC MOTOR (Monthly) 856
KLASSIKER (6 issues yearly) 874
NOSTALGIA (Monthly) 886

Music & Performing Arts

Cinema
BIOGUIDEN.SE 852
CINEMA (Monthly) 855
FILM INTERNATIONAL (6 issues yearly) 863
FILMKONST (6 issues yearly) 863
FILMRUTAN (Quarterly) 863
GREKER I NORDEN (Quarterly) 868
GRUFVAN (Half-yearly) 868
HEMMABIO (Monthly) 869
KÅRIREN (Quarterly) 873
MAGASIN1 (Monthly) 880
PRYLPORTALEN.SE (Daily) 891
RODEO (Quarterly) 893

Dance
DANSTIDNINGEN (6 issues yearly) 858
DANSTIDNINGEN; DANSTIDNINGEN.SE (Daily) 858

Music
DRAGSPELSNYTT (Quarterly) 859
FRIDA SPECIAL (Half-yearly) 865
FRIDA; WEBB (Daily) 865
FUZZ (Monthly) 866
GITARR OCH LUTA (Quarterly) 866
KINGSIZE MAGAZINE (6 issues yearly) 874
KOUNTRY KORRAL MAGAZINE (Quarterly) 875
KYRKOMUSIKERNAS TIDNING (Monthly) 876
LIRA MUSIKMAGASIN (Quarterly) 878
LIS-AKTUELLT (Quarterly) 878
LIVETS GODA (6 issues yearly) 878
MUSIKANT (Quarterly) 884
MUSIKINDUSTRIN, MI (Daily) 884
MUSIKTIDNINGEN MUSIKOMANEN (Half-yearly) 884
OPUS (6 issues yearly) 888
ORGELFORUM (Quarterly) 888
ORKESTER JOURNALEN - OM JAZZ (Monthly) 888
SONIC (6 issues yearly) 897
SPELMANNEN (Quarterly) 898
STUDIO (Monthly) 899
STUDIO; STUDIO.SE (Daily) 899
SWEDEN ROCK MAGAZINE (Monthly) 901
SYMFONI (Quarterly) 901
TIDIG MUSIK (Quarterly) 902
TIDNINGEN KÖRSÅNG (Quarterly) 903
TIDSKRIFTEN OPERA (Quarterly) 904
VECKO-REVYN; VECKOREVYN.COM (Daily) 908
ZERO MUSIC MAGAZINE (Quarterly) 911

Pop Music
CLOSE-UP MAGAZINE (6 issues yearly) 856
FÅR JAG LOV (6 issues yearly) 862
OKEJ (Monthly) 888

TV & Radio
FILM & TV (Quarterly) 863
SYDSVENSKAN; TV (Daily) 901

Theatre
DIALOGER (Quarterly) 858
ERGO; ERGO.NU (Daily) 861
FLM (Quarterly) 863
FOLKET I BILD / KULTURFRONT; FIB.SE (Daily) 864
JOURNAL (Half-yearly) 873
NÖJESGUIDEN; GÖTEBORG (Monthly) 885
NÖJESGUIDEN; MALMÖ/LUND 885
NÖJESGUIDEN; NOJESGUIDEN.SE (Daily) 885
RODEO; RODEO.NET (Daily) 893
SHERIFFI (Quarterly) 895
TEATERFORUM (6 issues yearly) 902
VÄRMLÄNDSK KULTUR (Daily) 908

National & International Periodicals

ALBA (6 times a year) 847
DITT & DATT (6 issues yearly) 859
ENTRÉ HALMSTAD (6 issues yearly) 861
FREEDOM (Half-yearly) 865
GALAGO (Half-yearly) 866
GRÖNKÖPINGS VECKOBLAD (Monthly) 868
I VÄREND OCH SUNNERBO (Quarterly) 871
NÖJESMIX (Monthly) 885
RETORIKMAGASINET (Quarterly) 893
RIG, KULTURHISTORISK TIDSKRIFT (Quarterly) 893
SAMHÄLLSTIDNINGEN RE:PUBLIC SERVICE (Quarterly) 894
SE & HÖR (Weekly) 894
TIDSKRIFTEN VÄSTERBOTTEN (Quarterly) 904

Other Classifications

Disability
ATT UNDERVISA (Quarterly) 850
DÖVAS TIDNING (6 issues yearly) 859
FÖRÄLDRAKONTAKTEN (Quarterly) 864
HANDIKAPPIDROTT (6 issues yearly) 869
KICK (Quarterly) 874
LIV (Quarterly) 878
NYA SYNVÄRLDEN (Quarterly) 887
SVENSK HANDIKAPPTIDSKRIFT, SHT (Monthly) 900
UNIK (6 issues yearly) 906
VÅR SYNPUNKT (6 issues yearly) 907

Expatriates
BERBANG (6 issues yearly) 851
NYHETSTIDNINGEN SESAM 887

Historic Buildings
BEBYGGELSEHISTORISK TIDSKRIFT (Half-yearly) 851

Miscellaneous
BYGD OCH NATUR (Quarterly) 854
FORSKNING & FRAMSTEG 864
POPULÄR HISTORIA (Monthly) 891

Paranormal
UFO-AKTUELLT (Quarterly) 906

Popular Science
ALLT OM HISTORIA (Monthly) 847
FORNVÄNNEN (Quarterly) 864
FRAMTIDER (Quarterly) 865
IDROTT & KUNSKAP (6 issues yearly) 871
NATIONAL GEOGRAPHIC (Monthly) 884
TELESCOPIUM (Quarterly) 902

Photography & Film Making

Photography
DIGITAL FOTO (Monthly) 858
DIGITALFOTO FÖR ALLA 858
DVDFORUM.NU (Daily) 859
FOTOGRAFISK TIDSKRIFT; WEBB (Daily) 865

Recreation & Leisure

Boating & Yachting
BÅTLIV (6 issues yearly) 851
BÅTLIV; BATLIV.SE (Daily) 851
BÅTNYTT (Monthly) 851
PÅ KRYSS (6 issues yearly) 889
PRAKTISKT BÅTÄGANDE (Monthly) 891
SEGLARBLADET (Quarterly) 894
SEGLING (Monthly) 894
SKÄRGÅRDSBÅTEN (Quarterly) 896
VI BÅTÄGARE (Monthly) 909

Camping & Caravanning
ALLT OM HUSVAGN & CAMPING (Monthly) 847
CARAVANBLADET (6 issues yearly) 855

Children & Youth
KAMRATPOSTEN (Monthly) 873
MOTDRAG (6 issues yearly) 883
OPSIS BARNKULTUR (Quarterly) 888
RESPONS UNGDOMSTIDNING (Half-yearly) 892
SCOUTEN (6 issues yearly) 894
STRUTEN (6 issues yearly) 898

Lifestyle
VICE (Monthly) 910

Recreation & Leisure Related
CAFÉ; CAFE.SE (Daily) 855
FRISKSPORT (6 issues yearly) 865
MÅ BRA; MABRA.COM (Daily) 880
RES (Monthly) 892
RESIDENCE (Monthly) 892
SCOUTING SPIRIT (6 issues yearly) 894
UTEMAGASINET (6 issues yearly) 906
UTEMAGASINET; WEBB (Daily) 906
VI BÅTÄGARE; WEBB (Daily) 909

Religious

AMOS (6 issues yearly) 849
BUDBÄRAREN - EFS MISSIONSTIDNING (Monthly) 854
EFS.NU (Quarterly) 860
ENIM (Quarterly) 861
FÖR (6 issues yearly) 864
IKON1931 (6 issues yearly) 871
JABBOK (Quarterly) 872
JUDISK KRÖNIKA (6 issues yearly) 873
KATOLSKT MAGASIN (Monthly) 874
KRISTEN FOSTRAN (6 issues yearly) 875
KVÄKARTIDSKRIFT (Quarterly) 876
KYRKA OCH FOLK (Weekly) 876
KYRKANS TIDNING (Weekly) 876
KYRKANS TIDNING; WEBB (Daily) 876
LEKMAN I KYRKAN (Quarterly) 877
LEVANDE STENAR - ELÄVÄT KIVET (Quarterly) 877
MEMENTO (Quarterly) 882
MENORAH (Quarterly) 882
RELIGION & LIVSFRÅGOR (Quarterly) 892
SÄNDAREN (26 issues yearly) 894
SIGNUM (6 issues yearly) 895
SIGNUM; SIGNUM.SE (Daily) 895
STRIDSROPET (26 issues yearly) 898
SVENSK KYRKOTIDNING (26 issues yearly) 900
SVENSK MISSIONSTIDSKRIFT (Quarterly) 900
SVENSK PASTORALTIDSKRIFT (26 issues yearly) 900
SVENSKA SÄNDEBUDET (Monthly) 901
TIDNINGEN SPIRA (6 issues yearly) 903
TIDSKRIFTEN TRO & LIV (6 issues yearly) 904
UPPDRAG MISSION (6 issues yearly) 906
VÄRLDEN IDAG (104 issues yearly) 907
VÄRLDEN IDAG; WEBB (Daily) 907
VÄRLDENS TIDNING (Quarterly) 907

Rural & Regional Interest

ANNONS-MARKNA'N (26 issues yearly) 849
BYAHORNET (Quarterly) 854
COMMERSEN (Daily) 856
EMMABODA TIDNING (Monthly) 860
GAGNEFSBLADET (Weekly) 866
GOTLÄNDSKA.SE (Daily) 867
HALLANDS AFFÄRER (Monthly) 868
HEMBYGDEN (Quarterly) 869
KALMARPOSTEN (Weekly) 873
KANAL 12 (Daily) 873
KH AKTUELLT (Monthly) 874
KIRUNA TIDNINGEN (Monthly) 874
KRISTINEHAMN-STORFORS AKTUELLT (Monthly) 875
LIDKÖPINGSNYTT.NU (Daily) 878
LIMHAMNS-TIDNINGEN (Quarterly) 878
LINKÖPINGS-POSTEN 878
LOKALTIDNINGEN KÄVLINGE NYA (26 issues yearly) 879
LOKALTIDNINGEN LOMMABLADET (26 issues yearly) 879
MAGASINET SKÅNE (6 issues yearly) 880
MÄLARÖARNAS NYHETER (26 issues yearly) 881
MALMÖTIDNINGEN (6 issues yearly) 881
MASEN (Weekly) 881
MET-AVIISI-TIDSKR. FÖR TORNEDALEN/ MALMFÄLTEN (Quarterly) 882
NORDMARKSBYGDEN (Monthly) 886
NYBRO-EXTRA 887
ÖRGRYTE-HÄRLANDA TIDNING (Monthly) 888
OXIEBLADET (Monthly) 889
PÅ TAL OM STOCKHOLM (Weekly) 889
PEJL PÅ BOTKYRKA (6 issues yearly) 890
SPEGELN SVEDALABLADET (Monthly) 898
STÅNGMÄRKET (6 issues yearly) 898
TORNEDALSBLADET (26 issues yearly) 904
TYRESÖ NYHETER (6 issues yearly) 905
VI PÅ NÄSET (6 issues yearly) 909

Rural Interest
GODS & GÅRDAR (Monthly) 867

Sport

Athletics
AFTONBLADET; SPORTMAGASINET (Monthly) 846
GOAL (Monthly) 867

Sweden: Consumer

Student Publications

The Arts & Literary

Women's Interest Consumer Magazines

NEO *(6 issues yearly)* 884
NK STIL *(Half-yearly)* 885
STUREPLAN.SE *(Daily)* 899
TIDSKRIFT FÖR GENUSVETENSKAP *(Quarterly)* 903
VEGAN *(Quarterly)* 908

Personal Finance
PRIVATA AFFÄRER PLACERINGSGUIDEN *(Monthly)* 891
SUNT FÖRNUFT *(6 issues yearly)* 899
VECKANS AFFÄRER; VA.SE *(Daily)* 908

Retirement
ÄLDREOMSORG *(6 issues yearly)* 847
I VÅRDEN *(6 issues yearly)* 871
PROPENSIONÄREN *(Monthly)* 891
SPRF-TIDNINGEN *(6 issues yearly)* 898
VETERANEN *(Monthly)* 909

Secretary & PA
DAGENS SEKRETERARE *(6 issues yearly)* 857

Slimming & Health
1,6 MILJONERKLUBBEN 845
AMELIA - KROPP & SKÖNHET *(Annual)* 849
BINDU *(Quarterly)* 852
BODY MAGAZINE; BODY.SE *(Daily)* 853
DOKTORN *(Quarterly)* 859
FREE *(6 issues yearly)* 865
FRISKISPRESSEN *(Quarterly)* 865
FYSIOTERAPI; WEBB *(Daily)* 866
HÄLSA - FÖR KROPP OCH SJÄL I BALANS *(Monthly)* 868
HÄLSA & VETENSKAP *(Quarterly)* 868
I FORM *(Monthly)* 871
KROPP & SJÄL *(Quarterly)* 875
LANDSTINGSNYTT *(Quarterly)* 876
LEVA MED DIABETES *(6 issues yearly)* 877
LEVA MED SMÄRTA *(6 issues yearly)* 877
MÅ BRA *(Monthly)* 880
NATURLIGT OM HÄLSA *(Quarterly)* 884
POPULÄR HÄLSA *(Quarterly)* 891
RESPONS FÖRETAGSTIDNING *(6 issues yearly)* 892
REUMATIKERVÄRLDEN *(6 issues yearly)* 893
TOPPHÄLSA *(Monthly)* 904
VÅRDGUIDEN *(Quarterly)* 907

Teenage
FRIDA *(26 issues yearly)* 865
JULIA SPECIAL *(Quarterly)* 873
KAMRATPOSTEN; KPWEBBEN.SE *(Daily)* 873
VECKO-REVYN *(26 issues yearly)* 908

Women's Interest
ALLT OM KLOCKOR OCH SMYCKEN *(Half-yearly)* 848
AMELIA *(26 issues yearly)* 848
AMELIA - SOMMAR *(Annual)* 849
BRÖLLOPSGUIDEN *(Half-yearly)* 854
COSMOPOLITAN *(Monthly)* 856
DAMERNAS VÄRLD *(Monthly)* 858
ELLE *(Monthly)* 860
FEMINA *(Monthly)* 862
FRED OCH FRIHET *(Quarterly)* 865
FRONTFACE MAGAZINE *(6 times a year)* 866
GLAZE *(Monthly)* 867
GO GIRL *(6 issues yearly)* 867
HÄNT EXTRA *(Weekly)* 869
JUNIA *(6 issues yearly)* 873
KÅRSORDET *(6 issues yearly)* 874
KUPÉ *(Monthly)* 876
MAMA MAGASIN *(Monthly)* 881
MODETTE.SE *(Daily)* 883
MORGONBRIS, S-KVINNORS TIDNING 883
NÖJESMAGASINET CITY; UMEÅ *(Monthly)* 885
PASSION FOR BUSINESS *(Quarterly)* 889
PETIT MAGAZINE *(Quarterly)* 890
PLAZA KVINNA *(Monthly)* 890
READER'S DIGEST *(Monthly)* 892
SATS MAGASIN *(Quarterly)* 894
SOLO *(Monthly)* 897
SVENSK DAMTIDNING *(Weekly)* 899
TARA *(Monthly)* 902

Women's Interest - Fashion
AMELIA - BRUD & BRÖLLOP *(Annual)* 848
AMELIA - HÅR & SKÖNHET *(Annual)* 848
BON MAGAZINE *(6 issues yearly)* 853
DAMERNAS VÄRLD - DV MODE *(Half-yearly)* 858
LIFESTYLE MAGAZINE *(Quarterly)* 878
NOLLTRETTON *(Monthly)* 885
SKOMAGAZINET *(6 issues yearly)* 896
TIDNINGEN ULLA *(Quarterly)* 903
TOVE HEM & TRÄDGÅRD *(Monthly)* 904
VECKANS NU *(26 issues yearly)* 908

Women's Interest Related
KVINNOTRYCK *(6 issues yearly)* 876

Switzerland

Business

Agriculture & Farming

Agriculture & Farming
AGRI *(Weekly)* 912
DIE GRÜNE *(26 issues yearly)* 923
SCHWEIZER BAUER *(104 issues yearly)* 934
ST. GALLER BAUER *(Weekly)* 938

Agriculture & Farming - Regional
THURGAUER BAUER *(Weekly)* 940

Applied Science & Laboratories

LABMED SCHWEIZ SUISSE SVIZZERA *(11 issues yearly)* 926
PSYCHOSCOPE *(10 issues yearly)* 932

Architecture & Building

Architecture
ARCHITEKTUR TECHNIK *(Monthly)* 914
ARCHITHESE *(6 issues yearly)* 914
EINFAMILIENHÄUSER *(Annual)* 920
HOCHPARTERRE *(10 issues yearly)* 924

Aviation & Aeronautics

Aviation & Aeronautics
AERO REVUE *(10 issues yearly)* 912
CARROSSIER *(8 issues yearly)* 918
COCKPIT *(Monthly)* 918
SKYNEWS.CH *(Monthly)* 937

Catering

Catering, Hotels & Restaurants
GASTRO JOURNAL *(Weekly)* 922

Chemicals

CHIMIA *(10 issues yearly)* 918
CR CHEMISCHE RUNDSCHAU *(10 issues yearly)* 919
SWISSPLASTICS *(10 issues yearly)* 939

Church & School Equipment & Education

Education
ECOLE ROMANDE *(6 issues yearly)* 919
DIE NEUE SCHULPRAXIS *(11 issues yearly)* 929
SCHULBLATT *(24 issues yearly)* 934
SCHULE KONKRET *(8 issues yearly)* 934

Education Teachers
WERKSPUREN *(Quarterly)* 943
ZEITSCHRIFT FÜR PÄDAGOGIK *(6 issues yearly)* 944

Clothing & Textiles

Clothing & Textiles
BULLETIN VSS/FDS *(Quarterly)* 917
SCHWEIZER SPORT & MODE SPORT & MODE SUISSE *(Quarterly)* 935

Commerce, Industry & Management

Commerce Related
ETH GLOBE *(Quarterly)* 920
MQ MANAGEMENT UND QUALITÄT *(10 issues yearly)* 928
SWISS ENGINEERING RTS *(10 issues yearly)* 938
TECHNISCHE RUNDSCHAU *(Monthly)* 939
TOP *(Annual)* 940

Commerce, Industry & Management
AUTO & WIRTSCHAFT *(10 issues yearly)* 915
BERNER KMU AKTUELL *(Monthly)* 916
BILAN *(22 issues yearly)* 916
FINANZ UND WIRTSCHAFT *(104 issues yearly)* 921
GDI IMPULS *(Quarterly)* 922
HANDELSZEITUNG & THE WALL STREET JOURNAL *(Weekly)* 923
IO NEW MANAGEMENT *(8 issues yearly)* 925
ORGANISATOR *(10 issues yearly)* 931
REFLEXIONEN *(6 issues yearly)* 933
SAFETY-PLUS *(Quarterly)* 934
SHAB.CH SCHWEIZERISCHES HANDELSAMTSBLATT FOSC.CH FEUILLE OFFICIELLE SUISSE DU COMMERCE FUSC.CH FOGLIO UFFICIALE SVIZZERO DI COMMERCIO *(252 issues yearly)* 936
SKO ASC ASQ LEADER *(5 issues yearly)* 937
UNTERNEHMER-ZEITUNG *(10 issues yearly)* 941
ZÜRCHER WIRTSCHAFT *(10 issues yearly)* 944

Training & Recruitment
PERSORAMA *(Quarterly)* 931
WIRTSCHAFTSPSYCHOLOGIE *(Quarterly)* 943

Communications, Advertising & Marketing

Communications, Advertising & Marketing
FORM *(6 issues yearly)* 921
MEDIA TREND JOURNAL *(Quarterly)* 928
MK MARKETING & KOMMUNIKATION *(Monthly)* 928

Press
WIRTSCHAFTSJOURNALIST *(6 issues yearly)* 943

Computers & Automation

COMPUTERWORLD *(22 issues yearly)* 918
PCTIPP *(Monthly)* 931
SIR MEDICAL *(6 issues yearly)* 937

Data Processing
COMPUTER SPECTRUM *(Quarterly)* 918

Data Transmission
PROFESSIONAL COMPUTING *(5 issues yearly)* 932

Multimedia
MEGALINK *(Monthly)* 928

Construction

General (Construction)
SCHWEIZER BAUWIRTSCHAFT *(24 issues yearly)* 934

Defence

ASMZ SICHERHEIT SCHWEIZ *(11 issues yearly)* 914
BAUEN & RETTEN *(Quarterly)* 915
SCHWEIZER SOLDAT *(11 issues yearly)* 935

Drinks & Licensed Trade

Licensed Trade, Wines & Spirits
SCHWEIZERISCHE WEINZEITUNG *(10 issues yearly)* 936
VINUM *(10 issues yearly)* 942

Electrical

ELECTRO REVUE *(24 issues yearly)* 920
ET ELEKTROTECHNIK *(11 issues yearly)* 920

Electronics

General (Electronics)
AKTUELLE TECHNIK *(Monthly)* 912

Energy, Fuel & Nuclear

BULLETIN *(16 issues yearly)* 917
ENERGIE & UMWELT *(Quarterly)* 920

Switzerland: Consumer

Music & Performing Arts

Music
ALPENROSEN *(6 issues yearly)* 912
DISSONANCE *(Quarterly)* 919
JAZZ TIME *(Monthly)* 925
TRUMPF-AS *(6 issues yearly)* 941

TV & Radio
RADIO MAGAZIN *(Weekly)* 933
TELE *(Weekly)* 939
TVSTAR *(Weekly)* 941

National & International Periodicals

7SKY MAG *(10 issues yearly)* 911
L' HEBDO *(Weekly)* 923
L' ILLUSTRÉ *(Weekly)* 924
NEBELSPALTER *(10 issues yearly)* 929
SCHWEIZER ILLUSTRIERTE *(Weekly)* 935
SÉLECTION *(Monthly)* 936

Other Classifications

Customer Magazines
COOP COOPZEITUNG *(Weekly)* 918
D IMPULS MAGAZIN *(8 issues yearly)* 919
DROGISTENSTERN *(10 issues yearly)* 919
VIA *(10 issues yearly)* 942

Disability
D-JOURNAL *(6 issues yearly)* 919
HANDICAPFORUM *(Quarterly)* 923

Miscellaneous
MANEGE *(6 issues yearly)* 911
ASTROLOGIE HEUTE *(6 issues yearly)* 914
BERNER ZEITSCHRIFT FÜR GESCHICHTE *(Quarterly)* 916
DAS GOETHEANUM *(45 issues yearly)* 923
MITTELALTER MOYEN AGE MEDIOEVO TEMP MEDIEVAL *(Quarterly)* 928
SCHWEIZERISCHES ARCHIV FÜR VOLKSKUNDE *(Half-yearly)* 936

Popular Science
ANIMAN *(6 issues yearly)* 913

Recreation & Leisure

Camping & Caravanning
CAMPCAR *(8 issues yearly)* 917
CAMPING REVUE *(9 issues yearly)* 917

Children & Youth
JUMI *(8 issues yearly)* 926

Religious

CHOISIR *(11 issues yearly)* 918
CHRISCHONA PANORAMA *(8 issues yearly)* 918
DIALOGUE *(Monthly)* 919
ESPOIR 920
ETHOS *(Monthly)* 920
FERMENT *(6 issues yearly)* 921
FORUM *(26 issues yearly)* 921
G2W *(11 issues yearly)* 922
HANDELN >>>>>> *(Quarterly)* 923
KIRCHE HEUTE *(41 issues yearly)* 926
REVUE JUIVE *(5 issues yearly)* 933
SIGRISTEN-VERBAND AKTUELL *(6 issues yearly)* 937
SONNTAG *(Weekly)* 937
WORT+WÄRCH *(Monthly)* 943

Rural & Regional Interest

AMTSBLATT *(Weekly)* 912
AMTSBLATT DES KANTONS AARGAU *(Weekly)* 912
AMTSBLATT DES KANTONS SOLOTHURN *(Weekly)* 912
AMTSBLATT DES KANTONS ST. GALLEN *(Weekly)* 912
AMTSBLATT DES KANTONS ZÜRICH *(Weekly)* 912
AZEIGER *(Weekly)* 915
KANTON URI AMTSBLATT *(Weekly)* 926
READER'S DIGEST SCHWEIZ *(Monthly)* 933
SCHULBLATT DES KANTONS ST. GALLEN *(11 issues yearly)* 934

Sport

Athletics
FIT FOR LIFE *(11 issues yearly)* 921

Flight
NACHRICHTEN AERO-CLUB OSTSCHWEIZ *(6 issues yearly)* 929

General (Sport)
GYM LIVE *(6 issues yearly)* 923
GYM LIVE *(6 issues yearly)* 923
GYM LIVE *(6 issues yearly)* 923
ZÜRISPORT *(Quarterly)* 945

Outdoor
DIE ALPEN *(Monthly)* 912
CLUBNACHRICHTEN SAC SEKTION BERN *(6 issues yearly)* 918
WANDERLAND *(6 issues yearly)* 942

Water Sports
YACHTING SWISS BOAT *(6 issues yearly)* 943

Student Publications

UNIJOURNAL *(6 issues yearly)* 941

The Arts & Literary

Arts
LA DISTINCTION *(5 issues yearly)* 919
DU *(10 issues yearly)* 919
INDUSTRIEARCHÄOLOGIE *(Quarterly)* 925
KUNST BULLETIN *(10 issues yearly)* 926

Women's Interest Consumer Magazines

Child Care
KIDY SWISS FAMILY *(6 issues yearly)* 926

Crafts
JOURNAL DES ARTS ET MÉTIERS *(Monthly)* 925

Food & Cookery
SAISON-KÜCHE *(Monthly)* 934
VINUM *(10 issues yearly)* 942

Home & Family
ATRIUM *(6 issues yearly)* 914
BON À SAVOIR *(11 issues yearly)* 917
K TIPP *(20 issues yearly)* 926
LEBEN & GLAUBEN *(Weekly)* 927
SCHWEIZER FAMILIE *(Weekly)* 934
WIR ELTERN *(11 issues yearly)* 943
WOHNREVUE *(Monthly)* 943

Home Purchase
DER SCHWEIZERISCHE HAUSEIGENTÜMER *(22 issues yearly)* 935
TOUT L'IMMOBILIER *(46 issues yearly)* 940
WOHNIWIRTSCHAFT *(10 issues yearly)* 943
DER ZÜRCHER HAUSEIGENTÜMER *(Monthly)* 944

Personal Finance
LA BORSA DELLA SPESA *(8 issues yearly)* 917
ÖKK MAGAZIN *(Quarterly)* 930

Retirement
ZEITLUPE *(10 issues yearly)* 944

Slimming & Health
NATÜRLICH LEBEN *(Monthly)* 929

Teenage
TEENSMAG *(6 issues yearly)* 939

Women's Interest
ANNABELLE *(22 issues yearly)* 913
BOLERO *(10 issues yearly)* 917
EDELWEISS *(11 issues yearly)* 919
GALATEA *(10 issues yearly)* 922
PROFIL *(6 issues yearly)* 932

Turkey

Business

Architecture & Building

Interior Design & Flooring
MOBILYA TEKSTIL *(Quarterly)* 946

Clothing & Textiles

Clothing & Textiles
TEKSTIL TEKNIK *(Monthly)* 946

Commerce, Industry & Management

Training & Recruitment
HUMAN RESOURCES *(Monthly)* 946

Communications, Advertising & Marketing

Communications, Advertising & Marketing
MARKETING TÜRKIYE *(24 issues yearly)* 946

Computers & Automation

Data Processing
CHIP *(Monthly)* 945

Personal Computers
PC NET *(Monthly)* 946

Professional Personal Computers
WINDOWS NET MAGAZINE *(Monthly)* 947

Electronics

Telecommunications
TELEPATI TELEKOM *(Monthly)* 946

Finance & Economics

Finance & Economics
CAPITAL *(Monthly)* 945
EKONOMIST *(Weekly)* 945

Food

General (Food)
GASTRONOMI *(6 issues yearly)* 945

Furnishings & Furniture

Furnishings & Furniture - Kitchens & Bathrooms
BANYO MUTFAK *(6 issues yearly)* 945

Health & Medical

Medical Equipment
MEDIKAL & TEKNIK *(Monthly)* 946

Heating & Ventilation

Industrial Heating & Ventilation
TERMODINAMIK *(Monthly)* 946
TESISAT MARKET *(Monthly)* 946

Local Government, Leisure & Recreation

Community Care & Social Services
ROTARY *(6 issues yearly)* 946

Turkey: Consumer

Willings Volume 2
Section 3

Newspapers Index

Newspapers in Europe listed by country, showing circulation figures where available.

Albania: Nationals

Title Circ. Page.

Albania

Nationals

ALBANIAN DAILY NEWS, 2,500 102
GAZETA ALBANIA, 5,000 102
PANORAMA, 25,000 102
SHEKULLI, 25,000 102
STANDARD, 10,000 102
TIRANA OBSERVER, 10,000 102

Andorra

Nationals

BONDIA, 8,000 102

Regional

DIARI D'ANDORRA, 3,200 102
EL PERIODIC D'ANDORRA, 7,700 102

Austria

Nationals

BÖRSEN-KURIER, 11,500 107
CITY, 60,000 108
CORPORAID MAGAZIN, 45,000 108
KRONEN ZEITUNG, 928,740 115
ÖSTERREICH, 303,630 120
DIE PRESSE, 97,418 122
DER STANDARD, 105,541 124
VIA, 27,500 127
WIENER BALLKALENDER, 80,000 128
WIENER JOURNAL, 53,000 128
WIENER ZEITUNG, 26,000 129
WIRTSCHAFTSBLATT, 36,812 129
WIRTSCHAFTSBLATT DELUXE, 50,000 129
WIRTSCHAFTSBLATT INVESTOR, 26,791 129

Regional

IMMO KURIER, 258,890 113
KLEINE ZEITUNG, 207,794 115
KURIER, 209,498 116
NEUE VORARLBERGER TAGESZEITUNG, 12,396 118
NEUES VOLKSBLATT, 23,500 118
OÖ NACHRICHTEN, 139,221 119
SALZBURGER NACHRICHTEN, 84,760 123
TIROLER TAGESZEITUNG 126
VN VORARLBERGER NACHRICHTEN, 69,642 127

Weekly/Local Newspapers

AMTSBLATT DER LANDESHAUPTSTADT LINZ, 850 104
BEZIRKSBLÄTTER KUFSTEIN, 36,387 106
BEZIRKSBLÄTTER PINZGAU, 31,018 106
BEZIRKSBLÄTTER REUTTE, 11,164 106
BEZIRKSBLÄTTER SCHWAZ, 34,211 106
BLUDENZER ANZEIGER, 13,374 107
ENNS STADTMAGAZIN, 35,000 109
DER ENNSTALER, 9,847 109
DIE FURCHE, 20,137 111
HALLER BLATT, 15,392 112
KLAGENFURT, 57,000 115
KURZ&BÜNDIG AMSTETTEN, 39,750 116
KURZ&BÜNDIG KREMS, 33,700 116
KURZ&BÜNDIG MELK-ERLAUFTAL, 40,200 116
KURZ&BÜNDIG ST. PÖLTEN, 49,350 116
LEOBEN STADTMAGAZIN, 16,700 116
LUST AUFS LAND, 496,000 116
MURTALER ZEITUNG, 15,500 118
NACHRICHTENBLATT MARKTGEMEINDE ARNOLDSTEIN, 2,700 118
OBERKÄRNTNER NACHRICHTEN, 46,700 119
OBERKÄRNTNER VOLLTREFFER, 33,100 119
OSTTIROLER BOTE, 17,000 121
R 19, 10,500 122
STEYR, 22,500 125
TELE, 1,215,281 125
TIPS FREISTADT, 25,500 125
TIPS LINZ, 142,400 125
TIPS VÖCKLABRUCK, 53,200 125
TREFFNER GEMEINDEZEITUNG, 2,020 126
UNSER ATTNANG-PUCHHEIM, 4,800 127
WALGAUBLATT, 15,222 128
WANN & WO AM SONNTAG, 126,023 128
WESTSTEIRISCHE RUNDSCHAU, 9,200 128
WIENER BEZIRKS BLATT, 650,000 128
WOCHE HARTBERGER BEZIRKSZEITUNG, 31,100 129
WOCHE OBERSTEIERMARK, 81,287 129
WOCHE VÖLKERMARKT & JAUNTAL, 14,798 129
WOCHE WEIZ & BIRKFELD, 37,685 129

Belarus

Nationals

7 DNEY, 40,000 130
BELGAZETA, 21,300 130
EXPRESS NOVOSTI, 7,000 130
NARODNAYA GAZETA, 40,000 131
SOVIETSKAYA BELORUSSIA, 417,966 131
VECHERNY MINSK, 40,000 131

Belgium

Nationals

7DIMANCHE, 250,000 131
7SUR7.BE 131
DE TIJD, 38,582 133
LA DERNIÈRE HEURE / LES SPORTS, 112,000 133
L' ECHO, 36,000 133
DE GENTENAAR - NIEUWSBLAD, 271,000 135
HEY NIEUWSBLAD OP ZONDAG, 50,000 135
HLN - HET LAATSTE NIEUWS / DE NIUEWE GAZET, 300,000 135
LESOIR.BE 136
LA LIBRE BELGIQUE - GAZETTE DE LIÈGE, 50,000 136
METRO, 290,000 137
LE SOIR, 150,000 139
DE STANDAARD, 100,010 139
DE ZONTAG, 645,000 141

Regional

HET BELANG VAN LIMBURG, 112,000 132
LA CAPITALE - REDACTION CENTRALE - BRUXELLES, 16,000 132
DEMORGEN.BE 133
GAZET VAN ANTWERPEN, 120,000 135
GRENZ-ECHO, 12,382 135
KRANT VAN WEST VLAANDEREN - SIEGE SOCIAL, 94,402 136
LA MEUSE SIEGE ADMINISTRATIF, 125,000 137
DE MORGEN, 70,000 137
NORD-ECLAIR - SIEGE ADMINISTRATIF 138
LA NOUVELLE GAZETTE SIEGE ADMINISTRATIF, 125,000 138
LA PROVINCE SIEGE ADMINISTRATIF, 150,000 138

Weekly/Local Newspapers

PASSE-PARTOUT, 5,000,000 138

Bosnia-Herzegovina

Nationals

DNEVNI AVAZ, 60,000 141
NEZAVISNE NEDJELJNE NOVINE, 20,000 141
NEZAVISNE NOVINE, 20,000 141
OSLOBODJENJE, 25,000 141

Bulgaria

Nationals

168 CHASSA, 65,000 142
24 CHASSA, 80,000 142
7 DNI SPORT, 30,000 142
ATAKA, 15,000 142
CAPITAL, 24,951 142
DNEVEN TRUD, 105,000 142
EUROFOOTBALL, 72,000 142
STANDART, 68,300 142
TELEGRAF, 66,000 142

Croatia

Nationals

JUTARNJI LIST, 115,000 142
NOVI LIST, 87,500 143
SLOBODNA DALMACIJA, 75,000 143

Regional

24SATA, 110,000 142

Cyprus

Nationals

ANTILOGOS, 6,500 143
CYPRUS MAIL, 8,000 143
CYPRUS OBSERVER 143
THE CYPRUS WEEKLY, 15,000 143
ERGATIKI PHONI, 12,000 143
ERGATIKO VIMA, 14,000 143
EVROPA-KIPR 143
HALKIN SESI, 2,000 143
KIBRISLI, 2,500 143
O PHILELEFTHEROS, 17,720 143
POLITIS, 11,000 144
POPKA, 3,500 144
I SIMERINI, 13,000 144
VESTNIK KIPRA, 4,000 144
YENIDÜZEN, 3,500 144

Czech Republic

Nationals

AHA! (DENÍK), 146,538 144
AHA! (NEDĚLNÍ), 137,258 144
BLESK 145
HOSPODÁŘSKÉ NOVINY, 60,848 149
LIDOVÉ NOVINY, 75,985 150
MLADÁ FRONTA DNES, 304,642 151
NEDĚLNÍ BLESK, 346,588 152
ŠÍP PLUS, 118,264 155

Regional

DENÍK ČECHY (SÍŤ), 181,300 147
DENÍK JIŽNÍ ČECHY (SÍŤ), 33,900 147
DENÍK SEVERNÍ ČECHY (SÍŤ), 48,865 147
DENÍK STŘEDNÍ ČECHY + PRAŽSKÝ DENÍK (SÍŤ), 37,900 147
DENÍK VÝCHODNÍ ČECHY (SÍŤ), 58,049 147
FAKTA PRESS, 35,000 148
JIŽNÍ LISTY (OSTRAVA), 48,000 149
KLADNO, 37,000 150
KRAJ VYSOČINA, 215,000 150
KRAJSKÉ LISTY, 132,000 150
KRAJSKÉ NOVINY, 40,000 150
LIBERECKÝ KRAJ, 182,000 150
MĚSÍC V REGIONU, 30,000 151
MĚSTSKÉ NOVINY (ÚSTÍ NAD LABEM), 44,500 151
METRO, 264,658 151
MORAVSKOSLEZSKÝ KRAJ, 490,000 152
MORAVSKÝ REGION, 400,000 152
NAŠE NOVINY (BRNO), 85,000 152
PÁTEK LIDOVÉ NOVINY, 110,918 153
PLZEŇSKÝ KRAJ, 255,400 153
PRAŽSKÝ DENÍK, 11,400 154
PRIO - PORUBSKÁ RADNICE INFORMUJE OBČANY, 35,000 154
PROBRNO, 50,000 154
REGIONÁLNÍ NOVINY ESO, 30,000 154
ŠESTKA, 56,000 155
TUČŇÁK, 71,500 157
U NÁS V KRAJI, 230,000 157

Weekly/Local Newspapers

KURÝR PRAHA, 300,000 150
LISTY HLAVNÍHO MĚSTA PRAHY, 60,000 150

Denmark

Nationals

BERLINGSKE, 102,640 159
BERLINGSKE REJSELIV, 122,933 159
BØRSEN, 72,086 160
B.T., 98,538 160
DEN BLÅ AVIS VEST, 80,000 162
EKSTRA BLADET NYHEDER, 108,478 163
ERHVERVSBLADET, 77,504 163
JYLLANDS POSTEN, 125,096 166
KRISTELIGT DAGBLAD, 26,145 166
LICITATIONEN, 4,111 167
POLITIKEN, 118,718 170

Regional

ÅRHUS STIFTSTIDENDE, 29,167 159
BORNHOLMS TIDENDE, 12,591 160
DAGBLADET HOLSTEBRO/STRUER, 10,906 161
DAGBLADET RINGSTED, 6,404 161
DAGBLADET ROSKILDE, 6,696 161
DR P4 BORNHOLM FORMIDDAG, 7,000 162
FOLKEBLADET LEMVIG, 3,118 164
FYENS STIFTSTIDENDE, 56,379 164
FYNS AMTS AVIS, 16,899 164
HELSINGØR DAGBLAD, 5,919 165
HERNING FOLKEBLAD, 12,626 165
HOLBÆK AMTS VENSTREBLAD, 14,257 165
HORSENS FOLKEBLAD, 15,708 165
MAGASINET MIDT, 40,000 168
MIDTJYLLANDS AVIS SILKEBORG, 14,863 168
MORSØ FOLKEBLAD, 5,547 169
NORDJYSKE STIFTSTIDENDE, 62,075 169
NORDJYSKE STIFTSTIDENDE AALBORG, 26,504 169
NORDJYSKE STIFTSTIDENDE HIMMERLAND, 9,482 169
NORDJYSKE STIFTSTIDENDE HJØRRING, 6,393 169
NORDSCHLESWIGER, 2,399 169
RANDERS AMTSAVIS, 10,922 170
SKIVE FOLKEBLAD, 11,840 171
THISTED DAGBLAD, 8,739 172
VIBORG STIFTS FOLKEBLAD, 10,721 174

Weekly/Local Newspapers

AABENRAA UGE-AVIS, 31,212 158
AARS AVIS, 16,825 158
ADRESSEAVISEN SYDDJURS, 23,427 158
ALBERTSLUND POSTEN, 17,520 159
ALLERØD NYT, 15,900 159
BAGSVÆRD/SØBORG BLADET, 41,297 159
BALLERUP BLADET, 43,234 159
BILLUND UGEAVIS, 18,600 160
BJERRINGBRO AVIS, 19,700 160
BRANDE BLADET, 16,002 160
BRØNSHØJ-HUSUM AVIS, 28,117 160
BUDSTIKKEN AABENRAA, 30,110 160
BUDSTIKKEN KOLDING, 43,147 160
BUDSTIKKEN SØNDERBORG, 38,194 160
CITY AVISEN, 26,361 161
DALUM-HJALLESE AVIS, 19,145 161
DJURSLANDSPOSTEN, 28,100 162

Estonia

Nationals

Title Circ. ... Page.

Finland

Nationals

Regional

Weekly/Local Newspapers

Finland: Weekly/Local Newspapers

Title Circ. ... Page.

PARGAS KUNGÖRELSER - PARAISTEN KUULUTUKSET, 4,854 ... 202
PARIKKALAN-RAUTJÄRVEN SANOMAT, 5,828 ... 202
PERHONJOKILAAKSO, 6,459 ... 203
PERNIÖNSEUDUN LEHTI, 4,208 ... 203
PETÄJÄVESI, 2,080 ... 203
PIEKSÄMÄEN LEHTI, 6,662 ... 203
PIELAVESI - KEITELE, 6,014 ... 203
PIELISJOKISEUTU, 3,652 ... 203
PIETARSAAREN SANOMAT, 2,612 ... 203
PITÄJÄLÄINEN, 4,446 ... 203
PITÄJÄNUUTISET, 5,570 ... 203
POGOSTAN SANOMAT, 5,477 ... 203
POHJANKYRÖ-LEHTI, 5,746 ... 204
POHJOIS-SATAKUNTA, 5,331 ... 204
PUNKALAITUMEN SANOMAT, 3,602 ... 205
PUOLANKA-LEHTI, 2,346 ... 205
PURUVESI, 6,643 ... 205
PUUMALA, 3,247 ... 205
PYHÄJÄRVEN SANOMAT, 4,327 ... 205
PYHÄJOKISEUTU, 6,409 ... 205
RAAHEN SEUTU, 8,760 ... 205
RANNIKKOSEUTU, 7,781 ... 206
RANTALAKEUS, 3,303 ... 206
RANTAPOHJA, 9,919 ... 206
RANTASALMEN LEHTI, 3,122 ... 206
REISJÄRVI, 2,068 ... 206
RUOVESI, 4,424 ... 207
SAMPO-LEHTI, 6,040 ... 207
SATAKUNNAN VIIKKO, 55,000 ... 208
SIEVILÄINEN, 2,727 ... 208
SIIKAJOKILAAKSO, 4,640 ... 208
SIPOON SANOMAT, 3,554 ... 208
SISÄ-SAVO, 7,213 ... 208
SISÄ-SUOMEN LEHTI, 7,412 ... 208
SOISALON SEUTU, 5,050 ... 208
SOMERO, 5,828 ... 209
SOMPIO, 3,482 ... 209
SOTKAMO-LEHTI, 5,794 ... 209
SULKAVA-LEHTI, 2,678 ... 209
SUUPOHJAN SANOMAT, 4,174 ... 210
SUUR-JYVÄSKYLÄN LEHTI, 81,000 ... 210
SUUR-KEURUU, 6,224 ... 210
SYDÄN-HÄMEEN LEHTI, 5,692 ... 211
SYDÄN-SATAKUNTA, 7,287 ... 211
TAMPERELAINEN, 142,000 ... 211
TEISKO-AITOLAHTI, 1,827 ... 212
TEJUKA, 4,047 ... 212
TERVAREITTI, 6,035 ... 212
TURKULAINEN, 118,100 ... 214
TURUN TIENOO, 5,852 ... 214
TYRVÄÄN SANOMAT, 9,110 ... 215
ULVILAN SEUTU, 3,072 ... 215
URJALAN SANOMAT, 5,231 ... 215
UUSI ESPOO, 103,700 ... 215
UUSI LAHTI, 54,500 ... 215
UUSI VANTAA, 85,500 ... 215
UUTIS ALASIN, 2,373 ... 215
UUTIS-JOUSI, 6,492 ... 215
VAAROJEN SANOMAT, 3,822 ... 216
VAKKA-SUOMEN SANOMAT, 8,545 ... 216
VALKEAKOSKEN SANOMAT, 7,510 ... 216
VANTAALAINEN, 58,000 ... 216
VANTAAN SANOMAT, 89,600 ... 216
VIIKKO POHJOIS-KARJALA, 7,193 ... 218
VIIKKO VAPAUS, 6,070 ... 218
VIIKKO-ETEENPÄIN, 5,435 ... 218
VIISKUNTA, 6,091 ... 218
VIISPIIKKINEN, 5,444 ... 218
VIITASAAREN SEUTU, 5,316 ... 218
VUOLIJOKI -LEHTI, 1,180 ... 218
YKKÖSSANOMAT, 3,563 ... 219
YLÄ-KAINUU, 7,980 ... 219
YLÄ-KARJALA, 5,471 ... 219
YLÄ-SATAKUNTA, 7,244 ... 219
YLÖJÄRVEN UUTISET, 6,828 ... 219

France

Nationals

AUJOURD'HUI EN FRANCE, 187,786 ... 222
LA CROIX, 104,901 ... 225
LES ECHOS, 125,984 ... 227
L' EQUIPE, 311,403 ... 228
L' EQUIPE MAGAZINE, 342,394 ... 228
LE FIGARO, 331,022 ... 229
LE FIGARO MAGAZINE, 444,150 ... 229
FRANCE DIMANCHE, 424,520 ... 230
FRANCE SOIR, 26,214 ... 230
L' HUMANITE, 52,456 ... 231
INTERNATIONAL HERALD TRIBUNE, 219,188 ... 232
INVESTIR, 77,639 ... 232
LE JOURNAL DU DIMANCHE, 267,659 ... 233
LIBERATION, 123,339 ... 234
LE MONDE, 319,418 ... 238
LE NOUVEL ECONOMISTE, 24,952 ... 240
LE PARISIEN - AUJOURD'HUI EN FRANCE, 499,269 ... 241
LA TRIBUNE, 78,463 ... 248

Regional

20 MINUTES PARIS, 658,920 ... 220
L' AISNE NOUVELLE, 19,004 ... 221
L' ALSACE, 105,795 ... 221
L' ALSACE EDITION DE GUEBWILLER ... 221
LE BERRY REPUBLICAIN, 30,168 ... 222
LE BIEN PUBLIC - S DEPECHES, 47,788 ... 222
CENTRE PRESSE, 22,350 ... 224
LA CHARENTE LIBRE, 38,228 ... 224
LA CHRONIQUE REPUBLICAINE, 15,202 ... 224
CORSE MATIN, 42,312 ... 225
LE COURRIER CAUCHOIS, 40,972 ... 225
LE COURRIER DE LA MAYENNE, 27,726 ... 225
LE COURRIER DE L'OUEST, 102,225 ... 225
LE COURRIER PICARD, 62,000 ... 225
LE DAUPHINE LIBERE, 241,867 ... 226
LE DAUPHINE LIBERE EDITION ISERE NORD BOURGOIN - VILLE NOUVELLE, 330,551 ... 226
LA DEPECHE DU MIDI, 190,875 ... 226
LA DEPECHE DU MIDI EDITION DE L'AUDE, 250,000 ... 226
LA DEPECHE DU MIDI EDITION DE L'AVEYRON, 223,067 ... 226
LA DEPECHE DU MIDI EDITION DU LOT-ET-GARONNE, 255,107 ... 226
LA DEPECHE DU MIDI EDITION DU TARN SUD, 192,075 ... 226
LA DEPECHE DU MIDI EDITION DU TARN-ET-GARONNE, 18,000 ... 226
DIMANCHE OUEST FRANCE, 350,055 ... 226
DIRECT MATIN PLUS, 350,000 ... 227
DIRECT SOIR, 303,162 ... 227
DNA - DERNIERES NOUVELLES D'ALSACE STRASBOURG, 196,301 ... 227
LA DORDOGNE LIBRE, 6,648 ... 227
L' ECHO REPUBLICAIN, 30,382 ... 227
L' ECLAIR PYRENEES, 8,960 ... 227
L' EST ECLAIR, 27,821 ... 229
L' EST REPUBLICAIN HOUDEMONT, 186,502 ... 229
L' EVEIL DE LA HAUTE LOIRE, 14,422 ... 229
LE HIC, 90,000 ... 231
L' INDEPENDANT BUREAU PARISIEN, 65,523 ... 232
L' INDEPENDANT RIVESALTES, 65,523 ... 232
LE JOURNAL DE LA HAUTE MARNE, 25,832 ... 233
LE JOURNAL DE SAONE ET LOIRE, 58,036 ... 233
LE JOURNAL DU CENTRE, 30,050 ... 233
LIBERATION CHAMPAGNE, 6,190 ... 234
LIBERTE DIMANCHE, 14,491 ... 234
LILLEPLUS, 50,853 ... 234
LYONPLUS, 62,519 ... 235
LE MAINE LIBRE - EDITION LE MANS, 46,117 ... 235
LA MARSEILISE, 139,000 ... 236
LA MARSEILLAISE EDITION DU VAR, 6,094 ... 237
METRO FRANCE (PARIS & LOCAL EDITIONS), 632,000 ... 237
MIDI LIBRE BUREAU PARISIEN, 180,000 ... 237
MIDI LIBRE MONTPELLIER, 147,392 ... 237
LA MONTAGNE CLERMONT-FERRAND, 191,639 ... 238
LA MONTAGNE NOIRE, 1,900 ... 238
NICE-MATIN NICE - SIEGE SOCIAL, 115,791 ... 239
NORD ÉCLAIR - ROUBAIX, 26,742 ... 239
NORD LITTORAL, 10,182 ... 239
LES NOUVEL DE TAHITI, 6,500 ... 240
LA NOUVELLE REPUBLIQUE DES PYRENEES, 12,867 ... 240
LA NOUVELLE REPUBLIQUE DU CENTRE-OUEST EDITION D'INDRE-ET-LOIRE TOURS ET LA BANLIEUE, 215,535 ... 240
OUEST FRANCE RENNES, 762,233 ... 240
PARIS NORMANDIE ROUEN, 61,425 ... 241
LE PARISIEN - PARIS, 311,483 ... 241
LE PETIT BU DU LOT ET GARONNE, 9,790 ... 241
LE POPULAIRE DU CENTRE: EDITION HAUTE-VIENNE, 42,858 ... 242
LA PRESSE DE MANCHE, 25,574 ... 242
PRESSE OCEAN NANTES, 45,204 ... 242
LE PROGRES EDITION LYON-VILLEURBANNE-CALUIRE, 222,570 ... 242
LA PROVENCE, 146,772 ... 242
LE REPUBLICAIN LORRAIN METZ, 145,475 ... 244
LA REPUBLIQUE DE SEINE ET MARNE, 22,063 ... 244
LA REPUBLIQUE DES PYRENEES, 32,465 ... 244
LA RÉPUBLIQUE DU CENTRE - EDITION DU LOIRET, 51,029 ... 244
SUD OUEST BORDEAUX, 313,031 ... 246
SUD OUEST DIMANCHE, 286,525 ... 246
LE TELEGRAMME DE BREST ET DE L'OUEST MORLAIX, 201,579 ... 247
LE TELEGRAMME DIMANCHE, 141,479 ... 247
LE TELEGRAMME DU FINISTERE NORD EDITIONS DE BREST OUEST BREST EST ET BREST, 215,000 ... 247
LA TRIBUNE LE PROGRES SAINT-ETIENNE ... 248
L' UNION REIMS, 106,384 ... 248
VAR-MATIN NICE-MATIN TOULON SIEGE SOCIAL, 75,520 ... 249
LA VOIX DU NORD EDITION DU NORD LILLE, 290,345 ... 250
VOSGES MATIN EPINAL, 50,000 ... 250
L' YONNE RÉPUBLICAINE AUXERRE, 36,682 ... 250
L' YONNE RÉPUBLICAINE: EDITION SUD, 36,682 ... 250

Weekly/Local Newspapers

A NOUS PARIS ... 220
LE TARN LIBRE, 25,000 ... 246

Germany

Nationals

AUDIOPHIL, 80,000 ... 270
BERLINER ZUGPFERDE, 450,000 ... 286
BILD, 2,917,454 ... 289
BILD AM SONNTAG, 1,533,020 ... 289
BILD.DE ... 290
BUCHJOURNAL, 267,502 ... 301
FAZ.NET ... 350
FEINE WELT, 32,000 ... 350
FEINE WELT, 32,000 ... 350
FEINE WELT, 47,000 ... 350
FEINE WELT, 35,000 ... 350
FINANCIAL TIMES DEUTSCHLAND, 102,188 ... 352
FRANKFURTER ALLGEMEINE, 396,793 ... 358
FRANKFURTER ALLGEMEINE SONNTAGSZEITUNG, 385,970 ... 358
FRANKFURTER RUNDSCHAU, 145,691 ... 359
HALBSTARK, 90,000 ... 384
HANDELSBLATT, 140,765 ... 387
HEIMSPIEL, 81,285 ... 392
ICON, 550,000 ... 399
INITIATIVBANKING, 185,800 ... 405
INTERNATIONAL HERALD TRIBUNE - FRANKFURT, 21,416 ... 406
JUNGE WELT, 18,500 ... 413
LUX, 494,000 ... 438
MAIN FEELING, 30,000 ... 440
LE MONDE DIPLOMATIQUE, 85,400 ... 457
NEUES DEUTSCHLAND, 35,872 ... 469
REISEWELT, 413,887 ... 503
SÜDDEUTSCHE ZEITUNG, 530,743 ... 533
SÜDDEUTSCHE ZEITUNG GOLF SPIELEN, 489,391 ... 533
SÜDDEUTSCHE ZEITUNG MAGAZIN, 585,693 ... 534
SÜDDEUTSCHE ZEITUNG WOHLFÜHLEN, 493,364 ... 534
SUEDDEUTSCHE.DE ... 534
DIE TAGESPOST, 11,658 ... 537
TAZ.DE ... 538
TAZ.DIE TAGESZEITUNG, 68,021 ... 538
VISAVIS WEB-BUSINESS, 120,000 ... 558
DIE WELT, 274,137 ... 563
WELT AKTUELL, 41,000 ... 563
WELT AM SONNTAG, 422,277 ... 563
WELT ONLINE ... 564
DIE ZEIT, 534,624 ... 579

Regional

AACHENER NACHRICHTEN, 129,569 ... 253
AACHENER ZEITUNG, 129,569 ... 253
AALENER NACHRICHTEN, 10,690 ... 253
AAR-BOTE, 63,127 ... 253
ABENDZEITUNG, 120,525 ... 253
ABENDZEITUNG.DE ... 253
ACHER- UND BÜHLER BOTE, 19,728 ... 254
ACHER-RENCH-ZEITUNG, 13,322 ... 254
ACHIMER KREISBLATT, 22,726 ... 254
AHLENER TAGEBLATT, 22,750 ... 257
AHLENER ZEITUNG, 7,119 ... 257
AICHACHER NACHRICHTEN, 6,195 ... 257
AICHACHER ZEITUNG, 9,059 ... 257
ALB BOTE, 130,526 ... 259
ALB BOTE, 5,063 ... 259
ALFELDER ZEITUNG, 7,705 ... 259
ALLER-ZEITUNG, 38,268 ... 259
ALLER-ZEITUNG.DE ... 259
ALLGÄUER ANZEIGEBLATT, 17,774 ... 259
ALLGÄUER ZEITUNG, 107,257 ... 259
ALLGEMEINE LABER-ZEITUNG - HEIMATAUSG. D. STRAUBINGER TAGBLATTS, 6,990 ... 260
ALLGEMEINE ZEITUNG, 109,123 ... 260
ALLGEMEINE ZEITUNG, 17,950 ... 260
ALLGEMEINE ZEITUNG DER LÜNEBURGER HEIDE, 17,804 ... 260
ALLGEMEINER ANZEIGER, 3,359 ... 260
ALL-IN.DE ... 261
ALSFELDER ALLGEMEINE, 3,578 ... 261
ALTENAER KREISBLATT, 3,879 ... 261
ALTLÄNDER TAGEBLATT, 8,969 ... 262
ALTMARK ZEITUNG, 18,581 ... 262
ALTMÜHL-BOTE, 8,178 ... 262
ALT-NEUÖTTINGER ANZEIGER, 20,257 ... 262
AMBERGER ZEITUNG, 26,411 ... 262
AN-ONLINE.DE ... 263
ANZEIGER FÜR HARLINGERLAND, 14,364 ... 264
AUGSBURGER ALLGEMEINE, 100,161 ... 271
AUGSBURGER ALLGEMEINE ONLINE ... 271
AZ NÜRNBERG, 15,920 ... 275
AZ-WEB.DE ... 275
BA BERGSTRÄSSER ANZEIGER, 14,515 ... 275
BACKNANGER KREISZEITUNG, 16,867 ... 276
BADEN ONLINE ... 276
BADISCHE NEUESTE NACHRICHTEN, 131,363 ... 276
BADISCHE ZEITUNG, 162,979 ... 277
BADISCHE ZEITUNG.DE ... 277
BADISCHES TAGBLATT, 34,973 ... 277
BARMSTEDTER ZEITUNG, 2,521 ... 278
BAYERISCHE RUNDSCHAU, 14,868 ... 281
DER BAYERWALD-BOTE, 17,847 ... 282
BAYERWALD-ECHO, 15,538 ... 282
BBV-NET ... 282
BEOBACHTER, 5,364 ... 283
BERCHTESGADENER ANZEIGER, 5,336 ... 284
BERGEDORFER ZEITUNG, 17,776 ... 284
BERGISCHE LANDESZEITUNG, 233,008 ... 284
BERGISCHE MORGENPOST, 13,432 ... 284
BERLINER KURIER, 174,579 ... 285
BERLINER KURIER AM SONNTAG, 174,579 ... 285
BERLINER MORGENPOST, 163,533 ... 285
BERLINER ZEITUNG, 185,825 ... 285
BERSENBRÜCKER KREISBLATT, 13,638 ... 286

Germany: Regional

Germany: Regional

Title Circ. Page.

Weekly/Local Newspapers

Germany: Weekly/Local Newspapers

Title Circ. Page.

Gibraltar

Nationals

Greece

Nationals

Regional

Hungary

Nationals

Regional

Italy: Nationals

Title Circ. Page.

IL MANIFESTO, 84,000 ... 640
IL MESSAGGERO, 400,000 ... 640
LA NAZIONE, 215,000 ... 642
LA REPUBBLICA, 597,694 ... 645
IL RESTO DEL CARLINO, 307,000 ... 645
SECOLO D'ITALIA, 35,000 ... 646
SETTE (CORRIERE DELLA SERA), 860,000 ... 647
IL SOLE 24 ORE, 500,000 ... 647
LA STAMPA, 470,000 ... 647
IL TEMPO, 100,000 ... 648
TUTTOSPORT, 205,000 ... 649
L' UNITA' ... 650
VIVIMILANO (CORRIERE DELLA SERA) . 650

Regional

IL CITTADINO LODI, 49,000 ... 629
LIBERTA', 38,000 ... 639
IL SECOLO XIX, 127,000 ... 646

Weekly/Local Newspapers

GIORNALE DI ERBA ... 636
IL GIORNALE DI LECCO, 17,000 ... 636
IL GIORNALE DI VIMERCATE, 10,000 ... 636

Latvia

Nationals

7 SEKRETOV, 34,000 ... 651
BIZNESS & BALTIJA, 12,000 ... 651
CHAS, 13,100 ... 651
DELOVYE VESTI, 38,000 ... 651
DIENA, 55,000 ... 651
DIENAS BIZNESS, 12,000 ... 651
LATVIJAS AVIZE, 48,000 ... 651
LATVIJAS SANTIMS, 170,000 ... 652
LATVIJAS VESTNESIS, 3,500 ... 652
NEATKARIGA RITA AVIZE, 35,000 ... 652
SUBBOTA, 46,150 ... 652
VESTI, 36,000 ... 652
VESTI SEGODNJA, 38,000 ... 652

Liechtenstein

Nationals

AUTO FRÜHLING, 11,000 ... 652
BAUEN WOHNEN, 11,000 ... 652
LIECHTENSTEINER VATERLAND, 10,373 ... 652
LIECHTENSTEINER VOLKSBLATT, 9,000 ... 653
LIECHTENSTEINS FUSSBALL ... 653
LIFESTYLE, 11,000 ... 653
PE CE, 11,000 ... 653
WEIHNACHTEN ... 653
WIRTSCHAFT REGIONAL ... 653

Regional

ABC-SCHÜTZEN ... 652

Weekly/Local Newspapers

DORFSPIEGEL TRIESENBERG, 1,400 ... 652
LIECHTENSTEINER VATERLAND, 20,145 ... 652
LIECHTENSTEINER VOLKSBLATT, 20,000 ... 653
NEUE LIEWO, 34,230 ... 653

Lithuania

Nationals

EKSPRESS NEDELIA, 68,000 ... 653
LAISVAS LAIKRASTIS, 32,400 ... 653
LIETUVOS RYTAS, 165,000 ... 653
LIETUVOS ZINIOS, 26,900 ... 654
LITOVSKIJ KURJER, 30,000 ... 654
OBZOR, 36,000 ... 654
RESPUBLIKA, 37,600 ... 654
VAKARO ZINIOS, 65,000 ... 654

Luxembourg

Nationals

352 LUXEMBOURG NEWS, 5,000 ... 654
D'LETZEBUERGER LAND, 7,500 ... 655
D'WORT (LUXEMBOURG), 82,327 ... 655
LËTZEBUERGER JOURNAL, 8,500 ... 656
LUX-POST, 140,000 ... 656
POINT 24, 72,000 ... 656
LE QUOTIDIEN, 8,500 ... 656
TAGEBLATT - ZEITUNG FIR LETZEBUERG, 27,000 ... 657
LA VOIX DU LUXEMBOURG, 8,578 ... 657
ZLV - ZEITUNG VUM LËTZEBUERGER VOLLEK, 9,000 ... 657

Regional

EXPRESS (ARDENER EXPRESS & LOKAL EXPRESS), 52,000 ... 655
SAUER ZEIDUNG, 14,000 ... 656

Macedonia

Nationals

DNEVNIK, 55,000 ... 657
MAKEDONSKI SPORT, 12,000 ... 657
NOVA MAKEDONIJA, 15,000 ... 657
UTRINSKI VESNIK, 25,000 ... 657
VECER, 10,000 ... 657

Malta

Nationals

KULLHADD, 20,000 ... 657
THE MALTA INDEPENDENT, 11,000 ... 657
THE MALTA INDEPENDENT ON SUNDAY, 20,000 ... 657
IL- MUMENT, 20,000 ... 658
IN- NAZZJON, 22,000 ... 658
L- ORIZZONT, 22,000 ... 658
THE SUNDAY TIMES, 40,000 ... 658
THE TIMES, 21,000 ... 658
IT- TORCA, 30,000 ... 658

Moldova

Nationals

COMERSANT PLUS, 3,000 ... 658
JURNAL DE CHIŞINĂU, 15,000 ... 658
KISINEVSKY OBOZREVATEL, 6,000 ... 658
MOLDAVSKIE VEDOMOSTI, 6,000 ... 658
NEZAVISIMAYA MOLDOVA, 17,000 ... 658
TIMPUL DE DIMINEAȚA, 19,227 ... 658

Monaco

Regional

MONACO-MATIN EDITION MONEGASQUE DE NICE-MATIN ... 659
L' OBSERVATEUR DE MONACO, 1,600 659

Weekly/Local Newspapers

MONACO HEBDO, 6,000 ... 659

Netherlands

Nationals

DAGBLAD DE PERS, 244,138 ... 669
NEDERLANDS DAGBLAD, 30,150 ... 690
NRC HANDELSBLAD, 200,723 ... 692
NRC WEEKBLAD, 229,285 ... 692
SPITS, 382,273 ... 705
DE TELEGRAAF, 648,958 ... 707
TROUW, 106,440 ... 710
DE VOLKSKRANT, 262,183 ... 714

Regional

AD GROENE HART, 40,574 ... 659
AD ROTTERDAMS DAGBLAD, 125,194 . 659
AD UTRECHTS NIEUWSBLAD, 55,932 .. 660
ALMERE VANDAAG, 78,153 ... 660
ALPHEN.CC, 19,241 ... 660
BN DESTEM, 112,074 ... 664
BRABANTS DAGBLAD, 129,216 ... 665
DAGBLAD DE LIMBURGER, 129,172 ... 669
DAGBLAD VAN HET NOORDEN, 137,813 ... 669
ED, 107,804 ... 671
DE GELDERLANDER, 148,592 ... 676
IJMUIDER COURANT, 6,918 ... 680
LIMBURGS DAGBLAD, 43,730 ... 685
HET PAROOL, 87,658 ... 696
PROVINCIALE ZEEUWSE COURANT, 54,570 ... 699
REFORMATORISCH DAGBLAD, 53,629 700
DE STENTOR, 130,828 ... 706

Weekly/Local Newspapers

BEDUMER NIEUWS EN ADVERTENTIEBLAD, 4,600 ... 663
DE BERGEN OP ZOOMSE BODE, 29,400 ... 663
DE BERGEN OP ZOOMSE BODE, ED. ZONDAG, 29,800 ... 663
DE BILDTSE POST, 18,600 ... 664
DE BREDASE BODE, 74,500 ... 665
BRIELS NIEUWSLAND, 7,800 ... 665
DE BUNSCHOTER (H.A.H.), 7,750 ... 666
'T CONTACT, 14,500 ... 668
CTR/DE POLDERBODE, 7,850 ... 669
DE DALFSER MARSKRAMER, 22,000 ... 669
DORPSKLANKEN, 4,500 ... 670
DE EEMSLANDER, 33,000 ... 671
EENDRACHTBODE, DE THOOLSE COURANT, 7,000 ... 671
ELNA, 8,900 ... 672
DE ETTEN-LEURSE BODE, 18,700 ... 673
EXTRA, 22,500 ... 673
GROOT HELLEVOET, 20,500 ... 677
GROOT WESTLAND, 47,000 ... 677
DE HAARLEMMER, 76,000 ... 677
DE HALDERBERGSE BODE, 13,500 ... 678
HEEMSTEEDSE COURANT, 27,645 ... 678
DE HERAUT, 22,500 ... 678
DE HOEKSE KRANT, 6,000 ... 678
HOOGEVEENSCHE COURANT, 10,300 . 679
HUIS AAN HUIS, 36,000 ... 679
DE IJSSELBODE, 24,000 ... 680
KATWIJK SPECIAAL, 18,000 ... 682
DE KATWIJKSCHE POST, 8,300 ... 682
DE KOGGENLANDER, 4,965 ... 683
LEIDERDORPS WEEKBLAD, 17,000 ... 684
LEIDS NIEUWSBLAD WEEKEND, 94,550 ... 684
MEDEMBLIKKER COURANT, 18,130 ... 687
DE MIDDENSTANDER, 31,000 ... 688
MONSTERSE COURANT, 9,500 ... 689
MONTFERLAND NIEUWS, 17,900 ... 689
DE NIEUWE SCHAKEL, 4,400 ... 691
NIEUWSBLAD VAN NOORD-OOST FRIESLAND, 7,500 ... 691
NIEUWSBLAD VOOR CASTRICUM, 17,500 ... 691
DE NOORDOOSTPOLDER, 61,400 ... 692
NOORDWIJKERHOUTS WEEKBLAD, 7,000 ... 692
ONS WEEKBLAD, 12,000 ... 694
HET OP ZONDAG, 107,000 ... 695
DE OVERSCHIESE KRANT, 12,800 ... 695
PEEL EN MAAS, 13,000 ... 696
DE POSTILJON, EDITIE ALEXANDERPOLDER E.O., 45,000 ... 698
DE POSTILJON, EDITIE ZOETERMEER, 68,000 ... 698
PRETTIG WEEKEND, 22,500 ... 698
RIJSSENS NIEUWSBLAD, 31,800 ... 701
DE ROOSENDAALSE BODE, 35,000 ... 702
DE ROOSENDAALSE BODE, ED. ZONDAG, 35,000 ... 702
DE ROSKAM, 10,000 ... 702
ROZENBURGSE COURANT DE SCHAKEL, 7,000 ... 702
DE RUCPHENSE BODE, 10,500 ... 702
SCHAAPSKOOI, 28,250 ... 703
SCHAGEN OP ZONDAG, 37,800 ... 703
HET SCHAGER WEEKBLAD, 30,500 ... 703
DE SCHELDEPOST, 5,500 ... 703
SNEEKER NIEUWSBLAD, 3,200 ... 704
DE STADSKRANT, 13,500 ... 705
STADSKRANT VEGHEL, 46,675 ... 705
STADSNIEUWS, 109,500 ... 705
DE TOREN, 52,000 ... 709
TROMPETTER ROERMOND WEEKEND, 69,500 ... 710
UDENS WEEKBLAD, 95,375 ... 711
VOORSTER NIEUWS, 13,500 ... 714
DE WASSENAARDER, 14,000 ... 715
WATERLAND WELZIJN, 51,000 ... 715
WEEKBLAD REGIO OSS, 49,300 ... 715
WEEKBLAD SPIJKENISSE, 44,000 ... 715
WESTFRIES WEEKBLAD, 86,120 ... 716
WESTVOORNSE COURANT, 14,000 ... 716
WIERINGER COURANT, 5,400 ... 716
WITTE WEEKBLAD EDITIE BADHOEVEDORP E.O., 7,500 ... 717
WITTE WEEKBLAD EDITIE HILLEGOM E.O., 11,300 ... 717
WITTE WEEKBLAD EDITIE TEYLINGEN & NOORDWIJKERHOUT, 19,925 ... 717
WITTE WEEKBLAD EDITIE ZWANENBURG E.O., 7,350 ... 717
DE WOENSDRECHTSE BODE, 9,800 ... 717
DE WOONBODE 'T GOOI, 138,020 ... 717
ZAANSTREEK OP ZONDAG, 74,900 ... 717
DE ZEEKANT, 11,350 ... 718
ZONDAG, WEEKBLAD VOOR WEST-FRIESLAND, 85,400 ... 718
ZONDAGOCHTENDBLAD BEVERWIJK/HEEMSKERK, 37,900 ... 718
ZONDAGOCHTENDBLAD HEILOO/CASTRICUM, 31,700 ... 718
DE ZUNDERTSE BODE, 9,300 ... 719
ZWARTSLUIZER REKLAMEBLAD, 2,425 719

Norway

Nationals

AFTENPOSTEN; DEBATTREDAKSJONEN, 250,179 ... 720
DAGBLADET; NYHETSREDAKSJONEN, 123,383 ... 725
DAGENS NÆRINGSLIV, 81,391 ... 725
DAGSAVISEN, 29,041 ... 725
NATIONEN, 15,670 ... 741
VÅRT LAND, 26,344 ... 753
VG, 284,414 ... 753

Regional

ADRESSEAVISEN, 75,835 ... 719
AGDERPOSTEN ... 720
AKERSHUS AMTSTIDENDE, 8,621 ... 720
ALTAPOSTEN, 5,505 ... 720
BERGENS TIDENDE, 83,086 ... 722
BUDSTIKKA, 28,264 ... 724
DAGEN, 10,842 ... 725
DALANE TIDENDE, 8,418 ... 725
FÆDRELANDSVENNEN, 41,326 ... 727
FARSUNDS AVIS, 6,103 ... 728
FINNMARK DAGBLAD, 8,813 ... 728
FINNMARKEN, 7,060 ... 728
FIRDA, 13,875 ... 728
FOSNA-FOLKET, 7,570 ... 730
FREDRIKSSTAD BLAD, 22,883 ... 730
FREMOVER, 8,835 ... 730
GJENGANGEREN, 6,173 ... 731
GLÅMDALEN, 19,370 ... 731
GUDBRANDSDØLEN DAGNINGEN, 26,458 ... 731
HADELAND, 7,487 ... 732
HALDEN ARBEIDERBLAD, 8,533 ... 732
HAMAR ARBEIDERBLAD, 26,677 ... 732
HARSTAD TIDENDE, 13,173 ... 732
HAUGESUNDS AVIS, 31,907 ... 732
HELGELAND ARBEIDERBLAD, 8,939 ... 732

Title Circ. Page.

Poland

Nationals

Regional

Weekly/Local Newspapers

Portugal

Nationals

Regional

Weekly/Local Newspapers

Romania

Nationals

Russian Federation

Nationals

Regional

Weekly/Local Newspapers

Title Circ. Page.

San Marino

Nationals

LA TRIBUNA SAMMARINESE ... 829

Serbia

Nationals

BORBA, 15,000 ... 829
DANAS, 30,000 ... 829
GLAS JAVNOSTI, 32,000 ... 829
POLITIKA, 85,000 ... 829
VECERNJE NOVOSTI, 200,000 ... 829

Slovakia

Nationals

HOSPODÁRSKE NOVINY, 32,000 ... 829
NOVÝ CAS, 210,000 ... 830
NOVY CAS VÍKEND, 330,000 ... 830
PRAVDA, 90,000 ... 830
THE SLOVAK SPECTATOR, 8,500 ... 830
SME, 92,369 ... 830
ÚJ SZÓ, 35,500 ... 830

Regional

KOSICKY DENNIK KORZAR, 22,153 ... 830
PRESOVKY DENNIK KORZAR, 12,200 ... 830
SPISSKY DENNIK KORZAR, 4,137 ... 830
TATRANSKY DENNIK KORZAR, 3,283 ... 830
ZEMPLINSKY DENNIK KORZAR, 5,021 ... 830

Slovenia

Nationals

DELO, 93,000 ... 830
DEMOKRACIJA, 11,000 ... 831
DIREKT, 18,000 ... 831
DNEVNIK, 59,000 ... 831
DRUŽINA, 53,000 ... 831
MLADINA, 9,544 ... 831
NEDELJSKI DNEVNIK, 148,000 ... 831
REPORTER, 15,000 ... 831
SLOVENIA TIMES, 10,000 ... 831

Regional

DOBRO JUTRO, 290,000 ... 831

Spain

Nationals

ABC, 359,842 ... 831
AS, 307,151 ... 832
CINCO DÍAS, 46,252 ... 833
EXPANSIÓN, 77,153 ... 837
LA GACETA DE LOS NEGOCIOS, 31,000 ... 837
MARCA, 527,478 ... 839
EL MUNDO DEL SIGLO VEINTIUNO, 401,902 ... 840
EL MUNDO DEPORTIVO, 100,737 ... 840
EL PAÍS, 597,407 ... 841
EL PERIÓDICO DE CATALUNYA, 236,000 ... 841
PÚBLICO, 132,441 ... 842
LA RAZÓN, 207,631 ... 842
SPORT, 182,258 ... 843
LA VANGUARDIA, 240,978 ... 844

Regional

EL 9 NOU D'OSONA I DEL RIPOLLÈS, 10,985 ... 831
EL 9 NOU-VALLES ORIENTAL, 5,431 ... 831
EL ADELANTADO DE SEGOVIA, 4,000 ... 832
EL ADELANTO DE SALAMANCA, 6,866 ... 832
ALERTA-EL DIARIO DE CANTABRIA, 26,610 ... 832
ATLÁNTICO DIARIO, 5,359 ... 832
AVUI+, 45,500 ... 833
CANARIAS 7, 30,152 ... 833
CIUDAD DE ALCOY, 5,200 ... 833
EL COMERCIO, 40,000 ... 834
CÓRDOBA, 17,294 ... 834
EL CORREO, 144,892 ... 834
EL CORREO DE ANDALUCÍA, 20,774 ... 834
EL CORREO DE BURGOS, 7,000 ... 834
EL CORREO GALLEGO, 20,000 ... 834
LA CRÓNICA DE LEÓN, 7,874 ... 834
DEIA, 26,365 ... 834
EL DÍA, 28,018 ... 834
EL DÍA DE CORDOBA, 200,000 ... 835
EL DÍA DE CUENCA, 8,500 ... 835
EL DÍA DE TOLEDO, 7,000 ... 835
DIARI DE BALEARES, 15,325 ... 835
DIARI DE GIRONA, 8,050 ... 835
DIARI DE SABADELL, 6,309 ... 835
DIARI DE TARRAGONA, 16,801 ... 835
DIARI DE TERRASSA, 6,488 ... 835
DIARIO DE ALCALÁ, 10,000 ... 835
DIARIO DE AVISOS, 16,484 ... 835
DIARIO DE BURGOS, 14,078 ... 835
DIARIO DE CÁDIZ, 34,638 ... 835
DIARIO DE IBIZA, 9,151 ... 835
DIARIO DE JEREZ, 13,000 ... 835
DIARIO DE LEÓN, 18,903 ... 835
DIARIO DE MALLORCA, 26,000 ... 835
DIARIO DE NAVARRA, 67,524 ... 835
DIARIO DE NOTICIAS DE NAVARRA, 24,006 ... 835
DIARIO DE PONTEVEDRA, 8,366 ... 835
DIARIO DE SEVILLA, 30,491 ... 835
DIARIO DE TERUEL, 4,000 ... 835
DIARIO DEL ALTO ARAGÓN, 9,250 ... 835
DIARIO MÁLAGA COSTA DEL SOL, 17,000 ... 835
EL DIARIO MONTAÑES, 38,078 ... 836
EL DIARIO PALENTINO, 5,114 ... 836
EL DIARIO VASCO, 95,000 ... 836
EQUIPO, 14,000 ... 836
ESTADIO DEPORTIVO, 11,774 ... 836
EUROPA SUR, 5,081 ... 836
EL FARO DE CEUTA, 3,500 ... 837
FARO DE VIGO, 49,800 ... 837
LA GACETA REGIONAL DE SALAMANCA, 15,033 ... 837
GENTE EN BURGOS, 50,000 ... 837
HERALDO DE ARAGÓN, 100,000 ... 837
HERALDO DE HUESCA, 5,819 ... 838
HERALDO DE SORIA 7 DÍAS, 4,199 ... 838
HOY - DIARIO DE EXTREMADURA, 25,892 ... 838
HUELVA INFORMACIÓN, 8,185 ... 838
IDEAL, 37,765 ... 838
EL IDEAL GALLEGO, 13,705 ... 838
INFORMACIÓN, 223,425 ... 838
JAÉN, 8,678 ... 838
LEVANTE DE CASTELLÓN, 6,200 ... 839
LEVANTE (EL MERCANTIL VALENCIANO), 70,000 ... 839
MAJORCA DAILY BULLETIN, 7,000 ... 839
LA MAÑANA, 7,358 ... 839
MENORCA DIARIO INSULAR, 7,000 ... 839
EL MUNDO CASTELLÓN AL DÍA, 6,500 ... 840
EL MUNDO DE ALICANTE, 14,302 ... 840
EL MUNDO DE ANDALUCIA, 286,685 ... 840
EL MUNDO DE CASTILLA Y LEÓN, 26,461 ... 840
EL MUNDO DE CATALUNYA, 26,000 ... 840
EL MUNDO DEL PAÍS VASCO, 22,000 ... 840
EL MUNDO DIARIO DE VALLADOLID, 9,368 ... 840
EL MUNDO / EL DIA DE BALEARES, 19,894 ... 840
EL MUNDO VALENCIA, 15,409 ... 840
EL MUNDO Y LA GACETA DE CANARIAS, 17,000 ... 840
EL NORTE DE CASTILLA, 40,000 ... 840
NUEVA ALCARRIA, 5,781 ... 841
LA NUEVA ESPAÑA, 60,000 ... 841
ODIEL INFORMACION, 5,001 ... 841
LA OPINIÓN A CORUÑA, 8,924 ... 841
LA OPINIÓN DE MÁLAGA, 20,948 ... 841
LA OPINIÓN DE MURCIA, 12,522 ... 841
LA OPINIÓN DE TENERIFE, 14,000 ... 841
LA OPINIÓN - EL CORREO DE ZAMORA, 7,325 ... 841
EL PERIÓDICO DE ARAGÓN, 18,656 ... 841
EL PERIÓDICO DE EXTREMADURA, 9,047 ... 841
EL PERIÓDICO LA VOZ DE ASTURIAS, 27,953 ... 841
EL PERIODICO MEDITERRÁNEO, 18,500 ... 841
EL PROGRESO, 18,889 ... 842
LA PROVINCIA, 56,000 ... 842
LAS PROVINCIAS, 53,000 ... 842
EL PUNT, 24,500 ... 842
REGIÓ 7, 9,778 ... 842
LA REGIÓN, 13,929 ... 842
LA RIOJA, 17,000 ... 843
SEGRE, 19,394 ... 843
SUR, 43,634 ... 843
LA TRIBUNA DE ALBACETE, 6,000 ... 844
LA TRIBUNA DE CIUDAD REAL, 5,000 ... 844
LA TRIBUNA DE LA COSTA DEL SOL, 15,000 ... 844
LA TRIBUNA DE SALAMANCA, 10,000 ... 844
ULTIMA HORA, 25,955 ... 844
LA VERDAD, 48,506 ... 844
LA VERDAD (ALBACETE), 3,662 ... 844
LA VERDAD (ALICANTE), 17,000 ... 844
LA VOZ DE ALMERÍA, 9,500 ... 845
LA VOZ DE AVILÉS - EL COMERCIO, 7,500 ... 845
LA VOZ DE GALICIA, 123,639 ... 845
XORNAL DE GALICIA, 15,000 ... 845

Weekly/Local Newspapers

EL 3 DE VUIT, 7,000 ... 831
CLAXON GARRAF PENEDES, 25,500 ... 833
CLAXON MANRESA, 40,000 ... 833
CLAXON TARRAGONA, 50,000 ... 833
LA COMARCA D'OLOT, 3,800 ... 833
DIARI DE VILANOVA, 7,500 ... 835
HORA NOVA, 4,500 ... 838
EL PUNT (VALENCIA), 8,000 ... 842
SETMANARI DE L'ALT EMPORDA, 5,300 ... 843
LA VEU DE L'ANOIA, 6,000 ... 844

Sweden

Nationals

8 SIDOR; 8SIDOR.SE ... 845
AFTONBLADET, 320,200 ... 846
AFTONBLADET; AFTONBLADET.SE ... 846
ALEKURIREN; ALEKURIREN.SE ... 847
ALINGSÅS TIDNING; ALINGSASTIDNING.SE ... 847
ARBETAREN; ARBETAREN.SE ... 849
ARVIKA NYHETER; ARVIKANYHETER.SE ... 850
BAROMETERN-OT; BAROMETERN.SE ... 851
BOHUSLÄNINGEN; BOHUSLANINGEN.SE ... 853
BORÅS TIDNING; BT.SE ... 853
DAGBLADET, NYA SAMHÄLLET; DAGBLADET.SE ... 857
DAGEN; DAGEN.SE ... 857
DAGENS INDUSTRI, 101,700 ... 857
DAGENS INDUSTRI; DI.SE ... 857
DAGENS NYHETER, 298,200 ... 857
DAGENS NYHETER; DN.SE ... 857
DAGENS NYHETER; FAMILJEREDAKTIONEN, 298,200 ... 857
DALABYGDEN; DALABYGDEN.SE ... 857
ENKÖPINGS-POSTEN; EPOSTEN.SE ... 861
ESKILSTUNA-KURIREN / STRENGNÄS TIDNING; WEBB ... 861
EXPRESSEN, 286,500 ... 861
EXPRESSEN; EXPRESSEN.SE ... 862
FILIPSTADS TIDNING; WEBB ... 863
FINNVEDEN NU; WEBB ... 863
FLAMMAN; FLAMMAN.SE ... 863
FOKUS; FOKUS.SE ... 864
FOLKBLADET; FOLKBLADET.SE ... 864
FOLKET; FOLKET.SE ... 864
FRYKSDALS-BYGDEN; FBYGDEN.SE ... 866
GÄSTRIKLANDS TIDNING; WEBB ... 866
GÖTEBORGS FRIA TIDNING; WEBB ... 867
GÖTEBORGS-POSTEN; GP.SE ... 867
GOTLANDS ALLEHANDA; HELAGOTLAND.SE ... 867
GT; GT.SE ... 868
HALLANDS NYHETER; WWW.HN.SE ... 868
HALLANDSPOSTEN; WEBB ... 868
HÄLLEKIS-KURIREN; WEBB ... 868
HELSINGBORGS DAGBLAD; HD.SE ... 869
HUDIKSVALLS TIDNING; HT.SE ... 870
INTERNATIONALEN; WEBB ... 872
JÖNKÖPING NU; WEBB ... 873
KALMAR LÄNS TIDNING / NYBRO TIDNING; WEBB ... 873
KARLSKOGA-KURIREN; WEBB ... 874
KATOLSKT MAGASIN; WEBB ... 874
KRISTDEMOKRATEN; WEBB ... 875
KVÄLLSPOSTEN; KVP.SE ... 876
LANDSKRONADIREKT.SE ... 876
LÄNS-POSTEN; LANSPOSTEN.SE ... 877
LÄNSTIDNINGEN SÖDERTÄLJE; LT.SE ... 877
LERUMS TIDNING; LERUMSTIDNING.COM ... 877
LIDINGÖ TIDNING; LT.NU ... 878
LJUSDALS-POSTEN; LJP.SE ... 878
LJUSNAN; LJUSNAN.SE ... 878
LOKALTIDNINGEN ÄNGELHOLM; WEBB ... 879
LOKALTIDNINGEN AVENYN; WEBB ... 879
LOKALTIDNINGEN BÅSTAD; WEBB ... 879
LOKALTIDNINGEN HELSINGBORG; WEBB ... 879
LOKALTIDNINGEN HÖGANÄS; WEBB ... 879
LOKALTIDNINGEN KÄVLINGE NYA; WEBB ... 879
LOKALTIDNINGEN KLIPPAN/PERSTORP/ BJUV/ÅSTORP/ÖRKELLJUNGA: WEBB ... 879
LOKALTIDNINGEN KRISTIANSTAD; WEBB ... 879
LOKALTIDNINGEN LAHOLM; WEBB ... 879
LOKALTIDNINGEN LANDSKRONA; WEBB ... 879
LOKALTIDNINGEN LOMMABLADET; WEBB ... 879
LOKALTIDNINGEN LUND; WEBB ... 879
LOKALTIDNINGEN MALMÖ; WEBB ... 879
LOKALTIDNINGEN MELLANSKÅNE; WEBB ... 879
LOKALTIDNINGEN SKURUP; WEBB ... 879
LOKALTIDNINGEN SVALÖV; WEBB ... 879
LOKALTIDNINGEN SVEDALA; WEBB ... 879
LOKALTIDNINGEN TRELLEBORG; WEBB ... 879
LOKALTIDNINGEN VÄSTBO ANDAN; WEBB ... 879
LOKALTIDNINGEN VELLINGE - NÄSET; WEBB ... 879
METRO.SE ... 882
MÖLNDALS-POSTEN; MOLNDALSPOSTEN.SE ... 883
MOTALA & VADSTENA TIDNING; MOTALATIDNING.SE ... 883
NACKA VÄRMDÖ POSTEN; NVP.SE ... 884
NORRA SKÅNE; NSK.SE ... 886
NORRKÖPINGS TIDNINGAR; NT.SE ... 886
NORRLÄNDSKA SOCIALDEMOKRATEN; NSD.SE ... 886
NU - DET LIBERALA NYHETSMAGASINET; WEBB ... 886
NYA KRISTINEHAMNS-POSTEN; NKP.SE ... 887
NYA LIDKÖPINGS-TIDNINGEN; NLT.SE ... 887
NYA WERMLANDS-TIDNINGEN; NWT.SE ... 887
NYHETSTIDNINGEN SESAM; SESAM.NU ... 887
NYNÄSHAMNS POSTEN; NHP.SE ... 887
OFFENSIV; WEBB ... 887
ÖLANDSBLADET; WEBB ... 888
ÖSTRAN / NYHETERNA ~ OSKARSHAMN; NYHETERNA.NET, 9,655 ... 889
ÖSTRAN / NYHETERNA; OSTRAN.SE ... 889
PITEÅ-TIDNINGEN; PITEA-TIDNINGEN.SE ... 890
PROLETÄREN; PROLETAREN.SE ... 891
SÄFFLE-TIDNINGEN; SAFFLETIDNING.SE ... 894
SÄNDAREN; SANDAREN.SE ... 894
SKARABORGSBYGDEN; SKARABORGSBYGDEN.SE ... 895
SKÄRGÅRDEN; SKARGARDEN.SE ... 895

Regional

Weekly/Local Newspapers

Switzerland

Nationals

Regional

Weekly/Local Newspapers

Switzerland: Weekly/Local Newspapers

Title Circ. Page.

NOVITATS, 4,669 930
OBERSEE NACHRICHTEN, 63,136 930
OBZ OBERBASELBIETER ZEITUNG, 42,433 930
PÖSCHTLI, 8,432 932
PRATTLER ANZEIGER, 3,339 932
REGION, 31,000 933
REGION, 6,000 933
LE REPUBLICAIN, 3,611 933
RHEINTALISCHE VOLKSZEITUNG, 28,466 933
RIGI ANZEIGER, 31,905 933
RIGI-POST, 3,290 933
RIVISTA DI LUGANO, 6,256 933
RUNDSCHAU RS, 18,700 934
RZ RHONE ZEITUNG, 37,303 934
SCHAFFHAUSER BOCK, 50,325 934
SCHAFFHAUSER NACHRICHTEN, 48,419 934
SEETALER BOTE, 5,204 936
DER SEETALER-DER LINDENBERG 936
SEMPACHER WOCHE, 2,711 936
SONNTAGS BLICK, 247,449 937
SONNTAGS ZEITUNG, 194,764 937
STADTANZEIGER, 48,000 938
STADT-ANZEIGER AARAU, 34,351 938
STADT-ANZEIGER BADEN, 45,104 938
SURSEER WOCHE, 8,528 938
LA VOCE DELLE VALLI/IL SAN BERNADINO, 1,026 942
VOGEL GRYFF, 29,000 942
VOLKSSTIMME, 20,060 942
WERDENBERGER & OBERTOGGENBURGER, 19,896 943
WINTERTHURER STADTANZEIGER, 66,312 943
WOCHEN-ZEITUNG, 2,600 943
WOZ DIE WOCHENZEITUNG, 17,000 943
ZUGER WOCHE, 43,618 944
ZÜRICHSEE-ZEITUNG 945
ZÜRICHSEE-ZEITUNG, 75,884 945

Turkey

Nationals

AKŞAM, 142,277 945
CUMHURIYET, 62,583 945
GÜNEŞ, 124,911 946
HÜRRIYET, 467,478 946
MILLIYET, 194,037 946
POSTA, 498,240 946
RADIKAL, 38,201 946
SABAH, 344,344 946
STAR, 113,214 946
TODAY S ZAMAN, 4,928 946
TURKISH DAILY NEWS, 2,535 946
TÜRKIYE, 140,927 946
YENI ŞAFAK, 104,129 947
ZAMAN, 873,954 947

Regional

TICARET GAZETESI, 4,970 946
YENI ASIR, 37,106 947

Ukraine

Nationals

DEN, 62,500 947
DONBASS, 22,000 947
FAKTY I KOMMENTARII, 784,275 947
KYIV POST, 25,000 947
LEVIY BEREG, 90,000 947
SEGODNYA, 135,000 947
UKRAINA MOLODA, 130,884 948
VECHIRNIY KYIV 100, 20,000 948
ZERKALO NEDELI, 57,515 948

Vatican City

Nationals

L' OSSERVATORE ROMANO, 40,000 948

Willings Volume 2
Section 4

Print Media Europe

Newspapers, Magazines and other Periodicals

Albania

Time Difference: GMT + 1 hr (CET - Central European Time)
National Telephone Code: +355
Continent: Europe
Capital: Tirana
Principal Language: Albanian
Population: 3600523
Monetary Unit: Lek (ALL)

EMBASSY HIGH

COMMISSION: Embassy of Albania: 33 St. George's Drive, London, SW1V 4DG, UK Tel:00442078288897; **Fax:** 00442078288869;

ALBANIAN DAILY NEWS
1841156AL65A-106
Editorial: "Dervish Hima" Street, ADA Tower, No. 1, TIRANA **Tel:** 4 256 112 **Fax:** 4 240 888
Email: editoradn@albnet.net **Web site:** http://www.albaniannews.com
Date Established: 1995; **Freq:** Daily; **Circ:** 2,500
Profile: Providing its readers with news, business, arts and entertainment information.
Language(s): English
ADVERTISING RATES:
Full Page Colour .... EUR 500.00
NATIONAL DAILY & SUNDAY NEWSPAPERS: National Daily Newspapers

GAZETA ALBANIA
1914705AL65A-109
Editorial: Rr. "Don Bosko" 5, Kulla Vizion Plus nr 2, TIRANE **Tel:** 4 22 29 243 **Fax:** 4 22 23 198
Email: albaniakryeredaktor@yahoo.com **Web site:** http://www.gazeta-albania.net
Date Established: 1995; **Freq:** Daily; **Cover Price:** ALL 0.30; **Circ:** 5,000
Usual Pagination: 24
Profile: National daily covering politics, economics, social issues and sports.
Language(s): Albanian
ADVERTISING RATES:
Full Page Colour .... ALL 30000.00
NATIONAL DAILY & SUNDAY NEWSPAPERS: National Daily Newspapers

PANORAMA
1846549AL65A-105
Editorial: Rr "Jordan Misja", behind Harry Fulltz School, Palace 1, Shk. 2/2, TIRANA **Tel:** 4 273 207 **Fax:** 4 273 206
Email: info@panorama.com.al **Web site:** http://www.panorama.com.al
Date Established: 2002; **Freq:** Daily; **Cover Price:** ALL 20.00; **Circ:** 25,000
Usual Pagination: 28
Profile: Daily newspaper covering social, economic, politic and cultural issues.
Language(s): English
ADVERTISING RATES:
Full Page Mono .... EUR 450.00
Full Page Colour .... EUR 600.00
NATIONAL DAILY & SUNDAY NEWSPAPERS: National Daily Newspapers

SHEKULLI
766182AL65A-101
Editorial: Rruga Ismail Qemali, Pallati Abissnet, TIRANE **Tel:** 4 256994 **Fax:** 4 256015
Email: kryeredaktor.shekulli@abissnet.al **Web site:** http://www.shekulli.com.al
Date Established: 1998; **Freq:** Daily - 7 days a week; **Cover Price:** ALL 20,00; **Circ:** 25,000
Profile: Newspaper covering politics, economy, education, health, culture, social events and sport, classified, recruitment, real estates, sell and buy business, travel offers, reportages, letters and comments, investigation.
Language(s): Albanian
Readership: General.
Supplement(s): SH2 - 52xY
NATIONAL DAILY & SUNDAY NEWSPAPERS: National Daily Newspapers

SPORTI SHQIPTAR
719169AL75A-1
Editorial: Rruga Aleksandër Moisiu, ish-Kinostudio, pranë A1 TV, TIRANE **Tel:** 43 68 322 **Fax:** 43 68 322
Email: www.sportishqiptar@live.com **Web site:** http://www.sportishqiptar.com.al
Date Established: 1935; **Freq:** Daily; **Cover Price:** ALL 30,00; **Circ:** 20,000
Editor: Baskhim Tufa; **Publisher:** Koço Kokëdhima
Profile: Newspaper covering sports news from Albania, especially football, international sport news.
Language(s): Albanian
CONSUMER: SPORT

STANDARD
1977929AL65A-116
Editorial: ad. rruga e Kavajes, nr.67, TIRANA
Tel: 4 2260695 **Fax:** 4 2255646
Email: info@standard.al **Web site:** http://www.standard.al
Date Established: 2005; **Freq:** Daily; **Cover Price:** ALL 20.00; **Circ:** 10,000
Profile: Newspaper covering daily news, politics, economics, social issues, culture, sports, with special reports and features. Presents right wing political views.
Language(s): Albanian
NATIONAL DAILY & SUNDAY NEWSPAPERS: National Daily Newspapers

TIRANA OBSERVER
1915989AL65A-114
Editorial: Rruga "Irfan Tomini", pallati "Biorn", Kati i 2-të, TIRANË **Tel:** 4 241 9001 **Fax:** 4 241 9000
Email: kontakti@tiranaobserver.com.al **Web site:** http://www.tiranaobserver.com.al
Freq: Daily - Not published on Mondays; **Circ:** 10,000
News Editor: Nikoleta Kovaçi
Profile: Informative daily paper distributed on all the territory of the Albanian Republic and Greece.
Language(s): Albanian
ADVERTISING RATES:
Full Page Mono .... ALL 40000.00
Full Page Colour .... ALL 50000.00
Mechanical Data: Type Area: 285x365mm
NATIONAL DAILY & SUNDAY NEWSPAPERS: National Daily Newspapers

Andorra

Time Difference: GMT + 1 hr (CET - Central European Time)
National Telephone Code: +376
Continent: Europe
Capital: Andorra la Vella
Principal Language: Catalan, Spanish, French
Population: 71822
Monetary Unit: Euro (EUR)

EMBASSY HIGH

COMMISSION: Embassy of the Principality of Andorra: 63 Westover Road, London SW18 2RF
Tel: 020 8874 4806
Fax: 020 8874 4902. Head of Mission: HE Mrs Maria Rosa Picart de Francis

7 DIES
53714AD80-5
Formerly: 7 Dias
Editorial: Avda. Riberaygua 39, 5° piso, AD 500, ANDORRA LA VELLA **Tel:** 87 74 77 **Fax:** 86 38 02
Email: diaridigital@diariandorra.ad **Web site:** http://www.diariandorra.ad
Freq: Weekly - Published on Wednesday; **Cover Price:** Free; **Circ:** 30,000
Editor: Rosa Mari Sorribes
Profile: Magazine focusing on news, politics and current affairs.
Language(s): Catalan
Readership: Aimed at residents and visitors.
CONSUMER: RURAL & REGIONAL INTEREST

ANDORRA MAGAZINE
53717AD80-30
Editorial: Verge del Pilar 5, 3° planta, dpcho 4, Aptdo. 1130, ANDORRA LA VELLA AD500
Tel: 86 78 88 **Fax:** 86 78 87
Email: lescomarques@lescomarques.com
Freq: Monthly; **Circ:** 5,000
Editor: Nuria Gras
Profile: Magazine for residents of Andorra.
Language(s): Spanish
CONSUMER: RURAL & REGIONAL INTEREST

BONDIA
1743222AD65A-1
Editorial: Carre Maria Pla 28, 1ª planta, ANDORRA LA VELLA **Tel:** 80 88 88 **Fax:** 82 88 88
Email: bondia@bondia.ad **Web site:** http://www.bondia.ad
Date Established: 2004; **Freq:** 260 issues yearly - Published Monday to Friday; **Cover Price:** Free; **Circ:** 8,000
Editor: Maria Baró; **Advertising Manager:** Riccardo Sandrini
Profile: Daily newspaper focusing on Andorra general news.
Language(s): Catalan
Average ad content per issue: 50%
NATIONAL DAILY & SUNDAY NEWSPAPERS: National Daily Newspapers

DIARI D'ANDORRA
53080AD67B-5
Editorial: Avda. Riberaygua 39, 5° piso, AD 50500, ANDORRA LA VELLA **Tel:** 87 74 77 **Fax:** 86 38 00
Email: redaccio@diariandorra.ad **Web site:** http://www.diariandorra.info
Date Established: 1991; **Freq:** Daily; **Cover Price:** EUR 1.00; **Circ:** 3,200
Editor: Toni Solanelles
Language(s): Catalan
Supplement(s): Informacions - 52xY.
REGIONAL DAILY & SUNDAY NEWSPAPERS: Regional Daily Newspapers

INFORMACIONS
53727AD80-10
Editorial: Avda. Riberaygua 39, 5° piso, ANDORRA LA VELLA AD 500 **Tel:** 87 74 77 **Fax:** 86 38 00
Email: redaccio@diariandorra.ad **Web site:** http://www.diariandorra.ad
Date Established: 2000; **Freq:** Weekly - Published on Sunday; **Circ:** 3,500
Usual Pagination: 32
Editor: Robert Pastor
Profile: Magazine containing information and local news about Andorra.
Language(s): Catalan
Readership: Aimed at visitors and residents of Andorra.
Supplement to: Diari d'Andorra - 365xY.
CONSUMER: RURAL & REGIONAL INTEREST

EL PERIODIC D'ANDORRA
53081AD67B-10
Editorial: Parc de la Mola, 10 Torre Caldea, 7° Piso, LES ESCALDES - ENGORDANY **Tel:** 73 62 00 **Fax:** 73 62 10
Email: redaccio@andorra.elperiodico.com **Web site:** http://www.elperiodico.com/andorra/default.asp
Date Established: 1997; **Freq:** Daily; **Cover Price:** EUR 1.00; **Circ:** 7,700
Editor: Roser Porta
Profile: General news about Andorra.
Language(s): Catalan
ADVERTISING RATES:
Full Page Mono .... EUR 862.93
Full Page Colour .... EUR 1188.75
REGIONAL DAILY & SUNDAY NEWSPAPERS: Regional Daily Newspapers

Austria

Time Difference: GMT + 1 hr (CET - Central European Time)
National Telephone Code: +43
Continent: Europe
Capital: Vienna
Principal Language: German
Population: 8199783
Monetary Unit: Euro (EUR)

EMBASSY HIGH

COMMISSION: Austrian Embassy: 18 Belgrave Mews West, London SW1X 8HU
Tel: 020 7235 3731
Fax: 020 7344 0292
Email: embassy@austria.org.uk
Website: http://www.austria.org.uk / Visa enquires: (020) 7245 6689 (2-4pm Mon-Fri) or 02030025936 (1-5 pm. Mon .Fri)

13ER-KURIER
1648422A40-646
Editorial: Kasernstr. 10, 4910 RIED
Tel: 502014431604 **Fax:** 502014417310
Freq: Quarterly; **Cover Price:** Free; **Circ:** 3,200
Profile: Magazine for the tank battalion in Ried.
Language(s): German

40 PLUS GUIDE
739123A74A-640
Editorial: Pillergasse 13/34, 1150 WIEN
Tel: 1 897486016 **Fax:** 1 897486022
Email: redaktion@mediamed.at **Web site:** http://www.myguides.at
Freq: Annual; **Cover Price:** Free; **Circ:** 80,000
Editor: Martha Proidl-Stachl; **Advertising Manager:** Nikolaus Angermayr
Profile: Magazine for women from 40 years of age onwards.
Language(s): German
ADVERTISING RATES:
Full Page Mono .... EUR 3300
Full Page Colour .... EUR 3300
Mechanical Data: Type Area: 178 x 120 mm
Copy instructions: *Copy Date:* 30 days prior to publication

4WD FOUR WHEEL DRIVE
1647545A77A-285
Editorial: Schloss Lichtenegg 1, 4600 WELS
Tel: 7242 6782310 **Fax:** 7242 29707
Email: 4wd@mmga.at **Web site:** http://www.4wd-international.at
Freq: 6 issues yearly; **Annual Sub.:** EUR 22,90; **Circ:** 25,000
Editor: Helmut Moser
Profile: Magazine about all aspects of four wheel driving in Austria.
Language(s): German
ADVERTISING RATES:
Full Page Colour .... EUR 4750
Copy instructions: *Copy Date:* 21 days prior to publication
Supplement(s): Green Clean Car

A3 BAU
719579A4E-20
Editorial: Wiener Str. 2/1/6, 2340 MÖDLING
Tel: 2236 4252836 **Fax:** 2236 26311
Email: s.mueller@a3verlag.com **Web site:** http://www.a3verlag.com
Freq: 10 issues yearly; **Annual Sub.:** EUR 38,00; **Circ:** 17,800
Editor: Sabine Müller-Hofstetter; **Advertising Manager:** Peter Mayer
Profile: Magazine focusing on the building industry, building equipment trade, read by architects and installation companies.
Language(s): German
ADVERTISING RATES:
Full Page Mono .... EUR 6970
Full Page Colour .... EUR 6970
Mechanical Data: Type Area: 250 x 185 mm, No. of Columns (Display): 4, Col Widths (Display): 43 mm
Copy instructions: *Copy Date:* 14 days prior to publication
Supplement(s): a3 Eco
BUSINESS: ARCHITECTURE & BUILDING: Building

A3 BOOM!
719580A2A-20
Editorial: Wiener Str. 2/1/6, 2340 MÖDLING
Tel: 2236 4252849 **Fax:** 650 26311
Email: c.krebs@a3verlag.com **Web site:** http://www.a3verlag.com
Freq: 10 issues yearly; **Annual Sub.:** EUR 38,00; **Circ:** 13,300
Editor: Christian Krebs; **Advertising Manager:** Hannes Walter
Profile: Austrian magazine for managers in marketing, advertising and media.
Language(s): German
ADVERTISING RATES:
Full Page Mono .... EUR 4400
Full Page Colour .... EUR 4400
Mechanical Data: Type Area: 250 x 185 mm, No. of Columns (Display): 4, Col Widths (Display): 43 mm
Copy instructions: *Copy Date:* 14 days prior to publication
Supplement(s): a3 Eco
BUSINESS: COMMUNICATIONS, ADVERTISING & MARKETING

A3 ECO
719582A14A-20
Editorial: Wiener Str. 2/1/6, 2340 MÖDLING
Tel: 2236 4252841 **Fax:** 2236 26311
Email: b.salomon@a3verlag.com **Web site:** http://www.a3verlag.com
Freq: Monthly; **Annual Sub.:** EUR 38,00; **Circ:** 80,000
Editor: Birgit Salomon; **Advertising Manager:** Michael Wolfbeisser
Profile: Economics magazine aimed at managers.
Language(s): German
ADVERTISING RATES:
Full Page Mono .... EUR 11250
Full Page Colour .... EUR 11250
Mechanical Data: Type Area: 250 x 185 mm, No. of Columns (Display): 3, Col Widths (Display): 60 mm
Copy instructions: *Copy Date:* 14 days prior to publication
Supplement to: a3 Bau, a3 Boom!, a3 Gast
BUSINESS: COMMERCE, INDUSTRY & MANAGEMENT

A3 EURO
765441A14A-2493
Editorial: Wiener Str. 2/1/6, 2340 MÖDLING
Tel: 2236 4252841 **Fax:** 2236 26311
Email: b.salomon@a3verlag.com **Web site:** http://www.a3verlag.com
Freq: Annual; **Annual Sub.:** EUR 38,00; **Circ:** 80,000
Editor: Birgit Salomon; **Advertising Manager:** Wolfgang Wolfbeiser
Profile: Business magazine.
Language(s): German
ADVERTISING RATES:
Full Page Colour .... EUR 11250
Mechanical Data: Type Area: 250 x 185 mm, No. of Columns (Display): 4, Col Widths (Display): 43 mm
Copy instructions: *Copy Date:* 7 days prior to publication

A LA CARTE
719914A74P-20
Editorial: Leberstr. 122, 1110 WIEN **Tel:** 1 74077878 **Fax:** 1 74077888

Email: redaktion@alacarte.at **Web site:** http://www.alacarte.at
Freq: Quarterly; **Cover Price:** EUR 5,00; **Circ:** 28,500
Editor: Christian Grünwald; **Advertising Manager:** Stefan W. Stumpf
Profile: Discerning connoisseurs and affluent, cultivated opinion leaders read the Gourmet magazine A La Carte. In the upscale restaurants at top winemakers and innovative beverage producers, it is as the lead medium.
Language(s): German
ADVERTISING RATES:
Full Page Colour .... EUR 5700
Mechanical Data: Type Area: 242 x 182 mm
Supplement(s): slow

A LA CARTE
719914A74P-288
Editorial: Leberstr. 122, 1110 WIEN **Tel:** 1 74077878 **Fax:** 1 74077888
Email: redaktion@alacarte.at **Web site:** http://www.alacarte.at
Freq: Quarterly; **Cover Price:** EUR 5,00; **Circ:** 28,500
Editor: Christian Grünwald; **Advertising Manager:** Stefan W. Stumpf
Profile: Discerning connoisseurs and affluent, cultivated opinion leaders read the Gourmet magazine A La Carte. In the upscale restaurants at top winemakers and innovative beverage producers, it is as the lead medium.
Language(s): German
ADVERTISING RATES:
Full Page Colour .... EUR 5700
Mechanical Data: Type Area: 242 x 182 mm
Supplement(s): slow

AB5ZIG
747383A74N-260
Editorial: Biberstr. 9, 1010 WIEN **Tel:** 1 51543600 **Fax:** 1 51543609
Email: wiener@seniorenbund.at **Web site:** http://www.ab5zig.at
Freq: 6 issues yearly; **Circ:** 70,000
Editor: Thomas Hos; **Advertising Manager:** Claudia Wlach
Profile: Magazine for the elderly concerning all aspects of retirement.
Language(s): German
Readership: Aimed at retired people in Vienna.
ADVERTISING RATES:
Full Page Mono .... EUR 2761
Full Page Colour .... EUR 3452
Mechanical Data: Type Area: 255 x 185 mm, No. of Columns (Display): 4, Col Widths (Display): 43 mm
Copy instructions: *Copy Date:* 35 days prior to publication
CONSUMER: WOMEN'S INTEREST CONSUMER MAGAZINES: Retirement

ABFALL & UMWELT
1849431A57-1164
Editorial: Schulweg 6, 2441 MITTERNDORF
Tel: 2234 74151 **Fax:** 2234 741554
Email: office@gvabaden.at **Web site:** http://www.gvabaden.at
Freq: Quarterly; **Circ:** 65,300
Profile: Magazine from the Communal Association for Waste Management and Public Charges for the administrative district of Baden.
Language(s): German

ACADEMIA
719491A82-3717
Editorial: Lerchenfelder Str. 14, 1080 WIEN
Tel: 1 405162230 **Fax:** 1 495162244
Email: academia@oevc.at **Web site:** http://www.oecv.at
Freq: 6 issues yearly; **Annual Sub.:** EUR 15,00; **Circ:** 13,000
Editor: Wolfgang Bamberg; **Advertising Manager:** Hildegrunde Metz
Profile: Magazine about politics, economics, religion and culture.
Language(s): German
ADVERTISING RATES:
Full Page Colour .... EUR 3200
Mechanical Data: Type Area: 255 x 175 mm
CONSUMER: CURRENT AFFAIRS & POLITICS

ACTA MECHANICA
1853165A19A-45
Editorial: Sachsenplatz 4, 1201 WIEN
Tel: 1 3302415532 **Fax:** 1 330242665
Email: silvia.schilgerius@springer.at **Web site:** http://www.springer.at
Freq: 28 issues yearly; **Circ:** 600
Editor: Silvia Schilgerius
Profile: Magazine containing technical articles concerning mechanical engineering.
Language(s): English
ADVERTISING RATES:
Full Page Mono .... EUR 1330
Full Page Colour .... EUR 2394
Mechanical Data: Type Area: 230 x 170 mm

ACTA NEUROCHIRURGICA
1852997A56A-2036
Editorial: Sachsenplatz 4, 1201 WIEN
Tel: 1 3302415532 **Fax:** 1 330242665
Email: silvia.schilgerius@springer.at **Web site:** http://www.springer.at
Freq: Monthly; **Circ:** 1,500
Editor: Silvia Schilgerius
Profile: European journal of neurosurgery.
Language(s): English
ADVERTISING RATES:
Full Page Mono .... EUR 1330
Full Page Colour .... EUR 2390
Mechanical Data: Type Area: 250 x 170 mm
Official Journal of: Organ d. European Association of Neurosurgical Societies

ACTIVE BEAUTY
1740607A74A-909
Editorial: Geiselbergstr. 15, 1110 WIEN
Tel: 1 601170 **Fax:** 1 60117190
Email: active@activebeauty.at **Web site:** http://www.activebeauty.at
Freq: 10 issues yearly; **Cover Price:** Free; **Circ:** 1,100,000
Editor: Peter Mosser
Language(s): German
ADVERTISING RATES:
Full Page Mono .... EUR 21600
Full Page Colour .... EUR 21600
Mechanical Data: Type Area: 242 x 174 mm
CONSUMER: WOMEN'S INTEREST CONSUMER MAGAZINES: Women's Interest

ADGAR
739439A2A-720
Editorial: Schellinggasse 1/7/3, 1010 WIEN
Tel: 1 9613888 **Fax:** 1 961388850
Email: office@starmuehler.at **Web site:** http://www.starmuehler.at
Freq: Annual; **Circ:** 10,000
Editor: Herbert Starmühler
Profile: Magazine to the Print Oscar Gala with topics around advertising and print media.
Language(s): German

ADVANTAGE
764299A73-382
Editorial: Bahnhofstr. 10, 9300 ST. VEIT
Tel: 4212 3323320 **Fax:** 4212 332336
Email: w.rumpler@advantage.at **Web site:** http://www.advantage.at
Freq: 6 issues yearly; **Cover Price:** Free; **Circ:** 17,500
Editor: Walter Rumpler
Profile: Regional magazine for opinion leaders about developments in economy and health issues.
Language(s): German
ADVERTISING RATES:
Full Page Mono .... EUR 2490
Full Page Colour .... EUR 2490
Mechanical Data: Type Area: 255 x 186 mm

AEP-INFORMATIONEN
719616A74A-40
Editorial: Müllerstr. 26, 6020 INNSBRUCK
Tel: 512 583698 **Fax:** 512 583698
Email: informationen@aep.at **Web site:** http://www.aep.at
Freq: Quarterly; **Annual Sub.:** EUR 18,00; **Circ:** 800
Editor: Monika Jarosch; **Advertising Manager:** Monika Jarosch
Profile: Feminist magazine about the relationship between the sexes and discrimination against women.
Language(s): German
Copy instructions: *Copy Date:* 30 days prior to publication

AERZTE STEIERMARK
743391A56A-1720
Editorial: Kaiserfeldgasse 29, 8010 GRAZ
Tel: 316 80440 **Fax:** 316 815671
Email: presse@aekstmk.or.at **Web site:** http://www.aekstmk.or.at
Freq: 11 issues yearly; Free to qualifying individuals
Annual Sub.: EUR 25,00; **Circ:** 6,600
Editor: Martin Novak
Profile: Magazine from the Medical Board of Steiermark.
Language(s): German
ADVERTISING RATES:
Full Page Mono .... EUR 1700
Full Page Colour .... EUR 2250
Mechanical Data: Type Area: 245 x 178 mm
Copy instructions: *Copy Date:* 14 days prior to publication
Supplement(s): ärzte Exklusiv

AGRAR POST
1655455A21A-1462
Editorial: Schulstr. 64, 2103 LANGENZERSDORF
Tel: 2244 46470 **Fax:** 2244 464723
Email: muellers.buero@speed.at
Freq: 10 issues yearly; **Circ:** 108,794
Editor: Bruno Müller
Profile: Magazine for rural regions about agricultural issues.
Language(s): German

AGRAR POST
1655455A21A-1511
Editorial: Schulstr. 64, 2103 LANGENZERSDORF
Tel: 2244 46470 **Fax:** 2244 464723
Email: muellers.buero@speed.at
Freq: 10 issues yearly; **Circ:** 108,794
Editor: Bruno Müller
Profile: Magazine for rural regions about agricultural issues.
Language(s): German

AGRAR TECHNIK ÖSTERREICH
733815A21E-1
Editorial: Lambrechtstr. 16, 1040 WIEN
Tel: 664 1342966 **Fax:** 1 9437900
Email: hannelore.wachter-sieg@dlv.de **Web site:** http://www.motorist.at
Freq: 6 issues yearly; **Circ:** 3,500
Editor: Hannelore Wachter-Sieg
Profile: Journal of the Federal Organisation of Agricultural Machine Operators and Traders.
Language(s): German
ADVERTISING RATES:
Full Page Mono .... EUR 1589
Full Page Colour .... EUR 2982
Mechanical Data: Type Area: 270 x 184 mm, No. of Columns (Display): 4, Col Widths (Display): 43 mm
BUSINESS: AGRICULTURE & FARMING: Agriculture - Machinery & Plant

AGRARISCHE RUNDSCHAU
719698A21A-60
Editorial: Franz-Josefs-Kai 13, 1010 WIEN
Tel: 1 253635029 **Fax:** 1 253635070
Email: info@oekosozial.at **Web site:** http://www.oekosozial.at
Freq: 6 issues yearly; **Annual Sub.:** EUR 49,10; **Circ:** 3,800
Editor: Klemens Riegler; **Advertising Manager:** Romana Hummer-Schierleitner
Profile: Official journal of the Austrian Agricultural Society.
Language(s): German
ADVERTISING RATES:
Full Page Mono .... EUR 2277
Full Page Colour .... EUR 2677
Mechanical Data: Type Area: 267 x 174 mm
BUSINESS: AGRICULTURE & FARMING

AGRO ZUCKER STÄRKE
719716A21A-80
Editorial: Marienheimgasse 4, 2460 BRUCK
Tel: 676 892612930 **Fax:** 2162 66404
Email: azas@dergampe.at **Web site:** http://www.agrana.com
Freq: Quarterly; **Cover Price:** EUR 1,00; **Circ:** 10,000
Editor: Brigitte Gampe; **Advertising Manager:** Brigitte Gampe
Profile: Magazine for the Austrian turnip, sugar and starch business.
Language(s): German
ADVERTISING RATES:
Full Page Mono .... EUR 1370
Full Page Colour .... EUR 1850
Mechanical Data: Type Area: 259 x 183 mm

AK TIP
744773A74M-180
Editorial: Bahnhofplatz 3, 9021 KLAGENFURT
Tel: 50477
Email: arbeiterkammer@akktn.at **Web site:** http://kaernten.arbeiterkammer.at
Freq: Quarterly; **Circ:** 150,000
Profile: Magazine containing information for consumers.
Language(s): German

AK TIROL TIROLER ARBEITERZEITUNG
719815A14L-160
Editorial: Maximilianstr. 7/II, 6010 INNSBRUCK
Tel: 512 5340 **Fax:** 512 53401290
Email: presse@ak-tirol.com **Web site:** http://www.ak-tirol.com
Freq: Quarterly; **Circ:** 200,000
Editor: Elmar Schiffkorn
Profile: Journal containing recent news about economic developments and training courses.
Language(s): German
BUSINESS: COMMERCE, INDUSTRY & MANAGEMENT: Trade Unions

AKTIV & GESUND
1641124A74M-243
Editorial: Arche-Noah-Gasse 8, 8020 GRAZ
Tel: 316 903312782 **Fax:** 316 903312754
Email: roswitha.jauk@cm-service.at **Web site:** http://www.cm-service.at
Freq: Half-yearly; **Cover Price:** Free; **Circ:** 56,000
Editor: Roswitha Jauk; **Advertising Manager:** Anton Reiter
Profile: Magazine of the health insurance company Gesundheits-Versicherung Merkur.
Language(s): German
ADVERTISING RATES:
Full Page Mono .... EUR 3900
Full Page Colour .... EUR 3900
Mechanical Data: Type Area: 297 x 210 mm

AKTUELL
1859583A21A-1512
Editorial: Schauflergasse 6/5, 1010 WIEN
Tel: 1 533022717 **Fax:** 1 5332104
Email: seifert@landforstbetriebe.at **Web site:** http://www.landforstbetriebe.at
Freq: Quarterly; **Circ:** 1,200
Editor: Karin Seifert; **Advertising Manager:** Karin Seifert
Profile: Official publication of the Austrian Association of Agriculture and Forestry.
Language(s): German

ALL4FAMILY
1660662A74C-796
Editorial: Brauhausstr. 8, 2320 SCHWECHAT
Tel: 1 7078191400 **Fax:** 1 707819133
Email: martina.krenn@all4family.at **Web site:** http://www.all4family.at
Freq: 6 issues yearly; **Annual Sub.:** EUR 13,20; **Circ:** 56,667
Editor: Martina Krenn; **Advertising Manager:** Martin Lagler
Language(s): German
ADVERTISING RATES:
Full Page Mono .... EUR 6590
Full Page Colour .... EUR 6590
Mechanical Data: Type Area: 240 x 172 mm
Copy instructions: *Copy Date:* 30 days prior to publication
CONSUMER: WOMEN'S INTEREST CONSUMER MAGAZINES: Home & Family

ALLES AUTO
719953A77A-40
Editorial: Beckgasse 24, 1130 WIEN **Tel:** 1 8779711 **Fax:** 1 87797114
Email: redaktion@allesauto.at **Web site:** http://www.allesauto.at
Freq: 10 issues yearly; **Annual Sub.:** EUR 19,00; **Circ:** 64,141
Editor: Enrico Falchetto; **Advertising Manager:** Franz Nistelberger
Profile: Magazine for car owners and motoring enthusiasts.
Language(s): German
ADVERTISING RATES:
Full Page Mono .... EUR 8900
Full Page Colour .... EUR 8900
Mechanical Data: Type Area: 260 x 190 mm
Copy instructions: *Copy Date:* 21 days prior to publication
CONSUMER: MOTORING & CYCLING: Motoring

DER ALM- UND BERGBAUER
720031A21A-140
Editorial: Postfach 73, 6010 INNSBRUCK
Tel: 680 1175560
Email: johann.jenewein@almwirtschaft.com **Web site:** http://www.almwirtschaft.com
Freq: 9 issues yearly; **Annual Sub.:** EUR 17,00; **Circ:** 6,450
Editor: Johann Jenewein; **Advertising Manager:** Johann Jenewein
Profile: Magazine containing information about livestock farming in the mountainous regions of Austria.
Language(s): German
Readership: Aimed at the agricultural community.
BUSINESS: AGRICULTURE & FARMING

ALPHA
1647515A74A-882
Editorial: Stubenbastei 12/14, 1010 WIEN
Tel: 1 5134800 **Fax:** 1 513480023
Email: dornerbrader@alphafrauen.org **Web site:** http://www.alphafrauen.org
Freq: 5 issues yearly; Free to qualifying individuals
Annual Sub.: EUR 15,00; **Circ:** 1,200
Editor: Eszter Dorner-Brader; **Advertising Manager:** Ulrike Hartl
Profile: Women's network.
Language(s): German
ADVERTISING RATES:
Full Page Mono .... EUR 500
Mechanical Data: Type Area: 250 x 180 mm, No. of Columns (Display): 2, Col Widths (Display): 60 mm
Copy instructions: *Copy Date:* 50 days prior to publication

ALT-NEUSTADT MITTEILUNGSBLATT
1600989A40-641
Editorial: Schwarzenbergplatz 1, 1010 WIEN
Tel: 1 7153759 **Fax:** 1 7121964
Email: office@alt-neustadt.at **Web site:** http://www.alt-neustadt.at
Freq: Quarterly; **Circ:** 1,500
Editor: Franz Lang; **Advertising Manager:** Franz Lang
Profile: Magazine containing reports about national defence and army policy in Austria.
Language(s): German

ALU FENSTER NEWS
1853312A4E-1338
Editorial: Praterstr. 74/3, 1020 WIEN **Tel:** 1 4929633 **Fax:** 1 4929633
Email: pr@bruggerdengg.at **Web site:** http://www.bruggerdengg.at
Freq: Annual; **Cover Price:** Free; **Circ:** 20,000
Editor: Hannelore Brugger-Dengg
Profile: Magazine for architects, planners, builders, investors and metal builders.
Language(s): German

AM DAS ÖSTERREICHISCHE AUTOMAGAZIN
720124A77A-60
Editorial: Grazer Str. 18, 8130 FROHNLEITEN
Tel: 3126 20088 **Fax:** 3126 2008855
Email: redaktion@automagazin.at **Web site:** http://www.automagazin.at
Freq: 6 issues yearly; **Circ:** 40,000
Editor: Karl W. Hartner
Profile: Austrian car magazine.

Language(s): German
ADVERTISING RATES:
Full Page Mono ...... EUR 3400
Full Page Colour ...... EUR 4600
Mechanical Data: No. of Columns (Display): 4, Col Widths (Display): 89 mm, Type Area: 255 x 187 mm
Copy instructions: *Copy Date:* 14 days prior to publication

AMINO ACIDS
1852998A37-266
Editorial: Sachsenplatz 4, 1201 WIEN
Tel: 1 3302415515 **Fax:** 1 330242665
Email: claudia.panuschka@springer.at **Web site:** http://www.springer.at
Freq: 10 issues yearly; **Circ:** 1,000
Editor: Gert Lubec
Profile: Scientific publication.
Language(s): English
ADVERTISING RATES:
Full Page Mono ...... EUR 1330
Full Page Colour ...... EUR 2394
Mechanical Data: Type Area: 230 x 170 mm

AMS-DIREKT
720161A14A-60
Editorial: Europaplatz 9, 4021 LINZ
Tel: 732 696320233 **Fax:** 732 696320290
Email: ams.oberoesterreich@ams.at **Web site:** http://www.ams.at/ooe
Freq: 11 issues yearly; **Cover Price:** Free; **Circ:** 7,000
Editor: Walter Kofler
Profile: Publication containing information for companies about the Upper Austrian labour market.
Language(s): German

AMTLICHE NACHRICHTEN NIEDERÖSTERREICH
720189A80-1654
Editorial: Landhausplatz 1, 3109 ST. PÖLTEN
Tel: 2742 900512173 **Fax:** 2742 900513550
Email: presse@noel.gv.at **Web site:** http://www.noel.gv.at
Freq: 24 issues yearly; **Annual Sub.:** EUR 13,00
Editor: Christian Salzmann
Profile: Journal providing local government news.
Language(s): German
CONSUMER: RURAL & REGIONAL INTEREST

AMTSBLATT DER LANDESHAUPTSTADT LINZ
720377A72-100
Editorial: Hauptplatz 1, 4041 LINZ **Tel:** 732 70701352
Fax: 732 70701313
Email: edith.prass@mag.linz.at **Web site:** http://www.linz.at
Freq: 24 issues yearly; **Annual Sub.:** EUR 40,80; **Circ:** 850
Editor: Karin Frohner
Profile: Magazine concerning Linz and the surrounding area.
Language(s): German
ADVERTISING RATES:
Full Page Mono ...... EUR 561
Mechanical Data: No. of Columns (Display): 2, Type Area: 260 x 170 mm, Col Widths (Display): 80 mm
Copy instructions: *Copy Date:* 14 days prior to publication
LOCAL NEWSPAPERS

ANALYSE
720715A56A-160
Editorial: Landgerichtsstr. 16, 1010 WIEN
Tel: 1 3108829 **Fax:** 1 319928227
Email: office@bsa.at **Web site:** http://www.analyse-online.at
Freq: Quarterly; **Cover Price:** EUR 0,80
Free to qualifying individuals ; **Circ:** 10,000
Editor: Margit Gstöttner
Profile: Publication of the Austrian Social-Democratic Doctors' Association.
Language(s): German
BUSINESS: HEALTH & MEDICAL

ANALYSE DER VERBRAUCHERPREISE
1644014A14A-2514
Editorial: Wiedner Hauptstr. 63, 1045 WIEN
Tel: 5909004103 **Fax:** 590900246
Email: statistik@wko.at **Web site:** http://www.wko.at/statistik
Freq: Monthly; **Cover Price:** Free; **Circ:** 20
Editor: Ulrike Oschischnig
Profile: Publication containing analyses of consumer prices.
Language(s): German

APOTHEKER KRONE
764251A37-261
Editorial: Seidengasse 9/1/1, 1070 WIEN
Tel: 1 40731110 **Fax:** 1 4073114
Email: apothekerkrone@medmedia.at **Web site:** http://www.medmedia.at
Freq: 24 issues yearly; **Circ:** 7,325
Editor: Wolfgang Exel; **Advertising Manager:** Thomas Schula
Profile: Magazine for pharmacists and pharmaceutical wholesale traders.

Language(s): German
ADVERTISING RATES:
Full Page Mono ...... EUR 3220
Full Page Colour ...... EUR 3220
Mechanical Data: No. of Columns (Display): 4, Col Widths (Display): 44 mm, Type Area: 263 x 190 mm

AQUA PRESS INTERNATIONAL
721030A42C-1
Editorial: Leberstr. 122, 1110 WIEN **Tel:** 1 74095544
Fax: 1 74095497
Email: hahn.zv@bohmann.at **Web site:** http://www.aquamedia.at
Freq: Quarterly; **Annual Sub.:** EUR 35,30; **Circ:** 8,000
Editor: Christof Hahn; **Advertising Manager:** Christof Hahn
Profile: Pan-European magazine focusing on the environmental consequences of water management. Includes infrastructure and traffic planning, political issues and reports of conferences.
Language(s): English; German
ADVERTISING RATES:
Full Page Mono ...... EUR 3420
Full Page Colour ...... EUR 4580
Mechanical Data: Type Area: 250 x 180 mm, No. of Columns (Display): 3, Col Widths (Display): 58 mm
BUSINESS: CONSTRUCTION: Water Engineering

ARBEIT & WIRTSCHAFT
721089A14L-320
Editorial: Johann-Böhm-Platz 1, 1020 WIEN
Tel: 1 5344439269 **Fax:** 1 5344100222
Email: sonja.adler@oegb.at **Web site:** http://www.arbeit-wirtschaft.at
Freq: 11 issues yearly; **Annual Sub.:** EUR 20,00; **Circ:** 28,000
Editor: Katharina Klee
Profile: Magazine about work and economy.
Language(s): German
BUSINESS: COMMERCE, INDUSTRY & MANAGEMENT: Trade Unions

ARCHITEKTUR
1648473A4E-1289
Editorial: Hochstr. 103, 2380 PERCHTOLDSDORF
Tel: 1 869582910 **Fax:** 1 869582920
Email: walter.laser@laserverlag.at **Web site:** http://www.architektur-online.com
Freq: 8 issues yearly; **Annual Sub.:** EUR 75,00; **Circ:** 10,500
Editor: Walter Laser; **Advertising Manager:** Nicolas Paga
Profile: Magazine focusing on the building business, planners, tenders and universities.
Language(s): German
ADVERTISING RATES:
Full Page Mono ...... EUR 2867
Full Page Colour ...... EUR 4908
Mechanical Data: Type Area: 277 x 187 mm
BUSINESS: ARCHITECTURE & BUILDING: Building

ARCHITEKTUR.AKTUELL
721124A4A-2
Editorial: Sachsenplatz 4, 1201 WIEN
Tel: 1 3302415330 **Fax:** 1 3302426350
Email: architektur.aktuell@springer.at **Web site:** http://www.architektur-aktuell.at
Freq: 10 issues yearly; **Annual Sub.:** EUR 136,40; **Circ:** 10,757
Editor: Matthias Boeckl; **Advertising Manager:** Bernd Mandl
Profile: European magazine covering all aspects of modern architecture.
Language(s): English; German
Readership: Read by architects and interior designers.
ADVERTISING RATES:
Full Page Mono ...... EUR 2920
Full Page Colour ...... EUR 4360
Mechanical Data: Type Area: 297 x 210 mm
BUSINESS: ARCHITECTURE & BUILDING: Architecture

ARCHITEKTURJOURNAL WETTBEWERBE
721128A4A-3
Editorial: Leberstr. 122, 1110 WIEN **Tel:** 1 74095559
Fax: 1 74095384
Email: redaktion@wettbewerbe-arch.com **Web site:** http://www.architekturweb.at
Freq: 5 issues yearly; **Annual Sub.:** EUR 75,00; **Circ:** 5,000
Editor: Josef R. Bahula; **Advertising Manager:** Roland Kanfer
Profile: Magazine focusing on all aspects of architecture.
Language(s): German
Readership: Read by architects and designers.
ADVERTISING RATES:
Full Page Mono ...... EUR 4200
Full Page Colour ...... EUR 4200
Mechanical Data: Type Area: 278 x 186 mm, No. of Columns (Display): 2, Col Widths (Display): 90 mm
Copy instructions: *Copy Date:* 21 days prior to publication

ARCHITEKTURJOURNAL WETTBEWERBE
721128A4A-5
Editorial: Leberstr. 122, 1110 WIEN **Tel:** 1 74095559
Fax: 1 74095384
Email: redaktion@wettbewerbe-arch.com **Web site:** http://www.architekturweb.at
Freq: 5 issues yearly; **Annual Sub.:** EUR 75,00; **Circ:** 5,000
Editor: Josef R. Bahula; **Advertising Manager:** Roland Kanfer
Profile: Magazine focusing on all aspects of architecture.
Language(s): German
Readership: Read by architects and designers.
ADVERTISING RATES:
Full Page Mono ...... EUR 4200
Full Page Colour ...... EUR 4200
Mechanical Data: Type Area: 278 x 186 mm, No. of Columns (Display): 2, Col Widths (Display): 90 mm
Copy instructions: *Copy Date:* 21 days prior to publication

ARD
721190A44-621
Editorial: Marxergasse 25, 1030 WIEN
Tel: 1 534521776 **Fax:** 1 53452140
Email: redaktion@lexisnexis.at **Web site:** http://ard.lexisnexis.at
Annual Sub.: EUR 615,00; **Circ:** 4,300
Editor: Barbara Tuma; **Advertising Manager:** Wolfgang Kreissl
Profile: Magazine focusing on employment, social security rights, taxation and legal issues.
Language(s): German
Readership: Read by social workers and members of the legal profession.
ADVERTISING RATES:
Full Page Mono ...... EUR 1930
Mechanical Data: Type Area: 250 x 165 mm
BUSINESS: LEGAL

ARWAG NEWS
1852933A4E-1330
Editorial: Würtzlerstr. 15, 1030 WIEN
Tel: 1 79700700 **Fax:** 1 79700790
Email: info@arwag.at **Web site:** http://www.arwag.at
Freq: Half-yearly; **Cover Price:** Free; **Circ:** 10,000
Editor: Stefan Hawla
Profile: Magazine for employees of ARWAG Holding-AG.
Language(s): German
ADVERTISING RATES:
Full Page Colour ...... EUR 727
Copy instructions: *Copy Date:* 30 days prior to publication

ARWAG NEWS
1852933A4E-1341
Editorial: Würtzlerstr. 15, 1030 WIEN
Tel: 1 79700700 **Fax:** 1 79700790
Email: info@arwag.at **Web site:** http://www.arwag.at
Freq: Half-yearly; **Cover Price:** Free; **Circ:** 10,000
Editor: Stefan Hawla
Profile: Magazine for employees of ARWAG Holding-AG.
Language(s): German
ADVERTISING RATES:
Full Page Colour ...... EUR 727
Copy instructions: *Copy Date:* 30 days prior to publication

ARZT+KIND
1746362A56A-1982
Editorial: Mühldorf 389, 8330 MÜHLDORF
Tel: 3152 39582 **Fax:** 1 9623359582
Email: k.deflorian@prometus.at **Web site:** http://www.prometus.at
Freq: 6 issues yearly; **Annual Sub.:** EUR 80,00; **Circ:** 8,125
Editor: Karin Deflorian; **Advertising Manager:** Robert Hlozek
Language(s): German
ADVERTISING RATES:
Full Page Mono ...... EUR 2890
Full Page Colour ...... EUR 2890
Mechanical Data: Type Area: 259 x 185 mm
BUSINESS: HEALTH & MEDICAL

ARZT+PATIENT
1746363A56A-1983
Editorial: Mühldorf 389, 8330 MÜHLDORF
Tel: 3152 39582 **Fax:** 1 9623359582
Email: k.deflorian@prometus.at **Web site:** http://www.prometus.at
Freq: 6 issues yearly; **Annual Sub.:** EUR 80,00; **Circ:** 11,000
Editor: Karin Deflorian; **Advertising Manager:** Robert Hlozek
Language(s): German
ADVERTISING RATES:
Full Page Mono ...... EUR 2890
Full Page Colour ...... EUR 2890
Mechanical Data: Type Area: 259 x 185 mm
BUSINESS: HEALTH & MEDICAL

ARZT & PRAXIS
721270A56A-240
Editorial: Hasenauerstr. 23, 1180 WIEN
Tel: 1 4790578 **Fax:** 1 479057830
Email: office@arztundpraxis.at **Web site:** http://www.arztundpraxis.at
Freq: 11 issues yearly; Free to qualifying individuals
Annual Sub.: EUR 35,00; **Circ:** 15,000
Advertising Manager: Manuela Moya
Profile: Journal containing articles about developments in practical medicine.
Language(s): German
Readership: Read by doctors in hospitals and private practice.
ADVERTISING RATES:
Full Page Colour ...... EUR 3290
Mechanical Data: Type Area: 270 x 185 mm
Copy instructions: *Copy Date:* 14 days prior to publication
BUSINESS: HEALTH & MEDICAL

ÄRZTE KRONE
1646155A56A-1943
Editorial: Seidengasse 9/1/1, 1070 WIEN
Tel: 1 407311130 **Fax:** 1 4073114
Email: aerztekrone@medmedia.at **Web site:** http://www.medmedia.at
Freq: 24 issues yearly; **Annual Sub.:** EUR 36,64; **Circ:** 13,500
Editor: Wolfgang Exel; **Advertising Manager:** Friedrich Tomaschek
Profile: Magazine on further education of physical doctors.
Language(s): German
ADVERTISING RATES:
Full Page Mono ...... EUR 3690
Full Page Colour ...... EUR 3690
Mechanical Data: No. of Columns (Display): 4, Col Widths (Display): 44 mm, Type Area: 263 x 190 mm
Copy instructions: *Copy Date:* 14 days prior to publication
Supplement(s): Wartezimmer Krone

ÄRZTE MAGAZIN
719632A56A-260
Editorial: Wiedner Hauptstr. 120, 1050 WIEN
Tel: 1 54600310 **Fax:** 1 54600730
Email: steiner@aerztemagazin.at **Web site:** http://www.aerztemagazin.at
Freq: 42 issues yearly; **Annual Sub.:** EUR 71,21; **Circ:** 16,500
Editor: Michaela Steiner; **Advertising Manager:** Reinhard Rosenberger
Profile: Magazine about the medical profession.
Language(s): German
Readership: Aimed at surgeons, doctors and nurses.
ADVERTISING RATES:
Full Page Colour ...... EUR 3980
Mechanical Data: Type Area: 297 x 210 mm
BUSINESS: HEALTH & MEDICAL

ÄRZTE WOCHE
719633A56A-280
Editorial: Sachsenplatz 4, 1201 WIEN **Tel:** 1 5131047
Fax: 1 5134783
Email: margarete.zupan@springer.at **Web site:** http://www.springermedizin.at
Freq: 44 issues yearly; **Annual Sub.:** EUR 57,50; **Circ:** 17,161
Editor: Margarete Zupan
Profile: Medical newspaper containing information about recent developments in medical practice.
Language(s): German
Readership: Aimed at members of the medical profession.
ADVERTISING RATES:
Full Page Mono ...... EUR 3352
Full Page Colour ...... EUR 4190
Mechanical Data: Type Area: 400 x 270 mm
Copy instructions: *Copy Date:* 5 days prior to publication
Supplement(s): hautnah; rheuma plus
BUSINESS: HEALTH & MEDICAL

ASOK ARBEITS- UND SOZIALRECHTSKARTEI
721298A44-622
Editorial: Scheydgasse 24, 1210 WIEN **Tel:** 1 246300
Fax: 1 2463051
Email: redaktion@lindeverlag.at **Web site:** http://www.asok.at
Freq: Monthly; **Annual Sub.:** EUR 181,50; **Circ:** 5,000
Editor: Eleonore Breitegger; **Advertising Manager:** Regina Erben-Hartig
Profile: Journal covering all aspects of Austrian law.
Language(s): German
Readership: Aimed at members of the legal profession.
ADVERTISING RATES:
Full Page Mono ...... EUR 999
Full Page Colour ...... EUR 1600
Mechanical Data: Type Area: 207 x 135 mm, No. of Columns (Display): 1, Col Widths (Display): 135 mm
Copy instructions: *Copy Date:* 14 days prior to publication
BUSINESS: LEGAL

ASSCOMPACT AUSTRIA
1749935A1C-166
Editorial: Kollingerfeld 9, 4563 MICHELDORF
Tel: 7582 511120 **Fax:** 7582 5111219
Email: aktuell@asscompact.at **Web site:** http://www.asscompact.at
Freq: Monthly; **Cover Price:** EUR 3,80; **Circ:** 10,000
Editor: Franz Waghubinger; **Advertising Manager:** Olaf Giessau
Profile: Magazine on investments.
Language(s): German
ADVERTISING RATES:
Full Page Colour ...... EUR 3450
Mechanical Data: Type Area: 257 x 170 mm
Copy instructions: *Copy Date:* 15 days prior to publication
BUSINESS: FINANCE & ECONOMICS: Banking

ASTRO WOCHE 1749622A94X-1674
Editorial: Wieninger Str. 1, 4780 SCHÄRDING
Tel: 7712 358500 **Fax:** 7712 3585021
Email: service@astrowoche.de **Web site:** http://www.astrowoche.de
Freq: Weekly; **Annual Sub.:** EUR 93,60; **Circ:** 48,119
Editor: Rudolf Kollböck
Profile: Million people read daily in newspapers, magazines or on the Internet their personal daily horoscope. More and more people are suffering, but these often superficial horoscopes. Astro Woche is the magazine for those who expect more. More horoscopes, more astrology, more counseling. Astro Woche is of no journal that is devoted to those who are already familiar with astrology. Week after week it manages the balancing act between depth horoscope analysis and tips that everyone can implement in his life. Astro Woche is also reading and, above all, a detailed health advice for those who want to live consciously and in harmony with their bodies.
Language(s): German
ADVERTISING RATES:
Full Page Mono .... EUR 2250
Full Page Colour .... EUR 2914
Mechanical Data: Type Area: 302 x 220 mm, No. of Columns (Display): 4, Col Widths (Display): 52 mm
Copy instructions: *Copy Date:* 21 days prior to publication
CONSUMER: OTHER CLASSIFICATIONS: Miscellaneous

ATG TANKSTELLEN- UND WERKSTÄTTENJOURNAL
721346A31A-1
Editorial: Leberstr. 122, 1110 WIEN **Tel:** 1 74095429
Fax: 1 74095430
Email: t.ableidinger@bohmann.at **Web site:** http://www.atg.at
Freq: 11 issues yearly; **Annual Sub.:** EUR 64,80; **Circ:** 10,000
Editor: Thomas Ableidinger; **Advertising Manager:** Markus Prikowitsch
Profile: Magazine for those working in garages and service stations, covering technical auto problems and their solutions, as well as new products and general information for the trade.
Language(s): German
ADVERTISING RATES:
Full Page Colour .... EUR 4100
Mechanical Data: Type Area: 270 x 182 mm
BUSINESS: MOTOR TRADE: Motor Trade Accessories

AUF 721388A74A-120
Editorial: Kleeblattgasse 7, 1010 WIEN
Tel: 1 5339164 **Fax:** 1 5326337
Email: auf@auf-einefrauenzeitschrift.at **Web site:** http://www.auf-einefrauenzeitschrift.at
Freq: Quarterly; Free to qualifying individuals
Annual Sub.: EUR 19,00; **Circ:** 2,500
Profile: Magazine of the Club to Support Feminist Projects.
Language(s): German

AUF 721388A74A-941
Editorial: Kleeblattgasse 7, 1010 WIEN
Tel: 1 5339164 **Fax:** 1 5326337
Email: auf@auf-einefrauenzeitschrift.at **Web site:** http://www.auf-einefrauenzeitschrift.at
Freq: Quarterly; Free to qualifying individuals
Annual Sub.: EUR 19,00; **Circ:** 2,500
Profile: Magazine of the Club to Support Feminist Projects.
Language(s): German

AUGENOPTIK & HÖRAKUSTIK
738271A56E-20
Editorial: Am Winterhafen 11, 4020 LINZ
Tel: 732 77422217 **Fax:** 732 77422250
Email: birgit.mayrhofer@como.at **Web site:** http://www.como.at
Freq: 6 issues yearly; Free to qualifying individuals
Annual Sub.: EUR 57,00; **Circ:** 1,700
Editor: Birgit Mayrhofer; **Advertising Manager:** Birgit Mayrhofer
Profile: Official journal of the Austrian Opticians' Association.
Language(s): German
ADVERTISING RATES:
Full Page Mono .... EUR 2100
Full Page Colour .... EUR 2100
Mechanical Data: Type Area: 250 x 170 mm
Copy instructions: *Copy Date:* 14 days prior to publication
BUSINESS: HEALTH & MEDICAL: Optics

AUSTRIA BÖRSENBRIEF
721524A1F-40
Editorial: Herzog-Odilo-Str. 52, 5310 MONDSEE
Tel: 6232 21051 **Fax:** 6232 210515
Email: redaktion@boersenbrief.at **Web site:** http://www.boersenbrief.at
Freq: Weekly; **Annual Sub.:** EUR 250,00; **Circ:** 5,000
Profile: Austrian stock exchange magazine.
Language(s): German
ADVERTISING RATES:
Full Page Mono .... EUR 1400
Full Page Colour .... EUR 1750
Mechanical Data: Type Area: 260 x 185 mm

AUSTRIA INNOVATIV 721528A14A-420
Editorial: Leberstr. 122, 1110 WIEN **Tel:** 1 74095435
Fax: 1 74095440
Email: klobucsar.zv@bohmann.at **Web site:** http://www.austriainnovativ.at
Freq: 6 issues yearly; **Annual Sub.:** EUR 47,90; **Circ:** 32,000
Editor: Christian Klobucsar; **Advertising Manager:** Gottfried Satek
Profile: Magazine about research, technology and business.
Language(s): German
ADVERTISING RATES:
Full Page Colour .... EUR 6380
Mechanical Data: Type Area: 260 x 193 mm
BUSINESS: COMMERCE, INDUSTRY & MANAGEMENT

AUSTRO CLASSIC 721538A77F-1
Editorial: Lenaugasse 10, 3412 KLOSTERNEUBURG
Tel: 2243 87476 **Fax:** 2243 87476
Email: office@austroclassic.com **Web site:** http://www.austroclassic.at
Freq: 6 issues yearly; **Annual Sub.:** EUR 39,00; **Circ:** 22,000
Editor: Wolfgang M. Buchta; **Advertising Manager:** Peter Kronberger
Profile: Magazine about classic cars.
Language(s): German
ADVERTISING RATES:
Full Page Mono .... EUR 1380
Full Page Colour .... EUR 1930
Mechanical Data: Type Area: 255 x 179 mm
Copy instructions: *Copy Date:* 30 days prior to publication
CONSUMER: MOTORING & CYCLING: Veteran Cars

AUSTROPACK 720971A35-22
Editorial: Geblergasse 95, 1170 WIEN
Tel: 1 906801112 **Fax:** 1 9068091112
Email: martin.oegg@austropack.at **Web site:** http://www.austropack.at
Freq: 11 issues yearly; **Annual Sub.:** EUR 63,00; **Circ:** 4,500
Editor: Martin Ögg; **Advertising Manager:** Martin Ögg
Profile: Magazine covering all aspects of packaging, warehousing, handling, transport and communications.
Language(s): German
Readership: Aimed at those involved in the handling industry.
ADVERTISING RATES:
Full Page Colour .... EUR 2396
Mechanical Data: Type Area: 257 x 175 mm, No. of Columns (Display): 3, Col Widths (Display): 55 mm
BUSINESS: PACKAGING & BOTTLING

AUTO AKTUELL 721561A77A-100
Editorial: Haydngasse 6, 1060 WIEN **Tel:** 1 5974985
Fax: 1 597498515
Email: office@autoaktuell.at **Web site:** http://www.autoaktuell.at
Freq: 5 issues yearly; **Annual Sub.:** EUR 14,00; **Circ:** 34,200
Editor: Christian Böhm; **Advertising Manager:** Christian Böhm
Profile: Magazine covering technical news, tuning, motor-sport and leisure.
Language(s): German
ADVERTISING RATES:
Full Page Mono .... EUR 4320
Full Page Colour .... EUR 5400
Mechanical Data: Type Area: 265 x 185 mm, No. of Columns (Display): 4, Col Widths (Display): 43 mm
Copy instructions: *Copy Date:* 10 days prior to publication
CONSUMER: MOTORING & CYCLING: Motoring

AUTO REVUE 1647381A77A-284
Editorial: Ferdinandstr. 4, 1020 WIEN
Tel: 1 863315201 **Fax:** 1 863315630
Email: redaktion@autorevue.at **Web site:** http://www.autorevue.at
Freq: Monthly; **Annual Sub.:** EUR 36,00; **Circ:** 65,445
Editor: Christian Kornherr; **Advertising Manager:** Mario Filipovic
Profile: Car magazine covering technology and sport.
Language(s): German
ADVERTISING RATES:
Full Page Mono .... EUR 10500
Full Page Colour .... EUR 10500
Mechanical Data: Type Area: 250 x 185 mm
Copy instructions: *Copy Date:* 21 days prior to publication

AUTO SERVICE 721622A31A-2
Editorial: Dresdner Str. 45, 1200 WIEN
Tel: 1 97000252 **Fax:** 1 970005252
Email: lutz.lischka@weka.at **Web site:** http://www.autoservice-online.at
Freq: 6 issues yearly; **Annual Sub.:** EUR 20,00; **Circ:** 8,700
Editor: Lutz Lischka; **Advertising Manager:** Karin Tober
Profile: Magazine containing information regarding the servicing and repair of motor vehicles.
Language(s): German
Readership: Aimed at mechanics, car dealers and owners of garages and motor companies.
ADVERTISING RATES:
Full Page Colour .... EUR 4450
Mechanical Data: Type Area: 267 x 180 mm
BUSINESS: MOTOR TRADE: Motor Trade Accessories

AUTO TOURING 721625A77E-40
Editorial: Tauchnergasse 5, 3400 KLOSTERNEUBURG **Tel:** 2243 4042701
Fax: 2243 4042721
Email: autotouring.redaktion@oeamtc.at **Web site:** http://www.autotouring.at
Freq: 11 issues yearly; **Circ:** 1,434,103
Editor: Peter Pisecker; **Advertising Manager:** Gerhard Schinhan
Profile: Magazine of the Austrian Automobile Touring Club.
Language(s): German
ADVERTISING RATES:
Full Page Mono .... EUR 14000
Full Page Colour .... EUR 21000
Mechanical Data: Type Area: 250 x 185 mm, No. of Columns (Display): 4, Col Widths (Display): 43 mm
CONSUMER: MOTORING & CYCLING: Club Cars

AUTO & WIRTSCHAFT
1655302A27-307
Editorial: Inkustr. 16, 3403 KLOSTERNEUBURG
Tel: 2243 368400 **Fax:** 2243 36840593
Email: lustig.gerhard@autoundwirtschaft.at **Web site:** http://www.autoundwirtschaft.at
Freq: 11 issues yearly; **Annual Sub.:** EUR 68,00; **Circ:** 12,500
Editor: Gerhard Lustig; **Advertising Manager:** Stefan Binder
Profile: Magazine on cars and economy including traffic, transportation, market, service and accessories.
Language(s): German
ADVERTISING RATES:
Full Page Mono .... EUR 3310
Full Page Colour .... EUR 4660
Mechanical Data: Type Area: 252 x 178 mm

AUTO & WIRTSCHAFT
1655302A27-322
Editorial: Inkustr. 16, 3403 KLOSTERNEUBURG
Tel: 2243 368400 **Fax:** 2243 36840593
Email: lustig.gerhard@autoundwirtschaft.at **Web site:** http://www.autoundwirtschaft.at
Freq: 11 issues yearly; **Annual Sub.:** EUR 68,00; **Circ:** 12,500
Editor: Gerhard Lustig; **Advertising Manager:** Stefan Binder
Profile: Magazine on cars and economy including traffic, transportation, market, service and accessories.
Language(s): German
ADVERTISING RATES:
Full Page Mono .... EUR 3310
Full Page Colour .... EUR 4660
Mechanical Data: Type Area: 252 x 178 mm

AWS REPORT 1856451A57-1171
Editorial: Hauptplatz 5, 2432 SCHWADORF
Tel: 2230 241812 **Fax:** 2230 24188
Email: m.kirchmeyer@avschwechat.at **Web site:** http://www.abfallverband.at/schwechat
Freq: Quarterly; **Cover Price:** Free; **Circ:** 29,000
Editor: Monika Kirchmeyer
Profile: Magazine with information about environment and waste.
Language(s): German

BANK & BÖRSE 1647524A1F-247
Editorial: Liebhartsgasse 36, 1160 WIEN
Tel: 1 4934945 **Fax:** 1 4934946
Email: office@bankundboerse.at **Web site:** http://www.bankundboerse.at
Freq: 46 issues yearly; **Annual Sub.:** EUR 220,00; **Circ:** 6,300
Editor: Werner Michael Szabo; **Advertising Manager:** Kurt Heinz
Profile: Magazine about the financial market in Austria.
Language(s): German
ADVERTISING RATES:
Full Page Mono .... EUR 2300
Full Page Colour .... EUR 2300
Mechanical Data: Type Area: 237 x 170 mm, No. of Columns (Display): 2, Col Widths (Display): 85 mm
Copy instructions: *Copy Date:* 5 days prior to publication

BANKARCHIV 1645461A1C-161
Editorial: Sachsenplatz 4, 1201 WIEN
Tel: 1 3302415450 **Fax:** 1 330242664
Email: edwin.schwarz@springer.at **Web site:** http://www.springer.at
Freq: Monthly; **Annual Sub.:** EUR 158,50; **Circ:** 3,500
Editor: Edwin W. Schwarz
Profile: Magazine about banking and the stock exchange .
Language(s): German
ADVERTISING RATES:
Full Page Mono .... EUR 1300
Full Page Colour .... EUR 2090
Mechanical Data: Type Area: 250 x 180 mm

DER BAUER 721977A21A-160
Editorial: Auf der Gugl 3, 4021 LINZ **Tel:** 5069021364
Fax: 5069021707
Email: ref-presse@lk-ooe.at **Web site:** http://www.lk-ooe.at
Freq: Weekly; Free to qualifying individuals
Annual Sub.: EUR 35,00; **Circ:** 41,700
Editor: Sandra Lengauer; **Advertising Manager:** Michael Schwabegger
Profile: Magazine concerning farming and forestry.
Language(s): German
ADVERTISING RATES:
Full Page Mono .... EUR 3700
Full Page Colour .... EUR 4440
Mechanical Data: Type Area: 260 x 196 mm, No. of Columns (Display): 4, Col Widths (Display): 45 mm
Copy instructions: *Copy Date:* 6 days prior to publication
Supplement(s): BauernJournal
BUSINESS: AGRICULTURE & FARMING

BAUERNBUND KALENDER
721982A21A-180
Editorial: Ferstlergasse 4, 3100 ST. PÖLTEN
Tel: 2742 9020200 **Fax:** 2742 9020240
Email: office@noebauernbund.at **Web site:** http://www.noebauernbund.at
Freq: Annual; **Circ:** 100,000
Profile: Calendar from the Lower Austrian Farmers Association.
Language(s): German

BAUERNBUND KALENDER
721982A21A-1509
Editorial: Ferstlergasse 4, 3100 ST. PÖLTEN
Tel: 2742 9020200 **Fax:** 2742 9020240
Email: office@noebauernbund.at **Web site:** http://www.noebauernbund.at
Freq: Annual; **Circ:** 100,000
Profile: Calendar from the Lower Austrian Farmers Association.
Language(s): German

BAUERNJOURNAL 1853442A21A-1507
Editorial: Schauflergasse 6, 1014 WIEN
Tel: 1 534418520
Email: office@lk-oe.at **Web site:** http://www.lk-oe.at
Freq: Monthly; **Circ:** 231,600
Profile: Magazine from the Austrian Chambers of Agriculture.
Language(s): German
Supplement to: Der Bauer, Die Information, Kärntner Bauer, Die Landwirtschaft, Landwirtschaftliche Blätter, Landwirtschaftliche Mitteilungen, mbl, Salzburger Bauer, Unser Ländle

BAUHANDBUCH 721996A4E-600
Editorial: Wiedner Hauptstr. 120, 1051 WIEN
Tel: 1 54664345 **Fax:** 1 54664520
Email: bauzeitung@wirtschaftsverlag.at **Web site:** http://www.bauforum.at
Freq: Annual; **Cover Price:** EUR 42,00; **Circ:** 2,800
Editor: Gisela Gary; **Advertising Manager:** Rudolf Reiter
Profile: Manual for the building sector, business, industry and associated business.
Language(s): German
ADVERTISING RATES:
Full Page Mono .... EUR 1300
Full Page Colour .... EUR 2086
Mechanical Data: Type Area: 180 x 140 mm

BAU-HOLZ 722001A4E-240
Editorial: Johann-Böhm-Platz 1, 1020 WIEN
Tel: 1 5344459260 **Fax:** 1 5344459900
Email: sonja.schmid@gbh.at **Web site:** http://www.bau-holz.at
Freq: 6 issues yearly; **Circ:** 101,000
Editor: Sonja Schmid
Profile: Journal containing news and information about safety methods in construction.
Language(s): German
Readership: Read by members of the Building and Carpenters' Trades Association.
BUSINESS: ARCHITECTURE & BUILDING: Building

BAURECHTLICHE BLÄTTER:BBL 1853174A4E-1336
Editorial: Kapitelgasse 5, 5020 SALZBURG
Fax: 662 8044303
Email: karim.giese@sbg.ac.at **Web site:** http://www.springer.at
Freq: 6 issues yearly; **Annual Sub.:** EUR 119,00; **Circ:** 5,000
Editor: Karim Giese
Profile: Magazine focusing on public works. Includes information on building legislation and regulations.
Language(s): German
ADVERTISING RATES:
Full Page Mono .... EUR 960
Full Page Colour .... EUR 1720
Mechanical Data: Type Area: 250 x 170 mm

BBB BAUMASCHINE BAUGERÄT BAUSTELLE
722192A42A-1
Editorial: Dresdner Str. 45, 1200 WIEN
Tel: 1 97000168 **Fax:** 1 970005168
Email: helmut.tober@weka.at **Web site:** http://www.bbb.co.at
Freq: 10 issues yearly; **Annual Sub.:** EUR 30,00; **Circ:** 8,680
Editor: Helmut Tober; **Advertising Manager:** Harald Dudas
Profile: Publication about building machinery and techniques, both in Austria and internationally.
Language(s): German
ADVERTISING RATES:
Full Page Colour .... EUR 5250
Mechanical Data: Type Area: 260 x 185 mm
Official Journal of: Organ d. Verb. Österr. Baumaschinenhändler
Supplement(s): topgebrauchte.at
BUSINESS: CONSTRUCTION

BERGAUF
720038A75L-20
Editorial: Olympiastr. 37, 6020 INNSBRUCK
Tel: 512 5954711 **Fax:** 512 575528
Email: redaktion@alpenverein.at **Web site:** http://www.bergauf-magazin.at
Freq: 5 issues yearly; Free to qualifying individuals
Annual Sub.: EUR 7,27; **Circ:** 230,000
Editor: Gerold Benedikter
Profile: Publication containing news from the Linz section of the Austrian Alpine Club.
Language(s): German
ADVERTISING RATES:
Full Page Mono .... EUR 5020
Full Page Colour .... EUR 6690
Mechanical Data: Type Area: 240 x 184 mm, No. of Columns (Display): 4, Col Widths (Display): 43 mm
Copy instructions: *Copy Date:* 35 days prior to publication
CONSUMER: SPORT: Outdoor

BERICHTE FÜR ÖKOLOGIE UND NATURSCHUTZ DER STADT LINZ
736973A57-1122
Editorial: Hauptstr. 1, 4041 LINZ **Tel:** 732 70701862
Fax: 732 70701874
Email: friedrich.schwarz@mag.linz.at **Web site:** http://www.linz.at/umwelt
Cover Price: EUR 28,00; **Circ:** 300
Editor: Friedrich Schwarz
Profile: Reports about ecology, nature conservation and environmental protection.
Language(s): German

BESSER WOHNEN
722581A74C-120
Editorial: Stelzhamergasse 4/9, 1030 WIEN
Tel: 1 712569214 **Fax:** 1 712569250
Email: redaktion@besser-wohnen.co.at **Web site:** http://www.besser-wohnen.co.at
Freq: 10 issues yearly; **Annual Sub.:** EUR 26,00; **Circ:** 60,383
Editor: Franz Klar; **Advertising Manager:** Franz Klar
Profile: Magazine with ideas on home furnishings and decoration.
Language(s): German
ADVERTISING RATES:
Full Page Colour .... EUR 7700
Mechanical Data: Type Area: 265 x 185 mm, No. of Columns (Display): 3, Col Widths (Display): 58 mm
Copy instructions: *Copy Date:* 28 days prior to publication
Supplement(s): besser Reisen
CONSUMER: WOMEN'S INTEREST CONSUMER MAGAZINES: Home & Family

BESSERES OBST
722577A26C-10
Editorial: Sturzgasse 1a, 1140 WIEN **Tel:** 1 98177163
Fax: 1 98177120
Email: g.luttenberger@agrarverlag.at **Web site:** http://www.besseres-obst.at
Freq: 11 issues yearly; **Annual Sub.:** EUR 85,90; **Circ:** 3,750
Editor: Gabriele Luttenberger; **Advertising Manager:** Romana Hummer-Schnierleitner
Profile: Official journal of the Austrian Association of Fruit Growers.
Language(s): German
ADVERTISING RATES:
Full Page Mono .... EUR 2121
Full Page Colour .... EUR 3159
Mechanical Data: Type Area: 260 x 175 mm, No. of Columns (Display): 4, Col Widths (Display): 40 mm
Copy instructions: *Copy Date:* 27 days prior to publication
Official Journal of: Organ d. Österr. Bundes-Obstbauverb.
BUSINESS: GARDEN TRADE

BESTSELLER
722599A2A-120
Editorial: Brunner Feldstr. 45, 2380 PERCHTOLDSDORF **Tel:** 1 86648601
Fax: 1 86648600
Email: bestseller@manstein.at **Web site:** http://www.horizont.at/bestseller
Freq: 6 issues yearly; **Annual Sub.:** EUR 65,00; **Circ:** 12,800
Editor: Sebastian Loudon; **Advertising Manager:** Martina Hofmann
Profile: Magazine focusing on marketing and sales, publicity and public relations.
Language(s): German
ADVERTISING RATES:
Full Page Mono .... EUR 2370
Full Page Colour .... EUR 4580
Mechanical Data: Type Area: 244 x 203 mm
Copy instructions: *Copy Date:* 25 days prior to publication
Supplement(s): trend Bestseller Medien spezial
BUSINESS: COMMUNICATIONS, ADVERTISING & MARKETING

BETON- UND STAHLBETONBAU
1775758A4E-1308
Editorial: Peter-Jordan-Str. 82, 1190 WIEN
Tel: 1 476545253 **Fax:** 1 476545292
Email: bust@iki.boku.ac.at
Freq: Monthly; **Annual Sub.:** EUR 426,93; **Circ:** 2,342
Editor: Konrad Bergmeister; **Advertising Manager:** Jost Lüddecke
Profile: Building industry magazine.
Language(s): German
ADVERTISING RATES:
Full Page Mono .... EUR 2740
Full Page Colour .... EUR 4285
Mechanical Data: Type Area: 260 x 181 mm, No. of Columns (Display): 4, Col Widths (Display): 42 mm
Copy instructions: *Copy Date:* 21 days prior to publication
BUSINESS: ARCHITECTURE & BUILDING: Building

BETONKALENDER
1749625A4E-1304
Editorial: Peter-Jordan-Str. 82, 1190 WIEN
Tel: 1 476545253 **Fax:** 1 476545292
Email: bust@iki.boku.ac.at
Freq: Annual; **Cover Price:** EUR 165,00; **Circ:** 14,000
Editor: Konrad Bergmeister; **Advertising Manager:** Norbert Schippel
Profile: Reference work for practitioners in structural engineering and coveted advertising medium of the construction industry.
Language(s): German
ADVERTISING RATES:
Full Page Mono .... EUR 2300
Full Page Colour .... EUR 3710
Mechanical Data: Type Area: 180 x 124 mm
Copy instructions: *Copy Date:* 50 days prior to publication

BEWUSST SEIN
722662A74G-15
Editorial: Postfach 36, 1042 WIEN **Tel:** 1 4709850
Fax: 1 9207080
Email: office@bewusst-sein.net **Web site:** http://www.bewusst-sein.net
Freq: 10 issues yearly; Free to qualifying individuals
Annual Sub.: EUR 13,00; **Circ:** 20,000
Editor: Margarete Frank
Profile: Magazine about health and nature including self-development, body awareness, human psychology, holistic medicine, environment and philosophy of nature.
Language(s): German
ADVERTISING RATES:
Full Page Mono .... EUR 505
Full Page Colour .... EUR 556
Mechanical Data: Type Area: 190 x 133 mm
CONSUMER: WOMEN'S INTEREST CONSUMER MAGAZINES: Slimming & Health

BEYARS.COM
1704521A7-1
Editorial: Hauptstr. 34/34a, 5202 NEUMARKT
Tel: 6216 20000
Email: office@beyars.com **Web site:** http://www.beyars.com
Freq: Daily; **Cover Price:** Paid; **Circ:** 84,407 Unique Users
Editor: Martin Pálffy
Language(s): German
BUSINESS: ANTIQUES

BEZIRKSBLÄTTER KUFSTEIN
722673A72-560
Editorial: Otto-Lasne-Str. 1, 6330 KUFSTEIN
Tel: 5372 64319 **Fax:** 5372 63022
Email: kufstein.red@bezirksblaetter.com **Web site:** http://www.bezirksblaetter.com
Freq: Weekly; **Cover Price:** Free; **Circ:** 36,387
Editor: Sieghard Krabichler; **Advertising Manager:** Manfred Gründler
Profile: Advertising journal (house-to-house) concentrating on local stories.
Language(s): German
ADVERTISING RATES:
Full Page Colour .... EUR 2195
Mechanical Data: Type Area: 260 x 200 mm, No. of Columns (Display): 6, Col Widths (Display): 31 mm
Copy instructions: *Copy Date:* 5 days prior to publication
LOCAL NEWSPAPERS

BEZIRKSBLÄTTER PINZGAU
722728A72-740
Editorial: Schmittenstr. 13, 5700 ZELL
Tel: 6542 72730 **Fax:** 6542 72730233
Email: pinzgau.red@bezirksblaetter.com **Web site:** http://www.bezirksblaetter.com
Freq: Weekly; **Cover Price:** Free; **Circ:** 31,018
Editor: Klaus Moser
Profile: Newspaper containing local news and information for the Pinzgau region.
Language(s): German
ADVERTISING RATES:
Full Page Mono .... EUR 2080
Full Page Colour .... EUR 2080
Mechanical Data: Type Area: 275 x 200 mm, No. of Columns (Display): 6, Col Widths (Display): 31 mm
Copy instructions: *Copy Date:* 5 days prior to publication
LOCAL NEWSPAPERS

BEZIRKSBLÄTTER REUTTE
723200A72-2160
Editorial: Lindenstr. 25/1, 6600 REUTTE
Tel: 5672 63464 **Fax:** 5672 63464233
Email: reutte.red@bezirksblaetter.com **Web site:** http://www.bezirksblaetter.com
Freq: Weekly; **Cover Price:** Free; **Circ:** 11,164
Editor: Sieghard Krabichler; **Advertising Manager:** Günther Reichel
Profile: Advertising journal (house-to-house) concentrating on local stories.
Language(s): German
ADVERTISING RATES:
Full Page Colour .... EUR 1176
Mechanical Data: Type Area: 260 x 200 mm, No. of Columns (Display): 6, Col Widths (Display): 31 mm
Copy instructions: *Copy Date:* 5 days prior to publication
LOCAL NEWSPAPERS

BEZIRKSBLÄTTER SCHWAZ
722677A72-640
Editorial: Münchner Str. 46, 6130 SCHWAZ
Tel: 5242 73186 **Fax:** 5242 73186233
Email: schwaz.red@bezirksblaetter.com **Web site:** http://www.bezirksblaetter.com
Freq: Weekly; **Cover Price:** Free; **Circ:** 34,211
Editor: Sieghard Krabichler; **Advertising Manager:** Wolfgang Engelhardt
Profile: Advertising journal (house-to-house) concentrating on local stories.
Language(s): German
ADVERTISING RATES:
Full Page Colour .... EUR 2018
Mechanical Data: Type Area: 260 x 200 mm, No. of Columns (Display): 6, Col Widths (Display): 31 mm
Copy instructions: *Copy Date:* 5 days prior to publication
LOCAL NEWSPAPERS

BHM BERG- UND HÜTTENMÄNNISCHE MONATSHEFTE
722773A30-1
Editorial: Polzergasse 29a, 8010 GRAZ
Fax: 316 382643
Email: peter.paschen@mueloben.at **Web site:** http://www.springer.at
Freq: Monthly; **Annual Sub.:** EUR 394,00; **Circ:** 3,500
Editor: Peter Paschen
Profile: Journal covering mining, quarrying and the iron and steel industries.
Language(s): German
ADVERTISING RATES:
Full Page Mono .... EUR 1520
Full Page Colour .... EUR 2730
Mechanical Data: Type Area: 250 x 170 mm
Official Journal of: Organ d. Montanuniv. Leoben, d. Eisenhütte Österr., d. Bergmänn. Verb. Österr. u. d. Fachverb. d. Bergwerke u. d. Eisen erzeugenden Industrie
BUSINESS: MINING & QUARRYING

BIBLOS
1685754A60B-45
Editorial: Josefsplatz 1, 1015 WIEN **Tel:** 1 53410642
Fax: 1 53410296
Email: christian.gastgeber@oeaw.ac.at **Web site:** http://www.onb.ac.at/biblos
Freq: Half-yearly; **Annual Sub.:** EUR 45,00; **Circ:** 600
Editor: Christian Gastgeber; **Advertising Manager:** Christian Gastgeber
Language(s): English; French; German; Italian
ADVERTISING RATES:
Full Page Mono .... EUR 500
Mechanical Data: Type Area: 195 x 105 mm, No. of Columns (Display): 2, Col Widths (Display): 61 mm
Copy instructions: *Copy Date:* 40 days prior to publication
BUSINESS: PUBLISHING: Libraries

BIENEN AKTUELL
720036A81G-1
Editorial: Riedl 16a, 6173 OBERPERFUSS
Tel: 5232 82313 **Fax:** 5232 82476
Email: info@walterschoepf.at **Web site:** http://www.bienenaktuell.com
Freq: 11 issues yearly; **Annual Sub.:** EUR 21,00; **Circ:** 21,000
Editor: Walter Schöpf; **Advertising Manager:** Manuela Jantscher
Profile: Magazine about the art of beekeeping.
Language(s): German
ADVERTISING RATES:
Full Page Mono .... EUR 818
Full Page Colour .... EUR 1500
Mechanical Data: Type Area: 252 x 176 mm, No. of Columns (Display): 4, Col Widths (Display): 41 mm
Copy instructions: *Copy Date:* 30 days prior to publication
CONSUMER: ANIMALS & PETS: Bees

BIKER IN ÖSTERREICH
722860A77A-180
Editorial: Oberwaltersdorferstr. 36, 2512 TRIBUSWINKEL **Tel:** 2252 259912 **Fax:** 2252 80204
Email: blacky@biker.at **Web site:** http://www.biker.at
Freq: 6 issues yearly; **Annual Sub.:** EUR 20,00; **Circ:** 20,000
Editor: Albert Schwarz; **Advertising Manager:** Gerhard Laber
Profile: Austrian biker magazine.
Language(s): German

BIO AUSTRIA
726488A21A-300
Editorial: Ellbognerstr. 60, 4020 LINZ
Tel: 732 654884 **Fax:** 732 65488440
Email: ingrid.schuler@bio-austria.at **Web site:** http://www.bio-austria.at
Freq: 6 issues yearly; **Annual Sub.:** EUR 22,00; **Circ:** 17,000
Editor: Ingrid Schuler-Knapp; **Advertising Manager:** Sylvie Hochwarter
Profile: Journal containing articles about organic farming, nutrition and healthy living.
Language(s): German
Readership: Read by farmers, doctors, staff and students in technical colleges and suppliers and retailers of organic foods.
ADVERTISING RATES:
Full Page Colour .... EUR 2093
Mechanical Data: Type Area: 257 x 178 mm
Copy instructions: *Copy Date:* 42 days prior to publication
BUSINESS: AGRICULTURE & FARMING

BIO AUSTRIA SALZBURG
740984A21A-1240
Editorial: Schwarzstr. 19, 5020 SALZBURG
Tel: 662 870571314 **Fax:** 662 878074
Email: salzburg@bio-austria.at **Web site:** http://www.bio-austria.at
Freq: Monthly; **Circ:** 2,400
Editor: Andreas Schwaighofer; **Advertising Manager:** Ingrid Angerer
Profile: Magazine about biological farming.
Language(s): German
ADVERTISING RATES:
Full Page Colour .... EUR 500
Mechanical Data: No. of Columns (Display): 3, Col Widths (Display): 60 mm, Type Area: 260 x 185 mm
Copy instructions: *Copy Date:* 12 days prior to publication

BK-AKTUELL
736713A21A-920
Editorial: St. Egidi 110, 8850 MURAU
Tel: 3532 21680 **Fax:** 3532 21685251
Email: bk-murau@lk-stmk.at **Web site:** http://www.agrarnet.info/murau
Freq: Quarterly; **Cover Price:** Free; **Circ:** 2,017
Editor: Franz Rodlauer; **Advertising Manager:** Thomas Wirnsberger
Profile: Magazine about agriculture and forestry in the region of Muru.
Language(s): German
ADVERTISING RATES:
Full Page Mono .... EUR 1600
Mechanical Data: Type Area: 247 x 160 mm, No. of Columns (Display): 2, Col Widths (Display): 75 mm
Copy instructions: *Copy Date:* 14 days prior to publication

BLICK INS LAND
723122A21A-1488
Editorial: Margaretenstr. 22/2/9, 1040 WIEN
Tel: 1 581289017 **Fax:** 1 581289023
Email: weber@blickinsland.at **Web site:** http://www.blickinsland.at
Freq: 11 issues yearly; **Annual Sub.:** EUR 6,00; **Circ:** 173,000
Editor: Bernhard Weber; **Advertising Manager:** Doris Orthaber-Dättel
Profile: Magazine covering all aspects of agriculture.
Language(s): German
ADVERTISING RATES:
Full Page Mono .... EUR 7950
Full Page Colour .... EUR 9400
Mechanical Data: Type Area: 264 x 200 mm, No. of Columns (Display): 6, Col Widths (Display): 31 mm
Copy instructions: *Copy Date:* 20 days prior to publication
BUSINESS: AGRICULTURE & FARMING

BLICKPUNKT LKW & BUS
723190A49B-1
Editorial: Schützenstr. 11, 6332 KUFSTEIN
Tel: 5372 623320 **Fax:** 5372 623324
Email: gamper-werbung@kufnet.at **Web site:** http://www.blickpunkt-lkw-bus.com
Freq: 8 issues yearly; **Annual Sub.:** EUR 33,00; **Circ:** 15,000
Editor: Helene Gamper; **Advertising Manager:** Helene Gamper
Profile: Magazine covering all aspects of the transport industry within Austria.
Language(s): German
Readership: Aimed at transport companies, haulage contractors, bus and HGV drivers.
ADVERTISING RATES:
Full Page Mono .... EUR 3290
Full Page Colour .... EUR 4900
Mechanical Data: Type Area: 262 x 189 mm, No. of Columns (Display): 4, Col Widths (Display): 43 mm

Copy instructions: *Copy Date:* 14 days prior to publication
BUSINESS: TRANSPORT: Bus & Coach Transport

BLUDENZER ANZEIGER
720920A72-220
Editorial: Rosengasse 5, 6800 FELDKIRCH
Tel: 5522 7233016 **Fax:** 5522 7233085
Email: andreas.feiertag@rzg.at **Web site:** http://www.rzg.at
Freq: Weekly; **Cover Price:** Free; **Circ:** 13,374
Editor: Andreas Feiertag; **Advertising Manager:** Peter Bertole
Profile: Advertising journal (house-to-house) concentrating on local stories.
Language(s): German
ADVERTISING RATES:
Full Page Mono .... EUR 987
Full Page Colour .... EUR 1325
Mechanical Data: Type Area: 265 x 210 mm, No. of Columns (Display): 4, Col Widths (Display): 48 mm
Copy instructions: *Copy Date:* 4 days prior to publication
LOCAL NEWSPAPERS

BLUM JOURNAL
723255A4E-1100
Editorial: Industriestr. 1, 6973 HÖCHST
Tel: 5578 7052320 **Fax:** 5578 70552320
Email: heimo.lubetz@blum.com **Web site:** http://www.blum.com
Freq: Quarterly; **Cover Price:** Free; **Circ:** 2,460
Editor: Heimo Lubetz
Profile: Magazine for employees of Haus- und Julius Blum GmbH.
Language(s): French

BLUM NEWS
723256A4E-1120
Editorial: Industriestr. 1, 6973 HÖCHST
Tel: 5578 7052320 **Fax:** 5578 70552320
Email: heimo.lubetz@blum.com **Web site:** http://www.blum.com
Freq: Quarterly; **Cover Price:** Free; **Circ:** 4,170
Editor: Heimo Lubetz
Profile: Magazine for employees of Haus- und Julius Blum GmbH.
Language(s): English

BLUM-BLÄTTLE
723257A4E-1140
Editorial: Industriestr. 1, 6973 HÖCHST
Tel: 5578 7052320 **Fax:** 5578 70552320
Email: heimo.lubetz@blum.com **Web site:** http://www.blum.com
Freq: Quarterly; **Cover Price:** Free; **Circ:** 45,000
Editor: Heimo Lubetz
Profile: Magazine for employees of Haus- und Julius Blum GmbH.
Language(s): German

BM BAUMAGAZIN
723269A4E-700
Editorial: Dresdner Str. 45, 1200 WIEN
Tel: 1 97000244 **Fax:** 1 970005244
Email: alexander.riell@weka.at **Web site:** http://www.bm-online.at
Freq: 6 issues yearly; **Annual Sub.:** EUR 22,00; **Circ:** 14,383
Editor: Alexander Riell; **Advertising Manager:** Harald Dudas
Profile: Magazine focusing on building techniques and equipment.
Language(s): German
ADVERTISING RATES:
Full Page Colour .... EUR 5870
Mechanical Data: Type Area: 261 x 184 mm
BUSINESS: ARCHITECTURE & BUILDING: Building

BÖRSEN-KURIER
723351A65J-1
Editorial: Lessinggasse 21, 1020 WIEN
Tel: 1 21322811 **Fax:** 1 21322800
Email: redaktion@boersen-kurier.at **Web site:** http://www.boersen-kurier.at
Freq: Weekly; **Annual Sub.:** EUR 83,90; **Circ:** 11,500
Editor: Marius Perger; **Advertising Manager:** Klaus Schweinegger
Profile: National daily containing stock market news and information.
Language(s): German
Mechanical Data: Type Area: 420 x 272 mm, No. of Columns (Display): 6, Col Widths (Display): 42 mm
Copy instructions: *Copy Date:* 6 days prior to publication
Official Journal of: Organ d. Zentralverb. Österr. AG'en u. Ges.'en mbH u. d. Interessenverb. f. Anleger
NATIONAL DAILY & SUNDAY NEWSPAPERS: National Weekly Newspapers

BOTE FÜR TIROL
723437A80-1665
Editorial: Neues Landhaus, 6020 INNSBRUCK
Tel: 512 5082184 **Fax:** 512 5082185
Email: bote@tirol.gv.at **Web site:** http://www.tirol.gv.at/bote
Freq: Weekly; **Annual Sub.:** EUR 23,00; **Circ:** 1,570
Editor: Alois Soraperra
Profile: Regional interest publication for the Austrian Tyrol.
Language(s): German

Readership: Aimed at officials with an interest in public affairs.
Mechanical Data: Type Area: 245 x 167 mm, No. of Columns (Display): 2, Col Widths (Display): 81 mm
Copy instructions: *Copy Date:* 5 days prior to publication
CONSUMER: RURAL & REGIONAL INTEREST

BRIGITTE
723629A74A-200
Editorial: Parkring 12, 1010 WIEN **Tel:** 1 512881031
Fax: 1 512881015
Email: brigitte.wien@guj.de
Freq: 26 issues yearly; **Cover Price:** EUR 2,80; **Circ:** 41,000
Editor: Elisabeth Habitzl; **Advertising Manager:** Maria Gepp
Profile: Women's interest magazine featuring fashion, beauty and lifestyle articles. German edition inclusive four pages for austria, editorial staff in Germany.
Language(s): German
ADVERTISING RATES:
Full Page Mono .... EUR 9400
Full Page Colour .... EUR 9400
Mechanical Data: Type Area: 257 x 185 mm
Copy instructions: *Copy Date:* 42 days prior to publication
CONSUMER: WOMEN'S INTEREST CONSUMER MAGAZINES: Women's Interest

BROT & ROSEN
1645913A74A-880
Editorial: Lindengasse 40, 1070 WIEN
Tel: 1 52125234 **Fax:** 1 5269119
Email: gruene.frauen.wien@gruene.at **Web site:** http://wien.gruene.at/gruenefrauen
Freq: Quarterly; **Cover Price:** Free; **Circ:** 7,000
Editor: Liesbeth Bijl
Profile: Magazine for women from the Green party in Vienna.
Language(s): German

BULLETIN
1605979A2A-923
Editorial: Margaretenstr. 1, 1040 WIEN
Tel: 1 58866326
Email: katja.horninger@austria.info **Web site:** http://www.austria.info/bulletin
Freq: 6 issues yearly; **Annual Sub.:** EUR 20,00; **Circ:** 14,000
Editor: Katja Horninger; **Advertising Manager:** Lucas-Michael Kopecky
Profile: Magazine with ideas and trends for the Austrian tourism business.
Language(s): German
ADVERTISING RATES:
Full Page Mono .... EUR 3000
Full Page Colour .... EUR 3000
Mechanical Data: Type Area: 232 x 184 mm
Copy instructions: *Copy Date:* 21 days prior to publication

BURGENLÄNDISCHE WIRTSCHAFT
723959A14A-540
Editorial: Robert-Graf-Platz 1, 7000 EISENSTADT
Tel: 5909074510 **Fax:** 5909074515
Email: redaktion@wkbgld.at **Web site:** http://wko.at/bgld
Freq: 15 issues yearly; **Circ:** 15,510
Editor: Harald Schermann
Profile: Magazine of the Austrian Business Society for the Burgenland.
Language(s): German
ADVERTISING RATES:
Full Page Mono .... EUR 1643
Full Page Colour .... EUR 2309
Mechanical Data: Type Area: 258 x 186 mm, No. of Columns (Display): 4, Col Widths (Display): 42 mm
BUSINESS: COMMERCE, INDUSTRY & MANAGEMENT

BURGENLÄNDISCHER FEIERABEND
723957A74N-40
Editorial: Ing.-Julius-Raab-Str. 7, 7000 EISENSTADT
Tel: 2682 79944 **Fax:** 2682 79945
Email: office.osb@oevp-burgenland.at **Web site:** http://www.bgld.seniorenbund.at
Freq: Quarterly; **Cover Price:** Free; **Circ:** 12,000
Profile: Magazine for the elderly covering health, travel, rights, politics and fashion.
Language(s): German
Readership: Aimed at the elderly.
ADVERTISING RATES:
Full Page Colour .... EUR 1309
Mechanical Data: Type Area: 270 x 200 mm, No. of Columns (Display): 4, Col Widths (Display): 45 mm
CONSUMER: WOMEN'S INTEREST CONSUMER MAGAZINES: Retirement

BÜRGERMEISTER ZEITUNG
1646239A32A-1127
Editorial: Kutschkergasse 42, 1180 WIEN
Tel: 1 476860 **Fax:** 1 4768621
Email: v.weege@webway.at **Web site:** http://www.buergermeisterzeitung.at
Freq: Monthly; **Annual Sub.:** EUR 154,00; **Circ:** 6,400
Editor: Volker Weege; **Advertising Manager:** Wolfgang Slaby
Profile: Magazine about communal economy, administration, politics and building.
Language(s): German

ADVERTISING RATES:
Full Page Mono .... EUR 3235
Full Page Colour .... EUR 4650
Mechanical Data: Type Area: 275 x 205 mm
Copy instructions: *Copy Date:* 5 days prior to publication
BUSINESS: LOCAL GOVERNMENT, LEISURE & RECREATION: Local Government

BUS & HOTEL REPORT INTERNATIONAL
724009A50-80
Editorial: Haydngasse 6, 1060 WIEN **Tel:** 1 5974985
Fax: 1 597498515
Email: cb@cbverlag.at **Web site:** http://www.cbverlag.at
Freq: Quarterly; **Cover Price:** EUR 2,60; **Circ:** 9,400
Editor: Christian Böhm
Profile: Magazine about coach tours in Europe. Includes bus and technology news.
Language(s): German
Readership: Aimed at coach tour companies, travel agencies and hotels.
ADVERTISING RATES:
Full Page Mono .... EUR 3600
Full Page Colour .... EUR 4500
Mechanical Data: Type Area: 265 x 185 mm, No. of Columns (Display): 4, Col Widths (Display): 43 mm
Copy instructions: *Copy Date:* 8 days prior to publication
BUSINESS: TRAVEL & TOURISM

BUSINESS BESTSELLER
1985713A14A-2657
Editorial: Europahaus, 6020 INNSBRUCK
Tel: 512 561740 **Fax:** 512 561741
Email: redaktion@business-bestseller.com **Web site:** http://www.business-bestseller.com
Freq: Quarterly; **Annual Sub.:** EUR 37,90; **Circ:** 22,000
Profile: Magazine containing book reviews about management literature.
Language(s): German
ADVERTISING RATES:
Full Page Mono .... EUR 1722
Full Page Colour .... EUR 1722
Mechanical Data: Type Area: 248 x 174 mm

BUSINESS PEOPLE
723996A14A-620
Editorial: Geiselbergstr. 15, 1110 WIEN
Tel: 1 60117311 **Fax:** 1 60117156
Email: michaela.stipsits@businesspeople.at **Web site:** http://www.businesspeople.at
Freq: Half-yearly; **Annual Sub.:** EUR 9,90; **Circ:** 23,000
Editor: Michaela Stipsits; **Advertising Manager:** Martin Wrana ,
Profile: Economy magazine.
Language(s): German
ADVERTISING RATES:
Full Page Mono .... EUR 6900
Full Page Colour .... EUR 6900
Mechanical Data: Type Area: 250 x 185 mm
BUSINESS: COMMERCE, INDUSTRY & MANAGEMENT

CAMPING REVUE
724071A91B-220
Editorial: Tauchnergasse 5, 3400 KLOSTERNEUBURG **Tel:** 2243 4042756
Fax: 2243 4042754
Email: office@campingclub.at **Web site:** http://www.campingclub.at
Freq: 6 issues yearly; **Circ:** 14,000
Editor: Roland Fibich
Profile: Publication of the Austrian Camping Club.
Language(s): German
Readership: Read by members of the camping club.
ADVERTISING RATES:
Full Page Mono .... EUR 2142
Full Page Colour .... EUR 2999
Mechanical Data: Type Area: 255 x 185 mm, No. of Columns (Display): 4, Col Widths (Display): 43 mm
Copy instructions: *Copy Date:* 14 days prior to publication
CONSUMER: RECREATION & LEISURE: Camping & Caravanning

C.A.S.H
724138A22A-40
Editorial: Brunner Feldstr. 45, 2380 PERCHTOLDSDORF **Tel:** 1 86648401
Fax: 1 86648400
Email: s.meissl@cash.at **Web site:** http://www.cash.at
Freq: 11 issues yearly; **Annual Sub.:** EUR 30,00; **Circ:** 27,000
Editor: Silvia Meißl; **Advertising Manager:** Karin Hasenhütl
Profile: Magazine concerning the food trade in Austria.
Language(s): German
ADVERTISING RATES:
Full Page Mono .... EUR 4750
Full Page Colour .... EUR 5150
Mechanical Data: Type Area: 267 x 180 mm, No. of Columns (Display): 4, Col Widths (Display): 40 mm
Copy instructions: *Copy Date:* 14 days prior to publication
Supplement(s): Kulinarium Bayern
BUSINESS: FOOD

CC JOURNAL
1641685A2A-926
Editorial: Zedlitzgasse 5/104, 1010 WIEN
Tel: 2236 8123304 **Fax:** 2236 8123300
Email: redaktion@mackcrossmedia.at **Web site:** http://www.ccjournal.at
Freq: Annual; **Annual Sub.:** EUR 25,00; **Circ:** 7,500
Editor: Renate Haiden; **Advertising Manager:** Georg Mack
Profile: Magazine about call centres, CRM and telecommunications.
Language(s): German
ADVERTISING RATES:
Full Page Mono .... EUR 3900
Full Page Colour .... EUR 3900
Mechanical Data: Type Area: 280 x 210 mm

CD AUSTRIA
724169A5F-1
Editorial: Tobra 9, 4320 PERG **Tel:** 7262 575570
Fax: 7262 5755744
Email: redaktion@cda-verlag.com **Web site:** http://www.cd-austria.at
Freq: Monthly; **Annual Sub.:** EUR 74,95; **Circ:** 16,030
Editor: Harald Gutzelnig
Profile: Computing magazine focusing on multimedia applications.
Language(s): German
Readership: Aimed at the general public.
ADVERTISING RATES:
Full Page Mono .... EUR 3990
Full Page Colour .... EUR 4990
Mechanical Data: Type Area: 240 x 170 mm
Copy instructions: *Copy Date:* 14 days prior to publication
Supplement(s): Schule Aktiv!
BUSINESS: COMPUTERS & AUTOMATION: Multimedia

CENTRAL EUROPEAN JOURNAL OF OPERATIONS RESEARCH
1804509A14A-2600
Editorial: Universitätsstr. 15/E3, 8010 GRAZ
Tel: 31 63803490 **Fax:** 31 63809560
Email: ulrike.leopold@uni-graz.at **Web site:** http://www.springerlink.com
Freq: Quarterly; **Annual Sub.:** EUR 338,00; **Circ:** 339
Editor: Ulrike Leopold-Wildburger
Profile: The Central European Journal of Operations Research provides an international readership with high quality papers that cover the theory and practice of OR and the relationship of OR methods to modern quantitative economics and business administration. The focus is on topics such as: - finance and banking - measuring productivity and efficiency in the public sector - environmental and energy issues - computational tools for strategic decision support - production management and logistics - planning and scheduling. The journal publishes theoretical papers as well as application-oriented contributions and practical case studies.
Language(s): English
ADVERTISING RATES:
Full Page Mono .... EUR 740
Full Page Colour .... EUR 1780
Mechanical Data: Type Area: 200 x 130 mm
Official Journal of: Organ d. Österr. Ges. f. Operations Research

CENTRAL EUROPEAN JOURNAL OF OPERATIONS RESEARCH
1804509A14A-2611
Editorial: Universitätsstr. 15/E3, 8010 GRAZ
Tel: 31 63803490 **Fax:** 31 63809560
Email: ulrike.leopold@uni-graz.at **Web site:** http://www.springerlink.com
Freq: Quarterly; **Annual Sub.:** EUR 338,00; **Circ:** 339
Editor: Ulrike Leopold-Wildburger
Profile: The Central European Journal of Operations Research provides an international readership with high quality papers that cover the theory and practice of OR and the relationship of OR methods to modern quantitative economics and business administration. The focus is on topics such as: - finance and banking - measuring productivity and efficiency in the public sector - environmental and energy issues - computational tools for strategic decision support - production management and logistics - planning and scheduling. The journal publishes theoretical papers as well as application-oriented contributions and practical case studies.
Language(s): English
ADVERTISING RATES:
Full Page Mono .... EUR 740
Full Page Colour .... EUR 1780
Mechanical Data: Type Area: 200 x 130 mm
Official Journal of: Organ d. Österr. Ges. f. Operations Research

CENTRALBLATT FÜR DAS GESAMTE FORSTWESEN
724193A46-1
Editorial: Sturzgasse 1a, 1140 WIEN **Tel:** 1 981770
Fax: 1 98177111
Email: office@agrarverlag.at **Web site:** http://www.agrarverlag.at
Freq: Quarterly; **Annual Sub.:** EUR 205,00
Editor: Hubert Hasenauer
Profile: Journal publishes scientific papers related to forest- and wood science, environmental science, natural protections as well as forest ecosystem research.
Language(s): German

Official Journal of: Organ d. Univ. f. Bodenkultur, Fachgruppe Forst- u. Holzwirtschaft u. d. Forstl. Bundesversuchsanstalt
BUSINESS: TIMBER, WOOD & FORESTRY

CHANGE MANAGEMENT
725675A14A-800
Editorial: Entenplatz 1a, 8020 GRAZ
Tel: 316 7189400 **Fax:** 316 71894040
Email: office@icg.eu.com **Web site:** http://www.icg.eu.com
Freq: Quarterly; **Cover Price:** Free; **Circ:** 5,310
Editor: Manfred Höfler
Profile: Customer magazine containing information and tips for managers.
Language(s): German

CHEFINFO
724235A14A-680
Editorial: Zamenhofstr. 9, 4020 LINZ
Tel: 732 6964453 **Fax:** 732 696441
Email: l.kruckenhauser@chefinfo.at **Web site:** http://www.chefinfo.at
Freq: 10 issues yearly; **Annual Sub.:** EUR 22,00; **Circ:** 21,150
Editor: Luzia Kruckenhauser-Klement; **Advertising Manager:** Christian Schüttengruber
Language(s): German
ADVERTISING RATES:
Full Page Mono .... EUR 3400
Full Page Colour .... EUR 3400
Mechanical Data: Type Area: 255 x 186 mm, No. of Columns (Display): 4, Col Widths (Display): 42 mm
BUSINESS: COMMERCE, INDUSTRY & MANAGEMENT

CHIRURGIE
724293A56A-340
Editorial: Hollandstr. 14, 1020 WIEN **Tel:** 1 5333542
Fax: 1 533354219
Email: chirurgie@aon.at **Web site:** http://www.boec.at
Freq: Quarterly; **Circ:** 5,500
Editor: Sebastian Roka; **Advertising Manager:** Katharina Moser
Profile: Magazine for surgeons and for members of the Surgeons' Professional Association.
Language(s): German
ADVERTISING RATES:
Full Page Colour .... EUR 2050
Mechanical Data: Type Area: 243 x 177 mm
Copy instructions: *Copy Date:* 28 days prior to publication

CITY
1861440A65A-80_101
Editorial: Leberstr. 122, 1110 WIEN **Tel:** 1 74095559
Fax: 1 74095384
Email: roland.kanfer@bohmann.at **Web site:** http://www.magazin-city.at
Freq: Quarterly; **Circ:** 60,000
Editor: Roland Kanfer
Profile: Reporting on the Vienna office buildings and architecture. Supplement in the Vienna edition of "Der Standard". Facebook: https://www.facebook.com/pages/city-das-magazin-f%C3%BCr-urbane-gestaltung/227876473899588.
Language(s): German
ADVERTISING RATES:
Full Page Mono .... EUR 12500
Full Page Colour .... EUR 12500
Mechanical Data: Type Area: 376 x 260 mm
Supplement to: Der Standard
NATIONAL DAILY & SUNDAY NEWSPAPERS: Unabhängiges konservatives MdEP

CLINICAL NEUROPATHOLOGY
724428G56A-2140
Editorial: Währinger Gürtel 18, 1097 WIEN
Email: johannes.hainfellner@meduniwien.ac.at
Freq: 6 issues yearly; **Annual Sub.:** EUR 205,00; **Circ:** 2,000
Editor: Johannes Hainfellner; **Advertising Manager:** Jörg Feistle
Profile: Journal publishes reviews and editorials, original papers, short communications and reports on recent advances in the entire field of clinical neuropathology.
Language(s): English
Mechanical Data: Type Area: 242 x 167 mm, No. of Columns (Display): 3, Col Widths (Display): 56 mm
Copy instructions: *Copy Date:* 28 days prior to publication
Official Journal of: Organ d. European Confederation of Neuropathological Societies

CLINICUM
724431A56A-360
Editorial: Wiedner Hauptstr. 120, 1050 WIEN
Tel: 1 54600330 **Fax:** 1 54600730
Email: beermann@clinicum.at **Web site:** http://www.clinicum.at
Freq: 10 issues yearly; **Annual Sub.:** EUR 44,00; **Circ:** 17,000
Editor: Birgit Beermann; **Advertising Manager:** Reinhard Rosenberger
Profile: Publication about modern medicine and hospitals.
Language(s): German
ADVERTISING RATES:
Full Page Colour .... EUR 3600
Mechanical Data: Type Area: 247 x 185 mm
Copy instructions: *Copy Date:* 14 days prior to publication
BUSINESS: HEALTH & MEDICAL

CLUB-NEWS
738690A2A-640
Editorial: Landstr. 31, 4020 LINZ **Tel:** 732 775634
Fax: 732 772016205
Email: ooe@presseclub.at **Web site:** http://www.presseclub.at
Freq: 22 issues yearly; **Circ:** 1,180
Editor: Helmuth K. Köhrer; **Advertising Manager:** Helmuth K. Köhrer
Profile: Magazine with event dates and reports of the Austrian press club.
Language(s): German
ADVERTISING RATES:
Full Page Mono .... EUR 1000
Full Page Colour .... EUR 2500
Mechanical Data: Type Area: 275 x 174 mm, No. of Columns (Display): 3, Col Widths (Display): 56 mm
Copy instructions: *Copy Date:* 10 days prior to publication

COMPUTERWELT
724569A5B-1
Editorial: Halbgasse 3, 1070 WIEN **Tel:** 1 523050818
Fax: 1 523050844
Email: edmund.lindau@itverlag.at **Web site:** http://www.computerwelt.at
Freq: 24 issues yearly; **Annual Sub.:** EUR 47,00; **Circ:** 18,000
Editor: Edmund E. Lindau; **Advertising Manager:** Manfred Zimmermann
Profile: Publication concerning the data processing industry.
Language(s): German
ADVERTISING RATES:
Full Page Mono .... EUR 9270
Full Page Colour .... EUR 9270
Mechanical Data: Type Area: 396 x 284 mm, No. of Columns (Display): 6, Col Widths (Display): 45 mm
Copy instructions: *Copy Date:* 14 days prior to publication
BUSINESS: COMPUTERS & AUTOMATION: Data Processing

CONNEX
724599A14K-1
Editorial: Heinestr. 38, 1020 WIEN **Tel:** 1 21300317
Fax: 1 21300327
Email: johannes.stern@as-institute.at **Web site:** http://www.as-institute.at
Freq: 6 issues yearly; **Cover Price:** EUR 3,50
Free to qualifying individuals ; **Circ:** 3,500
Editor: Johannes Stern
Profile: Journal from the Austrian Standards Institute about national, European and international standards.
Language(s): German
BUSINESS: COMMERCE, INDUSTRY & MANAGEMENT: Quality Assurance

CONTRACT
1644948A4E-1286
Editorial: Wiedner Hauptstr. 120, 1051 WIEN
Tel: 1 54664342 **Fax:** 1 5466450342
Email: contract@wirtschaftsverlag.at **Web site:** http://www.bauforum.at
Freq: 3 issues yearly; **Circ:** 12,500
Editor: Tom Cervinka; **Advertising Manager:** Franz-Michael Seidl
Profile: Magazine on interior building and design.
Language(s): German
ADVERTISING RATES:
Full Page Colour .... EUR 3000
Mechanical Data: Type Area: 255 x 185 mm
Copy instructions: *Copy Date:* 21 days prior to publication
Supplement to: Forum

CORPORAID MAGAZIN
1647288A32G-963
Editorial: Möllwaldplatz 5, 1040 WIEN **Tel:** 1 9690254
Fax: 1 96902545
Email: office@corporaid.at **Web site:** http://www.corporaid.at
Freq: 5 issues yearly; **Circ:** 45,000
Editor: Christoph Eder; **Advertising Manager:** Barbara Coudenhove-Kalergi
Profile: Magazine about the global fight against poverty from a social and economic perspective.
Language(s): German
ADVERTISING RATES:
Full Page Mono .... EUR 5900
Full Page Colour .... EUR 5900
Mechanical Data: Type Area: 240 x 183 mm
Supplement to: WirtschaftsBlatt

CORPORAID MAGAZIN
1647288A65A-121_103
Editorial: Möllwaldplatz 5, 1040 WIEN **Tel:** 1 9690254
Fax: 1 96902545
Email: office@corporaid.at **Web site:** http://www.corporaid.at
Freq: 5 issues yearly; **Circ:** 45,000
Editor: Christoph Eder; **Advertising Manager:** Barbara Coudenhove-Kalergi
Profile: Magazine about the global fight against poverty from a social and economic perspective.
Language(s): German
ADVERTISING RATES:
Full Page Mono .... EUR 5900
Full Page Colour .... EUR 5900
Mechanical Data: Type Area: 240 x 183 mm
Supplement to: WirtschaftsBlatt
NATIONAL DAILY & SUNDAY NEWSPAPERS: Unabhängiges konservatives MdEP

CREATION/PRODUCTION
724712A2A-180
Editorial: Marc-Aurel-Str. 9, 1011 WIEN
Tel: 1 536600 **Fax:** 1 53660935
Email: cp@falter.at **Web site:** http://www.creation-production.at
Freq: Annual; **Cover Price:** EUR 48,00; **Circ:** 7,000
Advertising Manager: Sigrid Johler
Profile: Directory about the creative branch in Austria.
Language(s): German
ADVERTISING RATES:
Full Page Mono .... EUR 1290
Full Page Colour .... EUR 1990
Mechanical Data: Type Area: 130 x 100 mm

DA DIE APOTHEKE
720985A74G-424
Editorial: Spitalgasse 31, 1090 WIEN
Tel: 1 402358826 **Fax:** 1 4085355
Email: redaktion@apoverlag.at **Web site:** http://www.apoverlag.at
Freq: Monthly; **Cover Price:** Free; **Circ:** 100,000
Editor: Monika Heinrich
Profile: Magazine concerning general pharmaceutical and health issues.
Language(s): German
ADVERTISING RATES:
Full Page Mono .... EUR 3400
Full Page Colour .... EUR 3400
Mechanical Data: Type Area: 271 x 188 mm, No. of Columns (Display): 4, Col Widths (Display): 44 mm
Copy instructions: *Copy Date:* 36 days prior to publication
CONSUMER: WOMEN'S INTEREST CONSUMER MAGAZINES: Slimming & Health

DACH WAND
724775A4E-720
Editorial: Wiedner Hauptstr. 120, 1051 WIEN
Tel: 1 54664353 **Fax:** 1 5466450353
Email: b.tegtbauer@wirtschaftsverlag.at **Web site:** http://www.dachwand.at
Freq: 6 issues yearly; **Annual Sub.:** EUR 48,00; **Circ:** 3,000
Editor: Birgit Tegtbauer; **Advertising Manager:** Franz-Michael Seidl
Profile: Magazine about roof and wall insulation.
Language(s): German
Readership: Read by decorators, plasterers and master builders.
ADVERTISING RATES:
Full Page Mono .... EUR 1795
Full Page Colour .... EUR 2565
Mechanical Data: Type Area: 255 x 185 mm
Copy instructions: *Copy Date:* 21 days prior to publication
BUSINESS: ARCHITECTURE & BUILDING: Building

DAVID
724844A87-520
Editorial: Hofgraben 1/1, 2490 EBENFURTH
Tel: 1 8886945 **Fax:** 1 8886945
Email: david_kultur@gmx.at **Web site:** http://www.davidkultur.at
Freq: Quarterly; Free to qualifying individuals
Annual Sub.: EUR 36,00; **Circ:** 10,750
Editor: Ilan Beresin; **Advertising Manager:** Ilan Beresin
Profile: Jewish cultural and religious magazine.
Language(s): German
ADVERTISING RATES:
Full Page Mono .... EUR 2000
Full Page Colour .... EUR 3000
Mechanical Data: Type Area: 262 x 180 mm
Copy instructions: *Copy Date:* 30 days prior to publication
CONSUMER: RELIGIOUS

DERPLAN
721187A4E-80
Editorial: Karlsgasse 9, 1040 WIEN **Tel:** 1 5051781
Fax: 1 5051005
Email: brigitte.groihofer@arching.at **Web site:** http://wien.arching.at
Freq: Quarterly; **Circ:** 4,500
Editor: Brigitte Groihofer; **Advertising Manager:** Brigitte Groihofer
Profile: Magazine for architects and engineers with professional, legal and economic issues.
Language(s): German
ADVERTISING RATES:
Full Page Mono .... EUR 2500
Full Page Colour .... EUR 3100
Mechanical Data: Type Area: 427 x 281 mm

DEUTSCHE ZEITSCHRIFT FÜR AKUPUNKTUR
1792755A56A-2004
Editorial: St.-Peter-Hauptstr. 31f, 8042 GRAZ
Email: t.ots@daegfa.de
Freq: Quarterly; **Annual Sub.:** EUR 167,00; **Circ:** 17,200
Editor: Thomas Ots
Profile: The Deutsche Zeitschrift für Akupunktur is the largest circulation magazine outside China for Acupuncture and Related Techniques (all forms of acupuncture, moxibustion, laser therapy, Neural therapy, reflex therapy, Tuina, dietetics, herbal medicine, homeopathy). It is the forum for scientific research and practical application of these techniques in clinic and practice.
Language(s): English; German
ADVERTISING RATES:
Full Page Mono .... EUR 2100
Full Page Colour .... EUR 3420
Mechanical Data: Type Area: 225 x 170 mm
Official Journal of: Organ d. Dt. Ärzteges. f. Akupunktur e.V., d. Österr. Ges. f. Akupunktur e.V., d. Dt. Ges. f. Akupunktur u. Neuraltherapie e.V., d. Österr. Wissenschaftl. Ärzteges. f. Akupunktur u. Association Luxembourgeoise d. Médecins-Acupuncteurs

DHK ASPEKTE
725196A63-100
Editorial: Schwarzenbergplatz 5/3/1, 1030 WIEN
Tel: 1 545141724 **Fax:** 1 5452259
Email: steffen.lenke@dhk.at **Web site:** http://www.dhk.at
Freq: 5 issues yearly; **Cover Price:** EUR 7,50
Free to qualifying individuals ; **Circ:** 10,000
Editor: Thomas Gindele; **Advertising Manager:** Corina Kaltenhauser
Profile: Publication of the German Chamber of Commerce in Austria, covering topics such as market trends, foreign trade, import and export and business news from Eastern Europe.
Language(s): German
ADVERTISING RATES:
Full Page Colour .... EUR 1700
Mechanical Data: Type Area: 250 x 175 mm, No. of Columns (Display): 4, Col Widths (Display): 40 mm
Copy instructions: *Copy Date:* 28 days prior to publication
BUSINESS: REGIONAL BUSINESS

DIABETES FORUM
1646165A56A-1944
Editorial: Seidengasse 9/1/1, 1070 WIEN
Tel: 1 407311126 **Fax:** 1 4073114
Email: a.brugger@medmedia.at **Web site:** http://www.medmedia.at
Freq: 5 issues yearly; **Cover Price:** EUR 9,50; **Circ:** 8,500
Editor: Christoph Schnack; **Advertising Manager:** Judith Hafner
Profile: Magazine from the Austrian Association of Diabetes.
Language(s): German
ADVERTISING RATES:
Full Page Colour .... EUR 3190
Mechanical Data: Type Area: 297 x 210 mm
Copy instructions: *Copy Date:* 14 days prior to publication

DINERS CLUB MAGAZIN
725310A94H-340
Editorial: Rainergasse 1/3, 1041 WIEN
Tel: 1 50135283
Email: s.schatz@mediaunit.at **Web site:** http://www.dinersclub.at
Freq: 5 issues yearly; **Cover Price:** EUR 3,50; **Circ:** 136,397
Editor: Stefan Schatz; **Advertising Manager:** Brigitte Cocyan-Mittermayer
Profile: Magazine for holders of Diners Club credit cards.
Language(s): German
ADVERTISING RATES:
Full Page Colour .... EUR 8740
Mechanical Data: Type Area: 235 x 179 mm
CONSUMER: OTHER CLASSIFICATIONS: Customer Magazines

DIRNDL REVUE
1852543A74A-944
Editorial: Streleweg 20, 6460 IMST **Tel:** 5412 69990
Fax: 5412 699954
Email: stapftextilimst@aon.at **Web site:** http://www.stapftextil.at
Freq: Annual; **Cover Price:** EUR 13,20; **Circ:** 18,000
Editor: Walter Paral
Profile: Magazine about homemade fashion.
Language(s): German

DISPO
725367A10-1
Editorial: Dresdner Str. 45, 1200 WIEN
Tel: 1 97000242 **Fax:** 1 970005242
Email: stefan.lenz@weka.at **Web site:** http://www.dispo.co.at
Freq: 10 issues yearly; **Annual Sub.:** EUR 34,00; **Circ:** 9,300
Editor: Stefan Lenz; **Advertising Manager:** Sebastian Wegmann
Profile: Publication about logistics.
Language(s): German
Readership: Aimed at managers of large and medium-sized businesses.
ADVERTISING RATES:
Full Page Colour .... EUR 4870
Mechanical Data: Type Area: 260 x 185 mm
BUSINESS: MATERIALS HANDLING

DIVA
725383A74B-2
Editorial: Geiselbergstr. 15, 1110 WIEN
Tel: 1 60117966 **Fax:** 1 60117240
Email: diva@diva-online.at **Web site:** http://www.diva-online.at
Freq: 9 issues yearly; **Annual Sub.:** EUR 29,00; **Circ:** 35,000

Editor: Karen Müller; **Advertising Manager:** Cornelia Steidl
Profile: High fashion magazine.
Language(s): German
ADVERTISING RATES:
Full Page Mono .... EUR 6200
Full Page Colour .... EUR 6200
Mechanical Data: Type Area: 278 x 210 mm
Copy instructions: *Copy Date:* 21 days prior to publication
CONSUMER: WOMEN'S INTEREST CONSUMER MAGAZINES: Women's Interest - Fashion

DOKTOR IN WIEN 747354A56A-1840
Editorial: Wiedner Hauptstr. 120, 1050 WIEN
Tel: 1 54600112 **Fax:** 1 54600710
Email: doktorinwien@medizin-medien.at **Web site:** http://www.medizin-medien.at
Freq: 11 issues yearly; **Annual Sub.:** EUR 46,00; **Circ:** 15,200
Editor: Jörg Hofmann; **Advertising Manager:** Reinhard Rosenberger
Profile: Journal concerning medical practice in Vienna.
Language(s): German
ADVERTISING RATES:
Full Page Mono .... EUR 2780
Full Page Colour .... EUR 2780
Mechanical Data: Type Area: 257 x 184 mm, No. of Columns (Display): 3, Col Widths (Display): 58 mm
Copy instructions: *Copy Date:* 25 days prior to publication
Supplement(s): ärzte Exklusiv
BUSINESS: HEALTH & MEDICAL

E & I 726600A17-60
Editorial: Krenngasse 37/1, 8010 GRAZ
Tel: 316 8737919 **Fax:** 316 8737917
Email: redaktion@ove.at **Web site:** http://www.springer.at
Freq: Monthly; **Circ:** 6,000
Editor: Peter Reichel
Profile: Magazine covering all aspects of electro and information technologies.
Language(s): German
ADVERTISING RATES:
Full Page Colour .... EUR 2900
Mechanical Data: Type Area: 250 x 170 mm

E&W 726602A43A-40
Editorial: Wilhelminenstr. 91/IIc, 1160 WIEN
Tel: 1 485314926 **Fax:** 1 486903230
Email: d.schebach@elektro.at **Web site:** http://www.elektro.at
Freq: 11 issues yearly; **Annual Sub.:** EUR 62,70; **Circ:** 13,034
Editor: Dominik Schebach
Profile: Magazine with specific information for the electronics branch.
Language(s): German
ADVERTISING RATES:
Full Page Mono .... EUR 4300
Full Page Colour .... EUR 5790
Mechanical Data: Type Area: 255 x 180 mm, No. of Columns (Display): 4, Col Widths (Display): 41 mm
BUSINESS: ELECTRICAL RETAIL TRADE

ECHO 725846A73-80
Editorial: Eduard-Bodem-Gasse 6, 6020 INNSBRUCK **Tel:** 512 342170 **Fax:** 512 34217020
Email: redaktion@echotirol.at **Web site:** http://www.echoonline.at
Freq: 11 issues yearly; **Annual Sub.:** EUR 22,00; **Circ:** 25,000
Editor: Armin Muigg; **Advertising Manager:** Birgit Steinlechner
Profile: Tyrolean illustrated magazine.
Language(s): German
ADVERTISING RATES:
Full Page Mono .... EUR 3255
Full Page Colour .... EUR 3255
Mechanical Data: Type Area: 250 x 184 mm
Copy instructions: *Copy Date:* 14 days prior to publication
Supplement(s): Echo Gesund & Leben; Echo Science

ECHO 1703345A73-408
Editorial: Carl-Zuckmayer-Str. 38, 5020 SALZBURG
Tel: 662 457090 **Fax:** 662 45709020
Email: redaktion@echosalzburg.at **Web site:** http://www.echoonline.at
Freq: 11 issues yearly; **Annual Sub.:** EUR 20,00; **Circ:** 18,000
Editor: Manfred Parzmayer
Profile: Tyrolean illustrated magazine.
Language(s): German
ADVERTISING RATES:
Full Page Mono .... EUR 2950
Full Page Colour .... EUR 2809
Mechanical Data: Type Area: 250 x 184 mm
Supplement(s): Echo Gesund & Leben; Echo Science

DER ECKART 725883A57-1121
Editorial: Fuhrmannsgasse 18a, 1080 WIEN
Tel: 1 4082273 **Fax:** 1 4022882
Email: redaktion@dereckart.at **Web site:** http://www.dereckart.at
Freq: 11 issues yearly; **Annual Sub.:** EUR 35,00; **Circ:** 5,600
Editor: Thomas Hüttner
Profile: Magazine focusing on Austrian environmental issues. Also includes news and reports about German speaking communities all over the world.
Language(s): German

DER ECKART 725883A57-1168
Editorial: Fuhrmannsgasse 18a, 1080 WIEN
Tel: 1 4082273 **Fax:** 1 4022882
Email: redaktion@dereckart.at **Web site:** http://www.dereckart.at
Freq: 11 issues yearly; **Annual Sub.:** EUR 35,00; **Circ:** 5,600
Editor: Thomas Hüttner
Profile: Magazine focusing on Austrian environmental issues. Also includes news and reports about German speaking communities all over the world.
Language(s): German

ECO.NOVA 725904A1A-221
Editorial: Hunoldstr. 20, 6020 INNSBRUCK
Tel: 512 2900880 **Fax:** 512 29008870
Email: loreck@econova.at **Web site:** http://www.econova.at
Freq: 14 issues yearly; **Annual Sub.:** EUR 19,00; **Circ:** 25,000
Editor: Christoph Loreck
Profile: Economics magazine.
Language(s): German

EHE UND FAMILIEN 725955A74C-140
Editorial: Spiegelgasse 3/3/9, 1010 WIEN
Tel: 1 515523201 **Fax:** 1 515523699
Email: luef@familie.at **Web site:** http://www.familie.at
Freq: 6 issues yearly; Free to qualifying individuals **Annual Sub.:** EUR 10,50; **Circ:** 40,000
Editor: Christina Luef
Profile: Magazine covering aspects of family life.
Language(s): German
ADVERTISING RATES:
Full Page Mono .... EUR 2800
Full Page Colour .... EUR 2800
Mechanical Data: Type Area: 272 x 191 mm, No. of Columns (Display): 2, Col Widths (Display): 90 mm
Copy instructions: *Copy Date:* 14 days prior to publication
CONSUMER: WOMEN'S INTEREST CONSUMER MAGAZINES: Home & Family

EHZ AUSTRIA 1645643A43A-61
Editorial: Ameisgasse 49, 1140 WIEN **Tel:** 1 4153927 **Fax:** 1 4153966
Email: w.franz@mbo-media.at **Web site:** http://www.ehzaustria.at
Freq: 11 issues yearly; **Annual Sub.:** EUR 32,00; **Circ:** 6,000
Editor: Wolfgang Franz; **Advertising Manager:** Stefan Wiza
Profile: Magazine for IT and telecommunications traders.
Language(s): German
ADVERTISING RATES:
Full Page Colour .... EUR 3500
Mechanical Data: Type Area: 245 x 182 mm
Copy instructions: *Copy Date:* 14 days prior to publication
BUSINESS: ELECTRICAL RETAIL TRADE

E.L.B.W. UMWELTTECHNIK 726119A57-180
Editorial: Walfischgasse 11/1/8, 1010 WIEN
Tel: 1 5131395 **Fax:** 1 5127369
Email: verlag@lisey.at **Web site:** http://www.lisey.at
Freq: 5 issues yearly; **Annual Sub.:** EUR 17,40; **Circ:** 7,700
Editor: Hedy Gruber; **Advertising Manager:** Hedy Gruber
Profile: Magazine about environmental techniques.
Language(s): German
ADVERTISING RATES:
Full Page Mono .... EUR 3444
Full Page Colour .... EUR 4387
Mechanical Data: Type Area: 266 x 183 mm
Copy instructions: *Copy Date:* 14 days prior to publication
BUSINESS: ENVIRONMENT & POLLUTION

ELEKTRO JOURNAL 764260A17-161
Editorial: Wiedner Hauptstr. 120, 1051 WIEN
Tel: 1 54664355 **Fax:** 1 54664520
Email: c.lanner@wirtschaftsverlag.at **Web site:** http://www.elektrojournal.at
Freq: 10 issues yearly; **Annual Sub.:** EUR 60,00; **Circ:** 12,530
Editor: Reinhard Ebner; **Advertising Manager:** Franz-Michael Seidl
Profile: Magazine from the Association of Electronic Technicians, Radio and Video Technicians.
Language(s): German
ADVERTISING RATES:
Full Page Colour .... EUR 4390
Mechanical Data: Type Area: 255 x 185 mm, No. of Columns (Display): 4, Col Widths (Display): 41 mm
BUSINESS: ELECTRICAL

ELEKTRONIK REPORT 1616542A18A-2
Editorial: Dresdner Str. 45, 1200 WIEN
Tel: 1 97000195 **Fax:** 1 970005195
Email: ronald.riska@weka.at **Web site:** http://www.elektronikreport.at
Freq: 10 issues yearly; **Annual Sub.:** EUR 37,00; **Circ:** 8,100
Editor: Ronald Riska; **Advertising Manager:** Stefan Teubel
Profile: Magazine with information about professional electronics, analysing and describing future trends as well as issues concerning further education in the electronics sector.
Language(s): German
ADVERTISING RATES:
Full Page Colour .... EUR 4760
Mechanical Data: Type Area: 270 x 190 mm
BUSINESS: ELECTRONICS

E-MEDIA 1647388A18B-585
Editorial: Taborstr. 1, 1020 WIEN **Tel:** 1 213120 **Fax:** 1 213202605
Email: schreibershofen.hadubrand@e-media.at **Web site:** http://www.e-media.at
Freq: 25 issues yearly; **Annual Sub.:** EUR 52,90; **Circ:** 66,892
Editor: Hadubrand Schreibershofen; **Advertising Manager:** Wolfgang Senn
Profile: Lifestyle magazine for the Internet generation.
Language(s): German
ADVERTISING RATES:
Full Page Mono .... EUR 11390
Full Page Colour .... EUR 11390
Mechanical Data: Type Area: 250 x 185 mm
Copy instructions: *Copy Date:* 21 days prior to publication

EMISSIONEN 1998523A57-1178
Editorial: Weierfing 68, 4971 AUROLZMÜNSTER
Tel: 7752 9050 **Fax:** 7752 905370
Email: office@scheuch.com **Web site:** http://www.scheuch.com
Freq: Half-yearly; **Circ:** 1,500
Profile: Company publication about ventilation and environmental technology.
Language(s): English

ENNS STADTMAGAZIN 726312A72-2520
Editorial: Lorcher Str. 4, 4470 ENNS
Tel: 7223 8262814 **Fax:** 7223 8262826
Email: ennser.stadtmagazin@med-holzinger-enns.at **Web site:** http://www.mt-i.com/ennser-stadtmagazin.ata
Freq: Monthly; **Cover Price:** Free; **Circ:** 35,000
Editor: Sandra Holzinger
Profile: Advertising journal (house-to-house) concentrating on local stories.
Language(s): German
ADVERTISING RATES:
Full Page Mono .... EUR 1768
Full Page Colour .... EUR 2080
Mechanical Data: Type Area: 266 x 200 mm
LOCAL NEWSPAPERS

DER ENNSTALER 726313A72-2560
Editorial: Mitterbergstr. 36, 8962 GRÖBMING
Tel: 3685 2212113 **Fax:** 3685 22321
Email: ennstaler@walligdruck.at **Web site:** http://www.derennstaler.at
Freq: Weekly; **Cover Price:** EUR 0,90; **Circ:** 9,847
Editor: Franz Wallig
Profile: Regional weekly covering politics, economics, sport, travel, technology and the arts.
Language(s): German
ADVERTISING RATES:
SCC .... EUR 29,00
Mechanical Data: Type Area: 320 x 226 mm, No. of Columns (Display): 4, Col Widths (Display): 54 mm
Copy instructions: *Copy Date:* 2 days prior to publication
LOCAL NEWSPAPERS

ERNEUERBARE ENERGIE 726484A58-100
Editorial: Feldgasse 19, 8200 GLEISDORF
Tel: 3112 5886
Email: office@aee.at **Web site:** http://www.aee.at
Freq: Quarterly; **Circ:** 7,500
Advertising Manager: Eva Steinmüller
Profile: Magazine about solar and wind energy.
Language(s): German

EUROPÄISCHE RUNDSCHAU 726654A82-820
Editorial: Ebendorferstr. 6/4, 1010 WIEN
Tel: 1 4083400 **Fax:** 1 408340011
Email: europ.rundschau@aon.at **Web site:** http://www.europaeische-rundschau.at
Freq: Quarterly; **Annual Sub.:** EUR 31,80; **Circ:** 2,800
Editor: Paul Lendvai
Profile: Magazine about European and international politics.
Language(s): German
ADVERTISING RATES:
Full Page Mono .... EUR 2180
Full Page Colour .... EUR 3270
Mechanical Data: Type Area: 193 x 127 mm
Copy instructions: *Copy Date:* 20 days prior to publication
CONSUMER: CURRENT AFFAIRS & POLITICS

EUROPEAN CIGAR JOURNAL 1753171A74P-276
Editorial: Heiligenstädter Str.43, 1190 WIEN
Tel: 1 90421410 **Fax:** 1 9042141440
Email: redaktion@cigar-cult.com **Web site:** http://www.cigar-cult.com
Freq: Quarterly; **Annual Sub.:** CHF 43,00; **Circ:** 35,000
Editor: Helmut Romé
Profile: Magazine for smokers.
Language(s): English; German
ADVERTISING RATES:
Full Page Mono .... CHF 4700
Full Page Colour .... CHF 4700
Mechanical Data: Type Area: 265 x 185 mm, No. of Columns (Display): 4
Copy instructions: *Copy Date:* 30 days prior to publication

EUROPEAN SURGERY 719515A56A-20
Editorial: Währinger Gürtel 18, 1090 WIEN
Fax: 1 404006898
Email: franz.riegler@meduniwien.ac.at **Web site:** http://www.springer.at
Freq: 6 issues yearly; **Circ:** 1,500
Editor: Franz Martin Riegler
Profile: Medical journal focusing on surgery.
Language(s): English; German
ADVERTISING RATES:
Full Page Mono .... EUR 2540
Full Page Colour .... EUR 3190
Mechanical Data: Type Area: 270 x 170 mm
Copy instructions: *Copy Date:* 28 days prior to publication
Official Journal of: Organ d. Austrian Society of Surgery u. d. Czech Surgical Society u. d. Slovenian Association of Surgeons
BUSINESS: HEALTH & MEDICAL

EUROTAX-AUTO-INFORMATION 726732A31A-3
Editorial: Dresdner Str. 89/3/9, 1200 WIEN
Tel: 1 3323000 **Fax:** 1 3323000100
Email: vienna@eurotax.com **Web site:** http://www.eurotaxglass.at
Freq: Weekly; **Annual Sub.:** EUR 625,00
Profile: Magazine covering all aspects of the motor trade.
Language(s): German
BUSINESS: MOTOR TRADE: Motor Trade Accessories

EWF EAST WEST FORUM 1847738A14C-188
Editorial: Klostergasse 9/10, 1180 WIEN
Tel: 1 4703850 **Fax:** 1 4703849
Email: eastwestforum@gmx.at **Web site:** http://www.east-west-forum.com
Freq: Quarterly; **Circ:** 7,800
Editor: Georg Messner
Profile: Magazine for executives about the economy and politics of East-West trade.
Language(s): English; German

EXPORTER'S 1789543A14C-186
Editorial: Otto-Bauer-Gasse 6, 1060 WIEN
Tel: 1 2351366555 **Fax:** 1 2351366999
Email: s.schatz@cpg.at **Web site:** http://www.newbusiness.at
Freq: 6 issues yearly; **Annual Sub.:** EUR 7,50; **Circ:** 25,000
Editor: Stefan Schatz; **Advertising Manager:** Lorin Polak
Profile: .
Language(s): German
ADVERTISING RATES:
Full Page Mono .... EUR 4000
Full Page Colour .... EUR 4000
Mechanical Data: Type Area: 280 x 210 mm
Copy instructions: *Copy Date:* 30 days prior to publication

EXTRADIENST 726882A2A-220
Editorial: Zieglergasse 1, 1072 WIEN **Tel:** 1 521310 **Fax:** 1 5239217
Email: extradienst@mucha.at **Web site:** http://www.extradienst.at
Freq: 10 issues yearly; **Annual Sub.:** EUR 99,00; **Circ:** 14,160
Editor: Christian W. Mucha
Profile: Magazine providing news from the communications, advertising and marketing industries.
Language(s): German
Readership: Aimed at events organisers, marketing and advertising managers.
ADVERTISING RATES:
Full Page Colour .... EUR 5750
Mechanical Data: Type Area: 243 x 180 mm, No. of Columns (Display): 4, Col Widths (Display): 42 mm

Copy instructions: *Copy Date:* 14 days prior to publication
BUSINESS: COMMUNICATIONS, ADVERTISING & MARKETING

FACTORY 763983A14A-2484

Editorial: Lindengasse 56, 1070 WIEN
Tel: 1 5859000 **Fax:** 1 585900016
Email: office@factorynet.at **Web site:** http://www.factorynet.at
Freq: 10 issues yearly; **Annual Sub.:** EUR 35,00; **Circ:** 13,280
Editor: Wolfgang R. Zissler
Profile: FACTORY is Austria's first magazine, which is made exclusively for the manufacturing industry. Monthly returns FACTORY makers valuable and cutting-edge information relating to the entire product creation process from planning and construction on the automation of production lines to the production and delivery. FACTORY At the same time also the first medium companies and decision makers offer all in one: information technology, automation, manufacturing know-how and logistics. The right program for technical decision makers and managers in industry and commerce.
Language(s): German
ADVERTISING RATES:
Full Page Mono .... EUR 3990
Full Page Colour .... EUR 3990
Mechanical Data: Type Area: 253 x 185 mm
Copy instructions: *Copy Date:* 14 days prior to publication
BUSINESS: COMMERCE, INDUSTRY & MANAGEMENT

FAHRGAST 726989A49A-586

Editorial: Magdalenenstr. 13/1/2, 1060 WIEN
Tel: 1 5871069 **Fax:** 1 5856269
Email: fahrgast@gmx.at **Web site:** http://www.fahrgast.at
Freq: Quarterly; Free to qualifying individuals
Annual Sub.: EUR 20,00; **Circ:** 1,500
Profile: Magazine with articles, providing a forum for discussions about transport, the improvement of public transport and green issues.
Language(s): German

FAKTEN DER RHEUMATOLOGIE 1859598A56A-2044

Editorial: Seidengasse 9/1/1, 1070 WIEN
Tel: 1 407311132 **Fax:** 1 4073114
Email: s.hinger@medmedia.at **Web site:** http://www.medmedia.at
Freq: Quarterly; **Annual Sub.:** EUR 10,45; **Circ:** 7,000
Editor: Susanne Hinger
Profile: Magazine about rheumatology.
Language(s): German
Mechanical Data: Type Area: 297 x 210 mm

FAKTUM. 727042A50-120

Editorial: Zieglergasse 1, 1072 WIEN **Tel:** 1 521310
Fax: 1 5239217
Email: faktum@mucha.at **Web site:** http://www.faktum.at
Freq: 10 issues yearly; **Annual Sub.:** EUR 28,00; **Circ:** 12,260
Editor: Verena Plank
Profile: Magazine for tour operators, travel agencies, airlines and the coach business.
Language(s): German
ADVERTISING RATES:
Full Page Colour .... EUR 5000
Mechanical Data: Type Area: 242 x 180 mm, No. of Columns (Display): 4, Col Widths (Display): 42 mm
Copy instructions: *Copy Date:* 14 days prior to publication

FALSTAFF 727048A89A-452

Editorial: Heiligenstädter Str. 43, 1190 WIEN
Tel: 1 90421410 **Fax:** 1 9042141450
Email: redaktion@falstaff.at **Web site:** http://www.falstaff.at
Freq: 8 issues yearly; **Annual Sub.:** EUR 44,80; **Circ:** 32,433
Editor: Peter Moser; **Advertising Manager:** Klaus Buttenhauser
Profile: Magazine containing articles about food, wines and travel. Facebook: http://www.facebook.com/Falstaff.Magazin This Outlet offers RSS (Really Simple Syndication).
Language(s): German
ADVERTISING RATES:
Full Page Mono .... EUR 6000
Full Page Colour .... EUR 6000
Mechanical Data: Type Area: 272 x 203 mm
CONSUMER: HOLIDAYS & TRAVEL: Travel

FALTER - AUSG. WIEN 727049A80-360

Editorial: Marc-Aurel-Str. 9, 1011 WIEN
Tel: 1 53660917 **Fax:** 1 53660912
Email: wienzeit@falter.at **Web site:** http://www.falter.at
Freq: Weekly; **Annual Sub.:** EUR 92,00
Editor: Armin Thurnher; **Advertising Manager:** Sigrid Johler
Profile: Magazine containing articles about politics and culture.
Language(s): German
ADVERTISING RATES:
Full Page Colour .... EUR 4950
Mechanical Data: Type Area: 315 x 216 mm, No. of Columns (Display): 4, Col Widths (Display): 51 mm
Copy instructions: *Copy Date:* 7 days prior to publication
Supplement(s): Durst; Falter Heureka; stadt.blicke
CONSUMER: RURAL & REGIONAL INTEREST

FALTER BEST OF VIENNA 727050A89A-120

Editorial: Marc-Aurel-Str. 9, 1011 WIEN
Tel: 1 53660995 **Fax:** 1 53660935
Email: platzgummer@falter.at **Web site:** http://www.falter.at
Freq: Half-yearly; **Cover Price:** EUR 4,90; **Circ:** 40,000
Editor: Stefanie Platzgummer; **Advertising Manager:** Sigrid Johler
Profile: Tourist magazine about Vienna.
Language(s): German
ADVERTISING RATES:
Full Page Colour .... EUR 4700
Mechanical Data: Type Area: 350 x 275 mm

FAMILIE & KINDERBETREUUNG 727055A74C-791

Editorial: Schulgasse 3, 3100 ST. PÖLTEN
Tel: 2742 77304 **Fax:** 2742 7730420
Email: gs@familienbund.at **Web site:** http://www.familienbund.at
Freq: Quarterly; Free to qualifying individuals
Annual Sub.: EUR 10,90; **Circ:** 30,000
Editor: Alice Pitzinger-Ryba
Profile: Journal about family and social policies.
Language(s): German
Readership: Read by members of the Austrian Familienbund.
ADVERTISING RATES:
Full Page Colour .... EUR 1600
Mechanical Data: Type Area: 297 x 210 mm
CONSUMER: WOMEN'S INTEREST CONSUMER MAGAZINES: Home & Family

FERTIGHAUS TRÄUME 727224A74C-340

Editorial: Ringstr. 44/1, 3500 KREMS
Tel: 2732 8200042 **Fax:** 2732 8200082
Email: bernhard.mayerhofer@lwmedia.at **Web site:** http://www.lwmedia.at
Freq: Annual; **Cover Price:** EUR 5,50; **Circ:** 140,000
Editor: Bernhard Mayerhofer; **Advertising Manager:** Karin Artner
Profile: Magazine about pre-fabricated housing.
Language(s): German
ADVERTISING RATES:
Full Page Colour .... EUR 8340
Mechanical Data: Type Area: 250 x 180 mm
Copy instructions: *Copy Date:* 21 days prior to publication
CONSUMER: WOMEN'S INTEREST CONSUMER MAGAZINES: Home & Family

FINANZ JOURNAL 1655365A1A-232

Editorial: Floßgasse 6, 1020 WIEN **Tel:** 1 2141715
Fax: 1 214171530
Email: info@finanzjournal.at **Web site:** http://www.finanzjournal.at
Freq: 11 issues yearly; **Annual Sub.:** EUR 174,85; **Circ:** 1,000
Editor: Martin Puchinger
Profile: Magazine for tax advisors, business trustees and lawyers.
Language(s): German
Mechanical Data: Type Area: 277 x 176 mm

FIRMENWAGEN 727396A49A-200

Editorial: Dresdner Str. 45, 1200 WIEN
Tel: 1 97000169 **Fax:** 1 970005169
Email: andreas.uebelbacher@weka.at **Web site:** http://www.firmenwagen.co.at
Freq: 6 issues yearly; **Annual Sub.:** EUR 30,00; **Circ:** 30,400
Editor: Andreas Übelbacher; **Advertising Manager:** Andreas Übelbacher
Profile: Magazine providing information about company cars. Focuses on servicing and repairs, new products and models on the market.
Language(s): German
Readership: Aimed at fleet managers and operators, retailers and distributors.
ADVERTISING RATES:
Full Page Colour .... EUR 6420
Mechanical Data: Type Area: 255 x 185 mm
BUSINESS: TRANSPORT

FLECKVIEH AUSTRIA 727451A21D-1

Editorial: Einsteinweg 5, 8160 WEIZ
Tel: 664 4857362
Email: ph.stueckler@tele2.at **Web site:** http://www.fleckvieh.at
Freq: 6 issues yearly; **Annual Sub.:** EUR 20,90; **Circ:** 14,000
Editor: Barbara Stückler
Profile: Agricultural magazine focusing on cattle farming.
Language(s): German
Readership: Aimed at cattle farmers.
ADVERTISING RATES:
Full Page Mono .... EUR 1350
Full Page Colour .... EUR 2010
Mechanical Data: Type Area: 260 x 190 mm, No. of Columns (Display): 4, Col Widths (Display): 46 mm
Copy instructions: *Copy Date:* 30 days prior to publication
BUSINESS: AGRICULTURE & FARMING: Livestock

FM 727558A50-140

Editorial: Zieglergasse 1, 1072 WIEN **Tel:** 1 521310
Fax: 1 5239217
Email: christian@mucha.at **Web site:** http://www.fm-online.at
Freq: Quarterly; **Annual Sub.:** EUR 28,00; **Circ:** 13,680
Editor: Christian W. Mucha
Profile: Magazine containing information about the tourism business.
Language(s): German
ADVERTISING RATES:
Full Page Mono .... EUR 6250
Full Page Colour .... EUR 6250
Mechanical Data: Type Area: 253 x 180 mm
BUSINESS: TRAVEL & TOURISM

FONDS EXKLUSIV - AUSG. DEUTSCHLAND 1790196A1F-261

Editorial: Donaufelder Str. 247, 1220 WIEN
Tel: 1 71370500 **Fax:** 1 713705040
Email: d.evensen@fondsverlag.com **Web site:** http://www.fondsverlag.com
Freq: Quarterly; **Annual Sub.:** EUR 11,00; **Circ:** 35,000
Editor: Daniel Evensen; **Advertising Manager:** Danja Bauer
Profile: Funds magazine.
Language(s): German
ADVERTISING RATES:
Full Page Mono .... EUR 5650
Full Page Colour .... EUR 5650
Mechanical Data: Type Area: 297 x 210 mm

FONDS EXKLUSIV - AUSG. ÖSTERR. 762204A1F-246

Editorial: Donaufelder Str. 247, 1220 WIEN
Tel: 1 71370500 **Fax:** 1 713705040
Email: d.evensen@fondsverlag.com **Web site:** http://www.fondsverlag.com
Freq: Quarterly; **Annual Sub.:** EUR 11,00; **Circ:** 27,096
Editor: Daniel Evensen; **Advertising Manager:** Danja Bauer
Profile: Funds magazine.
Language(s): German
ADVERTISING RATES:
Full Page Mono .... EUR 6990
Full Page Colour .... EUR 6990
Mechanical Data: Type Area: 297 x 210 mm
BUSINESS: FINANCE & ECONOMICS: Investment

FONDS PROFESSIONELL 1646209A1C-162

Editorial: Rechte Wienzeile 237/1, 1120 WIEN
Tel: 1 81554840 **Fax:** 1 815548418
Email: pankl@fondsprofessionell.com **Web site:** http://www.fondsprofessionell.at
Freq: Quarterly; **Circ:** 28,700
Editor: Gabriele Pankl
Profile: Magazine for independent financial service providers.
Language(s): German
ADVERTISING RATES:
Full Page Mono .... EUR 3290
Full Page Colour .... EUR 3290
Mechanical Data: Type Area: 250 x 182 mm

FORMAT 727623A14A-960

Editorial: Taborstr. 1, 1020 WIEN **Tel:** 1 217554112
Fax: 1 217554600
Email: redaktion@format.at **Web site:** http://www.format.at
Freq: Weekly; **Annual Sub.:** EUR 99,90; **Circ:** 59,914
Editor: Andreas Lampl; **Advertising Manager:** Susanne Seidelhuber
Profile: Economy magazine.
Language(s): German
ADVERTISING RATES:
Full Page Mono .... EUR 10190
Full Page Colour .... EUR 10190
Mechanical Data: Type Area: 250 x 185 mm
Copy instructions: *Copy Date:* 21 days prior to publication

FORSTZEITUNG 737986A46-4

Editorial: Sturzgasse 1a, 1140 WIEN **Tel:** 1 98177139
Fax: 1 98177130
Email: fischer@timber-online.net **Web site:** http://www.timber-online.net
Freq: Monthly; **Annual Sub.:** EUR 132,00; **Circ:** 3,500
Editor: Andreas Fischer; **Advertising Manager:** Christa Feichtner
Profile: Magazine covering the whole of the forestry industry and silviculture.
Language(s): German
ADVERTISING RATES:
Full Page Mono .... EUR 1416
Full Page Colour .... EUR 2281
Mechanical Data: Type Area: 262 x 185 mm
Copy instructions: *Copy Date:* 21 days prior to publication
BUSINESS: TIMBER, WOOD & FORESTRY

DER FORTSCHRITTLICHE LANDWIRT 727672A21A-320

Editorial: Hofgasse 5, 8010 GRAZ
Tel: 316 821636140 **Fax:** 316 835612
Email: wilhelm.tritscher@landwirt.com **Web site:** http://www.landwirt.com
Freq: 24 issues yearly; **Annual Sub.:** EUR 78,90; **Circ:** 43,000
Editor: Wilhelm Tritscher; **Advertising Manager:** Thomas Mühlbacher
Profile: Journal focusing on progressive farming.
Language(s): German
ADVERTISING RATES:
Full Page Mono .... EUR 2700
Full Page Colour .... EUR 3950
Mechanical Data: Type Area: 260 x 190 mm, No. of Columns (Display): 4, Col Widths (Display): 46 mm
Copy instructions: *Copy Date:* 30 days prior to publication
BUSINESS: AGRICULTURE & FARMING

FORUM 721130A4A-4

Editorial: Wiedner Hauptstr. 120, 1051 WIEN
Tel: 1 54664342 **Fax:** 1 5466450342
Email: t.cervinka@wirtschaftsverlag.at **Web site:** http://www.architektur-bauforum.at
Freq: 21 issues yearly; **Annual Sub.:** EUR 60,00; **Circ:** 10,559
Editor: Tom Cervinka; **Advertising Manager:** Franz-Michael Seidl
Profile: Magazine covering all aspects of architecture and building.
Language(s): German
Readership: Aimed at builders, architects and civil engineers.
ADVERTISING RATES:
Full Page Colour .... EUR 4036
Mechanical Data: Type Area: 432 x 292 mm
Copy instructions: *Copy Date:* 14 days prior to publication
Supplement(s): Contract; Skin
BUSINESS: ARCHITECTURE & BUILDING: Architecture

FORUM GAS WASSER WÄRME 729446A58-140

Editorial: Markgraf-Rüdiger-Str. 6, 1150 WIEN
Tel: 1 5480383 **Fax:** 1 5480385
Email: jobst@pjp.at **Web site:** http://www.ovgw.at
Freq: 6 issues yearly; **Annual Sub.:** EUR 35,00; **Circ:** 6,000
Editor: Hartwig M. Jobst
Profile: Energy magazine focusing on the gas and water industries.
Language(s): German
Readership: Read by people in the gas and water industries as well as by local authority employees, politicians and ÖVGW members.
ADVERTISING RATES:
Full Page Mono .... EUR 3200
Full Page Colour .... EUR 3200
Mechanical Data: Type Area: 238 x 179 mm
BUSINESS: ENERGY, FUEL & NUCLEAR

FORUM GESUNDHEIT 727718A74G-428

Editorial: Jahngasse 4, 6850 DORNBIRN
Tel: 5084551111 **Fax:** 50845581111
Email: forum.gesundheit@vgkk.at **Web site:** http://www.vgkk.at
Freq: Quarterly; **Cover Price:** Free; **Circ:** 28,000
Editor: Rose-Marie Mennel
Profile: Consumer magazine about health and medical care in the Vorarlberg region.
Language(s): German
Readership: Aimed at anyone with an interest in health matters including doctors, pharmacists, nurses and schools.
ADVERTISING RATES:
Full Page Mono .... EUR 880
Full Page Colour .... EUR 880
Mechanical Data: Type Area: 265 x 200 mm
Copy instructions: *Copy Date:* 28 days prior to publication
CONSUMER: WOMEN'S INTEREST CONSUMER MAGAZINES: Slimming & Health

FORUM GESUNDHEIT 1641912A74M-247

Editorial: Kempfstr. 8, 9021 KLAGENFURT
Tel: 5058552012 **Fax:** 50585582010
Email: direktion1@kgkk.at **Web site:** http://www.forumgesundheit.at
Freq: Quarterly; **Cover Price:** Free; **Circ:** 50,000
Editor: Heinz Macher
Profile: Customer magazine from the health insurance company Kärntner Gebietskrankenkasse.
Language(s): German
ADVERTISING RATES:
Full Page Mono .... EUR 2200
Full Page Colour .... EUR 2200
Mechanical Data: Type Area: 270 x 205 mm

FORUM GESUNDHEIT - AUSG. OBERÖSTERREICH 1842740A74M-268
Editorial: Gruberstr. 77, 4021 LINZ
Tel: 732 78072611 **Fax:** 732 78072692
Web site: http://www.ooegkk.at
Freq: 6 issues yearly; **Cover Price:** Free; **Circ:** 140,000
Editor: Heinz Macher; **Advertising Manager:** Norbert Wagner
Profile: Health magazine for Upper Austria.
Language(s): German
ADVERTISING RATES:
Full Page Mono .... EUR 3780
Full Page Colour .... EUR 3780
Mechanical Data: Type Area: 265 x 200 mm
Copy instructions: *Copy Date:* 21 days prior to publication

FORUM GESUNDHEIT - AUSG. SALZBURG 1842741A74M-269
Editorial: Engelbert-Weiß-Weg 10, 5021 SALZBURG
Tel: 662 88890 **Fax:** 662 88891058
Email: redaktion@sgkk.at **Web site:** http://www.sgkk.at
Freq: 6 issues yearly; **Cover Price:** Free; **Circ:** 53,000
Editor: Heinz Macher
Profile: Health magazine for Salzburg.
Language(s): German
ADVERTISING RATES:
Full Page Mono .... EUR 2108
Mechanical Data: Type Area: 265 x 200 mm

FORUM UMWELT 1837279A57-1160
Editorial: Mostviertelplatz 1, 3362 ÖHLING
Tel: 7475 53340200
Email: info@gvuam.at **Web site:** http://www.abfallverband.at/amstetten
Circ: 1,200
Editor: Wolfgang Lindorfer
Profile: Information from the waste management company Abfallverband Amstetten.
Language(s): German

FORUM.KSV 1856469A14A-2640
Editorial: Wagenseilgasse 7, 1120 WIEN
Tel: 5018708226 **Fax:** 501870991000
Email: stirner.karin@ksv.at **Web site:** http://www.ksv.at
Freq: 5 issues yearly; **Circ:** 24,000
Editor: Karin Stirner
Profile: Member magazine from the Association for Credit Protection.
Language(s): German

FRATZ&CO 727843A74C-380
Editorial: Altmannsdorfer Str. 104, 1120 WIEN
Tel: 1 2988888888 **Fax:** 1 2988883
Email: redaktion@zeit-fuer-mich.cc **Web site:** http://www.fratz.at
Freq: 6 issues yearly; **Annual Sub.:** EUR 13,40; **Circ:** 100,000
Editor: Marion Breiter-O'Donovan; **Advertising Manager:** Robert Herbst
Profile: Magazine for families.
Language(s): German
ADVERTISING RATES:
Full Page Mono .... EUR 6900
Full Page Colour .... EUR 6900
Mechanical Data: Type Area: 235 x 180 mm
CONSUMER: WOMEN'S INTEREST CONSUMER MAGAZINES: Home & Family

FREIE FAHRT 727910A77A-286
Editorial: Mariahilfer Str. 180, 1150 WIEN
Tel: 1 89121257 **Fax:** 1 89121227
Email: musil@freiefahrt.at **Web site:** http://www.freiefahrt.at
Freq: 8 issues yearly; **Circ:** 400,000
Editor: Leo Musil; **Advertising Manager:** Brigitte Lang
Profile: Journal of the Austrian Motorist, Motorcyclist and Cyclist Association. Contains tests of new models, comparisons, reports from motor fairs, motoring and safety tips.
Language(s): German
ADVERTISING RATES:
Full Page Mono .... EUR 8000
Full Page Colour .... EUR 12400
Mechanical Data: Type Area: 250 x 165 mm, No. of Columns (Display): 4, Col Widths (Display): 37 mm
Copy instructions: *Copy Date:* 22 days prior to publication
CONSUMER: MOTORING & CYCLING: Motoring

FREIZEIT-JOURNAL 727962A89A-453
Editorial: Ocwirkgasse 3, 1210 WIEN **Tel:** 1 27703
Fax: 1 2770326
Email: office@mildeverlag.at **Web site:** http://www.freizeit-journal.at
Freq: Quarterly; **Annual Sub.:** EUR 8,00; **Circ:** 12,200
Editor: Eva-Maria Milde
Profile: Magazine about travel and leisure, including items on health, cookery, fashion and culture.
Language(s): German
ADVERTISING RATES:
Full Page Mono .... EUR 2754
Full Page Colour .... EUR 3997
Mechanical Data: Type Area: 256 x 184 mm, No. of Columns (Display): 4, Col Widths (Display): 42 mm
Copy instructions: *Copy Date:* 14 days prior to publication
CONSUMER: HOLIDAYS & TRAVEL: Travel

FREUNDIN 1847740A74A-938
Editorial: Max-Schrems-Gasse 5/3/9, 2345 BRUNN
Tel: 2236 320068 **Fax:** 2236 320072
Email: office@weginger-media.at
Freq: 27 issues yearly; **Cover Price:** EUR 2,40; **Circ:** 55,000
Profile: Women's interest magazine. German edition inclusive four pages for austria, editorial staff in Germany.
Language(s): German

FSG DIREKT 747119A14L-1900
Editorial: Johann-Böhm-Platz 1, 1020 WIEN
Tel: 1 662329639738 **Fax:** 1 662329639793
Email: karin.stieber@oegbverlag.at **Web site:** http://www.fsg-direkt.at
Freq: 11 issues yearly; **Cover Price:** Free
Editor: Christoph Höllriegl
Profile: Journal about the politics and legislation of employment.
Language(s): German
BUSINESS: COMMERCE, INDUSTRY & MANAGEMENT: Trade Unions

DIE FURCHE 728187A72-2960
Editorial: Lobkowitzplatz 1, 1010 WIEN
Tel: 1 5125261 **Fax:** 1 5128215
Email: furche@furche.at **Web site:** http://www.furche.at
Freq: Weekly; **Annual Sub.:** EUR 97,00; **Circ:** 20,137
Editor: Claus Reitan; **Advertising Manager:** Margarita Stöber
Profile: National weekly covering politics, economics, sport, travel and the arts.
Language(s): German
Mechanical Data: Type Area: 411 x 275 mm
Copy instructions: *Copy Date:* 10 days prior to publication
Supplement(s): booklet
LOCAL NEWSPAPERS

DIE GANZE WOCHE 1647390A73-388
Editorial: Heiligenstädter Str. 121, 1190 WIEN
Tel: 1 29160290 **Fax:** 1 2916062
Email: redaktion@dgw.at **Web site:** http://www.ganzewoche.at
Freq: Weekly; **Annual Sub.:** EUR 51,00; **Circ:** 395,470
Editor: Burkhard Trummer
Profile: Weekly magazine featuring general interest subjects.
Language(s): German
ADVERTISING RATES:
Full Page Mono .... EUR 11400
Full Page Colour .... EUR 11400
Mechanical Data: Type Area: 290 x 215 mm
Copy instructions: *Copy Date:* 10 days prior to publication
Supplement(s): TV Dabei

GANZHEITSMEDIZIN 728293A56A-480
Editorial: Tannenweg 5, 2451 HOF **Tel:** 5354 52120
Email: oenr@acw.at **Web site:** http://www.neuraltherapie.at
Freq: Quarterly; **Annual Sub.:** EUR 26,00; **Circ:** 1,000
Editor: Robert Harsieber
Profile: Magazine on holistic medicine with focus on neuraltherapy.
Language(s): German
ADVERTISING RATES:
Full Page Mono .... EUR 250
Mechanical Data: Type Area: 205 x 155 mm

GARTEN + HAUS 728317A93-20
Editorial: Sturzgasse 1a, 1140 WIEN **Tel:** 1 98177171
Fax: 1 98177170
Email: g.stiptschitsch@agrarverlag.at **Web site:** http://www.garten-haus.at
Freq: 8 issues yearly; **Annual Sub.:** EUR 46,50; **Circ:** 50,000
Editor: Gerald Stiptschitsch; **Advertising Manager:** Gabriele Kautz
Profile: Magazine covering gardening matters and garden design. Published by the Austrian Horticultural Society.
Language(s): German
ADVERTISING RATES:
Full Page Mono .... EUR 3650
Full Page Colour .... EUR 4600
Mechanical Data: Type Area: 270 x 200 mm, No. of Columns (Display): 3, Col Widths (Display): 64 mm
Copy instructions: *Copy Date:* 28 days prior to publication
CONSUMER: GARDENING

GÄRTNER + FLORIST 728224A26C-20
Editorial: Sturzgasse 1a, 1140 WIEN **Tel:** 1 98177171
Fax: 1 98177120
Email: g.stiptschitsch@agrarverlag.at **Web site:** http://www.gaertner-florist.at
Freq: 24 issues yearly; **Annual Sub.:** EUR 115,00; **Circ:** 4,500
Editor: Gerald Stiptschitsch; **Advertising Manager:** Gabriele Kautz
Profile: Magazine providing information concerning the production, marketing and distribution of flowers and garden produce. Includes articles on plant care, environmental issues and growing conditions.
Language(s): German
Readership: Aimed at retail florists, wholesalers and professional gardeners.
ADVERTISING RATES:
Full Page Mono .... EUR 2100
Full Page Colour .... EUR 3510
Mechanical Data: Type Area: 260 x 191 mm, No. of Columns (Display): 4, Col Widths (Display): 44 mm
Copy instructions: *Copy Date:* 10 days prior to publication
BUSINESS: GARDEN TRADE

GASTRO 728346A11A-120
Editorial: Gersthofer Str. 87, 1180 WIEN
Tel: 1 4798430 **Fax:** 1 479843016
Email: schilling@gastroverlag.at **Web site:** http://www.gastroportal.at
Freq: Monthly; **Annual Sub.:** EUR 49,00; **Circ:** 18,440
Editor: Karl Schilling; **Advertising Manager:** Peter Bubenicek
Profile: Magazine focusing on gastronomical events and new food products.
Language(s): German
Readership: Aimed at those within the catering industry.
ADVERTISING RATES:
Full Page Mono .... EUR 4800
Full Page Colour .... EUR 5850
Mechanical Data: Type Area: 265 x 185 mm, No. of Columns (Display): 4, Col Widths (Display): 43 mm
Copy instructions: *Copy Date:* 14 days prior to publication
BUSINESS: CATERING: Catering, Hotels & Restaurants

GEBÄUDE INSTALLATION 737997A3D-120
Editorial: Wiedner Hauptstr. 120, 1051 WIEN
Tel: 1 54664351 **Fax:** 1 5466450351
Email: h.schmid@wirtschaftsverlag.at **Web site:** http://www.gebaeudeinstallation.at
Freq: 10 issues yearly; **Annual Sub.:** EUR 55,00; **Circ:** 11,000
Editor: Heinz Schmid; **Advertising Manager:** Franz Michael Seidl
Profile: Publication about gas, water, heating and air-conditioning.
Language(s): German
Readership: Read by plumbers, planners, architects and authorities.
ADVERTISING RATES:
Full Page Mono .... EUR 2862
Full Page Colour .... EUR 4090
Mechanical Data: Type Area: 255 x 185 mm
Copy instructions: *Copy Date:* 21 days prior to publication
BUSINESS: HEATING & VENTILATION: Heating & Plumbing

GEKO NEWS 728451A14A-1000
Editorial: Raffelspergergasse 33, 1190 WIEN
Tel: 1 4799127 **Fax:** 1 479912711
Circ: 2,700
Editor: Gerald Kotschwar
Profile: Company publication about marketing communications.
Language(s): German

DIE GEMEINDE 728499A87-900
Editorial: Seitenstettengasse 4, 1010 WIEN
Tel: 1 53104271 **Fax:** 1 53104279
Email: s.feiger@ikg-wien.at **Web site:** http://www.ikg-wien.at
Freq: 24 issues yearly; Free to qualifying individuals
Annual Sub.: EUR 25,00; **Circ:** 5,500
Editor: Sonia Feiger; **Advertising Manager:** Manuela Glamm
Profile: International journal of the Jewish community of Vienna.
Language(s): German
ADVERTISING RATES:
Full Page Mono .... EUR 1279
Full Page Colour .... EUR 2319
Mechanical Data: Type Area: 260 x 185 mm, No. of Columns (Display): 3, Col Widths (Display): 59 mm
Copy instructions: *Copy Date:* 15 days prior to publication
CONSUMER: RELIGIOUS

GEMÜSEBAUPRAXIS 728645A21A-340
Editorial: Gewerbestr. 10a, 2201 HAGENBRUNN
Tel: 2246 3489
Email: monika.vansorgen@bgvoe.at **Web site:** http://www.bgvoe.at
Freq: 6 issues yearly; **Annual Sub.:** EUR 17,00; **Circ:** 1,700
Editor: Monika van Sorgen; **Advertising Manager:** Sonja Niederwimmer
Profile: Official journal of the Austrian Association of Vegetable Growers.
Language(s): German
ADVERTISING RATES:
Full Page Mono .... EUR 1550
Full Page Colour .... EUR 1550
Mechanical Data: No. of Columns (Display): 3, Col Widths (Display): 58 mm, Type Area: 265 x 185 mm
Copy instructions: *Copy Date:* 21 days prior to publication

GEMÜSEBAUPRAXIS 728645A21A-1520
Editorial: Gewerbestr. 10a, 2201 HAGENBRUNN
Tel: 2246 3489
Email: monika.vansorgen@bgvoe.at **Web site:** http://www.bgvoe.at
Freq: 6 issues yearly; **Annual Sub.:** EUR 17,00; **Circ:** 1,700
Editor: Monika van Sorgen; **Advertising Manager:** Sonja Niederwimmer
Profile: Official journal of the Austrian Association of Vegetable Growers.
Language(s): German
ADVERTISING RATES:
Full Page Mono .... EUR 1550
Full Page Colour .... EUR 1550
Mechanical Data: No. of Columns (Display): 3, Col Widths (Display): 58 mm, Type Area: 265 x 185 mm
Copy instructions: *Copy Date:* 21 days prior to publication

GERIATRIE PRAXIS ÖSTERREICH 728725A56A-500
Editorial: Wiedner Hauptstr. 120, 1050 WIEN
Tel: 1 54600330 **Fax:** 1 54600730
Email: beermann@clinicum.at **Web site:** http://www.clinicum.at
Freq: 6 issues yearly; **Annual Sub.:** EUR 24,00; **Circ:** 12,000
Editor: Birgit Beermann; **Advertising Manager:** Reinhard Rosenberger
Profile: Medical journal focusing on geriatrics.
Language(s): German
Readership: Aimed at specialists in the field of geriatrics.
ADVERTISING RATES:
Full Page Colour .... EUR 3296
Mechanical Data: Type Area: 210 x mm, No. of Columns (Display): 297
Copy instructions: *Copy Date:* 21 days prior to publication
BUSINESS: HEALTH & MEDICAL

GESRZ DER GESELLSCHAFTER 728791A44-40
Editorial: Scheydgasse 24, 1210 WIEN **Tel:** 1 246300
Fax: 1 2463051
Email: redaktion@lindeverlag.at **Web site:** http://www.lindeverlag.at
Freq: 6 issues yearly; **Annual Sub.:** EUR 166,60; **Circ:** 3,000
Editor: Susanne Kalss; **Advertising Manager:** Regina Erben-Hartig
Profile: Journal covering the theory and practice of company law.
Language(s): German
ADVERTISING RATES:
Full Page Mono .... EUR 1100
Full Page Colour .... EUR 1600
Mechanical Data: Type Area: 242 x 167 mm
Copy instructions: *Copy Date:* 14 days prior to publication
BUSINESS: LEGAL

GESÜNDER LEBEN 728813A74G-100
Editorial: Siebenbrunngasse 17, 1050 WIEN
Tel: 1 3100700300 **Fax:** 1 3100700600
Email: bettina.kammerer@gesuender-leben.com
Web site: http://www.gesuender-leben.com
Freq: 10 issues yearly; **Circ:** 65,000
Editor: Bettina Kammerer; **Advertising Manager:** Brigitte Entremont
Profile: Magazine about a conscious and healthy way of living.
Language(s): German
ADVERTISING RATES:
Full Page Colour .... EUR 6290
Mechanical Data: Type Area: 248 x 180 mm
Copy instructions: *Copy Date:* 15 days prior to publication
CONSUMER: WOMEN'S INTEREST CONSUMER MAGAZINES: Slimming & Health

GESUNDHEIT 728823A74G-120
Editorial: Stoß im Himmel 1, 1010 WIEN
Tel: 1 532254016 **Fax:** 1 532254020
Email: goiser@gesundheit.co.at **Web site:** http://www.gesundheit.co.at
Freq: 10 issues yearly; **Annual Sub.:** EUR 36,00; **Circ:** 68,000
Editor: Roland Goiser; **Advertising Manager:** Karl Kohlbacher
Profile: Magazine about health and quality of life based on orthodox and alternative medicine.
Language(s): German
Readership: Read by women in the 20-50 age group.
ADVERTISING RATES:
Full Page Mono .... EUR 6999
Full Page Colour .... EUR 6999
Mechanical Data: Type Area: 264 x 190 mm
CONSUMER: WOMEN'S INTEREST CONSUMER MAGAZINES: Slimming & Health

Austria

GEWINN 728879A14A-1040
Editorial: Stiftgasse 31, 1071 WIEN **Tel:** 1 5212448 **Fax:** 1 5212430
Email: g.wailand@gewinn.com **Web site:** http://www.gewinn.com
Freq: 11 issues yearly; **Annual Sub.:** EUR 39,00; **Circ:** 85,291
Editor: Georg Wailand; **Advertising Manager:** Herbert Scheiblauer
Profile: Magazine about success in business.
Language(s): German
Readership: Read by people interested in personal success.
ADVERTISING RATES:
Full Page Mono .... EUR 7700
Full Page Colour .... EUR 13475
Mechanical Data: Type Area: 250 x 185 mm
BUSINESS: COMMERCE, INDUSTRY & MANAGEMENT

GIESSEREI RUNDSCHAU 728934A27-120
Editorial: Weitmosergasse 30, 1100 WIEN
Tel: 1 6172635 **Fax:** 1 6172635
Email: giesserei@verlag-strohmayer.at **Web site:** http://www.verlag-strohmayer.at
Freq: 6 issues yearly; **Annual Sub.:** EUR 61,00; **Circ:** 1,000
Editor: Erich Nechtelberger
Profile: Magazine for casting houses and supply companies.
Language(s): German
ADVERTISING RATES:
Full Page Mono .... EUR 1010
Full Page Colour .... EUR 1935
Mechanical Data: Type Area: 264 x 185 mm
Official Journal of: Organ d. Vereins Österr. Gießereifachleute, d. Fachverb. d. Gießereindustrie, d. Österr. Gießerei-Inst. u. d. Inst. f. Gießereikunde an d. Montanuniv.

GIESSEREI-PRAXIS 1775595A27-315
Editorial: Drosselweg 9, 8010 GRAZ **Tel:** 316 421335 **Fax:** 316 421448
Email: stephan.hasse@aon.at **Web site:** http://www.giesserei-praxis.de
Freq: 10 issues yearly; **Annual Sub.:** EUR 141,50; **Circ:** 3,500
Editor: Stephan Hasse; **Advertising Manager:** Hildegard Thüring
Profile: Facebook: http://www.facebook.com/pages/Special-Site-GIFA-12th-International-Foundry-Trade-Fair-presented-by/148652955154077.
Language(s): German
ADVERTISING RATES:
Full Page Mono .... EUR 1510
Full Page Colour .... EUR 2416
Mechanical Data: Type Area: 262 x 167 mm, No. of Columns (Display): 4, Col Widths (Display): 40 mm

GLOBAL NEWS 729001A57-240
Editorial: Neustiftgasse 36, 1070 WIEN
Tel: 1 8125730 **Fax:** 1 8125728
Email: globalnews@global2000.at **Web site:** http://www.global2000.at
Freq: Quarterly; **Circ:** 30,000
Editor: Astrid Breit
Profile: Magazine about the environment.
Language(s): German
Mechanical Data: Type Area: 250 x 183 mm

GOLF REVUE 729128A75D-120
Editorial: Ferdinandstr. 4, 1020 WIEN
Tel: 1 863315701 **Fax:** 1 863315640
Email: redaktion@golfrevue.at **Web site:** http://www.golfrevue.at
Freq: 7 issues yearly; **Annual Sub.:** EUR 24,90; **Circ:** 37,000
Editor: Klaus Nadizar
Profile: Magazine containing articles about golf.
Language(s): German
Readership: Read by golfers in Austria, South Germany and Switzerland.
ADVERTISING RATES:
Full Page Mono .... EUR 4790
Full Page Colour .... EUR 4790
Mechanical Data: Type Area: 250 x 185 mm, No. of Columns (Display): 4, Col Widths (Display): 43 mm
Copy instructions: *Copy Date:* 21 days prior to publication
Official Journal of: Organ d. Österr. Golfverb.
CONSUMER: SPORT: Golf

GOOD LIFE 729139A74Q-2
Editorial: Karl-Meißl-Str. 7/7, 1203 WIEN
Tel: 1 3326105 **Fax:** 1 332610533
Email: office@goodlife-magazin.com
Freq: Quarterly; **Annual Sub.:** EUR 15,00; **Circ:** 40,000
Editor: Johann Kercselics; **Advertising Manager:** Erica Schultz-Eulenburg
Profile: Magazine containing articles on how to achieve a better lifestyle and quality of life.
Language(s): German
Readership: Aimed at the general public.
ADVERTISING RATES:
Full Page Mono .... EUR 3600
Full Page Colour .... EUR 4950
Mechanical Data: Type Area: 252 x 190 mm
Copy instructions: *Copy Date:* 15 days prior to publication
CONSUMER: WOMEN'S INTEREST CONSUMER MAGAZINES: Lifestyle

GOURMETREISE 1772557A74P-277
Editorial: Reininghausstr. 13a, 8020 GRAZ
Tel: 316 58494651 **Fax:** 316 58494619
Email: michael.pech@gourmetreise.com **Web site:** http://www.gourmetreise.com
Freq: Quarterly; **Cover Price:** EUR 4,90; **Circ:** 55,067
Editor: Michael Pech; **Advertising Manager:** Silvana Zettinig
Language(s): German
ADVERTISING RATES:
Full Page Mono .... EUR 3890
Full Page Colour .... EUR 3890
Mechanical Data: Type Area: 258 x 188 mm
Copy instructions: *Copy Date:* 30 days prior to publication
CONSUMER: WOMEN'S INTEREST CONSUMER MAGAZINES: Food & Cookery

GRAPHISCHE REVUE ÖSTERREICHS 729189A41A-60
Editorial: Garbergasse 11/20, 1060 WIEN
Tel: 1 9437973
Email: knud.wassermann@chello.at **Web site:** http://www.bildungsverband.at
Freq: 7 issues yearly; **Annual Sub.:** EUR 32,00; **Circ:** 6,500
Editor: Knud Wassermann; **Advertising Manager:** Andrea Doubek
Profile: Magazine covering all aspects of the graphics and printing trade.
Language(s): German
ADVERTISING RATES:
Full Page Mono .... EUR 1800
Full Page Colour .... EUR 2900
Mechanical Data: Type Area: 265 x 160 mm
BUSINESS: PRINTING & STATIONERY: Printing

GRAWE AKTUELL 1996475A14A-2659
Editorial: Herrengasse 18, 8011 GRAZ
Tel: 316 80376765 **Fax:** 316 80376695
Email: davis.kumpusch@grawe.at **Web site:** http://www.grawe.at
Freq: Half-yearly; **Cover Price:** Free; **Circ:** 2,500
Editor: Karin Taferner-Bauer
Profile: Company publication from the Grazer Wechseitige Versicherung.
Language(s): German

DAS GRÜNE HAUS 729302A74G-180
Editorial: Gölsdorfgasse 2/2/13, 1010 WIEN
Tel: 1 5351256 **Fax:** 1 5351256
Email: redaktion@gruenehaus.at **Web site:** http://www.gesundheitswelten.com
Freq: 10 issues yearly; **Annual Sub.:** EUR 27,50; **Circ:** 81,000
Editor: Dieter Altermiller; **Advertising Manager:** Gertraud Altermiller
Profile: Family medical magazine, containing advice about a healthy lifestyle, alternative remedies and protecting the environment.
Language(s): German
ADVERTISING RATES:
Full Page Mono .... EUR 2800
Full Page Colour .... EUR 2800
Mechanical Data: Type Area: 256 x 191 mm, No. of Columns (Display): 4, Col Widths (Display): 44 mm
Copy instructions: *Copy Date:* 8 days prior to publication
CONSUMER: WOMEN'S INTEREST CONSUMER MAGAZINES: Slimming & Health

GRÜNE WELT 1655981A21A-1466
Editorial: Marco-d'Aviano-Gasse 1/1, 1015 WIEN
Tel: 1 512160110 **Fax:** 1 5139366
Email: doris.fischer@lak-noe.at **Web site:** http://www.landarbeiterkammer.at/noe
Freq: 8 issues yearly; **Circ:** 21,000
Editor: Doris Fischer
Profile: Magazine from the Lower Austrian Association of Employees in Agriculture and Forestry.
Language(s): German

GRÜNER BERICHT 1644064A21A-1453
Editorial: Stubenring 1, 1012 WIEN **Tel:** 1 711000 **Fax:** 1 711002140
Email: otto.hofer@bmlfuw.gv.at **Web site:** http://www.gruenerbericht.at
Freq: Annual; **Circ:** 3,500
Editor: Otto Hofer
Profile: National official paper about Austrian agriculture.
Language(s): German

GRÜNER SPIEGEL 729309A21A-420
Editorial: Herrengasse 13/I, 8010 GRAZ
Tel: 316 825325 **Fax:** 316 825325
Email: forstverein.steiermark@utanet.at **Web site:** http://www.steirischerwald.at
Freq: Quarterly; **Circ:** 1,500
Editor: Gerhard Pelzmann
Profile: Magazine from the Styrian Forestry Association.
Language(s): German
Copy instructions: *Copy Date:* 14 days prior to publication

GRÜNESLAND 1787524A21A-1484
Editorial: Landgutstr. 17, 4040 LINZ
Tel: 732 73940017 **Fax:** 732 73940099
Email: bauern@gruene.at **Web site:** http://www.bauern.gruene.at
Freq: Quarterly; Free to qualifying individuals
Annual Sub.: EUR 5,00; **Circ:** 10,000
Profile: Advertising journal (house-to-house) concentrating on local stories.
Language(s): German

GRÜNESLAND 1787524A21A-1491
Editorial: Landgutstr. 17, 4040 LINZ
Tel: 732 73940017 **Fax:** 732 73940099
Email: bauern@gruene.at **Web site:** http://www.bauern.gruene.at
Freq: Quarterly; Free to qualifying individuals
Annual Sub.: EUR 5,00; **Circ:** 10,000
Profile: Advertising journal (house-to-house) concentrating on local stories.
Language(s): German

GUSTO 1647394A74P-267
Editorial: Ferdinandstr. 4, 1020 WIEN
Tel: 1 863315301 **Fax:** 1 863315610
Email: redaktion@gusto.at **Web site:** http://www.gusto.at
Freq: Monthly; **Annual Sub.:** EUR 34,00; **Circ:** 69,550
Editor: Wolfgang Schlüter; **Advertising Manager:** Klaus Edelhofer
Profile: Magazine about cooking.
Language(s): German
ADVERTISING RATES:
Full Page Mono .... EUR 10600
Full Page Colour .... EUR 10600
Mechanical Data: Type Area: 250 x 185 mm
Copy instructions: *Copy Date:* 28 days prior to publication

GYN-AKTIV 729461A56A-520
Editorial: Seidengasse 9/1/1, 1070 WIEN
Tel: 1 40731110 **Fax:** 1 4073114
Email: p.lex@medmedia.at **Web site:** http://www.medmedia.at
Freq: 6 issues yearly; **Annual Sub.:** EUR 16,83; **Circ:** 8,500
Editor: Sepp Leodolter; **Advertising Manager:** Judith Hafner
Profile: Magazine on gynaecology and obstetrics.
Language(s): German
ADVERTISING RATES:
Full Page Colour .... EUR 3190
Mechanical Data: Type Area: 297 x 210 mm
Copy instructions: *Copy Date:* 14 days prior to publication
BUSINESS: HEALTH & MEDICAL

HABITAT 1641529A57-1124
Editorial: Gasometergasse 10, 9020 KLAGENFURT
Tel: 463 329666 **Fax:** 463 3296664
Email: office@arge-naturschutz.at **Web site:** http://www.arge-naturschutz.at
Freq: Half-yearly; **Circ:** 750
Editor: Klaus Krainer
Profile: Publication including information from the work group for environmental protection.
Language(s): German

HALLER BLATT 729510A72-3520
Editorial: Medienturm Saline Hall, 6060 HALL
Tel: 5223 5130 **Fax:** 5223 51320
Email: hallerblatt@ablinger-garber.at **Web site:** http://www.hallerblatt.at
Freq: Monthly; **Cover Price:** Free; **Circ:** 15,392
Editor: Walter Wurzer; **Advertising Manager:** Evelin Garber-Moisi
Profile: Newspaper containing information about Hall.
Language(s): German
ADVERTISING RATES:
Full Page Mono .... EUR 900
Full Page Colour .... EUR 999
Mechanical Data: Type Area: 273 x 190 mm, No. of Columns (Display): 4, Col Widths (Display): 45 mm
LOCAL NEWSPAPERS

HALLO INNSBRUCK 2002652A89A-520
Editorial: Eduard-Bodem-Gasse 6, 6020 INNSBRUCK **Tel:** 512 320703 **Fax:** 512 320720
Email: sonderprodukte.red@bezirksblaetter.com
Web site: http://www.bezirksblaetter.com
Freq: Quarterly; **Cover Price:** Free; **Circ:** 35,000
Editor: Karl Künstner
Profile: Tourist magazine about Innsbruck.
Language(s): French; Italian
ADVERTISING RATES:
Full Page Colour .... EUR 1800
Mechanical Data: Type Area: 242 x 184 mm
Copy instructions: *Copy Date:* 30 days prior to publication

HANDBUCH FÜR DIE SANITÄTSBERUFE ÖSTERREICHS 1859217A56A-2042
Editorial: Hernalser Hauptstr. 213, 1170 WIEN
Tel: 1 4864240 **Fax:** 1 4854902
Email: info@goeschl.co.at **Web site:** http://www.medizinprodukte.at
Freq: Annual; **Cover Price:** EUR 91,50; **Circ:** 4,000
Editor: Siegrid Göschl; **Advertising Manager:** Siegrid Göschl
Profile: Directory listing addresses of the Austrian healthcare system.
Language(s): German
Mechanical Data: Type Area: 180 x 120 mm

HANDBUCH WERBUNG 1829436A2A-955
Editorial: Schwarzenbergplatz 14/306, 1040 WIEN
Tel: 1 514503790 **Fax:** 1 51295483796
Email: werbungwien@wkw.at **Web site:** http://www.werbungwien.at
Freq: Annual; **Circ:** 10,000
Advertising Manager: Birgit Kloss
Profile: Directory about advertising and market communications.
Language(s): German
ADVERTISING RATES:
Full Page Mono .... EUR 2700
Full Page Colour .... EUR 2700
Mechanical Data: Type Area: 205 x 130 mm

HAUSARZT 729792A56A-560
Editorial: Kutschkergasse 26, 1180 WIEN
Tel: 1 5260501
Email: redaktionsbuero@mpv.co.at **Web site:** http://www.hausarzt-online.at
Freq: 10 issues yearly; Free to qualifying individuals
Annual Sub.: EUR 36,00; **Circ:** 7,898
Editor: Peter Pölzlbauer
Profile: Official journal of the Austrian Association of General Practitioners.
Language(s): German
ADVERTISING RATES:
Full Page Mono .... EUR 2220
Full Page Colour .... EUR 2970
Mechanical Data: Type Area: 270 x 185 mm, No. of Columns (Display): 3, Col Widths (Display): 6 mm
Copy instructions: *Copy Date:* 21 days prior to publication
Official Journal of: Organ d. Freier Berufsverb. f. Allgemeinmedizin
BUSINESS: HEALTH & MEDICAL

HAUTNAH 1645747A56A-1940
Editorial: Sachsenplatz 4, 1201 WIEN **Tel:** 1 5131047 **Fax:** 1 5134783
Email: margarete.zupan@springer.at **Web site:** http://www.springermedizin.at
Freq: Quarterly; **Annual Sub.:** EUR 42,00; **Circ:** 7,000
Editor: Margarete Zupan
Profile: Magazine for physical doctors and pharmacists on dermatology and allergology.
Language(s): German
ADVERTISING RATES:
Full Page Colour .... EUR 2475
Mechanical Data: Type Area: 270 x 170 mm
Copy instructions: *Copy Date:* 20 days prior to publication
Supplement to: Ärzte Woche

HGV PRAXIS 730563A11A-280
Editorial: Schrannengasse 2/3/2, 5027 SALZBURG
Tel: 662 87710829 **Fax:** 662 8771083
Email: h.lanzerstorfer@hgvpraxis.at **Web site:** http://www.hgvpraxis.at
Freq: 11 issues yearly; Free to qualifying individuals
Annual Sub.: EUR 38,00; **Circ:** 17,620
Editor: Harald Lanzerstorfer; **Advertising Manager:** Elisabeth Zillner
Profile: Magazine for the hotel, gastronomy and catering trade.
Language(s): German
ADVERTISING RATES:
Full Page Mono .... EUR 3900
Full Page Colour .... EUR 5300
Mechanical Data: Type Area: 261 x 190 mm, No. of Columns (Display): 4, Col Widths (Display): 43 mm
Copy instructions: *Copy Date:* 14 days prior to publication
BUSINESS: CATERING: Catering, Hotels & Restaurants

HLK HEIZUNG LÜFTUNG KLIMATECHNIK 1655373A3D-141
Editorial: Dresdner Str. 45, 1200 WIEN
Tel: 1 97000248 **Fax:** 1 970005248
Email: eberhard.herrmann@weka.at **Web site:** http://www.hlk.co.at
Freq: 9 issues yearly; **Annual Sub.:** EUR 35,00; **Circ:** 11,900
Editor: Eberhard Herrmann; **Advertising Manager:** Kerstin Hainzl
Profile: Magazine about heating, ventilation, cold air and air conditioning.
Language(s): German
ADVERTISING RATES:
Full Page Colour .... EUR 4850
Mechanical Data: Type Area: 260 x 186 mm
BUSINESS: HEATING & VENTILATION: Heating & Plumbing

HOLZDESIGN 730470A23A-40
Editorial: Sturzgasse 1a, 1140 WIEN **Tel:** 1 98177147
Fax: 1 98177130
Email: fingerlos@timber-online.net **Web site:** http://www.timber-online.net
Freq: 10 issues yearly; **Annual Sub.:** EUR 62,00; **Circ:** 7,400
Editor: Birgit Fingerlos; **Advertising Manager:** Sonja Wagner
Profile: Specialist magazine focusing on furniture production. Covers new trends, design, materials, industry news, market reports, furniture delivery and articles on flooring.
Language(s): German
Readership: Aimed at carpenters and people within the Austrian and international woodworking and furniture trade.
ADVERTISING RATES:
Full Page Mono .... EUR 2460
Full Page Colour .... EUR 3760
Mechanical Data: Type Area: 260 x 185 mm
Copy instructions: *Copy Date:* 14 days prior to publication
BUSINESS: FURNISHINGS & FURNITURE

HOLZKURIER 730480A46-3
Editorial: Sturzgasse 1a, 1140 WIEN **Tel:** 1 98177131
Fax: 1 98177130
Email: ebner@timber-online.net **Web site:** http://www.timber-online.net
Freq: Weekly; **Annual Sub.:** EUR 278,00; **Circ:** 4,250
Editor: Gerd Ebner; **Advertising Manager:** Sonja Wagner
Profile: Publication covering the forestry and wood industry.
Language(s): German
ADVERTISING RATES:
Full Page Mono .... EUR 1720
Full Page Colour .... EUR 2640
Mechanical Data: Type Area: 256 x 185 mm
Copy instructions: *Copy Date:* 8 days prior to publication
BUSINESS: TIMBER, WOOD & FORESTRY

L' HOMME 730502A86C-42
Editorial: Dr.-Karl-Lueger-Ring 1, 1010 WIEN
Tel: 1 427740813 **Fax:** 1 42779408
Email: lhomme.geschichte@univie.ac.at **Web site:** http://www.univie.ac.at/geschichte/lhomme
Freq: Half-yearly; **Annual Sub.:** EUR 34,90; **Circ:** 500
Advertising Manager: Julia Habersack
Profile: European Journal of Feminist History.
Language(s): German
ADVERTISING RATES:
Full Page Mono .... EUR 620
Mechanical Data: Type Area: 190 x 120 mm

HORIZONT 730528A2A-260
Editorial: Brunner Feldstr. 45, 2380 PERCHTOLDSDORF **Tel:** 1 86648601
Fax: 1 86648600
Email: horizont@manstein.at **Web site:** http://www.horizont.at
Freq: 46 issues yearly; **Annual Sub.:** EUR 85,00; **Circ:** 14,400
Editor: Sebastian Loudon; **Advertising Manager:** Martina Hofmann
Profile: Publication about marketing, advertising and the media.
Language(s): German
ADVERTISING RATES:
Full Page Mono .... EUR 3510
Full Page Colour .... EUR 5520
Mechanical Data: Type Area: 392 x 275 mm
Copy instructions: *Copy Date:* 8 days prior to publication
Supplement(s): trend Bestseller Medien spezial
BUSINESS: COMMUNICATIONS, ADVERTISING & MARKETING

HOTEL & TOURISTIK 730566A50-160
Editorial: Brunner Feldstr. 45, 2380 PERCHTOLDSDORF **Tel:** 1 86648421
Fax: 1 86648420
Email: s.lesjak-rasch@manstein.at **Web site:** http://www.hotelundtouristik.at
Freq: 9 issues yearly; **Annual Sub.:** EUR 35,00; **Circ:** 18,000
Editor: Sonja Lesjak-Rasch; **Advertising Manager:** Susanne Rehulka-Drechsler
Profile: Magazine on the hotel, gastronomy and tourism business.
Language(s): German
ADVERTISING RATES:
Full Page Mono .... EUR 3880
Full Page Colour .... EUR 6190
Mechanical Data: Type Area: 240 x 190 mm, No. of Columns (Display): 4, Col Widths (Display): 47 mm
Copy instructions: *Copy Date:* 14 days prior to publication
Supplement(s): Kulinarium Bayern
BUSINESS: TRAVEL & TOURISM

IBOMAGAZIN 730735A4E-780
Editorial: Alserbachstr. 5/8, 1090 WIEN
Tel: 1 3192005 **Fax:** 1 319200550
Email: tobias.waltjen@ibo.at **Web site:** http://www.ibo.at
Freq: Quarterly; Free to qualifying individuals
Annual Sub.: EUR 20,00; **Circ:** 6,000
Editor: Tobias Waltjen
Profile: Magazine for architects on building ecology and building biology.
Language(s): German
ADVERTISING RATES:
Full Page Mono .... EUR 3670
Full Page Colour .... EUR 5180
Mechanical Data: Type Area: 285 x 205 mm

IFK AKTUELL 1852461A40-663
Editorial: Stiftgasse 2a, 1070 WIEN
Tel: 502011028700 **Fax:** 502011017262
Email: lvak.ifk@bmlvs.gv.at **Web site:** http://www.bundesheer.at/organisation/beitraege/lvak/ifk/ifk.shtml
Freq: Quarterly; **Cover Price:** Free; **Circ:** 9,000
Editor: Walter Feichtinger
Profile: Magazine with information about safety policy.
Language(s): German

IM INSTITUTIONAL MONEY 1846365A1F-265
Editorial: Rechte Wienzeile 237/1, 1120 WIEN
Tel: 1 81554840 **Fax:** 1 815548418
Email: becker@institutional-money.com **Web site:** http://www.institutional-money.com
Freq: Quarterly; **Cover Price:** EUR 9,00; **Circ:** 23,000
Editor: Kurt Michael Becker
Profile: Magazine about institutional investment.
Language(s): German
ADVERTISING RATES:
Full Page Mono .... EUR 8390
Full Page Colour .... EUR 8390
Mechanical Data: Type Area: 250 x 182 mm

IMAGINATION 1643816A56A-1930
Editorial: Landhausgasse 2/44, 1010 WIEN
Email: imagination@oegatap.at **Web site:** http://www.oegatap.at
Freq: Quarterly; Free to qualifying individuals
Annual Sub.: EUR 34,00; **Circ:** 1,900
Editor: Josef Bittner
Profile: Magazine from the Austrian Association for Autogenic Training and General Psychotherapy.
Language(s): German
ADVERTISING RATES:
Full Page Mono .... EUR 350
Mechanical Data: Type Area: 197 x 120 mm

IMMO KURIER 1708519A67B-560_504
Editorial: Lindengasse 48, 1072 WIEN
Tel: 1 521002839 **Fax:** 1 521002263
Email: ela.angerer@kurier.at **Web site:** http://www.immomedia.at
Freq: Weekly; **Cover Price:** EUR 1,00; **Circ:** 258,890
Editor: Helmut Brandstätter
Language(s): German
ADVERTISING RATES:
Full Page Mono .... EUR 7380
Full Page Colour .... EUR 7380
Mechanical Data: Type Area: 246 x 190 mm, No. of Columns (Display): 4, Col Widths (Display): 45 mm
Copy instructions: *Copy Date:* 9 days prior to publication
Supplement to: Kurier
REGIONAL DAILY & SUNDAY NEWSPAPERS: Regional Daily Newspapers

IMMOBILIEN MAGAZIN 730920A74K-220
Editorial: Millennium Tower, Handelskai 94, 1020 WIEN **Tel:** 1 25254440 **Fax:** 1 25254320
Email: heimo.rollett@imv-medien.at **Web site:** http://www.immobilien-magazin.at
Freq: 8 issues yearly; **Annual Sub.:** EUR 39,00; **Circ:** 9,000
Editor: Heimo Rollett; **Advertising Manager:** Georg Linhart
Profile: Journal about real estate and investment.
Language(s): German
ADVERTISING RATES:
Full Page Mono .... EUR 3900
Full Page Colour .... EUR 3900
Mechanical Data: Type Area: 250 x 185 mm
CONSUMER: WOMEN'S INTEREST CONSUMER MAGAZINES: Home Purchase

IMMOLEX 730934A1A-60
Editorial: Johannesgasse 23, 1015 WIEN
Tel: 1 53161348 **Fax:** 1 53161181
Email: olga.kaser@manz.at **Web site:** http://www.immolex.at
Freq: 11 issues yearly; **Annual Sub.:** EUR 206,00; **Circ:** 1,500
Editor: Herbert Rainer; **Advertising Manager:** Heidrun R. Engel
Profile: Magazine for flat building cooperatives, agents, notaries and tax advisors.
Language(s): German
ADVERTISING RATES:
Full Page Mono .... EUR 1092
Full Page Colour .... EUR 1962
Mechanical Data: Type Area: 250 x 167 mm
Copy instructions: *Copy Date:* 28 days prior to publication

IMPULS 1843584A74M-270
Editorial: Schottenring 30, 1010 WIEN
Tel: 1 5035021336 **Fax:** 1 503509921039
Email: presseabteilung@staedtische.co.at **Web site:** http://www.wienerstaedtische.at
Freq: 3 issues yearly; **Cover Price:** Free; **Circ:** 130,000
Editor: Doris Taut
Profile: Customer magazine of Wiener Städtische Versicherung AG reaches customers with a class and life insurance premiums over a certain amount, with no age restriction. The edition will be sent individually addressed to more than 100,000 households in Austria.
Language(s): German

DIE INFORMATION 763525A21A-1442
Editorial: Gumpendorfer Str. 15, 1060 WIEN
Tel: 1 587952825 **Fax:** 1 587952821
Email: direktion@lk-wien.at **Web site:** http://www.lk-wien.at
Freq: Monthly; **Circ:** 1,400
Editor: Robert Fitzthum; **Advertising Manager:** Robert Fitzthum
Profile: Magazine from the Chamber of Agriculture for gardeners, wine growers and farmers and all interested in environment and agriculture.
Language(s): German
ADVERTISING RATES:
Full Page Mono .... EUR 2200
Full Page Colour .... EUR 2200
Mechanical Data: Type Area: 268 x 207 mm, No. of Columns (Display): 4, Col Widths (Display): 48 mm
Copy instructions: *Copy Date:* 21 days prior to publication
Supplement(s): BauernJournal

DIE INFORMATION 763525A21A-1492
Editorial: Gumpendorfer Str. 15, 1060 WIEN
Tel: 1 587952825 **Fax:** 1 587952821
Email: direktion@lk-wien.at **Web site:** http://www.lk-wien.at
Freq: Monthly; **Circ:** 1,400
Editor: Robert Fitzthum; **Advertising Manager:** Robert Fitzthum
Profile: Magazine from the Chamber of Agriculture for gardeners, wine growers and farmers and all interested in environment and agriculture.
Language(s): German
ADVERTISING RATES:
Full Page Mono .... EUR 2200
Full Page Colour .... EUR 2200
Mechanical Data: Type Area: 268 x 207 mm, No. of Columns (Display): 4, Col Widths (Display): 48 mm
Copy instructions: *Copy Date:* 21 days prior to publication
Supplement(s): BauernJournal

INFORMATION-DOKUMENTATION 731120A40-200
Editorial: Stiftgasse 2a, 1070 WIEN
Tel: 502011028630 **Fax:** 502011017109
Freq: Monthly; **Circ:** 800
Editor: Adolf Barton
Profile: Magazine from the armed forces academy.
Language(s): German

INFORMATION-DOKUMENTATION 1997368A40-665
Editorial: Stiftgasse 2a, 1070 WIEN
Tel: 502011028620 **Fax:** 502011017109
Email: helmut.huettl@bmlvs.gv.at
Freq: Monthly; **Circ:** 800
Editor: Helmut Hüttl
Profile: Magazine for political theory, safety policy and armed forces.
Language(s): German

INFORMATIV 731308A57-340
Editorial: Promenade 37, 4020 LINZ **Tel:** 732 779279
Fax: 732 785602
Email: ooenb@gmx.net **Web site:** http://www.naturschutzbund-ooe.at
Freq: Quarterly; **Circ:** 7,200
Editor: Martin Schwarz
Profile: Magazine of the Association for Nature Protection in Upper Austria.
Language(s): German

DER INGENIEUR 746613A19A-43
Editorial: Eschenbachgasse 9, 1010 WIEN
Tel: 1 5874198 **Fax:** 1 5868268
Email: voi@voi.at **Web site:** http://www.voi.at
Freq: Quarterly; **Circ:** 3,500
Editor: Diethelm C. Peschak
Profile: Official journal of the Association of Austrian Engineers.
Language(s): German
ADVERTISING RATES:
Full Page Mono .... EUR 810
Full Page Colour .... EUR 1300
Mechanical Data: Type Area: 264 x 180 mm
BUSINESS: ENGINEERING & MACHINERY

INJECTION 1859041A14A-2644
Editorial: Ludwig-Engel-Str. 1, 4311 SCHWERTBERG **Tel:** 506200
Email: gerd.liebig@engel.at **Web site:** http://www.engelglobal.com
Freq: Annual; **Circ:** 10,000
Editor: Gerd Liebig
Profile: Company publication published by Engel Austria.
Language(s): German

INNOVATIVES OBERÖSTERREICH 1743017A14A-2572
Editorial: Hafenstr. 47, 4020 LINZ
Tel: 732 798105013 **Fax:** 732 798105008
Email: info@tmg.at **Web site:** http://www.tmg.at
Freq: Half-yearly; **Cover Price:** Free; **Circ:** 20,000
Editor: Bruno Lindorfer; **Advertising Manager:** Karolin Solly
Profile: Content: Information on the region Oberösterreich (Austria) and to the Innovation Network Oberösterreich.
Language(s): English; German

DAS INSTALLATIONS-MAGAZIN 1645660A17-162
Editorial: Stockerauer Str. 43a/5, 2100 KORNEUBURG **Tel:** 32262 7465017
Fax: 2262 7465030
Email: thomas.altmann@i-magazin.at **Web site:** http://www.i-magazin.at
Freq: 10 issues yearly; **Annual Sub.:** EUR 22,00; **Circ:** 14,274
Editor: Thomas Altmann; **Advertising Manager:** Thomas Zoufal
Profile: Magazine about electro installations, light, edp networks, communications and alternative energy generation.
Language(s): German
ADVERTISING RATES:
Full Page Colour .... EUR 1900
Mechanical Data: Type Area: 260 x 185 mm

DAS INSTALLATIONS-MAGAZIN 1645660A17-167
Editorial: Stockerauer Str. 43a/5, 2100 KORNEUBURG **Tel:** 32262 7465017
Fax: 2262 7465030
Email: thomas.altmann@i-magazin.at **Web site:** http://www.i-magazin.at
Freq: 10 issues yearly; **Annual Sub.:** EUR 22,00; **Circ:** 14,274
Editor: Thomas Altmann; **Advertising Manager:** Thomas Zoufal
Profile: Magazine about electro installations, light, edp networks, communications and alternative energy generation.
Language(s): German
ADVERTISING RATES:
Full Page Colour .... EUR 1900
Mechanical Data: Type Area: 260 x 185 mm

INTENSIV-NEWS 731424A56A-660
Editorial: Koloman-Wallisch-Platz 12, 8600 BRUCK
Tel: 3862 56400 **Fax:** 3862 5640016
Email: wilfried.druml@meduniwien.ac.at **Web site:** http://www.medicom.cc
Freq: 6 issues yearly; **Annual Sub.:** EUR 60,00; **Circ:** 11,000
Editor: Wilfred Druml
Profile: Magazine for physical doctors.
Language(s): German

INTERN 731456A2A-300
Editorial: Brunner Feldstr. 45, 2380 PERCHTOLDSDORF **Tel:** 1 86648662
Fax: 1 86648620
Email: intern@manstein.at **Web site:** http://www.manstein.at
Freq: 47 issues yearly; **Annual Sub.:** EUR 285,00; **Circ:** 1,650
Editor: Milan Frühbauer
Profile: Information journal for the publicity and advertising sector.
Language(s): German

INTERN 731456A2A-958
Editorial: Brunner Feldstr. 45, 2380 PERCHTOLDSDORF **Tel:** 1 86648662
Fax: 1 86648620
Email: intern@manstein.at **Web site:** http://www.manstein.at
Freq: 47 issues yearly; **Annual Sub.:** EUR 285,00; **Circ:** 1,650
Editor: Milan Frühbauer
Profile: Information journal for the publicity and advertising sector.
Language(s): German

ISR INTERNATIONALE SEILBAHN-RUNDSCHAU 1643725A49E-201
Editorial: Leberstr. 122, 1110 WIEN **Tel:** 1 74095463
Fax: 1 74095183
Email: j.schramm@bohmann.at **Web site:** http://www.isr.at
Freq: 6 issues yearly; **Annual Sub.:** EUR 105,40; **Circ:** 5,125
Editor: Josef Schramm

Profile: Magazine for aerial railway companies, tourism, industry and economy.
Language(s): Chinese; English; French; German; Italian; Russian
ADVERTISING RATES:
Full Page Mono ..... EUR 2820
Full Page Colour ..... EUR 4600
Mechanical Data: Type Area: 270 x 185 mm
BUSINESS: TRANSPORT: Railways

IT&T BUSINESS 731635A14A-1240
Editorial: Scheibengasse 1, 1190 WIEN
Tel: 1 36980670 **Fax:** 1 369806722
Email: redaktion@itmedia.at **Web site:** http://www.itmedia.at
Freq: 10 issues yearly; **Annual Sub.:** EUR 35,00; **Circ:** 14,552
Editor: Adrienne Nikoll; **Advertising Manager:** Christian Stehno
Language(s): German
ADVERTISING RATES:
Full Page Mono ..... EUR 4240
Full Page Colour ..... EUR 4980
Mechanical Data: Type Area: 266 x 185 mm
BUSINESS: COMMERCE, INDUSTRY & MANAGEMENT

ITSELLER 1746676A43A-63
Editorial: Simmeringer Hauptstr. 152/19, 1110 WIEN
Tel: 664 8468645
Email: magazin@itseller.at **Web site:** http://www.itseller.at
Freq: 11 issues yearly; **Cover Price:** EUR 3,00; **Circ:** 12,900
Editor: Norbert Benesch
Language(s): German
ADVERTISING RATES:
Full Page Mono ..... EUR 2800
Full Page Colour ..... EUR 2800
Mechanical Data: Type Area: 2560 x 180 mm
BUSINESS: ELECTRICAL RETAIL TRADE

JAGD IN TIROL 731693A81B-2
Editorial: Adamgasse 7a/2, 6020 INNSBRUCK
Tel: 512 571093 **Fax:** 512 57109315
Email: info@tjv.at **Web site:** http://www.tjv.at
Freq: 11 issues yearly; **Circ:** 20,000
Editor: Helmuth Waldburger
Profile: European magazine of the Tyrol Hunters' Association.
Language(s): German
ADVERTISING RATES:
Full Page Colour ..... EUR 1775
Mechanical Data: Type Area: 242 x 184 mm
Copy instructions: *Copy Date:* 15 days prior to publication
CONSUMER: ANIMALS & PETS: Dogs

JATROS DIABETES & STOFFWECHSEL 731912A56A-700
Editorial: Markgraf-Rüdiger-Str. 8, 1150 WIEN
Tel: 1 876795634 **Fax:** 1 876795620
Email: katja.valent@universimed.com **Web site:** http://www.universimed.com
Freq: 5 issues yearly; **Circ:** 8,500
Editor: Katja Valent
Profile: Magazine on further education in diabetology from the Austrian Association of Diabetes.
Language(s): German
ADVERTISING RATES:
Full Page Mono ..... EUR 3220
Full Page Colour ..... EUR 3220
Mechanical Data: Type Area: 247 x 178 mm
Copy instructions: *Copy Date:* 28 days prior to publication
Official Journal of: Organ d. ÖDG u. d. ÖAG

JATROS HÄMATOLOGIE & ONKOLOGIE 1644649A56A-1932
Editorial: Markgraf-Rüdiger-Str. 8, 1150 WIEN
Tel: 1 876795654 **Fax:** 1 876795620
Email: alice.kment@universimed.com **Web site:** http://www.universimed.com
Freq: 6 issues yearly; **Circ:** 5,400
Editor: Alice Kment
Profile: Magazine for oncologists and haematologists.
Language(s): German
ADVERTISING RATES:
Full Page Mono ..... EUR 2640
Full Page Colour ..... EUR 2640
Mechanical Data: Type Area: 247 x 178 mm
Copy instructions: *Copy Date:* 28 days prior to publication

JATROS KARDIOLOGIE & GEFÄSSMEDIZIN 731915A56A-720
Editorial: Markgraf-Rüdiger-Str. 8, 1150 WIEN
Tel: 1 876795644 **Fax:** 1 876795620
Email: christian.fexa@universimed.com **Web site:** http://www.universimed.com
Freq: 5 issues yearly; **Circ:** 4,200
Editor: Christian Fexa
Profile: Magazine for internists and assorted practitioners.
Language(s): German
ADVERTISING RATES:
Full Page Mono ..... EUR 2640
Full Page Colour ..... EUR 2640
Mechanical Data: Type Area: 247 x 178 mm
Copy instructions: *Copy Date:* 28 days prior to publication
BUSINESS: HEALTH & MEDICAL

JATROS MEDIZIN FÜR DIE FRAU 731916A56A-740
Editorial: Markgraf-Rüdiger-Str. 8, 1150 WIEN
Tel: 1 876795644 **Fax:** 1 876795620
Email: christian.fexa@universimed.com **Web site:** http://www.universimed.com
Freq: Quarterly; **Annual Sub.:** EUR 22,00; **Circ:** 2,000
Editor: Christian Fexa
Profile: Magazine on gynaecology and obstetrics.
Language(s): English; German
ADVERTISING RATES:
Full Page Mono ..... EUR 2640
Full Page Colour ..... EUR 2640
Mechanical Data: Type Area: 247 x 178 mm
Copy instructions: *Copy Date:* 28 days prior to publication

JATROS NEUROLOGIE & PSYCHIATRIE 731918A56A-760
Editorial: Markgraf-Rüdiger-Str. 8, 1150 WIEN
Tel: 1 876795612 **Fax:** 1 876795620
Email: jan.sipos@universimed.com **Web site:** http://www.universimed.com
Freq: 8 issues yearly; **Circ:** 3,200
Editor: Jan Sipos
Profile: Magazine on neurology and psychiatry.
Language(s): German
ADVERTISING RATES:
Full Page Mono ..... EUR 2640
Full Page Colour ..... EUR 2640
Mechanical Data: Type Area: 247 x 178 mm
Copy instructions: *Copy Date:* 28 days prior to publication

JATROS ORTHOPÄDIE 731920A56A-780
Editorial: Markgraf-Rüdiger-Str. 8, 1150 WIEN
Tel: 1 876795616 **Fax:** 1 876795620
Email: christine.dominkus@universimed.com **Web site:** http://www.universimed.com
Freq: 6 issues yearly; **Circ:** 3,500
Editor: Christine Dominkus
Profile: Magazine for orthopaedists, emergency surgeons and rheumatologists.
Language(s): German
ADVERTISING RATES:
Full Page Mono ..... EUR 2640
Full Page Colour ..... EUR 2640
Mechanical Data: Type Area: 247 x 178 mm
Copy instructions: *Copy Date:* 28 days prior to publication
Official Journal of: Organ d. Österr. Ges. f. Orthopädie u. orthopäd. Chirurgie, d. Österr. Ges. f. orthopädische Fußchirurgie u. Fußmedizin, d. Österr. Ges. f. Wirbelsäulenchirurgie u. d. Österr. Ges. f. Tumororthopädie

JATROS VACCINES 731924A56A-820
Editorial: Markgraf-Rüdiger-Str. 8, 1150 WIEN
Tel: 1 87679560 **Fax:** 1 876795620
Email: friederike.hoerandl@universimed.com **Web site:** http://www.universimed.com
Freq: 3 issues yearly; **Circ:** 11,500
Editor: Friederike Hörandl
Profile: Magazine for general practitioners on immunisation.
Language(s): German
ADVERTISING RATES:
Full Page Mono ..... EUR 3220
Full Page Colour ..... EUR 3220
Mechanical Data: Type Area: 244 x 178 mm

JOURNAL FÜR GASTROENTEROLOGISCHE UND HEPATOLOGISCHE ERKRANKUNGEN 1645534A56A-1935
Editorial: Mozartgasse 10, 3003 GABLITZ
Tel: 2231 612580 **Fax:** 2231 6125810
Web site: http://www.kup.at/gastroenterologie
Freq: Quarterly; **Annual Sub.:** EUR 36,00; **Circ:** 3,500
Profile: Magazine about gastroenterological and hepatological diseases.
Language(s): German
ADVERTISING RATES:
Full Page Colour ..... EUR 2460
Mechanical Data: Type Area: 255 x 180 mm
Copy instructions: *Copy Date:* 30 days prior to publication

JOURNAL FÜR HYPERTONIE 732057A56A-880
Editorial: Mozartgasse 10, 3003 GABLITZ
Tel: 2231 612580 **Fax:** 2231 6125810
Email: katharina.grabner@kup.at **Web site:** http://www.kup.at/hypertonie
Freq: Quarterly; **Annual Sub.:** EUR 36,00; **Circ:** 3,200
Profile: Magazine about hypertonia.
Language(s): German
ADVERTISING RATES:
Full Page Colour ..... EUR 2500
Mechanical Data: Type Area: 255 x 180 mm
Copy instructions: *Copy Date:* 30 days prior to publication
Official Journal of: Organ d. Österr. Ges. f. Hypertensiologie

JOURNAL FÜR KARDIOLOGIE 732058A56A-900
Editorial: Mozartgasse 10, 3003 GABLITZ
Tel: 2231 612580 **Fax:** 2231 6125810
Email: gabriele.voss@kup.at **Web site:** http://www.kup.at/kardiologie
Freq: 6 issues yearly; **Annual Sub.:** EUR 60,00; **Circ:** 3,500
Editor: Kurt Huber
Profile: Magazine about cardiology.
Language(s): German
ADVERTISING RATES:
Full Page Mono ..... EUR 2500
Full Page Colour ..... EUR 2500
Mechanical Data: Type Area: 255 x 180 mm
Copy instructions: *Copy Date:* 21 days prior to publication

JOURNAL FÜR MINERALSTOFFWECHSEL 732062A56A-940
Editorial: Mozartgasse 10, 3003 GABLITZ
Tel: 2231 612580 **Fax:** 2231 6125810
Email: katharina.grabner@kup.at **Web site:** http://www.kup.at/mineralstoffwechsel
Freq: Quarterly; **Annual Sub.:** EUR 36,00; **Circ:** 4,500
Editor: Heinrich Resch
Profile: Magazine about orthopaedics, osteology and rheumatology.
Language(s): German
ADVERTISING RATES:
Full Page Colour ..... EUR 2710
Mechanical Data: Type Area: 255 x 180 mm
Copy instructions: *Copy Date:* 30 days prior to publication
Official Journal of: Organ d. Österr. Ges. z. Erforschung d. Knochens u. Mineralstoffwechsels u. d. Österr. Ges. f. Orthopädie u. Orthopäd. Chirurgie

JOURNAL FÜR NEUROLOGIE, NEUROCHIRURGIE UND PSYCHIATRIE 732064A56A-960
Editorial: Mozartgasse 10, 3003 GABLITZ
Tel: 2231 612580 **Fax:** 2231 6125810
Email: katharina.grabner@kup.at **Web site:** http://www.kup.at/neurologie
Freq: Quarterly; **Annual Sub.:** EUR 36,00; **Circ:** 2,300
Editor: K. Ungersböck
Profile: Magazine about diseases of the nervous system.
Language(s): German
ADVERTISING RATES:
Full Page Colour ..... EUR 2240
Mechanical Data: Type Area: 255 x 180 mm
Copy instructions: *Copy Date:* 30 days prior to publication

JOURNAL FÜR REPRODUKTIONSMEDIZIN UND ENDOKRINOLOGIE 1645535A56A-1936
Editorial: Mozartgasse 10, 3003 GABLITZ
Tel: 2231 612580 **Fax:** 2231 6125810
Email: gabriele.voss@kup.at **Web site:** http://www.kup.at/reproduktionsmedizin
Freq: 6 issues yearly; **Annual Sub.:** EUR 80,00; **Circ:** 1,600
Editor: Hermann M. Behre
Profile: Magazine about reproduction medicine and endocrinology.
Language(s): English; German
ADVERTISING RATES:
Full Page Colour ..... EUR 2880
Mechanical Data: Type Area: 255 x 180 mm
Copy instructions: *Copy Date:* 30 days prior to publication
Official Journal of: Organ d. Dachverb. Reproduktionsbiologie u. -medizin, d. Dt. Ges. f. Reproduktionsmedizin, d. Österr. Ges. f. Reproduktionsmedizin u. Endokrinologie, d. Dt. Ges. f. Andrologie, d. Bundesverb. Reproduktionsmedizin. Zentren Deutschlands, d. Dt. Ges. f. Gynäkolog. Endokrinologie u. Fortpflanzungsmedizin, d. ArGe Reproduktionsbiologie d. Menschen u. d. Sektion Reproduktionsbiologie u. -medizin d. Dt. Ges. f. Endokrinologie

JOURNAL FÜR UROLOGIE UND UROGYNÄKOLOGIE 732070A56A-980
Editorial: Mozartgasse 10, 3003 GABLITZ
Tel: 2231 612580 **Fax:** 2231 6125810
Email: katharina.grabner@kup.at **Web site:** http://www.kup.at/urologie
Freq: Quarterly; **Annual Sub.:** EUR 36,00; **Circ:** 1,800
Editor: H. Heidler
Profile: Magazine about urology and urogynaecology.
Language(s): German
ADVERTISING RATES:
Full Page Colour ..... EUR 2240
Mechanical Data: Type Area: 255 x 180 mm
Copy instructions: *Copy Date:* 30 days prior to publication

JOURNAL OF NEURAL TRANSMISSION 1853212A56A-2039
Editorial: Sachsenplatz 4, 1201 WIEN
Tel: 1 33024150 **Fax:** 1 3302426
Email: umamaheswari.chelladurai@springer.com **Web site:** http://www.springer.at
Freq: Monthly; **Circ:** 800
Editor: Peter Riederer
Profile: Magazine about neural transmission.
Language(s): English
ADVERTISING RATES:
Full Page Mono ..... EUR 1330
Full Page Colour ..... EUR 2394
Mechanical Data: Type Area: 230 x 170 mm
Official Journal of: Organ d. European Society for Clinical Neuropharmacology

JOURNAL OF PEST SCIENCE 720925G21R-80
Editorial: Technikerstr. 25, 6020 INNSBRUCK
Tel: 512 5075693 **Fax:** 512 5072817
Email: michael.traugott@uibk.ac.at **Web site:** http://www.springerlink.com
Freq: Quarterly; **Annual Sub.:** EUR 604,00; **Circ:** 94
Editor: Michael Traugott
Profile: Journal about pest control, plant and environmental protection.
Language(s): English; French; German
ADVERTISING RATES:
Full Page Mono ..... EUR 740
Full Page Colour ..... EUR 1780
Mechanical Data: Type Area: 240 x 175 mm
BUSINESS: AGRICULTURE & FARMING: Agriculture & Farming Related

JOURNALISTEN MEDIEN & PR-INDEX 732077A2A-320
Editorial: Frimmelgasse 41, 1190 WIEN
Tel: 1 3701577 **Fax:** 1 3704693
Email: redaktion@indexverlag.at **Web site:** http://www.indexverlag.at
Freq: Half-yearly; **Cover Price:** EUR 180,00; **Circ:** 2,800
Profile: Manual for advertising managers, PR experts and press offices.
Language(s): German
ADVERTISING RATES:
Full Page Mono ..... EUR 1417
Full Page Colour ..... EUR 1853
Mechanical Data: Type Area: 262 x 175 mm

JUNGE MEDIZINER 1655623A56A-1948
Editorial: Weihburggasse 10, 1010 WIEN
Tel: 1 515011276 **Fax:** 1 515011429
Email: stellenboerse@aekwien.at **Web site:** http://www.aekwien.at
Freq: 5 issues yearly; **Cover Price:** Free; **Circ:** 2,000
Profile: Magazine from the Medical Board of Vienna.
Language(s): German

JUNGE MEDIZINER 1655623A56A-2041
Editorial: Weihburggasse 10, 1010 WIEN
Tel: 1 515011276 **Fax:** 1 515011429
Email: stellenboerse@aekwien.at **Web site:** http://www.aekwien.at
Freq: 5 issues yearly; **Cover Price:** Free; **Circ:** 2,000
Profile: Magazine from the Medical Board of Vienna.
Language(s): German

KAMMER AKTUELL 732365A21A-480
Editorial: Scharitzerstr. 9, 4010 LINZ
Tel: 732 65638126 **Fax:** 732 65638129
Email: weingartner.harald@lak-ooe.at **Web site:** http://www.landarbeiterkammer.at/ooe
Freq: Quarterly; **Circ:** 12,000
Editor: Harald Weingartner; **Advertising Manager:** Harald Weingartner
Profile: Magazine about agriculture and forestry.
Language(s): German
ADVERTISING RATES:
Full Page Mono ..... EUR 1400
Full Page Colour ..... EUR 1400

KÄRNTNER ÄRZTEZEITUNG 732289A56A-1060
Editorial: St.-Veiter Str. 34, 9020 KLAGENFURT
Tel: 463 585626 **Fax:** 463 585644
Email: presse@aekktn.at **Web site:** http://www.kaerngesund.at
Freq: 10 issues yearly; Free to qualifying individuals
Annual Sub.: EUR 32,00; **Circ:** 3,200
Editor: Josef Huber
Profile: Newspaper of the Medical Chamber of Kärnten.
Language(s): German
ADVERTISING RATES:
Full Page Mono ..... EUR 760
Full Page Colour ..... EUR 1138
Mechanical Data: Type Area: 250 x 184 mm, No. of Columns (Display): 4, Col Widths (Display): 43 mm
Supplement(s): ärzte Exklusiv
BUSINESS: HEALTH & MEDICAL

KÄRNTNER BAUER 732290A21J-1
Editorial: Museumgasse 5, 9020 KLAGENFURT
Tel: 463 58501381 **Fax:** 463 58501389

Email: presse@lk-kaernten.at **Web site:** http://www.lk-kaernten.at
Freq: Weekly; Free to qualifying individuals
Annual Sub.: EUR 45,00; **Circ:** 25,000
Editor: Rudolf Fritzer
Profile: Farming magazine for the Kärnten region of Austria.
Language(s): German
ADVERTISING RATES:
Full Page Mono .... EUR 2280
Full Page Colour .... EUR 3192
Mechanical Data: No. of Columns (Display): 6, Col Widths (Display): 31 mm, Type Area: 263 x 200 mm
Copy instructions: *Copy Date:* 4 days prior to publication
Supplement(s): BauernJournal
BUSINESS: AGRICULTURE & FARMING: Agriculture & Farming - Regional

KÄRNTNER MONAT 1852557A73-419
Editorial: Eiskellerstr. 3/2, 9020 KLAGENFURT
Tel: 463 47858 **Fax:** 463 4785815
Email: wolfgang.kofler@monat.at **Web site:** http://www.monat.at
Freq: Monthly; **Annual Sub.:** EUR 22,00; **Circ:** 20,000
Editor: Wolfgang Kofler; **Advertising Manager:** Alexander Suppantschitsch
Profile: Magazine for the Kärnten region.
Language(s): German
ADVERTISING RATES:
Full Page Mono .... EUR 3600
Full Page Colour .... EUR 3600
Mechanical Data: Type Area: 266 x 193 mm
Copy instructions: *Copy Date:* 14 days prior to publication

KÄRNTNER SENIORENZEITUNG 732302A74N-60
Editorial: Bahnhofstr. 20/2, 9020 KLAGENFURT
Tel: 463 586242 **Fax:** 463 586243
Email: presse@seniorenbund.org **Web site:** http://www.seniorenbund.org
Freq: 8 issues yearly; **Circ:** 30,000
Editor: Franz Josef Martinz
Profile: Magazine of the Kärntner Senior Citizens' Association.
Language(s): German
ADVERTISING RATES:
Full Page Mono .... EUR 1550
Full Page Colour .... EUR 2400
Mechanical Data: Type Area: 265 x 200 mm
CONSUMER: WOMEN'S INTEREST CONSUMER MAGAZINES: Retirement

KFZWIRTSCHAFT 732538A31A-4
Editorial: Wiedner Hauptstr. 120, 1051 WIEN
Tel: 1 54664321 **Fax:** 1 5466450321
Email: w.bauer@wirtschaftsverlag.at **Web site:** http://www.kfz-wirtschaft.at
Freq: 11 issues yearly; **Annual Sub.:** EUR 60,00; **Circ:** 9,025
Editor: Wolfgang Bauer; **Advertising Manager:** Dieter Köllner-Gürsch
Profile: Journal covering the automotive industry, including articles on sales, repair and manufacture.
Language(s): German
ADVERTISING RATES:
Full Page Mono .... EUR 3124
Full Page Colour .... EUR 4462
Mechanical Data: Type Area: 255 x 185 mm
BUSINESS: MOTOR TRADE: Motor Trade Accessories

KIRCHE IN 732688A87-1340
Editorial: Keplergasse 8, 1100 WIEN **Tel:** 1 6035626
Fax: 1 60664104
Email: office@kirche-in.at **Web site:** http://www.kirche-in.at
Freq: Monthly; **Annual Sub.:** EUR 36,00; **Circ:** 20,000
Editor: Rudolf Schermann; **Advertising Manager:** Otto Neuberger
Profile: Magazine providing a forum for discussions about a more open church.
Language(s): German
ADVERTISING RATES:
Full Page Colour .... EUR 2500
Mechanical Data: Type Area: 250 x 187 mm, No. of Columns (Display): 3, Col Widths (Display): 56 mm
Copy instructions: *Copy Date:* 15 days prior to publication
CONSUMER: RELIGIOUS

KLAGENFURT 732762A72-3980
Editorial: Neuer Platz 1, 9010 KLAGENFURT
Tel: 463 5372271 **Fax:** 463 516990
Email: stadtzeitung@klagenfurt.at **Web site:** http://www.klagenfurt.at
Freq: 21 issues yearly; **Annual Sub.:** EUR 10,00; **Circ:** 57,000
Editor: Veronika Meissnitzer; **Advertising Manager:** Klaus Pikl
Profile: Local official paper.
Language(s): German
ADVERTISING RATES:
Full Page Mono .... EUR 1523
Full Page Colour .... EUR 1890
Mechanical Data: Type Area: 252 x 203 mm, No. of Columns (Display): 4, Col Widths (Display): 47 mm
LOCAL NEWSPAPERS

KLEINE ZEITUNG 732838A67B-520
Editorial: Schönaugasse 64, 8010 GRAZ
Tel: 316 8754001 **Fax:** 316 875404
Email: redaktion@kleinezeitung.at **Web site:** http://www.kleinezeitung.at
Freq: 312 issues yearly; **Circ:** 207,794
Editor: Hubert Patterer; **Advertising Manager:** Gerhard Valeskini
Profile: Regional daily newspaper covering politics, economics, sport, travel, technology and the arts.
Language(s): German
Mechanical Data: Type Area: 275 x 200 mm, No. of Columns (Display): 4, Col Widths (Display): 47 mm
Copy instructions: *Copy Date:* 1 day prior to publication
Supplement(s): Kleine Zeitung Ärzte-Führer; Kleine Zeitung Aufleben; Kleine Zeitung Uni; The Red Bulletin; Sieben Tage; tele; Uhren Schmuck Magazin
REGIONAL DAILY & SUNDAY NEWSPAPERS: Regional Daily Newspapers

KLEINGÄRTNER 737999A93-65
Editorial: Getreidemarkt 11, 1060 WIEN
Tel: 1 587078524 **Fax:** 1 587078530
Email: zvwien@kleingaertner.at **Web site:** http://www.kleingaertner.at
Freq: 11 issues yearly; **Annual Sub.:** EUR 12,00; **Circ:** 45,436
Profile: Publication about allotments and smallholdings.
Language(s): German
Readership: Aimed at people with an interest in gardening.
ADVERTISING RATES:
Full Page Mono .... EUR 2288
Full Page Colour .... EUR 3432
Mechanical Data: Type Area: 265 x 190 mm, No. of Columns (Display): 4, Col Widths (Display): 44 mm
Copy instructions: *Copy Date:* 21 days prior to publication
CONSUMER: GARDENING

KLIMABÜNDNIS 732870A57-380
Editorial: Hütteldorfer Str. 63, 1150 WIEN
Tel: 1 5815881 **Fax:** 1 5815880
Email: office@klimabuendnis.at **Web site:** http://www.klimabuendnis.at
Freq: Quarterly; **Circ:** 15,500
Advertising Manager: Elfriede Hecher
Profile: Magazine about climate protection.
Language(s): German
ADVERTISING RATES:
Full Page Mono .... EUR 1890
Full Page Colour .... EUR 1890
Mechanical Data: Type Area: 252 x 188 mm

KL!PP 1853341A73-422
Editorial: Friedhofgasse 20, 8020 GRAZ
Tel: 316 4260800 **Fax:** 316 426080122
Email: office@klippmagazin.at **Web site:** http://www.klippmagazin.at
Freq: 10 issues yearly; **Annual Sub.:** EUR 14,43; **Circ:** 10,000
Editor: Jürgen Lehner
Profile: Regional magazine with information on and from Styria. On the current day's events, Styria is well informed through newspapers and electronic media. KLIPP however looks regular, sustainable and effective Styrian behind the scenes, looks as a medium "for readers, which is not enough ostensible". KLIPP lights out as a regional magazine, which moves the Styrian backgrounds and contexts that come in daily to-date short. With honest journalism is in factual KLIPP dedicated focus to those issues that are of the Styrian. According to the features: What do the target groups, as they do, and why they do it? Target audience: decision makers and opinion leaders in business, finance and insurance, etc., in educational institutions (schools, colleges, universities), as well as doctors, lawyers, lawyers, civil engineers, accountants, trustees Facebook: http://www.facebook.com/pages/Steiermarkmagazin-Klipp/109818949067602.
Language(s): German
ADVERTISING RATES:
Full Page Mono .... EUR 1700
Full Page Colour .... EUR 1700
Mechanical Data: Type Area: 260 x 190 mm

KOCH & BACK JOURNAL 732940A74P-140
Editorial: Lindengasse 26, 1070 WIEN
Tel: 1 5261952 **Fax:** 1 526195246
Email: redaktion@kochundback.at **Web site:** http://www.kochundback.at
Freq: 10 issues yearly; **Annual Sub.:** EUR 27,66; **Circ:** 63,000
Editor: Rudolf Bruner; **Advertising Manager:** Rudolf Bruner
Profile: Magazine about cookery and baking.
Language(s): German
ADVERTISING RATES:
Full Page Mono .... EUR 6740
Full Page Colour .... EUR 6740
Mechanical Data: Type Area: 294 x 208 mm
Supplement(s): prima
CONSUMER: WOMEN'S INTEREST CONSUMER MAGAZINES: Food & Cookery

KOCHEN UND KÜCHE 1642363A74P-264
Editorial: Hofgasse 5, 8010 GRAZ
Tel: 316 821636169 **Fax:** 316 821636151
Email: redaktion@kochenundkueche.com **Web site:** http://www.kochenundkueche.com
Freq: Monthly; **Annual Sub.:** EUR 31,90; **Circ:** 48,000
Editor: Irmtraud Weishaupt-Orthofer; **Advertising Manager:** Reinhold Zötsch
Profile: Magazine about cooking and kitchens.
Language(s): German
ADVERTISING RATES:
Full Page Mono .... EUR 3990
Full Page Colour .... EUR 3990
Mechanical Data: Type Area: 253 x 185 mm

KÖF-INFORMATIONSDIENST 1852467A74A-943
Editorial: Krugerstr. 3, 1010 WIEN **Tel:** 1 5125800
Fax: 1 5128037
Email: wien@koef.at **Web site:** http://www.koef.at
Freq: Quarterly; **Cover Price:** Free; **Circ:** 50,000
Editor: Michaela Mojzis
Profile: Publication from the Emergency Aid of Austrian Women.
Language(s): German

KOLPING ÖSTERREICH 738040A87-1860
Editorial: Paulanergasse 11, 1040 WIEN
Tel: 1 58735420 **Fax:** 1 5879900
Email: w.engelmaier@kolping.at **Web site:** http://www.kolping.at
Freq: Quarterly; **Circ:** 16,000
Editor: Wolfgang Engelmaier; **Advertising Manager:** Susanne Friedl
Profile: Catholic magazine focusing on social issues.
Language(s): German
Readership: Aimed at members of the magazine, Catholic organisations and local authorities.
ADVERTISING RATES:
Full Page Mono .... EUR 1090
Full Page Colour .... EUR 1090
Mechanical Data: Type Area: 264 x 188 mm, No. of Columns (Display): 3, Col Widths (Display): 58 mm
Copy instructions: *Copy Date:* 7 days prior to publication
CONSUMER: RELIGIOUS

KOMMUNAL 733026A32A-320
Editorial: Löwelstr. 6/2, 1010 WIEN **Tel:** 1 532238816
Fax: 1 532238822
Email: hans.braun@kommunal.at **Web site:** http://www.kommunal.at
Freq: Monthly; **Circ:** 34,674
Editor: Hans Braun
Profile: Publication about municipal and local government in Austria. Focuses on the relationship between local government and international trade and industry.
Language(s): German
Readership: Aimed at mayors and other figures of authority in local governments.
ADVERTISING RATES:
Full Page Colour .... EUR 5800
Mechanical Data: Type Area: 256 x 180 mm, No. of Columns (Display): 3, Col Widths (Display): 60 mm
BUSINESS: LOCAL GOVERNMENT, LEISURE & RECREATION: Local Government

DER KOMMUNIKATOR 1659610A40-649
Editorial: Salzburgerstr. 3, 5600 ST. JOHANN
Tel: 502018231104 **Fax:** 502018217300
Email: fueub2.s5@bmlvs.gv.at
Freq: Quarterly; **Cover Price:** Free; **Circ:** 1,200
Editor: Markus Schlosser
Profile: Internal and external paper with information for and about the signals troop.
Language(s): German

KOMPACK 1655626A35-23
Editorial: Landstraßer Hauptstr. 141/3a/5, 1030 WIEN **Tel:** 1 7122036 **Fax:** 1 7122070
Email: werbeagentur.harald.eckert@chello.at **Web site:** http://www.kompack.info
Freq: 6 issues yearly; **Annual Sub.:** EUR 21,80; **Circ:** 11,000
Editor: Harald Eckert; **Advertising Manager:** Walter G. Klima
Profile: Magazine about packaging, transport, logistics, recycling and the environment.
Language(s): German

KOMPETENZ 733069A14A-2501
Editorial: Alfred-Dallinger-Platz 1, 1034 WIEN
Tel: 5030121228 **Fax:** 5030171215
Email: dwora.stein@gpa-djp.at **Web site:** http://www.gpa.at
Freq: 8 issues yearly; **Circ:** 230,000
Editor: Dwora Stein
Profile: Publication focusing on management. Also covers national and international politics, economics and business issues.
Language(s): German
ADVERTISING RATES:
Full Page Mono .... EUR 7770
Full Page Colour .... EUR 7770
Mechanical Data: Type Area: 240 x 185 mm
BUSINESS: COMMERCE, INDUSTRY & MANAGEMENT

KONSTRUKTIV 1852338A4E-1327
Editorial: Schottenfelgasse 72/2/5, 1070 WIEN
Tel: 1 52498030
Email: redaktion@daskonstruktiv.at **Web site:** http://www.daskonstruktiv.at
Freq: Quarterly; **Annual Sub.:** EUR 24,00; **Circ:** 15,000
Editor: Heide Linzer
Profile: Magazine covering all aspects of engineering.
Language(s): German
ADVERTISING RATES:
Full Page Colour .... EUR 5800
Mechanical Data: Type Area: 250 x 188 mm
Copy instructions: *Copy Date:* 21 days prior to publication

KONSUMENT 733103A74M-160
Editorial: Linke Wienzeile 18, 1060 WIEN
Tel: 1 588770 **Fax:** 1 5887774
Email: leserbriefe@konsument.at **Web site:** http://www.konsument.at
Freq: Monthly; **Annual Sub.:** EUR 45,00; **Circ:** 85,000
Editor: Gerhard Früholz
Profile: Magazine about product and service tests as well as consumer information.
Language(s): German

KR KERAMISCHE RUNDSCHAU 733522A4E-800
Editorial: Witthauergasse 6/2, 1180 WIEN
Tel: 1 478817013 **Fax:** 1 478817010
Email: r.hersey@impactmedia.at **Web site:** http://www.impactmedia.at
Freq: 11 issues yearly; **Annual Sub.:** EUR 81,00; **Circ:** 2,400
Editor: Regine Hersey; **Advertising Manager:** Erika Vaka
Profile: Magazine for tilers.
Language(s): German
ADVERTISING RATES:
Full Page Mono .... EUR 1770
Full Page Colour .... EUR 3200
Mechanical Data: Type Area: 297 x 210 mm
Supplement(s): werkzeug aktuell

KREBS:HILFE! 733262A56A-1100
Editorial: Wiedner Hauptstr. 120, 1050 WIEN
Tel: 1 54600330 **Fax:** 1 54600730
Email: beermann@clinicum.at **Web site:** http://www.clinicum.at
Freq: 6 issues yearly; **Annual Sub.:** EUR 24,00; **Circ:** 14,000
Editor: Birgit Beermann; **Advertising Manager:** Reinhard Rosenberger
Profile: Magazine on oncology.
Language(s): German
ADVERTISING RATES:
Full Page Colour .... EUR 3296
Mechanical Data: Type Area: 297 x 210 mm
Copy instructions: *Copy Date:* 21 days prior to publication

KRONEN ZEITUNG 1660625A65A-122
Editorial: Muthgasse 2, 1190 WIEN **Tel:** 1 360113475
Fax: 1 3698385
Email: chefredaktion@kronenzeitung.at **Web site:** http://www.krone.at
Freq: 156 issues yearly; **Circ:** 928,740
Editor: Christoph Dichand; **News Editor:** Biggi Egger-Musil
Profile: Tabloid-sized newspaper focusing on current affairs, technology and education. Includes articles about literature, the arts, leisure, health, society, travel and culture. Also covers sport, motoring, TV and entertainment.
Language(s): German
ADVERTISING RATES:
SCC .... EUR 345,00
Mechanical Data: Type Area: 265 x 198 mm, No. of Columns (Display): 6, Col Widths (Display): 31 mm
Copy instructions: *Copy Date:* 1 day prior to publication
NATIONAL DAILY & SUNDAY NEWSPAPERS: National Daily Newspapers

KULTURMAGAZIN DER WIENER FREMDENFÜHRER 1814422A89A-494
Editorial: Neulerchenfelder Str. 23/25, 1160 WIEN
Tel: 1 4029310
Email: office@guides-in-wien.at **Web site:** http://www.guides-in-wien.at
Freq: Annual; **Cover Price:** Free; **Circ:** 12,000
Advertising Manager: Christine Wirl
Profile: Cultural guide for Vienna.
Language(s): German
ADVERTISING RATES:
Full Page Colour .... EUR 2270
Mechanical Data: Type Area: 260 x 185 mm

KURIER
733595A67B-560

Editorial: Lindengasse 52, 1070 WIEN
Tel: 1 521002601 **Fax:** 1 521002263
Email: helmut.brandstaetter@kurier.at **Web site:** http://www.kurier.at
Freq: 156 issues yearly; **Circ:** 209,498
Editor: Helmut Brandstätter
Profile: Tabloid-sized newspaper covering national and international news and current affairs. Also provides information concerning politics, religion, economics, health and IT. Includes sports and entertainment reviews.
Language(s): German
Readership: Aimed at public sector employees.
ADVERTISING RATES:
SCC .... EUR 112,00
Mechanical Data: Type Area: 392 x 266 mm, No. of Columns (Display): 6, Col Widths (Display): 41 mm
Copy instructions: *Copy Date:* 1 day prior to publication
Supplement(s): Ärzte Kurier; Ball deluxe; Business Kurier; freizeit Kurier; Immo Kurier; Motor Kurier; The Red Bulletin; techno Kurier; tv.woche
REGIONAL DAILY & SUNDAY NEWSPAPERS: Regional Daily Newspapers

KURZ&BÜNDIG AMSTETTEN
763675A72-7308

Editorial: Gutenbergstr. 12, 3100 ST. PÖLTEN
Tel: 2742 744635554 **Fax:** 2742 744635522
Email: g.stubauer@kurz-und-buendig.at **Web site:** http://www.kurz-und-buendig.at
Freq: 26 issues yearly; **Cover Price:** Free; **Circ:** 39,750
Editor: Gerhard Stubauer; **Advertising Manager:** Christian Benedik
Profile: Advertising journal (house-to-house) concentrating on local stories.
Language(s): German
ADVERTISING RATES:
Full Page Colour .... EUR 1580
Mechanical Data: Type Area: 275 x 200 mm, No. of Columns (Display): 4, Col Widths (Display): 47 mm
LOCAL NEWSPAPERS

KURZ&BÜNDIG KREMS
763682A72-7315

Editorial: Gutenbergstr. 12, 3100 ST. PÖLTEN
Tel: 2742 744635554 **Fax:** 2742 744635522
Email: g.stubauer@kurz-und-buendig.at **Web site:** http://www.kurz-und-buendig.at
Freq: 26 issues yearly; **Cover Price:** Free; **Circ:** 33,700
Editor: Gerhard Stubauer; **Advertising Manager:** Christian Benedik
Profile: Advertising journal (house-to-house) concentrating on local stories.
Language(s): German
ADVERTISING RATES:
Full Page Colour .... EUR 1580
Mechanical Data: Type Area: 275 x 200 mm, No. of Columns (Display): 4, Col Widths (Display): 47 mm
LOCAL NEWSPAPERS

KURZ&BÜNDIG MELK-ERLAUFTAL
763683A72-7316

Editorial: Gutenbergstr. 12, 3100 ST. PÖLTEN
Tel: 2742 744635554 **Fax:** 2742 744635522
Email: g.stubauer@kurz-und-buendig.at **Web site:** http://www.kurz-und-buendig.at
Freq: 26 issues yearly; **Cover Price:** Free; **Circ:** 40,200
Editor: Gerhard Stubauer; **Advertising Manager:** Christian Benedik
Profile: Advertising journal (house-to-house) concentrating on local stories.
Language(s): German
ADVERTISING RATES:
Full Page Colour .... EUR 1580
Mechanical Data: Type Area: 275 x 200 mm, No. of Columns (Display): 4, Col Widths (Display): 47 mm
LOCAL NEWSPAPERS

KURZ&BÜNDIG ST. PÖLTEN
763687A72-7320

Editorial: Gutenbergstr. 12, 3100 ST. PÖLTEN
Tel: 2742 744635554 **Fax:** 2742 744635522
Email: g.stubauer@kurz-und-buendig.at **Web site:** http://www.kurz-und-buendig.at
Freq: 26 issues yearly; **Cover Price:** Free; **Circ:** 49,350
Editor: Gerhard Stubauer; **Advertising Manager:** Christian Benedik
Profile: Advertising journal (house-to-house) concentrating on local stories.
Language(s): German
ADVERTISING RATES:
Full Page Colour .... EUR 1580
Mechanical Data: Type Area: 275 x 200 mm, No. of Columns (Display): 4, Col Widths (Display): 47 mm
LOCAL NEWSPAPERS

LAND DER BERGE
733770A75L-160

Editorial: Ringstr. 44/1, 3500 KREMS
Tel: 2732 8200036 **Fax:** 2732 8200082
Email: klaus.haselboeck@lwmedia.at **Web site:** http://www.landderberge.at
Freq: 6 issues yearly; **Annual Sub.:** EUR 34,90; **Circ:** 25,000
Editor: Klaus Haselböck; **Advertising Manager:** Michael Linauer
Profile: Magazine for hikers, mountaineers and friends of nature.
Language(s): German
ADVERTISING RATES:
Full Page Mono .... EUR 3890
Full Page Colour .... EUR 3890
Mechanical Data: Type Area: 240 x 183 mm, No. of Columns (Display): 3, Col Widths (Display): 58 mm
Copy instructions: *Copy Date:* 21 days prior to publication
CONSUMER: SPORT: Outdoor

LAND DER BERGE SPECIAL
733772A75G-40

Editorial: Ringstr. 44/1, 3500 KREMS
Tel: 2732 8200036 **Fax:** 2732 8200082
Email: klaus.haselboeck@lwmedia.at **Web site:** http://www.landderberge.at
Freq: Annual; **Cover Price:** EUR 5,00; **Circ:** 70,000
Editor: Klaus Haselböck; **Advertising Manager:** Michael Linauer
Profile: Magazine about winter sport.
Language(s): German
ADVERTISING RATES:
Full Page Mono .... EUR 4590
Full Page Colour .... EUR 4590
Mechanical Data: Type Area: 240 x 183 mm
CONSUMER: SPORT: Winter Sports

LAND DER BERGE SPECIAL
733771A77C-20

Editorial: Ringstr. 44/1, 3500 KREMS
Tel: 2732 8200036 **Fax:** 2732 8200082
Email: klaus.haselboeck@lwmedia.at **Web site:** http://www.landderberge.at
Freq: Annual; **Cover Price:** EUR 5,00; **Circ:** 70,000
Editor: Klaus Haselböck; **Advertising Manager:** Michael Linauer
Profile: Austrian outdoor sports magazine with a focus on bicycling and trekking.
Language(s): German
ADVERTISING RATES:
Full Page Mono .... EUR 4590
Full Page Colour .... EUR 4590
Mechanical Data: Type Area: 240 x 183 mm
CONSUMER: MOTORING & CYCLING: Cycling

LAND- UND FORSTARBEIT HEUTE
733840A21A-520

Editorial: Raubergasse 20, 8010 GRAZ
Tel: 316 83250718 **Fax:** 316 83250720
Email: a.grimme@lak-stmk.at **Web site:** http://www.landarbeiterkammer.at/steiermark
Freq: 5 issues yearly; **Cover Price:** Free; **Circ:** 12,000
Editor: Albert Grimme; **Advertising Manager:** Albert Grimme
Profile: Magazine for farmers and forest workers.
Language(s): German
ADVERTISING RATES:
Full Page Colour .... EUR 1482
Mechanical Data: Type Area: 255 x 185 mm

LANDKALENDER
733803A21A-600

Editorial: Hofgasse 5, 8010 GRAZ **Tel:** 316 821636
Fax: 316 835612
Email: redaktion@landwirt.com **Web site:** http://www.landwirt.com
Freq: Annual; **Cover Price:** EUR 17,90; **Circ:** 15,000
Editor: Wilhelm Tritscher
Profile: Calendar for agriculture and forestry.
Language(s): German

LANDWIRTSCHAFTLICHE BLÄTTER
1647429A21A-1458

Editorial: Brixner Str. 1, 6021 INNSBRUCK
Tel: 592921051 **Fax:** 592921059
Email: presse@lk-tirol.at **Web site:** http://www.lk-tirol.info
Freq: Weekly; **Annual Sub.:** EUR 50,00; **Circ:** 21,500
Editor: Evelyn Darmann
Profile: Magazine from the Tyrolese Chambers of Agriculture.
Language(s): German
Supplement to: Österreichische BauernZeitung
Supplement(s): BauernJournal

LANDWIRTSCHAFTLICHES TAGEBUCH
1749906A21A-1480

Editorial: Geidorfgürtel 40, 8010 GRAZ
Tel: 316 711540 **Fax:** 316 718611
Email: redaktion@helguverlag.at
Freq: Annual; **Cover Price:** EUR 4,00; **Circ:** 70,000
Editor: Helmut G. Gugl
Profile: Magazine with agricultural information.
Language(s): German
ADVERTISING RATES:
Full Page Colour .... EUR 2092
Mechanical Data: Type Area: 270 x 185 mm
Copy instructions: *Copy Date:* 45 days prior to publication

LAUFSPORT MARATHON
733914A75J-20

Editorial: Ringstr. 44/1, 3500 KREMS
Tel: 2732 8200038 **Fax:** 2732 8200082
Email: gerhard.weber@lwmedia.at **Web site:** http://www.laufsport-marathon.at
Freq: 8 issues yearly; **Annual Sub.:** EUR 34,90; **Circ:** 20,000
Editor: Gerhard Weber; **Advertising Manager:** Michael Linauer
Profile: Sports magazine focusing on running.
Language(s): German
Readership: Read by running enthusiasts, both recreational and professional runners.
ADVERTISING RATES:
Full Page Mono .... EUR 2590
Full Page Colour .... EUR 2590
Mechanical Data: Type Area: 240 x 183 mm
CONSUMER: SPORT: Athletics

LEADERSHIP
1843595A14A-2621

Editorial: Lothringer Str. 12, 1030 WIEN
Tel: 1 7126510 **Fax:** 1 711352912
Email: r.graf@wdf.at **Web site:** http://www.wdf.at
Freq: 10 issues yearly; **Circ:** 3,500
Editor: Roland Graf
Profile: Journal covering business and industry management.
Language(s): German
ADVERTISING RATES:
Full Page Mono .... EUR 1090
Full Page Colour .... EUR 1450
Mechanical Data: Type Area: 240 x 180 mm
Copy instructions: *Copy Date:* 21 days prior to publication

LEOBEN STADTMAGAZIN
742767A72-6140

Editorial: Erzherzog-Johann-Str. 2, 8700 LEOBEN
Tel: 3842 4062258 **Fax:** 3842 4062327
Email: presse@leoben.at **Web site:** http://www.leoben.at
Freq: 10 issues yearly; **Cover Price:** Free; **Circ:** 16,700
Editor: Gerhard Lukasiewicz; **Advertising Manager:** Gerhard Lukasiewicz
Profile: Magazine for the town of Leoben.
Language(s): German
ADVERTISING RATES:
Full Page Mono .... EUR 672
Full Page Colour .... EUR 873
Mechanical Data: Type Area: 250 x 190 mm, No. of Columns (Display): 3, Col Widths (Display): 62 mm
Copy instructions: *Copy Date:* 15 days prior to publication
LOCAL NEWSPAPERS

LITERATUR UND KRITIK
734273A84B-304

Editorial: Ernest-Thun-Str. 11, 5020 SALZBURG
Tel: 662 8819740 **Fax:** 662 872387
Email: luk@omvs.at **Web site:** http://www.omvs.at
Freq: 5 issues yearly; **Annual Sub.:** EUR 33,00; **Circ:** 3,000
Editor: Karl-Markus Gauss
Profile: Magazine about contemporary Austrian and world literature and culture.
Language(s): German
Readership: Read by people interested in literature.
ADVERTISING RATES:
Full Page Mono .... EUR 581
Mechanical Data: Type Area: 190 x 120 mm
Copy instructions: *Copy Date:* 28 days prior to publication
CONSUMER: THE ARTS & LITERARY: Literary

LK DIE HANDELSZEITUNG
734304A22A-120

Editorial: Wiedner Hauptstr. 120, 1051 WIEN
Tel: 1 54664383 **Fax:** 1 5466450383
Email: g.jiresch@wirtschaftsverlag.at **Web site:** http://www.handelszeitung.at
Freq: 23 issues yearly; **Annual Sub.:** EUR 80,00; **Circ:** 15,758
Editor: Gabriele Jiresch; **Advertising Manager:** Alfred Vrej Minassian
Profile: Newspaper focusing on the Austrian food industry.
Language(s): German
ADVERTISING RATES:
Full Page Mono .... EUR 3822
Full Page Colour .... EUR 5460
Mechanical Data: Type Area: 325 x 223 mm
Copy instructions: *Copy Date:* 16 days prior to publication
BUSINESS: FOOD

LOGO
734364A21A-700

Editorial: Brixner Str. 1, 6020 INNSBRUCK
Tel: 512 5990020 **Fax:** 512 5990031
Email: tjblj@tiroler-bauernbund.at **Web site:** http://www.tjblj.at
Freq: 6 issues yearly; Free to qualifying individuals
Annual Sub.: EUR 11,00; **Circ:** 13,000
Editor: Thomas Kahn
Profile: Journal containing details of the activities of the Young Farmers' Association of the Tyrol.
Language(s): German
BUSINESS: AGRICULTURE & FARMING

LÜRZER'S ARCHIV - (DT. AUSG.)
1644495A2A-930

Editorial: Keinergasse 29/7, 1030 WIEN
Tel: 1 7152424 **Fax:** 1 7152470
Email: mw@luerzersarchive.com **Web site:** http://www.luerzersarchive.com
Freq: 6 issues yearly; **Annual Sub.:** EUR 80,00; **Circ:** 4,124
Editor: Michael Weinzetti; **Advertising Manager:** Sandra Lehnst
Profile: Archive containing advertisements and posters from all over the world.
Language(s): German
ADVERTISING RATES:
Full Page Mono .... EUR 2450
Full Page Colour .... EUR 2450
Mechanical Data: Type Area: 250 x 165 mm, No. of Columns (Display): 3, Col Widths (Display): 55 mm

LÜRZER'S ARCHIV - (DT. AUSG.)
1644495A2A-966

Editorial: Keinergasse 29/7, 1030 WIEN
Tel: 1 7152424 **Fax:** 1 7152470
Email: mw@luerzersarchive.com **Web site:** http://www.luerzersarchive.com
Freq: 6 issues yearly; **Annual Sub.:** EUR 80,00; **Circ:** 4,124
Editor: Michael Weinzetti; **Advertising Manager:** Sandra Lehnst
Profile: Archive containing advertisements and posters from all over the world.
Language(s): German
ADVERTISING RATES:
Full Page Mono .... EUR 2450
Full Page Colour .... EUR 2450
Mechanical Data: Type Area: 250 x 165 mm, No. of Columns (Display): 3, Col Widths (Display): 55 mm

LUST AUFS LAND
1660476A72-7545

Editorial: Harrachstr. 12, 4010 LINZ
Tel: 732 77386629 **Fax:** 732 784067
Email: redaktion@lustaufsland.at **Web site:** http://www.lustaufsland.at
Freq: Quarterly; **Cover Price:** Free; **Circ:** 496,000
Editor: Wolfgang Wallner
Profile: Upper Austrian customer magazine with information about nature, food, tourism and economy.
Language(s): German
ADVERTISING RATES:
Full Page Mono .... EUR 15600
Full Page Colour .... EUR 18960
Mechanical Data: Type Area: 395 x 274 mm, No. of Columns (Display): 5, Col Widths (Display): 52 mm
LOCAL NEWSPAPERS

LUST & LEBEN
1641139A74P-263

Editorial: Ignanz-Köck-Str. 17, 1210 WIEN
Tel: 1 29130423 **Fax:** 1 29130420
Email: willkommen@lustundleben.at **Web site:** http://www.lustundleben.at
Freq: Quarterly; **Annual Sub.:** EUR 18,00; **Circ:** 28,000
Editor: Daniela Pötzl; **Advertising Manager:** Günther Gapp
Profile: Publication focusing on guests, food and gastronomy.
Language(s): German
ADVERTISING RATES:
Full Page Mono .... EUR 4550
Full Page Colour .... EUR 4550
Mechanical Data: Type Area: 255 x 185 mm
Copy instructions: *Copy Date:* 12 days prior to publication

MACH MIT!
1646230A74N-323

Editorial: Ferstlergasse 4, 3109 ST. PÖLTEN
Tel: 2742 9020409 **Fax:** 2742 9020411
Email: presse@senioren-noe.at **Web site:** http://www.senioren-noe.at
Freq: 10 issues yearly; **Circ:** 50,000
Editor: Michael Satzinger; **Advertising Manager:** Thomas Hausner
Profile: Magazine for the elderly from the region of Niederösterreich.
Language(s): German
ADVERTISING RATES:
Full Page Mono .... EUR 3200
Full Page Colour .... EUR 3200
Mechanical Data: Type Area: 264 x 189 mm

MANUSKRIPTE
734768A60A-161

Editorial: Sackstr. 17, 8010 GRAZ **Tel:** 316 825608
Fax: 316 825605
Email: lz@manuskripte.at **Web site:** http://www.manuskripte.at
Freq: Quarterly; **Annual Sub.:** EUR 27,00; **Circ:** 2,500
Editor: Alfred Kolleritsch
Profile: Magazine concerning literature and the book trade.
Language(s): German
BUSINESS: PUBLISHING: Publishing & Book Trade

DER MARKT
734842A2A-360

Editorial: Augasse 2, 1090 WIEN **Tel:** 1 313364609
Fax: 1 31336732
Email: arne.floh@wu-wien.ac.at **Web site:** http://www.dermarkt.or.at

Freq: Quarterly; **Cover Price:** EUR 12,00; **Circ:** 800
Editor: Arne Floh; **Advertising Manager:** Thomas Salzberger
Profile: Magazine of the Austrian Society for Business Marketing, University of Economics, Vienna.
Language(s): English; German
Readership: Read by people working in the marketing sector.
BUSINESS: COMMUNICATIONS, ADVERTISING & MARKETING

MARTINUS
726079A87-780
Editorial: St.-Rochus-Str. 21, 7001 EISENSTADT
Tel: 2682 777243 **Fax:** 2682 777431
Email: walter.fikisz@martinus.at **Web site:** http://www.martinus.at
Freq: Weekly; **Annual Sub.:** EUR 47,50; **Circ:** 13,500
Editor: Walter Fikisz; **Advertising Manager:** Michaela Hellmann
Profile: Church publication for the Diocese of Eisenstadt.
Language(s): German
ADVERTISING RATES:
Full Page Mono .... EUR 1567
Full Page Colour .... EUR 2089
Mechanical Data: Type Area: 256 x 196 mm, No. of Columns (Display): 4, Col Widths (Display): 45 mm
Copy instructions: *Copy Date:* 8 days prior to publication
CONSUMER: RELIGIOUS

MAXIMA
734997A74A-580
Editorial: IZ NÖ Süd, Str. 3/16, 2355 WIENER NEUDORF **Tel:** 2236 6006730 **Fax:** 2236 6006770
Email: redaktion@maxima.co.at **Web site:** http://www.maxima.at
Freq: 10 issues yearly; **Cover Price:** EUR 1,00; **Circ:** 106,728
Editor: Brigitte Fuchs; **Advertising Manager:** Karin Tunkel
Profile: Magazine containing articles about fashion, beauty, family life, child care and home decoration.
Language(s): German
Readership: Aimed at women aged between 18 and 60 years.
ADVERTISING RATES:
Full Page Mono .... EUR 10000
Full Page Colour .... EUR 10000
Mechanical Data: Type Area: 300 x 230 mm
Supplement(s): maxima Rezeptheft
CONSUMER: WOMEN'S INTEREST CONSUMER MAGAZINES: Women's Interest

MBL
735017A21A-1457
Editorial: Esterházystr. 15, 7000 EISENSTADT
Tel: 2682 702102 **Fax:** 2682 702190
Email: matthias.leitgeb@lk-bgld.at **Web site:** http://www.lk-bgld.at
Freq: 22 issues yearly; **Circ:** 26,700
Editor: Matthias Leitgeb
Profile: Magazine about agriculture and rural regions.
Language(s): German
Mechanical Data: Type Area: 275 x 182 mm, No. of Columns (Display): 4, Col Widths (Display): 42 mm
Copy instructions: *Copy Date:* 10 days prior to publication
Supplement(s): BauernJournal

MBW MODELLBAHNWELT
735033A79B-80
Editorial: Wolfeggstr. 19, 6900 BREGENZ
Tel: 5574 46462 **Fax:** 5574 44033
Email: franz.steiner@vol.at **Web site:** http://www.modellbahnwelt.at
Freq: 6 issues yearly; **Annual Sub.:** EUR 37,50; **Circ:** 12,500
Editor: Franz Steiner
Profile: Publication about model railways.
Language(s): German
Readership: Aimed at people of all ages with an interest in model railways.
ADVERTISING RATES:
Full Page Mono .... EUR 710
Full Page Colour .... EUR 852
Mechanical Data: No. of Columns (Display): 3, Col Widths (Display): 60 mm, Type Area: 250 x 190 mm
Copy instructions: *Copy Date:* 23 days prior to publication
CONSUMER: HOBBIES & DIY: Models & Modelling

MEDIA BIZ
735070A2A-380
Editorial: Billrothstr. 55/8, 1190 WIEN
Tel: 1 40335830
Email: redaktion@mediabiz.at **Web site:** http://www.mediabiz.at
Freq: 8 issues yearly; **Annual Sub.:** EUR 36,00; **Circ:** 5,000
Editor: Wolfgang Ritzberger; **Advertising Manager:** Sylvia Bergmayer
Profile: Magazine for professionals covering television, radio, films, video and audio.
Language(s): German
ADVERTISING RATES:
Full Page Mono .... EUR 1440
Full Page Colour .... EUR 2130
Mechanical Data: Type Area: 244 x 187 mm
Copy instructions: *Copy Date:* 18 days prior to publication
BUSINESS: COMMUNICATIONS, ADVERTISING & MARKETING

MEDIA BIZ BRANCHENFÜHRER
735071A2A-400
Editorial: Billrothstr. 55/8, 1190 WIEN
Tel: 1 40335830
Email: redaktion@mediabiz.at **Web site:** http://www.mediabiz.at
Freq: Annual; **Cover Price:** EUR 26,00; **Circ:** 5,000
Editor: Wolfgang Ritzberger; **Advertising Manager:** Sylvia Bergmayer
Profile: Directory listing data from companies for the movie, event and media branches.
Language(s): German
ADVERTISING RATES:
Full Page Mono .... EUR 1440
Full Page Colour .... EUR 2130
Mechanical Data: Type Area: 244 x 187 mm
Copy instructions: *Copy Date:* 30 days prior to publication

MEDICAL TRIBUNE - AUSG. ÖSTERREICH
761580A56A-1921
Editorial: Wiedner Hauptstr. 120, 1050 WIEN
Tel: 1 54600320 **Fax:** 1 54600710
Email: redaktion@medical-tribune.at **Web site:** http://www.medical-tribune.at
Freq: Weekly; **Annual Sub.:** EUR 72,00; **Circ:** 16,000
Editor: Thomas Stodulka; **Advertising Manager:** Thomas Schmuttermeier
Profile: Magazine for general practitioners and internists, Austrian edition.
Language(s): German
ADVERTISING RATES:
Full Page Colour .... EUR 4180
Mechanical Data: Type Area: 390 x 286 mm, No. of Columns (Display): 5, Col Widths (Display): 54 mm
Copy instructions: *Copy Date:* 21 days prior to publication

MEDIEN UND RECHT
1852354A2A-962
Editorial: Danhauser Gasse 6, 1040 WIEN
Tel: 1 5052766 **Fax:** 1 505276615
Email: h.wittmann@medien-recht.com **Web site:** http://www.medien-recht.com
Freq: 8 issues yearly; **Annual Sub.:** EUR 195,00; **Circ:** 800
Editor: Heinz Wittmann
Profile: Magazine concerning media law. Includes information relating to the press, TV, film, radio and video.
Language(s): German
ADVERTISING RATES:
Full Page Mono .... EUR 800
Mechanical Data: Type Area: 254 x 173 mm, No. of Columns (Display): 2, Col Widths (Display): 85 mm
Copy instructions: *Copy Date:* 20 days prior to publication

MEDIENMANAGER
1638094A2A-924
Editorial: Grüngasse 16, 1050 WIEN **Tel:** 1 4053610
Fax: 1 405361027
Email: redaktion@medienmanager.at **Web site:** http://www.medienmanager.at
Freq: 10 issues yearly; **Annual Sub.:** EUR 40,00; **Circ:** 6,000
Editor: Helmut Spreitzer; **Advertising Manager:** Birgit Kloss
Profile: Magazine for newspaper publishers.
Language(s): German
ADVERTISING RATES:
Full Page Mono .... EUR 2880
Full Page Colour .... EUR 2880
Mechanical Data: Type Area: 373 x 267 mm, No. of Columns (Display): 5, Col Widths (Display): 50 mm
Supplement(s): director

MEDIZIN POPULÄR
735173A74G-280
Editorial: Nibelungengasse 13, 1010 WIEN
Tel: 1 512448628 **Fax:** 1 512448634
Email: k.kirschbichler@aerzteverlagshaus.at **Web site:** http://www.medizinpopulaer.at
Freq: 11 issues yearly; **Annual Sub.:** EUR 19,80; **Circ:** 86,200
Editor: Karin Kirschbichler; **Advertising Manager:** Christina Eva-Maria Hohenberg
Profile: Magazine for all people interested in medicine.
Language(s): German
ADVERTISING RATES:
Full Page Mono .... EUR 6700
Full Page Colour .... EUR 6700
Mechanical Data: Type Area: 248 x 183 mm
Copy instructions: *Copy Date:* 28 days prior to publication
CONSUMER: WOMEN'S INTEREST CONSUMER MAGAZINES: Slimming & Health

DER MEDIZINER
735158A56A-1160
Editorial: Steirer Str. 24, 9375 HÜTTENBERG
Tel: 4263 20034 **Fax:** 4263 20074
Email: office@mediziner.at **Web site:** http://www.mediziner.at
Freq: 10 issues yearly; **Annual Sub.:** EUR 39,00; **Circ:** 8,400
Editor: Peter Hübler
Profile: Medical journal.
Language(s): German
Readership: Aimed at hospital doctors.
ADVERTISING RATES:
Full Page Colour .... EUR 2400
Mechanical Data: Type Area: 251 x 179 mm
Copy instructions: *Copy Date:* 7 days prior to publication
BUSINESS: HEALTH & MEDICAL

MEDMIX
1646040A56A-1942
Editorial: Lange Gasse 20, 1080 WIEN
Tel: 1 4023555 **Fax:** 1 4060922
Email: alexander.fauland@afcom.at **Web site:** http://www.medmix.at
Freq: Quarterly; **Cover Price:** Free; **Circ:** 12,000
Editor: Peter Traxler; **Advertising Manager:** Alexander Fauland
Profile: Magazine for physical doctors.
Language(s): German
ADVERTISING RATES:
Full Page Mono .... EUR 2800
Full Page Colour .... EUR 2800
Mechanical Data: Type Area: 254 x 188 mm
Copy instructions: *Copy Date:* 3 days prior to publication
BUSINESS: HEALTH & MEDICAL

MEIN MONAT
735245A80-660
Editorial: Bahnhofstr. 24, 6410 TELFS
Tel: 5262 67491 **Fax:** 5262 6749113
Email: mo@meinmonat.at **Web site:** http://www.meinmonat.at
Freq: 16 issues yearly; **Cover Price:** Free; **Circ:** 13,527
Editor: Margit Offer; **Advertising Manager:** Günther Lechner
Profile: Business magazine for the Telfs region.
Language(s): German
ADVERTISING RATES:
Full Page Colour .... EUR 1088
Mechanical Data: Type Area: 274 x 196 mm, No. of Columns (Display): 4, Col Widths (Display): 46 mm
CONSUMER: RURAL & REGIONAL INTEREST

MEINE TANKSTELLE
1847275A33-83
Editorial: Plüddemanngasse 39, 8010 GRAZ
Tel: 316 475112 **Fax:** 316 466366
Email: redaktion@garms.co.at **Web site:** http://www.meine-tankstelle.at
Freq: 5 issues yearly; **Circ:** 3,600
Advertising Manager: Gerald Garms
Profile: Magazine for entrepreneurs and managers of gas stations, garages and service stations.
Language(s): German
ADVERTISING RATES:
Full Page Colour .... EUR 1880
Copy instructions: *Copy Date:* 20 days prior to publication

METALL
735376A27-220
Editorial: Wiedner Hauptstr. 120, 1051 WIEN
Tel: 1 54664340 **Fax:** 1 54664521
Email: e.fuchs@wirtschaftsverlag.at **Web site:** http://www.metallzeitung.at
Freq: 10 issues yearly; **Annual Sub.:** EUR 55,00; **Circ:** 8,400
Editor: Eberhard Fuchs; **Advertising Manager:** Franz-Michael Seidl
Profile: Magazine covering all aspects of the metal industry.
Language(s): German
ADVERTISING RATES:
Full Page Mono .... EUR 2205
Full Page Colour .... EUR 3150
Mechanical Data: Type Area: 255 x 185 mm
Copy instructions: *Copy Date:* 21 days prior to publication
BUSINESS: METAL, IRON & STEEL

MICROCHIMICA ACTA
1853222A37-267
Editorial: Sachsenplatz 4, 1201 WIEN
Tel: 1 3302415563 **Fax:** 1 330242665
Email: stephen.soehnlen@springer.at **Web site:** http://www.springer.at
Freq: 16 issues yearly; **Circ:** 800
Editor: Stephen Soehnlen
Profile: Publishes articles covering all aspects of modern micro-analytical sciences, including fundamental studies, practical applications and new instrumental approaches.
Language(s): English
ADVERTISING RATES:
Full Page Mono .... EUR 1330
Full Page Colour .... EUR 2394
Mechanical Data: Type Area: 230 x 170 mm

MISS
747368A74A-884
Editorial: Geiselbergstr. 15, 1110 WIEN
Tel: 1 60117993 **Fax:** 1 60117975
Email: miss@miss.at **Web site:** http://www.typischich.at
Freq: 10 issues yearly; **Annual Sub.:** EUR 17,00; **Circ:** 65,000
Editor: Julia Wagner; **Advertising Manager:** Mele Scherich
Profile: Magazine covering fashion, health and beauty and helping with relationship issues.
Language(s): German
Readership: Aimed at young women aged between 16 and 24 years old.
ADVERTISING RATES:
Full Page Mono .... EUR 5600
Full Page Colour .... EUR 5600
Mechanical Data: Type Area: 222 x 168 mm
Copy instructions: *Copy Date:* 23 days prior to publication
CONSUMER: WOMEN'S INTEREST CONSUMER MAGAZINES: Women's Interest

MITGLIEDER MAGAZIN
2078994A50-389
Editorial: Brixnerstr. 3, 6020 INNSBRUCK
Tel: 512 587748 **Fax:** 512 581144
Email: info@privatvermieter-tirol.at **Web site:** http://www.privatvermieter-tirol.at
Freq: Quarterly; **Circ:** 3,500
Profile: Quarterly newspaper members of the private landlord association of Tirol. The newspaper offers articles and insight into the association events.
Language(s): German

MITTEILUNGEN ÄRZTEKAMMER FÜR TIROL
719656A56A-60
Editorial: Anichstr. 7/IV, 6021 INNSBRUCK
Tel: 512 520580 **Fax:** 512 52058130
Email: kammer@aektirol.at **Web site:** http://www.aektirol.at
Freq: Quarterly; Free to qualifying individuals
Annual Sub.: EUR 30,00; **Circ:** 4,000
Editor: Artur Wechselberger
Profile: Journal from the Medical Board of Tirol.
Language(s): German
Supplement(s): ärzte Exklusiv
BUSINESS: HEALTH & MEDICAL

MM MASCHINENMARKT
1629392A14R-894
Editorial: Hietzinger Kai 175, 1130 WIEN
Tel: 1 876837910 **Fax:** 1 876837915
Email: m.gold@technik-medien.at **Web site:** http://www.maschinenmarkt.at
Freq: Monthly; **Annual Sub.:** EUR 49,00; **Circ:** 10,000
Editor: Martin Gold; **Advertising Manager:** Thomas Lunacek
Profile: Austrian industrial magazine.
Language(s): German
ADVERTISING RATES:
Full Page Mono .... EUR 4090
Full Page Colour .... EUR 4090
Mechanical Data: Type Area: 270 x 190 mm, No. of Columns (Display): 4, Col Widths (Display): 45 mm
Copy instructions: *Copy Date:* 21 days prior to publication
BUSINESS: COMMERCE, INDUSTRY & MANAGEMENT: Commerce Related

MOBILITÄT MIT ZUKUNFT
747884A49A-580
Editorial: Bräuhausgasse 7, 1050 WIEN
Tel: 1 8932697 **Fax:** 1 8932431
Email: vcoe@vcoe.at **Web site:** http://www.vcoe.at
Freq: Quarterly; **Cover Price:** EUR 25,00; **Circ:** 8,000
Advertising Manager: Christian Höller
Profile: Magazine with solutions to questions of transport security, transport planning, transport policies from an ecological, economical and social point of view.
Language(s): German
ADVERTISING RATES:
Full Page Mono .... EUR 4000
Full Page Colour .... EUR 4000
Mechanical Data: Type Area: 277 x 185 mm
Copy instructions: *Copy Date:* 21 days prior to publication

MODERN TIMES
736357A94C-1
Editorial: Palais Spittelwiese 8, 4020 LINZ
Tel: 732 795577 **Fax:** 732 795580
Email: linz@moderntimesmedia.at **Web site:** http://www.moderntimesmedia.at
Freq: Quarterly; **Annual Sub.:** EUR 32,00; **Circ:** 15,000
Editor: Markus Mahringer; **Advertising Manager:** Michaela Mahringer
Profile: Magazine for Gold MasterCard and Gold VISA holders, covering sport, fashion and leisure.
Language(s): German
ADVERTISING RATES:
Full Page Mono .... EUR 4500
Full Page Colour .... EUR 4500
Mechanical Data: Type Area: 300 x 230 mm
Copy instructions: *Copy Date:* 14 days prior to publication
CONSUMER: OTHER CLASSIFICATIONS: Credit Cards

MONATSHEFTE FÜR CHEMIE CHEMICAL MONTHLY
1853226A37-268
Editorial: Sachsenplatz 4, 1201 WIEN
Tel: 1 3302415515 **Fax:** 1 330242665
Email: claudia.panuschka@springer.at **Web site:** http://www.springer.at
Freq: Monthly; **Circ:** 800
Editor: Claudia Panuschka
Profile: International journal covering all branches of chemistry.
Language(s): English
ADVERTISING RATES:
Full Page Mono .... EUR 1330
Full Page Colour .... EUR 2394

Mechanical Data: Type Area: 230 x 170 mm
Official Journal of: Organ d. Österr. Akademie d. Wissenschaften, Mathemat.-Naturwissenschaftl. Klasse u. d. Ges. Österr. Chemiker

MONITOR
736424A5-400
Editorial: Leberstr. 122, 1110 WIEN **Tel:** 1 74095421 **Fax:** 1 74095427
Email: troger@monitor.co.at **Web site:** http://www.monitor.co.at
Freq: 9 issues yearly; **Annual Sub.:** EUR 30,00; **Circ:** 14,500
Editor: Dominik Troger; **Advertising Manager:** Katharina Lützelberger
Profile: IT magazine about the application of information technologies in companies.
Language(s): German
ADVERTISING RATES:
Full Page Mono .... EUR 5740
Full Page Colour .... EUR 5740
Mechanical Data: Type Area: 250 x 184 mm
BUSINESS: COMPUTERS & AUTOMATION

MORGEN
736449A84A-940
Editorial: Herrengasse 13, 1010 WIEN
Tel: 1 5338131
Email: office@morgen.at **Web site:** http://www.morgen.at
Freq: 6 issues yearly; **Annual Sub.:** EUR 24,00; **Circ:** 8,000
Editor: Hans Magenschab
Profile: Cultural magazine for the Niederösterreich region (Lower Austria).
Language(s): German
ADVERTISING RATES:
Full Page Mono .... EUR 3600
Full Page Colour .... EUR 3600
Mechanical Data: Type Area: 277 x 190 mm
Copy instructions: *Copy Date:* 14 days prior to publication
CONSUMER: THE ARTS & LITERARY: Arts

MOTOR FREIZEIT TRENDS
736486A77D-20
Editorial: Im Plattner 17, 6833 KLAUS
Tel: 5523 51581 **Fax:** 5523 51134
Email: redaktion@motor-freizeit-trends.at **Web site:** http://www.motor-freizeit-trends.at
Freq: 6 issues yearly; **Annual Sub.:** EUR 17,50; **Circ:** 22,000
Editor: Erich Scheiblauer; **Advertising Manager:** Erich Scheiblauer
Profile: Magazine featuring the latest trends and developments in motoring.
Language(s): German
ADVERTISING RATES:
Full Page Mono .... EUR 2995
Full Page Colour .... EUR 3215
Mechanical Data: Type Area: 277 x 190 mm, No. of Columns (Display): 4, Col Widths (Display): 45 mm
Copy instructions: *Copy Date:* 15 days prior to publication
CONSUMER: MOTORING & CYCLING: Motor Sports

MOTOR & MORE WIEN SÜD
2081152A77A-333
Editorial: Schönkirchnerstr. 4, 2231 STRASSHOF
Tel: 676 5440235
Email: office@motorandmore.at
Freq: 5 issues yearly; **Cover Price:** Free; **Circ:** 180,000
Editor: Johannes Gauglica
Profile: Free car magazine for Vienna South (10., 11., 12., 23. district and Schwechat, Zwölfaxing, Himberg, Maria Lanzendorf, Hennersdorf, Leopoldsdorf, Achau, Vösendorf, Perchtoldsdorf, Mödling, Maria Enzersdorf, Brunn a. Geb., Wr. Neudorf, Laxenburg, Biedermannsdorf, Breitenfurt, Kaltenleutgeben).
Language(s): German

MOTORRAD MAGAZIN
1655769A77B-2
Editorial: Geiselbergstr. 15, 1110 WIEN **Tel:** 1 60117 **Fax:** 1 60117680
Email: franz.sauer@motorrad-magazin.at **Web site:** http://www.styria-multi-media.com
Freq: 10 issues yearly; **Annual Sub.:** EUR 29,00; **Circ:** 32,000
Editor: Franz J. Sauer; **Advertising Manager:** Beate Kloda
Profile: Motorcycle magazine.
Language(s): German
ADVERTISING RATES:
Full Page Colour .... EUR 5600
Mechanical Data: Type Area: 278 x 210 mm

MOUNTAIN MANAGER
1832362A49A-596
Editorial: Habichtweg 16, 5211 LENGAU
Tel: 7746 2787 **Fax:** 7746 2787
Email: m.kalchgruber@aon.at
Freq: 8 issues yearly; **Annual Sub.:** EUR 64,00; **Circ:** 4,994
Editor: Markus Kalchgruber
Profile: Magazine for aerial railway operators, gastronomers in skiing regions and skiing schools.
Language(s): German

ADVERTISING RATES:
Full Page Mono .... EUR 2553
Full Page Colour .... EUR 3746
Mechanical Data: Type Area: 261 x 190 mm

MURTALER ZEITUNG
736718A72-4620
Editorial: Murtaler Platz 1, 8750 JUDENBURG
Tel: 3572 8580024 **Fax:** 3572 8580026
Email: murtaler.zeitung@styria.com **Web site:** http://www.murtalerzeitung.at
Freq: Weekly; **Circ:** 15,500
Editor: Wolfgang Pfister; **News Editor:** Wolfgang Pfister; **Advertising Manager:** Karl-Heinz Schellander
Profile: Regional weekly covering politics, economics, sport, travel, technology and the arts.
Language(s): German
Mechanical Data: Type Area: 275 x 200 mm, No. of Columns (Display): 4, Col Widths (Display): 47 mm
Copy instructions: *Copy Date:* 1 day prior to publication
LOCAL NEWSPAPERS

NACHRICHTENBLATT MARKTGEMEINDE ARNOLDSTEIN
736863A72-4740
Editorial: Gemeindeplatz 4, 9601 ARNOLDSTEIN
Tel: 4255 226011 **Fax:** 4255 226033
Email: siegfried.cesar@ktn.gde.at **Web site:** http://www.arnoldstein.gv.at
Freq: Quarterly; **Cover Price:** Free; **Circ:** 2,700
Editor: Siegfried Cesar
Profile: Magazine about the Arnoldstein area.
Language(s): German
ADVERTISING RATES:
Full Page Mono .... EUR 560
Full Page Colour .... EUR 780
Mechanical Data: Type Area: 254 x 176 mm, No. of Columns (Display): 3, Col Widths (Display): 55 mm
Copy instructions: *Copy Date:* 14 days prior to publication
LOCAL NEWSPAPERS

NATIONALPARK GESCHNATTER
736938A57-480
Editorial: Hauswiese, 7142 ILLMITZ **Tel:** 2175 34420 **Fax:** 2175 34424
Email: info@nationalpark-neusiedlersee-seewinkel.at **Web site:** http://www.nationalpark-neusiedlersee-seewinkel.at
Freq: Quarterly; **Annual Sub.:** EUR 10,00; **Circ:** 18,500
Editor: Alois Lang
Profile: Magazine about the environment.
Language(s): German
ADVERTISING RATES:
Full Page Mono .... EUR 545
Mechanical Data: Type Area: 430 x 260 mm, No. of Columns (Display): 4, Col Widths (Display): 60 mm
Copy instructions: *Copy Date:* 30 days prior to publication

NATUR UND LAND
736995A57-540
Editorial: Museumsplatz 2, 5020 SALZBURG
Tel: 662 64290913 **Fax:** 662 6437344
Email: natur-land@naturschutzbund.at **Web site:** http://www.naturschutzbund.at/publikationen.html
Freq: Quarterly; Free to qualifying individuals
Annual Sub.: EUR 19,00; **Circ:** 7,000
Editor: Ingrid Hagenstein; **Advertising Manager:** Ingrid Hagenstein
Profile: Official magazine of the Austrian League for the Preservation of Nature.
Language(s): German
ADVERTISING RATES:
Full Page Mono .... EUR 929
Full Page Colour .... EUR 1207
Mechanical Data: Col Widths (Display): 46 mm, Type Area: 234 x 146 mm, No. of Columns (Display): 3
Copy instructions: *Copy Date:* 42 days prior to publication
BUSINESS: ENVIRONMENT & POLLUTION

NATUR UND LANDSCHAFTSSCHUTZ IN DER STEIERMARK
1851203A57-1165
Editorial: Herdergasse 3, 8010 GRAZ
Tel: 316 32237713 **Fax:** 316 3223774
Email: werner.langs@naturschutzbundsteiermark.at
Web site: http://www.naturschutzbundsteiermark.at
Freq: Quarterly; Free to qualifying individuals
Annual Sub.: EUR 6,20; **Circ:** 15,000
Editor: Werner Langs
Profile: Magazine about nature protection in the Steiermark.
Language(s): German

NATUR & UMWELT IM PANNONISCHEN RAUM
1813058A57-1158
Editorial: Lisztgasse 2, 2491 NEUFELD
Tel: 2624 521025
Email: office@murczek-media.at **Web site:** http://www.murczek-media.at
Freq: Quarterly; **Circ:** 7,500

Profile: Official publication from the Burgenland Federal Environment Authority.
Language(s): German
ADVERTISING RATES:
Full Page Colour .... EUR 1200
Mechanical Data: Type Area: 265 x 180 mm
Copy instructions: *Copy Date:* 20 days prior to publication

NATURFREUND
736953A75L-422
Editorial: Viktoriagasse 6, 1150 WIEN
Tel: 1 892353431 **Fax:** 1 892353448
Email: pressestelle@naturfreunde.at **Web site:** http://www.naturfreunde.at
Freq: Quarterly; Free to qualifying individuals
Annual Sub.: EUR 10,00; **Circ:** 100,000
Editor: Doris Wenischnigger; **Advertising Manager:** Doris Wenischnigger
Profile: Magazine containing articles on hiking, climbing, mountain-biking, travel and nature in Austria.
Language(s): German
ADVERTISING RATES:
Full Page Mono .... EUR 2800
Full Page Colour .... EUR 3900
Mechanical Data: Type Area: 265 x 185 mm, No. of Columns (Display): 4, Col Widths (Display): 42 mm
Copy instructions: *Copy Date:* 42 days prior to publication
CONSUMER: SPORT: Outdoor

NEPHRO-NEWS
1656008A56A-1949
Editorial: Koloman-Wallisch-Platz 12, 8600 BRUCK
Tel: 3862 56400 **Fax:** 3862 5640016
Email: walter.hoerl@meduniwien.ac.at **Web site:** http://www.medicom.cc
Freq: 6 issues yearly; **Annual Sub.:** EUR 60,00; **Circ:** 4,000
Editor: Walter H. Hörl
Profile: Magazine containing information about nephrology and hypertensiology.
Language(s): German

NEPHROSCRIPT
1646171A56A-1945
Editorial: Seidengasse 9/1/1, 1070 WIEN
Tel: 1 40731110 **Fax:** 1 4073114
Email: walter.hoerl@meduniwien.ac.at **Web site:** http://www.medmedia.at
Freq: Quarterly; **Cover Price:** EUR 9,50; **Circ:** 8,000
Editor: Walter Hörl; **Advertising Manager:** Friederike Maierhofer
Profile: Magazine on interdisciplinary further education from the Austrian Association of Nephrology.
Language(s): German
ADVERTISING RATES:
Full Page Colour .... EUR 3190
Mechanical Data: Type Area: 297 x 210 mm
Copy instructions: *Copy Date:* 14 days prior to publication

DER NEUE KONDITOR
737134A8C-1
Editorial: Lenaugasse 5/11, 1080 WIEN
Tel: 1 40719910 **Fax:** 1 407199175
Email: redaktion@verlag-almer.at **Web site:** http://www.derneuekonditor.at
Freq: 15 issues yearly; **Annual Sub.:** EUR 52,00; **Circ:** 2,000
Profile: Magazine covering all aspects of the confectionery trade.
Language(s): German
ADVERTISING RATES:
Full Page Mono .... EUR 1980
Full Page Colour .... EUR 1980
Mechanical Data: Type Area: 260 x 180 mm, No. of Columns (Display): 2, Col Widths (Display): 72 mm
Copy instructions: *Copy Date:* 14 days prior to publication
BUSINESS: BAKING & CONFECTIONERY: Confectioners & Tobacconists

NEUE VORARLBERGER TAGESZEITUNG
737263A67B-780
Editorial: Gutenbergstr. 1, 6858 SCHWARZACH
Tel: 5572 501850 **Fax:** 5572 501860
Email: neue-redaktion@neue.vol.at **Web site:** http://www.neue.vol.at
Freq: 260 issues yearly; **Circ:** 12,396
Editor: Frank Andres; **Advertising Manager:** Gerard Hann
Profile: Regional daily newspaper covering politics, economics, sport, travel, technology and the arts.
Language(s): German
ADVERTISING RATES:
SCC .... EUR 82,00
Mechanical Data: Type Area: 270 x 208 mm, No. of Columns (Display): 6, Col Widths (Display): 33 mm
Copy instructions: *Copy Date:* 1 day prior to publication
Supplement(s): Vorarlberg Journal
REGIONAL DAILY & SUNDAY NEWSPAPERS: Regional Daily Newspapers

NEUES LAND
737226A21A-1446
Editorial: Reitschulgasse 3, 8011 GRAZ
Tel: 316 82636129 **Fax:** 316 82636116
Email: josef.kaltenegger@neuesland.at **Web site:** http://www.neuesland.at
Freq: Weekly; Free to qualifying individuals
Annual Sub.: EUR 62,00; **Circ:** 29,000

Editor: Josef Kaltenegger; **Advertising Manager:** Volker Bartl
Profile: Agricultural magazine concerning arable farming.
Language(s): German
ADVERTISING RATES:
Full Page Mono .... EUR 2964
Full Page Colour .... EUR 3848
Mechanical Data: Type Area: 260 x 200 mm, No. of Columns (Display): 4, Col Widths (Display): 47 mm
Copy instructions: *Copy Date:* 3 days prior to publication

NEUES VOLKSBLATT
737243A67B-820
Editorial: Hafenstr. 1, 4010 LINZ **Tel:** 732 76060 **Fax:** 732 779242
Web site: http://www.volksblatt.at
Freq: 312 issues yearly; **Circ:** 23,500
Editor: Werner Rohrhofer; **Advertising Manager:** Arno Perfaller
Profile: Regional daily newspaper covering politics, economics, sport, travel, technology and the arts.
Language(s): German
ADVERTISING RATES:
SCC .... EUR 46,20
Mechanical Data: Type Area: 265 x 197 mm, No. of Columns (Display): 6, Col Widths (Display): 30 mm
Copy instructions: *Copy Date:* 1 day prior to publication
Supplement(s): cabrio journal; hausruckviertel journal; innviertel journal; linzer stadt & land journal; motor journal; mühlviertel journal; Neues Volksblatt am Wochenende; Nutzfahrzeug & Logistik journal; tele; traunviertel journal
REGIONAL DAILY & SUNDAY NEWSPAPERS: Regional Daily Newspapers

NEUES VON LANG
2010188A4E-1352
Editorial: Alte Landstr. 44, 6123 TERFENS
Tel: 5242 6905148 **Fax:** 5242 65418
Email: alfred.lerchbaumer@langbau.at **Web site:** http://www.langbau.at
Freq: Annual; **Circ:** 2,200
Editor: Alfred Lerchbaumer
Profile: Magazine for employees.
Language(s): German

NEUROPSYCHIATRIE
1800401A56A-2006
Editorial: Anichstr. 35, 6020 INNSBRUCK
Tel: 512 50423668 **Fax:** 512 50423628
Email: ullrich.meise@uklibk.ac.at
Freq: Quarterly; **Annual Sub.:** EUR 99,50; **Circ:** 1,500
Editor: Ullrich Meise; **Advertising Manager:** Ullrich Meise
Profile: Journal about neurology and psychiatry.
Language(s): German
Official Journal of: Organ d. pro mente austria, d. Österr. Alzheimer Ges., d. Österr. Ges. f. Kinder- u. Jugendpsychiatrie u. d. Österr. Schizophrenieges.

NEVERTHELESS
2079123A73-433
Editorial: Gonzagagasse 12, 1010 WIEN
Tel: 1 5356762
Email: office@olschinsky.at **Web site:** http://www.nevertheless.at
Freq: Half-yearly; **Cover Price:** EUR 12,00; **Circ:** 1,000
Editor: Peter Olschinsky
Profile: Magazine for places, spaces, art, work, people, projects, reading, writing, fashion, design, photo, graphic and illustration. Facebook: http://www.facebook.com/pages/Nevertheless-Magazine/151911098180162.
Language(s): German
Mechanical Data: Type Area: 310 x 220 mm

NEW BUSINESS
737341A14A-1620
Editorial: Otto-Bauer-Gasse 6, 1060 WIEN
Tel: 1 2351366370 **Fax:** 1 2351366999
Email: reinhard.dorner@newbusiness.at **Web site:** http://www.newbusiness.at
Freq: 11 issues yearly; **Annual Sub.:** EUR 29,00; **Circ:** 55,000
Editor: Reinhard Dorner; **Advertising Manager:** Lorin Polak
Profile: Magazine concerning new commerce and industry in Austria.
Language(s): German
ADVERTISING RATES:
Full Page Mono .... EUR 4900
Full Page Colour .... EUR 4900
Mechanical Data: Type Area: 250 x 185 mm
Copy instructions: *Copy Date:* 21 days prior to publication
BUSINESS: COMMERCE, INDUSTRY & MANAGEMENT

NEWS
737360A73-220
Editorial: Taborstr. 1, 1020 WIEN **Tel:** 1 213121103 **Fax:** 1 213121650
Email: redaktion@news.at **Web site:** http://www.news.at
Freq: Weekly; **Annual Sub.:** EUR 79,90; **Circ:** 221,392
Editor: Peter Pelinka; **Advertising Manager:** Wolfgang Kröll

Profile: Austrian news magazine Facebook: http://www.facebook.com/NEWS.at Twitter: http://twitter.com/#!/NEWS_AT.
Language(s): German
ADVERTISING RATES:
Full Page Mono .... EUR 15890
Full Page Colour .... EUR 15890
Mechanical Data: Type Area: 250 x 185 mm
Copy instructions: *Copy Date:* 21 days prior to publication
Supplement(s): News exklusiv; Newsino; Niederösterreich News

NÖLP-NACHRICHTEN
737539A56A-1280
Editorial: Hauptstr. 22, 2326 MARIA-LANZENDORF
Tel: 2235 42965 **Fax:** 2235 44039
Email: noelp@aon.at **Web site:** http://www.psychotherapie.at/noelp
Freq: Half-yearly; **Circ:** 1,000
Editor: Winfrid Janisch
Profile: Magazine from the Austrian Association for Psychotherapy.
Language(s): German
ADVERTISING RATES:
Full Page Mono .... EUR 291

ÖAZ ÖSTERREICHISCHE APOTHEKER-ZEITUNG
737887A37-140
Editorial: Spitalgasse 31, 1090 WIEN
Tel: 1 402358837 **Fax:** 1 4085355
Email: redaktion@apoverlag.at **Web site:** http://www.oeaz.at
Freq: 26 issues yearly; **Annual Sub.:** EUR 113,30; **Circ:** 6,000
Editor: Monika Heinrich
Profile: Magazine providing information about the pharmaceutical industry.
Language(s): German
Readership: Aimed at pharmacists and their staff.
ADVERTISING RATES:
Full Page Mono .... EUR 2800
Full Page Colour .... EUR 2800
Mechanical Data: No. of Columns (Display): 3, Col Widths (Display): 56 mm, Type Area: 250 x 178 mm
Copy instructions: *Copy Date:* 10 days prior to publication
BUSINESS: PHARMACEUTICAL & CHEMISTS

OBERKÄRNTNER NACHRICHTEN
737796A72-5060
Editorial: 10.-Oktober-Str. 66, 9800 SPITTAL
Tel: 4762 4060 **Fax:** 4762 406014
Email: okn.schober@aon.at **Web site:** http://www.okn.at
Freq: 11 issues yearly; **Cover Price:** Free; **Circ:** 46,700
Editor: Peter Schober; **Advertising Manager:** Melanie Brunner-Thaler
Profile: Magazine covering local events.
Language(s): German
Readership: Aimed at residents and visitors to the area.
Mechanical Data: Type Area: 265 x 194 mm, No. of Columns (Display): 4, Col Widths (Display): 45 mm
Copy instructions: *Copy Date:* 9 days prior to publication
LOCAL NEWSPAPERS

OBERKÄRNTNER VOLLTREFFER
737797A72-7487
Editorial: Schweizer Gasse 26, 9900 LIENZ
Tel: 4852 6515131 **Fax:** 4852 65510
Email: redaktion@volltreffer.co.at **Web site:** http://www.osttirol-online.at
Freq: Weekly; **Cover Price:** Free; **Circ:** 33,100
Editor: Bernd Lenzer
Profile: Advertising journal (house-to-house) concentrating on local stories.
Language(s): German
ADVERTISING RATES:
Full Page Mono .... EUR 1923
Full Page Colour .... EUR 2500
Mechanical Data: Type Area: 270 x 190 mm, No. of Columns (Display): 4, Col Widths (Display): 45 mm
Copy instructions: *Copy Date:* 3 days prior to publication
LOCAL NEWSPAPERS

ÖBM DER ÖSTERREICHISCHE BAUSTOFFMARKT
737975A4R-140
Editorial: Witthauergasse 6/2, 1180 WIEN
Tel: 1 4788170 **Fax:** 1 478817010
Email: baustoff@impactmedia.at **Web site:** http://www.impactmedia.at
Freq: 8 issues yearly; Free to qualifying individuals
Annual Sub.: EUR 75,00; **Circ:** 5,500
Editor: Alois Fröstl; **Advertising Manager:** Silvia Baar
Profile: Journal about building supplies.
Language(s): German
Readership: Read by contractors and suppliers of building materials.
ADVERTISING RATES:
Full Page Mono .... EUR 2375
Full Page Colour .... EUR 3930
Mechanical Data: Type Area: 250 x 177 mm
Supplement(s): werkzeug aktuell
BUSINESS: ARCHITECTURE & BUILDING: Building Related

ÖBVAKTIV
1655190A14A-2529
Editorial: Grillparzerstr. 14, 1016 WIEN
Tel: 1 401201120 **Fax:** 1 401201001
Email: publicrelations@oebv.com **Web site:** http://www.oebv.com
Freq: Quarterly; **Cover Price:** Free; **Circ:** 7,000
Editor: Eva Enichlmayr
Profile: Company publication of the Österreichische Beamtenversicherung.
Language(s): German

OESTERREICHS ENERGIE
746148A58-240
Editorial: Brahmsplatz 3, 1040 WIEN
Tel: 1 50198260 **Fax:** 1 5051218
Email: e.brandstetter@oesterreichsenergie.at **Web site:** http://www.oesterreichsenergie.at
Freq: 10 issues yearly; **Annual Sub.:** EUR 135,00; **Circ:** 6,200
Editor: Ernst Brandstetter; **Advertising Manager:** Franz-Michael Seidl
Profile: Magazine covering all aspects of the electrical industry.
Language(s): German
ADVERTISING RATES:
Full Page Mono .... EUR 3350
Full Page Colour .... EUR 3350
Mechanical Data: Type Area: 233 x 173 mm

OESTERREICHS ENERGIE
746148A58-258
Editorial: Brahmsplatz 3, 1040 WIEN
Tel: 1 50198260 **Fax:** 1 5051218
Email: e.brandstetter@oesterreichsenergie.at **Web site:** http://www.oesterreichsenergie.at
Freq: 10 issues yearly; **Annual Sub.:** EUR 135,00; **Circ:** 6,200
Editor: Ernst Brandstetter; **Advertising Manager:** Franz-Michael Seidl
Profile: Magazine covering all aspects of the electrical industry.
Language(s): German
ADVERTISING RATES:
Full Page Mono .... EUR 3350
Full Page Colour .... EUR 3350
Mechanical Data: Type Area: 233 x 173 mm

DER OFFIZIER
1840093A40-656
Editorial: Schwarzenbergplatz 1, 1010 WIEN
Tel: 1 7121510 **Fax:** 1 7129963
Email: deroffizier@oeog.at **Web site:** http://www.oeog.at
Freq: Quarterly; **Circ:** 10,000
Editor: Manfred Gänsdorfer
Profile: Magazine from the Austrian Association of Army Officers.
Language(s): German
Mechanical Data: Type Area: 252 x 180 mm
Copy instructions: *Copy Date:* 14 days prior to publication

ÖGZ CAFÉ JOURNAL
724045A11A-60
Editorial: Wiedner Hauptstr. 120, 1051 WIEN
Tel: 1 54664364 **Fax:** 1 5466450364
Email: i.stelzmueller@wirtschaftsverlag.at **Web site:** http://www.cafejournal.at
Freq: 8 issues yearly; **Circ:** 21,291
Editor: Irene Stelzmüller; **Advertising Manager:** Gregory Kucera-Wurmehl
Profile: Magazine concerning cafes, patisseries and coffee-houses.
Language(s): German
ADVERTISING RATES:
Full Page Mono .... EUR 4123
Full Page Colour .... EUR 5890
Mechanical Data: Type Area: 358 x 245 mm
Official Journal of: Organ d. Fachverb. Gastronomie, Berufsgruppe d. Kaffeehausbetriebe
Supplement to: ÖGZ Österreichische Gastronomie- & Hotel-Zeitung
BUSINESS: CATERING: Catering, Hotels & Restaurants

ÖGZ ÖSTERREICHISCHE GASTRONOMIE- & HOTEL-ZEITUNG
737913A11A-421
Editorial: Wiedner Hauptstr. 120, 1051 WIEN
Tel: 1 54664360 **Fax:** 1 5466450360
Email: d.koffler@wirtschaftsverlag.at **Web site:** http://www.gast.at
Freq: 42 issues yearly; **Annual Sub.:** EUR 94,00; **Circ:** 21,762
Editor: Dieter Koffler; **Advertising Manager:** Gregory Kucera-Wurmehl
Profile: Newspaper about the hotel and catering business in Austria.
Language(s): German
ADVERTISING RATES:
Full Page Mono .... EUR 4123
Full Page Colour .... EUR 5890
Mechanical Data: Type Area: 400 x 266 mm, No. of Columns (Display): 5, Col Widths (Display): 50 mm
Copy instructions: *Copy Date:* 9 days prior to publication
Supplement(s): ÖGZ Café Journal; ÖGZ e.v.e.n.t.s.; ÖGZ spezial; ÖGZ Wein Journal; Unique
BUSINESS: CATERING: Catering, Hotels & Restaurants

ÖIAZ ÖSTERREICHISCHE INGENIEUR- UND ARCHITEKTEN-ZEITSCHRIFT
1853351A4E-1339
Editorial: Karlsplatz 13, 1040 WIEN
Tel: 1 5880122117 **Fax:** 1 5880122199
Email: h.brandl@tuwien.ac.at **Web site:** http://www.oiav.at
Freq: Quarterly; **Circ:** 4,500
Editor: Heinz Brandl; **Advertising Manager:** Gundula Forster
Profile: Official journal of the Austrian Architectural Engineers' Society.
Language(s): German
ADVERTISING RATES:
Full Page Mono .... EUR 1350
Full Page Colour .... EUR 2490
Mechanical Data: Type Area: 250 x 185 mm, No. of Columns (Display): 2, Col Widths (Display): 90 mm
Copy instructions: *Copy Date:* 14 days prior to publication

OIB AKTUELL
1843733A4E-1319
Editorial: Schenkenstr. 4, 1010 WIEN
Tel: 1 533655014 **Fax:** 1 5336423
Email: reisenhofer@oib.or.at **Web site:** http://www.oib.or.at
Freq: Quarterly; **Annual Sub.:** EUR 49,50; **Circ:** 5,000
Editor: Rainer Mikulits; **Advertising Manager:** Sylvia Reisenhofer
Profile: Magazine with information from the building industry in Austria and Europe and official organ of the Austrian Institute for Building Technology.
Language(s): German

OIZ ÖSTERREICHISCHE IMMOBILIEN ZEITUNG
737995A1E-100
Editorial: Rotenturmstr. 17, 1010 WIEN
Tel: 1 533326080 **Fax:** 1 533326015
Email: h.erdmann@fishmedia.at **Web site:** http://www.oiz.at
Freq: 11 issues yearly; **Annual Sub.:** EUR 110,00; **Circ:** 10,000
Editor: Heinz Erdmann; **Advertising Manager:** Mihai Starus
Profile: Real estate newspaper.
Language(s): German
Readership: Aimed at estate agents.
ADVERTISING RATES:
Full Page Mono .... EUR 4500
Full Page Colour .... EUR 4500
Mechanical Data: Type Area: 240 x 190 mm
BUSINESS: FINANCE & ECONOMICS: Property

ÖKO INVEST
737925A1F-200
Editorial: Schweizertalst. 8-10/5, 1130 WIEN
Tel: 1 8760501 **Fax:** 1 405717129
Email: oeko-invest@teleweb.at **Web site:** http://www.oeko-invest.de
Freq: 25 issues yearly; **Annual Sub.:** EUR 143,00; **Circ:** 1,500
Editor: Max Deml; **Advertising Manager:** Max Deml
Profile: Magazine that monitors the stock market and investment trends.
Language(s): German
Readership: Aimed at shareholderss and those with investments.
ADVERTISING RATES:
Full Page Mono .... EUR 1248
Full Page Colour .... EUR 1818
Mechanical Data: Type Area: 260 x 185 mm, No. of Columns (Display): 2
Copy instructions: *Copy Date:* 5 days prior to publication
BUSINESS: FINANCE & ECONOMICS: Investment

ÖKOENERGIE
737924A58-200
Editorial: Franz-Josefs-Kai 13, 1010 WIEN
Tel: 1 53307970 **Fax:** 1 533079790
Email: hofbauer@biomasseverband.at **Web site:** http://www.biomasseverband.at
Freq: Quarterly; **Cover Price:** Free; **Circ:** 140,000
Editor: Ernst Scheiber
Profile: Publication about renewable energy.
Language(s): German
BUSINESS: ENERGY, FUEL & NUCLEAR

ÖMP ÖSTERREICHISCHES MEDIZINPRODUKTE-HANDBUCH
1859238A56A-2043
Editorial: Hernalser Hauptstr. 213, 1170 WIEN
Tel: 1 4864240 **Fax:** 1 4854902
Email: info@goeschl.co.at **Web site:** http://www.medizinprodukte.at
Freq: Annual; **Cover Price:** EUR 25,00; **Circ:** 15,000
Editor: Siegrid Göschl; **Advertising Manager:** Siegrid Göschl
Profile: Directory listing Austrian supply companies for medical products.
Language(s): German
Mechanical Data: Type Area: 180 x 120 mm

ONRAIL
726619A89A-450
Editorial: Leberstr. 122, 1110 WIEN **Tel:** 1 74095555
Fax: 1 74095538
Email: christina.dany@bohmann.at **Web site:** http://www.onrail.at
Freq: 6 issues yearly; **Circ:** 85,000
Editor: Christina Dany; **Advertising Manager:** Marianne Kostandinovic
Profile: The travel magazine offers personally researched reports about interesting destinations and makes you want to vacation in Austria and Europe. In Premium and First Class Rail Jets, the magazine is distributed in person. Display in the second Class of Railjets, the IC / EC trains and six ÖBB club lounges.
Language(s): German
ADVERTISING RATES:
Full Page Mono .... EUR 8950
Full Page Colour .... EUR 8950
Mechanical Data: Type Area: 255 x 180 mm
CONSUMER: HOLIDAYS & TRAVEL: Travel

OÖ ÄRZTE
738242A56A-1360
Editorial: Dinghoferstr. 4, 4010 LINZ
Tel: 732 77837132 **Fax:** 732 783660323
Email: redaktion@aekooe.or.at **Web site:** http://www.gesundesooe.at
Freq: 10 issues yearly; **Circ:** 6,700
Editor: Susanne Sametinger
Profile: magazine of the Medical Board of Oberösterreich.
Language(s): German
Supplement(s): ärzte Exklusiv

OÖ NACHRICHTEN
738243A67B-1420
Editorial: Promenade 23, 4010 LINZ **Tel:** 732 78050
Fax: 732 7805329
Email: redaktion@nachrichten.at **Web site:** http://www.nachrichten.at
Freq: 260 issues yearly; **Circ:** 139,221
Editor: Gerald Mandlbauer; **News Editor:** Helmut Atteneder; **Advertising Manager:** Günther Plank
Profile: Regional daily newspaper covering politics, economics, sport, travel, technology and the arts.
Language(s): German
ADVERTISING RATES:
SCC .... EUR 77,00
Mechanical Data: Type Area: 410 x 270 mm, No. of Columns (Display): 8, Col Widths (Display): 32 mm
Copy instructions: *Copy Date:* 1 day prior to publication
Supplement(s): OÖ Fußball Nachrichten; The Red Bulletin; tele; Uhren Schmuck Magazin; wasistlos?
REGIONAL DAILY & SUNDAY NEWSPAPERS: Regional Daily Newspapers

OÖ WIRTSCHAFT
732367A63-200
Editorial: Hessenplatz 3, 4020 LINZ **Tel:** 5909093314
Fax: 5909093311
Email: medien@wkooe.at **Web site:** http://wko.at/ooe
Freq: 41 issues yearly; Free to qualifying individuals
Annual Sub.: EUR 70,00; **Circ:** 66,850
Editor: Günther Hosner
Profile: Publication from the Chamber of Commerce of Oberösterreich focusing on business in the Oberösterreich (North-West) region of Austria.
Language(s): German
ADVERTISING RATES:
Full Page Mono .... EUR 4706
Full Page Colour .... EUR 5459
Mechanical Data: Type Area: 258 x 192 mm, No. of Columns (Display): 4, Col Widths (Display): 45 mm
Copy instructions: *Copy Date:* 4 days prior to publication
BUSINESS: REGIONAL BUSINESS

ÖPV ÖSTERREICHISCHER PERSONENVERKEHR
737957A49A-587
Editorial: Wiedner Hauptstr. 120, 1051 WIEN
Tel: 1 54664324 **Fax:** 1 5466450324
Email: m.dittrich@wirtschaftsverlag.at **Web site:** http://www.wirtschaftsverlag.at
Freq: Monthly; **Annual Sub.:** EUR 60,00; **Circ:** 13,483
Editor: Marco Dittrich; **Advertising Manager:** Dieter Köllner-Gürsch
Profile: Official journal of the Trade Association of Transport Businesses and Vehicles.
Language(s): German
ADVERTISING RATES:
Full Page Mono .... EUR 3579
Full Page Colour .... EUR 5112
Mechanical Data: Type Area: 255 x 185 mm
Copy instructions: *Copy Date:* 21 days prior to publication
Official Journal of: Organ d. Personenbeförderungs- u. d. Autobusgewerbes
BUSINESS: TRANSPORT

OR SPECTRUM
738327G14A-5140
Editorial: Brünner Str. 72, 1210 WIEN
Email: stefan.minner@univie.ac.at **Web site:** http://www.springerlink.com
Freq: Quarterly; **Annual Sub.:** EUR 647,00; **Circ:** 1,061
Editor: Stefan Minner
Profile: Quantitative approaches in management.
Language(s): English; German
ADVERTISING RATES:
Full Page Mono .... EUR 920
Full Page Colour .... EUR 1960
Mechanical Data: Type Area: 200 x 130 mm
Official Journal of: Organ d. Ges. f. Operations Research

Austria

ORF NACHLESE 1647582A73-389
Editorial: Würzburggasse 30, 1136 WIEN
Tel: 1 8707712256 **Fax:** 1 8707713743
Email: nachlese@orf.at **Web site:** http://enterprise.orf.at
Freq: Monthly; **Annual Sub.:** EUR 21,00; **Circ:** 108,833
Editor: Katja Zinggl-Pokorny
Profile: Magazine of the ORF Broadcasting station.
Language(s): German
ADVERTISING RATES:
Full Page Mono .... EUR 7150
Full Page Colour .... EUR 7150
Mechanical Data: Type Area: 254 x 190 mm
Copy instructions: *Copy Date:* 30 days prior to publication
CONSUMER: NATIONAL & INTERNATIONAL PERIODICALS

ÖSTERREICH 1779835A65A-131
Editorial: Friedrichstr. 10, 1010 WIEN
Tel: 1 588111997 **Fax:** 1 5881199899
Email: redaktion@oe24.at **Web site:** http://www.oe24.at
Freq: 208 issues yearly; **Circ:** 303,630
Editor: Werner Schima; **Advertising Manager:** Hans Aschenbach
Profile: Nationwide Austrian daily newspaper.
Language(s): German
ADVERTISING RATES:
SCC .... EUR 127,00
Mechanical Data: Type Area: 315 x 216 mm, No. of Columns (Display): 5, Col Widths (Display): 40 mm
Copy instructions: *Copy Date:* 2 days prior to publication
Supplement(s): Immobilien Österreich; Life and Style; Madonna; Money.at; TV Austria
NATIONAL DAILY & SUNDAY NEWSPAPERS: National Daily Newspapers

ÖSTERREICH SPORT 738067A75A-400
Editorial: Prinz-Eugen-Str. 12, 1040 WIEN
Tel: 1 5044455 **Fax:** 1 504445566
Email: office@bso.or.at **Web site:** http://www.bso.or.at
Freq: 5 issues yearly; **Annual Sub.:** EUR 12,00; **Circ:** 10,000
Editor: Wolfgang Drabesch
Profile: Magazine concerning all types of sport.
Language(s): German
ADVERTISING RATES:
Full Page Mono .... EUR 1350
Full Page Colour .... EUR 1350
Mechanical Data: Type Area: 250 x 163 mm
Copy instructions: *Copy Date:* 30 days prior to publication
CONSUMER: SPORT

ÖSTERREICHISCHE ÄRZTEZEITUNG 737969A56A-1400
Editorial: Nibelungengasse 13, 1010 WIEN
Tel: 1 512448627 **Fax:** 1 512448664
Email: a.muehlgassner@aerzteverlagshaus.at **Web site:** http://www.aerztezeitung.at
Freq: 20 issues yearly; **Annual Sub.:** EUR 118,50; **Circ:** 40,600
Editor: Agnes M. Mühlgassner; **Advertising Manager:** Ulrich P. Pachernegg
Profile: Newspaper containing articles about new medical developments, research, medical conferences and related information.
Language(s): German
Readership: Read by members of the medical profession.
ADVERTISING RATES:
Full Page Mono .... EUR 3400
Full Page Colour .... EUR 4100
Mechanical Data: Type Area: 260 x 180 mm, No. of Columns (Display): 2, Col Widths (Display): 87 mm
Copy instructions: *Copy Date:* 21 days prior to publication
BUSINESS: HEALTH & MEDICAL

ÖSTERREICHISCHE BÄCKER ZEITUNG 737972A8A-60
Editorial: Lenaugasse 5/11, 1080 WIEN
Tel: 1 407199010 **Fax:** 1 407199175
Email: hans.almer@verlag-almer.at **Web site:** http://www.baeckerzeitung.at
Freq: Weekly; **Annual Sub.:** EUR 73,00; **Circ:** 2,600
Editor: Hans Almer; **Advertising Manager:** Heidi Zederbauer
Profile: Magazine concerning all aspects of the bakery trade.
Language(s): German
Readership: Read by bakers, pastry-cooks, trainees and authorities.
ADVERTISING RATES:
Full Page Mono .... EUR 1410
Full Page Colour .... EUR 2287
Mechanical Data: Type Area: 258 x 180 mm, No. of Columns (Display): 3, Col Widths (Display): 57 mm
BUSINESS: BAKING & CONFECTIONERY: Baking

ÖSTERREICHISCHE BAUERNZEITUNG 763534A21A-1444
Editorial: Schauflergasse 6, 1014 WIEN
Tel: 1 533144830 **Fax:** 1 533144833
Email: christine.demuth@bauernzeitung.at **Web site:** http://www.bauernzeitung.at
Freq: Monthly; **Annual Sub.:** EUR 70,00; **Circ:** 188,500
Editor: Christine Demuth; **Advertising Manager:** Christof Hillebrand
Profile: Austrian newspaper for farmers.
Language(s): German
ADVERTISING RATES:
Full Page Mono .... EUR 15761
Full Page Colour .... EUR 18131
Mechanical Data: Type Area: 395 x 274 mm, No. of Columns (Display): 6, Col Widths (Display): 42 mm
Supplement(s): Landwirtschaftliche Blätter
BUSINESS: AGRICULTURE & FARMING

ÖSTERREICHISCHE BAU.ZEITUNG 737977A4E-960
Editorial: Wiedner Hauptstr. 120, 1051 WIEN
Tel: 1 54664345 **Fax:** 1 5466450345
Email: g.gary@wirtschaftsverlag.at **Web site:** http://www.diebauzeitung.at
Freq: 42 issues yearly; **Annual Sub.:** EUR 130,00; **Circ:** 11,025
Editor: Gisela Gary; **Advertising Manager:** Franz-Michael Seidl
Profile: Magazine about all aspects of building in Austria.
Language(s): German
ADVERTISING RATES:
Full Page Mono .... EUR 3150
Full Page Colour .... EUR 4500
Mechanical Data: Type Area: 255 x 185 mm
Copy instructions: *Copy Date:* 10 days prior to publication
Official Journal of: Organ d. Bauwirtschaft, Baugewerbe, Fachv. d. Bauindustrie, d. Bundesinnung d. Bauhilfsgewerbe u. d. Steinmetzmeister, d. Fachverb. d. Stein- u. keram. Industrie, d. Verb. d. Baustoffhändler Österr., d. Verb. Österr. Beton- u. Fertigteilwerke, d. Güteverb. Transportbeton, d. Güteverb. Österr. Ziegelwerke, d. Vereinigung d. österr. Zementindustrie u. d. Vereinigung Österr Natursteinwerke
Supplement(s): Skin
BUSINESS: ARCHITECTURE & BUILDING: Building

ÖSTERREICHISCHE BETRIEBS TECHNIK 737979A14A-2534
Editorial: Walfischgasse 11/1/8, 1010 WIEN
Tel: 1 5131395 **Fax:** 1 5127369
Email: verlag@lisey.at **Web site:** http://www.lisey.at
Freq: 7 issues yearly; **Annual Sub.:** EUR 30,52; **Circ:** 8,000
Editor: Hedy Gruber
Profile: Magazine about all aspects of work and business.
Language(s): German
ADVERTISING RATES:
Full Page Mono .... EUR 3444
Full Page Colour .... EUR 4387
Mechanical Data: Type Area: 266 x 183 mm
Copy instructions: *Copy Date:* 14 days prior to publication
BUSINESS: COMMERCE, INDUSTRY & MANAGEMENT

ÖSTERREICHISCHE CHEMIE ZEITSCHRIFT 737982A13-200
Editorial: DOK IV NW 21, 2301 GROSS-ENZERSDORF **Tel:** 2249 4104 **Fax:** 2249 7481
Email: office@chemie-zeitschrift.at **Web site:** http://www.chemie-zeitschrift.at
Freq: Quarterly; Free to qualifying individuals
Annual Sub.: EUR 60,00; **Circ:** 6,400
Editor: Sepp Fischer; **Advertising Manager:** Marion Rimser
Profile: Magazine focusing on recent developments in chemistry.
Language(s): German
ADVERTISING RATES:
Full Page Mono .... EUR 2080
Full Page Colour .... EUR 3580
Mechanical Data: Type Area: 265 x 184 mm
Official Journal of: Organ d. Vereins Österr. Chemieingenieure u. Chemotechniker
BUSINESS: CHEMICALS

DIE ÖSTERREICHISCHE FEUERWEHR 737983A54A-160
Editorial: Leberstr. 122, 1110 WIEN **Tel:** 1 74095777
Fax: 1 74095183
Email: helmut.widmann@bohmann.at **Web site:** http://www.bohmann.at
Freq: 10 issues yearly; **Annual Sub.:** EUR 45,90; **Circ:** 6,800
Editor: Helmut Widmann; **Advertising Manager:** Gertrude Schöggl
Profile: Magazine for firefighters covering a variety of topics such as important developments and decisions within the industry, the development of technical equipment for tackling fires and safety for employees.
Language(s): German
ADVERTISING RATES:
Full Page Colour .... EUR 2900
Mechanical Data: Type Area: 250 x 185 mm
BUSINESS: SAFETY & SECURITY: Fire Fighting

ÖSTERREICHISCHE FLEISCHER ZEITUNG 737985A22D-40
Editorial: Wiedner Hauptstr. 120, 1051 WIEN
Tel: 1 54664368 **Fax:** 1 5466450368
Email: s.koestenbauer@wirtschaftsverlag.at **Web site:** http://www.fleischerzeitung.at
Freq: 25 issues yearly; **Annual Sub.:** EUR 75,00; **Circ:** 2,066
Editor: Stefan Köstenbauer
Profile: Newspaper of the Union of Butchers.
Language(s): German
ADVERTISING RATES:
Full Page Mono .... EUR 2550
Full Page Colour .... EUR 3600
Mechanical Data: Type Area: 400 x 275 mm, No. of Columns (Display): 5, Col Widths (Display): 51 mm
BUSINESS: FOOD: Meat Trade

DIE ÖSTERREICHISCHE FRAU 1856903A74A-947
Editorial: Lichtenfelsgasse 7, 1010 WIEN
Tel: 1 40126651 **Fax:** 1 4066245
Email: monika.posch@frauen.oevp.at **Web site:** http://www.frauenoffensive.at
Freq: Annual; **Circ:** 5,000
Editor: Monika Posch
Profile: Magazine shows statistical trends of Austrian females in education, family and occupation.
Language(s): German

DAS ÖSTERREICHISCHE GESUNDHEITSWESEN ÖKZ 1641607A56A-1926
Editorial: Wickenburggasse 32, 8010 GRAZ
Tel: 316 8205650 **Fax:** 316 82056520
Email: tschachler@schaffler-verlag.com **Web site:** http://www.oekz.at
Freq: 10 issues yearly; **Annual Sub.:** EUR 90,00; **Circ:** 14,000
Editor: Elisabeth Tschachler; **Advertising Manager:** Alexandra Pfisterer
Profile: Magazine about the Austrian health care system.
Language(s): German
ADVERTISING RATES:
Full Page Mono .... EUR 3370
Full Page Colour .... EUR 3370
Mechanical Data: Type Area: 245 x 180 mm

DER ÖSTERREICHISCHE HAUSBESITZ 737992A74K-260
Editorial: Bösendorfer Str. 2/4/13, 1010 WIEN
Tel: 1 5056177 **Fax:** 1 5056171
Email: andrea.reiber@eunet.at **Web site:** http://www.rv-hausbesitzer.at
Freq: 11 issues yearly; **Annual Sub.:** EUR 44,00; **Circ:** 3,000
Editor: Andrea Reiber
Profile: Journal of the Society of Austrian Landlords.
Language(s): German
Readership: Aimed at members.
ADVERTISING RATES:
Full Page Mono .... EUR 650
Mechanical Data: Type Area: 250 x 165 mm
Official Journal of: Organ d. LV Steiermark u. d. österr. Haus- u. Grundbesitzerbundes
CONSUMER: WOMEN'S INTEREST CONSUMER MAGAZINES: Home Purchase

DAS ÖSTERREICHISCHE INDUSTRIE MAGAZIN 1647397A14A-2522
Editorial: Lindengasse 56, 1070 WIEN
Tel: 1 5859000 **Fax:** 1 585900016
Email: rudolf.loidl@industriemagazin.at **Web site:** http://www.industriemagazin.at
Freq: 10 issues yearly; **Annual Sub.:** EUR 35,00; **Circ:** 25,700
Editor: Rudolf Loidl
Profile: Service magazine for managers and decision makers. Our target group are CEOs, executives and decision makers in manufacturing companies and the industry-related service industries. We deal every month with the latest management trends, with relevant economic developments and the assessment of the market. As a service to readers, we understand, prepare technical issues in the IT & telecom, automation and environmental technology and logistics so that they are understandable not only for highly specialized professionals. We want to bring them closer to those that help themselves by using new technologies work or increase the profits of their company do.
Language(s): German
ADVERTISING RATES:
Full Page Mono .... EUR 5990
Full Page Colour .... EUR 5990
Mechanical Data: Type Area: 253 x 185 mm
Copy instructions: *Copy Date:* 14 days prior to publication
BUSINESS: COMMERCE, INDUSTRY & MANAGEMENT

DER ÖSTERREICHISCHE INSTALLATEUR 737996A3D-100
Editorial: Leberstr. 122, 1110 WIEN **Tel:** 1 74095475
Fax: 1 74095490
Email: klaus.paukovits@bohmann.at **Web site:** http://www.derinstallateur.at
Freq: Monthly; **Annual Sub.:** EUR 72,70; **Circ:** 11,500
Editor: Klaus Paukovits; **Advertising Manager:** Andrea Traxler
Profile: Magazine about plumbing, heating and air conditioning.
Language(s): German
Readership: Aimed at plumbing and heating engineers.
ADVERTISING RATES:
Full Page Colour .... EUR 4580
Mechanical Data: Type Area: 270 x 185 mm
BUSINESS: HEATING & VENTILATION: Heating & Plumbing

DER ÖSTERREICHISCHE JOURNALIST 737998A2B-220
Editorial: Fliederweg 4, 5301 EUGENDORF
Tel: 6225 27000 **Fax:** 6225 270011
Email: georg.taitl@oberauer.com **Web site:** http://www.journalist.at
Freq: 6 issues yearly; **Annual Sub.:** EUR 42,00; **Circ:** 5,100
Editor: Georg Taitl; **Advertising Manager:** Margareta Uliarte
Profile: Magazine reflecting developments and background in journalism, photo-journalism and the media market. Includes news on tax, law, appointments and working techniques.
Language(s): German
ADVERTISING RATES:
Full Page Mono .... EUR 2660
Full Page Colour .... EUR 3591
Mechanical Data: Type Area: 252 x 188 mm, No. of Columns (Display): 4, Col Widths (Display): 44 mm
Copy instructions: *Copy Date:* 21 days prior to publication
BUSINESS: COMMUNICATIONS, ADVERTISING & MARKETING: Press

ÖSTERREICHISCHE KUNSTSTOFF ZEITSCHRIFT 738002A13-220
Editorial: Tribulzgasse 33, 1230 WIEN
Tel: 699 10401070
Email: k.sochor@kunststoff-zeitschrift.at **Web site:** http://www.kunststoff-zeitschrift.at
Freq: 6 issues yearly; **Annual Sub.:** EUR 60,20; **Circ:** 6,400
Editor: Kerstin Sochor; **Advertising Manager:** Kerstin Sochor
Profile: Official journal of the Association of the Development of Man-Made Substances and Chemicals.
Language(s): German
ADVERTISING RATES:
Full Page Mono .... EUR 2080
Full Page Colour .... EUR 3580
Mechanical Data: Type Area: 265 x 184 mm
Official Journal of: Organ d. Bundesinnung u. d. Landesinnungen d. Kunststoffverarbeiter
BUSINESS: CHEMICALS

ÖSTERREICHISCHE NOTARIATS ZEITUNG 738012A44-627
Editorial: Johannesgasse 23, 1015 WIEN
Tel: 1 531610 **Fax:** 1 53161181
Email: christopher.dietz@manz.at **Web site:** http://www.manz.at
Freq: Monthly; **Annual Sub.:** EUR 130,00; **Circ:** 1,600
Editor: Markus Kaspar; **Advertising Manager:** Heidrun R. Engel
Profile: Journal for practitioners in family, inheritance, land registry, contracts and company law.
Language(s): German
Readership: Aimed at notaries, legal executives, employers and all types of lawyers.
ADVERTISING RATES:
Full Page Mono .... EUR 967
Full Page Colour .... EUR 1837
Mechanical Data: Type Area: 260 x 170 mm
Copy instructions: *Copy Date:* 28 days prior to publication
BUSINESS: LEGAL

ÖSTERREICHISCHE PFLEGEZEITSCHRIFT 738001A56B-361
Editorial: Wilhelminenstr. 91/2e, 1160 WIEN
Tel: 1 47827100 **Fax:** 1 47827109
Email: bettina.surtmann@oegkv.at **Web site:** http://www.oegkv.at
Freq: 10 issues yearly; Free to qualifying individuals
Annual Sub.: EUR 30,00; **Circ:** 9,000
Editor: Bettina Surtmann; **Advertising Manager:** Ulrike Galuska
Profile: Journal of the Austrian Nursing Association.
Language(s): German
ADVERTISING RATES:
Full Page Colour .... EUR 1725
Mechanical Data: Type Area: 260 x 180 mm, No. of Columns (Display): 3, Col Widths (Display): 57 mm
Copy instructions: *Copy Date:* 30 days prior to publication
BUSINESS: HEALTH & MEDICAL: Nursing

ÖSTERREICHISCHE SPARKASSENZEITUNG 738042A1C-120
Editorial: Grimmelshausengasse 1, 1030 WIEN
Tel: 5010028414 **Fax:** 5010028571

Email: info@sv.sparkasse.at **Web site:** http://www.sparkasse.at/sparkassenzeitung
Freq: 11 issues yearly; **Annual Sub.:** EUR 96,00; **Circ:** 4,000
Editor: Michael Ikrath
Profile: Magazine from the Austrian Association of Savings Banks.
Language(s): German

ÖSTERREICHISCHE TEXTIL ZEITUNG
738051A47A-80
Editorial: Brunner Feldstr. 45, 2380 PERCHTOLDSDORF **Tel:** 1 86648219
Fax: 1 86648100
Email: b.medlin@textilzeitung.at **Web site:** http://www.textilzeitung.at
Freq: 24 issues yearly; **Annual Sub.:** EUR 55,00; **Circ:** 10,000
Editor: Brigitte Medlin; **Advertising Manager:** Claudia Jordan
Profile: Newspaper covering all aspects of the Austrian textiles industry.
Language(s): German
ADVERTISING RATES:
Full Page Colour .... EUR 6690
Mechanical Data: Type Area: 300 x 230 mm
Copy instructions: *Copy Date:* 14 days prior to publication
Official Journal of: Organ d. Bundes- u. d. Landesgremien d. Handels m. Textilwaren u. Bekleidung
Supplement(s): Mode in der Bel Etage
BUSINESS: CLOTHING & TEXTILES

ÖSTERREICHISCHE TRAFIKANTEN ZEITUNG
738053A8C-2
Editorial: Wiedner Hauptstr. 120, 1051 WIEN
Tel: 1 54664371 **Fax:** 1 5466450371
Email: p.hauer@wirtschaftsverlag.at **Web site:** http://www.trafikantenzeitung.at
Freq: Monthly; **Annual Sub.:** EUR 50,00; **Circ:** 5,000
Editor: Peter Hauer; **Advertising Manager:** Gregory Kucera-Wurmehl
Profile: Newspaper concerning the tobacconist trade.
Language(s): German
ADVERTISING RATES:
Full Page Colour .... EUR 3090
Mechanical Data: Type Area: 255 x 185 mm, No. of Columns (Display): 4, Col Widths (Display): 42 mm
Copy instructions: *Copy Date:* 21 days prior to publication
BUSINESS: BAKING & CONFECTIONERY: Confectioners & Tobacconists

ÖSTERREICHISCHE WASSER- UND ABFALLWIRTSCHAFT
738056A42C-2
Editorial: Marc-Aurel-Straße 5, 1010 WIEN
Tel: 1 535572086 **Fax:** 1 5354064
Email: randl@oewav.at **Web site:** http://www.oewav.at
Freq: 6 issues yearly; **Circ:** 5,000
Editor: Fritz Randl
Profile: Journal about water engineering and hydro-electric power.
Language(s): German
ADVERTISING RATES:
Full Page Mono .... EUR 2240
Full Page Colour .... EUR 2900
Mechanical Data: Type Area: 250 x 170 mm
BUSINESS: CONSTRUCTION: Water Engineering

ÖSTERREICHISCHER PENSIONISTEN-KALENDER
738024A74N-80
Editorial: Gentzgasse 129, 1180 WIEN **Tel:** 1 313720
Fax: 1 3137278
Email: office@pvoe.at **Web site:** http://www.pvoe.at
Freq: Annual; **Cover Price:** EUR 4,00; **Circ:** 88,000
Advertising Manager: Josef Hartl
Profile: Magazine for the elderly.
Language(s): German
ADVERTISING RATES:
Full Page Colour .... EUR 3000
Mechanical Data: Type Area: 186 x 130 mm, No. of Columns (Display): 2, Col Widths (Display): 62 mm
Copy instructions: *Copy Date:* 70 days prior to publication

ÖSTERREICHISCHES BAU- UND ENERGIESPAR HANDBUCH
729665A4E-760
Editorial: Bahnstr. 6, 2345 BRUNN **Tel:** 2236 31520
Fax: 2236 31529
Email: schmutzer@bauverlag.at **Web site:** http://www.bauverlag.at
Freq: Annual; **Circ:** 12,000
Profile: Manual for experts from the building sector.
Language(s): German
ADVERTISING RATES:
Full Page Mono .... EUR 1950
Mechanical Data: Type Area: 270 x 122 mm

ÖSTERREICHS FISCHEREI
738065A45B-50
Editorial: Scharfling 18, 5310 MONDSEE
Tel: 6232 3847 **Fax:** 6232 384733
Email: oester.fischerei@baw.at **Web site:** http://www.fischerei-verband.at
Freq: 8 issues yearly; **Annual Sub.:** EUR 33,00; **Circ:** 2,500
Editor: Albert Jagsch
Profile: European magazine containing news about the national and international fishing trade.
Language(s): German
Readership: Aimed at professional fishermen, scientists and fishing associations.
ADVERTISING RATES:
Full Page Mono .... EUR 392
Full Page Colour .... EUR 497
Mechanical Data: Type Area: 196 x 131 mm, No. of Columns (Display): 2, Col Widths (Display): 64 mm
BUSINESS: MARINE & SHIPPING: Commercial Fishing

ÖSTERREICHS WIRTSCHAFT
1775685A14A-2592
Editorial: Eschenbachgasse 11, 1010 WIEN
Tel: 1 5873633 **Fax:** 1 5870192
Web site: http://www.gewerbeverein.at
Freq: Quarterly; **Cover Price:** EUR 3,00
Free to qualifying individuals ; **Circ:** 54,000
Profile: Austrian economic magazine.
Language(s): German
ADVERTISING RATES:
Full Page Mono .... EUR 1200
Mechanical Data: Type Area: 280 x 210 mm
Copy instructions: *Copy Date:* 21 days prior to publication

ÖSTERREICHS WIRTSCHAFT
1775685A14A-2631
Editorial: Eschenbachgasse 11, 1010 WIEN
Tel: 1 5873633 **Fax:** 1 5870192
Web site: http://www.gewerbeverein.at
Freq: Quarterly; **Cover Price:** EUR 3,00
Free to qualifying individuals ; **Circ:** 54,000
Profile: Austrian economic magazine.
Language(s): German
ADVERTISING RATES:
Full Page Mono .... EUR 1200
Mechanical Data: Type Area: 280 x 210 mm
Copy instructions: *Copy Date:* 21 days prior to publication

OSTNEWS
1852837A49A-601
Editorial: Wiener Str. 26, 2326 MARIA-LANZENDORF
Tel: 1 797997922 **Fax:** 1 797997925
Email: ost-news@gw-world.com **Web site:** http://www.gw-world.com
Freq: Quarterly; **Cover Price:** Free; **Circ:** 5,000
Editor: Klaus Tumler
Profile: Magazine on logistics in Central and East Europe.
Language(s): German

OSTTIROLER BOTE
738414A72-5200
Editorial: Schweizer Gasse 26, 9900 LIENZ
Tel: 4852 651510 **Fax:** 4852 65510
Email: redaktion@osttirolerbote.at **Web site:** http://www.osttirol-online.at
Freq: Weekly; **Annual Sub.:** EUR 70,20; **Circ:** 17,000
Editor: Robert Hatzer; **Advertising Manager:** Maria Reiter
Profile: Regional weekly covering politics, economics, sport, travel, technology and the arts.
Language(s): German
Mechanical Data: Type Area: 270 x 190 mm, No. of Columns (Display): 4, Col Widths (Display): 45 mm
Copy instructions: *Copy Date:* 2 days prior to publication
Supplement(s): tv.woche
LOCAL NEWSPAPERS

ÖTZ ÖSTERREICHISCHE TAXIZEITUNG
738083A64G-2
Editorial: Hetzgasse 34/1/7, 1030 WIEN
Tel: 1 71549800 **Fax:** 1 715498012
Email: taxiverband@fachliste.at **Web site:** http://www.fachliste.at
Freq: Quarterly
Editor: Manfred Starzinger
Profile: Taxi trade journal.
Language(s): German
BUSINESS: OTHER CLASSIFICATIONS: Taxi Trade

ÖTZTAL INTERN
1844913A50-372
Editorial: Gemeindestr. 4, 6450 SÖLDEN **Tel:** 57200
Fax: 57200201
Email: info@oetztal.com **Web site:** http://www.oetztal.com
Freq: Half-yearly; **Circ:** 7,500
Editor: Carmen Fender
Profile: Magazine on all aspects of tourism.
Language(s): German
ADVERTISING RATES:
Full Page Colour .... EUR 5650

ÖTZTAL NATUR FÜHLEN CAMPING . . .
1843501A89A-503
Editorial: Gemeindestr. 4, 6450 SÖLDEN **Tel:** 57200
Fax: 57200201
Email: info@oetztal.com **Web site:** http://www.oetztal.com
Freq: Annual; **Cover Price:** Free; **Circ:** 18,000
Profile: Camping guide for the Oetztal region.
Language(s): English; German

OUT-OF-HOME
1826553A2A-953
Editorial: Roseggerweg 36, 2201 GERASDORF
Tel: 2246 21922 **Fax:** 2246 2192220
Email: dagmar.achter@workflows.at **Web site:** http://www.outofhome-online.at
Freq: 6 issues yearly; **Annual Sub.:** EUR 49,00; **Circ:** 8,500
Editor: Dagmar Achter; **Advertising Manager:** Bernd Klaus Achter
Profile: Magazine about large format printing advertising.
Language(s): German
ADVERTISING RATES:
Full Page Colour .... EUR 2570
Mechanical Data: Type Area: 270 x 185 mm
Copy instructions: *Copy Date:* 14 days prior to publication
Supplement(s): Digital Sign & Media; Point-of-Sale

PACKAGING AUSTRIA
764929A35-21
Editorial: Rotenmühlgasse 11/10, 1120 WIEN
Tel: 1 983064032 **Fax:** 1 983064018
Email: edit@packaging-austria.at **Web site:** http://www.packaging-austria.at
Freq: 6 issues yearly; **Annual Sub.:** EUR 40,70; **Circ:** 5,000
Editor: Michael Seidl
Profile: Magazine for the packaging industry.
Language(s): German
ADVERTISING RATES:
Full Page Mono .... EUR 1750
Full Page Colour .... EUR 250
Mechanical Data: No. of Columns (Display): 3, Col Widths (Display): 55 mm, Type Area: 265 x 175 mm

PÄDIATRIE & PÄDOLOGIE
738487A56A-1460
Editorial: Sachsenplatz 4, 1201 WIEN
Tel: 1 3302415285 **Fax:** 1 3302426260
Email: renate.hoehl@springer.at **Web site:** http://www.springer.at
Freq: 6 issues yearly; **Circ:** 7,300
Editor: Renate Höhl
Profile: Journal about children's health.
Language(s): German
ADVERTISING RATES:
Full Page Mono .... EUR 2540
Full Page Colour .... EUR 3190
Mechanical Data: Type Area: 270 x 170 mm
BUSINESS: HEALTH & MEDICAL

DIE PALETTE
1639229A1F-245
Editorial: Sturzgasse 1a, 1140 WIEN **Tel:** 1 98177121
Fax: 1 98177111
Email: h.schnedl@agrarverlag.at **Web site:** http://www.agrarverlag.at
Freq: Monthly; **Annual Sub.:** EUR 37,00; **Circ:** 27,000
Editor: Hartmut Schnedl; **Advertising Manager:** Johanna Kolbert
Profile: Magazine about financial investments, savings, building society savings as well as insurance and financial provisions for the pension products.
Language(s): German
ADVERTISING RATES:
Full Page Mono .... EUR 2647
Full Page Colour .... EUR 4299
Mechanical Data: Type Area: 260 x 175 mm, No. of Columns (Display): 3, Col Widths (Display): 55 mm

PANDAMAGAZIN
1655480A57-1134
Editorial: Ottakringer Str. 114, 1160 WIEN
Tel: 1 48817280 **Fax:** 1 48817278
Email: az@wwf.at **Web site:** http://www.wwf.at
Freq: Quarterly; **Circ:** 80,000
Editor: Andreas Zednicek; **Advertising Manager:** Ingrid Kaiser-Hackl
Profile: Magazine from the World Wide Fund For Nature.
Language(s): German
ADVERTISING RATES:
Full Page Mono .... EUR 10400
Full Page Colour .... EUR 10400
Mechanical Data: Type Area: 255 x 165 mm
BUSINESS: ENVIRONMENT & POLLUTION

PAPIER AUS ÖSTERREICH
738544A36-1
Editorial: Gumpendorfer Str. 6, 1061 WIEN
Tel: 1 58886209 **Fax:** 1 58886222
Email: dostal@austropapier.at **Web site:** http://www.austropapier.at
Freq: 10 issues yearly; **Annual Sub.:** EUR 75,00; **Circ:** 4,500
Editor: Ilse Dostal-Wanivenhaus; **Advertising Manager:** Lydia Fuchs
Profile: European journal for the Austrian pulp, paper and paperboard converting industry with investment, economic, technical, development and environmental information.
Language(s): German
Readership: Aimed at those who work in the supply and paper industries and customers.
ADVERTISING RATES:
Full Page Mono .... EUR 1630
Full Page Colour .... EUR 2570
Mechanical Data: Type Area: 257 x 192 mm
Copy instructions: *Copy Date:* 21 days prior to publication
BUSINESS: PAPER

PARNASS
738585A84A-1160
Editorial: Porzellangasse 43/19, 1090 WIEN
Tel: 1 3195375 **Fax:** 1 31953755
Email: office@parnass.at **Web site:** http://www.parnass.at
Freq: Quarterly; **Annual Sub.:** EUR 58,00; **Circ:** 9,700
Editor: Charlotte Kreuzmayr; **Advertising Manager:** Charlotte Kreuzmayr
Profile: Publication covering a variety of topics including art, design, architecture, music, theatre, literature and photography.
Language(s): German
ADVERTISING RATES:
Full Page Mono .... EUR 4000
Full Page Colour .... EUR 4000
Mechanical Data: Type Area: 251 x 191 mm
Copy instructions: *Copy Date:* 22 days prior to publication
CONSUMER: THE ARTS & LITERARY: Arts

PARTNER
738589A21J-3
Editorial: Leibnitzer Str. 76, 8403 LEBRING
Tel: 699 16004070 **Fax:** 3182 49406540
Email: info@partnerzeitung.at **Web site:** http://www.partnerzeitung.at
Freq: Monthly; **Annual Sub.:** EUR 10,00; **Circ:** 80,000
Editor: Ingrid Gady; **Advertising Manager:** Margit Krainer
Profile: Farming journal for the Leibnitz region.
Language(s): German
ADVERTISING RATES:
Full Page Mono .... EUR 2745
Full Page Colour .... EUR 3235
Mechanical Data: Col Widths (Display): 47 mm, Type Area: 264 x 200 mm, No. of Columns (Display): 4
Copy instructions: *Copy Date:* 8 days prior to publication
BUSINESS: AGRICULTURE & FARMING: Agriculture & Farming - Regional

PC NEWS
724173A5-100
Editorial: Tobra 9, 4320 PERG **Tel:** 7262 575570
Fax: 7262 5755744
Email: redaktion@cda-verlag.com **Web site:** http://www.pcnews-online.de
Freq: Monthly; **Cover Price:** EUR 4,99; **Circ:** 76,400
Editor: Harald Gutzelnig
Profile: Publication containing reports on CD-Roms, Software, Computers, Online and Multimedia.
Language(s): German
ADVERTISING RATES:
Full Page Mono .... EUR 3990
Full Page Colour .... EUR 4990
Mechanical Data: Type Area: 240 x 170 mm
Copy instructions: *Copy Date:* 14 days prior to publication
BUSINESS: COMPUTERS & AUTOMATION

PERSPEKTIVE
749060A62A-1020
Editorial: Rauhensteingasse 5/4, 1010 WIEN
Tel: 1 8130811 **Fax:** 1 8130815
Email: perspektive.zv@gmx.at **Web site:** http://www.zv-wien.at
Freq: Quarterly; Free to qualifying individuals
Annual Sub.: EUR 5,00
Profile: Journal concerning education and management in Vienna.
Language(s): German
Readership: Read by teachers in Vienna.
BUSINESS: CHURCH & SCHOOL EQUIPMENT & EDUCATION: Education

PERSPEKTIVEN
1998102A4E-1349
Editorial: Leberstr. 122, 1110 WIEN **Tel:** 1 74032764
Fax: 1 740327820
Email: c.divischek@redaktion-wien.at **Web site:** http://www.bohmann-verlag.at
Freq: 10 issues yearly; **Annual Sub.:** EUR 66,00; **Circ:** 12,000
Editor: Christoph Berndl; **Advertising Manager:** Gunther Pany
Profile: Journal about town planning.
Language(s): English; German
ADVERTISING RATES:
Full Page Mono .... EUR 2050
Full Page Colour .... EUR 3000

DER PFLANZENARZT
738884A26C-21
Editorial: Sturzgasse 1a, 1140 WIEN **Tel:** 1 98177163
Fax: 1 98177120
Email: redaktion1@agrarverlag.at **Web site:** http://www.agrarverlag.at
Freq: 8 issues yearly; **Annual Sub.:** EUR 55,20; **Circ:** 3,700
Editor: Gabriele Luttenberger; **Advertising Manager:** Romana Hummer-Schierleitner
Profile: Magazine about plant protection.
Language(s): German
Readership: Aimed at farmers and horticulturalists.

ADVERTISING RATES:
Full Page Mono .... EUR 3350
Full Page Colour .... EUR 3997
Mechanical Data: Type Area: 260 x 178 mm, No. of Columns (Display): 3, Col Widths (Display): 56 mm
Copy instructions: *Copy Date:* 14 days prior to publication
BUSINESS: GARDEN TRADE

PFM-MAGAZIN FÜR INFRASTRUKTUR UND TECHNOLOGIE
1666837A14A-2545
Editorial: Getreidemarkt 10, 1010 WIEN
Tel: 1 58120810 **Fax:** 1 581208199
Email: chefredaktion@pfm-magazin.at **Web site:** http://www.peterfmayer.at
Freq: 10 issues yearly; **Annual Sub.:** EUR 29,70; **Circ:** 25,000
Editor: Peter F. Mayer
Language(s): German
ADVERTISING RATES:
Full Page Colour .... EUR 5630
Mechanical Data: Type Area: 247 x 190 mm, No. of Columns (Display): 3, Col Widths (Display): 71 mm
Copy instructions: *Copy Date:* 10 days prior to publication
BUSINESS: COMMERCE, INDUSTRY & MANAGEMENT

PHARMAINFORMATION
738916A56A-1480
Editorial: Peter-Mayr-Str. 1a, 6020 INNSBRUCK
Tel: 512 5073700 **Fax:** 512 5072868
Web site: http://www.uibk.ac.at/c/c5/c515/pharmainfo.html
Freq: Quarterly; Free to qualifying individuals
Annual Sub.: EUR 8,80; **Circ:** 39,000
Editor: Hans Winkler
Profile: Magazine containing independent information about pharmaceutics for physicians and pharmacists.
Language(s): German

PHARMA-TIME
738922A37-180
Editorial: Teichgasse 20, 2325 HIMBERG
Tel: 2235 879431 **Fax:** 2235 879434
Email: redaktion@pharmatime.at **Web site:** http://www.pharmatime.at
Freq: 10 issues yearly; **Annual Sub.:** EUR 32,00; **Circ:** 8,000
Editor: Hans Jakesz; **Advertising Manager:** Hans Jakesz
Profile: Magazine covering all aspects of the pharmaceutical industry.
Language(s): German
ADVERTISING RATES:
Full Page Mono .... EUR 1860
Full Page Colour .... EUR 2740
Mechanical Data: Type Area: 224 x 190 mm, No. of Columns (Display): 3, Col Widths (Display): 61 mm
BUSINESS: PHARMACEUTICAL & CHEMISTS

PHARMIG INFO
738929A37-220
Editorial: Garnisongasse 4/1/6, 1090 WIEN
Tel: 1 4060290 **Fax:** 1 40602909
Email: kommunikation@pharmig.at **Web site:** http://www.pharmig.at
Freq: Quarterly; **Circ:** 6,800
Editor: Jan Oliver Huber
Profile: Official journal of the Austrian pharmaceutical trade.
Language(s): German
BUSINESS: PHARMACEUTICAL & CHEMISTS

PIN
739010A27-306
Editorial: 6600 REUTTE **Tel:** 5672 6002243
Email: denes.szechenyi@plansee.com **Web site:** http://www.plansee-group.com
Freq: Quarterly; **Circ:** 6,000
Editor: Dénes Széchényi
Profile: Magazine for employees of Plansee AG.
Language(s): German

PKA JOURNAL
739039A37-240
Editorial: Teichgasse 20, 2325 HIMBERG
Tel: 2235 879431 **Fax:** 2235 879434
Email: redaktion@pharmatime.at **Web site:** http://www.pharmatime.at
Freq: 6 issues yearly; **Annual Sub.:** EUR 13,00; **Circ:** 3,500
Editor: Christoph Jakesz; **Advertising Manager:** Christoph Jakesz
Profile: Magazine for pharmacists' sales assistants.
Language(s): German
ADVERTISING RATES:
Full Page Mono .... EUR 2153
Full Page Colour .... EUR 3122
Mechanical Data: No. of Columns (Display): 3, Col Widths (Display): 55 mm, Type Area: 244 x 174 mm

PLANET ALPEN
739055A57-800
Editorial: Knappensteig 12, 9500 VILLACH
Tel: 664 9762859
Email: planetalpen@gmx.at **Web site:** http://www.alpen-adria-planet.org
Freq: Quarterly; **Annual Sub.:** EUR 17,50; **Circ:** 12,600
Editor: Gerhard Leeb; **Advertising Manager:** Gerhard Leeb
Profile: Magazine about the environment.
Language(s): German
ADVERTISING RATES:
Full Page Mono .... EUR 1460
Full Page Colour .... EUR 1460
Mechanical Data: Type Area: 270 x 210 mm
Copy instructions: *Copy Date:* 20 days prior to publication

DIE PRESSE
739402A65A-40
Editorial: Hainburger Str. 33, 1030 WIEN
Tel: 1 514140 **Fax:** 1 51414400
Email: chefredaktion@diepresse.com **Web site:** http://www.diepresse.com
Freq: 260 issues yearly; **Circ:** 97,418
Editor: Michael Fleischhacker; **Advertising Manager:** Fritz Mühlbek
Profile: Tabloid-sized quality newspaper providing national and international news, political and economic information. Covers history, geography, commerce, IT, EU affairs and investment details.
Language(s): German
Readership: Aimed at decision-makers within business and industry, senior management, executives, civil servants and university students.
Mechanical Data: Type Area: 421 x 266 mm, No. of Columns (Display): 5, Col Widths (Display): 50 mm
Copy instructions: *Copy Date:* 1 day prior to publication
Supplement(s): Die Presse bauart; Die Presse ferienmagazin; Die Presse formart; Die Presse hightech special; Die Presse kompetent; Die Presse kultur spezial; Die Presse recht; Die Presse Schaufenster; Die Presse uhrenjournal; The Red Bulletin; tele; Wiener Stadtmagazin
NATIONAL DAILY & SUNDAY NEWSPAPERS: National Daily Newspapers

PRESSEHANDBUCH
739405A2A-700
Editorial: Johannesgasse 23, 1015 WIEN
Tel: 1 53161460 **Fax:** 1 53161666
Email: robert.keilhauer@manz.at **Web site:** http://www.pressehandbuch.at
Freq: Annual; **Cover Price:** EUR 100,00; **Circ:** 2,000
Editor: Robert Keilhauer; **Advertising Manager:** Heidrun R. Engel
Profile: Directory about the Austrian media.
Language(s): German
ADVERTISING RATES:
Full Page Colour .... EUR 3837
Mechanical Data: Type Area: 205 x 130 mm
Copy instructions: *Copy Date:* 67 days prior to publication

PRIMA
1643821A74P-265
Editorial: Lindengasse 26, 1070 WIEN
Tel: 1 5261952 **Fax:** 1 526195246
Email: redaktion@kochundback.at **Web site:** http://www.kochundback.at
Freq: Quarterly; **Circ:** 63,000
Editor: Rudolf Bruner; **Advertising Manager:** Rudolf Bruner
Profile: Magazine about enjoyment.
Language(s): German
ADVERTISING RATES:
Full Page Mono .... EUR 6740
Full Page Colour .... EUR 6740
Supplement to: Koch & Back Journal

PRINT & PUBLISHING
739437A41A-180
Editorial: Rotenmühlgasse 11/10, 1120 WIEN
Tel: 1 9830640 **Fax:** 1 983064018
Email: m.seidl@printernet.at **Web site:** http://www.printernet.at
Freq: 9 issues yearly; **Annual Sub.:** EUR 49,50; **Circ:** 6,500
Editor: Michael Seidl; **Advertising Manager:** Michael Seidl
Profile: Magazine focusing on the printing industry, including information on digital communication.
Language(s): German
ADVERTISING RATES:
Full Page Mono .... EUR 2660
Full Page Colour .... EUR 3800
Mechanical Data: Type Area: 260 x 185 mm, No. of Columns (Display): 3, Col Widths (Display): 50 mm
BUSINESS: PRINTING & STATIONERY: Printing

PROFIL
739559A73-260
Editorial: Hainburger Str. 33, 1030 WIEN
Tel: 1 534703502 **Fax:** 1 534703500
Email: redaktion@profil.at **Web site:** http://www.profil.at
Freq: Weekly; **Annual Sub.:** EUR 99,90; **Circ:** 91,000
Editor: Herbert Lackner; **Advertising Manager:** Christoph Gillissen
Profile: General news magazine.
Language(s): German
ADVERTISING RATES:
Full Page Mono .... EUR 12990
Full Page Colour .... EUR 12990
Mechanical Data: Type Area: 250 x 185 mm
Copy instructions: *Copy Date:* 21 days prior to publication
Supplement(s): Ball deluxe
CONSUMER: NATIONAL & INTERNATIONAL PERIODICALS

PROGENIO
1852844A14A-2636
Editorial: Böhmerwaldstr. 3, 4020 LINZ
Tel: 502838213 **Fax:** 502834212
Email: daniela.jung@ave.at **Web site:** http://www.ave.at
Freq: 3 issues yearly; **Circ:** 12,000
Advertising Manager: Oliver Olbrich
Profile: Company publication.
Language(s): German

PROP
739647A79B-100
Editorial: Prinz-Eugen-Str. 12, 1040 WIEN
Tel: 1 505102877 **Fax:** 1 5057923
Email: redaktion@prop.at **Web site:** http://www.prop.at
Freq: Quarterly; Free to qualifying individuals
Annual Sub.: EUR 30,00; **Circ:** 10,500
Editor: Manfred Dittmayer
Profile: Official publication of the model aircraft section of the Austrian Aero Club.
Language(s): German
Readership: Aimed at model aeroplane fliers in the Austrian Aero Club.
ADVERTISING RATES:
Full Page Colour .... EUR 770
Mechanical Data: Type Area: 297 x 210 mm
CONSUMER: HOBBIES & DIY: Models & Modelling

PSYCHOLOGISCHE MEDIZIN
739703A56A-1580
Editorial: Roseggerweg 50, 8036 GRAZ
Tel: 316 3853042 **Fax:** 316 3853608
Email: josef.egger@meduni-graz.at
Freq: Quarterly; Free to qualifying individuals
Annual Sub.: EUR 30,00; **Circ:** 900
Editor: Josef W. Egger
Profile: Magazine covering all aspects of psychological medicine.
Language(s): German
ADVERTISING RATES:
Full Page Mono .... EUR 330
Mechanical Data: Type Area: 262 x 182 mm
Official Journal of: Organ d. Integrativen Seminars f. Psychotherapie in Bad Gleichenberg, d. Internat. Seminars f. körperorientierte Psychotherapie u. Körpertherapie Bad Gleichenberg, d. Igler Tage f. Psychosomat. Medizin u. Sexualmedizin u. d. Forum f. d. PSY-Diplom-Fortbildung d. ÖÄK

PSYCHOPRAXIS
739708A56N-100
Editorial: Sachsenplatz 4, 1201 WIEN
Tel: 1 33024150 **Fax:** 1 3302426
Email: tanja.fabsits@springer.at **Web site:** http://www.springer.at
Freq: 6 issues yearly; **Circ:** 6,742
Editor: Tanja Fabsits
Profile: Magazine providing news, information and scientific articles about mental health. Focuses on psychiatry, neurology and psychotherapy, but also includes general medical details.
Language(s): German
ADVERTISING RATES:
Full Page Mono .... EUR 2540
Full Page Colour .... EUR 3190
Mechanical Data: Type Area: 270 x 170 mm
BUSINESS: HEALTH & MEDICAL: Mental Health

PUNKTUM
1655388A17-164
Editorial: Dresdner Str. 45, 1200 WIEN
Tel: 1 97000153 **Fax:** 1 970005153
Email: wolfgang.flegl@weka.at **Web site:** http://www.punktum.co.at
Freq: 10 issues yearly; **Annual Sub.:** EUR 35,00; **Circ:** 8,502
Editor: Wolfgang Flegl; **Advertising Manager:** Martin Wittmann
Profile: Magazine about electro installation, light and communications technologies.
Language(s): German
ADVERTISING RATES:
Full Page Colour .... EUR 3950
Mechanical Data: Type Area: 255 x 186 mm
BUSINESS: ELECTRICAL

Q-SPIRIT
1844648A49A-597
Editorial: Handelszentrum 3, 5101 BERGHEIM
Tel: 662 46800
Web site: http://www.quehenberger.com
Freq: 3 issues yearly; **Circ:** 10,000
Profile: Company publication about logistics and service solutions for trade and industry.
Language(s): English; German

QUALITAS
1642050A56A-1928
Editorial: Wickenburggasse 32, 8010 GRAZ
Tel: 316 8205650 **Fax:** 316 82056520
Email: roland@schaffler-verlag.com **Web site:** http://www.qualitas.at
Freq: Quarterly; **Annual Sub.:** EUR 30,00; **Circ:** 13,500
Editor: Roland Schaffler; **Advertising Manager:** Alexandra Pfisterer
Profile: Magazine about the quality and development of Austrian health institutions.
Language(s): German
ADVERTISING RATES:
Full Page Mono .... EUR 3370
Full Page Colour .... EUR 3370
Mechanical Data: Type Area: 218 x 180 mm

R 19
740537A72-5480
Editorial: Medienturm Saline Hall, 6060 HALL
Tel: 5223 5130 **Fax:** 5223 51320
Email: verlag@ablinger-garber.at **Web site:** http://www.r19.at
Freq: 10 issues yearly; **Cover Price:** Free; **Circ:** 10,500
Editor: Barbara Valentini-Konzert; **Advertising Manager:** Robert Ablinger
Profile: Regional newspaper containing information about the Tyrol.
Language(s): German
ADVERTISING RATES:
Full Page Mono .... EUR 750
Full Page Colour .... EUR 980
Mechanical Data: Type Area: 273 x 190 mm, No. of Columns (Display): 4, Col Widths (Display): 45 mm
Copy instructions: *Copy Date:* 10 days prior to publication
LOCAL NEWSPAPERS

RADTOUREN IN ÖSTERREICH.
739885A89A-240
Editorial: Freistädter Str. 119, 4041 LINZ
Tel: 732 7277100 **Fax:** 732 7277130
Email: tourismus@lto.at **Web site:** http://www.radtouren.at
Freq: Annual; **Cover Price:** Free; **Circ:** 100,000
Profile: Publication about cycling tours in Austria.
Language(s): German

RADTOUREN IN ÖSTERREICH.
739885A89A-508
Editorial: Freistädter Str. 119, 4041 LINZ
Tel: 732 7277100 **Fax:** 732 7277130
Email: tourismus@lto.at **Web site:** http://www.radtouren.at
Freq: Annual; **Cover Price:** Free; **Circ:** 100,000
Profile: Publication about cycling tours in Austria.
Language(s): German

RADWELT
739892A77C-60
Editorial: Ringstr. 44/1, 3500 KREMS
Tel: 2732 8200036 **Fax:** 2732 8200082
Email: klaus.haselboeck@lwmedia.at **Web site:** http://www.radwelt.at
Freq: 5 issues yearly; **Annual Sub.:** EUR 21,00; **Circ:** 18,000
Editor: Klaus Haselböck; **Advertising Manager:** Michael Linauer
Profile: Magazine focusing on cycling as a leisure activity.
Language(s): German
ADVERTISING RATES:
Full Page Mono .... EUR 2590
Full Page Colour .... EUR 2590
Mechanical Data: Type Area: 240 x 183 mm
CONSUMER: MOTORING & CYCLING: Cycling

RAIFFEISEN BLATT
738046A1C-140
Editorial: Am Stadtpark 9, 1030 WIEN
Tel: 1 717071270 **Fax:** 1 717072496
Email: andreas.pangl@rzb.at **Web site:** http://www.raiffeisenblatt.at
Freq: 11 issues yearly; **Annual Sub.:** EUR 74,00; **Circ:** 3,800
Editor: Andreas Pangl
Profile: Journal about Austrian savings bank practice and technology.
Language(s): German
Readership: Aimed at directors, business managers and those who work in or have an interest in banks.
ADVERTISING RATES:
Full Page Mono .... EUR 2630
Full Page Colour .... EUR 4169
Mechanical Data: Type Area: 241 x 165 mm
BUSINESS: FINANCE & ECONOMICS: Banking

RAIFFEISEN ZEITUNG
739927A21A-1160
Editorial: Friedrich-Wilhelm-Raiffeisen-Platz 1, 1020 WIEN **Tel:** 1 211362580 **Fax:** 1 211362551
Email: redaktion@raiffeisenzeitung.at **Web site:** http://www.raiffeisenzeitung.at
Freq: 45 issues yearly; **Annual Sub.:** EUR 27,00; **Circ:** 41,065
Editor: Edith Unger
Profile: Agricultural newspaper focusing on the economic and financial implications for farmers.
Language(s): German
Readership: Aimed at agricultural businesses and farming managers.
ADVERTISING RATES:
Full Page Mono .... EUR 6890
Full Page Colour .... EUR 6890
Mechanical Data: Type Area: 384 x 265 mm, No. of Columns (Display): 6, Col Widths (Display): 40 mm
Copy instructions: *Copy Date:* 10 days prior to publication
BUSINESS: AGRICULTURE & FARMING

RAINER
739932A94H-1020
Editorial: Wiedner Gürtel 3a, 1040 WIEN
Tel: 1 601660 **Fax:** 1 60166105
Email: georg.berner@rainer.co.at **Web site:** http://www.rainer.co.at
Freq: Quarterly; **Cover Price:** Free; **Circ:** 220,000
Editor: Georg Berner

Profile: Motoring and lifestyle magazine for clients of the Rainer motor dealership.
Language(s): German
CONSUMER: OTHER CLASSIFICATIONS: Customer Magazines

RAUM
1648383A4E-1288
Editorial: Franz-Josefs-Kai 27, 1010 WIEN
Tel: 1 533874721 **Fax:** 1 533874766
Email: neulinger@oir.at **Web site:** http://www.raum-on.at
Freq: Quarterly; **Annual Sub.:** EUR 35,00; **Circ:** 1,500
Editor: Johannes Steiner
Profile: Magazine informs about developments in land use planning and about regional politics in Austria and Europe.
Language(s): German
ADVERTISING RATES:
Full Page Mono .... EUR 1160
Mechanical Data: Type Area: 230 x 167 mm, No. of Columns (Display): 3, Col Widths (Display): 51 mm
Copy instructions: *Copy Date:* 30 days prior to publication

RDW ÖSTERREICHISCHES RECHT DER WIRTSCHAFT
740018A44-320
Editorial: Marxergasse 25, 1030 WIEN
Tel: 1 534521552 **Fax:** 1 53452146
Email: katharina.bacher@lexisnexis.at **Web site:** http://rdw.lexisnexis.at
Freq: Monthly; **Annual Sub.:** EUR 229,00; **Circ:** 3,800
Advertising Manager: Wolfgang Kreissl
Profile: Journal about business law.
Language(s): German
Readership: Aimed at solicitors, tax advisors, economists and chartered accountants.
ADVERTISING RATES:
Full Page Mono .... EUR 1830
Full Page Colour .... EUR 2620
Mechanical Data: Type Area: 252 x 172 mm
BUSINESS: LEGAL

RECHT DER UMWELT RDU
740040A44-380
Editorial: Johannesgasse 23, 1015 WIEN
Tel: 1 53161308 **Fax:** 1 53161666
Email: elisabeth.maier@manz.at **Web site:** http://www.manz.at
Freq: 6 issues yearly; **Annual Sub.:** EUR 126,00; **Circ:** 750
Editor: Wilhelm Bergthaler; **Advertising Manager:** Heidrun R. Engel
Profile: Publication about environmental law.
Language(s): German
ADVERTISING RATES:
Full Page Mono .... EUR 977
Full Page Colour .... EUR 1847
Mechanical Data: Type Area: 250 x 167 mm
Copy instructions: *Copy Date:* 28 days prior to publication
BUSINESS: LEGAL

REGAL
740109A53-2
Editorial: Floridsdorfer Hauptstr. 1, 1210 WIEN
Tel: 1 3686713 **Fax:** 1 368671318
Email: schuhmayer@regal.at **Web site:** http://www.regal.at
Freq: 11 issues yearly; **Annual Sub.:** EUR 26,00; **Circ:** 27,000
Editor: Harald-Gregor Schuhmayer; **Advertising Manager:** Stefanie Dähmlow
Profile: Magazine covering all aspects of the retail trade.
Language(s): German
ADVERTISING RATES:
Full Page Mono .... EUR 3510
Full Page Colour .... EUR 5395
Mechanical Data: Type Area: 270 x 180 mm
Copy instructions: *Copy Date:* 14 days prior to publication
BUSINESS: RETAILING & WHOLESALING

REGENWALD-NACHRICHTEN
1791982A57-1157
Editorial: Währinger Str. 182/24, 1180 WIEN
Tel: 1 4701935 **Fax:** 1 470193520
Email: info@regenwald.at **Web site:** http://www.regenwald.at
Freq: Half-yearly; **Circ:** 10,000
Editor: Michael Schnitzler
Profile: Information to support the safe theEsquinas rain forest in Costa Rica.
Language(s): German

REIMMICHLS VOLKSKALENDER
740187A73-280
Editorial: Exlgasse 20, 6020 INNSBRUCK
Tel: 512 2233202 **Fax:** 512 2233206
Email: buchverlag@tyrolia.at **Web site:** http://www.tyrolia-verlag.at
Freq: Annual; **Cover Price:** EUR 9,95; **Circ:** 30,000
Editor: Paul Muigg; **Advertising Manager:** Anna Hofer
Profile: Folklore calendar.
Language(s): German
ADVERTISING RATES:
Full Page Mono .... EUR 1500
Full Page Colour .... EUR 1600
Mechanical Data: Type Area: 210 x 145 mm

REISE AKTUELL
740194A89A-455
Editorial: Haydngasse 6, 1060 WIEN **Tel:** 1 5974985
Fax: 1 597498515
Email: news@reiseaktuell.at **Web site:** http://www.reiseaktuell.at
Freq: 3 issues yearly; **Annual Sub.:** EUR 11,50; **Circ:** 51,800
Editor: Christian Böhm; **Advertising Manager:** Christian Böhm
Profile: Travel magazine containing information about holiday destinations.
Language(s): German
ADVERTISING RATES:
Full Page Mono .... EUR 4960
Full Page Colour .... EUR 6200
Mechanical Data: Type Area: 265 x 185 mm, No. of Columns (Display): 4, Col Widths (Display): 43 mm
Copy instructions: *Copy Date:* 10 days prior to publication
CONSUMER: HOLIDAYS & TRAVEL: Travel

DER REITWAGEN
740235A77B-100
Editorial: Obertriesting 49, 2572 KAUMBERG
Tel: 2765 88033 **Fax:** 2765 88045
Email: zonko63@gmx.at **Web site:** http://www.reitwagen.at
Freq: 10 issues yearly; **Annual Sub.:** EUR 29,50; **Circ:** 45,000
Editor: Fritz Triendl
Profile: Motorcycle magazine.
Language(s): German
Readership: Aimed at motorcycle enthusiasts.
ADVERTISING RATES:
Full Page Mono .... EUR 5500
Full Page Colour .... EUR 6500
Mechanical Data: Type Area: 248 x 188 mm
CONSUMER: MOTORING & CYCLING: Motorcycling

RENOVATION
740262A4E-1290
Editorial: Dresdner Str. 45, 1200 WIEN
Tel: 1 97000244 **Fax:** 1 970005244
Email: alexander.riell@weka.at **Web site:** http://www.renovation.co.at
Freq: Quarterly; **Annual Sub.:** EUR 8,00; **Circ:** 30,000
Editor: Alexander Riell; **Advertising Manager:** Kerstin Hainzl
Profile: Publication concerning different aspects of building renovation and modernisation, both interior and exterior.
Language(s): German
ADVERTISING RATES:
Full Page Mono .... EUR 5900
Full Page Colour .... EUR 5900
Mechanical Data: Type Area: 248 x 184 mm
BUSINESS: ARCHITECTURE & BUILDING: Building

REPORT (+) PLUS
1648505A14A-2527
Editorial: Nattergasse 4, 1170 WIEN **Tel:** 1 9029913
Fax: 1 9029937
Email: flatscher@report.at **Web site:** http://www.report.at
Freq: Monthly; **Annual Sub.:** EUR 40,00; **Circ:** 50,000
Editor: Alfons Flatscher
Profile: Economics magazine.
Language(s): German
ADVERTISING RATES:
Full Page Mono .... EUR 8400
Full Page Colour .... EUR 8400
Mechanical Data: Type Area: 270 x 180 mm
Copy instructions: *Copy Date:* 7 days prior to publication
Supplement(s): bau + immobilien Report; energie Report; telekom + it Report

RETAIL
731140A14A-1220
Editorial: Kaiserstr. 50/10, 1070 WIEN
Tel: 1 9665848 **Fax:** 1 96658489
Email: mms@querverkehr.at **Web site:** http://www.retail.at
Freq: 5 issues yearly; **Cover Price:** Free; **Circ:** 4,000
Editor: Michael Schiebel
Profile: Magazine with information for trade and e-commerce.
Language(s): German
ADVERTISING RATES:
Full Page Mono .... EUR 2390
Full Page Colour .... EUR 2390
Mechanical Data: Type Area: 290 x 220 mm

RHEUMA PLUS
1645753A56A-1941
Editorial: Sachsenplatz 4, 1201 WIEN **Tel:** 1 5131047
Fax: 1 5134783
Email: margarete.zupan@springer.at **Web site:** http://www.springermedizin.at
Freq: Quarterly; **Circ:** 12,000
Editor: Margarete Zupan
Profile: Magazine on rheumatology.
Language(s): German
ADVERTISING RATES:
Full Page Mono .... EUR 1980
Full Page Colour .... EUR 2430
Mechanical Data: Type Area: 270 x 170 mm
Supplement to: Ärzte Woche

RUDERREPORT
740702A75M-40
Editorial: Teichtlgasse 2, 2105 OBERROHRBACH
Tel: 2266 80650 **Fax:** 2266 80650
Email: erwin.fuchs@aon.at
Freq: 8 issues yearly; **Cover Price:** EUR 2,20
Free to qualifying individuals ; **Circ:** 7,600
Editor: Erwin Fuchs; **Advertising Manager:** Erwin Fuchs
Profile: Magazine about rowing.
Language(s): German
CONSUMER: SPORT: Water Sports

RUNDSCHAU
740818A80-1060
Editorial: Riehlweg 515a, 6100 SEEFELD
Tel: 5212 4980
Email: oc@rundschau-seefeld.at **Web site:** http://www.rundschau-seefeld.at
Freq: Monthly; **Annual Sub.:** EUR 19,00; **Circ:** 10,250
Editor: Othmar Crepaz; **Advertising Manager:** Othmar Crepaz
Profile: Newspaper containing information about Telfs.
Language(s): German
ADVERTISING RATES:
Full Page Mono .... EUR 685
Full Page Colour .... EUR 905
Mechanical Data: Type Area: 274 x 196 mm, No. of Columns (Display): 4, Col Widths (Display): 46 mm
CONSUMER: RURAL & REGIONAL INTEREST

RUPERTUSBLATT
1643789A87-2594
Editorial: Kaigasse 8, 5020 SALZBURG
Tel: 662 872223 **Fax:** 662 87222313
Email: rupertusblatt@kommunikation.kirchen.net
Web site: http://www.kirchen.net/rupertusblatt
Freq: Weekly; **Annual Sub.:** EUR 33,00; **Circ:** 15,300
Editor: Karl Roithinger
Profile: Church paper form the diocese of Salzburg.
Language(s): German
ADVERTISING RATES:
Full Page Mono .... EUR 2012
Full Page Colour .... EUR 2683
Mechanical Data: Type Area: 262 x 196 mm, No. of Columns (Display): 4, Col Widths (Display): 46 mm
Copy instructions: *Copy Date:* 6 days prior to publication
CONSUMER: RELIGIOUS

RWZ RECHT & RECHNUNGSWESEN
1647309A14A-2519
Editorial: Marxergasse 25, 1030 WIEN
Tel: 1 534521562 **Fax:** 1 53452140
Email: evelyn.hahn@lexisnexis.at **Web site:** http://rwz.lexisnexis.at
Freq: Monthly; **Annual Sub.:** EUR 229,00; **Circ:** 1,800
Advertising Manager: Wolfgang Kreissl
Profile: Magazine about law and accountancy.
Language(s): German
ADVERTISING RATES:
Full Page Mono .... EUR 1480
Full Page Colour .... EUR 2270
Mechanical Data: Type Area: 252 x 172 mm

S&BT SEILBAHN BUS TOURISMUS
741742A49E-206
Editorial: Südtiroler Str. 16/1, 6240 RATTENBERG
Tel: 5337 62050 **Fax:** 5337 62060
Email: moser@mmga.at **Web site:** http://www.skigebietstest.at
Freq: 6 issues yearly; **Annual Sub.:** EUR 29,80; **Circ:** 8,000
Editor: Helmut Moser
Profile: Magazine with test results of cable cars within Austria, Germany, Switzerland and Italy.
Language(s): German
ADVERTISING RATES:
Full Page Colour .... EUR 3350
Copy instructions: *Copy Date:* 21 days prior to publication
BUSINESS: TRANSPORT: Railways

SALZBURGER KRIEGSOPFER
740987A94A-41
Editorial: Haunspergstr. 39, 5020 SALZBURG
Tel: 662 872240 **Fax:** 662 87224015
Email: skov@hostprofis.at
Freq: Half-yearly
Editor: Rupert Kobler
Profile: Newspaper of the Salzburg War Victims' Association.
Language(s): German
ADVERTISING RATES:
Full Page Mono .... EUR 581
Mechanical Data: Type Area: 230 x 180 mm, No. of Columns (Display): 3, Col Widths (Display): 63 mm
Copy instructions: *Copy Date:* 12 days prior to publication
CONSUMER: OTHER CLASSIFICATIONS: War Veterans

SALZBURGER NACHRICHTEN
740988A67B-1581
Editorial: Karolingerstr. 40, 5021 SALZBURG
Tel: 662 8373301 **Fax:** 662 8373399
Web site: http://www.salzburg.com
Freq: 208 issues yearly; **Circ:** 84,760
Editor: Manfred Perterer; **News Editor:** Viktor Hermann; **Advertising Manager:** Christian Strasser
Profile: National daily covering politics, economics, sport, travel and the arts.
Language(s): German
ADVERTISING RATES:
SCC .... EUR 105,40
Mechanical Data: Type Area: 410 x 270 mm, No. of Columns (Display): 6, Col Widths (Display): 43 mm
Copy instructions: *Copy Date:* 1 day prior to publication
Supplement(s): Gemeindeentwicklung; The Red Bulletin; Salzburg pur; tele; Uhren Schmuck Magazin
REGIONAL DAILY & SUNDAY NEWSPAPERS: Regional Daily Newspapers

SCHAFE & ZIEGEN AKTUELL
741153A21D-3
Editorial: Altirdning 11, 8952 IRDING
Tel: 3682 22451280
Email: schafe.aktuell@gmx.at **Web site:** http://www.landwirt.com
Freq: Quarterly; **Annual Sub.:** EUR 18,90; **Circ:** 6,000
Editor: Ferdinand Ringdorfer
Profile: Agricultural magazine focusing on sheep breeding.
Language(s): German
ADVERTISING RATES:
Full Page Mono .... EUR 990
Full Page Colour .... EUR 1868
Mechanical Data: Type Area: 260 x 190 mm
Official Journal of: Organ d. ArGe d. Schafzuchtverbände Österr.
BUSINESS: AGRICULTURE & FARMING: Livestock

SCHÖNER WOHNEN
721972A4E-1284
Editorial: Parkring 12, 1010 WIEN **Tel:** 1 512886832
Fax: 1 512886815
Email: schoenerwohnen.wien@guj.de
Freq: Annual; **Cover Price:** Free; **Circ:** 90,000
Editor: Edith Almhofer; **Advertising Manager:** Astrid Kiraly
Profile: Magazine about building and renovation. German edition inclusives four pages for austria, editorial staff in Germany.
Language(s): German
ADVERTISING RATES:
Full Page Mono .... EUR 10900
Full Page Colour .... EUR 10900
Mechanical Data: Type Area: 256 x 194 mm
Copy instructions: *Copy Date:* 42 days prior to publication
BUSINESS: ARCHITECTURE & BUILDING: Building

SCHÖNER WOHNEN
741352A74C-640
Editorial: Parkring 12, 1010 WIEN **Tel:** 1 512886832
Fax: 1 512886815
Email: schoenerwohnen.wien@guj.de
Freq: Monthly; **Cover Price:** EUR 4,80; **Circ:** 24,000
Editor: Edith Almhofer; **Advertising Manager:** Astrid Kiraly
Profile: Magazine containing features on houses and gardening. Includes information on building, decorating, furniture and furnishing. German edition inclusives four pages for austria, editorial staff in Germany.
Language(s): German
ADVERTISING RATES:
Full Page Mono .... EUR 9200
Full Page Colour .... EUR 9200
Mechanical Data: Type Area: 256 x 194 mm
CONSUMER: WOMEN'S INTEREST CONSUMER MAGAZINES: Home & Family

SCHRIFTTUM UND PRAXIS
741399A56A-1660
Editorial: Margaretenstr. 72, 1050 WIEN
Tel: 1 5866161
Freq: Half-yearly; **Circ:** 2,000
Editor: W. Brenner
Profile: Magazine for dermatologists.
Language(s): German

SCHUH & LEDERWAREN REVUE
741435A29-1
Editorial: Dresdner Str. 45, 1200 WIEN
Tel: 1 97000184 **Fax:** 1 970005184
Email: ute.held@weka.at **Web site:** http://www.schuhrevue.at
Freq: 7 issues yearly; **Annual Sub.:** EUR 14,00; **Circ:** 4,000
Editor: Ute Held; **Advertising Manager:** Ute Held
Profile: Magazine about the Austrian shoe business.
Language(s): German
ADVERTISING RATES:
Full Page Colour .... EUR 3180
Mechanical Data: Type Area: 255 x 185 mm
Official Journal of: Organ d. Bundesgremiums u. aller Landesgremien d. österr. Schuhhandels, d. Verb. d. Schuhindustrie, d. Bundesgremiums d. Lederwarenhandels, d. Verb. d. Lederwaren Österr., d. Landesgremiums Wien f. d. Einzelhandel m. Leder-, Galanterie- und Bijouteriewaren sowie kunstgewerbl. Artikeln u. d. Bundesinnung d. Lederwarenerzeuger, Taschner, Sattler u. Riemer
BUSINESS: FOOTWEAR

SCHWEISS- & PRÜFTECHNIK
741576A27-280

Editorial: Arsenal, Objekt 207, 1030 WIEN
Tel: 1 7982168 **Fax:** 1 7982168
Email: schweiss-prueftechnik@aon.at **Web site:** http://www.oegs.org
Freq: Monthly; Free to qualifying individuals
Annual Sub.: EUR 69,00; **Circ:** 1,150
Editor: Johann Wasserbauer; **Advertising Manager:** Susanne Mesaric
Profile: European magazine about equipment and testing technology.
Language(s): German
ADVERTISING RATES:
Full Page Mono .... EUR 1160
Full Page Colour .... EUR 1160
Mechanical Data: Type Area: 260 x 180 mm, No. of Columns (Display): 3, Col Widths (Display): 57 mm
Copy instructions: *Copy Date:* 25 days prior to publication

SCHWIMMBAD + THERME
721778A4E-220

Editorial: Wiedner Hauptstr. 120, 1051 WIEN
Tel: 1 54664351 **Fax:** 1 5466450351
Email: h.schmid@wirtschaftsverlag.at **Web site:** http://www.schwimmbad-therme.at
Freq: 6 issues yearly; Free to qualifying individuals
Annual Sub.: EUR 28,70; **Circ:** 7,380
Editor: Heinz Schmid; **Advertising Manager:** Franz-Michael Seidl
Profile: Magazine on swimming pool technology, laws, standards and reports for operators, communes and suppliers.
Language(s): German
ADVERTISING RATES:
Full Page Mono .... EUR 1792
Full Page Colour .... EUR 2560
Mechanical Data: Type Area: 255 x 185 mm
Copy instructions: *Copy Date:* 21 days prior to publication

SEITENBLICKE
764011A74A-865

Editorial: Heinrich-Collin-Str. 1, 1140 WIEN
Tel: 1 902210 **Fax:** 1 9022127930
Email: redaktion@seitenblicke.at **Web site:** http://www.seitenblicke.at
Freq: Weekly; **Annual Sub.:** EUR 59,90; **Circ:** 81,588
Editor: Andreas Wollinger; **Advertising Manager:** Angela Kindermann
Profile: Magazine for women.
Language(s): German
ADVERTISING RATES:
Full Page Mono .... EUR 7900
Full Page Colour .... EUR 7900
Mechanical Data: Type Area: 257 x 190 mm
CONSUMER: WOMEN'S INTEREST CONSUMER MAGAZINES: Women's Interest

SERVUS AM WÖRTHERSEE
741838A89C-358

Editorial: Kirchenstr. 11, 9220 VELDEN
Tel: 4274 3313 **Fax:** 4274 50710
Email: redaktion@veldnerzeitung.at **Web site:** http://www.veldnerzeitung.at
Freq: Annual; **Cover Price:** Free; **Circ:** 59,700
Editor: Peter Günzl; **Advertising Manager:** Renate Podesser
Profile: Independent magazine for holiday visitors to Velden.
Language(s): German
ADVERTISING RATES:
Full Page Mono .... EUR 3132
Full Page Colour .... EUR 3914
Mechanical Data: Type Area: 260 x 192 mm, No. of Columns (Display): 4, Col Widths (Display): 45 mm
Copy instructions: *Copy Date:* 30 days prior to publication
CONSUMER: HOLIDAYS & TRAVEL: Entertainment Guides

SERVUS IN STADT & LAND
2051097A74P-304

Editorial: Heinrich-Collin-Str. 1, 1140 WIEN
Tel: 1 902210 **Fax:** 1 9022127930
Email: office@servusmagazin.at **Web site:** http://www.servusmagazin.at
Freq: Monthly; **Annual Sub.:** EUR 39,90; **Circ:** 59,500
Editor: Andreas Kornhofer
Profile: Austrian lifestyle magazine: Nature and Garden, Food & Dining, Home & Comfort, Land & People, Tradition & Myths Facebook: http://www.facebook.com/Servus.in.Stadt.und.Land.
Language(s): German
ADVERTISING RATES:
Full Page Mono .... EUR 5900
Full Page Colour .... EUR 5900
Mechanical Data: Type Area: 300 x 230 mm

SHOP AKTUELL
741886A14A-1860

Editorial: Josef-Umdasch-Platz 1, 3300 AMSTETTEN
Tel: 7472 6050 **Fax:** 7472 63487
Email: shop.aktuell@umdasch.com **Web site:** http://www.umdasch-shop-concept.com
Freq: 5 issues yearly; **Cover Price:** EUR 6,00; **Circ:** 50,000
Profile: Magazine on interior design and marketing for shopkeepers.
Language(s): English; French; German; Italian

SI SEILBAHNEN INTERNATIONAL
742016A49E-160

Editorial: Kirchenstr. 25 A, 5301 EUGENDORF
Tel: 6225 7290 **Fax:** 6225 729014
Email: kw@simagazin.at **Web site:** http://www.simagazin.at
Freq: 7 issues yearly; **Annual Sub.:** EUR 95,00; **Circ:** 3,387
Editor: Kurt Wieser; **Advertising Manager:** Ottmar F. Steidl
Profile: Magazine with information about cable railways, includes new technology.
Language(s): German
ADVERTISING RATES:
Full Page Colour .... EUR 4050
Mechanical Data: Type Area: 260 x 184 mm
BUSINESS: TRANSPORT: Railways

SICHERE ARBEIT
741902A54B-1

Editorial: Leberstr. 122, 1110 WIEN **Tel:** 1 74095435
Fax: 1 74095440
Email: klobucsar.zv@bohmann.at **Web site:** http://www.sicherearbeit.at
Freq: 6 issues yearly; **Annual Sub.:** EUR 49,90; **Circ:** 13,000
Advertising Manager: Gertrude Schöggl
Profile: Magazine about occupational health and industrial safety.
Language(s): German
ADVERTISING RATES:
Full Page Colour .... EUR 4100
Mechanical Data: Type Area: 250 x 185 mm
BUSINESS: SAFETY & SECURITY: Safety

SIGNORA
741978A74A-700

Editorial: Mariahilfer Str. 89a, 1060 WIEN
Tel: 1 58040 **Fax:** 1 5804014
Email: barbara@diemucha.at **Web site:** http://www.signora.at
Freq: Quarterly; **Cover Price:** EUR 2,00; **Circ:** 50,000
Editor: Barbara Mucha; **Advertising Manager:** Barbara Mucha
Profile: Magazine for men and women from 40 years of age upwards about jobs, fashion, cosmetics, leisure time, health and finances.
Language(s): German
ADVERTISING RATES:
Full Page Colour .... EUR 7420
Mechanical Data: Type Area: 247 x 173 mm

SKIN
1644956A4E-1287

Editorial: Wiedner Hauptstr. 120, 1051 WIEN
Tel: 1 54664342 **Fax:** 1 5466450342
Email: skin@wirtschaftsverlag.at **Web site:** http://www.bauforum.at
Freq: Half-yearly; **Circ:** 12,300
Editor: Tom Cervinka; **Advertising Manager:** Franz-Michael Seidl
Profile: Magazine on planning and realising intelligent exterior architecture based on functional and physical aspects.
Language(s): German
ADVERTISING RATES:
Full Page Colour .... EUR 4555
Mechanical Data: Type Area: 255 x 185 mm
Copy instructions: *Copy Date:* 21 days prior to publication
Supplement to: Forum, Österreichische bau.zeitung

SKYLINES
742052A89D-2

Editorial: Karlsplatz 1/18, 1010 WIEN **Tel:** 1 8900881
Fax: 1 890088115
Email: gerald.sturz@diabla.at **Web site:** http://www.skylines.at
Freq: 6 issues yearly; **Cover Price:** Free; **Circ:** 120,000
Editor: Gerald Sturz; **Advertising Manager:** Andrea Fürnweger
Profile: In-flight magazine for Austrian Airlines.
Language(s): English; German
ADVERTISING RATES:
Full Page Mono .... EUR 10800
Full Page Colour .... EUR 10800
Mechanical Data: Type Area: 250 x 180 mm
CONSUMER: HOLIDAYS & TRAVEL: In-Flight Magazines

SLOW
2086906A74P-306

Editorial: Leberstr. 122, 1110 WIEN **Tel:** 1 740770
Fax: 1 74077888
Email: redaktion@alacarte.at **Web site:** http://www.alacarte.at
Freq: Quarterly; **Circ:** 30,000
Editor: Barbara van Melle; **Advertising Manager:** Stefan W. Stumpf
Profile: Magazine of the Austrian Slow Food convivium. It has plenty of background information, interesting facts and enjoyable entertainment. Renowned authors and journalists investigate and comment from the perspective of Slow Food recent developments in areas such as culinary arts, biodiversity, regional food cultures, environmental, food, sensor technology, sustainable food production, consumption, taste and well-being. Supplement to the A la Carte magazine and direct marketing to Slow Food members. Slow is an attractive science magazine for food lovers. For consumers who know that any purchase decision is a production decision, and wish to carefully deal with resources, because that is the basis for our quality of life. Want to know for people, the relationships and backgrounds, to buy intelligently and sustainably, to enjoy and live.
Language(s): German
ADVERTISING RATES:
Full Page Colour .... EUR 3900
Mechanical Data: Type Area: 280 x 210 mm
Supplement to: A la Carte

SLZ SALZBURGER LANDES-ZEITUNG
742064A80-1676

Editorial: Chiemseehof, 5010 SALZBURG
Tel: 662 80422048 **Fax:** 662 80422161
Email: landespressebuero@salzburg.gv.at **Web site:** http://www.salzburg.gv.at/pressebuero/lpb
Freq: 26 issues yearly; **Annual Sub.:** EUR 25,43; **Circ:** 2,000
Editor: Roland Floimair
Profile: Journal of the local government offices of Salzburg.
Language(s): German
ADVERTISING RATES:
Full Page Mono .... EUR 1599
Mechanical Data: Type Area: 410 x 276 mm
Copy instructions: *Copy Date:* 10 days prior to publication
CONSUMER: RURAL & REGIONAL INTEREST

SOL
1646258A57-1129

Editorial: Nr. 5, 7411 MARKT ALLHAU **Tel:** 3356 265
Fax: 1 878129283
Email: sol@nachhaltig.at **Web site:** http://www.nachhaltig.at
Freq: Quarterly; **Annual Sub.:** EUR 3,60; **Circ:** 4,000
Editor: Dan Jakubowicz; **Advertising Manager:** Dan Jakubowicz
Profile: Magazine about solidarity, ecology and lifestyle.
Language(s): German
ADVERTISING RATES:
Full Page Colour .... EUR 500
Mechanical Data: Type Area: 246 x 159 mm, No. of Columns (Display): 2, Col Widths (Display): 78 mm
Copy instructions: *Copy Date:* 30 days prior to publication

SOLID
1641459A4E-1285

Editorial: Lindengasse 56, 1070 WIEN
Tel: 1 585900018 **Fax:** 1 585900016
Email: priska.koiner@solidbau.at **Web site:** http://www.solidbau.at
Freq: 10 issues yearly; **Annual Sub.:** EUR 35,00; **Circ:** 15,200
Editor: Priska Koiner
Profile: Magazine for mercantile and technical executives of the Austrian Building business.
Language(s): German
ADVERTISING RATES:
Full Page Mono .... EUR 4990
Full Page Colour .... EUR 4990
Mechanical Data: Type Area: 253 x 185 mm
Copy instructions: *Copy Date:* 14 days prior to publication
BUSINESS: ARCHITECTURE & BUILDING: Building

SONNENZEITUNG
1644578A57-1127

Editorial: Neustiftgasse 115a/20, 1070 WIEN
Tel: 1 4039111 **Fax:** 1 403911133
Email: verlag@uranus.at **Web site:** http://www.sonnenzeitung.com
Freq: Quarterly; **Annual Sub.:** EUR 14,90; **Circ:** 55,000
Advertising Manager: Ute Stockhammer
Profile: Magazine about renewable energy.
Language(s): German
ADVERTISING RATES:
Full Page Colour .... EUR 3634
Mechanical Data: Type Area: 269 x 190 mm
Copy instructions: *Copy Date:* 14 days prior to publication

SONNTAG KIRCHENZEITUNG KATHOLISCHE KIRCHE KÄRNTEN
732296A87-1220

Editorial: Tarviser Str. 30, 9020 KLAGENFURT
Tel: 463 58772502
Email: sonntag@kath-kirche-kaernten.at **Web site:** http://www.sonntag-kaernten.at
Freq: Weekly; **Annual Sub.:** EUR 35,00; **Circ:** 10,000
Editor: Gerald Heschl
Profile: Communication member of the Carinthian Catholics, including discussions on church events and developments, and socio-political and cultural issues.
Language(s): German
CONSUMER: RELIGIOUS

SPEKTRUM DER AUGENHEILKUNDE
1853041A56A-2038

Editorial: Sachsenplatz 4, 1201 WIEN
Tel: 1 33024150 **Fax:** 1 330242664
Email: petra.naschenweng@springer.at **Web site:** http://www.springer.at
Freq: 6 issues yearly; **Circ:** 1,000
Editor: Susanne Binder
Profile: Journal of the Austrian Ophthalmologists' Association.
Language(s): German
ADVERTISING RATES:
Full Page Colour .... EUR 1795
Mechanical Data: Type Area: 260 x 180 mm

SPORT MAGAZIN
742539A75A-600

Editorial: Geiselbergstr. 15, 1110 WIEN
Tel: 1 60117226 **Fax:** 1 60117680
Email: redaktion@sportmagazin.at **Web site:** http://www.sport10.at
Freq: 11 issues yearly; **Annual Sub.:** EUR 35,00; **Circ:** 41,000
Editor: Fritz Hutter; **Advertising Manager:** Franz Fellner
Profile: Magazine containing articles on all types of sport.
Language(s): German
Readership: Read by people interested in sport between 20 and 35 years.
ADVERTISING RATES:
Full Page Colour .... EUR 9100
Mechanical Data: Type Area: 297 x 230 mm
Copy instructions: *Copy Date:* 21 days prior to publication
CONSUMER: SPORT

SPORTWOCHE
742587A75A-640

Editorial: Geiselbergstr. 15, 1110 WIEN
Tel: 1 60117226 **Fax:** 1 60117680
Email: redaktion@sportwoche.at **Web site:** http://www.sport10.at
Freq: Weekly; **Annual Sub.:** EUR 48,00; **Circ:** 63,000
Editor: Manfred Behr; **Advertising Manager:** Thomas Kohlweiss
Profile: Magazine containing articles on all types of sport.
Language(s): German
Readership: Aimed at sports enthusiasts.
ADVERTISING RATES:
Full Page Colour .... EUR 7500
Mechanical Data: Type Area: 280 x 200 mm
CONSUMER: SPORT

SPORTZEITUNG
737232A75A-320

Editorial: Linke Wienzeile 40/22, 1061 WIEN
Tel: 1 5855757404 **Fax:** 1 5855757411
Email: horst.hoetsch@lwmedia.at **Web site:** http://www.sportzeitung.at
Freq: Weekly; **Annual Sub.:** EUR 59,90; **Circ:** 33,384
Editor: Horst Hötsch; **Advertising Manager:** Alexandra Salvinetti
Profile: Austrian magazine about sport bets.
Language(s): German
ADVERTISING RATES:
Full Page Mono .... EUR 3690
Full Page Colour .... EUR 3690
Mechanical Data: No. of Columns (Display): 3, Col Widths (Display): 57 mm, Type Area: 270 x 195 mm
Copy instructions: *Copy Date:* 7 days prior to publication
CONSUMER: SPORT

DER STANDARD
743084A65A-80

Editorial: Herrengasse 19, 1010 WIEN **Tel:** 1 531700
Fax: 1 53170131
Email: chefredaktion@derstandard.at **Web site:** http://www.derstandarddigital.at
Freq: 260 issues yearly; **Circ:** 105,541
Editor: Oscar Bronner; **News Editor:** Otto Ranftl; **Advertising Manager:** Thomas Letz
Profile: Broadsheet-sized quality newspaper providing in-depth coverage of business, politics and culture. Includes reports concerning investment and covers the fields of insurance, education, science, technology and society. Facebook: http://www.facebook.com/derStandardat Twitter: http://twitter.com/#!/derstandardat This Outlet offers RSS (Really Simple Syndication).
Language(s): German
Readership: Aimed at company and financial directors, academics, managers, industrialists, business proprietors and university students.
Mechanical Data: Type Area: 420 x 266 mm, No. of Columns (Display): 5, Col Widths (Display): 50 mm
Copy instructions: *Copy Date:* 1 day prior to publication
Supplement(s): City; Hamburg: Das Magazin aus der Metropole; Rondo; SpielBurgSchau; tele; velosophie; Via; VIA International
NATIONAL DAILY & SUNDAY NEWSPAPERS: National Daily Newspapers

STARMÜHLER'S
738521A2A-620

Editorial: Schellinggasse 1/7/3, 1010 WIEN
Tel: 1 9613888 **Fax:** 1 961388850
Email: sonja.fehrer@starmuehler.at **Web site:** http://www.starmuehler.at
Freq: Quarterly; **Cover Price:** Free; **Circ:** 3,500
Editor: Sonja Fehrer
Profile: Magazine for agencies and public relations departments.
Language(s): German

STERNE-APARTMENTS, GASTHÖFE, PENSIONEN IN ÖSTERREICH
1772779A89A-488

Editorial: Wiedner Hauptstr. 120, 1051 WIEN
Tel: 1 54664263 **Fax:** 1 5466450263
Email: office@wirtschaftsverlag.at **Web site:** http://www.wirtschaftsverlag.at

Freq: Annual; **Cover Price:** Free; **Circ:** 40,000
Profile: Holidayinformation about Austria.
Language(s): German

STERNE-APARTMENTS, GASTHÖFE, PENSIONEN IN ÖSTERREICH 1772779A89A-516
Editorial: Wiedner Hauptstr. 120, 1051 WIEN
Tel: 1 54664263 **Fax:** 1 5466450263
Email: office@wirtschaftsverlag.at **Web site:** http://www.wirtschaftsverlag.at
Freq: Annual; **Cover Price:** Free; **Circ:** 40,000
Profile: Holidayinformation about Austria.
Language(s): German

STERNEHOTELS IN ÖSTERREICH 1772766A89A-487
Editorial: Wiedner Hauptstr. 120, 1051 WIEN
Tel: 1 54664263 **Fax:** 1 5466450263
Email: office@wirtschaftsverlag.at **Web site:** http://www.wirtschaftsverlag.at
Freq: Annual; **Cover Price:** Free; **Circ:** 45,000
Profile: Hotels in Austria.
Language(s): German

STERNEHOTELS IN ÖSTERREICH 1772766A89A-515
Editorial: Wiedner Hauptstr. 120, 1051 WIEN
Tel: 1 54664263 **Fax:** 1 5466450263
Email: office@wirtschaftsverlag.at **Web site:** http://www.wirtschaftsverlag.at
Freq: Annual; **Cover Price:** Free; **Circ:** 45,000
Profile: Hotels in Austria.
Language(s): German

STEYR 743493A72-6320
Editorial: Stadtplatz 27, 4400 STEYR
Tel: 7252 575445 **Fax:** 7252 48386
Email: presse@steyr.gv.at **Web site:** http://www.steyr.at
Freq: Monthly; **Annual Sub.:** EUR 16,00; **Circ:** 22,500
Editor: Michael Chvatal
Profile: Regional interest magazine for Steyr.
Language(s): German
Readership: Aimed at residents living in Steyr and the local area.
ADVERTISING RATES:
Full Page Colour .... EUR 1035
Mechanical Data: Type Area: 265 x 187 mm, No. of Columns (Display): 3, Col Widths (Display): 59 mm
Copy instructions: *Copy Date:* 15 days prior to publication
LOCAL NEWSPAPERS

STICHWORT-NEWSLETTER 743500A74A-720
Editorial: Diefenbachgasse 38/1, 1150 WIEN
Tel: 1 8129886 **Fax:** 1 8129886
Email: office@stichwort.or.at **Web site:** http://www.stichwort.or.at
Freq: Half-yearly; **Cover Price:** Free; **Circ:** 2,500
Profile: Feminist magazine.
Language(s): German

STOMATOLOGIE 743542A56D-60
Editorial: Sachsenplatz 4, 1201 WIEN
Tel: 1 3302415285 **Fax:** 1 3302426260
Email: renate.hoehl@springer.at **Web site:** http://www.springer.at
Freq: 8 issues yearly; **Circ:** 4,000
Editor: Gerwin V. Arnetzi
Profile: Journal about dentistry and oral hygiene.
Language(s): German
Readership: Aimed at those in the dental profession.
ADVERTISING RATES:
Full Page Colour .... EUR 2025
Mechanical Data: Type Area: 270 x 170 mm
BUSINESS: HEALTH & MEDICAL: Dental

STRASSENGÜTERVERKEHR 743563A49C-1
Editorial: Wiedner Hauptstr. 120, 1051 WIEN
Tel: 1 54664324 **Fax:** 1 5466450324
Email: m.dittrich@wirtschaftsverlag.at **Web site:** http://www.strassengueterverkehr.at
Freq: Monthly; **Annual Sub.:** EUR 60,00; **Circ:** 13,325
Editor: Marco Dittrich; **Advertising Manager:** Dieter Köllner-Gürsch
Profile: Journal about freight traffic.
Language(s): German
ADVERTISING RATES:
Full Page Mono .... EUR 3579
Full Page Colour .... EUR 5112
Mechanical Data: Type Area: 255 x 185 mm
Official Journal of: Organ d. Fachverb. u. d. Fachgruppen d. Güterbeförderungsgewerbes
BUSINESS: TRANSPORT: Freight

STYLE IN PROGRESS 743841A74B-1
Editorial: Salzweg 17, 5081 ANIF **Tel:** 6246 897999
Fax: 6246 897989
Email: stephan@ucm-verlag.at **Web site:** http://www.ucm-verlag.at
Freq: Quarterly; **Circ:** 10,200
Editor: Stephan Huber; **Advertising Manager:** Stephan Huber
Profile: Women's interest magazine focusing on fashion.
Language(s): German
Readership: Aimed at women.
ADVERTISING RATES:
Full Page Mono .... EUR 6320
Full Page Colour .... EUR 6320
Mechanical Data: Type Area: 300 x 220 mm
CONSUMER: WOMEN'S INTEREST CONSUMER MAGAZINES: Women's Interest - Fashion

STYLE IN PROGRESS 1739800A74B-3
Editorial: Salzweg 17, 5081 ANIF **Tel:** 6246 897999
Fax: 6246 897989
Email: stephan@ucm-verlag.at **Web site:** http://www.ucm-verlag.at
Freq: Quarterly; **Circ:** 7,900
Editor: Stephan Huber; **Advertising Manager:** Stephan Huber
Profile: Women's interest magazine focusing on fashion.
Language(s): English
ADVERTISING RATES:
Full Page Mono .... EUR 6320
Full Page Colour .... EUR 6320
Mechanical Data: Type Area: 300 x 220 mm

SÜDWIND 743960A82-3200
Editorial: Laudongasse 40, 1080 WIEN
Tel: 1 4055515 **Fax:** 1 4055519
Email: suedwind.magazin@suedwind.at **Web site:** http://www.suedwind-magazin.at
Freq: 10 issues yearly; **Annual Sub.:** EUR 38,00; **Circ:** 8,000
Editor: Irmgard Strach-Kirchner; **Advertising Manager:** Thomas Divis
Profile: Magazine containing information about political, economic, social and cultural development.
Language(s): German
Readership: Aimed at academics.
ADVERTISING RATES:
Full Page Mono .... EUR 1165
Full Page Colour .... EUR 1165
Mechanical Data: Type Area: 276 x 198 mm
Copy instructions: *Copy Date:* 21 days prior to publication
CONSUMER: CURRENT AFFAIRS & POLITICS

SVA AKTUELL 744063A1H-1
Editorial: Wiedner Hauptstr. 84, 1050 WIEN
Tel: 1 546543466
Email: gerhard.schumlits@svagw.at **Web site:** http://esv-sva.sozvers.at
Freq: Quarterly; **Circ:** 500,000
Editor: Gerhard Schumlits
Profile: Journal containing information about pensions and sickness benefit.
Language(s): German
BUSINESS: FINANCE & ECONOMICS: Pensions

S.W. SALZBURGER WIRTSCHAFT 740996A63-320
Editorial: Julius-Raab-Platz 1, 5027 SALZBURG
Tel: 662 8888345 **Fax:** 662 8888388
Email: salzburger-wirtschaft@wks.at **Web site:** http://wko.at/sbg
Freq: 42 issues yearly; Free to qualifying individuals
Annual Sub.: EUR 61,80; **Circ:** 35,805
Editor: Kurt Oberholzer
Profile: Journal of the Salzburg Chamber of Commerce.
Language(s): German
ADVERTISING RATES:
Full Page Mono .... EUR 2490
Full Page Colour .... EUR 3362
Mechanical Data: Type Area: 256 x 202 mm, No. of Columns (Display): 4, Col Widths (Display): 46 mm
Copy instructions: *Copy Date:* 3 days prior to publication
BUSINESS: REGIONAL BUSINESS

SWI STEUER & WIRTSCHAFT INTERNATIONAL 744128A1M-1
Editorial: Scheydgasse 24, 1210 WIEN **Tel:** 1 246300
Fax: 1 2463051
Email: redaktion@lindeverlag.at **Web site:** http://www.swi.at
Freq: Monthly; **Annual Sub.:** EUR 226,80; **Circ:** 4,000
Editor: Michael Lang; **Advertising Manager:** Regina Erben-Hartig
Profile: Tax and international business review.
Language(s): English; German
ADVERTISING RATES:
Full Page Mono .... EUR 999
Full Page Colour .... EUR 1600
Mechanical Data: Type Area: 207 x 135 mm, No. of Columns (Display): 1, Col Widths (Display): 135 mm
Copy instructions: *Copy Date:* 14 days prior to publication
BUSINESS: FINANCE & ECONOMICS: Taxation

SWK STEUER- UND WIRTSCHAFTSKARTEI 744129A14A-2000
Editorial: Scheydgasse 24, 1210 WIEN **Tel:** 1 246300
Fax: 1 2463051
Email: redaktion@lindeverlag.at **Web site:** http://www.swk.at
Freq: 36 issues yearly; **Annual Sub.:** EUR 309,90; **Circ:** 19,000
Editor: Eleonore Breitegger; **Advertising Manager:** Gabriele Hladik
Profile: Magazine focusing on finance, the economy and related legislation.
Language(s): German
Readership: Aimed at government officials, economics students and people working within the financial field.
ADVERTISING RATES:
Full Page Mono .... EUR 1978
Full Page Colour .... EUR 2554
Mechanical Data: Type Area: 207 x 135 mm, No. of Columns (Display): 1, Col Widths (Display): 135 mm
Copy instructions: *Copy Date:* 14 days prior to publication
BUSINESS: COMMERCE, INDUSTRY & MANAGEMENT

TAI TOURISMUSWIRTSCHAFT AUSTRIA & INTERNATIONAL 745226A50-320
Editorial: Weyrgasse 8/9, 1030 WIEN **Tel:** 1 5888150
Fax: 1 5888166
Email: verlag@tai.at **Web site:** http://www.tai.at
Freq: Weekly; **Annual Sub.:** EUR 72,00; **Circ:** 12,800
Editor: Christopher Norden; **Advertising Manager:** Gabriela Reichkendler
Profile: International magazine about leisure and business travel, tourism, hotel and guesthouse accommodation.
Language(s): German
Readership: Aimed at hotels, the catering trade, technical colleges, travel agencies, airports and international transport authorities.
ADVERTISING RATES:
Full Page Mono .... EUR 3800
Full Page Colour .... EUR 4800
Mechanical Data: Type Area: 407 x 272 mm, No. of Columns (Display): 5, Col Widths (Display): 52 mm
Copy instructions: *Copy Date:* 5 days prior to publication
BUSINESS: TRAVEL & TOURISM

TBA - (AUSG. ÖSTERR.) 1744711A76D-1185
Editorial: Favoritenstr. 4/10, 1040 WIEN
Tel: 1 9076766 **Fax:** 1 907676699
Email: office@tba-online.cc **Web site:** http://www.tba-online.cc
Freq: 11 issues yearly; **Annual Sub.:** EUR 15,00; **Circ:** 40,000
Editor: Thomas Heher; **Advertising Manager:** Thomas Weber
Language(s): German
ADVERTISING RATES:
Full Page Mono .... EUR 2200
Full Page Colour .... EUR 2200
Mechanical Data: Type Area: 260 x 190 mm
Supplement(s): GamingXP
CONSUMER: MUSIC & PERFORMING ARTS: Music

TECHNIK REPORT 1623556A14R-893
Editorial: Dresdner Str. 45, 1200 WIEN
Tel: 1 97000242 **Fax:** 1 970005242
Email: stefan.lenz@weka.at **Web site:** http://www.technikreport.at
Freq: 10 issues yearly; **Annual Sub.:** EUR 51,00; **Circ:** 8,573
Editor: Stefan Lenz; **Advertising Manager:** Mario Weber
Language(s): German
ADVERTISING RATES:
Full Page Colour .... EUR 4930
Mechanical Data: Type Area: 270 x 190 mm
BUSINESS: COMMERCE, INDUSTRY & MANAGEMENT: Commerce Related

TELE 744408A72-8190_700
Editorial: Lothringerstr. 14, 1030 WIEN **Tel:** 1 605900
Fax: 1 6059041
Email: redaktion@tele.at **Web site:** http://www.tele.at
Freq: Weekly; **Circ:** 1,215,281
Editor: Dieter Hauptmann; **Advertising Manager:** Hans Metzger
Profile: TV listings guide with features on celebrities and programmes.
Language(s): German
ADVERTISING RATES:
Full Page Mono .... EUR 31400
Full Page Colour .... EUR 31400
Mechanical Data: Type Area: 240 x 182 mm
Copy instructions: *Copy Date:* 12 days prior to publication
Supplement to: Badener Zeitung, Die Furche, Kleine Zeitung, Neue BVZ Eisenstadt, Neue BVZ Güssing/Jennersdorf, Neue BVZ Mattersburg, Neue BVZ Neusiedl, Neue BVZ Oberpullendorf, Neue BVZ Oberwart OZ Oberwarter Zeitung, Die neue Pinzgauer Post, Neues Volksblatt, Neue Vorarlberger Tageszeitung, NÖN Amstettner Zeitung, NÖN Baden/Bad Vöslau, NÖN Brucker Grenzbote, NÖN Erlaftal-Bote, NÖN Gmünder Zeitung, NÖN Herzogenburg-Traismauer, NÖN Hollabrunn, NÖN Horn-Eggenburg, NÖN Klosterneuburg, NÖN Korneuburg-Stockerau, NÖN Kremser Zeitung/Kamptal, NÖN Melker Zeitung, NÖN Mistelbach, NÖN Neunkirchen, NÖN Pielachtal, NÖN Purkersdorf, NÖN St. Pöltner Zeitung, NÖN Schwechat-Fischamend, NÖN Tullner Bezirksnachrichten, NÖN Waidhofner Zeitung, NÖN Wr. Neustädter Zeitung, NÖN Wienerwald, NÖN Ybbstal Zeitung Bote von der Ybbs, OÖ Nachrichten, Die Presse, Salzburger Nachrichten, Der Standard, SVZ Salzburger Volkszeitung, Tiroler Tageszeitung, VN Vorarlberger Nachrichten
LOCAL NEWSPAPERS

TELEKOM + IT REPORT 744432A18B-583
Editorial: Nattergasse 4, 1170 WIEN **Tel:** 1 902990
Fax: 1 9029937
Email: szelgrad@report.at **Web site:** http://www.report.at
Freq: 9 issues yearly; **Annual Sub.:** EUR 40,00; **Circ:** 13,000
Editor: Martin Szelgrad
Profile: Magazine containing information and advice about purchasing video equipment. Also includes features on mobile telecommunications and the Internet. Provides product reviews, tests and tips.
Language(s): German
ADVERTISING RATES:
Full Page Colour .... EUR 5300
Mechanical Data: Type Area: 253 x 175 mm
Copy instructions: *Copy Date:* 7 days prior to publication
Supplement to: Report (+) Plus
BUSINESS: ELECTRONICS: Telecommunications

TGA TECHNISCHE GEBÄUDEAUSRÜSTUNG 744529A4E-1291
Editorial: Dresdner Str. 45, 1200 WIEN
Tel: 1 97000233 **Fax:** 1 970005233
Email: barbara.fuerst@weka.at **Web site:** http://www.tga.at
Freq: 10 issues yearly; **Annual Sub.:** EUR 51,00; **Circ:** 10,100
Editor: Barbara Fürst-Jaklitsch; **Advertising Manager:** Marianne Schmidt
Profile: Journal for purchasers and operators of technical building equipment, manufacturers, designers and constructors.
Language(s): German
Readership: Aimed at architects, town planners, installers, builders and owners of large companies such as banks, shopping centres and cinemas.
ADVERTISING RATES:
Full Page Colour .... EUR 4700
Mechanical Data: Type Area: 270 x 190 mm
Official Journal of: Organ d. Österr. Kälte- u. Klimatechn. Vereins
BUSINESS: ARCHITECTURE & BUILDING: Building

TIPS FREISTADT 1645257A72-7406
Editorial: Eisengasse 5, 4240 FREISTADT
Tel: 7942 74100864 **Fax:** 7942 74100860
Email: tips-freistadt@tips.at **Web site:** http://www.tips.at
Freq: Weekly; **Cover Price:** Free; **Circ:** 25,500
Editor: Claudia Mayrhofer
Profile: Advertising journal (house-to-house) concentrating on local stories. Faceook: http://www.facebook.com/tips.at.
Language(s): German
ADVERTISING RATES:
Full Page Colour .... EUR 1570
Mechanical Data: Type Area: 262 x 196 mm, No. of Columns (Display): 6, Col Widths (Display): 31 mm
Copy instructions: *Copy Date:* 6 days prior to publication
LOCAL NEWSPAPERS

TIPS LINZ 1645271A72-7409
Editorial: Promenade 23, 4010 LINZ
Tel: 732 7895300 **Fax:** 732 785955
Email: tips-linz@tips.at **Web site:** http://www.tips.at
Freq: Weekly; **Cover Price:** Free; **Circ:** 142,400
Editor: Josef Gruber; **Advertising Manager:** Thomas Frühwirth
Profile: Advertising journal (house-to-house) concentrating on local stories. Faceook: http://www.facebook.com/tips.at.
Language(s): German
ADVERTISING RATES:
Full Page Colour .... EUR 4710
Mechanical Data: Type Area: 262 x 196 mm, No. of Columns (Display): 6, Col Widths (Display): 31 mm
Copy instructions: *Copy Date:* 6 days prior to publication
LOCAL NEWSPAPERS

TIPS VÖCKLABRUCK 1645273A72-7411
Editorial: Stadtplatz 37, 4840 VÖCKLABRUCK
Tel: 7672 7850680 **Fax:** 7672 78883
Email: tips-vbruck@tips.at **Web site:** http://www.tips.at
Freq: Weekly; **Cover Price:** Free; **Circ:** 53,200
Editor: Wolfgang Macherhammer
Profile: Advertising journal (house-to-house) concentrating on local stories. Faceook: http://www.facebook.com/tips.at.
Language(s): German
ADVERTISING RATES:
Full Page Colour .... EUR 2810
Mechanical Data: Type Area: 262 x 196 mm, No. of Columns (Display): 6, Col Widths (Display): 31 mm

Copy instructions: *Copy Date:* 6 days prior to publication
LOCAL NEWSPAPERS

TIROLER TAGESZEITUNG
745000A67B-1520
Editorial: Ing.-Etzel-Str. 30, 6021 INNSBRUCK
Tel: 504031600 **Fax:** 50403543
Email: redaktion@tt.com **Web site:** http://www.tt.com
Freq: 260 issues yearly
Editor: Mario Zenhäusern; **Advertising Manager:** Max Hafele
Profile: Regional daily newspaper covering politics, economics, sport, travel, technology and the arts.
Language(s): German
ADVERTISING RATES:
SCC .... EUR 206,90
Mechanical Data: Type Area: 430 x 284 mm, No. of Columns (Display): 8, Col Widths (Display): 32 mm
Copy instructions: *Copy Date:* 1 day prior to publication
Supplement(s): Gesund in Tirol; Mode und Mehr; The Red Bulletin; 6020; 6020 Extra; tele; TT Magazin; Uhren Schmuck Magazin; wissenswert
REGIONAL DAILY & SUNDAY NEWSPAPERS: Regional Daily Newspapers

TIROLER WIRTSCHAFT
745002A63-380
Editorial: Meinhardstr. 14, 6020 INNSBRUCK
Tel: 5909051482 **Fax:** 5909051461
Email: presse@wktirol.at **Web site:** http://www.tirolerwirtschaft.at
Freq: 26 issues yearly; **Cover Price:** Free; **Circ:** 41,102
Editor: Claus Meinert
Profile: Magazine of the Tyrol Chamber of Commerce.
Language(s): German
Readership: Aimed at employees of Wirtschaftskammer Tirol.
ADVERTISING RATES:
Full Page Colour .... EUR 9030
Mechanical Data: Type Area: 430 x 284 mm, No. of Columns (Display): 6, Col Widths (Display): 44 mm
Copy instructions: *Copy Date:* 7 days prior to publication
BUSINESS: REGIONAL BUSINESS

TIROLERIN
744995A74A-760
Editorial: Industriezone C6, 6166 FULPMES
Tel: 5225 63921 **Fax:** 5225 64196
Email: redaktion@tirolerin.at **Web site:** http://www.tirolerin.at
Freq: 10 issues yearly; **Annual Sub.:** EUR 22,00; **Circ:** 30,000
Editor: Christoph Ebead; **Advertising Manager:** Peter Schattanek
Profile: Regional magazine for the Tyrol area.
Language(s): German
Readership: Aimed at women living in the Tyrol.
ADVERTISING RATES:
Full Page Mono .... EUR 3780
Full Page Colour .... EUR 3780
Mechanical Data: Type Area: 260 x 190 mm
Copy instructions: *Copy Date:* 28 days prior to publication
CONSUMER: WOMEN'S INTEREST CONSUMER MAGAZINES: Women's Interest

TISCHLER JOURNAL
745008A46-100
Editorial: Wiedner Hauptstr. 120, 1051 WIEN
Tel: 1 54664352 **Fax:** 1 5466450352
Email: h.siebenbuerger@wirtschaftsverlag.at **Web site:** http://www.tischlerjournal.at
Freq: 11 issues yearly; **Annual Sub.:** EUR 70,00; **Circ:** 7,092
Editor: Harald Siebenbürger; **Advertising Manager:** Franz-Michael Seidl
Profile: Official publication of the Austrian Association of Carpenters.
Language(s): German
ADVERTISING RATES:
Full Page Mono .... EUR 2435
Full Page Colour .... EUR 3480
Mechanical Data: Type Area: 255 x 185 mm
Official Journal of: Organ d. Bundesinnung u. d. Landesinnung d. Tischler
BUSINESS: TIMBER, WOOD & FORESTRY

TOP AGRAR ÖSTERREICH
765400A21A-1447
Editorial: Südstadtzentrum 1/14/1, 2344 MARIA ENZERSDORF **Tel:** 2236 2870016
Fax: 2236 2870010
Email: redaktion@lv-topagrar.at **Web site:** http://www.topagrar.at
Freq: Monthly; **Circ:** 15,000
Editor: Torsten Altmann; **Advertising Manager:** Peter Wiggers
Profile: Agricultural journal for Austria.
Language(s): German
ADVERTISING RATES:
Full Page Mono .... EUR 1344
Full Page Colour .... EUR 2176
Mechanical Data: Type Area: 270 x 190 mm, No. of Columns (Display): 4, Col Widths (Display): 46 mm
Copy instructions: *Copy Date:* 20 days prior to publication

TOP GEWINN
745153A14A-2040
Editorial: Stiftgasse 31, 1071 WIEN **Tel:** 1 5212448
Fax: 1 5212430
Email: g.wailand@gewinn.com **Web site:** http://www.gewinn.com
Freq: 11 issues yearly; **Annual Sub.:** EUR 34,00; **Circ:** 45,000
Editor: Georg Wailand; **Advertising Manager:** Herbert Scheiblauer
Profile: Magazine containing information about recent business topics.
Language(s): German
ADVERTISING RATES:
Full Page Mono .... EUR 4420
Full Page Colour .... EUR 7735
Mechanical Data: Type Area: 250 x 185 mm

TOPGEBRAUCHTE.AT
1655358A49A-588
Editorial: Dresdner Str. 45, 1200 WIEN
Tel: 1 97000100 **Fax:** 1 970005100
Email: michael.watson@weka.at **Web site:** http://www.weka.at
Circ: 26,400
Advertising Manager: Michael Watson
Profile: Magazine about buying and selling used building equipment, pallet carriers, hoisting engines, commercial vehicles and vans.
Language(s): German
Supplement to: BBB Baumaschine Baugerät Baustelle, Traktuell
BUSINESS: TRANSPORT

TOPTIMES
764063A75A-801
Editorial: Belgiergasse 3, 8020 GRAZ
Tel: 316 903312780 **Fax:** 316 903312764
Email: gerhard.polzer@toptimes.at **Web site:** http://www.sport10.at
Freq: 6 issues yearly; **Annual Sub.:** EUR 12,90; **Circ:** 76,000
Editor: Gerhard Polzer; **Advertising Manager:** Bertram Taferner
Profile: The magazine is counselor and coach for all people in Austria who want to achieve through regular exercise, by amateur sports and fitness activities quality of life. The magazine offers technically sound reports on the topics of fitness, running, biking, golf, outdoor and other amateur sports. In addition, presents the title in the special section "Mittendrin" the biggest event platform for amateur sports in Austria.
Language(s): German
ADVERTISING RATES:
Full Page Mono .... EUR 7200
Full Page Colour .... EUR 720
Mechanical Data: Type Area: 280 x 200 mm
CONSUMER: SPORT

TOURISMUS INTERN
1996359A50-385
Editorial: Landhausplatz 1, 3109 ST. PÖLTEN
Tel: 2742 900516764
Email: d.mayer@noel.gv.at **Web site:** http://www.niederoesterreich.at
Freq: Quarterly; **Cover Price:** Free; **Circ:** 3,220
Editor: Doris Mayer
Profile: Magazine on tourism and for the leisure time business.
Language(s): German

TRAINING
745263A14A-2060
Editorial: Tautenhayngasse 21/3, 1150 WIEN
Tel: 1 786378114 **Fax:** 1 786378119
Email: wirl@magazintraining.at **Web site:** http://www.magazintraining.at
Freq: 8 issues yearly; **Annual Sub.:** EUR 35,00; **Circ:** 16,500
Editor: Eva Selan; **Advertising Manager:** Christine Wirl
Profile: Magazine for personnel developers, educational purchasing agents and trainers.
Language(s): German
ADVERTISING RATES:
Full Page Colour .... EUR 2800
Mechanical Data: Type Area: 260 x 188 mm, No. of Columns (Display): 3, Col Widths (Display): 60 mm

TRAKTUELL
731650A49A-300
Editorial: Dresdner Str. 45, 1200 WIEN
Tel: 1 97000180 **Fax:** 1 970005180
Email: florian.engel@weka.at **Web site:** http://www.traktuell.at
Freq: 10 issues yearly; **Annual Sub.:** EUR 30,00; **Circ:** 14,870
Editor: Florian Engel; **Advertising Manager:** Andreas Übelbacher
Profile: International publication mainly covering road transport, freight and commercial vehicles, but which also includes items on containerisation and shipping.
Language(s): German
ADVERTISING RATES:
Full Page Colour .... EUR 4995
Mechanical Data: Type Area: 260 x 185 mm
Official Journal of: Organ d. Organsiation "Truck of the Year" u. "Van of the Year"
Supplement(s): topgebrauchte.at
BUSINESS: TRANSPORT

TRANSFER
745281A2A-740
Editorial: Augasse 2, 1090 WIEN **Tel:** 1 313364617
Fax: 1 3176699
Email: guenter.schweiger@wu-wien.ac.at **Web site:** http://www.transfer-zeitschrift.net
Freq: Quarterly; Free to qualifying individuals
Annual Sub.: EUR 65,00; **Circ:** 5,500
Editor: Günter Schweiger; **Advertising Manager:** Thomas Biruhs
Profile: Information about advertising research.
Language(s): German
ADVERTISING RATES:
Full Page Mono .... EUR 2500
Full Page Colour .... EUR 2500
Mechanical Data: Type Area: 237 x 175 mm

TRANSPARENT
745292A81A-200
Editorial: Radetzkystr. 21, 1030 WIEN
Tel: 1 7130823 **Fax:** 1 713082310
Email: transparent@chello.at **Web site:** http://www.tierversuchsgegner.at
Freq: Quarterly; Free to qualifying individuals
Annual Sub.: EUR 6,54; **Circ:** 18,000
Editor: Gerda Matias
Profile: Anti-vivisection magazine.
Language(s): German
Readership: Read by members of anti-vivisection groups and those campaigning for animal rights.
ADVERTISING RATES:
Full Page Mono .... EUR 1497
Mechanical Data: Type Area: 257 x 190 mm
Copy instructions: *Copy Date:* 16 days prior to publication
CONSUMER: ANIMALS & PETS: Animals & Pets Protection

TRAVEL GUIDE
745314A89A-420
Editorial: Pillergasse 13/34, 1150 WIEN
Tel: 1 897486015 **Fax:** 1 897486022
Email: angermayr@mediamed.at **Web site:** http://www.myguides.at
Freq: Half-yearly; **Cover Price:** Free; **Circ:** 100,000
Editor: Nikolaus Angermayr; **Advertising Manager:** Nikolaus Angermayr
Profile: Travel guide.
Language(s): German
ADVERTISING RATES:
Full Page Mono .... EUR 4250
Full Page Colour .... EUR 4250
Mechanical Data: Type Area: 178 x 120 mm

TRAVELLER
745317A50-340
Editorial: Brunner Feldstr. 45, 2380 PERCHTOLDSDORF **Tel:** 1 86648435
Fax: 1 86648430
Email: redaktion@traveller-online.at **Web site:** http://www.traveller-online.at
Freq: Weekly; **Annual Sub.:** EUR 44,00; **Circ:** 8,500
Editor: Christa Oppenauer; **Advertising Manager:** Andreas Lorenz
Profile: Magazine for the tourism business in Austria.
Language(s): German
ADVERTISING RATES:
Full Page Mono .... EUR 2200
Full Page Colour .... EUR 3600
Mechanical Data: Type Area: 257 x 190 mm, No. of Columns (Display): 4, Col Widths (Display): 43 mm
Copy instructions: *Copy Date:* 4 days prior to publication

TRAVELLER
745317A50-373
Editorial: Brunner Feldstr. 45, 2380 PERCHTOLDSDORF **Tel:** 1 86648435
Fax: 1 86648430
Email: redaktion@traveller-online.at **Web site:** http://www.traveller-online.at
Freq: Weekly; **Annual Sub.:** EUR 44,00; **Circ:** 8,500
Editor: Christa Oppenauer; **Advertising Manager:** Andreas Lorenz
Profile: Magazine for the tourism business in Austria.
Language(s): German
ADVERTISING RATES:
Full Page Mono .... EUR 2200
Full Page Colour .... EUR 3600
Mechanical Data: Type Area: 257 x 190 mm, No. of Columns (Display): 4, Col Widths (Display): 43 mm
Copy instructions: *Copy Date:* 4 days prior to publication

TREFFNER GEMEINDEZEITUNG
745331A72-6720
Editorial: Marktplatz 2, 9521 TREFFEN
Tel: 4248 2805 **Fax:** 434248 280525
Email: treffen@ktn.gde.at **Web site:** http://www.treffen.at
Freq: 6 issues yearly; **Cover Price:** Free; **Circ:** 2,020
Editor: Helga Mayer
Profile: Newspaper for the Treffner region.
Language(s): German
ADVERTISING RATES:
Full Page Colour .... EUR 524
Mechanical Data: Type Area: 290 x 190 mm
LOCAL NEWSPAPERS

TREFFPUNKT WIR SENIOREN
747551A74N-280
Editorial: Obere Donaulände 7, 4010 LINZ
Tel: 732 775311712 **Fax:** 732 775311719
Email: wolfgang.lennert@ooe-seniorenbund.at **Web site:** http://www.ooe-seniorenbund.at
Freq: 10 issues yearly; **Circ:** 57,000
Editor: Wolfgang Lennert
Profile: Magazine of the Austrian Pensioners' Association.
Language(s): German
Readership: Read by senior citizens.
ADVERTISING RATES:
Full Page Mono .... EUR 3075
Full Page Colour .... EUR 3075
Mechanical Data: Type Area: 242 x 184 mm
CONSUMER: WOMEN'S INTEREST CONSUMER MAGAZINES: Retirement

TREND
745355A14A-2100
Editorial: Hainburger Str. 33, 1030 WIEN
Tel: 1 534703401 **Fax:** 1 534703410
Email: redaktion@trend.at **Web site:** http://www.trend.at
Freq: Monthly; **Annual Sub.:** EUR 44,90; **Circ:** 59,917
Editor: Stefan Klasmann; **Advertising Manager:** Wolfgang Kröll
Profile: Business and economics magazine.
Language(s): German
ADVERTISING RATES:
Full Page Mono .... EUR 12290
Full Page Colour .... EUR 12290
Mechanical Data: Type Area: 250 x 185 mm
Copy instructions: *Copy Date:* 21 days prior to publication
Supplement(s): trend Bestseller Medien spezial; trend Invest
BUSINESS: COMMERCE, INDUSTRY & MANAGEMENT

TRUCKER EXPRESS
745426A49D-125
Editorial: Wiedner Hauptstr. 120, 1051 WIEN
Tel: 1 54664322 **Fax:** 1 54664520
Email: trucker@wirtschaftsverlag.at **Web site:** http://www.automotive.co.at
Freq: Quarterly; **Cover Price:** Free; **Circ:** 23,500
Editor: Christina Andetsberger; **Advertising Manager:** Silvia Ruess
Profile: Magazine containing articles about trucks and truck driving.
Language(s): German
ADVERTISING RATES:
Full Page Colour .... EUR 2180
Mechanical Data: Type Area: 271 x 195 mm, No. of Columns (Display): 3, Col Widths (Display): 59 mm
Copy instructions: *Copy Date:* 21 days prior to publication
BUSINESS: TRANSPORT: Commercial Vehicles

TRUPPENDIENST
745438A40-600
Editorial: Rossauer Lände 1, 1090 WIEN
Tel: 502011031901 **Fax:** 502011017120
Email: truppendienst@bmlv.gv.at **Web site:** http://www.bmlv.gv.at/truppendienst/ausgaben/archiv.php
Freq: 6 issues yearly; **Annual Sub.:** EUR 26,00; **Circ:** 14,500
Editor: Jörg Aschenbrenner; **Advertising Manager:** Erwin Krall
Profile: Magazine about training in the Austrian army.
Language(s): German

TV DABEI
724760A76C-20
Editorial: Heiligenstädter Str. 121, 1190 WIEN
Tel: 1 29160252 **Fax:** 1 2916071
Email: a.duenhofen@dgw.at **Web site:** http://www.ganzewoche.at
Freq: Weekly; **Circ:** 400,000
Editor: Anna Dünhofen
Profile: TV programme supplement.
Language(s): German
ADVERTISING RATES:
Full Page Colour .... EUR 10000
Mechanical Data: Type Area: 180 x 230 mm
Copy instructions: *Copy Date:* 10 days prior to publication
Supplement to: Die ganze Woche
CONSUMER: MUSIC & PERFORMING ARTS: TV & Radio

TW ZEITSCHRIFT FÜR TOURISMUSWISSENSCHAFT
2036577A50-388
Editorial: Rudolfskai 42, 5020 SALZBURG
Tel: 662 80444109
Email: reinhard.bachleitner@sbg.ac.at **Web site:** http://www.zeitschriftarbeit.de
Freq: Half-yearly; Free to qualifying individuals
Annual Sub.: EUR 74,00; **Circ:** 300
Editor: Reinhard Bachleitner
Profile: The Journal of Tourism Research will focus on multidisciplinary and interdisciplinary questions about tourist phenomena. It is aimed at researchers and practitioners in equal measure, require sound information to the tourism-related problems.
Language(s): German
ADVERTISING RATES:
Full Page Mono .... EUR 380
Mechanical Data: Type Area: 195 x 120 mm

UG UNSERE GENERATION
739764A74N-100
Editorial: Gentzgasse 129, 1180 WIEN
Tel: 1 3137230 **Fax:** 1 3137278
Email: andy.wohlmuth@pvoe.at **Web site:** http://www.pvoe.at
Freq: 10 issues yearly; **Cover Price:** EUR 1,80,; **Circ:** 245,328
Editor: Andy Wohlmuth
Profile: Magazine for the elderly containing information, service and advice on wellness and leisure.
Language(s): German
ADVERTISING RATES:
Full Page Colour .... EUR 10500
Mechanical Data: Type Area: 252 x 187 mm, No. of Columns (Display): 3, Col Widths (Display): 60 mm
Copy instructions: *Copy Date:* 20 days prior to publication
Supplement(s): P Wir > 50
CONSUMER: WOMEN'S INTEREST CONSUMER MAGAZINES: Retirement

UHREN & JUWELEN
745659A52A-1
Editorial: Brunner Feldstr. 45, 2380 PERCHTOLDSDORF **Tel:** 1 86648219
Fax: 1 86648100
Email: b.medlin@manstein.at **Web site:** http://www.uhrenundjuwelen.at
Freq: 10 issues yearly; **Annual Sub.:** EUR 80,00; **Circ:** 3,680
Editor: Brigitte Medlin; **Advertising Manager:** Petra Gether-Schlacher
Profile: Journal of the Austrian watch, clock and jewellery trade.
Language(s): German
ADVERTISING RATES:
Full Page Mono .... EUR 3300
Full Page Colour .... EUR 3300
Mechanical Data: Type Area: 258 x 202 mm
BUSINESS: GIFT TRADE: Jewellery

ULTIMO
745685A74F-2
Editorial: Glockengasse 4c, 5020 SALZBURG
Tel: 662 849291 **Fax:** 662 84929116
Email: ultimo@akzente.net **Web site:** http://www.akzente.net
Freq: Quarterly; **Cover Price:** Free; **Circ:** 44,000
Editor: Marietta Oberrauch; **Advertising Manager:** Marietta Oberrauch
Profile: Magazine about Salzburg and the surrounding area.
Language(s): German
Readership: Aimed at people in the 15-21 age bracket in the Salzburg area.
CONSUMER: WOMEN'S INTEREST CONSUMER MAGAZINES: Teenage

UMWELT JOURNAL
745718A57-1000
Editorial: Geblergasse 95, 1170 WIEN
Tel: 1 906801126 **Fax:** 1 9068091199
Email: renate.storz@schendl.at **Web site:** http://www.umweltjournal.at
Freq: 8 issues yearly; **Annual Sub.:** EUR 15,40; **Circ:** 19,000
Editor: Renate Storz
Profile: Newspaper covering science, the environment, nature and related industrial matters.
Language(s): German
Readership: Aimed at the building and construction industry and the local authorities.
ADVERTISING RATES:
Full Page Mono .... EUR 3887
Full Page Colour .... EUR 4319
Mechanical Data: Type Area: 420 x 270 mm, No. of Columns (Display): 6, Col Widths (Display): 41 mm
BUSINESS: ENVIRONMENT & POLLUTION

UMWELTFORUM PRESSBAUM
1752686A57-1156
Editorial: Kaiserbrunnstr. 73, 3021 PRESSBAUM
Tel: 2233 55070 **Fax:** 2233 55070
Email: peter.samec@gruene.at **Web site:** http://www.ufo-pressbaum.at
Freq: Half-yearly; **Cover Price:** Free; **Circ:** 3,000
Editor: Sabine Pfau
Profile: Newspaper from the Political Party Die Grünen, section Pressbaum.
Language(s): German
Copy instructions: *Copy Date:* 30 days prior to publication

UMWELTSCHUTZ
745730A57-1040
Editorial: Leberstr. 122, 1110 WIEN **Tel:** 1 74095476
Fax: 1 74095497
Email: lisbeth.klein@bohmann.at **Web site:** http://www.umweltschutz.co.at
Freq: 6 issues yearly; **Annual Sub.:** EUR 35,10; **Circ:** 14,000
Editor: Lisbeth Klein; **Advertising Manager:** Fiala Scheherezade
Profile: Journal focusing on news, trends and developments in the environmental field.
Language(s): German
ADVERTISING RATES:
Full Page Mono .... EUR 4180
Full Page Colour .... EUR 5570
Mechanical Data: Type Area: 250 x 185 mm, No. of Columns (Display): 4, Col Widths (Display): 43 mm
BUSINESS: ENVIRONMENT & POLLUTION

UNISONO PLUS
745803A83-1140
Editorial: Universitätsstr. 65, 9020 KLAGENFURT
Tel: 463 27003901 **Fax:** 463 27009399
Email: lydia.kroemer@uni-klu.ac.at **Web site:** http://www.uni-klu.ac.at/unisonoonline
Freq: Quarterly; **Cover Price:** Free; **Circ:** 9,500
Editor: Lydia Krömer; **Advertising Manager:** Elfriede Steiner
Profile: Journal of Klagenfurt University.
Language(s): English; German
Mechanical Data: Type Area: 287 x 210 mm
Copy instructions: *Copy Date:* 15 days prior to publication
CONSUMER: STUDENT PUBLICATIONS

UNIVERSUM
745845A73-300
Editorial: Linke Wienzeile 40/2/22, 1060 WIEN
Tel: 1 5855757301 **Fax:** 1 5855757333
Email: juergen.hatzenbichler@lwmedia.at **Web site:** http://www.universum.co.at
Freq: 10 issues yearly; **Annual Sub.:** EUR 42,00; **Circ:** 42,000
Editor: Oliver Lehmann; **Advertising Manager:** Alexandra Salvinetti
Profile: Magazine covering the protection of wildlife and all natural history and conservation subjects.
Language(s): German
Readership: Aimed at young people.
ADVERTISING RATES:
Full Page Mono .... EUR 5690
Full Page Colour .... EUR 5690
Mechanical Data: Type Area: 240 x 184 mm
Copy instructions: *Copy Date:* 14 days prior to publication
Supplement(s): Das Naturhistorische
CONSUMER: NATIONAL & INTERNATIONAL PERIODICALS

UNIVERSUM INNERE MEDIZIN
1646185A56A-1947
Editorial: Seidengasse 9/1/1, 1070 WIEN
Tel: 1 407311115 **Fax:** 1 4073114
Email: g.kahlhammer@medmedia.at **Web site:** http://www.medmedia.at
Freq: 10 issues yearly; **Circ:** 10,393
Editor: Peter Fasching; **Advertising Manager:** Elisabeth Hönigschnabel
Profile: Magazine for physical doctors.
Language(s): German
ADVERTISING RATES:
Full Page Colour .... EUR 3020
Mechanical Data: Type Area: 297 x 210 mm
BUSINESS: HEALTH & MEDICAL

UNSER ATTNANG-PUCHHEIM
736844A72-4720
Editorial: Steinhüblstr. 1, 4800 ATTNANG-PUCHHEIM **Tel:** 7674 20666 **Fax:** 7674 20667
Email: office@pr-o.at **Web site:** http://www.pr-o.at
Freq: 6 issues yearly; **Cover Price:** Free; **Circ:** 4,800
Editor: Daniela Strasser
Profile: Magazine containing reports about environmental issues, sports, health, local cultural events, birth/marriages/deaths, local organisation activities and official news from the district council.
Language(s): German
Readership: Read by citizens of Attnang-Puchheim.
Mechanical Data: Type Area: 250 x 185 mm
LOCAL NEWSPAPERS

UNSER LAND
745923A21A-1340
Editorial: Wienerbergstr. 3, 1100 WIEN
Tel: 1 605155660 **Fax:** 1 605155679
Email: werner.jandl@rwa.at **Web site:** http://www.lagerhaus.at
Freq: 10 issues yearly; **Annual Sub.:** EUR 5,80; **Circ:** 115,000
Editor: Werner Jandl
Profile: Magazine about agriculture and related community matters.
Language(s): German
ADVERTISING RATES:
Full Page Colour .... EUR 7670
Mechanical Data: Type Area: 251 x 179 mm, No. of Columns (Display): 4, Col Widths (Display): 41 mm
Copy instructions: *Copy Date:* 21 days prior to publication
BUSINESS: AGRICULTURE & FARMING

UNSER LÄNDLE
745921A21J-150
Editorial: Montfortstr. 9, 6900 BREGENZ
Tel: 5574 400441 **Fax:** 5574 400600
Email: presse@lk-vbg.at **Web site:** http://www.diekammer.info
Freq: Weekly; **Annual Sub.:** EUR 35,00; **Circ:** 5,000
Editor: Bernhard Ammann
Profile: Farming journal for the Vorarlberg area.
Language(s): German
ADVERTISING RATES:
Full Page Mono .... EUR 1020
Full Page Colour .... EUR 1675
Mechanical Data: Type Area: 268 x 207 mm, No. of Columns (Display): 4, Col Widths (Display): 48 mm
Copy instructions: *Copy Date:* 4 days prior to publication
Supplement(s): BauernJournal
BUSINESS: AGRICULTURE & FARMING: Agriculture & Farming - Regional

UROLOGIK
746038A56A-1800
Editorial: Markgraf-Rüdiger-Str. 8, 1150 WIEN
Tel: 1 876795644 **Fax:** 1 876795620
Email: christian.fexa@universimed.com **Web site:** http://www.universimed.com
Freq: 5 issues yearly; **Circ:** 1,500
Editor: Christian Fexa
Profile: Magazine on urology.
Language(s): German
ADVERTISING RATES:
Full Page Mono .... EUR 2640
Full Page Colour .... EUR 2640
Mechanical Data: Type Area: 247 x 178 mm
Copy instructions: *Copy Date:* 28 days prior to publication
Official Journal of: Organ d. Berufsverb. d. Österr. Urologen
BUSINESS: HEALTH & MEDICAL

VCÖ-MAGAZIN
746108A49R-5
Editorial: Bräuhausgasse 7, 1050 WIEN
Tel: 1 8932697 **Fax:** 1 8932431
Email: christian.hoeller@vcoe.at **Web site:** http://www.vcoe.at
Freq: 6 issues yearly; Free to qualifying individuals
Annual Sub.: EUR 30,00; **Circ:** 22,000
Editor: Christian Höller; **Advertising Manager:** Christian Höller
Profile: Journal containing articles on negative effects of traffic on the environment. Gives possible solutions, both technical and political. Also covers the development of existing public transport systems.
Language(s): German
ADVERTISING RATES:
Full Page Mono .... EUR 4500
Full Page Colour .... EUR 5000
Mechanical Data: Type Area: 399 x 263 mm
Copy instructions: *Copy Date:* 21 days prior to publication
BUSINESS: TRANSPORT: Transport Related

VERKEHR
1772719A49A-595
Editorial: Leberstr. 122, 1110 WIEN **Tel:** 1 74095181
Fax: 1 74095430
Email: ernst.mueller@bohmann.at **Web site:** http://www.verkehr.co.at
Freq: Weekly; **Annual Sub.:** EUR 299,00; **Circ:** 10,000
Editor: Ernst F. Müller
Profile: Magazine covering all forms of transport and logistics.
Language(s): German
ADVERTISING RATES:
Full Page Colour .... EUR 5500
Mechanical Data: Type Area: 360 x 260 mm
Copy instructions: *Copy Date:* 10 days prior to publication
Official Journal of: Organ d. Österr. Verkehrswissenschaftl. Ges., d. Zentralverb. Spedition & Logistik, d. Österr. Möbeltransportverb., d. Verb. Österr. Fernfrächter u. d. Vereins d. Tarifeure
Supplement(s): Neue Bahn

VERORDNUNGSBLATT DES LANDESSCHULRATES FÜR NIEDERÖSTERREICH
746347A80-1680
Editorial: Rennbahnstr. 29, 3109 ST. PÖLTEN
Tel: 2742 2805115 **Fax:** 2742 2805199
Email: brigitte.diettrich@lsr-noe.gv.at **Web site:** http://www.lsr-noe.gv.at
Freq: Monthly
Editor: Brigitte Diettrich
Profile: Publication concerning schools and education in Lower Austria.
Language(s): German
Readership: Aimed at school inspectors in Lower Austria.
CONSUMER: RURAL & REGIONAL INTEREST

VIA
746475A65A-80_100
Editorial: Arche-Noah-Gasse 8, 8020 GRAZ
Tel: 316 903312769 **Fax:** 316 903312754
Email: daniela.gross@cm-service.at **Web site:** http://www.cm-service.at
Freq: Quarterly; **Cover Price:** Free; **Circ:** 27,500
Editor: Daniela Grundner-Gross; **Advertising Manager:** Anton Reiter
Profile: Magazine of Graz airport.
Language(s): German
ADVERTISING RATES:
Full Page Mono .... EUR 3600
Full Page Colour .... EUR 3600
Mechanical Data: Type Area: 297 x 225 mm
Supplement to: Der Standard
Supplement(s): VIA International
NATIONAL DAILY & SUNDAY NEWSPAPERS: Unabhängiges konservatives MdEP

VIA GASTROGUIDE
1641154A89A-460
Editorial: Arche-Noah-Gasse 8, 8020 GRAZ
Tel: 316 903312782 **Fax:** 316 903312754
Email: roswitha.jauk@cm-service.at **Web site:** http://www.graztourismus.at/cms/ziel/2873354/DE
Freq: Annual; **Cover Price:** Free; **Circ:** 70,000
Editor: Roswitha Jauk; **Advertising Manager:** Anton Reiter
Profile: Gastronomy guide for Graz.
Language(s): English; German; Italian
ADVERTISING RATES:
Full Page Mono .... EUR 2900
Full Page Colour .... EUR 2900
Mechanical Data: Type Area: 205 x 143 mm

VM DER VERSICHERUNGSMAKLER
1829937A1D-24
Editorial: Brunner Feldstr. 45, 2380 PERCHTOLDSDORF **Tel:** 1 86648140
Fax: 1 86648100
Email: m.fruehbauer@manstein.at **Web site:** http://www.ihrversicherungsmakler.at
Freq: 6 issues yearly; Free to qualifying individuals
Annual Sub.: EUR 25,00; **Circ:** 8,000
Editor: Milan Frühbauer; **Advertising Manager:** Karin Hasenhütl
Profile: Official magazine form the Association of Insurance Brokers.
Language(s): German
ADVERTISING RATES:
Full Page Mono .... EUR 2625
Full Page Colour .... EUR 3500
Mechanical Data: Type Area: 250 x 178 mm

VN VORARLBERGER NACHRICHTEN
746603A67B-1560
Editorial: Gutenbergstr. 1, 6858 SCHWARZACH
Tel: 5572 501993 **Fax:** 5572 501227
Email: redaktion@vn.vol.at **Web site:** http://www.vn.vol.at
Freq: 260 issues yearly; **Circ:** 69,642
Editor: Christian Ortner; **News Editor:** Sabrina Stauber; **Advertising Manager:** Gerard Hann
Profile: Regional daily newspaper covering politics, economics, sport, travel, technology and the arts. Facebook: http://www.facebook.com/VorarlbergerNachrichten Twitter: http://twitter.com/#!/VNChefredaktion.
Language(s): German
ADVERTISING RATES:
SCC .... EUR 96,00
Mechanical Data: Type Area: 425 x 278 mm, No. of Columns (Display): 8, Col Widths (Display): 33 mm
Copy instructions: *Copy Date:* 1 day prior to publication
Supplement(s): Heimat Bludenz; Heimat Bregenz; Heimat Bregenzerwald; Heimat Dornbirn; Heimat Feldkirch; Heimat Hofsteig; Heimat Kummenberg; Heimat Lustenau; Heimat Rankweil; Heimat Walgau; Leben & Wohnen; The Red Bulletin; tele; Vorarlberg Journal
REGIONAL DAILY & SUNDAY NEWSPAPERS: Regional Daily Newspapers

VOESTALPINE ANGESTELLTE
746618A27-300
Editorial: Kerpelystr. 199, 8700 LEOBEN
Tel: 50304253129 **Fax:** 50304653132
Email: alexander.lechner@voestalpine.com
Freq: Quarterly; **Circ:** 1,800
Editor: Alexander Lechner; **Advertising Manager:** Alexander Lechner
Profile: Magazine for works committee members of the Stahl Donanwith-Schienen-Draht-Bahnsysteme company.
Language(s): German
Copy instructions: *Copy Date:* 14 days prior to publication

VOESTALPINE ANGESTELLTE
746618A27-321
Editorial: Kerpelystr. 199, 8700 LEOBEN
Tel: 50304253129 **Fax:** 50304653132
Email: alexander.lechner@voestalpine.com
Freq: Quarterly; **Circ:** 1,800
Editor: Alexander Lechner; **Advertising Manager:** Alexander Lechner
Profile: Magazine for works committee members of the Stahl Donanwith-Schienen-Draht-Bahnsysteme company.
Language(s): German
Copy instructions: *Copy Date:* 14 days prior to publication

VORUM
1852119A4E-1325
Editorial: Binsenfeldstr. 6d, 6890 LUSTENAU
Tel: 5577 83713
Email: brigitte.boesch@prozessformen.at **Web site:** http://www.vorarlberg.at/gemeindeentwicklung
Freq: 5 issues yearly; **Cover Price:** Free; **Circ:** 6,500
Editor: Brigitte Bösch
Profile: Magazine about local developments in the Vorarlberg region.
Language(s): German

VÖWA WIRTSCHAFTSKURIER
1748232A14A-2582
Editorial: Teinfaltstr. 1, 1010 WIEN **Tel:** 1 53368760
Fax: 1 533687633
Email: office@voewa.at **Web site:** http://www.voewa.at
Freq: Quarterly; **Circ:** 4,000
Editor: Leo F. Aichhorn
Profile: Economy magazine.
Language(s): German
ADVERTISING RATES:
Full Page Mono .... EUR 1600
Full Page Colour .... EUR 1600
Mechanical Data: Type Area: 270 x 190 mm

VÖWA WIRTSCHAFTSKURIER
1748232A14A-2633
Editorial: Teinfaltstr. 1, 1010 WIEN **Tel:** 1 53368760
Fax: 1 533687633
Email: office@voewa.at **Web site:** http://www.voewa.at
Freq: Quarterly; **Circ:** 4,000
Editor: Leo F. Aichhorn
Profile: Economy magazine.
Language(s): German
ADVERTISING RATES:
Full Page Mono .... EUR 1600
Full Page Colour .... EUR 1600
Mechanical Data: Type Area: 270 x 190 mm

VÖZ AKTUELL
746621A2A-780
Editorial: Wipplingerstr. 15, 1010 WIEN
Tel: 1 53379790 **Fax:** 1 53379422
Email: office@voez.at **Web site:** http://www.voez.at
Circ: 160
Profile: Magazine with information from the Austrian Association of Newspaper Publishers about activities concerning media politics, law, business, economy and events.
Language(s): German

VRM PRESSEHANDBUCH
746762A2A-820
Editorial: Esterházygasse 4a/2/17, 1060 WIEN
Tel: 1 5857737 **Fax:** 1 585773737
Email: henrich@vrm.at **Web site:** http://www.vrm.at
Freq: Annual; **Cover Price:** Free; **Circ:** 5,500
Editor: Dieter Henrich; **Advertising Manager:** Dieter Henrich
Profile: Publication from the Austrian Regional Media Association.
Language(s): German
ADVERTISING RATES:
Full Page Colour .... EUR 1900
Mechanical Data: Type Area: 297 x 210 mm

WALGAUBLATT
746860A72-6960
Editorial: Rosengasse 5, 6800 FELDKIRCH
Tel: 5522 7233016 **Fax:** 5522 7233085
Email: andreas.feiertag@rzg.at **Web site:** http://www.walgaublatt.at
Freq: Weekly; **Cover Price:** Free; **Circ:** 15,222
Editor: Andreas Feiertag; **Advertising Manager:** Peter Bertole
Profile: Magazine for the Feldkirch region.
Language(s): German
ADVERTISING RATES:
Full Page Mono .... EUR 795
Full Page Colour .... EUR 1133
Mechanical Data: No. of Columns (Display): 4, Col Widths (Display): 48 mm, Type Area: 265 x 210 mm
LOCAL NEWSPAPERS

WANN & WO AM SONNTAG
746895A72-7000
Editorial: Gutenbergstr. 1, 6858 SCHWARZACH
Tel: 5572 501337 **Fax:** 5572 501155
Email: verena.daum@ww.vol.at **Web site:** http://www.ww.vol.at
Freq: Weekly; **Cover Price:** Free; **Circ:** 126,023
Editor: Verena Daum; **Advertising Manager:** Harald Schertler
Profile: Tabloid-style newspaper containing information of interest to young people.
Language(s): German
ADVERTISING RATES:
Full Page Mono .... EUR 3435
Full Page Colour .... EUR 4809
Mechanical Data: No. of Columns (Display): 6, Col Widths (Display): 33 mm, Type Area: 280 x 210 mm
Copy instructions: *Copy Date:* 3 days prior to publication
LOCAL NEWSPAPERS

WB WIRTSCHAFT IM BLICK
731996A14A-1280
Editorial: Mozartgasse 4, 1041 WIEN
Tel: 1 505479617 **Fax:** 1 505479640
Email: c.gruber@wirtschaftsbund.at **Web site:** http://www.wirtschaftsbund.at
Freq: Quarterly; **Circ:** 220,000
Editor: Cordula Gruber; **Advertising Manager:** Cordula Gruber
Profile: Magazine of the Austrian Business Association.
Language(s): German
ADVERTISING RATES:
Full Page Colour .... EUR 7500

WCM
746980A5-560
Editorial: Simmeringer Hauptstr. 152/19, 1110 WIEN
Tel: 664 8468645
Email: guido@wcm.at **Web site:** http://www.wcm.at
Freq: Monthly; **Annual Sub.:** EUR 29,90
Editor: Guido Fritdum; **Advertising Manager:** Lilla Leiter
Profile: Computer magazine.
Language(s): German
ADVERTISING RATES:
Full Page Mono .... EUR 4090
Full Page Colour .... EUR 4090
Mechanical Data: Type Area: 260 x 180 mm
BUSINESS: COMPUTERS & AUTOMATION

WEGE
747007A74Q-1
Editorial: Rankar 12, 4692 NIEDERTHALHEIM
Tel: 7676 7017
Email: redaktion@wege.at **Web site:** http://www.wege.at
Freq: Quarterly; **Annual Sub.:** EUR 19,00; **Circ:** 8,000
Editor: Eva Schreuer; **Advertising Manager:** Roman Schreuer
Profile: Magazine about holistical consciousness, thinking and acting.
Language(s): German
ADVERTISING RATES:
Full Page Mono .... EUR 970
Full Page Colour .... EUR 1503
Mechanical Data: Type Area: 252 x 180 mm, No. of Columns (Display): 3, Col Widths (Display): 57 mm
Copy instructions: *Copy Date:* 14 days prior to publication

WEIDWERK
738070A75F-140
Editorial: Wickenburggasse 3, 1080 WIEN
Tel: 1 405163630 **Fax:** 1 405163636
Email: redaktion@weidwerk.at **Web site:** http://www.weidwerk.at
Freq: Monthly; Free to qualifying individuals
Annual Sub.: EUR 56,00; **Circ:** 47,500
Editor: Hans-Friedemann Zedka
Profile: Illustrated magazine about hunting, fishing, shooting and nature protection.
Language(s): German
ADVERTISING RATES:
Full Page Mono .... EUR 2980
Full Page Colour .... EUR 3874
Mechanical Data: Type Area: 248 x 185 mm, No. of Columns (Display): 4, Col Widths (Display): 43 mm
Copy instructions: *Copy Date:* 21 days prior to publication
CONSUMER: SPORT: Shooting

WELLNESS MAGAZIN
747111A74G-432
Editorial: Ölzeltgasse 3, 1030 WIEN **Tel:** 1 4191095
Fax: 1 419109533
Email: redaktion@wellness-magazin.at **Web site:** http://www.wellness-magazin.at
Freq: Monthly; **Annual Sub.:** EUR 39,90; **Circ:** 95,000
Editor: Brigitta Grausam
Profile: Magazine about all aspects of medicine.
Language(s): German
ADVERTISING RATES:
Full Page Mono .... EUR 5990
Full Page Colour .... EUR 5990
Mechanical Data: Type Area: 255 x 184 mm
CONSUMER: WOMEN'S INTEREST CONSUMER MAGAZINES: Slimming & Health

WELSER MERKUR
2005873A14A-2662
Editorial: Ringstr. 27, 4600 WELS **Tel:** 7242 43074
Fax: 732 2100228101
Email: walter-christa.dannecker@liwest.at
Freq: Quarterly; **Circ:** 4,650
Editor: Walter Dannecker
Profile: Magazine from the Association of Former Students of the Federal Trade Academy.
Language(s): German

WELT DER FRAU
747122A74A-871
Editorial: Lustenauer Str. 21, 4020 LINZ
Tel: 732 77000112 **Fax:** 732 77000124
Email: christine.haiden@welt-der-frau.at **Web site:** http://www.welt-der-frau.at
Freq: 11 issues yearly; **Annual Sub.:** EUR 33,00; **Circ:** 61,487
Editor: Christine Haiden; **Advertising Manager:** Martin Bauer
Profile: General women's interest magazine.
Language(s): German
ADVERTISING RATES:
Full Page Colour .... EUR 4930
Mechanical Data: Type Area: 240 x 180 mm
Copy instructions: *Copy Date:* 14 days prior to publication
CONSUMER: WOMEN'S INTEREST CONSUMER MAGAZINES: Women's Interest

WESTPOINT
747300A89C-270
Editorial: Holzhammerstr. 15/3/1, 6020 INNSBRUCK
Tel: 664 3165777
Email: concerts@chello.at **Web site:** http://www.westpoint.at
Freq: 6 issues yearly; **Cover Price:** Free; **Circ:** 10,000
Editor: Kurt Herran
Profile: Concert and leisure magazine for West Austria.
Language(s): German
ADVERTISING RATES:
Full Page Mono .... EUR 1200
Full Page Colour .... EUR 1500
Mechanical Data: Type Area: 280 x 208 mm, No. of Columns (Display): 4, Col Widths (Display): 49 mm
CONSUMER: HOLIDAYS & TRAVEL: Entertainment Guides

WESTSTEIRISCHE RUNDSCHAU
747304A72-7080
Editorial: Fabrikstr. 15, 8530 DEUTSCHLANDSBERG
Tel: 3462 25240 **Fax:** 3462 252423
Email: rundschau@simadruck.at **Web site:** http://www.simadruck.at
Freq: Weekly; **Cover Price:** EUR 1,10; **Circ:** 9,200
Editor: Waltraud Weisi; **Advertising Manager:** Annemarie Aigner
Profile: Regional weekly covering politics, economics, sport, travel, technology and the arts.
Language(s): German
ADVERTISING RATES:
SCC .... EUR 35,00
Mechanical Data: Type Area: 385 x 275 mm, No. of Columns (Display): 11, Col Widths (Display): 24 mm
Copy instructions: *Copy Date:* 1 day prior to publication
LOCAL NEWSPAPERS

WIA WIRTSCHAFT IM ALPENRAUM
766171A14A-2496
Editorial: Rennweg 9, 6020 INNSBRUCK
Tel: 512 571985 **Fax:** 512 57198519
Email: pohl.partner@wianet.at **Web site:** http://www.wianet.at
Freq: 10 issues yearly; **Annual Sub.:** EUR 23,00; **Circ:** 28,000
Editor: Oliver Pohl
Profile: Regional business magazine.
Language(s): German
ADVERTISING RATES:
Full Page Mono .... EUR 2749
Full Page Colour .... EUR 2749
Mechanical Data: Type Area: 280 x 210 mm
Copy instructions: *Copy Date:* 14 days prior to publication

WIE GEHT'S
1644843A74M-249
Editorial: Esterhazyplatz 3, 7000 EISENSTADT
Tel: 2682 6080 **Fax:** 2682 6081041
Email: wie.gehts@bgkk.at **Web site:** http://www.bgkk.at
Freq: Quarterly; **Circ:** 100,000
Editor: Christian Moder
Profile: Magazine about health and wellness.
Language(s): German

WIEN EXCLUSIV MAGAZIN
747397A89C-360
Editorial: Emil-Kralik-Gasse 3/24, 1050 WIEN
Tel: 1 5452811 **Fax:** 1 54528115
Email: info@dirninger.com **Web site:** http://www.exclusiv-magazine.com
Freq: 3 issues yearly; **Cover Price:** Free; **Circ:** 24,000
Editor: Erika Moore; **Advertising Manager:** Reinhold Dirninger
Profile: Cultural and entertainment guide for visitors to Vienna.
Language(s): English; German
Mechanical Data: Type Area: 300 x 230 mm
CONSUMER: HOLIDAYS & TRAVEL: Entertainment Guides

WIEN, WIE ES ISST ...
1639940A89A-459
Editorial: Marc-Aurel-Str. 9, 1011 WIEN
Tel: 1 53660938 **Fax:** 1 53660935
Email: schwameis@falter.at **Web site:** http://www.falter.at
Freq: Annual; **Cover Price:** EUR 16,50; **Circ:** 25,000
Editor: Susanne Schwameis; **Advertising Manager:** Sigrid Johler
Profile: Gastronomy guide for Vienna.
Language(s): German
ADVERTISING RATES:
Full Page Mono .... EUR 2000
Full Page Colour .... EUR 3100
Mechanical Data: Type Area: 130 x 100 mm

WIENER
747353A86C-40
Editorial: Geiselbergstr. 15, 1110 WIEN
Tel: 1 60117232 **Fax:** 1 60117350
Email: wiener@wiener-online.at **Web site:** http://www.wienerpost.at
Freq: 11 issues yearly; **Annual Sub.:** EUR 24,00; **Circ:** 48,100
Editor: Helfried Bauer
Profile: Magazine containing celebrity interviews, product, book and film reviews and articles on sport, health, music and motoring.
Language(s): German
Readership: Aimed at men under the age of 35 years.
ADVERTISING RATES:
Full Page Mono .... EUR 7190
Full Page Colour .... EUR 7190
Mechanical Data: Type Area: 278 x 210 mm
Copy instructions: *Copy Date:* 21 days prior to publication
Supplement(s): Wiener Freizeit Guide; Wiener Stadtmagazin
CONSUMER: ADULT & GAY MAGAZINES: Men's Lifestyle Magazines

WIENER BALLKALENDER
1863811A65A-120_100
Editorial: Leberstr. 122, 1110 WIEN **Tel:** 1 74032255
Fax: 1 74032740
Email: d.borka@bohmann.at **Web site:** http://www.bohmann-verlag.at
Freq: Annual; **Cover Price:** EUR 1,10; **Circ:** 80,000
Advertising Manager: Gunther Pany
Profile: Programme of events.
Language(s): German
ADVERTISING RATES:
Full Page Colour .... EUR 3820
Mechanical Data: Type Area: 280 x 91 mm
Supplement to: Wiener Zeitung
NATIONAL DAILY & SUNDAY NEWSPAPERS: Unabhängiges konservatives MdEP

WIENER BEZIRKS BLATT
747356A72-7120
Editorial: Schottenfeldgasse 24, 1070 WIEN
Tel: 1 5247086 **Fax:** 1 5247086903
Email: redaktion@wienerbezirksblatt.at **Web site:** http://www.wienerbezirksblatt.at
Freq: Weekly; **Cover Price:** Free; **Circ:** 650,000
Editor: Thomas Landgraf
Profile: Magazine containing articles of interest to those living or working in Vienna.
Language(s): German
ADVERTISING RATES:
Full Page Mono .... EUR 9800
Full Page Colour .... EUR 14700
Mechanical Data: Type Area: 255 x 187 mm, No. of Columns (Display): 4, Col Widths (Display): 46 mm
Copy instructions: *Copy Date:* 12 days prior to publication
LOCAL NEWSPAPERS

WIENER JOURNAL
747370A65A-120_101
Editorial: Wiedner Gürtel 10, 1040 WIEN
Tel: 1 20699489 **Fax:** 1 20699592
Email: wienerjournal@wienerzeitung.at **Web site:** http://www.wienerzeitung.at
Freq: Weekly; **Circ:** 53,000
Editor: Brigitte Suchan; **Advertising Manager:** Harald Wegscheidler
Profile: Magazine focusing on politics, arts, literature, science and economics.
Language(s): German
Readership: Aimed at academics.
ADVERTISING RATES:
Full Page Mono .... EUR 2090
Full Page Colour .... EUR 2090
Mechanical Data: Type Area: 267 x 174 mm
Copy instructions: *Copy Date:* 11 days prior to publication
Supplement to: Wiener Zeitung
NATIONAL DAILY & SUNDAY NEWSPAPERS: National Daily Newspapers

WIENER KLINISCHE WOCHENSCHRIFT
747372A56A-1860
Editorial: Apollogasse 19, 1070 WIEN
Fax: 1 521031309
Email: marcus.koeller@meduniwien.ac.at **Web site:** http://www.springer.at
Freq: Monthly; **Circ:** 6,000
Editor: Marcus Köller
Profile: Magazine for Austrian physical doctors.
Language(s): German
ADVERTISING RATES:
Full Page Mono .... EUR 2600
Full Page Colour .... EUR 3350
Mechanical Data: Type Area: 270 x 170 mm
Official Journal of: Organ d. Österr. Ges. f. Innere Medizin u. d. Österr. Ges. f. Pneumologie

WIENER KLINISCHES MAGAZIN
747373A56A-1880
Editorial: Sachsenplatz 4, 1201 WIEN
Tel: 1 3302415222 **Fax:** 1 3302426260
Email: verena.kienast@springer.at **Web site:** http://www.springer.at
Freq: 6 issues yearly; **Circ:** 10,833
Editor: Verena Kienast
Profile: Publication covering all aspects of the pharmaceutical trade.
Language(s): German
ADVERTISING RATES:
Full Page Mono .... EUR 2600
Full Page Colour .... EUR 3350
Mechanical Data: Type Area: 270 x 170 mm
BUSINESS: HEALTH & MEDICAL

WIENER LOKALFÜHRER
1859266A89A-517
Editorial: Tenschertstr. 5, 1230 WIEN
Tel: 664 3236000 **Fax:** 664 2286000
Email: office@lokalfuehrer.at **Web site:** http://www.lokalfuehrer.at
Freq: Half-yearly; **Cover Price:** Free; **Circ:** 735,000
Advertising Manager: Margit Haas
Profile: Restaurant guide for Vienna.
Language(s): German
Mechanical Data: Type Area: 170 x 105 mm

WIENER NATURSCHUTZ-NACHRICHTEN 747380A57-1100
Editorial: Museumsplatz 1, Stiege 13, 1070 WIEN
Tel: 1 5223597 **Fax:** 1 5223597
Email: wien@naturschutzbund.at **Web site:** http://www.naturschutzbund.at
Freq: Quarterly; Free to qualifying individuals
Annual Sub.: EUR 16,00; **Circ:** 5,000
Editor: Hannes Minich
Profile: Magazine about nature and environmental protection.
Language(s): German

WIENER WIRTSCHAFT 747391A63-420
Editorial: Stubenring 8, 1010 WIEN **Tel:** 1 514501314
Fax: 1 514501470
Email: wienerwirtschaft@wkw.at **Web site:** http://www.wkw.at
Freq: 44 issues yearly; Free to qualifying individuals
Annual Sub.: EUR 54,00; **Circ:** 93,210
Advertising Manager: Erhard Witty
Profile: Official journal of the Vienna Chamber of Commerce.
Language(s): German
Readership: Aimed at all businesses in Vienna.
ADVERTISING RATES:
Full Page Mono .... EUR 4080
Full Page Colour .... EUR 6120
Mechanical Data: Type Area: 250 x 195 mm, No. of Columns (Display): 4, Col Widths (Display): 45 mm
Copy instructions: *Copy Date:* 7 days prior to publication
BUSINESS: REGIONAL BUSINESS

WIENER ZEITUNG 747395A65A-120
Editorial: Wiedner Gürtel 10, 1040 WIEN
Tel: 1 20699478 **Fax:** 1 20699592
Email: chefredaktion@wienerzeitung.at **Web site:** http://www.wienerzeitung.at
Freq: 260 issues yearly; **Annual Sub.:** EUR 198,00; **Circ:** 26,000
Editor: Reinhard Göweil; **Advertising Manager:** Harald Wegscheidler
Profile: A3-sized quality newspaper focusing on regional, national and international affairs, education, politics and economics. Includes stock market reports and articles covering the environment and developments in information technology.
Language(s): German
Readership: Aimed at judges, lawyers, economists and civil servants.
Mechanical Data: Type Area: 429 x 280 mm, No. of Columns (Display): 6, Col Widths (Display): 43 mm
Copy instructions: *Copy Date:* 2 days prior to publication
Supplement(s): ProgrammPunkte; tv.woche; wiener Journal
NATIONAL DAILY & SUNDAY NEWSPAPERS: National Daily Newspapers

WIENERIN 747366A74A-820
Editorial: Geiselbergstr. 15, 1110 WIEN
Tel: 1 60117936 **Fax:** 1 60117350
Email: wienerin@wienerin.at **Web site:** http://www.wienerin.at
Freq: Monthly; **Annual Sub.:** EUR 32,00; **Circ:** 97,000
Editor: Sylvia Margret Steinitz; **Advertising Manager:** Marena Kopic
Profile: Women's interest magazine.
Language(s): German
ADVERTISING RATES:
Full Page Mono .... EUR 9200
Full Page Colour .... EUR 9200
Mechanical Data: Type Area: 278 x 210 mm
Copy instructions: *Copy Date:* 21 days prior to publication
Supplement(s): Wienerin kocht; Wienerin mit Kind; Wienerin Spa Guide
CONSUMER: WOMEN'S INTEREST CONSUMER MAGAZINES: Women's Interest

WING BUSINESS 1641241A14A-2511
Editorial: Kopernikusgasse 24/3, 8010 GRAZ
Tel: 316 8737795 **Fax:** 316 8737797
Email: voessner@tugraz.at **Web site:** http://www.wing-online.at
Freq: Quarterly; Free to qualifying individuals
Annual Sub.: EUR 42,00; **Circ:** 2,500
Editor: Siegfried Vössner; **Advertising Manager:** Beatrice Freund
Profile: Magazine for technology and commercial managers.
Language(s): German
ADVERTISING RATES:
Full Page Mono .... EUR 870
Mechanical Data: Type Area: 258 x 178 mm

DER WINZER 747484A21H-3
Editorial: Sturzgasse 1a, 1140 WIEN **Tel:** 1 98177161
Fax: 1 98177120
Email: w.kaltzin@agrarverlag.at **Web site:** http://www.der-winzer.at
Freq: Monthly; **Annual Sub.:** EUR 87,50; **Circ:** 13,705
Editor: Walter Kaltzin; **Advertising Manager:** Romana Hummer-Schierleitner
Profile: Wine cultivation magazine of the Society of Austrian Winegrowers.
Language(s): German
ADVERTISING RATES:
Full Page Mono .... EUR 3650
Full Page Colour .... EUR 8650
Mechanical Data: Type Area: 260 x 175 mm, No. of Columns (Display): 4, Col Widths (Display): 40 mm
BUSINESS: AGRICULTURE & FARMING: Vine Growing

DIE WIRTSCHAFT 747564A14A-2280
Editorial: Wiedner Hauptstr. 120, 1051 WIEN
Tel: 1 54664380 **Fax:** 1 5466450380
Email: s.boeck@wirtschaftsverlag.at **Web site:** http://www.die-wirtschaft.at
Freq: 10 issues yearly; **Annual Sub.:** EUR 60,00; **Circ:** 75,000
Editor: Stefan Böck; **Advertising Manager:** Alfred Vrej Minassian
Profile: Magazine focusing on commerce and industry in Austria.
Language(s): German
ADVERTISING RATES:
Full Page Colour .... EUR 7990
Mechanical Data: Type Area: 240 x 180 mm
Copy instructions: *Copy Date:* 21 days prior to publication
BUSINESS: COMMERCE, INDUSTRY & MANAGEMENT

WIRTSCHAFT AKTIV 747566A14A-2320
Editorial: Franz-Josef-Str. 12, 5020 SALZBURG
Tel: 662 878147 **Fax:** 662 876649
Email: office@wirtschaftsliste.at **Web site:** http://www.wirtschaftsliste.at
Freq: Annual; **Cover Price:** Free; **Circ:** 34,500
Editor: Rudolf Pitterka; **Advertising Manager:** Rudolf Pitterka
Profile: Industry magazine for Salzburg.
Language(s): German
ADVERTISING RATES:
Full Page Colour .... EUR 2000
BUSINESS: COMMERCE, INDUSTRY & MANAGEMENT

WIRTSCHAFT & UMWELT 747847A57-1120
Editorial: Prinz-Eugen-Str. 20, 1040 WIEN
Tel: 1 501652629 **Fax:** 1 501652105
Email: wirtschaft.umwelt@akwien.at **Web site:** http://www.wirtschaftundumwelt.at
Freq: Quarterly; **Cover Price:** EUR 1,80
Free to qualifying individuals ; **Circ:** 15,000
Editor: Thomas Ritt
Profile: Magazine about environmental policy.
Language(s): German

WIRTSCHAFTS- UND SOZIALSTATISTISCHES TASCHENBUCH 747837A14A-2440
Editorial: Prinz-Eugen-Str. 20, 1040 WIEN
Tel: 1 501650
Email: statistik@akwien.at **Web site:** http://statistik.arbeiterkammer.at
Freq: Annual; **Cover Price:** EUR 13,10; **Circ:** 5,000
Editor: Margit Epler
Profile: Publication containing statistical data.
Language(s): German

WIRTSCHAFTSBLATT 747606A65A-121
Editorial: Geiselbergstr. 15, 1110 WIEN
Tel: 1 60117305 **Fax:** 1 60117259
Email: redaktion@wirtschaftsblatt.at **Web site:** http://www.wirtschaftsblatt.at
Freq: 208 issues yearly; **Circ:** 36,812
Editor: Wolfgang Unterhuber; **News Editor:** Günter Fritz; **Advertising Manager:** Dietmar Otti
Profile: Tabloid-sized quality newspaper providing business and financial news. Covers EU developments and legislation, the global economy, banking and stock exchange details. Also includes articles on information technology. Facebook: http://www.facebook.com/wirtschaftsblatt Twitter: http://twitter.com/#!/wiblatt.
Language(s): German
Readership: Read by members of the business community, IT and financial managers, investors, academics and civil servants.
Mechanical Data: No. of Columns (Display): 6, Col Widths (Display): 41 mm, Type Area: 410 x 266 mm
Copy instructions: *Copy Date:* 3 days prior to publication
Supplement(s): corporAid magazin; ECO Eco World Magazine; WirtschaftsBlatt deluxe; WirtschaftsBlatt investor
NATIONAL DAILY & SUNDAY NEWSPAPERS: National Daily Newspapers

WIRTSCHAFTSBLATT DELUXE 1809839A65A-121_100
Editorial: Geiselbergstr. 15, 1110 WIEN
Tel: 1 60117305 **Fax:** 1 60117259
Email: redaktion@wirtschaftsblatt.at **Web site:** http://www.wirtschaftsblatt.at/deluxe
Freq: 10 issues yearly; **Circ:** 50,000
Editor: Alexander Pfeffer; **Advertising Manager:** Heidi Dvoracek
Profile: Facebook: http://www.facebook.com/wirtschaftsblatt Twitter: http://twitter.com/#!/wiblatt.
Language(s): German
ADVERTISING RATES:
Full Page Mono .... EUR 5600
Full Page Colour .... EUR 5600
Mechanical Data: Type Area: 280 x 210 mm
Copy instructions: *Copy Date:* 13 days prior to publication
Supplement to: WirtschaftsBlatt
NATIONAL DAILY & SUNDAY NEWSPAPERS: Unabhängiges konservatives MdEP

WIRTSCHAFTSBLATT INVESTOR 1793903A65A-121_102
Editorial: Geiselbergstr. 15, 1110 WIEN
Tel: 1 60117305 **Fax:** 1 60117259
Email: redaktion@wirtschaftsblatt.at **Web site:** http://www.wirtschaftsblatt.at
Freq: Weekly; **Circ:** 26,791
Editor: Wolfgang Unterhuber
Profile: Facebook: http://www.facebook.com/wirtschaftsblatt Twitter: http://twitter.com/#!/wiblatt.
Language(s): German
ADVERTISING RATES:
Full Page Colour .... EUR 4990
Mechanical Data: Type Area: 260 x 185 mm
Copy instructions: *Copy Date:* 9 days prior to publication
Supplement to: WirtschaftsBlatt
NATIONAL DAILY & SUNDAY NEWSPAPERS: Unabhängiges konservatives MdEP

WIRTSCHAFTSNACHRICHTEN SÜD 747751A63-503
Editorial: Stempfergasse 3, 8010 GRAZ
Tel: 316 83402085 **Fax:** 316 83402010
Email: link@euromedien.at **Web site:** http://www.wn-online.at
Freq: 10 issues yearly; **Annual Sub.:** EUR 25,00; **Circ:** 15,500
Editor: Martin Link
Profile: Business magazine for the South Burgenland region.
Language(s): German
ADVERTISING RATES:
Full Page Colour .... EUR 4530
Mechanical Data: Type Area: 250 x 175 mm
Copy instructions: *Copy Date:* 14 days prior to publication
BUSINESS: REGIONAL BUSINESS

WIRTSCHAFTSREPORT 747392A63-502
Editorial: Lothringerstr. 14, 1030 WIEN
Tel: 1 5127631 **Fax:** 1 512763134
Email: m.langthaler@wirtschaftsbund-wien.at **Web site:** http://www.wirtschaftsbund-wien.at
Freq: Quarterly; **Circ:** 85,000
Editor: Markus Langthaler
Profile: Vienna business report.
Language(s): German
Readership: Aimed at businesses in Vienna.
ADVERTISING RATES:
Full Page Mono .... EUR 6000
Full Page Colour .... EUR 6000
Mechanical Data: Type Area: 283 x 193 mm
BUSINESS: REGIONAL BUSINESS

WMW WIENER MEDIZINISCHE WOCHENSCHRIFT 1645546A56A-1938
Editorial: Sachsenplatz 4, 1201 WIEN
Tel: 1 33024150 **Fax:** 1 3302426
Email: herbert.kurz@wienkav.at **Web site:** http://www.springer.at
Freq: Monthly; **Circ:** 4,150
Editor: Herbert Kurz
Profile: Magazine for general practitioners and physical doctors of Vienna.
Language(s): German
ADVERTISING RATES:
Full Page Mono .... EUR 2600
Full Page Colour .... EUR 3350
Mechanical Data: Type Area: 270 x 170 mm
Official Journal of: Organ d. Institute u. Kliniken d. Medizin. Fakultäten Graz, Innsbruck u. Wien u. d. Wissenschaftl. Ges. d. Ärzte in d. Steiermark

WOCHE HARTBERGER BEZIRKSZEITUNG 729887A72-3620
Editorial: Am Ökopark 9, 8230 HARTBERG
Tel: 3332 6239417 **Fax:** 3332 6239494
Email: alfred.mayer@woche.at **Web site:** http://www.woche.at/hbz
Freq: Weekly; **Cover Price:** Free; **Circ:** 31,100
Editor: Alfred Mayer; **Advertising Manager:** Waltraud Gotthard
Profile: Advertising journal (house-to-house) concentrating on local stories.
Language(s): German
ADVERTISING RATES:
Full Page Mono .... EUR 2600
Full Page Colour .... EUR 2600
Mechanical Data: Type Area: 260 x 200 mm, No. of Columns (Display): 4, Col Widths (Display): 47 mm
Copy instructions: *Copy Date:* 8 days prior to publication
LOCAL NEWSPAPERS

WOCHE OBERSTEIERMARK 737844A72-5100
Editorial: Grazer Str. 18, 8600 BRUCK
Tel: 3862 24707 **Fax:** 3862 24707255
Email: karl.doppelhofer@woche.at **Web site:** http://www.woche.at/obersteiermark
Freq: Weekly; **Cover Price:** Free; **Circ:** 81,287
Editor: Karl Doppelhofer; **Advertising Manager:** Gertrude Wolny
Profile: Advertising journal (house-to-house) concentrating on local stories.
Language(s): German
ADVERTISING RATES:
Full Page Mono .... EUR 3545
Full Page Colour .... EUR 3545
Mechanical Data: Type Area: 275 x 200 mm, No. of Columns (Display): 4, Col Widths (Display): 47 mm
Copy instructions: *Copy Date:* 7 days prior to publication
LOCAL NEWSPAPERS

WOCHE VÖLKERMARKT & JAUNTAL 1626774A72-7361
Editorial: Völkermarkter Ring 25/1, 9020 KLAGENFURT **Tel:** 676 845501643 **Fax:** 463 5800636
Email: uwe.sommersguter@woche.at **Web site:** http://www.woche.at
Freq: Weekly; **Cover Price:** Free; **Circ:** 14,798
Editor: Uwe Markus Sommersguter; **Advertising Manager:** Dieter Pucker
Profile: Advertising journal (house-to-house) concentrating on local stories.
Language(s): German
ADVERTISING RATES:
Full Page Colour .... EUR 1800
Mechanical Data: Type Area: 275 x 200 mm, No. of Columns (Display): 4, Col Widths (Display): 47 mm
Copy instructions: *Copy Date:* 6 days prior to publication
LOCAL NEWSPAPERS

WOCHE WEIZ & BIRKFELD 747098A72-7040
Editorial: Südtiroler Platz 2, 8160 WEIZ
Tel: 3172 379023 **Fax:** 3172 379021
Email: redaktion.weiz@woche.at **Web site:** http://www.woche.at/weiz
Freq: 44 issues yearly; **Cover Price:** Free; **Circ:** 37,685
Editor: Anneliese Grabenhofer; **Advertising Manager:** Andreas Rath
Profile: Advertising journal (house-to-house) concentrating on local stories.
Language(s): German
ADVERTISING RATES:
Full Page Mono .... EUR 2695
Full Page Colour .... EUR 2695
Mechanical Data: Type Area: 260 x 200 mm, No. of Columns (Display): 4, Col Widths (Display): 47 mm
Copy instructions: *Copy Date:* 7 days prior to publication
LOCAL NEWSPAPERS

WOHNKULTUR 748263A23A-100
Editorial: Weitmosergasse 30, 1100 WIEN
Tel: 1 6172635 **Fax:** 1 6172635
Email: wohnkultur@verlag-strohmayer.at **Web site:** http://www.wohnkultur.co.at
Freq: 6 issues yearly; Free to qualifying individuals
Annual Sub.: EUR 70,00; **Circ:** 7,000
Editor: Christian Lorenz
Profile: Journal for the furnishing, fixtures and fittings trade.
Language(s): German
ADVERTISING RATES:
Full Page Mono .... EUR 2490
Full Page Colour .... EUR 4100
Mechanical Data: Type Area: 275 x 185 mm
Official Journal of: Organ d. Bundesgremiums u. aller Landesgremien d. Einrichtungshandels
BUSINESS: FURNISHINGS & FURNITURE

WOHNTRAUM LIFESTYLE - (AUSG. LIEZEN) 748271A74C-780
Editorial: Werksgasse 71, 8786 ROTTENMANN
Tel: 3614 20330 **Fax:** 3614 20317
Email: office@idee-werbeagentur.at **Web site:** http://www.wohntraum.net
Freq: Monthly; **Cover Price:** Free; **Circ:** 42,953
Editor: Helmut Schaupensteiner; **Advertising Manager:** Helmut Schaupensteiner
Profile: Magazine containing suggestions for interior design and decoration.
Language(s): German
Mechanical Data: Type Area: 272 x 190 mm
CONSUMER: WOMEN'S INTEREST CONSUMER MAGAZINES: Home & Family

WOMAN 1647420A74A-881
Editorial: Taborstr. 1, 1020 WIEN **Tel:** 1 213129002
Fax: 1 21312290
Email: redaktion@woman.at **Web site:** http://www.woman.at
Freq: 25 issues yearly; **Annual Sub.:** EUR 45,90; **Circ:** 201,900
Editor: Euke Frank; **News Editor:** Katrin Kuba; **Advertising Manager:** Gabriele Kindl

Austria

Profile: Magazine for women.
Language(s): German
ADVERTISING RATES:
Full Page Mono .... EUR 14690
Full Page Colour .... EUR 14690
Mechanical Data: Type Area: 250 x 185 mm
Copy instructions: *Copy Date:* 21 days prior to publication
Supplement(s): man; woman business; woman Cuisine; woman Living; woman Luxury; woman's health; woman Shopping Guide

WT DER WIRTSCHAFTSTREUHÄNDER
1858589A1A-251
Editorial: Hainburger Str. 20/8, 1030 WIEN
Tel: 1 7153323 **Fax:** 1 712118520
Email: office@partner-kommunikation.at **Web site:** http://www.vwt.at
Freq: 6 issues yearly; Free to qualifying individuals
Annual Sub.: EUR 45,00; **Circ:** 11,000
Editor: Walter Holiczki
Profile: Magazine covering all aspects of accountancy.
Language(s): German
ADVERTISING RATES:
Full Page Colour .... EUR 2600
Mechanical Data: Type Area: 243 x 180 mm, No. of Columns (Display): 3, Col Widths (Display): 58 mm

WÜSTENROT MAGAZIN
748380A94H-1580
Editorial: Salzweg 17, 5081 ANIF **Tel:** 6246 897999
Fax: 6246 897989
Email: nz@ucm-verlag.at **Web site:** http://www.ucm-verlag.at
Freq: Half-yearly; **Circ:** 250,000
Editor: Nicolaus Zott; **Advertising Manager:** Manfred Jungwirth
Profile: Savings bank members' magazine.
Language(s): German
Readership: Aimed at bank members.
ADVERTISING RATES:
Full Page Mono .... EUR 7700
Full Page Colour .... EUR 7700
Mechanical Data: Type Area: 290 x 220 mm
CONSUMER: OTHER CLASSIFICATIONS: Customer Magazines

XUND
1641155A74M-245
Editorial: Arche-Noah-Gasse 8, 8020 GRAZ
Tel: 316 903312772 **Fax:** 316 903312754
Email: claudia.taucher@cm-service.at **Web site:** http://www.stgkk.at
Freq: Quarterly; **Cover Price:** Free; **Circ:** 390,000
Editor: Claudia Rief-Taucher
Profile: Magazine of the health insurance company Steiermärkische Gebietskrankenkasse.
Language(s): German
ADVERTISING RATES:
Full Page Mono .... EUR 7900
Full Page Colour .... EUR 7900
Mechanical Data: Type Area: 297 x 210 mm

YACHT INFO
748461A91A-1
Editorial: Mühlgasse 13, 2500 BADEN
Tel: 2252 88731 **Fax:** 2252 21700
Email: gerhard.maly@yachtinfo.at **Web site:** http://www.yachtinfo.at
Freq: Quarterly; **Annual Sub.:** EUR 14,00; **Circ:** 17,000
Editor: Gerhard Maly; **Advertising Manager:** Gerhard Maly
Profile: Magazine concerning all aspects of the sailing and motor yacht industry.
Language(s): German
Readership: Aimed at sailors and those who have an interest in sailing and motorboats.
ADVERTISING RATES:
Full Page Mono .... EUR 1200
Full Page Colour .... EUR 1800
Mechanical Data: Type Area: 250 x 185 mm, No. of Columns (Display): 4, Col Widths (Display): 42 mm
Copy instructions: *Copy Date:* 50 days prior to publication
CONSUMER: RECREATION & LEISURE: Boating & Yachting

ZAHN ARZT
748506A56D-80
Editorial: Sachsenplatz 4, 1201 WIEN **Tel:** 1 5131047
Fax: 1 5134783
Email: margarete.zupan@springer.at **Web site:** http://www.springermedizin.at
Freq: 10 issues yearly; **Annual Sub.:** EUR 33,00; **Circ:** 5,500
Editor: Margarete Zupan
Profile: Journal focusing on dentistry, oral hygiene and related products.
Language(s): German
Readership: Aimed at dentists, dental technicians and dental hygenists.
ADVERTISING RATES:
Full Page Colour .... EUR 2850
Mechanical Data: Type Area: 400 x 270 mm
BUSINESS: HEALTH & MEDICAL: Dental

ZEIT ZEICHEN
748800A87-2591
Editorial: Spiegelgasse 3/2, 1010 WIEN
Tel: 1 515523350 **Fax:** 1 515523764
Email: kab.office@kaoe.at
Freq: 5 issues yearly; **Annual Sub.:** EUR 10,00
Editor: Christoph Watz
Profile: Magazine of the Catholic Workers' Movement of Austria.
Language(s): German
ADVERTISING RATES:
Full Page Mono .... EUR 1165
Mechanical Data: Type Area: 270 x 185 mm, No. of Columns (Display): 3, Col Widths (Display): 59 mm
CONSUMER: RELIGIOUS

ZEITBÜHNE
748565A73-360
Editorial: Dr.-Josef-Ender-Str. 21, 4400 STEYR
Tel: 7252 50065 **Fax:** 7252 50065
Email: z.zeitbuehne@aon.at **Web site:** http://www.zeitbuehne.at
Freq: 6 issues yearly; Free to qualifying individuals
Annual Sub.: EUR 18,00; **Circ:** 8,000
Editor: Brigitte Zachl
Profile: Magazine about politics, the economy and culture.
Language(s): German
Mechanical Data: Type Area: 257 x 180 mm, No. of Columns (Display): 4, Col Widths (Display): 41 mm
Copy instructions: *Copy Date:* 14 days prior to publication
CONSUMER: NATIONAL & INTERNATIONAL PERIODICALS

ZEITSCHRIFT DER UNABHÄNGIGEN VERWALTUNGSSENATE
1641716A1A-226
Editorial: Bäckerstr. 1, 1010 WIEN **Tel:** 1 61077448
Fax: 1 61077419
Email: redaktion@verlagoesterreich.at **Web site:** http://www.verlagoesterreich.at
Freq: Quarterly; **Annual Sub.:** EUR 66,00; **Circ:** 1,030
Editor: Arnold Zotter
Profile: Magazine from the independent senates of administration about authoritative practice and application of law.
Language(s): German
ADVERTISING RATES:
Full Page Mono .... EUR 598
Mechanical Data: Type Area: 244 x 165 mm

ZEITSCHRIFT FÜR ABGABEN-, FINANZ- UND STEUERRECHT AFS
1641714A1A-225
Editorial: Bäckerstr. 1, 1010 WIEN **Tel:** 1 61077448
Fax: 1 61077419
Email: redaktion@verlagoesterreich.at **Web site:** http://www.verlagoesterreich.at
Freq: 10 issues yearly; **Annual Sub.:** EUR 124,00; **Circ:** 1,200
Profile: Magazine about tax law and concession tax law.
Language(s): German
ADVERTISING RATES:
Full Page Mono .... EUR 598
Mechanical Data: Type Area: 244 x 165 mm

ZEITSCHRIFT FÜR GESELLSCHAFTSRECHT UND ANGRENZENDES STEUERRECHT
1641687A1A-223
Editorial: Bäckerstr. 1, 1010 WIEN **Tel:** 1 61077448
Fax: 1 61077419
Email: redaktion@verlagoesterreich.at **Web site:** http://www.verlagoesterreich.at
Freq: 6 issues yearly; **Annual Sub.:** EUR 94,00; **Circ:** 1,150
Editor: Lukas Fanatur
Profile: Magazine about corporate and tax law.
Language(s): German
ADVERTISING RATES:
Full Page Mono .... EUR 598
Mechanical Data: Type Area: 244 x 165 mm
Copy instructions: *Copy Date:* 28 days prior to publication

ZEITSCHRIFT FÜR PSYCHOANALYTISCHE THEORIE UND PRAXIS
1775690A56A-1997
Editorial: Beckgasse 18, 1130 WIEN **Tel:** 1 8794265
Email: praxis@reiter.priv.at **Web site:** http://www.zptp.eu
Freq: Quarterly; **Annual Sub.:** EUR 78,00; **Circ:** 2,000
Editor: Bettina Reiter; **Advertising Manager:** Alexander Losse
Profile: Journal for discussion of clinical cases in psychoanalysis, psychoanalytic theory and history.
Language(s): German
ADVERTISING RATES:
Full Page Mono .... EUR 450
Mechanical Data: Type Area: 210 x 126 mm

ZEITSCHRIFT FÜR VERGABERECHT RPA
1641703A1A-224
Editorial: Bäckerstr. 1, 1010 WIEN **Tel:** 1 61077448
Fax: 1 61077419
Email: redaktion@verlagoesterreich.at **Web site:** http://www.verlagoesterreich.at
Freq: 6 issues yearly; **Annual Sub.:** EUR 128,90; **Circ:** 1,200
Profile: Magazine on contract acquisition law for lawyers, technicians, employees and institutions who deal with tenders.
Language(s): German
ADVERTISING RATES:
Full Page Mono .... EUR 598
Mechanical Data: Type Area: 244 x 165 mm

ZEK ZUKUNFTSENERGIE + KOMMUNALTECHNIK
1641290A58-244
Editorial: Lindaustr. 10, 4820 BAD ISCHL
Tel: 6235 20541 **Fax:** 6235 20541
Email: rg@zekmagazin.at **Web site:** http://www.zek.at
Freq: 6 issues yearly; **Annual Sub.:** EUR 57,00; **Circ:** 12,000
Editor: Roland Gruber; **Advertising Manager:** Günter Seefried
Profile: International magazine about renewable energies.
Language(s): German
ADVERTISING RATES:
Full Page Colour .... EUR 4720
Mechanical Data: Type Area: 262 x 186 mm

ZIK INSOLVENZRECHT & KREDITSCHUTZ
748876A44-631
Editorial: Marxergasse 25, 1030 WIEN
Tel: 1 534521552 **Fax:** 1 53452140
Email: katharina.bacher@lexisnexis.at **Web site:** http://zik.lexisnexis.at
Freq: 6 issues yearly; **Annual Sub.:** EUR 139,00; **Circ:** 1,800
Advertising Manager: Wolfgang Kreissl
Profile: Publication focusing on insolvency legislation and credit protection.
Language(s): German
ADVERTISING RATES:
Full Page Mono .... EUR 1510
Full Page Colour .... EUR 2300
Mechanical Data: Type Area: 252 x 172 mm
BUSINESS: LEGAL

ZIVILSCHUTZ AKTUELL
748894A54A-240
Editorial: Schottenfeldgasse 24, 1070 WIEN
Tel: 1 5247086 **Fax:** 1 5247086903
Email: ursula.hauer@echo.at **Web site:** http://www.echo.at
Freq: Quarterly; **Annual Sub.:** EUR 24,40; **Circ:** 30,000
Editor: Ursula Hauer
Profile: Publication containing information about civil defence.
Language(s): German
BUSINESS: SAFETY & SECURITY: Fire Fighting

ZUKUNFT
749030A82-3771
Editorial: Löwelstr. 18, 1014 WIEN **Tel:** 1 53427399
Fax: 431 53427363
Email: redaktion@diezukunft.at **Web site:** http://www.diezukunft.at
Freq: 11 issues yearly; **Annual Sub.:** EUR 44,00; **Circ:** 17,000
Editor: Caspar Einem
Profile: Socialist newspaper about politics, economics and culture.
Language(s): German
CONSUMER: CURRENT AFFAIRS & POLITICS

ZUKUNFTSBRANCHEN
749032A14A-2480
Editorial: Webgasse 29/26, 1060 WIEN
Tel: 1 8975349 **Fax:** 1 5955158
Email: haiden@publishfactory.at **Web site:** http://www.zukunftsbranchen.at
Freq: 8 issues yearly; **Annual Sub.:** EUR 24,75; **Circ:** 55,000
Editor: Renate Haiden; **Advertising Manager:** Harald Wurm
Profile: Magazine for job starters and jobseekers.
Language(s): German
ADVERTISING RATES:
Full Page Colour .... EUR 6500
Mechanical Data: No. of Columns (Display): 3, Col Widths (Display): 60 mm, Type Area: 252 x 190 mm
Copy instructions: *Copy Date:* 10 days prior to publication

Belarus

Time Difference: GMT + 2 hrs (EET - Eastern European Time)
National Telephone Code: +375
Continent: Europe
Capital: Minsk
Principal Language: Belarusian, Russian
Population: 9724723
Monetary Unit: Belarus Ruble (BYB)

EMBASSY HIGH COMMISSION: Embassy of the Republic of Belarus: 6 Kensington Court, London W8 5DL
Tel: 0207 937 32 88
Fax: 0207 361 00 05
Email: uk@belembassy.org
Website: http://www.belembassy.org/uk

7 DNEY
1615658BV65J-3
Editorial: ul. Engelsa 30, 220030 MINSK
Tel: 17 22 78 622 **Fax:** 17 22 78 622
Email: 7days@belta.by **Web site:** http://7days.belta.by
Date Established: 1990; **Freq:** Weekly - Published on Thursday; **Circ:** 40,000
Usual Pagination: 32
Editor: Viktor Chikin
Profile: A week's TV program, social events, sport, weather, film reviews, famous people, etc.
Language(s): Russian
NATIONAL DAILY & SUNDAY NEWSPAPERS: National Weekly Newspapers

AUTOBUSINESS WEEKLY
1202317BV31A-5
Formerly: AutoBusiness
Editorial: ul. Kalinovskogo 55, 220103 MINSK
Tel: 17 28 14 739 **Fax:** 17 28 14 741
Email: abw@abw.by **Web site:** http://abw.by
Date Established: 1993; **Freq:** Weekly - Published on Thursdays; **Circ:** 42,000
Usual Pagination: 144
Executive Editor: Sergey Mikhailov; **Editor-in-Chief:** Dimitriy Astashenko; **Advertising Manager:** Olga Shingaleyeva
Profile: Newspaper featuring news in motor trade industry, articles on cars testing, spare parts and used cars.
Language(s): Russian
ADVERTISING RATES:
Full Page Colour .... BYB 2183000.00
Mechanical Data: Page Width: 297mm, Col Length: 420mm, No. of Columns (Display): 5
Copy instructions: *Copy Date:* 1 week prior to publication date
Supplement(s): Truck.
BUSINESS: MOTOR TRADE: Motor Trade Accessories

BELGAZETA
766596BV65J-2
Editorial: ul. Kalvariskaya 17 A, office 616A, MINSK 220004 **Tel:** 17 200 40 50 **Fax:** 17 203 26 40
Email: bg@bg.org.by **Web site:** http://www.belgazeta.by
Date Established: 1995; **Freq:** Weekly - Published on Monday; **Circ:** 21,300
Usual Pagination: 40
Editor: Igor Vysotski; **Advertising Manager:** Elena Dubovnik; **Advertising Director:** Olga Popko
Profile: National newspaper focusing on news in economics, politics and society in Belarus and in the world.
Language(s): Russian
ADVERTISING RATES:
SCC .... BYB 8850.00
Mechanical Data: Type Area: A3
NATIONAL DAILY & SUNDAY NEWSPAPERS: National Weekly Newspapers

EXPRESS NOVOSTI
1800370BV65J-4
Editorial: pr. Nezavisimosti 77, 220013 MINSK
Tel: 17 29 26 405 **Fax:** 17 29 25 403
Email: info@expressnews.by **Web site:** http://www.expressnews.by
Date Established: 1997; **Freq:** Weekly; **Circ:** 7,000
Usual Pagination: 32
Profile: Analytical-informative newspaper.
Language(s): Belarusian; Russian
Readership: Aimed at businessmen, high calibre economists and industry leaders.

ADVERTISING RATES:
SCC .... BYB 1850.00
NATIONAL DAILY & SUNDAY NEWSPAPERS: National Weekly Newspapers

KOMPUTERNAYA GAZETA
714146BV5C-50
Editorial: P. O. Box 563, 220113 MINSK
Tel: 17 28 93 713 **Fax:** 17 33 44 476
Email: pumpur@nestormedia.com **Web site:** http://www.nestor.minsk.by/kg
Date Established: 1995; **Freq:** Weekly - Published on Mondays; **Circ:** 26,000
Usual Pagination: 24
Editor: Svetlana Pumpur; **Advertising Manager:** Elena Makarevich
Profile: Newspaper containing news, reviews, features general hardware and software information. Places emphasis on details about new and forthcoming products.
Language(s): Russian
Readership: Aimed at specialists and end users.
ADVERTISING RATES:
Full Page Mono .... BYB 2336400.00
Mechanical Data: Type Area: 255 x 330mm
BUSINESS: COMPUTERS & AUTOMATION: Professional Personal Computers

MC MOBILNAYA SVYAZ'
1840356BV18B-5
Editorial: pereulok Fedotova 14, MINSK
Tel: 17 29 15 885 **Fax:** 17 29 56 600
Email: info@mc.by **Web site:** http://mc.by
Date Established: 2003; **Freq:** Monthly; **Circ:** 25,000
Usual Pagination: 116
Advertising Director: Inna Vasilenko
Profile: Informative-analytical magazine about up-to-date technology andmobile connections in Belarus and abroad with news on cell phones, photo cameras, laptops, stereo systems, mp3 players, TV sets, video cameras and DVD players.
Language(s): Russian
ADVERTISING RATES:
Full Page Mono .... RUR 4620000.00
Mechanical Data: Type Area: 210 x 280mm
BUSINESS: ELECTRONICS: Telecommunications

NARODNAYA GAZETA
1202397BV65A-5
Editorial: ul. Khmelnitskogo 10A, Etazh 7, 220013 MINSK **Tel:** 17 28 71 870 **Fax:** 17 28 71 806
Email: info@ng.by **Web site:** http://www.ng.by
Date Established: 1990; **Freq:** Mornings - Published from Tuesday to Saturday; **Cover Price:** BYB 400,00; **Circ:** 40,000
Editor: Victor Leshchenko; **Editor-in-Chief:** Vladimir Andrievich
Profile: Newspaper covering national and international news with features on business and finance, culture, education and lifestyle.
Language(s): Belarusian; Russian
ADVERTISING RATES:
SCC .... BYB 2645.00
NATIONAL DAILY & SUNDAY NEWSPAPERS: National Daily Newspapers

RESPUBLIKA
763179BV14R-1
Editorial: ul. Bogdana Khmyalnitskogo 10a, MINSK 220013 **Tel:** 17 28 71 6 15 **Fax:** 17 28 71 6 12
Email: info@respublika.info **Web site:** http://respublika.info
Date Established: 1991; **Freq:** 250 issues yearly - Published 5 days a week; **Cover Price:** BYB 600.00
Annual Sub.: BYB 92400.00; **Circ:** 50,300
Editor: Anatoly Lemyeshyonok; **Advertising Director:** Vladimir Dolgih
Profile: Newspaper containing articles about official documents, legal acts, politics and news.
Language(s): Belarusian; Russian
Readership: Read by managers and directors.
ADVERTISING RATES:
Full Page Colour .... BYB 10913270.00
BUSINESS: COMMERCE, INDUSTRY & MANAGEMENT: Commerce Related

SOVIETSKAYA BELORUSSIA
766592BV65A-11
Editorial: vul. Khmelnitskogo 10A, 220013 MINSK
Tel: 17 29 25 101 **Fax:** 17 29 21 432
Email: admin@sb.by **Web site:** http://www.sb.by
Freq: 250 issues yearly - Published 5 times a week: from Tuesday to Saturday; **Annual Sub.:** BYB 108000.00; **Circ:** 417,966
Advertising Manager: Anatoliy Litvinski
Profile: Newspaper focusing on financial, economical and social-political issues.
Language(s): Russian
ADVERTISING RATES:
SCC .... BYB 6050.00
Mechanical Data: Type Area: 260 x 374mm
NATIONAL DAILY & SUNDAY NEWSPAPERS: National Daily Newspapers

VECHERNY MINSK
1201119BV65A-10
Editorial: Pr. Fr. Skoriny 44, 220005 MINSK
Tel: 17 28 45 944 **Fax:** 17 28 82 835
Email: vm@nsys.by **Web site:** http://www.newsvm.com
Date Established: 1967; **Freq:** Evenings; **Cover Price:** BYB 750.00; **Circ:** 40,000
Editor: Sergey Sverkunov; **Advertising Manager:** Marina Nesterova
Profile: Newspaper focusing on national and international news, politics and the economy, sport, culture and lifestyle.
Language(s): Russian
ADVERTISING RATES:
SCC .... EUR 2.60
NATIONAL DAILY & SUNDAY NEWSPAPERS: National Daily Newspapers

VIRTUAL JOYS
763133BV78D-400
Editorial: PO Box 563, 220113 MINSK
Tel: 17 28 93 713 **Fax:** 17 33 46 790
Email: nestorinfo@nestormedia.com **Web site:** http://www.nestor.minsk.by/vr
Date Established: 2000; **Freq:** Monthly; **Circ:** 25,000
Usual Pagination: 32
Editor: Marina Biryukova; **Advertising Manager:** Anatoly Kiryushkin
Profile: Newspaper containing information about computer games and related soft- and hardware.
Language(s): Russian
Supplement(s): Game News
CONSUMER: CONSUMER ELECTRONICS: Games

ZNAMYA YUNOSTI
1615909BV74F-1
Editorial: ul. Khmelnitskogo 10 A, 220013 MINSK
Tel: 17 28 71 684 **Fax:** 17 28 71 684
Email: zn@zn.by **Web site:** http://zn.by
Date Established: 1938; **Freq:** Weekly - Published on Friday; **Annual Sub.:** BYB 54000.00; **Circ:** 32,000
Usual Pagination: 34
Editor: Olga Pavlovna Yeroshenko; **Advertising Manager:** Aleksandr Alelurovich Bobokhin
Profile: Newspaper containing social-political news, articles on history, culture, show business and world-wide youth organisations.
Language(s): Russian
Readership: Aimed at young people aged 12 to 15 years.
CONSUMER: WOMEN'S INTEREST CONSUMER MAGAZINES: Teenage

Belgium

Time Difference: GMT + 1 hr (CET - Central European Time)
National Telephone Code: +32
Continent: Europe
Capital: Brussels
Principal Language: Dutch (Flemish), French, German
Population: 10392226
Monetary Unit: Euro (EUR)
EMBASSY HIGH COMMISSION: Belgian Embassy: 17 Grosvenor Crescent, London SW1X 7EE, UK
Tel: 020 7470 3700
Fax: 020 7470 3795/3710
Head of Mission: HE Mr Johan Verbeke,
Email: london@diplobel.fed.be
Website: http://www.diplomatie.be/london

7DIMANCHE
1704123B65B-6
Editorial: Avenue Léon Grosjean 92, 1140 EVERE
Tel: 2 730 33 11 **Fax:** 2 730 35 80
Email: red@7dimanche.be **Web site:** http://www.7dimanche.be
Date Established: 2005; **Freq:** Weekly - Belgium; **Cover Price:** Free; **Circ:** 250,000
Usual Pagination: 48
Language(s): French
Supplement(s): 7MAG (7DIMANCHE) - 4xY
NATIONAL DAILY & SUNDAY NEWSPAPERS: National Sunday Newspapers

7 DIMANCHE
2000816B74A-206
Tel: 2730 38 83 **Fax:** 27303580
Email: red@7dimanche.be **Web site:** http://www.7dimanche.be
Date Established: 2010; **Freq:** Quarterly - 01 05 09 12; **Circ:** 265,000
Language(s): French
Mechanical Data: Type Area: A4
Supplement to: 7 DIMANCHE
CONSUMER: WOMEN'S INTEREST CONSUMER MAGAZINES: Women's Interest

7SUR7.BE
1660212B65A-186
Editorial: Brusselsesteenweg 347, 1730 ASSE/KOBBEGEM **Tel:** 2454 26 16 **Fax:** 24542615
Email: info@7sur7.be **Web site:** http://www.7sur7.be
Language(s): French
NATIONAL DAILY & SUNDAY NEWSPAPERS: National Daily Newspapers

A MAGAZINE
1892924B84A-427
Editorial: Ijzerlaan 54-56, B-2060 ANTWERP
Email: info@amagazinecuratedby.com **Web site:** http://amagazinecuratedby.com
Date Established: 2004; **Freq:** Half-yearly; **Cover Price:** EUR 11; **Circ:** 15,000
Usual Pagination: 200
Editor-in-Chief: Daniel Thawley
Language(s): English; French
Mechanical Data: Type Area: 230 x 295
CONSUMER: THE ARTS & LITERARY: Arts

AFILIATYS
1469B74C-160
Editorial: Rue du Bâteau, 12 A, 1080 BRUXELLES
Tel: 2520 99 90 **Fax:** 2520 22 77
Email: info@special-editions.be **Web site:** http://www.afiliatysmag.eu
Date Established: 1997; **Freq:** 6 issues yearly; **Cover Price:** Free; **Circ:** 22,000
Usual Pagination: 100
Publisher: Léon Rusinek
Profile: Magazine containing articles and information about fittings, design and DIY for bathrooms.
Language(s): French
Readership: Aimed at people interested in DIY and home improvements.
ADVERTISING RATES:
Full Page Colour .... EUR 2.800
CONSUMER: WOMEN'S INTEREST CONSUMER MAGAZINES: Home & Family

AGENDA PLUS
2261B74Q-7
Editorial: Rue de la Terre Franche, 31, 5310 LONGCHAMPS **Tel:** 8143 24 80 **Fax:** 81432489
Email: info@agendaplus.be **Web site:** http://www.agendaplus.be
Date Established: 1996; **Freq:** Monthly - 1ère semaine du mois, sauf 01 08; **Cover Price:** Free; **Circ:** 40,000
Usual Pagination: 96
Editor: Jean Annet
Profile: Magazine focusing on natural health remedies, healthy lifestyle and the environment.
Language(s): French
ADVERTISING RATES:
Full Page Colour .... EUR 1130
Mechanical Data: Type Area: A5
CONSUMER: WOMEN'S INTEREST CONSUMER MAGAZINES: Lifestyle

AGORA MAGAZINE
1648148B14L-2
Editorial: Avenue des Gaulois, 36, 1040 BRUXELLES
Tel: 2733 98 00 **Fax:** 2733 05 33
Email: us@unionsyndicale.eu **Web site:** http://www.unionsyndicale.eu
Date Established: 1992; **Freq:** Quarterly; **Cover Price:** Free; **Circ:** 42,000
Usual Pagination: 32
Language(s): French
ADVERTISING RATES:
Full Page Colour .... EUR 1.300
BUSINESS: COMMERCE, INDUSTRY & MANAGEMENT: Trade Unions

ALLURE MAGAZINE
2421B80-5
Editorial: Raymond Stuyck Consultants, Koralenhoeve, 4, 2160 WONNELGEM
Tel: 3355 38 38 **Fax:** 3355 38 39
Email: contact@exlclusief.be **Web site:** http://www.exclusief.be
Date Established: 2003; **Freq:** Quarterly - 06 09 11 12; **Circ:** 32,000
Usual Pagination: 120
Profile: Regional fashion magazine, providing cultural and local news.
Language(s): Flemish; French
ADVERTISING RATES:
Full Page Mono .... EUR 1810
Full Page Colour .... EUR 2206
CONSUMER: RURAL & REGIONAL INTEREST

AMBIANCE CULINAIRE
2262B74P-236
Editorial: Katwilgweg, 2 - Bus 3, 2050 ANVERS
Tel: 3210 30 50 **Fax:** 32103051
Email: info@ambiance.be **Web site:** http://www.ambiance.be
Date Established: 1986; **Freq:** Monthly - Laatste dinsdag, niet in 01, 08; **Cover Price:** EUR 5.95
Annual Sub.: EUR 59.50; **Circ:** 42,000
Usual Pagination: 164
Editor: Dirk de Prins; **Publisher:** Bart Lodewijckx
Profile: Lifestyle magazine about food, wine and tourism.
Language(s): Flemish; French
Readership: Read by people who cook for pleasure and chefs.
Mechanical Data: Type Area: A 4
CONSUMER: WOMEN'S INTEREST CONSUMER MAGAZINES: Food & Cookery

ARCHI-NEWS
1892922B4A-165
Editorial: Dennedreef, 8 a, B-3721 KORTESEM
Tel: 11 37 56 13 **Fax:** 11 5607
Email: press@archi-news.com **Web site:** http://www.archi-news.com
Date Established: 2003; **Freq:** Monthly - Niet in 07 08; **Circ:** 115,000
Editor: Jacques Allard
Language(s): Flemish; French
BUSINESS: ARCHITECTURE & BUILDING: Architecture

ART ET DECORATION CAHIER BELGIQUE
2185B74C-15
Editorial: Place des Carabiniers, 15, 1030 BRUXELLES **Tel:** 2241 55 55 **Fax:** 22415533
Email: media.selling@euronet.be **Web site:** http://www.mediaselling.be
Date Established: 1898; **Freq:** Monthly - En 2009: 01/07 19/08 30/09 12/11; **Circ:** 41,000
Usual Pagination: 32
Profile: Magazine focusing on interior decoration and home improvement.
Language(s): French
ADVERTISING RATES:
Full Page Colour .... EUR 3950
Mechanical Data: Type Area: 300 x 232
CONSUMER: WOMEN'S INTEREST CONSUMER MAGAZINES: Home & Family

ATTITUDE
2213B74Q-20
Editorial: Pulsebaan, 50/1, 2242 PULDERBOS
Tel: 3466 00 66 **Fax:** 34660067
Email: info@attitude.be **Web site:** http://www.attitude.be
Date Established: 1984; **Freq:** 6 issues yearly - 02 04 06 09 11; **Circ:** 86,000
Usual Pagination: 85
Publisher: Bart De Landtsheer
Profile: Magazine covering lifestyle, fashion and culture. Separate editions for Antwerp, Brabant, Limburg and East and West Flanders.
Language(s): Flemish; French
Readership: Aimed at men and women aged between 28 and 65 years with a high disposable income.
ADVERTISING RATES:
Full Page Colour .... EUR 1795
Copy instructions: *Copy Date:* 28 days prior to publication date
CONSUMER: WOMEN'S INTEREST CONSUMER MAGAZINES: Lifestyle

AUTO LOISIRS
2378B77A-72
Editorial: Chaussée Romaine 186, Boîte 2, 4300 WAREMME **Tel:** 1933 16 00 **Fax:** 19331615
Email: autoloisirs@skynet.be **Web site:** http://www.autoloisirs.be
Freq: 6 issues yearly - le 20 du mois; **Cover Price:** EUR 450
Annual Sub.: EUR 30; **Circ:** 20,000
Profile: Magazine containing technical and financial information about cars.
Language(s): Flemish; French
ADVERTISING RATES:
Full Page Colour .... EUR 3350
Mechanical Data: Type Area: 310 x 220
CONSUMER: MOTORING & CYCLING: Motoring

AUTO MAX
1804266B77A-221
Editorial: Rue Petite Coyarde, 14, 1367 MONT SAINT ANDRE **Tel:** 8187 87 24 **Fax:** 8187 87 24
Email: redaction@automaxxx.be **Web site:** http://www.automaxxx.be
Date Established: 2006; **Freq:** 6 issues yearly; **Cover Price:** EUR 4
Annual Sub.: EUR 30; **Circ:** 20,000
Language(s): Flemish; French
ADVERTISING RATES:
Full Page Colour .... EUR 2.900
CONSUMER: MOTORING & CYCLING: Motoring

AUTOGIDS
1892979B77A-225
Editorial: Generaal Dumonceaulaan 56, 1190 BRUSSELS **Tel:** 2333 32 20 **Fax:** 23333261
Email: contact.aug@autogids.be **Web site:** http://www.autogids.be
Date Established: 1979; **Freq:** 26 issues yearly - Woensdag
Annual Sub.: EUR 65; **Circ:** 45,000
Usual Pagination: 200
Editor-in-Chief: Gaétan Philippe
Language(s): Flemish; French
Mechanical Data: Type Area: 297 x 210
CONSUMER: MOTORING & CYCLING: Motoring

AUTONEWS
2375B77A-40
Editorial: Walshoutenstraat, 63, 3401 LANDEN
Tel: 11 88 62 42 **Fax:** 56 55 88 21
Email: autonews@akynet.be **Web site:** http://www.autonews-magazine.com
Date Established: 1991; **Freq:** Monthly; **Cover Price:** EUR 5,95
Annual Sub.: EUR 59; **Circ:** 13,750
Usual Pagination: 80
Editor: Bernard Verstraete
Profile: Magazine focusing on cars and autosport.
Language(s): Flemish; French
Readership: Read by enthusiasts of motor sports.

Belgium

ADVERTISING RATES:
Full Page Colour .... EUR 2.290
CONSUMER: MOTORING & CYCLING: Motoring

AXELLE MAGAZINE
2163B74A-7
Editorial: Rue de la Poste, 111, 1030 BRUXELLES
Tel: 2227 13 19 **Fax:** 22230442
Email: axellemag@viefeminine.be **Web site:** http://www.axellemag.be
Date Established: 1998; **Freq:** Monthly - 26 du mois; **Annual Sub.:** EUR 24; **Circ:** 14,000
Usual Pagination: 48
Profile: Socio-cultural women's magazine.
Language(s): French
ADVERTISING RATES:
Full Page Colour .... EUR 950
Mechanical Data: Type Area: 220 x 285
CONSUMER: WOMEN'S INTEREST CONSUMER MAGAZINES: Women's Interest

BATIR
1647826B79A-257
Editorial: For all contact details see main record, KNACK, 1130 **Tel:** 2702 71 31 **Fax:** 27027132
Email: info@mediaoffice.be
Freq: Annual - Février; **Circ:** 280,000
Publisher: Bob De Meyer
Language(s): Flemish; French
ADVERTISING RATES:
Full Page Colour .... EUR 13083
Supplement to: KNACK
CONSUMER: HOBBIES & DIY

BE TV
2337B76C-30
Editorial: Chaussée de Louvain, 656, 1030 BRUXELLES **Tel:** 2730 02 11 **Fax:** 27300232
Email: abonnesweb@betv.be **Web site:** http://www.betv.be
Date Established: 1993; **Freq:** Monthly - Le 27 du mois; **Circ:** 156,045
Usual Pagination: 84
Managing Director: Frédéric Vandeschoor
Profile: Magazine containing information about films, music, sport, cinema and programmes on Canal Plus.
Language(s): French
Readership: Aimed at subscribers.
ADVERTISING RATES:
Full Page Colour .... EUR 4100
Mechanical Data: Type Area: 280 x 203
CONSUMER: MUSIC & PERFORMING ARTS: TV & Radio

BEAUTY
1647668B15A-201
Editorial: Rue Theophiel Roucourt, 38, 2600 BERCHEM **Tel:** 3230 09 09 **Fax:** 32302004
Email: info@gicom.be
Freq: Quarterly - 02 05 09 12; **Circ:** 150,000
Language(s): Flemish; French
ADVERTISING RATES:
Full Page Colour .... EUR 7125
BUSINESS: COSMETICS & HAIRDRESSING: Cosmetics

HET BELANG VAN LIMBURG
1880B67B-1000
Editorial: Herckenrodesingel 10, 3500 HASSELT
Tel: 1187 81 11 **Fax:** 1187 82 04
Email: hbvleindredactie@concentra.be **Web site:** http://www.hbvl.be
Date Established: 1879; **Freq:** Daily - 6 dagen/week; **Cover Price:** EUR 1.10
Annual Sub.: EUR 229; **Circ:** 112,000
Usual Pagination: 40
Editor: Ivo Vandekerckhove; **Editor-in-Chief:** Rik Van Puymbroeck
Language(s): Flemish; French
Mechanical Data: Type Area: 540 x 385
REGIONAL DAILY & SUNDAY NEWSPAPERS: Regional Daily Newspapers

BIOINFO
2222B74G-17
Editorial: Avenue Brugmann, 29, 1060 BRUXELLES
Tel: 2345 04 78 **Fax:** 2345 85 44
Email: bioinfo@skynet.be **Web site:** http://www.bioinfo.be
Date Established: 1998; **Freq:** Monthly - Chaque mois sauf janvier et août
Annual Sub.: EUR 20; **Circ:** 44,000
Usual Pagination: 68
Profile: Magazine focusing on healthy living and diet.
Language(s): Flemish; French
Readership: Read by customers of health shops and restaurants. Also read by health care workers.
ADVERTISING RATES:
Full Page Mono .... EUR 1300
Full Page Colour .... EUR 1500
Mechanical Data: Type Area: 275 x 195
Copy instructions: *Copy Date:* 20 days prior to publication date
CONSUMER: WOMEN'S INTEREST CONSUMER MAGAZINES: Slimming & Health

BLOEMEN & PLANTEN
2581B93-20
Editorial: Bredabaan 852, 2170 MERKSEM
Tel: 3645 42 94 **Fax:** 36450500
Email: redactie.benp@vipmedia.nl **Web site:** http://www.bloemenenplanten.be
Date Established: 1986; **Freq:** Monthly - 21ste van de maand; **Cover Price:** EUR 4.95
Annual Sub.: EUR 49.50; **Circ:** 50,000
Usual Pagination: 92
Editor: Jacqueline Leenders; **Editor-in-Chief:** Jeanine Hoogstraten
Profile: Magazine focusing on house and garden flowers and plants.
Language(s): Flemish; French
Readership: Aimed at gardening enthusiasts aged 30 to 60 years.
ADVERTISING RATES:
Full Page Mono .... EUR 1515
Full Page Colour .... EUR 2025
Copy instructions: *Copy Date:* 7 days prior to publication date
CONSUMER: GARDENING

BLOEMSCHIKKEN
1893170B93-162
Editorial: Pulsebaan, 50/1, 2242 PULDERBOS-ZANDHOVEN **Tel:** 3466 00 26 **Fax:** 34660067
Email: info.be@epninternational.be **Web site:** http://www.epninternational.com
Date Established: 1997; **Freq:** 26 issues yearly - 01 04 08 10; **Cover Price:** EUR 4.95; **Circ:** 76,000
Usual Pagination: 100
Editor: Nico Smout
Language(s): Flemish; French
CONSUMER: GARDENING

BOUWBEDRIJF - CONSTRUCTION
1554B42A-25
Editorial: Rue du Lombard 34-42, 1000 BRUXELLES
Tel: 2545 56 00 **Fax:** 2545 59 00
Email: info@confederatiebouw.be **Web site:** http://www.confederatiebouw.be
Date Established: 1945; **Freq:** Monthly - Début de mois; **Annual Sub.:** EUR 220; **Circ:** 17,000
Usual Pagination: 80
Editor: Peter Graller
Profile: Journal of the Confederation of Construction Companies.
Language(s): Flemish; French
Readership: Read by business executives, managers of building companies, architects, technical services officers and training personnel.
ADVERTISING RATES:
Full Page Mono .... EUR 1330
Full Page Colour .... EUR 2266
Mechanical Data: Type Area: A 4
Copy instructions: *Copy Date:* 31 days prior to publication date
BUSINESS: CONSTRUCTION

BOZARMAGAZINE
1648010B64P-1
Editorial: Palais des Beaux Arts, Rue Ravenstein, 23, 1000 BRUXELLES **Tel:** 2 507 84 54 **Fax:** 2 5078515
Email: publications@bozar.be **Web site:** http://www.bozar.be
Date Established: 2002; **Freq:** Monthly - Le 1er du mois; **Cover Price:** Free; **Circ:** 79,000
Usual Pagination: 50
Managing Director: Paul Dujardin
Language(s): English; Flemish; French
ADVERTISING RATES:
Full Page Colour .... EUR 4300
Mechanical Data: Type Area: 170 x 240
Copy instructions: *Copy Date:* 42 days prior to publication date
BUSINESS: OTHER CLASSIFICATIONS: Museums

(BRUID & BRUIDEGOM) DE FEESTGIDS
1745814B74L-158
Editorial: Schaliënstraat, 30-32, 2000 ANTWERPEN
Tel: 3281 21 00 **Fax:** 3281 12 84
Email: info@bruidenbruidegom.be **Web site:** http://www.bruidenbruidegom.be
Freq: Quarterly; **Cover Price:** EUR 3; **Circ:** 17,500
Managing Director: Eric Bogaert
Language(s): Flemish; French
ADVERTISING RATES:
Full Page Colour .... EUR 1.630
CONSUMER: WOMEN'S INTEREST CONSUMER MAGAZINES: Brides

BRUID & BRUIDEGOM MAGAZINE
1648088B74L-155
Editorial: Schaliënstraat 30-32, 2000 ANTWERP
Tel: 3281 21 00 **Fax:** 3281 12 84
Email: info@bruidenbruidegom.be **Web site:** http://www.bruidenbruidegom.be
Date Established: 1984; **Freq:** Quarterly - 03 06 09 12; **Circ:** 175,000
Usual Pagination: 180
Editor: Susan Lippe
Language(s): Flemish; French
ADVERTISING RATES:
Full Page Mono .... EUR 1185
Full Page Colour .... EUR 2168
CONSUMER: WOMEN'S INTEREST CONSUMER MAGAZINES: Brides

BUDGET & DROITS
1893046B1A-113
Editorial: Association des consommateurs, Rue de Hollande, 13, 1060 BRUXELLES **Tel:** 2542 35 55
Fax: 25423399
Email: membres@test-achats.be **Web site:** http://www.test-achats.be
Freq: 6 issues yearly - Fin de mois; **Circ:** 300,000
Language(s): French
BUSINESS: FINANCE & ECONOMICS

THE BULLETIN
2551B82-251
Editorial: Chaussée de Waterloo, 1038 BRUXELLES
Tel: 2373 83 26 **Fax:** 23759822
Email: thebulletin@ackroyd.be **Web site:** http://www.xpats.com
Date Established: 1962; **Freq:** Weekly - Jeudi;
Cover Price: EUR 4.50
Annual Sub.: EUR 110; **Circ:** 8,000
Usual Pagination: 84
Managing Director: Pascal Zoetart
Profile: Belgian newsweekly magazine in English that provides news and views on the political, economical, social and cultural scene in the Capital of Europe.
Language(s): English; French
ADVERTISING RATES:
Full Page Mono .... EUR 1800
Full Page Colour .... EUR 2250
Mechanical Data: Type Area: 275 x 205
CONSUMER: CURRENT AFFAIRS & POLITICS

BUNTER FADEN
2165B74A-35
Editorial: LFV, Talstrasse, 17A, 4701 KETTENIS
Tel: 8776 55 36 **Fax:** 8776 55 32
Email: lfv@skynet.be **Web site:** http://www.lfv.be
Freq: Monthly; **Cover Price:** Free; **Circ:** 2,300
Usual Pagination: 20
Editor: Chris Van Hoof
Profile: Publication of the women's association Landfrauenverband.
Language(s): Flemish; French
ADVERTISING RATES:
Full Page Colour .... EUR 850
CONSUMER: WOMEN'S INTEREST CONSUMER MAGAZINES: Women's Interest

BUSINESS LOGISTICS / SUPPLY CHAIN SOLUTIONS
630172B14A-40
Editorial: Jan van Gentstraat 1, Bus 102, 2000 ANTWERPEN **Tel:** 3 234 05 50
Email: barbara@businesslogistics.com **Web site:** http://www.businesslogistics.com
ISSN: 1372-875X
Date Established: 1994; **Freq:** Monthly - 3ème semaine, sauf 07 08; **Cover Price:** EUR 17
Annual Sub.: EUR 133; **Circ:** 12,000
Usual Pagination: 60
Profile: Magazine containing information about new high skill management concepts and strategies.
Language(s): Flemish; French
Readership: Read by senior managers, logistics and IT directors and production planners.
ADVERTISING RATES:
Full Page Mono .... EUR 2150
Full Page Colour .... EUR 3199
Mechanical Data: Type Area: A4
BUSINESS: COMMERCE, INDUSTRY & MANAGEMENT

LA CAPITALE - REDACTION CENTRALE - BRUXELLES
1873B67B-3600
Editorial: Rue Royale, 120, 1000 BRUXELLES
Tel: 2225 56 00 **Fax:** 22255913
Email: redaction.generale@sudpresse.be **Web site:** http://www.sudpresse.be
Date Established: 1944; **Freq:** Daily - Belgium; **Circ:** 16,000
Language(s): French
REGIONAL DAILY & SUNDAY NEWSPAPERS: Regional Daily Newspapers

CHE
706747B86C-15
Editorial: Oude Leeuwenrui, 8, Bus 2, 2000 ANTWERPEN **Tel:** 320 20 100 **Fax:** 320 20 140
Email: post@che.be **Web site:** http://www.che.be
Date Established: 2000; **Freq:** Monthly; **Cover Price:** EUR 4,90
Annual Sub.: EUR 54,00; **Circ:** 25,565
Editor: Günther Van Hassel
Profile: Male interest magazine.
Language(s): Flemish; French
Readership: Aimed at men between the ages of 18 and 45 years.
ADVERTISING RATES:
Full Page Colour .... EUR 3.950
CONSUMER: ADULT & GAY MAGAZINES: Men's Lifestyle Magazines

CINÉ TÉLÉ REVUE
1647681B76C-323
Editorial: Avenue Reine Marie-Henriette 101, 1190 BRUXELLES **Tel:** 2345 99 68 **Fax:** 23407443
Email: redaction@cinetelerevue.be **Web site:** http://www.cinetelerevue.be
Date Established: 1944; **Freq:** Weekly - Le jeudi;
Cover Price: EUR 125
Annual Sub.: EUR 6300; **Circ:** 350,459
Usual Pagination: 148
Language(s): French
ADVERTISING RATES:
Full Page Colour .... EUR 12200
Mechanical Data: Type Area: 300 x 235
CONSUMER: MUSIC & PERFORMING ARTS: TV & Radio

CITY MAG
1983671B74Q-373
Editorial: Rue Broodcoorensstraat 52, 1310 LA HULPE **Tel:** 2652 00 20 **Fax:** 26521129
Email: citymag@maxipress.be **Web site:** http://www.citynet.be/maxipress/presentation
Freq: Quarterly; **Cover Price:** Free; **Circ:** 35,000
Language(s): French
Copy instructions: *Copy Date:* 7 days prior to publication date
CONSUMER: WOMEN'S INTEREST CONSUMER MAGAZINES: Lifestyle

CLICKX MAGAZINE
2265B74Q-30
Editorial: Parklaan, 22, Bus 10, 2300 TURNHOUT
Tel: 1446 23 00 **Fax:** 1446 23 66
Email: redactie@clickx.be **Web site:** http://www.clickx.be
Date Established: 1997; **Freq:** Monthly - Vrijdag;
Cover Price: EUR 3.10
Annual Sub.: EUR 72; **Circ:** 42,000
Usual Pagination: 100
Editor: Bart Bettens; **Publisher:** Thomas Buytaert
Profile: Lifestyle magazine for Internet users in Belgium.
Language(s): Flemish; French
ADVERTISING RATES:
Full Page Colour .... EUR 3600
Mechanical Data: Type Area: 297 X 230
CONSUMER: WOMEN'S INTEREST CONSUMER MAGAZINES: Lifestyle

CLUBBRUGGE.BE
1706614B75B-156
Editorial: Club Brugge Koninklijke Voetbalvereniging, Olympialaan 74, 8200 BRUGGE **Tel:** 50 40 21 21
Fax: 50 38 10 23
Email: info@clubbrugge.be **Web site:** http://www.clubbrugge.be
Editor: Guy Jacobs
Language(s): English; Flemish; French
CONSUMER: SPORT: Football

CNAC INFO
2638B4E-200
Editorial: Rue Saint-Jean, 4, 1000 BRUXELLES
Tel: 2552 05 00 **Fax:** 25520505
Email: cnac@cnac.be **Web site:** http://www.cnac.be
Date Established: 1977; **Freq:** Quarterly - Fin 03 06 09 12; **Cover Price:** EUR 280
Annual Sub.: EUR 28; **Circ:** 50,000
Usual Pagination: 8
Managing Director: Carl Heyrman
Profile: Magazine containing information about safety procedures in construction.
Language(s): Flemish; French
Readership: Read by builders and architects.
ADVERTISING RATES:
Full Page Mono .... EUR 2500
Mechanical Data: Type Area: A3
BUSINESS: ARCHITECTURE & BUILDING: Building

COMBUSTIBLES
1739B58-20
Editorial: Féd. der Brandstoffenhandelaars, Rue L. Lepage, 4, 1000 BRUXELLES **Tel:** 2502 42 00
Fax: 25025446
Email: info@brafco.be **Web site:** http://www.brafco.be
Date Established: 1946; **Freq:** 6 issues yearly - Variable; **Circ:** 16,000
Usual Pagination: 40
Managing Director: Roger de Laet
Profile: Official journal of the Federation of Fuel Traders. Covers solid and liquid fuels, butane and propane.
Language(s): Flemish; French
Readership: Read by all fuel distributors in Belgium plus local and federal authorities.
ADVERTISING RATES:
Full Page Mono .... EUR 800
Full Page Colour .... EUR 1350
BUSINESS: ENERGY, FUEL & NUCLEAR

CONSTRUIRE OU RENOVER/ BOUWEN OF VERBOUWEN
1647837B4A-172
Editorial: Av. Lavoisier, 18C, 1300 WAVRE
Tel: 10 22 88 88 **Fax:** 10 238919
Email: info@marketingpress.be **Web site:** http://www.construire-renover.be
Date Established: 1985; **Freq:** Annual - Fin février; **Circ:** 70,000
Usual Pagination: 500
Managing Director: Roland Meers
Language(s): Flemish; French
ADVERTISING RATES:
Full Page Colour .... EUR 5250
BUSINESS: ARCHITECTURE & BUILDING: Architecture

CONTROL & AUTOMATION MAGAZINE
1252B5A-9
Editorial: Diamantstraat, 5, 2275 LILLE
Tel: 3326 56 16 **Fax:** 33265636
Email: info@mainpress.com **Web site:** http://www.mainpress.com
Date Established: 1993; **Freq:** 6 issues yearly - 03 05 06 09 12; **Annual Sub.:** EUR 36; **Circ:** 8,500
Usual Pagination: 52
Editor: Bert Belmans

Profile: Publication about the control automation and instrumentation industry.
Language(s): Flemish; French
Readership: Aimed at engineers.
ADVERTISING RATES:
Full Page Mono .... EUR 1775
Full Page Colour .... EUR 2370
Mechanical Data: Type Area: 295 x 210
Copy instructions: *Copy Date:* 15 days prior to publication date
BUSINESS: COMPUTERS & AUTOMATION: Automation & Instrumentation

LE COURRIER DU BOIS/ HOUTNIEUWS 1588B46-25

Editorial: Stationstraat, 108, 2800 MALINES
Tel: 2219 28 32 **Fax:** 25233962
Email: bois@decom.be **Web site:** http://www.lecourrierdubois.be
Date Established: 1961; **Freq:** Quarterly - 03 05 09 11; **Annual Sub.:** EUR 26; **Circ:** 23,000
Usual Pagination: 48
Publisher: Roger de Laet
Profile: Magazine containing news and information about forestry and the wood working industry. Covers technology, ecology and financial aspects.
Language(s): Flemish; French
Readership: Read by carpenters, joiners, foresters and other professionals within the trade.
ADVERTISING RATES:
Full Page Mono .... EUR 1785
Full Page Colour .... EUR 2500
Copy instructions: *Copy Date:* 31 days prior to publication date
BUSINESS: TIMBER, WOOD & FORESTRY

CULINAIRE SAISONNIER 2631B11A-131

Editorial: Picardielaan, 22, 2970 SCHILDE
Tel: 3380 17 00 **Fax:** 33801710
Email: info@saisonnier.net **Web site:** http://www.saisonnier.net
Date Established: 1996; **Freq:** Quarterly - 10/03 06 09 12; **Cover Price:** EUR 8.50
Annual Sub.: EUR 25; **Circ:** 24,000
Usual Pagination: 97
Profile: Seasonal catering magazine.
Language(s): Flemish; French
Readership: Read by restaurateurs and caterers.
ADVERTISING RATES:
Full Page Colour .... EUR 2640
Copy instructions: *Copy Date:* 62 days prior to publication date
BUSINESS: CATERING: Catering, Hotels & Restaurants

DAG ALLEMAAL 2187B74C-32

Editorial: Brandekensweg 2, 2627 SCHELLE
Tel: 3880 84 70 **Fax:** 38846152
Email: redactie@dagallemaal.be **Web site:** http://www.dagallemaal.be
Date Established: 1983; **Freq:** Weekly - Tuesday;
Cover Price: EUR 1.90
Annual Sub.: EUR 98; **Circ:** 486,692
Usual Pagination: 196
Editor: Ilse Beyers
Profile: Family magazine containing entertainment news, TV listings and interviews.
Language(s): Flemish; French
ADVERTISING RATES:
Full Page Colour .... EUR 12100
Mechanical Data: Type Area: 270 x 208
CONSUMER: WOMEN'S INTEREST CONSUMER MAGAZINES: Home & Family

DATA NEWS 1874453B5B-62

Editorial: Raketstraat 50, 1130 BRUSSELS
Tel: 2702 71 07 **Fax:** 2660 36 00
Email: lb@datanews.com **Web site:** http://www.datanews.be
Freq: Weekly - Vrijdag; **Cover Price:** EUR 29.99
Annual Sub.: EUR 99; **Circ:** 20,044
Usual Pagination: 50
Editor-in-Chief: Krista Vanhee
Language(s): Flemish; French
Mechanical Data: Type Area: 230 x 297
BUSINESS: COMPUTERS & AUTOMATION: Data Processing

DATANEWS CAREERS 1261B5B-40

Formerly: DATA NEWS CAREERS
Editorial: Firstmedia NV, Rues de la Fusée 50, 1130 BRUXELLES **Tel:** 51 26 66 67 **Fax:** 51 26 65 95
Email: info.jobs@roularta.be **Web site:** http://www.datanews.be
Date Established: 1979; **Freq:** Weekly - Vendredi;
Circ: 21,500
Profile: Magazine for electronic data-processing managers in Belgium, covering computer and telecommunications news.
Language(s): Flemish; French
ADVERTISING RATES:
Full Page Mono .... EUR 6800
BUSINESS: COMPUTERS & AUTOMATION: Data Processing

DE BIETPLANTER - LE BETTERAVIER 1455B21A-178

Editorial: Bd Anspach 111 - B 10, 1000 BRUXELLES
Tel: 2551 11 74 **Fax:** 25121988
Email: lebetteravier@cbb.be
Date Established: 1967; **Freq:** Monthly - Dernière semaine du mois; **Annual Sub.:** EUR 12; **Circ:** 12,000
Usual Pagination: 24
Profile: Journal of the Confederation of Belgian Beet Producers.
Language(s): Flemish; French
Readership: Read by beet and sugarbeet producers, cereal-growers and agriculturalists.
ADVERTISING RATES:
Full Page Mono .... EUR 1014
Full Page Colour .... EUR 1723.80
BUSINESS: AGRICULTURE & FARMING

DE BOND 2186B74C-20

Editorial: Troonstraat 125, 1050 BRUSSELS
Tel: 2507 89 22 **Fax:** 25078809
Email: redactiedebond@gezinsbond.be **Web site:** http://www.gezinsbond.be
Date Established: 1921; **Freq:** 104 issues yearly - vrijdag/vendredi; **Annual Sub.:** EUR 30; **Circ:** 287,800
Usual Pagination: 44
Editor: An Candaele
Profile: Family magazine.
Language(s): Flemish; French
ADVERTISING RATES:
Full Page Mono .... EUR 3930
Full Page Colour .... EUR 6205
Mechanical Data: Type Area: 350 x 235
CONSUMER: WOMEN'S INTEREST CONSUMER MAGAZINES: Home & Family

DE TIJD 1647698B65A-173

Editorial: Havenlaan 86 C, 1000 BRUSSELS
Tel: 2 423 18 39 **Fax:** 2 423 18 15
Email: hoofdredacteur@tijd.be **Web site:** http://www.tijd.be
ISSN: 0772-0809
Date Established: 1968; **Freq:** Daily - Belgium;
Cover Price: EUR 1.50
Annual Sub.: EUR 320; **Circ:** 38,582
Editor: Pierre Huylenbroeck; **Editor-in-Chief:** Roland Legrand
Language(s): Flemish; French
ADVERTISING RATES:
Full Page Mono .... EUR 14630
Full Page Colour .... EUR 17150
NATIONAL DAILY & SUNDAY NEWSPAPERS: National Daily Newspapers

DECO IDÉES 2188B74C-35

Editorial: Avenue Général Dumonceau 56, 1190 BRUXELLES **Tel:** 2333 32 11 **Fax:** 23333210
Email: contact@decoidees.be **Web site:** http://www.decoidees.be
Date Established: 1995; **Freq:** Monthly - Fin de mois; **Cover Price:** EUR 3.50
Annual Sub.: EUR 32; **Circ:** 37,000
Usual Pagination: 250
Profile: Magazine focusing on home furnishings and interior decoration.
Language(s): French
ADVERTISING RATES:
Full Page Colour .... EUR 4095
Mechanical Data: Type Area: 297 x 225
Copy instructions: *Copy Date:* 28 days prior to publication date
CONSUMER: WOMEN'S INTEREST CONSUMER MAGAZINES: Home & Family

DECODESIGN 1657995B4B-23

Editorial: Torhoutsesteenweg, 226, Bus 2, 8210 ZEDELGEM **Tel:** 5024 04 04 **Fax:** 50240445
Email: info@pmgroup.be **Web site:** http://www.decodesign.be
Date Established: 2004; **Freq:** Quarterly - 01 05 08 11; **Annual Sub.:** EUR 32; **Circ:** 5,000
Language(s): Flemish; French
ADVERTISING RATES:
Full Page Colour .... EUR 2800
BUSINESS: ARCHITECTURE & BUILDING: Interior Design & Flooring

DECORATIE 1233B4B-12

Formerly: DECORATIE - DECORATION
Editorial: Torhoutsesteenweg 226, Bus 2, 8210 ZEDELGEM **Tel:** 5024 04 04 **Fax:** 50240445
Email: info@pmg.be **Web site:** http://www.decosite.be
Date Established: 1994; **Freq:** 26 issues yearly;
Cover Price: EUR 6.25
Annual Sub.: EUR 51; **Circ:** 10,500
Usual Pagination: 65
Profile: Magazine about interior and exterior house decoration, including information about trends and new products.
Language(s): Flemish; French
Readership: Read by decorators, interior designers, suppliers and manufacturers.
ADVERTISING RATES:
Full Page Colour .... EUR 2800
BUSINESS: ARCHITECTURE & BUILDING: Interior Design & Flooring

DECORS 1234B4B-15

Editorial: NinOffices, Graanmarkt, 42 A1, 9400 NINOVE **Tel:** 5451 55 10 **Fax:** 54515515
Email: info@decors.be **Web site:** http://www.decors.be
ISSN: 0773-4034
Freq: Quarterly - Les 20 : 03 06 09 12; **Cover Price:** EUR 6.70
Annual Sub.: EUR 2300; **Circ:** 38,000
Usual Pagination: 192
Profile: Magazine focusing on design, architecture and decoration.
Language(s): Flemish; French
Readership: Read by interior designers, architects and the general public.
ADVERTISING RATES:
Full Page Mono .... EUR 2335
Full Page Colour .... EUR 2915
Mechanical Data: Type Area: 230 x 297
BUSINESS: ARCHITECTURE & BUILDING: Interior Design & Flooring

DECOSTYLE 601573B4B-17

Editorial: Redactiebureau INK, Stationstraat, 12, 8210 LOPPEM **Tel:** 5082 43 75 **Fax:** 50824380
Email: redactie@decostyle.info **Web site:** http://www.decostyle.info
Date Established: 1997; **Freq:** Quarterly - 31/03 - 30/06 - 10/09 - 27/12
Annual Sub.: EUR 40; **Circ:** 12,112
Usual Pagination: 56
Publisher: Jan Hoffman
Profile: Magazine containing information about new technologies and applications, market news, trends, technical and scientific analyses.
Language(s): Flemish; French
Readership: Read by interior designers, plasterers, joiners, decorators, wholesalers and suppliers.
ADVERTISING RATES:
Full Page Colour .... EUR 1995
Mechanical Data: Type Area: A4
BUSINESS: ARCHITECTURE & BUILDING: Interior Design & Flooring

DECOUVREZ LA FRANCE 1893404B89A-270

Editorial: Himalaya NV Kerkplein, 24, Bus 7, 1930 ZAVENTEM **Tel:** 2717 00 10 **Fax:** 27170011
Email: redactie@grande.be **Web site:** http://www.grande.be
Freq: Quarterly - 01 04 07 10; **Cover Price:** EUR 4.90; **Circ:** 50,000
Language(s): French
Copy instructions: *Copy Date:* 21 days prior to publication date
CONSUMER: HOLIDAYS & TRAVEL: Travel

DELICATESSE 601572B22A-20

Editorial: Torhoutsesteenweg, 226, Bus 2, 8210 ZEDELGEM **Tel:** 5024 04 04 **Fax:** 50240445
Email: info@pmgroup.be **Web site:** http://www.retail-deli.be
Date Established: 1999; **Freq:** 6 issues yearly - 03 06 09 11; **Cover Price:** EUR 6.25
Annual Sub.: EUR 41; **Circ:** 9,600
Usual Pagination: 44
Profile: Magazine containing articles and information about delicatessen food. Includes product and trade news, market trends, hygiene aspects, presentation, storage and marketing.
Language(s): Flemish; French
Readership: Aimed at chefs, food store supervisors, restaurant managers and other professionals within the field.
ADVERTISING RATES:
Full Page Colour .... EUR 2900
Copy instructions: *Copy Date:* 31 days prior to publication date
BUSINESS: FOOD

DEMORGEN.BE 1704126B67B-6032

Editorial: Brusselsesteenweg 347, 1730 ASSE/ KOBBEGEM **Tel:** 2556 68 11 **Fax:** 25203515
Email: journalist@demorgen.be **Web site:** http://www.demorgen.be
Date Established: 2003
Language(s): Flemish; French
REGIONAL DAILY & SUNDAY NEWSPAPERS: Regional Daily Newspapers

DER BAUER 1429B21A-40

Editorial: Diestsevest, 40, 3000 LEUVEN
Tel: 1628 63 02 **Fax:** 16286309
Email: boer&tuinder@boerenbond.be **Web site:** http://www.boerenbond.be
Date Established: 1893; **Freq:** Weekly - Vendredi;
Annual Sub.: EUR 75; **Circ:** 920
Usual Pagination: 16
Editor: Philippe Masscheleyn; **Publisher:** Sonja de Becker
Profile: Publication on agriculture, containing economic and technical information.
Language(s): Flemish; French
Readership: Read by farmers and people professionally linked with agriculture.
ADVERTISING RATES:
Full Page Mono .... EUR 260
Full Page Colour .... EUR 640
Mechanical Data: Type Area: A4
BUSINESS: AGRICULTURE & FARMING

LA DERNIÈRE HEURE / LES SPORTS 1813B65A-50

Editorial: Rue des Francs, 79, 1040 BRUXELLES
Tel: 2211 28 49 **Fax:** 2211 28 70
Email: dh.brabant@dh.be **Web site:** http://www.dhnet.be
Date Established: 1906; **Freq:** Daily - 6 jours / semaine; **Circ:** 112,000
Usual Pagination: 64
Profile: Tabloid-sized newspaper focusing mainly on sports items and interviews.
Language(s): French
Readership: Aimed at those with an interest in competitive sport.
Mechanical Data: Type Area: 385 x 239
NATIONAL DAILY & SUNDAY NEWSPAPERS: National Daily Newspapers

DIALOGUE & SANTE 2224B74G-25

Editorial: Rue du Bourdon, 100, 1180 BRUXELLES
Tel: 2333 34 11 **Fax:** 23323958
Web site: http://www.dialogueetsante.be
Date Established: 1983; **Freq:** Monthly - Le 10 du mois; **Cover Price:** Free; **Circ:** 230,000
Usual Pagination: 52
Profile: General health magazine distributed free in Belgian pharmacies.
Language(s): French
ADVERTISING RATES:
Full Page Colour .... EUR 6250
Mechanical Data: Type Area: 235 x 170
CONSUMER: WOMEN'S INTEREST CONSUMER MAGAZINES: Slimming & Health

DISTRIBUTION D'AUJOURD'HUI/ DISTRIBUTIE VANDAAG 1644B53-20

Editorial: Rue Marianne, 34, 1180 BRUXELLES
Tel: 2345 99 23 **Fax:** 2346 02 04
Email: info@cbd-bcd.be **Web site:** http://www.cbd-bcd.be
Date Established: 1959; **Freq:** Monthly - Vers le 20 du mois; **Circ:** 10,000
Usual Pagination: 108
Editor: Léon F. Wegnez
Profile: Magazine focusing on the distribution and retailing of the food and non food industry.
Language(s): Flemish; French
Readership: Aimed at manufacturers, retailers and wholesalers in the food and non food industry.
ADVERTISING RATES:
Full Page Mono .... EUR 2100
Full Page Colour .... EUR 2805
Copy instructions: *Copy Date:* 10 days prior to publication date
BUSINESS: RETAILING & WHOLESALING

DROIT BANCAIRE ET FINANCIER - BANK- EN FINANCIEEL RECHT 707115B44-20

Formerly: DROIT BANCAIRE/BANK-EN FINANCIEEL RECHT
Editorial: Coupure Rechts 298, 9000 GENT
Tel: 9269 97 96 **Fax:** 92699799
Email: info@uitgeverij.larcier.com **Web site:** http://ff.larcier.be
Freq: 6 issues yearly - Omstreeks de 15e vd maand
Annual Sub.: EUR 176; **Circ:** 580
Usual Pagination: 64
Profile: Magazine focusing on the law in connection with banking and finance.
Language(s): English; Flemish; French
Readership: Aimed at members of the legal profession, government, insurance, universities and financial specialists involved with companies.
ADVERTISING RATES:
Full Page Mono .... EUR 845
Full Page Colour .... EUR 1380
Mechanical Data: Type Area: A 4
BUSINESS: LEGAL

L' ECHO 1814B65A-70

Editorial: Avenue du port 86C, Boîte 309, 1000 BRUXELLES **Tel:** 2 423 17 11 **Fax:** 2 423 16 77
Email: redaction@lecho.be **Web site:** http://www.echo.be
Date Established: 1881; **Freq:** Daily - Belgium;
Cover Price: EUR 1.50
Annual Sub.: EUR 350; **Circ:** 36,000
Usual Pagination: 32
Publisher: Denis Laloy
Profile: Broadsheet-sized quality newspaper containing national and international news. Edited in two sections, one containing political information and the other concentrating on business/financial markets.
Language(s): French
Readership: Read by company directors, managers, senior executives and investors, 75 percent of whom live in the provinces of Liège and Brabant.
ADVERTISING RATES:
Full Page Mono .... EUR 9650
Full Page Colour .... EUR 11750
Mechanical Data: Type Area: 540 x 385
NATIONAL DAILY & SUNDAY NEWSPAPERS: National Daily Newspapers

EE TIMES EUROPE 1874554B18A-1

Editorial: 144 Avenue E. Plasky, 1030 BRUXELLES
Tel: 2 740 00 50 **Fax:** 2 740 00 59

Email: info@eetimes.be **Web site:** http://www.eetimes.eu
Freq: Monthly - 1er lundi du mois; **Cover Price:** Free; **Circ:** 70,000
Usual Pagination: 48
Editor: Christoph Hammerschmidt; **Publisher:** André Rousselot
Language(s): English; Flemish; French
ADVERTISING RATES:
Full Page Colour .... EUR 11525
Mechanical Data: Type Area: A4, Col Length: 277mm
Copy instructions: *Copy Date:* 14 days prior to publication date
BUSINESS: ELECTRONICS

ELECTRO-VENTE
1561B43A-15
Editorial: Edition Média Group, Gravendreef, 9 - Bus 8, 9120 BEVEREN **Tel:** 3750 90 20 **Fax:** 37509029
Email: info@emg-edit.be **Web site:** http://www.elctrovente.be
Date Established: 1965; **Freq:** Monthly - Le 20 du mois - Sauf 07; **Annual Sub.:** EUR 94; **Circ:** 8,000
Profile: Journal covering electrical appliances, heating, consumer electronics, lighting and security systems.
Language(s): Flemish; French
Readership: Read by wholesalers, retailers, manufacturers, installers and importers.
ADVERTISING RATES:
Full Page Mono .... EUR 2250
Full Page Colour .... EUR 2890
BUSINESS: ELECTRICAL RETAIL TRADE

ELEKTRO-VERKOOP
1892913B17-51
Editorial: Gravendreef, 9, Bus 8, 9120 BEVEREN
Tel: 3750 90 27 **Fax:** 37509029
Email: info@emg-edit.be **Web site:** http://www.elektroverkoop.be
ISSN: 0012-8066
Date Established: 1965; **Freq:** Monthly - Le 20 du mois - Sauf juillet
Annual Sub.: EUR 92; **Circ:** 7,500
Usual Pagination: 52
Editor: Linda Claeys
Language(s): Flemish; French
Mechanical Data: Type Area: A4
Copy instructions: *Copy Date:* 31 days prior to publication date
BUSINESS: ELECTRICAL

ELEKTRO-VISIE/ELECTRO VISION
1560B43A-10
Editorial: Nelectra, Station Lei, 78 - Boîte 1-1, 1800 VILVOORDE **Tel:** 2550 17 11 **Fax:** 25501729
Web site: http://www.nelectra.be
Date Established: 1989; **Freq:** Monthly - Niet en 01 07 08; **Circ:** 11,050
Usual Pagination: 50
Editor: Marc Van Hove; **Publisher:** Viviane Camphyn
Profile: Magazine containing articles and information covering the electronic goods trade and the electrical installation business.
Language(s): Flemish; French
Readership: Read by suppliers, retailers and installers.
ADVERTISING RATES:
Full Page Mono .... EUR 2025
Full Page Colour .... EUR 2700
BUSINESS: ELECTRICAL RETAIL TRADE

ELLE BELGIQUE DECORATION
2190B74C-45
Editorial: Chaussée de Louvain 431d, 1380 LASNE
Tel: 2379 29 90 **Fax:** 23792999
Email: elle.deco@ventures.be **Web site:** http://www.editionventures.be
Date Established: 1989; **Freq:** Monthly - Sauf 02 et 07; **Cover Price:** EUR 4.50
Annual Sub.: EUR 50; **Circ:** 17,500
Usual Pagination: 50
Profile: Magazine focusing on decoration and interior design.
Language(s): French
Readership: Aimed at home decoration enthusiasts.
ADVERTISING RATES:
Full Page Colour .... EUR 2465
Mechanical Data: Type Area: 29,7x22,7
Copy instructions: *Copy Date:* 21 days prior to publication date
CONSUMER: WOMEN'S INTEREST CONSUMER MAGAZINES: Home & Family

ELLE WMEN
1647692B74C-237
Editorial: Chaussée de Louvain, 431 D, 1380 LASNE
Tel: 2379 29 90 **Fax:** 23792999
Email: elle.wonen@ventures.be **Web site:** http://www.editionventures.be
Date Established: 1994; **Freq:** 6 issues yearly - 04 06 10 12; **Circ:** 9,500
Usual Pagination: 24
Language(s): Flemish; French
ADVERTISING RATES:
Full Page Colour .... EUR 1945
CONSUMER: WOMEN'S INTEREST CONSUMER MAGAZINES: Home & Family

ENTREPRISE AGRICOLE
1431B21A-85
Editorial: Geelseweg, 47 A, 2200 HERENTALS
Tel: 1428 60 80 **Fax:** 14214774
Email: info@rekad.be **Web site:** http://www.rekad.be
Date Established: 1993; **Freq:** Monthly - 1ère semaine du mois; **Annual Sub.:** EUR 36.50; **Circ:** 4,200
Usual Pagination: 48
Editor: Jan Ebinger
Profile: Magazine on farming containing information for farmers, foresters and local administrators.
Language(s): French
ADVERTISING RATES:
Full Page Mono .... EUR 1420
Mechanical Data: Type Area: 297 x 220
Copy instructions: *Copy Date:* 31 days prior to publication date
BUSINESS: AGRICULTURE & FARMING

EOS MAGAZINE
2608B94J-100
Editorial: Duboisstraat 50, 2060 ANTWERP
Tel: 3680 24 90 **Fax:** 3680 25 64
Email: redactie@eosmagazine.eu **Web site:** http://www.eosmagazine.eu
Date Established: 1983; **Freq:** Monthly - De 20ste, behalve Augustus; **Cover Price:** EUR 4.95
Annual Sub.: EUR 49.50; **Circ:** 47,432
Usual Pagination: 120
Editor-in-Chief: Liesbeth Gijsel; **Managing Director:** Kristine Ooms
Profile: Popular science and technology magazine.
Language(s): French
ADVERTISING RATES:
Full Page Colour .... EUR 3850
Mechanical Data: Type Area: 297 x 210
CONSUMER: OTHER CLASSIFICATIONS: Popular Science

EUROPEAN VOICE
2469B82-95
Editorial: International Press Centre, Résidence Palace, Rue de la Loi 155, Boite 6, 1040 BRUXELLES
Tel: 2540 90 90 **Fax:** 2540 90 71
Email: info@europeanvoice.com **Web site:** http://www.europeanvoice.com
Date Established: 1995; **Freq:** Weekly - jeudi; **Cover Price:** EUR 3.70
Annual Sub.: EUR 193; **Circ:** 20,000
Usual Pagination: 32
Editor: Jürgen Debusmann
Profile: Newspaper about European politics, business and current affairs.
Language(s): English; French
Readership: Read by business people and officials in the European Union.
ADVERTISING RATES:
Full Page Mono .... EUR 5810
Full Page Colour .... EUR 7750
Mechanical Data: Type Area: 400 x 290
CONSUMER: CURRENT AFFAIRS & POLITICS

L' ÉVÉNEMENT
707624B74Q-303
Editorial: Rue de Stalle 70-82, 1180 BRUXELLES
Tel: 2 333 07 00 **Fax:** 2 332 05 98
Email: evenement@mm.be **Web site:** http://www.dupedi.be
Date Established: 1979; **Freq:** Monthly - Le 7 du mois
Annual Sub.: EUR 42; **Circ:** 19,400
Usual Pagination: 280
Publisher: Jean-Pierre Dupuis
Profile: Publication dealing with new ideas in travel, home furnishing, fashion, lifestyle and decor.
Language(s): French
Readership: Read by women aged between 30 and 55 years.
ADVERTISING RATES:
Full Page Colour .... EUR 2850
Mechanical Data: Type Area: 217 x 284
CONSUMER: WOMEN'S INTEREST CONSUMER MAGAZINES: Lifestyle

EXPRESS.BE
1798980B14A-272
Editorial: Chaussée de La Hulpe, 150, 1170 WATERMAEL-BOITSFORT **Tel:** 3289 64 36
Fax: 37052778
Email: redactie@express.be **Web site:** http://www.express.be
Editor: Patrick De Schutter
Language(s): Flemish; French
BUSINESS: COMMERCE, INDUSTRY & MANAGEMENT

FEDERAUTO MAGAZINE
1495B31A-62
Editorial: Parc Artisanal 11-13, 4671 BARCHON
Tel: 2778 62 00 **Fax:** 27786222
Email: info@federauto.be **Web site:** http://www.federauto.be
ISSN: 0770-2302
Date Established: 1995; **Freq:** 6 issues yearly - Variable; **Annual Sub.:** EUR 42; **Circ:** 12,000
Usual Pagination: 68
Publisher: Philippe Pirson
Profile: Magazine containing articles and information concerning the car trade.
Language(s): Flemish; French
Readership: Aimed at managers of garages and body repair shops, dealers in second hand cars, distributors of car accessories and garage equipment.
ADVERTISING RATES:
Full Page Mono .... EUR 1345
Full Page Colour .... EUR 2245
Mechanical Data: Type Area: A 4
Copy instructions: *Copy Date:* 14 days prior to publication date
BUSINESS: MOTOR TRADE: Motor Trade Accessories

FEELING
2169B74A-60
Editorial: Uitbreidingsstraat 82, 2600 BERCHEM
Tel: 3290 13 51 **Fax:** 3290 13 52
Email: feeling@feeling.be **Web site:** http://www.feeling.be
Date Established: 1990; **Freq:** Monthly - Laatste woensdag van ecke maand; **Cover Price:** EUR 3.70
Annual Sub.: EUR 40.70; **Circ:** 121,670
Usual Pagination: 200
Editor: Lene Kemps
Profile: Magazine providing articles on lifestyle, health, fashion, beauty and career opportunities.
Language(s): Flemish; French
Readership: Aimed at modern Flemish women.
ADVERTISING RATES:
Full Page Colour .... EUR 9075
CONSUMER: WOMEN'S INTEREST CONSUMER MAGAZINES: Women's Interest

FEMMES D'AUJOURD'HUI
2170B74A-70
Editorial: Telecomlaan 5-7, 1831 DIEGEM
Tel: 2776 28 53 **Fax:** 2776 28 98
Email: femmesdaujourdhui@sanoma-magazines.be
Web site: http://www.femmesdaujourdhui.be
Date Established: 1933; **Freq:** Weekly - Le jeudi;
Cover Price: EUR 1.85
Annual Sub.: EUR 88.80; **Circ:** 130,000
Usual Pagination: 120
Profile: Magazine containing articles on fashion, beauty, health, housecraft and women's issues.
Language(s): French
Readership: Aimed at women aged between 20-55 years.
ADVERTISING RATES:
Full Page Colour .... EUR 4500
CONSUMER: WOMEN'S INTEREST CONSUMER MAGAZINES: Women's Interest

F.I.T. EXPRESS
1892963B14A-289
Formerly: FIT EXPRESS
Editorial: Gaucheretstraat 90, 1030 BRUSSELS
Tel: 2504 87 11 **Fax:** 25048899
Email: info@fitagency.be **Web site:** http://www.flandersinvestmentandtrade.be
Freq: Weekly - Le 10 du mois; **Circ:** 5,000
Usual Pagination: 12
Editor: Steffi Van Severen
Language(s): Flemish; French
Mechanical Data: Type Area: A4
BUSINESS: COMMERCE, INDUSTRY & MANAGEMENT

FLAIR
1893074B74A-184
Editorial: Rédaction Flair (magazine), Telecomlaan 5-7, 1831 DIEGEM **Tel:** 2 776 28 03 **Fax:** 2 776 28 48
Email: redaction@flair.be **Web site:** http://www.flair.be
Date Established: 1987; **Freq:** Weekly - Le mercredi;
Cover Price: EUR 1.85
Annual Sub.: EUR 78; **Circ:** 72,000
Usual Pagination: 96
Language(s): French
Mechanical Data: Type Area: 285 x 206
Copy instructions: *Copy Date:* 21 days prior to publication date
CONSUMER: WOMEN'S INTEREST CONSUMER MAGAZINES: Women's Interest

FLEET (EDITION NL)
1497B49D-2
Editorial: Z.I. Research Park, 20, 1731 ZELLIK
Tel: 2467 61 68 **Fax:** 24676162
Email: automotivemediacentre@effectivemedia.be
Web site: http://www.effectivemedia.be
Date Established: 2003; **Freq:** 6 issues yearly - 01 03 05 06 09 11; **Circ:** 27,600
Usual Pagination: 70
Profile: Magazine focusing on fleet management, including leasing of different models of cars.
Language(s): Flemish; French
Readership: Aimed at managers of company car fleets.
ADVERTISING RATES:
Full Page Mono .... EUR 3016
Full Page Colour .... EUR 4498
Mechanical Data: Type Area: 280 x 207
BUSINESS: TRANSPORT: Commercial Vehicles

FLEET & BUSINESS
1609B49A-20
Editorial: Complexe Arrobas, Parc Artisanal, 11-13, 4671 BARCHON **Tel:** 4387 87 87 **Fax:** 43879087
Email: info@mmm.be **Web site:** http://www.fleet-business.com
Freq: 6 issues yearly; **Annual Sub.:** EUR 52; **Circ:** 23,700
Profile: Magazine focusing on the management of company car and van fleets.
Language(s): Flemish; French
Readership: Aimed at car fleet managers, suppliers, car leasing managers and insurers.
ADVERTISING RATES:
Full Page Colour .... EUR 3990
Mechanical Data: Type Area: A4
BUSINESS: TRANSPORT

FOCUS KNACK
707274B76C-321
Editorial: Raketstraat 50, 1130 BRUSSELS
Tel: 2702 46 51 **Fax:** 2702 46 52
Email: focus@knack.be **Web site:** http://www.focusknack.be
Date Established: 1998; **Freq:** Weekly - Woensdag;
Circ: 140,000
Usual Pagination: 98
Editor: Patrick Duynslaegher; **Editor-in-Chief:** Barbara De Conninck; **Publisher:** Hans Maertens
Profile: Magazine focusing on radio, television, film, music, culture and celebrities.
Language(s): Flemish; French
ADVERTISING RATES:
Full Page Colour .... EUR 5500
CONSUMER: MUSIC & PERFORMING ARTS: TV & Radio

FOOD & MEAT DE SLAGER/LE BOUCHER
1466B22D-30
Editorial: Vlasstraat, 17, 8710 WIELSBEKE
Tel: 5660 73 33 **Fax:** 56610583
Email: info@evolution.be **Web site:** http://www.evolution.be
Date Established: 1987; **Freq:** Monthly - Le 20/02, 03,04,05,06,09,10,11; **Cover Price:** EUR 3.71
Annual Sub.: EUR 26; **Circ:** 7,900
Usual Pagination: 50
Profile: Journal about the meat and meat products trade.
Language(s): Flemish; French
ADVERTISING RATES:
Full Page Mono .... EUR 1485
Full Page Colour .... EUR 2120
Mechanical Data: Type Area: 297 x 210
Copy instructions: *Copy Date:* 21 days prior to publication date
BUSINESS: FOOD: Meat Trade

FORUM
1892794B88A-191
Editorial: Guimardstraat, 1, 1040 BRUSSEL
Tel: 2507 06 19 **Fax:** 2513 36 45
Email: forum@vsko.be **Web site:** http://www.vsko.be
Freq: Monthly; **Annual Sub.:** EUR 22,10; **Circ:** 5,000
Usual Pagination: 16
Editor: Willy Bombeek
Language(s): Flemish; French
CONSUMER: EDUCATION

GAEL
2175B74A-115
Editorial: Telecomlaan 5-7, 1831 DIEGEM
Tel: 2776 24 80 **Fax:** 2776 23 15
Email: gael@sanoma-magazines.be **Web site:** http://www.sanoma-magazines.be
Date Established: 1988; **Freq:** Monthly - Dernier mercredi du mois; **Cover Price:** EUR 3.20; **Circ:** 80,162
Usual Pagination: 200
Publisher: Anne Brouckmans
Profile: Magazine containing articles about style and fashion, home, gardening and cookery.
Language(s): French
Readership: Aimed at women with a high disposable income.
ADVERTISING RATES:
Full Page Colour .... EUR 5700
Copy instructions: *Copy Date:* 21 days prior to publication date
CONSUMER: WOMEN'S INTEREST CONSUMER MAGAZINES: Women's Interest

GAEL FOR MEN/MANNEN FEELING
1893194B86C-175
Editorial: Telecomlaan, 5-7, 1831 DIEGEM
Tel: 2776 24 80 **Fax:** 27762315
Email: gael@sanoma-magazines.be **Web site:** http://www.sanoma-magazines.be
Date Established: 2008; **Freq:** Half-yearly - Avril et octobre; **Cover Price:** Free; **Circ:** 80,000
Publisher: Anne Brouckmans
Language(s): French
Copy instructions: *Copy Date:* 21 days prior to publication date
CONSUMER: ADULT & GAY MAGAZINES: Men's Lifestyle Magazines

GAEL MAISON / FEELING WONEN
1605513B74C-191
Editorial: Telecomlaan, 5-7, 1831 DIEGEM
Tel: 2776 22 53 **Fax:** 2776 23 39
Email: gaelmaison@sanoma-magazines.be **Web site:** http://www.gaelmaison.be
Date Established: 1998; **Freq:** Monthly; **Cover Price:** EUR 3.40
Annual Sub.: EUR 27.90; **Circ:** 42,644
Usual Pagination: 134
Publisher: Marie-Anne de Temmerman
Profile: Magazine focusing on interior design, better living, house furnishing, practical tips and latest fashion in home improvements.
Language(s): Flemish; French
Readership: Magazine aimed at people with interest in home improvements.

ADVERTISING RATES:
Full Page Colour .... EUR 2750
CONSUMER: WOMEN'S INTEREST CONSUMER MAGAZINES: Home & Family

GAZET VAN ANTWERPEN
1871B67B-1800
Editorial: Katwilgweg 2, 2050 ANTWERP
Tel: 3 210 02 10 **Fax:** 3 219 40 41
Email: gvaachterkrant@concentra.be **Web site:** http://www.gva.be
Date Established: 1891; **Freq:** Daily - Belgium; **Cover Price:** EUR 1.10
Annual Sub.: EUR 267; **Circ:** 120,000
Usual Pagination: 36
Editor-in-Chief: Bart Huybens
Language(s): Flemish; French
Mechanical Data: Type Area: 538 x 385
REGIONAL DAILY & SUNDAY NEWSPAPERS: Regional Daily Newspapers

GENIETEN
1647707B74Q-365
Editorial: Rue de Stallestraat 70-82, 1180 BRUXELLES **Tel:** 2 333 07 00 **Fax:** 2 332 05 98
Email: redactie@genieten.be **Web site:** http://www.genieten.be
Date Established: 1999; **Freq:** Monthly - Eerste vrijdag v/d maand; **Cover Price:** EUR 4.95
Annual Sub.: EUR 54; **Circ:** 30,000
Usual Pagination: 140
Language(s): Flemish; French
ADVERTISING RATES:
Full Page Colour .... EUR 4000
Mechanical Data: Type Area: 298 x 210
CONSUMER: WOMEN'S INTEREST CONSUMER MAGAZINES: Lifestyle

DE GENTENAAR - NIEUWSBLAD
1818B65A-133
Formerly: DE GENTENAAR/NIEUWSBLAD
Editorial: Kouter 150, 9000 GENT **Tel:** 9 268 72 70 **Fax:** 9 268 72 71
Email: nieuws@gentenaar.be **Web site:** http://www.gentenaar.be
Freq: Daily - Belgium
Annual Sub.: EUR 264; **Circ:** 271,000
Usual Pagination: 40
Editor: Michel Vandersmissen
Profile: Broadsheet-sized newspaper containing national and international news, business reports and coverage of political events.
Language(s): Flemish; French
Readership: Read by company directors, managers and senior executives, university students and office personnel, the majority of whom live in Flanders.
NATIONAL DAILY & SUNDAY NEWSPAPERS: National Daily Newspapers

GENTLEMAN
1790984B86C-173
Editorial: Raketstraat 50, 1130 BRUXELLES
Tel: 5126 61 11
Email: info@roularta.be **Web site:** http://www.gentlemanmagazine.be
Date Established: 2006; **Freq:** 6 issues yearly - 02 04 05 09 10 11; **Circ:** 47,200
Publisher: Chantal Lepaige
Language(s): Flemish; French
ADVERTISING RATES:
Full Page Colour .... EUR 6250
Copy instructions: *Copy Date:* 31 days prior to publication date
CONSUMER: ADULT & GAY MAGAZINES: Men's Lifestyle Magazines

GEZOND THUIS
1647709B56A-269
Editorial: Ad. Lacombléaan 69-71, 1030 BRUSSELS
Tel: 2739 35 11 **Fax:** 27393599
Email: info@vlaanderen.wgk.be **Web site:** http://www.witgelekruis.be
Date Established: 1994; **Freq:** Quarterly - 03 06 09 12; **Circ:** 137,800
Usual Pagination: 32
Editor: Renild Wouters
Language(s): Flemish; French
ADVERTISING RATES:
Full Page Mono .... EUR 1842
Full Page Colour .... EUR 2694
Mechanical Data: Type Area: 297 x 210
BUSINESS: HEALTH & MEDICAL

GLAM-IT
1648301B74A-168
Editorial: Uitbreidingstraat, 82, 2600 BERCHEM
Tel: 3290 13 92 **Fax:** 3290 13 94
Email: info@glamit.be **Web site:** http://www.glamit.be
Date Established: 2003; **Freq:** Monthly - Elke 1ste dinsdag v/d maand; **Cover Price:** EUR 2.95
Annual Sub.: EUR 29.50; **Circ:** 61,000
Usual Pagination: 174
Editor: Pascale Baelden
Language(s): Flemish; French
ADVERTISING RATES:
Full Page Colour .... EUR 4500
CONSUMER: WOMEN'S INTEREST CONSUMER MAGAZINES: Women's Interest

GLOSSY
1655100B74A-170
Editorial: Katwilgweg 2 - B 5, 2050 ANTWERPEN
Tel: 3680 24 88 **Fax:** 36802564
Email: redactie3@cascade.be
Date Established: 2004; **Freq:** Monthly - Laatste donderdag vd maand; **Cover Price:** EUR 3.50; **Circ:** 10,000
Editor: Vic Dennis
Language(s): Flemish; French
ADVERTISING RATES:
Full Page Colour .... EUR 2500
CONSUMER: WOMEN'S INTEREST CONSUMER MAGAZINES: Women's Interest

GOED GEVOEL
2227B74G-35
Editorial: Brandekensweg 2, 2627 SCHELLE
Tel: 3880 84 50 **Fax:** 3844 61 52
Email: redactie@goedgevoel.be **Web site:** http://www.goedgevoel.be
Date Established: 1993; **Freq:** Monthly - Woe. voor laatste vrij v/d maand; **Cover Price:** EUR 3.50
Annual Sub.: EUR 37.80; **Circ:** 122,000
Usual Pagination: 200
Editor: Famke Robbrechts
Profile: Magazine covering health, well-being, beauty and home decorating.
Language(s): Flemish; French
ADVERTISING RATES:
Full Page Colour .... EUR 6000
Mechanical Data: Type Area: A 4
CONSUMER: WOMEN'S INTEREST CONSUMER MAGAZINES: Slimming & Health

GONDOLA MAGAZINE - RETAIL TODAY
1459B53-202
Editorial: Tervuursesteenweg, 605, 1982 ELEWIJT
Tel: 1562 79 00 **Fax:** 15627901
Email: info@gondola.be **Web site:** http://www.gondola.be
Date Established: 1993; **Freq:** Monthly - Vers le 20 du mois; **Cover Price:** EUR 15
Annual Sub.: EUR 125; **Circ:** 9,800
Usual Pagination: 50
Profile: Magazine about the production, marketing and distribution of consumer goods in supermarkets.
Language(s): Flemish; French
ADVERTISING RATES:
Full Page Colour .... EUR 3260
BUSINESS: RETAILING & WHOLESALING

GRAFISCH NIEUWS - NOUVELLES GRAPHIQUES
1892811B14J-3
Editorial: Rue de la Fusée 50, boîte 15, 1130 BRUXELLES **Tel:** 2 702 71 71 **Fax:** 2 702 71 72
Email: alfons.calders@roularta.be **Web site:** http://www.grafisch-nieuws.be
Date Established: 1950; **Freq:** Monthly - fin de mois; **Annual Sub.:** EUR 50; **Circ:** 6,000
Usual Pagination: 48
Editor: Alain Vermeire
Language(s): Flemish; French
Mechanical Data: Type Area: 297 x 210
BUSINESS: COMMERCE, INDUSTRY & MANAGEMENT: Commercial Design

GRANDE
707464B89A-261
Editorial: Himalaya sa/nv, Kerkplein 24, boîte 7, 1930 ZAVENTEM **Tel:** 2717 00 10 **Fax:** 27170011
Email: redaction@grande.be **Web site:** http://www.grande.be
Date Established: 2000; **Freq:** Monthly - Fin de mois; **Cover Price:** EUR 5.20
Annual Sub.: EUR 45; **Circ:** 50,000
Usual Pagination: 132
Profile: Magazine focusing on world travel. Each edition features a different country and highlights destinations, nature, culture and discovery.
Language(s): Flemish; French
Readership: Read by affluent members of Belgian society.
ADVERTISING RATES:
Full Page Colour .... EUR 6950
Copy instructions: *Copy Date:* 21 days prior to publication date
CONSUMER: HOLIDAYS & TRAVEL: Travel

GREENPEACE MAGAZINE
1874811B57-61
Editorial: Greenpeace Belgique, Chaussée de Haecht, 159, 1030 BRUXELLES **Tel:** 2274 02 00 **Fax:** 2274 02 30
Email: info@be.greenpeace.org **Web site:** http://www.greenpeace.be
Freq: Quarterly; **Circ:** 75,000
Language(s): Flemish; French
BUSINESS: ENVIRONMENT & POLLUTION

GRENZ-ECHO
1878B67B-2200
Editorial: Marktplatz, 8, 4700 EUPEN **Tel:** 8759 13 22 **Fax:** 87553457
Email: redaktion@grenzecho.be **Web site:** http://www.grenzecho.be
Date Established: 1927; **Freq:** Daily - Belgium; **Cover Price:** EUR 1.10
Annual Sub.: EUR 235; **Circ:** 12,382
Editor: Gérard Cremer
Language(s): French
ADVERTISING RATES:
Full Page Colour .... EUR 3600
Mechanical Data: Type Area: 420 x 288
REGIONAL DAILY & SUNDAY NEWSPAPERS: Regional Daily Newspapers

GUEST MAGAZINE
2001651B82-345
Editorial: Rue Royale 223, 1210 BRUXELLES
Tel: 2 209 63 70 **Fax:** 2 209 63 71
Email: info@firstmediapress.com **Web site:** http://www.guestmagazine.be
Freq: Monthly - 02 03 04 05 06 09 10 11 12; **Cover Price:** Free; **Circ:** 25,000
Editor: Mike Vandenvelde; **Publisher:** Emile Verschueren
Language(s): French
Mechanical Data: Type Area: 255 x 300
CONSUMER: CURRENT AFFAIRS & POLITICS

GUS
707481B86B-1
Editorial: Rue Fernand Bernier, 15, 1060 BRUXELLES **Tel:** 2544 10 44 **Fax:** 25379437
Email: editor@gusmag.net **Web site:** http://www.gusmag.net
Date Established: 2000; **Freq:** 6 issues yearly - 03 05 09 11
Annual Sub.: EUR 24; **Circ:** 20,000
Usual Pagination: 112
Publisher: Frédérick Boutry
Profile: Magazine focusing on gay lifestyle, aiming to promote a positive image of homosexuality.
Language(s): English; Flemish; French
ADVERTISING RATES:
Full Page Colour .... EUR 2600
Mechanical Data: Type Area: 305 x 225
Copy instructions: *Copy Date:* 14 days prior to publication date
CONSUMER: ADULT & GAY MAGAZINES: Gay & Lesbian Magazines

HEALTH AND FOOD
1675B56A-83
Editorial: Rue de Rixensart, 18, Bâtiment 17, Boite 3, 1332 GENVAL **Tel:** 2653 21 58 **Fax:** 26532158
Email: info@diffu-sciences.com **Web site:** http://www.healthandfood.be
Date Established: 1997; **Freq:** 6 issues yearly - 20-02, 04, 06, 09, 10, 12; **Annual Sub.:** EUR 25; **Circ:** 15,000
Usual Pagination: 24
Publisher: Danièle Degossely
Profile: Bulletin concerning dietetics and food in relation to health and medicine.
Language(s): French
Readership: Read by medical general practitioners and dieticians.
ADVERTISING RATES:
Full Page Mono .... EUR 2350
Full Page Colour .... EUR 3220
Mechanical Data: Type Area: A 4
BUSINESS: HEALTH & MEDICAL

HEY NIEUWSBLAD OP ZONDAG
1648324B65B-5
Editorial: Alfons Gossetlaan 28, 1702 GROOT BIJGAARDEN **Tel:** 2467 22 11 **Fax:** 24663093
Email: nieuws@nieuwsblad.be **Web site:** http://www.nieuwsblad.be
Date Established: 2003; **Freq:** Weekly - Belgium; **Circ:** 50,000
Editor: Geert Dewaele
Language(s): Flemish; French
NATIONAL DAILY & SUNDAY NEWSPAPERS: National Sunday Newspapers

HLN - HET LAATSTE NIEUWS / DE NIEUWE GAZET
1816B65A-108
Editorial: Brusselsesteenweg 347, 1730 ASSE/KOBBEGEM **Tel:** 2454 22 11 **Fax:** 24542801
Email: info@hln.be **Web site:** http://www.hln.be
Date Established: 2003; **Freq:** Daily - Belgium
Annual Sub.: EUR 216; **Circ:** 300,000
Editor-in-Chief: An Schoemans
Profile: Broadsheet-sized newspaper providing news and information covering politics, society, sport and regional issues.
Language(s): Flemish; French
Readership: Aimed at a broad sector of society, 90 percent of whom live in the Flemish part of Belgium.
ADVERTISING RATES:
Full Page Mono .... EUR 27450
Full Page Colour .... EUR 30500
Mechanical Data: Type Area: 540 x 385
NATIONAL DAILY & SUNDAY NEWSPAPERS: National Daily Newspapers

HOME SWEET HOME
1655037B74C-200
Editorial: Belgiëlaan 4b, 2200 HERENTALS
Tel: 1421 05 52 **Fax:** 1422 56 10
Email: info@homesweethome.be **Web site:** http://www.homesweethome.be
Date Established: 1992; **Freq:** Quarterly - 02 05 08 11
Annual Sub.: EUR 20; **Circ:** 30,000
Usual Pagination: 144
Language(s): Flemish; French
ADVERTISING RATES:
Full Page Colour .... EUR 1500
CONSUMER: WOMEN'S INTEREST CONSUMER MAGAZINES: Home & Family

HORECA REVUE
1305B11A-74
Editorial: Vlasstraat, 17, 8710 WIELSBEKE
Tel: 5660 73 33 **Fax:** 56610583
Email: info@evolution.be **Web site:** http://www.evolution.be
Date Established: 1974; **Freq:** 24 issues yearly - 02 03 04 05 06 09 10 11
Annual Sub.: EUR 32.50; **Circ:** 18,100
Usual Pagination: 56
Profile: Magazine for the hotel, restaurant and bar sector, covering management, culinary issues, trade fairs and exhibitions.
Language(s): Flemish; French
ADVERTISING RATES:
Full Page Mono .... EUR 1690
Full Page Colour .... EUR 2450
Mechanical Data: Type Area: 210 x 297
Copy instructions: *Copy Date:* 21 days prior to publication date
BUSINESS: CATERING: Catering, Hotels & Restaurants

HOTEL BUSINESS
1307B11A-76
Editorial: Vlasstraat, 17, 8710 WIELSBEKE
Tel: 5660 73 33 **Fax:** 56610583
Email: info@evolution.be **Web site:** http://www.evolution.be
Date Established: 1992; **Freq:** Quarterly - 03 06 09 11; **Cover Price:** EUR 3.71
Annual Sub.: EUR 12; **Circ:** 3,979
Usual Pagination: 48
Profile: Hotel magazine covering food and beverages, management, security, equipment, training and international exhibitions.
Language(s): Flemish; French
ADVERTISING RATES:
Full Page Mono .... EUR 795
Full Page Colour .... EUR 1215
Mechanical Data: Type Area: 210 x 297
Copy instructions: *Copy Date:* 21 days prior to publication date
BUSINESS: CATERING: Catering, Hotels & Restaurants

HUMO
2338B76C-50
Editorial: Harensesteenweg 226, 1800 VILVOORDE
Tel: 2303 3400 **Fax:** 2776 23 24
Email: redactie@humo.be **Web site:** http://www.humo.be
Date Established: 1936; **Freq:** Weekly - Dinsdag; **Cover Price:** EUR 2.20; **Circ:** 253,085
Usual Pagination: 187
Editor: Sam Degraeve; **Editor-in-Chief:** Davy Coolen
Profile: Magazine containing radio and television news.
Language(s): Flemish; French
ADVERTISING RATES:
Full Page Colour .... EUR 10580
Mechanical Data: Type Area: 270 x 205
CONSUMER: MUSIC & PERFORMING ARTS: TV & Radio

IKEA FAMILY LIVE
1790981B94H-25
Editorial: Weiveldlaan, 19, 1930 ZAVENTEM
Tel: 2719 19 66 **Fax:** 2721 46 21
Email: family.belgium@ikea.com **Web site:** http://www.ikea.be
Freq: Quarterly; **Cover Price:** Free; **Circ:** 200,000
Usual Pagination: 100
Editor: Olivier Baraille
Language(s): Flemish; French
CONSUMER: OTHER CLASSIFICATIONS: Customer Magazines

IMAGO
2151B74Q-364
Editorial: Ambachtenlaan 13, 3294 MOLENSTEDE-DIEST **Tel:** 13 78 07 90 **Fax:** 13 77 75 66
Email: jan.tuerlinckx@tuerlinckx.be **Web site:** http://www.imagomagazine.eu
Freq: Quarterly - 03 06 09 12; **Circ:** 66,000
Profile: General interest magazine containing articles and information concerning subjects such as economy, industry, finance, culture, tourism and health. Also contains interviews and personality profiles.
Language(s): Flemish; French
Readership: Aimed at affluent, influential people.
ADVERTISING RATES:
Full Page Colour .... EUR 6000
CONSUMER: WOMEN'S INTEREST CONSUMER MAGAZINES: Lifestyle

IMAGO PLUS
1893077B74A-187
Editorial: For all contact details see main record, IMAGO, 3294 **Tel:** 1378 07 90 **Fax:** 13777566
Email: sales@tuerlinckx.be **Web site:** http://www.imagomagazine.eu
Freq: Annual; **Circ:** 60,000
Language(s): Flemish; French
Mechanical Data: Type Area: 240 x 340
CONSUMER: WOMEN'S INTEREST CONSUMER MAGAZINES: Women's Interest

L' INDEPENDANT 1893017B14A-302

Editorial: Square Saintctelette, 11-12, 1000 BRUXELLES **Tel:** 2217 76 42 **Fax:** 22178841
Email: info@sninet.be **Web site:** http://www.sninet.be
Freq: 6 issues yearly - Les 1er et 15 du mois; **Cover Price:** Free; **Circ:** 42,000
Usual Pagination: 16
Language(s): French
Mechanical Data: Type Area: A4
BUSINESS: COMMERCE, INDUSTRY & MANAGEMENT

INFOTRAVEL 1629B50-75

Editorial: Vlasstraat 17, 8710 WIELSBEKE
Tel: 56 60 73 33 **Fax:** 56 61 05 83
Email: info@evolution.be **Web site:** http://www.evolution.be
Date Established: 1997; **Freq:** Monthly - 02 03 05 06 08 11 12; **Circ:** 5,500
Usual Pagination: 50
Profile: Professional magazine containing information about holidays and travel destinations.
Language(s): Flemish; French
Readership: Aimed at travel agents, tour operators and other professionals in tourism.
ADVERTISING RATES:
Full Page Mono .... EUR 1300
Full Page Colour .... EUR 1890
Mechanical Data: Type Area: A 4
BUSINESS: TRAVEL & TOURISM

INSIDE 1271B5E-30

Editorial: Rodenbachstraat 70, 1190 BRUSSELS
Tel: 2 349 35 50 **Fax:** 2 349 35 97
Email: abo@best.be **Web site:** http://www.digimedia.be/fr
Date Established: 1996; **Freq:** Monthly - 7 v/d maand
Annual Sub.: EUR 39; **Circ:** 19,000
Usual Pagination: 80
Editor: Boris Jancen
Profile: Magazine focusing on the internet. Includes guides to the best websites, expert advice and reviews.
Language(s): Flemish; French
ADVERTISING RATES:
Full Page Colour .... EUR 4000
BUSINESS: COMPUTERS & AUTOMATION: Data Transmission

I-TEL 1647989B14H-131

Editorial: I-Tel, Pastoor Schoeterstraat, 10, 2910 ESSEN **Tel:** 3677 24 56 **Fax:** 3677 10 92
Email: info@i-tel.be **Web site:** http://www.i-tel.be
Date Established: 2000; **Freq:** 26 issues yearly - 1e en 15de van de maand; **Annual Sub.:** EUR 25; **Circ:** 34,596
Language(s): Flemish; French
ADVERTISING RATES:
Full Page Colour .... EUR 4305.60
Mechanical Data: Type Area: Tabloïd
BUSINESS: COMMERCE, INDUSTRY & MANAGEMENT: Small Business

ITM - INDUSTRIE TECHNIQUE & MANAGEMENT - INDUSTRIE TECHNISCH & MANAGEMENT 1657984B14A-271

Editorial: Raketstraat 50, Bus 15, 1130 BRUXELLES
Tel: 2702 71 711 **Fax:** 27027174
Email: info.rpi@roularta.be **Web site:** http://www.industrie.be
Freq: 24 issues yearly - Niet in 01, 07, 08; **Annual Sub.:** EUR 50; **Circ:** 25,200
Usual Pagination: 160
Language(s): Flemish; French
ADVERTISING RATES:
Full Page Colour .... EUR 4500
BUSINESS: COMMERCE, INDUSTRY & MANAGEMENT

LES JARDINS DE FEMMES D'AUJOURD'HUI (SUPP. FEMMES D'AUJOURD'HUI) 1648183B93-152

Editorial: Femmes d'Aujourd'hui, Telecomlaan 5-7, B-1831 DIEGEM **Tel:** 2776 22 11 **Fax:** 2776 23 99
Email: femmesdaujourdhui@sanoma-magazines.be
Web site: http://www.femmesdaujourdhui.be
Date Established: 1993; **Freq:** Annual - 03; **Cover Price:** Free; **Circ:** 130,000
Language(s): French
ADVERTISING RATES:
Full Page Colour .... EUR 3300
Mechanical Data: Type Area: 285 x 220
Supplement to: FEMMES D'AUJOURD'HUI
CONSUMER: GARDENING

LES JARDINS D'EDEN-TUINEN VAN EDEN 2587B93-53

Editorial: Taxanderlei, 43, 2900 SCHOTEN
Tel: 3658 09 68 **Fax:** 36583708
Email: info@edenmagazine.be **Web site:** http://www.tuinenvaneden.be
Date Established: 1994; **Freq:** 3 issues yearly - 02 05 08 11; **Annual Sub.:** EUR 25; **Circ:** 45,000
Usual Pagination: 146
Editor: Jinge Lim
Profile: Magazine about gardening, garden decorations and architecture includes garden produce gastronomy.
Language(s): Flemish; French
Readership: Aimed at gardening enthusiasts and lovers of nature and landscapes.
ADVERTISING RATES:
Full Page Colour .... EUR 2210
CONSUMER: GARDENING

JARDINS & LOISIRS/ HOBBYTUIN 2586B93-55

Editorial: Geelseweg, 47 A, 2200 HERENTALS
Tel: 1428 60 80 **Fax:** 1421 47 74
Email: info@rekad.be **Web site:** http://www.rekad.be
Date Established: 1996; **Freq:** Monthly - Début du mois (sauf 01 08); **Cover Price:** EUR 395
Annual Sub.: EUR 3795; **Circ:** 12,000
Usual Pagination: 64
Profile: Magazine for gardening enthusiasts.
Language(s): Flemish; French
ADVERTISING RATES:
Full Page Colour .... EUR 2290
Mechanical Data: Type Area: 297 x 230
Copy instructions: *Copy Date:* 31 days prior to publication date
CONSUMER: GARDENING

LE JOURNAL DE L'ARCHITECTE - ARCHITECTENKRANT 1229B4A-80

Editorial: Aton Publishing, Rue Jules Lahaye 82, 1090 BRUXELLES **Tel:** 2772 40 47 **Fax:** 27719801
Email: info@atonpublishing.com **Web site:** http://www.lejournaldelarchitecte.be
ISSN: 1374-5352
Date Established: 1996; **Freq:** Monthly - Fin de mois (sauf 07); **Circ:** 9,700
Usual Pagination: 16
Profile: Magazine about architecture in Belgium and Luxembourg.
Language(s): Flemish; French
Readership: Aimed at architects and university students.
ADVERTISING RATES:
Full Page Mono .... EUR 2565
Full Page Colour .... EUR 2850
Mechanical Data: Type Area: 327 x 297
Copy instructions: *Copy Date:* 15 days prior to publication date
BUSINESS: ARCHITECTURE & BUILDING: Architecture

KAMPEERTOERIST 2569B91B-30

Editorial: Charles de Kerchovelaan, 11, 9000 GENT
Tel: 9223 77 91 **Fax:** 9223 93 86
Email: info@vkt.be **Web site:** http://www.vkt.be
Date Established: 1952; **Freq:** Monthly; **Cover Price:** EUR 4
Annual Sub.: EUR 42; **Circ:** 10,000
Usual Pagination: 52
Editor: Hilde Vanhoutte; **Publisher:** Dirk de Groot
Profile: Camping, caravanning and tourism magazine.
Language(s): Flemish; French
Readership: Read by people who enjoy camping and caravanning.
ADVERTISING RATES:
Full Page Colour .... EUR 775
CONSUMER: RECREATION & LEISURE: Camping & Caravanning

KIOSQUE 2554B89C-50

Editorial: ITI Publishing, Avenue Coghen, 119, 1180 BRUXELLES **Tel:** 2340 77 51 **Fax:** 23448770
Email: redaction@kiosque.be **Web site:** http://www.kiosque.be
Date Established: 1986; **Freq:** Monthly - Dernier vendredi du mois; **Cover Price:** EUR 175
Annual Sub.: EUR 1750; **Circ:** 15,000
Usual Pagination: 84
Publisher: Damien Vanheuverzwijn
Profile: Magazine covering leisure activities, entertainment and shows in Brussels.
Language(s): French
Readership: Aimed at residents and visitors to Brussels.
ADVERTISING RATES:
Full Page Colour .... EUR 1700
Mechanical Data: Type Area: 240 x 165
CONSUMER: HOLIDAYS & TRAVEL: Entertainment Guides

KLASSE VOOR LEERKRACHTEN 1752B62A-100

Editorial: Koning Albert II-laan 15, 1210 BRUSSELS
Tel: 2553 96 86 **Fax:** 25539685
Email: redactie.leraren@klasse.be **Web site:** http://www.klasse.be
Date Established: 1990; **Freq:** Monthly - Begin van de maand niet 07, 08; **Annual Sub.:** EUR 25; **Circ:** 200,000
Usual Pagination: 48
Profile: Educational journal for the Flanders region. Covers educational news from other countries and other parts of Belgium.
Language(s): Flemish; French
Readership: Read by teachers and educationalists.
ADVERTISING RATES:
Full Page Colour .... EUR 4628
Mechanical Data: Type Area: 203 x 280
BUSINESS: CHURCH & SCHOOL EQUIPMENT & EDUCATION: Education

KNACK 2152B82-338

Editorial: Raketstraat 50, 1130 BRUSSELS
Tel: 2 702 46 51 **Fax:** 2 702 46 52
Email: knack@knack.be **Web site:** http://www.knack.be
Date Established: 1971; **Freq:** Weekly - Woensdag;
Cover Price: EUR 3.50
Annual Sub.: EUR 134; **Circ:** 140,000
Editor: Karl Van den Broeck; **Editor-in-Chief:** Joost Albers
Profile: News magazine covering Belgian and international events, politics, sports and culture.
Language(s): Flemish; French
Readership: Aimed at the Dutch-speaking population in Belgium.
ADVERTISING RATES:
Full Page Colour .... EUR 9600
Mechanical Data: Type Area: 267 x 202
Copy instructions: *Copy Date:* 3 days prior to publication date
CONSUMER: CURRENT AFFAIRS & POLITICS

KRANT VAN WEST VLAANDEREN - SIEGE SOCIAL 1647979B67J-67

Editorial: Meiboomlaan, 33, 8800 ROESELARE
Tel: 5126 61 11 **Fax:** 51266587
Email: info@kw.be **Web site:** http://www.kw.be
Date Established: 1954; **Freq:** Weekly - Belgium;
Cover Price: EUR 2.50
Annual Sub.: EUR 100; **Circ:** 94,402
Usual Pagination: 50
Language(s): Flemish; French
ADVERTISING RATES:
Full Page Mono .... EUR 9120
Full Page Colour .... EUR 9720
Mechanical Data: Type Area: Tabloïd
REGIONAL DAILY & SUNDAY NEWSPAPERS: Regional Newspapers (excl. dailies)

LAN NEWS / ELECTRONICS HIGH-TECH 1263B5B-48

Editorial: Leemveldstraat, 42, 3090 OVERIJSE
Tel: 2785 02 80 **Fax:** 27319798
Email: info@lannews.be **Web site:** http://www.lannews.be
Date Established: 1995; **Freq:** 26 issues yearly - 02 04 05 09 11
Annual Sub.: EUR 72; **Circ:** 4,000
Usual Pagination: 48
Editor: Charles Carlier; **Publisher:** Karel Goorts
Profile: Magazine providing information concerning networking, data and telecommunications.
Language(s): Flemish; French
Readership: Read by network and telecom managers in large companies.
ADVERTISING RATES:
Full Page Colour .... EUR 2850
Mechanical Data: Type Area: A4
BUSINESS: COMPUTERS & AUTOMATION: Data Processing

LANDBOUW & TECHNIEK 1434B21A-120

Editorial: Diestsevest 40, 3000 LEUVEN
Tel: 1628 63 02 **Fax:** 16286309
Email: landbouwtechniek@boerenbond.be **Web site:** http://www.boerenbond.be
Date Established: 1996; **Freq:** 104 issues yearly - Maandag; **Annual Sub.:** EUR 118; **Circ:** 8,343
Usual Pagination: 48
Editor: Anne Vandenbosch
Profile: Magazine about agriculture, farming technology and equipment.
Language(s): Flemish; French
Readership: Read by farmers.
ADVERTISING RATES:
Full Page Mono .... EUR 900
Full Page Colour .... EUR 1300
Mechanical Data: Type Area: A4
BUSINESS: AGRICULTURE & FARMING

LESOIR.BE 1704155B65A-190

Editorial: Rue Royale, 100, 1000 BRUXELLES
Tel: 2225 54 32 **Fax:** 22255914
Email: internet@lesoir.be **Web site:** http://www.lesoir.be
Language(s): French
NATIONAL DAILY & SUNDAY NEWSPAPERS: National Daily Newspapers

LA LETTRE DU FNRS 1647738B55-152

Editorial: Rue d'Egmont, 5, 1000 BRUXELLES
Tel: 2504 92 11 **Fax:** 25049222
Web site: http://www.frs-fnrs.be
Date Established: 1990; **Freq:** Quarterly - 03, 06, 09, 12; **Cover Price:** Free; **Circ:** 50,000
Usual Pagination: 30
Publisher: Véronique Halloin
Language(s): French
ADVERTISING RATES:
Full Page Mono .... EUR 1800
Full Page Colour .... EUR 2000
Mechanical Data: Type Area: A 4
BUSINESS: APPLIED SCIENCE & LABORATORIES

LIBELLE 2176B74A-130

Editorial: Uitbreidingsstraat 82, 2600 BERCHEM
Tel: 3 290 14 42 **Fax:** 3 290 14 44
Email: libelle@libelle.be **Web site:** http://www.libelle.be
Date Established: 1945; **Freq:** Weekly - ab.woensdag, winkel donderdag
Annual Sub.: EUR 98; **Circ:** 273,451
Usual Pagination: 120
Editor-in-Chief: Miek Croonen
Profile: Magazine containing articles on fashion, beauty, health, housecraft and women's issues.
Language(s): Flemish; French
Readership: Aimed at the modern Belgian woman.
ADVERTISING RATES:
Full Page Colour .... EUR 10500
Mechanical Data: Type Area: A4
CONSUMER: WOMEN'S INTEREST CONSUMER MAGAZINES: Women's Interest

LIBELLE PROEVEN 1648188B74P-222

Editorial: Uitbreidingstraat, 82, 2600 BERCHEM
Tel: 3290 14 42 **Fax:** 3290 14 44
Email: libelle@libelle.be **Web site:** http://www.libelle.be
Date Established: 1994; **Freq:** Monthly - 02 04 05 07 09 11; **Cover Price:** EUR 3.50; **Circ:** 85,000
Usual Pagination: 116
Editor-in-Chief: Sofie Doms
Language(s): Flemish; French
ADVERTISING RATES:
Full Page Colour .... EUR 3300
Mechanical Data: Type Area: 285 x 220
Copy instructions: *Copy Date:* 28 days prior to publication date
CONSUMER: WOMEN'S INTEREST CONSUMER MAGAZINES: Food & Cookery

LIBELLE.BE 1660224B74A-171

Editorial: Uitbreidingsstraat, 82, 2600 BERCHEM
Tel: 3290 14 42 **Fax:** 32901444
Email: libelle@libelle.be **Web site:** http://www.libelle.be
Freq: Daily
Language(s): Flemish; French
CONSUMER: WOMEN'S INTEREST CONSUMER MAGAZINES: Women's Interest

LA LIBRE BELGIQUE - GAZETTE DE LIÈGE 1647740B65A-174

Editorial: Rue des Francs, 79, 1040 BRUXELLES
Tel: 2 211 27 11 **Fax:** 2 21128 32
Email: llb.gazettedeliege@lalibre.be **Web site:** http://www.lalibre.be
Date Established: 1840; **Freq:** Daily; **Cover Price:** EUR 1.10
Annual Sub.: EUR 235; **Circ:** 50,000
Usual Pagination: 64
Language(s): French
Mechanical Data: Type Area: Tabloïd
NATIONAL DAILY & SUNDAY NEWSPAPERS: National Daily Newspapers

LE LIGUEUR 1647742B82-254

Editorial: Avenue Émile de Beco 109, 1050 BRUXELLES **Tel:** 2507 72 11 **Fax:** 2507 72 00
Email: redaction@leligueur.be **Web site:** http://www.leligueur.be
Date Established: 1951; **Freq:** 26 issues yearly - 1 Mercredi sur 2; **Cover Price:** EUR 1.50
Annual Sub.: EUR 42.80; **Circ:** 85,000
Usual Pagination: 24
Language(s): French
Mechanical Data: Type Area: 420 x 310
CONSUMER: CURRENT AFFAIRS & POLITICS

LE LION - DE LEEUW 707628B74C-102

Editorial: Rue Osseghem 53, 1080 BRUXELLES
Tel: 2412 21 11 **Fax:** 24122099
Email: media@delhaizegroup.com **Web site:** http://www.delhaize.be
Date Established: 1986; **Freq:** 6 issues yearly - Le 1er jeudi de la saison; **Circ:** 500,000
Usual Pagination: 72
Publisher: Caroline Bruyninckx
Profile: Magazine focusing on all aspects of family life.
Language(s): Flemish; French
ADVERTISING RATES:
Full Page Colour .... EUR 19500
Copy instructions: *Copy Date:* 42 days prior to publication date
CONSUMER: WOMEN'S INTEREST CONSUMER MAGAZINES: Home & Family

LOOK-OUT 1647888B89C-205

Editorial: Ericalaan, 52, 2920 KALMTHOUT-HEIDE
Tel: 3248 58 38 **Fax:** 32484045
Email: info@look-out.be **Web site:** http://www.look-out.be
Date Established: 1986; **Freq:** Annual - Begin 03 09; **Circ:** 300,000
Editor: Wencke Dons
Language(s): Flemish; French

ADVERTISING RATES:
Full Page Colour .... EUR 2200
CONSUMER: HOLIDAYS & TRAVEL: Entertainment Guides

LOU MAGAZINE
1685603B74A-199
Editorial: Editions Ciné Revue, Av. Reine Marie-Henriette, 101, 1190 BRUXELLES **Tel:** 2290 04 80 **Fax:** 2343 12 72
Email: info@lou-mag.be **Web site:** http://www.lou-mag.be
Date Established: 2005; **Freq:** Monthly; **Cover Price:** EUR 2,50
Annual Sub.: EUR 22,50; **Circ:** 35,000
Usual Pagination: 132
Editor: Michel Leempoel
Language(s): French
ADVERTISING RATES:
Full Page Colour .... EUR 2.500
CONSUMER: WOMEN'S INTEREST CONSUMER MAGAZINES: Women's Interest

LOVING YOU FEESTZALENGIDS
1648023B74L-161
Editorial: EPN International, Pulsebaan, 50 - B1, 2242 PULDERBOS **Tel:** 3466 00 66 **Fax:** 34660067
Email: info@lovingyou.be **Web site:** http://www.lovingyou.be
Date Established: 1997; **Freq:** Half-yearly - 01 09; **Cover Price:** EUR 3.99; **Circ:** 40,000
Usual Pagination: 194
Language(s): Flemish; French
ADVERTISING RATES:
Full Page Colour .... EUR 3299
Mechanical Data: Type Area: 220 x 297
CONSUMER: WOMEN'S INTEREST CONSUMER MAGAZINES: Brides

LOVING YOU - LE MAGAZINE DU MARIAGE
2237B74L-40
Editorial: EPN International, Pulsebaan, 50 - B1, 2242 PULDERBOS **Tel:** 3466 00 66 **Fax:** 34660067
Email: info@lovingyou.be **Web site:** http://www.lovingyou.be
Date Established: 1989; **Freq:** Half-yearly - 09, 01; **Cover Price:** EUR 6.99
Annual Sub.: EUR 12.50; **Circ:** 120,000
Usual Pagination: 200
Editor: Bart De Landtscheer
Profile: Magazine focusing on wedding preparations and bridal wear.
Language(s): Flemish; French
Readership: Read by brides.
ADVERTISING RATES:
Full Page Colour .... EUR 3299
Mechanical Data: Type Area: 219 x 297
CONSUMER: WOMEN'S INTEREST CONSUMER MAGAZINES: Brides

LVZ KOERIER
1892962B14A-288
Editorial: Livornostraat 25, 1050 BRUSSELS
Tel: 2426 39 00 **Fax:** 24263417
Email: info@lvz.be **Web site:** http://www.lvz.be
Freq: Monthly - Second Tuesdays of the month;
Annual Sub.: EUR 110; **Circ:** 45,000
Usual Pagination: 24
Editor: Roni De Waele
Language(s): Flemish; French
Mechanical Data: Type Area: 350 x 250
BUSINESS: COMMERCE, INDUSTRY & MANAGEMENT

MAINTENANCE MAGAZINE
1412B19A-40
Editorial: Diamantstraat, 5, 2275 LILLE
Tel: 3326 56 16 **Fax:** 33265636
Email: info@mainpress.com **Web site:** http://www.mainpress.com
Date Established: 1992; **Freq:** 26 issues yearly - 03 05 06 09 12; **Annual Sub.:** EUR 39; **Circ:** 7,000
Usual Pagination: 52
Profile: Magazine about mechanical maintenance, electro and energy management, maintenance of buildings and facility management.
Language(s): Flemish; French
ADVERTISING RATES:
Full Page Mono .... EUR 1640
Full Page Colour .... EUR 2190
Mechanical Data: Type Area: 297x215 mm
BUSINESS: ENGINEERING & MACHINERY

MAMA
1996216B74C-243
Tel: 3680 25 68
Email: redactie@mama-magazine.be **Web site:** http://www.mama-magazine.be
Date Established: 2010; **Freq:** Monthly; **Cover Price:** EUR 4.95; **Circ:** 20,000
Usual Pagination: 124
Editor: Fleur Franssen
Language(s): Flemish
Mechanical Data: Type Area: 225 x 287
CONSUMER: WOMEN'S INTEREST CONSUMER MAGAZINES: Home & Family

MARIAGE.BE
1799013B74L-160
Editorial: Quai d'Aa, 6, 1070 BRUXELLES
Tel: 2526 93 25 **Fax:** 25245700
Email: info@ceremonie.com **Web site:** http://www.mariage.be
Language(s): French
CONSUMER: WOMEN'S INTEREST CONSUMER MAGAZINES: Brides

MARIAGES
2238B74L-50
Editorial: Clos des Lilas, 5, 1380 LASNE
Tel: 2660 69 40 **Fax:** 26600943
Email: cecile@dechamps-diffusions.be **Web site:** http://www.dechamps-diffusions.be
Freq: Half-yearly - 12; **Cover Price:** EUR 4.95; **Circ:** 12,000
Usual Pagination: 365
Profile: Magazine for couples getting married.
Language(s): French
ADVERTISING RATES:
Full Page Colour .... EUR 1725
Mechanical Data: Type Area: 185 x 235
Copy instructions: *Copy Date:* 42 days prior to publication date
CONSUMER: WOMEN'S INTEREST CONSUMER MAGAZINES: Brides

MARIE CLAIRE BELGIQUE
2177B74A-133
Editorial: Telecomlaan, 5-7, 1831 DIEGEM
Tel: 2776 22 11 **Fax:** 27762399
Email: marieclaire@sanoma-magazines.be **Web site:** http://www.sanoma-magazines.be
Date Established: 2003; **Freq:** Monthly - Milieu de mois; **Cover Price:** EUR 4.40; **Circ:** 66,000
Usual Pagination: 80
Profile: Magazine with articles on fashion, beauty, health, cookery and drink, interiors and worldwide socio-political issues.
Language(s): Flemish; French
ADVERTISING RATES:
Full Page Colour .... EUR 4100
Mechanical Data: Type Area: 215 x 270
Copy instructions: *Copy Date:* 35 days prior to publication date
CONSUMER: WOMEN'S INTEREST CONSUMER MAGAZINES: Women's Interest

MENZO SPORTS
706748B86C-130
Editorial: Wettersestraat, 64, 9260 SCHELLEBELLE
Tel: 9369 31 73 **Fax:** 93693293
Email: info@thinkmediamagazines.be **Web site:** http://www.menzo.be
Date Established: 2008; **Freq:** Monthly - laatste vrijdag vd maand; 2000
Annual Sub.: EUR 36; **Circ:** 20,000
Usual Pagination: 164
Editor: Jorn Van Besauw; **Editor-in-Chief:** Raf De Mot
Profile: Men's interest magazine, includes articles about cars, sport, motor bikes, films and literature.
Language(s): Flemish; French
Readership: Aimed at men, between 18 and 50 years old.
ADVERTISING RATES:
Full Page Colour .... EUR 3000
Mechanical Data: Type Area: 295 x 225
CONSUMER: ADULT & GAY MAGAZINES: Men's Lifestyle Magazines

METALLERIE
601570B27-50
Editorial: Torhoutsesteenweg 226, Bus 2, 8210 ZEDELGEM **Tel:** 50 24 04 04 **Fax:** 50 24 04 45
Email: info@pmg.be **Web site:** http://www.metallerie.be
Date Established: 1998; **Freq:** Monthly; **Cover Price:** EUR 6.25
Annual Sub.: EUR 68; **Circ:** 13,500
Profile: Magazine containing articles, news and information about the metal industry. Covers product and trade news, environmental issues, machinery and tool tests, finance and market analysis.
Language(s): Flemish; French
Readership: Aimed at suppliers, importers and exporters, engineers and other professionals within the field.
ADVERTISING RATES:
Full Page Colour .... EUR 3100
BUSINESS: METAL, IRON & STEEL

METRO
707736B65A-120
Editorial: S.A. Mass Transit Media, Galerie Ravenstein 4, 1000 BRUSSELS **Tel:** 2227 93 43 **Fax:** 2227 93 41
Email: metro@metrotime.be **Web site:** http://www.metrotime.be
Date Established: 2003; **Freq:** Daily - Lundi et vendredi; **Cover Price:** Free; **Circ:** 290,000
Usual Pagination: 24
Managing Director: Monique Raaffels
Profile: Tabloid-sized newspaper containing national and international news, sport and general information.
Language(s): Flemish; French
Readership: Read by commuters.
ADVERTISING RATES:
Full Page Mono .... EUR 12950
Full Page Colour .... EUR 15450
Mechanical Data: Type Area: 290 x 410
Copy instructions: *Copy Date:* 3 days prior to publication date
NATIONAL DAILY & SUNDAY NEWSPAPERS: National Daily Newspapers

METRO DELUXE
1983499B74Q-368
Editorial: Mass. Transit Media, Galerie Ravenstein, 4, 1000 BRUXELLES **Tel:** 2227 93 43 **Fax:** 2227 93 41
Email: metro@metrotime.be **Web site:** http://www.metrotime.be
Date Established: 2009; **Freq:** 6 issues yearly - 02 04 06 09 10 12; **Cover Price:** Free; **Circ:** 290,000
Editor-in-Chief: Arnaud Dujardin
Language(s): French
CONSUMER: WOMEN'S INTEREST CONSUMER MAGAZINES: Lifestyle

LA MEUSE SIEGE ADMINISTRATIF
1884B67B-4200
Editorial: Rue de Coquelet, 134, 5000 NAMUR
Tel: 81208 3 78 **Fax:** 81208372
Email: redaction.generale@sudpresse.be **Web site:** http://www.lameuse.be
Date Established: 2003; **Freq:** Daily - Belgium
Annual Sub.: EUR 202; **Circ:** 125,000
Usual Pagination: 64
Language(s): French
Mechanical Data: Type Area: 412 x 287
REGIONAL DAILY & SUNDAY NEWSPAPERS: Regional Daily Newspapers

MILLESIME 33
1308B11A-80
Editorial: Avenue d'Itterbeek, 388, 1070 ANDERLECHT **Tel:** 2241 66 21
Email: press.lerougedan@numericable.be **Web site:** http://www.millesime33.be
Date Established: 1984; **Freq:** Quarterly - 03, 06, 09, 12; **Cover Price:** EUR 3.10
Annual Sub.: EUR 12; **Circ:** 15,000
Usual Pagination: 32
Profile: Magazine about gastronomy and luxury travel.
Language(s): French
ADVERTISING RATES:
Full Page Mono .... EUR 979.18
Full Page Colour .... EUR 1412.99
Mechanical Data: Type Area: A 4
Copy instructions: *Copy Date:* 21 days prior to publication date
BUSINESS: CATERING: Catering, Hotels & Restaurants

MINE
2217B74F-14
Editorial: Fortis Banque Mine, 1AB1C, Montagne du Parc 3, 1000 BRUXELLES **Tel:** 2228 89 58 **Fax:** 25654285
Email: jeunes@fortis.com **Web site:** http://www.mine.be
Date Established: 1989; **Freq:** Quarterly - 01 05 09; **Cover Price:** Free; **Circ:** 320,000
Usual Pagination: 24
Profile: Magazine containing general news, articles and information of interest to young people.
Language(s): Flemish; French
Mechanical Data: Type Area: 260 x 185
CONSUMER: WOMEN'S INTEREST CONSUMER MAGAZINES: Teenage

MO* MONDIAAL NIEUWS
1648252B82-262
Editorial: Vlasfabriekstraat 11, 1060 BRUSSELS
Tel: 2536 19 64 **Fax:** 25361934
Email: info@mo.be **Web site:** http://www.MO.be
Date Established: 2003; **Freq:** Monthly - Laatste woensdag van de maand
Annual Sub.: EUR 30; **Circ:** 120,000
Usual Pagination: 68
Editor: Gie Goris
Language(s): Flemish; French
ADVERTISING RATES:
Full Page Mono .... EUR 6510
Mechanical Data: Type Area: 267 x 202
Copy instructions: *Copy Date:* 31 days prior to publication date
CONSUMER: CURRENT AFFAIRS & POLITICS

MODE DIT IS BELGISCH
2182B74B-45
Editorial: Raketstraat 50, bus 3, 1130 BRUSSELS
Tel: 2702 45 41 **Fax:** 27024542
Email: weekend@knack.be **Web site:** http://www.knackweekend.rnews.be
Date Established: 1984; **Freq:** Weekly - Le mercredi; **Circ:** 153,000
Editor: Trui Moerkerke
Profile: Magazine covering fashion and accessories.
Language(s): Flemish; French
Readership: Aimed at young people primarily women.
ADVERTISING RATES:
Full Page Colour .... EUR 6850
CONSUMER: WOMEN'S INTEREST CONSUMER MAGAZINES: Women's Interest - Fashion

LE MONITEUR AUTOMOBILE
2376B77A-75
Editorial: Avenue Général Dumonceau, 56, BP 1, 1190 BRUXELLES **Tel:** 2333 32 11 **Fax:** 23333261
Email: contact.mab@moniteurautomobile.be **Web site:** http://www.moniteurautomobile.be
Date Established: 1950; **Freq:** 26 issues yearly - Le mercredi
Annual Sub.: EUR 65; **Circ:** 45,000
Usual Pagination: 200
Profile: Magazine containing information about new and second-hand cars and the whole of the car industry. Includes new and second-hand prices, tests, comparisons and news.
Language(s): Flemish; French
Mechanical Data: Type Area: A 4
Copy instructions: *Copy Date:* 7 days prior to publication date
CONSUMER: MOTORING & CYCLING: Motoring

DE MORGEN
1874B67B-4600
Editorial: De Morgen, Arduinkaai 29, 1000 BRUSSELS **Tel:** 2 556 68 11 **Fax:** 2 520 35 15
Email: info@demorgen.be **Web site:** http://www.demorgen.be
Date Established: 1978; **Freq:** Daily - Sauf le dimanche
Annual Sub.: EUR 278; **Circ:** 70,000
Usual Pagination: 48
News Editor: Brecht Decaestecker; **Editor-in-Chief:** Wilfried Poelmans
Language(s): Flemish; French
ADVERTISING RATES:
Full Page Mono .... EUR 10620
Full Page Colour .... EUR 11800
Mechanical Data: Type Area: Berlinois
REGIONAL DAILY & SUNDAY NEWSPAPERS: Regional Daily Newspapers

MOTION CONTROL/ SNACKBLAD
1601255B5A-151
Editorial: Torhoutsesteenweg, 226, Bus 2, 8210 ZEDELGEM **Tel:** 5024 04 04 **Fax:** 50240445
Email: info@pmgroup.be **Web site:** http://www.motioncontrol.be
Date Established: 2002; **Freq:** 26 issues yearly;
Cover Price: EUR 6.25
Annual Sub.: EUR 56; **Circ:** 14,700
Usual Pagination: 68
Profile: Magazine focusing on news from the automation sector. Includes articles on techniques, economic climate, product information and training.
Language(s): Flemish; French
Readership: Aimed at engineers.
ADVERTISING RATES:
Full Page Colour .... EUR 3100
BUSINESS: COMPUTERS & AUTOMATION: Automation & Instrumentation

MOTO 80
2383B77B-60
Editorial: Rue Abbé Michel Renard, 15, 1400 NIVELLES **Tel:** 6749 36 36 **Fax:** 67493639
Email: moto80@moto80.be **Web site:** http://www.moto80.be
Date Established: 1980; **Freq:** Monthly - 1er vendredi du mois
Annual Sub.: EUR 40; **Circ:** 19,000
Usual Pagination: 100
Editor: Pierre Capart
Profile: Magazine containing articles and information about motorcycles.
Language(s): French
ADVERTISING RATES:
Full Page Mono .... EUR 1350
Full Page Colour .... EUR 1800
Mechanical Data: Type Area: A 4
Copy instructions: *Copy Date:* 14 days prior to publication date
CONSUMER: MOTORING & CYCLING: Motorcycling

NB MAGAZINE
1893087B74A-195
Editorial: For all contact details see main record, HET NIEUWSBLAD **Tel:** 2467 96 04 **Fax:** 24663093
Email: redactienbo@nieuwsblad.be **Web site:** http://www.nieuwsblad.be
Date Established: 2008; **Freq:** Weekly - Zaterdag;
Cover Price: EUR 1.25
Annual Sub.: EUR 255; **Circ:** 293,964
Usual Pagination: 44
Editor: Geert Dewaele; **Editor-in-Chief:** Julie Vallé
Language(s): French
CONSUMER: WOMEN'S INTEREST CONSUMER MAGAZINES: Women's Interest

NEST
1648221B74Q-315
Editorial: Raketstraat 50, 1130 BRUSSELS
Tel: 2 702 45 21 **Fax:** 2 702 45 42
Email: info@nest.be **Web site:** http://www.nest.be
Date Established: 2002; **Freq:** 26 issues yearly - 02 04 06 09 10 12
Annual Sub.: EUR 18; **Circ:** 188,417
Usual Pagination: 120
Editor: Peter Vandeweerdt; **Editor-in-Chief:** Marianne Bellens; **Publisher:** Chantal Lepaige
Language(s): Flemish; French
ADVERTISING RATES:
Full Page Colour .... EUR 9000
Copy instructions: *Copy Date:* 21 days prior to publication date
CONSUMER: WOMEN'S INTEREST CONSUMER MAGAZINES: Lifestyle

NETTO (SUPP. DE TIJD)
1648358B74M-4
Editorial: For all contact details see main record, DE TIJD, 1000 **Tel:** 2 349 35 50 **Fax:** 2 349 35 97
Email: redaction@monargent.be **Web site:** http://www.tijd.be
Date Established: 2006; **Freq:** Weekly - Le samedi; **Circ:** 60,000
Editor: Frank Demets
Language(s): Flemish
ADVERTISING RATES:
Full Page Colour .... EUR 6500
Mechanical Data: Type Area: 297 x 210
Supplement to: DE TIJD
CONSUMER: WOMEN'S INTEREST CONSUMER MAGAZINES: Personal Finance

NIGHTCODE
1648084B89C-207
Editorial: Rue Royale 100, 1000 BRUSSELS
Tel: 2528 18 12 **Fax:** 25281800
Email: info@nightcode.be **Web site:** http://www.nightcode.be
Date Established: 1992; **Freq:** Monthly - Début de mois; **Cover Price:** Free; **Circ:** 30,000
Usual Pagination: 48
Language(s): Flemish; French
ADVERTISING RATES:
Full Page Colour .... EUR 3000
Mechanical Data: Type Area: A5
CONSUMER: HOLIDAYS & TRAVEL: Entertainment Guides

NORD-ECLAIR - SIEGE ADMINISTRATIF
1887B67B-5000
Editorial: Rue de Coquelet, 134, 5000 NAMUR
Tel: 81208 2 11 **Fax:** 81208362
Email: redaction.generale@sudpresse.be **Web site:** http://www.sudpresse.be
Date Established: 2003; **Freq:** Daily - Belgium
Profile: Newspaper covering the Tournai, Mons and Charleroi areas.
Language(s): French
REGIONAL DAILY & SUNDAY NEWSPAPERS: Regional Daily Newspapers

LA NOUVELLE GAZETTE SIEGE ADMINISTRATIF
1875B67B-5200
Editorial: Rue de Coquelet, 134, 5000 NAMUR
Tel: 81208 2 11 **Fax:** 81208362
Email: redaction.generale@sudpresse.be **Web site:** http://www.nouvellegazette.be
Date Established: 2003; **Freq:** Daily - Belgium
Annual Sub.: EUR 202; **Circ:** 125,000
Language(s): French
ADVERTISING RATES:
Full Page Colour .... EUR 19300
Mechanical Data: Type Area: 540 x 385
REGIONAL DAILY & SUNDAY NEWSPAPERS: Regional Daily Newspapers

OKRA-MAGAZINE
1647690B74N-201
Editorial: Haachtsesteenweg 579, Schaarbeek, 1031 BRUSSELS **Tel:** 2246 44 41 **Fax:** 22464442
Web site: http://www.okra.be
Date Established: 1966; **Freq:** Monthly - 25e van de maand (Niet in 01 08); **Annual Sub.:** EUR 17.50; **Circ:** 175,000
Usual Pagination: 48
Editor: Lieve Demeester
Language(s): Flemish; French
ADVERTISING RATES:
Full Page Colour .... EUR 4125
Mechanical Data: Type Area: A4
CONSUMER: WOMEN'S INTEREST CONSUMER MAGAZINES: Retirement

OMICRON NV VAKTIJDSCHRIFT: GARDEN STYLE
1484B26D-27
Editorial: Omicron NV, Hoornstraat, 16 B, 8730 BEERNEM **Tel:** 50250 1 70 **Fax:** 50250171
Email: info@omicron-media.be **Web site:** http://www.omicron-media.be
Date Established: 1998; **Freq:** Quarterly - 02 05 09 11; **Annual Sub.:** EUR 35; **Circ:** 8,781
Usual Pagination: 72
Profile: Magazine containing information about the gardening sector, each issue profiles a landscape designer.
Language(s): Flemish; French
Readership: Read by managers of garden and garden tool centres, landscape gardeners, designers and groundsmen at sports grounds.
ADVERTISING RATES:
Full Page Mono .... EUR 1275
Full Page Colour .... EUR 1850
Mechanical Data: Type Area: A4
Copy instructions: *Copy Date:* 21 days prior to publication date
BUSINESS: GARDEN TRADE: Garden Trade Horticulture

OMTRENT
2502B84A-318
Editorial: Blijde Inkomststraat, 79-81, 3000 LEUVEN
Tel: 1631 06 00 **Fax:** 16310608
Email: omtrent@davidsfonds.be **Web site:** http://www.davidsfonds.be
Date Established: 1987; **Freq:** 26 issues yearly - 01, 03, 05, 08, 11
Annual Sub.: EUR 15; **Circ:** 68,000
Usual Pagination: 52
Profile: Magazine containing details of cultural activities.
Language(s): Flemish; French
Readership: Aimed at members of Davidsfonds.
ADVERTISING RATES:
Full Page Colour .... EUR 2140
Mechanical Data: Type Area: A 4
Copy instructions: *Copy Date:* 7 days prior to publication date
CONSUMER: THE ARTS & LITERARY: Arts

PAP.BE (DE PARTICULIER A PARTICULIER)
1706616B74K-132
Editorial: Chaussée de Vleurgat, 184, 1000 BRUXELLES **Tel:** 2655 04 65 **Fax:** 2655 04 60
Email: info@pap.be **Web site:** http://www.pap.be
Date Established: 2003; **Freq:** Monthly; **Cover Price:** EUR 2
Annual Sub.: EUR 35; **Circ:** 35,000 Unique Users
Managing Director: Vanessa Charon
Profile: Website of the magazine DE PARTICULIER A PARTICULIER focussing on commercial and residential property. Classified.
Language(s): French
CONSUMER: WOMEN'S INTEREST CONSUMER MAGAZINES: Home Purchase

PARIS MATCH
2155B73-80
Editorial: Rue des Francs, 79, 1040 BRUXELLES
Tel: 2211 31 48 **Fax:** 22113153
Date Established: 1977; **Freq:** Weekly - Jeudi;
Cover Price: EUR 235
Annual Sub.: EUR 9500; **Circ:** 46,787
Usual Pagination: 110
Profile: Magazine containing general information.
Language(s): French
ADVERTISING RATES:
Full Page Colour .... EUR 3750
Mechanical Data: Type Area: 297 x 230
CONSUMER: NATIONAL & INTERNATIONAL PERIODICALS

PARQUET/PARKET
1892743B4B-27
Editorial: Rue du Lombard, 34-42, 1000 BRUXELLES
Tel: 2 545 57 11 **Fax:** 2 545 58 59
Web site: http://www.magazinesconstruction.be
Freq: Quarterly - 03 06 09 12; **Circ:** 9,000
Language(s): Flemish; French
Mechanical Data: Type Area: A4
Copy instructions: *Copy Date:* 21 days prior to publication date
BUSINESS: ARCHITECTURE & BUILDING: Interior Design & Flooring

PASAR
1893409B89E-1
Editorial: Haachtsesteenweg 579, 1030 BRUSSELS
Tel: 2246 36 40 **Fax:** 22463669
Email: info@pasar.be **Web site:** http://www.pasar.be
ISSN: 0778-7871
Date Established: 2003; **Freq:** Monthly - Fin du mois; **Annual Sub.:** EUR 48; **Circ:** 40,000
Usual Pagination: 100
Editor: Gunther Ritsmans; **Editor-in-Chief:** Chris Van Minnebruggen; **Managing Director:** Michel Vandendriessche
Language(s): Flemish; French
Mechanical Data: Type Area: A 4
Copy instructions: *Copy Date:* 28 days prior to publication date
CONSUMER: HOLIDAYS & TRAVEL: Holidays

PASSE-PARTOUT
1660188B72-10
Editorial: Vaartdijk / Campus Remy, 3, BELGIË WIJGMAAL **Tel:** 8431 01 11 **Fax:** 84310112
Email: redac.marche@passe-partout.be **Web site:** http://www.passe-partout.be
Freq: Weekly; **Circ:** 5,000,000
Language(s): French
LOCAL NEWSPAPERS

PC MAGAZINE
1267B5B-58
Editorial: Parklaan 22, 2300 TURNHOUT
Tel: 1446 2300 **Fax:** 1444 23 66
Email: redactie@pcmagazine.be **Web site:** http://www.pcmagazine.be
Date Established: 1998; **Freq:** Monthly - Fin de mois
Annual Sub.: EUR 60; **Circ:** 60,000
Usual Pagination: 124
Editor: Bart Stoffels; **Editor-in-Chief:** Pieter-Jan Hellinckx
Profile: Magazine focusing on testing of hard- and software. Includes IT news, reviews, feature stories and articles on networking and multimedia.
Language(s): Flemish; French
Readership: Aimed at IT professionals.
ADVERTISING RATES:
Full Page Colour .... EUR 3600
Mechanical Data: Type Area: 297 x 210
Copy instructions: *Copy Date:* 21 days prior to publication date
BUSINESS: COMPUTERS & AUTOMATION: Data Processing

PC WORLD
1270B5D-100
Editorial: Rue Rodenbach 70, 1190 BRUXELLES
Tel: 2349 35 96 **Fax:** 23493597
Email: info@best.be **Web site:** http://www.pcworld.be
Date Established: 1998; **Freq:** Monthly - Le 29 du mois; **Cover Price:** EUR 4.90
Annual Sub.: EUR 49; **Circ:** 27,000
Usual Pagination: 112
Publisher: Jean de Gheldere
Profile: Magazine covering the purchase of computer systems. Includes tests, information about hard- and software and product reviews.
Language(s): French
Readership: Aimed at small business proprietors and home users.
ADVERTISING RATES:
Full Page Colour .... EUR 4000
BUSINESS: COMPUTERS & AUTOMATION: Personal Computers

PLEIN CHAMP
5157B21A-177
Editorial: Chaussée de Namur 47, 5030 GEMBLOUX
Tel: 8160 00 60 **Fax:** 81600446
Email: pleinchamp@fwa.be **Web site:** http://www.fwa.be
Date Established: 2001; **Freq:** Weekly - Jeudi;
Annual Sub.: EUR 50; **Circ:** 22,500
Usual Pagination: 25
Profile: International magazine containing articles concerning agriculture.
Language(s): French
Readership: Aimed at farmers and those involved in the agricultural sector.
ADVERTISING RATES:
Full Page Mono .... EUR 1242
Full Page Colour .... EUR 1750
Mechanical Data: Type Area: 230 x 330
Copy instructions: *Copy Date:* 7 days prior to publication date
BUSINESS: AGRICULTURE & FARMING

PLUS MAGAZINE
2248B74N-160
Editorial: Rue de la Fusée 50, Boite 10, 1130 BRUXELLES **Tel:** 2 702 49 01 **Fax:** 2 702 46 02
Email: redaction@plusmagazine.be **Web site:** http://www.plusmagazine.be
Date Established: 1988; **Freq:** Monthly - Entre le 19 et 24 de chaque mois; **Cover Price:** EUR 3.90
Annual Sub.: EUR 42; **Circ:** 166,464
Usual Pagination: 150
Managing Director: Hugues De Foucauld
Profile: Magazine containing practical features on holidays, legal issues, psychology, education, pensions, health, cookery and leisure activities.
Language(s): French
Readership: Aimed at active people aged 50 years and above.
ADVERTISING RATES:
Full Page Colour .... EUR 6550
Mechanical Data: Type Area: 267 x 202
Copy instructions: *Copy Date:* 21 days prior to publication date
CONSUMER: WOMEN'S INTEREST CONSUMER MAGAZINES: Retirement

P-MAGAZINE
2668B86C-165
Editorial: Oude Leeuwenrui, 8, Bus 2, 2000 ANTWERPEN **Tel:** 320 20 100 **Fax:** 320 20 110
Email: info@p-magazine.com **Web site:** http://www.p-magazine.com
Date Established: 1997; **Freq:** Weekly; **Cover Price:** EUR 2,10
Annual Sub.: EUR 104; **Circ:** 80,000
Usual Pagination: 162
Editor: Michaël Lescroart
Profile: General interest magazine, containing articles about lifestyle, entertainment, television, films, music, sports, cars, travel and politics.
Language(s): Flemish; French
Readership: Read by men aged between 18 and 45 years.
ADVERTISING RATES:
Full Page Colour .... EUR 4.950
CONSUMER: ADULT & GAY MAGAZINES: Men's Lifestyle Magazines

PME-KMO MAGAZINE
1362B14H-55
Editorial: Avenue du Pérou 77b, 1000 BRUXELLES
Tel: 1635 91 50 **Fax:** 16359158
Email: redaction@skrifta.eu **Web site:** http://www.pmekmo.eu
Date Established: 1981; **Freq:** Monthly - Le 20 du mois
Annual Sub.: EUR 45; **Circ:** 25,000
Usual Pagination: 64
Managing Director: Paul Eggerickx
Profile: Journal covering general business news and articles concerning management of small and medium sized businesses.
Language(s): French
Readership: Aimed at managers and directors of companies with between 5 and 100 employees.
ADVERTISING RATES:
Full Page Mono .... EUR 3640
Full Page Colour .... EUR 4990
Mechanical Data: Type Area: A 4
BUSINESS: COMMERCE, INDUSTRY & MANAGEMENT: Small Business

POPPUNT MAGAZINE
1893214B76D-169
Tel: 2504 99 00 **Fax:** 25049909
Email: info@poppunt.be **Web site:** http://www.poppunt.be
Date Established: 1999; **Freq:** Quarterly - 1/03 06 09 12; **Annual Sub.:** EUR 12; **Circ:** 6,000
Usual Pagination: 68
Editor: Joachim Wemel
Language(s): Flemish; French
Mechanical Data: Type Area: 230 x 170
CONSUMER: MUSIC & PERFORMING ARTS: Music

PREVENT MEMO
1893391B14F-9
Editorial: Gachardstraat 88, Bus 4, 1050 BRUSSELS
Tel: 2643 44 44 **Fax:** 26434440
Email: prevent@prevent.be **Web site:** http://www.prevent.be
Freq: Monthly - Sauf 07 08
Language(s): Flemish; French
BUSINESS: COMMERCE, INDUSTRY & MANAGEMENT: Training & Recruitment

PROEFTUINNIEUWS
1478B26C-45
Editorial: Diestsevest 40, 3000 LEUVEN
Tel: 1628 63 04 **Fax:** 16286349
Email: redactie@proeftuinnieuws.be **Web site:** http://www.proeftuinnieuws.be
ISSN: 0777-9844
Date Established: 1993; **Freq:** 104 issues yearly - Vendredi; **Annual Sub.:** EUR 95; **Circ:** 2,200
Usual Pagination: 48
Editor: Veerle Neefs
Profile: Journal containing articles, news, information and practical advice for fruit growing.
Language(s): Flemish; French
Readership: Aimed at professional growers of fruit and vegetables.
ADVERTISING RATES:
Full Page Mono .... EUR 420
Full Page Colour .... EUR 750
Mechanical Data: Type Area: A4
Copy instructions: *Copy Date:* 15 days prior to publication date
BUSINESS: GARDEN TRADE

PROMENADE MAGAZINE
1647769B74Q-306
Editorial: Meirebeekstraat 30, 9031 DRONGEN
Tel: 9375 32 75 **Fax:** 92214630
Email: info@media-productions.be **Web site:** http://www.media-productions.be
Date Established: 1982; **Freq:** 26 issues yearly - 02, 04, 09, 10, 11; **Annual Sub.:** EUR 991; **Circ:** 62,000
Usual Pagination: 88
Editor: Kristof Delombaerde
Language(s): Flemish; French
ADVERTISING RATES:
Full Page Colour .... EUR 2775
Mechanical Data: Type Area: A4
CONSUMER: WOMEN'S INTEREST CONSUMER MAGAZINES: Lifestyle

LA PROVINCE SIEGE ADMINISTRATIF
1876B67B-5600
Editorial: Rue de Coquelet, 134, 5000 NAMUR
Tel: 81208 416 **Fax:** 81208 362
Email: red.laprovince@sudpresse.be **Web site:** http://www.sudpresse.be
Date Established: 2003; **Freq:** Daily - Belgium
Annual Sub.: EUR 230; **Circ:** 150,000
Managing Director: Patrick Hurbain
Language(s): French
Mechanical Data: Type Area: 540 x 385
REGIONAL DAILY & SUNDAY NEWSPAPERS: Regional Daily Newspapers

PUB MAGAZINE
1195B2A-80
Editorial: Ragheno Business Park, Motstraat, 30, 2800 MECHELEN **Tel:** 1536 15 30 **Fax:** 15361899
Email: pub@kluwer.be **Web site:** http://www.pub.be
Date Established: 1976; **Freq:** 26 issues yearly - Variable; **Annual Sub.:** EUR 159; **Circ:** 5,000
Usual Pagination: 52
Editor: Mark Anthierens
Profile: Journal about media, advertising agencies and marketing.
Language(s): Flemish; French
Readership: Aimed at marketeers, media companies and PR agencies.
ADVERTISING RATES:
Full Page Mono .... EUR 2080
Full Page Colour .... EUR 2865
Copy instructions: *Copy Date:* 15 days prior to publication date
BUSINESS: COMMUNICATIONS, ADVERTISING & MARKETING

PUBLIMAT NEWS 1381B16A-90
Editorial: Omicron, Hoornstraat, 16 B, 8730 BEERNEM **Tel:** 5025 01 70 **Fax:** 50250171
Email: info@omicron-media.be **Web site:** http://www.omicron-media.be
Date Established: 2001; **Freq:** 6 issues yearly - 02 04 06 09 10 12
Annual Sub.: EUR 35; **Circ:** 5,367
Usual Pagination: 30
Profile: Magazine focusing on DIY, ironmongery and building within the European market.
Language(s): Flemish; French
Readership: Aimed ât wholesalers.
ADVERTISING RATES:
Full Page Colour .... EUR 1560
BUSINESS: DECORATING & PAINT

REISKRANT 1630B50-100
Editorial: Beenhouwersstraat, 9, 8000 BRUGGE
Tel: 5033 75 88 **Fax:** 50347467
Email: info@wegwijzer.be **Web site:** http://www.wegwijzer.be
Date Established: 1979; **Freq:** 26 issues yearly - 03 06 09 12
Annual Sub.: EUR 26; **Circ:** 10,000
Usual Pagination: 46
Editor: Lut d'Hondt
Profile: Magazine focusing on all aspects of the tourism trade including reviews of guides and maps.
Language(s): Flemish; French
Readership: Read by travel agents, tour operators, tourist boards and airline companies.
ADVERTISING RATES:
Full Page Colour .... EUR 1000
Mechanical Data: Type Area: 297 x 210
BUSINESS: TRAVEL & TOURISM

RETAIL 1601250B53-201
Editorial: Torhoutsesteenweg 226, Bus 2, 8210 ZEDELGEM **Tel:** 5024 04 04 **Fax:** 50240445
Email: info@pmg.be **Web site:** http://www.retail-pro.be
Date Established: 2002; **Freq:** Monthly; **Cover Price:** EUR 625
Annual Sub.: EUR 56; **Circ:** 10,166
Editor: Frank Verhue
Profile: Magazine focusing on retailing, includes beauty products, drinks, dried and fresh food, electrical and household items, hobby and leisure goods. Features trends, marketing, shop design and layout, also related legislation.
Language(s): Flemish; French
Readership: Read by managers of supermarkets and hypermarkets, in addition to general retailers.
ADVERTISING RATES:
Full Page Colour .... EUR 2900
BUSINESS: RETAILING & WHOLESALING

SANILEC 1213B3A-100
Editorial: Torhoutsesteenweg, 226, Bus 2, 8210 ZEDELGEM **Tel:** 5024 04 04 **Fax:** 50240445
Email: info@pmg.be **Web site:** http://www.sanilec.be
Date Established: 1995; **Freq:** Monthly - Variable; **Cover Price:** EUR 625
Annual Sub.: EUR 5600; **Circ:** 9,000
Usual Pagination: 76
Profile: Magazine containing product information about air conditioning, water treatment, central heating and humidifiers.
Language(s): Flemish; French
Readership: Read by installers of central heating systems, sanitary fittings, suppliers and wholesalers, and roofworkers.
ADVERTISING RATES:
Full Page Colour .... EUR 2900
BUSINESS: HEATING & VENTILATION: Domestic Heating & Ventilation

LA SANTE DE FEMMES D'AUJOURD'HUI 1660232B74A-172
Editorial: For all contact details see main record, FEMMES D'AUJOURD'HUI, 1831 **Tel:** 2776 28 53 **Fax:** 27762898
Email: femmesdaujourdhui@sanoma-magazines.be
Web site: http://www.femmesdaujourdhui.be
Freq: Half-yearly - 01 et 04; **Cover Price:** Free; **Circ:** 13,500
Language(s): French
ADVERTISING RATES:
Full Page Colour .... EUR 3300
Mechanical Data: Type Area: 285 x 220
CONSUMER: WOMEN'S INTEREST CONSUMER MAGAZINES: Women's Interest

SCIENCE CONNECTION 1893375B55-159
Editorial: Politique scientifique fédérale, Avenue Louise 231, 1050 BRUXELLES **Tel:** 2238 34 11 **Fax:** 22305912
Email: scienceconnection@belspo.be **Web site:** http://www.scienceconnection.be
Date Established: 2004; **Freq:** 6 issues yearly - 02 04 07 10 12; **Cover Price:** Free; **Circ:** 25,000
Usual Pagination: 60
Editor: Philippe Mettens
Language(s): French
Mechanical Data: Type Area: 225 x 300
BUSINESS: APPLIED SCIENCE & LABORATORIES

SEIZOEN 1892903B50-168
Editorial: Grasmarket 61, 1000 BRUSSELS
Tel: 2 504 03 00 **Fax:** 2 504 03 77
Email: communicatie@toerismevlaanderen.be **Web site:** http://www.toerismevlaanderen.be/seizoen
Date Established: 2006; **Freq:** Quarterly - 21/03 21/06 21/09 21/12; **Circ:** 3,000
Usual Pagination: 24
Language(s): Flemish; French
Mechanical Data: Type Area: A4
BUSINESS: TRAVEL & TOURISM

SENSA - GALERIA 707721B74Q-304
Editorial: Rue de la Fusée 50, Boîte 12, 1130 BRUXELLES **Tel:** 2702 47 56 **Fax:** 27024751
Web site: http://www.roularta.be
Date Established: 2000; **Freq:** Quarterly - 5/03 7/05 3/09 3/12; **Cover Price:** EUR 3.50; **Circ:** 260,468
Usual Pagination: 124
Profile: Publication focusing on lifestyle, family life and fashion.
Language(s): Flemish; French
Readership: Read mainly by women.
ADVERTISING RATES:
Full Page Colour .... EUR 6500
Mechanical Data: Type Area: A4
CONSUMER: WOMEN'S INTEREST CONSUMER MAGAZINES: Lifestyle

SHOES MAGAZINE 622565B29-70
Editorial: VDK Press, Zandstraat, 52-54, 8810 LICHTERVELDE **Tel:** 5024 04 04 **Fax:** 50240445
Email: info@pmg.be **Web site:** http://www.shoesportal.be
Date Established: 1997; **Freq:** Monthly - 02 03 08 09; **Cover Price:** EUR 15
Annual Sub.: EUR 50; **Circ:** 6,000
Usual Pagination: 100
Editor-in-Chief: Elisabeth Cornille
Profile: Magazine containing articles of interest for people in the shoe trade.
Language(s): Flemish; French
Readership: Aimed at shoe retailers.
ADVERTISING RATES:
Full Page Colour .... EUR 1850
BUSINESS: FOOTWEAR

LE SILLON BELGE - LANDBOUWLEVEN 1438B21A-170
Editorial: Avenue Léon Grosjean, 92, 1140 BRUXELLES **Tel:** 2730 34 00 **Fax:** 27303324
Email: erulu@euronet.be **Web site:** http://www.sillonbelge.be
Date Established: 1932; **Freq:** Weekly - Le vendredi;
Annual Sub.: EUR 47; **Circ:** 29,800
Usual Pagination: 50
Publisher: Joseph François
Profile: Magazine covering European farming and agriculture.
Language(s): Flemish; French
ADVERTISING RATES:
Full Page Mono .... EUR 1712
Full Page Colour .... EUR 2624
BUSINESS: AGRICULTURE & FARMING

SIMPLY YOU 1892884B94H-20
Editorial: Avenue des Olymiades, 20, 1140 BRUXELLES **Tel:** 2729 21 11
Email: simply-you@carrefour.com **Web site:** http://www.carrefour.eu/simplyyou
Freq: Monthly - Variable; **Cover Price:** Free; **Circ:** 800,000
Language(s): Flemish; French
CONSUMER: OTHER CLASSIFICATIONS: Customer Magazines

SMART BUSINESS STRATEGIES 707402B14A-250
Editorial: Minoc Business Press nv, Parklaan, 22 Bus 10, 2300 TURNHOUT **Tel:** 1446 23 00
Fax: 1446 23 66
Email: info@minoc.com **Web site:** http://www.minoc.com
Date Established: 2001; **Freq:** Monthly - Elke eerste dinsdag vd maand
Annual Sub.: EUR 39.95; **Circ:** 25,500
Usual Pagination: 68
Editor: William Visterin; **Publisher:** Caspar van Rhijn
Profile: Magazine containing information about the new economy, including IT technology, E-business and ICT.
Language(s): Flemish; French
Readership: Aimed at general managers, financial managers, marketing managers, ITEDP managers and web managers.
ADVERTISING RATES:
Full Page Colour .... EUR 5000
Mechanical Data: Type Area: 297 x 210
BUSINESS: COMMERCE, INDUSTRY & MANAGEMENT

SMILE 1648353B89A-263
Editorial: Decom Sa, Hofveld 6c4, Groot-Bijgaarden, 1702 BRUXELLES **Tel:** 2 325 64 64 **Fax:** 23256465
Email: info@decom.be **Web site:** http://www.decom.be
Date Established: 2003; **Freq:** Quarterly - 03 08 12; **Cover Price:** Free; **Circ:** 195,000
Managing Director: Roger de Laet
Language(s): Flemish; French
ADVERTISING RATES:
Full Page Colour .... EUR 4840
Mechanical Data: Type Area: 275 x 190
Copy instructions: *Copy Date:* 28 days prior to publication date
CONSUMER: HOLIDAYS & TRAVEL: Travel

LE SOIR 1819B65A-150
Editorial: Service Belgique, Rue Royale, 100, 1000 BRUXELLES **Tel:** 2225 54 32 **Fax:** 2225 59 14
Web site: http://www.lesoir.be
Date Established: 1887; **Freq:** Daily - 6 jours par semaine; **Cover Price:** EUR 1.20; **Circ:** 150,000
Usual Pagination: 40
Profile: Broadsheet-sized evening newspaper providing business and regional news. Also covers politics, culture, society, television and sport.
Language(s): French
Readership: Read by a broad sector of society, almost half of whom live in the Brussels area.
ADVERTISING RATES:
Full Page Colour .... EUR 21700
Mechanical Data: Type Area: 540 x 385
NATIONAL DAILY & SUNDAY NEWSPAPERS: National Daily Newspapers

LE SOIR MAGAZINE 2198B74C-150
Editorial: Rue Royale 100, 1000 BRUXELLES
Tel: 2225 57 70 **Fax:** 2225 59 11
Email: redaction@soirmag.be **Web site:** http://www.soirmag.be
Date Established: 1928; **Freq:** Weekly - Mercredi
Annual Sub.: EUR 84; **Circ:** 100,000
Usual Pagination: 100
Managing Director: Daniel Van Wylick; **Publisher:** Patrick Hurbain
Profile: Family magazine containing topical and general interest items, leisure features and a guide to TV programmes.
Language(s): French
ADVERTISING RATES:
Full Page Colour .... EUR 3950
Mechanical Data: Type Area: A4
Copy instructions: *Copy Date:* 10 days prior to publication date
CONSUMER: WOMEN'S INTEREST CONSUMER MAGAZINES: Home & Family

SOLUTIONS 1406B5B-60
Editorial: Avenue d'Overhem, 24, 1180 BRUXELLES
Tel: 2374 17 55 **Fax:** 23748809
Email: alain.de.fooz@skynet.be **Web site:** http://www.solutions-magazine.com
Date Established: 1993; **Freq:** Monthly - Le 20 du mois
Annual Sub.: EUR 50; **Circ:** 18,000
Usual Pagination: 56
Editor: Alain de Fooz
Profile: Magazine containing information and articles about data and image communications products for export, telecommunications in general, networking, computers and office automation and e-business.
Language(s): Flemish; French
Readership: Aimed at decision makers in larger companies.
ADVERTISING RATES:
Full Page Colour .... EUR 4800
BUSINESS: COMPUTERS & AUTOMATION: Data Processing

SOLUXIONS 1892895B18B-63
Editorial: Avenue d'Overhem, 24, 1180 BRUXELLES
Tel: 2374 17 55 **Fax:** 23748809
Email: alain.de.fooz@skynet.be **Web site:** http://www.soluxions-magazine.com
Freq: Monthly - Le 20 de chaque mois
Annual Sub.: EUR 30; **Circ:** 5,000
Usual Pagination: 56
Publisher: Alain de Fooz
Language(s): Flemish; French
BUSINESS: ELECTRONICS: Telecommunications

SPORT FOOT MAGAZINE 2283B75B-100
Editorial: Rue de la Fusée, 50, Boîte 5, 1130 BRUXELLES **Tel:** 2702 45 71 **Fax:** 27024572
Email: sportmagazine@roularta.be **Web site:** http://www.sportmagazine.be
Date Established: 1980; **Freq:** Weekly - Mercredi; **Cover Price:** EUR 2.90
Annual Sub.: EUR 129; **Circ:** 32,000
Editor: Dirk Lambrecht; **Publisher:** Amid Faljaoui
Profile: Magazine containing articles about football, tennis, volleyball and basketball, includes sporting news from Belgium and abroad. Provides in depth background information.
Language(s): Flemish; French
Readership: Aimed at the general public interested in sports.
ADVERTISING RATES:
Full Page Colour .... EUR 5500
Mechanical Data: Type Area: 267 x 202
Copy instructions: *Copy Date:* 14 days prior to publication date
CONSUMER: SPORT: Football

SPORT VOETBAL MAGAZINE 1892675B75A-178
Editorial: Rue de la Fusée, 50, Boîte 5, 1130 BRUXELLES **Tel:** 2702 45 71 **Fax:** 2702 45 72
Email: sportmagazine@roularta.be **Web site:** http://www.sportmagazine.be
Date Established: 1980; **Freq:** Weekly - Woensdag; **Cover Price:** EUR 2.90
Annual Sub.: EUR 129; **Circ:** 71,500
Editor: Dirk Lambrecht; **Managing Director:** Rik de Nolf
Language(s): Flemish; French
CONSUMER: SPORT

DE STANDAARD 1820B65A-160
Editorial: Gossetlaan 28, 1702 GROOT BIJGAARDEN **Tel:** 2467 25 52 **Fax:** 2 466 13 77
Email: binnenland@standaard.be **Web site:** http://www.standaard.be
Date Established: 1914; **Freq:** Daily - 6 Dagen per week; **Cover Price:** EUR 1.20
Annual Sub.: EUR 319; **Circ:** 100,010
Usual Pagination: 72
Editor: Bart Sturtewagen; **Editor-in-Chief:** Bert Bultinck
Profile: Broadsheet-sized newspaper containing regional, national and international news. Includes information on business, culture and society.
Language(s): Flemish; French
Readership: Aimed at managers, students, office personnel and factory workers.
Mechanical Data: Type Area: 300 x 410
NATIONAL DAILY & SUNDAY NEWSPAPERS: National Daily Newspapers

STORECHECK 1461B22A-100
Editorial: Gravendreef, 9 - B 8, 9120 BEVEREN
Tel: 3 750 90 20 **Fax:** 3 750 90 29
Email: stefan@storecheck.be **Web site:** http://www.emg-edit.be
ISSN: 1372-7346
Date Established: 1958; **Freq:** Monthly - De 4de - Niet in augustus
Annual Sub.: EUR 93; **Circ:** 8,000
Usual Pagination: 68
Editor: Stefan Van Rompaey
Profile: Magazine focusing on food retailing and distribution. First published in 1958, the publication has an average of 68 pages per issue. Aimed at professionals in the food sector, wholesalers, retailers and distributors. Local Translation: Onafhandelijk vaktijdschrift gericht tot de volledige voedingsdistributie (F1, F2 geïntegreerd, F2 niet-geïntegreerd, F3), speciaalzaken, groothandel en voedingsindustrie. alleen oop abonnement verkrijgbaar. Publication professionnelle s'adressant aux responsables des centrales, propriétaires et gérants de supermarchés.
Language(s): Flemish; French
Readership: Aimed at professionals in the food sector, wholesalers, retailers and distributors.
ADVERTISING RATES:
Full Page Mono .... EUR 2250
Full Page Colour .... EUR 2890
Mechanical Data: Type Area: A 4
Copy instructions: *Copy Date:* 28 days prior to publication date
BUSINESS: FOOD

SUPER MAGAZINE 1457B22A-105
Editorial: Tweekerkenstraat 29, 1000 BRUSSELS
Tel: 2238 05 57 **Fax:** 22380596
Email: info@supermagazine.be **Web site:** http://www.supermagazine.be
Date Established: 1949; **Freq:** 26 issues yearly - 02 04 05 06 09 11; **Circ:** 7,000
Usual Pagination: 55
Editor: Frank Verhue
Profile: Journal covering food retailing, processing, warehousing and distribution.
Language(s): Flemish; French
ADVERTISING RATES:
Full Page Mono .... EUR 1760
Full Page Colour .... EUR 2350
Mechanical Data: Type Area: A4
BUSINESS: FOOD

SYMBIOSES 1985550B57-62
Editorial: Rue Royale 266, 1210 BRUXELLES
Tel: 2286 95 70
Email: info@symbioses.be **Web site:** http://www.symbioses.be
Date Established: 1989; **Freq:** Quarterly; **Circ:** 4,000
Usual Pagination: 24
Publisher: Joëlle Van Den Berg
Language(s): French
BUSINESS: ENVIRONMENT & POLLUTION

SYNDICATS 1893394B14L-3
Editorial: Rue Haute 42, 1000 BRUSSELS
Tel: 2506 82 11 **Fax:** 25501404
Email: presse@fgtb.be **Web site:** http://www.abvv.be
Freq: 26 issues yearly - Vendredi sur 2; **Circ:** 320,000
Editor-in-Chief: Nicolas Errante
Language(s): French
BUSINESS: COMMERCE, INDUSTRY & MANAGEMENT: Trade Unions

TALKIES - STIJL 2278B74Q-180
Editorial: Rue de Stallestraat 70-82, 1180 BRUXELLES **Tel:** 2 333 07 00 **Fax:** 2 332 05 98
Email: talkies@mm.be **Web site:** http://www.talkiesmagazine.be
Date Established: 1986; **Freq:** Monthly - Begin van maand
Annual Sub.: EUR 55; **Circ:** 15,000
Usual Pagination: 146
Editor: Muriel Swartenbroeckx
Profile: Lifestyle magazine covering leisure, travel, fashion, cars and interior design.
Language(s): Flemish; French
ADVERTISING RATES:
Full Page Colour .... EUR 3900
Mechanical Data: Type Area: 217 x 284
CONSUMER: WOMEN'S INTEREST CONSUMER MAGAZINES: Lifestyle

TÉLÉ MOUSTIQUE 1647791B76C-324
Editorial: Telecomlaan 5-7, 1831 DIEGEM
Tel: 2776 25 20 **Fax:** 2776 23 99
Email: telemoustique@sanoma-magazines.be **Web site:** http://www.telemoustique.be
Date Established: 1924; **Freq:** Weekly - Mercredi;
Cover Price: EUR 1.80
Annual Sub.: EUR 88.40; **Circ:** 168,877
Usual Pagination: 186
Language(s): French
ADVERTISING RATES:
Full Page Colour .... EUR 4800
Mechanical Data: Type Area: 270 x 205
CONSUMER: MUSIC & PERFORMING ARTS: TV & Radio

TELE POCKET 2351B76C-260
Editorial: Telecomlaan, 5-7, 1831 DIEGEM
Tel: 2776 25 20 **Fax:** 27762314
Email: telepocket@sanoma-magazines.be **Web site:** http://www.telepocket.be
Date Established: 1994; **Freq:** Weekly - Mercredi
Annual Sub.: EUR 4080; **Circ:** 55,164
Usual Pagination: 105
Publisher: Marie-Anne de Temmerman
Profile: Magazine about forthcoming TV programmes and films.
Language(s): French
ADVERTISING RATES:
Full Page Colour .... EUR 1375
Mechanical Data: Type Area: 210 x 148
CONSUMER: MUSIC & PERFORMING ARTS: TV & Radio

TÉLÉPRO MAGAZINE 2349B76C-275
Editorial: Rue de la Fusée 50, Boîte 10, 1130 BRUXELLES **Tel:** 8730 87 61 **Fax:** 8731 35 37
Email: courrier@telepromagazine.be **Web site:** http://www.telepro.be
Date Established: 1954; **Freq:** Weekly - Mercredi;
Cover Price: EUR 1.30
Annual Sub.: EUR 64; **Circ:** 160,000
Usual Pagination: 124
Publisher: Hugues De Foucauld
Profile: Magazine containing television news.
Language(s): French
ADVERTISING RATES:
Full Page Colour .... EUR 3700
Mechanical Data: Type Area: 267 x 202
CONSUMER: MUSIC & PERFORMING ARTS: TV & Radio

TEVE BLAD 2352B76C-320
Editorial: Uitbreidingsstraat, 82, 2600 BERCHEM
Tel: 3290 14 81 **Fax:** 32901482
Email: info@teveblad.be **Web site:** http://www.teveblad.be
Date Established: 1981; **Freq:** Weekly - Dinsdag;
Cover Price: EUR 0.95
Annual Sub.: EUR 45.60; **Circ:** 170,000
Usual Pagination: 132
Editor: Jan Van der Vloedt
Profile: Magazine containing TV listings and programme features.
Language(s): Flemish; French
ADVERTISING RATES:
Full Page Colour .... EUR 3230
Mechanical Data: Type Area: 210 x 142
CONSUMER: MUSIC & PERFORMING ARTS: TV & Radio

THE PARLIAMENT MAGAZINE 1893250B82-326
Editorial: International Press Center, Bld Charlemagne, 1, 1041 BRUXELLES **Tel:** 2285 08 28
Fax: 22850823
Email: newsdesk@dods.eu **Web site:** http://www.theparliament.com
Freq: 26 issues yearly - Jeudi; **Annual Sub.:** EUR 97;
Circ: 5,000
Editor: Brian Johnson
Language(s): English; French
CONSUMER: CURRENT AFFAIRS & POLITICS

THIS IS IT 1983438B5C-1
Tel: 2 467 57 47 **Fax:** 2 4675841
Web site: http://datanews.rnews.be
Date Established: 2010; **Freq:** Quarterly; **Circ:** 64,000
Language(s): Flemish; French
Supplement to: DATA NEWS
BUSINESS: COMPUTERS & AUTOMATION: Professional Personal Computers

TOURING EXPLORER (FRENCH EDITION) 2379B77A-120
Formerly: TOURING EXPLORER (EDITION FRANCOPHONE)
Editorial: Rue de la Loi 44, 1040 BRUXELLES
Tel: 2233 24 72 **Fax:** 22332469
Email: redaction@touring.be **Web site:** http://www.touring.be
Date Established: 1948; **Freq:** Monthly - Sauf 01 et 08; **Circ:** 227,416
Usual Pagination: 108
Editor: Hedwig Teck
Profile: Magazine of the Royal Belgian Touring Club.
Language(s): French
ADVERTISING RATES:
Full Page Colour .... EUR 10500
Mechanical Data: Type Area: 295 x 220
Copy instructions: *Copy Date:* 15 days prior to publication date
CONSUMER: MOTORING & CYCLING: Motoring

TRANSPO 1614B49A-48
Editorial: Rue de l'Entrepôt, 5 A, 1020 BRUXELLES
Tel: 2421 51 70 **Fax:** 24261738
Email: transpo@transpo.org
Date Established: 1986; **Freq:** Monthly - Le 5 du mois (sauf 07-08); **Cover Price:** EUR 650
Annual Sub.: EUR 63; **Circ:** 10,000
Usual Pagination: 60
Profile: Journal of the Belgian Federation of Transporters containing social and juridical news, road tests and technical and statistical information.
Language(s): Flemish; French
Readership: Read by managers of road haulage companies.
ADVERTISING RATES:
Full Page Mono .... EUR 1500
Full Page Colour .... EUR 2300
Mechanical Data: Type Area: A4
BUSINESS: TRANSPORT

TRAVEL MAGAZINE 1632B50-164_50
Editorial: Hanswijkstraat 23, 2800 MECHELEN
Tel: 15 450 350 **Fax:** 15 450 360
Email: travmag@travel-magazine.be **Web site:** http://www.travel-magazine.be
Date Established: 1992; **Freq:** Monthly - Variable;
Annual Sub.: EUR 75; **Circ:** 7,000
Usual Pagination: 84
Profile: Magazine covering all aspects of the worldwide travel trade.
Language(s): Flemish; French
Readership: Read by travel agents, tour operators, travel personnel and tourism students.
ADVERTISING RATES:
Full Page Colour .... EUR 2410
Mechanical Data: Type Area: A 4
Copy instructions: *Copy Date:* 28 days prior to publication date
BUSINESS: TRAVEL & TOURISM

TRENDS - TENDENCES 1339B14A-169_30
Editorial: Raketstraat 50, 1130 BRUSSELS
Tel: 2702 48 00 **Fax:** 2702 48 02
Email: feedback@bizzmagazine.be **Web site:** http://www.trends.be
Date Established: 1975; **Freq:** Weekly - Donderdag;
Cover Price: EUR 4.50
Annual Sub.: EUR 192; **Circ:** 56,025
Editor: Amid Faljaoui; **Editor-in-Chief:** Roeland Byl
Profile: Business magazine covering marketing, management and finance.
Language(s): Flemish; French
ADVERTISING RATES:
Full Page Colour .... EUR 8000
Mechanical Data: Type Area: 267 x 202
BUSINESS: COMMERCE, INDUSTRY & MANAGEMENT

LA TRIBUNE 1657981B44-155
Editorial: Rue meyerbeer, 145, 1180 BRUXELLES
Tel: 2344 52 20 **Fax:** 23436172
Email: info@rpc.be **Web site:** http://www.rpc.be
Date Established: 2001; **Freq:** Quarterly - Les 15 : 03 06 09 12; **Circ:** 7,500
Usual Pagination: 40
Language(s): French
ADVERTISING RATES:
Full Page Mono .... EUR 1395
Full Page Colour .... EUR 1860
Mechanical Data: Type Area: A 4
Copy instructions: *Copy Date:* 15 days prior to publication date
BUSINESS: LEGAL

TURBO MAGAZINE (EDITION FRANCOPHONE) 2397B77D-80
Editorial: GALB sprl, rue des Combattants, 8, Fooz, 4340 LIEGE **Tel:** 4342 31 73 **Fax:** 43440400
Email: info@turbomagazine.be **Web site:** http://www.turbomagazine.be
Date Established: 1978; **Freq:** Monthly - Le 20 du mois
Annual Sub.: EUR 60; **Circ:** 12,000
Usual Pagination: 80
Editor: Geert Vermeerch
Profile: Magazine about national and international motor sports.
Language(s): French
ADVERTISING RATES:
Full Page Colour .... EUR 3250
Mechanical Data: Type Area: A 4
CONSUMER: MOTORING & CYCLING: Motor Sports

TV FAMILIE 2342B76C-80
Formerly: TV-FAMILIE - BLIK
Editorial: Brandekensweg 2, 2627 SCHELLE
Tel: 3 880 84 50 **Fax:** 3 844 61 52
Email: redactie@tvfamilie.be **Web site:** http://www.tvfamilie.be
Date Established: 1995; **Freq:** Weekly - Woensdag;
Cover Price: EUR 1.30; **Circ:** 193,000
Usual Pagination: 100
Editor: Isabelle Vandenberghe; **Editor-in-Chief:** Truus Genbrugge
Profile: TV listings magazine covering programme features and celebrity gossip.
Language(s): Flemish; French
ADVERTISING RATES:
Full Page Colour .... EUR 3600
Mechanical Data: Type Area: 270 x 208
CONSUMER: MUSIC & PERFORMING ARTS: TV & Radio

UITMAGAZINE 1634B77A-200
Editorial: Pastoor Coplaan 100, 2070 ZWIJNDRECHT **Tel:** 32 53 60 80 **Fax:** 32 53 60 90
Email: redactie@uit.be **Web site:** http://www.uit.be
ISSN: 0774-1324
Date Established: 1986; **Freq:** Monthly - Début de mois; **Cover Price:** EUR 3.50
Annual Sub.: EUR 25; **Circ:** 280,000
Usual Pagination: 120
Editor: Toni De Coninck; **Editor-in-Chief:** Ellen Van Damme
Profile: Magazine of the Flemish Automotive club. Covers cars, motorcycles, travel, tourism, food and wine, culture and leisure.
Language(s): Flemish; French
Readership: Read by travel and car enthusiasts.
ADVERTISING RATES:
Full Page Mono .... EUR 4200
Full Page Colour .... EUR 6200
Mechanical Data: Type Area: 198 X 275
Copy instructions: *Copy Date:* 21 days prior to publication date
CONSUMER: MOTORING & CYCLING: Motoring

UNION & ACTIONS 1165B1A-90
Editorial: Rue de la Pavée, 6, 5101 ERPENT
Tel: 8132 22 61 **Fax:** 8132 22 69
Email: ua@ucm.be **Web site:** http://www.ucm.be
Date Established: 1996; **Freq:** 24 issues yearly; **Circ:** 75,000
Usual Pagination: 16
Profile: Magazine focusing on social, fiscal, legal, economic and financial affairs.
Language(s): French
Readership: Aimed at company directors of small companies and self employed people, and also accountants.
ADVERTISING RATES:
Full Page Mono .... EUR 2.725
Full Page Colour .... EUR 3.420
BUSINESS: FINANCE & ECONOMICS

VERBONDSNIEUWS 1647804B26D-28
Editorial: AVBS, Denen 157, 9080 LOCHRISTI
Tel: 9326 72 10 **Fax:** 93267211
Email: info@avbs.be **Web site:** http://www.avbs.be
Date Established: 1956; **Freq:** 26 issues yearly - De 1ste en de 15 de; **Annual Sub.:** EUR 65; **Circ:** 2,000
Usual Pagination: 52
Editor: Willy De Geest; **Publisher:** Sonja de Becker
Language(s): Flemish; French
ADVERTISING RATES:
Full Page Mono .... EUR 280
Full Page Colour .... EUR 660
BUSINESS: GARDEN TRADE: Garden Trade Horticulture

VIB - VERENINING VOOR INKOOP EN BEDRIJFSLOGISTIEK 1893030B14A-313
Editorial: Filip Williotstraat 9, 2600 BERCHEM
Tel: 3286 80 90 **Fax:** 32868098
Email: vib@bevib.be **Web site:** http://www.bevib.be
Freq: Monthly - Le 25 du mois; **Circ:** 2,000
Editor: Greet Jansen
Language(s): Flemish; French
Copy instructions: *Copy Date:* 20 days prior to publication date
BUSINESS: COMMERCE, INDUSTRY & MANAGEMENT

LE VIF/L'EXPRESS 2161B82-336
Editorial: Rue de la Fusée 50, Boîte 6, 1130 BRUSSELS **Tel:** 2702 47 01 **Fax:** 2702 47 02
Email: levif@levif.be **Web site:** http://www.levif.be
Date Established: 1983; **Freq:** Weekly - Le vendredi;
Cover Price: EUR 3.70
Annual Sub.: EUR 185; **Circ:** 97,605
Usual Pagination: 112
Editor: Amid Faljaoui
Profile: News magazine for the French-speaking part of Belgium with articles and news items on Belgian, international, social, political, cultural and sports topics.
Language(s): French
ADVERTISING RATES:
Full Page Colour .... EUR 7400
Mechanical Data: Type Area: 266 x 202
CONSUMER: CURRENT AFFAIRS & POLITICS

VIGILES 1893252B44-169
Editorial: Galerie Ravenstein, 28, 1000 BRUXELLES
Tel: 2 289 26 10 **Fax:** 22892619
Email: info@politeia.be **Web site:** http://www.politeia.be
Date Established: 1995; **Freq:** Quarterly - 03 05 07 10 12; **Annual Sub.:** EUR 119; **Circ:** 2,000
Usual Pagination: 48
Editor: Frank Hutsebaut; **Publisher:** Martin De Loose
Language(s): Flemish; French
Mechanical Data: Type Area: A 4
BUSINESS: LEGAL

VILLAS 2199B4A-169
Editorial: Rue Golden Hope, 1, 1620 DROGENBOS
Tel: 2378 21 27 **Fax:** 2378 37 29
Email: info@villasdecoration.com **Web site:** http://www.villas-decoration.com
ISSN: 1370-6497
Date Established: 1971; **Freq:** Half-yearly; **Cover Price:** EUR 8,20; **Circ:** 40,000
Usual Pagination: 300
Editor: Raymond Naumann
Profile: Magazine about architecture, decoration and design for the general public, architects and professional decorators.
Language(s): Flemish; French
ADVERTISING RATES:
Full Page Mono .... EUR 2.600
Full Page Colour .... EUR 2.150
BUSINESS: ARCHITECTURE & BUILDING: Architecture

VINO MAGAZINE 1295B9C-10
Editorial: Rue de Merode, 60, (Saint Gilles), 1060 BRUXELLES **Tel:** 2533 27 60 **Fax:** 25332761
Email: vinopres@vinopres.com **Web site:** http://www.vinopres.be
Date Established: 1944; **Freq:** 6 issues yearly - Le 15 du mois; **Cover Price:** EUR 4.50
Annual Sub.: EUR 36; **Circ:** 18,500
Usual Pagination: 56
Editor: Baudouin Havaux
Profile: Journal about wines and spirits.
Language(s): Flemish; French
Readership: Read by professional wine and spirit traders, sommeliers and amateur wine lovers.
ADVERTISING RATES:
Full Page Mono .... EUR 1700
Full Page Colour .... EUR 2475
Mechanical Data: Type Area: A4
BUSINESS: DRINKS & LICENSED TRADE: Licensed Trade, Wines & Spirits

VITAT.BE 1665467B74Q-329
Editorial: Rue de l'Arbre Bénit, 93, 1050 BRUXELLES
Tel: 2646 71 30 **Fax:** 2502 40 24
Email: vivat.redaction@gmail.com **Web site:** http://www.vivat.be
Language(s): Flemish; French
CONSUMER: WOMEN'S INTEREST CONSUMER MAGAZINES: Lifestyle

VITAYA MAGAZINE 2226B74G-25_50
Editorial: Luchthavenlaan 20, 1800 VILVOORDE
Tel: 2 253 04 04 **Fax:** 2 257 91 50
Email: info@vitaya.be **Web site:** http://www.vitaya.be
Date Established: 1992; **Freq:** Monthly - Le 3ème mercredi du mois; **Cover Price:** EUR 3.70; **Circ:** 90,000
Usual Pagination: 164
Editor: Ann De Tremerie
Profile: Magazine about wellness and health for all the family. Also covers fashion, beauty, food and travel.
Language(s): Flemish; French
Readership: Read by women aged between 25 and 45 years old.
ADVERTISING RATES:
Full Page Colour .... EUR 3500
Mechanical Data: Type Area: 285 x 255
CONSUMER: WOMEN'S INTEREST CONSUMER MAGAZINES: Slimming & Health

VOTRE BEAUTE 2233B74H-200
Editorial: Clos des Lilas, 5, 1380 OHAIN
Tel: 2660 69 40 **Fax:** 26600943
Email: cecile@dechamps-diffusions.be **Web site:** http://www.dechamps-diffusions.be
Freq: Monthly - Le 25 du mois; **Cover Price:** EUR 3.50
Annual Sub.: EUR 35; **Circ:** 30,000
Usual Pagination: 180
Profile: Women's magazine focusing on beauty, health and fashion.
Language(s): French

ADVERTISING RATES:
Full Page Colour .... EUR 2825
Mechanical Data: Type Area: 210 x 275
Copy instructions: *Copy Date:* 42 days prior to publication date
CONSUMER: WOMEN'S INTEREST CONSUMER MAGAZINES: Hair & Beauty

VOYAGES VOYAGES - ELDERS EN ANDERS 2548B89A-260
Formerly: VOYAGES VOYAGES/ELDERS & ANDERS
Editorial: Rue de Stalle 70-82, 1180 BRUXELLES
Tel: 2333 07 00 **Fax:** 23320598
Email: voyages@mm.be **Web site:** http://www.voyagesvoyages.be
Date Established: 1996; **Freq:** Monthly - Le 15 du mois sauf 01 08; **Cover Price:** EUR 450
Annual Sub.: EUR 39; **Circ:** 15,000
Usual Pagination: 100
Editor-in-Chief: Liesbet Geboers; **Publisher:** Claude Dupuis
Profile: Magazine focusing on travel for all ages and budgets.
Language(s): Flemish; French
Mechanical Data: Type Area: A 4
CONSUMER: HOLIDAYS & TRAVEL: Travel

VRAAG & AANBOD 1351B14B-85
Editorial: Kluwer, Motstraat, 30, 2800 MECHELEN
Tel: 15 36 15 18 **Fax:** 15 36 18 99
Email: va@kluwer.be **Web site:** http://www.vraagenaanbod.be
Date Established: 1952; **Freq:** Weekly - Dinsdag/Mardi; **Annual Sub.:** EUR 151; **Circ:** 10,000
Usual Pagination: 28
Editor: Michel Verstrepen
Profile: Journal containing practical information on commerce, industry, technology and products.
Language(s): Flemish; French
ADVERTISING RATES:
Full Page Colour .... EUR 3024
Mechanical Data: Type Area: A3
BUSINESS: COMMERCE, INDUSTRY & MANAGEMENT: Industry & Factories

VROUW & WERELD 2179B74A-160
Editorial: Urbain Britsierslaan 5, 1030 BRUSSELS
Tel: 2246 51 11 **Fax:** 22465110
Email: redactie@kav.be **Web site:** http://www.kav.be
Date Established: 1929; **Freq:** Monthly - De 1ste. Niet in 08; **Annual Sub.:** EUR 25; **Circ:** 95,000
Usual Pagination: 60
Editor: Annick Geets; **Publisher:** Annemie Janssens
Profile: Socio-cultural women's magazine.
Language(s): Flemish; French
Readership: Aimed at active women aged between 30 and 49 years in the Flanders and Brussels area.
ADVERTISING RATES:
Full Page Colour .... EUR 3180
Mechanical Data: Type Area: 285 x 207
CONSUMER: WOMEN'S INTEREST CONSUMER MAGAZINES: Women's Interest

VROUWEN MET VAART 2166B74A-43
Editorial: Remylaan 4b, 3018 WIJGMAAL-LEUVEN
Tel: 1624 39 99 **Fax:** 16243909
Email: ledenblad@kvlv.be **Web site:** http://www.kvlv.be
Date Established: 1911; **Freq:** Monthly - De eerste; **Annual Sub.:** EUR 22; **Circ:** 109,000
Usual Pagination: 80
Editor: Annemie Morris
Profile: Socio-cultural magazine published by the Catholic Movement for Rural Women.
Language(s): Flemish; French
Readership: Read mainly by members of the movement.
ADVERTISING RATES:
Full Page Colour .... EUR 2650
Mechanical Data: Type Area: 297 x 210
CONSUMER: WOMEN'S INTEREST CONSUMER MAGAZINES: Women's Interest

WEEKEND KNACK 2279B74Q-250
Editorial: Raketstraat 50, boîte 6, 1130 BRUSSELS
Tel: 2 702 47 00 **Fax:** 2 702 47 69
Email: weekend@knack.be **Web site:** http://www.weekend.be
Date Established: 1985; **Freq:** Weekly - Woensdag
Annual Sub.: EUR 127; **Circ:** 126,654
Usual Pagination: 100
Editor: Trui Moerkerke; **Editor-in-Chief:** Leen Creve; **Publisher:** Chantal Lepaige
Profile: Lifestyle magazine containing features on fashion, beauty, food, wine, living in Europe, travel and leisure activities. Includes television programme listings.
Language(s): Flemish; French
ADVERTISING RATES:
Full Page Colour .... EUR 9600
Mechanical Data: Type Area: 267 x 202
CONSUMER: WOMEN'S INTEREST CONSUMER MAGAZINES: Lifestyle

WERELDWIJS 1893033B14A-316
Editorial: Gaucheretstraat 90, 1030 BRUSSELS
Tel: 2 504 87 11 **Fax:** 2 504 88 99
Email: wereldwijs@fitagency.be **Web site:** http://www.flandersinvestmentandtrade.be
Date Established: 2008; **Freq:** Monthly; **Circ:** 7,000
Usual Pagination: 32
Editor: Koen Allaert
Language(s): Flemish; French
Mechanical Data: Type Area: A4
BUSINESS: COMMERCE, INDUSTRY & MANAGEMENT

ZAP (SUPP. LE SOIR) 2220B74F-250
Editorial: For all contact details see main record, LE SOIR - SIEGE SOCIAL, 1000 **Tel:** 2225 54 32
Fax: 22255914
Email: culture@lesoir.be **Web site:** http://www.lesoir.be
Date Established: 2003; **Freq:** Weekly - vendredi; **Circ:** 110,000
Usual Pagination: 72
Publisher: Patrick Hurbain
Profile: Magazine featuring interviews, music, film and lifestyle.
Language(s): French
Readership: Aimed at teenagers aged 14 to 18 years.
Mechanical Data: Type Area: 285 x 210
CONSUMER: WOMEN'S INTEREST CONSUMER MAGAZINES: Teenage

DE ZONTAG 1648065B65B-1
Editorial: Meiboomlaan 33, 8800 ROESELARE
Tel: 51 26 61 11 **Fax:** 51 26 66 33
Email: redactie@roularta.be **Web site:** http://www.dezondag.be
Date Established: 1999; **Freq:** Weekly - Belgium; **Cover Price:** Free; **Circ:** 645,000
Language(s): Flemish; French
Mechanical Data: Type Area: 367 x 256
NATIONAL DAILY & SUNDAY NEWSPAPERS: National Sunday Newspapers

ZWERFAUTO MAGAZINE 2572B91B-60
Editorial: Postbus, 728, 8400 OOSTENDE
Tel: 59702 8 14 **Fax:** 59702834
Email: info@zwerfauto.info **Web site:** http://www.zwerfauto.info
ISSN: 0773-2473
Date Established: 1985; **Freq:** Monthly - Om de 6 weken; **Cover Price:** EUR 325
Annual Sub.: EUR 2375; **Circ:** 26,345
Usual Pagination: 64
Profile: Magazine focusing on camper vans and motor-homes.
Language(s): Flemish; French
Readership: Aimed at camping and caravan enthusiasts.
ADVERTISING RATES:
Full Page Mono .... EUR 909
Full Page Colour .... EUR 1155
Mechanical Data: Type Area: 303 x 213
CONSUMER: RECREATION & LEISURE: Camping & Caravanning

Bosnia-Herzegovina

Time Difference: GMT + 1 hr (CET - Central European Time)
National Telephone Code: +387
Continent: Europe
Capital: Sarajevo
Principal Language: Bosnian, Serbian, Croatian
Population: 3981239
Monetary Unit: Convertible Mark (KM)

EMBASSY HIGH

COMMISSION: Embassy of the Republic of Bosnia and Herzegovina: 5-7 Lexham Gardens, London, W8 5JJ
Tel: 020 7373 0867
Fax: 020 7373 0871
Website: http://www.bhembassy.co.uk
Email: embassy@bhembassy.co.uk

AUTO 1834426BA77A-1
Editorial: Šibenska 3/5, 71000 SARAJEVO
Tel: 33 26 26 00 **Fax:** 33 26 26 06
Email: redakcija@auto.ba **Web site:** http://www.auto.ba
ISSN: 1512-6137
Date Established: 1998; **Freq:** Monthly; **Cover Price:** KM 5.00; **Circ:** 15,000
Usual Pagination: 100
Editor-in-Chief: Mirko Gerh
Profile: Magazine about cars, cars' comparison and their technical characteristics, new car technologies and products.
Language(s): Bosnian
ADVERTISING RATES:
Full Page Colour .... EUR 800.00
Mechanical Data: Type Area: A4
CONSUMER: MOTORING & CYCLING: Motoring

DANI 766105BA82-2
Editorial: Skenderpašina 4, 71000 SARAJEVO
Tel: 33 22 04 62 **Fax:** 33 65 17 89
Email: bhdani@bih.net.ba **Web site:** http://www.bhdani.com
Date Established: 1992; **Freq:** Weekly - Published on Friday; **Cover Price:** KM 1,50
Annual Sub.: KM 115,00; **Circ:** 30,000
Usual Pagination: 90
Editor-in-Chief: Vildana Selimbegović
Profile: Magazine focusing on political and economic events.
Language(s): Bosnian
Readership: Aimed at anyone interested in political and economic events.
ADVERTISING RATES:
Full Page Colour .... EUR 1200.00
Agency Commission: 10-25%
Mechanical Data: Type Area: 230 x 300mm
Copy instructions: *Copy Date:* 1 week prior publication date
CONSUMER: CURRENT AFFAIRS & POLITICS

DNEVNI AVAZ 707957BA65A-40
Editorial: Tešanjska 24b, SARAJEVO 71000
Tel: 33 281 490 **Fax:** 33 281 441
Email: redakcija@avaz.ba **Web site:** http://www.avaz.ba
Freq: Daily; **Cover Price:** KM 1.00; **Circ:** 60,000
Usual Pagination: 72
Editor-in-Chief: Sejad Luckin
Profile: Newspaper with news on domestic and international politics, finance, culture, social issues, sport and entertainment.
Language(s): Bosnian
ADVERTISING RATES:
Full Page Mono .... KM 1000.00
Full Page Colour .... KM 1300.00
Mechanical Data: Type Area: 245 x 350mm
NATIONAL DAILY & SUNDAY NEWSPAPERS: National Daily Newspapers

MAXISTARS 1616247BA74Q-2
Formerly: MAX magazin
Editorial: Maršala Tita 30/V, 71000 SARAJEVO
Tel: 33 21 35 36 **Fax:** 33 21 35 72
Email: redakcija@maxi.co.ba **Web site:** http://www.maxi.co.ba
ISSN: 1840-2631
Date Established: 2007; **Freq:** Weekly - Published on Friday; **Cover Price:** KM 3.00; **Circ:** 20,000
Usual Pagination: 100
Editor-in-Chief: Berin Ekmečić; **Advertising Manager:** Adnan Havurdić
Profile: Lifestyle magazine with features, portraits and information from various spheres of life in the country and around the world.
Language(s): Bosnian
Readership: Aimed at readers of all ages.
ADVERTISING RATES:
Full Page Colour .... KM 1400.00
Mechanical Data: Type Area: 230 x 290mm
CONSUMER: WOMEN'S INTEREST CONSUMER MAGAZINES: Lifestyle

NEZAVISNE NEDJELJNE NOVINE 1664938BA65B-1
Editorial: Braće Pišteljića 1, 78000 BANJA LUKA
Tel: 51 33 18 00 **Fax:** 51 33 18 10
Email: desk@nezavisne.com **Web site:** http://www.nezavisne.com
Date Established: 2005; **Freq:** Sunday; **Cover Price:** KM 1.00; **Circ:** 20,000
Editor: Dragan Jerinić; **Managing Editor:** Dragan Jerinić
Profile: Newspaper focusing on national and international news, politics, economics, business, culture, lifestyle and sport.
Language(s): Bosnian
Readership: Aimed at readers in their 20s -70s.
NATIONAL DAILY & SUNDAY NEWSPAPERS: National Sunday Newspapers

NEZAVISNE NOVINE 766175BA65A-41
Editorial: Braće Pišteljića 1, 78000 BANJA LUKA
Tel: 51 33 18 00 **Fax:** 51 33 18 10
Email: desk@nezavisne.com **Web site:** http://www.nezavisne.com
Date Established: 1996; **Freq:** Daily - Published Monday to Saturday; **Cover Price:** EUR 0.5
Annual Sub.: EUR 160.00; **Circ:** 20,000
Editor: Dragan Jerinić; **Editor-in-Chief:** Borjana Radmanović-Petrović; **Managing Editor:** Dragan Jerinić; **Advertisement Director:** Sanja Blagojevic
Profile: Newspaper containing national and international news, current affairs and sport.
Language(s): Bosnian
ADVERTISING RATES:
Full Page Mono .... KM 900.00
Full Page Colour .... KM 1170.00
NATIONAL DAILY & SUNDAY NEWSPAPERS: National Daily Newspapers

OSLOBODJENJE 1600685BA65A-42
Editorial: Džemala Bijedića 185, 71000 SARAJEVO
Tel: 33 27 69 00 **Fax:** 33 46 80 54
Email: redaction@oslobodjenje.ba **Web site:** http://www.oslobodjenje.ba
Date Established: 1943; **Freq:** Daily; **Cover Price:** KM 1.00; **Circ:** 25,000
Editor-in-Chief: Faruk Boric
Profile: Newspaper focusing on national and international news, business, sport and current affairs.
Language(s): Bosnian
ADVERTISING RATES:
Full Page Mono .... KM 900.00
Full Page Colour .... KM 1180.00
Mechanical Data: Type Area: 250 x 350mm
NATIONAL DAILY & SUNDAY NEWSPAPERS: National Daily Newspapers

SLOBODNA BOSNA 766033BA82-4
Editorial: Čekaluša Čikma 6, 71000 SARAJEVO
Tel: 33 44 40 41 **Fax:** 33 44 48 95
Email: sl.bos@bih.net.ba **Web site:** http://www.slobodna-bosna.ba
ISSN: 1840-1201
Freq: Weekly - Published on Thursday; **Cover Price:** KM 3.00; **Circ:** 20,000
Editor: Senad Avdic
Profile: Magazine focusing on national and international news and current affairs.
Language(s): Bosnian
ADVERTISING RATES:
Full Page Colour .... KM 1800.00
Mechanical Data: Trim Size: 213 x 306mm
CONSUMER: CURRENT AFFAIRS & POLITICS

SPORT 707962BA75A-100
Editorial: Tešanjska 24b, 71000 SARAJEVO
Tel: 33 21 84 29 **Fax:** 33 28 14 06
Email: sport@avaz.ba **Web site:** http://www.avaz.ba
Freq: 104 issues yearly; **Circ:** 25,000
Usual Pagination: 40
Editor: Abdulah Campara
Profile: Magazine covering national and international sport events.
Language(s): Bosnian
Readership: Aimed at sport enthusiasts.
ADVERTISING RATES:
Full Page Mono .... KM 700.00
Mechanical Data: Type Area: 250 x 350mm
CONSUMER: SPORT

START BIH 765971BA82-3
Editorial: La Benevolencije 6, 71000 SARAJEVO
Tel: 33 26 02 10 **Fax:** 33 21 53 21
Email: redakcija@startbih.info **Web site:** http://www.startbih.info
Date Established: 1998; **Freq:** 26 issues yearly;
Annual Sub.: EUR 65.00 (Europe); **Circ:** 15,000
Usual Pagination: 88
Editor-in-Chief: Eldin Karic; **Advertisement Director:** Dario Novalic
Profile: News magazine covering politics, economics, sports and culture.
Language(s): Bosnian
Readership: Aimed at people in the age group between 22 and 60 years, with secondary school education (40 %) and highly educated readers (60%), who are in a position to decide in economy, business and politics.
ADVERTISING RATES:
Full Page Colour .... EUR 1000.00
Mechanical Data: Type Area: 210 x 290mm
CONSUMER: CURRENT AFFAIRS & POLITICS

Bulgaria

Bulgaria

Time Difference: GMT + 2 hrs (EET - Eastern European Time)
National Telephone Code: +359
Continent: Europe
Capital: Sofia
Principal Language: Bulgarian
Population: 726675
Monetary Unit: Lev (BGN)
EMBASSY HIGH COMMISSION: Embassy of the Republic of Bulgaria: 186-188 Queen's Gate, London SW7 5HL
Tel: 020 75 84 94 00
Fax: 020 75 84 49 48
Website: http://www.bulgarianembassy-london.org

168 CHASSA 1790704BG65J-84
Editorial: 47 Tsarigradsko Shose Blvd, 1504 SOFIA
Tel: 2 942 27 32 **Fax:** 2 942 28 24
Email: 168@press.zgb.bg
Freq: Weekly - Issued only on Friday; **Circ:** 65,000
Editor-in-Chief: Nikolay Penchev
Profile: National weekly newspaper including business, political and entertainment news and comments, mainly for intellectuals.
Language(s): Bulgarian
ADVERTISING RATES:
Full Page Mono .... BGN 3475.08
Full Page Colour .... BGN 4680.72
Mechanical Data: Type Area: 254 x 394 mm
NATIONAL DAILY & SUNDAY NEWSPAPERS: National Weekly Newspapers

24 CHASSA 1790695BG65A-260
Editorial: 47 Tsarigradsko Shose Blvd, 1504 SOFIA
Tel: 2 942 25 14 **Fax:** 2 942 28 19
Email: VGocheva@24chasa.bg **Web site:** http://www.24chasa.bg
Freq: Daily; **Circ:** 80,000
Editor-in-Chief: Venelina Gocheva
Profile: The second most circulated newspaper mainly for the average Bulgarian reader, strong opinion maker with eight regional editions in Varna, Plovdiv, Burgas, Stara Zagora, etc.
Language(s): Bulgarian
ADVERTISING RATES:
Full Page Mono .... BGN 10141.56
Full Page Colour .... BGN 13687.56
Mechanical Data: Type Area: 254 x 394 mm
NATIONAL DAILY & SUNDAY NEWSPAPERS: National Daily Newspapers

7 DNI SPORT 1790702BG65J-83
Editorial: 6 Al. Jendov St., Glavproekt, 1113 SOFIA
Tel: 2 807 65 85 **Fax:** 2 807 65 61
Email: 7sport@online.bg **Web site:** http://www.7sport.net/7sport
Freq: Daily; **Circ:** 30,000
Editor-in-Chief: July Moskov
Profile: Weekly newspaper for sports news from Bulgaria and the world.
Language(s): Bulgarian
ADVERTISING RATES:
Full Page Mono .... BGN 2836.8
Full Page Colour .... BGN 3782.4
Mechanical Data: Type Area: 254 x 394 mm
NATIONAL DAILY & SUNDAY NEWSPAPERS: National Weekly Newspapers

ATAKA 1790701BG65A-266
Editorial: 73 Yavorov District, ap.11, 1111 SOFIA
Tel: 2 971 11 72 **Fax:** 2 971 11 65
Email: ataka@vestnikataka.com **Web site:** http://www.vestnikataka.com
Freq: Daily - No edition on Sunday; **Circ:** 15,000
Editor-in-Chief: Kapka Siderova
Profile: Daily newspaper, official issue of the nationalists party Ataka.
Language(s): Bulgarian
ADVERTISING RATES:
Full Page Mono .... BGN 4048.2
Full Page Colour .... BGN 7979.4
Mechanical Data: Type Area: 260 x 390 mm
NATIONAL DAILY & SUNDAY NEWSPAPERS: National Daily Newspapers

AUTOKAZION 1695591BG49D-1
Editorial: 121 Tsarigradsko Shose Blv., 1784 SOFIA
Tel: 2 971 81 31 **Fax:** 2 971 81 31
Email: office@avtookazion-bg.com
Freq: 17 issues yearly - Issued each third week; **Circ:** 20,000
Editor-in-Chief: Radoslav Geshov
Profile: Magazine containing auto advertisements.
Language(s): Bulgarian
Readership: Aimed at international and domestic haulage companies, workshops, importers, dealers, drivers, technicians and travel businesses.
Mechanical Data: Type Area: 205 x 290 mm
BUSINESS: TRANSPORT: Commercial Vehicles

AVTOPAZAR 1790841BG31A-1
Editorial: 11-A Karnegi Str, 1000 SOFIA
Tel: 2 969 91 55 **Fax:** 2 969 91 68
Email: k.nanova@mobile.bg **Web site:** http://i.mobile.bg
Freq: Weekly; **Circ:** 18,000
Profile: Weekly newspaper for the automotive market in Bulgaria.
Language(s): Bulgarian
Mechanical Data: Type Area: 270 x 400 mm
BUSINESS: MOTOR TRADE: Motor Trade Accessories

BG MENU 1790878BG9A-1
Editorial: 65 B Manastirski Livadi, entrance B, floor 6, 1404 SOFIA **Tel:** 2 700 10 400
Email: office@bgmenu.com **Web site:** http://www.bgmenu.com
Freq: 6 issues yearly - Issued at interval of 60 days; **Circ:** 100,000
Profile: Paper issue for orders, contains all the articles offered by Road Runner's contractors. Road Runner is a company specialised in delivering food, catering and office subscription, as well as flowers and services such as dry-cleaning, to your home and office.
Language(s): Bulgarian
ADVERTISING RATES:
Full Page Colour .... BGN 1 320
Mechanical Data: Type Area: 165 x 240mm
BUSINESS: DRINKS & LICENSED TRADE: Drinks, Licensed Trade, Wines & Spirits

BUSINESS WEEK BULGARIA 1790798BG14A-6
Editorial: 5B Triaditsa St., 1000 SOFIA
Tel: 2 988 00 00 **Fax:** 2 988 55 15
Email: office@businessweek.bg **Web site:** http://www.businessweek.bg
Freq: Weekly; **Circ:** 16,500
Editor-in-Chief: Valeri Tsenkov
Profile: Weekly edition with tarnslated articles from the international edition and author's articles about economy, business, finances, technologies.
Language(s): Bulgarian
ADVERTISING RATES:
Full Page Mono .... BGN 3000
Full Page Colour .... BGN 3800
Mechanical Data: Type Area: 200 x 267 mm
BUSINESS: COMMERCE, INDUSTRY & MANAGEMENT

CAPITAL 765494BG65J-82
Editorial: 20 Ivan Vazov St., 1000 SOFIA
Tel: 2 937 61 22 **Fax:** 2 937 64 40
Email: editors@capital.bg **Web site:** http://www.capital.bg
Freq: Weekly - Issued only on Saturday; **Circ:** 24,951
Editor-in-Chief: Galya Prokopieva
Profile: Weekly mainly for intellectuals, decision-makers and economists. Premier source of financial and business reports and analyses. It's deemed to be the most powerful opinion maker in the country.
Language(s): Bulgarian; English
Readership: Read by decision makers from all spheres of business and public life.
ADVERTISING RATES:
Full Page Mono .... BGN 4900
Full Page Colour .... BGN 7350
Mechanical Data: Type Area: 255 x 390 mm
NATIONAL DAILY & SUNDAY NEWSPAPERS: National Weekly Newspapers

CULINARY JOURNAL FOR THE WOMAN 1790876BG74P-5
Editorial: 6 Alekdander Jendov, floor 6, 1113 SOFIA
Tel: 2 970 68 68 **Fax:** 2 970 68 31
Email: reporteri@sanomabliasak.bg
Freq: Monthly - Issued between 16th and 19th of every month; **Circ:** 100,000
Profile: Culinary magazine with new inspiring ideas and experience in cooking.
Language(s): Bulgarian
ADVERTISING RATES:
Full Page Colour .... BGN 2000
Mechanical Data: Type Area: 147 x 208 mm
CONSUMER: WOMEN'S INTEREST CONSUMER MAGAZINES: Food & Cookery

DNEVEN TRUD 1790694BG65A-259
Editorial: 119 Ekzarh Joseph St., 1000 SOFIA
Tel: 2 921 41 40 **Fax:** 2 943 39 40
Email: trud@zgb.bg **Web site:** http://www.trud.bg
Freq: Daily; **Circ:** 105,000
Editor-in-Chief: Tosho Toshev
Profile: The most circulated newspaper mainly for the average Bulgarian reader with eight regional editions in Varna, Plovdiv, Burgas, Stara Zagora, etc.
Language(s): Bulgarian
ADVERTISING RATES:
Full Page Mono .... BGN 13663.92
Full Page Colour .... BGN 18439.2
Mechanical Data: Type Area: 254 x 394 mm
NATIONAL DAILY & SUNDAY NEWSPAPERS: National Daily Newspapers

EUROFOOTBALL 1790735BG65J-90
Editorial: 1 Koloman St, 1618 SOFIA **Tel:** 2 818 91 75 **Fax:** 2 818 91 69
Email: euro_f@abv.bg **Web site:** http://www.eurofootball.bg
Freq: 104 issues yearly - Issued on Tuesday and Friday; **Circ:** 72,000
Editor-in-Chief: Ivaylo Stoimenov
Profile: The newspaper contains information on different sports and matches of world, national and club championships (football, basketball, Formula 1, hockey, tennis, volleyball, etc.).
Language(s): Bulgarian
ADVERTISING RATES:
Full Page Mono .... BGN 2574
Full Page Colour .... BGN 3510
Mechanical Data: Type Area: 255 x 390 mm
NATIONAL DAILY & SUNDAY NEWSPAPERS: National Weekly Newspapers

FORUM MEDIKUS 1790854BG74G-3
Editorial: 1 St. Georgi Sofiiski 1., 1431 SOFIA
Tel: 2 952 6303 **Fax:** 2 952 6314
Email: formed@interkraft.net **Web site:** http://forummedicus.hit.bg
Freq: Weekly; **Circ:** 100,000
Profile: The largest specialized newspaper for medicine.
Language(s): Bulgarian
CONSUMER: WOMEN'S INTEREST CONSUMER MAGAZINES: Slimming & Health

JOURNAL ZA JENATA 1790784BG74B-13
Editorial: 6 Alexander Jendov St., fl.6, 1113 SOFIA
Tel: 2 970 68 68 **Fax:** 2 970 68 31
Freq: Weekly; **Circ:** 108,000
Editor-in-Chief: Lyudmila Gribneva
Profile: Popular weekly edition mainly for housewives and famliy oriented women.
Language(s): Bulgarian
ADVERTISING RATES:
Full Page Colour .... BGN 3 900
Mechanical Data: Type Area: 213 x 278 mm
CONSUMER: WOMEN'S INTEREST CONSUMER MAGAZINES: Women's Interest - Fashion

MERIDIAN MATCH 1790703BG75B-2
Editorial: 113A Tsarigradsko Shose Blvd, 1784 SOFIA **Tel:** 2 975 25 96 **Fax:** 2 975 25 95
Email: editors@meridianmatch.bg **Web site:** http://www.meridianmatch.bg
Freq: Daily; **Circ:** 19,400
Editor-in-Chief: Vladimir Zarkov
Profile: The first newspaper for football news in Bulgaria.
Language(s): Bulgarian
ADVERTISING RATES:
Full Page Mono .... BGN 2730
Full Page Colour .... BGN 3822
Mechanical Data: Type Area: 262 x 390 mm
CONSUMER: SPORT: Football

NATIONAL GEOGRAPHIC BULGARIA 1790831BG94J-4
Editorial: 6 Alexander Zhendov Str., 1113 SOFIA
Tel: 2 970 6891 **Fax:** 2 970 6819
Email: nationalgeographic@sanomabliasak.bg **Web site:** http://www.ngm.bg
Freq: Monthly - Issued every month; **Circ:** 60,000
Editor-in-Chief: Emil Danailov
Profile: Monthly popular science magazine.
Language(s): Bulgarian
ADVERTISING RATES:
Full Page Colour .... BGN 11 000
Mechanical Data: Type Area: 175 x 254 mm
CONSUMER: OTHER CLASSIFICATIONS: Popular Science

REKLAMA 1790800BG2E-1
Editorial: 19-21 Drazki St., 9000 VARNA
Tel: 52 616 725 **Fax:** 52 615 891
Email: office@vestnikreklama.bg **Web site:** http://www.vestnikreklama.bg
Freq: Weekly - Issued only on Monday; **Circ:** 30,000
Editor-in-Chief: Natalia Georgieva
Profile: Free weekly issue for product advertising. Comes out every Monday.
Language(s): Bulgarian
ADVERTISING RATES:
Full Page Mono .... BGN 658
Mechanical Data: Type Area: 255 x 390 mm
BUSINESS: COMMUNICATIONS, ADVERTISING & MARKETING: Public Relations

STANDART 1790696BG65A-261
Editorial: 49 Bulgaria Blvd, Vitosha Business Center, 1404 SOFIA **Tel:** 2 818 23 11 **Fax:** 2 818 23 55
Email: office@standartnews.com **Web site:** http://www.standartnews.com
Freq: Daily; **Circ:** 68,300
Editor-in-Chief: Slavka Bozukova
Profile: National daily newspaper mainly for decision-makers and intellectuals. Edition of Standart News Ltd. Provides objective and fair view of daily issues in Bulgaria and worldwide. It includes 48 pages with interesting articles about politics, economy, sport, culture, humour and society.
Language(s): Bulgarian
ADVERTISING RATES:
Full Page Mono .... BGN 5673.6
Full Page Colour .... BGN 8983.2
Mechanical Data: Type Area: 257 x 394 mm
NATIONAL DAILY & SUNDAY NEWSPAPERS: National Daily Newspapers

TELEGRAF 1790697BG65A-262
Editorial: 113A Tsarigradsko Shose Blvd, 1784 SOFIA **Tel:** 2 960 22 12 **Fax:** 2 975 24 64
Email: telegraph@monitor.bg **Web site:** http://www.telegraph.bg
Freq: Daily; **Circ:** 66,000
Editor-in-Chief: Vladimir Yonchev
Profile: Daily newspaper for the average reader, covering general as well as subject specific news.
Language(s): Bulgarian
ADVERTISING RATES:
Full Page Mono .... BGN 9687.6
Full Page Colour .... BGN 6411.6
Mechanical Data: Type Area: 256 x 390 mm
NATIONAL DAILY & SUNDAY NEWSPAPERS: National Daily Newspapers

TRETA VAZRAST 1790732BG74N-1
Editorial: 47 A Tsarigradsko Shose Blvd, 1504 SOFIA
Tel: 2 846 74 64
Freq: Weekly; **Circ:** 309,900
Profile: Independent weekly newspaper for elderly people and their problems.
Language(s): Bulgarian
ADVERTISING RATES:
Full Page Mono .... BGN 795.6
Mechanical Data: Type Area: 25.5 x 37.5 cm
CONSUMER: WOMEN'S INTEREST CONSUMER MAGAZINES: Retirement

Croatia

Time Difference: GMT + 1 hr (CET - Central European Time)
National Telephone Code: +385
Continent: Europe
Capital: Zagreb
Principal Language: Croatian
Population: 4493312
Monetary Unit: Kuna (HRK)
EMBASSY HIGH COMMISSION: Embassy of the Republic of Croatia: 21 Conway Street, London W1T 5HL
Tel: 020 7387 2022
Fax: 020 7387 0310

24SATA 1705980HR67B-152
Editorial: Radnička cesta 210, 10 000 ZAGREB
Tel: 1 60 69 500 **Fax:** 1 60 69 660
Email: redakcija@24sata.hr **Web site:** http://www.24sata.hr
ISSN: 1845-3929
Freq: Daily; **Cover Price:** HRK 3
Annual Sub.: HRK 1080; **Circ:** 110,000
Usual Pagination: 64
News Editor: Ivan Buča; **Executive Editor:** Anamaria Todorić; **Editor-in-Chief:** Renato Ivanuš
Language(s): Croatian
Mechanical Data: Trim Size: 229x300mm
Supplement(s): PLAN 7, PLUS 7, TV TJEDAN
REGIONAL DAILY & SUNDAY NEWSPAPERS: Regional Daily Newspapers

JUTARNJI LIST 1202320HR65A-75
Editorial: Koranska 2, 10 000 ZAGREB
Tel: 1 61 03 100 **Fax:** 1 61 03 148
Email: jutarnji_list@eph.hr **Web site:** http://www.jutarnji.hr

ISSN: 1331-5692
Freq: Daily; **Circ:** 115,000
News Editor: Viktor Vresnik; **Executive Editor:** Ivica Buljan; **Features Editor:** Nada Mirković; **Editor-in-Chief:** Mladen Pleše
Profile: Newspaper covering national and international news, finance, business, culture, sports and in-depth background information. Twitter handle: http://twitter.com/Jutarnji. Facebook: http://www.facebook.com/jutarnji.list.
Language(s): Croatian
Mechanical Data: Trim Size: 265x386mm
Supplement(s): SPORT, AUTO, ONLINE, BESTSELER, STUDIO, GLORIA IN, MAGAZIN, NEKRETNINE, ZABAVNIK
NATIONAL DAILY & SUNDAY NEWSPAPERS: National Daily Newspapers

NOVI LIST 767183HR65A-15

Editorial: Zvonimirova 20a, 51 000 RIJEKA
Tel: 51 650-011 **Fax:** 51 672-114
Email: redakcija@novilist.hr **Web site:** http://www.novilist.hr
ISSN: 0350-4301
Freq: Daily; **Cover Price:** HRK 6
Annual Sub.: HRK 1920; **Circ:** 87,500
Usual Pagination: 48
Editor: Lucija Baretic; **Editor-in-Chief:** Ivica Dikic
Profile: Newspaper covering news, politics, culture and sports.
Language(s): Croatian
ADVERTISING RATES:
Full Page Mono .... EUR 2508.00
Full Page Colour .... EUR 3009.60
Mechanical Data: Trim Size: 290x420mm
Supplement(s): SPORT PONEDJELJKOM, ŠKOLSKI NOVI LIST, AUTO MOTO YACHT, POSLOVNI PRILOG, SPORTSKI PRILOG VIKTORIJA, ZABAVNO INFORMATIVNI PRILOG PETKOM, TV 7, POGLED, OBJEKTIV, LIFE, MEDITERAN, ZELENA NIT - KULTURA ŽIVLJENJA, PRIMORSKI NOVI LIST, OTOČNI NOVI LIST, GORANSKI NOVI LIST, LIBURNIJSKI NOVI LIST, LIČKI NOVI LIST, EUROPA, RIJEKA INFO, ŽMIGAVAC, KVARNER, PRIMORJE, OTOCI, GORJE
NATIONAL DAILY & SUNDAY NEWSPAPERS: National Daily Newspapers

SLOBODNA DALMACIJA

766917HR65A-12
Editorial: Hrvatske mornarice 4, 21 000 SPLIT
Tel: 21 352-888 **Fax:** 21 383-102
Email: redakcija@slobodnadalmacija.hr **Web site:** http://www.slobodnadalmacija.hr
ISSN: 0350-4662
Freq: Daily; **Cover Price:** HRK 6
Annual Sub.: HRK Split-1800; Hrvatska-2160; **Circ:** 75,000
Usual Pagination: 60
Executive Editor: Natasa Bakotic; **Editor-in-Chief:** Zoran Krzelj
Profile: Newspaper containing national and international news, politics, sports and culture.
Language(s): Croatian
ADVERTISING RATES:
Full Page Colour .... HRK 23100.00
Mechanical Data: Trim Size: 266x385mm
Supplement(s): STELLA, VRT, PORTAL, AUTO, REFLEKTOR, MORE, POMET, NEDJELJNA DALMACIJA
NATIONAL DAILY & SUNDAY NEWSPAPERS: National Daily Newspapers

Cyprus

Time Difference: GMT +2 hours
National Telephone Code: +357
Continent: Europe
Capital: Nicosia
Principal Language: Greek, English
Population: 788457
Monetary Unit: Euro (EUR)
EMBASSY HIGH COMMISSION: High Commission of the Republic of Cyprus: 13 St. Jame's Square, London SW1 4LB
Tel: 020 7321 4100 **Fax@** 020 7321 4164 **Web:** http://www.mfa.gov.cy/highcomlondon / cyphclondon@dial.pipex.com

ANTILOGOS 1639030CY65J-29

Editorial: 24 Elia Papakyriakou, Dafne Building, 1st floor, Acropoli, P.O.Box 28685, 2081 NICOSIA
Tel: 22 49 14 00 **Fax:** 22 49 12 30
Email: antilogos@cytanet.com.cy
Date Established: 1999; **Freq:** 38 issues yearly - Published on Fridays; **Cover Price:** EUR 1.00; **Circ:** 6,500
Profile: Weekly newspaper of general interest.
Language(s): Greek
NATIONAL DAILY & SUNDAY NEWSPAPERS: National Weekly Newspapers

THE BUYSELL MAGAZINE

1201159CY1E-2
Editorial: Office D 23-D 25, Coral Bay Plaza, 8575 PAFOS **Tel:** 26 20 00 00 **Fax:** 26 81 23 46
Email: info@buysellcyprus.com **Web site:** http://www.buysellcyprus.com
Date Established: 2002; **Freq:** Monthly; Free to qualifying individuals ; **Circ:** 40,000
Usual Pagination: 244
Profile: Provides people and businesses with power to search for properties in a simple effective way and educates people about buying and selling real estate in Cyprus, includes new and resale residential homes for sale and rent, developments for sale, land and plots for sale and commercial properties for sale and rent.
Language(s): English
Mechanical Data: Type Area: 349 x 260mm, Col Length: 349mm, Page Width: 260mm
Copy instructions: *Copy Date:* 10 days prior to publication date
BUSINESS: FINANCE & ECONOMICS: Property

CHRIMATISTIRIAKA NEA

1638966CY1F-1
Editorial: 169 Athalassas Ave., 1st floor, office 102, NICOSIA 2024 **Tel:** 22 31 31 06 **Fax:** 22 31 51 09
Email: famagdev@cytanet.com.cy
Date Established: 2000; **Freq:** Monthly; **Circ:** 10,000
Editor: Yianna Georgiou
Profile: Newspaper covering stock exchange news.
Language(s): Greek
ADVERTISING RATES:
Full Page Mono .... EUR 600.00
Full Page Colour .... EUR 1000.00
BUSINESS: FINANCE & ECONOMICS: Investment

CHRYSES EFKAIRIES 1893454CY2A-2

Editorial: 14 Spyrou Kyprianou Ave., Ag. Omologites, 2nd floor, P.O.Box 26560, 1075 NICOSIA
Tel: 22 469999 **Fax:** 22 469988
Email: eykairia@cytanet.com.cy
Date Established: 1994; **Freq:** Weekly; **Circ:** 18,000
Profile: Advertising Newspaper and Shopping Guide.
Language(s): Greek
ADVERTISING RATES:
Full Page Mono .... EUR 315.00
BUSINESS: COMMUNICATIONS, ADVERTISING & MARKETING

CITY FREE PRESS 1849758CY89C-3

Editorial: 31 Archangelos Avenue, P.O. Box 21836, 1513 NICOSIA **Tel:** 22 58 05 80 **Fax:** 22 58 04 25
Web site: http://www.dias.com.cy/city.asp
Freq: Weekly - Published on Fridays; **Cover Price:** Free; **Circ:** 40,000
Usual Pagination: 40
Advertising Manager: Georgia Toutouzian
Profile: Contains information on political, economic and sporting life of Cyprus, taste, music, cinema, theatre and shopping.
Language(s): Greek
ADVERTISING RATES:
Full Page Colour .... EUR 1500.00
CONSUMER: HOLIDAYS & TRAVEL: Entertainment Guides

CYPRUS MAIL 1201152CY65A-10

Editorial: 24 Vassilios Voulgaroktonos Str., PO Box 211 44, 1502 Nicosia, NICOSIA 1010 **Tel:** 22 81 85 85
Fax: 22 67 63 85
Email: mail@cyprus-mail.com **Web site:** http://www.cyprus-mail.com
Date Established: 1945; **Freq:** Mornings - Daily except Mondays; **Annual Sub.:** EUR 875.29; **Circ:** 8,000
Usual Pagination: 52
Editor: Jean Christou; **Advertising Manager:** Agathi Venizelou
Profile: Newspaper covering national and international news, politics, business, culture, entertainment and sport.
Language(s): English
Readership: Aimed at English-speaking Cypriots, diplomats, members of the international business community, British expatriates and tourists.
Mechanical Data: Type Area: 380 x 279mm
Supplement(s): Seven - 48xY
NATIONAL DAILY & SUNDAY NEWSPAPERS: National Daily Newspapers

CYPRUS OBSERVER 1846722CY65J-31

Editorial: 18 Aytekin Zekai Sok., Mersin 10, KYRENIA, NORTH CYPRUS **Tel:** 392 815 53 87
Fax: 392 815 55 85
Email: news@observercyprus.com **Web site:** http://www.observercyprus.com
Freq: Weekly - Published on Fridays
Editor: Umut Uras; **Executive Editor:** Hasan Ercakica; **Advertising Manager:** Burcu Aker;
Publisher: Can Ercakica
Profile: Weekly newspaper covering political, business, sports and society news.
Language(s): English
NATIONAL DAILY & SUNDAY NEWSPAPERS: National Weekly Newspapers

CYPRUS TODAY 1801370CY73-7

Editorial: PO Box 831, Lefkoşa, KIBRIS
Tel: 392 2252555 **Fax:** 392 2252934
Email: cyprustoday@yahoo.com
Freq: Weekly; **Cover Price:** YTL 1.000.000; **Circ:** 5,000
Profile: Newspaper reporting on events in the northern Cyprus region.
Language(s): Turkish
CONSUMER: NATIONAL & INTERNATIONAL PERIODICALS

THE CYPRUS WEEKLY

1201149CY65J-15
Editorial: PO Box 24977, NICOSIA 1306
Tel: 22 744400 **Fax:** 22 744400
Email: info@cyprusweekly.com.cy **Web site:** http://www.cyprusweekly.com.cy
Date Established: 1979; **Freq:** Weekly - Published on Friday; **Cover Price:** EUR 2.00
Annual Sub.: EUR 75.00; **Circ:** 15,000
Usual Pagination: 100
News Editor: Charlie Charalambous; **Executive Editor:** Martyn Henry; **Publisher:** Nicos Chr. Pattichis
Profile: Newspaper covering politics, economy, culture, sport, foreign and regional news.
Language(s): English
Readership: The newspaper is read by a cross-section of English-speaking people, mostly well-educated Cypriots, businessmen, diplomats and professionals.
ADVERTISING RATES:
Full Page Mono .... EUR 1300.00
Full Page Colour .... EUR 1800.00
Agency Commission: 20%
Copy instructions: *Copy Date:* 14 days prior to publication date
Average ad content per issue: 30%
Supplement(s): Choice - 52xY, Flair - 52xY, Flavour - 52xY, Home - 52xY
NATIONAL DAILY & SUNDAY NEWSPAPERS: National Weekly Newspapers

DIMOSSIOS YPALLILOS

1201589CY14L-5
Formerly: The Leader
Editorial: 3 Demosthenis Severis Avenue, 1066 NICOSIA **Tel:** 22 844444 **Fax:** 22 665199
Email: pasydy@spidernet.com.cy **Web site:** http://www.pasydy.org
Date Established: 1960; **Freq:** Weekly - Published on Thursdays; Free to qualifying individuals ; **Circ:** 13,500
Usual Pagination: 16
Profile: Journal covering public service, trade union and general affairs, providing news and comment about pubic service affairs and activities of the trade union of Cyprus Public Servants PASYDY and affiliates in Cyprus and Europe.
Language(s): Greek
Readership: Aimed at public officials in Cyprus and state authorities.
Copy instructions: *Copy Date:* 2 days prior to publication date
BUSINESS: COMMERCE, INDUSTRY & MANAGEMENT: Trade Unions

ERGATIKI PHONI 1639024CY65J-28

Editorial: P.O. Box 25 018, NICOSIA 1306
Tel: 22 84 98 49 **Fax:** 22 84 98 58
Email: sekxenis@cytanet.com.cy
Date Established: 1947; **Freq:** Weekly - Published on Wednesday; **Cover Price:** EUR 0.70; **Circ:** 12,000
Editor-in-Chief: Xenis Xenophontos
Profile: Newspaper of Cyprus Workers' Confederation covering politics, economy and social events.
Language(s): Greek
NATIONAL DAILY & SUNDAY NEWSPAPERS: National Weekly Newspapers

ERGATIKO VIMA 1600094CY65J-25

Editorial: PO Box 21185, 29 Archermos, 1045 NICOSIA **Tel:** 22 86 64 00 **Fax:** 22 86 64 81
Email: ergatiko-vima@peo.org.cy **Web site:** http://www.peo.org.cy
Date Established: 1956; **Freq:** Weekly - Published every Wednesday; **Cover Price:** EUR 0.51; **Circ:** 14,000
Editor: Andriana Michael; **Editor-in-Chief:** Neofitos Papalazarou; **Advertising Manager:** Savas Niciforou
Profile: Newspaper of the Cyprus Labour Federation (PEO) providing information on industrial relations, labour legislation, health and welfare funds, trade union news.
Language(s): Greek; Russian; Turkish
Readership: Aimed at workers.
NATIONAL DAILY & SUNDAY NEWSPAPERS: National Weekly Newspapers

EVROPA-KIPR 1881760CY65J-33

Tel: 25 581133 **Fax:** 25 582749
Email: avsi@cytanet.com.cy **Web site:** http://evropa-kipr.com
Date Established: 2004; **Freq:** Weekly - Published on Thursdays
Profile: Weekly newspaper providing useful information on life in Cyprus, property, tourism, economic and business news, Orthodox religion issues and entertainment.
Language(s): Russian
NATIONAL DAILY & SUNDAY NEWSPAPERS: National Weekly Newspapers

HALKIN SESI 1639088CY65A-36

Editorial: 172 Girne Caddesi, P.O. Box 339, Mersin 10, LEFKOSA **Tel:** 392 22 85 645 **Fax:** 392 22 72 612
Email: halkinsesi@superonline.com **Web site:** http://www.halkinsesicyprus.com
Date Established: 1942; **Freq:** Daily; **Cover Price:** YTL 1.00; **Circ:** 2,000
Editor: Sefa Karahasan; **Advertising Manager:** Fatoş Kizilyurek; **Publisher:** Mahmet Kucuk
Profile: Newspaper covering politics, economics, social and cultural events, sport.
Language(s): Turkish
NATIONAL DAILY & SUNDAY NEWSPAPERS: National Daily Newspapers

KARDIOLOGIKA NEA 1881721CY56A-1

Editorial: 26 Hytron Str., office 41, P.O.Box 26844, 1075 NICOSIA **Tel:** 22 762762 **Fax:** 22 757744
Email: cyheart@spidernet.com.cy **Web site:** http://www.heartfoundation.org.cy/act.htm
Freq: 6 issues yearly; **Cover Price:** Free; **Circ:** 35,000
Profile: Published with purpose of enlightenment and prevention against heart diseases.
Language(s): Greek
BUSINESS: HEALTH & MEDICAL

KIBRISLI 1639031CY65A-38

Editorial: Mecidiye Sok. No: 44, Mersin 10, LEFKOŞA **Tel:** 392 22 76 146 **Fax:** 90 22 75 703
Email: kibrisli@kktc.net **Web site:** http://www.kibrisligazetesi.net
Freq: Daily; **Circ:** 2,500
Editor: Kartal Harman
Profile: Newspaper covering politics, economics, culture and social events.
Language(s): Turkish
NATIONAL DAILY & SUNDAY NEWSPAPERS: National Daily Newspapers

MUST DECO 1638790CY4B-1

Editorial: Nicou Kranidiotis 7e, Engoni, NICOSIA 2411 **Tel:** 22 47 24 72 **Fax:** 22 66 48 60
Email: must@must-magazine.com **Web site:** http://www.must-magazine.com
Freq: 8 issues yearly - Not published regularly; **Cover Price:** EUR 6.50; **Circ:** 15,000
Editor-in-Chief: Avyie Savvidou; **Managing Director:** Avyie Savvidou
Profile: Magazine covering interior design, modern decoration and architecture in Cyprus, and new innovative concepts.
Language(s): Greek
ADVERTISING RATES:
Full Page Colour .... EUR 950.00
Agency Commission: 20%
Mechanical Data: Bleed Size: 305mm x 235mm, Trim Size: 285mm x 215mm, Type Area: 280mm x 215mm, Screen: 70lpc
BUSINESS: ARCHITECTURE & BUILDING: Interior Design & Flooring

O PHILELEFTHEROS

1201153CY65A-35
Editorial: PO Box 21094, 1 Diogenous Str., Engomi, NICOSIA 1501 **Tel:** 22 74 40 00 **Fax:** 22 59 01 22
Email: mailbox@phileleftheros.com **Web site:** http://www.phileleftheros.com
Date Established: 1955; **Freq:** Daily; **Cover Price:** EUR 1.00; **Circ:** 17,720
Usual Pagination: 40
Executive Editor: Kostas Venizelos; **Editor-in-Chief:** Aristos Michaelides; **Advertising Manager:** Renos Onoufrios; **Publisher:** Nicos Chr. Pattichis

Cyprus

Profile: Newspaper features news, politics, lifestyle from both a local and international perspective.
Language(s): Greek
ADVERTISING RATES:
Full Page Mono .... EUR 4508.00
Full Page Colour .... EUR 3315.00
Agency Commission: 15%
Mechanical Data: Col Widths (Display): 40mm, Screen: Mono: 30 lpc, Colour: 40 lpc, Film: Positive, right reading, emulsion side down
Copy instructions: *Copy Date:* 2 Days prior to publication
Average ad content per issue: 35%
Supplement(s): Economicos; Phileprosfores; O Philathlos; Akinita; Auto Mania; Kariera; Kali Zoi.
NATIONAL DAILY & SUNDAY NEWSPAPERS: National Daily Newspapers

POLITIS 1638624CY65A-33
Editorial: 8 Vassileiou Voulgaroktonou Str., NICOSIA 1524 **Tel:** 22 86 18 61 **Fax:** 22 86 18 71
Email: info@politis-news.com **Web site:** http://www.politis-news.com
ISSN: 1450-3913
Date Established: 1999; **Freq:** Mornings; **Cover Price:** EUR 1.00; **Circ:** 11,000
Editor: Sotiris Paroutis; **Publisher:** Yiannis Papadopoulos
Profile: Newspaper covering politics, current affairs, economy and sports news.
Language(s): Greek
NATIONAL DAILY & SUNDAY NEWSPAPERS: National Daily Newspapers

POPKA 1881763CY65J-34
Editorial: P.O.Box 41091, 6309 LARNAKA
Tel: 24 648090 **Fax:** 24 648089
Email: benzar@spidernet.com.cy **Web site:** http://www.popka-news.com
Date Established: 1999; **Freq:** Weekly - Published on Fridays; **Cover Price:** EUR 1.50; **Circ:** 3,500
Profile: Weekly newspaper providing news about life in Cyprus in Russian language, EU and world news, Russian TV programmes, advertisements, buy&sell section, literature and poetry.
Language(s): Russian
NATIONAL DAILY & SUNDAY NEWSPAPERS: National Weekly Newspapers

I SIMERINI 1201156CY65A-30
Editorial: 31 Archangelos Avenue, Strovolos, 2054 NICOSIA **Tel:** 22 58 05 80 **Fax:** 22 58 05 70
Email: mail@simerini.com **Web site:** http://www.simerini.com.cy
Date Established: 1976; **Freq:** Mornings - Online edition with more than 10000 unique daily visitors that generate more than 120000 hits; **Cover Price:** EUR 1.00; **Circ:** 13,000
Usual Pagination: 50
Advertising Manager: Ifigenia Liasi; **Advertising Director:** Maria Kyriakou
Profile: Newspaper covering politics, economy, culture and social events.
Language(s): Greek
ADVERTISING RATES:
Full Page Mono .... EUR 714.00
Full Page Colour .... EUR 1071.00
Agency Commission: 15%
Copy instructions: *Copy Date:* 1 week prior to publication date
Average ad content per issue: 30%
Supplement(s): OK! - 52xY, O Tiletheatis - 56xY
NATIONAL DAILY & SUNDAY NEWSPAPERS: National Daily Newspapers

SUNJET 1659705CY89D-6
Editorial: Kondilaki 6, 1090 NICOSIA **Tel:** 22 81 88 84 **Fax:** 22 87 36 32
Email: action@actionprgroup.com
Freq: Quarterly; **Cover Price:** Free; **Circ:** 75,000
Editor: Christos Christodoulou
Profile: In-flight magazine containing articles on travel, fashion, lifestyle, food and drink, business and financial issues.
Language(s): English
ADVERTISING RATES:
Full Page Mono .... EUR 2500.00
Full Page Colour .... EUR 3000.00
Mechanical Data: Bleed Size: 213 x 303mm
Official Journal of: Cyprus Airways
CONSUMER: HOLIDAYS & TRAVEL: In-Flight Magazines

SUNJET RUSSIAN EDITION 1881718CY89D-7
Editorial: PO Box 24676, 1302 NICOSIA
Tel: 22 81 88 84 **Fax:** 22 87 36 32
Email: action@actionprgroup.com **Web site:** http://www.parikia.com/cyprusmedia/cyprus_airways.html
Freq: Annual; **Cover Price:** Free; **Circ:** 75,000
Advertising Manager: Oriana Patala
Profile: Distributed to both Club and Economy class passengers on all Cyprus Airways flights to and from Russia.
Language(s): Russian
ADVERTISING RATES:
Full Page Colour .... EUR 3076.00
Mechanical Data: Type Area: 216x303mm
CONSUMER: HOLIDAYS & TRAVEL: In-Flight Magazines

O TILETHEATIS 767766CY76C-6
Editorial: 31 Archangelos Ave, Strovolos, 2054 NICOSIA **Tel:** 22 58 05 80 **Fax:** 22 58 06 74
Email: petroup@dias.com.cy **Web site:** http://www.dias.com.cy
Freq: 56 issues yearly - Published on Sunday; Free to qualifying individuals ; **Circ:** 140,000
Editor: Sophia Iona; **Advertising Manager:** Georgia Toutouzian
Profile: Magazine that combines a TV guide and features on entertainment and lifestyle, celebrity reviews and interviews, cooking and news from the world of music and entertainment.
Language(s): Greek
Readership: 62% of readers are women in age group 13-44 years. 65% of readers are of middle and higher education.
ADVERTISING RATES:
Full Page Colour .... EUR 1100.00
Supplement to: I Simerini
CONSUMER: MUSIC & PERFORMING ARTS: TV & Radio

TRAVEL NEWS EUROPE 1698333CY50-1
Editorial: 8 Vitsi Street, 1 floor, 2373 NICOSIA
Tel: 22 45 93 59 **Fax:** 22 45 93 61
Email: office@travelnewseurope.com **Web site:** http://www.travelnewseurope.com
Date Established: 2000; **Freq:** Monthly; **Cover Price:** Free
Annual Sub.: EUR 150.00; **Circ:** 18,000
Usual Pagination: 24
Editor: Victoria Geddes; **Managing Director:** Christos Agathocleous; **Publisher:** Christos Agathocleous
Profile: Magazine focusing on the world's travel industry.
Language(s): English
Readership: Aimed at travel trade professionals.
ADVERTISING RATES:
Full Page Colour .... EUR 7500.00
Mechanical Data: Type Area: 345 x 245 mm
BUSINESS: TRAVEL & TOURISM

TV MANIA 1638779CY76C-7
Editorial: PO Box 21094, Commercial Centre, 1 Diogenous, 3rd floor, Engomi, NICOSIA 1501
Tel: 22 744000 **Fax:** 22 590516
Email: tvmania@phileleftheros.com **Web site:** http://www.philenews.com
ISSN: 1450-3581
Freq: Weekly - Published on Saturdays; **Cover Price:** EUR 1.53; **Circ:** 68,000
Usual Pagination: 160
Editor: Linos Panagi
Profile: TV programme guide with entertainment.
Language(s): Greek
CONSUMER: MUSIC & PERFORMING ARTS: TV & Radio

VESTNIK KIPRA 1810387CY65J-30
Editorial: 14b Byron Str., 1 Park Tower, LIMASSOL
Tel: 25 58 21 20 **Fax:** 25 58 49 20
Email: info@vestnikkipra.com **Web site:** http://www.cyprusadvertiser.com
Date Established: 1995; **Freq:** 60 issues yearly; Free to qualifying individuals ; **Circ:** 4,000
Usual Pagination: 60
Editor: Alena Dolgyh
Profile: Covering political, economical and cultural life of Cyprus, Cyprus and Russian news, interviews with famous politicians, economists, artists, musicians, TV-programme.
Language(s): Russian
Readership: Aimed at Russian-speaking visitors and residents of Cyprus.
ADVERTISING RATES:
Full Page Mono .... EUR 550.00
Full Page Colour .... EUR 750.00
Mechanical Data: Type Area: 255 mm x 380 mm
NATIONAL DAILY & SUNDAY NEWSPAPERS: National Weekly Newspapers

YENIDÜZEN 1639090CY65A-34
Formerly: Yenidizen
Editorial: Yeni Sanayi Bölgesi, Mersin 10, LEFKOŞA-KIBRIS **Tel:** 392 22 56 658 **Fax:** 392 22 53 240
Email: yeniduzen@defne.net **Web site:** http://www.yeniduzengazetesi.com
Date Established: 1975; **Freq:** Daily; **Cover Price:** YTL 1.00; **Circ:** 3,500
Editor: Meltem Sonay; **News Editor:** Sevgül Uludag; **Editor-in-Chief:** Cenk Mutluyakali; **Advertising Manager:** Feryal Karakuş
Profile: Newspaper covering politics, economics and current affairs.
Language(s): Turkish
NATIONAL DAILY & SUNDAY NEWSPAPERS: National Daily Newspapers

Czech Republic

Time Difference: GMT + 1 hr (CET - Central European Time)
National Telephone Code: +420
Continent: Europe
Capital: Prague
Principal Language: Czech
Population: 10228744
Monetary Unit: Czech Koruna (CZK)

EMBASSY HIGH

COMMISSION: Embassy of the Czech Republic: 26-30 Kensington Palace Gardens, London W8 4QY
Tel: 020 7243 1115
Fax: 020 7727 9654
Email: london@embassy.mzv.cz
Website: http://www.mzv.cz/london

100+1 1202203CZ60B-5
Editorial: Karlovo náměstí 5, 12000 PRAHA 2
Email: manager@stoplus.cz **Web site:** http://www.stoplus.cz
ISSN: 0322-9629
Date Established: 01.01.1964; **Freq:** 26 issues yearly; **Cover Price:** CZK 28
Annual Sub.: CZK 728; **Circ:** 52,260
Usual Pagination: 68
Profile: Magazine with interesting information from all fields from the all world.
Language(s): Czech
Readership: Aimed at students and the general public interested in geography.
ADVERTISING RATES:
Full Page Colour .... CZK 115000
Mechanical Data: Type Area: 184 x 245mm
BUSINESS: PUBLISHING: Libraries

21. STOLETÍ 1699374CZ55-11
Editorial: Bohdalecká 6/1420, 10100 PRAHA 10 - MICHLE **Tel:** 281090657 **Fax:** 281090644
Email: jan.lidmansky@rf-hobby.cz **Web site:** http://www.rf-hobby.cz
ISSN: 1214-1097
Date Established: 18.04.03; **Freq:** Monthly; **Cover Price:** CZK 49; **Circ:** 73,997
Usual Pagination: 120
Editor: Jan Lukšík
Profile: Science and technology magazine reaching out to readers in a popular form.
Language(s): Czech
ADVERTISING RATES:
Full Page Colour .... CZK 195000
BUSINESS: APPLIED SCIENCE & LABORATORIES

3T - TEPLO, TECHNIKA, TEPLÁRENSTVÍ 1699377CZ3B-4
Editorial: Bělehradská 458, P.O.Box 17, 53009 PARDUBICE 9 **Tel:** 466414444 **Fax:** 466412737
Email: tscr@tscr.cz **Web site:** http://www.tscr.cz
ISSN: 1210-6003
Date Established: 01.01.93; **Freq:** 24 issues yearly; **Annual Sub.:** CZK 480; **Circ:** 1,500
Usual Pagination: 28
Editor: Olga Stará
Profile: Professional journal focused on heating, energy and engineering.
Language(s): Czech
ADVERTISING RATES:
Full Page Colour .... CZK 18000
BUSINESS: HEATING & VENTILATION: Industrial Heating & Ventilation

ACTIVE BEAUTY 1776559CZ74G-30
Editorial: Jeronýmova 1485/19, 37001 ČESKÉ BUDĚJOVICE
Email: dm@dm-drogeriemarkt.cz **Web site:** http://www.dm-drogeriemarkt.cz
Date Established: 01.01.06; **Freq:** 9 issues yearly; **Cover Price:** Free; **Circ:** 600,000
Usual Pagination: 64
Profile: Magazine about health and beauty.
Language(s): Czech
ADVERTISING RATES:
Full Page Colour .... CZK 176000
Mechanical Data: Type Area: 174 x 242mm
CONSUMER: WOMEN'S INTEREST CONSUMER MAGAZINES: Slimming & Health

AGROSPOJ 1699414CZ2-3
Editorial: Letohradská 48, 17000 PRAHA 7
Tel: 225278139 **Fax:** 225278140
Email: agrospoj@volny.cz
ISSN: 1213-7774
Date Established: 01.01.90; **Freq:** Weekly; **Annual Sub.:** CZK 476; **Circ:** 40,000
Usual Pagination: 64
Editor: Jana Větrovcová
Profile: Advertising newspaper for land workers.
Language(s): Czech
ADVERTISING RATES:
Full Page Colour .... CZK 18909
Mechanical Data: Type Area: 191 x 275mm
BUSINESS: COMMUNICATIONS, ADVERTISING & MARKETING

AHA! (DENÍK) 1776562CZ65A-25
Editorial: Komunardů 1584/42, 17000 PRAHA 7
Tel: 225977111
Email: david.saroch@ringier.cz **Web site:** http://www.ringier.cz
Date Established: 01.03.06; **Freq:** 312 issues yearly; **Cover Price:** CZK 7; **Circ:** 146,538
Usual Pagination: 16
Editor: Lubor Černohlávek
Profile: Tabloid newspaper.
Language(s): Czech
ADVERTISING RATES:
Full Page Colour .... CZK 191041,2
Mechanical Data: No. of Columns (Display): 7, Type Area: 263 x 380mm
NATIONAL DAILY & SUNDAY NEWSPAPERS: National Daily Newspapers

AHA! (NEDĚLNÍ) 1699415CZ65J-1
Editorial: Komunardů 1584/42, 17000 PRAHA 7
Email: david.saroch@ringier.cz **Web site:** http://www.ringier.cz
ISSN: 1214-8997
Date Established: 07.11.04; **Freq:** Weekly; **Cover Price:** CZK 11; **Circ:** 137,258
Usual Pagination: 48
Editor: Lubor Černohlávek
Profile: Tabloid newspaper.
Language(s): Czech
ADVERTISING RATES:
Full Page Colour .... CZK 135240
Mechanical Data: No. of Columns (Display): 5, Type Area: 204 x 276mm
NATIONAL DAILY & SUNDAY NEWSPAPERS: National Weekly Newspapers

AHA! TV MAGAZÍN 1776563CZ89C-34
Editorial: Komunardů 1584/42, 17000 PRAHA 7
Email: david.saroch@ringier.cz **Web site:** http://www.ringier.cz
Date Established: 02.03.06; **Freq:** Weekly; **Cover Price:** Free; **Circ:** 176,726
Usual Pagination: 64
Profile: Tabloid newspaper + TV guide.
Language(s): Czech
ADVERTISING RATES:
Full Page Colour .... CZK 129000
Mechanical Data: Type Area: 181 x 228mm
CONSUMER: HOLIDAYS & TRAVEL: Entertainment Guides

AHOJ BUDĚJOVICE 1699417CZ82-261
Editorial: Žerotínova 483/1, 37004 ČESKÉ BUDĚJOVICE **Tel:** 387843513 **Fax:** 387843518
Email: plm@plm.cz **Web site:** http://www.plm.cz
Date Established: 01.01.01; **Freq:** Monthly; **Cover Price:** Free; **Circ:** 60,000
Usual Pagination: 32
Editor: Petra Kubešová
Profile: Family magazine of Ceske Budejovice.
Language(s): Czech
ADVERTISING RATES:
Full Page Colour .... CZK 49400
Mechanical Data: Type Area: 190 x 271mm
CONSUMER: CURRENT AFFAIRS & POLITICS

ALARM REVUE HASIČŮ A ZÁCHRANÁŘŮ 1700197CZ54R-3
Editorial: Římská 45, 12000 PRAHA 2
Tel: 222518150 **Fax:** 222518150
Email: praha@hvp.cz **Web site:** http://www.hvp.cz
ISSN: 1211-099X
Date Established: 01.04.91; **Freq:** 24 issues yearly; **Cover Price:** CZK 50
Annual Sub.: CZK 234; **Circ:** 60,000
Usual Pagination: 52
Editor: Ivo Havlík
Profile: Revue for fire department and rescue workers.
Language(s): Czech
ADVERTISING RATES:
Full Page Colour .... CZK 39000
Mechanical Data: Type Area: 180 x 250mm
BUSINESS: SAFETY & SECURITY: Safety Related

ALBERT 1699431CZ74A-402
Editorial: Radlická 117, 15800 PRAHA 5 - NOVÉ BUTOVICE **Tel:** 234004338 **Fax:** 257297555
Email: info@ahold.cz **Web site:** http://www.ahold.cz
ISSN: 1211-1422
Date Established: 01.01.95; **Freq:** Monthly; **Cover Price:** Free; **Circ:** 750,000

Usual Pagination: 48
Editor: Jitka Maňáková
Profile: Magazine of supermarket Albert. Informs about cooking, schopping, cosmetics and family.
Language(s): Czech
ADVERTISING RATES:
Full Page Colour .... CZK 195000
Mechanical Data: Type Area: 201 x 261mm
CONSUMER: WOMEN'S INTEREST CONSUMER MAGAZINES: Women's Interest

AMATÉRSKÉ RADIO 1500125CZ18A-1
Editorial: Karlovo nám. 30, 12000 PRAHA 2
Tel: 257317314 **Fax:** 257317310
Email: pe@aradio.cz **Web site:** http://www.aradio.cz
ISSN: 0322-9572
Date Established: 01.01.1952; **Freq:** Monthly; **Cover Price:** CZK 50
Annual Sub.: CZK 504; **Circ:** 7,100
Usual Pagination: 52
Editor: Alan Kraus
Profile: Technical journal about electronics and radio.
Language(s): Czech
Readership: Aimed at those interested in amateur radio and electronics.
BUSINESS: ELECTRONICS

APETIT 1699452CZ74P-2
Editorial: Badeniho 1, 16000 PRAHA 6
Tel: 225354730 **Fax:** 225354759
Email: all@premiere.cz **Web site:** http://www.maxim.cz
ISSN: 1214-5599
Date Established: 19.03.04; **Freq:** Monthly; **Cover Price:** CZK 49; **Circ:** 67,350
Usual Pagination: 84
Editor: Hana Michopulu
Profile: Magazine about cooking.
Language(s): Czech
ADVERTISING RATES:
Full Page Colour .... CZK 160000
Mechanical Data: Type Area: 188 x 250mm
CONSUMER: WOMEN'S INTEREST CONSUMER MAGAZINES: Food & Cookery

ARCHITEKT 1500137CZ4A-5
Editorial: Heyrovského náměstí 7, 16200 PRAHA 6
Tel: 233931533 **Fax:** 233931508
Email: inzerce@architekt-casopis.cz **Web site:** http://www.architekt-casopis.cz
ISSN: 0862-7010
Date Established: 01.01.1954; **Freq:** Monthly; **Cover Price:** CZK 100
Annual Sub.: CZK 1200; **Circ:** 5,000
Usual Pagination: 130
Editor: Julius Macháček
Profile: Professional architecture magazine.
Language(s): Czech; English
Readership: Aimed at architects, surveyors and building contractors.
ADVERTISING RATES:
Full Page Colour .... CZK 87000
Mechanical Data: No. of Columns (Display): 4, Type Area: 195 x 277mm
BUSINESS: ARCHITECTURE & BUILDING: Architecture

AROMATERAPIE 1699468CZ74G-1
Editorial: Přemyslovců 653/24, 40007 ÚSTÍ NAD LABEM **Tel:** 475501321 **Fax:** 475500620
Email: hadek@hadek.cz **Web site:** http://www.ckhi.cz
Date Established: 01.01.93; **Freq:** Quarterly; **Annual Sub.:** CZK 75; **Circ:** 60,000
Usual Pagination: 60
Editor: Anastazie Skopalová
Profile: Aromaterapy magazine of Cosmetic Karl Hadek International company.
Language(s): Czech
ADVERTISING RATES:
Full Page Colour .... CZK 20000
CONSUMER: WOMEN'S INTEREST CONSUMER MAGAZINES: Slimming & Health

ASB (ČR) 1699471CZ4A-33
Editorial: Pražská 1279/18, 10200 PRAHA 10
Tel: 272767281 **Fax:** 284680482
Email: jagamedia@jagamedia.cz **Web site:** http://www.casopishome.cz
ISSN: 1214-7486
Date Established: 09.09.04; **Freq:** 8 issues yearly; **Cover Price:** CZK 79
Annual Sub.: CZK 549; **Circ:** 5,000
Usual Pagination: 96
Editor: Jitka Linhová
Profile: Review of Czech building industry, architecture, construction business and housing. It includes list of building materials, technology and machinery used by the industry.
Language(s): Czech
ADVERTISING RATES:
Full Page Colour .... CZK 84000
Mechanical Data: Type Area: 178 x 245mm
BUSINESS: ARCHITECTURE & BUILDING: Architecture

AUTO 7 1699485CZ77A-207
Editorial: U Krčského nádraží 36, 14000 PRAHA 4 - KRČ **Tel:** 241093443 **Fax:** 241721905
Email: motorpresse@motorpresse.cz **Web site:** http://www.motorpresse.cz
ISSN: 1214-6781
Date Established: 15.06.96; **Freq:** 26 issues yearly; **Cover Price:** CZK 29,90; **Circ:** 25,000
Usual Pagination: 52
Editor: Jan Blažek
Profile: Motorist magazine.
Language(s): Czech
ADVERTISING RATES:
Full Page Colour .... CZK 140000
Mechanical Data: Type Area: 190 x 259mm
CONSUMER: MOTORING & CYCLING: Motoring

AUTO FORUM 1699488CZ77B-2
Editorial: Na Třebešíně 10/1060, 10000 PRAHA 10
Tel: 274810306 **Fax:** 274810306
Email: khavlikova@autoforum.cz **Web site:** http://www.autoforum.cz
ISSN: 1212-351X
Date Established: 01.11.98; **Freq:** 24 issues yearly; **Cover Price:** CZK 44
Annual Sub.: CZK 402; **Circ:** 30,000
Usual Pagination: 100
Editor: Jaroslav Vavera
Profile: Motorist magazine.
Language(s): Czech
ADVERTISING RATES:
Full Page Colour .... CZK 85000
Mechanical Data: Type Area: 189 x 243mm
CONSUMER: MOTORING & CYCLING: Motorcycling

AUTO MOTOR A SPORT 1201739CZ77D-5
Editorial: U Krčského nádraží 36, 14000 PRAHA 4 - KRČ **Tel:** 241093444 **Fax:** 241721905
Email: motorpresse@motorpresse.cz **Web site:** http://www.motorpresse.cz
ISSN: 1212-1355
Date Established: 01.01.93; **Freq:** Monthly; **Cover Price:** CZK 69
Annual Sub.: CZK 660; **Circ:** 22,250
Usual Pagination: 100
Editor: Michal Kudela
Profile: Motorist magazine and motor-vehicle racing magazine.
Language(s): Czech
Readership: Aimed at motor sport enthusiasts.
ADVERTISING RATES:
Full Page Colour .... CZK 150000
Mechanical Data: Type Area: 175 x 230mm
CONSUMER: MOTORING & CYCLING: Motor Sports

AUTO PRŮVODCE 1776826CZ77A-281
Editorial: U Krčského nádraží 36, 14000 PRAHA 4 - KRČ **Tel:** 241093443 **Fax:** 241721905
Email: motorpresse@motorpresse.cz **Web site:** http://www.motorpresse.cz
ISSN: 1214-8342
Date Established: 01.01.94; **Freq:** Annual; **Cover Price:** CZK 325
Annual Sub.: CZK 267; **Circ:** 40,000
Usual Pagination: 300
Editor: Jan Blažek
Profile: Vehicle catalogue.
Language(s): Czech
ADVERTISING RATES:
Full Page Colour .... CZK 145000
Mechanical Data: Type Area: 175 x 230mm
CONSUMER: MOTORING & CYCLING: Motoring

AUTO TIP 764152CZ77A-10
Editorial: Dělnická 12, 17000 PRAHA 7
Tel: 266193173 **Fax:** 234692330
Email: inzerce@axelspringer.cz **Web site:** http://www.topdivka.cz
ISSN: 1210-1087
Date Established: 05.12.90; **Freq:** 26 issues yearly; **Cover Price:** CZK 29,90
Annual Sub.: CZK 507; **Circ:** 36,200
Usual Pagination: 76
Editor: Vítězslav Kodym
Profile: Motorist magazine.
Language(s): Czech
Readership: Aimed at young male motoring enthusiasts.
ADVERTISING RATES:
Full Page Colour .... CZK 130000
Mechanical Data: Type Area: 200 x 270mm
CONSUMER: MOTORING & CYCLING: Motoring

AUTOCAR 1699697CZ77A-232
Editorial: Drtinova 8, 15000 PRAHA 5
Tel: 234109598 **Fax:** 234109241
Email: esquire@stratosfera.cz **Web site:** http://www.stratosfera.cz
ISSN: 1213-9688
Date Established: 03.10.02; **Freq:** Weekly; **Cover Price:** CZK 29,90
Annual Sub.: CZK 1435; **Circ:** 9,055
Usual Pagination: 68
Editor: Jan Červenka
Profile: Car magazine mainly about middle class cars.
Language(s): Czech
ADVERTISING RATES:
Full Page Colour .... CZK 110000
CONSUMER: MOTORING & CYCLING: Motoring

AUTOHIT 1699499CZ77A-218
Editorial: Přemyslovská 2845/43, 13000 PRAHA 3
Tel: 222520617 **Fax:** 222522648
Email: inzerce@burda.cz **Web site:** http://www.burda.cz
ISSN: 1212-8791
Date Established: 23.02.00; **Freq:** 26 issues yearly; **Cover Price:** CZK 19,90
Annual Sub.: CZK 455; **Circ:** 24,750
Usual Pagination: 68
Editor: Jakub Rejlek
Profile: Motorist magazine.
Language(s): Czech
ADVERTISING RATES:
Full Page Colour .... CZK 95000
Mechanical Data: Type Area: 173 x 224mm
CONSUMER: MOTORING & CYCLING: Motoring

AUTOMOBIL REVUE 1699503CZ77A-221
Editorial: Nádražní 762/32, 15000 PRAHA 5
Tel: 225351155 **Fax:** 225351404
Email: info@bmczech.cz **Web site:** http://www.bmczech.cz
ISSN: 1211-9555
Date Established: 01.01.1957; **Freq:** Monthly; **Cover Price:** CZK 39
Annual Sub.: CZK 300; **Circ:** 18,780
Usual Pagination: 84
Editor: Tomáš Hyan
Profile: Motorist magazine.
Language(s): Czech
ADVERTISING RATES:
Full Page Colour .... CZK 111000
Mechanical Data: Type Area: 185 x 276mm
CONSUMER: MOTORING & CYCLING: Motoring

AUTOSPORT & TUNING 1699508CZ77A-225
Editorial: Svaté Anežky České 32, 53002 PARDUBICE **Tel:** 466530508 **Fax:** 466530508
Email: redakce@autosport-tuning.cz **Web site:** http://www.autosport-tuning.cz
ISSN: 1212-3773
Date Established: 01.01.99; **Freq:** Monthly; **Cover Price:** CZK 90
Annual Sub.: CZK 588; **Circ:** 26,650
Usual Pagination: 116
Editor: Vladimír Vrabec
Profile: Motor-vehicle racing magazine.
Language(s): Czech
ADVERTISING RATES:
Full Page Colour .... CZK 50000
Mechanical Data: Type Area: 178 x 248mm
CONSUMER: MOTORING & CYCLING: Motoring

AUTOTEC & AUTOSALON REVUE 1776831CZ77A-286
Editorial: Nádražní 762/32, 15000 PRAHA 5
Tel: 225351154 **Fax:** 225351404
Email: info@bmczech.cz **Web site:** http://www.bmczech.cz
Date Established: 01.01.02; **Freq:** Annual; **Cover Price:** Free; **Circ:** 60,000
Usual Pagination: 44
Editor: Pavel Olivík
Profile: Motorist magazine for Autotec.
Language(s): Czech
ADVERTISING RATES:
Full Page Colour .... CZK 158000
Mechanical Data: Type Area: 272 x 360mm
CONSUMER: MOTORING & CYCLING: Motoring

BÁJEČNÉ RECEPTY 1701378CZ74A-418
Editorial: Bohdalecká 6/1420, 10100 PRAHA 10 - MICHLE **Tel:** 281090640 **Fax:** 281090644
Email: jan.lidmansky@rf-hobby.cz **Web site:** http://www.rf-hobby.cz
ISSN: 1213-4767
Date Established: 01.01.02; **Freq:** 24 issues yearly; **Cover Price:** CZK 29,50; **Circ:** 33,051
Usual Pagination: 52
Editor: Lea Slámová
Profile: Women's magazine about healthy life.
Language(s): Czech
ADVERTISING RATES:
Full Page Colour .... CZK 89000
CONSUMER: WOMEN'S INTEREST CONSUMER MAGAZINES: Women's Interest

BAZÉN A SAUNA 1699534CZ23C-5
Editorial: Pod Štěpem 9a/1231, 10200 PRAHA 10
Tel: 272660101 **Fax:** 272650645
Email: redakce@bazen-sauna.cz **Web site:** http://www.bazen-sauna.cz
ISSN: 1211-541X
Date Established: 01.01.94; **Freq:** 24 issues yearly; **Cover Price:** CZK 52,50
Annual Sub.: CZK 315; **Circ:** 7,000
Usual Pagination: 32
Editor: Jiří Kouba
Profile: Magazine focused on saunas, swimming pools, bath tubs, solariums, also covers technology and equipment used for hydro therapy.
Language(s): Czech
ADVERTISING RATES:
Full Page Colour .... CZK 30000
Mechanical Data: Type Area: 196 x 281mm
BUSINESS: FURNISHINGS & FURNITURE: Furnishings & Furniture - Kitchens & Bathrooms

BETYNKA 1699556CZ74-1
Editorial: Přemyslovská 2845/43, 13000 PRAHA 3
Tel: 221589111 **Fax:** 222522648
Email: inzerce@burda.cz **Web site:** http://www.burda.cz
ISSN: 1212-0480
Date Established: 01.12.92; **Freq:** Monthly; **Cover Price:** CZK 29,90
Annual Sub.: CZK 348; **Circ:** 31,500
Usual Pagination: 132
Editor: Regina Rothová
Profile: Magazine for young mothers about care of children.
Language(s): Czech
ADVERTISING RATES:
Full Page Colour .... CZK 150000
Mechanical Data: Type Area: 165 x 220mm
CONSUMER: WOMEN'S INTEREST CONSUMER MAGAZINES

BIZ 1699569CZ1A-14
Editorial: Holandská 8, Spielberk Office Centre, 63900 BRNO **Tel:** 545113711 **Fax:** 545113712
Email: redakce@cpress.cz **Web site:** http://www.cpress.cz
ISSN: 1214-8431
Date Established: 19.05.00; **Freq:** Quarterly; **Cover Price:** CZK 49
Annual Sub.: CZK 499; **Circ:** 6,000
Usual Pagination: 100
Editor: Martin Chlouba
Profile: Magazine about e-business and new economy.
Language(s): Czech
ADVERTISING RATES:
Full Page Colour .... CZK 135000
BUSINESS: FINANCE & ECONOMICS

BLESK 1699572CZ65A-22
Editorial: Komunardů 1584/42, 17000 PRAHA 7
Tel: 225977616 **Fax:** 225977466
Email: david.saroch@ringier.cz **Web site:** http://www.ringier.cz
ISSN: 1210-5333
Date Established: 13.04.92; **Freq:** 312 times a year; **Cover Price:** Paid
Cover Price: CZK 9
Annual Sub.: CZK 1500; **Circ:** 500,953 Unique Users
Usual Pagination: 16
Editor: Vladimír Mužík
Profile: National tabloid newspaper.
Language(s): Czech
ADVERTISING RATES:
Full Page Colour .... CZK 707560
Mechanical Data: No. of Columns (Display): 7, Type Area: 263 x 380mm
NATIONAL DAILY & SUNDAY NEWSPAPERS: National Daily Newspapers

BLESK PRO ŽENY 1699576CZ74A-404
Editorial: Komunardů 1584/42, 17000 PRAHA 7
Tel: 225977140 **Fax:** 222713665
Email: david.saroch@ringier.cz **Web site:** http://www.ringier.cz
ISSN: 1214-6358
Date Established: 19.04.04; **Freq:** Weekly; **Cover Price:** CZK 10
Annual Sub.: CZK 416; **Circ:** 297,720
Usual Pagination: 56
Editor: Monika Mužíková
Profile: Weekly magazine for women.
Language(s): Czech
ADVERTISING RATES:
Full Page Colour .... CZK 160000
Mechanical Data: Type Area: 195 x 255mm
CONSUMER: WOMEN'S INTEREST CONSUMER MAGAZINES: Women's Interest

BLESK ZDRAVÍ 1776585CZ74G-32
Editorial: Komunardů 1584/42, 17000 PRAHA 7
Tel: 225977586 **Fax:** 222714641
Email: david.saroch@ringier.cz **Web site:** http://www.ringier.cz
ISSN: 1802-3738
Date Established: 22.03.06; **Freq:** Monthly; **Cover Price:** CZK 21; **Circ:** 57,205
Usual Pagination: 68
Editor: Bohumil Křeček
Profile: Magazine about health.
Language(s): Czech
ADVERTISING RATES:
Full Page Colour .... CZK 130000
Mechanical Data: Type Area: 185 x 250mm
CONSUMER: WOMEN'S INTEREST CONSUMER MAGAZINES: Slimming & Health

BOARD 1699581CZ75L-1
Editorial: 8. listopadu 871/53, 16200 PRAHA 6
Tel: 233357507 **Fax:** 233357507
Email: zdenek.svatos@dirtbiker.cz **Web site:** http://www.boardmag.cz
ISSN: 1212-4680
Date Established: 20.09.95; **Freq:** 9 issues yearly; **Cover Price:** CZK 69
Annual Sub.: CZK 440; **Circ:** 15,000
Usual Pagination: 180

Editor: Radek Hruška
Profile: Magazine about skateboarding, snowboarding, wakeboarding, biking and graffiti.
Language(s): Czech
ADVERTISING RATES:
Full Page Colour .... CZK 54600
CONSUMER: SPORT: Outdoor

BODY
1793060CZ74G-37
Editorial: Mozartova 24, 77200 OLOMOUC
Tel: 585203460 **Fax:** 585203460
Email: alenacikova@seznam.cz
Date Established: 01.09.06; **Freq:** Quarterly; **Cover Price:** CZK 45; **Circ:** 135,000
Usual Pagination: 72
Profile: Magazine about healthy lifestyle, fitness and body care.
Language(s): Czech
ADVERTISING RATES:
Full Page Colour .... CZK 77500
Mechanical Data: Type Area: 185 x 275mm
CONSUMER: WOMEN'S INTEREST CONSUMER MAGAZINES: Slimming & Health

BRAVO GIRL!
1699615CZ74B-1
Editorial: Victora Huga 6, P.O.Box 125, 15000 PRAHA 5 **Tel:** 225008271 **Fax:** 225008377
Email: inzerce@bauermedia.cz **Web site:** http://www.bauermedia.cz
ISSN: 1211-4308
Date Established: 27.02.96; **Freq:** 26 issues yearly; **Cover Price:** CZK 28
Annual Sub.: CZK 598; **Circ:** 71,934
Usual Pagination: 52
Editor: Mirka Srdínková
Profile: Magazine for teenage girls.
Language(s): Czech
ADVERTISING RATES:
Full Page Colour .... CZK 160000
Mechanical Data: Type Area: 198 x 249mm
CONSUMER: WOMEN'S INTEREST CONSUMER MAGAZINES: Women's Interest - Fashion

BUDEME MÍT MIMINKO - BABY GUIDE
1699640CZ74D-13
Editorial: Mikanova 3251/7, 10600 PRAHA 10
Tel: 603220960 **Fax:** 603806489
Email: cerna@casopis-miminko.cz **Web site:** http://www.casopis-miminko.cz
Date Established: 01.01.03; **Freq:** Half-yearly; **Cover Price:** Free; **Circ:** 100,000
Usual Pagination: 100
Editor: Romana Černá
Profile: Magazine about maternity.
Language(s): Czech
ADVERTISING RATES:
Full Page Colour .... CZK 99000
Mechanical Data: Type Area: 138 x 190mm
CONSUMER: WOMEN'S INTEREST CONSUMER MAGAZINES: Child Care

BURDA
1699677CZ74B-2
Editorial: Přemyslovská 2845/43, 13000 PRAHA 3
Tel: 222513525 **Fax:** 222522648
Email: inzerce@burda.cz **Web site:** http://www.burda.cz
Date Established: 01.04.91; **Freq:** Monthly; **Cover Price:** CZK 99
Annual Sub.: CZK 948; **Circ:** 24,000
Usual Pagination: 100
Editor: Eva Coufalová
Profile: Magazine about fashion, needlework.
Language(s): Czech
ADVERTISING RATES:
Full Page Colour .... CZK 115000
Mechanical Data: Type Area: 193 x 260mm
CONSUMER: WOMEN'S INTEREST CONSUMER MAGAZINES: Women's Interest - Fashion

BYDLENÍ
763960CZ74C-3
Editorial: Victora Huga 6, P.O.Box 125, 15000 PRAHA 5 **Tel:** 225008339 **Fax:** 225008341
Email: inzerce@bauermedia.cz **Web site:** http://www.bauermedia.cz
ISSN: 0232-0347
Date Established: 01.01.1979; **Freq:** Monthly; **Cover Price:** CZK 59
Annual Sub.: CZK 580; **Circ:** 22,869
Usual Pagination: 108
Editor: Martina Kotrbová
Profile: Magazine about housing.
Language(s): Czech
Readership: Aimed at DIY enthusiasts.
ADVERTISING RATES:
Full Page Colour .... CZK 89000
Mechanical Data: Type Area: 175 x 247mm
CONSUMER: WOMEN'S INTEREST CONSUMER MAGAZINES: Home & Family

BYDLENÍ STAVBY REALITY
1776594CZ74C-34
Editorial: Mezi Vodami 1952/9, 14300 PRAHA 4 - MODŘANY **Tel:** 225276253 **Fax:** 225276222
Email: inzerce@mf.cz **Web site:** http://www.mf.cz
ISSN: 1801-7533
Date Established: 01.01.06; **Freq:** Monthly; **Annual Sub.:** CZK 396; **Circ:** 60,000
Usual Pagination: 132
Editor: Jana Netopilová
Profile: Magazine about housing.
Language(s): Czech
ADVERTISING RATES:
Full Page Colour .... CZK 55000
Mechanical Data: Type Area: 180 x 260mm
CONSUMER: WOMEN'S INTEREST CONSUMER MAGAZINES: Home & Family

BYTY, DOMY, ZAHRADY
1793074CZ4B-8
Editorial: V Křovinách 1708/22, 14700 PRAHA 4
Tel: 241011082 **Fax:** 241011083
Email: group@nexus.cz **Web site:** http://www.novebydleni.cz
Date Established: 01.11.06; **Freq:** 24 issues yearly; **Cover Price:** Free; **Circ:** 50,000
Usual Pagination: 84
Editor: Ivan Hrabec
Profile: Magazine about housing.
Language(s): Czech
ADVERTISING RATES:
Full Page Colour .... CZK 69000
Mechanical Data: Type Area: 180 x 260mm
BUSINESS: ARCHITECTURE & BUILDING: Interior Design & Flooring

CAR TIP
1699696CZ77A-231
Editorial: Rokycanova 80, 61500 BRNO
Tel: 548530883 **Fax:** 548530883
Email: cartip@raz-dva.cz
Date Established: 01.01.94; **Freq:** Quarterly; **Cover Price:** Free; **Circ:** 110,000
Usual Pagination: 16
Editor: Petr Podroužek
Profile: Magazine about cars and motorcycles for region of Brno.
Language(s): Czech
ADVERTISING RATES:
Full Page Colour .... CZK 40000
Mechanical Data: Type Area: 204 x 291mm
CONSUMER: MOTORING & CYCLING: Motoring

ČEDOK REVUE
1699765CZ89A-6
Editorial: Na Příkopě 18, 11135 PRAHA 1
Email: exclusive@cedok.cz **Web site:** http://www.cedok.cz
Date Established: 01.01.02; **Freq:** 3 issues yearly; **Cover Price:** Free; **Circ:** 20,000
Usual Pagination: 40
Profile: Magazine of travel agency Cedok, about travelling.
Language(s): Czech
ADVERTISING RATES:
Full Page Colour .... CZK 36800
Mechanical Data: Type Area: 188 x 272mm
CONSUMER: HOLIDAYS & TRAVEL: Travel

CENTRAL & EASTERN EUROPEAN CIJ
1836444CZ42A-3
Editorial: Václavské náměstí 832/19, 11000 PRAHA 1
Tel: 224222307 **Fax:** 224222308
Email: vodrazkova@cijjournal.com **Web site:** http://www.construction.cz
ISSN: 1214-9896
Date Established: 01.01.95; **Freq:** Monthly; **Cover Price:** CZK 107
Annual Sub.: CZK 981; **Circ:** 18,000
Usual Pagination: 68
Editor: Robert McLean
Profile: Periodical focused on construction, building services and property development, contains information about new projects in Czech Republic and Slovakia. Also informs about current prices of commercial and residential properties. It is aimed at architects, building societies, investors, banks, developers, lawyers and advisors.
Language(s): English
ADVERTISING RATES:
Full Page Colour .... CZK 60000
BUSINESS: CONSTRUCTION

ČESKÁ A SLOVENSKÁ FARMACIE
1500165CZ37-5
Editorial: Sokolská 31, 12026 PRAHA 2
Tel: 224911420 **Fax:** 224266265
Email: medical@euronet.cz **Web site:** http://www.medical.cz
ISSN: 1210-7816
Date Established: 01.01.1951; **Freq:** 24 issues yearly; **Cover Price:** CZK 99
Annual Sub.: CZK 468; **Circ:** 680
Usual Pagination: 52
Profile: Magazine about pharmaceutical products and services.
Language(s): Czech; English; Slovak
Readership: Aimed at pharmacists, drug producers and specialists.
ADVERTISING RATES:
Full Page Colour .... CZK 29000
Mechanical Data: Type Area: 167 x 248mm
BUSINESS: PHARMACEUTICAL & CHEMISTS

ČESKÁ A SLOVENSKÁ OFTALMOLOGIE
1600816CZ56A-40
Editorial: Sokolská 31, 12026 PRAHA 2
Tel: 224911420 **Fax:** 224266265
Email: medical@euronet.cz **Web site:** http://www.medical.cz
ISSN: 1211-9059
Freq: 24 issues yearly; **Cover Price:** CZK 66
Annual Sub.: CZK 318; **Circ:** 2,700
Usual Pagination: 72
Profile: Professional medical magazine.
Language(s): Czech; English; Slovak
Readership: Aimed at all physicians engaged in ophthalmology and postgraduate students.
ADVERTISING RATES:
Full Page Colour .... CZK 27000
Mechanical Data: Type Area: 167 x 247mm
BUSINESS: HEALTH & MEDICAL

ČESKÉ MOTOCYKLOVÉ NOVINY (ČMN)
1699803CZ77B-3
Editorial: Vrbova 19/1427, 14700 PRAHA 4
Tel: 774707187 **Fax:** 244470663
Email: inzerce@bikes.cz **Web site:** http://www.bikes.cz
ISSN: 1212-4427
Date Established: 15.01.99; **Freq:** Weekly; **Cover Price:** CZK 23
Annual Sub.: CZK 950; **Circ:** 25,635
Usual Pagination: 16
Editor: Petr Hájek
Profile: Magazine about motorbikes a motorbike-rasing.
Language(s): Czech
ADVERTISING RATES:
Full Page Colour .... CZK 60000
Mechanical Data: Type Area: 267 x 388mm
CONSUMER: MOTORING & CYCLING: Motorcycling

ČESKOPIS
1776606CZ89A-46
Editorial: Pod Pekárnami 3, 18000 PRAH 8
Tel: 266312379 **Fax:** 266312379
Email: inzerce@ceskopis.cz **Web site:** http://www.ceskopis.cz
ISSN: 1801-7258
Date Established: 01.03.06; **Freq:** Monthly; **Cover Price:** CZK 38
Annual Sub.: CZK 280; **Circ:** 30,000
Usual Pagination: 84
Editor: Irena Pekovová
Profile: Magazine about Czech republic (geography, history, traveling).
Language(s): Czech
ADVERTISING RATES:
Full Page Colour .... CZK 82000
Mechanical Data: Type Area: 138 x 205mm
CONSUMER: HOLIDAYS & TRAVEL: Travel

ČESKO-SLOVENSKÁ PEDIATRIE
1201571CZ56A-95
Editorial: Sokolská 31, 12026 PRAHA 2
Tel: 224911420 **Fax:** 224266265
Email: medical@euronet.cz **Web site:** http://www.medical.cz
ISSN: 0069-2328
Date Established: 01.04.1946; **Freq:** Monthly; **Cover Price:** CZK 80
Annual Sub.: CZK 708; **Circ:** 2,000
Usual Pagination: 72
Editor: B. Binědová
Profile: Professional magazine of paediatrists.
Language(s): Czech; English; Slovak
Readership: Aimed at paediatricians, geneticists and paediatric surgeons and medical students.
ADVERTISING RATES:
Full Page Colour .... CZK 43500
Mechanical Data: Type Area: 167 x 247mm
BUSINESS: HEALTH & MEDICAL

CHEF GURMÁN
1776656CZ74P-20
Editorial: Belgická 38, 12085 PRAHA 2
ISSN: 1801-4917
Date Established: 10.11.05; **Freq:** Monthly; **Cover Price:** CZK 34; **Circ:** 40,068
Usual Pagination: 100
Editor: Martina Mecerová
Profile: Magazine about cooking.
Language(s): Czech
ADVERTISING RATES:
Full Page Colour .... CZK 150000
Mechanical Data: Type Area: 180 x 240mm
CONSUMER: WOMEN'S INTEREST CONSUMER MAGAZINES: Food & Cookery

CHEMAGAZÍN
1700298CZ13-1
Editorial: Boženy Němcové 2625, 53002 PARDUBICE **Tel:** 466411800 **Fax:** 466414161
Email: info@chemagazin.cz **Web site:** http://www.chemagazin.cz
ISSN: 1210-7409
Date Established: 01.01.91; **Freq:** 24 issues yearly; **Cover Price:** Free; **Circ:** 3,800
Usual Pagination: 40
Editor: Miloslav Rotrekl
Profile: Magazine about chemistry, chemical research and technology used within the chemical industries.
Language(s): Czech
ADVERTISING RATES:
Full Page Colour .... CZK 20000
Mechanical Data: Type Area: 180 x 268mm
BUSINESS: CHEMICALS

CHEMICKÉ LISTY
1201574CZ55-5
Editorial: Novotného lávka 200/5, 11668 PRAHA 1
Tel: 224354086 **Fax:** 224311082
Email: drasar@uochb.cas.cz **Web site:** http://www.csch.cz
ISSN: 0009-2770
Date Established: 01.01.1878; **Freq:** Monthly; **Cover Price:** CZK 170
Annual Sub.: CZK 1730; **Circ:** 1,250
Usual Pagination: 96
Editor: Bohumil Kratochvíl, Csc.
Profile: Newsletter about chemistry. News and information from scientific institute, univ.
Language(s): Czech; English; Slovak
Readership: Aimed at chemists, researchers and laboratory workers.
ADVERTISING RATES:
Full Page Colour .... CZK 25330
BUSINESS: APPLIED SCIENCE & LABORATORIES

CHIP
1700300CZ5B-19
Editorial: Přemyslovská 2845/43, 13000 PRAHA 3
Tel: 225018642 **Fax:** 221589600
Email: inzerce@burda.cz **Web site:** http://www.burda.cz
ISSN: 1210-0684
Date Established: 01.01.91; **Freq:** Monthly; **Cover Price:** CZK 198
Annual Sub.: CZK 4124; **Circ:** 36,500
Usual Pagination: 164
Editor: Josef Mika
Profile: Magazine about computers.
Language(s): Czech
ADVERTISING RATES:
Full Page Colour .... CZK 115000
Mechanical Data: Type Area: 173 x 260mm
BUSINESS: COMPUTERS & AUTOMATION: Data Processing

CHLAZENÍ A KLIMATIZACE
1700302CZ3B-3
Editorial: Ježkova 1, 13000 PRAHA 3
Tel: 222721164-5 **Fax:** 222722380
Email: cntl@cntl.cz **Web site:** http://www.cntl.cz
ISSN: 1211-1171
Date Established: 01.05.95; **Freq:** 24 issues yearly; **Cover Price:** CZK 42
Annual Sub.: CZK 402; **Circ:** 5,000
Usual Pagination: 40
Editor: Jiří Trapek
Profile: Professional magazine about ventilation and air conditioning.
Language(s): Czech
ADVERTISING RATES:
Full Page Colour .... CZK 48000
Mechanical Data: No. of Columns (Display): 3, Type Area: 185 x 250mm
BUSINESS: HEATING & VENTILATION: Industrial Heating & Ventilation

CIO BUSINESS WORLD
763796CZ14A-10
Editorial: Seydlerova 2451/11, 15500 PRAHA 5 - NOVÉ BUTOVICE **Tel:** 257088116 **Fax:** 257088174
Email: info@idg.cz **Web site:** http://www.idg.cz
ISSN: 1803-7321
Date Established: 01.10.99; **Freq:** Monthly; **Cover Price:** CZK 100
Annual Sub.: CZK 570; **Circ:** 10,000
Usual Pagination: 74
Editor: Lukáš Erben, Bsc.
Profile: Magazine for e-managers and IT-managers.
Language(s): Czech
Readership: Aimed at business managers and executives.
ADVERTISING RATES:
Full Page Colour .... CZK 85000
Mechanical Data: Type Area: 171 x 224mm
BUSINESS: COMMERCE, INDUSTRY & MANAGEMENT

CLAUDIA
1699722CZ74B-3
Editorial: Victora Huga 6, P.O.Box 125, 15000 PRAHA 5 **Tel:** 225008335 **Fax:** 225008347
Email: inzerce@bauermedia.cz **Web site:** http://www.bauermedia.cz
ISSN: 1214-4614
Date Established: 04.11.03; **Freq:** Weekly; **Cover Price:** CZK 10; **Circ:** 118,145
Usual Pagination: 40
Editor: Eva Stenglová
Profile: Magazine featuring fashion and beauty tips, recipes and crosswords.
Language(s): Czech
ADVERTISING RATES:
Full Page Colour .... CZK 135000
Mechanical Data: Type Area: 202 x 273mm
CONSUMER: WOMEN'S INTEREST CONSUMER MAGAZINES: Women's Interest - Fashion

CO JSME NAKOUPILI, TO SI UVAŘÍME
1699726CZ74P-4
Editorial: V Závětří 4, 17000 PRAHA 7
Tel: 266791550 **Fax:** 266791550
Email: cmveletrhy@etelnet.cz
Date Established: 01.01.02; **Freq:** 3 issues yearly; **Cover Price:** Free; **Circ:** 40,000
Usual Pagination: 32
Editor: Ladislava Bryknarová
Profile: Recipes and food-photograph.
Language(s): Czech

ADVERTISING RATES:
Full Page Colour .... CZK 21000
CONSUMER: WOMEN'S INTEREST CONSUMER MAGAZINES: Food & Cookery

COMPUTER 763798CZ5C-20
Editorial: Holandská 8, Spielberk Office Centre, 63900 BRNO **Tel:** 545113711 **Fax:** 545113712
Email: redakce@cpress.cz **Web site:** http://www.cpress.cz
ISSN: 1210-8790
Date Established: 29.04.94; **Freq:** 26 issues yearly; **Cover Price:** CZK 49
Annual Sub.: CZK 1199; **Circ:** 38,000
Usual Pagination: 116
Editor: Pavel Nygrýn
Profile: Original Czech periodical intended for improver as far as power user PC, software, circumference and services in areas computer techniques.
Language(s): Czech
Readership: Aimed at IT professionals and home PC owners.
ADVERTISING RATES:
Full Page Colour .... CZK 99000
BUSINESS: COMPUTERS & AUTOMATION: Professional Personal Computers

COMPUTERWORLD 1200785CZ5A-5
Editorial: Seydlerova 2451/11, 15500 PRAHA 5 - NOVÉ BUTOVICE **Tel:** 257088141 **Fax:** 257088174
Email: info@idg.cz **Web site:** http://www.idg.cz
ISSN: 1210-9924
Date Established: 18.05.90; **Freq:** 26 issues yearly; **Cover Price:** CZK 20
Annual Sub.: CZK 336; **Circ:** 10,000
Usual Pagination: 32
Editor: Petr Mandík
Profile: IT magazine for managers, IT managers and computer users.
Language(s): Czech; Slovak
Readership: Aimed at IT professionals.
ADVERTISING RATES:
Full Page Colour .... CZK 98000
Mechanical Data: Type Area: 212 x 275mm
BUSINESS: COMPUTERS & AUTOMATION: Automation & Instrumentation

CONNECT! 1201469CZ5B-10
Editorial: Pod Vinicí 23, 14311 PRAHA 4 - MODŘANY **Tel:** 225273930-3 **Fax:** 225273934
Email: redakce@cpress.cz **Web site:** http://www.cpress.cz
ISSN: 1211-3085
Date Established: 27.01.96; **Freq:** Monthly; **Cover Price:** CZK 79
Annual Sub.: CZK 680; **Circ:** 7,000
Usual Pagination: 76
Editor: Lukáš Honek
Profile: Magazine about communication, computer networks and open sources.
Language(s): Czech
Readership: Aimed at computer professionals and end-users.
ADVERTISING RATES:
Full Page Colour .... CZK 83000
BUSINESS: COMPUTERS & AUTOMATION: Data Processing

COSMOPOLITAN 766589CZ74A-401
Editorial: Drtinova 8, 15000 PRAHA 5
Tel: 234109133 **Fax:** 234109114
Email: cosmogirl@stratosfera.cz **Web site:** http://www.stratosfera.cz
ISSN: 1211-6459
Date Established: 25.08.94; **Freq:** Monthly; **Cover Price:** CZK 99,90
Annual Sub.: CZK 1099; **Circ:** 100,000
Usual Pagination: 148
Editor: Sabrina Karasová
Profile: Czech version of worldwide women's magazine.
Language(s): Czech
Readership: Aimed mainly at women.
ADVERTISING RATES:
Full Page Colour .... CZK 248000
CONSUMER: WOMEN'S INTEREST CONSUMER MAGAZINES: Women's Interest

C.O.T. BUSINESS 1699691CZ89A-3
Editorial: Opletalova 55, P.O.Box 772-HP, 11184 PRAHA 1 **Tel:** 221602242 **Fax:** 221602266
Email: redakce@cot.cz **Web site:** http://www.cot.cz
ISSN: 1212-4281
Date Established: 01.01.97; **Freq:** Monthly; **Cover Price:** CZK 94
Annual Sub.: CZK 924; **Circ:** 6,500
Usual Pagination: 82
Editor: Petr Ulrych
Profile: Magazine for businessmen in tourist industry.
Language(s): Czech; English
ADVERTISING RATES:
Full Page Colour .... CZK 42000
Mechanical Data: Type Area: 188 x 272mm
CONSUMER: HOLIDAYS & TRAVEL: Travel

LA CUCINA ITALIANA 1700762CZ74P-11
Editorial: Nad koupadly 1b, 14200 PRAHA 4 - LHOTKA **Tel:** 283870414 **Fax:** 283871636
Email: inzerce@omegagroup.cz **Web site:** http://www.omegagroup.cz
ISSN: 0214-8164
Date Established: 14.10.04; **Freq:** 8 issues yearly; **Cover Price:** CZK 59; **Circ:** 30,000
Usual Pagination: 132
Editor: Kateřina Růžičková
Profile: Magazine specialized in Italian cookery.
Language(s): Czech
ADVERTISING RATES:
Full Page Colour .... CZK 110000
Mechanical Data: Type Area: 189 x 252mm
CONSUMER: WOMEN'S INTEREST CONSUMER MAGAZINES: Food & Cookery

DENÍK ČECHY (SÍŤ) 1776588CZ67B-805
Editorial: Římská 14, 12085 PRAHA 2
Web site: http://www.vlp.cz
Date Established: 01.01.98; **Freq:** 312 issues yearly; **Cover Price:** CZK 11; **Circ:** 181,300
Profile: Regional daily newspaper (Vltava-Labe-Press company).
Language(s): Czech
ADVERTISING RATES:
Full Page Colour .... CZK 428778
Mechanical Data: Type Area: 278 x 415mm
REGIONAL DAILY & SUNDAY NEWSPAPERS: Regional Daily Newspapers

DENÍK ČESKÁ REPUBLIKA (SÍŤ) 1702443CZ73-264
Editorial: Římská 14, 12085 PRAHA 2
Tel: 221084506 **Fax:** 221084523
Web site: http://www.vlp.cz
Date Established: 01.01.01; **Freq:** 312 issues yearly; **Cover Price:** CZK 11; **Circ:** 274,988
Editor: Lída Rakušanová
Profile: Local newspapers net.
Language(s): Czech
ADVERTISING RATES:
Full Page Colour .... CZK 596106
Mechanical Data: Type Area: 278 x 415mm
CONSUMER: NATIONAL & INTERNATIONAL PERIODICALS

DENÍK JIŽNÍ ČECHY (SÍŤ) 1700513CZ67B-196
Editorial: Náměstí Přemysla Otakara II. 8/5, 37021 ČESKÉ BUDĚJOVICE **Tel:** 387411993
Fax: 387411825
Email: inzerce@1najihu.cz **Web site:** http://www.vlp.cz
Date Established: 19.05.1945; **Freq:** 312 issues yearly; **Cover Price:** CZK 11; **Circ:** 33,900
Editor: Petr Soukup
Profile: Network of southern regional daily newspapers.
Language(s): Czech
ADVERTISING RATES:
Full Page Colour .... CZK 122010
Mechanical Data: Type Area: 278 x 415mm
REGIONAL DAILY & SUNDAY NEWSPAPERS: Regional Daily Newspapers

DENÍK SEVERNÍ ČECHY (SÍŤ) 1701867CZ67B-547
Editorial: Klíšská 1702/25, 40001 ÚSTÍ NAD LABEM
Tel: 475212022 **Fax:** 475214348
Web site: http://www.vlp.cz
Date Established: 07.05.93; **Freq:** 312 issues yearly; **Circ:** 48,865
Editor: Miroslav Pakosta
Profile: Network of northern regional newspaper.
Language(s): Czech
ADVERTISING RATES:
Full Page Colour .... CZK 132468
Mechanical Data: Type Area: 278 x 415mm
REGIONAL DAILY & SUNDAY NEWSPAPERS: Regional Daily Newspapers

DENÍK STŘEDNÍ ČECHY + PRAŽSKÝ DENÍK (SÍŤ) 1702021CZ67B-572
Editorial: Římská 14, 12085 PRAHA 2
Tel: 221084506 **Fax:** 221084523
Web site: http://www.vlp.cz
Date Established: 01.05.99; **Freq:** 312 issues yearly; **Cover Price:** CZK 11; **Circ:** 37,900
Usual Pagination: 28
Editor: Alena Pancerová
Profile: Network of dailies in Prague and central Czech Republic.
Language(s): Czech
ADVERTISING RATES:
Full Page Colour .... CZK 108066
Mechanical Data: Type Area: 278 x 415mm
REGIONAL DAILY & SUNDAY NEWSPAPERS: Regional Daily Newspapers

DENÍK VÝCHODNÍ ČECHY (SÍŤ) 1702471CZ67B-677
Editorial: Kladská 17, P.O.Box 6, 50003 HRADEC KRÁLOVÉ **Tel:** 495800874 **Fax:** 495800875
Email: hradecke.noviny@denikybohemia.cz **Web site:** http://www.vlp.cz
Date Established: 26.04.1906; **Freq:** 312 issues yearly; **Cover Price:** CZK 11; **Circ:** 58,049
Editor: Jan Korbel
Profile: Network of regional dailies from eastern part of Czech republic.
Language(s): Czech
ADVERTISING RATES:
Full Page Colour .... CZK 146412
Mechanical Data: Type Area: 278 x 415mm
REGIONAL DAILY & SUNDAY NEWSPAPERS: Regional Daily Newspapers

DETAIL (BAŤA) 1699905CZ74B-6
Editorial: Nad Kazankou 37/708, 17100 PRAHA 7 - TRÓJA **Tel:** 244023201 **Fax:** 244023333
Email: info@bpublishing.cz **Web site:** http://www.bpublishing.cz
Date Established: 01.01.00; **Freq:** Quarterly; **Cover Price:** CZK 20; **Circ:** 145,000
Usual Pagination: 110
Editor: Jana Vodehnalová
Profile: Fashion magazine with offers of Bata company.
Language(s): Czech
ADVERTISING RATES:
Full Page Colour .... CZK 119000
CONSUMER: WOMEN'S INTEREST CONSUMER MAGAZINES: Women's Interest - Fashion

DIETA 1699921CZ74G-6
Editorial: Mezi Vodami 1952/9, 14300 PRAHA 4 - MODŘANY **Tel:** 225276213 **Fax:** 225276222
Email: inzerce@mf.cz **Web site:** http://www.mf.cz
ISSN: 1214-8784
Date Established: 23.11.04; **Freq:** Monthly; **Cover Price:** CZK 39
Annual Sub.: CZK 429; **Circ:** 50,000
Usual Pagination: 100
Editor: Petra Lamschová
Profile: Magazine about food, nutrition, bodybuilding and condition.
Language(s): Czech
ADVERTISING RATES:
Full Page Colour .... CZK 119000
Mechanical Data: Type Area: 183 x 245mm
CONSUMER: WOMEN'S INTEREST CONSUMER MAGAZINES: Slimming & Health

DIGIFOTO 1699922CZ85A-1
Editorial: Pod Vinicí 23, 14311 PRAHA 4 - MODŘANY **Tel:** 225273930 **Fax:** 225273934
Email: redakce@cpress.cz **Web site:** http://www.cpress.cz
ISSN: 1801-0873
Date Established: 01.01.02; **Freq:** 10 issues yearly; **Cover Price:** CZK 129
Annual Sub.: CZK 899; **Circ:** 11,000
Usual Pagination: 116
Editor: Petr Lindner
Profile: Magazine dealing with digital photos and videos.
Language(s): Czech
ADVERTISING RATES:
Full Page Colour .... CZK 95000
Mechanical Data: Type Area: 199 x 262mm
CONSUMER: PHOTOGRAPHY & FILM MAKING: Photography

DÍVKA 1699938CZ74F-2
Editorial: Victora Huga 6, P.O.Box 125, 15000 PRAHA 5 **Tel:** 225008334 **Fax:** 225008377
Email: inzerce@bauermedia.cz **Web site:** http://www.bauermedia.cz
ISSN: 1211-8265
Date Established: 01.06.91; **Freq:** Monthly; **Cover Price:** CZK 45
Annual Sub.: CZK 468; **Circ:** 47,378
Usual Pagination: 84
Editor: Michaela Kovářová
Profile: Magazine for teenage girls.
Language(s): Czech
ADVERTISING RATES:
Full Page Colour .... CZK 160000
Mechanical Data: Type Area: 200 x 265mm
CONSUMER: WOMEN'S INTEREST CONSUMER MAGAZINES: Teenage

DOMOV 1201728CZ74C-5
Editorial: Táborská 5/979, 14000 PRAHA 4
Tel: 226517950 **Fax:** 226517960
Email: zuzana.krausova@provolnycas.cz **Web site:** http://www.provolnycas.cz
ISSN: 0012-5369
Date Established: 01.01.1960; **Freq:** Monthly; **Cover Price:** CZK 59
Annual Sub.: CZK 649; **Circ:** 10,504
Usual Pagination: 92
Editor: Nada Ghani
Profile: Magazine about housing.
Language(s): Czech
Readership: Aimed at home owners.
CONSUMER: WOMEN'S INTEREST CONSUMER MAGAZINES: Home & Family

DOTEKY ŠTĚSTÍ 1699970CZ74R-2
Editorial: Bohdalecká 6/1420, 10100 PRAHA 10 - MICHLE **Tel:** 281090647 **Fax:** 281090644
Email: jan.lidmansky@rf-hobby.cz **Web site:** http://www.rf-hobby.cz
Date Established: 22.10.98; **Freq:** Monthly; **Cover Price:** CZK 24,50; **Circ:** 31,700
Usual Pagination: 54
Editor: Eva Dostálová
Profile: Magazine for women about human relationship between men and women.
Language(s): Czech
ADVERTISING RATES:
Full Page Mono .... CZK 18000
CONSUMER: WOMEN'S INTEREST CONSUMER MAGAZINES: Women's Interest Related

DOVOLENÁ PRO VÁS 1806126CZ89A-55
Editorial: Letohradská 48, 17000 PRAHA 7
Tel: 225278147 **Fax:** 233380336
Email: agro@cztisk.cz
Freq: Weekly; **Cover Price:** Free; **Circ:** 60,000
Editor: Michaela Poesová
Profile: Magazine about holiday leave.
Language(s): Czech
ADVERTISING RATES:
Full Page Colour .... CZK 7000
CONSUMER: HOLIDAYS & TRAVEL: Travel

DR. PALEČEK 1699977CZ56A-158
Editorial: V Jámě 1, 11000 PRAHA 1 **Tel:** 224162531
Fax: 224162591
Email: causasubita@praha.czcom.cz **Web site:** http://www.causa-subita.cz
ISSN: 1801-1896
Date Established: 02.05.05; **Freq:** Quarterly; **Cover Price:** Free; **Circ:** 80,000
Usual Pagination: 32
Editor: Marie Korcová
Profile: Magazine for parents of 3-12 yaers old children.
Language(s): Czech
ADVERTISING RATES:
Full Page Colour .... CZK 35000
BUSINESS: HEALTH & MEDICAL

DŘEVO, LESY, VODA 1699986CZ57-14
Editorial: náměstí W. Churchilla 2, 11359 PRAHA 3
Email: bernat.zdenek@cmkos.cz **Web site:** http://osdlv.cmkos.cz
ISSN: 0139-5432
Freq: Quarterly; **Annual Sub.:** CZK 26; **Circ:** 62,000
Usual Pagination: 4
Profile: Magazine about agriculture, ecology and forestry.
Language(s): Czech
BUSINESS: ENVIRONMENT & POLLUTION

DŮM A ZAHRADA 1699996CZ74C-15
Editorial: Lomnického 7/1705, 14079 PRAHA 4
Tel: 296162866 **Fax:** 296162767
Email: inzerce@homedeco.cz **Web site:** http://www.dumazahrada.cz
ISSN: 1211-7374
Date Established: 23.11.95; **Freq:** Monthly; **Cover Price:** CZK 69
Annual Sub.: CZK 696; **Circ:** 28,184
Usual Pagination: 188
Editor: Jiří Zázvorka
Profile: Magazine about housing and gardening.
Language(s): Czech
CONSUMER: WOMEN'S INTEREST CONSUMER MAGAZINES: Home & Family

EKONOM 1200758CZ1A-5
Editorial: Dobrovského 25, 17055 PRAHA 7
Tel: 233071301 **Fax:** 233072002
Email: michal.fialka@economia.cz **Web site:** http://www.economia.cz
ISSN: 1210-0714
Date Established: 01.10.91; **Freq:** Weekly; **Cover Price:** CZK 35
Annual Sub.: CZK 1352; **Circ:** 21,949
Usual Pagination: 68
Editor: Eva Hanáková
Profile: Economic magazine.
Language(s): Czech
Readership: Aimed at managers, government officials, economists, entrepreneurs and foreigners living in the Czech Republic.
ADVERTISING RATES:
Full Page Colour .... CZK 228000
Mechanical Data: Type Area: 190 x 259mm
BUSINESS: FINANCE & ECONOMICS

ELLE 1500198CZ74A-50
Editorial: Na Zátorce 3, 16000 PRAHA 6
Tel: 233023700 **Fax:** 233023701
Email: all@premiere.cz **Web site:** http://www.maxim.cz
ISSN: 1210-8480
Date Established: 01.04.94; **Freq:** Monthly; **Cover Price:** CZK 85
Annual Sub.: CZK 950; **Circ:** 58,600
Usual Pagination: 288
Editor: Andrea Běhounková
Profile: Czech version of worldwide women's magazine.
Language(s): Czech
Readership: Aimed at women aged between 18 and 26 years.
ADVERTISING RATES:
Full Page Colour .... CZK 235000
Mechanical Data: Type Area: 173 x 244mm
CONSUMER: WOMEN'S INTEREST CONSUMER MAGAZINES: Women's Interest

Czech Republic

ENERGETIKA
1201648CZ58-29
Editorial: Partyzánská 7, 17005 PRAHA 7 - HOLEŠOVICE **Tel:** 266753581 **Fax:** 266753580
Email: redakce.energetika@csze.cz **Web site:** http://www.volny.cz/casopis.energetika
ISSN: 0375-8842
Date Established: 01.01.1951; **Freq:** Monthly; **Cover Price:** CZK 25
Annual Sub.: CZK 300; **Circ:** 2,500
Usual Pagination: 36
Editor: František Petružalek
Profile: Magazine featuring articles on energy, power, production, measurement and control.
Language(s): Czech; Slovak
Readership: Aimed at researchers, university management, technicians and government department officials.
ADVERTISING RATES:
Full Page Colour .... CZK 30000
Mechanical Data: Type Area: 180 x 260mm
BUSINESS: ENERGY, FUEL & NUCLEAR

EPOCHA
1700030CZ74R-3
Editorial: Bohdalecká 6/1420, 10100 PRAHA 10 - MICHLE **Tel:** 281090679 **Fax:** 281090644
Email: jan.lidmansky@rf-hobby.cz **Web site:** http://www.rf-hobby.cz
ISSN: 1214-9519
Date Established: 06.04.05; **Freq:** 26 issues yearly; **Cover Price:** CZK 29,50; **Circ:** 98,070
Usual Pagination: 68
Editor: Pavel Přeučil
Profile: Magazine with interesting science news, reading about celebrities.
Language(s): Czech
ADVERTISING RATES:
Full Page Colour .... CZK 119000
CONSUMER: WOMEN'S INTEREST CONSUMER MAGAZINES: Women's Interest Related

ESQUIRE
1700037CZ86C-1
Editorial: Drtinova 8, 15000 PRAHA 5
Tel: 234109193 **Fax:** 234109101
Email: esquire@stratosfera.cz **Web site:** http://www.stratosfera.cz
ISSN: 1211-4006
Date Established: 25.04.96; **Freq:** Monthly; **Cover Price:** CZK 65
Annual Sub.: CZK 659; **Circ:** 41,500
Usual Pagination: 148
Editor: Antonin Herbeck
Profile: Magazine for men - lifestyle, cars, sport, music, travelling, electronics etc.
Language(s): Czech
ADVERTISING RATES:
Full Page Colour .... CZK 213000
CONSUMER: ADULT & GAY MAGAZINES: Men's Lifestyle Magazines

ESTETIKA
1793095CZ56A-159
Editorial: Branická 140/514, 14700 PRAHA 4
Tel: 222126141 **Fax:** 222518810
Email: estetika@estetika.cz **Web site:** http://www.zenaplus.cz
ISSN: 1802-0402
Date Established: 27.09.06; **Freq:** Monthly; **Cover Price:** CZK 59
Annual Sub.: CZK 670; **Circ:** 30,000
Usual Pagination: 100
Editor: Hana Profousová
Profile: Anaplasty magazine for everybody who wants to change himself.
Language(s): Czech
ADVERTISING RATES:
Full Page Colour .... CZK 140000
Mechanical Data: Type Area: 177 x 230mm
BUSINESS: HEALTH & MEDICAL

EURO
1700040CZ73-211
Editorial: Holečkova 103, P.O.Box 23, 15000 PRAHA 5 **Tel:** 251026101 **Fax:** 257328774
Email: vydavatelstvi@euro.cz **Web site:** http://www.euro.cz
ISSN: 1212-3129
Date Established: 26.10.98; **Freq:** Weekly; **Cover Price:** CZK 39
Annual Sub.: CZK 1622; **Circ:** 29,983
Usual Pagination: 94
Editor: István Léko
Profile: Economic weekly.
Language(s): Czech
ADVERTISING RATES:
Full Page Colour .... CZK 220000
Mechanical Data: Type Area: 184 x 244mm
CONSUMER: NATIONAL & INTERNATIONAL PERIODICALS

EUROFIRMA
1700043CZ1A-23
Editorial: Husitská 90, 13000 PRAHA 3
Tel: 222782670 **Fax:** 222780921
Email: info@eurofirma.cz **Web site:** http://www.eurofirma.cz
ISSN: 1214-1755
Date Established: 03.03.03; **Freq:** 26 issues yearly;
Annual Sub.: CZK 399; **Circ:** 50,000
Usual Pagination: 52
Editor: Petr Majcharčik
Profile: Magazine about companies in EU.
Language(s): Czech
ADVERTISING RATES:
Full Page Colour .... CZK 49000
Mechanical Data: Type Area: 189 x 277mm
BUSINESS: FINANCE & ECONOMICS

EVROPSKÉ NOVINY
1700055CZ82-210
Editorial: Kancelářská budova P8, č.p.80, 53353 PARDUBICE - SEMTÍN **Tel:** 466611139
Fax: 466611139
Email: redakce@bulvarpress.cz **Web site:** http://www.bulvarpress.cz
ISSN: 1214-696X
Date Established: 30.04.04; **Freq:** Monthly; **Cover Price:** CZK 15; **Circ:** 50,000
Usual Pagination: 8
Editor: Zuzana Nováková
Profile: Newspaper about EU (European Union), news, economy, politics, culture.
Language(s): Czech; English
ADVERTISING RATES:
Full Page Colour .... CZK 158038
Mechanical Data: Type Area: 276 x 409mm
CONSUMER: CURRENT AFFAIRS & POLITICS

EXPORTÉR
1700057CZ20-1
Editorial: Dobrovského 25, 17055 PRAHA 7
Tel: 233073003 **Fax:** 233072307
Email: economia@economia.cz **Web site:** http://www.economia.cz
Date Established: 01.10.03; **Freq:** Monthly; **Cover Price:** Free; **Circ:** 104,000
Usual Pagination: 40
Profile: Professional magazine focused on export and import.
Language(s): Czech
ADVERTISING RATES:
Full Page Colour .... CZK 168000
Mechanical Data: Type Area: 200 x 280mm
BUSINESS: IMPORT & EXPORT

EXTRA PC
1793097CZ5B-44
Editorial: Hrnčířská 23, 60200 BRNO **Tel:** 549210724
Fax: 549210724
Email: broza@epublishing.cz **Web site:** http://www.epublishing.cz
ISSN: 1802-1220
Date Established: 12.09.06; **Freq:** Monthly; **Cover Price:** CZK 69,90
Annual Sub.: CZK 499; **Circ:** 26,910
Usual Pagination: 108
Editor: Roman Kučera
Profile: IT magazine.
Language(s): Czech
ADVERTISING RATES:
Full Page Colour .... CZK 115000
Mechanical Data: Type Area: 204 x 260mm
BUSINESS: COMPUTERS & AUTOMATION: Data Processing

F1 - RACING
1700060CZ77D-12
Editorial: Drtinova 8, 15000 PRAHA 5
Tel: 234109261 **Fax:** 234109241
Email: esquire@stratosfera.cz **Web site:** http://www.stratosfera.cz
ISSN: 1213-0443
Date Established: 10.05.00; **Freq:** Monthly; **Cover Price:** CZK 65
Annual Sub.: CZK 659; **Circ:** 30,000
Usual Pagination: 100
Editor: Luděk Staněk
Profile: Czech version of F1 magazine.
Language(s): Czech
ADVERTISING RATES:
Full Page Colour .... CZK 87000
CONSUMER: MOTORING & CYCLING: Motor Sports

FAJN ŽIVOT
1700061CZ74Q-5
Editorial: Lomnického 7, 14000 PRAHA 4
Tel: 296162282 **Fax:** 224916965
Email: inzerce@sanomamag-praha.cz **Web site:** http://www.sanoma.cz
ISSN: 1214-9837
Date Established: 06.10.04; **Freq:** Monthly; **Cover Price:** CZK 19,90
Annual Sub.: CZK 234; **Circ:** 51,192
Usual Pagination: 60
Editor: Pavel Traub
Profile: Relaxation family magazine.
Language(s): Czech
ADVERTISING RATES:
Full Page Colour .... CZK 78000
Mechanical Data: Type Area: 185 x 245mm
CONSUMER: WOMEN'S INTEREST CONSUMER MAGAZINES: Lifestyle

FAKTA PRESS
1700062CZ67J-85
Editorial: Kapitána Nálepky 59, 58602 SVITAVY
Tel: 461533861 **Fax:** 461533861
Email: faktapress@seznam.cz **Web site:** http://www.faktapress.cz
Date Established: 01.01.02; **Freq:** Monthly; **Cover Price:** Free; **Circ:** 35,000
Usual Pagination: 8
Editor: Petr Roštlapil
Profile: Newspaper of region Svitavsko and Zdarsko.
Language(s): Czech
Mechanical Data: Type Area: 270 x 390mm
REGIONAL DAILY & SUNDAY NEWSPAPERS: Regional Newspapers (excl. dailies)

FHM
1831333CZ86C-11
Editorial: Drtinova 8, 15000 PRAHA 5
Email: esquire@stratosfera.cz **Web site:** http://www.stratosfera.cz
ISSN: 1802-9868
Date Established: 15.02.08; **Freq:** Monthly; **Cover Price:** CZK 59,90; **Circ:** 50,000
Usual Pagination: 150
Editor: Luděk Staněk
Profile: Magazine for men.
Language(s): Czech
ADVERTISING RATES:
Full Page Colour .... CZK 213000
CONSUMER: ADULT & GAY MAGAZINES: Men's Lifestyle Magazines

FINANČNÍ ZPRAVODAJ
1700086CZ1A-27
Editorial: Letenská 15, 11810 PRAHA 1
Tel: 257042500 **Fax:** 257042500
Email: zuzana.chocholova@mfcr.cz **Web site:** http://www.mfcr.cz
ISSN: 0322-9653
Date Established: 01.01.1967; **Freq:** Monthly; **Cover Price:** CZK 25
Annual Sub.: CZK 380; **Circ:** 32,800
Editor: Alena Šauerová
Profile: Newsletter of finance ministry.
Language(s): Czech
BUSINESS: FINANCE & ECONOMICS

FITNESS
1700094CZ75A-207
Editorial: Wintrova 11/1313, 53009 PARDUBICE
Tel: 466611314 **Fax:** 466611314
Email: rudzinskyj@pce.czcom.cz **Web site:** http://www.svetkulturistiky.cz
ISSN: 1212-2386
Date Established: 01.11.96; **Freq:** 24 issues yearly; **Cover Price:** CZK 68
Annual Sub.: CZK 340; **Circ:** 42,000
Usual Pagination: 86
Editor: Ivan Rudzinskyj
Profile: Magazine about body building, fitness etc.
Language(s): Czech
ADVERTISING RATES:
Full Page Colour .... CZK 28000
CONSUMER: SPORT

FITSTYL
1700095CZ74G-9
Editorial: Dolnoměcholupská 209/17, 10000 PRAHA 10 - HOSTIVAŘ **Tel:** 274777202
Email: zilkova@boremi.cz **Web site:** http://www.boremi.cz
ISSN: 1212-2629
Date Established: 01.11.97; **Freq:** Monthly; **Cover Price:** CZK 49
Annual Sub.: CZK 468; **Circ:** 42,000
Usual Pagination: 92
Editor: Miroslav Honsů
Profile: Magazine about healthy life style.
Language(s): Czech
ADVERTISING RATES:
Full Page Colour .... CZK 98000
Mechanical Data: Type Area: 153 x 204mm
CONSUMER: WOMEN'S INTEREST CONSUMER MAGAZINES: Slimming & Health

FLORA NA ZAHRADĚ
1700100CZ93-201
Editorial: Táborská 5/979, 14000 PRAHA 4
Tel: 226517911 **Fax:** 226517938
Email: hornova@casopisy2005.cz **Web site:** http://www.floranazahrade.cz
Date Established: 01.01.02; **Freq:** Monthly; **Cover Price:** CZK 35; **Circ:** 43,640
Usual Pagination: 84
Editor: Nataša Krempová
Profile: Magazine about flowers at home and in the garden.
Language(s): Czech
ADVERTISING RATES:
Full Page Colour .... CZK 78000
Mechanical Data: Type Area: 188 x 246mm
CONSUMER: GARDENING

FORD REVUE
1700110CZ77A-239
Editorial: Ostrovní 126/30, 11000 PRAHA 1
Tel: 222927104 **Fax:** 234648666
Email: dana.frumarova@crestcom.cz **Web site:** http://www.crestcom.cz
Freq: Monthly; **Cover Price:** Free; **Circ:** 50,000
Usual Pagination: 36
Editor: Dana Frumarová
Profile: Magazine of auto factory Ford.
Language(s): Czech
CONSUMER: MOTORING & CYCLING: Motoring

FOTOVIDEO
1700120CZ78A-3
Editorial: Velvarská 1626/45, 16000 PRAHA 6
Tel: 233025516 **Fax:** 233025502
Email: info@atemi.cz **Web site:** http://www.atemi.cz
ISSN: 1211-5312
Date Established: 01.01.97; **Freq:** Monthly; **Cover Price:** CZK 89
Annual Sub.: CZK 580; **Circ:** 13,000
Usual Pagination: 116
Editor: Rudolf Stáhlich
Profile: Professional journal about photography, audio, video camera, videorecorder and mulitmedia.
Language(s): Czech
ADVERTISING RATES:
Full Page Colour .... CZK 100000
Mechanical Data: Type Area: 173 x 232mm
CONSUMER: CONSUMER ELECTRONICS: Hi-Fi & Recording

FREUNDSCHAFT
1700129CZ62A-6
Editorial: Suchý vršek 2122, 15800 PRAHA 5
Tel: 235517837 **Fax:** 224491309
Email: janku@freundschaft.cz **Web site:** http://www.freundschaft.cz
ISSN: 0323-0384
Date Established: 01.01.1952; **Freq:** 10 issues yearly; **Cover Price:** CZK 16
Annual Sub.: CZK 160; **Circ:** 30,000
Usual Pagination: 16
Editor: Zuzana Janků
Profile: Magazine for education of german language.
Language(s): Czech; German
ADVERTISING RATES:
Full Page Colour .... CZK 12000
Mechanical Data: No. of Columns (Display): 3
BUSINESS: CHURCH & SCHOOL EQUIPMENT & EDUCATION: Education

G2010
1776861CZ75D-10
Editorial: Dopravákű 3, 18000 PRAHA 8
Tel: 284686779 **Fax:** 284688969
Email: office@beone.cz **Web site:** http://www.beone.cz
Date Established: 01.04.02; **Freq:** Annual; **Cover Price:** Free; **Circ:** 50,000
Usual Pagination: 222
Editor: Marko Zekič
Profile: Golf catalogue.
Language(s): Czech
ADVERTISING RATES:
Full Page Colour .... CZK 190000
Mechanical Data: Type Area: 130 x 210mm
CONSUMER: SPORT: Golf

GENERAL REALITY
1700149CZ1E-5
Editorial: Vítězné náměstí 10, 16000 PRAHA 6
Tel: 233344810 **Fax:** 233344810
Email: general@general.cz **Web site:** http://www.general.cz
Date Established: 01.09.03; **Freq:** 24 issues yearly; **Cover Price:** Free; **Circ:** 50,000
Usual Pagination: 16
Editor: Lucie Bílá
Profile: Magazine with offers of real estate agency General Invest Company.
Language(s): Czech
ADVERTISING RATES:
Full Page Colour .... CZK 30000
BUSINESS: FINANCE & ECONOMICS: Property

GEO
1776642CZ88R-4
Editorial: U Krčského nádraží 36, 14000 PRAHA 4 - KRČ **Tel:** 241093440 **Fax:** 241721905
Email: motorpresse@motorpresse.cz **Web site:** http://www.motorpresse.cz
ISSN: 1801-3201
Date Established: 27.10.05; **Freq:** Monthly; **Cover Price:** CZK 92; **Circ:** 21,100
Usual Pagination: 132
Editor: Martin Jaroš
Profile: Educational family magazine.
Language(s): Czech
ADVERTISING RATES:
Full Page Colour .... CZK 180000
Mechanical Data: Type Area: 178 x 238mm
CONSUMER: EDUCATION: Education Related

GLANC
1793105CZ74Q-25
Editorial: Přátelství 986, 10424 PRAHA 10 - UHŘÍNĚVES **Tel:** 222927221 **Fax:** 272700988
Email: i.valterova@tv-mag.cz **Web site:** http://www.tv-mag.cz
ISSN: 1802-0577
Date Established: 21.09.06; **Freq:** 26 issues yearly; **Cover Price:** CZK 29; **Circ:** 77,220
Usual Pagination: 108
Editor: Lubor Dobešek
Profile: Social and lifestyle magazine.
Language(s): Czech
ADVERTISING RATES:
Full Page Colour .... CZK 203000
Mechanical Data: Type Area: 180 x 240mm
CONSUMER: WOMEN'S INTEREST CONSUMER MAGAZINES: Lifestyle

GRAND AUTO
1700168CZ77A-241
Editorial: Vinohradská 174, 13000 PRAHA 3
Tel: 272107111 **Fax:** 272107000
Email: grandprinc@grandprinc.cz **Web site:** http://www.grandprinc.cz
Date Established: 24.09.02; **Freq:** Monthly; **Cover Price:** Free; **Circ:** 60,000
Usual Pagination: 52
Editor: Michal Busta
Profile: Professional car magazine.
Language(s): Czech
ADVERTISING RATES:
Full Page Colour .... CZK 60000
Mechanical Data: Type Area: 196 x 252mm
CONSUMER: MOTORING & CYCLING: Motoring

GRAND BIBLIO
1804179CZ84B-34
Editorial: Vinohradská 174, 13000 PRAHA 3
Tel: 272107111 **Fax:** 272107000
Email: grandprinc@grandprinc.cz **Web site:** http://www.grandprinc.cz
ISSN: 1802-3320
Date Established: 27.03.07; **Freq:** Monthly; **Cover Price:** Free; **Circ:** 50,000
Usual Pagination: 36
Editor: Jaroslav Císař
Profile: Magazine specialized in literary culture.
Language(s): Czech
ADVERTISING RATES:
Full Page Colour .... CZK 49000
Mechanical Data: Type Area: 196 x 252mm
CONSUMER: THE ARTS & LITERARY: Literary

GRAND DEVELOPER
1776645CZ1E-21
Editorial: Vinohradská 174, 13000 PRAHA 3
Tel: 272107111 **Fax:** 272107000
Email: grandprinc@grandprinc.cz **Web site:** http://www.grandprinc.cz
ISSN: 1802-3355
Date Established: 16.10.05; **Freq:** Quarterly; **Cover Price:** Free; **Circ:** 120,000
Usual Pagination: 36
Editor: Lenka Kerlová
Profile: Advertising magazine specialized in real estates.
Language(s): Czech
ADVERTISING RATES:
Full Page Colour .... CZK 120000
Mechanical Data: Type Area: 196 x 252mm
BUSINESS: FINANCE & ECONOMICS: Property

GRAND REALITY (PRAHA A STŘEDOČESKÝ KRAJ)
1700173CZ1E-7
Editorial: Vinohradská 174, 13000 PRAHA 3
Tel: 272107111 **Fax:** 272107000
Email: grandprinc@grandprinc.cz **Web site:** http://www.grandprinc.cz
Date Established: 15.01.02; **Freq:** 17 issues yearly; **Cover Price:** Free; **Circ:** 110,000
Usual Pagination: 108
Editor: Ahmed Chaibi
Profile: Magazine with offer of real estate agencies.
Language(s): Czech
ADVERTISING RATES:
Full Page Colour .... CZK 57000
Mechanical Data: Type Area: 196 x 252mm
BUSINESS: FINANCE & ECONOMICS: Property

GRAND ZDRAVÍ A KRÁSA
1700174CZ74G-10
Editorial: Vinohradská 174, 13000 PRAHA 3
Tel: 272107111 **Fax:** 272107000
Email: grandprinc@grandprinc.cz **Web site:** http://www.grandprinc.cz
Date Established: 27.09.04; **Freq:** Monthly; **Annual Sub.:** CZK 216; **Circ:** 30,000
Usual Pagination: 68
Editor: Iva Nováková
Profile: Magazine about life style, cosmetics etc.
Language(s): Czech
ADVERTISING RATES:
Full Page Colour .... CZK 60000
Mechanical Data: Type Area: 196 x 252mm
CONSUMER: WOMEN'S INTEREST CONSUMER MAGAZINES: Slimming & Health

HAIR & BEAUTY
1700186CZ74H-1
Editorial: Malířská 16, 17000 PRAHA 7
Tel: 233372877 **Fax:** 233372877
Email: redakce@vydavatelstvihs.cz **Web site:** http://www.vydavatelstvihs.cz
ISSN: 1211-8273
Date Established: 07.04.97; **Freq:** Monthly; **Cover Price:** CZK 69
Annual Sub.: CZK 474; **Circ:** 30,000
Usual Pagination: 64
Editor: Stanislava Stiborová
Profile: Magazine about fashion and cosmetics.
Language(s): Czech
ADVERTISING RATES:
Full Page Colour .... CZK 99000
Mechanical Data: Type Area: 182 x 262mm
CONSUMER: WOMEN'S INTEREST CONSUMER MAGAZINES: Hair & Beauty

HALENKY, SUKNĚ, KALHOTY (EDICE BURDA)
1700187CZ74B-11
Editorial: Přemyslovská 2845/43, 13000 PRAHA 3
Tel: 222513525 **Fax:** 222522648
Email: inzerce@burda.cz **Web site:** http://www.burda.cz
Date Established: 01.01.95; **Freq:** Half-yearly; **Cover Price:** Free; **Circ:** 40,000
Usual Pagination: 56
Editor: Eva Coufalová
Profile: Magazine about clothes and fashion.
Language(s): Czech
CONSUMER: WOMEN'S INTEREST CONSUMER MAGAZINES: Women's Interest - Fashion

HALÓ NOVINY
1700188CZ73-213
Editorial: Politických vězňů 9, P.O.Box 836, 11121 PRAHA 1 **Tel:** 224229740 **Fax:** 224224822
Email: inzerce@futura.cz **Web site:** http://www.halonoviny.cz
ISSN: 1210-1494
Date Established: 06.06.91; **Freq:** 312 issues yearly; **Cover Price:** CZK 10; **Circ:** 70,000
Usual Pagination: 16
Editor: Pavel Šafránek
Profile: Left-wing newspaper.
Language(s): Czech
ADVERTISING RATES:
Full Page Colour .... CZK 80000
Mechanical Data: Type Area: 296 x 433mm
CONSUMER: NATIONAL & INTERNATIONAL PERIODICALS

HAPPY BABY
1799458CZ74A-441
Editorial: Nad Údolím 3, 14700 PRAHA 4
Email: prosam@prosam.cz **Web site:** http://www.prosam.cz
Freq: Annual; **Cover Price:** Free; **Circ:** 115,000
Usual Pagination: 150
Profile: Magazine for mothers of newborn children.
Language(s): Czech
ADVERTISING RATES:
Full Page Colour .... CZK 130000
Mechanical Data: Type Area: 156 x 204mm
CONSUMER: WOMEN'S INTEREST CONSUMER MAGAZINES: Women's Interest

HARPER'S BAZAAR
1700194CZ74A-406
Editorial: Drtinova 8, 15000 PRAHA 5
Tel: 234109127-30 **Fax:** 234109114
Email: esquire@stratosfera.cz **Web site:** http://www.stratosfera.cz
ISSN: 1211-5371
Date Established: 15.11.96; **Freq:** Monthly; **Cover Price:** CZK 99,90
Annual Sub.: CZK 1099; **Circ:** 70,000
Usual Pagination: 148
Editor: Barbara Nesvadbová
Profile: Magazine for women - life style, fashion, cosmetics etc.
Language(s): Czech
ADVERTISING RATES:
Full Page Colour .... CZK 213000
CONSUMER: WOMEN'S INTEREST CONSUMER MAGAZINES: Women's Interest

HATTRICK
1700200CZ75B-5
Editorial: Roháčova 77, 13000 PRAHA 3
Tel: 271772197-8 **Fax:** 271770551
Email: hattrick@hattrick.cz **Web site:** http://www.hattrick.cz
ISSN: 1212-6756
Date Established: 05.10.99; **Freq:** Monthly; **Cover Price:** CZK 59,50; **Circ:** 50,000
Usual Pagination: 100
Editor: Martin Svoboda
Profile: Magazine about football.
Language(s): Czech
CONSUMER: SPORT: Football

HOSPODÁŘSKÉ NOVINY
1200761CZ65A-5
Editorial: Dobrovského 25, 17055 PRAHA 7
Tel: 233073001 **Fax:** 233072307
Web site: http://www.economia.cz
ISSN: 0862-9587
Date Established: 14.04.1957; **Freq:** 260 issues yearly; **Cover Price:** CZK 23
Annual Sub.: CZK 2848; **Circ:** 60,848
Usual Pagination: 10
Editor: Petr Šimůnek
Profile: Business and finance newspaper.
Language(s): Czech
Readership: Aimed at business professionals.
ADVERTISING RATES:
Full Page Colour .... CZK 495720
Mechanical Data: No. of Columns (Display): 6, Type Area: 295 x 425mm
NATIONAL DAILY & SUNDAY NEWSPAPERS: National Daily Newspapers

HOUSER
1700268CZ89C-7
Editorial: 5. května 63, 14200 PRAHA 4
Tel: 261222541 **Fax:** 261212524
Email: houser@houser.cz **Web site:** http://www.houser.cz
Date Established: 05.10.00; **Freq:** Weekly; **Cover Price:** Free; **Circ:** 70,000
Usual Pagination: 52
Editor: Ondřej Franta
Profile: Magazine with up-to date programs of culture events.
Language(s): Czech
ADVERTISING RATES:
Full Page Colour .... CZK 80000
Mechanical Data: Type Area: 131 x 180mm
CONSUMER: HOLIDAYS & TRAVEL: Entertainment Guides

HRM
1776653CZ14F-2
Editorial: Dobrovského 25, 17055 PRAHA 7
Tel: 233071634 **Fax:** 233072024
Email: economia@economia.cz **Web site:** http://www.economia.cz
ISSN: 1801-4690
Date Established: 21.11.05; **Freq:** 24 issues yearly; **Cover Price:** CZK 155
Annual Sub.: CZK 930; **Circ:** 10,000
Usual Pagination: 84
Editor: Alena Kazdová
Profile: Magazine for management about recruitment, employee motivation and education.
Language(s): Czech
ADVERTISING RATES:
Full Page Colour .... CZK 57000
Mechanical Data: Type Area: 143 x 216mm
BUSINESS: COMMERCE, INDUSTRY & MANAGEMENT: Training & Recruitment

INSTINKT
1700374CZ89C-8
Editorial: Panská 7/890, Kaunický palác, 11000 PRAHA 1 **Tel:** 296827110 **Fax:** 224239408
Email: tyden@tyden.cz **Web site:** http://www.tyden.cz
ISSN: 1213-774X
Date Established: 18.04.02; **Freq:** Weekly; **Cover Price:** CZK 29; **Circ:** 45,070
Usual Pagination: 76
Editor: Tomáš Skočdopole
Profile: Social periodical with reportage topics similar to German magazine Stern. Readership profile: 25 - 45 years, women 65%, men 35%, graduates, net monthly income over 20.000 CZK, available in larger towns.
Language(s): Czech
ADVERTISING RATES:
Full Page Colour .... CZK 159000
Mechanical Data: Type Area: 190 x 240,8mm
CONSUMER: HOLIDAYS & TRAVEL: Entertainment Guides

IRON MAN
1700397CZ75A-212
Editorial: Livornská 430, 10900 PRAHA 10
Tel: 605571745
Email: ronnie@ronnie.cz **Web site:** http://ironman.ronnie.cz
Date Established: 21.03.05; **Freq:** 24 issues yearly; **Cover Price:** CZK 99
Annual Sub.: CZK 470; **Circ:** 30,000
Usual Pagination: 168
Editor: Martin Jebas
Profile: Magazine about body-building and fitness.
Language(s): Czech
ADVERTISING RATES:
Full Page Colour .... CZK 50000
Mechanical Data: Type Area: 175 x 270mm
CONSUMER: SPORT

JACKIE
1700406CZ74Q-6
Editorial: Drtinova 8, 15000 PRAHA 5
Tel: 234109304 **Fax:** 234109241
Email: esquire@stratosfera.cz **Web site:** http://www.stratosfera.cz
ISSN: 1214-195X
Date Established: 09.04.03; **Freq:** Weekly; **Cover Price:** CZK 14,90; **Circ:** 110,000
Usual Pagination: 68
Editor: Denisa Kmeťová
Profile: Exclusive women's journal about life style.
Language(s): Czech
ADVERTISING RATES:
Full Page Colour .... CZK 179000
CONSUMER: WOMEN'S INTEREST CONSUMER MAGAZINES: Lifestyle

JAK NA POČÍTAČ
1700492CZ5B-24
Editorial: Holandská 8, Spielberk Office Centre, 63900 BRNO **Tel:** 545113711 **Fax:** 545113712
Email: redakce@cpress.cz **Web site:** http://www.cpress.cz
ISSN: 1214-1917
Date Established: 06.03.03; **Freq:** Monthly; **Cover Price:** CZK 49
Annual Sub.: CZK 499; **Circ:** 30,000
Usual Pagination: 68
Editor: Pavel Nygrýn
Profile: Computer magazine for beginners.
Language(s): Czech
ADVERTISING RATES:
Full Page Colour .... CZK 72000
BUSINESS: COMPUTERS & AUTOMATION: Data Processing

JEZDECTVÍ
1700507CZ81D-3
Editorial: Křižíkova 35 (2. patro), 18600 PRAHA 8
Tel: 221863306 **Fax:** 221863306
Email: shootmag@volny.cz **Web site:** http://www.strelecka-revue.cz
ISSN: 1210-5406
Date Established: 01.01.1953; **Freq:** Monthly; **Cover Price:** CZK 59
Annual Sub.: CZK 468; **Circ:** 25,390
Usual Pagination: 116
Editor: Zdeňka Motyginová
Profile: Magazine about horse riding.
Language(s): Czech; Slovak
ADVERTISING RATES:
Full Page Colour .... CZK 36000
Mechanical Data: Type Area: 179 x 260mm
CONSUMER: ANIMALS & PETS: Horses & Ponies

JIŽNÍ LISTY (OSTRAVA)
1700530CZ67B-208
Editorial: Na Poříčí 8, 11000 PRAHA 1
Tel: 558841880
Email: strategic@consultants.cz **Web site:** http://www.consultants.cz
Date Established: 01.01.00; **Freq:** Monthly; **Cover Price:** Free; **Circ:** 48,000
Usual Pagination: 16
Editor: Ivana Sachrová
Profile: Newsletter of region South Ostrava.
Language(s): Czech
ADVERTISING RATES:
Full Page Colour .... CZK 37500
Mechanical Data: Type Area: 182 x 264mm
REGIONAL DAILY & SUNDAY NEWSPAPERS: Regional Daily Newspapers

JOY
1700536CZ74-5
Editorial: Přemyslovská 2845/43, 13000 PRAHA 3
Tel: 221589141 **Fax:** 221589368
Email: inzerce@burda.cz **Web site:** http://www.burda.cz
Date Established: 01.10.05; **Freq:** Monthly; **Cover Price:** CZK 29; **Circ:** 78,500
Usual Pagination: 168
Profile: Women's magazine.
Language(s): Czech
ADVERTISING RATES:
Full Page Colour .... CZK 195000
Mechanical Data: Type Area: 138 x 190mm
CONSUMER: WOMEN'S INTEREST CONSUMER MAGAZINES

JUICY
1700538CZ74A-408
Editorial: Mezi Vodami 1952/9, 14300 PRAHA 4 - MODŘANY **Tel:** 225276111 **Fax:** 225276333
Email: inzerce@mf.cz **Web site:** http://www.mf.cz
Date Established: 01.10.03; **Freq:** Monthly; **Cover Price:** CZK 69
Annual Sub.: CZK 539; **Circ:** 45,000
Usual Pagination: 148
Editor: Eva Rýznerová
Profile: Magazine for women aged 25-35 years.
Language(s): Czech
ADVERTISING RATES:
Full Page Colour .... CZK 160000
Mechanical Data: Type Area: 183 x 235mm
CONSUMER: WOMEN'S INTEREST CONSUMER MAGAZINES: Women's Interest

K REVUE
1700541CZ84B-7
Editorial: Heranova 1550/1, P.O.Box 15, 15500 PRAHA 5 - STODŮLKY **Tel:** 224810146
Email: k-revue@sendme.cz
Date Established: 01.08.98; **Freq:** Monthly; **Cover Price:** Free; **Circ:** 30,000
Usual Pagination: 32
Editor: Jana Hamerníková - Dlouhá
Profile: Magazine about literature, book news.
Language(s): Czech
ADVERTISING RATES:
Full Page Colour .... CZK 10000
CONSUMER: THE ARTS & LITERARY: Literary

KALIMERA
1700552CZ89A-77
Editorial: Krakovská 18, 11000 PRAHA 1
Tel: 222211739 **Fax:** 222211739
Email: redakce@kalimera.cz **Web site:** http://www.studentskydiar.cz/onas/onas.html
ISSN: 1214-0775
Date Established: 01.01.00; **Freq:** Quarterly; **Annual Sub.:** CZK 75; **Circ:** 30,000
Usual Pagination: 8
Editor: Kateřina Sekyrková
Profile: Magazine about tourism and travel.
Language(s): Czech
Mechanical Data: Type Area: 271 x 380mm
CONSUMER: HOLIDAYS & TRAVEL: Travel

KAM V PRAZE
1776889CZ89C-44
Editorial: Jankovského 45, 17000 PRAHA 7
Tel: 266712487 **Fax:** 266712487
Email: ipr@volny.cz
Freq: Annual; **Cover Price:** Free; **Circ:** 40,000
Usual Pagination: 90
Editor: Jana Magličová
Profile: Prague quide.
Language(s): Czech
CONSUMER: HOLIDAYS & TRAVEL: Entertainment Guides

KATKA
763801CZ74A-100
Editorial: Přemyslovská 2845/43, 13000 PRAHA 3
Tel: 222520617 **Fax:** 222522648
Email: inzerce@burda.cz **Web site:** http://www.burda.cz
ISSN: 1211-1546
Date Established: 17.05.95; **Freq:** Weekly; **Cover Price:** CZK 10; **Circ:** 106,400
Usual Pagination: 84
Editor: Petra Fundová
Profile: Weekly for contemporary women with information from areas fashion, cosmetics, health and modern nutrition, living, with tips for beauty and wellbeing.
Language(s): Czech
Readership: Aimed at women.
ADVERTISING RATES:
Full Page Colour .... CZK 200000
Mechanical Data: Type Area: 173 x 224mm
CONSUMER: WOMEN'S INTEREST CONSUMER MAGAZINES: Women's Interest

Czech Republic

KATKA NÁŠ ÚTULNÝ BYT
1701108CZ74C-24
Editorial: Přemyslovská 2845/43, 13000 PRAHA 3
Tel: 222520617 **Fax:** 222522648
Email: inzerce@burda.cz **Web site:** http://www.burda.cz
ISSN: 1212-4788
Date Established: 01.03.99; **Freq:** Monthly; **Cover Price:** CZK 29,90
Annual Sub.: CZK 312; **Circ:** 38,000
Usual Pagination: 76
Editor: Petra Fundová
Profile: Magazine about housing.
Language(s): Czech
ADVERTISING RATES:
Full Page Colour .... CZK 75000
Mechanical Data: Type Area: 200 x 258mm
CONSUMER: WOMEN'S INTEREST CONSUMER MAGAZINES: Home & Family

KATKA NEJLEPŠÍ RECEPTY
1701149CZ74P-15
Editorial: Přemyslovská 2845/43, 13000 PRAHA 3
Tel: 222520617 **Fax:** 222522648
Email: inzerce@burda.cz **Web site:** http://www.burda.cz
ISSN: 1211-6254
Date Established: 01.01.97; **Freq:** Monthly; **Cover Price:** CZK 19
Annual Sub.: CZK 432; **Circ:** 27,000
Usual Pagination: 68
Editor: Jarmila Jarolímková
Profile: The best recipes for cooking.
Language(s): Czech
ADVERTISING RATES:
Full Page Colour .... CZK 95000
Mechanical Data: Type Area: 195 x 247mm
CONSUMER: WOMEN'S INTEREST CONSUMER MAGAZINES: Food & Cookery

KLADNO
1700603CZ67J-190
Editorial: náměstí Starosty Pavla 44, 27201 KLADNO, OKR. KLADNO
Email: noviny@mestokladno.cz **Web site:** http://www.mestokladno.cz
Date Established: 01.04.03; **Freq:** Monthly; **Cover Price:** Free; **Circ:** 37,000
Usual Pagination: 12
Profile: Newsletter of Kladno.
Language(s): Czech
ADVERTISING RATES:
Full Page Colour .... CZK 75300
Mechanical Data: Type Area: 285 x 435mm
REGIONAL DAILY & SUNDAY NEWSPAPERS: Regional Newspapers (excl. dailies)

KOKTEJL
1700632CZ89A-16
Editorial: Klíšská 1432/18, 40001 ÚSTÍ NAD LABEM
Tel: 475216177 **Fax:** 475207705
Email: magazin@koktejl.cz **Web site:** http://www.czech-press.cz
ISSN: 1210-4353
Date Established: 01.04.92; **Freq:** Monthly; **Cover Price:** CZK 69
Annual Sub.: CZK 690; **Circ:** 35,800
Usual Pagination: 148
Editor: Dagmar Cestrová
Profile: Social magazine, travelogues from interesting places.
Language(s): Czech
ADVERTISING RATES:
Full Page Colour .... CZK 185000
Mechanical Data: Type Area: 195 x 285mm
CONSUMER: HOLIDAYS & TRAVEL: Travel

KOKTEJL EXTRA PRO ŽENY
1776900CZ74P-21
Editorial: Klíšská 1432/18, 40001 ÚSTÍ NAD LABEM
Tel: 475216183 **Fax:** 475216182
Email: magazin@koktejl.cz **Web site:** http://www.czech-press.cz
Date Established: 01.01.06; **Freq:** Half-yearly; **Cover Price:** CZK 30; **Circ:** 30,000
Usual Pagination: 124
Editor: Barbora Literová
Profile: Magazine about gastronomy.
Language(s): Czech
ADVERTISING RATES:
Full Page Colour .... CZK 129000
Mechanical Data: Type Area: 158 x 249mm
CONSUMER: WOMEN'S INTEREST CONSUMER MAGAZINES: Food & Cookery

KOKTEJL SPECIÁL
1776668CZ89A-52
Editorial: Klíšská 1432/18, 40001 ÚSTÍ NAD LABEM
Tel: 475216177 **Fax:** 475207705
Email: magazin@koktejl.cz **Web site:** http://www.czech-press.cz
Date Established: 01.01.06; **Freq:** 5 issues yearly; **Cover Price:** CZK 29; **Circ:** 30,000
Usual Pagination: 100
Editor: Barbora Literová
Profile: Travel guide.
Language(s): Czech
ADVERTISING RATES:
Full Page Colour .... CZK 129000
Mechanical Data: Type Area: 158 x 249mm
CONSUMER: HOLIDAYS & TRAVEL: Travel

KONKURSNÍ NOVINY
1700647CZ44-10
Editorial: Pod křížkem 1774/2, 14100 PRAHA 4 - BRANÍK **Tel:** 241483161 **Fax:** 241481639
Email: knredakce@kn.cz **Web site:** http://www.kn.cz
ISSN: 1213-4023
Date Established: 01.01.97; **Freq:** 26 issues yearly; **Cover Price:** CZK 25
Annual Sub.: CZK 523; **Circ:** 5,000
Usual Pagination: 16
Editor: Karel Žitek
Profile: Newspaper focused on bankruptcy proceedings.
Language(s): Czech
ADVERTISING RATES:
Full Page Mono .... CZK 49000
Mechanical Data: Type Area: 280 x 412mm
BUSINESS: LEGAL

KONSTRUKCE
1700649CZ19E-3
Editorial: Českobratrská 1663/6, 70200 OSTRAVA
Tel: 595136028 **Fax:** 595136026
Email: redakce@konstrukce.cz **Web site:** http://www.konstrukce.cz
ISSN: 1213-8762
Date Established: 01.01.00; **Freq:** 24 issues yearly; **Cover Price:** CZK 100
Annual Sub.: CZK 606; **Circ:** 3,000
Usual Pagination: 74
Editor: Stanislav Cieslar
Profile: Professional magazine about metalworking industry and iron constructions.
Language(s): Czech
ADVERTISING RATES:
Full Page Colour .... CZK 48000
Mechanical Data: Type Area: 176 x 261mm
BUSINESS: ENGINEERING & MACHINERY: Machinery, Machine Tools & Metalworking

KRAJ VYSOČINA
1700680CZ67J-196
Editorial: Netín 306, 59444 RADOSTÍN NAD OSLAVOU **Tel:** 566545066 **Fax:** 566545066
Email: petros.martakidis@email.cz **Web site:** http://www.kr-vysocina.cz
Date Established: 30.01.04; **Freq:** Monthly; **Cover Price:** Free; **Circ:** 215,000
Usual Pagination: 12
Editor: Petros Martakidis
Profile: Newspaper of Vysocina.
Language(s): Czech
ADVERTISING RATES:
Full Page Colour .... CZK 164700
Mechanical Data: Type Area: 285 x 435mm
REGIONAL DAILY & SUNDAY NEWSPAPERS: Regional Newspapers (excl. dailies)

KRAJSKÉ LISTY
1700569CZ67J-184
Editorial: Husova 29, 30100 PLZEŇ **Tel:** 353565500
Fax: 353565500
Email: plzen@consultants.cz **Web site:** http://www.consultants.cz
Date Established: 01.09.03; **Freq:** Monthly; **Cover Price:** Free; **Circ:** 132,000
Usual Pagination: 8
Editor: Jaroslav Fikar
Profile: Newsletter of Karlovy Vary.
Language(s): Czech
ADVERTISING RATES:
Full Page Colour .... CZK 117600
Mechanical Data: Type Area: 285 x 435mm
REGIONAL DAILY & SUNDAY NEWSPAPERS: Regional Newspapers (excl. dailies)

KRAJSKÉ NOVINY
1700682CZ67J-197
Editorial: Kancelářská budova P8, č.p.80, 53353 PARDUBICE - SEMTÍN **Tel:** 466611139
Fax: 466611139
Email: redakce@bulvarpress.cz **Web site:** http://www.bulvarpress.cz
ISSN: 1213-9998
Date Established: 01.03.01; **Freq:** Monthly; **Cover Price:** CZK 15
Annual Sub.: CZK 180; **Circ:** 40,000
Usual Pagination: 12
Editor: Jarmila Kudláčková
Profile: Newspaper focused on politics, culture and regional economy in Pardubice and Hradec Kralove.
Language(s): Czech
ADVERTISING RATES:
Full Page Colour .... CZK 146749
Mechanical Data: Type Area: 276 x 409mm
REGIONAL DAILY & SUNDAY NEWSPAPERS: Regional Newspapers (excl. dailies)

KŘÍŽKOVÁ VÝŠIVKA (VELKÁ EDICE BURDA)
1700711CZ74E-2
Editorial: Přemyslovská 2845/43, 13000 PRAHA 3
Tel: 221589111 **Fax:** 222522648
Email: inzerce@burda.cz **Web site:** http://www.burda.cz
Date Established: 01.01.97; **Freq:** Half-yearly; **Annual Sub.:** CZK 160; **Circ:** 40,000
Profile: Magazine about needlework.
Language(s): Czech
CONSUMER: WOMEN'S INTEREST CONSUMER MAGAZINES: Crafts

KULTURA (PLZEŇ)
1700743CZ84A-27
Editorial: Kovářská 4, 30483 PLZEŇ **Tel:** 377168301
Fax: 377227215
Email: plzensky.denik@zapad.vlp.cz **Web site:** http://www.vlp.cz
Date Established: 01.01.95; **Freq:** Monthly; **Cover Price:** CZK 7; **Circ:** 31,000
Usual Pagination: 32
Editor: Jan Pertl
Profile: Magazine about culture activities in Plzen.
Language(s): Czech
ADVERTISING RATES:
Full Page Mono .... CZK 21600
Mechanical Data: Type Area: 205 x 280mm
CONSUMER: THE ARTS & LITERARY: Arts

KURÝR PRAHA
1776682CZ72-1
Editorial: Na jetelce 2/69, 19000 PRAHA 9
Email: kuryr@kuryr.org
Date Established: 19.04.06; **Freq:** Weekly; **Cover Price:** Free; **Circ:** 300,000
Usual Pagination: 16
Editor: Monika Čepeláková
Profile: Weekly newsletter distributed to residents in Prague.
Language(s): Czech
ADVERTISING RATES:
Full Page Colour .... CZK 172500
Mechanical Data: Type Area: 212 x 285mm
LOCAL NEWSPAPERS

KVALITA PRO ŽIVOT
1700494CZ14K-3
Editorial: Mariánské náměstí 480/5, 70928 OSTRAVA - MARIÁNSKÉ HORY **Tel:** 596625451
Fax: 596632267
Email: dto@ova.eridan.cz **Web site:** http://www.dtostrava.cz
ISSN: 1803-9138
Freq: Half-yearly; **Cover Price:** Free; **Circ:** 1,000
Usual Pagination: 70
Editor: Kateřina Látalová, Ph.D.
Profile: Magazine about quality and technical specifications.
Language(s): Czech
ADVERTISING RATES:
Full Page Colour .... CZK 7000
BUSINESS: COMMERCE, INDUSTRY & MANAGEMENT: Quality Assurance

LÉKY A LÉKÁRNA
1700777CZ74G-12
Editorial: Peckova 280/9, 18000 PRAHA 8 - KARLÍN
Tel: 224252435 **Fax:** 224516048
Email: edukafarm@edukafarm.cz **Web site:** http://www.edukafarm.cz
ISSN: 1214-5009
Date Established: 01.11.03; **Freq:** Quarterly; **Cover Price:** Free; **Circ:** 250,000
Usual Pagination: 24
Editor: Zdeněk Procházka
Profile: Magazine about health. It is distributed in doctors' waiting rooms, in policlinics and hospitals.
Language(s): Czech
ADVERTISING RATES:
Full Page Colour .... CZK 190000
CONSUMER: WOMEN'S INTEREST CONSUMER MAGAZINES: Slimming & Health

LESNICKÁ PRÁCE
1500449CZ46-10
Editorial: Zámek 1, P.O.Box 25, 28163 KOSTELEC NAD ČERNÝMI LESY **Tel:** 604211167
Fax: 321679413-4
Email: lesprace@iol.cz **Web site:** http://www.silvarium.cz
ISSN: 0322-9254
Date Established: 01.01.1922; **Freq:** Monthly; **Cover Price:** CZK 57,50
Annual Sub.: CZK 726; **Circ:** 4,200
Usual Pagination: 72
Editor: Jan Příhoda
Profile: Magazine about forestry.
Language(s): Czech
Readership: Aimed at the forestry community.
ADVERTISING RATES:
Full Page Colour .... CZK 30000
Mechanical Data: Type Area: 185 x 255mm
BUSINESS: TIMBER, WOOD & FORESTRY

LEVNÉ RECEPTY SPECIÁL
1700793CZ74P-12
Editorial: náměstí Antonie Bejdové 1791/5, 70800 OSTRAVA - PORUBA **Tel:** 596638024
Fax: 596638024
Email: vydav.suchy@volny.cz **Web site:** http://www.volny.cz/vydav.suchy
Date Established: 10.07.93; **Freq:** 24 issues yearly; **Cover Price:** CZK 35; **Circ:** 18,000
Usual Pagination: 36
Editor: Jarmila Suchá
Profile: Collection of recipes.
Language(s): Czech
ADVERTISING RATES:
Full Page Mono .... CZK 5000
CONSUMER: WOMEN'S INTEREST CONSUMER MAGAZINES: Food & Cookery

LIBERECKÝ KRAJ
1700798CZ67J-203
Editorial: Rumunská 655/9, 46001 LIBEREC 1
Email: obchod@genus.tv **Web site:** http://www.r1genus.cz
Date Established: 26.06.04; **Freq:** Monthly; **Cover Price:** Free; **Circ:** 182,000
Usual Pagination: 8
Profile: Newspaper focused on current affairs, cultural and sport events in Liberec region.
Language(s): Czech
ADVERTISING RATES:
Full Page Colour .... CZK 100000
Mechanical Data: Type Area: 280 x 420mm
REGIONAL DAILY & SUNDAY NEWSPAPERS: Regional Newspapers (excl. dailies)

LIDOVÉ NOVINY
1202624CZ65A-10
Editorial: Karla Engliše 519/11, 15000 PRAHA 5
Tel: 225067111 **Fax:** 225067199
Email: mfdnes@mfdnes.cz **Web site:** http://www.idnes.cz
ISSN: 0862-5921
Date Established: 02.04.92; **Freq:** 312 issues yearly; **Cover Price:** CZK 15
Annual Sub.: CZK 2512,5; **Circ:** 75,985
Usual Pagination: 24
Editor: Dalibor Balšínek
Profile: National newspaper.
Language(s): Czech
Readership: Aimed at those interested in current affairs.
ADVERTISING RATES:
Full Page Colour .... CZK 295974
Mechanical Data: No. of Columns (Display): 6, Type Area: 285 x 435mm
NATIONAL DAILY & SUNDAY NEWSPAPERS: National Daily Newspapers

LIDOVÉ RECEPTY SPECIÁL
1700806CZ74P-13
Editorial: Staňkova 18a, 70030 OSTRAVA 3
Tel: 596737053 **Fax:** 596737053
Email: recepty-sova@volny.cz
Freq: Quarterly; **Cover Price:** CZK 23,50; **Circ:** 56,000
Usual Pagination: 16
Editor: Zdeněk Kamenčák
Profile: Culinary magazine with recipes.
Language(s): Czech
CONSUMER: WOMEN'S INTEREST CONSUMER MAGAZINES: Food & Cookery

LIFESTYLE PRO MOU RODINU
1793143CZ74A-439
Editorial: Sladkovského nám. 302/5, 13000 PRAHA 3
Tel: 222780211 **Fax:** 222780211
Email: tee@free-dee.cz **Web site:** http://www.free-dee.cz
ISSN: 1802-1417
Date Established: 01.06.04; **Freq:** Quarterly; **Cover Price:** Free; **Circ:** 65,000
Usual Pagination: 164
Editor: Nicol Schlezáková
Profile: Family magazine about health care.
Language(s): Czech
ADVERTISING RATES:
Full Page Colour .... CZK 62400
CONSUMER: WOMEN'S INTEREST CONSUMER MAGAZINES: Women's Interest

LISTY HLAVNÍHO MĚSTA PRAHY
1700823CZ72J-223
Editorial: Vinohradská 1597/174, 13000 PRAHA 3
Tel: 272107323
Email: redakce@listypraha.cz **Web site:** http://www.tardus.cz
Date Established: 01.10.01; **Freq:** Monthly; **Cover Price:** Free; **Circ:** 60,000
Usual Pagination: 16
Editor: Vlastimil Svehna
Profile: Magazine about news in Prague.
Language(s): Czech
ADVERTISING RATES:
Full Page Colour .... CZK 170000
Mechanical Data: Type Area: 281 x 433mm
LOCAL NEWSPAPERS: Community Newsletters

LOBBY
1700847CZ1A-38
Editorial: Myslíkova 25, 11000 PRAHA 1
Tel: 221406221 **Fax:** 224930016
Email: redakce@lobby.cz **Web site:** http://www.lobby.cz
ISSN: 1212-4524
Date Established: 21.01.99; **Freq:** Monthly; **Cover Price:** CZK 29
Annual Sub.: CZK 453,6; **Circ:** 15,000
Usual Pagination: 36
Editor: Ivana Šmejdová
Profile: Magazine of Hospodarska komora Ceske republiky.
Language(s): Czech
ADVERTISING RATES:
Full Page Colour .... CZK 49000
Mechanical Data: Type Area: 205 x 252mm
BUSINESS: FINANCE & ECONOMICS

LOOK MAGAZINE
1700855CZ74A-443
Editorial: Legerova 26, 11000 PRAHA 1
Tel: 224262881 **Fax:** 224261589
Email: look@lookmagazine.cz **Web site:** http://www.lookmagazine.cz
ISSN: 1214-3405
Date Established: 01.10.03; **Freq:** 24 issues yearly; **Cover Price:** CZK 59; **Circ:** 15,500
Usual Pagination: 148
Editor: Renáta Vojtíšková

Profile: Lifestyle magazine for women.
Language(s): Czech
ADVERTISING RATES:
Full Page Colour .... CZK 140000
CONSUMER: WOMEN'S INTEREST CONSUMER MAGAZINES: Women's Interest

LOVE STAR
1700863CZ74A-444
Editorial: Drtinova 8, 15000 PRAHA 5
Tel: 234109194 **Fax:** 234109241
Email: esquire@stratosfera.cz **Web site:** http://www.stratosfera.cz
ISSN: 1801-3821
Date Established: 23.09.05; **Freq:** Monthly; **Cover Price:** CZK 21,90
Annual Sub.: CZK 219; **Circ:** 90,000
Usual Pagination: 172
Editor: Michaela Holinková - Popková
Profile: Women's magazine. It is divided into 3 parts: Miss (18-25 years), Woman (26-34 years) and Lady (35-45 years).
Language(s): Czech
ADVERTISING RATES:
Full Page Colour .... CZK 99000
CONSUMER: WOMEN'S INTEREST CONSUMER MAGAZINES: Women's Interest

LUXURY GUIDE
1700869CZ52C-1
Editorial: Na Maninách 14, 17000 PRAHA 7
Tel: 257312248 **Fax:** 257312248
Email: info@luxuryguide.cz **Web site:** http://www.luxuryguide.cz
Date Established: 01.04.01; **Freq:** Quarterly; **Cover Price:** CZK 99
Annual Sub.: CZK 396; **Circ:** 18,000
Usual Pagination: 200
Editor: Kateřina Daňková
Profile: Magazine dealing with luxury goods.
Language(s): Czech; English
BUSINESS: GIFT TRADE: Fancy Goods

MADAME RENÉE
1700872CZ74B-12
Editorial: Na Příkopě 25, 11000 PRAHA 1
Tel: 221967233 **Fax:** 221967233
Email: info@renee.cz **Web site:** http://www.renee.cz
ISSN: 1802-8586
Date Established: 30.03.05; **Freq:** Monthly; **Cover Price:** CZK 79
Annual Sub.: CZK 1100; **Circ:** 50,000
Usual Pagination: 196
Editor: Zdeněk Podhůrský
Profile: Exclusive fashion magazine for women aged 30+.
Language(s): Czech
ADVERTISING RATES:
Full Page Colour .... CZK 220000
Mechanical Data: Type Area: 190 x 253mm
CONSUMER: WOMEN'S INTEREST CONSUMER MAGAZINES: Women's Interest - Fashion

MAGAZÍN DNES + TV
1700877CZ73-230
Editorial: Karla Engliše 519/11, 15000 PRAHA 5
Tel: 225062206 **Fax:** 225062203
Email: mfdnes@mfdnes.cz **Web site:** http://www.idnes.cz
ISSN: 1210-1168
Date Established: 01.08.92; **Freq:** Weekly; **Circ:** 456,426
Usual Pagination: 60
Profile: Relaxation family magazine, culture, politics, TV chanels program.
Language(s): Czech
ADVERTISING RATES:
Full Page Colour .... CZK 377000
Mechanical Data: Type Area: 181 x 261mm
CONSUMER: NATIONAL & INTERNATIONAL PERIODICALS

MAGAZÍN ZLÍN
1700886CZ82-278
Editorial: Náměstí Míru 12, 76140 ZLÍN, OKR. ZLÍN
Tel: 577630342 **Fax:** 577630342
Email: muzlin@muzlin.cz **Web site:** http://www.zlin.cz
Date Established: 01.01.95; **Freq:** Monthly; **Cover Price:** Free; **Circ:** 34,500
Usual Pagination: 24
Editor: Irena Orságová
Profile: Magazine focused on current events in the town of Zlin.
Language(s): Czech
ADVERTISING RATES:
Full Page Colour .... CZK 38000
Mechanical Data: Type Area: 190 x 277mm
CONSUMER: CURRENT AFFAIRS & POLITICS

MÁMA A JÁ
1776690CZ74D-6
Editorial: Jaurisova 1499/23, 14000 PRAHA 4
Tel: 241401349 **Fax:** 241401485
Email: redakce@mamaaja.cz **Web site:** http://www.mamaaja.cz
ISSN: 1801-8769
Date Established: 01.06.06; **Freq:** Monthly; **Cover Price:** CZK 44; **Circ:** 50,000
Usual Pagination: 124
Editor: Hana Hoffmannová
Profile: Family magazine about children, childbirth, maternity etc.
Language(s): Czech
CONSUMER: WOMEN'S INTEREST CONSUMER MAGAZINES: Child Care

MAMINKA
1700897CZ74A-410
Editorial: Mezi Vodami 1952/9, 14300 PRAHA 4 - MODŘANY **Tel:** 225276239 **Fax:** 225276222
Email: inzerce@mf.cz **Web site:** http://www.mf.cz
ISSN: 1213-5100
Date Established: 01.02.98; **Freq:** Monthly; **Cover Price:** CZK 39
Annual Sub.: CZK 429; **Circ:** 60,000
Usual Pagination: 164
Editor: Markéta Behinová
Profile: Magazine for women-mothers.
Language(s): Czech
ADVERTISING RATES:
Full Page Colour .... CZK 145000
Mechanical Data: Type Area: 173 x 236mm
CONSUMER: WOMEN'S INTEREST CONSUMER MAGAZINES: Women's Interest

MAMITA
1700898CZ74D-4
Editorial: Vídeňská 800, 14000 PRAHA 12 - KUNRATICE **Tel:** 261082424 **Fax:** 261082424
Email: anna.mydlilova@ftn.cz **Web site:** http://www.mamita.cz
ISSN: 1214-1690
Date Established: 01.01.01; **Freq:** Quarterly; **Cover Price:** CZK 33
Annual Sub.: CZK 156; **Circ:** 30,000
Usual Pagination: 44
Editor: Anna Mydlilová
Profile: Magazine about maternity.
Language(s): Czech
ADVERTISING RATES:
Full Page Colour .... CZK 35000
Mechanical Data: Type Area: 190 x 260mm
CONSUMER: WOMEN'S INTEREST CONSUMER MAGAZINES: Child Care

MARATHON MAGAZINE
1776907CZ75A-241
Editorial: Záhořanského 3/1644, 12000 PRAHA 2
Tel: 224919209 **Fax:** 224923355
Email: marathon@pim.cz **Web site:** http://www.pim.cz
Date Established: 01.01.95; **Freq:** Annual; **Cover Price:** Free; **Circ:** 40,000
Usual Pagination: 80
Editor: Katerina Viglialoro
Profile: Magazine about running with sport actions.
Language(s): Czech; English
CONSUMER: SPORT

MARIANNE
1700904CZ74Q-9
Editorial: Na Zátorce 3, 16000 PRAHA 6
Tel: 233023750 **Fax:** 233023701
Email: all@premiere.cz **Web site:** http://www.maxim.cz
ISSN: 1213-1423
Date Established: 15.09.00; **Freq:** Monthly; **Cover Price:** CZK 59
Annual Sub.: CZK 540; **Circ:** 91,600
Usual Pagination: 172
Editor: Klára Olexová
Profile: Magazine for ambitious women - life style, fashion, career, cosmetics, child welfare.
Language(s): Czech
ADVERTISING RATES:
Full Page Colour .... CZK 225000
Mechanical Data: Type Area: 168 x 240mm
CONSUMER: WOMEN'S INTEREST CONSUMER MAGAZINES: Lifestyle

MARIANNE BYDLENÍ
1700905CZ74K-3
Editorial: Na Zátorce 3, 16000 PRAHA 6
Tel: 233023750 **Fax:** 233023701
Email: all@premiere.cz **Web site:** http://www.maxim.cz
ISSN: 1214-5580
Date Established: 12.03.04; **Freq:** Monthly; **Cover Price:** CZK 39; **Circ:** 35,850
Usual Pagination: 126
Editor: Pavlína Blahotová
Profile: Living magazine.
Language(s): Czech
ADVERTISING RATES:
Full Page Colour .... CZK 100000
Mechanical Data: Type Area: 188 x 250mm
CONSUMER: WOMEN'S INTEREST CONSUMER MAGAZINES: Home Purchase

MAXIM
1700921CZ86C-2
Editorial: Na Zátorce 3, 16000 PRAHA 6
Tel: 233023800 **Fax:** 233023801
Email: all@premiere.cz **Web site:** http://www.maxim.cz
ISSN: 1214-1569
Date Established: 29.04.97; **Freq:** Monthly; **Cover Price:** CZK 85
Annual Sub.: CZK 850; **Circ:** 69,900
Usual Pagination: 146
Editor: Pavel Vondráček
Profile: Social magazine for men.
Language(s): Czech
ADVERTISING RATES:
Full Page Colour .... CZK 195000
CONSUMER: ADULT & GAY MAGAZINES: Men's Lifestyle Magazines

MAXIMA MAGAZÍN
1700922CZ1E-9
Editorial: Washingtonova 5, 11000 PRAHA 1
Tel: 221110711 **Fax:** 221110555
Email: magazin@maxima.cz **Web site:** http://www.maxima.cz
Date Established: 01.11.98; **Freq:** Monthly; **Cover Price:** Free; **Circ:** 48,000
Usual Pagination: 28
Editor: Jana Joklová
Profile: Magazine of Maxima reality, property advertising.
Language(s): Czech
ADVERTISING RATES:
Full Page Colour .... CZK 55900
Mechanical Data: Type Area: 186 x 270mm
BUSINESS: FINANCE & ECONOMICS: Property

MEDICAL TRIBUNE
1700930CZ56R-57
Editorial: Na Moráni 5, 12800 PRAHA 2
Tel: 224923724 **Fax:** 224922436
Email: stepanovsky@medical-tribune.cz **Web site:** http://www.medical-tribune.cz
ISSN: 1214-8911
Date Established: 01.01.05; **Freq:** Weekly; **Cover Price:** CZK 24; **Circ:** 20,000
Usual Pagination: 24
Editor: Jaroslav Hořejší
Profile: Medical newspaper.
Language(s): Czech
ADVERTISING RATES:
Full Page Colour .... CZK 85000
Mechanical Data: Type Area: 281 x 388mm
BUSINESS: HEALTH & MEDICAL: Health Medical Related

MEDUŇKA
1700935CZ56R-58
Editorial: Krásova 6, 13000 PRAHA 3 **Tel:** 222722339
Fax: 222722339
Email: manolev@volny.cz
ISSN: 1214-4932
Freq: Monthly; **Cover Price:** CZK 25; **Circ:** 43,220
Usual Pagination: 52
Editor: Ilona Manolevská
Profile: Magazine about alternative posibilities of treatment.
Language(s): Czech
ADVERTISING RATES:
Full Page Colour .... CZK 30000
Mechanical Data: Type Area: 187 x 247mm
BUSINESS: HEALTH & MEDICAL: Health Medical Related

MEN ONLY / WOMAN ONLY
1812859CZ74Q-34
Editorial: Kováků 24, 15500 PRAHA 5
Tel: 225065207 **Fax:** 224215228
Email: sales@metro.cz **Web site:** http://www.metro.cz
Date Established: 16.07.07; **Freq:** Monthly; **Cover Price:** Free; **Circ:** 350,000
Usual Pagination: 112
Editor: Josef Rubeš
Profile: Lifestyle magazine for women and for men.
Language(s): Czech
ADVERTISING RATES:
Full Page Colour .... CZK 340000
Mechanical Data: Type Area: 178 x 255mm
CONSUMER: WOMEN'S INTEREST CONSUMER MAGAZINES: Lifestyle

MEN'S SPORTS
1818745CZ86C-10
Editorial: Šafaříkova 371/22, 12000 PRAHA 2
Tel: 222541049 **Fax:** 222541051
Email: tomiskova@geronia.cz
Date Established: 19.07.07; **Freq:** Weekly; **Cover Price:** CZK 39; **Circ:** 40,000
Usual Pagination: 16
Profile: Magazine for men about politics, culture, sports and society.
Language(s): Czech
ADVERTISING RATES:
Full Page Colour .... CZK 35000
CONSUMER: ADULT & GAY MAGAZINES: Men's Lifestyle Magazines

MĚSÍC V REGIONU
1812860CZ67J-221
Editorial: Mírové náměstí 152/25, 41201 LITOMĚŘICE
Email: ltv@seznam.cz
Date Established: 01.01.07; **Freq:** Monthly; **Cover Price:** Free; **Circ:** 30,000
Usual Pagination: 8
Profile: Monthly newsletter of Litoměřice.
Language(s): Czech
ADVERTISING RATES:
Full Page Colour .... CZK 64000
REGIONAL DAILY & SUNDAY NEWSPAPERS: Regional Newspapers (excl. dailies)

MĚSTSKÉ NOVINY (ÚSTÍ NAD LABEM)
1700957CZ67J-222
Editorial: Velká Hradební 2336/8, 40100 ÚSTÍ NAD LABEM **Tel:** 475241469 **Fax:** 475241830
Email: knotek@mag-ul.cz **Web site:** http://www.usti-nl.cz
Date Established: 01.06.00; **Freq:** 24 issues yearly; **Cover Price:** Free; **Circ:** 44,500
Usual Pagination: 16
Editor: Milan Knotek
Profile: Newspaper of region Usti nad Labem.
Language(s): Czech
ADVERTISING RATES:
Full Page Mono .... CZK 20000
REGIONAL DAILY & SUNDAY NEWSPAPERS: Regional Newspapers (excl. dailies)

METEOROLOGICKÉ ZPRÁVY
1700960CZ64N-3
Editorial: Na Šabatce 2050/17, 14306 PRAHA 4 - KOMOŘANY **Tel:** 244032722 **Fax:** 244032721
Email: horky@chmi.cz **Web site:** http://www.chmi.cz
ISSN: 0026-1173
Date Established: 01.01.1947; **Freq:** 24 issues yearly; **Cover Price:** CZK 20
Annual Sub.: CZK 180; **Circ:** 750
Usual Pagination: 36
Editor: Luboš Němec
Profile: Meteorological newsletter.
Language(s): Czech; English
ADVERTISING RATES:
Full Page Mono .... CZK 5000
BUSINESS: OTHER CLASSIFICATIONS: Weather

METRO
1700962CZ67B-854
Editorial: Kováků 24, 15500 PRAHA 5
Tel: 225065207 **Fax:** 224812602
Email: sales@metro.cz **Web site:** http://www.metro.cz
ISSN: 1211-7811
Date Established: 07.07.97; **Freq:** 260 issues yearly; **Cover Price:** Free; **Circ:** 264,658
Usual Pagination: 24
Editor: Josef Rubeš
Profile: Daily distributed free in Prague underground.
Language(s): Czech
ADVERTISING RATES:
Full Page Colour .... CZK 184680
Mechanical Data: No. of Columns (Display): 5, Type Area: 204 x 286mm
REGIONAL DAILY & SUNDAY NEWSPAPERS: Regional Daily Newspapers

MIMINKO
1700984CZ74D-11
Editorial: Mikanova 3251/7, 10600 PRAHA 10
Tel: 603220960 **Fax:** 603806489
Email: cerna@casopis-miminko.cz **Web site:** http://www.casopis-miminko.cz
Date Established: 01.01.03; **Freq:** Monthly; **Cover Price:** CZK 33; **Circ:** 39,000
Usual Pagination: 84
Editor: Romana Černá
Profile: Magazine for pregnant women and mothers till 3 years old children.
Language(s): Czech
ADVERTISING RATES:
Full Page Colour .... CZK 99000
Mechanical Data: Type Area: 137 x 210mm
CONSUMER: WOMEN'S INTEREST CONSUMER MAGAZINES: Child Care

MLADÁ FRONTA DNES
1202644CZ65A-15
Editorial: Karla Engliše 519/11, 15000 PRAHA 5
Tel: 225062206 **Fax:** 225062203
Email: mfdnes@mfdnes.cz **Web site:** http://www.idnes.cz
ISSN: 1210-1168
Date Established: 09.05.1945; **Freq:** 312 issues yearly; **Cover Price:** CZK 18
Annual Sub.: CZK 2772; **Circ:** 304,642
Usual Pagination: 32
Editor: Robert Čásenský
Profile: National newspaper.
Language(s): Czech
Readership: Aimed at those interested in current affairs.
NATIONAL DAILY & SUNDAY NEWSPAPERS: National Daily Newspapers

MOBILITY
1701010CZ5B-26
Editorial: Holandská 8, Spielberk Office Centre, 63900 BRNO **Tel:** 545113711 **Fax:** 545113712
Email: redakce@cpress.cz **Web site:** http://www.cpress.cz
ISSN: 1212-9879
Date Established: 18.01.99; **Freq:** Monthly; **Cover Price:** CZK 39
Annual Sub.: CZK 499; **Circ:** 23,000
Usual Pagination: 100
Editor: Tomáš Doseděl
Profile: Magazine about mobile telephones, notebooks, palmtops etc.
Language(s): Czech
ADVERTISING RATES:
Full Page Colour .... CZK 83000
BUSINESS: COMPUTERS & AUTOMATION: Data Processing

Czech Republic

MÓDA PRO DĚTI 1701013CZ74B-13
Editorial: Přemyslovská 2845/43, 13000 PRAHA 3
Email: inzerce@burda.cz **Web site:** http://www.burda.cz
Date Established: 01.01.01; **Freq:** Half-yearly; **Cover Price:** Free; **Circ:** 40,000
Profile: Magazine about fashion for small children.
Language(s): Czech
CONSUMER: WOMEN'S INTEREST CONSUMER MAGAZINES: Women's Interest - Fashion

MÓDA PRO DROBNÉ ŽENY 1701014CZ74B-14
Editorial: Přemyslovská 2845/43, 13000 PRAHA 3
Tel: 222513525 **Fax:** 222522648
Email: inzerce@burda.cz **Web site:** http://www.burda.cz
Date Established: 01.01.99; **Freq:** Half-yearly; **Cover Price:** Free; **Circ:** 40,000
Editor: Eva Coufalová
Profile: Magazine about fashion for slight women.
Language(s): Czech
Mechanical Data: Type Area: 194 x 253mm
CONSUMER: WOMEN'S INTEREST CONSUMER MAGAZINES: Women's Interest - Fashion

MÓDA PRO PLNOŠTÍHLÉ 1701015CZ74B-15
Editorial: Přemyslovská 2845/43, 13000 PRAHA 3
Tel: 221589111 **Fax:** 222522648
Email: inzerce@burda.cz **Web site:** http://www.burda.cz
Date Established: 01.01.94; **Freq:** Half-yearly; **Cover Price:** Free; **Circ:** 40,000
Usual Pagination: 60
Profile: Magazine about fashion for buxom women.
Language(s): Czech
CONSUMER: WOMEN'S INTEREST CONSUMER MAGAZINES: Women's Interest - Fashion

MODERNÍ BYT 1701019CZ74C-21
Editorial: Nádražní 762/32, 15000 PRAHA 5
Tel: 225351150 **Fax:** 225351153
Email: info@bmczech.cz **Web site:** http://www.bmczech.cz
ISSN: 1211-6637
Date Established: 25.04.97; **Freq:** Monthly; **Cover Price:** CZK 79,90
Annual Sub.: CZK 828; **Circ:** 20,870
Usual Pagination: 164
Editor: Petr Tschakert
Profile: Magazine about modern housing.
Language(s): Czech
ADVERTISING RATES:
Full Page Colour .... CZK 92000
Mechanical Data: Type Area: 192 x 261mm
CONSUMER: WOMEN'S INTEREST CONSUMER MAGAZINES: Home & Family

MODERNI OBCHOD 1202136CZ53-5
Editorial: Rosmarin Business Center, Dělnická 213/12, Praha 7 - Holešovice, 17000 PRAGUE
Tel: 270003961 **Fax:** 270003977
Email: mobchod@con-praha.cz **Web site:** http://www.mobchod.cz
ISSN: 1210-4094
Date Established: 01; **Freq:** Monthly - měsíčník; **Cover Price:** CZK 80
Annual Sub.: CZK 840; **Circ:** 11,200
Usual Pagination: 74
Editor-in-Chief: Štefan Weber
Profile: Professional magazine for traders.
Language(s): Czech; Slovak
Readership: Aimed at decision makers in purchasing and sales departments, branch and district managers, managing directors and independent retailers in the consumer and capital goods industries.
ADVERTISING RATES:
Full Page Colour .... CZK 100000
Mechanical Data: Type Area: 175 x 258mm, Col Length: 258mm
BUSINESS: RETAILING & WHOLESALING

MOJE GENERACE 40+ 1701034CZ74Q-10
Editorial: Šlikova 62, 16900 PRAHA 6
Tel: 220513184 **Fax:** 233108103
Email: inzerce@mojegenerace.cz **Web site:** http://www.mojegenerace.cz
ISSN: 1214-1453
Date Established: 01.01.03; **Freq:** 24 issues yearly; **Cover Price:** CZK 49
Annual Sub.: CZK 210; **Circ:** 8,000
Usual Pagination: 56
Editor: Marta Csontosová
Profile: Magazine for people 45 years and older.
Language(s): Czech
ADVERTISING RATES:
Full Page Colour .... CZK 59000
Mechanical Data: Type Area: 170 x 245mm
CONSUMER: WOMEN'S INTEREST CONSUMER MAGAZINES: Lifestyle

MOJE PSYCHOLOGIE 1793128CZ56R-124
Editorial: Mezi Vodami 1952/9, 14300 PRAHA 4 - MODŘANY **Tel:** 225276245 **Fax:** 225276222
Email: inzerce@mf.cz **Web site:** http://www.mf.cz
ISSN: 1802-2073
Date Established: 15.11.06; **Freq:** Monthly; **Cover Price:** CZK 69
Annual Sub.: CZK 690; **Circ:** 50,000
Usual Pagination: 140
Editor: Martina Švecová
Profile: Lifestyle magazine about psychology.
Language(s): Czech
ADVERTISING RATES:
Full Page Colour .... CZK 160000
Mechanical Data: Type Area: 173 x 236mm
BUSINESS: HEALTH & MEDICAL: Health Medical Related

MOJE ZDRAVÍ 1701035CZ74G-14
Editorial: Mezi Vodami 1952/9, 14300 PRAHA 4 - MODŘANY **Tel:** 225276294 **Fax:** 225276222
Email: inzerce@mf.cz **Web site:** http://www.mf.cz
ISSN: 1214-3871
Date Established: 01.07.03; **Freq:** Monthly; **Cover Price:** CZK 29
Annual Sub.: CZK 319; **Circ:** 120,000
Usual Pagination: 84
Editor: Marie Hejlová
Profile: Magazine about drug products.
Language(s): Czech
ADVERTISING RATES:
Full Page Colour .... CZK 129000
Mechanical Data: Type Area: 184 x 265mm
CONSUMER: WOMEN'S INTEREST CONSUMER MAGAZINES: Slimming & Health

MORAVSKOSLEZSKÝ KRAJ 1701046CZ67J-226
Editorial: Vítkovická 1, 70200 OSTRAVA
Tel: 596638510 **Fax:** 596638510 596638510
Email: ostrava@consultants.cz **Web site:** http://www.consultants.cz
Date Established: 01.05.03; **Freq:** Monthly; **Cover Price:** Free; **Circ:** 490,000
Usual Pagination: 8
Editor: Šárka Swiderová
Profile: Newspaper of Moravian and Silesian region.
Language(s): Czech
ADVERTISING RATES:
Full Page Colour .... CZK 211700
REGIONAL DAILY & SUNDAY NEWSPAPERS: Regional Newspapers (excl. dailies)

MORAVSKÝ REGION 1701051CZ67J-224
Editorial: Velehradská 507, 76701 KROMĚŘÍŽ
Tel: 573335577 **Fax:** 573336406
Email: redakce@mregion.cz **Web site:** http://www.mregion.cz
Date Established: 01.01.03; **Freq:** Monthly; **Cover Price:** Free; **Circ:** 400,000
Usual Pagination: 16
Editor: Radka Skácelová
Profile: Advertising newspaper of 6 regions in Moravia: Zlin, Kromeriz, South Moravia, Vsetin, Brno - Olomouc and Prerov.
Language(s): Czech
ADVERTISING RATES:
Full Page Mono .... CZK 27200
Mechanical Data: Type Area: 215 x 286mm
REGIONAL DAILY & SUNDAY NEWSPAPERS: Regional Newspapers (excl. dailies)

MORAVSKÝ VETERÁN 1701056CZ77F-1
Editorial: Nemilany - Heská čtvrť 28, 78302 OLOMOUC 19 **Tel:** 585414639
Freq: 3 issues yearly; **Cover Price:** CZK 16; **Circ:** 20
Usual Pagination: 16
Editor: Jan Opálka
Profile: Bulletin about veteran motor cars in Moravia and Silesia, for members only.
Language(s): Czech
CONSUMER: MOTORING & CYCLING: Veteran Cars

MOTOCYKL 1200771CZ77D-10
Editorial: U Krčského nádraží 36, 14000 PRAHA 4 - KRČ **Tel:** 241093445 **Fax:** 241721905
Email: motorpresse@motorpresse.cz **Web site:** http://www.motorpresse.cz
ISSN: 1213-7138
Date Established: 01.01.91; **Freq:** Monthly; **Cover Price:** CZK 79
Annual Sub.: CZK 504; **Circ:** 15,600
Usual Pagination: 116
Editor: Richard Šimer
Profile: Magazine about motorbikes.
Language(s): Czech
Readership: Aimed at motorcyclists and spectators of sports events.
ADVERTISING RATES:
Full Page Colour .... CZK 85000
Mechanical Data: Type Area: 192 x 252mm
CONSUMER: MOTORING & CYCLING: Motor Sports

MOTOCYKL PRŮVODCE 1776916CZ77B-14
Editorial: U Krčského nádraží 36, 14000 PRAHA 4 - KRČ **Tel:** 241093445 **Fax:** 241721905
Email: motorpresse@motorpresse.cz **Web site:** http://www.motorpresse.cz
ISSN: 1212-0537
Date Established: 01.01.96; **Freq:** Annual; **Cover Price:** CZK 229
Annual Sub.: CZK 199; **Circ:** 30,000
Usual Pagination: 180
Editor: Richard Šimer
Profile: Motobikes directory.
Language(s): Czech
ADVERTISING RATES:
Full Page Colour .... CZK 80000
Mechanical Data: Type Area: 192 x 252mm
CONSUMER: MOTORING & CYCLING: Motorcycling

MOTOHOUSE KATALOG AUTOMOBILŮ 1776917CZ77A-290
Editorial: Záhřebská 41, 12000 PRAHA 2
Tel: 296361654 **Fax:** 296202084
Web site: http://www.motohouse.cz
Date Established: 01.01.99; **Freq:** Annual; **Cover Price:** CZK 199; **Circ:** 50,000
Usual Pagination: 300
Editor: Miroslav Mihálik
Profile: Motor-vehicle catalogue.
Language(s): Czech
ADVERTISING RATES:
Full Page Colour .... CZK 119000
CONSUMER: MOTORING & CYCLING: Motoring

MOTORKÁŘ 1701067CZ77B-8
Editorial: Vrbova 19/1427, 14700 PRAHA 4
Tel: 244471640 **Fax:** 244470663
Email: inzerce@bikes.cz **Web site:** http://www.bikes.cz
Date Established: 10.03.04; **Freq:** Annual; **Cover Price:** CZK 69; **Circ:** 30,000
Usual Pagination: 164
Profile: Magazine about motorbikes.
Language(s): Czech
ADVERTISING RATES:
Full Page Colour .... CZK 59000
Mechanical Data: Type Area: 190 x 270mm
CONSUMER: MOTORING & CYCLING: Motorcycling

MŮJ DŮM 1701074CZ74C-22
Editorial: Nádražní 762/32, 15000 PRAHA 5
Tel: 225351300 **Fax:** 225351622
Email: info@bmczech.cz **Web site:** http://www.bmczech.cz
ISSN: 1210-7654
Date Established: 17.10.93; **Freq:** Monthly; **Cover Price:** CZK 88
Annual Sub.: CZK 936; **Circ:** 21,560
Usual Pagination: 210
Editor: Michal Wernisch
Profile: Magazine about housing.
Language(s): Czech
ADVERTISING RATES:
Full Page Colour .... CZK 92000
Mechanical Data: Type Area: 200 x 252mm
CONSUMER: WOMEN'S INTEREST CONSUMER MAGAZINES: Home & Family

MYSLIVOST 1701085CZ75F-2
Editorial: Seifertova 81, 13000 PRAHA 3
Tel: 222780010 **Fax:** 222780010
Email: myslivost@anet.cz **Web site:** http://www.myslivost.cz
ISSN: 0323-214X
Date Established: 01.01.1923; **Freq:** Monthly; **Cover Price:** CZK 50
Annual Sub.: CZK 564; **Circ:** 50,000
Usual Pagination: 52
Editor: Jiří Kasina
Profile: Magazine about hunting.
Language(s): Czech; Slovak
ADVERTISING RATES:
Full Page Colour .... CZK 44000
CONSUMER: SPORT: Shooting

NA CESTĚ 1701090CZ77A-252
Editorial: Bucharova 1186/16, 15500 PRAHA 5
Tel: 251025363 **Fax:** 251626965
Email: info@hyundaimotor.cz **Web site:** http://www.hyundaimotorcz.cz
Date Established: 12.03.03; **Freq:** Half-yearly; **Cover Price:** Free; **Circ:** 30,000
Usual Pagination: 36
Editor: Veronika Jakubcová
Profile: Magazine of auto factory Hyundai.
Language(s): Czech
ADVERTISING RATES:
Full Page Colour .... CZK 45000
CONSUMER: MOTORING & CYCLING: Motoring

NA DOMA 1701091CZ74P-27
Editorial: Thámova 18, 18000 PRAHA 8 - KARLÍN
Tel: 224071604 **Fax:** 224071124
Email: info@nadoma.cz **Web site:** http://www.unilever.cz
Date Established: 01.01.02; **Freq:** Half-yearly; **Cover Price:** Free; **Circ:** 110,000
Usual Pagination: 52
Editor: Veronika Kulichová
Profile: Woman magazine about cooking and family.
Language(s): Czech
CONSUMER: WOMEN'S INTEREST CONSUMER MAGAZINES: Food & Cookery

NAPSÁNO ŽIVOTEM 1701098CZ74A-412
Editorial: Victora Huga 6, P.O.Box 125, 15000 PRAHA 5 **Tel:** 225008244 **Fax:** 225008306
Email: inzerce@bauermedia.cz **Web site:** http://www.bauermedia.cz
ISSN: 1211-6505
Date Established: 14.02.97; **Freq:** 26 issues yearly; **Cover Price:** CZK 17
Annual Sub.: CZK 416; **Circ:** 71,821
Usual Pagination: 36
Editor: Pavla Liebichová
Profile: Relaxation family magazine.
Language(s): Czech
ADVERTISING RATES:
Full Page Colour .... CZK 40000
Mechanical Data: Type Area: 185 x 252mm
CONSUMER: WOMEN'S INTEREST CONSUMER MAGAZINES: Women's Interest

NAŠE KRÁSNÁ ZAHRADA 1701114CZ93-202
Editorial: Přemyslovská 2845/43, 13000 PRAHA 3
Tel: 222520617 **Fax:** 222522648
Email: inzerce@burda.cz **Web site:** http://www.burda.cz
ISSN: 1211-4995
Date Established: 01.08.96; **Freq:** Monthly; **Cover Price:** CZK 42
Annual Sub.: CZK 420; **Circ:** 38,400
Usual Pagination: 68
Editor: Jiří Dvořák
Profile: Magazine about gardening.
Language(s): Czech
ADVERTISING RATES:
Full Page Colour .... CZK 80000
Mechanical Data: Type Area: 188 x 250mm
CONSUMER: GARDENING

NAŠE NOVINY (BRNO) 1701120CZ67J-223
Editorial: Vychodilova 2531/13, 63500 BRNO - ŽABOVŘESKY **Tel:** 541231322 **Fax:** 549255480
Email: nasenoviny@volny.cz **Web site:** http://nasenoviny.unas.cz
Date Established: 15.06.94; **Freq:** Monthly; **Cover Price:** Free; **Circ:** 85,000
Usual Pagination: 4
Editor: Vratislav Mlčoch
Profile: Newsletter of Brno - Kurim, Veverska Bityska etc.
Language(s): Czech
REGIONAL DAILY & SUNDAY NEWSPAPERS: Regional Newspapers (excl. dailies)

NATIONAL GEOGRAPHIC 1701131CZ57-31
Editorial: Lomnického 7, 14000 PRAHA 4
Tel: 296162849 **Fax:** 224921732
Email: inzerce@sanomamag-praha.cz **Web site:** http://www.sanoma.cz
ISSN: 1213-9394
Date Established: 26.09.02; **Freq:** Monthly; **Cover Price:** CZK 95
Annual Sub.: CZK 799; **Circ:** 43,200
Usual Pagination: 156
Editor: Tomáš Tureček
Profile: Travelogue magazine.
Language(s): Czech
ADVERTISING RATES:
Full Page Colour .... CZK 205000
Mechanical Data: Type Area: 141 x 223mm
BUSINESS: ENVIRONMENT & POLLUTION

NEDĚLNÍ BLESK 1701139CZ65B-1
Editorial: Komunardů 1584/42, 17000 PRAHA 7
Tel: 225977586 **Fax:** 222714641
Email: david.saroch@ringier.cz **Web site:** http://www.ringier.cz
ISSN: 1210-8774
Date Established: 21.03.93; **Freq:** Weekly; **Cover Price:** CZK 12
Annual Sub.: CZK 1500; **Circ:** 346,588
Usual Pagination: 48
Editor: Jiří Fabián
Profile: Sunday tabloid weekly.
Language(s): Czech
NATIONAL DAILY & SUNDAY NEWSPAPERS: National Sunday Newspapers

NEDĚLNÍ SPORT 1701140CZ75A-217
Editorial: Komunardů 1584/42, 17000 PRAHA 7
Tel: 225975111 **Fax:** 225977653
Email: david.saroch@ringier.cz **Web site:** http://www.ringier.cz
Date Established: 04.09.05; **Freq:** Weekly; **Cover Price:** CZK 10; **Circ:** 61,422
Editor: Lukáš Tomek
Profile: Sport Sunday weekly.
Language(s): Czech

ADVERTISING RATES:
Full Page Colour .... CZK 139080
Mechanical Data: No. of Columns (Display): 6, Type Area: 256 x 380mm
CONSUMER: SPORT

O2 ARENA 1699459CZ89C-2
Editorial: Chodovecké náměstí 8, 14100 PRAHA 4 - CHODOV
Email: entre@entre.cz **Web site:** http://www.entre.cz
Date Established: 23.04.04; **Freq:** Half-yearly; **Cover Price:** Free; **Circ:** 12,000
Usual Pagination: 24
Profile: Life-style magazine and culture program of Sazka arena.
Language(s): Czech
ADVERTISING RATES:
Full Page Colour .... CZK 70000
Mechanical Data: Type Area: 180 x 267mm
CONSUMER: HOLIDAYS & TRAVEL: Entertainment Guides

OBCHODNÍ TÝDENÍK 1701271CZ1A-47
Editorial: Mezi Vodami 1952/9, 14300 PRAHA 4 - MODŘANY **Tel:** 225276223 **Fax:** 225276333
Email: inzerce@mf.cz **Web site:** http://www.mf.cz
ISSN: 1214-6579
Date Established: 27.04.04; **Freq:** 26 issues yearly; **Annual Sub.:** CZK 198; **Circ:** 57,000
Usual Pagination: 32
Editor: Olga Novotná
Profile: B2B and economic magazine.
Language(s): Czech
ADVERTISING RATES:
Full Page Colour .... CZK 54000
Mechanical Data: Type Area: 189 x 277mm
BUSINESS: FINANCE & ECONOMICS

O.K. TIP 1701257CZ75A-219
Editorial: Politických vězňů 156, 26601 BEROUN
Tel: 311633177 **Fax:** 311633111
Email: tipsport@tipsport.cz **Web site:** http://www.tipsport.cz
Date Established: 25.09.92; **Freq:** Weekly; **Cover Price:** CZK 30; **Circ:** 15,000
Usual Pagination: 96
Editor: Miloš Klíma
Profile: Magazine for clients of bettign shop Tipsport.
Language(s): Czech
ADVERTISING RATES:
Full Page Colour .... CZK 20000
CONSUMER: SPORT

OKNO DO KRAJE 1776716CZ82-275
Editorial: Pekárenská 42, 76001 ZLÍN - PŘÍLUKY
Tel: 577043111 **Fax:** 577011480
Email: info@hexxa.cz **Web site:** http://www.hexxa.cz
Date Established: 01.12.05; **Freq:** Monthly; **Cover Price:** Free; **Circ:** 260,000
Usual Pagination: 16
Profile: Regional magazine.
Language(s): Czech
CONSUMER: CURRENT AFFAIRS & POLITICS

OPAVSKÉ REKLAMNÍ NOVINY 1701313CZ2-67
Editorial: Domky 319, 74781 OTICE, OKR. OPAVA
Tel: 553762226 **Fax:** 553762226
Email: novinyopava@volny.cz **Web site:** http://www.volny.cz/novinyopava
Date Established: 01.01.93; **Freq:** Monthly; **Cover Price:** Free; **Circ:** 45,000
Usual Pagination: 12
Editor: Robert Zorek
Profile: Advertising newspaper of region Opava.
Language(s): Czech
BUSINESS: COMMUNICATIONS, ADVERTISING & MARKETING

OPEL MAGAZÍN 1701318CZ77A-254
Editorial: Nádražní 762/32, 15000 PRAHA 5
Tel: 606956320 **Fax:** 225351404
Email: info@bmczech.cz **Web site:** http://www.bmczech.cz
ISSN: 1212-7213
Date Established: 01.12.97; **Freq:** Quarterly; **Cover Price:** CZK 55; **Circ:** 15,000
Usual Pagination: 60
Editor: Martin Hejral
Profile: Magazine of auto factory Opel.
Language(s): Czech
ADVERTISING RATES:
Full Page Colour .... CZK 78000
Mechanical Data: Type Area: 185 x 270mm
CONSUMER: MOTORING & CYCLING: Motoring

OPTICA MODA 1793134CZ56E-7
Editorial: Washingtonova 9, 11000 PRAHA 1
Tel: 272940325
Email: eif@eiffeloptic.cz **Web site:** http://www.eiffeloptic.cz
Freq: Quarterly; **Cover Price:** Free; **Circ:** 50,000
Usual Pagination: 36
Editor: Hana Havlíčková
Profile: Custom-magazine of Eiffel Optic company.
Language(s): Czech
BUSINESS: HEALTH & MEDICAL: Optics

PANEL PLUS 1701374CZ74K-4
Editorial: Koněvova 2660/141, 13083 PRAHA 3
Tel: 296566214 **Fax:** 296566213
Email: j.chara@panelplus.cz **Web site:** http://www.panelplus.cz
ISSN: 1214-4150
Date Established: 10.10.03; **Freq:** 24 issues yearly; **Cover Price:** CZK 45
Annual Sub.: CZK 225; **Circ:** 40,000
Usual Pagination: 96
Editor: Jan Chára
Profile: Magazine focused on blocks of flats, reconstruction, design, innovation of exterior and interior.
Language(s): Czech
ADVERTISING RATES:
Full Page Colour .... CZK 69000
Mechanical Data: Type Area: 192 x 261mm
CONSUMER: WOMEN'S INTEREST CONSUMER MAGAZINES: Home Purchase

PANELÁK DOMOV MŮJ 1701375CZ74C-25
Editorial: V Závětří 4, 17000 PRAHA 7
Tel: 266791550 **Fax:** 266791550
Email: cmveletrhy@etelnet.cz
Freq: 3 issues yearly; **Cover Price:** Free; **Circ:** 40,000
Usual Pagination: 32
Editor: Ladislava Bryknarová
Profile: Magazine about prefabricated houses.
Language(s): Czech
ADVERTISING RATES:
Full Page Colour .... CZK 28000
CONSUMER: WOMEN'S INTEREST CONSUMER MAGAZINES: Home & Family

PANÍ DOMU 1701376CZ74A-416
Editorial: Bohdalecká 6/1420, 10100 PRAHA 10 - MICHLE **Tel:** 281090667 **Fax:** 281090644
Email: jan.lidmansky@rf-hobby.cz **Web site:** http://www.rf-hobby.cz
ISSN: 1213-4767
Date Established: 01.10.01; **Freq:** Monthly; **Cover Price:** CZK 24,50
Annual Sub.: CZK 468; **Circ:** 41,752
Usual Pagination: 86
Editor: Lenka Korandová
Profile: Magazine for women about housing and solutions of daily problems with family life.
Language(s): Czech
ADVERTISING RATES:
Full Page Colour .... CZK 89000
CONSUMER: WOMEN'S INTEREST CONSUMER MAGAZINES: Women's Interest

PAPARAZZI REVUE 1793139CZ74Q-32
Editorial: Bohdalecká 6/1420, 10100 PRAHA 10 - MICHLE **Tel:** 281000757 **Fax:** 281090623
Email: jan.lidmansky@rf-hobby.cz **Web site:** http://www.rf-hobby.cz
ISSN: 1802-1158
Date Established: 18.10.06; **Freq:** 26 issues yearly; **Cover Price:** CZK 25; **Circ:** 54,300
Usual Pagination: 52
Editor: Petr Casanova
Profile: Weekly yellow press.
Language(s): Czech
ADVERTISING RATES:
Full Page Colour .... CZK 89000
CONSUMER: WOMEN'S INTEREST CONSUMER MAGAZINES: Lifestyle

PAPÍR A CELULÓZA 1201565CZ36-5
Editorial: K Hrušovu 292/4, 10223 PRAHA 10
Tel: 271081131 **Fax:** 271081136
Email: redakce@sppac.cz **Web site:** http://www.sppac.cz
ISSN: 0031-1421
Date Established: 01.12.1946; **Freq:** Monthly; **Cover Price:** CZK 50
Annual Sub.: CZK 600; **Circ:** 1,400
Usual Pagination: 40
Editor: Miloš Leśikar
Profile: Professional magazine about wood-processing industry, papers, cellulose and technology.
Language(s): Czech; English; Slovak
Readership: Aimed at paper mill professionals, consumers of paper and producers of packaging.
ADVERTISING RATES:
Full Page Colour .... CZK 35000
Mechanical Data: Type Area: 173 x 257mm
BUSINESS: PAPER

PÁTEK LIDOVÉ NOVINY 1701398CZ67H-1
Editorial: Karla Engliše 519/11, 15000 PRAHA 5
Tel: 225067111 **Fax:** 225067199
Email: mfdnes@mfdnes.cz **Web site:** http://www.idnes.cz
Date Established: 01.10.96; **Freq:** Weekly; **Cover Price:** Free; **Circ:** 110,918
Usual Pagination: 56
Profile: Magazine for relaxing, TV chanels program.
Language(s): Czech
ADVERTISING RATES:
Full Page Colour .... CZK 159000
Mechanical Data: Type Area: 181 x 261mm
REGIONAL DAILY & SUNDAY NEWSPAPERS: Regional Colour Supplements

PATRIOT 1701399CZ77R-2
Editorial: Suchardova 515, 27201 KLADNO
Tel: 220611308 **Fax:** 220611310
Email: patriot@patriot-cz.com **Web site:** http://www.patriot-cz.com
Date Established: 01.06.01; **Freq:** Monthly; **Cover Price:** Free; **Circ:** 45,000
Usual Pagination: 36
Editor: Petr Kojzar
Profile: Magazine for motorists about feature of society.
Language(s): Czech
ADVERTISING RATES:
Full Page Colour .... CZK 160000
CONSUMER: MOTORING & CYCLING: Motoring & Cycling Related

PES PŘÍTEL ČLOVĚKA 1701425CZ81B-4
Editorial: Křížikova 35 (2. patro), 18600 PRAHA 8
Tel: 221863402 **Fax:** 221863401
Email: shootmag@volny.cz **Web site:** http://www.strelecka-revue.cz
ISSN: 0231-5424
Date Established: 01.01.1957; **Freq:** Monthly; **Cover Price:** CZK 49
Annual Sub.: CZK 420; **Circ:** 38,500
Usual Pagination: 104
Editor: Zuzana Trankovská
Profile: Magazine about rearing and training dogs.
Language(s): Czech; Slovak
ADVERTISING RATES:
Full Page Colour .... CZK 37800
Mechanical Data: Type Area: 182 x 265mm
CONSUMER: ANIMALS & PETS: Dogs

PESTRÝ SVĚT 1701426CZ74Q-11
Editorial: Victora Huga 6, P.O.Box 125, 15000 PRAHA 5 **Tel:** 225008368 **Fax:** 257327103
Email: inzerce@bauermedia.cz **Web site:** http://www.bauermedia.cz
ISSN: 1214-8253
Date Established: 02.09.04; **Freq:** Weekly; **Cover Price:** CZK 14
Annual Sub.: CZK 624; **Circ:** 320,021
Usual Pagination: 32
Editor: Barbora Štenglová
Profile: Magazine about social life, celebrities, recipes, health, crosswords.
Language(s): Czech
ADVERTISING RATES:
Full Page Colour .... CZK 125000
Mechanical Data: Type Area: 202 x 265mm
CONSUMER: WOMEN'S INTEREST CONSUMER MAGAZINES: Lifestyle

PETROLMAGAZÍN 1701427CZ58-10
Editorial: Na dlouhém lánu 508/41, 16000 PRAHA 6
Tel: 224305350 **Fax:** 224305335
Email: petrolmagazin@petrol.cz **Web site:** http://www.petrol.cz
Date Established: 01.09.00; **Freq:** 24 issues yearly; **Cover Price:** Free; **Circ:** 4,000
Usual Pagination: 100
Editor: Tomáš Mikšovský
Profile: Professional petrochemistry and petrol station magazine.
Language(s): Czech; Slovak
ADVERTISING RATES:
Full Page Colour .... CZK 40000
Mechanical Data: Type Area: 184 x 260mm
BUSINESS: ENERGY, FUEL & NUCLEAR

PEUGEOT STYLE 1701430CZ31A-2
Editorial: Na strži 40, 14000 PRAHA 4
Tel: 244118800 **Fax:** 244118801
Web site: http://www.peugeot.cz
Date Established: 01.01.99; **Freq:** 3 issues yearly; **Cover Price:** Free; **Circ:** 40,000
Usual Pagination: 68
Profile: Magazine of auto factory Peugeot.
Language(s): Czech
ADVERTISING RATES:
Full Page Colour .... CZK 39000
Mechanical Data: Type Area: 175 x 254mm
BUSINESS: MOTOR TRADE: Motor Trade Accessories

PLAYBOY 1701454CZ86A-33
Editorial: Dělnická 12, 17000 PRAHA 7
Tel: 234692233 **Fax:** 234692239
Email: playboy@playpress.cz **Web site:** http://www.playpress.cz
ISSN: 0862-9374
Date Established: 01.05.91; **Freq:** Monthly; **Cover Price:** CZK 99
Annual Sub.: CZK 999; **Circ:** 23,000
Usual Pagination: 164
Editor: Vladimír Olexa
Profile: Luxury magazine for men.
Language(s): Czech; Slovak
ADVERTISING RATES:
Full Page Colour .... CZK 155000
Mechanical Data: Type Area: 173 x 248mm
CONSUMER: ADULT & GAY MAGAZINES: Adult Magazines

PLZEŇSKÝ KRAJ 1701465CZ67J-174
Editorial: Husova 29, 30100 PLZEŇ **Tel:** 377322973
Fax: 377322972
Email: plzen@consultants.cz **Web site:** http://www.consultants.cz
Date Established: 01.06.03; **Freq:** Monthly; **Cover Price:** Free; **Circ:** 255,400
Usual Pagination: 8
Editor: Richard Beneš
Profile: Advertising newspaper of region Plzen.
Language(s): Czech
ADVERTISING RATES:
Full Page Colour .... CZK 126500
Mechanical Data: Type Area: 285 x 435mm
REGIONAL DAILY & SUNDAY NEWSPAPERS: Regional Newspapers (excl. dailies)

POČÍTAČ PRO KAŽDÉHO 1701472CZ5B-32
Editorial: Přemyslovská 2845/43, 13000 PRAHA 3
Tel: 225018708 **Fax:** 225018600
Email: inzerce@burda.cz **Web site:** http://www.burda.cz
ISSN: 1212-0723
Date Established: 08.04.98; **Freq:** 26 issues yearly; **Cover Price:** CZK 55
Annual Sub.: CZK 995; **Circ:** 25,849
Usual Pagination: 64
Editor: Ivan Heisler
Profile: Computer magazine for common users.
Language(s): Czech
ADVERTISING RATES:
Full Page Colour .... CZK 95000
Mechanical Data: Type Area: 173 x 260mm
BUSINESS: COMPUTERS & AUTOMATION: Data Processing

PODNIKÁNÍ A OBCHOD 1701482CZ1A-51
Editorial: Košťálkova 1105/1, 18200 PRAHA 8 - KOBYLISY **Tel:** 284683898 **Fax:** 284683898
Email: podnikaniaobchod.richter@atlas.cz
ISSN: 1211-0841
Date Established: 01.01.96; **Freq:** Monthly; **Cover Price:** Free; **Circ:** 120,000
Usual Pagination: 8
Editor: Ivan Richter
Profile: Monthly magazine about economy and law services.
Language(s): Czech
ADVERTISING RATES:
Full Page Mono .... CZK 28000
Mechanical Data: Type Area: 265 x 375mm
BUSINESS: FINANCE & ECONOMICS

PORADCE 1701506CZ1A-56
Editorial: Štefánikova 2, 73701 ČESKÝ TĚŠÍN
Tel: 558731125-7 **Fax:** 558731128
Email: poradce@i-poradce.cz **Web site:** http://www.i-poradce.cz
ISSN: 1211-2437
Date Established: 01.09.96; **Freq:** Monthly; **Cover Price:** CZK 96
Annual Sub.: CZK 998; **Circ:** 50,000
Usual Pagination: 250
Editor: Eugenie Dokoupilová
Profile: Professional journal for businessmen about new legislation and law.
Language(s): Slovak
Mechanical Data: Type Area: 118 x 183mm
BUSINESS: FINANCE & ECONOMICS

POŠLI RECEPT 1809512CZ74P-25
Editorial: Přemyslovská 2845/43, 13000 PRAHA 3
Email: inzerce@burda.cz **Web site:** http://www.burda.cz
Date Established: 06.04.07; **Freq:** Monthly; **Cover Price:** CZK 5; **Circ:** 590,000
Usual Pagination: 68
Profile: Recipes from readers.
Language(s): Czech
ADVERTISING RATES:
Full Page Colour .... CZK 135000
Mechanical Data: Type Area: 133 x 183mm
CONSUMER: WOMEN'S INTEREST CONSUMER MAGAZINES: Food & Cookery

PRACOVNÍ LÉKAŘSTVÍ 1600824CZ56A-120
Editorial: Sokolská 31, 12026 PRAHA 2
Tel: 224911420 **Fax:** 224266265
Email: medical@euronet.cz **Web site:** http://www.medical.cz
ISSN: 0032-6739
Date Established: 01.01.1948; **Freq:** Quarterly; **Cover Price:** CZK 97
Annual Sub.: CZK 308; **Circ:** 750
Usual Pagination: 48
Profile: Professional medical magazine.
Language(s): Czech; English; Slovak
Readership: Aimed at doctors from orthopaedics, neurology, ENT and dermatology branches.
ADVERTISING RATES:
Full Page Colour .... CZK 22000

Mechanical Data: Type Area: 167 x 247mm
BUSINESS: HEALTH & MEDICAL

PRAKTICKÁ ŽENA 1701540CZ74E-4
Editorial: Lomnického 7, 14000 PRAHA 4
Tel: 296162255 **Fax:** 296162420
Email: inzerce@sanomamag-praha.cz **Web site:** http://www.sanoma.cz
ISSN: 0231-6471
Date Established: 01.01.1951; **Freq:** Monthly; **Cover Price:** CZK 55
Annual Sub.: CZK 468; **Circ:** 50,493
Usual Pagination: 100
Editor: Jiřina Köppelová
Profile: Magazine for women about needlework, housing, gardening.
Language(s): Czech
ADVERTISING RATES:
Full Page Colour .... CZK 120000
Mechanical Data: Type Area: 193 x 245mm
CONSUMER: WOMEN'S INTEREST CONSUMER MAGAZINES: Crafts

PRAKTICKÝ PORADCE V DAŇOVÝCH OTÁZKÁCH 1701544CZ1M-9
Editorial: Na Příkopě 18, P.O.Box 756, 11121 PRAHA 1 **Tel:** 224197333 **Fax:** 224197555
Email: info@dashofer.cz **Web site:** http://www.dashofer.cz
ISSN: 1210-5813
Date Established: 01.01.93; **Freq:** 26 issues yearly;
Annual Sub.: CZK 3160; **Circ:** 4,000
Usual Pagination: 40
Editor: Markéta Nováková
Profile: Professional magazine about tax accounting.
Language(s): Czech
BUSINESS: FINANCE & ECONOMICS: Taxation

PRAKTIK 1701545CZ74C-27
Editorial: Křižíkova 35 (2. patro), 18600 PRAHA 8
Tel: 221863403 **Fax:** 221863403
Email: shootmag@volny.cz **Web site:** http://www.strelecka-revue.cz
ISSN: 1211-5533
Date Established: 01.03.96; **Freq:** Monthly; **Cover Price:** CZK 29
Annual Sub.: CZK 300; **Circ:** 20,000
Usual Pagination: 52
Editor: Jaroslava Medková
Profile: Magazine for pottering at home and in the garden.
Language(s): Czech
ADVERTISING RATES:
Full Page Colour .... CZK 42900
Mechanical Data: Type Area: 184 x 273mm
CONSUMER: WOMEN'S INTEREST CONSUMER MAGAZINES: Home & Family

PRAŽSKÝ DENÍK 1793142CZ67B-814
Editorial: Římská 14, 12085 PRAHA 2
Tel: 221084506 **Fax:** 221084523
Web site: http://www.vlp.cz
Date Established: 18.09.06; **Freq:** 312 issues yearly; **Cover Price:** CZK 11; **Circ:** 11,400
Usual Pagination: 32
Editor: Alena Pancerová
Profile: Regional newsletter of Prague.
Language(s): Czech
ADVERTISING RATES:
Full Page Colour .... CZK 59262
Mechanical Data: Type Area: 278 x 415mm
REGIONAL DAILY & SUNDAY NEWSPAPERS: Regional Daily Newspapers

PRIO - PORUBSKÁ RADNICE INFORMUJE OBČANY 1701511CZ67J-172
Editorial: Klimkovická 28/55, 70856 OSTRAVA - PORUBA **Tel:** 599480291 **Fax:** 599480212
Email: info@moporuba.cz **Web site:** http://www.moporuba.cz
Date Established: 01.01.91; **Freq:** Monthly; **Circ:** 35,000
Usual Pagination: 16
Editor: Lumír Palyza
Profile: Newsletter of Ostrava-Poruba.
Language(s): Czech
ADVERTISING RATES:
Full Page Colour .... CZK 32900
Mechanical Data: Type Area: 182 x 264mm
REGIONAL DAILY & SUNDAY NEWSPAPERS: Regional Newspapers (excl. dailies)

PRO FOOTBALL 1701600CZ75B-9
Editorial: Žirovnická 3124, 10600 PRAHA 10
Tel: 224800751 **Fax:** 272770044
Email: egmontcr@egmont.cz **Web site:** http://www.egmont.cz
ISSN: 1212-818X
Date Established: 18.01.00; **Freq:** Monthly; **Cover Price:** CZK 63
Annual Sub.: CZK 693; **Circ:** 21,000
Usual Pagination: 68
Editor: Gabriel Oman
Profile: World football magazine.
Language(s): Czech
ADVERTISING RATES:
Full Page Colour .... CZK 40000
CONSUMER: SPORT: Football

PRO HOCKEY 1701608CZ75G-2
Editorial: Žirovnická 3124, 10600 PRAHA 10
Tel: 224800751 **Fax:** 272770044
Email: egmontcr@egmont.cz **Web site:** http://www.egmont.cz
ISSN: 1212-3986
Date Established: 01.09.98; **Freq:** Monthly; **Cover Price:** CZK 63
Annual Sub.: CZK 536; **Circ:** 21,000
Usual Pagination: 68
Editor: Petter Jennervall
Profile: Magazine about hockey, especially NHL.
Language(s): Czech
ADVERTISING RATES:
Full Page Colour .... CZK 40000
CONSUMER: SPORT: Winter Sports

PROBRNO 1701586CZ67J-167
Editorial: Zelný trh 12, 60200 BRNO **Tel:** 542210210
Fax: 542211982
Email: bures@bbpress.cz **Web site:** http://www.vasesance.cz
Date Established: 01.01.02; **Freq:** 26 issues yearly; **Cover Price:** Free; **Circ:** 50,000
Usual Pagination: 32
Editor: Petra Štelclová
Profile: Cultural and advertising newspaper of region Brno.
Language(s): Czech
ADVERTISING RATES:
Full Page Colour .... CZK 18000
Mechanical Data: Type Area: 190 x 274mm
REGIONAL DAILY & SUNDAY NEWSPAPERS: Regional Newspapers (excl. dailies)

PROČ NE?! 1701587CZ74Q-13
Editorial: Dobrovského 25, 17055 PRAHA 7
Tel: 233073002 **Fax:** 233072002
Email: economia@economia.cz **Web site:** http://www.economia.cz
Date Established: 07.04.05; **Freq:** 10 issues yearly; **Cover Price:** Free; **Circ:** 80,000
Usual Pagination: 68
Editor: Petr Šimůnek
Profile: Lifestyle magazine.
Language(s): Czech
ADVERTISING RATES:
Full Page Colour .... CZK 202000
Mechanical Data: Type Area: 212 x 279mm
CONSUMER: WOMEN'S INTEREST CONSUMER MAGAZINES: Lifestyle

PROFIT 1701599CZ1A-63
Editorial: Francouzská 284/94, 10100 PRAHA 10
Tel: 225010378 **Fax:** 225010377
Email: vesely@profit.cz **Web site:** http://www.profit.cz
ISSN: 1212-3498
Date Established: 01.09.90; **Freq:** Weekly; **Cover Price:** CZK 34
Annual Sub.: CZK 1173; **Circ:** 23,000
Usual Pagination: 68
Editor: Petr Korbel
Profile: Magazine about finance, trade, economy.
Language(s): Czech
ADVERTISING RATES:
Full Page Colour .... CZK 177000
Mechanical Data: Type Area: 184 x 242mm
BUSINESS: FINANCE & ECONOMICS

PROGRAM (NAKLADATELSTVÍ MISE) 1701602CZ89C-19
Editorial: Prokopa Velikého 30, 70300 OSTRAVA - VÍTKOVICE **Tel:** 595693060 **Fax:** 595693050
Email: mise@applet.cz **Web site:** http://www.mise.cz
Date Established: 01.01.94; **Freq:** Monthly; **Cover Price:** Free; **Circ:** 134,000
Usual Pagination: 40
Editor: Hana Marušáková
Profile: Advertising monthly with cultural, society and sport offers for 3 regions: Ostrava, Opava and Frydek - Mistek.
Language(s): Czech
ADVERTISING RATES:
Full Page Colour .... CZK 51700
Mechanical Data: Type Area: 190 x 276mm
CONSUMER: HOLIDAYS & TRAVEL: Entertainment Guides

PULS 1701660CZ74Q-14
Editorial: Dolnoměcholupská 209/17, 10000 PRAHA 10 - HOSTIVAŘ
Email: zilkova@boremi.cz **Web site:** http://www.boremi.cz
ISSN: 1211-7404
Date Established: 17.04.97; **Freq:** Monthly; **Cover Price:** CZK 49
Annual Sub.: CZK 468; **Circ:** 16,423
Usual Pagination: 84
Profile: Magazine about healthy life style and fashion.
Language(s): Czech
ADVERTISING RATES:
Full Page Colour .... CZK 70000
Mechanical Data: Type Area: 153 x 204mm
CONSUMER: WOMEN'S INTEREST CONSUMER MAGAZINES: Lifestyle

RALLY 1701696CZ77D-14
Editorial: Kotěrova 5543, 76001 ZLÍN
Tel: 577430164 **Fax:** 577211998
Email: redakce@rally.cz **Web site:** http://www.alitron.cz
ISSN: 1212-9836
Date Established: 01.03.00; **Freq:** 10 issues yearly; **Cover Price:** CZK 65; **Circ:** 20,000
Usual Pagination: 78
Editor: Tomáš Plachý
Profile: Motor-vehicle rallye magazine.
Language(s): Czech
ADVERTISING RATES:
Full Page Colour .... CZK 48000
CONSUMER: MOTORING & CYCLING: Motor Sports

RAZ DVA TŘI 1701700CZ88E-2
Editorial: Františka Křížka 1, 17030 PRAHA 7
Tel: 220412221 **Fax:** 220412206
Email: redakce@moje1noviny.cz **Web site:** http://www.moje1noviny.cz
ISSN: 1214-9616
Date Established: 01.01.05; **Freq:** Monthly; **Cover Price:** CZK 20; **Circ:** 50,000
Usual Pagination: 44
Editor: Jiří Sedláček
Profile: English language education for children and youth.
Language(s): Czech; English
CONSUMER: EDUCATION: Preparatory & Junior Education

REAL SPEKTRUM 1701710CZ1E-14
Editorial: Lidická 77/718, 60200 BRNO
Tel: 541219500 **Fax:** 541212474
Email: rs@realspektrum.cz **Web site:** http://www.realspektrum.cz
Freq: Quarterly; **Cover Price:** Free; **Circ:** 200,000
Usual Pagination: 4
Editor: Pavel Daněk
Profile: Newsletter with offers of estate agency.
Language(s): Czech
BUSINESS: FINANCE & ECONOMICS: Property

REAL-CITY (SEVERNÍ MORAVA A VALAŠSKO) 1701709CZ1E-13
Editorial: Slévárenská 412/10, 70900 OSTRAVA - MARIÁNSKÉ HORY **Tel:** 596943310 **Fax:** 596943310
Email: info.ostrava@realcity.cz **Web site:** http://www.real-city.cz
Date Established: 01.11.02; **Freq:** 17 issues yearly; **Cover Price:** Free; **Circ:** 40,000
Usual Pagination: 16
Editor: Gabriela Neuwirthová
Profile: Magazine with offers of real estates agencies.
Language(s): Czech
ADVERTISING RATES:
Full Page Colour .... CZK 107090
Mechanical Data: Type Area: 210 x 271mm
BUSINESS: FINANCE & ECONOMICS: Property

RECEPTÁŘ PRO ZDRAVÍ 1804222CZ74G-40
Editorial: V Celnici 1031/4, 11000 PRAHA 1
Email: vyber@vyber.cz **Web site:** http://www.vyber.cz
Date Established: 07.02.07; **Freq:** Quarterly; **Cover Price:** CZK 19; **Circ:** 50,000
Usual Pagination: 60
Profile: Magazine specialized in style of life, health, cosmetics and sports.
Language(s): Czech
ADVERTISING RATES:
Full Page Colour .... CZK 75000
Mechanical Data: Type Area: 181 x 254mm
CONSUMER: WOMEN'S INTEREST CONSUMER MAGAZINES: Slimming & Health

RECEPTY PRIMA NÁPADŮ 1701721CZ74P-16
Editorial: Vinohradská 138, 13000 PRAHA 3
Tel: 272107111
Email: info@medialaboratory.cz **Web site:** http://www.medialaboratory.cz
ISSN: 1213-8967
Date Established: 12.03.02; **Freq:** Monthly; **Cover Price:** CZK 29
Annual Sub.: CZK 676; **Circ:** 60,000
Usual Pagination: 84
Editor: Ivana Hudcová
Profile: Magazine about cooking with many recipes.
Language(s): Czech
ADVERTISING RATES:
Full Page Colour .... CZK 90000
Mechanical Data: Type Area: 191 x 252mm
CONSUMER: WOMEN'S INTEREST CONSUMER MAGAZINES: Food & Cookery

RECEPTY RECEPTÁŘE 1793146CZ74P-23
Editorial: V Celnici 1031/4, 11000 PRAHA 1
Email: vyber@vyber.cz **Web site:** http://www.vyber.cz
Date Established: 31.08.06; **Freq:** Quarterly; **Cover Price:** CZK 29; **Circ:** 50,000
Usual Pagination: 44
Profile: Recipe magazine.
Language(s): Czech
ADVERTISING RATES:
Full Page Colour .... CZK 45000
Mechanical Data: Type Area: 181 x 254mm
CONSUMER: WOMEN'S INTEREST CONSUMER MAGAZINES: Food & Cookery

REFLEX 763787CZ82-200
Editorial: Komunardů 1584/42, 17000 PRAHA 7
Tel: 267097441 **Fax:** 222582013
Email: david.saroch@ringier.cz **Web site:** http://www.ringier.cz
ISSN: 0862-6634
Date Established: 03.04.90; **Freq:** Weekly; **Cover Price:** CZK 35
Annual Sub.: CZK 1040; **Circ:** 97,312
Usual Pagination: 76
Editor: Pavel Šafr
Profile: Magazine focusing on current affairs, politics, lifestyle and celebrity.
Language(s): Czech
ADVERTISING RATES:
Full Page Colour .... CZK 230000
Mechanical Data: Type Area: 196 x 259mm
CONSUMER: CURRENT AFFAIRS & POLITICS

REGENA 1701725CZ74G-17
Editorial: V Hodkovičkách 2/20, 14700 PRAHA 4
Tel: 241768555-8 **Fax:** 241768561
Email: pragma@pragma.cz **Web site:** http://www.pragma.cz
Date Established: 01.01.90; **Freq:** Monthly; **Cover Price:** CZK 24
Annual Sub.: CZK 200; **Circ:** 31,000
Usual Pagination: 44
Editor: Kateřina Drmlová
Profile: Magazine about alternative methods od medicine.
Language(s): Czech
ADVERTISING RATES:
Full Page Colour .... CZK 37000
Mechanical Data: Type Area: 194 x 260mm
CONSUMER: WOMEN'S INTEREST CONSUMER MAGAZINES: Slimming & Health

REGENERACE 1701726CZ74G-18
Editorial: Starostřešovická 79/15, 16200 PRAHA 6
Tel: 233313708 **Fax:** 233313708
Email: regenerace@regenerace.cz **Web site:** http://www.regenerace.cz
ISSN: 1210-6631
Date Established: 01.10.93; **Freq:** Monthly; **Cover Price:** CZK 35
Annual Sub.: CZK 258; **Circ:** 32,435
Usual Pagination: 80
Editor: Jakub Malina
Profile: Magazine about health and medical care.
Language(s): Czech
ADVERTISING RATES:
Full Page Colour .... CZK 42000
Mechanical Data: Type Area: 173 x 241mm
CONSUMER: WOMEN'S INTEREST CONSUMER MAGAZINES: Slimming & Health

REGIONÁLNÍ NOVINY ESO 1701740CZ67J-160
Editorial: Purkyňova 55 (u autobusového nádraží), 56802 SVITAVY **Tel:** 461541123 **Fax:** 461541123
Email: eso@unet.cz
Freq: 26 issues yearly; **Cover Price:** Free; **Circ:** 30,000
Usual Pagination: 12
Editor: Jaroslava Šimková
Profile: Regional newspaper.
Language(s): Czech
REGIONAL DAILY & SUNDAY NEWSPAPERS: Regional Newspapers (excl. dailies)

REHABILITACE A FYZIKÁLNÍ LÉKAŘSTVÍ 1600823CZ56A-135
Editorial: Sokolská 31, 12026 PRAHA 2
Tel: 224911420 **Fax:** 224266265
Email: medical@euronet.cz **Web site:** http://www.medical.cz
ISSN: 1211-2658
Date Established: 01.01.93; **Freq:** Quarterly; **Cover Price:** CZK 91
Annual Sub.: CZK 292; **Circ:** 1,650
Usual Pagination: 48
Profile: Professional medical magazine.
Language(s): Czech; English; Slovak
Readership: Aimed at general practitioners, specialists, physiotherapists, ergotherapists, psychologists, social workers, ergonomists and those interested in myoskeletal medicine and therapy.
ADVERTISING RATES:
Full Page Colour .... CZK 29000
Mechanical Data: Type Area: 167 x 248mm
BUSINESS: HEALTH & MEDICAL

RESPEKT
1701753CZ82-236
Editorial: Dobrovského 1278/25, 17055 PRAHA 7
Tel: 224930792 **Fax:** 226216799
Email: redakce@respekt.cz **Web site:** http://www.respekt.cz
ISSN: 0862-6545
Date Established: 01.01.90; **Freq:** Weekly; **Cover Price:** CZK 35
Annual Sub.: CZK 1040; **Circ:** 43,537
Usual Pagination: 76
Editor: Erik Tabery
Profile: Political and social weekly sight on comments, interview, coverage, reporting inland also from abroad.
Language(s): Czech; Slovak
ADVERTISING RATES:
Full Page Colour .... CZK 155000
Mechanical Data: Type Area: 204 x 268mm
CONSUMER: CURRENT AFFAIRS & POLITICS

REVUE ČESKÉ LÉKAŘSKÉ SPOLEČNOSTI J. E. PURKYNĚ
1701759CZ56R-121
Editorial: Sokolská 31, 12026 PRAHA 2
Fax: 224266226
Email: medical@euronet.cz **Web site:** http://www.medical.cz
ISSN: 1214-6889
Date Established: 01.01.04; **Freq:** Quarterly; **Cover Price:** Free; **Circ:** 31,500
Usual Pagination: 36
Editor: Jaroslav Blahoš, DrSc.
Profile: Magazine of CLS JEP.
Language(s): Czech
ADVERTISING RATES:
Full Page Colour .... CZK 25000
BUSINESS: HEALTH & MEDICAL: Health Medical Related

RODIČE
1701774CZ74C-41
Editorial: Americká 17, 12000 PRAHA 2
Tel: 222521286 **Fax:** 222518655
Email: redakcerodice@volny.cz **Web site:** http://www.rodice.com
ISSN: 1211-880X
Date Established: 01.11.97; **Freq:** Monthly; **Cover Price:** CZK 36
Annual Sub.: CZK 320; **Circ:** 30,000
Usual Pagination: 84
Editor: Magda Friedrichová
Profile: Magazine about young families, about their problems and solutions.
Language(s): Czech
ADVERTISING RATES:
Full Page Colour .... CZK 65000
CONSUMER: WOMEN'S INTEREST CONSUMER MAGAZINES: Home & Family

RODINNÉ DOMY - PROJEKTY A REALIZACE
1776962CZ4D-6
Editorial: Tiskařská 10/257, 10800 PRAHA 10
Tel: 56884500 **Fax:** 568840182
Email: info@gservis.cz **Web site:** http://www.gservis.cz
Date Established: 01.01.95; **Freq:** Half-yearly; **Cover Price:** CZK 179; **Circ:** 30,000
Usual Pagination: 500
Editor: Jiří Maňák
Profile: Catalog of houses project.
Language(s): Czech
ADVERTISING RATES:
Full Page Colour .... CZK 87000
BUSINESS: ARCHITECTURE & BUILDING: Planning & Housing

RODINNÉ DOMY SE SNÍŽENOU SPOTŘEBOU ENERGIÍ
1776963CZ4D-7
Editorial: Havlíčkova 304, 53803 HEŘMANŮV MĚSTEC **Tel:** 777555860 **Fax:** 469633617
Email: cruxsro@gmail.com **Web site:** http://www.ceskaenergetika.com
ISSN: 1214-7291
Date Established: 08.09.04; **Freq:** Annual; **Cover Price:** CZK 89; **Circ:** 40,000
Usual Pagination: 90
Editor: Markéta Strnadová
Profile: Catalogue of houses with energetics and energy savings.
Language(s): Czech
ADVERTISING RATES:
Full Page Colour .... CZK 59000
Mechanical Data: Type Area: 270 x 190mm
BUSINESS: ARCHITECTURE & BUILDING: Planning & Housing

RODINNÝ DŮM
1701778CZ4D-9
Editorial: Nádražní 762/32, 15000 PRAHA 5
Tel: 225351630 **Fax:** 225351622
Email: info@bmczech.cz **Web site:** http://www.bmczech.cz
ISSN: 1214-5181
Date Established: 04.03.04; **Freq:** Monthly; **Cover Price:** CZK 35
Annual Sub.: CZK 280; **Circ:** 27,230
Usual Pagination: 112
Editor: Michal Wernisch
Profile: Magazine about housing and building houses.
Language(s): Czech
ADVERTISING RATES:
Full Page Colour .... CZK 81000
Mechanical Data: Type Area: 184 x 235mm
BUSINESS: ARCHITECTURE & BUILDING: Planning & Housing

ROZHLEDY V CHIRURGII
1600791CZ56A-140
Editorial: Sokolská 31, 12026 PRAHA 2
Tel: 224911420 **Fax:** 224266265
Email: medical@euronet.cz **Web site:** http://www.medical.cz
ISSN: 0035-9351
Date Established: 01.01.1921; **Freq:** Monthly; **Cover Price:** CZK 92
Annual Sub.: CZK 912; **Circ:** 1,500
Usual Pagination: 56
Profile: Professional medical magazine.
Language(s): Czech; English; Slovak
Readership: Aimed at surgeons, surgical staff and postgraduate students.
ADVERTISING RATES:
Full Page Colour .... CZK 36000
Mechanical Data: Type Area: 168 x 248mm
BUSINESS: HEALTH & MEDICAL

RYBÁŘSTVÍ
1701815CZ92-4
Editorial: Akademická 688/1, 10800 PRAHA 10
Tel: 274781562 **Fax:** 274784048
Email: urban@rybar-sro.cz **Web site:** http://www.rybar-sro.cz
ISSN: 0373-675X
Date Established: 01.01.1897; **Freq:** Monthly; **Cover Price:** CZK 70; **Circ:** 40,000
Usual Pagination: 100
Editor: Vladimír Urban
Profile: Magazine about fishing.
Language(s): Czech
ADVERTISING RATES:
Full Page Colour .... CZK 50000
Mechanical Data: Type Area: 185 x 263mm
CONSUMER: ANGLING & FISHING

RYTMUS ŽIVOTA
764035CZ74A-280
Editorial: Victora Huga 6, P.O.Box 125, 15000 PRAHA 5 **Tel:** 225008303 **Fax:** 225008340
Email: inzerce@bauermedia.cz **Web site:** http://www.bauermedia.cz
ISSN: 1211-5649
Date Established: 13.11.96; **Freq:** Weekly; **Cover Price:** CZK 20
Annual Sub.: CZK 1014; **Circ:** 361,562
Usual Pagination: 56
Editor: Jiřina Pavlíková
Profile: Tabloid magazine covering social topics.
Language(s): Czech
Readership: Aimed at women aged between 20 and 50 years.
ADVERTISING RATES:
Full Page Colour .... CZK 210000
Mechanical Data: Type Area: 202 x 259mm
CONSUMER: WOMEN'S INTEREST CONSUMER MAGAZINES: Women's Interest

SALON
1701377CZ74A-417
Editorial: Bohdalecká 6/1420, 10100 PRAHA 10 - MICHLE **Tel:** 281090640 **Fax:** 281090644
Email: jan.lidmansky@rf-hobby.cz **Web site:** http://www.rf-hobby.cz
Date Established: 01.01.04; **Freq:** Quarterly; **Cover Price:** CZK 49; **Circ:** 46,843
Usual Pagination: 118
Editor: Lea Slámová
Profile: Women's magazine about healthy life.
Language(s): Czech
ADVERTISING RATES:
Full Page Colour .... CZK 89000
CONSUMER: WOMEN'S INTEREST CONSUMER MAGAZINES: Women's Interest

SANQUIS
1701835CZ56R-134
Editorial: Španělská 1073/10, 12000 PRAHA 2
Tel: 221180195 **Fax:** 221180280
Email: info@sanquis.cz **Web site:** http://www.sanquis.cz
ISSN: 1212-6535
Date Established: 01.12.99; **Freq:** Monthly; **Cover Price:** CZK 95
Annual Sub.: CZK 950; **Circ:** 10,000
Usual Pagination: 84
Editor: Irena Jirků
Profile: Professional magazine about medicine with culture and art.
Language(s): Czech
ADVERTISING RATES:
Full Page Colour .... CZK 55000
Mechanical Data: Type Area: 194 x 270mm
BUSINESS: HEALTH & MEDICAL: Health Medical Related

SANTÉ
1701836CZ74G-20
Editorial: Jakobiho 326, 10900 PRAHA 10
Tel: 274861189 **Fax:** 274861189
Email: pharmanews@pharmanews.cz **Web site:** http://www.pharmanews.cz
Date Established: 01.05.03; **Freq:** Half-yearly; **Cover Price:** Free; **Circ:** 550,000
Usual Pagination: 16
Editor: Jana Jokešová
Profile: Class magazine about health and lifestyle.
Language(s): Czech
ADVERTISING RATES:
Full Page Colour .... CZK 99000
Mechanical Data: Type Area: 190 x 277mm
CONSUMER: WOMEN'S INTEREST CONSUMER MAGAZINES: Slimming & Health

SECURITY WORLD
1701406CZ5B-28
Editorial: Seydlerova 2451/11, 15500 PRAHA 5 - NOVÉ BUTOVICE **Tel:** 257088110 **Fax:** 235520812
Email: info@idg.cz **Web site:** http://www.idg.cz
ISSN: 1802-4505
Date Established: 15.09.04; **Freq:** Quarterly; **Cover Price:** CZK 49
Annual Sub.: CZK 160; **Circ:** 10,000
Usual Pagination: 52
Editor: Petr Mandík
Profile: Magazine about computer safety.
Language(s): Czech
ADVERTISING RATES:
Full Page Colour .... CZK 85000
Mechanical Data: Type Area: 180 x 253mm
BUSINESS: COMPUTERS & AUTOMATION: Data Processing

ŠESTKA
1702099CZ67J-145
Editorial: Politických vězňů 10, 11000 PRAHA 1
Tel: 22192409
Email: bachora@volny.cz **Web site:** http://www.sestka.cz
Date Established: 01.01.94; **Freq:** Monthly; **Cover Price:** Free; **Circ:** 56,000
Usual Pagination: 24
Editor: Jaroslav Bachora
Profile: Newsletter of Prague 6.
Language(s): Czech
ADVERTISING RATES:
Full Page Colour .... CZK 39111
Mechanical Data: Type Area: 208 x 259mm
REGIONAL DAILY & SUNDAY NEWSPAPERS: Regional Newspapers (excl. dailies)

SETKÁNÍ (AUTOMOBILY A STK)
1701864CZ77A-262
Editorial: Mistřínská 394, 15521 PRAHA 5
Tel: 235318694 **Fax:** 235318694
Email: osmium.praha@volny.cz
Date Established: 01.01.04; **Freq:** Quarterly; **Cover Price:** Free; **Circ:** 100,000
Usual Pagination: 20
Editor: Otakar Štajf
Profile: Motorist magazine.
Language(s): Czech
ADVERTISING RATES:
Full Page Colour .... CZK 90000
Mechanical Data: Type Area: 188 x 272mm
CONSUMER: MOTORING & CYCLING: Motoring

ŠÍP PLUS
1776774CZ65A-26
Editorial: Přátelství 986, 10424 PRAHA 10 - UHŘÍNĚVES **Tel:** 221999111 **Fax:** 221999520
Email: i.valterova@tv-mag.cz **Web site:** http://www.tv-mag.cz
ISSN: 1801-478X
Date Established: 17.10.05; **Freq:** Weekly; **Cover Price:** CZK 14; **Circ:** 118,264
Usual Pagination: 48
Editor: Michal Brož
Profile: Nationwide yellow press (except for Praha).
Language(s): Czech
ADVERTISING RATES:
Full Page Colour .... CZK 110000
Mechanical Data: Type Area: 225 x 265mm
NATIONAL DAILY & SUNDAY NEWSPAPERS: National Daily Newspapers

ŠKODA MAGAZÍN
1699928CZ77A-237
Editorial: Václava Klementa 869/II, 29360 MLADÁ BOLESLAV **Tel:** 326817338 **Fax:** 326812302
Email: info@skoda-auto.cz **Web site:** http://www.skoda-auto.cz
ISSN: 1802-2561
Date Established: 01.01.02; **Freq:** Quarterly; **Cover Price:** Free; **Circ:** 50,000
Usual Pagination: 40
Editor: Jana Skočdopolová
Profile: Magazine for members of Skoda motor Club.
Language(s): Czech
ADVERTISING RATES:
Full Page Colour .... CZK 70000
Mechanical Data: Type Area: 198 x 286mm
CONSUMER: MOTORING & CYCLING: Motoring

ŠKOLA PLETENÍ (EDICE BURDA)
1777001CZ74E-8
Editorial: Přemyslovská 2845/43, 13000 PRAHA 3
Tel: 221589111 **Fax:** 222522648
Email: inzerce@burda.cz **Web site:** http://www.burda.cz
Date Established: 01.01.96
Cover Price: Free; **Circ:** 40,000
Usual Pagination: 99
Profile: Magazine about needlework.
Language(s): Czech
CONSUMER: WOMEN'S INTEREST CONSUMER MAGAZINES: Crafts

SNPLUS
1701992CZ42R-3
Editorial: Radlická 2, 15000 PRAHA 5
Tel: 251560513 **Fax:** 251560513
Email: premisa@premisa.cz **Web site:** http://www.premisa.cz
Date Established: 10.12.93; **Freq:** Monthly; **Annual Sub.:** CZK 238; **Circ:** 60,000
Editor: Ivana Zedníková
Profile: Advertising newspaper about building industry.
Language(s): Czech
ADVERTISING RATES:
Full Page Colour .... CZK 40339
BUSINESS: CONSTRUCTION: Construction Related

SOUDCE
1701934CZ44-29
Editorial: Vlašská 6, 11800 PRAHA 1 **Tel:** 257223009
Fax: 257223010
Email: sekretariat@brainteam.cz **Web site:** http://www.brainteam.cz
ISSN: 1211-5347
Date Established: 01.01.99; **Freq:** Monthly; **Annual Sub.:** CZK 2280; **Circ:** 3,500
Usual Pagination: 40
Editor: Karel Havlíček
Profile: Professional magazine of law courts in Czech Republic.
Language(s): Czech
ADVERTISING RATES:
Full Page Colour .... CZK 20000
BUSINESS: LEGAL

SPEED
1701948CZ77A-263
Editorial: Drtinova 8, 15000 PRAHA 5
Tel: 234109126 **Fax:** 234109241
Email: esquire@stratosfera.cz **Web site:** http://www.stratosfera.cz
ISSN: 1212-4583
Date Established: 01.04.99; **Freq:** Monthly; **Cover Price:** CZK 75,
Annual Sub.: CZK 749; **Circ:** 40,000
Usual Pagination: 100
Editor: Jan Červenka
Profile: Magazine about sport cars.
Language(s): Czech
ADVERTISING RATES:
Full Page Colour .... CZK 118000
CONSUMER: MOTORING & CYCLING: Motoring

SPIRIT
1701955CZ74R-9
Editorial: Ve Stromkách 460/10, P.O.Box 114, 40021 ÚSTÍ NAD LABEM 2 **Tel:** 472741989 **Fax:** 472741989
Email: inzerce@spirit.cz **Web site:** http://www.spirit.cz
Date Established: 01.01.90; **Freq:** Weekly; **Cover Price:** CZK 14; **Circ:** 90,000
Usual Pagination: 8
Editor: Marcela Zlatohlávková
Profile: Crosswords, fun topics, natural medicaments.
Language(s): Czech
ADVERTISING RATES:
Full Page Mono .... CZK 66000
Mechanical Data: No. of Columns (Display): 5, Type Area: 260 x 390mm
CONSUMER: WOMEN'S INTEREST CONSUMER MAGAZINES: Women's Interest Related

SPORT
763633CZ75A-200
Editorial: Komunardů 1584/42, 17000 PRAHA 7
Tel: 225975111 **Fax:** 225977653
Email: david.saroch@ringier.cz **Web site:** http://www.ringier.cz
ISSN: 1210-8383
Date Established: 01.01.1953; **Freq:** 312 issues yearly; **Cover Price:** CZK 13; **Circ:** 78,204
Usual Pagination: 24
Editor: Lukáš Tomek
Profile: Nationwide sport daily.
Language(s): Czech
Readership: Aimed at those interested in sport.
ADVERTISING RATES:
Full Page Colour .... CZK 249891,6
Mechanical Data: No. of Columns (Display): 6, Type Area: 285 x 419mm
CONSUMER: SPORT

SPORT MAGAZÍN
1701960CZ75A-226
Editorial: Komunardů 1584/42, 17000 PRAHA 7
Tel: 225975111 **Fax:** 225975476
Email: david.saroch@ringier.cz **Web site:** http://www.ringier.cz
ISSN: 1214-3677
Date Established: 28.02.97; **Freq:** Weekly; **Cover Price:** CZK 16; **Circ:** 98,238
Usual Pagination: 32
Editor: Lukáš Tomek
Profile: Supplement of SPORT.
Language(s): Czech
ADVERTISING RATES:
Full Page Colour .... CZK 125000
Mechanical Data: Type Area: 190 x 264mm
CONSUMER: SPORT

Czech Republic

SPY
763791CZ74Q-1

Editorial: Drtinova 8, 15000 PRAHA 5
Tel: 234109450 **Fax:** 234109431
Email: esquire@stratosfera.cz **Web site:** http://www.stratosfera.cz
ISSN: 1212-2645
Date Established: 15.09.98; **Freq:** Weekly; **Cover Price:** CZK 31
Annual Sub.: CZK 1488; **Circ:** 170,000
Usual Pagination: 60
Editor: Leoš Mareš
Profile: Tabloid weekly about celebrities, scandals etc.
Language(s): Czech
Readership: Aimed mainly at women.
ADVERTISING RATES:
Full Page Colour .... CZK 215000
CONSUMER: WOMEN'S INTEREST CONSUMER MAGAZINES: Lifestyle

SREALITY
1701972CZ1E-39

Editorial: Radlická 608/2, 15000 PRAHA 5
Tel: 234694451-2 **Fax:** 234694459
Email: obchod@firma.seznam.cz **Web site:** http://www.seznam.cz
Date Established: 14.03.03; **Freq:** 10 issues yearly; **Cover Price:** Free; **Circ:** 480,000
Usual Pagination: 42
Editor: Ivana Michálková
Profile: Advertising magazine specialized in real estates.
Language(s): Czech
ADVERTISING RATES:
Full Page Colour .... CZK 45000
Mechanical Data: Type Area: 184 x 256mm
BUSINESS: FINANCE & ECONOMICS: Property

STAVBA
1701988CZ4A-29

Editorial: Nádražní 762/32, 15000 PRAHA 5
Tel: 225351351 **Fax:** 225351104
Email: info@bmczech.cz **Web site:** http://www.bmczech.cz
ISSN: 1210-9568
Date Established: 01.05.94; **Freq:** 24 issues yearly; **Cover Price:** CZK 99
Annual Sub.: CZK 474; **Circ:** 6,000
Usual Pagination: 114
Editor: Milena Sršňová
Profile: Magazine about building industry.
Language(s): Czech
ADVERTISING RATES:
Full Page Colour .... CZK 92000
Mechanical Data: Type Area: 185 x 254mm
BUSINESS: ARCHITECTURE & BUILDING: Architecture

STAVEBNICTVÍ (PONTIUM)
1776996CZ4R-6

Editorial: Brněnská 700/25, 50006 HRADEC KRÁLOVÉ **Tel:** 495541949 **Fax:** 495541949
Date Established: 01.01.01; **Freq:** Annual; **Cover Price:** Free; **Circ:** 30,000
Usual Pagination: 76
Editor: Petr Dastlík
Profile: Specialized building industry directory of companies in individual regions of Bohemia and Moravia.
Language(s): Czech
BUSINESS: ARCHITECTURE & BUILDING: Building Related

STAVOSPOJ
1702000CZ4R-1

Editorial: Letohradská 48, 17000 PRAHA 7
Tel: 225278147 **Fax:** 233380336
Email: agro@cztisk.cz
Date Established: 01.11.03; **Freq:** Weekly; **Annual Sub.:** CZK 686,4; **Circ:** 30,000
Usual Pagination: 64
Editor: Michaela Poesová
Profile: Magazine about building industry.
Language(s): Czech
ADVERTISING RATES:
Full Page Colour .... CZK 30000
Mechanical Data: Type Area: 190 x 275mm
BUSINESS: ARCHITECTURE & BUILDING: Building Related

STEREO & VIDEO
1702002CZ78A-5

Editorial: Pernerova 35a, 18600 PRAHA 8 - KARLÍN
Tel: 225386575 **Fax:** 225386555
Email: tlp@tlp.cz **Web site:** http://www.tlp.cz
ISSN: 1210-7026
Date Established: 20.09.93; **Freq:** Monthly; **Cover Price:** CZK 199
Annual Sub.: CZK 4666; **Circ:** 14,600
Usual Pagination: 120
Editor: Luboš Horčic
Profile: Magazine about audio and video technics.
Language(s): Czech
ADVERTISING RATES:
Full Page Colour .... CZK 150000
Mechanical Data: Type Area: 179 x 250mm
CONSUMER: CONSUMER ELECTRONICS: Hi-Fi & Recording

ŠTĚSTÍ A NESNÁZE
1702115CZ74Q-17

Editorial: Victora Huga 6, P.O.Box 125, 15000 PRAHA 5 **Tel:** 225008245 **Fax:** 257327103
Email: inzerce@bauermedia.cz **Web site:** http://www.bauermedia.cz
Date Established: 31.03.04; **Freq:** 24 issues yearly; **Cover Price:** CZK 20
Annual Sub.: CZK 114; **Circ:** 28,448
Usual Pagination: 36
Editor: Iveta Cichrová
Profile: Magazine for women with stories from life and about love.
Language(s): Czech
ADVERTISING RATES:
Full Page Colour .... CZK 35000
Mechanical Data: Type Area: 185 x 252mm
CONSUMER: WOMEN'S INTEREST CONSUMER MAGAZINES: Lifestyle

STORY
1702009CZ74Q-27

Editorial: Lomnického 7, 14000 PRAHA 4
Tel: 296162250 **Fax:** 296162420
Email: inzerce@sanomamag-praha.cz **Web site:** http://www.sanoma.cz
ISSN: 1211-1848
Date Established: 28.04.94; **Freq:** Weekly; **Cover Price:** CZK 33; **Circ:** 63,064
Usual Pagination: 84
Editor: Daniela Prokopová
Profile: Tabloid social magazine.
Language(s): Czech
ADVERTISING RATES:
Full Page Colour .... CZK 199000
Mechanical Data: Type Area: 210 x 262mm
CONSUMER: WOMEN'S INTEREST CONSUMER MAGAZINES: Lifestyle

STŘELECKÁ REVUE
1702024CZ75F-3

Editorial: Křižíkova 35 (2. patro), 18600 PRAHA 8
Tel: 221863404 **Fax:** 221863404
Email: shootmag@volny.cz **Web site:** http://www.strelecka-revue.cz
ISSN: 0322-7650
Date Established: 01.01.1970; **Freq:** Monthly; **Cover Price:** CZK 67
Annual Sub.: CZK 660; **Circ:** 27,000
Usual Pagination: 100
Editor: Přemysl Liška
Profile: Magazine about munitions, firearms and history.
Language(s): Czech
ADVERTISING RATES:
Full Page Colour .... CZK 29000
Mechanical Data: Type Area: 175 x 253mm
CONSUMER: SPORT: Shooting

STUFF
1702040CZ86C-9

Editorial: Drtinova 8, 15000 PRAHA 5
Tel: 234109261 **Fax:** 234109241
Email: esquire@stratosfera.cz **Web site:** http://www.stratosfera.cz
ISSN: 1214-2603
Date Established: 12.09.03; **Freq:** Monthly; **Cover Price:** CZK 65
Annual Sub.: CZK 659; **Circ:** 35,000
Usual Pagination: 100
Editor: Tomáš Suchomel
Profile: "Magazine dealing with technical ""toys"" for men.".
Language(s): Czech
ADVERTISING RATES:
Full Page Colour .... CZK 110000
CONSUMER: ADULT & GAY MAGAZINES: Men's Lifestyle Magazines

STYLE
1702041CZ74B-16

Editorial: Drtinova 8, 15000 PRAHA 5
Tel: 234109195 **Fax:** 234109192
Email: esquire@stratosfera.cz **Web site:** http://www.stratosfera.cz
ISSN: 1213-1067
Date Established: 01.09.00; **Freq:** Monthly; **Cover Price:** CZK 59,90
Annual Sub.: CZK 879; **Circ:** 70,000
Usual Pagination: 148
Editor: Simona Matásková
Profile: Magazine about celebrities.
Language(s): Czech
ADVERTISING RATES:
Full Page Colour .... CZK 187000
CONSUMER: WOMEN'S INTEREST CONSUMER MAGAZINES: Women's Interest - Fashion

SUPER INFO
1702045CZ2A-44

Editorial: Tylova 57, 30100 PLZEŇ, OKR. PLZEŇ
Tel: 377382339 **Fax:** 377383600
Email: plzen@superinfo.cz **Web site:** http://www.superinfo.cz
Date Established: 20.06.95; **Freq:** 26 issues yearly; **Cover Price:** Free; **Circ:** 900,000
Usual Pagination: 8
Editor: Jana Labudová
Profile: Advertising newspaper.
Language(s): Czech
Mechanical Data: Type Area: 200 x 280mm
BUSINESS: COMMUNICATIONS, ADVERTISING & MARKETING

SVĚT
1799483CZ82-260

Editorial: Hrnčířská 23, 60200 BRNO **Tel:** 549210724
Fax: 549210724
Email: broza@epublishing.cz **Web site:** http://www.epublishing.cz
ISSN: 1802-2278
Date Established: 24.11.06; **Freq:** Monthly; **Cover Price:** CZK 49,90
Annual Sub.: CZK 399; **Circ:** 22,150
Usual Pagination: 100
Editor: Igor Mahal
Profile: Magazine about the worldwide news.
Language(s): Czech
ADVERTISING RATES:
Full Page Colour .... CZK 115000
Mechanical Data: Type Area: 204 x 260mm
CONSUMER: CURRENT AFFAIRS & POLITICS

SVĚT BALENÍ
1812864CZ35-1

Editorial: Dělnická 213/12, Rosmarin Business Center, 17000 PRAHA 7 -HOLEŠOVICE
Tel: 270003945 **Fax:** 270003977
Email: con@con-praha.cz **Web site:** http://www.con-praha.cz
ISSN: 1212-7809
Date Established: 01.01.07; **Freq:** 24 issues yearly; **Cover Price:** CZK 80
Annual Sub.: CZK 400; **Circ:** 7,000
Usual Pagination: 52
Editor: Ladislava Caisová
Profile: Profesional magazine specialized in pack and packing technologies.
Language(s): Czech
ADVERTISING RATES:
Full Page Colour .... CZK 60000
Mechanical Data: Type Area: 175 x 262mm
BUSINESS: PACKAGING & BOTTLING

SVĚT KOUPELEN
1702064CZ23C-1

Editorial: Nádražní 762/32, 15000 PRAHA 5
Tel: 225351150 **Fax:** 225351153
Email: info@bmczech.cz **Web site:** http://www.bmczech.cz
Date Established: 15.03.00; **Freq:** Quarterly; **Cover Price:** CZK 49
Annual Sub.: CZK 528; **Circ:** 6,600
Usual Pagination: 100
Editor: Petr Tschakert
Profile: Magazine about bathrooms.
Language(s): Czech
ADVERTISING RATES:
Full Page Colour .... CZK 49000
Mechanical Data: Type Area: 192 x 261mm
BUSINESS: FURNISHINGS & FURNITURE: Furnishings & Furniture - Kitchens & Bathrooms

SVĚT KUCHYNÍ
1702065CZ23C-2

Editorial: Nádražní 762/32, 15000 PRAHA 5
Tel: 225351150 **Fax:** 225351153
Email: info@bmczech.cz **Web site:** http://www.bmczech.cz
Date Established: 15.02.00; **Freq:** Quarterly; **Cover Price:** CZK 49
Annual Sub.: CZK 528; **Circ:** 14,260
Usual Pagination: 100
Editor: Petr Tschakert
Profile: Magazine about kitchens.
Language(s): Czech
ADVERTISING RATES:
Full Page Colour .... CZK 49000
Mechanical Data: Type Area: 192 x 261mm
BUSINESS: FURNISHINGS & FURNITURE: Furnishings & Furniture - Kitchens & Bathrooms

SVĚT KULTURISTIKY
1702066CZ75P-1

Editorial: Wintrova 11/1313, 53009 PARDUBICE
Tel: 466611314 **Fax:** 466611314
Email: rudzinskyj@pce.czcom.cz **Web site:** http://www.svetkulturistiky.cz
ISSN: 1210-289X
Date Established: 01.04.90; **Freq:** Monthly; **Cover Price:** CZK 78
Annual Sub.: CZK 780; **Circ:** 39,000
Usual Pagination: 100
Editor: Ivan Rudzinskyj
Profile: Body-building magazine.
Language(s): Czech
ADVERTISING RATES:
Full Page Colour .... CZK 35000
CONSUMER: SPORT: Fitness/Bodybuilding

SVĚT MOTORŮ
1702071CZ77A-264

Editorial: Dělnická 12, 17000 PRAHA 7
Tel: 234692312 **Fax:** 234692329
Email: inzerce@axelspringer.cz **Web site:** http://www.topdivka.cz
ISSN: 0039-7016
Date Established: 01.01.1946; **Freq:** Weekly; **Cover Price:** CZK 22
Annual Sub.: CZK 780; **Circ:** 45,818
Usual Pagination: 52
Editor: Zbyšek Pechr
Profile: Popular magazine bringing information about the world of rally and F1. Also features advice, test reviews and news from motoring industries around the world.
Language(s): Czech
ADVERTISING RATES:
Full Page Colour .... CZK 140000
Mechanical Data: Type Area: 200 x 270mm
CONSUMER: MOTORING & CYCLING: Motoring

SVĚT PSŮ
1702077CZ81B-6

Editorial: Říčanská 10/1923, 10100 PRAHA 10 - VINOHRADY **Tel:** 272742611 **Fax:** 271732458
Email: minerva@i-minerva.cz **Web site:** http://www.i-minerva.cz
ISSN: 1211-2976
Date Established: 01.06.94; **Freq:** Monthly; **Cover Price:** CZK 47
Annual Sub.: CZK 492; **Circ:** 30,000
Usual Pagination: 96
Editor: Petr Dvořák
Profile: Magazine about dogs.
Language(s): Czech
ADVERTISING RATES:
Full Page Colour .... CZK 36000
Mechanical Data: Type Area: 192 x 263mm
CONSUMER: ANIMALS & PETS: Dogs

SVĚT ŽENY
1702081CZ74A-421

Editorial: Přemyslovská 2845/43, 13000 PRAHA 3
Tel: 222520617 **Fax:** 222522648
Email: inzerce@burda.cz **Web site:** http://www.burda.cz
ISSN: 1213-757X
Date Established: 08.04.02; **Freq:** Monthly; **Cover Price:** CZK 12; **Circ:** 250,000
Usual Pagination: 124
Editor: Markéta Vavřinová
Profile: Magazine for contemporary dynamic women which is bringing a lot of periodic column.
Language(s): Czech
ADVERTISING RATES:
Full Page Colour .... CZK 225000
Mechanical Data: Type Area: 173 x 220mm
CONSUMER: WOMEN'S INTEREST CONSUMER MAGAZINES: Women's Interest

SVĚTLO
1702083CZ17-2

Editorial: Pod Vodárenskou věží 1143/4, 18208 PRAHA 8 **Tel:** 286583011-2 **Fax:** 284683022
Email: inzerce@fccgroup.cz **Web site:** http://www.fccgroup.cz
ISSN: 1212-0812
Date Established: 01.01.98; **Freq:** 24 issues yearly; **Cover Price:** CZK 52
Annual Sub.: CZK 312; **Circ:** 2,300
Usual Pagination: 56
Editor: Jiří Novotný
Profile: Magazine for lighting technicians.
Language(s): Czech
ADVERTISING RATES:
Full Page Colour .... CZK 36000
Mechanical Data: Type Area: 180 x 248mm
BUSINESS: ELECTRICAL

TATRANSKÉ PUTOVÁNÍ
1799486CZ89A-54

Editorial: Hradčany 86, 28906 HRADČANY
Email: a.schellenberg@email.cz **Web site:** http://www.schellenberg.cz
Date Established: 01.01.06; **Freq:** Quarterly; **Cover Price:** Free; **Circ:** 40,000
Usual Pagination: 52
Profile: Magazine about Tatry mountain.
Language(s): Czech
ADVERTISING RATES:
Full Page Colour .... CZK 45000
Mechanical Data: Type Area: 196 x 252mm
CONSUMER: HOLIDAYS & TRAVEL: Travel

TERRA
1702165CZ46-15

Editorial: Dolní náměstí 172/16, 77900 OLOMOUC
Tel: 585224318 **Fax:** 585224318
Email: redakce@terrapolis.cz **Web site:** http://www.terrapolis.cz
Date Established: 01.01.92; **Freq:** 10 issues yearly; **Cover Price:** CZK 18
Annual Sub.: CZK 432; **Circ:** 30,000
Usual Pagination: 60
Editor: Václav Dostál
Profile: Magazine about wood-processing industry.
Language(s): Czech
ADVERTISING RATES:
Full Page Colour .... CZK 27000
Mechanical Data: Type Area: 218 x 312mm
BUSINESS: TIMBER, WOOD & FORESTRY

TESCOMA MAGAZÍN
1702166CZ74P-17

Editorial: Nádražní 762/32, 15000 PRAHA 5
Email: info@bmczech.cz **Web site:** http://www.bmczech.cz
Date Established: 01.03.05; **Freq:** Quarterly; **Cover Price:** Free; **Circ:** 35,000
Usual Pagination: 66
Profile: Magazine about gastronomy.
Language(s): Czech
ADVERTISING RATES:
Full Page Colour .... CZK 25000
Mechanical Data: Type Area: 193 x 236mm
CONSUMER: WOMEN'S INTEREST CONSUMER MAGAZINES: Food & Cookery

TINA
1702184CZ74A-422

Editorial: Victora Huga 6, P.O.Box 125, 15000 PRAHA 5 **Tel:** 225008250 **Fax:** 257324072
Email: inzerce@bauermedia.cz **Web site:** http://www.bauermedia.cz
ISSN: 1801-7398
Date Established: 01.01.91; **Freq:** Weekly; **Cover Price:** CZK 11
Annual Sub.: CZK 520; **Circ:** 139,838
Usual Pagination: 52
Editor: Renáta Fialová
Profile: Magazine for women, about cosmetics, cooking, fashion, children, medicine, travelling, crosswords.
Language(s): Czech
ADVERTISING RATES:
Full Page Colour .... CZK 220000
Mechanical Data: Type Area: 208 x 299mm
CONSUMER: WOMEN'S INTEREST CONSUMER MAGAZINES: Women's Interest

TOP DÍVKY
1702205CZ74F-3

Editorial: Dělnická 12, 17000 PRAHA 7
Tel: 234692220 **Fax:** 234692229
Email: inzerce@axelspringer.cz **Web site:** http://www.topdivka.cz
ISSN: 1214-3804
Date Established: 01.01.94; **Freq:** Monthly; **Cover Price:** CZK 43,90; **Circ:** 59,625
Usual Pagination: 68
Editor: Marie Písecká
Profile: Magazine for teenage girls.
Language(s): Czech
ADVERTISING RATES:
Full Page Colour .... CZK 150000
Mechanical Data: Type Area: 190 x 275mm
CONSUMER: WOMEN'S INTEREST CONSUMER MAGAZINES: Teenage

TOP GEAR
1776784CZ77A-278

Editorial: Drtinova 8, 15000 PRAHA 5
Tel: 234109598 **Fax:** 234109241
Email: esquire@stratosfera.cz **Web site:** http://www.stratosfera.cz
ISSN: 1212-4583
Date Established: 29.05.06; **Freq:** Monthly; **Cover Price:** CZK 85
Annual Sub.: CZK 879; **Circ:** 45,000
Usual Pagination: 148
Editor: Jan Červenka
Profile: Car magazine.
Language(s): Czech
ADVERTISING RATES:
Full Page Colour .... CZK 100000
CONSUMER: MOTORING & CYCLING: Motoring

TRAVEL IN THE CZECH REPUBLIC
1702219CZ89A-32

Editorial: Mezi Vodami 1952/9, 14300 PRAHA 4 - MODŘANY **Tel:** 225276111 **Fax:** 225276222
Email: inzerce@mf.cz **Web site:** http://www.mf.cz
ISSN: 1214-388X
Date Established: 01.01.03; **Freq:** 24 issues yearly;
Annual Sub.: CZK 499; **Circ:** 30,000
Usual Pagination: 100
Editor: Jan Schlindenbuch
Profile: Magazine presenting the Czech republic to foreigners.
Language(s): Czech; English
ADVERTISING RATES:
Full Page Colour .... CZK 59000
CONSUMER: HOLIDAYS & TRAVEL: Travel

TRUCKER
1702244CZ49D-2

Editorial: Nádražní 762/32, 15000 PRAHA 5
Tel: 225351501 **Fax:** 225351404
Email: info@bmczech.cz **Web site:** http://www.bmczech.cz
ISSN: 1335-5431
Date Established: 01.01.91; **Freq:** Monthly; **Cover Price:** CZK 48
Annual Sub.: CZK 432; **Circ:** 13,540
Usual Pagination: 76
Editor: Boris Dacko
Profile: Magazine about trucks and traffic.
Language(s): Czech; Slovak
BUSINESS: TRANSPORT: Commercial Vehicles

TRUCKSALON
1777010CZ49C-11

Editorial: Dělnická 12, 17000 PRAHA 7
Tel: 234692340 **Fax:** 234692340
Email: inzerce@axelspringer.cz **Web site:** http://www.topdivka.cz
ISSN: 1212-334X
Date Established: 01.01.99; **Freq:** Annual; **Cover Price:** CZK 89; **Circ:** 30,000
Usual Pagination: 100
Profile: Truck catalogue.
Language(s): Czech
ADVERTISING RATES:
Full Page Colour .... CZK 75000
Mechanical Data: Type Area: 200 x 270mm
BUSINESS: TRANSPORT: Freight

TUČŇÁK
1702256CZ67J-105

Editorial: Na Poříčí 8, 11000 PRAHA 1
Tel: 224816821 **Fax:** 224816818
Email: strategic@consultants.cz **Web site:** http://www.consultants.cz
Date Established: 01.01.91; **Freq:** Monthly; **Cover Price:** Free; **Circ:** 71,500
Usual Pagination: 32
Editor: Martin Dudek
Profile: Newspaper of Prague 4.
Language(s): Czech
ADVERTISING RATES:
Full Page Colour .... CZK 56400
Mechanical Data: Type Area: 182 x 264mm
REGIONAL DAILY & SUNDAY NEWSPAPERS: Regional Newspapers (excl. dailies)

TUNING MAGAZINE
1702260CZ77A-268

Editorial: Jandova 3/10, 19000 PRAHA 9
Tel: 234639954 **Fax:** 234639954
Email: inzerce@tuning-magazine.cz **Web site:** http://www.tuning-magazine.cz
ISSN: 1214-2964
Date Established: 23.06.03; **Freq:** Monthly; **Cover Price:** CZK 89
Annual Sub.: CZK 780; **Circ:** 25,000
Usual Pagination: 108
Editor: Robert Bezouška
Profile: Magazine about auto tuning.
Language(s): Czech
ADVERTISING RATES:
Full Page Colour .... CZK 32000
CONSUMER: MOTORING & CYCLING: Motoring

TV PLUS
1702270CZ89C-29

Editorial: Victora Huga 6, P.O.Box 125, 15000 PRAHA 5 **Tel:** 225008709 **Fax:** 257327103
Email: inzerce@bauermedia.cz **Web site:** http://www.bauermedia.cz
ISSN: 1212-6500
Date Established: 14.09.99; **Freq:** Weekly; **Cover Price:** CZK 9; **Circ:** 69,006
Usual Pagination: 40
Editor: Tamara Dobrovolná
Profile: TV channels programme and film guide.
Language(s): Czech
ADVERTISING RATES:
Full Page Colour .... CZK 95000
Mechanical Data: Type Area: 184 x 253mm
CONSUMER: HOLIDAYS & TRAVEL: Entertainment Guides

TV POHODA
1702271CZ89C-30

Editorial: V Olšinách 75, 10000 PRAHA 10
Tel: 281002205 **Fax:** 274775492
Email: j.davidkova@tv-pohoda.cz **Web site:** http://www.tv-pohoda.cz
ISSN: 1801-352X
Date Established: 19.09.05; **Freq:** Weekly; **Cover Price:** CZK 9; **Circ:** 217,565
Usual Pagination: 36
Editor: Zuzana Horešovská
Profile: TV channels programme and film guide.
Language(s): Czech
ADVERTISING RATES:
Full Page Colour .... CZK 140000
Mechanical Data: Type Area: 200 x 285mm
CONSUMER: HOLIDAYS & TRAVEL: Entertainment Guides

TV REVUE
1702272CZ89C-31

Editorial: Victora Huga 6, P.O.Box 125, 15000 PRAHA 5 **Tel:** 225008709 **Fax:** 257327103
Email: inzerce@bauermedia.cz **Web site:** http://www.bauermedia.cz
ISSN: 1212-2998
Date Established: 01.10.99; **Freq:** Weekly; **Cover Price:** CZK 13
Annual Sub.: CZK 494; **Circ:** 52,569
Usual Pagination: 48
Editor: Tamara Dobrovolná
Profile: TV channels programme and film guide.
Language(s): Czech
ADVERTISING RATES:
Full Page Colour .... CZK 130000
Mechanical Data: Type Area: 193 x 263mm
CONSUMER: HOLIDAYS & TRAVEL: Entertainment Guides

TV STAR
1776794CZ76C-210

Editorial: Přátelství 986, 10424 PRAHA 10 - UHŘÍNĚVES **Tel:** 272015326 **Fax:** 272015259
Email: i.valterova@tv-mag.cz **Web site:** http://www.tv-mag.cz
ISSN: 1801-4860
Date Established: 14.11.05; **Freq:** 26 issues yearly; **Cover Price:** CZK 20; **Circ:** 196,748
Usual Pagination: 116
Editor: Alice Mackeová
Profile: TV channels programme and film guide.
Language(s): Czech
ADVERTISING RATES:
Full Page Colour .... CZK 145000
Mechanical Data: Type Area: 190 x 251mm
CONSUMER: MUSIC & PERFORMING ARTS: TV & Radio

TVŮJ SVĚT
1793355CZ74B-25

Editorial: Victora Huga 6, P.O.Box 125, 15000 PRAHA 5 **Tel:** 225008244 **Fax:** 257327103
Email: inzerce@bauermedia.cz **Web site:** http://www.bauermedia.cz
ISSN: 1802-1824
Date Established: 06.11.06; **Freq:** Monthly; **Cover Price:** CZK 14; **Circ:** 37,832
Usual Pagination: 40
Editor: Iveta Cichrová
Profile: Women's magazine about lifestyle, health, cosmetics and psychology.
Language(s): Czech
ADVERTISING RATES:
Full Page Colour .... CZK 110000
Mechanical Data: Type Area: 199 x 255mm
CONSUMER: WOMEN'S INTEREST CONSUMER MAGAZINES: Women's Interest - Fashion

TÝDEN
1702276CZ82-247

Editorial: Panská 7/890, Kaunický palác, 11000 PRAHA 1 **Tel:** 296827110 **Fax:** 224239408
Email: tyden@tyden.cz **Web site:** http://www.tyden.cz
ISSN: 1210-9940
Date Established: 01.09.94; **Freq:** Weekly; **Cover Price:** CZK 30; **Circ:** 65,573
Usual Pagination: 100
Editor: František Nachtigall
Profile: Magazine containing information about actual politics, economics a social life.
Language(s): Czech
ADVERTISING RATES:
Full Page Colour .... CZK 225000
Mechanical Data: Type Area: 183 x 253mm
CONSUMER: CURRENT AFFAIRS & POLITICS

TÝDENÍK KVĚTY
1702285CZ74A-423

Editorial: Lomnického 7, 14000 PRAHA 4
Tel: 296162522 **Fax:** 224920131
Email: inzerce@sanomamag-praha.cz **Web site:** http://www.sanoma.cz
ISSN: 0862-898X
Date Established: 01.01.1834; **Freq:** Weekly; **Cover Price:** CZK 30; **Circ:** 100,533
Usual Pagination: 92
Editor: Pavel Traub
Profile: Social and fun magazine.
Language(s): Czech
ADVERTISING RATES:
Full Page Colour .... CZK 225000
Mechanical Data: Type Area: 190 x 262mm
CONSUMER: WOMEN'S INTEREST CONSUMER MAGAZINES: Women's Interest

TÝDENÍK ROZHLAS
1702292CZ89C-32

Editorial: Olšanská 3/54, 13000 PRAHA 3
Tel: 272096302 **Fax:** 272096314
Email: casopis.rozhlas@rozhlas.cz **Web site:** http://www.rozhlas.cz
ISSN: 0231-6811
Date Established: 01.01.1925; **Freq:** Weekly; **Cover Price:** CZK 25
Annual Sub.: CZK 624; **Circ:** 30,000
Usual Pagination: 68
Editor: Milan Pokorný
Profile: Culture newspaper with TV and radio channels program.
Language(s): Czech
ADVERTISING RATES:
Full Page Colour .... CZK 34000
Mechanical Data: Type Area: 184 x 246mm
CONSUMER: HOLIDAYS & TRAVEL: Entertainment Guides

TYPOGRAFIA
1702299CZ41A-10

Editorial: Bolívarova 23, 16900 PRAHA 6
Tel: 220960098 **Fax:** 220961441
Email: marsova.typografia@tercie.cz
ISSN: 0322-9068
Date Established: 01.01.1888; **Freq:** Monthly; **Cover Price:** CZK 60
Annual Sub.: CZK 700; **Circ:** 3,500
Usual Pagination: 36
Editor: Vladislav Najbrt
Profile: Professional journal about printing services and typography.
Language(s): Czech
ADVERTISING RATES:
Full Page Colour .... CZK 30000
Mechanical Data: Type Area: 195 x 270mm
BUSINESS: PRINTING & STATIONERY: Printing

U NÁS V KRAJI
1702303CZ67J-102

Editorial: Wonkova 1142, 50002 HRADEC KRÁLOVÉ
Tel: 495817111 **Fax:** 495817336
Email: unasvkraji@kr-kralovehradecky.cz **Web site:** http://www.kr-kralovehradecky.cz
Date Established: 01.09.02; **Freq:** Quarterly; **Cover Price:** Free; **Circ:** 230,000
Usual Pagination: 8
Editor: Jiří Vambera
Profile: Regional newspaper.
Language(s): Czech
ADVERTISING RATES:
Full Page Colour .... CZK 44000
Mechanical Data: Type Area: 285 x 435mm
REGIONAL DAILY & SUNDAY NEWSPAPERS: Regional Newspapers (excl. dailies)

UČITELSKÝ ZPRAVODAJ
1776800CZ62A-17

Editorial: Pobřežní 34, 18600 PRAHA 8
Tel: 234705573 **Fax:** 234705505
Email: scio@scio.cz **Web site:** http://www.scio.cz
Date Established: 02.09.06
Cover Price: Free; **Circ:** 150,000
Usual Pagination: 24
Editor: Bohumil Kartous
Profile: Magazine for teachers about education and about children rearing.
Language(s): Czech
ADVERTISING RATES:
Full Page Colour .... CZK 99000
BUSINESS: CHURCH & SCHOOL EQUIPMENT & EDUCATION: Education

VADEMECUM ZDRAVÍ
1776802CZ74G-35

Editorial: Novorossijská 16, 10000 PRAHA 10
Tel: 271752381 **Fax:** 245008229
Email: info@granit-publishing.cz **Web site:** http://www.vademecum-zdravi.cz
ISSN: 1802-3959
Date Established: 01.01.05; **Freq:** Half-yearly;
Annual Sub.: CZK 60; **Circ:** 30,000
Usual Pagination: 50
Editor: Jiří Prinz, DiS.
Profile: Health magazine.
Language(s): Czech
ADVERTISING RATES:
Full Page Colour .... CZK 60000
Mechanical Data: Type Area: 178 x 240mm
CONSUMER: WOMEN'S INTEREST CONSUMER MAGAZINES: Slimming & Health

VAŘÍME
1702185CZ74P-18

Editorial: Victora Huga 6, P.O.Box 125, 15000 PRAHA 5 **Tel:** 225008250 **Fax:** 257324072
Email: inzerce@bauermedia.cz **Web site:** http://www.bauermedia.cz
ISSN: 1211-4316
Date Established: 26.09.03; **Freq:** Quarterly; **Cover Price:** CZK 30
Annual Sub.: CZK 118; **Circ:** 35,713
Usual Pagination: 52
Editor: Miroslava Mazáčková
Profile: Magazine about cooking.
Language(s): Czech
ADVERTISING RATES:
Full Page Colour .... CZK 75000
Mechanical Data: Type Area: 208 x 271mm
CONSUMER: WOMEN'S INTEREST CONSUMER MAGAZINES: Food & Cookery

VÁŠ OSOBNÍ LÉKAŘ
1702379CZ74G-24

Editorial: V Pátém 226, 19014 PRAHA 9
Tel: 222517772 **Fax:** 281961461
Email: o.sladek@cbox.cz
ISSN: 1212-8467
Date Established: 01.01.94; **Freq:** Monthly; **Cover Price:** CZK 6; **Circ:** 30,000
Usual Pagination: 8
Editor: Bohumil Ždichynec, Csc.
Profile: Magazine about medical prevention.
Language(s): Czech
CONSUMER: WOMEN'S INTEREST CONSUMER MAGAZINES: Slimming & Health

VČELAŘSTVÍ
1702383CZ81G-2

Editorial: Křemencova 177/8, 11524 PRAHA 1
Tel: 224934082 **Fax:** 224934478
Email: uvcsvpha@login.cz **Web site:** http://www.beekeeping.cz
ISSN: 0042-2924
Date Established: 01.01.1947; **Freq:** Monthly; **Cover Price:** Free; **Circ:** 48,000
Usual Pagination: 36
Editor: Petr Prokeš
Profile: Professional magazine about beekeeping.
Language(s): Czech
CONSUMER: ANIMALS & PETS: Bees

VERENA
1702399CZ74E-6

Editorial: Přemyslovská 2845/43, 13000 PRAHA 3
Tel: 222513525 **Fax:** 222522648
Email: inzerce@burda.cz **Web site:** http://www.burda.cz
Date Established: 01.01.99; **Freq:** Half-yearly; **Cover Price:** CZK 99; **Circ:** 50,000
Usual Pagination: 100
Editor: Eva Coufalová
Profile: Magazine about needlework for women.
Language(s): Czech
ADVERTISING RATES:
Full Page Colour .... CZK 58000
Mechanical Data: Type Area: 194 x 253mm
CONSUMER: WOMEN'S INTEREST CONSUMER MAGAZINES: Crafts

VESELÝ VÝLET
1702405CZ89A-40

Editorial: Temný Důl 46, 54226 HORNÍ MARŠOV
Tel: 499736130 **Fax:** 499736131
Email: info@veselyvylet.cz **Web site:** http://www.veselyvylet.cz
Date Established: 06.06.92; **Freq:** Half-yearly; **Cover Price:** Free; **Circ:** 60,000
Usual Pagination: 28
Editor: Pavel Klimeš
Profile: Tourist magazine of mountain Krkonoše.
Language(s): Czech
ADVERTISING RATES:
Full Page Colour .... CZK 14000

Czech Republic

Mechanical Data: Type Area: 180 x 230mm
CONSUMER: HOLIDAYS & TRAVEL: Travel

VETERINÁRNÍ LÉKAŘ
1857264CZ64H-10
Editorial: Třebohostická 564/9, 10000 PRAHA 10
Email: info@tigis.cz **Web site:** http://www.tigis.cz
Date Established: 01.12.06; **Freq:** Quarterly; **Cover Price:** CZK 60
Annual Sub.: CZK 260
Profile: Professional magazine for veterinarians.
Language(s): Czech
ADVERTISING RATES:
Full Page Colour .... CZK 20000
BUSINESS: OTHER CLASSIFICATIONS: Veterinary

VITALAND
1702432CZ74G-25
Editorial: Na Pankráci 1618/30, 14000 PRAHA 4
Tel: 234633460 **Fax:** 234633480
Email: info@vitaland.cz **Web site:** http://www.vitaland.cz
Freq: 24 issues yearly; **Cover Price:** Free; **Circ:** 70,000
Usual Pagination: 40
Editor: Daniela Kramulová
Profile: Magazine for leisure time about health and lifestyle.
Language(s): Czech
ADVERTISING RATES:
Full Page Colour .... CZK 75000
Mechanical Data: Type Area: 196 x 277mm
CONSUMER: WOMEN'S INTEREST CONSUMER MAGAZINES: Slimming & Health

---

VLASTA
763807CZ74A-300
Editorial: Lomnického 7, 14000 PRAHA 4
Tel: 296162255 **Fax:** 296162420
Email: inzerce@sanomamag-praha.cz **Web site:** http://www.sanoma.cz
ISSN: 0139-6617
Date Established: 01.01.1947; **Freq:** Weekly; **Cover Price:** CZK 28
Annual Sub.: CZK 816; **Circ:** 103,436
Usual Pagination: 84
Editor: Jiřina Köppelová
Profile: Women's magazine about life.
Language(s): Czech
Readership: Aimed at women.
CONSUMER: WOMEN'S INTEREST CONSUMER MAGAZINES: Women's Interest

---

VNITŘNÍ LÉKAŘSTVÍ
1600792CZ56A-145
Editorial: Václavské nám. 832/19, 11000 PRAHA 1
Email: info@mhw.cz **Web site:** http://www.medicahealthworld.cz
ISSN: 0042-773X
Date Established: 01.01.1954; **Freq:** Monthly; **Cover Price:** CZK 109
Annual Sub.: CZK 1308; **Circ:** 1,500
Usual Pagination: 84
Editor: Petr Svačina
Profile: Professional journal about internal medicine..
Language(s): Czech; English; Slovak
Readership: Aimed at postgraduates training in all disciplines of internal medicine and general practitioners.
ADVERTISING RATES:
Full Page Colour .... CZK 50000
BUSINESS: HEALTH & MEDICAL

VOLKSWAGEN MAGAZÍN
1702451CZ77A-270
Editorial: Čistovická 249/11, 16300 PRAHA 6
Tel: 220513680 **Fax:** 220518209
Email: vwmagazin@accpr.cz **Web site:** http://www.accpr.cz
ISSN: 1213-4058
Freq: Quarterly; **Cover Price:** CZK 59; **Circ:** 30,000
Usual Pagination: 84
Editor: Jan Klíma
Profile: Magazine of auto factory Volkswagen.
Language(s): Czech
ADVERTISING RATES:
Full Page Colour .... CZK 60000
Mechanical Data: Type Area: 200 x 280mm
CONSUMER: MOTORING & CYCLING: Motoring

VŠE PRO DÍTĚ
1702460CZ56R-105
Editorial: Orelská 18, 10100 PRAHA 10
Tel: 271720898 **Fax:** 271720898
Email: prm@prm.cz **Web site:** http://www.prm.cz
Date Established: 01.04.99; **Freq:** Annual; **Cover Price:** Free; **Circ:** 30,000
Usual Pagination: 88
Profile: Magazine for parents children till 15 years in Prague. Medical guide Prague.
Language(s): Czech
ADVERTISING RATES:
Full Page Colour .... CZK 28200
Mechanical Data: Type Area: 132 x 196mm
BUSINESS: HEALTH & MEDICAL: Health Medical Related

VŠE PRO DŮM - BYT - ZAHRADU - HOBBY
1702461CZ74C-32
Editorial: U topíren 860/2, 17041 PRAHA 7
Tel: 220416165 **Fax:** 220416163
Email: office@antisa.cz **Web site:** http://www.antisa.cz
ISSN: 1214-8210
Freq: Monthly; **Cover Price:** CZK 39
Annual Sub.: CZK 360; **Circ:** 30,000
Usual Pagination: 92
Editor: Lenka Fenclová
Profile: Magazine about housing, building houses, about gardening.
Language(s): Czech
ADVERTISING RATES:
Full Page Colour .... CZK 49000
Mechanical Data: Type Area: 186 x 272mm
CONSUMER: WOMEN'S INTEREST CONSUMER MAGAZINES: Home & Family

VÝCHODOČESKÉ STAVEBNÍ NOVINY
1702472CZ2-102
Editorial: Veverkova 1343, 50002 HRADEC KRÁLOVÉ 2 **Tel:** 498500228 **Fax:** 498500228
Email: informart@post.cz **Web site:** http://www.stavo-info.cz
Date Established: 01.01.00; **Freq:** Monthly; **Cover Price:** Free; **Circ:** 45,000
Usual Pagination: 8
Editor: Ladislav Sobolík
Profile: Advertising newspaper with presentation of architecture companies and products.
Language(s): Czech
Mechanical Data: Type Area: 188 x 270mm
BUSINESS: COMMUNICATIONS, ADVERTISING & MARKETING

VZORY PRO RUČNÍ PLETENÍ (EDICE BURDA)
1777027CZ74E-9
Editorial: Přemyslovská 2845/43, 13000 PRAHA 3
Tel: 221589111 **Fax:** 222522648
Email: inzerce@burda.cz **Web site:** http://www.burda.cz
Date Established: 01.01.96
Cover Price: Free; **Circ:** 40,000
Profile: Magazine about needlework.
Language(s): Czech
CONSUMER: WOMEN'S INTEREST CONSUMER MAGAZINES: Crafts

XANTYPA
1702498CZ74A-425
Editorial: Holečkova 31, 15095 PRAHA 5
Tel: 257312206 **Fax:** 257312729
Email: sekretariat@xantypa.cz **Web site:** http://www.xantypa.cz
ISSN: 1211-7587
Date Established: 01.09.95; **Freq:** Monthly; **Cover Price:** CZK 69
Annual Sub.: CZK 650; **Circ:** 21,000
Usual Pagination: 112
Editor: Magdalena Dietlová
Profile: Social journal about celebrities.
Language(s): Czech
ADVERTISING RATES:
Full Page Colour .... CZK 125000
CONSUMER: WOMEN'S INTEREST CONSUMER MAGAZINES: Women's Interest

---

ZAHRÁDKÁŘ
763767CZ93-200
Editorial: Rokycanova 318/15, 13000 PRAHA 3
Tel: 222781773 **Fax:** 222782711
Web site: http://www.zahradkari.cz
ISSN: 0139-7781
Date Established: 01.01.1968; **Freq:** Monthly; **Cover Price:** CZK 29
Annual Sub.: CZK 240; **Circ:** 100,000
Usual Pagination: 48
Editor: Jan Stanzel, Csc.
Profile: Magazine about gardening.
Language(s): Czech
Readership: Aimed at gardening enthusiasts and allotment owners as well as professional gardeners.
ADVERTISING RATES:
Full Page Colour .... CZK 80000
Mechanical Data: Type Area: 184 x 260mm
CONSUMER: GARDENING

ZBOŽÍ & PRODEJ
1702534CZ53-6
Editorial: Holečkova 657/29, 15095 PRAHA 5
Tel: 246007200 **Fax:** 246007201
Email: josef.broz@atoz.cz **Web site:** http://www.atoz.cz
ISSN: 1802-1662
Date Established: 01.12.93; **Freq:** Monthly; **Cover Price:** CZK 80
Annual Sub.: CZK 840; **Circ:** 12,000
Usual Pagination: 84
Editor: Jana Lysáková
Profile: Magazine about marketing and distribution of food, consumer goods and pharmaceutical goods.
Language(s): Czech
ADVERTISING RATES:
Full Page Colour .... CZK 100000
Mechanical Data: Type Area: 220 x 320mm
BUSINESS: RETAILING & WHOLESALING

ZDRAVÍ
1702537CZ74G-27
Editorial: Táborská 5/979, 14000 PRAHA 4
Tel: 226517935 **Fax:** 226517938
Email: hornova@casopisy2005.cz **Web site:** http://www.floranazahrade.cz
ISSN: 0139-5629
Date Established: 01.01.1953; **Freq:** Monthly; **Cover Price:** CZK 35
Annual Sub.: CZK 384; **Circ:** 35,000
Usual Pagination: 100
Editor: Ivana Závozdová
Profile: Family magazine about health and natural food.
Language(s): Czech
ADVERTISING RATES:
Full Page Colour .... CZK 78000
Mechanical Data: Type Area: 186 x 236mm
CONSUMER: WOMEN'S INTEREST CONSUMER MAGAZINES: Slimming & Health

---

ŽENA A ŽIVOT
763952CZ74A-400
Editorial: Victora Huga 6, P.O.Box 125, 15000 PRAHA 5 **Tel:** 225008260 **Fax:** 257323287
Email: inzerce@bauermedia.cz **Web site:** http://www.bauermedia.cz
ISSN: 1210-8235
Date Established: 28.03.94; **Freq:** 26 issues yearly; **Cover Price:** CZK 29
Annual Sub.: CZK 616; **Circ:** 110,497
Usual Pagination: 116
Editor: Michaela Kramárová
Profile: Women's magazine covering recipes for cooking, needlework, gardening etc.
Language(s): Czech
Readership: Aimed at women aged between 20 and 50 years.
ADVERTISING RATES:
Full Page Colour .... CZK 270000
Mechanical Data: Type Area: 175 x 249mm
CONSUMER: WOMEN'S INTEREST CONSUMER MAGAZINES: Women's Interest

---

ŽENA & KUCHYNĚ
1702714CZ74G-29
Editorial: Lomnického 7, 14000 PRAHA 4
Tel: 296162255 **Fax:** 296162420
Email: inzerce@sanomamag-praha.cz **Web site:** http://www.sanoma.cz
ISSN: 1801-3791
Date Established: 12.10.05; **Freq:** Monthly; **Cover Price:** CZK 38; **Circ:** 67,408
Usual Pagination: 84
Editor: Jiřina Köppelová
Profile: Magazine featuring recipes, table settings, innovations for kitchen. Aimed at modern women.
Language(s): Czech
ADVERTISING RATES:
Full Page Colour .... CZK 99000
Mechanical Data: Type Area: 190 x 250mm
CONSUMER: WOMEN'S INTEREST CONSUMER MAGAZINES: Slimming & Health

---

ŽIJEME NA PLNÝ PLYN
1702717CZ94H-55
Editorial: Novodvorská 803/82, 14200 PRAHA 4
Tel: 241027106 **Fax:** 241027106
Email: stp@stp.cz **Web site:** http://www.stp.cz
Date Established: 01.04.04; **Freq:** Quarterly; **Cover Price:** Free; **Circ:** 130,000
Usual Pagination: 8
Editor: Alena Petríková
Profile: Client magazine of gas companies.
Language(s): Czech
CONSUMER: OTHER CLASSIFICATIONS: Customer Magazines

ZOOM
1702566CZ84A-63
Editorial: Mezi Vodami 1952/9, 14300 PRAHA 4 - MODŘANY **Tel:** 225276361 **Fax:** 225276222
Email: inzerce@mf.cz **Web site:** http://www.mf.cz
ISSN: 1214-3987
Date Established: 01.04.03; **Freq:** Weekly; **Annual Sub.:** CZK 198; **Circ:** 30,000
Editor: Štěpán Sedláček
Profile: Magazine about Prague for young people.
Language(s): Czech
ADVERTISING RATES:
Full Page Colour .... CZK 70000
CONSUMER: THE ARTS & LITERARY: Arts

ZPRAVODAJ VOJENSKÉ ZDRAVOTNÍ POJIŠŤOVNY ČESKÉ REPUBLIKY
1702689CZ94H-28
Editorial: Drahobejlova 1404/4, 19003 PRAHA 9
Tel: 266311911 **Fax:** 284824194
Email: info@vozp.cz **Web site:** http://www.vozp.cz
Date Established: 01.01.95; **Freq:** Half-yearly; **Cover Price:** Free; **Circ:** 400,000
Usual Pagination: 48
Profile: Newsletter of Army Health Insurance Company in Czech Republic.
Language(s): Czech
CONSUMER: OTHER CLASSIFICATIONS: Customer Magazines

Denmark

Time Difference: GMT + 1 hr (CET - Central European Time)
National Telephone Code: +45
Continent: Europe
Capital: Copenhagen
Principal Language: Danish
Population: 5468120
Monetary Unit: Danish Krone (DKK)

EMBASSY HIGH COMMISSION: Royal Danish Embassy: 55 Sloane St, London SW1X 9SR
Tel: 020 7333 0200
Fax: 020 7333 0270
Email: lonamb@um.dk
Website: http://www.amblondon.um.dk/en

&MÆLK
1791652D22A-116
Editorial: Frederiks Allé 22, 8000 ÅRHUS
Tel: 87 31 20 00 **Fax:** 87 31 20 01
Email: lwi@mejeri.dk **Web site:** http://www.mejeri.dk
Freq: Quarterly; **Circ:** 110,000
Editor: Lars Winther
Language(s): Danish
BUSINESS: FOOD

24TIMER FORBRUG
1836451D14A-271
Editorial: Bygmestervej 61, 2400 COPENHAGEN
Tel: 77 30 57 57
Email: forbrug@24timer.dk **Web site:** http://www.24timer.dk
Freq: Daily - 5 gange om ugen - mandag til fredag; **Cover Price:** Free; **Circ:** 500,000
Language(s): Danish
BUSINESS: COMMERCE, INDUSTRY & MANAGEMENT

AABENRAA UGE-AVIS
630352D72-26
Editorial: Ramsherred 47, 6200 AABENRAA
Tel: 74 62 60 00 **Fax:** 74 63 25 34
Email: red.au@b-l.dk **Web site:** http://www.aabenraaugeavis.dk
Freq: Weekly; **Cover Price:** Free; **Circ:** 31,212
Executive Editor: Jan Sternkopf
Language(s): Danish
ADVERTISING RATES:
Full Page Colour .... DKK 14274
SCC .... DKK 52
LOCAL NEWSPAPERS

AARS AVIS
630356D72-1176
Editorial: Himmerlandsgade 150, 9600 AARS
Tel: 98 62 17 11 **Fax:** 98 62 27 99
Email: redaktion@aarsavis.dk **Web site:** http://www.aarsavis.dk
Freq: Weekly; **Cover Price:** Free; **Circ:** 16,825
Editor: Thorkil Christensen
Language(s): Danish
ADVERTISING RATES:
Full Page Colour .... DKK 9240
SCC .... DKK 31,5
LOCAL NEWSPAPERS

ADRESSEAVISEN SYDDJURS
630358D72-1175
Editorial: Grenåvej 10A, 8410 RØNDE
Tel: 86 37 10 28 **Fax:** 86 37 11 91
Email: mail@adresseavisen.dk **Web site:** http://www.adresseavisen.dk
Freq: Weekly; **Cover Price:** Free; **Circ:** 23,427
Language(s): Danish
ADVERTISING RATES:
Full Page Colour .... DKK 7161
SCC .... DKK 31
LOCAL NEWSPAPERS

ÆLDRE SAGEN NU
3625D74N-20
Editorial: Nørregade 49, 1165 KØBENHAVN K
Tel: 33 96 86 86 **Fax:** 33 96 86 87
Email: aeldresagen@aeldresagen.dk **Web site:** http://www.aeldresagen.dk
Freq: 6 issues yearly; **Circ:** 370,000
Editor: Sanna Kjær Hansen
Profile: Magazine for members of the National Association for Elderly People.
Language(s): Danish
CONSUMER: WOMEN'S INTEREST CONSUMER MAGAZINES: Retirement

AGROLOGISK 3076D21A-128
Editorial: Birk Centerpark 36, 7400 HJØRRING
Tel: 96 26 52 87 **Fax:** 76 20 79 60
Email: agrologisk@agrar.dk **Web site:** http://www.agrologisk.dk
Freq: Monthly; **Circ:** 3,385
Editor: Ivan Cordes; **Executive Editor:** Niels Damsgaard Hansen
Profile: Journal containing articles on arable farming and agricultural research.
Language(s): Danish
Readership: Read by farmers and agricultural students.
ADVERTISING RATES:
Full Page Colour .... DKK 22300
BUSINESS: AGRICULTURE & FARMING

AKTIONÆREN 3795D1F-10
Editorial: Amagertorv 9, 3.sal, Postboks 1140, 1010 COPENHAGEN **Tel:** 45 82 15 91 **Fax:** 45 41 15 90
Email: daf@shareholders.dk **Web site:** http://www.shareholders.dk
Date Established: 1990; **Freq:** Monthly; **Circ:** 16,500
Executive Editor: Jens Møller Nielsen
Profile: Magazine of the Danish Shareholders' Association.
Language(s): Danish
Readership: Aimed at members of the Association.
ADVERTISING RATES:
Full Page Colour .... DKK 27500
SCC .... DKK 286.70
BUSINESS: FINANCE & ECONOMICS: Investment

AKTUEL SIKKERHED 3265D54B-5
Editorial: Glostrup Torv 6 Box 162, 2600 GLOSTRUP
Tel: 43 43 51 12 **Fax:** 43431513
Email: akt-sik@aktuel-sikkerhed.dk **Web site:** http://www.aktuel-sikkerhed.dk
Freq: 6 issues yearly; **Circ:** 9,192
Profile: Magazine about safety practice and equipment in the workplace.
Language(s): Danish
BUSINESS: SAFETY & SECURITY: Safety

ALBERTSLUND POSTEN
625000D72-25
Editorial: Stationsporten 9, 2620 ALBERTSLUND
Tel: 45 90 82 26 **Fax:** 45 90 82 31
Email: michael.sandholt@lokalavisen.dk **Web site:** http://www.albertslundposten.dk
Freq: Weekly; **Cover Price:** Free; **Circ:** 17,520
Language(s): Danish
ADVERTISING RATES:
Full Page Colour .... DKK 15333,50
SCC .... DKK 65,0
LOCAL NEWSPAPERS

ALLERØD NYT 630236D72-1174
Editorial: M.D Madsensvej 13, 3450 ALLERØD
Tel: 70 13 11 00 **Fax:** 45 90 82 23
Email: redaktion@allerodnyt.dk **Web site:** http://www.allerodnyt.dk
Freq: Weekly; **Cover Price:** Free; **Circ:** 15,900
Language(s): Danish
ADVERTISING RATES:
Full Page Colour .... DKK 12951
SCC .... DKK 55
LOCAL NEWSPAPERS

ALT FOR DAMERNE 3585D74A-10
Editorial: Hellerupvej 51, 2900 HELLERUP
Tel: 39 45 75 00
Email: alt@altfordamerne.dk **Web site:** http://www.altfordamerne.dk
Freq: Weekly; **Circ:** 58,000
Executive Editor: Camilla Frank
Profile: Magazine containing articles of general interest and features on fashion, beauty, health and work.
Language(s): Danish
Readership: Aimed at women between 20 and 49 years of age.
ADVERTISING RATES:
Full Page Colour .... DKK 59800
SCC .... DKK 533.90
CONSUMER: WOMEN'S INTEREST CONSUMER MAGAZINES: Women's Interest

---

ALT OM DATA 2978D5B-5
Editorial: Sejrøgade 7-9, 2100 KØBENHAVN Ø
Tel: 33 74 71 33 **Fax:** 33 74 71 91
Email: redaktion@altomdata.dk **Web site:** http://www.altomdata.dk
Date Established: 1985; **Freq:** Monthly; **Circ:** 12,066
Editor: Carsten Sørensen; **Executive Editor:** Lars Bennetzen
Profile: Publication concerning the whole data-communications field.
Language(s): Danish
ADVERTISING RATES:
Full Page Colour .... DKK 23000
SCC .... DKK 213
BUSINESS: COMPUTERS & AUTOMATION: Data Processing

ALT OM HAVEN 3781D93-10
Editorial: Bistrup Park 40, 3460 BIRKERØD
Tel: 45 81 29 32 **Fax:** 70 27 11 56
Web site: http://www.altomhaven.dk
Date Established: 1983; **Freq:** Monthly; **Circ:** 17,123
Editor: Marian Haugaard Steffensen
Profile: Magazine covering all aspects of gardening. Includes product reviews and articles on plants and shrubs of all kinds.
Language(s): Danish
Readership: Aimed at people who enjoy gardening.
ADVERTISING RATES:
Full Page Colour .... DKK 25500
CONSUMER: GARDENING

ANDERS AND & CO 1791724D73-225
Editorial: Vognmagergade 11, 1148 KBH K
Tel: 33 30 57 13 **Fax:** 33 30 57 60
Email: kat@tsf.egmont.com **Web site:** http://www.disney.dk/andersand
Freq: Weekly; **Circ:** 48,101
Language(s): Danish
CONSUMER: NATIONAL & INTERNATIONAL PERIODICALS

ANTIK & AUKTION 3684D79K-15
Editorial: Vigerslev Alle 18, 2500 VALBY
Tel: 36 15 20 00 **Fax:** 36 15 27 91
Email: aa@madogbolig.dk **Web site:** http://www.antikogauktion.dk
Date Established: 1997; **Freq:** 6 issues yearly; **Circ:** 18,799
Editor: Thomas Bendix; **Executive Editor:** Søren Anker Madsen
Profile: Journal covering articles, news and information about auctions and antiques.
Language(s): Danish
Readership: Aimed at people interested in antiques auctions, art and classic modernist design.
CONSUMER: HOBBIES & DIY: Collectors Magazines

ARBEJDSMILJØ 3266D54B-10
Editorial: Lersø Parkallé 105, 2100 KØBENHAVN Ø
Tel: 39 16 54 94 **Fax:** 39 16 52 01
Email: videnscenter@ami.dk **Web site:** http://www.arbejdsmiljo.dk
Freq: Monthly; **Circ:** 85,633
Executive Editor: Hannah Maimin Weil
Profile: Journal focusing on safety in the workplace, includes information about environmentally friendly machinery, tools, ventilation systems and noise reduction equipment.
Language(s): Danish
Readership: Read by members of safety committees, trade unions, local authorities and managers of construction companies.
ADVERTISING RATES:
Full Page Colour .... DKK 22600
BUSINESS: SAFETY & SECURITY: Safety

ARENA 1791991D73-263
Editorial: Finsensvej 6 D, 2000 FREDERIKSBERG
Tel: 70 22 02 55 **Fax:** 70 22 02 56
Email: arena@benjamin.dk **Web site:** http://www.arena-magazine.dk
Freq: Monthly; **Circ:** 21,137
Executive Editor: Troels Evold Widding
Language(s): Danish
ADVERTISING RATES:
Full Page Colour .... DKK 39700
SCC .... DKK 464,30
CONSUMER: NATIONAL & INTERNATIONAL PERIODICALS

ÅRHUS STIFTSTIDENDE
3404D67B-1600
Editorial: Banegårdspladsen 11, 8000 ÅRHUS C
Tel: 87 40 10 10 **Fax:** 87 40 13 21
Email: red@stiften.dk **Web site:** http://www.stiften.dk
Freq: Daily; **Circ:** 29,167
Executive Editor: Flemming Hvidtfeldt
Language(s): Danish
ADVERTISING RATES:
Full Page Colour .... DKK 23711
SCC .... DKK 102,6
REGIONAL DAILY & SUNDAY NEWSPAPERS: Regional Daily Newspapers

---

ARKITEKTEN 2956D4A-10
Editorial: Overgaden oven Vandet 10, 1, 1415 KØBENHAVN K **Tel:** 32 83 69 53
Email: red@arkfo.dk **Web site:** http://www.arkfo.dk
Freq: Monthly; **Circ:** 8,175
Editor: Erik Juul
Profile: Magazine covering all aspects of architecture.
Language(s): Danish
ADVERTISING RATES:
Full Page Colour .... DKK 22900
SCC .... DKK 181,80
BUSINESS: ARCHITECTURE & BUILDING: Architecture

ARKITEKTUR DK 2957D4A-20
Editorial: Overgaden oven Vandet 10, 1., 1415 KØBENHAVN K **Tel:** 32 83 69 56
Email: red@arkfo.dk **Web site:** http://www.arkfo.dk
Date Established: 1957
Circ: 4,671
Editor: Martin Keiding
Profile: Review of modern Danish architecture.
Language(s): Danish; English; German
Readership: Read by architects, engineers and contractors.

ASSURANDØR KREDSEN
2918D1D-10
Editorial: APPLEBYS PLADS 5, DK-1411 COPENHAGEN **Tel:** 32 66 1357
Email: bes@finansforbundet.dk **Web site:** http://www.assurandorkredsen.dk
Freq: Quarterly; **Circ:** 2,000
Editor: Carsten Jørgensen
Profile: Magazine covering all aspects of insurance.
Language(s): Danish
Readership: Aimed at insurance agents and brokers.
BUSINESS: FINANCE & ECONOMICS: Insurance

AUTOMATIK 3071D19J-10
Editorial: Glostrup Torv 6, Postbox 162, 2600 GLOSTRUP **Tel:** 43 46 67 00 **Fax:** 43 43 15 13
Email: jb@folkebladet.dk **Web site:** http://www.teknisk-udvikling.dk
Freq: Monthly; **Circ:** 25,500
Editor: Elo Thorndahl
Profile: Computing newspaper, includes applications of automation, electronics and computing in industry.
Language(s): Danish
Readership: Readers include engineers, chief mechanics, foremen, managers, electricians and plumbers in industrial establishments and the metalworking industry.
ADVERTISING RATES:
Full Page Colour .... DKK 26300
SCC .... DKK 121,80
BUSINESS: ENGINEERING & MACHINERY: CAD & CIM (Computer Integrated Manufacture)

BÅDMAGASINET 3768D91A-20
Editorial: Rungsted Havn 1D, 2960 RUNGSTED KYST **Tel:** 88 77 00 00
Email: jette@baadmagasinet.dk **Web site:** http://www.baadmagasinet.dk
Date Established: 1992; **Freq:** Monthly; **Circ:** 11,044
Profile: General boating magazine. Includes details of sailing, yachting and motor boats.
Language(s): Danish
CONSUMER: RECREATION & LEISURE: Boating & Yachting

BAGSVÆRD/SØBORG BLADET
625009D72-53
Editorial: centrumgade 7, 2750 BALLERUP
Tel: 44 60 03 30 **Fax:** 44 60 03 31
Email: red.bsb@b-l.dk **Web site:** http://www.bagsvaerdbladet.dk
Freq: Weekly; **Cover Price:** Free; **Circ:** 41,297
Editor: Lars Schmidt; **Executive Editor:** Jørgen Nielsen
Language(s): Danish
ADVERTISING RATES:
Full Page Colour .... DKK 22287
SCC .... DKK 95
LOCAL NEWSPAPERS

BALLERUP BLADET 625010D72-60
Editorial: Centrumgade 7, 2750 BALLERUP
Tel: 44 60 03 30 **Fax:** 44 60 03 31
Email: red.bsb@b-l.dk **Web site:** http://www.ballerupbladet.dk
Date Established: 1910; **Freq:** Weekly; **Cover Price:** Free; **Circ:** 43,234
Executive Editor: Jørgen Nielsen
Language(s): Danish
ADVERTISING RATES:
Full Page Colour .... DKK 22518
SCC .... DKK 95
LOCAL NEWSPAPERS

BAZAR 713237D74A-15
Editorial: Havneholmen 33, 1561 COPENHAGEN
Tel: 72 34 20 00
Email: bazar@bazaronline.dk **Web site:** http://www.bazaronline.dk
Freq: Monthly; **Circ:** 44,076
Executive Editor: Kathrine Member
Profile: Magazine covering all subjects of interest and lifestyle, fashion trends and entertainment.
Language(s): Danish
ADVERTISING RATES:
Full Page Colour .... DKK 32800
SCC .... DKK 292.80
CONSUMER: WOMEN'S INTEREST CONSUMER MAGAZINES: Women's Interest

---

BEBOERBLADET 3590D74C-5
Editorial: Studiestræde 50, 1554 KØBENHAVN V
Tel: 33 76 20 00 **Fax:** 33 96 20 01
Email: presse@bl.dk **Web site:** http://www.beboerbladet.dk
Freq: Quarterly; **Circ:** 552,000
Profile: Magazine for tenants living in non-profit housing. Contains news and information about improvements, problems and changes to premises, regulations and proposals.
Language(s): Danish
ADVERTISING RATES:
Full Page Colour .... DKK 32500
CONSUMER: WOMEN'S INTEREST CONSUMER MAGAZINES: Home & Family

BERLINGSKE 3387D65A-66
Editorial: Pilestræde 34, 1147 KØBENHAVN K
Tel: 33 75 75 75 **Fax:** 33 75 20 20
Email: redaktionen@berlingske.dk **Web site:** http://www.b.dk
Freq: Daily; **Circ:** 102,640
Profile: Broadsheet-sized quality newspaper providing in-depth coverage of national and international news, politics, events, features, culture, business and sports.
Language(s): Danish
Readership: Read by a broad range of the population.
ADVERTISING RATES:
Full Page Colour .... DKK 95312
SCC .... DKK 435.20
Copy instructions: *Copy Date:* 30 days prior to publication date
NATIONAL DAILY & SUNDAY NEWSPAPERS: National Daily Newspapers

---

BERLINGSKE NYHEDSMAGASIN 1792005D73-266
Editorial: Pilestræde 34, 1147 COPENHAGEN
Tel: 33 75 74 00 **Fax:** 33 75 20 20
Email: redaktion@bny.dk **Web site:** http://www.b.dk
Freq: Weekly; **Circ:** 13,675
Editor: Pia Fuglsang Bach
Language(s): Danish
ADVERTISING RATES:
Full Page Colour .... DKK 35000
SCC .... DKK 466.70
CONSUMER: NATIONAL & INTERNATIONAL PERIODICALS

BERLINGSKE REJSELIV
758982D65A-126
Editorial: Pilestræde 34, 1147 COPENHAGEN
Tel: 33 75 21 60 **Fax:** 33 75 20 20
Email: rejseliv@berlingske.dk **Web site:** http://www.b.dk
Freq: Weekly - Denmark; **Circ:** 122,933
Editor: Lars Johansen
Language(s): Danish
Copy instructions: *Copy Date:* 15 days prior to publication date
NATIONAL DAILY & SUNDAY NEWSPAPERS: National Daily Newspapers

---

BILAVISEN 3661D77A-13_50
Editorial: Værkmestergade 11, 2. sal, 8000 ÅRHUS C
Tel: 87 69 69 69 **Fax:** 86 12 73 90
Email: cs@aarhusmedia.dk **Web site:** http://www.aarhusmedia.dk/bilavisen.htm
Freq: Weekly; **Circ:** 65,000
Editor: Christian Schacht
Profile: Magazine containing articles and information about cars and other vehicles. Covers news, products, road tests, events and practical advice.
Language(s): Danish
ADVERTISING RATES:
Full Page Colour .... DKK 8640
SCC .... DKK 37
CONSUMER: MOTORING & CYCLING: Motoring

BILLED-BLADET 3591D74C-10
Editorial: Otto Mønstedsgade 3, 1506 KØBENHAVN V **Tel:** 36 15 35 00 **Fax:** 36 15 35 01
Email: bb@billed-bladet.dk **Web site:** http://www.billedbladet.dk
Freq: Weekly; **Circ:** 193,000
Editor: Kristian Bo Eriksen; **Executive Editor:** Annemette Krakau
Profile: Magazine for the whole family, containing television listings and general interest articles.
Language(s): Danish
ADVERTISING RATES:
Full Page Colour .... DKK 55000
SCC .... DKK 491,10
CONSUMER: WOMEN'S INTEREST CONSUMER MAGAZINES: Home & Family

BILLEDKUNSTNEREN 3182D38-5
Editorial: Vingårdstræde 21, 1070 KØBENHAVN K
Tel: 33 12 81 72
Email: bkf@bkf.dk **Web site:** http://www.bkf.dk
Freq: Quarterly; **Circ:** 1,800
Editor: Miriam Katz
Profile: Magazine about the photography trade.
Language(s): Danish
BUSINESS: PHOTOGRAPHIC TRADE

Denmark

BILLUND UGEAVIS 630373D72-70
Editorial: Højmarksvej 5, 7190 BILLUND
Tel: 75 33 12 18 **Fax:** 75 35 37 08
Email: redaktionen@billund-ugeavis.dk **Web site:** http://www.billund-ugeavis.dk
Freq: Weekly; **Cover Price:** Free; **Circ:** 18,600
Editor: Keld Stampe
Language(s): Danish
ADVERTISING RATES:
Full Page Colour .... DKK 8476,50
SCC .... DKK 35
LOCAL NEWSPAPERS

BILMAGASINET 3662D77A-15
Editorial: Finsensvej 6 D, 2000 FREDERIKSBERG
Tel: 70 22 02 55 **Fax:** 70 22 02 56
Email: bilmagasinet@benjamin.dk **Web site:** http://www.bilmagasinet.dk
Freq: Monthly; **Circ:** 41,596
Executive Editor: Mikkel Thomsager
Profile: Magazine covering all aspects of motoring.
Language(s): Danish
Readership: Aimed at motoring enthusiasts between 18 and 40 years of age.
ADVERTISING RATES:
Full Page Colour .... DKK 36000
SCC .... DKK 404
CONSUMER: MOTORING & CYCLING: Motoring

BILSNAK 3665D77A-25
Editorial: Park Allé 355, 2605 BRØNDBY
Tel: 43 28 82 00
Email: redaktion@bilsnak.dk **Web site:** http://www.volkswagendanmark.dk
Date Established: 1976; **Freq:** Quarterly; **Cover Price:** Free; **Circ:** 195,000
Profile: Publication containing general information about cars.
Language(s): Danish
Readership: Read by car owners and people interested in cars.
CONSUMER: MOTORING & CYCLING: Motoring

BIOENERGI 1819957D14A-268
Editorial: Sdr. Tingvej 10, 6630 RØDDING
Tel: 73 84 85 45
Email: kv@vmarketing.dk **Web site:** http://www.bioenergi.dk
Freq: 6 issues yearly; **Circ:** 3,500
Language(s): Danish
Copy instructions: *Copy Date:* 19 days prior to publication date
BUSINESS: COMMERCE, INDUSTRY & MANAGEMENT

BJERRINGBRO AVIS 630375D72-82
Editorial: Banegårdspladsen 3, 8850 BJERRINGBRO
Tel: 86 68 17 55 **Fax:** 86 68 03 87
Email: redaktion@bjerringbro-avis.dk **Web site:** http://www.bjerringbro-avis.dk
Freq: Weekly; **Cover Price:** Free; **Circ:** 19,700
Editor: Christine K. Hansen
Language(s): Danish
ADVERTISING RATES:
Full Page Colour .... DKK 9041,50
SCC .... DKK 40
LOCAL NEWSPAPERS

BO BEDRE 3592D74C-11
Editorial: Strandboulevarden 130, 2100 COPENHAGEN **Tel:** 39 17 20 00 **Fax:** 39 29 01 99
Email: bobedre@bobedre.dk **Web site:** http://www.bobedre.dk
Date Established: 1961; **Freq:** Monthly; **Circ:** 86,096
Executive Editor: Erik Rimmer
Profile: Magazine covering interior design, furniture and furnishings, gardening, cookery and related information concerning home decoration.
Language(s): Danish
Readership: Aimed at people with a high income aged between 25 and 55 years.
ADVERTISING RATES:
Full Page Colour .... DKK 72600
SCC .... DKK 611.60
Copy instructions: *Copy Date:* 35 days prior to publication date
CONSUMER: WOMEN'S INTEREST CONSUMER MAGAZINES: Home & Family

BOLIG MAGASINET 3782D93-17
Editorial: Finsensvej 6 D, 2000 FREDERIKSBERG
Tel: 39 10 30 09 **Fax:** 70 22 02 56
Email: louisele@benjamin.dk **Web site:** http://boligmagasinet.dk
Freq: Monthly; **Circ:** 30,111
Executive Editor: Louise Lehrmann
Profile: Magazine concerning the home and garden.
Language(s): Danish
Readership: Aimed at the general public.
ADVERTISING RATES:
Full Page Colour .... DKK 33000
SCC .... DKK 574.90
Copy instructions: *Copy Date:* 30 days prior to publication date
CONSUMER: GARDENING

BOLIGEN 2961D4D-10
Editorial: Studiestræde 50, 1554 KØBENHAVN V
Tel: 33 76 20 00 **Fax:** 33 76 20 01
Email: boligen@bl.dk **Web site:** http://www.blboligen.dk
Date Established: 1933; **Freq:** Monthly; **Cover Price:** Free; **Circ:** 30,000
Profile: Publication providing details concerning house planning.
Language(s): Danish
ADVERTISING RATES:
Full Page Colour .... DKK 23500
BUSINESS: ARCHITECTURE & BUILDING: Planning & Housing

BOLIGLIV 1792268D73-300
Editorial: Hellerupvej 51, 2900 HELLERUP
Tel: 39 45 75 51
Email: redaktion@boligliv.dk **Web site:** http://www.boligliv.dk
Freq: Monthly; **Circ:** 26,822
Executive Editor: Iben Nielsen
Language(s): Danish
ADVERTISING RATES:
Full Page Colour .... DKK 31900
SCC .... DKK 379.80
CONSUMER: NATIONAL & INTERNATIONAL PERIODICALS

BØRN & UNGE 3157D32G-35
Editorial: Blegdamsvej 124, DK-2100 COPENHAGEN
Tel: 35 46 50 00 **Fax:** 35465039
Email: bogu@bupl.dk **Web site:** http://www.boernogunge.dk
Freq: Weekly -, hver torsdag; **Circ:** 69,633
Profile: Magazine of the Child and Youth Welfare Workers' Association.
Language(s): Danish
BUSINESS: LOCAL GOVERNMENT, LEISURE & RECREATION: Community Care & Social Services

BORNHOLMS TIDENDE 3425D67B-1800
Editorial: Nørregade 11-19, 3700 RØNNE
Tel: 56 90 30 00 **Fax:** 56 95 31 65
Email: redaktion@bornholmstidende.dk **Web site:** http://www.bornholmstidende.dk
Date Established: 1866; **Freq:** Daily; **Circ:** 12,591
Editor: Dan Qvitzau
Language(s): Danish
ADVERTISING RATES:
Full Page Colour .... DKK 22052
SCC .... DKK 45
REGIONAL DAILY & SUNDAY NEWSPAPERS: Regional Daily Newspapers

BØRSEN 3388D65A-35
Editorial: Møntergade 19, 1140 KØBENHAVN K
Tel: 33 32 01 02 **Fax:** 33 12 24 45
Email: redaktionen@borsen.dk **Web site:** http://www.borsen.dk
Freq: Daily; **Circ:** 72,086
Profile: Tabloid-sized quality newspaper covering business news, finance, economics and politics.
Language(s): Danish
Readership: Read by the business community, financial executives and decision makers within both the private and the public sector.
ADVERTISING RATES:
Full Page Colour .... DKK 85080
SCC .... DKK 388.50
NATIONAL DAILY & SUNDAY NEWSPAPERS: National Daily Newspapers

BØRSEN PLEASURE.DK 1837120D4B-306
Editorial: Møntergade 19, 1140 COPENHAGEN
Tel: 33 32 01 02 **Fax:** 33 12 24 45
Email: redaktionen@borsen.dk **Web site:** http://www.pleasure.dk
Freq: Daily; **Circ:** 31,785 Unique Users
Language(s): Danish
BUSINESS: ARCHITECTURE & BUILDING: Interior Design & Flooring

BØRSEN UDLAND 1810318D14F-113
Editorial: Møntergade 19, 1140 COPENHAGEN
Tel: 72 42 34 00 **Fax:** 33 12 24 45
Email: redaktionen@borsen.dk **Web site:** http://www.borsen.dk
Freq: Daily; **Circ:** 70,503
Language(s): Danish
BUSINESS: COMMERCE, INDUSTRY & MANAGEMENT: Training & Recruitment

BØRSEN VÆKST DANMARK 1840527D14C-46
Editorial: Møntergade 19, 1140 COPENHAGEN
Tel: 33 76 94 91 **Fax:** 33 12 24 45
Email: vaekstdanmark@borsen.dk **Web site:** http://www.borsen.dk
Freq: Weekly; **Circ:** 70,503
Editor: Kim Betak Pedersen
Language(s): Danish
ADVERTISING RATES:
Full Page Colour .... DKK 85080
SCC .... DKK 388.50
BUSINESS: COMMERCE, INDUSTRY & MANAGEMENT: International Commerce

BRANDE BLADET 630381D72-92
Editorial: Storegade 25, Posboks 169, 7330 BRANDE **Tel:** 97 18 28 38 **Fax:** 97 18 00 93
Email: post@brande-bladet.dk **Web site:** http://www.brandebladet.dk
Freq: Weekly; **Cover Price:** Free; **Circ:** 16,002
Executive Editor: Erik Lauritzen
Language(s): Danish
ADVERTISING RATES:
Full Page Colour .... DKK 8316
SCC .... DKK 36
LOCAL NEWSPAPERS

BRICKS 1810010D14A-260
Editorial: Valby Langgade 19, 2500 VALBY
Tel: 36 16 60 33 **Fax:** 36 160818
Email: kaff@kfum-kfuk.dk **Web site:** http://www.bricksnet.dk
Freq: Quarterly; **Circ:** 2,000
Editor: Anna Møller Olsen
Language(s): Danish
BUSINESS: COMMERCE, INDUSTRY & MANAGEMENT

BROEN 3774D91D-20
Editorial: Arsenalvej 10, 1436 KØBENHAVN K
Tel: 32 64 00 50 **Fax:** 32 64 00 75
Email: broen@dds.dk **Web site:** http://www.issuu.com/spejder
Freq: Quarterly; **Circ:** 12,000
Profile: Magazine for scouts.
Language(s): Danish
CONSUMER: RECREATION & LEISURE: Children & Youth

BRØNSHØJ-HUSUM AVIS 625023D72-95
Editorial: Frederikssundsvej 322 A, 2700 BRØNSHØJ **Tel:** 38 60 30 03 **Fax:** 38 60 01 47
Email: red@bha.dk **Web site:** http://www.bha.dk
Freq: Weekly; **Cover Price:** Free; **Circ:** 28,117
Language(s): Danish
ADVERTISING RATES:
Full Page Colour .... DKK 16045
SCC .... DKK 69,5
LOCAL NEWSPAPERS

BRYLLUPSMAGASINET 3622D74L-80
Editorial: Enrum Slot, Strandvejen 341, 2940 VEDBÆK **Tel:** 38 76 01 98 **Fax:** 70 21 42 14
Email: info@bryllupsmagasinet.dk **Web site:** http://www.bryllupsmagasinet.dk
Freq: Half-yearly; **Circ:** 25,000
Profile: Publication for brides-to-be.
Language(s): Danish
ADVERTISING RATES:
Full Page Colour .... DKK 15800
SCC .... DKK 196.50
CONSUMER: WOMEN'S INTEREST CONSUMER MAGAZINES: Brides

B.T. 3386D65A-20
Editorial: Pilestræde 34, 1147 COPENHAGEN
Tel: 33 75 75 33 **Fax:** 33752033
Email: bt@bt.dk **Web site:** http://www.bt.dk
Date Established: 1916; **Freq:** Daily - Denmark; **Circ:** 98,538
Executive Editor: Olav Skaaning Andersen
Profile: Tabloid-sized newspaper containing news, sports and entertainment features.
Language(s): Danish
Readership: Read mainly by skilled and manual workers.
ADVERTISING RATES:
Full Page Colour .... DKK 75161
SCC .... DKK 343.20
NATIONAL DAILY & SUNDAY NEWSPAPERS: National Daily Newspapers

BUDSTIKKEN AABENRAA 630385D72-1173
Editorial: Nørreport 5, 6200 ÅBENRÅ
Tel: 74 62 12 75 **Fax:** 74 62 12 76
Email: red-aab@budstikken.com **Web site:** http://www.budstikken.com
Freq: Weekly; **Cover Price:** Free; **Circ:** 30,110
Language(s): Danish
ADVERTISING RATES:
Full Page Colour .... DKK 13167
SCC .... DKK 57
LOCAL NEWSPAPERS

BUDSTIKKEN KOLDING 630390D72-97
Editorial: Bredgade 33, 1. sal, 6000 KOLDING
Tel: 75 50 24 20 **Fax:** 75 50 55 20
Email: red-kol@budstikken.com **Web site:** http://www.budstikken.com
Freq: Weekly; **Cover Price:** Free; **Circ:** 43,147
Language(s): Danish
ADVERTISING RATES:
Full Page Colour .... DKK 15246
SCC .... DKK 66
LOCAL NEWSPAPERS

BUDSTIKKEN SØNDERBORG 630389D72-98
Editorial: Perlegade 4, 1. sal, 6400 SØNDERBORG
Tel: 74 42 18 01 **Fax:** 74 42 55 01
Email: red-sdb@budstikken.com **Web site:** http://www.budstikken.com
Freq: Weekly; **Cover Price:** Free; **Circ:** 38,194
Language(s): Danish
ADVERTISING RATES:
Full Page Colour .... DKK 14899,5
SCC .... DKK 64,5
LOCAL NEWSPAPERS

BUREAUBIZ.DK 1840528D2A-102
Editorial: Sophus Falcks Alle 28, 2791 DRAGOER
Tel: 40 31 00 38
Email: finn@bureaubiz.dk **Web site:** http://www.bureaubiz.dk
Freq: Daily; **Cover Price:** Free; **Circ:** 63,936 Unique Users
Language(s): Danish
BUSINESS: COMMUNICATIONS, ADVERTISING & MARKETING

BUSINESS TRAVELLER DENMARK 1791606D74R-4
Editorial: Rymarksvej 46, 2900 HELLERUP
Tel: 33 11 44 13 **Fax:** 33 114414
Email: info@btdk.dk **Web site:** http://www.businesstravellerdenmark.com
Freq: 6 issues yearly - Hver sjette uge; **Circ:** 10,000
Editor: Anders Nielsen; **Executive Editor:** Michael Bøjes
Language(s): Danish
CONSUMER: WOMEN'S INTEREST CONSUMER MAGAZINES: Women's Interest Related

BY OG LAND 2959D4A-40
Editorial: Borgergade 111, 1022 KØBENHAVN K
Tel: 70 22 12 99 **Fax:** 70 22 12 90
Email: mail@byogland.dk **Web site:** http://www.byogland.dk
Freq: Quarterly; **Circ:** 9,000
Profile: Magazine about the restoration of buildings and building heritage.
Language(s): Danish
Readership: Aimed at architects, builders, craftsmen and those generally interested in building heritage.
ADVERTISING RATES:
Full Page Colour .... DKK 4000
BUSINESS: ARCHITECTURE & BUILDING: Architecture

BYG TEK 1792534D73-368
Editorial: Stationsparken 25, 2600 GLOSTRUP
Tel: 43 43 29 00 **Fax:** 43 43 13 28
Email: odsgard@odsgard.dk **Web site:** http://www.odsgard.dk/default.asp?pageid=bygtek
Freq: Monthly; **Circ:** 21,702
Language(s): Danish
ADVERTISING RATES:
Full Page Colour .... DKK 43804
SCC .... DKK 307,70
CONSUMER: NATIONAL & INTERNATIONAL PERIODICALS

BYGGE & ANLÆGSAVISEN 2964D4E-20
Editorial: Trommesalen 5, 2. sal, DK-1614 COPENHAGEN **Tel:** 31 21 26 28
Email: jens@bygge-anlaegsavisen.dk **Web site:** http://www.bygge-anlaegsavisen.dk
Freq: Quarterly; **Circ:** 15,000
Executive Editor: Jens Nørgaard
Profile: Newspaper concerning building and construction.
Language(s): Danish
ADVERTISING RATES:
Full Page Colour .... DKK 29600
SCC .... DKK 255
BUSINESS: ARCHITECTURE & BUILDING: Building

BYGGEAVISEN 1791504D4E-182
Editorial: Værkmestergade 11, 8000 ÅRHUS C
Tel: 87 69 69 69 **Fax:** 86 12 73 90
Email: akn@aarhusmedia.dk **Web site:** http://www.aarhusmedia.dk/byggeavisen.htm
Freq: Monthly; **Circ:** 35,000
Editor: Anne Kathrine Nielsen
Language(s): Danish
BUSINESS: ARCHITECTURE & BUILDING: Building

BYGGEMAGASINET 2965D4E-22
Editorial: Søren Frichs Vej 18, 8100 ÅRHUS
Tel: 89 34 34 34
Email: info@stark.dk **Web site:** http://www.bygge-avisen.dk
Freq: Quarterly; **Circ:** 1,600,000
Profile: Magazine for professionals in the building industry.
Language(s): Danish
BUSINESS: ARCHITECTURE & BUILDING: Building

BYGGEPLADS 1792493D73-357
Editorial: Solvang 23, Postboks 146, 3450 ALLERØD
Tel: 48 17 0078
Email: info@byggeplads.dk **Web site:** http://www.byggeplads.dk
Freq: 6 issues yearly; **Circ:** 12,850
Executive Editor: Kim Sejr
Language(s): Danish
ADVERTISING RATES:
Full Page Colour .... DKK 23300
SCC .... DKK 215.70
Copy instructions: *Copy Date:* 30 days prior to publication date
CONSUMER: NATIONAL & INTERNATIONAL PERIODICALS

BYGGERI 2968D4E-85
Editorial: Stationsparken 25, 2600 GLOSTRUP
Tel: 43 43 29 00 **Fax:** 43 43 13 28
Email: byggeri@byggeri.dk **Web site:** http://www.byggeri.dk
Freq: Monthly; **Cover Price:** Paid; **Circ:** 8,663 Unique Users
Executive Editor: Klaus Tøttrup
Profile: Magazine about building policy, planning and projects.
Language(s): Danish
ADVERTISING RATES:
Full Page Colour .... DKK 20400
SCC .... DKK 194,60
BUSINESS: ARCHITECTURE & BUILDING: Building

BYGGERIET 2969D4E-90
Editorial: Nr. Voldgade 106, Postboks 2125, 1055 KØBENHAVN K **Tel:** 72 16 00 00 **Fax:** 72 16 00 10
Email: red@danskbyggeri.dk **Web site:** http://www.danskbyggeri.dk/presse+-c12-+politik/magasinet+byggeriet
Freq: Monthly; **Circ:** 11,500
Editor: Martin K. I. Christensen
Profile: Magazine published by the Building Employers' Organisation covering all building crafts.
Language(s): Danish
BUSINESS: ARCHITECTURE & BUILDING: Building

BYGGETEKNIK 2970D4E-100
Editorial: Birk Centerpark 36, 7400 HERNING
Tel: 96 26 52 82 **Fax:** 96 26 52 96
Email: redaktion@byggeteknik.dk **Web site:** http://www.byggeteknik.dk
Freq: Monthly; **Circ:** 29,643
Editor: Bjarne Madsen
Profile: Magazine for the building and foundation industry. Also covers the wood, electronics and sanitation trades.
Language(s): Danish
ADVERTISING RATES:
Full Page Colour .... DKK 29512
SCC .... DKK 136,60
BUSINESS: ARCHITECTURE & BUILDING: Building

BYPLAN NYT 2962D4D-50
Editorial: Nørregade 36, 1165 KØBENHAVN K
Tel: 33 17 72 81
Email: nwo@byplanlab.dk **Web site:** http://www.byplanlab.dk
Freq: 6 issues yearly; **Circ:** 900
Profile: Journal about municipal and regional planning.
Language(s): Danish
Readership: Aimed at town planners.
ADVERTISING RATES:
Full Page Colour .... DKK 9200

C3 MAGASINET OM LEDELSE OG ØKONOMI 3013D14A-25
Editorial: Søtorvet 5, Postboks 2043, 1012 KØBENHAVN K **Tel:** 36 91 91 11 **Fax:** 33 14 11 49
Email: cad@c3.dk **Web site:** http://www.c3.dk
Freq: 6 issues yearly; **Circ:** 17,000
Editor: Christina Adler Jensen
Profile: Publication containing news, information and articles about economy and trade, human resources, marketing and general management.
Language(s): Danish
Readership: Read by graduates (and students) in economics and business administration.
ADVERTISING RATES:
Full Page Colour .... DKK 17500
BUSINESS: COMMERCE, INDUSTRY & MANAGEMENT

CAMPING-FRITID 3772D91B-10
Editorial: Korsdalsvej 134, 2605 BRØNDBY
Tel: 33 21 06 00 **Fax:** 33 21 01 08
Email: info@dcu.dk **Web site:** http://www.dcu.dk
Freq: Monthly; **Circ:** 60,000
Executive Editor: Jørgen W. G. Fröhlich
Profile: Magazine of the Danish Camping Union.
Language(s): Danish
ADVERTISING RATES:
Full Page Colour .... DKK 19000
SCC .... DKK 190
CONSUMER: RECREATION & LEISURE: Camping & Caravanning

CAMPISTEN 3773D91B-20
Editorial: DK-Camp, Industrivej 5 D, 7120 VEJLE Ø
Tel: 75 71 29 60 **Fax:** 75 71 29 66
Email: info@dk-camp.dk **Web site:** http://www.dk-camp.dk
Freq: Half-yearly; **Cover Price:** Free; **Circ:** 50,000
Profile: Magazine containing advice and information about camping. Includes product reviews, details of particular venues and excursions.
Language(s): Danish
Readership: Aimed at people who enjoy outdoor activities.
CONSUMER: RECREATION & LEISURE: Camping & Caravanning

CHAUFFØREN 3245D49B-35
Editorial: Svanevej 22, 2400 KØBENHAVN NV
Tel: 88 92 27 66 **Fax:** 38 14 06 09
Email: per.thomasen@3f.dk **Web site:** http://www.3f.dk/koebenhavns-chauffoerer/Fagbladet+Chauff%c3%b8ren.aspx
Freq: Monthly; **Circ:** 8,207
Editor: Torben Joconde
Profile: Journal covering the Scandinavian transport industry.
Language(s): Danish
Readership: Aimed at bus, coach and lorry drivers.
BUSINESS: TRANSPORT: Bus & Coach Transport

CHAUFFØRNYT 3244D49B-30
Editorial: Postboks 596, 2200 KØBENHAVN N
Tel: 21 48 19 27 **Fax:** 35 35 51 60
Email: per@samfundskontakt.dk **Web site:** http://chauffoernyt.dk
Date Established: 1961; **Freq:** 6 issues yearly; **Circ:** 22,000
Editor: Per S. Grove-Stephensen
Profile: Publication for drivers of buses, coaches, trucks, lorries and cars.
Language(s): Danish
BUSINESS: TRANSPORT: Bus & Coach Transport

CHECK-IN BILLUND 3883D50-10
Editorial: Vesterbrogade 19, 1620 KØBENHAVN V
Tel: 33 26 84 00 **Fax:** 33 26 84 01
Email: charlotte@standby.dk **Web site:** http://www.bll.dk/Generel%20info/Check_in_Billund.aspx
Freq: 6 issues yearly; **Cover Price:** Free; **Circ:** 32,000
Language(s): Danish

CHILI MAGAZINE 3708D83-20
Editorial: Otto Mønsteds Gade 3, 1571 COPENHAGEN **Tel:** 72 341200 **Fax:** 72 341201
Email: chilibladet@chiligroup.dk **Web site:** http://www.chilinet.dk
Date Established: 1985; **Freq:** Monthly; **Cover Price:** Free; **Circ:** 80,000
Executive Editor: Søren McGuere
Profile: Student magazine covering culture, education, leisure time, extreme sports and topical subjects concerning young people in society.
Language(s): Danish; Swedish
Readership: Distributed free in high schools, business colleges and universities throughout Denmark. Aimed primarily at students of 15 to 25 years.
ADVERTISING RATES:
Full Page Colour .... DKK 42300
SCC .... DKK 354.90
CONSUMER: STUDENT PUBLICATIONS

CITY AVISEN 625026D72-100
Editorial: Øster Alle 42, 2100 COPENHAGEN
Tel: 35 42 25 15 **Fax:** 35428151
Email: red.parken@b-l.dk **Web site:** http://www.cityavisen.dk
Freq: Weekly; **Cover Price:** Free; **Circ:** 26,361
Language(s): Danish
ADVERTISING RATES:
Full Page Colour .... DKK 15015
SCC .... DKK 65
LOCAL NEWSPAPERS

CO-INDUSTRI MAGASINET 758749D14A-145
Editorial: Vester Søgade 12, 2. sal, 1790 COPENHAGEN **Tel:** 33 63 80 00 **Fax:** 33 63 80 90
Email: co@co-industri.dk **Web site:** http://www.co-industri.dk
Freq: Monthly - undtagen juli; **Circ:** 24,800
Language(s): Danish
BUSINESS: COMMERCE, INDUSTRY & MANAGEMENT

COSTUME 1792131D73-284
Editorial: Finsensvej 6D, 2000 FREDERIKSBERG
Tel: 39 10 30 22 **Fax:** 70 22 02 56
Email: costume@benjamin.dk **Web site:** http://www.costume.dk
Freq: Monthly; **Circ:** 44,258
Executive Editor: Rikke Agnete Dam
Language(s): Danish
ADVERTISING RATES:
Full Page Colour .... DKK 43500
SCC .... DKK 395.40
Copy instructions: *Copy Date:* 30 days prior to publication date
CONSUMER: NATIONAL & INTERNATIONAL PERIODICALS

CRN 1791510D73-193
Editorial: Hørkær 18, 2730 HERLEV **Tel:** 77 30 02 70
Email: a.thestrup@idg.dk **Web site:** http://www.crn.dk
Freq: Monthly; **Circ:** 10,200
Editor: Allan Thestrup
Language(s): Danish
ADVERTISING RATES:
Full Page Colour .... DKK 36500
SCC .... DKK 357
Copy instructions: *Copy Date:* 7 days prior to publication date
CONSUMER: NATIONAL & INTERNATIONAL PERIODICALS

CS-BLADET 3187D40-10
Editorial: Centralforeningen for Stampersonel, Trommesalen 3, 1614 KØBENHAVN V
Tel: 36 90 89 39 **Fax:** 33 31 10 33
Email: csbladet@cs.dk **Web site:** http://www.cs.dk
Freq: Monthly; **Circ:** 11,000
Profile: Magazine for enlisted personnel and NCOs in the Army, Navy and Air Force.
Language(s): Danish
Readership: Read by members of the union, politicians and leading members of the community.
BUSINESS: DEFENCE

CSR 634343D57-24
Editorial: Center Boulevard 5, 2300 KØBENHAVN S
Tel: 32 47 32 30 **Fax:** 32 47 32 39
Email: info@horisontgruppen.dk **Web site:** http://www.horisontgruppen.dk
Date Established: 1994; **Freq:** Monthly; **Circ:** 5,718
Editor: Anette Lykke Rasmussen
Profile: Magazine covering environmental issues.
Language(s): Danish
BUSINESS: ENVIRONMENT & POLLUTION

CYKLISTER 3670D77C-30
Editorial: Rømersgade 7, 1362 KØBENHAVN K
Tel: 33 32 31 21 **Fax:** 33 32 76 83
Email: rrn@dcf.dk **Web site:** http://www.dcf.dk
Date Established: 1935; **Freq:** 6 issues yearly; **Circ:** 15,200
Profile: Magazine of the Danish Cyclist Federation. Includes articles on bicycle transport policy, legislation, news, touring and test reports.
Language(s): Danish
Readership: Read by members.
CONSUMER: MOTORING & CYCLING: Cycling

DÆK-MAGASINET 3241D49A-5
Editorial: Hans Edvard Teglers Vej 5, 2920 CHARLOTTENLUND **Tel:** 39 63 97 79
Fax: 39 63 92 79
Email: daekbranchen@mail.dk **Web site:** http://www.dsl-tyres.dk
Date Established: 1928; **Freq:** Monthly -, 10 gange årligt; **Circ:** 1,000
Profile: Magazine covering the transport and tyre industry.
Language(s): Danish

DAGBLADET HOLSTEBRO/ STRUER 3414D67B-2000
Editorial: Lægårdsvej 86, 7500 HOLSTEBRO
Tel: 99 12 84 10 **Fax:** 97 41 03 20
Email: holstebro@bergske.dk **Web site:** http://www.dagbladet-holstebro-struer.dk
Date Established: 1881; **Freq:** Daily; **Circ:** 10,906
Editor: Torben Pedersen
Language(s): Danish
ADVERTISING RATES:
Full Page Colour .... DKK 12969
SCC .... DKK 51
REGIONAL DAILY & SUNDAY NEWSPAPERS: Regional Daily Newspapers

DAGBLADET RINGSTED 3424D67B-2200
Editorial: Søgade 4-12, 4100 RINGSTED
Tel: 57 61 25 00 **Fax:** 57 61 06 22
Email: dagbladet@sj-medier.dk **Web site:** http://www.dagbladetonline.dk
Freq: Daily; **Circ:** 6,404
Editor: Jørgen Søhuus; **Executive Editor:** Torben Dalby Larsen
Language(s): Danish
ADVERTISING RATES:
Full Page Colour .... DKK 17696
SCC .... DKK 38,50
REGIONAL DAILY & SUNDAY NEWSPAPERS: Regional Daily Newspapers

DAGBLADET ROSKILDE 3426D67B-2300
Editorial: Hersegade 22, 4000 ROSKILDE
Tel: 46 35 85 00 **Fax:** 46 35 80 40
Email: dagbladet@sj-medier.dk **Web site:** http://www.dagbladetonline.dk
Freq: Daily; **Circ:** 6,696
Editor: Finn Sinding Yde
Language(s): Danish
ADVERTISING RATES:
Full Page Colour .... DKK 17696
SCC .... DKK 38,50
REGIONAL DAILY & SUNDAY NEWSPAPERS: Regional Daily Newspapers

DAGENS MEDICIN 3272D56A-65
Editorial: Christian IX's Gade 3, 1. sal; Postboks 194, 1006 KØBENHAVN K **Tel:** 33 32 44 00
Fax: 33 18 86 66
Email: dm@dagensmedicin.dk **Web site:** http://www.dagensmedicin.dk
Date Established: 1997; **Freq:** Weekly; **Circ:** 22,904
Executive Editor: Kristian Lund
Profile: Journal concerning the latest research and developments within the medical field.
Language(s): Danish
Readership: Aimed at professionals within the medical field.
ADVERTISING RATES:
Full Page Colour .... DKK 29000
SCC .... DKK 125,54
BUSINESS: HEALTH & MEDICAL

DALUM-HJALLESE AVIS 630398D72-110
Editorial: Banegårdspladsen, 5100 ODENSE C
Tel: 66 14 14 10 **Fax:** 66 12 22 00
Email: red@dh-avis.dk **Web site:** http://www.ugeavisen-odense.dk
Freq: Weekly; **Cover Price:** Free; **Circ:** 19,145
Language(s): Danish
ADVERTISING RATES:
Full Page Colour .... DKK 11665,50
SCC .... DKK 50,50
LOCAL NEWSPAPERS

DANISH OFFSHORE INDUSTRY 1791470D73-184
Editorial: Lerbjergstien 18, 3460 BIRKERØD
Tel: 48 17 62 82 **Fax:** 48 177880
Email: fmk@fmkpresse.dk **Web site:** http://www.offshorecontacts.com
Freq: Annual - Næste gang 8. februar 2008; **Circ:** 6,000
Editor: Frede Madsen
Language(s): Danish
CONSUMER: NATIONAL & INTERNATIONAL PERIODICALS

DANMARKS TRANSPORT-TIDENDE 3225D45C-30
Editorial: Jernbanegade 18, 6330 PADBORG
Tel: 70 10 05 06 **Fax:** 74 67 40 47
Email: dtt@transporttidende.com **Web site:** http://www.transporttidende.com
Freq: 26 issues yearly; **Circ:** 4,622
Executive Editor: Gwyn Nissen
Profile: Journal providing articles, news and information about the transport and shipping trades.
Language(s): Danish
Readership: Read by shipping and forwarding agents and haulage contractors.
ADVERTISING RATES:
Full Page Colour .... DKK 18995
SCC .... DKK 82.23
Copy instructions: *Copy Date:* 7 days prior to publication date
BUSINESS: MARINE & SHIPPING: Maritime Freight

DANSK ARTILLERI-TIDSSKRIFT 3188D40-30
Editorial: Hjertingvej 127, 6800 VARDE
Tel: 76 95 50 00 **Fax:** 76 95 54 14
Email: justdb2000@yahoo.dk **Web site:** http://www.artilleriet.dk
Freq: Quarterly; **Circ:** 500
Profile: Journal for artillery officers.
Language(s): Danish

DANSK BRIDGE 3680D79F-50
Editorial: Smedevej 1, 9340 ASAA **Tel:** 32 55 52 13
Fax: 48 47 62 13

Email: dansk@bridge.dk **Web site:** http://www.bridge.dk
Date Established: 1941; **Freq:** Monthly; **Circ:** 22,643
Editor: Henrik Kruse Petersen
Profile: Magazine for bridge players.
Language(s): Danish
CONSUMER: HOBBIES & DIY: Games & Puzzles

DANSK GOLF 3631D75D-30

Editorial: Idrættens Hus Brøndby Stadion 20, 2605 BRØNDBY **Tel:** 43 26 27 00 **Fax:** 43 26 27 01
Email: tve@dgu.org **Web site:** http://www.golf.dk
Date Established: 1943; **Freq:** 6 issues yearly; **Circ:** 102,000
Profile: Magazine containing articles, news and information about Danish golf. Also covers international golfing news.
Language(s): Danish
Readership: Read by Members of the Danish Golf Union.
CONSUMER: SPORT: Golf

DANSK HANDELSBLAD 3260D53-20

Editorial: Fenrisvej 11, 8230 ÅBYHØJ
Tel: 86 15 80 11 **Fax:** 86 158252
Email: info@danskhandelsblad.dk **Web site:** http://www.danskhandelsblad.dk
Freq: Weekly -, fredag; **Circ:** 7,127
Profile: National journal for merchants, wholesale and retail grocers, chain stores, supermarkets and department stores, importers and the brand industry.
Language(s): Danish
ADVERTISING RATES:
Full Page Colour .... DKK 23500
SCC .... DKK 10.73

DANSK MUSIK TIDSSKRIFT

3652D76D-30
Editorial: Strandvejen 100 D, 3070 SNEKKERSTEN
Tel: 33 24 42 48 **Fax:** 33 24 42 46
Email: info@danskmusiktidsskrift.dk **Web site:** http://www.danskmusiktidsskrift.dk
Freq: 6 issues yearly; **Circ:** 1,100
Profile: Magazine about classical and modern music, composers and musicians.
Language(s): Danish
CONSUMER: MUSIC & PERFORMING ARTS: Music

DANSKE MÆLKEPRODUCENTER

3090D21C-12
Editorial: Vestergade 19, 7600 STRUER
Tel: 97 84 13 80 **Fax:** 97 84 13 70
Email: borsmark@bors-mark.dk **Web site:** http://www.maelkeproducenter.dk
Freq: Monthly; **Circ:** 4,641
Profile: Publication focusing on milk production and dairy products.
Language(s): Danish
Readership: Read by milk, calf and cattle producers.
BUSINESS: AGRICULTURE & FARMING: Dairy Farming

DANSKE OFFICERER 3191D40-35

Editorial: Olof Palmes Gade 10, 2100 KØBENHAVN Ø **Tel:** 33 15 02 33 **Fax:** 33 14 46 26
Email: lahrmann@hod.dk **Web site:** http://www.hod.dk
Date Established: 1992; **Freq:** Monthly; **Circ:** 6,800
Editor: Henning Lahrmann
Profile: Publication about officers in the defence forces.
Language(s): Danish; English
Readership: Aimed at people in military professions.

DANSKE REVISORER 2913D1B-3

Editorial: Munkehatten 32, 5220 ODENSE
Tel: 65 93 25 00 **Fax:** 65 93 25 08
Email: carsten@fdr.dk **Web site:** http://www.fdr.dk
Freq: Quarterly - Medio marts, juni, september, december; **Circ:** 1,200
Editor: Carsten Klint
Profile: Journal of the Danish Auditors' and Accountants' Association.
Language(s): Danish
ADVERTISING RATES:
Full Page Colour .... DKK 6500
BUSINESS: FINANCE & ECONOMICS: Accountancy

DATATID 2981D5B-15

Editorial: Sejrøgade 7-9, 2100 COPENHAGEN
Tel: 33 91 28 33 **Fax:** 33 747191
Email: redaktionen@datatid.dk **Web site:** http://www.datatid.dk
Freq: Monthly; **Circ:** 7,654
Editor: Aksel Brinck
Profile: Computer magazine containing product reviews and tests.
Language(s): Danish
Readership: Aimed at small businesses and people working within the IT industry.
ADVERTISING RATES:
Full Page Colour .... DKK 17500
SCC .... DKK 162
BUSINESS: COMPUTERS & AUTOMATION: Data Processing

DAU BLADET 758874D14A-155

Editorial: Hannemanns Alle 25, 2300 COPENHAGEN
Tel: 39 90 39 55
Email: dau@dau.dk **Web site:** http://www.dau.dk
Freq: Quarterly; **Circ:** 1,400
Language(s): Danish
BUSINESS: COMMERCE, INDUSTRY & MANAGEMENT

DEN BLÅ AVIS VEST 624992D65A-63

Editorial: Marselisborg, Havnevej 26 Box 180, 8100 ÅRHUS C **Tel:** 87 31 31 31 **Fax:** 87 31 31 91
Email: piam@dba.dk **Web site:** http://www.dba.dk
Freq: Weekly; **Cover Price:** Free; **Circ:** 80,000
Language(s): Danish
ADVERTISING RATES:
Full Page Colour .... DKK 38750
SCC .... DKK 167,7
NATIONAL DAILY & SUNDAY NEWSPAPERS: National Daily Newspapers

DI BUSINESS 1792526D73-364

Editorial: Hannemanns Alle 25, 2300 COPENHAGEN
Tel: 33 77 33 77 **Fax:** 33 773300
Email: redaktion@di.dk **Web site:** http://www.di.dk
Freq: Weekly - 4x /mdr. undtagen i juli; **Circ:** 15,878
Editor: Rolf Ejlertsen
Language(s): Danish
ADVERTISING RATES:
Full Page Colour .... DKK 25100
SCC .... DKK 193.10
CONSUMER: NATIONAL & INTERNATIONAL PERIODICALS

DIABETES 3273D56A-80

Editorial: Rytterkasernen 1, 5000 ODENSE C
Tel: 66 12 90 06 **Fax:** 65 91 49 08
Email: df@diabetesforeningen.dk **Web site:** http://www.diabetes.dk
Date Established: 1940; **Freq:** 6 issues yearly; **Circ:** 66,000
Editor: Helen H. Heidemann
Profile: Publication of the Diabetes Association.
Language(s): Danish
BUSINESS: HEALTH & MEDICAL

DIÆTISTEN 3274D56A-80_25

Editorial: Landmærket 10, 1012 KØBENHAVN K
Tel: 33 32 00 39 **Fax:** 38 71 03 22
Email: post@diaetist.dk **Web site:** http://www.diaetist.dk
Freq: 6 issues yearly; **Circ:** 650
Editor: Ulla Mortensen
Profile: Publication concerning food and nutrition.
Language(s): Danish
Readership: Aimed at dieticians and food and nutrition experts.

DIGITAL FOTO 1791773D73-234

Editorial: Strandboulevarden 130, 2100 KØBENHAVN Ø **Tel:** 39 17 20 00 **Fax:** 39 17 23 09
Email: redaktionen@digitalfotoonline.dk **Web site:** http://www.digitalfotoonline.dk
Freq: Monthly; **Circ:** 17,557
Executive Editor: Klaus Nygaard
Language(s): Danish
ADVERTISING RATES:
Full Page Colour .... DKK 19000
SCC .... DKK 172,10
CONSUMER: NATIONAL & INTERNATIONAL PERIODICALS

DJØF BLADET 3811D44-100

Editorial: Gothersgade 133, Postboks 2126, 1123 COPENHAGEN **Tel:** 33 95 97 00 **Fax:** 33959991
Email: mik@djoef.dk **Web site:** http://www.djoef.dk
Freq: 26 issues yearly - fredag; **Circ:** 45,304
Profile: Journal of the Danish Association of Lawyers and Economists.
Language(s): Danish
Readership: Aimed at members of the Association.
BUSINESS: LEGAL

DJURSLANDSPOSTEN

630409D72-115
Editorial: Østerbrogade 45, 8500 GRENÅ
Tel: 87 58 55 00 **Fax:** 87 58 55 16
Email: redaktion@djurslandsposten.dk **Web site:** http://www.djurslandsposten.dk
Freq: Weekly; **Cover Price:** Free; **Circ:** 28,100
Language(s): Danish
ADVERTISING RATES:
Full Page Colour .... DKK 9471
SCC .... DKK 41
LOCAL NEWSPAPERS

DKUUG-NYT 2980D5B-12

Editorial: Fruebjergvej 3, 2100 KØBENHAVN Ø
Tel: 39 17 99 44
Email: dkuug-nyt@dkuug.dk **Web site:** http://www.dkuug.dk
Freq: Monthly; **Circ:** 1,500
Editor: Keld Simonsen
Profile: Magazine providing news and information about operating systems, programming languages, de-bugging, IT and general issues concerning computers.
Language(s): Danish
Readership: Aimed at professional PC users and IT administrators.
BUSINESS: COMPUTERS & AUTOMATION: Data Processing

DL MAGASINET 3282D56A-81_75

Editorial: P.O. Box 1297, 7500 HOLSTEBRO
Tel: 97 41 13 54 **Fax:** 97 40 43 54
Email: niels@stoktoft.dk **Web site:** http://www.dl-hk.dk
Freq: Monthly; **Cover Price:** Free; **Circ:** 10,581
Profile: Magazine of the Danish Association of Medical Secretaries.
Language(s): Danish
ADVERTISING RATES:
Full Page Colour .... DKK 9800
SCC .... DKK 155,55
BUSINESS: HEALTH & MEDICAL

DLG NYT 3083D21A-90

Editorial: Axelborg, Vesterbrogade 4A, 1503 KØBENHAVN V **Tel:** 33 68 30 00 **Fax:** 33 68 87 28
Email: info@dlg.dk **Web site:** http://www.dlg.dk
Freq: Monthly; **Circ:** 104,000
Profile: Publication about production and foodstuffs.
Language(s): Danish
Readership: Read by farmers.
BUSINESS: AGRICULTURE & FARMING

DMC BLADET 3667D77B-40

Editorial: Haverslevvej 47, Ersted, 9520 SKØRPING
Tel: 98 37 36 93 **Fax:** 98 37 28 81
Email: skovloekke@dmc-org.dk **Web site:** http://www.dmc-org.dk
Freq: Quarterly; **Circ:** 2,000
Editor: Rolf Skovløkke
Profile: Magazine for members of Danish motorcycle clubs.
Language(s): Danish
ADVERTISING RATES:
Full Page Colour .... DKK 1750

DR NYHEDER TV AVISEN 21.00

1863717D82-319
Editorial: DR Byen, Emil Holms Kanal 20, 0999 KØBENHAVN C **Tel:** 35 20 45 20 **Fax:** 35 20 46 46
Email: tva@dr.dk **Web site:** http://www.dr.dk
Freq: Daily; **Circ:** 750,000
Language(s): Danish
ADVERTISING RATES:
SCC .... DKK 100272
CONSUMER: CURRENT AFFAIRS & POLITICS

DR P4 BORNHOLM FORMIDDAG 1864007D67B-8407

Editorial: Åkirkebyvej 52, 3700 RØNNE
Tel: 56 94 37 00 **Fax:** 56 94 37 37
Email: bornholm@dr.dk **Web site:** http://www.dr.dk/bornholm
Freq: Daily; **Circ:** 7,000
Language(s): Danish
ADVERTISING RATES:
SCC .... DKK 247
REGIONAL DAILY & SUNDAY NEWSPAPERS: Regional Daily Newspapers

DRC-BLADET / RESTAURANT & CAFÉ 3004D11A-15

Editorial: Islands Brygge 26, 2300 KØBENHAVN S
Tel: 33 25 1011 **Fax:** 33 25 3099
Email: bladet@d-r-c.dk **Web site:** http://www.d-r-c.dk
Date Established: 1939; **Freq:** Monthly - minus juli; **Circ:** 15,000
Editor: Carsten Kruuse
Profile: Magazine about cafés, hotels, restaurants, grills, bars and self-service catering. Published by the Danish Restaurant and Cafeteria Association.
Language(s): Danish
BUSINESS: CATERING: Catering, Hotels & Restaurants

DS-BLADET 1834441D14A-270

Editorial: Magnoliavej 2, 5250 ODENSE SV
Tel: 66 17 33 33
Email: oan@ds-net.dk **Web site:** http://www.ds-net.dk/OmDS/DSbladet/tabid/95/Default.aspx
Freq: Monthly; **Circ:** 3,500
Editor: Ole Andersen
Language(s): Danish
ADVERTISING RATES:
Full Page Colour .... DKK 10840
SCC .... DKK 10840
BUSINESS: COMMERCE, INDUSTRY & MANAGEMENT

DTL MAGASINET 3248D49D-20

Editorial: Grønningen 17, Postboks 2250, 1019 COPENHAGEN **Tel:** 70 15 95 00 **Fax:** 70159522
Email: dtl@dtl.eu **Web site:** http://www.dtl.eu/nyheder/dtl_magasinet.aspx
Freq: Monthly; **Circ:** 5,010
Editor: John Larsen
Profile: Journal for the owners of trucks and lorries.
Language(s): Danish
ADVERTISING RATES:
Full Page Colour .... DKK 19200
SCC .... DKK 220.68

DTU AVISEN 1791842D14A-250

Editorial: Anker Engelunds Vej 1, Bygning 101, 2800 LYNGBY **Tel:** 45 25 10 76 **Fax:** 45 88 80 40
Email: redaktion@dtuavisen.dk **Web site:** http://www.dtu.dk
Freq: Monthly - (minus juli og august); **Circ:** 7,000
Editor: Peter Hoffmann
Language(s): Danish
ADVERTISING RATES:
Full Page Colour .... DKK 10500
BUSINESS: COMMERCE, INDUSTRY & MANAGEMENT

DYK 3646D75M-150

Editorial: Rentemestervej 64, 2400 KØBENHAVN NV
Tel: 70 26 30 15 **Fax:** 70 26 90 15
Email: redaktion@dyk.net **Web site:** http://www.dyk.net
Freq: Monthly; **Circ:** 10,000
Executive Editor: Martin Örnroth
Profile: Magazine covering all aspects of recreational scuba diving and related topics.
Language(s): Danish; Swedish
CONSUMER: SPORT: Water Sports

DYREVENNEN 630420D81A-60

Editorial: Alhambravej 15, 1826 FREDERIKSBERG C
Tel: 33 28 70 00 **Fax:** 33 25 14 60
Email: hk@dyrenes-beskyttelse.dk **Web site:** http://www.dyrenes-beskyttelse.dk
Freq: 6 issues yearly; **Circ:** 71,499
Editor: Helene Kemp
Profile: Magazine focusing on animal protection.
Language(s): Danish
CONSUMER: ANIMALS & PETS: Animals & Pets Protection

EFFEKTIVT LANDBRUG

3077D21A-20
Editorial: Odensevej 29, 5550 LANGESKOV
Tel: 70 15 12 37 **Fax:** 70 15 12 47
Email: redaktion@effektivtlandbrug.dk **Web site:** http://www.effektivtlandbrug.dk
Freq: Daily; **Circ:** 17,000
Profile: Journal about animal husbandry, cattle and pig breeding, farm buildings, machinery and mechanisation.
Language(s): Danish
Readership: Read by farmers and suppliers.
ADVERTISING RATES:
Full Page Colour .... DKK 21764
SCC .... DKK 91,50
BUSINESS: AGRICULTURE & FARMING

EJENDOMSAVISEN HORSENS POSTEN 3618D74K-70

Editorial: Søndergade 47, 8700 HORSENS
Tel: 76 27 20 00
Email: info@ejendoms-avisen.dk **Web site:** http://www.horsens-folkeblad.dk/?an=ea
Date Established: 1997; **Freq:** Weekly - onsdag; **Cover Price:** Free; **Circ:** 60,104
Editor: Christina Juel-Klitsgaard
Profile: Regional property magazine providing articles and news for people interested in house purchasing.
Language(s): Danish
ADVERTISING RATES:
Full Page Colour .... DKK 17651
SCC .... DKK 76.50
CONSUMER: WOMEN'S INTEREST CONSUMER MAGAZINES: Home Purchase

EJENDOMSMÆGLEREN

2923D1E-20
Editorial: Islands Brygge 43, 2300 COPENHAGEN
Tel: 70 25 09 99 **Fax:** 32 64 45 99
Email: de@de.dk **Web site:** http://www.de.dk/Bladet
Freq: Monthly - 11 gange årligt, minus juli; **Circ:** 5,700
Editor: Lise Westphal
Profile: Publication of the Danish Estate Agents' Association.
Language(s): Danish
Readership: Read by real-estate agents, lawyers and building society personnel.
BUSINESS: FINANCE & ECONOMICS: Property

EKSTRA BLADET NYHEDER
3389D65A-67
Editorial: Rådhuspladsen 37, 1785 COPENHAGEN
Tel: 33 11 13 13 **Fax:** 33 14 10 00
Email: redaktionen@eb.dk **Web site:** http://www.ekstrabladet.dk
Date Established: 1904; **Freq:** Daily - Denmark; **Circ:** 108,478
Editor: Mogens Bille
Profile: Tabloid-sized newspaper covering mostly national sports news, events, features and travel information.
Language(s): Danish
Readership: Read mainly by skilled and manual workers.
ADVERTISING RATES:
Full Page Colour .... DKK 72380
SCC .... DKK 313.30
NATIONAL DAILY & SUNDAY NEWSPAPERS: National Daily Newspapers

EKSTRA-POSTEN
630427D80-60
Editorial: Papirfabrikken 18, 8600 SILKEBORG
Tel: 86 82 13 00 **Fax:** 86 82 13 60
Email: redaktion@ekstraposten.dk **Web site:** http://www.midtjyllandsavis.dk
Freq: Weekly; **Cover Price:** Free; **Circ:** 47,293
Editor: Peter Bruvik-Hansen
Profile: Local newspaper for Silkeborg.
Language(s): Danish
Readership: Read by local residents.
CONSUMER: RURAL & REGIONAL INTEREST

ELECTRA
3051D17-15
Editorial: Paul Bergsøes Vej 6, 2600 GLOSTRUP
Tel: 77 42 42 23 **Fax:** 43 43 21 03
Email: electra@tekniq.dk **Web site:** http://www.electra.dk
Freq: Monthly; **Circ:** 4,226
Editor: Amalie Mathiassen
Profile: Journal for electrical contractors, manufacturers, consulting engineers, electrical wholesalers and students in technical schools.
Language(s): Danish
ADVERTISING RATES:
Full Page Colour .... DKK 15350
SCC .... DKK 195,30

ELEKTRIKEREN
3052D17-20
Editorial: Vodroffsvej 26, 1900 FREDERIKSBERG C
Tel: 33 29 70 00 **Fax:** 33 29 70 70
Email: def@def.dk **Web site:** http://www.def.dk
Date Established: 1908; **Freq:** 6 issues yearly; **Circ:** 31,000
Editor: Jim Jæger
Profile: Journal containing articles of interest to electricians. Publication of the Danish Electricians' Union.
Language(s): Danish
Readership: Members of the Union.
ADVERTISING RATES:
Full Page Colour .... DKK 23400
SCC .... DKK 242,90
BUSINESS: ELECTRICAL

ELEKTRONIK & DATA
3056D18A-45
Editorial: Stationsparken 25, 2600 GLOSTRUP
Tel: 43 45 10 63 **Fax:** 43 43 13 28
Email: elek-data@odsgard.dk **Web site:** http://www.elek-data.dk
Date Established: 1990; **Freq:** Monthly - 13 gange årligt; **Circ:** 7,041
Executive Editor: Lars Kristiansen
Profile: Magazine about the electronics and data-communications trade.
Language(s): Danish
Readership: Read by electronics, data and production engineers and by distributors and retailers of electronic equipment and components.
BUSINESS: ELECTRONICS

ELTEKNIK
3053D17-40
Editorial: Naverland 35, 2600 GLOSTRUP
Tel: 43 24 26 28 **Fax:** 43 24 26 26
Email: am@techmedia.dk **Web site:** http://www.techmedia.dk/default.asp?Action=Details&Item=1497
Freq: Monthly - 10 gange årligt; **Circ:** 3,450
Profile: Journal offering technical information and news covering both low and heavy current engineering. Official journal of the Electrotechnical Association.
Language(s): Danish
ADVERTISING RATES:
Full Page Colour .... DKK 25800
SCC .... DKK 252.90
Copy instructions: *Copy Date:* 21 days prior to publication date

ENTREPRENØREN
2971D4E-110
Editorial: Traverbanevej 10, 2920 CHARLOTTENLUND **Tel:** 35 25 34 00
Fax: 35 25 34 04
Email: entreprenoeren@forlaget-coronet.dk **Web site:** http://www.entreprenoeren.dk
Freq: Monthly - minus januar og juli; **Circ:** 4,335
Editor: Carsten Stæhr
Profile: Magazine for building contractors, concerning the building industry.
Language(s): Danish

ERHVERVSAVISEN FOR LOLLAND, FALSTER, SYDSJÆLLAND OG MØN
1812795D73-410
Editorial: Frederik Den VII's Gade 10, 4800 NYKØBING F **Tel:** 54 85 11 85 **Fax:** 54 82 74 00
Email: redaktion@erhvervsavisen.com **Web site:** http://www.erhvervsavisen.com
Freq: Monthly; **Cover Price:** Free; **Circ:** 5,400
Language(s): Danish
ADVERTISING RATES:
Full Page Colour .... DKK 9124,50
SCC .... DKK 39,50
CONSUMER: NATIONAL & INTERNATIONAL PERIODICALS

ERHVERVSBLADET
3016D65A-65
Editorial: Pilestræde 34, 1147 COPENHAGEN
Tel: 33 75 38 01 **Fax:** 33 75 38 96
Email: red@erhvervsbladet.dk **Web site:** http://www.erhvervsbladet.dk
Freq: Daily - Denmark; **Circ:** 77,504
Editor: Morten Asmussen
Profile: Newspaper containing financial and marketing news.
Language(s): Danish
ADVERTISING RATES:
Full Page Colour .... DKK 31996
SCC .... DKK 138.50
NATIONAL DAILY & SUNDAY NEWSPAPERS: National Daily Newspapers

EUROINVESTOR.DK
1842214D14A-272
Editorial: Øster Allé 42, 5., 2100 COPENHAGEN
Email: info@euroinvestor.com **Web site:** http://www.euroinvestor.dk
Freq: Daily; **Circ:** 39,281 Unique Users
Language(s): Danish
BUSINESS: COMMERCE, INDUSTRY & MANAGEMENT

EUROMAN
3732D86C-60
Editorial: Hellerupvej 51, 2900 HELLERUP
Tel: 39 45 75 00
Email: nfo@euroman.dk **Web site:** http://www.euroman.dk
Freq: Monthly; **Circ:** 23,906
Executive Editor: Mads Lange
Profile: Lifestyle magazine for men interested in fashion, sport, culture, films and current affairs.
Language(s): Danish
ADVERTISING RATES:
Full Page Colour .... DKK 43500
SCC .... DKK 486.60
Copy instructions: *Copy Date:* 28 days prior to publication date
CONSUMER: ADULT & GAY MAGAZINES: Men's Lifestyle Magazines

EUROWOMAN
3890D74B-30
Editorial: Hellerupvej 51, 2900 HELLERUP
Tel: 39 45 77 70 **Fax:** 39 46 77 80
Email: info@eurowoman.dk **Web site:** http://www.eurowoman.dk
Freq: Monthly; **Circ:** 29,761
Executive Editor: Anne Lose
Profile: Magazine focusing on fashion and beauty. Also contains interviews with celebrities and others.
Language(s): Danish
Readership: Aimed at women between 18 and 35 years of age.
ADVERTISING RATES:
Full Page Colour .... DKK 43500
SCC .... DKK 486.60
CONSUMER: WOMEN'S INTEREST CONSUMER MAGAZINES: Women's Interest - Fashion

EXTRA POSTEN
630436D72-170
Editorial: Nygade 30, 4900 NAKSKOV
Tel: 54 92 48 00 **Fax:** 54 95 10 20
Email: post@extraposten.dk **Web site:** http://www.extra-posten.dk
Freq: Weekly; **Cover Price:** Free; **Circ:** 20,543
Language(s): Danish
ADVERTISING RATES:
Full Page Colour .... DKK 10979
SCC .... DKK 41
LOCAL NEWSPAPERS

F BLADET
3149D32A-70
Editorial: Knabrostræde 12, Postboks 1114, 1210 COPENHAGEN **Tel:** 33 18 86 00 **Fax:** 33 15 87 60
Email: fbf@forbrugsforeningen.dk **Web site:** http://www.forbrugsforeningen.dk
Freq: Quarterly; **Circ:** 173,000
Profile: Publication for buyers in public administration and institutions.
Language(s): Danish
BUSINESS: LOCAL GOVERNMENT, LEISURE & RECREATION: Local Government

FAGBLADET FARMA
3180D37-10
Editorial: Rygårds Alle 1, 2900 HELLERUP
Tel: 39 46 36 00 **Fax:** 39 46 36 39
Email: ak@pharmadanmark.dk **Web site:** http://www.pharmadanmark.dk
Freq: 26 issues yearly; **Circ:** 5,000
Profile: Publication providing information concerning the pharmaceutical industry.
Language(s): Danish
ADVERTISING RATES:
Full Page Colour .... DKK 13400
SCC .... DKK 336,50
BUSINESS: PHARMACEUTICAL & CHEMISTS

FAGBLADET FOA
3040D14L-80
Editorial: Staunings Plads 1-3, 1790 COPENHAGEN
Tel: 46 97 26 26
Email: foa@foa.dk **Web site:** http://www.foa.dk
Freq: Monthly - 11 gange årligt; **Circ:** 205,565
Profile: Magazine of the Public Employees' Union.
Language(s): Danish
BUSINESS: COMMERCE, INDUSTRY & MANAGEMENT: Trade Unions

FAGBLADET TIB
758834D4E-175
Editorial: Mimersgade 41, 2200 KÆ **Tel:** 88 18 70 00
Fax: 88 18 71 10
Email: fagbladet@tib.dk **Web site:** http://www.tib.dk
Freq: Monthly; **Circ:** 70,000
Language(s): Danish
BUSINESS: ARCHITECTURE & BUILDING: Building

FAGLIGT FORSVAR
758891D14A-170
Editorial: Kronprinsensgade 8, 1114 KØBENHAVN K
Tel: 33 93 65 22 **Fax:** 33 93 65 23
Email: mj@hkkf.dk **Web site:** http://www.hkkf.dk
Freq: Monthly; **Circ:** 7,300
Language(s): Danish
BUSINESS: COMMERCE, INDUSTRY & MANAGEMENT

FAIR NOK
1810242D73-394
Editorial: Nørregade 15, 4. sal, 1165 COPENHAGEN
Tel: 70 23 13 45
Email: info@maxhavelaar.dk **Web site:** http://www.fairtrade-maerket.dk/MAGASINET_br_/FAIR_NOK.aspx
Freq: Quarterly; **Circ:** 100,000
Language(s): Danish
CONSUMER: NATIONAL & INTERNATIONAL PERIODICALS

FAMILIE JOURNAL
3596D74C-20
Editorial: Postboks 420, 0900 COPENHAGEN
Tel: 72 34 22 22
Email: redaktionen@familiejournalen.dk **Web site:** http://www.familiejournalen.dk
Freq: Weekly; **Circ:** 204,443
Executive Editor: Anette Kokholm
Profile: Magazine with items of interest to all members of the family.
Language(s): Danish
ADVERTISING RATES:
Full Page Colour .... DKK 62700
SCC .... DKK 559.80
CONSUMER: WOMEN'S INTEREST CONSUMER MAGAZINES: Home & Family

FARMACI
3181D37-25
Editorial: Bredgade 54, 1260 KØBENHAVN K
Tel: 33 76 76 00 **Fax:** 33 76 76 97
Email: farmaci@apotekerforeningen.dk **Web site:** http://www.farmaci.dk
Freq: Monthly; **Circ:** 1,600
Editor: Peter Arends
Profile: Journal of the Danish Pharmaceutical Association.
Language(s): Danish
Readership: Read by pharmacists, pharmacy technicians, the medical industry and scientific institutions.
BUSINESS: PHARMACEUTICAL & CHEMISTS

DE FARVER
1792288D4E-188
Editorial: Islands Brygge 26, Postboks 1989, 2300 KØBENHAVN S **Tel:** 32 63 03 70 **Fax:** 32 63 03 99
Email: redaktionen@malermestre.dk **Web site:** http://www.malermestre.dk
Freq: Quarterly; **Circ:** 7,449
Language(s): Danish
BUSINESS: ARCHITECTURE & BUILDING: Building

FAXE BUGTEN
630441D72-1172
Editorial: Torvegade 6, 4640 FAKSE **Tel:** 56 71 32 31
Fax: 56 71 38 08
Email: kontor@faxebugten.dk **Web site:** http://www.faxebugten.dk
Date Established: 1903; **Freq:** Weekly; **Cover Price:** Free; **Circ:** 16,500
Editor: Torkild Svane Kraft
Language(s): Danish
ADVERTISING RATES:
Full Page Colour .... DKK 12012
SCC .... DKK 52
LOCAL NEWSPAPERS

FEMINA
3587D74A-20
Editorial: Postboks 420, 0900 COPENHAGEN
Tel: 36 15 23 23 **Fax:** 36 15 23 99
Email: redaktionen@femina.dk **Web site:** http://www.femina.dk
Freq: Weekly; **Circ:** 69,000
Profile: Magazine providing articles on fashion, beauty, health and cookery.
Language(s): Danish
Readership: Aimed at women between 20 and 49 years of age.
ADVERTISING RATES:
Full Page Colour .... DKK 53000
SCC .... DKK 473.20
CONSUMER: WOMEN'S INTEREST CONSUMER MAGAZINES: Women's Interest

FHM
1791706D73-222
Editorial: Finsensvej 6D, 2000 FREDERIKSBERG
Tel: 70 22 02 55 **Fax:** 70 22 02 56
Email: sorenb@benjamin.dk **Web site:** http://www.fhm.dk
Freq: Monthly; **Circ:** 28,553
Executive Editor: Søren Baastrup
Language(s): Danish
ADVERTISING RATES:
Full Page Colour .... DKK 46366
SCC .... DKK 386,40
CONSUMER: NATIONAL & INTERNATIONAL PERIODICALS

FILM GUIDE
3816D76A-61
Editorial: Borgergade 14, 4. sal, 1300 KØBENHAVN K **Tel:** 33 32 54 00 **Fax:** 33 15 71 70
Email: filmguide@drf.dk **Web site:** http://www.drf.dk
Freq: Monthly; **Circ:** 185,000
Editor: Christa Bjørklund
Language(s): Danish
CONSUMER: MUSIC & PERFORMING ARTS: Cinema

FINANS
3041D14L-100
Editorial: Applebys Plads 5, Postboks 1960, 1411 COPENHAGEN **Tel:** 32 96 46 00 **Fax:** 32 961225
Email: cjo@finansforbundet.dk **Web site:** http://www.finansforbundet.dk/?mId=3866
Freq: Monthly - 1. fredag i måneden - undtagen i juli; **Circ:** 52,443
Executive Editor: Lotte Ustrup
Profile: Publication for members of the Danish Finance Union.
Language(s): Danish
BUSINESS: COMMERCE, INDUSTRY & MANAGEMENT: Trade Unions

FINANS/INVEST
2926D1F-50
Editorial: Holmstrupgårdvej 140, 8210 ÅRHUS
Tel: 86 24 29 90 **Fax:** 86 24 30 42
Email: mail@finansinvest.dk **Web site:** http://www.finansinvest.dk
Freq: 6 issues yearly - 8 gange årligt; **Circ:** 1,000
Editor: Anders Grosen
Profile: Magazine for financial and investment managers, advisers, analysts and auditors.
Language(s): Danish
BUSINESS: FINANCE & ECONOMICS: Investment

FINANSRÅDETS NYHEDSBREV
1791784D1A-141
Editorial: Finansrådets Hus, Amaliegade 7, 1256 KØBENHAVN K **Tel:** 33 70 10 00
Email: miw@finansraadet.dk **Web site:** http://www.finansraadet.dk
Freq: Monthly; **Cover Price:** Free
Editor: Mikael Winkler
Language(s): Danish
BUSINESS: FINANCE & ECONOMICS

FISK & FRI
3778D92-50
Editorial: Christians Brygge 28, st. tv., 1559 KØBENHAVN V **Tel:** 33 11 14 88 **Fax:** 33 93 81 70
Email: jb@fiskogfri.dk **Web site:** http://www.fiskogfri.com
Freq: Monthly; **Circ:** 17,000
Executive Editor: Søren Blok Honoré
Profile: Magazine providing information and advice about fishing.
Language(s): Danish
Readership: Aimed at angling enthusiasts.
CONSUMER: ANGLING & FISHING

FISKE AVISEN
3779D92-70
Editorial: Vestskellet 21, 3250 GILLELEJE
Tel: 48 30 13 68 **Fax:** 48 35 44 54
Email: info@fiskeavisen.dk **Web site:** http://www.fiskeavisen.dk
Freq: Monthly; **Circ:** 17,200
Profile: Magazine about fishing and sailing.
Language(s): Danish
CONSUMER: ANGLING & FISHING

FITNEWS MAGAZINE
1819900D53-43
Editorial: Dronnings Tværgade 8 A, 1302 COPENHAGEN **Tel:** 36 92 70 70

Email: info@fitnews.dk **Web site:** http://www.fitnews.dk
Freq: Monthly; **Circ:** 25,400
Executive Editor: Steen Broford
Language(s): Danish
ADVERTISING RATES:
Full Page Colour .... DKK 17300
SCC .... DKK 230.60
BUSINESS: RETAILING & WHOLESALING

FOCUS DENMARK
3029D14C-45
Editorial: Danmarks Exportråd, Asiatisk Plads 2, 1448 KØBENHAVN K **Tel:** 33 92 00 00
Fax: 32 54 19 18
Email: focusdenmark@um.dk **Web site:** http://www.eksportraadet.dk
Date Established: 1987; **Freq:** Quarterly; **Circ:** 18,431
Profile: International magazine published by the Ministry for Foreign Affairs promoting Danish trade.
Language(s): Chinese; English; German; Spanish
BUSINESS: COMMERCE, INDUSTRY & MANAGEMENT: International Commerce

FOLKEBLADET FOR GLOSTRUP, BRØNDBY OG VALLENSBÆK
625117D72-190
Editorial: Glostrup Torv 6, 2600 GLOSTRUP
Tel: 43 96 00 31 **Fax:** 43 63 28 41
Email: folkebladet@folkebladet.dk **Web site:** http://www.folkebladet.dk
Freq: Weekly; **Cover Price:** Free; **Circ:** 36,232
Language(s): Danish
ADVERTISING RATES:
Full Page Colour .... DKK 29658
SCC .... DKK 66
LOCAL NEWSPAPERS

FOLKEBLADET LEMVIG
630242D67B-5450
Editorial: Bredgade 20, 7620 LEMVIG
Tel: 96 63 04 00 **Fax:** 96 63 04 18
Email: lemvig@bergske.dk **Web site:** http://www.lemvig-folkeblad.dk
Freq: Daily; **Circ:** 3,118
Editor: Lars Kamstrup; **Executive Editor:** Erik Møller
Language(s): Danish
ADVERTISING RATES:
Full Page Colour .... DKK 12969
SCC .... DKK 51
REGIONAL DAILY & SUNDAY NEWSPAPERS: Regional Daily Newspapers

FOLKESKOLEN
3357D62C-60
Editorial: P.O. Box 2139, 1015 KØBENHAVN K
Tel: 33 69 63 00 **Fax:** 33 69 64 26
Email: folkeskolen@dlf.org **Web site:** http://www.folkeskolen.dk
Freq: 26 issues yearly; **Circ:** 88,299
Editor: Stine Grynberg Andersen; **Executive Editor:** Hanne Birgitte Jørgensen
Profile: Magazine covering primary education.
Language(s): Danish
Readership: Aimed at primary school teachers, members of school governing bodies and local authorities.
ADVERTISING RATES:
Full Page Colour .... DKK 22600
SCC .... DKK 206,40
BUSINESS: CHURCH & SCHOOL EQUIPMENT & EDUCATION: Junior Education

FORÆLDRE & BØRN
1791971D73-260
Editorial: Vigerslev Allé 18, 2500 VALBY
Tel: 36 15 21 41 **Fax:** 36152698
Email: redaktionen@fb.aller.dk **Web site:** http://www.mama.dk
Freq: Monthly; **Circ:** 9,465
Editor: Ulla Johanne Johansson; **Executive Editor:** Charlotte Riparbelli
Language(s): Danish
ADVERTISING RATES:
Full Page Colour .... DKK 34300
SCC .... DKK 329.80
CONSUMER: NATIONAL & INTERNATIONAL PERIODICALS

FORMANDSBLADET
2972D4E-115
Editorial: Prags Boulevard 45, 2300 COPENHAGEN
Tel: 32 96 56 22 **Fax:** 32 96 58 22
Email: kbm@danskformand.dk **Web site:** http://www.danskformand.dk
Freq: 6 issues yearly; **Circ:** 3,299
Editor: Kim Bøje Madsen
Profile: Magazine for foremen and supervisors in the building industry.
Language(s): Danish
ADVERTISING RATES:
Full Page Colour .... DKK 15800
BUSINESS: ARCHITECTURE & BUILDING: Building

FREDERIKSBERG BLADET
625125D72-200
Editorial: Solbjergvej 2A . Erhvervsplan, 2000 FREDERIKSBERG C **Tel:** 33 88 88 88
Fax: 33 88 88 99
Email: red.fb@b-l.dk **Web site:** http://www.frederiksbergbladet.dk
Freq: Weekly; **Cover Price:** Free; **Circ:** 58,225
Executive Editor: Peter Erlitz
Language(s): Danish
ADVERTISING RATES:
Full Page Colour .... DKK 24304
SCC .... DKK 105
LOCAL NEWSPAPERS

FREDERIKSVÆRK UGEBLAD, HALSNÆS POSTEN
630142D72-1171
Editorial: Valseværksgade 6, 3300 FREDERIKSVÆRK **Tel:** 47 77 14 14 **Fax:** 47 76 05 00
Email: red.fu@b-l.dk **Web site:** http://www.frederiksvaerkugeblad.dk
Freq: Weekly; **Cover Price:** Free; **Circ:** 21,758
Language(s): Danish
ADVERTISING RATES:
Full Page Colour .... DKK 13341,50
SCC .... DKK 57,75
LOCAL NEWSPAPERS

FREELANCENØGLEN
2009983D14A-288
Tel: 33 42 80 00
Email: melgaard@dj-freelance.dk **Web site:** http://www.dj-freelance.dk
Freq: Annual; **Circ:** 10,000
Language(s): Danish
ADVERTISING RATES:
Full Page Colour .... DKK 12900
BUSINESS: COMMERCE, INDUSTRY & MANAGEMENT

FRIE
758719D14A-175
Editorial: Paghs Gård, Overstræde 2b, 5100 ODENSE C **Tel:** 63 13 85 50 **Fax:** 63 13 85 55
Email: bbb@f-f.dk **Web site:** http://www.f-f.dk
Freq: Quarterly; **Circ:** 25,000
Editor: Bente Bærentzen
Language(s): Danish
BUSINESS: COMMERCE, INDUSTRY & MANAGEMENT

FRIII
1792114D73-282
Editorial: Langagervej 1, DK-9220 AALBORG
Tel: 99 35 33 00
Email: flemming.kristensen@nordjyske.dk **Web site:** http://www.friii.dk
Freq: Weekly; **Circ:** 69,258 Unique Users
Editor: Helle Madsen
Language(s): Danish
CONSUMER: NATIONAL & INTERNATIONAL PERIODICALS

FRIKVARTER
3653D76E-30
Editorial: Bispevej 4, 2.sal, 2400 COPENHAGEN
Tel: 33 38 63 33 **Fax:** 33386300
Email: frikvarter@frikvarter.dk **Web site:** http://www.frikvarter.dk
Date Established: 1995; **Freq:** Monthly; **Circ:** 69,307
Profile: Magazine for teenagers about music.
Language(s): Danish
ADVERTISING RATES:
Full Page Colour .... DKK 28800
SCC .... DKK 257.10
CONSUMER: MUSIC & PERFORMING ARTS: Pop Music

FRITIDSLIV
3645D75L-70
Editorial: Kultorvet 7, 1, 1175 KØBENHAVN K
Tel: 33 12 11 65
Email: dvl@dvl.dk **Web site:** http://www.dvl.dk
Date Established: 1930; **Freq:** 6 issues yearly; **Circ:** 14,000
Editor: Michala Mentze
Profile: Magazine of the Danish Walkers' Association. Contains articles and information on walking in Denmark and abroad.
Language(s): Danish
CONSUMER: SPORT: Outdoor

FYENS STIFTSTIDENDE
3422D67B-3200
Editorial: Banegårdspladsen, 5100 ODENSE C
Tel: 66 11 11 11 **Fax:** 65 45 52 88
Email: redaktion@fyens.dk **Web site:** http://www.fyens.dk
Date Established: 1772; **Freq:** Daily; **Circ:** 56,379
Editor: Hans Kiel; **Executive Editor:** Per Westergård
Language(s): Danish
ADVERTISING RATES:
Full Page Colour .... DKK 55347
SCC .... DKK 135,50
REGIONAL DAILY & SUNDAY NEWSPAPERS: Regional Daily Newspapers

FYNS AMTS AVIS
3430D67B-3400
Editorial: Sankt Nicolai Gade 3, BOX 40, 5700 SVENDBORG **Tel:** 62 21 46 21 **Fax:** 62 22 06 10
Email: post@faa.dk **Web site:** http://www.fynsamtsavis.dk
Freq: Daily; **Circ:** 16,899
Editor: Hans Jensen; **Executive Editor:** Jørgen Krebs
Language(s): Danish
ADVERTISING RATES:
Full Page Colour .... DKK 35360
SCC .... DKK 85
REGIONAL DAILY & SUNDAY NEWSPAPERS: Regional Daily Newspapers

FYSIOTERAPEUTEN
758752D56A-225
Editorial: Nørre Voldgade 90, 1358 KØBENHAVN K
Tel: 33 41 46 29 **Fax:** 33 41 46 14
Email: redaktionen@fysio.dk **Web site:** http://www.fysio.dk
Freq: 26 issues yearly; **Circ:** 10,366
Editor: Vibeke Pilmark
Profile: Journal of the Danish Association of Physiotherapists.
Language(s): Danish

GAFFA
3654D76E-40
Editorial: Enghavevej 40, 1674 COPENHAGEN
Tel: 70 27 06 00 **Fax:** 86 189222
Email: redaktion@gaffa.dk **Web site:** http://www.gaffa.dk
Freq: Monthly; **Cover Price:** Free; **Circ:** 70,000
Profile: Magazine covering all aspects of popular music. Distributed free in record shops, schools, leisure centres, discotheques, bars, cafés and clubs in Denmark.
Language(s): Danish
ADVERTISING RATES:
Full Page Colour .... DKK 32500
SCC .... DKK 216.71
CONSUMER: MUSIC & PERFORMING ARTS: Pop Music

GAMEREACTOR
1791605D73-213
Editorial: Strandvejen 72, 2900 COPENHAGEN
Tel: 45 88 76 00
Email: info@gamereactor.dk **Web site:** http://www.gamereactor.dk
Freq: Monthly; **Cover Price:** Free; **Circ:** 29,431
Language(s): Danish
CONSUMER: NATIONAL & INTERNATIONAL PERIODICALS

GASTEKNIK
3122D24-20
Editorial: Dr. Neergaards Vej 5B, 2970 HØRSHOLM
Tel: 97 51 45 95 **Fax:** 97 51 33 95
Email: redaktion@gasteknik.dk **Web site:** http://www.gasteknik.dk
Date Established: 1912; **Freq:** 6 issues yearly; **Circ:** 3,475
Profile: Official magazine of the Danish Gas Association.
Language(s): Danish
Readership: Aimed at managers and employees in gas companies, gas scientist centres, public technical administration, advisors, heat- and power plants, lager industrial gas consumers, vendors to the gas industry and gas heating engineers.
ADVERTISING RATES:
Full Page Colour .... DKK 1325
SCC .... DKK 115

GASTRO
1791454D73-182
Editorial: Hellerupvej 51, 2900 HELLERUP
Tel: 39 45 75 00
Email: info@gastro.dk **Web site:** http://www.gastro.dk
Freq: Monthly; **Circ:** 11,521
Executive Editor: Jesper Uhrup Jensen
Language(s): Danish
CONSUMER: NATIONAL & INTERNATIONAL PERIODICALS

GIVE AVIS
630241D72-210
Editorial: Vestergade 7 E, 7323 GIVE
Tel: 75 73 22 00 **Fax:** 75 73 23 46
Email: gb@give-avis.dk **Web site:** http://www.give-avis.dk
Freq: Weekly; **Cover Price:** Free; **Circ:** 21,352
Editor: Heidi Kiilerich Kristensen
Language(s): Danish
ADVERTISING RATES:
Full Page Colour .... DKK 7090,50
SCC .... DKK 30,50
LOCAL NEWSPAPERS

GLADSAXE BLADET
625126D72-220
Editorial: Søborg Hovedgade 119, 4 sal, 2860 SØBORG **Tel:** 39 56 12 75 **Fax:** 39 56 14 35
Email: gb@gladsaxebladet.dk **Web site:** http://www.gladsaxebladet.dk
Freq: Weekly; **Cover Price:** Free; **Circ:** 38,989
Language(s): Danish
ADVERTISING RATES:
Full Page Colour .... DKK 18697,50
SCC .... DKK 81
LOCAL NEWSPAPERS

GOAL
3629D75B-70
Editorial: Vognmagergade 11, 1148 KØBENHAVN K
Tel: 70 20 50 35 **Fax:** 33 30 57 60
Email: tj@goal.dk **Web site:** http://www.goal.dk
Freq: Monthly; **Circ:** 16,000
Editor: Michael Søgaard; **Executive Editor:** Tony Jørgensen
Profile: Football magazine.
Language(s): Danish
CONSUMER: SPORT: Football

GOLFMAGASINET
3632D75D-60
Editorial: Otto Mønsteds Gade 3, 1571 KØBENHAVN K **Tel:** 36 15 33 00 **Fax:** 36 15 33 02
Email: info@golfmagasinet.dk **Web site:** http://www.golfmagasinet.dk
Date Established: 1998; **Freq:** 6 issues yearly; **Circ:** 79,000
Editor: Astrid Ellemo; **Executive Editor:** Ole Høy Hansen
Profile: Magazine for golfers.
Language(s): Danish
ADVERTISING RATES:
Full Page Colour .... DKK 27700
SCC .... DKK 318,3
CONSUMER: SPORT: Golf

GØR DET SELV
3678D79A-50
Editorial: Strandboulevarden 130, 2100 COPENHAGEN **Tel:** 39 17 20 00 **Fax:** 39 17 23 07
Email: gds@bp.bonnier.dk **Web site:** http://www.goerdetselv.dk
Freq: Monthly; **Circ:** 39,426
Executive Editor: Rune Michaelsen
Profile: Magazine for DIY enthusiasts in Scandinavia.
Language(s): Danish; Finnish; Norwegian; Swedish
ADVERTISING RATES:
Full Page Colour .... DKK 26000
SCC .... DKK 306.20
Copy instructions: *Copy Date:* 30 days prior to publication date
CONSUMER: HOBBIES & DIY

GRAFISK FREMTID
1902441D2A-107
Editorial: Røgelvej 1, 8220 BRABRAND
Tel: 86 25 59 77 **Fax:** 86 25 59 78
Email: kontakt@degrafiske.dk **Web site:** http://www.degrafiske.dk/hvem-er-vi-(1).aspx
Freq: 6 issues yearly; **Cover Price:** Free; **Circ:** 1,600
Language(s): Danish
BUSINESS: COMMUNICATIONS, ADVERTISING & MARKETING

GRAVID - ALT OM DIG
3893D74D-60
Editorial: Hellerupvej 51, 2900 HELLERUP
Tel: 39 45 75 00 **Fax:** 39457404
Email: vif@egmontmagasiner.dk **Web site:** http://www.egmontmagasiner.dk
Freq: Quarterly; **Circ:** 20,000
Executive Editor: Christina Bølling
Profile: Magazine containing articles and information concerning the care and development of babies and young children. Covers pregnancy, health, nutrition, behaviour, fashion and accessories.
Language(s): Danish
Readership: Aimed at pregnant women and new mothers.
CONSUMER: WOMEN'S INTEREST CONSUMER MAGAZINES: Child Care

GRENAA BLADET
630252D72-1170
Editorial: Storegade 37, 8500 GRENÅ
Tel: 86 32 16 77 **Fax:** 86 32 46 11
Email: redaktion@grenaabladet.dk **Web site:** http://www.grenaabladet.dk
Freq: Weekly; **Cover Price:** Free; **Circ:** 22,771
Editor: Henrik Dolmer
Language(s): Danish
ADVERTISING RATES:
Full Page Colour .... DKK 7774,5
SCC .... DKK 35,50
LOCAL NEWSPAPERS

HÅND & VÆRK
3021D14A-65
Editorial: Dronningens Tværgade 2 A, 1302 KØBENHAVN K **Tel:** 48 48 17 88 **Fax:** 33 14 16 25
Email: post@adampade.dk **Web site:** http://www.hvfkbh.dk
Freq: Monthly; **Circ:** 3,500
Editor: Adam Pade
Profile: Magazine of the Association of Craftsmen in Copenhagen.
Language(s): Danish
Readership: Read by artisans, members of the Guild of Craftsmen, contractors and merchants.
BUSINESS: COMMERCE, INDUSTRY & MANAGEMENT

HANDICAP-NYT
3313D56L-30
Editorial: Hans Knudsens Plads 1A, 2100 KØBENHAVN Ø **Tel:** 39 29 35 55 **Fax:** 39 29 39 48
Email: handicap-nyt@dhf-net.dk **Web site:** http://dhf-net.dk/handicap-nyt
Date Established: 1925; **Freq:** 6 issues yearly; **Cover Price:** Free; **Circ:** 30,000
Editor: Solveig Andersen

Profile: Magazine containing articles, news and information about disability.
Language(s): Danish
ADVERTISING RATES:
Full Page Colour .... DKK 12500
BUSINESS: HEALTH & MEDICAL: Disability & Rehabilitation

HARDWAREONLINE.DK
1791678D5C-5
Editorial: Fåborgvej 51, 4700 NÆSTVED
Tel: 70 22 38 20
Email: presse@hardwareonline.dk **Web site:** http://www.hardwareonline.dk
Cover Price: Paid; **Circ:** 7,000 Unique Users
Executive Editor: Thomas Eriksen
Language(s): Danish
BUSINESS: COMPUTERS & AUTOMATION: Professional Personal Computers

HASLEV POSTEN
630320D72-228
Editorial: Jernbanegade 12, 1. sal, 4690 HASLEV
Tel: 56 31 11 12 **Fax:** 56 31 60 61
Email: hp@haslev-posten.dk **Web site:** http://www.haslev-posten.dk
Freq: Weekly; **Cover Price:** Free; **Circ:** 18,379
ADVERTISING RATES:
Full Page Colour .... DKK 12936
SCC .... DKK 56
LOCAL NEWSPAPERS

HAVEBLADET
3132D26D-50
Editorial: Frederikssundsvej 304 A, 2700 BRØNSHØJ **Tel:** 38 28 87 50 **Fax:** 38 28 83 50
Email: info@kolonihave.dk **Web site:** http://www.kolonihave.dk/bladet.htm
Freq: Quarterly; **Circ:** 40,500
Editor: Grethe Bjerregaard
Profile: Publication of the Danish Association of Allotment Owners.
Language(s): Danish
BUSINESS: GARDEN TRADE: Garden Trade Horticulture

HAVEN
3783D93-50
Editorial: Clausholmvej 316, 8370 HADSTEN
Tel: 86 49 17 33 **Fax:** 86 49 17 35
Email: haven@haven.dk **Web site:** http://www.haveselskab.dk
Date Established: 1901; **Freq:** Monthly; **Circ:** 42,000
Editor: Frank Kirkegaard Hansen
Profile: Magazine for gardening enthusiasts.
Language(s): Danish
ADVERTISING RATES:
Full Page Colour .... DKK 17900
CONSUMER: GARDENING

HAVENYT.DK
1810469D73-409
Editorial: Vestenskovvej 11, 4900 NAKSKOV
Tel: 70 20 83 81
Email: redaktionen@havenyt.dk **Web site:** http://www.havenyt.dk
Freq: Daily; **Cover Price:** Paid; **Circ:** 825,000 Unique Users
Language(s): Danish
CONSUMER: NATIONAL & INTERNATIONAL PERIODICALS

HELSE
3613D74G-35
Editorial: Frederiksberg Runddel 1, 2000 FREDERIKSBERG **Tel:** 35 25 05 25 **Fax:** 35 26 87 60
Email: helse@helse.dk **Web site:** http://www.helse.dk
Freq: Monthly; **Cover Price:** Free; **Circ:** 310,000
Editor: Jesper Bo Bendtsen
Profile: Family health magazine.
Language(s): Danish
ADVERTISING RATES:
Full Page Colour .... DKK 55500
CONSUMER: WOMEN'S INTEREST CONSUMER MAGAZINES: Slimming & Health

HELSE GOOD FOOD
1896587D22A-119
Editorial: Frederiksberg Runddel 1, 2000 FREDERIKSBERG **Tel:** 35 25 05 25
Email: helse@helse.dk **Web site:** http://www.helse.dk
Freq: 6 issues yearly; **Circ:** 12,000
Editor: Jesper Bo Bendtsen
Language(s): Danish
ADVERTISING RATES:
Full Page Colour .... DKK 16900
SCC .... DKK 194,25
BUSINESS: FOOD

HELSINGØR DAGBLAD
3409D67B-3800
Editorial: Klostermosevej 101, 3000 HELSINGØR
Tel: 49 22 21 10 **Fax:** 49 26 65 05
Email: redaktionen@hdnet.dk **Web site:** http://www.helsingordagblad.dk
Freq: Daily; **Circ:** 5,919
Executive Editor: Klaus Dalgas
Language(s): Danish
ADVERTISING RATES:
Full Page Colour .... DKK 12231
SCC .... DKK 49
REGIONAL DAILY & SUNDAY NEWSPAPERS: Regional Daily Newspapers

HENDES VERDEN
3588D74A-40
Editorial: Hellerupvej 51, 2900 HELLERUP
Tel: 39 45 75 00
Email: hv@hendesverden.dk **Web site:** http://www.hendesverden.dk
Date Established: 1937; **Freq:** Weekly; **Circ:** 47,836
Executive Editor: Iben Nielsen
Profile: Magazine covering fashion, beauty, crafts, cookery and health.
Language(s): Danish
Readership: Aimed at women over 35 years of age.
ADVERTISING RATES:
Full Page Colour .... DKK 22700
SCC .... DKK 202.70
CONSUMER: WOMEN'S INTEREST CONSUMER MAGAZINES: Women's Interest

HER OG NU
3895D76C-30
Editorial: Hellerupvej 51, 2900 HELLERUP
Tel: 39 45 77 00 **Fax:** 39 45 77 17
Email: herognu@herognu.com **Web site:** http://www.herognu.com
Date Established: 1998; **Freq:** Weekly; **Circ:** 109,365
Executive Editor: Michael Rasmussen
Profile: Television magazine containing gossip and news about Danish and international celebrities.
Language(s): Danish
ADVERTISING RATES:
Full Page Colour .... DKK 31400
SCC .... DKK 280,40
CONSUMER: MUSIC & PERFORMING ARTS: TV & Radio

HERLEV BLADET
625287D72-235
Editorial: Herlev Bygade 39, 2730 HERLEV
Tel: 44 94 10 10 **Fax:** 44 94 13 63
Email: redaktion@herlevbladet.dk **Web site:** http://www.herlevbladet.dk
Freq: Weekly; **Cover Price:** Free; **Circ:** 25,907
Editor: Britt Spangsberg
Language(s): Danish
ADVERTISING RATES:
Full Page Colour .... DKK 26669
SCC .... DKK 59,50
LOCAL NEWSPAPERS

HERNING BLADET
630330D72-237
Editorial: Bredgade 33, 2. sal, 7400 HERNING
Tel: 97 12 15 00 **Fax:** 97 22 20 42
Email: redaktion@herningbladet.dk **Web site:** http://www.herningbladet.dk
Freq: Weekly; **Cover Price:** Free; **Circ:** 50,000
Language(s): Danish
ADVERTISING RATES:
Full Page Colour .... DKK 11133
SCC .... DKK 51
LOCAL NEWSPAPERS

HERNING FOLKEBLAD
3410D67B-4000
Editorial: Østergade 25, 7400 HERNING
Tel: 96 26 37 00 **Fax:** 97 22 36 00
Email: herning@herningfolkeblad.dk **Web site:** http://www.herningfolkeblad.dk
Date Established: 1869; **Freq:** Daily; **Circ:** 12,626
Executive Editor: Vibeke Larsen
Language(s): Danish
ADVERTISING RATES:
Full Page Colour .... DKK 22812
SCC .... DKK 50
REGIONAL DAILY & SUNDAY NEWSPAPERS: Regional Daily Newspapers

HEST OG RYTTER
3696D81D-40
Editorial: Hejreskovvej 20, 3490 KVISTGÅRD
Tel: 49 13 92 00 **Fax:** 49 13 85 00
Email: mail@hest-rytter.dk **Web site:** http://www.hest-rytter.dk
Freq: Monthly; **Circ:** 24,400
Profile: Magazine containing information about horses. Includes articles on breeding, feeding, injuries and riding. Also contains details of forthcoming shows and events, results and showjumping techniques. Provides a section dedicated to ponies.
Language(s): Danish
Readership: Aimed at horse breeders and riders of all standards.
CONSUMER: ANIMALS & PETS: Horses & Ponies

HILLERØD POSTEN
630334D72-1165
Editorial: Møllestræde 9, 3400 HILLERØD
Tel: 70 13 11 00 **Fax:** 48 24 16 16
Email: redaktion@hip.dk **Web site:** http://hilleroed.lokalavisen.dk/apps/pbcs.dll/forside
Freq: Weekly; **Cover Price:** Free; **Circ:** 34,924
Editor: John Jessen Hansen
Language(s): Danish
ADVERTISING RATES:
Full Page Colour .... DKK 16835
SCC .... DKK 72,87
LOCAL NEWSPAPERS

HISTORIE
1791760D73-230
Editorial: Strandboulevarden 122, 2100 KØBENHAVN Ø **Tel:** 39 17 20 00
Email: redaktionen@historiebladet.dk **Web site:** http://historienet.dk
Freq: Monthly; **Circ:** 28,000
Executive Editor: Sebastian Relster
Language(s): Danish
ADVERTISING RATES:
Full Page Colour .... DKK 19600
CONSUMER: NATIONAL & INTERNATIONAL PERIODICALS

HJEMMET
3598D74C-60
Editorial: Hellerupvej 51, 2900 HELLERUP
Tel: 39 45 76 00
Email: red@hjemmet.dk **Web site:** http://www.hjemmet.dk
Freq: Weekly; **Circ:** 157,550
Executive Editor: Bjarne Ravnsted
Profile: Magazine containing articles about family life. Includes short stories, puzzles and television reviews, information on home decoration and crafts, interviews and recipes.
Language(s): Danish
Readership: Aimed at women aged 35 and over.
ADVERTISING RATES:
Full Page Colour .... DKK 50600
SCC .... DKK 451.80
CONSUMER: WOMEN'S INTEREST CONSUMER MAGAZINES: Home & Family

HJERTENYT
3277D56A-235
Editorial: Hausers Plads 10, 1127 COPENHAGEN
Tel: 33 93 17 88
Email: post@hjerteforeningen.dk **Web site:** http://www.hjerteforeningen.dk
Freq: Half-yearly; **Circ:** 86,158
Editor: Morten Bonde Pedersen
Profile: Journal about heart surgery, disease prevention and research.
Language(s): Danish
ADVERTISING RATES:
Full Page Colour .... DKK 28300
BUSINESS: HEALTH & MEDICAL

HK KOMMUNALBLADET
1792457D73-337
Editorial: Weidekampsgade 8, 0900 KØBENHAVN C
Tel: 33 30 43 85 **Fax:** 33 30 44 49
Email: redaktionen@kommunalbladet.dk **Web site:** http://www.hkkommunal.dk
Freq: 26 issues yearly; **Circ:** 66,540
Language(s): Danish
CONSUMER: NATIONAL & INTERNATIONAL PERIODICALS

HK/STAT MAGASINET
3172D32K-70
Editorial: Weidekampsgade 8, PostBoks 470, 0900 KØBENHAVN C **Tel:** 33 30 43 43 **Fax:** 33 30 42 22
Email: hkstat@hk.dk **Web site:** http://www.hkstatmagasinet.dk
Freq: Monthly; **Circ:** 32,613
Editor: Tom Gotfred
Profile: Publication for and about people employed by the government.
Language(s): Danish
ADVERTISING RATES:
Full Page Colour .... DKK 23300
BUSINESS: LOCAL GOVERNMENT, LEISURE & RECREATION: Civil Service

HOBRO AVIS
630362D72-240
Editorial: Adelgade 56, 9500 HOBRO
Tel: 98 52 70 30 **Fax:** 98 51 18 88
Email: hobroavis@nordjyske.dk **Web site:** http://www.nordjyskeugeaviser.dk
Freq: Weekly; **Cover Price:** Free; **Circ:** 21,142
Editor: Peter V. Andersen; **Executive Editor:** Per Lyngby
Language(s): Danish
ADVERTISING RATES:
Full Page Colour .... DKK 10231,50
SCC .... DKK 44,30
LOCAL NEWSPAPERS

HOLBÆK AMTS VENSTREBLAD
3413D67B-4200
Editorial: Bladhuset i Holbæk, Ahlgade 1, 4300 HOLBÆK **Tel:** 88 88 43 00 **Fax:** 59 44 50 34
Email: red.hav@nordvest.dk **Web site:** http://www.venstrebladet.dk
Freq: Daily; **Circ:** 14,257
Editor: Lars Qvist Skjøde; **Executive Editor:** Mogens Flyvholm
Language(s): Danish
ADVERTISING RATES:
Full Page Colour .... DKK 11998
SCC .... DKK 42
REGIONAL DAILY & SUNDAY NEWSPAPERS: Regional Daily Newspapers

HØRELSEN
3315D56L-40
Editorial: Kløverprisvej 10 B, 2650 HVIDOVRE
Tel: 61 38 54 94 **Fax:** 36 38 85 80
Email: hoerelsen@hoereforeningen.dk **Web site:** http://www.lbh.dk
Freq: Monthly; **Circ:** 12,000
Profile: Magazine containing information concerning hearing difficulties.
Language(s): Danish
Readership: Aimed at manufacturers of hearing aids and equipment, hospital and social workers.
ADVERTISING RATES:
Full Page Colour .... DKK 16800
BUSINESS: HEALTH & MEDICAL: Disability & Rehabilitation

HORSENS FOLKEBLAD
3415D67B-4400
Editorial: Bojsens Gård, Søndergade 47, 8700 HORSENS **Tel:** 76 27 20 00 **Fax:** 75 61 07 97
Email: redaktionen@horsens-folkeblad.dk **Web site:** http://www.horsens-folkeblad.dk
Date Established: 1863; **Freq:** Daily; **Circ:** 15,708
Editor: Sven Grønborg
Language(s): Danish
ADVERTISING RATES:
Full Page Colour .... DKK 34913
SCC .... DKK 73
REGIONAL DAILY & SUNDAY NEWSPAPERS: Regional Daily Newspapers

HUNDEN
3694D81B-50
Editorial: Mediehuset Wiegården, Postboks 315, 9500 HOBRO **Tel:** 98 51 20 66 **Fax:** 98 51 20 06
Email: hunden-redaktionen@wiegaarden.dk **Web site:** http://www.dansk-kennel-klub.dk/885
Date Established: 1897; **Freq:** Monthly; **Circ:** 30,100
Editor: Marlene Hedegaard
Profile: Magazine for members of the Danish Kennel Club.
Language(s): Danish
CONSUMER: ANIMALS & PETS: Dogs

HUS & HAVE AVISEN
1792027D4B-302
Editorial: Traverbanevej 10, 2920 CHARLOTTENLUND **Tel:** 70 20 01 82
Fax: 36 70 50 63
Email: jg@husoghaveavisen.dk **Web site:** http://www.husoghaveavisen.dk
Freq: Quarterly; **Cover Price:** Free; **Circ:** 1,317,282
Editor: Jeanet Gugic Stæhr
Language(s): Danish
ADVERTISING RATES:
Full Page Colour .... DKK 40887
SCC .... DKK 177
Copy instructions: *Copy Date:* 30 days prior to publication date
BUSINESS: ARCHITECTURE & BUILDING: Interior Design & Flooring

HUSET
2924D1E-60
Editorial: Nørre Voldgade 2, 4. sal, 1358 COPENHAGEN **Tel:** 33 12 03 30 **Fax:** 33 12 62 75
Email: rik@ejendomsforeningen.dk **Web site:** http://www.ejendomsf.dk
Freq: Monthly - 10 gange årligt minus januar og juli; **Circ:** 4,581
Profile: Magazine providing information on new property developments, financial issues and commercial premises.
Language(s): Danish
ADVERTISING RATES:
Full Page Colour .... DKK 18300
BUSINESS: FINANCE & ECONOMICS: Property

HUSFLID
3599D74C-62
Editorial: Tyrebakken 11, 5300 KERTEMINDE
Tel: 63 32 20 96 **Fax:** 63 32 20 97
Email: dansk@husflid.dk **Web site:** http://www.husflid.dk
Date Established: 1871; **Freq:** 6 issues yearly; **Circ:** 5,000
Editor: Finn Glibstrup
Profile: Magazine about home decoration and handicrafts.
Language(s): Danish
Readership: Aimed at people interested in improving their home environment.
CONSUMER: WOMEN'S INTEREST CONSUMER MAGAZINES: Home & Family

HVIDOVRE AVIS
625304D72-250
Editorial: Hvidovrevej 301, 2650 HVIDOVRE
Tel: 36 49 55 55 **Fax:** 36 77 25 55
Email: red@hvidovre-avis.dk **Web site:** http://www.hvidovreavis.dk
Freq: Weekly; **Cover Price:** Free; **Circ:** 27,338
Executive Editor: Niels Erik Madsen
Language(s): Danish
ADVERTISING RATES:
Full Page Colour .... DKK 29976
SCC .... DKK 67
LOCAL NEWSPAPERS

Denmark

I FORM
32356D74G-116
Editorial: Strandboulevarden 130, 2100 COPENHAGEN **Tel:** 39 17 20 00 **Fax:** 39 17 23 11
Email: iform@iform.dk **Web site:** http://www.iform.dk
Date Established: 1988; **Freq:** Monthly; **Circ:** 63,089
Editor: Karen Lyager Horve
Profile: Magazine focusing on lifestyle, healthy food, fitness and fashion.
Language(s): Danish; Norwegian
Readership: Read mainly by women aged between 18 and 40 years.
ADVERTISING RATES:
Full Page Colour .... DKK 39100
SCC .... DKK 337.06
Copy instructions: *Copy Date:* 31 days prior to publication date
CONSUMER: WOMEN'S INTEREST CONSUMER MAGAZINES: Slimming & Health

IDÉNYT
3600D74C-63
Editorial: Strandboulevarden 130, 2100 COPENHAGEN **Tel:** 39 17 20 00
Email: ali@idenyt.dk **Web site:** http://www.idenyt.dk
Freq: Monthly; **Cover Price:** Free; **Circ:** 1,712,634
Editor: Per Handberg; **Executive Editor:** Anna-Lise Aaen
Profile: Magazine containing news and information concerning the home and garden. Covers maintenance, decoration and new products, along with ideas and advice on related legal and financial matters.
Language(s): Danish
Readership: Distributed free to all Danish homeowners.
ADVERTISING RATES:
Full Page Colour .... DKK 244900
SCC .... DKK 2186.60
CONSUMER: WOMEN'S INTEREST CONSUMER MAGAZINES: Home & Family

IDRÆTSLIV
3642D75A-150
Editorial: Idrættens Hus, Brøndby Stadion 20, 2605 BRØNDBY **Tel:** 43 26 26 26 **Fax:** 43 26 26 30
Email: idraetsliv@dif.dk **Web site:** http://www.dif.dk
Date Established: 1923; **Freq:** Monthly; **Circ:** 19,000
Editor: Hanna Britt Milling
Profile: Magazine providing news and information about all sports. Covers training, nutrition, health, and competitions, also includes politics and economics.
Language(s): Danish
Readership: Aimed at politicians, leaders and trainers.
ADVERTISING RATES:
Full Page Colour .... DKK 12000
CONSUMER: SPORT

ILLUSTRERET VIDENSKAB
3791D55-51
Editorial: Strandboulevarden 130, 2100 COPENHAGEN **Tel:** 39 17 20 00 **Fax:** 39172300
Email: redaktion@illvid.dk **Web site:** http://www.illustreretvidenskab.dk
Freq: Monthly; **Circ:** 67,863
Editor: Christian Bækgaard
Profile: Scandinavian popular science magazine containing articles and information.
Language(s): Danish
BUSINESS: APPLIED SCIENCE & LABORATORIES

INBUSINESS
2943D2F-80
Editorial: Nørre Farimagsgade 49, 1364 COPENHAGEN **Tel:** 33 74 02 00 **Fax:** 33 74 0290
Email: inbusiness@businessdanmark.dk **Web site:** http://www.businessdanmark.dk
Freq: Monthly; **Circ:** 26,396
Profile: Journal focusing on sales promotions, training, new cars and products to be used by the sales professional.
Language(s): Danish
Readership: Read by salesmen and sales managers.
ADVERTISING RATES:
Full Page Colour .... DKK 15800
SCC .... DKK 257.95
BUSINESS: COMMUNICATIONS, ADVERTISING & MARKETING: Selling

INGENIØREN
3061D19A-50
Editorial: Skelbækgade 4, 1717 KØBENHAVN V
Tel: 33 26 53 00 **Fax:** 33 26 53 01
Email: redaktion@ing.dk **Web site:** http://www.ing.dk
Date Established: 1894; **Freq:** Weekly; **Circ:** 66,048
Profile: Journal of the Society of Danish Engineers. Publishes wide-ranging information about technical developments in Denmark and abroad.
Language(s): Danish
ADVERTISING RATES:
Full Page Colour .... DKK 50700
SCC .... DKK 230
BUSINESS: ENGINEERING & MACHINERY

INSPI
2914D1B-5
Editorial: Revifora, Kronprinsessegade 8, 1306 KØBENHAVN K **Tel:** 33 15 15 19 **Fax:** 33 93 15 19
Email: inspi@revifora.dk **Web site:** http://www.revifora.dk
Freq: Monthly; **Circ:** 3,148
Profile: Accountancy and auditing journal.
Language(s): Danish
ADVERTISING RATES:
Full Page Colour .... DKK 17000
SCC .... DKK 198,85
BUSINESS: FINANCE & ECONOMICS: Accountancy

INSTALLATIONS NYT
3054D17-50
Editorial: Naverland 35, 2600 GLOSTRUP
Tel: 43 24 26 28 **Fax:** 43 24 26 26
Email: dbj@techmedia.dk **Web site:** http://www.techmedia.dk/default.asp?Action=Details&Item=3652
Freq: Monthly; **Circ:** 3,995
Profile: Journal for electro-technical engineers.
Language(s): Danish
ADVERTISING RATES:
Full Page Colour .... DKK 24900
SCC .... DKK 325,49

ISABELLAS
1792488D73-353
Editorial: Hesede Hovedgård 3, 4690 HASLEV
Tel: 70 70 14 14
Email: charlotte.riparbelli@isabellas.dk **Web site:** http://www.isabellasmith.com
Freq: 6 issues yearly; **Circ:** 38,515
Executive Editor: Charlotte Riparbelli
Language(s): Danish
ADVERTISING RATES:
Full Page Colour .... DKK 35700
SCC .... DKK 318.80
CONSUMER: NATIONAL & INTERNATIONAL PERIODICALS

JÆGER
3633D75F-20
Editorial: Højnæsvej 56, 2610 RØDOVRE
Tel: 36 73 05 00 **Fax:** 36 72 09 11
Email: red@jaegerne.dk **Web site:** http://www.jaegerne.dk
Date Established: 1884; **Freq:** Monthly; **Circ:** 82,831
Editor: Maria Metzger
Profile: Magazine covering all aspects of hunting.
Language(s): Danish
ADVERTISING RATES:
Full Page Colour .... DKK 34400
SCC .... DKK 380,81
CONSUMER: SPORT: Shooting

JOURNALISTEN
3042D14L-150
Editorial: Gl. Strand 46, 1202 KØBENHAVN K
Tel: 33 42 80 00 **Fax:** 33 42 80 08
Email: journalisten@journalisten.dk **Web site:** http://www.journalisten.dk
Freq: 26 issues yearly; **Circ:** 14,287
Executive Editor: Jakob Elkjær
Profile: Magazine about the media in Denmark, primarily the development of journalism. Published by the Danish Union of Journalists.
Language(s): Danish
ADVERTISING RATES:
Full Page Colour .... DKK 19100
SCC .... DKK 146,60
BUSINESS: COMMERCE, INDUSTRY & MANAGEMENT: Trade Unions

JYDERUP POSTEN
630391D72-350
Editorial: Industrivej 1 B, Postboks 70, 4450 JYDERUP **Tel:** 88 88 44 50 **Fax:** 59 27 76 67
Email: red.jp@nordvest.dk **Web site:** http://www.venstrebladet.dk/hav/default.asp?action=ugeaviser&ugeavis=jypost
Freq: Weekly; **Cover Price:** Free; **Circ:** 18,920
Editor: Rita Sørensen
Language(s): Danish
ADVERTISING RATES:
Full Page Colour .... DKK 9268
SCC .... DKK 40
LOCAL NEWSPAPERS

JYLLANDS POSTEN
3392D65A-68
Editorial: Rådhuspladsen 37, 1785 COPENHAGEN
Tel: 87 38 38 38 **Fax:** 87 38 3 99
Email: jp@jp.dk **Web site:** http://www.jp.dk
Freq: Daily; **Circ:** 125,096
Editor: Knud Refsing Andersen
Profile: Broadsheet-sized newspaper covering national and international news, politics and sports.
Language(s): Danish
Readership: Read by a wide cross-section of the population.
ADVERTISING RATES:
Full Page Colour .... DKK 127050
SCC .... DKK 550
NATIONAL DAILY & SUNDAY NEWSPAPERS: National Daily Newspapers

JYLLANDS-POSTEN, MORGENAVISEN; GISMO
1841160D5C-20
Editorial: St. Kongensgade 14, 1., 2164 KØBENHAVN K **Tel:** 33 30 82 62
Email: info@gismo-online.dk **Web site:** http://www.gismo-online.dk
Freq: Monthly; **Circ:** 140,000
Editor: Mette Gert
Language(s): Danish
BUSINESS: COMPUTERS & AUTOMATION: Professional Personal Computers

KABEL OG LINIEMESTEREN
3329D58-50
Editorial: Ørbækvej 47, 7330 BRANDE
Tel: 97 18 03 77 **Fax:** 97 18 13 53
Email: redaktor@kogl.dk **Web site:** http://www.kogl.dk
Freq: Monthly; **Circ:** 705
Profile: Magazine providing information about the Danish electricity industry.
Language(s): Danish
Readership: Aimed at technicians of Danish electricity supply boards.
ADVERTISING RATES:
Full Page Colour .... DKK 6150
SCC .... DKK 84

KATOLSK ORIENTERING
3737D87-60
Editorial: Gl. Kongevej 15, 1610 KØBENHAVN V
Tel: 33 55 60 40 **Fax:** 33 24 49 75
Email: redaktion@katolskorientering.dk **Web site:** http://www.katolskorientering.dk
Date Established: 1975; **Freq:** 26 issues yearly; **Circ:** 7,700
Profile: Newspaper containing cultural and religious articles.
Language(s): Danish
Readership: Distributed free to all members of the Catholic Church.
CONSUMER: RELIGIOUS

KENTAUR
3190D40-50
Editorial: Hærens Kampskole, 6840 OKSBØL
Tel: 76 54 12 00 **Fax:** 76 54 14 09
Email: hks@mil.dk **Web site:** http://forsvaret.dk/HKS/Kentaur/Pages/default.aspx
Date Established: 1954; **Freq:** Quarterly; **Circ:** 1,500
Profile: Military journal concerned with materials and training methods used within the infantry and armoury divisions.
Language(s): Danish
Readership: Military personnel.
ADVERTISING RATES:
Full Page Colour .... DKK 4100
SCC .... DKK 47,12

KIG IND
3584D73-100
Editorial: Vigerslev Allé 18, 2500 VALBY
Tel: 36 15 20 00 **Fax:** 36 15 20 49
Email: kigind@aller.dk **Web site:** http://www.kigind.com
Freq: Weekly; **Circ:** 50,000
Editor: Malene Fich Weischer; **Executive Editor:** Michael Hansen
Profile: Magazine containing articles and information of interest to the whole family. Also covers listings of radio and television programmes.
Language(s): Danish
ADVERTISING RATES:
Full Page Colour .... DKK 28000
SCC .... DKK 250
CONSUMER: NATIONAL & INTERNATIONAL PERIODICALS

KIROPRAKTOREN
3280D56A-80_90
Editorial: Vendersgade 6, 2.tv, 1011 KØBENHAVN K
Tel: 33 93 04 00 **Fax:** 33 93 04 89
Email: dkf@kiropraktor-foreningen.dk **Web site:** http://www.kiropraktor-foreningen.dk
Freq: Monthly; **Circ:** 500
Editor: Ole Rasmussen
Profile: Journal of the Danish Chiropractors' Association.
Language(s): Danish
ADVERTISING RATES:
Full Page Colour .... DKK 2600
SCC .... DKK 29,88

KØGE ONSDAG
630412D72-380
Editorial: Torvet 10, 4600 KØGE **Tel:** 56 65 10 05
Fax: 56 65 07 12
Email: koege.onsdag.red@sj-medier.dk **Web site:** http://www.koege-onsdag.dk
Freq: Weekly; **Cover Price:** Free; **Circ:** 42,639
Editor: Arne Egaa
Language(s): Danish
ADVERTISING RATES:
Full Page Colour .... DKK 17784
SCC .... DKK 77
LOCAL NEWSPAPERS

KOMPUTER FOR ALLE
2984D5D-200
Editorial: Strandboulevarden 130, 2100 KØBENHAVN Ø **Tel:** 39 17 20 00 **Fax:** 39 17 23 09
Web site: http://www.komputer.dk
Date Established: 1997; **Freq:** Monthly; **Circ:** 47,238
Executive Editor: Leif Jonasson
Profile: Magazine about all aspects of computers and data processing.
Language(s): Danish; Finnish; Norwegian; Swedish
Readership: Aimed at home PC users.
ADVERTISING RATES:
Full Page Colour .... DKK 33600
SCC .... DKK 304,30
BUSINESS: COMPUTERS & AUTOMATION: Personal Computers

KRISTELIGT DAGBLAD
3391D65A-45
Editorial: Rosengården 14, 1174 COPENHAGEN
Tel: 33 48 05 00 **Fax:** 33480502
Email: kristeligt-dagblad@kristeligt-dagblad.dk **Web site:** http://www.kristeligt-dagblad.dk
Date Established: 1896; **Freq:** Daily - Denmark; **Circ:** 26,145
Profile: Broadsheet-sized religious newspaper covering national and international news, current affairs, culture and features.
Language(s): Danish
Readership: Read mainly by Christian people and those interested in religious issues.
ADVERTISING RATES:
Full Page Colour .... DKK 21680
SCC .... DKK 48.39
NATIONAL DAILY & SUNDAY NEWSPAPERS: National Daily Newspapers

KROP & FYSIK
3311D56L-18
Editorial: Vejrøvænget 85, 5500 MIDDELFART
Tel: 75 85 80 90
Email: redaktionen@krop-fysik.dk **Web site:** http://www.krop-fysik.dk
Freq: 6 issues yearly; **Circ:** 18,000
Editor: Marianne Nørup
Profile: Journal covering physical health-care and physiotherapy.
Language(s): Danish
ADVERTISING RATES:
Full Page Colour .... DKK 24400
SCC .... DKK 266.92
Copy instructions: *Copy Date:* 21 days prior to publication date
BUSINESS: HEALTH & MEDICAL: Disability & Rehabilitation

KRYDSFELT
1819960D14A-269
Editorial: Anker Engelundsvej 1, DTU bygn. 101E, 2800 KGS. LYNGBY **Tel:** 77 42 44 17
Email: redaktion@krydsfelt.dk **Web site:** http://www.krydsfelt.dk
Freq: 6 issues yearly; **Circ:** 4,000
Language(s): Danish
ADVERTISING RATES:
Full Page Colour .... DKK 8000
SCC .... DKK 94,33
BUSINESS: COMMERCE, INDUSTRY & MANAGEMENT

KULØR
1791813D73-244
Editorial: Otto Mønsteds Gade 3, 1571 COPENHAGEN **Tel:** 72 341200
Email: red@kuloer.dk **Web site:** http://www.kuloer.dk
Freq: Monthly - 12 gange årligt; **Cover Price:** Free; **Circ:** 81,342
Executive Editor: Louise Voller
Language(s): Danish
ADVERTISING RATES:
Full Page Colour .... DKK 33200
SCC .... DKK 463.40
Copy instructions: *Copy Date:* 33 days prior to publication date
CONSUMER: NATIONAL & INTERNATIONAL PERIODICALS

KULTURMAGASINET SKOPET
3627D74Q-50
Editorial: Kjellerupsgade 16-18, 9000 AALBORG
Tel: 98 16 70 82 **Fax:** 98 16 70 52
Email: redak@skopet.dk **Web site:** http://www.skopet.dk
Freq: 6 issues yearly; **Circ:** 8,000
Editor: Lone Nedergaard
Profile: Magazine containing lifestyle articles and cultural information about Denmark.
Language(s): Danish
CONSUMER: WOMEN'S INTEREST CONSUMER MAGAZINES: Lifestyle

LÆGEMAGASINET
3839D56A-81
Editorial: Emiliekildevej 35, 2930 KLAMPENBORG
Tel: 39 90 80 00 **Fax:** 39 90 82 80
Email: tbv@scanpublisher.dk **Web site:** http://www.laegemagasinet.dk
Freq: 6 issues yearly; **Circ:** 5,200
Profile: Magazine focusing on new medicines, treatments and diagnostic methods.
Language(s): Danish
Readership: Read by general practitioners and pharmacists.
ADVERTISING RATES:
Full Page Colour .... DKK 17500
SCC .... DKK 277,7

LAND & LIV
3110D21J-15
Editorial: Vester Farimagsgade 6, 2. sal, 1606 KØBENHAVN V **Tel:** 33 39 47 00 **Fax:** 33 39 47 39
Email: fogtmann@landogliv.dk **Web site:** http://www.landogliv.dk
Freq: 26 issues yearly; **Circ:** 113,082
Executive Editor: Henrik Lisberg
Profile: Publication about Danish agriculture.
Language(s): Danish
ADVERTISING RATES:
Full Page Colour .... DKK 28000
SCC .... DKK 121,21
BUSINESS: AGRICULTURE & FARMING: Agriculture & Farming - Regional

LANDBRUG FYN 3111D21A-126
Editorial: Odensevej 29, 5550 LANGESKOV
Tel: 70 15 12 37 **Fax:** 65 38 33 37
Email: fyn@landbrugnet.dk **Web site:** http://www.landbrugnet.dk
Date Established: 1969; **Freq:** Weekly; **Circ:** 16,555
Profile: Journal containing articles and information of interest to farmers in Denmark and Europe.
Language(s): Danish
Readership: All farms with more than 50 hectares, more than 60 cows, more than 80 sows, more than 4.000 finishers and all farm managers, all farm machine co-ops, farm machine dealers, advisorycentres and other Danish agricultural businesses, as well as subscribers.
ADVERTISING RATES:
Full Page Colour .... DKK 12187
SCC .... DKK 56,40
BUSINESS: AGRICULTURE & FARMING

LANDBRUG NORD 1810404D14A-266
Editorial: Østre Allé, 9530 STØVRING
Tel: 98 35 12 37 **Fax:** 98 33 12 37
Email: post@landbrugnord.dk **Web site:** http://www.landbrugnet.dk
Freq: Weekly; **Circ:** 37,719
Editor: Anne-Marie Glistrup
Language(s): Danish
BUSINESS: COMMERCE, INDUSTRY & MANAGEMENT

LANDBRUG ØST 1810403D14A-265
Editorial: Huginsvej 11, 4100 RINGSTED
Tel: 55 50 12 37 **Fax:** 55 50 12 31
Email: post@landbrugoest.dk **Web site:** http://www.landbrugnet.dk
Freq: Weekly; **Circ:** 26,184
Editor: Torben Andersen
Language(s): Danish
BUSINESS: COMMERCE, INDUSTRY & MANAGEMENT

LANDBRUG SYD 3112D21J-52
Editorial: Skolegade 1A, 6650 BRØRUP
Tel: 75 38 15 00 **Fax:** 75 38 15 16
Email: syd@landbrugnet.dk **Web site:** http://www.landbrugnet.dk
Date Established: 1993; **Freq:** Weekly; **Circ:** 25,420
Executive Editor: John Ankersen
Profile: Publication for farmers in South Jutland.
Language(s): Danish
ADVERTISING RATES:
Full Page Colour .... DKK 13051
SCC .... DKK 60,40
BUSINESS: AGRICULTURE & FARMING: Agriculture & Farming - Regional

LANDBRUGSAVISEN 1834363D21A-127
Editorial: Vester Farimagsgade 6, 2.sal, 1606 KØBENHAVN V **Tel:** 33 39 47 00 **Fax:** 33 39 47 49
Email: post@landbrugsavisen.dk **Web site:** http://www.landbrugsavisen.dk
Freq: Weekly; **Circ:** 54,000
Executive Editor: Henrik Lisberg
Language(s): Danish
ADVERTISING RATES:
Full Page Colour .... DKK 33500
SCC .... DKK 153
BUSINESS: AGRICULTURE & FARMING

LANDBRUGSAVISEN LANDBRUGSAVISEN.DK 3081D21A-70
Editorial: Vester Farimagsgade 6, 2.sal, 1606 KØBENHAVN V **Tel:** 33 39 47 00 **Fax:** 33 39 47 49
Email: post@landbrugsavisen.dk **Web site:** http://www.landbrugsavisen.dk
Freq: Daily; **Cover Price:** Paid; **Circ:** 13,000 Unique Users
Editor: Henning Laen Sørensen; **Executive Editor:** Henrik Lisberg
Profile: Magazine containing general articles and information about farming.
Language(s): Danish
Readership: Read by farmers.
ADVERTISING RATES:
SCC .... DKK 30,6
BUSINESS: AGRICULTURE & FARMING

LANDBRUGS-NYT 3113D21J-55
Editorial: Marrebæk Norvej 1, 4873 VÆGGERLØSE
Tel: 54 17 73 00 **Fax:** 54 17 73 43
Email: es@landbrugs-nyt.dk **Web site:** http://www.landbrugs-nyt.dk
Freq: Weekly; **Circ:** 23,420
Profile: Publication containing news and information about agriculture and farming in Sjaelland.
Language(s): Danish
BUSINESS: AGRICULTURE & FARMING: Agriculture & Farming - Regional

LASTBIL MAGASINET 3833D49A-17
Editorial: Kongensgade 72, 1. sal, 5000 ODENSE C
Fax: 66 16 01 47
Email: redaktionen@lastbilmagasinet.dk **Web site:** http://www.lastbilmagasinet.dk
Date Established: 1997; **Freq:** Monthly; **Circ:** 10,600
Executive Editor: Rasmus Haargaard
Profile: Magazine focusing on transport, including lorries and commercial vehicles.
Language(s): Danish
ADVERTISING RATES:
Full Page Colour .... DKK 14900
SCC .... DKK 139,50

LEDELSE I DAG LEDELSEIDAG.DK 3024D14A-200
Editorial: Vermlandsgade 65, DK-2300 COPENHAGEN **Tel:** 32 83 32 83 **Fax:** 32 833284
Email: lid@lederne.dk **Web site:** http://www.ledelseidag.dk
Freq: Weekly; **Circ:** 4,100 Unique Users
Profile: Magazine concerning the management of private companies and public authorities.
Language(s): Danish
BUSINESS: COMMERCE, INDUSTRY & MANAGEMENT

LEDERNE 3025D14A-120
Editorial: Vermlandsgade 65, 2300 COPENHAGEN
Tel: 32 83 32 83 **Fax:** 32833284
Email: lh@lederne.dk **Web site:** http://www.lederne.dk
Freq: Monthly; **Circ:** 83,431
Profile: Journal for management in trade, service and industry.
Language(s): Danish
ADVERTISING RATES:
Full Page Colour .... DKK 26300
SCC .... DKK 339.08
BUSINESS: COMMERCE, INDUSTRY & MANAGEMENT

LEDSAGER 1810292D14A-264
Editorial: Gentoftegade 118, 2820 GENTOFTE
Tel: 39 77 80 14
Email: redaktion@gigtforeningen.dk **Web site:** http://www.gigtforeningen.dk
Freq: 6 issues yearly; **Circ:** 72,182
Editor: Morten Linnemann
Language(s): Danish
ADVERTISING RATES:
Full Page Colour .... DKK 18.400
SCC .... DKK 227,16
BUSINESS: COMMERCE, INDUSTRY & MANAGEMENT

LEDSAGER - ALT OM GIGT OG GODE VANER 1791433D73-176
Editorial: Gentoftegade 118, 2820 GENTOFTE
Tel: 39 77 80 14 **Fax:** 39 65 11 96
Email: redaktion@gigtforeningen.dk **Web site:** http://www.gigtforeningen.dk
Freq: 6 issues yearly; **Circ:** 98,000
Editor: Michael Søby Andersen
Language(s): Danish
ADVERTISING RATES:
Full Page Colour .... DKK 18800
CONSUMER: NATIONAL & INTERNATIONAL PERIODICALS

LEVENDE NATUR 3693D81A-70
Editorial: WWF Verdensnaturfonden, Ryesgade 3F, 2200 KØBENHAVN N **Tel:** 35 36 36 35
Fax: 35 24 78 68
Email: levende.natur@wwf.dk **Web site:** http://www.wwf.dk
Freq: Quarterly; **Circ:** 20,500
Editor: Karoline Rahbek
Profile: Official journal of the World Wide Fund for Nature.
Language(s): Danish
Readership: Read by members, journalists and decision makers.
ADVERTISING RATES:
Full Page Colour .... DKK Har ikke annoncer
CONSUMER: ANIMALS & PETS: Animals & Pets Protection

LEVNEDSMIDDEL & FØDEVARE MAGASINET 3834D22A-65
Editorial: Tinggårdsvej 4, 4130 VIBY **Tel:** 82 30 75 00
Email: info@lodfmagasinet.dk **Web site:** http://www.logfmagasinet.dk
Date Established: 1994; **Freq:** Quarterly; **Circ:** 7,000
Profile: Magazine focusing on the food and beverage industry.
Language(s): Danish
Readership: Read by caterers and professionals within the food and beverage industry, and the retail-/wholesale market.
ADVERTISING RATES:
Full Page Colour .... DKK 24000
SCC .... DKK 269.36
BUSINESS: FOOD

LICITATIONEN 3202D65A-69
Editorial: Marielundvej 46D, Postbox 537, 2730 HERLEV **Tel:** 70 15 02 22 **Fax:** 44 85 89 19
Email: licitationen@licitationen.dk **Web site:** http://www.licitationen.dk
Freq: Daily; **Circ:** 4,111
Executive Editor: Claus Michael Nielsen
Profile: Newspaper concerning all aspects of construction and the building industry.
Language(s): Danish
ADVERTISING RATES:
Full Page Colour .... DKK 20550
SCC .... DKK 88,96
NATIONAL DAILY & SUNDAY NEWSPAPERS: Unabhängiges konservatives MdEP

LIME 1792260D73-299
Editorial: Otto Mønsteds Gade 3, 1571 COPENHAGEN **Tel:** 72 34 12 00
Email: lvo@chiligroup.dk **Web site:** http://www.chiligroup.dk
Freq: Monthly; **Cover Price:** Free; **Circ:** 201,442
Executive Editor: Louise Voller
Language(s): Danish
ADVERTISING RATES:
Full Page Colour .... DKK 43900
SCC .... DKK 374.10
Copy instructions: *Copy Date:* 31 days prior to publication date
CONSUMER: NATIONAL & INTERNATIONAL PERIODICALS

LIVING DESIGN 1792253D73-298
Editorial: Vigerslev Allé 18, 2500 VALBY
Tel: 36 15 20 00
Email: livingdesign@aller.dk **Web site:** http://www.livingdesignmag.dk
Freq: Quarterly; **Circ:** 7,720
Executive Editor: Thomas Bendix
Language(s): Danish
ADVERTISING RATES:
Full Page Colour .... DKK 31200
SCC .... DKK 278,60
CONSUMER: NATIONAL & INTERNATIONAL PERIODICALS

LOKALAVISEN FREDERIKSHAVN 630162D72-1162
Editorial: Tordenskjoldsgade 2, 9900 FREDERIKSHAVN **Tel:** 99 20 33 33 **Fax:** 99 20 33 60
Email: lokalavisen@nordjyske.dk **Web site:** http://www.nordjyskeugeaviser.dk
Date Established: 1975; **Freq:** Weekly; **Cover Price:** Free; **Circ:** 22,927
Language(s): Danish
ADVERTISING RATES:
Full Page Colour .... DKK 11375,50
SCC .... DKK 49
LOCAL NEWSPAPERS

LOKALAVISEN KALØ VIG 630165D72-1163
Editorial: Tingvej 36, 8543 HORNSLET
Tel: 86 99 45 11 **Fax:** 86 99 55 49
Email: mail@lokalavisen.dk **Web site:** http://kaloevig.lokalavisen.dk
Freq: Weekly; **Cover Price:** Free; **Circ:** 25,130
Editor: Lars Norman Thomsen
Language(s): Danish
ADVERTISING RATES:
Full Page Colour .... DKK 7161
SCC .... DKK 3,1
LOCAL NEWSPAPERS

LOKALAVISEN NORDSJÆLLAND 630170D72-457
Editorial: Klostermosevej 101, 3000 HELSINGØR
Tel: 49 22 21 10 **Fax:** 49 22 11 08
Email: redaktionen@nsnet.dk **Web site:** http://www.nsnet.dk
Freq: Weekly; **Cover Price:** Free; **Circ:** 37,451
Language(s): Danish
ADVERTISING RATES:
Full Page Colour .... DKK 16170
SCC .... DKK 70
LOCAL NEWSPAPERS

LOKALAVISEN UGE NYT 630195D72-459
Editorial: Stenløse Center 69, 3660 STENLØSE
Tel: 47 17 00 49 **Fax:** 47 17 27 27
Email: red@ugenyt.dk **Web site:** http://www.ugenyt.dk
Freq: Weekly; **Cover Price:** Free; **Circ:** 31,084
Language(s): Danish
ADVERTISING RATES:
Full Page Colour .... DKK 14296,50
SCC .... DKK 61,88
LOCAL NEWSPAPERS

LOKALPOSTEN LEM UGEAVIS 630214D72-1158
Editorial: Falkevej 4, 6920 VIDEBÆK
Tel: 97 17 11 22 **Fax:** 97 17 31 11
Email: post@videbaek-bogtrykkeri.dk **Web site:** http://www.danske-lokalaviser.dk/blade/LokalpostenLem/LokalpostenLem.htm
Freq: Weekly; **Cover Price:** Free; **Circ:** 3,800
Language(s): Danish
ADVERTISING RATES:
Full Page Colour .... DKK 5504,50
SCC .... DKK 23,80
LOCAL NEWSPAPERS

LOLLANDS POSTEN 630218D72-1146
Editorial: Banegårdspladsen 2, 4930 MARIBO
Tel: 54 76 04 88 **Fax:** 54 88 03 61
Email: redaktionen@lollands-posten.dk **Web site:** http://www.lollands-posten.dk
Freq: Weekly; **Cover Price:** Free; **Circ:** 21,913
Editor: Jens Bang
Language(s): Danish
ADVERTISING RATES:
Full Page Colour .... DKK 20170
SCC .... DKK 45
LOCAL NEWSPAPERS

LØRDAGSAVISEN KØGE 630223D72-1149
Editorial: Søndre Alle 1, 4600 KØGE **Tel:** 56 65 82 00
Fax: 56 65 93 09
Email: redaktion@kmc-as.dk **Web site:** http://www.loerdagsavisen.dk
Date Established: 1981; **Freq:** Weekly; **Cover Price:** Free; **Circ:** 44,700
Editor: Per Møller
Language(s): Danish
ADVERTISING RATES:
Full Page Colour .... DKK 17784
SCC .... DKK 77
LOCAL NEWSPAPERS

LUKSUS 1791587D73-209
Editorial: Vesterbrogade 74, 4, 1620 KØBENHAVN N
Tel: 29 71 61 75
Email: info@luksusmag.dk **Web site:** http://www.luksusonline.dk
Freq: 6 issues yearly; **Cover Price:** Free; **Circ:** 20,000
Language(s): Danish
ADVERTISING RATES:
Full Page Colour .... DKK 16300
SCC .... DKK 143
CONSUMER: NATIONAL & INTERNATIONAL PERIODICALS

LUNGEFORENINGEN BOSERUP MINDE 3837D56A-82_50
Editorial: Old Gyde 74, 5620 GLAMSBJERG
Tel: 64 72 13 57 **Fax:** 64 72 13 77
Email: bm-bladet@boserup-minde.dk **Web site:** http://www.boserup-minde.dk
Date Established: 1942; **Freq:** 6 issues yearly; **Circ:** 5,600
Profile: Medical publication focusing on lung diseases.
Language(s): Danish

M! 3733D86C-80
Editorial: Finsensvej 6D, 2000 FREDERIKSBERG
Tel: 39 10 30 06
Email: m@benjamin.dk **Web site:** http://mmm.dk
Date Established: 1997; **Freq:** Monthly; **Circ:** 45,367
Profile: Magazine containing articles and information about lifestyle, travel, motoring, fashion, personal finance and related topics.
Language(s): Danish
Readership: Aimed at men aged between 15-35 years.
ADVERTISING RATES:
Full Page Colour .... DKK 44500
SCC .... DKK 374.60
CONSUMER: ADULT & GAY MAGAZINES: Men's Lifestyle Magazines

MAD! 1810744D53-41
Editorial: Postboks 420, 0900 COPENHAGEN
Tel: 72 34 20 00
Email: iben.rouw@magasinetmad.dk **Web site:** http://www.magasinetmad.dk
Freq: Monthly; **Circ:** 25,000
Executive Editor: Charlotte Riparbelli
Language(s): Danish
ADVERTISING RATES:
Full Page Colour .... DKK 28400
SCC .... DKK 332.20
BUSINESS: RETAILING & WHOLESALING

MAD OG BOLIG 3601D74C-66
Editorial: Havneholmen 33, 1561 COPENHAGEN
Tel: 72 34 20 00
Email: rie.duun@madogbolig.dk **Web site:** http://www.madogbolig.dk
Date Established: 1991; **Freq:** Monthly; **Circ:** 40,179
Executive Editor: Søren Anker Madsen
Profile: Magazine includes articles about wine, cookery, homes, gardens, interior decor, furnishings and travel.
Language(s): Danish
ADVERTISING RATES:
Full Page Colour .... DKK 40100
SCC .... DKK 358
CONSUMER: WOMEN'S INTEREST CONSUMER MAGAZINES: Home & Family

MAD&VENNER 1977723D22A-138
Editorial: Dortheavej 59, 2400 COPENHAGEN
Tel: 32 71 12 00
Email: info@jslpublications.dk **Web site:** http://www.madogvenner.dk
Freq: Monthly; **Circ:** 64,000
Editor: Ole Høy Hansen
Language(s): Danish
BUSINESS: FOOD

MAGASIN K 1882027D2A-105
Editorial: Gl. Strand 46, 1202 KØBENHAVN K
Tel: 33 40 80 00
Email: magasin-k@journalistforbundet.dk **Web site:** http://www.journalistforbundet.dk
Freq: Quarterly; **Circ:** 16,500
Editor: Karin Sloth; **Executive Editor:** Dennis Christiansen
Language(s): Danish
ADVERTISING RATES:
Full Page Colour .... DKK 20100
BUSINESS: COMMUNICATIONS, ADVERTISING & MARKETING

MAGASINET 759407D1P-305
Editorial: Nørregade 13, 1165 KØBENHAVN K
Tel: 33 15 28 00 **Fax:** 33 18 78 16
Email: ph@dca.dk **Web site:** http://www.noedhjaelp.dk
Freq: Monthly; **Circ:** 129,900
Editor: Marianne Lemvig
Language(s): Danish
BUSINESS: FINANCE & ECONOMICS: Fundraising

MAGASINET DIGITALT 1894705D5C-26
Editorial: Christiansborggade 1, 1558 KØBENHAVN V **Tel:** 33 32 90 66
Email: redaktion@magasinetdigitalt.dk **Web site:** http://www.magasinetdigitalt.dk
Freq: Monthly; **Circ:** 5,800
Language(s): Danish
ADVERTISING RATES:
Full Page Colour .... DKK 20495
SCC .... DKK 235,50
BUSINESS: COMPUTERS & AUTOMATION: Professional Personal Computers

MAGASINET HEST 3101D21D-40
Editorial: Vester Farimagsgade 6, 2.sal, 1606 KØBENHAVN V **Tel:** 33 39 47 82 **Fax:** 33 39 47 49
Email: hest@magasinethest.dk **Web site:** http://www.magasinethest.dk
Freq: Monthly; **Circ:** 7,861
Editor: Mette Boas
Profile: Magazine about horse breeding.
Language(s): Danish
ADVERTISING RATES:
Full Page Colour .... DKK 10800
SCC .... DKK 124,13
BUSINESS: AGRICULTURE & FARMING: Livestock

MAGASINET KVALITET 758827D14A-195
Editorial: Jersie Solvænge 16, 2680 SOLRØD STRAND **Tel:** 70 20 32 13 **Fax:** 70 20 32 23
Email: dfk@dfk.dk **Web site:** http://www.dfk.dk
Freq: Quarterly; **Circ:** 1,348
Editor: Ib Orlamundt
Language(s): Danish
ADVERTISING RATES:
Full Page Colour .... DKK 11040
SCC .... DKK 138,86
BUSINESS: COMMERCE, INDUSTRY & MANAGEMENT

MAGASINET MIDT 1934356D67B-8432
Editorial: Region Midtjylland, Tingvej 15, 8800 VIBORG **Tel:** 87 28 58 12
Email: magasinetmidt@rm.dk **Web site:** http://www.rm.dk/om+regionen/aktuelt/magasinet+midt
Freq: Quarterly; **Cover Price:** Free; **Circ:** 40,000
Editor: Anne Domino
Language(s): Danish
ADVERTISING RATES:
Full Page Colour .... DKK 23500
REGIONAL DAILY & SUNDAY NEWSPAPERS: Regional Daily Newspapers

MAGISTERBLADET 3361D62F-100
Editorial: Nimbusparken 16, 2000 FREDERIKSBERG
Tel: 38 15 66 25 **Fax:** 38 15 66 65
Email: magisterbladet@dm.dk **Web site:** http://www.magisterbladet.dk
Date Established: 1918; **Freq:** 26 issues yearly; **Circ:** 28,689
Profile: Journal covering educational issues concerning organisation, administration, current affairs, politics, research and science.
Language(s): Danish
Readership: Read by lecturers and researchers at educational institutions and in the private sector.
ADVERTISING RATES:
Full Page Colour .... DKK 21500
SCC .... DKK 235,63
BUSINESS: CHURCH & SCHOOL EQUIPMENT & EDUCATION: Adult Education

MALEREN 759117D14A-205
Editorial: Lersø Park Allé 109, 2100 KØBENHAVN Ø
Tel: 39 16 79 00 **Fax:** 39 16 79 10
Email: maler@maler.dk **Web site:** http://www.maler.dk/default.asp?id=9
Freq: Monthly; **Circ:** 15,000
Editor: Allan Larsen
Language(s): Danish
BUSINESS: COMMERCE, INDUSTRY & MANAGEMENT

MÅNEDSMAGASINET ERHVERV 3376D63-150
Editorial: Jernbanegade 18, 6700 ESBJERG
Tel: 75 15 52 00 **Fax:** 75 13 82 77
Email: info@maanedsmagasinet.dk **Web site:** http://www.maanedsmagasinet.dk
Freq: Monthly; **Circ:** 95,958
Profile: Magazine providing business news, articles and financial information about the Western parts of Denmark.
Language(s): Danish
ADVERTISING RATES:
Full Page Colour .... DKK 24950
SCC .... DKK 252,29
BUSINESS: REGIONAL BUSINESS

MÅNEDSSKRIFT FOR PRAKTISK LÆGEGERNING 3284D56A-83
Editorial: Stockholmsgade 55, 2100 KØBENHAVN Ø
Tel: 35 26 67 85 **Fax:** 35 26 04 15
Email: mpl@mpl.dk **Web site:** http://www.mpl.dk/composite-244.htm
Date Established: 1922; **Freq:** Monthly; **Circ:** 6,500
Profile: Publication of the Medical Association in Denmark.
Language(s): Danish
ADVERTISING RATES:
Full Page Colour .... DKK 17200
SCC .... DKK 197,70

MARK 3082D21A-75
Editorial: Vester Farimagsgade 6, 2.sal, 1606 KØBENHAVN V **Tel:** 33 39 47 00 **Fax:** 33 39 47 49
Email: post@landbrugsavisen.dk **Web site:** http://www.landbrugsavisen.dk
Freq: Daily; **Cover Price:** Paid; **Circ:** 7,200 Unique Users
Editor: Stig Bundgaard
Profile: Magazine focusing on arable farming.
Language(s): Danish
Readership: Read by farmers.
ADVERTISING RATES:
SCC .... DKK 30,6
BUSINESS: AGRICULTURE & FARMING

MARKEDSFØRING 2933D2A-50
Editorial: Postboks 40, 2000 FREDERIKSBERG
Tel: 38 11 87 87 **Fax:** 38118747
Email: redaktion@markedsforing.dk **Web site:** http://www.markedsforing.dk
Freq: 26 issues yearly - excl. juli; **Circ:** 6,905
Profile: Magazine about marketing and communication.
Language(s): Danish
ADVERTISING RATES:
Full Page Colour .... DKK 28410
SCC .... DKK 128
BUSINESS: COMMUNICATIONS, ADVERTISING & MARKETING

MASKIN AKTUELT 3069D19F-60
Editorial: Naverland 35, 2600 GLOSTRUP
Tel: 43 24 26 28 **Fax:** 43 24 26 26
Email: pf@techmedia.dk **Web site:** http://www.techmedia.dk/default.asp?Action=Details&Item=1491
Freq: 6 issues yearly; **Circ:** 8,200
Profile: Journal concerning the iron, metal and engineering industries, providing news on products and services. Also covers related political and economic information.
Language(s): Danish
Readership: Read by sales and production managers in mechanical- engineering companies.
ADVERTISING RATES:
Full Page Colour .... DKK 21400
SCC .... DKK 246

MASKIN & MATERIAL MAGASINET 3841D19E-75
Editorial: Gustav Wieds Vej 53, 8600 SILKEBORG
Tel: 86 80 44 99 **Fax:** 86 80 44 49
Email: mmm@mail.dk **Web site:** http://www.mmm-online.dk
Freq: Monthly; **Circ:** 13,330
Profile: Magazine focusing on industrial materials, machinery and logistics.
Language(s): Danish
Readership: Read by managers and decision makers.
ADVERTISING RATES:
SCC .... DKK 12.25

MASKINBLADET 3107D21E-25
Editorial: Birk Centerpark 36, 7400 HERNING
Tel: 96 26 52 66 **Fax:** 96 26 52 96
Email: redaktion@maskinbladet.dk **Web site:** http://www.maskinbladet.dk
Date Established: 1980; **Freq:** Monthly; **Circ:** 53,562
Profile: Publication about farming and farm-equipment.
Language(s): Danish; English; German
Readership: Read by Danish farmers.
ADVERTISING RATES:
Full Page Colour .... DKK 34305
SCC .... DKK 158.80
BUSINESS: AGRICULTURE & FARMING: Agriculture - Machinery & Plant

MEDIAWATCH MEDIAWATCH.DK 759072D2B-50
Editorial: St. Regnegade 12, 1.sal, 1100 COPENHAGEN **Tel:** 70 27 90 70 **Fax:** 31 410191
Email: redaktion@mediawatch.dk **Web site:** http://www.mediawatch.dk
Freq: Daily; **Circ:** 1,787 Unique Users
Language(s): Danish
BUSINESS: COMMUNICATIONS, ADVERTISING & MARKETING: Press

MENIGHEDSRÅDENES BLAD 3738D87-70
Editorial: Vesterport 3, 1., 8000 ÅRHUS C
Tel: 87 32 21 33 **Fax:** 86 19 80 40
Email: kontor@menighedsraad.dk **Web site:** http://www.menighedsraad.dk
Freq: Monthly; **Circ:** 25,000
Profile: Magazine providing news and information about church councils.
Language(s): Danish
ADVERTISING RATES:
Full Page Colour .... DKK 8090
SCC .... DKK 104,78
CONSUMER: RELIGIOUS

MERKONOMBLADET 2934D2A-55
Editorial: Ramsingsvej 28 A, stuen, 2500 VALBY
Tel: 31 22 25 77 **Fax:** 31 22 25 32
Email: merkonom@sam.dk **Web site:** http://www.mh.dk
Freq: 6 issues yearly; **Circ:** 18,398
Profile: Magazine covering marketing and advertising.
Language(s): Danish
ADVERTISING RATES:
Full Page Colour .... DKK 12200
SCC .... DKK 147.87
BUSINESS: COMMUNICATIONS, ADVERTISING & MARKETING

MESTER & SVEND 3229D46-10
Editorial: Stationsparken 25, 2600 GLOSTRUP
Tel: 43 43 29 00 **Fax:** 43 43 13 28
Email: redaktion@odsgard.dk **Web site:** http://www.mester-svend.dk
Freq: Quarterly; **Circ:** 26,152
Editor: Michael Rughede; **Executive Editor:** Klaus Tøttrup
Profile: Magazine for the building industry. Contains articles about tools, floors, doors, windows and walls.
Language(s): Danish
Readership: Aimed at joiners, carpenters and craftsmen.
ADVERTISING RATES:
Full Page Colour .... DKK 33200
SCC .... DKK 143,37
BUSINESS: TIMBER, WOOD & FORESTRY

MESTER TIDENDE 3203D42A-25
Editorial: Marielundsvej 46 E, 2730 HERLEV
Tel: 70 11 59 57 **Fax:** 44 85 10 13
Email: mt@mestertidende.dk **Web site:** http://www.mestertidende.dk
Freq: Monthly; **Circ:** 35,578
Profile: Building and construction newspaper.
Language(s): Danish
Readership: Read by engineers, civil engineers, architects and builders.
ADVERTISING RATES:
Full Page Colour .... DKK 44000
SCC .... DKK 227.70
BUSINESS: CONSTRUCTION

METALMAGASINET 3136D27-50
Editorial: Nyropsgade 38, Postboks 308, 1780 KØBENHAVN V **Tel:** 33 63 20 00 **Fax:** 33 63 21 51
Email: metal@danskmetal.dk **Web site:** http://www.danskmetal.dk/Nyheder%20og%20presse/MetalMagasinet.aspx
Freq: 6 issues yearly; **Circ:** 143,678
Profile: Publication about the metal industry.
Language(s): Danish
ADVERTISING RATES:
Full Page Colour .... DKK 20000
SCC .... DKK 168,40
BUSINESS: METAL, IRON & STEEL

MIDTJYLLANDS AVIS SILKEBORG 3427D67B-5600
Editorial: Papirfabrikken 18, 8600 SILKEBORG
Tel: 86 82 13 00 **Fax:** 86 81 35 77
Email: silkeborg@mja.dk **Web site:** http://www.midtjyllandsavis.dk
Freq: Daily; **Circ:** 14,863
Editor: Bent Nørgaard; **Executive Editor:** Steffen Lange
Language(s): Danish
ADVERTISING RATES:
Full Page Colour .... DKK 31172
SCC .... DKK 74,90
REGIONAL DAILY & SUNDAY NEWSPAPERS: Regional Daily Newspapers

MIDTJYSK UGEAVIS 630243D72-1152
Editorial: Jernbanegade 25, 7200 GRINDSTED
Tel: 75 32 05 00 **Fax:** 75 32 31 95
Email: redaktion@midtjyskugeavis.dk **Web site:** http://www.midtjyskugeavis.dk
Freq: Weekly; **Cover Price:** Free; **Circ:** 20,890
Language(s): Danish
ADVERTISING RATES:
Full Page Colour .... DKK 9471
SCC .... DKK 41
LOCAL NEWSPAPERS

MIDTSJÆLLANDS FOLKBLAD 630246D72-1151
Editorial: Kvarmløsevej 36, 4340 TØLLØSE
Tel: 59 18 51 57 **Fax:** 59 18 57 39
Email: folkeblad@midttryk.dk **Web site:** http://www.midttryk.dk
Freq: Weekly; **Cover Price:** Free; **Circ:** 27,500
Language(s): Danish
ADVERTISING RATES:
Full Page Colour .... DKK 10785,60
SCC .... DKK 46,70
LOCAL NEWSPAPERS

MIDT-VEST AVIS 630237D72-1155
Editorial: Langagervej 1, 9220 AALBORG Ø
Tel: 99 35 35 35 **Fax:** 99 35 35 34
Email: nordjyske@nordjyske.dk **Web site:** http://www.nordjyske.dk
Freq: Weekly; **Cover Price:** Free; **Circ:** 42,629
Editor: Ole Skouboe
Language(s): Danish
ADVERTISING RATES:
Full Page Colour .... DKK 15243
SCC .... DKK 66
LOCAL NEWSPAPERS

MILJØAVISEN HVIDOVRE 3842D57-68
Editorial: Hvidovrevej 278, 2650 HVIDOVRE
Tel: 36 39 35 00 **Fax:** 36 39 36 58
Email: teknik@hvidovre.dk **Web site:** http://www.hvidovre.dk
Freq: Quarterly; **Circ:** 800
Language(s): Danish

MILJØDANMARK 630497D57-27
Editorial: Højbro Plads 4, 1200 KØBENHAVN K
Tel: 33 92 76 00 **Fax:** 32 66 04 79
Email: miljoedanmark@mim.dk **Web site:** http://www.mim.dk/udgivelser/miljødanmark
Freq: 6 issues yearly; **Circ:** 16,000
Editor: Carsten Engedal
Profile: Magazine containing information on environmental issues.
Language(s): Danish

MIT HUS 3619D74K-100
Editorial: Kjærstrupvej 36, 2500 VALBY
Tel: 38 74 76 88 **Fax:** 38 74 76 12
Email: sekretariat@parcelhus.dk **Web site:** http://www.parcelhus.dk
Date Established: 1980; **Freq:** Quarterly; **Circ:** 30,000
Executive Editor: Allan Malskaer
Profile: Magazine about home owning associations.
Language(s): Danish
Readership: Read by members.
ADVERTISING RATES:
Full Page Colour .... DKK 14400
SCC .... DKK 177,7
CONSUMER: WOMEN'S INTEREST CONSUMER MAGAZINES: Home Purchase

MOBIL 707817D18B-60
Editorial: Carl Jacobsens vej 16, 2500 VALBY
Tel: 47 10 81 66 **Fax:** 47 10 83 66
Email: danmark@mobil.nu **Web site:** http://www.mobil.nu
Date Established: 2000; **Freq:** Monthly; **Circ:** 15,000
Profile: Magazine covering all aspects of mobile communications.
Language(s): Danish
ADVERTISING RATES:
Full Page Colour .... DKK 27300
SCC .... DKK 231,30
BUSINESS: ELECTRONICS: Telecommunications

MOBILSIDEN.DK 1792285D18B-201
Editorial: Pærehaven 12, 5320 AGEDRUP
Tel: 35 35 09 40
Email: nyheder@mobilsiden.dk **Web site:** http://www.mobilsiden.dk
Cover Price: Paid; **Circ:** 27,500 Unique Users
Language(s): Danish
ADVERTISING RATES:
SCC .... DKK 180
BUSINESS: ELECTRONICS: Telecommunications

MOMENT 1792294D73-305
Editorial: Gothersgade 11, 1123 KØBENHAVN K
Tel: 70 20 18 35 **Fax:** 33 11 10 88
Email: redaktion@moment.dk **Web site:** http://www.moment.dk/om/default.asp?id=16
Freq: Quarterly; **Cover Price:** Free; **Circ:** 39,880
Editor: Thomas Elmegård
Language(s): Danish
ADVERTISING RATES:
Full Page Colour .... DKK 21500
SCC .... DKK 247,12
CONSUMER: NATIONAL & INTERNATIONAL PERIODICALS

MONITOR 1810014D14A-261
Editorial: Sdr. Strandvej 18, 3000 HELSINGØR
Tel: 70 20 98 38
Email: henrik@monitordk.dk **Web site:** http://www.monitordk.dk
Freq: Monthly; **Circ:** 7,500
Language(s): Danish
ADVERTISING RATES:
Full Page Colour .... DKK 22775
SCC .... DKK 261,78
BUSINESS: COMMERCE, INDUSTRY & MANAGEMENT

MORSØ FOLKEBLAD 3421D67B-5800
Editorial: Elsøvej 105, 7900 NYKØBING MORS
Tel: 97 72 10 00 **Fax:** 97 72 10 10
Email: redaktion@mf.dk **Web site:** http://www.mf.dk
Freq: Daily; **Circ:** 5,547
Editor: Anders Holmgaard
Language(s): Danish
ADVERTISING RATES:
Full Page Colour .... DKK 9600
SCC .... DKK 43,80
REGIONAL DAILY & SUNDAY NEWSPAPERS: Regional Daily Newspapers

MORSØ FOLKEBLADS UGEAVIS 630277D72-460
Editorial: Elsøvej 105, 7900 NYKØBING M
Tel: 97 72 10 00 **Fax:** 97 72 10 10
Email: ugeavis@mf.dk **Web site:** http://www.mf.dk
Freq: Weekly; **Cover Price:** Free; **Circ:** 18,690
Language(s): Danish
ADVERTISING RATES:
Full Page Colour .... DKK 10866
SCC .... DKK 47
LOCAL NEWSPAPERS

MOTOR 3666D77A-50
Editorial: Firskovvej 32, 2800 KGS. LYNGBY
Tel: 45 27 07 07 **Fax:** 45270989
Email: motor@fdm.dk **Web site:** http://www.fdm.dk
Date Established: 1906; **Freq:** Monthly; **Circ:** 240,450
Editor: Leif Nielsen
Profile: Motoring magazine containing tests and reviews of new models available on the market.
Language(s): Danish
Readership: Membership magazine of FDM, the Federation of Danish Motorists.
ADVERTISING RATES:
Full Page Colour .... DKK 46200
SCC .... DKK 530
CONSUMER: MOTORING & CYCLING: Motoring

MUSIKKALENDEREN 3909D76D-200
Editorial: Wilders Plads 15C, 1403 KØBENHAVN K
Tel: 32 96 06 12 **Fax:** 32 96 06 21
Email: mbr@mbr.dk **Web site:** http://www.mbr.dk
Freq: Monthly; **Circ:** 49,167
Editor: Steffen Lund
Profile: Magazine providing information and dates for live concerts in Copenhagen and the surrounding area.
Language(s): Danish
CONSUMER: MUSIC & PERFORMING ARTS: Music

NÆSTVED-BLADET 630296D72-470
Editorial: Ringstedgade 11, 4700 NÆSTVED
Tel: 55 73 50 00 **Fax:** 55 73 55 79
Email: redaktion@naestved-bladet.dk **Web site:** http://www.naestved-bladet.dk
Freq: Weekly; **Cover Price:** Free; **Circ:** 42,107
Editor: Tove Gurresø
Language(s): Danish
ADVERTISING RATES:
Full Page Colour .... DKK 13609
SCC .... DKK 59
LOCAL NEWSPAPERS

NATIONAL GEOGRAPHIC DENMARK 719329D73-150
Editorial: Strandboulevarden 130, 2100 KØBENHAVN Ø **Tel:** 39 17 20 00 **Fax:** 39 17 23 01
Email: national.geographic@bp.bonnier.dk **Web site:** http://www.bonnier.dk
Date Established: 2001; **Freq:** Monthly; **Circ:** 17,714
Executive Editor: Birgitte Engen
Profile: Magazine providing geographic information articles concerning natural history and society. Also includes news of general interest from around the world.
Language(s): Danish
Readership: Read mainly by people aged 25 to 35 years.
ADVERTISING RATES:
Full Page Colour .... DKK 34300
SCC .... DKK 394

NATUR OG MILJØ 759447D57-90
Editorial: Masnedøgade 20, 2100 KØBENHAVN Ø
Tel: 39 17 40 00 **Fax:** 39 17 41 41
Email: dn@dn.dk **Web site:** http://www.dn.dk
Freq: Quarterly; **Circ:** 155,000
Editor: Kristian Ørsted Pedersen
Language(s): Danish
ADVERTISING RATES:
Full Page Colour .... DKK 17380
SCC .... DKK 199,77
BUSINESS: ENVIRONMENT & POLLUTION

NEWZ NEWZ.DK 1834025D5C-18
Editorial: Jernbanegade 27, 6000 KOLDING
Tel: 70 23 70 03
Email: presse@newz.dk **Web site:** http://www.newz.dk
Freq: Daily; **Cover Price:** Paid; **Circ:** 12,331 Unique Users
Editor: Peter Rechnagel
Language(s): Danish
ADVERTISING RATES:
SCC .... DKK 39,08
BUSINESS: COMPUTERS & AUTOMATION: Professional Personal Computers

NNF-ARBEJDEREN 3117D22C-50
Editorial: C.F. Richs vej 103, DK-2000 FREDERIKSBERG **Tel:** 38 18 72 72 **Fax:** 38 18 72 30
Email: redaktionen@nnf.dk **Web site:** http://www.nnf.dk
Freq: Daily; **Circ:** 52,000
Profile: Publication for workers in the food-processing industry.
Language(s): Danish
BUSINESS: FOOD: Food Processing & Packaging

NORDEN NU 3377D63-160
Editorial: Malmøgade 3, 2100 KØBENHAVN Ø
Tel: 35 42 63 25 **Fax:** 35 42 80 88
Email: redaktion@foreningen-norden.dk **Web site:** http://www.foreningen-norden.dk
Freq: Quarterly; **Circ:** 11,000
Executive Editor: Preben Sørensen
Profile: Publication of the Nordic Association in Denmark, the Nordic Council and the Nordic Council of Ministers. Contains information concerning business, culture, current-affairs and politics in the Nordic countries.
Language(s): Danish
BUSINESS: REGIONAL BUSINESS

NORDJYSKE STIFTSTIDENDE 3403D67B-6200
Editorial: Langagervej 1, 9220 AALBORG ØST
Tel: 99 35 35 35 **Fax:** 99 35 33 75
Email: nordjyske@nordjyske.dk **Web site:** http://www.nordjyske.dk
Freq: Daily; **Circ:** 62,075
Editor: Jørgen la Cour-Harbo; **Executive Editor:** Lars Jespersen
Language(s): Danish
ADVERTISING RATES:
Full Page Colour .... DKK 75936
SCC .... DKK 169,50
REGIONAL DAILY & SUNDAY NEWSPAPERS: Regional Daily Newspapers

NORDJYSKE STIFTSTIDENDE AALBORG 630275D67B-6220
Editorial: Langagervej 1, 9220 AALBORG
Tel: 99 35 35 35 **Fax:** 99 31 95 55
Email: aalborg@nordjyske.dk **Web site:** http://www.nordjyske.dk
Freq: Daily; **Circ:** 26,504
Editor: Ole Skouboe
Language(s): Danish
ADVERTISING RATES:
Full Page Colour .... DKK 31592
SCC .... DKK 314
REGIONAL DAILY & SUNDAY NEWSPAPERS: Regional Daily Newspapers

NORDJYSKE STIFTSTIDENDE FREDERIKSHAVN 630295D72-475
Editorial: Tordenskjoldsgade 2, 9900 FREDRIKSHAVN **Tel:** 99 20 33 33 **Fax:** 99 20 33 03
Email: frederikshavn@nordjyske.dk **Web site:** http://www.nordjyske.dk
Freq: Daily; **Circ:** 6,939
Editor: Carl C. Madsen
Language(s): Danish
ADVERTISING RATES:
Full Page Colour .... DKK 13046
SCC .... DKK 56,47
LOCAL NEWSPAPERS

NORDJYSKE STIFTSTIDENDE HIMMERLAND 630298D67B-6230
Editorial: Adelgade 56, 9500 HOBRO
Tel: 98 52 70 00 **Fax:** 98 52 70 15
Email: hobro@nordjyske.dk **Web site:** http://www.nordjyske.dk
Freq: Daily; **Circ:** 9,482
Language(s): Danish
ADVERTISING RATES:
Full Page Colour .... DKK 13046
SCC .... DKK 56,47
REGIONAL DAILY & SUNDAY NEWSPAPERS: Regional Daily Newspapers

NORDJYSKE STIFTSTIDENDE HJØRRING 630304D67B-6240
Editorial: Frederikshavnsvej 81, 9800 HJØRRING
Tel: 99 24 50 60 **Fax:** 99 24 51 05
Email: hjoerring@nordjyske.dk **Web site:** http://www.nordjyske.dk
Freq: Daily; **Circ:** 6,393
Language(s): Danish
ADVERTISING RATES:
Full Page Colour .... DKK 13046
SCC .... DKK 56,47
REGIONAL DAILY & SUNDAY NEWSPAPERS: Regional Daily Newspapers

NORDSCHLESWIGER 3402D67B-6400
Editorial: Skibbroen 4, 6200 AABENRAA
Tel: 74 62 38 80 **Fax:** 74 62 94 30
Email: redaktion@nordschleswiger.dk **Web site:** http://www.nordschleswiger.dk
Freq: Daily; **Circ:** 2,399
Executive Editor: Siegfried Matlok
Language(s): Danish
REGIONAL DAILY & SUNDAY NEWSPAPERS: Regional Daily Newspapers

NØRRESUNDBY AVIS 630314D72-484
Editorial: Langagervej 1, 9220 AALBORG Ø
Tel: 99 35 33 80 **Fax:** 99 35 35 34
Email: susanne.justsen@nordjyske.dk **Web site:** http://www.nordjyskeugeaviser.dk
Freq: Weekly; **Cover Price:** Free; **Circ:** 30,775
Language(s): Danish
ADVERTISING RATES:
Full Page Colour .... DKK 12055,50
SCC .... DKK 52,10
LOCAL NEWSPAPERS

NPINVESTOR NPINVESTOR.DK 1792284D14A-257
Editorial: Kigkurren 8 D, 3t.h., 2300 COPENHAGEN
Tel: 83 30 00 00
Email: redaktion@netposten.dk **Web site:** http://www.netposten.dk
Freq: Daily; **Circ:** 4,289 Unique Users
Editor: Lars Persson
Language(s): Danish
BUSINESS: COMMERCE, INDUSTRY & MANAGEMENT

NYT 759457D56A-265
Editorial: Generatorvej 2A, 2730 HERLEV
Tel: 44 85 60 30 **Fax:** 44 85 60 99
Email: dbcent@dbcent.dk **Web site:** http://www.dbcent.dk
Freq: Quarterly; **Cover Price:** Free; **Circ:** 1,800
Editor: Bettina Ugelvig Møller
Profile: Magazine with news from the Centre for deaf and blind.
Language(s): Danish

ODSHERREDS KYSTEN 630204D72-490
Editorial: Grønnehavestræde 1, 4500 NYKØBING S
Tel: 88 88 45 10 **Fax:** 59 91 22 32
Email: red.ok@nordvest.dk **Web site:** http://www.odsherreds-kysten.dk
Freq: Weekly; **Cover Price:** Free; **Circ:** 24,696
Language(s): Danish
ADVERTISING RATES:
Full Page Colour .... DKK 10465
SCC .... DKK 45,30
LOCAL NEWSPAPERS

ONSDAGSAVISEN HORSENS 630217D72-493
Editorial: Nørregade 22, 8700 HORSENS
Tel: 75 61 28 77 **Fax:** 75 61 20 30
Email: info@onsdags-avisen.dk **Web site:** http://www.onsdags-avisen.dk
Freq: Weekly; **Cover Price:** Free; **Circ:** 43,000
Language(s): Danish
ADVERTISING RATES:
Full Page Colour .... DKK 16450
SCC .... DKK 11,75
LOCAL NEWSPAPERS

OPLANDSAVISEN 630222D72-500
Editorial: Gravensgade 42, 9700 BRØNDERSLEV
Tel: 96 45 55 65 **Fax:** 96 45 55 60
Email: oplandsavisen@nordjyske.dk **Web site:** http://www.nordjyskeugeaviser.dk/Default.aspx?tabid=74
Freq: Weekly; **Cover Price:** Free; **Circ:** 30,616
Language(s): Danish
ADVERTISING RATES:
Full Page Colour .... DKK 11709
SCC .... DKK 50,68
LOCAL NEWSPAPERS

ØSTERBRO AVIS 630190D72-503
Editorial: Aldersrogade 6A, 2100 KØBENHAVN Ø
Tel: 35 42 25 15 **Fax:** 35 42 81 51
Email: red.oa@b-l.dk **Web site:** http://www.oesterbroavis.dk
Freq: Weekly; **Cover Price:** Free; **Circ:** 50,531
Language(s): Danish
ADVERTISING RATES:
Full Page Colour .... DKK 21480
SCC .... DKK 92.98
LOCAL NEWSPAPERS

PACKMARKEDET 3179D35-50
Editorial: Nørregade 36 B, 3 Sal, 1165 KØBENHAVN K **Tel:** 70 25 35 00 **Fax:** 70 25 35 95
Email: info@packm.dk **Web site:** http://packmarkedet.dk
Freq: Monthly; **Circ:** 4,085
Profile: Magazine covering all aspects of the packaging industry.
Language(s): Danish
ADVERTISING RATES:
Full Page Colour .... DKK 22900
SCC .... DKK 197,41

PC PLANET 624209D5D-480
Editorial: Hellerupvej 51, 2900 HELLERUP
Tel: 39 45 75 00 **Fax:** 39 45 77 37
Email: pc-planet@pc-planet.dk **Web site:** http://www.pc-planet.dk
Freq: Monthly; **Circ:** 8,097
Editor: Thomas Berger; **Executive Editor:** Jørn Thinggaard Laursen
Profile: Magazine containing information about PCs.
Language(s): Danish
Readership: Read by users and potential purchasers.
ADVERTISING RATES:
Full Page Colour .... DKK 13500
SCC .... DKK 114
BUSINESS: COMPUTERS & AUTOMATION: Personal Computers

PC PLAYER 4029D5D-500
Editorial: Stefansgade 7, Baghuset, st., 2200 KØBENHAVN N **Tel:** 33 91 30 32 **Fax:** 33 91 30 36
Email: morten.skovgaard@pcplayer.dk **Web site:** http://www.pcplayer.dk
Freq: Monthly; **Circ:** 10,000
Editor: Kim Dorff Hansen; **Executive Editor:** Morten Skovgaard
Profile: Magazine focusing on all aspects of PCs.
Language(s): Danish
Readership: Aimed at PC users of all ages.
BUSINESS: COMPUTERS & AUTOMATION: Personal Computers

PCWORLD.DK 2988D5D-550
Editorial: Carl Jacobsens Vej 25, 2500 VALBY
Tel: 77 30 03 00 **Fax:** 77300304
Email: presse@pcworld.dk **Web site:** http://www.pcworld.dk
Date Established: 1984; **Freq:** Daily; **Circ:** 18,232 Unique Users
Profile: Magazine containing tests on both software and hardware, previews, features and news.
Language(s): Danish
BUSINESS: COMPUTERS & AUTOMATION: Personal Computers

PENGE & PRIVATØKONOMI 3624D74M-40
Editorial: Strandboulevarden 130, 2100 COPENHAGEN **Tel:** 39 10 30 73
Email: info@penge.dk **Web site:** http://www.penge.dk/cm/1.811
Freq: Monthly; **Circ:** 33,696
Executive Editor: Søren Verup
Profile: Magazine providing advice and information about money and private investment.
Language(s): Danish

Readership: Aimed at anyone interested in personal finance.
ADVERTISING RATES:
Full Page Colour .... DKK 42400
SCC .... DKK 343.40
Copy instructions: *Copy Date:* 30 days prior to publication date
CONSUMER: WOMEN'S INTEREST CONSUMER MAGAZINES: Personal Finance

PLAST PANORAMA 3185D39-10
Editorial: Naverland 35, 2600 GLOSTRUP
Tel: 43 24 26 01 **Fax:** 43 24 26 26
Email: jc@techmedia.dk **Web site:** http://www.techmedia.dk/plast
Freq: Monthly; **Circ:** 3,289
Profile: Magazine containing news of materials, machinery, products and processes in the plastics and rubber industry.
Language(s): Danish
ADVERTISING RATES:
Full Page Colour .... DKK 22700

PLAYRIGHT PLAYRIGHT.DK 3677D78D-100
Editorial: Vognmagergade 9, 1148 KØBENHAVN K
Tel: 33 30 50 00 **Fax:** 33 30 55 50
Email: psm@tsf.egmont.com **Web site:** http://www.playright.dk
Date Established: 1999; **Freq:** Daily; **Cover Price:** Paid; **Circ:** 20,000 Unique Users
Editor: Rune J. Keller; **Executive Editor:** Svend Skytte
Profile: Magazine containing information, articles and news about Playstation games and computer software.
Language(s): Danish
Readership: Aimed at home PC users.
CONSUMER: CONSUMER ELECTRONICS: Games

POLITIKEN 3393D65A-60
Editorial: Rådhuspladsen 37, 1785 COPENHAGEN
Tel: 33 11 85 11 **Fax:** 33154117
Email: presse@pol.dk **Web site:** http://www.politiken.dk
Freq: Daily - Denmark; **Circ:** 118,718
Editor: Thomas Borberg; **Executive Editor:** Tøger Seidenfaden
Profile: Broadsheet-sized newspaper providing in-depth coverage of national and international news, politics, sports and features.
Language(s): Danish
Readership: Read by academics, politicians, managers and office workers.
ADVERTISING RATES:
Full Page Colour .... DKK 113006
SCC .... DKK 310.40
NATIONAL DAILY & SUNDAY NEWSPAPERS: National Daily Newspapers

POLITISK HORISONT 759466D82-275
Editorial: Nyhavn 4, 1051 KØBENHAVN K
Tel: 33 13 41 40 **Fax:** 33 93 37 73
Email: horisont@konservative.dk **Web site:** http://www.konservative.dk
Freq: Quarterly; **Circ:** 27,000
Editor: Rikke Egelund
Language(s): Danish
CONSUMER: CURRENT AFFAIRS & POLITICS

PRACTICUS 3846D56A-130
Editorial: Øster Farimagsgade 5, Postboks 2099, 1014 KØBENHAVN K **Tel:** 35 32 65 90
Fax: 35 32 65 91
Email: practicus@dsam.dk **Web site:** http://www.epracticus.dk
Freq: 6 issues yearly; **Circ:** 3,700
Editor: Karen Kjær Larsen; **Executive Editor:** Claus Rendtorff
Profile: Magazine about general medicine.
Language(s): Danish
Readership: Members of DSAM.

PROSABLADET 2987D5B-70
Editorial: Ahlefeldtsgade 16, 1359 KØBENHAVN K
Tel: 33 36 41 41 **Fax:** 33 91 90 44
Email: prosabladet@prosa.dk **Web site:** http://www.prosa.dk/aktuelt/prosabladet/alle-numre
Freq: Monthly; **Circ:** 11,984
Profile: Magazine focusing on electronic data processing.
Language(s): Danish
ADVERTISING RATES:
Full Page Colour .... DKK 19500
BUSINESS: COMPUTERS & AUTOMATION: Data Processing

PROSIT 1810017D14A-262
Editorial: Overgade 54, 5000 ODENSE
Tel: 66 17 72 11
Email: prosit@prosa.dk **Web site:** http://www.prosa.dk/aktuelt/prosit
Freq: 6 issues yearly; **Circ:** 5,500
Language(s): Danish
BUSINESS: COMMERCE, INDUSTRY & MANAGEMENT

PSYKOLOGI 1792487D73-352
Editorial: Havneholmen 33, 1561 COPENHAGEN
Tel: 72 34 20 00
Email: psykologi@aller.dk **Web site:** http://www.psykologimagasinet.dk
Freq: 6 issues yearly; **Circ:** 18,090
Editor: Charlotte Heje Haase
Language(s): Danish
CONSUMER: NATIONAL & INTERNATIONAL PERIODICALS

PUFF 3231D46-30
Editorial: Stationsparken 25, 2600 GLOSTRUP
Tel: 43 43 29 00 **Fax:** 43 43 13 28
Email: puff@odsgard.dk **Web site:** http://www.odsgard.dk
Freq: Monthly; **Circ:** 2,003
Profile: Journal containing articles and personnel news concerning the timber and building markets.
Language(s): Danish
ADVERTISING RATES:
Full Page Colour .... DKK 14560
SCC .... DKK 185,20

RADIOTELEGRAFEN 3058D18B-90
Editorial: Havnegade 55, 1058 KØBENHAVN K
Tel: 33 14 19 17
Email: raf1917@cs.dk **Web site:** http://www.raf1917.dk
Freq: 6 issues yearly; **Circ:** 1,200
Executive Editor: Jan Preisler
Profile: Publication of the Danish Radio Officers' Union.
Language(s): Danish
BUSINESS: ELECTRONICS: Telecommunications

RANDERS AMTSAVIS 630366D67B-6600
Editorial: Nørregade 7, 8900 RANDERS
Tel: 87 12 20 00 **Fax:** 87 12 20 10
Email: redaktion@amtsavisen.dk **Web site:** http://www.amtsavisen.dk
Freq: Daily; **Circ:** 10,922
Executive Editor: Turid Fennefoss Nielsen
Language(s): Danish
ADVERTISING RATES:
Full Page Colour .... DKK 14692,50
SCC .... DKK 57,50
REGIONAL DAILY & SUNDAY NEWSPAPERS: Regional Daily Newspapers

RENS & VASK 3139D28-50
Editorial: Naverland 35, 2600 GLOSTRUP
Tel: 43 24 26 28 **Fax:** 43 24 26 26
Email: benno@techmedia.dk **Web site:** http://www.techmedia.dk/default.asp?Action=Details&Item=1476
Freq: Monthly; **Circ:** 3,340
Profile: Magazine for laundries and dry cleaners in Denmark.
Language(s): Danish
Readership: Magazine aimed for laundries and dry cleaners in Denmark.
ADVERTISING RATES:
Full Page Colour .... DKK 18400
SCC .... DKK 211,49

RESERVEN 3192D40-120
Editorial: Rigensgade 9, 1316 KØBENHAVN K
Tel: 33 14 16 01
Email: mail@hprd.dk **Web site:** http://www.roid.dk
Date Established: 1948; **Freq:** Quarterly; **Circ:** 3,000
Editor: Bengt Laier
Profile: Publication of the Reserve Officers' Association.
Language(s): Danish; English; German
ADVERTISING RATES:
Full Page Colour .... DKK 9000

REVISION & REGNSKABSVÆSEN 2915D1B-10
Editorial: Nytorv 5, 1450 COPENHAGEN
Tel: 33 74 07 00 **Fax:** 33 12 16 36
Email: flemming.bach@thomson.com **Web site:** http://www.thomson.dk
Date Established: 1931; **Freq:** Monthly; **Circ:** 4,950
Profile: Magazine focusing on all areas of accountancy, tax and business law.
Language(s): Danish
Readership: Aimed at accountants, civil servants and decision makers within the business world.
ADVERTISING RATES:
Full Page Colour .... DKK 22600
SCC .... DKK 218.80
BUSINESS: FINANCE & ECONOMICS: Accountancy

REVISORBLADET 2916D1B-20
Editorial: Åmarksvej 1, 2650 HVIDOVRE
Tel: 36 34 44 22 **Fax:** 36 344444
Email: fsr@fsr.dk **Web site:** http://www.drefo.dk
Freq: Quarterly; **Circ:** 2,600
Editor: Jan Wie
Profile: Journal about general accountancy.
Language(s): Danish
ADVERTISING RATES:
Full Page Colour .... DKK 13900
SCC .... DKK 170
BUSINESS: FINANCE & ECONOMICS: Accountancy

ROAD LIFE MAGAZINE 4034D77A-75
Editorial: Klostermosevej 140, 3000 HELSINGØR
Tel: 49 22 37 00 **Fax:** 49 22 37 46
Email: fw@williams.dk **Web site:** http://www.roadlife.dk
Freq: 6 issues yearly; **Circ:** 14,200
Editor: Finn Williams
Profile: Magazine for truck drivers containing articles about heavy goods vehicles, technical information and life on the road.
Language(s): Danish
ADVERTISING RATES:
Full Page Colour .... DKK 10800
SCC .... DKK 124,13

RUCNYT 1810209D14A-263
Editorial: Postboks 260, 4000 ROSKILDE
Tel: 46 74 20 13
Email: rucnyt@ruc.dk **Web site:** http://www.ruc.dk/om-universitetet/nyhedsportal/rucnyt
Freq: Monthly; **Circ:** 2,300
Language(s): Danish
ADVERTISING RATES:
Full Page Colour .... DKK 3075
BUSINESS: COMMERCE, INDUSTRY & MANAGEMENT

RYTTERKNÆGTEN 630303D72-548
Editorial: Nørregade 11-19, 3700 RØNNE
Tel: 56 90 30 00 **Fax:** 56 90 30 91
Email: redaktion@bornholmstidende.dk **Web site:** http://www.bornholmstidende.dk
Freq: Weekly; **Cover Price:** Free; **Circ:** 22,912
Editor: Dan Qvitzau; **Executive Editor:** Dan Qvitzau
Language(s): Danish
ADVERTISING RATES:
Full Page Colour .... DKK 12685
SCC .... DKK 54,91
LOCAL NEWSPAPERS

SAMFUNDSØKONOMEN 2912D1A-100
Editorial: Gothersgade 133, P.O. Box 2126, 1015 KØBENAVHN K **Tel:** 33 95 97 00 **Fax:** 33 95 99 99
Email: djoef@djoef.dk **Web site:** http://www.djoef.dk/Udgivelser/Samfundsoekonomen.aspx
Freq: 6 issues yearly; **Circ:** 1,000
Editor: Niels Ploug
Profile: Official magazine of the Association of Danish Lawyers and Economists. Provides financial and economic news and information.
Language(s): Danish
BUSINESS: FINANCE & ECONOMICS

SAMVIRKE 3602D74C-70
Editorial: Ragnesminde, Vallensbæk Torvevej 9, 2620 ALBERTSLUND **Tel:** 39 47 00 31
Fax: 39 47 00 01
Email: samvirke@fdb.dk **Web site:** http://www.fdb.dk/samvirke
Freq: Monthly; **Circ:** 380,000
Editor: Lotte Malmgren; **Executive Editor:** Flemming Jørgensen
Profile: Magazine published by the FDB, United Danish Co-operative Stores. Contains articles on all aspects of family life, cultural news and information concerning the environment, food, health and lifestyle. Also covers recruitment.
Language(s): Danish
Readership: Aimed at people of all ages.
ADVERTISING RATES:
Full Page Colour .... DKK 90000
SCC .... DKK 1034,4
CONSUMER: WOMEN'S INTEREST CONSUMER MAGAZINES: Home & Family

SCANDINAVIAN FOOD & DRINK 4077D22A-113
Editorial: Naverland 35, 2600 GLOSTRUP
Tel: 43 24 26 28 **Fax:** 43 24 26 26
Email: kh@techmedia.dk **Web site:** http://www.techmedia.dk/default.asp?Action=Details&Item=1481
Freq: Monthly; **Circ:** 7,538
Profile: Magazine focusing on food processing. Includes articles on raw materials, ingredients, machinery and laboratory equipment.
Language(s): Danish; English
ADVERTISING RATES:
Full Page Colour .... DKK 25000
SCC .... DKK 287.35
Copy instructions: *Copy Date:* 45 days prior to publication date
BUSINESS: FOOD

SCANDINAVIAN PROPERTY MAGAZINE 1937357D1E-103
Editorial: Ndr. Strandvej 119C, 3150 HELLERUP
Tel: 42 76 00 20
Email: sevel@magasinetejendom.dk **Web site:** http://www.scandinavianpropertymagazine.com
Freq: Annual; **Cover Price:** Free; **Circ:** 2,500
Language(s): Danish
ADVERTISING RATES:
Full Page Colour .... DKK 14000
Copy instructions: *Copy Date:* 15 days prior to publication date
BUSINESS: FINANCE & ECONOMICS: Property

SCENARIO 3020D14A-64_50
Editorial: Nørre Farimagsgade 65, 1364 COPENHAGEN **Tel:** 33 11 71 76
Email: cha@iff.dk **Web site:** http://www.cifs.dk/dk/tidsskrift.asp
Freq: 6 issues yearly - 6 gange om året; **Circ:** 3,000
Editor: Christine Højlund Andersen; **Executive Editor:** Morten Grønborg
Profile: Publication for management and decision makers in the public and private sector about prevailing and future work practices.
Language(s): Danish
BUSINESS: COMMERCE, INDUSTRY & MANAGEMENT

SCM 759465D14A-220
Editorial: Center Boulevard 5, 2300 KØBENHAVN S
Tel: 32 47 32 30 **Fax:** 32 47 32 39
Email: info@horisontgruppen.dk **Web site:** http://www.scm.dk
Date Established: 1962; **Freq:** Monthly; **Circ:** 12,000
Editor: Ulla Bechsgaard
Profile: Trade magazine covering modern industrial production, workshop techniques and new materials.
Language(s): Danish
Readership: Decision makers, production managers, engineers, technical schools.
ADVERTISING RATES:
Full Page Colour .... DKK 24300
SCC .... DKK 279
BUSINESS: COMMERCE, INDUSTRY & MANAGEMENT

SE OG HØR 3651D76C-180
Editorial: Vigerslev Allé 18, 2500 VALBY
Tel: 36 15 20 00 **Fax:** 36152499
Email: redaktionen@seoghoer.dk **Web site:** http://www.seoghoer.dk
Freq: Weekly; **Circ:** 195,881
Profile: General and family interest magazine, including listings of radio and television programmes.
Language(s): Danish
ADVERTISING RATES:
Full Page Colour .... DKK 75800
SCC .... DKK 676.90
CONSUMER: MUSIC & PERFORMING ARTS: TV & Radio

SERVICE 3173D32K-103
Editorial: Upsalagade 20, 2100 KØBENHAVN Ø
Tel: 70 15 04 00 **Fax:** 70 15 04 05
Email: ltf@dff-s.dk **Web site:** http://www.dff-s.dk
Freq: Monthly; **Circ:** 25,323
Profile: Publication for civil servants.
Language(s): Danish
ADVERTISING RATES:
Full Page Colour .... DKK 10000
SCC .... DKK 115
BUSINESS: LOCAL GOVERNMENT, LEISURE & RECREATION: Civil Service

SIRENE 707794D74A-100
Editorial: Hellerupvej 51, 2900 HELLERUP
Tel: 39 45 75 00 **Fax:** 33305760
Email: sirene@sirene.dk **Web site:** http://www.sirene.dk
Date Established: 2001; **Freq:** Monthly; **Circ:** 24,103
Profile: Magazine covering all subjects of interest and lifestyle, fashion trends and entertainment.
Language(s): Danish
Readership: Read by teenage girls.
ADVERTISING RATES:
Full Page Colour .... DKK 32500
SCC .... DKK 296.80
CONSUMER: WOMEN'S INTEREST CONSUMER MAGAZINES: Women's Interest

SKATTEREVISOREN 3854D1M-90
Editorial: Alperosevej 11, 4600 KØGE
Tel: 21 75 22 92
Email: skatterevisoren@hotmail.com **Web site:** http://www.srf.dk
Freq: 6 issues yearly; **Circ:** 2,300
Profile: Magazine about taxation and finance.
Language(s): Danish
ADVERTISING RATES:
Full Page Colour .... DKK 12000
SCC .... DKK 138
BUSINESS: FINANCE & ECONOMICS: Taxation

SKIPPEREN 1792291D73-303
Editorial: Rederiforeningen for Mindre Skibe, Amaliegade 33, 1256 KØBENHAVN K
Tel: 33 11 40 88 **Fax:** 33 11 62 10
Email: minship@danmarksrederiforening.dk **Web site:** http://www.danmarksrederiforening.dk
Freq: Monthly; **Circ:** 400
Editor: Michael Wengel-Nielsen
Language(s): Danish
CONSUMER: NATIONAL & INTERNATIONAL PERIODICALS

SKIVE FOLKEBLAD 3429D67B-7400
Editorial: Gemsevej 7-9, 7800 SKIVE
Tel: 97 51 34 11 **Fax:** 97 51 28 35
Email: redaktion@skivefolkeblad.dk **Web site:** http://www.skivefolkeblad.dk
Freq: Daily; **Cover Price:** Free; **Circ:** 11,840
Editor: Merete Just
Language(s): Danish
ADVERTISING RATES:
Full Page Colour .... DKK 19366
SCC .... DKK 54,50
REGIONAL DAILY & SUNDAY NEWSPAPERS: Regional Daily Newspapers

SKO, SHOES & MORE 3140D29-10
Editorial: Langebrogade 5, 1411 COPENHAGEN
Tel: 33 91 46 07
Email: bm@skohandlerforening.dk **Web site:** http://www.skohandlerforening.dk
Freq: 6 issues yearly - 9 gange årligt - hvoraf 4 udstillingsnumre i forbindelse med skomesser; **Circ:** 1,200
Editor: Marianne Müller
Profile: Journal about shoes and leather accessories.
Language(s): Danish
ADVERTISING RATES:
Full Page Colour .... DKK 9200
SCC .... DKK 105.75

SKOLEBØRN 3349D62A-180
Editorial: Gammel Kongevej 140 A, 1850 FREDERIKSBERG C **Tel:** 33 26 17 21
Fax: 33 26 17 22
Email: redaktionen@skole-samfund.dk **Web site:** http://www.skole-samfund.dk/sw48882.asp
Date Established: 1935; **Freq:** Monthly; **Circ:** 14,100
Editor: Claus Engelund
Profile: Magazine providing a forum for discussion regarding the improvement of education for children aged between 6 and 17 years.
Language(s): Danish
Readership: Read by teachers, school administrators, politicians and parents.
ADVERTISING RATES:
Full Page Colour .... DKK 8000
SCC .... DKK 130
BUSINESS: CHURCH & SCHOOL EQUIPMENT & EDUCATION: Education

SKOV & LAND 3085D46-38
Editorial: Emdrupvej 28A, 2100 KØBENHAVN Ø
Tel: 33 23 00 45 **Fax:** 38 71 03 23
Email: dsl@skovogland.dk **Web site:** http://www.skovogland.dk
Freq: Monthly; **Circ:** 1,185
Executive Editor: Marianne Tinggaard
Profile: Magazine containing articles and information about forestry and nature management. Covers issues of interest to members of the Association of Danish Foresters and Surveyors.
Language(s): Danish
Readership: Aimed at foresters, surveyors, administrators and gardeners.
ADVERTISING RATES:
Full Page Colour .... DKK 8170
SCC .... DKK 163,40

SKOVEN 3230D46-15
Editorial: Amalievej 20, 1875 FREDERIKSBERG C
Tel: 33 78 52 15 **Fax:** 33 24 02 42
Email: sf@skovforeningen.dk **Web site:** http://www.skovforeningen.dk
Date Established: 1916; **Freq:** Monthly; **Circ:** 4,400
Profile: Journal providing longer articles and information about all aspects of forestry.
Readership: Read by forestry professionals and researchers.
ADVERTISING RATES:
Full Page Colour .... DKK 9300
SCC .... DKK 117

SKYTTEBLADET 3635D75F-100
Editorial: Idrættens Hus, Brøndby Stadion 20, 2605 BRØNDBY **Tel:** 43 26 26 26 **Fax:** 43 26 23 55
Email: info@skytteunion.dk **Web site:** http://www.skytteunion.dk
Freq: 6 issues yearly; **Circ:** 2,000
Profile: Magazine of the Danish Shooting Union.
Language(s): Danish
CONSUMER: SPORT: Shooting

SKYTTEN 3855D75F-120
Editorial: Vingstedvej 27, 7182 BREDSTEN
Tel: 75 86 42 22 **Fax:** 75 86 54 75
Email: dds@skytten.dk **Web site:** http://www.skytten.dk
Freq: 6 issues yearly; **Circ:** 8,000
Profile: Magazine focusing on shooting spot (pistols and guns).
Language(s): Danish
ADVERTISING RATES:
Full Page Colour .... DKK 7200
SCC .... DKK 144
CONSUMER: SPORT: Shooting

SLÆGTSGAARDEN 3086D21A-105
Editorial: Skælskør Landevej 83, Lundforlund, 4200 SLAGELSE **Tel:** 58 58 40 16
Email: ogn@mail.tele.dk **Web site:** http://www.slaegtsgaardsforeningen.dk
Freq: 6 issues yearly; **Circ:** 2,200
Editor: Ole G Nielsen
Profile: Magazine of the Danish Family Farmers' Association.
Language(s): Danish
BUSINESS: AGRICULTURE & FARMING

SLØJD 3233D46-55
Editorial: Møldrupvej 53 A, 9510 ARDEN
Tel: 98 56 53 43
Email: slojdblad@gmail.com **Web site:** http://www.slojd.dk
Date Established: 1972; **Freq:** 6 issues yearly; **Circ:** 2,087
Editor: Karsten Bjerregaard
Profile: Magazine published by the Danish Woodwork Teachers' Association.
Language(s): Danish

SMAG & BEHAG 3008D11A-49
Editorial: Abildgårdsparken 5, 3460 BIRKERØD
Tel: 33 97 43 43 **Fax:** 33 111762
Email: kontor@smag-behag.dk **Web site:** http://www.smag-behag.dk
Freq: Monthly; **Circ:** 11,043
Profile: Magazine providing information concerning gastronomy and wine. Includes features on lifestyle and travel, industry news and product reviews.
Language(s): Danish
Readership: Aimed at restaurateurs, owners and managers of wine bars and wine retailers in Denmark.
ADVERTISING RATES:
Full Page Colour .... DKK 16900
SCC .... DKK 139.40
BUSINESS: CATERING: Catering, Hotels & Restaurants

SOCIALDEMOKRATEN 3707D82-150
Editorial: Danasvej 7, 1910 FREDERIKSBERG
Tel: 72 30 08 00 **Fax:** 33 93 67 70
Email: socialdemokraten@partikontoret.dk **Web site:** http://socialdemokraterne.dk/default.aspx?func=search.content&q=SOCIALDEMOKRATEN
Date Established: 1991; **Freq:** Quarterly; **Circ:** 5,500
Editor: Nina Juhl Østergaard
Profile: Publication of the Social Democratic Party.
Language(s): Danish
ADVERTISING RATES:
Full Page Colour .... DKK 15000
SCC .... DKK 172,41
CONSUMER: CURRENT AFFAIRS & POLITICS

SOCIALPÆDAGOGEN 3167D32G-105
Editorial: Brolæggerstræde 9, 1211 KØBENHAVN K
Tel: 72 48 60 00 **Fax:** 72 48 60 01
Email: redaktionen@sl.dk **Web site:** http://www.socialpaedagogen.dk
Freq: 26 issues yearly; **Circ:** 42,864
Editor: Jens Nielsen
Profile: Magazine covering social issues and education.
Language(s): Danish
Readership: Aimed at social workers, institutions and authorities.
BUSINESS: LOCAL GOVERNMENT, LEISURE & RECREATION: Community Care & Social Services

SØNDAG 3604D74C-100
Editorial: Havneholmen 33, 1561 KØBENHAVN V
Tel: 72 34 20 00 **Fax:** 72 34 20 05
Email: soendag@soendag.dk **Web site:** http://www.soendag.dk
Freq: Weekly; **Circ:** 74,000
Editor: Stinne Bjerre
Profile: Family magazine including news, interviews and features on clothes, cosmetics, food, health and fiction.
Language(s): Danish
ADVERTISING RATES:
Full Page Colour .... DKK 33500
SCC .... DKK 299.10
CONSUMER: WOMEN'S INTEREST CONSUMER MAGAZINES: Home & Family

SØNDAGSAVISEN CENTRALREDAKTIONEN
630434D72-610
Editorial: Gladsaxe Møllevej 28, 2860 SØBORG
Tel: 39 57 75 00 **Fax:** 39577600
Email: redak@sondagsavisen.dk **Web site:** http://www.sondagsavisen.dk
Freq: Weekly; **Cover Price:** Free; **Circ:** 2,177,571
Executive Editor: Søren Krogsgaard
Language(s): Danish
ADVERTISING RATES:
Full Page Colour .... DKK 36263
SCC .... DKK 156.70
LOCAL NEWSPAPERS

SØNDERBORG UGEAVIS
630443D72-615
Editorial: Østergade 3, 1.sal, 6400 SØNDERBORG
Tel: 87 54 25 42 **Fax:** 87 54 25 43
Email: info.su@b-l.dk **Web site:** http://www.sonderborgugeavis.dk
Freq: Weekly; **Cover Price:** Free; **Circ:** 38,923
Language(s): Danish
ADVERTISING RATES:
Full Page Colour .... DKK 15431
SCC .... DKK 66,80
LOCAL NEWSPAPERS

SORØ AVIS 630363D80-145
Editorial: Absalonsgade 1 A, 4281 SORØ
Tel: 57 83 47 77 **Fax:** 57 83 48 42
Email: red.soa@b-l.dk **Web site:** http://www.soroeavis.dk
Freq: Weekly; **Cover Price:** Free; **Circ:** 17,552
Editor: Bjarne Stenbæk
Profile: Local newspaper for Sorø.
Language(s): Danish
Readership: Read by local residents.
ADVERTISING RATES:
Full Page Colour .... DKK 11340
SCC .... DKK 49
CONSUMER: RURAL & REGIONAL INTEREST

SPASTIKEREN 4049D56A-273
Editorial: Spastikerforeningen, Flintholm Allé 8, 2000 FREDERIKSBERG **Tel:** 38 88 45 75 **Fax:** 38 88 45 76
Email: info@spastikeren.dk **Web site:** http://www.spastikerforeningen.dk
Freq: 6 issues yearly; **Circ:** 6,500
Editor: Benjamin Steengaard Rasmussen; **Executive Editor:** Frands Havaleschka
Profile: Official publication of the Danish Society for Cerebral Palsy.
Language(s): Danish

SPILDEVANDSTEKNISK TIDSSKRIFT 3325D57-40
Editorial: Bøgevej 12, 8660 SKANDERBORG
Tel: 86 52 41 08
Email: red@stf.dk **Web site:** http://www.stf.dk
Freq: Quarterly; **Circ:** 1,880
Profile: Magazine containing information concerning the sewage and waste water industry.
Language(s): Danish

SPIS BEDRE 1792020D73-268
Editorial: Store Kongensgade 72, 1264 COPENHAGEN **Tel:** 50 80 02 91
Email: redaktionen@spis-bedre.dk **Web site:** http://www.spis-bedre.dk
Freq: Monthly; **Circ:** 29,574
Executive Editor: Chanet Deleuran
Language(s): Danish
CONSUMER: NATIONAL & INTERNATIONAL PERIODICALS

SPORTSFISKEREN 3780D92-100
Editorial: Worsåesgade 1, 7100 VEJLE
Tel: 75 82 06 99 **Fax:** 75 82 02 09
Email: ow@sportsfiskerforbundet.dk **Web site:** http://www.sportsfiskeren.dk
Date Established: 1926; **Freq:** Monthly; **Circ:** 32,000
Editor: Orla Bertram Nielsen
Profile: Magazine providing angling information.
Language(s): Danish
CONSUMER: ANGLING & FISHING

SR-SKAT 759429D1A-135
Editorial: Nytorv 5, 1450 COPENHAGEN
Tel: 33 74 07 00 **Fax:** 33 12 16 36
Email: thomson@thomson.dk **Web site:** http://www.thomson.dk
Freq: 6 issues yearly - 6-7 gange om måneden; **Circ:** 3,700
Language(s): Danish
ADVERTISING RATES:
Full Page Colour .... DKK 6700
BUSINESS: FINANCE & ECONOMICS

STAND BY 3254D50-95
Editorial: Carl Jacobsens Vej 20, 1. sal, 2500 VALBY
Tel: 33 26 84 00 **Fax:** 33 26 84 01
Email: standby@standby.dk **Web site:** http://www.standby.dk
Date Established: 1982; **Freq:** Monthly; **Circ:** 21,000
Editor: Henrik Baumgarten; **Executive Editor:** Anne Orholt
Profile: Journal for the Scandinavian travel trade.
Language(s): Danish; Norwegian; Swedish
ADVERTISING RATES:
Full Page Colour .... DKK 26900
SCC .... DKK 122.80
BUSINESS: TRAVEL & TOURISM

STAT & KOMMUNE INDKØB
3154D32A-140
Editorial: Glostrup Torv 6, 2600 GLOSTRUP
Tel: 43 43 31 21 **Fax:** 43 43 15 13
Email: saki@saki.dk **Web site:** http://www.saki.dk
Circ: 8,341
Profile: Publication with municipal information on all topics.
Language(s): Danish
ADVERTISING RATES:
Full Page Colour .... DKK 19900
SCC .... DKK 86,14
BUSINESS: LOCAL GOVERNMENT, LEISURE & RECREATION: Local Government

STREET BOYS 1810745D53-42
Editorial: Havneholmen 33, 1561 COPENHAGEN
Tel: 44 85 88 08
Web site: http://www.streetboys.dk
Freq: 6 issues yearly; **Circ:** 27,000
Editor: Caroline Wilhejlm; **Executive Editor:** Tina Appelt
Language(s): Danish
BUSINESS: RETAILING & WHOLESALING

STUDY ABROAD 3858D62A-200
Editorial: Faendediget 1A, 2, 4600 KØGE
Tel: 56 27 64 44 **Fax:** 56 27 65 29
Email: study-abroad@ksi.dk **Web site:** http://www.study-abroad.dk
Freq: Quarterly; **Circ:** 86,215
Profile: Magazine providing information about studying abroad.
Language(s): Danish
BUSINESS: CHURCH & SCHOOL EQUIPMENT & EDUCATION: Education

SUKKERROE NYT 759421D21A-125
Editorial: Axelborg, Axeltorv 3, 1., 1609 KØBENHAVN K **Tel:** 33 39 40 00 **Fax:** 33 39 41 51
Email: ks@landbrug.dk **Web site:** http://www.danskesukkerroedyrkere.dk
Freq: Quarterly; **Circ:** 3,000
Profile: A members magazine for sugar beet growers and others involved in the business.
Language(s): Danish
Readership: A members magazine aimed for sugar beet growers and others involved in the business.
BUSINESS: AGRICULTURE & FARMING

SUNDHEDSGUIDEN.DK
1842836D37-28
Editorial: Hollandsvej 12, 2800 LYNGBY
Tel: 39 13 10 10
Email: info@sundhedsguiden.dk **Web site:** http://www.sundhedsguiden.dk
Freq: Daily; **Cover Price:** Free; **Circ:** 11,312 Unique Users
Language(s): Danish
ADVERTISING RATES:
SCC .... DKK 23,91
BUSINESS: PHARMACEUTICAL & CHEMISTS

SUNDHEDSPLEJERSKEN
3860D56A-167
Editorial: G. C. Amdrupsvej 12, 8200 ÅRHUS
Tel: 86 91 25 15 **Fax:** 86 16 71 36
Email: lisbetnissen@fs10.dk **Web site:** http://www.dsr.dk/msite/text.asp?id=57&TextID=688
Date Established: 1979; **Freq:** 6 issues yearly; **Circ:** 3,000
Editor: Lisbet Nissen
Profile: Magazine focusing on health care issues.
Language(s): Danish
Readership: Aimed at health visitors.

SUPER AVISEN 1792491D73-355
Editorial: Grønholmsvej 12, 4340 TØLLØSE
Tel: 59 18 54 30 **Fax:** 59 18 58 12
Email: administrationen@superavisen.dk **Web site:** http://www.superavisen.dk
Freq: 26 issues yearly; **Circ:** 8,991
Editor: Gitte Ackermann; **Executive Editor:** Jørn Ackermann
Language(s): Danish
ADVERTISING RATES:
Full Page Colour .... DKK 17060
SCC .... DKK 103.90
Copy instructions: *Copy Date:* 15 days prior to publication date
CONSUMER: NATIONAL & INTERNATIONAL PERIODICALS

SVEJSNING 3138D27-120
Editorial: c/o Dansk Svejseteknisk Landsforening, Park Allé 345, 2605 BRØNDBY **Tel:** 40 61 30 90
Fax: 43 26 70 11
Email: bly.bi-press@mail.tele.dk **Web site:** http://dslsvejs.dk
Freq: 6 issues yearly; **Circ:** 2,000
Editor: Birthe Lyngsø
Profile: Journal of the Danish Welding Society.
Language(s): Danish
ADVERTISING RATES:
Full Page Colour .... DKK 8750

SYDSJÆLLANDS TIDENDE
630422D72-700
Editorial: Torvestræde 4, 4760 VORDINBORG
Tel: 55 37 00 09 **Fax:** 55 34 00 11
Email: redaktion@sydtid.dk **Web site:** http://www.sydtid.dk
Freq: Weekly; **Cover Price:** Free; **Circ:** 30,800
Editor: Henrik Ekberg
Language(s): Danish
ADVERTISING RATES:
Full Page Colour .... DKK 11817,50
SCC .... DKK 51,15
LOCAL NEWSPAPERS

SYGEPLEJERSKEN
3292D56B-10
Editorial: Sankt Annæ Plads 30, postboks 1084, 1008 KØBENHAVN K **Tel:** 33 15 15 55
Fax: 33 15 18 41
Email: redaktionen@dsr.dk **Web site:** http://www.sygeplejersken.dk
Date Established: 1901; **Freq:** 26 issues yearly; **Circ:** 75,154
Editor: Søren Palsbo; **Executive Editor:** Sigurd Nissen-Petersen
Profile: Official journal of the Danish Nurses' Association.
Language(s): Danish
Readership: Magazine aimed for politicians, nurses and others.
ADVERTISING RATES:
Full Page Colour .... DKK 24750
SCC .... DKK 238
BUSINESS: HEALTH & MEDICAL: Nursing

TÆNK PENGE
630483D14R-150
Editorial: Fiolstræde 17, Postbox 2188, 1017 KØBENHAVN K **Tel:** 77 41 77 41 **Fax:** 77 41 77 42
Email: red@fbr.dk **Web site:** http://www.taenk.dk
Freq: Monthly; **Circ:** 90,000
Executive Editor: Lis Hornø
Language(s): Danish
ADVERTISING RATES:
Full Page Colour .... DKK 20000
SCC .... DKK 224.50
BUSINESS: COMMERCE, INDUSTRY & MANAGEMENT: Commerce Related

TAKE OFF TAKEOFF.DK
3255D50-100
Editorial: Vester Voldgade 83,3, 1553 KØBENHAVN V **Tel:** 33 26 8400 **Fax:** 33 26 8401
Email: info@takeoff.dk **Web site:** http://www.takeoff.dk
Circ: 12,500 Unique Users
Editor: Henrik Baumgarten; **Executive Editor:** Anne Orholt
Profile: Magazine providing information on all aspects of the travel trade.
Language(s): Danish
Readership: Read by hoteliers, airline executives, tourist information officers, travel agents and tour operators.
BUSINESS: TRAVEL & TOURISM

TÅRNBY BLADET
630478D80-148
Editorial: Englandsvej 290, Postboks 34, 2770 KASTRUP **Tel:** 32 50 92 90 **Fax:** 32 50 92 93
Email: redaktionen@taarnbybladet.dk **Web site:** http://www.taarnbybladet.dk
Freq: Monthly; **Cover Price:** Free; **Circ:** 21,000
Editor: Arne Olsen
Profile: Local newspaper for Kastrup.
Language(s): English
Readership: Read by local residents.
ADVERTISING RATES:
Full Page Colour .... DKK 4500
SCC .... DKK 85
CONSUMER: RURAL & REGIONAL INTEREST

TEGL
2975D4E-160
Editorial: Lille Strandstræde 20C, 1254 KØBENHAVN K **Tel:** 33 32 34 84 **Fax:** 33 32 22 97
Email: tegl@muro.dk **Web site:** http://www.muro.dk
Date Established: 1897; **Freq:** Quarterly; **Circ:** 2,500
Editor: Susanne Ulrik
Profile: Magazine focusing on bricks and tiles.
Language(s): Danish
Readership: Aimed at builders and architects.
ADVERTISING RATES:
Full Page Colour .... DKK 12500
SCC .... DKK 189

TEKNIKEREN
3065D19A-120
Editorial: Nørre Voldgade 12, 1358 KØBENHAVN K
Tel: 33 43 65 00 **Fax:** 33 43 66 67
Email: teknikeren@tl.dk **Web site:** http://www.tl.dk/nyheder/teknikeren
Date Established: 1919; **Freq:** Monthly; **Circ:** 31,381
Editor: Susanne Bruun
Profile: Magazine for technical assistants, architects, engineers and draughtsmen.
Language(s): Danish
ADVERTISING RATES:
Full Page Colour .... DKK 19600
SCC .... DKK 96,60
BUSINESS: ENGINEERING & MACHINERY

TEKNISK NYT
3070D19F-130
Editorial: Naverland 35, 2600 GLOSTRUP
Tel: 43 24 26 28 **Fax:** 43 24 26 26
Email: hfn@techmedia.dk **Web site:** http://www.techmedia.dk
Freq: Monthly; **Circ:** 10,080
Profile: Magazine containing information about new products and techniques within design, automation and process control. Includes regular coverage of CAD/CAM.
Language(s): Danish
Readership: Aimed at mechanical and design engineers.
ADVERTISING RATES:
Full Page Colour .... DKK 27500
SCC .... DKK 516,70

TELEKOMMUNIKATION
3059D18B-200
Editorial: Stationsparken 25, 2600 GLOSTRUP
Tel: 43 43 29 00 **Fax:** 43 43 13 28
Email: redaktion@telekommunikation.dk **Web site:** http://www.telekommunikation.dk
Date Established: 1998; **Freq:** Monthly - minus januar, juni og juli; **Circ:** 5,327
Editor: Per Danielsen
Profile: Magazine containing articles and information about IT and the telecommunications industry.
Language(s): Danish
Readership: Read by telephone, mobile phone and Internet operators, installers of computers and electronics equipment, suppliers and manufacturers.
ADVERTISING RATES:
Full Page Colour .... DKK 17500
SCC .... DKK 262.80
BUSINESS: ELECTRONICS: Telecommunications

THISTED DAGBLAD
3431D67B-7600
Editorial: Sydhavnsvej 5, 7700 THISTED
Tel: 99 19 93 00 **Fax:** 99 19 94 08
Email: thisted@nordjyske.dk **Web site:** http://www.nordjyske.dk/thisted/forside.aspx
Freq: Daily; **Circ:** 8,739
Editor: Hans Peter Kragh; **Executive Editor:** Hans Peter Kragh
Language(s): Danish
ADVERTISING RATES:
Full Page Colour .... DKK 17932
SCC .... DKK 81,90
REGIONAL DAILY & SUNDAY NEWSPAPERS: Regional Daily Newspapers

THISTED POSTEN
630456D72-720
Editorial: Sydhavnsvej 5, 7700 THISTED
Tel: 99 19 93 99 **Fax:** 99 19 93 27
Email: thisted.posten@nordjyske.dk **Web site:** http://www.nordjyskeugeaviser.dk/Default.aspx?tabid=112
Date Established: 1973; **Freq:** Weekly; **Cover Price:** Free; **Circ:** 24,262
Editor: Leif Damsgaard Jensen
Language(s): Danish
ADVERTISING RATES:
Full Page Colour .... DKK 10971
SCC .... DKK 47,50
LOCAL NEWSPAPERS

TID & TENDENSER
630518D74B-250
Editorial: Bitsovvej 2, 7400 HERNING
Tel: 97 11 89 00 **Fax:** 97 11 85 11
Email: info@pejgruppen.dk **Web site:** http://www.pejgruppen.dk
Date Established: 1980; **Freq:** 6 issues yearly; **Circ:** 1,000
Executive Editor: Helle Mathiesen
Profile: Magazine covering fashion news and trends. Also includes lifestyle and design.
Language(s): Danish
ADVERTISING RATES:
Full Page Colour .... DKK 18000
CONSUMER: WOMEN'S INTEREST CONSUMER MAGAZINES: Women's Interest - Fashion

TIDSSKRIFT FOR DANSK SUNDHEDSVÆSEN
3864D56A-170
Editorial: Niels Bohrs Vej 30, 9200 AALBORG
Tel: 99 27 27 30
Email: freefyn@mail.tele.dk **Web site:** http://www.dssnet.dk
Date Established: 1924; **Freq:** Monthly; **Circ:** 1,600
Editor: Hans Peder Graversen
Profile: Magazine concerning all aspects of the health care sector.
Language(s): Danish
Readership: Aimed at managers in the health care sector.
ADVERTISING RATES:
Full Page Colour .... DKK 12400

TIDSSKRIFT FOR SKATTER OG AFGIFTER
2931D1M-130
Editorial: Palægade 4, 1261 COPENHAGEN
Tel: 70 20 33 14 **Fax:** 33 96 01 01
Email: magnus@magnus.dk **Web site:** http://www.magnus.dk
Freq: Weekly; **Circ:** 3,100
Executive Editor: Dorte Carlsson
Profile: Financial publication for professionals in the tax field.
Language(s): Danish
ADVERTISING RATES:
Full Page Colour .... DKK 18315
BUSINESS: FINANCE & ECONOMICS: Taxation

TIPSBLADET
3630D75B-200
Editorial: Kristen Bernikowsgade 4, 3. sal, 1105 KØBENHAVN K **Tel:** 49 70 89 00 **Fax:** 49 70 88 30
Email: redaktion@tipsbladet.dk **Web site:** http://www.tipsbladet.dk
Freq: 104 issues yearly; **Circ:** 8,324
Executive Editor: Thomas Færch Kvist
Profile: Football magazine.
Language(s): Danish
ADVERTISING RATES:
Full Page Colour .... DKK 22500
SCC .... DKK 87,30
CONSUMER: SPORT: Football

TJECK MAGAZINE
3609D74F-65
Editorial: Øresundsvej 49, 4 t.v., 2300 COPENHAGEN **Tel:** 60 7777 61
Email: torben@tjeck.dk **Web site:** http://www.tjeck.dk
Date Established: 1992; **Freq:** Monthly; **Cover Price:** Free; **Circ:** 110,000
Executive Editor: Kristian Falkenberg
Profile: Magazine covering all lifestyle issues in relation to young people. Focuses on current affairs and culture, including information on religion, politics and human rights. Also provides articles on music, films and fashion.
Language(s): Danish
Readership: Distributed free in schools, cafés, bars, cinemas and other social meeting places. Read predominantly by people aged between 15 and 24 years.
ADVERTISING RATES:
Full Page Colour .... DKK 19000
SCC .... DKK 354
CONSUMER: WOMEN'S INTEREST CONSUMER MAGAZINES: Teenage

TORPARE BLADET
3809D89A-40
Editorial: Landskronagade 82, 2100 KØBENHAVN Ø
Tel: 39 29 52 82 **Fax:** 39 29 59 82
Email: redaktion@danske-torpare.dk **Web site:** http://www.danske-torpare.dk/index1.asp
Date Established: 1981; **Freq:** Quarterly; **Circ:** 5,200
Profile: Magazine containing information of interest to those with a second or holiday home in Sweden.
Language(s): Danish
ADVERTISING RATES:
Full Page Colour .... DKK 3840
SCC .... DKK 96

TOURING NYT
3669D77B-160
Editorial: Markvangen 6, 8260 VIBY J
Tel: 86 11 62 00 **Fax:** 86 11 62 59
Email: tn@mctouringclub.dk **Web site:** http://www.mctouringclub.dk
Date Established: 1971; **Freq:** 6 issues yearly; **Circ:** 29,000
Profile: Magazine containing articles, travel information, interviews and product news for motorcycle owners.
Language(s): Danish
ADVERTISING RATES:
Full Page Colour .... DKK 7780
SCC .... DKK 155,60
CONSUMER: MOTORING & CYCLING: Motorcycling

TRÆ- & MØBELINDUSTRI
3234D46-90
Editorial: Naverland 35, 2600 GLOSTRUP
Tel: 43 24 26 16 **Fax:** 43 24 26 26
Email: pf@techmedia.dk **Web site:** http://www.techmedia.dk
Freq: Monthly; **Circ:** 6,229
Profile: Magazine for specialists in the woodworking and furniture trade. Informs on new machinery, tools, storage and transportation.
Language(s): Danish
ADVERTISING RATES:
Full Page Colour .... DKK 26900
SCC .... DKK 358,67

TRANS INFORM
3247D49C-50
Editorial: Jernbanegade 18, 6330 PADBORG
Tel: 70 10 05 06 **Fax:** 74 67 40 47
Email: info@transinform.com **Web site:** http://www.transinform.com
Freq: Monthly; **Circ:** 3,629
Executive Editor: Gwyn Nissen
Profile: Magazine covering transport, cargo handling and removals.
Language(s): Danish
ADVERTISING RATES:
Full Page Colour .... DKK 16945
SCC .... DKK 214,54

TRANSPORTMAGASINET
3243D49A-40
Editorial: Marielundvej 46 D, Box 536, 2730 HERLEV
Tel: 70 11 51 01 **Fax:** 44 85 10 13
Email: info@transportmagasinet.dk **Web site:** http://www.transportmagasinet.dk
Freq: 26 issues yearly; **Circ:** 12,140
Profile: Journal for haulage contractors, transportation companies, construction firms, wholesale and service companies, public administration, refuse collectors and students of technical schools.
Language(s): Danish
ADVERTISING RATES:
Full Page Colour .... DKK 25250
SCC .... DKK 110
BUSINESS: TRANSPORT

TURENGAARTIL.DK
1810301D73-401
Editorial: Rådhuspladsen 37, 1785 COPENHAGEN
Tel: 33 47 25 65
Email: info@tgt.dk **Web site:** http://tgt.dk
Circ: 15,591 Unique Users
Language(s): Danish
CONSUMER: NATIONAL & INTERNATIONAL PERIODICALS

TV 2 / DANMARK NYHEDERNE; 18.00
1864023D82-330
Editorial: Rugaardsvej 25, 5100 ODENSE C
Tel: 65 91 91 91 **Fax:** 65 91 33 22
Email: nyhederne@tv2.dk **Web site:** http://www.nyhederne.tv2.dk
Freq: Daily; **Circ:** 532,000
Language(s): Danish
ADVERTISING RATES:
SCC .... DKK 71126
CONSUMER: CURRENT AFFAIRS & POLITICS

TV 2 FINANS FINANS.TV2.DK
1791785D1A-142
Editorial: Teglholm Allé 16, 2450 COPENHAGEN
Tel: 39 75 75 75 **Fax:** 39 75 75 00
Email: finans@tv2.dk **Web site:** http://finans.tv2.dk
Editor: Dorthe Duvander
Language(s): Danish
BUSINESS: FINANCE & ECONOMICS

UD & SE
3752D89E-200
Editorial: Sølvgade 40, 1349 KØBENHAVN K
Tel: 33 54 44 76 **Fax:** 33 54 42 40
Email: udogse@dsb.dk **Web site:** http://www.dsb.dk/Om-DSB/DSB-i-medierne/Ud-og-Se
Freq: Monthly; **Cover Price:** Free; **Circ:** 194,860
Editor: Andreas Fugl Thøgersen
Profile: Magazine focusing on travel by Danish State Railways.
Language(s): Danish
ADVERTISING RATES:
Full Page Colour .... DKK 45700
CONSUMER: HOLIDAYS & TRAVEL: Holidays

UDDANNELSESAVISEN
3747D62A-225
Editorial: Fændediget 1A, 2. sal, Postboks 293, 4600 KØGE **Tel:** 56 27 64 44 **Fax:** 56 27 65 29
Email: christina@ksi.dk **Web site:** http://www.uddannelses-avisen.dk
Freq: 6 issues yearly; **Circ:** 128,400
Editor: Christina Qvistgaard
Profile: Newspaper concerning all aspects of education.
Language(s): Danish
Readership: Aimed at students, student councillors and personnel managers.
ADVERTISING RATES:
Full Page Colour .... DKK 67440
SCC .... DKK 292
BUSINESS: CHURCH & SCHOOL EQUIPMENT & EDUCATION: Education

UDE OG HJEMME
3603D74C-88
Editorial: Havneholmen 33, 1561 COPENHAGEN
Tel: 72 34 20 56
Email: redaktionen@udeoghjemme.dk **Web site:** http://www.udeoghjemme.dk
Freq: Weekly; **Circ:** 174,874
Profile: Magazine containing articles and information concerning leisure activities for all the family.
Language(s): Danish
ADVERTISING RATES:
Full Page Colour .... DKK 52800
SCC .... DKK 471.40
CONSUMER: WOMEN'S INTEREST CONSUMER MAGAZINES: Home & Family

UGE NYT SLAGELSE
630481D72-1145
Editorial: Klingeberg 14, 4200 SLAGELSE
Tel: 58 53 32 22 **Fax:** 58 52 90 88
Email: ugenyt@sondagsavisen.dk **Web site:** http://www.sondagsavisen.dk
Freq: Weekly; **Cover Price:** Free; **Circ:** 59,960
Language(s): Danish
ADVERTISING RATES:
Full Page Colour .... DKK 13972,50
SCC .... DKK 60,48
LOCAL NEWSPAPERS

UGEAVISEN FOR BRAMMING OG OMEGN
630499D72-756
Editorial: Sct. Knuds Alle 3, 6740 BRAMMING
Tel: 75 17 40 00 **Fax:** 75 17 37 87
Email: im@ugeavisen-bramming.dk **Web site:** http://www.ugeavisen-bramming.dk
Freq: Weekly; **Cover Price:** Free; **Circ:** 15,767
Language(s): Danish
ADVERTISING RATES:
Full Page Colour .... DKK 10635
SCC .... DKK 46,03
LOCAL NEWSPAPERS

UGEAVISEN FOR RIBE OG OMEGN
630527D72-1060
Editorial: Grønnegade 14, 6760 RIBE
Tel: 75 42 23 66 **Fax:** 75 42 25 66
Email: redaktion@ugeavisen-ribe.dk **Web site:** http://www.ugeavisen-ribe.dk
Date Established: 1970; **Freq:** Weekly; **Cover Price:** Free; **Circ:** 24,999
Language(s): Danish
ADVERTISING RATES:
Full Page Colour .... DKK 11105
SCC .... DKK 48,07
LOCAL NEWSPAPERS

UGEAVISEN NORDFYN
630212D72-497
Editorial: Østergade 14, 5400 BOGENSE
Tel: 65 45 57 00 **Fax:** 64 86 11 45
Email: uanredaktion@fynskemedier.dk **Web site:** http://www.ugeavisennordfyn.dk
Freq: Weekly; **Cover Price:** Free; **Circ:** 22,447
Language(s): Danish
ADVERTISING RATES:
Full Page Colour .... DKK 13860
SCC .... DKK 60
LOCAL NEWSPAPERS

UGEAVISEN ODENSE
630560D72-748
Editorial: Vestergade 70-74, 5100 ODENSE C
Tel: 66 14 14 10 **Fax:** 66 12 22 00
Email: redaktionen@ugeavisen-odense.dk **Web site:** http://www.ugeavisen-odense.dk
Freq: Weekly; **Cover Price:** Free; **Circ:** 117,161
Language(s): Danish
ADVERTISING RATES:
Full Page Colour .... DKK 22888,50
SCC .... DKK 99,08
LOCAL NEWSPAPERS

UGEAVISEN SVENDBORG
630552D72-749
Editorial: Sankt Nicolai Gade 1A, 5700 SVENDBORG
Tel: 62 21 73 21 **Fax:** 62 22 30 09
Email: red@ugeavisen-svendborg.dk **Web site:** http://ugeavisensvendborg.dk
Freq: Weekly; **Cover Price:** Free; **Circ:** 33,868
Editor: Michael Thorbjørnsen
Language(s): Danish
ADVERTISING RATES:
Full Page Colour .... DKK 13167
SCC .... DKK 57
LOCAL NEWSPAPERS

UGEAVISEN SVENSTRUP
630556D72-750
Editorial: Godthåbsvej 7, 9230 SVENSTRUP
Tel: 98 38 14 77 **Fax:** 98 38 19 65
Email: tekst@uge-avisen.com **Web site:** http://www.delokaleugeaviser.dk/dd/default.aspx?template=blad&id=4&area=&bladid=289&layout=2
Freq: Weekly; **Circ:** 35,000
Language(s): Danish
ADVERTISING RATES:
Full Page Colour .... DKK 13167
SCC .... DKK 57
LOCAL NEWSPAPERS

UGEAVISEN VEJLE
630548D72-753
Editorial: Bugattivej 8, 7100 VEJLE **Tel:** 75 83 10 00
Fax: 75 72 17 27
Email: kl@ugeavisenvejle.dk **Web site:** http://www.ugeavisenvejle.dk
Freq: Weekly; **Cover Price:** Free; **Circ:** 71,843
Language(s): Danish
ADVERTISING RATES:
Full Page Colour .... DKK 15246
SCC .... DKK 66
LOCAL NEWSPAPERS

UGEBLADET FOR MØN
630549D72-1070
Editorial: Lille Kirkestræde 2, 4780 STEGE
Tel: 55 81 40 34 **Fax:** 55 81 40 35
Email: redaktion@ugebladet-for-moen.dk **Web site:** http://www.ugebladet-for-moen.dk
Freq: Weekly; **Cover Price:** Free; **Circ:** 7,630
Language(s): Danish
ADVERTISING RATES:
Full Page Colour .... DKK 7852,50
SCC .... DKK 33,99
LOCAL NEWSPAPERS

UGEBLADET NÆSTVED OG OMEGN
630553D72-1141
Editorial: Dania 38, 4700 NÆSTVED **Tel:** 72 45 11 00
Fax: 72 45 12 19
Email: ugebladet@sj-medier.dk **Web site:** http://www.sj-medier.dk
Freq: Weekly; **Cover Price:** Free; **Circ:** 47,587
Editor: Per Witt
Language(s): Danish
ADVERTISING RATES:
Full Page Colour .... DKK 19057,50
SCC .... DKK 82,50
LOCAL NEWSPAPERS

UGEBLADET SYDSJÆLLAND
630544D72-765
Editorial: Adelgade 70, 4720 PRÆSTØ
Tel: 55 99 21 21 **Fax:** 55 99 33 28
Email: redaktion-ubs@sj-medier.dk **Web site:** http://www.sj-medier.dk
Freq: Weekly; **Cover Price:** Free; **Circ:** 21,859
Editor: Niels Bangild; **Executive Editor:** Helge Wedel
Language(s): Danish
ADVERTISING RATES:
Full Page Colour .... DKK 14782,50
SCC .... DKK 39,00
LOCAL NEWSPAPERS

UGEBLADET VESTSJÆLLAND
630542D72-761
Editorial: Centervej 33, 4270 HØNG **Tel:** 88 88 42 90
Fax: 58 85 20 75
Email: red.ubv@nordvest.dk **Web site:** http://www.venstrebladet.dk
Date Established: 1916; **Freq:** Weekly; **Cover Price:** Free; **Circ:** 22,045
Language(s): Danish
ADVERTISING RATES:
Full Page Colour .... DKK 9854
SCC .... DKK 42,65
LOCAL NEWSPAPERS

UGEBREVET MEALS
759400D14A-235
Editorial: Gl. Bregnerødvej 12, 3520 FARUM
Tel: 44 99 90 01
Email: mail@meals.dk **Web site:** http://www.meals.dk
Freq: Weekly; **Circ:** 5,000
Language(s): Danish
BUSINESS: COMMERCE, INDUSTRY & MANAGEMENT

UGE-NYT FREDENSBORG
630461D72-1144
Editorial: Chr. Boecks Vej 3, 3480 FREDENSBORG
Tel: 45 90 80 70 **Fax:** 48 48 52 08
Email: redaktionen@uge-nyt.dk **Web site:** http://www.uge-nyt.dk
Freq: Weekly; **Cover Price:** Free; **Circ:** 21,400
Language(s): Danish
ADVERTISING RATES:
Full Page Colour .... DKK 15823,50
SCC .... DKK 68,50
LOCAL NEWSPAPERS

UGEPOSTEN SKJERN
630536D72-768
Editorial: Bergs plads 5, 6900 SKJERN
Tel: 96 81 53 13 **Fax:** 96 81 53 01
Email: skjern.annonce@bergske.dk **Web site:** http://midtjyskemedier.dk/default.asp?s=kontakt#ugeaviser-ugeposten%20skjern
Freq: Weekly; **Cover Price:** Free; **Circ:** 25,000
Editor: Jørgen Baungaard
Language(s): Danish
ADVERTISING RATES:
Full Page Colour .... DKK 10278
SCC .... DKK 44,49
LOCAL NEWSPAPERS

UGESKRIFT FOR LÆGER
3288D56A-180
Editorial: Trondhjemsgade 9, 2100 KØBENHAVN Ø
Tel: 35 44 85 00 **Fax:** 35 44 85 02
Email: ufl@dadl.dk **Web site:** http://www.ugeskriftet.dk
Freq: Weekly; **Circ:** 24,600
Editor: John Sahl Andersen; **Executive Editor:** Torben Kitaj
Profile: Magazine covering all aspects of the medical profession.
Language(s): Danish
Readership: Aimed at doctors.
ADVERTISING RATES:
Full Page Colour .... DKK 33200
SCC .... DKK 394,70
BUSINESS: HEALTH & MEDICAL

UNDERVISERE
1810474D14A-267
Editorial: Vandkunsten 12, 1015 KØBENHAVN K
Tel: 33 69 63 00 **Fax:** 33 69 64 26
Email: folkeskolen@dlf.org **Web site:** http://www.undervisere.dk/Content.aspx?ContentId=1
Freq: Monthly; **Circ:** 89,403
Editor: Stine Grynberg Andersen; **Executive Editor:** Thorkild Thejsen
Language(s): Danish
ADVERTISING RATES:
Full Page Colour .... DKK 24400
SCC .... DKK 280
BUSINESS: COMMERCE, INDUSTRY & MANAGEMENT

UNIVERSITETSAVISEN
3714D83-200
Editorial: Københavns Universitet, Nørregade 10, 1005 KØBENHAVN K **Tel:** 35 32 28 98
Fax: 35 32 29 20
Email: uni-avis@adm.ku.dk **Web site:** http://www.ku.dk/universitetsavisen
Freq: 26 issues yearly; **Circ:** 53,000
Profile: Magazine covering all aspects of university life.
Language(s): Danish
Readership: Read by students and personnel of Copenhagen University.
ADVERTISING RATES:
Full Page Colour .... DKK 25100
SCC .... DKK 108,65
CONSUMER: STUDENT PUBLICATIONS

VÆDDELØBSBLADET
3919D75E-300
Editorial: Traverbanevej 10, 2920 CHARLOTTENLUND **Tel:** 39 96 20 20
Fax: 39 63 91 65
Email: vb@trav.dk **Web site:** http://www.travoggalop.dk
Freq: Monthly; **Circ:** 5,000
Profile: Publication containing news about horse racing.
Language(s): Danish
Readership: Aimed at breeders, owners and trainers.
CONSUMER: SPORT: Horse Racing

VÆRN OM SYNET
3304D56E-120
Editorial: Ny Kongensgade 20, 1557 KØBENHAVN K
Tel: 33 69 11 00 **Fax:** 33 69 11 01
Email: el@vos.dk **Web site:** http://www.vos.dk
Freq: Quarterly; **Circ:** 35,000
Editor: Erik Lohmann
Profile: Magazine about research and developments in combatting diseases of the eye.
Language(s): Danish
ADVERTISING RATES:
Full Page Colour .... DKK 14800
BUSINESS: HEALTH & MEDICAL: Optics

VAGABOND REJS
3753D89E-205
Editorial: Bregnerødvej 132, 3460 BIRKERØD
Tel: 70 22 44 36 **Fax:** 48131507
Email: mail@vagabond.info **Web site:** http://www.vagabond.info/default.asp?id=37
Freq: Quarterly; **Circ:** 30,000
Profile: Travel magazine providing detailed guides and information on backpacking and package holidays.
Language(s): Danish
Readership: Aimed at the independent traveller.
ADVERTISING RATES:
Full Page Colour .... DKK 26425
SCC .... DKK 230.20
Copy instructions: *Copy Date:* 30 days prior to publication date
CONSUMER: HOLIDAYS & TRAVEL: Holidays

VALBY BLADET
630526D72-771
Editorial: Solbjergvej 2A . Erhvervsplan, 2000 FREDERIKSBERG C **Tel:** 33 88 88 88
Fax: 33 88 89 99
Email: red.va@b-l.dk **Web site:** http://www.valbybladet.dk
Freq: Weekly; **Cover Price:** Free; **Circ:** 28,381
Executive Editor: Peter Erlitz
Language(s): Danish
ADVERTISING RATES:
Full Page Colour .... DKK 20054,50
SCC .... DKK 86,81
LOCAL NEWSPAPERS

VEDVARENDE ENERGI & MILJØ
4051D58-107
Editorial: Dannebrogsgade 8 A, 8000 ÅRHUS
Tel: 86 76 04 44 **Fax:** 86 76 05 44
Email: vem@ve.dk **Web site:** http://www.energi-miljo.dk
Freq: 6 issues yearly; **Circ:** 4,000
Profile: Publication about renewable energy sources and environment.
Language(s): Danish
ADVERTISING RATES:
Full Page Colour .... DKK 6215
SCC .... DKK 71.50

VEJEN AVIS
630532D72-775
Editorial: Vestergade 2D, 6600 VEJEN
Tel: 75 36 00 22 **Fax:** 75 36 03 90
Email: vejenavis@jv.dk **Web site:** http://www.vejenavis.dk
Date Established: 1941; **Freq:** Weekly; **Cover Price:** Free; **Circ:** 36,128
Editor: Jørgen Schultz
Language(s): Danish
ADVERTISING RATES:
Full Page Colour .... DKK 10624,50
SCC .... DKK 46
LOCAL NEWSPAPERS

VEJGAARD AVIS
630534D72-778
Editorial: Langagervej 1, 9330 AALBORG Ø
Tel: 99 35 35 35 **Fax:** 99 35 35 34
Email: aalborg@nordjyske.dk **Web site:** http://www.nordjyskeugeaviser.dk/Default.aspx?tabid=78
Freq: Weekly; **Cover Price:** Free; **Circ:** 33,762
Language(s): Danish
ADVERTISING RATES:
Full Page Colour .... DKK 12286,50
SCC .... DKK 53,18
LOCAL NEWSPAPERS

VENDELBO POSTEN
630525D72-790
Editorial: Frederikshavnvej 81, 9800 HJØRRING
Tel: 99 24 50 60 **Fax:** 99 24 50 35
Email: inge.steen@nordjyske.dk **Web site:** http://www.nordjyskeugeaviser.dk/Default.aspx?tabid=79
Freq: Weekly; **Cover Price:** Free; **Circ:** 35,857
Language(s): Danish
ADVERTISING RATES:
Full Page Colour .... DKK 12217,50
SCC .... DKK 52,88
LOCAL NEWSPAPERS

VESTEGNEN
630521D72-793
Editorial: Mosede Strandvej 11, 2670 GREVE
Tel: 70 20 64 01 **Fax:** 70 20 64 02
Email: redaktion@vestegnen.dk **Web site:** http://www.vestegnen.dk
Freq: Weekly; **Cover Price:** Free; **Circ:** 153,147
Language(s): Danish
ADVERTISING RATES:
Full Page Colour .... DKK 28373,50
SCC .... DKK 122,82
LOCAL NEWSPAPERS

VESTERBROBLADET
630144D80-200
Editorial: Solbjergvej 2A, 2000 FREDERIKSBERG
Tel: 33 88 88 88 **Fax:** 33888899
Email: red.vb@b-l.dk **Web site:** http://www.vesterbrobladet.dk
Freq: Weekly; **Cover Price:** Free; **Circ:** 23,365
Profile: Publication focusing on local news and events in Vesterbro.
Language(s): Danish
Readership: Read by residents.
ADVERTISING RATES:
Full Page Colour .... DKK 18518.50
SCC .... DKK 80.16
CONSUMER: RURAL & REGIONAL INTEREST

VI FORÆLDRE
3917D74D-140
Editorial: Vognmagergade 11, 1148 COPENHAGEN
Tel: 39 45 75 00
Email: mia.hessner@egmontmagasiner.dk **Web site:** http://www.viforaeldre.dk
Date Established: 1999; **Freq:** Monthly; **Circ:** 15,110
Executive Editor: Mille Collin Flaherty
Profile: Magazine focusing on children and childcare.
Language(s): Danish
Readership: Aimed at parents with children aged between 0 and 6 years.
ADVERTISING RATES:
Full Page Colour .... DKK 24700
SCC .... DKK 220.50
CONSUMER: WOMEN'S INTEREST CONSUMER MAGAZINES: Child Care

VI LEJERE
3620D74K-150
Editorial: Reventlowsgade 14, 1651 KØBENHAVN V
Tel: 33 86 09 10 **Fax:** 33 86 09 20
Email: kjhammer@mail.dk **Web site:** http://www.lejerneslo.dk
Freq: Quarterly; **Circ:** 93,000
Executive Editor: Kjeld Hammer
Profile: Magazine of the Danish Tenants' Association.
Language(s): Danish
ADVERTISING RATES:
Full Page Colour .... DKK 15620
SCC .... DKK 150
CONSUMER: WOMEN'S INTEREST CONSUMER MAGAZINES: Home Purchase

VI MED HUND
1792490D73-354
Editorial: Dortheavej 59, 2400 KØBENHAVN NV
Tel: 32 71 12 00 **Fax:** 32 71 12 12
Email: redaktion@vimedhund.dk **Web site:** http://www.vimedhund.dk
Freq: Monthly; **Circ:** 16,052
Editor: Anette Hvidkjær
Language(s): Danish
ADVERTISING RATES:
Full Page Colour .... DKK 31800
CONSUMER: NATIONAL & INTERNATIONAL PERIODICALS

VI UNGE
3611D74F-80
Editorial: Havneholmen 33, 1561 COPENHAGEN
Tel: 72 34 20 03
Email: redaktionen@viunge.dk **Web site:** http://www.viunge.dk

Denmark

Date Established: 1962; **Freq:** Monthly; **Circ:** 45,065
Editor: Julie Rosendahl
Profile: Magazine for teenage girls and young women.
Language(s): Danish
Readership: Read by girls aged between 13 and 24 years old.
ADVERTISING RATES:
Full Page Colour .... DKK 29000
SCC .... DKK 271.50
CONSUMER: WOMEN'S INTEREST CONSUMER MAGAZINES: Teenage

VIBORG NYT 630158D72-803
Editorial: Vesterbrogade 8, 8800 VIBORG
Tel: 89 27 63 00 **Fax:** 89 27 63 70
Email: viborgnyt@bergske.dk **Web site:** http://www.delokaleugeaviser.dk/dd/default.asp?template=blad&id=4&area=&bladid=98&layout=2
Freq: Weekly; **Cover Price:** Free; **Circ:** 41,630
Editor: Søren Brogaard
Language(s): Danish
ADVERTISING RATES:
Full Page Colour .... DKK 11352
SCC .... DKK 49,14
LOCAL NEWSPAPERS

VIBORG STIFTS FOLKEBLAD 3433D67B-8200
Editorial: Vesterbrogade 8, 8800 VIBORG
Tel: 89 27 63 00 **Fax:** 89 27 64 80
Email: viborg@bergske.dk **Web site:** http://www.viborg-folkeblad.dk
Freq: Daily; **Circ:** 10,721
Editor: Jane Gisselmann; **Executive Editor:** Lars Norup
Language(s): Danish
ADVERTISING RATES:
Full Page Colour .... DKK 10807,50
SCC .... DKK 42,50
REGIONAL DAILY & SUNDAY NEWSPAPERS: Regional Daily Newspapers

VILLABYERNE 630160D72-810
Editorial: Ordrupvej 101 3. sal, 2920 CHARLOTTENLUND **Tel:** 39 63 51 11
Fax: 39 63 81 36
Email: redaktion@villabyerne.dk **Web site:** http://www.villabyerne.dk
Freq: 104 issues yearly; **Cover Price:** Free; **Circ:** 37,695
Language(s): Danish
ADVERTISING RATES:
Full Page Colour .... DKK 44368
SCC .... DKK 99
LOCAL NEWSPAPERS

VINBLADET 758842D22A-115
Editorial: Postboks 75, Vandværksvej 11, 5690 TOMMERUP **Tel:** 64 75 22 84 **Fax:** 64 75 28 44
Email: vinbladet@vinbladet.dk **Web site:** http://www.vinbladet.dk
Date Established: 1992; **Freq:** 6 issues yearly; **Circ:** 5,000
Language(s): Danish
BUSINESS: FOOD

VISITOR 3005D11A-30
Editorial: HORESTA, Vodroffsvej 32, 1900 FREDERIKSBERG C **Tel:** 35 24 80 80
Fax: 35 24 80 85
Email: vistor@horesta.dk **Web site:** http://www.horesta.dk/Service/Om%20Horesta/Medier/VISITOR.aspx
Freq: Monthly; **Circ:** 18,885
Profile: Magazine for those involved in the hotel, catering and tourist industries.
Language(s): Danish
ADVERTISING RATES:
Full Page Colour .... DKK 20100
SCC .... DKK 341
BUSINESS: CATERING: Catering, Hotels & Restaurants

VOGNMALEREN 1791815D14A-249
Editorial: Lersø Park Allé 109, DK-2100 KØBENHAVN Ø **Tel:** 39 16 79 00 **Fax:** 39 16 79 10
Email: maler@maler.dk **Web site:** http://www.maler.dk
Freq: Quarterly; **Circ:** 2,000
Language(s): Danish
BUSINESS: COMMERCE, INDUSTRY & MANAGEMENT

VORES BØRN 3606D74D-150
Editorial: Oxygen A/S, Thoravej 13, 3.sal, 2400 COPENHAGEN **Tel:** 39 16 26 16
Email: voresborn@oxygen.dk **Web site:** http://www.voresborn.dk
Date Established: 1989; **Freq:** Monthly; **Circ:** 25,000
Executive Editor: Katrine Boyer
Profile: Magazine covering all aspects of pregnancy and parenthood.
Language(s): Danish
Readership: Aimed at mothers-to-be and parents with children aged up to 7 years.
ADVERTISING RATES:
Full Page Colour .... DKK 28500
SCC .... DKK 259.80
Copy instructions: *Copy Date:* 30 days prior to publication date
CONSUMER: WOMEN'S INTEREST CONSUMER MAGAZINES: Child Care

VORT LANDBOBLAD 630174D72-885
Editorial: Himmerlandsgade 150, 9600 AARS
Tel: 98 62 17 11 **Fax:** 98 62 27 99
Email: redaktion@aarsavis.dk **Web site:** http://www.aarsavis.dk
Freq: Weekly; **Cover Price:** Free; **Circ:** 18,902
Editor: Torkil Christensen
Language(s): Danish
ADVERTISING RATES:
Full Page Colour .... DKK 8902,20
SCC .... DKK 38,53
LOCAL NEWSPAPERS

WASTE MANAGEMENT & RESEARCH 3326D57-50
Editorial: Overgaden Oven Vandet 48 E, DK-1415 COPENHAGEN **Tel:** 32 96 15 88 **Fax:** 32 96 15 84
Email: wmr@iswa.org **Web site:** http://wmr.sagepub.com
Freq: 6 issues yearly; **Circ:** 2,000
Profile: International journal published by the International Solid Waste Association, containing articles related to waste management, book reviews and research papers.
Language(s): English
Readership: Read by scientists, researchers and practitioners within the field.

WASTE MANAGEMENT WORLD 3156D32B-120
Editorial: Vesterbrogade 74, 3rd floor, 1620 KØBENHAVN V **Tel:** 32 96 15 88 **Fax:** 32 96 15 84
Email: iswa@iswa.dk **Web site:** http://www.iswa.org
Freq: 6 times a year; **Cover Price:** Free; **Circ:** 12,000 Unique Users
Editor: Peter Hurup
Profile: International magazine covering all aspects of waste management. Includes news and information from around the world, book reviews and a calendar of forthcoming meetings and events.
Language(s): English
Readership: Aimed at companies involved in waste management, university professors and students.
ADVERTISING RATES:
Full Page Colour .... DKK 31800
SCC .... DKK 365
BUSINESS: LOCAL GOVERNMENT, LEISURE & RECREATION: Public Health & Cleaning

WENDY 3698D81D-200
Editorial: Vognmagergade 11, 1148 KØBENHAVN K
Tel: 70 20 50 35 **Fax:** 33 30 57 60
Email: wendy@tsf.egmont.com **Web site:** http://www.wendy.dk
Freq: 26 issues yearly; **Circ:** 29,000
Editor: Lene Fabricius Christensen
Profile: Publication for young people interested in horses.
Language(s): Danish
Readership: Aimed mainly at girls aged between 6 and 16 years old.
CONSUMER: ANIMALS & PETS: Horses & Ponies

WHERE2GO 1792485D73-351
Editorial: Otto Mønsteds gade 3, 1571 COPENHAGEN **Tel:** 72 34 12 00 **Fax:** 72 34 12 01
Web site: http://www.where2go.dk
Freq: Monthly; **Circ:** 47,143
Executive Editor: Søren McGuire
Language(s): Danish
ADVERTISING RATES:
Full Page Colour .... DKK 30800
SCC .... DKK 358.10
CONSUMER: NATIONAL & INTERNATIONAL PERIODICALS

WINDPOWER MONTHLY 758843D58-115
Editorial: P.O. Box 100, 8250 EGAA **Tel:** 86 36 54 65
Fax: 86 36 56 26
Email: mail@windpower-monthly.com **Web site:** http://www.windpower-monthly.com
Freq: Monthly; **Circ:** 5,000
Language(s): Danish
ADVERTISING RATES:
Full Page Colour .... DKK 27600
SCC .... DKK 368
BUSINESS: ENERGY, FUEL & NUCLEAR

WOMAN 630492D74A-150
Editorial: Finsensvej 6 D, 2000 FREDERIKSBERG
Tel: 70 22 00 55
Email: metten@benjamin.dk **Web site:** http://www.woman.dk
Date Established: 2000; **Freq:** Monthly; **Circ:** 51,010
Executive Editor: Helle Blok
Profile: Women's interest magazine featuring fashion, beauty and lifestyle articles.
Language(s): Danish
Readership: Aimed at young women aged between 18 and 35 years.
ADVERTISING RATES:
Full Page Colour .... DKK 49500
SCC .... DKK 416
Copy instructions: *Copy Date:* 30 days prior to publication date
CONSUMER: WOMEN'S INTEREST CONSUMER MAGAZINES: Women's Interest

ZONETERAPEUTEN 3289D56A-200
Editorial: Dyrehavevej 90, 5800 NYBORG
Tel: 65 31 28 85 **Fax:** 70 27 99 50
Email: zoneterapeuten@fdz.dk **Web site:** http://www.fdz.dk
Freq: Monthly; **Circ:** 2,000
Profile: Publication about zone therapy.
Language(s): Danish
ADVERTISING RATES:
Full Page Colour .... DKK 5000
SCC .... DKK 126,13

Estonia

Time Difference: GMT + 2 hrs (EET - Eastern European Time)
National Telephone Code: +372
Continent: Europe
Capital: Tallinn
Principal Language: Estonian, English, Finnish, Russian, Ukrainian
Population: 1315912
Monetary Unit: Kroon (EEK)
EMBASSY HIGH
COMMISSION: Embassy of the Republic of Estonia: 16 Hyde Park Gate, Kensington, London, SW7 5DG
Tel: 020 7589 3428
Fax: 020 7589 3430
Email: london@mfa.ee,
Website: http://www.estonia.gov.uk

ÄRIPÄEV 1202461EE65A-5
Editorial: Pärnu mnt. 105, 19094 TALLINN
Tel: 6 67 01 11 **Fax:** 6 67 02 65
Email: aripaev@aripaev.ee **Web site:** http://www.ap3.ee
Date Established: 1989; **Freq:** Daily - Published Monday to Friday; **Circ:** 20,340
Profile: Business newspaper with emphasis on business news from Estonia and news from financial markets. Includes surveys of currency rates, banking services and stock prices. Each issue dedicates two pages for news from abroad and features a selection of interviews, surveys, problem stories, reports and personal or corporate profiles.
Language(s): Estonian
Readership: Aimed at corporate executives and business managers.
ADVERTISING RATES:
Full Page Colour .... EEK 64900.00
Mechanical Data: Type Area: 367 x 277mm, Col Length: 367mm, Film: Positive, No. of Columns (Display): 6, Print Process: Offset, Page Width: 277mm
Copy instructions: *Copy Date:* Deadline for booking adspace is until 3 pm 2 working days prior to publication
Supplement(s): Puhkepäev - 52xY
NATIONAL DAILY & SUNDAY NEWSPAPERS: National Daily Newspapers

THE BALTIC GUIDE 1600375EE89A-1
Editorial: L. Koidula 5, 10125 TALLINN
Tel: 6 01 33 35 **Fax:** 6 01 33 24
Email: editorial@balticguide.ee **Web site:** http://www.balticguide.ee
Date Established: 1993; **Freq:** Monthly; **Cover Price:** Free; **Circ:** 70,000
Usual Pagination: 50
Editor: Mari Tuovinen; **Advertising Manager:** Marge Kato
Profile: Magazine featuring information on travel, tourism and entertainment.
Language(s): Estonian; Finnish
CONSUMER: HOLIDAYS & TRAVEL: Travel

DEN ZA DNJOM 762360EE65J-1
Editorial: Peterburi mnt 53, TALLINN 11415
Tel: 6 78 82 88 **Fax:** 6 78 82 90
Email: toimetus@dzd.ee **Web site:** http://www.dzd.ee
Freq: Weekly - Published on Friday; **Cover Price:** EEK 15,9; **Circ:** 14,000
Profile: Newspaper focusing on national news, politics, business and sport.
Language(s): Estonian; Russian
ADVERTISING RATES:
Full Page Colour .... EEK 33600.00
Mechanical Data: Type Area: 260 x 372mm
NATIONAL DAILY & SUNDAY NEWSPAPERS: National Weekly Newspapers

EESTI EKSPRESS 1202518EE65J-2
Editorial: Narva mnt. 11 E, 10151 TALLINN
Tel: 66 98 030 **Fax:** 66 98 154
Email: ekspress@ekspress.ee **Web site:** http://www.ekspress.ee
ISSN: 1406-1104
Date Established: 1989; **Freq:** Weekly - Published on Wednesday; **Cover Price:** EEK 19.80; **Circ:** 40,900
Editor-in-Chief: Priit Hõbemägi; **Publisher:** Hans Luik
Profile: Newspaper focusing on national and international news, politics, entertainment and sport.
Language(s): Estonian
ADVERTISING RATES:
Full Page Colour .... EEK 4200.00
Mechanical Data: Type Area: 260 x 348mm, Bleed Size: 292 x 390mm
NATIONAL DAILY & SUNDAY NEWSPAPERS: National Weekly Newspapers

EESTI PÄEVALEHT 1202538EE65A-15
Editorial: Narva mnt. 13, 10151 TALLINN
Tel: 6 80 44 00 **Fax:** 6 80 44 01
Email: mail@epl.ee **Web site:** http://www.epl.ee
Date Established: 1905; **Freq:** Daily - Published Monday - Saturday; **Cover Price:** EEK 10.00; **Circ:** 35,500
Editor: Lea Larin; **Managing Director:** Mihkel Reinsalu; **Advertising Director:** Mihkel Reinsalu; **Publisher:** Mihkel Reinsalu
Profile: Newspaper covering national and international news, business, finance, culture and sport.
Language(s): Estonian
ADVERTISING RATES:
Full Page Colour $4200.00
Mechanical Data: Type Area: 562 x 348mm, Col Length: 536mm, Film: Positive, emulsion side down, Print Process: Offset, Screen: 34 lpc, Page Width: 348mm
Copy instructions: *Copy Date:* 2 days prior to publication date
Supplement(s): Ärileht - 52xY
NATIONAL DAILY & SUNDAY NEWSPAPERS: National Daily Newspapers

KOMSOMOLSKAJA PRAVDA 1858423EE65J-10
Editorial: Läänemere tee 70/1, office 30, TALLINN 13914 **Tel:** 622 8990 **Fax:** 6228991
Email: info@kompravda.eu **Web site:** http://www.kompravda.eu
Freq: Weekly; **Circ:** 12,900
Editor-in-Chief: Oleg Samorodni; **Publisher:** Igor Teterin
Profile: Newspaper focusing on national and international news, culture, history, social life, tourism and sport.
Language(s): Russian
NATIONAL DAILY & SUNDAY NEWSPAPERS: National Weekly Newspapers

KROONIKA 1600438EE74Q-50
Editorial: Maakri 23 A, 10145 TALLINN
Tel: 66 62 660 **Fax:** 66 62 564
Email: kroonika@kroonika.ee **Web site:** http://www.kroonika.ee
Date Established: 1996; **Freq:** Weekly - Published every Wednesday; **Annual Sub.:** EEK 540.00; **Circ:** 45,000
Editor: Aive Lauriste
Profile: Magazine focusing on celebrities and lifestyle.
Language(s): Estonian
Readership: Aimed primarily at women.
CONSUMER: WOMEN'S INTEREST CONSUMER MAGAZINES: Lifestyle

KULDNE BÖRS 1644267EE2A-2
Editorial: Parnu 102c, 11312 TALLINN
Tel: 6 20 88 01 **Fax:** 6 20 88 11
Email: kuldnebors@sanoma.ee **Web site:** http://www.kuldnebors.ee/index.mec
Freq: Quarterly; **Circ:** 15,000
Profile: Magazine of advertisements.
Language(s): Estonian
BUSINESS: COMMUNICATIONS, ADVERTISING & MARKETING

MAALEHT 1600363EE80-200
Editorial: Toompuiestee 16, 10137 TALLINN
Tel: 661 3300 **Fax:** 661 3344
Email: ml@maaleht.ee **Web site:** http://www.maaleht.ee
Date Established: 1987; **Freq:** Weekly - Published on Thursday; **Annual Sub.:** EEK 560.00; **Circ:** 50,000

Editor: Lii Sammler; **Editor-in-Chief:** Sulev Valner; **Advertising Manager:** Kaja Prügi; **Publisher:** Kadi Lambot
Profile: Newspaper focusing on rural life.
Language(s): Estonian
CONSUMER: RURAL & REGIONAL INTEREST

MK-ESTONIA 1858421EE65J-9

Editorial: Pärnu mnt 139f, 11317 TALLINN
Tel: 654 1640 **Fax:** 654 1650
Email: mke@sky.ee **Web site:** http://www.mk-est.ee/
Freq: Weekly; **Circ:** 12,000
Editor: Liana Turpakova; **Editor-in-Chief:** Pavel Ivanov; **Publisher:** Margus Merima
Profile: Newspaper focusing on national and international news, culture, history, social life, tourism and sport.
Language(s): Estonian
NATIONAL DAILY & SUNDAY NEWSPAPERS: National Weekly Newspapers

---

MOLODJOZ ESTONIJ 1202494EE65A-32

Editorial: Tartu mnt. 53, 10115 TALLINN
Tel: 62 30 144 **Fax:** 62 30 171
Email: moles@moles.ee **Web site:** http://www.moles.ee
Date Established: 1997; **Freq:** Daily - Published Monday to Saturday; **Circ:** 7,800
Profile: Newspaper focusing on national and international news, politics, business and sport.
Language(s): Russian
NATIONAL DAILY & SUNDAY NEWSPAPERS: National Daily Newspapers

---

NAISED 1896484EE74A-102

Editorial: Maakri 23a, 10145 TALLINN **Tel:** 6662120
Email: inga.raitar@kirjastus.ee **Web site:** http://ajakirinaised.naistemaailm.ee/
Circ: 50,000
Editor: Kaire Kenk; **Managing Editor:** Pille-Mai Helemae
Profile: Magazine focused on women's interests.
Language(s): Estonian
CONSUMER: WOMEN'S INTEREST CONSUMER MAGAZINES: Women's Interest

---

POSTIMEES 1202506EE65A-30

Editorial: Maakri 23 A, 10145 TALLINN
Tel: 6 66 22 02 **Fax:** 6 66 22 01
Email: postimees@postimees.ee **Web site:** http://www.postimees.ee
Date Established: 1857; **Freq:** Daily - Published Monday to Saturday; **Circ:** 63,000
Editor: Eva Tammsaar; **News Editor:** Britt Rosen; **Executive Editor:** Aarne Seppel; **Advertising Manager:** Liis Idavain; **Advertising Director:** Marika Jahilo
Profile: National newspaper focusing on national and international news, politics, business and sport.
Language(s): Estonian
ADVERTISING RATES:
Full Page Colour .... EEK 68000.00
Agency Commission: 10%
Mechanical Data: Type Area: 289 x 381mm, Col Widths (Display): 44mm, No. of Columns (Display): 6
Supplement(s): Arter - 52xY Televisioon - 52xY Luup - 26xY.
NATIONAL DAILY & SUNDAY NEWSPAPERS: National Daily Newspapers

---

POSTIMEES (RUSSIAN EDITION) 1852862EE65A-34

Editorial: Maakri 23a, TALLINN 10145
Tel: 6 66 22 02 **Fax:** 6 66 22 01
Email: vene@postimees.ee **Web site:** http://rus.postimees.ee
Date Established: 2005; **Freq:** Daily - Published five days a week, from Monday to Friday; **Circ:** 15,000
Editor: Stanislav Bulganin; **Advertising Director:** Marika Jahilo
Profile: Includes stories translated from Estonian-language Postimees as well as original stories by Russian-language editorial board. Published on Fridays is Postimees vene keeles Extra with chalk paper covers and its own TV guide.
Language(s): Russian
ADVERTISING RATES:
Full Page Colour .... EUR 4349.99
Mechanical Data: Type Area: 289 x 381mm
NATIONAL DAILY & SUNDAY NEWSPAPERS: National Daily Newspapers

---

PRIVAT-INFO 1644383EE2A-3

Editorial: Pärnu mnt 67 A, 15043 TALLINN
Tel: 6 30 47 04 **Fax:** 6 46 14 97
Email: privat@privatinfo.ee **Web site:** http://www.privatinfo.ee
Freq: Weekly; **Circ:** 11,500
Profile: Magazine of free advertisements, companies contacts etc.
Language(s): Estonian
BUSINESS: COMMUNICATIONS, ADVERTISING & MARKETING

SEKRETAR.EE 1644461EE14G-1

Formerly: Sekretar
Editorial: Lootse 2B, 11415 TALLINN **Tel:** 5680 90 86
Email: sekretar@sekretar.ee **Web site:** http://www.sekretar.ee
Freq: Quarterly; **Circ:** 10,000
Profile: Magazine about company secretaries.
Language(s): Estonian
BUSINESS: COMMERCE, INDUSTRY & MANAGEMENT: Company Secretaries

---

SL ÕHTULEHT 1201182EE65A-25

Formerly: Õhtuleht
Editorial: Narva mnt 13 III korrus, 10502 TALLINN
Tel: 6 14 40 00 **Fax:** 6 14 40 01
Email: leht@ohtuleht.ee **Web site:** http://www.ohtuleht.ee
ISSN: 1406-1236
Date Established: 1944; **Freq:** Daily - Published Monday to Saturday; **Circ:** 62,000
Managing Director: Kristjan Mauer; **Advertising Manager:** Toomas Tõlp
Profile: Tabloid newspaper focusing on entertainment, sports, national and international news and politics.
Language(s): Estonian
NATIONAL DAILY & SUNDAY NEWSPAPERS: National Daily Newspapers

---

SOOV 1644472EE2A-4

Editorial: Maakri 23A, TALLINN 10145 **Tel:** 6 662001
Fax: 6 662003
Email: soov@soov.ee **Web site:** http://www.soov.ee
Freq: 104 issues yearly; **Circ:** 8,700
Profile: Magazine of advertisments.
Language(s): Estonian
BUSINESS: COMMUNICATIONS, ADVERTISING & MARKETING

TALLINN THIS WEEK 1600456EE89A-2

Editorial: Maakri 23 A, 10145 TALLINN
Tel: 6 66 26 73 **Fax:** 6 66 25 64
Email: ttw@hot.ee **Web site:** http://www.ttw.ee
Date Established: 1989; **Freq:** 6 issues yearly; **Circ:** 65,000
Managing Editor: Liina Teder
Profile: Magazine featuring tourist information about Tallinn.
Language(s): English
Readership: Read by tourists.
CONSUMER: HOLIDAYS & TRAVEL: Travel

TERVIS PLUSS 1644533EE56A-1

Editorial: Maakri 23 a, 10145 TALLINN
Tel: 6 66 26 00 **Fax:** 6 66 25 57
Email: sirje.maasikmae@kirjastus.ee **Web site:** http://www.tervispluss.ee
Freq: Monthly; **Circ:** 22,000
Profile: Magazine about healthcare and medical news.
Language(s): Estonian
BUSINESS: HEALTH & MEDICAL

Finland

Time Difference: GMT + 2 hrs (EET - Eastern European Time)
National Telephone Code: +358
Continent: Europe
Capital: Helsinki
Principal Language: Finnish, Swedish
Population: 5238460
Monetary Unit: Euro (EUR)

EMBASSY HIGH COMMISSION: Finnish Embassy: 38 Chesham Place, London SW1X 8HW,
Tel: 020 7838 6200
Fax: 020 7235 3680
Email: sanomat.lon@formin.fi
Website: http://www.finemb.org.uk

---

60 DEGREES NORTH 706029L21A-41

Formerly: Luonnonvara
Editorial: PL 30/ Hallituskatu 3 A, 00023 VALTIONEUVOSTO **Tel:** 9 16 05 33 26
Fax: 9 16 05 42 02
Email: tiedotus@mmm.fi **Web site:** http://60north.mmm.fi
ISSN: 1239-5862
Date Established: 1997; **Freq:** Half-yearly; **Cover Price:** Free; **Circ:** 3,000
Usual Pagination: 32
Editor-in-Chief: Pekka Väisänen; **Managing Editor:** Mervi Ukkonen
Profile: Customer and personnel magazine by the Ministry of Forestry and Agriculture.
Language(s): English; Finnish

---

7 PÄIVÄÄ 15238L73-20

Editorial: PL 124/ Pursimiehenkatu 29-31 A, 00151 HELSINKI **Tel:** 9 86 21 70 00 **Fax:** 9 86 21 71 77
Email: toimitus@seiska.fi **Web site:** http://www.seiska.fi
ISSN: 1236-2409
Date Established: 1992; **Freq:** Weekly; **Circ:** 211,707
Usual Pagination: 90
Editor-in-Chief: Eeva-Helena Jokitaipale; **Managing Editor:** Jari Peltomäki
Profile: Magazine focusing on gossip and rumours concerning celebrities. Also contains TV-guide.
Language(s): Finnish
Readership: Men and women aged 20 to 44 years.
ADVERTISING RATES:
Full Page Colour .... EUR 8300
SCC .... EUR 74.10
Agency Commission: 15%
Mechanical Data: Type Area: 192 x 265mm, Col Length: 207mm, Page Width: 280mm, Print Process: offset, Screen: 60 lpc, Film: negative
CONSUMER: NATIONAL & INTERNATIONAL PERIODICALS

@CSC-SIVUSTO 753112L5B-1

Editorial: PL 405/ Keilaranta 14, 02101 ESPOO
Tel: 9 45 72 001 **Fax:** 9 45 72 302
Email: paavo.ahonen@csc.fi **Web site:** http://www.csc.fi/csc/julkaisut/atcsc
ISSN: 1238-4798
Date Established: 2001; **Freq:** Quarterly; **Cover Price:** Free; **Circ:** 3,500 Unique Users
Usual Pagination: 52
Profile: Magazine that provides information about CSC's networks, computers and scientific computing services.
Language(s): Finnish
BUSINESS: COMPUTERS & AUTOMATION: Data Processing

A & O 749152L87-1_50

Editorial: Kalastajankatu 1 B, 20100 TURKU
Tel: 2 25 15 385 **Fax:** 2 25 15 384
Email: tiedotus@ao-media.net **Web site:** http://www.ao-media.net
ISSN: 1457-375X
Date Established: 2000; **Freq:** Quarterly; **Cover Price:** Free; **Circ:** 65,000
Usual Pagination: 20
Editor-in-Chief: Kimmo Jalonen; **Managing Director:** Kimmo Jalonen
Profile: Magazine about religious matters in the Turku and Pori region.
Language(s): Finnish
ADVERTISING RATES:
Full Page Colour .... EUR 1750.00
SCC .... EUR 12.50
CONSUMER: RELIGIOUS

A. VOGELIN TERVEYSUUTISET 705306L37-40

Formerly: A. Vogelin terveydenhoitouutiset
Editorial: Purjeentekijänkuja 7 B 15, 00210 HELSINKI
Tel: 9 45 59 17 24 **Fax:** 9 45 59 17 23
Email: elisa@rosenberg.fi **Web site:** http://www.terveydenhoitouutiset.fi
ISSN: 0357-2226
Date Established: 1944; **Freq:** Quarterly; **Circ:** 25,000
Usual Pagination: 40
Profile: Journal about pharmaceutical products based on herbs and plants.
Language(s): Finnish
ADVERTISING RATES:
Full Page Colour .... EUR 700
Mechanical Data: Type Area: 160 x 246mm, Print Process: offset
BUSINESS: PHARMACEUTICAL & CHEMISTS

AAMULEHTI 15219L67B-20

Editorial: PL 327, 33101 TAMPERE **Tel:** 10 66 51 11
Fax: 10 66 53 140
Email: al.kotimaa@aamulehti.fi **Web site:** http://www.aamulehti.fi
ISSN: 0355-6913
Date Established: 1881; **Freq:** Daily; **Circ:** 131,539
Usual Pagination: 30
Editor: Markku Huotari; **Editor-in-Chief:** Jorma Pokkinen; **Managing Editor:** Kari Ikonen
Profile: Regional newspaper mainly for the Tampere region.
Language(s): Finnish
ADVERTISING RATES:
Full Page Colour .... EUR 21756
SCC .... EUR 51.80
Mechanical Data: Col Length: 525mm, No. of Columns (Display): 8, Col Widths (Display): 44mm, Page Width: 380mm
Editions:
Aamulehti Ajankohtaistoimitus
Aamulehti Kulttuuritoimitus
Aamulehti Taloustoimitus
Aamulehti Ulkomaantoimitus
Aamulehti Urheilutoimitus
Aamulehti Uutistoimitus
Aamulehti Verkkotoimitus
REGIONAL DAILY & SUNDAY NEWSPAPERS: Regional Daily Newspapers

---

AAMULEHTI MÄNTTÄ 705854L67E-2

Editorial: Seppälänpuistotie 8, 35800 MÄNTTÄ
Tel: 10 66 53 250
Email: sirkka.iso-ettala@aamulehti.fi **Web site:** http://www.aamulehti.fi
Profile: Mänttä the regional office of Aamulehti.
Language(s): Finnish
REGIONAL DAILY & SUNDAY NEWSPAPERS: Regional Offices

AAMULEHTI MORO 712938L67H-4

Editorial: PL 327/ Itäinenkatu 11, 33101 TAMPERE
Tel: 10 66 51 11 **Fax:** 10 66 53 140
Email: moro@aamulehti.fi **Web site:** http://www.aamulehti.fi
Circ: 138,403
Usual Pagination: 24
Profile: Special city edition of Aamulehti.
Language(s): Finnish
ADVERTISING RATES:
Full Page Colour .... EUR 4700.16
SCC .... EUR 26.20
Mechanical Data: No. of Columns (Display): 5, Col Widths (Display): 44mm, Col Length: 380mm, Page Width: 236mm, Type Area: 236mm x 360mm
REGIONAL DAILY & SUNDAY NEWSPAPERS: Regional Colour Supplements

---

AAMULEHTI ORIVESI 706123L67E-4

Editorial: Keskustie 41 B 14, 35300 ORIVESI
Tel: 10 66 53 250 **Fax:** 3 33 57 019
Email: paula.latva@aamulehti.fi **Web site:** http://www.aamulehti.fi
Profile: Orivesi regional office of Aamulehti.
Language(s): Finnish
REGIONAL DAILY & SUNDAY NEWSPAPERS: Regional Offices

AAMULEHTI PARKANO 705710L67E-6

Editorial: PL 47/ Viinikanrinne 1 A 5, 39701 PARKANO **Tel:** 10 66 53 248 **Fax:** 3 44 80 368
Email: aulis.alatalo@aamulehti.fi **Web site:** http://www.aamulehti.fi
Profile: Parkano regional office of Aamulehti.
Language(s): Finnish
REGIONAL DAILY & SUNDAY NEWSPAPERS: Regional Offices

AAMULEHTI VALKEAKOSKI 705774L67E-10

Editorial: Valtakatu 12, 37600 VALKEAKOSKI
Tel: 10 66 51 11 **Fax:** 3 58 42 780
Email: juha.karilainen@aamulehti.fi **Web site:** http://www.aamulehti.fi
Profile: Valkeakoski regional office of Aamulehti.
Language(s): Finnish
REGIONAL DAILY & SUNDAY NEWSPAPERS: Regional Offices

AAMULEHTI VALO 712939L67H-2

Formerly: Aamulehti Allakka
Editorial: PL 327/ Itäinenkatu 11, 33101 TAMPERE
Tel: 10 66 51 11 **Fax:** 10 66 53 130
Email: al.valo@aamulehti.fi **Web site:** http://valo.aamulehti.fi
Freq: Weekly - Friday; **Circ:** 138,403
Usual Pagination: 40
Editor: Kaija Toivonen; **Editor-in-Chief:** Jorma Pokkinen
Profile: Special Tampere city events-guide with film, TV and radio information.
Language(s): Finnish
ADVERTISING RATES:
Full Page Colour .... EUR 4700.16
Mechanical Data: Type Area: 236mm x 360mm, Col Length: 380mm, Page Width: 260mm, No. of Columns (Display): 5
REGIONAL DAILY & SUNDAY NEWSPAPERS: Regional Colour Supplements

---

AAMULEHTI VAMMALA 705587L67E-12

Formerly: Aamulehti Sastamala
Editorial: Puistokatu 28, 38200 VAMMALA
Tel: 3 51 12 382 **Fax:** 35142048
Email: riitta-liisa.pirttikoski@aamulehti.fi **Web site:** http://www.aamulehti.fi
Profile: Vammala and Sastamala regional office of Aamulehti.
Language(s): Finnish
REGIONAL DAILY & SUNDAY NEWSPAPERS: Regional Offices

AAMUPOSTI 15214L67B-6700

Formerly: Riihimäen Sanomat
Editorial: PL 14/ Kauppakatu 12, 11101 RIIHIMAKI
Tel: 20 77 03 462

Email: toimitus.aamuposti@lehtiyhtyma.fi **Web site:** http://www.aamuposti.fi
ISSN: 0356-1674
Date Established: 1914
Circ: 22,212
Usual Pagination: 20
Managing Editor: Pekka Liukka
Profile: Regional newspaper issued in Riihimäki, Hausjärvi, Loppi, Janakkala, Nurmijärvi, Tuusula, Hyvinkää and Tervakoski.
Language(s): Finnish
ADVERTISING RATES:
Full Page Colour .... EUR 7828
SCC .... EUR 19
Agency Commission: 15%
Mechanical Data: Page Width: 380mm, No. of Columns (Display): 8, Col Widths (Display): 44mm, Col Length: 515mm, Print Process: offset
REGIONAL DAILY & SUNDAY NEWSPAPERS: Regional Daily Newspapers

AAMUPOSTI HYVINKÄÄ
1834447L67E-7
Editorial: PL 93/ Kauppalankatu 7-11, 05801 HYVINKÄÄ **Tel:** 20 77 03 461 **Fax:** 20 77 03 025
Email: toimitus.aamuposti@lehtiyhtyma.fi **Web site:** http://www.aamuposti.fi
Circ: 22,174
Managing Editor: Eero Pulkkinen
Profile: Regional newspaper issued in Riihimäki, Hausjärvi, Loppi, Janakkala, Nurmijärvi, Tuusula, Hyvinkää and Tervakoski.
Language(s): Finnish
ADVERTISING RATES:
Full Page Colour .... EUR 7622
SCC .... EUR 18.50
Mechanical Data: Col Length: 515mm, Page Width: 380mm
REGIONAL DAILY & SUNDAY NEWSPAPERS: Regional Offices

AAMUSET
705085L72-10
Editorial: PL 600/ Yliopistonkatu 14, 20101 TURKU
Tel: 2 26 93 900 **Fax:** 2 26 94 51
Email: aamuset@aamuset.fi **Web site:** http://www.aamuset.fi
Date Established: 1981; **Freq:** 104 issues yearly; **Cover Price:** Free; **Circ:** 136,600
Usual Pagination: 36
Editor-in-Chief: Lasse Virtanen
Profile: Newspaper distributed in Turku, Raisio, Kieto, Naantali, Kaarina, Masku, Nousiainen, Merimasku, Rymättylä, Rusko, Vahto, Piikkiö and Parainen.
Language(s): Finnish
ADVERTISING RATES:
Full Page Colour .... EUR 7227
SCC .... EUR 33
Agency Commission: 15%
Mechanical Data: Type Area: 254 x 365mm, No. of Columns (Display): 6, Col Widths (Display): 39mm, Col Length: 365mm, Page Width: 254mm
Copy instructions: *Copy Date:* 5 days prior to publication date
LOCAL NEWSPAPERS

AARRE
1852036L46-203
Editorial: PL 440/Simonkatu 6, 00101 HELSINKI
Tel: 20 41 32 155 **Fax:** 20 41 62 233
Email: toimitus@aarrelehti.fi **Web site:** http://www.aarrelehti.fi
Date Established: 2008; **Freq:** Monthly - Published 10/year; **Circ:** 16,575
Editor-in-Chief: Mari Ikonen
Profile: Magazine about forestry.
Language(s): Finnish
Readership: Forest owners.
ADVERTISING RATES:
Full Page Colour .... EUR 3300
SCC .... EUR 28.40
Copy instructions: *Copy Date:* 20 days prior to publication date

ABO
761345L56P-9
Formerly: Sydämestä sydämeen
Editorial: Veripalvelu, Kivihaantie 7, 00310 HELSINKI
Tel: 9 58 011 **Fax:** 9 58 01 329
Email: toimitus@mediafocus.fi **Web site:** http://www.veripalvelu.fi/www/abo
ISSN: 0785-5796
Freq: Annual; **Cover Price:** Free; **Circ:** 60,000
Usual Pagination: 24
Editor-in-Chief: Satu Pastila
Profile: Magazine about blood donating.
Language(s): Finnish
Readership: Customers of Finnish Red Cross.
BUSINESS: HEALTH & MEDICAL: Casualty & Emergency

ÅBO UNDERRÄTTELSER
15220L67B-2100
Editorial: PB 211/ Auragatan 1 B, 3 vån, 20101 ÅBO
Tel: 2 27 49 900 **Fax:** 2 23 11 394
Email: nyheter@fabsy.fi **Web site:** http://www.abounderrattelser.fi
ISSN: 0785-398X
Date Established: 1824
Circ: 7,500
Usual Pagination: 24
Profile: Independent newspaper issued in Turku, Kaarina, Naantali, Raisio, Parainen, Nauvo, Korppoo, Houtskari, Iniö, Kemiö, Dragsfjärd, Västanfjärd and Särkisalo.
Language(s): Swedish
ADVERTISING RATES:
Full Page Colour .... EUR 2500
SCC .... EUR 11.40
Agency Commission: 15%
Mechanical Data: Page Width: 260mm, Col Widths (Display): 40mm, No. of Columns (Display): 6, Type Area: 260 x 355mm, Film: negative, Screen: 34 lpc
Copy instructions: *Copy Date:* 10 days prior to publication date
Editions:
Åbo Underrättelser Internetredaktionen
REGIONAL DAILY & SUNDAY NEWSPAPERS: Regional Daily Newspapers

AESCULAPIUS
763808L56A-1
Editorial: PL 65/ Orionintie 1A, 02101 ESPOO
Tel: 10 42 61 **Fax:** 10 42 62 020
Email: corpcom@orion.fi **Web site:** http://www.orion.fi
ISSN: 0400-6747
Date Established: 1953; **Freq:** Monthly; **Circ:** 37,000
Usual Pagination: 44
Editor-in-Chief: Pekka Järvensivu
Profile: Customer-magazine by Orion about medicine.
Language(s): Finnish
Readership: Aesculapius is aimed at doctors, Galenos at pharmacies, Orion at share-holders.

AGENDA
1793711L14C-1
Editorial: PL 123, 00531 HELSINKI **Tel:** 45 63 85 302
Email: articles@agendafin.com **Web site:** http://www.agendafin.com
Date Established: 2006; **Freq:** Quarterly; **Circ:** 2,000
Editor-in-Chief: Denisa Udroiu
Profile: Business-like magazine, covering Finnish politics, Finnish social topics, Finnish culture and lifestyle. In every issue, a new country is presented.
Language(s): English
Readership: International business people and travllers.
ADVERTISING RATES:
Full Page Colour .... EUR 1750.00
Mechanical Data: Type Area: 210 x 280mm

AGRIFORUM
1638121L21B-10
Editorial: Mäntyläntie 16 A 4, 80220 JOENSUU
Tel: 500 67 43 12 **Fax:** 13 89 73 94
Email: toimitus@forumlehdet.fi **Web site:** http://www.forumlehdet.fi
Date Established: 1996; **Freq:** 6 issues yearly; **Circ:** 27,000
Usual Pagination: 24
Managing Editor: Sirkku Mikkonen
Profile: Magazine about entrepreneurship in agriculture and forestry.
Language(s): Finnish

AHJO
705329L14L-2_5
Editorial: PL 107/ Hakaniemenranta 1, 6 krs, 00531 HELSINKI **Tel:** 20 77 40 01 **Fax:** 20 77 41 240
Email: ahjo@metallililitto.fi **Web site:** http://www.ahjo.fi
ISSN: 0355-922X
Freq: 26 issues yearly; **Circ:** 173,000
Usual Pagination: 32
Editor-in-Chief: Heikki Piskonen
Profile: Journal of the Union of Metal Workers.
Language(s): Finnish; Swedish
Readership: Read by members.
ADVERTISING RATES:
Full Page Colour .... EUR 3200.00
SCC .... EUR 26.60
Agency Commission: 15%
Mechanical Data: Print Process: offset, Bleed Size: 225 x 300mm, Type Area: 225 x 300mm, No. of Columns (Display): 4, Col Widths (Display): 47mm
BUSINESS: COMMERCE, INDUSTRY & MANAGEMENT: Trade Unions

AHT-TEKNISET
706012L49C-5
Editorial: Selkämerenkuja 1A, 00180 HELSINKI
Tel: 50 44 49 908 **Fax:** 9 69 48 043
Email: kai.nieminen@aht-tekniset.fi **Web site:** http://www.aht-tekniset.fi
Freq: Quarterly; **Circ:** 1,500
Usual Pagination: 12
Editor-in-Chief: Kai Nieminen
Profile: Journal for members of the Technical Employees in Stevedoring and Forwarding Branch Union.
Language(s): Finnish

AJA HYVIN / PEUGEOT
705855L31R-5
Editorial: Tiilenpolttajankuja 5 A, 01720 VANTAA
Tel: 10 76 86 200 **Fax:** 10 76 86 330
Email: riitta.luomala@peugeot.fi **Web site:** http://www.peugeot.fi/peugeot_suomessa/aja_hyvin_lehti
ISSN: 1795-2093
Freq: Half-yearly; **Cover Price:** Free; **Circ:** 120,000
Usual Pagination: 68
Editor-in-Chief: Riitta Luomala
Profile: Magazine focusing on Peugeot automobiles.
Language(s): Finnish
BUSINESS: MOTOR TRADE: Motor Trade Related

AJAN FAKTA
752815L87-210
Editorial: Chydenius Center, 67100 KOKKOLA
Tel: 6 83 12 222 **Fax:** 6 83 12 466
Email: savokarjalan.ajanfakta@gmail.com **Web site:** http://www.ajanfakta.fi
ISSN: 1237-4091
Date Established: 1994; **Freq:** Quarterly; **Cover Price:** Free; **Circ:** 40,000
Usual Pagination: 16
Editor: Jarkko Malinen; **Editor-in-Chief:** Reijo Ruotsalainen
Profile: Baptist news magazine about religious affairs in central Ostrobothnia.
Language(s): Finnish
ADVERTISING RATES:
SCC .... EUR 10.00
Mechanical Data: No. of Columns (Display): 6, Col Widths (Display): 40mm
CONSUMER: RELIGIOUS

AJASSA
622644L1C-3
Formerly: Avainasiakas
Editorial: Alma 360 Asiakasmedia, PL 502/ Munkkiniemen puistotie 35, 5 krs, 00101 HELSINKI
Tel: 10 66 51 02 **Fax:** 10 66 52 533
Email: riitta.ekholm@alma360.fi **Web site:** http://www.digipaper.fi/ajassa
Freq: Quarterly; Free to qualifying individuals ; **Circ:** 465,000
Usual Pagination: 28
Profile: Magazine by Nordea Bank containing articles and information about personal finance.
Language(s): Finnish; Swedish
Readership: Aimed at families with investment opportunities.
Agency Commission: 15%
Mechanical Data: Type Area: 205 x 265mm
BUSINESS: FINANCE & ECONOMICS: Banking

AJOLINJA
15071L49B-30
Editorial: Nuijamiestentie 5 A, 00400 HELSINKI
Tel: 9 54 76 21 **Fax:** 9 54 76 22 46
Email: jouni.hievanen@boy.fi **Web site:** http://www.ajolinja.fi
ISSN: 0359-3010
Date Established: 1983; **Freq:** 6 issues yearly - Published 8/year; **Circ:** 23,100
Usual Pagination: 72
Profile: Publication for truck drivers. Includes technical and general information.
Language(s): Finnish
Readership: Aimed at truck drivers and those in the transport and logistics fields.
ADVERTISING RATES:
Full Page Colour .... EUR 3390
SCC .... EUR 31
Agency Commission: 15%
Mechanical Data: Print Process: Offset, Screen: 60 lpc, Trim Size: 275 x 210mm, Type Area: 253 x 187mm, Col Length: 250mm, Page Width: 185mm, Film: positive
Copy instructions: *Copy Date:* 7 days prior to publication date

AKAAN SEUTU
704916L72-20
Editorial: PL 60 /Alventie 4, 37801 TOIJALA
Tel: 3 54 09 600 **Fax:** 3 54 09 630
Email: toimitus@akaanseutu.fi **Web site:** http://www.akaanseutu.fi
ISSN: 1239-4343
Date Established: 1916; **Freq:** 104 issues yearly; **Circ:** 6,009
Usual Pagination: 12
Editor-in-Chief: Juha Kosonen
Profile: Newspaper issued in Toijala, Viiala, Kylmäkoski, Saarioispuoli and Kalvola.
Language(s): Finnish
ADVERTISING RATES:
Full Page Colour .... EUR 3049
SCC .... EUR 12.10
Mechanical Data: Bleed Size: 292 x 420mm, No. of Columns (Display): 6, Col Widths (Display): 45mm, Print Process: offset, Page Width: 290mm, Col Length: 420mm
Editions:
Akaan Seutu Verkkotoimitus
LOCAL NEWSPAPERS

AKT
705331L49A-2
Formerly: Auto- ja Kuljetusala
Editorial: PL 313/ John Stenbergin ranta 6, 00531 HELSINKI **Tel:** 9 61 31 12 38 **Fax:** 9 61 31 12 97
Email: toimitus@akt.fi **Web site:** http://www.akt.fi
Date Established: 1958; **Freq:** Monthly - Published 15/year; **Circ:** 52,000
Usual Pagination: 24
Profile: Journal for members of the Car and Transport Worker's Union.
Language(s): Finnish
ADVERTISING RATES:
Full Page Colour .... EUR 2800
SCC .... EUR 15.40
Agency Commission: 15%
Mechanical Data: Type Area: 255 x 363mm, Col Length: 412mm, Print Process: offset, Screen: 34 lpc, Col Widths (Display): 47mm, No. of Columns (Display): 5
BUSINESS: TRANSPORT

ÅLAND
15205L67B-2200
Editorial: PB 50/ Strandgatan 16, 22101 MARIEHAMN **Tel:** 18 26 026 **Fax:** 18 15 755
Email: 15000@alandstidningen.ax **Web site:** http://www.tidningen.aland.net
Date Established: 1891
Circ: 9,167
Usual Pagination: 32
Managing Editor: Jörgen Pettersson
Profile: The main newspapers on the Aaland (Ahvenanmaa) Islands.
Language(s): Swedish
ADVERTISING RATES:
Full Page Colour .... EUR 6329
SCC .... EUR 28.90
Agency Commission: 15%
Mechanical Data: Type Area: 252 x 370mm, Col Widths (Display): 38.1mm, No. of Columns (Display): 6, Col Length: 370mm, Screen: 34 pc, Print Process: offset
Editions:
Åland Internetredaktionen
REGIONAL DAILY & SUNDAY NEWSPAPERS: Regional Daily Newspapers

ALARA
706013L58-2
Editorial: Purotie 1 B, 00380 HELSINKI
Tel: 9 22 45 210 **Fax:** 9 22 45 211
Web site: http://www.stuk.fi/julkaisut_maaraykset/alara/fi_FI/alara
ISSN: 1235-1970
Date Established: 1991; **Freq:** Quarterly; **Circ:** 2,000
Usual Pagination: 32
Editor-in-Chief: Elina Martikka
Profile: The magazine gives information on radon and uv-radioation health impacts and on mobile phone, computer, microwave oven and solarium radiation impacts. Further issues are nuclear safety in Finland and nearby regions, nuclear waste handling and radiation use in health care.
Language(s): Finnish
ADVERTISING RATES:
Full Page Colour .... EUR 1200.00
Mechanical Data: Type Area: 186 x 274mm, Bleed Size: 210 x 297mm, Print Process: offset, Screen: 60 lpc

ALASATAKUNTA
704943L72-40
Editorial: PL 19/ Eurantie 6, 27511 EURA
Tel: 2 83 87 92 00 **Fax:** 2 86 51 961
Email: toimitus@alasatakunta.fi **Web site:** http://www.alasatakunta.fi
ISSN: 0782-5684
Date Established: 1949; **Freq:** 104 issues yearly; **Circ:** 10,228
Usual Pagination: 20
Profile: Newspaper issued in Kiukainen, Köyliö, Lappi TL, Eura, Yläne and Säkylä.
Language(s): Finnish
ADVERTISING RATES:
Full Page Colour .... EUR 2628
SCC .... EUR 12
Agency Commission: 10-15%
Mechanical Data: Print Process: offset, Screen: 30 lpc, Type Area: 260 x 365mm, No. of Columns (Display): 6, Col Widths (Display): 40mm, Col Length: 365mm, Page Width: 260mm
Editions:
Alasatakunta Verkkotoimitus
LOCAL NEWSPAPERS

ALAVIESKA
704993L72-45
Editorial: PL 20 / Pääskyntie 1, 85201 ALAVIESKA
Tel: 8 43 01 59 **Fax:** 8 43 12 40
Email: alavieskalehti@kotinet.com **Web site:** http://alavieskanviri.sporttisaitti.com/alavieska-lehti
Date Established: 1983; **Freq:** Weekly; **Circ:** 1,683
Usual Pagination: 12
Profile: Newspaper issued in Alavieska.
Language(s): Finnish
ADVERTISING RATES:
SCC .... EUR 6.50
LOCAL NEWSPAPERS

ALIBI
15394L94X-10
Editorial: Esterinportti 1, 00015 OTAVAMEDIA
Tel: 9 15 665 **Fax:** 9 15 66 62 06
Email: alibi-toimitussihteerit@otavamedia.fi **Web site:** http://www.alibi.fi
ISSN: 0357-542X
Date Established: 1980; **Freq:** Monthly; **Circ:** 37,104
Usual Pagination: 88
Editor-in-Chief: Mika Lahtonen
Profile: Magazine about criminal cases and investigations.
Language(s): Finnish
Readership: Read by members of the general public and those with a specific interest in crime.
ADVERTISING RATES:
Full Page Colour .... EUR 2250
SCC .... EUR 20
Mechanical Data: Bleed Size: 280 x 217mm, Film: Digital, Print Process: offset, Col Widths (Display): 45mm, Film: positive, Screen: 54 lpc
CONSUMER: OTHER CLASSIFICATIONS: Miscellaneous

ALLERGIA & ASTMA
15093L56A-5
Editorial: Paciuksenkatu 19, 00270 HELSINKI
Tel: 9 47 33 51 **Fax:** 9 47 33 53 30
Email: toimitus@allergia.fi **Web site:** http://www.allergia.com
ISSN: 1238-3902
Date Established: 1970; **Freq:** Quarterly; **Circ:** 28,684
Usual Pagination: 72

Editor-in-Chief: Tari Haahtela; **Managing Editor:** Annukka Lehto
Profile: Medical journal relating to allergies and asthmatic conditions.
Language(s): Finnish
ADVERTISING RATES:
Full Page Colour .... EUR 3200.00
SCC .... EUR 26.90
Mechanical Data: Bleed Size: 210 x 297mm, Type Area: 185 x 270mm, No. of Columns (Display): 2/3, Col Widths (Display): 37.5/80mm, Print Process: offset, Film: negative, Screen: 48 lpc
BUSINESS: HEALTH & MEDICAL

ALMA MEDIAN HELSINGIN TOIMITUS 705723L67E-8
Formerly: Alma Median politiikan toimitus
Editorial: PL 1364/ Eteläesplanadi 20, 6. krs, 00101 HELSINKI **Tel:** 10 66 52 800 **Fax:** 10 66 52 423
Email: kl.toimitus@kauppalehti.fi **Web site:** http://www.almamedia.fi/helsingin_toimitus
Freq: Daily
Profile: Joint Helsinki and political office of Alma Media newspapers.
Language(s): Finnish
REGIONAL DAILY & SUNDAY NEWSPAPERS: Regional Offices

AMMATTIAUTOT 706024L49A-52
Formerly: Kevyt Kuljetuskalusto
Editorial: Takojankatu 11, 33540 TAMPERE
Tel: 3 38 07 700 **Fax:** 3 38 07 701
Email: ammattiautot@ammattiautot.fi **Web site:** http://www.ammattiautot.fi
ISSN: 1455-7088
Date Established: 1996; **Freq:** Monthly; **Circ:** 44,112
Usual Pagination: 64
Profile: Magazine about light transport vehicles.
Language(s): Finnish
ADVERTISING RATES:
Full Page Colour .... EUR 2656
SCC .... EUR 22.30
Agency Commission: 15%
Mechanical Data: Type Area: 210 x 297mm, Col Widths (Display): 43mm, No. of Columns (Display): 4, Print Process: heatset offset rotation, Screen: 48 lpc, colour 60 lpc, Trim Size: 187 x 265mm
BUSINESS: TRANSPORT

AMMATTISOTILAS 705786L40-75
Formerly: Puol'väli
Editorial: Ratamestarinkatu 11, 7.krs, 00520 HELSINKI **Tel:** 9 14 86 915 **Fax:** 9 27 87 854
Email: petteri.leino@aliupseeriliitto.fi **Web site:** http://www.aliupseeriliitto.fi
ISSN: 0786-3985
Date Established: 1988; **Freq:** Quarterly; **Circ:** 1,600
Usual Pagination: 40
Editor-in-Chief: Petteri Leino
Profile: Journal of the Finnish Soldiers' Union.
Language(s): Finnish
Readership: Read by members.
ADVERTISING RATES:
Full Page Mono .... EUR 860.00
Full Page Colour .... EUR 1500.00

ANNA 15244L74A-20
Editorial: Maistraatinportti 1, 00015 OTAVAMEDIA
Tel: 9 15 661 **Fax:** 9 14 82 025
Email: anna@otavamedia.fi **Web site:** http://www.anna.fi
ISSN: 0355-3035
Date Established: 1962; **Freq:** Weekly; **Circ:** 111,465
Usual Pagination: 108
Editor-in-Chief: Hanna Jensen; **Managing Editor:** Sanna Wirtavuori
Profile: Women's magazine focusing on lifestyle, entertainment and culture.
Language(s): Finnish
ADVERTISING RATES:
Full Page Colour .... EUR 6690
SCC .... EUR 59.70
Mechanical Data: Bleed Size: 280 x 230mm, Print Process: Offset, Film: Digital, Screen: 60 lpc, No. of Columns (Display): 4, Col Widths (Display): 47mm, Film: positive
Copy instructions: *Copy Date:* 13 days prior to publication date
CONSUMER: WOMEN'S INTEREST CONSUMER MAGAZINES: Women's Interest

APOLLO 749482L82-1_50
Editorial: Apollonkatu 11 a, 00100 HELSINKI
Tel: 400 90 90 13 **Fax:** 10 28 97 240
Email: helsinki@keskusta.fi **Web site:** http://www.helsinginkeskusta.fi
Freq: Half-yearly; **Cover Price:** Free; **Circ:** 10,000
Usual Pagination: 24
Profile: Finnish Center Party newspaper about Helsinki matters.
Language(s): Finnish
CONSUMER: CURRENT AFFAIRS & POLITICS

APOTEEKKI 2002759L56A-205
Editorial: PL 100/ Lapinmäentie 1, 00040 SANOMA MAGAZINES **Tel:** 9 12 01 **Fax:** 9 12 05 988
Email: liisa.kuittinen@sanomamagazines.fi **Web site:** http://www.avainapteekit.fi/avainapteekit/apoteekki-lehti
Freq: 6 issues yearly; **Cover Price:** Free; **Circ:** 340,000
Profile: Customer magazine of Avainapteekit.
Language(s): Finnish

APTEEKIN HYLLYLTÄ 1609342L37-7
Editorial: Valimotie 7, 00380 HELSINKI
Tel: 9 54 20 46
Email: katariina.kalsta@yliopistonapteekki.fi **Web site:** http://www.yliopistonapteekki.fi
ISSN: 1455-0423
Freq: Quarterly - Published 5/year; **Cover Price:** Free; **Circ:** 450,000
Usual Pagination: 24
Profile: Magazine about pharmacies, medicine, beauty, cosmetics, health and healthy food.
Language(s): Finnish
Readership: Customers of pharmacy chain Yliopiston Apteekki.
ADVERTISING RATES:
Full Page Colour .... EUR 7100
SCC .... EUR 94.60
Copy instructions: *Copy Date:* 44 days prior to publication date
BUSINESS: PHARMACEUTICAL & CHEMISTS

APTEEKKARI 15025L37-25
Formerly: Apteekkarilehti
Editorial: Pieni Roobertinkatu 14 C, 00120 HELSINKI
Tel: 9 22 87 11 **Fax:** 9 64 82 43
Email: toimitus@apteekkari.fi **Web site:** http://www.apteekkari.fi
ISSN: 0355-533X
Date Established: 1912; **Freq:** Monthly; Free to qualifying individuals ; **Circ:** 2,143
Usual Pagination: 40
Managing Editor: Inkeri Koskela
Profile: Publication of the Association of Finnish Pharmacies works mainly as a discussion forum for the pharmacies and their personnel.
Language(s): Finnish
Readership: Pharmacy owners and their staff.
ADVERTISING RATES:
Full Page Colour .... EUR 1750
SCC .... EUR 20.10
Agency Commission: 15%
Mechanical Data: Bleed Size: 210 x 297mm, Type Area: 183 x 261mm, No. of Columns (Display): 2/3/4, Col Widths (Display): 85/55/40mm, Print Process: offset, Screen: 60 lpc, Film: negative
BUSINESS: PHARMACEUTICAL & CHEMISTS

APU 15255L73-21
Editorial: Risto Rytin tie 33, 00081 A-LEHDET
Tel: 9 75 961 **Fax:** 9 75 98 31 01
Email: apu@a-lehdet.fi **Web site:** http://www.apu.fi
ISSN: 0355-3051
Date Established: 1933; **Freq:** Weekly; **Circ:** 168,780
Usual Pagination: 120
Profile: Family magazine providing information and articles on the Finnish lifestyle. Covers home, society and hobbies.
Language(s): Finnish
ADVERTISING RATES:
Full Page Colour .... EUR 2500
SCC .... EUR 63.90
Mechanical Data: Col Widths (Display): 44mm, Type Area: 240 x 196mm, Bleed Size: 265 x 216mm, No. of Columns (Display): 4, Screen: 70 lpc, Film: negative, Col Length: 240mm, Page Width: 190mm
Editions:
Apu.fi
CONSUMER: NATIONAL & INTERNATIONAL PERIODICALS

ARBETARBLADET 704864L82-2
Editorial: PB 140/ Aspnäsgatan 7-9, 00531 HELSINGFORS **Tel:** 9 77 32 844 **Fax:** 9 70 18 845
Email: siv.astrand@arbetarbladet.fi **Web site:** http://www.arbetarbladet.fi
ISSN: 0789-8274
Date Established: 1919; **Freq:** Daily. Published on Thursday; **Circ:** 2,093 Unique Users
Usual Pagination: 8
Profile: Current-affairs from the Swedish-speaking worker's point of view.
Language(s): Swedish
CONSUMER: CURRENT AFFAIRS & POLITICS

ARBETSPENSION 706183L74N-2
Editorial: Kirjurinkatu 3, 00065 ELÄKETURVAKESKUS **Tel:** 10 75 11
Fax: 10 75 02 176
Email: pia.hansson@etk.fi **Web site:** http://www.etk.fi
ISSN: 0355-2748
Date Established: 1967; **Freq:** Half-yearly; **Annual Sub.:** EUR 8.00; **Circ:** 1,500
Usual Pagination: 36
Editor-in-Chief: Kati Kalliomäki
Profile: Magazine about retirement and pension security.
Language(s): Swedish

ARKKITEHTI 14890L4A-10
Editorial: Runeberginkatu 5 A, 00100 HELSINKI
Tel: 9 58 44 48 **Fax:** 958444222
Web site: http://www.safa.fi/ark
ISSN: 0783-3660
Date Established: 1903; **Freq:** 6 issues yearly; **Circ:** 4,473
Usual Pagination: 90
Profile: Magazine containing articles about architecture.
Language(s): English; Finnish
Readership: Read by architects, interior designers, engineers, builders and contractors, policymakers and industry managers.
ADVERTISING RATES:
Full Page Colour .... EUR 3575
SCC .... EUR 33.20
Agency Commission: 15%
Mechanical Data: Trim Size: 297 x 240mm, Print Process: Offset, Screen: Mono: 54 lpc, Colour: 60 lpc, Film: Digital material. See: www.artprint.fi, Type Area: 258 x 207mm, Col Length: 258mm, Page Width: 207mm, No. of Columns (Display): 4
Copy instructions: *Copy Date:* 14 days prior to publication date
BUSINESS: ARCHITECTURE & BUILDING: Architecture

ARKKITEHTIUUTISET-ARKITEKTNYTT 705192L4A-3
Editorial: Runeberginkatu 5 A, 00100 HELSINKI
Tel: 9 58 44 48 **Fax:** 958444222
Email: au@safa.fi **Web site:** http://www.safa.fi
ISSN: 0044-8915
Date Established: 1948; **Freq:** Monthly; **Circ:** 4,487
Usual Pagination: 40
Profile: Magazine of the Finnish Association of Architects.
Language(s): Finnish; Swedish
Readership: Read by architects, designers and students.
ADVERTISING RATES:
Full Page Colour .... EUR 2100
SCC .... EUR 51.20
Agency Commission: 15%
Mechanical Data: Type Area: 138 x 172mm, Print Process: offset, No. of Columns (Display): 2, Col Widths (Display): 67mm, Col Length: 189mm, Bleed Size: 169 x 210mm, Film: positive, Screen: 60 lpc
BUSINESS: ARCHITECTURE & BUILDING: Architecture

ARVO 706408L14L-4
Formerly: AY -lehti
Editorial: c/o Alma 360 Asiakasmedia, PL 502/ Munkkiniemen puistotie 25, 5 krs, 00101 HELSINKI
Tel: 10 66 51 02 **Fax:** 10 66 52 533
Email: arvoposti@alma360.fi **Web site:** http://www.arvo-lehti.fi
ISSN: 1458-3356
Freq: Quarterly - Published 5/year; **Cover Price:** Free; **Circ:** 110,000
Usual Pagination: 48
Editor-in-Chief: Sanni Halla-aho
Profile: Journal of the Central Organisation of Finnish Trade Unions.
Language(s): Finnish
Readership: Read by members of age 18-25.
ADVERTISING RATES:
Full Page Colour .... EUR 2600
BUSINESS: COMMERCE, INDUSTRY & MANAGEMENT: Trade Unions

ARVOPAPERI 14880L1F-4
Editorial: PL 920/ Annankatu 34-36 B, 00101 HELSINKI **Tel:** 20 44 240 **Fax:** 20 44 24 677
Email: toimitus@arvopaperi.fi **Web site:** http://www.arvopaperi.fi
ISSN: 0782-6060
Date Established: 1983; **Freq:** Monthly; **Circ:** 24,264
Usual Pagination: 76
Editor-in-Chief: Eljas Repo; **Managing Editor:** Karo Hämäläinen
Profile: Magazine containing information about the Finnish stocks and equities market.
Language(s): Finnish
Readership: Read by investors.
ADVERTISING RATES:
Full Page Colour .... EUR 4020
SCC .... EUR 34.50
Agency Commission: 5-15%
Mechanical Data: Type Area: 210 x 297mm, No. of Columns (Display): 4, Col Widths (Display): 42mm, Print Process: offset, Film: positive, Screen: 60/ 70 lpc
Copy instructions: *Copy Date:* 10 days prior to publication date
Editions:
Arvopaperi.fi
BUSINESS: FINANCE & ECONOMICS: Investment

ASEMAN LAPSET 706639L74C-2
Editorial: Vuorikatu 8 A 14, 00100 HELSINKI
Tel: 9 65 47 40 **Fax:** 9 68 42 05 10
Email: toimitus@asemanlapset.fi **Web site:** http://www.asemanlapset.fi
ISSN: 1457-3113
Date Established: 1993; **Freq:** Quarterly; **Circ:** 5,000
Usual Pagination: 44
Editor-in-Chief: Vuokko Ahti
Profile: Magazine to enhance better living condition for children, youngsters and their families.
Language(s): Finnish
ADVERTISING RATES:
Full Page Colour .... EUR 1200.00
Mechanical Data: Type Area: 210 x 295mm, Screen: 60 lpc
CONSUMER: WOMEN'S INTEREST CONSUMER MAGAZINES: Home & Family

ASKEL 705461L87-4
Editorial: PL 279/ Hietalahdenranta 13, 00181 HELSINKI **Tel:** 20 75 42 257
Email: askel.toimitus@kotimaa.fi **Web site:** http://www.askellehti.fi
ISSN: 0780-9972
Freq: Monthly; **Circ:** 17,818
Usual Pagination: 64
Profile: Christian periodical current-affairs-magazine.
Language(s): Finnish
ADVERTISING RATES:
Full Page Colour .... EUR 1900
SCC .... EUR 17.70
Agency Commission: 15%
Mechanical Data: Type Area: 210 x 297mm, No. of Columns (Display): 4, Col Widths (Display): 42mm, Screen: 40 lpc, Print Process: offset rotation
Copy instructions: *Copy Date:* 16 days prior to publication date
CONSUMER: RELIGIOUS

ÄSSÄ 705211L53-2
Editorial: PL 1/ Fleminginkatu 34, 00088 S-RYHMÄ
Tel: 10 76 80 11 **Fax:** 10 76 80 380
Email: assa@sok.fi **Web site:** http://www.s-kanava.fi/web/s-kanava-medialle/lehdet
ISSN: 0781-7347
Date Established: 1915; **Freq:** Monthly; **Cover Price:** Free; **Circ:** 46,362
Usual Pagination: 56
Profile: Magazine about the business activities and personnel management of retail trade group S-ryhmä.
Language(s): Finnish
ADVERTISING RATES:
Full Page Colour .... EUR 4350
SCC .... EUR 39.80
Agency Commission: 15%
Mechanical Data: Col Widths (Display): 45mm, No. of Columns (Display): 4, Type Area: 210 x 273mm, Print Process: offset, Screen: 60 lpc
BUSINESS: RETAILING & WHOLESALING

ASTRA NOVA 15245L74A-25
Editorial: Tallbergsgatan 1/175, 00180 HELSINGFORS **Tel:** 50 57 23 579 **Fax:** 9 44 29 26
Email: astranovaredaktion@gmail.com **Web site:** http://www.astranova.fi
ISSN: 1238-1837
Date Established: 1919; **Freq:** 6 issues yearly; **Circ:** 1,500
Usual Pagination: 60
Editor-in-Chief: Karmela Bélinki
Profile: Magazine about women, society and culture.
Language(s): Swedish
ADVERTISING RATES:
Full Page Colour .... EUR 1050.00
CONSUMER: WOMEN'S INTEREST CONSUMER MAGAZINES: Women's Interest

ASU JA RAKENNA 706015L4D-5
Editorial: PL 35/ Kasarminkatu 25, 00023 VALTIONEUVOSTO **Tel:** 9 16 03 96 10
Email: anna-maija.vainio@stellatum.fi **Web site:** http://www.ymparisto.fi
ISSN: 1237-0703
Date Established: 1993; **Freq:** 6 issues yearly; **Annual Sub.:** EUR 52.00; **Circ:** 2,500
Usual Pagination: 36
Profile: Magazine focusing on living, it contains information about legal matters. Ecological building, retailing, house planning and living politics are also subjects.
Language(s): Finnish
ADVERTISING RATES:
Full Page Colour .... EUR 1500.00
SCC .... EUR 18.20

ASUKAS 705393L4D-10
Editorial: PL 40/ Mannerheimintie 168, 00301 HELSINKI **Tel:** 20 50 83 300
Web site: http://www.vvo.fi
ISSN: 1456-0569
Date Established: 1975; **Freq:** Quarterly; **Cover Price:** Free; **Circ:** 65,000
Usual Pagination: 64
Editor-in-Chief: Marjaana Kivioja; **Managing Editor:** Jari Kallio
Profile: Magazine containing information on construction and maintenance of properties.
Language(s): Finnish
Readership: Read by clients of VVO.
Mechanical Data: Bleed Size: 210 x 297mm, No. of Columns (Display): 3, Col Widths (Display): 55mm, Screen: 52 lpc, Type Area: 185 x 264mm
BUSINESS: ARCHITECTURE & BUILDING: Planning & Housing

ASUKKI 719252L4D-11
Editorial: Kinaporinkatu 2, 00500 HELSINKI
Tel: 10 54 81 900 **Fax:** 10 54 81 999
Email: asukki@vvary.fi **Web site:** http://www.vvary.fi
ISSN: 0783-6783
Date Established: 1987; **Freq:** Quarterly; **Circ:** 3,500
Usual Pagination: 36
Profile: Magazine about homeless people and about the planning for cheaper apartments.
Language(s): Finnish

ASUNTOINFO.NET 1606904L74K-6
Editorial: Sinikalliontie 11, 02630 ESPOO
Tel: 9 42 47 38 60 **Fax:** 9 45 22 206
Email: info@asuntoinfo.net **Web site:** http://www.asuntoinfo.net
ISSN: 1459-8396
Freq: Quarterly - Published 5/year; Free to qualifying individuals ; **Circ:** 100,000
Usual Pagination: 68
Profile: Magazine about home purchase, building, repair and interior-design.
Language(s): Finnish
ADVERTISING RATES:
Full Page Colour .... EUR 4900
SCC .... EUR 54.90
Agency Commission: 15%
Mechanical Data: Bleed Size: 230 x 297mm, Print Process: offset
CONSUMER: WOMEN'S INTEREST CONSUMER MAGAZINES: Home Purchase

ASUNTOLEHTI - BOSTADSBLADET 754249L74K-8
Editorial: Gerbyntie 18, 65230 VAASA
Tel: 6 32 18 017 **Fax:** 6 32 18 001
Web site: http://www.bostadsbladet.com
Date Established: 2001; **Freq:** Weekly; **Cover Price:** Free; **Circ:** 44,283
Usual Pagination: 12
Editor-in-Chief: Sture Udd
Profile: Magazine with ads for home purchase in the Vasa region.
Language(s): Finnish; Swedish
ADVERTISING RATES:
Full Page Colour .... EUR 680.00
CONSUMER: WOMEN'S INTEREST CONSUMER MAGAZINES: Home Purchase

ASUNTOMEDIA 705455L74K-15
Formerly: Etuovi.com
Editorial: PL 368/ Aleksanterinkatu 9, 00101 HELSINKI **Tel:** 10 66 51 05 **Fax:** 10 66 55 019
Email: etuovi.toimitus@etuovi.com **Web site:** http://www.etuovi.com
ISSN: 0782-8179
Freq: 26 issues yearly - Published on Saturday; **Cover Price:** Free; **Circ:** 380,000
Usual Pagination: 24
Profile: Journal about purchasing homes.
Language(s): Finnish
Readership: All households in Kuopio, Jyväskylä, Oulu, Helsinki and Pori.
CONSUMER: WOMEN'S INTEREST CONSUMER MAGAZINES: Home Purchase

ATS YDINTEKNIIKKA 706534L58-3
Editorial: Säteilyturvakeskus, PL 14, 00881 HELSINKI
Email: paatoimittaja@ats-ydintekniikka.fi **Web site:** http://www.ATS-FNS.fi
Date Established: 1972; **Freq:** Quarterly; **Circ:** 900
Usual Pagination: 36
Editor-in-Chief: Riku Mattila
Profile: Magazine about radiation safety and nuclear energy use.
Language(s): Finnish
ADVERTISING RATES:
Full Page Colour .... EUR 700.00

AURANMAAN VIIKKOLEHTI 704887L72-80
Editorial: PL 15 / Kehityksentie 3, 21801 KYRÖ
Tel: 2 48 64 950 **Fax:** 2 48 68 053
Email: toimitus@auranmaanviikkolehti.fi **Web site:** http://www.auranmaanviikkolehti.fi
ISSN: 1455-920X
Date Established: 1926; **Freq:** 104 issues yearly; **Circ:** 8,752
Usual Pagination: 16
Profile: Newspaper issued in Aura, Karinainen, Koski TL, Marttila, Mellilä, Oripää, Pöytyä, Tarvasjoki and Yläne.
Language(s): Finnish
ADVERTISING RATES:
Full Page Colour .... EUR 3247
SCC .... EUR 13.20
Agency Commission: 15%
Mechanical Data: Page Width: 284mm, Col Length: 410mm, Col Widths (Display): 44mm, No. of Columns (Display): 6, Print Process: offset rotation
Copy instructions: *Copy Date:* 5 days prior to publication date
LOCAL NEWSPAPERS

AUTO BILD SUOMI 1640639L77A-160
Editorial: PL 100/ Lapinmäentie 1, 00040 SANOMA MAGAZINES **Tel:** 9 12 05 911 **Fax:** 9 12 05 795
Email: toimitus@autobild.fi **Web site:** http://www.autobild.fi
ISSN: 1459-949X
Date Established: 2004; **Freq:** 26 issues yearly - Published on Friday; **Circ:** 46,850
Usual Pagination: 84
Editor-in-Chief: Jarmo Markkanen; **Managing Editor:** Juha Koski
Profile: Magazine about cars and motoring.
Language(s): Finnish
ADVERTISING RATES:
Full Page Colour .... EUR 4350
SCC .... EUR 36.60
Mechanical Data: Type Area: 230 x 297mm, Screen: 60 lpc
Copy instructions: *Copy Date:* 10 days prior to publication date
CONSUMER: MOTORING & CYCLING: Motoring

AUTO & KULJETUS 1613624L49A-1
Editorial: Rihvelimäki 3 D 36, 02770 ESPOO
Tel: 9 85 93 001
Email: g.spare@kolumbus.fi
Date Established: 1998; **Freq:** 6 issues yearly; **Circ:** 12,000
Editor-in-Chief: Gustav Spåre
Profile: Magazine about commercial vehicles and transport.
Language(s): Finnish
Mechanical Data: Type Area: 165 x 257mm, Bleed Size: 210 x 297mm, Film: positive, Print Process: offset, Screen: 60 lpc

AUTO, TEKNIIKKA JA KULJETUS 15069L49A-50
Editorial: Nuijamiestentie 5 A, 00400 HELSINKI
Tel: 9 54 76 21 **Fax:** 9 54 76 22 46
Email: autotekniikka@boy.fi **Web site:** http://www.autotekniikka.fi
ISSN: 0357-4466
Date Established: 1979; **Freq:** Monthly - Published 10/year; **Circ:** 21,000
Usual Pagination: 96
Managing Editor: Harri Onnila
Profile: Publication focusing on the economic and logistic aspects of commercial transportation. Includes information on trucks, buses, coaches, cars and vans.
Language(s): Finnish
Readership: Aimed at decision makers in commerce and industry.
ADVERTISING RATES:
Full Page Colour .... EUR 4590
SCC .... EUR 23.70
Agency Commission: 15%
Mechanical Data: Print Process: Offset, Trim Size: 275 x 210mm, Type Area: 253 x 187mm, Screen: 60 lpc, Col Length: 250mm, Page Width: 185mm
Copy instructions: *Copy Date:* 7 days prior to publication date

AUTOPOKKARI 706503L31A-2
Editorial: Takojankatu 11, 33540 TAMPERE
Tel: 3 38 07 700 **Fax:** 3 38 07 701
Email: toimitus@autopokkari.com **Web site:** http://www.autopokkari.com
ISSN: 1456-8500
Date Established: 1999; **Freq:** 26 issues yearly; **Cover Price:** Free; **Circ:** 180,000
Usual Pagination: 56
Editor-in-Chief: Mikko Hietamäki; **Managing Director:** Janne Virtanen
Profile: Magazine with car, boat, caravan and motoring ads.
Language(s): Finnish
ADVERTISING RATES:
Full Page Colour .... EUR 3102.00
Agency Commission: 15%
Mechanical Data: Bleed Size: 260 x 380mm, Type Area: 243 x 366mm, Print Process: offset, Screen: 40 lpc
BUSINESS: MOTOR TRADE: Motor Trade Accessories

AUTOSOUND TECHNICAL MAGAZINE 706598L77A-4
Editorial: Olarinluoma 15, 02200 ESPOO
Tel: 10 77 86 404 **Fax:** 10 77 86 410
Email: toimitus@autosound.fi **Web site:** http://www.autosound.fi
ISSN: 1456-4157
Date Established: 1998; **Freq:** 6 issues yearly; **Circ:** 4,600
Usual Pagination: 60
Editor-in-Chief: Teppo Hirvikunnas; **Managing Editor:** Mauri Eronen
Profile: Magazine about hi-fi equipment in cars.
Language(s): Finnish
ADVERTISING RATES:
Full Page Colour .... EUR 1190.00
SCC .... EUR 10.00
Mechanical Data: Bleed Size: 210 x 297mm, Print Process: offset, Screen: 60 lpc

AUTOT 1998871L91D-171
Editorial: Lapinmäentie 1, 00350 HELSINKI
Tel: 9 12 06 20 **Fax:** 91205569
Web site: http://www.sanomamagazines.fi
Freq: Monthly; **Circ:** 11,285
Editor-in-Chief: Paula Antila
Profile: Magazine for children covering comic strips, games and ideas for car games.
Language(s): Finnish
Readership: 4-7-vuotaat lapset. / Children aged 4-7 years.
ADVERTISING RATES:
Full Page Colour .... EUR 1590
CONSUMER: RECREATION & LEISURE: Children & Youth

AVAIN 15111L56R-50
Formerly: Avain-Nyckeln-lehti
Editorial: PL 15/ Seppäläntie 90, 21251 MASKU
Tel: 2 43 92 111 **Fax:** 2 43 92 133
Email: tiedotus@ms-liitto.fi **Web site:** http://www.ms-liitto.fi
ISSN: 1455-898X
Date Established: 1971; **Freq:** 6 issues yearly - Published 7/year; **Circ:** 9,969
Usual Pagination: 64
Managing Editor: Saija Suominen
Profile: Official publication of the Finnish MS Society.
Language(s): Finnish; Swedish
Readership: Read by members of the society as well as professionals within social welfare and the medical sector.
ADVERTISING RATES:
Full Page Colour .... EUR 1550
SCC .... EUR 19.10
Agency Commission: 15%
Mechanical Data: Bleed Size: 210 x 297mm, Type Area: 185 x 270mm, No. of Columns (Display): 2/3/4, Col Widths (Display): 40/54/83mm, Print Process: offset, Film: negative, Screen: 56 lpc
Copy instructions: *Copy Date:* 21 days prior to publication date
BUSINESS: HEALTH & MEDICAL: Health Medical Related

AVH 705779L56R-2
Formerly: Afasia
Editorial: Suvilinnantie 2, 20900 TURKU
Tel: 2 21 38 200 **Fax:** 2 21 38 210
Email: paivi.leppa-seppala@stroke.fi **Web site:** http://www.stroke.fi
ISSN: 0782-8578
Date Established: 1979; **Freq:** Quarterly; **Circ:** 6,923
Usual Pagination: 40
Editor-in-Chief: Tiina Viljanen; **Managing Editor:** Päivi Leppä-Seppälä
Profile: Magazine about stroke patients.
Language(s): Finnish
ADVERTISING RATES:
Full Page Colour .... EUR 2150.00
Mechanical Data: Bleed Size: 210 x 275mm, Type Area: 185 x 255mm, Print Process: offset, Screen: 48 lpc mono, 53 lpc colour
BUSINESS: HEALTH & MEDICAL: Health Medical Related

AVOTAKKA 15257L23A-2
Editorial: Risto Rytin tie 33, 00081 A-LEHDET
Tel: 9 75 961 **Fax:** 9 75 98 31 10
Email: avotakka@a-lehdet.fi **Web site:** http://www.avotakka.fi
ISSN: 0355-2950
Date Established: 1967; **Freq:** Monthly; **Circ:** 85,104
Usual Pagination: 100
Editor-in-Chief: Johanna Falck; **Managing Editor:** Miia Kauhanen
Profile: Magazine focusing on all aspects of interior design. Featuring reports on the latest trends, ideas and products available.
Language(s): Finnish
ADVERTISING RATES:
Full Page Colour .... EUR 7200
SCC .... EUR 67.40
Mechanical Data: Type Area: 267 x 190mm, Bleed Size: 273 x 230mm, Screen: 60 lpc, No. of Columns (Display): 4, Print Process: Offset, Film: Digital, Col Length: 267mm, Page Width: 190mm
Copy instructions: *Copy Date:* 16 days prior to publication date
BUSINESS: FURNISHINGS & FURNITURE

AVUN MAAILMA 15123L32G-91
Formerly: Punainen Risti
Editorial: PL 168/Tehtaankatu 1 a, 00141 HELSINKI
Tel: 20 70 12 000 **Fax:** 20 70 12 310
Email: kimmo.holopainen@punainenristi.fi **Web site:** http://www.redcross.fi
ISSN: 1236-4770
Freq: Quarterly; **Circ:** 90,000
Usual Pagination: 32
Editor-in-Chief: Hannu-Pekka Laiho
Profile: Official publication of the Finnish Red Cross.
Language(s): Finnish; Swedish
ADVERTISING RATES:
Full Page Colour .... EUR 2450
Mechanical Data: Type Area: 200 x 260mm, No. of Columns (Display): 4, Col Widths (Display): 45mm, Print Process: offset, Film: negative, Screen: 54 lpc, Bleed Size: 230 x 297mm
BUSINESS: LOCAL GOVERNMENT, LEISURE & RECREATION: Community Care & Social Services

BENSIINIUUTISET 15019L33-20
Editorial: Mannerheimintie 40 D 84, 00100 HELSINKI
Tel: 9 75 19 55 00 **Fax:** 9 75 19 55 25
Email: hannu.laitinen@arvonanto.fi **Web site:** http://www.bensiinikauppiaat.fi
ISSN: 0045-1738
Date Established: 1957; **Freq:** 6 issues yearly; **Circ:** 3,000
Usual Pagination: 40
Editor-in-Chief: Hannu Laitinen
Profile: Journal of the Association of Finnish Petrol Retailers.
Language(s): Finnish
ADVERTISING RATES:
Full Page Colour .... EUR 2950.00
SCC .... EUR 24.80
Mechanical Data: Type Area: 185 x 265mm, Bleed Size: 210 x 297mm, No. of Columns (Display): 4, Col Widths (Display): 43mm, Print Process: offset, Screen: 54-60 lpc

BIKE 15320L77B-20
Editorial: Sulankuja 3, 04300 TUUSULA
Tel: 10 42 04 120 **Fax:** 9 27 31 301
Email: info@bike.fi **Web site:** http://www.bikelehti.fi
ISSN: 1455-1861
Date Established: 1984; **Freq:** Monthly - Published 10/year; **Circ:** 12,132
Usual Pagination: 98
Profile: Magazine covering motorcycles. Also includes information about scooters.
Language(s): Finnish
ADVERTISING RATES:
Full Page Colour .... EUR 2346
SCC .... EUR 21.80
Agency Commission: 15%
Mechanical Data: Col Widths (Display): 44mm, Col Length: 191mm, Film: Negative, Print Process: Offset rotation, No. of Columns (Display): 4, Page Width: 215mm
CONSUMER: MOTORING & CYCLING: Motorcycling

BIRKA 705118L74C-3
Editorial: PL 410/ Risto Rytin tie 33, 00811 HELSINGFORS **Tel:** 9 42 42 73 30 **Fax:** 9 42 42 73 33
Email: pirkka@dialogi.fi **Web site:** http://www.pirkka.fi
ISSN: 0780-4784
Date Established: 1976; **Freq:** Monthly - 10 issues/year; Free to qualifying individuals ; **Circ:** 80,539
Usual Pagination: 48
Editor-in-Chief: Minna Järvenpää
Profile: Customer-magazine of food retail group K-ryhmä (Kesko Oyj).
Language(s): Swedish
ADVERTISING RATES:
Full Page Colour .... EUR 4500
SCC .... EUR 46.80
Agency Commission: 15%
Mechanical Data: No. of Columns (Display): 4, Col Widths (Display): 45mm, Screen: 70 lpc, Type Area: 190 x 240mm, Print Process: offset
CONSUMER: WOMEN'S INTEREST CONSUMER MAGAZINES: Home & Family

BLUE WINGS 15372L89D-20
Editorial: PL 100/ Lapinmäentie 1, 00040 SANOMA MAGAZINES **Tel:** 9 12 01 **Fax:** 9 12 05 988
Email: bluewings@sanomamagazines.fi **Web site:** http://www.sanomamagazines.fi
ISSN: 0358-7703
Date Established: 1980; **Freq:** Monthly - Published 10/year; **Cover Price:** Free; **Circ:** 70,000
Usual Pagination: 148
Managing Editor: Anu Virnes-Karjalainen
Profile: General interest in-flight magazine.
Language(s): English; Finnish
Readership: Read by Finnair passengers.
ADVERTISING RATES:
Full Page Colour .... EUR 8530
SCC .... EUR 71.80
Mechanical Data: Type Area: 194 x 248mm, Bleed Size: 230 x 297mm, Screen: 60 lpc, Print Process: offset
Copy instructions: *Copy Date:* 18 days prior to publication date
CONSUMER: HOLIDAYS & TRAVEL: In-Flight Magazines

BORGÅBLADET 15179L67B-2300
Editorial: PB 200 / Mannerheimgatan 9-11, 06101 BORGÅ **Tel:** 20 75 69 622 **Fax:** 19 53 48 244
Email: redaktion@bbl.fi **Web site:** http://www.bbl.fi
ISSN: 0358-6294
Date Established: 1860
Circ: 7,798
Usual Pagination: 24
Profile: Regional newspaper distributed in Porvoo, Sipoo, Pernaja, Loviisa, Liljendal, Lapinjärvi, Myrskylä and Ruotsinpyhtää.
Language(s): Swedish
ADVERTISING RATES:
Full Page Colour .... EUR 4061
SCC .... EUR 18.80
Agency Commission: 5-15%
Mechanical Data: Page Width: 253mm, Col Length: 365mm, No. of Columns (Display): 5, Col Widths (Display): 47mm, Screen: 85 lpi, Print Process: offset, Type Area: 251 x 350mm
Editions:
Borgåbladet Internetredaktionen
REGIONAL DAILY & SUNDAY NEWSPAPERS: Regional Daily Newspapers

BOTNIA ECHO 767558L36-40
Formerly: Me Botnialaiset
Editorial: PL 165, 26101 RAUMA **Tel:** 10 46 68 999
Fax: 10 46 68 372
Email: saija.tuomikoski@botnia.com **Web site:** http://www.botnia.com
ISSN: 1455-8297
Freq: Half-yearly; **Cover Price:** Free; **Circ:** 4,500
Usual Pagination: 24
Editor-in-Chief: Saija Tuomikoski; **Managing Editor:** Leena Salminen
Profile: Customer magazine about paper manufacturing published in English, German and Finnish.
Language(s): Finnish; German
Readership: Customers of Oy Metsä-Botnia Ab.

BUSINESS FINLAND 2035393L14A-162
Editorial: Purpuripolku 6, 00420 HELSINKI
Tel: 9 42 82 10 00 **Fax:** 9 42 82 10 30
Email: info@perhemediat.fi **Web site:** http://www.perhemediat.fi
Freq: 6 issues yearly; **Circ:** 12,000
Profile: Magazine covering Finnish economics.
Language(s): Finnish
Readership: Kansainväliset päättäjät ja liikemiehet. / International decision makers as well as business men.
ADVERTISING RATES:
Full Page Colour .... EUR 6400
SCC .... EUR 82

BUSINESS NETWORKS 1641904L5E-110
Editorial: PL 128/ Sinikalliontie 16, 02631 ESPOO
Tel: 9 42 43 55 55 **Fax:** 9 50 23 840
Email: juhani.leskinen@lanwan.fi **Web site:** http://www.lanwan.fi
Freq: Annual; **Circ:** 15,000
Usual Pagination: 16
Managing Editor: Juhani Leskinen
Profile: Magazine about information networks and information security.
Language(s): Finnish

BUSSIAMMATTILAINEN 705216L49B-35
Editorial: Lauttasaarentie 8, 00200 HELSINKI
Tel: 20 71 05 000 **Fax:** 20 71 05 484
Email: saara.remes@bak.fi **Web site:** http://www.linja-autoliitto.fi
ISSN: 0789-6921
Date Established: 1966; **Freq:** 6 issues yearly; **Circ:** 7,000
Usual Pagination: 56
Editor-in-Chief: Saara Remes
Profile: Journal for members of the Finnish Coach Union.
Language(s): Finnish
ADVERTISING RATES:
Full Page Colour .... EUR 2950.00
SCC .... EUR 24.80
Mechanical Data: Col Widths (Display): 43mm, No. of Columns (Display): 4, Type Area: 210 x 297mm, Print Process: offset, Screen: 60 lpc

CAD-Q NEWS 768061L5E-120
Formerly: CadQ.News
Editorial: Ruosilankuja 3 A, 00390 HELSINKI
Tel: 9 54 22 65 00 **Fax:** 9 54 22 66 00
Email: info@cadi.fi **Web site:** http://www.cadigroup.fi
Freq: Half-yearly; **Cover Price:** Free; **Circ:** 17,000
Usual Pagination: 20
Profile: Magazine about information administration planning, IT and Autodesk planning.
Language(s): Finnish
Readership: Customers of CADi Oy.
Mechanical Data: Screen: 60 lpc, Type Area: 210 x 297mm, Film: negative, Print Process: offset

CAMPUS.FI 706539L83-18_50
Formerly: Academica
Editorial: Erottajankatu 15-17, 00130 HELSINKI
Tel: 20 74 39 900 **Fax:** 20 74 39 909
Email: info@acacom.com **Web site:** http://www.acacom.com
ISSN: 1459-9643
Date Established: 1997; **Freq:** Quarterly; **Cover Price:** Free; **Circ:** 100,000
Usual Pagination: 68
Managing Editor: Anna Malk
Profile: Magazine for students that are about to graduate.
Language(s): Finnish
ADVERTISING RATES:
Full Page Colour .... EUR 5135.00
Agency Commission: 15%
Mechanical Data: Bleed Size: 210 x 297mm, Screen: 60 lpc, Print Process: offset
CONSUMER: STUDENT PUBLICATIONS

CARAVAN 15379L91B-50
Editorial: Viipurintie 58, 13210 HÄMEENLINNA
Tel: 3 61 53 140 **Fax:** 3 61 53 162
Email: pekka.heinonen@caravan-lehti.fi **Web site:** http://www.caravan-lehti.fi
ISSN: 0356-2468
Date Established: 1965; **Freq:** 6 issues yearly; **Circ:** 56,918
Usual Pagination: 128
Profile: Magazine about caravans and caravanning.
Language(s): Finnish; Swedish
Readership: Members of the Finnish Federation of Caravanning.
ADVERTISING RATES:
Full Page Colour .... EUR 2725
SCC .... EUR 24.80
Agency Commission: 15%
Mechanical Data: Type Area: 187 x 269mm, Col Widths (Display): 43mm, Screen: 54 lpc, Print Process: offset, Film: positive, No. of Columns (Display): 4
CONSUMER: RECREATION & LEISURE: Camping & Caravanning

CHARTER CLUB 706266L49B-40
Editorial: Hauenkoukku 14 as 9, 70700 KUOPIO
Tel: 45 67 65 865
Email: lehti@tilausajokuljettajat.fi **Web site:** http://www.tilausajokuljettajat.fi
Date Established: 1981; **Freq:** Quarterly; **Cover Price:** Free; **Circ:** 3,500
Usual Pagination: 36
Editor-in-Chief: Timo Rinnekari
Profile: Magazine about coach and mini-bus chartering.
Language(s): Finnish
ADVERTISING RATES:
Full Page Colour .... EUR 1000.00

CHYDENIUS 706536L1C-5
Editorial: Munkkiniemen puistotie 25, 00330 HELSINKI **Tel:** 10 66 51 02 **Fax:** 10 66 52 533
Web site: http://www.op.fi
ISSN: 1457-3253
Date Established: 2000; **Freq:** Quarterly; **Cover Price:** Free; **Circ:** 34,500
Usual Pagination: 36
Editor-in-Chief: Stina Suominen
Profile: Magazine of the banking group OP-Pohjola-ryhmä containing views on economic prospects.
Language(s): Finnish
Readership: Read by clients of the banking group OP-Pohjola-ryhmä.
BUSINESS: FINANCE & ECONOMICS: Banking

CIRCLE 1641477L5E-130
Editorial: Keilaranta 7, 02150 ESPOO **Tel:** 9 52 55 01
Email: i-teijal@microsoft.com
ISSN: 1459-7357
Freq: Half-yearly; **Cover Price:** Free; **Circ:** 90,000
Usual Pagination: 40
Editor-in-Chief: Teija Laine; **Managing Editor:** Jukka Jänönen
Profile: Magazine about information networks and computers.
Language(s): Finnish
Readership: Customers, organisations and people involved with Microsoft Finland.
Mechanical Data: Type Area: 210 x 297mm, Screen: 60 lpc
BUSINESS: COMPUTERS & AUTOMATION: Data Transmission

CITY-HELSINKI 15370L72-95
Formerly: City Lehti
Editorial: PL 80/ Hankasuontie 3, 00391 HELSINKI
Tel: 9 56 15 63 00 **Fax:** 9 56 15 63 21
Email: city@citypress.fi **Web site:** http://www.city.fi
Date Established: 1986; **Freq:** 26 issues yearly; **Cover Price:** Free; **Circ:** 85,000
Usual Pagination: 80
Profile: Magazine containing information and news about Helsinki. Also provides details of events and entertainment.
Language(s): Finnish
ADVERTISING RATES:
Full Page Colour .... EUR 6500
SCC .... EUR 28.80
Agency Commission: 15%
Mechanical Data: Trim Size: 280 x 400mm, Type Area: 260 x 375mm, Print Process: offset, Screen: 40 lpc, Col Length: 375mm, Page Width: 254mm, No. of Columns (Display): 6
Copy instructions: *Copy Date:* 7 days prior to publication date
LOCAL NEWSPAPERS

CITY-JYVÄSKYLÄ 705111L72-105
Editorial: PL 115, 40101 JYVÄSKYLÄ
Tel: 14 33 82 459
Email: jyvaskyla@citypress.fi **Web site:** http://www.city.fi
Freq: Monthly; **Cover Price:** Free; **Circ:** 20,000
Profile: Events, restaurants, music and news about famous people in the Jyväskylä region.
Language(s): Finnish
ADVERTISING RATES:
Full Page Colour .... EUR 1920
Mechanical Data: Type Area: 375 x 260mm, Print Process: offset rotation, Screen: 30 lpc mono, 34 lpc colour, Film: negative, Col Length: 375mm, Page Width: 254mm, No. of Columns (Display): 6
LOCAL NEWSPAPERS

CLUB ONE 706204L45A-3
Formerly: Meriviesti; Merellä - Till Havs
Editorial: Markkinointiviestintä Dialogi, PL 410/ Risto Rytin tie 33, 00811 HELSINKI **Tel:** 9 42 42 73 30
Fax: 9 42 42 73 33
Web site: http://www.tallinksilja.com/clubone
Freq: Quarterly; **Cover Price:** Free; **Circ:** 220,000
Usual Pagination: 52
Editor-in-Chief: Hanna Michelsson
Profile: Magazine about special offers, cruises, food and drink and tax free issues.
Language(s): Finnish; Swedish
Readership: Frequent passengers of cruise-ship group Tallink Silja.
BUSINESS: MARINE & SHIPPING

COSMOPOLITAN 706409L74A-26
Editorial: PL 100/ Lapinmäentie 1, 00040 SANOMA MAGAZINES **Tel:** 9 12 01 **Fax:** 9 12 05 259
Email: cosmopolitan@sanomamagazines.fi **Web site:** http://www.cosmopolitan.fi
ISSN: 1456-5234
Date Established: 1999; **Freq:** Monthly; **Circ:** 78,502
Usual Pagination: 132
Editor-in-Chief: Miina Lange; **Managing Editor:** Katariina Kivimäki
Profile: Magazine about fashion and beauty.
Language(s): Finnish
Readership: Women of age 18-30.
ADVERTISING RATES:
Full Page Colour .... EUR 6200
SCC .... EUR 73.80
Mechanical Data: Bleed Size: 210 x 280mm, Type Area: 210 x 280mm, No. of Columns (Display): 3, Col Widths (Display): 60mm, Print Process: offset, Film: positive, Screen: 60 lpc
CONSUMER: WOMEN'S INTEREST CONSUMER MAGAZINES: Women's Interest

CRUISE BUSINESS REVIEW 2041366L49A-132
Editorial: Palokuja 6 A 17, 04250 KERAVA
Tel: 50 51 49 085
Email: cruise.media@netlife.fi **Web site:** http://www.cruisebusiness.com
Freq: Half-yearly - 3/ a year; **Circ:** 6,500
Publisher: Teijo Niemelä
Profile: Magazine covering monitoring the development and analyzing the cruise industry worldwide.
Language(s): Finnish
Readership: The management of cruise and shipping lines as well as port authorities and shipyards.
ADVERTISING RATES:
Full Page Colour .... EUR 3270.00

CSC NEWS 705163L5B-2
Editorial: PL 405/ Keilaranta 14, 02101 ESPOO
Tel: 9 45 72 001 **Fax:** 9 45 72 302
Email: ari.turunen@csc.fi **Web site:** http://www.csc.fi/lehdet/cscnews
ISSN: 0787-7536
Freq: Quarterly; **Cover Price:** Free; **Circ:** 5,000
Usual Pagination: 16
Editor-in-Chief: Ari Turunen
Profile: Magazine about scientific information technology.
Language(s): English
Readership: Customers of CSC.
BUSINESS: COMPUTERS & AUTOMATION: Data Processing

DEKO 1643547L23C-2
Editorial: Maistraatinportti 1, 00015 OTAVAMEDIA
Tel: 9 15 661 **Fax:** 9 15 66 602
Email: deko@otavamedia.fi **Web site:** http://www.dekolehti.fi
ISSN: 1459-7128
Date Established: 2004; **Freq:** Monthly - Published 10/year; **Circ:** 37,833
Usual Pagination: 124
Profile: Magazine about interior-design and home furnishing.
Language(s): Finnish
Readership: 19-39-year-olds.
ADVERTISING RATES:
Full Page Colour .... EUR 5500
SCC .... EUR 46.20
Mechanical Data: Type Area: 230 x 280mm
Copy instructions: *Copy Date:* 19 days prior to publication date
BUSINESS: FURNISHINGS & FURNITURE: Furnishings & Furniture - Kitchens & Bathrooms

DEMETER-LEHTI 14978L21A-2
Editorial: Uudenmaankatu 25 A 4, 00120 HELSINKI
Tel: 9 64 41 60 **Fax:** 9 68 02 591
Email: info@biodyn.fi **Web site:** http://www.biodyn.fi
ISSN: 0355-8789
Date Established: 1964; **Freq:** Quarterly; **Annual Sub.:** EUR 27.00; **Circ:** 1,000
Usual Pagination: 28
Editor-in-Chief: Pirkko Okkonen
Profile: Journal about organic agriculture and food.
Language(s): Finnish

DEMI 706387L74F-1_50
Editorial: Risto Rytin tie 33, 00081 A-LEHDET
Tel: 9 75 961 **Fax:** 9 75 98 31 15
Email: demi@a-lehdet.fi **Web site:** http://www.demi.fi
ISSN: 1456-1433
Date Established: 1998; **Freq:** Monthly; **Circ:** 52,236
Usual Pagination: 100
Editor-in-Chief: Satu Koivisto; **Managing Editor:** Kati Toivanen
Profile: Magazine about lifestyle, pop music and interesting beauty issues for teenage girls.
Language(s): Finnish
Readership: Girls of age 12-19.
ADVERTISING RATES:
Full Page Colour .... EUR 4200
SCC .... EUR 43.50
Mechanical Data: Type Area: 187 x 241mm, No. of Columns (Display): 4, Print Process: offset, Screen: 60 lpc, Film: positive
Copy instructions: *Copy Date:* 10 days prior to publication date
CONSUMER: WOMEN'S INTEREST CONSUMER MAGAZINES: Teenage

DEUTSCH-FINNISCHER HANDEL 706272L14C-3
Editorial: PL 83/ Mikonkatu 25, 00101 HELSINKI
Tel: 9 61 22 120 **Fax:** 9 64 28 59
Email: info@dfhk.fi **Web site:** http://www.dfhk.fi
ISSN: 1236-360X
Freq: Quarterly; **Cover Price:** Free; **Circ:** 2,000
Usual Pagination: 40
Editor-in-Chief: Bernd Fischer
Profile: Journal covering issues on (possible) business between Finland and Germany.
Language(s): Finnish; German
ADVERTISING RATES:
Full Page Colour .... EUR 1590.00
SCC .... EUR 17.80
Mechanical Data: Col Length: 260mm, Trim Size: 130 x 260mm, No. of Columns (Display): 3, Type Area: 210 x 297mm, Print Process: offset, Screen: 60 lpc

DIABETES 15094L56R-6
Editorial: Kirjoniementie 15, 33680 TAMPERE
Tel: 3 28 60 111 **Fax:** 3 28 60 422
Email: lehdet@diabetes.fi **Web site:** http://www.diabetes.fi
ISSN: 0046-0192
Date Established: 1949; **Freq:** Monthly - Published 9/year; **Circ:** 63,015
Usual Pagination: 40
Profile: Magazine of the Finnish Diabetes Association.
Language(s): Finnish; Swedish
Readership: Aimed at people with diabetes and health care personnel.
ADVERTISING RATES:
Full Page Colour .... EUR 3245
SCC .... EUR 29.30
Agency Commission: 15%
Mechanical Data: Col Widths (Display): 48mm, No. of Columns (Display): 4, Type Area: 297 x 210mm, Trim Size: 276 x 195mm, Print Process: offset, Screen: 48 lpc, 4-colours 54-60 lpc
Average ad content per issue: 30%
BUSINESS: HEALTH & MEDICAL: Health Medical Related

DIGIKUVA 1657471L85A-3
Editorial: Siltasaarenkatu 18-20 A, 00530 HELSINKI
Tel: 20 76 08 500 **Fax:** 20 76 08 520
Email: toimitus@digi-kuva.fi **Web site:** http://www.digi-kuva.fi
ISSN: 1795-3081
Date Established: 2004; **Freq:** Monthly - Published 18/year; **Circ:** 6,311
Usual Pagination: 84
Profile: Magazine about digital photography.
Language(s): Finnish
ADVERTISING RATES:
Full Page Colour .... EUR 2650
SCC .... EUR 32
Agency Commission: 15%
Mechanical Data: Type Area: 205 x 276mm, Screen: 54 lpc, Print Process: offset
CONSUMER: PHOTOGRAPHY & FILM MAKING: Photography

DIVAANI 1828244L4B-50
Editorial: Siltasaarenkatu 18-20 A, 00530 HELSINKI
Tel: 20 76 08 500 **Fax:** 20 76 08 520
Email: divaani@bonnier.fi **Web site:** http://www.divaanilehti.fi
Date Established: 2008; **Freq:** Monthly - Published 10/year; **Circ:** 29,563
Managing Editor: Anna Vartiainen
Profile: Magazine about interior-design.
Language(s): Finnish
Readership: Women of age 35-55.
ADVERTISING RATES:
Full Page Colour .... EUR 4750
SCC .... EUR 53.30
Agency Commission: 15%
Mechanical Data: Type Area: 230 x 297mm
Copy instructions: *Copy Date:* 15 days prior to publication date
BUSINESS: ARCHITECTURE & BUILDING: Interior Design & Flooring

DOSIS 15026L37-10
Editorial: Iso Roobertinkatu 7 A, 00120 HELSINKI
Tel: 9 69 62 270 **Fax:** 9 60 51 12
Email: jouni.hirvonen@helsinki.fi **Web site:** http://www.farmasialiitto.fi
ISSN: 0783-4233
Freq: Quarterly; Free to qualifying individuals ; **Circ:** 7,500
Usual Pagination: 72
Managing Editor: Leena Männynoksa-Ollila
Profile: Magazine of the Finnish Pharmacists' Association.
Language(s): English; Finnish
ADVERTISING RATES:
Full Page Colour .... EUR 2500
SCC .... EUR 54.10
Agency Commission: 15%
Mechanical Data: Type Area: 256 x 179mm, Print Process: Offset, Screen: 60 lpc, Col Length: 250mm, Page Width: 170mm, Bleed Size: 176 x 250mm, No. of Columns (Display): 2, Col Widths (Display): 70mm

DYSFASIA 754431L56R-200
Editorial: Suvilinnantie 2, 20900 TURKU
Tel: 2 21 38 200 **Fax:** 2 21 38 210

Email: paivi.seppa-lassila@stroke.fi **Web site:** http://www.stroke.fi
ISSN: 1458-6363
Date Established: 2002; **Freq:** Quarterly; **Circ:** 2,644
Usual Pagination: 40
Editor-in-Chief: Tiina Viljanen
Profile: Magazine about oral and language development problem.
Language(s): Finnish
ADVERTISING RATES:
Full Page Colour .... EUR 2150.00
Mechanical Data: Bleed Size: 210 x 275mm, Type Area: 185 x 255mm, Print Process: offset, Screen: 48 lpc mono, 53 lpc colour
BUSINESS: HEALTH & MEDICAL: Health Medical Related

EEVA 15246L74A-29
Editorial: Risto Rytin tie 33, 00081 A-LEHDET
Tel: 9 75 961 **Fax:** 9 75 98 31 05
Email: eeva@a-lehdet.fi **Web site:** http://www.eeva.fi
ISSN: 0358-8351
Date Established: 1934; **Freq:** Monthly; **Circ:** 101,403
Usual Pagination: 132
Managing Editor: Outi Rastas
Profile: Women's interest magazine with celebrity interviews, life management and family therapy issues.
Language(s): Finnish
Readership: Aimed at professional women.
ADVERTISING RATES:
Full Page Colour .... EUR 6300
SCC .... EUR 58.90
Mechanical Data: Type Area: 241 x 187mm, Bleed Size: 273 x 230mm, No. of Columns (Display): 4, Print Process: Offset, Film: Digital, Screen: 60 lpc, Col Length: 241mm, Page Width: 190mm, Col Widths (Display): 44mm
CONSUMER: WOMEN'S INTEREST CONSUMER MAGAZINES: Women's Interest

EKO-ASIAA 706128L57-2
Editorial: PL 181/ Kuulojankatu 1, 11101 RIIHIMÄKI
Tel: 10 75 51 000 **Fax:** 10 75 51 368
Email: teuvo.heinonen@ekokem.fi **Web site:** http://www.ekokem.fi
ISSN: 1239-5390
Date Established: 1986; **Freq:** Quarterly; **Cover Price:** Free; **Circ:** 33,000
Usual Pagination: 40
Editor-in-Chief: Teuvo Heinonen
Profile: Customer-magazine from Ekokem Oy Ab, which handles chemical waste.
Language(s): Finnish; Swedish

EKONOMI 14864L1A-5
Editorial: Kynämies, Köydenpunojankatu 2 aD, 00180 HELSINKI **Tel:** 9 15 66 85 10
Fax: 9 15 66 86 00
Email: toimitus.ekonomi@kynamies.fi **Web site:** http://www.ekonomilehti.com
ISSN: 0783-2613
Date Established: 1935; **Freq:** 6 issues yearly - Published 9/year; Free to qualifying individuals ; **Circ:** 43,676
Usual Pagination: 58
Managing Editor: Leena Leppänen
Profile: Magazine containing news, interviews and educational information for business administration professionals.
Language(s): Finnish
Readership: Read by members of the Finnish Association of Graduates in Economics and Business Administration.
ADVERTISING RATES:
Full Page Colour .... EUR 3110
SCC .... EUR 27.70
Mechanical Data: Type Area: 217 x 280mm, No. of Columns (Display): 4, Col Widths (Display): 43mm, Print Process: offset, Screen: 60 lpc
BUSINESS: FINANCE & ECONOMICS

EKONOMISKA SAMFUNDETS TIDSKRIFT 14865L1A-10
Editorial: ISES/ Åbo Akademi, Fänriksgatan 3 B, 20500 ÅBO **Tel:** 2 21 54 163
Web site: http://www.ekonomiskasamfundet.fi
ISSN: 0013-3183
Date Established: 1913; **Freq:** Half-yearly - Published 3/year; **Annual Sub.:** EUR 25; **Circ:** 1,400
Usual Pagination: 60
Profile: Theoretical research in the field of economics. Essays presented during meetings of the Economic Society of Finland are also published in the magazine.
Language(s): Swedish
Readership: Aimed at academics and members of the business community.
ADVERTISING RATES:
Full Page Colour .... EUR 330
BUSINESS: FINANCE & ECONOMICS

ELÄINMAAILMA KOIRAT 1698256L81B-25
Editorial: PL 1269/ Vuorikatu 14 A, 00101 HELSINKI
Tel: 20 13 32 222 **Fax:** 20 13 32 360
Email: koirat@egmontkustannus.fi **Web site:** http://www.koirat.fi
ISSN: 1795-780X
Date Established: 2005; **Freq:** 6 issues yearly; **Circ:** 10,320
Usual Pagination: 80
Editor-in-Chief: Virpi Kaivonen
Profile: Magazine about dogs.
Language(s): Finnish
ADVERTISING RATES:
Full Page Colour .... EUR 2200
Mechanical Data: Type Area: 210 x 297mm
Copy instructions: *Copy Date:* 45 days prior to publication date
CONSUMER: ANIMALS & PETS: Dogs

ELÄKELÄINEN 705403L74N-4
Editorial: Mechelininkatu 20 A 1, 00100 HELSINKI
Tel: 20 74 33 610 **Fax:** 20 74 33 619
Email: elakelainen-lehti@elakelaiset.fi **Web site:** http://www.elakelaiset.fi
ISSN: 0355-8290
Freq: 6 issues yearly; **Circ:** 42,000
Usual Pagination: 34
Editor-in-Chief: Hannu Partanen
Profile: Magazine about leisure, rehabilitation, health and legal rights issues for retired people.
Language(s): Finnish
ADVERTISING RATES:
SCC .... EUR 17.00
Agency Commission: 15%
Mechanical Data: No. of Columns (Display): 6, Col Widths (Display): 40mm, Col Length: 365mm, Print Process: offset
CONSUMER: WOMEN'S INTEREST CONSUMER MAGAZINES: Retirement

ELÄKKEENSAAJA 705404L74N-6
Editorial: PL 168/ Haapaniemenkatu 14, 2 krs, 00531 HELSINKI **Tel:** 9 61 26 840 **Fax:** 9 17 06 99
Email: ekl@elakkeensaajat.fi **Web site:** http://www.elakkeensaajat.fi/palvelut/elakkeensaaja-lehti
ISSN: 0355-6557
Date Established: 1971; **Freq:** 6 issues yearly - Published 8/year; **Cover Price:** Free; **Circ:** 45,000
Usual Pagination: 32
Profile: Magazine about retirement and pensions.
Language(s): Finnish
ADVERTISING RATES:
Full Page Colour .... EUR 3182
SCC .... EUR 16.90
Mechanical Data: Type Area: 284 x 412mm, No. of Columns (Display): 6, Print Process: offset, Col Widths (Display): 44mm, Screen: 32 lpc mono, 48 lpc colour
CONSUMER: WOMEN'S INTEREST CONSUMER MAGAZINES: Retirement

ELÄMÄSSÄ - MITT I ALLT 15288L74N-50
Formerly: Kelan Sanomat
Editorial: PL 450, 00101 HELSINKI **Tel:** 20 63 411
Fax: 20 63 45 058
Email: toimitus@kela.fi **Web site:** http://www.kela.fi
ISSN: 0787-8370
Date Established: 1968; **Freq:** Quarterly; **Cover Price:** Free; **Circ:** 2,700,000
Usual Pagination: 32
Editor-in-Chief: Seija Kauppinen
Profile: Magazine concerning social issues. Includes information on sickness, disability, health, unemployment, social benefits and retirement.
Language(s): Finnish
CONSUMER: WOMEN'S INTEREST CONSUMER MAGAZINES: Retirement

ELIMÄEN SANOMAT 704951L72-140
Editorial: PL 10/Vanhamaantie 7, 47201 ELIMÄKI
Tel: 5 74 00 500 **Fax:** 57400510
Email: toimitus@elimaensanomat.fi **Web site:** http://www.elimaensanomat.fi
Date Established: 1976; **Freq:** Weekly; **Circ:** 2,777
Usual Pagination: 16
Editor-in-Chief: Raija Anttila
Profile: Local weekly newspaper issued in Elimäki.
Language(s): Finnish
ADVERTISING RATES:
Full Page Colour .... EUR 2090
SCC .... EUR 11.30
Agency Commission: 15%
Mechanical Data: Type Area: 255 x 370mm, Col Length: 370mm, Page Width: 255mm, Col Widths (Display): 47mm, No. of Columns (Display): 5
LOCAL NEWSPAPERS

ELONKEHÄ 706077L57-3
Editorial: Kauppakartanonkatu 7 A 27, 00930 HELSINKI **Tel:** 44 20 32 439
Email: elonkeha@estelle.fi **Web site:** http://www.elonkeha.fi
ISSN: 1238-7460
Date Established: 1995; **Freq:** Monthly; **Annual Sub.:** EUR 25.00; **Circ:** 600
Usual Pagination: 8
Editor-in-Chief: Elias Hämäläinen
Profile: Ecological culture magazine about the state of the environment.
Language(s): Finnish

EL-SANOMAT 705401L74N-5
Formerly: Eläkeliitto-lehti
Editorial: Kalevankatu 61, 00180 HELSINKI
Tel: 9 72 57 11 00 **Fax:** 9 72 57 11 98
Email: vesa.toikka@elakeliitto.fi **Web site:** http://www.elakeliitto.fi
Date Established: 1970; **Freq:** 6 issues yearly; **Circ:** 82,887
Usual Pagination: 32
Profile: Magazine about retired people's benefits and pensions.
Language(s): Finnish
ADVERTISING RATES:
Full Page Colour .... EUR 2990
SCC .... EUR 14
Agency Commission: 15%
Mechanical Data: Type Area: 284 x 420mm, No. of Columns (Display): 6, Col Length: 420mm, Print Process: offset, Screen: 34-40 lpc, Col Widths (Display): 44mm
Copy instructions: *Copy Date:* 18 days prior to publication date
CONSUMER: WOMEN'S INTEREST CONSUMER MAGAZINES: Retirement

ENERGIA JA YMPÄRISTÖ 1745282L58-53
Formerly: Energian kulutus
Editorial: Vanha Turuntie 371, 03150 HUHMARI
Tel: 9 41 39 73 00
Email: aikakauslehdet@karprint.fi **Web site:** http://www.karprint.fi
ISSN: 1796-3389
Date Established: 2006; **Freq:** 6 issues yearly; **Circ:** 8,000
Usual Pagination: 84
Profile: Magazine about cost-effective consumption of energy.
Language(s): Finnish
Readership: Energy consuming households.
ADVERTISING RATES:
Full Page Colour .... EUR 1780
SCC .... EUR 19.60
Agency Commission: 15%
Copy instructions: *Copy Date:* 18 days prior to publication date

ENERGIAUUTISET 15131L58-75
Editorial: PL 1427/ Fredrikinkatu 51-53 B 5. krs, 00101 HELSINKI **Tel:** 9 53 05 27 00
Fax: 9 53 05 27 01
Email: petri.sallinen@energia.fi **Web site:** http://www.energiauutiset.fi
ISSN: 1237-6388
Date Established: 1989; **Freq:** 6 issues yearly - Published 7/year; **Circ:** 5,000
Usual Pagination: 66
Editor-in-Chief: Pekka Tiusanen; **Managing Editor:** Petri Sallinen
Profile: Publication about energy production, installation and use.
Language(s): Finnish
Readership: Aimed all those involved in the energy sector, including trade associations, research institutes, engineers, electrical and industrial companies.
ADVERTISING RATES:
Full Page Colour .... EUR 3000
SCC .... EUR 25.20
Agency Commission: 15%
Mechanical Data: Trim Size: 3mm, Col Widths (Display): 42.5, No. of Columns (Display): 4, Film: Positive, Type Area: 267 x 180mm, Bleed Size: 297 x 210mm, Screen: 60 lpc, Col Length: 276mm, Page Width: 180mm, Print Process: offset
Copy instructions: *Copy Date:* 14 days prior to publication date
Average ad content per issue: 20%

ENERGIAVIRTAA 764869L58-76
Editorial: PL 95/ Peltolantie 27, 01301 VANTAA
Tel: 9 82 901 **Fax:** 9 82 65 17
Email: mari.lehtinen@vantaanenergia.fi **Web site:** http://www.vantaanenergia.fi
ISSN: 1456-7091
Date Established: 1998; **Freq:** Quarterly; **Cover Price:** Free; **Circ:** 98,000
Usual Pagination: 32
Editor-in-Chief: Mari Lehtinen
Profile: Magazine about energy and electricity.
Language(s): Finnish
Readership: Customers of Vantaan Energia.
BUSINESS: ENERGY, FUEL & NUCLEAR

ERÄ 15304L75L-20
Editorial: Esterinportti 1, 00015 OTAVAMEDIA
Tel: 9 15 661 **Fax:** 9 15 66 62 10
Email: era@otavamedia.fi **Web site:** http://www.eralehti.fi
ISSN: 0356-3464
Date Established: 1977; **Freq:** Monthly - Published 14/year; **Circ:** 45,185
Usual Pagination: 100
Editor-in-Chief: Jari Kaalikoski
Profile: Magazine covering different sports, including angling, shooting and hunting, outdoor and adventure sports.
Language(s): Finnish
ADVERTISING RATES:
Full Page Colour .... EUR 2720
SCC .... EUR 24.20
Mechanical Data: Film: Digital, Print Process: Offset, Bleed Size: 280 x 217mm, Col Widths (Display): 45mm, Film: positive, Screen: 60 lpc, Type Area: 217 x 280mm
Copy instructions: *Copy Date:* 19 days prior to publication date
CONSUMER: SPORT: Outdoor

ERNIE 1639678L1B-70
Editorial: Elielinaukio 5 B, 00100 HELSINKI
Tel: 20 72 80 190
Web site: http://www.ey.com/fi
ISSN: 1459-7802
Freq: Quarterly; **Cover Price:** Free; **Circ:** 10,000
Usual Pagination: 16
Editor-in-Chief: Hannele Lindell
Profile: Magazine about accounting, taxation and finance administration.
Language(s): Finnish
Readership: Customers of Ernst & Young Oy.
BUSINESS: FINANCE & ECONOMICS: Film

ESSE 706131L87-22
Formerly: Espoon Seurakuntasanomat
Editorial: PL 200/ Kirkkokatu 1, 02771 ESPOO
Tel: 20 75 42 000 **Fax:** 9 80 50 22 85
Email: esse.toimitus@kotimaa.fi **Web site:** http://www.esse.fi
ISSN: 1455-2310
Freq: Weekly - Published on Thursday; Free to qualifying individuals ; **Circ:** 81,300
Usual Pagination: 20
Editor-in-Chief: Simo Repo
Profile: Journal about religious events in Espoo parish.
Language(s): Finnish
ADVERTISING RATES:
Full Page Colour .... EUR 2850
SCC .... EUR 18
Agency Commission: 15%
Mechanical Data: No. of Columns (Display): 5, Col Widths (Display): 47mm, Type Area: 255 x 355mm, Screen: 34 lpc, Print Process: offset
CONSUMER: RELIGIOUS

ESSELLOO EXPRÈS 705166L17-4_50
Editorial: PL 88/ Ritakuja 2, 01741 VANTAA
Tel: 10 28 311 **Fax:** 102832010
Email: sari.bamberg@slo.fi **Web site:** http://www.slo.fi
ISSN: 0789-709X
Freq: Quarterly - Published 3/ year; **Cover Price:** Free; **Circ:** 11,140
Usual Pagination: 20
Profile: Product news magazine from electrical appliances wholesaler SLO to energy companies, telecommunications companies, industry, engineers and architects.
Language(s): Finnish
ADVERTISING RATES:
Full Page Colour .... EUR 2000
SCC .... EUR 22.40
Mechanical Data: Bleed Size: 210 x 297mm, Type Area: 192 x 272mm, Col Widths (Display): 45mm, No. of Columns (Display): 4, Print Process: offset, Screen: 70 lpc

ETELÄ-POHJANMAA 704856L67B-2301
Editorial: PL 60/Koulukatu 10, 60101 SEINÄJOKI
Tel: 6 24 77 865 **Fax:** 6 24 77 869
Email: uutiset@epari.fi **Web site:** http://www.epari.fi
Date Established: 1926; **Freq:** Weekly; **Cover Price:** Free; **Circ:** 44,500
Editor-in-Chief: Markku Leiwo
Profile: Regional newspaper distributed in Seinäjoki, Nurmo and the Finnish speaking region of southern Ostrobothnia.
Language(s): Finnish
ADVERTISING RATES:
SCC .... EUR 13.30
Mechanical Data: Print Process: offset, Screen: 40 lpc, Col Length: 365mm, No. of Columns (Display): 6, Col Widths (Display): 40mm, Type Area: 260 x 365mm, Page Width: 260mm
Editions:
Etelä-Pohjanmaa Verkkotoimitus
REGIONAL DAILY & SUNDAY NEWSPAPERS: Regional Daily Newspapers

ETELÄ-SAIMAA 15201L67B-2350
Editorial: PL 3/Lauritsalantie 1, 53501 LAPPEENRANTA **Tel:** 5 53 88 13 **Fax:** 5 53 88 32 07
Email: uutinen@esaimaa.fi **Web site:** http://www.esaimaa.fi
ISSN: 0357-0975
Date Established: 1885; **Freq:** Daily; **Circ:** 30,288
Usual Pagination: 24
Editor-in-Chief: Pekka Lakka; **Managing Editor:** Petri Karjalainen
Profile: Politically independent newspaper issued mainly in the town of Lappeenranta in southeastern Finland.
Language(s): Finnish
ADVERTISING RATES:
Full Page Colour .... EUR 8652
SCC .... EUR 21
Mechanical Data: Page Width: 380mm, Col Length: 515mm, No. of Columns (Display): 8, Col Widths (Display): 44mm
Editions:
Etelä-Saimaa Urheilutoimitus
Etelä-Saimaa Verkkotoimitus
REGIONAL DAILY & SUNDAY NEWSPAPERS: Regional Daily Newspapers

ETELÄ-SAIMAA IMATRA 705590L67E-20
Editorial: Lappeentie 24, 55100 IMATRA
Tel: 5 53 88 31 **Fax:** 5 53 88 34 66

Email: toimitus.imatra@esaimaa.fi **Web site:** http://www.esaimaa.fi
Freq: Daily
Profile: Imatra regional office of newspaper Etelä-Saimaa.
Language(s): Finnish
REGIONAL DAILY & SUNDAY NEWSPAPERS: Regional Offices

ETELÄ-SUOMEN SANOMAT
15200L67B-2400
Editorial: PL 80/ Ilmarisentie 7, 15101 LAHTI
Tel: 3 75 751 **Fax:** 3 75 75 469
Email: toimitus@ess.fi **Web site:** http://www.ess.fi
ISSN: 0359-5056
Date Established: 1900; **Freq:** Daily; **Circ:** 58,400
Usual Pagination: 32
Editor-in-Chief: Heikki Hakala; **Managing Editor:** Tarja Koljonen
Profile: Newspaper mainly issued in Lahti, Heinola, Hollola, Orimattila, Askola, Joutsa, Mäntsälä and Pukkila.
Language(s): Finnish
ADVERTISING RATES:
Full Page Colour .... EUR 14471
SCC .... EUR 33.50
Agency Commission: 15%
Mechanical Data: Col Widths (Display): 44mm, No. of Columns (Display): 8, Type Area: 380 x 540mm, Col Length: 540mm, Page Width: 380mm
Editions:
Etelä-Suomen Sanomat Verkkotoimitus
REGIONAL DAILY & SUNDAY NEWSPAPERS: Regional Daily Newspapers

ETERA
706028L1D-52
Formerly: LEL-Uutiset
Editorial: PL 20/Palkkatilanportti 1, 00241 HELSINKI
Tel: 10 55 33 00 **Fax:** 10 55 33 477
Email: riitta.heinonen@etera.fi **Web site:** http://www.etera.fi
Freq: Quarterly; **Cover Price:** Free; **Circ:** 40,000
Usual Pagination: 20
Profile: Journal about work pensions, pension insurance and social security.
Language(s): Finnish
BUSINESS: FINANCE & ECONOMICS: Insurance

ETEVÄ-SAVO
2059549L14A-164
Editorial: Patteristonkatu 2 C, 50100 MIKKELI
Tel: 15 33 70 111
Email: mikkeli@chamber.fi **Web site:** http://www.southsavo.chamber.fi
Freq: 6 issues yearly; **Cover Price:** Free; **Circ:** 45,000
Editor-in-Chief: Markku Kakriainen
Profile: Etelä-Savo commercial chamber's magazine.
Language(s): Finnish
Readership: Distributed as a supplement to Itä-Savo and Länsi-Savo newspapers.
ADVERTISING RATES:
SCC .... EUR 15.50

ETIKETTI
705202L9A-10
Editorial: Sanoma Magazines Finland Oy, PL 100, 00040 SANOMA MAGAZINES **Tel:** 9 12 05 853
Fax: 9 12 05 988
Email: etiketti@sanomamagazines.fi **Web site:** http://www.alko.fi
ISSN: 0780-508X
Date Established: 1964; **Freq:** Quarterly; **Cover Price:** Free
Free to qualifying individuals
Annual Sub.: EUR 19.00; **Circ:** 275,000
Usual Pagination: 52
Editor-in-Chief: Sari Askola; **Managing Editor:** Sirkka Järvenpää
Profile: Magazine featuring articles on wines, wines in cookery and other alcoholic beverages.
Language(s): Finnish; Swedish
Readership: Finnish customers of Alko interested in wines and alcoholic beverages.
ADVERTISING RATES:
Full Page Colour .... EUR 4896.00
SCC .... EUR 68.00
Agency Commission: 15%
Mechanical Data: Bleed Size: 210 x 297mm, Page Width: 210mm
BUSINESS: DRINKS & LICENSED TRADE: Drinks, Licensed Trade, Wines & Spirits

ET-LEHTI
15287L74N-20
Editorial: PL 100/ Lapinmäentie 1, 00040 SANOMA MAGAZINES **Tel:** 9 12 01 **Fax:** 9 12 05 460
Email: et-lehti@sanomamagazines.fi **Web site:** http://www.et-lehti.fi
ISSN: 0785-0913
Date Established: 1973; **Freq:** Monthly - Published 20/year; **Circ:** 237,265
Usual Pagination: 140
Editor-in-Chief: Maija Toppila; **Managing Editor:** Aira Väisänen
Profile: Magazine covering retirement issues also culture and new interests for the mature generation.
Language(s): Finnish
Readership: Aimed at those aged over 50 years.
ADVERTISING RATES:
Full Page Colour .... EUR 9300
SCC .... EUR 83
Mechanical Data: Type Area: 194 x 248mm, Col Widths (Display): 47mm, Print Process: offset, Film: positive, Screen: 54 lpc, Bleed Size: 230 x 273mm, No. of Columns (Display): 4
CONSUMER: WOMEN'S INTEREST CONSUMER MAGAZINES: Retirement

ETUMATKAA
706018L31R-15
Editorial: Hitsaajankatu 9 B, 00810 HELSINKI
Tel: 20 42 828 **Fax:** 9 75 94 20 11
Email: tarja@tietoputki.fi **Web site:** http://www.tietoputki.fi
Freq: Quarterly; **Cover Price:** Free; **Circ:** 325,000
Usual Pagination: 44
Editor-in-Chief: Lauri Haapala
Profile: Magazine for owners of Volkswagen, Audi and Seat cars.
Language(s): Finnish
BUSINESS: MOTOR TRADE: Motor Trade Related

EURO & TALOUS
706203L1A-6
Editorial: PL 160, 00101 HELSINKI **Tel:** 10 83 11
Fax: 9 65 84 24
Email: info@bof.fi **Web site:** http://www.bof.fi
ISSN: 1456-4718
Date Established: 1993; **Freq:** 6 issues yearly; **Cover Price:** Free
Usual Pagination: 50
Profile: Magazine of the Bank of Finland containing articles about currency, general economic issues and about economic prospects.
Language(s): Finnish
BUSINESS: FINANCE & ECONOMICS

EUROMETALLI
1639208L27-1
Formerly: Europörssin Metalli
Editorial: Tampereentie 484, 33880 LEMPÄÄLÄ
Tel: 20 75 79 595 **Fax:** 20 75 79 591
Email: ep@eurometalli.com **Web site:** http://www.eurometalli.com
Date Established: 2003; **Freq:** Monthly; **Circ:** 30,000
Usual Pagination: 68
Editor-in-Chief: Petri Kuhlman
Profile: Magazine about metals and machinery.
Language(s): Finnish
ADVERTISING RATES:
Full Page Colour .... EUR 1783.00
SCC .... EUR 16.80
Agency Commission: 15%
Mechanical Data: Type Area: 185 x 265mm, No. of Columns (Display): 4, Col Widths (Display): 43mm, Screen: 48 lpc, 4-colour 54-60lpc

EUROMETRI
1642258L82-5
Editorial: PL 332, 00121 HELSINKI **Tel:** 46 98 08 227
Email: posti@suomeneurooppaliike.fi **Web site:** http://www.suomeneurooppaliike.fi/eurometri
Date Established: 1995; **Freq:** Quarterly; **Circ:** 100,000
Usual Pagination: 28
Editor-in-Chief: Pauli Kivipensas
Profile: Magazine about the Finnish European matters.
Language(s): Finnish
CONSUMER: CURRENT AFFAIRS & POLITICS

EUROOPAN TIEDE JA TEKNOLOGIA
706133L1R-5
Formerly: Eurotutkimus
Editorial: PL 69/ Kyllikinportti 2, 00101 HELSINKI
Tel: 10 60 55 055 **Fax:** 10 60 55 904
Web site: http://www.tekes.fi/eu/fin/julkaisut/ett/index.html
ISSN: 1459-4862
Freq: Quarterly; **Cover Price:** Free
Usual Pagination: 32
Profile: Publication of Finnish Development Centre for Technology focuses on EU financing of projects. A version of the publication is issued in English once a year.
Language(s): Finnish
BUSINESS: FINANCE & ECONOMICS: Financial Related

EUROPÖRSSI
705164L49C-10
Editorial: Tampereentie 484, 33880 LEMPÄÄLÄ
Tel: 20 75 79 700 **Fax:** 20 75 79 701
Web site: http://www.europorssi.com
ISSN: 1238-7924
Freq: Monthly; **Circ:** 51,650
Usual Pagination: 76
Editor-in-Chief: Petri Kuhlman
Profile: Journal about mining, building and environment services, vehicles, spare parts and forest machines.
Language(s): Finnish
ADVERTISING RATES:
Full Page Colour .... EUR 1783.00
Agency Commission: 15%
Mechanical Data: Bleed Size: 210 x 297mm, Type Area: 185 x 265mm, No. of Columns (Display): 4, Col Widths (Display): 43mm, Print Process: Heatset rotation, Screen: 48 lpc mono; 54-60 lpc colour
BUSINESS: TRANSPORT: Freight

EXCLUSIVE
1615381L73-260
Editorial: PL 100/ Lapinmäentie 1, 00040 SANOMA MAGAZINES **Tel:** 9 12 05 911 **Fax:** 9 12 05 988
Email: sirkka.jarvenpaa@sanomamagazines.fi **Web site:** http://www.stockmann.fi
ISSN: 1459-2002
Date Established: 2003; **Freq:** Quarterly; **Cover Price:** Free; **Circ:** 130,000
Usual Pagination: 68
Editor-in-Chief: Maaret Kuisma
Profile: Magazine about luxury products, current affairs and issues of interest for shoppers.
Language(s): Finnish; Swedish
Readership: Loyal customers of department store Stockmann.
ADVERTISING RATES:
Full Page Colour .... EUR 6500.00
SCC .... EUR 77.30
Mechanical Data: Print Process: offset, Type Area: 210 x 280mm, Screen: 60 lpc
CONSUMER: NATIONAL & INTERNATIONAL PERIODICALS

EXPRESSI
1655612L49B-50
Editorial: OSG Viestintä, Aurakatu 14 B, 20100 TURKU **Tel:** 20 78 06 853
Email: pramedia@pramedia.fi **Web site:** http://www.expressbus.fi/expressi-asiakaslehti
Freq: Quarterly; **Cover Price:** Free; **Circ:** 45,600
Usual Pagination: 16
Editor-in-Chief: Saara Remes
Profile: Magazine about bus travel.
Language(s): Finnish
Readership: Customers of ExpressBus.
ADVERTISING RATES:
Full Page Colour .... EUR 3000.00
BUSINESS: TRANSPORT: Bus & Coach Transport

FAKTA
14924L14A-5
Editorial: PL 920/ Annankatu 34-36 B, 00101 HELSINKI **Tel:** 20 44 240 **Fax:** 20 44 24 650
Email: fakta@talentum.fi **Web site:** http://www.fakta.fi
ISSN: 0358-626X
Date Established: 1981; **Freq:** Monthly; **Circ:** 18,030
Usual Pagination: 60
Managing Editor: Heikki Nivaro
Profile: Business magazine covering management, development and entrepreneurship.
Language(s): Finnish
Readership: Read by decision makers, corporate management and executives.
ADVERTISING RATES:
Full Page Colour .... EUR 3910
SCC .... EUR 32.90
Agency Commission: 5-15%
Mechanical Data: Screen: 70 lpc, Print Process: Offset, Film: Digital, Type Area: 220 x 297mm, No. of Columns (Display): 4, Col Length: 297mm, Page Width: 220mm
Copy instructions: *Copy Date:* 9 days prior to publication date
Editions:
Fakta.fi
BUSINESS: COMMERCE, INDUSTRY & MANAGEMENT

FAKTORI
15035L60A-10
Editorial: Museokatu 13 A 4, 00100 HELSINKI
Tel: 9 45 42 18 40 **Fax:** 9496276
Web site: http://www.faktori.fi
ISSN: 0355-676X
Date Established: 1915; **Freq:** Quarterly - Published 5/year; **Annual Sub.:** EUR 50; **Circ:** 2,986
Usual Pagination: 56
Profile: Publication of the Association of Finnish Print and Media Managers.
Language(s): Finnish
ADVERTISING RATES:
Full Page Colour .... EUR 1930
SCC .... EUR 21.60
Agency Commission: 15%
Mechanical Data: Type Area: 180 x 265mm, Print Process: Offset, Screen: 54/60 lpc, Col Widths (Display): 54mm, Col Length: 265mm, Page Width: 170mm, Film: negative, No. of Columns (Display): 3
BUSINESS: PUBLISHING: Publishing & Book Trade

FANBÄRAREN
719251L40-1
Editorial: Nylands Brigad, 10640 DRAGSVIK
Tel: 19 18 14 739 **Fax:** 19 18 14 741
Email: fanbararen@mil.fi **Web site:** http://www.nylandsbrigadsgille.fi
ISSN: 0358-1268
Date Established: 1935; **Freq:** Quarterly; **Circ:** 4,000
Usual Pagination: 44
Editor-in-Chief: Anders Gardberg
Profile: Magazine about traditions in the Swedish-speaking military institution Nylands Brigad.
Language(s): Swedish

FARMASIA
15028L37-20
Formerly: Semina
Editorial: Iso Roobertinkatu 7 A, 00120 HELSINKI
Tel: 9 69 62 270 **Fax:** 9 60 51 12
Email: farmasia@farmasialiitto.fi **Web site:** http://www.farmasialiitto.fi
ISSN: 1796-6116
Date Established: 1917; **Freq:** Monthly - Double issue for October and a special issue in November; **Circ:** 7,800
Usual Pagination: 32
Managing Editor: Leena Männynoksa-Ollila
Profile: Magazine of the Finnish Pharmacists' Association for internal communication.
Language(s): Finnish
ADVERTISING RATES:
Full Page Colour .... EUR 2950
SCC .... EUR 35.30
Agency Commission: 15%
Mechanical Data: Type Area: 217 x 278mm, No. of Columns (Display): 3, Col Widths (Display): 55mm, Screen: 60/48 lpc, Col Length: 278mm, Page Width: 217mm
Average ad content per issue: 10%

FARMI
706542L21A-3_10
Formerly: Farmi-Uutiset
Editorial: Liisankatu 11 C 69, 28100 PORI
Tel: 2 63 24 310 **Fax:** 2 63 24 313
Email: farmi@countrymedia.fi **Web site:** http://www.countrymedia.fi
ISSN: 1238-1586
Date Established: 1983; **Freq:** 6 issues yearly - Published 9/year; **Circ:** 20,000
Editor-in-Chief: Katja Simonen
Profile: Magazine about entrepreneurship on the countryside.
Language(s): Finnish
ADVERTISING RATES:
Full Page Colour .... EUR 2300
SCC .... EUR 21.50
Agency Commission: 15%
Mechanical Data: Col Widths (Display): 40mm, No. of Columns (Display): 6, Type Area: 186 x 267mm, Screen: 36-48 lpc
Editions:
Farmi verkkotoimitus

FENNIA
706455L1D-130
Formerly: Y-Fennia
Editorial: 00017 FENNIA **Tel:** 10 50 31
Fax: 10 50 36 690
Email: fennialehti@fennia.fi **Web site:** http://www.fennia.fi
ISSN: 1456-1891
Freq: Quarterly; **Cover Price:** Free; **Circ:** 50,000
Usual Pagination: 36
Editor: Pia Kuorikoski; **Editor-in-Chief:** Eliisa Anttila
Profile: Customer-magazine for private household customers of insurance company Fennia Oy.
Language(s): Finnish
BUSINESS: FINANCE & ECONOMICS: Insurance

FINLANDS NATUR
706080L57-5
Editorial: Annegatan 26, 00100 HELSINGFORS
Tel: 9 61 22 290 **Fax:** 9 61 22 29 10
Email: fn@naturochmiljo.fi **Web site:** http://www.naturochmiljo.fi
ISSN: 0356-4509
Date Established: 1941; **Freq:** 6 issues yearly; **Circ:** 5,000
Usual Pagination: 40
Editor-in-Chief: Magnus Östman
Profile: Magazine about biology, nature and environment protection in Finland.
Language(s): Swedish
ADVERTISING RATES:
Full Page Colour .... EUR 1200.00
Mechanical Data: Type Area: 210 x 297mm, Film: negative, Screen: 28-32 lpc mono, 48 lpc colour

FINN NICHE
713681L14C-6
Editorial: WTC/ Aleksanterinkatu 17, Thame, 00100 HELSINKI **Tel:** 50 30 00 579
Email: markku@finn-niche.com **Web site:** http://www.finn-niche.com
ISSN: 0955-6087
Date Established: 1989; **Freq:** Quarterly; **Cover Price:** Free; **Circ:** 5,000
Usual Pagination: 32
Editor-in-Chief: Markku Vartiainen
Profile: Magazine to promote business and cultural relations between Finland and Great Britain.
Language(s): English; Finnish
ADVERTISING RATES:
Full Page Colour .... EUR 1950.00
Mechanical Data: Bleed Size: 220 x 307mm, Trim Size: 210 x 297mm

FINNET KOTIASIAKASLEHTI
705268L18B-4
Formerly: Kotipuhelin
Editorial: PL 949/Sinebrychoffinkatu 11, 00101 HELSINKI **Tel:** 9 31 53 15 **Fax:** 9 31 53 82 44
Email: riittamaija.stahle@finnet.fi **Web site:** http://www.finnet.fi/index.html
ISSN: 0780-9565
Date Established: 1976; **Freq:** Quarterly; **Cover Price:** Free; **Circ:** 180,000
Usual Pagination: 16
Managing Editor: Riittamaija Ståhle
Profile: Customer-magazine about telecommunications and information technology. About 30 local versions of the magazine are produced throughout the country.
Language(s): Finnish
ADVERTISING RATES:
Full Page Colour .... EUR 4700.00
Agency Commission: 15%
Mechanical Data: Bleed Size: 210 x 297mm, Type Area: 194 x 267mm
BUSINESS: ELECTRONICS: Telecommunications

FINNET YRITYSASIAKASLEHTI
705254L18B-120

Formerly: Yrittäjän Puhelin
Editorial: PL 949/Sinebrychoffinkatu 11, 00101 HELSINKI **Tel:** 9 31 53 15 **Fax:** 9 31 53 82 44
Email: riittamaija.stahle@finnet.fi **Web site:** http://www.finnet.fi/index.html
ISSN: 1239-7237
Date Established: 1994; **Freq:** Quarterly; **Cover Price:** Free; **Circ:** 11,000
Usual Pagination: 24
Managing Editor: Riittamaija Ståhle
Profile: Magazine about information technology solutions, services and products for small and medium-sized companies.
Language(s): Finnish
ADVERTISING RATES:
Full Page Colour .... EUR 3200.00
Agency Commission: 15%
Mechanical Data: Type Area: 194 x 267mm
BUSINESS: ELECTRONICS: Telecommunications

FINPRO IN FRONT
718005L14C-8

Editorial: Viestintätoimisto Sanakunta Oy, Kristiinankatu 3 B, 20100 TURKU **Tel:** 20 46 951
Web site: http://www.finpro.fi
ISSN: 1456-6524
Freq: Quarterly; **Cover Price:** Free; **Circ:** 8,000
Usual Pagination: 38
Managing Editor: Maarit Niemi
Profile: Magazine by Finpro, an organisation that helps businesses with international issues.
Language(s): Finnish
ADVERTISING RATES:
Full Page Colour .... EUR 2440
SCC .... EUR 29
Mechanical Data: Type Area: 182 x 260mm, No. of Columns (Display): 2/3, Col Widths (Display): 85mm/ 55mm, Print Process: offset, Screen: 70 lpc

FINSKA LÄKARESÄLLSKAPETS HANDLINGAR
706543L56A-4

Editorial: PB 82/ Johannesbergsvägen 8, 00251 HELSINGFORS **Tel:** 9 47 76 80 90 **Fax:** 9 43 62 055
Email: kansliet@fls.fi **Web site:** http://www.fls.fi
ISSN: 0015-2501
Date Established: 1841; **Freq:** Half-yearly; **Circ:** 2,000
Usual Pagination: 58
Editor-in-Chief: Johan Lundin
Profile: Magazine about recent medical research.
Language(s): Swedish

FIT
706430L75P-25

Formerly: Fitness
Editorial: Pursimiehenkatu 29-31 A, 00150 HELSINKI **Tel:** 9 86 21 70 00 **Fax:** 9 86 21 71 39
Email: toimitus@fit.fi **Web site:** http://www.fit.fi
ISSN: 1236-2247
Date Established: 1992; **Freq:** Monthly - Published 10/year; **Circ:** 21,250
Usual Pagination: 84
Editor-in-Chief: Taru Marjamaa; **Managing Editor:** Anne Luhtala
Profile: Magazine about fitness and body-care.
Language(s): Finnish
ADVERTISING RATES:
Full Page Colour .... EUR 2990
SCC .... EUR 35.50
Agency Commission: 15%
Mechanical Data: Type Area: 217 x 280mm, Print Process: offset
Copy instructions: *Copy Date:* 14 days prior to publication date
CONSUMER: SPORT: Fitness/Bodybuilding

FORMA & FURNITURE
14998L4B-3

Formerly: Forma Uutiset
Editorial: Mannerheimintie 40 D 82, 00100 HELSINKI **Tel:** 10 82 09 800 **Fax:** 10 82 09 806
Email: forma@formamessut.fi **Web site:** http://www.formamessut.fi
ISSN: 1795-3715
Date Established: 1979; **Freq:** 6 issues yearly; **Circ:** 8,000
Usual Pagination: 44
Editor-in-Chief: Arja Tammi
Profile: Magazine about household goods and furnishings.
Language(s): Finnish
Readership: Read by manufacturers, retailers and designers.
ADVERTISING RATES:
Full Page Colour .... EUR 3375.00
SCC .... EUR 32.40
Agency Commission: 15%
Mechanical Data: Type Area: 191 x 243mm, Bleed Size: 210 x 280mm, No. of Columns (Display): 4, Col Widths (Display): 48.75mm, Print Process: offset, Screen: 70 lpc

FORSSAN LEHTI
15181L67B-2500

Editorial: PL 38/ Esko Aaltosen katu 2, 30101 FORSSA **Tel:** 3 41 551 **Fax:** 3 41 55 724
Email: toimitus@forssanlehti.fi **Web site:** http://www.forssanlehti.fi
ISSN: 0782-663X
Date Established: 1917
Circ: 13,455
Usual Pagination: 18
Profile: Regional newspaper issued in Forssa, Tammela, Jokioinen, Humppila, Ypäjä, Somero and Urjala.
Language(s): Finnish
ADVERTISING RATES:
Full Page Colour .... EUR 7654
SCC .... EUR 18.40
Mechanical Data: Col Length: 520mm, No. of Columns (Display): 8, Col Widths (Display): 43mm, Print Process: 4-colouroffsetrotation, Screen: 34 lpc b/w, 40 lpc colour, Page Width: 379mm
Editions:
Forssan Lehti Urheilutoimitus
Forssan Lehti Verkkotoimitus
REGIONAL DAILY & SUNDAY NEWSPAPERS: Regional Daily Newspapers

FORUM 24
749279L72-175

Editorial: Lekatie 6, 90510 OULU **Tel:** 20 75 45 700 **Fax:** 20 75 45 701
Email: toimitus@forum24.fi **Web site:** http://www.forum24.fi
ISSN: 1458-4042
Date Established: 2001; **Freq:** 104 issues yearly; **Cover Price:** Free; **Circ:** 94,000
Usual Pagination: 24
Editor-in-Chief: Martti Turunen; **Managing Editor:** Risto Kenttä
Profile: Newspaper distributed in Oulu.
Language(s): Finnish
ADVERTISING RATES:
Full Page Colour .... EUR 5324
SCC .... EUR 25.50
Mechanical Data: Type Area: 248 x 348mm, Bleed Size: 280 x 400mm, Page Width: 280mm, Col Length: 348mm, No. of Columns (Display): 6
LOCAL NEWSPAPERS

FORUM FÖR EKONOMI OCH TEKNIK
14926L1R-15

Editorial: Mannerheimvägen 20 A, 7 vån, 00100 HELSINGFORS **Tel:** 9 54 95 55 00 **Fax:** 9 54 95 55 77
Email: redaktionen@forum.fi **Web site:** http://www.forum-fet.fi
ISSN: 0533-070X
Date Established: 1967; **Freq:** Monthly; **Circ:** 10,947
Usual Pagination: 60
Managing Editor: Heidi Furu
Profile: Publication containing articles on technology and business economics.
Language(s): Swedish
Readership: Read by people involved in business and technology.
ADVERTISING RATES:
Full Page Colour .... EUR 3540
SCC .... EUR 42.10
Agency Commission: 15%
Mechanical Data: Screen: 60 lpc, Type Area: 185 x 254mm, Print Process: Offset, Col Length: 280mm, Page Width: 212mm, Bleed Size: 212 x 280mm, No. of Columns (Display): 3-4, Col Widths (Display): 40-54mm
Copy instructions: *Copy Date:* 14 days prior to publication date
Average ad content per issue: 20%
BUSINESS: FINANCE & ECONOMICS: Financial Related

FREDSPOSTEN
706082L40-2

Editorial: c/o Christian Lång, Hörnvägen 2 A 7, 64200 NÄRPES **Tel:** 9 31 04 94 84
Web site: http://www.fredsposten.fi
Date Established: 1926; **Freq:** Quarterly; **Annual Sub.:** EUR 18.00; **Circ:** 1,500
Usual Pagination: 16
Editor-in-Chief: Christian Lång
Profile: Magazine about peace, understanding, anti-nuclear justice in our world.
Language(s): Swedish
ADVERTISING RATES:
Full Page Colour .... EUR 170.00

FRISK BRIS
705357L91A-3

Editorial: Blåbergsvägen 5 B, 02630 ESBO **Tel:** 9 50 23 490 **Fax:** 95023486
Email: kari.wilen@seakari.fi **Web site:** http://www.friskbris.fi
ISSN: 0359-6648
Date Established: 1903; **Freq:** 6 issues yearly - Published 7/year; **Circ:** 2,111
Usual Pagination: 48
Profile: Magazine about boating and yachting.
Language(s): Swedish
ADVERTISING RATES:
Full Page Colour .... EUR 960
Agency Commission: 15%
Mechanical Data: Type Area: 175 x 250mm, No. of Columns (Display): 3/4, Print Process: offset, Screen: 60 lpc
CONSUMER: RECREATION & LEISURE: Boating & Yachting

FUTURE MAAILMA
706259L5R-7

Editorial: Sahaajankatu 26 A, 00880 HELSINKI **Tel:** 9 47 85 400 **Fax:** 9 47 85 45 00
Email: info@futurecad.fi **Web site:** http://www.futurecad.fi
Freq: Quarterly; **Cover Price:** Free; **Circ:** 24,000
Usual Pagination: 40
Editor-in-Chief: Jukka Koskinen
Profile: Future Cad Oy is a leading marketing and consulting company for information applications. The company-magazine is a tool for business enhancement.
Language(s): Finnish
Mechanical Data: Print Process: offset, Bleed Size: 210 x 297mm, Film: negative, Screen: 60 lpc
BUSINESS: COMPUTERS & AUTOMATION: Computers Related

GEO
1831466L73-60

Editorial: PL 100/ Lapinmäentie 1, 00040 SANOMA MAGAZINES **Tel:** 9 12 05 949 **Fax:** 9 12 05 758
Email: geo@sanomamagazines.fi **Web site:** http://www.geo-lehti.fi
ISSN: 1797-3600
Date Established: 2008; **Freq:** Monthly - Published 11/year; **Circ:** 25,154
Usual Pagination: 116
Profile: Magazine about society, history, medicine, psychology, ecology and environment.
Language(s): Finnish
ADVERTISING RATES:
Full Page Colour .... EUR 3510
SCC .... EUR 32.50
CONSUMER: NATIONAL & INTERNATIONAL PERIODICALS

GLORIA
15247L74A-29_9

Editorial: PL 100/ Lapinmäentie 1, 00040 SANOMA MAGAZINES **Tel:** 9 12 01 **Fax:** 9 12 05 427
Email: gloria@sanomamagazines.fi **Web site:** http://www.gloria.fi
ISSN: 0783-6856
Date Established: 1987; **Freq:** Monthly; **Circ:** 52,367
Usual Pagination: 220
Editor-in-Chief: Sami Sykkö; **Managing Editor:** Eeva-Liisa Pere
Profile: Women's interest magazine.
Language(s): Finnish
Readership: Aimed at women aged 30 to 50 years old.
ADVERTISING RATES:
Full Page Colour .... EUR 8230
SCC .... EUR 69.20
Mechanical Data: Type Area: 195 x 267mm, No. of Columns (Display): 4, Col Widths (Display): 45mm, Print Process: offset, Film: positive, Screen: 60 lpc
Copy instructions: *Copy Date:* 21 days prior to publication date
CONSUMER: WOMEN'S INTEREST CONSUMER MAGAZINES: Women's Interest

GLORIAN ANTIIKKI
14912L7-50

Editorial: PL 100/ Lapinmäentie 1, 00040 SANOMA MAGAZINES **Tel:** 9 12 01 **Fax:** 9 12 05 427
Email: glorianantiikki@sanomamagazines.fi **Web site:** http://www.glorianantiikki.fi
ISSN: 1238-5654
Date Established: 1993; **Freq:** Monthly - Published 10/year; **Circ:** 29,069
Usual Pagination: 100
Editor-in-Chief: Pia Maria Montonen
Profile: Magazine about antique and antiquities.
Language(s): Finnish
Readership: Read by antiquaries and antique dealers.
ADVERTISING RATES:
Full Page Colour .... EUR 4500
SCC .... EUR 37.80
Mechanical Data: Type Area: 195 x 267mm, Bleed Size: 230 x 297mm, No. of Columns (Display): 4, Col Widths (Display): 45mm, Film: positive, Print Process: offset, Screen: 60 lpc
Copy instructions: *Copy Date:* 16 days prior to publication date
BUSINESS: ANTIQUES

GLORIAN KOTI
705856L74C-20

Editorial: PL 100/ Lapinmäentie 1, 00040 SANOMA MAGAZINES **Tel:** 9 12 01 **Fax:** 9 12 05 427
Email: gloriankoti@sanomamagazines.fi **Web site:** http://www.gloriankoti.fi
ISSN: 1455-1284
Date Established: 1996; **Freq:** Monthly; **Circ:** 47,192
Usual Pagination: 124
Editor-in-Chief: Minna Juti; **Managing Editor:** Sanna Tyry
Profile: Magazine covering trends in Finnish homes, lifestyle and decoration. Features ideas on decorating homes and gardens.
Language(s): Finnish
Readership: Aimed at people interested in home decoration.
ADVERTISING RATES:
Full Page Colour .... EUR 5600
SCC .... EUR 47.10
Mechanical Data: Type Area: 194 x 267mm, Col Widths (Display): 45mm, No. of Columns (Display): 4, Bleed Size: 230 x 297mm, Film: positive, Screen: 60 lpc, Print Process: offset
Copy instructions: *Copy Date:* 20 days prior to publication date
CONSUMER: WOMEN'S INTEREST CONSUMER MAGAZINES: Home & Family

GLORIAN RUOKA & VIINI
706506L74P-30

Editorial: PL 100/ Lapinmäentie 1, 00040 SANOMA MAGAZINES **Tel:** 9 12 01 **Fax:** 9 12 05 427
Email: glorianruoka&viini@sanomamagazines.fi **Web site:** http://www.glorianruokajaviini.fi
ISSN: 1457-0769
Date Established: 1999; **Freq:** 6 issues yearly - Published 8/year; **Circ:** 34,699
Usual Pagination: 116
Editor-in-Chief: Sanna Maskulin
Profile: Magazine about gourmet food and fine wines.
Language(s): Finnish
ADVERTISING RATES:
Full Page Colour .... EUR 555C
SCC .... EUR 69.2C
Mechanical Data: Bleed Size: 230 x 297mm, Type Area: 195 x 267mm, Film: negative, Print Process: offset
Copy instructions: *Copy Date:* 20 days prior to publication date
CONSUMER: WOMEN'S INTEREST CONSUMER MAGAZINES: Food & Cookery

GOD TID
705407L74N-8

Editorial: PB 129/ Annegatan 25 A, 3 vån, 00101 HELSINGFORS **Tel:** 20 72 88 810 **Fax:** 9 72 88 82 15
Email: ulf.wahlstrom@spfpension.fi **Web site:** http://www.spfpension.fi
ISSN: 0359-8969
Date Established: 1973; **Freq:** 6 issues yearly; **Circ:** 16,000
Usual Pagination: 16
Editor-in-Chief: Ulf Wahlström
Profile: Journal covering current information on retirement issues, union events, travel, culture, social politics, health and medicine.
Language(s): Swedish
Readership: Aimed at Swedish-speaking elderly people living along the Finnish coastline, including the Ahvenanmaa Islands.
ADVERTISING RATES:
SCC .... EUR 19.00
Agency Commission: 15%
Mechanical Data: Type Area: 250 x 350mm, No. of Columns (Display): 5, Col Widths (Display): 46mm, Screen: 34 lpc, Print Process: offset, Bleed Size: 280 x 395mm

GRIFFIN
712711L46-100

Editorial: PL 380/ Eteläesplanadi 2, 00101 HELSINKI **Tel:** 20 41 51 11
Web site: http://www.upm-kymmene.com/thegriffin
ISSN: 1239-4645
Date Established: 1996; **Freq:** Half-yearly; **Cover Price:** Free; **Circ:** 10,000
Usual Pagination: 48
Editor-in-Chief: Monica Krabbe
Profile: Griffin is the voice of UPM-Kymmene Paper Industry and is a source of technical updates, international comment and the latest news from the company.
Language(s): English; French; German

GTI-MAGAZINE
706604L77A-6

Editorial: PL 100/ Lapinmäentie 1, 00040 SANOMA MAGAZINES **Tel:** 9 12 01 **Fax:** 9 12 05 795
Email: gti-toimitus@sanomamagazines.fi **Web site:** http://www.gti.fi
ISSN: 1457-6058
Date Established: 2000; **Freq:** Monthly - Published 11/year; **Circ:** 35,827
Usual Pagination: 92
Editor: Lauri Setälä; **Editor-in-Chief:** Jarmo Markkanen; **Managing Editor:** Ilja Ojala
Profile: Magazine about car tuning.
Language(s): Finnish
Readership: Young men.
ADVERTISING RATES:
Full Page Colour .... EUR 3150
SCC .... EUR 35.30
Mechanical Data: Bleed Size: 210 x 297mm, Type Area: 191 x 274mm, Print Process: offset, Film: positive
Copy instructions: *Copy Date:* 21 days prior to publication date
CONSUMER: MOTORING & CYCLING: Motoring

GULA BLADET
713465L19R-50

Editorial: PB 75/ Banvaktsgatan 2, 00521 HELSINGFORS **Tel:** 9 47 67 717 **Fax:** 9 47 67 73 33
Email: kansli@diff.fi **Web site:** http://gulabladet.tidskrift.fi
Freq: Monthly; **Cover Price:** Free; **Circ:** 7,500
Editor-in-Chief: Lars Engström
Profile: Journal for Swedish-speaking members of the Civil Engineering Union.
Language(s): Swedish

HAAPAVESI-LEHTI
1626470L72-180

Editorial: Tähtelänkuja 2, 86600 HAAPAVESI **Tel:** 20 75 04 640 **Fax:** 207504641
Email: toimitus@haapavesi-lehti.fi **Web site:** http://www.haapavesi-lehti.fi
ISSN: 1456-033X
Date Established: 2003; **Freq:** Weekly; **Circ:** 3,102
Usual Pagination: 8
Editor-in-Chief: Katariina Anttila
Profile: Newspaper distributed in the Haapavesi region.
Language(s): Finnish
ADVERTISING RATES:
SCC .... EUR 7.40
Mechanical Data: Type Area: 258 x 365mm, Col Length: 365mm, Print Process: offset, Page Width: 258mm, No. of Columns (Display): 6, Col Widths (Display): 38mm
LOCAL NEWSPAPERS

HÄÄT JA JUHLAT 1668291L74L-8
Editorial: Vattuniemenranta 2, 00210 HELSINKI
Tel: 9 32 95 11 00 **Fax:** 9 32 95 11 09
Email: info@haatjajuhlat.fi **Web site:** http://www.haatjajuhlat.fi
Date Established: 2005; **Freq:** Half-yearly; **Circ:** 25,000
Usual Pagination: 246
Editor-in-Chief: Sofia Boij
Profile: Magazine about weddings and party organizing.
Language(s): Finnish
ADVERTISING RATES:
Full Page Colour .... EUR 2180.00
Mechanical Data: Type Area: 225 x 298mm

HÄÄT-LEHTI 706021L74L-5
Editorial: Meritullinkatu 11 K, 00170 HELSINKI
Tel: 9 26 00 470 **Fax:** 9 26 00 471
Email: haat@editus.fi **Web site:** http://www.haat-lehti.fi
ISSN: 1237-1904
Date Established: 1994; **Freq:** Half-yearly; **Circ:** 25,000
Usual Pagination: 100
Editor-in-Chief: Sari Yli-Salomäki
Profile: Women's interest magazine specialising in wedding arrangements.
Language(s): Finnish
Readership: People that are planning their wedding day.
ADVERTISING RATES:
Full Page Colour .... EUR 2830.00
SCC .... EUR 27.70
Agency Commission: 15%
Mechanical Data: Type Area: 217 x 280mm, Trim Size: 185 x 255mm, No. of Columns (Display): 4, Col Widths (Display): 44mm, Print Process: offset, Screen: 60 lpc

HALLINTO 705137L14A-11
Editorial: Purotie 1 B, 00380 HELSINKI
Tel: 9 54 21 01 00
Email: anna-maija.vainio@stellatum.fi **Web site:** http://www.stellatum.fi
ISSN: 0355-7448
Date Established: 1960; **Freq:** 6 issues yearly; **Circ:** 2,000
Usual Pagination: 40
Editor-in-Chief: Silja Hiironniemi; **Managing Editor:** Anna-Maija Vainio
Profile: Hallinto provides a forum for the Finnish public administration and its development. It contains articles written by professionals and society decision makers and also news concerning administration.
Language(s): Finnish
ADVERTISING RATES:
Full Page Colour .... EUR 1600.00
Mechanical Data: Bleed Size: 210 x 297mm, Print Process: offset, Screen: 60 lpc, Type Area: 180 x 255mm

HÄMEEN SANOMAT 15182L67B-3650
Editorial: PL 530/ Vanajatie 7, 13111 HÄMEENLINNA
Tel: 3 61 511 **Fax:** 3 61 51 492
Email: toimitus@hameensanomat.fi **Web site:** http://www.hameensanomat.fi
ISSN: 0356-2751
Date Established: 1879; **Freq:** Daily; **Circ:** 28,296
Usual Pagination: 24
Editor-in-Chief: Pauli Uusi-Kilponen; **Managing Editor:** Tapio Lahtinen
Profile: Newspaper issued in Hämeenlinna, Hattula, Hauho, Janakkala, Kalvola, Lammi, Renko and Tuulos.
Language(s): Finnish
ADVERTISING RATES:
Full Page Colour .... EUR 10608
SCC .... EUR 26
Agency Commission: 15%
Mechanical Data: Page Width: 380mm, Col Length: 510mm, No. of Columns (Display): 8, Col Widths (Display): 44mm, Print Process: offset
Editions:
Hämeen Sanomat Verkkotoimitus
REGIONAL DAILY & SUNDAY NEWSPAPERS:
Regional Daily Newspapers

HÄMEEN SANOMAT RIIHIMÄKI 705611L67E-117
Editorial: Kauppakatu 12, 11130 RIIHIMAKI
Tel: 19 72 39 45 **Fax:** 19 71 96 90
Email: riihimaki@hameensanomat.fi **Web site:** http://www.hameensanomat.fi
Date Established: 1879; **Freq:** Daily
Profile: Riihimäki regional office of newspaper Hämeen Sanomat.
Language(s): Finnish
REGIONAL DAILY & SUNDAY NEWSPAPERS:
Regional Offices

HÄMEENKYRÖN SANOMAT 704900L72-185
Editorial: PL 13 / Nuijamiestentie 1, 39101 HÄMEENKYRÖ **Tel:** 3 31 43 31 00 **Fax:** 3 37 15 788
Email: toimitus@hameenkyronsanomat.fi **Web site:** http://www.hameenkyronsanomat.fi
ISSN: 0789-662X
Date Established: 1922; **Freq:** 104 issues yearly; **Circ:** 5,619
Usual Pagination: 12
Managing Director: Kari Silvola
Profile: Newspaper issued in Hämeenkyrö and Viljakkala.
Language(s): Finnish
ADVERTISING RATES:
Full Page Colour .... EUR 3951
SCC .... EUR 13.60
Agency Commission: 15%
Mechanical Data: No. of Columns (Display): 7, Col Length: 430mm, Type Area: 290 x 430mm, Col Widths (Display): 38.5mm, Print Process: offset, Page Width: 290mm
Editions:
Hämeenkyrön Sanomat Verkkotoimitus
LOCAL NEWSPAPERS

HANKASALMEN SANOMAT 704920L72-200
Editorial: PL 12/Keskustie 32, 41521 HANKASALMI
Tel: 14 84 11 45 **Fax:** 14841961
Email: toimitus@hankasalmensanomat.fi **Web site:** http://www.hankasalmensanomat.fi
Date Established: 1963; **Freq:** Weekly; **Circ:** 3,575
Editor-in-Chief: Arja Korpela
Profile: Local newspaper issued in Hankasalmi.
Language(s): Finnish
ADVERTISING RATES:
SCC .... EUR 8.60
Agency Commission: 15%
Mechanical Data: No. of Columns (Display): 6, Col Widths (Display): 40mm, Col Length: 370mm, Print Process: offset
Editions:
Hankasalmen Sanomat Verkkotoimitus
LOCAL NEWSPAPERS

HANKINTAVINKIT 705217L19E-3
Editorial: Hämeenpuisto 44, 33200 TAMPERE
Tel: 3 22 34 380 **Fax:** 3 22 34 381
Email: toimitus@hankintavinkit.fi **Web site:** http://www.hankintavinkit.fi
ISSN: 1238-1950
Date Established: 1985; **Freq:** Monthly; **Circ:** 19,500
Usual Pagination: 40
Profile: Magazine about building, forestry and real estate machinery.
Language(s): Finnish
ADVERTISING RATES:
Full Page Colour .... EUR 3154
SCC .... EUR 14.80
Mechanical Data: Type Area: 260 x 355mm, Bleed Size: 280 x 400mm, Col Widths (Display): 40mm, No. of Columns (Display): 6

HEINÄVEDEN LEHTI 704962L72-215
Editorial: PL 23 / Kermantie 24 A, 79701 HEINÄVESI
Tel: 17 56 25 71 **Fax:** 17562573
Email: uutiset@heinavedenlehti.fi **Web site:** http://www.heinavedenlehti.fi
ISSN: 0782-5781
Date Established: 1969; **Freq:** Weekly; **Circ:** 3,557
Usual Pagination: 12
Editor-in-Chief: Eija Kosunen
Profile: Newspaper issued in Heinävesi.
Language(s): Finnish
ADVERTISING RATES:
SCC .... EUR 8.90
Agency Commission: 15%
Mechanical Data: No. of Columns (Display): 6, Col Length: 370mm, Page Width: 255mm, Col Widths (Display): 40mm, Print Process: offset, Film: negative, Screen: 34/48 lpc
LOCAL NEWSPAPERS

HELEN 706192L58-85
Editorial: Kampinkuja 2, 00090 HELEN **Tel:** 9 61 71
Fax: 9 61 72 360
Email: helsingin.energia@helsinginenergia.fi **Web site:** http://www.helsinginenergia.fi
ISSN: 1455-9528
Freq: Quarterly; **Cover Price:** Free; **Circ:** 330,000
Usual Pagination: 24
Editor-in-Chief: Seija Uusitalo
Profile: Customer-magazine for private household by Helsinki Energy Company.
Language(s): Finnish
BUSINESS: ENERGY, FUEL & NUCLEAR

HELEN B. 706546L58-90
Editorial: Kampinkuja 2, 00090 HELEN **Tel:** 9 61 71
Fax: 9 61 72 360
Email: helsingin.energia@helsinginenergia.fi **Web site:** http://www.helsinginenergia.fi
ISSN: 1456-7849
Freq: Half-yearly; **Cover Price:** Free; **Circ:** 23,000
Usual Pagination: 16
Editor-in-Chief: Seija Uusitalo
Profile: Customer-magazine by Helsinki Energy Company for company clients.
Language(s): Finnish

HELSINGIN RESERVIN SANOMAT 705857L40-3
Editorial: Döbelninkatu 2, 00260 HELSINKI
Tel: 9 40 56 20 80 **Fax:** 9 44 86 59
Email: reservinsanomat@helresp.fi **Web site:** http://www.reservilaisliitto.fi
ISSN: 0355-824X
Date Established: 1969; **Freq:** Monthly - Published 10/year; Free to qualifying individuals ; **Circ:** 12,279
Usual Pagination: 20
Profile: Journal for people interested in voluntary defence.
Language(s): Finnish
ADVERTISING RATES:
Full Page Colour .... EUR 1400
BUSINESS: DEFENCE

HELSINGIN SANOMAT 15162L65A-27
Editorial: PL 85, 00089 SANOMA **Tel:** 9 12 21
Fax: 9 12 22 366
Email: hs.talous@hs.fi **Web site:** http://www.hs.fi
ISSN: 0355-2047
Date Established: 1889; **Freq:** Daily; **Circ:** 383,361
Usual Pagination: 100
Managing Editor: Reetta Räty
Profile: Broadsheet-sized quality newspaper providing in-depth coverage of national and international news, politics, economics, business, events, culture and sport.
Language(s): Finnish
Readership: Read by private households over the whole of Finland.
ADVERTISING RATES:
Full Page Colour .... EUR 23621
SCC .... EUR 56.20
Mechanical Data: Film: Positive, Print Process: Offset, Screen: 54 lpc, Col Length: 560mm, Page Width: 400mm, No. of Columns (Display): 8, Col Widths (Display): 44mm
Copy instructions: *Copy Date:* 21 days prior to publication date
Sections:
Helsingin Sanomat Kaupunkitoimitus
Helsingin Sanomat Kotimaantoimitus
Helsingin Sanomat Matkailu
Helsingin Sanomat Sunnuntaitoimitus
Helsingin Sanomat Taloustoimitus
NATIONAL DAILY & SUNDAY NEWSPAPERS:
National Daily Newspapers

HELSINGIN SANOMAT KAUPUNKITOIMITUS 706479L65A-27_103
Editorial: PL 65/ Töölönlahdenkatu 2, 00089 SANOMA **Tel:** 9 12 22 511 **Fax:** 9 12 26 22
Email: hs.kaupunki@hs.fi **Web site:** http://www.hs.fi
Freq: Daily
Profile: Helsinki city edition of national newspaper Helsingin Sanomat.
Language(s): Finnish
Section of: Helsingin Sanomat
NATIONAL DAILY & SUNDAY NEWSPAPERS:
National Daily Newspapers

HELSINGIN SANOMAT KOTIMAANTOIMITUS 706480L65A-27_109
Editorial: PL 65/ Töölönlahdenkatu 2, 00089 SANOMA **Tel:** 9 12 22 452 **Fax:** 9 12 26 57
Email: hs.kotimaa@hs.fi **Web site:** http://www.hs.fi
Freq: Daily
Profile: Domestic affairs part of national newspaper Helsingin Sanomat.
Language(s): Finnish
Section of: Helsingin Sanomat
NATIONAL DAILY & SUNDAY NEWSPAPERS:
National Daily Newspapers

HELSINGIN SANOMAT KUOPIO 705599L65C-135
Editorial: Kauppakatu 39 A, 70100 KUOPIO
Tel: 17 21 13 333 **Fax:** 17 21 13 334
Email: hs.kuopio@hs.fi **Web site:** http://www.hs.fi
Freq: Daily
Profile: Kuopio regional office of national newspaper Helsingin Sanomat.
Language(s): Finnish
NATIONAL DAILY & SUNDAY NEWSPAPERS:
National Daily Regional Offices

HELSINGIN SANOMAT KUUKAUSILIITE 705107L65H-5
Editorial: PL 80/ Töölönlahdenkatu 2, 00089 SANOMA **Tel:** 9 12 21 **Fax:** 9 12 22 624
Email: hs.kuukausiliite@hs.fi **Web site:** http://www.hs.fi/kuukausiliite
ISSN: 0780-0096
Date Established: 1983; **Freq:** Monthly - Finland; **Circ:** 474,726
Usual Pagination: 108
Profile: Monthly general-interest colour-supplement of national newspaper Helsingin Sanomat.
Language(s): Finnish
ADVERTISING RATES:
Full Page Colour .... EUR 13526
SCC .... EUR 164.30
Mechanical Data: Type Area: 235 x 280mm, Print Process: offset, Screen: FM, Bleed Size: 258 x 300mm, Col Length: 269mm, Page Width: 233mm
Supplement to: Helsingin Sanomat
NATIONAL DAILY & SUNDAY NEWSPAPERS:
National Colour Supplements

HELSINGIN SANOMAT LAPPEENRANTA 705598L65C-145
Editorial: Ilkankatu 1, 53100 LAPPEENRANTA
Tel: 5 54 47 400 **Fax:** 5 54 47 420
Email: hs.lappeenranta@hs.fi **Web site:** http://www.hs.fi
Freq: Daily
Profile: Lappeenranta and southeastern regional office of national newspaper Helsingin Sanomat.
Language(s): Finnish
NATIONAL DAILY & SUNDAY NEWSPAPERS:
National Daily Regional Offices

HELSINGIN SANOMAT MATKAILU 749161L65A-27_111
Editorial: PL 65/ Töölönlahdenkatu 2, 00089 SANOMA **Tel:** 9 12 21 **Fax:** 9 12 22 278
Email: hs.matkailu@hs.fi **Web site:** http://www.hs.fi
Freq: Weekly - Published on a Saturday
Profile: Travel desk of national newspaper Helsingin Sanomat.
Language(s): Finnish
Section of: Helsingin Sanomat
NATIONAL DAILY & SUNDAY NEWSPAPERS:
National Daily Newspapers

HELSINGIN SANOMAT NYT-VIIKKOLIITE 705880L65H-10
Editorial: PL 85/ Töölönlahdenkatu 2, 00089 SANOMA **Tel:** 9 12 21 **Fax:** 9 12 22 456
Web site: http://nyt.hs.fi
ISSN: 1238-9838
Freq: Weekly - Finland; **Circ:** 410,392
Usual Pagination: 56
Profile: Supplement of national newspaper Helsingin Sanomat is about freetime activities, events and TV programmes mainly from the Helsinki point of view.
Language(s): Finnish
ADVERTISING RATES:
Full Page Colour .... EUR 9405
Mechanical Data: Type Area: 235 x 355mm, Print Process: offset, Screen: 40 lpc, Bleed Size: 260 x 380mm, Col Length: 325mm, Page Width: 260mm
Supplement to: Helsingin Sanomat
NATIONAL DAILY & SUNDAY NEWSPAPERS:
National Colour Supplements

HELSINGIN SANOMAT OULU 705602L65C-155
Editorial: Kauppurienkatu 23, 90100 OULU
Tel: 8 31 20 800 **Fax:** 8 31 20 804
Email: hs.oulu@hs.fi **Web site:** http://www.hs.fi
Freq: Daily
Profile: Oulu regional office of national newspaper Helsingin Sanomat.
Language(s): Finnish
NATIONAL DAILY & SUNDAY NEWSPAPERS:
National Daily Regional Offices

HELSINGIN SANOMAT SUNNUNTAITOIMITUS 706484L65A-27_113
Editorial: PL 85/ Töölönlahdenkatu 2, 00089 SANOMA **Tel:** 9 12 22 443 **Fax:** 9 12 22 448
Email: hs.sunnuntai@hs.fi **Web site:** http://www.hs.fi
Freq: Weekly - Sunday; **Annual Sub.:** EUR 150; **Circ:** 435,152
Profile: Sunday edition of national newspaper Helsingin Sanomat.
Language(s): Finnish
ADVERTISING RATES:
Full Page Colour .... EUR 31117
SCC .... EUR 84.70
Section of: Helsingin Sanomat
NATIONAL DAILY & SUNDAY NEWSPAPERS:
National Daily Newspapers

HELSINGIN SANOMAT TALOUSTOIMITUS 706485L65A-27_110
Editorial: PL 75/ Töölönlahdenkatu 2, 00089 SANOMA **Tel:** 9 12 22 682
Email: hs.talous@hs.fi **Web site:** http://www.hs.fi
Freq: Daily
Profile: Finance division of national newspaper Helsingin Sanomat.
Language(s): Finnish
Section of: Helsingin Sanomat
NATIONAL DAILY & SUNDAY NEWSPAPERS:
National Daily Newspapers

HELSINGIN SANOMAT TAMPERE VAASA 705604L65C-170
Editorial: Tuomiokirkonkatu 17 B 31, 33100 TAMPERE **Tel:** 3 22 31 257 **Fax:** 3 21 27 055
Email: hs.tampere@hs.fi **Web site:** http://www.hs.fi
Freq: Daily
Profile: Tampere and Vaasa regional office of national newspaper Helsingin Sanomat.
Language(s): Finnish
NATIONAL DAILY & SUNDAY NEWSPAPERS:
National Daily Regional Offices

HELSINGIN SANOMAT TURKU 705858L65C-175
Editorial: Kauppiaskatu 11 C 24, 20100 TURKU
Tel: 2 25 16 655 **Fax:** 2 23 32 021
Email: hs.turku@hs.fi **Web site:** http://www.hs.fi
Freq: Daily

Profile: Turku regional office of national newspaper Helsingin Sanomat.
Language(s): Finnish
NATIONAL DAILY & SUNDAY NEWSPAPERS: National Daily Regional Offices

HELSINGIN SANOMAT VERKKOLIITE 624488L65A-29
Formerly: Helsingin Sanomat (Online)
Editorial: PL 85/ Töölönlahdenkatu 2, 00089 SANOMA **Tel:** 9 12 21 **Fax:** 9 12 27 535
Email: verkkoliite@hs.fi **Web site:** http://www.hs.fi
ISSN: 1239-257X
Date Established: 1996; **Freq:** Daily. Web site is updated continuously; **Circ:** 1,231,000 Unique Users
Managing Editor: Paula Salovaara
Profile: Internet version of the broadsheet-sized quality newspaper, providing in-depth coverage of national and international news, politics, economics, business, events, culture and sport.
Language(s): Finnish
Readership: Read predominantly by university students, academics, civil servants, politicians and managers.
NATIONAL DAILY & SUNDAY NEWSPAPERS: National Daily Newspapers

HELSINKI THIS WEEK 15367L89C-100
Editorial: Pohjoinen Makasiinikatu 4, 00130 HELSINKI **Tel:** 9 22 88 13 33 **Fax:** 9 22 88 13 99
Email: helsinkithisweek@helsinkiexpert.fi **Web site:** http://www.helsinkithisweek.fi
ISSN: 0356-2778
Date Established: 1956; **Freq:** 6 issues yearly - Published 8/year; Free to qualifying individuals ; **Circ:** 77,000
Usual Pagination: 96
Managing Director: Timo Orilähde; **Managing Editor:** Pirjo Kauppinen
Profile: Magazine containing details of events in Helsinki. Covers festivals, concerts, art exhibitions, theatre, opera, famous sights, museums, shops, restaurants and transport.
Language(s): English; Russian
Readership: Aimed at tourists in Helsinki. Distributed via hotels, tourist information centres, congresses, travel agencies, airport info desks, ferry companies, currency exchange offices and shops.
ADVERTISING RATES:
Full Page Colour .... EUR 2940
Agency Commission: 15%
Mechanical Data: Trim Size: 210 x 148mm, Film: Send digital material to htw@a5.notenet.fi For details contact Mark Granath at 358 3-27 15 240 or see http://aineisto.notenet.fi, Print Process: offset, Type Area: 175 x 125mm, Col Length: 175mm, Page Width: 125mm, Screen: 60-70 lpc
Average ad content per issue: 40%
CONSUMER: HOLIDAYS & TRAVEL: Entertainment Guides

HELSINKI-INFO 706442L72-220
Formerly: Helsingin kaupunki tiedottaa
Editorial: PL 1/ Pohjoisesplanadi 11-13, 00099 HELSINGIN KAUPUNKI **Tel:** 9 31 01 641
Fax: 9 31 03 65 85
Web site: http://www.hel.fi/helsinki-info
ISSN: 0782-0453
Date Established: 1976; **Freq:** 6 issues yearly; **Cover Price:** Free; **Circ:** 356,675
Usual Pagination: 24
Editor-in-Chief: Rita Ekelund
Profile: Magazine about what is going on in Helsinki.
Language(s): Finnish; Swedish
Readership: Private households in Helsinki.
Mechanical Data: Col Length: 360mm, Page Width: 278mm, No. of Columns (Display): 5
LOCAL NEWSPAPERS

HENGITYS 15116L56R-17
Formerly: Hyvä Hengitys
Editorial: PL 40/ Oltermannintie 8, 00621 HELSINKI
Tel: 20 75 75 000
Email: tuula.hakkarainen@heli.fi **Web site:** http://www.hengitysliitto.fi
ISSN: 1458-5871
Date Established: 1945; **Freq:** 6 issues yearly; **Circ:** 34,799
Usual Pagination: 56
Managing Editor: Tuula Hakkarainen
Profile: Official publication of the Association for the Pulmonary Disabled, and contains information for personnel and decision makers.
Language(s): Finnish
ADVERTISING RATES:
Full Page Colour .... EUR 2700
SCC .... EUR 34.60
Agency Commission: 15%
Mechanical Data: Type Area: 210 x 297mm, Trim Size: 210 x 297mm, Print Process: offset, Screen: 60 lpc
BUSINESS: HEALTH & MEDICAL: Health Medical Related

HENKI & ELÄMÄ 706577L87-94_30
Formerly: Seurakuntaviesti
Editorial: Yliopistokatu 12 B, 40100 JYVÄSKYLÄ
Tel: 14 63 67 80 **Fax:** 14 63 67 85
Email: jklsrk.lehti@evl.fi **Web site:** http://www.jyvaskylanseurakunta.fi/henki_elama
ISSN: 1235-2802
Date Established: 1950; **Freq:** 26 issues yearly - Published 20/year; **Circ:** 60,000
Profile: Magazine by the Jyväskylä parish.
Language(s): Finnish
ADVERTISING RATES:
Full Page Colour .... EUR 2500
SCC .... EUR 16
Agency Commission: 10-15%
Mechanical Data: Type Area: 280 x 400mm, No. of Columns (Display): 5, Col Widths (Display): 44mm, Print Process: offset, Screen: 34 lpc
Copy instructions: *Copy Date:* 8 days prior to publication date
CONSUMER: RELIGIOUS

HETKY 705950L5R-10
Formerly: Hetkyn Tietosanomat
Editorial: Lars Sonckin kaari 12, 02600 ESPOO
Tel: 400 83 26 98 **Fax:** 20 74 19 889
Email: hetky@ttlry.fi **Web site:** http://www.hetky.fi
ISSN: 1458-4816
Date Established: 1982; **Freq:** Quarterly; **Circ:** 10,000
Usual Pagination: 32
Editor-in-Chief: Pipsa Ylä-Mononen; **Managing Editor:** Elina Ylppö
Profile: The Helsinki Information Technology Association (HITA) is the local member association of the Finnish Information Processing Association (FIPA) and with this magazine the members can follow advances within the field of business.
Language(s): Finnish
ADVERTISING RATES:
Full Page Colour .... EUR 2082.00
SCC .... EUR 26.80
Agency Commission: 15%
Mechanical Data: Bleed Size: 215 x 297mm, No. of Columns (Display): 3, Col Widths (Display): 57/70mm, Film: positive, Screen: 64 lpc, Print Process: offset, Type Area: 178 x 258mm
BUSINESS: COMPUTERS & AUTOMATION: Computers Related

HEVOSHULLU 706139L81D-4
Editorial: PL 1269/ Vuorikatu 14 A, 00101 HELSINKI
Tel: 20 13 32 222 **Fax:** 20 13 32 278
Email: hevoshullu@egmontkustannus.fi **Web site:** http://www.hevoshullu.fi
ISSN: 0356-5483
Date Established: 1972; **Freq:** 26 issues yearly; **Circ:** 9,821
Usual Pagination: 52
Editor-in-Chief: Marjo Kylmänen
Profile: Magazine about horses as a hobby. It also contains comics.
Language(s): Finnish
Readership: Young horse owners.
ADVERTISING RATES:
Full Page Colour .... EUR 1600
CONSUMER: ANIMALS & PETS: Horses & Ponies

HEVOSURHEILU 15293L75E-40
Editorial: Tulkinkuja 3, 02650 ESPOO
Tel: 20 76 05 300 **Fax:** 20 76 05 390
Email: hevosurheilu@hevosurheilu.fi **Web site:** http://www.hevosurheilu.fi
ISSN: 0787-5274
Date Established: 1934; **Freq:** 104 issues yearly - Published Wednesday and Friday; **Circ:** 24,776
Usual Pagination: 24
Editor-in-Chief: Jorma Kemiläinen; **Managing Editor:** Jari-Pekka Rättyä
Profile: Publication focusing on horse racing.
Language(s): Finnish
ADVERTISING RATES:
Full Page Colour .... EUR 3391.60
SCC .... EUR 23.80
Agency Commission: 10-15%
Mechanical Data: Type Area: 290 x 390mm, Col Length: 375mm, No. of Columns (Display): 6, Col Widths (Display): 45mm, Print Process: offset, Screen: 34-40 lpc, Film: negative
Copy instructions: *Copy Date:* 7 days prior to publication date
CONSUMER: SPORT: Horse Racing

HIPPO 705428L91D-8
Editorial: Kids Factory Oy, PL 209/ Särkiniementie 3 b, 00201 HELSINKI **Tel:** 41 53 70 04
Web site: http://www.hippo.fi
Date Established: 1980; **Freq:** Quarterly; **Cover Price:** Free; **Circ:** 199,836
Editor-in-Chief: Satu Piha-Kujala
Profile: Junior-magazine by Co-operatives Bank in Finland.
Language(s): Finnish
Readership: Children of age 5-11.
Mechanical Data: Type Area: 190 x 275mm, Bleed Size: 210 x 297mm, Page Width: 210mm, Print Process: offset, No. of Columns (Display): 4, Screen: 60 lpc
CONSUMER: RECREATION & LEISURE: Children & Youth

HIRSITALO 1615660L46-170
Editorial: PL 56, 08101 LOHJA **Tel:** 44 30 01 070
Fax: 19 33 33 13
Email: hirsitalo@saarimedia.fi **Web site:** http://www.saarimedia.fi
ISSN: 1459-4005
Date Established: 2003; **Freq:** Quarterly; **Circ:** 35,000
Usual Pagination: 76
Editor-in-Chief: Jorma Välimaa
Profile: Magazine about using timber in house building.
Language(s): Finnish
Readership: People building leisure timber houses.
ADVERTISING RATES:
Full Page Colour .... EUR 2450.00
SCC .... EUR 28.10

HITSAUSTEKNIIKKA-SVETSTEKNIK 15002L27-50
Formerly: Hitsaustekniikka
Editorial: Mäkelänkatu 36 A 2, 00510 HELSINKI
Tel: 9 77 32 199 **Fax:** 9 77 32 661
Email: shy@co.inet.fi **Web site:** http://www.shy-hitsaus.net
ISSN: 0437-6056
Date Established: 1951; **Freq:** 6 issues yearly; **Circ:** 4,500
Usual Pagination: 88
Editor-in-Chief: Juha Lukkari
Profile: Journal containing theoretical and practical information about welding technology and related topics.
Language(s): Finnish; Swedish
Readership: Read by engineers, technicians, supervisors and training staff in the industry.
ADVERTISING RATES:
Full Page Colour .... EUR 1600.00
SCC .... EUR 20.00
Agency Commission: 15%
Mechanical Data: Type Area: 178 x 266mm, Col Widths (Display): 56mm, No. of Columns (Display): 3, Print Process: offset, Screen: 54 lpc

HITSAUSUUTISET 1601508L27-51
Editorial: Ruosilantie 18, 00390 HELSINKI
Tel: 9 54 77 61 **Fax:** 9 54 77 773
Email: esab@esab.fi **Web site:** http://www.esab.fi/fi/fi/news/asiakaslehti.cfm
Date Established: 1967; **Freq:** Quarterly; **Cover Price:** Free; **Circ:** 16,000
Usual Pagination: 24
Editor-in-Chief: Juha Lukkari
Profile: Magazine about industrial ventilation, metal cutting and welding.
Language(s): Finnish

HOIVAPALVELUT 2051407L56A-204
Editorial: Virmantie 7, 90830 HAUKIPUDAS
Tel: 40 57 41 237
Email: heikki.lantto@pp.inet.fi **Web site:** http://www.hoivapalvelut-lehti.fi
Freq: Monthly; **Circ:** 3,000
Profile: Publication covering elderly care.
Language(s): Finnish
Readership: Companies providing social services and public social services. / Kuntien sosiaalitoimi, hoivapalveluja tuottavat yritykset ja järjestöt.
ADVERTISING RATES:
Full Page Colour .... EUR 1350.00
SCC .... EUR 15.10

HORISONT 15239L73-70
Editorial: Hörnvägen 2 A 7, 64200 NÄRPES
Tel: 50 37 14 963
Email: sofie@horisont.fi **Web site:** http://www.horisont.fi
ISSN: 0439-5530
Date Established: 1954; **Freq:** Quarterly; **Circ:** 1,000
Usual Pagination: 80
Editor-in-Chief: Peter Björkman
Profile: Literary journal containing cultural articles from Finland and Sweden.
Language(s): Swedish
ADVERTISING RATES:
Full Page Colour .... EUR 300.00

HUFVUDSTADSBLADET 15163L65A-25
Editorial: PB 217/ Mannerheimvägen 18, 00101 HELSINGFORS **Tel:** 9 12 531 **Fax:** 9 64 29 30
Email: nyheter@hbl.fi **Web site:** http://www.hbl.fi
ISSN: 0356-0724
Date Established: 1864; **Freq:** Daily; **Circ:** 48,046
Usual Pagination: 20
Profile: Tabloid-sized quality newspaper providing national and international news and articles on politics, business, economics, culture, sport and events.
Language(s): Swedish
Readership: Read by Swedish-speaking people throughout Finland.
ADVERTISING RATES:
Full Page Colour .... EUR 5500
SCC .... EUR 25.10
Agency Commission: 5-15%
Mechanical Data: No. of Columns (Display): 6, Col Widths (Display): 38mm, Col Length: 365mm, Print Process: offset, Screen: 34 lpc, Page Width: 253mm
Editions:
Hufvudstadsbladet Internetredaktionen
NATIONAL DAILY & SUNDAY NEWSPAPERS: National Daily Newspapers

HUILI 2022443L74Q-70
Editorial: Rauhankatu 16 A 26, 65100 VAASA
Tel: 6 35 77 750 **Fax:** 6 35 77 791
Email: riikka.suominen@kraftkultur.com **Web site:** http://www.huililehti.fi
Freq: 6 issues yearly; **Circ:** 30,000
Profile: Customer magazine covering anything related to ecology and ecological lifestyle as well as culture, travel, time management and new phenomena. Also available for purchase as single copies from books shops.
Language(s): Finnish
Readership: Customer's of Kraft & Kultur and also readers interested in ecology. / Kraft & Kulturin asiakkaat sekä ekologisuudesta kiinnostuneet lukijat.
ADVERTISING RATES:
Full Page Colour .... EUR 2200.00
SCC .... EUR 20.30

HUOLTOVIESTI 705885L40-5
Editorial: PL 600/ Ratamestarinkatu 9 C, 00521 HELSINKI **Tel:** 2 25 88 394 **Fax:** 2 25 88 792
Email: huoltoviesti@kol.inet.fi **Web site:** http://www.kolry.fi
Date Established: 1945; **Freq:** Quarterly; **Annual Sub.:** EUR 20.00; **Circ:** 2,700
Editor-in-Chief: Matti Höök
Profile: Magazine for widows of war-veterans.
Language(s): Finnish

HUOMISTA TEHDÄÄN 753109L1G-4
Formerly: Kuntarahoitus
Editorial: PL 744/ Antinkatu 3 C, 5. krs, 00101 HELSINKI **Tel:** 9 68 03 56 66 **Fax:** 9 68 03 56 69
Email: pekka.averio@kuntarahoitus.fi **Web site:** http://www.kuntarahoitus.fi
Freq: Quarterly; **Cover Price:** Free
Usual Pagination: 8
Editor-in-Chief: Pekka Averio
Profile: Magazine about credit trading for local government.
Language(s): Finnish
BUSINESS: FINANCE & ECONOMICS: Credit Trading

HYMY 15240L73-80
Formerly: Hymy Lehti
Editorial: Maistraatinportti 1, 00015 OTAVAMEDIA
Tel: 9 15 661 **Fax:** 9 15 66 212
Email: hymy@otavamedia.fi **Web site:** http://www.hymy.fi
ISSN: 0355-4317
Date Established: 1960; **Freq:** Monthly; **Circ:** 88,637
Usual Pagination: 80
Editor-in-Chief: Mika Lahtonen; **Managing Editor:** Juha-Tapio Tuomela
Profile: General interest magazine with information on current affairs, lifestyle, culture and society.
Language(s): Finnish
ADVERTISING RATES:
Full Page Colour .... EUR 3550
SCC .... EUR 29.80
Mechanical Data: Bleed Size: 320 x 217mm, Film: Digital, No. of Columns (Display): 4, Col Widths (Display): 44mm, Film: positive, Screen: 60 lpc, Type Area: 230 x 300mm
CONSUMER: NATIONAL & INTERNATIONAL PERIODICALS

HYVÄ KAUPPA 706549L53-3
Editorial: Metsärinne 4, 01760 VANTAA
Tel: 500 45 60 96
Email: vaisto.hyvakauppa@kolumbus.fi **Web site:** http://www.hyvakauppa.com
ISSN: 1457-2176
Date Established: 2000; **Freq:** 6 issues yearly; **Cover Price:** Free; **Circ:** 60,000
Usual Pagination: 56
Editor-in-Chief: Markku Väistö; **Publisher:** Markku Väistö
Profile: Magazine about retailing and commerce.
Language(s): Finnish
ADVERTISING RATES:
Full Page Colour .... EUR 4550.00
SCC .... EUR 20.70
Agency Commission: 15%
Mechanical Data: No. of Columns (Display): 6, Type Area: 253 x 365mm, Col Widths (Display): 38mm, Screen: 40 lpc, Print Process: offset, Col Length: 365mm
BUSINESS: RETAILING & WHOLESALING

HYVÄ TERVEYS 15279L74G-30
Editorial: PL 100/ Lapinmäentie 1, 00040 SANOMA MAGAZINES **Tel:** 9 12 01 **Fax:** 9 12 05 456
Email: hyva.terveys@sanomamagazines.fi **Web site:** http://www.hyvaterveys.fi
ISSN: 1236-3081
Date Established: 1985; **Freq:** Monthly - Published 16/year; **Circ:** 127,522
Usual Pagination: 80
Editor-in-Chief: Taina Risto
Profile: Consumer health magazine.
Language(s): Finnish
ADVERTISING RATES:
Full Page Colour .... EUR 6050
SCC .... EUR 50.90
Mechanical Data: Bleed Size: 230 x 273mm, Type Area: 194 x 248mm, No. of Columns (Display): 4, Col Widths (Display): 45mm, Print Process: offset, Film: positive, Screen: 60 lpc
CONSUMER: WOMEN'S INTEREST CONSUMER MAGAZINES: Slimming & Health

HYVINVOINTI 705290L56A-42
Editorial: PL 242/ Haapaniemenkatu 7-9 B, 10 krs, 00531 HELSINKI **Tel:** 10 23 99 080 **Fax:** 10 23 99 089
Email: pasi.ylitalo@sal-lomat.net **Web site:** http://www.sal-lomat.net
Freq: Half-yearly; **Cover Price:** Free; **Circ:** 15,000
Usual Pagination: 16
Editor-in-Chief: Pasi Ylitalo
Profile: Magazine about vacation, health, exercises, nutrition, mental health and life administration.
Language(s): Finnish
Readership: Members of the Finnish Trade Union Federation.
ADVERTISING RATES:
Full Page Colour .... EUR 1570.00
Mechanical Data: Type Area: 255 x 380mm

IDÄNTUTKIMUS 761586L20-7
Editorial: Aleksanteri-instituutti, PL 42/ Unioninkatu 33, 00014 HELSINGIN YLIOPISTO **Tel:** 9 19 12 41 75
Fax: 9 19 12 36 15
Email: markku.kangaspuro@helsinki.fi **Web site:** http://www.helsinki.fi/idantutkimus
ISSN: 1237-6051
Date Established: 1994; **Freq:** Quarterly; **Annual Sub.:** EUR 28; **Circ:** 500
Usual Pagination: 90
Editor: Mikko Ylikangas; **Editor-in-Chief:** Markku Kangaspuro
Profile: Magazine about research in Russian and Eastern European issues.
Language(s): Finnish
ADVERTISING RATES:
Full Page Mono .... EUR 170

IIJOKISEUTU 705016L72-255
Editorial: PL 24 / Puistotie 2, 93100 PUDASJÄRVI
Tel: 8 86 00 715 **Fax:** 8 86 00 731
Email: toimitus@iijokiseutu.fi **Web site:** http://www.iijokiseutu.fi
ISSN: 0782-6753
Date Established: 1969; **Freq:** 104 issues yearly; **Circ:** 4,634
Usual Pagination: 16
Profile: Newspaper issued in Pudasjärvi and Taivalkoski.
Language(s): Finnish
ADVERTISING RATES:
Full Page Colour .... EUR 3986
SCC .... EUR 18.20
Agency Commission: 15-17.5%
Mechanical Data: Print Process: offset, Type Area: 255 x 365mm, Col Widths (Display): 47mm, No. of Columns (Display): 5
Editions:
Iijokiseutu Verkkotoimitus
LOCAL NEWSPAPERS

IISALMEN SANOMAT 15186L67B-3800
Editorial: PL 11/Kilpivirrantie 7, 74101 IISALMI
Tel: 17 83 51 311 **Fax:** 17 83 51 401
Email: toimitus@iisalmensanomat.fi **Web site:** http://www.iisalmensanomat.fi
ISSN: 0356-2298
Date Established: 1925
Circ: 12,686
Usual Pagination: 20
Managing Editor: Jorma Tikkanen
Profile: Newspaper mainly issued in Pyhäntä, Pyhäsalmi, Kiuruvesi, Vieremä, Keitele, Pielavesi, Iisalmi, Sonkajärvi, Lapinlahti, Varpaisjärvi and Rautavaara.
Language(s): Finnish
ADVERTISING RATES:
Full Page Colour .... EUR 3460
SCC .... EUR 15.80
Agency Commission: 10-15%
Mechanical Data: No. of Columns (Display): 6, Col Widths (Display): 40mm, Print Process: offset, Col Length: 365mm, Page Width: 254mm
Editions:
Iisalmen Sanomat Urheilutoimitus
Iisalmen Sanomat Verkkotoimitus
REGIONAL DAILY & SUNDAY NEWSPAPERS: Regional Daily Newspapers

IITINSEUTU 704952L72-260
Editorial: PL 37/ Kauppakatu 6, 47401 KAUSALA
Tel: 5 32 60 355 **Fax:** 53260321
Email: voitto.ruohonen@iitinseutulehti.fi **Web site:** http://www.iitinseutulehti.fi
ISSN: 0357-9107
Date Established: 1954; **Freq:** 104 issues yearly; **Circ:** 3,491
Usual Pagination: 6
Profile: Newspaper issued in Iitti and Jaala.
Language(s): Finnish
ADVERTISING RATES:
SCC .... EUR 11.20
Agency Commission: 15%
Mechanical Data: Type Area: 380 x 540mm, No. of Columns (Display): 8, Col Widths (Display): 44mm
LOCAL NEWSPAPERS

IKÄPLUS 1927106L32G-301
Editorial: Vanha Turuntie 371, 03150 HUHMARI
Tel: 9 41 39 73 00 **Fax:** 9 41 39 74 01
Email: aikakauslehdet@karprint.fi **Web site:** http://www.karprint.fi
Date Established: 2009; **Freq:** 6 issues yearly - Published 8/year; **Circ:** 25,000
Profile: Magazine about aging.
Language(s): Finnish
Readership: Men and women of age 50+.
ADVERTISING RATES:
Full Page Colour .... EUR 1957
SCC .... EUR 16.20
Copy instructions: *Copy Date:* 19 days prior to publication date

IKÄPLUS 1927106L74N-91
Editorial: Vanha Turuntie 371, 03150 HUHMARI
Tel: 9 41 39 73 00 **Fax:** 9 41 39 74 01
Email: aikakauslehdet@karprint.fi **Web site:** http://www.karprint.fi
Date Established: 2009; **Freq:** 6 issues yearly - Published 8/year; **Circ:** 25,000
Profile: Magazine about aging.
Language(s): Finnish
Readership: Men and women of age 50+.
ADVERTISING RATES:
Full Page Colour .... EUR 1957
SCC .... EUR 16.20
Copy instructions: *Copy Date:* 19 days prior to publication date

IKKUNAPAIKKA 15075L50-50
Editorial: Raisiontie 6 D, 00280 HELSINKI
Tel: 9 62 22 500 **Fax:** 3 61 25 500
Email: leena.tolvanen@ikkunapaikka.fi **Web site:** http://www.ikkunapaikka.fi
ISSN: 0786-7867
Date Established: 1989; **Freq:** 6 issues yearly - Published 8/year; **Circ:** 5,000
Usual Pagination: 24
Profile: Journal concerning the travel industry.
Language(s): Finnish
Readership: Aimed at those employed in the travel industry.
ADVERTISING RATES:
Full Page Colour .... EUR 6840
SCC .... EUR 30
Agency Commission: 15%
Mechanical Data: Print Process: Offset, Type Area: 277 x 380mm, Screen: Mono: 54 lpc, Colour: 60 lpc, Col Length: 420mm, No. of Columns (Display): 6, Page Width: 297mm, Bleed Size: 297 x 420mm
Average ad content per issue: 40%
BUSINESS: TRAVEL & TOURISM

ILKKA 15218L67B-3820
Editorial: PL 60/ Koulukatu 10, 60101 SEINÄJOKI
Tel: 6 24 77 830 **Fax:** 6 24 77 855
Email: toimitus@ilkka.fi **Web site:** http://www.ilkka.fi
ISSN: 0356-1283
Date Established: 1906; **Freq:** Daily; **Circ:** 53,768
Usual Pagination: 24
Editor-in-Chief: Matti Kalliokoski; **Managing Editor:** Kauko Palola
Profile: Newspaper issued in southern Ostrobotnia (Seinäjoki, Kauhajoki, Kristiinankaupunki and Vaasa).
Language(s): Finnish
ADVERTISING RATES:
Full Page Colour .... EUR 14070
SCC .... EUR 33.50
Agency Commission: 5%
Mechanical Data: Screen: 40 lpc, Type Area: 380 x 535mm, Col Length: 525mm, No. of Columns (Display): 8, Print Process: offset, Col Widths (Display): 44mm, Page Width: 380mm
Editions:
Ilkka Kulttuuritoimitus
Ilkka Taloustoimitus
Ilkka Urheilutoimitus
Ilkka Verkkotoimitus
REGIONAL DAILY & SUNDAY NEWSPAPERS: Regional Daily Newspapers

ILKKA ALAVUS 705692L67E-152
Formerly: Ilkka Suomenselkä
Editorial: Kirjapainonkuja 2, 63300 ALAVUS
Tel: 6 24 77 576 **Fax:** 6 24 77 864
Email: tarja.riihimaki@ilkka.fi **Web site:** http://www.ilkka.fi
Freq: Daily
Profile: Suomenselkä and Järviseutu regional office of newspaper Ilkka.
Language(s): Finnish
REGIONAL DAILY & SUNDAY NEWSPAPERS: Regional Offices

ILKKA KAUHAJOKI 705693L67E-154
Formerly: Ilkka Suupohja
Editorial: Topeeka 21, 61800 KAUHAJOKI
Tel: 6 24 77 574 **Fax:** 6 24 77 859
Email: jukka.svenstrom@ilkka.fi **Web site:** http://www.ilkka.fi
Freq: Daily
Profile: Suupohja and Kauhajoki regional office of newspaper Ilkka.
Language(s): Finnish
REGIONAL DAILY & SUNDAY NEWSPAPERS: Regional Offices

ILMAJOKI-LEHTI 704995L72-265
Editorial: PL 12 / Mikontie 3, 60801 ILMAJOKI
Tel: 6 42 44 800 **Fax:** 6 42 44 834
Email: toimitus@ilmajoki-lehti.fi **Web site:** http://www.ilmajoki-lehti.fi
ISSN: 0768-5511
Date Established: 1929; **Freq:** 104 issues yearly; **Circ:** 4,984
Profile: Newspaper issued in Ilmajoki.
Language(s): Finnish
ADVERTISING RATES:
Full Page Colour .... EUR 1944
SCC .... EUR 90
Mechanical Data: Col Length: 360mm, Page Width: 260mm, No. of Columns (Display): 6, Col Widths (Display): 43mm, Print Process: offset
LOCAL NEWSPAPERS

ILMANSUOJELU 705688L57-7
Editorial: PL 136, 00251 HELSINKI **Tel:** 40 75 09 225
Email: aira.saloniemi@uta.fi **Web site:** http://www.isy.fi
ISSN: 0786-5899
Date Established: 1976; **Freq:** Quarterly; **Circ:** 700
Usual Pagination: 40
Editor-in-Chief: Aira Saloniemi
Profile: Magazine of the Finnish Air Pollution Prevention Society.
Language(s): Finnish
ADVERTISING RATES:
Full Page Colour .... EUR 250.00

ILMARINEN 753086L1D-50_50
Formerly: Ilmarinen Uutiset
Editorial: Porkkalankatu 1, 00018 ILMARINEN
Tel: 10 28 411 **Fax:** 10 28 42 580
Email: asiakaslehti@ilmarinen.fi **Web site:** http://www.ilmarinen.fi
ISSN: 1239-050X
Date Established: 2001; **Freq:** Quarterly; **Cover Price:** Free; **Circ:** 90,000
Usual Pagination: 32
Editor-in-Chief: Päivi Sihvola
Profile: Magazine for the Ilmarinen insurance customers.
Language(s): Finnish
BUSINESS: FINANCE & ECONOMICS: Insurance

ILMATORJUNTAUPSEERI 706145L40-6
Editorial: PL 5, 04301 TUUSULA **Tel:** 9 18 16 24 94
Fax: 9 18 16 24 89
Web site: http://www.ilmatorjuntaupseeriyhdistys.fi
ISSN: 1235-3434
Date Established: 1955; **Freq:** Quarterly; **Cover Price:** Free; **Circ:** 2,500
Editor-in-Chief: Jussi Ylimartimo
Profile: Magazine about aerial defence.
Language(s): Finnish

ILTALEHTI 704849L65A-33
Editorial: PL 372/ Aleksanterinkatu 9, 00101 HELSINKI **Tel:** 10 66 51 00 **Fax:** 9 17 73 13
Email: il.toimitus@iltalehti.fi **Web site:** http://www.iltalehti.fi
ISSN: 0355-5461
Date Established: 1980; **Freq:** Daily - Published Monday-Saturday; **Circ:** 107,052
Usual Pagination: 62
Editor-in-Chief: Kari Kivelä; **Managing Editor:** Elina Schüller
Profile: National evening newspaper with news and celebrity comments. E.
Language(s): Finnish
ADVERTISING RATES:
Full Page Colour .... EUR 5431
SCC .... EUR 24.80
Agency Commission: 15%
Mechanical Data: Type Area: 253 x 365mm, Page Width: 253mm, Col Length: 365mm, No. of Columns (Display): 6, Col Widths (Display): 38mm, Screen: 40 lpc, Print Process: offset
Sections:
Iltalehti Ilona
Iltalehti Online
NATIONAL DAILY & SUNDAY NEWSPAPERS: National Daily Newspapers

ILTALEHTI ILONA 1605508L65A-33_100
Formerly: Iltalehti Helmi / Ilona
Editorial: PL 372/ Aleksanterinkatu 9, 00101 HELSINKI **Tel:** 10 66 51 00 **Fax:** 10 66 52 097
Email: ilona.toimitus@ililona.fi **Web site:** http://www.iltalehti.fi/nainen
ISSN: 1796-3354
Freq: Daily - Ilona is issued weekly on Wednesday; **Circ:** 100,000
Profile: The Helmi section of Iltalehti concerns women's issues, such as fitness, cosmetics, fashion and leisure.
Language(s): Finnish
ADVERTISING RATES:
Full Page Colour .... EUR 3270
SCC .... EUR 27.50
Mechanical Data: Page Width: 230mm, Col Length: 257mm
Section of: Iltalehti
NATIONAL DAILY & SUNDAY NEWSPAPERS: Unabhängiges konservatives MdEP

ILTALEHTI ONLINE 624613L65A-33_101
Editorial: PL 372/ Aleksanterinkatu 9, 00101 HELSINKI **Tel:** 40 77 84 854 **Fax:** 9 17 73 13
Email: iltalehti.online@iltalehti.fi **Web site:** http://www.iltalehti.fi
Freq: Daily. Web site is updated 5 days a week; **Cover Price:** Free; **Circ:** 1,833,000 Unique Users
Profile: Internet version of the tabloid-sized evening newspaper. Covers national and international news, culture, sport, fashion, entertainment and interviews.
Language(s): Finnish
Readership: Aimed at young, educated people living in the city.
Section of: Iltalehti
NATIONAL DAILY & SUNDAY NEWSPAPERS: National Daily Newspapers

ILTALEHTI TURKU 705612L65C-225
Editorial: Kuuvuorenkatu 7, 20540 TURKU
Tel: 10 66 52 001 **Fax:** 2 25 42 246
Email: markku.haapio@iltalehti.fi **Web site:** http://www.iltalehti.fi
Freq: Daily
Profile: Turku regional office of national evening newspaper Iltalehti.
Language(s): Finnish
NATIONAL DAILY & SUNDAY NEWSPAPERS: National Daily Regional Offices

ILTA-SANOMAT 15164L65A-30
Editorial: PL 45/ Töölönlahdenkatu 2, 00089 SANOMA **Tel:** 9 12 21 **Fax:** 9 12 23 419
Email: uutiset@iltasanomat.fi **Web site:** http://www.iltasanomat.fi
ISSN: 0355-2055
Date Established: 1932; **Freq:** Daily - Published Monday to Saturday; **Circ:** 150,351
Usual Pagination: 40
Managing Editor: Kari Ylänne; **Publisher:** Tapio Sadeoja
Profile: Tabloid-sized evening newspaper covering a broad range of national and international news, events, entertainment, sports and features.
Language(s): Finnish
Readership: Read by a broad range of the population.
ADVERTISING RATES:
Full Page Colour .... EUR 6250
SCC .... EUR 28
Agency Commission: 15%
Mechanical Data: Type Area: 365 x 253mm, Print Process: Offset litho, Screen: Mono: 28 lpc. Colour: 34 lpc, No. of Columns (Display): 6, Col Widths (Display): 38mm, Col Length: 365mm, Page Width: 253mm
Copy instructions: *Copy Date:* 2 days prior to publication date
Average ad content per issue: 20%
Sections:
Ilta-Sanomat Plus
NATIONAL DAILY & SUNDAY NEWSPAPERS: National Daily Newspapers

ILTA-SANOMAT PLUS 1605367L65A-30_100
Formerly: Ilta-Sanomat Viikonvaihdetoimitus
Editorial: PL 45/ Töölönlahdenkatu 2, 00089 SANOMA **Tel:** 9 12 23 417 **Fax:** 9 12 23 419
Email: plus@iltasanomat.fi **Web site:** http://www.iltasanomat.fi
ISSN: 1795-1798
Freq: Weekly; **Circ:** 185,332
Usual Pagination: 64
Managing Editor: Iina Artima-Kyrki
Profile: Weekend edition of Ilta-Sanomat.
Language(s): Finnish
ADVERTISING RATES:
Full Page Colour .... EUR 6545
Mechanical Data: Page Width: 260mm, Col Length: 380mm
Section of: Ilta-Sanomat
NATIONAL DAILY & SUNDAY NEWSPAPERS: National Daily Newspapers

ILVES MURISEE 705364L75B-60
Editorial: Rievàkatu 2, 33540 TAMPERE
Tel: 207 48 26 80 **Fax:** 3 26 12 614
Email: risto.valkeala@ilves.fi **Web site:** http://www.ilves.fi
Freq: Half-yearly; **Cover Price:** Free; **Circ:** 100,000
Editor-in-Chief: Risto Valkeala
Profile: Magazine about football and icehockey in Tampere team Ilves.
Language(s): Finnish
ADVERTISING RATES:
Full Page Colour .... EUR 2000.00
CONSUMER: SPORT: Football

IMAGE 15241L74Q-10
Editorial: PL 212/ Risto Rytin tie 33, 00811 HELSINKI
Tel: 9 75 96 779 **Fax:** 9 75 98 38 04
Email: image@imagekustannus.fi **Web site:** http://www.image.fi
ISSN: 0782-3614
Date Established: 1985; **Freq:** Monthly; **Circ:** 31,000
Usual Pagination: 100
Editor-in-Chief: Mikko Numminen; **Managing Editor:** Pekka Hiltunen
Profile: Magazine covering fashion, entertainment, culture and lifestyle issues.
Language(s): Finnish
Readership: Young urban adults.
ADVERTISING RATES:
Full Page Colour .... EUR 4800
SCC .... EUR 40
Agency Commission: 15%
Mechanical Data: Type Area: 300 x 230mm, Col Length: 300mm, Page Width: 230mm, Print Process: Offset. Rotative, Film: Positive. Digital, Screen: 70 lpc

Finland

Copy instructions: *Copy Date:* 15 days prior to publication date
Editions:
Image.fi

IMPROBATUR 705859L83-26
Editorial: Erottajankatu 15-17, 00130 HELSINKI
Tel: 20 74 39 900 **Fax:** 20 74 39 909
Email: improbatur@lukio.fi **Web site:** http://www.lukio.fi
ISSN: 0784-705X
Freq: Quarterly; **Cover Price:** Free; **Circ:** 50,000
Usual Pagination: 36
Editor-in-Chief: Venla Pöyliö
Profile: Magazine by the Union of High School Students.
Language(s): Finnish
ADVERTISING RATES:
Full Page Colour .... EUR 3150.00
Mechanical Data: Type Area: 215 x 280mm, Screen: 60 lpc, Print Process: offset
CONSUMER: STUDENT PUBLICATIONS

INTERNET-UUTISET 1646090L5E-141
Editorial: Kantolankatu 7, 13110 HÄMEENLINNA
Tel: 3 65 700 **Fax:** 3 63 36 430
Email: webinfo@webinfo.fi **Web site:** http://www.infocenter.fi
Freq: Quarterly; **Cover Price:** Free; **Circ:** 85,000
Usual Pagination: 8
Editor-in-Chief: Markku Vettenniemi
Profile: Magazine about Internet and online-registers.
Language(s): Finnish
BUSINESS: COMPUTERS & AUTOMATION: Data Transmission

INTIIM 1934357L84B-202
Editorial: PL 324 / Siltasaarenkatu 2, 00531 HELSINKI **Tel:** 9 77 39 71 **Fax:** 9 75 38 511
Email: intiim@teamliitto.fi **Web site:** http://www.teamliitto.fi/tiedotus/intiim-lehti
Freq: Monthly - 14/ a year; **Circ:** 70,000
Editor-in-Chief: Tuomo Lilja
Language(s): Finnish
ADVERTISING RATES:
Full Page Colour .... EUR 3000.00
SCC .... EUR 16.00
CONSUMER: THE ARTS & LITERARY: Literary

INTRESSI 718077L1G-15
Formerly: Perintätieto
Editorial: PL 47/ Hitsaajankatu 20, 00811 HELSINKI
Tel: 9 22 91 11 **Fax:** 9 22 91 19 11
Email: intressi@intrum.com **Web site:** http://www.intrum.fi
ISSN: 1459-0530
Date Established: 1984; **Freq:** Quarterly; **Cover Price:** Free; **Circ:** 17,500
Usual Pagination: 16
Editor-in-Chief: Katja Luotola
Profile: Magazine about credit management and collecting.
Language(s): Finnish
Readership: Customers of credit management company Intrum Justitia.
BUSINESS: FINANCE & ECONOMICS: Credit Trading

IT INVALIDITYÖ 705736L56L-4
Editorial: Omnipress Oy, Hämeentie 13 B, 00530 HELSINKI **Tel:** 9 75 99 620 **Fax:** 9 75 99 62 30
Email: fmd@invalidiliitto.fi **Web site:** http://www.it-lehti.fi
ISSN: 0356-7249
Date Established: 1941; **Freq:** Monthly - Published 10/year; **Circ:** 31,180
Usual Pagination: 96
Managing Editor: Tapio Rusanen
Profile: Magazine about people with physical disabilities.
Language(s): Finnish; Swedish
Readership: Disabled people and people working in the social and health sector.
ADVERTISING RATES:
Full Page Colour .... EUR 2540
SCC .... EUR 23.50
Agency Commission: 15%
Mechanical Data: No. of Columns (Display): 2-4, Type Area: 187 x 270mm, Col Widths (Display): 58/ 35mm, Print Process: offset, Film: negative, Screen: 60 lpc
Copy instructions: *Copy Date:* 38 days prior to publication date
BUSINESS: HEALTH & MEDICAL: Disability & Rehabilitation

ITÄ-HÄME 15184L67B-3900
Editorial: PL 10/Lampikatu 8, 18101 HEINOLA
Tel: 3 75 75 05 **Fax:** 3 75 75 765
Email: iha.toimitus@itahame.fi **Web site:** http://www.itahame.fi
ISSN: 0359-5064
Date Established: 1927
Circ: 10,719
Usual Pagination: 28
Profile: Regional newspaper issued in Heinola, Heinolan mlk, Sysmä, Hartola Luhanka, Pertunmaa and Joutsa.
Language(s): Finnish
ADVERTISING RATES:
Full Page Colour .... EUR 3744
SCC .... EUR 17.10
Agency Commission: 15%
Mechanical Data: No. of Columns (Display): 6, Col Widths (Display): 39mm, Type Area: 254 x 365mm, Screen: 40 lpc, Print Process: offset, Col Length: 365mm, Page Width: 260mm
Copy instructions: *Copy Date:* 7 days prior to publication date
Editions:
Itä-Häme Verkkotoimitus
REGIONAL DAILY & SUNDAY NEWSPAPERS: Regional Daily Newspapers

ITÄ-SAVO 15217L67B-3920
Editorial: PL 101/ Olavinkatu 60, 57101 SAVONLINNA **Tel:** 15 35 03 400 **Fax:** 15 35 03 444
Email: toimitus@ita-savo.fi **Web site:** http://www.ita-savo.fi
ISSN: 0356-4444
Date Established: 1907
Circ: 16,674
Usual Pagination: 20
Managing Editor: Janne Tiainen
Profile: Newspaper issued in Savonlinna, Enonkoski, Kerimäki, Punkaharju, Savonranta, Sulkava, Rantasalmi, Parikkala, Saari and Uukuniemi.
Language(s): Finnish
ADVERTISING RATES:
Full Page Colour .... EUR 4778
SCC .... EUR 18.10
Mechanical Data: Col Widths (Display): 44mm, Type Area: 284 x 420mm, No. of Columns (Display): 6, Print Process: offset, Page Width: 284mm, Col Length: 440mm
Editions:
Itä-Savo Verkkotoimitus
REGIONAL DAILY & SUNDAY NEWSPAPERS: Regional Daily Newspapers

ITUA 705308L21A-85
Formerly: ProAgria Etelä-Pohjanmaa; Terve Maaseutu
Editorial: Huhtalantie 2, 60220 SEINÄJOKI
Tel: 6 41 63 111 **Fax:** 6 41 63 448
Email: tiina.kolunsarka@proagria.fi **Web site:** http://www.proagria.fi/ep
Freq: Quarterly; **Circ:** 10,000
Usual Pagination: 24
Editor-in-Chief: Antti Siljamäki
Profile: Journal about agriculture and co-operative affairs in southern Ostrobotnia.
Language(s): Finnish
ADVERTISING RATES:
Full Page Colour .... EUR 1600.00
SCC .... EUR 9.40
Mechanical Data: Print Process: offset, No. of Columns (Display): 6, Col Widths (Display): 40mm, Col Length: 370mm, Page Width: 260mm

ITVIIKKO 601399L5B-60
Editorial: PL 45/ Töölönlahdenkatu 2, 00089 SANOMA **Tel:** 9 12 21 **Fax:** 9 12 24 179
Email: itviikko@sanoma.fi **Web site:** http://www.itviikko.fi
ISSN: 0359-4947
Date Established: 1999; **Freq:** Daily; **Cover Price:** Free; **Circ:** 85,000 Unique Users
Usual Pagination: 32
Profile: Web site containing information on all aspects of the IT sector.
Language(s): Finnish
Readership: Aimed at IT professionals and business executives.
Mechanical Data: Type Area: 375 x 254mm, Print Process: Offset rotation, Screen: 34 lpc, Bleed Size: 400 x 280mm, Col Length: 365mm, Film: Positive, No. of Columns (Display): 6, Col Widths (Display): 39mm
BUSINESS: COMPUTERS & AUTOMATION: Data Processing

JÄÄKIEKKOLEHTI 705365L75A-15
Editorial: PL 1269/ Vuorikatu 14 A, 00101 HELSINKI
Tel: 20 13 32 222 **Fax:** 20 13 32 360
Email: jaakiekkolehti@egmontkustannus.fi **Web site:** http://www.jaakiekkolehti.fi
ISSN: 1238-0903
Date Established: 1993; **Freq:** Monthly - Published 10/year; **Circ:** 14,791
Usual Pagination: 84
Editor-in-Chief: Jukka Torvinen
Profile: Magazine about events, players, results and stars from the world of ice-hockey.
Language(s): Finnish
Readership: Men of age 20-35.
ADVERTISING RATES:
Full Page Colour .... EUR 2400
SCC .... EUR 23.70
Agency Commission: 15%
Mechanical Data: Type Area: 210 x 273mm, Bleed Size: 210 x 297mm, Col Widths (Display): 45mm, Film: positive, Print Process: offset
CONSUMER: SPORT

JÄGAREN 15296L75F-30
Editorial: Fantsvägen 13-14, 00890 HELSINGFORS
Tel: 9 27 27 81 16 **Fax:** 9 27 27 81 30
Email: mkj@riista.fi **Web site:** http://www.riista.fi
ISSN: 0355-2683
Date Established: 1951; **Freq:** 6 issues yearly; **Cover Price:** Free; **Circ:** 18,547
Usual Pagination: 64
Managing Editor: Klaus Ekman
Profile: Magazine concerning all aspects of hunting.
Language(s): Finnish; Swedish
ADVERTISING RATES:
Full Page Colour .... EUR 6000
Agency Commission: 15%
Mechanical Data: Type Area: 185 x 271mm, No. of Columns (Display): 4, Col Widths (Display): 43mm, Print Process: offset, Screen: 48 lpc b/w, 54 lpc colour, Film: negative
CONSUMER: SPORT: Shooting

JAHTI - JAKT 705386L75L-26
Editorial: PL 91/ Kinturinkuja 4, 11101 RIIHIMAKI
Tel: 10 84 10 050 **Fax:** 10 84 10 051
Web site: http://www.metsastajaliitto.fi
ISSN: 1234-3090
Date Established: 1952; **Freq:** Quarterly; Free to qualifying individuals ; **Circ:** 150,000
Usual Pagination: 176
Profile: Magazine about hunting, wild animals and dog training.
Language(s): Finnish; Swedish
ADVERTISING RATES:
Full Page Colour .... EUR 2600
Mechanical Data: Col Widths (Display): 40mm, No. of Columns (Display): 4, Screen: 54 lpc, Type Area: 175 x 270mm, Print Process: offset
CONSUMER: SPORT: Outdoor

JÄMSÄN SEUTU 15188L72-535
Formerly: Koillis-Häme
Editorial: Lindemaninkatu 3, 42100 JÄMSÄ
Tel: 10 66 55 149 **Fax:** 10 66 55 152
Email: js.toimitus@sps.fi **Web site:** http://www.jamsanseutu.fi
ISSN: 0786-2202
Date Established: 1921; **Freq:** Daily; **Circ:** 7,114
Usual Pagination: 20
Profile: Newspaper issued in Jämsä, Jämsänkoski, Korpilahti, Kuhmoinen, Längelmäki and Kuorevesi.
Language(s): Finnish
ADVERTISING RATES:
Full Page Colour .... EUR 3019
SCC .... EUR 13.60
Agency Commission: 15%
Mechanical Data: Bleed Size: 260 x 375mm, No. of Columns (Display): 6, Col Widths (Display): 40mm, Print Process: 4-colour offset, Col Length: 370mm, Page Width: 260mm
Editions:
Jämsän Seutu Verkkotoimitus
LOCAL NEWSPAPERS

JANAKKALAN SANOMAT 704929L72-605
Formerly: Kotokulma; Janakkalan-Rengon Sanomat
Editorial: PL 5/ Harvialantie 7 A, 14201 TURENKI
Tel: 10 66 56 050 **Fax:** 106656056
Email: toimitus.janakkalansanomat@sps.fi **Web site:** http://www.janakkalansanomat.fi
ISSN: 1457-7205
Date Established: 1964; **Freq:** Weekly; **Circ:** 4,695
Usual Pagination: 16
Profile: Newspaper issued in Renko and Janakkala.
Language(s): Finnish
ADVERTISING RATES:
Full Page Colour .... EUR 2842
SCC .... EUR 12.80
Agency Commission: 15%
Mechanical Data: No. of Columns (Display): 6, Col Widths (Display): 45mm, Col Length: 420mm, Type Area: 290 x 420mm, Screen: 34 lpc, Print Process: offset rotation
Editions:
Janakkalan Sanomat Verkkotoimitus
Supplement(s): Janakkalan Ilves 12/year, circulation 15.000
LOCAL NEWSPAPERS

JÄRVISEUDUN SANOMAT 704998L72-300
Editorial: PL 29/ Maneesintie 4, 62601 LAPPAJÄRVI
Tel: 20 79 40 510 **Fax:** 20 79 40 512
Email: toimitus@jarviseudunsanomat.fi **Web site:** http://www.jarviseudunsanomat.fi
ISSN: 1235-9963
Date Established: 1962; **Freq:** Weekly; **Circ:** 8,178
Usual Pagination: 16
Profile: Newspaper issued in Evijärvi, Kortesjärvi, Lappajärvi and Vimpeli.
Language(s): Finnish
ADVERTISING RATES:
Full Page Colour .... EUR 4488
SCC .... EUR 11
Agency Commission: 17.5%
Mechanical Data: Col Widths (Display): 44mm, No. of Columns (Display): 8, Col Length: 520mm, Print Process: offset, Page Width: 380mm
LOCAL NEWSPAPERS

JÄRVISEUTU 704999L72-305
Editorial: PL 33 / Hoiskontie 4, 62901 ALAJÄRVI
Tel: 6 24 77 890 **Fax:** 6 24 77 899
Email: toimitus@jarviseutu-lehti.fi **Web site:** http://www.jarviseutu-lehti.fi
Date Established: 1937; **Freq:** Weekly; **Circ:** 5,472
Usual Pagination: 8
Profile: Newspaper issued in Alajärvi, Soini, Lehtimäki, Vimpeli and Lappajärvi.
Language(s): Finnish
ADVERTISING RATES:
Full Page Colour .... EUR 3307
SCC .... EUR 15.10
Mechanical Data: Col Widths (Display): 40mm, No. of Columns (Display): 6, Col Length: 365mm, Print Process: offset, Screen: 28-34 lpc, Page Width: 260mm
Editions:
Järviseutu Verkkotoimitus
LOCAL NEWSPAPERS

JOHDIN 706055L18B-3_5
Editorial: PL 419/ Metsänneidonkuja 8, 02130 ESPOO **Tel:** 10 56 61 **Fax:** 10 56 63 400
Email: eeva.aunesluoma@draka.com **Web site:** http://www.draka.fi
ISSN: 0356-6129
Freq: Half-yearly; **Cover Price:** Free; **Circ:** 7,500
Usual Pagination: 28
Editor-in-Chief: Eeva Aunesluoma
Profile: Newsletter covering all aspects of telecommunications and e-commerce, including cable and fibre production.
Language(s): Finnish
Readership: Aimed at customers of Draka Oy.
BUSINESS: ELECTRONICS: Telecommunications

JOROISTEN LEHTI 704964L72-320
Editorial: Joroisniementie 4, 79600 JOROINEN
Tel: 15 35 03 154 **Fax:** 15 35 03 151
Email: toimitus@joroistenlehti.fi **Web site:** http://www.joroistenlehti.fi
ISSN: 0782-5994
Date Established: 1948; **Freq:** Weekly; **Circ:** 2,462
Usual Pagination: 16
Profile: Newspaper issued in Joroinen.
Language(s): Finnish
ADVERTISING RATES:
Full Page Colour .... EUR 2719
SCC .... EUR 10.30
Agency Commission: 15%
Mechanical Data: No. of Columns (Display): 6, Col Widths (Display): 44mm, Type Area: 253 x 370mm, Print Process: offset, Screen: 34 lpc, Col Length: 365mm
LOCAL NEWSPAPERS

JOUTSAN SEUTU 704924L72-325
Editorial: PL 15/ Jousitie 31, 19651 JOUTSA
Tel: 20 18 76 100 **Fax:** 20 18 76 101
Email: konttori@joutsanseutu.fi **Web site:** http://www.joutsanseutu.fi
ISSN: 0782-6001
Date Established: 1971; **Freq:** Weekly; **Circ:** 5,088
Usual Pagination: 12
Profile: Newspaper issued in Joutsa, Leivonmäki and Luhanka.
Language(s): Finnish
ADVERTISING RATES:
Full Page Colour .... EUR 2119
SCC .... EUR 11.30
Agency Commission: 15%
Mechanical Data: No. of Columns (Display): 5, Col Widths (Display): 48mm, Col Length: 380mm, Page Width: 257mm
Editions:
Joutsan Seutu Verkkotoimitus
LOCAL NEWSPAPERS

JOUTSENO 704953L72-330
Editorial: Keskuskatu 7, 54100 JOUTSENO
Tel: 5 21 00 25 00 **Fax:** 5 41 32 004
Email: toimitus@joutsenolehti.fi **Web site:** http://www.joutsenolehti.fi
ISSN: 0357-0983
Date Established: 1966; **Freq:** Weekly; **Circ:** 3,264
Usual Pagination: 12
Profile: Newspaper issued in Joutseno.
Language(s): Finnish
ADVERTISING RATES:
Full Page Colour .... EUR 2540
SCC .... EUR 11.60
Agency Commission: 15%
Mechanical Data: Print Process: offset, Col Widths (Display): 39mm, No. of Columns (Display): 6, Col Length: 360mm
LOCAL NEWSPAPERS

JP KUNNALLISSANOMAT 704996L72-295
Formerly: Jalasjärven-Peräseinäjoen Kunnallissanomat
Editorial: PL 53 / Torikuja 9, 61601 JALASJÄRVI
Tel: 6 45 65 100 **Fax:** 6 45 61 420
Email: toimitus@jp-kunnallissanomat.fi **Web site:** http://www.jp-kunnallissanomat.fi
Date Established: 1955; **Freq:** 104 issues yearly; **Circ:** 6,353
Usual Pagination: 16
Profile: Newspaper distributed in Jalasjärvi and Peräseinäjoki.
Language(s): Finnish
ADVERTISING RATES:
Full Page Colour .... EUR 1624
SCC .... EUR 8.90
Agency Commission: 15-17.5%
Mechanical Data: Type Area: 260 x 365mm, No. of Columns (Display): 5, Col Length: 365mm, Col Widths (Display): 49mm, Screen: 25-34 lpc, Print Process: offset, Page Width: 260mm
LOCAL NEWSPAPERS

JULKAISIJA
15135L2A-2
Editorial: PL 23/ Hietakummuntie 18, 00701 HELSINKI **Tel:** 44 07 00 401 **Fax:** 9 22 45 148
Email: toimitus@julkaisija.fi **Web site:** http://www.julkaisija.fi
ISSN: 1236-519X
Date Established: 1993; **Freq:** 6 issues yearly; **Circ:** 3,500
Usual Pagination: 52
Profile: Magazine containing information on desk-top publishing.
Language(s): Finnish
Readership: Read by communication and publishing professionals.
ADVERTISING RATES:
Full Page Colour .... EUR 2438
SCC .... EUR 29
Mechanical Data: Type Area: 220 x 285mm, Col Length: 285mm, Page Width: 220mm, Print Process: Offset, Film: Digital
Copy instructions: *Copy Date:* 21 days prior to publication date

JUOKSIJA
15309L75J-5
Formerly: Juoksija Lehti
Editorial: Olympiastadion, Eteläkaarre B 10, 00250 HELSINKI **Tel:** 9 43 42 040 **Fax:** 9 43 42 04 44
Email: toimitus@juoksija-lehti.fi **Web site:** http://www.juoksija-lehti.fi
ISSN: 0782-4971
Date Established: 1970; **Freq:** Monthly - Published 10/year; **Circ:** 19,257
Usual Pagination: 96
Managing Director: Harri Hänninen
Profile: Publication focusing on endurance sports including triathlon, running, swimming, cross-country skiing, cycling and orienteering.
Language(s): Finnish
ADVERTISING RATES:
Full Page Colour .... EUR 2790
SCC .... EUR 24.90
Mechanical Data: Type Area: 190 x 272mm, No. of Columns (Display): 4, Print Process: offset, Screen: 60 lpc
CONSUMER: SPORT: Athletics

JURVAN SANOMAT
704997L72-340
Editorial: Hahdonkuja 2, 66300 JURVA
Tel: 6 24 77 875 **Fax:** 62477877
Email: toimitus@jurvansanomat.fi **Web site:** http://www.jurvansanomat.fi
ISSN: 0782-6427
Date Established: 1976; **Freq:** Weekly; **Circ:** 2,256
Usual Pagination: 8
Profile: Newspaper issued in Jurva.
Language(s): Finnish
ADVERTISING RATES:
Full Page Colour .... EUR 3964
SCC .... EUR 11.90
Agency Commission: 17.5%
Mechanical Data: Col Widths (Display): 40mm, No. of Columns (Display): 6, Print Process: offset, Col Length: 365mm
Editions:
Jurvan Sanomat Verkkotoimitus
LOCAL NEWSPAPERS

JUURIKASSARKA
14980L21A-3_50
Editorial: Toivonlinnantie 518, 21500 PIIKKIÖ
Tel: 10 43 10 62 **Fax:** 2 73 76 409
Email: marte.romer-lindroos@danisco.com **Web site:** http://www.sjt.fi
ISSN: 0789-2667
Date Established: 1988; **Freq:** Quarterly; **Circ:** 4,400
Usual Pagination: 40
Profile: Journal containing information on Sugar Beet Research.
Language(s): Finnish; Swedish

JUVAN LEHTI
704965L72-345
Editorial: PL 27 / Koulutie 6 A 2, 51901 JUVA
Tel: 15 35 03 172 **Fax:** 15 35 03 171
Email: toimitus@juvanlehti.fi **Web site:** http://www.juvanlehti.fi
ISSN: 0784-1663
Date Established: 1956; **Freq:** Weekly; **Circ:** 4,220
Usual Pagination: 8
Profile: Newspaper issued in Juva.
Language(s): Finnish
ADVERTISING RATES:
Full Page Colour .... EUR 2686
SCC .... EUR 12.10
Mechanical Data: Page Width: 285mm, Col Length: 410mm, No. of Columns (Display): 6, Col Widths (Display): 40mm, Print Process: 4-colour offset rotation, Bleed Size: 285 x 410mm
LOCAL NEWSPAPERS

JYTY
705246L32A-55
Formerly: Kunnan Ammattilaiset
Editorial: Asemamiehenkatu 4, 00520 HELSINKI
Tel: 20 78 93 799 **Fax:** 20 78 93 790
Email: kari.hietamaki@jytyliitto.fi **Web site:** http://www.jytyliitto.fi
Freq: Monthly; **Circ:** 64,000
Usual Pagination: 36
Editor-in-Chief: Kari Hietamäki
Profile: Journal about benefits for people working in the municipal sector.
Language(s): Finnish
ADVERTISING RATES:
Full Page Colour .... EUR 2520.00
Agency Commission: 15%
Mechanical Data: Print Process: offset, Type Area: 185 x 275mm, Screen: 54 lpc
BUSINESS: LOCAL GOVERNMENT, LEISURE & RECREATION: Local Government

KAAKONKULMA
704955L72-360
Editorial: PL 20/ Mäkitie 3, 49901 VIROLAHTI
Tel: 5 35 71 040 **Fax:** 5 35 71 560
Email: toimitus@kaakonkulma.fi **Web site:** http://www.kaakonkulma.fi
ISSN: 1236-8865
Date Established: 1968; **Freq:** Weekly; **Circ:** 4,868
Usual Pagination: 12
Profile: Newspaper issued in Miehikkälä, Vironlahti and Ylämaa.
Language(s): Finnish
ADVERTISING RATES:
SCC .... EUR 11.10
Agency Commission: 15%
Mechanical Data: No. of Columns (Display): 6, Col Widths (Display): 39mm, Col Length: 370mm, Print Process: offset, Page Width: 256mm
LOCAL NEWSPAPERS

KAARINA
704886L72-365
Editorial: PL 73/Pyhän Katariinantie 7, 20781 KAARINA **Tel:** 2 58 88 600 **Fax:** 22743610
Email: toimitus@kaarina-lehti.fi **Web site:** http://www.kaarina-lehti.fi
Date Established: 1985; **Freq:** Weekly; **Circ:** 4,665
Usual Pagination: 16
Editor-in-Chief: Teija Uurinmäki
Profile: Newspaper issued in Kaarina.
Language(s): Finnish
ADVERTISING RATES:
Full Page Colour .... EUR 4618
SCC .... EUR 20.80
Mechanical Data: Col Length: 410mm, Page Width: 284mm, No. of Columns (Display): 6, Col Widths (Display): 44mm
LOCAL NEWSPAPERS

KAASUJALKA
1791246L77A-7
Editorial: PL 235, 01301 VANTAA **Tel:** 400 77 77 97
Email: mika.salomaa@wheelmedia.fi **Web site:** http://www.kaasujalka.fi
Date Established: 2006; **Freq:** Monthly; **Cover Price:** Free; **Circ:** 100,000
Usual Pagination: 24
Editor-in-Chief: Mika Salomaa
Profile: Magazine about cars with tests and ads.
Language(s): Finnish
Readership: Households in eastern Helsinki and Vantaa.
ADVERTISING RATES:
Full Page Colour .... EUR 1300.00
CONSUMER: MOTORING & CYCLING: Motoring

KAINUUN SANOMAT
15191L67B-4400
Editorial: PL 150/ Kauppakatu 11, 87101 KAJAANI
Tel: 8 61 66 333 **Fax:** 8 62 34 00
Email: ks.toimitus@kainuunsanomat.fi **Web site:** http://www.kainuunsanomat.fi
ISSN: 0356-3502
Date Established: 1918; **Freq:** Daily; **Circ:** 20,265
Usual Pagination: 10
Editor-in-Chief: Matti Piirainen; **Managing Editor:** Pekka Vasala
Profile: Newspaper issued mainly in Kajaani, Vuolijoki, Vaala, Paltamo, Sotkamo, Kuhmo, Ristijärvi, Puolanka, Hyrynsalmi and Suomussalmi.
Language(s): Finnish
ADVERTISING RATES:
Full Page Colour .... EUR 4590
SCC .... EUR 20.90
Agency Commission: 15%
Mechanical Data: No. of Columns (Display): 8, No. of Columns (Display): 44mm, Page Width: 380mm, Print Process: offset, Film: negative, Screen: 25-34 lpc, Col Length: 510mm
Editions:
Kainuun Sanomat Kulttuuritoimitus
Kainuun Sanomat Urheilutoimitus
Kainuun Sanomat Verkkotoimitus
REGIONAL DAILY & SUNDAY NEWSPAPERS: Regional Daily Newspapers

KAKSPLUS
15270L74D-20
Editorial: Maistraatinportti 1, 00015 OTAVAMEDIA
Tel: 9 15 66 592 **Fax:** 9 15 66 550
Email: kaksplus@otavamedia.fi **Web site:** http://www.kaksplus.fi
ISSN: 0355-4252
Date Established: 1969; **Freq:** Monthly; **Circ:** 28,760
Usual Pagination: 110
Managing Editor: Matilda Katajamäki
Profile: Magazine covering pregnancy, birth and child care. Also includes features on food, fashion, interior decoration and beauty.
Language(s): Finnish
Readership: Aimed at women with babies and young children.
ADVERTISING RATES:
Full Page Colour .... EUR 4490
SCC .... EUR 37.70
Mechanical Data: Bleed Size: 280 x 230mm, Print Process: Offset, Film: Digital, Screen: 60 lpc
Copy instructions: *Copy Date:* 19 days prior to publication date
CONSUMER: WOMEN'S INTEREST CONSUMER MAGAZINES: Child Care

KALAJOEN SEUTU
706198L72-370
Editorial: Kalajoentie 4, 85100 KALAJOKI
Tel: 8 46 01 66 **Fax:** 8460543
Email: toimitus@kalajoenseutu.fi **Web site:** http://www.kalajoenseutu.fi
ISSN: 1455-2965
Date Established: 1997; **Freq:** Weekly; **Circ:** 2,767
Usual Pagination: 16
Profile: Local newspaper issued in Kalajoki.
Language(s): Finnish
ADVERTISING RATES:
Full Page Colour .... EUR 1836
SCC .... EUR 18.50
Mechanical Data: Page Width: 260mm, Col Length: 360mm
Editions:
Kalajoen Seutu Verkkotoimitus
LOCAL NEWSPAPERS

KALAJOKI
705000L72-375
Editorial: PL 14/Kalajoentie 29 L 11, 85101 KALAJOKI **Tel:** 8 46 21 00 **Fax:** 8 46 08 30
Email: anne.mattila@kalajokilehti.fi **Web site:** http://www.kalajokilehti.fi
ISSN: 0782-6214
Date Established: 1976; **Freq:** Weekly; **Circ:** 2,147
Usual Pagination: 24
Profile: Newspaper issued in Kalajoki.
Language(s): Finnish
ADVERTISING RATES:
Full Page Colour .... EUR 3413
SCC .... EUR 15.80
Agency Commission: 15%
Mechanical Data: Page Width: 250mm, Col Length: 360mm, No. of Columns (Display): 6, Col Widths (Display): 38mm, Print Process: offset
Editions:
Kalajoki Verkkotoimitus
LOCAL NEWSPAPERS

KALAJOKILAAKSO
15229L72-380
Editorial: PL 7/Kartanotie 3, 84101 YLIVIESKA
Tel: 20 75 04 600 **Fax:** 20 75 04 618
Email: toimitus@kalajokilaakso.fi **Web site:** http://www.kalajokilaakso-lehti.fi
ISSN: 0784-3647
Date Established: 1927; **Freq:** Daily; **Circ:** 7,095
Usual Pagination: 10
Managing Editor: Liisa Ängeslevä
Profile: Newspaper issued in Ylivieska.
Language(s): Finnish
ADVERTISING RATES:
Full Page Colour .... EUR 7072
SCC .... EUR 17
Agency Commission: 15%
Mechanical Data: Col Length: 520mm, No. of Columns (Display): 8, Col Widths (Display): 44mm, Print Process: offset, Page Width: 380mm
LOCAL NEWSPAPERS

KALEVA
15207L67B-4440
Editorial: PL 170/ Lekatie 1, 90401 OULU
Tel: 8 53 77 111 **Fax:** 8 53 77 195
Email: toimitus@kaleva.fi **Web site:** http://www.kaleva.fi
ISSN: 0356-1356
Date Established: 1899
Circ: 78,216
Usual Pagination: 36
Editor-in-Chief: Markku Mantila; **Managing Editor:** Kyösti Karvonen
Profile: The biggest newspaper in northern Finland.
Language(s): Finnish
ADVERTISING RATES:
Full Page Colour .... EUR 15582
SCC .... EUR 37.10
Agency Commission: 15%
Mechanical Data: Print Process: offset, No. of Columns (Display): 8, Screen: 34 lpc, Col Widths (Display): 44mm, Col Length: 525mm, Page Width: 380mm
Editions:
Kaleva Ajankohtaistoimitus
Kaleva Kulttuuritoimitus
Kaleva Kuntatoimitus
Kaleva Politiikantoimitus
Kaleva Taloustoimitus
Kaleva Ulkomaantoimitus
Kaleva Urheilutoimitus
Kaleva Uutistoimitus
Kaleva Verkkopalvelut
REGIONAL DAILY & SUNDAY NEWSPAPERS: Regional Daily Newspapers

KALEVA KEMI-TORNIO
705618L67E-416
Editorial: Valtakatu 27-29, 94100 KEMI
Tel: 44 79 49 783 **Fax:** 16 25 04 31
Email: jouni.knihtila@kaleva.fi **Web site:** http://www.kaleva.fi
Profile: Kemi-Tornio regional office of newspaper Kaleva.
Language(s): Finnish
REGIONAL DAILY & SUNDAY NEWSPAPERS: Regional Offices

KALEVA KUUSAMO
705619L67E-418
Editorial: Kitkantie 19, 93600 KUUSAMO
Tel: 44 79 49 785 **Fax:** 8 86 60 084
Email: anne.hentila@kaleva.fi **Web site:** http://www.kaleva.fi
Profile: Kuusamo regional office of newspaper Kaleva.
Language(s): Finnish
REGIONAL DAILY & SUNDAY NEWSPAPERS: Regional Offices

KALEVA RAAHE
705620L67E-420
Editorial: Kauppakatu 42, 92100 RAAHE
Tel: 44 79 49 787 **Fax:** 8 22 28 12
Email: timo.myllykoski@kaleva.fi **Web site:** http://www.kaleva.fi
Profile: Raahe regional office of newspaper Kaleva.
Language(s): Finnish
REGIONAL DAILY & SUNDAY NEWSPAPERS: Regional Offices

KALEVA VAALA
705623L67E-424
Editorial: Asematie 2 A 8, 91700 VAALA
Tel: 400 95 60 45 **Fax:** 8 53 61 035
Email: petri.hakkarainen@kaleva.fi **Web site:** http://www.kaleva.fi
Profile: Vaala regional office of newspaper Kaleva.
Language(s): Finnish
REGIONAL DAILY & SUNDAY NEWSPAPERS: Regional Offices

KALEVA YLIVIESKA
705624L67E-426
Editorial: Kartanontie 1, 84100 YLIVIESKA
Tel: 44 79 49 790 **Fax:** 8 42 30 80
Email: liisa.lehto-peippo@kaleva.fi **Web site:** http://www.kaleva.fi
Profile: Ylivieska regional office of newspaper Kaleva.
Language(s): Finnish
REGIONAL DAILY & SUNDAY NEWSPAPERS: Regional Offices

KÄLVIÄN SEUDUN SANOMAT
704931L72-395
Editorial: Kälviäntie 36, 68300 KÄLVIÄ
Tel: 6 82 43 822 **Fax:** 68243848
Email: toimitus@kalviansanomat.com **Web site:** http://www.kalviansanomat.com
ISSN: 0786-4604
Date Established: 1988; **Freq:** Weekly; **Circ:** 1,699
Usual Pagination: 8
Profile: Newspaper issued in Kälviä, Lohtaja and Ullava.
Language(s): Finnish
ADVERTISING RATES:
Full Page Colour .... EUR 2080
SCC .... EUR 9.50
Mechanical Data: Col Widths (Display): 46mm, No. of Columns (Display): 6, Col Length: 410mm
LOCAL NEWSPAPERS

KAMERA-LEHTI
15030L85A-5
Editorial: Lastenkodinkatu 5, 00180 HELSINKI
Tel: 9 68 11 490 **Fax:** 9 69 40 166
Email: asko.vivolin@kamera-lehti.fi **Web site:** http://www.kamera-lehti.fi
ISSN: 0022-8133
Date Established: 1950; **Freq:** 6 issues yearly - Published 8/year; **Circ:** 12,029
Usual Pagination: 68
Profile: Magazine concerning photographic, video and digital imaging.
Language(s): Finnish
Readership: Aimed at retailers of photographic equipment and professional and amateur photographers.
ADVERTISING RATES:
Full Page Colour .... EUR 3300
SCC .... EUR 37
Mechanical Data: Type Area: 210 x 297mm, Screen: 80 lpc, Print Process: offset, Film: positive
Copy instructions: *Copy Date:* 21 days prior to publication date
CONSUMER: PHOTOGRAPHY & FILM MAKING: Photography

KANAVA
15339L84B-60
Editorial: Maistraatinportti 1, 00015 OTAVAMEDIA
Tel: 9 15 66 537 **Fax:** 9 15 66 63 45
Email: kanava@otavamedia.fi **Web site:** http://www.kuvalehdet.fi/kanava
ISSN: 0355-0303
Date Established: 1972; **Freq:** 6 issues yearly - Published 8/year; **Circ:** 7,019
Usual Pagination: 80
Profile: Magazine about political, social and cultural issues.
Language(s): Finnish
Readership: Written by managers in the Finnish culture, financial and science field of business.
ADVERTISING RATES:
Full Page Colour .... EUR 830
SCC .... EUR 16.70
Mechanical Data: Bleed Size: 248 x 188mm, Print Process: Offset, Film: Digital positive, Screen: 54 lpc, Page Width: 188mm, Col Length: 248mm
CONSUMER: THE ARTS & LITERARY: Literary

KANGASALAN SANOMAT
704901L72-415
Editorial: PL 40/Myllystenpohjantie 2, 36201 KANGASALA **Tel:** 3 37 76 900 **Fax:** 3 37 70 668

Web site: http://www.kangasalansanomat.fi
ISSN: 0782-596X
Date Established: 1918; **Freq:** 104 issues yearly; **Circ:** 7,981
Usual Pagination: 24
Profile: Newspaper issued in Kangasala.
Language(s): Finnish
ADVERTISING RATES:
Full Page Colour .... EUR 4284
SCC .... EUR 17
Agency Commission: 15%
Mechanical Data: No. of Columns (Display): 6, Col Widths (Display): 40mm, Col Length: 420mm, Print Process: offset, Page Width: 315mm
LOCAL NEWSPAPERS

KANGASNIEMEN KUNNALLISLEHTI
704966L72-420
Editorial: PL 115 / Otto Mannisen tie 13, 51201 KANGASNIEMI **Tel:** 15 35 03 160 **Fax:** 153503161
Email: toimitus@kangasniemen-kunnallislehti.fi **Web site:** http://www.kangasniemen-kunnallislehti.fi
ISSN: 0782-6354
Date Established: 1953; **Freq:** Weekly; **Circ:** 4,350
Usual Pagination: 12
Profile: Newspaper issued in Kangasniemi.
Language(s): Finnish
ADVERTISING RATES:
Full Page Colour .... EUR 1693
SCC .... EUR 8.30
Agency Commission: 10-15%
Mechanical Data: No. of Columns (Display): 5, Col Widths (Display): 47mm, Col Length: 375mm, Bleed Size: 290 x 420mm, Page Width: 290mm
Editions:
Kangasniemen Kunnallislehti Verkkotoimitus
LOCAL NEWSPAPERS

KANKAANPÄÄN SEUTU
704944L72-425
Editorial: PL 16 / Linnankatu 1, 38701 KANKAANPÄÄ
Tel: 10 66 55 763 **Fax:** 10 66 55 776
Email: kas.toimitus@sps.fi **Web site:** http://www.kankaanpaanseutu.fi
ISSN: 0355-8754
Date Established: 1968; **Freq:** 104 issues yearly; **Circ:** 9,857
Usual Pagination: 20
Profile: Newspaper issued in Honkajoki, Jämijärvi, Kankaanpää, Karvia, Lavia, Pomarkku, Siikainen and Suodenniemi.
Language(s): Finnish
ADVERTISING RATES:
Full Page Colour .... EUR 2606
SCC .... EUR 11.90
Agency Commission: 15%
Mechanical Data: Page Width: 260mm, Col Length: 365mm, No. of Columns (Display): 6, Col Widths (Display): 40mm, Print Process: offset
LOCAL NEWSPAPERS

KANSAN TAHTO
15208L67B-4500
Editorial: PL 61/Mäkelininkatu 29, 90101 OULU
Tel: 8 53 71 724 **Fax:** 8 37 13 14
Email: toimitus@kansantahto.fi **Web site:** http://www.kansantahto.fi
Date Established: 1906
Circ: 6,965
Usual Pagination: 16
Profile: Left-wing regional newspaper issued in Oulu, Lapland and Kainuu in northern Finland.
Language(s): Finnish
ADVERTISING RATES:
Full Page Colour .... EUR 5325
SCC .... EUR 25
Agency Commission: 15%
Mechanical Data: No. of Columns (Display): 6, Col Widths (Display): 40mm, Col Length: 355mm, Page Width: 257mm
REGIONAL DAILY & SUNDAY NEWSPAPERS: Regional Daily Newspapers

KANSAN UUTISET JYVÄSKYLÄ
705904L67E-445
Editorial: Väinönkatu 28 B 14, 40100 JYVÄSKYLÄ
Tel: 9 75 96 02 51 **Fax:** 975960319
Email: jarkko.manttari@kansanuutiset.fi **Web site:** http://www.kansanuutiset.fi
Freq: Daily
Profile: Jyväskylä regional office of political newspaper Kansan Uutiset.
Language(s): Finnish
REGIONAL DAILY & SUNDAY NEWSPAPERS: Regional Offices

KANSAN UUTISET TAMPERE
705903L67E-450
Editorial: Kauppakatu 11 C, 2krs, huone 5, 33200 TAMPERE **Tel:** 9 75 96 02 53 **Fax:** 975960319
Email: sirpa.koskinen@kansanuutiset.fi **Web site:** http://www.kansanuutiset.fi
Freq: Daily
Profile: Tampere regional office of a political newspaper.
Language(s): Finnish
REGIONAL DAILY & SUNDAY NEWSPAPERS: Regional Offices

KANSAN UUTISET TURKU
705902L67E-455
Editorial: Humalistonkatu 14 C, 20100 TURKU
Tel: 9 75 96 02 52 **Fax:** 975960319
Email: pekka.helminen@kansanuutiset.fi **Web site:** http://www.kansanuutiset.fi
Freq: Daily
Profile: Turku regional office of political newspaper Kansan Uutiset.
Language(s): Finnish
REGIONAL DAILY & SUNDAY NEWSPAPERS: Regional Offices

KANSAN UUTISET VERKKOLEHTI
15166L67B-4501
Editorial: PL 64/ Vilhonvuorenkatu 11 C 7, 00501 HELSINKI **Tel:** 9 75 96 01 **Fax:** 975960319
Email: ku@kansanuutiset.fi **Web site:** http://www.kansanuutiset.fi
ISSN: 0357-1521
Freq: Daily; **Circ:** 7,361 Unique Users
Usual Pagination: 24
Managing Editor: Kai Hirvasnoro
Profile: Tabloid-sized left-wing newspaper turned into web publication covering national and international business and political news.
Language(s): Finnish
Readership: Read by politically active workers and trade union members.
Agency Commission: 15%
Mechanical Data: Type Area: 256 x 365mm, No. of Columns (Display): 7, Col Widths (Display): 34mm, Print Process: offset, Screen: 28-34 lpc
REGIONAL DAILY & SUNDAY NEWSPAPERS: Regional Daily Newspapers

KANSAN UUTISET VIIKKOLEHTI
1994342L82-168
Editorial: PL 64/ Vilhonvuorenkatu 11 C 7, 00501 HELSINKI **Tel:** 9 75 96 01 **Fax:** 9 75 96 03 19
Email: ku@kansanuutiset.fi **Web site:** http://www.kansanuutiset.fi
Freq: Weekly; **Circ:** 14,663
Managing Editor: Kai Hirvasnoro
Language(s): Finnish
ADVERTISING RATES:
Full Page Colour .... EUR 4836
SCC .... EUR 26.50
CONSUMER: CURRENT AFFAIRS & POLITICS

KANSANTALOUDELLINEN AIKAKAUSKIRJA
14866L1A-15
Editorial: Palkansaajien tutkimuslaitos, Pitkänsillanranta 3 A, 00530 HELSINKI
Tel: 9 25 35 73 55
Email: aila.mustonen@labour.fi **Web site:** http://www.taloustieteellinenyhdistys.fi/julkaisut/kak
ISSN: 0022-8427
Date Established: 1905; **Freq:** Quarterly; **Circ:** 2,100
Usual Pagination: 150
Editor-in-Chief: Matti Pohjola
Profile: Journal includes articles on economic research, comments on economic policy, information about doctoral dissertations, seminar presentations and book reviews.
Language(s): Finnish
BUSINESS: FINANCE & ECONOMICS

KARJALAINEN
15189L67B-4695
Editorial: PL 99/ Kosti Aaltosen tie 9, 80141 JOENSUU **Tel:** 10 23 08 080 **Fax:** 10 23 08 081
Email: toimitus@karjalainen.fi **Web site:** http://www.karjalainen.fi
ISSN: 0358-1705
Date Established: 1874; **Freq:** Daily; **Circ:** 45,584
Usual Pagination: 32
Editor-in-Chief: Pasi Koivumaa; **Managing Editor:** Kari Kontkanen
Profile: Karjalainen is a newspaper emphasizing on northern Karelia.
Language(s): Finnish
Readership: Read by people in North Karelia.
ADVERTISING RATES:
Full Page Colour .... EUR 12158
SCC .... EUR 29.80
Agency Commission: 3/15%
Mechanical Data: Col Widths (Display): 44mm, No. of Columns (Display): 8, Page Width: 380mm, Print Process: offset, Col Length: 510mm
Editions:
Karjalainen Kulttuuritoimitus
Karjalainen Taloustoimitus
Karjalainen Urheilutoimitus
Karjalainen Verkkotoimitus
REGIONAL DAILY & SUNDAY NEWSPAPERS: Regional Daily Newspapers

KARJALAINEN KESÄLAHTI
705627L67E-434
Editorial: Lehmisavuntie 21, 59800 KESÄLAHTI
Tel: 10 23 08 131
Email: sirpa.suomalainen@karjalainen.fi **Web site:** http://www.karjalainen.fi
Freq: Daily
Profile: Kesälahti regional office of newspaper Karjalainen.
Language(s): Finnish
REGIONAL DAILY & SUNDAY NEWSPAPERS: Regional Offices

KARJALAINEN KITEE
705626L67E-436
Editorial: Pokentie 2 as 4, 82500 KITEE
Tel: 10 23 08 132
Email: anja.itkonen@karjalainen.fi **Web site:** http://www.karjalainen.fi
Freq: Daily
Profile: Kitee, Tohmajärvi, Värtsilä, Rääkkylä and Kesälahti regional office of newspaper Karjalainen.
Language(s): Finnish
REGIONAL DAILY & SUNDAY NEWSPAPERS: Regional Offices

KARJALAINEN LIEKSA
705628L67E-437
Editorial: Siltakatu 1, 81700 LIEKSA
Tel: 10 23 08 134
Email: veikko.huotari@karjalainen.fi **Web site:** http://www.karjalainen.fi
Profile: Lieksa regional office of newspaper Karjalainen.
Language(s): Finnish
REGIONAL DAILY & SUNDAY NEWSPAPERS: Regional Offices

KARJALAINEN NURMES
705629L67E-438
Editorial: Pappilansuora 15, 75500 NURMES
Tel: 10 23 08 130
Email: toimitus@karjalainen.fi **Web site:** http://www.karjalainen.fi
Freq: Daily
Profile: Nurmes, Valtimo and Juuka regional office of newspaper Karjalainen.
Language(s): Finnish
REGIONAL DAILY & SUNDAY NEWSPAPERS: Regional Offices

KARJALAN MAA
15190L67B-4700
Editorial: PL 98/Pankakoskentie 8, 80101 JOENSUU
Email: toimitus@karjalanmaa.fi **Web site:** http://www.karjalanmaa.fi
ISSN: 1357-1378
Date Established: 1917; **Freq:** Weekly - Finland; **Circ:** 3,423
Usual Pagination: 16
Profile: Regional newspaper issued mainly in northern Carelia.
Language(s): Finnish
ADVERTISING RATES:
Full Page Colour .... EUR 3692
SCC .... EUR 17
Mechanical Data: No. of Columns (Display): 6, Col Widths (Display): 40mm
REGIONAL DAILY & SUNDAY NEWSPAPERS: Regional Daily Newspapers

KÄSIKÄDESSÄ
706416L56N-3
Editorial: Malmin kauppatie 26, 00700 HELSINKI
Tel: 9 56 57 730 **Fax:** 956577334
Email: kasikadessa.lehti@mtkl.fi **Web site:** http://www.mtkl.fi
ISSN: 1236-780X
Date Established: 1972; **Freq:** 6 issues yearly; **Circ:** 11,249
Usual Pagination: 64
Profile: Journal about taking care of people with mental problems.
Language(s): Finnish
ADVERTISING RATES:
Full Page Colour .... EUR 2150
SCC .... EUR 19.60
Mechanical Data: Type Area: 210 x 273mm, No. of Columns (Display): 4, Col Widths (Display): 45mm, Film: negative, Screen: 54 lpc
Copy instructions: *Copy Date:* 34 days prior to publication date
BUSINESS: HEALTH & MEDICAL: Mental Health

KÄTILÖLEHTI
15102L56A-43
Formerly: Kätilölehti - Tidskrift för Barnmorskor
Editorial: PL 100/ Asemamiehenkatu 4, 00060 TEHY
Tel: 9 54 22 74 91 **Fax:** 961500268
Email: toimisto@suomenkatiloliitto.fi **Web site:** http://www.suomenkatiloliitto.fi
ISSN: 0022-9415
Date Established: 1896; **Freq:** 6 issues yearly - Published 7/year; **Circ:** 4,000
Usual Pagination: 40
Profile: Medical journal focusing on midwifery.
Language(s): Finnish; Swedish
ADVERTISING RATES:
Full Page Colour .... EUR 1150
SCC .... EUR 12.90
Agency Commission: 15%
Mechanical Data: Type Area: 152 x 220mm, Print Process: offset, Film: negative, Screen: 60 lpc
Copy instructions: *Copy Date:* 30 days prior to publication date

KATSASTUSLEHTI
706643L77A-8
Editorial: PL 510/ Vetokuja 4, 01601 VANTAA
Tel: 75 32 32 000 **Fax:** 75 32 32 003
Email: toimitus@a-katsastus.fi **Web site:** http://www.katsastuslehti.fi
ISSN: 1239-4092
Date Established: 1996; **Freq:** Half-yearly; **Cover Price:** Free; **Circ:** 12,000
Usual Pagination: 16
Editor-in-Chief: Outi Arola
Profile: Magazine about obligatory car inspection.
Language(s): Finnish; Swedish

KATSO!
15310L76C-100
Editorial: PL 124/ Pursimiehenkatu 29-31 A, 00151 HELSINKI **Tel:** 9 86 21 70 00 **Fax:** 9 86 21 71 39
Email: katso@katso.fi **Web site:** http://www.katso.fi
ISSN: 0355-2969
Date Established: 1960; **Freq:** Weekly; **Circ:** 33,264
Usual Pagination: 100
Editor-in-Chief: Kirsi Lindh-Mansikka
Profile: TV and radio magazine. Includes features on films, videos and entertainment.
Language(s): Finnish
ADVERTISING RATES:
Full Page Colour .... EUR 3600
SCC .... EUR 32.10
Mechanical Data: Type Area: 280 x 207mm, Bleed Size: 302 x 230mm, Print Process: Offset, No. of Columns (Display): 4, Screen: 60 lpc, Col Length: 280mm, Page Width: 204mm, Film: positive, Col Widths (Display): 49mm
CONSUMER: MUSIC & PERFORMING ARTS: TV & Radio

KAUHAJOKI-LEHTI
705001L72-460
Formerly: Kauhajoen Kunnallislehti
Editorial: PL 5 / Puistotie 25, 61801 KAUHAJOKI
Tel: 6 23 57 100 **Fax:** 6 23 12 210
Email: toimitus@kauhajoenkunnallislehti.fi **Web site:** http://www.kauhajoenkunnallislehti.fi
ISSN: 0782-5587
Date Established: 1925; **Freq:** 104 issues yearly; **Circ:** 7,075
Usual Pagination: 12
Profile: Newspaper issued in Kauhajoki.
Language(s): Finnish
ADVERTISING RATES:
Full Page Colour .... EUR 2786
SCC .... EUR 12.90
Agency Commission: 15-17.5%
Mechanical Data: Print Process: offset, Type Area: 260 x 360mm, No. of Columns (Display): 6, Col Widths (Display): 40mm, Col Length: 360mm, Page Width: 260mm
LOCAL NEWSPAPERS

KAUNEUS & TERVEYS
15283L74G-31
Editorial: Risto Rytin tie 33, 00081 A-LEHDET
Tel: 9 75 961 **Fax:** 9 75 98 31 06
Email: kauneusjaterveys@a-lehdet.fi **Web site:** http://www.kauneusjaterveys.fi
ISSN: 0047-3308
Date Established: 1956; **Freq:** Monthly - Published 16/year; **Circ:** 79,529
Usual Pagination: 148
Editor-in-Chief: Titta Kiuru; **Managing Editor:** Iina Soininen
Profile: Magazine containing professional advice for women conscious of their health and appearance. It features instructions and expert articles on how to attain beauty, style and well-being.
Language(s): Finnish
ADVERTISING RATES:
Full Page Colour .... EUR 6850
SCC .... EUR 64.10
Mechanical Data: Print Process: Offset, No. of Columns (Display): 4, Screen: 60 lpc, Col Length: 267mm, Page Width: 190mm, Type Area: 190 x 267mm, Film: positive, Col Widths (Display): 44mm
Copy instructions: *Copy Date:* 15 days prior to publication date
CONSUMER: WOMEN'S INTEREST CONSUMER MAGAZINES: Slimming & Health

KAUNIIT KODIT
2009991L4B-51
Editorial: Sahaajankatu 20-22 D, 00880 HELSINKI
Tel: 9 42 41 34 10
Email: toimitus@kauniitkodit.fi **Web site:** http://www.kauniitkodit.fi
Freq: Monthly; **Circ:** 30,000
Profile: Magazine covering interior design and decoration.
Language(s): Finnish
ADVERTISING RATES:
Full Page Colour .... EUR 3925
SCC .... EUR 45.10

KAUPAN MAAILMA
15086L53-200
Formerly: Vähittäiskauppa
Editorial: PL3/ Laturinkuja 10, 02601 ESPOO
Tel: 9 54 21 01 00 **Fax:** 9 54 21 01 32
Email: km-toimitus@bbm.fi **Web site:** http://www.bbm.fi
ISSN: 1459-9325
Date Established: 1990; **Freq:** 6 issues yearly - Published 8/year; **Circ:** 15,000
Usual Pagination: 72
Managing Editor: Piia Kunnas
Profile: Magazine concerning the retail trade, providing information and news.
Language(s): Finnish
Readership: Aimed at owners and managers of shops, supermarket chains and market stalls.
ADVERTISING RATES:
Full Page Colour .... EUR 4337
SCC .... EUR 36.70
Agency Commission: 15%
Mechanical Data: Type Area: 220 x 295mm
Copy instructions: *Copy Date:* 15 days prior to publication date

KAUPPA JA TEOLLISUUS
749150L14A-13_40
Editorial: Kölikatu 14, 20810 TURKU **Tel:** 2 23 96 616
Email: helina.vuori@media-tori.fi **Web site:** http://www.media-tori.fi/kauppateollisuus.html
Date Established: 1977; **Freq:** 6 issues yearly; **Cover Price:** Free; **Circ:** 15,000
Usual Pagination: 20
Editor-in-Chief: Helinä Vuori
Profile: Magazine about business, commerce and industry in the Turku region.
Language(s): Finnish
ADVERTISING RATES:
Full Page Colour .... EUR 3942.00
SCC .... EUR 18.00
Mechanical Data: No. of Columns (Display): 6, Type Area: 255 x 370mm, Col Widths (Display): 39mm, Print Process: offset

KAUPPALEHTI
15167L65A-40
Editorial: PL 189 / Eteläesplanadi 20, 00101 HELSINKI **Tel:** 10 66 51 01
Email: kl.toimitus@kauppalehti.fi **Web site:** http://www.kauppalehti.fi
ISSN: 0451-5560
Date Established: 1898; **Freq:** Daily - Published Monday - Friday; **Circ:** 70,118
Usual Pagination: 32
Editor-in-Chief: Hannu Leinonen; **Managing Editor:** Juha Ruonala
Profile: Tabloid-sized quality newspaper containing financial and business news.
Language(s): Finnish
Readership: Read by the business community, financial executives, business managers and academics.
ADVERTISING RATES:
Full Page Colour .... EUR 14700
SCC .... EUR 67.10
Agency Commission: 15%
Mechanical Data: Type Area: 253 x 365mm, No. of Columns (Display): 6, Col Widths (Display): 38mm, Print Process: offset rotation, Screen: 40 lpc, Page Width: 276mm, Col Length: 365mm
NATIONAL DAILY & SUNDAY NEWSPAPERS: National Daily Newspapers

KAUPPALEHTI OPTIO
705147L1A-9_10
Editorial: PL 189 / Eteläesplanadi 20, 00101 HELSINKI **Tel:** 10 66 51 01
Email: kl.optio@kauppalehti.fi **Web site:** http://www.kauppalehti.fi
ISSN: 1238-4895
Date Established: 1987; **Freq:** 26 issues yearly - Published 19/year; Free to qualifying individuals ; **Circ:** 86,654
Usual Pagination: 92
Managing Editor: Jussi Jalkanen
Profile: Weekly financial magazine is at the same time a supplement to national finance newspaper Kauppalehti.
Language(s): Finnish
ADVERTISING RATES:
Full Page Colour .... EUR 8500
SCC .... EUR 71.50
Agency Commission: 15%
Mechanical Data: Type Area: 220 x 297mm, No. of Columns (Display): 10, Col Widths (Display): 47mm, Print Process: offset, Screen: 60 lpc
Copy instructions: *Copy Date:* 13 days prior to publication date
BUSINESS: FINANCE & ECONOMICS

KAUPPAPOLITIIKKA
14944L14C-20
Editorial: PL 481/ Kanavakatu 3 C, 00023 VALTIONEUVOSTO **Tel:** 9 16 005
Email: jari.sinkari@formin.fi **Web site:** http://www.kauppapolitiikka.fi
ISSN: 0783-490X
Freq: 6 issues yearly; **Cover Price:** Free; **Circ:** 11,000
Usual Pagination: 36
Editor-in-Chief: Kimmo Laukkanen; **Managing Editor:** Mikko Taivainen
Profile: Publication about foreign trade policy.
Language(s): Finnish
Readership: Read by business people and policymakers.
ADVERTISING RATES:
Full Page Colour .... EUR 1950.00
SCC .... EUR 13.20
Mechanical Data: Type Area: 195 x 270mm, Bleed Size: 210 x 297mm, Print Process: offset

KAUPPATEKNIKKO
705205L14A-13_50
Editorial: c/o Mika Bohm, Kirkkokatu 11 B 27, 15110 LAHTI **Tel:** 3 61 78 200
Web site: http://www.kauppateknikkoliitto.fi
Freq: Quarterly; **Annual Sub.:** EUR 35.00; **Circ:** 2,000
Editor-in-Chief: Mika Bohm
Profile: Journal of the Union for people working in Trade, Service, Industry and Business Administration.
Language(s): Finnish
Readership: Read by members.
ADVERTISING RATES:
Full Page Colour .... EUR 650.00
Agency Commission: 15%
Mechanical Data: Bleed Size: 210 x 297mm, Type Area: 178 x 260mm, No. of Columns (Display): 4, Col Widths (Display): 40mm, Print Process: offset, Screen: 54 lpc

KAUPPIAS
705206L53-4
Editorial: Kruunuvuorenkatu 5 A, 00160 HELSINKI
Tel: 10 53 010 **Fax:** 105336206
Email: riitta.kilgast@k-kauppiasliitto.fi **Web site:** http://www.k-kauppiasliitto.fi
Freq: Monthly - Published 16/year; Free to qualifying individuals ; **Circ:** 1,800
Managing Editor: Kirsi Suurnäkki-Vuorinen
Profile: Magazine about retail trade competition.
Language(s): Finnish
ADVERTISING RATES:
Full Page Colour .... EUR 2100
Agency Commission: 5-15%
Mechanical Data: Type Area: 246 x 360mm, Bleed Size: 295 x 420mm, No. of Columns (Display): 6, Col Widths (Display): 37mm, Print Process: offset, Screen: 54 lpc, Trim Size: 245 x 355mm

KAUPUNKISANOMAT
706306L72-480
Editorial: PL 203/ Mannerheimintie 94, 00531 HELSINKI **Tel:** 45 13 800 **Fax:** 9 43 65 00 13
Email: toimitus@kaupunkisanomat.fi **Web site:** http://www.kaupunkisanomat.fi
Date Established: 1995; **Freq:** Weekly; **Cover Price:** Free; **Circ:** 20,000
Usual Pagination: 20
Editor-in-Chief: Merja Nordbäck-Raunio
Profile: Newspaper distributed in different city parts of Helsinki.
Language(s): Finnish
Readership: 20-45 year old active consumers in the Helsinki region.
ADVERTISING RATES:
Full Page Colour .... EUR 1490
SCC .... EUR 10
Agency Commission: 15%
Mechanical Data: Type Area: 255 x 370mm, Bleed Size: 280 x 400mm, Col Length: 370mm, No. of Columns (Display): 6, Print Process: offset, Col Widths (Display): 38mm, Screen: 34 lpc, Page Width: 400mm
LOCAL NEWSPAPERS

KÄYTÄNNÖN MAAMIES
14981L21A-5
Editorial: Esterinportti 1 A, 00015 OTAVAMEDIA
Tel: 9 15 661 **Fax:** 9 15 66 735
Email: pentti.torma@otavamedia.fi **Web site:** http://www.kaytannonmaamies.fi
ISSN: 0022-9571
Date Established: 1951; **Freq:** Monthly - Published 15/year; **Circ:** 20,362
Usual Pagination: 84
Managing Editor: Esa Mustonen
Profile: Journal covering all aspects of agriculture, including farm economy, financing, investing, taxation, crop husbandry and protection, harvesting and harvesting technology, animal breeding, forestry and information technology.
Language(s): Finnish
ADVERTISING RATES:
Full Page Colour .... EUR 2770
SCC .... EUR 24.70
Mechanical Data: Bleed Size: 280 x 217mm, Print Process: Offset, Film: Digital positive, Col Widths (Display): 44mm, Screen: 60 lpc
Copy instructions: *Copy Date:* 21 days prior to publication date
BUSINESS: AGRICULTURE & FARMING

KD
15340L87-65
Formerly: Kristityn Vastuu
Editorial: Karjalankatu 2 C, 7 krs, 00520 HELSINKI
Tel: 9 34 88 22 30 **Fax:** 9 34 88 22 38
Email: kdtoimitus@kd.fi **Web site:** http://www.kristillisdemokraatit.fi
ISSN: 0356-3545
Date Established: 1966; **Freq:** Weekly; **Circ:** 3,515
Usual Pagination: 16
Editor-in-Chief: Kristiina Kunnas
Profile: Magazine of the Finnish Christian Democrats.
Language(s): Finnish; Swedish
Readership: All people interested in the development of the society from Christian democratic point of view.
ADVERTISING RATES:
Full Page Colour .... EUR 2700.00
SCC .... EUR 11.30
Agency Commission: 15%
Mechanical Data: Col Widths (Display): 48mm, No. of Columns (Display): 5, Print Process: offset
Editions:
Kd Verkkotoimitus
CONSUMER: RELIGIOUS

KEHITTYVÄ KAUPPA
15080L53-35
Editorial: Kruunuvuorenkatu 5 A, 00160 HELSINKI
Tel: 10 53 010 **Fax:** 10 53 36 206
Email: riitta.kilgast@k-kauppiasliitto.fi **Web site:** http://www.k-kauppiasliitto.fi
ISSN: 0783-5167
Date Established: 1907; **Freq:** Monthly - Published 10/year; **Circ:** 20,286
Usual Pagination: 72
Managing Editor: Riitta Kilgast
Profile: Business magazine published by the Finnish Retailers' Association.
Language(s): Finnish
Readership: Read by management and staff within the retail trade.
ADVERTISING RATES:
Full Page Colour .... EUR 3800
SCC .... EUR 31.90
Agency Commission: 15%
Mechanical Data: Bleed Size: 297 x 210mm, Trim Size: 287 x 200mm, No. of Columns (Display): 4, Col Widths (Display): 43mm, Print Process: Offset rotation, Film: Positive, Screen: 54 lpc, Type Area: 210 x 297mm
Copy instructions: *Copy Date:* 21 days prior to publication date
BUSINESS: RETAILING & WHOLESALING

KEHITYS-UTVECKLING
14929L14C-23
Editorial: PL 456/ Kanavakatu 3, 00023 VALTIONEUVOSTO **Tel:** 9 16 005 **Fax:** 9 16 05 63 75
Email: milma.kettunen@formin.fi **Web site:** http://global.finland.fi
ISSN: 0787-0418
Freq: Quarterly; **Cover Price:** Free; **Circ:** 9,000
Usual Pagination: 48
Editor-in-Chief: Milma Kettunen
Profile: Publication of the Department for International Development Cooperation of the Finnish Ministry for Foreign Affairs.
Language(s): Finnish; Swedish

KEKSINTÖUUTISET
706307L14B-2
Editorial: Radiokatu 20, 2 krs, 00240 HELSINKI
Tel: 9 27 80 00 02 **Fax:** 9 27 22 037
Email: keksintouutiset@kekery.fi **Web site:** http://www.kekery.fi
ISSN: 0359-0291
Date Established: 1972; **Freq:** Quarterly; **Annual Sub.:** EUR 40.00; **Circ:** 2,000
Usual Pagination: 32
Editor-in-Chief: Kauko Kareinen
Profile: Journal of the Finnish Inventors' Union.
Language(s): Finnish
Readership: Read by members.
ADVERTISING RATES:
Full Page Colour .... EUR 1270.00
SCC .... EUR 16.70
Mechanical Data: Col Widths (Display): 56mm, No. of Columns (Display): 3, Bleed Size: 210 x 297mm, Type Area: 180 x 252mm, Screen: 60 lpc

KELTAINEN PÖRSSI
705347L94X-24
Editorial: PL 66/ Pyhäranta 7, 33211 TAMPERE
Tel: 3 25 24 299 **Fax:** 3 25 24 211
Email: toimitus.keltainenporssi@sanoma.fi **Web site:** http://www.keltainenporssi.fi
Date Established: 1983; **Freq:** Weekly; **Circ:** 14,915
Usual Pagination: 104
Profile: Magazine with free ads for people that want to sell or buy things.
Language(s): Finnish
ADVERTISING RATES:
Full Page Colour .... EUR 1920
Agency Commission: 15%
Mechanical Data: Col Length: 365mm, Page Width: 255mm, Print Process: offset, Screen: 34 lpc, No. of Columns (Display): 6, Col Widths (Display): 38mm
CONSUMER: OTHER CLASSIFICATIONS: Miscellaneous

KESKI-HÄME
704926L72-505
Editorial: Lamminraitti 25, 16900 LAMMI
Fax: 3 63 32 382
Email: toimitus@keski-hame.fi **Web site:** http://www.keski-hame.fi
Date Established: 1956; **Freq:** Weekly; **Circ:** 5,326
Usual Pagination: 12
Profile: Local newspaper issued in Hämeenkoski, Lammi, Tuulos and Hauho.
Language(s): Finnish
ADVERTISING RATES:
Full Page Colour .... EUR 2588
SCC .... EUR 11.50
Agency Commission: 15%
Mechanical Data: Type Area: 261 x 385mm, No. of Columns (Display): 6, Col Widths (Display): 41mm, Col Length: 375mm, Page Width: 260mm
LOCAL NEWSPAPERS

KESKILAAKSO
704950L72-65
Formerly: Anjalankosken Sanomat
Editorial: PL 20 / Valtatie 12, 46901 INKEROINEN
Tel: 5 21 00 25 70 **Fax:** 5 36 73 600
Email: toimitus@keskilaakso.fi **Web site:** http://www.keskilaakso.fi
ISSN: 0357-9301
Date Established: 1931; **Freq:** 104 issues yearly; **Circ:** 5,171
Usual Pagination: 16
Profile: Newspaper issued in Anjalankoski, Kaipiainen, Myllykoski, Sippola, Inkeroinen and Anjala.
Language(s): Finnish
ADVERTISING RATES:
Full Page Colour .... EUR 2716
SCC .... EUR 12.40
Agency Commission: 3-15%
Mechanical Data: Page Width: 254mm, Col Length: 365mm, No. of Columns (Display): 6, Col Widths (Display): 39mm, Print Process: offset
LOCAL NEWSPAPERS

KESKIPOHJANMAA
15195L67B-4850
Editorial: PL 45/ Rantakatu 10, 67101 KOKKOLA
Tel: 20 75 04 400 **Fax:** 20 75 04 444
Email: toimitus@kpk.fi **Web site:** http://www.keskipohjanmaa.net
ISSN: 0788-8325
Date Established: 1917
Circ: 25,479
Usual Pagination: 28
Editor-in-Chief: Lassi Jaakkola; **Managing Editor:** Hannu Lehto
Profile: Newspaper issued mainly in central Ostrobothnia (Pohjanmaa).
Language(s): Finnish
ADVERTISING RATES:
Full Page Colour .... EUR 11856
SCC .... EUR 28.50
Mechanical Data: Print Process: 4-colour offset rotation, No. of Columns (Display): 8, Col Widths (Display): 44mm, Col Length: 520mm, Page Width: 380mm
Editions:
Keskipohjanmaa Urheilutoimitus
Keskipohjanmaa Verkkotoimitus
REGIONAL DAILY & SUNDAY NEWSPAPERS: Regional Daily Newspapers

KESKIPOHJANMAA HAAPAJÄRVI
705632L67E-170
Editorial: Ståhlberginkatu 2-4, 85800 HAAPAJÄRVI
Tel: 20 75 04 455 **Fax:** 20 75 04 446
Email: ylivieska@kpk.fi **Web site:** http://www.keskipohjanmaa.net
Freq: Daily
Profile: Haapajärvi regional office of newspaper Keskipohjanmaa.
Language(s): Finnish
REGIONAL DAILY & SUNDAY NEWSPAPERS: Regional Offices

KESKIPOHJANMAA KALAJOKI
705633L67E-172
Editorial: Pohjankyläntie 1, 85100 KALAJOKI
Tel: 20 75 04 456 **Fax:** 20 75 04 447
Email: ylivieska@kpk.fi **Web site:** http://www.keskipohjanmaa.net
Freq: Daily
Profile: Kalajoki regional office of newspaper Keskipohjanmaa.
Language(s): Finnish
REGIONAL DAILY & SUNDAY NEWSPAPERS: Regional Offices

KESKIPOHJANMAA PIETARSAARI
705634L67E-174
Editorial: Kanavapuistikko 19 A, 68600 PIETARSAARI **Tel:** 20 75 04 400
Email: pietarsaari@kpk.fi **Web site:** http://www.keskipohjanmaa.net
Freq: Daily
Profile: Pietarsaari regional off of newspaper Keskipohjanmaa.
Language(s): Finnish
REGIONAL DAILY & SUNDAY NEWSPAPERS: Regional Offices

KESKIPOHJANMAA VETELI
705635L67E-176
Editorial: Kirkkotie 3, 69700 VETELI
Tel: 20 75 04 457 **Fax:** 20 75 04 676
Email: veteli@kpk.fi **Web site:** http://www.keskipohjanmaa.net
Freq: Daily
Profile: Veteli regional office of newspaper Keskipohjanmaa.
Language(s): Finnish
REGIONAL DAILY & SUNDAY NEWSPAPERS: Regional Offices

KESKIPOHJANMAA YLIVIESKA
705636L67E-178
Editorial: PL 16/ Kartanotie 3, 84101 YLIVIESKA
Tel: 20 75 04 400 **Fax:** 20 75 04 445
Email: ylivieska@kpk.fi **Web site:** http://www.keskipohjanmaa.net
Freq: Daily
Profile: Ylivieska regional office of newspaper Keskipohjanmaa.
Language(s): Finnish
REGIONAL DAILY & SUNDAY NEWSPAPERS: Regional Offices

KESKISUOMALAINEN
15168L67B-4900
Editorial: PL 159/ Aholaidantie 3, 40101 JYVÄSKYLÄ
Tel: 14 62 20 00 **Fax:** 14 62 22 72
Email: talous@keskisuomalainen.fi **Web site:** http://www.ksml.fi
ISSN: 1458-5529
Date Established: 1871
Circ: 68,880
Usual Pagination: 28
Editor-in-Chief: Pekka Mervola
Profile: Broadsheet-sized quality newspaper providing in-depth coverage of national and international news, politics, finance, culture and sport.
Language(s): Finnish
Readership: Read by all sectors of society.
ADVERTISING RATES:
Full Page Colour .... EUR 12444
SCC .... EUR 30.50
Agency Commission: 15%

Mechanical Data: Col Length: 510mm, No. of Columns (Display): 8, Type Area: 510 x 380mm, Print Process: Web offset, Screen: 40 lpc, Page Width: 380mm, Col Widths (Display): 44mm
Copy instructions: *Copy Date:* 2 days prior to publication date
Average ad content per issue: 30%
Editions:
Keskisuomalainen Kotimaantoimitus
Keskisuomalainen Kulttuuritoimitus
Keskisuomalainen Taloustoimitus
Keskisuomalainen Ulkomaantoimitus
Keskisuomalainen Urheilutoimitus
Keskisuomalainen Verkkotoimitus
REGIONAL DAILY & SUNDAY NEWSPAPERS: Regional Daily Newspapers

KESKISUOMALAINEN ÄÄNEKOSKI
705643L67E-250
Editorial: Kauppakatu 1, 44100 ÄÄNEKOSKI
Tel: 14 52 21 34 89 563 36 **Fax:** 14 34 89 561
Email: pekka.tiihonen@keskisuomalainen.fi **Web site:** http://www.ksml.fi
Profile: Äänekoski regional office of newspaper Keskisuomalainen.
Language(s): Finnish
REGIONAL DAILY & SUNDAY NEWSPAPERS: Regional Offices

KESKISUOMALAINEN JÄMSÄ
705637L67E-252
Editorial: Talvialantie 2, 42100 JÄMSÄ
Tel: 14 71 80 71 **Fax:** 14 71 85 74
Email: hannu.karjalainen@keskisuomalainen.fi **Web site:** http://www.ksml.fi
Profile: Jämsä regional office of newspaper Keskisuomalainen.
Language(s): Finnish
REGIONAL DAILY & SUNDAY NEWSPAPERS: Regional Offices

KESKISUOMALAINEN KEURUU
705639L67E-260
Editorial: Kippavuorentie 7, 42700 KEURUU
Tel: 14 72 03 61 **Fax:** 14 72 20 61
Email: rainer.liimatainen@keskisuomalainen.fi **Web site:** http://www.ksml.fi
Profile: Keuruu and Virrat regional office of newspaper Keskisuomalainen.
Language(s): Finnish
REGIONAL DAILY & SUNDAY NEWSPAPERS: Regional Offices

KESKISUOMALAINEN SAARIJÄRVI
705640L67E-262
Editorial: Myllyperäntie 1, 43100 SAARIJÄRVI
Tel: 14 42 24 47 **Fax:** 14 42 44 83
Email: maarit.vaaherkumpu@keskisuomalainen.fi **Web site:** http://www.ksml.fi
Profile: Saarijärvi regional office of newspaper Keskisuomalainen.
Language(s): Finnish
REGIONAL DAILY & SUNDAY NEWSPAPERS: Regional Offices

KESKI-SUOMEN VIIKKO
704870L72-510
Editorial: PL 273/ Vasarakatu 1, 40101 JYVÄSKYLÄ
Tel: 10 42 34 900 **Fax:** 10 42 34 909
Email: toimitus@ksviikko.fi **Web site:** http://www.ksviikko.fi
ISSN: 1455-6227
Date Established: 1981; **Freq:** Weekly; **Circ:** 6,227
Usual Pagination: 16
Profile: Newspaper issued in central Finland.
Language(s): Finnish
ADVERTISING RATES:
Full Page Colour .... EUR 4305
SCC .... EUR 17.50
Agency Commission: 15%
Mechanical Data: Col Widths (Display): 44mm, No. of Columns (Display): 6, Col Length: 410mm, Screen: 34 lpc
LOCAL NEWSPAPERS

KESKI-UUSIMAA
15223L67B-4800
Editorial: PL 52/ Klaavolantie 5, 04301 TUUSULA
Tel: 20 77 03 101 **Fax:** 20 77 03 000
Email: toimitus.keskiuusimaa@lehtiyhtyma.fi **Web site:** http://www.keskiuusimaa.fi
ISSN: 0357-2021
Date Established: 1920
Circ: 20,444
Usual Pagination: 18
Managing Editor: Laura Liski
Profile: Newspaper issued mainly in Järvenpää, Kerava, Tuusula, Nurmijärvi, Sipoo and partly in Vantaa and Mäntsälä.
Language(s): Finnish
ADVERTISING RATES:
Full Page Colour .... EUR 7828
SCC .... EUR 19
Mechanical Data: Type Area: 380 x 520mm, Print Process: offset, Screen: 34 lpc, Col Length: 520mm, No. of Columns (Display): 8, Col Widths (Display): 44mm

Editions:
Keski-Uusimaa Verkkotoimitus
REGIONAL DAILY & SUNDAY NEWSPAPERS: Regional Daily Newspapers

KG
1611074L74G-50
Formerly: Painonvartijat
Editorial: Maistraatinportti 1, 00015 OTAVAMEDIA
Tel: 9 15 661 **Fax:** 9145650
Email: paivi.laakso@otavamedia.fi **Web site:** http://www.kglehti.fi
ISSN: 1796-7163
Date Established: 2003; **Freq:** 6 issues yearly - Published 7/year; **Circ:** 26,508
Usual Pagination: 108
Editor-in-Chief: Päivi Laakso
Profile: Magazine about slimming.
Language(s): Finnish
ADVERTISING RATES:
Full Page Colour .... EUR 4040
SCC .... EUR 34
Mechanical Data: Bleed Size: 230 x 280mm, Print Process: offset
Copy instructions: *Copy Date:* 19 days prior to publication date
CONSUMER: WOMEN'S INTEREST CONSUMER MAGAZINES: Slimming & Health

KIERROSSA
706555L36-2
Formerly: Encore / Kierrossa
Editorial: PL 143/ Porkkalankatu 20 a, 3. krs, 00181 HELSINKI **Tel:** 9 22 81 91 **Fax:** 9 17 71 09
Web site: http://www.paperinkerays.fi
ISSN: 1236-1488
Date Established: 1993; **Freq:** Half-yearly - Published 3/year; **Cover Price:** Free; **Circ:** 8,000
Usual Pagination: 24
Editor-in-Chief: Kyösti Pöyry; **Managing Editor:** Elina Mikkola
Profile: Magazine about recycled paper.
Language(s): Finnish
ADVERTISING RATES:
SCC .... EUR 17.70
Mechanical Data: Screen: 54 lpc, Film: positive

KIINA SANOIN JA KUVIN
706309L89A-2
Editorial: Ludviginkatu 3-5 A 52, 00130 HELSINKI
Tel: 9 60 58 12 **Fax:** 9 60 53 15
Email: kiinaseura@lasipalatsi.fi **Web site:** http://kiinaseura.lasipalatsi.fi
Date Established: 1956; **Freq:** Quarterly; **Circ:** 2,800
Usual Pagination: 16
Editor-in-Chief: Veli Rosenberg
Profile: Magazine about travel to and business-relations with China.
Language(s): Finnish
ADVERTISING RATES:
Full Page Colour .... EUR 600.00

KIINTEISTÖ JA ISÄNNÖINTI
705193L4D-15
Formerly: Kiinteistö ja isännöitsijä
Editorial: Vanha Turuntie 371, 03150 HUHMARI
Tel: 9 41 39 73 00 **Fax:** 9 41 39 74 05
Email: ki.toimitus@karprint.fi **Web site:** http://www.kiinteistojaisannoitsija.fi
ISSN: 0782-7911
Date Established: 1983; **Freq:** Monthly; **Circ:** 13,000
Usual Pagination: 100
Profile: Magazine on real estate.
Language(s): Finnish
Readership: Aimed at real estate professionals.
ADVERTISING RATES:
Full Page Colour .... EUR 2163
SCC .... EUR 17.90
Agency Commission: 15%
Mechanical Data: Bleed Size: 213 x 302mm, Type Area: 192 x 262mm, Col Widths (Display): 44mm, No. of Columns (Display): 4, Print Process: offset, Screen: 54 lpc
Copy instructions: *Copy Date:* 21 days prior to publication date

KIINTEISTÖPOSTI
705194L4D-20
Editorial: Pisteenkaari 4, 03100 NUMMELA
Tel: 9 22 38 560 **Fax:** 9 22 26 515
Email: toimitus@kiinteistoposti.fi **Web site:** http://www.kiinteistoposti.fi
ISSN: 1237-6965
Date Established: 1994; **Freq:** Monthly; **Circ:** 60,928
Usual Pagination: 48
Editor-in-Chief: Riina Takala
Profile: Magazine about maintenance of properties, includes information on regulations, safety, garbage disposal and control.
Language(s): Finnish
Readership: Aimed at representatives of construction and renovation companies and house-managers.
ADVERTISING RATES:
Full Page Colour .... EUR 4100.00
SCC .... EUR 37.90
Agency Commission: 15%
Mechanical Data: Bleed Size: 210 x 297mm, Type Area: 185 x 270mm, Screen: 60 lpc
BUSINESS: ARCHITECTURE & BUILDING: Planning & Housing

KIINTEISTÖSEKTORI
753071L4D-26
Editorial: Pihlajistonkuja 4, 00710 HELSINKI
Tel: 9 72 51 55 00 **Fax:** 9 72 51 55 99
Email: suomen.talokeskus@suomentalokeskus.fi
Web site: http://www.suomentalokeskus.fi
Freq: Half-yearly; **Cover Price:** Free; **Circ:** 17,000
Usual Pagination: 36
Editor-in-Chief: Jani Saarinen
Profile: Magazine about house-keeping, repairs and building.
Language(s): Finnish
Readership: Customers of Suomen Talokeskus Oy.

KIPPARI
15375L91A-28
Editorial: Maistraatinportti 1, 00015 OTAVAMEDIA
Tel: 9 15 661 **Fax:** 9 15 66 62 10
Email: kippari.toimitus@otavamedia.fi **Web site:** http://www.kipparilehti.fi
ISSN: 0780-5373
Date Established: 1986; **Freq:** Monthly; **Circ:** 20,525
Usual Pagination: 100
Profile: Magazine including information on boating, engines, servicing, repairs and accessories.
Language(s): Finnish
Readership: Aimed at those interested in boating, especially motorboat owners who use their boats in summer months.
ADVERTISING RATES:
Full Page Colour .... EUR 1970
SCC .... EUR 16.70
Mechanical Data: Bleed Size: 280 x 217mm, Print Process: Offset, Film: Digital, Col Widths (Display): 42mm, Film: positive, Screen: 60 lpc, Type Area: 217 x 280mm
Copy instructions: *Copy Date:* 20 days prior to publication date
CONSUMER: RECREATION & LEISURE: Boating & Yachting

KIRKKO & KAUPUNKI
15358L87-50
Editorial: PL 279/ Hietalahdenranta 13, 00181 HELSINKI **Tel:** 20 75 42 000 **Fax:** 20 75 42 343
Email: kirkkojakaupunki@kotimaa.fi **Web site:** http://www.kirkkojakaupunki.fi
ISSN: 1458-431X
Date Established: 1942; **Freq:** Weekly - Published on Wednesday; Free to qualifying individuals ; **Circ:** 199,393
Usual Pagination: 24
Editor-in-Chief: Seppo Simola; **Managing Editor:** Marja Kuparinen
Profile: Magazine concerning all aspects of religion in Finland, especially in Helsinki.
Language(s): Finnish
ADVERTISING RATES:
Full Page Colour .... EUR 3950
SCC .... EUR 26
Agency Commission: 10-15%
Mechanical Data: Type Area: 255 x 355mm, Screen: 34 lpc, No. of Columns (Display): 5, Col Widths (Display): 47mm, Bleed Size: 280 x 400mm
CONSUMER: RELIGIOUS

KIRKKO JA KOTI
706556L87-51
Editorial: PL 1064/ Suokatu 22, 70101 KUOPIO
Tel: 17 15 81 11 **Fax:** 17 15 82 88
Email: kirkkojakoti@evl.fi **Web site:** http://www.kirkkojakoti.net
Date Established: 1913; **Freq:** 26 issues yearly - Published on Friday; Free to qualifying individuals ; **Circ:** 60,000
Profile: Magazine issued by the Kuopio parish.
Language(s): Finnish
ADVERTISING RATES:
Full Page Colour .... EUR 2600
SCC .... EUR 14.60
Agency Commission: 15%
Mechanical Data: Bleed Size: 250 x 360mm, Type Area: 280 x 405mm, No. of Columns (Display): 5, Col Widths (Display): 47mm, Screen: 34 lpc, Print Process: offset
CONSUMER: RELIGIOUS

KIRKKO JA ME, KYRKAN OCH VI
15359L87-55
Formerly: Kirkko ja Me
Editorial: PL 922/ Eerikinkatu 3, 20101 TURKU
Tel: 2 26 17 111 **Fax:** 2 26 17 289
Email: mervi.sipila-koski@evl.fi **Web site:** http://www.turunsrk.fi
Date Established: 1965; **Freq:** Monthly - Published 11/ year; **Cover Price:** Free; **Circ:** 115,000
Usual Pagination: 16
Editor-in-Chief: Paula Heino
Profile: Magazine of the Union of the Lutheran parishes of Turku and Kaarina.
Language(s): English; Finnish; Swedish
ADVERTISING RATES:
Full Page Colour .... EUR 3100
SCC .... EUR 16
CONSUMER: RELIGIOUS

KIRKONSEUTU
706560L87-69
Formerly: Lahden Kotikirkko
Editorial: PL 84/ Vapaudenkatu 6, 15111 LAHTI
Tel: 3 89 111 **Fax:** 3 78 30 891
Email: kirkonseutu@evl.fi **Web site:** http://www.evl.fi/lahti
ISSN: 1459-2363
Date Established: 2003; **Freq:** 26 issues yearly; **Cover Price:** Free; **Circ:** 93,600
Usual Pagination: 16
Editor-in-Chief: Markku Jalava
Profile: Newspaper distributed to members of the Lahti parish.
Language(s): Finnish
ADVERTISING RATES:
SCC .... EUR 11.00
Agency Commission: 15%
Mechanical Data: Type Area: 285 x 400mm, No. of Columns (Display): 6, Col Widths (Display): 39mm, Print Process: offset, Screen: 34 lpc
CONSUMER: RELIGIOUS

KIURUVESI
704969L72-530
Editorial: PL 69/ Hovinpelto 3, 74701 KIURUVESI
Tel: 17 77 07 700 **Fax:** 17 77 07 770
Email: toimitus@kiuruvesilehti.fi **Web site:** http://www.kiuruvesilehti.fi
Date Established: 1953; **Freq:** Weekly; **Circ:** 6,458
Usual Pagination: 12
Profile: Newspaper issued in Kiuruvesi.
Language(s): Finnish
ADVERTISING RATES:
Full Page Colour .... EUR 2940
SCC .... EUR 8.50
Agency Commission: 17.5%
Mechanical Data: Col Length: 390mm, No. of Columns (Display): 7, Col Widths (Display): 39mm, Type Area: 294 x 390mm, Bleed Size: 315 x 430mm, Screen: 40 lpc, Film: negative
LOCAL NEWSPAPERS

KIVI
713543L30-4
Formerly: Suomalainen Kivi
Editorial: Unioninkatu 14, 00131 HELSINKI
Tel: 9 12 99 300 **Fax:** 9 12 99 414
Email: kiviteollisuusliitto@finstone.fi **Web site:** http://www.finstone.com/liitto/lehti
ISSN: 0784-5510
Freq: Quarterly; **Annual Sub.:** EUR 24.00; **Circ:** 4,000
Usual Pagination: 48
Editor-in-Chief: Pekka Jauhiainen
Profile: Publication of the Finnish Natural Stone Association.
Language(s): English; Finnish; German
ADVERTISING RATES:
Full Page Colour .... EUR 2102.00
SCC .... EUR 23.50
Agency Commission: 15%
Mechanical Data: Bleed Size: 210 x 297mm, Print Process: offset

KLUBI
717511L75B-100
Editorial: Sonera Stadium, Urheilukatu 5, 00250 HELSINKI **Tel:** 9 74 21 66 00 **Fax:** 9 74 21 66 66
Email: hjk@hjk.fi **Web site:** http://www.hjk.fi
Freq: Half-yearly; **Cover Price:** Free; **Circ:** 100,000
Usual Pagination: 32
Editor-in-Chief: Kari Haapiainen
Profile: Magazine about the activities of Helsinki Football Club.
Language(s): Finnish
Readership: Fans, players and investors of Helsinki Football Club.
CONSUMER: SPORT: Football

KM VET
705957L81A-4
Editorial: Esterinportti 1, 00015 OTAVAMEDIA
Tel: 9 15 661 **Fax:** 9 15 66 735
Email: pentti.torma@otavamedia.fi **Web site:** http://www.kaytannonmaamies.fi/kmvet
ISSN: 1239-0429
Date Established: 1996; **Freq:** 6 issues yearly - Published 7/year; **Circ:** 5,153
Usual Pagination: 32
Profile: Magazine about protection and health supervision of cattle.
Language(s): Finnish
Readership: Veterinaries and others interested in cattle protection.
ADVERTISING RATES:
Full Page Colour .... EUR 1440
SCC .... EUR 12.80
Mechanical Data: Type Area: 217 x 280mm, Col Widths (Display): 44mm, Print Process: offset, Film: positive, Screen: 60 lpc
CONSUMER: ANIMALS & PETS: Animals & Pets Protection

KMV-LEHTI
704903L72-645
Formerly: Kuorevesi-Mänttä-Vilppula
Editorial: PL 33 / Ratakatu 5, 35801 MÄNTTÄ
Tel: 10 66 55 630 **Fax:** 3 47 47 518
Email: kmvtoimitus@sps.fi **Web site:** http://www.kmvlehti.fi
ISSN: 0782-7076
Date Established: 1925; **Freq:** 104 issues yearly; **Circ:** 7,040
Usual Pagination: 16
Profile: Local newspaper issued in Kuorevesi, Mänttä, Vilppula and Juupajoki.
Language(s): Finnish
ADVERTISING RATES:
Full Page Colour .... EUR 2398
SCC .... EUR 10.80
Agency Commission: 15%
Mechanical Data: Col Widths (Display): 40mm, No. of Columns (Display): 6, Type Area: 260 x 370mm, Print Process: offset
LOCAL NEWSPAPERS

KODIN KUVALEHTI 15260L74C-40

Editorial: PL 100/ Lapinmäentie 1, 00040 SANOMA MAGAZINES **Tel:** 9 12 01
Email: kodin.kuvalehti@sanomamagazines.fi **Web site:** http://www.kodinkuvalehti.fi
ISSN: 0023-2610
Date Established: 1967; **Freq:** 26 issues yearly; **Circ:** 174,710
Usual Pagination: 130
Editor-in-Chief: Minna McGill
Profile: Illustrated magazine about the home. Includes features on DIY and decoration.
Language(s): Finnish
ADVERTISING RATES:
Full Page Colour .... EUR 9400
SCC .... EUR 79.10
Mechanical Data: Bleed Size: 230 x 297mm, Type Area: 195 x 267mm, Page Width: 230mm, No. of Columns (Display): 4, Col Widths (Display): 45mm, Print Process: offset, Film: positive, Screen: 60 lpc
CONSUMER: WOMEN'S INTEREST CONSUMER MAGAZINES: Home & Family

KODIN PELLERVO 14986L74C-41

Formerly: Pellervo
Editorial: PL 77/ Simonkatu 6, 00101 HELSINKI
Tel: 9 47 67 501 **Fax:** 9 69 48 845
Email: toimisto@pellervo.fi **Web site:** http://www.pellervo.fi/kodinpellervo
ISSN: 1456-7210
Date Established: 1899; **Freq:** Monthly; **Circ:** 33,817
Usual Pagination: 76
Editor-in-Chief: Teemu Pakarinen; **Managing Editor:** Anna-Liisa Huhtala-Fiskars
Profile: Magazine covering all aspects of country living in Finland. Contains recipes, short stories about rural communities, features on country houses, home decoration and lifestyle.
Language(s): Finnish
Readership: Aimed at women aged between 40 and 60 years, living in rural areas of Finland.
ADVERTISING RATES:
Full Page Colour .... EUR 2556
SCC .... EUR 23.60
Agency Commission: 15%
Mechanical Data: Col Length: 270mm, Col Widths (Display): 43mm, Film: Digital material, Type Area: 270 x 185mm, Print Process: Offset, Screen: 54-60 lpc, Page Width: 185mm, No. of Columns (Display): 4
Copy instructions: *Copy Date:* 14 days prior to publication date
CONSUMER: WOMEN'S INTEREST CONSUMER MAGAZINES: Home & Family

KODINRAKENTAJA 1657707L74K-41

Formerly: Osaava Kodinrakentaja
Editorial: PL 44/ Hämeentie 33, 00501 HELSINKI
Tel: 9 12 01 **Fax:** 20 74 18 622
Email: toimitus@kodinrakentaja.fi **Web site:** http://www.kodinrakentaja.fi
ISSN: 1795-391X
Date Established: 2004; **Freq:** Monthly - Published 10/year; **Circ:** 38,836
Usual Pagination: 100
Editor-in-Chief: Veijo Käyhty; **Managing Editor:** Heikki Heikkonen
Profile: Magazine about home repairs and building.
Language(s): Finnish
ADVERTISING RATES:
Full Page Colour .... EUR 4010
SCC .... EUR 45
Mechanical Data: Print Process: offset, Screen: 60 lpc, Type Area: 230 x 297mm
CONSUMER: WOMEN'S INTEREST CONSUMER MAGAZINES: Home Purchase

KOILLIS-LAPPI 704871L72-540

Editorial: PL 19 / Hallituskatu 1, 98101 KEMIJÄRVI
Tel: 10 66 57 922 **Fax:** 16812777
Email: koillislappi@koillislappi.fi **Web site:** http://www.koillislappi.fi
ISSN: 0782-5579
Date Established: 1957; **Freq:** 104 issues yearly; **Circ:** 3,605
Usual Pagination: 16
Profile: Newspaper issued in Kemijärvi, Salla, Savukoski and Pelkosenniemi.
Language(s): Finnish
ADVERTISING RATES:
Full Page Colour .... EUR 3066
SCC .... EUR 14
Agency Commission: 15%
Mechanical Data: Page Width: 280mm, No. of Columns (Display): 6, Col Widths (Display): 38mm, Col Length: 365mm, Print Process: 4-colour offset
LOCAL NEWSPAPERS

KOILLISSANOMAT 15199L72-555

Editorial: Kitkantie 31-33, 93600 KUUSAMO
Tel: 8 86 00 620 **Fax:** 8 86 00 621
Email: toimitus@koillissanomat.fi **Web site:** http://www.koillissanomat.fi
ISSN: 0356-4886
Date Established: 1950; **Freq:** Daily; **Circ:** 7,155
Usual Pagination: 12
Managing Editor: Ulla Ingalsuo
Profile: Newspaper issued in Kuusamo, Posio and Taivalkoski.
Language(s): Finnish
ADVERTISING RATES:
Full Page Colour .... EUR 7140
SCC .... EUR 17
Agency Commission: 15%
Mechanical Data: Type Area: 380 x 525mm, Col Length: 525mm, No. of Columns (Display): 8, Col Widths (Display): 44mm, Print Process: offset, Screen: 34 lpc, Page Width: 380mm
Editions:
Koillissanomat Verkkotoimitus
LOCAL NEWSPAPERS

KOILLIS-SAVO 704970L72-545

Editorial: PL 31/ Kaavintie 3, 73601 KAAVI
Tel: 17 28 87 721 **Fax:** 17 28 87 733
Email: uutiset@koillis-savo.fi **Web site:** http://www.koillis-savo.fi
ISSN: 1236-8407
Date Established: 1963; **Freq:** 104 issues yearly; **Circ:** 6,035
Usual Pagination: 16
Profile: Newspaper distributed in Juankoski, Kaavi, Tuusniemi and Riistavesi.
Language(s): Finnish
ADVERTISING RATES:
Full Page Colour .... EUR 2686
SCC .... EUR 12.10
Agency Commission: 15%
Mechanical Data: Print Process: offset, Page Width: 254mm, Col Length: 370mm, Col Widths (Display): 40mm, No. of Columns (Display): 6
LOCAL NEWSPAPERS

KOIRAMME - VÅRA HUNDAR 705477L81B-30

Editorial: Torikatu 2 B 12, 14200 TURENKI
Tel: 3 68 50 80 **Fax:** 3 68 50 816
Email: info@kennelliitto.fi **Web site:** http://www.kennelliitto.fi
ISSN: 0355-7235
Date Established: 1896; **Freq:** Monthly - 10/ year; **Circ:** 134,305
Usual Pagination: 132
Profile: Koiramme gives information for people interested in dogs.
Language(s): Finnish; Swedish
ADVERTISING RATES:
Full Page Colour .... EUR 3980
SCC .... EUR 40.60
Agency Commission: 15%
Mechanical Data: Bleed Size: 230 x 273mm, Col Widths (Display): 43mm, No. of Columns (Display): 4, Screen: 54 lpc, Print Process: offset, Type Area: 203 x 244mm
Editions:
Koirauutiset
CONSUMER: ANIMALS & PETS: Dogs

KOIVUNLEHTI 717990L1C-18

Editorial: Yliopistonkatu 7, 00100 HELSINKI
Tel: 9 68 11 700
Email: helena.hujala@osg.fi **Web site:** http://www.paikallisosuuspankit.fi
Freq: Quarterly; **Cover Price:** Free; **Circ:** 170,000
Usual Pagination: 12
Editor-in-Chief: Vesa Huttunen
Profile: Membership and customer-magazine by the Local Co-operatives Bank Group in Finland.
Language(s): Finnish
Readership: Customers and members of the Local Co-operatives Bank Group in Finland.
BUSINESS: FINANCE & ECONOMICS: Banking

KONE & KULJETUS 706460L49A-70

Editorial: Larin Kyöstin katu 16, 13130 HÄMEENLINNA **Tel:** 3 65 65 005 **Fax:** 20 74 12 249
Email: info@supermedia.fi **Web site:** http://www.supermedia.fi
Freq: 6 issues yearly; **Circ:** 7,900
Editor-in-Chief: Jorma Yrjölä
Profile: Magazine about machines, transport and motoring.
Language(s): Finnish
ADVERTISING RATES:
Full Page Colour .... EUR 1498.00
Mechanical Data: Type Area: 210 x 297mm, Col Widths (Display): 44mm, No. of Columns (Display): 4, Print Process: offset, Screen: 60 lpc

KONEIKKUNA 1641400L27-60

Formerly: Konekauppa Ikkuna
Editorial: Koulukatu 10 A, 53100 LAPPEENRANTA
Tel: 5 54 12 245 **Fax:** 5 54 12 246
Email: olavi.ahtiainen@koneikkuna.fi **Web site:** http://www.koneikkuna.fi
ISSN: 1456-2200
Date Established: 1998; **Freq:** 6 issues yearly; **Cover Price:** Free; **Circ:** 13,500
Usual Pagination: 32
Editor-in-Chief: Olavi Ahtiainen
Profile: Magazine about metals and machinery.
Language(s): Finnish
ADVERTISING RATES:
Full Page Colour .... EUR 1950.00
Mechanical Data: Type Area: 284 x 435mm, Screen: 42 lpc, Col Widths (Display): 44mm, No. of Columns (Display): 6

KONEKURIIRI 705207L19E-6

Editorial: Hämeenpuisto 44, 33200 TAMPERE
Tel: 3 22 34 034 **Fax:** 3 22 34 882
Email: toimitus@konekuriiri.fi **Web site:** http://www.konekuriiri.fi
Date Established: 1981; **Freq:** Monthly; **Cover Price:** Free; **Circ:** 16,000
Usual Pagination: 32
Editor-in-Chief: Arto Räikkönen
Profile: Magazine about machinery in metal and engineering companies.
Language(s): Finnish
ADVERTISING RATES:
Full Page Colour .... EUR 2840.00
Mechanical Data: Type Area: 260 x 355mm, No. of Columns (Display): 6, Col Widths (Display): 40mm, Bleed Size: 280 x 400mm

KONEPÖRSSI 14915L19E-7

Editorial: Takojankatu 11, 33540 TAMPERE
Tel: 3 38 07 700 **Fax:** 3 38 07 701
Email: koneporssi@koneporssi.com **Web site:** http://www.koneporssi.com
ISSN: 0359-209X
Date Established: 1982; **Freq:** Monthly; **Circ:** 45,000
Usual Pagination: 166
Editor-in-Chief: Jussi Lehtonen
Profile: Publication containing information about machinery and heavy transportation.
Language(s): Finnish
ADVERTISING RATES:
Full Page Colour .... EUR 2953
SCC .... EUR 24.80
Agency Commission: 15%
Mechanical Data: Type Area: 210 x 297mm, Col Widths (Display): 43mm, No. of Columns (Display): 4, Print Process: offset, Screen: 48-60 lpc
Copy instructions: *Copy Date:* 9 days prior to publication date

KONETYÖ 1609428L49C-11

Formerly: Finntrans
Editorial: Larin Kyöstin katu 16, 13130 HÄMEENLINNA **Tel:** 3 65 65 005 **Fax:** 20 74 12 249
Email: info@supermedia.fi **Web site:** http://www.supermedia.fi
Freq: 6 issues yearly; **Circ:** 7,800
Editor-in-Chief: Jorma Yrjölä
Profile: Magazine about freight and machinery.
Language(s): Finnish
ADVERTISING RATES:
Full Page Colour .... EUR 1498.00
Mechanical Data: Type Area: 210 x 297mm, Screen: 60 lpc, Col Widths (Display): 44mm, No. of Columns (Display): 4, Print Process: offset

KONEVIESTI 14992L21E-50

Editorial: PL 480/ Simonkatu 6, 00101 HELSINKI
Tel: 20 41 32 110 **Fax:** 20 41 32 209
Email: newsdesk@koneviesti.fi **Web site:** http://www.koneviesti.fi
ISSN: 0355-0729
Date Established: 1952; **Freq:** Monthly - Published 18/year; **Circ:** 33,002
Usual Pagination: 54
Editor-in-Chief: Uolevi Oristo
Profile: Publication concerning farm and forestry machinery.
Language(s): Finnish
Readership: Read by farmers and foresters.
ADVERTISING RATES:
Full Page Colour .... EUR 3640
SCC .... EUR 24.40
Agency Commission: 15%
Mechanical Data: Print Process: Offset, Col Length: 355mm, Type Area: 225 x 300mm, Col Widths (Display): 38mm, No. of Columns (Display): 5
BUSINESS: AGRICULTURE & FARMING: Agriculture - Machinery & Plant

KONEYRITTÄJÄ 14916L21E-55

Editorial: Sitratie 7, 00420 HELSINKI
Tel: 40 90 09 410 **Fax:** 9 56 30 329
Email: toimitus@koneyrittajat.fi **Web site:** http://www.koneyrittajat.fi
ISSN: 0788-9860
Date Established: 1969; **Freq:** Monthly - Published 10/year; **Circ:** 5,115
Usual Pagination: 62
Editor-in-Chief: Erkki Eilavaara
Profile: Publication about earth-moving, forestry and harvesting machinery.
Language(s): Finnish
Readership: Read by contractors.
ADVERTISING RATES:
Full Page Colour .... EUR 1980
SCC .... EUR 18.50
Agency Commission: 15%
Mechanical Data: Type Area: 183 x 267mm, Bleed Size: 210 x 297mm, No. of Columns (Display): 4, Col Widths (Display): 42mm, Screen: 60 lpc, Film: positive, Print Process: offset
Copy instructions: *Copy Date:* 17 days prior to publication date
BUSINESS: AGRICULTURE & FARMING: Agriculture - Machinery & Plant

KONTAKT 706311L89A-2_50

Editorial: PL 194/ Haapaniemenkatu 7-9 B, 12. krs, 00531 HELSINKI **Tel:** 9 69 38 31 **Fax:** 9 69 38 630
Email: svs@venajaseura.com **Web site:** http://www.venajaseura.com
ISSN: 1238-1363
Date Established: 1971; **Freq:** Quarterly; **Circ:** 10,000
Usual Pagination: 16
Editor-in-Chief: Merja Hannus
Profile: Magazine with information about Finland for Russian associations and Russian travellers.
Language(s): Russian
Readership: Mailed only to members of the Finnish-Russian Association.

KORPELA PLUS 762200L58-96

Editorial: PL 13/ Junkalantie 15, 69101 KANNUS
Tel: 6 87 47 311 **Fax:** 6 87 04 08
Email: margetta.santala@korpelanvoima.fi **Web site:** http://www.korpelanvoima.fi
ISSN: 1456-0712
Date Established: 1998; **Freq:** Half-yearly; **Cover Price:** Free; **Circ:** 17,000
Usual Pagination: 20
Editor-in-Chief: Margetta Santala
Profile: Customer-magazine about electricity.
Language(s): Finnish
Readership: Customers of Korpelan Voima.

KORPILAHTI 704927L72-570

Editorial: Kokkotie 11 C 17, 41800 KORPILAHTI
Tel: 40 19 77 400 **Fax:** 14822471
Email: toimitus@korpilahtilehti.fi **Web site:** http://www.korpilahtilehti.fi
ISSN: 0782-5608
Date Established: 1971; **Freq:** Weekly; **Circ:** 3,030
Usual Pagination: 8
Profile: Newspaper issued in Korpilahti.
Language(s): Finnish
ADVERTISING RATES:
Full Page Colour .... EUR 1971
SCC .... EUR 90
Mechanical Data: No. of Columns (Display): 6, Col Widths (Display): 49mm, Type Area: 255 x 375mm
LOCAL NEWSPAPERS

KOTI 705479L21R-15

Editorial: PL 251/ Urheilutie 6, 01301 VANTAA
Tel: 20 74 72 400 **Fax:** 20 74 72 401
Email: toimitus@koti-lehti.fi **Web site:** http://www.koti-lehti.fi
ISSN: 0355-1555
Date Established: 1939; **Freq:** Monthly - Published 10/year; **Circ:** 11,186
Usual Pagination: 48
Profile: Journal about taking care of big co-operatives and farms.
Language(s): Finnish
Readership: Housewives of farms.
ADVERTISING RATES:
Full Page Colour .... EUR 1950
SCC .... EUR 20.40
Agency Commission: 15%
Mechanical Data: Type Area: 190 x 238mm, No. of Columns (Display): 2/4, Col Widths (Display): 43mm/ 92mm, Screen: 60 lpc, Print Process: offset, Bleed Size: 220 x 270mm
BUSINESS: AGRICULTURE & FARMING: Agriculture & Farming Related

KOTI JA KEITTIÖ 705907L74C-42_5

Editorial: PL 222/ Pursimiehenkatu 29-31 A, 00151 HELSINKI **Tel:** 9 86 21 70 00 **Fax:** 9 86 21 71 39
Email: koti@aller.fi **Web site:** http://www.kotijakeittio.fi
ISSN: 1458-3755
Date Established: 1996; **Freq:** Monthly - Published 10/year; **Circ:** 63,624
Usual Pagination: 100
Editor-in-Chief: Anna-Liisa Hämäläinen; **Managing Editor:** Eija Erkkilä
Profile: Magazine about decoration, home, gardening, food and travel.
Language(s): Finnish
Readership: Young families and women of age 30-49.
ADVERTISING RATES:
Full Page Colour .... EUR 4950
SCC .... EUR 41.60
Agency Commission: 15%
Mechanical Data: Type Area: 207 x 280mm, Print Process: offset, Screen: 60 lpc, Film: negative, No. of Columns (Display): 4
Copy instructions: *Copy Date:* 13 days prior to publication date
CONSUMER: WOMEN'S INTEREST CONSUMER MAGAZINES: Home & Family

KOTIAVAIN 1665781L74K-20

Editorial: Finlaysoninkuja 22, 33210 TAMPERE
Tel: 3 22 38 688 **Fax:** 3 22 38 680
Email: toimitus@kotiavain.com **Web site:** http://www.kotiavain.com
Date Established: 2005; **Freq:** 26 issues yearly; **Cover Price:** Free; **Circ:** 143,000
Usual Pagination: 36
Editor-in-Chief: Kari Lahtinen
Profile: Magazine with home purchase ads.
Language(s): Finnish
ADVERTISING RATES:
Full Page Colour .... EUR 1870.00
Agency Commission: 15%
Mechanical Data: Type Area: 254 x 370mm, Screen: 48 lpc
CONSUMER: WOMEN'S INTEREST CONSUMER MAGAZINES: Home Purchase

KOTI-KARJALA 704968L72-580

Editorial: PL 34 / Pokentie 8, 82501 KITEE
Tel: 13 68 48 411 **Fax:** 13 41 45 93
Email: toimitus@kotikarjala.fi **Web site:** http://www.kotikarjala.fi
ISSN: 1236-4495

Date Established: 1960; **Freq:** 104 issues yearly; **Circ:** 6,477
Usual Pagination: 16
Profile: Newspaper issued in Kitee, Kesälahti, Rääkkylä, Tohmajärvi and Värtsilä.
Language(s): Finnish
ADVERTISING RATES:
Full Page Colour .... EUR 3488
SCC .... EUR 15.50
Agency Commission: 3-15%
Mechanical Data: No. of Columns (Display): 6, Col Widths (Display): 40mm, Col Length: 375mm, Page Width: 264mm
LOCAL NEWSPAPERS

KOTILÄÄKÄRI 15280L56A-45
Editorial: Maistraatinportti 1, 00015 OTAVAMEDIA
Tel: 9 15 661 **Fax:** 9 15 66 507
Email: kotilaakari@otavamedia.fi **Web site:** http://www.kotilaakari.fi
ISSN: 0787-9385
Date Established: 1975; **Freq:** Monthly; **Circ:** 39,326
Usual Pagination: 100
Managing Editor: Eija Niemeläinen
Profile: Magazine focusing on health, nutrition, psychology, fitness, beauty and medical matters.
Language(s): Finnish
ADVERTISING RATES:
Full Page Colour .... EUR 3700
SCC .... EUR 33
Mechanical Data: Bleed Size: 230 x 280mm, Film: Digital positive, Print Process: Offset, Type Area: 230 x 280mm, No. of Columns (Display): 4
Copy instructions: *Copy Date:* 19 days prior to publication date
BUSINESS: HEALTH & MEDICAL

KOTILIESI 15248L74C-42_10
Editorial: Maistraatinportti 1, 00015 OTAVAMEDIA
Tel: 9 15 661 **Fax:** 9 14 77 24
Email: kotiliesi@otavamedia.fi **Web site:** http://www.kotiliesi.fi
ISSN: 0023-4281
Date Established: 1922; **Freq:** 26 issues yearly; **Circ:** 141,520
Usual Pagination: 120
Editor-in-Chief: Leeni Peltonen; **Managing Editor:** Sari Salonen
Profile: Women's magazine covering food, fashion, beauty, health, the environment and interior design.
Language(s): Finnish
Readership: Well educated families.
ADVERTISING RATES:
Full Page Colour .... EUR 6780
SCC .... EUR 57
Mechanical Data: Bleed Size: 280 x 230mm, Print Process: Offset, Film: Digital, Screen: 60 lpc
Copy instructions: *Copy Date:* 18 days prior to publication date
CONSUMER: WOMEN'S INTEREST CONSUMER MAGAZINES: Home & Family

KOTIMAA 15169L87-60_40
Editorial: PL 279/ Hietalahdenranta 13, 00181 HELSINKI **Tel:** 20 75 42 000
Email: toimitus@kotimaa.fi **Web site:** http://www.kotimaa.fi
ISSN: 0356-1135
Date Established: 1905; **Freq:** Weekly - Published on Friday; **Circ:** 38,563
Usual Pagination: 28
Managing Editor: Annmari Salmela
Profile: Tabloid-sized religious magazine covering a broad range of national and international news and current affairs from a Protestant viewpoint.
Language(s): Finnish
Readership: Read mainly by the working class.
ADVERTISING RATES:
Full Page Colour .... EUR 3900
SCC .... EUR 25
Agency Commission: 10-15%
Mechanical Data: Col Widths (Display): 47mm, No. of Columns (Display): 5, Type Area: 255 x 355mm, Screen: 34 lpc, Bleed Size: 280 x 400mm, Print Process: offset
Copy instructions: *Copy Date:* 8 days prior to publication date
Editions:
Kotimaa Verkkotoimitus
CONSUMER: RELIGIOUS

KOTIMIKRO 706086L5D-35
Formerly: Kompuutteri Kaikille
Editorial: Siltasaarenkatu 18-20 A, 00530 HELSINKI
Tel: 3 21 34 776 **Fax:** 3 36 64 998
Email: toimitus@kotimikro.fi **Web site:** http://www.kotimikro.fi
ISSN: 1795-3138
Date Established: 1997; **Freq:** Monthly - Published 18/year; **Circ:** 10,389
Usual Pagination: 84
Profile: Magazine about personal computers for ordinary home users.
Language(s): Finnish
ADVERTISING RATES:
Full Page Colour .... EUR 2250
SCC .... EUR 43.20
Agency Commission: 15%
Mechanical Data: Type Area: 185 x 260mm, Bleed Size: 210 x 297mm, Screen: 54 lpc, Film: positive, Print Process: offset
Copy instructions: *Copy Date:* 20 days prior to publication date
BUSINESS: COMPUTERS & AUTOMATION: Personal Computers

KOTIPUUTARHA 15390L93-60
Editorial: Viljatie 4 C, 00700 HELSINKI
Tel: 9 58 41 66 **Fax:** 9 58 41 65 55
Email: kotipuutarha@puutarhaliitto.fi **Web site:** http://www.kotipuutarha.fi
ISSN: 0355-8673
Date Established: 1940; **Freq:** Monthly - Published 10/year; **Circ:** 32,210
Usual Pagination: 116
Editor-in-Chief: Maija Stenman
Profile: Magazine focusing on gardening. Provides articles and information on ornamental plants, the cultivation of fruit and vegetables, new products and equipment. Also includes interviews and profiles of gardens.
Language(s): Finnish
Readership: Aimed at amateur gardeners.
ADVERTISING RATES:
Full Page Colour .... EUR 3365
SCC .... EUR 32.30
Agency Commission: 15%
Mechanical Data: Type Area: 260 x 189mm, Bleed Size: 282 x 226mm, Trim Size: 276 x 220mm, Col Length: 260mm, Page Width: 189mm, Print Process: offset, Screen: 60 lpc, Film: negative, Col Widths (Display): 44mm, No. of Columns (Display): 4
Average ad content per issue: 25%
CONSUMER: GARDENING

KOTISEUDUN SANOMAT 704928L72-585
Editorial: Keskustie 8, 44800 PIHTIPUDAS
Tel: 20 79 31 620 **Fax:** 14 56 25 28
Email: toimitus@kotiseudunsanomat.fi **Web site:** http://www.kotiseudunsanomat.fi
ISSN: 0359-7067
Date Established: 1961; **Freq:** Weekly; **Circ:** 5,089
Usual Pagination: 16
Profile: Newspaper issued in Pihtipudas and Kinnula.
Language(s): Finnish
ADVERTISING RATES:
Full Page Colour .... EUR 1796
SCC .... EUR 8.20
Agency Commission: 15%
Mechanical Data: Page Width: 260mm, Col Length: 365mm, No. of Columns (Display): 6, Col Widths (Display): 45mm, Print Process: 4-colour offset
Editions:
Kotiseudun Sanomat Verkkotoimitus
LOCAL NEWSPAPERS

KOTISEUTU-UUTISET 704971L72-590
Editorial: PL 14 / Keskustie 20, 83101 LIPERI
Tel: 10 66 66 081 **Fax:** 132525013
Email: toimitus@kotiseutu-uutiset.fi **Web site:** http://www.kotiseutu-uutiset.com
ISSN: 0782-5625
Date Established: 1966; **Freq:** 104 issues yearly; **Circ:** 3,234
Usual Pagination: 20
Managing Editor: Riitta Parkkinen
Profile: Newspaper issued in Liperi and Rääkkylä.
Language(s): Finnish
ADVERTISING RATES:
Full Page Colour .... EUR 3441
SCC .... EUR 15.50
Agency Commission: 17.5%
Mechanical Data: Type Area: 240 x 370mm, No. of Columns (Display): 5, Col Widths (Display): 44mm, Print Process: offset
LOCAL NEWSPAPERS

KOTITALO 1663944L4D-16
Formerly: Kehittyvä Kiinteistö
Editorial: PL 1370, 00101 HELSINKI **Tel:** 9 56 58 310
Fax: 9 27 87 364
Email: toimitus@kotitalolehti.fi **Web site:** http://www.kotitalolehti.fi
ISSN: 1795-3960
Date Established: 2005; **Freq:** 6 issues yearly - Published 8/year; **Circ:** 9,574
Usual Pagination: 60
Profile: Magazine about property maintenance.
Language(s): Finnish
Readership: People interested in maintaining real-estate investments.
ADVERTISING RATES:
Full Page Colour .... EUR 2400
SCC .... EUR 30.70
Agency Commission: 15%
Mechanical Data: Screen: 60 lpc, No. of Columns (Display): 3, Col Widths (Display): 53mm, Print Process: offset, Type Area: 210 x 297mm

KOTIVINKKI 15262L74C-43
Editorial: Elimäenkatu 17-19, 6 krs., 00510 HELSINKI
Tel: 9 77 39 51 **Fax:** 9 77 39 53 21
Email: toimitus.kotivinkki@forma.fi **Web site:** http://www.kotivinkki.fi
ISSN: 0359-8713
Freq: Monthly - Published 21/year; **Circ:** 97,512
Usual Pagination: 124
Editor-in-Chief: Outi Gyldén; **Managing Editor:** Jonna Hietala
Profile: Family and home magazine for women.
Language(s): Finnish
Readership: Women aged 20 to 44 years.
ADVERTISING RATES:
Full Page Colour .... EUR 7320
SCC .... EUR 61.60
Agency Commission: 15%
Mechanical Data: Type Area: 217 x 280mm, Print Process: offset, Film: positive, Screen: 54 lpc
CONSUMER: WOMEN'S INTEREST CONSUMER MAGAZINES: Home & Family

KOULULAINEN 15382L88E-30
Editorial: Maistraatinportti 1, 00015 OTAVAMEDIA
Tel: 9 15 661 **Fax:** 9 15 66 788
Email: koululainen@otavamedia.fi **Web site:** http://www.koululainen.fi
ISSN: 0357-2714
Freq: Monthly - Double issue in June/July; **Circ:** 39,196
Usual Pagination: 56
Managing Editor: Leea Puranen
Profile: Magazine including features on animals, music, sport and hobbies, along with puzzles and games.
Language(s): Finnish
Readership: Aimed at school children between 7 and 12 years of age.
ADVERTISING RATES:
Full Page Colour .... EUR 2330
SCC .... EUR 27.70
Mechanical Data: Bleed Size: 280 x 217mm, Print Process: Offset, Film: Digital positive, No. of Columns (Display): 3, Col Widths (Display): 58mm, Screen: 60 lpc, Type Area: 217 x 280mm
Copy instructions: *Copy Date:* 19 days prior to publication date
CONSUMER: EDUCATION: Preparatory & Junior Education

KOUVOLAN SANOMAT 15197L67B-5000
Editorial: PL 40/Lehtikaari 1, 45101 KOUVOLA
Tel: 5 28 00 14 **Fax:** 5 28 00 47 06
Email: toimitus@kouvolansanomat.fi **Web site:** http://www.kouvolansanomat.fi
ISSN: 0357-9298
Freq: Daily; **Circ:** 27,273
Usual Pagination: 20
Managing Editor: Petri Karjalainen
Profile: Newspaper issued mainly in Kouvola in the southeastern part of Finland.
Language(s): Finnish
ADVERTISING RATES:
Full Page Colour .... EUR 9105
SCC .... EUR 22.10
Agency Commission: 3-10%
Mechanical Data: Col Length: 515mm, Col Widths (Display): 44mm, No. of Columns (Display): 8, Page Width: 380mm, Print Process: offset
Editions:
Kouvolan Sanomat Verkkotoimitus
REGIONAL DAILY & SUNDAY NEWSPAPERS: Regional Daily Newspapers

KOUVOLAN SANOMAT VALKEALA 705649L67E-288
Editorial: Kustaa III tie 8, 45379 VALKEALA
Tel: 5 28 00 44 61
Email: tapio.lainesalo@kouvolansanomat.fi **Web site:** http://www.kouvolansanomat.fi
Freq: Daily
Profile: Valkeala local office of Kouvolan Sanomat.
Language(s): Finnish
REGIONAL DAILY & SUNDAY NEWSPAPERS: Regional Offices

KUHMOISTEN SANOMAT 704930L72-620
Editorial: PL 8 / Toritie 52, 17801 KUHMOINEN
Tel: 3 55 51 437 **Fax:** 3 55 56 538
Email: toimitus@kuhmoistensanomat.fi **Web site:** http://www.kuhmoistensanomat.fi
ISSN: 0356-228X
Date Established: 1950; **Freq:** Weekly; **Circ:** 2,933
Usual Pagination: 8
Profile: Newspaper issued in Kuhmoinen and its surroundings.
Language(s): Finnish
ADVERTISING RATES:
Full Page Colour .... EUR 2246
SCC .... EUR 10.20
Agency Commission: 15%
Mechanical Data: Col Length: 367mm, No. of Columns (Display): 6, Col Widths (Display): 40mm
LOCAL NEWSPAPERS

KUHMOLAINEN 705017L72-625
Editorial: Kainuuntie 103, 88900 KUHMO
Tel: 8 63 25 30 **Fax:** 8 63 25 334
Email: ku.toimitus@sps.fi **Web site:** http://www.kuhmolainen.fi
ISSN: 0787-5312
Date Established: 1959; **Freq:** 104 issues yearly; **Circ:** 3,935
Usual Pagination: 16
Profile: Newspaper issued in Kuhmo.
Language(s): Finnish
ADVERTISING RATES:
Full Page Colour .... EUR 2518
SCC .... EUR 11.50
Agency Commission: 15%
Mechanical Data: No. of Columns (Display): 6, Col Widths (Display): 40mm, Col Length: 365mm, Page Width: 260mm, Print Process: offset
Copy instructions: *Copy Date:* 10 days prior to publication date
Editions:
Kuhmolainen Verkkotoimitus
LOCAL NEWSPAPERS

KULJETUS JA LOGISTIIKKA 1637855L10-50
Editorial: Artturinkatu 2, 20200 TURKU
Tel: 2 24 44 110 **Fax:** 2 23 22 382
Email: lehti@kuljetusjalogistiikka.com **Web site:** http://www.kuljetusjalogistiikka.com
ISSN: 1458-1086
Freq: 6 issues yearly; **Circ:** 14,600
Usual Pagination: 40
Editor-in-Chief: M-T Saarinen
Profile: Magazine about transport, logistics and materials-handling.
Language(s): Finnish
ADVERTISING RATES:
Full Page Colour .... EUR 1900.00
Mechanical Data: Col Widths (Display): 48mm, No. of Columns (Display): 4, Type Area: 190 x 270mm

KULJETUS-VARASTO-LOGISTIIKKA 1609429L10-100
Formerly: Varastouutiset
Editorial: Larin Kyöstin katu 16, 13130 HÄMEENLINNA **Tel:** 20 74 12 240 **Fax:** 20 74 12 249
Email: info@supermedia.fi **Web site:** http://www.supermedia.fi
Freq: Quarterly; **Annual Sub.:** EUR 40.00; **Circ:** 8,000
Editor-in-Chief: Jorma Yrjölä
Profile: Magazine about storage, logistics and warehousing.
Language(s): Finnish
ADVERTISING RATES:
Full Page Colour .... EUR 1498.00
Mechanical Data: Type Area: 210 x 297mm, Col Widths (Display): 44mm, No. of Columns (Display): 4, Screen: 60 lpc, Print Process: offset

KULJETUSYRITTÄJÄ 15072L49D-20
Editorial: PL 38 /Nuijamiestentie 7, 00401 HELSINKI
Tel: 9 47 89 99 **Fax:** 9 58 78 520
Email: toimitus@skal.fi **Web site:** http://www.skal.fi
ISSN: 1236-066X
Date Established: 1993; **Freq:** Monthly - Published 10/year; **Circ:** 8,350
Usual Pagination: 80
Managing Editor: Anneli Similä
Profile: Journal of the Finnish Trucking Association, covering transport economy, technology, product news, taxation and legislation.
Language(s): Finnish; Swedish
Readership: Read by independent transport operators.
ADVERTISING RATES:
Full Page Colour .... EUR 2950
SCC .... EUR 24.80
Agency Commission: 15%
Mechanical Data: Trim Size: 297 x 210mm, Type Area: 270 x 185mm, Print Process: Heat offset, Screen: 60 lpc, Col Length: 270mm, Page Width: 185mm, Film: Colour separated positive films or digital material in PC format, No. of Columns (Display): 4, Col Widths (Display): 43mm
Copy instructions: *Copy Date:* 14 days prior to publication date
Average ad content per issue: 20%
BUSINESS: TRANSPORT: Commercial Vehicles

KULTAJYVÄ 705314L21A-8
Editorial: PL 308/ Teollisuuskatu 1b, 00101 HELSINKI **Tel:** 10 25 20 10
Web site: http://www.op.fi
ISSN: 0788-8511
Date Established: 1974; **Freq:** Half-yearly; **Cover Price:** Free; **Circ:** 93,000
Usual Pagination: 32
Editor-in-Chief: Kari Vartiainen; **Managing Editor:** Paavo Tuovinen
Profile: Magazine about the financing aspects of agriculture and forestry.
Language(s): Finnish
Readership: Customers of OP-Pohjola-ryhmä.
Mechanical Data: Print Process: offset, Col Widths (Display): 43mm, Screen: 54-60 lpc
BUSINESS: AGRICULTURE & FARMING

KULTTUURIHAITARI 706492L84A-8
Editorial: PL 164, 20101 TURKU **Tel:** 20 71 21 254
Fax: 20 71 21 251
Email: info@kulttuurihaitari.fi **Web site:** http://www.kulttuurihaitari.fi
ISSN: 1456-5587
Date Established: 1998; **Freq:** Quarterly; Free to qualifying individuals ; **Circ:** 28,000
Usual Pagination: 48
Editor-in-Chief: Jaakko Amperla; **Managing Editor:** Annika Selänniemi
Profile: Magazine about cultural events and related persons.
Language(s): Finnish
Readership: Distributed during cultural events to people interested in culture.
ADVERTISING RATES:
Full Page Colour .... EUR 2510
SCC .... EUR 17.80
Agency Commission: 15%
Mechanical Data: Type Area: 205 x 280mm, No. of Columns (Display): 5, Col Widths (Display): 38mm, Print Process: offset
CONSUMER: THE ARTS & LITERARY: Arts

KULTTUURINTUTKIMUS
706090L74Q-30
Editorial: Nykykulttuurin tutkimuskeskus, PL 35, 40014 JYVÄSKYLÄN YLIOPISTO **Tel:** 14 26 01 317 **Fax:** 14 26 01 311
Email: minna.m.nerg@jyu.fi **Web site:** http://www.jyu.fi/kulttuurintutkimus
ISSN: 0781-5751
Date Established: 1984; **Freq:** Quarterly; **Annual Sub.:** EUR 28; **Circ:** 750
Usual Pagination: 66
Profile: Magazine by the Research Centre for Contemporary Culture.
Language(s): Finnish

KUMIVIESTI
719257L39-3
Editorial: PL 13/ Nokiankatu 1, 38211 SASTAMALA
Tel: 3 51 911 **Fax:** 3 51 91 33 30
Email: sinikka.sisto@teknikum.com **Web site:** http://www.teknikum.com
ISSN: 0039-1697
Date Established: 1954; **Freq:** Half-yearly; **Cover Price:** Free; **Circ:** 2,500
Usual Pagination: 16
Profile: Magazine about rubber and chemicals.
Language(s): Finnish
Readership: Customers of Teknikum Co.

KUNNALLISLEHTI PAIMIO-SAUVO-KAARINA
704888L72-635
Formerly: Kunnallislehti Paimio-Sauvo-Piikkiö
Editorial: PL 29/Vistantie 38, 21531 PAIMIO
Tel: 2 47 76 66 **Fax:** 2 47 76 600
Email: toimitus@kunnallislehti.fi **Web site:** http://www.kuntsari.fi
Date Established: 1916; **Freq:** 104 issues yearly; **Circ:** 6,502
Usual Pagination: 12
Profile: Local newspaper in Piikkiö, Sauvo ja Paimio.
Language(s): Finnish
ADVERTISING RATES:
Full Page Colour .... EUR 2290
SCC .... EUR 10.60
Agency Commission: 17.5%
Mechanical Data: Print Process: offset rotation, Page Width: 255mm, Col Length: 360mm, No. of Columns (Display): 6, Col Widths (Display): 40mm, Type Area: 255 x 360mm
Copy instructions: *Copy Date:* 4 days prior to publication date
LOCAL NEWSPAPERS

KUNTA JA INVESTOINNIT
705247L32C-10
Editorial: PL 313/ Linnanrakentajantie 4, 00811 HELSINKI **Tel:** 50 57 67 062
Email: wasenius@wippies.fi
Freq: Quarterly - Published 5/year; **Circ:** 19,598
Editor-in-Chief: Olli Wasenius
Profile: Journal about building, real estates, community planning and investments from the local government point of view.
Language(s): Finnish
BUSINESS: LOCAL GOVERNMENT, LEISURE & RECREATION: Local Government Finance

KUNTALEHTI
15007L32A-60
Editorial: Toinen linja 14, 00530 HELSINKI
Tel: 9 77 11
Email: kuntalehti@kuntalehti.fi **Web site:** http://www.kuntalehti.fi
ISSN: 1236-0066
Date Established: 1993; **Freq:** 26 issues yearly - Published 16/year; **Circ:** 12,729
Usual Pagination: 60
Editor-in-Chief: Hannu Kataja
Profile: Magazine covering many different aspects of work in the public services and local administration sector - housing, planning, finance, the environment, traffic, public funding, local government and affairs relating to the European Union.
Language(s): Finnish
Readership: Aimed at city and municipal directors and managers, MPs, councillors, managers of private enterprises associated with local authorities and universities.
ADVERTISING RATES:
Full Page Colour .... EUR 3950
SCC .... EUR 35.20
Mechanical Data: Type Area: 195 x 255mm, Bleed Size: 215 x 280mm, No. of Columns (Display): 4, Col Widths (Display): 45mm, Print Process: offset, Film: positive, Screen: 54 lpc
Copy instructions: *Copy Date:* 14 days prior to publication date
Editions:
Kuntalehti.fi
BUSINESS: LOCAL GOVERNMENT, LEISURE & RECREATION: Local Government

KUNTATEKNIIKKA
705174L4D-40
Formerly: Kuntatekniikka - Kommunteknik
Editorial: Toinen linja 14, 00530 HELSINKI
Tel: 9 77 11 **Fax:** 9 77 12 486
Email: toimitus@kuntatekniikka.fi **Web site:** http://www.kuntatekniikka.fi
ISSN: 1238-125X
Date Established: 1946; **Freq:** 6 issues yearly - Published 8/year; Free to qualifying individuals ; **Circ:** 5,000
Usual Pagination: 64
Profile: Magazine containing information on the technical planning of local projects in building, road construction, energy supply, harbor activities, plumbing and town planning.
Language(s): Finnish
Readership: Read by local government policymakers, engineers, technicians, designers and users of local facilities.
ADVERTISING RATES:
Full Page Colour .... EUR 3150
SCC .... EUR 26.50
Agency Commission: 15%
Mechanical Data: Type Area: 185 x 264mm, No. of Columns (Display): 4, Col Widths (Display): 43mm, Print Process: offset, Screen: 60 lpc, Film: positive
Copy instructions: *Copy Date:* 25 days prior to publication date

KUNTO PLUS
705480L74G-33
Editorial: c/o Raija Kivinen, PL 78, 02211 ESPOO
Tel: 40 54 10 696
Email: toimitus@kuntoplus.fi **Web site:** http://www.kuntoplus.fi
ISSN: 0788-348X
Date Established: 1987; **Freq:** Monthly - Published 18/year; **Circ:** 19,306
Usual Pagination: 84
Profile: Magazine for people interested in health and physical well-being.
Language(s): Finnish
Readership: Well educated 19-39-year-old health-conscious people.
ADVERTISING RATES:
Full Page Colour .... EUR 4100
SCC .... EUR 39.40
Agency Commission: 15%
Mechanical Data: Bleed Size: 205 x 276mm, Type Area: 185 x 260mm, Print Process: offset, Film: negative, Screen: 54 lpc, No. of Columns (Display): 4, Col Widths (Display): 56mm
CONSUMER: WOMEN'S INTEREST CONSUMER MAGAZINES: Slimming & Health

KURIKKA-LEHTI
705005L72-655
Editorial: PL 50 / Laulajantie 4, 61301 KURIKKA
Tel: 6 45 15 500 **Fax:** 6 45 15 532
Email: toimitus@kurikka-lehti.fi **Web site:** http://www.kurikka-lehti.fi
ISSN: 1795-9748
Date Established: 1928; **Freq:** 104 issues yearly; **Circ:** 5,084
Usual Pagination: 12
Managing Editor: Ulla Antila-Bamichas
Profile: Local newspaper issued in Kurikka.
Language(s): Finnish
ADVERTISING RATES:
Full Page Colour .... EUR 3348
SCC .... EUR 15.50
Mechanical Data: Type Area: 260 x 360mm, No. of Columns (Display): 6, Col Widths (Display): 40mm, Print Process: offset
LOCAL NEWSPAPERS

KURIREN
15264L73-82
Editorial: Skeppsgatan 3, 65101 VASA
Tel: 6 31 81 900 **Fax:** 6 31 81 911
Email: material@kuriren.net **Web site:** http://www.kuriren.net
Date Established: 1959; **Freq:** Monthly - Published 18/year; **Circ:** 9,814
Usual Pagination: 64
Editor-in-Chief: Frejvid Weegar; **Managing Editor:** Maria Toivola
Profile: Magazine about the home and family matters.
Language(s): Swedish
ADVERTISING RATES:
Full Page Colour .... EUR 1807
SCC .... EUR 18.40
Agency Commission: 15%
Mechanical Data: Bleed Size: 220 x 275mm, Type Area: 200 x 247mm, Col Widths (Display): 48mm, No. of Columns (Display): 4, Print Process: offset, Film: positive, Screen: 60 lpc, Col Length: 247mm
Average ad content per issue: 10%

KYLKIRAUTA
705126L40-8
Editorial: Eino Leinonkatu 12 E 64, 00250 HELSINKI
Tel: 9 49 09 32 **Fax:** 9 44 62 62
Email: marko.laaksonen@mil.fi **Web site:** http://www.kadettikunta.fi
ISSN: 0454-7357
Date Established: 1921; **Freq:** Quarterly; **Circ:** 6,200
Usual Pagination: 68
Editor-in-Chief: Marko Laaksonen
Profile: Magazine by the Finnish Cadet Society about defence, leadership and ethics.
Language(s): Finnish
ADVERTISING RATES:
Full Page Colour .... EUR 1400.00
Mechanical Data: Type Area: 165 x 260mm, Print Process: offset

KYLVÖSIEMEN
14982L21A-35
Editorial: Metsontie 20, 32210 LOIMAA
Tel: 50 52 10 560
Email: raimo.nordman@kylvosiemen.fi **Web site:** http://www.kylvosiemen.fi
ISSN: 0355-0435
Date Established: 1961; **Freq:** Quarterly; **Circ:** 3,200
Usual Pagination: 28
Editor-in-Chief: Raimo Nordman
Profile: Publication of the Finnish Agricultural Producers' Service.
Language(s): Finnish
ADVERTISING RATES:
Full Page Colour .... EUR 1227.00

KYMEN SANOMAT
15196L67B-5100
Editorial: PL 27/Tornatorintie 3, 48101 KOTKA
Tel: 5 21 00 15 **Fax:** 5 21 00 52 06
Email: uutiset@kymensanomat.fi **Web site:** http://www.kymensanomat.fi
ISSN: 0789-6700
Date Established: 1902
Circ: 23,208
Usual Pagination: 28
Managing Editor: Markku Kumpunen
Profile: Newspaper distributed mainly in Kotka, Hamina and Vehkalahti.
Language(s): Finnish
ADVERTISING RATES:
Full Page Colour .... EUR 9682
SCC .... EUR 23.50
Agency Commission: 10%
Mechanical Data: No. of Columns (Display): 8, Col Widths (Display): 44mm, Col Length: 515mm, Bleed Size: 380 x 515mm
Editions:
Kymen Sanomat Verkkotoimitus
REGIONAL DAILY & SUNDAY NEWSPAPERS: Regional Daily Newspapers

KYMEN SANOMAT HAMINA
718319L67E-457
Editorial: Pikkuympyräkatu 22-24, 49400 HAMINA
Tel: 5 21 00 15 **Fax:** 5 34 44 908
Email: antti.larvio@kymensanomat.fi **Web site:** http://www.kymensanomat.fi
Circ: 24,927
Profile: Hamina regional office of Kymen Sanomat.
Language(s): Finnish
REGIONAL DAILY & SUNDAY NEWSPAPERS: Regional Offices

KYMPPI
1645312L17-41
Editorial: PL 29/ Töölönkatu 4, 00101 HELSINKI
Tel: 10 21 02 10 **Fax:** 10 21 02 15
Email: info@kymppivoima.fi **Web site:** http://www.kymppivoima.fi
ISSN: 1457-2761
Date Established: 2000; **Freq:** Quarterly; **Cover Price:** Free; **Circ:** 364,000
Usual Pagination: 48
Editor-in-Chief: Anu Koskenkorva
Profile: Magazine about electrical services.
Language(s): Finnish; Swedish
Readership: Customers of Kymppivoima Oy.
ADVERTISING RATES:
Full Page Colour .... EUR 2950.00
Mechanical Data: Type Area: 220 x 270mm
BUSINESS: ELECTRICAL

KYRKPRESSEN
705464L87-66
Editorial: Mannerheimvägen 16 A 9, 00100 HELSINGFORS **Tel:** 9 61 26 15 49 **Fax:** 9 27 84 138
Email: redaktionen@kyrkpressen.fi **Web site:** http://www.kyrkpressen.fi
Date Established: 1969; **Freq:** Weekly - Published on Thursday; **Circ:** 100,513
Usual Pagination: 16
Profile: Finlandssvensk kyrklig tidning.
Language(s): Swedish
ADVERTISING RATES:
Full Page Colour .... EUR 2850
SCC .... EUR 13
Mechanical Data: Type Area: 364 x 251mm, Screen: 34 lpc, Col Widths (Display): 38mm, No. of Columns (Display): 6, Print Process: offset
CONSUMER: RELIGIOUS

KYRÖNMAA-LEHTI
705004L72-680
Editorial: PL 61/Ruutintie 2 C, 66401 LAIHIA
Tel: 6 47 76 116 **Fax:** 64776114
Email: toimitus@kyronmaa-lehti.fi **Web site:** http://www.kyronmaa-lehti.fi
ISSN: 1795-3073
Date Established: 1956; **Freq:** 104 issues yearly; **Circ:** 3,028
Usual Pagination: 16
Managing Editor: Erkki Tuori
Profile: Newspaper issued in Laihia, Isokyrö, Vähäkyrö and Ylistaro.
Language(s): Finnish
ADVERTISING RATES:
Full Page Colour .... EUR 2700
SCC .... EUR 12.50
LOCAL NEWSPAPERS

LÄÄKÄRISANOMAT
1601118L56A-51
Editorial: Mäkikatu 3 B 50-51, 70110 KUOPIO
Tel: 17 36 20 389
Email: maj@laakarisanomat.fi
ISSN: 1455-9374
Date Established: 1998; **Freq:** Quarterly; **Circ:** 27,000
Usual Pagination: 32
Profile: Magazine for members of the Finnish Medical Association.
Language(s): Finnish
ADVERTISING RATES:
Full Page Colour .... EUR 2657
SCC .... EUR 10.80

LÄÄKETIETEELLINEN AIKAKAUSKIRJA DUODECIM
15095L56A-50
Formerly: Duodecim
Editorial: PL 713/ Kalevankatu 11 A, 00101 HELSINKI **Tel:** 9 61 88 51 **Fax:** 9 61 88 52 59
Email: pekka.lahdenne@duodecim.fi **Web site:** http://www.duodecimlehti.fi
ISSN: 0012-7183
Date Established: 1885; **Freq:** 26 issues yearly; **Circ:** 22,500
Usual Pagination: 86
Editor-in-Chief: Jussi Huttunen; **Managing Director:** Pekka Mustonen
Profile: Educational journal for medical doctors.
Language(s): Finnish
ADVERTISING RATES:
Full Page Colour .... EUR 3250.00
SCC .... EUR 65.00
Mechanical Data: Trim Size: 256 x 182mm, Type Area: 250 x 176mm, Film: Digital accepted
Copy instructions: *Copy Date:* 3 weeks prior to publication

LAATU
705931L14K-3
Formerly: Laatuviesti; eXBa
Editorial: Keilaranta 12, 02150 ESPOO
Tel: 20 77 91 470 **Fax:** 20 77 91 499
Email: info@laatukeskus.fi **Web site:** http://www.laatukeskus.fi
ISSN: 1458-137X
Date Established: 1987; **Freq:** Quarterly; **Cover Price:** Free; **Circ:** 80,000
Usual Pagination: 44
Editor-in-Chief: Margit Lindholm
Profile: Suomen Laatuyhdistys is a neutral organization to develop quality thinking in Finnish companies and organizations by quality assurance TQM.
Language(s): Finnish
ADVERTISING RATES:
Full Page Colour .... EUR 2920.00
SCC .... EUR 32.70
Mechanical Data: Type Area: 185 x 265mm, Print Process: offset
BUSINESS: COMMERCE, INDUSTRY & MANAGEMENT: Quality Assurance

LÄHETYSSANOMAT
15365L87-98
Formerly: Suomen Lähetyssanomat
Editorial: PL 154/ Tähtitorninkatu 18, 00141 HELSINKI **Tel:** 9 12 971 **Fax:** 9 12 97 294
Email: sls@mission.fi **Web site:** http://www.mission.fi/julkaisut/index.html
ISSN: 0780-8313
Date Established: 1859; **Freq:** Monthly; **Circ:** 10,553
Usual Pagination: 48
Managing Editor: Pirre Saario
Profile: Magazine of the Finnish Evangelical Lutheran Mission, concerning religious missions. Also includes details on third world development and refugee work.
Language(s): Finnish
Readership: Aimed at people interested in mission work, third world countries, religion and culture.
ADVERTISING RATES:
Full Page Colour .... EUR 1300
SCC .... EUR 11.90
Mechanical Data: Type Area: 273 x 230mm, Col Length: 273mm, Page Width: 230mm, Bleed Size: 230 x 273mm, No. of Columns (Display): 4, Print Process: offset, Film: negative, Screen: 54 lpc, Col Widths (Display): 45mm
CONSUMER: RELIGIOUS

LÄHIS
15081L53-37
Formerly: Ketjuviesti
Editorial: PL 1/ Sörnäistenkatu 2, 00581 HELSINKI
Tel: 20 70 03 00 **Fax:** 20 70 03 570
Web site: http://www.lahikauppa.fi/fi/etusivu
ISSN: 1239-5013
Freq: 6 issues yearly; **Circ:** 9,000
Usual Pagination: 40
Profile: Personnel magazine for the Suomen Lähikauppa retail company. Includes information on personal skill development and general retail news.
Language(s): Finnish
Readership: Partners and personnel of Suomen Lähikauppa Oy.
ADVERTISING RATES:
Full Page Colour .... EUR 3360
Agency Commission: 15%
Mechanical Data: Bleed Size: 210 x 297mm, No. of Columns (Display): 2-4, Print Process: offset, Screen: 70 lpc

LAHTIWATTI
754462L58-97
Formerly: Lahti Energia
Editorial: PL96/ Kauppakatu 31, 15141 LAHTI
Tel: 3 82 300 **Fax:** 3 82 34 567
Web site: http://www.lahtienergia.fi
ISSN: 1458-6258
Freq: Half-yearly; **Cover Price:** Free; **Circ:** 76,500
Usual Pagination: 16
Editor-in-Chief: Jaana Lehtovirta
Profile: Customer-magazine by energy company Lahti Energia Oy.
Language(s): Finnish
BUSINESS: ENERGY, FUEL & NUCLEAR

LAITILAN SANOMAT 704891L72-690

Editorial: PL 8/Keskuskatu 2, 23801 LAITILA
Tel: 2 85 006 **Fax:** 2 85 008
Email: toimitus@laitilansanomat.fi **Web site:** http://www.laitilansanomat.fi
ISSN: 0782-5595
Date Established: 1925; **Freq:** 104 issues yearly; **Circ:** 4,967
Usual Pagination: 16
Profile: Newspaper distributed in Laitila, Pyhäranta and Kodisjoki.
Language(s): Finnish
ADVERTISING RATES:
Full Page Colour .... EUR 2738
SCC .... EUR 12.50
Agency Commission: 15%
Mechanical Data: Col Length: 365mm, No. of Columns (Display): 6, Page Width: 255mm, Col Widths (Display): 40mm, Print Process: offset
Copy instructions: *Copy Date:* 5 days prior to publication date
LOCAL NEWSPAPERS

LAKIMIESUUTISET-JURISTNYTT 15047L44-10

Formerly: Lakimiesuutiset
Editorial: Uudenmaankatu 4-6 B 10, 00120 HELSINKI **Tel:** 9 85 61 03 00 **Fax:** 9 85 61 03 06
Email: lakimiesuutiset@lakimiesliitto.fi **Web site:** http://www.lakimiesuutiset.fi
ISSN: 0023-7361
Date Established: 1945; **Freq:** 6 issues yearly; **Circ:** 14,159
Usual Pagination: 64
Editor-in-Chief: Jorma Tilander; **Managing Editor:** Juha Mikkonen
Profile: Magazine aiming to look after the social and economic interests of lawyers and associates.
Language(s): English; Finnish; Swedish
Readership: Read by professionals in the legal field.
ADVERTISING RATES:
Full Page Colour .... EUR 2050.00
SCC .... EUR 29.90
Mechanical Data: Type Area: 278 x 215mm, Col Length: 278mm, Trim Size: 280 x 210mm, Print Process: Offset, Screen: 48-60 lpc, Page Width: 215mm, No. of Columns (Display): 3, Col Widths (Display): 55/85mm
BUSINESS: LEGAL

LÄMMÖLLÄ 706563L3A-100

Editorial: Öljyalan Palvelukeskus Oy, Eteläranta 8, 00130 HELSINKI **Tel:** 9 62 26 150 **Fax:** 9 62 22 042
Email: lammolla@vca.fi **Web site:** http://www.lammolla.fi
ISSN: 1457-1277
Date Established: 1996; **Freq:** Quarterly; **Cover Price:** Free; **Circ:** 250,000
Usual Pagination: 64
Editor-in-Chief: Eero Otsonen
Profile: Magazine on heating by using oil, housing and maintenance.
Language(s): Finnish
Readership: Aimed at property owners using oil for heating.
ADVERTISING RATES:
Full Page Colour .... EUR 8900.00
SCC .... EUR 74.17
Mechanical Data: Bleed Size: 210 x 297mm, Print Process: offset
BUSINESS: HEATING & VENTILATION: Domestic Heating & Ventilation

LANDSBYGDENS FOLK 14983L21A-40

Editorial: Fredriksgatan 61 A 34, 00100 HELSINGFORS **Tel:** 9 58 60 460 **Fax:** 9 69 41 358
Email: redaktion.lf@slc.fi **Web site:** http://www.landsbygdensfolk.fi
ISSN: 0023-8011
Date Established: 1947; **Freq:** Weekly; **Circ:** 9,956
Usual Pagination: 20
Editor-in-Chief: Micke Godtfredssen
Profile: Magazine of the Swedish Farmers' Association in Finland.
Language(s): Swedish
ADVERTISING RATES:
Full Page Colour .... EUR 2890.00
SCC .... EUR 16.50
Agency Commission: 15%
Mechanical Data: Page Width: 251mm, Col Length: 350mm, Type Area: 251 x 350mm, No. of Columns (Display): 5, Col Widths (Display): 46mm, Screen: 28 lpc mono, 34 lpc colour, Print Process: offset
BUSINESS: AGRICULTURE & FARMING

LÄNSI-SAIMAAN SANOMAT 704961L72-1640

Formerly: Yhteissanomat
Editorial: Peltoinlahdentie 24, 54800 SAVITAIPALE
Tel: 5 67 73 300 **Fax:** 5 47 72 211
Email: toimitus@lansisaimaa.fi **Web site:** http://www.lansisaimaa.fi
ISSN: 0782-601X
Date Established: 1950; **Freq:** 104 issues yearly; **Circ:** 4,901
Usual Pagination: 12
Profile: Newspaper issued in Savitaipale, Lemi, Suomenniemi and Taipalsaari.
Language(s): Finnish
ADVERTISING RATES:
Full Page Colour .... EUR 2409
SCC .... EUR 11
Mechanical Data: No. of Columns (Display): 6, Col Widths (Display): 47.5mm, Print Process: offset, Col Length: 365mm, Page Width: 280mm
LOCAL NEWSPAPERS

LÄNSI-SAVO 15206L67B-5780

Editorial: PL 6/ Teollisuuskatu 2-6, 50101 MIKKELI
Tel: 15 35 01
Email: toimitus@lansi-savo.fi **Web site:** http://www.lansi-savo.fi
ISSN: 0356-1623
Date Established: 1889; **Freq:** Daily; **Circ:** 25,018
Usual Pagination: 20
Editor-in-Chief: Tapio Honkamaa
Profile: Newspaper issued mainly in the Mikkeli region.
Language(s): Finnish
ADVERTISING RATES:
Full Page Colour .... EUR 4963
SCC .... EUR 18.80
Mechanical Data: Print Process: offset, Page Width: 284mm, Col Length: 440mm
Editions:
Länsi-Savo Verkkotoimitus
REGIONAL DAILY & SUNDAY NEWSPAPERS: Regional Daily Newspapers

LÄNSI-SAVO PIEKSÄMÄKI 705658L67E-496

Editorial: Häyrisentie 6, 76100 PIEKSÄMÄKI
Tel: 15 35 03 504
Email: elisa.salste@lansi-savo.fi **Web site:** http://www.lansi-savo.fi
Freq: Daily
Profile: Pieksämäki, Jäppilä and Virtasalmi regional office of newspaper Länsi-Savo.
Language(s): Finnish
REGIONAL DAILY & SUNDAY NEWSPAPERS: Regional Offices

LÄNSI-SUOMI 15213L67B-5800

Editorial: PL 5/ Susivuorentie 2, 26101 RAUMA
Tel: 10 83 361 **Fax:** 10 83 36 659
Email: toimitus@lansi-suomi.fi **Web site:** http://www.lansi-suomi.fi
ISSN: 0782-6419
Date Established: 1905
Circ: 15,750
Usual Pagination: 18
Managing Editor: Mikko Soini
Profile: Newspaper issued mainly in Rauma and its surroundings in western Finland.
Language(s): Finnish
ADVERTISING RATES:
Full Page Colour .... EUR 10037
SCC .... EUR 24.60
Mechanical Data: No. of Columns (Display): 8, Col Widths (Display): 44mm, Screen: 28-34 lpc, Print Process: offset, Type Area: 380 x 510mm, Page Width: 380mm, Col Length: 510mm
Editions:
Länsi-Suomi Urheilutoimitus
Länsi-Suomi Verkkotoimitus
REGIONAL DAILY & SUNDAY NEWSPAPERS: Regional Daily Newspapers

LÄNSI-UUSIMAA 15202L67B-5600

Editorial: PL 60/ Suurlohjankatu 10, 08101 LOHJA
Tel: 20 61 00 130 **Fax:** 20 77 03 048
Email: lu.toimitus@lehtiyhtyma.fi **Web site:** http://www.lansi-uusimaa.fi
ISSN: 0783-3261
Date Established: 1915
Circ: 13,432
Usual Pagination: 16
Managing Editor: Päivi Kallo
Profile: Non-political newspaper issued in Lohja and its neighbouring municipalities.
Language(s): Finnish
ADVERTISING RATES:
Full Page Colour .... EUR 9435
SCC .... EUR 22.90
Mechanical Data: Screen: 38 lpc, Col Widths (Display): 45mm, No. of Columns (Display): 8, Col Length: 530mm, Print Process: offset
Editions:
Länsi-Uusimaa Verkkotoimitus
REGIONAL DAILY & SUNDAY NEWSPAPERS: Regional Daily Newspapers

LÄNSIVÄYLÄ 705066L72-710

Editorial: PL 350/ Rälssitie 7 A, 01511 VANTAA
Tel: 20 61 00 110 **Fax:** 20 77 03 016
Email: lv.toimitus@lehtiyhtyma.fi **Web site:** http://www.lansivayla.fi
ISSN: 0356-2352
Date Established: 1954; **Freq:** 104 issues yearly; **Cover Price:** Free; **Circ:** 119,000
Usual Pagination: 20
Editor-in-Chief: Risto Hietanen
Profile: Newspaper distributed in Espoo, Kauniainen and Kirkkonummi.
Language(s): Finnish
ADVERTISING RATES:
Full Page Colour .... EUR 9110
SCC .... EUR 21.90
Agency Commission: 15%
Mechanical Data: Type Area: 380 x 510mm, Col Length: 520mm, No. of Columns (Display): 8-10, Col Widths (Display): 44mm, Print Process: offset rotation, Screen: 34 lpc, Page Width: 380mm
Editions:
Länsiväylä Verkkotoimitus
LOCAL NEWSPAPERS

LAPIN KANSA 15215L67B-5700

Editorial: Veitikantie 2-8, 96100 ROVANIEMI
Tel: 10 66 50 22 **Fax:** 10 66 57 725
Email: lktoimitus@lapinkansa.fi **Web site:** http://www.lapinkansa.fi
ISSN: 0359-6753
Date Established: 1928; **Freq:** Daily; **Circ:** 32,691
Usual Pagination: 20
Editor-in-Chief: Antti Kokkonen; **Managing Editor:** Jouko Kurppa
Profile: Newspaper issued in Lapland, northern Finland.
Language(s): Finnish
ADVERTISING RATES:
Full Page Colour .... EUR 5891
SCC .... EUR 26.90
Agency Commission: 15%
Mechanical Data: No. of Columns (Display): 8, Col Widths (Display): 44mm, Col Length: 520mm, Page Width: 380mm, Print Process: offset
Editions:
Lapin Kansa Verkkotoimitus
REGIONAL DAILY & SUNDAY NEWSPAPERS: Regional Daily Newspapers

LAPIN KANSA INARI-UTSJOKI 706461L67E-460

Editorial: Inarintie 34, 99800 INARI **Tel:** 10 66 57 845
Fax: 16 67 15 08
Email: veikko.vaananen@lapinkansa.fi **Web site:** http://www.lapinkansa.fi
Freq: Daily
Profile: Inari and Utsjoki local office of regional newspaper Lapin Kansa.
Language(s): Finnish
REGIONAL DAILY & SUNDAY NEWSPAPERS: Regional Offices

LAPIN KANSA KEMIJÄRVI-SALLA-PELKOSENNIEMI 705650L67E-465

Editorial: Hallituskatu 1, 98100 KEMIJÄRVI
Tel: 10 66 57 638 **Fax:** 16 81 27 77
Email: lkkemijarvi@lapinkansa.fi **Web site:** http://www.lapinkansa.fi
Freq: Daily
Profile: Kemijärvi, Pelkosenniemi, Salla and Savukoski local office of regional newspaper Lapin Kansa.
Language(s): Finnish
REGIONAL DAILY & SUNDAY NEWSPAPERS: Regional Offices

LAPIN KANSA KITTILÄ-MUONIO-ENONTEKIÖ 705652L67E-470

Editorial: Valtatie 27, 99100 KITTILÄ
Tel: 10 66 57 846 **Fax:** 16 64 21 02
Email: antti.sallinen@lapinkansa.fi **Web site:** http://www.lapinkansa.fi
Freq: Daily
Profile: Kittilä, Muonio and Enontekiö local office of regional newspaper Lapin Kansa.
Language(s): Finnish
REGIONAL DAILY & SUNDAY NEWSPAPERS: Regional Offices

LAPIN KANSA SODANKYLÄ 705651L67E-485

Editorial: Ojennustie 3, 99600 SODANKYLÄ
Tel: 10 66 57 870 **Fax:** 16 61 28 48
Email: paula.hakala@lapinkansa.fi **Web site:** http://www.lapinkansa.fi
Freq: Daily
Profile: Sodankylä local office of regional newspaper Lapin Kansa.
Language(s): Finnish
REGIONAL DAILY & SUNDAY NEWSPAPERS: Regional Offices

LAPSEMME 15012L74D-22

Editorial: PL 141/Toinen Linja 17, 00531 HELSINKI
Tel: 75 32 451 **Fax:** 75 32 45 403
Email: lapsemme@mll.fi **Web site:** http://www.mll.fi
ISSN: 0358-7908
Date Established: 1971; **Freq:** Quarterly; **Circ:** 51,301
Usual Pagination: 52
Profile: Official publication of the Mannerheim League for Child Welfare.
Language(s): Finnish
Readership: Read by families with children.
ADVERTISING RATES:
Full Page Colour .... EUR 2415
SCC .... EUR 22.30
Agency Commission: 15%
Mechanical Data: Type Area: 210 x 285mm, Print Process: offset, Screen: 54 lpc
CONSUMER: WOMEN'S INTEREST CONSUMER MAGAZINES: Child Care

LAPSEN MAAILMA 705412L74D-23

Editorial: Armfeltintie 1, 00150 HELSINKI
Tel: 9 32 96 011 **Fax:** 9 32 96 02 99
Email: lapsen.maailma@lskl.fi **Web site:** http://www.lapsenmaailma-lehti.fi
ISSN: 0786-0188
Date Established: 1938; **Freq:** Monthly; **Circ:** 21,263
Usual Pagination: 52
Managing Editor: Anu Jämsén
Profile: Journal about raising children and teenagers.
Language(s): Finnish
ADVERTISING RATES:
Full Page Colour .... EUR 3250
SCC .... EUR 18.90
Agency Commission: 15%
Mechanical Data: Type Area: 210 x 297mm, No. of Columns (Display): 4, Col Widths (Display): 43mm, Print Process: offset, Film: negative, Screen: 54 lpc
CONSUMER: WOMEN'S INTEREST CONSUMER MAGAZINES: Child Care

LAPUAN SANOMAT 705006L72-725

Editorial: Sanomatie 1, 62100 LAPUA
Tel: 6 43 87 352 **Fax:** 6 43 38 901
Email: toimitus@lapuansanomat.fi **Web site:** http://www.lapuansanomat.fi
ISSN: 0782-5773
Date Established: 1932; **Freq:** 104 issues yearly; **Circ:** 6,546
Usual Pagination: 20
Profile: Newspaper issued in Lapua.
Language(s): Finnish
ADVERTISING RATES:
Full Page Colour .... EUR 2384
SCC .... EUR 11.10
Agency Commission: 15%
Mechanical Data: Print Process: offset, Screen: 34 lpc, No. of Columns (Display): 6, Col Widths (Display): 39mm, Col Length: 355mm, Page Width: 249mm, Type Area: 249 x 355mm
LOCAL NEWSPAPERS

LASTENTARHA 705250L74D-25

Editorial: Rautatieläisenkatu 6, 00520 HELSINKI
Tel: 20 74 89 400 **Fax:** 9 14 27 20
Email: toimitus@lastentarha.fi **Web site:** http://www.lastentarha.fi
ISSN: 0355-5070
Date Established: 1937; **Freq:** Quarterly; **Cover Price:** Free; **Circ:** 14,865
Usual Pagination: 64
Editor-in-Chief: Anne Liimola
Profile: Lastentarha is a magazine for child-care professionals.
Language(s): Finnish
ADVERTISING RATES:
Full Page Colour .... EUR 1753.00
Mechanical Data: Type Area: 190 x 270mm, Col Widths (Display): 56/41mm, No. of Columns (Display): 3/4, Screen: 54 lpc, Print Process: offset, Bleed Size: 210 x 297mm
Average ad content per issue: 10-20%
CONSUMER: WOMEN'S INTEREST CONSUMER MAGAZINES: Child Care

LATU JA POLKU 15305L75L-28

Editorial: Radiokatu 20, 00240 HELSINKI
Tel: 44 72 26 300 **Fax:** 9663376
Email: latujapolku@suomenlatu.fi **Web site:** http://www.suomenlatu.fi
ISSN: 0356-2395
Date Established: 1940; **Freq:** 6 issues yearly - Published 8/year; **Circ:** 51,231
Usual Pagination: 52
Profile: Magazine about sports, travel, camping, mountaineering, hiking, skiing and outdoor pursuits.
Language(s): Finnish
ADVERTISING RATES:
Full Page Colour .... EUR 2650
SCC .... EUR 22.30
Agency Commission: 15%
Mechanical Data: Type Area: 210 x 297mm, No. of Columns (Display): 3/4, Col Widths (Display): 42mm, Print Process: offset, Film: negative, Screen: 60 lpc
Copy instructions: *Copy Date:* 31 days prior to publication date
CONSUMER: SPORT: Outdoor

LAUKAA-KONNEVESI 704932L72-730

Editorial: PL 1/Laukaantie 26, 41341 LAUKAA
Tel: 14 33 97 400 **Fax:** 14 33 97 401
Email: toimitus@laukaa-konnevesi.fi **Web site:** http://www.laukaa-konnevesi.fi
Date Established: 1964; **Freq:** Weekly; **Circ:** 7,583
Usual Pagination: 24
Profile: Local newspaper issued in Laukaa and Konnevesi.
Language(s): Finnish
ADVERTISING RATES:
Full Page Colour .... EUR 3150
SCC .... EUR 12.50
Agency Commission: 15%
Mechanical Data: Col Length: 420mm, No. of Columns (Display): 6, Col Widths (Display): 44mm, Print Process: offset
Editions:
Laukaa-Konnevesi Verkkotoimitus
LOCAL NEWSPAPERS

LAUTTAKYLÄ 704905L72-735

Editorial: PL 36/Karpintie 13, 32701 HUITTINEN
Tel: 2 55 54 200 **Fax:** 2 55 54 220

Email: toimitus@lauttakyla.fi **Web site:** http://www.lauttakyla.fi
ISSN: 1238-7045
Date Established: 1913; **Freq:** 104 issues yearly; **Circ:** 5,385
Usual Pagination: 10
Profile: Newspaper issued in Huittinen, Vampula and Äetsä.
Language(s): Finnish
ADVERTISING RATES:
Full Page Colour .... EUR 2774
SCC .... EUR 11.50
Agency Commission: 15%
Mechanical Data: No. of Columns (Display): 6, Col Widths (Display): 40mm, Print Process: offset, Page Width: 280mm, Col Length: 402mm
LOCAL NEWSPAPERS

LEHTIPISTEUUTISET 705213L53-41
Editorial: PL 1/ Koivuvaarankuja 2, 01641 VANTAA
Tel: 9 85 281 **Fax:** 9 85 28 444
Email: pirjoliisa.lauren@lehtipiste.fi **Web site:** http://www.lehtipiste.fi
ISSN: 0783-7518
Date Established: 1968; **Freq:** Monthly; **Cover Price:** Free; **Circ:** 10,000
Usual Pagination: 32
Profile: Magazine about magazine supplies for retailers and publishers.
Language(s): English; Finnish; Swedish
ADVERTISING RATES:
Full Page Colour .... EUR 2060
SCC .... EUR 34.60

LEIPÄ LEVEÄMMÄKSI 705702L21R-25
Editorial: PL 900/ Mechelininkatu 1 A, 00181 HELSINKI **Tel:** 10 21 51 11 **Fax:** 10 21 52 126
Email: leipa.leveammaksi@yara.com **Web site:** http://www.yara.fi
ISSN: 0356-0813
Date Established: 1953; **Freq:** Quarterly; **Cover Price:** Free; **Circ:** 65,000
Usual Pagination: 60
Editor-in-Chief: Seija Luomanperä; **Managing Editor:** Tuulikki Suihkonen
Profile: Customer-magazine for farmers about fertilisers, soil improvement and plant protection.
Language(s): Finnish
Readership: Customers of Yara Suomi, former Kemira GrowHow Oyj.
BUSINESS: AGRICULTURE & FARMING: Agriculture & Farming Related

LEIPURI 14913L8A-10
Editorial: PL 115/ Pasilankatu 2, 00241 HELSINKI
Tel: 9 14 88 73 00 **Fax:** 9 14 88 73 01
Email: elina.matikainen@leipuriliitto.fi **Web site:** http://www.leipuriliitto.fi
ISSN: 0024-0699
Date Established: 1903; **Freq:** 6 issues yearly; **Circ:** 1,379
Usual Pagination: 40
Editor-in-Chief: Mika Väyrynen; **Managing Editor:** Elina Matikainen
Profile: Magazine about baking and confectionery.
Language(s): Finnish
Readership: Read by people working in the baking and confectionery industry.
ADVERTISING RATES:
Full Page Colour .... EUR 1950.00
SCC .... EUR 23.90
Agency Commission: 15%
Mechanical Data: Type Area: 260 x 185mm, Screen: 60 lpc, Trim Size: 297 x 210mm, Page Width: 185mm, Print Process: Offset, Col Length: 271mm, Film: Positive or digital material, Col Widths (Display): 90mm, No. of Columns (Display): 2
Copy instructions: *Copy Date:* 4 weeks prior to publication
BUSINESS: BAKING & CONFECTIONERY: Baking

LEMMIKKI 15338L81X-50
Editorial: Maistraatinportti 1, 00015 OTAVAMEDIA
Tel: 9 15 661 **Fax:** 9 15 66 788
Email: lemmikki@otavamedia.fi **Web site:** http://www.otavamedia.fi/web/guest/lemmikki
ISSN: 0787-6424
Date Established: 1990; **Freq:** Monthly; **Circ:** 19,343
Usual Pagination: 64
Profile: Magazine about animals, particularly domestic pets.
Language(s): Finnish
Readership: Aimed at young people in Finland.
ADVERTISING RATES:
Full Page Colour .... EUR 1400
SCC .... EUR 16.60
Mechanical Data: Bleed Size: 280 x 217mm, Print Process: Offset, Film: Digital negative, Type Area: 217 x 280mm
Copy instructions: *Copy Date:* 19 days prior to publication date
CONSUMER: ANIMALS & PETS

LEMPÄÄLÄN-VESILAHDEN SANOMAT 704906L72-745
Editorial: PL 38 / Tampereentie 17, 37501 LEMPÄÄLÄ **Tel:** 3 34 29 000 **Fax:** 3 34 29 030
Email: toimitus@lvs.fi **Web site:** http://www.lvs.fi
Date Established: 1931; **Freq:** 104 issues yearly; **Circ:** 7,131
Usual Pagination: 12
Managing Editor: Satu Lehtonen
Profile: Newspaper issued in Lempäälä and Vesilahti.
Language(s): Finnish
ADVERTISING RATES:
Full Page Colour .... EUR 3312
SCC .... EUR 3.30
Mechanical Data: Col Length: 365mm, No. of Columns (Display): 6, Col Widths (Display): 40mm, Print Process: offset, Page Width: 260mm
LOCAL NEWSPAPERS

LEPPIS 705434L91D-67
Editorial: Maistraatinportti 1, 00015 OTAVAMEDIA
Tel: 9 15 661 **Fax:** 9 15 66 788
Email: leppis@otavamedia.fi **Web site:** http://www.otavamedia.fi
ISSN: 0784-2546
Date Established: 1996; **Freq:** Monthly - Published 8/year; **Circ:** 11,791
Usual Pagination: 40
Managing Editor: Leea Puranen
Profile: Magazine with fairy tales, plays and games for small children and their parents.
Language(s): Finnish
Readership: Children of age 2-7.
ADVERTISING RATES:
Full Page Colour .... EUR 1390
Mechanical Data: Type Area: 230 x 260mm, Print Process: offset, Film: positive, Screen: 60 lpc
CONSUMER: RECREATION & LEISURE: Children & Youth

LESTIJOKI 705007L72-755
Formerly: Lestinjoki
Editorial: PL 1 / Valtakatu 9, 69101 KANNUS
Tel: 20 75 04 650 **Fax:** 20 75 04 659
Email: toimitus@lestijoki-lehti.fi **Web site:** http://www.lestijoki-lehti.fi
ISSN: 0782-5617
Date Established: 1975; **Freq:** Weekly; **Circ:** 5,045
Usual Pagination: 16
Profile: Newspaper issued in Kannus, Toholampi, Lestijärvi, Himanka and Lohtaja.
Language(s): Finnish
ADVERTISING RATES:
Full Page Colour .... EUR 2409
SCC .... EUR 11
Agency Commission: 15%
Mechanical Data: Col Length: 365mm, Page Width: 255mm, Col Widths (Display): 39mm, No. of Columns (Display): 6
Editions:
Lestijoki Verkkotoimitus
LOCAL NEWSPAPERS

LEVI. NYT! 706616L89A-3
Editorial: Luhtapolku 7, 99140 KÖNGÄS
Tel: 16 65 31 55 **Fax:** 16 65 31 55
Email: levi.nyt@gmail.com **Web site:** http://www.levinyt.fi
ISSN: 1457-6813
Date Established: 2000; **Freq:** 26 issues yearly - Issued weekly until May, after that sporadically throughout the year; Free to qualifying individuals ; **Circ:** 12,000
Usual Pagination: 12
Profile: Magazine about travel activities in winter resort Levi.
Language(s): English; Finnish
Readership: Tourists and cabin owners in Levi.
ADVERTISING RATES:
Full Page Colour .... EUR 2376
SCC .... EUR 11
Mechanical Data: No. of Columns (Display): 6, Col Widths (Display): 44.5mm
Copy instructions: *Copy Date:* 28 days prior to publication date

LIEKSAN LEHTI 704973L72-760
Editorial: PL 22/ Siltakatu 1, 81701 LIEKSA
Tel: 10 23 08 650 **Fax:** 10 23 08 690
Email: toimitus@lieksanlehti.fi **Web site:** http://www.lieksanlehti.fi
ISSN: 0782-6397
Date Established: 1954; **Freq:** 104 issues yearly; **Circ:** 6,454
Usual Pagination: 12
Profile: Newspaper issued in Lieksa.
Language(s): Finnish
ADVERTISING RATES:
Full Page Colour .... EUR 3373
SCC .... EUR 15.80
Agency Commission: 15%
Mechanical Data: Col Widths (Display): 38.75mm, Col Length: 365mm, No. of Columns (Display): 6, Type Area: 240 x 360mm, Print Process: offset, Page Width: 255mm
LOCAL NEWSPAPERS

LIHALEHTI 14995L22D-50
Editorial: Vuorikatu 8 A 19, 00100 HELSINKI
Tel: 9 41 88 76 32 **Fax:** 941887634
Email: veli.saarenheimo@lihakeskusliitto.fi **Web site:** http://www.lihalehti.fi
ISSN: 0786-9444
Date Established: 1936; **Freq:** 6 issues yearly - Published 8/year; **Circ:** 4,675
Usual Pagination: 64
Editor-in-Chief: Veli Saarenheimo; **Managing Editor:** Mari Hannuksela
Profile: Journal for the meat industry and food trade.
Language(s): Finnish
Readership: Read by decision-makers in top and middle management of the Finnish meat, food and catering industries.
ADVERTISING RATES:
Full Page Colour .... EUR 1890
SCC .... EUR 18.10
Mechanical Data: Bleed Size: 210 x 297mm, Type Area: 177 x 260mm, No. of Columns (Display): 4, Col Widths (Display): 41mm, Screen: 60 lpc, Film: positive, Print Process: offset
Average ad content per issue: 30%
BUSINESS: FOOD: Meat Trade

LIHATALOUS 14996L21D-3
Editorial: PL 77, 00101 HELSINKI **Fax:** 9 69 48 845
Web site: http://www.ltk.fi
ISSN: 1236-1895
Date Established: 1943; **Freq:** 6 issues yearly - Published 8/year; **Annual Sub.:** EUR 96; **Circ:** 2,481
Usual Pagination: 52
Managing Editor: Vesa Jääskeläinen
Profile: Publication dealing with farm management and cattle, includes environmental and veterinary issues concerning meat production.
Language(s): Finnish
Readership: Read by farmers, veterinarians and experts of the meat industry.
ADVERTISING RATES:
Full Page Colour .... EUR 1650
SCC .... EUR 21.40
Agency Commission: 15%
Mechanical Data: Type Area: 230 x 273mm, No. of Columns (Display): 4/3, Col Widths (Display): 46mm/63mm, Print Process: Offset, Col Length: 273mm, Page Width: 230mm, Bleed Size: 230 x 273mm, Screen: 54-60 lpc, Film: negative
Copy instructions: *Copy Date:* 15 days prior to publication date
BUSINESS: AGRICULTURE & FARMING: Livestock

LIIKETALOUDELLINEN AIKAKAUSKIRJA 705143L1A-9_30
Editorial: PL 1210/ Runeberginkatu 22-24, 00101 HELSINKI **Tel:** 9 43 13 84 69 **Fax:** 9 43 13 86 78
Email: LTA@hse.fi **Web site:** http://lta.hse.fi
ISSN: 0024-3469
Date Established: 1952; **Freq:** Quarterly; **Annual Sub.:** EUR 31.00; **Circ:** 1,500
Usual Pagination: 180
Profile: The Association for Business Studies Administration aims to promote and support the research for business science and business economics of enterprises in Finland.
Language(s): English; Finnish; Swedish
BUSINESS: FINANCE & ECONOMICS

LIIKETALOUS 14949L14A-14
Formerly: LTA Liiketalous
Editorial: Asemamiehenkatu 2, 00520 HELSINKI
Tel: 9 22 94 71 71 **Fax:** 9 86 83 42 50
Email: toimitus@liiketaloudenliitto.fi **Web site:** http://www.liiketalous.fi
ISSN: 1239-6044
Date Established: 1958; **Freq:** Quarterly; **Circ:** 6,735
Usual Pagination: 32
Editor-in-Chief: Annina Antell
Profile: Publication about the business world.
Language(s): Finnish
Readership: Read by graduates from commercial colleges.
BUSINESS: COMMERCE, INDUSTRY & MANAGEMENT

LINNANMÄKI-UUTISET 706320L91D-68
Editorial: PL 37/ Tivolikuja 1, 00101 HELSINKI
Tel: 9 77 39 91
Web site: http://www.linnanmaki.fi
Freq: Annual; **Circ:** 500,000
Profile: Magazine about activities in the amusement park Linnanmäki.
Language(s): Finnish
CONSUMER: RECREATION & LEISURE: Children & Youth

LION/LEIJONA 705737L64C-300
Editorial: Kirkonkyläntie 10, 00700 HELSINKI
Tel: 9 56 55 95 11 **Fax:** 9 56 55 95 55
Email: toimitus@lions.fi **Web site:** http://www.lions.fi
ISSN: 0356-5149
Date Established: 1955; **Freq:** 6 issues yearly; **Cover Price:** Free; **Circ:** 28,205
Usual Pagination: 64
Editor: Bo Lindberg; **Editor-in-Chief:** Raimo Naumanen
Profile: Magazine focusing on various activities available to members of the Lions organisation.
Language(s): Finnish; Swedish
ADVERTISING RATES:
Full Page Colour .... EUR 2250.00
Agency Commission: 15%
Mechanical Data: Col Widths (Display): 44mm, Type Area: 188 x 271mm, No. of Columns (Display): 4, Screen: 60 lpc, Print Process: offset
BUSINESS: OTHER CLASSIFICATIONS: Clubs

LOCUS 706095L4D-50
Editorial: Annankatu 24, 2. krs., 00100 HELSINKI
Tel: 9 41 66 76 500 **Fax:** 9 64 87 45
Email: lasse.talvitie@locuslehti.fi **Web site:** http://www.locuslehti.fi
ISSN: 1455-7215
Date Established: 1997; **Freq:** Quarterly; **Circ:** 5,000
Usual Pagination: 52
Editor-in-Chief: Lasse Talvitie
Profile: Magazine on real estate and construction industry. Focus on company management personnel.
Language(s): Finnish
ADVERTISING RATES:
Full Page Colour .... EUR 2650
SCC .... EUR 35.30
Agency Commission: 15%
Mechanical Data: Col Length: 262mm, Type Area: 177 x 262mm, No. of Columns (Display): 4, Col Widths (Display): 41mm, Print Process: offset

LOG ON 762045L49C-20
Formerly: KHT
Editorial: Asemamiehenkatu 4, 00520 HELSINKI
Tel: 20 11 30 200 **Fax:** 20 11 30 201
Email: ritva.vayrynen@erto.fi **Web site:** http://www.logistiikantoimihenkilot.fi
ISSN: 0788-026X
Date Established: 1990; **Freq:** Quarterly; **Cover Price:** Free; **Circ:** 5,000
Usual Pagination: 8
Editor-in-Chief: Ritva Väyrynen
Profile: Magazine about working in the transport and logistics business.
Language(s): Finnish

LOGISTIIKKA 14917L10-60
Editorial: Särkiniementie 3, 00210 HELSINKI
Tel: 9 69 63 752 **Fax:** 9 63 16 72
Email: logistiikka@logy.fi **Web site:** http://www.logy.fi
ISSN: 1238-6022
Date Established: 1995; **Freq:** 6 issues yearly; **Circ:** 6,000
Usual Pagination: 68
Editor-in-Chief: Mikko Melasniemi
Profile: Journal of the Finnish Association of Logistics, covering materials handling, packing, transport services and logistics. Also features new products and national and world news.
Language(s): English; Finnish; German
Readership: Aimed at decision makers in purchasing and logistic services.
ADVERTISING RATES:
Full Page Colour .... EUR 2930.00
SCC .... EUR 35.20
Mechanical Data: Screen: 60 lpc, Type Area: 277 x 200mm, Bleed Size: 297 x 220mm
Copy instructions: *Copy Date:* 10 days prior to publication date

LOIMAAN LEHTI 704892L72-765
Editorial: PL 2/Kartanomäenkatu 4, 32201 LOIMAA
Tel: 2 58 88 000 **Fax:** 2 76 31 233
Email: toimitus@loimaanlehti.fi **Web site:** http://www.loimaanlehti.fi
ISSN: 0358-9161
Date Established: 1915; **Freq:** 104 issues yearly; **Circ:** 8,717
Usual Pagination: 12
Profile: Newspaper issued in Loimaa, Alastaro, Mellilä and Oripää.
Language(s): Finnish
ADVERTISING RATES:
Full Page Colour .... EUR 4477
SCC .... EUR 18.20
Agency Commission: 15%
Mechanical Data: Col Length: 410mm, Page Width: 315mm, Bleed Size: 315 x 460mm, Col Widths (Display): 44mm, No. of Columns (Display): 6, Print Process: offset
Editions:
Loimaan Lehti Verkkotoimitus
LOCAL NEWSPAPERS

LÖÖPPI 2056568L2A-32
Editorial: Hietalahdenkatu 2 B 23, 00180 HELSINKI
Tel: 9 61 10 55
Web site: http://www.sal-info.org
Freq: Quarterly; **Circ:** 3,000
Editor-in-Chief: Ismo Lehtonen
Profile: Magazine for the members of The Finnish Association of Magazine Editors.
Language(s): Finnish
Readership: Liiton jäsenet, aikakauslehti- ja kustannustoimittajat. / Members of the association.
ADVERTISING RATES:
Full Page Colour .... EUR 800.00

LOUNAISRANTA SYDVÄSTBLADET 14867L1A-60
Formerly: Talous 2000 Business News
Editorial: PL 275/ Yliopistonkatu 23 A, 2 krs, 20101 TURKU **Tel:** 2 25 01 738
Email: lounaisranta@pelipeitto.fi **Web site:** http://www.pelipeitto.fi
ISSN: 0787-0590
Date Established: 1991; **Freq:** Quarterly; **Cover Price:** Free; **Circ:** 28,000
Usual Pagination: 12
Profile: Magazine containing articles and information on finance and economics.
Language(s): Finnish
Readership: Read by managers in business and industry.
ADVERTISING RATES:
SCC .... EUR 13
Agency Commission: 15%

Mechanical Data: No. of Columns (Display): 6, Col Widths (Display): 41mm, Col Length: 385mm, Type Area: 260 x 385mm, Film: negative
BUSINESS: FINANCE & ECONOMICS

LOVIISAN SANOMAT 15203L72-780
Editorial: PL 42 / Sibeliuksenkatu 10, 07901 LOVIISA
Tel: 19 53 27 01 **Fax:** 19 53 27 06
Email: toimitus@lovari.fi **Web site:** http://www.loviisansanomat.net
ISSN: 0356-1291
Date Established: 1916; **Freq:** 104 issues yearly; **Circ:** 4,417
Usual Pagination: 20
Editor-in-Chief: Arto Henriksson; **Managing Editor:** Auli Silmäri
Profile: Newspaper issued in Loviisa, Lapinjärvi, Liljendal, Pernaja and Ruotsinpyhtää.
Language(s): Finnish
ADVERTISING RATES:
Full Page Colour .... EUR 3172
SCC .... EUR 14.10
Agency Commission: 15%
Mechanical Data: Page Width: 255mm, Col Length: 375mm, No. of Columns (Display): 6, Col Widths (Display): 40mm, Print Process: offset
Editions:
Loviisan Sanomat Verkkotoimitus
Supplement(s): Pyhtäänlehti - Pyttisbladet - 26xY
LOCAL NEWSPAPERS

LUONNONSUOJELIJA 15125L57-50
Editorial: Kotkankatu 9, 00510 HELSINKI
Tel: 9 22 80 81 **Fax:** 922808200
Web site: http://www.sll.fi/jasensivut/luonnonsuojelija
ISSN: 0788-8708
Date Established: 1975; **Freq:** 6 issues yearly; **Circ:** 34,400
Usual Pagination: 12
Editor-in-Chief: Matti Nieminen
Profile: Official journal of the Finnish Association for Nature Conservation.
Language(s): Finnish
Readership: Aimed at the members of the Association.
ADVERTISING RATES:
Full Page Colour .... EUR 2500
SCC .... EUR 13.80

LUONNONTIETEIDEN AKATEEMISET 14923L55-15
Formerly: Kemisti Kemisten
Editorial: Pohjoinen Makasiinikatu 6 A, 4. kerros, 00130 HELSINKI **Tel:** 9 25 11 16 60
Fax: 9 25 11 16 71
Email: anna.melkas@luonnontieteilijat.fi **Web site:** http://www.luonnontieteilijat.fi
ISSN: 1457-9936
Date Established: 1958; **Freq:** 6 issues yearly; **Circ:** 6,312
Usual Pagination: 32
Editor-in-Chief: Anna Melkas
Profile: Magazine containing professional and social information about scientists and reviews of the chemical and biotechnological industry. Published by the Finnish Union of experts of Science.
Language(s): Finnish
ADVERTISING RATES:
Full Page Colour .... EUR 1500.00
SCC .... EUR 21.30
Mechanical Data: Bleed Size: 210 x 270mm, Type Area: 175 x 230mm, No. of Columns (Display): 2/3, Col Widths (Display): 55/84mm, Print Process: offset, Screen: 60 lpc, Film: negative
BUSINESS: APPLIED SCIENCE & LABORATORIES

LUONTAISTUNTIJA 705414L37-80
Editorial: Laivanvarustajankatu 9 A, 00140 HELSINKI
Tel: 9 80 94 481 **Fax:** 9 80 94 482
Web site: http://www.luontaistuntijat.fi
ISSN: 0785-0433
Freq: 6 issues yearly; **Cover Price:** Free
Free to qualifying individuals
Annual Sub.: EUR 10.00; **Circ:** 500,000
Usual Pagination: 24
Editor-in-Chief: Marjut Myllymäki
Profile: Magazine about alternative medicine retail chain.
Language(s): Finnish
ADVERTISING RATES:
Full Page Colour .... EUR 5390.00
SCC .... EUR 50.40
BUSINESS: PHARMACEUTICAL & CHEMISTS

LUOTEISVÄYLÄ 704945L72-1495
Formerly: Uutismarkku
Editorial: Finpyyntie 9, 29600 NOORMARKKU
Tel: 10 66 55 640 **Fax:** 2 64 18 282
Email: toimitus.luoteisvayla@sps.fi **Web site:** http://www.uutismarkku.fi
ISSN: 1239-1093
Date Established: 1978; **Freq:** Weekly; **Circ:** 2,939
Usual Pagination: 12
Editor-in-Chief: Teijo Mäki
Profile: Newspaper issued in Noormarkku and Pomarkku.
Language(s): Finnish
ADVERTISING RATES:
Full Page Colour .... EUR 2321
SCC .... EUR 10.60
Agency Commission: 15%

Mechanical Data: No. of Columns (Display): 6, Type Area: 260 x 380mm, Col Widths (Display): 40mm
LOCAL NEWSPAPERS

LUOTTOLISTA 705144L1G-5
Editorial: PL 16/ Työpajankatu 10 A, 00581 HELSINKI **Tel:** 10 27 07 000 **Fax:** 10 27 07 338
Email: ville.kauppi@asiakastieto.fi **Web site:** http://www.asiakastieto.fi
ISSN: 0787-9873
Date Established: 1983; **Freq:** 26 issues yearly; **Circ:** 5,230
Usual Pagination: 16
Editor-in-Chief: Ville Kauppi
Profile: Magazine of Suomen Asiakastieto, containing information on their credit business.
Language(s): Finnish
Readership: Read by customers and prospects.
ADVERTISING RATES:
Full Page Colour .... EUR 1400.00
Agency Commission: 15%
Mechanical Data: Type Area: 192 x 275mm, Col Widths (Display): 57mm, Print Process: offset, Film: negative, Screen: 54 lpc, No. of Columns (Display): 4
BUSINESS: FINANCE & ECONOMICS: Credit Trading

LUPPI 705964L57-51
Editorial: Mechelininkatu 36, 00260 HELSINKI
Tel: 9 44 63 13 **Fax:** 9 44 66 04
Email: lup@luontoliitto.fi **Web site:** http://www.luontoliitto.fi/luppi
Freq: Half-yearly; **Cover Price:** Free; **Circ:** 1,800
Usual Pagination: 12
Editor-in-Chief: Petro Pynnönen
Profile: Magazine for environmental activists in the Uusimaa region.
Language(s): Finnish

LUUMÄEN LEHTI 704956L72-800
Editorial: Linnalantie 53, 54500 TAAVETTI
Tel: 5 45 72 301 **Fax:** 5 45 72 303
Web site: http://www.luumaenlehti.fi
ISSN: 1457-7372
Date Established: 1963; **Freq:** Weekly; **Circ:** 3,572
Usual Pagination: 12
Profile: Newspaper issued in Luumäki.
Language(s): Finnish
ADVERTISING RATES:
Full Page Colour .... EUR 2786
SCC .... EUR 12.90
Agency Commission: 15%
Mechanical Data: No. of Columns (Display): 6, Col Length: 370mm, Type Area: 249 x 370mm, Col Widths (Display): 37.5mm, Print Process: offset, Page Width: 249mm
LOCAL NEWSPAPERS

LXRY MAGAZINE 1841178L74Q-61
Editorial: PL 1421, 00101 HELSINKI
Tel: 44 95 63 308
Email: info@lxry.fi **Web site:** http://www.lxry.fi
Date Established: 2008; **Freq:** Quarterly; **Circ:** 20,000
Editor-in-Chief: Charles Kuhlman
Profile: Magazine about luxury lifestyle.
Language(s): Finnish
Readership: Urban, wealthy people of age 28-55.
ADVERTISING RATES:
Full Page Colour .... EUR 4800.00
SCC .... EUR 58.30

MAAILMANKAUPPALEHTI 716248L14C-22
Editorial: c/o Saloranta, Huugontie 8, 40900 SÄYNÄTSALO **Tel:** 45 67 05 645
Web site: http://www.maailmankaupat.fi
ISSN: 1455-6987
Date Established: 1984; **Freq:** Quarterly; **Circ:** 15,000
Usual Pagination: 20
Editor-in-Chief: Anastasia Lapintie
Profile: Magazine about fair trade between the Western and the Third World.
Language(s): Finnish

MAALI! 15291L75B-50
Formerly: Futari
Editorial: PL 410/ Risto Rytin tie 33, 00811 HELSINKI
Tel: 9 42 42 73 30 **Fax:** 9 42 42 73 33
Web site: http://www.palloliitto.fi/viestinta/maali_spl_n_jasenlehti
ISSN: 0359-4378
Date Established: 1982; **Freq:** Quarterly; **Circ:** 80,000
Usual Pagination: 56
Editor-in-Chief: Sami Terävä; **Managing Editor:** Jouko Vuorela
Profile: Publication of the Football Association of Finland.
Language(s): Finnish
Readership: Read by registered players and friends of the Association, also enthusiasts.
ADVERTISING RATES:
Full Page Colour .... EUR 3740
Mechanical Data: Type Area: 188 x 273mm, No. of Columns (Display): 4, Print Process: Offset, Screen: 60 lpc
CONSUMER: SPORT: Football

MAALLA 1930446L74C-108
Editorial: Maistraatinportti 1, 00015 OTAVAMEDIA
Tel: 9 15 661 **Fax:** 9 14 77 24
Email: maalla@otavamedia.fi **Web site:** http://www.maalla.fi
Freq: Quarterly; **Circ:** 86,594
Editor-in-Chief: Erja Salovaara; **Managing Editor:** Ann-Mari Lehtonen
Language(s): Finnish
ADVERTISING RATES:
Full Page Colour .... EUR 4550
SCC .... EUR 38.20
Copy instructions: *Copy Date:* 20 days prior to publication date
CONSUMER: WOMEN'S INTEREST CONSUMER MAGAZINES: Home & Family

MAANOMISTAJA 705316L21A-42
Editorial: Urheilutie 6 D, 01370 VANTAA
Tel: 9 13 56 511 **Fax:** 9 13 57 100
Email: toimisto@maanomistajainliitto.fi **Web site:** http://www.maanomistajainliitto.fi
ISSN: 0355-0478
Freq: Quarterly; **Annual Sub.:** EUR 20.00; **Circ:** 3,000
Usual Pagination: 12
Editor-in-Chief: Tuija Nummela
Profile: Magazine about the rights and benefits of farm owners.
Language(s): Finnish
ADVERTISING RATES:
Full Page Colour .... EUR 970.00
Mechanical Data: Bleed Size: 280 x 400mm, Type Area: 250 x 365mm, No. of Columns (Display): 4, Col Widths (Display): 60mm, Print Process: offset

MAASELKÄ 705018L72-810
Editorial: PL 74/ Puistokatu 37, 85801 HAAPAJÄRVI
Tel: 8 77 27 500 **Fax:** 87727555
Email: toimitus@maaselkalehti.fi **Web site:** http://www.maaselkalehti.fi
ISSN: 0789-8150
Date Established: 1961; **Freq:** 104 issues yearly; **Circ:** 4,416
Usual Pagination: 24
Profile: Newspaper issued in Haapajärvi and Reisjärvi.
Language(s): Finnish
ADVERTISING RATES:
Full Page Colour .... EUR 2208
SCC .... EUR 9.20
Agency Commission: 15%
Mechanical Data: Page Width: 284mm, Col Length: 410mm, No. of Columns (Display): 6, Col Widths (Display): 44mm, Print Process: offset
Copy instructions: *Copy Date:* 10 days prior to publication date
Editions:
Maaselkä Verkkotoimitus
LOCAL NEWSPAPERS

MAASEUDUN TULEVAISUUS 14985L65A-41
Editorial: PL 440/ Simonkatu 6, 00101 HELSINKI
Tel: 20 41 32 100 **Fax:** 9 69 43 717
Email: toimitus@maaseuduntulevaisuus.fi **Web site:** http://www.maaseuduntulevaisuus.fi
ISSN: 0355-3787
Date Established: 1916; **Freq:** 104 issues yearly - Published Monday, Wednesday and Friday; **Circ:** 83,158
Usual Pagination: 16
Editor-in-Chief: Lauri Kontro; **Managing Editor:** Jussi Martikainen
Profile: Official newspaper of the Finnish Farmers' Union.
Language(s): Finnish
ADVERTISING RATES:
Full Page Colour .... EUR 16925
SCC .... EUR 42
Agency Commission: 15%
Mechanical Data: Screen: 34-40 lpc, Print Process: Offset, No. of Columns (Display): 8, Col Widths (Display): 44mm, Col Length: 510mm, Page Width: 380mm
Copy instructions: *Copy Date:* 10 days prior to publication date
Editions:
Maaseudun Tulevaisuus Verkkotoimitus
NATIONAL DAILY & SUNDAY NEWSPAPERS: National Daily Newspapers

MAATILAN PELLERVO 623241L21A-57
Editorial: PL 77/ Simonkatu 6, 00101 HELSINKI
Tel: 9 47 67 501 **Fax:** 96948845
Email: toimisto@pellervo.fi **Web site:** http://www.pellervo.fi
ISSN: 1456-7229
Freq: Monthly - Published 10/year; **Circ:** 16,050
Usual Pagination: 76
Editor-in-Chief: Teemu Pakarinen; **Managing Editor:** Markku Nummi
Profile: Magazine containing information on agriculture in Finland.
Language(s): Finnish
Readership: Aimed at farmers in Finland.
ADVERTISING RATES:
Full Page Colour .... EUR 3179
SCC .... EUR 29.40
Agency Commission: 15%
Mechanical Data: Type Area: 270 x 185mm, Print Process: Offset, Trim Size: 297 x 210mm, Col Widths (Display): 43mm, No. of Columns (Display): 4, Screen: 54-60 lpc, Film: Digital material, Col Length: 270mm, Page Width: 185mm
Copy instructions: *Copy Date:* 14 days prior to publication date
BUSINESS: AGRICULTURE & FARMING

MAATILAN PIRKKA - ÅKER BIRKA 15083L21E-65
Editorial: PL 410/ Risto Rytin tie 33, 00811 HELSINKI
Tel: 9 42 42 73 30 **Fax:** 9 42 42 73 33
Email: maatilanpirkka@dialogi.fi **Web site:** http://www.maatilan.pirkka.fi
Date Established: 1972; **Freq:** Quarterly - Published 5/year; **Cover Price:** Free; **Circ:** 49,055
Usual Pagination: 64
Editor-in-Chief: Anne Penttilä
Profile: Publication covering farming, farming technology and animal husbandry.
Language(s): Finnish; Swedish
Readership: Aimed at Finnish farmers.
ADVERTISING RATES:
Full Page Colour .... EUR 2468
SCC .... EUR 27.70
Agency Commission: 15%
Mechanical Data: Type Area: 270 x 190mm, Bleed Size: 297 x 210mm, Film: Positive, right reading, emulsion side down, Screen: 54 lpc, Col Length: 270mm, Page Width: 190mm
BUSINESS: AGRICULTURE & FARMING: Agriculture - Machinery & Plant

MAAVIESTI 705319L21A-58
Editorial: PL 106/ Kauppurienkatu 23, 90101 OULU
Tel: 8 31 68 611 **Fax:** 8 37 30 75
Email: ella.karttimo@proagria.fi **Web site:** http://www.oulunmaaseutukeskus.fi
ISSN: 0788-0979
Date Established: 1946; **Freq:** Quarterly; **Cover Price:** Free; **Circ:** 12,000
Usual Pagination: 32
Editor-in-Chief: Vesa Nuolioja; **Managing Editor:** Ella Karttimo
Profile: Magazine about farming, forestry and fishery.
Language(s): Finnish
Readership: Agriculture households in Kainuu and Oulu.
ADVERTISING RATES:
Full Page Colour .... EUR 1600.00
SCC .... EUR 20.00
Agency Commission: 15%
Mechanical Data: Bleed Size: 280 x 400mm, Type Area: 252 x 366mm, No. of Columns (Display): 6, Col Widths (Display): 37.5mm, Screen: 32 lpc, Film: negative, Print Process: offset

MADE IN EU 2029450L14A-161
Editorial: Pengerkatu 2, 67100 KOKKOLA
Tel: 46 57 48 571
Email: info@zonetradeservices.eu **Web site:** http://www.zonetradeservices.eu
Freq: Quarterly; **Circ:** 28,000
Profile: Magazine informing importers outside the EU of companies operating within the EU.
Language(s): English; Finnish
Readership: Entrepreneurs as well as management of import/export companies.
ADVERTISING RATES:
Full Page Colour .... EUR 1000.00

MAINE 752655L2A-3
Editorial: Antbackantie 4 D 22, 02400 KIRKKONUMMI **Tel:** 400 39 26 60
Email: pekka.virolainen@mainemedia.fi **Web site:** http://www.maine-lehti.fi
Date Established: 2001; **Freq:** Half-yearly; **Circ:** 8,000
Usual Pagination: 40
Editor-in-Chief: Pekka Virolainen; **Publisher:** Kimmo Korpijaakko
Profile: Magazine about communications by using company cases.
Language(s): Finnish
Readership: People working in the communications and IR sector.
ADVERTISING RATES:
Full Page Colour .... EUR 3250.00
SCC .... EUR 36.40
Mechanical Data: Type Area: 225 x 310mm

MAINOSTAJA 1623218L2A-8
Editorial: Erottajankatu 19 B, 00130 HELSINKI
Tel: 9 68 60 840 **Fax:** 9 68 60 84 20
Email: ml@mainostajat.fi **Web site:** http://www.mainostajat.fi
ISSN: 1459-4811
Date Established: 2003; **Freq:** Quarterly; **Circ:** 4,500
Usual Pagination: 56
Editor-in-Chief: Janne Häivälä
Profile: Magazine about advertising and marketing.
Language(s): Finnish
Readership: Members of the Association of Finnish Advertisers.
ADVERTISING RATES:
Full Page Colour .... EUR 1990.00
Mechanical Data: Type Area: 320 x 300mm, Print Process: offset, Screen: 54 lpc

MAKU 1614097L74P-50
Editorial: Risto Rytin tie 33, 00081 A-LEHDET
Tel: 9 75 961 **Fax:** 9 75 98 31 18

Email: maku@a-lehdet.fi **Web site:** http://www.maku.fi
ISSN: 1459-4447
Date Established: 2003; **Freq:** 6 issues yearly; **Circ:** 49,855
Usual Pagination: 100
Editor-in-Chief: Marita Joutjärvi; **Managing Editor:** Helena Saine-Laitinen
Profile: Magazine about food and cookery.
Language(s): Finnish
ADVERTISING RATES:
Full Page Colour .... EUR 5100
SCC .... EUR 47.70
Mechanical Data: Bleed Size: 230 x 273mm, Type Area: 190 x 267mm, No. of Columns (Display): 4, Print Process: offset, Screen: 60 lpc
Copy instructions: *Copy Date:* 14 days prior to publication date
CONSUMER: WOMEN'S INTEREST CONSUMER MAGAZINES: Food & Cookery

MÄNTSÄLÄ 704882L72-820

Formerly: Mäntsälä-Lehti
Editorial: Keskuskatu 4, 04601 MÄNTSÄLÄ
Tel: 20 61 00 152 **Fax:** 20 77 03 019
Email: toimitus@lehtiyhtyma.fi **Web site:** http://www.mantsalalehti.fi
ISSN: 0782-6206
Date Established: 1972; **Freq:** 104 issues yearly; **Circ:** 3,745
Usual Pagination: 16
Editor-in-Chief: Katri Hämäläinen
Profile: Newspaper issued in Mäntsälä, Pornainen and Pukkila.
Language(s): Finnish
ADVERTISING RATES:
Full Page Colour .... EUR 2131
SCC .... EUR 9.60
Agency Commission: 15%
Mechanical Data: No. of Columns (Display): 5, Col Length: 370mm, Page Width: 255mm, Col Widths (Display): 47mm
Editions:
Mäntsälä Verkkotoimitus
LOCAL NEWSPAPERS

MARKKINAVIESTI 1983560L53-204

Editorial: PL 58, 29201 HARJAVALTA
Tel: 20 74 98 707 **Fax:** 20 74 98 701
Email: markkinaviesti@markkina.net **Web site:** http://www.markkina.net/markkinaviesti
Freq: 6 issues yearly - 9/year; **Circ:** 4,500
Editor-in-Chief: Ari Kallas
Profile: Magazine for event organisers and market controllers.
Language(s): Finnish
Readership: Kauppiaat, kaupunkien ja kuntien tori- ja markkinavastaavat sekä markkina- ja messujärjestäjät. / Traders, market responsibles of cities and boroughs as well as market and fair organisers.
ADVERTISING RATES:
Full Page Colour .... EUR 1062.00

MARKKINOINTI & MAINONTA 14884L2-15

Editorial: PL 920/ Annankatu 34-36 B, 00101 HELSINKI **Tel:** 20 44 240 **Fax:** 20 44 24 102
Email: toimitus@marmai.fi **Web site:** http://www.marmai.fi
ISSN: 1237-6655
Date Established: 1996; **Freq:** Weekly; **Circ:** 9,470
Usual Pagination: 32
Editor-in-Chief: Reijo Ruokanen; **Managing Editor:** Mattias Erkkilä
Profile: Magazine about marketing, emphasising advertising and the media.
Language(s): Finnish
Readership: Read by people working in marketing.
ADVERTISING RATES:
Full Page Colour .... EUR 7300
SCC .... EUR 62
Agency Commission: 5-15%
Mechanical Data: Trim Size: 260 x 380mm, Screen: 40 lpc, Print Process: Offset, Col Length: 380mm, Page Width: 260mm, No. of Columns (Display): 5, Col Widths (Display): 47mm
Editions:
Marmai.fi
BUSINESS: COMMUNICATIONS, ADVERTISING & MARKETING

MARTAT 15259L74A-29_5

Formerly: Emäntälehti Martat
Editorial: Lapinlahdenkatu 3 A, 00180 HELSINKI
Tel: 10 83 85 500 **Fax:** 10 83 85 601
Email: lehti@martat.fi **Web site:** http://www.martat.fi
ISSN: 0014-6522
Date Established: 1902; **Freq:** 6 issues yearly - Published 8/year; **Circ:** 36,360
Usual Pagination: 48
Managing Editor: Helena Kokkonen
Profile: Magazine containing information on home economics, consumer matters and gardening.
Language(s): Finnish
Readership: Aimed at women aged 30 to 70 years.
ADVERTISING RATES:
Full Page Colour .... EUR 2250
SCC .... EUR 30
Agency Commission: 15%
Mechanical Data: Trim Size: 280 x 215mm, Print Process: Offset, Screen: 60 lpc, Type Area: 182 x 250mm, Col Length: 253mm, Page Width: 200mm, Col Widths (Display): 58mm, No. of Columns (Display): 3
Copy instructions: *Copy Date:* 21 days prior to publication date
CONSUMER: WOMEN'S INTEREST CONSUMER MAGAZINES: Women's Interest

MARTHA 15265L74A-59

Formerly: Marthabladet
Editorial: Lönnrotsgatan 3 A 7, 00120 HELSINGFORS **Tel:** 10 27 97 250 **Fax:** 9 68 01 188
Email: marthabladet@martha.fi **Web site:** http://www.marthaforbundet.fi
ISSN: 1457-5922
Date Established: 1903; **Freq:** 6 issues yearly; **Circ:** 5,200
Usual Pagination: 40
Editor-in-Chief: Christel Raunio; **Managing Editor:** Mikaela Groop
Profile: Magazine containing articles on home, family, society and consumer issues.
Language(s): Swedish
Readership: Read by women.
ADVERTISING RATES:
Full Page Colour .... EUR 1765.00
SCC .... EUR 22.10
Agency Commission: 15%
Mechanical Data: Type Area: 265 x 190mm, Bleed Size: 297 x 210mm, Screen: Mono: 48 lpc, Colour: 54 lpc, Col Widths (Display): 42mm, No. of Columns (Display): 4, Print Process: Offset, Film: Negative, Col Length: 265mm, Page Width: 190mm
CONSUMER: WOMEN'S INTEREST CONSUMER MAGAZINES: Women's Interest

MATERIA 706524L30-5

Formerly: Vuoriteollisuus - Bergshanteringen
Editorial: Kaskilaaksontie 3 D 108, 02360 ESPOO
Tel: 9 81 34 758 **Fax:** 9 81 34 758
Email: u-r.lahtinen@vuorimiesyhdistys.fi **Web site:** http://www.vuorimiesyhdistys.fi
ISSN: 1459-9694
Date Established: 1945; **Freq:** Quarterly; **Circ:** 4,000
Usual Pagination: 64
Editor-in-Chief: Jouko Härkki
Profile: Journal for the Finnish Association of Mining and Metallurgical Engineers.
Language(s): Finnish; Swedish
ADVERTISING RATES:
Full Page Colour .... EUR 1995.00
SCC .... EUR 23.10
Mechanical Data: Type Area: 210 x 287mm, Print Process: offset, Screen: 54-60 lpc

MATKAAN 15374L49E-15

Editorial: Alma 360 Asiakasmedia, PL 502/ Munkkiniemen puistotie 25, 5.krs, 00101 HELSINKI
Tel: 10 66 51 02 **Fax:** 10 66 52 533
Email: sami.turunen@alma360.fi **Web site:** http://www.vr.fi
ISSN: 1236-2433
Freq: Monthly; **Cover Price:** Free; **Circ:** 75,000
Usual Pagination: 24
Editor-in-Chief: Heikki Ruuhijärvi
Profile: Customer magazine for travellers on VR, Finnish Railways.
Language(s): Finnish; Swedish
Readership: Available free on trains, at railway stations and travel agencies.
ADVERTISING RATES:
Full Page Colour .... EUR 2500
SCC .... EUR 16.80
Mechanical Data: Type Area: 245 x 360mm, Bleed Size: 273 x 396mm, No. of Columns (Display): 4, Screen: 40 lpc, Col Widths (Display): 57mm
BUSINESS: TRANSPORT: Railways

MATKAILUSILMÄ 15076L50-75

Editorial: PL 625/Töölönkatu 11, 00101 HELSINKI
Tel: 10 60 58 00 **Fax:** 10 60 58 333
Email: mek@mek.fi **Web site:** http://www.mek.fi
ISSN: 0355-5194
Freq: Quarterly; **Circ:** 3,000
Usual Pagination: 24
Editor-in-Chief: Matti Linnoila
Profile: Magazine of the Finnish Tourist Board.
Language(s): Finnish
Readership: Read by travel agents, tour operators and people working in tourist information offices.
BUSINESS: TRAVEL & TOURISM

MATKAOPAS 706443L89A-4

Editorial: PL 100/ Lapinmäentie 1, 00040 SANOMA MAGAZINES **Tel:** 9 12 01 **Fax:** 9 12 05 352
Email: matkaopas@sanomamagazines.fi **Web site:** http://www.matkaopaslehti.fi
ISSN: 1456-419X
Date Established: 1999; **Freq:** 6 issues yearly - Published 8/year; **Circ:** 41,457
Usual Pagination: 84
Profile: Magazine with tips about interesting travel destinations for both private households and business travellers.
Language(s): Finnish
Readership: Active, well educated Finns with passion for travel and high purchasing power.
ADVERTISING RATES:
Full Page Colour .... EUR 4050
SCC .... EUR 36.10
Mechanical Data: Bleed Size: 215 x 280mm, Screen: 60 lpc, Film: positive, Print Process: offset, Type Area: 190 x 250mm
Copy instructions: *Copy Date:* 19 days prior to publication date
Editions:
Matkaopaslehti.fi
CONSUMER: HOLIDAYS & TRAVEL: Travel

MATTI JA LIISA 704974L72-830

Editorial: PL 21 / Juhani Ahontie 2, 73101 LAPINLAHTI **Tel:** 17 73 15 40 **Fax:** 17 73 15 31
Email: matti.liisa@mattijaliisa.fi **Web site:** http://www.mattijaliisa.fi
ISSN: 0356-2328
Date Established: 1970; **Freq:** Weekly; **Circ:** 5,228
Usual Pagination: 24
Profile: Newspaper issued in Lapinlahti and Varpaisjärvi.
Language(s): Finnish
ADVERTISING RATES:
SCC .... EUR 11.80
Agency Commission: 15%
Mechanical Data: No. of Columns (Display): 6, Col Widths (Display): 40mm, Print Process: offset, Type Area: 254 x 370mm, Page Width: 251mm, Col Length: 370mm
LOCAL NEWSPAPERS

MAZDA 705220L31R-45

Formerly: Startti
Editorial: Vetokuja 1, 01610 VANTAA
Tel: 20 77 04 300
Email: erja.aalto@alma360.fi **Web site:** http://www.mazda.fi
ISSN: 0781-7711
Freq: Quarterly; **Cover Price:** Free; **Circ:** 90,000
Usual Pagination: 40
Editor-in-Chief: Edvard Duncker
Profile: Magazine focusing on Mazda cars.
Language(s): Finnish
BUSINESS: MOTOR TRADE: Motor Trade Related

MDS 15027L37-15

Editorial: PL 56/ Viikinkaari 5, 00014 HELSINGIN YLIOPISTO **Tel:** 9 37 45 273 **Fax:** 9 22 43 18 77
Email: mds@yfk.fi **Web site:** http://www.helsinki.fi/jarj/yfk
ISSN: 0024-8045
Date Established: 1901; **Freq:** Quarterly; **Annual Sub.:** EUR 18.00; **Circ:** 600
Usual Pagination: 40
Editor-in-Chief: Tiia Metiäinen
Profile: Magazine concerning all aspects of the pharmaceutical industry.
Language(s): Finnish
Readership: Aimed at pharmacies, medical companies and pharmacy students at the University of Helsinki.
ADVERTISING RATES:
Full Page Colour .... EUR 605.00
Mechanical Data: No. of Columns (Display): 1-2, Print Process: offset

ME 15266L73-84

Formerly: Me-lehti
Editorial: PL 1/ Sörnäistenkatu 2, 00581 HELSINKI
Tel: 20 70 03 00
Email: me.lehti@lahikauppa.fi **Web site:** http://www.lahikauppa.fi
ISSN: 0025-6269
Date Established: 1917; **Freq:** Monthly; Free to qualifying individuals ; **Circ:** 832,309
Usual Pagination: 72
Editor-in-Chief: Jaana Huttunen; **Managing Editor:** Outi Jaakkola
Profile: Magazine for loyalty members of the Suomen Lähikauppa Oy.
Language(s): Finnish
ADVERTISING RATES:
Full Page Colour .... EUR 6990
SCC .... EUR 66.40
Agency Commission: 15%
Mechanical Data: Trim Size: 217 x 270mm, Screen: 60 lpc
CONSUMER: NATIONAL & INTERNATIONAL PERIODICALS

ME NAISET 15249L74A-60

Editorial: PL 100/ Lapinmäentie 1, 00040 SANOMA MAGAZINES **Tel:** 9 12 01 **Fax:** 9 12 05 414
Email: menaiset@sanomamagazines.fi **Web site:** http://www.menaiset.fi
ISSN: 0025-6277
Date Established: 1952; **Freq:** Weekly - Published on Friday; **Circ:** 147,354
Usual Pagination: 100
Editor-in-Chief: Marjo Vuorinen; **Managing Editor:** Sari Parkkonen
Profile: Women's general interest magazine.
Language(s): Finnish
ADVERTISING RATES:
Full Page Colour .... EUR 7550
SCC .... EUR 63.50
Mechanical Data: Type Area: 194 x 248mm, No. of Columns (Display): 4, Col Widths (Display): 45mm, Print Process: offset, Film: positive, Screen: 60 lpc
CONSUMER: WOMEN'S INTEREST CONSUMER MAGAZINES: Women's Interest

MEDBORGARBLADET 705396L82-10

Editorial: Nordinfo Ab, Lillviksvägen 6, 02360 ESPOO
Tel: 9 88 86 017 **Fax:** 9 88 86 019
Email: redaktion@sfp.fi **Web site:** http://www.sfp.fi
Date Established: 1945; **Freq:** 6 issues yearly; **Circ:** 35,000
Usual Pagination: 20
Editor-in-Chief: Peter Nordling; **Managing Editor:** Victor Grandell
Profile: Political newspaper for members of the Swedish Speakers' Party in Finland.
Language(s): Swedish
ADVERTISING RATES:
Full Page Colour .... EUR 1200.00
Mechanical Data: Type Area: 251 x 357mm, Col Widths (Display): 45mm, No. of Columns (Display): 5, Print Process: offset, Screen: 30 lpc, Bleed Size: 280 x 395mm
CONSUMER: CURRENT AFFAIRS & POLITICS

MEDIUUTISET 706325L37-16

Editorial: PL 500/ Annankatu 34 - 36 B, 00101 HELSINKI **Tel:** 20 44 240 **Fax:** 20 44 24 699
Email: toimitus@mediuutiset.fi **Web site:** http://www.mediuutiset.fi
ISSN: 1456-1484
Date Established: 1998; **Freq:** Weekly - Published on Friday; **Circ:** 27,000
Usual Pagination: 48
Profile: Magazine about health care, pharmacies and social services.
Language(s): Finnish
ADVERTISING RATES:
Full Page Colour .... EUR 4950
SCC .... EUR 33.60
Agency Commission: 5-15%
Mechanical Data: Type Area: 252 x 368mm, Screen: 40 lpc, Col Widths (Display): 44mm, Print Process: offset, Col Length: 365mm, No. of Columns (Display): 5
Copy instructions: *Copy Date:* 3 days prior to publication date
Editions:
Mediuutiset.fi
BUSINESS: PHARMACEUTICAL & CHEMISTS

MEHILÄINEN 705410L56A-81

Editorial: Pohjoinen Hesperiankatu 17 C, 00260 HELSINKI **Tel:** 10 41 43 036 **Fax:** 10 41 43 095
Email: terveydenhuoltoa.yksityisesti@mehilainen.fi
Web site: http://www.mehilainen.fi
ISSN: 1235-6352
Date Established: 1991; **Freq:** Half-yearly; **Cover Price:** Free; **Circ:** 930,900
Usual Pagination: 32
Editor-in-Chief: Jarmo Karpakka; **Managing Editor:** Karina Vikman
Profile: Magazine about health services and health issues.
Language(s): Finnish
Readership: All households in the Helsinki region.
BUSINESS: HEALTH & MEDICAL

MEIDÄN MÖKKI 706158L89E-30

Editorial: Risto Rytin tie 33, 00081 A-LEHDET
Tel: 9 75 961 **Fax:** 9 75 98 31 12
Email: meidanmokki@a-lehdet.fi **Web site:** http://www.meidanmokki.fi
ISSN: 1456-6257
Date Established: 1997; **Freq:** 6 issues yearly - Published 9/year; **Circ:** 46,564
Usual Pagination: 100
Editor-in-Chief: Päivi Anttila
Profile: Magazine on leisure housing, includes information on summer cottages.
Language(s): Finnish
ADVERTISING RATES:
Full Page Colour .... EUR 4700
SCC .... EUR 48.70
Mechanical Data: Bleed Size: 230 x 273mm, Page Width: 230mm, Type Area: 187 x 241mm, Print Process: offset, Screen: 60 lpc, No. of Columns (Display): 4
Copy instructions: *Copy Date:* 13 days prior to publication date
CONSUMER: HOLIDAYS & TRAVEL: Holidays

MEIDÄN PERHE 1639716L74C-50

Editorial: PL 100, 00040 SANOMA MAGAZINES
Tel: 9 12 01 **Fax:** 9 12 05 352
Email: meidanperhe@sanomamagazines.fi **Web site:** http://www.perhe.fi
ISSN: 1459-9929
Date Established: 2004; **Freq:** Monthly; **Circ:** 50,522
Usual Pagination: 100
Editor-in-Chief: Satu Vasantola; **Managing Editor:** Liina Putkonen
Profile: Magazine about family and home.
Language(s): Finnish
ADVERTISING RATES:
Full Page Colour .... EUR 5900
SCC .... EUR 70.20
Mechanical Data: Type Area: 215 x 280mm, Print Process: offset, Screen: 60 lpc
CONSUMER: WOMEN'S INTEREST CONSUMER MAGAZINES: Home & Family

MEIDÄN SUOMI 1689456L91R-60

Editorial: PL 106/ Pitäjänmäentie 14, 00381 HELSINKI **Tel:** 9 50 34 41 **Fax:** 9 50 34 499
Email: meidansuomi@valitutpalat.fi **Web site:** http://www.meidansuomi.fi
ISSN: 1795-6358
Date Established: 2005; **Freq:** Quarterly - Published 5/year; **Circ:** 54,323
Usual Pagination: 132

Finland

Editor-in-Chief: Ilkka Virtanen; **Publisher:** Jukka Reinikainen
Profile: Magazine about leisure activities in Finland during different seasons.
Language(s): Finnish
ADVERTISING RATES:
Full Page Colour .... EUR 2850
SCC .... EUR 34.40
Agency Commission: 5-15%
Mechanical Data: Type Area: 222 x 276mm
CONSUMER: RECREATION & LEISURE: Recreation & Leisure Related

MEIDÄN TALO 14893L74K-30
Formerly: Meidän Talo & Koti
Editorial: Risto Rytin tie 33, 00081 A-LEHDET
Tel: 9 75 961 **Fax:** 9 75 98 31 11
Email: meidantalo@a-lehdet.fi **Web site:** http://www.meidantalo.fi
ISSN: 1237-1130
Date Established: 1959; **Freq:** Monthly; **Circ:** 58,654
Usual Pagination: 112
Editor-in-Chief: Timo Pääsky; **Managing Editor:** Merja Halme
Profile: Journal concerning house construction, repair and furnishing.
Language(s): Finnish
Readership: Read by architects, building and construction engineers and home owners.
ADVERTISING RATES:
Full Page Colour .... EUR 5600
SCC .... EUR 58
Mechanical Data: Type Area: 241 x 187mm, Bleed Size: 273 x 230mm, No. of Columns (Display): 4, Print Process: Offset, Screen: 60 lpc, Col Length: 241mm, Page Width: 187mm
Copy instructions: *Copy Date:* 15 days prior to publication date
Editions:
Meidän Talo Verkkotoimitus
CONSUMER: WOMEN'S INTEREST CONSUMER MAGAZINES: Home Purchase

MEKLARI 1639714L1C-13
Editorial: Acacom Print Oy, Erottajankatu 15-17, 00130 HELSINKI **Tel:** 20 74 39 900
Email: info@acacom.com **Web site:** http://www.eq.fi
ISSN: 1459-1251
Freq: Quarterly; **Cover Price:** Free; **Circ:** 50,000
Usual Pagination: 68
Managing Editor: Henna Tanskanen
Profile: Magazine about personal-finance, investment, funds and banking.
Language(s): Finnish
Readership: Customers of eQ Bank.
ADVERTISING RATES:
Full Page Colour .... EUR 4580
Agency Commission: 15%
Mechanical Data: Type Area: 210 x 280mm, Screen: 60 lpc, Print Process: offset

MENNÄÄN NAIMISIIN 706327L74L-20
Editorial: Puolikuu 5 B-C, 02210 ESPOO
Tel: 9 88 70 840 **Fax:** 9 88 70 84 66
Email: liisa.silla@malisilla.fi **Web site:** http://www.mennaannaimisiin.fi
ISSN: 1239-4513
Date Established: 1995; **Freq:** Half-yearly; **Circ:** 25,000
Usual Pagination: 100
Editor-in-Chief: Liisa Silla
Profile: Wedding magazine issued partly for a yearly wedding fair.
Language(s): Finnish
ADVERTISING RATES:
Full Page Colour .... EUR 2850.00
SCC .... EUR 27.90
Mechanical Data: Bleed Size: 250 x 345mm, Type Area: 200 x 290mm, Print Process: offset, Film: positive, Screen: 60 lpc

MERCEDES 1702771L31R-28
Editorial: Salomonkatu 17 B, 00100 HELSINKI
Tel: 10 56 92 202 **Fax:** 10 56 92 208
Email: johanna.talvela@acacom.com **Web site:** http://www.veho.fi
ISSN: 1459-0239
Freq: Quarterly; **Cover Price:** Free; **Circ:** 60,000
Usual Pagination: 68
Editor-in-Chief: Kenneth Strömsholm; **Managing Editor:** Johanna Talvela
Profile: Magazine about Mercedes-Benz cars.
Language(s): Finnish
ADVERTISING RATES:
Full Page Colour .... EUR 5880.00
Agency Commission: 15%
Mechanical Data: Type Area: 215 x 280mm, Screen: 60 lpc, Print Process: offset
BUSINESS: MOTOR TRADE: Motor Trade Related

MERIKARVIALEHTI 704893L72-840
Editorial: PL 3/Kauppatie 36, 29901 MERIKARVIA
Tel: 2 55 11 272 **Fax:** 2 55 12 271
Email: toimitus.merikarvialehti@sps.fi **Web site:** http://www.merikarvialehti.fi
Date Established: 1982; **Freq:** Weekly; **Circ:** 3,431
Usual Pagination: 8
Profile: Newspaper issued in Merikarvia and Siikainen.
Language(s): Finnish
ADVERTISING RATES:
Full Page Colour .... EUR 1892
SCC .... EUR 8.30

Agency Commission: 15%
Mechanical Data: Col Length: 390mm, No. of Columns (Display): 6, Col Widths (Display): 40mm
LOCAL NEWSPAPERS

MESTARI-INSINÖÖRI 706037L4E-4
Formerly: Rakennusmestari ja -insinööri
Editorial: Rahakamarinportti 3 A, 00240 HELSINKI
Tel: 9 87 70 650 **Fax:** 9 14 70 80
Email: rakennusmestarit@rkl.fi **Web site:** http://www.rkl.fi
ISSN: 1795-5823
Date Established: 1905; **Freq:** Quarterly; **Circ:** 9,000
Usual Pagination: 20
Editor-in-Chief: Hannu Ahokanto
Profile: Magazine about building engineers and workmen.
Language(s): Finnish
Mechanical Data: Type Area: 205 x 290mm, No. of Columns (Display): 4, Col Widths (Display): 41mm, Screen: 70 lpc, Print Process: offset

METALLITEKNIIKKA 14976L27-70
Editorial: PL 920/ Annankatu 34-36 B, 00101 HELSINKI **Tel:** 20 44 240 **Fax:** 20 44 24 105
Email: metallitekniikka@talentum.fi **Web site:** http://www.metallitekniikka.fi
ISSN: 1237-6663
Date Established: 1948; **Freq:** Monthly; **Circ:** 8,581
Usual Pagination: 68
Editor-in-Chief: Terho Puustinen; **Managing Editor:** Mika Hämäläinen
Profile: Journal of the Technology Industries of Finland.
Language(s): Finnish
Readership: Read by professionals in the metal industry.
ADVERTISING RATES:
Full Page Colour .... EUR 4280
SCC .... EUR 36
Agency Commission: 5-15%
Mechanical Data: Type Area: 279 x 190mm, Trim Size: 297 x 210mm, Bleed Size: 307 x 215mm, Print Process: Offset, No. of Columns (Display): 4, Screen: Mono: 54 lpc, Colour: 54-60 lpc, Col Length: 279mm, Page Width: 190mm, Col Widths (Display): 44.5mm
Copy instructions: *Copy Date:* 15 days prior to publication date
Editions:
Metallitekniikka.fi
BUSINESS: METAL, IRON & STEEL

METRO 706464L72-850
Editorial: PL 300/ Martinkyläntie 11 A, 01621 VANTAA **Tel:** 9 12 24 351 **Fax:** 9 12 24 442
Email: metro@sanoma.fi **Web site:** http://www.metrolive.fi
Date Established: 1999; **Freq:** Daily; **Cover Price:** Free; **Circ:** 160,000
Usual Pagination: 16
Editor-in-Chief: Janne Kaijärvi; **Managing Editor:** Ismo Uusitupa
Profile: Free local newspaper distributed at news stands in Helsinki and surroundings, Tampere, Turku and Lahti.
Language(s): Finnish
ADVERTISING RATES:
Full Page Colour .... EUR 5982
SCC .... EUR 27.30
Agency Commission: 15%
Mechanical Data: Type Area: 254 x 370mm, Col Widths (Display): 39mm, No. of Columns (Display): 6, Col Length: 365mm, Page Width: 254mm
LOCAL NEWSPAPERS

METROPOLI 761881L89C-150
Formerly: Ekas
Editorial: Joukahaisenkatu 67, 53500 LAPPEENRANTA **Tel:** 50 30 31 000
Email: marko@metrotuotanto.com **Web site:** http://www.metropoli.net
ISSN: 1458-1981
Freq: Monthly - Published 10/year; **Cover Price:** Free; **Circ:** 120,000
Usual Pagination: 24
Managing Director: Marko Haapahuhta; **Managing Editor:** Teemu Siltanen
Profile: Entertainment newspaper issued in different Finnish cities.
Language(s): Finnish
Readership: 16-40 year old urban people.
ADVERTISING RATES:
Full Page Colour .... EUR 2000
SCC .... EUR 11.10
Agency Commission: 15%
Mechanical Data: Bleed Size: 280 x 400mm, Type Area: 250 x 360mm, Print Process: offset, Screen: 40 lpc colour
Copy instructions: *Copy Date:* 7 days prior to publication date
CONSUMER: HOLIDAYS & TRAVEL: Entertainment Guides

METSÄALAN AMMATTILEHTI 1639908L46-195
Editorial: Vironkatu 9, 00170 HELSINKI
Tel: 9 69 80 442 **Fax:** 9 68 13 07 11
Email: janne.jokela@ammattilehti.fi **Web site:** http://www.ammattilehti.fi
Date Established: 1986; **Freq:** 6 issues yearly; Free to qualifying individuals ; **Circ:** 16,000
Usual Pagination: 72

Profile: Magazine about forest machinery, transport and industry.
Language(s): Finnish
ADVERTISING RATES:
Full Page Colour .... EUR 1620
SCC .... EUR 10.30
Mechanical Data: Type Area: 221 x 312mm, No. of Columns (Display): 5, Col Widths (Display): 41mm

METSÄ.FI 718827L46-54_50
Formerly: Metsävaltio
Editorial: PL 94/ Vernissakatu 4, 01301 VANTAA
Tel: 20 56 41 00 **Fax:** 20 56 45 050
Email: hanna.kaurala@metsa.fi **Web site:** http://www.metsafi-lehti.fi
ISSN: 1235-0060
Date Established: 1956; **Freq:** 6 issues yearly;
Cover Price: Free; **Circ:** 12,400
Usual Pagination: 18
Editor-in-Chief: Juha Mäkinen
Profile: Personnel magazine for people working in the Forestry Board.
Language(s): Finnish

METSÄLEHTI 15056L46-20
Editorial: Soidinkuja 4, 00700 HELSINKI
Tel: 20 77 29 120 **Fax:** 20 77 29 139
Email: toimitus@metsalehti.fi **Web site:** http://www.metsalehti.fi
ISSN: 0355-0893
Date Established: 1933; **Freq:** 26 issues yearly; **Circ:** 37,854
Usual Pagination: 28
Profile: Official journal of the Forestry Development Centre.
Language(s): Finnish
ADVERTISING RATES:
Full Page Colour .... EUR 3250
SCC .... EUR 17.10
Agency Commission: 15%
Mechanical Data: Bleed Size: 315 x 420mm, Type Area: 254 x 375mm, No. of Columns (Display): 5, Col Widths (Display): 48mm, Print Process: offset, Film: negative, Screen: 40 lpc
Editions:
Metsälehti.fi
BUSINESS: TIMBER, WOOD & FORESTRY

METSÄLIITON VIESTI 15057L46-30
Editorial: PL 10/ Revontulentie 6, 02020 METSÄ
Tel: 10 46 54 737 **Fax:** 10 46 54 553
Email: sirkku.vanhatalo@metsaliitto.fi **Web site:** http://www.metsaliitto.fi
Date Established: 1949; **Freq:** Quarterly; **Cover Price:** Free; **Circ:** 130,000
Usual Pagination: 52
Editor-in-Chief: Anne-Mari Achrén
Profile: Magazine of the cooperative of Finnish forest owners.
Language(s): Finnish
ADVERTISING RATES:
Full Page Colour .... EUR 2980.00
SCC .... EUR 33.40
Agency Commission: 15%
Mechanical Data: Type Area: 186 x 272mm, Bleed Size: 210 x 297mm, No. of Columns (Display): 3, Col Widths (Display): 58mm, Print Process: offset, Screen: 60 lpc, Film: negative
BUSINESS: TIMBER, WOOD & FORESTRY

METSÄNHOITAJA 15058L46-50
Editorial: Kruunuvuorenkatu 5 F 25, 00160 HELSINKI
Tel: 9 68 40 810 **Fax:** 9 68 40 81 22
Email: johanna.hristov@metsanhoitajat.fi **Web site:** http://www.metsanhoitajat.fi
Date Established: 1951; **Freq:** Quarterly; **Annual Sub.:** EUR 35.00; **Circ:** 3,000
Usual Pagination: 48
Editor-in-Chief: Tapio Hankala
Profile: Journal of The Society of Finnish Professional Foresters.
Language(s): English; Finnish; Swedish
Readership: Aimed at members as well as employees of forest organisations and companies.
ADVERTISING RATES:
Full Page Colour .... EUR 1200.00
SCC .... EUR 15.60
Agency Commission: 10%
Mechanical Data: Type Area: 182 x 255mm, Col Widths (Display): 57mm, No. of Columns (Display): 3, Screen: 48-54 lpc, Print Process: offset

METSÄRAHA 705321L46-52
Editorial: Virkkalantie 12-16 B 13, 08700 LOHJA
Tel: 19 31 22 95
Web site: http://www.op.fi
ISSN: 0788-8511
Freq: Half-yearly; **Cover Price:** Free; **Circ:** 173,000
Usual Pagination: 32
Editor-in-Chief: Martti Tynkkynen; **Managing Editor:** Paavo Tuovinen
Profile: Magazine about the financing of forestry.
Language(s): Finnish
Readership: Forestry customers of OP-Pohjola-ryhmä.
Mechanical Data: Print Process: offset, Film: positive, Col Widths (Display): 43mm, Screen: 54-60 lpc
BUSINESS: TIMBER, WOOD & FORESTRY

METSÄSTÄJÄ 15297L75A-65
Editorial: Fantsintie 13-14, 00890 HELSINKI
Tel: 9 27 27 810 **Fax:** 927278130
Email: mkj@riista.fi **Web site:** http://www.riista.fi
ISSN: 0047-6989
Date Established: 1951; **Freq:** 6 issues yearly; **Circ:** 303,241
Usual Pagination: 64
Managing Editor: Klaus Ekman
Profile: Magazine of the Hunters' Central Organisation in Finland.
Language(s): Finnish
Readership: Aimed at people interested in hunting.
ADVERTISING RATES:
Full Page Colour .... EUR 6000
Agency Commission: 15%
Mechanical Data: Type Area: 185 x 272mm, No. of Columns (Display): 4, Col Widths (Display): 43mm, Print Process: offset rotation, Screen: 54 lpc, Film: negative
CONSUMER: SPORT

METSÄSTYS JA KALASTUS 15298L92-62
Editorial: Maistraatinportti 1, 00015 OTAVAMEDIA
Tel: 9 15 661 **Fax:** 9 14 81 721
Email: metsastys.kalastus@otavamedia.fi **Web site:** http://www.otavamedia.fi
ISSN: 0026-1629
Freq: Monthly; **Circ:** 46,397
Usual Pagination: 108
Profile: Magazine for hunters, fishermen and outdoor enthusiasts.
Language(s): Finnish
ADVERTISING RATES:
Full Page Colour .... EUR 2820
SCC .... EUR 25.10
Mechanical Data: Print Process: Offset, Film: Digital. positive, Bleed Size: 280 x 217mm, Col Widths (Display): 45mm, Screen: 60 lpc, Type Area: 217 x 280mm
Copy instructions: *Copy Date:* 19 days prior to publication date
CONSUMER: ANGLING & FISHING

METSÄTALOUS-FORESTRY 705967L46-53
Editorial: Hietalahdenkatu 8 A, 00180 HELSINKI
Tel: 9 61 26 55 15 **Fax:** 9 61 26 55 30
Email: pirjo.korhonen@metsatalous.fi **Web site:** http://www.metsatalous.fi
ISSN: 1239-677X
Date Established: 1998; **Freq:** 6 issues yearly; **Circ:** 10,200
Usual Pagination: 36
Editor-in-Chief: Pirjo Korhonen
Profile: Magazine focusing on all aspects of forestry.
Language(s): Finnish
ADVERTISING RATES:
Full Page Colour .... EUR 1919.00
SCC .... EUR 23.50
Agency Commission: 15%
Mechanical Data: Type Area: 189 x 272mm, No. of Columns (Display): 3/4, Col Widths (Display): 60/ 44mm, Screen: 54-70 lpc, Print Process: offset, Film: negative

METSÄTIETEEN AIKAKAUSKIRJA 706330L46-54
Editorial: PL 18/ Jokiniemenkuja 1, 01301 VANTAA
Tel: 10 21 11 **Fax:** 10 21 12 101
Email: silva.fennica@metla.fi **Web site:** http://www.metla.fi/aikakauskirja
ISSN: 1455-2515
Date Established: 1994; **Freq:** Quarterly; **Annual Sub.:** EUR 60.00; **Circ:** 500
Usual Pagination: 96
Editor-in-Chief: Eeva Korpilahti
Profile: Publication of the Finnish Forest Research Institute covering all aspects of forest research.
Language(s): Finnish; Swedish

METSÄTRANS 768337L46-200
Editorial: Myllärinkatu 21 A, 65100 VAASA
Tel: 6 31 82 820 **Fax:** 6 31 82 821
Email: toimitus@metsatrans.com **Web site:** http://www.metsatrans.com
ISSN: 1457-2656
Date Established: 1997; **Freq:** 6 issues yearly; **Circ:** 6,500
Usual Pagination: 116
Editor-in-Chief: Seppo Ala-Kutsi
Profile: Magazine about wood manufacturing and the transport of timber.
Language(s): Finnish
Readership: Professionals within forestry.
ADVERTISING RATES:
Full Page Colour .... EUR 1460.00
SCC .... EUR 13.50
Agency Commission: 15%
Mechanical Data: Bleed Size: 210 x 297mm, Type Area: 185 x 270mm, Col Widths (Display): 43mm, No. of Columns (Display): 4, Print Process: offset, Screen: 60 lpc

METSÄVIESTI 706331L46-55
Editorial: Pitkänsillankatu 20 c, 67100 KOKKOLA
Tel: 6 83 14 175 **Fax:** 6 82 24 164
Web site: http://www.mhy.fi/keskipohjanmaa
Freq: Half-yearly; **Circ:** 6,300
Usual Pagination: 20

Editor-in-Chief: Timo Heikkilä
Profile: Magazine about local forest research.
Language(s): Finnish

MIELENTERVEYS 15119L56N-50
Editorial: Maistraatinportti 4 A, 00240 HELSINKI
Tel: 9 61 55 16 **Fax:** 961551770
Email: kristina.salonen@mielenterveysseura.fi **Web site:** http://www.mielenterveysseura.fi
ISSN: 0303-2558
Date Established: 1961; **Freq:** 6 issues yearly; **Circ:** 3,924
Usual Pagination: 56
Profile: Magazine of the Finnish Association for Mental Health. Covers mental health in general.
Language(s): Finnish
Readership: Read by social and mental health workers, and those who are interested in mental health issues.
ADVERTISING RATES:
Full Page Colour .... EUR 1282
SCC .... EUR 15.80
Mechanical Data: Bleed Size: 230 x 275mm, Type Area: 183 x 240mm, No. of Columns (Display): 4, Col Widths (Display): 42mm, Print Process: offset, Film: negative, Screen: 48-54 lpc
BUSINESS: HEALTH & MEDICAL: Mental Health

MIILU 704992L72-855
Editorial: PL 5/ Kallentie 1, 74301 SONKAJÄRVI
Tel: 17 76 13 12 **Fax:** 17761341
Email: miilu@miilu.fi **Web site:** http://www.miilu.fi
ISSN: 0789-0192
Date Established: 1972; **Freq:** Weekly; **Circ:** 3,732
Usual Pagination: 16
Profile: Newspaper issued in Sonkajärvi and Vieremä.
Language(s): Finnish
ADVERTISING RATES:
SCC .... EUR 11.70
Agency Commission: 15%
Mechanical Data: Col Length: 253mm, No. of Columns (Display): 6
LOCAL NEWSPAPERS

MIKROBITTI 14906L5D-25
Editorial: PL 100/ Lapinmäentie 1, 00040 SANOMA MAGAZINES **Tel:** 9 12 01 **Fax:** 9 12 05 705
Email: toimitus@mikrobitti.fi **Web site:** http://www.mbnet.fi
ISSN: 0781-2078
Date Established: 1984; **Freq:** Monthly; **Circ:** 79,626
Usual Pagination: 140
Editor-in-Chief: Otto Aalto; **Managing Editor:** Pasi Andrejeff
Profile: Magazine covering different aspects of home computing.
Language(s): Finnish
Readership: Read by PC owners.
ADVERTISING RATES:
Full Page Colour .... EUR 5750
SCC .... EUR 48.40
Agency Commission: 15%
Mechanical Data: Trim Size: 297 x 230mm, No. of Columns (Display): 4, Print Process: Offset, Film: Positive, Screen: 54 lpc
Copy instructions: *Copy Date:* 17 days prior to publication date
Average ad content per issue: 20%
BUSINESS: COMPUTERS & AUTOMATION: Personal Computers

MIKROPC 14905L5D-26
Formerly: Mikro PC
Editorial: PL 920/ Annankatu 34-36 B, 00101 HELSINKI **Tel:** 20 44 24 263 **Fax:** 20 44 24 103
Email: mikropc@talentum.fi **Web site:** http://www.mikropc.net
ISSN: 0785-9988
Date Established: 1983; **Freq:** Monthly; **Circ:** 28,446
Usual Pagination: 90
Editor-in-Chief: Antti Oksanen
Profile: Magazine providing articles and information on Personal Computers, includes tests and comparisons of hardware, software and services of different manufacturers. Also contains information on mobile communication.
Language(s): Finnish
Readership: Aimed at IT professionals and users.
ADVERTISING RATES:
Full Page Colour .... EUR 6575
SCC .... EUR 59.70
Agency Commission: 5-15%
Mechanical Data: Type Area: 275 x 175mm, Bleed Size: 307 x 215mm, Trim Size: 297 x 210mm, Screen: 54 lpc, Print Process: Offset, No. of Columns (Display): 4, Col Length: 275mm, Page Width: 175mm, Col Widths (Display): 42mm
Copy instructions: *Copy Date:* 10 days prior to publication date
BUSINESS: COMPUTERS & AUTOMATION: Personal Computers

MISS MIX 706332L74F-20
Formerly: MIX
Editorial: PL 173/Pursimiehenkatu 29-31 A, 00151 HELSINKI **Tel:** 9 86 21 70 00 **Fax:** 9 86 21 71 77
Email: missmix@aller.fi **Web site:** http://www.missmix.fi
ISSN: 1796-7198
Date Established: 1998; **Freq:** Monthly; **Circ:** 27,731
Usual Pagination: 92
Profile: Magazine about trends, movies, music, relationships, outlook, fashion, video, Internet and teenage subjects.
Language(s): Finnish
Readership: 12-19 year-old boys and girls.
ADVERTISING RATES:
Full Page Colour .... EUR 2400
SCC .... EUR 21.40
Agency Commission: 15%
Mechanical Data: Screen: 60 lpc, Print Process: offset, Type Area: 207 x 280mm, Film: negative
CONSUMER: WOMEN'S INTEREST CONSUMER MAGAZINES: Teenage

MISSION 15361L87-70
Editorial: PB 154/ Observatoriegatan 18, 00141 HELSINGFORS **Tel:** 9 12 971 **Fax:** 9 12 97 294
Email: sls@mission.fi **Web site:** http://www.mission.fi
ISSN: 0357-296X
Date Established: 1859; **Freq:** Quarterly; **Cover Price:** Free
Annual Sub.: EUR 33.00; **Circ:** 1,766
Usual Pagination: 32
Editor-in-Chief: Outi Laukkanen
Profile: Magazine of the Finnish Lutheran Mission. Covers world missions, religion and culture.
Language(s): Swedish
Readership: Aimed at people interested in mission work, third world countries, religion and culture.
ADVERTISING RATES:
Full Page Mono .... EUR 589.00
Full Page Colour .... EUR 841.00
Mechanical Data: Bleed Size: 219 x 280mm, Type Area: 219 x 280mm, No. of Columns (Display): 8, Col Widths (Display): 50mm, Print Process: offset, Film: negative
CONSUMER: RELIGIOUS

MOBILISTI 15325L77A-10
Editorial: Niittyläntie 11, 00620 HELSINKI
Tel: 9 27 27 100 **Fax:** 9 27 27 10 27
Email: toimitus@mobilisti.fi **Web site:** http://www.mobilisti.fi
ISSN: 0783-4616
Date Established: 1979; **Freq:** 6 issues yearly; **Circ:** 17,941
Usual Pagination: 96
Editor-in-Chief: Jan Enqvist
Profile: Publication about veteran cars.
Language(s): Finnish
ADVERTISING RATES:
Full Page Colour .... EUR 1600.00
CONSUMER: MOTORING & CYCLING: Motoring

MODA 15273L74E-70
Formerly: Novita
Editorial: Maistraatinportti 1, 00015 OTAVAMEDIA
Tel: 9 15 661 **Fax:** 9 15 66 550
Email: moda@otavamedia.fi **Web site:** http://www.modalehti.fi
ISSN: 1259-692X
Date Established: 1993; **Freq:** 6 issues yearly; **Circ:** 41,980
Usual Pagination: 116
Profile: Magazine focusing on all aspects of knitwear and related fashion.
Language(s): Finnish
Readership: Aimed at women.
ADVERTISING RATES:
Full Page Colour .... EUR 3100
SCC .... EUR 26
Mechanical Data: Bleed Size: 280 x 230mm, Print Process: Offset, Film: Digital positive, Screen: 60 lpc, Type Area: 230 x 297mm, Col Length: 280mm
Copy instructions: *Copy Date:* 19 days prior to publication date
CONSUMER: WOMEN'S INTEREST CONSUMER MAGAZINES: Crafts

MODIN 15065L47A-20
Formerly: Kenkäalusikka
Editorial: Mannerheimintie 76 B, 00250 HELSINKI
Tel: 9 68 44 73 21 **Fax:** 9 68 44 73 44
Email: modin@muotikaupanliitto.fi **Web site:** http://www.muotikaupanliitto.fi
ISSN: 1457-554X
Date Established: 2000; **Freq:** 6 issues yearly;
Annual Sub.: EUR 80; **Circ:** 4,629
Usual Pagination: 68
Editor-in-Chief: Yrjö Gorski
Profile: Magazine forecasting the trends and presenting the collections for the coming season in the fashion industry. Covers clothing, textiles, shoes, bags and sportswear.
Language(s): Finnish
Readership: Read by members of the Fashion Retailers' Association, wholesalers, fashion manufacturers, agents and buyers.
ADVERTISING RATES:
Full Page Colour .... EUR 2300
SCC .... EUR 25.80
Agency Commission: 15%
Mechanical Data: Film: Negative, Print Process: Offset, Screen: 60 lpc, Trim Size: 297 x 210mm, Type Area: 297 x 210mm, Col Length: 265mm, Page Width: 190mm, No. of Columns (Display): 1-3
Copy instructions: *Copy Date:* 30 days prior to publication date
Average ad content per issue: 25%
BUSINESS: CLOTHING & TEXTILES

MONDO 706031L89A-3_50
Formerly: Matkamedia
Editorial: PL 212/ Risto Rytin tie 33, 00811 HELSINKI
Tel: 9 75 96 779 **Fax:** 9 75 98 38 04
Email: mondo@imagekustannus.fi **Web site:** http://www.mondo.fi
ISSN: 1459-0964
Date Established: 1997; **Freq:** Monthly - Published 10/year; **Circ:** 26,000
Usual Pagination: 68
Editor-in-Chief: Heikki Valkama; **Managing Editor:** Kati Kelola
Profile: Magazine featuring articles on specialised travel information, current phenomenon and geographical cultures.
Language(s): Finnish
Readership: Aimed at well-travelled women aged between 35 and 55 years.
ADVERTISING RATES:
Full Page Colour .... EUR 4000
SCC .... EUR 33.30
Agency Commission: 15%
Mechanical Data: Type Area: 230 x 300mm, Print Process: offset, Film: positive, Screen: 70 lpc
Copy instructions: *Copy Date:* 10 days prior to publication date
Editions:
Mondo.fi

MOOTTORI 15317L77A-40
Editorial: Köydenpunojankatu 2 a D, 00180 HELSINKI **Tel:** 9 15 661 **Fax:** 9 15 66 86 00
Email: moottori@kynamies.fi **Web site:** http://www.moottori.fi
ISSN: 0359-7636
Date Established: 1925; **Freq:** Monthly - 10/ a year; **Circ:** 93,747
Usual Pagination: 100
Managing Editor: Timo Toiviainen
Profile: Magazine for automobile owners and mobile home owners.
Language(s): Finnish
ADVERTISING RATES:
Full Page Colour .... EUR 5000
SCC .... EUR 35.70
Agency Commission: 15%
Mechanical Data: Type Area: 280 x 215mm, Print Process: Offset, Screen: 60 lpc, Col Length: 280mm, Page Width: 215mm
Copy instructions: *Copy Date:* 20 days prior to publication date
CONSUMER: MOTORING & CYCLING: Motoring

MOOTTORITURISTI 766877L77B-55
Editorial: Karstulantie 4, 00550 HELSINKI
Tel: 9 77 34 573
Email: toimitus@tfmk.com **Web site:** http://www.tfmk.com
Freq: Quarterly; **Annual Sub.:** EUR 17.00; **Circ:** 1,000
Usual Pagination: 32
Profile: Magazine about travelling by motorcycle.
Language(s): Finnish
Readership: Members of Touring Finlandia MK ry.
ADVERTISING RATES:
Full Page Colour .... EUR 180.00

MOTIIVI 705335L32A-56
Formerly: Kunta ja Me - Kommunen och Vi
Editorial: PL 101/ Sörnäisten rantatie 23, 00531 HELSINKI **Tel:** 10 77 031 **Fax:** 107703410
Email: motiivi.lehti@jhl.fi **Web site:** http://www.jhl.fi
ISSN: 1795-7249
Date Established: 1956; **Freq:** Monthly - Published 13/year; **Circ:** 215,558
Usual Pagination: 56
Managing Editor: Airi Immonen
Profile: Journal for members of the Municipality Workers' Union.
Language(s): Finnish; Swedish
ADVERTISING RATES:
Full Page Colour .... EUR 3800
SCC .... EUR 35.40
Agency Commission: 15%
Mechanical Data: Bleed Size: 230 x 273mm, Type Area: 204 x 268mm, No. of Columns (Display): 4, Col Widths (Display): 48mm, Screen: 54 lpc, Print Process: offset
BUSINESS: LOCAL GOVERNMENT, LEISURE & RECREATION: Local Government

MOTIVA XPRESS 706395L58-110
Editorial: PL 489/ Urho Kekkosenkatu 4-6 A, 00101 HELSINKI **Tel:** 424 28 11 **Fax:** 424 28 12 99
Email: motiva@motiva.fi **Web site:** http://www.motiva.fi
ISSN: 1237-3125
Freq: Quarterly; **Cover Price:** Free; **Circ:** 7,000
Usual Pagination: 16
Editor-in-Chief: Iiris Lappalainen
Profile: Magazine on energy saving in building, construction and planning.
Language(s): Finnish
Readership: Aimed at new landlords, people who obtained a building license on their property and the officials dealing with licences.

MOTORISTI 760044L77B-60
Editorial: Niilontie 1 B 6, 35600 HALLI
Tel: 50 52 89 239
Email: motoristi@mp69.fi **Web site:** http://www.mp69.fi
Freq: Quarterly; **Circ:** 2,000
Editor-in-Chief: Oiva Lepola
Profile: Club magazine about motorcycling.
Language(s): Finnish
Readership: Motorcycle club members.

MOTO-YKKÖNEN 712888L77B-50
Formerly: Moto-Lehti
Editorial: Ahdekallionkatu 46, 05820 HYVINKÄÄ
Tel: 10 61 72 410 **Fax:** 10 29 61 841
Email: pekka.neste@moto-lehti.com **Web site:** http://www.moto1.fi
ISSN: 1795-9071
Date Established: 1977; **Freq:** 6 issues yearly; **Circ:** 12,000
Usual Pagination: 68
Editor-in-Chief: Pekka Neste
Profile: Magazine covering all aspects of motorcycling, including history, technology and road tests.
Language(s): Finnish
ADVERTISING RATES:
Full Page Colour .... EUR 1850.00
SCC .... EUR 16.90
Mechanical Data: Type Area: 210 x 297mm

MP MAAILMA 753105L77B-70
Formerly: Offroad Sanomat
Editorial: Jäspilänkatu 28 D, 04250 KERAVA
Tel: 9 85 61 93 00 **Fax:** 9 85 61 93 01
Web site: http://www.mpmaailma.fi
ISSN: 1457-151X
Date Established: 1999; **Freq:** 6 issues yearly - Published 10/year; **Circ:** 9,039
Usual Pagination: 64
Editor-in-Chief: Markus Ström; **Managing Editor:** Janne Huhtala
Profile: Magazine about Enduro-bikes, motocross and trial.
Language(s): Finnish
ADVERTISING RATES:
Full Page Colour .... EUR 2157
SCC .... EUR 18.10
Mechanical Data: Bleed Size: 210 x 297mm
CONSUMER: MOTORING & CYCLING: Motorcycling

MTK-VIESTI 14953L21A-45
Formerly: Maataloustuottaja
Editorial: PL 510/ Simonkatu 6, 00101 HELSINKI
Tel: 20 41 31 **Fax:** 20 41 32 425
Email: virpi.siitonen@mtk.fi **Web site:** http://www.mtk.fi
ISSN: 0355-0494
Date Established: 1928; **Freq:** 6 issues yearly; **Circ:** 8,000
Usual Pagination: 32
Editor-in-Chief: Matti Voutilainen
Profile: Publication containing information for Agricultural Producers and Forest Owners.
Language(s): Finnish
Readership: Read by members of the Central Union of Agricultural Producers and Forest Owners.
ADVERTISING RATES:
Full Page Colour .... EUR 1900.00
Agency Commission: 15%
Mechanical Data: Type Area: 210 x 297mm, Screen: 48 - 60 lpc

MUOTIMAAILMA 705868L74A-63
Editorial: Mikkolantie 1 A, 00640 HELSINKI
Tel: 9 75 21 469 **Fax:** 9 75 21 439
Email: muotimaailma@muotimaailma.fi **Web site:** http://www.muotimaailma.fi
ISSN: 1238-5638
Date Established: 1995; **Freq:** 6 issues yearly; **Circ:** 5,000
Usual Pagination: 120
Managing Director: Tomi Viitanen
Profile: Magazine about the fashion industry in Finland and abroad.
Language(s): Finnish; Russian
Readership: Clothing retailers, sportswear, footwear and fabrics retailers, textile and ready to wear industry.
ADVERTISING RATES:
Full Page Colour .... EUR 2338
SCC .... EUR 24.10
Agency Commission: 15%
Mechanical Data: Bleed Size: 220 x 315mm, Type Area: 200 x 285mm, Print Process: offset, Col Widths (Display): 48mm
Copy instructions: *Copy Date:* 14 days prior to publication date
CONSUMER: WOMEN'S INTEREST CONSUMER MAGAZINES: Women's Interest

MUOVI-PLAST 705180L39-5
Editorial: Pälkäneentie 18, 00510 HELSINKI
Tel: 9 86 89 910 **Fax:** 986899115
Email: muovi-plast@muoviyhdistys.fi **Web site:** http://www.muoviyhdistys.fi
ISSN: 0788-8430
Date Established: 1989; **Freq:** 6 issues yearly; **Circ:** 1,600
Usual Pagination: 40
Profile: Magazine focusing on the Finnish plastics industry.
Language(s): Finnish
Readership: Read by professionals at companies which produce plastic products and those which provide the plastic raw materials, semi-finished products and machinery.

Finland

ADVERTISING RATES:
Full Page Colour .... EUR 1800
SCC .... EUR 17.30
Mechanical Data: Bleed Size: 210 x 297mm, Type Area: 185 x 270mm, Print Process: offset, Screen: 54-60 lpc

MYYNTI & MARKKINOINTI
705145L2A-4
Formerly: Markkinointi-Myyntimiehet
Editorial: PL 1100/ Töölönkatu 11 A, 5 krs, 00101 HELSINKI **Tel:** 9 47 80 77 00 **Fax:** 9 47 80 77 30
Email: oili.valkila@smkj.fi **Web site:** http://www.myyntijamarkkinointi.fi
ISSN: 1458-5162
Date Established: 1932; **Freq:** 6 issues yearly - Published 9/year; **Circ:** 27,175
Usual Pagination: 84
Managing Editor: Oili Valkila
Profile: Magazine containing articles about sales, marketing and advertising.
Language(s): Finnish
Readership: Read by professionals in sales, buying and marketing.
ADVERTISING RATES:
Full Page Colour .... EUR 4200
SCC .... EUR 47.10
Agency Commission: 15%
Mechanical Data: Bleed Size: 210 x 297mm, Print Process: offset, Type Area: 185 x 248mm, No. of Columns (Display): 3, Col Widths (Display): 58mm, Film: negative, Screen: 60 lpc
BUSINESS: COMMUNICATIONS, ADVERTISING & MARKETING

NAISTUTKIMUS - KVINNOFORSKNING
15289L74A-64
Editorial: PL 1000, Historian laitos, 90014 OULUN YLIOPISTO **Tel:** 40 51 15 039
Email: naistutkimuslehti@oulu.fi **Web site:** http://www.nt-suns.org/nt-lehti/ntlehti.html
ISSN: 0784-3844
Date Established: 1988; **Freq:** Quarterly; **Annual Sub.:** EUR 45.00; **Circ:** 1,000
Usual Pagination: 88
Editor-in-Chief: Seija Jalagin
Profile: Magazine looking at the women's movement and women's studies in Finland today. Featuring feminist theory and critical gender research.
Language(s): Finnish; Swedish
Readership: Read by people interested in current research and debate in women's studies.
ADVERTISING RATES:
Full Page Colour .... EUR 250.00
Mechanical Data: Col Length: 195mm, Type Area: 195 x 132mm, Print Process: Offset, Page Width: 172mm, No. of Columns (Display): 2
Copy instructions: *Copy Date:* 15th of the month prior to publication date
CONSUMER: WOMEN'S INTEREST CONSUMER MAGAZINES: Women's Interest

NÄKÖALOJA
1606010L12B-140
Editorial: Kaitilankatu 11, 45130 KOUVOLA
Tel: 20 74 03 200 **Fax:** 20 74 03 300
Email: info@lumon.fi **Web site:** http://www.lumon.fi
ISSN: 1459-0352
Freq: Half-yearly; **Cover Price:** Free; **Circ:** 55,000
Usual Pagination: 40
Editor-in-Chief: Jyrki Hutri
Profile: Magazine about glass and aluminium building, especially balconies.
Language(s): Finnish
Readership: Customers of Lumon Oy.
BUSINESS: CERAMICS, POTTERY & GLASS: Glass

NATIONAL GEOGRAPHIC
706671L94J-50
Editorial: Siltasaarenkatu 18-20 A, 00530 HELSINKI
Tel: 20 76 08 568 **Fax:** 20 76 08 520
Email: toimitus@ngsuomi.com **Web site:** http://www.nationalgeographic-suomi.com
ISSN: 1457-5981
Date Established: 2001; **Freq:** Monthly - Published 14/year; **Circ:** 11,560
Usual Pagination: 124
Profile: Magazine about science, geography and travel.
Language(s): Finnish
ADVERTISING RATES:
Full Page Colour .... EUR 4100
SCC .... EUR 78.70
Agency Commission: 15%
Mechanical Data: Bleed Size: 175 x 254mm, Print Process: offset, Film: positive, Screen: 54 lpc
CONSUMER: OTHER CLASSIFICATIONS: Popular Science

NAUTIC
15378L91A-53
Formerly: Navigare
Editorial: Westendinkatu 7, 02160 ESPOO
Tel: 20 79 64 200 **Fax:** 20 79 64 111
Email: nautic@purjehtija.fi **Web site:** http://www.purjehtija.fi
ISSN: 1796-0576
Date Established: 1986; **Freq:** 6 issues yearly - Published 7/year; **Circ:** 50,000
Usual Pagination: 84
Profile: Magazine for members of the Finnish Boating Association.
Language(s): Finnish
ADVERTISING RATES:
Full Page Colour .... EUR 3600
SCC .... EUR 39.80
Agency Commission: 15%
Mechanical Data: Type Area: 210 x 280mm, Print Process: offset
CONSUMER: RECREATION & LEISURE: Boating & Yachting

NET
705181L5D-27
Editorial: Alma Media Lehdentekijät Oy, PL 502/ Munkkiniemen puistotie 25, 5.krs, 00101 HELSINKI
Tel: 10 66 51 02 **Fax:** 10 66 52 533
Email: net@fi.fujitsu.com **Web site:** http://www.net-lehti.com
ISSN: 0782-8217
Date Established: 1970; **Freq:** Quarterly; **Cover Price:** Free; **Circ:** 97,000
Usual Pagination: 16
Editor-in-Chief: Satu Pelttari
Profile: Current affairs and future views on information technology for work life and society. Net also presents applications and program products.
Language(s): Finnish
ADVERTISING RATES:
Full Page Colour .... EUR 4500.00
SCC .... EUR 40.10
Agency Commission: 15%
Mechanical Data: Type Area: 265 x 390mm, Print Process: coldset, Screen: 40 lpc
BUSINESS: COMPUTERS & AUTOMATION: Personal Computers

NEW HORIZONS
754884L73-85
Editorial: Katajanokanlaituri 5, 00160 HELSINKI
Tel: 9 62 29 640 **Fax:** 9 62 29 64 64
Email: info@ostromedia.fi **Web site:** http://www.newhorizons.fi
ISSN: 1459-8179
Date Established: 1999; **Freq:** 6 issues yearly; **Circ:** 15,000
Usual Pagination: 96
Profile: Current-affairs magazine about the northern hemisphere: politics, finance, science, technology, culture, history, fashion, travel, leisure and holidays.
Language(s): Russian
Readership: Russian-speakers in Finland, Sweden, Norway, Denmark, Germany, Estonia, Latvia, Lithuania and Russia.
ADVERTISING RATES:
Full Page Colour .... EUR 3060.00
SCC .... EUR 35.10
Agency Commission: 15%
Mechanical Data: Print Process: offset, Film: positive, Page Width: 217mm, Col Length: 290mm, No. of Columns (Display): 3, Type Area: 215 x 290mm

NIVALA-LEHTI
705008L72-885
Editorial: PL 2/ Kalliontie 30, 85501 NIVALA
Tel: 20 75 04 710 **Fax:** 20 75 04 719
Email: toimitus@nivala-lehti.fi **Web site:** http://www.nivala-lehti.fi
Date Established: 1949; **Freq:** 104 issues yearly; **Circ:** 5,954
Usual Pagination: 20
Profile: Newspaper issued in Nivala.
Language(s): Finnish
ADVERTISING RATES:
Full Page Colour .... EUR 2080
SCC .... EUR 9.50
Agency Commission: 17.5%
Mechanical Data: Page Width: 280mm, Col Length: 365mm, No. of Columns (Display): 6, Col Widths (Display): 39mm, Print Process: offset
Editions:
Nivala-lehti Verkkotoimitus
LOCAL NEWSPAPERS

NIVELTIETO
1687081L56K-1
Editorial: c/o Jyrki Laakso, Pajutie 16, 07940 LOVIISA **Tel:** 44 55 44 555
Email: jyrki.laakso@niveltieto.net **Web site:** http://www.tekonivel.net
Freq: Quarterly; **Circ:** 9,462
Profile: Magazine about nodes and reumatism treatment.
Language(s): Finnish
ADVERTISING RATES:
Full Page Colour .... EUR 2300
Mechanical Data: Type Area: 180 x 255mm
BUSINESS: HEALTH & MEDICAL: Chiropody

NLP-MIELILEHTI
705971L74Q-40
Editorial: Kalliokuja 4, 13100 HÄMEENLINNA
Tel: 3 61 21 827 **Fax:** 3 61 21 428
Web site: http://www.suomennlp-yhdistys.fi/lehti.html
Date Established: 1990; **Freq:** Quarterly; **Annual Sub.:** EUR 35.00; **Circ:** 1,200
Usual Pagination: 36
Editor-in-Chief: Riitta Asikainen
Profile: Magazine about a healthy, positive way of living to make better results in life.
Language(s): Finnish
ADVERTISING RATES:
Full Page Colour .... EUR 260.00

NOKIAN UUTISET
704858L72-890
Editorial: PL 13/ Välimäenkatu 23, 37101 NOKIA
Tel: 10 66 51 10 **Fax:** 3 31 43 14 44
Email: nu.toimitus@sps.fi **Web site:** http://www.nokianuutiset.fi
ISSN: 0782-5560
Date Established: 1913; **Freq:** 104 issues yearly; **Circ:** 8,955
Usual Pagination: 12
Profile: Newspaper issued in Nokia.
Language(s): Finnish
ADVERTISING RATES:
Full Page Colour .... EUR 4314
SCC .... EUR 19.70
Agency Commission: 15%
Mechanical Data: Col Widths (Display): 44mm, No. of Columns (Display): 6, Type Area: 284 x 420mm, Screen: 34 lpc, Print Process: offset, Page Width: 315mm, Col Length: 460mm
LOCAL NEWSPAPERS

NORDICUM
706343L1A-9_40
Editorial: Pälkäneentie 19 A, 00510 HELSINKI
Tel: 9 68 66 250 **Fax:** 9 68 52 940
Email: info@publico.com **Web site:** http://www.nordicum.com
ISSN: 1236-3839
Date Established: 1993; **Freq:** 6 issues yearly; **Circ:** 15,000
Usual Pagination: 90
Profile: Scandinavian business magazine focusing on logistics, environment, biotechnology, energy, real estate, pulp and paper, packaging and forest industry.
Language(s): English
ADVERTISING RATES:
Full Page Colour .... EUR 4700
SCC .... EUR 61.40
Mechanical Data: Type Area: 210 x 277mm, Film: positive, Screen: 60 lpc
BUSINESS: FINANCE & ECONOMICS

NUORI LÄÄKÄRI - YNGRE LÄKARE
705297L56A-54
Editorial: PL 49/ Mäkelänkatu 2 A, 5 krs, 00501 HELSINKI **Tel:** 9 39 30 873 **Fax:** 9 39 30 773
Web site: http://www.nly.fi/nuori-laakari
ISSN: 0355-3973
Date Established: 1964; **Freq:** 6 issues yearly - Published 8/year; **Circ:** 20,000
Usual Pagination: 82
Profile: Magazine about doctors' education, health politics and international medical issues.
Language(s): Finnish
ADVERTISING RATES:
Full Page Colour .... EUR 1670
SCC .... EUR 19.80
Mechanical Data: Print Process: offset, Type Area: 210 x 280mm

NYA ÅLAND
15403L67B-6200
Editorial: PB 21/Uppgårdsvägen 6, 22101 MARIEHAMN **Tel:** 18 23 444 **Fax:** 18 23 449
Email: redaktion@nyan.ax **Web site:** http://www.nyan.ax
ISSN: 0359-1414
Date Established: 1981
Circ: 6,769
Usual Pagination: 20
Profile: Politically neutral newspaper is issued on the Åland (Ahvenanmaa) Islands.
Language(s): Swedish
ADVERTISING RATES:
Full Page Colour .... EUR 5952
SCC .... EUR 24.80
Agency Commission: 15%
Mechanical Data: No. of Columns (Display): 6, Page Width: 290mm, Col Length: 400mm, Col Widths (Display): 45mm, Screen: 40 lpc, Film: negative, Print Process: offset
Editions:
Nya Åland Internetredaktionen
REGIONAL DAILY & SUNDAY NEWSPAPERS: Regional Daily Newspapers

NYKYPÄIVÄ
705397L82-15
Editorial: Runeberginkatu 5 B, 7. krs, 00100 HELSINKI **Tel:** 20 74 88 488 **Fax:** 20 74 88 507
Email: nypa@nykypaiva.fi **Web site:** http://www.nykypaiva.fi
ISSN: 0783-1668
Date Established: 1955; **Freq:** Weekly - Published on Friday; **Circ:** 22,475
Usual Pagination: 28
Managing Editor: Eero Iloniemi
Profile: Official journal of the National Coalition Party containing articles on politics, economics, social affairs.
Language(s): Finnish
ADVERTISING RATES:
Full Page Colour .... EUR 2910
SCC .... EUR 12.90
Agency Commission: 15%
Mechanical Data: Type Area: 254 x 375mm, Bleed Size: 290 x 420mm, Print Process: offset, No. of Columns (Display): 6, Col Widths (Display): 39mm, Screen: 40 lpc
CONSUMER: CURRENT AFFAIRS & POLITICS

NYKY-TAMPERE
705743L72-910
Editorial: Kuninkaankatu 13 B, 33210 TAMPERE
Tel: 50 56 45 054
Email: plentys@saunalahti.fi **Web site:** http://www.tamperelainenkokoomus.fi/nykytampere-lehdet
Freq: Quarterly; **Cover Price:** Free; **Circ:** 88,000
Usual Pagination: 12
Editor-in-Chief: Harri Airaksinen
Profile: Local newspaper issued in Tampere by The Finnish Coalition Party.
Language(s): Finnish
ADVERTISING RATES:
SCC .... EUR 22
Mechanical Data: Col Widths (Display): 42mm, No. of Columns (Display): 6, Type Area: 265 x 385mm
LOCAL NEWSPAPERS

O & P
14870L1C-15
Formerly: Osuuspankkilainen
Editorial: PL 308, 00101 HELSINKI **Tel:** 10 25 20 10 **Fax:** 10 25 22 298
Email: viestinta@op.fi **Web site:** http://www.nordinfo.fi/fi/op.html
ISSN: 0475-1647
Freq: 6 issues yearly; Free to qualifying individuals ; **Circ:** 27,405
Managing Editor: Peter Nordling
Profile: Magazine to support the personnel and other interest groups of the Central Union of Cooperative Banks with bank news and views on national economy.
Language(s): Finnish
ADVERTISING RATES:
Full Page Colour .... EUR 2278
Mechanical Data: Type Area: 190 x 250mm, No. of Columns (Display): 4, Col Widths (Display): 40mm, Print Process: offset, Screen: 54-60 lpc
BUSINESS: FINANCE & ECONOMICS: Banking

OHUTLEVY
705182L27-2
Editorial: PL 10/ Eteläranta 10, 00131 HELSINKI
Tel: 9 45 12 706 **Fax:** 9 62 44 62
Email: tuire.mikluha@hut.fi **Web site:** http://www.ohutlevy.com
ISSN: 1239-4122
Freq: Half-yearly; **Annual Sub.:** EUR 25.00; **Circ:** 1,500
Usual Pagination: 48
Editor-in-Chief: Simo Mäkimattila
Profile: Magazine of the Technology Industries of Finland.
Language(s): Finnish
Readership: Read by members.
ADVERTISING RATES:
Full Page Colour .... EUR 1200.00
SCC .... EUR 11.30
Mechanical Data: Print Process: offset, Type Area: 170 x 260mm, Bleed Size: 180 x 265mm, Screen: 60 lpc, Film: positive

OLE HYVÄ!
1687083L1E-70
Editorial: Iso Roobertinkatu 43 A, 00120 HELSINKI
Tel: 9 68 44 550 **Fax:** 9 60 70 42
Email: pekka.porko@plus-ryhma.fi **Web site:** http://www.olehyva-lehti.fi
ISSN: 1795-7184
Date Established: 2005; **Freq:** 6 issues yearly; **Cover Price:** Free; **Circ:** 100,000
Usual Pagination: 64
Editor-in-Chief: Pekka Porko
Profile: Magazine about home improvement, interior-design and gardening.
Language(s): Finnish
Readership: Customers of K-Rauta.
ADVERTISING RATES:
Full Page Colour .... EUR 5930.00
Mechanical Data: Type Area: 210 x 297mm, Print Process: offset
BUSINESS: FINANCE & ECONOMICS: Property

OLIVIA
1791245L74B-50
Editorial: Siltasaarenkatu 18-20 A, 00530 HELSINKI
Tel: 20 76 08 500 **Fax:** 20 76 08 520
Email: olivia@bonnier.fi **Web site:** http://www.olivialehti.fi
ISSN: 1796-7066
Date Established: 2007; **Freq:** Monthly; **Circ:** 46,333
Usual Pagination: 188
Editor-in-Chief: Niina Leino; **Managing Editor:** Mari Paalosalo-Jussinmäki
Profile: Magazine about women's interest.
Language(s): Finnish
Readership: 30-40-year old women.
ADVERTISING RATES:
Full Page Colour .... EUR 5600
SCC .... EUR 62.80
Agency Commission: 15%
Mechanical Data: Bleed Size: 230 x 297mm, Print Process: offset, Screen: 60 lpc
Copy instructions: *Copy Date:* 15 days prior to publication date
CONSUMER: WOMEN'S INTEREST CONSUMER MAGAZINES: Women's Interest - Fashion

OMA KOTI KULLAN KALLIS
1828246L4B-8
Editorial: Simonkatu 12 B 13, 00100 HELSINKI
Tel: 10 38 78 700 **Fax:** 10 38 78 788
Email: info@omakotilehti.fi **Web site:** http://www.omakotilehti.fi
ISSN: 1796-8992
Date Established: 2007; **Freq:** Monthly - Published 10/year; **Circ:** 33,727
Usual Pagination: 124
Profile: Magazine about home and interior-design.
Language(s): Finnish
ADVERTISING RATES:
Full Page Colour .... EUR 3750
SCC .... EUR 34.70

Mechanical Data: Type Area: 190 x 270mm, Bleed Size: 210 x 297mm, Print Process: offset
Copy instructions: *Copy Date:* 30 days prior to publication date
BUSINESS: ARCHITECTURE & BUILDING: Interior Design & Flooring

OMA LIIKUNTA 715030L75A-47
Formerly: Liikunta Extra; FIX Liikunta
Editorial: Helsinginkatu 25, 00510 HELSINKI
Tel: 9 34 88 600 **Fax:** 9 34 88 64 00
Email: mona.helin@urheiluhallit.fi **Web site:** http://www.urheiluhallit.fi
ISSN: 1459-0409
Freq: Half-yearly; **Cover Price:** Free; **Circ:** 135,000
Usual Pagination: 24
Editor-in-Chief: Eija Holmala
Profile: Publication about different sports activities in the Helsinki region.
Language(s): Finnish
Readership: All households in the Helsinki region.
CONSUMER: SPORT

OMAKOTISANOMAT 705053L74K-35
Editorial: Maailman-Matti 2 A 2, 02230 ESPOO
Tel: 9 54 07 310 **Fax:** 95031810
Email: omakotisanomat@kolumbus.fi **Web site:** http://www.omakotisanomat.fi
ISSN: 1797-1829
Date Established: 1979; **Freq:** Quarterly - Published 5/year; **Circ:** 18,000
Usual Pagination: 36
Profile: Magazine about small flat housing in the Helsinki region.
Language(s): Finnish
ADVERTISING RATES:
Full Page Colour .... EUR 1950
SCC .... EUR 18
Mechanical Data: Print Process: offset, Screen: 54-60 lpc, Type Area: 188 x 270mm
Copy instructions: *Copy Date:* 12 days prior to publication date
CONSUMER: WOMEN'S INTEREST CONSUMER MAGAZINES: Home Purchase

OMISTAJA & SIJOITTAJA 706421L1F-60
Editorial: Kynämies Oy, Köydenpunojankatu 2 aD, 00180 HELSINKI **Tel:** 9 15 661 **Fax:** 915668600
Web site: http://www.omistajaonline.fi
ISSN: 1239-7105
Freq: Half-yearly; **Cover Price:** Free; **Circ:** 12,000 Unique Users
Usual Pagination: 8
Profile: Publication of the Ministry of Trade and Industry is about ownership and investments.
Language(s): Finnish; Swedish
BUSINESS: FINANCE & ECONOMICS: Investment

OODI 706075L56F-3
Editorial: PL 365/ Uusikatu 50, 90101 OULU
Tel: 10 34 52 000
Web site: http://www.odl.fi
ISSN: 1457-8412
Freq: Quarterly; **Circ:** 100,000
Usual Pagination: 16
Editor-in-Chief: Seppo Rajaniemi
Profile: Magazine about health care and social-services.
Language(s): Finnish
Readership: Customers in northern Finland.
BUSINESS: HEALTH & MEDICAL: Health Education

OOPPERASANOMAT 753127L76F-98
Editorial: PL 176/ Helsinginkatu 58, 00251 HELSINKI
Tel: 9 40 30 21 **Fax:** 9 40 30 22 95
Email: press@operafin.fi **Web site:** http://www.ooppera.fi
Freq: Half-yearly; **Cover Price:** Free; **Circ:** 80,000
Usual Pagination: 32
Managing Editor: Heidi Almi
Profile: Publication by the Finnish National Opera about performances.
Language(s): Finnish
CONSUMER: MUSIC & PERFORMING ARTS: Opera

OOPPERAUUTISET 705761L76F-100
Editorial: Olavinkatu 27, 57130 SAVONLINNA
Tel: 15 47 67 50 **Fax:** 15 47 67 540
Email: info@operafestival.fi **Web site:** http://www.operafestival.fi
ISSN: 0786-342X
Freq: Quarterly; **Cover Price:** Free; **Circ:** 65,000
Usual Pagination: 64
Profile: Magazine about the opera festival in Savonlinna.
Language(s): Finnish
Readership: Opera enthusiasts.
CONSUMER: MUSIC & PERFORMING ARTS: Opera

OPAS-GUIDE 15077L50-90
Editorial: Verkatehtaankatu 2, 33100 TAMPERE
Tel: 3 21 10 802 **Fax:** 3 21 10 802
Email: toimisto@suomenopasliitto.fi **Web site:** http://www.suomenopasliitto.fi
ISSN: 0788-2386
Date Established: 1982; **Freq:** Quarterly; **Annual Sub.:** EUR 14.00; **Circ:** 3,000
Usual Pagination: 24
Editor-in-Chief: Margit Sellberg
Profile: Journal of the Federation of Finnish Tourist Guide Associations.
Language(s): Finnish; Swedish
Readership: Read by tourist guides based in Scandinavia and employees in travel agencies and organisations.
ADVERTISING RATES:
Full Page Mono .... EUR 504.00
Agency Commission: 15%
Mechanical Data: Type Area: 180 x 260mm
BUSINESS: TRAVEL & TOURISM

OPETTAJA 15148L62B-11
Editorial: PL 94/ Rautatieläisenkatu 6, 00521 HELSINKI **Tel:** 20 74 89 600 **Fax:** 20 74 89 760
Email: opettaja@oaj.fi **Web site:** http://www.opettaja.fi
ISSN: 0355-3965
Date Established: 1906; **Freq:** Weekly; Free to qualifying individuals ; **Circ:** 97,642
Usual Pagination: 88
Editor-in-Chief: Hannu Laaksola; **Managing Editor:** Annu Somppi
Profile: Magazine for teachers in Finnish comprehensive schools, vocational schools and colleges.
Language(s): Finnish
ADVERTISING RATES:
Full Page Colour .... EUR 3950
SCC .... EUR 33.20
Agency Commission: 15%
Mechanical Data: Trim Size: 217 x 280mm, Print Process: Offset, Col Widths (Display): 44mm, No. of Columns (Display): 4, Type Area: 217 x 280mm, Film: positive, Screen: 54 lpc
BUSINESS: CHURCH & SCHOOL EQUIPMENT & EDUCATION: Education Teachers

OP-POHJOLA 624052L1C-10
Formerly: Kultaraha
Editorial: Markkinointiviestintä Dialogi Oy, PL 410, 00081 A-LEHDET **Tel:** 9 42 42 73 30 **Fax:** 942427333
Email: asiakaslehdet@dialogi.fi **Web site:** http://www.op.fi
ISSN: 1459-7675
Date Established: 1939; **Freq:** Quarterly; **Cover Price:** Free; **Circ:** 871,294
Usual Pagination: 48
Managing Editor: Katarina Cygnel-Nuortie
Profile: Magazine containing information about economic and investment matters, also includes current affairs.
Language(s): Finnish
Readership: Read by private investors.
ADVERTISING RATES:
Full Page Colour .... EUR 8320
SCC .... EUR 115.50
Mechanical Data: Type Area: 200 x 267mm, Bleed Size: 230 x 297mm, Print Process: Offset, Film: Digital, Screen: 60 lpc, No. of Columns (Display): 3, Col Length: 267mm, Page Width: 200mm
BUSINESS: FINANCE & ECONOMICS: Banking

OP-POHJOLA-NYTT 705231L1C-2
Formerly: Andelsbanknytt
Editorial: Nordinfo Ab, Lillviksvägen 6, 02360 ESBO
Tel: 9 88 86 017 **Fax:** 9 88 86 019
Email: redaktionen@nordinfo.fi **Web site:** http://www.nordinfo.fi
ISSN: 1235-0958
Date Established: 1929; **Freq:** Quarterly; **Cover Price:** Free; **Circ:** 30,498
Usual Pagination: 16
Profile: Customer-magazine of the bank group OP-Pohjola-ryhmä and sent to Swedish-speaking members, customers and employees mainly in the Helsinki and coast line region.
Language(s): Swedish
Mechanical Data: Col Widths (Display): 40mm, No. of Columns (Display): 4, Type Area: 210 x 270mm, Screen: 54-60 lpc, Print Process: offset
BUSINESS: FINANCE & ECONOMICS: Banking

ORIMATTILAN SANOMAT 704935L72-915
Editorial: PL 5 / Erkontie 17, 16301 ORIMATTILA
Tel: 3 87 66 78 **Fax:** 37774244
Email: toimitus@orimattilansanomat.fi **Web site:** http://www.orimattilansanomat.fi
ISSN: 1236-6609
Date Established: 1951; **Freq:** 104 issues yearly; **Circ:** 4,588
Usual Pagination: 16
Profile: Newspaper issued in Orimattila, Artjärvi, Pukkila and Myrskylä.
Language(s): Finnish
ADVERTISING RATES:
Full Page Colour .... EUR 6674
SCC .... EUR 16.20
Mechanical Data: Print Process: offset rotation, No. of Columns (Display): 8, Col Widths (Display): 44mm, Type Area: 380 x 515mm
Copy instructions: *Copy Date:* 10 days prior to publication date
LOCAL NEWSPAPERS

ORIVEDEN SANOMAT 704907L72-925
Editorial: PL 33 / Lehmilaidantie 6, 35301 ORIVESI
Tel: 3 35 89 500 **Fax:** 3 35 89 535
Email: toimitus@orivedensanomat.fi **Web site:** http://www.orivedensanomat.fi
ISSN: 0789-8126
Date Established: 1926; **Freq:** 104 issues yearly; **Circ:** 5,344
Usual Pagination: 12
Profile: Newspaper issued in Orivesi, Juupajoki and Längelmä.
Language(s): Finnish
ADVERTISING RATES:
Full Page Colour .... EUR 3951
SCC .... EUR 13.60
Agency Commission: 15%
Mechanical Data: Col Length: 415mm, No. of Columns (Display): 7, Col Widths (Display): 39mm, Screen: 34 lpc, Film: negative, Print Process: offset rotation
LOCAL NEWSPAPERS

ÖSTERBOTTENS TIDNING 15187L67B-4000
Formerly: Jakobstads Tidning
Editorial: PB 22/Jakobsgatan 13, 68601 JAKOBSTAD **Tel:** 6 78 48 800 **Fax:** 6 78 48 883
Email: nyheter@ot.fi **Web site:** http://www.ot.fi
ISSN: 1791-5492
Date Established: 1898
Circ: 14,603
Usual Pagination: 12
Editor-in-Chief: Margareta Björklund; **Managing Editor:** Lars Hedman
Profile: Third biggest Swedish-language newspaper in Finland is issued mainly in northern Ostrobotnia on the west coast.
Language(s): Swedish
ADVERTISING RATES:
Full Page Colour .... EUR 9996
SCC .... EUR 24.50
Agency Commission: 15%
Mechanical Data: No. of Columns (Display): 8, Col Widths (Display): 44mm, Col Length: 515mm, Print Process: 4-colour offset rotation
Copy instructions: *Copy Date:* 8 days prior to publication date
Editions:
Österbottens Tidning Internetredaktionen
REGIONAL DAILY & SUNDAY NEWSPAPERS: Regional Daily Newspapers

ÖSTERBOTTENS TIDNING NYKARLEBY 708202L67E-202
Formerly: Jakobstads Tidning Nykarleby
Editorial: Bankgatan 12, 66900 NYKARLEBY
Tel: 6 78 48 470
Email: britt.sund@ot.fi **Web site:** http://www.ot.fi
Profile: Nykarleby local office of Österbottens Tidning.
Language(s): Swedish
REGIONAL DAILY & SUNDAY NEWSPAPERS: Regional Offices

ÖSTRA NYLAND 15204L67B-6400
Formerly: Östra Nyland - Kotka Nyheter
Editorial: PB 58/ Alexandersgatan 8, 07901 LOVISA
Tel: 19 55 73 41 **Fax:** 19 53 17 59
Email: red@on.fi **Web site:** http://www.on.fi
ISSN: 0356-5653
Date Established: 1881
Circ: 3,816
Usual Pagination: 28
Profile: Regional newspaper issued in Loviisa, Pernaja, Porvoo and Kotka.
Language(s): Swedish
ADVERTISING RATES:
Full Page Colour .... EUR 3176
SCC .... EUR 14.50
Agency Commission: 15%
Mechanical Data: Type Area: 255 x 370mm, Col Length: 370mm, Page Width: 255mm, No. of Columns (Display): 5, Col Widths (Display): 47mm, Print Process: offset, Screen: 100 lpi
REGIONAL DAILY & SUNDAY NEWSPAPERS: Regional Daily Newspapers

OULU-LEHTI 705041L72-930
Editorial: PL 52 / Lekatie 4, 90101 OULU
Tel: 8 53 70 022 **Fax:** 8 53 70 327
Email: toimitus@oululehti.fi **Web site:** http://www.oululehti.fi
ISSN: 1236-7524
Date Established: 1959; **Freq:** 104 issues yearly; **Cover Price:** Free; **Circ:** 100,000
Usual Pagination: 8
Editor-in-Chief: Mirja Rintala
Profile: Newspaper distributed in Oulu.
Language(s): Finnish
ADVERTISING RATES:
Full Page Colour .... EUR 2050
SCC .... EUR 22
Mechanical Data: Col Length: 365mm, No. of Columns (Display): 9, Col Widths (Display): 39mm, Print Process: offset rotation, Screen: 34 lpc, Page Width: 255mm
LOCAL NEWSPAPERS

OULUN SANOMAT 705106L72-940
Editorial: PL 18, 90400 OULU **Tel:** 40 55 50 239
Fax: 8 31 15 540
Email: toimitus@oulunsanomat.fi **Web site:** http://www.oulunsanomat.fi
ISSN: 0783-9774
Date Established: 1987; **Freq:** Weekly; **Cover Price:** Free; **Circ:** 62,000
Editor-in-Chief: Veera Visuri
Profile: Local newspaper issued in Oulu.
Language(s): Finnish
ADVERTISING RATES:
SCC .... EUR 22
Mechanical Data: Col Widths (Display): 38mm, No. of Columns (Display): 7, Col Length: 360mm, Page Width: 257mm
LOCAL NEWSPAPERS

OUTOKUMMUN SEUTU 704976L72-955
Editorial: PL 7 / Koulukatu 2, 83501 OUTOKUMPU
Tel: 10 23 08 850 **Fax:** 10 23 08 860
Email: toimitus@outokummunseutu.fi **Web site:** http://www.outokummunseutu.fi
ISSN: 0357-1386
Date Established: 1968; **Freq:** 104 issues yearly; **Circ:** 4,721
Usual Pagination: 12
Profile: Newspaper issued in Outokumpu and Polvijärvi.
Language(s): Finnish
ADVERTISING RATES:
Full Page Colour .... EUR 2738
SCC .... EUR 12.50
Mechanical Data: No. of Columns (Display): 5, Col Widths (Display): 47mm, Col Length: 365mm
Editions:
Outokummun Seutu Verkkotoimitus
LOCAL NEWSPAPERS

PÄÄKAUPUNKISEUDUN AUTOUUTISET 706218L31R-30
Editorial: Nuijatie 11 B, 01650 VANTAA
Tel: 3 85 53 260 **Fax:** 38532009
Email: tuulenkyla@legenda.fi **Web site:** http://www.autouutiset.com
Date Established: 1994; **Freq:** 6 issues yearly; **Cover Price:** Free; **Circ:** 157,000
Usual Pagination: 20
Profile: Magazine about cars, spare parts and car repair services.
Language(s): Finnish
ADVERTISING RATES:
Full Page Colour .... EUR 3260
SCC .... EUR 15
Mechanical Data: Bleed Size: 289 x 405mm, Type Area: 255 x 360mm, Print Process: offset, Screen: 40 lpc, No. of Columns (Display): 5-6
BUSINESS: MOTOR TRADE: Motor Trade Related

PÄÄLLYSTÖLEHTI 15032L40-70
Editorial: Laivastokatu 1 b, 00160 HELSINKI
Tel: 50 35 57 289 **Fax:** 9 72 62 299
Email: toimisto@paallystoliitto.fi **Web site:** http://www.paallystoliitto.fi
ISSN: 0788-8554
Date Established: 1930; **Freq:** 6 issues yearly; **Circ:** 6,000
Usual Pagination: 36
Editor-in-Chief: Ari Pakarinen
Profile: Magazine containing information of interest to soldiers involved in frontier defence.
Language(s): Finnish
ADVERTISING RATES:
Full Page Colour .... EUR 700.00
Agency Commission: 15%
Mechanical Data: Type Area: 185 x 260mm, No. of Columns (Display): 3, Col Widths (Display): 59mm, Screen: 48 lpc mono, 60 lpc colour, Print Process: offset

PADASJOEN SANOMAT 704934L72-960
Editorial: PL 3/ Koivutie 8, 17501 PADASJOKI
Tel: 3 55 27 500 **Fax:** 3 55 27 525
Email: toimitus@padasjoensanomat.fi **Web site:** http://www.padasjoensanomat.fi
ISSN: 0784-6568
Date Established: 1950; **Freq:** Weekly; **Circ:** 3,640
Usual Pagination: 12
Profile: Newspaper issued in Lahti and Padasjoki.
Language(s): Finnish
ADVERTISING RATES:
Full Page Colour .... EUR 2622
SCC .... EUR 11.50
Agency Commission: 15%
Mechanical Data: Page Width: 260mm, Col Length: 380mm, No. of Columns (Display): 6, Col Widths (Display): 40mm
LOCAL NEWSPAPERS

PAIKALLISLIIKENNE 764847L49B-100
Editorial: Unioninkatu 22, 3. krs, 00130 HELSINKI
Tel: 9 22 89 95 10 **Fax:** 922899550
Email: pekka.aalto@pllry.fi **Web site:** http://www.paikallisliikenneliitto.com
ISSN: 0788-6365
Freq: Half-yearly; **Circ:** 4,500
Usual Pagination: 32
Profile: Magazine about public transport in Finland.
Language(s): Finnish
ADVERTISING RATES:
Full Page Colour .... EUR 1200

Finland

PAIKALLISUUTISET 704925L72-975
Editorial: PL 40/ Savonmäentie 1, 40801 VAAJAKOSKI **Tel:** 40 54 75 111 **Fax:** 201876103
Email: toimitus@paikallisuutiset.fi **Web site:** http://www.paikallisuutiset.fi
ISSN: 1456-2952
Date Established: 1964; **Freq:** Weekly; **Circ:** 1,675
Usual Pagination: 12
Profile: Newspaper issued in Toivakka, Uurainen and Jyväskylän maalaiskunta.
Language(s): Finnish
ADVERTISING RATES:
Full Page Colour .... EUR 2964
SCC .... EUR 13
Agency Commission: 15%
Mechanical Data: No. of Columns (Display): 6, Col Widths (Display): 40mm, Screen: 28-34 lpc
LOCAL NEWSPAPERS

PAINOMAAILMA 15037L41A-120
Editorial: Markkinointiviestintä Dialogi Oy, PL 410, 00811 HELSINKI **Tel:** 9 42 42 73 30 **Fax:** 942427333
Email: ari.malmberg@dialogi.fi **Web site:** http://www.painomaailma.fi
ISSN: 1235-905X
Date Established: 1906; **Freq:** 6 issues yearly - Published 8/year; **Annual Sub.:** EUR 110; **Circ:** 2,967
Usual Pagination: 66
Managing Editor: Ari Malmberg
Profile: Magazine focusing on all aspects of the graphic arts industry.
Language(s): Finnish
Readership: Read by graphic artists and the graphic arts industry.
ADVERTISING RATES:
Full Page Colour .... EUR 2920
SCC .... EUR 24.50
Mechanical Data: Bleed Size: 210 x 297mm, No. of Columns (Display): 4, Col Widths (Display): 42mm, Print Process: offset, Screen: 60 lpc, Type Area: 203 x 267mm
Copy instructions: *Copy Date:* 22 days prior to publication date
BUSINESS: PRINTING & STATIONERY: Printing

PAKKAUS 15023L35-10
Editorial: Ritarikatu 3 b A, 00170 HELSINKI
Tel: 9 68 40 340 **Fax:** 968403410
Email: roger.bagge@pakkaus.com **Web site:** http://www.pakkaus.com
ISSN: 0031-0131
Date Established: 1964; **Freq:** 6 issues yearly - Published 8/year; **Annual Sub.:** EUR 75; **Circ:** 2,500
Usual Pagination: 48
Profile: Journal focusing on the packaging and manufacturing industry.
Language(s): Finnish
Readership: Members of the Finnish Packaging Association.
ADVERTISING RATES:
Full Page Colour .... EUR 2335
SCC .... EUR 22.80
Agency Commission: 15%
Mechanical Data: Type Area: 265 x 185mm, Trim Size: 297 x 210mm, Screen: 60 lpc, Print Process: Offset, Col Length: 265mm, Page Width: 185mm, Col Widths (Display): 57/42mm, No. of Columns (Display): 3/4
Copy instructions: *Copy Date:* 16 days prior to publication date

PAM 706620L14L-103
Editorial: PL 54/ Paasivuorenkatu 4-6 A, 2 krs, 00531 HELSINKI **Tel:** 20 77 40 02 **Fax:** 207742055
Email: toimitus@pam.fi **Web site:** http://www.pam-lehti.fi
ISSN: 1457-2133
Date Established: 2000; **Freq:** 26 issues yearly - Published 20/year; **Annual Sub.:** EUR 30; **Circ:** 185,000
Usual Pagination: 36
Editor-in-Chief: Auli Kivenmaa
Profile: Union membership journal for people working in the private service business field.
Language(s): Finnish; Swedish
ADVERTISING RATES:
Full Page Colour .... EUR 3620
SCC .... EUR 22
Agency Commission: 15%
Mechanical Data: No. of Columns (Display): 5, Print Process: offset, Col Widths (Display): 40mm, Trim Size: 240 x 340mm, Bleed Size: 245 x 350mm
BUSINESS: COMMERCE, INDUSTRY & MANAGEMENT: Trade Unions

PANDAN POLKU 708086L57-60
Formerly: WWF Uutiset
Editorial: Lintulahdenkatu 10, 00500 HELSINKI
Tel: 9 77 40 100 **Fax:** 9 77 40 21 39
Web site: http://www.wwf.fi
ISSN: 1458-5308
Date Established: 1991; **Freq:** Quarterly; **Circ:** 18,700
Usual Pagination: 24
Editor-in-Chief: Anne Brax
Profile: Magazine for Finnish environment and animal-protection supporters of World Wide Foundation.
Language(s): Finnish
ADVERTISING RATES:
Full Page Colour .... EUR 2495.00
SCC .... EUR 30.80
Mechanical Data: Type Area: 210 x 270mm

PAPERI JA PUU 15059L46-60
Formerly: Paperi ja Puu - Paper and Timber
Editorial: Melkonkatu 28 D, 00210 HELSINKI
Email: carita.paivanen@legendium.fi **Web site:** http://www.paperijapuu.fi
ISSN: 0031-1243
Date Established: 1919; **Freq:** Quarterly; **Circ:** 4,000
Usual Pagination: 64
Editor-in-Chief: Jouni Törrönen; **Managing Editor:** Carita Päivänen
Profile: Journal covering the paper and timber industries.
Language(s): English; Finnish
ADVERTISING RATES:
Full Page Colour .... EUR 2900
SCC .... EUR 28.50
Agency Commission: 15%
Mechanical Data: Trim Size: 297 x 210mm, Screen: 60 lpc, Print Process: Sheetfed offset, Type Area: 271 x 184mm, Col Length: 271mm, Page Width: 184mm, No. of Columns (Display): 3/4, Col Widths (Display): 58/43mm, Film: positive
Editions:
Paperijapuu.fi

PAPERI JA PUU 15059L46-204
Formerly: Paperi ja Puu - Paper and Timber
Editorial: Melkonkatu 28 D, 00210 HELSINKI
Email: carita.paivanen@legendium.fi **Web site:** http://www.paperijapuu.fi
ISSN: 0031-1243
Date Established: 1919; **Freq:** Quarterly; **Circ:** 4,000
Usual Pagination: 64
Editor-in-Chief: Jouni Törrönen; **Managing Editor:** Carita Päivänen
Profile: Journal covering the paper and timber industries.
Language(s): English; Finnish
ADVERTISING RATES:
Full Page Colour .... EUR 2900
SCC .... EUR 28.50
Agency Commission: 15%
Mechanical Data: Trim Size: 297 x 210mm, Screen: 60 lpc, Print Process: Sheetfed offset, Type Area: 271 x 184mm, Col Length: 271mm, Page Width: 184mm, No. of Columns (Display): 3/4, Col Widths (Display): 58/43mm, Film: positive
Editions:
Paperijapuu.fi

PAPERI JA PUU 15059L46-204
Formerly: Paperi ja Puu - Paper and Timber
Editorial: Melkonkatu 28 D, 00210 HELSINKI
Email: carita.paivanen@legendium.fi **Web site:** http://www.paperijapuu.fi
ISSN: 0031-1243
Date Established: 1919; **Freq:** Quarterly; **Circ:** 4,000
Usual Pagination: 64
Editor-in-Chief: Jouni Törrönen; **Managing Editor:** Carita Päivänen
Profile: Journal covering the paper and timber industries.
Language(s): English; Finnish
ADVERTISING RATES:
Full Page Colour .... EUR 2900
SCC .... EUR 28.50
Agency Commission: 15%
Mechanical Data: Trim Size: 297 x 210mm, Screen: 60 lpc, Print Process: Sheetfed offset, Type Area: 271 x 184mm, Col Length: 271mm, Page Width: 184mm, No. of Columns (Display): 3/4, Col Widths (Display): 58/43mm, Film: positive
Editions:
Paperijapuu.fi

PAPERILIITTO-LEHTI 15024L36-50
Formerly: Paperiliitto
Editorial: PL 326/ Paasivuorenkatu 4-6 A, 00531 HELSINKI **Tel:** 9 70 891 **Fax:** 9 70 12 279
Email: tiedotus@paperiliitto.fi **Web site:** http://www.paperiliitto.fi
Freq: Monthly; **Cover Price:** Free; **Circ:** 50,800
Usual Pagination: 16
Editor-in-Chief: Jouko Ahonen
Profile: Newspaper concerning the paper industry. Contains trade news, leisure, economics, union and government information.
Language(s): Finnish
Readership: Aimed at workers in the paper industry.
ADVERTISING RATES:
Full Page Colour .... EUR 2550.00
SCC .... EUR 23.60
Agency Commission: 15%
Mechanical Data: Type Area: 230 x 270mm, Col Widths (Display): 49mm, No. of Columns (Display): 4, Col Length: 248mm, Print Process: offset
BUSINESS: PAPER

PAPPER 1708435L74Q-42
Editorial: Box 217/ Mannerheimvägen 18, 00101 HELSINGFORS **Tel:** 50 55 58 494
Email: peppar@peppar.fi **Web site:** http://www.papper.fi
ISSN: 1795-9233
Date Established: 2006; **Freq:** Monthly - Published 9/ a year; **Cover Price:** Free; **Circ:** 140,000
Usual Pagination: 40
Editor-in-Chief: Jeanette Öhman
Profile: Lifestyle-magazine about youth issues.
Language(s): Swedish
Readership: Young people of age 15-35 in the Swedish-speaking regions of Finland.
ADVERTISING RATES:
Full Page Colour .... EUR 5400
SCC .... EUR 37
Agency Commission: 15%
Mechanical Data: Type Area: 251 x 364mm, Screen: 34 lpc, Bleed Size: 280 x 395mm
CONSUMER: WOMEN'S INTEREST CONSUMER MAGAZINES: Lifestyle

PARDIANYT 1667001L14L-104
Editorial: Ratamestarinkatu 11, 00520 HELSINKI
Tel: 75 32 47 575 **Fax:** 75 32 47 576
Email: riitta.nieminen@pardia.fi **Web site:** http://www.pardia.fi
ISSN: 1795-5475
Date Established: 2005; **Freq:** Quarterly; **Cover Price:** Free; **Circ:** 38,316
Usual Pagination: 48
Editor-in-Chief: Riitta Nieminen
Profile: Trade-union membership magazine.
Language(s): Finnish
BUSINESS: COMMERCE, INDUSTRY & MANAGEMENT: Trade Unions

PARGAS KUNGÖRELSER - PARAISTEN KUULUTUKSET 704894L72-985
Editorial: Strandvägen 24, 21600 PARGAS
Tel: 2 45 44 118 **Fax:** 24544119
Email: leena.lehtonen@fabsy.fi **Web site:** http://www.pku.fi
ISSN: 0785-3998
Date Established: 1913; **Freq:** Weekly; **Circ:** 4,854
Usual Pagination: 16
Profile: Newspaper issued in Parainen/ Pargas.
Language(s): Finnish; Swedish
ADVERTISING RATES:
Full Page Colour .... EUR 1500
SCC .... EUR 6.80
Agency Commission: 15%
Mechanical Data: Col Length: 365mm, Page Width: 260mm, No. of Columns (Display): 6, Col Widths (Display): 44mm
LOCAL NEWSPAPERS

PARIKKALAN-RAUTJÄRVEN SANOMAT 704977L72-990
Formerly: Parikkalan Sanomat
Editorial: Parikkalantie 18, 59100 PARIKKALA
Tel: 10 23 08 900 **Fax:** 5 43 00 83
Email: toimitus@parikkalan-rautjarvensanomat.fi
Web site: http://www.parikkalan-rautjarvensanomat.fi
ISSN: 1236-7974
Date Established: 1908; **Freq:** 104 issues yearly; **Circ:** 5,828
Usual Pagination: 8
Profile: Newspaper issued in Parikkala, Saari, Simpele, Rautjärvi and Uukuniemi.
Language(s): Finnish
ADVERTISING RATES:
Full Page Colour .... EUR 3154
SCC .... EUR 14.40
Agency Commission: 15%
Mechanical Data: Col Widths (Display): 38.75mm, Col Length: 365mm, No. of Columns (Display): 6, Print Process: offset, Page Width: 255mm
LOCAL NEWSPAPERS

PARKINSON-POSTIA 705914L56R-75
Editorial: PL 905/ Suvilinnantie 2, 20101 TURKU
Tel: 2 27 40 400 **Fax:** 2 27 40 444
Email: parkinson-liitto@parkinson.fi **Web site:** http://www.parkinson.fi
ISSN: 0784-0004
Date Established: 1987; **Freq:** Quarterly - Published 5/year; **Circ:** 7,593
Usual Pagination: 64
Profile: Journal about the Parkinson disease.
Language(s): Finnish
ADVERTISING RATES:
Full Page Colour .... EUR 2000
Copy instructions: *Copy Date:* 39 days prior to publication date
BUSINESS: HEALTH & MEDICAL: Health Medical Related

PARNASSO 15354L84B-150
Editorial: Maistraatinportti 1, 00015 KUVALEHDET
Tel: 9 15 661 **Fax:** 9144076
Email: parnasso@otavamedia.fi **Web site:** http://www.parnasso.fi
Date Established: 1951; **Freq:** 6 issues yearly - Published 7/year; **Circ:** 7,152
Usual Pagination: 72
Profile: Magazine about literature and culture in Finland.
Language(s): Finnish
ADVERTISING RATES:
Full Page Colour .... EUR 1040
SCC .... EUR 13
Mechanical Data: Print Process: Offset, Film: Digital positive, Type Area: 200 x 265mm, Screen: 60 lpc
CONSUMER: THE ARTS & LITERARY: Literary

PARTIO 15384L91D-100
Editorial: Töölönkatu 55, 00250 HELSINKI
Tel: 9 88 65 11 00 **Fax:** 988651199
Email: partio-lehti@partio.fi **Web site:** http://www.partio.fi
ISSN: 0556-3488
Freq: 6 issues yearly; **Circ:** 43,596
Usual Pagination: 48
Profile: Magazine concerning the guide and scouting movement in Finland.
Language(s): Finnish
Readership: Aimed at guides and scouts aged from 7 to 17 years.
ADVERTISING RATES:
Full Page Colour .... EUR 2415
Mechanical Data: Type Area: 213 x 280mm, No. of Columns (Display): 3, Col Widths (Display): 56mm, Print Process: offset, Film: positive
CONSUMER: RECREATION & LEISURE: Children & Youth

PATINA 705415L74N-60
Editorial: Kansakoulukatu 5 A 6, 00100 HELSINKI
Tel: 20 74 88 444 **Fax:** 9 75 30 931
Email: hannele.vuori@senioriliitto.fi **Web site:** http://www.senioriliitto.fi
ISSN: 1235-5259
Date Established: 1978; **Freq:** 6 issues yearly - Published 7/year; **Circ:** 30,000
Usual Pagination: 26
Profile: Journal about retirement, pensions and benefits for elderly people.
Language(s): Finnish
ADVERTISING RATES:
Full Page Colour .... EUR 2590
SCC .... EUR 14
Agency Commission: 15%
Mechanical Data: Type Area: 254 x 375mm, No. of Columns (Display): 6, Col Widths (Display): 39mm, Print Process: offset, Screen: 10 lpc mono, 24 lpc colour
Copy instructions: *Copy Date:* 4 days prior to publication date

PAX 706102L40-72
Editorial: Rauhanasema, Veturitori 3, 00520 HELSINKI **Tel:** 9 14 27 03 **Fax:** 9 14 72 97
Email: toimisto@sadankomitea.org **Web site:** http://www.pax.fi
ISSN: 0781-8971
Freq: Quarterly; **Annual Sub.:** EUR 20.00; **Circ:** 2,000
Usual Pagination: 16
Editor-in-Chief: Olli Alm
Profile: Magazine about international peace movement, the Finnish foreign and security policies, military duties and European defence.
Language(s): Finnish

PELAA! 1666592L78D-85
Editorial: PL 1378/ Museokatu 44 C 115, 00101 HELSINKI **Tel:** 9 43 69 37 57 **Fax:** 9 43 69 37 58
Email: janne@pelaa.info **Web site:** http://www.pelaa.info
ISSN: 1795-7001
Date Established: 2005; **Freq:** 6 issues yearly; **Cover Price:** Free; **Circ:** 40,000
Usual Pagination: 32
Editor-in-Chief: Janne Pyykkönen
Profile: Magazine about computer-games.
Language(s): Finnish
Readership: Young, urban people.
ADVERTISING RATES:
Full Page Colour .... EUR 2600.00
SCC .... EUR 33.30
Agency Commission: 15%
Mechanical Data: Type Area: 190 x 260mm, Bleed Size: 200 x 270mm
CONSUMER: CONSUMER ELECTRONICS: Games

PELASTUSTIETO-RÄDDNING 15087L54B-2
Editorial: Pasilankatu 8, 00240 HELSINKI
Tel: 9 22 93 380 **Fax:** 9 22 93 38 33
Email: toimitus@pelastustieto.fi **Web site:** http://www.pelastustieto.com
ISSN: 1236-8369
Date Established: 1950; **Freq:** Monthly - Published 10/year; **Circ:** 5,583
Usual Pagination: 60
Profile: Magazine focusing on fire fighting and fire safety.
Language(s): Finnish; Swedish
Readership: Aimed at professionals at fire brigades, fire safety officers, builders and insurance company managers.
ADVERTISING RATES:
Full Page Colour .... EUR 2300
SCC .... EUR 21.20
Mechanical Data: Type Area: 185 x 275mm, Col Widths (Display): 43mm, No. of Columns (Display): 4, Print Process: offset, Screen: 60 lpc, Film: positive
Copy instructions: *Copy Date:* 14 days prior to publication date
BUSINESS: SAFETY & SECURITY: Safety

PELIT 15385L78D-100
Formerly: Peliasema and Konsolipelaaja
Editorial: PL 100/ Lapinmäentie 1, 00040 SANOMA MAGAZINES **Tel:** 9 12 01 **Fax:** 9 12 05 758
Email: toimitus@pelit.fi **Web site:** http://www.pelit.fi
ISSN: 1235-1199
Date Established: 1992; **Freq:** Monthly - Published 13/ a year; **Circ:** 27,893
Usual Pagination: 100
News Editor: Tuomas Honkala
Profile: Magazine focusing on PC games, providing articles on related hardware and new releases.
Language(s): Finnish
Readership: Read principally by males between 16 and 18 years of age.

ADVERTISING RATES:
Full Page Colour .... EUR 3200
SCC .... EUR 29.90
Mechanical Data: Type Area: 267 x 195mm, Col Length: 267mm, Bleed Size: 297 x 230mm, Print Process: Offset, Film: Positive, Screen: 60 lpc
Copy instructions: *Copy Date:* 20 days prior to publication date
CONSUMER: CONSUMER ELECTRONICS: Games

PERHONJOKILAAKSO
705010L72-995
Editorial: Kirkkotanhua 3, 69700 VETELI
Tel: 20 75 04 670
Web site: http://www.perhonjokilaakso.fi
ISSN: 0782-5676
Date Established: 1970; **Freq:** Weekly; **Circ:** 6,459
Usual Pagination: 16
Profile: Newspaper issued in the villages of Halsua, Perho, Veteli and the town of Kaustinen.
Language(s): Finnish
ADVERTISING RATES:
Full Page Colour .... EUR 2518
SCC .... EUR 11.50
Mechanical Data: No. of Columns (Display): 6, Col Widths (Display): 38.5mm, Col Length: 365mm, Page Width: 280mm
LOCAL NEWSPAPERS

PERNIÖNSEUDUN LEHTI
704895L72-1000
Editorial: PL 35 / Salontie 2, 25501 PERNIÖ
Tel: 2 73 52 301 **Fax:** 27352284
Email: toimitus@pernionseudunlehti.fi **Web site:** http://www.pernionseudunlehti.fi
ISSN: 0782-5714
Date Established: 1944; **Freq:** Weekly; **Circ:** 4,208
Usual Pagination: 8
Profile: Local newspaper issued in Perniö and Särkisalo.
Language(s): Finnish
ADVERTISING RATES:
Full Page Colour .... EUR 2142
SCC .... EUR 8.50
Agency Commission: 15%
Mechanical Data: Type Area: 290 x 420mm, No. of Columns (Display): 6, Col Widths (Display): 45mm
LOCAL NEWSPAPERS

PETÄJÄVESI
704921L72-1005
Editorial: Asematie 6, 41900 PETÄJÄVESI
Tel: 14 85 42 40 **Fax:** 14854904
Email: toimitus@petajavesi.net **Web site:** http://www.petajavesi.net
Date Established: 1961; **Freq:** Weekly; **Circ:** 2,080
Usual Pagination: 8
Managing Director: Inkeri Niiles
Profile: Newspaper issued in Petäjävesi.
Language(s): Finnish
ADVERTISING RATES:
SCC .... EUR 70
Mechanical Data: Type Area: 255 x 375mm, No. of Columns (Display): 5, Col Widths (Display): 48mm
Editions:
Petäjävesi Verkkotoimitus
LOCAL NEWSPAPERS

PIEKSÄMÄEN LEHTI
704978L72-1010
Editorial: Hallipussi 2, 76100 PIEKSÄMÄKI
Tel: 15 34 81 722 **Fax:** 15 34 14 21
Email: toimitus@pieksamaenlehti.fi **Web site:** http://www.pieksamaenlehti.fi
ISSN: 0356-6447
Date Established: 1925; **Freq:** 104 issues yearly; **Circ:** 6,662
Usual Pagination: 20
Profile: Newspaper issued in Pieksämäki, Pieksämäen mlk, Haukivuori, Jäppilä and Virtasalmi.
Language(s): Finnish
ADVERTISING RATES:
Full Page Colour .... EUR 3574
SCC .... EUR 16.10
Agency Commission: 15%
Mechanical Data: Type Area: 254 x 370mm, Page Width: 254mm, Col Length: 370mm, No. of Columns (Display): 6, Col Widths (Display): 39mm
LOCAL NEWSPAPERS

PIELAVESI - KEITELE
704979L72-1015
Editorial: Laaksotie 28, 72400 PIELAVESI
Tel: 17 28 87 781 **Fax:** 17 28 87 787
Email: pieke@pielavesi-keitele.fi **Web site:** http://www.pielavesi-keitele.fi
ISSN: 0780-7392
Date Established: 1961; **Freq:** Weekly; **Circ:** 6,014
Usual Pagination: 20
Profile: Newspaper issued in Pielavesi and Keitele.
Language(s): Finnish
ADVERTISING RATES:
SCC .... EUR 11.20
Agency Commission: 15%
Mechanical Data: Page Width: 251mm, No. of Columns (Display): 5, Col Widths (Display): 47mm, Print Process: offset, Type Area: 251 x 370mm, Col Length: 370mm
LOCAL NEWSPAPERS

PIELISJOKISEUTU
704980L72-1020
Editorial: Liikekeskus, 81200 ENO **Tel:** 10 23 08 700 **Fax:** 10 23 08 760
Email: toimitus@pielisjokiseutu.fi **Web site:** http://www.pielisjokiseutu.fi
ISSN: 0357-6906
Date Established: 1963; **Freq:** Weekly; **Circ:** 3,652
Usual Pagination: 12
Editor-in-Chief: Sami Tolvanen
Profile: Newspaper issued in Eno and Kontiolahti.
Language(s): Finnish
ADVERTISING RATES:
Full Page Colour .... EUR 2956
SCC .... EUR 13.50
Agency Commission: 17.5%
Mechanical Data: Type Area: 240 x 368mm, Col Length: 365mm, Page Width: 240mm, Col Widths (Display): 44mm, No. of Columns (Display): 5, Print Process: offset
Editions:
Pielisjokiseutu Verkkotoimitus
LOCAL NEWSPAPERS

PIETARSAAREN SANOMAT
705009L72-1025
Editorial: PL 105/Jaakonkatu 13, 68601 PIETARSAARI **Tel:** 6 78 48 603 **Fax:** 67848885
Email: ps@pietarsaarensanomat.fi **Web site:** http://www.pietarsaarensanomat.fi
ISSN: 0784-428X
Date Established: 1984; **Freq:** 104 issues yearly; **Annual Sub.:** EUR 110; **Circ:** 2,612
Usual Pagination: 16
Profile: Newspaper issued in Kokkola, Kruunupyy, Luoto, Pedersöre, Pietarsaari, Uusikaarlepyy and Oravainen.
Language(s): Finnish
ADVERTISING RATES:
Full Page Colour .... EUR 6732
SCC .... EUR 16.50
Agency Commission: 15%
Mechanical Data: No. of Columns (Display): 8, Col Widths (Display): 44mm, Col Length: 510mm, Print Process: 4-colour offset rotation
Copy instructions: *Copy Date:* 5 days prior to publication date
Editions:
Pietarsaaren Sanomat Verkkotoimitus
LOCAL NEWSPAPERS

PILKE
15383L91D-85
Formerly: Nuorten Sarka
Editorial: Suomen 4H-liitto/4H-Pilke-lehti, Karjalankatu 2 A, 00520 HELSINKI **Tel:** 9 75 12 42 00 **Fax:** 9 75 12 42 55
Email: pilke@4h.fi **Web site:** http://www.4h.fi
ISSN: 1459-4463
Date Established: 1945; **Freq:** 6 issues yearly - Published 8/year; **Circ:** 18,952
Usual Pagination: 40
Managing Editor: Satu Mellanen
Profile: Magazine containing general interest information, news and short stories.
Language(s): Finnish
Readership: Aimed at young people in Finland between 7 and 21 years of age.
ADVERTISING RATES:
Full Page Colour .... EUR 1300
SCC .... EUR 11.40
Agency Commission: 15%
Mechanical Data: Type Area: 230 x 273mm, Screen: 60 lpc, Print Process: offset, Col Widths (Display): 49mm, No. of Columns (Display): 4, Film: negative
CONSUMER: RECREATION & LEISURE: Children & Youth

PIRKANMAAN KIINTEISTÖVIESTI
705460L4D-59
Editorial: Plenty's Oy, PL 8, 33501 TAMPERE
Tel: 3 26 10 850 **Fax:** 3 26 10 855
Email: aineistot@plentys.fi **Web site:** http://www.pirkanmaankiinteistoyhdistys.fi
ISSN: 0785-9058
Date Established: 1988; **Freq:** Quarterly; **Circ:** 5,300
Usual Pagination: 40
Editor-in-Chief: Jorma Koutonen
Profile: Magazine covering all aspects of housing management.
Language(s): Finnish
Readership: Aimed at house managers within the Pirkanmaa area.
ADVERTISING RATES:
Full Page Colour .... EUR 1090.00
Mechanical Data: Screen: 60 lpc, Film: positive, Bleed Size: 210 x 297mm, Type Area: 185 x 270mm, Col Widths (Display): 43mm, Col Length: 270mm, Print Process: offset, No. of Columns (Display): 4

PIRKANMAAN YRITTÄJÄ
705092L63-41
Editorial: PL 7/ Kehräsaari B, 2. krs., 33201 TAMPERE **Tel:** 3 25 16 500 **Fax:** 32516516
Email: ville.kulmala@py-lehti.fi **Web site:** http://www.py-lehti.fi
Date Established: 1948; **Freq:** Monthly - 11/ a year; **Cover Price:** Free; **Circ:** 157,000
Usual Pagination: 44
Profile: Company interest journal is distributed to companies mainly in the Pirkanmaa region of Finland.
Language(s): Finnish
ADVERTISING RATES:
Full Page Colour .... EUR 4410
SCC .... EUR 19.80
Agency Commission: 15%
Mechanical Data: No. of Columns (Display): 6, Col Widths (Display): 41mm, Col Length: 370mm, Type Area: 260 x 370mm, Print Process: offset, Screen: 35-40 lpc
Copy instructions: *Copy Date:* 7 days prior to publication date
BUSINESS: REGIONAL BUSINESS

PIRKKA
15267L74C-65
Editorial: PL 410/ Risto Rytin tie 33, 00811 HELSINKI
Tel: 9 42 42 73 30 **Fax:** 9 42 42 73 33
Email: pirkka@dialogi.fi **Web site:** http://www.pirkka.fi
ISSN: 0032-0242
Date Established: 1933; **Freq:** Monthly - 10 issues/ a year; **Circ:** 1,720,139
Usual Pagination: 100
Profile: Magazine of the Kesko retail chain covering shopping, food, clothes and other topics.
Language(s): Finnish
ADVERTISING RATES:
Full Page Colour .... EUR 18200
SCC .... EUR 189.50
Agency Commission: 15%
Mechanical Data: Film: Negative, right reading, emulsion side down, Type Area: 240 x 190mm, Print Process: Offset rotation, Screen: 70 lpc, Bleed Size: 265 x 216mm, Col Length: 240mm, No. of Columns (Display): 4, Page Width: 190mm
Copy instructions: *Copy Date:* 23 days prior to publication date
Average ad content per issue: 25%
Editions:
Pirkka.fi
CONSUMER: WOMEN'S INTEREST CONSUMER MAGAZINES: Home & Family

PISTE
1605390L5F-55
Editorial: Täsmäviestintä, Karstuntie 20 A 1, 08100 LOHJA **Tel:** 19 32 38 31 **Fax:** 19 32 38 41
Email: kta@kta.fi **Web site:** http://www.kta.fi
Date Established: 1980; **Freq:** Quarterly; **Cover Price:** Free; **Circ:** 2,800
Usual Pagination: 8
Editor-in-Chief: Annette Lindahl
Profile: Magazine about computer graphics and printer devices.
Language(s): Finnish
Readership: Customers of KTA-Yhtiöt Oy and Data Engineering.

PITÄJÄLÄINEN
704975L72-1040
Editorial: PL 18 / Nilsiäntie 71, 73301 NILSIÄ
Tel: 17 28 87 790 **Fax:** 172887799
Email: uutiset@pitajalainen.fi **Web site:** http://www.pitajalainen.fi
ISSN: 1236-8652
Date Established: 1976; **Freq:** 104 issues yearly; **Circ:** 4,446
Usual Pagination: 12
Profile: Newspaper issued in Rautavaara and Nilsiä.
Language(s): Finnish
ADVERTISING RATES:
SCC .... EUR 11.70
Agency Commission: 15%
Mechanical Data: Col Widths (Display): 40mm, No. of Columns (Display): 6, Page Width: 254mm, Col Length: 375mm, Print Process: heatset
LOCAL NEWSPAPERS

PITÄJÄNUUTISET
704981L72-1045
Editorial: PL 5 / Pentinpolku 1, 52701 MÄNTYHARJU
Tel: 15 34 66 00 **Fax:** 15 34 66 10
Email: toimitus@pitajanuutiset.fi **Web site:** http://www.pitajanuutiset.fi
Date Established: 1956; **Freq:** 104 issues yearly; **Circ:** 5,570
Usual Pagination: 12
Editor-in-Chief: Esa Hirvonen
Profile: Newspaper issued in Mäntyharju and Pertunmaa.
Language(s): Finnish
ADVERTISING RATES:
Full Page Colour .... EUR 2584
SCC .... EUR 11.80
Agency Commission: 15%
Mechanical Data: Screen: 34 lpc, Type Area: 292 x 409mm, No. of Columns (Display): 6, Col Length: 400mm, Print Process: offset, Col Widths (Display): 40.5mm, Page Width: 281mm
LOCAL NEWSPAPERS

PLAANI
705886L17-5
Formerly: INFO-lehti (Sähkösuunnittelijat)
Editorial: Alppikatu 13 B 15, 00530 HELSINKI
Tel: 9 70 14 611 **Fax:** 9 76 82 45
Email: webmaster@nssoy.fi **Web site:** http://www.nssoy.fi
ISSN: 1457-0246
Freq: Quarterly; **Annual Sub.:** EUR 80; **Circ:** 4,000
Usual Pagination: 40
Editor-in-Chief: Risto Hiltunen; **Managing Editor:** Virpi Kumpulainen
Profile: Publication of the Association of Consulting Electrical Engineers.
Language(s): Finnish
ADVERTISING RATES:
Full Page Colour .... EUR 2000
Mechanical Data: Type Area: 180 x 260mm
Copy instructions: *Copy Date:* 30 days prior to publication date

PLAZAKOTI
1752565L74C-67
Editorial: Simonkatu 12 B 13, 00100 HELSINKI
Tel: 10 38 78 704 **Fax:** 10 38 78 788
Email: anne.melart@plazakoti.com **Web site:** http://www.plazakoti.fi
ISSN: 1796-3370
Date Established: 2006; **Freq:** Monthly; **Circ:** 50,000
Usual Pagination: 164
Profile: Magazine about home and interior-design.
Language(s): Finnish
ADVERTISING RATES:
Full Page Colour .... EUR 4150
SCC .... EUR 81
Agency Commission: 5-15%
Mechanical Data: Type Area: 200 x 256mm, Bleed Size: 225 x 290mm, Print Process: offset
Copy instructions: *Copy Date:* 31 days prior to publication date
CONSUMER: WOMEN'S INTEREST CONSUMER MAGAZINES: Home & Family

PODIUM
2044578L56A-203
Editorial: Varraskuja 1, 15880 HOLLOLA
Tel: 10 32 07 200
Email: toimitus@podium.fi **Web site:** http://www.podium.fi
Freq: Quarterly - Published 5/year; **Circ:** 5,000
Editor-in-Chief: Elina Puska
Profile: Medicine and hospital equipment trade magazine. Publishes the content on their website, too.
Language(s): Finnish
Readership: Alan yritysten johto, työntekijät sekä sidosryhmät. / Management, employees and partners.
ADVERTISING RATES:
Full Page Colour .... EUR 2975.00
SCC .... EUR 33.30

POGOSTAN SANOMAT
704982L72-1050
Editorial: PL 41/ Kauppatie 29, 82901 ILOMANTSI
Tel: 10 23 08 800 **Fax:** 10 23 08 802
Email: toimitus@pogostansanomat.fi **Web site:** http://www.pogostansanomat.fi
ISSN: 0782-5765
Date Established: 1966; **Freq:** 104 issues yearly; **Circ:** 5,477
Usual Pagination: 8
Profile: Newspaper issued in Ilomantsi and Tuupovaara.
Language(s): Finnish
ADVERTISING RATES:
SCC .... EUR 12.20
Agency Commission: 15%
Mechanical Data: No. of Columns (Display): 6, Col Widths (Display): 38.75mm, Col Length: 365mm, Print Process: offset
LOCAL NEWSPAPERS

POHJALAINEN
15224L67B-6250
Formerly: Pohjalainen (Vaasa)
Editorial: PL 37/ Hietasaarenkatu 19, 65101 VAASA
Tel: 6 24 77 930 **Fax:** 6 24 77 945
Email: toimitus@pohjalainen.fi **Web site:** http://www.pohjalainen.fi
ISSN: 0789-0737
Date Established: 1903; **Freq:** Daily; **Circ:** 25,517
Usual Pagination: 20
Editor: Jukka-Pekka Porola; **Editor-in-Chief:** Kalle Heiskanen; **Managing Editor:** Kauko Palola
Profile: Newspaper distributed mainly in the Vaasa region.
Language(s): Finnish
ADVERTISING RATES:
Full Page Colour .... EUR 12936
SCC .... EUR 30.80
Agency Commission: 5%
Mechanical Data: Page Width: 380mm, Col Length: 525mm
Editions:
Pohjalainen Kulttuuritoimitus
Pohjalainen Taloustoimitus
Pohjalainen Urheilutoimitus
Pohjalainen Verkkotoimitus
REGIONAL DAILY & SUNDAY NEWSPAPERS: Regional Daily Newspapers

POHJALAINEN PIETARSAARI
705660L67E-530
Editorial: Raatihuoneenkatu 7, 68600 PIETARSAARI
Tel: 6 24 77 581 **Fax:** 6 24 77 957
Email: toimitus@pohjalainen.fi **Web site:** http://www.pohjalainen.fi
Freq: Daily
Profile: Pietarsaari regional office of newspaper Pohjalainen.
Language(s): Finnish
REGIONAL DAILY & SUNDAY NEWSPAPERS: Regional Offices

POHJALAINEN SEINÄJOKI
705661L67E-532
Editorial: PL 139/ Koulukatu 10, 60101 SEINÄJOKI
Tel: 6 24 77 862 **Fax:** 6 24 77 855
Email: toimitus@pohjalainen.fi **Web site:** http://www.pohjalainen.fi
Freq: Daily
Profile: Seinäjoki regional office of newspaper Pohjalainen.

Language(s): Finnish
REGIONAL DAILY & SUNDAY NEWSPAPERS: Regional Offices

POHJALAINEN SUUPOHJA
705659L67E-534
Editorial: Topeeka 21, 61800 KAUHAJOKI
Tel: 6 24 77 930 **Fax:** 6 24 77 859
Email: toimitus@pohjalainen.fi **Web site:** http://www.pohjalainen.fi
Freq: Daily
Profile: Suupohja regional office of Pohjalainen.
Language(s): Finnish
REGIONAL DAILY & SUNDAY NEWSPAPERS: Regional Offices

POHJANKYRÖ-LEHTI
705011L72-1055
Editorial: Pohjankyröntie 128, 61501 ISOKYRÖ
Tel: 6 47 15 214 **Fax:** 6 47 14 400
Email: toimitus@pohjankyro-lehti.fi **Web site:** http://www.pohjankyro-lehti.fi
ISSN: 0782-6656
Date Established: 1950; **Freq:** 104 issues yearly; **Circ:** 5,746
Usual Pagination: 16
Managing Editor: Arto Erkkilä
Profile: Newspaper issued in Vähäkyrö, Isokyrö, Ylistaro and Laihia.
Language(s): Finnish
ADVERTISING RATES:
Full Page Colour .... EUR 2851
SCC .... EUR 13.20
Agency Commission: 15%
Mechanical Data: Page Width: 260mm, Col Length: 360mm, No. of Columns (Display): 6, Col Widths (Display): 40mm, Print Process: offset, Type Area: 260 x 360mm
LOCAL NEWSPAPERS

POHJOIS-SATAKUNTA
704909L72-1070
Editorial: PL 24 / Keskisenkatu 1, 39501 IKAALINEN
Tel: 3 45 89 300 **Fax:** 3 45 87 736
Email: toimitus@pohjoissatakuntalehti.fi **Web site:** http://www.pohjoissatakuntalehti.fi
ISSN: 0782-579X
Date Established: 1914; **Freq:** 104 issues yearly; **Circ:** 5,331
Usual Pagination: 12
Profile: Local newspaper issued in Ikaalinen and the region of northern Satakunta.
Language(s): Finnish
ADVERTISING RATES:
Full Page Colour .... EUR 3788
SCC .... EUR 13.20
Agency Commission: 15%
Mechanical Data: No. of Columns (Display): 7, Col Widths (Display): 38mm, Page Width: 290mm, Col Length: 410mm
LOCAL NEWSPAPERS

POHJOLAN LUOMU
1865392L21A-95
Editorial: Kankurinkatu 4-6, 05800 HYVINKÄÄ
Tel: 40 30 11 230 **Fax:** 40 30 11 239
Email: marika.salmi@pohjolanluomu.fi **Web site:** http://www.pohjolanluomu.fi/lehti
Date Established: 2002; **Freq:** Quarterly; **Circ:** 4,000
Editor-in-Chief: Marika Salmi
Profile: Magazine about ecological agriculture.
Language(s): Finnish
ADVERTISING RATES:
Full Page Colour .... EUR 1490.00

POHJOLAN SANOMAT
15193L67B-6260
Editorial: Sairaalakatu 2, 94100 KEMI
Tel: 10 66 56 276 **Fax:** 10 66 56 300
Email: ps.toimitus@pohjolansanomat.fi **Web site:** http://www.pohjolansanomat.fi
ISSN: 0782-372X
Date Established: 1915; **Freq:** Daily; **Circ:** 20,070
Usual Pagination: 24
Managing Editor: Juhani Tapio
Profile: Newspaper issued mainly in Enontekiö, Muonio, Kolari, Pello, Ylitornio, Tervola, Tornio, Haaparanta, Keminmaa, Kemi, Simo and Kuivaniemi (all north-west Finland).
Language(s): Finnish
ADVERTISING RATES:
Full Page Colour .... EUR 5146
SCC .... EUR 23.50
Agency Commission: 15%
Mechanical Data: Page Width: 380mm, No. of Columns (Display): 8, Col Widths (Display): 44mm, Print Process: offset, Col Length: 520mm, Type Area: 380 x 520mm
Editions:
Pohjolan Sanomat Verkkotoimitus
REGIONAL DAILY & SUNDAY NEWSPAPERS: Regional Daily Newspapers

POHJOLAN SANOMAT KOLARI
705663L67E-540
Editorial: 95900 KOLARI **Tel:** 10 66 56 442
Email: heikki.liimatainen@pohjolansanomat.fi **Web site:** http://www.pohjolansanomat.fi
Freq: Daily
Profile: Kolari regional office of newspaper Pohjolan Sanomat.
Language(s): Finnish
REGIONAL DAILY & SUNDAY NEWSPAPERS: Regional Offices

POHJOLAN SANOMAT PELLO
705664L67E-542
Editorial: Nivanpääntie 2, 95700 PELLO
Tel: 10 66 56 441
Email: helena.lessing@pohjolansanomat.fi **Web site:** http://www.pohjolansanomat.fi
Freq: Daily
Profile: Pello regional office of newspaper Pohjolan Sanomat.
Language(s): Finnish
REGIONAL DAILY & SUNDAY NEWSPAPERS: Regional Offices

POHJOLAN SANOMAT TORNIO
705666L67E-544
Editorial: Hallituskatu 6, 95400 TORNIO
Tel: 10 66 56 393
Email: sari.pelttari-heikka@pohjolansanomat.fi **Web site:** http://www.pohjolansanomat.fi
Profile: Tornio regional office of newspaper Pohjolan Sanomat.
Language(s): Finnish
REGIONAL DAILY & SUNDAY NEWSPAPERS: Regional Offices

POHJOLAN SANOMAT YLITORNIO
705714L67E-546
Editorial: Alkkulanraitti 55 A, 95600 YLITORNIO
Tel: 10 66 56 440
Email: tuulikki.kourilehto@pohjolansanomat.fi **Web site:** http://www.pohjolansanomat.fi
Freq: Daily
Profile: Ylitornio regional office of newspaper Pohjolan Sanomat.
Language(s): Finnish
REGIONAL DAILY & SUNDAY NEWSPAPERS: Regional Offices

POHJOLAN TYÖ
704859L67B-6401
Editorial: PL 43/ Limingantie 5, 90101 OULU
Tel: 8 31 16 688 **Fax:** 8 31 15 540
Email: toimitus@pohjolantyo.fi **Web site:** http://www.pohjolantyo.fi
ISSN: 0782-5390
Date Established: 1938
Circ: 5,832
Usual Pagination: 20
Profile: Local newspaper issued in Oulu, Kemi and Tornio.
Language(s): Finnish
ADVERTISING RATES:
Full Page Colour .... EUR 6460
SCC .... EUR 29.50
Agency Commission: 15%
Mechanical Data: Print Process: 4-colour offset rotation, No. of Columns (Display): 7, Col Widths (Display): 38mm, Col Length: 420mm, Type Area: 264 x 395mm
REGIONAL DAILY & SUNDAY NEWSPAPERS: Regional Daily Newspapers

PORRAS
15097L56A-60
Editorial: Läntinen Pitkäkatu 35, 20100 TURKU
Tel: 2 27 39 700 **Fax:** 2 27 39 701
Email: susanna.hakuni@lihastautiliitto.fi **Web site:** http://www.lihastautiliitto.fi
ISSN: 0359-2928
Date Established: 1981; **Freq:** 6 issues yearly; Free to qualifying individuals
Annual Sub.: EUR 23.55; **Circ:** 4,500
Usual Pagination: 44
Editor-in-Chief: Leena Koikkalainen
Profile: Magazine of the Finnish Association for Muscular Disorders. Contains general, medical and rehabilitation news.
Language(s): Finnish; Swedish
Readership: Read by doctors and members of the Association.
ADVERTISING RATES:
Full Page Colour .... EUR 2150.00

PORTAALI
15022L34-200
Formerly: Uudistuva Konttori
Editorial: Taipaleentie 380, 31640 HUMPPILA
Tel: 10 42 26 590 **Fax:** 34378591
Email: toimitus@portaalilehti.fi **Web site:** http://www.portaalilehti.fi
ISSN: 1459-6636
Date Established: 1975; **Freq:** 6 issues yearly - Published 8/year; **Annual Sub.:** EUR 74; **Circ:** 19,000
Usual Pagination: 48
Editor-in-Chief: Risto Anttila
Profile: Magazine concerning office equipment and technology.
Language(s): Finnish
Readership: Read by managing directors, chiefs, secretaries and office workers.
ADVERTISING RATES:
Full Page Colour .... EUR 2650
SCC .... EUR 24
Agency Commission: 15%
Mechanical Data: Col Length: 275mm, Col Widths (Display): 45mm, Film: Negative, No. of Columns (Display): 4, Type Area: 275 x 194mm, Print Process: Offset, Screen: 60 lpc, Trim Size: 297 x 210mm, Page Width: 194mm
Copy instructions: *Copy Date:* 14 days prior to publication date

POSITIO
712636L4A-50
Editorial: Maanmittauslaitos, PL 84/ Opastinsilta 12 C, 00521 HELSINKI **Tel:** 20 54 15 345
Fax: 20 54 15 598
Email: positio@maanmittauslaitos.fi **Web site:** http://www.maanmittauslaitos.fi/Positio
ISSN: 1236-1070
Freq: Quarterly; **Annual Sub.:** EUR 28.00; **Circ:** 1,100
Usual Pagination: 34
Editor-in-Chief: Kirsi Mäkinen
Profile: POSITIO is an information channel for producers, users, application planners and builders of location technology.
Language(s): Finnish
Readership: Read by government officials, teachers, and representatives within the location and geography private sector.
ADVERTISING RATES:
Full Page Colour .... EUR 900.00
SCC .... EUR 11.30

POSTIA SINULLE
705974L2R-25
Editorial: PL 6, 00011 ITELLA **Tel:** 20 45 15 641
Fax: 20 45 14 765
Email: postiasinulle@posti.fi **Web site:** http://www.itella.com
ISSN: 1234-5678
Freq: Half-yearly; **Cover Price:** Free; **Circ:** 2,500,000
Usual Pagination: 48
Editor-in-Chief: Riitta Vuorenmaa; **Managing Editor:** Lea Elo-Vehman
Profile: Magazine of Finnish Post.
Language(s): Finnish
Readership: Aimed at all Finnish households.
BUSINESS: COMMUNICATIONS, ADVERTISING & MARKETING: Communications Related

POWER
708039L19E-1
Formerly: ABB Asiakas
Editorial: PL 210, 00381 HELSINKI **Tel:** 10 22 11
Email: jaana.nikkari@fi.abb.com **Web site:** http://www.abb.fi
ISSN: 1799-5213
Date Established: 1984; **Freq:** Half-yearly - Published 3/year; **Circ:** 11,000
Usual Pagination: 16
Profile: Magazine of Swedish conglomerate ABB Finnish branch.
Language(s): Finnish

PRETAX
1605509L1B-120
Editorial: Antinkatu 3 C, 3. krs, 00100 HELSINKI
Tel: 20 74 42 300
Web site: http://www.pretax.net
ISSN: 1458-9354
Freq: Half-yearly; **Cover Price:** Free; **Circ:** 80,000
Usual Pagination: 20
Profile: Magazine about finance administration and salary services.
Language(s): Finnish
Readership: Customers of Pretax Oy.
BUSINESS: FINANCE & ECONOMICS: Accountancy

PRO TOIMIHENKILÖUNIONI
705341L14L-106
Formerly: Rakennustekniset
Editorial: PL 36/ Kaupintie 16 A, 3 krs, 00441 HELSINKI **Tel:** 9 41 33 44 00 **Fax:** 9 41 33 44 33
Email: pro@unionimedia.fi **Web site:** http://www.toimihenkilounioni.fi
ISSN: 1458-3453
Date Established: 2001; **Freq:** 6 issues yearly; **Circ:** 118,000
Usual Pagination: 68
Editor-in-Chief: Jaana Aaltonen; **Managing Editor:** Jaana Pohja
Profile: Magazine for members of the Union of Salaried Employees.
Language(s): Finnish
ADVERTISING RATES:
Full Page Colour .... EUR 2700.00
SCC .... EUR 30.30
Mechanical Data: Type Area: 210 x 297mm, Col Widths (Display): 52,8mm, No. of Columns (Display): 3, Screen: 60 lpc, Print Process: offset
BUSINESS: COMMERCE, INDUSTRY & MANAGEMENT: Trade Unions

PROAGRIA ITÄ-SUOMI
705310L21A-3_20
Formerly: Järvi-Suomen Maaseutulehti
Editorial: PL 5/ Koskikatu 11 C, 80101 JOENSUU
Tel: 13 25 83 311 **Fax:** 132583399
Email: anu.pesonen@proagria.fi **Web site:** http://www.proagria.fi/ek
Date Established: 1995; **Freq:** Quarterly; **Circ:** 36,000
Usual Pagination: 12
Editor-in-Chief: Eero Parviainen
Profile: Magazine about agriculture, forestry and fishery for professionals in northern Carelia.
Language(s): Finnish
ADVERTISING RATES:
Full Page Colour .... EUR 2396
SCC .... EUR 17
Mechanical Data: Type Area: 292 x 375mm, No. of Columns (Display): 6, Col Widths (Display): 39mm

PROAGRIA KESKI-POHJANMAA
705311L21A-6
Formerly: Keski-Pohjanmaan Maaseutukeskus
Editorial: Ristirannankatu 1, 67100 KOKKOLA
Tel: 20 74 73 250 **Fax:** 20 74 73 299
Email: ritva-liisa.nisula@proagria.fi **Web site:** http://www.proagria.fi/kp
ISSN: 1235-838X
Freq: Quarterly; **Annual Sub.:** EUR 10.00; **Circ:** 6,000
Usual Pagination: 18
Editor-in-Chief: Tapio Kurki; **Managing Editor:** Ritva-Liisa Nisula
Profile: Magazine about agriculture for farmers in central Ostrobothnia.
Language(s): Finnish
ADVERTISING RATES:
SCC .... EUR 12.00
Mechanical Data: Type Area: 237 x 360mm, Screen: 40 lpc, No. of Columns (Display): 5, Col Widths (Display): 45mm, Print Process: offset

PROAGRIA SATOA
14993L21A-44
Formerly: Maaseutuyrittäjä
Editorial: Vanajantie 10 B, 13110 HÄMEENLINNA
Tel: 20 74 73 000
Email: paivi.meronen@proagria.fi **Web site:** http://www.proagria.fi/hame/index.html
ISSN: 1238-1713
Freq: Quarterly; **Circ:** 33,000
Usual Pagination: 20
Editor-in-Chief: Lassi Uotila
Profile: Journal containing farming news for the southern region of Finland.
Language(s): Finnish
ADVERTISING RATES:
Full Page Colour .... EUR 1600
SCC .... EUR 15
Mechanical Data: Type Area: 185 x 265mm, Print Process: 40 lpc

PROINTERIOR
1664375L4B-10
Editorial: Pälkäneentie 19 A, 00510 HELSINKI **Tel:** 9 68 66 250 **Fax:** 9 68 52 940
Email: prointerior@publico.com **Web site:** http://www.prointerior.fi
ISSN: 1457-0955
Date Established: 2004; **Freq:** Quarterly; **Circ:** 10,000
Usual Pagination: 54
Editor-in-Chief: Sami Anteroinen; **Managing Editor:** Paul Charpentier
Profile: Magazine about professional interior-design.
Language(s): Finnish
Readership: Professionals within the interior-design industry.
Mechanical Data: Type Area: 175 x 242mm, Bleed Size: 210 x 277mm

PROJEKTIUUTISET
705197L4D-60
Editorial: Ruukinkuja 3, 02330 ESPOO
Tel: 9 80 99 11 **Fax:** 9 80 99 14 00
Email: eeva.maukola@rpt.fi **Web site:** http://www.projektiuutiset.fi
ISSN: 0786-8081
Date Established: 1988; **Freq:** 6 issues yearly; **Circ:** 11,000
Usual Pagination: 116
Editor-in-Chief: Kari Mäkinen; **Managing Editor:** Eeva Maukola
Profile: Magazine containing information and new ideas on how and with whom to carry out big construction projects.
Language(s): Finnish
Readership: Aimed at decision makers in the construction industry and in business.
ADVERTISING RATES:
Full Page Colour .... EUR 3360
SCC .... EUR 41.40
Agency Commission: 15%
Mechanical Data: Bleed Size: 210 x 297mm, Type Area: 178 x 270mm, Col Widths (Display): 56mm, No. of Columns (Display): 3, Print Process: offset, Screen: 70 lpc
Copy instructions: *Copy Date:* 27 days prior to publication date

PROSESSORI
14968L5C-5
Editorial: PL 100/ Lapinmäentie 1, 00040 SANOMA MAGAZINES **Tel:** 9 12 01 **Fax:** 9 12 05 758
Email: toimitus@prosessori.fi **Web site:** http://www.prosessori.fi
ISSN: 0357-4121
Date Established: 1979; **Freq:** Monthly; **Circ:** 8,451
Usual Pagination: 108
Editor-in-Chief: Jari Peltoniemi; **Managing Editor:** Seppo Lindstedt
Profile: Journal about electronics, computers, data communications and automation.
Language(s): Finnish
Readership: Read by IT professionals and enthusiasts.
ADVERTISING RATES:
Full Page Colour .... EUR 3500
SCC .... EUR 33.60
Mechanical Data: Type Area: 260 x 185mm, Trim Size: 297 x 210mm, Col Length: 260mm, Film: Positive, Print Process: Offset, Screen: 60 lpc

Copy instructions: *Copy Date:* 19 days prior to publication date
Editions:
Prosessori.fi
BUSINESS: COMPUTERS & AUTOMATION: Professional Personal Computers

PROVIISORI 706065L37-30
Formerly: Suomen Proviisorilehti
Editorial: Kaisaniemenkatu 1 B a, 7 krs, 00100 HELSINKI **Tel:** 9 17 77 71 **Fax:** 9 68 43 99 11
Email: toimisto@proviisoriyhdistys.net **Web site:** http://www.proviisoriyhdistys.net
Freq: Quarterly; **Circ:** 4,300
Usual Pagination: 24
Editor-in-Chief: Ville-Matti Mäkinen
Profile: Magazine about current pharmaceutical issues.
Language(s): Finnish
ADVERTISING RATES:
Full Page Colour .... EUR 2300.00
SCC .... EUR 27.60
Agency Commission: 15%
Mechanical Data: Bleed Size: 210 x 297mm, Type Area: 190 x 277mm, No. of Columns (Display): 3, Col Widths (Display): 57mm, Screen: 60 lpc, Print Process: offset, Film: negative

PUNKALAITUMEN SANOMAT 704910L72-1085
Editorial: PL 1 / Lauttakyläntie 4, 31901 PUNKALAIDUN **Tel:** 2 76 74 256 **Fax:** 27674225
Email: toimitus@punkalaitumensanomat.fi **Web site:** http://www.punkalaitumensanomat.fi
ISSN: 1236-8415
Date Established: 1908; **Freq:** Weekly; **Circ:** 3,602
Usual Pagination: 8
Profile: Newspaper issued in Punkalaidun.
Language(s): Finnish
ADVERTISING RATES:
Full Page Colour .... EUR 1425
SCC .... EUR 7.50
Agency Commission: 15%
Mechanical Data: Col Length: 380mm, No. of Columns (Display): 5, Col Widths (Display): 48mm, Screen: offset rotation, Page Width: 260mm
LOCAL NEWSPAPERS

PUOLANKA-LEHTI 705019L72-1090
Editorial: PL 15 / Kajaanintie 5, 89201 PUOLANKA
Tel: 8 65 32 200 **Fax:** 86532229
Email: toimitus@puolanka-lehti.fi **Web site:** http://www.puolanka-lehti.fi
Date Established: 1983; **Freq:** Weekly; **Circ:** 2,346
Usual Pagination: 12
Profile: Newspaper issued in Puolanka.
Language(s): Finnish
ADVERTISING RATES:
SCC .... EUR 10.40
Agency Commission: 15%
Mechanical Data: Type Area: 390 x 295mm, No. of Columns (Display): 6, Col Widths (Display): 45mm, Bleed Size: 440 x 289mm
LOCAL NEWSPAPERS

PURUVESI 704983L72-1100
Editorial: PL 2 / Kauppatie 16, 58501 PUNKAHARJU
Tel: 15 35 03 410 **Fax:** 15 35 03 411
Email: uutiset@puruvesi.net **Web site:** http://www.puruvesi.net
Date Established: 1964; **Freq:** 104 issues yearly; **Circ:** 6,643
Usual Pagination: 16
Editor-in-Chief: Tiina Strandén
Profile: Newspaper issued in Enonkoski, Kerimäki, Kesälahti, Punkaharju and Savonranta.
Language(s): Finnish
ADVERTISING RATES:
Full Page Colour .... EUR 2772
SCC .... EUR 10.50
Agency Commission: 15%
Mechanical Data: No. of Columns (Display): 6, Col Widths (Display): 39mm, Col Length: 369mm, Page Width: 254mm
LOCAL NEWSPAPERS

PUU 705199L46-56
Editorial: Snellmaninkatu 13, 00170 HELSINKI
Tel: 9 68 65 450 **Fax:** 9 68 65 45 30
Email: info@puuinfo.fi **Web site:** http://www.puuinfo.fi/kirjasto/puu-lehti
ISSN: 0357-9484
Date Established: 1980; **Freq:** Quarterly; **Cover Price:** Free; **Circ:** 13,500
Usual Pagination: 50
Editor-in-Chief: Pekka Heikkinen; **Managing Editor:** Marja Korpivaara
Profile: Magazine about Finnish wood architecture and building with wood.
Language(s): English; Finnish; French; German
ADVERTISING RATES:
Full Page Colour .... EUR 2600
Agency Commission: 15%
Mechanical Data: Type Area: 180 x 270mm, No. of Columns (Display): 3-4, Col Widths (Display): 41/57mm, Print Process: offset, Screen: 60 lpc

PUU & TEKNIIKKA 15061L46-80
Formerly: Puutekniikka
Editorial: Faktapro Oy, PL 4, 02941 ESPOO
Tel: 9 54 79 74 10 **Fax:** 9 51 22 033
Email: toimitus@puutekniikka.fi **Web site:** http://www.puutekniikka.fi
ISSN: 0783-5442
Date Established: 1986; **Freq:** Monthly; **Cover Price:** Free; **Circ:** 11,500
Usual Pagination: 48
Editor-in-Chief: Maija-Liisa Saksa
Profile: Professional journal for the woodworking industry. Includes information on machinery, supplies and new technological advances.
Language(s): Finnish
ADVERTISING RATES:
Full Page Colour .... EUR 3600
SCC .... EUR 15.50
Mechanical Data: Bleed Size: 289 x 410mm, Type Area: 262 x 386mm, Col Widths (Display): 49mm, No. of Columns (Display): 5, Film: negative, Print Process: offset, Screen: 54-60 lpc

PUUMALA 704957L72-1110
Editorial: PL 12 / Kenttätie 7, 52201 PUUMALA
Tel: 15 46 81 225 **Fax:** 154681833
Email: toimitus@puumalalehti.fi **Web site:** http://www.puumalalehti.fi
ISSN: 0782-5935
Date Established: 1954; **Freq:** Weekly; **Circ:** 3,247
Usual Pagination: 8
Profile: Newspaper issued in Puumala.
Language(s): Finnish
ADVERTISING RATES:
Full Page Colour .... EUR 2331
SCC .... EUR 12.60
Agency Commission: 17.5%
Mechanical Data: Bleed Size: 420 x 289mm, No. of Columns (Display): 5, Page Width: 255mm, Col Length: 370mm, Col Widths (Display): 48mm, Print Process: offset
LOCAL NEWSPAPERS

PUUMIES 15060L46-70
Editorial: Keskustie 20 D, 40100 JYVÄSKYLÄ
Tel: 14 21 56 36 **Fax:** 14 21 56 52
Email: toimisto@puumies.fi **Web site:** http://www.puumies.fi
ISSN: 0355-953X
Date Established: 1955; **Freq:** Monthly; **Circ:** 3,600
Usual Pagination: 58
Editor-in-Chief: Ritva Varis
Profile: Journal focusing on forestry, sawmills and the wood industry.
Language(s): Finnish
Readership: Aimed at members of the Finnish Society of Forestry Technicians and those involved in the timber trade.
ADVERTISING RATES:
Full Page Colour .... EUR 2500.00
SCC .... EUR 23.10
Mechanical Data: Type Area: 186 x 270mm, No. of Columns (Display): 4, Col Widths (Display): 43mm, Screen: 60 lpc, Print Process: offset

PUUTARHA & KAUPPA 14999L26C-5
Editorial: Larin Kyöstintie 6, 00650 HELSINKI
Tel: 9 72 88 210 **Fax:** 9 72 88 21 28
Email: pk.toimitus@hortimedia.fi **Web site:** http://www.puutarhakauppa.fi
ISSN: 1239-8691
Date Established: 1996; **Freq:** 26 issues yearly - Published 21/year; **Circ:** 3,193
Usual Pagination: 30
Profile: Publication of the Finnish Glasshouse Growers' Association.
Language(s): Finnish
ADVERTISING RATES:
Full Page Colour .... EUR 1658
SCC .... EUR 15.60
Agency Commission: 15%
Mechanical Data: Type Area: 265 x 185mm, Col Length: 265mm, Page Width: 185mm, Trim Size: 297 x 210mm, Bleed Size: 6mm, Col Widths (Display): 42mm, No. of Columns (Display): 4, Print Process: Offset, Screen: 70 lpc, Film: positive
Copy instructions: *Copy Date:* 14 days prior to publication date
Average ad content per issue: 21%
BUSINESS: GARDEN TRADE

PUUVENE 705976L46-81
Editorial: Hämeentie 153 B, 00560 HELSINKI
Tel: 9 66 15 11 **Fax:** 9 66 15 21
Email: puuvene@klippidm.fi **Web site:** http://www.puuvene.fi
ISSN: 1238-2841
Date Established: 1995; **Freq:** Quarterly; **Annual Sub.:** EUR 38.00; **Circ:** 1,500
Usual Pagination: 68
Editor-in-Chief: Yrjö Klippi; **Managing Editor:** Juha Aromaa
Profile: Magazine about Finnish traditions associated with wooden boats.
Language(s): Finnish
ADVERTISING RATES:
Full Page Colour .... EUR 500.00
Mechanical Data: Type Area: 185 x 265mm

PYHÄJÄRVEN SANOMAT 704984L72-1115
Editorial: PL 41/ Asematie 2, 86801 PYHÄSALMI
Tel: 8 77 29 000 **Fax:** 8 77 29 040
Email: toimitus@pyhajarvensanomat.fi **Web site:** http://www.pyhajarvensanomat.fi
Date Established: 1955; **Freq:** Weekly; **Circ:** 4,327
Usual Pagination: 16
Profile: Local newspaper in Pyhäjärvi.
Language(s): Finnish
ADVERTISING RATES:
Full Page Colour .... EUR 1555
SCC .... EUR 7.20
Agency Commission: 17.5%
Mechanical Data: Type Area: 256 x 370mm, Screen: 34 lpc, Page Width: 280mm, Col Length: 380mm, No. of Columns (Display): 6, Col Widths (Display): 39mm, Print Process: offset
Editions:
Pyhäjärven Sanomat Verkkotoimitus
LOCAL NEWSPAPERS

PYHÄJOKISEUTU 705020L72-1125
Editorial: PL 1/ Asemakatu 1, 86301 OULAINEN
Tel: 10 66 55 145 **Fax:** 8 47 95 125
Email: pjs.toimitus@sps.fi **Web site:** http://www.pyhajokiseutu.fi
ISSN: 0356-2492
Date Established: 1954; **Freq:** 104 issues yearly; **Circ:** 6,409
Usual Pagination: 12
Profile: Newspaper issued in Pyhäjoki, Merijärvi, Haapavesi, Kärsämäki, Vihanti and Oulainen.
Language(s): Finnish
ADVERTISING RATES:
Full Page Colour .... EUR 3132
SCC .... EUR 14.30
Agency Commission: 15%
Mechanical Data: Type Area: 284 x 415mm, Screen: 34 lpc, Col Length: 415mm, No. of Columns (Display): 6, Col Widths (Display): 44mm, Print Process: offset
Editions:
Pyhäjokiseutu Verkkotoimitus
LOCAL NEWSPAPERS

RAAHEN SEUTU 704860L72-1140
Editorial: PL 61/ Fellmaninpuistokatu 4, 92101 RAAHE **Tel:** 10 66 55 185 **Fax:** 8 22 07 02
Email: rstoimitus@sps.fi **Web site:** http://www.raahenseutu.fi
Date Established: 1919; **Freq:** Daily; **Circ:** 8,760
Usual Pagination: 12
Profile: Local newspaper issued in Raahe, Pattijoki, Pyhäjoki, Ruukki, Siikajoki and Vihanti.
Language(s): Finnish
ADVERTISING RATES:
Full Page Colour .... EUR 4205
SCC .... EUR 19.20
Agency Commission: 15%
Mechanical Data: No. of Columns (Display): 6, Type Area: 315 x 460mm, Print Process: offset rotation, Col Widths (Display): 44mm, Col Length: 365mm, Page Width: 400mm
LOCAL NEWSPAPERS

RADIOGRAFIA 706674L56A-55
Editorial: PL 140/ Asemamiehenkatu 4, 00060 TEHY
Tel: 9 54 22 75 22 **Fax:** 9 61 50 02 67
Email: toimisto@suomenrontgenhoitajaliitto.fi **Web site:** http://www.suomenrontgenhoitajaliitto.fi
ISSN: 1455-688X
Freq: Quarterly; **Annual Sub.:** EUR 48.00; **Circ:** 3,500
Usual Pagination: 44
Editor-in-Chief: Ulla Nikupaavo; **Managing Editor:** Katariina Kortelainen
Profile: Magazine by the Finnish Radiographers Union.
Language(s): Finnish
ADVERTISING RATES:
Full Page Colour .... EUR 900.00
Mechanical Data: Type Area: 180 x 260mm, Print Process: offset, No. of Columns (Display): 3, Col Widths (Display): 51mm

RAHTARIT 705221L49C-15
Editorial: Pitkäniemenkatu 11, 33330 TAMPERE
Tel: 3 34 33 710 **Fax:** 33433752
Email: rahtarit@rahtarit.fi **Web site:** http://www.rahtarit.fi
ISSN: 1238-5549
Date Established: 1973; **Freq:** 6 issues yearly - 5/ a year; **Circ:** 28,950
Usual Pagination: 68
Profile: Magazine about trucking and freight vehicles.
Language(s): Finnish
ADVERTISING RATES:
Full Page Colour .... EUR 1450
SCC .... EUR 16.20
Mechanical Data: Screen: 56-60 lpc, Film: positive, Type Area: 210 x 297mm

RAJAMME VARTIJAT 15033L40-80
Editorial: PL 3/ Korkeavuorenkatu 21, 00131 HELSINKI **Tel:** 71 87 21 333 **Fax:** 71 87 21 009
Email: rajavartiolaitos@raja.fi **Web site:** http://www.raja.fi
ISSN: 0483-9080
Date Established: 1934; **Freq:** 6 issues yearly; **Cover Price:** Free; **Circ:** 23,296
Usual Pagination: 32
Editor-in-Chief: Päivi Kaasinen
Profile: Publication about soldiers working as frontier guards on the border of Finland.
Language(s): Finnish; Swedish

RAJASEUTU 705128L21A-62
Editorial: Tunturikatu 6 A 19, 00100 HELSINKI
Tel: 9 44 42 38 **Fax:** 9493701
Email: tarmo.salo@rajaseutuliitto.fi **Web site:** http://www.rajaseutuliitto.fi
ISSN: 0355-452X
Date Established: 1923; **Freq:** Quarterly; **Annual Sub.:** EUR 10; **Circ:** 6,000
Usual Pagination: 32
Profile: Magazine about development in border areas.
Language(s): Finnish
ADVERTISING RATES:
Full Page Mono .... EUR 590

RAKENNA OIKEIN 705198L4D-65
Editorial: Ruukinkuja 3, 02330 ESPOO
Tel: 9 80 99 11 **Fax:** 980991400
Email: rakennaoikein@reedbusiness.fi **Web site:** http://www.rakennaoikein.fi
Freq: Annual - Issued in February; **Circ:** 50,000
Profile: Supplement about repairing and building real estates.
Language(s): Finnish
ADVERTISING RATES:
Full Page Colour .... EUR 3560
Mechanical Data: Bleed Size: 210 x 297mm, Type Area: 178 x 280mm, Col Widths (Display): 58mm, No. of Columns (Display): 3, Print Process: offset, Screen: 70 lpc
Supplement to: Projektiuutiset

RAKENNUSINSINÖÖRI JA - ARKKITEHTI RIA 15040L4A-4
Formerly: Rakennusinsinööri ja Arkkitehti
Editorial: PL 357/ Albertinkatu 23 A 13, 00121 HELSINKI **Tel:** 9 61 22 770 **Fax:** 961227733
Email: markku.rekola@ria.fi **Web site:** http://www.ria.fi/ria-lehti/ria-lehti.html
ISSN: 0356-0775
Date Established: 1966; **Freq:** Monthly; **Circ:** 12,000
Usual Pagination: 92
Profile: Journal about civil engineering and architecture.
Language(s): Finnish
Readership: Read by engineers and architects.
ADVERTISING RATES:
Full Page Colour .... EUR 2300
SCC .... EUR 21.60
Agency Commission: 15%
Mechanical Data: Type Area: 182 x 265mm, No. of Columns (Display): 3/4, Col Widths (Display): 58/43mm, Print Process: offset, Screen: 60 lpc
Copy instructions: *Copy Date:* 23 days prior to publication date

RAKENNUSLEHTI 14895L4D-75
Editorial: PL 44/ Hämeentie 33, 00501 HELSINKI
Tel: 20 74 18 600 **Fax:** 207418622
Email: toimitus@rakennuslehti.fi **Web site:** http://www.rakennuslehti.fi
ISSN: 0033-9121
Date Established: 1966; **Freq:** Weekly; **Circ:** 33,755
Usual Pagination: 20
Managing Editor: Seppo Mölsä
Profile: Magazine for the building and construction sector.
Language(s): Finnish
Readership: Read by civil engineers, architects, construction managers, financial and technical directors and other authorities in contracting.
ADVERTISING RATES:
Full Page Colour .... EUR 10080
SCC .... EUR 44.80
Mechanical Data: Screen: 34 lpc mono; 42-52 lpc colour, Print Process: Offset, Trim Size: 410 x 304mm, Type Area: 278 x 375mm, Film: Negative, Col Length: 375mm, Page Width: 278mm, No. of Columns (Display): 7, Col Widths (Display): 38mm
Copy instructions: *Copy Date:* 7 days prior to publication date
Editions:
Rakennuslehti.fi
Supplement(s): Korjausplussa - 8xY.
BUSINESS: ARCHITECTURE & BUILDING: Planning & Housing

RAKENNUSSANOMAT 14894L4D-70
Editorial: PL 387/ Yliopistokatu 23 A, 20101 TURKU
Tel: 2 25 01 738 **Fax:** 2 23 33 309
Email: rakennussanomat@pelipeitto.fi **Web site:** http://www.pelipeitto.fi
ISSN: 0784-3399
Date Established: 1976; **Freq:** Monthly; **Annual Sub.:** EUR 18.00; **Circ:** 27,000
Usual Pagination: 20
Editor-in-Chief: Harri Kumpulainen
Profile: Magazine containing news from the building sector.
Language(s): Finnish
ADVERTISING RATES:
Full Page Colour .... EUR 3233.00
SCC .... EUR 14.00
Agency Commission: 15%
Mechanical Data: No. of Columns (Display): 6, Col Widths (Display): 40mm, Col Length: 385mm, Type Area: 260 x 385mm, Film: negative, Screen: 30-40 lpc

Finland

RAKENNUSTAITO 14896L4D-80
Editorial: PL 1004/ Runeberginkatu 5, 00101 HELSINKI **Tel:** 20 74 76 405 **Fax:** 207476390
Email: rakennustaito@rakennustieto.fi **Web site:** http://www.rakennustaito.fi
ISSN: 0048-6663
Date Established: 1905; **Freq:** Monthly - Published 10/year; **Annual Sub.:** EUR 65; **Circ:** 12,000
Usual Pagination: 60
Profile: Journal of the Central Association of Construction Engineers and the Finnish Building Information Institute. Contains features on materials, methods, management and projects.
Language(s): Finnish
Readership: Read by building contractors, civil and construction engineers and architects.
ADVERTISING RATES:
Full Page Colour .... EUR 3285
SCC .... EUR 40.50
Agency Commission: 15%
Mechanical Data: Type Area: 270 x 180mm, Trim Size: 297 x 210mm, Col Widths (Display): 42mm, Screen: 60 lpc, Print Process: Offset, Film: Positive-charge for film. Digital preferred. E-mail fkp@fossankp.fi. ISDN Leonardo 03-435 9030, Col Length: 270mm, No. of Columns (Display): 3, Page Width: 180mm
Copy instructions: *Copy Date:* 21 days prior to publication date

---

RAKENNUSTEKNIIKKA 14897L4D-85
Editorial: Töölönkatu 4, 1.krs, 00100 HELSINKI
Tel: 20 71 20 600 **Fax:** 20 71 20 619
Email: helena.soimakallio@ril.fi **Web site:** http://www.ril.fi
ISSN: 0033-913X
Date Established: 1945; **Freq:** Quarterly; **Annual Sub.:** EUR 60.00; **Circ:** 7,000
Usual Pagination: 68
Editor-in-Chief: Helena Soimakallio
Profile: Publication about building and construction, includes information on real estate, roads, town planning, water building and bridges.
Language(s): Finnish
Readership: Aimed at decision makers in the construction industry, people working for the (local) government, universities and research institutes.
ADVERTISING RATES:
Full Page Colour .... EUR 2673.00
SCC .... EUR 22.50
Agency Commission: 15%
Mechanical Data: Print Process: offset, Bleed Size: 210 x 297mm, Type Area: 185 x 270mm, No. of Columns (Display): 3, Col Widths (Display): 58mm, Screen: 54-60 lpc, mono 48 lpc
Supplement(s): Rakennusinsinööri - 5xY

RAKENTAJA 14898L4E-80
Editorial: PL 307/ Siltasaarenkatu 4, 00531 HELSINKI
Tel: 20 77 40 03 **Fax:** 20 77 43 061
Email: paatoimittaja@rakennusliitto.fi **Web site:** http://www.rakennusliitto.fi/rakentaja-lehti
ISSN: 0355-8614
Freq: Monthly; **Circ:** 85,000
Usual Pagination: 32
Editor-in-Chief: Jukka Nissinen
Profile: Magazine about building.
Language(s): Finnish
Readership: Read by architects, engineers and constructors.
ADVERTISING RATES:
Full Page Colour .... EUR 2800.00
SCC .... EUR 19.40
Agency Commission: 15%
Mechanical Data: Type Area: 252 x 360mm, Print Process: offset, Screen: 34 lpc colour, No. of Columns (Display): 4, Col Widths (Display): 51mm
BUSINESS: ARCHITECTURE & BUILDING: Building

RAKENTAJAPOSTI 714420L4D-87
Editorial: Kreetankuja 2, 2120 RAISIO
Tel: 2 27 78 080 **Fax:** 2 27 78 099
Email: info@kustantamo.fi **Web site:** http://www.kustantamo.fi
ISSN: 0781-7762
Date Established: 1984; **Freq:** 6 issues yearly; **Cover Price:** Free; **Circ:** 60,000
Usual Pagination: 36
Editor-in-Chief: Keijo Asikainen
Profile: Magazine featuring various information on architecture, home building, decoration, finance and planning.
Language(s): Finnish
ADVERTISING RATES:
Full Page Colour .... EUR 1600.00
Agency Commission: 15%
Mechanical Data: Type Area: 255 x 365mm, Bleed Size: 280 x 400mm, Col Widths (Display): 47mm, Print Process: offset, Screen: 34 lpc b&w; 40 lpc colour
BUSINESS: ARCHITECTURE & BUILDING: Planning & Housing

RAKKAUDESTA RUOKAAN 753099L11A-33_50
Editorial: PL 37/ Laulukuja 6, 00421 HELSINKI
Tel: 20 72 96 000 **Fax:** 20 72 96 012
Email: laura.totterman@fazer.com **Web site:** http://www.amica.fi/Ravintolat/Reseptit/Rakkaudesta-ruokaan
Date Established: 1998; **Freq:** Annual - Published in February; **Cover Price:** Free; **Circ:** 150,000
Usual Pagination: 52
Editor: Laura Tötterman
Profile: Magazine with recipes and news for company clients.
Language(s): Finnish
BUSINESS: CATERING: Catering, Hotels & Restaurants

RANNIKKOSEUTU 704896L72-1145
Editorial: PL 7/ Tornikatu 2, 21201 RAISIO
Tel: 10 66 55 220 **Fax:** 2 43 97 137
Email: toimitus.rannikkoseutu@sps.fi **Web site:** http://www.rannikkoseutu.fi
ISSN: 0782-5544
Date Established: 1932; **Freq:** 104 issues yearly; **Circ:** 7,781
Usual Pagination: 28
Profile: Newspaper issued in Raisio, Naantali, Rymättylä, Masku, Merimasku, Askainen and Lemu.
Language(s): Finnish
ADVERTISING RATES:
Full Page Colour .... EUR 2509
SCC .... EUR 11.30
Agency Commission: 15%
Mechanical Data: Print Process: offset, No. of Columns (Display): 6, Col Length: 370mm, Page Width: 260mm, Col Widths (Display): 41mm
Editions:
Rannikkoseutu Verkkotoimitus
LOCAL NEWSPAPERS

RANNIKON PUOLUSTAJA 749347L40-82
Editorial: Jollaksentie 30, 00850 HELSINKI
Tel: 40 51 11 851
Web site: http://www.rannikonpuolustaja.fi
ISSN: 1239-0445
Date Established: 1958; **Freq:** Quarterly; **Circ:** 5,000
Usual Pagination: 80
Editor-in-Chief: Pekka Kurvinen
Profile: Magazine about the Finnish coastal defence.
Language(s): Finnish
Mechanical Data: Screen: 60 lpc, Type Area: 147 x 215mm

RANTALAKEUS 705021L72-1150
Editorial: PL 21/Limingan Säästökeskus, 91901 LIMINKA **Tel:** 8 38 16 85 **Fax:** 8 38 12 69
Email: toimitus@rantalakeus.fi **Web site:** http://www.rantalakeus.fi
Date Established: 1976; **Freq:** Weekly; **Circ:** 3,303
Usual Pagination: 20
Profile: Newspaper distributed in Hailuoto, Kempele, Liminka, Lumijoki, Oulunsalo, Temmes and Tyrnävä.
Language(s): Finnish
ADVERTISING RATES:
SCC .... EUR 12.70
Agency Commission: 15-17.5%
Mechanical Data: No. of Columns (Display): 5, Col Widths (Display): 46.5mm, Page Width: 250mm, Col Length: 370mm, Screen: 40 lpc
Editions:
Rantalakeus Verkkotoimitus
LOCAL NEWSPAPERS

RANTAPOHJA 705022L72-1155
Editorial: PL 15/Huvipolku 6, 90831 HAUKIPUDAS
Tel: 8 56 37 200 **Fax:** 8 54 72 433
Email: toimitus@rantapohja.fi **Web site:** http://www.rantapohja.fi
ISSN: 0358-478X
Date Established: 1969; **Freq:** 104 issues yearly; **Circ:** 9,919
Usual Pagination: 16
Profile: Newspaper issued in Haukipudas, Kiiminki, Ylikiiminki, Ii, Yli-Ii, Kuivaniemi and Pateniemi.
Language(s): Finnish
ADVERTISING RATES:
Full Page Colour .... EUR 1747
SCC .... EUR 8.20
Agency Commission: 15-17.5%
Mechanical Data: Col Length: 370mm, Page Width: 255mm, Col Widths (Display): 39mm, No. of Columns (Display): 6, Print Process: offset rotation
LOCAL NEWSPAPERS

RANTASALMEN LEHTI 704985L72-1160
Editorial: PL 4 / Kylätie 37, 58901 RANTASALMI
Tel: 15 44 07 51 **Fax:** 15440775
Web site: http://www.rantasalmenlehti.fi
ISSN: 0359-3002
Date Established: 1966; **Freq:** Weekly; **Circ:** 3,122
Usual Pagination: 8
Editor-in-Chief: Arto Ylhävaara
Profile: Newspaper issued in Rantasalmi.
Language(s): Finnish
ADVERTISING RATES:
Full Page Colour .... EUR 1748
SCC .... EUR 9.50
Mechanical Data: Col Length: 400mm, No. of Columns (Display): 5, Col Widths (Display): 50mm
LOCAL NEWSPAPERS

RASKASSARJA 753134L49A-53
Editorial: Rydöntie 24, 20360 TURKU
Tel: 2 23 84 223 **Fax:** 22383335
Email: toimitus@raskassarja.fi **Web site:** http://www.raskassarja.fi
ISSN: 0789-8428
Freq: Quarterly - Published 5/year; **Circ:** 19,000
Profile: Magazine about trucks and heavy transportation.
Language(s): Finnish
ADVERTISING RATES:
Full Page Colour .... EUR 1550
SCC .... EUR 14.20
Agency Commission: 15%
Mechanical Data: Type Area: 185 x 272mm, Screen: 52 lpc, Col Widths (Display): 44mm, No. of Columns (Display): 4

RAUHAN TERVEHDYS 705517L87-92
Editorial: PL 102/ Isokatu 19 B, 2 krs, 90101 OULU
Tel: 8 56 26 400 **Fax:** 8 56 26 444
Email: toimitus@rauhantervehdys.fi **Web site:** http://www.rauhantervehdys.fi
ISSN: 0356-2840
Date Established: 1907; **Freq:** Weekly - Published on Thursday; Free to qualifying individuals ; **Circ:** 93,747
Usual Pagination: 20
Profile: Magazine for the Lutheran parishes in the Oulu region.
Language(s): Finnish
ADVERTISING RATES:
Full Page Colour .... EUR 3130
SCC .... EUR 17
Mechanical Data: Type Area: 250 x 360mm, No. of Columns (Display): 4-6, Col Widths (Display): 59mm/46mm/38mm
CONSUMER: RELIGIOUS

RAUHANTURVAAJA 705490L40-100
Formerly: Sinibaretti
Editorial: Aittastentie 138, 27320 IHODE
Tel: 44 51 23 944
Email: palaute@rauhanturvaajalehti.fi **Web site:** http://www.rauhanturvaajalehti.fi
Date Established: 1980; **Freq:** 6 issues yearly; **Annual Sub.:** EUR 16.70; **Circ:** 5,000
Editor-in-Chief: Asko Tanhuanpää
Profile: Magazine about defence for the Finnish Military Area organisation and UN forces.
Language(s): Finnish
ADVERTISING RATES:
Full Page Colour .... EUR 950.00
Mechanical Data: Screen: 54 lpc, Type Area: 185 x 270mm, No. of Columns (Display): 4, Print Process: offset

---

REFINE 1687299L58-115
Editorial: Alma Media Lehdentekijät Oy, Munkkiniemen puistotie 25, 00330 HELSINKI
Tel: 10 66 51 02 **Fax:** 10 66 52 533
Web site: http://www.nesteoil.fi
ISSN: 1795-6773
Date Established: 2005; **Freq:** Quarterly; **Cover Price:** Free; **Circ:** 50,000
Usual Pagination: 38
Editor-in-Chief: Heikki Kilander
Profile: Magazine about oil and refineries.
Language(s): English; Finnish
Readership: Customers and target groups of Neste Oil Oyj.
BUSINESS: ENERGY, FUEL & NUCLEAR

REGINA 15355L74A-66
Editorial: PL 246/Lekatie 6, 90101 OULU
Tel: 8 53 70 033 **Fax:** 8 53 06 118
Email: regina.toimitus@kolmiokirja.fi **Web site:** http://www.reginainen.fi
ISSN: 0355-841X
Freq: 26 issues yearly; **Circ:** 18,000
Usual Pagination: 76
Editor-in-Chief: Eeva Vainikainen
Profile: Magazine with stories and articles for young women.
Language(s): Finnish
ADVERTISING RATES:
Full Page Colour .... EUR 2400.00
SCC .... EUR 20.50
Agency Commission: 15%
Mechanical Data: Bleed Size: 200 x 260mm, Screen: 40 lpc b&w, 60 lpc colour
CONSUMER: WOMEN'S INTEREST CONSUMER MAGAZINES: Women's Interest

---

REHUMAKASIINI 706576L21A-63
Editorial: PL 101, 21201 RAISIO **Tel:** 2 44 32 111
Fax: 2 44 32 137
Email: marjo.keskikastari@raisio.com **Web site:** http://www.rehuraisio.com
ISSN: 1456-6826
Date Established: 1975; **Freq:** Quarterly; **Cover Price:** Free; **Circ:** 28,500
Usual Pagination: 54
Editor-in-Chief: Bengt-Erik Rosin
Profile: Magazine about food for livestock and poultry.
Language(s): Finnish; Swedish
Readership: Customers of Raisio Group.

REISJÄRVI 704873L72-1165
Editorial: PL 2/ Kirkkotie 3 H, 85901 REISJÄRVI
Tel: 8 77 70 20 **Fax:** 8777021
Email: toimitus@reisjarvilehti.fi **Web site:** http://www.reisjarvilehti.fi
ISSN: 0785-5907
Date Established: 1988; **Freq:** Weekly; **Circ:** 2,068
Usual Pagination: 12
Profile: Newspaper issued in Reisjärvi.
Language(s): Finnish
ADVERTISING RATES:
SCC .... EUR 7.50
Agency Commission: 17.5%
Mechanical Data: No. of Columns (Display): 6, Page Width: 263mm, Col Length: 400mm, Col Widths (Display): 40mm, Print Process: offset
LOCAL NEWSPAPERS

RESERVILÄINEN 15034L40-90
Editorial: Döbelninkatu 2, 00260 HELSINKI
Tel: 9 40 56 20 16 **Fax:** 9 40 56 20 96
Email: toimitus@reservilainen.fi **Web site:** http://www.reservilainen.fi
ISSN: 0557-8477
Date Established: 1933; **Freq:** 6 issues yearly; **Cover Price:** Free; **Circ:** 57,717
Usual Pagination: 28
Editor-in-Chief: Mirva Brola; **Managing Editor:** Jarmo Riikonen
Profile: Newspaper for members of the reservist forces.
Language(s): Finnish
ADVERTISING RATES:
Full Page Colour .... EUR 3200.00
SCC .... EUR 14.00
Agency Commission: 15%
Mechanical Data: No. of Columns (Display): 6, Col Widths (Display): 45mm, Type Area: 290 x 380mm, Print Process: offset, Bleed Size: 317 x 418mm, Film: negative, Screen: 54 lpc
BUSINESS: DEFENCE

REUMA 705418L56R-95
Editorial: Iso Roobertinkatu 20-22 A, 00120 HELSINKI **Tel:** 9 47 61 55 **Fax:** 9 64 22 86
Email: riitta.katko@reumaliitto.fi **Web site:** http://www.reumaliitto.fi
ISSN: 0787-5223
Date Established: 1952; **Freq:** Quarterly; **Circ:** 54,645
Usual Pagination: 32
Editor-in-Chief: Riitta Katko
Profile: Magazine about rheumatism.
Language(s): Finnish
ADVERTISING RATES:
Full Page Colour .... EUR 4622.00
SCC .... EUR 17.00
Agency Commission: 15%
Mechanical Data: Print Process: offset, Type Area: 297 x 411mm, No. of Columns (Display): 6, Col Widths (Display): 42mm, Screen: heatset 48-54 lpc, coldset 34 lpc, Film: negative
BUSINESS: HEALTH & MEDICAL: Health Medical Related

REVANSSI 1614458L56N-65
Editorial: Ratakatu 9, 00120 HELSINKI
Tel: 9 56 57 730 **Fax:** 9 56 57 73 34
Email: timo.peltovuori@mtkl.fi **Web site:** http://www.mtkl.fi
ISSN: 1458-4522
Freq: Quarterly; **Circ:** 15,261
Usual Pagination: 16
Profile: Magazine about mental health.
Language(s): Finnish
Readership: Members of the Central Association for Mental Health.
ADVERTISING RATES:
SCC .... EUR 15
Mechanical Data: Type Area: 260 x 380mm, No. of Columns (Display): 5, Col Widths (Display): 46mm, Print Process: offset, Screen: 40 lpc
BUSINESS: HEALTH & MEDICAL: Mental Health

RISK CONSULTING 1633008L1N-100
Editorial: Niittyportti 4 A, 00025 IF **Tel:** 10 19 15 15
Email: juha.ettala@if.fi **Web site:** http://www.if.fi
ISSN: 1459-3904
Freq: Half-yearly; **Cover Price:** Free; **Circ:** 11,000
Usual Pagination: 32
Editor-in-Chief: Juha Ettala
Profile: Magazine about risk management and insurance.
Language(s): English; Finnish; Swedish
Readership: Clients of IF Suurasiakkaat.

RONDO-CLASSICA 15140L61-2
Formerly: Musiikkilehti Rondo
Editorial: Ilmalankuja 2 L, 00240 HELSINKI
Tel: 9 72 51 40 11
Web site: http://www.rondolehti.fi
ISSN: 0355-5054
Date Established: 1963; **Freq:** Monthly; **Circ:** 6,539
Usual Pagination: 80
Profile: Magazine covering articles on Finnish classical music, people and events.
Language(s): Finnish
Readership: Aimed at Members of the Finnish Music Teacher's Union and musicians in general.
ADVERTISING RATES:
Full Page Colour .... EUR 1850
SCC .... EUR 17.50
Mechanical Data: Type Area: 195 x 250mm, Bleed Size: 230 x 280mm, Print Process: offset, Screen: 60 lpc
BUSINESS: MUSIC TRADE

RUKA-KUUSAMO 1746527L89A-6

Formerly: Ruka! News
Editorial: Torangintaival 2, 93600 KUUSAMO
Tel: 8 85 21 300 **Fax:** 8 85 21 305
Email: tuija.rytkonen@rukakuusamo.fi **Web site:** http://www.ruka.fi
Freq: Annual; **Cover Price:** Free; **Circ:** 50,000
Usual Pagination: 24
Profile: Magazine about travel activities in winter resort Ruka.
Language(s): Finnish
Readership: Tourists and cabin owners in Ruka.
ADVERTISING RATES:
Full Page Colour .... EUR 3700.00
Agency Commission: 15%
Mechanical Data: Type Area: 250 x 336mm, Bleed Size: 280 x 400mm
CONSUMER: HOLIDAYS & TRAVEL: Travel

RUOTUVÄKI 706225L40-95

Editorial: PL 25/ Korkeavuorenkatu 21, 00131 HELSINKI **Tel:** 9 18 12 24 32 **Fax:** 9 18 12 24 68
Email: ruotuvaki@mil.fi **Web site:** http://www.mil.fi/ruotuvaki
ISSN: 0057-4897
Date Established: 1962; **Freq:** 26 issues yearly; **Circ:** 30,000
Usual Pagination: 16
Editor-in-Chief: Mikko Ilkko
Profile: News magazine about Finnish defence.
Language(s): Finnish
Editions:
Ruotuväki Verkkotoimitus

RUOVESI 704911L72-1205

Editorial: PL 2/ Honkalantie 2, 2 krs, 34601 RUOVESI
Tel: 3 47 61 400 **Fax:** 3 47 61 424
Email: toimitus@ruovesi-lehti.fi **Web site:** http://www.ruovesi-lehti.fi
ISSN: 1235-810X
Date Established: 1920; **Freq:** Weekly; **Circ:** 4,424
Usual Pagination: 12
Editor-in-Chief: Kalevi Tiitinen
Profile: Newspaper issued in Ruovesi.
Language(s): Finnish
ADVERTISING RATES:
Full Page Colour .... EUR 1998
SCC .... EUR 90
Agency Commission: 15%
Mechanical Data: Film: negative, No. of Columns (Display): 6, Col Widths (Display): 40mm, Type Area: 260 x 375mm, Print Process: offset, Screen: 34 lpc
Copy instructions: *Copy Date:* 10 days prior to publication date
LOCAL NEWSPAPERS

RUSKALEHTI 705419L74N-65

Editorial: Fredrikinkatu 62 A 1, 00100 HELSINKI
Tel: 9 49 27 43 **Fax:** 9 40 66 67
Email: suomen.ruskaliitto@kolumbus.fi **Web site:** http://www.kolumbus.fi/suomen.ruskaliitto.ry
Freq: Quarterly; **Annual Sub.:** EUR 10.00; **Circ:** 3,200
Usual Pagination: 14
Editor-in-Chief: Elsa Stenroos
Profile: Magazine about senior-citizens and their social and economic well-being.
Language(s): Finnish
ADVERTISING RATES:
Full Page Mono .... EUR 588.00
Mechanical Data: Type Area: 255 x 370mm, No. of Columns (Display): 5, Col Widths (Display): 47mm

RY RAKENNETTU YMPÄRISTÖ 15041L4C-5

Formerly: Rakennusvalvonta
Editorial: Rakennustieto Oy, PL 1004, 00101 HELSINKI **Tel:** 20 74 76 400 **Fax:** 207476320
Email: lauri.jaaskelainen@hel.fi **Web site:** http://www.rakennustieto.fi/ry
ISSN: 1457-9510
Date Established: 1964; **Freq:** Quarterly; **Annual Sub.:** EUR 41; **Circ:** 3,281
Usual Pagination: 96
Profile: Journal of the Finnish Association of Building Inspectors.
Language(s): English; Finnish
Readership: Read by officials and professionals dealing with construction licensing, planning and inspecting.
ADVERTISING RATES:
Full Page Colour .... EUR 1680
SCC .... EUR 31.10
Agency Commission: 15%
Mechanical Data: Type Area: 180 x 270mm, No. of Columns (Display): 2, Col Widths (Display): 72mm, Print Process: offset, Film: positive, Screen: 60 lpc
Copy instructions: *Copy Date:* 28 days prior to publication date
BUSINESS: ARCHITECTURE & BUILDING: Surveying

SAARISTOUUTISET 706063L89A-7

Editorial: Kirkonkyläntie 12, 23200 VINKKILÄ
Tel: 20 71 21 254 **Fax:** 20 71 21 259
Email: info@saaristouutiset.fi **Web site:** http://www.saaristouutiset.fi
Date Established: 1994; **Freq:** 6 issues yearly; **Circ:** 24,000
Usual Pagination: 100
Editor-in-Chief: Jaakko Amperla; **Managing Editor:** Tiina Amperla-Hirvonen
Profile: Leisure magazine about the Finnish archipelago and coastline, includes local services and travel information.
Language(s): Finnish
ADVERTISING RATES:
Full Page Colour .... EUR 2510.00
Agency Commission: 15%
CONSUMER: HOLIDAYS & TRAVEL: Travel

SÄÄSTÖPANKKI 14871L1C-17

Editorial: PL 68/ Linnoitustie 9, 02601 ESPOO
Tel: 9 54 80 51 **Fax:** 20 60 29 108
Email: jenni.pekkinen@saastopankki.fi
ISSN: 0036-2123
Date Established: 1903; **Freq:** 6 issues yearly; **Circ:** 4,000
Usual Pagination: 24
Editor-in-Chief: Jenni Pekkinen
Profile: Magazine containing information on banking and savings.
Language(s): Finnish; Swedish
Readership: Read by banking personnel, customers of banking products and policy makers.
BUSINESS: FINANCE & ECONOMICS: Banking

SAHAYRITTÄJÄ 705322L46-82

Editorial: Kiljavantie 6 rak.12, 05200 RAJAMÄKI
Tel: 40 82 18 238
Email: info@sahayrittajat.fi **Web site:** http://www.sahayrittajat.fi
Date Established: 1946; **Freq:** Quarterly; **Annual Sub.:** EUR 25.00; **Circ:** 1,000
Editor-in-Chief: Raimo Etelä
Profile: Magazine issued by the Finnish Saw Entrepeneurs.
Language(s): Finnish
ADVERTISING RATES:
Full Page Colour .... EUR 420.00

SÄHKÖ & TELE 14963L17-35

Formerly: Sähkö ja Tele
Editorial: Merikasarminkatu 7, 00160 HELSINKI
Tel: 9 66 89 850 **Fax:** 9 65 75 62
Email: sil@sil.fi **Web site:** http://www.sil.fi
ISSN: 0789-676X
Date Established: 1927; **Freq:** 6 issues yearly - Published 8/year; **Circ:** 10,000
Usual Pagination: 72
Profile: Journal of the Finnish Association of Electrical Engineers.
Language(s): Finnish
Readership: Decision-makers, engineers, technicians, researchers and teachers in the fields of electrotechnics and electronics.
ADVERTISING RATES:
Full Page Colour .... EUR 2950
SCC .... EUR 33.10
Agency Commission: 15%
Mechanical Data: Type Area: 200 x 290mm, No. of Columns (Display): 3, Col Widths (Display): 55mm, Print Process: offset, Screen: 60 lpc, Film: negative

SÄHKÖALA 14964L17-22

Editorial: PL 55/ Harakantie 18, 02601 ESPOO
Tel: 9 54 76 10 **Fax:** 954761310
Email: sahkoala@sahkoinfo.fi **Web site:** http://www.sahkoala.fi
ISSN: 0789-5437
Date Established: 1958; **Freq:** Monthly - Published 10/year; **Circ:** 1,999
Usual Pagination: 68
Editor-in-Chief: Olli-Heikki Kyllönen
Profile: Magazine of the Finnish Electrical Contractors' Association. Articles concern electrical and installation technology, product news, economic issues, labour market questions, management issues and union activities.
Language(s): Finnish
ADVERTISING RATES:
Full Page Colour .... EUR 3000
SCC .... EUR 26.70
Agency Commission: 15%
Mechanical Data: Type Area: 270 x 185mm, Trim Size: 297 x 210mm, Screen: Mono: 48 lpc, Colour: 60 lpc, Print Process: Offset, Film: Offset material; diskette, hard copy, mechanicals, ready-to-print screened positive film, Col Length: 270mm, Page Width: 185mm, Col Widths (Display): 45mm, No. of Columns (Display): 4
Copy instructions: *Copy Date:* 18 days prior to publication date
Average ad content per issue: 30%
BUSINESS: ELECTRICAL

SÄHKÖMAAILMA 14965L17-30

Editorial: PL 55/ Harakantie 18, 02601 ESPOO
Tel: 9 54 76 10 **Fax:** 954761310
Email: sahkomaailma@stul.fi **Web site:** http://www.sahkoala.fi
ISSN: 0781-8556
Date Established: 1986; **Freq:** Monthly; **Circ:** 4,866
Usual Pagination: 32
Editor-in-Chief: Olli-Heikki Kyllönen
Profile: Magazine containing information about current events in the electrical industry. Articles include details on company ownership changes, international activity, contractor provisions, new products and training events.
Language(s): Finnish
Readership: Read by employees of contractor firms, power plants and planning offices.
ADVERTISING RATES:
Full Page Colour .... EUR 4250
SCC .... EUR 16.80
Agency Commission: 15%
Mechanical Data: Type Area: 420 x 290mm, Col Widths (Display): 38mm, Screen: Mono: 48 lpc, Colour: 64 lpc, Print Process: Offset, Col Length: 380mm, Page Width: 256mm, No. of Columns (Display): 6, Film: negative
Average ad content per issue: 30%
BUSINESS: ELECTRICAL

SÄHKÖVIESTI 14966L17-40

Editorial: PL 1427/ Fredrikinkatu 51-53 B 5. krs, 00101 HELSINKI **Tel:** 9 53 05 27 00
Fax: 9 53 05 28 01
Email: ari.vesa@energia.fi **Web site:** http://www.adato.fi
ISSN: 0355-5356
Date Established: 1939; **Freq:** Quarterly; **Cover Price:** Free; **Circ:** 300,000
Usual Pagination: 24
Profile: Customer-magazine published by the Finnish Electricity Association about saving power, electricity use and activities. Covers national news and information from 50 local electricity companies.
Language(s): Finnish; Swedish
BUSINESS: ELECTRICAL

SAIRAANHOITAJA - SJUKSKÖTERSKAN 705301L56B-8

Editorial: Asemamiehenkatu 2, 00520 HELSINKI
Tel: 9 22 90 020 **Fax:** 922900240
Email: toimitus@sairaanhoitajaliitto.fi **Web site:** http://www.sairaanhoitajalehti.fi
ISSN: 0785-7527
Date Established: 1927; **Freq:** Monthly; **Circ:** 42,132
Usual Pagination: 60
Profile: The voice of the Finnish Nurse Union emphasizes current affairs in nursing and examines possibilities to develop the skills of nurses.
Language(s): Finnish; Swedish
Readership: Read by nurses, special nurses, midwives, researchers and students.
ADVERTISING RATES:
Full Page Colour .... EUR 2210
SCC .... EUR 24.80
Mechanical Data: Type Area: 186 x 268mm, Print Process: offset, No. of Columns (Display): 4, Col Widths (Display): 43.5mm
Copy instructions: *Copy Date:* 25 days prior to publication date
BUSINESS: HEALTH & MEDICAL: Nursing

SALON SEUDUN SANOMAT 15216L67B-7000

Editorial: PL 117/ Örninkatu 14, 24101 SALO
Tel: 2 77 021 **Fax:** 2 77 02 300
Email: toimitus@sss.fi **Web site:** http://www.sss.fi
ISSN: 0782-5404
Date Established: 1919
Circ: 21,828
Usual Pagination: 28
Editor-in-Chief: Ville Pohjonen; **Managing Editor:** Jarmo Lehto
Profile: Independent newspaper mainly distributed in the Salo-Somero region.
Language(s): Finnish
ADVERTISING RATES:
Full Page Colour .... EUR 4600
SCC .... EUR 10.90
Agency Commission: 5-15%
Mechanical Data: Col Length: 525mm, Col Widths (Display): 44mm, No. of Columns (Display): 8, Page Width: 380mm
Copy instructions: *Copy Date:* 10 days prior to publication date
Editions:
Salon Seudun Sanomat Kulttuuritoimitus
Salon Seudun Sanomat Mielipidetoimitus
Salon Seudun Sanomat Taloustoimitus
Salon Seudun Sanomat Urheilutoimitus
Salon Seudun Sanomat Verkkotoimitus
Salon Seudun Sanomat Viikonlopputoimitus
REGIONAL DAILY & SUNDAY NEWSPAPERS: Regional Daily Newspapers

SAMPO-LEHTI 704938L72-1225

Editorial: PL 46/ Kauppakatu 5, 43101 SAARIJÄRVI
Tel: 14 42 14 60 **Fax:** 14 42 50 80
Email: toimitus@sampolehti.fi **Web site:** http://www.sampolehti.fi
ISSN: 0782-5919
Date Established: 1943; **Freq:** Weekly; **Circ:** 6,040
Usual Pagination: 20
Profile: Newspaper issued in Saarijärvi, Kannonkoski and Pylkönmäki.
Language(s): Finnish
ADVERTISING RATES:
Full Page Colour .... EUR 2153
SCC .... EUR 9.70
Agency Commission: 15%
Mechanical Data: No. of Columns (Display): 6, Print Process: offset, Col Widths (Display): 40mm, Col Length: 370mm
LOCAL NEWSPAPERS

SANA 705469L87-94

Editorial: Kaisaniemenkatu 8, 4. krs, 00100 HELSINKI **Tel:** 20 76 81 700
Email: toimitus@sana.fi **Web site:** http://www.sana.fi
ISSN: 0356-5025
Date Established: 1945; **Freq:** Weekly; **Circ:** 20,467
Usual Pagination: 24
Managing Editor: Freija Özcan
Profile: Spiritual magazine by the Finnish Biblical Society.
Language(s): Finnish
ADVERTISING RATES:
Full Page Colour .... EUR 3100
SCC .... EUR 18.70
Agency Commission: 15%
Mechanical Data: No. of Columns (Display): 5, Col Widths (Display): 43mm, Col Length: 335mm
CONSUMER: RELIGIOUS

SARA. 1774723L74A-69

Editorial: PL 100/ Lapinmäentie 1, 00040 SANOMA MAGAZINES **Tel:** 9 12 01 **Fax:** 9 12 05 414
Email: sara@sanomamagazines.fi **Web site:** http://www.sara-lehti.fi
ISSN: 1796-6213
Date Established: 2006; **Freq:** Monthly - Published 10/year; **Circ:** 50,505
Usual Pagination: 112
Editor-in-Chief: Kristiina Dragon
Profile: Magazine for mature women.
Language(s): Finnish
Readership: Women of age 40 +.
ADVERTISING RATES:
Full Page Colour .... EUR 5960
SCC .... EUR 66.80
Mechanical Data: Bleed Size: 230 x 297mm, Type Area: 195 x 267mm, Page Width: 195mm, Col Length: 267mm, Print Process: offset, Screen: 60 lpc
CONSUMER: WOMEN'S INTEREST CONSUMER MAGAZINES: Women's Interest

SÄRMÄ 14957L14L-107_6

Editorial: PL 318/Haapaniemenkatu 7-9 B, 00531 HELSINKI **Tel:** 9 61 51 61 **Fax:** 97532506
Email: tiedotus@puuliitto.fi **Web site:** http://www.puuliitto.fi
ISSN: 1236-5564
Date Established: 1906; **Freq:** Monthly - Published 15/year; **Circ:** 41,246
Usual Pagination: 22
Profile: Publication of the Finnish Wood and Allied Workers' Union.
Language(s): Finnish; Swedish
Readership: Read by members.
ADVERTISING RATES:
Full Page Colour .... EUR 4944
SCC .... EUR 20
Agency Commission: 15%
Mechanical Data: Type Area: 284 x 412mm, No. of Columns (Display): 6, Col Widths (Display): 44mm, Screen: 34-40 lpc, Print Process: offset, Bleed Size: 315 x 460mm
BUSINESS: COMMERCE, INDUSTRY & MANAGEMENT: Trade Unions

SATAKUNNAN KANSA 15210L67B-7095

Editorial: PL 58/ Pohjoisranta 11 E, 28101 PORI
Tel: 10 66 58 318 **Fax:** 10 66 58 330
Email: sk.toimitus@satakunnankansa.fi **Web site:** http://www.satakunnankansa.fi
ISSN: 0355-8746
Date Established: 1873; **Freq:** Daily; **Circ:** 52,370
Usual Pagination: 24
Editor: Pertti Heikkilä; **Editor-in-Chief:** Petri Hakala
Profile: Newspaper issued in Satakunta, western Finland, mainly around the city of Pori.
Language(s): Finnish
ADVERTISING RATES:
Full Page Colour .... EUR 6252
SCC .... EUR 25.20
Mechanical Data: Screen: 34 lpc colour, No. of Columns (Display): 8, Col Widths (Display): 44mm, Type Area: 380 x 525mm, Page Width: 380mm, Print Process: offset, Col Length: 525mm
Editions:
Satakunnan Kansa Kulttuuritoimitus
Satakunnan Kansa Urheilutoimitus
Satakunnan Kansa Verkkotoimitus
REGIONAL DAILY & SUNDAY NEWSPAPERS: Regional Daily Newspapers

SATAKUNNAN KANSA EURA 705667L67E-560

Editorial: Eurantie 4, 27510 EURA **Tel:** 10 66 58 346
Email: sk.eura@satakunnankansa.fi **Web site:** http://www.satakunnankansa.fi
Freq: Daily
Profile: Eura and Rauma regional office of newspaper Satakunnan Kansa.
Language(s): Finnish
REGIONAL DAILY & SUNDAY NEWSPAPERS: Regional Offices

SATAKUNNAN KANSA HUITTINEN 705668L67E-562

Editorial: PL 18/Risto Rytinkatu 30, 32701 HUITTINEN **Tel:** 10 66 58 344
Email: sk.huittinen@satakunnankansa.fi **Web site:** http://www.satakunnankansa.fi
Freq: Daily
Profile: Huittinen regional office of newspaper Satakunnan Kansa.
Language(s): Finnish
REGIONAL DAILY & SUNDAY NEWSPAPERS: Regional Offices

SATAKUNNAN KANSA KANKAANPÄÄ 705669L67E-564
Editorial: Torikatu 13 A 3, 38700 KANKAANPÄÄ
Tel: 10 66 58 340
Email: paivi.leppilahti@satakunnankansa.fi **Web site:** http://www.satakunnankansa.fi
Freq: Daily
Profile: Kankaanpää regional office of newspaper Satakunnan Kansa.
Language(s): Finnish
REGIONAL DAILY & SUNDAY NEWSPAPERS: Regional Offices

SATAKUNNAN TYÖ 15211L67B-7100
Editorial: PL 41/ Eteläpuisto 14, 28101 PORI
Tel: 2 63 03 200 **Fax:** 2 63 03 240
Email: toimitus@satakunnantyo.fi **Web site:** http://www.satakunnantyo.fi
ISSN: 0356-2239
Date Established: 1946
Circ: 2,680
Usual Pagination: 12
Profile: Workers and employers newspaper distributed in Pori, Ulvila and Noormarkku of Satakunta.
Language(s): Finnish
ADVERTISING RATES:
Full Page Colour .... EUR 4944
SCC .... EUR 20
Agency Commission: 15%
Mechanical Data: No. of Columns (Display): 6, Col Length: 385mm, Print Process: offset, Page Width: 265mm, Col Widths (Display): 40mm, Type Area: 265 x 385mm
Editions:
Satakunnan Työ Verkkotoimitus
REGIONAL DAILY & SUNDAY NEWSPAPERS: Regional Daily Newspapers

SATAKUNNAN VIIKKO 706625L72-1230
Editorial: Teljänkatu 8, 28130 PORI **Tel:** 2 63 44 563
Fax: 2 63 44 511
Web site: http://www.satakunnanviikko.net
ISSN: 1457-9561
Date Established: 1999; **Freq:** Weekly; Free to qualifying individuals ; **Circ:** 55,000
Usual Pagination: 20
Editor-in-Chief: Kim Huovinlahti
Profile: Local newspaper distributed in Pori, Ulvila, Luvia and Noormarkku in western Finland. Publishes newspaper with housing ads every other Friday.
Language(s): Finnish
ADVERTISING RATES:
Full Page Colour .... EUR 3774
SCC .... EUR 17.20
Mechanical Data: Type Area: 260 x 380mm, No. of Columns (Display): 6, Col Widths (Display): 40mm, Print Process: offset, Screen: 40 lpc, Film: negative
LOCAL NEWSPAPERS

SAVON SANOMAT 15198L67B-7150
Editorial: PL 68/Vuorikatu 21, 70101 KUOPIO
Tel: 17 30 31 11 **Fax:** 17 30 33 47
Email: uutiset@savonsanomat.fi **Web site:** http://www.savonsanomat.fi
ISSN: 0356-3510
Date Established: 1908
Circ: 61,546
Usual Pagination: 32
Features Editor: Seppo Kononen; **Editor-in-Chief:** Jari Tourunen; **Managing Editor:** Seppo Rönkkö
Profile: Newspaper issued mainly in the city of Kuopio and in the Savo region.
Language(s): Finnish
ADVERTISING RATES:
Full Page Colour .... EUR 12281
SCC .... EUR 30.10
Mechanical Data: No. of Columns (Display): 8, Col Length: 510mm, Print Process: offset, Col Widths (Display): 44mm, Page Width: 380mm
Editions:
Savon Sanomat Ajankohtaistoimitus
Savon Sanomat Urheilutoimitus
Savon Sanomat Verkkotoimitus
Savon Sanomat Yhteiskuntatoimitus
REGIONAL DAILY & SUNDAY NEWSPAPERS: Regional Daily Newspapers

SAVON SANOMAT KESKI-SAVON ALUETOIMITUS 705673L67E-586
Formerly: Savon Sanomat Varkaus
Editorial: PL 197/ Pirnankatu 4, 78201 VARKAUS
Fax: 17 28 87 773
Email: varkaus@savonsanomat.fi **Web site:** http://www.savonsanomat.fi
Profile: Varkaus regional office of newspaper Savon Sanomat.
Language(s): Finnish
REGIONAL DAILY & SUNDAY NEWSPAPERS: Regional Offices

SAVON SANOMAT PIEKSÄMÄKI 705500L67E-584
Editorial: Keskuskatu 15, 76100 PIEKSÄMÄKI
Tel: 15 34 16 00 **Fax:** 15 34 16 04
Email: pieksamaki@savonsanomat.fi **Web site:** http://www.savonsanomat.fi
Profile: Pieksämäki regional office of newspaper Savon Sanomat.
Language(s): Finnish
REGIONAL DAILY & SUNDAY NEWSPAPERS: Regional Offices

SAVON SANOMAT YLÄ-SAVON ALUETOIMITUS 705671L67E-580
Formerly: Savon Sanomat Iisalmi
Editorial: Kilpivirrantie 7, 2 krs, 74120 IISALMI
Tel: 17 83 51 480 **Fax:** 17 83 51 489
Email: iisalmi@savonsanomat.fi **Web site:** http://www.savonsanomat.fi
Profile: Iisalmi regional office of newspaper Savon Sanomat.
Language(s): Finnish
REGIONAL DAILY & SUNDAY NEWSPAPERS: Regional Offices

SCANDINAVIAN JOURNAL OF SURGERY SJS 705286L56A-2
Formerly: Annales Chirurgiae Et Gynaecologiae
Editorial: PL 49/ Mäkelänkatu 2 A, 00501 HELSINKI
Tel: 9 39 30 91 **Fax:** 9 39 30 794
Email: sjs@fimnet.fi **Web site:** http://www.fimnet.fi/sjs
ISSN: 0355-9521
Date Established: 1946; **Freq:** Quarterly; **Circ:** 2,000
Usual Pagination: 90
Editor: Hannu Aro; **Editor-in-Chief:** Esko Kemppainen
Profile: Journal focusing on surgery and related fields.
Language(s): English
Readership: Read mostly by surgeons and specialists of related fields.
ADVERTISING RATES:
Full Page Colour .... EUR 1515.00
Mechanical Data: Bleed Size: 210 x 280mm, Type Area: 180 x 245mm, Print Process: offset, Film: positive, Screen: 54 lpc

SCANDINAVIAN MAGAZINE 706636L73-350
Formerly: Scandinavian World
Editorial: Haraldsby, 22410 GODBY **Tel:** 18 41 869
Email: info@scandinavianmagazine.com **Web site:** http://www.scandinavianmagazine.com
Freq: Half-yearly; **Circ:** 80,000
Usual Pagination: 100
Editor: Janna Johansson
Profile: Entertainment news magazine about the culture of Scandinavia and the archipelago.
Language(s): English
Readership: People interested in the archipelago of the Baltic Sea.
Mechanical Data: Type Area: 245 x 355mm, Film: negative
CONSUMER: NATIONAL & INTERNATIONAL PERIODICALS

SCANIA MAAILMA 705895L49D-23
Editorial: PL 59/ Muonamiehentie 1, 00391 HELSINKI
Tel: 10 55 50 10 **Fax:** 10 55 55 317
Email: seppo.salmi@scania.fi **Web site:** http://www.scania.fi
ISSN: 1457-8484
Freq: Quarterly; **Cover Price:** Free; **Circ:** 20,000
Usual Pagination: 24
Editor-in-Chief: Seppo Salmi
Profile: Magazine about trucks, lorries and other commercial vehicles mainly provided by Scania Ab.
Language(s): Finnish

SEURA 15269L73-88
Editorial: Maistraatinportti 1, 00015 OTAVAMEDIA
Tel: 9 15 661 **Fax:** 9 14 96 472
Email: seura@otavamedia.fi **Web site:** http://www.seura.fi
ISSN: 0358-8017
Date Established: 1934; **Freq:** Weekly; **Circ:** 165,051
Usual Pagination: 96
Editor-in-Chief: Saija Hakoniemi; **Managing Editor:** Ari Korvola
Profile: Magazine of interest to all members of the family. Covers entertainment, every day drama, economics and politics.
Language(s): Finnish
ADVERTISING RATES:
Full Page Colour .... EUR 7370
SCC .... EUR 52.60
Mechanical Data: Film: Digital. positive, Bleed Size: 280 x 217mm, Type Area: 280 x 217mm, Screen: 70 lpc
Copy instructions: *Copy Date:* 10 days prior to publication date
Editions:
Seura.fi
CONSUMER: NATIONAL & INTERNATIONAL PERIODICALS

SIC! 2056563L56A-206
Editorial: PL 55, 00301 HELSINKI **Tel:** 9 47 33 41
Email: sic@fimea.fi **Web site:** http://sic.fimea.fi
Freq: Quarterly; **Circ:** 40,000
Editor-in-Chief: Sinikka Rajaniemi
Profile: Pharmaceutical publication covering new medicine reviews, medication, adverse effects, herbal medicine, animal and biological medication.
Language(s): Finnish
Readership: Professionals in pharmaceutics. / Lääkealan ammattilaiset.

SIEVILÄINEN 705012L72-1255
Editorial: PL 23/Haikolantie 23, 85411 SIEVI
Tel: 8 48 02 78 **Fax:** 8480278
Email: sievilainen-lehti@kolumbus.fi **Web site:** http://www.sievilainenlehti.fi
Date Established: 1979; **Freq:** Weekly; **Circ:** 2,727
Usual Pagination: 12
Profile: Newspaper issued in Sievi, Nivala, Ylivieska, Kannus, Toholampi and Reisjärvi.
Language(s): Finnish
ADVERTISING RATES:
SCC .... EUR 70
Agency Commission: 17.5%
LOCAL NEWSPAPERS

SIIKAJOKILAAKSO 705023L72-1260
Editorial: PL 22/Pekkalantie 3, 92401 RUUKKI
Tel: 8 27 07 400 **Fax:** 8 27 07 411
Email: toimitus@siikkis.fi **Web site:** http://www.siikkis.fi
ISSN: 0787-4987
Date Established: 1966; **Freq:** 104 issues yearly; **Circ:** 4,640
Usual Pagination: 12
Profile: Newspaper issued in Siikajoki, Ruukki, Rantsila, Kestilä, Pulkkila, Piippola and Pyhäntä.
Language(s): Finnish
ADVERTISING RATES:
Full Page Colour .... EUR 3000
SCC .... EUR 13.70
Agency Commission: 15-17.5%
Mechanical Data: Col Widths (Display): 40mm, No. of Columns (Display): 6, Print Process: offset rotation, Col Length: 365mm, Page Width: 255mm, Film: negative
LOCAL NEWSPAPERS

SILTA-BRÜCKE 753064L89A-75
Editorial: Pohjoinen Makasiinikatu 7, 00130 HELSINKI **Tel:** 9 62 27 02 00 **Fax:** 9 62 27 02 77
Email: info@ssyl.fi **Web site:** http://www.ssyl.fi
ISSN: 0781-5824
Date Established: 1984; **Freq:** Quarterly; **Circ:** 7,000
Usual Pagination: 48
Editor-in-Chief: Pirjo Luoto
Profile: Magazine about culture, history, travel and news concerning both Finland and Germany.
Language(s): Finnish; German
Readership: Members of the Union of Finnish-German Associations.

SILVA FENNICA 15062L46-85
Editorial: PL 18/ Jokiniemenkuja 1, 01301 VANTAA
Tel: 10 21 11 **Fax:** 10 21 12 101
Email: silva.fennica@metla.fi **Web site:** http://www.metla.fi/silvafennica
ISSN: 0037-5330
Date Established: 1926; **Freq:** Quarterly; **Annual Sub.:** EUR 200.00; **Circ:** 1,050
Usual Pagination: 112
Editor-in-Chief: Eeva Korpilahti
Profile: International Journal of the Finnish Society of Forest Science and the Finnish Forest Research Institute. Covers all aspects of forest research.
Language(s): English
Readership: Aimed at researchers and academics within forestry and related disciplines.
Supplement(s): Silva Fennica Monographs.

SIPOON SANOMAT 704883L72-1265
Editorial: PL 11/Iso Kylätie 20, 04131 SIPOO
Tel: 20 61 00 101 **Fax:** 207703007
Email: sipoon.sanomat@lehtiyhtyma.fi **Web site:** http://www.sipoonsanomat.fi
Date Established: 1980; **Freq:** Weekly; **Circ:** 3,554
Usual Pagination: 12
Profile: Newspaper issued in Sipoo.
Language(s): Finnish
ADVERTISING RATES:
Full Page Colour .... EUR 5150
SCC .... EUR 12.50
Agency Commission: 15%
Mechanical Data: Col Length: 520mm, No. of Columns (Display): 6, Col Widths (Display): 44mm, Screen: 34 lpc, Film: negative
LOCAL NEWSPAPERS

SISÄ-SAVO 706174L72-1270
Formerly: Sisä-Savon Sanomat
Editorial: PL 14/ Iisvedentie 3, 77601 SUONENJOKI
Tel: 17 28 87 700 **Fax:** 17 28 87 755
Email: uutiset@sisa-savolehti.fi **Web site:** http://www.sisa-savonsanomat.fi
ISSN: 1456-3002
Date Established: 1965; **Freq:** 104 issues yearly; **Circ:** 7,213
Usual Pagination: 20
Profile: Newspaper issued in Karttula, Rautalampi, Suonenjoki, Tervo and Vesanto.
Language(s): Finnish
ADVERTISING RATES:
Full Page Colour .... EUR 2686
SCC .... EUR 12.10
Agency Commission: 15%
Mechanical Data: Page Width: 255mm, Col Length: 370mm, No. of Columns (Display): 6, Col Widths (Display): 40mm, Print Process: offset
LOCAL NEWSPAPERS

SISÄ-SUOMEN LEHTI 15178L72-1275
Editorial: PL 15/ Kauppakatu 1, 44101 ÄÄNEKOSKI
Tel: 14 34 89 500 **Fax:** 14 34 89 513
Email: toimitus@sisasuomenlehti.fi **Web site:** http://www.sisasuomenlehti.fi
ISSN: 0356-3103
Date Established: 1960; **Freq:** 104 issues yearly; **Circ:** 7,412
Usual Pagination: 32
Profile: Local newspaper issued in Äänekoski, Suolahti, Sumiainen and Konnevesi.
Language(s): Finnish
ADVERTISING RATES:
Full Page Colour .... EUR 2531
SCC .... EUR 11.40
Mechanical Data: No. of Columns (Display): 6, Col Widths (Display): 40 mm/1 column, Type Area: 254 x 370mm
Editions:
Sisä-Suomen Lehti Verkkotoimitus
LOCAL NEWSPAPERS

SISUSTA. 706256L1E-2
Formerly: Sisustajan Asunto
Editorial: Innova Magazines Oy, Käenkuja 8 C, 00500 HELSINKI **Tel:** 9 42 41 34 10 **Fax:** 9 42 41 34 11
Email: toimitus@sisustalehti.fi **Web site:** http://www.sisustalehti.fi
ISSN: 1796-4644
Date Established: 2000; **Freq:** Quarterly; **Annual Sub.:** EUR 56.00; **Circ:** 16,000
Usual Pagination: 116
Editor-in-Chief: Inkeri Ala-Peijari
Profile: Magazine containing information on buying a property or building, includes legal aspects and advice but also interior-design.
Language(s): Finnish
ADVERTISING RATES:
Full Page Colour .... EUR 3200.00
SCC .... EUR 57.10
Agency Commission: 15%
Mechanical Data: Bleed Size: 230 x 280mm, Col Widths (Display): 90mm, No. of Columns (Display): 2, Screen: 70 lpc, Type Area: 230 x 280mm, Print Process: offset
BUSINESS: FINANCE & ECONOMICS: Property

SIX DEGREES 1616456L89D-55
Editorial: Vilhonvuorenkatu 11 B, 00500 HELSINKI
Tel: 9 68 96 74 20 **Fax:** 9 68 96 74 21
Email: info@6d.fi **Web site:** http://www.6d.fi
ISSN: 1459-5680
Date Established: 2003; **Freq:** Monthly - Published 10/year; Free to qualifying individuals ; **Circ:** 50,000
Usual Pagination: 24
Editor-in-Chief: Alexis Kouros; **Managing Editor:** Laura Seppälä
Profile: Magazine about the Finnish culture in a world of global cultures.
Language(s): English; Finnish
Readership: People coming to Finland as tourists, guest workers, refugees and interesting in the Finnish way of living.
ADVERTISING RATES:
Full Page Colour .... EUR 2400
SCC .... EUR 16.60
Mechanical Data: Type Area: 255 x 370mm, Bleed Size: 280 x 400mm, Screen: 40 lpc, Print Process: offset
CONSUMER: HOLIDAYS & TRAVEL: In-Flight Magazines

SKOGSBRUKET 15063L46-90
Editorial: Orrspelsgränden 4 A, 00700 HELSINGFORS **Tel:** 20 77 29 000 **Fax:** 207729008
Email: skogsbruket@tapio.fi **Web site:** http://www.skogsbruket.fi
ISSN: 0037-6434
Date Established: 1931; **Freq:** Monthly; **Annual Sub.:** EUR 36; **Circ:** 4,000
Usual Pagination: 32
Editor-in-Chief: Klaus Yrjönen
Profile: Journal containing information about forestry.
Language(s): Swedish
Readership: Read by Swedish-speaking Finnish forest owners.
ADVERTISING RATES:
Full Page Colour .... EUR 1735
SCC .... EUR 16.30
Agency Commission: 15%
Mechanical Data: Bleed Size: 210 x 297mm, Type Area: 185 x 265mm, No. of Columns (Display): 4, Col Widths (Display): 41mm, Print Process: offset
Average ad content per issue: 40%

SOISALON SEUTU 704972L72-1280
Editorial: PL 32 / Savonkatu 32, 79101 LEPPÄVIRTA
Tel: 17 28 87 741 **Fax:** 17 28 87 754
Web site: http://www.soisalonseutu.fi
Date Established: 1962; **Freq:** 104 issues yearly; **Circ:** 5,050
Usual Pagination: 24
Profile: Leppävirrassa ja Vehmersalmella ilmestyvä paikallislehti.
Language(s): Finnish
ADVERTISING RATES:
Full Page Colour .... EUR 2997
SCC .... EUR 13.50

Mechanical Data: Page Width: 254mm, Col Length: 370mm, No. of Columns (Display): 6, Col Widths (Display): 39.5mm, Print Process: offset
LOCAL NEWSPAPERS

SOMERO 704897L72-1285
Editorial: PL 11/Kiiruuntie 1, 31401 SOMERO
Tel: 2 58 88 561 **Fax:** 2 74 88 658
Email: toimitus@somerolehti.fi **Web site:** http://www.somerolehti.fi
ISSN: 0356-200X
Date Established: 1924; **Freq:** 104 issues yearly; **Circ:** 5,828
Usual Pagination: 16
Profile: Newspaper issued in Ypäjä, Tammela, Nummi-Pusula, Kiikala, Kuusjoki and Koski Tl.
Language(s): Finnish
ADVERTISING RATES:
Full Page Colour .... EUR 2497
SCC .... EUR 11.40
Agency Commission: 15%
Mechanical Data: Col Widths (Display): 40mm, No. of Columns (Display): 6, Page Width: 255mm, Col Length: 370mm
Copy instructions: *Copy Date:* 15 days prior to publication date
LOCAL NEWSPAPERS

SOMPIO 705726L72-1290
Editorial: Unarintie 23 A, 99600 SODANKYLÄ
Tel: 10 66 64 140 **Fax:** 16 61 30 00
Email: toimitus@sompio.fi **Web site:** http://www.sompio.fi
ISSN: 1237-4040
Date Established: 1993; **Freq:** 104 issues yearly; **Annual Sub.:** EUR 62.00; **Circ:** 3,482
Usual Pagination: 12
Editor-in-Chief: Kari Lindholm
Profile: Newspaper issued in Sodankylä.
Language(s): Finnish
ADVERTISING RATES:
SCC .... EUR 12.10
Mechanical Data: No. of Columns (Display): 6, Col Widths (Display): 41.5mm, Col Length: 400mm, Screen: 34 lpc
LOCAL NEWSPAPERS

SOSIAALILÄÄKETIETEELLINEN AIKAKAUSLEHTI 715915L56A-70
Editorial: Siirtolaisuusinstituutti, Eerikinkatu 34, 20100 TURKU **Tel:** 2 28 40 453
Email: toimitussihteeri@socialmedicine.fi **Web site:** http://ojs.tsv.fi/index.php/SA/index
ISSN: 0355-5097
Date Established: 1963; **Freq:** Quarterly; **Annual Sub.:** EUR 39.00; **Circ:** 1,500
Usual Pagination: 128
Editor-in-Chief: Kristiina Manderbacka
Profile: Journal of social medicine.
Language(s): Finnish

SOTAVETERAANI - KRIGSVETERANEN 15392L94A-20
Formerly: Sotaveteraani
Editorial: PL 600/ Ratamestarinkatu 9 C, 00521 HELSINKI **Tel:** 9 61 26 200 **Fax:** 9 61 26 20 20
Email: toimitus@sotaveteraaniliitto.fi **Web site:** http://www.sotaveteraaniliitto.fi
ISSN: 0782-8543
Date Established: 1958; **Freq:** 6 issues yearly; **Annual Sub.:** EUR 15.00; **Circ:** 68,225
Usual Pagination: 56
Editor-in-Chief: Markku Seppä
Profile: Magazine of the Finnish War Veterans' Federation.
Language(s): Finnish; Swedish
ADVERTISING RATES:
Full Page Colour .... EUR 3200.00
SCC .... EUR 17.50
Mechanical Data: Type Area: 252 x 365mm, No. of Columns (Display): 5, Col Widths (Display): 46mm, Print Process: offset, Screen: 40 lpc
CONSUMER: OTHER CLASSIFICATIONS: War Veterans

SOTILASAIKAKAUSLEHTI 705919L40-110
Editorial: Laivastokatu 1 B, 00160 HELSINKI
Tel: 9 66 89 40 16 **Fax:** 9 66 89 40 20
Email: varama@upseeriliitto.fi **Web site:** http://www.upseeriliitto.fi
ISSN: 0038-1675
Date Established: 1925; **Freq:** Monthly; **Annual Sub.:** EUR 60.00; **Circ:** 7,000
Usual Pagination: 80
Editor-in-Chief: Martti Lehto
Profile: Journal for members of the Military Officers' Union containing articles on employment news, defence, security and politics.
Language(s): Finnish
ADVERTISING RATES:
Full Page Colour .... EUR 1500.00
SCC .... EUR 21.00
Mechanical Data: Film: negative, Print Process: offset, Type Area: 164 x 237mm, Bleed Size: 200 x 270mm

SOTILASKOTI 15290L40-115
Editorial: Simonkatu 12 A 9, 00100 HELSINKI
Tel: 9 56 57 20 22 **Fax:** 9 56 57 20 25
Email: toimitus@sotilaskotiliitto.fi **Web site:** http://www.sotilaskotiliitto.fi
ISSN: 0355-9343
Date Established: 1967; **Freq:** 6 issues yearly; **Annual Sub.:** EUR 8.40; **Circ:** 7,000
Usual Pagination: 32
Editor-in-Chief: Karoliina Hofmann
Profile: Journal about women's voluntary work for the welfare of soldiers.
Language(s): English; Finnish; Swedish
ADVERTISING RATES:
Full Page Colour .... EUR 900.00
Mechanical Data: Type Area: 151 x 223mm, Bleed Size: 175 x 250mm, No. of Columns (Display): 3, Col Widths (Display): 46mm, Print Process: offset

SOTKAMO-LEHTI 705024L72-1300
Editorial: Keskuskatu 10, 88600 SOTKAMO
Tel: 10 66 56 000 **Fax:** 10 66 56 003
Email: sot.toimitus@sps.fi **Web site:** http://www.sotkamolehti.fi
ISSN: 0787-5320
Date Established: 1962; **Freq:** 104 issues yearly; **Circ:** 5,794
Usual Pagination: 16
Profile: Local newspaper issued in Sotkamo.
Language(s): Finnish
ADVERTISING RATES:
Full Page Colour .... EUR 2518
SCC .... EUR 11.50
Agency Commission: 15%
Mechanical Data: Type Area: 260 x 365mm, No. of Columns (Display): 6, Col Widths (Display): 40mm, Page Width: 260mm, Print Process: offset, Film: negative, Screen: 25-34 lpc
Editions:
Sotkamo-lehti Verkkotoimitus
LOCAL NEWSPAPERS

SPORT 706156L74G-37
Editorial: PL 100/ Lapinmäentie 1, 00040 SANOMA MAGAZINES **Tel:** 9 12 01 **Fax:** 91205414
Email: sport@sanomamagazines.fi **Web site:** http://www.sport-lehti.fi
ISSN: 1458-7122
Date Established: 2002; **Freq:** Monthly - Published 10/year; **Circ:** 42,207
Usual Pagination: 132
Profile: Magazine about good health, nutrition and well-being of women.
Language(s): Finnish
ADVERTISING RATES:
Full Page Colour .... EUR 5100
SCC .... EUR 60.70
Mechanical Data: Bleed Size: 210 x 280mm, Print Process: offset, Film: negative
Copy instructions: *Copy Date:* 19 days prior to publication date
CONSUMER: WOMEN'S INTEREST CONSUMER MAGAZINES: Slimming & Health

STOP IN FINLAND 752926L89A-80
Editorial: Koulukatu 10 B, 53100 LAPPEENRANTA
Tel: 5 41 85 101 **Fax:** 5 41 85 102
Email: maria.danilova@stopinfin.ru **Web site:** http://www.stopinfin.ru
Date Established: 2001; **Freq:** 6 issues yearly; **Cover Price:** Free; **Circ:** 25,000
Usual Pagination: 48
Editor-in-Chief: Maria Danilova
Profile: Magazine about tourism in Finland, tax free issues and events.
Language(s): Russian
Readership: Russians travelling to Finland by car.
ADVERTISING RATES:
SCC .... EUR 2860.00
Agency Commission: 15%
Mechanical Data: Type Area: 210 x 297mm, Print Process: offset

STTK-LEHTI 14939L14B-75
Formerly: STTK-FTFC-lehti
Editorial: PL 421/ Mikonkatu 8 A, 6 krs, 00101 HELSINKI **Tel:** 9 13 15 21 **Fax:** 9 65 23 67
Email: marja-liisa.rajakangas@sttk.fi **Web site:** http://www.sttk.fi/fi-FI/Lehti
ISSN: 1237-9921
Date Established: 1975; **Freq:** 6 issues yearly; **Circ:** 26,488
Usual Pagination: 32
Editor-in-Chief: Marja-Liisa Rajakangas
Profile: Journal of the Finnish Confederation of Salaried Employees.
Language(s): Finnish
Readership: Read by nurses, healthcare, municipal and industrial union employees.
ADVERTISING RATES:
Full Page Colour .... EUR 4000.00
SCC .... EUR 36.70
Agency Commission: 15%
Mechanical Data: Type Area: 187 x 272mm, Bleed Size: 230 x 273mm, Print Process: offset, No. of Columns (Display): 4, Col Widths (Display): 43mm, Screen: 54 lpc
BUSINESS: COMMERCE, INDUSTRY & MANAGEMENT: Industry & Factories

SUE 706109L76D-28
Editorial: Yliopistonkatu 12 a A 402, 20100 TURKU
Tel: 2 25 10 899
Email: toimitus@sue.fi **Web site:** http://www.sue.fi
ISSN: 1238-1853
Date Established: 1994; **Freq:** Monthly; **Cover Price:** Free; **Circ:** 60,000
Usual Pagination: 48
Editor-in-Chief: Kimmo Nurminen; **Managing Editor:** AriVäntänen
Profile: Magazine about indie, rock and punk music.
Language(s): Finnish
ADVERTISING RATES:
Full Page Colour .... EUR 2920.00
Agency Commission: 15%
Mechanical Data: Type Area: 240 x 350mm, Trim Size: 265 x 380mm
Average ad content per issue: 25-40%
Editions:
Sue.fi
CONSUMER: MUSIC & PERFORMING ARTS: Music

SULKAKYNÄ 15285L14G-15
Editorial: Eerikinkatu 20 C 37, 00100 HELSINKI
Tel: 9 58 65 020 **Fax:** 9 58 65 021
Email: sulkakyna@tradenomihsosihteerit.fi **Web site:** http://www.tradenomihsosihteerit.fi
ISSN: 0783-4942
Date Established: 1971; **Freq:** Quarterly; **Annual Sub.:** EUR 42.00; **Circ:** 2,767
Usual Pagination: 32
Editor-in-Chief: Marina Paulaharju
Profile: Magazine of the Helsinki Secretarial College.
Language(s): Finnish
Readership: Aimed at secretaries, personal assistants and managers.
ADVERTISING RATES:
Full Page Colour .... EUR 1425.00
Agency Commission: 15%
Mechanical Data: Bleed Size: 210 x 295mm, Type Area: 184 x 270mm, No. of Columns (Display): 3, Col Widths (Display): 55mm, Print Process: offset, Film: positive, Screen: 60 lpc
BUSINESS: COMMERCE, INDUSTRY & MANAGEMENT: Company Secretaries

SULKAVA-LEHTI 704987L72-1305
Editorial: Uitonrinne 18, 58700 SULKAVA
Tel: 15 47 15 44 **Fax:** 15 67 63 26
Email: sulkava.lehti@co.inet.fi
ISSN: 0782-6583
Date Established: 1963; **Freq:** Weekly; **Annual Sub.:** EUR 37.00; **Circ:** 2,678
Usual Pagination: 8
Editor-in-Chief: Kalle Keränen
Profile: Newspaper issued in Sulkava.
Language(s): Finnish
ADVERTISING RATES:
Full Page Colour .... EUR 1850.00
SCC .... EUR 10.00
Agency Commission: 15%
Mechanical Data: Col Length: 390mm, No. of Columns (Display): 5, Col Widths (Display): 48mm, Page Width: 255mm, Print Process: offset
LOCAL NEWSPAPERS

SUNNUNTAISUOMALAINEN 706250L67H-180
Editorial: PL 159/ Aholaidantie 3, 40101 JYVÄSKYLÄ
Tel: 14 62 20 00 **Fax:** 14622414
Email: satu.takala@sunnuntaisuomalainen.fi **Web site:** http://www.sunnuntaisuomalainen.fi
Freq: Weekly - Finland
Editor: Terhi Nevalainen
Profile: Sunday suppliment to Ilkka, Karjalainen, Keskisuomalainen, Pohjalainen and Savon Sanomat newspapers covering general interest.
Language(s): Finnish
ADVERTISING RATES:
Full Page Colour .... EUR 5900
Supplement to: Keskisuomalainen
REGIONAL DAILY & SUNDAY NEWSPAPERS: Regional Colour Supplements

SUOMALAINEN MAASEUTU 705326L21A-65
Editorial: Rautatiekatu 15, 84100 YLIVIESKA
Tel: 20 41 33 120 **Fax:** 20 41 33 121
Email: jouko.hannula@mtk.fi **Web site:** http://www.suomalainenmaaseutu.fi
ISSN: 0788-8457
Date Established: 1987; **Freq:** Monthly; **Circ:** 85,000
Editor-in-Chief: Jouko Hannula
Profile: Magazine supplement about the development of the countryside.
Language(s): Finnish
ADVERTISING RATES:
SCC .... EUR 37.50
Mechanical Data: Print Process: coldset rotation, Bleed Size: 280 x 400mm, Type Area: 255 x 370mm, No. of Columns (Display): 6, Col Widths (Display): 40mm, Screen: 34-40 lpc, Page Width: 260mm
BUSINESS: AGRICULTURE & FARMING

SUOMELA 752819L74K-43
Editorial: Lapinrinne 3, 00100 HELSINKI
Tel: 9 61 55 15 **Fax:** 9 61 55 18 00
Email: suomela@suoramedia.fi **Web site:** http://www.suomela.net
Freq: 6 issues yearly - Published 6/year; **Cover Price:** Free; **Circ:** 980,000
Usual Pagination: 52
Profile: News magazine about home purchase, house auctions and home repair.
Language(s): Finnish
ADVERTISING RATES:
Full Page Colour .... EUR 22700
SCC .... EUR 207.80
Mechanical Data: Type Area: 185 x 255mm, Bleed Size: 203 x 273mm
Copy instructions: *Copy Date:* 30 days prior to publication date
CONSUMER: WOMEN'S INTEREST CONSUMER MAGAZINES: Home Purchase

SUOMEN GOLFLEHTI 705379L75D-50
Editorial: Viestintä Tarmio Oy, Kivenlahdenkatu 1 B, 5 krs, 02320 ESPOO **Tel:** 9 80 16 849
Fax: 9 80 16 806
Email: toimitus@suomengolflehti.fi **Web site:** http://www.golf.fi
ISSN: 0784-5502
Date Established: 1957; **Freq:** 6 issues yearly - Published 8/year; **Circ:** 87,251
Usual Pagination: 130
Editor-in-Chief: Janne Tarmio; **Managing Editor:** Janne Knuuti
Profile: Magazine by the Finnish Golf Association.
Language(s): Finnish
ADVERTISING RATES:
Full Page Colour .... EUR 5000
SCC .... EUR 66.50
Agency Commission: 15%
Mechanical Data: Bleed Size: 217 x 280mm, Type Area: 180 x 248mm, No. of Columns (Display): 3-4, Print Process: offset, Film: positive, Screen: 60 lpc
CONSUMER: SPORT: Golf

SUOMEN KALANKASVATTAJA 15054L22G-105
Formerly: Suomen Kalankasvattaja - Fiskodlaren
Editorial: Malmin kauppatie 26, 00700 HELSINKI
Tel: 50 52 48 582 **Fax:** 9 68 44 59 59
Email: lehti@kalankasvatus.fi **Web site:** http://www.kalankasvattajaliitto.fi
ISSN: 0787-9008
Freq: Quarterly; **Annual Sub.:** EUR 42.00; **Circ:** 707
Usual Pagination: 60
Editor-in-Chief: Mikko Poskiparta
Profile: Official publication of the Finnish Fish Farmers' Association.
Language(s): Finnish; Swedish
Readership: Read by pisciculturists, fish scientists and wholesalers.
ADVERTISING RATES:
Full Page Colour .... EUR 1780.00
Agency Commission: 15%
Mechanical Data: Film: Negative, Bleed Size: 297 x 210mm, Screen: 60 lpc, Type Area: 180 x 265mm, Col Widths (Display): 57mm, No. of Columns (Display): 3, Print Process: offset
BUSINESS: FOOD: Fish Trade

SUOMEN KALASTUSLEHTI 15055L22G-110
Editorial: Malmin kauppatie 26, 00700 HELSINKI
Tel: 9 68 44 590 **Fax:** 9 68 44 59 59
Email: kalastus@ahven.net **Web site:** http://www.ahven.net
ISSN: 0039-5528
Date Established: 1892; **Freq:** 6 issues yearly; **Annual Sub.:** EUR 33.00; **Circ:** 4,167
Usual Pagination: 48
Editor-in-Chief: Markku Myllylä
Profile: Journal of the Federation of Finnish Fisheries Associations, providing scientific articles and results of research projects.
Language(s): Finnish
Readership: Read by fish farmers, biologists, fish wholesalers and commercial fishermen.
ADVERTISING RATES:
Full Page Colour .... EUR 1150.00
Mechanical Data: Type Area: 158 x 230mm, No. of Columns (Display): 3, Col Widths (Display): 49mm, Print Process: offset, Film: negative, Screen: 65 lpc
BUSINESS: FOOD: Fish Trade

SUOMEN KIINTEISTÖLEHTI 14879L1E-100
Editorial: Annankatu 24 A 4 krs, 00100 HELSINKI
Tel: 9 16 67 65 00 **Fax:** 9 64 87 45
Email: jukka.siren@kiinteistolehti.fi **Web site:** http://www.kiinteistolehti.fi
ISSN: 0355-7537
Date Established: 1925; **Freq:** Monthly - Published 10/year; **Circ:** 32,467
Usual Pagination: 82
Profile: Publication of the Finnish Real Estate Federation covering the real estate management and renovation sector. Subjects include finance, insurance, maintenance, renovation and legislation.
Language(s): Finnish
Readership: Read by board members and other elected officials at housing and real estate companies, the managing directors of agencies for maintenance management as well as staff with responsibilities related to maintenance management within commercial and industrial organizations.
ADVERTISING RATES:
Full Page Colour .... EUR 2900
SCC .... EUR 26.80
Agency Commission: 15%
Mechanical Data: Type Area: 190 x 270mm, Bleed Size: 210 x 297mm, No. of Columns (Display): 4, Col Widths (Display): 43mm, Print Process: offset, Film: positive, Screen: 60 lpc
BUSINESS: FINANCE & ECONOMICS: Property

SUOMEN KUVALEHTI 15242L73-200
Editorial: Maistraatinportti 1, 00015 OTAVAMEDIA
Tel: 9 15 661 **Fax:** 9 14 40 76
Email: suomen.kuvalehti@otavamedia.fi **Web site:** http://www.suomenkuvalehti.fi
ISSN: 0039-5552
Date Established: 1916; **Freq:** Weekly; **Circ:** 88,667
Usual Pagination: 96
Editor-in-Chief: Tapani Ruokanen; **Managing Editor:** Jari Lindholm
Profile: Magazine providing information on the latest news stories.
Language(s): Finnish
ADVERTISING RATES:
Full Page Colour .... EUR 6310
SCC .... EUR 56.30
Mechanical Data: Bleed Size: 280 x 217mm, Type Area: 280 x 217mm, Col Widths (Display): 45mm, Film: positive, Screen: 60 lpc
Editions:
Suomenkuvalehti.fi
CONSUMER: NATIONAL & INTERNATIONAL PERIODICALS

SUOMEN LÄÄKÄRILEHTI 15098L56A-80
Editorial: PL 49/Mäkelänkatu 2 A, 00501 HELSINKI
Tel: 9 39 30 91 **Fax:** 9 39 30 795
Email: laakarilehti@fimnet.fi **Web site:** http://www.laakarilehti.fi
ISSN: 0039-5560
Date Established: 1922; **Freq:** Weekly; **Circ:** 25,994
Usual Pagination: 120
Managing Editor: Esa Ilmolahti
Profile: Publication of the Finnish Medical Association.
Language(s): Finnish
Readership: Read by medical professionals and others working at health stations.
ADVERTISING RATES:
Full Page Colour .... EUR 3500
SCC .... EUR 41.60
Mechanical Data: Type Area: 245 x 170mm, Col Length: 245mm, Page Width: 170mm, Trim Size: 280 x 210mm, Print Process: Offset, Col Widths (Display): 40mm, No. of Columns (Display): 4

SUOMEN LEHDISTÖ - FINLANDS PRESS 14887L2B-90
Formerly: Suomen Lehdistö
Editorial: PL 415/Lönnrotinkatu 11, 00121 HELSINKI
Tel: 9 22 87 73 00 **Fax:** 9 60 79 89
Email: suomen.lehdisto@sanomalehdet.fi **Web site:** http://www.sanomalehdet.fi/suomenlehdisto
ISSN: 0039-5587
Date Established: 1931; **Freq:** Monthly - Published 10/year; **Circ:** 2,722
Usual Pagination: 54
Profile: Specialist magazine for people working in communications agencies and newspapers, such as newspaper publishers, journalists, advertising and publicity personnel.
Language(s): Finnish; Swedish
Readership: Read by newspaper publishers, journalists, advertising and publicity personnel.
ADVERTISING RATES:
Full Page Colour .... EUR 2760
SCC .... EUR 16.40
Agency Commission: 15%
Mechanical Data: Type Area: 230 x 334mm, Bleed Size: 260 x 370mm, Screen: 48 lpc, Print Process: Offset, Col Length: 334mm, Page Width: 230mm
Copy instructions: *Copy Date:* 12 days prior to publication date
Average ad content per issue: 15%
BUSINESS: COMMUNICATIONS, ADVERTISING & MARKETING: Press

SUOMEN LUONTO 15126L57-70
Editorial: Kotkankatu 9, 00510 HELSINKI
Tel: 9 22 80 81 **Fax:** 9 22 80 82 32
Web site: http://www.suomenluonto.fi
ISSN: 0356-0678
Date Established: 1942; **Freq:** Monthly - Published 10/year; **Circ:** 25,033
Usual Pagination: 68
Editor-in-Chief: Jorma Laurila; **Managing Editor:** Antti Halkka
Profile: Magazine containing information about nature and environmental protection. Includes articles on ecology, biology, nature protection, climate changes and the relationship between man and nature.
Language(s): Finnish
ADVERTISING RATES:
Full Page Colour .... EUR 2375
SCC .... EUR 19.90
Agency Commission: 15%
Mechanical Data: Col Length: 275mm, No. of Columns (Display): 4, Print Process: offset, Film: Digital material. positive, Type Area: 184 x 271mm, Col Widths (Display): 43mm, Screen: 60 lpc
Average ad content per issue: 10%
BUSINESS: ENVIRONMENT & POLLUTION

SUOMEN MATKAILULEHTI 712583L89A-3_40
Formerly: Matkailu ja Retkeilylehti
Editorial: Kreetankuja 2, 21200 RAISIO
Tel: 2 27 78 071 **Fax:** 2 27 78 099
Email: info@kustantamo.fi **Web site:** http://www.kustantamo.fi
ISSN: 1457-9375
Freq: Quarterly; **Cover Price:** Free; **Circ:** 250,000
Usual Pagination: 48
Editor-in-Chief: Keijo Asikainen
Profile: Domestic and foreign travel destinations, coming events and travel fairs are presented during the different seasons.
Language(s): Finnish
ADVERTISING RATES:
Full Page Colour .... EUR 1943.00
Agency Commission: 15%
Mechanical Data: Type Area: 255 x 365mm, Bleed Size: 280 x 400mm, Col Widths (Display): 47mm, Print Process: offset, Screen: 34 lpc mpno, 40 lpc colour
CONSUMER: HOLIDAYS & TRAVEL: Travel

SUOMEN OMAKOTILEHTI 705130L4E-85
Editorial: Sompiontie 1, 00730 HELSINKI
Tel: 9 68 03 710 **Fax:** 9 68 03 71 55
Email: olli-pekka.laine@omakotiliitto.fi **Web site:** http://www.omakotiliitto.fi
ISSN: 1236-178X
Date Established: 1995; **Freq:** Quarterly - Published 5/year; **Circ:** 72,000
Usual Pagination: 40
Editor-in-Chief: Olli-Pekka Laine
Profile: Magazine covering all aspects of home ownership.
Language(s): Finnish
Readership: Aimed at private house owners.
ADVERTISING RATES:
Full Page Colour .... EUR 3800
SCC .... EUR 27.80
Agency Commission: 15%
Mechanical Data: Type Area: 204 x 274mm, Print Process: offset, Screen: 60 lpc, No. of Columns (Display): 5
BUSINESS: ARCHITECTURE & BUILDING: Building

SUOMEN SILTA 15393L94D-250
Editorial: Mariankatu 8 B c 15, 00170 HELSINKI
Tel: 9 68 41 210 **Fax:** 9 68 41 21 40
Email: info@suomi-seura.fi **Web site:** http://www.suomi-seura.fi
ISSN: 0039-5625
Date Established: 1927; **Freq:** 6 issues yearly; **Circ:** 17,500
Usual Pagination: 56
Editor-in-Chief: Leena Isbom
Profile: Magazine containing news about Finland, along with articles on culture, society and political issues.
Language(s): English; Finnish; German; Swedish
Readership: Aimed at Finnish emigrants and their relatives in Finland.
ADVERTISING RATES:
Full Page Colour .... EUR 1900.00
Agency Commission: 15%
Mechanical Data: Print Process: Offset, No. of Columns (Display): 3, Type Area: 270 x 183mm, Col Length: 270mm, Film: Negative, Bleed Size: 297 x 210mm, Screen: 54 lpc, Page Width: 183mm, Col Widths (Display): 57mm
CONSUMER: OTHER CLASSIFICATIONS: Expatriates

SUOMEN SOTILAS 705131L40-120
Editorial: Döbelninkatu 2, 00260 HELSINKI
Tel: 10 42 38 380 **Fax:** 10 42 38 389
Email: toimitus@suomensotilas.fi **Web site:** http://www.suomensotilas.fi
ISSN: 1237-8704
Date Established: 1919; **Freq:** 6 issues yearly; **Circ:** 13,864
Usual Pagination: 64
Editor-in-Chief: Jaakko Puuperä; **Managing Editor:** Petri Välkki
Profile: Magazine about military traditions and the civilian work among soldiers.
Language(s): Finnish
ADVERTISING RATES:
Full Page Colour .... EUR 1650.00
Agency Commission: 15%
Mechanical Data: Type Area: 186 x 270mm, Bleed Size: 210 x 297mm, No. of Columns (Display): 4, Col Widths (Display): 43mm, Print Process: offset, Screen: 45 lpc
BUSINESS: DEFENCE

SUOMEN YRITTÄJÄSANOMAT 14932L14H-20
Formerly: Suomen Yrittäjät
Editorial: PL 999/ Mannerheimintie 76 A, 00101 HELSINKI **Tel:** 9 22 92 21 **Fax:** 9 22 92 29 99
Email: jouko.lantto@yrittajat.fi **Web site:** http://www.yrittajat.fi
ISSN: 1795-7982
Freq: Monthly - Published 10/year; **Circ:** 84,751
Usual Pagination: 44
Editor-in-Chief: Anssi Kujala
Profile: The magazine enhances interest supervision by small-scale firms, gives the entrepreneur point of view about current affairs and informs about current events.
Language(s): Finnish
Readership: SYKL (Confederation of Finnish Entrepreneurs) member companies.
ADVERTISING RATES:
Full Page Colour .... EUR 8450
SCC .... EUR 20.50
Mechanical Data: Type Area: 380 x 515mm, No. of Columns (Display): 8, Col Widths (Display): 44mm, Screen: 34 lpc, Print Process: offset
Copy instructions: *Copy Date:* 7 days prior to publication date
BUSINESS: COMMERCE, INDUSTRY & MANAGEMENT: Small Business

SUOMENMAA 15209L65A-42
Editorial: PL 1070/ Apollonkatu 11 A, 00101 HELSINKI **Tel:** 44 73 70 262 **Fax:** 8 33 83 53
Email: uutiset@suomenmaa.fi **Web site:** http://www.suomenmaa.fi
ISSN: 0356-3588
Date Established: 1906; **Freq:** 156 issues yearly - Published Tuesday, Wednesday and Friday; **Circ:** 11,032
Usual Pagination: 32
Profile: Main newspaper of the Centre Party. Once a month a special issue called Maa- ja metsätalous is distributed to all households of northern Finland, where the Centre Party is strong. Incorporating a monthly suppliment Sentteri.
Language(s): Finnish
ADVERTISING RATES:
Full Page Colour .... EUR 6771
SCC .... EUR 30.50
Agency Commission: 15%
Mechanical Data: Col Length: 370mm, Page Width: 255mm, No. of Columns (Display): 6, Print Process: offset, Screen: 40 lpc, Col Widths (Display): 39mm
Editions:
Suomenmaa Verkkotoimitus
NATIONAL DAILY & SUNDAY NEWSPAPERS: National Daily Newspapers

SUOMENMAA OULUN TOIMITUS 705876L65C-585
Editorial: PL 52/ Lekatie 4, 90101 OULU
Tel: 8 53 70 011 **Fax:** 8 33 83 53
Email: toimitus@suomenmaa.fi **Web site:** http://www.suomenmaa.fi
ISSN: 0356-3588
Date Established: 1908; **Freq:** 156 issues yearly - Published Tuesday, Wednesday and Friday; **Circ:** 2,468
Usual Pagination: 32
Editor-in-Chief: Juha Määttä; **Managing Editor:** Pirkko Wilén
Profile: Main newspaper of the Centre Party in Finland. This is the rural edition of the same newspaper that also is issued as a national newspaper from Helsinki.
Language(s): Finnish
ADVERTISING RATES:
SCC .... EUR 30.50
Agency Commission: 15%
Mechanical Data: Col Length: 370mm, No. of Columns (Display): 6, Col Widths (Display): 39mm, Print Process: offset
NATIONAL DAILY & SUNDAY NEWSPAPERS: National Daily Regional Offices

SUOMI+ 1902200L73-351
Formerly: Lue!
Editorial: Vanha Turuntie 371, 03150 HUHMARI
Tel: 9 41 39 73 00
Email: suomiplus@karprint.fi **Web site:** http://www.lue-lehti.fi
ISSN: 1798-2960
Date Established: 2009; **Freq:** Monthly - Published 10/year; **Circ:** 40,000
Usual Pagination: 100
Editor-in-Chief: Juha Ahola
Profile: Magazine about people, gossip and general-interest interviews.
Language(s): Finnish
Readership: Readers older than 40 years old.
ADVERTISING RATES:
Full Page Colour .... EUR 2100
SCC .... EUR 17.30

SUOMI-UNKARI 719174L89A-7_50
Editorial: Kaisaniemenkatu 10, 00100 HELSINKI
Tel: 9 85 69 85 66
Web site: http://www.suomiunkari.fi
Date Established: 1980; **Freq:** Quarterly; **Annual Sub.:** EUR 10.00; **Circ:** 8,000
Usual Pagination: 20
Editor-in-Chief: Marjatta Manni-Hämäläinen
Profile: Magazine about the travel and business enhancement between Finland and Hungary.
Language(s): Finnish
ADVERTISING RATES:
SCC .... EUR 10.00

SUOSIKKI 15315L76E-200
Editorial: Maistraatinportti 1, 00015 OTAVAMEDIA
Tel: 9 15 661 **Fax:** 9 14 45 95
Email: suosikki@otavamedia.fi **Web site:** http://www.suosikki.fi
ISSN: 0355-4260
Date Established: 1961; **Freq:** Monthly; **Circ:** 24,366
Usual Pagination: 96
Managing Editor: Mikko Merilinna
Profile: Magazine providing information about popular music. Includes celebrity news and interviews.
Language(s): Finnish
Readership: Young people interested in pop and rock music.
ADVERTISING RATES:
Full Page Colour .... EUR 4580
SCC .... EUR 40.80
Mechanical Data: Bleed Size: 280 x 230mm, Print Process: Offset, Film: Digital positive, Page Width: 230mm, Screen: 60 lpc, No. of Columns (Display): 4, Col Widths (Display): 45mm, Type Area: 230 x 280mm
Copy instructions: *Copy Date:* 19 days prior to publication date
CONSUMER: MUSIC & PERFORMING ARTS: Pop Music

SUPER 705287L56B-9
Editorial: Ratamestarinkatu 12, 00520 HELSINKI
Tel: 9 27 27 910 **Fax:** 9 27 27 91 20
Email: super-lehti@superliitto.fi **Web site:** http://www.superliitto.fi
ISSN: 0784-6975
Date Established: 1953; **Freq:** Monthly; **Circ:** 70,922
Usual Pagination: 52
Profile: Journal for members of the Nurses' Trade Union.
Language(s): Finnish; Swedish
Readership: Women of average age 37.
ADVERTISING RATES:
Full Page Colour .... EUR 2895
SCC .... EUR 56.30
Agency Commission: 15%
Mechanical Data: Type Area: 170 x 257mm, No. of Columns (Display): 2, Col Widths (Display): 82mm, Print Process: offset, Screen: 60 lpc
BUSINESS: HEALTH & MEDICAL: Nursing

SUUPOHJAN SANOMAT 705013L72-1320
Editorial: PL 4/Läntinen Pitkäkatu 15, 64101 KRISTIINANKAUPUNKI **Tel:** 6 24 77 880
Fax: 62477889
Email: toimitus@suupohjansanomat.fi **Web site:** http://www.suupohjansanomat.fi
ISSN: 0787-6742
Date Established: 1897; **Freq:** 104 issues yearly; **Circ:** 4,174
Usual Pagination: 12
Managing Editor: Tauno Riihiluoma
Profile: Newspaper distributed in Kristiinankaupunki, Isojoki, Karijoki, Kaskinen, Närpiö and Teuva.
Language(s): Finnish
ADVERTISING RATES:
Full Page Colour .... EUR 3197
SCC .... EUR 14.60
Agency Commission: 15%
Mechanical Data: Type Area: 260 x 365mm, Page Width: 260mm, Col Length: 365mm, No. of Columns (Display): 6, Col Widths (Display): 40mm, Print Process: offset, Film: negative, Screen: 40 lpc
Editions:
Suupohjan Sanomat Verkkotoimitus
LOCAL NEWSPAPERS

SUURI KÄSITYÖLEHTI 15274L47A-21
Editorial: PL 100/ Lapinmäentie 1, 00040 SANOMA MAGAZINES **Tel:** 9 12 01 **Fax:** 9 12 05 352
Email: suuri.kasityolehti@sanomamagazines.fi **Web site:** http://www.suurikasityo.fi
ISSN: 1236-3855
Date Established: 1974; **Freq:** Monthly - Published 11/year; **Circ:** 68,179
Usual Pagination: 84
Editor-in-Chief: Heidi Laaksonen; **Managing Editor:** Helena Ahopelto
Profile: Magazine focusing on dress-making with features on knitting, sewing, weaving, embroidery, crochet and other crafts.
Language(s): Finnish
ADVERTISING RATES:
Full Page Colour .... EUR 5900
SCC .... EUR 49.60
Mechanical Data: Bleed Size: 230 x 273mm, Type Area: 194 x 248mm, No. of Columns (Display): 4, Col Widths (Display): 45mm, Print Process: offset, Film: positive, Screen: 60 lpc
Copy instructions: *Copy Date:* 17 days prior to publication date
BUSINESS: CLOTHING & TEXTILES

SUUR-JYVÄSKYLÄN LEHTI 705035L72-1330
Editorial: PL 115/ Kauppakatu 41 A, 40101 JYVÄSKYLÄ **Tel:** 14 33 82 421 **Fax:** 14 33 82 490
Email: toimitus@sjl.fi **Web site:** http://www.suur-jyvaskylanlehti.fi
Date Established: 1959; **Freq:** 104 issues yearly; **Cover Price:** Free; **Circ:** 81,000
Usual Pagination: 24
Editor-in-Chief: Tapani Markkanen
Profile: Newspaper issued in the Jyväskylä, Muurame, Säynätsalo and Laukaan Tiituspohja area.
Language(s): Finnish
ADVERTISING RATES:
Full Page Colour .... EUR 4157
SCC .... EUR 18.50
Agency Commission: 15%
Mechanical Data: No. of Columns (Display): 6, Col Length: 370mm, Col Widths (Display): 38mm, Print Process: offset, Screen: 40 lpc, Page Width: 254mm
LOCAL NEWSPAPERS

SUUR-KEURUU 15194L72-1335
Editorial: PL 31 / Niilontie 1, 42701 KEURUU
Tel: 10 66 55 186 **Fax:** 14 77 28 19
Email: suur-keuruu.toimitus@sps.fi **Web site:** http://www.suurkeuruu.fi
ISSN: 0738-3709
Date Established: 1922; **Freq:** 104 issues yearly; **Circ:** 6,224

Usual Pagination: 16
Profile: Newspaper issued in Keuruu, Multia, Mänttä, Vilppula and Petäjävesi.
Language(s): Finnish
ADVERTISING RATES:
Full Page Colour .... EUR 2575
SCC .... EUR 11.60
Agency Commission: 15%
Mechanical Data: Type Area: 260 x 370mm, No. of Columns (Display): 6, Col Widths (Display): 40mm, Print Process: offset
Editions:
Suur-Keuruu Verkkotoimitus
LOCAL NEWSPAPERS

SYDÄN 15099L56R-105
Editorial: PL 50/ Oltermannintie 8, 00621 HELSINKI
Tel: 9 75 27 521
Email: marja.kytomaki@sydanliitto.fi **Web site:** http://www.sydan.fi
ISSN: 0039-7571
Date Established: 1957; **Freq:** Quarterly - Published 5/year; **Circ:** 81,153
Usual Pagination: 48
Profile: Magazine about cardiovascular diseases. Includes information and opinions on measures, treatment, rehabilitation and the activities of the various heart disease organisations in Finland.
Language(s): Finnish; Swedish
Readership: Read by the general public interested in their health and of others especially members of the Finnish Heart Association.
ADVERTISING RATES:
Full Page Colour .... EUR 3000
SCC .... EUR 28.30
Agency Commission: 15%
Mechanical Data: Type Area: 184 x 265mm, Bleed Size: 210 x 297mm, Col Widths (Display): 43mm, No. of Columns (Display): 4, Print Process: offset, Screen: 54 lpc
BUSINESS: HEALTH & MEDICAL: Health Medical Related

SYDÄN-HÄMEEN LEHTI 704902L72-1340
Editorial: PL 16 / Onkkaalantie 58, 36601 PÄLKÄNE
Tel: 3 53 99 800 **Fax:** 3 53 99 888
Email: toimitus@shl.fi **Web site:** http://www.shl.fi
ISSN: 0788-8279
Date Established: 1929; **Freq:** 104 issues yearly; **Circ:** 5,692
Usual Pagination: 12
Profile: Newspaper issued in Kuhmolahti, Luopioinen, Pälkänen and Sahalahti.
Language(s): Finnish
ADVERTISING RATES:
Full Page Colour .... EUR 2696
SCC .... EUR 10.70
Agency Commission: 15%
Mechanical Data: Bleed Size: 290 x 420mm, Page Width: 290mm, Col Length: 428mm, No. of Columns (Display): 6, Col Widths (Display): 45mm, Print Process: offset, Screen: 34 lpc
LOCAL NEWSPAPERS

SYDÄN-SATAKUNTA 706519L72-1345
Editorial: PL 34/ Kilkunkatu 12, 32801 KOKEMÄKI
Tel: 10 66 55 700 **Fax:** 10 66 55 712
Email: ss.toimitus@sps.fi **Web site:** http://www.sydansatakunta.fi
ISSN: 1456-9337
Date Established: 1999; **Freq:** 104 issues yearly; **Circ:** 7,287
Usual Pagination: 16
Profile: Newspaper issued in Harjavalta, Kokemäki, Kiukainen and Nakkila.
Language(s): Finnish
ADVERTISING RATES:
Full Page Colour .... EUR 2668
SCC .... EUR 11.70
Agency Commission: 15%
Mechanical Data: No. of Columns (Display): 6, Type Area: 260 x 365mm, Col Length: 365mm, Col Widths (Display): 40mm, Print Process: offset
Editions:
Sydän-Satakunta Verkkotoimitus
LOCAL NEWSPAPERS

SYD-ÖSTERBOTTEN 704867L67B-7101
Editorial: PB 6/ Närpesvägen 4, 64201 NÄRPES
Tel: 6 78 48 700 **Fax:** 6 78 48 887
Email: redaktion@sydin.fi **Web site:** http://www.sydin.fi
ISSN: 0358-2434
Date Established: 1903
Circ: 7,149
Usual Pagination: 16
Profile: Regional newspaper distributed in Korsnäs, Närpiö, Kaskinen and Kristiinankaupunki.
Language(s): Swedish
ADVERTISING RATES:
Full Page Colour .... EUR 3816
SCC .... EUR 21.50
Agency Commission: 10-15%
Mechanical Data: Type Area: 255 x 370mm, No. of Columns (Display): 5, Col Widths (Display): 47mm, Col Length: 355mm, Screen: 34 lpc, Print Process: 4-colouroffset
Copy instructions: *Copy Date:* 5 days prior to publication date
REGIONAL DAILY & SUNDAY NEWSPAPERS: Regional Daily Newspapers

SYÖPÄ-CANCER 706433L56B-10
Editorial: Pieni Roobertinkatu 9, 00130 HELSINKI
Tel: 9 13 53 31 **Fax:** 9 13 51 093
Email: toimitus@cancer.fi **Web site:** http://www.cancer.fi
ISSN: 0356-3081
Date Established: 1972; **Freq:** 6 issues yearly; Free to qualifying individuals ; **Circ:** 120,000
Usual Pagination: 32
Managing Editor: Satu Lipponen
Profile: Magazine about cancer and the treatment of patients with cancer.
Language(s): Finnish; Swedish
BUSINESS: HEALTH & MEDICAL: Nursing

TAKOJA 15349L74Q-45
Editorial: Uudenmaankatu 25 A 4, 00120 HELSINKI
Tel: 9 69 62 520 **Fax:** 9 68 02 591
Web site: http://www.antropos.fi
ISSN: 1239-3142
Date Established: 1972; **Freq:** Quarterly; **Annual Sub.:** EUR 26.00; **Circ:** 900
Usual Pagination: 44
Editor-in-Chief: Pentti Aaltonen
Profile: Anthrophosophically oriented cultural magazine covering art and literature and related spiritual development.
Language(s): Finnish
Readership: Aimed at those interested in anthroposophy and spiritual development.
ADVERTISING RATES:
Full Page Colour .... EUR 330.00
Mechanical Data: Type Area: 183 x 261mm

TALO & KOTI 706520L74K-45
Editorial: Elimäenkatu 17-19, 6 krs., 00510 HELSINKI
Tel: 9 77 39 51 **Fax:** 9 77 39 53 99
Email: toimitus.talo-koti@forma.fi **Web site:** http://www.talokoti.fi
ISSN: 1457-3911
Date Established: 2000; **Freq:** Monthly - Published 10/year; **Circ:** 49,816
Usual Pagination: 124
Editor: Atso Mikkola; **Editor-in-Chief:** Kirsi Turunen;
Managing Editor: Hanna Sandström
Profile: Magazine about home purchase, interior-design and do-it-yourself-repairs.
Language(s): Finnish
ADVERTISING RATES:
Full Page Colour .... EUR 4320
SCC .... EUR 36.30
Agency Commission: 15%
Mechanical Data: Type Area: 217 x 280mm, Bleed Size: 217 x 280mm, Print Process: offset, Film: negative, Screen: 54 lpc
CONSUMER: WOMEN'S INTEREST CONSUMER MAGAZINES: Home Purchase

TALOMESTARI 15328L4D-90
Editorial: Vanha Turuntie 371, 03150 HUHMARI
Tel: 9 41 39 73 00 **Fax:** 9 41 39 74 05
Email: talomestari@karprint.fi **Web site:** http://www.talomestari-lehti.fi
ISSN: 0785-6318
Date Established: 1977; **Freq:** 6 issues yearly; **Circ:** 40,000
Usual Pagination: 84
Profile: Magazine containing articles on building, renovating and decorating, includes practical advices. Publishes the content of Sisustuvinkki magazine that ceased publication in 2010 covering interior design.
Language(s): Finnish
Readership: Read by people in the construction and renovation industry.
ADVERTISING RATES:
Full Page Colour .... EUR 1800
SCC .... EUR 14.90
Agency Commission: 15%
Mechanical Data: Type Area: 192 x 262mm, Bleed Size: 213 x 302mm, No. of Columns (Display): 4, Col Widths (Display): 44mm, Print Process: offset, Screen: 54 lpc

TALOTEKNIIKKA 14889L3B-10
Editorial: Lönnrotinkatu 4 B, 00120 HELSINKI
Tel: 20 74 35 760 **Fax:** 20 74 35 761
Email: eeva.vartiainen@talotekniikka-lehti.fi **Web site:** http://www.talotekniikka-lehti.fi
ISSN: 1236-5173
Date Established: 1993; **Freq:** 6 issues yearly - Published 8/year; **Circ:** 6,077
Usual Pagination: 100
Managing Editor: Jaana Ahti-Virtanen
Profile: Magazine containing information on heating, ventilating and air-conditioning. Summer issue aimed at consumers too and distributed at the annual housing fair.
Language(s): Finnish
Readership: Aimed at manufacturers, industrial designers and constructors.
ADVERTISING RATES:
Full Page Colour .... EUR 2795
SCC .... EUR 25.80
Agency Commission: 15%
Mechanical Data: Type Area: 270 x 185mm, Col Length: 270mm, Page Width: 185mm, Trim Size: 297 x 210mm, Screen: 54-60 lpc, Print Process: Offset, No. of Columns (Display): 2-4, Col Widths (Display): 42/58/87mm, Film: negative
BUSINESS: HEATING & VENTILATION: Industrial Heating & Ventilation

TALOUS & YHTEISKUNTA 719176L1A-65
Editorial: Pitkänsillanranta 3 A, 6 krs, 00530 HELSINKI **Tel:** 9 25 35 73 30 **Fax:** 9 25 35 73 32
Email: Heikki.Taimio@labour.fi **Web site:** http://www.labour.fi
ISSN: 1236-7206
Date Established: 1973; **Freq:** Quarterly; **Annual Sub.:** EUR 22.00; **Circ:** 3,000
Usual Pagination: 48
Editor-in-Chief: Jaakko Kiander
Profile: Magazine with forecasts and studies concerning economics, work and society.
Language(s): Finnish
BUSINESS: FINANCE & ECONOMICS

TALOUSELÄMÄ 14934L1A-70
Editorial: PL 920/ Annankatu 34-36 B, 00101 HELSINKI **Tel:** 20 44 240 **Fax:** 20 44 24 108
Email: te@talentum.fi **Web site:** http://www.talouselama.fi
ISSN: 0356-5106
Date Established: 1938; **Freq:** Weekly - Published 44/ a year; **Circ:** 79,406
Usual Pagination: 60
Managing Editor: Jouni Luotonen
Profile: Business magazine containing articles about big national and international companies, covering issues on trade, industry, personnel, finance, and market developments.
Language(s): Finnish
Readership: Read by executives, middle management and private investors in Finland.
ADVERTISING RATES:
Full Page Colour .... EUR 10045
SCC .... EUR 84.50
Agency Commission: 5-15%
Mechanical Data: Trim Size: 297 x 220mm, No. of Columns (Display): 4, Screen: 54 lpc, Print Process: offset, Col Widths (Display): 47mm
Copy instructions: *Copy Date:* 42 days prior to publication date
Editions:
Talouselama.fi
BUSINESS: FINANCE & ECONOMICS

TALOUSELÄMÄ PLATINUM 2036062L74Q-71
Editorial: PL 920/ Annankatu 34-36 B, 00101 HELSINKI **Tel:** 20 44 240 **Fax:** 20 44 24 108
Email: te@talentum.fi **Web site:** http://www.talouselama.fi/platinum
Freq: Quarterly; **Circ:** 110,000
Editor-in-Chief: Reijo Ruokanen
Profile: Magazine covering consuming issues and new products and services, including luxury products.
Language(s): Finnish
Readership: Korkeasti koulutetut, hyvin toimeen tulevat ja kulutuskykyiset lukijat. / Readers with higher education and high income interested in consumption.
ADVERTISING RATES:
Full Page Colour .... EUR 11000

TALOUSSANOMAT 706066L65A-101
Editorial: PL 35/ Töölönlahdenkatu 2, 00089 SANOMA **Tel:** 9 12 21
Email: taloussanomat@sanoma.fi **Web site:** http://www.taloussanomat.fi
ISSN: 1455-6308
Date Established: 1997; **Freq:** Daily. Published Tuesday-Saturday; **Cover Price:** Free; **Circ:** 676,000 Unique Users
Managing Editor: Anneli Koistinen
Profile: Business and financial web site.
Language(s): Finnish
Agency Commission: 15%
Mechanical Data: Type Area: 253 x 365mm, No. of Columns (Display): 6, Col Widths (Display): 39mm, Print Process: offset, Screen: 34 lpc
NATIONAL DAILY & SUNDAY NEWSPAPERS: National Daily Newspapers

TALOUSTAITO 14882L1M-50
Editorial: Kalevankatu 4, 00100 HELSINKI
Tel: 9 61 88 71 **Fax:** 9604435
Email: antti.marttinen@veronmaksajat.fi **Web site:** http://www.taloustaito.fi
ISSN: 0788-9135
Date Established: 1948; **Freq:** Monthly; **Circ:** 239,965
Usual Pagination: 68
Managing Editor: Riitta Rimmi
Profile: Journal of the Finnish Taxpayers' Association. Focuses on private and public finance and taxation.
Language(s): Finnish
ADVERTISING RATES:
Full Page Colour .... EUR 5310
SCC .... EUR 44.60
Agency Commission: 15%
Mechanical Data: Col Length: 280mm, Type Area: 260 x 192mm, Print Process: Offset rotation, Screen: 54-60 lpc, Bleed Size: 280 x 210mm, No. of Columns (Display): 3, Page Width: 192mm
Average ad content per issue: 15%
BUSINESS: FINANCE & ECONOMICS: Taxation

TALOUSTAITO YRITYS 14881L1M-50_5
Formerly: Finanssi
Editorial: Kalevankatu 4, 00100 HELSINKI
Tel: 9 61 88 71 **Fax:** 9 60 80 87
Email: antti.marttinen@veronmaksajat.fi **Web site:** http://www.taloustaito.fi
ISSN: 0789-6778
Date Established: 1992; **Freq:** 6 issues yearly - Published 5/year; **Circ:** 46,364
Usual Pagination: 68
Managing Editor: Riitta Rimmi
Profile: Journal of the Finnish Taxpayers' Association, mainly dealing with leadership, business, marketing and corporation tax.
Language(s): Finnish
Readership: Read by (financial) directors and entrepreneurs.
ADVERTISING RATES:
Full Page Colour .... EUR 3440
SCC .... EUR 40.90
Agency Commission: 15%
Mechanical Data: Col Length: 280mm, Type Area: 275 x 192mm, Print Process: Offset rotation, Screen: 54-60 lpc, Bleed Size: 280 x 210mm, Page Width: 192mm, No. of Columns (Display): 3
BUSINESS: FINANCE & ECONOMICS: Taxation

TAMPEREEN KIRKKOSANOMAT 705471L87-99_30
Editorial: PL 226/ Näsilinnankatu 26, 33101 TAMPERE **Tel:** 3 21 90 274 **Fax:** 3 21 90 388
Email: toimitus@tampereenkirkkosanomat.fi **Web site:** http://www.tampereenkirkkosanomat.fi
Date Established: 1954; **Freq:** 26 issues yearly; **Cover Price:** Free; **Circ:** 102,800
Usual Pagination: 16
Editor-in-Chief: Marja Rautanen
Profile: Magazine about internationality, mission, human rights and the diaconate from the Tampere parish point of view.
Language(s): Finnish
ADVERTISING RATES:
Full Page Colour .... EUR 3100.00
SCC .... EUR 19.00
Agency Commission: 10-15%
Mechanical Data: No. of Columns (Display): 5, Col Widths (Display): 47mm, Screen: 34 lpc, Print Process: offset, Type Area: 289 x 419mm
CONSUMER: RELIGIOUS

TAMPERELAINEN 705094L72-1360
Editorial: PL 375/ Mustanlahdenkatu 3-7, 33101 TAMPERE **Tel:** 20 61 00 170 **Fax:** 20 77 03 040
Email: tre.toimitus@lehtiyhtyma.fi **Web site:** http://www.tamperelainen.fi
Date Established: 1957; **Freq:** 104 issues yearly; **Cover Price:** Free; **Circ:** 142,000
Usual Pagination: 32
Editor-in-Chief: Jari Niemelä
Profile: Newspaper issued in Tampere, Nokia, Ylöjärvi, Pirkkala, Kangasala and Lempäälä.
Language(s): Finnish
ADVERTISING RATES:
Full Page Colour .... EUR 4707
SCC .... EUR 22.60
Agency Commission: 15%
Mechanical Data: Col Widths (Display): 40mm, No. of Columns (Display): 9, Print Process: offset, Screen: 28-34 lpc, Col Length: 515mm, Page Width: 380mm
LOCAL NEWSPAPERS

TANSSIVIIHDE 1794990L76G-4
Editorial: PL 57, 33711 TAMPERE **Tel:** 50 56 91 969
Email: tanssiviihde@tanssiviihde.fi **Web site:** http://www.tanssiviihde.fi
ISSN: 1796-7120
Date Established: 2007; **Freq:** Quarterly; **Cover Price:** Free; **Circ:** 125,000
Usual Pagination: 20
Editor-in-Chief: Jaana Vuorenpää
Profile: Magazine about dance music.
Language(s): Finnish
ADVERTISING RATES:
Full Page Colour .... EUR 3558.00
Mechanical Data: Type Area: 290 x 390mm, Print Process: offset, No. of Columns (Display): 6, Col Widths (Display): 45mm
CONSUMER: MUSIC & PERFORMING ARTS: Dance

TAPATURMAVAKUUTUS 760050L1D-110
Editorial: PL 275/ Bulevardi 28, 00121 HELSINKI
Tel: 9 68 04 01 **Fax:** 9 68 04 05 14
Web site: http://www.tvl.fi
ISSN: 0785-7292
Date Established: 1928; **Freq:** Quarterly; **Annual Sub.:** EUR 20.00; **Circ:** 3,300
Usual Pagination: 40
Editor-in-Chief: Tapani Miettinen
Profile: Magazine about work accident insurance.
Language(s): Finnish

TAPIOLA OMA TALOUS 706041L1D-92
Editorial: Revontulentie 7, 02010 TAPIOLA
Tel: 9 45 31 **Fax:** 9 45 32 929
Email: tapiola@sanomamagazines.fi **Web site:** http://www.tapiola.fi
ISSN: 1795-9020

Date Established: 1983; **Freq:** Half-yearly; **Cover Price:** Free; **Circ:** 50,000
Usual Pagination: 40
Editor: Tiina Niemi; **Editor-in-Chief:** Jyrki Antikainen; **Managing Editor:** Tiina Riippa
Profile: Customer-magazine of insurance and financial group Tapiola.
Language(s): Finnish
BUSINESS: FINANCE & ECONOMICS: Insurance

TEATTERIIN 705877L76B-10
Editorial: Ensi Linja 2, 00530 HELSINKI **Tel:** 9 39 401 **Fax:** 9 39 40 404
Web site: http://www.hkt.fi
ISSN: 1455-8009
Freq: Quarterly; **Cover Price:** Free; **Circ:** 270,000
Usual Pagination: 24
Editor-in-Chief: Asko Sarkola; **Managing Editor:** Olli Eljaala
Profile: Magazine with information about shows and performers of Helsinki City Theatre.
Language(s): Finnish
CONSUMER: MUSIC & PERFORMING ARTS: Theatre

TEE ITSE 15329L79A-50
Editorial: Siltasaarenkatu 18-20 A, 00530 HELSINKI **Tel:** 20 76 08 500 **Fax:** 20 76 08 520
Email: teeitse@gmail.com **Web site:** http://www.teeitse.com
ISSN: 1457-5512
Date Established: 1987; **Freq:** Monthly - Published 17/year; **Circ:** 12,782
Usual Pagination: 80
Profile: Magazine for the do-it-yourself enthusiast.
Language(s): Finnish
ADVERTISING RATES:
Full Page Colour .... EUR 3000
SCC .... EUR 57.60
Agency Commission: 15%
Mechanical Data: Bleed Size: 205 x 276mm, Type Area: 185 x 260mm, Screen: 54 lpc, Film: positive, Print Process: offset
CONSUMER: HOBBIES & DIY

TEHO 14987L21A-80
Editorial: PL 5/ Kiljavantie 6, 05201 RAJAMÄKI
Tel: 9 29 04 12 00 **Fax:** 9 51 29 07 20
Email: teho@tts.fi **Web site:** http://www.tts.fi
ISSN: 0355-2527
Date Established: 1946; **Freq:** 6 issues yearly; **Circ:** 2,134
Usual Pagination: 40
Editor-in-Chief: Tarmo Luoma
Profile: Journal focusing on agriculture, forestry and home economics.
Language(s): Finnish
Readership: Read by farmers and students of adult education institutes.
ADVERTISING RATES:
Full Page Colour .... EUR 1650
SCC .... EUR 18.50
Agency Commission: 15%
Mechanical Data: Type Area: 175 x 256mm, No. of Columns (Display): 3, Col Widths (Display): 55mm, Screen: 54 lpc, Print Process: offset, Film: positive
BUSINESS: AGRICULTURE & FARMING

TEHY-LEHTI 15100L56C-55
Editorial: PL 10/Asemamiehenkatu 4, 00060 TEHY
Tel: 9 54 22 70 00 **Fax:** 9 61 50 02 73
Email: tehy.lehti@tehy.fi **Web site:** http://www.tehy.fi
ISSN: 0358-4038
Date Established: 1981; **Freq:** Monthly - Published 16/year; **Circ:** 119,805
Usual Pagination: 62
Profile: Publication for members of the Union of Health Professionals.
Language(s): Finnish; Swedish
ADVERTISING RATES:
Full Page Colour .... EUR 3930
SCC .... EUR 39.30
Mechanical Data: Col Widths (Display): 44mm, No. of Columns (Display): 4, Type Area: 250 x 191mm, Col Length: 250mm, Page Width: 191mm, Trim Size: 280 x 217mm, Print Process: Offset, Screen: 54 lpc
Copy instructions: *Copy Date:* 12 days prior to publication date
BUSINESS: HEALTH & MEDICAL: Hospitals

TEISKO-AITOLAHTI 704913L72-1370
Editorial: PL 2/ Runoilijankulma, Honkalantie 2, 2 krs, 34601 RUOVESI **Tel:** 3 47 61 400 **Fax:** 3 47 61 424
Email: teisko.aitolahti@ruovesi-lehti.fi **Web site:** http://www.ruovesi-lehti.fi
ISSN: 1457-8999
Date Established: 1926; **Freq:** Weekly; **Circ:** 1,827
Usual Pagination: 8
Editor-in-Chief: Kalevi Tiitinen
Profile: Newspaper issued in Teisko and Aitolahti.
Language(s): Finnish
ADVERTISING RATES:
Full Page Colour .... EUR 1776
SCC .... EUR 80
Agency Commission: 15%
Mechanical Data: No. of Columns (Display): 6, Type Area: 260 x 375mm, Col Widths (Display): 40mm, Print Process: offset, Screen: 34 lpc
Copy instructions: *Copy Date:* 10 days prior to publication date
LOCAL NEWSPAPERS

TEJUKA 705014L72-1375
Editorial: PL 16 / Tiilitie 2, 64701 TEUVA
Tel: 6 24 74 300 **Fax:** 62474321
Email: toimitus@tejuka-lehti.fi **Web site:** http://www.tejuka-lehti.fi
ISSN: 0782-582X
Date Established: 1950; **Freq:** Weekly; **Circ:** 4,047
Usual Pagination: 16
Managing Editor: Mauno Filppula
Profile: Local newspaper in Teuva and Jurva.
Language(s): Finnish
ADVERTISING RATES:
SCC .... EUR 10.50
Mechanical Data: Type Area: 260 x 365mm, No. of Columns (Display): 6, Col Widths (Display): 40mm, Print Process: offset
LOCAL NEWSPAPERS

TEK 14972L19A-45
Formerly: TEK Tekniikan Akateemiset
Editorial: Ratavartijankatu 2, 00520 HELSINKI
Tel: 9 22 91 21 **Fax:** 9 22 91 29 11
Email: tek-lehti@tek.fi **Web site:** http://www.tek.fi
ISSN: 1459-1898
Date Established: 1980; **Freq:** 6 issues yearly - Published 7/year; Free to qualifying individuals ; **Circ:** 67,823
Usual Pagination: 48
Managing Editor: Helena Andersson
Profile: Magazine for members of the Finnish Association of Graduate Engineers.
Language(s): Finnish
ADVERTISING RATES:
Full Page Colour .... EUR 3200
SCC .... EUR 26.90
Agency Commission: 15%
Mechanical Data: Col Length: 280mm, Print Process: Offset rotation, Bleed Size: 280 x 210mm, Trim Size: 274 x 214mm, Screen: 60 lpc, No. of Columns (Display): 4, Page Width: 210mm, Type Area: 213 x 286mm, Film: positive, Col Widths (Display): 43mm
Average ad content per issue: 10%
BUSINESS: ENGINEERING & MACHINERY

TEKNIIKAN MAAILMA 15333L78R-20
Editorial: Maistraatinportti 1, 00015 OTAVAMEDIA
Tel: 9 15 661 **Fax:** 9 15 66 63 13
Email: tekniikan.maailma@otavamedia.fi **Web site:** http://www.tekniikanmaailma.fi
ISSN: 0355-4287
Date Established: 1953; **Freq:** 26 issues yearly - Published 22/year; **Circ:** 138,322
Usual Pagination: 140
Editor: Jari Kujala; **Editor-in-Chief:** Velimatti Honkanen; **Managing Editor:** Raimo Haapaniemi
Profile: Magazine carrying out tests on cars, motor cycles, home electronics and appliances, cameras and photographic equipment.
Language(s): Finnish
ADVERTISING RATES:
Full Page Colour .... EUR 8510
SCC .... EUR 75.90
Mechanical Data: Bleed Size: 280 x 217mm, Film: Digital. positive, Type Area: 217 x 280mm, Col Widths (Display): 45mm, Screen: 60 lpc
Copy instructions: *Copy Date:* 16 days prior to publication date
Editions:
Tekniikanmaailma.fi
CONSUMER: CONSUMER ELECTRONICS: Consumer Electronics Related

TEKNIIKAN WAIHEITA 705184L19A-50
Editorial: Tieteiden Talo, Kirkkokatu 6, 00170 HELSINKI **Tel:** 40 72 75 335
Email: terhi.ketolainen@kolumbus.fi **Web site:** http://www.ths.fi
ISSN: 0780-5772
Date Established: 1983; **Freq:** Quarterly; **Annual Sub.:** EUR 31.00; **Circ:** 1,200
Usual Pagination: 80
Editor-in-Chief: Sampsa Kaataja
Profile: Magazine about the history of engineering, machinery and technical science.
Language(s): Finnish
ADVERTISING RATES:
Full Page Colour .... EUR 600.00
Mechanical Data: Print Process: offset, Type Area: 175 x 245mm

TEKNIIKKA & TALOUS 14973L14A-72
Editorial: PL 920/ Annankatu 34-36 B, 00101 HELSINKI **Tel:** 20 44 240
Email: tektal@talentum.fi **Web site:** http://www.tekniikkatalous.fi
ISSN: 0785-997X
Date Established: 1961; **Freq:** Weekly - Published on Friday; **Circ:** 95,690
Usual Pagination: 24
Profile: Magazine containing information about developments in technology, economics and industry.
Language(s): Finnish
Readership: Read by technically educated management.
ADVERTISING RATES:
Full Page Colour .... EUR 10050
SCC .... EUR 45.80
Agency Commission: 5-15%
Mechanical Data: Type Area: 365 x 253mm, Trim Size: 400 x 280mm, Screen: 40 lpc, No. of Columns (Display): 6, Col Widths (Display): 38mm, Print Process: Rotation offset, Col Length: 365mm, Page Width: 253mm
Editions:
Tekniikkatalous.fi
BUSINESS: COMMERCE, INDUSTRY & MANAGEMENT

TEKSTIVIESTIT OY 706368L5B-6
Editorial: Köydenpunojankatu 4 a D, 00180 HELSINKI **Tel:** 9 60 25 44 **Fax:** 9 61 16 70
Email: toimitus@tekstiviestit.fi **Web site:** http://www.tekstiviestit.fi
Freq: Daily
Profile: Tekstiviestit Oy is a production company that delivers articles about information, office and consumer technology to magazines including Kotimikro, Sihteeri & Assistentti, Mikro PC, Yhteishyvä, Suomela and Kuluttaja.
Language(s): Finnish
BUSINESS: COMPUTERS & AUTOMATION: Data Processing

TELMA 706592L14E-35
Formerly: Työyhteisöviesti - Arbetsplatsinfo
Editorial: Lönnrotinkatu 4 B, 00120 HELSINKI
Tel: 9 61 62 61 **Fax:** 9 61 21 287
Email: telma@telma-lehti.fi **Web site:** http://www.telma-lehti.fi
ISSN: 1239-0925
Freq: Quarterly; **Cover Price:** Free; **Circ:** 113,500
Usual Pagination: 56
Managing Editor: Eija Åback
Profile: Magazine about safety at work.
Language(s): Finnish; Swedish
Readership: Customers of the Centre for Occupational Safety.
BUSINESS: COMMERCE, INDUSTRY & MANAGEMENT: Work Study

TEOLLISUUS NYT 713040L4E-100
Editorial: Ruukinkuja 3, 02330 ESPOO
Tel: 9 80 99 11 **Fax:** 9 80 99 12 00
Email: teollisuusnyt@rpt.fi **Web site:** http://www.teollisuusnyt.fi
ISSN: 1457-7437
Date Established: 2000; **Freq:** Half-yearly - Published 5/year; **Circ:** 13,000
Usual Pagination: 100
Profile: Magazine specialising in industry and building information.
Language(s): Finnish
Readership: Read by people responsible for industry investments and undertakers.
ADVERTISING RATES:
Full Page Colour .... EUR 2990
SCC .... EUR 57
Mechanical Data: Type Area: 174 x 262mm, Bleed Size: 210 x 297mm, Col Widths (Display): 72mm, No. of Columns (Display): 2, Print Process: offset, Screen: 70 lpc

TEOLLISUUSSANOMAT 705156L14A-73
Formerly: Wolyymi Sanomat
Editorial: Kreetankuja 2, 21200 RAISIO
Tel: 2 27 78 080 **Fax:** 2 27 78 099
Email: info@kustantamo.fi **Web site:** http://www.kustantamo.fi
ISSN: 1458-4166
Freq: 6 issues yearly; **Cover Price:** Free; **Circ:** 20,000
Usual Pagination: 32
Editor-in-Chief: Kejio Asikainen
Profile: Teollisuussanomat is a news magazine about production technology and trade. Trade decision-makers and officials and company presidents are among the readers.
Language(s): Finnish
ADVERTISING RATES:
Full Page Colour .... EUR 1680.00
SCC .... EUR 9.20
Agency Commission: 15%
Mechanical Data: Type Area: 255 x 365mm, Bleed Size: 280 x 400mm, Col Widths (Display): 47mm, Print Process: offset, Screen: 34 lpc b&w; 40 lpc colour

TEOLLISUUSSIJOITUS 1754728L1F-80
Editorial: PL 685/ Kalevankatu 9 A, 00101 HELSINKI
Tel: 9 68 03 680 **Fax:** 9 61 21 680
Email: tapio.kivisto@sanomamagazines.fi **Web site:** http://www.teollisuussijoitus.fi
ISSN: 1796-0266
Freq: Half-yearly; **Cover Price:** Free; **Circ:** 3,000
Usual Pagination: 20
Editor-in-Chief: Juha Marjosola
Profile: Magazine about investment in the industry sector.
Language(s): Finnish

TEOLLISUUSSUOMI 766503L14A-75
Editorial: Itkonniemenkatu 13 A, 70500 KUOPIO
Tel: 17 36 86 000
Email: aineisto@ammattiviestit.fi **Web site:** http://www.ammattiviestit.fi
ISSN: 1458-3259
Date Established: 2002; **Freq:** Quarterly - Published 7/year; **Cover Price:** Free; **Circ:** 7,000
Usual Pagination: 40
Profile: News magazine about industry and commerce in Finland.
Language(s): Finnish
Readership: People interested in novelties in Finnish industry.
ADVERTISING RATES:
Full Page Colour .... EUR 1150
SCC .... EUR 7.90
Mechanical Data: Type Area: 268 x 388mm, Print Process: offset

TERÄSRAKENNE 705200L27-3
Editorial: PL 381/ Unioninkatu 14, 4. kerros, 00131 HELSINKI **Tel:** 9 12 99 514 **Fax:** 9 12 99 214
Email: info@terasrakenneyhdistys.fi **Web site:** http://www.terasrakenneyhdistys.fi
ISSN: 0782-0941
Date Established: 1978; **Freq:** Quarterly; **Circ:** 13,300
Usual Pagination: 44
Profile: Magazine about using steel as building material.
Language(s): English; Finnish
ADVERTISING RATES:
Full Page Colour .... EUR 2250
SCC .... EUR 20.80
Agency Commission: 15%
Mechanical Data: Type Area: 185 x 270mm, Screen: 90 lpc, Col Length: 270mm, Page Width: 185mm, No. of Columns (Display): 4, Col Widths (Display): 42mm, Print Process: offset

TERVAREITTI 705025L72-1380
Editorial: PL 63/ Aaronkuja 5, 91501 MUHOS
Tel: 8 53 13 700 **Fax:** 8 53 32 179
Email: toimitus@tervareitti.fi **Web site:** http://www.tervareitti.fi
ISSN: 0789-8142
Date Established: 1959; **Freq:** 104 issues yearly; **Circ:** 6,035
Usual Pagination: 16
Profile: Tervareitti is a local newspaper issued in Muhos, Utajärvi and Vaala.
Language(s): Finnish
ADVERTISING RATES:
Full Page Colour .... EUR 2299
SCC .... EUR 10.50
Agency Commission: 15%
Mechanical Data: Page Width: 260mm, Col Length: 365mm, No. of Columns (Display): 6, Col Widths (Display): 40mm
Editions:
Tervareitti Verkkotoimitus
LOCAL NEWSPAPERS

TERVE METSÄ 706631L46-92
Editorial: PL 486, 00101 HELSINKI **Tel:** 20 46 24 971 **Fax:** 20 46 21 364
Email: terve.metsa@storaenso.com **Web site:** http://www.storaenso.com/metsa
ISSN: 1235-1687
Date Established: 1989; **Freq:** Quarterly; **Cover Price:** Free; **Circ:** 50,000
Usual Pagination: 28
Editor-in-Chief: Juha Hanni
Profile: Magazine focusing on all aspects of forestry.
Language(s): Finnish
BUSINESS: TIMBER, WOOD & FORESTRY

TERVE POTILAS 1833336L56A-82
Editorial: Kumppania Oy, Pohjoisranta 11, 28100 PORI **Tel:** 9 23 16 31 21
Email: emilii.malmi@fimnet.fi **Web site:** http://www.tervepotilas.fi
Date Established: 2008; **Freq:** Quarterly; **Cover Price:** Free; **Circ:** 250,000
Usual Pagination: 56
Editor-in-Chief: Emilii Malmi
Profile: Magazine about health and nutrition.
Language(s): Finnish
ADVERTISING RATES:
Full Page Colour .... EUR 6500.00
SCC .... EUR 58.00
Agency Commission: 15%
Mechanical Data: Type Area: 217 x 280mm, Print Process: offset
BUSINESS: HEALTH & MEDICAL

TERVE TALO 719170L4E-65
Formerly: Luomurakentaja
Editorial: Keskitie 5, 36760 LUOPIOINEN
Tel: 40 53 59 417
Email: keskus@luomura.com **Web site:** http://www.luomura.com
ISSN: 1795-0481
Date Established: 2000; **Freq:** Annual; **Annual Sub.:** EUR 24.00; **Circ:** 3,000
Usual Pagination: 16
Editor-in-Chief: Mikko Tuononen
Profile: Magazine about building houses in an ecological way.
Language(s): Finnish
ADVERTISING RATES:
Full Page Mono .... EUR 650.00
Full Page Colour .... EUR 800.00
Mechanical Data: Type Area: 178 x 252mm

TERVEYDEKSI! 705493L74G-102
Editorial: Otavamedia/ Kynämies Oy, Köydenpunojankatu 2 a D, 3 krs, 00180 HELSINKI
Tel: 9 15 66 85 10 **Fax:** 9 64 82 43

Email: tiina.kuosa@apteekkariliitto.fi **Web site:** http://www.terveydeksi.fi
ISSN: 0781-5867
Date Established: 1984; **Freq:** Quarterly - Published in March, June, September and December; **Cover Price:** Free; **Circ:** 450,000
Usual Pagination: 60
Managing Editor: Jari Kallio
Profile: Customer-magazine with aim to enhance health, care and prevention of illnesses and to provide information on medicine and pharmacy services.
Language(s): Finnish; Swedish
ADVERTISING RATES:
Full Page Colour .... EUR 7800
SCC .... EUR 154.10
Agency Commission: 15%
Mechanical Data: Type Area: 217 x 280mm, Print Process: offset, Screen: 70 lpc, Trim Size: 200 x 253mm
Copy instructions: *Copy Date:* 42 days prior to publication date
CONSUMER: WOMEN'S INTEREST CONSUMER MAGAZINES: Slimming & Health

TERVEYSUUTISET 706297L37-11
Formerly: Hyvän Mielen Terveiset
Editorial: TK-Mediatalo Oy, Hämeenkatu 14, 3 krs, 11100 RIIHIMÄKI **Tel:** 10 42 15 000
Email: timo.kivioja@tkmediatalo.fi **Web site:** http://www.hyvanmielenapteekit.fi
Date Established: 1996; **Freq:** Half-yearly; **Cover Price:** Free; **Circ:** 680,000
Usual Pagination: 24
Editor-in-Chief: Eeva Teitti; **Managing Editor:** Timo Kivioja
Profile: Magazine about pharmaceutical news and services.
Language(s): Finnish
ADVERTISING RATES:
Full Page Colour .... EUR 8976
SCC .... EUR 74.8
Mechanical Data: Screen: 40 lpc, Type Area: 252 x 362mm
BUSINESS: PHARMACEUTICAL & CHEMISTS

TESO-LEHTI 1983557L56A-202
Editorial: Tullikatu 10, 33100 TAMPERE
Tel: 3 21 10 363 **Fax:** 3 35 68 097
Email: tesory@tesory.com **Web site:** http://www.tesory.com
Freq: Quarterly - 2-4 times/year; **Circ:** 7,000
Editor-in-Chief: Tuula Savonen
Profile: Magazine for members of Terveys- ja Sosiaalialan Yrittäjät ry.
Language(s): Finnish
Readership: Yhdistyksen jäsenet, alan yrittäjät, viranhaltijat sekä opiskelijat. / Members of the Teso ry as well as those who work within healthcare and students.
ADVERTISING RATES:
Full Page Colour .... EUR 1500.00

TIE JA LIIKENNE 15043L49A-54
Editorial: PL 55/ Kaupintie 16 A, 00441 HELSINKI
Tel: 20 78 61 000 **Fax:** 20 78 61 009
Email: tieyhdistys@tieyhdistys.fi **Web site:** http://www.tieyhdistys.fi
ISSN: 0355-7855
Date Established: 1917; **Freq:** 6 issues yearly; **Circ:** 4,200
Usual Pagination: 40
Editor-in-Chief: Jaakko Rahja; **Managing Editor:** Liisi Vähätalo
Profile: Magazine published by the Finnish Road Association to promote road construction and road traffic. Includes information on international developments in road technology.
Language(s): English; Finnish
ADVERTISING RATES:
Full Page Colour .... EUR 2200.00
SCC .... EUR 21.40
Agency Commission: 15%
Mechanical Data: Bleed Size: 210 x 297mm, Type Area: 196 x 278mm, Film: positive, Screen: 48 lpc mono, 60 lpc colour, Print Process: offset, Col Widths (Display): 43mm, No. of Columns (Display): 4

TIEDE 15399L94J-60
Formerly: Tiede 2000
Editorial: PL 100/ Lapinmäentie 1, 00040 SANOMA MAGAZINES **Tel:** 9 12 01 **Fax:** 9 12 05 352
Email: tiede@sanomamagazines.fi **Web site:** http://www.tiede.fi
ISSN: 1457-9030
Date Established: 1980; **Freq:** Monthly; **Circ:** 63,117
Usual Pagination: 68
Editor-in-Chief: Jukka Ruukki; **Managing Editor:** Annikka Mutanen
Profile: Magazine providing information on scientific advances.
Language(s): Finnish
Readership: Aimed at people with an interest in science.
ADVERTISING RATES:
Full Page Colour .... EUR 3900
SCC .... EUR 35.70
Mechanical Data: Type Area: 194 x 248mm, Bleed Size: 230 x 273mm, No. of Columns (Display): 4, Col Widths (Display): 45mm, Print Process: offset, Film: positive, Screen: 60 lpc
Editions:
Tiede.fi
CONSUMER: OTHER CLASSIFICATIONS: Popular Science

TIEDOSTA 705694L5E-13
Formerly: Edisty
Editorial: Salomonkatu 17 A, 10 krs., 00100 HELSINKI **Tel:** 9 47 63 04 00 **Fax:** 9 47 63 03 99
Email: tieke@tieke.fi **Web site:** http://www.tieke.fi/tiedosta-lehti
ISSN: 1795-5351
Freq: Quarterly; **Circ:** 3,000
Usual Pagination: 52
Editor-in-Chief: Eppie Eloranta
Profile: Official publication of TIEKE, the Centre for Development of Information Technology, focusing on electronic information distribution.
Language(s): Finnish
Readership: Read by IT-professionals.
ADVERTISING RATES:
Full Page Colour .... EUR 700.00
SCC .... EUR 8.40
BUSINESS: COMPUTERS & AUTOMATION: Data Transmission

TIETEEN KUVALEHTI 705389L94J-65
Editorial: Siltasaarenkatu 18-20 A, 00530 HELSINKI
Tel: 20 76 08 563 **Fax:** 207608520
Web site: http://www.tieteenkuvalehti.com
ISSN: 0109-2456
Date Established: 1986; **Freq:** Monthly - Published 17/year; **Circ:** 41,537
Usual Pagination: 84
Publisher: Jens Henneberg
Profile: Magazine about current social and environmental scientific affairs for a broad range of public.
Language(s): Finnish
Readership: People interested in different sciences.
ADVERTISING RATES:
Full Page Colour .... EUR 3800
SCC .... EUR 76
Agency Commission: 15%
Mechanical Data: Bleed Size: 205 x 276mm, Type Area: 185 x 250mm, Screen: 54 lpc, Film: positive, Print Process: offset
CONSUMER: OTHER CLASSIFICATIONS: Popular Science

TIETEEN TIETOTEKNIIKKA 705233L5B-150
Formerly: Tietoyhteys
Editorial: PL 405/ Keilaranta 14, 02101 ESPOO
Tel: 9 45 72 001 **Fax:** 9 45 72 302
Email: tommi.kutilainen@csc.fi **Web site:** http://www.csc.fi/lehdet/tietoyhteys
ISSN: 1239-9248
Date Established: 1997; **Freq:** Quarterly; **Cover Price:** Free; **Circ:** 4,500
Usual Pagination: 32
Editor-in-Chief: Ari Turunen
Profile: Magazine about super computers and digital accounting services for research purposes in universities.
Language(s): Finnish
Agency Commission: 15%
Mechanical Data: Type Area: 190 x 249mm, No. of Columns (Display): 4, Col Widths (Display): 44mm, Screen: 54 lpc, Print Process: offset
BUSINESS: COMPUTERS & AUTOMATION: Data Processing

TIETOA MAASTA 749551L4C-10
Editorial: PL 84, Opastinsilta 12 C, 00521 HELSINKI
Tel: 20 54 15 335 **Fax:** 20 54 15 454
Email: tietoamaasta@maanmittauslaitos.fi **Web site:** http://www.maanmittauslaitos.fi
ISSN: 1457-9367
Date Established: 2001; **Freq:** Quarterly; **Cover Price:** Free; **Circ:** 12,000
Usual Pagination: 16
Editor-in-Chief: Liisa Kallela
Profile: Magazine about the services of the Finnish Land Measurement Institution.
Language(s): Finnish

TIETOKONE 14907L5C-6
Editorial: PL 100, 00040 SANOMA MAGAZINES
Tel: 9 12 01 **Fax:** 9 12 05 799
Email: toimitus@tietokone.fi **Web site:** http://www.tietokone.fi
ISSN: 0359-4947
Date Established: 1982; **Freq:** Monthly; **Circ:** 38,396
Usual Pagination: 140
Editor-in-Chief: Harri Lindfors; **Managing Editor:** Toni Stubin
Profile: Magazine covering all aspects of personal computing. Includes articles on hardware, software, the Internet, programming and networks.
Language(s): Finnish
ADVERTISING RATES:
Full Page Colour .... EUR 6600
SCC .... EUR 84.60
Agency Commission: 15%
Mechanical Data: No. of Columns (Display): 3, Print Process: Offset, Trim Size: 297 x 210mm, Type Area: 260 x 185mm, Col Length: 260mm, Col Widths (Display): 58mm, Film: Positive, Screen: 60 lpc
Copy instructions: *Copy Date:* 16 days prior to publication date
Editions:
Tietokone.fi
BUSINESS: COMPUTERS & AUTOMATION: Professional Personal Computers

TIETOTEKNIIKAN TUOTEUUTISET 706042L5C-7
Editorial: Lammaslammentie 13, 01710 VANTAA
Tel: 9 70 12 565 **Fax:** 9 85 56 559
Email: aineisto@tuoteuutiset.com **Web site:** http://www.tuoteuutiset.fi
ISSN: 1235-4023
Date Established: 1987; **Freq:** 6 issues yearly; **Cover Price:** Free; **Circ:** 35,000
Usual Pagination: 68
Editor-in-Chief: Jari Siebenberg
Profile: Magazine about new products in the computer business by ads and product presentation.
Language(s): Finnish
Readership: The magazine is sent to 20000 selected people responsible for company computer purchases.
ADVERTISING RATES:
Full Page Colour .... EUR 2700.00
SCC .... EUR 50.50
Mechanical Data: Type Area: 210 x 297mm
BUSINESS: COMPUTERS & AUTOMATION: Professional Personal Computers

TIETOVIIKKO 14903L5C-9
Editorial: PL 920/ Annankatu 34-36 B, 00101 HELSINKI **Tel:** 20 44 240 **Fax:** 20 44 24 106
Email: tietoviikko@talentum.fi **Web site:** http://www.tietoviikko.fi
ISSN: 0359-8543
Date Established: 1983; **Freq:** Weekly - Published 20/ year; **Circ:** 36,700
Usual Pagination: 24
Editor-in-Chief: Antti Oksanen; **Managing Editor:** Jonna Vuokola
Profile: Magazine covering computing and IT.
Language(s): Finnish
Readership: Read by IT-professionals and enthusiasts.
ADVERTISING RATES:
Full Page Colour .... EUR 9280
SCC .... EUR 42.30
Agency Commission: 5-15%
Mechanical Data: Type Area: 365 x 253mm, Trim Size: 400 x 280mm, No. of Columns (Display): 6, Col Widths (Display): 38mm, Screen: 40 lpc, Print Process: Rotation offset, Col Length: 365mm, Page Width: 253mm
Copy instructions: *Copy Date:* 15 days prior to publication date
Editions:
Tietoviikko.fi
BUSINESS: COMPUTERS & AUTOMATION: Professional Personal Computers

TILINTARKASTUS 705132L1B-2
Formerly: Tilintarkastus - Revision
Editorial: Fredrikinkatu 61 A 35, 00100 HELSINKI
Tel: 9 69 44 064 **Fax:** 9 69 49 215
Email: toimitus@tilintarkastuslehti.fi **Web site:** http://www.tilintarkastuslehti.fi
ISSN: 0383-0017
Date Established: 1957; **Freq:** 6 issues yearly; **Circ:** 5,000
Usual Pagination: 68
Profile: The subjects of the magazine are accounting and finance administration.
Language(s): Finnish
Readership: Most of the readers work in the field of account and internal revision.
ADVERTISING RATES:
Full Page Colour .... EUR 1400
SCC .... EUR 16.90
Agency Commission: 15%
Mechanical Data: Bleed Size: 210 x 297mm, Print Process: offset
BUSINESS: FINANCE & ECONOMICS: Accountancy

TILISANOMAT 14869L1B-50
Editorial: MCI Press Oy, Mikonkatu 18 B, 00100 HELSINKI **Tel:** 9 68 50 57 55 **Fax:** 9 69 49 596
Email: toimitus@tilisanomat.fi **Web site:** http://www.tilisanomat.fi
ISSN: 0358-111X
Date Established: 1980; **Freq:** 6 issues yearly; **Circ:** 11,470
Usual Pagination: 70
Profile: Magazine focusing on finance and accounting.
Language(s): Finnish
Readership: Read by members of the Finnish Association of Accountancy firms.
ADVERTISING RATES:
Full Page Colour .... EUR 2790
SCC .... EUR 48.90
Agency Commission: 15%
Mechanical Data: Bleed Size: 215 x 285mm, Type Area: 175 x 238mm, No. of Columns (Display): 2, Screen: 60 lpc, Print Process: offset, Col Widths (Display): 60mm
BUSINESS: FINANCE & ECONOMICS: Accountancy

TM RAKENNUSMAAILMA 1703207L4R-42
Editorial: Maistraatinportti 1, 00015 KUVALEHDET
Tel: 9 15 661 **Fax:** 9 15 66 63 13
Email: rakennusmaailma@otavamedia.fi **Web site:** http://www.rakennusmaailma.fi
ISSN: 1459-1839
Date Established: 2005; **Freq:** Monthly - Published 11/year; **Circ:** 58,538
Usual Pagination: 100
Editor-in-Chief: Juho Huttula
Profile: Magazine about building and construction.
Language(s): Finnish
ADVERTISING RATES:
Full Page Colour .... EUR 4470
SCC .... EUR 39.90
Mechanical Data: Type Area: 217 x 280mm
Copy instructions: *Copy Date:* 19 days prior to publication date
BUSINESS: ARCHITECTURE & BUILDING: Building Related

TORI 1696849L74Q-60
Formerly: Vippi
Editorial: Kynämies Oy, Köydenpunojankatu 2 a D, 00180 HELSINKI **Tel:** 9 15 66 85 10
Fax: 9 15 66 86 00
Email: teija.laakso@kynamies.fi **Web site:** http://www.kayttoluotto.fi
ISSN: 1459-9902
Freq: Quarterly; **Cover Price:** Free; **Circ:** 185,000
Usual Pagination: 34
Editor-in-Chief: Tuula Mattila; **Managing Editor:** Teija Laakso
Profile: Lifestyle-magazine about credits and shopping.
Language(s): Finnish
Readership: Customers of Nordea Finance.
ADVERTISING RATES:
SCC .... EUR 35.83
Mechanical Data: Type Area: 217 x 280mm, Screen: 60 lpc
CONSUMER: WOMEN'S INTEREST CONSUMER MAGAZINES: Lifestyle

TOSI ELÄMÄÄ 705124L73-202
Editorial: PL 246/Lekatie 6, 90101 OULU
Tel: 8 53 70 033 **Fax:** 8 53 06 118
Web site: http://www.joutsenmedia.fi/tuotteet-ja-palvelut/tosi-elamaa.html
Freq: Monthly; **Circ:** 14,000
Usual Pagination: 48
Editor-in-Chief: Eeva Vainikainen
Profile: Periodical for elderly people.
Language(s): Finnish
ADVERTISING RATES:
Full Page Colour .... EUR 1500.00
Agency Commission: 15%
Mechanical Data: Bleed Size: 200 x 260mm, Screen: 40 lpc b&w; 60 lpc colour

TOSIMIES 752889L86C-30
Editorial: PL 4/ Jänismäki 1 A, 02941 ESPOO
Tel: 9 54 79 74 10 **Fax:** 9 51 22 033
Email: toimitus@tosimies-lehti.fi **Web site:** http://www.tosimies-lehti.fi
ISSN: 1458-3224
Date Established: 2002; **Freq:** 6 issues yearly; **Circ:** 5,000
Usual Pagination: 56
Profile: Magazine with Christian values and men's lifestyle.
Language(s): Finnish
ADVERTISING RATES:
Full Page Colour .... EUR 1600
SCC .... EUR 15.10
Mechanical Data: Bleed Size: 210 x 264mm, Type Area: 192 x 264mm, No. of Columns (Display): 4, Col Widths (Display): 43mm, Print Process: offset, Film: negative, Screen: 54-60 lpc

TOYOTA PLUS 705993L31R-55
Editorial: PL 12/ Korpivaarantie 1, 01451 VANTAA
Tel: 9 85 181 **Fax:** 9 85 18 22 21
Web site: http://www.toyota.fi
ISSN: 1238-9102
Freq: Quarterly; **Cover Price:** Free; **Circ:** 201,000
Usual Pagination: 36
Editor-in-Chief: Heikki Freund
Profile: Magazine focusing on Toyota cars. Covers automotive news, new models, car design, safety, motor sport, culture, tourism and sponsorship.
Language(s): Finnish
Readership: Read by Toyota car owners.
BUSINESS: MOTOR TRADE: Motor Trade Related

TRACTOR POWER 1813186L49C-70
Editorial: Kehävuorenkuja 16, 01690 VANTAA
Tel: 50 32 34 794
Email: toimitus@tractorpower.fi **Web site:** http://www.tractorpower.fi
Date Established: 2007; **Freq:** 6 issues yearly; **Circ:** 25,000
Editor-in-Chief: Vesa Jääskeläinen
Profile: Magazine about tractors.
Language(s): Finnish
ADVERTISING RATES:
Full Page Colour .... EUR 1780.00

TRANSPORT NEWS 1614211L49A-120
Editorial: PL 68/ Tiurinsaarenkatu 8, 49401 HAMINA
Tel: 50 40 75 212
Email: aarnio.news@co.inet.fi **Web site:** http://www.transportnews.fi
ISSN: 1457-7542
Freq: 6 issues yearly; **Circ:** 4,000
Usual Pagination: 28
Profile: Magazine about logistics in and between countries in EU and eastern Europe.
Language(s): Finnish

ADVERTISING RATES:
Full Page Colour .... EUR 3200
SCC .... EUR 21.90

TRAVEL ROVANIEMI 706655L89A-8
Editorial: Katajaranta 24, 96400 ROVANIEMI
Tel: 16 31 16 11 **Fax:** 16 31 28 45
Email: anneli.aula@matkalehti.fi **Web site:** http://www.matkalehti.fi
ISSN: 0789-5631
Date Established: 1993; **Freq:** Half-yearly; **Cover Price:** Free; **Circ:** 40,000
Usual Pagination: 48
Editor-in-Chief: Jorma Aula
Profile: Magazine about travel activities in Rovaniemi.
Language(s): Finnish
ADVERTISING RATES:
Full Page Colour .... EUR 2956.00
Mechanical Data: Bleed Size: 210 x 292mm, Type Area: 210 x 292mm, Screen: 54 lpc, Trim Size: 190 x 268mm
CONSUMER: HOLIDAYS & TRAVEL: Travel

TRENDI 15254L74A-67
Editorial: Elimäenkatu 17-19, 6. krs., 00510 HELSINKI **Tel:** 9 77 39 51 **Fax:** 9 77 39 53 21
Email: trendi.toimitus@forma.fi **Web site:** http://www.trendi.fi
ISSN: 0786-9282
Date Established: 1989; **Freq:** Monthly; **Circ:** 47,394
Usual Pagination: 132
Editor-in-Chief: Elina Tanskanen; **Managing Editor:** Tia Nikkinen
Profile: Lifestyle magazine covering fashion, beauty, health, relationships, popular culture, food, travel and women around the world.
Language(s): Finnish
Readership: Aimed at women aged between 20 and 35 years.
ADVERTISING RATES:
Full Page Colour .... EUR 5230
SCC .... EUR 58.60
Mechanical Data: Type Area: 217 x 280mm, Print Process: offset, Film: positive, Screen: 54 lpc
Copy instructions: *Copy Date:* 18 days prior to publication date
CONSUMER: WOMEN'S INTEREST CONSUMER MAGAZINES: Women's Interest

TS. 705994L76C-110
Formerly: Treffi -viikkoliite
Editorial: PL 95/ Kauppiaskatu 5, 20101 TURKU
Tel: 2 26 93 311
Email: tspiste@ts.fi **Web site:** http://www.ts.fi
Freq: Weekly
Profile: Supplement with TV and radio programme information.
Language(s): Finnish
ADVERTISING RATES:
Full Page Colour .... EUR 3150
Mechanical Data: Type Area: 252 x 365mm, No. of Columns (Display): 6, Col Widths (Display): 39.5mm, Print Process: offset, Col Length: 365mm, Page Width: 252mm
CONSUMER: MUSIC & PERFORMING ARTS: TV & Radio

TUKILINJA 712956L94F-50
Editorial: Pasilanraitio 5, 00240 HELSINKI
Tel: 9 41 55 15 00
Email: toimitus@tukilinja.fi **Web site:** http://www.tukilinja.fi
ISSN: 1458-6304
Date Established: 1996; **Freq:** 6 issues yearly - Published 8/year; **Circ:** 50,000
Usual Pagination: 38
Editor-in-Chief: Iris Tenhunen
Profile: Magazine aims to give information about disability, education and fitting into the society.
Language(s): Finnish
Readership: The wide public with social orientation and will to help. Also professional readers and people with handicaps or people otherwise involved with handicapped persons.
CONSUMER: OTHER CLASSIFICATIONS: Disability

TULLIVIESTI 705282L20-20
Editorial: PL 512/ Erottajankatu 2, 00101 HELSINKI
Tel: 9 61 41 **Fax:** 20 49 22 852
Email: reijo.virtanen@tulli.fi **Web site:** http://www.tulli.fi
ISSN: 0789-0001
Freq: Quarterly; **Cover Price:** Free; **Circ:** 6,200
Usual Pagination: 40
Editor-in-Chief: Jarkko Saksa
Profile: Customer-magazine of the Finnish toll about import, export and new regulations.
Language(s): Finnish
Agency Commission: 15%
Mechanical Data: Screen: 54 lpc, Col Widths (Display): 56mm, No. of Columns (Display): 3, Type Area: 213 x 280mm

TUOTTAVA PERUNA 705327L21A-90
Editorial: Ruosuontie 156, 16900 LAMMI
Tel: 3 65 63 00 **Fax:** 3 65 63 030
Email: info@petla.fi **Web site:** http://www.petla.fi
Freq: Quarterly; **Circ:** 1,500
Usual Pagination: 32
Editor-in-Chief: Paavo Kuisma
Profile: Publication by the Potato Research Center.
Language(s): Finnish

TURKULAINEN 705088L72-1400
Editorial: PL 396/ Läntinen Pitkäkatu 34, 4.krs, 20101 TURKU **Tel:** 20 61 00 160 **Fax:** 20 77 03 038
Email: tku.toimitus@lehtiyhtyma.fi **Web site:** http://www.turkulainen.fi
Date Established: 1958; **Freq:** 104 issues yearly; **Cover Price:** Free; **Circ:** 118,100
Usual Pagination: 24
Editor-in-Chief: Antti-Pekka Pietilä; **Managing Editor:** Teija Uitto
Profile: Newspaper issued in the Turku region.
Language(s): Finnish
ADVERTISING RATES:
Full Page Colour .... EUR 4707
SCC .... EUR 23
Agency Commission: 15%
Mechanical Data: No. of Columns (Display): 10, Type Area: 388 x 530mm, Col Widths (Display): 40mm, Print Process: offset, Col Length: 515mm, Page Width: 380mm
LOCAL NEWSPAPERS

TURUN OMAKOTILEHTI 706589L4D-100
Editorial: PL 943/ Itäinen Rantakatu 68 C 48, 20101 TURKU **Tel:** 2 23 66 790 **Fax:** 2 23 66 790
Email: turunomakotilehti@pp.inet.fi
Date Established: 1971; **Freq:** 6 issues yearly; **Circ:** 3,000
Usual Pagination: 12
Editor-in-Chief: Pirjo Holmstén
Profile: Magazine about housing in the Turku region.
Language(s): Finnish
ADVERTISING RATES:
SCC .... EUR 8.70

TURUN SANOMAT 15222L67B-7400
Editorial: PL 95/ Kauppiaskatu 5, 20101 TURKU
Tel: 2 26 93 311 **Fax:** 2 26 93 274
Email: ts.uutiset@ts.fi **Web site:** http://www.ts.fi
ISSN: 0356-133X
Date Established: 1905; **Freq:** Daily; **Circ:** 107,199
Usual Pagination: 80
Managing Editor: Veikko Valtonen
Profile: Newspaper that covers the Turku region, southwest of Finland.
Language(s): Finnish
ADVERTISING RATES:
Full Page Colour .... EUR 19824
SCC .... EUR 47.20
Agency Commission: 15%
Mechanical Data: Col Length: 525mm, Film: Negative, No. of Columns (Display): 8, Type Area: 525 x 380mm, Print Process: Offset litho, Page Width: 380mm, Screen: 40 lpc, Col Widths (Display): 44mm
Average ad content per issue: 39%
Editions:
Turun Sanomat Kuntatoimitus
Turun Sanomat Ulkomaantoimitus
Turun Sanomat Verkkotoimitus
REGIONAL DAILY & SUNDAY NEWSPAPERS: Regional Daily Newspapers

TURUN SANOMAT HUITTINEN 705676L67E-622
Editorial: Veteraanikatu, 32700 HUITTINEN
Tel: 2 56 14 73 **Fax:** 2 56 66 04
Email: erja.hyytiainen@ts.fi **Web site:** http://www.ts.fi
Profile: Huittinen regional office of Turun Sanomat.
Language(s): Finnish
REGIONAL DAILY & SUNDAY NEWSPAPERS: Regional Offices

TURUN SANOMAT LOHJA 705677L67E-624
Editorial: PL 66, 08101 LOHJA **Tel:** 50 52 32 254
Fax: 19 32 52 18
Email: merja.ilpala@ts.fi **Web site:** http://www.ts.fi
Profile: Lohja regional office of Turun Sanomat.
Language(s): Finnish
REGIONAL DAILY & SUNDAY NEWSPAPERS: Regional Offices

TURUN SANOMAT LOIMAA 705678L67E-626
Editorial: Kartanomäenkatu 4, 32200 LOIMAA
Tel: 50 51 20 112 **Fax:** 2 76 22 279
Email: anne.savolainen@ts.fi **Web site:** http://www.ts.fi
Profile: Loimaa regional office of Turun Sanomat.
Language(s): Finnish
REGIONAL DAILY & SUNDAY NEWSPAPERS: Regional Offices

TURUN SANOMAT RAUMA 705679L67E-628
Editorial: Seminaarinkatu 5, 26100 RAUMA
Tel: 2 82 11 570 **Fax:** 2 83 37 571
Email: jari.rantanen@ts.fi **Web site:** http://www.ts.fi
Profile: Rauma regional office of Turun Sanomat.
Language(s): Finnish
REGIONAL DAILY & SUNDAY NEWSPAPERS: Regional Offices

TURUN SANOMAT SÄKYLÄ 705681L67E-630
Editorial: Lehtikallentie 2, 27800 SÄKYLÄ
Tel: 2 86 70 940 **Fax:** 2 86 70 717
Email: jorma.pihlava@ts.fi **Web site:** http://www.ts.fi
Profile: Säkylä regional office of Turun Sanomat.
Language(s): Finnish
REGIONAL DAILY & SUNDAY NEWSPAPERS: Regional Offices

TURUN SANOMAT SALO 705680L67E-629
Editorial: Katrineholminkatu 7, 24240 SALO
Tel: 2 73 15 255 **Fax:** 2 73 13 355
Email: paivi.palm@ts.fi **Web site:** http://www.ts.fi
Profile: Salo regional office of Turun Sanomat.
Language(s): Finnish
REGIONAL DAILY & SUNDAY NEWSPAPERS: Regional Offices

TURUN SANOMAT SUNNUNTAITOIMITUS 1604989L67B-8542
Editorial: PL 95/Kauppiaskatu 5, 20101 TURKU
Tel: 2 26 93 311 **Fax:** 2 26 93 274
Email: ts.sunnuntai@ts.fi **Web site:** http://www.ts.fi
Circ: 119,700
Profile: Sunday section of Turun Sanomat.
Language(s): Finnish
REGIONAL DAILY & SUNDAY NEWSPAPERS: Regional Daily Newspapers

TURUN SANOMAT UUSIKAUPUNKI 705682L67E-632
Editorial: Alinenkatu 29, 23500 UUSIKAUPUNKI
Tel: 2 84 51 14 51 **Fax:** 2 84 51 14 53
Email: jaakko.louhivuori@ts.fi **Web site:** http://www.ts.fi
Profile: Uusikaupunki regional office of Turun Sanomat.
Language(s): Finnish
REGIONAL DAILY & SUNDAY NEWSPAPERS: Regional Offices

TURUN TIENOO 704898L72-1410
Editorial: Elotie 26, 21360 LIETO AS. **Tel:** 2 48 92 00
Fax: 2 48 92 099
Email: toimitus@turuntienoo.fi **Web site:** http://www.turuntienoo.fi
ISSN: 0782-5986
Date Established: 1954; **Freq:** 104 issues yearly; **Circ:** 5,852
Usual Pagination: 12
Profile: Newspaper distributed in Lieto, Maaria, Paattinen, Rusko and Vahto.
Language(s): Finnish
ADVERTISING RATES:
Full Page Colour .... EUR 2878
SCC .... EUR 11.70
LOCAL NEWSPAPERS

TURVALLISUUS & RISKIENHALLINTA 15090L54B-4
Formerly: Turvallisuus
Editorial: Kumitehtaankatu 5, 04260 KERAVA
Tel: 40 58 40 212 **Fax:** 10 42 19 601
Email: toimitus@turvallisuus.com **Web site:** http://www.turvallisuus.com
ISSN: 0782-7571
Date Established: 1984; **Freq:** 6 issues yearly; **Circ:** 6,234
Usual Pagination: 52
Profile: Magazine covering all aspects of company security.
Language(s): Finnish
ADVERTISING RATES:
Full Page Colour .... EUR 2520
SCC .... EUR 21.20
Mechanical Data: Type Area: 185 x 260mm, Bleed Size: 210 x 297mm, Print Process: offset, Film: positive, Screen: 60 lpc
BUSINESS: SAFETY & SECURITY: Safety

TUULET 2056569L50-101
Editorial: Huvilakatu 8, 06100 PORVOO
Email: info@tuulet.fi **Web site:** http://www.tuulet.fi
Freq: Half-yearly - 3/ year; **Circ:** 5,000
Editor: Taila Groth-Sulosalmi; **Editor-in-Chief:** Tuula Lukić
Profile: Special publication covering tourism and travel in Southern Finland.
Language(s): Finnish
ADVERTISING RATES:
Full Page Colour .... EUR 1800.00

TUULILASI 15318L77A-50
Editorial: Risto Rytin tie 33, 00081 A-LEHDET
Tel: 9 75 961 **Fax:** 9 75 98 31 18
Email: tuulilasi@a-lehdet.fi **Web site:** http://www.tuulilasi.fi
ISSN: 0041-4468
Date Established: 1963; **Freq:** Monthly - Published 16/year; **Circ:** 77,895
Usual Pagination: 116
Editor-in-Chief: Lauri Larmela; **Managing Editor:** Tapio Ketonen
Profile: Motoring magazine containing tests and comparisons on the latest vehicles arriving in Finland. Also includes details on car accessories, tyres and spare parts, service advice and a used car guide.
Language(s): Finnish
Readership: Read mainly by male motoring enthusiasts.
ADVERTISING RATES:
Full Page Colour .... EUR 7100
SCC .... EUR 69.80
Mechanical Data: Type Area: 254 x 194mm, Bleed Size: 280 x 217mm, No. of Columns (Display): 4, Print Process: Offset, Screen: 60 lpc, Col Length: 254mm, Page Width: 194mm
Copy instructions: *Copy Date:* 13 days prior to publication date
Editions:
Tuulilasi.fi
CONSUMER: MOTORING & CYCLING: Motoring

TV RADIO BLADET 705351L76C-120
Formerly: Vision
Editorial: PB 217/ Mannerheimvägen 18, 00101 HELSINGFORS **Tel:** 9 12 531 **Fax:** 9 12 53 500
Email: vision@hbl.fi **Web site:** http://www.hbl.fi
Freq: Weekly; Free to qualifying individuals ; **Circ:** 50,853
Profile: TV- and radio guide of national Swedish-speaking newspaper Hufvudstadsbladet.
Language(s): Swedish
CONSUMER: MUSIC & PERFORMING ARTS: TV & Radio

TV-MAAILMA 706404L76C-115
Editorial: Maistraatinportti 1, 00015 OTAVAMEDIA
Tel: 9 15 661 **Fax:** 91566756
Email: tv@otavamedia.fi
ISSN: 1456-2006
Date Established: 1998; **Freq:** Weekly; Free to qualifying individuals ; **Circ:** 227,119
Usual Pagination: 40
Managing Editor: Iina Alanko
Profile: TV listings magazine, contains programme reviews and interviews with celebrities.
Language(s): Finnish
Readership: Readers of Suomen Kuvalehti and Seura.
ADVERTISING RATES:
Full Page Colour .... EUR 5080
SCC .... EUR 47
Mechanical Data: Bleed Size: 217 x 270mm, No. of Columns (Display): 4, Col Widths (Display): 44mm, Print Process: offset, Film: positive, Screen: 60 lpc
CONSUMER: MUSIC & PERFORMING ARTS: TV & Radio

TYÖ TERVEYS TURVALLISUUS 15089L56A-83
Editorial: Topeliuksenkatu 41 a A, 00250 HELSINKI
Tel: 30 47 41 **Fax:** 30 47 42 478
Email: info-ttt@ttl.fi **Web site:** http://www.ttl.fi
ISSN: 0041-4816
Date Established: 1971; **Freq:** 6 issues yearly - Published 8/year; **Circ:** 61,624
Usual Pagination: 48
Managing Editor: Merja Karjalainen
Profile: Journal specialising in occupational safety and health.
Language(s): English; Finnish
Readership: Read by office and facility managers.
ADVERTISING RATES:
Full Page Colour .... EUR 5540
SCC .... EUR 75.60
Agency Commission: 15%
Mechanical Data: Col Length: 266mm, Type Area: 209 x 266mm, Print Process: Offset, No. of Columns (Display): 4, Page Width: 209mm, Col Widths (Display): 49mm, Screen: 40-54 lpc
Average ad content per issue: 9.5%
BUSINESS: HEALTH & MEDICAL

TYÖELÄKE 706244L74N-70
Editorial: Kirjurinkatu 3, 00065 ELÄKETURVAKESKUS **Tel:** 10 75 11
Fax: 10 75 02 176
Email: kati.kalliomaki@etk.fi **Web site:** http://www.etk.fi
ISSN: 0564-5808
Date Established: 1966; **Freq:** Quarterly; **Cover Price:** Free; **Circ:** 13,500
Usual Pagination: 32
Editor-in-Chief: Kati Kalliomäki; **Managing Editor:** Anne Iivonen
Profile: Magazine about work pensions.
Language(s): Finnish

TYÖTERVEYSLÄÄKÄRI 15101L56A-100
Formerly: Työterveyslääkäri
Editorial: PL 713/ Kalevankatu 11 A, 00101 HELSINKI **Tel:** 9 61 88 52 11 **Fax:** 9 61 88 52 60
Email: riitta.keinanen@duodecim.fi **Web site:** http://www.terveysportti.fi/stly
ISSN: 0780-2218

Date Established: 1983; **Freq:** Quarterly; **Circ:** 2,300
Usual Pagination: 60
Editor-in-Chief: Selina Selin
Profile: Publication of the Finnish Association of Industrial Medicine.
Language(s): Finnish
ADVERTISING RATES:
Full Page Colour .... EUR 2400.00
SCC .... EUR 31.30
Mechanical Data: Type Area: 210 x 280mm, Print Process: offset, Screen: 48 lpc mono, 60 lpc colour

TYÖVOITTO
706614L74N-55
Formerly: Korvamerkki
Editorial: Kirjurinkatu 3, 00065 ELÄKETURVAKESKUS **Tel:** 10 75 11 **Fax:** 10 75 12 205
Email: kimmo.kontio@etk.fi **Web site:** http://www.etk.fi
Date Established: 1999; **Freq:** Half-yearly; **Cover Price:** Free; **Circ:** 800,000
Usual Pagination: 8
Editor-in-Chief: Kati Kalliomäki; **Managing Editor:** Kimmo Kontio
Profile: Magazine about pensions and retirement.
Language(s): Finnish
CONSUMER: WOMEN'S INTEREST CONSUMER MAGAZINES: Retirement

TYRVÄÄN SANOMAT
704914L72-1415
Editorial: PL 21 / Onkiniemenkatu 18, 38201 SASTAMALA **Tel:** 10 66 55 781 **Fax:** 3 51 41 921
Email: tyrvis.toimitus@sps.fi **Web site:** http://www.tyrvaansanomat.fi
ISSN: 0359-0305
Date Established: 1894; **Freq:** 104 issues yearly; **Circ:** 9,110
Usual Pagination: 12
Editor-in-Chief: Minna Ala-Heikkilä
Profile: Newspaper issued in Vammala, Kiikoinen and Äetsä.
Language(s): Finnish
ADVERTISING RATES:
Full Page Colour .... EUR 2935
SCC .... EUR 13.40
Agency Commission: 15%
Mechanical Data: Col Widths (Display): 43mm, No. of Columns (Display): 6, Type Area: 283 x 415mm, Col Length: 460mm, Page Width: 315mm
Editions:
Tyrvään Sanomat Verkkotoimitus
LOCAL NEWSPAPERS

ULKOPOLITIIKKA
14947L14C-120
Editorial: PL 400/ Kruunuvuorenkatu 4, 00161 HELSINKI **Tel:** 9 43 27 700
Email: toimitus@ulkopolitiikka.fi **Web site:** http://www.ulkopolitiikka.fi
ISSN: 0501-0659
Date Established: 1961; **Freq:** Quarterly; **Circ:** 4,000
Usual Pagination: 130
Editor-in-Chief: Teija Tiilikainen; **Managing Editor:** Joonas Pörsti
Profile: Journal dealing with topics relevant to foreign policy and security policy.
Language(s): English; Finnish
Readership: Read by politicians, government officials, students and other people interested in international politics.
ADVERTISING RATES:
Full Page Colour .... EUR 1210
SCC .... EUR 21.60
Agency Commission: 15%
Mechanical Data: Type Area: 210 x 280mm, Col Widths (Display): 68mm, No. of Columns (Display): 2, Print Process: Offset, Screen: 60 lpc

ULTRA
705123L94E-28
Editorial: Salojärventie 36, 17950 KYLÄMÄ **Tel:** 3 55 58 101 **Fax:** 3 55 58 111
Email: toimitus@ultra-lehti.com **Web site:** http://www.ultra-lehti.com
ISSN: 0357-2846
Date Established: 1972; **Freq:** Monthly - Published 10/year; **Circ:** 4,660
Usual Pagination: 40
Managing Editor: Arja Kuningas
Profile: Magazine about paranormal phenomena in Finland and abroad.
Language(s): Finnish
ADVERTISING RATES:
Full Page Colour .... EUR 922
SCC .... EUR 8.60
CONSUMER: OTHER CLASSIFICATIONS: Paranormal

ULVILAN SEUTU
704949L72-1420
Editorial: PL 11/ Friitalantie 13, 28401 ULVILA **Tel:** 2 53 11 721 **Fax:** 25311710
Email: toimitus@ulvilanseutu.fi **Web site:** http://www.ulvilanseutu.fi
Date Established: 1979; **Freq:** Weekly; **Circ:** 3,072
Usual Pagination: 16
Profile: Newspaper issued in Ulvila and Kullaa.
Language(s): Finnish
ADVERTISING RATES:
SCC .... EUR 90
Agency Commission: 17.5%
Mechanical Data: Col Length: 410mm, No. of Columns (Display): 6, Page Width: 284mm, Col Widths (Display): 44mm
Supplement(s): MeriPorilainen 4/year
LOCAL NEWSPAPERS

UN WOMEN -UUTISET
715905L74A-100
Formerly: Unifem Akseli
Editorial: Töölöntorinkatu 2 B, 8 krs, 00260 HELSINKI **Tel:** 9 69 40 944 **Fax:** 9 69 40 990
Email: toimisto@unifem.fi **Web site:** http://www.unifem.fi
ISSN: 1457-2338
Freq: Quarterly; **Cover Price:** Free; **Circ:** 7,000
Usual Pagination: 12
Managing Editor: Tomi Kuhanen
Profile: Publication about feminism and women's matters.
Language(s): Finnish
ADVERTISING RATES:
Full Page Colour .... EUR 1400.00
Mechanical Data: Type Area: 255 x 380mm, Print Process: offset, Screen: 34 lpc, Col Widths (Display): 48mm, No. of Columns (Display): 5
CONSUMER: WOMEN'S INTEREST CONSUMER MAGAZINES: Women's Interest

URAKOINTI-UUTISET
1805074L49C-80
Editorial: Takojankatu 11, 33540 TAMPERE **Tel:** 3 38 07 700 **Fax:** 3 38 07 701
Email: uutoimitus@urakointiuutiset.fi **Web site:** http://www.urakointiuutiset.fi
ISSN: 1796-637X
Date Established: 2007; **Freq:** Monthly; **Cover Price:** Free; **Circ:** 70,800
Usual Pagination: 36
Editor-in-Chief: Seppo Rentti
Profile: Magazine about tractors and work machines.
Language(s): Finnish
Readership: Professionals within the tractor business.
ADVERTISING RATES:
Full Page Colour .... EUR 2980.00
SCC .... EUR 64.20
Agency Commission: 15%
Mechanical Data: Type Area: 255 x 375mm, Trim Size: 280 x 400mm, Col Widths (Display): 40mm, No. of Columns (Display): 6, Print Process: offset, Screen: 40 lpc
BUSINESS: TRANSPORT: Freight

URATIE
706247L14F-9
Editorial: PL 920/ Annankatu 34-36 B, 00101 HELSINKI **Tel:** 20 44 240 **Fax:** 20 44 24 108
Email: uratie@talentum.com **Web site:** http://www.uratie.fi
Freq: Weekly - Published on Friday; **Cover Price:** Free; **Circ:** 79,684
Usual Pagination: 16
Profile: Magazine containing news about personnel matters, appointments and vacancies, mainly of the business sector.
Language(s): Finnish
ADVERTISING RATES:
Full Page Colour .... EUR 15850
Agency Commission: 5-15%
Mechanical Data: Type Area: 220 x 297mm, Screen: 54 lpc, Print Process: offset, No. of Columns (Display): 4
BUSINESS: COMMERCE, INDUSTRY & MANAGEMENT: Training & Recruitment

URHEILULEHTI
705385L75A-85
Editorial: Risto Rytin tie 33, 00081 A-LEHDET **Tel:** 9 75 961 **Fax:** 9 75 98 31 17
Email: urheilulehti@a-lehdet.fi **Web site:** http://www.urheilulehti.fi
ISSN: 0355-6085
Date Established: 1898; **Freq:** Weekly - Published on Friday; **Circ:** 36,350
Usual Pagination: 64
Managing Editor: Lauri Karppinen
Profile: Magazine covering popular sports. Urheilulehti-Extra is a special issue published when there is a major sports event.
Language(s): Finnish
ADVERTISING RATES:
Full Page Colour .... EUR 2500
SCC .... EUR 34.50
Agency Commission: 15%
Mechanical Data: Bleed Size: 230 x 273mm, No. of Columns (Display): 5, Type Area: 187 x 241mm, Print Process: offset rotation, Col Widths (Display): 48mm, Screen: 60 lpc, Film: positive
CONSUMER: SPORT

URJALAN SANOMAT
704915L72-1425
Editorial: PL 61/ Urjalantie 26, 31761 URJALA **Tel:** 40 18 13 020 **Fax:** 3 54 66 660
Email: toimitus@urjalansanomat.fi **Web site:** http://www.urjalansanomat.fi
ISSN: 0782-5258
Date Established: 1917; **Freq:** Weekly; **Circ:** 5,231
Usual Pagination: 12
Profile: Newspaper issued in Urjala and Kylmäkoski.
Language(s): Finnish
ADVERTISING RATES:
Full Page Colour .... EUR 1634
SCC .... EUR 8.60
Agency Commission: 15%
Mechanical Data: No. of Columns (Display): 5, Type Area: 255 x 380mm, Col Widths (Display): 47mm, Print Process: offset rotation
LOCAL NEWSPAPERS

UUDENKAUPUNGIN SANOMAT
704861L67B-7601
Editorial: PL 68/ Alinenkatu 29, 23501 UUSIKAUPUNKI **Tel:** 2 58 88 302 **Fax:** 2 84 24 940
Email: toimitus@uudenkaupunginsanomat.fi **Web site:** http://www.uudenkaupunginsanomat.fi
ISSN: 0356-1860
Date Established: 1893
Circ: 7,424
Usual Pagination: 12
Profile: Newspaper in western Finland issued in Uusikaupunki, Laitila, Vehmaa, Taivalsalo, Pyhätanta and Kustavi.
Language(s): Finnish
ADVERTISING RATES:
Full Page Colour .... EUR 3635
SCC .... EUR 16.60
Agency Commission: 15%
Mechanical Data: Page Width: 255mm, Col Length: 365mm, No. of Columns (Display): 6, Col Widths (Display): 40mm, Screen: 34 lpc, Print Process: offset
REGIONAL DAILY & SUNDAY NEWSPAPERS: Regional Daily Newspapers

UUDENMAAN ALUEEN INSINÖÖRI
705188L19A-60
Editorial: Tietäjäntie 4, 02130 ESPOO **Tel:** 9 47 74 540 **Fax:** 9 47 74 54 42
Email: ins@unionimedia.fi **Web site:** http://www.helins.fi
ISSN: 1796-1211
Date Established: 1977; **Freq:** 6 issues yearly; **Circ:** 15,344
Usual Pagination: 48
Editor-in-Chief: Pekka Laakso
Profile: Magazine about technical development and its influence on society.
Language(s): Finnish
Readership: Engineers and people specialised in technical development.
ADVERTISING RATES:
Full Page Colour .... EUR 1100.00
SCC .... EUR 13.50
Agency Commission: 15%
Mechanical Data: Type Area: 185 x 270mm, Bleed Size: 210 x 297mm, Col Widths (Display): 90mm, No. of Columns (Display): 3, Print Process: offset, Screen: 60 lpc
BUSINESS: ENGINEERING & MACHINERY

UUDET TUULET
715903L74N-73
Editorial: Hämeentie 58-60 A, 00500 HELSINKI **Tel:** 9 77 45 900 **Fax:** 9 70 15 474
Web site: http://www.valli.fi
ISSN: 1238-5204
Date Established: 1993; **Freq:** 6 issues yearly; **Circ:** 3,000
Usual Pagination: 32
Editor-in-Chief: Marja-Liisa Kunnas
Profile: Publication about taking care of senior citizens at home.
Language(s): Finnish
ADVERTISING RATES:
Full Page Colour .... EUR 1450.00
SCC .... EUR 18.50
Agency Commission: 15%
Mechanical Data: Type Area: 185 x 260mm, Print Process: offset, Screen: 60 lpc

UUSI AIKA
704855L67B-7602
Editorial: PL 205/Kuninkaanlahdenkatu 7, 28101 PORI **Tel:** 44 73 00 200 **Fax:** 2 63 00 280
Email: ua.toimitus@uusiaika-lehti.fi **Web site:** http://www.uusiaika-lehti.fi
ISSN: 0789-8169
Date Established: 1907
Circ: 6,283
Usual Pagination: 16
Profile: Regional newspaper distributed in the Satakunta region.
Language(s): Finnish
ADVERTISING RATES:
Full Page Colour .... EUR 5191
SCC .... EUR 21
Mechanical Data: Page Width: 284mm, Col Length: 412mm, No. of Columns (Display): 6, Col Widths (Display): 44mm, Print Process: offset
REGIONAL DAILY & SUNDAY NEWSPAPERS: Regional Daily Newspapers

UUSI ESPOO
705075L72-1430
Editorial: Itäportti 4 A, 02210 ESPOO **Tel:** 20 74 88 521 **Fax:** 9 85 50 586
Email: mika.airinen@kokoomus.fi **Web site:** http://www.kokoomus.fi/espoo
Freq: Half-yearly; **Cover Price:** Free; **Circ:** 103,700
Usual Pagination: 16
Editor-in-Chief: Mika Airinen
Profile: Newspaper issued by the Coalition Party in Espoo.
Language(s): Finnish
ADVERTISING RATES:
SCC .... EUR 24.50
Mechanical Data: Col Widths (Display): 40mm, No. of Columns (Display): 6, Col Length: 368mm, Page Width: 280mm
LOCAL NEWSPAPERS

UUSI INSINÖÖRI
705170L19A-2
Formerly: Insinööri
Editorial: Ratavartijankatu 2 A, 8krs, 00520 HELSINKI **Tel:** 20 18 01 801 **Fax:** 20 18 01 880
Email: ilona.maenpaa@uil.fi **Web site:** http://www.insinoori-lehti.fi
ISSN: 1457-3636
Freq: 6 issues yearly - Published 8/year; **Circ:** 60,995
Usual Pagination: 36
Editor-in-Chief: Ilona Mäenpää
Profile: Insinööri is a union magazine for engineers and building architects. The magazine reports about the Finnish Engineering Union activities.
Language(s): Finnish
ADVERTISING RATES:
Full Page Colour .... EUR 3000
SCC .... EUR 33.60
Agency Commission: 15%
Mechanical Data: Type Area: 210 x 297mm, No. of Columns (Display): 3, Col Widths (Display): 58.5mm, Col Length: 264mm, Screen: 60 lpc, Print Process: offset, Film: negative
BUSINESS: ENGINEERING & MACHINERY

UUSI LAHTI
705084L72-1435
Editorial: Vapaudenkatu 8 A 6, 4. krs., 15110 LAHTI **Tel:** 3 87 68 76 **Fax:** 3 78 28 457
Email: toimitus@uusilahti.fi **Web site:** http://www.uusilahti.fi
ISSN: 0358-8483
Date Established: 1982; **Freq:** 104 issues yearly; Free to qualifying individuals ; **Circ:** 54,500
Usual Pagination: 40
Editor-in-Chief: Tommi Berg
Profile: Newspaper issued in Lahti and Hollola.
Language(s): Finnish
ADVERTISING RATES:
Full Page Colour .... EUR 3723
SCC .... EUR 17
Mechanical Data: No. of Columns (Display): 6, Col Widths (Display): 42mm, Type Area: 267 x 370mm, Screen: 40 lpc, Col Length: 365mm, Page Width: 267mm
Editions:
Uusi Lahti Verkkotoimitus
LOCAL NEWSPAPERS

UUSI VANTAA
705076L72-1465
Editorial: Pakkalankuja 5, 01510 VANTAA **Tel:** 20 74 88 523
Email: kim.zilliacus@kokoomus.fi **Web site:** http://www.vantaankokoomus.fi
Date Established: 1971; **Freq:** Half-yearly; **Cover Price:** Free; **Circ:** 85,500
Editor-in-Chief: Kim Zilliacus
Profile: Newspaper distributed by the Coalition Party in Vantaa.
Language(s): Finnish
ADVERTISING RATES:
SCC .... EUR 30
Mechanical Data: Col Length: 370mm, Page Width: 255mm, Screen: 34 lpc, Print Process: offset
LOCAL NEWSPAPERS

UUSIMAA
15212L67B-7620
Editorial: PL 15/Teollisuustie 19, 06151 PORVOO **Tel:** 20 61 00 140 **Fax:** 20 77 03 021
Email: toimitus.uusimaa@lehtiyhtyma.fi **Web site:** http://www.uusimaa.fi
ISSN: 0357-1858
Date Established: 1894
Circ: 12,849
Usual Pagination: 16
Profile: Regional newspaper influencing Porvoo, Askola, Pornainen, Pukkila, Myrskylä, Pernaja, Sipoo, Mäntsälä, Porvoon mlk, Loviisa and Liljendal.
Language(s): Finnish
ADVERTISING RATES:
Full Page Colour .... EUR 7210
SCC .... EUR 17.50
Agency Commission: 15%
Mechanical Data: Page Width: 381mm, Col Length: 525mm, Col Widths (Display): 44mm, No. of Columns (Display): 8, Film: negative, Screen: 30-35 lpc
Editions:
Uusimaa Verkkotoimitus
REGIONAL DAILY & SUNDAY NEWSPAPERS: Regional Daily Newspapers

UUTIS ALASIN
704988L72-1385
Formerly: Tohmajärven - Värtsilän Lehti
Editorial: PL 6 / Asemantie 2, 82601 TOHMAJÄRVI **Tel:** 10 42 24 000 **Fax:** 104224005
Email: toimitus@uutisalasin.fi **Web site:** http://www.uutisalasin.fi
ISSN: 1239-2251
Date Established: 1980; **Freq:** Weekly; **Annual Sub.:** EUR 68; **Circ:** 2,373
Usual Pagination: 12
Profile: Local newspaper issued in Tohmajärvi and Värtsilä.
Language(s): Finnish
ADVERTISING RATES:
SCC .... EUR 15.20
Agency Commission: 10%
Mechanical Data: Col Length: 375mm, Page Width: 260mm, No. of Columns (Display): 6, Col Widths (Display): 40mm, Screen: 34 lpc
LOCAL NEWSPAPERS

UUTIS-JOUSI
704989L72-1480
Editorial: Asematie 2, 71800 SIILINJÄRVI **Tel:** 17 28 77 800 **Fax:** 17 28 77 833
Email: uutiset@uutis-jousi.fi **Web site:** http://www.uutis-jousi.fi
ISSN: 0789-8347

Date Established: 1967; **Freq:** 104 issues yearly; **Circ:** 6,492
Usual Pagination: 16
Profile: Newspaper issued in Siilinjärvi and Maaninka.
Language(s): Finnish
ADVERTISING RATES:
Full Page Colour .... EUR 3796
SCC .... EUR 17.10
Agency Commission: 15%
Mechanical Data: Col Length: 370mm, No. of Columns (Display): 6, Col Widths (Display): 40mm, Print Process: offset
LOCAL NEWSPAPERS

UUTISPÄIVÄ DEMARI 712735L65A-130

Editorial: PL 338/ Haapaniemenkatu 7-9 B, 00531 HELSINKI **Tel:** 9 70 10 41 **Fax:** 9 70 10 567
Email: toimitus@demari.fi **Web site:** http://www.demari.fi
ISSN: 1457-9545
Date Established: 1895; **Freq:** 260 issues yearly - Published Monday-Friday; **Circ:** 14,119
Usual Pagination: 32
Profile: Social-democrat newspaper with national news of interest for working-class people.
Language(s): Finnish
ADVERTISING RATES:
Full Page Colour .... EUR 5694
SCC .... EUR 26
Agency Commission: 15%
Mechanical Data: Type Area: 255 x 365mm, No. of Columns (Display): 6, Col Widths (Display): 39mm, Col Length: 365mm, Screen: 34 lpc, Page Width: 255mm
Editions:
Uutispäivä Demari Verkkotoimitus
NATIONAL DAILY & SUNDAY NEWSPAPERS: National Daily Newspapers

UUTISPÄIVÄ DEMARI TAMPERE 713463L65C-665

Editorial: Hämeenpuisto 28, 5 krs., 33200 TAMPERE
Tel: 3 21 29 330 **Fax:** 3 21 26 555
Email: anna-liisa.blomberg@demari.fi **Web site:** http://www.demari.fi
Freq: 260 issues yearly - Mon thru Fri
Profile: The Tampere regional office of social-democrat newspaper Uutispäivä Demari.
Language(s): Finnish
NATIONAL DAILY & SUNDAY NEWSPAPERS: National Daily Regional Offices

UUTISPÄIVÄ DEMARI TURKU 713472L65C-667

Editorial: Linnankatu 13 a B 31, 20100 TURKU
Tel: 2 27 70 471 **Fax:** 2 27 70 499
Email: turku.toimitus@demari.fi **Web site:** http://www.demari.fi
Freq: 260 issues yearly - Mon thru Fri
Profile: The Turku regional office of social-democrat newspaper Uutispäivä Demari.
Language(s): Finnish
NATIONAL DAILY & SUNDAY NEWSPAPERS: National Daily Regional Offices

UUTISPÄIVÄ DEMARI VAASA 713476L65C-669

Editorial: Korsholmanpuistikko 6-8, 65100 VAASA
Tel: 6 31 74 104 **Fax:** 6 31 73 771
Email: sirpa.taskinen@demari.fi **Web site:** http://www.demari.fi
Freq: 260 issues yearly - Mon thru Fri
Profile: The Pohjanmaa regional office of social-democrat newspaper Uutispäivä Demari.
Language(s): Finnish
NATIONAL DAILY & SUNDAY NEWSPAPERS: National Daily Regional Offices

V8-MAGAZINE 15319L77A-90

Editorial: PL 100/ Lapinmäentie 1, 00040 SANOMA MAGAZINES **Tel:** 9 12 01 **Fax:** 9 12 05 795
Email: v8-toimitus@sanomamagazines.fi **Web site:** http://www.veekasi.net
ISSN: 0780-2102
Date Established: 1978; **Freq:** Monthly - Published 10/year; **Circ:** 30,358
Usual Pagination: 128
Managing Editor: Petri Laulajainen
Profile: Magazine devoted to American cars and hot-rods. Covers new models, parts, new products and sporting events.
Language(s): Finnish
ADVERTISING RATES:
Full Page Colour .... EUR 2750
SCC .... EUR 33.40
Mechanical Data: Type Area: 191 x 274mm, Bleed Size: 210 x 297mm, Print Process: offset, Screen: 60 lpc, Film: positive
Copy instructions: *Copy Date:* 21 days prior to publication date
CONSUMER: MOTORING & CYCLING: Motoring

VAAROJEN SANOMAT 704990L72-1505

Editorial: Juuantie 9 A, 83900 JUUKA
Tel: 10 83 54 004 **Fax:** 132481310
Email: varpu.strengell@vaarojensanomat.com **Web site:** http://www.juukaseura.fi/fi/Vaarojen+Sanomat.html
ISSN: 1236-7796
Date Established: 1968; **Freq:** 104 issues yearly; **Circ:** 3,822
Usual Pagination: 12
Profile: Newspaper issued in Juuka and Koli.
Language(s): Finnish
ADVERTISING RATES:
SCC .... EUR 13.50
Agency Commission: 15%
Mechanical Data: No. of Columns (Display): 5, Col Widths (Display): 46mm, Print Process: offset, Col Length: 375mm
Supplement(s): Pohjolan Pariisi Juuka 12/year
LOCAL NEWSPAPERS

VAKKA-SUOMEN SANOMAT 704862L72-1515

Editorial: PL 84/ Rauhankatu 8 A, 23501 UUSIKAUPUNKI **Tel:** 2 84 26 300 **Fax:** 2 84 16 142
Email: toimitus@vakka.fi **Web site:** http://www.vakkass.fi
Date Established: 1950; **Freq:** 104 issues yearly; **Circ:** 8,545
Usual Pagination: 20
Profile: Newspaper issued in the Uusikaupunki region in southwestern Finland.
Language(s): Finnish
ADVERTISING RATES:
Full Page Colour .... EUR 4050
SCC .... EUR 18
Agency Commission: 3-15%
Mechanical Data: Page Width: 260mm, Print Process: offset, Type Area: 260 x 375mm, No. of Columns (Display): 6, Col Length: 375mm, Col Widths (Display): 40mm, Screen: 34 lpc
LOCAL NEWSPAPERS

VAKUUTUSVÄKI - FÖRSÄKRINGSMANNABLADET 14877L1D-120

Editorial: Asemamiehenkatu 2, 00520 HELSINKI
Tel: 9 85 67 24 00 **Fax:** 9 85 67 24 01
Email: satu.lehmuskoski@vvl.fi **Web site:** http://www.vvl.fi
ISSN: 0355-9254
Date Established: 1949; **Freq:** 6 issues yearly; **Circ:** 10,500
Usual Pagination: 28
Editor-in-Chief: Sirpa Komonen
Profile: Insurance news, interviews and salary negotiations from the employee perspective.
Language(s): Finnish; Swedish
Readership: Members of the Union of Insurance Employees.
ADVERTISING RATES:
Full Page Colour .... EUR 2160.00
SCC .... EUR 12.00
Agency Commission: 15%
Mechanical Data: Type Area: 370 x 250mm, Print Process: Offset rotation, Col Widths (Display): 45mm, No. of Columns (Display): 5, Screen: 85 lpc, Col Length: 370mm, Page Width: 250mm
BUSINESS: FINANCE & ECONOMICS: Insurance

VALITUT PALAT 15243L73-250

Editorial: PL 106/ Pitäjämäentie 14, 00381 HELSINKI
Tel: 9 50 34 41 **Fax:** 9 50 34 499
Email: lehtitoimitus@valitutpalat.fi **Web site:** http://www.valitutpalat.fi
ISSN: 0042-2290
Date Established: 1945; **Freq:** Monthly; **Circ:** 187,404
Usual Pagination: 190
Editor-in-Chief: Ilkka Virtanen; **Managing Editor:** Anni-Marja Riikinsaari
Profile: Magazine containing articles of general interest, specially commissioned or reprinted from national and international publications.
Language(s): Finnish
Readership: Customers of Reader's Digest.
ADVERTISING RATES:
Full Page Colour .... EUR 7130
SCC .... EUR 193.70
Agency Commission: 5-15%
Mechanical Data: Col Length: 184mm, Col Widths (Display): 54mm, Film: Digital material: PDF, No. of Columns (Display): 2, Type Area: 134 x 184mm, Print Process: Offset rotation, Screen: FM-screen, Bleed Size: 192 x 138mm, Trim Size: 184 x 134mm, Page Width: 134mm
Average ad content per issue: 12%
CONSUMER: NATIONAL & INTERNATIONAL PERIODICALS

VALKEAKOSKEN SANOMAT 15227L72-1520

Editorial: Valtakatu 9-11, 4 krs, 37600 VALKEAKOSKI **Tel:** 10 66 55 730 **Fax:** 10 66 55 733
Email: vs.toimitus@sps.fi **Web site:** http://www.valkeakoskensanomat.fi
Date Established: 1921; **Freq:** Daily; **Circ:** 7,510
Usual Pagination: 12
Profile: Newspaper issued in Valkeakoski.
Language(s): Finnish
ADVERTISING RATES:
Full Page Colour .... EUR 4314
SCC .... EUR 19.70
Agency Commission: 15%

Mechanical Data: Page Width: 281mm, Col Length: 635mm, No. of Columns (Display): 7, Print Process: offset
LOCAL NEWSPAPERS

VALO 706499L17-26

Editorial: Särkiniementie 3, 00210 HELSINKI
Tel: 400 86 93 39
Web site: http://www.valosto.com
ISSN: 1237-3907
Date Established: 1994; **Freq:** Half-yearly; **Circ:** 5,000
Usual Pagination: 52
Editor-in-Chief: Tapio Kallasjoki; **Managing Director:** Heikki Härkönen; **Managing Editor:** Markku Varsila
Profile: Magazine about illumination, electricity and interior-architecture.
Language(s): Finnish
Readership: Members of the Illuminating Engineering Society of Finland.
ADVERTISING RATES:
Full Page Colour .... EUR 2750.00
Mechanical Data: Type Area: 180 x 267mm, Print Process: offset, Film: negative, Screen: 60 lpc

VANHUSTYÖ - SENIORARBETE 705284L74N-75

Editorial: Malmin kauppatie 26, 00700 HELSINKI
Tel: 9 35 08 600 **Fax:** 9 35 08 60 10
Email: info@vtkl.fi **Web site:** http://www.vanhustyonkeskusliitto.fi
ISSN: 0358-7304
Freq: 6 issues yearly; **Circ:** 2,700
Usual Pagination: 34
Editor-in-Chief: Pirkko Karjalainen
Profile: Journal about caring of senior citizens.
Language(s): Finnish; Swedish
Readership: People working with services for elderly people.
ADVERTISING RATES:
Full Page Colour .... EUR 2150.00
SCC .... EUR 26.50
Agency Commission: 15%
Mechanical Data: Type Area: 185 x 270mm, Print Process: offset, Screen: 60 lpc

VANTAALAINEN 705077L72-1540

Editorial: Lehdokkitie 2, 2 krs, 01300 VANTAA
Tel: 9 82 30 595 **Fax:** 9 82 30 596
Email: vantaakj@sdp.fi **Web site:** http://www.vantaandemarit.fi
Freq: Quarterly; **Cover Price:** Free; **Circ:** 58,000
Usual Pagination: 8
Profile: Local social democrat newspaper issued in Vantaa.
Language(s): Finnish
LOCAL NEWSPAPERS

VANTAAN LAURI 705926L87-108_50

Editorial: PL 56/ Unikkotie 5 B, 01301 VANTAA
Tel: 9 83 06 274 **Fax:** 9 82 30 136
Email: vantaan.lauri@evl.fi **Web site:** http://www.vantaanlauri.fi
ISSN: 1799-9022
Date Established: 1996; **Freq:** Weekly - Published 43/ year; **Cover Price:** Free; **Circ:** 83,100
Usual Pagination: 16
Editor-in-Chief: Pauli Juusela; **Managing Editor:** Heli Kulmavuori
Profile: News magazine from the Vantaa parish to Vantaa households belonging to the Evangelical Lutheran Church.
Language(s): Finnish
ADVERTISING RATES:
Full Page Colour .... EUR 2850
SCC .... EUR 18
Agency Commission: 10-15%
Mechanical Data: Type Area: 255 x 355mm, No. of Columns (Display): 5, Col Widths (Display): 47mm, Bleed Size: 290 x 410mm, Screen: 34 lpc, Print Process: offset
Copy instructions: *Copy Date:* 8 days prior to publication date
CONSUMER: RELIGIOUS

VANTAAN SANOMAT 704875L72-1550

Editorial: PL 350/ Rälssitie 7 A, 01511 VANTAA
Tel: 20 61 00 110 **Fax:** 20 77 03 014
Email: vantaan.sanomat@lehtiyhtyma.fi **Web site:** http://www.vantaansanomat.fi
ISSN: 1236-0392
Date Established: 1967; **Freq:** 104 issues yearly; Free to qualifying individuals ; **Circ:** 89,600
Usual Pagination: 14
Editor-in-Chief: Risto Hietanen
Profile: Newspaper issued in Vantaa.
Language(s): Finnish
ADVERTISING RATES:
Full Page Colour .... EUR 2560
SCC .... EUR 10.10
Agency Commission: 15%
Mechanical Data: Print Process: offset, Type Area: 380 x 520mm, Screen: 28 lpc mono, 34 lpc colour, No. of Columns (Display): 8, Col Length: 515mm, Col Widths (Display): 44mm, Page Width: 380mm
LOCAL NEWSPAPERS

VAPAA AJATTELIJA 706120L74Q-50

Formerly: Vapaa-ajattelija - Fritänkaren
Editorial: Neljäs linja 1, 00530 HELSINKI
Tel: 44 71 56 01 **Fax:** 9 71 56 02
Web site: http://www.vapaa-ajattelijat.fi/liitto/lehti
ISSN: 0355-8703
Date Established: 1945; **Freq:** 6 issues yearly; **Annual Sub.:** EUR 22; **Circ:** 2,700
Usual Pagination: 32
Editor-in-Chief: Robert Brotherus
Profile: Politically and economically neutral journal about free thinking, atheism and humanism.
Language(s): Finnish; Swedish
ADVERTISING RATES:
Full Page Colour .... EUR 235

VAPAA-AJAN KALASTAJA 15388L92-60

Formerly: Kalamies
Editorial: Vanha Talvitie 2-6 A 11, 00580 HELSINKI
Tel: 9 22 89 130 **Fax:** 9 68 49 904
Email: vapaa-ajankalastaja@vapaa-ajankalastaja.fi
Web site: http://www.vapaa-ajankalastaja.fi
ISSN: 1795-5033
Freq: 6 issues yearly; **Circ:** 49,893
Usual Pagination: 20
Editor-in-Chief: Veli-Matti Saksi
Profile: Information magazine about fishing, fishing equipment, fish water maintenance, legislation, fish dishes and news concerning sport fishing.
Language(s): Finnish
ADVERTISING RATES:
Full Page Colour .... EUR 3235.00
Agency Commission: 15%
Mechanical Data: Type Area: 240 x 344mm, No. of Columns (Display): 5, Col Widths (Display): 44mm, Bleed Size: 260 x 380mm, Screen: 40 lpc, Print Process: offset
CONSUMER: ANGLING & FISHING

VAPAAT TOIMITILAT 715892L34-250

Editorial: Annankatu 25 5. krs, 00100 HELSINKI
Tel: 9 41 30 06 00 **Fax:** 9 41 30 06 01
Email: vapaat@toimitilat.fi **Web site:** http://www.toimitilat.fi
Date Established: 1986; **Freq:** 6 issues yearly; **Cover Price:** Free; **Circ:** 70,000
Usual Pagination: 20
Editor-in-Chief: Mikael Eklund
Profile: Publication about office space for rent.
Language(s): Finnish
ADVERTISING RATES:
Full Page Colour .... EUR 4515.00
SCC .... EUR 28.50
Mechanical Data: Screen: 38-40 lpc, Type Area: 248 x 363mm, Col Widths (Display): 38mm, No. of Columns (Display): 6
BUSINESS: OFFICE EQUIPMENT

VARMA 706405L1D-125

Formerly: Varma-Sampo
Editorial: PL 1/ Salmisaarenranta 11, 00098 VARMA
Tel: 10 24 40 **Fax:** 10 24 45 037
Email: info@varma.fi **Web site:** http://www.varma.fi
ISSN: 1456-209X
Date Established: 1998; **Freq:** Quarterly; **Cover Price:** Free; **Circ:** 65,000
Usual Pagination: 40
Editor-in-Chief: Satu Perälampi
Profile: Mutual pension insurance company Varma customer-magazine for clients and company interest groups.
Language(s): Finnish; Swedish
BUSINESS: FINANCE & ECONOMICS: Insurance

VARUSMIES 705134L40-130

Editorial: PL 1303/ Asemapäällikönkatu 1, 00101 HELSINKI **Fax:** 9 77 41 833
Web site: http://www.varusmiesliitto.fi
Date Established: 1970; **Freq:** Half-yearly; Free to qualifying individuals ; **Circ:** 9,000
Usual Pagination: 12
Profile: Journal issued for people doing their military duty.
Language(s): Finnish

VASABLADET 15226L67B-7700

Editorial: PB 52/ Sandögatan 20, 65101 VASA
Tel: 6 78 48 200 **Fax:** 6 78 48 881
Email: nyheter@vasabladet.fi **Web site:** http://www.vasabladet.fi
ISSN: 0356-1844
Date Established: 1856
Circ: 21,529
Usual Pagination: 18
Editor-in-Chief: Lars Hedman
Profile: Regional newspapers for Swedish-speakers mainly in Ostrobotnia on the Finnish western coastline.
Language(s): Swedish
ADVERTISING RATES:
Full Page Colour .... EUR 10404
SCC .... EUR 25.50
Agency Commission: 15%
Mechanical Data: No. of Columns (Display): 8, Col Length: 510mm, Screen: 34 lpc, Print Process: offset, Col Widths (Display): 44mm, Page Width: 380mm
Copy instructions: *Copy Date:* 5 days prior to publication date

Editions:
Vasabladet Internetredaktionen
REGIONAL DAILY & SUNDAY NEWSPAPERS: Regional Daily Newspapers

VASABLADET HELSINGFORS
705721L67E-650
Editorial: PB 179/ Estnäsgatan 10 C, 00171 HELSINGFORS **Tel:** 9 69 48 583 **Fax:** 9 69 48 458
Email: henrik.stenback@vasabladet.fi **Web site:** http://www.vasabladet.fi
Profile: Local Helsinki office of Swedish-language regional newspaper Vasabladet.
Language(s): Swedish
REGIONAL DAILY & SUNDAY NEWSPAPERS: Regional Offices

VASABLADET JAKOBSTAD-NYKARLEBY
705716L67E-652
Editorial: Jakobsgatan 13, 68600 JAKOBSTAD
Tel: 6 78 48 803
Email: kenneth.myntti@vasabladet.fi **Web site:** http://www.vasabladet.fi
Profile: Local Jakobstad and Nykarleby office of Swedish-language regional newspaper Vasabladet.
Language(s): Swedish
REGIONAL DAILY & SUNDAY NEWSPAPERS: Regional Offices

VASABLADET KARLEBY
705715L67E-653
Editorial: Karlebygatan 22, 67100 KARLEBY
Tel: 6 78 48 803
Email: yrsa.slotte@vasabladet.fi **Web site:** http://www.vasabladet.fi
Profile: Local Karleby office of Swedish-language regional newspaper Vasabladet.
Language(s): Swedish
REGIONAL DAILY & SUNDAY NEWSPAPERS: Regional Offices

VASABLADET MALAX KORSNÄS
705718L67E-655
Editorial: Erkustået 17, 66140 ÖVERMALAX
Tel: 6 78 48 203
Email: kerstin.nordman@vasabladet.fi **Web site:** http://www.vasabladet.fi
Profile: Local Malax and Korsnäs office of Swedish-language regional newspaper Vasabladet.
Language(s): Swedish
REGIONAL DAILY & SUNDAY NEWSPAPERS: Regional Offices

VASABLADET NÄRPES
705719L67E-660
Editorial: Närpesvägen 4, 64200 NÄRPES
Tel: 6 78 48 700
Email: nyheter@vasabladet.fi **Web site:** http://www.vasabladet.fi
Profile: Local Närpes office of Swedish-language regional newspaper Vasabladet.
Language(s): Swedish
REGIONAL DAILY & SUNDAY NEWSPAPERS: Regional Offices

VASABLADET ORAVAIS-VÖRÅ-MAXMO
705717L67E-665
Editorial: Eljasusvägen 49, 66830 ORAVAIS
Tel: 6 78 48 203
Email: karin.sundstrom@vasabladet.fi **Web site:** http://www.vasabladet.fi
Profile: Local Oravais, Vörå and Maxmo office of Swedish-language regional newspaper Vasabladet.
Language(s): Swedish
REGIONAL DAILY & SUNDAY NEWSPAPERS: Regional Offices

VASAMA
705343L14L-114_4
Editorial: PL 747/Aleksanterinkatu 15, 33101 TAMPERE **Tel:** 3 25 20 111 **Fax:** 3 25 20 210
Email: vasamalehti@sahkoliitto.fi **Web site:** http://www.sahkoliitto.fi
Date Established: 1957; **Freq:** Monthly; **Circ:** 31,420
Usual Pagination: 16
Editor-in-Chief: Paavo Holi
Profile: Journal of the Electrical Workers' Union.
Language(s): Finnish
Readership: Read by members.
ADVERTISING RATES:
Full Page Colour .... EUR 3746.00
SCC .... EUR 18.10
Agency Commission: 15%
Mechanical Data: Type Area: 257 x 345mm, No. of Columns (Display): 6, Col Widths (Display): 40mm, Col Length: 370mm, Print Process: offset rotation, Screen: 28-34 lpc
BUSINESS: COMMERCE, INDUSTRY & MANAGEMENT: Trade Unions

VÄSTRA NYLAND
15180L67B-8000
Editorial: PB 26/ Genvägen 4, 10601 EKENÄS
Tel: 19 22 28 22 **Fax:** 19 22 28 14
Email: vnred@vastranyland.fi **Web site:** http://www.vastranyland.fi
ISSN: 0782-6559
Date Established: 1881
Circ: 10,837
Usual Pagination: 16
Managing Director: Tommy Westerlund
Profile: Regional Swedish-language newspaper issued mainly in Western Uusimaa on the south coast of Finland.
Language(s): Swedish
ADVERTISING RATES:
Full Page Colour .... EUR 3685
SCC .... EUR 16.80
Agency Commission: 15%
Mechanical Data: Col Length: 390mm, Col Widths (Display): 45mm, No. of Columns (Display): 6, Screen: 34 lpc b/w; 40 lpc colour, Print Process: offset
Editions:
Västra Nyland Internetredaktionen
REGIONAL DAILY & SUNDAY NEWSPAPERS: Regional Daily Newspapers

VÄSTRA NYLAND HANGÖ
708206L67E-674
Editorial: Berggatan 19, 10900 HANGÖ
Tel: 19 24 82 287 **Fax:** 19 24 87 130
Email: eva.hagman@vastranyland.fi **Web site:** http://www.vastranyland.fi
Profile: Hanko local office of newspaper Västra Nyland.
Language(s): Swedish
REGIONAL DAILY & SUNDAY NEWSPAPERS: Regional Offices

VÄSTRA NYLAND KARIS
708211L67E-675
Editorial: Torggatan 1-3, 10300 KARIS
Tel: 50 54 97 917 **Fax:** 19 23 02 40
Email: marit.lundstrom@vastranyland.fi **Web site:** http://www.vastranyland.fi
Profile: Local Karis, Pojo, Ingå and Lojo office of Swedish-language regional newspaper Västra Nyland.
Language(s): Swedish
REGIONAL DAILY & SUNDAY NEWSPAPERS: Regional Offices

VÄSTRA NYLAND KYRKSLÄTT
708214L67E-676
Editorial: PB 66/ Torgvägen 1 A 1, 02401 KYRKSLÄTT **Tel:** 29 08 01 305 **Fax:** 9 29 89 232
Email: olle.hakala@vastranyland.fi **Web site:** http://www.vastranyland.fi
Profile: Kyrkslätt and Sjundeå local office of newspaper Västra Nyland.
Language(s): Swedish
REGIONAL DAILY & SUNDAY NEWSPAPERS: Regional Offices

VASTUULLINEN VAIKUTTAJA
1638073L14C-5
Formerly: FiBS
Editorial: Mikonkatu 17, 5 krs, 00100 HELSINKI
Tel: 400 87 78 89
Web site: http://www.fibsry.fi
ISSN: 1458-6355
Freq: Half-yearly; **Cover Price:** Free; **Circ:** 5,000
Editor-in-Chief: Mikko Routti
Profile: Magazine about society ethics and companies.
Language(s): Finnish
Readership: Members of the Finnish Business & Society.
ADVERTISING RATES:
Full Page Colour .... EUR 1200.00

VAUHDIN MAAILMA
15322L77A-95
Editorial: Esterinportti 1 A, 00015 KUVALEHDET
Tel: 9 15 661 **Fax:** 915666210
Email: vauhdin.maailma@otavamedia.fi **Web site:** http://www.vauhdinmaailma.fi
ISSN: 0355-4295
Date Established: 1965; **Freq:** Monthly; **Circ:** 22,068
Usual Pagination: 120
Managing Editor: Tuomo Kiisseli
Profile: Motor sport magazine including technical and general information on cars, bikes and all motor sports.
Language(s): Finnish
Readership: Aimed at those interested in motorsports and driving.
ADVERTISING RATES:
Full Page Colour .... EUR 2500
SCC .... EUR 21
Agency Commission: 15%
Mechanical Data: Col Length: 280mm, Col Widths (Display): 45mm, No. of Columns (Display): 4, Type Area: 280 x 217mm, Print Process: Offset, Screen: 60 lpc, Trim Size: 272 x 209mm, Film: Digital positive, Page Width: 217mm
Copy instructions: *Copy Date:* 21 days prior to publication date
Average ad content per issue: 25%
CONSUMER: MOTORING & CYCLING: Motoring

VAUVA
15271L74D-100
Editorial: PL 100/ Lapinmäentie 1, 00040 SANOMA MAGAZINES **Tel:** 9 12 01 **Fax:** 9 12 05 352
Email: vauva@sanomamagazines.fi **Web site:** http://www.vauva.fi
ISSN: 0789-9238
Date Established: 1992; **Freq:** Monthly; **Circ:** 39,601
Usual Pagination: 116
Managing Editor: Maria Tuominen
Profile: Magazine for parents-to-be and those with children under six years.
Language(s): Finnish
ADVERTISING RATES:
Full Page Colour .... EUR 4900
SCC .... EUR 49
Mechanical Data: Bleed Size: 215 x 280mm, Trim Size: 267 x 195mm, Type Area: 190 x 250mm, No. of Columns (Display): 4, Col Widths (Display): 45mm, Print Process: offset, Film: positive, Screen: 60 lpc
Copy instructions: *Copy Date:* 18 days prior to publication date
CONSUMER: WOMEN'S INTEREST CONSUMER MAGAZINES: Child Care

VEGAIA
718170L74P-100
Editorial: Hämeentie 48, 00500 HELSINKI
Tel: 50 34 49 524 **Fax:** 9 22 15 696
Email: vegaia@vegaaniliitto.fi **Web site:** http://www.vegaaniliitto.fi/vegaia
ISSN: 1237-3184
Date Established: 1994; **Freq:** Quarterly; **Annual Sub.:** EUR 12.00; **Circ:** 1,500
Usual Pagination: 32
Editor-in-Chief: Johanna Kaipiainen
Profile: Magazine about vegetarianism and healthy food.
Language(s): Finnish
ADVERTISING RATES:
Full Page Colour .... EUR 150.00

VEIKKAAJA
705353L94X-120
Formerly: IS Veikkaaja
Editorial: PL 45/ Töölönlahdenkatu 2, 00089 SANOMA **Tel:** 9 12 23 563 **Fax:** 9 12 23 419
Email: veikkaaja@iltasanomat.fi **Web site:** http://www.veikkaaja.fi
ISSN: 0786-9339
Date Established: 1949; **Freq:** Weekly - Published on Tuesday; **Circ:** 45,411
Usual Pagination: 100
Managing Editor: Antti Virolainen
Profile: Magazine containing information on sports, gambling, betting and the lottery.
Language(s): Finnish
ADVERTISING RATES:
Full Page Colour .... EUR 3900
SCC .... EUR 26.20
Agency Commission: 15%
Mechanical Data: Col Widths (Display): 38mm, No. of Columns (Display): 6, Screen: 32 lpc, Type Area: 253 x 365mm, Print Process: offset
CONSUMER: OTHER CLASSIFICATIONS: Miscellaneous

VENÄJÄN AIKA
706500L14C-150
Editorial: Kaupintie 16 B 16, 00440 HELSINKI
Tel: 9 85 45 320 **Fax:** 9 85 45 32 50
Email: novomedia@novomedia.fi **Web site:** http://www.venajanaika.fi
ISSN: 1455-0520
Date Established: 1997; **Freq:** Quarterly; **Circ:** 10,000
Usual Pagination: 80
Editor-in-Chief: Aleksander Borodavkin
Profile: Magazine about current affairs in Russia influencing Finnish companies.
Language(s): Finnish
ADVERTISING RATES:
Full Page Colour .... EUR 1600.00
SCC .... EUR 17.10
Mechanical Data: Type Area: 215 x 300mm, Print Process: offset rotation, Screen: 60 lpc

VENE
15377L91A-50
Editorial: Maistraatinportti 1, 00015 OTAVAMEDIA
Tel: 9 15 661 **Fax:** 9 15 66 62 10
Email: vene@otavamedia.fi **Web site:** http://www.venelehti.fi/venelehti
Date Established: 1966; **Freq:** Monthly; **Circ:** 22,054
Usual Pagination: 132
Profile: Magazine about yachting, boats and navigation.
Language(s): Finnish
Readership: Aimed at sailing enthusiasts and people who own motor-boats.
ADVERTISING RATES:
Full Page Colour .... EUR 2720
SCC .... EUR 24.20
Mechanical Data: Bleed Size: 280 x 217mm, Film: Digital. positive, Print Process: Offset, Type Area: 217 x 280mm, Col Widths (Display): 42mm, Screen: 60 lpc
Copy instructions: *Copy Date:* 19 days prior to publication date
CONSUMER: RECREATION & LEISURE: Boating & Yachting

VEROTUS
705255L1M-51
Editorial: PL 223/ Paasitie 12 A 1, 00101 HELSINKI
Tel: 50 91 76 866 **Fax:** 9 66 20 06
Email: webmaster@verotus-lehti.fi **Web site:** http://www.verotus-lehti.fi
ISSN: 0357-2331
Date Established: 1950; **Freq:** Quarterly; **Circ:** 4,500
Usual Pagination: 140
Editor-in-Chief: Olli Nykänen
Profile: Magazine about national and international developments in corporate and private tax issues.
Language(s): Finnish
Readership: Aimed at tax professionals and people interested in taxation.
ADVERTISING RATES:
Full Page Colour .... EUR 550.00
Mechanical Data: Bleed Size: B5, Type Area: 145 x 210mm, Col Widths (Display): 70mm, No. of Columns (Display): 2, Print Process: offset
BUSINESS: FINANCE & ECONOMICS: Taxation

VEROUUTISET
706178L1M-52
Editorial: Kalevankatu 4, 00100 HELSINKI
Tel: 9 61 88 71 **Fax:** 9 60 80 87
Email: veronmaksajat@veronmaksajat.fi **Web site:** http://www.verotieto.fi
Freq: Monthly; **Annual Sub.:** EUR 145.00
Editor-in-Chief: Juha-Pekka Huovinen; **Managing Editor:** Riitta Rimmi
Profile: Verouutiset journal is distributed to members of Taxpayers' Central Union and it contains information about taxation from the taxpayer's point of view.
Language(s): Finnish
BUSINESS: FINANCE & ECONOMICS: Taxation

VEROVÄKI
705793L1M-53
Formerly: Verovirkailija
Editorial: Ratamestarinkatu 11, 00520 HELSINKI
Tel: 9 22 93 36 33 **Fax:** 9 22 93 36 36
Email: kirsi.huhtamaki-nasri@verovl.fi **Web site:** http://www.verovl.fi
Date Established: 1981; **Freq:** Quarterly; **Cover Price:** Free; **Circ:** 6,500
Usual Pagination: 20
Editor-in-Chief: Kirsi Huhtamäki-Nasri
Profile: Journal of the Finnish Union of taxation officials.
Language(s): Finnish
Readership: Read by members.
BUSINESS: FINANCE & ECONOMICS: Taxation

VIA LEADERSHIP
1809820L14A-150
Editorial: Westendinkatu 7, 02160 ESPOO
Tel: 20 74 02 800 **Fax:** 20 74 02 830
Email: info@viagroup.fi **Web site:** http://www.viagroup.fi
Freq: Half-yearly; **Cover Price:** Free; **Circ:** 12,500
Profile: Magazine about management.
Language(s): Finnish
Readership: Decision-makers.
Mechanical Data: Type Area: 235 x 275mm

VIHERPIHA
15391L93-200
Editorial: Risto Rytin tie 33, 00081 A-LEHDET
Tel: 9 75 961 **Fax:** 9 75 98 31 13
Email: viherpiha@a-lehdet.fi **Web site:** http://www.viherpiha.fi
Date Established: 1994; **Freq:** Monthly - Published 10/year; **Circ:** 90,906
Usual Pagination: 100
Editor-in-Chief: Auli Honkanen; **Managing Editor:** Liisa Häkli
Profile: Magazine featuring a broad range of articles from basic garden design and care, to the latest plants and cultivation methods. Includes features on balcony and indoor plants.
Language(s): Finnish
Readership: Aimed at amateur gardeners.
ADVERTISING RATES:
Full Page Colour .... EUR 5600
SCC .... EUR 58
Mechanical Data: Screen: 60 lpc, Print Process: Offset, Bleed Size: 273 x 230mm, Type Area: 241 x 187mm, No. of Columns (Display): 4, Col Length: 241mm, Page Width: 187mm
CONSUMER: GARDENING

VIHREÄ LANKA
15127L82-105
Editorial: Fredrikinkatu 33, 3 krs, 00120 HELSINKI
Tel: 9 58 60 41 23 **Fax:** 9 58 60 41 24
Email: toimitus@vihrealanka.fi **Web site:** http://www.vihrealanka.fi
ISSN: 0780-9417
Date Established: 1983; **Freq:** 26 issues yearly - Published on Friday; **Circ:** 7,065
Usual Pagination: 16
Managing Editor: Laura Häkli
Profile: Publication concerning the economic and political aspects of ecological and green issues.
Language(s): Finnish
Readership: Read by politically green people and environment professionals in organizations and companies.
ADVERTISING RATES:
Full Page Colour .... EUR 3400
SCC .... EUR 18.90
Agency Commission: 15%
Mechanical Data: Type Area: 254 x 380mm, No. of Columns (Display): 5, Bleed Size: 290 x 410mm, Screen: 28-34 lpc, Film: negative, Col Widths (Display): 48mm
Editions:
Vihrealanka.fi
CONSUMER: CURRENT AFFAIRS & POLITICS

VIIHTYISÄ KOTI
706048L74K-50
Editorial: Vetotie 3 A, 01610 VANTAA
Tel: 20 73 12 310 **Fax:** 20 73 12 319

Finland

Email: jukka.jaakkola@prkk.fi **Web site:** http://www.viihtyisakoti.fi
ISSN: 1239-887X
Date Established: 1996; **Freq:** 6 issues yearly; **Cover Price:** Free; **Circ:** 165,000
Usual Pagination: 48
Editor-in-Chief: Jukka Jaakkola
Profile: Magazine about interior-design, building and living.
Language(s): Finnish
ADVERTISING RATES:
Full Page Colour .... EUR 5490.00
SCC .... EUR 51.20
Mechanical Data: Print Process: offset, Film: negative, Screen: 48-56 lpc, Type Area: 180 x 268mm, Bleed Size: 210 x 300mm
CONSUMER: WOMEN'S INTEREST CONSUMER MAGAZINES: Home Purchase

VIIKKO POHJOIS-KARJALA
704854L72-1577
Editorial: PL 97/ Niskakatu 7, 80101 JOENSUU
Tel: 13 73 75 811 **Fax:** 13 74 33 07
Email: toimitus@viikkopk.fi **Web site:** http://www.viikkopk.fi
Date Established: 1906; **Freq:** Weekly; **Circ:** 7,193
Usual Pagination: 20
Profile: Local weekly newspaper issued in Joensuu and its surroundings in northern Carelia.
Language(s): Finnish
ADVERTISING RATES:
Full Page Colour .... EUR 5922
SCC .... EUR 23.50
Agency Commission: 15%
Mechanical Data: No. of Columns (Display): 6, Type Area: 284 x 416mm, Col Widths (Display): 44mm, Screen: 200 pixels/inch, Col Length: 416mm, Print Process: offset
LOCAL NEWSPAPERS

VIIKKO VAPAUS
704869L72-1555
Formerly: Vapaus
Editorial: PL 228/Porrassalmenkatu 2, 50101 MIKKELI **Tel:** 15 32 13 70 **Fax:** 15 36 03 27
Email: toimitus@vapauslehti.com **Web site:** http://www.vapauslehti.com
Date Established: 1906; **Freq:** Weekly; **Circ:** 6,070
Usual Pagination: 20
Profile: Newspaper issued in the Mikkeli region.
Language(s): Finnish
ADVERTISING RATES:
Full Page Colour .... EUR 2988
SCC .... EUR 12
Agency Commission: 15%
Mechanical Data: No. of Columns (Display): 6, Col Widths (Display): 44mm, Type Area: 315 x 461mm, Col Length: 415mm, Print Process: offset
LOCAL NEWSPAPERS

VIIKKO-ETEENPÄIN
704960L72-155
Formerly: Eteenpäin
Editorial: PL 140/ Kymenlaaksonkatu 10, 48101 KOTKA **Tel:** 5 22 51 122 **Fax:** 5 21 81 157
Email: eteenpain@etp.kymp.net **Web site:** http://www.eteenpain.fi
ISSN: 0786-4612
Date Established: 1905; **Freq:** Weekly; **Circ:** 5,435
Usual Pagination: 24
Profile: Newspaper issued in the Kymi region.
Language(s): Finnish
ADVERTISING RATES:
Full Page Colour .... EUR 4756
SCC .... EUR 19.10
Mechanical Data: Type Area: 289 x 415mm, No. of Columns (Display): 6, Col Widths (Display): 44mm, Print Process: offset, Col Length: 415mm, Page Width: 289mm
LOCAL NEWSPAPERS

VIIKKO-HÄME
704857L67B-7800
Editorial: PL 108/ Birger Jarlin katu 11 C, 13101 HÄMEENLINNA **Tel:** 3 62 85 50 **Fax:** 36171269
Email: toimitus@viikko-hame.fi **Web site:** http://www.viikko-hame.fi
ISSN: 1457-8921
Date Established: 1906
Circ: 8,334
Usual Pagination: 20
Profile: This local newspaper is a merger of Lounais-Häme, Riihimäen Seutu, Hämeen Kansa and Päijätseutu.
Language(s): Finnish
ADVERTISING RATES:
Full Page Colour .... EUR 4308
SCC .... EUR 17.30
Agency Commission: 15%
Mechanical Data: Type Area: 284 x 415mm, No. of Columns (Display): 6, Col Widths (Display): 44mm, Print Process: offset, Screen: 85 lpi, Col Length: 415mm
REGIONAL DAILY & SUNDAY NEWSPAPERS: Regional Daily Newspapers

VIIKKO-HÄME LAHTI
1834448L67E-670
Editorial: Aleksanterinkatu 26 a, 15140 LAHTI
Tel: 3 78 28 762 **Fax:** 37823219
Email: toimitus@viikko-hame.fi **Web site:** http://www.viikko-hame.fi
Circ: 8,334
Profile: This local newspaper is a merger of Lounais-Häme, Riihimäen Seutu, Hämeen Kansa and Päijätseutu.
Language(s): Finnish
ADVERTISING RATES:
Full Page Colour .... EUR 4048
SCC .... EUR 17.30
REGIONAL DAILY & SUNDAY NEWSPAPERS: Regional Offices

VIISARI
715895L74C-72
Formerly: Vesainen
Editorial: Asemapäällikönkatu 1, 00520 HELSINKI
Tel: 20 75 52 696 **Fax:** 20 75 52 627
Web site: http://www.vesaiset.fi
ISSN: 0357-9875
Date Established: 1979; **Freq:** Half-yearly; **Annual Sub.:** EUR 10.00
Usual Pagination: 32
Editor-in-Chief: Jyrki Nurmi
Profile: Publication about children and family life.
Language(s): Finnish
Readership: Families with children aged 4-14.
CONSUMER: WOMEN'S INTEREST CONSUMER MAGAZINES: Home & Family

VIISAS RAHA
1830170L1F-100
Editorial: PL 502, 00100 HELSINKI **Tel:** 10 66 51 02
Fax: 10 66 52 533
Email: viisasraha@alma360.fi **Web site:** http://www.osakeliitto.fi
ISSN: 1797-3503
Date Established: 2008; **Freq:** Monthly - Published 10/year; **Circ:** 16,000
Managing Editor: Helena Ranta-aho
Profile: Osakesäästäjien Keskusliiton sijoituslehti.
Language(s): Finnish
ADVERTISING RATES:
Full Page Colour .... EUR 2750
SCC .... EUR 49.10
Mechanical Data: Type Area: 215 x 280mm, Print Process: offset
BUSINESS: FINANCE & ECONOMICS: Investment

VIISKUNTA
705015L72-1605
Editorial: PL 11/Kirjapainokuja 2, 63301 ALAVUS
Tel: 6 24 77 870 **Fax:** 6 24 77 874
Email: toimitus@viiskunta.fi **Web site:** http://www.viiskunta.fi
Date Established: 1954; **Freq:** 104 issues yearly; **Circ:** 6,091
Usual Pagination: 12
Profile: Newspaper issued in Alavus, Kuortane, Lehtimäki, Töysä and Ähtäri.
Language(s): Finnish
ADVERTISING RATES:
Full Page Colour .... EUR 3986
SCC .... EUR 18.20
Mechanical Data: Col Widths (Display): 44mm, Col Length: 525mm, Print Process: offset, Screen: 28-34 lpc
Editions:
Viiskunta Verkkotoimitus
LOCAL NEWSPAPERS

VIISPIIKKINEN
704941L72-1575
Formerly: Viiden Kunnan Sanomat
Editorial: PL 41/ Virastotie 3, 43501 KARSTULA
Tel: 14 41 77 300
Email: toimitus@viispiikkinen.fi **Web site:** http://www.viispiikkinen.fi
Date Established: 1949; **Freq:** Weekly; **Circ:** 5,444
Usual Pagination: 24
Profile: Local newspaper issued in Karstula, Kannonkoski, Kivijärvi, Kyyjärvi and Pylkönmäki.
Language(s): Finnish
ADVERTISING RATES:
Full Page Colour .... EUR 2080
SCC .... EUR 9.50
Agency Commission: 15%
Mechanical Data: Col Widths (Display): 40mm, No. of Columns (Display): 6, Col Length: 365mm, Print Process: offset rotation
Editions:
Viispiikkinen Verkkotoimitus
LOCAL NEWSPAPERS

VIITASAAREN SEUTU
704942L72-1615
Editorial: PL 61 / Keskitie 7, 44501 VIITASAARI
Tel: 14 33 97 100 **Fax:** 14 33 97 111
Email: seutu.toimitus@keskisuomalainen.fi **Web site:** http://www.viitasaarenseutu.fi
ISSN: 0356-1410
Date Established: 1934; **Freq:** Weekly; **Circ:** 5,316
Usual Pagination: 16
Profile: Local newspaper issued in the Viitasaari area.
Language(s): Finnish
ADVERTISING RATES:
Full Page Colour .... EUR 1953
SCC .... EUR 9.30
Agency Commission: 15%
Mechanical Data: No. of Columns (Display): 6, Col Length: 370mm, Col Widths (Display): 41mm, Print Process: offset
Editions:
Viitasaaren Seutu Verkkotoimitus
LOCAL NEWSPAPERS

VILLIVARSA
15336L81D-100
Editorial: Maistraatinportti 1, 00015 OTAVAMEDIA
Tel: 9 15 661 **Fax:** 9 15 66 788
Email: villivarsa@otavamedia.fi **Web site:** http://www.otavamedia.fi
ISSN: 0781-5638
Date Established: 1983; **Freq:** Monthly; **Circ:** 14,643
Usual Pagination: 72
Profile: Magazine about horses.
Language(s): Finnish
Readership: Aimed at young people interested in horses and ponies.
ADVERTISING RATES:
Full Page Colour .... EUR 1100
Mechanical Data: Bleed Size: 265 x 190mm, Print Process: Offset, Type Area: 190 x 265mm, Film: positive, Screen: 48 lpc
Copy instructions: *Copy Date:* 20 days prior to publication date
CONSUMER: ANIMALS & PETS: Horses & Ponies

VIRO.NYT
764848L14C-160
Editorial: PL 464/ Mariankatu 8 b C 12, 00171 HELSINKI **Tel:** 9 68 42 84 64 **Fax:** 9 68 42 84 65
Email: svyl@svyl.net **Web site:** http://www.svyl.net
ISSN: 1459-2134
Date Established: 2001; **Freq:** Quarterly; **Annual Sub.:** EUR 20.00; **Circ:** 3,500
Usual Pagination: 24
Managing Editor: Terhi Pääskylä
Profile: Magazine about the economic and cultural exchange between Finland and Estonia.
Language(s): Finnish
Readership: Finns interested in Estonia.
ADVERTISING RATES:
Full Page Colour .... EUR 300.00

VIVA
1698174L74N-90
Editorial: Maistraatinportti 1, 00015 OTAVAMEDIA
Tel: 9 15 661 **Fax:** 9 14 96 445
Email: viva@otavamedia.fi **Web site:** http://www.vivalehti.fi
ISSN: 1795-9950
Date Established: 2005; **Freq:** Monthly - Published 14/year; **Circ:** 47,420
Usual Pagination: 140
Managing Editor: Veli-Matti Jusi
Profile: Magazine about aging and enjoying life.
Language(s): Finnish
Readership: Middle-aged people.
ADVERTISING RATES:
Full Page Colour .... EUR 4340
SCC .... EUR 51.60
Mechanical Data: Type Area: 230 x 280mm, Screen: 60 lpc, Print Process: offset
CONSUMER: WOMEN'S INTEREST CONSUMER MAGAZINES: Retirement

VOI HYVIN
15282L74G-250
Editorial: Risto Rytin tie 33, 00081 A-LEHDET
Tel: 9 75 961 **Fax:** 9 75 98 31 09
Email: voihyvin@a-lehdet.fi **Web site:** http://www.voihyvin.fi
ISSN: 0780-1122
Date Established: 1986; **Freq:** 6 issues yearly - Published 8/year; **Circ:** 48,414
Usual Pagination: 112
Profile: Magazine focusing on well-being and self development through natural health and beauty. Features articles on alternative medicine and vegetarian food.
Language(s): Finnish
Readership: Aimed at women aged between 35 and 65 years.
ADVERTISING RATES:
Full Page Colour .... EUR 4500
SCC .... EUR 46.60
Mechanical Data: Type Area: 241 x 187mm, Bleed Size: 273 x 230mm, No. of Columns (Display): 4, Print Process: Offset, Screen: 60 lpc, Col Length: 241mm, Page Width: 187mm
CONSUMER: WOMEN'S INTEREST CONSUMER MAGAZINES: Slimming & Health

VOILÀ CITROËN
1611077L31R-59
Editorial: PL 115, 01511 VANTAA **Tel:** 10 56 97 41
Fax: 10 56 97 294
Email: voila@acacom.com **Web site:** http://www.citroen.fi
ISSN: 1239-2960
Freq: Quarterly; **Cover Price:** Free; **Circ:** 50,000
Usual Pagination: 24
Editor-in-Chief: Pekka Koski; **Managing Editor:** Niina Käkelä
Profile: Customer-magazine of Citroën.
Language(s): Finnish
Agency Commission: 15%
Mechanical Data: Type Area: 210 x 297mm, Screen: 60 lpc, Print Process: offset
BUSINESS: MOTOR TRADE: Motor Trade Related

VOIMA
706523L82-130
Editorial: Hämeentie 48, 00500 HELSINKI
Tel: 9 77 44 31 20 **Fax:** 9 77 32 328
Email: voima@voima.fi **Web site:** http://www.voima.fi
ISSN: 1457-1005
Date Established: 1999; **Freq:** Monthly - Published 10/year; Free to qualifying individuals ; **Circ:** 60,000
Usual Pagination: 48
Managing Editor: Susanna Kuparinen
Profile: Publication containing articles about culture, current-affairs, environment and politics.
Language(s): Finnish
ADVERTISING RATES:
Full Page Colour .... EUR 3223
SCC .... EUR 17.10
Agency Commission: 15%
Mechanical Data: Type Area: 254 x 375mm
Editions:
Voima.fi
CONSUMER: CURRENT AFFAIRS & POLITICS

VOIMA JA KÄYTTÖ - KRAFT OCH DRIFT
15051L45D-25
Formerly: Voima ja Käyttö
Editorial: Lastenkodinkuja 1, 00180 HELSINKI
Tel: 9 58 60 48 10 **Fax:** 9 69 48 798
Email: leif.wikstrom@konepaallystoliitto.fi **Web site:** http://www.konepaallystoliitto.fi
ISSN: 0355-7081
Date Established: 1903; **Freq:** 6 issues yearly; **Circ:** 5,221
Usual Pagination: 40
Editor-in-Chief: Leif Wikström
Profile: Journal covering the shipping industry.
Language(s): English; Finnish; Swedish
Readership: Read by engineers and managers of shipping companies.
ADVERTISING RATES:
Full Page Colour .... EUR 1990.00
SCC .... EUR 25.00
Agency Commission: 15%
Mechanical Data: Bleed Size: 210 x 297mm, Type Area: 180 x 260mm, No. of Columns (Display): 3, Col Widths (Display): 58.7mm, Print Process: offset, Film: negative, Screen: 54-60 lpc
BUSINESS: MARINE & SHIPPING: Marine Engineering Equipment

VOLVO VIESTI
705226L31R-60
Editorial: c/o Alma 360 Asiakasmedia, PL 502, 00101 HELSINKI **Tel:** 10 665 01
Email: volvoviesti@alma360.fi **Web site:** http://www.volvocars.fi
ISSN: 0356-3952
Date Established: 1932; **Freq:** Quarterly; **Cover Price:** Free; **Circ:** 140,000
Usual Pagination: 36
Editor-in-Chief: Petri Castrén; **Managing Editor:** Matti Sovijärvi
Profile: Customer-magazine for owners of Volvo cars.
Language(s): Finnish
Agency Commission: 15%
Mechanical Data: Type Area: 220 x 280mm
BUSINESS: MOTOR TRADE: Motor Trade Related

VOLVO VISIITTI
1611044L49D-50
Editorial: PL 50/ Vetokuja 1 E, 01611 VANTAA
Tel: 10 65 500 **Fax:** 10 65 55 895
Email: eija-liisa.tilli@volvo.com **Web site:** http://magazine.volvotrucks.com/fi
ISSN: 1458-7602
Date Established: 2002; **Freq:** Quarterly; **Cover Price:** Free; **Circ:** 25,000
Usual Pagination: 36
Editor-in-Chief: Eija-Liisa Tilli
Profile: Magazine about Volvo trucks and lorries.
Language(s): Finnish
Readership: Customers of Volvo Trucking.
ADVERTISING RATES:
Full Page Colour .... EUR 2600.00
Mechanical Data: Type Area: 189 x 239mm, Print Process: offset, Bleed Size: 217 x 280mm

VUOLIJOKI -LEHTI
706635L72-1620
Editorial: Sairaalatie 8, 88300 PALTAMO
Tel: 8 87 19 99 **Fax:** 8 87 20 21
Email: aineistot@paltamonkirjapaino.fi **Web site:** http://www.paltamonkirjapaino.fi/vuolijoki
Date Established: 1991; **Freq:** Weekly; **Annual Sub.:** EUR 46.00; **Circ:** 1,180
Usual Pagination: 8
Editor-in-Chief: Tuula Keränen
Profile: Local newspaper issued in Vuolijoki.
Language(s): Finnish
ADVERTISING RATES:
SCC .... EUR 10.50
Mechanical Data: Type Area: 385 x 255mm, No. of Columns (Display): 5, Col Widths (Display): 47mm
LOCAL NEWSPAPERS

WARKAUDEN LEHTI
15228L67B-8500
Editorial: Pirnankatu 4, 78200 VARKAUS
Tel: 17 77 83 631 **Fax:** 17 55 22 375
Email: toimitus@warkaudenlehti.fi **Web site:** http://www.warkaudenlehti.fi
ISSN: 0356-0996
Date Established: 1919
Circ: 10,590
Usual Pagination: 12
Managing Editor: Antti Aho
Profile: Regional newspaper issued in Joroinen, Kangaslampi, Varkaus, Heinävesi, Jäppilä, Leppävirta and Rantasalmi.
Language(s): Finnish
ADVERTISING RATES:
Full Page Colour .... EUR 6963
SCC .... EUR 16.90
Mechanical Data: Col Widths (Display): 43mm, Col Length: 515mm, No. of Columns (Display): 8, Page Width: 410mm, Type Area: 379 x 515mm, Bleed Size: 410 x 580mm, Print Process: offset

Average ad content per issue: 25%
REGIONAL DAILY & SUNDAY NEWSPAPERS: Regional Daily Newspapers

WATTIVIESTI
1664533L17-42
Editorial: PL 9/ Radanvarsi 2, 28101 PORI
Tel: 2 62 12 233
Email: porienergia@porienergia.fi **Web site:** http://www.porienergia.fi
Freq: Quarterly; **Cover Price:** Free; **Circ:** 80,000
Usual Pagination: 16
Editor-in-Chief: Matti Rintanen
Profile: Magazine about local electrical services.
Language(s): Finnish
Readership: Customers of Pori Energia Oy.
BUSINESS: ELECTRICAL

WELCOME TO FINLAND
1813181L89D-60
Editorial: Henry Fordin katu 5 H 5 krs, 00150 HELSINKI **Tel:** 9 61 16 80
Email: toimisto@susamuru.fi **Web site:** http://www.welcometofinland.fi
Date Established: 1984; **Freq:** Quarterly; Free to qualifying individuals ; **Circ:** 45,000
Profile: Magazine with information about Finland.
Language(s): English
ADVERTISING RATES:
Full Page Colour .... EUR 9500
CONSUMER: HOLIDAYS & TRAVEL: In-Flight Magazines

WOODWORKING PUUNTYÖSTÖ
15064L46-120
Editorial: PL 211/ Puistokatu 9 A, 15101 LAHTI
Tel: 3 73 31 501 **Fax:** 37331511
Email: woodworking@kolumbus.fi **Web site:** http://www.puuntyosto.com
ISSN: 1239-047X
Date Established: 1990; **Freq:** Monthly - Published 10/year; **Annual Sub.:** EUR 48; **Circ:** 3,300
Usual Pagination: 56
Profile: Magazine for the woodworking, furniture and sawmill industry in Finland. Contains reports on all aspects of the wood industry including tools, machines and production processes and the latest developments in technology and markets.
Language(s): English; Finnish
Readership: Read by people working in woodworking, furniture and sawmill industry.
ADVERTISING RATES:
Full Page Colour .... EUR 2190
SCC .... EUR 20.80
Agency Commission: 15%
Mechanical Data: No. of Columns (Display): 2/3, Type Area: 262 x 180 mm, Trim Size: 297 x 210mm, Col Widths (Display): 57/87mm, Print Process: Offset, Screen: 60 lpc, Film: Digital
Copy instructions: *Copy Date:* 15 days prior to publication date

X-LEHTI
1703861L74M-70
Editorial: Alma 360 Asiakasmedia, PL 502/ Munkkiniemen puistotie 25, 00101 HELSINKI
Tel: 10 66 51 02
Email: sami.turunen@alma360.fi **Web site:** http://www.veikkaus.fi
ISSN: 1796-0231
Date Established: 2005; **Freq:** Quarterly; **Cover Price:** Free; **Circ:** 302,637
Usual Pagination: 52
Profile: Magazine about gambling and social issues.
Language(s): Finnish
Readership: Customers of Veikkaus Oy.
CONSUMER: WOMEN'S INTEREST CONSUMER MAGAZINES: Personal Finance

YHDYSKUNTASUUNNITTELU
706594L4D-105
Formerly: Yhteiskuntasuunnittelu
Editorial: Tieteiden talo, Kirkkokatu 6, 00170 HELSINKI **Tel:** 9 22 86 92 70
Email: yss@yss.fi **Web site:** http://www.yss.fi
ISSN: 0788-1010
Date Established: 1963; **Freq:** Quarterly; **Annual Sub.:** EUR 40.00; **Circ:** 600
Usual Pagination: 88
Editor-in-Chief: Pasi Mäenpää
Profile: Magazine containing information on town planning, building and urban studies.
Language(s): Finnish
ADVERTISING RATES:
Full Page Colour .... EUR 250.00

YHTEENVETO
705346L14L-115
Editorial: Maistraatinportti 4 A, 6 krs, 00240 HELSINKI **Tel:** 20 12 35 340 **Fax:** 9 14 72 42
Email: anna.joutsenniemi@akavanerityisalat.fi **Web site:** http://www.akavanerityisalat.fi
ISSN: 0780-7058
Date Established: 1983; **Freq:** 6 issues yearly; Free to qualifying individuals ; **Circ:** 24,993
Usual Pagination: 32
Editor-in-Chief: Anna Joutsenniemi
Profile: Journal of the Confederation of Unions for Academic Professionals in Finland.
Language(s): Finnish
Readership: Read by members.
ADVERTISING RATES:
Full Page Colour .... EUR 2500
SCC .... EUR 34.70
Agency Commission: 15%
Mechanical Data: Bleed Size: 210 x 297mm, Type Area: 195 x 240mm, No. of Columns (Display): 3, Col Widths (Display): 62mm, Print Process: offset, Screen: 60 lpc
BUSINESS: COMMERCE, INDUSTRY & MANAGEMENT: Trade Unions

YHTEISHYVÄ
705119L74C-75
Editorial: Alma 360 Asiakasmedia Oy, PL 502/ Munkkiniemen puistotie 25, 5. krs, 00101 HELSINKI
Tel: 10 66 51 02 **Fax:** 10 66 52 533
Email: tanja.eranto@sok.fi **Web site:** http://www.yhteishyva.fi
ISSN: 0044-0396
Date Established: 1904; **Freq:** Monthly; Free to qualifying individuals ; **Circ:** 1,720,658
Usual Pagination: 132
Managing Editor: Sanna Autio
Profile: Customer-magazine about private household finance administration, health and food planning.
Language(s): Finnish; Swedish
ADVERTISING RATES:
Full Page Colour .... EUR 12990
SCC .... EUR 118.90
Agency Commission: 15%
Mechanical Data: Type Area: 210 x 273mm, No. of Columns (Display): 4, Col Widths (Display): 43mm, Print Process: offset, Screen: 54 lpc
CONSUMER: WOMEN'S INTEREST CONSUMER MAGAZINES: Home & Family

YKKÖSSANOMAT
704884L72-1650
Editorial: Riikantie 2, 09810 NUMMI **Tel:** 19 37 10 76
Fax: 19 37 10 21
Email: ykkossanomat@ykkossanomat.fi **Web site:** http://www.ykkossanomat.fi
ISSN: 0784-0373
Date Established: 1986; **Freq:** Weekly; **Circ:** 3,563
Usual Pagination: 16
Profile: Newspaper issued in Nummi-Pusula, Sammatti, Karjalohja, Suomusjärvi.
Language(s): Finnish
ADVERTISING RATES:
Full Page Colour .... EUR 2109
SCC .... EUR 9.50
Agency Commission: 15%
Mechanical Data: No. of Columns (Display): 6, Bleed Size: 255 x 370mm, Col Length: 370mm, Page Width: 255mm, Col Widths (Display): 40mm
LOCAL NEWSPAPERS

YLÄ-KAINUU
705027L72-1655
Editorial: PL 63 / Kauppakatu 10 A 1, 89601 SUOMUSSALMI **Tel:** 8 63 30 00 **Fax:** 8 63 30 030
Email: yla.toimitus@sps.fi **Web site:** http://www.ylakainuu.fi
Date Established: 1965; **Freq:** 104 issues yearly; **Circ:** 7,980
Usual Pagination: 16
Profile: Newspaper issued in Suomussalmi, Hyrynsalmi and Puolanka.
Language(s): Finnish
ADVERTISING RATES:
Full Page Colour .... EUR 2584
SCC .... EUR 11.80
Agency Commission: 15%
Mechanical Data: Col Widths (Display): 40mm, No. of Columns (Display): 6, Col Length: 360mm, Print Process: offset
LOCAL NEWSPAPERS

YLÄ-KARJALA
704991L72-1660
Editorial: PL 5/Pappilansuora 15, 75501 NURMES
Tel: 10 23 08 600 **Fax:** 10 23 08 620
Email: toimitus@ylakarjala.fi **Web site:** http://www.ylakarjala.fi
ISSN: 0782-5382
Date Established: 1929; **Freq:** 104 issues yearly; **Circ:** 5,471
Usual Pagination: 6
Profile: Newspaper issued in Nurmes and Valtimo.
Language(s): Finnish
ADVERTISING RATES:
Full Page Colour .... EUR 3635
SCC .... EUR 16.60
Agency Commission: 3-15%
Mechanical Data: Page Width: 255mm, Col Widths (Display): 38.75mm, No. of Columns (Display): 6, Col Length: 365mm, Print Process: offset
LOCAL NEWSPAPERS

YLÄ-SATAKUNTA
704917L72-1665
Editorial: PL 6 / Parkanontie 63, 39701 PARKANO
Tel: 3 44 381 **Fax:** 3 44 38 44
Email: toimittajat@ylasatakunta.fi **Web site:** http://www.ylasatakunta.fi
ISSN: 0358-1934
Date Established: 1933; **Freq:** 104 issues yearly; **Circ:** 7,244
Usual Pagination: 16
Profile: Newspaper issued in Karvia, Parkano and Kihniö.
Language(s): Finnish
ADVERTISING RATES:
Full Page Colour .... EUR 1799
SCC .... EUR 7.90
Agency Commission: 15%
Mechanical Data: Col Widths (Display): 44mm, No. of Columns (Display): 6, Print Process: offset, Type Area: 284 x 375mm, Col Length: 375mm, Film: negative
Editions:
Ylä-Satakunta Verkkotoimitus
LOCAL NEWSPAPERS

YLEISLÄÄKÄRI
705293L56A-46
Formerly: Kunnallislääkäri-Kommunalläkaren
Editorial: PL 49 / Mäkelänkatu 2, 00501 HELSINKI
Tel: 9 39 30 758 **Fax:** 9 39 30 773
Email: paivi-maarit.luukkonen@fimnet.fi **Web site:** http://www.yleislaakarit.fi
ISSN: 1796-2889
Date Established: 1922; **Freq:** 6 issues yearly - Published 8/year; **Circ:** 10,400
Usual Pagination: 56
Profile: Magazine with medical, educational and health political information for doctors working in municipalities.
Language(s): Finnish
ADVERTISING RATES:
Full Page Colour .... EUR 3150
SCC .... EUR 37.50
Mechanical Data: Bleed Size: 210 x 280mm, Print Process: offset, Screen: 54-60 lpc, Film: negative

YLÖJÄRVEN UUTISET
704918L72-1675
Editorial: PL 26/ Mikkolantie 7, 33471 YLÖJÄRVI
Tel: 3 34 77 200 **Fax:** 3 34 77 221
Web site: http://www.ylojarvenuutiset.fi
ISSN: 1457-103X
Date Established: 1934; **Freq:** Weekly; **Circ:** 6,828
Usual Pagination: 24
Profile: Newspaper issued in Ylöjärvi.
Language(s): Finnish
ADVERTISING RATES:
Full Page Colour .... EUR 3828
SCC .... EUR 14.50
Agency Commission: 15%
Mechanical Data: Bleed Size: 315 x 460mm, Type Area: 291 x 420mm, Col Length: 440mm, No. of Columns (Display): 6, Col Widths (Display): 46mm, Print Process: offset
Editions:
Ylöjärven Uutiset Verkkotoimitus
LOCAL NEWSPAPERS

YMPÄRISTÖ
15128L57-110
Editorial: PL 140/ Mechelininkatu 34 A, 00251 HELSINKI **Tel:** 20 61 01 23
Web site: http://www.ymparisto.fi
ISSN: 1237-0711
Date Established: 1987; **Freq:** 6 issues yearly; **Circ:** 5,000
Usual Pagination: 24
Editor-in-Chief: Leena Rantajärvi
Profile: Magazine containing articles and discussions on environmental issues featuring research, legislation and the protection and planning of land.
Language(s): Finnish
Readership: Read by professionals and specialists of environmental matters in national and local authorities and private companies, students.
ADVERTISING RATES:
Full Page Colour .... EUR 1600.00
SCC .... EUR 15.20
Mechanical Data: Type Area: 186 x 274mm, Bleed Size: 210 x 297mm, Screen: 60 lpc, Print Process: offset

YMPÄRISTÖASIANTUNTIJA
706008L57-73
Formerly: YKL-posti
Editorial: Vuorikatu 22 A 15, 00100 HELSINKI
Tel: 9 62 26 850 **Fax:** 9 62 26 85 50
Email: tuula.kilpelainen@ykl.fi **Web site:** http://www.ykl.fi
ISSN: 1459-515X
Freq: Quarterly; **Circ:** 5,200
Usual Pagination: 24
Editor-in-Chief: Tuula Kilpeläinen
Profile: Journal for members of the Environment Specialists' Union.
Language(s): Finnish
ADVERTISING RATES:
Full Page Colour .... EUR 800.00
Mechanical Data: Bleed Size: 210 x 297mm, No. of Columns (Display): 3, Col Widths (Display): 56mm, Print Process: offset, Film: negative, Screen: 70 lpc, Type Area: 183 x 267mm

YRITTÄJÄ
14935L14A-90
Editorial: PL 999/ Mannerheimintie 76 A. 3.krs, 00101 HELSINKI **Tel:** 9 22 92 21 **Fax:** 9 22 92 29 99
Email: toimitus@yrittajat.fi **Web site:** http://www.yrittajat.fi
ISSN: 1237-2234
Date Established: 1981; **Freq:** 6 issues yearly; **Circ:** 27,729
Usual Pagination: 76
Editor-in-Chief: Jarmo Hyytiäinen
Profile: Journal of the Confederation of Finnish Entrepreneurs.
Language(s): Finnish
Readership: Read by entrepreneurs.
ADVERTISING RATES:
Full Page Colour .... EUR 4200
SCC .... EUR 37.50
Mechanical Data: Type Area: 175 x 257mm, Col Widths (Display): 45mm, Print Process: offset, Screen: 60 lpc
BUSINESS: COMMERCE, INDUSTRY & MANAGEMENT

YRITYSMAAILMA
705893L63-100
Editorial: Teollisuuskatu 11, 80100 JOENSUU
Tel: 10 82 05 700 **Fax:** 10 82 05 750
Email: joensuun.kustannus@yritma.fi **Web site:** http://www.yritma.fi
Freq: 6 issues yearly; **Cover Price:** Free; **Circ:** 500,000
Usual Pagination: 28
Editor-in-Chief: Risto Käyhkö
Profile: Magazine with company presentation and issued in local versions.
Language(s): Finnish
Readership: It is distributed to companies and official institutions in local versions.
ADVERTISING RATES:
SCC .... EUR 12.70
Mechanical Data: Page Width: 258mm, Col Length: 380mm, No. of Columns (Display): 6, Col Widths (Display): 39mm, Print Process: heatset, Film: negative, Screen: b&w 26-30 lpc, colour 45-55 lpc
BUSINESS: REGIONAL BUSINESS

YRITYSMAAKUNTA
705140L14A-118
Formerly: Yrityssuomalainen
Editorial: PL 159/ Aholaidantie 3, 40101 JYVÄSKYLÄ
Tel: 14 62 20 00 **Fax:** 14 62 24 02
Email: talous@keskisuomalainen.fi **Web site:** http://www.ksml.fi
ISSN: 1458-5529
Freq: Monthly; **Circ:** 73,900
Profile: A joint supplement between small companies in central Finland and the Central Chamber of Commerce issued in the national newspaper Keskisuomalainen.
Language(s): Finnish
Readership: Aimed at small-companies in central Finland.
BUSINESS: COMMERCE, INDUSTRY & MANAGEMENT

YTIMEKÄS
1692282L14A-130
Editorial: Teollisuuden Voima, Olkiluoto, 27160 EURAJOKI **Tel:** 2 83 811 **Fax:** 2 83 81 52 09
Email: tiedotus@tvo.fi **Web site:** http://www.tvo.fi
Freq: Quarterly; **Cover Price:** Free; **Circ:** 4,000
Usual Pagination: 32
Editor-in-Chief: Anneli Nikula
Profile: Magazine about energy for industry needs.
Language(s): Finnish
Readership: Customers of Teollisuuden Voima Oy.

France

Time Difference: GMT + 1 hr (CET - Central European Time)
National Telephone Code: +33
Continent: Europe
Capital: Paris
Principal Language: French
Population: 61875822
Monetary Unit: Euro (EUR)

EMBASSY HIGH COMMISSION: French Embassy: 58 Knightsbridge, London SW1X 7JT
Tel: 020 7201 1000
Fax: 020 7201 1004 Head of Mission: HE Monsieur Gerard Errera
Email: info-londres@diplomatie.fr or consulat.londres-fslt@diplomatie.fr
Website: http://www.ambafrance-uk.org

01 INFORMATIQUE
4637F5B-10
Editorial: 12 rue d'Oradour S/Glane, 75015 PARIS
Tel: 1 71 18 54 00 **Fax:** 1 71 18 52 50
Email: redaction@groupe01.fr **Web site:** http://www.01net.com
ISSN: 0398-1169
Freq: Weekly
Annual Sub.: EUR 228; **Circ:** 55,394
Usual Pagination: 104
Managing Director: Marc Laufer
Profile: Magazine covering all aspects of data processing.
Language(s): French

Readership: Read by professionals and management within the field.
ADVERTISING RATES:
Full Page Colour .... EUR 29200
Mechanical Data: Type Area: 28,5 x 35
BUSINESS: COMPUTERS & AUTOMATION: Data Processing

1,2,3... DETENTE
1817559F94H-512
Editorial: 163 quai du Docteur-Dervaux, 92601, CEDEX ASNIERES **Tel:** 1 41 32 73 15
Fax: 141327305
Email: 123detente@aprr.fr **Web site:** http://www.aprr.fr
ISSN: 1956-7308
Date Established: 2007; **Freq:** Half-yearly - 15 janvier et 15 juin; **Cover Price:** Free; **Circ:** 800,000
Usual Pagination: 32
Editor: Pascal Devertu
Profile: Customer magazine focussing on motorways including family, regional interest, agenda, activities, children, news and road safety. Circulated in the APRR highways.
Language(s): French
Mechanical Data: Type Area: 21 x 29,7
Copy instructions: *Copy Date:* 31 days prior to publication date
CONSUMER: OTHER CLASSIFICATIONS: Customer Magazines

20 MINUTES PARIS
1619401F67B-8401
Editorial: 50-52 boulevard Haussmann, CS 10300, 75427 CEDEX 09 PARIS **Tel:** 1 53 26 65 65
Fax: 1 53 26 65 68
Email: redaction@20minutes.fr **Web site:** http://www.20minutes.fr
ISSN: 1632-1022
Date Established: 2002; **Freq:** Daily - du lundi au vendredi; **Cover Price:** Free; **Circ:** 658,920
Usual Pagination: 32
Publisher: Mathias Cena
Profile: Daily newspaper of general information on the Paris region.
Language(s): French
ADVERTISING RATES:
Full Page Colour .... EUR 55100
Mechanical Data: Type Area: tabloïd
REGIONAL DAILY & SUNDAY NEWSPAPERS: Regional Daily Newspapers

60
1696573F32A-1086
Editorial: Conseil Général, 1 rue Cambry, BP 941 CEDEX, 60024 BEAUVAIS **Tel:** 3 44 06 60 60
Fax: 3 44 06 60 26
Email: carole.michel@cg60.fr **Web site:** http://www.oise.fr
Date Established: 2004; **Freq:** Monthly - Le 15 du mois; **Cover Price:** Free; **Circ:** 325,000
Usual Pagination: 36
Profile: Publication focussing on local government and department issues.
Language(s): French
Mechanical Data: Type Area: A4
BUSINESS: LOCAL GOVERNMENT, LEISURE & RECREATION: Local Government

60 MILLIONS DE CONSOMMATEURS
1617999F74C-451
Editorial: 80 rue Lecourbe, 75015 PARIS
Tel: 1 45 66 20 98 **Fax:** 1 45 67 05 93
Email: mj.husset@inc60.fr **Web site:** http://www.60millions-mag.com
ISSN: 1267-8066
Date Established: 1970; **Freq:** Monthly - fin de mois; **Cover Price:** EUR 4.20
Annual Sub.: EUR 39; **Circ:** 190,000
Usual Pagination: 76
Language(s): French
ADVERTISING RATES:
Full Page Colour .... EUR 16491
Mechanical Data: Type Area: 215 x 275
CONSUMER: WOMEN'S INTEREST CONSUMER MAGAZINES: Home & Family

A NOUS PARIS
754750F72-50
Editorial: 23 rue de Châteaudun, CEDEX 09, 75308 PARIS **Tel:** 1 75 55 10 00 **Fax:** 1 75 55 12 61
Email: redaction@anous.fr **Web site:** http://www.anous.fr
ISSN: 1294-4572
Date Established: 1999; **Freq:** Weekly; **Cover Price:** Free; **Circ:** 284,000 Unique Users
Usual Pagination: 56
Editor: Rik De Nolf; **Managing Director:** Bruno Zaro
Profile: Newspaper focusing on news and events in Paris. Cultural information on the city of Paris: Concert dates, art shows, movie and book review, restaurant addresses. Distributed for free in the Metro and RER network.
Language(s): French
Readership: Read by commuters.
LOCAL NEWSPAPERS

A PARIS VILLE DE PARIS
6992F32A-1097
Editorial: 4 rue de Lobau, 75196, CEDEX 4 PARIS
Tel: 1 42 76 79 82 **Fax:** 142767995
Email: magazineaparis@paris.fr **Web site:** http://www.paris.fr
Date Established: 2002; **Freq:** Quarterly - 03 06 09 12; **Cover Price:** Free; **Circ:** 1,150,000
Usual Pagination: 44
Editor: Anne Sylvie Schneider
Profile: Magazine providing regional and municipal information for Paris.
Language(s): French
Mechanical Data: Type Area: 21 x 27
BUSINESS: LOCAL GOVERNMENT, LEISURE & RECREATION: Local Government

A TOULOUSE
1618570F32A-611
Editorial: MAIRIE, 17 rue de Rémusat, CEDEX 6, 31040 TOULOUSE **Tel:** 5 61 22 21 02
Fax: 5 61 22 21 20
Email: atoulouse@mairie-toulouse.fr **Web site:** http://www.toulouse.fr
Date Established: 1980; **Freq:** Monthly - 1ers lundis de chaque mois; **Cover Price:** Free; **Circ:** 300,000
Usual Pagination: 80
Profile: Municipal publication focussing on local information.
Language(s): French
Mechanical Data: Type Area: 215x 270
BUSINESS: LOCAL GOVERNMENT, LEISURE & RECREATION: Local Government

ACCENTS BOUCHES DU RHONE
1617136F32R-1
Editorial: Conseil Général - Hôtel département, Service communication, 52 avenue Saint Just CEDEX 20, 13256 MARSEILLE **Tel:** 4 91 21 15 37
Fax: 4 91 21 15 90
Email: accents@cg13.fr **Web site:** http://www.cg13.fr
Date Established: 1995; **Freq:** 24 issues yearly - 1ère quinzaine du mois; **Cover Price:** Free; **Circ:** 780,000
Usual Pagination: 40
Profile: Publication focussing on local government and department issues, including economics, events, leisure, cultural and social issues.
Language(s): French
Mechanical Data: Type Area: A 4
BUSINESS: LOCAL GOVERNMENT, LEISURE & RECREATION: Local Government Related

ACTION COMMERCIALE
4808F14A-25
Editorial: 13 rue Louis Pasteur, CEDEX, 92513 BOULOGNE BILLANCOURT **Tel:** 1 46 99 93 93
Fax: 1 46 99 81 40 97 71
Email: lbischoff@editialis.fr **Web site:** http://www.actionco.fr
ISSN: 0752-5192
Date Established: 1982; **Freq:** Monthly - début de mois; **Cover Price:** EUR 7.50
Annual Sub.: EUR 115; **Circ:** 15,674
Usual Pagination: 84
Profile: Magazine containing articles and information concerning commerce and management.
Language(s): French
Readership: Aimed at commercial and marketing directors.
ADVERTISING RATES:
Full Page Mono .... EUR 4012
Full Page Colour .... EUR 5350
Mechanical Data: Type Area: 23 x 30
BUSINESS: COMMERCE, INDUSTRY & MANAGEMENT

L' ACTION FRANCAISE 2000
6366F73-3
Editorial: 10 rue Croix des Petits Champs, 75001 PARIS **Tel:** 1 40 39 92 06 **Fax:** 1 40 26 31 63
Email: fromentouxmi@wanadoo.fr **Web site:** http://action.francaise.free.fr
ISSN: 1166-3286
Date Established: 1947; **Freq:** 26 issues yearly - 1er et 3e jeudi du mois
Annual Sub.: EUR 76; **Circ:** 30,000
Usual Pagination: 16
Profile: Magazine about aspects of contemporary French life.
Language(s): French
Mechanical Data: Type Area: Tabloïd
CONSUMER: NATIONAL & INTERNATIONAL PERIODICALS

ACTIVES, LES PAYS DE SAVOIE
6394F74A-10
Editorial: 7 route de Nanfray, 74960 CRAN-GEVRIER
Tel: 4 50 33 35 35 **Fax:** 4 50 52 11 06
Email: actives@ecosavoie.fr **Web site:** http://www.activesmag.fr
ISSN: 1244-8613
Date Established: 1992; **Freq:** Monthly - 1er samedi de chaque mois; **Cover Price:** Free; **Circ:** 20,000
Usual Pagination: 100
Profile: Magazine for the well-informed French woman. Features include contemporary problems in society, working women, business, families and leisure.
Language(s): French
ADVERTISING RATES:
Full Page Colour .... EUR 1490
Mechanical Data: Type Area: 230 x 300
Copy instructions: *Copy Date:* 10 days prior to publication date
CONSUMER: WOMEN'S INTEREST CONSUMER MAGAZINES: Women's Interest

AD - ARCHITECTURAL DIGEST
624294F74C-10
Editorial: 26 rue Cambacérès, 75008 PARIS
Tel: 1 53 43 61 72 60 00 **Fax:** 1 53 43 61 70
Email: oduboy@condenast.fr
Date Established: 2000; **Freq:** Monthly - First Month; **Cover Price:** EUR 4.90
Annual Sub.: EUR 39.30; **Circ:** 101,295
Usual Pagination: 188
Profile: Magazine containing information about homes, decoration, architecture and lifestyle.
Language(s): French
Readership: Aimed at the general public.
ADVERTISING RATES:
Full Page Mono .... EUR 9010
Full Page Colour .... EUR 10600
Mechanical Data: Type Area: 212 x 275
Copy instructions: *Copy Date:* 31 days prior to publication date
CONSUMER: WOMEN'S INTEREST CONSUMER MAGAZINES: Home & Family

LES AEROPORTS DE PARIS MAGAZINE
1691242F89D-207
Editorial: 6 rue Daru, 75379 CEDEX 08 PARIS
Tel: 1 44 15 30 00
Web site: http://www.prismapub.com
ISSN: 1954-5321
Date Established: 2005; **Freq:** Monthly - tous les mois; **Cover Price:** Free; **Circ:** 250,000
Usual Pagination: 84
Profile: Airport publication focussing on culture, shopping, fashion, society and local information. Bilingual French and English.
Language(s): English; French
Mechanical Data: Type Area: 205x270
Copy instructions: *Copy Date:* 31 days prior to publication date
CONSUMER: HOLIDAYS & TRAVEL: In-Flight Magazines

AFFICHES D'ALSACE LORRAINE MONITEUR DES SOUMISSIONS ET VENTES DE BOIS DE L'EST
5472F44-20
Editorial: 3 rue Saint-Pierre-le-Jeune, BP 50238, 67006 STRASBOURG **Tel:** 3 88 21 59 79
Fax: 388235624
Email: redaction@affiches-moniteur.com **Web site:** http://www.affiches-moniteur.com
ISSN: 1169-2634
Date Established: 1919; **Freq:** 104 issues yearly - mardi et vendredi; **Cover Price:** EUR 0.80
Annual Sub.: EUR 49; **Circ:** 10,000
Usual Pagination: 40
Editor: Gilbert Brézillon
Profile: Professional journal monitoring the wood industry in the Bas-Rhin and Moselle region. Focuses on juridical and economic information.
Language(s): French
Mechanical Data: Type Area: A 4
Copy instructions: *Copy Date:* 15 days prior to publication date
BUSINESS: LEGAL

AFRIQUE AGRICULTURE
4990F21A-50
Editorial: ATC, 23 rue Dupont des Loges, BP 90 146 CEDEX 1, 57004 METZ **Tel:** 3 87 69 18 18
Fax: 3 87 69 18 14
Email: redac@groupe-atc.com
ISSN: 0337-9515
Date Established: 1975; **Freq:** 24 issues yearly - début de mois; **Cover Price:** EUR 7.60
Annual Sub.: EUR 39.50; **Circ:** 8,000
Usual Pagination: 80
Profile: Publication about African farming methods including articles on agriculture, livestock, horticulture, machinery, hydraulics, forestry and fishing.
Language(s): French
ADVERTISING RATES:
Full Page Mono .... EUR 1650
Full Page Colour .... EUR 2675
Mechanical Data: Type Area: 210 x 297
BUSINESS: AGRICULTURE & FARMING

L' AGEFI
4465F1A-50
Editorial: 8 rue du Sentier, CEDEX 02, 75082 PARIS
Tel: 1 53 00 27 03 **Fax:** 1 53 00 27 28
Email: agarabedian@agefi.fr **Web site:** http://www.agefi.fr
ISSN: 1777-165X
Date Established: 2005; **Freq:** Daily; **Cover Price:** EUR 6.50; **Circ:** 15,000
Usual Pagination: 68
Profile: Magazine focussing on finance, investment, asset management, banking and insurance. Aimed at financial professionals and advisers. Local Translation: Journal quotidien électronique spécialisé en économie et finances. Traite en profondeur de la stratégie des entreprises financières, et dissèque leurs innovations et nouveaux produits.
Language(s): French
ADVERTISING RATES:
Full Page Colour .... EUR 12500
Mechanical Data: Type Area: 21 x 27
BUSINESS: FINANCE & ECONOMICS

AGIR EN PICARDIE
1617213F32A-1070
Editorial: Direction de la communication, 11 mail Albert 1er, BP 2616 CEDEX, 80026 AMIENS
Tel: 3 22 97 37 37 **Fax:** 3 22 97 19 34
Email: lsivignon@cr-picardie.fr
ISSN: 0293-4663
Date Established: 1986; **Freq:** 24 issues yearly - 1er du mois; **Cover Price:** Free; **Circ:** 840,000
Usual Pagination: 44
Profile: Publication focussing on local government and department issues.
Language(s): French
Mechanical Data: Type Area: 230 x 285
BUSINESS: LOCAL GOVERNMENT, LEISURE & RECREATION: Local Government

AGRA PRESSE HEBDO
4992F21A-110
Editorial: 84 boulevard de Sébastopol, 75003 PARIS
Tel: 1 42 74 28 00 **Fax:** 1 42 74 29 36
Email: fxsimon@agra-presse.be **Web site:** http://www.agrapresse.fr
ISSN: 0183-7656
Date Established: 1949; **Freq:** Weekly - lundi; **Annual Sub.:** EUR 1585; **Circ:** 1,500
Usual Pagination: 54
Profile: Agricultural magazine.
Language(s): French
ADVERTISING RATES:
Full Page Colour .... EUR 2000
BUSINESS: AGRICULTURE & FARMING

AGRANDIR ET PROTEGER SA MAISON
6438F74C-20
Editorial: 27 rue Pétion de Villeneuve, 75011 PARIS
Tel: 1 43 79 07 37 **Fax:** 1 43 79 76 88
Email: redaction@decoration-francaise.fr
ISSN: 0753-1818
Date Established: 1984; **Freq:** Quarterly - les mois 01 02 07 10
Annual Sub.: EUR 80; **Circ:** 30,000
Usual Pagination: 100
Profile: Pan-European magazine about decoration, art and design.
Language(s): French
Readership: Aimed at people with an interest in design and home decoration.
ADVERTISING RATES:
Full Page Mono .... EUR 3400
Full Page Colour .... EUR 5564
Mechanical Data: Type Area: 21 x 29,7
Copy instructions: *Copy Date:* 10 days prior to publication date
CONSUMER: WOMEN'S INTEREST CONSUMER MAGAZINES: Home & Family

AGRICULTEURS DE FRANCE
4993F21A-300
Editorial: 8 rue d'Athènes, 75009 PARIS
Tel: 1 44 53 15 15 **Fax:** 1 44 53 15 25
Email: saf@saf.asso.fr
ISSN: 0339-4433
Date Established: 1837; **Freq:** 24 issues yearly - le 15 de 02-04-06-08-10-12
Annual Sub.: EUR 46; **Circ:** 4,000
Usual Pagination: 36
Editor-in-Chief: Valery Elisseeff
Profile: Journal covering all aspects of French agriculture in relation to economics.
Language(s): French
ADVERTISING RATES:
Full Page Mono .... EUR 1525
Full Page Colour .... EUR 2687
Mechanical Data: Type Area: 210 x 297
Copy instructions: *Copy Date:* 15 days prior to publication date
BUSINESS: AGRICULTURE & FARMING

AIR ACTUALITES
5408F40-5
Editorial: SIRPA AIR, 5 bis avenue de la Porte de Sèvres, CEDEX 15, 75509 PARIS **Tel:** 1 45 52 90 80
Fax: 1 45 52 90 65
Email: magazine@air-actualites.com **Web site:** http://www.defense.gouv.fr/air
ISSN: 0002-2152
Freq: Monthly - 1ère semaine du mois; **Cover Price:** EUR 4.20
Annual Sub.: EUR 33; **Circ:** 33,000
Usual Pagination: 68
Profile: Journal focusing on the air-force and aeronautics.
Language(s): French
ADVERTISING RATES:
Full Page Colour .... EUR 3350
Mechanical Data: Type Area: 200 x 300
BUSINESS: DEFENCE

AIR ET COSMOS
1617564F6A-303
Editorial: 1 bis avenue de la République, 75011 PARIS **Tel:** 1 49 29 32 00 **Fax:** 1 49 29 32 01
Email: air-cosmos@air-cosmos.com **Web site:** http://www.air-cosmos.com
ISSN: 1240-3113
Date Established: 1963; **Freq:** Weekly - vendredi; **Cover Price:** EUR 4.50
Annual Sub.: EUR 177; **Circ:** 23,737
Usual Pagination: 50
Profile: Publication focussing on aeronautics including industry, technology, civil and military applications and space.
Language(s): French
ADVERTISING RATES:
Full Page Mono .... EUR 4400

Full Page Colour .... EUR 7600
Mechanical Data: Type Area: A 4
Copy instructions: *Copy Date:* 10 days prior to publication date
BUSINESS: AVIATION & AERONAUTICS

AIR FRANCE MADAME 6413F74A-258
Editorial: 5 rue d'Aguesseau, 75008 PARIS
Tel: 1 53 43 60 00 **Fax:** 1 53 43 61 90
Email: mpointurier@condenast.fr
ISSN: 0980-7519
Date Established: 1986; **Freq:** 24 issues yearly - 1er du mois; **Cover Price:** Free; **Circ:** 263,949
Usual Pagination: 196
Profile: Women's magazine containing features on beauty, fashion and accessories, decoration, art, culture, and tourism.
Language(s): French
ADVERTISING RATES:
Full Page Mono .... EUR 12000
Full Page Colour .... EUR 15000
Mechanical Data: Type Area: 210 x 285
Copy instructions: *Copy Date:* 21 days prior to publication date
CONSUMER: WOMEN'S INTEREST CONSUMER MAGAZINES: Women's Interest

AIR FRANCE MAGAZINE
7221F89D-10
Editorial: Rédaction, 5 rue Sébastien Bottin, 75007 PARIS **Tel:** 1 49 54 16 42 **Fax:** 1 49 54 16 40
Email: valerie.degivry@gallimard.fr
ISSN: 1290-1563
Date Established: 1997; **Freq:** Monthly - le 1er du mois; **Cover Price:** Free; **Circ:** 390,271
Usual Pagination: 293
Profile: In-flight magazine of Air France. Includes reviews and articles on travel, cinema, music and hotels.
Language(s): French
ADVERTISING RATES:
Full Page Mono .... EUR 16264
Full Page Colour .... EUR 20300
Mechanical Data: Type Area: 195x260
Copy instructions: *Copy Date:* 62 days prior to publication date
CONSUMER: HOLIDAYS & TRAVEL: In-Flight Magazines

L' AISNE CONSEIL GENERAL DE L'AISNE 1617164F32A-1028
Editorial: Hôtel-du-Département, Rue Paul-Doumer, 02013 CEDEX LAON **Tel:** 3 23 24 62 80
Fax: 323246284
Email: servicecom@cg02.fr **Web site:** http://www.aisne.com
ISSN: 1262-5256
Date Established: 1993; **Freq:** 6 issues yearly - 1ère quinzaine des mois impairs; **Cover Price:** Free; **Circ:** 245,000
Usual Pagination: 32
Editor: Yves Daudigny
Profile: Publication focussing on local government and department issues, including economics, culture, heath, tourism and sport.
Language(s): French
Mechanical Data: Type Area: 23 x 30
BUSINESS: LOCAL GOVERNMENT, LEISURE & RECREATION: Local Government

L' AISNE NOUVELLE 6207F67B-2100
Editorial: 10 Boulevard Henri Martin, BP 149, CEDEX, 2103 SAINT-QUENTIN **Tel:** 3 23 06 36 36
Fax: 3 23 64 26 06
Email: redactionstq@aisnenouvelle.fr **Web site:** http://aisnenouvelle.fr
ISSN: 1770-1546
Date Established: 1944; **Freq:** Daily - lundi mardi jeudi samedi; **Cover Price:** EUR 0.80
Annual Sub.: EUR 129; **Circ:** 19,004
Usual Pagination: 24
Profile: L'Aines Nouvelle is a current events newspaper covering the Aisne department and its region. It offers also regular magazine columns (Cars, cultural life, horse races). Thursday price including TV Guide: 1,05 €.
Language(s): French
ADVERTISING RATES:
Full Page Mono .... EUR 2714
REGIONAL DAILY & SUNDAY NEWSPAPERS: Regional Daily Newspapers

ALPES MAGAZINE 7171F89A-29
Editorial: Savoie Technolac, 12 allée du Lac de Garde, BP 308 CEDEX, 73377 LE BOURGET DU LAC
Tel: 4 79 26 28 26 **Fax:** 4 79 26 27 89
Email: alpes@milan.fr **Web site:** http://www.alpesmagazine.com
Date Established: 1989; **Freq:** 24 issues yearly - fin 02 04 06 08 10 12; **Cover Price:** EUR 5.95
Annual Sub.: EUR 43; **Circ:** 24,626
Usual Pagination: 100
Profile: Magazine promoting the Alps.
Language(s): French
ADVERTISING RATES:
Full Page Colour .... EUR 4300
Mechanical Data: Type Area: 21 x 27
Copy instructions: *Copy Date:* 62 days prior to publication date
CONSUMER: HOLIDAYS & TRAVEL: Travel

L' ALSACE 1619420F67B-8420
Editorial: 18 rue de Thann, CEDEX 9, 68945 MULHOUSE **Tel:** 3 89 32 70 00 **Fax:** 3 89 32 11 26
Email: redaction@lalsace.fr **Web site:** http://www.lalsace.fr
ISSN: 0245-662X
Date Established: 1945; **Freq:** Daily - chaque matin; **Cover Price:** EUR 0.90
Annual Sub.: EUR 321; **Circ:** 105,795
Usual Pagination: 40
Profile: Daily regional newspaper covering general, regional and local current events and sports. Saturday price: 1.60 €.
Language(s): French
ADVERTISING RATES:
Full Page Mono .... EUR 6797
Full Page Colour .... EUR 8496
Copy instructions: *Copy Date:* 2 days prior to publication date
REGIONAL DAILY & SUNDAY NEWSPAPERS: Regional Daily Newspapers

L' ALSACE EDITION DE GUEBWILLER 6195F67B-2200
Editorial: 85-87 rue de la République, BP 84, 68502 GUEBWILLER **Tel:** 3 89 76 81 05 **Fax:** 389748242
Email: redaction-gu@lalsace.fr **Web site:** http://www.lalsace.fr
ISSN: 0245-662X
Date Established: 1944; **Freq:** Daily - Haut-Rhin (68); **Cover Price:** EUR 0.90
Annual Sub.: EUR 321
Usual Pagination: 48
Profile: Daily regional newspaper covering general, regional and local current events and sports. 6 to 8 local news pages.
Language(s): French
REGIONAL DAILY & SUNDAY NEWSPAPERS: Regional Daily Newspapers

ALTERNATIVES ECONOMIQUES 6367F73-10
Editorial: 28 rue du Sentier, 75002 PARIS
Tel: 1 44 88 28 90
Email: redaction@alternatives-economiques.fr **Web site:** http://www.alternatives-economiques.fr
ISSN: 0247-3739
Date Established: 1980; **Freq:** Monthly - Early in the month; **Cover Price:** EUR 3.80
Annual Sub.: EUR 34; **Circ:** 115,186
Usual Pagination: 100
Profile: International magazine for the general public covering topical economic subjects in an easy-to-understand format. Includes Europe, the Euro, globalisation, health, urbanisation, environment, education, management and the effect of new technology.
Language(s): French
Readership: Read by economists, lecturers and students.
ADVERTISING RATES:
Full Page Colour .... EUR 6300
Mechanical Data: Type Area: A 4
Copy instructions: *Copy Date:* 10 days prior to publication date
CONSUMER: NATIONAL & INTERNATIONAL PERIODICALS

L' AMATEUR DE BORDEAUX
6579F74P-15
Editorial: 22 rue Letellier, cedex 15, 75739 PARIS
Tel: 1 43 23 45 72 **Fax:** 1 43 23 04 95
Email: degustation@lamateurdevin.com **Web site:** http://www.lamateurdevin.com
ISSN: 2102-4200
Date Established: 1981; **Freq:** Quarterly - 03-06-09-12; **Cover Price:** EUR 6.80
Annual Sub.: EUR 26; **Circ:** 38,000
Usual Pagination: 96
Profile: Magazine containing articles about Bordeaux wine, including profiles of regions and tasting events coverage.
Language(s): English; French
ADVERTISING RATES:
Full Page Colour .... EUR 4400
Mechanical Data: Type Area: 190 x 285
Copy instructions: *Copy Date:* 31 days prior to publication date
CONSUMER: WOMEN'S INTEREST CONSUMER MAGAZINES: Food & Cookery

L' AMATEUR DE CIGARE
7120F86C-5
Editorial: 2 avenue du Général Leclerc, 75014 PARIS
Tel: 1 45 87 14 88 **Fax:** 1 47 07 50 47
Email: redaction@amateurdecigare.com **Web site:** http://www.amateurdecigare.com
ISSN: 1254-6798
Date Established: 1994; **Freq:** 24 issues yearly - 02 04 06 08 10 12; **Cover Price:** EUR 5.50
Annual Sub.: EUR 25; **Circ:** 20,000
Usual Pagination: 86
Profile: Magazine containing articles and information about cigars, including the history and tradition, also reviews different brands of cigar.
Language(s): French
Readership: Aimed at cigar smokers.
ADVERTISING RATES:
Full Page Colour .... EUR 7000
Mechanical Data: Type Area: 220 x 285
Copy instructions: *Copy Date:* 21 days prior to publication date
CONSUMER: ADULT & GAY MAGAZINES: Men's Lifestyle Magazines

AMC - LE MONITEUR ARCHITECTURE 4581F4A-10
Editorial: 17 rue d'Uzès, CEDEX 02, 75108 PARIS
Tel: 1 40 13 30 30 **Fax:** 1 40 13 32 02
Email: amc@groupemoniteur.fr **Web site:** http://www.groupemoniteur.fr
ISSN: 0998-4194
Date Established: 1980; **Freq:** Monthly - vers le 5 du mois; **Cover Price:** EUR 23
Annual Sub.: EUR 164; **Circ:** 14,411
Usual Pagination: 148
Editor-in-Chief: Jean-François Drevon
Profile: Journal covering architecture, design, urban planning and construction.
Language(s): French
ADVERTISING RATES:
Full Page Mono .... EUR 5200
Full Page Colour .... EUR 6500
Mechanical Data: Type Area: 300 x 230
Copy instructions: *Copy Date:* 31 days prior to publication date
BUSINESS: ARCHITECTURE & BUILDING: Architecture

L' AMI DES JARDINS ET DE LA MAISON 6440F74C-30
Editorial: Immeuble Trait d'Union, 8 rue François Ory, 92120 MONTROUGE **Tel:** 1 46 48 48 06
Fax: 1 46 48 48 60
Email: amidesjardins@mondadori.fr **Web site:** http://www.mondadoripub.fr
ISSN: 1277-7765
Date Established: 1930; **Freq:** Monthly - le 15 du mois; **Cover Price:** EUR 4.30; **Circ:** 155,770
Usual Pagination: 140
Profile: Magazine specialising in garden and house renovation, including product news, methods and materials.
Language(s): French
ADVERTISING RATES:
Full Page Colour .... EUR 12500
Mechanical Data: Type Area: A 4
Copy instructions: *Copy Date:* 15 days prior to publication date
CONSUMER: WOMEN'S INTEREST CONSUMER MAGAZINES: Home & Family

AMINA 6395F74A-15
Editorial: 11 rue de Téhéran, 75008 PARIS
Tel: 1 45 62 74 76 **Fax:** 1 45 63 22 48
Email: amina9@wanadoo.fr
ISSN: 0244-0008
Date Established: 1972; **Freq:** Monthly - le 28 du mois précédent
Annual Sub.: EUR 22; **Circ:** 50,767
Usual Pagination: 192
Profile: This magazine covers fashion, beauty, health, education and family matters. It is aimed at women of the African-Caribbean community.
Language(s): French
Readership: Aimed at women of the African-Caribbean community.
ADVERTISING RATES:
Full Page Mono .... EUR 1350
Full Page Colour .... EUR 2000
Mechanical Data: Type Area: 21 x 27,5
CONSUMER: WOMEN'S INTEREST CONSUMER MAGAZINES: Women's Interest

ANGELINE'S MAG 1618066F74B-223
Editorial: 83 avenue de Clichy, 75017 PARIS
Email: fadyelkhoury@yahoo.com
ISSN: 1143-6395
Date Established: 1992; **Freq:** Quarterly - début de trimestre (01 04 07 10)
Annual Sub.: EUR 22.87; **Circ:** 200,000
Usual Pagination: 82
Language(s): French
Mechanical Data: Type Area: 226 x 297
Copy instructions: *Copy Date:* 14 days prior to publication date
CONSUMER: WOMEN'S INTEREST CONSUMER MAGAZINES: Women's Interest - Fashion

LES ANNEES LASER 6887F78A-40
Editorial: 20 passage Turquetil, 75011 PARIS
Tel: 1 55 25 80 00 **Fax:** 1 55 25 80 08
Email: patrick.marteau@annees-laser.com **Web site:** http://www.annees-laser.com
ISSN: 1157-7002
Date Established: 1990; **Freq:** Monthly - variable; **Cover Price:** EUR 4.60
Annual Sub.: EUR 49; **Circ:** 85,000
Usual Pagination: 140
Profile: International magazine focusing on DVD home cinema.
Language(s): French
ADVERTISING RATES:
Full Page Colour .... EUR 4950
Mechanical Data: Type Area: 210 x 297
CONSUMER: CONSUMER ELECTRONICS: Hi-Fi & Recording

AP - HP MAGAZINE 5789F56C-15
Editorial: Assistance Publique Hôpitaux Paris, 10 rue des Fossés St Marcel, 75005 PARIS
Tel: 1 40 27 52 86 **Fax:** 1 40 27 43 59
Email: jean-michel.forestier@sap.aphp.fr
ISSN: 1153-4494
Date Established: 1990; **Freq:** 24 issues yearly - 01 03 05 07 09 et 11; **Cover Price:** Free; **Circ:** 120,000
Usual Pagination: 32
Profile: Journal containing information about Parisian hospitals and the health and social security services.
Language(s): French
ADVERTISING RATES:
Full Page Colour .... EUR 6800
Mechanical Data: Type Area: A 4
Copy instructions: *Copy Date:* 31 days prior to publication date
BUSINESS: HEALTH & MEDICAL: Hospitals

APRES-VENTE AUTOMOBILE
5267F31A-95
Editorial: 40 rue Edith Cavell, 92400 COURBEVOIE
Tel: 1 41 88 09 00 **Fax:** 1 41 88 09 19
Email: jmpierret@publi-expert.fr
ISSN: 1779-0174
Date Established: 2006; **Freq:** Monthly - le 10 du mois; **Cover Price:** EUR 4.50
Annual Sub.: EUR 38; **Circ:** 38,566
Usual Pagination: 56
Profile: Journal concerning spare parts for cars and lorries. Official journal of the Car Distribution Association.
Language(s): French
Readership: Aimed at distributors and suppliers of car spare parts.
ADVERTISING RATES:
Full Page Colour .... EUR 6700
Mechanical Data: Type Area: 230 x 300
BUSINESS: MOTOR TRADE: Motor Trade Accessories

L' AQUITAINE CONSEIL REGIONAL D'AQUITAINE
1617219F32A-1072
Editorial: 14 rue François-de-Sourdis, 33077 BORDEAUX CEDEX **Tel:** 5 57 57 02 80
Fax: 5 57 57 02 47
Email: laquitaine@aquitaine.fr **Web site:** http://journal.aquitaine.fr
ISSN: 1634-2917
Date Established: 2002; **Freq:** 6 issues yearly - Variable; **Cover Price:** Free; **Circ:** 1,350,000
Usual Pagination: 24
Editor: Alain Rousset
Profile: Publication focussing on local government and department issues.
Language(s): French
Mechanical Data: Type Area: tabloïd
Copy instructions: *Copy Date:* pas de publicité
BUSINESS: LOCAL GOVERNMENT, LEISURE & RECREATION: Local Government

ARABIES 7033F82-15_50
Editorial: 18 rue de Varize, 75016 PARIS
Tel: 1 47 66 46 00 **Fax:** 1 43 80 73 62
Email: catherine@arabies.com **Web site:** http://www.arabies.com
ISSN: 0983-1509
Date Established: 1987; **Freq:** Monthly - le 29-30 du mois; **Cover Price:** EUR 4.50
Annual Sub.: EUR 48; **Circ:** 46,900
Usual Pagination: 68
Profile: Magazine containing economic, political and cultural information for the Arab world.
Language(s): French
ADVERTISING RATES:
Full Page Mono .... EUR 3800
Full Page Colour .... EUR 5300
Mechanical Data: Type Area: 22 x 27
CONSUMER: CURRENT AFFAIRS & POLITICS

L' ARBORICULTURE FRUITIERE
5220F26C-10
Editorial: 23 rue Dupont des Loges, BP 90146, CEDEX 1, 57004 METZ **Tel:** 3 87 69 18 18
Fax: 3 87 69 18 14
Email: arbo@groupe-atc.com
ISSN: 0003-794X
Freq: Monthly - beginnig of the month; **Cover Price:** EUR 5.30
Annual Sub.: EUR 52.90; **Circ:** 6,213
Usual Pagination: 48
Profile: This magazine covers fruit production and the economy.
Language(s): French
ADVERTISING RATES:
Full Page Mono .... EUR 1570
Full Page Colour .... EUR 2635
Mechanical Data: Type Area: 210 x 297
BUSINESS: GARDEN TRADE

L' ARGUS DE ASSURANCE
1617015F1D-123
Editorial: Antony Parc 2, 10 place du Général de Gaulle, 92160 ANTONY **Tel:** 1 77 92 92 92
Fax: 1 77 92 98 19
Email: redac@largusdelassurance.com **Web site:** http://www.argusdelassurance.com
ISSN: 1626-4428
Date Established: 1877; **Freq:** Weekly
Annual Sub.: EUR 149; **Circ:** 21,797
Usual Pagination: 70
Profile: Publication focussing on insurance including technical and legal issues.
Language(s): French
ADVERTISING RATES:
Full Page Colour .... EUR 5060
Mechanical Data: Type Area: A 4

Copy instructions: *Copy Date:* 7 days prior to publication date
BUSINESS: FINANCE & ECONOMICS: Insurance

L' ARGUS DE AUTOMOBILE

5259F77A-10
Editorial: 52 rue de la Victoire, 75009 PARIS
Tel: 1 53 29 11 00 **Fax:** 1 49 27 09 50
Email: dlaurent@argusauto.com **Web site:** http://www.argusauto.com
ISSN: 0751-5545
Date Established: 1927; **Freq:** Weekly - jeudi; **Cover Price:** EUR 2.95
Annual Sub.: EUR 95; **Circ:** 44,663
Usual Pagination: 163
Profile: This car magazine covers new and second hand cars. Topics include fixtures, valuations, test reports, repairs and advice on selling and buying vehicles.
Language(s): French
ADVERTISING RATES:
Full Page Mono .... EUR 8400
Full Page Colour .... EUR 11950
Mechanical Data: Type Area: 29,7 x 23
CONSUMER: MOTORING & CYCLING: Motoring

LES ARMEES D'AUJOURD'HUI

5411F40-36
Editorial: DICOD - Ecole Militaire, 1 place Joffre, 75007 PARIS **Tel:** 1 44 42 43 01 **Fax:** 1 44 42 58 89
Email: olivier.destefanis@dicod.defense.gouv.fr **Web site:** http://www.defense.gouv.fr
ISSN: 0338-3520
Date Established: 1975; **Freq:** Monthly - 1ère semaine du mois
Annual Sub.: EUR 20; **Circ:** 100,000
Usual Pagination: 68
Profile: Review of the French armed forces.
Language(s): French
ADVERTISING RATES:
Full Page Colour .... EUR 5000
Mechanical Data: Type Area: 200 x 280
BUSINESS: DEFENCE

L' ART ET DECORATION

6441F74C-40
Editorial: 149 rue Anatole France, CEDEX, 92534 LEVALLOIS PERRET **Tel:** 1 41 34 67 38
Email: artdeco@lagardere-active.com **Web site:** http://www.art-decoration.fr
ISSN: 0004-3168
Date Established: 1897; **Freq:** Monthly
Annual Sub.: EUR 32; **Circ:** 315,965
Usual Pagination: 248
Profile: International magazine about home renovation and decoration.
Language(s): French
ADVERTISING RATES:
Full Page Colour .... EUR 25500
Mechanical Data: Type Area: 23 x 30
Copy instructions: *Copy Date:* 62 days prior to publication date
CONSUMER: WOMEN'S INTEREST CONSUMER MAGAZINES: Home & Family

ART PRESS

7074F84A-50
Editorial: 8 rue François Villon, 75015 PARIS
Tel: 1 53 68 65 65 **Fax:** 1 53 68 65 77
Email: c.millet@artpress.fr **Web site:** http://www.art-press.fr
ISSN: 0245-5676
Date Established: 1972; **Freq:** Monthly - the 22nd of the month; **Cover Price:** EUR 6.50
Annual Sub.: EUR 66.50; **Circ:** 50,000
Profile: Magazine focusing on contemporary art, including plastic art, architecture, dance, literature, music, theatre and media.
Language(s): French
ADVERTISING RATES:
Full Page Mono .... EUR 2286
Full Page Colour .... EUR 3430
Copy instructions: *Copy Date:* 31 days prior to publication date
CONSUMER: THE ARTS & LITERARY: Arts

ARTS ET METIERS MAG

1618269F19F-38
Editorial: 9 bis avenue d'Iéna, CEDEX 16, 75783 PARIS **Tel:** 1 40 69 27 47 00 **Fax:** 1 40 20 58 46
Email: amm@arts-et-metiers.asso.fr **Web site:** http://www.artsetmetiersmagazine.com
ISSN: 0999-4084
Date Established: 1847; **Freq:** Monthly - vers le 07 du mois
Annual Sub.: EUR 30; **Circ:** 12,857
Usual Pagination: 84
Profile: Publication focussing on industry and engineering.
Language(s): French
ADVERTISING RATES:
Full Page Colour .... EUR 6000
Mechanical Data: Type Area: 22 x 28
Copy instructions: *Copy Date:* 15 days prior to publication date
BUSINESS: ENGINEERING & MACHINERY: Production & Mechanical Engineering

AUJOURD'HUI EN FRANCE

1619399F65A-161
Editorial: 25 avenue Michelet, 93408 SAINT-OUEN
Tel: 1 40 10 30 30 **Fax:** 1 40 10 35 17
Web site: http://www.leparisien.fr
ISSN: 1247-4282
Date Established: 1994; **Freq:** Daily - matin; **Cover Price:** EUR 0.90
Annual Sub.: EUR 249.60; **Circ:** 187,786
Usual Pagination: 45
Editor: Marie-Odile Amaury; **Managing Director:** Jean Hornain
Profile: Daily national newspaper providing articles of general interest and covering politics, finance, current affairs, lifestyle and culture.
Language(s): French
ADVERTISING RATES:
Full Page Mono .... EUR 44300
Full Page Colour .... EUR 61800
Mechanical Data: Type Area: Tabloïd
NATIONAL DAILY & SUNDAY NEWSPAPERS: National Daily Newspapers

L' AUTO JOURNAL

6813F77A-50_50
Editorial: Immeuble Trait d'Union, 8 rue François Ory, 92120 MONTROUGE **Tel:** 1 41 33 50 00
Fax: 1 41 33 57 04
Email: autojournal@mondadori.fr **Web site:** http://www.autojournal.fr
ISSN: 1252-5634
Date Established: 1950; **Freq:** 26 issues yearly - 1 jeudi sur 2; **Cover Price:** EUR 3.30
Annual Sub.: EUR 64; **Circ:** 110,831
Managing Director: Jean-Luc Breysse
Profile: Magazine focusing on all aspects of motoring.
Language(s): French
Readership: Aimed at the general public.
ADVERTISING RATES:
Full Page Colour .... EUR 10350
CONSUMER: MOTORING & CYCLING: Motoring

AUTO MOTO

6805F77A-5
Editorial: 149 rue Anatole France, 92300 LEVALLOIS PERRET **Tel:** 1 41 34 60 00 **Fax:** 1 41 34 95 26
Email: christophe.boulain@lagardere-active.com
Web site: http://www.autonews.fr
Date Established: 1994; **Freq:** Monthly - le 20
Annual Sub.: EUR 30; **Circ:** 269,059
Usual Pagination: 136
Publisher: Franck Espiasse-Cabau
Profile: Magazine containing information about new cars, including road tests and a buyers guide.
Language(s): French
ADVERTISING RATES:
Full Page Mono .... EUR 18800
Full Page Colour .... EUR 18800
Mechanical Data: Type Area: 215 x 287
CONSUMER: MOTORING & CYCLING: Motoring

AUTO PLUS

6815F77A-54
Editorial: Immeuble Trait d'Union, 8 rue François Ory, 92120 MONTROUGE **Tel:** 1 41 33 50 00
Fax: 1 41 33 57 06
Web site: http://www.autoplus.fr
ISSN: 0092-8154
Date Established: 1988; **Freq:** Weekly - le mardi;
Cover Price: EUR 1.90
Annual Sub.: EUR 79; **Circ:** 305,614
Usual Pagination: 72
Profile: Magazine providing general motoring news, advice and information.
Language(s): French
Readership: Aimed at car enthusiasts.
ADVERTISING RATES:
Full Page Colour .... EUR 19250
Mechanical Data: Type Area: 227 x 327
Copy instructions: *Copy Date:* 28 days prior to publication date
CONSUMER: MOTORING & CYCLING: Motoring

AUTO-HEBDO

6812F77D-127
Editorial: SFEP, 48/50 Boulevard Sénard, 92210 SAINT CLOUD **Tel:** 1 47 11 20 43 **Fax:** 1 46 02 09 10
Email: courrier@autoh.hommell.com **Web site:** http://www.autohebdo.fr
ISSN: 0395-4366
Date Established: 1976; **Freq:** Weekly; **Cover Price:** EUR 3.20
Annual Sub.: EUR 99; **Circ:** 32,370
Usual Pagination: 76
Profile: Motoring magazine including industry news, tests, new products, national and international motor sport news.
Language(s): French
ADVERTISING RATES:
Full Page Colour .... EUR 4500
Mechanical Data: Type Area: 300 x 225
CONSUMER: MOTORING & CYCLING: Motor Sports

L' AUTOMOBILE & ENTREPRISE

5264F49D-2
Editorial: Immeuble Parc II, 10 place du Général de Gaulle, 92160 ANTONY **Tel:** 1 77 92 92 92
Fax: 1 77 92 98 26
Email: redactionae@etai.fr **Web site:** http://www.automobile-entreprise.com
ISSN: 1259-3095
Date Established: 1994; **Freq:** Monthly - 4ème semaine du mois précédent; **Cover Price:** EUR 12
Annual Sub.: EUR 84; **Circ:** 15,500
Usual Pagination: 60
Profile: Magazine containing advice about the management of company car fleets, including vehicle tests.
Language(s): French
ADVERTISING RATES:
Full Page Colour .... EUR 6950
Mechanical Data: Type Area: 210 x 297
BUSINESS: TRANSPORT: Commercial Vehicles

L' AUTOMOBILE MAGAZINE

6818F77A-65
Editorial: 12 rue Rouget de Lisle, CEDEX, 92442 ISSY LES MOULINEAUX **Tel:** 1 41 33 37 37
Fax: 1 41 33 37 99
Email: amopinions@motorpresse.fr **Web site:** http://www.automobile-magazine.fr
ISSN: 0758-6957
Date Established: 1946; **Freq:** Monthly - variable;
Cover Price: EUR 3.60
Annual Sub.: EUR 39; **Circ:** 145,421
Usual Pagination: 148
Profile: Magazine containing motoring news and advice.
Language(s): French
ADVERTISING RATES:
Full Page Colour .... EUR 14400
Mechanical Data: Type Area: 225x287
CONSUMER: MOTORING & CYCLING: Motoring

L' AUTOMOBILISTE

6807F77A-30
Editorial: 5 avenue de la Paix, BP 10164, CEDEX, 67000 STRASBOURG **Tel:** 3 88 36 04 34
Fax: 3 88 36 00 63
Email: revue@automobileclub.org **Web site:** http://www.automobileclub.org
ISSN: 1296-3739
Freq: Monthly - fin de mois; **Cover Price:** EUR 1.80
Annual Sub.: EUR 16; **Circ:** 35,800
Usual Pagination: 24
Profile: Magazine containing articles on cars and motorbikes, motoring news and tourism.
Language(s): French
ADVERTISING RATES:
Full Page Colour .... EUR 2825
Mechanical Data: Type Area: 230 x 297
Copy instructions: *Copy Date:* 28 days prior to publication date
CONSUMER: MOTORING & CYCLING: Motoring

LES AVANTAGES

6396F74A-20
Editorial: 10 boulevard des Frères Voisin, CEDEX 9, 92792 ISSY LES MOULINEAUX **Tel:** 1 41 46 89 03 88 88 **Fax:** 1 41 46 87 77
Email: avaredac@gmc.tm.fr **Web site:** http://www.magazine-avantages.fr
ISSN: 0992-9967
Date Established: 1988; **Freq:** Monthly - 10 du mois
Annual Sub.: EUR 19; **Circ:** 453,680
Usual Pagination: 221
Profile: Magazine covering cookery, beauty and fashion.
Language(s): French
ADVERTISING RATES:
Full Page Mono .... EUR 20200
Full Page Colour .... EUR 27200
Mechanical Data: Type Area: 21 x 27
CONSUMER: WOMEN'S INTEREST CONSUMER MAGAZINES: Women's Interest

BEAUX ARTS MAGAZINE

7076F84A-145
Editorial: T.T.M. Editions, 101 boulevard Murat, 75016 PARIS **Tel:** 1 53 84 31 50 **Fax:** 1 53 84 31 99
Email: courrier@beauxartsmagazine.com **Web site:** http://www.beauxartsmagazine.com
ISSN: 0757-2271
Date Established: 1982; **Freq:** Monthly - End of the Month; **Cover Price:** EUR 6.30
Annual Sub.: EUR 53; **Circ:** 61,325
Usual Pagination: 132
Editor-in-Chief: Fabrice Bousteau; **Publisher:** Claude Pommereau
Profile: Magazine focusing on all aspects of art and culture.
Language(s): French
ADVERTISING RATES:
Full Page Mono .... EUR 8400
Full Page Colour .... EUR 8400
Mechanical Data: Type Area: 285 x 220
Copy instructions: *Copy Date:* 15 days prior to publication date
CONSUMER: THE ARTS & LITERARY: Arts

BELLE SANTE

6498F74G-20
Editorial: HAMARNILS, BP 8, 77520 DONNEMARIE-DONTILLY **Tel:** 1 64 01 37 08
Web site: http://www.belle-sante.com
ISSN: 1249-2868
Date Established: 1998; **Freq:** Monthly - le 20 du mois précédent; **Cover Price:** EUR 3.80
Annual Sub.: EUR 34; **Circ:** 160,000
Usual Pagination: 116
Profile: Pan-European health and beauty magazine focusing on natural products, healing techniques and remedies.
Language(s): French
Readership: Aimed at women aged between 40 and 70 years.
ADVERTISING RATES:
Full Page Colour .... EUR 3750
Mechanical Data: Type Area: 215 x 299
Copy instructions: *Copy Date:* 40 days prior to publication date
CONSUMER: WOMEN'S INTEREST CONSUMER MAGAZINES: Slimming & Health

LE BERRY REPUBLICAIN

6162F67B-2400
Editorial: 1 rue du Général Ferrié, CEDEX, 18023 BOURGES **Tel:** 2 48 27 63 63 **Fax:** 2 48 27 63 65
Email: redaction.berry@centrefrance.com **Web site:** http://www.leberry.fr
ISSN: 0988-8357
Freq: Daily - le matin; **Cover Price:** EUR 0.80
Annual Sub.: EUR 305; **Circ:** 30,168
Usual Pagination: 26
Profile: Regional and local newspaper. 1 edition with multiple offices. 1 supplement every day: Monday: Berry Sports - Tuesday: Berry de l'Economie + finance pages - Wednesday: Berry du Cinéma + Berry Livres - Thursday: Sports Club - Friday: Berry Passions + going out page - Saturday: Berry du week-end - Sunday: Berry dimanche with Centre France, TV magazine, Version Fémina. Sunday price: 1,60 €. Subscription: Weekdays only: 223 € - Including Sunday and supplements: 305 €.
Language(s): French
ADVERTISING RATES:
Full Page Colour .... EUR 6519
REGIONAL DAILY & SUNDAY NEWSPAPERS: Regional Daily Newspapers

LE BETTERAVIER FRANCAIS

4998F21A-600
Editorial: 43/45 rue de Naples, 75008 PARIS
Tel: 1 44 69 40 40 **Fax:** 1 44 69 40 49
Email: lebetteravier@wanadoo.fr **Web site:** http://www.lebetteravier.com
ISSN: 0405-6701
Date Established: 1946; **Freq:** 26 issues yearly - le mardi en début et fin de mois; **Annual Sub.:** EUR 64;
Circ: 28,000
Usual Pagination: 44
Profile: Journal focusing on sugar-beet growing. Covers culture, politics, markets, agriculture, and general information.
Language(s): French
Readership: Read by producers and processors.
ADVERTISING RATES:
Full Page Colour .... EUR 8660
Mechanical Data: Type Area: 350 x 280
BUSINESS: AGRICULTURE & FARMING

BIBA

6397F74A-30
Editorial: Immeuble Trait d'Union, 8 rue François Ory, 92120 MONTROUGE **Tel:** 1 46 48 48 48
Fax: 1 46 48 18 47
Email: redac-chef.biba@mondadori.fr **Web site:** http://www.bibamagazine.fr
ISSN: 0221-7996
Date Established: 1980; **Freq:** Monthly - autour du 05 de chaque mois; **Cover Price:** EUR 1.50
Annual Sub.: EUR 19.80; **Circ:** 308,531
Usual Pagination: 252
Managing Director: Ernesto Mauri
Profile: Magazine containing articles on fashion, beauty and topics of general interest to women.
Language(s): French
ADVERTISING RATES:
Full Page Colour .... EUR 16600
Mechanical Data: Type Area: 215 x 282
CONSUMER: WOMEN'S INTEREST CONSUMER MAGAZINES: Women's Interest

BIEN ETRE ET SANTE

6499F74G-30
Editorial: 107 rue Armand Silvestre, 92400 COURBEVOIE **Tel:** 1 49 97 01 00 **Fax:** 1 49 97 01 11
Email: d.galibert@santecom.fr
ISSN: 0154-893X
Freq: Monthly - début de mois (dble 12/1 et 7/8);
Cover Price: EUR 2.50; **Circ:** 536,942
Usual Pagination: 44
Profile: Magazine about health and fitness.
Language(s): French
ADVERTISING RATES:
Full Page Colour .... EUR 20000
Mechanical Data: Type Area: 200 x 270
Copy instructions: *Copy Date:* 21 days prior to publication date
CONSUMER: WOMEN'S INTEREST CONSUMER MAGAZINES: Slimming & Health

LE BIEN PUBLIC - S DEPECHES

6168F67B-2500
Editorial: 7 boulevard du Chanoine Kir, BP 21 550, CEDEX, 21015 DIJON **Tel:** 3 80 42 42 42
Fax: 3 80 42 42 10
Email: redaction@lebienpublic.fr **Web site:** http://www.bienpublic.com
ISSN: 0998-4593
Date Established: 1868; **Freq:** Daily - 4-5 h
Annual Sub.: EUR 396.76; **Circ:** 47,788
Usual Pagination: 65
Editor-in-Chief: Jean-Louis Pierre
Profile: National and regional current events newspaper. Friday price including Loisirs supplement): 0,92 €. Sunday price (including the supplements): 1,50 €. Weekday subscription (300 issues): 250 € - Sunday subscription (52 issues): 78 €.
Language(s): French
ADVERTISING RATES:
Full Page Mono .... EUR 4312

Full Page Colour .... EUR 5217
Mechanical Data: Type Area: Tabloïd
REGIONAL DAILY & SUNDAY NEWSPAPERS: Regional Daily Newspapers

---

BIENSUR SANTE 1743265F74G-306
Editorial: BIEN SUR SANTE EDITIONS, 144 avenue Charles de Gaulle, 92200 NEUILLY SUR SEINE
Tel: 6 80 58 40 51
Email: magazine@biensur-sante.com **Web site:** http://www.biensur-sante.com
ISSN: 1964-4663
Date Established: 2006; **Freq:** 24 issues yearly - 1ère semaine 01 03 05 07 09 11; **Cover Price:** Free; **Circ:** 297,313
Usual Pagination: 52
Profile: Publication focussing on health including news, environment, interviews, reviews and consumer issues.
Language(s): French
ADVERTISING RATES:
Full Page Colour .... EUR 16500
Mechanical Data: Type Area: 200 x 260
Copy instructions: *Copy Date:* 31 days prior to publication date
CONSUMER: WOMEN'S INTEREST CONSUMER MAGAZINES: Slimming & Health

---

BILANS HEBDOMADAIRES 7034F1A-70
Editorial: 13 avenue de l'Opéra, CEDEX 01, 75039 PARIS **Tel:** 1 40 15 17 89 **Fax:** 1 40 15 17 15
Email: redacpol@sgpresse.fr
ISSN: 0755-2238
Date Established: 1946; **Freq:** Weekly; **Cover Price:** EUR 15
Annual Sub.: EUR 600; **Circ:** 350
Usual Pagination: 50
Profile: Magazine containing French and world political, economic and social news.
Language(s): French
Readership: Read by bankers, insurers and investment advisers.
Mechanical Data: Type Area: A 4
BUSINESS: FINANCE & ECONOMICS

BOOST TUNING 6823F77A-160
Editorial: BP 337, CEDEX, 80103 ABBEVILLE
Tel: 3 22 20 15 63 **Fax:** 3 22 24 90 27
Email: boost.tuning@wanadoo.fr
Date Established: 1996; **Freq:** Monthly - le 12du mois; **Cover Price:** EUR 4.95
Annual Sub.: EUR 36; **Circ:** 80,000
Usual Pagination: 192
Editor-in-Chief: Evens Stievenart
Profile: Magazine about cars, maintenance and engine tuning.
Language(s): French
Readership: Aimed at general motoring enthusiasts.
ADVERTISING RATES:
Full Page Colour .... EUR 3060
Mechanical Data: Type Area: 222 x 297
Copy instructions: *Copy Date:* 15 days prior to publication date
CONSUMER: MOTORING & CYCLING: Motoring

BOTANIC 1664704F94H-507
Editorial: Botanic IBP Archamps, BP 64106, 74161 CEDEX SAINT-JULIEN-EN-GENEVOIS
Tel: 4 50 31 27 00 **Fax:** 450312701
Email: contact@botanic.com **Web site:** http://www.botanic.com
Date Established: 2004; **Freq:** Quarterly - fin des mois 02 05 09 11; **Circ:** 300,000
Usual Pagination: 34
Managing Director: Eric Bouchet
Profile: Customer magazine focussing on botanic and gardening including flowers, plants, trees, pets items, home decoration, environment, news, tips, techniques, new products and events. Circulated in the Botanic shops.
Language(s): French
Mechanical Data: Type Area: 205 x 255
CONSUMER: OTHER CLASSIFICATIONS: Customer Magazines

BRETAGNE MAGAZINE 6968F80-235
Editorial: Le Grand large, Quai de la Douane, 29200 BREST **Tel:** 2 98 80 99 14 **Fax:** 2 98 43 09 48
Email: bretagne-magazine@letelegramme.fr **Web site:** http://www.bretagnemagazine.com
ISSN: 1289-5954
Date Established: 1998; **Freq:** 24 issues yearly - les mois impairs; **Cover Price:** EUR 5.95
Annual Sub.: EUR 49.60; **Circ:** 29,241
Usual Pagination: 130
Profile: Magazine concerned with all aspects of the Brittany region. Includes articles on history, folklore, nature and tours.
Language(s): French
ADVERTISING RATES:
Full Page Colour .... EUR 4437
Mechanical Data: Type Area: 21 x 27
Copy instructions: *Copy Date:* 15 days prior to publication date
CONSUMER: RURAL & REGIONAL INTEREST

BULLETIN DE L'ORDRE NATIONAL 1618449F56A-778
Editorial: 180 Boulevard Haussmann, 75008 PARIS
Tel: 1 53 89 32 80 **Fax:** 1 53 89 32 81
Email: conseil-national@cn.medecin.fr **Web site:** http://www.conseil-national.medecin.fr
ISSN: 0030-4565
Freq: 24 issues yearly - fin des mois impairs; **Annual Sub.:** EUR 32; **Circ:** 230,000
Usual Pagination: 16
Profile: Publication focussing on health and medicine including general practice, news, legal and professional issues.
Language(s): French
BUSINESS: HEALTH & MEDICAL

BURDA 6425F74B-20
Editorial: 26 avenue de l'Europe, BP 60052, CEDEX, 67013 STRASBOURG **Tel:** 3 88 19 25 25
Fax: 3 88 19 40 76
Email: elisabeth.gallan@burda.com **Web site:** http://www.burda.fr
Freq: Monthly - vers le 20 du mois
Annual Sub.: EUR 65.40; **Circ:** 70,000
Usual Pagination: 104
Profile: Magazine containing advice and patterns for home-dressmaking. Also covers beauty, cookery and home decoration.
Language(s): French
ADVERTISING RATES:
Full Page Colour .... EUR 6700
Mechanical Data: Type Area: 215 x 280
Copy instructions: *Copy Date:* 15 days prior to publication date
CONSUMER: WOMEN'S INTEREST CONSUMER MAGAZINES: Women's Interest - Fashion

---

CA M'INTERESSE 7036F82-20
Editorial: 13 rue Henri Barbusse, 92624 GENNEVILLIERS **Tel:** 1 73 05 60 24
Email: caminteresse@prisma-presse.com **Web site:** http://www.caminteresse.fr
ISSN: 0243-1335
Date Established: 1981; **Freq:** Monthly - début de mois; **Cover Price:** EUR 3.50
Annual Sub.: EUR 35.95; **Circ:** 255,310
Usual Pagination: 118
Publisher: Martin Trautmann
Profile: Magazine containing articles on current affairs, society, science, health and history.
Language(s): French
Readership: Aimed at the general public.
ADVERTISING RATES:
Full Page Mono .... EUR 10800
Full Page Colour .... EUR 14400
Mechanical Data: Type Area: 283 x 225
Copy instructions: *Copy Date:* 31 days prior to publication date
CONSUMER: CURRENT AFFAIRS & POLITICS

LES CAHIERS DU CINEMA 6722F76A-50
Editorial: 65 rue Montmartre, 75002 PARIS
Tel: 1 53 44 75 75 **Fax:** 1 43 43 95 04
Email: sdelorme@cahiersducinema.com **Web site:** http://www.cahiersducinema.com
ISSN: 0008-011X
Date Established: 1951; **Freq:** Monthly - premier mercredi de chaque mois; **Cover Price:** EUR 5.90
Annual Sub.: EUR 63; **Circ:** 20,845
Usual Pagination: 100
Profile: Magazine with actor interviews and behind-the-scenes information.
Language(s): French
ADVERTISING RATES:
Full Page Colour .... EUR 6500
Mechanical Data: Type Area: 210 x 270
CONSUMER: MUSIC & PERFORMING ARTS: Cinema

CAMPAGNE DECORATION 623467F74C-464
Editorial: 124 rue Danton, 92300 LEVALLOIS PERRET **Tel:** 1 41 34 60 00 **Fax:** 1 41 34 95 59
Email: anne.gastineau@lagardere-active.com
ISSN: 1299-2585
Date Established: 2000; **Freq:** 24 issues yearly - mois impairs; **Cover Price:** EUR 4.30
Annual Sub.: EUR 20; **Circ:** 150,000
Usual Pagination: 124
Publisher: Philippe Khyr
Profile: Magazine about interior design, decoration and styles for country houses.
Language(s): French
ADVERTISING RATES:
Full Page Mono .... EUR 7650
Full Page Colour .... EUR 10200
Mechanical Data: Type Area: 230 x 285
Copy instructions: *Copy Date:* 31 days prior to publication date
CONSUMER: WOMEN'S INTEREST CONSUMER MAGAZINES: Home & Family

CAMPING CAR MAGAZINE 7255F91B-10
Editorial: 12 rue Rouget de Lisle, CEDEX, 92442 ISSY LES MOULINEAUX **Tel:** 1 41 33 37 37
Fax: 1 41 33 47 67
Email: svend.meyzonnier@motorpresse.fr **Web site:** http://www.motorpresse.fr
ISSN: 0769-3249
Date Established: 1978; **Freq:** Monthly - Milieu du mois; **Cover Price:** EUR 4.80
Annual Sub.: EUR 42; **Circ:** 60,684
Usual Pagination: 200
Profile: Magazine focusing on motor caravans.
Language(s): French
ADVERTISING RATES:
Full Page Mono .... EUR 4400
Full Page Colour .... EUR 7575
Mechanical Data: Type Area: 21 x 29
CONSUMER: RECREATION & LEISURE: Camping & Caravanning

CAMPING ET CARAVANING - LE CARAVANIER 1616796F91B-27
Editorial: 12 rue Rouget de Lisle, CEDEX, 92442 ISSY LES MOULINEAUX **Tel:** 1 41 33 37 37
Fax: 1 41 33 47 67
Email: marc.lacoste@motorpresse.fr **Web site:** http://www.motorpresse.fr
Freq: Monthly - Milieu de mois; **Cover Price:** EUR 4.20
Annual Sub.: EUR 27; **Circ:** 18,469
Usual Pagination: 160
Publisher: Marc Lacoste
Profile: Publication focussing on camping and caravanning including tourism and vehicles.
Language(s): French
ADVERTISING RATES:
Full Page Mono .... EUR 4060
Full Page Colour .... EUR 6040
Mechanical Data: Type Area: 21 x 29
Copy instructions: *Copy Date:* 10 days prior to publication date
CONSUMER: RECREATION & LEISURE: Camping & Caravanning

CAMPUS MAG 7063F83-30
Editorial: 56 rue Gabriel Péri, 92120 MONTROUGE
Tel: 1 41 63 29 80 **Fax:** 1 41 63 29 89
Email: redaction@campusmag.fr **Web site:** http://www.planetecampus.com
ISSN: 1267-7876
Date Established: 1980; **Freq:** Monthly - début de mois; **Cover Price:** Free; **Circ:** 144,500
Usual Pagination: 60
Profile: Student magazine including cultural and career news, as well as local information.
Language(s): French
Readership: Read by students.
ADVERTISING RATES:
Full Page Colour .... EUR 9000
Mechanical Data: Type Area: A 4
Copy instructions: *Copy Date:* 10 days prior to publication date
CONSUMER: STUDENT PUBLICATIONS

CANAL 31 1617141F32R-6
Editorial: Conseil Général, 1 boulevard de la Marquette, CEDEX 9, 31090 TOULOUSE
Tel: 5 34 33 32 31 **Fax:** 5 34 33 30 28
Email: webmestrecg31@cg31.fr
ISSN: 2108-8551
Date Established: 1986; **Freq:** 6 issues yearly - 02 04 06 09 12; **Cover Price:** Free; **Circ:** 400,000
Usual Pagination: 32
Profile: Publication focussing on local government and department issues.
Language(s): French
Mechanical Data: Type Area: A 4
BUSINESS: LOCAL GOVERNMENT, LEISURE & RECREATION: Local Government Related

---

CANALSAT - LE MAGAZINE DES ABONNES 1674291F76C-232
Editorial: 35 rue du Pont, 92200 NEUILLY-SUR-SEINE **Tel:** 1 47 47 13 03
Web site: http://www.canalsat.fr
ISSN: 1620-1191
Freq: Monthly - 25-30 de chaque mois sf aoû; **Cover Price:** Free; **Circ:** 2,932,000
Usual Pagination: 40
Editor: Guy Lafarge
Profile: Publication focussing on Canalsatellite TV programmes.
Language(s): French
ADVERTISING RATES:
Full Page Colour .... EUR 39100
Mechanical Data: Type Area: 170 x 220
CONSUMER: MUSIC & PERFORMING ARTS: TV & Radio

LE CANARD ENCHAINE 1618253F73-336
Editorial: 173 rue Saint Honoré, 75001 PARIS
Tel: 1 42 60 31 36
Web site: http://www.lecanardenchaine.fr
Date Established: 1916; **Freq:** Weekly - mercredi; **Cover Price:** EUR 1.20
Annual Sub.: EUR 54.90; **Circ:** 550,000
Usual Pagination: 8
Profile: Publication focussing on news and current affairs including satire, politics, economics and culture.
Language(s): French
Mechanical Data: Type Area: tabloïd
CONSUMER: NATIONAL & INTERNATIONAL PERIODICALS

CANARD PC 1773069F78D-253
Editorial: PRESSE NON-STOP, 122 avenue Jean Lolive, 93500 PANTIN
Email: casque@canardpc.com **Web site:** http://www.canardpc.com
ISSN: 1764-5107
Date Established: 2003; **Freq:** 26 issues yearly - le 1er et le 15 chaque mois; **Cover Price:** EUR 4.30
Annual Sub.: EUR 78; **Circ:** 30,000
Usual Pagination: 64
Profile: Publication focussing on computer games including PC, news, material and tests.
Language(s): French
ADVERTISING RATES:
Full Page Colour .... EUR 1700
Mechanical Data: Type Area: A4
Copy instructions: *Copy Date:* 8 days prior to publication date
CONSUMER: CONSUMER ELECTRONICS: Games

CAPITAL 6561F74M-32
Editorial: 13 rue Henri Barbusse, 92624 GENNEVILLIERS **Tel:** 1 73 05 47 00
Fax: 1 73 05 48 57
Email: capital@prisma-presse.com **Web site:** http://www.capital.fr
ISSN: 1162-6704
Date Established: 1991; **Freq:** Monthly - dernier jeudi du mois; **Cover Price:** EUR 3.50
Annual Sub.: EUR 27.50; **Circ:** 367,226
Usual Pagination: 140
Publisher: Martin Trautmann
Profile: Magazine about personal finance and economics.
Language(s): French
ADVERTISING RATES:
Full Page Mono .... EUR 28125
Full Page Colour .... EUR 37500
Mechanical Data: Type Area: 21 x 27
CONSUMER: WOMEN'S INTEREST CONSUMER MAGAZINES: Personal Finance

---

CAPITAL FINANCE 601365F1F-20
Editorial: 16 rue du 4 septembre, CEDEX 02, 75112 PARIS **Tel:** 1 49 53 64 40 **Fax:** 1 49 53 68 62
Email: capitalfinance@lesechos.fr **Web site:** http://www.capitalfinance.eu
ISSN: 0999-5978
Date Established: 1989; **Freq:** Weekly - le lundi
Annual Sub.: EUR 1519; **Circ:** 1,100
Usual Pagination: 16
Profile: Finance magazine containing information on investment, stock market prices, mergers and acquisitions.
Language(s): French
Readership: Aimed at professionals in the finance sector.
ADVERTISING RATES:
Full Page Colour .... EUR 4500
Mechanical Data: Type Area: A 4
BUSINESS: FINANCE & ECONOMICS: Investment

CARAC MAGAZINE 1618955F94H-517
Editorial: CARAC, 2 ter rue du Château, CEDEX, 92577 NEUILLY SUR SEINE **Tel:** 1 55 61 55 61
Fax: 1 55 61 55 64
Email: finglese@carac.fr **Web site:** http://www.carac.fr
ISSN: 1269-5408
Date Established: 2005; **Freq:** Quarterly - janvier avril juillet octobre; **Cover Price:** EUR 0.46
Annual Sub.: EUR 1.52; **Circ:** 298,100
Usual Pagination: 20
Language(s): French
Mechanical Data: Type Area: 210 x 297
CONSUMER: OTHER CLASSIFICATIONS: Customer Magazines

CARDIOLOGIE PRATIQUE 5658F56A-90
Editorial: AXIS SANTE, 15 rue des Sablons, 75116 PARIS **Tel:** 1 47 55 31 41 **Fax:** 1 47 55 31 32
Email: info@axis-sante.com
ISSN: 0766-3633
Date Established: 1985; **Freq:** Weekly - mercredi (sauf juillet-août); **Cover Price:** EUR 1.83
Annual Sub.: EUR 54; **Circ:** 9,050
Usual Pagination: 20
Profile: Medical newspaper focusing on cardiology and problems related to the heart.
Language(s): French
ADVERTISING RATES:
Full Page Mono .... EUR 5300
Full Page Colour .... EUR 6500
Mechanical Data: Type Area: 290 x 430
Copy instructions: *Copy Date:* 8 days prior to publication date
BUSINESS: HEALTH & MEDICAL

LES CARNETS DU YOGA 6501F74G-45
Editorial: 3 rue Aubriot, 75004 PARIS
Tel: 1 42 78 03 05 **Fax:** 1 42 78 06 27
Email: laffez-jean-pierre@wanadoo.fr
ISSN: 0221-3532
Freq: Monthly - 1ère semaine du mois
Annual Sub.: EUR 48; **Circ:** 1,350
Usual Pagination: 50
Editor-in-Chief: Jean-Pierre Laffez
Profile: Publication of the French Yoga Association.

Language(s): French
Mechanical Data: Type Area: 21 x 15
CONSUMER: WOMEN'S INTEREST CONSUMER MAGAZINES: Slimming & Health

CARREFOUR SAVOIRS
623479F94H-522
Editorial: Agence Ipanema, 10 rue Pergolèse, 75016 PARIS **Tel:** 1 44 17 34 34 **Fax:** 1 44 17 34 39
Web site: http://www.agence-ipanema.fr
ISSN: 1631-2562
Date Established: 1999; **Freq:** Monthly - 1er du mois; **Cover Price:** Free; **Circ:** 500,000
Usual Pagination: 64
Editor: Michel Duplessier
Profile: Magazine focusing on: shows, music, multimedia, cinema and books.
Language(s): French
Readership: Distributed to customers of the supermarket chain Carrefour.
Mechanical Data: Type Area: A 4
CONSUMER: OTHER CLASSIFICATIONS: Customer Magazines

CENTRE PRESSE
6202F67B-2600
Editorial: 5 rue Victor Hugo, BP 299, CEDEX, 86007 POITIERS **Tel:** 5 49 55 55 70 **Fax:** 5 49 60 36 60
Email: redaction@centre-presse.fr **Web site:** http://www.centre-presse.fr
ISSN: 1144-4134
Freq: Daily - Mornings except Sunday; **Cover Price:** EUR 0.90
Annual Sub.: EUR 269.45; **Circ:** 22,350
Usual Pagination: 30
Editor-in-Chief: Richard Lavigne
Profile: News on the Vienne area.
Language(s): French
ADVERTISING RATES:
Full Page Mono .... EUR 7777
Full Page Colour .... EUR 10110
Mechanical Data: Type Area: 271 x 400
REGIONAL DAILY & SUNDAY NEWSPAPERS: Regional Daily Newspapers

CFDT MAGAZINE
1616942F14L-303
Editorial: 4 Boulevard de la Villette, CEDEX 19, 75955 PARIS **Tel:** 1 42 03 82 00 **Fax:** 1 53 72 85 68
Email: magazine@cfdt.fr **Web site:** http://www.cfdt.fr
ISSN: 0395-5621
Date Established: 1960; **Freq:** Monthly - milieu de mois; **Cover Price:** EUR 2.80
Annual Sub.: EUR 39; **Circ:** 600,000
Usual Pagination: 48
Profile: Publication focussing on trade unions including European and international social issues, practical information, culture and leisure.
Language(s): French
ADVERTISING RATES:
Full Page Colour .... EUR 6100
Mechanical Data: Type Area: 210 x 290
BUSINESS: COMMERCE, INDUSTRY & MANAGEMENT: Trade Unions

CGA CONTACT
1647473F14H-126
Editorial: 2 rue Meissonier, 75017 PARIS
Tel: 1 42 67 98 09 **Fax:** 1 47 66 14 08
Email: info@cgadiffusion.com **Web site:** http://www.cgadiffusion.com
ISSN: 0291-7637
Date Established: 1997; **Freq:** 24 issues yearly - variable; **Annual Sub.:** EUR 3.80; **Circ:** 170,000
Usual Pagination: 20
Language(s): French
ADVERTISING RATES:
Full Page Colour .... EUR 7320
Mechanical Data: Type Area: A4
Copy instructions: *Copy Date:* 31 days prior to publication date
BUSINESS: COMMERCE, INDUSTRY & MANAGEMENT: Small Business

CHALLENGES
4816F14A-80_3
Editorial: 33 rue Vivienne, 75002 PARIS
Tel: 1 58 65 03 03 **Fax:** 1 58 65 03 04
Email: redaction@challenges.fr **Web site:** http://www.challenges.fr
ISSN: 0751-4417
Date Established: 2005; **Freq:** Weekly - le jeudi; **Cover Price:** EUR 2.50
Annual Sub.: EUR 58; **Circ:** 275,577
Usual Pagination: 90
Profile: Business magazine containing financial and economic information.
Language(s): French
ADVERTISING RATES:
Full Page Colour .... EUR 19000
Mechanical Data: Type Area: 21 x 26,5
Copy instructions: *Copy Date:* 15 days prior to publication date
BUSINESS: COMMERCE, INDUSTRY & MANAGEMENT

CHALLENGES HAUTE MARNE
5991F14A-800
Editorial: CCI, 55 rue du Président Carnot, CEDEX, 52115 SAINT-DIZIER **Tel:** 3 25 07 32 00
Fax: 3 25 07 32 19
Email: saint-dizier@haute-marne.cci.fr **Web site:** http://www.haute-marne.cci.fr
ISSN: 1148-9634
Freq: Quarterly - 03 06 09 12
Annual Sub.: EUR 15; **Circ:** 6,000
Usual Pagination: 24
Profile: Journal of the Chamber of Commerce and Industry of Haute-Marne.
Language(s): French
Mechanical Data: Type Area: A4
BUSINESS: COMMERCE, INDUSTRY & MANAGEMENT

LA CHARENTE LIBRE
6157F67B-2700
Editorial: ZI n° 3, CEDEX 9, 16903 ANGOULEME
Tel: 5 45 94 16 00 **Fax:** 5 45 94 17 19 16 19
Email: charente@charentelibre.fr **Web site:** http://www.charentelibre.fr
ISSN: 0247-7823
Date Established: 1944; **Freq:** Daily - 7j/7 sauf dimanche et 01/05; **Cover Price:** EUR 0.85
Annual Sub.: EUR 236; **Circ:** 38,228
Usual Pagination: 56
Profile: Regional and local news.
Language(s): French
ADVERTISING RATES:
Full Page Mono .... EUR 4533
Full Page Colour .... EUR 5220
Mechanical Data: Type Area: tabloid
REGIONAL DAILY & SUNDAY NEWSPAPERS: Regional Daily Newspapers

CHASSEUR D'IMAGES
7107F85A-20
Editorial: BP 100, CEDEX, 86101 CHATELLERAULT
Tel: 5 49 85 49 85 **Fax:** 5 49 85 49 99
Email: redac@photim.com **Web site:** http://www.photim.com
ISSN: 0396-8235
Date Established: 1976; **Freq:** Monthly - le 15 du mois pour mois suivant; **Cover Price:** EUR 4.95
Annual Sub.: EUR 43; **Circ:** 99,494
Usual Pagination: 220
Profile: Magazine containing advice about photography, includes tests and reviews of new cameras.
Language(s): French
ADVERTISING RATES:
Full Page Mono .... EUR 6750
Full Page Colour .... EUR 7600
Mechanical Data: Type Area: 230 x 297
Copy instructions: *Copy Date:* 21 days prior to publication date
CONSUMER: PHOTOGRAPHY & FILM MAKING: Photography

LE CHASSEUR FRANCAIS
6630F75F-9
Editorial: Immeuble Trait d'Union, 8 rue François Ory, 92120 MONTROUGE **Tel:** 1 41 33 22 20
Fax: 1 41 33 22 90
Email: lechasseur.francais@mondadori.fr **Web site:** http://www.mondadoripub.fr
ISSN: 0750-3334
Date Established: 1885; **Freq:** Monthly - dernier mardi du mois; **Cover Price:** EUR 2.90
Annual Sub.: EUR 27.30; **Circ:** 422,702
Usual Pagination: 160
Profile: Magazine about hunting, shooting and fishing.
Language(s): French
ADVERTISING RATES:
Full Page Colour .... EUR 19700
Mechanical Data: Type Area: 185 x 255
Copy instructions: *Copy Date:* 31 days prior to publication date
CONSUMER: SPORT: Shooting

CHEMINEES MAGAZINE
6443F74C-60
Editorial: 27 rue Pétion de Villeneuve, 75011 PARIS
Tel: 1 43 79 07 37 **Fax:** 1 43 79 76 88
Email: redaction@decoration-francaise.fr **Web site:** http://www.cheminees-magazine.fr
ISSN: 0242-2409
Date Established: 1979; **Freq:** Quarterly - les mois 03 06 09 12
Annual Sub.: EUR 80; **Circ:** 30,000
Usual Pagination: 100
Editor-in-Chief: Olivier De Tiliere
Profile: Pan-European review specialising in chimneys, fireplaces, hearths and barbecues.
Language(s): French
Readership: Aimed at people interested in DIY and home improvement.
Mechanical Data: Type Area: 22 x 29,7
Copy instructions: *Copy Date:* 15 days prior to publication date
CONSUMER: WOMEN'S INTEREST CONSUMER MAGAZINES: Home & Family

LA CHRONIQUE REPUBLICAINE
1619205F67J-83
Editorial: 39 rue de Nantes, BP 30162, CEDEX, 35301 FOUGERES **Tel:** 2 99 99 12 15
Fax: 2 99 99 77 24
ISSN: 0751-5901
Date Established: 1837; **Freq:** Weekly; **Cover Price:** EUR 1.20
Annual Sub.: EUR 60; **Circ:** 15,202
Usual Pagination: 52
Profile: Local news, local sports news + 1 page "Madame Chronique".
Language(s): French
ADVERTISING RATES:
Full Page Mono .... EUR 2808
Full Page Colour .... EUR 3900
Mechanical Data: Type Area: 255 x 390
REGIONAL DAILY & SUNDAY NEWSPAPERS: Regional Newspapers (excl. dailies)

CINEMA CHEZ SOI
6898F78B-25
Editorial: 4 rue des Beaumonts, 94120 FONTENAY-SOUS-BOIS **Tel:** 1 71 33 15 88
Email: redaction@cinemachezsoi.com
ISSN: 1291-6579
Date Established: 1995; **Freq:** Monthly - le 29 du mois
Annual Sub.: EUR 45; **Circ:** 65,000
Usual Pagination: 116
Profile: Magazine containing articles on home entertainment equipment. Focuses on sound and image equipment for home cinemas.
Language(s): French
Readership: Aimed at those interested in equipment and technology for home cinemas and home entertainment systems.
ADVERTISING RATES:
Full Page Mono .... EUR 1980
Full Page Colour .... EUR 2745
Mechanical Data: Type Area: 21 x 29,7
CONSUMER: CONSUMER ELECTRONICS: Video & DVD

CIRCUITS CULTURE
5032F21B-5
Editorial: 23 rue Dupont des Loges, BP 90 146, CEDEX 1, 57004 METZ **Tel:** 3 87 69 18 18
Fax: 3 87 69 18 14
Email: circuits-culture@groupe-atc.com
ISSN: 0751-6037
Freq: Monthly - le 1er du mois; **Cover Price:** EUR 7.26
Annual Sub.: EUR 65.40; **Circ:** 5,500
Usual Pagination: 66
Profile: Review of commerce and distribution of agricultural products and supplies.
Language(s): French
Readership: Read by suppliers and wholesalers of agricultural products.
ADVERTISING RATES:
Full Page Mono .... EUR 2510
Full Page Colour .... EUR 3340
Mechanical Data: Type Area: 210 x 297
BUSINESS: AGRICULTURE & FARMING: Agriculture - Supplies & Services

CIRCULER AUTREMENT
5551F49A-50
Editorial: 6 avenue Hoche, 75008 PARIS
Tel: 1 44 15 27 00 **Fax:** 1 44 15 27 40
Email: circuler@preventionroutiere.asso.fr **Web site:** http://www.preventionroutiere.asso.fr
ISSN: 1956-9629
Date Established: 1986; **Freq:** Quarterly - janvier avril juillet octobre; **Circ:** 95,000
Usual Pagination: 20
Profile: Magazine focusing on transport, road management and accident prevention.
Language(s): French
Mechanical Data: Type Area: A 4
BUSINESS: TRANSPORT

CITIZEN K
1618072F74B-227
Editorial: 18 rue Séguier, 75006 PARIS
Tel: 1 55 42 20 20 **Fax:** 1 55 42 20 21
Email: redaction@citizen-k.com **Web site:** http://www.citizen-k.com
ISSN: 1366-8285
Date Established: 1994; **Freq:** Quarterly - early months 03 06 09 12
Annual Sub.: EUR 40; **Circ:** 114,877
Usual Pagination: 230
Language(s): French
ADVERTISING RATES:
Full Page Colour .... EUR 17000
Mechanical Data: Type Area: 206 x 275
Copy instructions: *Copy Date:* 31 days prior to publication date
CONSUMER: WOMEN'S INTEREST CONSUMER MAGAZINES: Women's Interest - Fashion

CLASSE EXPORT MAGAZINE
4989F20-30
Editorial: 100 route de Paris, 69260 CHARBONNIERES **Tel:** 4 72 59 10 10
Fax: 4 72 59 03 16
Email: redaction@classe-export.com **Web site:** http://www.classe-export.com
ISSN: 1254-1737
Date Established: 1990; **Freq:** Monthly - le 20 du mois
Annual Sub.: EUR 89; **Circ:** 7,500
Usual Pagination: 64
Profile: Magazine about the international export trade. Also covers national and international commerce, business and markets.
Language(s): French
ADVERTISING RATES:
Full Page Colour .... EUR 3300
Mechanical Data: Type Area: A 4
BUSINESS: IMPORT & EXPORT

CLOSER
1691394F74Q-222
Editorial: Immeuble Trait d'Union, 8 rue François Ory, 92120 MONTROUGE **Tel:** 1 41 86 18 15
Fax: 1 41 86 16 87
Email: courrier@closermag.fr **Web site:** http://www.closermag.fr
ISSN: 1774-7201
Date Established: 2005; **Freq:** Weekly - le samedi;
Cover Price: EUR 1.30
Annual Sub.: EUR 56; **Circ:** 499,977
Usual Pagination: 88
Profile: Publication focussing on celebrities including news, gossips, lifestyle, fashion, beauty, decoration, shopping, cookery and TV guide.
Language(s): French
ADVERTISING RATES:
Full Page Colour .... EUR 14000
Mechanical Data: Type Area: 220 x 300
CONSUMER: WOMEN'S INTEREST CONSUMER MAGAZINES: Lifestyle

COMMUNES DE FRANCE
5293F32A-30
Editorial: Rédaction - Administration, 8 bis rue de Solférino, 75007 PARIS **Tel:** 1 42 81 41 36
Fax: 1 48 74 00 78
Email: redaction@mde-communes-de-france.fr
ISSN: 1165-9408
Date Established: 1959; **Freq:** Monthly - le 12-15 du mois; **Cover Price:** EUR 9.90
Annual Sub.: EUR 99; **Circ:** 4,916
Usual Pagination: 52
Profile: Magazine concerning local government in France.
Language(s): French
Readership: Aimed at elected representatives of regional communities.
ADVERTISING RATES:
Full Page Mono .... EUR 3310
Full Page Colour .... EUR 5204
Mechanical Data: Type Area: 230 x 300
BUSINESS: LOCAL GOVERNMENT, LEISURE & RECREATION: Local Government

COMPUTER ARTS
4986F19J-46
Editorial: 101/109 rue Jean Jaurès, 92300 LEVALLOIS PERRET **Tel:** 1 41 27 38 38
Fax: 1 41 27 38 39
Email: jean-david.hernandez@yellowmedia.fr
Date Established: 1998; **Freq:** Monthly - vers le 15 de chaque mois; **Cover Price:** EUR 7.90
Annual Sub.: EUR 56; **Circ:** 14,439
Usual Pagination: 114
Profile: Magazine focusing on all aspects of graphic art and design. Includes articles on 3D imaging, the use of the Internet and how to digitally enhance graphics.
Language(s): French
Readership: Aimed at graphic designers, artists and those generally interested in computer aided graphics and design.
ADVERTISING RATES:
Full Page Colour .... EUR 5000
Mechanical Data: Type Area: 300 x 220
Copy instructions: *Copy Date:* 21 days prior to publication date
BUSINESS: ENGINEERING & MACHINERY: CAD & CIM (Computer Integrated Manufacture)

CONFORTIQUE MAGAZINE - LE MAGAZINE
5461F43A-10
Editorial: 8 quai de Bir Hakeim, CEDEX, 94417 SAINT MAURICE **Tel:** 1 43 97 95 23
Fax: 1 43 97 20 07
Email: i.lejeune@fr.oleane.com **Web site:** http://www.confortique-news.com
ISSN: 0989-1706
Date Established: 1988; **Freq:** Monthly - le 10 du mois suivant; **Cover Price:** EUR 15
Annual Sub.: EUR 125; **Circ:** 10,000
Usual Pagination: 120
Profile: Professional review of electrical appliances including television, hi-fi and video.
Language(s): French
ADVERTISING RATES:
Full Page Colour .... EUR 6590
Mechanical Data: Type Area: A 4
Copy instructions: *Copy Date:* 10 days prior to publication date
BUSINESS: ELECTRICAL RETAIL TRADE

CONNAISSANCE DES ARTS
7077F84A-220
Editorial: 16 rue du Quatre-Septembre, CEDEX 2, 75112 PARIS **Tel:** 1 44 88 55 00 **Fax:** 1 44 88 51 88
Email: cda@cdesarts.com **Web site:** http://www.connaissancedesarts.com
ISSN: 0293-9274
Date Established: 1952; **Freq:** Monthly - fin du mois;
Cover Price: EUR 9.60
Annual Sub.: EUR 69; **Circ:** 45,841
Usual Pagination: 150
Profile: Art review.
Language(s): French
Readership: Read by members of the French Society of Artistic Promotion.
ADVERTISING RATES:
Full Page Colour .... EUR 9000
Mechanical Data: Type Area: 215 x 285
CONSUMER: THE ARTS & LITERARY: Arts

CONSEIL GENERAL VAR MAGAZINE

1617145F32R-10

Editorial: Conseil Général, 390 avenue des Lices, BP 1303 CEDEX, 83076 TOULON **Tel:** 4 94 18 62 65 **Fax:** 4 94 18 65 05
Email: varmag@cg83.fr **Web site:** http://www.cg83.fr
ISSN: 1260-6162
Date Established: 1994; **Freq:** Monthly - La 1ère semaine du mois; **Cover Price:** Free; **Circ:** 475,000
Usual Pagination: 24
Profile: Publication focussing on local government and department issues, including economics, solidarity, events, local news, cultural and social issues. Also published in Braille.
Language(s): French
Mechanical Data: Type Area: 30 x 22
BUSINESS: LOCAL GOVERNMENT, LEISURE & RECREATION: Local Government Related

CONSOLES +

6903F78D-30

Editorial: 101/109 rue Jean Jaurès, 92300 LEVALLOIS PERRET **Tel:** 1 41 27 38 38 **Fax:** 1 41 27 38 39
Email: vincent.oms@yellowmedia.fr **Web site:** http://www.consolesplus.fr
ISSN: 1162-8669
Date Established: 1991; **Freq:** Monthly - 25th of the month; **Cover Price:** EUR 6.50
Annual Sub.: EUR 62.40; **Circ:** 14,732
Usual Pagination: 196
Editor-in-Chief: Vincent Oms
Profile: Magazine about console games.
Language(s): French
ADVERTISING RATES:
Full Page Colour .... EUR 2900
Mechanical Data: Type Area: 23 x 30
CONSUMER: CONSUMER ELECTRONICS: Games

CONTACT

1617116F78R-81

Editorial: 18 rue Balard, 75015 PARIS
Tel: 1 40 58 35 35 **Fax:** 1 45 75 47 39
Email: aseidel@francoallemand.com **Web site:** http://www.francoallemand.com
ISSN: 1148-6678
Date Established: 1954; **Freq:** 24 issues yearly - variable; **Cover Price:** Free; **Circ:** 5,000
Usual Pagination: 60
Profile: Customer magazine focussing on culture and consumer electronics including CD, books, DVD, CDRom, new products, hi-fi, telecommunication, mobile phones, computing and technology. Circulated in the FNAC shops.
Language(s): French
Mechanical Data: Type Area: A 5
CONSUMER: CONSUMER ELECTRONICS: Consumer Electronics Related

CONVERGENCE

1656867F1P-51

Editorial: 9/11 rue Froissart, CEDEX 03, 75140 PARIS **Tel:** 1 44 78 21 00 **Fax:** 1 44 78 21 88
Email: convergence@secourspopulaire.fr **Web site:** http://www.secourspopulaire.fr
ISSN: 0293-3292
Date Established: 1981; **Freq:** Monthly - entre le 1er et le 05 du mois
Annual Sub.: EUR 10; **Circ:** 320,000
Usual Pagination: 24
Language(s): French
ADVERTISING RATES:
Full Page Mono .... EUR 3213
Full Page Colour .... EUR 3780
BUSINESS: FINANCE & ECONOMICS: Fundraising

LA CORRESPONDANCE ECONOMIQUE

4466F1A-80

Editorial: 13 avenue de l'Opéra, CEDEX 01, 75039 PARIS **Tel:** 1 40 15 17 89 **Fax:** 1 40 15 17 15
Email: redaceco@sgpresse.fr
ISSN: 1621-3920
Date Established: 1945; **Freq:** Daily - le matin du lundi au vendredi; **Cover Price:** EUR 22
Annual Sub.: EUR 4500; **Circ:** 1,050
Usual Pagination: 24
Profile: Journal containing social and economic news.
Language(s): French
Readership: Read by economists and financiers.
ADVERTISING RATES:
Full Page Mono .... EUR 3300
Full Page Colour .... EUR 3950
Mechanical Data: Type Area: A 4
BUSINESS: FINANCE & ECONOMICS

CORSE MATIN

1619402F67B-8402

Editorial: 2 rue Sergent Casalonga, 20000 AJACCIO
Tel: 4 95 51 74 00 **Fax:** 4 95 51 74 01
Email: redacchef@nicematin.fr **Web site:** http://www.corsematin.com
Date Established: 1944; **Freq:** Daily - le matin;
Cover Price: EUR 0.85
Annual Sub.: EUR 349; **Circ:** 42,312
Usual Pagination: 48
Profile: Local and regional news. Corsica edition of Nice Matin. Sport supplement for the Sunday and Monday edition, real estate supplement on Tuesday. Friday price: 1,20 € (La Corse, votre hebdo supplement). Saturday Price: 1,50 € (TV hebdo et Version Fémina supplement).
Language(s): French
ADVERTISING RATES:
Full Page Mono .... EUR 2311
Full Page Colour .... EUR 2889
Mechanical Data: Type Area: 320 X 470
REGIONAL DAILY & SUNDAY NEWSPAPERS: Regional Daily Newspapers

COSMETIQUE MAGAZINE

4900F15A-16

Editorial: Forum 55, 52 rue Camille Desmoulins, 92448 ISSY LES MOULINEAUX **Tel:** 1 46 29 46 29
Email: pthouanel@reedbusiness.fr **Web site:** http://www.cosmetiquemag.fr
ISSN: 1297-4773
Date Established: 1999; **Freq:** Monthly - entre le 5 et 8 du mois; **Cover Price:** EUR 14
Annual Sub.: EUR 90; **Circ:** 9,866
Usual Pagination: 120
Profile: Journal covering product distribution in the hygiene, beauty and health sector.
Language(s): French
ADVERTISING RATES:
Full Page Mono .... EUR 5500
Full Page Colour .... EUR 7100
Mechanical Data: Type Area: A 4
Copy instructions: *Copy Date:* 10 days prior to publication date
BUSINESS: COSMETICS & HAIRDRESSING: Cosmetics

COSMOPOLITAN

6400F74A-110

Editorial: 10 boulevard des Frères Voisin, CEDEX 9, 92792 ISSY LES MOULINEAUX **Tel:** 1 41 46 88 88 **Fax:** 1 41 46 85 56
Email: cosmoredaction@gmc.tm.fr **Web site:** http://www.cosmopolitan.fr
ISSN: 1161-2258
Date Established: 1973; **Freq:** Monthly - entre le 5-10 du mois précédent
Annual Sub.: EUR 20; **Circ:** 418,141
Usual Pagination: 180
Profile: Magazine aimed at young, professional women covering fashion, beauty, health, travel and work.
Language(s): French
ADVERTISING RATES:
Full Page Mono .... EUR 16450
Full Page Colour .... EUR 23500
Mechanical Data: Type Area: 28 x 20
Copy instructions: *Copy Date:* 31 days prior to publication date
CONSUMER: WOMEN'S INTEREST CONSUMER MAGAZINES: Women's Interest

COTE D'OR MAGAZINE

1617147F32R-12

Editorial: Conseil Général - Hôtel du département, 53 bis rue de la Préfecture, BP 1601 CEDEX, 21035 DIJON **Tel:** 3 80 63 30 05 **Fax:** 3 80 63 65 34
Email: cotedor-magazine@cg21.fr **Web site:** http://www.cotedor.fr
Date Established: 1989; **Freq:** Monthly - Début des mois; **Cover Price:** Free; **Circ:** 245,000
Usual Pagination: 24
Profile: Publication focussing on local government and department issues.
Language(s): French
Mechanical Data: Type Area: A 4
BUSINESS: LOCAL GOVERNMENT, LEISURE & RECREATION: Local Government Related

COTE MOMES

1772516F74D-286

Editorial: 6 rue Sadi Carnot, 93170 BAGNOLET
Email: redaction@cote-momes.com **Web site:** http://www.cote-momes.com
ISSN: 1960-7474
Date Established: 2006; **Freq:** 24 issues yearly - vers le 6 du mois; **Cover Price:** Free; **Circ:** 500,000
Usual Pagination: 100
Language(s): French
ADVERTISING RATES:
Full Page Colour .... EUR 39000
Mechanical Data: Type Area: 190 x 230
Copy instructions: *Copy Date:* 7 days prior to publication date
CONSUMER: WOMEN'S INTEREST CONSUMER MAGAZINES: Child Care

COTE SANTE

1692881F74G-301

Editorial: 6 rue Faidherbe, 94160 SAINT-MANDE
Tel: 1 48 12 35 31 **Fax:** 1 48 12 35 52
Email: redaction@cotesante.fr
ISSN: 1778-0756
Date Established: 2005; **Freq:** Monthly - le 20 de chaque mois; **Cover Price:** EUR 2.80
Annual Sub.: EUR 19; **Circ:** 80,000
Usual Pagination: 116
Profile: Publication focussing on good health including fitness, beauty, sexuality, environment, education and psychology.
Language(s): French
ADVERTISING RATES:
Full Page Colour .... EUR 10800
Mechanical Data: Type Area: 21 x 27
Copy instructions: *Copy Date:* 15 days prior to publication date
CONSUMER: WOMEN'S INTEREST CONSUMER MAGAZINES: Slimming & Health

COTES D'ARMOR

1617148F32A-1017

Editorial: Conseil général, 9 place du Général de Gaulle, BP 2371 CEDEX 1, 22023 SAINT-BRIEUC
Tel: 2 96 62 85 41 **Fax:** 2 96 62 50 06
Email: lemagazine@cg22.fr **Web site:** http://www.cotesdarmor.fr
ISSN: 1283-5048
Freq: Monthly - Début du mois; **Cover Price:** Free; **Circ:** 280,000
Usual Pagination: 32
Profile: Publication focussing on local government and department issues, including economics, events, leisure, cultural heritage, culture and social issues.
Language(s): French
Mechanical Data: Type Area: 23 x 30
BUSINESS: LOCAL GOVERNMENT, LEISURE & RECREATION: Local Government

COURRIER CADRES

1617270F94K-5

Editorial: 1 rue des Entrepreneurs, 93400 SAINT OUEN **Tel:** 1 40 11 44 44 **Fax:** 1 40 11 55 50
Email: courriercadres@clubtouati.com **Web site:** http://www.courriercadres.com
ISSN: 0220-6994
Date Established: 1977; **Freq:** Monthly - 1st Thursday of the month
Annual Sub.: EUR 39; **Circ:** 121,128
Usual Pagination: 100
Language(s): French
ADVERTISING RATES:
Full Page Colour .... EUR 12800
Mechanical Data: Type Area: 200 x 267
Copy instructions: *Copy Date:* 21 days prior to publication date
CONSUMER: OTHER CLASSIFICATIONS: Job Seekers

LE COURRIER CAUCHOIS

1619271F67J-145

Editorial: 2 rue Edmond Labbé, BP 129, CEDEX, 76194 YVETOT **Tel:** 2 35 56 29 64 **Fax:** 2 35 56 30 82
Email: redaction@lecourriercauchois.fr **Web site:** http://www.lecourriercauchois.fr
Freq: Weekly; **Cover Price:** EUR 140
Annual Sub.: EUR 70; **Circ:** 40,972
Usual Pagination: 180
Profile: Regional news.
Language(s): French
ADVERTISING RATES:
Full Page Colour .... EUR 2028
Mechanical Data: Type Area: tabloïd
REGIONAL DAILY & SUNDAY NEWSPAPERS: Regional Newspapers (excl. dailies)

LE COURRIER DE LA MAYENNE

1619276F67J-150

Editorial: 108 rue Victor Boissel, BP 529, CEDEX, 53005 LAVAL **Tel:** 2 43 59 10 40 **Fax:** 2 43 49 03 91
Email: redaction@courrierdelamayenne.com **Web site:** http://www.courriermayenne.com
ISSN: 0750-4020
Date Established: 1944; **Freq:** Weekly; **Cover Price:** EUR 1.20
Annual Sub.: EUR 55; **Circ:** 27,726
Usual Pagination: 64
Profile: Weekly local newspaper.
Language(s): French
ADVERTISING RATES:
Full Page Mono .... EUR 3408
Mechanical Data: Type Area: tabloïd
REGIONAL DAILY & SUNDAY NEWSPAPERS: Regional Newspapers (excl. dailies)

LE COURRIER DE L'OUEST

6156F67B-2800

Editorial: Boulevard Albert Blanchoin, BP 10728, CEDEX 01, 49007 ANGERS **Tel:** 2 41 68 86 88 **Fax:** 2 41 44 31 43
Email: secretariat.redac-chef.angers@courrier-ouest.com
ISSN: 2102-6882
Freq: Daily - tous les matins; **Cover Price:** EUR 0.75
Annual Sub.: EUR 238.89; **Circ:** 102,225
Profile: General and regional Maine-et-Loire and Deux-Sèvres area news.
Language(s): French
ADVERTISING RATES:
Full Page Mono .... EUR 12095
Full Page Colour .... EUR 15893
REGIONAL DAILY & SUNDAY NEWSPAPERS: Regional Daily Newspapers

LE COURRIER DES MAIRES

5294F32A-34

Editorial: 17 rue d'Uzès, CEDEX 02, 75108 PARIS
Tel: 1 40 13 30 30 **Fax:** 1 40 13 51 06
Email: redaccourrier@courrierdesmaires.fr **Web site:** http://www.courrierdesmaires.fr
ISSN: 1252-1574
Date Established: 1993; **Freq:** Monthly - le 10 ou 15 du mois; **Cover Price:** EUR 13
Annual Sub.: EUR 112; **Circ:** 10,000
Usual Pagination: 100
Profile: Journal covering town planning, development, communication, social affairs, transport, sport and culture.
Language(s): French
Readership: Read by elected members and decision makers of local councils.
ADVERTISING RATES:
Full Page Colour .... EUR 4620
Mechanical Data: Type Area: 300 x 230
Copy instructions: *Copy Date:* 20 days prior to publication date
BUSINESS: LOCAL GOVERNMENT, LEISURE & RECREATION: Local Government

LE COURRIER DU GRAND PARIS

6025F14A-820

Editorial: CCIP, 27 avenue de Friedland, 75008 PARIS **Tel:** 1 55 65 55 65 **Fax:** 1 55 65 70 67
Email: ibrunetdebaines@ccip.fr **Web site:** http://www.ccip.fr
ISSN: 1162-3802
Date Established: 1991; **Freq:** 6 issues yearly - 01 03 05 09 11; **Cover Price:** EUR 2.50
Annual Sub.: EUR 22.50; **Circ:** 270,000
Usual Pagination: 56
Profile: Journal of the Chamber of Commerce of Paris.
Language(s): French
Mechanical Data: Type Area: 205 x 280
BUSINESS: COMMERCE, INDUSTRY & MANAGEMENT

LE COURRIER INTERNATIONAL

7039F82-35

Editorial: 6/8 rue Jean Antoine de Baïf, 75013 PARIS
Tel: 1 46 46 16 00 **Fax:** 1 46 46 16 01 02
Email: courrier@iway.fr **Web site:** http://www.courrierinternational.com
ISSN: 1154-516X
Date Established: 1990; **Freq:** Weekly - jeudi; **Cover Price:** EUR 3.50
Annual Sub.: EUR 94.50; **Circ:** 217,664
Usual Pagination: 60
Profile: Magazine providing translations of the most important news from the world's press.
Language(s): French
ADVERTISING RATES:
Full Page Colour .... EUR 13200
Mechanical Data: Type Area: 40 x 30
CONSUMER: CURRENT AFFAIRS & POLITICS

LE COURRIER PICARD

6155F67B-2900

Editorial: 29 rue de la République, BP 1021, CEDEX 1, 80010 AMIENS **Tel:** 3 22 82 60 00 **Fax:** 3 22 82 60 11
Email: courrier@courrier-picard.fr **Web site:** http://www.courrier-picard.fr
ISSN: 1285-8668
Date Established: 1944; **Freq:** Daily - matin; **Cover Price:** EUR 0.90
Annual Sub.: EUR 318; **Circ:** 62,000
Usual Pagination: 52
Profile: Regional and local newspaper.
Language(s): French
ADVERTISING RATES:
Full Page Mono .... EUR 6535
Full Page Colour .... EUR 8169
Mechanical Data: Type Area: tabloïd
REGIONAL DAILY & SUNDAY NEWSPAPERS: Regional Daily Newspapers

CREA LE MAG COMMUNAUTE D'AGGLOMERATION DE ROUEN ELBEUF AUSTREBERTHE

1648603F80-857

Editorial: Norwich House, 14 bis avenue Pasteur, BP 589, 76006 CEDEX 1 ROUEN **Tel:** 2 35 52 68 10 **Fax:** 235712595
Email: mag@la-crea.fr **Web site:** http://www.agglo-de-rouen.fr
ISSN: 1269-3855
Freq: Monthly - Première semaine du mois; **Circ:** 225,000
Usual Pagination: 28
Profile: Publication focussing on local community information.
Language(s): French
Mechanical Data: Type Area: 200 X 260
CONSUMER: RURAL & REGIONAL INTEREST

LA CROIX

6088F65A-20

Editorial: 18 rue Barbès, CEDEX, 92128 MONTROUGE **Tel:** 1 74 31 60 60 **Fax:** 1 74 31 60 01
Web site: http://www.la-croix.com
ISSN: 0242-6056
Date Established: 1883; **Freq:** Daily - du lundi au vendredi + sam.dim; **Cover Price:** EUR 1.20
Annual Sub.: EUR 312; **Circ:** 104,901
Usual Pagination: 32
Profile: Tabloid-sized quality newspaper, covering a broad range of news and current affairs from a Catholic viewpoint.
Language(s): French
Readership: Read by senior executives, academics, managers and the business community, a large proportion of whom are retired.
ADVERTISING RATES:
Full Page Mono .... EUR 17000
Full Page Colour .... EUR 22300
Mechanical Data: Type Area: 40 x 28
NATIONAL DAILY & SUNDAY NEWSPAPERS: National Daily Newspapers

LA CUISINE ACTUELLE

6581F74P-80

Editorial: 13 rue Henri Barbusse, 92624 GENNEVILLIERS **Tel:** 1 73 05 65 98 67 00

Email: cuisineactuelle@prisma-presse.com **Web site:** http://www.cuisineactuelle.fr
ISSN: 0989-3091
Freq: Monthly - milieu du mois précédent; **Cover Price:** EUR 1.95
Annual Sub.: EUR 18; **Circ:** 202,199
Profile: Magazine about cookery and food.
Language(s): French
Readership: Aimed at people with passion for cooking.
ADVERTISING RATES:
Full Page Mono .... EUR 10500
Full Page Colour .... EUR 14000
Copy instructions: *Copy Date:* 31 days prior to publication date
CONSUMER: WOMEN'S INTEREST CONSUMER MAGAZINES: Food & Cookery

CUISINE ET VINS DE FRANCE
6580F74P-95
Editorial: 43/47 rue du Gouverneur Général Eboué, CEDEX, 92137 ISSY LES MOULINEAUX
Tel: 1 41 46 84 39 **Fax:** 1 41 46 84 68
Email: cvfredac@gmc.tm.fr **Web site:** http://www.cuisineetvinsdefrance.com
ISSN: 1761-3531
Date Established: 1947; **Freq:** 24 issues yearly; **Cover Price:** EUR 3.30
Annual Sub.: EUR 16; **Circ:** 153,152
Usual Pagination: 100
Profile: Magazine about French wine and cuisine.
Language(s): French
ADVERTISING RATES:
Full Page Mono .... EUR 7280
Full Page Colour .... EUR 9100
Mechanical Data: Type Area: 225 x 285
Copy instructions: *Copy Date:* 31 days prior to publication date
CONSUMER: WOMEN'S INTEREST CONSUMER MAGAZINES: Food & Cookery

CUISINE GOURMANDE
6582F74P-100
Editorial: 13 rue Henri Barbusse, 92624 GENNEVILLIERS **Tel:** 1 73 05 65 98 67 00
Email: cuisinegourmande@prisma-presse.com **Web site:** http://www.cuisinegourmande.fr
ISSN: 1952-7802
Freq: 24 issues yearly - 01-03-04-07-09-11; **Cover Price:** EUR 3.20
Annual Sub.: EUR 14.50; **Circ:** 41,584
Usual Pagination: 124
Profile: Magazine about gourmet cuisine.
Language(s): French
ADVERTISING RATES:
Full Page Mono .... EUR 4500
Full Page Colour .... EUR 6000
Copy instructions: *Copy Date:* 31 days prior to publication date
CONSUMER: WOMEN'S INTEREST CONSUMER MAGAZINES: Food & Cookery

CULTURE LEGUMIERE
5222F26C-30
Editorial: AT COMMUNICATION - Cité de l'Agriculture, 13 avenue des Droits de l'Homme, CEDEX 9, 45921 ORLEANS **Tel:** 2 38 52 00 11
Fax: 2 38 52 00 21
Email: h.sauvage@groupe-atc.com
ISSN: 1248-0525
Freq: 24 issues yearly - the 15th of even months; **Cover Price:** EUR 7.20
Annual Sub.: EUR 48.80; **Circ:** 9,600
Usual Pagination: 48
Profile: This magazine covers topics focusing on vegetable growing, production and the economy.
Language(s): French
ADVERTISING RATES:
Full Page Mono .... EUR 1910
Full Page Colour .... EUR 2780
Mechanical Data: Type Area: 210 x 297
Copy instructions: *Copy Date:* 15 days prior to publication date
BUSINESS: GARDEN TRADE

CULTURES MARINES
5511F45B-41
Editorial: ZI Rennes Chantepie, 13 rue du Breil, CS 46305 CEDEX, 35063 RENNES **Tel:** 2 99 32 58 80
Fax: 2 99 32 58 88
Email: redaction@infomer.fr **Web site:** http://www.infomer.fr
ISSN: 0297-4932
Date Established: 1986; **Freq:** Monthly - le 1er du mois (sauf 01 & 08); **Cover Price:** EUR 6.50
Annual Sub.: EUR 49; **Circ:** 4,500
Usual Pagination: 40
Profile: Magazine about oyster farming.
Language(s): French
ADVERTISING RATES:
Full Page Mono .... EUR 1710
Full Page Colour .... EUR 2570
Mechanical Data: Type Area: 210 x 297
Copy instructions: *Copy Date:* 15 days prior to publication date
BUSINESS: MARINE & SHIPPING: Commercial Fishing

CUS-MAGAZINE
1648615F80-869
Editorial: 1 parc de l'Etoile, CEDEX, 67076 STRASBOURG **Tel:** 3 88 60 93 45 **Fax:** 3 88 60 93 90
Email: cus.magazine@cus-strasbourg.net
ISSN: 0008-5472
Date Established: 1996; **Freq:** 6 issues yearly - variable; **Cover Price:** Free; **Circ:** 252,500
Usual Pagination: 32
Profile: Publication focussing on local community information.
Language(s): French
Mechanical Data: Type Area: 300 x 420
CONSUMER: RURAL & REGIONAL INTEREST

D'A (D'ARCHITECTURES)
4587F4A-31
Editorial: 1 place Boieldieu, 75002 PARIS
Tel: 1 48 24 08 97 **Fax:** 1 42 47 00 76
Email: e.caille@innovapresse.com **Web site:** http://www.innovapresse.com
ISSN: 1145-0835
Date Established: 1989; **Freq:** Monthly - début de mois; **Cover Price:** EUR 9.50
Annual Sub.: EUR 82; **Circ:** 5,156
Usual Pagination: 100
Profile: Magazine concerning all aspects of architecture.
Language(s): French
Readership: Read by architects and designers.
ADVERTISING RATES:
Full Page Colour .... EUR 6030
Mechanical Data: Type Area: 230 x 300
Copy instructions: *Copy Date:* 21 days prior to publication date
BUSINESS: ARCHITECTURE & BUILDING: Architecture

DANS L'AIR DU TEMPS
1774805F74N-126
Editorial: ADT Communication, 450 route de Nîmes, 34920 LE CRES **Tel:** 4 67 87 05 60
Fax: 4 67 87 02 36
Email: redac.adt@orange.fr **Web site:** http://www.danslairdutemps.com
Date Established: 1997; **Freq:** Monthly; **Cover Price:** Free; **Circ:** 250,000
Editor: Christine Clémentz
Language(s): French
CONSUMER: WOMEN'S INTEREST CONSUMER MAGAZINES: Retirement

LE DAUPHINE LIBERE
6172F67B-3000
Editorial: Les Iles Cordées, CEDEX, 38913 VEUREY
Tel: 4 76 88 71 00 **Fax:** 4 76 85 80 20
Email: jean-pierre.souchon@ledauphine.com **Web site:** http://www.ledauphine.com
ISSN: 1760-6314
Date Established: 1945; **Freq:** Daily - tous les jours; **Cover Price:** EUR 0.85
Annual Sub.: EUR 243; **Circ:** 241,867
Usual Pagination: 32
Profile: Daily regional newspaper covering national, regional and local current events. The head editorial office produces the pages common to all editions. Sunday price: 1,50 € (including TV Magazine and Version Fémina).
Language(s): French
ADVERTISING RATES:
Full Page Mono .... EUR 10959
Full Page Colour .... EUR 14247
Mechanical Data: Type Area: 330 x 500
REGIONAL DAILY & SUNDAY NEWSPAPERS: Regional Daily Newspapers

LE DAUPHINE LIBERE EDITION ISERE NORD BOURGOIN - VILLE NOUVELLE
1619544F67B-8544
Editorial: 19 avenue du Grand-Tissage, BP 223, 38305 BOURGOIN-JALLIEU **Tel:** 4 74 28 03 00
Fax: 4 74 28 89 95
Email: centre.bourgoin@ledauphine.com **Web site:** http://www.ledauphine.com
Freq: Daily - tous les jours; **Cover Price:** EUR 0.85
Annual Sub.: EUR 243; **Circ:** 330,551
Usual Pagination: 30
Profile: Daily regional newspaper covering national, regional and local current events.
Language(s): French
ADVERTISING RATES:
Full Page Mono .... EUR 5453
Mechanical Data: Type Area: 410 x 590
REGIONAL DAILY & SUNDAY NEWSPAPERS: Regional Daily Newspapers

DECISION ACHATS
4822F14A-139
Editorial: 13 rue Louis Pasteur, CEDEX, 92513 BOULOGNE BILLANCOURT **Tel:** 1 46 99 93 93
Fax: 1 46 99 97 71
Email: sdeboisfleury@editialis.fr **Web site:** http://www.decision-achats.fr
ISSN: 1960-1379
Date Established: 1994; **Freq:** Monthly - variable; **Cover Price:** EUR 7.50
Annual Sub.: EUR 120; **Circ:** 30,000
Usual Pagination: 108
Profile: Review of consumer products and services for business, with topical and product news, buyers guide, and practical pages.
Language(s): French
ADVERTISING RATES:
Full Page Colour .... EUR 5500
Mechanical Data: Type Area: 21 x 28,5
Copy instructions: *Copy Date:* 15 days prior to publication date
BUSINESS: COMMERCE, INDUSTRY & MANAGEMENT

LA DEPECHE DU MIDI
6210F67B-3100
Editorial: A Paris, 5 rue du Hanovre, 75002 PARIS
Tel: 5 62 11 33 00 **Fax:** 5 62 11 34 59
Email: yann.bouffin@ladepeche.fr **Web site:** http://www.ladepeche.fr
Freq: Daily - le matin; **Cover Price:** EUR 0.90
Annual Sub.: EUR 220.97; **Circ:** 190,875
Usual Pagination: 30
Managing Director: José Biosca
Profile: Daily newspaper. Local news and Magazine. Sunday price: 1,50 €.
Language(s): French
ADVERTISING RATES:
Full Page Mono .... EUR 6100
Full Page Colour .... EUR 7625
Mechanical Data: Type Area: berlinois
REGIONAL DAILY & SUNDAY NEWSPAPERS: Regional Daily Newspapers

LA DEPECHE DU MIDI EDITION DE L'AUDE
753047F67B-8752
Editorial: 20 place Carnot, 11000 CARCASSONNE
Tel: 4 68 11 90 11 **Fax:** 4 68 11 90 12
Email: redaction.castelnaudary@ladepeche.fr **Web site:** http://www.ladepeche.fr
ISSN: 0181-7981
Date Established: 1870; **Freq:** Daily - Aude (11); **Cover Price:** EUR 0.90
Annual Sub.: EUR 343.21; **Circ:** 250,000
Usual Pagination: 40
Profile: General news covering the Aude region.
Language(s): French
REGIONAL DAILY & SUNDAY NEWSPAPERS: Regional Daily Newspapers

LA DEPECHE DU MIDI EDITION DE L'AVEYRON
753048F67B-8754
Editorial: 20 rue Lamartine, 12700 CAPDENAC-GARE **Tel:** 5 65 63 81 30 **Fax:** 5 65 64 80 97
Email: redaction.decazeville@ladepeche.fr **Web site:** http://www.ladepeche.fr
ISSN: 0181-7981
Freq: Daily - le matin tous les jours; **Cover Price:** EUR 0.90
Annual Sub.: EUR 293.51; **Circ:** 223,067
Profile: Regional newspaper focussing on news, current affairs, economics, politics, culture and sport. One part general and one regional.
Language(s): French
Mechanical Data: Type Area: berlinois
REGIONAL DAILY & SUNDAY NEWSPAPERS: Regional Daily Newspapers

LA DEPECHE DU MIDI EDITION DU LOT-ET-GARONNE
753059F67B-8753
Editorial: 109 boulevard Carnot, BP 59, 47003 CEDEX AGEN **Tel:** 5 53 48 05 10 **Fax:** 5 53 66 77 73
Email: redaction.villeneuve@ladepeche.fr **Web site:** http://www.ladepeche.fr
ISSN: 0181-7981
Freq: Daily - tous les jours; **Cover Price:** EUR 0.90
Annual Sub.: EUR 293.51; **Circ:** 255,107
Profile: Regional and local news covering the Lot-et-Garonne region.
Language(s): French
REGIONAL DAILY & SUNDAY NEWSPAPERS: Regional Daily Newspapers

LA DEPECHE DU MIDI EDITION DU TARN SUD
753060F67B-8759
Editorial: 4 quai Miredames, 81100 CASTRES
Tel: 5 63 51 42 10 **Fax:** 5 63 51 11 54
Email: redaction.castres@ladepeche.fr **Web site:** http://www.ladepeche.fr
Freq: Daily - tous les matins; **Cover Price:** EUR 0.90
Annual Sub.: EUR 293.51; **Circ:** 192,075
Profile: National, regional and local news.
Language(s): French
REGIONAL DAILY & SUNDAY NEWSPAPERS: Regional Daily Newspapers

LA DEPECHE DU MIDI EDITION DU TARN-ET-GARONNE
753061F67B-8758
Editorial: 3 rue de la république, 82200 MOISSAC
Tel: 5 63 04 02 24 **Fax:** 5 63 04 32 27
Email: redaction.moissac@ladepeche.fr **Web site:** http://www.ladepeche.fr
Freq: Daily - le matin; **Cover Price:** EUR 0.90
Annual Sub.: EUR 293.51; **Circ:** 18,000
Profile: National, regional and local news.
Language(s): French
REGIONAL DAILY & SUNDAY NEWSPAPERS: Regional Daily Newspapers

DERMATOLOGIE PRATIQUE
5665F56A-170
Editorial: LEN MEDICAL, 15 rue des Sablons, 75116 PARIS **Tel:** 1 47 55 31 31 **Fax:** 1 47 55 32 32
Email: phumbert@len-medical.fr
ISSN: 0982-8567
Date Established: 1987; **Freq:** Monthly - le 25 chaque mois; **Cover Price:** EUR 460
Annual Sub.: EUR 39; **Circ:** 4,850
Usual Pagination: 16
Managing Director: Stéphane Elgozi
Profile: Magazine containing articles about the treatment of skin diseases.
Language(s): French
ADVERTISING RATES:
Full Page Mono .... EUR 5300
Full Page Colour .... EUR 6500
Mechanical Data: Type Area: 290 x 430
BUSINESS: HEALTH & MEDICAL

DETENTE JARDIN
7285F93-30
Editorial: 22 rue Letellier, CEDEX 15, 75739 PARIS
Tel: 1 43 23 45 72 **Fax:** 1 43 23 04 95
Email: catherine.delvaux@uni-editions.com
ISSN: 1253-8280
Date Established: 1996; **Freq:** 24 issues yearly - dernière semaine des mois pairs; **Cover Price:** EUR 2.40
Annual Sub.: EUR 15.60; **Circ:** 381,487
Usual Pagination: 52
Profile: Magazine dedicated to gardening.
Language(s): French
ADVERTISING RATES:
Full Page Colour .... EUR 8600
Mechanical Data: Type Area: 21 x 27
Copy instructions: *Copy Date:* 31 days prior to publication date
CONSUMER: GARDENING

DETOURS EN FRANCE
7176F89A-42
Editorial: 22 rue Letellier, 75739 CEDEX 15 PARIS
Tel: 1 43 23 45 72 **Fax:** 1 57 72 02 54
ISSN: 1264-5044
Date Established: 1991; **Freq:** Monthly - 01 03 04 06 09 10 11 et 12; **Cover Price:** EUR 5.95
Annual Sub.: EUR 71.40; **Circ:** 78,574
Usual Pagination: 100
Managing Director: Jacques Brière
Profile: Magazine focusing on French culture and heritage.
Language(s): French
ADVERTISING RATES:
Full Page Colour .... EUR 8800
Mechanical Data: Type Area: 220 x 285
Copy instructions: *Copy Date:* 62 days prior to publication date
CONSUMER: HOLIDAYS & TRAVEL: Travel

DIAPASON
6890F78A-120
Editorial: Immeuble Trait d'Union, 8 rue François Ory, 92120 MONTROUGE **Tel:** 1 41 33 57 36
Fax: 1 41 33 57 18
Web site: http://www.diapasonmag.fr
ISSN: 0224-4950
Date Established: 1956; **Freq:** Monthly - fin mois pour mois suivant; **Cover Price:** EUR 5.90; **Circ:** 36,466
Usual Pagination: 164
Managing Director: Ernesto Mauri
Profile: Magazine covering all aspects of classical music.
Language(s): French
ADVERTISING RATES:
Full Page Mono .... EUR 4390
Full Page Colour .... EUR 3450
Mechanical Data: Type Area: 220 x 280
Copy instructions: *Copy Date:* 21 days prior to publication date
CONSUMER: CONSUMER ELECTRONICS: Hi-Fi & Recording

DIMANCHE OUEST FRANCE
1619403F67B-8403
Editorial: 10 rue du Breil, ZI Sud Est, 35051 CEDEX 9 RENNES **Tel:** 2 99 32 67 26 **Fax:** 2 99 32 62 63
Email: dimanche@ouest-france.fr **Web site:** http://www.ouest-france.fr
ISSN: 1285-7688
Date Established: 1997; **Freq:** Weekly - le dimanche; **Cover Price:** EUR 0.90
Annual Sub.: EUR 43; **Circ:** 350,055
Usual Pagination: 64
Profile: General, regional and local information newspaper. Divided in 4 parts: News, family, sports and local events guide. Family booklet with 4 pages dedicated to children "Dimoitou" News, comics, games, experiments, DIY, jokes).
Language(s): French
ADVERTISING RATES:
Full Page Mono .... EUR 1800
Full Page Colour .... EUR 2340
Mechanical Data: Type Area: 225 x 315
REGIONAL DAILY & SUNDAY NEWSPAPERS: Regional Daily Newspapers

DIRECT AFFAIRES
1772788F21A-2647
Editorial: 2 avenue du Pays-de-Caen, Colombelles, 14902 CEDEX 9 CAEN **Tel:** 2 31 35 77 00
Fax: 2 31 35 77 18
Email: commercial@direct-affaires.fr **Web site:** http://www.direct-affaires.fr
Freq: 26 issues yearly - milieu de mois; **Cover Price:** Free; **Circ:** 240,000
Usual Pagination: 24
Managing Director: Marc Jourdan

Profile: Publication focussing on agriculture including rural interest and classified.
Language(s): French
Copy instructions: *Copy Date:* 4 days prior to publication date
BUSINESS: AGRICULTURE & FARMING

DIRECT MATIN PLUS
1800013F67B-8805
Editorial: 31-32 quai de Dion Bouton, 92800 PUTEAUX **Tel:** 1 46 96 31 00 **Fax:** 1 46 96 40 94
Email: s.planas@direct8.fr **Web site:** http://www.matinplus.net
ISSN: 1771-2459
Date Established: 2007; **Freq:** Daily - matin; **Cover Price:** Free; **Circ:** 350,000
Profile: Free regional daily newspaper focussing on regional, national and international news and current affairs including sport, leisure, TV guide, classifieds, games and weather forecast.
Language(s): French
ADVERTISING RATES:
Full Page Colour .... EUR 49500
REGIONAL DAILY & SUNDAY NEWSPAPERS: Regional Daily Newspapers

DIRECT SOIR
1752998F67B-8798
Editorial: 31-32 quai de Dion Bouton, 92800 PUTEAUX **Tel:** 1 46 96 431 00 **Fax:** 1 46 96 40 94
Email: redac@directsoir.net **Web site:** http://www.directsoir.net
ISSN: 1771-2092
Date Established: 2006; **Freq:** Daily - le soir, du lundi au vendredi; **Cover Price:** Free; **Circ:** 303,162
Usual Pagination: 28
Profile: First free evening daily newspaper dedicated to current events, entertainment, culture and celebrities. Distributed in the following cities: Agen, Aix-en-Provence, Avignon, Balma, Bordeaux, Grenoble, Lille, Lyon, Marseille, Paris, Roubaix, Saint-Etienne, Saint-Denis, Toulon and Toulouse.
Language(s): French
ADVERTISING RATES:
Full Page Colour .... EUR 45000
Mechanical Data: Type Area: 298 x 390
REGIONAL DAILY & SUNDAY NEWSPAPERS: Regional Daily Newspapers

DISTRIBUTIQUE.COM
4644F5B-38
Editorial: 40 boulevard Henri-Sellier, 92150 SURESNES **Tel:** 1 41 97 02 02 **Fax:** 1 41 97 02 01
Email: redac_webdistri@it-news-info.com **Web site:** http://www.distributique.com
Date Established: 1997
Circ: 80,000 Unique Users
Profile: Business magazine for direct and indirect sales of computing and telecommunications products and services for office or home.
Language(s): French
ADVERTISING RATES:
Full Page Colour .... EUR 4900
BUSINESS: COMPUTERS & AUTOMATION: Data Processing

DNA - DERNIERES NOUVELLES D'ALSACE STRASBOURG
1619405F67B-8405
Editorial: 17-21 rue de la Nuée-Bleue, BP 406, 67077 CEDEX STRASBOURG **Tel:** 3 88 21 55 00
Fax: 3 88 21 55 15
Email: a.latham@dna.fr **Web site:** http://www.dna.fr
ISSN: 0150-397X
Freq: Daily - le matin; **Cover Price:** EUR 0.90
Annual Sub.: EUR 294.59; **Circ:** 196,301
Managing Director: Jean-Claude Bonnaud
Profile: Local, regional, national and international information newspaper. Price on Friday: 1,50 €, because of the Tv Guide and the Fémina Version supplements.
Language(s): French
ADVERTISING RATES:
Full Page Mono .... EUR 12510
Mechanical Data: Type Area: 31 x 47
REGIONAL DAILY & SUNDAY NEWSPAPERS: Regional Daily Newspapers

LA DORDOGNE LIBRE
6160F67B-3300
Editorial: 4 allée d'Aquitaine, BP 3053, CEDEX, 24003 PERIGUEUX **Tel:** 5 53 35 59 00
Fax: 5 53 09 49 18
Email: redactiondl@dordogne.com **Web site:** http://www.dordogne.com
Date Established: 1945; **Freq:** Daily - ts les jours sauf dim. et fêtes; **Cover Price:** EUR 0.65
Annual Sub.: EUR 182; **Circ:** 6,648
Usual Pagination: 32
Profile: Local news. Editing supplements sold with the daily newspaper.
Language(s): French
ADVERTISING RATES:
Full Page Mono .... EUR 2584
Full Page Colour .... EUR 3037
Mechanical Data: Type Area: tabloïd
REGIONAL DAILY & SUNDAY NEWSPAPERS: Regional Daily Newspapers

LE DOSSIER FAMILIAL
1618003F74C-452
Editorial: 22 rue Letellier, CEDEX 15, 75739 PARIS
Tel: 1 43 23 45 72 **Fax:** 1 43 23 61 12
Email: yves.george@uni-editions.com **Web site:** http://www.dossierfamilial.com
ISSN: 0182-5100
Date Established: 1973; **Freq:** Monthly - entre le 25 et le 30 du mois; **Cover Price:** EUR 3.05
Annual Sub.: EUR 39.60; **Circ:** 1,359,644
Usual Pagination: 76
Language(s): French
Mechanical Data: Type Area: 15 x 22
Copy instructions: *Copy Date:* 31 days prior to publication date
CONSUMER: WOMEN'S INTEREST CONSUMER MAGAZINES: Home & Family

DREAMS
1617027F74B-1
Editorial: 72 boulevard Berthier, 75017 PARIS
Tel: 1 47 63 90 95 48 00 **Fax:** 1 47 63 49 08
Email: fjdaehn@monsieur.fr **Web site:** http://www.dreams-magazine.com
ISSN: 1958-170X
Date Established: 1999; **Freq:** Quarterly - 03 06 09 11
Annual Sub.: EUR 18; **Circ:** 20,000
Usual Pagination: 200
Profile: Publication focussing on watches, jewellery and luxury goods including interviews, designers, and new trends.
Language(s): French
ADVERTISING RATES:
Full Page Colour .... EUR 5150
Mechanical Data: Type Area: 225 x 297
Copy instructions: *Copy Date:* 21 days prior to publication date
CONSUMER: WOMEN'S INTEREST CONSUMER MAGAZINES: Women's Interest - Fashion

LA DROME
1617169F32A-1032
Editorial: Conseil Général - Hôtel du Département, 26 avenue du Président Herriot, CEDEX 9, 26026 VALENCE **Tel:** 4 75 79 26 23 **Fax:** 4 75 79 26 29
Email: communication@ladrome.fr **Web site:** http://www.ladrome.fr
ISSN: 0981-2075
Freq: 24 issues yearly - mois impairs; **Cover Price:** Free; **Circ:** 220,000
Usual Pagination: 32
Profile: Publication focussing on local government and department issues, including economics, culture and social issues.
Language(s): French
Mechanical Data: Type Area: A 4
BUSINESS: LOCAL GOVERNMENT, LEISURE & RECREATION: Local Government

DU COTE DE CHEZ VOUS
1641346F94H-506
Editorial: TEXTUEL, 146 rue du Faubourg Poissonnière, 75010 PARIS **Tel:** 1 53 21 21 00
Fax: 1 53 21 22 49
Email: rvincent@leroymerlin.fr
ISSN: 1297-3696
Date Established: 2004; **Freq:** 24 issues yearly - 1ère semaine du mois; **Circ:** 354,052
Usual Pagination: 100
Profile: Publication focussing on home & style including tips, ideas, refurbishment, fitting decoration and interior design.
Language(s): French
ADVERTISING RATES:
Full Page Colour .... EUR 20000
Mechanical Data: Type Area: 212 x 280
Copy instructions: *Copy Date:* 21 days prior to publication date
CONSUMER: OTHER CLASSIFICATIONS: Customer Magazines

L' ECHO DU PAS DE CALAIS
1660708F80-934
Editorial: 5 place Jean Jaurès, BP 139, CEDEX, 62194 LILLERS **Tel:** 3 21 54 35 75 **Fax:** 3 21 54 34 89
Email: contact@echo62.com **Web site:** http://www.echo62.com
ISSN: 1254-5171
Date Established: 1976; **Freq:** Monthly - le 1er lundi du mois; **Cover Price:** Free; **Circ:** 625,893
Usual Pagination: 32
Profile: Regional publication focussing on local news and current affairs including rural interest, cultural heritage, tourism, sport, arts, shows, events and student interest.
Language(s): French
ADVERTISING RATES:
Full Page Colour .... EUR 10000
Mechanical Data: Type Area: tabloïd
Copy instructions: *Copy Date:* 21 days prior to publication date
CONSUMER: RURAL & REGIONAL INTEREST

L' ECHO REPUBLICAIN
6166F67B-3700
Editorial: 21 rue Vincent Chevard, BP 50189, 28004 CHARTRES **Tel:** 2 37 88 88 88
Email: lucette.dihars@lechorepublicain.presse.fr **Web site:** http://lechorepublicain.fr
ISSN: 0758-3311
Date Established: 1929; **Freq:** Daily - tous les jours; **Cover Price:** EUR 0.85
Annual Sub.: EUR 252; **Circ:** 30,382
Usual Pagination: 40
Editor-in-Chief: Hugues De Lestapis
Profile: Regional and local news.
Language(s): French
ADVERTISING RATES:
Full Page Mono .... EUR 4552
Full Page Colour .... EUR 5684
Mechanical Data: Type Area: Tabloïd
REGIONAL DAILY & SUNDAY NEWSPAPERS: Regional Daily Newspapers

L' ECHO TOURISTIQUE
5579F50-40
Editorial: Antony Parc 2, 10 place du Général de Gaulle, BP 20156 CEDEX, 92186 ANTONY
Tel: 1 77 92 92 92 **Fax:** 1 77 92 98 33
Email: lrousseau@gisi.fr **Web site:** http://www.lechotouristique.com
ISSN: 0150-6560
Freq: Weekly; **Cover Price:** EUR 2.50
Annual Sub.: EUR 53; **Circ:** 13,071
Usual Pagination: 48
Profile: Journal for travel and tourism professionals.
Language(s): French
ADVERTISING RATES:
Full Page Mono .... EUR 3900
Full Page Colour .... EUR 6500
BUSINESS: TRAVEL & TOURISM

LES ECHOS
6089F65A-30
Editorial: 16 rue du 4 septembre, CEDEX 02, 75112 PARIS **Tel:** 1 49 53 65 65
Email: hgibier@lesechos.fr **Web site:** http://www.lesechos.fr
ISSN: 0153-4831
Date Established: 1908; **Freq:** Daily - du lundi au vendredi; **Cover Price:** EUR 1.40
Annual Sub.: EUR 383; **Circ:** 125,984
Usual Pagination: 64
Profile: Tabloid-sized quality newspaper focusing on financial and economic news. Also covers national and international news, politics, culture and sport.
Language(s): French
Readership: Read by company directors, senior executives, middle managers and students.
ADVERTISING RATES:
Full Page Mono .... EUR 41000
Full Page Colour .... EUR 64000
Mechanical Data: Type Area: berlinois
NATIONAL DAILY & SUNDAY NEWSPAPERS: National Daily Newspapers

L' ECLAIR PYRENEES
1619713F67B-8711
Editorial: 6-8 rue Despourrins, 64000 PAU
Tel: 5 59 82 29 29 **Fax:** 5 59 27 79 31
Email: redaction-pp@pyrenees.com
ISSN: 2109-0874
Date Established: 1944; **Freq:** Daily - Every morning except Sunday; **Cover Price:** EUR 0.80
Annual Sub.: EUR 218; **Circ:** 8,960
Usual Pagination: 56
Profile: Daily general and regional newspaper. The journalists from "Pyrénées Presse" are working for 2 newspapers: "La République des Pyrénées" and "L'Éclair".
Language(s): French
ADVERTISING RATES:
Full Page Mono .... EUR 4347
Full Page Colour .... EUR 4706
Mechanical Data: Type Area: tabloïd
REGIONAL DAILY & SUNDAY NEWSPAPERS: Regional Daily Newspapers

ECO DES PAYS DE SAVOIE
6003F14A-808
Editorial: 7 route de Nanfray, 74960 CRAN-GEVRIER
Tel: 4 50 33 35 35 **Fax:** 4 50 52 11 06
Email: redaction@ecosavoie.fr **Web site:** http://www.ecosavoie.fr
ISSN: 1287-4779
Date Established: 1869; **Freq:** Weekly - vendredi
Annual Sub.: EUR 80; **Circ:** 14,000
Usual Pagination: 56
Profile: Magazine focusing on regional business and economics.
Language(s): French
ADVERTISING RATES:
Full Page Colour .... EUR 1300
Mechanical Data: Type Area: 23 x 30
BUSINESS: COMMERCE, INDUSTRY & MANAGEMENT

ECRAN TOTAL
4562F2D-29
Editorial: Immeuble Sirius, 9 allée Jean Prouvé, CEDEX, 92387 CLICHY **Tel:** 1 41 40 33 33
Fax: 1 47 40 31 00
Email: redac.et@editions-lariviere.fr **Web site:** http://www.ecran-total.fr
ISSN: 1165-8045
Date Established: 1993; **Freq:** Weekly - mercredi
Annual Sub.: EUR 343; **Circ:** 10,000
Usual Pagination: 38
Profile: Magazine focusing on the audio-visual field, with creative, economic and technical features.
Language(s): French
Readership: Read by managers of recording studios and technicians.
ADVERTISING RATES:
Full Page Mono .... EUR 2150
Full Page Colour .... EUR 3500
BUSINESS: COMMUNICATIONS, ADVERTISING & MARKETING: Broadcasting

EDGAR
623477F86C-12
Editorial: 4 rue Reyer, CEDEX, 6414 CANNES
Tel: 4 97 06 95 95 **Fax:** 4 97 06 95 96
Email: i.garnerone@luxmediagroup.com
ISSN: 1621-613X
Date Established: 2000; **Freq:** 24 issues yearly - the 10th of even months; **Circ:** 71,221
Usual Pagination: 162
Profile: Men's interest magazine covering a wide range of subjects. Also contains views of the rich and famous.
Language(s): French
ADVERTISING RATES:
Full Page Colour .... EUR 9200
Mechanical Data: Type Area: 23 x 28
CONSUMER: ADULT & GAY MAGAZINES: Men's Lifestyle Magazines

ELECTRONIC PRODUCT NEWS
1394F18A-182
Editorial: Forum 55, 52 rue Camille Desmoulins, 92448 ISSY LES MOULINEAUX **Tel:** 1 46 29 46 29
Fax: 1 46 29 23 50
Email: epn@reedbusiness.fr **Web site:** http://www.epn-online.com
ISSN: 1763-7384
Date Established: 1973; **Freq:** Monthly - 1ère semaine du mois; **Cover Price:** Free; **Circ:** 50,000
Usual Pagination: 44
Profile: Pan-European journal covering new electronic components and instruments from manufacturers worldwide.
Language(s): French
ADVERTISING RATES:
Full Page Colour .... EUR 20500
Mechanical Data: Type Area: tabloïd
Copy instructions: *Copy Date:* 21 days prior to publication date
BUSINESS: ELECTRONICS

ELECTRONIQUES
4631F5A-20
Editorial: 12 rue d'Oradour S/Glane, CEDEX 15, 75504 PARIS **Tel:** 1 71 18 54 00 **Fax:** 1 71 18 52 50
Email: electroniques@groupe01.fr **Web site:** http://www.electroniques.biz
ISSN: 1157-1152
Date Established: 2010; **Freq:** Monthly. vers le 15 du mois; **Cover Price:** EUR 12.20
Annual Sub.: EUR 110; **Circ:** 8,205 Unique Users
Usual Pagination: 100
Profile: Magazine focusing on automation and electronics.
Language(s): French
Readership: Aimed at design engineers.
ADVERTISING RATES:
Full Page Mono .... EUR 5149
Full Page Colour .... EUR 5420
Mechanical Data: Type Area: 23 x 29,7
Copy instructions: *Copy Date:* 15 days prior to publication date
BUSINESS: COMPUTERS & AUTOMATION: Automation & Instrumentation

ELECTRONIQUES.BIZ
4929F18A-38
Editorial: 12 rue d'Oradour-sur-Glane, CEDEX 15, 75504 PARIS **Tel:** 1 71 18 54 00 **Fax:** 145575039
Email: eih@groupe-tests.fr **Web site:** http://www.electronique.biz
Date Established: 1991; **Freq:** Daily. Continuous;
Circ: 15,000 Unique Users
Usual Pagination: 45
Profile: Journal covering development of products and electronic systems.
Language(s): French
Mechanical Data: Type Area: A 3
BUSINESS: ELECTRONICS

ELLE
6403F74A-130
Editorial: 149 rue Anatole France, CEDEX, 92534 LEVALLOIS PERRET **Tel:** 1 41 34 60 00
Fax: 1 41 34 74 92
Email: peggy.michelon@lagardere-active.com **Web site:** http://www.elle.fr
ISSN: 0013-6298
Date Established: 1945; **Freq:** Weekly - vendredi
Annual Sub.: EUR 85; **Circ:** 386,173
Usual Pagination: 266
Publisher: Franck Espiasse-Cabau
Profile: Magazine with fashion, beauty, health and articles on women's issues.
Language(s): French
ADVERTISING RATES:
Full Page Mono .... EUR 22000
Full Page Colour .... EUR 27500
Mechanical Data: Type Area: 227 x 297
Copy instructions: *Copy Date:* 21 days prior to publication date
CONSUMER: WOMEN'S INTEREST CONSUMER MAGAZINES: Women's Interest

ELLE A TABLE
7352F74P-451
Editorial: 149 rue Anatole France, CEDEX, 92534 LEVALLOIS PERRET **Tel:** 1 41 34 66 87
Fax: 1 41 34 67 10

Email: courrierelleatable@hfp.fr
ISSN: 1293-5948
Date Established: 1999; **Freq:** 24 issues yearly - tous les 2 mois; **Cover Price:** EUR 3.50
Annual Sub.: EUR 17; **Circ:** 176,786
Usual Pagination: 136
Publisher: Philippe Khyr
Profile: Magazine containing articles on all types of cuisine includes recipes and cooking styles from different countries.
Language(s): French
ADVERTISING RATES:
Full Page Mono .... EUR 10400
Full Page Colour .... EUR 13000
Mechanical Data: Type Area: 285 x 220
Copy instructions: *Copy Date:* 28 days prior to publication date
CONSUMER: WOMEN'S INTEREST CONSUMER MAGAZINES: Food & Cookery

ELLE DECORATION 6445F74C-95
Editorial: 149 rue Anatole France, CEDEX, 92534 LEVALLOIS PERRET **Tel:** 1 41 34 60 00 65 95
Fax: 1 41 34 71 94
Email: courrierelledeco@hfp.fr
ISSN: 0988-1476
Date Established: 1987; **Freq:** Monthly - 01 02 03 04 05 06 09 10 11 12; **Cover Price:** EUR 4.50
Annual Sub.: EUR 32; **Circ:** 191,438
Usual Pagination: 180
Publisher: Philippe Khyr
Profile: Magazine containing interior decorating ideas.
Language(s): French
Readership: Read by home owners aged between 25 and 50 years.
ADVERTISING RATES:
Full Page Mono .... EUR 10300
Full Page Colour .... EUR 15800
Copy instructions: *Copy Date:* 31 days prior to publication date
CONSUMER: WOMEN'S INTEREST CONSUMER MAGAZINES: Home & Family

L' ELU D'AUJOURD'HUI 5297F32A-65
Editorial: 10 rue Parmentier, CEDEX, 93189 MONTREUIL **Tel:** 1 48 51 15 79 78 78
Fax: 1 48 51 50 72
Email: elu@elunet.org
ISSN: 0181-2736
Date Established: 1979; **Freq:** Monthly - entre le 12 et le 15
Annual Sub.: EUR 75; **Circ:** 12,000
Usual Pagination: 56
Profile: Journal of the National Association of Communist and Republican Elected Councillors.
Language(s): French
ADVERTISING RATES:
Full Page Mono .... EUR 3940
Full Page Colour .... EUR 5170
Mechanical Data: Type Area: 210 x 297
BUSINESS: LOCAL GOVERNMENT, LEISURE & RECREATION: Local Government

EMBALLAGES MAGAZINE
5356F35-60
Editorial: Antony Parc 2, 10 place du Général de Gaulle, 92160 ANTONY **Tel:** 1 77 92 92 92
Fax: 1 77 92 98 25
Email: hsaporta@gisi.fr **Web site:** http://www.emballagesmagazine.com
ISSN: 0013-6573
Date Established: 1932; **Freq:** Monthly - 10 du mois (sf janvier et août)
Annual Sub.: EUR 149; **Circ:** 10,000
Usual Pagination: 8
Editor-in-Chief: Henri Saporta
Profile: Professional magazine about packaging and conditioning.
Language(s): French
ADVERTISING RATES:
Full Page Mono .... EUR 2730
Full Page Colour .... EUR 4240
Copy instructions: *Copy Date:* 14 days prior to publication date
BUSINESS: PACKAGING & BOTTLING

EN ALSACE 1616817F89A-336
Editorial: 18 rue de Thann, CEDEX 9, 68945 MULHOUSE
Email: redaction@en-alsace.fr
ISSN: 1634-3859
Date Established: 1996; **Freq:** 24 issues yearly - début des mois 03 06 08 10 12; **Cover Price:** EUR 6.50; **Circ:** 25,000
Usual Pagination: 116
Editor-in-Chief: Christophe Nagyos
Language(s): French
ADVERTISING RATES:
Full Page Colour .... EUR 2500
Mechanical Data: Type Area: 21 x 28,7
Copy instructions: *Copy Date:* 21 days prior to publication date
CONSUMER: HOLIDAYS & TRAVEL: Travel

ENERGIE PLUS 5919F58-49
Editorial: 47 avenue Laplace, CEDEX, 94117 ARCUEIL **Tel:** 1 46 56 35 44 **Fax:** 1 49 85 06 27
Email: energieplus@atee.fr **Web site:** http://www.energie-plus.com
ISSN: 0292-1731
Date Established: 1981; **Freq:** 26 issues yearly - 1er et 15 du mois; **Annual Sub.:** EUR 130; **Circ:** 2,527
Usual Pagination: 56
Profile: Technical and professional journal about all aspects of the energy sector.
Language(s): French
ADVERTISING RATES:
Full Page Mono .... EUR 1337
Full Page Colour .... EUR 2465
Mechanical Data: Type Area: A 4
Copy instructions: *Copy Date:* 10 days prior to publication date
BUSINESS: ENERGY, FUEL & NUCLEAR

ENFANT MAGAZINE 6477F74D-40
Editorial: 18 rue Barbès, CEDEX, 92128 MONTROUGE **Tel:** 1 74 31 58 88 60 60
Fax: 1 74 31 60 29
Email: enfant.magazine@bayard-presse.com **Web site:** http://www.enfant.com
ISSN: 0397-4820
Date Established: 1976; **Freq:** Monthly - 6-8 du mois; **Cover Price:** EUR 2.90
Annual Sub.: EUR 20.60; **Circ:** 131,233
Usual Pagination: 148
Profile: Practical childcare magazine for expectant mothers and parents of children of up to 2 years. Covers health and hygiene, growing up, young fashion, baby accessories and toys.
Language(s): French
ADVERTISING RATES:
Full Page Mono .... EUR 13200
Full Page Colour .... EUR 16500
Mechanical Data: Type Area: 285 x 225
CONSUMER: WOMEN'S INTEREST CONSUMER MAGAZINES: Child Care

ENJEUX - LES ECHOS 4468F1A-140
Editorial: 16 rue du 4 septembre, CEDEX 02, 75112 PARIS **Tel:** 1 49 53 65 65
Email: mlopez@lesechos.fr **Web site:** http://www.lesechos.fr
ISSN: 1167-2196
Date Established: 1992; **Freq:** Monthly - début de mois - vendredi; **Circ:** 119,481
Usual Pagination: 150
Profile: Magazine of financial and economic analysis and prospects.
Language(s): French
ADVERTISING RATES:
Full Page Colour .... EUR 22000
Mechanical Data: Type Area: 21,5 x 29
BUSINESS: FINANCE & ECONOMICS

L' ENSEIGNANT 5975F62J-90
Editorial: SE-UNSA, 209 boulevard Saint Germain, 75007 PARIS **Tel:** 1 44 39 23 89 **Fax:** 1 44 39 23 83
Email: secteur.communication@se-unsa.org
ISSN: 1241-039X
Freq: Monthly - mardi-mercredi
Annual Sub.: EUR 36; **Circ:** 115,598
Usual Pagination: 48
Profile: Publication of the French Syndicate of Teachers.
Language(s): French
ADVERTISING RATES:
Full Page Mono .... EUR 6125
Full Page Colour .... EUR 8450
Mechanical Data: Type Area: 205 x 280
Copy instructions: *Copy Date:* 10 days prior to publication date
BUSINESS: CHURCH & SCHOOL EQUIPMENT & EDUCATION: Teachers & Education Management

L' ENSEIGNEMENT PUBLIC
5952F62A-70
Editorial: UNSA EDUCATION, 87 bis avenue Georges Gosnat, CEDEX, 94853 IVRY SUR SEINE
Tel: 1 56 20 29 50 **Fax:** 1 56 20 29 89
Email: national@unsa-education.org
Freq: Quarterly - 15 des mois 03 06 10 12; **Cover Price:** EUR 4.60
Annual Sub.: EUR 18.40; **Circ:** 91,338
Usual Pagination: 32
Profile: Journal of the National Federation of Education.
Language(s): French
Readership: Read by members of the teaching profession.
ADVERTISING RATES:
Full Page Mono .... EUR 7695
Full Page Colour .... EUR 8550
Mechanical Data: Type Area: 205 x 280
Copy instructions: *Copy Date:* 14 days prior to publication date
BUSINESS: CHURCH & SCHOOL EQUIPMENT & EDUCATION: Education

ENTREPRENDRE 4826F14A-280_10
Editorial: CAHETEL, 70 avenue de Strasbourg, 94300 VINCENNES **Tel:** 1 49 57 99 46
Fax: 1 70 79 06 23
Email: i.goubier@lafontpresse.fr **Web site:** http://www.lafontpresse.fr
ISSN: 1145-5764
Date Established: 1984; **Freq:** Monthly - le 20 du mois; **Cover Price:** EUR 2.10; **Circ:** 18,255
Usual Pagination: 110
Profile: Business magazine for managers and directors.
Language(s): French
ADVERTISING RATES:
Full Page Colour .... EUR 7300
Mechanical Data: Type Area: 21 x 29,7
BUSINESS: COMMERCE, INDUSTRY & MANAGEMENT

L' ENTREPRISE 1617572F14H-121
Editorial: 29 rue de Châteaudun, CEDEX 09, 75308 PARIS **Tel:** 1 75 55 10 00 43 13 **Fax:** 1 75 55 41 20
Email: redaction@lentreprise.com **Web site:** http://www.lentreprise.com
ISSN: 1243-4167
Date Established: 1985; **Freq:** Monthly - first Wednesday of the month; **Cover Price:** EUR 3.50
Annual Sub.: EUR 24; **Circ:** 79,845
Usual Pagination: 180
Profile: Business publication focussing on economics, social, marketing, finance and management.
Language(s): French
ADVERTISING RATES:
Full Page Colour .... EUR 18300
Mechanical Data: Type Area: 205 x 280
Copy instructions: *Copy Date:* 10 days prior to publication date
BUSINESS: COMMERCE, INDUSTRY & MANAGEMENT: Small Business

ENTREPRISE ET CARRIERES
4870F14F-45
Editorial: 1 rue Eugène et Armand Peugeot, Case Postale 706, CEDEX, 92856 RUEIL MALMAISON
Tel: 1 76 73 33 01 **Fax:** 1 76 73 48 85
Email: gderosa@groupeliaisons.fr **Web site:** http://www.wk-rh.fr
ISSN: 1955-5687
Date Established: 1989; **Freq:** Weekly - tous les mardi; **Cover Price:** EUR 3.80
Annual Sub.: EUR 252.19; **Circ:** 17,613
Usual Pagination: 50
Profile: Magazine about management and human resources.
Language(s): French
ADVERTISING RATES:
Full Page Mono .... EUR 6700
Full Page Colour .... EUR 9600
Mechanical Data: Type Area: A 4
BUSINESS: COMMERCE, INDUSTRY & MANAGEMENT: Training & Recruitment

ENTRETIEN DES TEXTILES ET NETTOYAGE 5249F28-10
Editorial: CTTN - IREN, Avenue Guy de Collongue, BP 41 CEDEX, 69131 ECULLY **Tel:** 4 78 33 08 61
Fax: 4 78 43 34 12
Email: secretariat@cttn-iren.fr **Web site:** http://www.cttn-iren.fr
ISSN: 0181-8120
Freq: 24 issues yearly - début des mois 02 04 06 08 10 12; **Annual Sub.:** EUR 61; **Circ:** 3,000
Usual Pagination: 32
Profile: Review of textile cleaning and maintenance.
Language(s): French
ADVERTISING RATES:
Full Page Mono .... EUR 664
Full Page Colour .... EUR 1129
Mechanical Data: Type Area: A 4
BUSINESS: LAUNDRY & DRY CLEANING

L' ENTREVUE 7122F86C-25
Editorial: SCPE, 14 bis rue de la Faisanderie, CEDEX, 75116 PARIS **Tel:** 1 70 39 71 00
Fax: 1 45 53 17 10
Email: redac@entrevue.fr **Web site:** http://www.entrevue.fr
ISSN: 1169-5463
Date Established: 1992; **Freq:** Monthly - dernier mardi de chaque mois
Annual Sub.: EUR 28; **Circ:** 335,334
Usual Pagination: 148
Profile: Men's interest magazine containing interviews, human interest stories and information on television.
Language(s): French
Readership: Aimed at men aged between 18 to 35 years.
ADVERTISING RATES:
Full Page Colour .... EUR 25500
Mechanical Data: Type Area: 215 x 270
Copy instructions: *Copy Date:* 31 days prior to publication date
CONSUMER: ADULT & GAY MAGAZINES: Men's Lifestyle Magazines

ENVIRONNEMENT ET TECHNIQUE 5908F57-23
Editorial: SAP, 9 rue de l'Arbre Sec, 69001 LYON
Tel: 4 72 98 26 60 **Fax:** 4 72 98 26 80
Email: chateauvieux@dpe-edition.com **Web site:** http://www.pro-environnement.com
ISSN: 0986-2943
Date Established: 1980; **Freq:** Monthly - The 4th or 5th of the month; **Cover Price:** EUR 10.50
Annual Sub.: EUR 102; **Circ:** 7,550
Usual Pagination: 76
Profile: Magazine covering articles and information about pollution and all forms of waste disposal, providing industrial cleaning solutions.
Language(s): French
ADVERTISING RATES:
Full Page Mono .... EUR 1890
Full Page Colour .... EUR 2700
Mechanical Data: Type Area: A 4
Copy instructions: *Copy Date:* 15 days prior to publication date
BUSINESS: ENVIRONMENT & POLLUTION

ENVIRONNEMENT MAGAZINE
5905F57-184
Editorial: 38 rue Croix des Petits Champs, 75001 PARIS **Tel:** 1 53 45 89 00 **Fax:** 1 53 45 89 11
Email: d.bomstein@victoires-editions.fr **Web site:** http://www.environnement-magazine.fr
ISSN: 1163-2720
Date Established: 1845; **Freq:** Monthly; **Cover Price:** EUR 14
Annual Sub.: EUR 196; **Circ:** 13,887
Usual Pagination: 80
Profile: Magazine containing information, analysis and solutions on the environment. Also covers technology and the law relating to the environment.
Language(s): French
ADVERTISING RATES:
Full Page Mono .... EUR 3500
Full Page Colour .... EUR 4795
Mechanical Data: Type Area: A 4
Copy instructions: *Copy Date:* 21 days prior to publication date
BUSINESS: ENVIRONMENT & POLLUTION

L' EQUIPE 6090F65A-35
Editorial: 4 cours de l'Ile-Seguin, BP 10302, CEDEX, 92102 BOULOGNE BILLANCOURT
Tel: 1 40 93 20 20 **Fax:** 1 40 93 20 08
Web site: http://www.lequipe.fr
ISSN: 0153-1069
Date Established: 1948; **Freq:** Daily - 7 jours sur 7; **Cover Price:** EUR 0.85
Annual Sub.: EUR 309; **Circ:** 311,403
Managing Director: François Moriniere
Profile: Broadsheet-sized newspaper covering all aspects of competitive sport and motoring news. Political outlook: Independent.
Language(s): French
Readership: Read by a wide range of the general public and those of all ages particularly interested in sport and motoring.
Mechanical Data: Type Area: 39 x 57,5
NATIONAL DAILY & SUNDAY NEWSPAPERS: National Daily Newspapers

L' EQUIPE MAGAZINE 6102F65H-40
Editorial: 4 cour de l'Ile-Seguin, BP 10302, CEDEX, 92102 BOULOGNE BILLANCOURT
Tel: 1 40 93 20 20 **Fax:** 1 40 93 24 92
Email: magazine@lequipe.presse.fr **Web site:** http://www.lequipe.fr
ISSN: 0245-3312
Date Established: 1980; **Freq:** Weekly - France; **Circ:** 342,394
Usual Pagination: 106
Managing Director: François Moriniere
Profile: Magazine focusing exclusively on sport.
Language(s): French
ADVERTISING RATES:
Full Page Colour .... EUR 25000
Mechanical Data: Type Area: 220 x 290
NATIONAL DAILY & SUNDAY NEWSPAPERS: National Colour Supplements

L' ESPRIT SHOPI 1617123F94H-501
Editorial: TEXTUEL, 146 rue du Faubourg Poissonnière, 75010 PARIS **Tel:** 1 53 21 21 00
Fax: 1 53 21 22 33
Email: fdisant@textuel.fr
ISSN: 1270-3214
Date Established: 1996; **Freq:** Weekly - mercredi; **Cover Price:** Free; **Circ:** 400,000
Usual Pagination: 32
Profile: Customer magazine focussing on Shopi products including TV programmes, practical information, TV gossip, horoscope, health, fitness, beauty, tourism, leisure, cookery, and CDRom.. Circulated in the Shopi supermarkets.
Language(s): French
Mechanical Data: Type Area: A 4
Copy instructions: *Copy Date:* 49 days prior to publication date
CONSUMER: OTHER CLASSIFICATIONS: Customer Magazines

L' ESSENTIEL DE AUTO
1617652F77A-373
Editorial: Rédaction, BP 60460, CEDEX, 56174 QUIBERON **Tel:** 2 97 29 53 29
Email: redaction.auto@wanadoo.fr **Web site:** http://www.lafontpresse.fr
ISSN: 1620-5154
Date Established: 1999; **Freq:** 24 issues yearly - milieu de mois pairs; **Cover Price:** EUR 4.50; **Circ:** 80,000
Usual Pagination: 100
Profile: Publication focussing on cars and motorcycles including interviews, tests, used vehicles, legal, shopping, camping cars, classic vehicles, tourism, guide and classifieds.
Language(s): French
ADVERTISING RATES:
Full Page Mono .... EUR 5110
Full Page Colour .... EUR 7100
Mechanical Data: Type Area: 210 x 297
CONSUMER: MOTORING & CYCLING: Motoring

' ESSENTIEL DE LA MAROQUINERIE

1619891F52D-102

Editorial: DGT Associés, 46 rue du Général Chanzy, 4130 NOGENT-SUR-MARNE **Tel:** 1 48 77 37 06
ax: 1 48 77 37 36
mail: gilles@lessentiel.com **Web site:** http://www.essentiel.com
SSN: 1295-9502
ate Established: 1999; **Freq:** Quarterly - 01 04 08); **Cover Price:** EUR 8.50
nnual Sub.: EUR 28; **Circ:** 5,000
sual Pagination: 80
rofile: Publication focussing on leather industry including new products, distribution, selling points nd practical information.
anguage(s): French
DVERTISING RATES:
ull Page Mono .... EUR 915
ull Page Colour .... EUR 1525
echanical Data: Type Area: 21,5 x 28
USINESS: GIFT TRADE: Leather

' ESSENTIEL DU MOBILE

1663481F18B-102

ditorial: ITEC PRESSE, 34 port des Champs lysées, 75008 PARIS **Tel:** 1 42 66 53 31
mail: redaction@essentiel-mobile.fr **Web site:** ttp://www.essentiel-mobile.fr
SSN: 1771-379X
ate Established: 2004; **Freq:** 24 issues yearly - 0th of the month; **Cover Price:** EUR 5.20
nnual Sub.: EUR 22.30; **Circ:** 40,000
sual Pagination: 100
rofile: Publication focussing on telecommunication nd mobile phones including reviews, tests, omparisons, news, practical information and buyers uide.
anguage(s): French
DVERTISING RATES:
ull Page Colour .... EUR 2400
echanical Data: Type Area: 210 x 275
USINESS: ELECTRONICS: Telecommunications

ESSENTIEL SANTE MAGAZINE

1774716F1D-179

ditorial: Harmonie Mutuelles, 8 boulevard de eaumont, CS 11241 CEDEX, 35012 RENNES
el: 2 23 25 24 00 **Fax:** 2 23 25 24 27
mail: essentielsantemagazine@harmonie-mutuelles. **Web site:** http://www.harmonie-mutuelles.fr
SSN: 1771-2718
ate Established: 2006; **Freq:** 24 issues yearly - 02-4-06-09-11; **Cover Price:** EUR 0.51
nnual Sub.: EUR 2.55; **Circ:** 2,171,400
sual Pagination: 32
anguage(s): French
echanical Data: Type Area: 200 x 260
USINESS: FINANCE & ECONOMICS: Insurance

' EST ECLAIR

6212F67B-3900

ditorial: BP 532, CEDEX, 10081 TROYES
el: 3 25 71 75 75 **Fax:** 3 25 79 58 54
mail: redaction@lest-eclair.fr **Web site:** http://www.est-eclair.fr
ate Established: 1945; **Freq:** Daily - matin; **Cover rice:** EUR 0.80
nnual Sub.: EUR 208; **Circ:** 27,821
sual Pagination: 64
rofile: General, regional and departmental news.
anguage(s): French
DVERTISING RATES:
ull Page Mono .... EUR 4166
ull Page Colour .... EUR 5832
EGIONAL DAILY & SUNDAY NEWSPAPERS: egional Daily Newspapers

' EST MAGAZINE

1619143F80-822

ditorial: L'Est Républicain, Rue Théophraste-enaudot, 54185 CEDEX HEILLECOURT
el: 3 83 59 09 15 **Fax:** 383598013
mail: estmagazine@estrepublicain.fr
SSN: 1760-4958
ate Established: 2000; **Freq:** Weekly - dimanche; **irc:** 350,000
sual Pagination: 32
ditor: Jean Bletner
rofile: Regional publication focussing on local news nd current affairs including tourism, cars, otorcycles, cinema, music, books, fashion, trends, onsumption, gastronomy, wine, table decoration, oney, multimedia, collectables, genealogy, xhibitions, animals, environment, youth interest and ulture.
anguage(s): French
echanical Data: Type Area: 21 x 28,5
ONSUMER: RURAL & REGIONAL INTEREST

L' EST REPUBLICAIN HOUDEMONT

1619437F67B-8437

ditorial: Rue Théophraste-Renaudot, Houdemont, 4185 CEDEX HEILLECOURT **Tel:** 3 83 59 88 01
mail: lerdirredac@estrepublicain.fr **Web site:** http://www.estrepublicain.fr
SSN: 1760-4958
ate Established: 1889; **Freq:** Daily - matin
nnual Sub.: EUR 330.50; **Circ:** 186,502
sual Pagination: 40
rofile: Daily regional and general information ewspaper. Supplements: TV guide, "Version émina" and "Est Magazine" included in Sunday ssue. Sunday price: 1.60€.

Language(s): French
ADVERTISING RATES:
Full Page Mono .... EUR 6889
Full Page Colour .... EUR 8611
REGIONAL DAILY & SUNDAY NEWSPAPERS: Regional Daily Newspapers

ESTETICA FRANCE

4913F15B-40

Editorial: 5 rue Boudreau, 75009 PARIS
Tel: 1 42 60 25 61 **Fax:** 1 42 60 24 40
Email: mpeyramond@orange.fr
ISSN: 1244-9709
Date Established: 1994; **Freq:** Quarterly - 10 des mois 03 06 09 12
Annual Sub.: EUR 50; **Circ:** 11,000
Usual Pagination: 180
Profile: Magazine containing information about the hairdressing trade.
Language(s): French
Readership: Aimed at hairdressers.
ADVERTISING RATES:
Full Page Colour .... EUR 2900
Mechanical Data: Type Area: 216 x 288
BUSINESS: COSMETICS & HAIRDRESSING: Hairdressing

ETUDES

7921F87-221

Editorial: 14 rue d'Assas, 75006 PARIS
Tel: 1 44 39 48 48 **Fax:** 1 44 39 48 17
Email: chloe.salvan@ser-sa.com **Web site:** http://www.revue-etudes.com
ISSN: 0014-1941
Date Established: 1856; **Freq:** Monthly - 1er du mois; **Cover Price:** EUR 11
Annual Sub.: EUR 92; **Circ:** 15,500
Usual Pagination: 144
Managing Director: Antoine Corman
Profile: Publication focussing on cultural studies including news, philosophy, science, religion, arts, literature, theatre, media, cinema, exhibitions, music and literature.
Language(s): French
ADVERTISING RATES:
Full Page Mono .... EUR 1067
Mechanical Data: Type Area: 235 x 155
CONSUMER: RELIGIOUS

L' ETUDIANT

7067F83-62

Editorial: 23 rue de Châteaudun, CEDEX 09, 75308 PARIS **Tel:** 1 75 55 40 40
Email: edavidenkoff@letudiant.fr **Web site:** http://www.letudiant.fr
ISSN: 0766-6330
Date Established: 1977; **Freq:** Monthly - Middle of the month; **Cover Price:** EUR 3.90
Annual Sub.: EUR 39.90; **Circ:** 120,000
Usual Pagination: 120
Profile: Magazine providing information on general matters, education, training and employment.
Language(s): French
Readership: Aimed at students between the ages of 15 and 24 years.
ADVERTISING RATES:
Full Page Mono .... EUR 5617
Full Page Colour .... EUR 7268
Mechanical Data: Type Area: tabloïd
Copy instructions: *Copy Date:* 15 days prior to publication date
CONSUMER: STUDENT PUBLICATIONS

L' EVEIL DE LA HAUTE LOIRE

6175F67B-8712

Editorial: 9 place Michelet, BP 24, CEDEX, 43001 LE PUY-EN-VELAY **Tel:** 4 71 09 32 14
Fax: 4 71 02 94 08
Email: redaction@leveil.fr **Web site:** http://www.leveil.fr
ISSN: 0249-5775
Freq: Daily - 15 h 30; **Cover Price:** EUR 0.55
Annual Sub.: EUR 157; **Circ:** 14,422
Usual Pagination: 20
Editor-in-Chief: Jean-Luc Broc
Profile: General, regional and local news. Friday price: 0,80 € (TV supplement). Including supplements.
Language(s): French
ADVERTISING RATES:
Full Page Colour .... EUR 2940
Mechanical Data: Type Area: tabloïd
REGIONAL DAILY & SUNDAY NEWSPAPERS: Regional Daily Newspapers

L' EXPANSION

4831F14A-283

Editorial: 29 rue de Châteaudun, CEDEX 09, 75308 PARIS **Tel:** 1 75 55 10 00
Email: alouyot@lexpansion.com **Web site:** http://www.lexpansion.com
ISSN: 0014-4703
Date Established: 1967; **Freq:** Monthly - dernier mercredi du mois
Annual Sub.: EUR 26; **Circ:** 156,708
Usual Pagination: 130
Profile: Magazine about business matters.
Language(s): French
Readership: Read by managers and decision makers throughout all business sectors.
ADVERTISING RATES:
Full Page Colour .... EUR 20100
Mechanical Data: Type Area: 270 x 209
BUSINESS: COMMERCE, INDUSTRY & MANAGEMENT

L' EXPRESS

6371F73-40

Editorial: 29 rue de Châteaudun, CEDEX 09, 75308 PARIS **Tel:** 1 75 55 10 00
Email: cbarbier@lexpress.fr **Web site:** http://www.lexpress.fr
ISSN: 0014-5270
Date Established: 1953; **Freq:** Weekly - mercredi
Annual Sub.: EUR 104; **Circ:** 546,181
Usual Pagination: 175
Profile: General information magazine.
Language(s): French
ADVERTISING RATES:
Full Page Mono .... EUR 16700
Full Page Colour .... EUR 25700
Mechanical Data: Type Area: 20 x 27
Copy instructions: *Copy Date:* 10 days prior to publication date
CONSUMER: NATIONAL & INTERNATIONAL PERIODICALS

FAMILI

6478F74D-65

Editorial: 10 boulevard des Frères Voisin, CEDEX 9, 92792 ISSY LES MOULINEAUX **Tel:** 1 41 46 88 88
Fax: 1 41 46 80 05
Email: familiredac@gmc.tm.fr **Web site:** http://www.famili.fr
ISSN: 1246-3299
Date Established: 1993; **Freq:** Monthly - vers le 15 des mois pairs; **Cover Price:** EUR 2.50
Annual Sub.: EUR 20; **Circ:** 125,114
Usual Pagination: 171
Publisher: Fredrik Edstrom
Profile: Covers motherhood and family and parenting. Offers advice to new mothers, tips on raising children, information on nutrition, health, beauty and grooming, new products and other topics.
Language(s): French
ADVERTISING RATES:
Full Page Mono .... EUR 10290
Full Page Colour .... EUR 14700
Mechanical Data: Type Area: 225 x 285
CONSUMER: WOMEN'S INTEREST CONSUMER MAGAZINES: Child Care

FAMILLE CHRETIENNE

6447F74C-110

Editorial: EDIFA, 15/27 rue Moussorgski, CEDEX 18, 75895 PARIS **Tel:** 1 53 26 35 00 **Fax:** 1 53 26 35 05
Email: redaction@famillechretienne.fr **Web site:** http://www.famillechretienne.fr
ISSN: 0154-6821
Date Established: 1978; **Freq:** Weekly - Saturday; **Cover Price:** EUR 3.20
Annual Sub.: EUR 120; **Circ:** 60,607
Usual Pagination: 84
Profile: Magazine containing family and Christian news and information.
Language(s): French
ADVERTISING RATES:
Full Page Mono .... EUR 2500
Full Page Colour .... EUR 3500
Mechanical Data: Type Area: 21 x 29,7
CONSUMER: WOMEN'S INTEREST CONSUMER MAGAZINES: Home & Family

FAMILLE ET EDUCATION

7156F88A-63

Editorial: 277 rue Saint Jacques, CEDEX 5, 75240 PARIS **Tel:** 1 53 73 73 90 **Fax:** 1 53 73 74 00
Email: catherine.bonnin@apelnationale.fr **Web site:** http://www.apel.asso.fr
ISSN: 1249-2329
Date Established: 1947; **Freq:** 24 issues yearly - 01/02 03/04 05/06 09/10 11/12
Annual Sub.: EUR 4.50; **Circ:** 779,240
Usual Pagination: 92
Profile: Magazine containing information about school subjects and education in general.
Language(s): French
Readership: Aimed at the parents of school children.
ADVERTISING RATES:
Full Page Colour .... EUR 14200
Mechanical Data: Type Area: A 4
Copy instructions: *Copy Date:* 62 days prior to publication date
CONSUMER: EDUCATION

FASHION DAILY NEWS

5537F47B-80

Editorial: Espace Clichy - Immeuble Sirius, 9 allée Jean Prouvé, CEDEX, 92587 CLICHY
Tel: 1 41 40 34 77 33 33 **Fax:** 1 41 40 31 17
Email: jean-paul.leroy@editions-lariviere.fr **Web site:** http://www.fashion-dailynews.com
Date Established: 2000; **Freq:** Weekly - Monday
Annual Sub.: EUR 125; **Circ:** 17,547
Usual Pagination: 32
Publisher: Stéphanie Casasnovas
Profile: International review covering lingerie, corsets, swimwear, night-clothes and home/leisure-wear.
Language(s): French
ADVERTISING RATES:
Full Page Mono .... EUR 4270
Full Page Colour .... EUR 6400
Mechanical Data: Type Area: 28 x 37
BUSINESS: CLOTHING & TEXTILES: Lingerie, Hosiery/Swimwear

LA FEMME ACTUELLE

6406F74A-160

Editorial: 13 rue Henri Barbusse, 92624 GENNEVILLIERS **Tel:** 1 73 05 67 46
Fax: 1 47 92 66 60
Email: femactu@prisma-presse.com **Web site:** http://www.femmeactuelle.fr
ISSN: 0764-0021
Date Established: 1984; **Freq:** Weekly - lundi; **Cover Price:** EUR 1.30
Annual Sub.: EUR 53; **Circ:** 976,660
Profile: Women's magazine covering fashion, travel, interior decor, home furnishings, cookery, gardening and celebrities.
Language(s): French
ADVERTISING RATES:
Full Page Colour .... EUR 37650
CONSUMER: WOMEN'S INTEREST CONSUMER MAGAZINES: Women's Interest

FERRARI CLUB

1647470F77E-88

Editorial: FINK MEDIA GROUPE, 6 rue Roquépine, 75008 PARIS **Tel:** 1 47 05 01 01 **Fax:** 1 47 05 90 20
Email: info@fink-presse.fr
Date Established: 2004; **Freq:** 24 issues yearly - variable; **Cover Price:** EUR 8.90
Annual Sub.: EUR 53; **Circ:** 10,198
Usual Pagination: 132
Profile: Publication of Ferrari focussing on motor sports including cars, design, techniques, history, tests, quotes, collectors, classic cars, models and classified.
Language(s): French
ADVERTISING RATES:
Full Page Colour .... EUR 7500
Mechanical Data: Type Area: A4
Copy instructions: *Copy Date:* 7 days prior to publication date
CONSUMER: MOTORING & CYCLING: Club Cars

LE FIGARO

6091F65A-40

Editorial: 14 boulevard Haussmann, 75009 PARIS
Tel: 1 57 08 50 00
Email: jmsalvator@lefigaro.fr **Web site:** http://www.lefigaro.fr
ISSN: 0182-5852
Date Established: 1826; **Freq:** Daily - matin; **Cover Price:** EUR 1.30; **Circ:** 331,022
Usual Pagination: 50
Profile: Broadsheet-sized quality newspaper. Provides in-depth coverage of national, international, financial and economic news, culture, the arts and sport.
Language(s): French
Readership: Read by decision makers, senior executives, managers, office personnel and students.
ADVERTISING RATES:
Full Page Mono .... EUR 76000
Full Page Colour .... EUR 102000
Mechanical Data: Type Area: berlinois
NATIONAL DAILY & SUNDAY NEWSPAPERS: National Daily Newspapers

LE FIGARO MAGAZINE

6104F65H-80

Editorial: 14 boulevard Haussmann, 75009 PARIS
Tel: 1 57 08 50 00 **Fax:** 1 57 08 57 94
Email: figmag@lefigaro.fr **Web site:** http://www.lefigaro.fr
ISSN: 0184-9336
Freq: Weekly - France; **Circ:** 444,150
Usual Pagination: 162
Editor-in-Chief: Arnauld Dingreville
Profile: Colour supplement giving details on current affairs and general information.
Language(s): French
ADVERTISING RATES:
Full Page Colour .... EUR 33000
Mechanical Data: Type Area: 215 x 280
NATIONAL DAILY & SUNDAY NEWSPAPERS: National Colour Supplements

LE FIGAROSCOPE

7195F89C-30

Editorial: Coursiers, 3 rue Pillet-Will, 75009 PARIS
Tel: 1 57 08 50 00 **Fax:** 1 57 08 59 08
Email: bjacquot@lefigaro.fr **Web site:** http://www.figaroscope.fr
ISSN: 1279-6212
Date Established: 1987; **Freq:** Weekly - mercredi matin; **Cover Price:** Free; **Circ:** 215,000
Usual Pagination: 64
Profile: Magazine about culture, leisure and travel in and around Paris.
Language(s): French
ADVERTISING RATES:
Full Page Mono .... EUR 24600
Full Page Colour .... EUR 30900
Mechanical Data: Type Area: 264 x 355
Copy instructions: *Copy Date:* 21 days prior to publication date
CONSUMER: HOLIDAYS & TRAVEL: Entertainment Guides

LE FIL DES ANS

1692346F32G-202

Editorial: BP 300, CEDEX, 6800 CAGNES-SUR-MER
Tel: 4 92 13 78 74
Email: v.driot@probtp.com

Date Established: 1967; **Freq:** 24 issues yearly - le 15 mois pairs; **Cover Price:** EUR 0.76
Annual Sub.: EUR 4.56; **Circ:** 900,000
Usual Pagination: 40
Profile: Publication focussing on social interest including law, health, holidays and retirement for construction workers.
Language(s): French
Mechanical Data: Type Area: 210 x 297
BUSINESS: LOCAL GOVERNMENT, LEISURE & RECREATION: Community Care & Social Services

LE FILM FRANCAIS 6081F64K-87

Editorial: Immeuble Trait d'Union, 8 rue François Ory, 92120 MONTROUGE **Tel:** 1 41 33 50 01
Fax: 1 41 86 16 91
Email: lefilmfrancais@mondadori.fr **Web site:** http://www.lefilmfrancais.com
ISSN: 0759-0385
Date Established: 1945; **Freq:** Weekly - vendredi
Annual Sub.: EUR 320; **Circ:** 13,000
Usual Pagination: 32
Profile: Magazine concerning the cinema trade. Includes statistics, reports, analysis, technical and economic information, news on forthcoming events and film festivals.
Language(s): French
Readership: Aimed at audiovisual professionals.
ADVERTISING RATES:
Full Page Colour .... EUR 4600
Mechanical Data: Type Area: 250 x 340
BUSINESS: OTHER CLASSIFICATIONS: Cinema Entertainment

FINISTERE PENN AR BED 1617154F32A-1020

Editorial: Conseil Général du Finistère, 1 allée Truffaut, CEDEX, 29196 QUIMPER **Tel:** 2 98 76 26 75
Fax: 2 98 76 24 70
Email: jean-emmanuel.bouley@cg29.fr **Web site:** http://www.cg29.fr
ISSN: 1953-6968
Freq: 24 issues yearly - 02 04 06 09 11; **Cover Price:** Free; **Circ:** 380,000
Usual Pagination: 20
Profile: Publication focussing on local government and department issues, including economics, events, cultural and social issues.
Language(s): French
Mechanical Data: Type Area: A 4
BUSINESS: LOCAL GOVERNMENT, LEISURE & RECREATION: Local Government

FIRST CLASS PARIS 7196F89C-40

Editorial: 17 rue Jean Mermoz, 75008 PARIS
Tel: 1 42 25 26 25 **Fax:** 1 53 75 30 95
Email: direction@firstclass.fr **Web site:** http://www.firstclass.fr
ISSN: 0983-1193
Date Established: 1984; **Freq:** Weekly - Mondays
Annual Sub.: EUR 200; **Circ:** 35,000
Usual Pagination: 78
Profile: Guide to Paris for international business and leisure travellers.
Language(s): French
Readership: Aimed at business people and travellers.
ADVERTISING RATES:
Full Page Colour .... EUR 2600
Mechanical Data: Type Area: 15 x 21
Copy instructions: *Copy Date:* 15 days prior to publication date
CONSUMER: HOLIDAYS & TRAVEL: Entertainment Guides

FLD - FRUITS ET LEGUMES 5225F26C-65

Editorial: 84 Boulevard de Sébastopol, 75003 PARIS
Tel: 1 42 74 28 00 **Fax:** 1 42 74 28 33
Email: omasbou@siac.fr **Web site:** http://www.fldhebdo.fr
ISSN: 1287-1516
Date Established: 1987; **Freq:** Weekly - mardi;
Cover Price: EUR 4.86
Annual Sub.: EUR 238; **Circ:** 4,000
Usual Pagination: 162
Profile: Publication for professionals concerned with the marketing of fruit and vegetables.
Language(s): French
ADVERTISING RATES:
Full Page Colour .... EUR 4000
Mechanical Data: Type Area: 210 x 297
BUSINESS: GARDEN TRADE

FLUVIAL 7244F91A-100

Editorial: 36 boulevard de la Bastille, 75012 PARIS
Tel: 1 40 19 90 00 **Fax:** 1 40 19 09 72
Email: info@fluvialnet.com **Web site:** http://www.fluvialnet.com
ISSN: 0755-5180
Date Established: 1983; **Freq:** Monthly - The end of the month; **Cover Price:** EUR 5.30
Annual Sub.: EUR 48; **Circ:** 36,000
Usual Pagination: 96
Profile: Journal concerning inland waterways, narrow boats, motor cruisers and barges. Includes features on tourism, equipment, motorisation and construction.
Language(s): French
ADVERTISING RATES:
Full Page Mono .... EUR 1940
Full Page Colour .... EUR 2300
Mechanical Data: Type Area: A4
CONSUMER: RECREATION & LEISURE: Boating & Yachting

FMP MUTUALITE 1618949F1D-132

Editorial: 19 Cité Voltaire, 75011 PARIS
Tel: 1 40 46 12 65 **Fax:** 1 40 46 10 80
Email: fmpmut.camus@fr.oleane.com **Web site:** http://www.fmp.fr
ISSN: 0293-9916
Freq: 24 issues yearly - le 25 mois impairs (sauf 07-08); **Annual Sub.:** EUR 11.16; **Circ:** 150,000
Usual Pagination: 32
Language(s): French
ADVERTISING RATES:
Full Page Mono .... EUR 4000
Full Page Colour .... EUR 5000
Mechanical Data: Type Area: 300 x 230
BUSINESS: FINANCE & ECONOMICS: Insurance

LE FRANCAIS DANS MONDE 7158F88A-70

Editorial: 9 bis rue Abel Hovelacque, 75013 PARIS
Tel: 1 72 36 30 67 **Fax:** 1 45 87 43 18
Email: fdlm@fdlm.org **Web site:** http://www.fdlm.org
ISSN: 0015-9395
Date Established: 1961; **Freq:** 24 issues yearly - les mois 01 03 05 09 11; **Cover Price:** EUR 13
Annual Sub.: EUR 80; **Circ:** 10,000
Usual Pagination: 65
Profile: Educational review.
Language(s): French
ADVERTISING RATES:
Full Page Colour .... EUR 1510
Mechanical Data: Type Area: 285 x 210
Copy instructions: *Copy Date:* 21 days prior to publication date
CONSUMER: EDUCATION

LA FRANCE AGRICOLE 5006F21A-1050

Editorial: 8 Cité Paradis, CEDEX 10, 75493 PARIS
Tel: 1 40 22 79 00 **Fax:** 1 40 22 70 80
Email: redaction@lafranceagricole.fr **Web site:** http://www.lafranceagricole.fr
ISSN: 0046-4899
Date Established: 1945; **Freq:** Weekly - vendredi;
Cover Price: EUR 4.30
Annual Sub.: EUR 114; **Circ:** 155,855
Usual Pagination: 100
Managing Director: Michel Collonge
Profile: Agricultural magazine containing pages on the cultivation of beet, soya, potatoes, sorghum, vines, fruit, vegetables and sections on cattle, dairy herds, pigs, poultry and rabbits. Also includes a section on machinery and equipment.
Language(s): French
ADVERTISING RATES:
Full Page Mono .... EUR 10200
Full Page Colour .... EUR 14500
Mechanical Data: Type Area: 200 x 270
Copy instructions: *Copy Date:* 15 days prior to publication date
BUSINESS: AGRICULTURE & FARMING

FRANCE DIMANCHE 6098F65B-10

Editorial: 149 rue Anatole France, CEDEX, 92534 LEVALLOIS PERRET **Tel:** 1 41 34 85 30
Fax: 1 41 34 90 25 85 81
Email: philippe.bonnel@lagardere-active.com
ISSN: 0015-9549
Date Established: 1946; **Freq:** Weekly - vendredi;
Cover Price: EUR 1.20
Annual Sub.: EUR 49.90; **Circ:** 424,520
Usual Pagination: 50
Publisher: Oscar Becerra
Profile: Tabloid newspaper covering news, current events, sport, employment vacancies, celebrities, showbiz, cooking, tourism + pages on themes such as medical.
Language(s): French
Readership: Widely read throughout France, especially by retired people and those currently unemployed.
ADVERTISING RATES:
Full Page Mono .... EUR 9200
Full Page Colour .... EUR 11160
Mechanical Data: Type Area: 312 x 230
Copy instructions: *Copy Date:* 15 days prior to publication date
NATIONAL DAILY & SUNDAY NEWSPAPERS: National Sunday Newspapers

FRANCE FOOTBALL 6607F75B-75

Editorial: 4 cour de l'Ile-Seguin, BP 10302, CEDEX, 92102 BOULOGNE BILLANCOURT
Tel: 1 40 93 20 20 **Fax:** 1 40 93 24 05
Email: dchaumier@lequipe.presse.fr **Web site:** http://www.francefootball.fr
ISSN: 0015-9557
Date Established: 1947; **Freq:** 26 issues yearly - mardi et vendredi
Annual Sub.: EUR 96; **Circ:** 146,493
Usual Pagination: 50
Managing Director: François Moriniere
Profile: Magazine about French football.
Language(s): French
ADVERTISING RATES:
Full Page Colour .... EUR 13000
Mechanical Data: Type Area: 263 x 350
Copy instructions: *Copy Date:* 7 days prior to publication date
CONSUMER: SPORT: Football

FRANCE GRAPHIQUE 5423F41A-70

Editorial: Parc Antony II, 10 place du Général de Gaulle, 92160 ANTONY **Tel:** 1 77 92 92 92
Fax: 1 77 92 98 20
Email: gbregeras@etai.fr **Web site:** http://www.francegraphique.com
ISSN: 0015-9565
Date Established: 1947; **Freq:** Monthly - début de mois
Annual Sub.: EUR 65; **Circ:** 8,000
Usual Pagination: 66
Profile: Magazine for the arts and graphics industries.
Language(s): French
ADVERTISING RATES:
Full Page Mono .... EUR 2710
Full Page Colour .... EUR 4164
Mechanical Data: Type Area: A 4
Copy instructions: *Copy Date:* 21 days prior to publication date
BUSINESS: PRINTING & STATIONERY: Printing

FRANCE SOIR 6092F65A-50

Editorial: 100 avenue des Champs-Elysées, 75008 PARIS **Tel:** 1 56 21 00 00 **Fax:** 1 56 21 07 50
Email: redaction@francesoir.fr **Web site:** http://www.francesoir.fr
ISSN: 0182-5860
Date Established: 1944; **Freq:** Daily - matin; **Cover Price:** EUR 0.50
Annual Sub.: EUR 156; **Circ:** 26,214
Usual Pagination: 40
Profile: Tabloid-sized evening newspaper covering news, finance, entertainment, sport, accommodation and employment vacancies.
Language(s): French
Readership: Read by a broad range of the population, almost half of whom live or work in Paris and one third of whom are either retired or currently unemployed.
ADVERTISING RATES:
Full Page Mono .... EUR 10500
Full Page Colour .... EUR 15800
Mechanical Data: Type Area: 290 X 360
NATIONAL DAILY & SUNDAY NEWSPAPERS: National Daily Newspapers

FRANCHISE MAGAZINE 4833F14A-289

Editorial: 6 bis rue Gambetta, CEDEX, 92022 NANTERRE **Tel:** 1 46 69 11 33 **Fax:** 1 46 69 11 98
Email: franchise@groupe-icf.com **Web site:** http://www.franchise-magazine.com
ISSN: 1255-6629
Date Established: 1982; **Freq:** 24 issues yearly - les 20 / 01 03 05 07 09 11 12; **Cover Price:** EUR 4.80
Annual Sub.: EUR 32; **Circ:** 8,254
Usual Pagination: 200
Profile: Commercial news magazine providing advice and practical information, with examples of specific cases and strategies about franchising.
Language(s): French
ADVERTISING RATES:
Full Page Colour .... EUR 3200
Mechanical Data: Type Area: A4
Copy instructions: *Copy Date:* 15 days prior to publication date
BUSINESS: COMMERCE, INDUSTRY & MANAGEMENT

GALA 6373F74Q-274

Editorial: 13 rue Henri Barbusse, 92624 GENNEVILLIERS **Tel:** 1 73 05 47 00
Fax: 1 56 99 51 50
Email: mgurtler@prisma-presse.com **Web site:** http://www.gala.fr
ISSN: 1243-6070
Date Established: 1993; **Freq:** Weekly - lundi; **Cover Price:** EUR 2.20
Annual Sub.: EUR 75; **Circ:** 296,461
Usual Pagination: 100
Publisher: Philippe Labi
Profile: Magazine focusing on show business, crowned heads and celebrities. Includes articles on fashion, beauty, cuisine and tourism.
Language(s): French
ADVERTISING RATES:
Full Page Colour .... EUR 19200
Mechanical Data: Type Area: 24 X 33
Copy instructions: *Copy Date:* 28 days prior to publication date
CONSUMER: WOMEN'S INTEREST CONSUMER MAGAZINES: Lifestyle

LA GAZETTE DES COMMUNES 5301F32A-90

Editorial: 17 rue d'Uzès, CEDEX 02, 75108 PARIS
Tel: 1 40 13 30 30 31 11 **Fax:** 1 40 13 51 06
Email: redacgazette@lagazettedescommunes.com
Web site: http://www.lagazettedescommunes.com
ISSN: 0769-3508
Date Established: 1934; **Freq:** Weekly - Monday
Annual Sub.: EUR 174; **Circ:** 34,972
Usual Pagination: 200
Profile: Journal concerning all aspects of local community life.
Language(s): French
ADVERTISING RATES:
Full Page Colour .... EUR 580
Mechanical Data: Type Area: 230 x 297
BUSINESS: LOCAL GOVERNMENT, LEISURE & RECREATION: Local Government

LA GAZETTE DES JARDINS 7286F93-4

Editorial: Alpha Comédia, 23 avenue du Parc Robiony, 6200 NICE **Tel:** 4 93 96 16 13
Email: redaction@gazettedesjardins.com **Web site:** http://www.gazettedesjardins.com
ISSN: 1261-7202
Date Established: 1995; **Freq:** 24 issues yearly - le 15 01/03/05/07/09/11
Annual Sub.: EUR 25; **Circ:** 30,000
Usual Pagination: 32
Profile: Magazine about Mediterranean style gardens and their upkeep.
Language(s): French
ADVERTISING RATES:
Full Page Mono .... EUR 254
Full Page Colour .... EUR 318
Mechanical Data: Type Area: 420 x 297
CONSUMER: GARDENING

LA GAZETTE HOTELIERE 4774F11A-12

Editorial: 6 Place de Bordeaux, CEDEX, 67080 STRASBOURG **Tel:** 3 88 25 05 15 **Fax:** 3 88 25 08 4
Email: info@g-h-r-d.com
ISSN: 1141-3301
Date Established: 1920; **Freq:** Monthly - début du mois; **Cover Price:** EUR 4.96
Annual Sub.: EUR 45; **Circ:** 1,382
Usual Pagination: 32
Profile: Review for the hotel and catering trade in the Alsace and Moselle regions of France.
Language(s): French
ADVERTISING RATES:
Full Page Colour .... EUR 115
Mechanical Data: Type Area: 21 x 29,7
Copy instructions: *Copy Date:* 15 days prior to publication date
BUSINESS: CATERING: Catering, Hotels & Restaurants

LA GAZETTE OFFICIELLE DU TOURISME 5582F50-4

Editorial: Antenne à Paris, 3 rue Séguier, 75006 PARIS **Tel:** 5 59 52 55 33 **Fax:** 5 59 52 84 01
Email: gazette-tourisme@edi-pole.com **Web site:** http://www.edi-pole.com
ISSN: 0016-5573
Date Established: 1950; **Freq:** Weekly - mercredi suivant
Annual Sub.: EUR 260; **Circ:** 4,500
Usual Pagination: 16
Profile: Magazine covering all aspects of the national and international tourist trade.
Language(s): French
ADVERTISING RATES:
Full Page Mono .... EUR 134
Mechanical Data: Type Area: 210 x 297
BUSINESS: TRAVEL & TOURISM

GAZOLINE 628844F77F-12

Editorial: PIXEL PRESS, 1 Parc des Fontenelles, 78870 BAILLY **Tel:** 1 30 56 65 05 **Fax:** 1 34 62 05 07
Email: ecrire@gazoline.net **Web site:** http://gazoline.net
ISSN: 1262-4357
Date Established: 1995; **Freq:** Monthly - 4e mardi de chaque mois; **Cover Price:** EUR 3.80
Annual Sub.: EUR 33; **Circ:** 112,800
Usual Pagination: 148
Profile: Magazine dedicated to collectible old cars from the years 1950 to 1975. Features articles on maintenance, restoration and purchase guides.
Language(s): French
Readership: Read by people who have an interest in classic cars.
ADVERTISING RATES:
Full Page Colour .... EUR 225
Mechanical Data: Type Area: 23 x 30
CONSUMER: MOTORING & CYCLING: Veteran Cars

LE GENERALISTE 5885F56A-827

Editorial: 21 rue Camille Desmoulins, CEDEX 9, 92789 ISSY LES MOULINEAUX **Tel:** 1 73 28 14 70
Fax: 1 73 28 14 71
Email: jean.paillard@fr.cmpmedica.com **Web site:** http://www.legeneraliste.fr
ISSN: 01834568
Date Established: 1975; **Freq:** Weekly - vendredi;
Annual Sub.: EUR 80; **Circ:** 45,000
Usual Pagination: 90
Profile: Journal about continued medical training and professional news.
Language(s): French
ADVERTISING RATES:
Full Page Mono .... EUR 6800
Full Page Colour .... EUR 9000
Mechanical Data: Type Area: 230 X 297
Copy instructions: *Copy Date:* 8 days prior to publication date
BUSINESS: HEALTH & MEDICAL

GEO 1617361F73-327
Editorial: 13 rue Henri Barbusse, 92624 GENNEVILLIERS **Tel:** 1 73 05 60 61
Email: lecteurs@geo.presse.fr **Web site:** http://www.geomagazine.fr
ISSN: 0220-8245
Date Established: 1979; **Freq:** Monthly - end of month; **Circ:** 299,564
Usual Pagination: 146
Managing Director: Pierre Riandet
Profile: Publication focussing on geography and nature including country reviews, news, science and environment.
Language(s): French
ADVERTISING RATES:
Full Page Mono .... EUR 20025
Full Page Colour .... EUR 26700
Mechanical Data: Type Area: 213 x 270
Copy instructions: *Copy Date:* 31 days prior to publication date
CONSUMER: NATIONAL & INTERNATIONAL PERIODICALS

GESTION DE FORTUNE 4470F1A-170
Editorial: 35 rue de Liège, 75008 PARIS
Tel: 1 44 70 66 66 **Fax:** 1 44 70 66 69
Email: redaction@gestiondefortune.com **Web site:** http://www.gestiondefortune.com
ISSN: 1163-720X
Date Established: 1991; **Freq:** Monthly - fin du mois; **Cover Price:** EUR 5.50
Annual Sub.: EUR 60; **Circ:** 30,000
Usual Pagination: 100
Profile: Publication about finance, wealth management and French business.
Language(s): French
ADVERTISING RATES:
Full Page Mono .... EUR 4924
Full Page Colour .... EUR 7200
Mechanical Data: Type Area: 21 x 29,7
BUSINESS: FINANCE & ECONOMICS

GLAMOUR 1639520F74A-819
Editorial: 26 rue Cambacérès, 75008 PARIS
Tel: 1 53 43 60 00 **Fax:** 1 53 43 68 20
Email: magazine-glamour@condenast.fr **Web site:** http://www.glamourparis.com
ISSN: 0990-6479
Date Established: 2004; **Freq:** Monthly - 1ère semaine du mois; **Cover Price:** EUR 1.80
Annual Sub.: EUR 14.40; **Circ:** 390,051
Usual Pagination: 256
Language(s): French
ADVERTISING RATES:
Full Page Mono .... EUR 17200
Full Page Colour .... EUR 21500
Mechanical Data: Type Area: 170 x 220
Copy instructions: *Copy Date:* 62 days prior to publication date
CONSUMER: WOMEN'S INTEREST CONSUMER MAGAZINES: Women's Interest

GOLF SENIOR 6622F75D-110
Editorial: 13 rue Prémayac, BP 170, 33390 BLAYE
Tel: 5 57 42 69 05 **Fax:** 5 57 42 69 09
Email: golfsenior@wanadoo.fr **Web site:** http://www.golfsenior.fr
ISSN: 1283-7415
Date Established: 1997; **Freq:** Quarterly - 10/03-30/06-30/08-30/11; **Cover Price:** Free; **Circ:** 40,000
Usual Pagination: 116
Profile: Magazine covering all aspects of golf as a hobby. Includes articles on equipment, courses and techniques.
Language(s): French
Readership: Aimed at retired golf enthusiasts over 50 years of age.
ADVERTISING RATES:
Full Page Colour .... EUR 3000
Mechanical Data: Type Area: 225 x 297
CONSUMER: SPORT: Golf

GRAND LYON MAGAZINE COMMUNAUTE URBAINE DE LYON 1618634F80-845
Editorial: 20 rue du Lac, BP 3103, 69399 CEDEX 3 LYON **Tel:** 4 78 63 46 19 **Fax:** 478634605
Email: magazine@grandlyon.org **Web site:** http://www.grandlyon.com
ISSN: 1636-3493
Date Established: 2002; **Freq:** 6 issues yearly - début de mois impairs; **Cover Price:** Free; **Circ:** 614,000
Usual Pagination: 24
Profile: Publication focussing on local community information.
Language(s): French
Mechanical Data: Type Area: 227 x 298
CONSUMER: RURAL & REGIONAL INTEREST

GRAND TOULOUSE INFOS COMMUNAUTE D'AGGLOMERATION DU GRAND TOULOUSE 1648696F80-913
Editorial: 1 place de la Légion-d'Honneur, BP 5821, 31505 CEDEX 5 TOULOUSE **Tel:** 5 34 41 59 00
Fax: 534415901
Email: contact@grandtoulouse.org **Web site:** http://www.grandtoulouse.fr
ISSN: 1772-3477
Date Established: 2002; **Freq:** Half-yearly - mars et octobre; **Circ:** 300,000
Usual Pagination: 16
Editor: Pierre Cohen
Profile: Publication focussing on local community information.
Language(s): French
Mechanical Data: Type Area: 21 x 29,7
CONSUMER: RURAL & REGIONAL INTEREST

GRANDS REPORTAGES 7234F89E-50
Editorial: 6 rue Irvoy, CEDEX 1, 38027 GRENOBLE
Tel: 4 76 70 92 60 **Fax:** 4 76 70 54 12
Email: infos@grands-reportages.com **Web site:** http://www.grands-reportages.com
ISSN: 0182-0346
Date Established: 1978; **Freq:** Monthly - End of the month; **Cover Price:** EUR 4.90
Annual Sub.: EUR 46; **Circ:** 51,721
Usual Pagination: 132
Profile: Travel magazine providing reports on regions, countries, people, food and customs.
Language(s): French
ADVERTISING RATES:
Full Page Colour .... EUR 8700
Mechanical Data: Type Area: 210 x 277
CONSUMER: HOLIDAYS & TRAVEL: Holidays

HAPPY FEW 7235F89E-60
Editorial: 40 avenue Niel, 75017 PARIS
Tel: 1 43 80 31 25 **Fax:** 9 56 72 16 82
Email: guycouloubrier@free.fr **Web site:** http://happyfewmag.free.fr
ISSN: 0756-3558
Date Established: 1982; **Freq:** Half-yearly - 21 juin, fin novembre; **Annual Sub.:** EUR 55; **Circ:** 40,000
Usual Pagination: 120
Profile: Pan-European magazine about international travel and luxury goods.
Language(s): French
ADVERTISING RATES:
Full Page Mono .... EUR 6300
Full Page Colour .... EUR 9800
Mechanical Data: Type Area: 23 x 31
Copy instructions: *Copy Date:* 21 days prior to publication date
CONSUMER: HOLIDAYS & TRAVEL: Holidays

HARMONIE COMMUNAUTE D'AGGLOMERATION DE MONTPELLIER 1648621F80-875
Editorial: 50 place Zeus - CS 39556, BP 9531, 34961 MONTPELLIER CEDEX 2 **Tel:** 4 67 13 60 00
Fax: 4 67 13 64 00
Email: contact@montpellier-agglo.com **Web site:** http://www.montpellier-agglo.com
Freq: Monthly; **Cover Price:** Free; **Circ:** 220,000
Usual Pagination: 48
Editor: Jean-Pierre Moure
Profile: Publication focussing on local community information including news, local services, reviews and local life.
Language(s): French
CONSUMER: RURAL & REGIONAL INTEREST

HAUTE-VIENNE LE MAGAZINE CONSEIL GENERAL DE LA HAUTE- VIENNE 1617178F32A-1038
Editorial: Hôtel-du-Département, 43 avenue de la Libération, 87031 CEDEX LIMOGES
Tel: 5 55 45 12 54 **Fax:** 555795781
Email: magazine@cg87.fr **Web site:** http://www.cg87.fr
ISSN: 0769-7651
Freq: 6 issues yearly - 02 05 07 09 12; **Cover Price:** Free; **Circ:** 178,000
Usual Pagination: 24
Editor: Anne-Catherine Farges
Profile: Publication focussing on local government and department issues, including economics, tourism, cultural and social issues.
Language(s): French
Mechanical Data: Type Area: A 4
BUSINESS: LOCAL GOVERNMENT, LEISURE & RECREATION: Local Government

HAUT-RHIN MAGAZINE CONSEIL GENERAL DU HAUT-RHIN 1693269F32A-1082
Editorial: Hôtel-du-Département, 100 avenue d'Alsace, BP 20351, 68006 CEDEX COLMAR
Tel: 3 89 30 60 70 **Fax:** 389217285
Email: communication@cg68,fr **Web site:** http://www.cg68.fr
ISSN: 1772-3361
Date Established: 2005; **Freq:** Quarterly - variable; **Cover Price:** Free; **Circ:** 332,000
Usual Pagination: 44
Editor: Charles Buttner
Profile: Publication focussing on local government and department issues, including economics, solidarity, environment, cultural and social issues.
Language(s): French
Mechanical Data: Type Area: 230 x 280
BUSINESS: LOCAL GOVERNMENT, LEISURE & RECREATION: Local Government

L' HERAULT LE MAGAZINE DU DÉPARTEMENT 1617177F32A-1037
Editorial: Conseil Général, 1000 rue d'Alco, CEDEX 4, 34087 MONTPELLIER **Tel:** 4 67 67 74 41
Fax: 4 67 67 72 71
Email: vgirard@cg34.fr
ISSN: 1155-1259
Freq: Monthly - le 20 du mois; **Cover Price:** Free; **Circ:** 500,000
Usual Pagination: 32
Profile: Publication focussing on local government and department issues.
Language(s): French
Mechanical Data: Type Area: 297 x 210
BUSINESS: LOCAL GOVERNMENT, LEISURE & RECREATION: Local Government

HI FI VIDEO HOME CINEMA 5464F43B-40
Editorial: TRANSOCEANIC, 3 boulevard Ney, 75018 PARIS **Tel:** 1 44 65 80 80 **Fax:** 1 44 65 80 90
Email: a.bellamy@orange-business.fr
ISSN: 1281-1548
Date Established: 1969; **Freq:** Monthly - le 30 du mois; **Cover Price:** EUR 4.50
Annual Sub.: EUR 39; **Circ:** 40,000
Usual Pagination: 116
Profile: Magazine about hi-fi and video equipment.
Language(s): French
ADVERTISING RATES:
Full Page Colour .... EUR 3600
Mechanical Data: Type Area: A 4
Copy instructions: *Copy Date:* 21 days prior to publication date
BUSINESS: ELECTRICAL RETAIL TRADE: Radio & Hi-Fi

LE HIC 1619288F67J-162
Editorial: 70 rue de Lorraine, BP 1205, CEDEX, 49312 CHOLET **Tel:** 2 41 49 02 34 **Fax:** 2 41 49 02 39
Email: redaction@lehic.com
ISSN: 0397118X
Date Established: 1972; **Freq:** Weekly - mercredi; **Cover Price:** Free; **Circ:** 90,000
Usual Pagination: 46
Profile: Local current events, association and cultural newspaper. 4 editions: Cholet, Saumur, Bressuire and Sablé-la-Flèche. Total circulation including all editions: 261920 issues.
Language(s): French
ADVERTISING RATES:
Full Page Mono .... EUR 1755
Full Page Colour .... EUR 2094
Mechanical Data: Type Area: 290 x 420
REGIONAL DAILY & SUNDAY NEWSPAPERS: Regional Newspapers (excl. dailies)

L' HISTOIRE 7800F88R-286
Editorial: 74 avenue du Maine, 75014 PARIS
Tel: 1 44 10 10 10 **Fax:** 1 44 10 54 47
Email: courrier@histoire.presse.fr **Web site:** http://www.histoire.presse.fr
ISSN: 0182-2411
Date Established: 1978; **Freq:** Monthly - fin de mois
Annual Sub.: EUR 59; **Circ:** 72,753
Usual Pagination: 100
Profile: Magazine containing historical information.
Language(s): French
ADVERTISING RATES:
Full Page Mono .... EUR 6800
Full Page Colour .... EUR 8000
Mechanical Data: Type Area: 200 x 280
Copy instructions: *Copy Date:* 21 days prior to publication date
CONSUMER: EDUCATION: Education Related

L' HOTELIER DE PLEIN AIR 5583F50-45
Editorial: 12 rue Rouget de Lisle, CEDEX, 92442 ISSY LES MOULINEAUX **Tel:** 1 41 33 37 37
Fax: 1 41 33 47 67
Email: jean-baptiste.treboul@motorpresse.fr **Web site:** http://www.motorpresse.fr
Freq: 24 issues yearly - début des mois pairs; **Cover Price:** EUR 10.65
Annual Sub.: EUR 61; **Circ:** 7,000
Usual Pagination: 50
Publisher: Marc Lacoste
Profile: Journal focusing on the management of camping and caravan sites and leisure parks.
Language(s): French
Readership: Read by managers of camp-sites.
ADVERTISING RATES:
Full Page Colour .... EUR 1840
Mechanical Data: Type Area: 21 x 29,7
Copy instructions: *Copy Date:* 15 days prior to publication date
BUSINESS: TRAVEL & TOURISM

L' HOTELLERIE - RESTAURATION 4778F11A-140
Editorial: 5 rue Antoine Bourdelle, CEDEX 15, 75737 PARIS **Tel:** 1 45 48 64 64 **Fax:** 1 45 48 04 23
Email: redaction@lhotellerie-restauration.fr **Web site:** http://www.lhotellerie-restauration.fr
ISSN: 1151-2601
Date Established: 1923; **Freq:** Weekly
Annual Sub.: EUR 43; **Circ:** 56,112
Usual Pagination: 36
Profile: Magazine focusing on the hotel and catering trade.
Language(s): French
ADVERTISING RATES:
Full Page Mono .... EUR 6500
Full Page Colour .... EUR 9000
Mechanical Data: Type Area: 290 x 385
Copy instructions: *Copy Date:* 7 days prior to publication date
BUSINESS: CATERING: Catering, Hotels & Restaurants

HTR - EUROTRENDS & MARKETING 4776F11A-125
Editorial: 5 rue de Dantzig, 75015 PARIS
Tel: 1 56 56 87 77 **Fax:** 1 56 56 87 78
Email: redaction@hotelhebdo.com **Web site:** http://www.htrmagazine.com
ISSN: 1274-2341
Date Established: 1994; **Freq:** Monthly - 1ère semaine du mois
Annual Sub.: EUR 145; **Circ:** 6,500
Usual Pagination: 92
Profile: Pan-European magazine concerning the hotel and tourist trade.
Language(s): French
ADVERTISING RATES:
Full Page Colour .... EUR 2745
Mechanical Data: Type Area: A 4
BUSINESS: CATERING: Catering, Hotels & Restaurants

L' HUMANITE 6093F65A-60
Editorial: 164 rue Ambroise Croizat, CEDEX, 93528 SAINT-DENIS **Tel:** 1 49 22 72 72
Email: papel-muller@humanite.fr **Web site:** http://www.humanite.fr
ISSN: 0242-6870
Date Established: 1904; **Freq:** Daily - le matin; **Cover Price:** EUR 1.20
Annual Sub.: EUR 336; **Circ:** 52,456
Usual Pagination: 28
Profile: Tabloid-sized newspaper of the French Communist Party. Covers news, politics, culture, sport, entertainment and employment vacancies.
Language(s): French
Readership: Read by a broad range of the population.
ADVERTISING RATES:
Full Page Mono .... EUR 12650
Full Page Colour .... EUR 17650
Mechanical Data: Type Area: 390 x 280
NATIONAL DAILY & SUNDAY NEWSPAPERS: National Daily Newspapers

L' HYDROCARBURE 5348F33-30
Editorial: Association ENSPM, 228-232 av. Napoléon Bonaparte, CEDEX, 92852 RUEIL MALMAISON
Tel: 1 47 52 71 12 **Fax:** 1 47 52 72 21
Email: diane.cournord@ifp.fr
Date Established: 1925; **Freq:** Quarterly - les mois 04 07 12; **Cover Price:** EUR 6.50; **Circ:** 2,500
Usual Pagination: 44
Profile: Magazine focusing on the production and distribution of petrol.
Language(s): French
ADVERTISING RATES:
Full Page Mono .... EUR 1450
Full Page Colour .... EUR 2050
Mechanical Data: Type Area: A 4
Copy instructions: *Copy Date:* 15 days prior to publication date
BUSINESS: OIL & PETROLEUM

ICI PARIS 6374F73-90
Editorial: 149 rue Anatole France, CEDEX, 92534 LEVALLOIS PERRET **Tel:** 1 41 34 88 10
Fax: 1 41 34 89 34
Email: docicip@hfp.fr
ISSN: 0249-6054
Date Established: 1945; **Freq:** Weekly - mardi; **Cover Price:** EUR 1.20
Annual Sub.: EUR 48; **Circ:** 370,010
Usual Pagination: 50
Profile: Topical news magazine focusing mainly on show business.
Language(s): French
ADVERTISING RATES:
Full Page Colour .... EUR 9070
Mechanical Data: Type Area: 29 x 23
Copy instructions: *Copy Date:* 15 days prior to publication date
CONSUMER: NATIONAL & INTERNATIONAL PERIODICALS

IDEAT 1618084F74B-235
Editorial: 12/14 rue Jules César, 75012 PARIS
Tel: 1 44 75 79 40 **Fax:** 1 44 75 79 49
Email: laurentblanc@ideat.fr **Web site:** http://www.ideat.fr
ISSN: 1294-9485
Date Established: 1999; **Freq:** Monthly - 8 issues yearly; **Cover Price:** EUR 4.90
Annual Sub.: EUR 16; **Circ:** 71,787
Usual Pagination: 245
Profile: Publication focussing on home & style including decoration, interior and contemporary design.
Language(s): French
ADVERTISING RATES:
Full Page Mono .... EUR 6800
Full Page Colour .... EUR 10300

Mechanical Data: Type Area: 215 x 275
CONSUMER: WOMEN'S INTEREST CONSUMER MAGAZINES: Women's Interest - Fashion

IMAGINE TON FUTUR
1732100F74F-225
Editorial: 16 rue de l'Arbalète, 75005 PARIS
Tel: 1 79 85 01 00 **Fax:** 1 79 85 01 09
Email: contacts@imaginetonfutur.com **Web site:** http://www.imaginetonfutur.com
ISSN: 1969-1521
Date Established: 2005; **Freq:** 24 issues yearly - le 25 des mois impairs; **Cover Price:** Free; **Circ:** 208,125
Usual Pagination: 40
Profile: Youth publication (12-25 years) focussing on teenage lifestyle, career and counselling.
Language(s): French
ADVERTISING RATES:
Full Page Colour .... EUR 17500
Mechanical Data: Type Area: 200 x 260
Copy instructions: *Copy Date:* 14 days prior to publication date
CONSUMER: WOMEN'S INTEREST CONSUMER MAGAZINES: Teenage

IMPACT MEDECINE
5690F56R-313
Editorial: 152 avenue de Malakoff, 75116 PARIS
Tel: 1 53 93 36 00 **Fax:** 1 53 93 37 75
Email: jschenckery@impactmedecine.fr **Web site:** http://www.impactmedecine.fr
ISSN: 1635-3420
Date Established: 1976; **Freq:** Weekly - le jeudi; **Annual Sub.:** EUR 79; **Circ:** 45,800
Usual Pagination: 102
Managing Director: Claudine Du Fontenioux
Profile: Magazine for medical finalists, specialists and hospital doctors.
Language(s): French
ADVERTISING RATES:
Full Page Mono .... EUR 11100
Full Page Colour .... EUR 13950
Mechanical Data: Type Area: 365 x 273
BUSINESS: HEALTH & MEDICAL: Health Medical Related

L' INDEPENDANT BUREAU PARISIEN
1619447F67B-8447
Editorial: 80 boulevard Auguste-Blanqui, 75683 CEDEX 14 PARIS **Tel:** 1 44 71 80 44 **Fax:** 144718046
Email: redac.paris@midilibre.com **Web site:** http://www.lindependant.com
ISSN: 0220-0058
Date Established: 1948; **Freq:** Daily - Aude (11); **Cover Price:** EUR 0.85
Annual Sub.: EUR 232; **Circ:** 65,523
Profile: The Paris office is dedicated to the Indépendant issue of the Midi Libre et Centre Presse.
Language(s): French
REGIONAL DAILY & SUNDAY NEWSPAPERS: Regional Daily Newspapers

L' INDEPENDANT RIVESALTES
1619448F67B-8448
Editorial: Mas de la Garrigue, 2 avenue Alfred-Sauvy, BP 105, 66605 CEDEX RIVESALTES
Tel: 4 68 64 88 88 **Fax:** 468648840
Email: direction.redaction@lindependant.com **Web site:** http://www.lindependant.com
ISSN: 0220-0058
Date Established: 1846; **Freq:** Daily - Aude (11); **Cover Price:** EUR 0.85
Annual Sub.: EUR 232; **Circ:** 65,523
Usual Pagination: 40
Editor: Alain Plombat
Profile: Daily regional newspaper. Local news is about 70% of the editorial content.
Language(s): French
ADVERTISING RATES:
Full Page Colour .... EUR 8658
Mechanical Data: Type Area: berlinois
REGIONAL DAILY & SUNDAY NEWSPAPERS: Regional Daily Newspapers

L' INDUSTRIE HOTELIERE
4779F11A-160
Editorial: 9 rue Labie, CEDEX 17, 75838 PARIS
Tel: 1 45 74 21 62 **Fax:** 1 45 74 01 03
Email: industriehoteliere@lechef.com **Web site:** http://www.lechef.com
ISSN: 1141-0078
Date Established: 1951; **Freq:** Monthly - le 10 du mois suivant; **Cover Price:** EUR 5.50
Annual Sub.: EUR 38; **Circ:** 35,787
Usual Pagination: 64
Profile: Journal containing information concerning the hotel and catering trade.
Language(s): French
Readership: Aimed at professionals in the hotel and catering industry.
ADVERTISING RATES:
Full Page Mono .... EUR 5800
Full Page Colour .... EUR 7800
Mechanical Data: Type Area: A4
BUSINESS: CATERING: Catering, Hotels & Restaurants

L' INFFO FORMATION
1619860F14F-169
Editorial: Centre INFFO, 4 avenue du Stade de France, CEDEX, 93218 LA PLAINE SAINT DENIS
Tel: 1 55 93 91 91 **Fax:** 1 49 46 96 91
Email: contact@centre-inffo.fr **Web site:** http://www.centre-inffo.fr
ISSN: 0397-3301
Date Established: 1976; **Freq:** 26 issues yearly - entre 16-31 du mois; **Annual Sub.:** EUR 130; **Circ:** 3,173
Usual Pagination: 24
Language(s): French
ADVERTISING RATES:
Full Page Colour .... EUR 2500
Mechanical Data: Type Area: 210 x 297
Copy instructions: *Copy Date:* 14 days prior to publication date
BUSINESS: COMMERCE, INDUSTRY & MANAGEMENT: Training & Recruitment

INFO CHIMIE MAGAZINE
4804F13-132
Editorial: Antony Parc II, 10 place du Général de Gaulle, 92160 ANTONY **Tel:** 1 77 92 95 86
Email: slatieule@etai.fr **Web site:** http://www.france-chimie.com
Date Established: 1964; **Freq:** Monthly - variable; **Cover Price:** EUR 31
Annual Sub.: EUR 215; **Circ:** 3,500
Usual Pagination: 80
Profile: Journal with information on the chemical industry, including pharmaceuticals, cosmetics and food.
Language(s): French
ADVERTISING RATES:
Full Page Colour .... EUR 4660
Mechanical Data: Type Area: A 4
Copy instructions: *Copy Date:* 31 days prior to publication date
BUSINESS: CHEMICALS

INFO MAGAZINE CLERMONT-FERRAND
1619151F80-1103
Editorial: 7 place de Jaude, 63038, CEDEX 1 CLERMONT-FERRAND **Tel:** 4 73 43 50 50
Fax: 473342997
Email: redac63@infomagazine.com **Web site:** http://www.yakinfo.com
ISSN: 0766-8171
Date Established: 1985; **Freq:** Weekly - lundi; **Cover Price:** Free; **Circ:** 200,000
Usual Pagination: 72
Editor: Daniel Voissier
Profile: Reports, investigations, cinema, driving tests, shows, fashion, beauty... Info Magazine has also local editions in the Allier, the Haute-Vienne and the Corrèze regions, corresponding to a total of 550,000 copies/week with local editorial offices for each edition but with an identical basic structure.
Language(s): French
ADVERTISING RATES:
Full Page Mono .... EUR 3614
Full Page Colour .... EUR 4780
Mechanical Data: Type Area: 27 x 40
CONSUMER: RURAL & REGIONAL INTEREST

L' INFO METROPOLE
1618661F32A-700
Editorial: 4 avenue Henri Fréville, CS 20723, CEDEX 2, 35207 RENNES **Tel:** 2 99 86 62 82
Fax: 2 99 86 62 61
Email: linfo@agglo-rennesmetropole.fr
ISSN: 1297-3491
Date Established: 1990; **Freq:** Monthly - le 1er du mois; **Cover Price:** Free; **Circ:** 205,000
Usual Pagination: 40
Profile: Municipal publication focussing on local government news, sports, associations, culture and leisure.
Language(s): French
Mechanical Data: Type Area: 23 x 30
BUSINESS: LOCAL GOVERNMENT, LEISURE & RECREATION: Local Government

INFO SANTE
1618141F74G-265
Editorial: 152 avenue de Malakoff, 75116 PARIS
Tel: 1 53 93 36 00 **Fax:** 1 53 93 37 75
Email: dmagnien@impactmedecine.fr **Web site:** http://www.impactmedecine.fr
ISSN: 0399-6689
Freq: Monthly - début du mois (sauf août déc.); **Cover Price:** Free; **Circ:** 800,000
Usual Pagination: 4
Managing Director: Claudine Du Fontenioux
Profile: Publication focussing on health including pharmaceutics, health prevention and education.
Language(s): French
Mechanical Data: Type Area: A 4
CONSUMER: WOMEN'S INTEREST CONSUMER MAGAZINES: Slimming & Health

L' INFORMATION DENTAIRE
5817F56D-80
Editorial: 40 avenue Bugeaud, CEDEX 16, 75784 PARIS **Tel:** 1 56 26 50 00 **Fax:** 1 56 26 50 01
Email: info@information-dentaire.fr **Web site:** http://www.information-dentaire.com
ISSN: 0020-0018
Date Established: 1919; **Freq:** Weekly - mercredi; **Cover Price:** EUR 5.50
Annual Sub.: EUR 172; **Circ:** 13,950
Usual Pagination: 64
Profile: Dentistry journal containing general and professional information. Also contains conference and training details.
Language(s): French
Readership: Read by dental surgeons.
ADVERTISING RATES:
Full Page Colour .... EUR 2600
Mechanical Data: Type Area: 21 x 27
Copy instructions: *Copy Date:* 7 days prior to publication date
BUSINESS: HEALTH & MEDICAL: Dental

LES INROCKUPTIB
6782F76E-100
Editorial: Les Editions Indépendantes, 24 rue Saint Sabin, 75011 PARIS **Tel:** 1 42 44 16 16
Fax: 1 42 44 16 00
Email: jean-marc.lalanne@inrocks.com **Web site:** http://www.lesinrocks.com
ISSN: 0298-3788
Date Established: 1986; **Freq:** Weekly - Wednesday; **Cover Price:** EUR 2.50
Annual Sub.: EUR 98; **Circ:** 40,534
Usual Pagination: 148
Profile: Magazine which specialises in the different forms of rock culture - music, photo, cinema, literature and theatre.
Language(s): French
ADVERTISING RATES:
Full Page Colour .... EUR 8000
Mechanical Data: Type Area: 214 x 280
CONSUMER: MUSIC & PERFORMING ARTS: Pop Music

INTER REGIONS
6014F14A-815
Editorial: 219 Boulevard Saint Germain, 75007 PARIS **Tel:** 1 42 22 35 29 **Fax:** 1 45 49 91 49
Email: cner@cner-france.com **Web site:** http://www.cner-france.com
ISSN: 0240-9925
Date Established: 1979; **Freq:** 24 issues yearly - début 02 04 06 08 09 12
Annual Sub.: EUR 46; **Circ:** 900
Usual Pagination: 44
Profile: Magazine focusing on regional expansion and development.
Language(s): French
ADVERTISING RATES:
Full Page Colour .... EUR 1000
Mechanical Data: Type Area: 210 x 270
BUSINESS: COMMERCE, INDUSTRY & MANAGEMENT

INTERNATIONAL HERALD TRIBUNE
1639772F65A-164
Editorial: 6 bis rue des Graviers, CEDEX, 92521 NEUILLY SUR SEINE **Tel:** 1 41 43 93 00
Fax: 1 41 43 92 12
Email: asmale@iht.com **Web site:** http://www.iht.com
Date Established: 1887; **Freq:** Daily - Africa; **Circ:** 219,188
Usual Pagination: 24
Editor-in-Chief: Tom Redburn
Profile: Newspaper focusing on national and international news, business, politics, culture, sport and entertainment.
Language(s): English
ADVERTISING RATES:
Full Page Mono .... EUR 59053
NATIONAL DAILY & SUNDAY NEWSPAPERS: National Daily Newspapers

INTERNET & ENTREPRISE
601023F5B-90
Editorial: 20 rue de la Banque, 75002 PARIS
Tel: 1 55 35 38 90
Email: redaction@i-entreprise.com **Web site:** http://www.i-entreprise.com
ISSN: 1298-3209
Date Established: 1999; **Freq:** Monthly - fin des mois pairs
Annual Sub.: EUR 49; **Circ:** 58,200
Usual Pagination: 100
Profile: Computer magazine aiming to help businesses to make the most of new information technology.
Language(s): French
Readership: Aimed at general and IT managers in small and medium sized companies.
ADVERTISING RATES:
Full Page Colour .... EUR 9900
Mechanical Data: Type Area: 210 x 285
Copy instructions: *Copy Date:* 15 days prior to publication date
BUSINESS: COMPUTERS & AUTOMATION: Data Processing

L' INTERNET PRATIQUE
628859F5E-128
Editorial: 101/109 rue Jean Jaurès, 92300 LEVALLOIS PERRET **Tel:** 1 41 27 38 38
Fax: 1 41 27 38 39
Email: pierre.bielande@skynet.be
ISSN: 1635-2610
Date Established: 2000; **Freq:** Monthly - le 15 du mois; **Cover Price:** EUR 7.50
Annual Sub.: EUR 38.50; **Circ:** 21,723
Usual Pagination: 100
Editor-in-Chief: Pierre Bielande
Profile: Magazine focusing on the Internet.
Language(s): French
Readership: Aimed at Internet enthusiasts.
ADVERTISING RATES:
Full Page Colour .... EUR 420
Mechanical Data: Type Area: 210 x 284
BUSINESS: COMPUTERS & AUTOMATION: Data Transmission

INTRAMUROS
4595F4B-10
Editorial: 29 rue de Meaux, 75019 PARIS
Tel: 1 42 03 95 95 **Fax:** 1 42 03 95 77
Email: info@intramuros.fr **Web site:** http://www.intramuros.fr
ISSN: 0769-3710
Date Established: 1985; **Freq:** 24 issues yearly - 01 03 05 07 09 11; **Cover Price:** EUR 12
Annual Sub.: EUR 62; **Circ:** 30,000
Usual Pagination: 124
Profile: Magazine covering design and architecture.
Language(s): English; French
Readership: Aimed at architects, designers, industrialists and distributors. Also the general public interested in design.
ADVERTISING RATES:
Full Page Mono .... EUR 720
Full Page Colour .... EUR 720
Mechanical Data: Type Area: 300 x 225
Copy instructions: *Copy Date:* 30 days prior to publication date
BUSINESS: ARCHITECTURE & BUILDING: Interior Design & Flooring

INVESTIR
4523F6J-2
Editorial: 16 rue du 4 Septembre, 75002 PARIS
Tel: 1 44 88 48 00 **Fax:** 1 44 88 48 02
Email: investir@investir.fr **Web site:** http://www.investir.fr
ISSN: 0759-7673
Date Established: 1974; **Freq:** Weekly - samedi pour la semaine suivante; **Cover Price:** EUR 3.90
Annual Sub.: EUR 112; **Circ:** 77,639
Usual Pagination: 68
Profile: Newspaper containing topical investment analysis and economic conjecture. Also provides information on the stock market.
Language(s): French
Readership: Aimed at investment advisers.
ADVERTISING RATES:
Full Page Mono .... EUR 2120
Full Page Colour .... EUR 2720
Mechanical Data: Type Area: 285 x 390
NATIONAL DAILY & SUNDAY NEWSPAPERS: National Weekly Newspapers

INVESTIR MAGAZINE
4524F1F-55
Editorial: 16 rue du 4 Septembre, 75002 PARIS
Tel: 1 44 88 48 00 **Fax:** 1 44 88 48 02
Email: tbogaty@investir.fr **Web site:** http://www.investir.fr
ISSN: 0994-6845
Date Established: 1988; **Freq:** Monthly - vers le 15 du mois; **Cover Price:** EUR 3.90
Annual Sub.: EUR 25; **Circ:** 91,959
Usual Pagination: 112
Profile: Financial journal giving details and advice about all types of investment, stocks and shares.
Language(s): French
Readership: Read by estate agents and investment advisers.
ADVERTISING RATES:
Full Page Mono .... EUR 14400
Full Page Colour .... EUR 18500
Mechanical Data: Type Area: 205 x 280
Copy instructions: *Copy Date:* 7 days prior to publication date
BUSINESS: FINANCE & ECONOMICS: Investment

ISERE MAGAZINE
1617162F32A-1027
Editorial: Hôtel du Département, 7 rue Fantin Latour, BP 1096 CEDEX 1, 38022 GRENOBLE
Tel: 4 76 00 38 38 **Fax:** 4 76 00 38 09
Email: v.granger@cg38.fr **Web site:** http://www.isere.fr
ISSN: 0757-990X
Freq: Monthly - Vers le 20 du mois; **Cover Price:** Free; **Circ:** 538,000
Usual Pagination: 48
Profile: Publication focussing on local government and department issues.
Language(s): French
Mechanical Data: Type Area: A 4
BUSINESS: LOCAL GOVERNMENT, LEISURE & RECREATION: Local Government

IT, INDUSTRIE ET TECHNOLOGIES
4852F14B-110
Editorial: Antony Parc 2, 10 place du Général-de-Gaulle, BP 20156, 92186 ANTONY **Tel:** 1 77 92 92 92
Fax: 1 77 92 98 51
Web site: http://www.industrie.com/it
ISSN: 1633-7107
Date Established: 1958; **Freq:** Monthly - mid month publication; **Cover Price:** EUR 11
Annual Sub.: EUR 105; **Circ:** 8,075
Usual Pagination: 116
Profile: Publication focusing on new technology and its application in modern industry.
Language(s): French
Readership: Read by engineers, technicians and executives.
ADVERTISING RATES:
Full Page Mono .... EUR 5070
Full Page Colour .... EUR 8795

lechanical Data: Type Area: 23 x 29,7
opy instructions: *Copy Date:* 15 days prior to
ublication date
USINESS: COMMERCE, INDUSTRY & MANAGEMENT: Industry & Factories

ALOU GALLERY
6430F74B-70
ditorial: 10 rue du Plâtre, 75004 PARIS **Tel:** 1-53-1-10-30 **Fax:** 1-53-01-11-93
/eb site: http://www.jalougallery.com
SSN: 1281-0282
ate Established: 1997; **Freq:** Monthly - publishes etween the 20th and 25th of the month; **Circ:** 81,140
sual Pagination: 148
ditor: Jennifer Eymère; **Editor-in-Chief:** Laure mbroise; **Advertising Manager:** Anna Lucas
rofile: High fashion magazine for women.
anguage(s): French
eadership: Read by women aged between 18 and 0 years.
DVERTISING RATES:
ull Page Mono .... EUR 11118
ull Page Colour .... EUR 12750
lechanical Data: Type Area: 220 x 285
opy instructions: *Copy Date:* 20 days prior to ublication date
ONSUMER: WOMEN'S INTEREST CONSUMER MAGAZINES: Women's Interest - Fashion

ARDIN PRATIQUE
7289F93-60
ditorial: 8 rue François Villon, 75015 PARIS
el: 1 53 68 65 65 **Fax:** 1 53 68 65 75
mail: jardinpratique@wanadoo.fr
SSN: 0762-9699
ate Established: 1984; **Freq:** 24 issues yearly - le 0 des mois pairs
nnual Sub.: EUR 28.50; **Circ:** 90,000
sual Pagination: 64
rofile: Magazine providing advice and information bout gardening.
anguage(s): French
DVERTISING RATES:
ull Page Mono .... EUR 2068
ull Page Colour .... EUR 2625
lechanical Data: Type Area: 180 x 250
opy instructions: *Copy Date:* 31 days prior to ublication date
ONSUMER: GARDENING

JARDINERIES
5216F26A-55
ditorial: 11 route de la Butte du Moulin, 78125 POIGNY LA FORET **Tel:** 1 34 84 70 60
ax: 1 34 84 70 55
mail: contacts@groupej-sas.com **Web site:** http://www.jardineries.com
SSN: 0151-4695
Date Established: 1976; **Freq:** Monthly - 1er jeudi du nois; **Cover Price:** EUR 6.13
nnual Sub.: EUR 91.50; **Circ:** 7,500
Jsual Pagination: 56
rofile: Publication about the sale of fruit and egetables includes distribution and market aluation.
anguage(s): French
DVERTISING RATES:
ull Page Mono .... EUR 3540
ull Page Colour .... EUR 4500
lechanical Data: Type Area: 230 x 297
opy instructions: *Copy Date:* 7 days prior to ublication date
BUSINESS: GARDEN TRADE: Market Garden raders

JAZZ MAGAZINE
6766F76D-75
ditorial: 15 rue Duphot, 75001 PARIS
el: 1 56 88 17 73 **Fax:** 1 49 53 08 31
mail: franckbergerot@jazzmagazine.com **Web site:** http://www.jazzmagazine.com
SSN: 1965-1740
Date Established: 1954; **Freq:** Monthly - 30th of each month; **Circ:** 25,000
Jsual Pagination: 84
rofile: Magazine about the history of jazz and urrent music trends.
anguage(s): French
DVERTISING RATES:
ull Page Mono .... EUR 2014
ull Page Colour .... EUR 2877
Mechanical Data: Type Area: 220 x 285
CONSUMER: MUSIC & PERFORMING ARTS: Music

JE BOUQUINE
601329F91D-90
ditorial: 18 rue Barbès, CEDEX, 92128 MONTROUGE **Tel:** 1 74 31 60 60 **Fax:** 1 74 31 60 80
mail: veronique.girard@bayard-presse.com **Web site:** http://www.jebouquine.com
SSN: 0756-564X
Date Established: 1984; **Freq:** Monthly - vers le 25 our le mois suivant; **Cover Price:** EUR 6.50
nnual Sub.: EUR 64.80; **Circ:** 32,905
Jsual Pagination: 102
Profile: Magazine containing children's stories, artoon extracts, games and information about CD-ROMs and computer games.
Language(s): French
Readership: Aimed at youngsters between 10 and 15 years.
ADVERTISING RATES:
Full Page Colour .... EUR 6750
Mechanical Data: Type Area: 195 x 223

Copy instructions: *Copy Date:* 62 days prior to publication date
CONSUMER: RECREATION & LEISURE: Children & Youth

JEUX VIDEO MAGAZINE
628851F78D-197
Editorial: 101/109 rue Jean Jaurès, 92300 LEVALLOIS PERRET **Tel:** 1 41 27 38 38
Fax: 1 41 27 38 39
Email: cyrille.tessier@yellowmedia.fr **Web site:** http://www.jvn.com
ISSN: 1625-449X
Date Established: 2000; **Freq:** Monthly - toutes les 4 semaines; **Cover Price:** EUR 2.99
Annual Sub.: EUR 16.50; **Circ:** 77,262
Usual Pagination: 148
Profile: Magazine containing video game guides; tested and rated.
Language(s): French
Readership: Read by people who enjoy video games.
ADVERTISING RATES:
Full Page Colour .... EUR 6400
Mechanical Data: Type Area: 23 x 29,2
Copy instructions: *Copy Date:* 28 days prior to publication date
CONSUMER: CONSUMER ELECTRONICS: Games

JOGGING INTERNATIONAL
6663F75J-100
Editorial: 12 rue Rouget de l'Isle, CEDEX, 92442 ISSY LES MOULINEAUX **Tel:** 1 41 33 37 37
Fax: 1 41 33 47 67
Email: bruno.lacroix@motorpresse.fr **Web site:** http://www.motorpresse.fr
Date Established: 1993; **Freq:** Monthly - vers le 01 - 10 de chaque mois; **Cover Price:** EUR 4.95
Annual Sub.: EUR 39.60; **Circ:** 34,978
Usual Pagination: 190
Profile: Magazine about jogging, running and marathons.
Language(s): French
ADVERTISING RATES:
Full Page Colour .... EUR 6820
Mechanical Data: Type Area: 210 x 285
Copy instructions: *Copy Date:* 20 days prior to publication date
CONSUMER: SPORT: Athletics

LE JOURNAL DE LA CUB
1739770F80-970
Editorial: Communauté urbaine de Bordeaux, Esplanade Charles de Gaulle, CEDEX, 33076 BORDEAUX **Tel:** 5 56 93 67 29
Email: nsevenet@cu-bordeaux.fr
ISSN: 1779-4889
Date Established: 2006; **Freq:** Quarterly - variable; **Cover Price:** Free; **Circ:** 360,000
Usual Pagination: 32
Profile: Publication focussing on local community information.
Language(s): French
Mechanical Data: Type Area: 230 X 300
CONSUMER: RURAL & REGIONAL INTEREST

LE JOURNAL DE LA HAUTE MARNE
6167F67B-4700
Editorial: 14 rue du Patronage Laïque, BP 2057, CEDEX 9, 52902 CHAUMONT **Tel:** 3 25 03 86 40
Fax: 3 25 03 86 52
Email: jhmdir@graphycom.com **Web site:** http://www.jhm.fr
ISSN: 1168-9668
Freq: Daily - tous les matins; **Cover Price:** EUR 0.80
Annual Sub.: EUR 270; **Circ:** 25,832
Usual Pagination: 40
Profile: General and local news focussing on economy, health and politics.
Language(s): French
ADVERTISING RATES:
Full Page Mono .... EUR 2972
Full Page Colour .... EUR 3715
REGIONAL DAILY & SUNDAY NEWSPAPERS: Regional Daily Newspapers

LE JOURNAL DE LA MAISON
6450F74C-160
Editorial: 124 rue Danton, 92300 LEVALLOIS PERRET **Tel:** 1 41 34 60 00 62 28 **Fax:** 1 41 34 95 59
Email: anne.gastineau@lagardere-active.com
ISSN: 0750-3288
Date Established: 1968; **Freq:** Monthly - Le 15 du mois
Annual Sub.: EUR 30; **Circ:** 179,390
Usual Pagination: 140
Publisher: Philippe Khyr
Profile: Magazine covering house construction, renovation, decoration and equipment, with ideas, applications and prices.
Language(s): French
Readership: Aimed at people seeking to improve their home surroundings.
ADVERTISING RATES:
Full Page Mono .... EUR 11040
Full Page Colour .... EUR 13800
Mechanical Data: Type Area: 212 x 285
CONSUMER: WOMEN'S INTEREST CONSUMER MAGAZINES: Home & Family

LE JOURNAL DE LA VENDEE CONSEIL GENERAL DE LA VENDEE
1617209F32A-1067
Editorial: 40 rue Maréchal-Foch, 85923 CEDEX 9 LA ROCHE-SUR-YON **Tel:** 2 51 44 79 10
Fax: 251447911
Email: journalvendee@gmail.com **Web site:** http://www.vendee.fr
ISSN: 1957-0112
Date Established: 2003; **Freq:** 26 issues yearly - un lundi sur deux; **Cover Price:** Free; **Circ:** 285,000
Usual Pagination: 12
Editor: Joël Sarlot
Profile: Publication focussing on local government and department issues, including economics, culture, computing, tourism, training, social, sport and environment.
Language(s): French
Mechanical Data: Type Area: Tabloïd
BUSINESS: LOCAL GOVERNMENT, LEISURE & RECREATION: Local Government

LE JOURNAL DE L'AUTOMOBILE
5275F31A-150
Editorial: EDITION COPROSAS, 89 rue du Gouverneur Général Eboué, 92130 ISSY LES MOULINEAUX **Tel:** 1 46 90 20 00 **Fax:** 1 46 90 09 39
Email: herve.daigueperce@journalauto.com **Web site:** http://www.journalauto.com
ISSN: 0242-0805
Date Established: 1979; **Freq:** Weekly - le vendredi; **Cover Price:** EUR 7.50
Annual Sub.: EUR 99; **Circ:** 5,061
Usual Pagination: 56
Managing Director: François Schiettecatte
Profile: Magazine concerning the automobile industry. Includes information on markets, car models and distribution.
Language(s): French
Readership: Aimed at professionals in the automobile industry.
ADVERTISING RATES:
Full Page Colour .... EUR 5190
Mechanical Data: Type Area: 245 x 340
Copy instructions: *Copy Date:* 14 days prior to publication date
BUSINESS: MOTOR TRADE: Motor Trade Accessories

LE JOURNAL DE MICKEY
754747F91D-105
Editorial: 10 rue Thierry Le Luron, CEDEX, 92592 LEVALLOIS PERRET **Tel:** 1 41 34 85 00
Fax: 1 41 34 88 61
Email: edith.rieubon@lagardere-active.com
Date Established: 1934; **Freq:** Weekly - mercredi; **Cover Price:** EUR 1.90
Annual Sub.: EUR 98.80; **Circ:** 145,158
Usual Pagination: 76
Profile: Magazine featuring the cartoon world of Walt Disney.
Language(s): French
Readership: Read by children of all ages.
ADVERTISING RATES:
Full Page Colour .... EUR 9200
Mechanical Data: Type Area: 195 x 278
Copy instructions: *Copy Date:* 20 days prior to publication date
CONSUMER: RECREATION & LEISURE: Children & Youth

LE JOURNAL DE SAONE ET LOIRE
6164F67B-4800
Editorial: 9-15 rue des Tonneliers, BP 30134, CEDEX, 71104 CHALON-SUR-SAONE
Tel: 3 85 90 68 00 **Fax:** 3 85 93 02 96
Email: infos@lejsl.fr **Web site:** http://www.lejsl.com
ISSN: 1620-8943
Date Established: 1826; **Freq:** Daily - le matin
Annual Sub.: EUR 291.20; **Circ:** 58,036
Usual Pagination: 68
Profile: Regional news. Friday price:1,10 € - Sunday price: 1,50 € - Number of issues per year: 312 (Weekday) and 52 (Sunday). Annual subscription: 291,20 € (Weekday) and 78 € (Sunday).
Language(s): French
ADVERTISING RATES:
Full Page Mono .... EUR 4548
Full Page Colour .... EUR 5504
Mechanical Data: Type Area: tabloid
REGIONAL DAILY & SUNDAY NEWSPAPERS: Regional Daily Newspapers

LE JOURNAL DES ARTS
7085F84A-350
Editorial: 8 rue Borromée, 75015 PARIS
Tel: 1 48 42 90 00 **Fax:** 1 48 42 90 01
Email: contact@artclair.com **Web site:** http://www.artclair.com
ISSN: 1245-1495
Date Established: 1994; **Freq:** 26 issues yearly - un vendredi sur deux; **Cover Price:** EUR 5.90
Annual Sub.: EUR 88; **Circ:** 25,000
Usual Pagination: 36
Profile: Magazine focusing on all aspects of the arts.
Language(s): French
ADVERTISING RATES:
Full Page Colour .... EUR 6500
Mechanical Data: Type Area: 300 x 420
Copy instructions: *Copy Date:* 14 days prior to publication date
CONSUMER: THE ARTS & LITERARY: Arts

LE JOURNAL DES FINANCES
4471F1A-200
Editorial: 14 boulevard Haussmann, CEDEX 09, 75438 PARIS **Tel:** 1 57 08 73 00 **Fax:** 1 57 08 73 47
Email: roland.laskine@jdf.com **Web site:** http://www.jdf.com
ISSN: 0021-8049
Date Established: 1867; **Freq:** Weekly; **Cover Price:** EUR 3.80
Annual Sub.: EUR 109; **Circ:** 55,046
Usual Pagination: 56
Managing Director: Jean-Guillaume D' Ornano;
Publisher: François De Pirey
Profile: Journal covering economics and finance.
Language(s): French
Readership: Read by senior officials and business executives.
ADVERTISING RATES:
Full Page Mono .... EUR 18390
Full Page Colour .... EUR 24390
Mechanical Data: Type Area: 47 x 32
BUSINESS: FINANCE & ECONOMICS

LE JOURNAL DES MAIRES
5306F32A-150
Editorial: 22 rue Cambacérès, 75008 PARIS
Tel: 1 42 65 58 94 **Fax:** 1 47 42 87 57
Web site: http://www.journaldesmaires.com
Date Established: 1857; **Freq:** Monthly - le 15 du mois
Annual Sub.: EUR 90; **Circ:** 17,406
Usual Pagination: 100
Profile: Journal concerned with the organisation and day to day running of small and medium sized towns and villages.
Language(s): French
Readership: Aimed at the mayors of small and medium sized towns and villages.
ADVERTISING RATES:
Full Page Colour .... EUR 3400
Mechanical Data: Type Area: 210 x 297
Copy instructions: *Copy Date:* 15 days prior to publication date
BUSINESS: LOCAL GOVERNMENT, LEISURE & RECREATION: Local Government

LE JOURNAL DES PLAGES
1819089F89A-325
Editorial: 240 rue Le Corbusier, 30000 NIMES
Tel: 4 66 26 88 95 **Fax:** 466756931
Email: redaction@lejournaldesplages.com **Web site:** http://www.lejournaldesplages.com
Freq: Monthly - le samedi pendant les mois de juillet et aout; **Cover Price:** Free; **Circ:** 960,000
Usual Pagination: 28
Editor: François Ory
Profile: Publication focussing on tourism including French beaches, practical information, agenda, events, interviews, beauty and fashion.
Language(s): French
Copy instructions: *Copy Date:* 10 days prior to publication date
CONSUMER: HOLIDAYS & TRAVEL: Travel

LE JOURNAL DU CALVADOS CONSEIL GENERAL DU CALVADOS
1617179F32A-1039
Editorial: Conseil Général du Calvados, 9 rue Saint-Laurent, BP 20520, 14035 CEDEX 1 CAEN
Tel: 2 31 57 11 07 **Fax:** 231571139
Email: communication@cg14.fr **Web site:** http://www.cg14.fr
ISSN: 0767-0567
Date Established: 1984; **Freq:** Quarterly - printemps, été, automne, hiver; **Cover Price:** Free; **Circ:** 310,000
Usual Pagination: 48
Editor: Jean-Marie Agnès
Profile: Publication focussing on local government and department issues, including economics, cultural heritage, environment, tourism, cultural and social issues.
Language(s): French
Mechanical Data: Type Area: 23 x 30
BUSINESS: LOCAL GOVERNMENT, LEISURE & RECREATION: Local Government

LE JOURNAL DU CENTRE
6198F67B-4900
Editorial: 3 rue du Chemin de Fer, BP 106, CEDEX, 58001 NEVERS **Tel:** 3 86 71 45 00 **Fax:** 3 86 71 45 20
Email: redaction.jdc@centrefrance.com **Web site:** http://www.lejdc.fr
Date Established: 1944; **Freq:** Daily - le matin;
Cover Price: EUR 0.90
Annual Sub.: EUR 251; **Circ:** 30,050
Usual Pagination: 60
Profile: General, regional and local news. Everyday life pages.
Language(s): French
ADVERTISING RATES:
Full Page Mono .... EUR 5007
Mechanical Data: Type Area: 40 x 28
REGIONAL DAILY & SUNDAY NEWSPAPERS: Regional Daily Newspapers

LE JOURNAL DU DIMANCHE
6099F65B-11
Editorial: 149 rue Anatole France, CEDEX, 92534 LEVALLOIS PERRET **Tel:** 1 41 34 60 00
Fax: 1 41 34 97 16

Web site: http://www.lejdd.fr
ISSN: 0242-3065
Freq: Weekly - samedi et dimanche; **Cover Price:** EUR 1.50
Annual Sub.: EUR 49; **Circ:** 267,659
Usual Pagination: 32
Profile: Broadsheet-sized newspaper covering a broad range of news and current affairs.
Language(s): French
Readership: Read largely by people living in the Ile-de-France region.
ADVERTISING RATES:
Full Page Mono .... EUR 52800
Full Page Colour .... EUR 66000
Mechanical Data: Type Area: berlinois
Copy instructions: *Copy Date:* 2 days prior to publication date
NATIONAL DAILY & SUNDAY NEWSPAPERS: National Sunday Newspapers

LE JOURNAL DU TEXTILE
5530F47A-170
Editorial: 61 rue de Malte, CEDEX 11, 75541 PARIS **Tel:** 1 43 57 21 89 **Fax:** 1 47 00 08 35
Email: contact@journaldutextile.com **Web site:** http://www.journaldutextile.com
ISSN: 0293-0757
Date Established: 1964; **Freq:** Weekly - mardi;
Cover Price: EUR 6.70
Annual Sub.: EUR 175; **Circ:** 14,164
Usual Pagination: 78
Profile: This Magazine covers topics about new store openings, launch of new commercial concepts, new sales methods, organization techniques, management tools and technologies. Also monitors personnel changes.
Language(s): French
Readership: Aimed at those in the textile and garment trades.
ADVERTISING RATES:
Full Page Mono .... EUR 3955
Full Page Colour .... EUR 6155
Mechanical Data: Type Area: 305 x 400
Copy instructions: *Copy Date:* 15 days prior to publication date
BUSINESS: CLOTHING & TEXTILES

LA JOURNEE VINICOLE
4750F21H-191
Editorial: Parc d'activité le Cresse Saint Martin, 34660 COURNONSEC **Tel:** 4 67 07 52 66
Fax: 4 67 71 76 88
Email: contact@journee-vinicole.com **Web site:** http://www.journee-vinicole.com
ISSN: 0151-4393
Date Established: 1927; **Freq:** Daily - du lundi au vendredi; **Annual Sub.:** EUR 178.37; **Circ:** 16,000
Usual Pagination: 24
Profile: Newspaper concerning the French and international wine industry.
Language(s): French
ADVERTISING RATES:
Full Page Colour .... EUR 1992
Mechanical Data: Type Area: Tabloïd
BUSINESS: AGRICULTURE & FARMING: Vine Growing

JULIE
7269F91D-110
Editorial: 300 rue Léon Joulin, CEDEX 9, 31101 TOULOUSE **Tel:** 5 61 76 64 64 **Fax:** 5 61 76 64 00
Email: ssa@milan.fr **Web site:** http://www.leblogdejulie.com
ISSN: 1288-3557
Date Established: 1998; **Freq:** Monthly - Once a Month; **Cover Price:** EUR 4.95
Annual Sub.: EUR 53; **Circ:** 65,105
Usual Pagination: 68
Profile: Magazine containing articles on life, health, music, culture and famous people.
Language(s): French
Readership: Aimed at girls aged 8-12 years.
ADVERTISING RATES:
Full Page Colour .... EUR 7155
Mechanical Data: Type Area: A 4
Copy instructions: *Copy Date:* 31 days prior to publication date
CONSUMER: RECREATION & LEISURE: Children & Youth

JURIS TOURISME
5499F44-164_50
Editorial: 75 bis rue de Sèze, 69006 LYON
Tel: 4 72 98 18 40 **Fax:** 4 78 28 93 83
Email: infojuris@dalloz.fr **Web site:** http://www.juriseditions.fr
ISSN: 1290-0559
Date Established: 1998; **Freq:** Monthly - the 10th of the month; **Cover Price:** EUR 18
Annual Sub.: EUR 155; **Circ:** 3,000
Usual Pagination: 52
Profile: Magazine providing legal news and information concerning the leisure and tourist industries.
Language(s): French
ADVERTISING RATES:
Full Page Mono .... EUR 1450
Full Page Colour .... EUR 2060
Mechanical Data: Type Area: 190 x 240
BUSINESS: LEGAL

KID'S MAG
1617122F91D-327
Editorial: DHP, 10 rue Thierry Le Luron, CEDEX, 92592 LEVALLOIS PERRET **Tel:** 1 41 34 88 73
Fax: 1 41 34 88 61
Email: mariejosee.azcuenaga@lagardere-active.com
ISSN: 0040-781X
Date Established: 2010; **Freq:** Monthly - le 1er du mois; **Cover Price:** Free; **Circ:** 500,000
Usual Pagination: 52
Profile: Customer magazine focussing on youth including news, reviews, leisure, cinema, books, computer games, comics, shopping, nature and animals.
Language(s): French
Mechanical Data: Type Area: 21 x 28
CONSUMER: RECREATION & LEISURE: Children & Youth

LAND
1616912F77A-355
Editorial: 61 avenue Gambetta, 94100 SAINT MAUR DES FOSSES **Tel:** 1 77 01 83 00 **Fax:** 1 77 01 83 19
Email: landmag@groupeoffroads.com
ISSN: 0279-6503
Date Established: 1998; **Freq:** Monthly - toutes les 6 semaines; **Cover Price:** EUR 4.90
Annual Sub.: EUR 34.90; **Circ:** 18,007
Usual Pagination: 140
Profile: Publication focussing on off-road and 4x4 cars including news, travel, car tests and classifieds.
Language(s): French
ADVERTISING RATES:
Full Page Mono .... EUR 1890
Full Page Colour .... EUR 3300
Mechanical Data: Type Area: 215 x 290
Copy instructions: *Copy Date:* 20 days prior to publication date
CONSUMER: MOTORING & CYCLING: Motoring

LEMONDE.FR
601374F5F-350
Editorial: LE MONDE INTERACTIF, 80 boulevard Auguste Blanqui, 75013 PARIS **Tel:** 1 53 38 42 60
Fax: 1 53 38 42 96
Email: actu@lemonde.fr **Web site:** http://www.lemonde.fr
Date Established: 1999; **Freq:** Daily; **Circ:** 6,273,864 Unique Users
Profile: E-zine focusing on new information technology. Includes information on e-commerce, the Internet and telecommunications.
Language(s): French
BUSINESS: COMPUTERS & AUTOMATION: Multimedia

LA LETTRE DE LA REGION CONSEIL REGIONAL PROVENCE-ALPES-COTE D'AZUR
1617233F32A-1078
Editorial: Hôtel-de-Région, 27 place Jules-Guesde, 13481 CEDEX 20 MARSEILLE **Tel:** 4 91 57 50 57
Fax: 491575205
Email: info@regionpaca.fr **Web site:** http://www.regionpaca.fr
ISSN: 0991-0107
Date Established: 1982; **Freq:** Monthly - Variable;
Cover Price: Free; **Circ:** 362,000
Usual Pagination: 25
Editor: Nathalie Bonsignori
Profile: Publication focussing on local government and department issues, including economics, regional news, events, cultural heritage, culture and social issues.
Language(s): French
Mechanical Data: Type Area: 26,5 x 35
BUSINESS: LOCAL GOVERNMENT, LEISURE & RECREATION: Local Government

LA LETTRE DU LIMOUSIN - MAGAZINE
1617222F32A-1073
Editorial: Conseil Régional, 27 Boulevard Corderie, CEDEX 1, 87031 LIMOGES **Tel:** 5 55 45 00 59
Fax: 5 55 45 17 48
Email: lalettredulimousin@cr-limousin.fr
ISSN: 0151-2587
Date Established: 1986; **Freq:** 24 issues yearly - Variable; **Cover Price:** Free; **Circ:** 355,000
Usual Pagination: 20
Profile: Publication focussing on local government and department issues, including economics, environment, tourism, agriculture, sustainable development agribusiness, cultural and social issues.
Language(s): French
Mechanical Data: Type Area: A 4
BUSINESS: LOCAL GOVERNMENT, LEISURE & RECREATION: Local Government

LIBERATION
6094F65A-80
Editorial: 11 rue Béranger, CEDEX 03, 75154 PARIS
Tel: 1 42 76 17 89
Email: sergent@liberation.fr **Web site:** http://www.liberation.fr
ISSN: 0335-1793
Date Established: 1978; **Freq:** Daily - le matin à partir de 4 heures; **Cover Price:** EUR 1.30; **Circ:** 123,339
Usual Pagination: 30
Profile: Tabloid-sized newspaper covering national and international news, economics, culture, sport, accommodation and travel. Political outlook: Left wing.
Language(s): French

Readership: Read by a wide range of the French society, over half of whom live in the Ile-de-France region.
ADVERTISING RATES:
Full Page Mono .... EUR 31600
Full Page Colour .... EUR 49600
Mechanical Data: Type Area: 390 x 290
NATIONAL DAILY & SUNDAY NEWSPAPERS: National Daily Newspapers

LIBERATION CHAMPAGNE
6213F67B-5100
Editorial: 39 place Jean Jaurès, BP 713, CEDEX, 10003 TROYES **Tel:** 3 25 82 68 50 **Fax:** 3 25 73 79 29
Email: redaction@liberation-champagne.fr **Web site:** http://www.liberation-champagne.fr
ISSN: 0988-3134
Date Established: 1945; **Freq:** Daily - tous les jours;
Cover Price: EUR 0.80
Annual Sub.: EUR 208; **Circ:** 6,190
Usual Pagination: 64
Profile: Regional daily newspaper focussing on news and current affairs including reviews, event guide, regional interest, women's interest, sports and TV guide.
Language(s): French
REGIONAL DAILY & SUNDAY NEWSPAPERS: Regional Daily Newspapers

LIBERTE DIMANCHE
6216F67C-110
Editorial: 33 rue des Grosses-Pierres, 76250 DEVILLE-LES-ROUEN **Tel:** 2 32 08 37 39
Fax: 2 32 08 37 34
Email: redaction.liberte@presse-normande.com
Date Established: 1944; **Freq:** Weekly - Calvados (14)
Annual Sub.: EUR 48; **Circ:** 14,491
Usual Pagination: 32
Profile: Regional newspaper focussing on local news and current affairs including leisure, sport and internet.
Language(s): French
ADVERTISING RATES:
Full Page Mono .... EUR 8800
Full Page Colour .... EUR 10560
Mechanical Data: Type Area: 39 x 28
REGIONAL DAILY & SUNDAY NEWSPAPERS: Regional Sunday Newspapers

LIEN HORTICOLE
5234F26D-70
Editorial: Rédaction - Parc Club du Millénaire - Bât 9, 1025 rue Henri Becquerel, 34000 MONTPELLIER
Tel: 4 67 50 42 60 **Fax:** 4 67 50 19 02
Email: ginestet@lienhorticole.fr
ISSN: 0293-6852
Date Established: 1964; **Freq:** Weekly - mercredi;
Annual Sub.: EUR 85; **Circ:** 6,779
Usual Pagination: 36
Managing Director: Michel Collonge
Profile: Magazine covering all aspects of the horticultural industry. Includes general, technical, social, economic and professional information.
Language(s): French
Readership: Aimed at those in the horticultural sector.
ADVERTISING RATES:
Full Page Mono .... EUR 2990
Full Page Colour .... EUR 3370
Mechanical Data: Type Area: 290 x 400
Copy instructions: *Copy Date:* 8 days prior to publication date
BUSINESS: GARDEN TRADE: Garden Trade Horticulture

LILLE METROPOLE INFO
1648640F80-940
Editorial: Communauté Urbaine de Lille, 1 rue du Ballon, CEDEX, 59034 LILLE **Tel:** 3 20 21 65 48
Fax: 3 20 21 21 49
Email: infometropole@lillemetropole.fr **Web site:** http://www.lillemetropole.fr
ISSN: 1639-9269
Date Established: 2003; **Freq:** Monthly - début du mois; **Cover Price:** Free; **Circ:** 485,000
Usual Pagination: 32
Profile: Publication focussing on local community information.
Language(s): French
CONSUMER: RURAL & REGIONAL INTEREST

LILLEPLUS
1641392F67B-8769
Editorial: PGLM, 29 rue Esquermoise, 59000 LILLE
Tel: 3 20 44 80 00 **Fax:** 3 20 44 33 55
Email: contact@directlille.com **Web site:** http://www.directlille.com
ISSN: 1969-8143
Date Established: 2004; **Freq:** Daily - du lundi au vendredi; **Cover Price:** Free; **Circ:** 50,853
Usual Pagination: 32
Profile: Free regional daily newspaper focussing on general, local, regional, national and international news and current affairs.
Language(s): French
ADVERTISING RATES:
Full Page Colour .... EUR 2659
REGIONAL DAILY & SUNDAY NEWSPAPERS: Regional Daily Newspapers

LINEAIRES
5199F22E-3
Editorial: 13 square du Chêne Germain, CS 77711, CEDEX, 35577 CESSON-SEVIGNE **Tel:** 2 99 32 21 21
Fax: 2 99 32 14 17
Email: fvacheret@editionsduboisbaudry.fr **Web site:** http://www.lineaires.com
ISSN: 0981-4183
Date Established: 1986; **Freq:** Monthly - le 1er du mois; **Annual Sub.:** EUR 95; **Circ:** 12,507
Usual Pagination: 140
Profile: Magazine about distribution of fresh and frozen food products.
Language(s): French
ADVERTISING RATES:
Full Page Mono .... EUR 466
Full Page Colour .... EUR 666
Mechanical Data: Type Area: A 4
BUSINESS: FOOD: Frozen Food

LIRE
7099F84B-10
Editorial: 29 rue de Châteaudun, CEDEX 09, 75308 PARIS **Tel:** 1 75 55 10 00 **Fax:** 1 75 55 41 16
Email: redaction@lire.fr **Web site:** http://www.lire.fr
ISSN: 0338-5019
Date Established: 1975; **Freq:** Monthly - 1er ou dernier jeudi du mois; **Cover Price:** EUR 5.90
Annual Sub.: EUR 40; **Circ:** 82,733
Usual Pagination: 132
Publisher: Eric Matton
Profile: Magazine focusing on books and literature.
Language(s): French
ADVERTISING RATES:
Full Page Mono .... EUR 600
Full Page Colour .... EUR 890
Mechanical Data: Type Area: 205 x 270
CONSUMER: THE ARTS & LITERARY: Literary

LIVRES HEBDO - L'HEBDOMADAIRE
5931F60A-7
Editorial: 35 rue Grégoire de Tours, 75006 PARIS
Tel: 1 44 41 28 00 **Fax:** 1 43 29 77 85
Email: livreshebdo@electre.com **Web site:** http://www.livreshebdo.com
ISSN: 0294-0000
Date Established: 1979; **Freq:** Weekly - tous les vendredis
Annual Sub.: EUR 390; **Circ:** 9,000
Usual Pagination: 120
Profile: Magazine about publishing, books and libraries.
Language(s): French
ADVERTISING RATES:
Full Page Mono .... EUR 155
Full Page Colour .... EUR 232
Mechanical Data: Type Area: 230 x 297
BUSINESS: PUBLISHING: Publishing & Book Trade

LOIRE ATLANTIQUE - LE MAGAZINE
1617188F32A-1048
Editorial: Conseil Général, 3 quai Ceineray, BP 94109 CEDEX 1, 44041 NANTES **Tel:** 2 40 99 10 00
Fax: 2 40 99 11 85
Email: magazine44@loire-atlantique.fr **Web site:** http://www.loire-atlantique.fr
ISSN: 1281-2919
Date Established: 1996; **Freq:** Monthly - début de mois; **Cover Price:** Free; **Circ:** 546,000
Usual Pagination: 24
Profile: Publication focussing on local government and department issues, including economics, sports, leisure, environment, cultural and social issues.
Language(s): French
Mechanical Data: Type Area: A 4
BUSINESS: LOCAL GOVERNMENT, LEISURE & RECREATION: Local Government

LOIRE MAGAZINE
1617187F32A-1047
Editorial: Conseil Général de la Loire, 2 rue Charles de Gaulle, CEDEX 1, 42022 SAINT-ETIENNE
Tel: 4 77 48 40 67 **Fax:** 4 77 48 40 16
Email: carine.bar@cg42.fr **Web site:** http://www.loire.fr
ISSN: 1959-9145
Date Established: 1996; **Freq:** 24 issues yearly - janv-mars-mai-juillet-sept-nov; **Cover Price:** Free;
Circ: 330,000
Usual Pagination: 32
Profile: Publication focussing on local government and department issues, including economics, tourism, cultural and social issues.
Language(s): French
Mechanical Data: Type Area: 23 x 30
BUSINESS: LOCAL GOVERNMENT, LEISURE & RECREATION: Local Government

LORRAINE ET VOUS CONSEIL REGIONAL DE LORRAINE
1746512F32A-1089
Editorial: 1 place Gabriel-Hocquard, BP 81004, 57036 METZ CEDEX 1 **Tel:** 3 87 33 60 00
Fax: 3 87 33 61 57
Email: dc@lorraine.eu **Web site:** http://www.lorraineetvous.fr
ISSN: 1299-5061
Date Established: 2005; **Freq:** Quarterly; **Cover Price:** Free; **Circ:** 1,190,000
Usual Pagination: 16
Editor: Jean-Pierre Masseret

Profile: Publication focussing on local government and department issues, including economics, regional news, events, culture and social issues.
Language(s): French
BUSINESS: LOCAL GOVERNMENT, LEISURE & RECREATION: Local Government

LSA 4540F2A-48
Editorial: Antony - Parc 2, 10 place du Général de Gaulle, 92160 ANTONY **Tel:** 1 77 92 92 92
Email: ypuget@lsa.fr **Web site:** http://www.lsa.fr
ISSN: 0024-2632
Freq: Weekly - jeudi
Annual Sub.: EUR 199; **Circ:** 26,497
Usual Pagination: 88
Profile: Magazine about mass marketing.
Language(s): French
Readership: Aimed at marketing and advertising executives.
ADVERTISING RATES:
Full Page Mono .... EUR 4620
Full Page Colour .... EUR 7690
Mechanical Data: Type Area: 22 x 28,5
Copy instructions: *Copy Date:* 10 days prior to publication date
BUSINESS: COMMUNICATIONS, ADVERTISING & MARKETING

LYCEE MAG 634129F83-90
Editorial: 23 rue de Châteaudun, CEDEX 09, 75308 PARIS **Tel:** 1 75 55 43 05
Email: sdetarle@letudiant.fr
Date Established: 2000; **Freq:** Half-yearly - mars et mai; **Cover Price:** Free; **Circ:** 120,000
Usual Pagination: 84
Profile: Magzine covering important issues for students such as available courses, cultural news and societies.
Language(s): French
Readership: Aimed at students aged between 15 and 18 years.
ADVERTISING RATES:
Full Page Mono .... EUR 5617
Full Page Colour .... EUR 7268
Mechanical Data: Type Area: A 4
Copy instructions: *Copy Date:* 15 days prior to publication date
CONSUMER: STUDENT PUBLICATIONS

LYON CITOYEN 6981F80-438
Editorial: Hôtel de Ville, CEDEX 01, 69205 LYON
Tel: 4 72 10 30 30 **Fax:** 4 72 10 30 45
Email: severine.andrieu@mairie-lyon.fr **Web site:** http://www.lyon.fr
ISSN: 1245-1711
Date Established: 2001; **Freq:** Monthly - 1er lundi du mois; **Cover Price:** Free; **Circ:** 276,000
Usual Pagination: 48
Profile: Information magazine for the town of Lyons covering culture, sport, daily and social matters.
Language(s): French
Mechanical Data: Type Area: 22 x 28,5
Copy instructions: *Copy Date:* 15 days prior to publication date
CONSUMER: RURAL & REGIONAL INTEREST

LYON POCHE 7200F89C-90
Editorial: 3 rue de la Claire, 69009 LYON
Tel: 4 78 64 84 64 **Fax:** 4 78 43 49 51
Email: lyonpoche@lyonpoche.com **Web site:** http://www.lyonpoche.com
ISSN: 1169-8098
Date Established: 1973; **Freq:** Weekly - mercredi; **Circ:** 13,347
Usual Pagination: 112
Profile: Magazine containing cultural and leisure news for Lyons and the surrounding area.
Language(s): French
ADVERTISING RATES:
Full Page Mono .... EUR 1300
Full Page Colour .... EUR 1900
Mechanical Data: Type Area: 138 x 215
Copy instructions: *Copy Date:* 9 days prior to publication date
CONSUMER: HOLIDAYS & TRAVEL: Entertainment Guides

LYONPLUS 1641294F67B-8768
Editorial: 4 rue Montrochet, 69002 LYON
Tel: 4 78 14 77 91
Email: info@lyonplus.com **Web site:** http://www.lyonplus.com
ISSN: 1969-8305
Date Established: 2004; **Freq:** Daily - du lundi au vendredi; **Cover Price:** Free; **Circ:** 62,519
Usual Pagination: 24
Profile: Free regional daily newspaper focussing on general, local, regional, national and international news and current affairs including multimedia, high tech, news technologies, tourism, leisure, practical information, fashion, celebrities, sport, culture, exhibitions, cinema and theatre.
Language(s): French
ADVERTISING RATES:
Full Page Colour .... EUR 6000
REGIONAL DAILY & SUNDAY NEWSPAPERS: Regional Daily Newspapers

MA REGION HAUTE-NORMANDIE CONSEIL REGIONAL 1617227F32A-1074
Editorial: 5 rue Robert Schuman, BP 1129, 76174 ROUEN CEDEX 1 **Tel:** 2 35 52 56 82
Fax: 2 35 52 57 97
Web site: http://www.region-haute-normandie.fr
ISSN: 1294-8578
Date Established: 1999; **Freq:** Monthly - la 1ère semaine du mois; **Cover Price:** Free; **Circ:** 780,000
Usual Pagination: 16
Editor: Alain Le Vern
Profile: Publication focussing on local government and department issues.
Language(s): French
Mechanical Data: Type Area: 210 x 297
Copy instructions: *Copy Date:* pas de publicité
BUSINESS: LOCAL GOVERNMENT, LEISURE & RECREATION: Local Government

MACHINES PRODUCTION 4978F19E-50
Editorial: Editions SOFETEC, 66 rue Escudier, 92100 BOULOGNE BILLANCOURT **Tel:** 1 48 25 50 30
Fax: 1 48 25 90 54
Email: bc@machpro.fr **Web site:** http://www.machpro.fr
ISSN: 0047-536X
Date Established: 1971; **Freq:** 26 issues yearly - 15 et 30 de chaque mois
Annual Sub.: EUR 130; **Circ:** 6,915
Usual Pagination: 68
Profile: Pan-European journal concerned with mechanical engineering.
Language(s): French
ADVERTISING RATES:
Full Page Colour .... EUR 3100
Mechanical Data: Type Area: A 4
BUSINESS: ENGINEERING & MACHINERY: Machinery, Machine Tools & Metalworking

MADAME FIGARO 6412F74A-250
Editorial: Coursiers, 3 rue Pillet-Will, 75009 PARIS
Tel: 1 57 08 50 00 **Fax:** 1 57 08 57 97
Email: afschmitt@lefigaro.fr **Web site:** http://madame.lefigaro.fr
ISSN: 0246-5205
Date Established: 1980; **Freq:** Weekly - samedi; **Circ:** 437,846
Usual Pagination: 164
Profile: Magazine covering women's interests in fashion, beauty and social life.
Language(s): French
ADVERTISING RATES:
Full Page Colour .... EUR 29500
Mechanical Data: Type Area: 21 X 28
Copy instructions: *Copy Date:* 21 days prior to publication date
CONSUMER: WOMEN'S INTEREST CONSUMER MAGAZINES: Women's Interest

LE MAGAZINE DES CINEMAS GAUMONT 6728F94H-519
Editorial: SEC Colisée, 2 rue Lamennais, 75008 PARIS **Tel:** 1 71 72 30 00 **Fax:** 1 71 72 30 82
Email: claudine.felix@europalaces.com **Web site:** http://www.cinemasgaumontpathe.com
ISSN: 1760-0243
Date Established: 1992; **Freq:** Monthly - 1er mercredi du mois; **Cover Price:** Free; **Circ:** 467,913
Usual Pagination: 36
Profile: Magazine presenting film news and information of the Gaumont cinema chain.
Language(s): French
ADVERTISING RATES:
Full Page Colour .... EUR 18900
Mechanical Data: Type Area: 175 X 250
Copy instructions: *Copy Date:* 15 days prior to publication date
CONSUMER: OTHER CLASSIFICATIONS: Customer Magazines

LE MAGAZINE D'ORPHEOPOLIS 1618954F1D-137
Editorial: ORPHEOPOLIS, 44 rue Roger Salengro, CEDEX, 94126 FONTENAY-SOUS-BOIS
Tel: 1 49 74 22 22 **Fax:** 1 49 74 22 01
Email: lbarlet@orpheopolis.fr **Web site:** http://www.orpheopolis.fr
ISSN: 1769-0129
Date Established: 1927; **Freq:** Quarterly - fin de mois 01 04 07 10; **Annual Sub.:** EUR 7.62; **Circ:** 89,000
Usual Pagination: 20
Language(s): French
Mechanical Data: Type Area: 210 x 297
BUSINESS: FINANCE & ECONOMICS: Insurance

LE MAGAZINE DU CONSEIL GENERAL 1617176F32A-1036
Editorial: Conseil Général de l'Essonne, Direction de la Communication, Boulevard de France CEDEX, 91012 EVRY **Tel:** 1 60 91 91 06
Email: contact@essonne.fr **Web site:** http://www.essonne.fr
ISSN: 1274-4689
Date Established: 1999; **Freq:** Monthly - La 2ème semaine du mois; **Cover Price:** Free; **Circ:** 460,000
Usual Pagination: 48
Profile: Publication focussing on local government and department issues.
Language(s): French
Mechanical Data: Type Area: 28 x 23
BUSINESS: LOCAL GOVERNMENT, LEISURE & RECREATION: Local Government

LE MAGAZINE DU CONSEIL GENERAL DE LA GIRONDE 1617180F32A-1040
Editorial: Hôtel-du-Département, Esplanade Charles-de-Gaulle, 33074 CEDEX BORDEAUX
Tel: 5 56 99 33 10 **Fax:** 556993399
Email: mag-gironde@cg33.fr **Web site:** http://www.gironde.fr
ISSN: 1141-5932
Date Established: 1990; **Freq:** 6 issues yearly - 01 03 05 07 09 11; **Cover Price:** Free; **Circ:** 612,000
Usual Pagination: 24
Profile: Publication focussing on local government and department issues.
Language(s): French
Mechanical Data: Type Area: A 4
BUSINESS: LOCAL GOVERNMENT, LEISURE & RECREATION: Local Government

LE MAGAZINE DU MOUVEMENT POPULAIRE 1619102F82-278
Editorial: 55 rue La Boétie, 75384 CEDEX 08 PARIS
Tel: 1 40 74 08 00 **Fax:** 140740780
Email: umpmagazine@club-internet.fr
ISSN: 1638-7504
Date Established: 2003; **Freq:** Quarterly - 15 de 02-05-08-11
Annual Sub.: EUR 10; **Circ:** 250,000
Usual Pagination: 24
Editor: Eric Césari
Profile: Publication of the UMP party focussing on politics including life and activities of the party.
Language(s): French
CONSUMER: CURRENT AFFAIRS & POLITICS

LE MAINE LIBRE - EDITION LE MANS 6186F67B-5400
Editorial: 28/30 place de l'Eperon, 72013 CEDEX 2 LE MANS **Tel:** 2-43-83-72-30 **Fax:** 2-43-28-28-19
Email: redaction@maine-libre.com **Web site:** http://www.lemainelibre.fr
ISSN: 0246-4225
Freq: Daily - matin lundi au dimanche inclus; **Cover Price:** EUR 0.75
Annual Sub.: EUR 253; **Circ:** 46,117
Usual Pagination: 30
Profile: Daily general, regional and local newspaper: Saturday price: 0,90 € (including TV guide supplement). Sunday price: 0,90 € (including women supplement Version Fémina).
Language(s): French
ADVERTISING RATES:
Full Page Mono .... EUR 10072
Full Page Colour .... EUR 12590
Copy instructions: *Copy Date:* 2 days prior to publication date
REGIONAL DAILY & SUNDAY NEWSPAPERS: Regional Daily Newspapers

MAINE-ET-LOIRE LE MAGAZINE DU CONSEIL GENERAL DE MAINE-ET-LOIRE 1617189F32A-1049
Editorial: Hôtel-du-Département, Place Michel-Debré, BP 94104, 49941 ANGERS CEDEX 09
Tel: 2 41 81 43 86 **Fax:** 2 41 81 49 94
Email: info@cg49.fr **Web site:** http://www.cg49.fr
ISSN: 1295-5329
Date Established: 1999; **Freq:** Monthly - Le 25 de chaques mois; **Cover Price:** Free; **Circ:** 345,000
Usual Pagination: 24
Editor: Christophe Béchu
Profile: Publication focussing on local government and department issues.
Language(s): French
Mechanical Data: Type Area: A 4
Copy instructions: *Copy Date:* 1 mois avant parution
BUSINESS: LOCAL GOVERNMENT, LEISURE & RECREATION: Local Government

MAISON BRICOLAGE ET DECORATION 6921F79A-100
Editorial: 67 rue de Dunkerque, 75009 PARIS
Tel: 1 53 63 10 27 **Fax:** 1 53 63 82 38
Email: maisonbricolage@editions-burda.fr **Web site:** http://www.editions-burda.fr
ISSN: 1766-4381
Date Established: 1985; **Freq:** Monthly - variable; **Cover Price:** EUR 3.50; **Circ:** 100,848
Usual Pagination: 144
Profile: Magazine covering DIY in the home. Includes articles on renovation, repair and decoration.
Language(s): French
ADVERTISING RATES:
Full Page Mono .... EUR 8320
Full Page Colour .... EUR 10500
Mechanical Data: Type Area: A 4
Copy instructions: *Copy Date:* 62 days prior to publication date
CONSUMER: HOBBIES & DIY

LA MAISON CREATIVE 1618382F74C-469
Editorial: 22 rue Letellier, CEDEX 15, 75739 PARIS
Tel: 1 43 23 20 35 **Fax:** 1 43 23 04 95
Email: celine.costantini@uni-editions.com
ISSN: 1624-8694
Date Established: 2001; **Freq:** 24 issues yearly - 20-25 des mois impairs; **Cover Price:** EUR 3.90
Annual Sub.: EUR 19.90; **Circ:** 434,186
Usual Pagination: 132
Profile: Publication focussing on home & style including decoration, lifestyle, news, exhibitions, fairs, stores, shopping, books, multimedia, new products, gardens, DIY, buyers guide, interior design, home improvement, recycling, restoration, gardens, maintenance, trends, travel, international interest, news, agenda and designers.
Language(s): French
ADVERTISING RATES:
Full Page Mono .... EUR 7100
Full Page Colour .... EUR 9500
Mechanical Data: Type Area: 230 x 300
Copy instructions: *Copy Date:* 31 days prior to publication date
CONSUMER: WOMEN'S INTEREST CONSUMER MAGAZINES: Home & Family

LA MAISON ET TRAVAUX 6452F74C-210
Editorial: 149 rue Anatole France, CEDEX, 92534 LEVALLOIS PERRET **Tel:** 1 41 34 67 66
Email: patrick.demontalivet@lagardere-active.com
Web site: http://www.maison-travaux.fr
ISSN: 0244-1136
Date Established: 1981; **Freq:** Monthly - les mois 01 02 04 05 07 08 10 11
Annual Sub.: EUR 28; **Circ:** 201,499
Usual Pagination: 128
Profile: Magazine about house renovation, decoration and fittings, also contains a product guide.
Language(s): French
ADVERTISING RATES:
Full Page Colour .... EUR 16000
Mechanical Data: Type Area: 300 x 232
Copy instructions: *Copy Date:* 31 days prior to publication date
CONSUMER: WOMEN'S INTEREST CONSUMER MAGAZINES: Home & Family

MAISON FRANCAISE 6454F74C-220
Editorial: 29 rue de Châteaudun, CEDEX 09, 75308 PARIS **Tel:** 1 75 55 10 00
Email: iforestier@maisonfrancaise.com **Web site:** http://www.maisonfrancaise.fr
ISSN: 0960-7773
Date Established: 1946; **Freq:** 24 issues yearly - 02 04 06 09 10 12; **Cover Price:** EUR 4.50
Annual Sub.: EUR 28; **Circ:** 126,407
Usual Pagination: 220
Profile: Magazine about home living and decoration.
Language(s): French
ADVERTISING RATES:
Full Page Mono .... EUR 10300
Full Page Colour .... EUR 13600
Mechanical Data: Type Area: 220 x 280
Copy instructions: *Copy Date:* 28 days prior to publication date
CONSUMER: WOMEN'S INTEREST CONSUMER MAGAZINES: Home & Family

MAISON MAGAZINE 6456F74C-230
Editorial: 29 rue de Châteaudun, CEDEX 09, 75308 PARIS **Tel:** 1 75 55 10 00 **Fax:** 1 75 55 11 46
Email: jaumont@maisonmagazine.com
ISSN: 0150-6439
Date Established: 1974; **Freq:** 24 issues yearly - Months: 01 03 06 08 10 12; **Cover Price:** EUR 3.30
Annual Sub.: EUR 15; **Circ:** 137,275
Usual Pagination: 156
Profile: Magazine about house renovation, construction and decoration.
Language(s): French
ADVERTISING RATES:
Full Page Colour .... EUR 11700
Mechanical Data: Type Area: 220 X 287
Copy instructions: *Copy Date:* 21 days prior to publication date
CONSUMER: WOMEN'S INTEREST CONSUMER MAGAZINES: Home & Family

MAISONS COTE EST 6459F74C-233_50
Editorial: 29 rue de Châteaudun, CEDEX 09, 75309 PARIS **Tel:** 1 75 55 16 92 90 **Fax:** 1 75 55 11 47
Email: vdesaint-vaulry@groupe-exp.com **Web site:** http://www.cotemaison.fr
Date Established: 1999; **Freq:** Quarterly - 20-25 des mois pairs; **Cover Price:** EUR 5.50
Annual Sub.: EUR 20; **Circ:** 54,439
Profile: Magazine concerning houses, home decoration, architecture and regional and cultural differences in Eastern France.
Language(s): French
ADVERTISING RATES:
Full Page Mono .... EUR 5025
Full Page Colour .... EUR 6700
Copy instructions: *Copy Date:* 62 days prior to publication date
CONSUMER: WOMEN'S INTEREST CONSUMER MAGAZINES: Home & Family

MAISONS COTE OUEST
6460F74C-234
Editorial: 29 rue de Châteaudun, CEDEX 09, 75309 PARIS **Tel:** 1 75 55 16 90 92 **Fax:** 1 75 55 11 47
Email: cmesnil@groupe-exp.com **Web site:** http://www.cotemaison.fr
ISSN: 1252-2570
Date Established: 1994; **Freq:** 24 issues yearly - 02 04 06 08 10 12; **Cover Price:** EUR 5.50
Annual Sub.: EUR 27; **Circ:** 83,027
Usual Pagination: 170
Profile: Magazine focusing on home decor and lifestyle.
Language(s): French
ADVERTISING RATES:
Full Page Mono .... EUR 7913
Full Page Colour .... EUR 10550
Mechanical Data: Type Area: A 4
Copy instructions: *Copy Date:* 31 days prior to publication date
CONSUMER: WOMEN'S INTEREST CONSUMER MAGAZINES: Home & Family

MAISONS COTE SUD
6461F74C-235
Editorial: 16 impasse du 11 Novembre, CEDEX, 6414 CANNES **Tel:** 4 92 92 57 57 **Fax:** 4 92 92 57 58
Email: slapauze@cotesud.com **Web site:** http://www.cotemaison.fr
ISSN: 1292-6434
Date Established: 1990; **Freq:** 24 issues yearly - Mid February April June August October December
Annual Sub.: EUR 33; **Circ:** 119,232
Usual Pagination: 240
Profile: Magazine focusing on home decoration and the art of living on the French South coast.
Language(s): French
ADVERTISING RATES:
Full Page Mono .... EUR 10350
Full Page Colour .... EUR 13800
Copy instructions: *Copy Date:* 62 days prior to publication date
CONSUMER: WOMEN'S INTEREST CONSUMER MAGAZINES: Home & Family

LES MAISONS DE CAMPAGNE
1618387F74C-474
Editorial: 111 avenue Victor-Hugo, 75016 PARIS
Tel: 1 47 55 63 63 **Fax:** 1 47 55 63 53
Email: md@vip-international.fr
ISSN: 0241-6948
Date Established: 1999; **Freq:** 6 issues yearly - début des mois pairs; **Cover Price:** EUR 4.30
Annual Sub.: EUR 20; **Circ:** 60,188
Usual Pagination: 132
Editor: Philippe Aubry
Profile: Publication focussing on country homes & style including decoration, interior design, flowers, gardening, practical information, DIY, new products, architecture, gastronomy and tips.
Language(s): French
ADVERTISING RATES:
Full Page Colour .... EUR 9000
Mechanical Data: Type Area: 211 x 280
Copy instructions: *Copy Date:* 15 days prior to publication date
CONSUMER: WOMEN'S INTEREST CONSUMER MAGAZINES: Home & Family

MAISONS ET DECORS
6465F74C-255
Editorial: Europarc Pichaury, Bât.C 10 - Av. Guillibert de la Lauzière, BP 439 CEDEX 3, 13591 AIX-EN-PROVENCE **Tel:** 4 42 37 14 50 **Fax:** 4 42 24 28 26
Email: redaction@maisonsetdecors.com
ISSN: 0180-4561
Date Established: 1975; **Freq:** 24 issues yearly - entre les 1er/6 des mois pairs; **Cover Price:** EUR 4.60
Annual Sub.: EUR 23.50; **Circ:** 62,625
Usual Pagination: 164
Profile: Magazine focusing on Mediterranean housing and furnishing.
Language(s): French
ADVERTISING RATES:
Full Page Colour .... EUR 4270
Mechanical Data: Type Area: 22 x 30
Copy instructions: *Copy Date:* 30 days prior to publication date
CONSUMER: WOMEN'S INTEREST CONSUMER MAGAZINES: Home & Family

MAISONS NORMANDES
6548F74K-190
Editorial: 111 avenue Victor-Hugo, 75016 PARIS
Tel: 1 47 55 63 63 **Fax:** 147556353
Email: m.a.beni@wanadoo.fr
Date Established: 1992; **Freq:** 6 issues yearly - début des mois pairs; **Cover Price:** EUR 5.30
Annual Sub.: EUR 26; **Circ:** 45,000
Usual Pagination: 140
Editor: Philippe Aubry
Profile: Magazine focusing on property in the Normandy region. Includes sales information and articles on decoration and furnishing.
Language(s): French
ADVERTISING RATES:
Full Page Colour .... EUR 3360
Mechanical Data: Type Area: 230 x 300
Copy instructions: *Copy Date:* 7 days prior to publication date
CONSUMER: WOMEN'S INTEREST CONSUMER MAGAZINES: Home Purchase

MAMAN !
1618016F74D-259
Editorial: BLEUCOM, 10-12 villa Thoreton, 75015 PARIS **Tel:** 1 45 71 75 00
Email: costa@bleucom.net **Web site:** http://mamanmagazine.com
ISSN: 1626-7427
Date Established: 2000; **Freq:** Monthly - 20-25 du mois daté mois suivant; **Cover Price:** EUR 2.99
Annual Sub.: EUR 18; **Circ:** 63,259
Usual Pagination: 124
Language(s): French
ADVERTISING RATES:
Full Page Colour .... EUR 9293
Mechanical Data: Type Area: 215 x 285
Copy instructions: *Copy Date:* 31 days prior to publication date
CONSUMER: WOMEN'S INTEREST CONSUMER MAGAZINES: Child Care

MANAGEMENT
4829F14A-420
Editorial: 13 rue Henri Barbusse, 92624 GENNEVILLIERS **Tel:** 1 73 05 47 00
Fax: 1 56 99 48 49
Email: management@prisma-presse.com **Web site:** http://www.capital.fr/carriere-management
ISSN: 1263-7807
Date Established: 1995; **Freq:** Monthly - 3ème jeudi du mois; **Cover Price:** EUR 3.50
Annual Sub.: EUR 31.50; **Circ:** 124,375
Usual Pagination: 140
Publisher: Martin Trautmann
Profile: Management magazine.
Language(s): French
ADVERTISING RATES:
Full Page Colour .... EUR 18700
Mechanical Data: Type Area: 21,3 x 27
BUSINESS: COMMERCE, INDUSTRY & MANAGEMENT

MANCHE MAG' CONSEIL GÉNÉRAL DE LA MANCHE
1693800F32A-1085
Editorial: 98 route de Candol, 50008 CEDEX SAINT-LO **Tel:** 2 33 05 95 00 **Fax:** 233059565
Email: manchemag@manche.fr **Web site:** http://www.manche.fr
ISSN: 1771-4486
Date Established: 2005; **Freq:** Monthly - 2ème lundi de chaque mois; **Cover Price:** Free; **Circ:** 223,000
Usual Pagination: 8
Editor: Jean-François Le Grand
Profile: Publication focussing on local government and department issues.
Language(s): French
Mechanical Data: Type Area: A 4
BUSINESS: LOCAL GOVERNMENT, LEISURE & RECREATION: Local Government

MANIERE DE VOIR
1619103F82-960
Editorial: 1 avenue Stéphen-Pichon, 75013 PARIS
Tel: 1 53 94 96 01 **Fax:** 153969626
Email: secretariat@monde-diplomatique.fr **Web site:** http://www.monde-diplomatique.fr
ISSN: 1241-6290
Date Established: 1988; **Freq:** 6 issues yearly - autour du 15 des mois impairs
Annual Sub.: EUR 34; **Circ:** 39,676
Usual Pagination: 100
Editor: Serge Halimi
Profile: Publication focussing on politics including geopolitics, international issues, analysis, economics, social issues, trends and science.
Language(s): French
ADVERTISING RATES:
Full Page Colour .... EUR 3100
Mechanical Data: Type Area: 230 x 285
Copy instructions: *Copy Date:* 7 days prior to publication date
CONSUMER: CURRENT AFFAIRS & POLITICS

LES MARCHES
5190F22A-245
Editorial: 84 boulevard de Sébastopol, 75003 PARIS
Tel: 1 42 74 28 00 **Fax:** 1 42 74 28 55
Email: redac.lesmarches@siac.fr **Web site:** http://www.lequotidienlesmarches.fr
ISSN: 0989-8662
Date Established: 1966; **Freq:** Daily - tous les jours à 13h; **Annual Sub.:** EUR 615
Profile: Publication about the distribution of farm-produce, and including the economic and commercial aspects.
Language(s): French
ADVERTISING RATES:
Full Page Mono .... EUR 2040
Full Page Colour .... EUR 2600
BUSINESS: FOOD

MARIANNE
6376F73-140
Editorial: 32 rue René Boulanger, CEDEX 10, 75484 PARIS **Tel:** 1 53 72 29 00 **Fax:** 1 53 72 29 72
Web site: http://www.marianne2.fr
ISSN: 1275-7500
Date Established: 1997; **Freq:** Weekly - samedi; **Cover Price:** EUR 2.50
Annual Sub.: EUR 78; **Circ:** 272,959
Usual Pagination: 92
Profile: Periodical about news, current affairs, science, economics and culture.
Language(s): French
ADVERTISING RATES:
Full Page Mono .... EUR 12200
Full Page Colour .... EUR 12200
Mechanical Data: Type Area: 205 x 270
Copy instructions: *Copy Date:* 21 days prior to publication date
CONSUMER: NATIONAL & INTERNATIONAL PERIODICALS

MARIE CLAIRE
6414F74A-260
Editorial: 10 Boulevard des Frères Voisin, CEDEX 9, 92792 ISSY LES MOULINEAUX **Tel:** 1 41 46 88 88
Fax: 1 41 46 84 32
Email: mcredac@gmc.tm.fr **Web site:** http://www.marieclaire.fr
ISSN: 0025-3049
Date Established: 1954; **Freq:** Monthly - milieu du mois précédent; **Cover Price:** EUR 2.50
Annual Sub.: EUR 22; **Circ:** 484,858
Usual Pagination: 330
Profile: Magazine covering fashion, beauty, topical and cultural news of interest to women. Includes Parisian and regional editions.
Language(s): French
ADVERTISING RATES:
Full Page Mono .... EUR 23520
Full Page Colour .... EUR 33600
Mechanical Data: Type Area: 207 x 280
Copy instructions: *Copy Date:* 31 days prior to publication date
CONSUMER: WOMEN'S INTEREST CONSUMER MAGAZINES: Women's Interest

MARIE CLAIRE IDEES
6466F74A-265
Editorial: 10 Boulevard des Frères Voisin, CEDEX 9, 92792 ISSY LES MOULINEAUX **Tel:** 1 41 46 88 88 87 79 **Fax:** 1 41 46 84 76
Email: mciredac@gmc.tm.fr **Web site:** http://www.marieclaireidees.com
ISSN: 1164-0316
Date Established: 1991; **Freq:** 24 issues yearly - les mois pairs; **Cover Price:** EUR 4.60; **Circ:** 307,051
Usual Pagination: 170
Publisher: Fredrik Edstrom
Profile: Magazine covering beauty, fashion, cookery, floral art, decoration and DIY.
Language(s): French
ADVERTISING RATES:
Full Page Mono .... EUR 16640
Full Page Colour .... EUR 20800
Mechanical Data: Type Area: 230 X 297
Copy instructions: *Copy Date:* 42 days prior to publication date
CONSUMER: WOMEN'S INTEREST CONSUMER MAGAZINES: Women's Interest

MARIE CLAIRE MAISON
6467F74C-258
Editorial: 10 Boulevard des Frères Voisin, CEDEX 9, 92792 ISSY LES MOULINEAUX **Tel:** 1 41 46 88 88
Fax: 1 41 46 84 36
Email: mcmredaction@gmc.tm.fr **Web site:** http://www.marieclairemaison.com
ISSN: 0542-1594
Date Established: 1967; **Freq:** Monthly - 12/01-2/03-04-5/06-7/08-09-10-11; **Cover Price:** EUR 4.50
Annual Sub.: EUR 36.59; **Circ:** 131,822
Usual Pagination: 124
Publisher: Fredrik Edstrom
Profile: Magazine containing features on homes and gardens.
Language(s): French
ADVERTISING RATES:
Full Page Mono .... EUR 11600
Full Page Colour .... EUR 14500
Mechanical Data: Type Area: 230 x 297
Copy instructions: *Copy Date:* 31 days prior to publication date
CONSUMER: WOMEN'S INTEREST CONSUMER MAGAZINES: Home & Family

MARIE FRANCE
6415F74A-280
Editorial: 10 boulevard des Frères Voisin, CEDEX 9, 92792 ISSY LES MOULINEAUX **Tel:** 1 41 46 83 77
Fax: 1 41 46 89 06
Email: mfredac@gmc.tm.fr **Web site:** http://www.groupemarieclaire.com
ISSN: 1259-5225
Date Established: 1995; **Freq:** Monthly - le 12
Annual Sub.: EUR 24; **Circ:** 192,848
Usual Pagination: 180
Profile: High-class lifestyle magazine.
Language(s): French
Readership: Read by women aged 35 years and over.
ADVERTISING RATES:
Full Page Colour .... EUR 16300
Mechanical Data: Type Area: 21,5 x 27
Copy instructions: *Copy Date:* 31 days prior to publication date
CONSUMER: WOMEN'S INTEREST CONSUMER MAGAZINES: Women's Interest

MARIONS NOUS !
6557F74L-112
Editorial: 5 bis rue Faÿs, 94160 SAINT-MANDE
Tel: 1 41 74 10 00 **Fax:** 1 41 74 11 21
Email: contact@lesitedumariage.com **Web site:** http://www.lesitedumariage.com
Date Established: 1998; **Freq:** Quarterly - 20/02 20/05 20/08 20/11; **Cover Price:** EUR 4.50
Annual Sub.: EUR 15; **Circ:** 56,000
Usual Pagination: 160
Profile: Magazine concerning all aspects of wedding organisation.
Language(s): French
Readership: Aimed at those planning a wedding.
ADVERTISING RATES:
Full Page Colour .... EUR 3800
Mechanical Data: Type Area: 225 x 310
CONSUMER: WOMEN'S INTEREST CONSUMER MAGAZINES: Brides

MARKET - JOURNAL DU COMMERCE
5462F43A-100
Editorial: 163-165 avenue Charles de Gaulle, 92200 NEUILLY SUR SEINE **Tel:** 1 41 43 22 80
Fax: 1 47 45 06 01
Email: journal.market@wanadoo.fr
ISSN: 1161-8787
Freq: Monthly - 5-7/year
Annual Sub.: EUR 59; **Circ:** 14,100
Usual Pagination: 52
Profile: Magazine focusing on equipment for the home.
Language(s): French
Readership: Read by interior designers and retailers.
ADVERTISING RATES:
Full Page Mono .... EUR 4777
Full Page Colour .... EUR 7141
Mechanical Data: Type Area: A 4
BUSINESS: ELECTRICAL RETAIL TRADE

MARKETING DIRECT
4542F2A-50_50
Editorial: 13 rue Louis Pasteur, CEDEX, 92513 BOULOGNE BILLANCOURT **Tel:** 1 41 31 72 66
Fax: 1 41 31 72 62
Email: frouffiac@editialis.fr **Web site:** http://www.e-marketing.fr
ISSN: 1261-9523
Date Established: 1995; **Freq:** Monthly - Beginning of the month; **Cover Price:** EUR 7.50
Annual Sub.: EUR 85; **Circ:** 9,341
Usual Pagination: 68
Profile: Magazine containing information, analysis and discussion on the strategy and techniques of direct marketing.
Language(s): French
Readership: Read by marketing and advertising personnel.
ADVERTISING RATES:
Full Page Mono .... EUR 5650
Full Page Colour .... EUR 6050
Mechanical Data: Type Area: 215 x 285
Copy instructions: *Copy Date:* 21 days prior to publication date
BUSINESS: COMMUNICATIONS, ADVERTISING & MARKETING

MARKETING MAGAZINE
4543F2A-50_60
Editorial: 13 rue Louis Pasteur, CEDEX, 92513 BOULOGNE BILLANCOURT **Tel:** 1 41 31 72 66
Fax: 1 41 31 72 62
Email: frouffiac@editialis.fr **Web site:** http://www.e-marketing.fr
ISSN: 1261-9515
Date Established: 1995; **Freq:** Monthly - fin de mois; **Cover Price:** EUR 7.50
Annual Sub.: EUR 50; **Circ:** 10,811
Usual Pagination: 116
Profile: Publication covering general marketing issues in France and abroad. Provides details of new products for drawing and design and product launches. Also contains analysis and reflection on the problems and techniques used in direct marketing.
Language(s): French
ADVERTISING RATES:
Full Page Mono .... EUR 5650
Full Page Colour .... EUR 6050
Mechanical Data: Type Area: 215 x 285
Copy instructions: *Copy Date:* 21 days prior to publication date
BUSINESS: COMMUNICATIONS, ADVERTISING & MARKETING

LA MARNE LE MAG CONSEIL GENERAL DE LA MARNE
1812834F32A-1095
Editorial: Hôtel-du-Département, 40 rue Carnot, 51038 CEDEX CHALONS-EN-CHAMPAGNE
Tel: 3 26 69 51 51 **Fax:** 326214981
Web site: http://www.marne.fr
ISSN: 1779 4226
Freq: 6 issues yearly - Début de mois; **Cover Price:** Free; **Circ:** 300,000
Usual Pagination: 24
Editor: René-Paul Savary
Profile: Publication focussing on local government and department issues, including economics, sports, cultural and social issues.
Language(s): French
Mechanical Data: Type Area: A4
BUSINESS: LOCAL GOVERNMENT, LEISURE & RECREATION: Local Government

LA MARSEILISE
6187F67B-5500
Editorial: 19 cours d'Estienne d'Orves, BP 91862, CEDEX 01, 13222 MARSEILLE **Tel:** 4 91 57 75 00
Fax: 4 91 57 75 25 99
Email: lamars@lamarseillaise.fr **Web site:** http://www.journal-lamarseillaise.com
ISSN: 0247-4204
Date Established: 1944; **Freq:** Daily - 7 jours sur 7 sauf le 1er mai; **Cover Price:** EUR 0.85
Annual Sub.: EUR 195; **Circ:** 139,000
Usual Pagination: 48
Profile: Regional daily newspaper focussing on local and regional news and current affairs.

Language(s): French
ADVERTISING RATES:
Full Page Mono .... EUR 5670
Full Page Colour .... EUR 7371
Mechanical Data: Type Area: tabloïd
REGIONAL DAILY & SUNDAY NEWSPAPERS: Regional Daily Newspapers

LA MARSEILLAISE EDITION DU VAR
6188F67B-5600
Editorial: 10 rue Berny, (entrée rue Parmentier), 83500 LA SEYNE-SUR-MER **Tel:** 4 94 94 76 67
Fax: 4 94 94 82 63
Email: aglaseyne@lamarseillaise.fr **Web site:** http://www.lamarseillaise.fr
Freq: Daily - 7 jours sur 7 sauf le 1er mai; **Cover Price:** EUR 0.85
Annual Sub.: EUR 195; **Circ:** 6,094
Usual Pagination: 32
Profile: Left wing daily regional newspaper. Regional and local news. Only one edition for the Var region, the Seyne-sur-Mer office covering the west of the region.
Language(s): French
ADVERTISING RATES:
Full Page Mono .... EUR 3990
Full Page Colour .... EUR 5897
Mechanical Data: Type Area: tabloïd
REGIONAL DAILY & SUNDAY NEWSPAPERS: Regional Daily Newspapers

MAXI
6416F74A-285
Editorial: 30/32 rue de Chabrol, 75010 PARIS
Tel: 1 40 22 75 00 **Fax:** 1 48 24 08 40
Email: bonino@maxi.presse.fr **Web site:** http://www.editions-bauer.fr
Date Established: 1986; **Freq:** Weekly - tous les lundis; **Cover Price:** EUR 1.10
Annual Sub.: EUR 49.50; **Circ:** 487,090
Usual Pagination: 68
Profile: Women's magazine discussing practical subjects and matters relating to daily life.
Language(s): French
ADVERTISING RATES:
Full Page Colour .... EUR 17000
Mechanical Data: Type Area: 23 x 29
Copy instructions: *Copy Date:* 42 days prior to publication date
CONSUMER: WOMEN'S INTEREST CONSUMER MAGAZINES: Women's Interest

MAXI CUISINE
6590F74P-300
Editorial: 30-32 rue de Chabrol, 75010 PARIS
Tel: 1 40 22 75 00 **Fax:** 1 48 24 08 40
Email: accueil@editions-bauer.fr **Web site:** http://www.editions-bauer.fr
ISSN: 1287-4035
Date Established: 2001; **Freq:** 6 issues yearly - première semaine mois impairs; **Cover Price:** EUR 1.80
Annual Sub.: EUR 18; **Circ:** 236,694
Usual Pagination: 76
Editor: Detlef Tyra
Profile: Cookery magazine focusing on simple French cuisine.
Language(s): French
Readership: Aimed at those interested in cookery.
ADVERTISING RATES:
Full Page Colour .... EUR 10500
Mechanical Data: Type Area: 210 x 280
CONSUMER: WOMEN'S INTEREST CONSUMER MAGAZINES: Food & Cookery

MAXIMOTO
1618486F77B-314
Editorial: 40 rue de Paradis, 75010 PARIS
Tel: 1 53 34 98 00 **Fax:** 1 53 34 98 05
Email: pboisvert@maxi-moto.com
ISSN: 1628-2124
Date Established: 2001; **Freq:** Monthly - dernier jeudi du mois; **Cover Price:** EUR 5.20
Annual Sub.: EUR 43; **Circ:** 33,064
Usual Pagination: 132
Profile: Publication focussing on motorcycling including interviews, tests, contact, evolution, reviews, interviews, buyers guide and practical information.
Language(s): French
ADVERTISING RATES:
Full Page Colour .... EUR 2990
Mechanical Data: Type Area: 21x28,6
CONSUMER: MOTORING & CYCLING: Motorcycling

MEDECINS SANS FRONTIERES INFOS
1617624F32G-192
Editorial: 8 rue Saint Sabin, CEDEX 11, 75544 PARIS
Tel: 1 40 21 29 29 **Fax:** 1 48 06 68 68
Email: office@paris.msf.org **Web site:** http://www.msf.fr
ISSN: 1146-2930
Date Established: 1987; **Freq:** 24 issues yearly - irrégulier; **Circ:** 500,000
Usual Pagination: 16
Language(s): French
Mechanical Data: Type Area: 150 x 210
BUSINESS: LOCAL GOVERNMENT, LEISURE & RECREATION: Community Care & Social Services

LES MESSAGES DU SECOURS CATHOLIQUE
7141F87-130
Editorial: 106 rue du Bac, CEDEX 07, 75341 PARIS
Tel: 1 45 49 73 36 **Fax:** 1 45 49 52 33
Email: dept.info@secours-catholique.org
ISSN: 0026-0290
Date Established: 1947; **Freq:** Monthly - 1er du mois (1 numéro 07-08); **Cover Price:** Free; **Circ:** 500,000
Usual Pagination: 24
Profile: Journal providing religious information on projects, surveys and topical subjects. Contains information on poverty in France and rest of the world.
Language(s): French
Readership: Read by people who donate to the Catholic Church.
Mechanical Data: Type Area: 230 x 280
CONSUMER: RELIGIOUS

MESURES
4633F5A-40
Editorial: Immeuble Europaris, 12 rue d'Oradour S/ Glane, CEDEX 15, 75504 PARIS **Tel:** 1 71 18 54 00
Email: redaction@mesures.presse.fr **Web site:** http://www.mesures.com
ISSN: 0755-219X
Date Established: 1936; **Freq:** Monthly - début du mois; **Cover Price:** EUR 12.20
Annual Sub.: EUR 105; **Circ:** 9,562
Usual Pagination: 90
Managing Director: Marc Laufer
Profile: Magazine covering instrumentation and automation analysis, test, control and trials.
Language(s): French
ADVERTISING RATES:
Full Page Colour .... EUR 4935
BUSINESS: COMPUTERS & AUTOMATION: Automation & Instrumentation

METRO FRANCE (PARIS & LOCAL EDITIONS)
1619601F67B-8601
Editorial: 35, rue Greneta, 75002 PARIS
Tel: 1 55 34 45 00 **Fax:** 1 55 34 45 03
Email: metrofrance@gmail.com **Web site:** http://www.metrofrance.com
ISSN: 1632-1065
Date Established: 2002; **Freq:** 260 issues yearly - Mon thru Fri; **Cover Price:** Free; **Circ:** 632,000
Usual Pagination: 24
Profile: Free regional daily newspaper focussing on general news and current affairs.
Language(s): French
ADVERTISING RATES:
Full Page Mono .... EUR 43400
Full Page Colour .... EUR 62000
Mechanical Data: Type Area: 290 x 385
Copy instructions: *Copy Date:* 2 days prior to publication date
REGIONAL DAILY & SUNDAY NEWSPAPERS: Regional Daily Newspapers

LA MG ACTUALITES
1618971F1D-154
Editorial: La Mutuelle Générale, 6 rue Vandrezanne, CEDEX 13, 75634 PARIS **Tel:** 1 40 78 08 10
Fax: 1 40 78 08 13
Email: contact@lamutuellegenerale.fr **Web site:** http://www.lamutuellegenerale.fr
ISSN: 0996-5955
Freq: Quarterly - 01 04 07 10; **Cover Price:** EUR 0.53; **Circ:** 900,000
Usual Pagination: 16
Language(s): French
Mechanical Data: Type Area: 170 x 250
BUSINESS: FINANCE & ECONOMICS: Insurance

MIAM - MAGAZINE D'INFORMATIONS SUR L'AUVERGNE EN MOUVEMENT
1617214F32A-1071
Editorial: 13-15 avenue de Fontmaure, BP 60, 63402 CEDEX CHAMALIERES **Tel:** 4 73 31 86 38
Fax: 473318623
Email: miam@cr-auvergne.fr **Web site:** http://www.auvergne.org
ISSN: 1774-1939
Date Established: 2005; **Freq:** Quarterly - Variable; **Cover Price:** Free; **Circ:** 620,000
Usual Pagination: 16
Editor: René Souchon
Profile: Publication focussing on local government and department issues.
Language(s): French
BUSINESS: LOCAL GOVERNMENT, LEISURE & RECREATION: Local Government

MICRO ACTUEL
1665494F5D-256
Editorial: 101/109 rue Jean Jaurès, 92300 LEVALLOIS PERRET **Tel:** 1 41 27 38 38
Fax: 1 41 27 38 39
Email: juliette.paoli@yellowmedia.fr **Web site:** http://www.microactuel.com
ISSN: 1773-6064
Date Established: 2005; **Freq:** Monthly - fin de mois; **Cover Price:** EUR 2.99
Annual Sub.: EUR 24.70; **Circ:** 103,144
Usual Pagination: 135
Profile: Publication focussing on computing including user guide, tips, internet, games, material, techniques, news, reviews, hardware, software, multimedia and mobile computing and telecommunication.
Language(s): French

ADVERTISING RATES:
Full Page Colour .... EUR 8600
Mechanical Data: Type Area: 21 x 29,7
BUSINESS: COMPUTERS & AUTOMATION: Personal Computers

MICRO HEBDO
4682F5D-73
Editorial: 26 rue d'Oradour sur Glane, CEDEX 15, 75504 PARIS **Tel:** 1 44 25 30 01 38 26
Fax: 1 45 57 43 75
Email: redaction@microhebdo.com **Web site:** http://www.01net.com
ISSN: 1276-549X
Date Established: 1998; **Freq:** Weekly - le jeudi; **Cover Price:** EUR 1.95
Annual Sub.: EUR 69; **Circ:** 156,705
Usual Pagination: 60
Profile: Magazine concerning computing. Includes articles on PCs, games and the Internet.
Language(s): French
Readership: Aimed at those interested in computing.
ADVERTISING RATES:
Full Page Colour .... EUR 11100
Mechanical Data: Type Area: 230 x 298
BUSINESS: COMPUTERS & AUTOMATION: Personal Computers

MICRO PRATIQUE
4684F5D-75
Editorial: Immeuble Sirius, 9 allée Jean Prouvé, CEDEX, 92587 CLICHY **Tel:** 1 41 40 31 65
Fax: 1 41 40 32 50
Email: herve.blanchard@editions-lariviere.fr
ISSN: 1253-1022
Date Established: 1996; **Freq:** Monthly - autour du 15
Annual Sub.: EUR 51; **Circ:** 65,000
Usual Pagination: 116
Editor-in-Chief: Hervé Blanchard; **Publisher:** Frédéric De Watrigant
Profile: Magazine containing information about personal computing.
Language(s): French
Readership: Aimed at those wishing to develop their skills.
ADVERTISING RATES:
Full Page Colour .... EUR 2600
Mechanical Data: Type Area: 285 x 210
BUSINESS: COMPUTERS & AUTOMATION: Personal Computers

MIDI LIBRE BUREAU PARISIEN
6193F67B-5700
Editorial: 89 rue du Faubourg-Saint-Honoré, 75008 PARIS **Tel:** 1 44 71 80 44 **Fax:** 1 44 71 80 46
Email: redac.paris@midilibre.com **Web site:** http://www.midilibre.com
ISSN: 0397-2550
Date Established: 1944; **Freq:** Daily - tous les jours; **Cover Price:** EUR 0.85
Annual Sub.: EUR 325; **Circ:** 180,000
Usual Pagination: 48
Profile: Regional office of the daily newspaper focussing on news and current affairs.
Language(s): French
Mechanical Data: Type Area: berlinois
REGIONAL DAILY & SUNDAY NEWSPAPERS: Regional Daily Newspapers

MIDI LIBRE MONTPELLIER
1619611F67B-8611
Editorial: rue du Mas-de-Grille, 34438 CEDEX SAINT-JEAN-DE-VEDAS **Tel:** 4 67 07 67 07
Fax: 4 67 07 68 57
Email: midiloisirs@midilibre.com **Web site:** http://www.midilibre.com
ISSN: 0397-2550
Date Established: 1944; **Freq:** Daily - le matin; **Cover Price:** EUR 0.85
Annual Sub.: EUR 325; **Circ:** 147,392
Usual Pagination: 48
Editor: Philippe Palat
Profile: Regional daily newspaper focussing on local, regional and national news and current affairs including leisure and shopping.
Language(s): French
ADVERTISING RATES:
Full Page Colour .... EUR 14882
Mechanical Data: Type Area: 420 x 290
REGIONAL DAILY & SUNDAY NEWSPAPERS: Regional Daily Newspapers

MIDI MUT
6986F80-469_50
Editorial: 16 La Canebière, BP 31866, CEDEX 01, 13221 MARSEILLE **Tel:** 4 91 00 76 44
Fax: 4 91 00 29 92
Email: mireille.nistasos@ag2rlamondiale.fr
ISSN: 0398-1444
Date Established: 1976; **Freq:** 24 issues yearly - fin 02 04 06 08 10 mi 12; **Cover Price:** EUR 0.58
Annual Sub.: EUR 3.48; **Circ:** 39,552
Usual Pagination: 36
Profile: Magazine focusing on health and social welfare. Includes articles on local industry, the economy and tourism in the South West of France.
Language(s): French
Mechanical Data: Type Area: 210 x 297
Copy instructions: *Copy Date:* 35 days prior to publication date
CONSUMER: RURAL & REGIONAL INTEREST

MIEUX VIVRE VOTRE ARGENT
6565F74M-50
Editorial: 29 rue de Châteaudun, 75009 PARIS
Tel: 1 75 55 10 00 **Fax:** 1 75 55 11 40
Email: jffilliatre@mieuxvivre.fr **Web site:** http://www.votreargent.fr
ISSN: 1291-2549
Date Established: 1979; **Freq:** Monthly - le dernier samedi du mois; **Cover Price:** EUR 3.90
Annual Sub.: EUR 20; **Circ:** 243,233
Usual Pagination: 128
Profile: Magazine about personal investment and money management.
Language(s): French
ADVERTISING RATES:
Full Page Mono .... EUR 12875
Full Page Colour .... EUR 17600
Mechanical Data: Type Area: 21 x 27,5
Copy instructions: *Copy Date:* 15 days prior to publication date
CONSUMER: WOMEN'S INTEREST CONSUMER MAGAZINES: Personal Finance

MITI NEWS
4648F5B-145
Editorial: 5 rue François-Ponsard, 75116 PARIS
Tel: 1 55 74 62 00 **Fax:** 155746210
Email: topix.redaction@wanadoo.fr **Web site:** http://www.mitinews.info
ISSN: 0247-039X
Date Established: 2000
Editor: Bernard Marx
Profile: Magazine concerning the use of information technology and telecommunications in the public sector.
Language(s): French
ADVERTISING RATES:
Full Page Mono .... EUR 2900
Mechanical Data: Type Area: A4
BUSINESS: COMPUTERS & AUTOMATION: Data Processing

MNH REVUE
1618974F1D-157
Editorial: 331 avenue d'Antibes, AMILLY, CEDEX, 45213 MONTARGIS **Tel:** 2 38 90 78 50
Fax: 2 38 90 75 72
Email: jean.gaultier@mnh.fr **Web site:** http://www.mnh.fr
ISSN: 1164-4869
Freq: Quarterly - 1er 02-05 - fin 08 - début 11; **Cover Price:** EUR 0.76
Annual Sub.: EUR 3.04; **Circ:** 750,000
Usual Pagination: 36
Language(s): French
Mechanical Data: Type Area: 210 x 280
BUSINESS: FINANCE & ECONOMICS: Insurance

MOBILES MAGAZINE
4949F18B-50
Editorial: 168-170 rue Raymond Losserand, 75014 PARIS **Tel:** 1 44 78 93 00 **Fax:** 1 44 78 97 67 98 34
Email: info@oracom.fr **Web site:** http://www.oracom.fr/ww.mobicity.com
ISSN: 1253-4560
Date Established: 1997; **Freq:** Monthly - by the 5th of the month; **Cover Price:** EUR 5.20
Annual Sub.: EUR 49; **Circ:** 50,000
Usual Pagination: 116
Profile: Guide to buying and comparing mobile phones.
Language(s): French
ADVERTISING RATES:
Full Page Colour .... EUR 7100
Mechanical Data: Type Area: 215 x 285
Copy instructions: *Copy Date:* 14 days prior to publication date
BUSINESS: ELECTRONICS: Telecommunications

MODES ET TRAVAUX
6434F74B-110
Editorial: Immeuble Trait d'Union, 8 rue François Ory, 92120 MONTROUGE **Tel:** 1 46 48 48 48
Fax: 1 46 48 19 00
Email: patricia.wagner@mondadori.fr **Web site:** http://www.mondadoripub.fr
ISSN: 0026-8739
Date Established: 1919; **Freq:** Monthly - 1ère semaine du mois
Annual Sub.: EUR 23; **Circ:** 405,455
Usual Pagination: 152
Publisher: Alexandre Dutreil
Profile: Magazine covering all aspects of fashion.
Language(s): French
ADVERTISING RATES:
Full Page Mono .... EUR 18900
Full Page Colour .... EUR 21000
Mechanical Data: Type Area: 200 x 270
Copy instructions: *Copy Date:* 93 days prior to publication date
CONSUMER: WOMEN'S INTEREST CONSUMER MAGAZINES: Women's Interest - Fashion

MON JARDIN ET MA MAISON
6468F74C-260
Editorial: Immeuble Delta, 124 rue Danton, CEDEX, 92538 LEVALLOIS PERRET **Tel:** 1 41 34 60 00
Fax: 1 41 34 95 81
Email: christiane.rivallin@lagardere-active.com
ISSN: 0026-9166
Date Established: 1958; **Freq:** Monthly - published between the 17th and 25th of the month; **Cover Price:** EUR 4.30
Annual Sub.: EUR 39; **Circ:** 159,416
Usual Pagination: 140
Publisher: Philippe Khyr

Profile: Magazine giving advice and information on the subject of house and garden.
Language(s): French
Readership: Aimed at DIY enthusiasts.
ADVERTISING RATES:
Full Page Mono .... EUR 10800
Full Page Colour .... EUR 13500
Mechanical Data: Type Area: 285 x 212
Copy instructions: *Copy Date:* 31 days prior to publication date
CONSUMER: WOMEN'S INTEREST CONSUMER MAGAZINES: Home & Family

MON QUOTIDIEN
7272F91D-150
Editorial: Play Bac Presse, 14 bis rue des Minimes, CEDEX 03, 75140 PARIS **Tel:** 1 53 01 23 60
Fax: 1 53 01 23 99
Email: f.dufour@playbac.fr **Web site:** http://www.playbacpresse.fr
ISSN: 1258-6447
Date Established: 1995; **Freq:** Daily - tous les matins; **Cover Price:** EUR 0.48
Annual Sub.: EUR 90; **Circ:** 65,000
Usual Pagination: 8
Editor-in-Chief: François Dufour
Profile: Publication containing topical news and sports items.
Language(s): French
Readership: Read by children aged 10 to 15 years.
ADVERTISING RATES:
Full Page Colour .... EUR 3000
Mechanical Data: Type Area: 230 x 310
CONSUMER: RECREATION & LEISURE: Children & Youth

LE MONDE
6095F65A-100
Editorial: 80 boulevard Auguste Blanqui, CEDEX 13, 75707 PARIS **Tel:** 1 57 28 20 00 **Fax:** 1 57 28 21 21
Email: kajman@lemonde.fr **Web site:** http://www.lemonde.fr
ISSN: 0395-2037
Date Established: 1944; **Freq:** Daily - 12h (Paris) - 17h (province); **Cover Price:** EUR 1.40
Annual Sub.: EUR 301.85; **Circ:** 319,418
Usual Pagination: 30
Editor-in-Chief: Eric Le Boucher; **Publisher:** Michel Sfeir
Profile: Tabloid-sized quality newspaper providing in-depth coverage of economics, current affairs, cultural and political issues. Political outlook: Centre-left.
Language(s): French
Readership: Readership includes senior managers and executives, decision makers, civil servants, university students and academics.
ADVERTISING RATES:
Full Page Mono .... EUR 89000
Full Page Colour .... EUR 116800
Mechanical Data: Type Area: berlinois
Editions:
Le Monde (UK Office)
NATIONAL DAILY & SUNDAY NEWSPAPERS: National Daily Newspapers

LE MONDE DE LA TECHNOLOGIE
4967F19A-170
Editorial: 106 avenue Félix Faure, 75015 PARIS
Tel: 1 45 54 54 54 **Fax:** 1 45 54 31 63
Email: info@france-intec.asso.fr **Web site:** http://www.france-intec.asso.fr
Date Established: 1974; **Freq:** Quarterly - mars juin octobre et septembre
Annual Sub.: EUR 20; **Circ:** 2,000
Usual Pagination: 16
Profile: Magazine for engineers and technicians.
Language(s): French
ADVERTISING RATES:
Full Page Colour .... EUR 720
Mechanical Data: Type Area: A 4
BUSINESS: ENGINEERING & MACHINERY

LE MONDE DES ARTISANS
4840F14H-123
Editorial: EDIMETIERS, 137 quai de Valmy, 75010 PARIS **Tel:** 1 40 05 23 23 **Fax:** 1 40 05 23 24
Email: c.saintignon@groupe-atc.com
Date Established: 1991; **Freq:** 24 issues yearly - 13/9 8/11 13/12 1/3 30/4 1/6
Annual Sub.: EUR 40; **Circ:** 350,000
Usual Pagination: 48
Profile: Magazine about business for professionals and entrepreneurs.
Language(s): French
ADVERTISING RATES:
Full Page Colour .... EUR 9430
Mechanical Data: Type Area: A 4
Copy instructions: *Copy Date:* 31 days prior to publication date
BUSINESS: COMMERCE, INDUSTRY & MANAGEMENT: Small Business

LE MONDE DES LIVRES SUPPLEMENT DU QUOTIDIEN LE MONDE
7103F84B-165
Editorial: 80 boulevard Auguste-Blanqui, 75707 CEDEX 13 PARIS **Tel:** 1 57 28 20 00
Fax: 1 57 28 21 05
Web site: http://www.lemonde.fr
ISSN: 0395-2037
Freq: Weekly - le jeudi; **Circ:** 400,000
Profile: Publication providing critical discussion about books, including reviews of new books.
Language(s): French
ADVERTISING RATES:
Full Page Mono .... EUR 44700
Full Page Colour .... EUR 60300
Copy instructions: *Copy Date:* 7 days prior to publication date
CONSUMER: THE ARTS & LITERARY: Literary

LE MONDE DIPLOMATIQUE
7047F82-140
Editorial: 1 avenue Stephen Pichon, 75013 PARIS
Tel: 1 53 94 96 01 07 **Fax:** 1 53 94 96 26
Email: secretariat@monde-diplomatique.fr **Web site:** http://www.monde-diplomatique.fr
ISSN: 0026-9395
Date Established: 1954; **Freq:** Monthly - 1er du mois; **Cover Price:** EUR 4.50
Annual Sub.: EUR 45; **Circ:** 163,703
Usual Pagination: 28
Profile: Magazine containing political, social and economic analysis and comment.
Language(s): French
ADVERTISING RATES:
Full Page Mono .... EUR 13400
Full Page Colour .... EUR 19400
Mechanical Data: Type Area: 325 x 475
CONSUMER: CURRENT AFFAIRS & POLITICS

LE MONDE DU CAMPING CAR
7258F91B-25
Editorial: Espace Clichy - Immeuble Sirius, 9 allée Jean Prouvé, CEDEX, 92587 CLICHY
Tel: 1 41 40 33 10 33 33 **Fax:** 1 41 40 33 34 35
Email: camping-car@editions-lariviere.fr **Web site:** http://www.editions-lariviere.fr
ISSN: 1962-4751
Date Established: 1988; **Freq:** Monthly - Between the 12th and 15th of the month; **Cover Price:** EUR 4.50
Annual Sub.: EUR 50; **Circ:** 70,000
Usual Pagination: 260
Publisher: Karim Khaldi
Profile: Magazine about caravans, camper vans and other leisure vehicles.
Language(s): French
Readership: Read by camping enthusiasts.
ADVERTISING RATES:
Full Page Mono .... EUR 3136
Full Page Colour .... EUR 5521
Mechanical Data: Type Area: A 4
CONSUMER: RECREATION & LEISURE: Camping & Caravanning

LE MONDE DU PIN AIR
7256F91B-15
Editorial: Espace Clichy - Immeuble Sirius, 9 allée Jean Prouvé, CEDEX, 92587 CLICHY
Tel: 1 41 40 33 10 33 33 **Fax:** 1 41 40 33 34 35
Email: caravmag@editions-lariviere.fr **Web site:** http://www.editions-lariviere.fr
Freq: 24 issues yearly - le 20/01 03 05 07 08 09;
Cover Price: EUR 4.20
Annual Sub.: EUR 24.60; **Circ:** 55,000
Usual Pagination: 116
Publisher: Karim Khaldi
Profile: Magazine about caravans and other vehicles used in leisure pursuits.
Language(s): French
ADVERTISING RATES:
Full Page Mono .... EUR 3004
Full Page Colour .... EUR 5265
Mechanical Data: Type Area: A 4
CONSUMER: RECREATION & LEISURE: Camping & Caravanning

LE MONDE ECONOMIE SUPPLEMENT DU QUOTIDIEN LE MONDE
1617917F1A-416
Editorial: 80 boulevard Auguste-Blanqui, 75707 CEDEX 13 PARIS **Tel:** 1 57 28 29 61 **Fax:** 157282173
Web site: http://www.lemonde.fr
ISSN: 0763-5508
Freq: Weekly - le lundi; **Circ:** 514,000
Usual Pagination: 8
Profile: Business publication, supplement of the daily newspaper Le Monde focussing on economics and business.
Language(s): French
ADVERTISING RATES:
Full Page Mono .... EUR 45300
Full Page Colour .... EUR 62300
BUSINESS: FINANCE & ECONOMICS

LE MONDE EDUCATION SUPPLEMENT DU QUOTIDIEN LE MONDE
7326F62A-85
Editorial: 80 boulevard Auguste-Blanqui, CEDEX 13, 75707 PARIS **Tel:** 1 57 28 20 00 **Fax:** 1 57 28 38 12
Email: lemonde.education@lemonde.fr **Web site:** http://www.lemonde.fr/mde
Date Established: 1974; **Freq:** Monthly - 2ème mardi de chaque mois
Usual Pagination: 100
Editor: Eric Fottorino
Profile: Newspaper containing information on all aspects of primary and secondary education.
Language(s): French
Readership: Aimed at teachers and others interested in educational issues.
ADVERTISING RATES:
Full Page Mono .... EUR 6000
Full Page Colour .... EUR 8800
Mechanical Data: Type Area: A4
BUSINESS: CHURCH & SCHOOL EQUIPMENT & EDUCATION: Education

MONDE ET VIE
7048F82-160
Editorial: 14 rue Edmond Valentin, 75007 PARIS
Tel: 1 47 05 10 42
Email: mondevie@monde-vie.com **Web site:** http://www.monde-vie.com
ISSN: 0335-3788
Date Established: 1973; **Freq:** 26 issues yearly - samedi; **Cover Price:** EUR 4.20
Annual Sub.: EUR 62; **Circ:** 10,000
Usual Pagination: 32
Profile: Magazine containing opinions and information focusing on politics, economics, religion, current affairs and the arts.
Language(s): French
ADVERTISING RATES:
Full Page Colour .... EUR 850
Mechanical Data: Type Area: 23 x 30
CONSUMER: CURRENT AFFAIRS & POLITICS

LE MONDE MAGAZINE
754328F82-265
Editorial: 80 boulevard Auguste Blanqui, CEDEX 13, 75707 PARIS **Tel:** 1 57 28 25 61 **Fax:** 1 57 28 35 99
Email: lemonde2@lemonde.fr
ISSN: 0395-2037
Date Established: 2000; **Freq:** Weekly - vendredi Paris, samedi province; **Cover Price:** EUR 2.50; **Circ:** 271,291
Usual Pagination: 116
Profile: General news and photojournalism magazine.
Language(s): French
ADVERTISING RATES:
Full Page Colour .... EUR 20500
Mechanical Data: Type Area: 230 x 290
CONSUMER: CURRENT AFFAIRS & POLITICS

LE MONITEUR DES PHARMACIES
5376F37-110
Editorial: 1 rue Eugène et Armand Peugeot, Case Postale 802, CEDEX, 92856 RUEIL MALMAISON
Tel: 1 76 73 30 00 **Fax:** 1 76 73 48 60
Email: llefort@groupeliaisons.fr **Web site:** http://www.moniteurpharmacies.com
ISSN: 0026-9689
Date Established: 1947; **Freq:** Weekly - Saturday;
Cover Price: EUR 6.95
Annual Sub.: EUR 238; **Circ:** 22,512
Usual Pagination: 100
Profile: Magazine containing information about pharmaceutical products.
Language(s): French
ADVERTISING RATES:
Full Page Mono .... EUR 4390
Full Page Colour .... EUR 6270
Mechanical Data: Type Area: 21 x 29,7
Copy instructions: *Copy Date:* 15 days prior to publication date
BUSINESS: PHARMACEUTICAL & CHEMISTS

LE MONITEUR DES TRAVAUX PUBLICS
5445F42A-350
Editorial: 17 rue d'Uzès, CEDEX 02, 75108 PARIS
Tel: 1 40 13 30 30 **Fax:** 1 40 41 94 95
Email: redac@groupemoniteur.fr **Web site:** http://www.lemoniteur-expert.com
ISSN: 0026-9700
Date Established: 1903; **Freq:** Weekly
Annual Sub.: EUR 339; **Circ:** 57,899
Usual Pagination: 350
Managing Director: Guillaume Prot; **Publisher:** Olivier De La Chaise
Profile: Journal about building and public works.
Language(s): French
ADVERTISING RATES:
Full Page Mono .... EUR 8640
Full Page Colour .... EUR 10800
Mechanical Data: Type Area: 23 x 30
Copy instructions: *Copy Date:* 15 days prior to publication date
BUSINESS: CONSTRUCTION

LE MONITEUR DU COMMERCE INTERNATIONAL
4863F14C-28
Editorial: 11 rue de Milan, CEDEX 09, 75440 PARIS
Tel: 1 53 80 74 00
Web site: http://www.lemoci.com
ISSN: 0026-9719
Date Established: 1883; **Freq:** 26 issues yearly - Thursdays
Annual Sub.: EUR 305; **Circ:** 6,514
Usual Pagination: 84
Profile: Journal providing economic analyses, articles on export techniques and information about foreign markets.
Web site: www.motomag.com
Language(s): French
ADVERTISING RATES:
Full Page Mono .... EUR 4700
Full Page Colour .... EUR 6800
Mechanical Data: Type Area: 185 x 251
Copy instructions: *Copy Date:* 15 days prior to publication date
BUSINESS: COMMERCE, INDUSTRY & MANAGEMENT: International Commerce

MONSIEUR MAGAZINE
7124F86C-50
Editorial: 72 boulevard Berthier, 75017 PARIS
Tel: 1 47 63 48 00 **Fax:** 1 47 63 49 08
Email: fjdaehn@monsieur.fr **Web site:** http://www.monsieur.fr
ISSN: 1265-0080
Date Established: 1995; **Freq:** 24 issues yearly - Comb. JUN/JUL; **Cover Price:** EUR 4.80
Annual Sub.: EUR 20; **Circ:** 35,000
Usual Pagination: 100
Profile: Magazine for the modern man with features on fashion, sport and lifestyle.
Language(s): French
ADVERTISING RATES:
Full Page Colour .... EUR 6550
Mechanical Data: Type Area: 23 x 30
Copy instructions: *Copy Date:* 21 days prior to publication date
CONSUMER: ADULT & GAY MAGAZINES: Men's Lifestyle Magazines

LA MONTAGNE CLERMONT-FERRAND
1619470F67B-8470
Editorial: 45 rue du Clos-Four, BP 83, 63056 CEDEX 2 CLERMONT-FERRAND **Tel:** 4 73 17 17 17
Fax: 4 73 17 18 19
Email: locale@centrefrance.com **Web site:** http://www.lamontagne.fr
Freq: Daily - 7 jours sur 7; **Cover Price:** EUR 0.90
Annual Sub.: EUR 251; **Circ:** 191,639
Usual Pagination: 28
Profile: Regional newspaper - Sports - Current events.
Language(s): French
ADVERTISING RATES:
Full Page Mono .... EUR 10990
REGIONAL DAILY & SUNDAY NEWSPAPERS: Regional Daily Newspapers

LA MONTAGNE NOIRE
6191F67B-5800
Editorial: 30 boulevard du Thoré, 81200 AUSSILLON
Tel: 5 63 97 57 10 **Fax:** 5 63 61 70 37
Email: redaction@lamontagnenoire.fr
ISSN: 0995-4201
Date Established: 1914; **Freq:** Daily - le matin : mar-mer-jeu-ven; **Cover Price:** EUR 0.50
Annual Sub.: EUR 80; **Circ:** 1,900
Usual Pagination: 6
Profile: Local news, 4 issues /week. Published on: Tuesday, Wednesday, Thursday and Friday. 8 Pages on Friday.
Language(s): French
ADVERTISING RATES:
Full Page Mono .... EUR 755
Full Page Colour .... EUR 990
REGIONAL DAILY & SUNDAY NEWSPAPERS: Regional Daily Newspapers

MOSELLE MAGAZINE
1617191F32A-1050
Editorial: Conseil Général de la Moselle, 1 rue du Pont-Moreau, BP 11096 CEDEX 1, 57036 METZ
Tel: 3 87 37 57 06 **Fax:** 3 87 37 58 09
Email: webmestre@cg57.fr **Web site:** http://www.cg57.fr
ISSN: 1274-3119
Date Established: 1996; **Freq:** 24 issues yearly - 01 03 05 07 09 11; **Cover Price:** Free; **Circ:** 445,000
Usual Pagination: 24
Profile: Publication focussing on local government and department issues, including economics, sports, cultural and social issues.
Language(s): French
Mechanical Data: Type Area: 230 x 297
BUSINESS: LOCAL GOVERNMENT, LEISURE & RECREATION: Local Government

MOTO JOURNAL
6845F77B-98
Editorial: 12 rue Rouget de Lisle, CEDEX, 92442 ISSY LES MOULINEAUX **Tel:** 1 41 33 37 37
Fax: 1 41 33 38 13
Email: motojournal@motorpresse.fr **Web site:** http://www.moto-journal.tv
ISSN: 0751-591X
Date Established: 1971; **Freq:** Weekly - jeudi (sauf mi-juillet mi-août); **Cover Price:** EUR 3.20
Annual Sub.: EUR 141; **Circ:** 34,320
Usual Pagination: 84
Profile: Magazine about all aspects of motorcycling.
Language(s): French
ADVERTISING RATES:
Full Page Mono .... EUR 3075
Full Page Colour .... EUR 4540
Mechanical Data: Type Area: A 4
CONSUMER: MOTORING & CYCLING: Motorcycling

MOTO MAGAZINE
6847F77B-99
Editorial: 35 rue des Messiers, 93100 MONTREUIL
Tel: 1 55 86 18 00 **Fax:** 1 48 58 02 98
Email: mmoutalbi@motomag.com **Web site:** http://www.motomag.com
ISSN: 0241-8932
Date Established: 1983; **Freq:** Monthly - last Thursday of the month; **Cover Price:** EUR 4.50
Annual Sub.: EUR 32; **Circ:** 117,295
Usual Pagination: 148
Editor-in-Chief: Alain Corroler
Profile: This magazine covers motorcycles and motorcycling.

Language(s): French
Readership: Read by motorcycling enthusiasts.
ADVERTISING RATES:
Full Page Mono .... EUR 2828
Full Page Colour .... EUR 4876
Mechanical Data: Type Area: A 4
CONSUMER: MOTORING & CYCLING: Motorcycling

MOTO REVUE 6848F77B-100
Editorial: Espace Clichy - Immeuble Agéna, 12 rue Mozart, CEDEX, 92587 CLICHY Tel: 1 41 40 31 76 32 32 Fax: 1 41 40 32 50
Email: alain.lecorre@editions-lariviere.fr Web site: http://www.motorevue.com
ISSN: 9782-9142
Freq: Weekly - jeudi; Cover Price: EUR 3.20; Circ: 70,000
Usual Pagination: 96
Publisher: Philippe Budillon
Profile: Motorcycling review with news, tests, sports and sponsorship.
Language(s): French
ADVERTISING RATES:
Full Page Mono .... EUR 2680
Full Page Colour .... EUR 4250
Mechanical Data: Type Area: A 4
CONSUMER: MOTORING & CYCLING: Motorcycling

LE MOUVEMENT HOTELIER ET TOURISTIQUE 4783F11A-195
Editorial: 221 avenue de Lyon, BP 448, CEDEX, 73004 CHAMBERY Tel: 4 79 69 26 18
Fax: 4 79 62 68 33
Email: mouvhotel@wanadoo.fr
ISSN: 1169-8217
Date Established: 1968; Freq: 24 issues yearly - fin des mois 02 04 06 08 10 12
Annual Sub.: EUR 37; Circ: 4,500
Usual Pagination: 24
Profile: Magazine for professionals in the hotel and catering trade.
Language(s): French
ADVERTISING RATES:
Full Page Colour .... EUR 500
Mechanical Data: Type Area: 30 x 22
Copy instructions: *Copy Date:* 7 days prior to publication date
BUSINESS: CATERING: Catering, Hotels & Restaurants

MOVING MAGAZINE 1646389F74G-296
Editorial: 60 rue de Miromesnil, 75008 PARIS
Tel: 1 56 43 35 30 Fax: 1 56 43 35 29
Web site: http://www.moving.fr
Freq: Quarterly; Cover Price: EUR 2; Circ: 200,000
Usual Pagination: 36
Managing Director: Lionel Bourillon
Profile: Publication focussing on good health and fitness including news, beauty and well being.
Language(s): French
ADVERTISING RATES:
Full Page Colour .... EUR 6200.00
CONSUMER: WOMEN'S INTEREST CONSUMER MAGAZINES: Slimming & Health

MPS - MIDI PRESSE SERVICE TOULOUSE 6024F14A-819
Editorial: Dépêche Mag, Avenue Jean-Baylet, CEDEX 1, 31095 TOULOUSE Tel: 5 62 11 96 00
Fax: 5 62 11 96 01
Email: redaction-mps@depechemag.com Web site: http://www.midipresse.fr
ISSN: 0395-6431
Date Established: 1974; Freq: Weekly. vendredi;
Cover Price: EUR 10.67
Annual Sub.: EUR 420; Circ: 2,600 Unique Users
Usual Pagination: 16
Profile: Newsletter containing economic news and information for the Midi-Pyrénées.
Language(s): French
Readership: Aimed at lawyers, directors, local government officials and bank managers.
ADVERTISING RATES:
Full Page Mono .... EUR 1360
Full Page Colour .... EUR 1970
Mechanical Data: Type Area: A 4
BUSINESS: COMMERCE, INDUSTRY & MANAGEMENT

MULTIMEDIA A LA UNE 4706F5F-385
Editorial: 45 rue de l'Est, 92100 BOULOGNE BILLANCOURT Tel: 1 48 25 11 33 Fax: 1 48 25 47 42
Email: psouplet@multimedialaune.com Web site: http://www.multimedialaune.com
ISSN: 1267-7663
Date Established: 1995; Freq: Monthly - around the 10th of the month
Annual Sub.: EUR 33; Circ: 10,000
Usual Pagination: 72
Editor-in-Chief: Philippe Souplet
Profile: Magazine about the latest developments in multimedia.
Language(s): French
Readership: Aimed at professionals within the field.
ADVERTISING RATES:
Full Page Colour .... EUR 4900
Mechanical Data: Type Area: 230 x 300
BUSINESS: COMPUTERS & AUTOMATION: Multimedia

LE MUTUALISTE 1618959F1D-142
Editorial: 8 Terrasse du Front du Médoc, CEDEX, 33054 BORDEAUX Tel: 5 56 01 57 57
Fax: 5 56 24 74 94
Email: daniel.paloumet@ociane.fr
ISSN: 1163-3735
Date Established: 1950; Freq: Quarterly - début 01-04-07-10; Cover Price: EUR 0.60
Annual Sub.: EUR 2.40; Circ: 280,000
Usual Pagination: 16
Language(s): French
Mechanical Data: Type Area: tabloïd
BUSINESS: FINANCE & ECONOMICS: Insurance

NANTES METROPOLE COMMUNAUTE D'AGGLOMERATION DE NANTES 1804258F80-1048
Editorial: 2 cours du Champ-de-Mars, 44923 CEDEX 9 NANTES Tel: 2 40 99 48 27 Fax: 240994800
Email: david.pouilloux@nantesmetropole.fr Web site: http://www.nantesmetropole.fr
ISSN: 2107-6677
Date Established: 2006; Freq: 6 issues yearly - début des mois impairs; Cover Price: Free; Circ: 275,000
Editor: Jean-Marc Ayrault
Profile: Publication focussing on local community information.
Language(s): French
Mechanical Data: Type Area: 21 x 29,7
CONSUMER: RURAL & REGIONAL INTEREST

NANTES PASSION 6988F32A-1100
Editorial: Mairie, 2 rue de l'Hôtel de Ville, CEDEX 1, 44094 NANTES Tel: 2 40 41 67 00 Fax: 2 40 41 59 39
Email: infonantes@mairie-nantes.fr Web site: http://www.mairie-nantes.fr
ISSN: 1164-4125
Date Established: 1989; Freq: Monthly - début du mois; Cover Price: Free; Circ: 171,700
Usual Pagination: 84
Profile: Magazine for the town of Nantes.
Language(s): French
Readership: Read by visitors and residents.
BUSINESS: LOCAL GOVERNMENT, LEISURE & RECREATION: Local Government

NATIONAL GEOGRAPHIC FRANCE 1617363F73-328
Editorial: 13 rue Henri Barbusse, 92624 GENNEVILLIERS Tel: 1 73 05 60 96
Fax: 1 47 92 67 00
Email: nationalgeographic@ngm-f.com Web site: http://www.nationalgeographic.fr
ISSN: 1297-1715
Date Established: 1999; Freq: Monthly - fin ou début du mois; Cover Price: EUR 4.90
Annual Sub.: EUR 39; Circ: 123,727
Usual Pagination: 186
Profile: Publication focussing on geography and nature including travel, landscapes and adventure.
Language(s): French
ADVERTISING RATES:
Full Page Mono .... EUR 10875
Full Page Colour .... EUR 14500
Mechanical Data: Type Area: 175 x 255
Copy instructions: *Copy Date:* 31 days prior to publication date
CONSUMER: NATIONAL & INTERNATIONAL PERIODICALS

NEGOCE 4621F4E-337_50
Editorial: 17 rue d'Uzès, 75002 PARIS
Tel: 1 40 13 30 30 34 80 Fax: 1 40 13 51 02
Email: redac.negoce@groupemoniteur.fr Web site: http://www.lemoniteur.fr
ISSN: 0767-4430
Freq: 26 issues yearly - le 1er et le 15 du mois; Cover Price: EUR 11
Annual Sub.: EUR 104; Circ: 13,000
Usual Pagination: 72
Managing Director: Olivier De La Chaise
Profile: Magazine containing articles about building methods.
Language(s): French
Readership: Aimed at builders merchants, do-it-yourself and decorating retailers and wholesalers.
ADVERTISING RATES:
Full Page Mono .... EUR 5325
Full Page Colour .... EUR 7100
Mechanical Data: Type Area: 246 x 320
Copy instructions: *Copy Date:* 31 days prior to publication date
BUSINESS: ARCHITECTURE & BUILDING: Building

NEO RESTAURATION MAGAZINE 4784F11A-200
Editorial: Antony Parc 2, 10 place du Général de Gaulle, 92160 ANTONY Tel: 1 77 92 92 92
Fax: 1 77 92 98 54
Email: ypuget@neorestauration.com Web site: http://www.neorestauration.com
ISSN: 1145-377X
Date Established: 1972; Freq: Monthly - 1ère semaine du mois
Annual Sub.: EUR 77; Circ: 18,957
Usual Pagination: 120
Profile: Magazine covering all aspects of the restaurant trade.
Language(s): French
ADVERTISING RATES:
Full Page Mono .... EUR 3860
Full Page Colour .... EUR 5200
Mechanical Data: Type Area: A 4
BUSINESS: CATERING: Catering, Hotels & Restaurants

NEUF MOIS MAGAZINE 1618017F74A-404
Editorial: BLEUCOM, 10-12 villa Thoreton, 75015 PARIS Tel: 1 45 71 75 00
Email: costa@bleucom.net Web site: http://www.neufmois.fr
ISSN: 1999-1929
Date Established: 2000; Freq: Monthly - dernier samedi daté mois suivant
Annual Sub.: EUR 21.95; Circ: 51,098
Usual Pagination: 114
Language(s): French
ADVERTISING RATES:
Full Page Colour .... EUR 9293
Mechanical Data: Type Area: 225 x 300
CONSUMER: WOMEN'S INTEREST CONSUMER MAGAZINES: Women's Interest

NICE-MATIN NICE - SIEGE SOCIAL 6199F67B-5900
Editorial: 214 route de Grenoble, 06290 CEDEX 3 NICE Tel: 4 93 18 28 38 Fax: 4 93 18 29 51
Email: redacchef@nicematin.fr Web site: http://www.nicematin.com
Date Established: 1944; Freq: Daily - Chaque jour sauf le 1er mai; Cover Price: EUR 0.85
Annual Sub.: EUR 309; Circ: 115,791
Usual Pagination: 34
Profile: Regional newspaper for Nice and surrounding area, containing four pages devoted specifically to Monaco.
Language(s): French
ADVERTISING RATES:
Full Page Colour .... EUR 33096
Mechanical Data: Type Area: Tabloïd
REGIONAL DAILY & SUNDAY NEWSPAPERS: Regional Daily Newspapers

NINTENDO - LE MAGAZINE OFFICIEL 1617531F78D-205
Editorial: 101/109 rue Jean Jaurès, 92300 LEVALLOIS PERRET Tel: 1 41 27 38 38
Fax: 1 41 27 38 39
Email: filipe.canelas@yellowmedia.fr Web site: http://www.jvn.com
ISSN: 1633-0684
Date Established: 2002; Freq: Monthly - dernier mercredi du mois
Annual Sub.: EUR 84; Circ: 20,826
Usual Pagination: 100
Profile: Publication focussing on computer games including Nintendo DS and Wii, news, previews, products, tests and tips.
Language(s): French
ADVERTISING RATES:
Full Page Colour .... EUR 3100
Mechanical Data: Type Area: 23 x 28
CONSUMER: CONSUMER ELECTRONICS: Games

NITRO 6884F77F-200
Editorial: 48/50 Boulevard Sénard, 92210 SAINT CLOUD Tel: 1 47 11 20 00 Fax: 1 49 11 02 77
Email: clefebvre@nitro.hommell.com Web site: http://www.nitromag.fr
ISSN: 0248-7888
Date Established: 1981; Freq: 24 issues yearly - le 25 des mois impairs
Annual Sub.: EUR 26; Circ: 19,470
Usual Pagination: 100
Managing Director: Jean-Claude Lebon
Profile: Magazine about American cars of the 1950s and 60s, hot rods, customised cars and dragsters.
Language(s): French
ADVERTISING RATES:
Full Page Colour .... EUR 1900
Mechanical Data: Type Area: A 4
CONSUMER: MOTORING & CYCLING: Veteran Cars

LE NORD 1617182F32A-1042
Editorial: Conseil Général du Nord, 2 rue Jacquemars-Giélée, CEDEX, 59047 LILLE
Tel: 3 59 73 59 59 Fax: 3 59 73 83 69
Email: lenord@cg59.fr
ISSN: 1169-4947
Freq: Monthly - début de mois; Cover Price: Free;
Circ: 1,100,000
Usual Pagination: 32
Profile: Publication focussing on local government and department issues.
Language(s): French
Mechanical Data: Type Area: A4
BUSINESS: LOCAL GOVERNMENT, LEISURE & RECREATION: Local Government

NORD ÉCLAIR - ROUBAIX 6205F67B-6000
Editorial: 42 rue du Général-Sarrail, 59100 ROUBAIX
Tel: 3 20 25 62 37 Fax: 3 20 25 62 98
Email: region@nordeclair.fr Web site: http://www.nordeclair.fr
Date Established: 1944; Freq: Daily - matin 7j/7;
Cover Price: EUR 0.75; Circ: 26,742
Managing Director: Jean-René Lore
Profile: Regional daily newspaper focussing on news and current affairs including local events.
Language(s): French
ADVERTISING RATES:
Full Page Mono .... EUR 5460
Full Page Colour .... EUR 7371
Copy instructions: *Copy Date:* 2 days prior to publication date
REGIONAL DAILY & SUNDAY NEWSPAPERS: Regional Daily Newspapers

NORD LITTORAL 6163F67B-6100
Editorial: 91 boulevard Jacquard, BP 108, CEDEX, 62102 CALAIS Tel: 3 21 19 12 13 12
Fax: 3 21 19 12 10
Email: courrier@nord-littoral.fr Web site: http://www.nordlittoral.fr
ISSN: 0989-8492
Freq: Daily - 7 jours/7; Cover Price: EUR 0.95
Annual Sub.: EUR 301.60; Circ: 10,182
Usual Pagination: 32
Profile: Regional daily newspaper focussing on news and current affairs including TV guide.
Language(s): French
ADVERTISING RATES:
Full Page Mono .... EUR 1069
Full Page Colour .... EUR 1437
Mechanical Data: Type Area: 270 x 400
REGIONAL DAILY & SUNDAY NEWSPAPERS: Regional Daily Newspapers

NOTRE TEMPS MAGAZINE 6574F74N-40
Editorial: 18 rue Barbès, 92128 MONTROUGE
Tel: 1 74 31 60 60
Email: redaction@notretemps.com Web site: http://www.notretemps.com
ISSN: 0029-456X
Date Established: 1968; Freq: Monthly - autour du 15 du mois; Cover Price: EUR 3.30
Annual Sub.: EUR 36.60; Circ: 899,551
Usual Pagination: 175
Profile: Magazine for retired people featuring news about health, travel, cookery and the home.
Language(s): French
ADVERTISING RATES:
Full Page Mono .... EUR 28350
Full Page Colour .... EUR 31500
Mechanical Data: Type Area: Magazine
Copy instructions: *Copy Date:* 62 days prior to publication date
CONSUMER: WOMEN'S INTEREST CONSUMER MAGAZINES: Retirement

NOUS DEUX 6417F74A-288
Editorial: Immeuble Trait d'Union, 8 rue François Ory, 92120 MONTROUGE Tel: 1 46 48 48 48
Fax: 1 46 48 43 20
Email: marion.minuit@mondadori.fr Web site: http://www.mondadori.fr
ISSN: 0299-7061
Date Established: 1947; Freq: Weekly - mardi;
Cover Price: EUR 1.95
Annual Sub.: EUR 93.90; Circ: 324,514
Usual Pagination: 84
Profile: Magazine containing articles about health, tourism, new products, practical advice, animals, education, cookery, beauty and fashion.
Language(s): French
Readership: Read by women.
ADVERTISING RATES:
Full Page Mono .... EUR 7380
Full Page Colour .... EUR 9980
Mechanical Data: Type Area: 209 x 268
Copy instructions: *Copy Date:* 28 days prior to publication date
CONSUMER: WOMEN'S INTEREST CONSUMER MAGAZINES: Women's Interest

NOUS, VOUS ILLE 1617192F32A-1051
Editorial: Conseil Général - Hôtel du Département, 1 avenue de la Préfecture, CS 24218 CEDEX, 35042 RENNES Tel: 2 99 02 35 35 Fax: 2 99 02 39 25
Email: nousvousille@cg35.fr
ISSN: 0764-3926
Date Established: 1986; Freq: Quarterly - mi10 pour2010et fin 01et 04/2011; Cover Price: Free;
Circ: 468,000
Usual Pagination: 52
Profile: Publication focussing on local government and department issues, including economics, society, environment, cultural heritage, culture and social issues.
Language(s): French
Mechanical Data: Type Area: 23 x 30
BUSINESS: LOCAL GOVERNMENT, LEISURE & RECREATION: Local Government

LE NOUVEAU DETECTIVE 6379F73-170
Editorial: 26 rue Vercingétorix, CEDEX 14, 75685 PARIS Tel: 1 40 64 31 31 Fax: 1 40 64 31 30
Email: caroline.canavarian@nuitetjour.fr
ISSN: 0221-4709
Date Established: 1928; Freq: Weekly - mercredi;
Cover Price: EUR 1.50
Annual Sub.: EUR 59; Circ: 270,947
Usual Pagination: 36

Profile: Magazine containing information on various topics of interest.
Language(s): French
ADVERTISING RATES:
Full Page Mono .... EUR 6150
Full Page Colour .... EUR 7590
Mechanical Data: Type Area: 334 x 245
CONSUMER: NATIONAL & INTERNATIONAL PERIODICALS

LES NOUVEL DE TAHITI

1800089PF67B-2
Editorial: SELN - Immeuble Sarateva, Carrefour de Fautaua, BP 629, 98713 PAPEETE - POLYNESIE FRANCAISE **Tel:** 689 47 52 00 **Fax:** 689 47 52 09
Email: redac@lesnouvelles.pf **Web site:** http://www.lesnouvelles.pf
Freq: Daily - French Polynesia; **Circ:** 6,500
Profile: Daily Papeete and Tahiti region current events newspaper. Columns: Femua news, all pictures, society, politics, Oceania, time to live, France World, sports news, press release, leisure, today on TV, community information, weather forecast.
Language(s): French
Readership: Companies, civil service, popa'a (France expatriates).
REGIONAL DAILY & SUNDAY NEWSPAPERS: Regional Daily Newspapers

LE NOUVEL ECONOMISTE

4474F65J-3
Editorial: 5 passage Piver, 75011 PARIS
Tel: 1 58 30 64 64 **Fax:** 1 58 30 64 65
Web site: http://www.nouveleconomiste.fr
ISSN: 0395-6458
Date Established: 1976; **Freq:** Weekly - jeudi
Annual Sub.: EUR 149; **Circ:** 24,952
Usual Pagination: 32
Profile: Journal containing economic and financial news, includes personal finance, regional reports and current affairs.
Language(s): French
Readership: Readership includes senior executives and those interested in current affairs.
ADVERTISING RATES:
Full Page Colour .... EUR 4900
Mechanical Data: Type Area: 290x410
NATIONAL DAILY & SUNDAY NEWSPAPERS: National Weekly Newspapers

LE NOUVEL OBSERVATEUR

6380F73-180
Editorial: 10/12 place de la Bourse, CEDEX 02, 75081 PARIS **Tel:** 1 44 88 34 34
Email: mlabro@nouvelobs.com **Web site:** http://www.nouvelobs.com
ISSN: 0029-4713
Date Established: 1964; **Freq:** Weekly - jeudi; **Cover Price:** EUR 3.20
Annual Sub.: EUR 120; **Circ:** 525,547
Usual Pagination: 132
Profile: News magazine with articles of general interest.
Language(s): French
ADVERTISING RATES:
Full Page Colour .... EUR 29300
CONSUMER: NATIONAL & INTERNATIONAL PERIODICALS

LA NOUVELLE REPUBLIQUE DES PYRENEES

6209F67B-6200
Editorial: 48 avenue Bertrand Barère, BP 730, CEDEX, 65007 TARBES **Tel:** 5 62 44 05 05
Fax: 5 62 44 05 24
Email: jean-louis.toulouze@nrpyrenees.com **Web site:** http://www.nrpyrenees.com
ISSN: 1146-447X
Date Established: 1944; **Freq:** Daily; **Cover Price:** EUR 0.80
Annual Sub.: EUR 229; **Circ:** 12,867
Usual Pagination: 36
Profile: National and local daily newspaper. Sports, culture, agriculture, consumption, health, legal ads and obituaries. Weekly TV guide on Thursdays (price: 1,15 €).
Language(s): French
ADVERTISING RATES:
Full Page Mono .... EUR 2580
Mechanical Data: Type Area: berlinois
REGIONAL DAILY & SUNDAY NEWSPAPERS: Regional Daily Newspapers

LA NOUVELLE REPUBLIQUE DU CENTRE-OUEST EDITION D'INDRE-ET-LOIRE TOURS ET LA BANLIEUE

6211F67B-6300
Editorial: 232 avenue de Grammont, 37048 CEDEX 1 TOURS **Tel:** 2 47 31 70 00 **Fax:** 2 47 31 70 70
Email: nr.joue@nrco.fr **Web site:** http://www.lanouvellerepublique.fr
ISSN: 0152-2590
Freq: Daily - quotidienne; **Cover Price:** EUR 0.80
Annual Sub.: EUR 246.15; **Circ:** 215,535
Usual Pagination: 140
Editor: Olivier Saint-Cricq
Profile: Local, regional and national news: covering politics, finance, art, entertainment, sports, leisure, practical information, and associative life. General news: Sports supplement on Monday - Motor Car supplement on Saturday (Free) - Leisure supplement on Friday.
Language(s): French
ADVERTISING RATES:
Full Page Mono .... EUR 8685
Full Page Colour .... EUR 12004
Mechanical Data: Type Area: Tabloid
REGIONAL DAILY & SUNDAY NEWSPAPERS: Regional Daily Newspapers

NUMERO

1623286F74A-804
Editorial: 53 avenue Victor Hugo, 75116 PARIS
Tel: 1 56 88 98 00 **Fax:** 1 56 88 98 32
Email: vham@groupe-ayache.com **Web site:** http://www.numero-magazine.com
ISSN: 1292-6213
Date Established: 1999; **Freq:** Monthly - Last Friday of the month
Annual Sub.: EUR 45; **Circ:** 85,000
Usual Pagination: 260
Language(s): English; French
ADVERTISING RATES:
Full Page Colour .... EUR 12950
Mechanical Data: Type Area: 30 x 23
Copy instructions: *Copy Date:* 21 days prior to publication date
CONSUMER: WOMEN'S INTEREST CONSUMER MAGAZINES: Women's Interest

L' OEIL

7088F84A-450
Editorial: 8 rue Borromée, 75015 PARIS
Tel: 1 48 42 90 00 **Fax:** 1 48 42 90 01
Email: contact@artclair.com **Web site:** http://www.artclair.com
ISSN: 0029-862X
Date Established: 1955; **Freq:** Monthly - dernier jeudi du mois; **Cover Price:** EUR 6.90
Annual Sub.: EUR 58; **Circ:** 30,000
Usual Pagination: 132
Profile: Magazine focusing on art.
Language(s): French
ADVERTISING RATES:
Full Page Colour .... EUR 4200
Mechanical Data: Type Area: 300 x 230
CONSUMER: THE ARTS & LITERARY: Arts

L' OFFICIEL

6435F74B-130
Editorial: 10 rue du Plâtre, 75004 PARIS
Tel: 1 53 01 10 30 **Fax:** 1 42 72 65 95
Email: v.bellugeon@editionsjalou.com **Web site:** http://www.jalougallery.com
ISSN: 0030-0403
Date Established: 1921; **Freq:** Monthly - the 20th of each month; **Cover Price:** EUR 4.50; **Circ:** 87,668
Usual Pagination: 200
Profile: Magazine containing information about Paris haute couture.
Language(s): French
Readership: Read by women with a high disposable income.
ADVERTISING RATES:
Full Page Mono .... EUR 13000
Full Page Colour .... EUR 14000
Mechanical Data: Type Area: A 3
Copy instructions: *Copy Date:* 10 days prior to publication date
CONSUMER: WOMEN'S INTEREST CONSUMER MAGAZINES: Women's Interest - Fashion

L' OFFICIEL DES TERRAINS DE CAMPINGS

5585F50-65
Editorial: 12 rue Rouget-de-Lisle, 92442 ISSY-LES-MOULINEAUX **Tel:** 1 41 33 47 22 **Fax:** 141334767
Web site: http://www.campingfrance.com
ISSN: 0987-321X
Date Established: 1972; **Freq:** Monthly - Début de mois sauf 07 08; **Cover Price:** EUR 7.90
Annual Sub.: EUR 68; **Circ:** 13,000
Profile: Professional review for camp site managers.
Language(s): French
ADVERTISING RATES:
Full Page Mono .... EUR 1390
Full Page Colour .... EUR 2290
Mechanical Data: Type Area: A 4
BUSINESS: TRAVEL & TOURISM

OKAPI

7273F91D-180
Editorial: 18 rue Barbès, CEDEX, 92128 MONTROUGE **Tel:** 1 74 31 60 60 **Fax:** 1 74 31 60 80
Email: francois.blaise@bayard-presse.com **Web site:** http://www.okapi.bayardpresse.fr
ISSN: 0751-6002
Date Established: 1971; **Freq:** 26 issues yearly - le 1er et le 15 du mois; **Cover Price:** EUR 5.20
Annual Sub.: EUR 89.80; **Circ:** 67,886
Usual Pagination: 52
Profile: Topical world news magazine.
Language(s): French
Readership: Aimed at young people between 11 and 15 years.
ADVERTISING RATES:
Full Page Mono .... EUR 4978
Full Page Colour .... EUR 7230
Mechanical Data: Type Area: 220 x 297
Copy instructions: *Copy Date:* 62 days prior to publication date
CONSUMER: RECREATION & LEISURE: Children & Youth

L' OPTIMUM

1618398F86C-255
Editorial: 10 rue du Plâtre, 75004 PARIS
Tel: 1 53 01 10 30 **Fax:** 1 53 01 10 35
Email: a.mantoux@editionsjalou.com **Web site:** http://www.jalougallery.com
ISSN: 1284-2079
Date Established: 1996; **Freq:** Monthly - Last Saturday of the month
Annual Sub.: EUR 18; **Circ:** 50,037
Usual Pagination: 164
Profile: Publication focussing on men's interest including reviews, interviews, politics, fashion, beauty, consumption, restaurants, bars, cars, watches, perfume, alcoholic drinks, wine and tourism.
Language(s): French
ADVERTISING RATES:
Full Page Mono .... EUR 10700
Full Page Colour .... EUR 12200
Mechanical Data: Type Area: 227 x 275
Copy instructions: *Copy Date:* 21 days prior to publication date
CONSUMER: ADULT & GAY MAGAZINES: Men's Lifestyle Magazines

L' OPTION FINANCE

4475F1A-250
Editorial: 91 bis rue Cherche-Midi, 75006 PARIS
Tel: 1 53 63 55 55 **Fax:** 1 53 63 55 50
Email: sylvie.alinc@optionfinance.fr
ISSN: 0989-1900
Date Established: 1988; **Freq:** Weekly - le lundi;
Cover Price: EUR 7.90
Annual Sub.: EUR 486; **Circ:** 20,000
Usual Pagination: 60
Profile: Magazine about all aspects of finance and economics.
Language(s): French
Readership: Aimed at professionals working in banks and financial institutions.
ADVERTISING RATES:
Full Page Mono .... EUR 9100
Full Page Colour .... EUR 11500
Mechanical Data: Type Area: 20,4 x 28
BUSINESS: FINANCE & ECONOMICS

L' ORDINATEUR INDIVIDUEL

4669F5C-90
Editorial: 12 rue d'Oradour S/Glane, CEDEX 15, 75504 PARIS **Tel:** 1 71 18 53 99 **Fax:** 1 71 18 52 60
Email: redaction@ordinateur-individuel.presse.fr **Web site:** http://www.01net.com
ISSN: 0183-570X
Date Established: 1978; **Freq:** Monthly - 3rd Thursday of the month; **Cover Price:** EUR 2.90; **Circ:** 127,410
Usual Pagination: 160
Managing Director: Marc Laufer
Profile: Magazine containing information about micro-computing.
Language(s): French
Readership: Read by retailers and users.
ADVERTISING RATES:
Full Page Colour .... EUR 11600
Copy instructions: *Copy Date:* 31 days prior to publication date
BUSINESS: COMPUTERS & AUTOMATION: Professional Personal Computers

OUEST FRANCE RENNES

6204F67B-6400
Editorial: 10 rue du Breil, ZI Sud Est, 35051 CEDEX 9 RENNES **Tel:** 2 99 32 60 00 **Fax:** 2 99 32 60 25
Email: redaction.multimedia@ouest-france.fr **Web site:** http://www.ouest-france.fr
ISSN: 0999-2138
Date Established: 1944; **Freq:** Daily - le matin;
Cover Price: EUR 0.80
Annual Sub.: EUR 213; **Circ:** 762,233
Usual Pagination: 44
Profile: Regional daily newspaper focussing on local and regional news and current affairs.
Language(s): French
ADVERTISING RATES:
Full Page Mono .... EUR 14740
Full Page Colour .... EUR 17688
Mechanical Data: Type Area: tabloïd
REGIONAL DAILY & SUNDAY NEWSPAPERS: Regional Daily Newspapers

OUI MAGAZINE

6558F74L-20
Editorial: 3 avenue de l'Opéra, 75001 PARIS
Tel: 1 55 35 06 71 **Fax:** 1 55 35 06 88
Email: redaction@ouimagazine.net **Web site:** http://www.ouimagazine.net
ISSN: 1259-0355
Date Established: 1995; **Freq:** Quarterly - 3ème semaine mois 02 05 08 11; **Cover Price:** EUR 5.50
Annual Sub.: EUR 20; **Circ:** 9,918
Usual Pagination: 216
Profile: Magazine dedicated to wedding preparations. Also discusses topics relevant to newlyweds.
Language(s): French
ADVERTISING RATES:
Full Page Mono .... EUR 4500
Full Page Colour .... EUR 5700
Mechanical Data: Type Area: 230 x 297
Copy instructions: *Copy Date:* 31 days prior to publication date
CONSUMER: WOMEN'S INTEREST CONSUMER MAGAZINES: Brides

PANORAMA DU MEDECIN

5734F56A-573
Editorial: 114 avenue Charles de Gaulle, CEDEX, 92522 NEUILLY SUR SEINE **Tel:** 1 55 62 68 00
Fax: 1 55 62 68 29
Email: cleborgne@gmsante.fr **Web site:** http://www.egora.fr
ISSN: 0299-3286
Freq: Weekly - chaque mardi; **Annual Sub.:** EUR 65; **Circ:** 40,000
Usual Pagination: 44
Profile: Magazine containing information of interest to doctors in general practice.
Language(s): French
ADVERTISING RATES:
Full Page Mono .... EUR 8000
Full Page Colour .... EUR 10500
Mechanical Data: Type Area: 230 x 297
BUSINESS: HEALTH & MEDICAL

PARENTS

6481F74D-100
Editorial: 10 rue Thierry Le Luron, CEDEX, 92592 LEVALLOIS PERRET **Tel:** 1 41 34 60 00
Fax: 1 41 34 70 79
Email: mag@parents.fr **Web site:** http://parents.fr
ISSN: 0833-1936
Date Established: 1969; **Freq:** Monthly - entre le 7 et le 10 du mois; **Cover Price:** EUR 2.20
Annual Sub.: EUR 19; **Circ:** 293,475
Usual Pagination: 130
Profile: Childcare magazine, including paediatric and psychological information, also items on beauty, fashion, cookery and leisure.
Language(s): French
Readership: Read by parents of children up to 15 years.
ADVERTISING RATES:
Full Page Mono .... EUR 23600
Full Page Colour .... EUR 29500
Mechanical Data: Type Area: A 4
Copy instructions: *Copy Date:* 28 days prior to publication date
CONSUMER: WOMEN'S INTEREST CONSUMER MAGAZINES: Child Care

LES PARENTS & ENFANTS SUPPLEMENT HEBDOMADAIRE DU JOURNAL LA CROIX

1618018F74C-631
Editorial: 18 rue Barbès, 92128 CEDEX MONTROUGE **Tel:** 1 74 31 60 60 **Fax:** 1 74 31 60 01
Web site: http://www.la-croix.com/parents-enfants
ISSN: 2125-2009
Date Established: 1995; **Freq:** Weekly - mercredi de la semaine suivante; **Circ:** 177,944
Usual Pagination: 4
Editor: Georges Sanerot
Profile: Supplement part of the Christian publication La Croix focussing on parenting issues.
Language(s): French
ADVERTISING RATES:
Full Page Mono .... EUR 20200
Full Page Colour .... EUR 25500
Mechanical Data: Type Area: 40 x 28
CONSUMER: WOMEN'S INTEREST CONSUMER MAGAZINES: Home & Family

PARIS CAPITALE

6994F80-560
Editorial: BUZZ, 13-15 rue Lamennais, 75008 PARIS
Tel: 1 44 20 08 90 **Fax:** 1 53 96 00 13
Email: redaction@pariscapitale.com **Web site:** http://www.pariscapitale.com
Date Established: 1989; **Freq:** Monthly - le 6-8 du mois
Annual Sub.: EUR 26; **Circ:** 65,000
Usual Pagination: 200
Managing Director: David Slama
Profile: Magazine for and about Paris.
Language(s): French
Readership: Read by residents and visitors to Paris.
ADVERTISING RATES:
Full Page Colour .... EUR 13000
Mechanical Data: Type Area: 210 X 275
Copy instructions: *Copy Date:* 20 days prior to publication date
CONSUMER: RURAL & REGIONAL INTEREST

PARIS MATCH

6381F73-190
Editorial: 149 rue Anatole France, CEDEX, 92534 LEVALLOIS PERRET **Tel:** 1 41 34 60 00
Fax: 1 41 34 71 23
Email: fanny.payet@lagardere-active.com **Web site:** http://www.parismatch.com
ISSN: 0397-1635
Date Established: 1949; **Freq:** Weekly - mercredi;
Cover Price: EUR 2.30
Annual Sub.: EUR 99; **Circ:** 688,359
Usual Pagination: 134
Publisher: Franck Espiasse-Cabau
Profile: Magazine focusing on celebrities, lifestyle, and general news. Also publish regional French editions and international editions.
Language(s): French
ADVERTISING RATES:
Full Page Colour .... EUR 33600
Mechanical Data: Type Area: 23 x 29,7
Copy instructions: *Copy Date:* 10 days prior to publication date
CONSUMER: NATIONAL & INTERNATIONAL PERIODICALS

PARIS NORMANDIE ROUEN
6206F67B-6500
Editorial: 78 rue Jeanne d'Arc, 76000 ROUEN
Tel: 2 35 14 56 56 **Fax:** 2 32 08 47 96
Email: redaction.rouen@presse-normande.com **Web site:** http://www.paris-normandie.fr
ISSN: 0999-2154
Freq: Daily - toute la semaine même dimanche; **Cover Price:** EUR 0.90
Annual Sub.: EUR 269; **Circ:** 61,425
Usual Pagination: 38
Editor-in-Chief: Sophie Bloch; **Publisher:** Michel Lepinay
Profile: This regional daily newspaper covers news and current affairs including beauty, leisure, cookery, culture, cinema, books, fashion, sport, economics, TV guide and w omen's interests.
Language(s): French
REGIONAL DAILY & SUNDAY NEWSPAPERS: Regional Daily Newspapers

PARISCOPE
7208F89C-168
Editorial: 10 rue Thierry Le Luron, CEDEX, 92592 LEVALLOIS PERRET **Tel:** 1 41 34 73 47
Fax: 1 41 34 73 26
Email: nathalie.pejicic@lagardere-active.com
ISSN: 1287-0633
Date Established: 1968; **Freq:** Weekly; **Cover Price:** EUR 0.40
Annual Sub.: EUR 65; **Circ:** 65,434
Usual Pagination: 250
Profile: City and entertainment guide for Paris with listings for theatres, restaurants, clubs, bars, art galleries, museums, concerts and tourist attractions.
Language(s): French
ADVERTISING RATES:
Full Page Mono .... EUR 3960
Mechanical Data: Type Area: 215 x 130
CONSUMER: HOLIDAYS & TRAVEL: Entertainment Guides

LE PARISIEN - AUJOURD'HUI EN FRANCE
6096F65A-120
Editorial: 25 avenue Michelet, CEDEX, 93408 SAINT OUEN **Tel:** 1 40 10 30 30 **Fax:** 1 40 10 35 17
Email: jlallain@leparisien.presse.fr **Web site:** http://www.leparisien.fr
Freq: Daily - France; **Cover Price:** EUR 0.80
Annual Sub.: EUR 249.60; **Circ:** 499,269
Usual Pagination: 30
Editor-in-Chief: Stéphane Albouy
Profile: Newspaper providing articles of general interest, topical news, politics, culture, art, sport, events and television listings.
Language(s): French
Readership: Read predominantly in the Ile-de-France region.
Mechanical Data: Type Area: Tabloid
NATIONAL DAILY & SUNDAY NEWSPAPERS: National Daily Newspapers

LE PARISIEN - AUJOURD'HUI EN FRANCE ECONOMIE SUPPLEMENT DU QUOTIDIEN LE PARISIEN
1696183F1A-461
Editorial: 25 avenue Michelet, 93408 SAINT-OUEN
Tel: 1 40 10 30 30 **Fax:** 1 40 10 30 51
Web site: http://www.leparisien.fr
Date Established: 2005; **Freq:** Weekly - lundi
Usual Pagination: 35
Profile: Business publication, supplement of the newspapers Le Parisien and Aujourd'hui en France focussing on economics and business.
Language(s): French
ADVERTISING RATES:
Full Page Colour .... EUR 76700
Mechanical Data: Type Area: Tabloid
BUSINESS: FINANCE & ECONOMICS

LE PARISIEN - PARIS
1619570F67B-8570
Editorial: 25 avenue Michelet, 93408 CEDEX SAINT-OUEN **Tel:** 1 40 10 30 30 **Fax:** 1 40 10 34 28
Email: transports@leparisien.presse.fr **Web site:** http://www.leparisien.fr
ISSN: 0767-3558
Date Established: 1944; **Freq:** Daily - du lundi au dimanche
Annual Sub.: EUR 299; **Circ:** 311,483
Usual Pagination: 48
Editor: Marie-Odile Amaury; **Managing Director:** Jean Hornain
Profile: First regional newspaper for the Parisian region and the Oise area with 10 editions covering general and local news including topics such as sports, economy, social, society, politics, arts, entertainment, culture, banks, finance, Europe, foreign policy and current affairs.
Language(s): French
ADVERTISING RATES:
Full Page Mono .... EUR 39900
Full Page Colour .... EUR 55700
Mechanical Data: Type Area: tabloid
REGIONAL DAILY & SUNDAY NEWSPAPERS: Regional Daily Newspapers

LE PARTICULIER
6567F74M-60
Editorial: 14 boulevard Haussmann, 75009 PARIS
Tel: 1 57 08 58 00 **Fax:** 1 57 08 73 88
Email: plepetit@leparticulier.fr **Web site:** http://www.leparticulier.fr
ISSN: 1167-6078
Date Established: 1949; **Freq:** Monthly - fin de mois; **Cover Price:** EUR 3.90
Annual Sub.: EUR 58; **Circ:** 461,766
Usual Pagination: 98
Managing Director: Jean-Guillaume D' Ornano
Profile: Publication containing information about financial matters.
Language(s): French
ADVERTISING RATES:
Full Page Colour .... EUR 30000
Mechanical Data: Type Area: 172 X 250
CONSUMER: WOMEN'S INTEREST CONSUMER MAGAZINES: Personal Finance

PAS DE CALAIS, LE JOURNAL
1617193F32A-1052
Editorial: Conseil Général - Hôtel département, Direction de la communication, Rue Ferdinand Buisson CEDEX 9, 62018 ARRAS **Tel:** 3 21 21 91 01
Fax: 3 21 21 62 96
Email: pasdecalais.lejournal@cg62.fr **Web site:** http://www.pasdecalais.fr
ISSN: 0989-5167
Date Established: 1985; **Freq:** Quarterly - 03 06 09 12; **Cover Price:** Free; **Circ:** 639,000
Usual Pagination: 24
Profile: Publication focussing on local government and department issues.
Language(s): French
Mechanical Data: Type Area: A 4
BUSINESS: LOCAL GOVERNMENT, LEISURE & RECREATION: Local Government

PAYS BASQUE MAGAZINE
7935F80-796
Editorial: 300 rue Léon-Joulin, CEDEX 9, 31101 TOULOUSE **Tel:** 5 61 76 65 31 **Fax:** 561766304
Email: paysbasque@milan.fr **Web site:** http://www.paysbasquemagazine.com
ISSN: 1268-3884
Date Established: 1996; **Freq:** Quarterly - 03 06 09 12; **Cover Price:** EUR 6.50
Annual Sub.: EUR 29; **Circ:** 18,221
Usual Pagination: 100
Language(s): French
ADVERTISING RATES:
Full Page Colour .... EUR 2500
Copy instructions: *Copy Date:* 62 days prior to publication date
CONSUMER: RURAL & REGIONAL INTEREST

PAYS COMTOIS
7181F89A-171
Editorial: 18 rue de Thann, CEDEX 9, 68945 MULHOUSE
Email: redaction@pays-comtois.fr
ISSN: 1266-1341
Date Established: 1995; **Freq:** 24 issues yearly - autour du 20 des mois impairs; **Cover Price:** EUR 6.50
Annual Sub.: EUR 34; **Circ:** 25,000
Usual Pagination: 100
Profile: Magazine focusing on the Franche-Comté region.
Language(s): French
Readership: Magazine for tourists and visitors to the Franche-Comté region.
ADVERTISING RATES:
Full Page Colour .... EUR 2500
Mechanical Data: Type Area: 210 x 287
Copy instructions: *Copy Date:* 31 days prior to publication date
CONSUMER: HOLIDAYS & TRAVEL: Travel

PAYS DU NORD
7183F89A-180
Editorial: 229 rue Solférino, CEDEX, 59000 LILLE
Tel: 3 20 15 99 41 **Fax:** 3 20 42 00 13
Email: redac@pays-du-nord.fr **Web site:** http://www.pays-du-nord.fr
ISSN: 1263-8730
Date Established: 1994; **Freq:** 24 issues yearly - 1ère semaine d01/03/05/07/09/11
Annual Sub.: EUR 35; **Circ:** 20,225
Usual Pagination: 100
Profile: Magazine containing information on holidays and travel in Northern France. Covers tourism, nature, environment, gastronomy, architecture, literature, history and local traditions.
Language(s): French
ADVERTISING RATES:
Full Page Colour .... EUR 3950
Mechanical Data: Type Area: 210 x 287
Copy instructions: *Copy Date:* 21 days prior to publication date
CONSUMER: HOLIDAYS & TRAVEL: Travel

PAYSAN BRETON
5148F21J-920
Editorial: 18 rue de la Croix, BP 224, CEDEX, 22192 PLERIN **Tel:** 2 96 74 40 40 **Fax:** 2 96 74 59 02
Email: paysan-breton@paysan-breton.fr **Web site:** http://www.paysan-breton.fr
ISSN: 1145-6639
Date Established: 1945; **Freq:** Weekly - vendredi;
Annual Sub.: EUR 38; **Circ:** 52,872
Usual Pagination: 28
Profile: Regional agricultural magazine for Brittany.
Language(s): French
ADVERTISING RATES:
Full Page Mono .... EUR 6786
Full Page Colour .... EUR 10179
Mechanical Data: Type Area: 410 x 289
BUSINESS: AGRICULTURE & FARMING: Agriculture & Farming - Regional

PC ACHAT
4687F5D-78
Editorial: 101/109 rue Jean Jaurès, 92300 LEVALLOIS PERRET **Tel:** 1 41 27 38 38
Fax: 1 41 27 38 39
Email: jean.loi@yellowmedia.fr **Web site:** http://pcachat.fr
ISSN: 1278-6101
Freq: Monthly - fin du mois
Annual Sub.: EUR 27; **Circ:** 27,605
Usual Pagination: 300
Profile: Magazine guide to buying a PC.
Language(s): French
ADVERTISING RATES:
Full Page Colour .... EUR 5300
Mechanical Data: Type Area: 210 x 285
Copy instructions: *Copy Date:* 21 days prior to publication date
BUSINESS: COMPUTERS & AUTOMATION: Personal Computers

PC JEUX
6911F78D-148
Editorial: 101/109 rue Jean Jaurès, 92300 LEVALLOIS PERRET **Tel:** 1 41 27 38 38
Fax: 1 41 27 38 39
Email: jean-pierre.abidal@yellowmedia.fr **Web site:** http://www.jvn.com
ISSN: 1284-8611
Date Established: 1997; **Freq:** Monthly - toutes les 4 semaines; **Cover Price:** EUR 6.50
Annual Sub.: EUR 67.60; **Circ:** 31,846
Usual Pagination: 160
Profile: Magazine focusing on PC games.
Language(s): French
Readership: Read by computer games enthusiasts.
ADVERTISING RATES:
Full Page Colour .... EUR 4700
Mechanical Data: Type Area: 30 x 22
Copy instructions: *Copy Date:* 28 days prior to publication date
CONSUMER: CONSUMER ELECTRONICS: Games

PEI - PRODUITS EQUIPEMENTS INDUSTRIELS
4855F14B-160
Editorial: 15/17 rue de Vanves, 92100 BOULOGNE BILLANCOURT **Tel:** 1 41 31 74 50 **Fax:** 1 57 67 12 41
Email: info@pei-france.com **Web site:** http://www.pei-france.com
ISSN: 0999-4297
Date Established: 1989; **Freq:** Monthly - 2ème quinzaine du mois; **Annual Sub.:** EUR 77; **Circ:** 34,753
Usual Pagination: 32
Publisher: Daniel Cardon
Profile: Technical magazine concerning industrial equipment. Includes information on new products and materials.
Language(s): French
Readership: Aimed at producers and people involved in selling industrial technical equipment.
ADVERTISING RATES:
Full Page Mono .... EUR 9495
Full Page Colour .... EUR 11165
Mechanical Data: Type Area: tabloïd
BUSINESS: COMMERCE, INDUSTRY & MANAGEMENT: Industry & Factories

PELERIN
6382F87-255
Editorial: 18 rue Barbès, CEDEX, 92128 MONTROUGE **Tel:** 1 74 31 60 60
Web site: http://www.pelerin.info
ISSN: 0764-4663
Date Established: 1873; **Freq:** Weekly - jeudi; **Cover Price:** EUR 2.50
Annual Sub.: EUR 130; **Circ:** 247,413
Usual Pagination: 92
Profile: General interest magazine, includes religion.
Language(s): French
ADVERTISING RATES:
Full Page Mono .... EUR 8640
Full Page Colour .... EUR 9600
Mechanical Data: Type Area: 205 x 272
CONSUMER: RELIGIOUS

PERSPECTIVES AGRICOLES
5015F21A-1615
Editorial: 23/25 avenue de Neuilly, 75116 PARIS
Tel: 1 44 31 10 20 00 **Fax:** 1 47 20 10 59
Email: e.fabre@arvalisinstitutduvegetal.fr **Web site:** http://www.perspectives-agricoles.com
ISSN: 0399-8533
Date Established: 1977; **Freq:** Monthly - 1ère semaine du mois; **Cover Price:** EUR 8.50
Annual Sub.: EUR 64; **Circ:** 12,000
Usual Pagination: 80
Profile: Technical journal concerning agriculture. Emphasis on cereal production and agricultural products.
Language(s): French
Readership: Aimed at farmers and agricultural technicians.
ADVERTISING RATES:
Full Page Mono .... EUR 1800
Full Page Colour .... EUR 3000
Mechanical Data: Type Area: 210 x 297
BUSINESS: AGRICULTURE & FARMING

LE PETIT BU DU LOT ET GARONNE
6154F67B-6700
Editorial: 113/115 Boulevard Carnot, BP 162, CEDEX, 47005 AGEN **Tel:** 5 53 77 06 70
Fax: 5 53 48 03 42
Email: redaction@petit-bleu.fr
ISSN: 0759-609X
Freq: Daily - Lot-et-Garonne (47); **Cover Price:** EUR 0.80; **Circ:** 9,790
Usual Pagination: 32
Profile: Regional and local news. International and national pages.
Language(s): French
Mechanical Data: Type Area: berlinois
REGIONAL DAILY & SUNDAY NEWSPAPERS: Regional Daily Newspapers

LES PHARMACEUTIQUES
5380F37-130
Editorial: 91 rue Jean Jaurès, CEDEX, 92807 PUTEAUX **Tel:** 1 43 34 73 00 **Fax:** 1 43 34 73 24
Email: redaction@pharmaceutiques.com **Web site:** http://www.pharmaceutiques.com
ISSN: 1240-0866
Date Established: 1992; **Freq:** Monthly - première semaine du mois suivant; **Cover Price:** EUR 14.50
Annual Sub.: EUR 127; **Circ:** 6,000
Usual Pagination: 100
Editor-in-Chief: Jean-Jacques Cristofari
Profile: International magazine containing information about the pharmaceutical industry.
Language(s): French
Readership: Read by management of pharmaceutical companies and healthcare decision makers.
ADVERTISING RATES:
Full Page Colour .... EUR 2500
Mechanical Data: Type Area: A4
BUSINESS: PHARMACEUTICAL & CHEMISTS

LE PHARMACIEN DE FRANCE
5385F37-200
Editorial: 13 rue Ballu, CEDEX 09, 75311 PARIS
Tel: 1 42 81 15 96 **Fax:** 1 42 81 96 61
Email: lsimon@lepharmacien.fr
ISSN: 0031-6938
Date Established: 1930; **Freq:** Monthly - le 30 du mois; **Cover Price:** EUR 12
Annual Sub.: EUR 90; **Circ:** 12,565
Usual Pagination: 64
Profile: Journal of the Federation of Pharmacists of France. General and scientific information.
Language(s): French
ADVERTISING RATES:
Full Page Mono .... EUR 3100
Full Page Colour .... EUR 4700
Mechanical Data: Type Area: 230 x 297
Copy instructions: *Copy Date:* 9 days prior to publication date
BUSINESS: PHARMACEUTICAL & CHEMISTS

LE PHARMACIEN HOSPITALIER
5384F37-190
Editorial: 62 rue Camille Desmoulins, CEDEX, 92442 ISSY LES MOULINEAUX **Tel:** 1 71 16 55 00
Fax: 1 71 16 51 99
Email: b.edouard@ccml.fr **Web site:** http://www.lepharmacienhospitalier.fr
ISSN: 0768-9179
Date Established: 1966; **Freq:** Quarterly - 30th of the month; **Annual Sub.:** EUR 127; **Circ:** 1,100
Usual Pagination: 60
Editor-in-Chief: Bruno Edouard
Profile: Magazine containing details of recent developments in the pharmaceutical industry.
Language(s): French
Readership: Read by private and hospital pharmacists.
ADVERTISING RATES:
Full Page Mono .... EUR 3500
Full Page Colour .... EUR 5800
Mechanical Data: Type Area: A 4
BUSINESS: PHARMACEUTICAL & CHEMISTS

PHOTO
7109F85A-65
Editorial: 149 rue Anatole France, CEDEX, 92534 LEVALLOIS PERRET **Tel:** 1 41 34 73 27 60 00
Email: photo@hfp.fr **Web site:** http://www.photo.fr
ISSN: 0399-8568
Date Established: 1967; **Freq:** Monthly - début de mois
Annual Sub.: EUR 40.50; **Circ:** 35,619
Usual Pagination: 100
Profile: Magazine containing information about photography, includes new techniques, exhibitions and festivals.
Language(s): French
ADVERTISING RATES:
Full Page Colour .... EUR 7800
Mechanical Data: Type Area: 300 x 230
Copy instructions: *Copy Date:* 31 days prior to publication date
CONSUMER: PHOTOGRAPHY & FILM MAKING: Photography

PICSOU MAGAZINE
754748F91D-185
Editorial: 10 rue Thierry Le Luron, CEDEX, 92592 LEVALLOIS PERRET **Tel:** 1 41 34 85 00
Fax: 1 41 34 88 61
Email: pascal.pierrey@lagardere-active.com

Date Established: 1972; **Freq:** Monthly - 1er mercredi du mois; **Cover Price:** EUR 3.50
Annual Sub.: EUR 42; **Circ:** 121,201
Usual Pagination: 140
Profile: Magazine featuring the cartoon world of Donald Duck.
Language(s): French
Readership: Read by children of all ages.
ADVERTISING RATES:
Full Page Colour .... EUR 9200
Mechanical Data: Type Area: 278 x 195
Copy instructions: *Copy Date:* 31 days prior to publication date
CONSUMER: RECREATION & LEISURE: Children & Youth

LA PLEINE VIE 6575F74N-60

Editorial: Editions Taitbout - Pleine Vie, 8 rue François Ory, CEDEX, 92543 MONTROUGE
Tel: 1 41 33 50 01 **Fax:** 1 41 33 10 67
Email: jeanne.thiriet@mondadori.fr **Web site:** http://www.pleinevie.fr
ISSN: 0753-2164
Date Established: 1981; **Freq:** Monthly - entre le 10 et le 15 du mois
Annual Sub.: EUR 36; **Circ:** 898,443
Usual Pagination: 204
Managing Director: Ernesto Mauri
Profile: Magazine for the active retired, giving social, financial and legal information.
Language(s): French
ADVERTISING RATES:
Full Page Mono .... EUR 25020
Full Page Colour .... EUR 27800
Mechanical Data: Type Area: 207 X 273
Copy instructions: *Copy Date:* 35 days prior to publication date
CONSUMER: WOMEN'S INTEREST CONSUMER MAGAZINES: Retirement

PLUS LE MAGAZINE DES ABONNES DE CANAL+ 6740F76C-33

Editorial: 35 rue du Pont, 92200 NEUILLY-SUR-SEINE **Tel:** 1 47 47 13 03
ISSN: 1624-690X
Date Established: 1984; **Freq:** Monthly - tous les mois sauf août; **Cover Price:** Free; **Circ:** 4,000,000
Usual Pagination: 44
Editor: Rodolphe Belmer
Profile: Magazine providing information on forthcoming programmes on Canal Plus. Also includes features on actors and celebrities.
Language(s): French
ADVERTISING RATES:
Full Page Colour .... EUR 75500
Mechanical Data: Type Area: 250 x 200
CONSUMER: MUSIC & PERFORMING ARTS: TV & Radio

LE POINT 6383F73-200

Editorial: 74 avenue du Maine, CEDEX 14, 75682 PARIS **Tel:** 1 44 10 10 10 **Fax:** 1 43 21 43 24
Email: courrier@lepoint.fr **Web site:** http://www.lepoint.fr
ISSN: 0242-6005
Date Established: 1972; **Freq:** Weekly - jeudi; **Cover Price:** EUR 3.50
Annual Sub.: EUR 129; **Circ:** 429,521
Usual Pagination: 130
Profile: Publication including economic, business, financial and political news. Also publish a weekly international edition under the same title.
Language(s): French
ADVERTISING RATES:
Full Page Colour .... EUR 22250
Mechanical Data: Type Area: 28,6 x 20
CONSUMER: NATIONAL & INTERNATIONAL PERIODICALS

LE POINT DE VUE 6384F73-220

Editorial: 23 rue de Châteaudun, CEDEX 09, 75308 PARIS **Tel:** 1 75 55 17 00 **Fax:** 1 75 55 10 22
Email: sloison@pointdevue.fr **Web site:** http://www.pointdevue.fr
ISSN: 0750-0475
Date Established: 1945; **Freq:** Weekly - mercredi; **Cover Price:** EUR 2.20
Annual Sub.: EUR 85; **Circ:** 259,121
Usual Pagination: 90
Profile: Magazine covering international current affairs, debates, opinions and politics.
Language(s): French
ADVERTISING RATES:
Full Page Mono .... EUR 9900
Full Page Colour .... EUR 13300
Mechanical Data: Type Area: 230 x 287
CONSUMER: NATIONAL & INTERNATIONAL PERIODICALS

POINTS DE VENTE 4565F2F-35

Editorial: 90 avenue des Ternes, 75017 PARIS
Tel: 1 55 37 24 10
Email: cdevars@pointsdevente.fr **Web site:** http://www.pointsdevente.fr
ISSN: 0150-1844
Date Established: 1962; **Freq:** 26 issues yearly - 1 lundi sur 2; **Cover Price:** EUR 7.50
Annual Sub.: EUR 190; **Circ:** 11,191
Usual Pagination: 100
Profile: Journal for professionals in the distribution and mass marketing fields.
Language(s): French
ADVERTISING RATES:
Full Page Colour .... EUR 7700
Mechanical Data: Type Area: A 4
Copy instructions: *Copy Date:* 15 days prior to publication date
BUSINESS: COMMUNICATIONS, ADVERTISING & MARKETING: Selling

LA POLLUTION ATMOSPHERIQUE 5909F57-40

Editorial: 10 rue Pierre Brossolette, 94270 LE KREMLIN BICETRE **Tel:** 1 42 11 15 00
Fax: 1 42 11 15 01
Email: revuepa@appa.asso.fr
ISSN: 0032-3632
Date Established: 1963; **Freq:** Quarterly - les mois 03 06 09 12; **Cover Price:** EUR 41
Annual Sub.: EUR 160; **Circ:** 2,000
Usual Pagination: 150
Profile: International technical and scientific review focusing on air pollution.
Language(s): French
Readership: Aimed at manufacturers and users of equipment for measuring pollution, also officials in central and local authorities, health agencies and managers of industrial companies.
ADVERTISING RATES:
Full Page Mono .... EUR 1046
Full Page Colour .... EUR 1848
Mechanical Data: Type Area: 21 x 29,7
BUSINESS: ENVIRONMENT & POLLUTION

LE POPULAIRE DU CENTRE: EDITION HAUTE-VIENNE 6180F67B-6800

Editorial: 15 rue du Général-Catroux, BP 541, 87011 CEDEX 1 LIMOGES **Tel:** 5 55 58 59 60
Fax: 5 55 58 59 77
Email: lepopulaire.bellac@centrefrance.com **Web site:** http://www.lepopulaire.fr
Date Established: 1905; **Freq:** Daily - tous les matins; **Cover Price:** EUR 0.90
Annual Sub.: EUR 251; **Circ:** 42,858
Usual Pagination: 56
Editor: Alain Védrine
Profile: International, national, regional and local news. 3 issues: Haute-Vienne, Corrèze and Creuse. 2 supplements: sport (Monday), leisure (Friday). 1 "Pays d'Ouest" supplement every Wednesday covering Saint-Junien and Rochechouart regions.
Language(s): French
ADVERTISING RATES:
Full Page Mono .... EUR 4370
Mechanical Data: Type Area: 40 x 27
REGIONAL DAILY & SUNDAY NEWSPAPERS: Regional Daily Newspapers

POSITIF 6730F76A-240

Editorial: 38 rue Milton, 75009 PARIS
Tel: 1 43 26 17 80 **Fax:** 1 43 26 29 77
Email: posed@wanadoo.fr **Web site:** http://www.revue-positif.net
ISSN: 0048-4911
Date Established: 1952; **Freq:** Monthly - 1ère semaine du mois
Annual Sub.: EUR 60.98; **Circ:** 25,000
Usual Pagination: 104
Editor: Michel Ciment
Profile: Magazine about the cinema.
Language(s): French
ADVERTISING RATES:
Full Page Mono .... EUR 2500
Full Page Colour .... EUR 3220
Mechanical Data: Type Area: 210 x 297
CONSUMER: MUSIC & PERFORMING ARTS: Cinema

PREFMAG 1640595F86B-817

Editorial: 64 rue Anatole France, 92300 LEVALLOIS PERRET **Tel:** 1 40 87 10 70
Email: info@preferencesmag.com **Web site:** http://www.prefmag.com
ISSN: 1766-5752
Date Established: 2004; **Freq:** 24 issues yearly - The last Thursday of even months
Annual Sub.: EUR 25; **Circ:** 80,000
Usual Pagination: 176
Profile: Publication focussing on men's interest including gay interest, news, society, economics, tourism, lifestyle, culture, fashion, new technologies, urban lifestyle, decoration and beauty.
Language(s): French
ADVERTISING RATES:
Full Page Colour .... EUR 7000
Mechanical Data: Type Area: 23 x 30
Copy instructions: *Copy Date:* 20 days prior to publication date
CONSUMER: ADULT & GAY MAGAZINES: Gay & Lesbian Magazines

PRESENCES 6033F14A-826

Editorial: CCI, 1 Place André Malraux, BP 297 CEDEX 1, 38016 GRENOBLE **Tel:** 4 76 28 28 76
Fax: 4 76 28 28 60
Email: presences@grenoble.cci.fr **Web site:** http://www.presences-grenoble.fr
ISSN: 0981-1869
Date Established: 1989; **Freq:** Monthly - début de mois; **Cover Price:** EUR 380
Annual Sub.: EUR 35; **Circ:** 34,000
Usual Pagination: 64
Profile: Publication of the Grenoble Chamber of Commerce and Industry.
Language(s): French
Mechanical Data: Type Area: A4
BUSINESS: COMMERCE, INDUSTRY & MANAGEMENT

LA PRESSE DE MANCHE 1619721F67B-8719

Editorial: 9 rue Gambetta, BP 408, CEDEX, 50104 CHERBOURG **Tel:** 2 33 97 16 16 **Fax:** 2 33 97 16 18
Email: redaction.locale@lapressedelamanche.fr
Freq: Daily - Monday to Sunday; **Cover Price:** EUR 0.70
Annual Sub.: EUR 224; **Circ:** 25,574
Usual Pagination: 28
Profile: General and local news.
Language(s): French
ADVERTISING RATES:
Full Page Mono .... EUR 6640
Full Page Colour .... EUR 10624
Mechanical Data: Type Area: 365 x 560
REGIONAL DAILY & SUNDAY NEWSPAPERS: Regional Daily Newspapers

PRESSE OCEAN NANTES 6197F67B-6900

Editorial: 8-12 rue Santeuil, 44024 CEDEX 1 NANTES
Tel: 2 40 44 24 00 **Fax:** 2 40 44 24 40
Email: redac.locale.nantes@presse-ocean.com **Web site:** http://www.presseocean.fr
ISSN: 1144-3596
Freq: Daily - matin; **Cover Price:** EUR 0.73
Annual Sub.: EUR 222.58; **Circ:** 45,204
Usual Pagination: 32
Profile: Regional daily newspaper focussing on news and current affairs including TV guide.
Language(s): French
Mechanical Data: Type Area: tabloïd
REGIONAL DAILY & SUNDAY NEWSPAPERS: Regional Daily Newspapers

PREVENTION BTP 1617693F4E-471

Editorial: OPPBTP, 25 avenue du Général Leclerc, CEDEX, 92660 BOULOGNE BILLANCOURT
Tel: 1 46 09 26 54 **Fax:** 1 46 09 26 52
Email: gerard.larpent@oppbtp.fr **Web site:** http://www.oppbtp.fr
ISSN: 1287-7778
Date Established: 1998; **Freq:** Monthly - 1ère semaine du mois; **Cover Price:** EUR 6.80
Annual Sub.: EUR 42; **Circ:** 20,975
Usual Pagination: 68
Editor-in-Chief: Guillaume Mangeas
Profile: Magazine focussing on safety issues in the construction sector.
Language(s): French
ADVERTISING RATES:
Full Page Mono .... EUR 2280
Full Page Colour .... EUR 3595
Mechanical Data: Type Area: A 4
Copy instructions: *Copy Date:* 15 days prior to publication date
BUSINESS: ARCHITECTURE & BUILDING: Building

PRIMA 6419F74A-300

Editorial: 13 rue Henri Barbusse, 92624 GENNEVILLIERS **Tel:** 1 73 05 67 01
Fax: 1 44 90 67 21
Email: lperez@prisma-presse.com **Web site:** http://www.prima.fr
ISSN: 0293-2407
Date Established: 1982; **Freq:** Monthly - début du mois précédent; **Cover Price:** EUR 2.10
Annual Sub.: EUR 20; **Circ:** 497,064
Usual Pagination: 200
Managing Director: Pierre Riandet; **Publisher:** Loïc Guilloux
Profile: Magazine for practically-minded women with features on crafts, cookery, fashion, beauty, homecare and decorating.
Language(s): French
ADVERTISING RATES:
Full Page Colour .... EUR 23800
Mechanical Data: Type Area: A 4
Copy instructions: *Copy Date:* 31 days prior to publication date
CONSUMER: WOMEN'S INTEREST CONSUMER MAGAZINES: Women's Interest

PRIONS EN EGLISE 7146F87-169

Editorial: 18 rue Barbès, 92128 CEDEX MONTROUGE **Tel:** 1 74 31 60 60
Email: prions.eneglise@bayard-presse.com **Web site:** http://www.prionseneglise.fr
ISSN: 0383-8285
Date Established: 1987; **Freq:** Monthly - début de mois
Annual Sub.: EUR 32; **Circ:** 480,000
Usual Pagination: 260
Editor: Georges Sanerot
Profile: Magazine concerning the Catholic religion and the Catholic mass.
Language(s): French
Readership: Aimed at catholics and those interested in the Catholic religion.
Mechanical Data: Type Area: 12 x 13
CONSUMER: RELIGIOUS

PROCESS ALIMENTAIRE 5195F22C-40

Editorial: 13 square du Chêne Germain, CS 77711, CEDEX, 35577 CESSON-SEVIGNE **Tel:** 2 99 32 21 21
Fax: 2 99 32 14 17 89 20
Email: fmorel@editionsduboisbaudry.fr **Web site:** http://www.processalimentaire.com
ISSN: 0998-6650
Freq: Monthly - 15th of the month; **Cover Price:** EUR 17
Annual Sub.: EUR 115; **Circ:** 7,966
Usual Pagination: 100
Editor-in-Chief: François Morel
Profile: Magazine containing information on technology, manufacturing processes, equipment and supplies for the food and dairy industry.
Language(s): French
ADVERTISING RATES:
Full Page Mono .... EUR 2500
Full Page Colour .... EUR 3300
Mechanical Data: Type Area: 220 x 295
Copy instructions: *Copy Date:* 31 days prior to publication date
BUSINESS: FOOD: Food Processing & Packaging

PRODUITS DE LA MER 5201F22G-200

Editorial: ZI Rennes Chantepie, 13 rue du Breil, CS 46305 CEDEX, 35063 RENNES **Tel:** 2 99 32 58 80 44
Fax: 2 99 32 58 88
Email: redaction@infomer.fr **Web site:** http://www.infomer.fr
ISSN: 1150-7680
Date Established: 1990; **Freq:** 24 issues yearly - 5-10 des mois pairs
Annual Sub.: EUR 91; **Circ:** 8,000
Usual Pagination: 120
Profile: Review focussing on the processing, marketing and distribution of fish and other sea food.
Language(s): French
ADVERTISING RATES:
Full Page Mono .... EUR 2450
Full Page Colour .... EUR 3440
Mechanical Data: Type Area: 210 x 297
BUSINESS: FOOD: Fish Trade

LE PROGRES EDITION LYON-VILLEURBANNE-CALUIRE 6184F67B-7000

Editorial: 4 rue Paul-Montrochet, 69002 LYON
Tel: 4 72 22 23 23 **Fax:** 4 78 14 77 10
Email: economie@leprogres.fr **Web site:** http://www.leprogres.fr
Freq: Daily; **Cover Price:** EUR 0.90
Annual Sub.: EUR 249; **Circ:** 222,570
Managing Director: Pierre Fanneau
Profile: Daily regional newspaper. Main editorial office based in Lyon and head office based in Chassieu. Weekly subscription + Sunday: 327 €.
Language(s): French
ADVERTISING RATES:
Full Page Mono .... EUR 21812
Full Page Colour .... EUR 24110
REGIONAL DAILY & SUNDAY NEWSPAPERS: Regional Daily Newspapers

LA PROVENCE 6190F67B-7100

Editorial: 248 avenue Roger Salengro, CEDEX 20, 13902 MARSEILLE **Tel:** 4 91 84 45 45
Fax: 4 91 84 49 95
Email: jmamiel@laprovence-presse.fr **Web site:** http://www.laprovence.com
ISSN: 1280-9810
Freq: Daily - tous les jours; **Cover Price:** EUR 0.90
Annual Sub.: EUR 299; **Circ:** 146,772
Usual Pagination: 28
Profile: Regional and local news.
Language(s): French
ADVERTISING RATES:
Full Page Mono .... EUR 11000
Full Page Colour .... EUR 13750
REGIONAL DAILY & SUNDAY NEWSPAPERS: Regional Daily Newspapers

PSM3 1617540F78D-214

Editorial: 101/109 rue Jean Jaurès, 92300 LEVALLOIS PERRET **Tel:** 1 41 27 38 38
Fax: 1 41 27 38 39
Email: jean-charles.daguinot@yellowmedia.fr **Web site:** http://www.jvn.com
ISSN: 1956-7324
Date Established: 2007; **Freq:** Monthly - autour du 20 de chaque mois; **Cover Price:** EUR 6.95
Annual Sub.: EUR 36.90; **Circ:** 14,159
Usual Pagination: 100
Profile: Publication focussing on computer games including PlayStation 3, news, reviews and tests.
Language(s): French
ADVERTISING RATES:
Full Page Colour .... EUR 3000
Mechanical Data: Type Area: 22 x 31
CONSUMER: CONSUMER ELECTRONICS: Games

PSYCHOLOGIES MAGAZINE 6513F74G-140

Editorial: 149-151 rue Anatole France, CEDEX, 92534 LEVALLOIS PERRET **Tel:** 1 41 34 60 00
Email: magazine@psychologies.com **Web site:** http://www.psychologies.com
ISSN: 0032-1583
Date Established: 1970; **Freq:** Monthly - le 28 de chaque mois

Annual Sub.: EUR 36; **Circ:** 373,113
Usual Pagination: 276
Profile: Magazine promoting health and well-being using psychological means.
Language(s): French
ADVERTISING RATES:
Full Page Mono .... EUR 22100
Full Page Colour .... EUR 26000
Mechanical Data: Type Area: 21,5 x 28
CONSUMER: WOMEN'S INTEREST CONSUMER MAGAZINES: Slimming & Health

PUBLIC 1626499F74A-935
Editorial: 149 rue Anatole France, CEDEX, 92534 LEVALLOIS PERRET **Tel:** 1 41 34 92 37 85 00
Fax: 1 41 34 90 98
Email: npigasse@hfp.fr **Web site:** http://www.public.fr
ISSN: 1761-659X
Date Established: 2003; **Freq:** Weekly - vendredi; **Cover Price:** EUR 1.40; **Circ:** 483,251
Usual Pagination: 96
Profile: Publication focussing on celebrities including women's interest, fashion and TV guide.
Language(s): French
ADVERTISING RATES:
Full Page Colour .... EUR 11200
Mechanical Data: Type Area: 230 X 285
Copy instructions: *Copy Date:* 10 days prior to publication date
CONSUMER: WOMEN'S INTEREST CONSUMER MAGAZINES: Women's Interest

LES QUATRE SAISONS DU JARDIN BIO 7292F93-120
Editorial: Domaine de Raud, 38710 MENS
Tel: 4 76 34 80 80 **Fax:** 4 76 34 84 02
Email: info@terrevivante.org **Web site:** http://www.terrevivante.org
ISSN: 0242-4959
Date Established: 1980; **Freq:** 24 issues yearly - début mois impairs; **Cover Price:** EUR 5.95
Annual Sub.: EUR 31; **Circ:** 80,000
Usual Pagination: 96
Profile: Practical review of organic gardening and ecology.
Language(s): French
Readership: Aimed at gardeners.
ADVERTISING RATES:
Full Page Mono .... EUR 1005
Full Page Colour .... EUR 1270
Mechanical Data: Type Area: 155 x 217
Copy instructions: *Copy Date:* 62 days prior to publication date
CONSUMER: GARDENING

QUE CHOISIR 626736F74C-320
Editorial: 233 boulevard Voltaire, CEDEX 11, 75555 PARIS **Tel:** 1 43 48 55 48 **Fax:** 1 43 48 44 35
Email: redaction@quechoisir.org **Web site:** http://www.quechoisir.org
ISSN: 0033-5932
Date Established: 1961; **Freq:** Monthly - dernier mardi de chaque mois; **Cover Price:** EUR 4.20
Annual Sub.: EUR 40.40; **Circ:** 510,000
Usual Pagination: 68
Profile: Magazine containing information about different products and services, includes comparative tests on products.
Language(s): French
Readership: Read by members of the general public aged between 35 and 65 years.
CONSUMER: WOMEN'S INTEREST CONSUMER MAGAZINES: Home & Family

QUESTIONS DE FEMMES 6420F74A-305
Editorial: 117 rue de la Tour, 75116 PARIS
Tel: 1 45 03 80 00 **Fax:** 1 45 03 80 23
Email: lfialaix@groupe-ayache.com **Web site:** http://www.questionsdefemmes.com
ISSN: 1270-8887
Date Established: 1996; **Freq:** Monthly - 3rd Thursday of the month
Annual Sub.: EUR 18; **Circ:** 300,000
Usual Pagination: 132
Profile: Magazine containing star interviews, fashion, beauty, cookery, health and travel features.
Language(s): French
Readership: Aimed at women.
ADVERTISING RATES:
Full Page Mono .... EUR 10500
Full Page Colour .... EUR 15000
Mechanical Data: Type Area: 205 x 275
Copy instructions: *Copy Date:* 15 days prior to publication date
CONSUMER: WOMEN'S INTEREST CONSUMER MAGAZINES: Women's Interest

LE QUOTIDIEN DU MEDECIN 5740F56A-610
Editorial: 21 rue Camille Desmoulins, CEDEX 9, 92789 ISSY LES MOULINEAUX **Tel:** 1 73 28 12 70
Fax: 1 73 28 12 71
Email: redaction@quotimed.com **Web site:** http://www.quotimed.com
ISSN: 0399-2659
Date Established: 1971; **Freq:** Daily - le matin du lundi au vendredi; **Annual Sub.:** EUR 168; **Circ:** 72,982
Usual Pagination: 24
Profile: Journal containing general medical information.
Language(s): French
Readership: Read by members of the medical profession.
ADVERTISING RATES:
Full Page Mono .... EUR 10440
Full Page Colour .... EUR 14200
Mechanical Data: Type Area: tabloïd
BUSINESS: HEALTH & MEDICAL

LE QUOTIDIEN DU PHARMACIEN 5388F37-250
Editorial: 21 rue Camille Desmoulins, CEDEX 9, 92789 ISSY LES MOULINEAUX **Tel:** 1 73 28 14 40
Fax: 1 73 28 14 41
Email: tborsa@quotimed.com **Web site:** http://www.quotipharm.com
ISSN: 0764-5104
Date Established: 1985; **Freq:** 26 issues yearly - lundi et jeudi; **Cover Price:** EUR 1.34
Annual Sub.: EUR 120; **Circ:** 22,000
Usual Pagination: 28
Profile: Newspaper covering all aspects of the pharmacy business.
Language(s): French
ADVERTISING RATES:
Full Page Mono .... EUR 6600
Full Page Colour .... EUR 9280
Mechanical Data: Type Area: Tabloïd
BUSINESS: PHARMACEUTICAL & CHEMISTS

LE QUOTIDIEN DU TOURISME 5587F50-69
Editorial: Espace Clichy - Immeuble Sirius, 9 allée Jean Prouvé, CEDEX, 92587 CLICHY
Tel: 1 41 40 33 33 **Fax:** 1 41 40 34 17
Email: quotidien@quotidiendutourisme.com **Web site:** http://www.quotidiendutourisme.com
ISSN: 1152-8729
Date Established: 1990; **Freq:** 26 issues yearly - Comb. Tues/Weds and Thurs/Fri issues
Annual Sub.: EUR 119; **Circ:** 10,205
Usual Pagination: 16
Publisher: Frédéric De Watrigant
Profile: Publication containing information about the travel and tourism trade.
Language(s): French
Readership: Read by travel agents and tour operators.
ADVERTISING RATES:
Full Page Colour .... EUR 5900
Mechanical Data: Type Area: Tabloïd, Page Width: 43cm
Copy instructions: *Copy Date:* 2 days prior to publication date
BUSINESS: TRAVEL & TOURISM

RAPPELS 1646391F76B-202
Editorial: 76 Champs-Elysées, 75008 PARIS
Tel: 1 40 18 92 19
Email: rappels@nomade.fr
ISSN: 1631-8218
Date Established: 2001; **Freq:** Monthly - début de mois; **Cover Price:** Free; **Circ:** 250,000
Usual Pagination: 36
Profile: Publication focussing on theatre including latest releases, critics, reviews and agenda.
Language(s): French
ADVERTISING RATES:
Full Page Colour .... EUR 9900
Mechanical Data: Type Area: 210 x 300
Copy instructions: *Copy Date:* 15 days prior to publication date
CONSUMER: MUSIC & PERFORMING ARTS: Theatre

RAYON BOISSONS 7643F9A-124
Editorial: 13 square du Chêne Germain, CS 77711, CEDEX, 35577 CESSON-SEVIGNE **Tel:** 2 99 32 21 21
Fax: 2 99 32 89 20
Email: bmoreau@editionsduboisbaudry.fr **Web site:** http://www.rayon-boissons.com
ISSN: 1247-2077
Date Established: 1993; **Freq:** Monthly - le 10 du mois
Annual Sub.: EUR 60; **Circ:** 7,500
Usual Pagination: 122
Profile: Trade publication focussing on drinks including economics, distribution, commerce and marketing.
Language(s): French
ADVERTISING RATES:
Full Page Colour .... EUR 4980
Mechanical Data: Type Area: 210 x 285
Copy instructions: *Copy Date:* 21 days prior to publication date
BUSINESS: DRINKS & LICENSED TRADE: Drinks, Licensed Trade, Wines & Spirits

RCA MAG REGION CHAMPAGNE-ARDENNE 1617231F32A-1076
Editorial: 5 rue de Jéricho, 51037 CHALONS-EN-CHAMPAGNE CEDEX **Tel:** 3 26 70 31 33
Fax: 3 26 70 66 60
Email: com@cr-champagne-ardenne.fr **Web site:** http://www.cr-champagne-ardenne.fr
ISSN: 1157-1462
Date Established: 1990; **Freq:** Quarterly - printemps, été, automne, hiver; **Cover Price:** Free; **Circ:** 588,000
Usual Pagination: 44
Editor: Jean-Paul Bachy
Profile: Publication focussing on local government and department issues.
Language(s): French
Mechanical Data: Type Area: A4
Copy instructions: *Copy Date:* pas de publicité
BUSINESS: LOCAL GOVERNMENT, LEISURE & RECREATION: Local Government

READER'S DIGEST SELECTION 1618263F73-344
Editorial: 1-7 avenue Louis-Pasteur, 92220 CEDEX BAGNEUX **Tel:** 1 77 75 29 01 **Fax:** 1 46 74 85 75
Web site: http://www.selectionclic.com
ISSN: 0037-1386
Date Established: 1947; **Freq:** Monthly - fin de mois
Annual Sub.: EUR 44.95; **Circ:** 318,157
Usual Pagination: 162
Profile: Publication focussing on news and current affairs including French and international news.
Language(s): French
ADVERTISING RATES:
Full Page Mono .... EUR 15400
Full Page Colour .... EUR 18000
Mechanical Data: Type Area: 134 x 184
Copy instructions: *Copy Date:* 30 days prior to publication date
CONSUMER: NATIONAL & INTERNATIONAL PERIODICALS

LA RECHERCHE 5635F55-67
Editorial: 74 avenue du Maine, 75014 PARIS
Tel: 1 44 10 10 10
Email: courrier@larecherche.fr **Web site:** http://www.larecherche.fr
ISSN: 0029-5671
Date Established: 1970; **Freq:** Monthly - dernier jeudi du mois; **Cover Price:** EUR 6.40
Annual Sub.: EUR 52.60; **Circ:** 49,431
Usual Pagination: 100
Profile: International technical and scientific review.
Language(s): French
ADVERTISING RATES:
Full Page Mono .... EUR 6545
Full Page Colour .... EUR 7700
Mechanical Data: Type Area: 210 x 287
BUSINESS: APPLIED SCIENCE & LABORATORIES

RECYCLAGE RECUPERATION MAGAZINE 5323F32B-100
Editorial: 38 rue Croix des Petits Champs, 75001 PARIS **Tel:** 1 53 45 89 00 **Fax:** 1 53 45 96 66
Email: m.chartier@victoires-editions.fr **Web site:** http://www.recyclage-recuperation.fr
ISSN: 1156-962X
Date Established: 1909; **Freq:** Weekly - vendredi
Annual Sub.: EUR 139; **Circ:** 2,579
Usual Pagination: 20
Profile: Journal about waste recycling, methods of reprocessing waste, its treatment and redevelopment. Includes information on industrial waste.
Language(s): French
ADVERTISING RATES:
Full Page Mono .... EUR 1877
Full Page Colour .... EUR 3025
Mechanical Data: Type Area: A 4
BUSINESS: LOCAL GOVERNMENT, LEISURE & RECREATION: Public Health & Cleaning

REFLETS 1617232F32A-1077
Editorial: Conseil régional - Abbaye aux Dames, Place Reine Mathilde, BP 523 CEDEX 1, 14035 CAEN
Tel: 2 31 06 98 55 **Fax:** 2 31 06 97 95
Email: reflets@crbn.fr **Web site:** http://www.region-basse-normandie.fr
ISSN: 1621-9554
Freq: 24 issues yearly - 02 04 06 10 12; **Cover Price:** Free; **Circ:** 700,000
Usual Pagination: 40
Profile: Publication focussing on local government and department issues, including economics, agriculture, regional development, cultural and social issues.
Language(s): French
Mechanical Data: Type Area: 23 x 30
BUSINESS: LOCAL GOVERNMENT, LEISURE & RECREATION: Local Government

LES REFLETS D'ALLIER 1617197F32A-1055
Editorial: Conseil Général de l'Allier, 1 avenue Victor Hugo, BP 1669 CEDEX, 3016 MOULINS
Tel: 4 70 34 40 03 **Fax:** 4 70 34 41 72
Email: reflets-allier@cg03.fr **Web site:** http://www.allier.fr
ISSN: 1280-4169
Date Established: 1999; **Freq:** Monthly - dernier mardi de chaque mois; **Cover Price:** Free; **Circ:** 175,000
Usual Pagination: 32
Profile: Publication focussing on local government and department issues, including economics, sports, leisure, environment, cultural and social issues.
Language(s): French
Mechanical Data: Type Area: 229 x 297
Copy instructions: *Copy Date:* 31 days prior to publication date
BUSINESS: LOCAL GOVERNMENT, LEISURE & RECREATION: Local Government

REFLETS DU LOIRET CONSEIL GENERAL DU LOIRET 1617198F32A-1056
Editorial: Hôtel-du-Département, 15 rue Eugène-Vignat, BP 2019, 45010 CEDEX 1 ORLEANS
Tel: 2 38 25 43 25 **Fax:** 238254347
Email: dircom@cg45.fr **Web site:** http://www.loiret.com
ISSN: 0769-5241
Freq: 6 issues yearly - milieu de mois impairs; **Cover Price:** EUR 0.30; **Circ:** 330,000
Usual Pagination: 32
Editor: Jean-Noël Cardoux
Profile: Publication focussing on local government and department issues, including economics, tourism, sports, cultural and social issues.
Language(s): French
Mechanical Data: Type Area: 27 x 21,5
BUSINESS: LOCAL GOVERNMENT, LEISURE & RECREATION: Local Government

REGAL 1656500F74P-489
Editorial: 22 rue Letellier, CEDEX 15, 75739 PARIS
Tel: 1 43 23 45 72 **Fax:** 1 43 23 04 95
Email: martine.soliman@uni-editions.com
ISSN: 1769-3977
Date Established: 2004; **Freq:** 24 issues yearly - publishes around the 20th of every other month;
Cover Price: EUR 3.90
Annual Sub.: EUR 19; **Circ:** 292,576
Usual Pagination: 132
Profile: Covers wine and gastronomy. Offers recipes, culinary news, product reviews, regional food markets.
Language(s): French
ADVERTISING RATES:
Full Page Colour .... EUR 7000
Mechanical Data: Type Area: 210 x 275
Copy instructions: *Copy Date:* 31 days prior to publication date
CONSUMER: WOMEN'S INTEREST CONSUMER MAGAZINES: Food & Cookery

REGION ALSACE CONSEIL REGIONAL 1617234F32A-1079
Editorial: 1 place du Wacken, BP 91006, 67070, CEDEX STRASBOURG **Tel:** 3 88 15 68 67
Fax: 388156815
Email: contact@region-alsace.eu **Web site:** http://www.region-alsace.eu
ISSN: 1142-9259
Date Established: 2000; **Freq:** 6 issues yearly - 01 03 06 09 11; **Cover Price:** Free; **Circ:** 733,000
Usual Pagination: 16
Editor: André Reichardt
Profile: Publication focussing on local government and department issues, including economics, environment, training, tourism, agriculture, land settlement, transport, education, tourism, international relations, sports, cultural and social issues.
Language(s): French
Mechanical Data: Type Area: A4
BUSINESS: LOCAL GOVERNMENT, LEISURE & RECREATION: Local Government

RELATION CLIENT 4936F18B-2_4
Editorial: 13 rue Louis Pasteur, CEDEX, 92513 BOULOGNE BILLANCOURT **Tel:** 1 41 31 72 66
Fax: 1 41 31 72 62
Email: frouffiac@editialis.fr **Web site:** http://www.relationclientmag.fr
ISSN: 1287-7603
Date Established: 1998; **Freq:** 24 issues yearly - 1ère/2ème semaine des mois pairs; **Cover Price:** EUR 7.50
Annual Sub.: EUR 68; **Circ:** 6,000
Usual Pagination: 90
Profile: Telecommunications magazine focusing on all aspects of call centres and call centre management.
Language(s): French
Readership: Aimed at call centre managers and those providing call centre equipment, services and back-up.
ADVERTISING RATES:
Full Page Mono .... EUR 5650
Full Page Colour .... EUR 6050
Mechanical Data: Type Area: A4
Copy instructions: *Copy Date:* 14 days prior to publication date
BUSINESS: ELECTRONICS: Telecommunications

REPONSE A TOUT 6385F73-225
Editorial: 117 rue de la Tour, 75116 PARIS
Tel: 1 45 03 80 00 **Fax:** 1 45 03 80 23
Email: vham@groupe-ayache.com **Web site:** http://www.reponseatout.com
Date Established: 1990; **Freq:** Monthly - dernier vendredi du mois
Annual Sub.: EUR 30; **Circ:** 128,712
Usual Pagination: 88
Profile: General information magazine.
Language(s): French
ADVERTISING RATES:
Full Page Mono .... EUR 11900
Full Page Colour .... EUR 15000

Mechanical Data: Type Area: 210 x 272
CONSUMER: NATIONAL & INTERNATIONAL PERIODICALS

REPONSES PHOTO
7111F85A-120
Editorial: Immeuble Trait d'Union, 8 rue François Ory, 92120 MONTROUGE **Tel:** 1 41 86 17 12
Fax: 1 41 86 17 11
Email: sylvie.hugues@mondadori.fr **Web site:** http://www.mondadoripub.fr
ISSN: 1167-844X
Date Established: 1992; **Freq:** Monthly - 10-15 du mois; **Cover Price:** EUR 4.80
Annual Sub.: EUR 47; **Circ:** 58,951
Usual Pagination: 172
Profile: Magazine covering all aspects of photography.
Language(s): French
ADVERTISING RATES:
Full Page Colour .... EUR 7100
Mechanical Data: Type Area: A 4
CONSUMER: PHOTOGRAPHY & FILM MAKING: Photography

LE REPUBLICAIN LORRAIN METZ
6192F67B-7300
Editorial: 24 rue Serpenoise, 57000 METZ
Tel: 3 87 38 58 00 **Fax:** 3 87 38 58 01
Email: redaction.metz@republicain-lorrain.fr **Web site:** http://www.republicain-lorrain.fr
Date Established: 1919; **Freq:** Daily - quotidienne;
Cover Price: EUR 0.85
Annual Sub.: EUR 271.97; **Circ:** 145,475
Usual Pagination: 40
Editor: Pierre Wicker
Profile: International, national, regional and local news, magazine. 11 issues covering 2 departments. Supplements published (school counselling, housing) according to the current events including 1 at the end of the year.
Language(s): French
ADVERTISING RATES:
Full Page Mono .... EUR 6240
Full Page Colour .... EUR 8112
REGIONAL DAILY & SUNDAY NEWSPAPERS: Regional Daily Newspapers

LA REPUBLIQUE DE SEINE ET MARNE
1619237F67J-114
Editorial: 3 boulevard Victor Hugo, BP 22, CEDEX, 77001 MELUN **Tel:** 1 64 87 50 00 **Fax:** 1 64 52 14 92
Email: redaction@larepublique.com **Web site:** http://www.larepublique.com
ISSN: 0768-7893
Date Established: 1894; **Freq:** Weekly - lundi; **Cover Price:** EUR 1.20
Annual Sub.: EUR 57.60; **Circ:** 22,063
Usual Pagination: 74
Publisher: Thomas Martin
Profile: Regional and local news (Society, sports, economy, politics, associations, leisure, internet). National information relating to local news. ISSN numbers: 0768-7893 - 0765-9105 - 0760-9113.
Language(s): French
Mechanical Data: Type Area: tabloïd
REGIONAL DAILY & SUNDAY NEWSPAPERS: Regional Newspapers (excl. dailies)

LA REPUBLIQUE DES PYRENEES
1619722F67B-8720
Editorial: 6/8 rue Despourrins, CEDEX, 64002 PAU
Tel: 5 59 82 20 00 **Fax:** 5 59 82 20 11
Email: jp.cassagne@pyrenees.com **Web site:** http://www.pyrenees.com
Date Established: 1944; **Freq:** Daily - matin sauf le dimanche et jf; **Cover Price:** EUR 0.80
Annual Sub.: EUR 218; **Circ:** 32,465
Usual Pagination: 56
Profile: Regional and local current events. The journalists from "Pyrénées Presse" are working for 2 publications: "La République des Pyrénées" and "L'Éclair".
Language(s): French
ADVERTISING RATES:
Full Page Mono .... EUR 4347
Full Page Colour .... EUR 4706
Mechanical Data: Type Area: tabloïd
REGIONAL DAILY & SUNDAY NEWSPAPERS: Regional Daily Newspapers

LA RÉPUBLIQUE DU CENTRE - EDITION DU LOIRET
6171F67B-7400
Editorial: Rue de la Halte, BP 93035, 45403 CEDEX FLEURY-LES-AUBRAIS **Tel:** 2 38 78 79 80
Fax: 2 38 78 79 79
Email: agence.orleans@larep.com **Web site:** http://www.larep.com
ISSN: 0221-1750
Date Established: 1944; **Freq:** Daily - matin; **Cover Price:** EUR 0.80
Annual Sub.: EUR 213; **Circ:** 51,029
Usual Pagination: 28
Profile: Current events, economy, politics, social life.
Language(s): French
Mechanical Data: Type Area: Tabloïd
REGIONAL DAILY & SUNDAY NEWSPAPERS: Regional Daily Newspapers

RESIDENCES DECORATION
6471F74C-360
Editorial: Nice Leader - Hermès, 66 route de Grenoble, BP 3024 CEDEX 3, 6201 NICE
Tel: 4 93 72 11 88 **Fax:** 4 93 72 04 25
Email: residences@smc-france.com
ISSN: 1254-8278
Date Established: 1994; **Freq:** 24 issues yearly - 10th of every even month; **Cover Price:** EUR 4.90
Annual Sub.: EUR 23; **Circ:** 175,000
Usual Pagination: 176
Profile: International magazine about the home, garden and interior design.
Language(s): French
ADVERTISING RATES:
Full Page Colour .... EUR 12900
Mechanical Data: Type Area: 227 x 296
Copy instructions: *Copy Date:* 21 days prior to publication date
CONSUMER: WOMEN'S INTEREST CONSUMER MAGAZINES: Home & Family

RESTAURER SA MAISON
6472F74C-380
Editorial: 3 route des Moulins, 27120 HARDENCOURT-COCHEREL **Tel:** 2 32 26 50 14
Fax: 1 47 55 63 53
Email: m.a.beni@wanadoo.fr
ISSN: 1274-8838
Freq: 6 issues yearly - mois impairs
Annual Sub.: EUR 25; **Circ:** 100,000
Usual Pagination: 116
Editor: Philippe Aubry
Profile: Magazine containing practical advice on home restoration.
Language(s): French
ADVERTISING RATES:
Full Page Colour .... EUR 5900
Mechanical Data: Type Area: 21 x 28
Copy instructions: *Copy Date:* 15 days prior to publication date
CONSUMER: WOMEN'S INTEREST CONSUMER MAGAZINES: Home & Family

REUSSIR - GRANDES CULTURES
5020F21A-1700
Editorial: 2 avenue du Pays de Caen, Colombelles, CEDEX 9, 14902 CAEN **Tel:** 2 31 35 77 00
Fax: 2 31 82 29 63
Email: n.ouvrard@reussir.tm.fr **Web site:** http://www.reussir-grandes-cultures.com
ISSN: 0996-858X
Date Established: 1987; **Freq:** Monthly - le 5 du mois; **Cover Price:** EUR 7.60
Annual Sub.: EUR 67; **Circ:** 66,500
Usual Pagination: 108
Profile: Journal covering cereal cultivation.
Language(s): French
Readership: Read by farmers and those connected with the processing of grain.
ADVERTISING RATES:
Full Page Mono .... EUR 4067
Full Page Colour .... EUR 8134
Mechanical Data: Type Area: 210 x 297
BUSINESS: AGRICULTURE & FARMING

REUSSIR - LAIT
5040F21C-42
Editorial: 2 avenue du Pays de Caen, Colombelles, CEDEX 9, 14902 CAEN **Tel:** 2 31 35 77 00
Fax: 2 31 82 29 63
Email: a.conte@reussir.tm.fr **Web site:** http://www.reussir-lait.com
ISSN: 0995-6492
Date Established: 1987; **Freq:** Monthly - le 5 du mois; **Cover Price:** EUR 7.80
Annual Sub.: EUR 64; **Circ:** 56,800
Usual Pagination: 140
Profile: Journal containing technical and economic information about milk production. Includes information on dairy cattle breeding.
Language(s): French
Readership: Read by dairy farmers.
ADVERTISING RATES:
Full Page Mono .... EUR 3612
Full Page Colour .... EUR 6140
Mechanical Data: Type Area: 210 x 297
BUSINESS: AGRICULTURE & FARMING: Dairy Farming

REUSSIR - VIGNE
5083F21H-87
Editorial: 2 avenue du Pays de Caen, Colombelles, CEDEX 9, 14902 CAEN **Tel:** 2 31 35 77 00
Fax: 2 31 82 29 63
Email: m.ivaldi@reussir.tm.fr **Web site:** http://www.reussir-vigne.com
ISSN: 1261-0208
Date Established: 1994; **Freq:** Monthly - milieu de mois; **Cover Price:** EUR 7.30
Annual Sub.: EUR 67; **Circ:** 23,700
Usual Pagination: 48
Profile: Magazine covering vine growing in all regions of France.
Language(s): French
ADVERTISING RATES:
Full Page Mono .... EUR 2297
Full Page Colour .... EUR 4028
Mechanical Data: Type Area: 210 x 297
BUSINESS: AGRICULTURE & FARMING: Vine Growing

LE REVENU LE MENSUEL CONSEIL POUR VOS PLACEMENTS
4476F1A-300
Editorial: 1 bis avenue de la République, 75011 PARIS **Tel:** 1 49 29 30 00 **Fax:** 1 49 29 30 98
Email: redaction@lerevenu.com **Web site:** http://www.lerevenu.com
Date Established: 1968; **Freq:** Monthly - before the last Friday of the month; **Circ:** 81,902
Usual Pagination: 100
Editor: Laurent Grassin; **Editor-in-Chief:** Gilles Pouzin
Profile: Publication about finance, investment and the economy. Also includes articles on property and the stockmarket.
Language(s): French
ADVERTISING RATES:
Full Page Mono .... EUR 12500
Full Page Colour .... EUR 16500
Mechanical Data: Type Area: 23 x 29,7
BUSINESS: FINANCE & ECONOMICS

LE REVENU L'HEBDO CONSEIL DE LA BOURSE
1618045F1A-437
Editorial: 1 bis avenue de la République, 75011 PARIS **Tel:** 1 49 29 30 00
Email: pub@lerevenu.com **Web site:** http://www.lerevenu.com
ISSN: 1293-4259
Date Established: 1994; **Freq:** Weekly - Friday;
Cover Price: EUR 3.50
Annual Sub.: EUR 103; **Circ:** 168,701
Usual Pagination: 40
Profile: Magazine focussing on economics, stock exchange, investments and financial consultancy.
Language(s): French
ADVERTISING RATES:
Full Page Mono .... EUR 12100
Full Page Colour .... EUR 16500
Mechanical Data: Type Area: 285x390
BUSINESS: FINANCE & ECONOMICS

REVUE BANQUE
4491F1C-20
Editorial: 18 rue La Fayette, 75009 PARIS
Tel: 1 48 00 54 10 **Fax:** 1 48 24 12 97
Email: hauvette@revue-banque.fr **Web site:** http://www.revue-banque.fr
ISSN: 0005-5581
Freq: Monthly - fin de mois
Annual Sub.: EUR 275; **Circ:** 6,933
Profile: Professional and technical journal concerning all aspects of banking. Includes information on markets, accountancy, finance, economics, bank management, law and the Internet.
Language(s): French
Readership: Aimed at those in the banking and finance sectors.
ADVERTISING RATES:
Full Page Mono .... EUR 3700
Full Page Colour .... EUR 5500
Mechanical Data: Type Area: A 4
BUSINESS: FINANCE & ECONOMICS: Banking

REVUE DE L'ELECTRICITE
4925F17-170
Editorial: SEE, 17 rue de l'Amiral Hamelin, CEDEX 16, 75783 PARIS **Tel:** 1 56 90 37 17
Fax: 1 56 90 37 19
Email: redacree@see.asso.fr **Web site:** http://www.see.asso.fr
ISSN: 1265-6534
Date Established: 1995; **Freq:** Monthly - 1ère semaine du mois; **Cover Price:** EUR 18
Annual Sub.: EUR 165; **Circ:** 4,000
Usual Pagination: 96
Profile: Magazine focusing on industrial electricity and electronics.
Language(s): French
Readership: Aimed at engineers, researchers and technicians.
ADVERTISING RATES:
Full Page Colour .... EUR 2500
Mechanical Data: Type Area: A 4
Copy instructions: *Copy Date:* 21 days prior to publication date
BUSINESS: ELECTRICAL

LA REVUE DES COMPTOIRS
4789F11A-262
Editorial: 16 rue Saint Fiacre, 75002 PARIS
Tel: 1 42 36 51 02 **Fax:** 1 42 36 04 62
Email: redactioncomptoirs@groupembc.com
ISSN: 1271-4836
Date Established: 1996; **Freq:** Monthly - Début de mois
Annual Sub.: EUR 38; **Circ:** 37,500
Usual Pagination: 64
Profile: Magazine for proprietors of French cafés, bars and brasseries.
Language(s): French
ADVERTISING RATES:
Full Page Colour .... EUR 5800
Mechanical Data: Type Area: 21 x 29,7
BUSINESS: CATERING: Catering, Hotels & Restaurants

LA REVUE DES DEUX MONDES
7056F82-215
Editorial: 97 rue de Lille, 75007 PARIS
Tel: 1 47 53 61 94 **Fax:** 1 47 53 61 99
Email: mcrepu@fimalac.com **Web site:** http://www.revuedesdeuxmondes.fr
ISSN: 0750-9278
Date Established: 1829; **Freq:** Monthly - début du mois suivant; **Cover Price:** EUR 11
Annual Sub.: EUR 7550; **Circ:** 12,000
Usual Pagination: 192
Profile: Magazine containing political, cultural and economic articles and news.
Language(s): French
CONSUMER: CURRENT AFFAIRS & POLITICS

LA REVUE DES MONTRES
6958F79K-300
Editorial: 10 rue du Plâtre, 75004 PARIS
Tel: 1 53 01 10 30 **Fax:** 1 42 72 65 75
Email: c.matthieussent@editionsjalou.com **Web site:** http://www.larevuedesmontres.com
ISSN: 11480483
Date Established: 1991; **Freq:** Monthly - le 25 du mois; **Cover Price:** EUR 5.50
Annual Sub.: EUR 36; **Circ:** 16,378
Usual Pagination: 84
Profile: Magazine concerning all types of watches.
Language(s): French
Readership: Aimed at collectors of old and new watches.
ADVERTISING RATES:
Full Page Mono .... EUR 6000
Full Page Colour .... EUR 7400
Mechanical Data: Type Area: A 4
CONSUMER: HOBBIES & DIY: Collectors Magazines

REVUE DES OENOLOGUES
4754F9C-94
Editorial: Château de Chaintré, Cidex 453 Bis, 71570 CHAINTRE **Tel:** 3 85 37 43 21 **Fax:** 3 85 37 19 83
Email: infos@mail.oeno.tm.fr **Web site:** http://www.oeno.tm.fr
ISSN: 0760-9868
Date Established: 1975; **Freq:** Quarterly - 01 04 07 10 11
Annual Sub.: EUR 62; **Circ:** 15,000
Usual Pagination: 72
Profile: Publication which covers the technical and scientific aspects of wine culture and production.
Language(s): French
Readership: Aimed at professionals within the wine industry.
ADVERTISING RATES:
Full Page Mono .... EUR 1580
Full Page Colour .... EUR 2200
Mechanical Data: Type Area: 220 x 305
BUSINESS: DRINKS & LICENSED TRADE: Licensed Trade, Wines & Spirits

LA REVUE DES PARENTS
6483F74D-170
Editorial: 108/110 avenue Ledru-Rollin, CEDEX 11, 75544 PARIS **Tel:** 1 43 57 16 16 **Fax:** 1 43 57 40 78
Email: fcpecom@fcpe.asso.fr **Web site:** http://www.fcpe.asso.fr
ISSN: 0223-0232
Date Established: 1946; **Freq:** 24 issues yearly - tous les 2 mois; **Cover Price:** EUR 2.29
Annual Sub.: EUR 60; **Circ:** 250,000
Usual Pagination: 36
Profile: Review for parents of children in state schools.
Language(s): French
ADVERTISING RATES:
Full Page Colour .... EUR 5340
Mechanical Data: Type Area: 205 x 285
Copy instructions: *Copy Date:* 15 days prior to publication date
CONSUMER: WOMEN'S INTEREST CONSUMER MAGAZINES: Child Care

LA REVUE DES TABACS
5596F51-50
Editorial: Rédaction, 16 rue Saint Fiacre, 75002 PARIS **Tel:** 1 42 36 51 02 95 59 **Fax:** 1 42 36 04 62 83 24
Email: revuedestabacs@groupembc.com
ISSN: 0753-1605
Date Established: 1925; **Freq:** Monthly - entre le 3 et le 10 du mois
Annual Sub.: EUR 53; **Circ:** 35,000
Usual Pagination: 70
Profile: Magazine focusing on the cultivation, preparation and distribution of tobacco products.
Language(s): French
Readership: Read by tobacconists.
ADVERTISING RATES:
Full Page Colour .... EUR 6400
Mechanical Data: Type Area: A 4
BUSINESS: TOBACCO

LA REVUE DU VIN DE FRANCE
6591F74P-320
Editorial: 43/47 rue du Gouverneur Général Eboué, CEDEX, 92137 ISSY LES MOULINEAUX
Tel: 1 41 40 23 00 **Fax:** 1 41 40 23 09
Email: dsaverot@gmc.tm.fr **Web site:** http://www.larvf.com
ISSN: 1634-7625

Date Established: 1927; **Freq:** Monthly - between 20 and 25; **Cover Price:** EUR 5.90
Annual Sub.: EUR 65; **Circ:** 80,000
Usual Pagination: 152
Profile: Publication providing information concerning French wines.
Language(s): French
ADVERTISING RATES:
Full Page Mono .... EUR 7000
Full Page Colour .... EUR 7000
Mechanical Data: Type Area: 215 x 285
Copy instructions: *Copy Date:* 31 days prior to publication date
CONSUMER: WOMEN'S INTEREST CONSUMER MAGAZINES: Food & Cookery

REVUE GENERALE NUCLEAIRE
5922F58-120
Editorial: SFEN, 5 rue des Morillons, 75015 PARIS
Tel: 1 53 58 32 10 **Fax:** 1 53 58 32 11
Email: sfen@sfen.fr **Web site:** http://www.sfen.org
ISSN: 0335-5004
Date Established: 1972; **Freq:** 24 issues yearly - milieu mois 01 03 05 07 10 11; **Cover Price:** EUR 16
Annual Sub.: EUR 90; **Circ:** 4,000
Usual Pagination: 88
Profile: Official journal of the French Nuclear Energy Society. Covers all the subjects connected with the peaceful use of nuclear energy.
Language(s): French
ADVERTISING RATES:
Full Page Mono .... EUR 1600
Full Page Colour .... EUR 2450
Mechanical Data: Type Area: A 4
Copy instructions: *Copy Date:* 31 days prior to publication date
BUSINESS: ENERGY, FUEL & NUCLEAR

LA REVUE VINICOLE INTERNATIONALE
4753F9C-90
Editorial: 84 boulevard de Sébastopol, 75003 PARIS
Tel: 1 43 96 16 16 **Fax:** 1 43 96 16 16
Email: fhermine@larvi.com **Web site:** http://www.larvi.fr
ISSN: 0035-4368
Freq: Monthly - 1er du mois; **Cover Price:** EUR 12.70
Annual Sub.: EUR 105; **Circ:** 8,000
Usual Pagination: 76
Editor: Vladimir Kauffmann
Profile: Magazine containing information and articles about wine, spirits, soft drinks and beer.
Language(s): French
Readership: Read by managers of clubs, bars and restaurateurs.
ADVERTISING RATES:
Full Page Colour .... EUR 4650
Mechanical Data: Type Area: 205 x 270
BUSINESS: DRINKS & LICENSED TRADE: Licensed Trade, Wines & Spirits

RHONE-ALPES CONSEIL REGIONAL RHONE-ALPES
1786565F32A-1093
Editorial: 78 route de Paris, BP 19, 69751 CHARBONNIERES-LES-BAINS CEDEX
Tel: 4 72 59 40 00 **Fax:** 4 72 59 42 18
Web site: http://www.rhonealpes.fr
Date Established: 2006; **Freq:** Quarterly; **Cover Price:** Free; **Circ:** 400,000
Usual Pagination: 24
Profile: Publication focussing on local government and department issues, including economics, politics, cultural heritage, culture and social issues.
Language(s): French
BUSINESS: LOCAL GOVERNMENT, LEISURE & RECREATION: Local Government

RIA - REVUE DE L'INDUSTRIE
5182F21R-195
Editorial: 8 Cité Paradis, CEDEX 10, 75493 PARIS
Tel: 1 40 22 79 00 **Fax:** 1 40 22 70 72
Email: l.benard@gfa.fr
ISSN: 0035-4244
Date Established: 1953; **Freq:** Monthly - 7-15 du mois; **Cover Price:** EUR 17
Annual Sub.: EUR 149; **Circ:** 8,925
Usual Pagination: 90
Editor-in-Chief: Laurent Benard; **Managing Director:** Michel Collonge
Profile: Journal concerning agri-business. Includes articles on procedures, products, agri-business economics and logistics.
Language(s): French
Readership: Aimed at those in the agri-business sector and related trades.
ADVERTISING RATES:
Full Page Colour .... EUR 3740
Mechanical Data: Type Area: 220 x 285
Copy instructions: *Copy Date:* 31 days prior to publication date
BUSINESS: AGRICULTURE & FARMING: Agriculture & Farming Related

ROCK & FOLK
6791F76E-250
Editorial: Espace Clichy - Immeuble Agéna, 12 rue Mozart, CEDEX, 92587 CLICHY **Tel:** 1 41 40 32 99 33 33 **Fax:** 1 41 40 34 71
Email: rock&folk@editions-lariviere.fr **Web site:** http://www.rocknfolk.com
ISSN: 0750-7852
Date Established: 1966; **Freq:** Monthly - le 18-20 du mois
Annual Sub.: EUR 54.25; **Circ:** 42,901
Usual Pagination: 132
Publisher: Philippe Budillon
Profile: Magazine about all types of music.
Language(s): French
Readership: Aimed at all music enthusiasts.
ADVERTISING RATES:
Full Page Mono .... EUR 4650
Full Page Colour .... EUR 6800
Mechanical Data: Type Area: 210 x 297
CONSUMER: MUSIC & PERFORMING ARTS: Pop Music

RUSTICA
7293F93-150
Editorial: 15-27 rue Moussorgski, CEDEX 18, 75895 PARIS **Tel:** 1 53 26 33 00 **Fax:** 1 53 26 33 01
Email: j.dorbeaux@rustica.fr **Web site:** http://www.rustica.fr
ISSN: 0338-5353
Date Established: 1928; **Freq:** Weekly - mercredi;
Cover Price: EUR 2.20
Annual Sub.: EUR 59; **Circ:** 234,281
Usual Pagination: 52
Managing Director: Eric De Montlivault
Profile: Gardening magazine.
Language(s): French
ADVERTISING RATES:
Full Page Mono .... EUR 8490
Full Page Colour .... EUR 12570
Mechanical Data: Type Area: 202 x 290
Copy instructions: *Copy Date:* 21 days prior to publication date
CONSUMER: GARDENING

SANTE & TECHNOLOGIES
5896F56R-160
Editorial: MSO COMMUNICATION, 50 rue de Paradis, 75010 PARIS **Tel:** 1 45 23 22 34
Fax: 1 45 23 22 33
Email: mso.com@wanadoo.fr
ISSN: 1292-3516
Date Established: 1998; **Freq:** 24 issues yearly - fin 02 04 06 08 10 12; **Cover Price:** EUR 18
Annual Sub.: EUR 85; **Circ:** 5,000
Usual Pagination: 40
Profile: Health and technology journal.
Language(s): French
ADVERTISING RATES:
Full Page Colour .... EUR 5000
Mechanical Data: Type Area: A 4
Copy instructions: *Copy Date:* 7 days prior to publication date
BUSINESS: HEALTH & MEDICAL: Health Medical Related

SANTE MAGAZINE
6516F74G-153
Editorial: UNI EDITIONS, 22 rue Letellier, 75015 PARIS **Tel:** 1 43 23 45 72 **Fax:** 1 43 23 04 95
Email: pascale.guyader@uni-editions.com **Web site:** http://www.santemagazine.fr
ISSN: 0397-0329
Date Established: 1976; **Freq:** Monthly - 1ère semaine du mois; **Cover Price:** EUR 2.80
Annual Sub.: EUR 29; **Circ:** 286,174
Usual Pagination: 180
Profile: Journal concerning medicine and health matters.
Language(s): French
Readership: Aimed at the general public.
ADVERTISING RATES:
Full Page Mono .... EUR 16500
Full Page Colour .... EUR 21000
Mechanical Data: Type Area: A 4
Copy instructions: *Copy Date:* 31 days prior to publication date
CONSUMER: WOMEN'S INTEREST CONSUMER MAGAZINES: Slimming & Health

SAONE & LOIRE INFO CONSEIL GENERAL DE SAONE-ET-LOIRE
1617200F32A-1058
Editorial: Hôtel-du-Département, Rue de Lingendes, 71026 CEDEX 9 MACON **Tel:** 3 85 39 66 90
Fax: 385396666
Email: com@cg71.fr **Web site:** http://www.cg71.fr
ISSN: 0753-3454
Date Established: 1990; **Freq:** Monthly - le 15 de chaque mois; **Cover Price:** Free; **Circ:** 267,000
Usual Pagination: 32
Profile: Publication focussing on local government and department issues, including economics, agriculture, tourism, events, leisure, cultural and social issues.
Language(s): French
Mechanical Data: Type Area: 230 x 300
BUSINESS: LOCAL GOVERNMENT, LEISURE & RECREATION: Local Government

LE SAPEUR POMPIER
5615F54A-50
Editorial: 32 rue Bréguet, 75011 PARIS
Tel: 1 49 23 18 24 **Fax:** 1 49 23 18 15
Email: spmag@pompiers.fr **Web site:** http://www.lesapeurpompier.fr
ISSN: 0036-469X
Date Established: 1889; **Freq:** Monthly - le 5 de chaque mois; **Cover Price:** EUR 4.20
Annual Sub.: EUR 28.20; **Circ:** 80,000
Usual Pagination: 92
Editor-in-Chief: Richard Labeviere
Profile: Official newspaper of the French Federation of Fire Fighters.
Language(s): French
Readership: Read by federation members.
ADVERTISING RATES:
Full Page Colour .... EUR 3148
Mechanical Data: Type Area: A 4
Copy instructions: *Copy Date:* 31 days prior to publication date
BUSINESS: SAFETY & SECURITY: Fire Fighting

LA SARTHE CONSEIL GENERAL DE LA SARTHE
1617174F32A-1034
Editorial: Hôtel-du-Département, Place Aristide-Briand, 72072 CEDEX 9 LE MANS **Tel:** 2 43 54 70 26
Fax: 2 43 54 70 31
Web site: http://www.cg72.fr
ISSN: 1260-9862
Freq: 6 issues yearly - Milieu du mois; **Cover Price:** Free; **Circ:** 250,000
Usual Pagination: 32
Editor: Roland du Luart
Profile: Publication focussing on local government and department issues, including economics, sports, leisure, environment, cultural and social issues.
Language(s): French
Mechanical Data: Type Area: 22,4 x 30
BUSINESS: LOCAL GOVERNMENT, LEISURE & RECREATION: Local Government

SATELLIFAX (NEWSLETTER)
714189F2D-132
Editorial: 9 rue Charlot, 75003 PARIS
Tel: 1 44 78 04 78 **Fax:** 1 42 78 70 36
Email: redaction@satellifax.com **Web site:** http://www.satellifax.com
Date Established: 1995; **Freq:** Daily. 7h (fax) - 3h (e-mail); **Cover Price:** EUR 11
Annual Sub.: EUR 2380
Usual Pagination: 14
Editor: Joël Wirsztel
Profile: Publication focussing on audiovisual news.
Language(s): French
Mechanical Data: Type Area: A4
BUSINESS: COMMUNICATIONS, ADVERTISING & MARKETING: Broadcasting

SAVEURS
6592F74P-400
Editorial: 67 rue de Dunkerque, 75009 PARIS
Tel: 1 53 63 10 15 **Fax:** 1 53 63 82 38
Email: saveurs@editions-burda.fr **Web site:** http://www.editions-burda.fr/magazine-saveurs
ISSN: 0998-4623
Date Established: 1989; **Freq:** 24 issues yearly;
Cover Price: EUR 4.80
Annual Sub.: EUR 38.60; **Circ:** 89,359
Usual Pagination: 132
Profile: Magazine about food, drink and travel.
Language(s): French
ADVERTISING RATES:
Full Page Colour .... EUR 8300
Mechanical Data: Type Area: 230x280
Copy instructions: *Copy Date:* 62 days prior to publication date
CONSUMER: WOMEN'S INTEREST CONSUMER MAGAZINES: Food & Cookery

SAVOIE MAGAZINE
1617201F32A-1059
Editorial: Conseil Général de la Savoie, Hôtel du département - Château des Ducs, BP 1802 CEDEX, 73018 CHAMBERY **Tel:** 4 79 96 73 27
Fax: 4 79 96 88 87
Email: savoiemagazine@cg73.fr
ISSN: 1136-7733
Date Established: 2001; **Freq:** 24 issues yearly - Mois pairs; **Cover Price:** Free; **Circ:** 190,000
Usual Pagination: 24
Profile: Publication focussing on local government and department issues.
Language(s): French
Mechanical Data: Type Area: 23x29,7
BUSINESS: LOCAL GOVERNMENT, LEISURE & RECREATION: Local Government

LA SCIENCE & VIE
7112F94J-250
Editorial: Immeuble Trait d'Union, 8 rue François Ory, 92120 MONTROUGE **Tel:** 1 46 48 48 48
Fax: 1 46 48 48 67
Email: svmendoc@mondadori.fr **Web site:** http://www.science-et-vie.com
ISSN: 0036-8369
Date Established: 1913; **Freq:** Monthly - fin de mois;
Cover Price: EUR 3.90
Annual Sub.: EUR 39.80; **Circ:** 329,661
Usual Pagination: 160
Profile: Magazine focusing on news and developments in science and technology. Covers science, medical research, the environment, archaeology and astrophysics.
Language(s): French
ADVERTISING RATES:
Full Page Colour .... EUR 17800
Mechanical Data: Type Area: 183 x 242
Copy instructions: *Copy Date:* 31 days prior to publication date
CONSUMER: OTHER CLASSIFICATIONS: Popular Science

SCIENCE & VIE JUNIOR
1618328F91D-371
Editorial: Immeuble Trait d'Union, 8 rue François Ory, 92120 MONTROUGE **Tel:** 1 46 48 48 48 49 74
Fax: 1 46 48 49 91
Email: courriersvj@mondadori.fr **Web site:** http://www.svjlesite.fr
ISSN: 0992-5899
Date Established: 1989; **Freq:** Monthly - autour du 20 du même mois; **Cover Price:** EUR 4.50
Annual Sub.: EUR 45.80; **Circ:** 169,871
Usual Pagination: 100
Managing Director: Ernesto Mauri
Profile: Youth publication (12-25 years) focussing on science, general news, health and medicine, physics, astronomy, computing, biology, culture, exhibitions, society, consumption and DVDs.
Language(s): French
ADVERTISING RATES:
Full Page Colour .... EUR 11400
Mechanical Data: Type Area: 230 x 275
Copy instructions: *Copy Date:* 15 days prior to publication date
CONSUMER: RECREATION & LEISURE: Children & Youth

SCIENCE-ENVIRONNEMENT.INFO
5325F57-90
Editorial: 5 rue François Ponsard, 75116 PARIS
Tel: 1 55 74 62 00 **Fax:** 1 55 74 62 10
Email: topix.redaction@wanadoo.fr **Web site:** http://www.science-environnement.info
Date Established: 2000; **Freq:** Daily; **Cover Price:** Free
Profile: Magazine covering developments in environmental technology.
Language(s): French
Readership: Aimed at people involved in decisions concerning the environment.
ADVERTISING RATES:
Full Page Colour .... EUR 3380
BUSINESS: ENVIRONMENT & POLLUTION

LES SCIENCES ET AVENIR
6387F73-229
Editorial: 33 rue Vivienne, CEDEX 2, 75083 PARIS
Tel: 1 55 35 56 00 **Fax:** 1 55 35 56 04
Email: redaction@sciences-et-avenir.com **Web site:** http://www.sciences-et-avenir.com
ISSN: 0036-8636
Date Established: 1947; **Freq:** Monthly - dernier jeudi du mois précédent
Annual Sub.: EUR 35; **Circ:** 268,429
Usual Pagination: 116
Profile: Magazine focusing on science, technology and the future.
Language(s): French
ADVERTISING RATES:
Full Page Colour .... EUR 16400
Mechanical Data: Type Area: 200 x 270
Copy instructions: *Copy Date:* 15 days prior to publication date
CONSUMER: NATIONAL & INTERNATIONAL PERIODICALS

SECURITE INFORMATIQUE
4657F5B-186
Editorial: 47 rue Aristide-Briand, 92300 LEVALLOIS-PERRET **Tel:** 1 41 49 93 60 **Fax:** 1 47 57 37 25
Email: a.fraumont@publi-news.fr **Web site:** http://www.publi-news.fr
Freq: 26 times a year. 2ième et 4ième mardi du mois;
Annual Sub.: EUR 635; **Circ:** 1,000 Unique Users
Usual Pagination: 8
Editor: Ange Galula
Profile: Technical magazine concerning computing, with particular emphasis on information and computing security.
Language(s): French
ADVERTISING RATES:
Full Page Mono .... EUR 1380
Copy instructions: *Copy Date:* 7 days prior to publication date
BUSINESS: COMPUTERS & AUTOMATION: Data Processing

SEINE ET MARNE MAGAZINE
1617203F32A-1061
Editorial: Conseil Général, Hôtel du Département, CEDEX, 77010 MELUN **Tel:** 1 64 14 70 58 70 48
Fax: 1 64 14 70 46
Email: magazine@cg77.fr **Web site:** http://www.seine-et-marne.fr
ISSN: 1147-9337
Freq: Monthly - 1er lundi du mois; **Cover Price:** Free;
Circ: 500,000
Usual Pagination: 32
Profile: Publication focussing on local government and department issues, including economics, agriculture, tourism, events, leisure, cultural and social issues.
Language(s): French
Mechanical Data: Type Area: A 4
BUSINESS: LOCAL GOVERNMENT, LEISURE & RECREATION: Local Government

France

SEINE SAINT DENIS.FR LE MAGAZINE
1617202F32A-1060

Editorial: Conseil Général, Hôtel du Département, CEDEX, 93006 BOBIGNY **Tel:** 1 43 93 94 67
Fax: 1 43 93 94 50
Email: mag93@cg93.fr
ISSN: 1274-1043
Date Established: 1996; **Freq:** Monthly - début de mois; **Cover Price:** Free; **Circ:** 600,000
Usual Pagination: 44
Profile: Publication focussing on local government and department issues, including economics, sports, leisure, environment, cultural and social issues.
Language(s): French
Mechanical Data: Type Area: 23 x 30
BUSINESS: LOCAL GOVERNMENT, LEISURE & RECREATION: Local Government

SEINE-MARITIME LE MAGAZINE CONSEIL GENERAL DE SEINE-MARITIME
1617196F32A-1054

Editorial: Hôtel-du-Département, Quai Jean-Moulin, 76101 CEDEX 1 ROUEN **Tel:** 2 35 03 54 17
Fax: 235036774
Email: mag@cg76.fr **Web site:** http://www.seinemaritime.net
ISSN: 1176-5991
Date Established: 2005; **Freq:** Monthly - dernière semaine du mois; **Cover Price:** Free; **Circ:** 550,000
Usual Pagination: 50
Editor: Jean-François Bernard
Profile: Publication focussing on local government and department issues, including economics, culture and social issues.
Language(s): French
Mechanical Data: Type Area: 180 x 240
BUSINESS: LOCAL GOVERNMENT, LEISURE & RECREATION: Local Government

SFR MINIMAG
1617132F18B-94

Editorial: SFR - Tour Séquoia, 1 place Carpeaux, 92915 PARIS-LA-DEFENSE **Tel:** 1 71 08 32 96
Fax: 1 71 08 90 34
Email: francoise.marechal@sfr.com **Web site:** http://www.sfr.fr
ISSN: 1629-2278
Date Established: 2001; **Freq:** Monthly - tous les 15 du mois; **Cover Price:** Free; **Circ:** 8,000,000
Usual Pagination: 5
Editor: Cécile Berger
Profile: Customer magazine focussing on telecommunication and mobile phones. Circulated in the SFR selling points.
Language(s): French
Mechanical Data: Type Area: 94 x198
Copy instructions: *Copy Date:* pas de publicité
BUSINESS: ELECTRONICS: Telecommunications

SITES COMMERCIAUX
4520F1E-250

Editorial: 70 boulevard Magenta, 75010 PARIS
Tel: 1 40 34 15 15 **Fax:** 1 40 38 41 28
Email: alain.boutigny@enseigne-et-sites.com
Date Established: 1990; **Freq:** Monthly - le 5 du mois
Annual Sub.: EUR 74; **Circ:** 12,000
Usual Pagination: 48
Profile: Property magazine containing information on commercial sites, trading estates, shopping malls, hypermarkets and town centres.
Language(s): French
Mechanical Data: Type Area: 24 x 32
BUSINESS: FINANCE & ECONOMICS: Property

SONO MAGAZINE
5948F61-190

Editorial: 2/12 rue de Bellevue, CEDEX 19, 75940 PARIS **Tel:** 1 44 84 84 84 **Fax:** 1 44 84 84 67
Email: redaction@sonomag.com **Web site:** http://www.sonomag.com
Date Established: 1978; **Freq:** Monthly - 10 du mois;
Cover Price: EUR 4.60
Annual Sub.: EUR 40.70; **Circ:** 13,268
Usual Pagination: 164
Profile: Magazine concerning sound and lighting for the music industry. Includes technical articles and information on exhibitions and concerts.
Language(s): French
Readership: Aimed at lighting and sound technicians in the music sector.
ADVERTISING RATES:
Full Page Mono .... EUR 2360
Full Page Colour .... EUR 3340
Mechanical Data: Type Area: 225 x 287
BUSINESS: MUSIC TRADE

SONOVISION VIDEO BROADCAST
5466F43C-70

Editorial: EDITIONS TRANSOCEANIC, 3 boulevard Ney, 75018 PARIS **Tel:** 1 44 65 80 80
Fax: 1 44 65 80 69 90
Email: lionel@sonovision.com **Web site:** http://www.sonovision.com
ISSN: 0299-4690
Date Established: 1971; **Freq:** Monthly - vers le 5 du mois
Annual Sub.: EUR 77; **Circ:** 20,000
Usual Pagination: 130
Profile: Technical and professional magazine about the audiovisual sector. Includes information on audiovisual techniques and equipment, also production and programmes.
Language(s): French
ADVERTISING RATES:
Full Page Colour .... EUR 3075
Mechanical Data: Type Area: 230 x 300
BUSINESS: ELECTRICAL RETAIL TRADE: TV

SORTIR TELERAMA SUPPLEMENT DE TELERAMA
1616764F89C-358

Editorial: 8 rue Jean-Antoine-de-Baïf, 75212 CEDEX 13 PARIS **Tel:** 1 55 30 55 62 **Fax:** 1 45 22 08 45
Email: sortir@telerama.fr **Web site:** http://www.telerama.fr
ISSN: 0040-2699
Freq: Weekly - le mercredi; **Cover Price:** Free; **Circ:** 300,000
Usual Pagination: 40
Profile: Publication focussing on events in the Paris area including going out, concerts, theatre, exhibition, dance, cinema and practical information.
Language(s): French
ADVERTISING RATES:
Full Page Colour .... EUR 19300
Mechanical Data: Type Area: 214 x 280
CONSUMER: HOLIDAYS & TRAVEL: Entertainment Guides

SPECTACLES A NANCY
7215F89C-250

Editorial: 22 rue François de Neufchâteau, BP 43722, CEDEX, 54098 NANCY **Tel:** 3 83 92 42 42
Fax: 3 83 94 02 87
Email: info@spectaclespublications.com **Web site:** http://www.spectacles-publications.com
ISSN: 1259-1971
Date Established: 1984; **Freq:** Monthly - fin de mois;
Cover Price: Free; **Circ:** 29,950
Usual Pagination: 64
Profile: Magazine providing entertainment listings and general information for Nancy and the surrounding region. Includes articles on books, records, video, multimedia and health and beauty.
Language(s): French
ADVERTISING RATES:
Full Page Mono .... EUR 1250
Full Page Colour .... EUR 2030
Mechanical Data: Type Area: 235 x 300
CONSUMER: HOLIDAYS & TRAVEL: Entertainment Guides

SPORT ET STYLE
1656953F86C-274

Editorial: 4 cours de l'Ile Seguin, BP 10302, 92102 BOULOGNE BILLANCOURT **Tel:** 1 40 93 20 20
Fax: 1 40 93 27 78
Email: eseydi@condenast.fr
ISSN: 1769-437X
Date Established: 2004; **Freq:** Quarterly - les mois 03 06 09 12; **Cover Price:** Free; **Circ:** 480,000
Usual Pagination: 138
Publisher: Louis Gillet
Profile: Upscale publication focussing on men's interest including fashion, sport and luxury.
Language(s): French
ADVERTISING RATES:
Full Page Colour .... EUR 32000
Mechanical Data: Type Area: 225 x 295
Copy instructions: *Copy Date:* 31 days prior to publication date
CONSUMER: ADULT & GAY MAGAZINES: Men's Lifestyle Magazines

STRATEGIES
4550F2A-90

Editorial: Forum 55, 52 rue Camille Desmoulins, BP 62, 92448 ISSY LES MOULINEAUX
Tel: 1 46 29 46 29 **Fax:** 1 46 29 46 09
Email: redaction@strategies.fr **Web site:** http://www.strategies.fr
ISSN: 0180-6424
Date Established: 1971; **Freq:** Weekly - Thursday;
Cover Price: EUR 5.80
Annual Sub.: EUR 190; **Circ:** 13,769
Usual Pagination: 50
Editor-in-Chief: Olivier Mongeau
Profile: Journal providing information about marketing, publicity and communication. Online version is up-dated daily.
Language(s): French
ADVERTISING RATES:
Full Page Colour .... EUR 7550
Mechanical Data: Type Area: magazine
BUSINESS: COMMUNICATIONS, ADVERTISING & MARKETING

STUDYRAMAG
7197F89C-70

Editorial: 34/38 rue Camille Pelletan, CEDEX, 92309 LEVALLOIS PERRET **Tel:** 1 41 06 59 00
Fax: 1 41 06 59 09
Email: redaction@vocatis.fr **Web site:** http://www.studyrama.com
ISSN: 1146-3171
Date Established: 1989; **Freq:** Monthly - 1ère semaine du mois; **Cover Price:** Free; **Circ:** 200,000
Usual Pagination: 70
Profile: Magazine containing information about Paris reflecting student interests.
Language(s): French
Readership: Aimed at young people between 18 and 26 years.
ADVERTISING RATES:
Full Page Colour .... EUR 5000
Mechanical Data: Type Area: A 5
Copy instructions: *Copy Date:* 15 days prior to publication date
CONSUMER: HOLIDAYS & TRAVEL: Entertainment Guides

SUD OUEST BORDEAUX
6161F67B-7600

Editorial: 23 quai de Queyries, 33094 BORDEAUX
Tel: 5 35 31 31 31
Email: contact@sudouest.com **Web site:** http://www.sudouest.fr
ISSN: 1760-6454
Date Established: 1944; **Freq:** Daily - le matin du lundi au samedi; **Cover Price:** EUR 0.85
Annual Sub.: EUR 242; **Circ:** 313,031
Profile: Regional daily newspaper focussing on local and regional news and current affairs including politics, aeronautics, science, economics, Europe, employment, employees, social, health, culture, law, sport, fashion, beauty, tourism, regional interest, social studies, wine and news in brief.
Language(s): French
ADVERTISING RATES:
Full Page Mono .... EUR 8238
Full Page Colour .... EUR 9550
Mechanical Data: Type Area: tabloïd
Copy instructions: *Copy Date:* 2 days prior to publication date
REGIONAL DAILY & SUNDAY NEWSPAPERS: Regional Daily Newspapers

SUD OUEST DIMANCHE
1619694F67C-111

Editorial: 23, quai de Queyries, 33094 CEDEX BORDEAUX **Tel:** 5 35 31 31 31
Email: dimanche@sudouest.com **Web site:** http://www.sudouest.com
ISSN: 7116-0941
Date Established: 1949; **Freq:** Weekly - dimanche;
Cover Price: EUR 1.50
Annual Sub.: EUR 71.35; **Circ:** 286,525
Profile: Sunday edition of the regional daily newspaper focussing on news and current affairs.
Language(s): French
ADVERTISING RATES:
Full Page Mono .... EUR 12631
Full Page Colour .... EUR 13890
Mechanical Data: Type Area: tabloïd
REGIONAL DAILY & SUNDAY NEWSPAPERS: Regional Sunday Newspapers

SUPER PICSOU GEANT
1618337F91D-372

Editorial: 10 rue Thierry-Le-Luron, 92592 CEDEX LEVALLOIS-PERRET **Tel:** 1 41 34 89 31
Fax: 141348861
Web site: http://www.picsou.fr
ISSN: 1291-9039
Freq: 6 issues yearly - le premier mercredi mois impairs; **Cover Price:** EUR 390
Annual Sub.: EUR 1950; **Circ:** 205,562
Usual Pagination: 196
Profile: Youth publication (12-25 years) focussing on Disney comics and games.
Language(s): French
ADVERTISING RATES:
Full Page Colour .... EUR 5991
Mechanical Data: Type Area: 190 x 275
Copy instructions: *Copy Date:* 62 days prior to publication date
CONSUMER: RECREATION & LEISURE: Children & Youth

SYSTEME D
6922F79A-150

Editorial: 15 à 27 rue Moussorgski, 75018 PARIS
Tel: 1 53 26 30 06 **Fax:** 1 53 26 33 03
Email: redac@systemed.fr **Web site:** http://www.systemed.fr
ISSN: 1554-2829
Date Established: 1924; **Freq:** Monthly - fin de mois;
Cover Price: EUR 4.50
Annual Sub.: EUR 40.50; **Circ:** 141,692
Usual Pagination: 132
Managing Director: Benoît Pollet
Profile: DIY and hobby magazine including features about carpentry, masonry, electronics, mechanics, car maintenance, boat building, photography, film-making, gardening and decorating.
Language(s): French
ADVERTISING RATES:
Full Page Colour .... EUR 13750
Mechanical Data: Type Area: 225 x 272
Copy instructions: *Copy Date:* 31 days prior to publication date
CONSUMER: HOBBIES & DIY

SYSTEMES SOLAIRES
5925F58-170

Editorial: OBSERV'ER, 146 rue de l'Université, 75007 PARIS **Tel:** 1 44 18 00 80 **Fax:** 1 44 18 00 36
Email: systemes.solaires@energies-renouvelables.org **Web site:** http://www.energies-renouvelables.org
ISSN: 0295-5873
Date Established: 1985; **Freq:** 24 issues yearly - 15th of the month; **Cover Price:** EUR 22
Annual Sub.: EUR 79; **Circ:** 6,000
Usual Pagination: 96
Editor-in-Chief: Yves-Bruno Civel
Profile: Magazine focusing on renewable energy. Includes information about solar energy, wind, biomass, micro and hydro-electricity and geothermal energy.
Language(s): French
ADVERTISING RATES:
Full Page Colour .... EUR 2600
Mechanical Data: Type Area: 21 x 29,7
Copy instructions: *Copy Date:* 7 days prior to publication date
BUSINESS: ENERGY, FUEL & NUCLEAR

LE TARN LIBRE
5161F72-1201

Editorial: Rue Alain Colas, BP 24, CEDEX 9, 81027 ALBI **Tel:** 5 63 48 75 48 **Fax:** 5 63 48 75 49
Email: redaction@letarnlibre.com **Web site:** http://www.letarnlibre.com
Date Established: 1835; **Freq:** Weekly; **Cover Price:** EUR 1.20
Annual Sub.: EUR 57; **Circ:** 25,000
Usual Pagination: 48
Profile: Regional news.
Language(s): French
ADVERTISING RATES:
Full Page Mono .... EUR 2400
Full Page Colour .... EUR 3590
Mechanical Data: Type Area: 44 x 29
LOCAL NEWSPAPERS

TECHNIKART MAGAZINE
7090F84A-525

Editorial: Passage du Cheval Blanc, 2 rue de la Roquette, 75011 PARIS **Fax:** 1 43 14 33 39 40
Email: rturcat@technikart.com **Web site:** http://www.technikart.com
ISSN: 1162-8732
Date Established: 1991; **Freq:** Monthly - Last Thursday of the month; **Cover Price:** EUR 4.90
Annual Sub.: EUR 39.20; **Circ:** 41,270
Usual Pagination: 132
Profile: Magazine focusing on the arts and culture. Includes information on art, sculpture and photography.
Language(s): French
Readership: Aimed at the general public.
ADVERTISING RATES:
Full Page Mono .... EUR 6800
Full Page Colour .... EUR 8500
Mechanical Data: Type Area: 230 x 300
CONSUMER: THE ARTS & LITERARY: Arts

TELE 2 SEMAINES
1639292F76C-209

Editorial: 14 boulevard du Général Leclerc, CEDEX, 92527 NEUILLY SUR SEINE **Tel:** 1 73 05 57 00
Fax: 1 76 68 57 40
Email: cantonin@prisma-presse.com **Web site:** http://www.tele2semaines.fr
ISSN: 1763-5640
Date Established: 2003; **Freq:** 26 issues yearly - 1 lundi sur 2; **Cover Price:** EUR 1.30
Annual Sub.: EUR 28; **Circ:** 1,102,116
Usual Pagination: 208
Publisher: Philippe Labi
Profile: Publication focussing on TV and radio programmes including cable, satellite, celebrities, reviews, sport and games.
Language(s): French
ADVERTISING RATES:
Full Page Mono .... EUR 22290
Full Page Colour .... EUR 29100
Mechanical Data: Type Area: 210 x 256
CONSUMER: MUSIC & PERFORMING ARTS: TV & Radio

TELE 7 JOURS
6746F76C-80

Editorial: Immeuble Europa, 149 rue Anatoie France, CEDEX, 92534 LEVALLOIS PERRET
Tel: 1 41 34 60 00 **Fax:** 1 41 34 68 92
Email: claude.bosle@lagardere-active.com **Web site:** http://www.tele7.fr
ISSN: 0153-0747
Date Established: 1960; **Freq:** Weekly - lundi; **Cover Price:** EUR 0.99
Annual Sub.: EUR 48; **Circ:** 1,513,771
Usual Pagination: 152
Profile: Television listings magazine.
Language(s): French
ADVERTISING RATES:
Full Page Mono .... EUR 26767
Full Page Colour .... EUR 37650
Mechanical Data: Type Area: 20 x 28
CONSUMER: MUSIC & PERFORMING ARTS: TV & Radio

TELE LOISIRS
6749F76C-120

Editorial: 14 boulevard du Général Leclerc, CEDEX, 92527 NEUILLY SUR SEINE **Tel:** 1 76 68 57 00
Fax: 1 76 68 58 50 58 29
Email: tele-loisirs@prisma-presse.com **Web site:** http://www.teleloisirs.fr
ISSN: 0297-8695
Date Established: 1986; **Freq:** Weekly - lundi; **Cover Price:** EUR 1.10
Annual Sub.: EUR 49.90; **Circ:** 1,110,013
Usual Pagination: 156
Publisher: Philippe Labi
Profile: Television listings magazine containing news, discussion and information.
Language(s): French
ADVERTISING RATES:
Full Page Mono .... EUR 22100
Full Page Colour .... EUR 28875
Mechanical Data: Type Area: 220 x 270
Copy instructions: *Copy Date:* 20 days prior to publication date
CONSUMER: MUSIC & PERFORMING ARTS: TV & Radio

TELE LOISIRS GUIDE CUISINE
6589F74P-280
Editorial: 13 rue Henri Barbusse, 92624 GENNEVILLIERS **Tel:** 1 73 05 65 98 67 00
Email: guidecuisine@prisma-presse.com **Web site:** http://www.guidecuisine.fr
ISSN: 1264-7306
Freq: Monthly - autour du 10 du mois précédent; **Cover Price:** EUR 1.80
Annual Sub.: EUR 18; **Circ:** 77,063
Profile: Practical guide to cooking and eating.
Language(s): French
ADVERTISING RATES:
Full Page Mono .... EUR 10500
Full Page Colour .... EUR 14000
Copy instructions: *Copy Date:* 21 days prior to publication date
CONSUMER: WOMEN'S INTEREST CONSUMER MAGAZINES: Food & Cookery

TELE MAGAZINE
6751F76C-130
Editorial: 68 rue Marjolin, CEDEX, 92309 LEVALLOIS PERRET **Tel:** 1 45 19 58 00 **Fax:** 1 45 19 58 16
Email: redaction@telemagazine.fr **Web site:** http://www.telemagazine.fr
ISSN: 0759-6669
Date Established: 1955; **Freq:** Weekly - jeudi
Annual Sub.: EUR 44.95; **Circ:** 360,812
Usual Pagination: 114
Profile: TV guide to forthcoming French programmes.
Language(s): French
ADVERTISING RATES:
Full Page Colour .... EUR 7500
Copy instructions: *Copy Date:* 15 days prior to publication date
CONSUMER: MUSIC & PERFORMING ARTS: TV & Radio

TELE POCHE
6752F76C-140
Editorial: Immeuble Trait d'Union, 8 rue François Ory, 92120 MONTROUGE **Tel:** 1 41 33 50 02 53 27
Fax: 1 41 33 57 49
Email: eric.pavon@mondadori.fr **Web site:** http://www.telepoche.fr
ISSN: 1274-9192
Date Established: 1966; **Freq:** Weekly - lundi suivant; **Cover Price:** EUR 0.99
Annual Sub.: EUR 43.90; **Circ:** 588,466
Usual Pagination: 204
Profile: Television programme magazine with news and commentary.
Language(s): French
Readership: Aimed at children.
ADVERTISING RATES:
Full Page Mono .... EUR 14408
Full Page Colour .... EUR 16950
Mechanical Data: Type Area: 170 x 210
CONSUMER: MUSIC & PERFORMING ARTS: TV & Radio

TELE STAR
6755F76C-160
Editorial: Immeuble Trait d'Union, 8 rue François Ory, 92120 MONTROUGE **Tel:** 1 41 33 58 02
Fax: 1 41 33 58 80
Email: fabrice.dupreuilh@mondadori.fr **Web site:** http://www.telestar.fr
ISSN: 0150-2581
Date Established: 1976; **Freq:** Weekly - chaque lundi; **Cover Price:** EUR 1.10
Annual Sub.: EUR 54.60; **Circ:** 1,197,456
Usual Pagination: 160
Profile: Magazine containing TV listings and celebrity profiles and interviews.
Language(s): French
ADVERTISING RATES:
Full Page Mono .... EUR 23987
Full Page Colour .... EUR 28220
CONSUMER: MUSIC & PERFORMING ARTS: TV & Radio

TELE Z
6756F76C-165
Editorial: 10 avenue de Messine, 75008 PARIS
Tel: 1 53 83 93 40 **Fax:** 1 42 89 97 73
Email: info@telez.fr **Web site:** http://www.telez.fr
ISSN: 0753-695X
Date Established: 1982; **Freq:** Weekly - lundi; **Cover Price:** EUR 0.39
Annual Sub.: EUR 17; **Circ:** 1,614,772
Usual Pagination: 130
Profile: Television listings magazine.
Language(s): French
ADVERTISING RATES:
Full Page Mono .... EUR 22290
Full Page Colour .... EUR 33900
Copy instructions: *Copy Date:* 7 days prior to publication date
CONSUMER: MUSIC & PERFORMING ARTS: TV & Radio

TELECABLE SAT HEBDO
6747F76C-98
Editorial: 48/50 Boulevard Sénard, 92210 SAINT CLOUD **Tel:** 1 47 11 20 00 **Fax:** 1 46 02 31 51
Email: courrier@telecable.hommell.com **Web site:** http://www.telecablesat.fr
ISSN: 1280-6617
Date Established: 1990; **Freq:** Weekly - Monday; **Cover Price:** EUR 1.40
Annual Sub.: EUR 67; **Circ:** 636,736
Usual Pagination: 166
Managing Director: Christian Castellani
Profile: Magazine detailing cable and satellite TV programmes.
Language(s): French
ADVERTISING RATES:
Full Page Colour .... EUR 14000
Mechanical Data: Type Area: 205 x 270
Copy instructions: *Copy Date:* 11 days prior to publication date
CONSUMER: MUSIC & PERFORMING ARTS: TV & Radio

LE TELEGRAMME DE BREST ET DE L'OUEST MORLAIX
6194F67B-7700
Editorial: 7 voie d'Accès-au-Port, BP 67243, 29672 CEDEX MORLAIX **Tel:** 2 98 62 11 33
Fax: 2 98 63 20 99
Email: economie@letelegramme.fr **Web site:** http://www.letelegramme.com
ISSN: 0751-5928
Freq: Daily; **Cover Price:** EUR 0.80
Annual Sub.: EUR 244.70; **Circ:** 201,579
Usual Pagination: 30
Profile: International, national, regional and local news. Supplements published: sport on Monday, classified ads on Tuesday, cultural current events on Wednesday, TV guide on Saturday, women's interests on Sunday. Available on the website: daily news in video.
Language(s): French
ADVERTISING RATES:
Full Page Mono .... EUR 30930
Full Page Colour .... EUR 37988
Mechanical Data: Type Area: tabloïd
REGIONAL DAILY & SUNDAY NEWSPAPERS: Regional Daily Newspapers

LE TELEGRAMME DIMANCHE
1619588F67B-8588
Editorial: 7 voie d'Accès-au-Port, BP 67243, Cedex, 29672 MORLAIX **Tel:** 2 98 62 11 33
Fax: 2 98 63 45 45
Email: telegramme@letelegramme.fr **Web site:** http://www.letelegramme.com
ISSN: 0751-5928
Date Established: 1998; **Freq:** Weekly - Côtes-d'Armor (22); **Circ:** 141,479
Usual Pagination: 44
Profile: 16 sport report removable pages. International, national and regional news, including several special columns on top of the daily national news: games, celebrities, TV guide... The magazine 'Version Fémina' (published by Hachette Filipacchi Médias) is included as supplément. 4 editions: Nord Finistère, Sud Finistère, Côtes d'Armor and Morbihan.
Language(s): French
Mechanical Data: Type Area: tabloïd
REGIONAL DAILY & SUNDAY NEWSPAPERS: Regional Daily Newspapers

LE TELEGRAMME DU FINISTERE NORD EDITIONS DE BREST OUEST BREST EST ET BREST
1619592F67B-8592
Editorial: 19 rue Jean-Macé, CS 91957, 29219 CEDEX 1 BREST **Tel:** 2 98 33 74 31
Fax: 2 98 80 35 36
Email: brest@letelegramme.fr **Web site:** http://www.letelegramme.com
Freq: Daily - tous les jours; **Cover Price:** EUR 0.80
Annual Sub.: EUR 244.70; **Circ:** 215,000
Usual Pagination: 50
Profile: International, national, regional and local news. Saturday and Sunday price: 0,90 €.
Language(s): French
Mechanical Data: Type Area: tabloïd
REGIONAL DAILY & SUNDAY NEWSPAPERS: Regional Daily Newspapers

TELEOBS PARIS - TELE CINE OBS
1616784F76A-400
Editorial: 10-12 place de la Bourse, 75081 CEDEX 02 PARIS **Tel:** 1 44 88 35 70 **Fax:** 1 44 88 35 15
Web site: http://www.teleobs.com
ISSN: 1622-9207
Date Established: 1993; **Freq:** Weekly - jeudi; **Circ:** 185,000
Usual Pagination: 108
Editor: Claude Perdriel
Profile: Publication focussing on cinema, TV, video and digital space.
Language(s): French
ADVERTISING RATES:
Full Page Mono .... EUR 14400
Full Page Colour .... EUR 18000
Mechanical Data: Type Area: 230 x 300
Copy instructions: *Copy Date:* 10 days prior to publication date
CONSUMER: MUSIC & PERFORMING ARTS: Cinema

TELERAMA
6757F76C-200
Editorial: 6/8 rue Jean Antoine de Baïf, CEDEX 13, 75212 PARIS **Tel:** 1 55 30 55 30
Email: pascaud.f@telerama.fr **Web site:** http://www.telerama.fr
ISSN: 0040-2699
Date Established: 1950; **Freq:** Weekly - mercredi
Annual Sub.: EUR 74.90; **Circ:** 650,446
Usual Pagination: 160
Profile: Cultural magazine covering television, radio, cinema, music and books.
Language(s): French
ADVERTISING RATES:
Full Page Colour .... EUR 30400
Mechanical Data: Type Area: 214 x 280
Copy instructions: *Copy Date:* 15 days prior to publication date
CONSUMER: MUSIC & PERFORMING ARTS: TV & Radio

TENTATION
7179F89A-225
Editorial: 19 bis rue de Villeneuve, 92380 GARCHES
Tel: 1 47 01 95 95 **Fax:** 1 47 01 95 99
Email: magazine.tentation@wanadoo.fr
ISSN: 0269-1191
Date Established: 1990; **Freq:** Quarterly - January, April, July and October
Annual Sub.: EUR 24; **Circ:** 90,000
Usual Pagination: 120
Editor-in-Chief: Bruno Lecoq
Profile: Magazine concerning tourism, leisure, art and other leisure activities.
Language(s): French
ADVERTISING RATES:
Full Page Colour .... EUR 7050
Mechanical Data: Type Area: 215 x 300
CONSUMER: HOLIDAYS & TRAVEL: Travel

LA TERRASSE
7216F89C-270
Editorial: 4 avenue de Corbéra, 75012 PARIS
Tel: 1 53 02 06 60 **Fax:** 1 43 44 07 08
Email: la.terrasse@wanadoo.fr **Web site:** http://www.journal-laterrasse.fr
ISSN: 1241-5715
Date Established: 1992; **Freq:** Monthly - le 1er mercredi du mois; **Cover Price:** Free; **Circ:** 73,800
Usual Pagination: 40
Profile: Magazine detailing cultural events taking place in the l'Ile-de-France region.
Language(s): French
ADVERTISING RATES:
Full Page Mono .... EUR 2920
Full Page Colour .... EUR 3980
Mechanical Data: Type Area: A3
CONSUMER: HOLIDAYS & TRAVEL: Entertainment Guides

LA TERRE
5023F21A-1820
Editorial: 164 rue Ambroise Croizat, CEDEX, 93207 SAINT-DENIS **Tel:** 1 49 22 72 00 35
Fax: 1 49 22 73 80
Email: laterre@laterre.fr **Web site:** http://www.laterre.fr
ISSN: 0040-3814
Date Established: 1937; **Freq:** Weekly - mercredi
Annual Sub.: EUR 98; **Circ:** 110,000
Usual Pagination: 24
Profile: Agricultural publication of the French Communist Party.
Language(s): French
ADVERTISING RATES:
Full Page Mono .... EUR 5590
Full Page Colour .... EUR 8870
Mechanical Data: Type Area: 640 x 860
Copy instructions: *Copy Date:* 5 days prior to publication date
BUSINESS: AGRICULTURE & FARMING

LA TERRE DE CHEZ NOUS
5163F21J-1275
Editorial: 130 bis rue de Belfort, BP 939, CEDEX, 25021 BESANCON **Tel:** 3 81 65 52 03 52
Fax: 3 81 50 07 42
Email: terre.de.chez.nous@wanadoo.fr
ISSN: 0242-147X
Date Established: 1948; **Freq:** Weekly - samedi; **Cover Price:** EUR 1.50
Annual Sub.: EUR 74; **Circ:** 7,853
Usual Pagination: 24
Profile: Agricultural and rural life magazine for the Doubs region.
Language(s): French
ADVERTISING RATES:
Full Page Mono .... EUR 2000
Full Page Colour .... EUR 3030
Mechanical Data: Type Area: A3
BUSINESS: AGRICULTURE & FARMING: Agriculture & Farming - Regional

TERRE INFORMATION MAGAZINE
5419F40-80
Editorial: SIRPA TERRE, 14 rue Saint Dominique, 75700 PARIS SP 07 **Tel:** 1 72 69 25 50
Fax: 1 72 69 25 51
Email: sirpat-comecrite.emat@terre-net.defense.gouv.fr **Web site:** http://www.defense.gouv.fr/terre
ISSN: 0995-6999
Date Established: 1988; **Freq:** Monthly - début de mois
Annual Sub.: EUR 26.50; **Circ:** 95,000
Usual Pagination: 80
Profile: Magazine containing information about the army.
Language(s): French
ADVERTISING RATES:
Full Page Mono .... EUR 2500
Full Page Colour .... EUR 4000
Mechanical Data: Type Area: 200 x 300
Copy instructions: *Copy Date:* 15 days prior to publication date
BUSINESS: DEFENCE

TERRITOIRE MUTUEL
1618987F1D-170
Editorial: 7 rue Bergère, 75009 PARIS
Tel: 1 44 83 12 34 **Fax:** 1 44 83 12 00
Email: mntweb@mnt.fr
ISSN: 1163-3824
Date Established: 1985; **Freq:** Quarterly - mars juin septembre décembre; **Cover Price:** EUR 0.76
Annual Sub.: EUR 3.04; **Circ:** 750,000
Usual Pagination: 20
Language(s): French
Mechanical Data: Type Area: 200 x 280
Copy instructions: *Copy Date:* 31 days prior to publication date
BUSINESS: FINANCE & ECONOMICS: Insurance

TERRITOIRES
5318F32A-450
Editorial: 1 rue Sainte Lucie, 75015 PARIS
Tel: 1 43 55 40 05 **Fax:** 1 55 28 30 21
Email: territoires@adels.org **Web site:** http://www.adels.org
ISSN: 0223-5951
Date Established: 1959; **Freq:** Monthly - début de mois; **Cover Price:** EUR 7.50
Annual Sub.: EUR 55; **Circ:** 8,000
Usual Pagination: 58
Profile: Magazine covering rural policies. Includes information on local life, local development and town planning.
Language(s): French
Readership: Aimed at local communities.
ADVERTISING RATES:
Full Page Mono .... EUR 1000
Mechanical Data: Type Area: 260 x 200
Copy instructions: *Copy Date:* 14 days prior to publication date
BUSINESS: LOCAL GOVERNMENT, LEISURE & RECREATION: Local Government

TETU
7119F86B-160
Editorial: 6 bis rue Campagne Première, 75014 PARIS **Tel:** 1 56 80 20 80 **Fax:** 1 56 80 20 85
Email: redaction@tetu.com **Web site:** http://www.tetu.com
ISSN: 1265-3578
Date Established: 1995; **Freq:** Monthly - Third Wednesday of the month
Annual Sub.: EUR 49; **Circ:** 47,009
Usual Pagination: 213
Profile: Magazine concerning gay and lesbian issues. Also contains information about fashion, leisure time and current topical subjects.
Language(s): French
Readership: Aimed at the French gay community.
ADVERTISING RATES:
Full Page Colour .... EUR 7200
Mechanical Data: Type Area: 230 x 300
CONSUMER: ADULT & GAY MAGAZINES: Gay & Lesbian Magazines

LE TGV MAGAZINE
7231F89E-40
Editorial: TEXTUEL, 146 rue du Faubourg Poissonnière, 75010 PARIS **Tel:** 1 53 21 21 00
Fax: 1 53 21 21 53
Email: sylvain.fanet@textuel-lamine.com
ISSN: 1287-6232
Freq: Monthly - début de mois; **Cover Price:** Free; **Circ:** 293,819
Usual Pagination: 100
Profile: Tourism magazine for Paris and the rest of France. Includes information on tourism, leisure time, culture, business and lifestyles.
Language(s): French
Readership: Available when travelling on high speed trains.
ADVERTISING RATES:
Full Page Colour .... EUR 16400
Mechanical Data: Type Area: 200 x 260
Copy instructions: *Copy Date:* 62 days prior to publication date
CONSUMER: HOLIDAYS & TRAVEL: Holidays

TOP SANTE
6521F74G-160
Editorial: Immeuble Trait d'Union, 8 rue François Ory, 92120 MONTROUGE **Tel:** 1 46 48 48 48
Fax: 1 46 48 43 50
Email: sophie.delaugere@mondadori.fr **Web site:** http://www.topsante.com
ISSN: 1152-7137
Date Established: 1990; **Freq:** Monthly - autour du 25 du mois; **Cover Price:** EUR 2.70
Annual Sub.: EUR 30; **Circ:** 372,162
Usual Pagination: 120
Managing Director: Ernesto Mauri
Profile: Health and beauty magazine.
Language(s): French
ADVERTISING RATES:
Full Page Colour .... EUR 20500
Mechanical Data: Type Area: 200 x 270
Copy instructions: *Copy Date:* 31 days prior to publication date
CONSUMER: WOMEN'S INTEREST CONSUMER MAGAZINES: Slimming & Health

TOULON PROVENCE MEDITERRANEE COMMUNAUTE D'AGGLOMERATION 1648712F80-928

Editorial: 20 rue Nicolas-Peiresc, BP 536, 83041 TOULON CEDEX 9 **Tel:** 4 94 93 83 00
Fax: 4 94 93 83 22
Email: mag@tpmed.org **Web site:** http://www.tpm-agglo.fr
ISSN: 1767-9753
Date Established: 2004; **Freq:** Quarterly; **Circ:** 223,000
Usual Pagination: 36
Editor: Marc Giraud
Profile: Publication focussing on local community information.
Language(s): French
CONSUMER: RURAL & REGIONAL INTEREST

TOUR HEBDO 5588F50-81

Editorial: 1 rue Eugène et Armand Peugeot, CEDEX, 92856 RUEIL MALMAISON **Tel:** 1 76 73 30 00
Fax: 1 55 02 90 92
Email: vdennemont@wolters-kluwer.fr **Web site:** http://pros-du-tourisme.com/tourhebdo
ISSN: 1282-478X
Date Established: 1979; **Freq:** Weekly; **Cover Price:** EUR 2.60
Annual Sub.: EUR 71.50; **Circ:** 8,537
Usual Pagination: 52
Profile: Magazine providing information about the tourism industry in France, Belgium, Switzerland and Luxembourg.
Language(s): French
ADVERTISING RATES:
Full Page Mono .... EUR 4300
Full Page Colour .... EUR 6400
Mechanical Data: Type Area: 230 x 300
BUSINESS: TRAVEL & TOURISM

TOUT LE BAS RHIN CONSEIL GENERAL DU BAS-RHIN 1617206F32A-1064

Editorial: Hôtel-du-Département, Place du Quartier-Blanc, 67964 CEDEX 9 STRASBOURG
Tel: 3 88 76 67 67 **Fax:** 388766917
Email: tlbr@cg67.fr **Web site:** http://www.cg67.fr
ISSN: 1296-7920
Freq: 6 issues yearly - début 01 03 05 07 09 11; **Cover Price:** Free; **Circ:** 462,000
Usual Pagination: 32
Editor: Guy-Dominique Kennel
Profile: Publication focussing on local government and department issues, including economics, transport, education, environment, tourism, cultural and social issues.
Language(s): French
Mechanical Data: Type Area: 23 x 30
BUSINESS: LOCAL GOVERNMENT, LEISURE & RECREATION: Local Government

TOUTE LA MAISON 1618392F74C-479

Editorial: 111 avenue Victor-Hugo, 75016 PARIS
Tel: 1 47 55 63 63 **Fax:** 1 47 55 63 53
Email: md@vip-international.fr
Date Established: 1996; **Freq:** 6 issues yearly - fin de mois pairs
Annual Sub.: EUR 10; **Circ:** 46,382
Usual Pagination: 84
Editor: Philippe Aubry
Profile: Publication focussing on home & style including decoration, gardens, safety, books, exhibitions and new products.
Language(s): French
ADVERTISING RATES:
Full Page Colour .... EUR 7000
Mechanical Data: Type Area: 280 x 210
Copy instructions: *Copy Date:* 20 days prior to publication date
CONSUMER: WOMEN'S INTEREST CONSUMER MAGAZINES: Home & Family

TRAITEMENTS & MATERIAUX 4974F19C-60

Editorial: 16/18 place de la Chapelle, 75018 PARIS
Tel: 1 53 26 48 00 **Fax:** 1 53 26 48 01
Email: info@pyc.fr **Web site:** http://www.pyc.fr
ISSN: 0041-0950
Date Established: 1963; **Freq:** 24 issues yearly - les mois 01 03 05 08 10 12; **Cover Price:** EUR 22.50
Annual Sub.: EUR 145; **Circ:** 2,000
Usual Pagination: 48
Profile: Journal focusing on finishing treatments. Also provides information for the metal industry.
Language(s): French
Readership: Aimed at people within the engineering industry.
ADVERTISING RATES:
Full Page Mono .... EUR 1125
Full Page Colour .... EUR 2335
Mechanical Data: Type Area: A 4
Copy instructions: *Copy Date:* 31 days prior to publication date
BUSINESS: ENGINEERING & MACHINERY: Finishing

TRANSFAC - L'EXPRESS 1617331F83-237

Editorial: 23 rue de Châteaudun, CEDEX 09, 75308 PARIS **Tel:** 1 75 55 40 40
Email: stavennec@letudiant.fr
ISSN: 1158-0933
Date Established: 1985; **Freq:** Quarterly - début de mois; **Cover Price:** Free; **Circ:** 201,628
Usual Pagination: 64
Editor-in-Chief: Philippe Mandry
Language(s): French
ADVERTISING RATES:
Full Page Mono .... EUR 5617
Full Page Colour .... EUR 7268
Mechanical Data: Type Area: A4
Copy instructions: *Copy Date:* 7 days prior to publication date
CONSUMER: STUDENT PUBLICATIONS

TRAVAIL ET SECURITE 5629F54C-170

Editorial: 30 rue Olivier Noyer, CEDEX 14, 75680 PARIS **Tel:** 1 40 44 31 54 **Fax:** 1 40 44 30 41
Email: ts@inrs.fr **Web site:** http://www.travail-et-securite.fr
ISSN: 0373-1944
Freq: Monthly - début de mois; **Cover Price:** EUR 5.10
Annual Sub.: EUR 45; **Circ:** 98,000
Usual Pagination: 56
Profile: Magazine containing articles about accident prevention at work.
Language(s): French
Mechanical Data: Type Area: A 4
BUSINESS: SAFETY & SECURITY: Security

LA TRIBUNE 6097F65A-160

Editorial: 26 rue d'Oradour sur Glane, 75015 PARIS
Tel: 1 44 82 16 16
Web site: http://www.latribune.fr
ISSN: 0989-1922
Freq: Daily - le lendemain matin; **Cover Price:** EUR 1.30
Annual Sub.: EUR 385; **Circ:** 78,463
Usual Pagination: 32
Profile: Tabloid-sized quality newspaper focusing exclusively on financial and business news, company analyses and reports.
Language(s): French
Readership: Aimed at leaders in the financial and business sectors, senior executives, managers and university students.
ADVERTISING RATES:
Full Page Mono .... EUR 29800
Full Page Colour .... EUR 37900
Mechanical Data: Type Area: tabloid
NATIONAL DAILY & SUNDAY NEWSPAPERS: National Daily Newspapers

LA TRIBUNE LE PROGRES SAINT-ETIENNE 6185F67B-7800

Editorial: 2 place Jean-Jaurès, 42000 SAINT-ETIENNE **Tel:** 4 77 45 10 10 **Fax:** 4 77 45 10 29
Email: chefinfo42@leprogres.fr **Web site:** http://www.leprogres.fr
ISSN: 0999-2219
Freq: Daily; **Cover Price:** EUR 0.85
Annual Sub.: EUR 249
Usual Pagination: 32
Profile: National, regional and local news. Sunday price: 1,50 € - Full week subscription including Sunday: 327 €.
Language(s): French
ADVERTISING RATES:
Full Page Mono .... EUR 3717
REGIONAL DAILY & SUNDAY NEWSPAPERS: Regional Daily Newspapers

LA TUTELAIRE 1618989F1D-172

Editorial: 45 rue Eugène-Oudiné, 75013 PARIS
Tel: 1 44 06 89 42 **Fax:** 144239567
Email: contact@tutelaire.fr **Web site:** http://www.tutelaire.fr
ISSN: 1279-3019
Freq: Quarterly - janvier avril juillet octobre; **Cover Price:** EUR 0.32; **Circ:** 530,000
Usual Pagination: 20
Language(s): French
Mechanical Data: Type Area: 210 x 297
BUSINESS: FINANCE & ECONOMICS: Insurance

TV GRANDES CHAINES 1642311F76C-213

Editorial: 14 boulevard du Général Leclerc, CEDEX, 92527 NEUILLY SUR SEINE **Tel:** 1 76 68 57 00 58 64
Fax: 1 76 68 59 39
Email: rpernele@prisma-presse.com **Web site:** http://www.tvgrandeschaines.fr
ISSN: 1767-0519
Date Established: 2004; **Freq:** 26 issues yearly - un lundi sur deux; **Cover Price:** EUR 0.95
Annual Sub.: EUR 23.40; **Circ:** 1,121,202
Usual Pagination: 160
Publisher: Philippe Labi
Profile: Publication focussing on aerial channels TV programmes only including celebrities, cinema, DVD, books, cookery, health, horoscope, games and TV series.
Language(s): French
ADVERTISING RATES:
Full Page Mono .... EUR 14200
Full Page Colour .... EUR 18500
Mechanical Data: Type Area: 225 x 273
Copy instructions: *Copy Date:* 21 days prior to publication date
CONSUMER: MUSIC & PERFORMING ARTS: TV & Radio

TV MAGAZINE 6745F76C-60

Editorial: 14 boulevard Haussmann, CEDEX 09, 75438 PARIS **Tel:** 1 57 08 72 00 **Fax:** 1 57 08 72 22
Email: f.tauriac@tvmag.com **Web site:** http://www.tvmag.com
ISSN: 0184-9336
Date Established: 1987; **Freq:** Weekly - mercredi ou samedi; **Circ:** 4,587,082
Publisher: François Tauriac
Profile: Magazine containing television listings and information about television stars.
Language(s): French
ADVERTISING RATES:
Full Page Colour .... EUR 83500
Mechanical Data: Type Area: 220 x 290
Copy instructions: *Copy Date:* 21 days prior to publication date
CONSUMER: MUSIC & PERFORMING ARTS: TV & Radio

L' UNION GIRONDINE DES VINS 5085F21H-90

Editorial: 1 cours du 30 Juillet, 33000 BORDEAUX
Tel: 5 56 00 22 98 **Fax:** 5 56 48 53 79
Email: contact@union-girondine.com **Web site:** http://fgvb.monaoc.com
ISSN: 0242-6706
Date Established: 1922; **Freq:** Monthly - le 25 de chaque mois
Annual Sub.: EUR 45; **Circ:** 6,500
Usual Pagination: 48
Profile: Official newspaper of the wine-producing region of Bordeaux, with economic, technical and legislative information.
Language(s): French
Readership: Read by vine growers and wine producers.
ADVERTISING RATES:
Full Page Mono .... EUR 1270
Full Page Colour .... EUR 2050
Mechanical Data: Type Area: 210 x 297
Copy instructions: *Copy Date:* 31 days prior to publication date
BUSINESS: AGRICULTURE & FARMING: Vine Growing

L' UNION REIMS 6203F67B-7900

Editorial: 5 rue de Talleyrand, 51083 CEDEX REIMS
Tel: 3 26 50 50 50 **Fax:** 3 26 47 45 45
Email: dirgen@journal-lunion.fr **Web site:** http://www.lunion.presse.fr
ISSN: 1628-1128
Date Established: 1944; **Freq:** Daily - matin; **Cover Price:** EUR 0.80
Annual Sub.: EUR 273.04; **Circ:** 106,384
Profile: National, regional and local news. Current events. Fémina and TV guide supplements on Saturday.
Language(s): French
ADVERTISING RATES:
Full Page Mono .... EUR 13059
Mechanical Data: Type Area: tabloïd
REGIONAL DAILY & SUNDAY NEWSPAPERS: Regional Daily Newspapers

L' UNIVERS DES ARTS 7092F84A-650

Editorial: 8 rue Ducouëdic, 75014 PARIS
Tel: 1 43 27 57 98
Email: info@univers-des-arts.com
ISSN: 1261-7164
Date Established: 1994; **Freq:** Monthly - fin de mois (n° dble 7/8 - 12/1)
Annual Sub.: EUR 50; **Circ:** 35,000
Usual Pagination: 84
Profile: International magazine containing topical news and in-depth articles on the world of art.
Language(s): French
ADVERTISING RATES:
Full Page Colour .... EUR 1550
Mechanical Data: Type Area: 220 x 285
Copy instructions: *Copy Date:* 15 days prior to publication date
CONSUMER: THE ARTS & LITERARY: Arts

L' UNIVERS DES VOYAGES 1620434F50-189

Editorial: 71 rue Desnouettes, 75015 PARIS
Tel: 1 44 19 90 81 **Fax:** 1 48 28 39 50
Email: pgeoffroy@pvm.fr
ISSN: 1278-6306
Date Established: 1996; **Freq:** Monthly - 03-05-07-09-11-01; **Cover Price:** EUR 3.50
Annual Sub.: EUR 29; **Circ:** 8,142
Usual Pagination: 68
Publisher: Didier Bahers
Profile: Trade publication focussing on tourism including travel agents, hotels, restaurants, commercial analysis, products, destinations, services and production.
Language(s): French
ADVERTISING RATES:
Full Page Mono .... EUR 5150
Full Page Colour .... EUR 6250
Mechanical Data: Type Area: 220x285
BUSINESS: TRAVEL & TOURISM

URBANISME 4601F4D-200

Editorial: 176 rue du Temple, 75003 PARIS
Tel: 1 45 45 45 00 **Fax:** 1 45 45 60 37
Email: urbanisme@urbanisme.fr **Web site:** http://www.urbanisme.fr
ISSN: 1240-0874
Date Established: 1932; **Freq:** 24 issues yearly - 15-20 des mois 01 03 05 07 09 11; **Cover Price:** EUR 18
Annual Sub.: EUR 96; **Circ:** 8,000
Usual Pagination: 100
Publisher: Thierry Paquot
Profile: International magazine about town-planning.
Language(s): French
Readership: Read by architects and town planners.
Mechanical Data: Type Area: 225 x 300
Copy instructions: *Copy Date:* 21 days prior to publication date
BUSINESS: ARCHITECTURE & BUILDING: Planning & Housing

L' USINE NOUVELLE 4857F14B-290

Editorial: Antony Parc II, 10 place du Général de Gaulle, BP 20156 CEDEX, 92186 ANTONY
Tel: 1 77 92 92 92
Web site: http://www.usinenouvelle.com
ISSN: 0042-126X
Freq: Weekly; **Cover Price:** EUR 3.50
Annual Sub.: EUR 180; **Circ:** 58,270
Usual Pagination: 104
Profile: Publication containing articles and topical industrial news with special emphasis on new products and technologies.
Language(s): French
ADVERTISING RATES:
Full Page Mono .... EUR 7220
Full Page Colour .... EUR 12950
Mechanical Data: Type Area: 22 x 28,5
BUSINESS: COMMERCE, INDUSTRY & MANAGEMENT: Industry & Factories

VAL DE MARNE 1617144F32R-9

Editorial: Conseil Général, Hôtel du Département, CEDEX, 94011 CRETEIL **Tel:** 1 43 99 71 33
Email: cvm@cg94.fr **Web site:** http://www.cg94.fr
ISSN: 0758-3524
Date Established: 1990; **Freq:** Monthly - début du mois; **Cover Price:** Free; **Circ:** 581,000
Usual Pagination: 44
Profile: Publication focussing on local government and department issues.
Language(s): French
Mechanical Data: Type Area: A 4
BUSINESS: LOCAL GOVERNMENT, LEISURE & RECREATION: Local Government Related

VALEURS ACTUELLES 7061F82-250

Editorial: 3/5 rue Saint Georges, 75009 PARIS
Tel: 1 40 54 11 00 **Fax:** 1 40 54 12 85
Email: branca@valmonde.fr **Web site:** http://www.valeursactuelles.com
ISSN: 0049-5749
Date Established: 1966; **Freq:** Weekly; **Cover Price:** EUR 3.20
Annual Sub.: EUR 120; **Circ:** 92,923
Usual Pagination: 90
Profile: Magazine containing political and financial information.
Language(s): French
ADVERTISING RATES:
Full Page Colour .... EUR 10000
Mechanical Data: Type Area: 208 x 290
CONSUMER: CURRENT AFFAIRS & POLITICS

VALEURS MUTUALISTES 1618990F32G-196

Editorial: MGEN, 3 square Max Hymans, CEDEX 15, 75748 PARIS **Tel:** 1 40 47 20 20 **Fax:** 1 40 47 20 25
Email: jdumay@mgen.fr **Web site:** http://www.mgen.fr
ISSN: 1241-8935
Date Established: 1947; **Freq:** 24 issues yearly - 01 03 04 07 09 11; **Cover Price:** EUR 0.60
Annual Sub.: EUR 3.80; **Circ:** 1,800,000
Usual Pagination: 36
Language(s): French
Mechanical Data: Type Area: 210 x 297
BUSINESS: LOCAL GOVERNMENT, LEISURE & RECREATION: Community Care & Social Services

VALEURS VERTES 5916F57-150

Editorial: 21 avenue de la Motte Picquet, 75007 PARIS **Tel:** 1 40 62 96 49 **Fax:** 1 40 62 94 99
Email: contact@valeursvertes.com **Web site:** http://www.valeursvertes.com
ISSN: 1167-3435
Date Established: 1992; **Freq:** 24 issues yearly - 1ère quinzaine mois impairs
Annual Sub.: EUR 36; **Circ:** 15,000
Usual Pagination: 60
Profile: Magazine about the environment. Focuses on economic details.
Language(s): French
ADVERTISING RATES:
Full Page Mono .... EUR 4100
Full Page Colour .... EUR 4800
Mechanical Data: Type Area: A 4
Copy instructions: *Copy Date:* 15 days prior to publication date
BUSINESS: ENVIRONMENT & POLLUTION

VAR-MATIN NICE-MATIN TOULON SIEGE SOCIAL
6200F67B-8100
Editorial: 15 boulevard de Strasbourg, BP 806, 83051 CEDEX TOULON **Tel:** 4 94 93 31 50
Fax: 4 94 93 31 51
Email: redacchef@nicematin.fr **Web site:** http://www.varmatin.com
Freq: Daily - chaque jour sauf le 1er mai; **Cover Price:** EUR 0.85
Annual Sub.: EUR 309; **Circ:** 75,520
Profile: Regional daily newspaper focussing on news and current affairs.
Language(s): French
ADVERTISING RATES:
Full Page Colour .... EUR 19656
Mechanical Data: Type Area: Tabloïd
REGIONAL DAILY & SUNDAY NEWSPAPERS: Regional Daily Newspapers

VAUCLUSE CONSEIL GENERAL DE VAUCLUSE
1617208F32A-1066
Editorial: Hôtel-du-Département, Rue Viala, 84909 CEDEX 9 AVIGNON **Tel:** 4 90 16 11 12
Fax: 490161117
Email: dircom@cg84.fr **Web site:** http://www.vaucluse.fr
ISSN: 1165-5267
Date Established: 1992; **Freq:** 6 issues yearly - début de mois; **Cover Price:** Free; **Circ:** 230,000
Usual Pagination: 20
Editor: Jean-Pierre Lambertin
Profile: Publication focussing on local government and department issues.
Language(s): French
Mechanical Data: Type Area: A 4
BUSINESS: LOCAL GOVERNMENT, LEISURE & RECREATION: Local Government

VEGETABLE
5223F26C-50
Editorial: 1405 route de Noves, BP 12, 84310 MORIERES-LES-AVIGNON **Tel:** 4 90 33 56 56
Fax: 4 90 33 51 51
Email: j.harzig@vegetable.fr **Web site:** http://www.vegetable.fr
ISSN: 1779-4390
Date Established: 1985; **Freq:** Monthly - le 15 du mois
Annual Sub.: EUR 70; **Circ:** 8,000
Usual Pagination: 92
Profile: Pan-European journal covering fruit and vegetable production and marketing.
Language(s): French
Readership: Read by fruit and vegetable producers, wholesalers and supermarket retailers.
ADVERTISING RATES:
Full Page Colour .... EUR 3300
Mechanical Data: Type Area: 210 x 297
BUSINESS: GARDEN TRADE

VEILLE
4848F14A-700
Editorial: 134 avenue Henri-Ginoux, 92120 MONTROUGE **Tel:** 1 46 65 55 37 **Fax:** 1 78 76 51 20
Email: contact@veillemag.com **Web site:** http://www.veillemag.com
ISSN: 1281-1114
Date Established: 1997; **Freq:** 26 issues yearly - le 10 du mois; **Cover Price:** EUR 17; **Circ:** 5,000
Usual Pagination: 36
Editor: Philippe Souhiard
Profile: Magazine concerning economic intelligence. Includes information on the analysis of sources of information and how effective strategic monitoring systems can be put in place.
Language(s): French
Readership: Aimed at managing directors, all managers, engineers and document services and departments.
ADVERTISING RATES:
Full Page Mono .... EUR 1900
Full Page Colour .... EUR 2500
Mechanical Data: Type Area: A4
BUSINESS: COMMERCE, INDUSTRY & MANAGEMENT

VERSION FEMINA
6404F74A-147
Editorial: Rédaction, 124 rue Danton, TSA 31002 CEDEX, 92538 LEVALLOIS PERRET
Tel: 1 41 34 86 16 00 **Fax:** 1 41 34 91 30
Email: annie.gomez@lagardere-active.com **Web site:** http://www.femina.fr
ISSN: 0100-7254
Date Established: 2002; **Freq:** Weekly - dimanche; **Circ:** 3,586,052
Usual Pagination: 50
Profile: Magazine containing articles on cooking, decoration, fashion, health and beauty.
Language(s): French
Readership: Aimed at women.
ADVERTISING RATES:
Full Page Colour .... EUR 73200
Copy instructions: *Copy Date:* 62 days prior to publication date
CONSUMER: WOMEN'S INTEREST CONSUMER MAGAZINES: Women's Interest

VERTITUDE MAGAZINE
634200F57-175
Editorial: 9 rue de l'Arbre-Sec, 69281 CEDEX 01 LYON **Tel:** 4 72 98 26 60 **Fax:** 4 72 98 26 80
Web site: http://www.pro-environnement.com
ISSN: 1295-2869
Date Established: 1994; **Freq:** Half-yearly - début juin et décembre; **Cover Price:** EUR 12
Annual Sub.: EUR 45; **Circ:** 4,000
Usual Pagination: 32
Editor-in-Chief: Bruno Mortgat
Profile: Magazine concerning environmental management and security, focusing on new technological advances.
Language(s): French
Readership: Aimed at professionals in environmental management and security.
ADVERTISING RATES:
Full Page Colour .... EUR 2390
Mechanical Data: Type Area: A 4
Copy instructions: *Copy Date:* 15 days prior to publication date
BUSINESS: ENVIRONMENT & POLLUTION

LA VIE
6391F73-310
Editorial: 80 boulevard Auguste Blanqui, CEDEX 13, 75707 PARIS **Tel:** 1 48 88 46 00 **Fax:** 1 48 88 46 01
Email: jp.denis@lavie.fr **Web site:** http://www.lavie.fr
ISSN: 0151-2323
Date Established: 1945; **Freq:** Weekly; **Cover Price:** EUR 2.90
Annual Sub.: EUR 114; **Circ:** 146,788
Usual Pagination: 100
Profile: Christian news magazine.
Language(s): French
ADVERTISING RATES:
Full Page Mono .... EUR 7430
Full Page Colour .... EUR 9010
Mechanical Data: Type Area: 220 x 280
CONSUMER: NATIONAL & INTERNATIONAL PERIODICALS

LA VIE DU RAIL MAGAZINE
1619931F49A-234
Editorial: 11 rue de Milan, CEDEX 09, 75440 PARIS
Tel: 1 49 70 12 00 **Fax:** 1 42 81 92 61
Email: francois.dumont@laviedurail.com **Web site:** http://www.laviedurail.com
ISSN: 0042-5478
Date Established: 1945; **Freq:** Weekly - mercredi; **Cover Price:** EUR 2.50
Annual Sub.: EUR 99; **Circ:** 88,125
Usual Pagination: 68
Profile: Publication focussing on railway, road, maritime and air transport and logistics.
Language(s): French
ADVERTISING RATES:
Full Page Mono .... EUR 8000
Full Page Colour .... EUR 9000
Mechanical Data: Type Area: 21 x 27
Copy instructions: *Copy Date:* 10 days prior to publication date
BUSINESS: TRANSPORT

LA VIE MUTUALISTE EN BLEU
1618956F1D-139
Editorial: Mutuelle Bleue, 68 rue du Rocher, CEDEX 08, 75396 PARIS **Tel:** 1 53 42 59 59
Fax: 1 53 42 58 38
ISSN: 1638-8631
Date Established: 2003; **Freq:** Quarterly - février-mai- août-novembre; **Cover Price:** Free; **Circ:** 608,000
Usual Pagination: 8
Managing Director: Olivier Raimbault
Language(s): French
Mechanical Data: Type Area: 210 x 297
BUSINESS: FINANCE & ECONOMICS: Insurance

VIE PRATIQUE FEMININ
1740319F74A-857
Editorial: COM-PRESSE, 6 rue Tarnac, 47220 ASTAFFORT **Tel:** 5 53 48 17 60 **Fax:** 5 53 66 71 64
Email: info@com-presse.fr **Web site:** http://www.com-presse.fr
ISSN: 1950-4314
Date Established: 2006; **Freq:** Monthly - Around the 15th of the month; **Circ:** 101,904
Usual Pagination: 100
Language(s): French
ADVERTISING RATES:
Full Page Colour .... EUR 8500
Mechanical Data: Type Area: 170 x 252
CONSUMER: WOMEN'S INTEREST CONSUMER MAGAZINES: Women's Interest

VIE PRATIQUE GOURMAND
1647623F74P-487
Editorial: COM-PRESSE, 6 rue Tarnac, 47220 ASTAFFORT **Tel:** 5 53 48 17 60 **Fax:** 5 53 66 71 64
Email: info@com-presse.fr **Web site:** http://www.com-presse.fr
ISSN: 1638-8690
Freq: 26 issues yearly - tous les 15 jours; **Cover Price:** EUR 2.50
Annual Sub.: EUR 49; **Circ:** 199,455
Usual Pagination: 100
Profile: Publication focussing on gastronomy including cooking, recipes and tourism.
Language(s): French
ADVERTISING RATES:
Full Page Colour .... EUR 8000
Mechanical Data: Type Area: 180 x 265
Copy instructions: *Copy Date:* 31 days prior to publication date
CONSUMER: WOMEN'S INTEREST CONSUMER MAGAZINES: Food & Cookery

LES VIES DE FAMILLE
6474F74C-420
Editorial: Forum 55-52 rue Camille Desmoulins, 92448 ISSY LES MOULINEAUX **Tel:** 1 46 29 46 29
Email: gpayet@reedbusiness.fr
ISSN: 1294-0607
Date Established: 1950; **Freq:** 24 issues yearly - tous les mois sauf 04 07 08 12; **Cover Price:** Free; **Circ:** 5,049,723
Usual Pagination: 19
Profile: Magazine concerning all aspects of family life.
Language(s): French
ADVERTISING RATES:
Full Page Colour .... EUR 65000
Mechanical Data: Type Area: 21 x 28
CONSUMER: WOMEN'S INTEREST CONSUMER MAGAZINES: Home & Family

LA VIGNE
5086F21H-100
Editorial: 8 Cité Paradis, CEDEX 10, 75493 PARIS
Tel: 1 40 22 79 00 10 **Fax:** 1 40 22 73 18
Email: bertrand.collard@gfa.fr
ISSN: 1145-5799
Date Established: 1990; **Freq:** Monthly; **Circ:** 20,525
Usual Pagination: 94
Managing Director: Michel Collonge
Profile: Magazine containing economic and trade news of vine growing, includes reviews of wines worldwide, discussion of production methods and commonly found problems.
Language(s): French
Readership: Read by vine growers.
Mechanical Data: Type Area: 210 x 297
BUSINESS: AGRICULTURE & FARMING: Vine Growing

VITI
5091F21H-170
Editorial: 23 rue Dupont des Loges, BP 90 146, CEDEX 1, 57004 METZ **Tel:** 3 87 69 18 18
Fax: 3 87 69 18 14
Email: viti@groupe-atc.com
ISSN: 0757-4673
Freq: Monthly - beginning of the month; **Cover Price:** EUR 5.30
Annual Sub.: EUR 52.90; **Circ:** 25,177
Usual Pagination: 56
Profile: This magazine covers the wine industry and business management.
Language(s): French
Readership: Aimed at those involved in the wine industry.
ADVERTISING RATES:
Full Page Mono .... EUR 3050
Full Page Colour .... EUR 4970
Mechanical Data: Type Area: 230 x 300
Copy instructions: *Copy Date:* 15 days prior to publication date
BUSINESS: AGRICULTURE & FARMING: Vine Growing

VIVA - ENTRE NOUS LA VIE
6392F73-320
Editorial: 3/5 rue de Vincennes, 93100 MONTREUIL
Tel: 1 49 88 53 30 **Fax:** 1 49 88 53 70
Email: viva@viva.presse.fr **Web site:** http://www.viva.presse.fr
ISSN: 0984-4376
Date Established: 1986; **Freq:** Monthly - début du mois; **Cover Price:** EUR 2.17
Annual Sub.: EUR 22.40; **Circ:** 591,772
Usual Pagination: 92
Profile: General interest magazine.
Language(s): French
ADVERTISING RATES:
Full Page Colour .... EUR 8800
Mechanical Data: Type Area: 180 x 240
CONSUMER: NATIONAL & INTERNATIONAL PERIODICALS

VIVRE
1617036F56R-222
Editorial: LNCC, 14 rue Corvisart, 75013 PARIS
Tel: 1 53 55 24 27 **Fax:** 1 53 55 25 53
Email: lerouxc@ligue-cancer.net **Web site:** http://www.ligue-cancer.net
ISSN: 0249-0358
Date Established: 1923; **Freq:** Quarterly - fin 03 06 09 12
Annual Sub.: EUR 50; **Circ:** 1,952,000
Usual Pagination: 76
Profile: Publication focussing on cancer research including news, interviews, prevention and screening.
Language(s): French
Mechanical Data: Type Area: 170 x 250
BUSINESS: HEALTH & MEDICAL: Health Medical Related

VIVRE EN PERIGORD
1617151F32A-1018
Editorial: Hôtel du département, 2 rue Paul Louis Courier, CEDEX, 24019 PERIGUEUX
Tel: 5 53 02 20 20 **Fax:** 5 53 08 88 27
Email: n.platon@dordogne.fr **Web site:** http://www.cg24.fr
ISSN: 1779-0700
Date Established: 1994; **Freq:** 24 issues yearly - fin de mois impairs; **Cover Price:** Free; **Circ:** 196,500
Usual Pagination: 24
Profile: Publication focussing on local government and department issues.
Language(s): French
Mechanical Data: Type Area: 21 x 29,7
BUSINESS: LOCAL GOVERNMENT, LEISURE & RECREATION: Local Government

VIVRE EN SOMME CONSEIL GENERAL DE LA SOMME
1752689F32A-1090
Editorial: 53, rue de la république, BP 32615, 80026 AMIENS CEDEX 1 **Tel:** 3 22 71 97 16
Fax: 3 22 71 83 50
Email: i.dewazieres@somme.fr **Web site:** http://www.somme.fr
Date Established: 2005; **Freq:** Monthly; **Cover Price:** Free; **Circ:** 276,000
Usual Pagination: 32
Editor: Paul Delomel
Profile: Publication focussing on local government and department issues, including economics, sports, leisure, environment, cultural and social issues.
Language(s): French
BUSINESS: LOCAL GOVERNMENT, LEISURE & RECREATION: Local Government

VOGUE
6436F74B-170
Editorial: 56 A rue du Faubourg Saint Honoré, 75008 PARIS **Tel:** 1 53 43 60 00 **Fax:** 1 53 43 60 60
Email: mbulteau@condenast.fr **Web site:** http://www.vogue.fr
ISSN: 0750-3628
Date Established: 1920; **Freq:** Monthly; **Cover Price:** EUR 4.90
Annual Sub.: EUR 36; **Circ:** 151,419
Usual Pagination: 250
Profile: Magazine focusing on fashion and beauty.
Language(s): French
ADVERTISING RATES:
Full Page Colour .... EUR 17500
Mechanical Data: Type Area: 220 x 285
Copy instructions: *Copy Date:* 31 days prior to publication date
CONSUMER: WOMEN'S INTEREST CONSUMER MAGAZINES: Women's Interest - Fashion

VOGUE HOMMES INTERNATIONAL
7361F86C-262
Editorial: 56 A rue du Faubourg Saint Honoré, 75008 PARIS **Tel:** 1 53 43 60 00 **Fax:** 1 53 43 61 00
Email: mbulteau@condenast.fr
ISSN: 0750-3628
Date Established: 1997; **Freq:** Half-yearly - mi-mars et mi-septembre
Annual Sub.: EUR 9.60; **Circ:** 60,841
Usual Pagination: 240
Publisher: Delphine Royant
Profile: Men's interest magazine focusing on fashion. Magazine de mode et beauté masculine diffusé dans 50 pays et publié en 2 langues: français, anglais. Toute l'actualité de la mode masculine internationale à travers les plus grands couturiers de Paris, New-York ou Milan : nouvelles boutiques, défilés, accessoires, portrait d'une star.
Language(s): French
ADVERTISING RATES:
Full Page Mono .... EUR 9600
Full Page Colour .... EUR 11000
Mechanical Data: Type Area: A 4
Copy instructions: *Copy Date:* 31 days prior to publication date
CONSUMER: ADULT & GAY MAGAZINES: Men's Lifestyle Magazines

VOICI
6424F74A-350
Editorial: 13 rue Henri Barbusse, 92624 GENNEVILLIERS **Tel:** 1 73 05 45 45
Fax: 1 56 99 48 20
Email: voici@prisma-presse.com **Web site:** http://www.voici.fr
ISSN: 0245-5803
Date Established: 1987; **Freq:** Weekly - le samedi; **Cover Price:** EUR 1.50
Annual Sub.: EUR 69; **Circ:** 443,132
Usual Pagination: 96
Publisher: Philippe Labi
Profile: Magazine containing information and topical news of interest to women. Includes articles on celebrities and astrology.
Language(s): French
ADVERTISING RATES:
Full Page Mono .... EUR 10500
Full Page Colour .... EUR 14000
Mechanical Data: Type Area: 230x 285
Copy instructions: *Copy Date:* 15 days prior to publication date
CONSUMER: WOMEN'S INTEREST CONSUMER MAGAZINES: Women's Interest

VOILES ET VOILIERS
7252F91A-250
Editorial: 21 rue du Faubourg Saint Antoine, CEDEX 11, 75550 PARIS **Tel:** 1 44 87 87 87
Fax: 1 44 87 87 79
Email: redaction@voilesetvoiliers.com **Web site:** http://www.voilesetvoiliers.com
ISSN: 0751-5405
Date Established: 1971; **Freq:** Monthly - vers le 18 du mois; **Cover Price:** EUR 5.50
Annual Sub.: EUR 62.20; **Circ:** 57,417

France

Usual Pagination: 196
Managing Director: Pierre Lavialle
Profile: Publication about races, cruises, charter and commercial crafts, luxury yachts, sailing dinghies and sportsboats.
Language(s): French
ADVERTISING RATES:
Full Page Mono .... EUR 3570
Full Page Colour .... EUR 5600
Mechanical Data: Type Area: 23 x 30
CONSUMER: RECREATION & LEISURE: Boating & Yachting

LA VOIX DES ENTREPRISES CLERMONT-FERRAND
5993F14A-802
Editorial: CCI de Clermont-Ferrand-Issoire, 148 boulevard Lavoisier, 63037 CLERMONT-FERRAND CEDEX 1 **Tel:** 4 73 43 43 43 **Fax:** 4 73 43 43 42
Email: cci@clermont-fd.cci.fr **Web site:** http://www.clermont-fd.cci.fr
Freq: 24 issues yearly - un jeudi sur deux; **Circ:** 90,000
Usual Pagination: 2
Editor: Bernard Chanelle
Profile: Magazine focusing on trade and industry in the Clermont-Ferrand area. Includes articles on training, business ventures, projects and European affairs.
Language(s): French
Mechanical Data: Type Area: tabloïd
Copy instructions: *Copy Date:* pas de publicité
BUSINESS: COMMERCE, INDUSTRY & MANAGEMENT

LA VOIX DU NORD EDITION DU NORD LILLE
6176F67B-8200
Editorial: 8 place du Général-de-Gaulle, BP 549, 59023 CEDEX LILLE **Tel:** 3 20 78 40 40
Fax: 3 20 78 42 44
Email: lille@lavoixdunord.fr **Web site:** http://www.lavoixdunord.fr
ISSN: 0999-2189
Freq: Daily - le matin du lundi au dimanche; **Cover Price:** EUR 0.85
Annual Sub.: EUR 258; **Circ:** 290,345
Usual Pagination: 56
Managing Director: Jacques Hardoin
Profile: Daily regional current events newspaper covering the North, Pas-de-Calais, Somme and Aisne regions.
Language(s): French
ADVERTISING RATES:
Full Page Mono .... EUR 4648
Full Page Colour .... EUR 6275
Mechanical Data: Type Area: tabloïd
Copy instructions: *Copy Date:* 3 days prior to publication date
REGIONAL DAILY & SUNDAY NEWSPAPERS: Regional Daily Newspapers

VOSGES MATIN EPINAL
6170F67B-5200
Editorial: 40 quai des Bons-Enfants, BP 273, 88026 CEDEX EPINAL **Tel:** 29 82 98 00 **Fax:** 3 29 82 99 29
Email: redaction.web@vosgesmatin.fr **Web site:** http://www.vosgesmatin.fr
Date Established: 2009; **Freq:** Daily - le matin;
Cover Price: EUR 0.90
Annual Sub.: EUR 214; **Circ:** 50,000
Usual Pagination: 32
Profile: Regional and local news. Sunday price: 1.52 € (including TV Magazine, Version Fémina and Est Magazine) - Subscription price including Sunday supplements: 292 €.
Language(s): French
ADVERTISING RATES:
Full Page Mono .... EUR 5694
Full Page Colour .... EUR 7118
Mechanical Data: Type Area: 500 x 370
Copy instructions: *Copy Date:* 2 days prior to publication date
REGIONAL DAILY & SUNDAY NEWSPAPERS: Regional Daily Newspapers

VOTRE BEAUTE
6533F74B-273
Editorial: 10 boulevard des Frères Voisin, CEDEX 9, 92792 ISSY LES MOULINEAUX **Tel:** 1 41 46 88 88
Fax: 1 41 46 81 80
Email: cblancaneaux@gmc.tm.fr **Web site:** http://www.groupemarieclaire.com
ISSN: 0042-8965
Date Established: 1933; **Freq:** Monthly - between 15 to 20 months ahead
Annual Sub.: EUR 24.39; **Circ:** 83,393
Usual Pagination: 132
Profile: Magazine specialising in beauty, health and fashion. This magazine covers beauty, health and fashion.
Language(s): French
ADVERTISING RATES:
Full Page Mono .... EUR 12560
Full Page Colour .... EUR 15700
Mechanical Data: Type Area: 210 x 275
CONSUMER: WOMEN'S INTEREST CONSUMER MAGAZINES: Women's Interest - Fashion

VOTRE DIETETIQUE
6526F74G-220
Editorial: 30 rue Agricol Perdiguier, 42100 SAINT-ETIENNE **Tel:** 4 77 81 38 13 **Fax:** 4 77 81 30 71
Email: votredietetique@trenta.fr **Web site:** http://www.votredietetique.com
Date Established: 1993; **Freq:** 24 issues yearly - fin de mois impairs; **Cover Price:** Free; **Circ:** 40,000
Usual Pagination: 32
Editor-in-Chief: Roland Reymondier
Profile: Magazine about diet, food, sport, beauty, health and fitness.
Language(s): French
ADVERTISING RATES:
Full Page Colour .... EUR 2170
Mechanical Data: Type Area: 23 x 29,7
CONSUMER: WOMEN'S INTEREST CONSUMER MAGAZINES: Slimming & Health

VOTRE MAISON - VOTRE JARDIN
6475F74C-450
Editorial: 15-27 rue Moussorgski, CEDEX 18, 75895 PARIS **Tel:** 1 53 26 30 04 **Fax:** 1 53 26 33 03
Email: m.gerardin@rustica.fr **Web site:** http://www.rustica.fr
ISSN: 0042-8973
Date Established: 1949; **Freq:** 24 issues yearly;
Cover Price: EUR 3.80
Annual Sub.: EUR 17.90; **Circ:** 52,551
Usual Pagination: 116
Managing Director: Eric De Montlivault
Profile: Magazine providing advice on home decoration and garden maintenance.
Language(s): French
Readership: Read mainly by those in the 40 to 50 year old age group with a high disposable income.
ADVERTISING RATES:
Full Page Mono .... EUR 11000
Full Page Colour .... EUR 11000
Mechanical Data: Type Area: 220 x 300
Copy instructions: *Copy Date:* 31 days prior to publication date
CONSUMER: WOMEN'S INTEREST CONSUMER MAGAZINES: Home & Family

LES VOYAGES D'AFFAIRES
5592F89A-332
Editorial: 6 cité Paradis, 75010 PARIS
Tel: 1 53 24 24 00
Email: redaction@voyages-d-affaires.com **Web site:** http://www.voyages-d-affaires.com
ISSN: 0995-4228
Date Established: 1988; **Freq:** 24 issues yearly - end of months 01 03 05 06 09 11
Annual Sub.: EUR 42; **Circ:** 60,898
Usual Pagination: 110
Publisher: Bruno Collentier
Profile: Journal about business travel, meetings, seminars, incentives and management.
Language(s): French
Readership: Aimed at managers and business travellers.
ADVERTISING RATES:
Full Page Colour .... EUR 8900
Mechanical Data: Type Area: A 4
Copy instructions: *Copy Date:* 15 days prior to publication date
CONSUMER: HOLIDAYS & TRAVEL: Travel

VSB - VINS SPIRITUEUX BOISSONS
4756F9C-106
Editorial: 84 boulevard de Sébastopol, 75003 PARIS
Tel: 1 42 74 28 00 **Fax:** 1 42 74 20 63
Email: jmpeyronnet@siac.fr **Web site:** http://www.vsb-lalettre.fr
ISSN: 0247-9591
Freq: Weekly - le vendredi; **Annual Sub.:** EUR 730;
Circ: 1,000
Usual Pagination: 10
Editor-in-Chief: Michel De Saint-Albin
Profile: Newsletter focusing on the drinks industry. Contains information about new products and developments within the sector.
Language(s): French
Readership: Aimed at drinks manufacturers.
Mechanical Data: Type Area: 210 x 297
BUSINESS: DRINKS & LICENSED TRADE: Licensed Trade, Wines & Spirits

VSD
6390F73-300
Editorial: 13 rue Henri Barbusse, 92624 GENNEVILLIERS **Tel:** 1 73 05 60 24
Email: ocabrera@vsd.fr **Web site:** http://www.vsd.fr
ISSN: 1278-916X
Date Established: 1977; **Freq:** Weekly; **Cover Price:** EUR 2.40
Annual Sub.: EUR 95; **Circ:** 146,794
Usual Pagination: 88
Profile: Weekend magazine of topical news including leisure and cultural information.
Language(s): French
ADVERTISING RATES:
Full Page Mono .... EUR 9750
Full Page Colour .... EUR 13000
Mechanical Data: Type Area: 245 x 332
Copy instructions: *Copy Date:* 10 days prior to publication date
CONSUMER: NATIONAL & INTERNATIONAL PERIODICALS

VU DU DOUBS
1617211F32A-1069
Editorial: Conseil Général du Doubs - Dion Communi, 7 avenue de la Gare d'Eau, CEDEX, 25031 BESANCON **Tel:** 3 81 25 80 42 **Fax:** 3 81 25 80 41
Email: vududoubs@doubs.fr **Web site:** http://www.doubs.fr
ISSN: 0294-0329
Date Established: 1982; **Freq:** Monthly - 1ère semaine du mois; **Cover Price:** Free; **Circ:** 232,000
Usual Pagination: 36
Profile: Publication focussing on local government and department issues, including economics, cultural heritage, environment, tourism, cultural and social issues.
Language(s): French
Mechanical Data: Type Area: 33 x 27
BUSINESS: LOCAL GOVERNMENT, LEISURE & RECREATION: Local Government

WHERE PARIS
7218F89C-300
Editorial: 35 rue des Mathurins, 75008 PARIS
Tel: 1 43 12 56 56 **Fax:** 1 43 12 56 57
Email: sandra.iskander@wheremagazine.com **Web site:** http://www.wheremagazine.com
ISSN: 1241-8625
Date Established: 1992; **Freq:** Monthly - début du mois
Annual Sub.: EUR 65; **Circ:** 55,143
Profile: Guide to attractions and events in Paris.
Language(s): French
ADVERTISING RATES:
Full Page Mono .... EUR 3380
Full Page Colour .... EUR 4780
Mechanical Data: Type Area: 254 x 178
Copy instructions: *Copy Date:* 35 days prior to publication date
CONSUMER: HOLIDAYS & TRAVEL: Entertainment Guides

WINDOWS NEWS
4662F5B-260
Editorial: 101/109 rue Jean Jaurès, 92300 LEVALLOIS PERRET **Tel:** 1 41 27 38 38
Fax: 1 41 27 38 39
Email: thierry.outrebon@yellowmedia.fr **Web site:** http://www.windowsnews.fr
ISSN: 1266-8044
Date Established: 1995; **Freq:** Monthly - début de mois; **Cover Price:** EUR 5.90
Annual Sub.: EUR 45.50; **Circ:** 52,265
Usual Pagination: 110
Profile: Publication covering the Windows sector. Contains articles and news about programs, comparative products, user-advice and implementation.
Language(s): French
ADVERTISING RATES:
Full Page Colour .... EUR 7000
Mechanical Data: Type Area: 285 x 210
Copy instructions: *Copy Date:* 21 days prior to publication date
BUSINESS: COMPUTERS & AUTOMATION: Data Processing

WWD
6437F74B-220
Editorial: 9 rue Royale, 75008 PARIS
Tel: 1 44 51 13 00 **Fax:** 1 42 68 16 41
Email: chantal.goupil@fairchildpub.com **Web site:** http://www.fairchildpub.com
ISSN: 1274-350X
Freq: Monthly - le 20 du mois; **Cover Price:** EUR 9.15; **Circ:** 459,500
Usual Pagination: 200
Editor: Stefano Tonchi
Profile: Magazine covering fashion, beauty and the art of living.
Language(s): French
ADVERTISING RATES:
Full Page Mono .... EUR 55270
Full Page Colour .... EUR 69552
Copy instructions: *Copy Date:* 62 days prior to publication date
CONSUMER: WOMEN'S INTEREST CONSUMER MAGAZINES: Women's Interest - Fashion

L' YONNE RÉPUBLICAINE AUXERRE
6158F67B-8400
Editorial: 8-12 avenue Jean-Moulin, 89025 CEDEX AUXERRE **Tel:** 3 86 49 52 15 **Fax:** 3 86 46 99 90
Email: secretaire.yr@centrefrance.com **Web site:** http://www.lyonne.fr
ISSN: 0247-8293
Date Established: 1944; **Freq:** Daily - le matin sauf dimanche et JF; **Cover Price:** EUR 0.90
Annual Sub.: EUR 243; **Circ:** 36,682
Usual Pagination: 48
Managing Director: Laurent Couronne
Profile: National, regional and local news. Wednesday price: 1 € (including Version Fémina supplement). Saturday price: 1,50 € (including Yonne Mag and TV Magazine supplements).
Language(s): French
ADVERTISING RATES:
Full Page Mono .... EUR 3330
Full Page Colour .... EUR 3996
Mechanical Data: Type Area: tabloid
REGIONAL DAILY & SUNDAY NEWSPAPERS: Regional Daily Newspapers

L' YONNE RÉPUBLICAINE: EDITION SUD
1619715F67B-8714
Editorial: 6 rue de Paris, 89200 AVALLON
Tel: 3 86 34 99 15 **Fax:** 3 86 34 99 14
Email: stfargeau.yr@centrefrance.com **Web site:** http://www.lyonne.fr
Date Established: 1944; **Freq:** Daily - le matin sauf dimanche; **Cover Price:** EUR 0.90
Annual Sub.: EUR 259; **Circ:** 36,682
Usual Pagination: 50
Profile: National, regional and local news. Including Version Fémina on Wednesday (1 €) and TV Mag on Saturday (1,50 €).
Language(s): French
Mechanical Data: Type Area: tabloid
REGIONAL DAILY & SUNDAY NEWSPAPERS: Regional Daily Newspapers

Germany

Time Difference: GMT + 1 hr (CET - Central European Time)
National Telephone Code: +49
Continent: Europe
Capital: Berlin
Principal Language: German
Population: 82424609
Monetary Unit: Euro (EUR)
EMBASSY HIGH
COMMISSION: Embassy of the Federal Republic of Germany: 23 Belgrave Sq, London SW1X 8PZ
Tel: 020 7824 1300
Fax: 020 7824 1449
Email: mail@german-embassy.org.uk
Website: http://www.german-embassy.org.uk

+ROSEBUD
1849403G19B-116
Editorial: Pelzetleite 65, 90614 AMMERNDORF
Tel: 172 8942290 **Fax:** 9127 577581
Email: ask@rosebudmagazine.com **Web site:** http://www.rosebudmagazine.com
Freq: Annual; **Cover Price:** EUR 36,00; **Circ:** 4,000
Editor: Ralf Herms; **Advertising Manager:** Ralf Herms
Profile: Design magazine.
Language(s): English

.COMDIRECT
1661168G1F-1587
Editorial: Pascalkehre 15, 25451 QUICKBORN
Tel: 4106 7040 **Fax:** 4106 7042508
Web site: http://www.comdirect.de
Freq: Daily; **Cover Price:** Paid; **Circ:** 180,000,000 Unique Users
Profile: Homepage of the comdirect bank Aktiengesellschaft.
Language(s): German
BUSINESS: FINANCE & ECONOMICS: Investment

...TEXTIL...
744508G62B-60
Editorial: Bismarckstr. 10, 76133 KARLSRUHE
Tel: 721 9254656 **Fax:** 721 9254657
Email: waltraud.rusch@ph-karlsruhe.de **Web site:** http://www.ph-karlsruhe.de
Freq: Quarterly; **Annual Sub.:** EUR 50,30; **Circ:** 900
Editor: Waltraud Rusch; **Advertising Manager:** Ulrich Schneider
Profile: Magazine about career prospects, training and employment in the fashion and textiles industries.
Language(s): German
ADVERTISING RATES:
Full Page Mono .... EUR 520
Full Page Colour .... EUR 1400
Mechanical Data: Type Area: 256 x 172 mm
Copy instructions: *Copy Date:* 42 days prior to publication
BUSINESS: CHURCH & SCHOOL EQUIPMENT & EDUCATION: Education Teachers

0-100 STREET PERFORMANCE
2037682G77A-2958
Editorial: Gögginger Str. 2, 72505 KRAUCHENWIES
Tel: 7576 961850 **Fax:** 7576 9618599
Email: info@streetperformance.de **Web site:** http://www.streetperformance.de
Freq: 6 issues yearly; **Annual Sub.:** EUR 15,90; **Circ:** 70,000
Editor: Mathias R. Albert; **Advertising Manager:** Jennifer Reitz
Profile: Facebook: http://www.facebook.com/0100streetperformance.
Language(s): German
ADVERTISING RATES:
Full Page Mono .... EUR 2900
Full Page Colour .... EUR 2900
Mechanical Data: Type Area: 268 x 183 mm

[030]
737739G80-14212
Editorial: Askanischer Platz 3, 10963 BERLIN
Tel: 30 2902144009 **Fax:** 30 29021514

Email: 030@zitty.de **Web site:** http://www.berlin030.de
Freq: 26 issues yearly; **Annual Sub.:** EUR 25,00; **Circ:** 34,895
Editor: Stefan Sauerbrey; **Advertising Manager:** Jan Linkersdorff
Profile: 030 gives its readers a comprehensive insight into the new, young scene of Berlin. In addition to the nightlife scene, the editors favour the Berlin music scene in particular. The event calendar for 14 days and nights is the largest section in the 030 Berlin Magazine. 030 also provides information about youth culture in Berlin, restarts in the cinema and fashion trends. In the section 030 Guide the 030 Berlin magazine published in each issue the six most interesting districts of Berlin with maps, addresses and overview articles on restaurants, shopping, fitness and styling.
Language(s): German
ADVERTISING RATES:
Full Page Mono .... EUR 3500
Full Page Colour .... EUR 4100
Mechanical Data: Type Area: 225 x 164 mm, No. of Columns (Display): 5, Col Widths (Display): 30 mm
Copy instructions: *Copy Date:* 9 days prior to publication
CONSUMER: RURAL & REGIONAL INTEREST

11 FREUNDE
1609394G75A-3558
Editorial: Palisadenstr. 48, 10243 BERLIN
Tel: 30 4039360 **Fax:** 30 403936122
Email: redaktion@11freunde.de **Web site:** http://www.11freunde.de
Freq: Monthly; **Annual Sub.:** EUR 40,00; **Circ:** 75,871
Editor: Philipp Köster
Profile: Founded in 2000, is "11 Freunde", magazine for football culture, the long overdue implementation of a nationwide and from associations independent magazine for football culture. Intelligent, entertaining, exciting, amusing and packed in an aesthetic layout. In the tradition of English magazines such as "When Saturday Comes" illuminated "11 Freunde" rather than producing just faceless statistics and match reports, football with subtle, but fresh reports that make the passion of the writers on the sport experience. According to reader analysis is "11 Freunde" so read by an above-average educated, predominantly male audience aged 20 to 35 years to a one: the love of football. The editors, based in Berlin gathered football fans from all over the Republic. Whether fans of Arminia Bielefeld, Bayern Munich and Fortuna Dusseldorf - the club is not as important to the passion that counts. "11 Freunde" can look out of the turn onto the field, integrating into position. For the fans and for the game. Twitter: http://twitter.com/11Freunde_Feed.
Language(s): German
ADVERTISING RATES:
Full Page Mono .... EUR 10500
Full Page Colour .... EUR 10500
Mechanical Data: No. of Columns (Display): 4, Col Widths (Display): 50 mm, Type Area: 280 x 210 mm
Copy instructions: *Copy Date:* 21 days prior to publication
Supplement(s): 11 Freundinnen
CONSUMER: SPORT

20 PRIVATE WOHNTRÄUME
749070G74C-20
Editorial: Rosenkavalierplatz 14, 81925 MÜNCHEN
Tel: 89 9100930 **Fax:** 89 91009353
Email: h.teschner@ipm-verlag.de **Web site:** http://www.ipm-verlag.de
Freq: 6 issues yearly; **Annual Sub.:** EUR 29,00; **Circ:** 23,528
Editor: Hannah Teschner; **Advertising Manager:** Rüdiger Knapp
Profile: The magazine is beautifully designed and interesting houses or apartments with their owners and their experiences in the construction, renovation or purchase of their property.
Language(s): German
Readership: Aimed at home owners.
ADVERTISING RATES:
Full Page Mono .... EUR 7100
Full Page Colour .... EUR 7100
Mechanical Data: Type Area: 260 x 186 mm
Copy instructions: *Copy Date:* 45 days prior to publication
CONSUMER: WOMEN'S INTEREST CONSUMER MAGAZINES: Home & Family

24/7
1863890G33-349
Editorial: Wittener Str. 45, 44789 BOCHUM
Tel: 234 3153625
Email: beate.muellmann@aral.com **Web site:** http://www.aral.de
Freq: 11 issues yearly; **Cover Price:** Free; **Circ:** 18,000
Editor: Beate Müllmann
Profile: Magazine for employees of the Aral company gas stations.
Language(s): German
ADVERTISING RATES:
Full Page Mono .... EUR 1930
Full Page Colour .... EUR 3705
Mechanical Data: Type Area: 255 x 185 mm

2 DIE ZWEI
749071G74A-20
Editorial: Münchener Str. 101, 85737 ISMANING
Tel: 89 272707211 **Fax:** 89 272707290
Email: redaktion@die2.de **Web site:** http://www.gonginfo.de
Freq: Weekly; **Annual Sub.:** EUR 57,20; **Circ:** 107,445
Editor: Carsten Pfefferkorn
Profile: Women's magazine with information about household, fashion and health, lifestyle articles, interviews, as well as TV listings.
Language(s): German
ADVERTISING RATES:
Full Page Mono .... EUR 4040
Full Page Colour .... EUR 4040
Mechanical Data: Type Area: 260 x 196 mm, No. of Columns (Display): 4, Col Widths (Display): 46 mm
Copy instructions: *Copy Date:* 23 days prior to publication
CONSUMER: WOMEN'S INTEREST CONSUMER MAGAZINES: Women's Interest

37
1665723G80-14488
Editorial: Am Leinekanal 4, 37073 GÖTTINGEN
Tel: 551 5042818 **Fax:** 551 5042819
Email: info@stadtmagazin37.de **Web site:** http://www.stadtmagazin37.de
Freq: 10 issues yearly; **Cover Price:** Free; **Circ:** 10,299
Editor: Sonja Grzeganek; **Advertising Manager:** Christoph Berlinecke
Language(s): German
ADVERTISING RATES:
Full Page Mono .... EUR 1560
Full Page Colour .... EUR 1560
Mechanical Data: Type Area: 261 x 194 mm, No. of Columns (Display): 3, Col Widths (Display): 50 mm
Copy instructions: *Copy Date:* 14 days prior to publication
CONSUMER: RURAL & REGIONAL INTEREST

3R
740574G58-1280
Editorial: Huyssenallee 52, 45128 ESSEN
Tel: 201 8200233 **Fax:** 201 8200240
Email: n.huelsdau@vulkan-verlag.de **Web site:** http://www.vulkan-verlag.de
Freq: 9 issues yearly; **Annual Sub.:** EUR 290,00; **Circ:** 2,881
Editor: Nico Hülsdau; **Advertising Manager:** Helga Pelzer
Profile: The pipeline's journal 3R covers the areas pipe manufacturing, pipe processing, pipeline construction and technical, economic and legal issues of transportation of liquid, gaseous and solid substances in pipelines. In focus topics books, experts of the subject in each case an overview of achievements, experiences and trends in key segments of the tube manufacturing and the construction and operation of pipelines. To provide a society in the future with safe energy and water and pay the resulting wastewater to efficient distribution networks are required. Play of the construction, operation and maintenance of these networks an essential role. 3R is the leading technical journal, which deals with these issues across all industries. With current contributions are reported on the latest technical developments of piping, components and processes in the field of gas and water supply, sewage disposal, district heating supply, plant construction and pipeline technology. With the two English-speaking special-editions "3R international," the magazine as an advertising medium opens up export markets in all continents.
Language(s): English; German
ADVERTISING RATES:
Full Page Mono .... EUR 2500
Full Page Colour .... EUR 3805
Mechanical Data: Type Area: 250 x 182 mm, No. of Columns (Display): 3, Col Widths (Display): 58 mm
Copy instructions: *Copy Date:* 10 days prior to publication
Official Journal of: Organ d. Fachbereichs Rohrleitungen im Fachverb. Dampfkessel-, Behälter- u. Rohrleitungsbau e.V., d. Fachverb. Kathod. Korrosionsschutz e.V., d. Frontinus-Ges. e.V., d. Kunststoffrohrverb. e.V., d. Rohrleitungsbauverb. e.V., d. Rohrleitungssanierungsverb. e.V. u. d. Verb. d. Dt. Hersteller v. Gasdruck-Regelgeräten, Gasmeß- u. Gasregelanlagen e.V.
BUSINESS: ENERGY, FUEL & NUCLEAR

3R INTERNATIONAL
2098387G58-1851
Editorial: Huyssenallee 52, 45128 ESSEN
Tel: 201 8200233 **Fax:** 201 8200240
Email: n.huelsdau@vulkan-verlag.de **Web site:** http://www.vulkan-verlag.de
Freq: 9 issues yearly; **Annual Sub.:** EUR 290,00; **Circ:** 2,881
Editor: Nico Hülsdau; **Advertising Manager:** Helga Pelzer
Profile: The pipeline's journal 3R covers the areas pipe manufacturing, pipe processing, pipeline construction and technical, economic and legal issues of transportation of liquid, gaseous and solid substances in pipelines. In focus topics books, experts of the subject in each case an overview of achievements, experiences and trends in key segments of the tube manufacturing and the construction and operation of pipelines. To provide a society in the future with safe energy and water and pay the resulting wastewater to efficient distribution networks are required. Play of the construction, operation and maintenance of these networks an essential role. 3R is the leading technical journal, which deals with these issues across all industries. With current contributions are reported on the latest technical developments of piping, components and processes in the field of gas and water supply, sewage disposal, district heating supply, plant construction and pipeline technology. With the two English-speaking special-editions "3R international," the magazine as an advertising medium opens up export markets in all continents.
Language(s): English
ADVERTISING RATES:
Full Page Mono .... EUR 2500
Full Page Colour .... EUR 3805
Mechanical Data: Type Area: 250 x 182 mm, No. of Columns (Display): 3, Col Widths (Display): 58 mm
Copy instructions: *Copy Date:* 10 days prior to publication

60PLUSMINUS - AUSG. DRESDEN
2001686G74N-1014
Editorial: Juri-Gagarin-Ring 68, 99084 ERFURT
Tel: 361 6633632 **Fax:** 361 6028502
Email: susann.deluca@cala-verlag.de **Web site:** http://www.60plusminus.de
Freq: Quarterly; **Cover Price:** Free; **Circ:** 15,000
Editor: Susann de Luca; **Advertising Manager:** Carsten Franke
Profile: Regional magazine for active people over 50 in the Dresden region. With calendar of events and exhibitions.
Language(s): German
ADVERTISING RATES:
Full Page Mono .... EUR 980
Full Page Colour .... EUR 980
Mechanical Data: Type Area: 260 x 182 mm
Copy instructions: *Copy Date:* 11 days prior to publication

60PLUSMINUS - AUSG. THÜRINGEN
2001685G74N-1013
Editorial: Juri-Gagarin-Ring 68, 99084 ERFURT
Tel: 361 6633632 **Fax:** 361 6028502
Email: susann.deluca@cala-verlag.de **Web site:** http://www.60plusminus.de
Freq: Quarterly; **Cover Price:** Free; **Circ:** 20,000
Editor: Susann de Luca; **Advertising Manager:** Carsten Franke
Profile: Regional magazine for active people over 50 in the region of Thuringia. With calendar of events and exhibitions.
Language(s): German
ADVERTISING RATES:
Full Page Mono .... EUR 1100
Full Page Colour .... EUR 1100
Mechanical Data: Type Area: 260 x 182 mm
Copy instructions: *Copy Date:* 11 days prior to publication

65ER NACHRICHTEN DER STADT SIEGBURG
1655414G74N-847
Editorial: Nogenter Platz 10, 53721 SIEGBURG
Tel: 2241 102290 **Fax:** 2241 102284
Email: rathaus@siegburg.de **Web site:** http://www.siegburg.de
Freq: Quarterly; **Cover Price:** Free; **Circ:** 8,000
Editor: Heinz-Dieter Gessner
Profile: Magazine for the elderly from the city of Siegburg.
Language(s): German
ADVERTISING RATES:
Full Page Mono .... EUR 300
Copy instructions: *Copy Date:* 50 days prior to publication

7 TAGE
741943G74A-40
Editorial: Rotweg 8, 76532 BADEN-BADEN
Tel: 7221 3501501 **Fax:** 7221 3501599
Email: 7tage@klambt.de
Freq: Weekly; **Annual Sub.:** EUR 91,00; **Circ:** 96,280
Editor: Peter Viktor Kulig; **Advertising Manager:** Martin Fischer
Profile: 7 Tage is the current women's magazine with great entertainment and value. In modern, fully colored look, with an interesting mix of topics. 7 Tage reported each week on the small and big secrets of the celebrities of this world. Recent reports and detailed reports are always very close to the lives of celebrities and the offspring of prominent personalities from the nobility and show business, from film and television, sports and society. And under the motto "For you thereby" report 7 Tage-reporters each week, from the exceptional events, the stage for the organizers and protagonists in the show business to see and be seen. Practical advice with a high value guarantee service topics in 7 Tage. With emphasis on the fields health / medicine and a current medical series, fashion and beauty, holidays and travel, nature, home and garden, Law and Council and new cooking and baking recipes. Rounding out the issue a mixture with the novel and the window with the current buy recommendations and a puzzle part with attractive prizes, a weekly TV-overview and a horoscope.
Language(s): German
ADVERTISING RATES:
Full Page Mono .... EUR 2577
Full Page Colour .... EUR 2577
Mechanical Data: Type Area: 260 x 195 mm, No. of Columns (Display): 4, Col Widths (Display): 45 mm
Copy instructions: *Copy Date:* 28 days prior to publication
CONSUMER: WOMEN'S INTEREST CONSUMER MAGAZINES: Women's Interest

DIE 80 BESTEN GRATINS WOCHE DER FRAU
2086891G74P-1391
Editorial: Rotweg 8, 76532 BADEN-BADEN
Tel: 7221 3501131 **Fax:** 7221 3501304
Email: wochederfrau@klambt.de
Freq: Annual; **Circ:** 80,000
Advertising Manager: Martin Fischer
Profile: Au gratin dishes, casseroles and baked dishes are always good. They are unbeatable because they are so well prepared and easy to prepare. Fine supplements fall into the baking dish, like hearty conjure with and without meat or sweet main dishes: delicious with crispy crust, oven-hits with pasta, moussaka, lasagne & Co., sweet saturated maker.
Language(s): German
ADVERTISING RATES:
Full Page Mono .... EUR 5370
Full Page Colour .... EUR 5370
Mechanical Data: Type Area: 250 x 195 mm, No. of Columns (Display): 4, Col Widths (Display): 45 mm
Copy instructions: *Copy Date:* 28 days prior to publication

DIE 80 BESTEN GRILL-REZEPTE WOCHE DER FRAU
2086892G74P-1392
Editorial: Rotweg 8, 76532 BADEN-BADEN
Tel: 7221 3501131 **Fax:** 7221 3501304
Email: wochederfrau@klambt.de
Freq: Annual; **Circ:** 80,000
Advertising Manager: Martin Fischer
Profile: What would a summer without the smell of charcoal and delicious grilled meat? Only half as good! For a barbecue fun in gregarious company we keep lots of ideas for delicious grilled ready: Spicy marinades for every taste, poultry and fish from the grill: Light and delicious! Crisp grilled vegetables: More than just a garnish, delicious spit-and much more!.
Language(s): German
ADVERTISING RATES:
Full Page Mono .... EUR 5370
Full Page Colour .... EUR 5370
Mechanical Data: Type Area: 250 x 195 mm, No. of Columns (Display): 4, Col Widths (Display): 45 mm
Copy instructions: *Copy Date:* 28 days prior to publication

DIE 80 BESTEN PASTA-REZEPTE WOCHE DER FRAU
2086893G74P-1393
Editorial: Rotweg 8, 76532 BADEN-BADEN
Tel: 7221 3501131 **Fax:** 7221 3501304
Email: wochederfrau@klambt.de
Freq: Annual; **Circ:** 80,000
Advertising Manager: Martin Fischer
Profile: Noodles make you happy - are prepared quickly and easily. No matter how you love noodles, this leaves nothing to be desired: Enjoyment of the fork - Spaghetti variations, noodle dishes from the oven, delicious pasta salads, pasta for the very rushed. Delicious for many occasions.
Language(s): German
ADVERTISING RATES:
Full Page Mono .... EUR 5370
Full Page Colour .... EUR 5370
Mechanical Data: Type Area: 250 x 195 mm, No. of Columns (Display): 4, Col Widths (Display): 45 mm
Copy instructions: *Copy Date:* 28 days prior to publication

DIE 80 BESTEN SCHNITZEL-REZEPTE WOCHE DER FRAU
2086894G74P-1394
Editorial: Rotweg 8, 76532 BADEN-BADEN
Tel: 7221 3501131 **Fax:** 7221 3501304
Email: wochederfrau@klambt.de
Freq: Annual; **Circ:** 80,000
Advertising Manager: Martin Fischer
Profile: Quick made and dearly loved: cutlet for every taste - from classic to exotic variations: Wiener Schnitzel & Co., quick cutlet dishes, fruity and spicy cutlet-pleasure and tasty easy chicken cutlet.
Language(s): German
ADVERTISING RATES:
Full Page Mono .... EUR 5370
Full Page Colour .... EUR 5370
Mechanical Data: Type Area: 250 x 195 mm, No. of Columns (Display): 4, Col Widths (Display): 45 mm
Copy instructions: *Copy Date:* 28 days prior to publication

9ELF
1812830G77A-2808
Editorial: Schrempfstr. 8, 70597 STUTTGART
Tel: 711 24897600 **Fax:** 711 24897628
Email: 9elf@mo-web.de **Web site:** http://www.mo-web.de
Freq: 6 issues yearly; **Cover Price:** EUR 5,90; **Circ:** 22,000
Editor: Jürgen Gassebner; **Advertising Manager:** Sabine Schermer
Profile: 9ELF begins where others leave off with the topic of Automobile Magazine Porsche. Staying well researched, lavishly illustrated and features high quality, the magazine presents the fascinating technology, history and dynamics of sports and racing cars from Zuffenhausen. Background reports on Porsche and racing activities, new services and accessories from the market as well as news 9ELF make an indispensable medium for all Porsche enthusiasts.
Language(s): German
ADVERTISING RATES:
Full Page Mono .... EUR 3655
Full Page Colour .... EUR 6140
Mechanical Data: Type Area: 262 x 184 mm, No. of Columns (Display): 4, Col Widths (Display): 43 mm

:INFO
731025G56A-11179

Editorial: Johannes-Weyer-Str. 1, 40227 DÜSSELDORF **Tel:** 211 7709541 **Fax:** 211 7709545
Email: yvonne.hochtritt@duesseldorf.aidshilfe.de
Web site: http://www.duesseldorf.aidshilfe.de
Freq: 3 issues yearly; **Cover Price:** Free; **Circ:** 1,500
Editor: Yvonne Hochtritt
Profile: Magazine from the Düsseldorf AIDS-Hilfe.
Language(s): German
Mechanical Data: Type Area: 263 x 173 mm
Copy instructions: *Copy Date:* 30 days prior to publication

:K
1659662G19E-1878

Editorial: Talhofstr. 24b, 82205 GILCHING
Tel: 8105 385382 **Fax:** 8105 385311
Email: m.kleine@verlag-henrich.de **Web site:** http://www.k-magazin.de
Freq: 8 issues yearly; **Annual Sub.:** EUR 84,00; **Circ:** 23,775
Editor: Michael Kleine; **Advertising Manager:** Siegfried Kunert
Profile: :K is a practical, solution oriented industry journal that provides impulses for every phase of the design process and offers concrete, comprehensive support. In doing so, :K takes into account all aspects of design – mechanical, electrical, software – as well as a view of operational-economical aspects, and all of that in a unique and goal-oriented journalistic combination. The production process is always kept in the foreground. :K reaches out to all groups involved in the decision-making process in a realistic mix. :K is the initiator of the Mechatronik working group, which counts leading representatives from various firms among its members. This permanently open dialog delivers a completely current and highly accurate view of the market, which in turn flows into the journal.
Language(s): German
ADVERTISING RATES:
Full Page Mono .... EUR 5150
Full Page Colour .... EUR 6580
Mechanical Data: Type Area: 282 x 200 mm, No. of Columns (Display): 4, Col Widths (Display): 47 mm
Copy instructions: *Copy Date:* 28 days prior to publication
BUSINESS: ENGINEERING & MACHINERY: Machinery, Machine Tools & Metalworking

:OTTO
1651751G14A-9611

Editorial: Am Alten Theater 1, 39104 MAGDEBURG
Tel: 391 5870 **Fax:** 391 5871551
Email: info@sw-magdeburg.de **Web site:** http://www.sw-magdeburg.de
Freq: Half-yearly; **Circ:** 1,500
Editor: Anne-Kathrin Beyer
Profile: Company publication for selected customers of the Städtische Werke Magdeburg.
Language(s): German

:ZEITPUNKT
1892851G14A-10274

Editorial: Ottoplatz 1, 50679 KÖLN
Tel: 221 92547721 **Fax:** 221 92547799
Email: goeddertz@regionale2010.de **Web site:** http://www.regionale2010.de
Freq: Annual; **Circ:** 10,000
Editor: Manfred Kasper
Profile: Regional political magazine.
Language(s): German

<KES>
732514G5E-11

Editorial: Lise-Meitner-Str. 4, 55435 GAU-ALGESHEIM **Tel:** 6725 93040 **Fax:** 6725 5994
Email: redaktion.kes@secumedia.de **Web site:** http://www.kes.info
Freq: 6 issues yearly; **Annual Sub.:** EUR 127,00; **Circ:** 7,820
Editor: Norbert Luckhardt; **Advertising Manager:** Birgit Eckert
Profile: Journal focusing on data communications and data protection.
Language(s): German
ADVERTISING RATES:
Full Page Mono .... EUR 1920
Full Page Colour .... EUR 2920
Mechanical Data: No. of Columns (Display): 3, Col Widths (Display): 50 mm, Type Area: 245 x 164 mm
Official Journal of: Organ d. Bundesamtes f. Sicherheit in d. Informationstechnik
BUSINESS: COMPUTERS & AUTOMATION: Data Transmission

> E ENERGIESPEKTRUM
726272G58-260

Editorial: Talhofstr. 24b, 82205 GILCHING
Tel: 8105 385336 **Fax:** 8105 385311
Email: v.tisken@verlag-henrich.de **Web site:** http://www.energiespektrum.de
Freq: 10 issues yearly; **Annual Sub.:** EUR 135,00; **Circ:** 16,255
Editor: Volker Tisken; **Advertising Manager:** Diana Beatrice Schmidt
Profile: Magazine for decision makers in the energy sector. Middle of the market reports> e-energy spectrum of the monthly technology of today and tomorrow's trends. The topics range from the economical power generation, distribution and application, as well as energy management and energy policy. Furthermore, competition and regulation of the energy market, energy trading and information technology solutions are regularly the focus.
Language(s): German
ADVERTISING RATES:
Full Page Mono .... EUR 4098
Full Page Colour .... EUR 5478
Mechanical Data: Type Area: 282 x 200 mm, No. of Columns (Display): 4, Col Widths (Display): 47 mm
Copy instructions: *Copy Date:* 28 days prior to publication
Supplement(s): i Quadrat
BUSINESS: ENERGY, FUEL & NUCLEAR

>>ÄSTHETISCHE DERMATOLOGIE & KOSMETOLOGIE
1900071G56A-11600

Editorial: Tiergartenstr. 17, 69121 HEIDELBERG
Tel: 6221 4878322 **Fax:** 6221 48768322
Email: sonja.kempinski@springer.com **Web site:** http://www.springermedizin.de
Freq: 6 issues yearly; **Annual Sub.:** EUR 180,00; **Circ:** 4,800
Editor: Sonja Kempinski; **Advertising Manager:** Sabine Weidner
Profile: The magazine 'ästhetische dermatologie & kosmetologie' offers the latest training for office-based dermatologists. Content of scientific and practical knowledge and experience of aesthetic dermatology are taught. The focus is to obtain a training post of 3 CME points and the current coverage of conferences. Original papers delve into each issue an aesthetic and dermatological issue, the usefulness for the daily practice of the reader in the foreground.
Language(s): German
ADVERTISING RATES:
Full Page Mono .... EUR 2590
Full Page Colour .... EUR 3630
Mechanical Data: Type Area: 240 x 174 mm
Copy instructions: *Copy Date:* 21 days prior to publication
Official Journal of: Organ d. ArGe f. ästhet. Dermatologie u. Kosmetologie

>COMPASS
727143G94H-14275

Editorial: Richard-Wagner-Str. 10, 50674 KÖLN
Email: kontakt@redaktionshaus-koeln.de **Web site:** http://www.comdirect.de
Freq: Quarterly; **Circ:** 308,350
Editor: Thomas Licher; **Advertising Manager:** Heiko Hager
Profile: Magazine about financial investments.
Language(s): German
ADVERTISING RATES:
Full Page Mono .... EUR 13100
Full Page Colour .... EUR 13100
Mechanical Data: Type Area: 249 x 183 mm
CONSUMER: OTHER CLASSIFICATIONS: Customer Magazines

>>DLR DEUTSCHE LEBENSMITTEL-RUNDSCHAU
725028G22R-51

Editorial: Lessingstr. 2, 74405 GAILDORF
Tel: 7971 978604 **Fax:** 7971 978607
Email: dlr@behrs.de **Web site:** http://www.behrs.de
Freq: Monthly; **Annual Sub.:** EUR 384,13; **Circ:** 1,050
Editor: Gabriele Lauser; **Advertising Manager:** Markus Wenzel
Profile: Magazine covering all aspects of food chemistry, food technology and food law.
Language(s): English; German
Readership: Read by university lecturers and caterers dealing with food technology.
ADVERTISING RATES:
Full Page Mono .... EUR 1430
Full Page Colour .... EUR 2840
Mechanical Data: Type Area: 252 x 175 mm, No. of Columns (Display): 3, Col Widths (Display): 53 mm
Copy instructions: *Copy Date:* 21 days prior to publication
BUSINESS: FOOD: Food Related

>>EXTRACTA GYNAECOLOGICA
1852548G56A-11563

Editorial: Tiergartenstr. 17, 69121 HEIDELBERG
Tel: 6221 4878322 **Fax:** 6221 48768322
Email: sonja.kempinski@springer.com **Web site:** http://www.extracta-gynaecologica.de
Freq: 6 issues yearly; **Annual Sub.:** EUR 174,00; **Circ:** 9,587
Editor: Sonja Kempinski; **Advertising Manager:** Odette Thomßen
Profile: >>Extracta gynaecologica principally addresses practitioners in the field of gynaecology and obstetrics. The aim of this journal is to provide the reader with a continuous overview of practice-relevant information and state-of-the-art knowledge, thereby keeping the reader informed of up-to-date developments in this field. The contents cover all areas of applied gynaecology relevant to the medical practice - from obstetrics to oncology, endocrinology and reproductive medicine. Each issue contains interesting case reports, information about practice management and law, journal clubs and congress news. Qualified experts of the advisory board guarantee a high professional standard of the journal. Each issue offers several opportunities for further education of the highest standard: Articles in the section CME-Continuing Medical Education offer established knowledge and make comprehensive medical experience accessible for daily use in the medical practice. After reading the articles, the reader may verify the acquired knowledge and collect CME credits online. Further, he is invited to refresh his knowledge in colposcopy and ultrasound in special courses.
Language(s): German
ADVERTISING RATES:
Full Page Mono .... EUR 3800
Full Page Colour .... EUR 3800
Mechanical Data: Type Area: 240 x 174 mm

>>EXTRACTA ORTHOPAEDICA
1852549G56A-11564

Editorial: Tiergartenstr. 17, 69121 HEIDELBERG
Tel: 6221 4878322 **Fax:** 6221 48768322
Email: sonja.kempinski@springer.com **Web site:** http://www.springermedizin.de
Freq: 6 issues yearly; **Annual Sub.:** EUR 174,00; **Circ:** 5,581
Editor: Sonja Kempinski; **Advertising Manager:** Noëla Krischer-Janka
Profile: >>Extracta orthopaedica principally addresses practitioners in the field of orthopaedics. The aim of this journal is to provide the reader with a continuous overview of practice-relevant information and state-of-the-art knowledge, thereby keeping the reader informed of up-to-date developments in this field. The contents provide information about current developments in all areas of applied orthopaedics relevant to the medical practice. Each issue contains interesting case reports, information about practice management and law, journal clubs and congress news. Qualified experts of the advisory board guarantee a high professional standard of the journal. Each issue offers several opportunities for further education of the highest standard: Articles in the section 'CME-Continuing Medical Education' offer established knowledge and make comprehensive medical experience accessible for daily use in the medical practice. After reading the articles, the reader may verify the acquired knowledge and collect CME credits online. Further, he is invited to refresh his knowledge in sports medicine and childrens orthopaedics in special courses.
Language(s): German
ADVERTISING RATES:
Full Page Mono .... EUR 3280
Full Page Colour .... EUR 3280
Mechanical Data: Type Area: 240 x 174 mm

Ã APICIUS
2098183G74P-1409

Editorial: Gut Pottscheidt, 53639 KÖNIGSWINTER
Tel: 2223 92300 **Fax:** 2223 923013
Email: d.henkel@heel-verlag.de **Web site:** http://www.heel-verlag.de
Freq: Half-yearly; **Annual Sub.:** EUR 70,00; **Circ:** 5,000
Editor: Denia Henkel; **Advertising Manager:** Jasmin Noorani
Profile: Discover exciting products, future-oriented philosophies, visions and creative culinary recipes of the best international chefs - Apicius is the platform for the culinary avant-garde and now finally appears also in German.
Language(s): German
ADVERTISING RATES:
Full Page Mono .... EUR 3300
Full Page Colour .... EUR 3300
Mechanical Data: Type Area: 297 x 210 mm

A AUTOMATION
727469G5A-3

Editorial: Talhofstr. 24b, 82205 GILCHING
Tel: 8105 385376 **Fax:** 8105 385311
Email: m.lind@verlag-henrich.de **Web site:** http://www.automationnet.de
Freq: 6 issues yearly; **Annual Sub.:** EUR 80,00; **Circ:** 20,295
Editor: Michael Lind; **Advertising Manager:** Siegfried Kunert
Profile: Magazine about solutions, processes and products for the effective rationalization in all operational areas of manufacturing Industrie.Im are reporting application-oriented focus of automation solutions. Reports, market and industry analysis, company profiles, interviews and the idea of process and product engineering and new developments.
Language(s): German
ADVERTISING RATES:
Full Page Mono .... EUR 4860
Full Page Colour .... EUR 6240
Mechanical Data: Type Area: 282 x 200 mm, No. of Columns (Display): 4, Col Widths (Display): 47 mm
Supplement(s): i Quadrat
BUSINESS: COMPUTERS & AUTOMATION: Automation & Instrumentation

A DIE AKTUELLE
719565G74A-391

Editorial: Münchener Str. 101, 85737 ISMANING
Tel: 89 272707211 **Fax:** 89 272707290
Email: kontakt@die-aktuelle.de **Web site:** http://www.aktuelle.de
Freq: Weekly; **Annual Sub.:** EUR 78,00; **Circ:** 388,071
Editor: Anne Hoffmann
Profile: News People magazine reports on VIPs, stars and other lifestyle, exciting and emotional conversation, extensive spa, beauty and health issues, recipes and tips for Deco ideas and the current kitchen, large travel section and an extra puzzle magazine with 18 pages.
Language(s): German
ADVERTISING RATES:
Full Page Mono .... EUR 9800
Full Page Colour .... EUR 9800
Mechanical Data: Type Area: 260 x 196 mm, No. of Columns (Display): 4, Col Widths (Display): 46 mm
Copy instructions: *Copy Date:* 27 days prior to publication
CONSUMER: WOMEN'S INTEREST CONSUMER MAGAZINES: Women's Interest

A DIE AKTUELLE LIEBE & SCHICKSAL
1623360G74A-3384

Editorial: Münchener Str. 101/Geb. 09, 85737 ISMANING **Tel:** 89 272707811 **Fax:** 89 272707890
Email: info@raetsel.de **Web site:** http://www.raetsel.de
Freq: 6 issues yearly; **Cover Price:** EUR 1,75; **Circ:** 75,000
Editor: Bernd Koophamel
Profile: Novel Issue: Exciting stories about love, lust and passion. The magazine offers modern love stories, everyday stories turbulent and romantic love novels.
Language(s): German
ADVERTISING RATES:
Full Page Mono .... EUR 1500
Full Page Colour .... EUR 1500
Mechanical Data: Type Area: 275 x 215 mm

A DIE AKTUELLE PREIS RÄTSEL MAGAZIN
719566G79F-60

Editorial: Münchener Str. 101/Geb. 09, 85737 ISMANING **Tel:** 89 272707811 **Fax:** 89 272707890
Email: info@raetsel.de **Web site:** http://www.raetsel.de
Freq: Monthly; **Annual Sub.:** EUR 21,60; **Circ:** 128,000
Editor: Bernd Koophamel
Profile: Magazine containing crossword puzzles and lifestyle articles.
Language(s): German
Readership: Aimed at women.
ADVERTISING RATES:
Full Page Mono .... EUR 1100
Full Page Colour .... EUR 1400
Mechanical Data: Type Area: 275 x 215 mm
Copy instructions: *Copy Date:* 42 days prior to publication
CONSUMER: HOBBIES & DIY: Games & Puzzles

À LA CARTE
719911G74P-20

Editorial: Höfeweg 40, 33619 BIELEFELD
Tel: 521 911110 **Fax:** 521 9111112
Email: info@klocke-verlag.de **Web site:** http://www.klocke-verlag.de
Freq: Monthly; **Annual Sub.:** EUR 72,00; **Circ:** 33,277
Editor: Thomas Klocke; **Advertising Manager:** Wolfgang Pohl
Profile: One of the leading food magazines in Germany, is hosting a monthly variety of recommended hotels and restaurants of Sylt to Tegernsee. The editorial concept is based on an objective, neutral presentation of the addresses and the offer, which the guests expected both culinary and the ambience here, we do not "restaurant test " and are not a "restaurant critic". Instead, we wish town or region based publish tips for going out and enjoying a beer garden can be like a cocktail bar or a 3-star restaurant, a family-run country hotel, where a 5-star home.
Language(s): German
ADVERTISING RATES:
Full Page Mono .... EUR 4750
Full Page Colour .... EUR 8400
Mechanical Data: Type Area: 252 x 172 mm
Copy instructions: *Copy Date:* 63 days prior to publication
CONSUMER: WOMEN'S INTEREST CONSUMER MAGAZINES: Food & Cookery

À LA CARTE
740712G89C-3440

Editorial: Markt 10, 18528 BERGEN
Tel: 3838 809970 **Fax:** 3838 809977
Email: info@apmarketing.de **Web site:** http://www.apmarketing.de
Freq: 7 issues yearly; **Cover Price:** Free; **Circ:** 29,950
Editor: Christina Wuitschik; **Advertising Manager:** Britta Rosengarth
Profile: Free publication for the Rügen area available from tourist boards, hotels and restaurants.
Language(s): German
ADVERTISING RATES:
Full Page Mono .... EUR 994
Full Page Colour .... EUR 1057
Mechanical Data: Type Area: 270 x 180 mm, No. of Columns (Display): 4, Col Widths (Display): 40 mm
Copy instructions: *Copy Date:* 20 days prior to publication
CONSUMER: HOLIDAYS & TRAVEL: Entertainment Guides

A TAVOLA!
1775557G74P-1222

Editorial: Junkernstr. 3, 29320 HERMANNSBURG
Tel: 5052 912118 **Fax:** 5052 912119
Email: redaktion@a-tavola.info **Web site:** http://www.a-tavola.info
Freq: 6 issues yearly; **Annual Sub.:** EUR 18,00; **Circ:** 32,000
Editor: Manuel Silzer
Profile: Specialists and guest magazine for Italian cuisine and lifestyle.
Language(s): German
ADVERTISING RATES:
Full Page Mono .... EUR 3200
Full Page Colour .... EUR 3200
Mechanical Data: Type Area: 297 x 210 mm

Copy instructions: *Copy Date:* 30 days prior to publication

A&D
721447G5A-2
Editorial: Nymphenburger Str. 86, 80636 MÜNCHEN
Tel: 89 50038321 **Fax:** 89 50038310
Email: aud.news@publish-industry.net **Web site:** http://www.aud24.net
Freq: 10 issues yearly; **Annual Sub.:** EUR 107,00; **Circ:** 19,496
Editor: Mathis Bayerdörfer; **Advertising Manager:** Caroline Häfner
Profile: The magazine carried competence and know-how in industrial automation - from the manufacturer to the user, and comprising all along the value chain. Journalistic quality management articles and thoroughly researched technology contributions presenting the latest trends and innovations, supported by strong imagery and contemporary layout. Informative applications as example of success inspire the reader to optimize the workplace, at. An important guide also provide reports on key trends in the markets of machine and plant construction. A&D offers a variety of solutions for a best-of-class production in the discrete manufacturing. It shows the benefits, for the production operator from the multidisciplinary optimization of the automated results. A&D represents for technology users and suppliers a fixed point in the regular assessment and technology is the reader in both print and e-paper edition is available.
Language(s): German
Readership: Read by designers, engineers and technicians.
ADVERTISING RATES:
Full Page Mono .... EUR 5338
Full Page Colour .... EUR 6280
Mechanical Data: Type Area: 232 x 178 mm, No. of Columns (Display): 4, Col Widths (Display): 42 mm
Supplement(s): A&D Messe-Taschenbuch
BUSINESS: COMPUTERS & AUTOMATION: Automation & Instrumentation

A&I ANÄSTHESIOLOGIE & INTENSIVMEDIZIN
1748974G56A-11406
Editorial: Roritzerstr. 27, 90419 NÜRNBERG
Tel: 911 9337812 **Fax:** 911 3938195
Email: anaesth.intensivmed@dgai-ev.de **Web site:** http://www.ai-online.info
Freq: 11 issues yearly; Free to qualifying individuals
Annual Sub.: EUR 250,38; **Circ:** 23,177
Editor: Alexandra Hisom; **Advertising Manager:** Pia Engelhardt
Language(s): German
ADVERTISING RATES:
Full Page Mono .... EUR 2060
Full Page Colour .... EUR 3470
Mechanical Data: Type Area: 223 x 180 mm, No. of Columns (Display): 3, Col Widths (Display): 55 mm
Copy instructions: *Copy Date:* 20 days prior to publication
Official Journal of: Organ d. Dt. Ges. f. Anästhesiologie u. Intensivmedizin, d. Berufsverb. Dt. Anästhesisten, d. Dt. Akademie f. Anästhesiolog. Fortbildung u. d. Dt. Interdisziplinären Vereinigung f. Intensiv- u. Notfallmedizin
BUSINESS: HEALTH & MEDICAL

A & W ARCHITEKTUR & WOHNEN
721449G74C-40
Editorial: Poßmoorweg 2, 22301 HAMBURG
Tel: 40 27173700 **Fax:** 40 27172073
Email: redaktion@awmagazin.de **Web site:** http://www.awmagazin.de
Freq: 6 issues yearly; **Annual Sub.:** EUR 45,00; **Circ:** 98,504
Editor: Barbara Friedrich; **Advertising Manager:** Sabine Rethmeier
Profile: "A & W Architektur & Wohnen" reportes widely, competent and entertaining at the same time about trends and tendencies in the field of housing, architecture, interior and product design, in garden design. The title provides background knowledge of international architecture projects and observe the art from its specific perspective. "A & W Architektur & Wohnen" does not only reflect the aesthetic trends of our time, but creates styles so proves its role as an opinion leader. "A & W Architektur & Wohnen" is conceived as a popular magazine and also recognized among experts.
Language(s): German
Readership: Aimed at women with a home and family.
ADVERTISING RATES:
Full Page Mono .... EUR 17900
Full Page Colour .... EUR 17900
Mechanical Data: Type Area: 258 x 188 mm, No. of Columns (Display): 4, Col Widths (Display): 44 mm
Copy instructions: *Copy Date:* 48 days prior to publication
CONSUMER: WOMEN'S INTEREST CONSUMER MAGAZINES: Home & Family

AACHENER NACHRICHTEN
719426G67B-20
Editorial: Dresdener Str. 3, 52068 AACHEN
Tel: 241 5101310 **Fax:** 241 5101360
Email: redaktion@zeitungsverlag-aachen.de **Web site:** http://www.an-online.de
Freq: 312 issues yearly; **Circ:** 129,569
Editor: Bernd Mathieu; **News Editor:** Peter Pappert;
Advertising Manager: Christian Kretschmer
Profile: Newspaper covering politics, economics, sport, travel and technology. Facebook: http://facebook.com/aachenernachrichten This Outlet offers RSS (Really Simple Syndication).
Language(s): German
ADVERTISING RATES:
SCC .... EUR 246,80
Mechanical Data: Type Area: 480 x 324 mm, No. of Columns (Display): 7, Col Widths (Display): 44 mm
Copy instructions: *Copy Date:* 1 day prior to publication
Supplement(s): prisma
REGIONAL DAILY & SUNDAY NEWSPAPERS: Regional Daily Newspapers

AACHENER WOCHE SUPER MITTWOCH
719427G72-96
Editorial: Dresdener Str. 3, 52068 AACHEN
Tel: 241 5101591 **Fax:** 241 5101550
Email: info@supermittwoch.de
Freq: Weekly; **Cover Price:** Free; **Circ:** 102,710
Editor: Astrid van Megeren; **Advertising Manager:** Jürgen Carduck
Profile: Advertising journal (house-to-house) concentrating on local stories.
Language(s): German
ADVERTISING RATES:
Full Page Mono .... EUR 6587
Full Page Colour .... EUR 9222
Mechanical Data: Type Area: 430 x 282 mm, No. of Columns (Display): 7, Col Widths (Display): 38 mm
Copy instructions: *Copy Date:* 2 days prior to publication
LOCAL NEWSPAPERS

AACHENER ZEITUNG
719428G67B-40
Editorial: Dresdener Str. 3, 52068 AACHEN
Tel: 241 5101310 **Fax:** 241 5101360
Email: redaktion@zeitungsverlag-aachen.de **Web site:** http://www.aachener-zeitung.de
Freq: 312 issues yearly; **Circ:** 129,569
Editor: Bernd Mathieu; **News Editor:** Peter Pappert;
Advertising Manager: Christian Kretschmer
Profile: Newspaper covering politics, economics, sport, travel and technology. Facebook: http://facebook.com/aachenerzeitung This Outlet offers RSS (Really Simple Syndication).
Language(s): German
ADVERTISING RATES:
SCC .... EUR 246,80
Mechanical Data: Type Area: 480 x 324 mm, No. of Columns (Display): 7, Col Widths (Display): 44 mm
Copy instructions: *Copy Date:* 1 day prior to publication
Supplement(s): prisma
REGIONAL DAILY & SUNDAY NEWSPAPERS: Regional Daily Newspapers

AALENER NACHRICHTEN
719431G67B-60
Editorial: Rudolf-Roth-Str. 18, 88299 LEUTKIRCH
Tel: 7561 800 **Fax:** 7561 80134
Email: redaktion@schwaebische-zeitung.de **Web site:** http://www.schwaebische.de
Freq: 312 issues yearly; **Circ:** 10,690
Profile: In its edition provides the "Aalener Nachrichten" its readers daily with the latest information from government, business, sports, culture and food from the local environment. Twitter: https://twitter.com/AalenerNachr This Outlet offers RSS (Really Simple Syndication).
Language(s): German
ADVERTISING RATES:
SCC .... EUR 63,20
Mechanical Data: Type Area: 480 x 320 mm, No. of Columns (Display): 7, Col Widths (Display): 44 mm
Copy instructions: *Copy Date:* 1 day prior to publication
REGIONAL DAILY & SUNDAY NEWSPAPERS: Regional Daily Newspapers

AAR-BOTE
719439G67B-80
Editorial: Langgasse 21, 65183 WIESBADEN
Tel: 611 3490 **Fax:** 611 3492233
Freq: 312 issues yearly; **Circ:** 63,127
Advertising Manager: Gerhard Müller
Profile: Daily newspaper with regional news and a local sports section.
Language(s): German
ADVERTISING RATES:
SCC .... EUR 143,20
Mechanical Data: Type Area: 480 x 325 mm, No. of Columns (Display): 7, Col Widths (Display): 45 mm
Copy instructions: *Copy Date:* 1 day prior to publication
Supplement(s): Untertaunus anzeiger
REGIONAL DAILY & SUNDAY NEWSPAPERS: Regional Daily Newspapers

AB ARCHIV DES BADEWESENS
719447G32E-1
Editorial: Alfredstr. 73, 45130 ESSEN
Tel: 201 8796912 **Fax:** 201 8796921
Email: info@baederportal.com **Web site:** http://www.baederportal.com
Freq: Monthly; Free to qualifying individuals
Annual Sub.: EUR 67,00; **Circ:** 4,500
Editor: Joachim Heuser; **Advertising Manager:** Sebastian Friedrich
Profile: Magazine with information about public swimming pools.
Language(s): German
Readership: Aimed at architects, engineers and technologists.
ADVERTISING RATES:
Full Page Mono .... EUR 1220
Full Page Colour .... EUR 1814
Mechanical Data: Type Area: 251 x 177 mm, No. of Columns (Display): 3, Col Widths (Display): 57 mm
Copy instructions: *Copy Date:* 15 days prior to publication
BUSINESS: LOCAL GOVERNMENT, LEISURE & RECREATION: Swimming Pools

ABBOTT TIMES
719448G56A-20
Editorial: Max-Planck-Ring 2, 65205 WIESBADEN
Tel: 6122 581744 **Fax:** 6122 581277
Web site: http://www.abbottdiagnostik.de
Freq: Half-yearly; **Annual Sub.:** EUR 18,41; **Circ:** 8,000
Editor: Karl-Heinz Pick
Profile: Magazine for physical doctors and pharmacists.
Language(s): German

ABENDZEITUNG
719453G67B-100
Editorial: Rundfunkplatz 4, 80335 MÜNCHEN
Tel: 89 23770 **Fax:** 89 2377729
Email: redaktion@abendzeitung.de **Web site:** http://www.abendzeitung.de
Freq: 312 issues yearly; **Circ:** 120,525
Editor: Arno Makowsky; **News Editor:** Frank Müller
Profile: Regional daily newspaper covering politics, economics, culture, sports, travel and technology. Facebook: http://www.facebook.com/abendzeitung Twitter: http://twitter.com/Abendzeitung This Outlet offers RSS (Really Simple Syndication).
Language(s): German
ADVERTISING RATES:
SCC .... EUR 207,50
Mechanical Data: Type Area: 485 x 325 mm, No. of Columns (Display): 7, Col Widths (Display): 45 mm
Copy instructions: *Copy Date:* 1 day prior to publication
Supplement(s): Anpfiff; mehr Freude am Leben; TV-Woche
REGIONAL DAILY & SUNDAY NEWSPAPERS: Regional Daily Newspapers

ABENDZEITUNG.DE
1620695G67B-16501
Editorial: Rundfunkplatz 4, 80335 MÜNCHEN
Tel: 89 26020692
Email: info@az-digital.de **Web site:** http://www.abendzeitung.de
Freq: Daily; **Cover Price:** Paid; **Circ:** 2,089,770 Unique Users
Editor: Gunnar Jans
Profile: Online presence of the regional daily newspaper, news from Munich, Nürnberg and Bavaria, sports, local, domestic and foreign policy, money, culture (literature, cinema, theater and pop / rock), people (parties and events of the Munich Society), Panorama (Issues & people who are on everyone's lips) and Boulevard. Facebook: http://www.facebook.com/abendzeitung Twitter: http://twitter.com/Abendzeitung This Outlet offers RSS (Really Simple Syndication).
Language(s): German
REGIONAL DAILY & SUNDAY NEWSPAPERS: Regional Daily Newspapers

ABENTEUER UND REISEN
1622371G89A-12151
Editorial: Dieselstr. 36, 63071 OFFENBACH
Tel: 69 98190430 **Fax:** 69 98190412
Email: kontakt@abenteuer-reisen.de **Web site:** http://www.abenteuer-reisen.de
Freq: Weekly; **Cover Price:** Paid; **Circ:** 59,926 Unique Users
Editor: Peter Pfänder; **Advertising Manager:** Sabine Nieth
Profile: Ezine: abenteuer-reisen.de is the Internet portal of Germany's wellestablished print magazine, abenteuer und reisen. It provides multimedia enjoyment to suit a modern, mobile lifestyle. Hundreds of first-class reports with a wide range of photos, more than 850 videoclips of the best destinations plus a large number of insider tips are included in comprehensive interactive travel guides. All contents can be easily found using the navigation markers on the interactive maps and search windows. abenteuer und reisen usersppublish their travel experiences, reports and photos in the Community section. Facebook: http://www.facebook.com/abenteuerundreisen.
Language(s): German
CONSUMER: HOLIDAYS & TRAVEL: Travel

ABENTEUER UND REISEN
1638087G89A-12162
Editorial: Dieselstr. 36, 63071 OFFENBACH
Tel: 69 98190430 **Fax:** 89 98190412
Email: kontakt@abenteuer-reisen.de **Web site:** http://www.abenteuer-reisen.de
Freq: 10 issues yearly; **Annual Sub.:** EUR 45,00; **Circ:** 81,846
Editor: Peter Pfänder; **Advertising Manager:** Volker Andres
Profile: abenteuer und reisen is the travel magazine, which reports throughout the world ten times per year. The writers and photographers research between Alaska and Cyprus, Arctic and Zimbabwe. There are always acknowledged country experts and credible reporters. abenteuer und reisen is the info-magazine that offers animation and above all information - in terms of tourist life support and service information. Insider tips from first-hand, always thoroughly researched, critically examined and personally tested. Facebook: http://www.facebook.com/abenteuerundreisen.
Language(s): German
ADVERTISING RATES:
Full Page Mono .... EUR 11800
Full Page Colour .... EUR 11800
Mechanical Data: Type Area: 246 x 182 mm, No. of Columns (Display): 4, Col Widths (Display): 43 mm
Copy instructions: *Copy Date:* 47 days prior to publication
CONSUMER: HOLIDAYS & TRAVEL: Travel

ABFALLR ZEITSCHRIFT FÜR DAS RECHT DER ABFALLWIRTSCHAFT
1828368G1A-3693
Editorial: Güntzelstr. 63, 10717 BERLIN
Tel: 30 81450616 **Fax:** 30 81450622
Email: kessels@lexxion.de **Web site:** http://www.lexxion.de
Freq: 6 issues yearly; **Annual Sub.:** EUR 181,46; **Circ:** 1,000
Editor: Vivian Keßels
Profile: Magazine for jurists.
Language(s): German
ADVERTISING RATES:
Full Page Mono .... EUR 920
Mechanical Data: Type Area: 248 x 175 mm
Copy instructions: *Copy Date:* 21 days prior to publication

ABFALLWIRTSCHAFTLICHER INFORMATIONSDIENST
719460G57-20
Editorial: Kurfürstenstr. 17, 10785 BERLIN
Tel: 30 2619854 **Fax:** 30 2616300
Email: redaktion@rhombos.de **Web site:** http://www.abfallinfodienst.de
Freq: Quarterly; **Annual Sub.:** EUR 250,00; **Circ:** 1,000
Editor: Bernhard Reiser; **Advertising Manager:** Steffi Nerlinger
Profile: Magazine with news and announcements relating to the waste business and national and international environmental politics.
Language(s): German
ADVERTISING RATES:
Full Page Mono .... EUR 410
Full Page Colour .... EUR 1175
Mechanical Data: Type Area: 270 x 190 mm
Copy instructions: *Copy Date:* 30 days prior to publication
BUSINESS: ENVIRONMENT & POLLUTION

ABI AKTUELLE BERICHTE UND INFORMATIONEN FÜR ARCHITEKTEN UND INGENIEURE
1833359G4E-7218
Editorial: Rheinstr. 129c, 76275 ETTLINGEN
Tel: 7243 39396 **Fax:** 7243 39395
Email: info@ingenieurverlag.de **Web site:** http://www.ingenieurverlag.de
Freq: 6 issues yearly; **Annual Sub.:** EUR 31,00; **Circ:** 700
Editor: Wolfgang Staubach
Profile: Magazine for architecs and engineers.
Language(s): German

ABI AKTUELLE BERICHTE UND INFORMATIONEN FÜR ARCHITEKTEN UND INGENIEURE
1833359G4E-7313
Editorial: Rheinstr. 129c, 76275 ETTLINGEN
Tel: 7243 39396 **Fax:** 7243 39395
Email: info@ingenieurverlag.de **Web site:** http://www.ingenieurverlag.de
Freq: 6 issues yearly; **Annual Sub.:** EUR 31,00; **Circ:** 700
Editor: Wolfgang Staubach
Profile: Magazine for architecs and engineers.
Language(s): German

ABI-TECHNIK
719472G60B-20
Editorial: Paul-Gerhardt-Allee 46, 81245 MÜNCHEN
Tel: 89 31890544 **Fax:** 89 31890553
Email: abi@vnmonline.de **Web site:** http://www.abi-technik.de
Freq: Quarterly; **Annual Sub.:** EUR 145,00; **Circ:** 2,920
Editor: Berndt Dugall; **Advertising Manager:** Elke Zimmermann
Profile: German language only nationwide, internationally quoted scientific journal for the specialty areas of automation, construction and technology in the archive, library and information science. Updates on new products and technologies. Continuous four-color, high image quality. The subtitle, "Journal of Automation, construction and technology in the archive, library and information science" illustrates the issues dealt with by the journal. The focus is on contributions to library buildings and equipment (includes IT and technical equipment), but there are also many technical papers on general library issues, eg Development and business processes. The magazine is aimed at professionals in libraries and archives and to adjacent

industries (construction, engineering, warehousing, logistics). Immediately following the heading "technical contribution" is found the heading "News", announcements regarding new construczion projects and especially interiors.
Language(s): German
ADVERTISING RATES:
Full Page Mono .... EUR 945
Full Page Colour .... EUR 1627
Mechanical Data: Type Area: 260 x 185 mm, No. of Columns (Display): 3, Col Widths (Display): 54 mm
Copy instructions: *Copy Date:* 28 days prior to publication
BUSINESS: PUBLISHING: Libraries

DER ABITURIENT 1613628G91D-9781
Editorial: Carl-Bertelsmann-Str. 33, 33311 GÜTERSLOH **Tel:** 5241 234800 **Fax:** 5241 23480215
Email: focken@derabiturient.de **Web site:** http://www.derabiturient.de
Freq: Quarterly; **Cover Price:** Free; **Circ:** 178,029
Editor: Christian Focken
Profile: The newspaper has a young and open-minded audience useful and interesting content on the topics of high school preparation, study and career choices, leisure activities and careers. The newspaper is for high school students and graduates an important medium through which they learn about occupations, industries and businesses. Der Abiturient assists in one of the hardest decisions in life: What should I be? The medium is the information platform for and about universities and companies.
Language(s): German
ADVERTISING RATES:
Full Page Mono .... EUR 6900
Full Page Colour .... EUR 6900
Mechanical Data: No. of Columns (Display): 4, Col Widths (Display): 58 mm, Type Area: 370 x 247 mm
Copy instructions: *Copy Date:* 21 days prior to publication
CONSUMER: RECREATION & LEISURE: Children & Youth

ABSATZWIRTSCHAFT 719483G2A-60
Editorial: Grafenberger Allee 293, 40237 DÜSSELDORF **Tel:** 211 8871423 **Fax:** 211 8871420
Email: absatzwirtschaft@fachverlag.de **Web site:** http://www.absatzwirtschaft.de
Freq: Monthly; Free to qualifying individuals
Annual Sub.: EUR 111,00; **Circ:** 25,262
Editor: Christoph Berdi; **Advertising Manager:** Regina Hamdorf
Profile: absatzwirtschaft is Germany's largest circulation monthly magazine for marketing. Researched and written for executives in the companies it covers all the practical issues of modern marketing and sales and provides information on trends, best practices, new methods and the development on the part of the media and marketing services. The magazine supports and promotes the development of modern sales and marketing. It gives the practitioners in the business ideas and practices, where it appears the editors offered constructive criticism. Carefully researched, journalistic articles, interviews and articles offering the high-profile authors absatzwirtschaft in a modern, independent magazine layout dar. The magazine is divided into five departments: Global Marketing - focusing on the international perspective Strategy & Innovation - the department for the transfer of knowledge between practice, science and Consulting Media & Communication - the route for daily operations and direct impact on media and marketing budget CRM & distribution - with the facts for customer relationship management and distribution Marketing-Life - the issue end with stories written marketing, away from the specialized information.
Language(s): German
ADVERTISING RATES:
Full Page Mono .... EUR 6370
Full Page Colour .... EUR 6370
Mechanical Data: Type Area: 256 x 180 mm, No. of Columns (Display): 4, Col Widths (Display): 42 mm
Copy instructions: *Copy Date:* 20 days prior to publication
Official Journal of: Organ d. Verein Dt. Ingenieure e.V., Ges. Produkt- u. Prozessgestaltung
BUSINESS: COMMUNICATIONS, ADVERTISING & MARKETING

ABSEITS-DENKSTE 1616461G74N-820
Editorial: Rachelstr. 6, 93413 CHAM **Tel:** 9971 78291 **Fax:** 9971 845291
Email: senioren@lra.landkreis-cham.de **Web site:** http://www2.landkreis-cham.de
Freq: Half-yearly; **Cover Price:** Free; **Circ:** 7,000
Profile: Magazine for the elderly from the region of Cham.
Language(s): German

ABSOLUT|REPORT 1696125G1F-1647
Editorial: Große Elbstr. 277a, 22767 HAMBURG
Tel: 40 3037790 **Fax:** 40 30377915
Email: redaktion@absolut-report.de **Web site:** http://www.absolut-report.de
Freq: 6 issues yearly; **Annual Sub.:** EUR 957,65; **Circ:** 8,000
Editor: Ellen Hörth; **Advertising Manager:** Augustina Nebelthau
Profile: Trade publication for institutional investors in Germany, Austria and Switzerland. The focus is on innovative asset management concepts and all the institutional issues surrounding the investment.
Language(s): German
ADVERTISING RATES:
Full Page Mono .... EUR 9000
Full Page Colour .... EUR 9000
Mechanical Data: Type Area: 297 x 210 mm, No. of Columns (Display): 3, Col Widths (Display): 55 mm
Copy instructions: *Copy Date:* 15 days prior to publication

ABZ ALLGEMEINE BÄCKERZEITUNG 719992G8A-20
Editorial: Silberburgstr. 122, 70176 STUTTGART
Tel: 711 2133305 **Fax:** 711 2133280
Email: m.fischer@matthaes.de **Web site:** http://www.abzonline.de
Freq: 25 issues yearly; **Annual Sub.:** EUR 216,00; **Circ:** 11,956
Editor: Manfred Fischer; **Advertising Manager:** Nicole M. Felger
Profile: The ABZ Allgemeine BäckerZeitung aimed at managers and decision makers in the baking industry. Through detailed reports on new trends and important markets, baking technology and machine technology, marketing and sales concepts get our readers with valuable information for their professional success. Other key topics of the ABZ Allgemeine BäckerZeitung include business and company news, industry policy and the comprehensive reports on trade fairs, congresses and events in the baking industry. Who wants to know about important events, businesses, news and technical subjects know who reads the ABZ Allgemeine BäckerZeitung. Through the nationwide spread of ABZ Allgemeine BäckerZeitung you reach with your advertising decision makers in the bakery trade.
Language(s): German
Readership: Aimed at bakers and chefs.
ADVERTISING RATES:
Full Page Mono .... EUR 6404
Full Page Colour .... EUR 6404
Mechanical Data: Type Area: 364 x 254 mm, No. of Columns (Display): 5, Col Widths (Display): 48 mm
Copy instructions: *Copy Date:* 10 days prior to publication
Official Journal of: Organ d. Bäckerinnungsverbände Baden-Württemberg, Südwest, Saarland, Hessen
BUSINESS: BAKING & CONFECTIONERY: Baking

ABZ ALLGEMEINE BAUZEITUNG 719994G4E-461
Editorial: Alter Flughafen 15, 30179 HANNOVER
Tel: 511 6740860 **Fax:** 511 6740853
Email: abz-oschuetz@patzer-verlag.de **Web site:** http://www.abznet.de
Freq: Weekly; **Annual Sub.:** EUR 127,40; **Circ:** 32,163
Editor: Rainer Oschütz
Profile: ABZ Allgemeine Bauzeitung is the current trade magazine for the entire construction industry. Weekly on Friday with the latest news from construction policy, construction and civil engineering. Permanent expert Information on construction equipment, construction machinery, construction materials, architecture, construction and building research, reports, analysis and building site reports.
Language(s): German
Readership: Aimed at architects and people in the building and construction industry.
ADVERTISING RATES:
Full Page Mono .... EUR 16474
Full Page Colour .... EUR 28829
Mechanical Data: Type Area: 528 x 371 mm, No. of Columns (Display): 8, Col Widths (Display): 45 mm
Copy instructions: *Copy Date:* 3 days prior to publication
Official Journal of: Organ d. Bundesverb. Gerüstbau, Güteschutzverb. Stahlgerüstbau, Betonbohren u. -sägen u. d. Dt. Abbruchverb.
BUSINESS: ARCHITECTURE & BUILDING: Building

ACADEMIA 719490G83-200
Editorial: Steinbügelstr. 9, 76228 KARLSRUHE
Tel: 721 405129 **Fax:** 721 401256
Email: j.leclerque@t-online.de **Web site:** http://www.cartellverband.de
Freq: 6 issues yearly; **Annual Sub.:** EUR 12,50; **Circ:** 29,293
Editor: Johannes Leclerque
Profile: Magazine about academic education, politics, religion and history.
Language(s): German
Readership: Aimed at students.
ADVERTISING RATES:
Full Page Mono .... EUR 1540
Full Page Colour .... EUR 2020
Mechanical Data: Type Area: 237 x 183 mm, No. of Columns (Display): 3, Col Widths (Display): 58 mm
Copy instructions: *Copy Date:* 42 days prior to publication
CONSUMER: STUDENT PUBLICATIONS

ACE LENKRAD 719496G77E-20
Editorial: Schmidener Str. 227, 70374 STUTTGART
Tel: 711 5303201 **Fax:** 711 5303210
Email: redaktion@ace-lenkrad.de **Web site:** http://www.ace-lenkrad.de
Freq: Monthly; Free to qualifying individuals
Annual Sub.: EUR 24,00; **Circ:** 544,182
Editor: Klaus-Michael Schaal; **Advertising Manager:** Jörg Eisenach
Profile: ACE LENKRAD is the member magazine of the ACE Auto Club Europa, reaching 550,000 ACE members, totaling nearly one million readers. For them, ACE LENKRAD is an important source of information that is widely used. 67 per cent of the members read the magazine intensively and regularly, and another 24 percent occasionally. The content of ACE LENKRAD is tailored month by month to the needs of the constant and stable targeted readership. Mobility and varied interest play the main role. The continuous selection of topics includes sound reviews and current launches in the automotive sector, large travel reports and reports on the two-wheeler segment as well as camping and caravanning. ACE LENKRAD presents the entire range of issues around cars, mobility, leisure and travel at the same time it is informative and entertaining. In particular, the utility value quality and service-oriented guide issues across all departments and steadily attract attention - with lots of cash tips, informative product tests and well-founded recommendation to buy, are a highlight in every issue of ACE LENKRAD.
Language(s): German
Readership: Aimed at members of ACE and all car and camper drivers.
ADVERTISING RATES:
Full Page Colour .... EUR 19500
Mechanical Data: Type Area: 247 x 185 mm, No. of Columns (Display): 4, Col Widths (Display): 43 mm
Copy instructions: *Copy Date:* 30 days prior to publication
CONSUMER: MOTORING & CYCLING: Club Cars

ACHER- UND BÜHLER BOTE 719499G67B-160
Editorial: Linkenheimer Landstr. 133, 76149 KARLSRUHE **Tel:** 721 7890 **Fax:** 721 789155
Email: redaktion@bnn.de **Web site:** http://www.bnn.de
Freq: 312 issues yearly; **Circ:** 19,728
Advertising Manager: Gerhard Fautz
Profile: The Badische Neueste Nachrichten with a paid circulation of about 150,000 copies and 400,000 readers every day one of the major daily newspapers in the state of Baden-Wuerttemberg. This newspaper is understood in the concert of the leaves the country as a not to be hearing voices of Baden and the Palatinate region between and Ortenau, between the Black Forest and Rhine valley. Nine local editions in the distribution area in the Karlsruhe, Pforzheim and Bruchsal, Baden resources emphasize the character of this newspaper as Baden regional newspaper. On this image editing with a full working day with about 90 editors. Most of the editorial staff but provided in the local editors at ten locations in the distribution area the readers with local news. In addition to the BNN output Karlsruhe, Rastatt, Baden-Baden, Ettlingen arise then the Pforzheimer Kurier, the Bruchsaler Rundschau, the Brettener Nachrichten and not least the Acher- und Bühler Bote. Although the focus of reporting is very strong locally and regionally, the Badische Neueste Nachrichten offer their readers a broad and comprehensive news coverage.
Language(s): German
ADVERTISING RATES:
SCC .... EUR 54,00
Mechanical Data: Type Area: 480 x 360 mm, No. of Columns (Display): 8, Col Widths (Display): 43 mm
Copy instructions: *Copy Date:* 1 day prior to publication
REGIONAL DAILY & SUNDAY NEWSPAPERS: Regional Daily Newspapers

ACHER-RENCH-ZEITUNG 719497G67B-140
Editorial: Am Marktplatz 4, 77704 OBERKIRCH
Tel: 7802 80424 **Fax:** 7802 80441
Email: lokales.oberkirch@reiff.de **Web site:** http://www.baden-online.de
Freq: 312 issues yearly; **Circ:** 13,322
Advertising Manager: Gebhard Schnurr
Profile: Regional daily newspaper with news on politics, economy, culture, sports, travel, technology, etc. The Mittelbadische Presse, that are Offenburger Tageblatt, Kehler Zeitung, Lahrer Zeitung and Acher-Rench-Zeitung. With a total circulation of about 60,000 specimens come from the media company Reiff, "the" home of the newspapers Ortenau. Partly for nearly 200 years we have * Absolute readers around because the reader is with us in the self-Journal * Regional expertise * Information Platform of the events and life in the region * instrument of human communication, commerce, economics and politics in the Ortenau and therefore ideal promotional tool. Newspapers are, six days a week: * News * Independent * unique - they are always subject.
Language(s): German
ADVERTISING RATES:
SCC .... EUR 32,50
Mechanical Data: Type Area: 420 x 284 mm, No. of Columns (Display): 6, Col Widths (Display): 44 mm
Copy instructions: *Copy Date:* 1 day prior to publication
REGIONAL DAILY & SUNDAY NEWSPAPERS: Regional Daily Newspapers

ACHIMER KREISBLATT 719501G67B-180
Editorial: Am Ristedter Weg 17, 28857 SYKE
Tel: 4242 58300 **Fax:** 4242 58332
Email: redaktion@kreiszeitung.de **Web site:** http://www.kreiszeitung.de
Freq: 312 issues yearly; **Circ:** 22,726
Advertising Manager: Axel Berghoff
Profile: The Kreiszeitung publishing group is the fifth largest newspaper in Niedersachsen, with a daily circulation of over 82,000 copies. Regional daily newspaper covering politics, economics, sport, travel and technology. Facebook: http://www.facebook.com/pages/Kreiszeitung Twitter: http://twitter.com/kreiszeitung This Outlet offers RSS (Really Simple Syndication).
Language(s): German
ADVERTISING RATES:
SCC .... EUR 64,80
Mechanical Data: Type Area: 472 x 325 mm, No. of Columns (Display): 7, Col Widths (Display): 45 mm
Copy instructions: *Copy Date:* 1 day prior to publication
REGIONAL DAILY & SUNDAY NEWSPAPERS: Regional Daily Newspapers

ACKERPLUS 2080653G21A-4475
Editorial: Bopserstr. 17, 70180 STUTTGART
Tel: 711 2140141 **Fax:** 711 2360232
Email: redaktion-lw@bwagrar.de **Web site:** http://www.ackerplus.de
Freq: 6 issues yearly; **Annual Sub.:** EUR 44,00; **Circ:** 59,511
Editor: Heiner Krehl; **Advertising Manager:** Gerhard Kretschmer
Profile: Ackerplus is the new modern medium for the cultivation and cattle professionals: 6 times a year as a high quality print magazine, 6 x as an interactive e-paper, and always online!. Ackerplus provides competent and independent of all relevant agricultural issues. The combination of print, online and e-paper uses the entire mix of modern information dissemination. The qualified controlled circulation allows for highly targeted approach of the agricultural professionals - with virtually no losses and a high range. This innovative concept, we offer customized solutions for successful communication. The range of topics: seeds and varieties, plant protection, fertilization, soil preparation, sowing and harvesting, renewable energy, best practices, technology, management, new products, news and events.
Language(s): German
ADVERTISING RATES:
Full Page Mono .... EUR 4780
Full Page Colour .... EUR 6880
Mechanical Data: Type Area: 252 x 180 mm, No. of Columns (Display): 4, Col Widths (Display): 45 mm
Copy instructions: *Copy Date:* 6 days prior to publication

ACP ARBEITSKREIS CHRISTLICHER PUBLIZISTEN 1861061G2A-5785
Editorial: Schöne Aussicht 8, 34305 NIEDENSTEIN
Tel: 5624 5259 **Fax:** 5624 6921
Email: info@acp-international.de **Web site:** http://www.acp-international.de
Freq: 5 issues yearly; Free to qualifying individuals
Annual Sub.: EUR 10,00; **Circ:** 8,000
Editor: Heinz Matthias
Profile: The magazine reports on current issues of Christianity, especially on such topics that are important for the media coverage. An important section are interviews with personalities from political, social or cultural life of the place occupied by questions of Christian values.
Language(s): German
ADVERTISING RATES:
Full Page Mono .... EUR 500

ACQUISA 719509G2F-1
Editorial: Munzinger Str. 9, 79111 FREIBURG
Tel: 761 8983031 **Fax:** 761 8983112
Email: redaktion@acquisa.de **Web site:** http://www.acquisa.de
Freq: Monthly; **Annual Sub.:** EUR 116,00; **Circ:** 24,131
Editor: Christoph Pause; **Advertising Manager:** Michael Reischke
Profile: Journal covering sales theory and practice, with trade information and tips.
Language(s): German
ADVERTISING RATES:
Full Page Mono .... EUR 6320
Full Page Colour .... EUR 6320
Mechanical Data: Type Area: 249 x 176 mm, No. of Columns (Display): 3, Col Widths (Display): 56 mm
Copy instructions: *Copy Date:* 20 days prior to publication
Supplement(s): acquisa update; direkt marketing
BUSINESS: COMMUNICATIONS, ADVERTISING & MARKETING: Selling

ACTA NEUROPATHOLOGICA 1638470G56A-11273
Editorial: Domagkstr. 19, 48149 MÜNSTER
Tel: 251 8356967 **Fax:** 251 8356971
Email: subscriptions@springer.com **Web site:** http://www.springerlink.com
Freq: 6 issues yearly; **Annual Sub.:** EUR 6457,00; **Circ:** 292
Editor: Werner Paulus
Profile: Organ of the Research Group for Neuropathology.
Language(s): German
ADVERTISING RATES:
Full Page Mono .... EUR 740
Full Page Colour .... EUR 1780
Mechanical Data: Type Area: 240 x 175 mm

ACTIVE WOMAN 1810918G74A-3551
Editorial: Greflingerstr. 3, 93055 REGENSBURG
Tel: 941 796070 **Fax:** 941 7960710
Email: info@active-woman.de **Web site:** http://www.activewoman.de

Freq: 6 issues yearly; **Annual Sub.:** EUR 15,90; **Circ:** 43,354
Editor: Gerda Obermeier; **Advertising Manager:** Michael Wagner
Profile: Sports magazine for women with reports to industry talk, people, VIP-News, Drive and Fun, technology firsthand Drive Products, Travel, Style Drive, motor sports and legal tips. Facebook: http://www.facebook.com/activwoman This Outlet offers RSS (Really Simple Syndication).
Language(s): German
ADVERTISING RATES:
Full Page Mono .... EUR 5327
Full Page Colour .... EUR 6179
Mechanical Data: Type Area: 240 x 175 mm, No. of Columns (Display): 4, Col Widths (Display): 40 mm
Copy instructions: *Copy Date:* 29 days prior to publication
Supplement(s): active woman drive&style

ACV PROFIL
719539G77E-40
Editorial: Vilbeler Landstr. 45a, 60388 FRANKFURT
Tel: 6109 734130 **Fax:** 6109 734145
Email: martina.pocke@t-online.de **Web site:** http://www.acv.de
Freq: 10 issues yearly; **Circ:** 266,697
Profile: Magazine of the German Automobil-Club Verkehr.
Language(s): German
Readership: Read by the club members.
ADVERTISING RATES:
Full Page Mono .... EUR 4114
Full Page Colour .... EUR 6171
Mechanical Data: Type Area: 262 x 182 mm, No. of Columns (Display): 3, Col Widths (Display): 58 mm
Copy instructions: *Copy Date:* 30 days prior to publication
CONSUMER: MOTORING & CYCLING: Club Cars

AD ARCHITECTURAL DIGEST
719540G74C-60
Editorial: Unter den Linden 10, 10117 BERLIN
Tel: 30 2014440 **Fax:** 30 201444152
Email: leserbriefe@ad-magazin.de **Web site:** http://www.ad-magazin.de
Freq: 10 issues yearly; **Annual Sub.:** EUR 52,00; **Circ:** 98,406
Editor: Oliver Jahn; **Advertising Manager:** Anja Grewe
Profile: AD ARCHITECTURAL DIGEST is the premium magazine for architecture, interior design and lifestyle in Germany. Each issue fascinates by its high level of quality and originality with stunning images and excellently researched stories. Sophisticated architecture, luxurious interior, smart living concepts - the diversity of AD shows the whole cosmos of themes from modern life. Of art, design and installation of tableware, garden design and lifestyle topics as fashion, jewelry and travel in style - AD informs and entertains the sophisticated readers. For years, received awards as the prestigious Lead Award "Bestes Wohnmagazin" and awards for individual contributions, show the special position of AD as a style-and opinion-forming magazine. To keep an eye on the beautiful and important, to keep an eye open for quality and innovation and inspire it with lots of charm and knowledge - this concept of true luxury is AD's philosophy and addresses the modern style elite directly. AD will therefore not only be the key medium for private users, but for all design professionals: architects, designers, gallery owners and managers in cultural business as well as creative retailers of furniture, precious fabrics and home accessories and manufacturer of high quality kitchens and bathrooms.
Language(s): German
ADVERTISING RATES:
Full Page Mono .... EUR 18000
Full Page Colour .... EUR 18000
Mechanical Data: Type Area: 252 x 190 mm, No. of Columns (Display): 4, Col Widths (Display): 44 mm
Copy instructions: *Copy Date:* 41 days prior to publication
CONSUMER: WOMEN'S INTEREST CONSUMER MAGAZINES: Home & Family

ADAC BUNGALOW MOBILHEIM FÜHRER
1655132G89A-11869
Editorial: Leonhard-Moll-Bogen 1, 81373 MÜNCHEN
Tel: 89 76760 **Fax:** 89 76762836
Email: accf@adac.de **Web site:** http://www.adac.de
Freq: Annual; **Cover Price:** EUR 16,90; **Circ:** 40,000
Editor: Stefan Thurn; **Advertising Manager:** Gabriele Möbius
Profile: Directory of the General German Automobile Club (ADAC) eV with addresses from bungalows, chalets, mobile homes and other rental accommodation in and outside of campsites across Europe.
Language(s): German
ADVERTISING RATES:
Full Page Mono .... EUR 4250
Full Page Colour .... EUR 4250
Mechanical Data: Type Area: 204 x 116 mm
Copy instructions: *Copy Date:* 93 days prior to publication

ADAC CAMPING CARAVANING FÜHRER
719542G89A-80
Editorial: Leonhard-Moll-Bogen 1, 81373 MÜNCHEN
Tel: 89 76762942 **Fax:** 89 76762836
Email: accf@adac.de **Web site:** http://www.adac.de/campingfuehrer
Freq: Annual; **Cover Price:** EUR 19,95; **Circ:** 67,639
Editor: Stefan Thurn; **Advertising Manager:** Gabriele Möbius
Profile: The ADAC Camping-Caravaning Guide (Edition Germany & Northern Europe) offers detailed and clearly prepared information on the most attractive tourist campsites in Europe. Year after year, is a trained team of incorruptible inspectors throughout Europe on the move to examine the campsites on the heart and kidneys. The tested plants are classified by the editor with the unique and highly transparent ADAC Camping-profile. For all tested campsites are available detailed descriptions, such as Sanitary equipment, stall design, supply, recreational facilities, entertainment and recreation programs. Of course, opening times and all relevant contact information, descriptions and access the current price by the ADAC comparison price for the season. Newly developed recreational icons show campers immediately where they are lifted with their individual holiday wishes particularly well places for families with young children, nude holidaymakers, walkers and riders are just as stressed plants, the special offers for boaters, surfers and Wellness Camper ready.
Language(s): German
ADVERTISING RATES:
Full Page Mono .... EUR 5310
Full Page Colour .... EUR 7930
Mechanical Data: Type Area: 204 x 116 mm
Copy instructions: *Copy Date:* 90 days prior to publication
CONSUMER: HOLIDAYS & TRAVEL: Travel

ADAC CAMPING CARAVANING FÜHRER
719543G89A-100
Editorial: Leonhard-Moll-Bogen 1, 81373 MÜNCHEN
Tel: 89 76762942 **Fax:** 89 76762836
Email: accf@adac.de **Web site:** http://www.adac.de/campingfuehrer
Freq: Annual; **Cover Price:** EUR 19,95; **Circ:** 110,000
Editor: Stefan Thurn; **Advertising Manager:** Gabriele Möbius
Profile: The ADAC Camping-Caravaning Guide (Edition Southern Europe) offers detailed and clearly prepared information on the most attractive tourist campsites in Europe. Year after year, is a trained team of incorruptible inspectors throughout Europe on the move to examine the campsites on the heart and kidneys. The tested plants are classified by the editor with the unique and highly transparent ADAC Camping-profile. For all tested campsites are available detailed descriptions, such as Sanitary equipment, stall design, supply, recreational facilities, entertainment and recreation programs. Of course, opening times and all relevant contact information, descriptions and access the current price by the ADAC comparison price for the season. Newly developed recreational icons show campers immediately where they are lifted with their individual holiday wishes particularly well places for families with young children, nude holidaymakers, walkers and riders are just as stressed plants, the special offers for boaters, surfers and Wellness Camper ready.
Language(s): German
ADVERTISING RATES:
Full Page Mono .... EUR 5560
Full Page Colour .... EUR 8280
Mechanical Data: Type Area: 204 x 116 mm
Copy instructions: *Copy Date:* 90 days prior to publication
CONSUMER: HOLIDAYS & TRAVEL: Travel

ADAC MOTORWELT
719547G77A-2645
Editorial: Leonhard-Moll-Bogen 1, 81373 MÜNCHEN
Tel: 89 76760 **Fax:** 89 76762500
Email: adac@adac.de **Web site:** http://www.adac.de
Freq: Monthly; **Circ:** 13,674,319
Editor: Michael Ramstetter; **Advertising Manager:** Ulrich Witt
Profile: ADAC MOTORWELT - the current club magazine of the ADAC. The ADAC eV has 17 million members, the largest motorist community in Europe. Its exceptionally positive image is based on the values ??of security and confidence and on the quality of its services for the mobile lif. Communication to members of the ADAC is based centrally on the ADAC Motorwelt. It is therefore the most widely and regularly used power of the ADAC. Among the members the ADAC Motorwelt has an important role as an information medium. They value the club magazine in particular for: - the credibility of editorial content - thematic independence, which is based solely on the interests of the club and its members - the ADAC test expertise - and the modern, reader-friendly layout With this specific brand, the ADAC has a unique position in the German magazine market. In surveys, the ADAC members regularly confirm their strong interest in the magazine and the intensive use of the content. And 88% regular readers suggest that the Club magazine is well received.
Language(s): German
ADVERTISING RATES:
Full Page Mono .... EUR 80960
Full Page Colour .... EUR 111040
Mechanical Data: Type Area: 244 x 184 mm, No. of Columns (Display): 4, Col Widths (Display): 43 mm
Copy instructions: *Copy Date:* 28 days prior to publication
CONSUMER: MOTORING & CYCLING: Motoring

ADAC REISEMAGAZIN
719549G89A-12106
Editorial: Leonhard-Moll-Bogen 1, 81373 MÜNCHEN
Tel: 89 76760 **Fax:** 89 76767699
Email: redaktion.reisemagazin@adac.de **Web site:** http://www.adac.de/reisemagazin
Freq: 6 issues yearly; **Annual Sub.:** EUR 39,90; **Circ:** 140,831
Editor: Michael Ramstetter; **Advertising Manager:** Ulrich Witt
Profile: Mono Thematic travel magazine. Features tour by car, bicycle or on foot to bring the reader closer to the travel destination and provide insights into the landscape, cultures and regional characteristics. Renowned writers write exclusively for the travel magazine about their homeland. The reporters are devoted to interesting topics from the fields of architecture, theater, art and music. The magazine shows the special restaurants of the region as well as local specialties and presents the most beautiful hotels. To this end it provides photographs speak for themselves, travel info, shopping tips and much more. The travel magazine is popular with his readers in order to get suggestions for new objectives, plan trips and to follow local recommendations. Because of their high educational and income levels are among the readers of travel magazine about the status of elites in Germany. They are extremely mobile and on new trends are particularly interested. In her large circle of friends, you act as opinion leaders and trendsetters. Holidays are an important issue for them. This is just a competent travel preparations such as the high quality demands on the holiday destination and the tourism service providers. Particularly like to make the readers of the travel magazine Holiday in Europe and in long-haul countries. But Short travel are among her favorite leisure activities.
Language(s): German
ADVERTISING RATES:
Full Page Mono .... EUR 18640
Full Page Colour .... EUR 18640
Mechanical Data: Type Area: 252 x 184 mm
Copy instructions: *Copy Date:* 56 days prior to publication
CONSUMER: HOLIDAYS & TRAVEL: Travel

ADAC REISEMAGAZIN SKI
719550G89A-11522
Editorial: Leonhard-Moll-Bogen 1, 81373 MÜNCHEN
Tel: 89 76760 **Fax:** 89 76766799
Email: redaktion.reisemagazin@adac.de **Web site:** http://www.adac.de/reisemagazin
Freq: Annual; **Cover Price:** EUR 6,95; **Circ:** 90,000
Editor: Michael Ramstetter; **Advertising Manager:** Lutz Sonntag
Profile: Ski Magazine: Buying advice, tips and trends, data and prices around the winter sport. Also: great features on top destinations in the Alps and in America.
Language(s): German
ADVERTISING RATES:
Full Page Mono .... EUR 6510
Full Page Colour .... EUR 6510
Mechanical Data: Type Area: 252 x 184 mm, No. of Columns (Display): 4, Col Widths (Display): 43 mm
Copy instructions: *Copy Date:* 42 days prior to publication

ADAC SKIGUIDE
719552G89A-140
Editorial: Leonhard-Moll-Bogen 1, 81373 MÜNCHEN
Tel: 89 76760 **Fax:** 89 76764243
Email: skiguide@adac.de **Web site:** http://www.adac.de/skiguide
Freq: Annual; **Cover Price:** EUR 24,90; **Circ:** 50,000
Editor: Thomas Biersack; **Advertising Manager:** Ulrich Witt
Profile: The ski guide offers as a market leader at around 800 pages a complete overview of the most attractive ski resorts in the Alps and worldwide. On the competence of the ADAC, the largest automobile club in Europe can trust when it comes to winter holidays and Skiing: The ski guide in-depth reports provide the most interesting ski resorts and exclusive ADAC tests in winter tourism - and complies with all the information gaps claims. In large part guide all ADAC tests of ski helmets and goggles to snow chains and snow tires are presented. Extensive market surveys Relation to pass, ski hire, flights to the Alps as well as useful supplements such as Overview of over 4,000 ski pass prices, the great Alpine ADAC card and the unique SkiGuide search engine on DVD.
Language(s): German
ADVERTISING RATES:
Full Page Mono .... EUR 8990
Full Page Colour .... EUR 8990
Mechanical Data: No. of Columns (Display): 3, Col Widths (Display): 53 mm, Type Area: 267 x 185 mm
Copy instructions: *Copy Date:* 60 days prior to publication

ADAC SPECIAL GEBRAUCHTWAGEN
755555G77A-2522
Editorial: Leonard-Moll-Bogen 1, 81373 MÜNCHEN
Tel: 89 76760 **Fax:** 89 76762500
Email: redaktion@adac-special.de **Web site:** http://www.adac.de/special
Freq: Annual; **Cover Price:** EUR 6,90; **Circ:** 120,000
Editor: Joachim Negwer; **Advertising Manager:** Ulrich Witt
Profile: Magazine for used motor cars.
Language(s): German
ADVERTISING RATES:
Full Page Mono .... EUR 7260
Full Page Colour .... EUR 10200
Mechanical Data: Type Area: 252 x 184 mm
Copy instructions: *Copy Date:* 60 days prior to publication

ADAC STELLPLATZ FÜHRER
1656879G89A-11875
Editorial: Leonhard-Moll-Bogen 1, 81373 MÜNCHEN
Tel: 89 76762311 **Fax:** 89 76762310
Email: aspf@adac.de **Web site:** http://www.adac.de
Freq: Annual; **Cover Price:** EUR 19,95; **Circ:** 45,000
Editor: Thomas Nitsch; **Advertising Manager:** Gabriele Möbius
Profile: Travel guide for mobile home drivers from the German Automobile Club ADAC for Germany-Europa (Andorra, Belgium, Denmark, Estonia, Finland, France, Great Britain, Ireland, Italy, Croatia, Latvia, Lithuania, Luxembourg, Netherlands, Norway, Austria, Poland, Portugal, Sweden, Switzerland, Slovenia, Spain, Czech Republic, Hungary) pitches. With description of 3800 parking spaces described.
Language(s): German
ADVERTISING RATES:
Full Page Mono .... EUR 4250
Full Page Colour .... EUR 4250
Mechanical Data: Type Area: 204 x 116 mm
Copy instructions: *Copy Date:* 76 days prior to publication

ADEL AKTUELL
1841646G74A-3608
Editorial: Rotweg 8, 76532 BADEN-BADEN
Tel: 7221 3501501 **Fax:** 7221 3501599
Email: kontakt@klambt.de **Web site:** http://www.klambt.de
Freq: Monthly; **Cover Price:** EUR 0,80; **Circ:** 250,000
Editor: Peter Viktor Kulig; **Advertising Manager:** Martin Fischer
Profile: Adel aktuell is the first German-speaking aristocracy magazine. A success story among the entertaining women's magazines. Adel aktuell shows each month dazzling world of royalty. Glamorous events are reflected in magnificent color features. Exclusive report obsequious and uncritical reporting on the life and loves of the nobility, reveal secrets and scandals. The magazine shows how Highnesses live, reveals the recipes from the royal kitchens, the health problems known behind palace walls, is hosting royal fashion. Target group: women, 30 years plus.
Language(s): German
ADVERTISING RATES:
Full Page Mono .... EUR 6200
Full Page Colour .... EUR 6200
Mechanical Data: Type Area: 250 x 195 mm, No. of Columns (Display): 4, Col Widths (Display): 45 mm

ADEL EXKLUSIV
1848156G74A-3622
Editorial: Burchardstr. 11, 20095 HAMBURG
Tel: 40 30194123 **Fax:** 40 30194133
Email: birgit.haase@bauerredaktionen.de **Web site:** http://adel-exklusiv.wunderweib.de
Freq: 8 issues yearly; **Cover Price:** EUR 0,69; **Circ:** 170,000
Editor: Hansjörn Muder
Profile: Magazine covering German and international current affairs, news, opinion and social trends. Also includes features on travel, health, personal finance, quizzes, stories and horoscopes.
Language(s): German
Mechanical Data: Type Area: 226 x 180 mm

ADENAUER WOCHENSPIEGEL
719560G72-120
Editorial: Bossardstr. 5, 53474 BAD NEUENAHR-AHRWEILER **Tel:** 2641 902827 **Fax:** 2641 902829
Email: red-adenau@weiss-verlag.de **Web site:** http://www.wochenspiegellive.de
Freq: Weekly; **Cover Price:** Free; **Circ:** 6,365
Editor: Alexander Lenders
Profile: Advertising journal (house-to-house) concentrating on local stories.
Language(s): German
ADVERTISING RATES:
Full Page Mono .... EUR 1626
Full Page Colour .... EUR 2288
Mechanical Data: Type Area: 430 x 290 mm, No. of Columns (Display): 7, Col Widths (Display): 38 mm
Copy instructions: *Copy Date:* 2 days prior to publication
LOCAL NEWSPAPERS

ADESSO
719562G88B-20
Editorial: Fraunhoferstr. 22, 82152 PLANEGG
Tel: 89 856810 **Fax:** 89 85681360
Email: adesso@spotlight-verlag.de **Web site:** http://www.adesso-online.de
Freq: Monthly; **Annual Sub.:** EUR 69,60,; **Circ:** 30,844
Editor: Rossella Dimola; **Advertising Manager:** Axel Zettler
Profile: Magazine for Italian learners. Adesso is the magazine for lovers of Italian life, the culture, enjoyment and language are inextricably linked. Looking forward to a month more than 30,000 Italian fans on the colorful abundance of exciting travel features, varied lifestyle reports and current background reports. The topics range from the jewels of art and culture on food and drink to regular travel ideas, politics, society, film, fashion and design.
Language(s): German; Italian
ADVERTISING RATES:
Full Page Mono .... EUR 3056
Full Page Colour .... EUR 5095
Mechanical Data: Type Area: 246 x 186 mm, No. of Columns (Display): 4, Col Widths (Display): 43 mm
Copy instructions: *Copy Date:* 35 days prior to publication
Supplement(s): evviva!
CONSUMER: EDUCATION: Adult Education

ADHÄSION KLEBEN & DICHTEN
719563G13-20

Editorial: Abraham-Lincoln-Str. 46, 65189 WIESBADEN **Tel:** 611 7878283 **Fax:** 611 7878495
Email: marlene.doobe@springer.com **Web site:** http://www.adhaesion.com
Freq: 10 issues yearly; **Annual Sub.:** EUR 235,00; **Circ:** 3,454
Editor: Marlene Doobe; **Advertising Manager:** Britta Dolch
Profile: Only German-language journal for industrial sealing and adhesive bonding technology. It speaks to manufacturers and users of adhesives and sealants and creates cross-industry synergies. The reader is given practical information on the topics of raw materials, adhesives and sealants, equipment engineering and plant technology, applications and research and development. The magazine points to market trends and reports on product developments. Information on major exhibitions and events round out the coverage.
Language(s): English; German
ADVERTISING RATES:
Full Page Mono .... EUR 2483
Full Page Colour .... EUR 4313
Mechanical Data: Type Area: 240 x 175 mm, No. of Columns (Display): 4, Col Widths (Display): 40 mm
Copy instructions: *Copy Date:* 23 days prior to publication
BUSINESS: CHEMICALS

ADIEU TRISTESSE
1794942G89A-12287

Editorial: Immanuelkirchstr. 38, 10405 BERLIN
Tel: 30 443519440 **Fax:** 30 443519420
Email: info@at-reisemagazin.de **Web site:** http://www.at-reisemagazin.de
Freq: 5 issues yearly; **Cover Price:** EUR 4,80; **Circ:** 105,000
Editor: Michael Steineck; **Advertising Manager:** Michael Steineck
Profile: Travel journal with critical reporting and authentic background reports.
Language(s): German
ADVERTISING RATES:
Full Page Colour .... EUR 6290
Mechanical Data: Type Area: 258 x 160 mm
Copy instructions: *Copy Date:* 27 days prior to publication

ADIPOSITAS
1865494G56A-11580

Editorial: Hölderlinstr. 3, 70174 STUTTGART
Tel: 711 2298736 **Fax:** 711 2298765
Email: redaktion@adipositas-journal.de **Web site:** http://www.adipositas-journal.de
Freq: Quarterly; **Annual Sub.:** EUR 96,00; **Circ:** 3,800
Advertising Manager: Jasmin Thurner
Profile: The current topic obesity is the focus of the journal Adipositas - Causes, complications, therapy. To meet the growing interest of quite different subjects at the central health issue "obesity" meet and bring together the many facets of the phenomenon, the magazine is designed as a multidisciplinary medium. The primary goal: Evidence-based medicine from the latest scientific knowledge into practice out in particular to convey the resident physician. Given the healthy economic and social importance of the issue of obesity and related diseases, the magazine Adipositas will also appeal to health and social ministries, and health insurance.
Language(s): German
ADVERTISING RATES:
Full Page Mono .... EUR 2125
Full Page Colour .... EUR 3265
Mechanical Data: Type Area: 243 x 179 mm, No. of Columns (Display): 3, Col Widths (Display): 57 mm
Copy instructions: *Copy Date:* 40 days prior to publication
Official Journal of: Organ d. Dt. Adipositas-Ges. e.V.

ADLERSHOF JOURNAL
1772680G14A-9913

Editorial: Rudower Chaussee 17, 12489 BERLIN
Tel: 30 63922238 **Fax:** 30 63922236
Email: nitschke@wista.de **Web site:** http://www.adlershof.de/journal
Freq: 6 issues yearly; **Annual Sub.:** EUR 20,00; **Circ:** 3,000
Editor: Sylvia Nitschke
Profile: Information about science, economy and media.
Language(s): German
Mechanical Data: Type Area: 262 x 170 mm
Copy instructions: *Copy Date:* 21 days prior to publication

ADVANCED ENGINEERING MATERIALS
719596G19A-1051

Editorial: Boschstr. 12, 69469 WEINHEIM
Tel: 6201 606235 **Fax:** 6201 606500
Email: aem@wiley-vch.de **Web site:** http://www.wiley-vch.de
Freq: Monthly; **Annual Sub.:** EUR 2063,00; **Circ:** 4,996
Editor: Jörn Ritterbusch; **Advertising Manager:** Patricia Filler
Profile: Interdisciplinary magazine about engineering materials.
Language(s): English; German
ADVERTISING RATES:
Full Page Mono .... EUR 2300
Full Page Colour .... EUR 3230
Mechanical Data: Type Area: 260 x 180 mm, No. of Columns (Display): 4, Col Widths (Display): 41 mm

ADVANCED FUNCTIONAL MATERIALS
719597G19A-1052

Editorial: Boschstr. 12, 69469 WEINHEIM
Tel: 6201 606531 **Fax:** 6201 606500
Email: afm@wiley-vch.de **Web site:** http://www.afm-journal.de
Freq: 24 issues yearly; **Annual Sub.:** EUR 4466,00; **Circ:** 1,000
Editor: David Flanagan; **Advertising Manager:** Marion Schulz
Profile: Magazine for chemists, physicians, scientists and engineers.
Language(s): English
ADVERTISING RATES:
Full Page Mono .... EUR 2300
Full Page Colour .... EUR 3230
Mechanical Data: Type Area: 260 x 180 mm, No. of Columns (Display): 2, Col Widths (Display): 88 mm
Copy instructions: *Copy Date:* 24 days prior to publication

ADVANCED MATERIALS
719598G55-3983

Editorial: Boschstr. 12, 69469 WEINHEIM
Tel: 6201 606235 **Fax:** 6201 606500
Email: advmat@wiley-vch.de **Web site:** http://www.advmat.de
Freq: Weekly; **Annual Sub.:** EUR 7041,00; **Circ:** 1,000
Editor: Peter Gregory; **Advertising Manager:** Marion Schulz
Profile: Research and development journal focusing on the applications of high-tech materials including polymers, ceramics, liquid crystals, alloys, semi-conductors and super-conductors.
Language(s): English
ADVERTISING RATES:
Full Page Mono .... EUR 2300
Full Page Colour .... EUR 3230
Mechanical Data: Type Area: 260 x 180 mm, No. of Columns (Display): 2, Col Widths (Display): 90 mm
Copy instructions: *Copy Date:* 24 days prior to publication
BUSINESS: APPLIED SCIENCE & LABORATORIES

ADVOICE
719604G1A-3498

Editorial: Littenstr. 11, 10179 BERLIN
Tel: 30 7261520 **Fax:** 30 26152195
Email: advoiceredaktion@davforum.de **Web site:** http://www.davforum.de
Freq: Quarterly; Free to qualifying individuals
Annual Sub.: EUR 51,00; **Circ:** 12,500
Editor: Tobias Sommer
Profile: Database for young lawyers.
Language(s): German
ADVERTISING RATES:
Full Page Mono .... EUR 1650
Full Page Colour .... EUR 2445
Mechanical Data: Type Area: 267 x 190 mm
Copy instructions: *Copy Date:* 26 days prior to publication

AE ARBEITSRECHTLICHE ENTSCHEIDUNGEN
1696428G1A-3613

Editorial: Budapester Str. 40, 10787 BERLIN
Tel: 30 25459155 **Fax:** 30 25459166
Email: kontakt@advocati.de
Freq: Quarterly; Free to qualifying individuals
Annual Sub.: EUR 107,60; **Circ:** 3,500
Editor: Hans-Georg Meier
Profile: Magazine for lawyers.
Language(s): German
ADVERTISING RATES:
Full Page Mono .... EUR 1210
Full Page Colour .... EUR 2080
Mechanical Data: Type Area: 260 x 186 mm, No. of Columns (Display): 2, Col Widths (Display): 90 mm

AERO INTERNATIONAL
719621G6A-20

Editorial: Im Tal 14, 28870 OTTERSBERG
Tel: 4205 394510 **Fax:** 4205 394522
Email: redaktion@aerointernational.de **Web site:** http://www.aerointernational.de
Freq: Monthly; **Annual Sub.:** EUR 68,40; **Circ:** 26,450
Editor: Dietmar Plath; **Advertising Manager:** Klaus Macholz
Profile: Magazine on the subject of civil aviation for the entire German-speaking countries. Focus: Industry and Technology, airline, airport, helicopters and business travel and private air travel, portraits of airports, airlines and aircraft types as well as interviews with personalities from the industry. Readership: specialists and executives in the aviation industry, airlines and air cargo, airports, ground handling services and the business aviation as well as people who have an intense interest in civil aviation.
Language(s): German
ADVERTISING RATES:
Full Page Mono .... EUR 4035
Full Page Colour .... EUR 6714
Mechanical Data: Type Area: 248 x 185 mm, No. of Columns (Display): 4, Col Widths (Display): 45 mm
Copy instructions: *Copy Date:* 27 days prior to publication
BUSINESS: AVIATION & AERONAUTICS

AEROKURIER
719622G6A-40

Editorial: Ubierstr. 83, 53173 BONN
Tel: 228 9565222 **Fax:** 228 9565246
Email: redaktion@aerokurier.de **Web site:** http://www.aerokurier.de
Freq: Monthly; **Annual Sub.:** EUR 54,90; **Circ:** 20,743
Editor: Volker K. Thomalla
Profile: International Journal of pilots for pilots. It informes as a trade magazine for the international civil aviation on the topics of general and business aviation, powered flight, air sports and aeronautical engineering. As a recognized trade journal, aerokurier published each month with reviews of general aviation aircraft. aerokurier contributes with expert reporting, transparent presentation of the market and in-depth research to increase public acceptance of aviation at. The readers covers the challenging editorial concept, the need for information on all aspects of civil aviation. Several times a year ideas are published as a booklet in the magazine. Topics include flight training, helicopters, maintenance, and business aviation. aerokurier appeals to the people who are interested in the whole spectrum of civil aviation and largely self aeronautically active. Facebook: www.facebook.com/aerokurier Twitter: http://twitter.com/aerokurier This Outlet offers RSS (Really Simple Syndication).
Language(s): German
ADVERTISING RATES:
Full Page Mono .... EUR 3600
Full Page Colour .... EUR 6660
Mechanical Data: Type Area: 248 x 185 mm, No. of Columns (Display): 4, Col Widths (Display): 43 mm
Copy instructions: *Copy Date:* 35 days prior to publication
Official Journal of: Organ d. Verb. d. Allg. Luftfahrt e.V. u. d. Club d. Luftfahrt v. Deutschland e.V.
BUSINESS: AVIATION & AERONAUTICS

AEÜ INTERNATIONAL JOURNAL OF ELECTRONICS AND COMMUNICATION
719658G18A-221

Editorial: 01062 DRESDEN **Tel:** 351 46333942
Fax: 351 46337163
Email: aeue@ifn.et.tu-dresden.de
Freq: Monthly; **Annual Sub.:** EUR 430,00
Editor: Ralf Lehnert
Profile: Journal about all aspects of electronics and communications.
Language(s): English
BUSINESS: ELECTRONICS

AFRICA POSITIVE
1622667G73-491

Editorial: Rheinische Str. 147, 44147 DORTMUND
Tel: 231 7978590 **Fax:** 231 72592735
Email: veye.tatah@africa-positive.de **Web site:** http://www.africa-positive.de
Freq: Quarterly; Free to qualifying individuals
Annual Sub.: EUR 18,00; **Circ:** 10,000
Editor: Veye Tatah
Profile: Magazine about African countries, people, politics, economy and culture.
Language(s): German
ADVERTISING RATES:
Full Page Mono .... EUR 1200
Full Page Colour .... EUR 1200
Mechanical Data: Type Area: 270 x 186 mm, No. of Columns (Display): 3, Col Widths (Display): 58 mm
Copy instructions: *Copy Date:* 40 days prior to publication

THE AFRICAN TIMES
1895856G14A-10281

Editorial: Tempelhofer Ufer 23, 10963 BERLIN
Tel: 30 21505422 **Fax:** 30 21505447
Email: info@african-times.com **Web site:** http://www.african-times.com
Freq: Monthly; **Cover Price:** EUR 2,00; **Circ:** 10,000
Editor: Bruno Waltert; **Advertising Manager:** Janine Kulbrock
Profile: Provides information for business executives on the world of politics, economy and science in Africa..
Language(s): English
ADVERTISING RATES:
Full Page Mono .... EUR 23000
Full Page Colour .... EUR 23000
Mechanical Data: Type Area: 530 x 290 mm
Copy instructions: *Copy Date:* 5 days prior to publication

AFTER DARK
719676G89C-4781

Editorial: Marienstr. 3, 24534 NEUMÜNSTER
Tel: 4321 559590 **Fax:** 4321 5595914
Email: info@afterdark.de **Web site:** http://www.afterdark.de
Freq: Monthly; **Cover Price:** Free; **Circ:** 13,095
Editor: Jörg Stoeckicht; **Advertising Manager:** Insa Scheibel
Profile: After Dark will appear in Central Holstein, Neumünster, Rendsburg and Bad Segeberg. Through more than 370 Beuth - even in rural areas - to After Dark has established itself as the only event magazine in the region between the cities of Kiel, Lübeck and Hamburg. In addition to the regular special issues the target group especially appreciates the extensive part of date with indications.
Language(s): German
ADVERTISING RATES:
Full Page Mono .... EUR 590
Full Page Colour .... EUR 1150
Mechanical Data: Type Area: 185 x 125 mm
Copy instructions: *Copy Date:* 15 days prior to publication
CONSUMER: HOLIDAYS & TRAVEL: Entertainment Guides

AFZ ALLGEMEINE FLEISCHER ZEITUNG
719677G22D-20

Editorial: Mainzer Landstr. 251, 60326 FRANKFURT
Tel: 69 75951551 **Fax:** 69 75951550
Email: red-afz@dfv.de **Web site:** http://www.fleischwirtschaft.de
Freq: Weekly; **Annual Sub.:** EUR 362,00; **Circ:** 10,599
Editor: Renate Kühlcke; **Advertising Manager:** Claudia Besand-Groth
Profile: Official journal of the German Meat Association.
Language(s): German
ADVERTISING RATES:
Full Page Mono .... EUR 11835
Full Page Colour .... EUR 13611
Mechanical Data: Type Area: 428 x 282 mm, No. of Columns (Display): 5, Col Widths (Display): 52 mm
Copy instructions: *Copy Date:* 9 days prior to publication
Official Journal of: Organ d. DFV
Supplement(s): afz journal
BUSINESS: FOOD: Meat Trade

AFZ DER WALD ZUSAMMEN MIT FORST UND HOLZ
719678G46-1

Editorial: Muskatstr. 4, 70619 STUTTGART
Tel: 711 448270 **Fax:** 711 4482777
Email: redaktion@afz-derwald.de **Web site:** http://www.forstpraxis.de
Freq: 24 issues yearly; **Annual Sub.:** EUR 173,00; **Circ:** 5,211
Editor: Bernd-Gunther Encke; **Advertising Manager:** Thomas Herrmann
Profile: Leading national and united independent forestry magazine for decision makers in the administration of state forestry agencies and the major forest owners, for forestry experts, planners, forestry training centers, tree nurseries, arborists, the timber trade as well as for forestry services and outfitters.
Language(s): German
Readership: Read by forestry owners and workers also wood turners.
ADVERTISING RATES:
Full Page Mono .... EUR 1966
Full Page Colour .... EUR 2948
Mechanical Data: Type Area: 270 x 184 mm, No. of Columns (Display): 4, Col Widths (Display): 43 mm
Copy instructions: *Copy Date:* 21 days prior to publication
BUSINESS: TIMBER, WOOD & FORESTRY

AG DIE AKTIENGESELLSCHAFT
719681G1C-20

Editorial: Gustav-Heinemann-Ufer 58, 50968 KÖLN
Tel: 221 93738561 **Fax:** 221 93738954
Email: dieaktiengesellschaft@otto-schmidt.de **Web site:** http://www.die-aktiengesellschaft.de
Freq: 22 issues yearly; **Annual Sub.:** EUR 441,90; **Circ:** 1,840
Editor: Bastian Schoppe; **Advertising Manager:** Thorsten Deuse
Profile: Magazine on German, European and international stock exchange.
Language(s): German
ADVERTISING RATES:
Full Page Mono .... EUR 2425
Full Page Colour .... EUR 4200
Mechanical Data: Type Area: 260 x 180 mm, No. of Columns (Display): 2, Col Widths (Display): 88 mm

AGD VIERTEL
719682G14J-3

Editorial: Steinstr. 3, 38100 BRAUNSCHWEIG
Tel: 531 16757 **Fax:** 531 16989
Email: info@agd.de **Web site:** http://www.agd.de
Freq: Quarterly; Free to qualifying individuals
Annual Sub.: EUR 25,00; **Circ:** 5,000
Editor: Christina Sahr; **Advertising Manager:** Roswitha Wendhof
Profile: The editorial team presents extraordinary works by fellow designers, helpful information for the respective topic and corresponding guest contributions of various articles.
Language(s): German
Readership: Aimed at self-employed designers.
ADVERTISING RATES:
Full Page Mono .... EUR 2180
Full Page Colour .... EUR 2180
Mechanical Data: Type Area: 274 x 210 mm
Copy instructions: *Copy Date:* 60 days prior to publication
BUSINESS: COMMERCE, INDUSTRY & MANAGEMENT: Commercial Design

AGP-MITTEILUNGEN
719692G14A-100

Editorial: Wilhelmshöher Allee 283a, 34131 KASSEL
Tel: 561 9324250 **Fax:** 561 9324252
Email: info@agpev.de **Web site:** http://www.agpev.de
Freq: Quarterly; Free to qualifying individuals
Annual Sub.: EUR 15,00; **Circ:** 4,000
Editor: Heinrich Beyer; **Advertising Manager:** Heinrich Beyer
Profile: The "AGP-Mitteilungen" contain the latest information on all aspects of employee participation in theory and practice. New operational models, field reports from the company, concepts of profit sharing and equity participation, including instruments of performance management, succession planning opportunities, reorganization and privatization, legal and tax regulations, political developments, events, meetings.

Language(s): German
ADVERTISING RATES:
Full Page Mono .... EUR 480
Full Page Colour .... EUR 1580
Mechanical Data: Type Area: 277 x 175 mm, No. of Columns (Display): 4
Copy instructions: *Copy Date:* 15 days prior to publication
BUSINESS: COMMERCE, INDUSTRY & MANAGEMENT

AGRAR TECHNIK 719709G21E-1
Editorial: Werner-von-Siemens-Str. 55a, 97076 WÜRZBURG **Tel:** 931 279970 **Fax:** 931 2799777
Email: agrartechnik@dlv.de **Web site:** http://www.agrartechnikonline.de
Freq: Monthly; **Annual Sub.:** EUR 104,00; **Circ:** 12,707
Editor: Dieter Dänzer; **Advertising Manager:** Thomas Herrmann
Profile: Leading and largest circulation German magazine for trade and service for specialized companies with a focus on "agricultural, forestry, municipal, energy technology, engine instrumentation, construction machinery technology".
Language(s): German
ADVERTISING RATES:
Full Page Mono .... EUR 3618
Full Page Colour .... EUR 5173
Mechanical Data: Type Area: 270 x 184 mm, No. of Columns (Display): 4, Col Widths (Display): 43 mm
Copy instructions: *Copy Date:* 23 days prior to publication
Official Journal of: Organ d. Bundesverb. LandBauTechnik und der Bundesfachgruppe Motorgeräte im Bundesverb. LandBauTechnik
BUSINESS: AGRICULTURE & FARMING: Agriculture - Machinery & Plant

AGRAR- UND UMWELTRECHT 719707G44-40
Editorial: Siebengebirgsstr. 200, 53229 BONN
Tel: 228 7031483 **Fax:** 228 703191483
Email: volkmar.nies@lwk.nrw.de **Web site:** http://www.aur-net.de
Freq: Monthly; **Annual Sub.:** EUR 192,00; **Circ:** 1,150
Editor: Volkmar Nies; **Advertising Manager:** Gabriele Wittkowski
Profile: Pan-European magazine covering agricultural business and law.
Language(s): German
Readership: Aimed at judges, solicitors and administrators.
ADVERTISING RATES:
Full Page Mono .... EUR 1074
Full Page Colour .... EUR 1770
Mechanical Data: Type Area: 270 x 190 mm, No. of Columns (Display): 4, Col Widths (Display): 46 mm
Copy instructions: *Copy Date:* 21 days prior to publication
BUSINESS: LEGAL

AGRARGEWERBLICHE WIRTSCHAFT 719696G21A-120
Editorial: Wollgrasweg 31, 70599 STUTTGART
Tel: 711 167790 **Fax:** 711 4586093
Email: info@vdaw.de **Web site:** http://www.vdaw.de
Freq: Monthly; Free to qualifying individuals
Annual Sub.: EUR 100,00; **Circ:** 1,650
Editor: Erich Reich; **Advertising Manager:** Claudia Denzinger
Profile: Magazine for the agricultural business.
Language(s): German
ADVERTISING RATES:
Full Page Mono .... EUR 800
Full Page Colour .... EUR 1200
Mechanical Data: Type Area: 270 x 195 mm, No. of Columns (Display): 2, Col Widths (Display): 92 mm
Copy instructions: *Copy Date:* 5 days prior to publication

AGRARMETEOROLOGISCHER MONATSBERICHT FÜR BAYERN 755560G21A-4201
Editorial: Alte Akademie 16, Weihenstephaner Berg, 85354 FREISING **Tel:** 8161 537690
Fax: 8161 5376950
Email: lw.weihenstephan@dwd.de **Web site:** http://www.dwd.de
Freq: Monthly; **Annual Sub.:** EUR 56,90; **Circ:** 350
Profile: Magazine on agrarmeteorologics for the German federal state of Bayern.
Language(s): German

AGRARMETEOROLOGISCHER MONATSBERICHT FÜR BAYERN 755560G21A-4471
Editorial: Alte Akademie 16, Weihenstephaner Berg, 85354 FREISING **Tel:** 8161 537690
Fax: 8161 5376950
Email: lw.weihenstephan@dwd.de **Web site:** http://www.dwd.de
Freq: Monthly; **Annual Sub.:** EUR 56,90; **Circ:** 350
Profile: Magazine on agrarmeteorologics for the German federal state of Bayern.
Language(s): German

AGRARZEITUNG 719712G22A-120
Editorial: Mainzer Landstr. 251, 60326 FRANKFURT
Tel: 69 75951581 **Fax:** 69 75951580
Email: angela.werner@dfv.de **Web site:** http://www.agrarzeitung.de
Freq: Weekly; **Annual Sub.:** EUR 415,00; **Circ:** 7,688
Editor: Angela Werner; **Advertising Manager:** Dirk Armbruster
Profile: Magazine on farming, agrarian trade, grain, wholesale and export trade.
Language(s): German
ADVERTISING RATES:
Full Page Mono .... EUR 3700
Full Page Colour .... EUR 5400
Mechanical Data: Type Area: 371 x 251 mm, No. of Columns (Display): 5, Col Widths (Display): 47 mm
Copy instructions: *Copy Date:* 7 days prior to publication
BUSINESS: FOOD

AHLENER TAGEBLATT 719727G67B-200
Editorial: Engelbert-Holterdorf-Str. 4, 59302 OELDE
Tel: 2522 730 **Fax:** 2522 73166
Email: redaktion@die-glocke.de **Web site:** http://www.die-glocke.de
Freq: 312 issues yearly; **Circ:** 22,750
Advertising Manager: Hans-Georg Hippel
Profile: Daily newspaper with regional news and a local sports section.
Language(s): German
ADVERTISING RATES:
SCC .... EUR 61,60
Mechanical Data: Type Area: 480 x 320 mm, No. of Columns (Display): 7, Col Widths (Display): 44 mm
Copy instructions: *Copy Date:* 1 day prior to publication
Supplement(s): prisma
REGIONAL DAILY & SUNDAY NEWSPAPERS: Regional Daily Newspapers

AHLENER ZEITUNG 719728G67B-220
Editorial: An der Hansalinie 1, 48163 MÜNSTER
Tel: 251 6900 **Fax:** 251 690717
Email: redaktion@westfaelische-nachrichten.de **Web site:** http://www.westfaelische-nachrichten.de
Freq: 312 issues yearly; **Circ:** 7,119
Profile: Daily newspaper with regional news and a local sports section. Facebook: http://www.facebook.com/wnonline.
Language(s): German
ADVERTISING RATES:
SCC .... EUR 24,00
Mechanical Data: Type Area: 488 x 324 mm, No. of Columns (Display): 7, Col Widths (Display): 44 mm
Copy instructions: *Copy Date:* 1 day prior to publication
Supplement(s): lenz; prisma; yango family
REGIONAL DAILY & SUNDAY NEWSPAPERS: Regional Daily Newspapers

AHRTALER WOCHENSPIEGEL 719730G72-132
Editorial: Bossardstr. 5, 53474 BAD NEUENAHR-AHRWEILER **Tel:** 2641 902828 **Fax:** 2641 902829
Email: red-ahrtal@weiss-verlag.de **Web site:** http://www.wochenspiegellive.de
Freq: Weekly; **Cover Price:** Free; **Circ:** 39,761
Editor: Alexander Lenders
Profile: Advertising journal (house-to-house) concentrating on local stories.
Language(s): German
ADVERTISING RATES:
Full Page Mono .... EUR 3071
Full Page Colour .... EUR 4305
Mechanical Data: Type Area: 430 x 290 mm, No. of Columns (Display): 7, Col Widths (Display): 38 mm
Copy instructions: *Copy Date:* 2 days prior to publication
LOCAL NEWSPAPERS

AIB ARBEITSRECHT IM BETRIEB 721075G14L-220
Editorial: Gerolsteiner Str. 67, 50937 KÖLN
Tel: 221 3557699 **Fax:** 221 3557761
Email: eva-maria.stoppkotte@bund-verlag.de **Web site:** http://www.aib-web.de
Freq: 11 issues yearly; **Annual Sub.:** EUR 129,60; **Circ:** 17,744
Editor: Eva-Maria Stoppkotte; **Advertising Manager:** Peter Beuther
Profile: For over 30 years, the AiB Arbeitsrecht im Betrieb provides practical and understandable the legal possibilities of action of the works council. The Journal informed of the basics of the works council work and the most important decisions of labor courts for works councils.
Language(s): German
ADVERTISING RATES:
Full Page Mono .... EUR 3985
Full Page Colour .... EUR 4982
Mechanical Data: Type Area: 260 x 180 mm
Copy instructions: *Copy Date:* 20 days prior to publication
Supplement(s): AiBplus
BUSINESS: COMMERCE, INDUSTRY & MANAGEMENT: Trade Unions

AICHACHER NACHRICHTEN 719735G67B-240
Editorial: Curt-Frenzel-Str. 2, 86167 AUGSBURG
Tel: 821 7770 **Fax:** 821 7772067
Email: redaktion@augsburger-allgemeine.de **Web site:** http://www.augsburger-allgemeine.de
Freq: 312 issues yearly; **Circ:** 6,195
Advertising Manager: Herbert Dachs
Profile: Daily newspaper with regional news and a local sports section. Facebook: http://www.facebook.com/AugsburgerAllgemeine Twitter: http://twitter.com/AZ_Augsburg This Outlet offers RSS (Really Simple Syndication).
Language(s): German
ADVERTISING RATES:
SCC .... EUR 26,10
Mechanical Data: Type Area: 480 x 327 mm, No. of Columns (Display): 7, Col Widths (Display): 45 mm
Copy instructions: *Copy Date:* 1 day prior to publication
Supplement(s): CiA City News
REGIONAL DAILY & SUNDAY NEWSPAPERS: Regional Daily Newspapers

AICHACHER ZEITUNG 719737G67B-260
Editorial: Oberbernbacher Weg 7, 86551 AICHACH
Tel: 8251 880142 **Fax:** 8251 880149
Email: redaktion@aichacher-zeitung.de **Web site:** http://www.aichacher-zeitung.de
Freq: 312 issues yearly; **Circ:** 9,059
Profile: Daily newspaper with regional news and a local sports section. Facebook: http://www.facebook.com/pages/Aichacher-Zeitung/106491819403255.
Language(s): German
ADVERTISING RATES:
SCC .... EUR 11,40
Mechanical Data: Type Area: 440 x 284 mm, No. of Columns (Display): 6, Col Widths (Display): 44 mm
Copy instructions: *Copy Date:* 1 day prior to publication
Supplement(s): rtv
REGIONAL DAILY & SUNDAY NEWSPAPERS: Regional Daily Newspapers

AINS ANÄSTHESIOLOGIE INTENSIVMEDIZIN NOTFALLMEDIZIN SCHMERZTHERAPIE 1614847G56A-11196
Editorial: Rüdigerstr. 14, 70469 STUTTGART
Tel: 711 89310 **Fax:** 711 8931298
Email: carolin.freye@thieme.de **Web site:** http://www.thieme.de/ains
Freq: 10 issues yearly; **Annual Sub.:** EUR 330,80; **Circ:** 5,700
Editor: Carolin Freye
Profile: AINS Anästhesiologie Intensivmedizin Notfallmedizin Schmerztherapie provides date knowledge and offers training. AINS has set itself the goal to provide the readers (specialists and training assistants in anesthesiology) are always practical value and maximum support. In the category expertise revolves around the four pillars of anesthesia: in the CME articles, in case reports, in reviews and in the main topic that illuminates in every issue an issue from multiple perspectives. The research section presents news from science - short and concise. The sections management and focus provide information on patient, self and quality management and the latest news about professional politics and health policy. In addition, the AINS supplied to the reader with useful information such as addresses and events, personalia, book recommendations or answers legal questions. Each issue of AINS provides valuable CME credits.
Language(s): German
ADVERTISING RATES:
Full Page Mono .... EUR 1860
Full Page Colour .... EUR 3030
Mechanical Data: Type Area: 248 x 175 mm, No. of Columns (Display): 3, Col Widths (Display): 55 mm
Official Journal of: Organ d. Dt. Ges. f. Anästhesiologie u. Intensivmedizin u. d. Österr. Ges. f. Anaesthesiologie, Reanimation u. Intensivmedizin

AIT ARCHITEKTUR INNENARCHITEKTUR TECHNISCHER AUSBAU 719763G4E-40
Editorial: Fasanenweg 18, 70771 LEINFELDEN-ECHTERDINGEN **Tel:** 711 7591286
Fax: 711 7591410
Email: ait-red@ait-online.de **Web site:** http://www.ait-online.de
Freq: 3 issues yearly; Free to qualifying individuals ; **Circ:** 24,753
Editor: Dietmar Danner; **Advertising Manager:** Judith Hageloch
Profile: The main issues seem to be abit on the subject of office and administration buildings, banks, insurance companies and government agencies with expanded editorial section for workplace design and furnishings. Recipient of the ABIT are: • Architecture and architects • Interior architects and interior designers • Members of: BDIA (Bund Deutscher Innenarchitekten) BÖIA (Bund Österreichischer Innenarchitekten) VSI.ASAI. (Vereinigung Schweizer Innenarchitekten) creative inneneinrichter e.V. and national organizations that are members of the ECIA (European Council of Interior Architects) • Furnishers • Interior designers, shop fitters and exhibition stand builders • Planning agencies • Engineers, civil engineers for building services, consulting engineers and specialists.
Language(s): German
ADVERTISING RATES:
Full Page Mono .... EUR 5185
Full Page Colour .... EUR 7645
Mechanical Data: Type Area: 280 x 212 mm, No. of Columns (Display): 4, Col Widths (Display): 50 mm
Copy instructions: *Copy Date:* 30 days prior to publication
Official Journal of: Organ d. Bundes Dt. Innenarchitekten

AIT ARCHITEKTUR INNENARCHITEKTUR TECHNISCHER AUSBAU ARCHITECTURE INTERIOR TECHNICAL SOLUTIONS 719764G4B-689
Editorial: Fasanenweg 18, 70771 LEINFELDEN-ECHTERDINGEN **Tel:** 711 7591318
Fax: 711 7591410
Email: ait-red@ait-online.de **Web site:** http://www.ait-online.de
Freq: 7 issues yearly; Free to qualifying individuals
Annual Sub.: EUR 142,80; **Circ:** 21,661
Editor: Dietmar Danner; **Advertising Manager:** Judith Hageloch
Profile: The review provides an architectural journal in the context of holistic architectural approach than other the room its importance. In the field of interior design and interior construction is their special competence. Besides the design, specifically in commercial, industrial and public buildings, she brings in a special compartment of explicitly their technical development. Recipient of the AIT are: • Architecture and architects • Interior architects and interior designers • Members of: BDIA (Bund Deutscher Innenarchitekten) BÖIA (Bund Österreichischer Innenarchitekten) VSI.ASAI. (Vereinigung Schweizer Innenarchitekten) creative inneneinrichter e.V. and national organizations that are members of the ECIA (European Council of Interior Architects) • Furnishers • Interior designers, shop fitters and exhibition stand builders • Planning agencies • Engineers, civil engineers for building services, consulting engineers and specialists.
Language(s): English; German
ADVERTISING RATES:
Full Page Mono .... EUR 4190
Full Page Colour .... EUR 6335
Mechanical Data: Type Area: 280 x 212 mm, No. of Columns (Display): 4, Col Widths (Display): 50 mm
Copy instructions: *Copy Date:* 30 days prior to publication
Official Journal of: Organ d. Bundes Dt. Innenarchitekten
BUSINESS: ARCHITECTURE & BUILDING: Interior Design & Flooring

AKADEMIE 719770G14A-9392
Editorial: Mönchelsstr. 16a, 99867 GOTHA
Tel: 3621 505566 **Fax:** 3621 505567
Email: der@aschenbrenner.tv
Freq: Quarterly; Free to qualifying individuals
Annual Sub.: EUR 11,00; **Circ:** 13,122
Editor: Rainer Aschenbrenner; **Advertising Manager:** Monika Droege
Profile: Journal focusing on management training.
Language(s): German
Readership: Aimed at business executives.
ADVERTISING RATES:
Full Page Mono .... EUR 914
Full Page Colour .... EUR 1965
Mechanical Data: Type Area: 234 x 186 mm
Copy instructions: *Copy Date:* 21 days prior to publication
BUSINESS: COMMERCE, INDUSTRY & MANAGEMENT

DER AKTIONÄR 719810G1F-100
Editorial: Am Eulenhof 14, 95326 KULMBACH
Tel: 9221 90510 **Fax:** 9221 90514119
Email: aktionaer@boersenmedien.de **Web site:** http://www.deraktionaer.de
Freq: Weekly; **Annual Sub.:** EUR 196,50; **Circ:** 26,794
Editor: Frank Phillips
Profile: The stock market magazine for private and institutional investors, offers every week the best stock market tips on stocks, funds and Derivaten. Der Aktionär is not only newspaper is printed in all major German stock exchanges. It also stands for an Internet platform that is on the analysis of the action on the floor in an instant and comments. Or collect for stock reports, the selected topics, countries or sectors in all its depth. Not to mention the independent TV format in the Deutsche Anleger Fernsehen (DAF). It also publishes the magazine now also as an app on the iPhone the tips of the Der Aktionär on the move. Facebook: http://www.facebook.com/aktionaer Twitter: https://twitter.com/#!/aktionaer This Outlet offers RSS (Really Simple Syndication).
Language(s): German
ADVERTISING RATES:
Full Page Colour .... EUR 6900
Mechanical Data: Type Area: 252 x 180 mm, No. of Columns (Display): 3, Col Widths (Display): 56 mm
Copy instructions: *Copy Date:* 10 days prior to publication
BUSINESS: FINANCE & ECONOMICS: Investment

DER AKTIONÄR 1620717G1F-1508
Editorial: Am Eulenhof 14, 95326 KULMBACH
Tel: 9221 9051150 **Fax:** 9221 90514119
Email: info@boersenmedien.de **Web site:** http://www.deraktionaer.de
Freq: 250 times a year; **Cover Price:** Paid; **Circ:** 1,039,733 Unique Users
Editor: Frank Phillipps
Profile: Ezine: Opinion and recommendation portal for stock market and finance. The focus is on specific buy or sell recommendations and the assessment of current news and commentary. A 20-strong editorial team follows every trading day, the financial markets and extracts the important information. The information is clear, simple and comments presented. Facebook: http://www.facebook.com/aktionaer Twitter: https://twitter.com/#!/aktionaer This Outlet offers RSS (Really Simple Syndication).
Language(s): German
BUSINESS: FINANCE & ECONOMICS: Investment

AKTIONÄRSREPORT 755565G1F-1466
Editorial: Hackenstr. 7b, 80331 MÜNCHEN
Tel: 89 20208460 **Fax:** 89 202084610
Email: rotter@sdk.org **Web site:** http://www.sdk.org
Freq: 10 issues yearly; Free to qualifying individuals
Annual Sub.: EUR 50,00; **Circ:** 3,500
Editor: Harald Rotter
Profile: Magazine from the Schutzgemeinschaft der Kapitalanleger about shares and shareholder protection.
Language(s): German

AKTIV 719816G74N-60
Editorial: René-Schickele-Str. 10, 53123 BONN
Tel: 228 367930 **Fax:** 228 3679390
Email: harms@medcominternational.de **Web site:** http://www.deutsche-seniorenliga.de
Freq: Quarterly; **Circ:** 25,000
Editor: Dorit Harms; **Advertising Manager:** Dorit Harms
Profile: Magazine for the elderly dealing with medicine, politics and society.
Language(s): German
ADVERTISING RATES:
Full Page Mono .... EUR 1800
Full Page Colour .... EUR 3045
Mechanical Data: Type Area: 252 x 175 mm
Copy instructions: *Copy Date:* 15 days prior to publication

AKTIV FRAUEN IN BADEN-WÜRTTEMBERG 1935225G74A-3729
Editorial: Postfach 103443, 70029 STUTTGART
Tel: 711 1230 **Fax:** 711 1233999
Web site: http://www.frauen-aktiv.de
Freq: Quarterly; **Cover Price:** Free; **Circ:** 19,500
Editor: Anita Wochner
Profile: ACTIVE offers insights into the broad spectrum of women's political Topics. Each magazine focuses on a key issue, which is illuminated from different angles. It concludes with in-depth information and advice to women politically interesting events, addresses, books, exhibitions, prizes and scholarships.
Language(s): German
ADVERTISING RATES:
Full Page Mono .... EUR 900
Mechanical Data: Type Area: 277 x 190 mm
Copy instructions: *Copy Date:* 25 days prior to publication

AKTIV IM LEBEN 1861540G74N-967
Editorial: Uhlandstr. 104, 73614 SCHORNDORF
Tel: 7181 253231 **Fax:** 7181 258878
Email: redaktion@baumeister-verlag.de **Web site:** http://www.baumeister-verlag.de
Freq: 6 issues yearly; **Annual Sub.:** EUR 18,00; **Circ:** 43,479
Editor: Stefan Raab; **Advertising Manager:** Beate Heibel
Profile: Best-Ager-Magazine offers reviews, interviews and reports on the topics of fitness, travel, art, culture, health, housing, portraits of prominent personalities.
Language(s): German
ADVERTISING RATES:
Full Page Mono .... EUR 2980
Full Page Colour .... EUR 2980
Mechanical Data: Type Area: 260 x 185 mm, No. of Columns (Display): 4, Col Widths (Display): 43 mm

AKTIV IM RUHESTAND 719826G74N-872
Editorial: Postfach 1464, 55004 MAINZ
Tel: 6131 223371 **Fax:** 6131 225625
Email: post@brh.de **Web site:** http://www.brh.de
Freq: 10 issues yearly; **Cover Price:** EUR 2,50; **Circ:** 53,512
Editor: Heike Eichmeier
Profile: Magazine focusing on activities for pensioners. It addresses policy issues and officials to learn new information, such as changes in officials and utility law. The high utility of the information guarantees high compliance values.
Language(s): German
Readership: Read by pensioners.
ADVERTISING RATES:
Full Page Mono .... EUR 3070
Full Page Colour .... EUR 4570
Mechanical Data: Type Area: 270 x 185 mm, No. of Columns (Display): 4, Col Widths (Display): 43 mm
CONSUMER: WOMEN'S INTEREST CONSUMER MAGAZINES: Retirement

AKTIV LAUFEN 1663375G75J-481
Editorial: Machabäerstr. 3, 50668 KÖLN
Tel: 221 922790 **Fax:** 221 9227979
Email: hensen@cng-media.de **Web site:** http://www.aktiv-laufen.de
Freq: 6 issues yearly; **Annual Sub.:** EUR 21,00; **Circ:** 28,182
Editor: Norbert Hensen; **Advertising Manager:** Frank Krauthäuser
Profile: Magazine for running, fitness, endurance, nutrition, counseling and a lot of tips in training, dress and running style.
Language(s): German
ADVERTISING RATES:
Full Page Mono .... EUR 4500
Full Page Colour .... EUR 4500
Mechanical Data: Type Area: 248 x 185 mm, No. of Columns (Display): 4, Col Widths (Display): 43 mm
CONSUMER: SPORT: Athletics

AKTIV RADFAHREN 719827G77C-20
Editorial: Fraunhoferstr. 9, 85737 ISMANING
Tel: 89 41615400 **Fax:** 89 416154019
Email: info@aktiv-radfahren.de **Web site:** http://www.radfahren.de
Freq: 8 issues yearly; **Annual Sub.:** EUR 42,80; **Circ:** 55,000
Editor: Daniel Oliver Fikuart; **Advertising Manager:** Albertus Mehler
Profile: Magazine providing information, product news and articles concerning cycling.
Language(s): German
Readership: Aimed at cycling enthusiasts.
ADVERTISING RATES:
Full Page Mono .... EUR 3495
Full Page Colour .... EUR 4388
Mechanical Data: Type Area: 250 x 200 mm, No. of Columns (Display): 4, Col Widths (Display): 46 mm
Copy instructions: *Copy Date:* 35 days prior to publication
CONSUMER: MOTORING & CYCLING: Cycling

AKTIVER RUHESTAND 720072G74N-100
Editorial: Silcherstr. 7, 70176 STUTTGART
Tel: 711 210300
Email: michael@rux-online.de **Web site:** http://www.gew-bw.de
Freq: Quarterly; **Cover Price:** EUR 1,00
Free to qualifying individuals ; **Circ:** 7,000
Editor: Michael Rux; **Advertising Manager:** Rainer Dahlem
Profile: Magazine of the German education trade-union for pensioners and bereaved.
Language(s): German
ADVERTISING RATES:
Full Page Mono .... EUR 700
Mechanical Data: Type Area: 270 x 188 mm, No. of Columns (Display): 3, Col Widths (Display): 60 mm
Copy instructions: *Copy Date:* 21 days prior to publication

AKTUALITÄTSLEXIKON UMWELTSCHUTZ 1928108G57-2935
Editorial: Postfach 1420, 65764 KELKHEIM
Tel: 172 6712118 **Fax:** 6195 65118
Email: presse-lutz@gmx.net
Freq: Annual; **Circ:** 10,000
Profile: Magazine bibliography on environmental protection.
Language(s): German
Mechanical Data: Type Area: 204 x 145 mm
Copy instructions: *Copy Date:* 30 days prior to publication

DER AKTUAR 1932687G1A-3804
Editorial: Hohenstaufenring 47, 50674 KÖLN
Tel: 221 9125540 **Fax:** 221 91255444
Email: info@aktuar.de **Web site:** http://www.aktuar.de
Freq: Quarterly; **Annual Sub.:** EUR 18,00; **Circ:** 3,800
Editor: Michael Steinmetz; **Advertising Manager:** Benjamin Bittmann
Profile: Magazine from the German Actuary Association.
Language(s): German
ADVERTISING RATES:
Full Page Mono .... EUR 1850
Full Page Colour .... EUR 3238
Mechanical Data: Type Area: 266 x 185 mm, No. of Columns (Display): 3, Col Widths (Display): 58 mm

AKTUAR AKTUELL 719833G1A-60
Editorial: Hohenstaufenring 47, 50674 KÖLN
Tel: 221 9125540 **Fax:** 221 91255444
Email: info@aktuar.de **Web site:** http://www.aktuar.de
Freq: Quarterly; **Circ:** 3,500
Editor: Michael Steinmetz
Profile: Magazine from the German Actuary Association.
Language(s): German
ADVERTISING RATES:
Full Page Mono .... EUR 1850
Full Page Colour .... EUR 3238
Mechanical Data: Type Area: 266 x 185 mm, No. of Columns (Display): 3, Col Widths (Display): 58 mm
Copy instructions: *Copy Date:* 14 days prior to publication

AKTUELL 1698785G40-976
Editorial: Stauffenbergstr. 18, 10785 BERLIN
Tel: 30 200429030 **Fax:** 30 200429036
Email: aktuell@bundeswehr.de **Web site:** http://www.aktuell.bundeswehr.de
Freq: Weekly; **Circ:** 60,000
Editor: Frank Pflüger
Profile: Official weekly newspaper of the armed forces. The members of the armed forces use the newspaper as an information source for news, current background information, news and interviews from the armed forces and areas as well as for security, defense and military policy.
Language(s): German

AKTUELL FÜR DIE FRAU 1841647G74A-3609
Editorial: Ziegelkamp 9, 21635 JORK
Tel: 7222 9311110
Email: redaktion@ms-medienteam.de
Freq: Monthly; **Cover Price:** EUR 0,79; **Circ:** 182,762
Editor: Michael Stange; **Advertising Manager:** Michael Stange
Profile: aktuell für die Frau - is the magazine, standing in the middle of life, with great diversity entertains and informs. The trends in fashion, beauty, wellness and food will be presented by experts and celebrity chefs. aktuell für die Frau's direct link to national and international stars, who answer questions are added. Travel reports regularly kidnap the readers of the most beautiful destinations at home and abroad. They also focus on the areas Guides, Tips and Health, which are distinguished thanks to the cooperation with TV-renowned fashion, beauty and health professionals with high competence and credibility. Magazine concept is complemented by real-life reports and good entertainment.
Language(s): German
ADVERTISING RATES:
Full Page Mono .... EUR 7450
Full Page Colour .... EUR 7450
Mechanical Data: Type Area: 276 x 200 mm

AKTUELLE DERMATOLOGIE 719859G56A-140
Editorial: Rüdigerstr. 14, 70469 STUTTGART
Tel: 711 8931281 **Fax:** 711 8931408
Email: grit.vollmer@thieme.de **Web site:** http://www.thieme.de/derma
Freq: 10 issues yearly; **Annual Sub.:** EUR 254,80; **Circ:** 4,377
Editor: Grit Vollmer
Profile: The entire Dermatology, Venereology and Andrology in a journal: Current information from the experts in our subject area, relevant original and review articles and interesting case reports, from the roots of our subject, Histologic Quiz - Test your knowledge, news from diagnosis and treatment have view, Certified didactic training, highlights from international journals.
Language(s): German
ADVERTISING RATES:
Full Page Mono .... EUR 2160
Full Page Colour .... EUR 3300
Mechanical Data: Type Area: 248 x 175 mm, No. of Columns (Display): 4, Col Widths (Display): 40 mm
Official Journal of: Organ d. Dt. Ges. f. Photobiologie
BUSINESS: HEALTH & MEDICAL

AKTUELLE ERNÄHRUNGSMEDIZIN 719860G56A-160
Editorial: Rüdigerstr. 14, 70469 STUTTGART
Tel: 711 8931502 **Fax:** 711 8931408
Email: marion.rukavina@thieme.de **Web site:** http://www.thieme.de/akternmed
Freq: 6 issues yearly; Free to qualifying individuals
Annual Sub.: EUR 226,80; **Circ:** 3,930
Editor: Marion Rukavina
Profile: Expertise: The original work in the fields of metabolic research, clinical nutrition, dietetics Practical: Information for the dietary advice News in brief: Latest research news In addition: dates, society news and convention speeches.
Language(s): German
ADVERTISING RATES:
Full Page Mono .... EUR 1830
Full Page Colour .... EUR 2970
Mechanical Data: Type Area: 248 x 175 mm, No. of Columns (Display): 3, Col Widths (Display): 55 mm
Official Journal of: Organ d. Dt. Ges. f. Ernährungsmedizin, d. Österr. ArGe f. klin. Ernährung, d. Ges. f. klin. Ernährung d. Schweiz u. d. Dt. Akademie f. Ernährungsmedizin
BUSINESS: HEALTH & MEDICAL

DAS AKTUELLE FÜR ÄRZTE, HEIL- UND PFLEGEBERUFE 1665045G1M-171
Editorial: Portastr. 2, 32423 MINDEN **Tel:** 571 23729
Fax: 571 28768
Email: info@wiadok.de **Web site:** http://www.wiadok.de
Freq: Quarterly; **Circ:** 3,600
Editor: von Knobelsdorf
Profile: Magazine for tax law professionals.
Language(s): German

DAS AKTUELLE GMBH UND IHRE GESELLSCHAFTER 1664551G1A-3598
Editorial: Portastr. 2, 32423 MINDEN **Tel:** 571 23729
Fax: 571 28768
Email: info@wiadok.de **Web site:** http://www.wiadok.de
Freq: 6 issues yearly; **Circ:** 1,650
Editor: Ulbrich
Profile: Magazine for tax law professionals.
Language(s): German

AKTUELLE NEPHROLOGIE 755552G56A-11081
Editorial: Podbielskistr. 380, 30659 HANNOVER
Tel: 511 9060 **Fax:** 511 9063367
Freq: Quarterly; **Annual Sub.:** EUR 36,00; **Circ:** 2,200
Editor: Jens Bahlmann
Profile: Magazine about nephrology.
Language(s): German

AKTUELLE RHEUMATOLOGIE 719869G56A-200
Editorial: Rüdigerstr. 14, 70469 STUTTGART
Tel: 711 8931287 **Fax:** 711 8931623
Email: daniela.erhardl@thieme.de **Web site:** http://www.thieme.de/rheuma
Freq: 6 issues yearly; **Annual Sub.:** EUR 236,90; **Circ:** 4,050
Editor: Daniela Erhard
Profile: Aktuelle Rheumatologie published the latest trial and research results of clinical invetisgations from all areas of rheumatology. In focal point books specialists of respective research publish their latest findings. Rounding out the Aktuelle Rheumatologie by a magazine-like editorial section, which echoes the diversity of the subject and reports on practical developments as well as diagnostic and therapeutic indications.
Language(s): German
ADVERTISING RATES:
Full Page Mono .... EUR 1860
Full Page Colour .... EUR 3030
Mechanical Data: Type Area: 248 x 175 mm, No. of Columns (Display): 3, Col Widths (Display): 55 mm
Supplement(s): Current congress
BUSINESS: HEALTH & MEDICAL

DER AKTUELLE STEUERRATGEBER 719873G74M-20
Editorial: Haus an der Eisernen Brücke, 93059 REGENSBURG **Tel:** 941 5684100 **Fax:** 941 5684111
Email: walhalla@walhalla.de **Web site:** http://www.walhalla.de
Freq: Annual; **Cover Price:** EUR 9,50; **Circ:** 7,500
Editor: Dieter Kattenbeck
Profile: Tax advisor with payroll tax tables, an extensive tax glossary and all important tax-saving tips.
Language(s): German

DER AKTUELLE STEUERRATGEBER ÖFFENTLICHER DIENST 719874G74M-40
Editorial: Haus an der Eisernen Brücke, 93059 REGENSBURG **Tel:** 941 5684100 **Fax:** 941 5684111
Email: walhalla@walhalla.de **Web site:** http://www.walhalla.de
Freq: Annual; **Cover Price:** EUR 9,50; **Circ:** 2,000
Editor: Dieter Kattenbeck
Profile: Magazine on taxes.
Language(s): German

DAS AKTUELLE UMSATZSTEUER 1665046G1M-172
Editorial: Portastr. 2, 32423 MINDEN **Tel:** 571 23729
Fax: 571 28768
Email: info@wiadok.de **Web site:** http://www.wiadok.de
Freq: Quarterly; **Circ:** 4,200
Editor: von Knobelsdorf
Profile: Magazine for tax law professionals.
Language(s): German

AKTUELLE UROLOGIE 719878G56A-240
Editorial: Rüdigerstr. 14, 70469 STUTTGART
Tel: 711 8931287 **Fax:** 711 8931623
Email: daniela.erhard@thieme.de **Web site:** http://www.thieme.de/uro
Freq: 6 issues yearly; **Annual Sub.:** EUR 277,90; **Circ:** 1,120
Editor: Daniela Erhard
Profile: Information about current urological issues, problems of daily practice and interesting research reports are the main points. Contributions on novel and standardized methods of diagnosis and treatment are commented. Much diligence to the

editors at papers that give a quick overview of progress in urology and border areas. Each issue contains a richly illustrated article "Surgical Techniques".
Language(s): German
ADVERTISING RATES:
Full Page Mono .... EUR 1480
Full Page Colour .... EUR 2575
Mechanical Data: Type Area: 248 x 175 mm, No. of Columns (Display): 3, Col Widths (Display): 55 mm
Supplement(s): Current congress
BUSINESS: HEALTH & MEDICAL

AKUSTIK GITARRE 719892G76D-200
Editorial: Karlstr. 17, 64546 MÖRFELDEN-WALLDORF **Tel:** 6105 272793 **Fax:** 6105 272794
Email: redaktionsteam@akustik-gitarre.com **Web site:** http://www.akustik-gitarre.com
Freq: 6 issues yearly; **Annual Sub.:** EUR 22,80; **Circ:** 30,000
Editor: Andreas Schulz
Profile: Akustik Gitarre is the largest trade magazine for acoustic guitar players. About 150 pages news and feature articles, reviews, workshops, CD and DVD reviews, book reviews, manufacturer portraits as well as exhibition and event reports.Akustik Gitarre magazine for fingerstyle, Singer / Songwriter, Folk, Blues, Pop, Jazz, Latin, rock and classical music. Facebook: http://www.facebook.com/pages/akustik-gitarrecom/150260138325733.
Language(s): German
ADVERTISING RATES:
Full Page Mono .... EUR 1730
Full Page Colour .... EUR 2730
Mechanical Data: Type Area: 254 x 185 mm, No. of Columns (Display): 4, Col Widths (Display): 43 mm
Copy instructions: *Copy Date:* 30 days prior to publication
CONSUMER: MUSIC & PERFORMING ARTS: Music

AKUT 719893G56A-300
Editorial: Am Köllnischen Park 1, 10179 BERLIN
Tel: 30 7001300 **Fax:** 30 700130340
Email: akut@berlin.msf.org **Web site:** http://www.aerzte-ohne-grenzen.de
Freq: Quarterly; **Circ:** 300,000
Editor: Frauke Ossig
Profile: Magazine about donations to the humane project Ärzte ohne Grenzen. Facebook: http://www.facebook.com/aerzteohnegrenzenMSF.
Language(s): German

AKZENT 719899G80-140
Editorial: Moltkestr. 2, 78467 KONSTANZ
Tel: 7531 9914810 **Fax:** 7531 9914870
Email: m.hotz@akzent-magazin.com **Web site:** http://www.akzent-magazin.com
Freq: Monthly; **Annual Sub.:** EUR 40,00; **Circ:** 25,000
Editor: Markus Hotz; **Advertising Manager:** Markus Hotz
Profile: Regional magazine for the Bodensee area.
Language(s): German
ADVERTISING RATES:
Full Page Mono .... EUR 1740
Full Page Colour .... EUR 1740
Mechanical Data: Type Area: 276 x 188 mm
Copy instructions: *Copy Date:* 15 days prior to publication
CONSUMER: RURAL & REGIONAL INTEREST

AKZENTE 719900G14C-60
Editorial: Dag-Hammarskjöld-Weg 1, 65760 ESCHBORN **Tel:** 6196 790 **Fax:** 6196 791115
Email: info@giz.de **Web site:** http://www.giz.de
Freq: Quarterly; **Cover Price:** Free; **Circ:** 10,000
Editor: Wolfgang Barina
Profile: Efficient, effective and partner-oriented, so we help people and societies in developing, transition and industrialized countries to develop own perspectives and to improve their living conditions.
Language(s): German

ALB BOTE 719918G67B-280
Editorial: Gutenbergstr. 1, 72525 MÜNSINGEN
Tel: 7381 18730 **Fax:** 7381 18735
Email: alb-bote.redaktion@swp.de **Web site:** http://www.suedwest-aktiv.de
Freq: 312 issues yearly; **Circ:** 5,063
Advertising Manager: Helmut Schepper
Profile: Daily newspaper with regional news and a local sports section. Twitter: http://twitter.com/SWPde This Outlet offers RSS (Really Simple Syndication).
Language(s): German
ADVERTISING RATES:
SCC .... EUR 28,60
Mechanical Data: Type Area: 480 x 320 mm, No. of Columns (Display): 7, Col Widths (Display): 44 mm
Copy instructions: *Copy Date:* 1 day prior to publication
REGIONAL DAILY & SUNDAY NEWSPAPERS: Regional Daily Newspapers

ALB BOTE 719919G67B-300
Editorial: Max-Stromeyer-Str. 178, 78467 KONSTANZ **Tel:** 7531 9990 **Fax:** 7531 9991576
Email: thomas.satinsky@suedkurier.de **Web site:** http://www.suedkurier.de
Freq: 312 issues yearly; **Circ:** 130,526
Advertising Manager: Michael Beyer
Profile: Daily newspaper with regional news and a local sports section. Facebook: http://www.facebook.com/pages/SUDKURIER/346232178065 Twitter: http://twitter.com/SUEDKURIER This Outlet offers RSS (Really Simple Syndication).
Language(s): German
ADVERTISING RATES:
SCC .... EUR 240,60
Mechanical Data: No. of Columns (Display): 6, Col Widths (Display): 45 mm, Type Area: 435 x 280 mm
Copy instructions: *Copy Date:* 1 day prior to publication
REGIONAL DAILY & SUNDAY NEWSPAPERS: Regional Daily Newspapers

ALFELDER ZEITUNG 719931G67B-320
Editorial: Ravenstr. 45, 31061 ALFELD
Tel: 5181 800230 **Fax:** 5181 800247
Email: redaktion@alfelder-zeitung.de **Web site:** http://www.alfelder-zeitung.de
Freq: 312 issues yearly; **Circ:** 7,705
Editor: Olaf Groß; **Advertising Manager:** Manfred Bombelka
Profile: Daily newspaper with regional news and a local sports section.
Language(s): German
ADVERTISING RATES:
SCC .... EUR 27,20
Mechanical Data: Type Area: 430 x 277 mm, No. of Columns (Display): 6, Col Widths (Display): 45 mm
Copy instructions: *Copy Date:* 1 day prior to publication
REGIONAL DAILY & SUNDAY NEWSPAPERS: Regional Daily Newspapers

ALL4ENGINEERS 1704272G31A-323
Editorial: Abraham-Lincoln-Str. 46, 65189 WIESBADEN **Tel:** 611 7878284 **Fax:** 611 787878284
Email: julia.ehl@gwv-fachverlage.de **Web site:** http://www.all4engineers.com
Freq: Monthly; **Cover Price:** Paid; **Circ:** 9,000 Unique Users
Editor: Thomas Jungmann; **Advertising Manager:** Mandy Krause
Profile: Ezine: International magazine focusing on the automobile industry, includes new products and technology.
Language(s): German
BUSINESS: MOTOR TRADE: Motor Trade Accessories

ALL ABOUT SOURCING 1860051G14A-10211
Editorial: Kemptener Str. 2f, 86163 AUGSBURG
Tel: 821 66109326 **Fax:** 821 66109327
Email: redaktion@allaboutsourcing.de **Web site:** http://www.allaboutsourcing.de
Freq: 9 issues yearly; **Annual Sub.:** EUR 32,40; **Circ:** 22,306
Advertising Manager: Ulrich Abele
Profile: Magazine is aimed at managers and decision makers in purchasing, logistics, materials management in German firms, covers all major supply chain areas. Board members, directors and managers from purchasing, logistics and materials management, see All about Sourcing exclusively researched technical articles, market reports, shopping, product and supplier surveys, guide, and much more.
Language(s): German
ADVERTISING RATES:
Full Page Mono .... EUR 6750
Full Page Colour .... EUR 6750
Mechanical Data: Type Area: 351 x 251 mm
Copy instructions: *Copy Date:* 28 days prior to publication

ALL ARABIAN PRODUCT & BUYER'S GUIDE 1799110G56A-11455
Editorial: Theodor-Althoff-Str. 39, 45133 ESSEN
Tel: 201 8712673 **Fax:** 201 87126940
Email: a.parr@vva.de **Web site:** http://www.arab-medico.com
Freq: Annual; **Cover Price:** Free; **Circ:** 21,000
Editor: Andrea Parr; **Advertising Manager:** Andrea Parr
Profile: Information on medical and pharmaceutical products. Information for all decision makers in the Arab countries: Ministries, Health Authorities, Hospitals and Private Clinics.
Language(s): Arabic; English
ADVERTISING RATES:
Full Page Colour .... EUR 3500
Mechanical Data: Type Area: 262 x 190 mm
Copy instructions: *Copy Date:* 30 days prior to publication

ALLERGIE KONKRET 719946G94F-100
Editorial: Fliethstr. 114, 41061 MÖNCHENGLADBACH **Tel:** 2161 814940
Fax: 2161 8149430
Email: info@daab.de **Web site:** http://www.daab.de
Freq: Quarterly; Free to qualifying individuals
Annual Sub.: EUR 18,00; **Circ:** 25,000
Editor: Andrea Wallrafen; **Advertising Manager:** Bettina Burghardt
Profile: Patient magazine issued by the German Allergy and Asthma Association.
Language(s): German
ADVERTISING RATES:
Full Page Mono .... EUR 2050
Full Page Colour .... EUR 3588
Mechanical Data: Type Area: 270 x 189 mm, No. of Columns (Display): 3, Col Widths (Display): 60 mm
Copy instructions: *Copy Date:* 28 days prior to publication
CONSUMER: OTHER CLASSIFICATIONS: Disability

ALLERGIKUS 1748950G94F-1908
Editorial: Gezelinallee 37, 51375 LEVERKUSEN
Tel: 214 310570 **Fax:** 214 3105719
Email: info@gfmk.com **Web site:** http://www.gfmk.com
Freq: Quarterly; **Cover Price:** Free; **Circ:** 59,644
Editor: Anke Tennemann; **Advertising Manager:** Hilda Kesisoglu
Profile: Magazine for people with allergies, neurodermitis, asthma, COPD or similar skin or Respiratory diseases. Reports of medicine and research, a better life with the disease and from the self-help.
Language(s): German
ADVERTISING RATES:
Full Page Mono .... EUR 4045
Full Page Colour .... EUR 6068
Mechanical Data: Type Area: 240 x 178 mm, No. of Columns (Display): 3, Col Widths (Display): 48 mm
CONSUMER: OTHER CLASSIFICATIONS: Disability

ALLERGO JOURNAL 719947G56A-320
Editorial: Aschauer Str. 30, 81549 MÜNCHEN
Tel: 89 2030431401 **Fax:** 89 2030431399
Email: markus.seidl@springer.com **Web site:** http://www.allergo-journal.de
Freq: 8 issues yearly; Free to qualifying individuals
Annual Sub.: EUR 99,00; **Circ:** 6,865
Editor: Markus Seidl; **Advertising Manager:** Kornelia Echsel
Profile: The „Allergo Journal" publishes original articles and guidelines and position papers on allergy, immunology and environmental health problems. The editorial section with papers from the international literature and conference proceedings informs all allergologically working doctors on the latest advances in diagnosis, therapy and prevention, and deals with the professional and professional policy issues. A training module enables the acquisition of CME credits.
Language(s): English; German
ADVERTISING RATES:
Full Page Mono .... EUR 2730
Full Page Colour .... EUR 4230
Mechanical Data: Type Area: 240 x 174 mm
Copy instructions: *Copy Date:* 21 days prior to publication
Official Journal of: Organ d. Dt. Ges. f. Allergologie u. klin. Immunologie u. d. Ärzteverb. Dt. Allergologen
BUSINESS: HEALTH & MEDICAL

ALLERGOLOGIE 1929831G56A-11649
Editorial: Ricklinger Str. 5, 30449 HANNOVER
Tel: 511 9246276
Email: werfel.thomas@mh-hannover.de
Freq: Monthly; **Annual Sub.:** EUR 193,00; **Circ:** 4,600
Editor: Thomas Werfel; **Advertising Manager:** Christian Graßl
Profile: Allergologie published overviews, original articles, case reports, current comments, questions from practice/reader questions, Focus, Clinical Immunology - what's new, letters to the editor, interviews, legal issues, professional policies, professional issues, announcements of relevant companies and also personal details, congress announcements, book reviews, etc. from all areas of experimental and clinical allergy and immunology.
Language(s): German
ADVERTISING RATES:
Full Page Mono .... EUR 2130
Full Page Colour .... EUR 3120
Mechanical Data: Type Area: 242 x 167 mm, No. of Columns (Display): 3, Col Widths (Display): 56 mm
Copy instructions: *Copy Date:* 28 days prior to publication

ALLER-ZEITUNG 719950G67B-340
Editorial: Steinweg 73, 38518 GIFHORN
Tel: 5371 808125 **Fax:** 5371 808164
Email: redaktion@aller-zeitung.de **Web site:** http://www.aller-zeitung.de
Freq: 312 issues yearly; **Circ:** 38,268
Editor: Carsten Baschin; **Advertising Manager:** Hans-Jürgen Dölves
Profile: Daily newspaper with regional news and a local sports section. This Outlet offers RSS (Really Simple Syndication).
Language(s): German
ADVERTISING RATES:
SCC .... EUR 51,40
Mechanical Data: Type Area: 430 x 277 mm, No. of Columns (Display): 6, Col Widths (Display): 45 mm
Copy instructions: *Copy Date:* 1 day prior to publication
REGIONAL DAILY & SUNDAY NEWSPAPERS: Regional Daily Newspapers

ALLER-ZEITUNG.DE 1620778G67B-16509
Editorial: Steinweg 73, 38518 GIFHORN
Tel: 5371 80883 **Fax:** 5371 808164
Email: redaktion@aller-zeitung.de **Web site:** http://www.aller-zeitung.de
Freq: Daily; **Cover Price:** Paid; **Circ:** 380,000 Unique Users
Editor: Carsten Baschin; **Advertising Manager:** Hans-Jürgen Dölves
Profile: Website of Aller-Zeitung with news on politics, economy, culture, sport, travel, technology, etc. Facebook: http://www.facebook.com/allerzeitung Twitter: http://twitter.com/#!/azgifhorn This Outlet offers RSS (Really Simple Syndication).
Language(s): German
REGIONAL DAILY & SUNDAY NEWSPAPERS: Regional Daily Newspapers

ALLES FÜR DIE FRAU 1687090G74A-3469
Editorial: Meßberg 1, 20095 HAMBURG
Tel: 40 30195219 **Fax:** 40 30195417
Email: afdf@bauerredaktionen.de **Web site:** http://www.bauermedia.com
Freq: Weekly; **Annual Sub.:** EUR 36,40; **Circ:** 203,079
Editor: Viola Wallmüller
Profile: Alles für die Frau stands for a wide range of topics. With 100 tips with each episode booklet helps the magazine to make life and save time. In addition, the title offers medical news, fashion, beauty and decoration.
Language(s): German
ADVERTISING RATES:
Full Page Mono .... EUR 13700
Full Page Colour .... EUR 13700
Mechanical Data: Type Area: 258 x 206 mm, Col Widths (Display): 39 mm, No. of Columns (Display): 5
Copy instructions: *Copy Date:* 19 days prior to publication
CONSUMER: WOMEN'S INTEREST CONSUMER MAGAZINES: Women's Interest

ALLGÄUER ANZEIGEBLATT 719979G67B-360
Editorial: Jahnstr. 4, 87509 IMMENSTADT
Tel: 8323 8020 **Fax:** 8323 802180
Email: redaktion@allgaeuer-anzeigeblatt.net **Web site:** http://www.allgaeuer-anzeigeblatt.de
Freq: 312 issues yearly; **Circ:** 17,774
Advertising Manager: Peter Fuchs
Profile: Daily newspaper with regional news and a local sports section. Facebook: http://www.allgaeuer-anzeigeblatt.de/index.shtml?life_style.
Language(s): German
ADVERTISING RATES:
SCC .... EUR 59,90
Mechanical Data: Type Area: 480 x 327 mm, No. of Columns (Display): 7, Col Widths (Display): 45 mm
Copy instructions: *Copy Date:* 2 days prior to publication
Supplement(s): Allgäu-Dribbler; allgäu weit; allgäu weit Allgäuer Kultursommer; allgäu weit Gesundheit; allgäu weit Sommer; allgäu weit Winter; Golfregion Allgäu; Hütten-Freizeit; ImmobilienReport Oberallgäu mit Finanzjournal; Life & Style; rtv; Die Schwäbische Bäderstrasse Kraft-Quellen; Sommer Paradies
REGIONAL DAILY & SUNDAY NEWSPAPERS: Regional Daily Newspapers

ALLGÄUER BAUERNBLATT 719981G21J-15
Editorial: Porschestr. 2, 87437 KEMPTEN
Tel: 831 5714223 **Fax:** 831 79008
Email: bauernblatt@ava-verlag.de **Web site:** http://www.allgaeuer-bauernblatt.de
Freq: Weekly; **Annual Sub.:** EUR 105,80; **Circ:** 9,972
Editor: Johann Stich; **Advertising Manager:** Karl König
Profile: Whether current events from the Allgäu, background information on agricultural policy, scholarly articles about animal breeding, animal husbandry, animal feeding, dairy farming, grassland or forestry - the »Allgäuer Bauernblatt« is a valuable source of information for the modern farm manager simply irreplaceable. Useful gardening tips all year round, attractive recipes for every occasion and useful health guide to make the "green sheet" for the entire family especially popular.
Language(s): German
ADVERTISING RATES:
Full Page Mono .... EUR 3996
Full Page Colour .... EUR 5584
Mechanical Data: Type Area: 270 x 187 mm, No. of Columns (Display): 4, Col Widths (Display): 45 mm
Copy instructions: *Copy Date:* 3 days prior to publication
BUSINESS: AGRICULTURE & FARMING: Agriculture & Farming - Regional

ALLGÄUER ZEITUNG 719984G67B-380
Editorial: Heisinger Str. 14, 87437 KEMPTEN
Tel: 831 206439 **Fax:** 831 206123
Email: redaktion@azv.de **Web site:** http://www.all-in.de
Freq: 312 issues yearly; **Circ:** 107,257
Editor: Hermann König; **News Editor:** Jürgen Gerstenmaier; **Advertising Manager:** Reinhard Melder
Profile: Daily newspaper with regional news and a local sports section. Twitter: http://twitter.com/allgaeu This Outlet offers RSS (Really Simple Syndication).
Language(s): German
ADVERTISING RATES:
SCC .... EUR 265,50

Germany

Mechanical Data: Type Area: 480 x 327 mm, No. of Columns (Display): 7, Col Widths (Display): 45 mm
Copy instructions: *Copy Date:* 2 days prior to publication
Supplement(s): Allgäu-Dribbler; Allgäu-Dribbler; allgäu weit; allgäu weit Allgäuer Kultursommer; allgäu weit Gesundheit; allgäu weit Sommer; allgäu weit Winter; doppio; Golfregion Allgäu; Hütten-Freizeit; rtv; Die Schwäbische Bäderstrasse Kraft-Quellen
REGIONAL DAILY & SUNDAY NEWSPAPERS: Regional Daily Newspapers

ALLGEMEIN- UND VISZERALCHIRURGIE UP2DATE
1826703G56A-11527
Editorial: Rüdigerstr. 14, 70469 STUTTGART
Tel: 711 8931648 **Fax:** 711 8931499
Email: nicole.karbe@thieme.de **Web site:** http://www.thieme.de/fz/avc-u2d.html
Freq: 6 issues yearly; **Annual Sub.:** EUR 194,40; **Circ:** 2,950
Editor: Heinz Becker
Profile: Allgemein- und Viszeralchirurgie up2date is the first magazine devoted exclusively to the CME-certified training in general and visceral surgery. Four high-quality color designed individual contributions per issue, which are bound separately and can be stored individually by the subscribers in a ring binder.
Language(s): German
ADVERTISING RATES:
Full Page Mono .... EUR 1590
Full Page Colour .... EUR 2760
Mechanical Data: Type Area: 256 x 180 mm, No. of Columns (Display): 2, Col Widths (Display): 88 mm

DER ALLGEMEINARZT
719990G56A-360
Editorial: Talstr. 5, 93152 NITTENDORF
Tel: 9404 952011 **Fax:** 9404 952020
Email: seifert@der-allgemeinarzt.com **Web site:** http://www.allgemeinarzt-online.de
Freq: 20 issues yearly; Free to qualifying individuals **Annual Sub.:** EUR 59,40; **Circ:** 49,672
Editor: Vera Seifert; **Advertising Manager:** Björn Lindenau
Profile: Training journal for general practitioners with solid base among the practitioners of the annual training conference Practica, Europe's largest house continuing medical education. 20 issues a year cover several topics per issue from the entire spectrum of treatment the family doctor.
Language(s): German
ADVERTISING RATES:
Full Page Mono .... EUR 5660
Full Page Colour .... EUR 5660
Mechanical Data: Type Area: 245 x 178 mm, No. of Columns (Display): 4, Col Widths (Display): 40 mm
Copy instructions: *Copy Date:* 28 days prior to publication
Official Journal of: Organ d. Dt. Hausärzteverb. e.V. u. d. practica Fortbildung z. Mitmachen
BUSINESS: HEALTH & MEDICAL

ALLGEMEINE HOMÖOPATHISCHE ZEITUNG
719996G56A-380
Editorial: Oswald-Hesse-Str. 50, 70469 STUTTGART
Tel: 711 8931732 **Fax:** 711 8931748
Email: daniela.elsasser@medizinverlage.de **Web site:** http://www.medizinverlage.de
Freq: 6 issues yearly; Free to qualifying individuals **Annual Sub.:** EUR 99,95; **Circ:** 4,100
Editor: Daniela Elsasser; **Advertising Manager:** Nancy Ruhland
Profile: Lots of practical information: thematic issues, mainly devoted to an indication; Latest news about research and practice of homeopathy; detailed and well-documented case reports that provide much inspiration for their own choices, new extra-heading "Drug tests and images", a service section with book reviews, conference reports and schedules. The AHZ stands for the direction of horizontal technical discussion, because the selection of papers representing the various tendencies within homeopathy. The AHZ is the oldest, still published medical journal. Unchanged but its goal: to provide an ideology-free knowledge, to question the nature benevolent and critically and to provide guidance to a reflective and self-conscious practice.
Language(s): German
ADVERTISING RATES:
Full Page Mono .... EUR 1240
Full Page Colour .... EUR 2145
Mechanical Data: Type Area: 241 x 175 mm
Copy instructions: *Copy Date:* 35 days prior to publication
Official Journal of: Organ d. Dt. Zentralvereins homöopath. Ärzte
BUSINESS: HEALTH & MEDICAL

ALLGEMEINE HOTEL- UND GASTRONOMIE-ZEITUNG
719997G11A-60
Editorial: Silberburgstr. 122, 70176 STUTTGART
Tel: 711 2133321 **Fax:** 711 2133366
Email: h.markgraf@matthaes.de **Web site:** http://www.ahgz.de
Freq: Weekly; **Circ:** 16,491
Editor: Hendrik Markgraf; **Advertising Manager:** Klaus Wendt
Profile: The Allgemeine Hotel- und Gastronomie-Zeitung is the only weekly newspaper for the hospitality industry in Germany. With a current market activity on the focused, practical coverage AHGZ is essential for the successful hoteliers and restaurateurs. With news, analysis and background reports on everything related to competition, customer trends, sales and marketing, food & beverage, equipment and technology and tourism has to be done. In addition to information about the hospitality industry in the regions. Facebook: http://www.facebook.com/pages/AHGZ-Allgemeine-Hotel-und-Gastronomie-Zeitung/294417568037.
Language(s): German
ADVERTISING RATES:
Full Page Mono .... EUR 7800
Full Page Colour .... EUR 10260
Mechanical Data: Type Area: 426 x 282 mm, No. of Columns (Display): 6, Col Widths (Display): 45 mm
Copy instructions: *Copy Date:* 5 days prior to publication
Official Journal of: Organ d. Dt. Hotel- u. Gaststättenverb. e.V.
Supplement(s): AHGZ spezial; der hotelier
BUSINESS: CATERING: Catering, Hotels & Restaurants

ALLGEMEINE LABER-ZEITUNG - HEIMATAUSG. D. STRAUBINGER TAGBLATTS
720001G67B-420
Editorial: Ludwigsplatz 30, 94315 STRAUBING
Tel: 9421 9404601 **Fax:** 9421 9404609
Email: landkreis@straubinger-tagblatt.de **Web site:** http://www.idowa.de
Freq: 312 issues yearly; **Circ:** 6,990
Advertising Manager: Klaus Huber
Profile: Regional daily newspaper with news on politics, economics, culture, sports, travel, technology, etc. She is a local issue by Straubinger Tagblatt for old County Mallersdorf and the County Kelheim. Twitter: http://twitter.com/idowa This Outlet offers RSS (Really Simple Syndication).
Language(s): German
ADVERTISING RATES:
SCC .... EUR 20,90
Mechanical Data: Type Area: 430 x 282 mm, No. of Columns (Display): 6, Col Widths (Display): 45 mm
Copy instructions: *Copy Date:* 1 day prior to publication
Supplement(s): Zuhause
REGIONAL DAILY & SUNDAY NEWSPAPERS: Regional Daily Newspapers

ALLGEMEINE ZEITUNG
720011G67B-440
Editorial: Rosenstr. 2, 48653 COESFELD
Tel: 2541 921151 **Fax:** 2541 921155
Email: redaktion@azonline.de **Web site:** http://www.azonline.de
Freq: 312 issues yearly; **Circ:** 17,950
Advertising Manager: Ralf Bohlje
Profile: Daily newspaper with regional news and a local sports section.
Language(s): German
ADVERTISING RATES:
SCC .... EUR 38,50
Mechanical Data: Type Area: 488 x 324 mm, No. of Columns (Display): 7, Col Widths (Display): 44 mm
Copy instructions: *Copy Date:* 1 day prior to publication
Supplement(s): prisma
REGIONAL DAILY & SUNDAY NEWSPAPERS: Regional Daily Newspapers

ALLGEMEINE ZEITUNG
720012G67B-460
Editorial: Erich-Dombrowski-Str. 2, 55127 MAINZ
Tel: 6131 485805 **Fax:** 6131 485833
Web site: http://www.allgemeine-zeitung.de
Freq: 312 issues yearly; **Circ:** 109,123
Editor: Friedrich Roeingh; **Advertising Manager:** Gerhard Müller
Profile: Regional daily newspaper covering politics, economics, sport, travel and technology. Facebook: http://www.facebook.com/pages/Allgemeine-Zeitung/255951758912 Twitter: http://twitter.com/aznachrichten This Outlet offers RSS (Really Simple Syndication).
Language(s): German
ADVERTISING RATES:
SCC .... EUR 214,70
Mechanical Data: Type Area: 480 x 325 mm, No. of Columns (Display): 7, Col Widths (Display): 45 mm
Copy instructions: *Copy Date:* 1 day prior to publication
Supplement(s): extra Familie; extra Gesundheit; extra Sport; extra Wissen; pepper; schaufenster akktuell KastellKostheim; TheaterZeitung
REGIONAL DAILY & SUNDAY NEWSPAPERS: Regional Daily Newspapers

ALLGEMEINE ZEITUNG DER LÜNEBURGER HEIDE
720013G67B-480
Editorial: Gr. Liederner Str. 45, 29525 UELZEN
Tel: 581 80891202 **Fax:** 581 80891290
Email: redaktion.az@cbeckers.de **Web site:** http://www.az-online.de
Freq: 312 issues yearly; **Circ:** 17,804
Editor: Andreas Becker; **Advertising Manager:** Heike Köhn
Profile: Daily newspaper with regional news and a local sports section. Facebook: http://www.facebook.com/pages/az-online/428840365229 Twitter: http://twitter.com/AZUelzen This Outlet offers RSS (Really Simple Syndication).
Language(s): German
ADVERTISING RATES:
SCC .... EUR 73,20
Mechanical Data: Type Area: 435 x 285 mm, No. of Columns (Display): 6, Col Widths (Display): 45 mm
Copy instructions: *Copy Date:* 2 days prior to publication
Supplement(s): Ambiente Exklusiv; Ausbildung und Beruf; Auto Das Magazin; AZ-Anpfiff; Eltern-Ratgeber; Faszination Bauen; Das Gesundheitsmagazin Sprechstunde; Golf in der Region; Stadtmagazin Uelzen; Top Uelzens erfolgreichste Sportler; Uelzen informativ
REGIONAL DAILY & SUNDAY NEWSPAPERS: Regional Daily Newspapers

ALLGEMEINER ANZEIGER
720003G67B-500
Editorial: Schillerstr. 20, 58511 LÜDENSCHEID
Tel: 2351 1580 **Fax:** 2351 158223
Email: ln@come-on.de **Web site:** http://www.come-on.de
Freq: 312 issues yearly; **Circ:** 3,359
Advertising Manager: Guido Schröder
Profile: Daily newspaper with regional news and a local sports section. Facebook: http://www.facebook.com/westfaelischer.anzeiger Twitter: http://twitter.com/wa_online This Outlet offers RSS (Really Simple Syndication).
Language(s): German
ADVERTISING RATES:
SCC .... EUR 30,80
Mechanical Data: Type Area: 466 x 317 mm, No. of Columns (Display): 7, Col Widths (Display): 43 mm
Copy instructions: *Copy Date:* 1 day prior to publication
Supplement(s): prisma
REGIONAL DAILY & SUNDAY NEWSPAPERS: Regional Daily Newspapers

ALLGEMEINER ANZEIGER
1704271G72-19479
Editorial: Gottstedter Landstr. 6, 99092 ERFURT
Tel: 361 2274 **Fax:** 361 2275034
Email: redaktion@allgemeiner-anzeiger.de **Web site:** http://www.allgemeiner-anzeiger.de
Freq: Daily; **Cover Price:** Paid; **Circ:** 14,971 Unique Users
Editor: Emanuel Beer
Profile: Ezine: Advertising journal (house-to-house) concentrating on local stories.
Language(s): German
LOCAL NEWSPAPERS

ALLGEMEINER ANZEIGER EICHSFELD
719409G72-32
Editorial: Wilhelmstr. 66, 37308 HEILIGENSTADT
Tel: 3606 555714 **Fax:** 3606 555720
Email: p.schindler@allgemeiner-anzeiger.de **Web site:** http://www.allgemeiner-anzeiger.de
Freq: Weekly; **Cover Price:** Free; **Circ:** 44,825
Editor: Peter Schindler; **Advertising Manager:** Klaus-Peter Apel
Profile: Advertising journal (house-to-house) concentrating on local stories.
Language(s): German
ADVERTISING RATES:
Full Page Mono .... EUR 2890
Full Page Colour .... EUR 3901
Mechanical Data: Type Area: 480 x 326 mm, No. of Columns (Display): 7, Col Widths (Display): 44 mm
Copy instructions: *Copy Date:* 2 days prior to publication
LOCAL NEWSPAPERS

ALLGEMEINER ANZEIGER EISENACH
719410G72-36
Editorial: Sophienstr. 40a, 99817 EISENACH
Tel: 3691 683661 **Fax:** 3691 683668
Email: w.kaiser@allgemeiner-anzeiger.de **Web site:** http://www.allgemeiner-anzeiger.de
Freq: Weekly; **Cover Price:** Free; **Circ:** 48,385
Editor: Werner Kaiser; **Advertising Manager:** Karlheinz Uth
Profile: Advertising journal (house-to-house) concentrating on local stories.
Language(s): German
ADVERTISING RATES:
Full Page Mono .... EUR 2890
Full Page Colour .... EUR 3901
Mechanical Data: Type Area: 480 x 326 mm, No. of Columns (Display): 7, Col Widths (Display): 44 mm
Copy instructions: *Copy Date:* 2 days prior to publication
LOCAL NEWSPAPERS

ALLGEMEINER ANZEIGER ERFURT
719411G72-40
Editorial: Meyfartstr. 19, 99084 ERFURT
Tel: 361 5550561 **Fax:** 361 5550569
Email: h.floeckner@allgemeiner-anzeiger.de **Web site:** http://www.allgemeiner-anzeiger.de
Freq: Weekly; **Cover Price:** Free; **Circ:** 118,900
Editor: Helke Floeckner; **Advertising Manager:** Sylvia Aniol
Profile: Advertising journal (house-to-house) concentrating on local stories.
Language(s): German
ADVERTISING RATES:
Full Page Mono .... EUR 5242
Full Page Colour .... EUR 7077
Mechanical Data: Type Area: 480 x 326 mm, No. of Columns (Display): 7, Col Widths (Display): 44 mm
Copy instructions: *Copy Date:* 2 days prior to publication
LOCAL NEWSPAPERS

ALLGEMEINER ANZEIGER GERA/SCHMÖLLN
719412G72-44
Editorial: Puschkinplatz 6, 07545 GERA
Tel: 365 55247112 **Fax:** 365 55247120
Email: s.weiss@allgemeiner-anzeiger.de **Web site:** http://www.allgemeiner-anzeiger.de
Freq: Weekly; **Cover Price:** Free; **Circ:** 88,850
Editor: Steffen Weiß; **Advertising Manager:** Marcus Hlawatsch
Profile: Advertising journal (house-to-house) concentrating on local stories.
Language(s): German
ADVERTISING RATES:
Full Page Mono .... EUR 4268
Full Page Colour .... EUR 5761
Mechanical Data: Type Area: 480 x 326 mm, No. of Columns (Display): 7, Col Widths (Display): 44 mm
Copy instructions: *Copy Date:* 2 days prior to publication
LOCAL NEWSPAPERS

ALLGEMEINER ANZEIGER GOTHA
719413G72-48
Editorial: Hauptmarkt 40, 99867 GOTHA
Tel: 3621 419718 **Fax:** 3621 419729
Email: uj.igel@allgemeiner-anzeiger.de **Web site:** http://www.allgemeiner-anzeiger.de
Freq: Weekly; **Cover Price:** Free; **Circ:** 58,610
Editor: Uwe-Jens Igel; **Advertising Manager:** Martina Weymann
Profile: Advertising journal (house-to-house) concentrating on local stories.
Language(s): German
ADVERTISING RATES:
Full Page Mono .... EUR 3596
Full Page Colour .... EUR 4854
Mechanical Data: Type Area: 480 x 326 mm, No. of Columns (Display): 7, Col Widths (Display): 44 mm
Copy instructions: *Copy Date:* 2 days prior to publication
LOCAL NEWSPAPERS

ALLGEMEINER ANZEIGER HOLZLANDBOTE
719414G72-52
Editorial: Eisenberger Str. 79a, 07629 HERMSDORF
Tel: 36601 89521 **Fax:** 36601 89529
Email: k.viererbe@allgemeiner-anzeiger.de **Web site:** http://www.allgemeiner-anzeiger.de
Freq: Weekly; **Cover Price:** Free; **Circ:** 28,720
Editor: Kerrin Viererbe; **Advertising Manager:** Marcus Hlawatsch
Profile: Advertising journal (house-to-house) concentrating on local stories.
Language(s): German
ADVERTISING RATES:
Full Page Mono .... EUR 2671
Full Page Colour .... EUR 3539
Mechanical Data: Type Area: 480 x 326 mm, No. of Columns (Display): 7, Col Widths (Display): 44 mm
Copy instructions: *Copy Date:* 2 days prior to publication
LOCAL NEWSPAPERS

ALLGEMEINER ANZEIGER JENA
719416G72-60
Editorial: Leutragraben 2, 07743 JENA
Tel: 3641 520617 **Fax:** 3641 520610
Email: b.hausdoerfer@allgemeiner-anzeiger.de **Web site:** http://www.allgemeiner-anzeiger.de
Freq: Weekly; **Cover Price:** Free; **Circ:** 60,200
Editor: Bernd Hausdörfer; **Advertising Manager:** Steffi Voigt
Profile: Advertising journal (house-to-house) concentrating on local stories.
Language(s): German
ADVERTISING RATES:
Full Page Mono .... EUR 3528
Full Page Colour .... EUR 4763
Mechanical Data: Type Area: 480 x 326 mm, No. of Columns (Display): 7, Col Widths (Display): 44 mm
Copy instructions: *Copy Date:* 2 days prior to publication
LOCAL NEWSPAPERS

ALLGEMEINER ANZEIGER MÜHLHAUSEN/BAD LANGENSALZA
719417G72-64
Editorial: Obermarkt 5, 99974 MÜHLHAUSEN
Tel: 3601 880242 **Fax:** 3601 880244
Email: w.rewicki@allgemeiner-anzeiger.de **Web site:** http://www.allgemeiner-anzeiger.de
Freq: Weekly; **Cover Price:** Free; **Circ:** 52,750
Editor: Wolfgang Rewicki; **Advertising Manager:** Sabine Jentczak
Profile: Advertising journal (house-to-house) concentrating on local stories.
Language(s): German
ADVERTISING RATES:
Full Page Mono .... EUR 3293
Full Page Colour .... EUR 4446

Mechanical Data: Type Area: 480 x 326 mm, No. of Columns (Display): 7, Col Widths (Display): 44 mm
Copy instructions: *Copy Date:* 2 days prior to publication
LOCAL NEWSPAPERS

ALLGEMEINER ANZEIGER NORDHAUSEN/SONDERSHAUSEN 719418G72-68
Editorial: Bahnhofstr. 35, 99734 NORDHAUSEN
Tel: 3631 605864 **Fax:** 3631 605866
Email: h.fischer@allgemeiner-anzeiger.de **Web site:** http://www.allgemeiner-anzeiger.de
Freq: Weekly; **Cover Price:** Free; **Circ:** 64,200
Editor: Heidrun Fischer; **Advertising Manager:** Klaus-Peter Apel
Profile: Advertising journal (house-to-house) concentrating on local stories.
Language(s): German
ADVERTISING RATES:
Full Page Mono .... EUR 3797
Full Page Colour .... EUR 5126
Mechanical Data: Type Area: 480 x 326 mm, No. of Columns (Display): 7, Col Widths (Display): 44 mm
Copy instructions: *Copy Date:* 2 days prior to publication
LOCAL NEWSPAPERS

ALLGEMEINER ANZEIGER SAALFELD/RUDOLSTADT/PÖSSNECK 719419G72-72
Editorial: Am Blankenburger Tor 1a, 07318 SAALFELD **Tel:** 3671 4559022 **Fax:** 3671 4559018
Email: a.abendroth@allgemeiner-anzeiger.de **Web site:** http://www.allgemeiner-anzeiger.de
Freq: Weekly; **Cover Price:** Free; **Circ:** 79,972
Editor: Andreas Abendroth; **Advertising Manager:** Stefan Saalmann
Profile: Advertising journal (house-to-house) concentrating on local stories.
Language(s): German
ADVERTISING RATES:
Full Page Mono .... EUR 3629
Full Page Colour .... EUR 4899
Mechanical Data: Type Area: 480 x 326 mm, No. of Columns (Display): 7, Col Widths (Display): 44 mm
Copy instructions: *Copy Date:* 2 days prior to publication
LOCAL NEWSPAPERS

ALLGEMEINER ANZEIGER SÖMMERDA/ARTERN 719421G72-80
Editorial: Lange Str. 16, 99610 SÖMMERDA
Tel: 3634 687814 **Fax:** 3634 687812
Email: s.rosenkranz@allgemeiner-anzeiger.de **Web site:** http://www.allgemeiner-anzeiger.de
Freq: Weekly; **Cover Price:** Free; **Circ:** 47,240
Editor: Sandra Rosenkranz; **Advertising Manager:** Sylvia Aniol
Profile: Advertising journal (house-to-house) concentrating on local stories.
Language(s): German
ADVERTISING RATES:
Full Page Mono .... EUR 2991
Full Page Colour .... EUR 4038
Mechanical Data: Type Area: 480 x 326 mm, No. of Columns (Display): 7, Col Widths (Display): 44 mm
Copy instructions: *Copy Date:* 2 days prior to publication
LOCAL NEWSPAPERS

ALLGEMEINER ANZEIGER THÜRINGER VOGTLAND 719424G72-92
Editorial: Greizer Str. 10, 07937 ZEULENRODA-TRIEBES **Tel:** 36628 43316 **Fax:** 36628 43329
Email: ag.marsch@allgemeiner-anzeiger.de **Web site:** http://www.allgemeiner-anzeiger.de
Freq: Weekly; **Cover Price:** Free; **Circ:** 55,078
Editor: Antje-Gesine Marsch; **Advertising Manager:** Marina Görsch
Profile: Advertising journal (house-to-house) concentrating on local stories.
Language(s): German
ADVERTISING RATES:
Full Page Mono .... EUR 3495
Full Page Colour .... EUR 4718
Mechanical Data: Type Area: 480 x 326 mm, No. of Columns (Display): 7, Col Widths (Display): 44 mm
Copy instructions: *Copy Date:* 2 days prior to publication
LOCAL NEWSPAPERS

ALLGEMEINER ANZEIGER WEIMAR/APOLDA 719423G72-88
Editorial: Goetheplatz 9a, 99423 WEIMAR
Tel: 3643 558433 **Fax:** 3643 558440
Email: s.schulter@allgemeiner-anzeiger.de **Web site:** http://www.allgemeiner-anzeiger.de
Freq: Weekly; **Cover Price:** Free; **Circ:** 65,850
Editor: Simone Schulter; **Advertising Manager:** Steffi Voigt
Profile: Advertising journal (house-to-house) concentrating on local stories.
Language(s): German
ADVERTISING RATES:
Full Page Mono .... EUR 3629
Full Page Colour .... EUR 4899
Mechanical Data: Type Area: 480 x 326 mm, No. of Columns (Display): 7, Col Widths (Display): 44 mm

Copy instructions: *Copy Date:* 2 days prior to publication
LOCAL NEWSPAPERS

ALLIANZ FIRMEN INFO 1660456G14A-9653
Editorial: Fritz-Schäffer-Str. 9, 81737 MÜNCHEN
Tel: 89 38002712 **Fax:** 89 380082712
Email: firmeninfo@allianz.de **Web site:** http://www.allianz.de
Freq: Quarterly; **Cover Price:** Free; **Circ:** 136,000
Editor: Karin Hauk
Profile: Customer magazine from the insurance company 'Allianz'.
Language(s): German

ALLIGATOR 720017G57-40
Editorial: Greifswalder Str. 4, 10405 BERLIN
Tel: 30 2044745 **Fax:** 30 2044468
Email: alligator@grueneliga.de **Web site:** http://www.grueneliga.de
Freq: 6 issues yearly; Free to qualifying individuals
Annual Sub.: EUR 18,00; **Circ:** 1,100
Editor: Oliver C. Pfannenstiel; **Advertising Manager:** Katrin Kusche
Profile: Magazine on environmental protection from the Grüne Liga.
Language(s): German
ADVERTISING RATES:
Full Page Mono .... EUR 300
Full Page Colour .... EUR 550
Mechanical Data: Type Area: 268 x 184 mm, No. of Columns (Display): 3, Col Widths (Display): 50 mm
Copy instructions: *Copy Date:* 14 days prior to publication

ALL-IN.DE 1620730G67B-16504
Editorial: Heisinger Str. 14, 87437 KEMPTEN
Tel: 831 206394 **Fax:** 831 2065117
Email: content@rta-design.de **Web site:** http://www.all-in.de
Freq: Daily; **Cover Price:** Paid; **Circ:** 781,387 Unique Users
Editor: Markus Niessner; **Advertising Manager:** Kathrin Sommer
Profile: Ezine: all-in.de is the news portal of the Allgäuer Zeitung. However, all-in.de is more than the newspaper on the web. The portal combines the information from all over Bavaria and prepares them for diverse and demanding. With all-in.de you will find news and Allgäu-videos, television news reports from TV Allgäu, police reports, leisure tips and picture galleries. all-in.de has the great Allgäuer online yellow pages, maps the Allgäuer advertising market and provides information on current weather and events in the Allgäu. A third of all-in.de users are not newspaper readers. To create your online advertising to all-in.de additional coverage. Twitter: http://twitter.com/allgaeu This Outlet offers RSS (Really Simple Syndication).
Language(s): German
REGIONAL DAILY & SUNDAY NEWSPAPERS: Regional Daily Newspapers

ALMANAC 1865045G37-1860
Editorial: Silberstreifen 4, 76287 RHEINSTETTEN
Tel: 721 51610 **Fax:** 721 517101
Email: marcom@bruker-biospin.de **Web site:** http://www.bruker-biospin.de
Freq: Annual; **Cover Price:** Free; **Circ:** 9,000
Editor: Thorsten Thiel
Profile: Company publication published by Bruker Biospin.
Language(s): English

DER ALMBAUER 720029G21A-401
Editorial: Postfach 200523, 80005 MÜNCHEN
Tel: 89 53098950
Freq: 11 issues yearly; **Annual Sub.:** EUR 29,00; **Circ:** 2,526
Editor: Johannes Urban; **Advertising Manager:** Thomas Herrmann
Profile: Journal about alpine, mountain and meadowland farming.
Language(s): German
ADVERTISING RATES:
Full Page Mono .... EUR 1220
Full Page Colour .... EUR 1966
Mechanical Data: Type Area: 270 x 184 mm, No. of Columns (Display): 4, Col Widths (Display): 43 mm
Copy instructions: *Copy Date:* 21 days prior to publication
BUSINESS: AGRICULTURE & FARMING

ALPENADRIA 1615134G89A-12141
Editorial: Hastener Str. 140, 42349 WUPPERTAL
Tel: 202 94600246 **Fax:** 202 94600247
Email: redaktion@alpenadria.eu **Web site:** http://www.alpenadria.eu
Freq: Half-yearly; **Annual Sub.:** EUR 10,00; **Circ:** 42,000
Editor: Snezana Simicic; **Advertising Manager:** Stephan Fennel
Profile: Magazine for travel, pleasure, culture and lifestyle - reported from the Alpine area and the countries along the Adriatic. With two mono-thematic issues per year (spring and autumn), which focus on a selected area and its diversity of themes and present it in detail. Facebook: http://www.facebook.com/motourmedia.

Language(s): German
ADVERTISING RATES:
Full Page Mono .... EUR 4000
Full Page Colour .... EUR 4900
Mechanical Data: No. of Columns (Display): 3, Col Widths (Display): 60 mm, Type Area: 273 x 195 mm
Copy instructions: *Copy Date:* 28 days prior to publication

ALPIN 720043G75L-60
Editorial: Planegger Str. 15, 82131 GAUTING
Tel: 89 8931600 **Fax:** 89 89316019
Email: info@alpin.de **Web site:** http://www.alpin.de
Freq: Monthly; **Annual Sub.:** EUR 58,80; **Circ:** 34,765
Editor: Bene Benedikt; **Advertising Manager:** Axel Nieber
Profile: ALPIN presents understandable know-how and makes expert knowledge directly usable. Service issues define our profile. Focus is on the test that we perform at neutral test institutes and in real use at the mountain. Clearly prepared practical issues take a large space: Equipment market overviews, "basic " knowledge, know-how, security, medicine, orientation by GPS, food, books, guides, movies, tourism. Each month ALPIN introduces product news in detail and tests the most interesting parts. As big additions, the ALPIN-Panorama and the ALPIN-EXTRA. The ALPIN-Panorama, an eight-page gatefold sheet on extra thick paper, lead the reader into the most fascinating mountain landscapes of the earth. The mega-inserts ALPIN-EXTRA are large-format guides with 30 to 40 tour tips from an area or prepare a mountain theme compact and precise. Topics such as mountain biking, cross country, climbing, ski tour security or well-being places of the Alps. Facebook: http://www.facebook.com/pages/Alpinde/151033891587334.
Language(s): German
ADVERTISING RATES:
Full Page Mono .... EUR 4350
Full Page Colour .... EUR 4350
Mechanical Data: Type Area: 260 x 194 mm, No. of Columns (Display): 4, Col Widths (Display): 45 mm
Copy instructions: *Copy Date:* 36 days prior to publication
CONSUMER: SPORT: Outdoor

ALPS ALPINE LEBENSART 2034448G89A-12578
Editorial: Hildegardstr. 9, 80539 MÜNCHEN
Tel: 89 24207505 **Fax:** 89 24207504
Email: cs@alps-magazine.com **Web site:** http://www.alps-magazine.com
Freq: 6 issues yearly; **Annual Sub.:** EUR 27,00; **Circ:** 100,000
Editor: Charlotte Seeling
Profile: Facebook: http://www.facebook.com/alpsmagazine.
Language(s): German
ADVERTISING RATES:
Full Page Mono .... EUR 10000
Full Page Colour .... EUR 10000
Mechanical Data: Type Area: 260 x 176 mm

ALSFELDER ALLGEMEINE 720046G67B-520
Editorial: Marburger Str. 18, 35390 GIESSEN
Tel: 641 30030 **Fax:** 641 3003305
Email: redaktion@giessener-allgemeine.de **Web site:** http://www.giessener-allgemeine.de
Freq: 312 issues yearly; **Circ:** 3,578
Advertising Manager: Wilfried Kämpf
Profile: Regional daily newspaper with news on politics, economy, culture, sports, travel, technology, etc. The Alsfelder Allgemeine is the local edition of Giessener Allgemeine. Facebook: http://www.facebook.com/pages/Giessener-Allgemeine-Zeitung/142861707245 This Outlet offers RSS (Really Simple Syndication).
Language(s): German
ADVERTISING RATES:
SCC .... EUR 12,00
Mechanical Data: Type Area: 430 x 282 mm, No. of Columns (Display): 6, Col Widths (Display): 45 mm
Copy instructions: *Copy Date:* 1 day prior to publication
REGIONAL DAILY & SUNDAY NEWSPAPERS: Regional Daily Newspapers

ALSTERTAL MAGAZIN 720051G72-296
Editorial: Barkhausenweg 11, 22339 HAMBURG
Tel: 40 5389300 **Fax:** 40 53893011
Email: redaktion@alster-net.de **Web site:** http://www.alster-net.de
Freq: Monthly; **Cover Price:** Free; **Circ:** 51,000
Editor: Kai Wehl
Profile: Magazine containing articles about culture, politics and events in the Alster district of Hamburg.
Language(s): German
ADVERTISING RATES:
Full Page Mono .... EUR 2223
Full Page Colour .... EUR 2363
Mechanical Data: Type Area: 280 x 195 mm, No. of Columns (Display): 4, Col Widths (Display): 45 mm
Copy instructions: *Copy Date:* 11 days prior to publication
Supplement(s): Alstertal Einkaufs-Zentrum Das Center-Magazin; Doc Alstertal; Handwerk der besonderen Art
LOCAL NEWSPAPERS

ALT? NA UND! 1616257G74N-814
Editorial: Bergstr. 1, 45479 MÜLHEIM
Email: redaktion@alt-na-und.de **Web site:** http://www.alt-na-und.de
Freq: Quarterly; **Cover Price:** Free; **Circ:** 6,500
Editor: Gabriele Strauß-Blumberg
Profile: Magazine for the elderly from the elderly of the city of Mülheim.
Language(s): German

ALTBAYERISCHE HEIMATPOST 720055G80-720
Editorial: Gabelsbergerstr. 4, 83308 TROSTBERG
Tel: 8621 80827 **Fax:** 8621 80843
Email: altbayerische@erdl-verlag.de **Web site:** http://www.chiemgau-online.de
Freq: Weekly; **Circ:** 12,245
Editor: Herbert Reichgruber; **Advertising Manager:** Christian von Hobe
Profile: The Altbayerische Heimatpost is the weekly newspaper for Bavaria. With reports on life in Bavaria and its people. The tabloid published Author Journal provides weekly an exciting mix of Bavarian history, culture, traditions and customs - for over 60 years. Integral part of the blade approach is an exclusive serialized novel and an extensive calendar of events.
Language(s): German
Mechanical Data: Type Area: 288 x 203 mm, No. of Columns (Display): 3, Col Widths (Display): 65 mm
Copy instructions: *Copy Date:* 14 days prior to publication
CONSUMER: RURAL & REGIONAL INTEREST

ALTENAER KREISBLATT 720062G67B-560
Editorial: Lennestr. 48, 58762 ALTENA
Tel: 2352 91870 **Fax:** 2352 918713
Email: ak@come-on.de **Web site:** http://www.come-on.de
Freq: 312 issues yearly; **Circ:** 3,879
Advertising Manager: Guido Schröder
Profile: Daily newspaper with regional news and a local sports section. This Outlet offers RSS (Really Simple Syndication).
Language(s): German
ADVERTISING RATES:
SCC .... EUR 34,80
Mechanical Data: Type Area: 466 x 317 mm, No. of Columns (Display): 7, Col Widths (Display): 43 mm
Copy instructions: *Copy Date:* 1 day prior to publication
Supplement(s): prisma
REGIONAL DAILY & SUNDAY NEWSPAPERS: Regional Daily Newspapers

ALTENHEIM 720064G56B-80
Editorial: Plathnerstr. 4c, 30175 HANNOVER
Tel: 511 9910110 **Fax:** 511 9910119
Email: monika.gaier@vincentz.net **Web site:** http://www.altenheim.vincentz.net
Freq: Monthly; **Annual Sub.:** EUR 112,00; **Circ:** 8,933
Editor: Monika Gaier; **Advertising Manager:** Thomas Veitschegger
Profile: For four out of five leaderships of the elderly and nursing homes, residential facilities and some assisted living facilities include Altenheim for a monthly must-read. Altenheim is the leading trade magazine for the home management and informed current and practical about the successful strategies of corporate management, the proper use of new laws and regulations, the most important advice regarding law, the most sought-care schemes and offers that are most helpful tools for personnel management. Each issue contains projects and concepts from the field, the latest news from the provinces, from health and professional politics, quotes opinions from the industry, reports on special events and conferences, provides books and product innovations and provides information on important events and seminars.
Language(s): German
ADVERTISING RATES:
Full Page Mono .... EUR 2560
Full Page Colour .... EUR 4390
Mechanical Data: Type Area: 250 x 175 mm, No. of Columns (Display): 4, Col Widths (Display): 42 mm
Copy instructions: *Copy Date:* 19 days prior to publication
BUSINESS: HEALTH & MEDICAL: Nursing

ALTENPFLEGE 720067G56B-1644
Editorial: Plathnerstr. 4c, 30175 HANNOVER
Tel: 511 9910120 **Fax:** 511 9910119
Email: holger.jenrich@vincentz.net **Web site:** http://www.altenpflege.vincentz.net
Freq: Monthly; **Annual Sub.:** EUR 55,00; **Circ:** 18,420
Editor: Holger Jenrich; **Advertising Manager:** Thomas Veitschegger
Profile: Altenpflege is on the German market, the trade magazine for professionals and executives in the elderly. Its primary target group are nurses in senior and executive positions. Over 19,000 readers every month its get. Altenpflege is subscribed to by 85% of all inpatient facilities and 54% of all outpatient facilities. Two-thirds of all nurses in nursing homes read Altenpflege regularly. It is by far the leading sheet in the industry. The magazine always offers current information and relevant expertise around the organization and implementation of care for older people. Topics in the news and distances, in technical papers and training modules in all those areas are treated, which are relevant in the work of professional personnel are as follows: dementia and palliative care, care management and nursing practice, law and medicine. The readers benefit will

further enhances current product information, books tips, education opportunities, a long-distance training, additional services on the Internet and a regular job market.
Language(s): German
ADVERTISING RATES:
Full Page Mono .... EUR 2650
Full Page Colour .... EUR 4570
Mechanical Data: Type Area: 250 x 175 mm, No. of Columns (Display): 4, Col Widths (Display): 42 mm
Copy instructions: *Copy Date:* 19 days prior to publication
BUSINESS: HEALTH & MEDICAL: Nursing

ÄLTER WERDEN IM LANDKREIS SAARLOUIS
1643473G74N-843
Editorial: Kaiser-Wilhelm-Str. 4, 66740 SAARLOUIS
Tel: 6831 444226 **Fax:** 6831 444620
Email: amt59@kreis-saarlouis.de **Web site:** http://www.kreis-saarlouis.de
Freq: Half-yearly; **Cover Price:** Free; **Circ:** 10,000
Profile: Magazine for the elderly in the region of Saarlouis.
Language(s): German

ALTHAUS MODERNISIEREN
720076G79A-10
Editorial: Höhenstr. 17, 70736 FELLBACH
Tel: 711 5206274 **Fax:** 711 5206300
Email: althaus@fachschriften.de **Web site:** http://www.renovieren.de
Freq: 6 issues yearly; **Annual Sub.:** EUR 15,00; **Circ:** 24,448
Editor: Kurt Jeni; **Advertising Manager:** Wolfgang Loges
Profile: Magazine about the renovation of old properties.
Language(s): German
Readership: Aimed at home owners.
ADVERTISING RATES:
Full Page Colour .... EUR 9550
Mechanical Data: Type Area: 247 x 187 mm, No. of Columns (Display): 4, Col Widths (Display): 43 mm
Copy instructions: *Copy Date:* 40 days prior to publication
Supplement(s): baugui.de; Energ!e Extra-Heft dämmen + dichten; Energ!e Extra-Heft Lüftung und Klima; Energ!e Extra-Heft Solar Energie
CONSUMER: HOBBIES & DIY

ALTLÄNDER TAGEBLATT
720079G67B-580
Editorial: Glückstädter Str. 10, 21682 STADE
Tel: 4141 9360 **Fax:** 4141 936294
Email: redaktion-std@tageblatt.de **Web site:** http://www.tageblatt.de
Freq: 312 issues yearly; **Circ:** 8,969
Advertising Manager: Georg Lempke
Profile: Daily newspaper with regional news and a local sports section.
Language(s): German
ADVERTISING RATES:
SCC .... EUR 41,80
Mechanical Data: Type Area: 487 x 324 mm, No. of Columns (Display): 7, Col Widths (Display): 45 mm
Copy instructions: *Copy Date:* 1 day prior to publication
Supplement(s): Ferienjournal; Stader Buxtehuder Altländer Tageblatt Freizeit Magazin; Stader Buxtehuder Altländer Tageblatt Steilpass
REGIONAL DAILY & SUNDAY NEWSPAPERS: Regional Daily Newspapers

ALTLASTEN SPEKTRUM
720080G57-60
Editorial: Grenzstr. 18c, 15732 EICHWALDE
Tel: 340 21033064 **Fax:** 721 151343857
Email: redaktion@altlastenspektrum-itva.de **Web site:** http://www.altlastenspektrum-itva.de
Freq: 6 issues yearly; Free to qualifying individuals
Annual Sub.: EUR 74,17; **Circ:** 2,200
Editor: Jörg Frauenstein; **Advertising Manager:** Peter Taprogge
Profile: Magazine accompanies the scientific, technical, legal and economic development of the exploration, acquisition, assessment and remediation of contaminated sites.
Language(s): German
ADVERTISING RATES:
Full Page Mono .... EUR 1560
Full Page Colour .... EUR 2460
Mechanical Data: Type Area: 254 x 185 mm, No. of Columns (Display): 2, Col Widths (Display): 84 mm
Copy instructions: *Copy Date:* 24 days prior to publication
BUSINESS: ENVIRONMENT & POLLUTION

ALTMARK ZEITUNG
720085G67B-600
Editorial: Vor dem Neuperver Tor 4, 29410 SALZWEDEL **Tel:** 3901 831493100
Fax: 3901 831493790
Email: redaktion.saw@cbeckers.de **Web site:** http://www.az-online.de
Freq: 312 issues yearly; **Circ:** 18,581
Editor: Ulrike Meineke
Profile: Regional daily newspaper covering politics, economics, sport, travel and technology. Facebook: http://www.facebook.com/pages/az-online/428840365229.
Language(s): German
ADVERTISING RATES:
SCC .... EUR 79,60
Mechanical Data: Type Area: 430 x 282 mm, No. of Columns (Display): 6, Col Widths (Display): 45 mm
Copy instructions: *Copy Date:* 1 day prior to publication
Supplement(s): AZ-Anpfiff
REGIONAL DAILY & SUNDAY NEWSPAPERS: Regional Daily Newspapers

ALTMÜHL-BOTE
720086G67B-620
Editorial: Marktplatz 47, 91710 GUNZENHAUSEN
Tel: 9831 50080 **Fax:** 9831 500841
Email: redaktion@altmuehl-bote.de **Web site:** http://www.altmuehl-bote.de
Freq: 312 issues yearly; **Circ:** 8,178
Profile: Daily newspaper with regional news and a local sports section.
Language(s): German
ADVERTISING RATES:
SCC .... EUR 24,10
Mechanical Data: Type Area: 430 x 280 mm, No. of Columns (Display): 6, Col Widths (Display): 45 mm
Copy instructions: *Copy Date:* 2 days prior to publication
REGIONAL DAILY & SUNDAY NEWSPAPERS: Regional Daily Newspapers

ALT-NEUÖTTINGER ANZEIGER
720087G67B-540
Editorial: Medienstr. 5, 94036 PASSAU
Tel: 851 8020 **Fax:** 851 802256
Email: pnp@vgp.de **Web site:** http://www.pnp.de
Freq: 312 issues yearly; **Circ:** 20,257
Advertising Manager: Gerhard Koller
Profile: Daily newspaper with regional news and a local sports section. Twitter: http://twitter.com/pnp_online This Outlet offers RSS (Really Simple Syndication).
Language(s): German
ADVERTISING RATES:
SCC .... EUR 55,50
Mechanical Data: Type Area: 482 x 325 mm, No. of Columns (Display): 7, Col Widths (Display): 45 mm
Copy instructions: *Copy Date:* 2 days prior to publication
REGIONAL DAILY & SUNDAY NEWSPAPERS: Regional Daily Newspapers

ALTONAER WOCHENBLATT
720089G72-332
Editorial: Harburger Rathausstr. 40, 21073 HAMBURG **Tel:** 40 85322933 **Fax:** 40 85322939
Email: post@wochenblatt-redaktion.de **Web site:** http://www.altonaer-wochenblatt.de
Freq: Weekly; **Cover Price:** Free; **Circ:** 64,885
Editor: Olaf Zimmermann; **Advertising Manager:** Jürgen Müller
Profile: Advertising journal (house-to-house) concentrating on local stories.
Language(s): German
ADVERTISING RATES:
Full Page Mono .... EUR 4696
Full Page Colour .... EUR 4816
Mechanical Data: Type Area: 430 x 282 mm, No. of Columns (Display): 6, Col Widths (Display): 45 mm
Copy instructions: *Copy Date:* 2 days prior to publication
Supplement(s): Elbe-Einkaufszentrum Aktuell
LOCAL NEWSPAPERS

ALTÖTTINGER LIEBFRAUENBOTE
720088G87-320
Editorial: Neuöttinger Str. 5, 84503 ALTÖTTING
Tel: 8671 927320 **Fax:** 8671 927329
Email: terhoerst@liebfrauenbote.de **Web site:** http://www.liebfrauenbote.de
Freq: Weekly; **Circ:** 16,917
Editor: Wolfgang Terhörst; **Advertising Manager:** Barbara Kieswimmer
Profile: Theological Sunday paper for the Catholic citizens of the community of Altötting.
Language(s): German
ADVERTISING RATES:
Full Page Mono .... EUR 1344
Full Page Colour .... EUR 2624
Mechanical Data: Type Area: 280 x 214 mm, No. of Columns (Display): 4, Col Widths (Display): 53 mm
Copy instructions: *Copy Date:* 10 days prior to publication
CONSUMER: RELIGIOUS

ALUMINIUM
720100G27-40
Editorial: Hans-Böckler-Allee 9, 30173 HANNOVER
Tel: 511 73040 **Fax:** 511 7304157
Email: vkarow@online.de **Web site:** http://www.alu-web.de
Freq: 10 issues yearly; **Annual Sub.:** EUR 289,00; **Circ:** 4,521
Editor: Volker Karow
Profile: Publication containing facts, information and articles about aluminium.
Language(s): English; German
ADVERTISING RATES:
Full Page Mono .... EUR 2140
Full Page Colour .... EUR 3130
Mechanical Data: Type Area: 272 x 188 mm, No. of Columns (Display): 4, Col Widths (Display): 44 mm
Copy instructions: *Copy Date:* 14 days prior to publication
BUSINESS: METAL, IRON & STEEL

ALUMINIUM KURIER NEWS
1902493G27-3110
Editorial: Kirchplatz 8, 82538 GERETSRIED
Tel: 8171 911888 **Fax:** 8171 60974
Email: elgass@pse-redaktion.de **Web site:** http://www.alu-news.de
Freq: 6 issues yearly; **Annual Sub.:** EUR 51,65; **Circ:** 8,942
Editor: Stefan Elgaß; **Advertising Manager:** Monika Wagner
Profile: Aluminium Kurier News in 1996 as the first trade magazine for the production, processing and handling of materials aluminum and magnesium formed. Today, will virtually all light-treated and non-ferrous metals.The content is targeted at the technical implementation of the applications of materials and the industry-specific marketing. As a trade organ for the countries Austria, Switzerland and Germany, takes Aluminium Kurier News a leading market position. This claim is underscored by an international team of authors. Readers will appreciate the professional, market- and company-independent and, above all, a user-oriented reporting. The editorial staff also manages the magazine metallbau. A particularly intense research for the construction applications of aluminum is given. Thanks to a unique mix of topics with each issue, subscribers will receive the opportunity far beyond one's "own backyard". Innovative applications in other industrial and craft areas open to the readers the opportunity, proven technologies to improve their own production use.
Language(s): German
ADVERTISING RATES:
Full Page Mono .... EUR 1990
Full Page Colour .... EUR 3990
Mechanical Data: Type Area: 418 x 265 mm, No. of Columns (Display): 5, Col Widths (Display): 49 mm
Official Journal of: Organ d. Aluminium-Verbände Österr., Schweiz, Deutschland

ALUMINIUM LIEFERVERZEICHNIS
720103G27-80
Editorial: Am Bonneshof 5, 40474 DÜSSELDORF
Tel: 211 4796423 **Fax:** 211 4796424
Email: c.czech@alu-media.de **Web site:** http://www.alu-media.de
Freq: Annual; **Cover Price:** EUR 16,50; **Circ:** 20,000
Editor: Christiane Czech; **Advertising Manager:** Christiane Czech
Profile: Directory for aluminium processing.
Language(s): English; German
ADVERTISING RATES:
Full Page Mono .... EUR 2100
Full Page Colour .... EUR 3200
Mechanical Data: Type Area: 218 x 173 mm, No. of Columns (Display): 3, Col Widths (Display): 55 mm
Copy instructions: *Copy Date:* 45 days prior to publication

ALUMINIUM PRAXIS
720104G27-100
Editorial: Hans-Böckler-Allee 9, 30173 HANNOVER
Tel: 511 73040 **Fax:** 511 7304157
Email: alwin.schmitt@t-online.de **Web site:** http://www.alu-web.de
Freq: 10 issues yearly; **Annual Sub.:** EUR 68,00; **Circ:** 7,975
Editor: Alwin Schmitt; **Advertising Manager:** Dennis Roß
Profile: Magazine about the components, manufacture, uses and products of aluminium.
Language(s): German
Readership: Aimed at those involved in the metal industry.
ADVERTISING RATES:
Full Page Mono .... EUR 2080
Full Page Colour .... EUR 3070
Mechanical Data: Type Area: 385 x 270 mm, No. of Columns (Display): 6, Col Widths (Display): 40 mm
Copy instructions: *Copy Date:* 14 days prior to publication
Supplement(s): kataloge orange
BUSINESS: METAL, IRON & STEEL

ALZEYER WOCHENBLATT
720108G72-340
Editorial: Antoniterstr. 37, 55232 ALZEY
Tel: 6731 961356 **Fax:** 6731 961359
Email: redaktion@alzeyer-wochenblatt.de **Web site:** http://www.alzeyer-wochenblatt.de
Freq: Weekly; **Cover Price:** Free; **Circ:** 37,042
Editor: Rüdiger Benda; **Advertising Manager:** Rainer Baumann
Profile: Advertising journal (house-to-house) concentrating on local stories.
Language(s): German
ADVERTISING RATES:
Full Page Mono .... EUR 3495
Full Page Colour .... EUR 4704
Mechanical Data: Type Area: 480 x 325 mm, No. of Columns (Display): 7, Col Widths (Display): 45 mm
Copy instructions: *Copy Date:* 2 days prior to publication
LOCAL NEWSPAPERS

AMBERGER ZEITUNG
720117G67B-660
Editorial: Mühlgasse 2, 92224 AMBERG
Tel: 9621 306257 **Fax:** 9621 306250
Email: redaz@zeitung.org **Web site:** http://www.oberpfalznetz.de
Freq: 312 issues yearly; **Circ:** 26,411
Profile: Regional daily newspaper with news on politics, economy, culture, sports, travel, technology, etc. It is a regional edition of the newspaper "Der neue Tag". Facebook: http://www.facebook.com/oberpfalznetz Twitter: http://twitter.com/oberpfalznetz This Outlet offers RSS (Really Simple Syndication).
Language(s): German
ADVERTISING RATES:
SCC .... EUR 49,50
Mechanical Data: Type Area: 430 x 284 mm, No. of Columns (Display): 6, Col Widths (Display): 45 mm
Copy instructions: *Copy Date:* 1 day prior to publication
REGIONAL DAILY & SUNDAY NEWSPAPERS: Regional Daily Newspapers

AMERICA JOURNAL
720125G89A-11523
Editorial: Geisbergstr. 39, 10777 BERLIN
Tel: 30 28878980 **Fax:** 30 288789817
Email: redaktion@americajournal.de **Web site:** http://www.americajournal.de
Freq: 6 issues yearly; **Annual Sub.:** EUR 24,00; **Circ:** 31,500
Editor: Julia A. Latka; **Advertising Manager:** Benno M. Wildemann
Profile: Magazine about travel to and in North America, both for business and pleasure.
Language(s): German
Readership: Read by frequent travellers.
ADVERTISING RATES:
Full Page Mono .... EUR 3715
Full Page Colour .... EUR 4980
Mechanical Data: Type Area: 256 x 178 mm, No. of Columns (Display): 4, Col Widths (Display): 43 mm
Copy instructions: *Copy Date:* 30 days prior to publication
CONSUMER: HOLIDAYS & TRAVEL: Travel

AMG OWNERS CLUB
1826734G77A-2827
Editorial: Mariental 12, 99817 EISENACH
Tel: 3691 296336 **Fax:** 3691 296363
Email: info@amg-owners-club.org **Web site:** http://www.amg-owners-club.org
Freq: Half-yearly; **Cover Price:** EUR 4,00
Free to qualifying individuals ; **Circ:** 5,000
Editor: Frank Bode
Profile: Magazine on exclusive cars.
Language(s): German
ADVERTISING RATES:
Full Page Colour .... EUR 1295
Mechanical Data: Type Area: 297 x 210 mm, No. of Columns (Display): 3, Col Widths (Display): 62 mm
Copy instructions: *Copy Date:* 14 days prior to publication

AMG OWNERS CLUB
1826734G77A-2954
Editorial: Mariental 12, 99817 EISENACH
Tel: 3691 296336 **Fax:** 3691 296363
Email: info@amg-owners-club.org **Web site:** http://www.amg-owners-club.org
Freq: Half-yearly; **Cover Price:** EUR 4,00
Free to qualifying individuals ; **Circ:** 5,000
Editor: Frank Bode
Profile: Magazine on exclusive cars.
Language(s): German
ADVERTISING RATES:
Full Page Colour .... EUR 1295
Mechanical Data: Type Area: 297 x 210 mm, No. of Columns (Display): 3, Col Widths (Display): 62 mm
Copy instructions: *Copy Date:* 14 days prior to publication

AMICA
1620736G74A-3360
Editorial: Steinhauser Str. 1, 81677 MÜNCHEN
Tel: 89 92502404
Email: amica@tomorrow-focus.de **Web site:** http://www.amica.de
Cover Price: Paid; **Circ:** 255,183 Unique Users
Editor: Jochen Wegner
Profile: Ezine: Magazine covering fashion, health, beauty and women's lifestyle.
Language(s): German
CONSUMER: WOMEN'S INTEREST CONSUMER MAGAZINES: Women's Interest

AMPEL
1983782G1D-502
Editorial: Orensteinstr. 10, 56626 ANDERNACH
Tel: 2632 960459 **Fax:** 2632 960100
Email: info@ukrlp.de **Web site:** http://www.ukrlp.de
Freq: Quarterly; **Circ:** 9,000
Editor: Gerlinde Weidner-Theisen
Profile: Publication from the insurance company Unfallkasse Rheinland-Pfalz.
Language(s): German

AMTSBLATT
720263G80-14021
Editorial: Marktplatz 8, 97753 KARLSTADT
Tel: 9353 793113 **Fax:** 9353 793252
Email: poststelle@lramsp.de **Web site:** http://www.mainspessart.de
Freq: 28 issues yearly; **Circ:** 180
Profile: Official gazette from the communities of Landkreis Main-Spessart.
Language(s): German
CONSUMER: RURAL & REGIONAL INTEREST

AMZ AUTO MOTOR ZUBEHÖR
720708G31A-312
Editorial: Finkenstr. 2, 97264 HELMSTADT
Tel: 9369 9982171 **Fax:** 9369 9982172
Email: rinn@schluetersche.de **Web site:** http://www.amz.de
Freq: 10 issues yearly; Free to qualifying individuals
Annual Sub.: EUR 62,00; **Circ:** 25,794
Editor: Jürgen Rinn; **Advertising Manager:** Christian Welc
Profile: The trade magazine amz informed the executives and decision makers in the automotive industry and aftermarket about news from automotive technology, workshop technology and equipment. Furthermore amz provides tips, advice and reports from management, service marketing and sales. As a member of GVA amz reported on the automotive parts market as well as accessories and components industry.
Language(s): German
Readership: Read by manufacturers, distributors, wholesalers and retailers of automotive parts, accessories and workshop equipment.
ADVERTISING RATES:
Full Page Mono .... EUR 4865
Full Page Colour .... EUR 5975
Mechanical Data: Type Area: 272 x 188 mm, No. of Columns (Display): 3, Col Widths (Display): 60 mm
Copy instructions: *Copy Date:* 21 days prior to publication
Official Journal of: Organ d. Gesamtverb. Autoteilehandel e.V.
BUSINESS: MOTOR TRADE: Motor Trade Accessories

DER ANAESTHESIST
720713G56A-460
Editorial: Tiergartenstr. 17, 69121 HEIDELBERG
Tel: 6221 4878618 **Fax:** 6221 48768618
Email: werner.roessling@springer.com **Web site:** http://www.springermedizin.de
Freq: Monthly; **Annual Sub.:** EUR 352,00; **Circ:** 6,800
Advertising Manager: Odette Thomßen
Profile: Comprehensive review articles on selected topics access to anesthesiology-clinical problems. They also reflect the multidisciplinary environment in pharmacotherapy, intensive care, emergency medicine, regional anesthesia, pain management and medical law. In addition to the provision of relevant background knowledge, the focus is on the assessment of scientific results in the light of practical experience. The original papers presenting relevant clinical studies and serve the scientific exchange. Case reports show interesting case studies.
Language(s): German
Readership: Read by anaesthetists.
ADVERTISING RATES:
Full Page Mono .... EUR 1900
Full Page Colour .... EUR 3480
Mechanical Data: Type Area: 240 x 174 mm
Official Journal of: Organ d. Österr. Ges. f. Anästhesiologie, Reanimation u. Intensivtherapie, d. Dt. Ges. f. Anästhesiologie u. Intensivmedizin, d. Schweizer. Ges. f. Anästhesiologie u. Reanimation u. d. European Society of Anaesthesiology
BUSINESS: HEALTH & MEDICAL

ANALYTICAL AND BIOANALYTICAL CHEMISTRY
727978G55-3891
Editorial: Tiergartenstr. 17, 69121 HEIDELBERG
Tel: 6221 4878377 **Fax:** 6221 4878629
Email: abc@springer.com **Web site:** http://www.springerlink.com
Freq: 24 issues yearly; **Annual Sub.:** EUR 6219,00; **Circ:** 550
Editor: Christina E. Dyllick
Profile: Publication about analytical chemistry.
Language(s): English
ADVERTISING RATES:
Full Page Mono .... EUR 830
Full Page Colour .... EUR 1870
Mechanical Data: Type Area: 240 x 175 mm
BUSINESS: APPLIED SCIENCE & LABORATORIES

ANALYTISCHE KINDER- UND JUGENDLICHEN-PSYCHOTHERAPIE
720720G56A-480
Editorial: Kirschgartenstr. 1, 65719 HOFHEIM
Tel: 6192 21876
Email: redaktion-akjp@gmx.de
Freq: Quarterly; **Annual Sub.:** EUR 64,00; **Circ:** 2,500
Editor: Beate Kunze; **Advertising Manager:** Roland Apsel
Profile: Journal on psychoanalysis with children and adolescents.
Language(s): English; German
ADVERTISING RATES:
Full Page Mono .... EUR 680
Mechanical Data: Type Area: 180 x 110 mm
Copy instructions: *Copy Date:* 24 days prior to publication

ANDRÉ CITROËN-CLUB RUNDBRIEF
720743G77A-80
Editorial: Rheingauer Str. 8, 55122 MAINZ
Tel: 6131 41818 **Fax:** 6131 41817
Email: citroen-club@t-online.de **Web site:** http://www.andre-citroen-club.de
Freq: 6 issues yearly; Free to qualifying individuals
Annual Sub.: EUR 28,00; **Circ:** 4,100
Editor: Ulrich Brenken; **Advertising Manager:** Ulrich Brenken
Profile: Fan club magazine for Citroën automobiles.
Language(s): German
ADVERTISING RATES:
Full Page Mono .... EUR 390
Full Page Colour .... EUR 500
Mechanical Data: Type Area: 275 x 185 mm, No. of Columns (Display): 3, Col Widths (Display): 59 mm
Copy instructions: *Copy Date:* 30 days prior to publication

ANDROLOGIA
1639474G56A-11281
Editorial: Rotherstr. 21, 10245 BERLIN
Tel: 30 47031450 **Fax:** 30 47031410
Email: klaus.mickus@wiley.com **Web site:** http://www.wiley.com
Freq: 6 issues yearly; **Circ:** 1,100
Advertising Manager: Tobias Trinkel
Profile: Journal provides an international forum for original papers in English on the current clinical, morphological, biochemical, and experimental status of organic male infertility and sexual disorders in men.
Language(s): English
ADVERTISING RATES:
Full Page Mono .... EUR 920
Full Page Colour .... EUR 1700
Mechanical Data: Type Area: 240 x 170 mm, No. of Columns (Display): 2, Col Widths (Display): 80 mm
Copy instructions: *Copy Date:* 28 days prior to publication

ANGEWANDTE ARBEITSWISSENSCHAFT
753683G14A-170
Editorial: Uerdinger Str. 56, 40474 DÜSSELDORF
Tel: 211 5422628 **Fax:** 211 54226337
Email: p.blinn@ifaa-mail.de **Web site:** http://www.arbeitswissenschaft.net
Freq: Quarterly; **Annual Sub.:** EUR 18,20; **Circ:** 3,600
Editor: Petra Blinn
Profile: Magazine for business executives.
Language(s): German

ANGEWANDTE CHEMIE
720750G13-60
Editorial: Boschstr. 12, 69469 WEINHEIM
Tel: 6201 606315 **Fax:** 6201 606331
Email: angewandte@wiley-vch.de **Web site:** http://www.angewandte.de
Freq: Weekly; **Annual Sub.:** EUR 5941,71; **Circ:** 3,352
Editor: Peter Gölitz; **Advertising Manager:** Marion Schulz
Profile: The world's most renowned under the chemical trade journals give the reader an overview of new developments across the chemical. As a "Must" for everyone in the chemical research and development and for all who want to know today, such as the chemical products of tomorrow, reports it first-hand about the key findings of major research laboratories around the world, both in text and highlights / essays as well as in summary papers. Facebook: http://www.facebook.com/AngewandteChemie Twitter: http://twitter.com/#!/angew_chem This Outlet offers RSS (Really Simple Syndication).
Language(s): German
ADVERTISING RATES:
Full Page Mono .... EUR 3310
Full Page Colour .... EUR 4990
Mechanical Data: Type Area: 260 x 180 mm, No. of Columns (Display): 4, Col Widths (Display): 45 mm
Copy instructions: *Copy Date:* 17 days prior to publication
Supplement(s): ChemMedChem
BUSINESS: CHEMICALS

ANGEWANDTE SCHMERZTHERAPIE UND PALLIATIVMEDIZIN
1835225G56A-11548
Editorial: Aschauer Str. 30, 81549 MÜNCHEN
Tel: 89 2030431300 **Fax:** 89 2030431399
Email: doris.berger@springer.com **Web site:** http://www.astup.de
Freq: Quarterly; Free to qualifying individuals
Annual Sub.: EUR 85,50; **Circ:** 4,800
Editor: Doris Berger
Profile: The Journal of „Angewandte Schmerztherapie und Palliativmedizin" is distinguished by its holistic and interdisciplinary character. In well-understood contributions summarized the essence of original scientific publications for the day. The integration of the Deutschen Schmerzhilfe is using the journal link and communicator between therapists and those affected.
Language(s): German
ADVERTISING RATES:
Full Page Mono .... EUR 2210
Full Page Colour .... EUR 3400
Mechanical Data: Type Area: 240 x 174 mm
Official Journal of: Organ d. Dt. Akademie f. Ganzheitl. Schmerztherapie

ANNALISA
1818828G89A-12363
Editorial: Am Kanal, Geb. 59, 15749 MITTENWALDE
Tel: 33764 23000 **Fax:** 33764 23001
Email: info@annalisa.info **Web site:** http://www.annalisa.info
Freq: Half-yearly; **Cover Price:** EUR 4,80; **Circ:** 32,000
Editor: Anna L. Kern; **Advertising Manager:** Christoph Dietrich
Profile: Recommended beauty and wellness hotels, spas and holiday destinations in Europe.
Language(s): German
ADVERTISING RATES:
Full Page Colour .... EUR 1250
Mechanical Data: Type Area: 262 x 186 mm, No. of Columns (Display): 3, Col Widths (Display): 59 mm
Copy instructions: *Copy Date:* 30 days prior to publication

ANNALS OF FINANCE
1832416G14A-10125
Editorial: Tiergartenstr. 17, 69121 HEIDELBERG
Tel: 6221 4870 **Fax:** 6221 4878366
Email: werner.mueller@springer.com **Web site:** http://www.springerlink.com
Freq: Quarterly; **Annual Sub.:** EUR 338,00; **Circ:** 94
Editor: Charalambos D. Aliprantis
Profile: Economic theory.
Language(s): English
ADVERTISING RATES:
Full Page Mono .... EUR 740
Full Page Colour .... EUR 1780
Mechanical Data: Type Area: 200 x 130 mm

ANNALS OF HEMATOLOGY
720792G56A-600
Editorial: Carl-Neuberg-Str. 1, 30625 HANNOVER
Fax: 511 5328041
Email: ganser.arnold@mh-hannover.de **Web site:** http://www.springerlink.com
Freq: Monthly; **Annual Sub.:** EUR 2324,00; **Circ:** 320
Editor: Arnold Ganser
Profile: Magazine for medical professionals.
Language(s): English
ADVERTISING RATES:
Full Page Mono .... EUR 740
Full Page Colour .... EUR 1780
Mechanical Data: Type Area: 240 x 175 mm
Official Journal of: Organ d. Dt. u. d. Österr. Ges. f. Hämatologie u. Onkologie u. d. Ges. f. Thrombose u. Hämostaseforschung

ANNUAL MULTIMEDIA
720809G5F-35
Editorial: Schiffbauerdamm 5, 10117 BERLIN
Tel: 30 27572911 **Fax:** 30 27572920
Email: annual-multimedia@walhalla.de **Web site:** http://www.annual-multimedia.de
Freq: Annual; **Cover Price:** EUR 79,00; **Circ:** 3,000
Editor: Rebecca Roloff; **Advertising Manager:** Rebecca Roloff
Profile: The Annual Multimedia jury selects the best new-media productions of the year and commented on trends and ideas.
Language(s): German
ADVERTISING RATES:
Full Page Mono .... EUR 1300
Full Page Colour .... EUR 2300
Mechanical Data: Type Area: 240 x 180 mm

AN-ONLINE.DE
1620745G67B-16507
Editorial: Dresdener Str. 3, 52068 AACHEN
Tel: 241 5101357 **Fax:** 241 5101360
Email: u.kutsch@zva-digital.de **Web site:** http://www.an-online.de
Freq: Daily; **Cover Price:** Paid; **Circ:** 508,029 Unique Users
Editor: Ulrich Kutsch; **Advertising Manager:** Frank Mantler
Profile: Ezine: Regional daily newspaper covering politics, economics, culture, sports, travel and technology. Facebook: http://facebook.com/aachenernachrichten Twitter: http://twitter.com/#!/an_topnews This Outlet offers RSS (Really Simple Syndication).
Language(s): German
REGIONAL DAILY & SUNDAY NEWSPAPERS: Regional Daily Newspapers

ANSICHT
721660G32G-240
Editorial: Blücherstr. 62, 10961 BERLIN
Tel: 30 263094553 **Fax:** 30 26309324553
Email: awo-ansicht@awo.org **Web site:** http://www.awo.org
Freq: 6 issues yearly; **Annual Sub.:** EUR 6,42
Editor: Peter Kuleßa; **Advertising Manager:** Peter Kuleßa
Profile: Journal of the Arbeiterwohlfahrt with interviews, profiles, reports and reports from the field and in each case deals with a social and socio-political issue intensively.
Language(s): German
Mechanical Data: Type Area: 265 x 185 mm, No. of Columns (Display): 4, Col Widths (Display): 43 mm
BUSINESS: LOCAL GOVERNMENT, LEISURE & RECREATION: Community Care & Social Services

ANTRIEB
720849G45D-1
Editorial: Senator-Bömers-Str. 4, 28197 BREMEN
Tel: 421 5288314 **Fax:** 421 544949
Freq: Quarterly; Free to qualifying individuals
Annual Sub.: EUR 27,00; **Circ:** 1,400
Editor: Friedrich Eils; **Advertising Manager:** Friedrich Eils
Profile: Magazine focusing on shipping, shipyards and the maritime trade. Official journal of the Bremen Shipping Engineers' Society.
Language(s): German
Readership: Read by marine engineers.
ADVERTISING RATES:
Full Page Mono .... EUR 750
Full Page Colour .... EUR 1209
Mechanical Data: Type Area: 246 x 170 mm, No. of Columns (Display): 2, Col Widths (Display): 85 mm
Copy instructions: *Copy Date:* 21 days prior to publication
Official Journal of: Organ d. Vereins d. Schiffsingenieure in Bremen u. d. Vereinigung Dt. Schiffsingenieure
BUSINESS: MARINE & SHIPPING: Marine Engineering Equipment

ANTRIEBS PRAXIS
1703699G14R-6138
Editorial: Justus-von-Liebig-Str. 1, 86899 LANDSBERG **Tel:** 8191 125401 **Fax:** 8191 125483
Email: franz.graf@mi-verlag.de **Web site:** http://www.antriebspraxis.de
Freq: 7 issues yearly; **Annual Sub.:** EUR 68,00; **Circ:** 14,474
Editor: Franz Graf; **Advertising Manager:** Stefan Pilz
Language(s): German
ADVERTISING RATES:
Full Page Mono .... EUR 4690
Full Page Colour .... EUR 5450
Mechanical Data: Type Area: 257 x 178 mm, No. of Columns (Display): 4, Col Widths (Display): 41 mm
Copy instructions: *Copy Date:* 28 days prior to publication
BUSINESS: COMMERCE, INDUSTRY & MANAGEMENT: Commerce Related

ANTRIEBSTECHNIK
720850G19E-30
Editorial: Lise-Meitner-Str. 2, 55129 MAINZ
Tel: 6131 992345 **Fax:** 6131 992100
Email: d.schaar@vfmz.de **Web site:** http://www.industrie-service.de
Freq: 11 issues yearly; **Annual Sub.:** EUR 150,00; **Circ:** 15,575
Editor: Dirk Schaar; **Advertising Manager:** Oliver Jennen
Profile: antriebstechnik is for nearly 50 years the technical competent magazine for all ranges of the mechanical, thermal and electric drives as well as their controls and regulations. antriebstechnik is the most important platform for technical designers, operational fund technical designers as well as development engineers within the ranges production development, automation (above all Motion control and assembly and operations technology), as well as wider drivenear ranges was firmly established. In addition for example the renewable energies or also safe drive technology count. The annual extra charge Marktübersicht antriebstechnik provides a singular overview over the offer German and other European companies. Meaningfully structured tables with important technical data of individual products make this object to a unique working document.
Language(s): German
ADVERTISING RATES:
Full Page Mono .... EUR 4620
Full Page Colour .... EUR 5850
Mechanical Data: Type Area: 265 x 185 mm, No. of Columns (Display): 4, Col Widths (Display): 41 mm
Copy instructions: *Copy Date:* 14 days prior to publication
Official Journal of: Organ d. Forschungsvereinigung Antriebstechnik e.V.
BUSINESS: ENGINEERING & MACHINERY: Machinery, Machine Tools & Metalworking

ANWALT24.DE
1704275G74M-788
Editorial: Feldstiege 100, 48161 MÜNSTER
Tel: 2533 9300740 **Fax:** 2533 930015
Email: info@anwalt24.de **Web site:** http://www.anwalt24.de
Cover Price: Paid; **Circ:** 299,223 Unique Users
Profile: Web site with lawyers' and legal search engine and specialized information.
Language(s): German
CONSUMER: WOMEN'S INTEREST CONSUMER MAGAZINES: Personal Finance

ANWALTSBLATT
720855G44-3085
Editorial: Littenstr. 11, 10179 BERLIN
Tel: 30 726152141 **Fax:** 30 726152191
Email: anwaltsblatt@anwaltverein.de **Web site:** http://www.anwaltsblatt.de
Freq: 11 issues yearly; Free to qualifying individuals
Annual Sub.: EUR 132,00; **Circ:** 69,703
Editor: Nicolas Lührig
Profile: The Anwaltsblatt of attorney is a legal journal from the German Bar Association. Advocates inform lawyers about the latest developments in all areas of law. Focus is on the right lawyer, the lawyer and the lawyer liability compensation.
Language(s): German
ADVERTISING RATES:
Full Page Mono .... EUR 3950
Full Page Colour .... EUR 5450
Mechanical Data: Type Area: 252 x 175 mm, No. of Columns (Display): 3, Col Widths (Display): 55 mm
Copy instructions: *Copy Date:* 28 days prior to publication
BUSINESS: LEGAL

ANZEIGER EXTRA
720904G72-1468
Editorial: Franz-Tuczek-Weg 1, 35039 MARBURG
Tel: 6421 409243 **Fax:** 6421 409117
Email: info@mymedia.de **Web site:** http://www.mymedia.de

Cover Price: Free
Advertising Manager: Roger Schneider
Profile: Advertising journal (house-to-house) concentrating on local stories.
Language(s): German
LOCAL NEWSPAPERS

ANZEIGER FÜR BODENWERDER 720905G72-1472
Editorial: Große Str. 63, 37619 BODENWERDER
Tel: 5533 97460 **Fax:** 5533 9746633
Email: bodenwerder@dewezet.de
Freq: 14 issues yearly; **Cover Price:** Free; **Circ:** 8,350
Editor: Edda Dreyer; **Advertising Manager:** Michael Steuer
Profile: Newspaper containing information about Bodenwerder.
Language(s): German
ADVERTISING RATES:
Full Page Mono .... EUR 1729
Full Page Colour .... EUR 2761
Mechanical Data: Type Area: 430 x 281 mm, No. of Columns (Display): 6, Col Widths (Display): 45 mm
Copy instructions: *Copy Date:* 4 days prior to publication
LOCAL NEWSPAPERS

ANZEIGER FÜR DIE SEELSORGE 720921G87-800
Editorial: Hermann-Herder-Str. 4, 79104 FREIBURG
Tel: 761 2717407 **Fax:** 761 2717285
Email: anzeiger@herder.de **Web site:** http://www.anzeiger-fuer-die-seelsorge.de
Freq: 11 issues yearly; **Annual Sub.:** EUR 42,25; **Circ:** 10,391
Editor: Klaus Vellguth; **Advertising Manager:** Friederike Ward
Profile: Magazine about Catholic pastoral care.
Language(s): German
ADVERTISING RATES:
Full Page Mono .... EUR 1500
Full Page Colour .... EUR 2070
Mechanical Data: Type Area: 242 x 178 mm
CONSUMER: RELIGIOUS

ANZEIGER FÜR HARLINGERLAND 720924G67B-2100
Editorial: Am Markt 18, 26409 WITTMUND
Tel: 4462 989180 **Fax:** 4462 989199
Email: redaktion@harlinger.de **Web site:** http://www.harlinger.de
Freq: 312 issues yearly; **Annual Sub.:** EUR 25,20; **Circ:** 14,364
Editor: Klaus-Dieter Heimann; **Advertising Manager:** Horst-Wilhelm Lamberti
Profile: Daily newspaper with regional news and a local sports section.
Language(s): German
ADVERTISING RATES:
SCC .... EUR 35,40
Mechanical Data: Type Area: 420 x 282 mm, No. of Columns (Display): 6, Col Widths (Display): 45 mm
Copy instructions: *Copy Date:* 1 day prior to publication
Supplement(s): Kinderblatt; Moin Moin; Moin Moin; Moin Moin
REGIONAL DAILY & SUNDAY NEWSPAPERS: Regional Daily Newspapers

DER AO STEUER-BERATER 1609346G1A-3488
Editorial: Gustav-Heinemann-Ufer 58, 50968 KÖLN
Tel: 221 93738151 **Fax:** 221 93738902
Email: verlag@otto-schmidt.de **Web site:** http://www.aostb.de
Freq: Monthly; **Annual Sub.:** EUR 146,90; **Circ:** 1,258
Editor: Annette Stuhldreier; **Advertising Manager:** Thorsten Deuse
Profile: Magazine for tax advisors.
Language(s): German
ADVERTISING RATES:
Full Page Mono .... EUR 595
Full Page Colour .... EUR 1042
Mechanical Data: No. of Columns (Display): 2, Col Widths (Display): 88 mm, Type Area: 260 x 180 mm
BUSINESS: FINANCE & ECONOMICS

AOL.DE 1704276G18B-2123
Editorial: Zirkusweg 1, 20359 HAMBURG
Tel: 40 361590 **Fax:** 40 361597060
Email: aolkontakt@aol.com **Web site:** http://www.aol.de
Cover Price: Paid; **Circ:** 58,372,494 Unique Users
Editor: Andreas Demuth
Language(s): German
BUSINESS: ELECTRONICS: Telecommunications

AP APOTHEKEN PRAXIS 720995G37-1735
Editorial: Birkenwaldstr. 44, 70191 STUTTGART
Tel: 711 2582238 **Fax:** 711 2582290
Email: daz@deutscher-apotheker-verlag.de **Web site:** http://www.deutscher-apotheker-verlag.de
Freq: 6 issues yearly; **Circ:** 30,262
Editor: Peter Ditzel
Profile: Magazine containing information, interviews, health and product news, reports, comment and sales and marketing concepts concerning the pharmaceutical industry.
Language(s): German
Readership: Aimed at pharmacists.
Supplement to: DAZ Deutsche ApothekerZeitung

APÉRO 1792748G74P-1225
Editorial: Baumstr. 4, 80469 MÜNCHEN
Tel: 89 2002713 **Fax:** 89 20027150
Email: apero@fp-food.de **Web site:** http://www.apero-magazin.de
Freq: Quarterly; **Annual Sub.:** EUR 66,00; **Circ:** 25,000
Editor: Mechthild Piepenbrock-Fischer
Profile: Magazine for people who like to enjoy all facets of recipes, travel tips and portraits of interesting people.
Language(s): German
ADVERTISING RATES:
Full Page Mono .... EUR 5500
Full Page Colour .... EUR 5500
Mechanical Data: Type Area: 300 x 230 mm
Copy instructions: *Copy Date:* 46 days prior to publication

APHVMAGAZIN 736847G79C-4
Editorial: Vogelsrather Weg 27, 41366 SCHWALMTAL **Tel:** 2163 49760
Email: aphv@phil-creativ.de **Web site:** http://www.aphv.de
Freq: 11 issues yearly; **Circ:** 700
Editor: Wolfgang Maaßen
Profile: Magazine of the Association of German Stamp Traders.
Language(s): German
ADVERTISING RATES:
Full Page Mono .... EUR 240
Full Page Colour .... EUR 300
Mechanical Data: Type Area: 185 x 125 mm
Copy instructions: *Copy Date:* 21 days prior to publication
CONSUMER: HOBBIES & DIY: Philately

APOTHEKE + MARKETING 755595LI37-1
Editorial: Am Forsthaus Gravenbruch 5, 63263 NEU-ISENBURG **Tel:** 6102 5060 **Fax:** 6102 506394
Email: am-redaktion@springer.com **Web site:** http://www.apotheke-und-marketing.de
Freq: Monthly; **Annual Sub.:** EUR 50,00; **Circ:** 22,620
Editor: Gabi Kannamüller; **Advertising Manager:** Marion Bornemann
Profile: Journal aimed at the professionals in the community pharmacy, with particular attention on the magazine's professional information needs of the pharmacy manager. apotheke + marketing helps him with a strong service-oriented mix of targeted adequately prepared contributions to to establish the areas of marketing, management and business administration, his pharmacy as a health and counseling center and close to the future. In addition, the magazine offers the pharmacist the opportunity to qualify by attending a certified training in marketing and pharmaceutical industry, to continue professionally.
Language(s): German
ADVERTISING RATES:
Full Page Colour .... EUR 4390
Mechanical Data: Type Area: 242 x 176 mm, No. of Columns (Display): 2, Col Widths (Display): 88 mm
Copy instructions: *Copy Date:* 21 days prior to publication
BUSINESS: PHARMACEUTICAL & CHEMISTS

APOTHEKE.COM 1704277G94F-1888
Editorial: Neckarstr. 131, 70376 STUTTGART
Tel: 711 577190 **Fax:** 711 57719790
Email: redaktion@apotheke.com **Web site:** http://www.apotheke.com
Cover Price: Paid; **Circ:** 55,847 Unique Users
Language(s): German
CONSUMER: OTHER CLASSIFICATIONS: Disability

APOTHEKEN KURIER 720993G94H-520
Editorial: Gutenbergstr. 3, 99869 GÜNTHERSLEBEN-WECHMAR **Tel:** 36256 280130
Fax: 36256 280132
Email: stheinert@apothekenkurier.de **Web site:** http://www.apothekenkurier.de
Freq: Monthly; **Circ:** 215,412
Editor: Roswitha Eichhorn
Profile: Customer magazine distributed in pharmacies focusing on health and wellness.
Language(s): German
ADVERTISING RATES:
Full Page Mono .... EUR 7160
Full Page Colour .... EUR 9995
Mechanical Data: Type Area: 260 x 185 mm, No. of Columns (Display): 4, Col Widths (Display): 43 mm
CONSUMER: OTHER CLASSIFICATIONS: Customer Magazines

APOTHEKEN MAGAZIN 720994G37-420
Editorial: Duisburger Str. 375/C-Geb., 46049 OBERHAUSEN **Tel:** 208 8480224 **Fax:** 208 8480242
Email: birgit.voelkel@storckverlag.de **Web site:** http://www.storckverlag.de
Freq: 10 issues yearly; **Annual Sub.:** EUR 30,00; **Circ:** 21,262
Editor: Wilhelm Gössling
Profile: Magazine focusing on pharmaceutical matters.
Language(s): German
Readership: Aimed at pharmacists.
ADVERTISING RATES:
Full Page Mono .... EUR 3540
Full Page Colour .... EUR 3540
Mechanical Data: Type Area: 267 x 185 mm
Copy instructions: *Copy Date:* 42 days prior to publication
BUSINESS: PHARMACEUTICAL & CHEMISTS

APOTHEKEN RÄTSEL MAGAZIN 50+ 720997G94H-540
Editorial: Duisburger Str. 375/C-Geb., 46049 OBERHAUSEN **Tel:** 208 8480224 **Fax:** 208 8480242
Email: birgit.voelkel@storckverlag.de **Web site:** http://www.storckverlag.de
Freq: Monthly; **Cover Price:** Free; **Circ:** 91,700
Editor: Wilhelm Gössling; **Advertising Manager:** Birgit Völkel
Profile: Pharmacies - Customer magazine for diabetics and people aged 50 Age.
Language(s): German
ADVERTISING RATES:
Full Page Mono .... EUR 3500
Full Page Colour .... EUR 3500
Mechanical Data: Type Area: 180 x 133 mm, No. of Columns (Display): 3, Col Widths (Display): 40 mm
Copy instructions: *Copy Date:* 45 days prior to publication
CONSUMER: OTHER CLASSIFICATIONS: Customer Magazines

APOTHEKEN UMSCHAU - AUSG. A 720999G94H-580
Editorial: Konradshöhe, 82065 BAIERBRUNN
Tel: 89 744330 **Fax:** 89 74433330
Email: au@wortundbildverlag.de **Web site:** http://www.apotheken-umschau.de
Freq: Monthly; **Cover Price:** Free; **Circ:** 5,024,614
Editor: Peter Kanzler; **Advertising Manager:** Brigitta Hackmann
Profile: Customer magazine distributed in pharmacies focusing on health and wellness.
Language(s): German
ADVERTISING RATES:
Full Page Mono .... EUR 61850
Full Page Colour .... EUR 61850
Mechanical Data: Type Area: 256 x 184 mm, No. of Columns (Display): 4, Col Widths (Display): 40 mm
Copy instructions: *Copy Date:* 48 days prior to publication
CONSUMER: OTHER CLASSIFICATIONS: Customer Magazines

APOTHEKEN-DEPESCHE 720989G37-380
Editorial: Paul-Wassermann-Str. 15, 81829 MÜNCHEN **Tel:** 89 68073811 **Fax:** 89 681043
Email: monikawalter@t-online.de **Web site:** http://www.gfi-medien.de
Freq: 10 issues yearly; **Annual Sub.:** EUR 30,00; **Circ:** 21,649
Editor: Monika Walter; **Advertising Manager:** Jutta Jüttner
Profile: Magazine containing information, advice and details of new products.
Language(s): German
Readership: Aimed at pharmacists and chemist shop employees.
ADVERTISING RATES:
Full Page Mono .... EUR 2340
Full Page Colour .... EUR 3580
Mechanical Data: Type Area: 258 x 185 mm, No. of Columns (Display): 3, Col Widths (Display): 59 mm
Copy instructions: *Copy Date:* 21 days prior to publication
BUSINESS: PHARMACEUTICAL & CHEMISTS

APOTHEKENMANAGER 720860G37-180
Editorial: Solmsstr. 25, 60486 FRANKFURT
Tel: 69 79203372 **Fax:** 69 770638910
Email: sabine.lange@anzag.de **Web site:** http://www.anzag.de
Freq: 6 issues yearly; **Cover Price:** Free; **Circ:** 10,000
Editor: Sabine Lange
Profile: Magazine about pharmacy-marketing and management.
Language(s): German
ADVERTISING RATES:
Full Page Mono .... EUR 3900
Full Page Colour .... EUR 3900
Mechanical Data: Type Area: 220 x 200 mm

APOTHEKERKAMMER NACHRICHTEN 721002G37-540
Editorial: An der Markuskirche 4, 30163 HANNOVER
Tel: 511 390990 **Fax:** 511 3909936
Email: info@apothekerkammer-nds.de **Web site:** http://www.apothekerkammer-niedersachsen.de
Freq: Monthly; **Circ:** 6,800
Profile: Magazine containing news of the Pharmacist's Association of Lower Saxony.
Language(s): German
BUSINESS: PHARMACEUTICAL & CHEMISTS

APOTHEKERPLUS 1841069G56A-11553
Editorial: Am Forsthaus Gravenbruch 5, 63263 NEU-ISENBURG **Tel:** 6102 5060 **Fax:** 6102 58740
Email: info@aerztezeitung.de **Web site:** http://www.aerztezeitung.de
Freq: Monthly; **Circ:** 85,000
Editor: Christoph Winnat; **Advertising Manager:** Ute Krille
Profile: The interdisciplinary journal for pharmacists and physicians is a supplement of the Ärzte Zeitung. This Outlet offers RSS (Really Simple Syndication).
Language(s): German
ADVERTISING RATES:
Full Page Mono .... EUR 9230
Full Page Colour .... EUR 10950
Mechanical Data: Type Area: 390 x 286 mm
Copy instructions: *Copy Date:* 7 days prior to publication
Supplement to: Ärzte Zeitung

APPLIED CARDIOPULMONARY PATHOPHYSIOLOGY 1850029G56A-11555
Editorial: Ratzeburger Allee 160, 23538 LÜBECK
Email: m.heringlake@pabst-publishers.com
Freq: Quarterly; **Annual Sub.:** EUR 30,00; **Circ:** 1,900
Editor: M. Heringlake; **Advertising Manager:** Wolfgang Pabst
Profile: Journal on applied cardiopulmonary pathophysiology.
Language(s): English
ADVERTISING RATES:
Full Page Mono .... EUR 767
Full Page Colour .... EUR 1023
Mechanical Data: Type Area: 215 x 160 mm, No. of Columns (Display): 2, Col Widths (Display): 77 mm

APPLIED ECONOMICS QUARTERLY 733082G1R-2200
Editorial: Mohrenstr. 58, 10119 BERLIN
Tel: 30 89789227 **Fax:** 30 89789305
Email: cwey@diw.de **Web site:** http://aeq.diw.de
Freq: Quarterly; **Annual Sub.:** EUR 98,00; **Circ:** 330
Editor: Christian Wey; **Advertising Manager:** Arlett Günther
Profile: Journal about economics, contributing to rational economic policy on the basis of current theoretical and empirical findings.
Language(s): English
ADVERTISING RATES:
Full Page Mono .... EUR 450
Mechanical Data: Type Area: 185 x 115 mm
BUSINESS: FINANCE & ECONOMICS: Financial Related

APR AKTUELLE PAPIER-RUNDSCHAU 721021G36-1
Editorial: Industriestr. 2, 63150 HEUSENSTAMM
Tel: 6104 606111 **Fax:** 6104 606145
Email: g.brucker@kepplermediengruppe.de **Web site:** http://www.a-p-r.de
Freq: Monthly; **Annual Sub.:** EUR 198,00; **Circ:** 4,590
Editor: Gerhard W. Brucker; **Advertising Manager:** Marion Apitz
Profile: The apr is the overall highest circulation paper magazine in Germany and an indispensable magazine for decision makers in the paper business, providing commercial and technical terms. It impresses with timeliness, is independent, has economic vision, and is written by professionals for professionals. The extensive job market of the German paper magazine shows the acceptance and importance in the market.
Language(s): German
ADVERTISING RATES:
Full Page Colour .... EUR 3880
Mechanical Data: Type Area: 257 x 188 mm, No. of Columns (Display): 4, Col Widths (Display): 43 mm
BUSINESS: PAPER

APUS 721027G57-2705
Editorial: Postfach 730107, 06045 HALLE
Web site: http://www.osa-internet.de
Freq: 3 issues yearly; Free to qualifying individuals
Annual Sub.: EUR 25,00; **Circ:** 600
Editor: Robert Schönbrodt; **Advertising Manager:** Mark Schönbrodt
Profile: Regional magazine on environmental protection.
Language(s): German
Mechanical Data: Type Area: 200 x 134 mm, No. of Columns (Display): 2, Col Widths (Display): 64 mm

AQUA FORUM 1828671G57-2853
Editorial: Hauptstr. 19, 84168 AHAM
Tel: 8744 96120 **Fax:** 8744 961222
Email: info@wit-bayern.de **Web site:** http://www.wit-bayern.de
Freq: Half-yearly; **Circ:** 5,000
Editor: Bernd König
Profile: Customer magazine from the water supplier Wasser-Info-Team Bayern.
Language(s): German

AQUARISTIK VEREINT MIT AQUARIUM LIVE 721032G81E-2

Editorial: Weideweg 41, 49744 GEESTE
Tel: 5937 91553 **Fax:** 5937 91532
Email: f.bitter@daehne.de **Web site:** http://www.aquaristik-online.de
Freq: 6 issues yearly; **Annual Sub.:** EUR 29,50; **Circ:** 20,082
Editor: Friedrich Bitter; **Advertising Manager:** Thomas Heinen
Profile: aquaristik vereint mit Aquarium live is an attractive and practical magazine for every aquarist. The journal offers sound, reliable and easy to understand at the same contribution to all Issues of fresh water aquariums. Topics range from maintenance and breeding of ornamental fish species of aquarium words to trip reports and Shopping tips. We are regularly publish the authors recognized the aquarium. It lays great emphasis on the magazine a spacious and beautiful illustrations Photos. Vivid and informative, it is aimed at both beginners and professional aquarium lovers.
Language(s): German
ADVERTISING RATES:
Full Page Mono .... EUR 1415
Full Page Colour .... EUR 2945
Mechanical Data: Type Area: 250 x 189 mm, No. of Columns (Display): 4, Col Widths (Display): 43 mm
Copy instructions: *Copy Date:* 35 days prior to publication
CONSUMER: ANIMALS & PETS: Fish

ARA MAGAZIN 1615933G57-2674

Editorial: August-Bebel-Str. 16, 33602 BIELEFELD
Tel: 521 65943 **Fax:** 521 64975
Email: ara@araonline.de **Web site:** http://www.araonline.de
Freq: Quarterly; Free to qualifying individuals
Annual Sub.: EUR 10,00; **Circ:** 3,000
Editor: Wolfgang Kuhlmann
Profile: Publication containing information about projects supporting environmentally and socially compatible developments.
Language(s): German
ADVERTISING RATES:
Full Page Mono .... EUR 400
Full Page Colour .... EUR 400
Copy instructions: *Copy Date:* 20 days prior to publication

ARAB MEDICO 1654897G56A-11303

Editorial: Hülsdonker Str. 45b, 47441 MOERS
Email: bashar@assassa.de **Web site:** http://www.arab-medico.com
Freq: Quarterly; **Annual Sub.:** EUR 24,00; **Circ:** 21,000
Editor: Bashar Assassa; **Advertising Manager:** Andrea Parr
Profile: Medical journal in the Arabic language for patients and medical tourism.
Language(s): Arabic
ADVERTISING RATES:
Full Page Mono .... EUR 4680
Full Page Colour .... EUR 4680
Mechanical Data: Type Area: 250 x 178 mm, No. of Columns (Display): 2, Col Widths (Display): 67 mm
Copy instructions: *Copy Date:* 30 days prior to publication

ARAL AUTO-ATLAS 1740094G89A-12220

Editorial: Schleefstr. 1, 44287 DORTMUND
Tel: 231 444770 **Fax:** 231 4447777
Email: hauptredaktion@busche.de **Web site:** http://www.busche.de
Freq: Annual; **Cover Price:** EUR 15,95; **Circ:** 45,000
Advertising Manager: Jörg Leu
Profile: Groundbreaking and currently is the Aral Auto-Atlas. From Gibraltar to Riga and Dublin to Palermo: No line and no goal in Europe remains with the reliable "paper pilots" hidden. Motorways, highways, border crossings, tunnels and ferries are always clearly marked and fit in one - even for beginners - easy to read cartographic picture.
Language(s): German
ADVERTISING RATES:
Full Page Colour .... EUR 5600
Mechanical Data: Type Area: 295 x 210 mm

ARAL DEUTSCHLAND-ATLAS 1740095G89A-12221

Editorial: Schleefstr. 1, 44287 DORTMUND
Tel: 231 444770 **Fax:** 231 4447777
Email: hauptredaktion@busche.de **Web site:** http://www.busche.de
Freq: Annual; **Cover Price:** EUR 15,95; **Circ:** 52,379
Advertising Manager: Jörg Leu
Profile: The Aral Deutschland-Atlas is published annually, a major update and includes a universal maps, ideal for travel in business, on holiday or for leisure. The cartography offers the main roads and smaller roads and scenic routes. In all large cities and autonomous municipalities, the districts are called. Over 30,000 icons lead to selected attractions - Germany.
Language(s): German
Mechanical Data: Type Area: 295 x 210 mm

ARAL STRASSEN-ATLAS 1740096G89A-12222

Editorial: Schleefstr. 1, 44287 DORTMUND
Tel: 231 444770 **Fax:** 231 4447777
Email: hauptredaktion@busche.de **Web site:** http://www.busche.de
Freq: Annual; **Cover Price:** EUR 7,95; **Circ:** 180,000
Advertising Manager: Jörg Leu
Profile: The atlas is published annually, completely updated. The cartography is despite a wealth of information very easy to read. An ideal complement to the travel card Germany, the area maps. They provide a wide-ranging overview in busy areas with difficult road guides. Numerous City plans round out the product.
Language(s): German
Mechanical Data: Type Area: 297 x 210 mm

ARBEIT 721043G14R-6093

Editorial: Evinger Platz 17, 44339 DORTMUND
Tel: 231 8596241 **Fax:** 231 8596100
Email: ammon@sfs-dortmund.de **Web site:** http://www.zeitschriftarbeit.de
Freq: Quarterly; **Annual Sub.:** EUR 100,00; **Circ:** 500
Editor: Ursula Ammon
Profile: Publication which deals with work development, planning and work politics.
Language(s): German
ADVERTISING RATES:
Full Page Mono .... EUR 400
Mechanical Data: Type Area: 210 x 160 mm
Copy instructions: *Copy Date:* 35 days prior to publication
BUSINESS: COMMERCE, INDUSTRY & MANAGEMENT: Commerce Related

ARBEIT UND ARBEITSRECHT 721081G14A-9393

Editorial: Am Friedrichshain 22, 10407 BERLIN
Tel: 30 42151238 **Fax:** 30 42151300
Email: aua.redaktion@hussberlin.de **Web site:** http://www.arbeit-und-arbeitsrecht.de
Freq: Monthly; **Annual Sub.:** EUR 166,80; **Circ:** 7,914
Editor: Volker Hassel; **Advertising Manager:** Udo Magister
Profile: The journal „Arbeit und Arbeitsrecht" (AuA) is intended as a practical and indispensable guide to the modern human resource practices to meet the needs of executives. It plays a leading role among the major professional journals. Well-known authors, all practitioners, to report on current developments in the priority topics of labor law, personnel practices, wage and salary and social security law. AuA combines new trends in personnel management with comprehensive information to current case law and new regulations. The magazine provides experience from the corporate world and provides employment assistance in the form of checklists, model contracts, operating agreements, etc.
Language(s): German
ADVERTISING RATES:
Full Page Mono .... EUR 2350
Full Page Colour .... EUR 3520
Mechanical Data: Type Area: 260 x 185 mm
Copy instructions: *Copy Date:* 19 days prior to publication
BUSINESS: COMMERCE, INDUSTRY & MANAGEMENT

ARBEITNEHMER 721048G63-1758

Editorial: Fritz-Dobisch-Str. 6, 66111 SAARBRÜCKEN **Tel:** 681 4005402 **Fax:** 681 4005401
Email: presse@arbeitskammer.de **Web site:** http://www.arbeitnehmer-online.de
Freq: 8 issues yearly; **Annual Sub.:** EUR 7,50; **Circ:** 25,000
Editor: Peter Riede; **Advertising Manager:** Christina Baltes
Profile: Informative reports from the working world, interviews with experts on issues relating to the Saar workers, tips and information for the daily work. It also contains a lot of reading and knowing the labor and social rights, education, politics and cultural life.
Language(s): German
Readership: Read by members of the local business community.
ADVERTISING RATES:
Full Page Mono .... EUR 971
Full Page Colour .... EUR 971
Mechanical Data: Type Area: 247 x 178 mm
Copy instructions: *Copy Date:* 14 days prior to publication
BUSINESS: REGIONAL BUSINESS

ARBEITSMEDIZIN SOZIALMEDIZIN UMWELTMEDIZIN 721074G56A-620

Editorial: Forststr. 131, 70193 STUTTGART
Tel: 711 63672848 **Fax:** 711 63672711
Email: asu@gentnerverlag.de **Web site:** http://www.asu-arbeitsmedizin.com
Freq: Monthly; **Annual Sub.:** EUR 166,20; **Circ:** 3,306
Editor: Gerhard Triebig; **Advertising Manager:** Angela Grüssner
Profile: Arbeitsmedizin Sozialmedizin Umwelt (ASU) is the dominant medium in occupational medicine. Its quality is assured with a scientific editorial board, an advisory board and the recognized authors from science and practice. ASU provides information on current and advanced topics in Scientific and Practical occupational medicine.
Language(s): German
ADVERTISING RATES:
Full Page Mono .... EUR 2090
Full Page Colour .... EUR 3035
Mechanical Data: Type Area: 260 x 185 mm, No. of Columns (Display): 4, Col Widths (Display): 45 mm
Copy instructions: *Copy Date:* 25 days prior to publication
Official Journal of: Organ d. Dt. Ges. f. Arbeits- u. Umweltmedizin e.V., d. Österr. Ges. f. Arbeitsmedizin, d. Verb. Dt. Betriebs- u. Werkärzte e.V., d. Berufsverb. Dt. Arbeitsmediziner, d. Vereinigung Schweizer. Betriebsärzte, d. Vereinigung Dt. Staatl. Gewerbeärzte e.V., d. Akademie f. Arbeitsmedizin u. Gesundheitsschutz in d. Ärztekammer Berlin, d. Bayer. Akademie f. Arbeits-, Sozial- u. Umweltmedizin Mü., d. Sächs. Akademie f. ärztl. Fortbildung u. d. Sozial- u. Arbeitsmedizin. Akademie Baden-Württemberg e.V.
Supplement(s): ASUprotect; baua: Aktuell
BUSINESS: HEALTH & MEDICAL

DER ARBEITS-RECHTS-BERATER 755600G1A-3441

Editorial: Gustav-Heinemann-Ufer 58, 50968 KÖLN
Tel: 221 93738186 **Fax:** 221 93738906
Email: arbeitsrechtsberater@otto-schmidt.de **Web site:** http://www.arbrb.de
Freq: Monthly; **Annual Sub.:** EUR 156,90; **Circ:** 2,140
Editor: Petra Rülfing; **Advertising Manager:** Thorsten Deuse
Profile: Magazine containing information for lawyers specialised in labour law.
Language(s): German
ADVERTISING RATES:
Full Page Mono .... EUR 595
Full Page Colour .... EUR 1042
Mechanical Data: No. of Columns (Display): 2, Col Widths (Display): 88 mm, Type Area: 260 x 180 mm

ARCADE 721094G23A-15

Editorial: Weidestr. 120a, 22083 HAMBURG
Tel: 40 63201833 **Fax:** 40 6307510
Email: brit.dieckvoss@holzmann.de **Web site:** http://www.arcade-xxl.de
Freq: 6 issues yearly; **Annual Sub.:** EUR 51,36; **Circ:** 7,528
Editor: Brit Dieckvoß; **Advertising Manager:** Pia Russell
Profile: arcade is the premium magazine in the design-oriented interiors and covers the entire range of textile equipment, floor, lighting, furniture, over outdoor to the bathroom. Designers, industry players, trade fairs - national and international - Trends, Awards or scene, arcade is in reports, interviews and analysis on the market. And this in a sophisticated design environment - in XXL format. With its overarching concept that has created its own magazines genre, stands arcade as the only and unmistakable. You can reach with arcade an attention-grabbing image-laden advertising campaign that allows you to position your product targeted at the top interior designers, architects and planners of the upscale residential, property and office area as well as the high-quality retailers. The distribution is inter alia held in collaboration with the BDA and BDIA in Germany and the German-speaking countries.
Language(s): German
ADVERTISING RATES:
Full Page Mono .... EUR 4560
Full Page Colour .... EUR 6180
Mechanical Data: Type Area: 359 x 257 mm, No. of Columns (Display): 4, Col Widths (Display): 59 mm
Copy instructions: *Copy Date:* 30 days prior to publication
BUSINESS: FURNISHINGS & FURNITURE

ARCGUIDE.DE 1604958G4E-6892

Editorial: Ernst-Mey-Str. 8, 70771 LEINFELDEN-ECHTERDINGEN **Tel:** 711 7594334
Fax: 711 7594405
Email: jennifer.buehling@konradin.de **Web site:** http://www.arcguide.de
Freq: Quarterly; **Cover Price:** Free; **Circ:** 50,000
Editor: Jennifer Bühling
Profile: Magazine for architects, building engineers and students. Twitter: http://twitter.com/arcguide.
Language(s): German

ARCH+ 721186G4A-4

Editorial: Kurbrunnenstr. 22, 52066 AACHEN
Tel: 241 508302 **Fax:** 241 54831
Email: aachen@archplus.net **Web site:** http://www.archplus.net
Freq: Quarterly; **Annual Sub.:** EUR 49,00; **Circ:** 7,668
Editor: Sabine Kraft; **Advertising Manager:** Gabriele Lauscher-Dreess
Profile: Arch+ is an independent, conceptual magazine for architecture and urbanism. The name is also the program: more than architecture. Each issue is examined in depth a particular theme, and draws on current discussions in other disciplines in terms of architecture and urban issues. Founded in the wake of the 1968 upheaval, the focus of Arch+ on the critical reflection of social entitlement of architecture. The magazine sees itself as a catalyst experimental practices. Against this background, the redesign of Arch+ in 2008 the result of a substantive preparatory work began as part of the magazine project of Documenta 12, with the editors gradually the question of today's self-understanding and the potential of a critical architectural magazine as a mediator between architectural, cultural, political and social discourse has approached. So that goes against the backdrop of the Arch+ digital ubiquity of networked knowledge, again in search of new forms of knowledge to negotiate socially relevant architectural and urban problems. Arch+ now operates as a discourse platform in the fusion of different media such as magazine and exhibitions, prizes, symposia and event series, co.
Language(s): German
ADVERTISING RATES:
Full Page Mono .... EUR 2710
Full Page Colour .... EUR 4555
Mechanical Data: Type Area: 278 x 211 mm, No. of Columns (Display): 4, Col Widths (Display): 50 mm
Copy instructions: *Copy Date:* 21 days prior to publication
BUSINESS: ARCHITECTURE & BUILDING: Architecture

ARCHÄOLOGIE IN DEUTSCHLAND 721098G94X-600

Editorial: Reinsburgstr. 104, 70197 STUTTGART
Tel: 711 621803 **Fax:** 711 6150340
Email: wais@wais-und-partner.de **Web site:** http://www.aid-magazin.de
Freq: 8 issues yearly; **Annual Sub.:** EUR 69,90; **Circ:** 11,115
Editor: André Wais; **Advertising Manager:** Esther Herzhauser
Profile: The magazine reports on the cutting edge of archaeological research and lets sensational discoveries and fascinating insights, the distant worlds of our ancestors are alive again. The time frame of our modern science magazine is broad. It extends from the Incarnation up to Romans, Celts and Teutons, the Sky Disc of Nebra to the Cold War and it makes one thing clear: The Archeology of the 21 Century with all its many facets and disciplines is a high-tech science that can plunge, thanks to modern scientific method ever deeper into the mysteries of our distant past. In addition to a thematic focus in each issue we highlight the regularly appearing categories research, international, focus, reportage, news, and the window of Europe all aspects of the archaeological spectrum. In the comprehensive part "News from the Department of Archaeology," we report on the latest discoveries on your doorstep. Unique profile of the magazine is alive, her profound bridge the gap between science and the public. All reports are from first-hand by the excavators and researchers themselves, and are implemented by a competent editorial in clear, easily understandable and varied contributions.
Language(s): German
ADVERTISING RATES:
Full Page Mono .... EUR 1390
Full Page Colour .... EUR 1990
Mechanical Data: Type Area: 254 x 190 mm, No. of Columns (Display): 3, Col Widths (Display): 51 mm
Copy instructions: *Copy Date:* 75 days prior to publication
CONSUMER: OTHER CLASSIFICATIONS: Miscellaneous

ARCHÄOLOGISCHES NACHRICHTENBLATT 721111G94J-711

Editorial: Schloß Charlottenburg, Langhansbau, 14059 BERLIN **Tel:** 30 32674816 **Fax:** 30 32674812
Email: pdva-berlin@t-online.de **Web site:** http://anb.akademie-verlag.de
Freq: Quarterly; **Annual Sub.:** EUR 66,80; **Circ:** 1,000
Editor: Heino Neumayer; **Advertising Manager:** Christina Gericke
Profile: Magazine containing news and information about archaeology.
Language(s): German
ADVERTISING RATES:
Full Page Mono .... EUR 880
Mechanical Data: Type Area: 202 x 131 mm
Official Journal of: Organ d. dt. Verbände f. Archäologie
CONSUMER: OTHER CLASSIFICATIONS: Popular Science

DIE ARCHE 1829966G57-2855

Editorial: Heilig-Kreuz-Str. 6, 86152 AUGSBURG
Tel: 821 37695 **Fax:** 821 514787
Email: bn_kg_augsburg@augustakom.net **Web site:** http://www.bund-naturschutz-augsburg.de
Freq: Half-yearly; **Circ:** 5,000
Editor: Paul Reisbacher
Profile: Witg Die Arche, the group in Augsburg will take care of the natural order and thus the health of people in the county and the city of Augsburg. Our big concern is, nature protection is human protection. If the soil, air and water by human interventions are not overused, can we get in our future livelihood.
Language(s): German

DIE ARCHE 1829966G57-2940

Editorial: Heilig-Kreuz-Str. 6, 86152 AUGSBURG
Tel: 821 37695 **Fax:** 821 514787
Email: bn_kg_augsburg@augustakom.net **Web site:** http://www.bund-naturschutz-augsburg.de
Freq: Half-yearly; **Circ:** 5,000
Editor: Paul Reisbacher
Profile: Witg Die Arche, the group in Augsburg will take care of the natural order and thus the health of people in the county and the city of Augsburg. Our big concern is, nature protection is human protection. If the soil, air and water by human interventions are not overused, can we get in our future livelihood.
Language(s): German

DER ARCHITEKT 1833364G4A-243

Editorial: Köpenicker Str. 48, 10179 BERLIN
Tel: 30 27879917 **Fax:** 30 27879915

Email: redaktion@bdada.de **Web site:** http://www.bdada.de
Freq: 6 issues yearly; Free to qualifying individuals
Annual Sub.: EUR 49,90; **Circ:** 6,228
Editor: Andreas Denk
Profile: „der architekt" is the journal of the Association of German Architects BDA. It reaches all members of the BDA, all the architecture professors, the senior staff of the planning and building departments of government, heads of the building departments of large companies, banks, insurance companies and property developers, but also executives in particular the construction, financial and real estate industry and the interested public.
Language(s): German
ADVERTISING RATES:
Full Page Mono .... EUR 2800
Full Page Colour .... EUR 2800
Mechanical Data: Type Area: 255 x 184 mm
Copy instructions: *Copy Date:* 20 days prior to publication

ARCHIV DER PHARMAZIE

721141G37-560
Editorial: Max-von-Laue-Str. 9, 60438 FRANKFURT
Tel: 69 79829302 **Fax:** 69 79829258
Email: h.stark@pharmchem.uni-frankfurt.de **Web site:** http://www.archpharm.de
Freq: Monthly; **Annual Sub.:** EUR 1523,00; **Circ:** 700
Editor: Holger Stark; **Advertising Manager:** Prisca Henheik
Profile: Journal on research and development in pharmaceutical chemistry.
Language(s): English
Official Journal of: Organ d. Pharmazeut. Ges., d. Ges. Dt. Chemiker, Fachgruppe Medizin. Chemie

ARCHIV FÜR LEBENSMITTELHYGIENE

721172G22R-20
Editorial: Schönleuthnerstr. 8, 85764 OBERSCHLEISSHEIM
Email: milchhygiene@mh.vetmed.uni-muenchen.de
Freq: 6 issues yearly; **Annual Sub.:** EUR 146,80; **Circ:** 924
Editor: Erwin Märtlbauer; **Advertising Manager:** Bettina Kruse
Profile: Publication focusing on meat, fish and milk hygiene.
Language(s): German
Readership: Read by veterinarians, scientists and others involved in hygiene and food research as well as town and district administrators.
ADVERTISING RATES:
Full Page Mono .... EUR 928
Full Page Colour .... EUR 1400
Mechanical Data: Type Area: 297 x 210 mm, No. of Columns (Display): 4, Col Widths (Display): 44 mm
Copy instructions: *Copy Date:* 21 days prior to publication
Official Journal of: Organ d. Arbeitsgebietes Lebensmittelhygiene d. DVG
BUSINESS: FOOD: Food Related

ARCHIVE OF APPLIED MECHANICS

721146G19A-60
Editorial: Postfach 330440, 28334 BREMEN
Email: aam_eic@mechanik.uni-bremen.de **Web site:** http://www.springerlink.com
Freq: Monthly; **Annual Sub.:** EUR 2476,00; **Circ:** 125
Editor: Reinhold Kienzler
Profile: Archive of applied mechanics.
Language(s): English
ADVERTISING RATES:
Full Page Mono .... EUR 740
Full Page Colour .... EUR 1780
Mechanical Data: Type Area: 240 x 175 mm

ARCHIVES OF DERMATOLOGICAL RESEARCH

721151G56A-640
Editorial: Schittenhelmstr. 7, 24105 KIEL
Email: umrowietz@dermatology.uni-kiel.de **Web site:** http://www.springerlink.com
Freq: 10 issues yearly; **Annual Sub.:** EUR 1817,00; **Circ:** 302
Editor: Ulrich Mrowietz
Profile: Archives of dermatological research.
Language(s): English
ADVERTISING RATES:
Full Page Mono .... EUR 830
Full Page Colour .... EUR 1870
Mechanical Data: Type Area: 240 x 175 mm

ARCHIVES OF GYNECOLOGY AND OBSTETRICS

1638471G56A-11274
Editorial: Tiergartenstr. 17, 69121 HEIDELBERG
Tel: 6221 4870 **Fax:** 6221 4878366
Email: subscriptions@springer.com **Web site:** http://www.springerlink.com
Freq: Monthly; **Annual Sub.:** EUR 2325,00; **Circ:** 72
Editor: H. Ludwig
Profile: Archives of gynaecology and obstetrics.
Language(s): English
ADVERTISING RATES:
Full Page Mono .... EUR 740
Full Page Colour .... EUR 1780
Mechanical Data: Type Area: 240 x 175 mm
Official Journal of: Organ d. Dt. Ges. f. Gynäkologie u. Geburtshilfe

ARCHIVES OF ORTHOPAEDIC AND TRAUMA SURGERY

721154G56A-680
Editorial: Tiergartenstr. 17, 69121 HEIDELBERG
Tel: 6221 4870 **Fax:** 6221 4878366
Email: gabriele.schroeder@springer.com **Web site:** http://www.springerlink.com
Freq: Monthly; **Annual Sub.:** EUR 3252,00; **Circ:** 348
Editor: J. Goldhahn
Profile: "Archives of Orthopaedic and Trauma Surgery" is a rich source of instruction and information for physicians in clinical practice and research in the extensive field of orthopaedics and traumatology. The journal publishes papers that deal with diseases and injuries of the musculoskeletal system from all fields and aspects of medicine. The journal is particularly interested in papers that satisfy the information needs of orthopaedic clinicians and practitioners. The journal places special emphasis on clinical relevance.
Language(s): English
ADVERTISING RATES:
Full Page Mono .... EUR 740
Full Page Colour .... EUR 1780
Mechanical Data: Type Area: 240 x 175 mm
Official Journal of: Official journal of the German Speaking Arthroscopy Association

ARCHIVES OF TOXICOLOGY

721155G56A-700
Editorial: Ardeystr. 67, 44139 DORTMUND
Fax: 231 1084403
Email: archtox@ifado.de **Web site:** http://www.springerlink.com
Freq: Monthly; **Annual Sub.:** EUR 3527,00; **Circ:** 133
Editor: J. G. Hengstler
Profile: Archives of toxicology.
Language(s): English
ADVERTISING RATES:
Full Page Mono .... EUR 740
Full Page Colour .... EUR 1780
Mechanical Data: Type Area: 240 x 175 mm

ARCHIVES OF WOMEN'S MENTAL HEALTH

1852999A56A-2037
Editorial: Tiergartenstr. 17, 69121 HEIDELBERG
Tel: 6221 4878335 **Fax:** 6221 4878658
Email: hilde.haala@springer.com **Web site:** http://www.springer.com
Freq: 6 issues yearly; **Circ:** 1,000
Editor: M. Steiner
Profile: Journal of the Section on Women's Mental Health of the World Psychiatric Association.
Language(s): English
ADVERTISING RATES:
Full Page Mono .... EUR 1330
Full Page Colour .... EUR 2394
Mechanical Data: Type Area: 230 x 170 mm

ARCOR MAGAZIN

721189G18B-100
Editorial: Alfred-Herrhausen-Allee 1, 65760 ESCHBORN **Tel:** 69 21693211 **Fax:** 69 21693027
Email: michael.peter@arcor.net **Web site:** http://www.presse.arcor.net
Freq: 3 issues yearly; **Circ:** 25,000
Editor: Michael Peter
Profile: Company publication published by Arcor.
Language(s): German
ADVERTISING RATES:
Full Page Mono .... EUR 3100
Full Page Colour .... EUR 3100
Mechanical Data: No. of Columns (Display): 2, Col Widths (Display): 71 mm, Type Area: 228 x 175 mm
Copy instructions: *Copy Date:* 14 days prior to publication

ARD BUFFET

1659535G74P-1144
Editorial: Büschstr. 2, 20354 HAMBURG
Tel: 40 30706411 **Fax:** 40 32526481
Email: ardbuffet@burda.com **Web site:** http://www.ard-buffet.de
Freq: Monthly; **Annual Sub.:** EUR 29,40; **Circ:** 171,599
Editor: Angelika Puls
Profile: On TV (Monday to Friday over a million viewers per show) and as a printed magazine - ARD Buffet attracts many years a large fan base in their spell. ARD Buffet magazine, the monthly companion magazine to the broadcast, is enjoying increasing popularity and now occupies a top position in the food and beverage magazines. The focus of the large-format specifications are the creative and easily implementable recipes: fresh, seasonal ingredients are combined in a surprising new and classic recipe to do a revival. Current decorating ideas for home, garden and table decorations give suggestions to relax and enjoy. The great advice section provides comprehensive information on health issues, clarifies the latest jurisdictions and offer tips on home and garden. We also provide you in every issue from an interesting destination, and a report on our ARD experts and knowledge about traditional crafts. This offers an interesting view ARD Buffet behind the scenes - a man and artist from the show and introduce yourself, what they stand for. And that's just quality of life - a boon for body and soul. Facebook: http://www.facebook.com/pages/ARD-Buffet/175685132455134.
Language(s): German
ADVERTISING RATES:
Full Page Mono .... EUR 11000
Full Page Colour .... EUR 11000
Mechanical Data: Type Area: 284 x 214 mm
CONSUMER: WOMEN'S INTEREST CONSUMER MAGAZINES: Food & Cookery

ARD JAHRBUCH

721195G2A-5411
Editorial: Bertramstr. 8, 60320 FRANKFURT
Tel: 69 15687211 **Fax:** 69 15687100
Email: ardjahrbuch@hr-online.de **Web site:** http://www.dra.de
Freq: Annual; **Cover Price:** EUR 9,00; **Circ:** 19,000
Editor: Doris Rehme-Lauer
Profile: Every year is the new ARD Jahrbuch a summary overview of what's happening in and around the ARD, during the previous year. Whatever happened in importance in the Chronicle, the Section "competitions and events" and the various reports in a concentrated form it is read again, of political and financial issues to the program events and reforms. Whatever manifests itself in figures - finances, program output, the media research data - is in the "Statistics" documents. The section "Organization and Personnel" is like every year the current "Who's Who" of ARD dar. Here are the addresses, legal bases and identities of the ARD, its members, community programs and facilities, advertising and daughters look up investments. Useful as usual: the sections entitled "Document" and "register" the ARD Jahrbuch. The index can be around 2,500 people, nearly 1,000 program titles and more than 1,100 issues from the entire book.
Language(s): German

ARGUMENTE + FAKTEN DER MEDIZIN

721207G56A-720
Editorial: Friedensallee 30, 63263 NEU-ISENBURG
Tel: 6102 71570 **Fax:** 6102 715771
Email: redaktion@linguamed.de **Web site:** http://www.linguamed.de
Freq: Monthly; **Annual Sub.:** EUR 29,95; **Circ:** 10,833
Editor: Karin Wilbrand; **Advertising Manager:** Karin Wilbrand
Profile: Since April 1991, regularly published a magazine for the young general practitioners and internists: "Argumente + Fakten der Medizin". The magazine is sent to a selected medical audience. Category A doctors' offices (more than 4 employees), year of birth of the practice owner after 1950, specialized in general medicine physicians and internists are the underlying selection criteria. Argumente + Fakten der Medizin contains practical information on new research findings of the medical and pharmaceutical products, mainly found the pathophysiology of the particular disease and the pharmacologically influenced pathomechanisms strong consideration. The magazine is an indispensable resource for practitioners who can learn in short and concise articles particularly time-saving on the current trends in medical and pharmacological research.
Language(s): German
Readership: Read by internists and people working in the medical profession.
ADVERTISING RATES:
Full Page Mono .... EUR 2570
Full Page Colour .... EUR 3815
Mechanical Data: Type Area: 255 x 174 mm, No. of Columns (Display): 3, Col Widths (Display): 54 mm
Copy instructions: *Copy Date:* 21 days prior to publication
BUSINESS: HEALTH & MEDICAL

ARIVA.DE

1660890G1C-1451
Editorial: Walkerdamm 17, 24103 KIEL
Tel: 431 971080 **Fax:** 431 9710829
Email: info@ariva.de **Web site:** http://www.ariva.de
Freq: Daily; **Cover Price:** Paid; **Circ:** 4,907,505 Unique Users
Language(s): German
BUSINESS: FINANCE & ECONOMICS: Banking

ARMBAND UHREN

721224G79K-100
Editorial: Friesenheimer Str. 18, 68169 MANNHEIM
Tel: 621 712202 **Fax:** 621 3214459
Email: p.braun@heel-verlag.de
Freq: 7 issues yearly; **Annual Sub.:** EUR 54,00; **Circ:** 12,470
Editor: Peter Braun; **Advertising Manager:** Sabine Blüm
Profile: Journal for friends and collectors of fine wristwatches, imagination v. News and classics. Positioned in the segment of sophisticated special-interest publication for high-profile men target groups.
Language(s): German
Readership: Read by watch collectors.
ADVERTISING RATES:
Full Page Mono .... EUR 3650
Full Page Colour .... EUR 5150
Mechanical Data: Type Area: 256 x 175 mm, No. of Columns (Display): 4, Col Widths (Display): 43 mm
Copy instructions: *Copy Date:* 35 days prior to publication
CONSUMER: HOBBIES & DIY: Collectors Magazines

ART

721238G84A-360
Editorial: Am Baumwall 11, 20459 HAMBURG
Tel: 40 37030 **Fax:** 40 37035618
Email: kunst@art-magazin.de **Web site:** http://www.art-magazin.de
Freq: Monthly; **Annual Sub.:** EUR 86,40; **Circ:** 51,524
Editor: Tim Sommer; **Advertising Manager:** André Freiheit
Profile: Magazine containing information about all aspects of art. Twitter: http://twitter.com/art_magazin.
Language(s): German
ADVERTISING RATES:
Full Page Mono .... EUR 13200
Full Page Colour .... EUR 13200
Mechanical Data: Type Area: 252 x 178 mm
Copy instructions: *Copy Date:* 42 days prior to publication
CONSUMER: THE ARTS & LITERARY: Arts

ARTHRITIS + RHEUMA

721245G56A-740
Editorial: Hölderlinstr. 3, 70174 STUTTGART
Tel: 711 2298735 **Fax:** 711 2298765
Email: claudia.stein@schattauer.de **Web site:** http://www.arthritis-und-rheuma-online.de
Freq: 6 issues yearly; **Annual Sub.:** EUR 126,00; **Circ:** 7,606
Editor: Claudia Stein; **Advertising Manager:** Christoph Brocker
Profile: For a rapid transfer of knowledge from the clinic in the practice sets the arthritis + rheuma to latest research findings in the fields of orthopedics / traumatology and rheumatology / immunology into understandable, practical training. Carefully designed special issues in the form of scientific original and review articles or exemplary case reports reliably inform readers about the latest diagnostic and therapeutic developments of major diseases. Particularly relevant topics are picked on arthritis + rheuma also in regular series. For quick orientation are short, topical conference reports, literature reports of the most reputable publications, and respectable news from research and industry.
Language(s): German
Readership: Read by the members of the medical profession.
ADVERTISING RATES:
Full Page Mono .... EUR 1895
Full Page Colour .... EUR 3085
Mechanical Data: Type Area: 243 x 179 mm, No. of Columns (Display): 3, Col Widths (Display): 57 mm
Copy instructions: *Copy Date:* 40 days prior to publication
Official Journal of: Organ d. VRA (Verb. Rheumatolog. Akutkliniken e.V.) u. d. GKJR (Ges. f. Kinder- u. Jugendrheumatologie)
BUSINESS: HEALTH & MEDICAL

ARTHROSE NACHRICHTEN

1898897G56A-11597
Editorial: Otto-Hahn-Str. 7, 50997 KÖLN
Tel: 2236 376562 **Fax:** 2236 376101
Email: hoefele@biermann.net **Web site:** http://www.biermann.net
Freq: Half-yearly; **Cover Price:** Free; **Circ:** 10,000
Editor: Felix Höfele
Profile: The magazine „Arthrose Nachrichten" based in part on patients and their relatives, which will help the content to understand the disease arthritis better and cope better with it. Second, to general practitioners and specialists are will informed. The journal is published semi-annually to the two major congresses of Orthopedics and Traumatology.
Language(s): German
ADVERTISING RATES:
Full Page Mono .... EUR 2995
Full Page Colour .... EUR 2995
Mechanical Data: Type Area: 242 x 162 mm
Copy instructions: *Copy Date:* 53 days prior to publication

ARTHROSE NACHRICHTEN

1898897G56A-11721
Editorial: Otto-Hahn-Str. 7, 50997 KÖLN
Tel: 2236 376562 **Fax:** 2236 376101
Email: hoefele@biermann.net **Web site:** http://www.biermann.net
Freq: Half-yearly; **Cover Price:** Free; **Circ:** 10,000
Editor: Felix Höfele
Profile: The magazine „Arthrose Nachrichten" based in part on patients and their relatives, which will help the content to understand the disease arthritis better and cope better with it. Second, to general practitioners and specialists are will informed. The journal is published semi-annually to the two major congresses of Orthopedics and Traumatology.
Language(s): German
ADVERTISING RATES:
Full Page Mono .... EUR 2995
Full Page Colour .... EUR 2995
Mechanical Data: Type Area: 242 x 162 mm
Copy instructions: *Copy Date:* 53 days prior to publication

ARTHROSKOPIE

721247G56A-780
Editorial: Tiergartenstr. 17, 69121 HEIDELBERG
Tel: 6221 4878731 **Fax:** 6221 48768731
Email: isabelle.duerk@springer.com **Web site:** http://www.springermedizin.de
Freq: Quarterly; **Annual Sub.:** EUR 217,00; **Circ:** 3,450
Editor: Andreas B. Imhoff; **Advertising Manager:** Noëla Krischer-Janka
Profile: Arthroskopie offers up-to-date review articles and original papers for all medical doctors and scientists working in the field of arthroscopy. The focus is on current developments regarding endoscopic examination and surgery of the joints, diagnostic and therapeutic possibilities of related methods, e.g. minimal invasive surgery. Freely submitted original papers allow the presentation of important clinical studies and serve scientific

exchange. Comprehensive reviews on a specific topical issue provide evidenced based information on diagnostics and therapy.
Language(s): German
ADVERTISING RATES:
Full Page Mono .... EUR 1812
Full Page Colour .... EUR 2852
Mechanical Data: Type Area: 240 x 174 mm
Official Journal of: Organ d. Dt.-sprachigen ArGe f. Arthroskopie u. d. Bundesverb. f. ambulante Arthroskopie e.V.

ARZNEIMFORSCH DRUGRES ARZNEIMITTEL FORSCHUNG DRUG RESEARCH
721259G37-600
Editorial: Baendelstockweg 20, 88326 AULENDORF
Tel: 7525 940122 **Fax:** 7525 940127
Email: redaktion@ecv.de **Web site:** http://www.ecv.de
Freq: Monthly; **Annual Sub.:** EUR 384,00; **Circ:** 1,158
Editor: Hans-Georg Classen; **Advertising Manager:** Judith Scheller
Profile: Journal focusing on biotechnology in drug research.
Language(s): English; German
Readership: Aimed at those within the pharmaceutical sector.
ADVERTISING RATES:
Full Page Mono .... EUR 850
Full Page Colour .... EUR 1750
Mechanical Data: Type Area: 270 x 187 mm, No. of Columns (Display): 4, Col Widths (Display): 46 mm
BUSINESS: PHARMACEUTICAL & CHEMISTS

ARZNEIMITTEL ZEITUNG
721261G37-580
Editorial: Am Forsthaus Gravenbruch 5, 63263 NEU-ISENBURG **Tel:** 6102 506136 **Fax:** 6102 506220
Email: info@aerztezeitung.de **Web site:** http://www.aerztezeitung.de
Freq: Monthly; **Annual Sub.:** EUR 50,00; **Circ:** 3,600
Editor: Bertold Schmitt-Feuerbach; **Advertising Manager:** Ute Krille
Profile: The Arzneimittel Zeitung is the newspaper for makers and employees in the pharmaceutical industry. Industry-specific it informed about health and pharmaceutical policies, to companies and associations, markets and products, management, marketing and sales, advertising and public relations, research and approval.
Language(s): German
Readership: Aimed at pharmacists and chemists.
ADVERTISING RATES:
Full Page Mono .... EUR 4800
Full Page Colour .... EUR 5700
Mechanical Data: Type Area: 408 x 291 mm, No. of Columns (Display): 5, Col Widths (Display): 55 mm
Copy instructions: *Copy Date:* 7 days prior to publication
Supplement(s): Pharma Kommunikation
BUSINESS: PHARMACEUTICAL & CHEMISTS

DER ARZNEIMITTELBRIEF
721258G56A-840
Editorial: Potsdamer Str. 17, 12205 BERLIN
Tel: 30 84314361 **Fax:** 30 84314362
Email: info@der-arzneimittelbrief.de **Web site:** http://www.der-arzneimittelbrief.de
Freq: Monthly; **Annual Sub.:** EUR 48,00; **Circ:** 15,000
Editor: Dietrich von Herrath
Profile: Der Arzneimittelbrief informs physicians, medical students, pharmacists and other health professionals about the benefits and risks of medicines. Der Arzneimittelbrief appears as an independent journal without advertisements of the pharmaceutical industry. It is funded solely by its readers, ie by the subscribers.
Language(s): German
Readership: Aimed at doctors in clinics and practices, pharmacists and medical students.
BUSINESS: HEALTH & MEDICAL

ARZNEIMITTELTHERAPIE
720169G56A-420
Editorial: Birkenwaldstr. 44, 70191 STUTTGART
Tel: 711 2582234 **Fax:** 711 2582283
Email: amt@wissenschaftliche-verlagsgesellschaft.de **Web site:** http://www.arzneimitteltherapie.de
Freq: 11 issues yearly; **Annual Sub.:** EUR 92,90; **Circ:** 17,080
Editor: Heike Oberpichler-Schwenk; **Advertising Manager:** Kornelia Wind
Profile: Arzneimitteltherapie is concerned mainly with all aspects of drug therapy in the clinic. Arzneimitteltherapie is aimed primarily at chief and senior physicians in clinics and hospital pharmacy managers, so the clinic that is determined and represented in the therapy of the Drug Commission of the clinic.
Language(s): German
ADVERTISING RATES:
Full Page Mono .... EUR 2999
Full Page Colour .... EUR 4407
Mechanical Data: Type Area: 262 x 182 mm, No. of Columns (Display): 3, Col Widths (Display): 56 mm
Copy instructions: *Copy Date:* 15 days prior to publication
Supplement(s): Neue Arzneimittel
BUSINESS: HEALTH & MEDICAL

DER ARZT
721263G56A-860
Editorial: Gorkistr. 142, 13509 BERLIN
Tel: 30 40208060 **Fax:** 30 40208059
Email: der-arzt@inter.net **Web site:** http://www.der-arzt.de
Freq: Annual; **Cover Price:** EUR 53,00; **Circ:** 3,000
Advertising Manager: Gabriele Stöckel
Profile: Includes as an indispensable handbook for the practice, the addresses with telephone and fax numbers, office hours, Internet and e-mail addresses of all doctors (including psychological psychotherapists, orthodontists, dentists and veterinarians), hospitals, pharmacies, respiratory therapists, occupational therapists, midwives, physiotherapists, speech therapists, masseurs, podiatrists, etc., in Berlin. Moreover, in a special chapter on all medical and professional organizations, trade associations, health plans, associations, working groups and the appropriate state offices, etc. are listed. It is equipped with a convenient tab and arranged within the twelve administrative districts of Berlin alphabetically by subject areas, the work is complemented by a complete alphabetical list.
Language(s): German
ADVERTISING RATES:
Full Page Mono .... EUR 1080
Full Page Colour .... EUR 1230
Mechanical Data: Type Area: 184 x 112 mm, No. of Columns (Display): 2, Col Widths (Display): 54 mm
Copy instructions: *Copy Date:* 90 days prior to publication

ARZT + AUTO
721268G56A-900
Editorial: Langer Weg 18, 60489 FRANKFURT
Tel: 69 97843251 **Fax:** 69 97843253
Email: kvda.de@t-online.de **Web site:** http://www.kvda-online.de
Freq: 6 issues yearly; **Cover Price:** EUR 3,00
Free to qualifying individuals ; **Circ:** 6,000
Editor: Eckart Wernicke
Profile: Journal of General Practice, traffic, emergency, and travel medicine, car and travel.
Language(s): German
ADVERTISING RATES:
Full Page Mono .... EUR 1280
Full Page Colour .... EUR 2480
Mechanical Data: Type Area: 260 x 185 mm
BUSINESS: HEALTH & MEDICAL

ARZT UND KRANKENHAUS
1841431G56A-11554
Editorial: Tersteegenstr. 9, 40476 DÜSSELDORF
Tel: 211 454990 **Fax:** 211 4541914
Email: info@vlk-online.de **Web site:** http://www.vlk-online.de
Freq: Monthly; Free to qualifying individuals
Annual Sub.: EUR 61,80; **Circ:** 4,977
Editor: Gerd Norden; **Advertising Manager:** Michael Menzer
Profile: Trade journal for senior hospital doctors.
Language(s): German
ADVERTISING RATES:
Full Page Mono .... EUR 1400
Full Page Colour .... EUR 2150
Mechanical Data: Type Area: 252 x 176 mm, No. of Columns (Display): 3, Col Widths (Display): 55 mm

ARZT & WIRTSCHAFT
721274G56A-980
Editorial: Justus-von-Liebig-Str. 1, 86899 LANDSBERG **Tel:** 8191 125143 **Fax:** 8191 125868
Email: aw@mi-verlag.de **Web site:** http://www.auw.de
Freq: Monthly; **Annual Sub.:** EUR 79,00; **Circ:** 59,263
Editor: Hans-Joachim Hofmann; **Advertising Manager:** Maximilian Schriewersmann
Profile: The magazine is now after over 43 years of market presence of the special business permits within the medical press. He turns directly to physicians, particularly internists and family physicians in practicing. Expect from the magazine and receive medical information and assistance with legal, corporate and business problems. Only practical and value determine the editorial selection of topics. The concise and clearly structured editorial assures the reader a quick time-ridden issue with the overview and specific medical information behavior into account.
Language(s): German
ADVERTISING RATES:
Full Page Mono .... EUR 4690
Full Page Colour .... EUR 6550
Mechanical Data: Type Area: 257 x 178 mm, No. of Columns (Display): 3, Col Widths (Display): 53 mm
Copy instructions: *Copy Date:* 33 days prior to publication
BUSINESS: HEALTH & MEDICAL

ARZT ZAHNARZT & NATURHEILVERFAHREN
721275G56D-80
Editorial: Heupenmühle, 53539 KELBERG
Tel: 2692 931960 **Fax:** 2692 9319077
Email: azn-redaktion@t-online.de **Web site:** http://www.azn-naturheilkunde.de
Freq: Quarterly; **Annual Sub.:** EUR 30,00; **Circ:** 6,146
Editor: Alfred Dietrich; **Advertising Manager:** Heike Müller-Wüstenfeld
Profile: Magazine for dentists focusing on recent developments in diagnosis and methods of treatment.
Language(s): German
ADVERTISING RATES:
Full Page Mono .... EUR 2370
Full Page Colour .... EUR 3510
Mechanical Data: Type Area: 245 x 176 mm, No. of Columns (Display): 3, Col Widths (Display): 55 mm
Copy instructions: *Copy Date:* 42 days prior to publication
BUSINESS: HEALTH & MEDICAL: Dental

ÄRZTE ZEITUNG
719635G56A-1020
Editorial: Am Forsthaus Gravenbruch 5, 63263 NEU-ISENBURG **Tel:** 6102 5060 **Fax:** 6102 506203
Email: info@aerztezeitung.de **Web site:** http://www.aerztezeitung.de
Freq: 260 issues yearly; **Annual Sub.:** EUR 153,50; **Circ:** 57,933
Editor: Wolfgang van den Bergh; **Advertising Manager:** Ute Krille
Profile: The Ärzte Zeitung is Germany's only daily newspaper for doctors and delivers Monday through Friday, a quick overview of current issues and developments in health care. The articles from the fields of medicine, health policy, practice management, business and social attention to the needs of the target group of GPs. Regular sections such as diabetes in mind, Best Agers or bur-services to enrich the range of topics. This Outlet offers RSS (Really Simple Syndication).
Language(s): German
Mechanical Data: Type Area: 415 x 291 mm, No. of Columns (Display): 5, Col Widths (Display): 51 mm
Copy instructions: *Copy Date:* 1 day prior to publication
Supplement(s): Apothekerplus; ArztOnline; ArztRaum; Forschung und Praxis
BUSINESS: HEALTH & MEDICAL

ÄRZTE ZEITUNG FÜR NEUROLOGEN UND PSYCHIATER
1833015G56A-11545
Editorial: Am Forsthaus Gravenbruch 5, 63263 NEU-ISENBURG **Tel:** 6102 5060 **Fax:** 6102 58870
Email: info@aerztezeitung.de **Web site:** http://www.aerztezeitung.de
Freq: Monthly; **Annual Sub.:** EUR 21,40; **Circ:** 6,841
Editor: Wolfgang van den Bergh; **Advertising Manager:** Ute Krille
Profile: The special edition of specialist neurologists and psychiatrists, the high quality of the Ärzte Zeitung - separately for the subject area. The medical issues are specific to the subject. Reporting on current health policy, tips on job security and economic success as well as relevant, immediately actionable information on the economic issues are also available for the reader. Special treat: In every issue there is an attractive CME module.
Language(s): German
ADVERTISING RATES:
Full Page Mono .... EUR 2950
Full Page Colour .... EUR 4200
Mechanical Data: Type Area: 390 x 286 mm, No. of Columns (Display): 5, Col Widths (Display): 54 mm

ÄRZTE ZEITUNG KLINIKREPORT
719637G56A-1060
Editorial: Am Forsthaus Gravenbruch 5, 63263 NEU-ISENBURG **Tel:** 6102 5060 **Fax:** 6102 58740
Email: info@aerztezeitung.de **Web site:** http://www.aerztezeitung.de
Freq: 11 issues yearly; **Annual Sub.:** EUR 42,80; **Circ:** 16,725
Editor: Wolfgang van den Bergh; **Advertising Manager:** Ute Krille
Profile: The „Ärzte Zeitung Klinikreport" provides decision makers at the clinic a quick overview of job-relevant topics. It provides comprehensive information on public health, medical, economic and socio-political developments. The „Klinikreport" offers a mix of current news coverage here and classify background information and commentary.
Language(s): German
Readership: Read by doctors, surgeons and hospital managers.
ADVERTISING RATES:
Full Page Mono .... EUR 5300
Full Page Colour .... EUR 6070
Mechanical Data: Type Area: 415 x 291 mm, No. of Columns (Display): 5, Col Widths (Display): 51 mm
Copy instructions: *Copy Date:* 10 days prior to publication
Supplement(s): ArztRaum
BUSINESS: HEALTH & MEDICAL

ÄRZTE ZEITUNG ONLINE
1620704G56A-11215
Editorial: Am Forsthaus Gravenbruch 5, 63263 NEU-ISENBURG **Tel:** 6102 506304 **Fax:** 6102 58870
Email: gabriele.wagner@aerztezeitung.de **Web site:** http://www.aerztezeitung.de
Freq: 230 times a year; **Cover Price:** Paid; **Circ:** 768,110 Unique Users
Editor: Gabriele Wagner; **Advertising Manager:** Ute Krille
Profile: Ezine: National daily specialising in medicine and health.
Language(s): German
BUSINESS: HEALTH & MEDICAL

ÄRZTEBLATT BADEN-WÜRTTEMBERG
719606G56A-60
Editorial: Jahnstr. 38a, 70597 STUTTGART
Tel: 711 7698945 **Fax:** 711 76989859
Web site: http://www.aerzteblatt-bw.de
Freq: Monthly; Free to qualifying individuals
Annual Sub.: EUR 112,80; **Circ:** 48,209
Editor: Oliver Erens; **Advertising Manager:** Angela Grüssner
Profile: Official publication of the Medical board of Baden-Württemberg.
Language(s): German
ADVERTISING RATES:
Full Page Mono .... EUR 2965
Full Page Colour .... EUR 4765
Mechanical Data: Type Area: 260 x 185 mm, No. of Columns (Display): 4, Col Widths (Display): 45 mm
Copy instructions: *Copy Date:* 25 days prior to publication
Official Journal of: Organ d. Landesärztekammer sowie aller KV'en u. Bezirksärztekammern Baden-Württemberg
BUSINESS: HEALTH & MEDICAL

ÄRZTEBLATT MECKLENBURG-VORPOMMERN
719626G56A-1080
Editorial: August-Bebel-Str. 9a, 18055 ROSTOCK
Tel: 381 4928016 **Fax:** 381 4928080
Email: aerzteblatt@aek-mv.de **Web site:** http://www.aek-mv.de
Freq: Monthly; Free to qualifying individuals
Annual Sub.: EUR 88,50; **Circ:** 9,350
Editor: Andreas Crusius; **Advertising Manager:** Melanie Bölsdorff
Profile: Already since January 1991 is published the "Ärzteblatt Mecklenburg-Vorpommern" as the official newsletter of the Medical Council. Topics of medicine, professional politics, science and research, but also literary and cultural contributions are presented here each month.
Language(s): German
ADVERTISING RATES:
Full Page Mono .... EUR 1280
Full Page Colour .... EUR 2195
Mechanical Data: Type Area: 252 x 185 mm, No. of Columns (Display): 3, Col Widths (Display): 58 mm
Copy instructions: *Copy Date:* 20 days prior to publication
BUSINESS: HEALTH & MEDICAL

ÄRZTEBLATT RHEINLAND-PFALZ
755558G56A-11083
Editorial: Deutschhausplatz 3, 55116 MAINZ
Tel: 6131 2882225 **Fax:** 6131 2882289
Email: engelmohr@laek-rlp.de **Web site:** http://www.laek-rlp.de
Freq: Monthly; Free to qualifying individuals
Annual Sub.: EUR 133,00; **Circ:** 19,500
Editor: Ines Engelmohr; **Advertising Manager:** Livia Kummer
Profile: The Ärzteblatt Rheinland-Pfalz is the official publication organ of the State Medical Association, the District Medical Associations, the physicians' association and the Academy for Medical Training. For members of the State Medical Association the subscription is paid for by membership dues. In our Ärzteblatt we regularly publish educational texts.
Language(s): German
ADVERTISING RATES:
Full Page Mono .... EUR 1500
Full Page Colour .... EUR 2610
Mechanical Data: Type Area: 252 x 185 mm, No. of Columns (Display): 3, Col Widths (Display): 58 mm
Copy instructions: *Copy Date:* 20 days prior to publication
Official Journal of: Organ d. Landesärztekammer, d. Bezirksärztekammern u. d. Kassenärztl. Vereinigungen Rheinland-Pfalz

ÄRZTEBLATT SACHSEN
719627G56A-1100
Editorial: Schützenhöhe 16, 01099 DRESDEN
Tel: 351 8267161 **Fax:** 351 8267162
Email: redaktion@slaek.de **Web site:** http://www.slaek.de
Freq: Monthly; Free to qualifying individuals
Annual Sub.: EUR 113,00; **Circ:** 20,000
Editor: Winfried Klug; **Advertising Manager:** Silke El Gendy-Johne
Profile: Magazine covering news, reports and information for general practitioners in the region of Saxon.
Language(s): German
ADVERTISING RATES:
Full Page Mono .... EUR 1465
Full Page Colour .... EUR 2350
Mechanical Data: Type Area: 252 x 185 mm, No. of Columns (Display): 3, Col Widths (Display): 58 mm
Copy instructions: *Copy Date:* 20 days prior to publication
BUSINESS: HEALTH & MEDICAL

ÄRZTEBLATT SACHSEN-ANHALT
719628G56A-1120
Editorial: Doctor-Eisenbart-Ring 2, 39120 MAGDEBURG **Tel:** 391 60547800 **Fax:** 391 60547850
Email: redaktion@aeksa.de **Web site:** http://www.aerzteblatt-sachsen-anhalt.de
Freq: Monthly; Free to qualifying individuals
Annual Sub.: EUR 48,00; **Circ:** 9,800
Editor: H. Friebel
Profile: Content of the magazine: current status of priority political and professional issues, general

interest technical articles, cultural and medical historical articles, training and continuing education articles, training events calendar, job listings. Aims of the Journal: rapid job-specific information to all licensed physicians in Saxony-Anhalt. Opinion on interest nationwide professional issues, continuing education and training tasks.
Language(s): German
ADVERTISING RATES:
Full Page Mono .... EUR 1200
Full Page Colour .... EUR 2100
Mechanical Data: Type Area: 248 x 175 mm, No. of Columns (Display): 2, Col Widths (Display): 85 mm
Copy instructions: *Copy Date:* 25 days prior to publication
BUSINESS: HEALTH & MEDICAL

ÄRZTEBLATT THÜRINGEN
719629G56A-1140
Editorial: Im Semmicht 33, 07751 JENA
Tel: 3641 614103 **Fax:** 3641 614108
Email: aerzteblatt@laek-thueringen.de **Web site:** http://www.laek-thueringen.de
Freq: 11 issues yearly; Free to qualifying individuals
Annual Sub.: EUR 108,00; **Circ:** 11,400
Editor: Mathias Wesser; **Advertising Manager:** Anne Gentzsch
Profile: Journal of the Medical Board of Thüringen.
Language(s): German
ADVERTISING RATES:
Full Page Mono .... EUR 1785
Full Page Colour .... EUR 3300
Mechanical Data: No. of Columns (Display): 4, Col Widths (Display): 45 mm, Type Area: 252 x 185 mm
Copy instructions: *Copy Date:* 20 days prior to publication
BUSINESS: HEALTH & MEDICAL

ÄRZTIN
719638G56A-1180
Editorial: Herbert-Lewin-Platz 1, 10623 BERLIN
Tel: 30 400456540 **Fax:** 30 400456541
Email: gundel.koebke@t-online.de **Web site:** http://www.aerztinnenbund.de
Freq: 3 issues yearly; Free to qualifying individuals
Annual Sub.: EUR 9,00; **Circ:** 2,300
Editor: Gundel Köbke
Profile: Magazine focusing on the advantages and disadvantages of various treatments, also contains information from the Association.
Language(s): German
Readership: Read by members of the German Association of Women Doctors (Deutsche Ärztins Bund).
ADVERTISING RATES:
Full Page Mono .... EUR 800
Full Page Colour .... EUR 1200
Mechanical Data: Type Area: 258 x 185 mm, No. of Columns (Display): 3, Col Widths (Display): 59 mm
BUSINESS: HEALTH & MEDICAL

ÄRZTLICHE PRAXIS GYNÄKOLOGIE
719643G56A-1260
Editorial: Otto-Hahn-Str. 7, 50997 KÖLN
Tel: 2236 376408 **Fax:** 2236 376999
Email: dk@biermann.net **Web site:** http://www.biermann.net
Freq: 6 issues yearly; **Annual Sub.:** EUR 49,50; **Circ:** 10,953
Editor: Dieter Kaulard; **Advertising Manager:** Isabelle Becker
Profile: Ärztliche Praxis Gynäkologie provides the gynecologist everything he needs for the practice of everyday life: a quick overview of new medical knowledge, practice-relevant information on all major indications in his field and tips if the fee cap and pushes the budget is too tight. Always with a certified training.
Language(s): German
ADVERTISING RATES:
Full Page Mono .... EUR 2590
Full Page Colour .... EUR 3590
Mechanical Data: Type Area: 233 x 180 mm
BUSINESS: HEALTH & MEDICAL

ÄRZTLICHE PRAXIS NEUROLOGIE PSYCHIATRIE
719644G56A-1280
Editorial: Otto-Hahn-Str. 7, 50997 KÖLN
Tel: 2236 376456 **Fax:** 2236 376999
Email: nec@biermann.net **Web site:** http://www.biermann.net
Freq: Monthly; **Annual Sub.:** EUR 99,00; **Circ:** 7,032
Editor: Nadine Eckert; **Advertising Manager:** Isabelle Becker
Profile: Practically relevant issues and current research results - the actual magazine for neurologists and psychiatrists. Ideal for permanent residents who also appreciate tips on accounting. Ärztliche Praxis Neurologie Psychiatrie appears with tailored information from the fields of medicine, economics and politics. Always with a certified training.
Language(s): German
ADVERTISING RATES:
Full Page Mono .... EUR 2180
Full Page Colour .... EUR 3140
Mechanical Data: Type Area: 233 x 180 mm
Copy instructions: *Copy Date:* 21 days prior to publication
BUSINESS: HEALTH & MEDICAL

ÄRZTLICHE PRAXIS ONKOLOGIE
1862250G56A-11576
Editorial: Otto-Hahn-Str. 7, 50997 KÖLN
Tel: 2236 376408 **Fax:** 2236 376999
Email: dk@biermann.net **Web site:** http://www.biermann.net
Freq: 6 issues yearly; **Annual Sub.:** EUR 56,50; **Circ:** 7,834
Editor: Dieter Kaulard; **Advertising Manager:** Isabelle Becker
Profile: Ärztliche Praxis Onkologie, the oncology journal of Biermann Medizin. It is aimed at relevant prescribers and therapists in hospitals, cancer centers and oncology practices, as well as to therapists in the areas of psycho-oncology (physicians, psychologists, psychotherapists), aftercare, rehabilitation and palliative care and with oncology health economics dealing People in research, clinical practice, practice, administration, management, health policy, in associations, organizations, industry and health insurance companies.
Language(s): German
ADVERTISING RATES:
Full Page Mono .... EUR 2890
Full Page Colour .... EUR 4000
Mechanical Data: Type Area: 233 x 180 mm
Copy instructions: *Copy Date:* 21 days prior to publication

ÄRZTLICHE PSYCHOTHERAPIE UND PSYCHOSOMATISCHE MEDIZIN
1792689G56A-11436
Editorial: Hölderlinstr. 3, 70174 STUTTGART
Tel: 711 2298754 **Fax:** 711 2298765
Email: jan.hueber@schattauer.de **Web site:** http://www.schattauer.de
Freq: Quarterly; **Annual Sub.:** EUR 98,00; **Circ:** 2,600
Editor: Jan Hueber; **Advertising Manager:** Klaus Jansch
Profile: The last decades have shown that medical psychotherapy is an essential part of the services become our healthcare system. The journal Ärztliche Psychotherapie und Psychosomatische Medizin offers a forum for the medical practice of psychotherapy. Including the professional associations they fully informed about the latest research and treatment developments in the field. As part of a multidisciplinary approach to social and political conditions of the professional practice of psychotherapy discussed and debated subject-specific developments in the future. A special focus is practice-relevant contributions (cash reports, treatment pitfalls, integration of additional PT-procedures, adjuvant pharmacotherapy).
Language(s): German
ADVERTISING RATES:
Full Page Mono .... EUR 1740
Full Page Colour .... EUR 2865
Mechanical Data: Type Area: 242 x 174 mm
Copy instructions: *Copy Date:* 40 days prior to publication
Official Journal of: Organ d. Dt. Ges. f. Psychosomat. Medizin u. Ärztl. Psychotherapie, d. Vereinigung psychotherapeut. tätiger Kassenärzte, d. Dt. Ges. f. klin. Psychotherapie u. Psychotherap. Rehabilitation, d. Chefarztkonferenz Psychosomat.-Psychotherapeut. Krankenhäuser u. Abteilungen, d. Dt. Ges. psychosomat. Frauenheilkunde u. Geburtshilfe u. d. Internat. Federation for Psychotherapy

ÄRZTLICHER RATGEBER FÜR WERDENDE UND JUNGE ELTERN
719648G74D-20
Editorial: Konradshöhe, 82065 BAIERBRUNN
Tel: 89 744330 **Fax:** 89 74433333
Email: kontakt@wortundbildverlag.de **Web site:** http://www.wortundbild-media.de
Freq: 3 issues yearly; **Cover Price:** Free; **Circ:** 251,872
Editor: Stefanie Becker; **Advertising Manager:** Brigitta Hackmann
Profile: Magazine focusing on the first five years of a baby's life.
Language(s): German
Readership: Aimed at new parents.
ADVERTISING RATES:
Full Page Mono .... EUR 21400
Full Page Colour .... EUR 21400
Mechanical Data: Type Area: 256 x 184 mm, No. of Columns (Display): 2, Col Widths (Display): 88 mm
Copy instructions: *Copy Date:* 49 days prior to publication
CONSUMER: WOMEN'S INTEREST CONSUMER MAGAZINES: Child Care

ÄRZTLICHES JOURNAL REISE & MEDIZIN
719651G56A-1400
Editorial: Arnulfstr. 10, 80335 MÜNCHEN
Tel: 89 54584517 **Fax:** 89 54584520
Email: reichenberger@ohv-online.de **Web site:** http://www.aerztliches-journal.de
Freq: Monthly; **Annual Sub.:** EUR 42,50; **Circ:** 54,730
Editor: Soheyla Reichenberger; **Advertising Manager:** Edeltraud Koller
Profile: Travel magazine for practicing internists, general practitioners and practitioners. The magazine is divided into two parts: the weather forecast and cultural contributions, including specific tips and advice on country-specific characteristics such as climate, housing and vaccinations. In addition, hands-on medical training and convention reports, case reports, interviews and comprehensive presentation of current medical issues.
Language(s): German
ADVERTISING RATES:
Full Page Mono .... EUR 4400
Full Page Colour .... EUR 6140
Mechanical Data: Type Area: 257 x 185 mm, No. of Columns (Display): 4, Col Widths (Display): 43 mm
Copy instructions: *Copy Date:* 30 days prior to publication
Supplement(s): patienten journal reise & gesundheit
BUSINESS: HEALTH & MEDICAL

ÄRZTLICHES JOURNAL REISE & MEDIZIN NEUROLOGIE/ PSYCHIATRIE
719649G56A-1360
Editorial: Arnulfstr. 10, 80335 MÜNCHEN
Tel: 89 54584514 **Fax:** 89 54584520
Email: reichenberger@ohv-online.de **Web site:** http://www.aerztliches-journal.de
Freq: 6 issues yearly; **Annual Sub.:** EUR 21,00; **Circ:** 5,678
Editor: Soheyla Reichenberger; **Advertising Manager:** Edeltraud Koller
Profile: Travel magazine for practicing for neurologists, psychiatrists and neurologists. The magazine is divided into two parts: the weather forecast and cultural contributions, including specific tips and advice on country-specific characteristics such as climate, housing and vaccinations. In addition, hands-on medical training and convention reports, case reports, interviews and comprehensive presentation of current medical issues.
Language(s): German
ADVERTISING RATES:
Full Page Mono .... EUR 2020
Full Page Colour .... EUR 3070
Mechanical Data: Type Area: 257 x 185 mm, No. of Columns (Display): 4, Col Widths (Display): 43 mm
Copy instructions: *Copy Date:* 30 days prior to publication
Supplement(s): patienten journal reise & gesundheit
BUSINESS: HEALTH & MEDICAL

ÄRZTLICHES JOURNAL REISE & MEDIZIN ONKOLOGIE
1796331G56A-11453
Editorial: Arnulfstr. 10, 80335 MÜNCHEN
Tel: 89 54584517 **Fax:** 89 54584520
Email: weber@ohv-online.de **Web site:** http://www.aerztliches-journal.de
Freq: 6 issues yearly; **Annual Sub.:** EUR 21,00; **Circ:** 6,904
Editor: Soheyla Reichenberger; **Advertising Manager:** Edeltraud Koller
Profile: Travel journal of oncology physicians working in clinics and practices. The magazine is divided into two parts: the weather forecast and cultural contributions, including specific tips and advice on country-specific characteristics such as climate, housing and vaccinations. In addition, hands-on medical training and convention reports, case reports, interviews and comprehensive presentation of current medical issues.
Language(s): German
ADVERTISING RATES:
Full Page Mono .... EUR 2390
Full Page Colour .... EUR 3440
Mechanical Data: Type Area: 257 x 185 mm, No. of Columns (Display): 4, Col Widths (Display): 43 mm
Copy instructions: *Copy Date:* 30 days prior to publication
Supplement(s): patienten journal reise & gesundheit

ÄRZTLICHES JOURNAL REISE & MEDIZIN ORTHOPÄDIE/ RHEUMATOLOGIE
719650G56A-1380
Editorial: Arnulfstr. 10, 80335 MÜNCHEN
Tel: 89 54584514 **Fax:** 89 54584520
Email: weber@ohv-online.de **Web site:** http://www.aerztliches-journal.de
Freq: 6 issues yearly; **Annual Sub.:** EUR 21,00; **Circ:** 4,203
Editor: Soheyla Reichenberger; **Advertising Manager:** Edeltraud Koller
Profile: Travel magazine for orthopedic surgeons and rheumatologists. The magazine is divided into two parts: the weather forecast and cultural contributions, including specific tips and advice on country-specific characteristics such as climate, housing and vaccinations. In addition, hands-on medical training and convention reports, case reports, interviews and comprehensive presentation of current medical issues.
Language(s): German
ADVERTISING RATES:
Full Page Mono .... EUR 1740
Full Page Colour .... EUR 2790
Mechanical Data: Type Area: 257 x 185 mm, No. of Columns (Display): 4, Col Widths (Display): 43 mm
Copy instructions: *Copy Date:* 30 days prior to publication
Supplement(s): patienten journal reise & gesundheit
BUSINESS: HEALTH & MEDICAL

ARZTONLINE
721266G56A-880
Editorial: Am Forsthaus Gravenbruch 5, 63263 NEU-ISENBURG **Tel:** 6102 5060 **Fax:** 6102 506178
Email: wi@aerztezeitung.de **Web site:** http://www.aerztezeitung.de
Freq: Quarterly; **Circ:** 59,823
Editor: Wolfgang van den Bergh; **Advertising Manager:** Ute Krille
Profile: Computer supplement of a doctor's magazine.
Language(s): German
ADVERTISING RATES:
Full Page Mono .... EUR 9230
Full Page Colour .... EUR 10950
Mechanical Data: Type Area: 390 x 286 mm
Copy instructions: *Copy Date:* 7 days prior to publication
Supplement to: Ärzte Zeitung

ARZTRAUM
1924004G56A-11617
Editorial: Am Forsthaus Gravenbruch 5, 63263 NEU-ISENBURG **Tel:** 6102 5060 **Fax:** 6102 58870
Email: info@aerztezeitung.de **Web site:** http://www.aerztezeitung.de
Freq: Quarterly; **Circ:** 94,000
Editor: Wolfgang van den Bergh
Profile: Construction and furnishing of the Ärzte Zeitung for practice and clinic.
Language(s): German
ADVERTISING RATES:
Full Page Mono .... EUR 9230
Full Page Colour .... EUR 10950
Mechanical Data: Type Area: 390 x 286 mm
Supplement to: Ärzte Zeitung, Ärzte Zeitung Klinikreport

ARZTRECHT
721267G56A-1420
Editorial: Fiduciastr. 2, 76227 KARLSRUHE
Tel: 721 4538880 **Fax:** 721 4538888
Email: verlag@arztrecht.org **Web site:** http://www.arztrecht.org
Freq: Monthly; **Annual Sub.:** EUR 62,00; **Circ:** 3,100
Editor: Bernhard Debong; **Advertising Manager:** Rosemarie Fitterer
Profile: To account for the medical and legal issues properly, doctors and lawyers together to create the content of the magazine. As time has ArztRecht to the Compendium of the whole law of medicine developed. Since the first issue, ArztRecht readers practical informed and up to date by the publication of court decisions and essays. Here are legal advice and design recommendations for behavior in the foreground. Thus, for example created along with the Association for Medical Law a model for chief physician service contracts and regularly reviewed. Questions and feedback from readers give many suggestions for shaping the form and content of the magazine. There is no doctor legal question that has not yet dealt with since the founding of the journal ArztRecht.
Language(s): German
ADVERTISING RATES:
Full Page Mono .... EUR 1500
Full Page Colour .... EUR 2100
Mechanical Data: Type Area: 252 x 175 mm, No. of Columns (Display): 3, Col Widths (Display): 55 mm
Copy instructions: *Copy Date:* 16 days prior to publication
Official Journal of: Organ d. ArGe f. Arztrecht
BUSINESS: HEALTH & MEDICAL

AS AKTIVE SENIOREN
1609431G74N-811
Editorial: Westhellweg 23, 58239 SCHWERTE
Tel: 2304 13647 **Fax:** 2304 13647
Email: info@as.citynetz.com **Web site:** http://www.as.citynetz.com
Freq: Quarterly; **Cover Price:** Free; **Circ:** 4,500
Editor: Horst Reinhard Haake
Profile: Regional magazine for the elderly in the city of Schwerte.
Language(s): German

AS AKTIVE SENIOREN
1609431G74N-932
Editorial: Westhellweg 23, 58239 SCHWERTE
Tel: 2304 13647 **Fax:** 2304 13647
Email: info@as.citynetz.com **Web site:** http://www.as.citynetz.com
Freq: Quarterly; **Cover Price:** Free; **Circ:** 4,500
Editor: Horst Reinhard Haake
Profile: Regional magazine for the elderly in the city of Schwerte.
Language(s): German

ASB MAGAZIN
721278G56R-160
Editorial: Sülzburgstr. 140, 50937 KÖLN
Tel: 221 47605324 **Fax:** 221 47605297
Email: magazin@asb.de **Web site:** http://www.asb.de
Freq: Quarterly; **Circ:** 996,364
Editor: Alexandra Valentino
Profile: The ASB magazine is the magazine for members of the Workers' Samaritan Federation Germany eV, it informed the members four times a year about how the ASB uses its membership dues. It also reports on current issues and provides helpful tips on topics of health, nutrition and family. Exciting reports give an insight into the projects of the ASB in Germany and worldwide. Reports access to major social issue, experts provide valuable consumer tips and interviews to know the readers more about the ASB'ler behind the scenes. Price entertaining puzzles, brain teasers and special services for ASB members complete the reading range.
Language(s): German
Readership: Read by member of the Samaritans.
ADVERTISING RATES:
Full Page Colour .... EUR 13929
Mechanical Data: Type Area: 250 x 180 mm, No. of Columns (Display): 4, Col Widths (Display): 42 mm

Copy instructions: *Copy Date:* 42 days prior to publication
BUSINESS: HEALTH & MEDICAL: Health Medical Related

ASCHAFFENBURGER STADT MAGAZIN 721283G80-820
Editorial: Weichertstr. 20, 63741 ASCHAFFENBURG
Tel: 6021 396145 **Fax:** 6021 396150
Email: redaktion@aschaffenburger-stadtmagazin.de **Web site:** http://www.aschaffenburger-stadtmagazin.de
Freq: Monthly; **Cover Price:** Free; **Circ:** 22,000
Editor: Thomas Giegerich; **Advertising Manager:** Herbert Bäck
Profile: Magazine about the region of Aschaffenburg.
Language(s): German
ADVERTISING RATES:
Full Page Mono .... EUR 1095
Full Page Colour .... EUR 1640
Mechanical Data: Type Area: 270 x 190 mm, No. of Columns (Display): 4, Col Widths (Display): 44 mm
Copy instructions: *Copy Date:* 7 days prior to publication
CONSUMER: RURAL & REGIONAL INTEREST

ASC-KURIER 1927051G14A-10367
Editorial: Hamburger Allee 26, 30161 HANNOVER
Tel: 511 33617930 **Fax:** 511 336179355
Email: info@asc-hannover.de
Freq: Monthly; **Cover Price:** Free; **Circ:** 7,000
Editor: Uwe Wawrzynowicz
Profile: Magazine for employers.
Language(s): German

ASIA BRIDGE 721292G14A-340
Editorial: Rudolfstr. 22, 60327 FRANKFURT
Tel: 69 6656320 **Fax:** 69 66563222
Email: charlotte.wolff@asiavision.de **Web site:** http://www.maerkte-weltweit.de
Freq: Monthly; **Annual Sub.:** EUR 228,00; **Circ:** 8,941
Advertising Manager: Shezad Malik
Profile: Asian business magazine. The geographic range extends from India through Southeast Asia to the economic giants China and Japan. In addition to graphics and charts supported by exclusive background reports and in-depth analysis the magazine contains further contact information. The reporting is done in collaboration with the bfai.
Language(s): German
ADVERTISING RATES:
Full Page Mono .... EUR 2150
Full Page Colour .... EUR 3000
Mechanical Data: Type Area: 287 x 200 mm
BUSINESS: COMMERCE, INDUSTRY & MANAGEMENT

THE ASIA PACIFIC TIMES 1895857G14A-10282
Editorial: Tempelhofer Ufer 23, 10963 BERLIN
Tel: 30 21505422 **Fax:** 30 21505447
Email: info@asia-pacific-times.com **Web site:** http://www.asia-pacific-times.com
Freq: Monthly; **Circ:** 30,000
Editor: Peter H. Koepf; **Advertising Manager:** Janine Kulbrok
Profile: Magazine for executives from government, industry and academia in Asia. The magazine wants to help ensure that develops between the old and the new Asia, a ratio that is not of rivalry or even confrontation is determined, but of partnership.
Language(s): English
ADVERTISING RATES:
Full Page Mono .... EUR 23000
Full Page Colour .... EUR 23000
Mechanical Data: Type Area: 530 x 290 mm
Copy instructions: *Copy Date:* 5 days prior to publication

ASIA & MIDDLE EAST FOOD TRADE 721291G14C-80
Editorial: Heilsbachstr. 17, 53123 BONN
Tel: 228 919320 **Fax:** 228 9193217
Email: editor@ameft.de **Web site:** http://www.ameft.de
Freq: Quarterly; **Annual Sub.:** EUR 40,00; **Circ:** 17,818
Editor: Gabriele D. Ingwersen; **Advertising Manager:** Monika Huber
Profile: Since foundation, Asia & Middle East Food Trade has been an invaluable link between suppliers and buyers around the globe. In four comprehensive issues per annum, Asia & Middle East Food Trade provides expert information, carefully tailored to match reader requirements. Each issue contains a dedicated "Markets" section with latest market intelligence from the Middle East and Asia along with interviews with leading local food and beverage manufacturers. A special focus on the "Ingredients" industry as well as "Processing & Packaging" features introduce new raw materials and latest technology. They also provide insights into specific applications, case studies and introduce renowned suppliers. In its "Events" section Asia & Middle East Food Trade looks at the product range available at leading food industry shows, providing a choice of select events as well as a useful overview of the wide variety of exhibitions available for anyone seeking new sales channels or supplier platforms.
Language(s): English
ADVERTISING RATES:
Full Page Mono .... EUR 2940
Full Page Colour .... EUR 3960
Mechanical Data: Type Area: 256 x 178 mm, No. of Columns (Display): 4, Col Widths (Display): 41 mm
Copy instructions: *Copy Date:* 21 days prior to publication

ASP AUTO SERVICE PRAXIS 721623G31R-13
Editorial: Aschauer Str. 30, 81549 MÜNCHEN
Tel: 89 2030431286 **Fax:** 89 2030431218
Email: autoservicepraxis@springer.com **Web site:** http://www.autoservicepraxis.de
Freq: Monthly; **Annual Sub.:** EUR 77,90; **Circ:** 24,672
Editor: Frank Schlieben; **Advertising Manager:** Michael Harms
Profile: Magazine for independent motor vehicle master and technical managers in workshops and car dealerships. Automotive technology, workshop technology and business practice are the three main headings of the journal. As TÜV Partner magazine is asp Auto Service practice is also an important information tool for the more than 17,000 service centers that collaborate with the TÜV Twitter: http://twitter.com/#!/autoserviceprax.
Language(s): German
Readership: Read by personnel in car dealer showrooms and workshops.
ADVERTISING RATES:
Full Page Mono .... EUR 5830
Full Page Colour .... EUR 7900
Mechanical Data: Type Area: 240 x 175 mm
BUSINESS: MOTOR TRADE: Motor Trade Related

ASP AUTOSERVICEPRAXIS.DE 1622553G31R-37
Editorial: Aschauer Str. 30, 81549 MÜNCHEN
Tel: 89 2030431287 **Fax:** 89 2030431205
Email: presse.dienste@springer.com **Web site:** http://www.autoservicepraxis.de
Freq: Daily; **Cover Price:** Paid; **Circ:** 63,410 Unique Users
Editor: Niko Ganzer; **Advertising Manager:** Michael Harms
Profile: Ezine: Magazine containing practical and technical information about the servicing of cars. Twitter:http://twitter.com/#!/autoserviceprax.
Language(s): German
BUSINESS: MOTOR TRADE: Motor Trade Related

ASPHALT 721305G42B-1
Editorial: Düppenberg 61, 45357 ESSEN
Tel: 201 8681064 **Fax:** 201 8681065
Email: m_sutor@yahoo.com **Web site:** http://www.giesel.de
Freq: 8 issues yearly; Free to qualifying individuals
Annual Sub.: EUR 99,00; **Circ:** 6,078
Editor: Maike Sutor-Fiedler; **Advertising Manager:** Berko Härtel
Profile: As an organ of the strongest association in Europe is "asphalt" Europe's largest and leading specialist journal for asphalt manufacture, installation and use. Its fully informed about all aspects of asphalt road construction including the production of asphalt. In addition, all application areas of the building material asphalt are entering the editorial area, such as airport construction, landfill and hydraulic engineering and railway track construction. A whole range of information connects the major industries in the manufacturing plants for asphalt, the Kies-/Sand-Industrie, civil engineering and road construction companies and the construction machine industry.
Language(s): German
ADVERTISING RATES:
Full Page Mono .... EUR 2538
Full Page Colour .... EUR 3808
Mechanical Data: Type Area: 248 x 160 mm, No. of Columns (Display): 3, Col Widths (Display): 50 mm
Copy instructions: *Copy Date:* 20 days prior to publication
Official Journal of: Organ d. Dt. Asphaltverb. e.V. u. d. Dt. Asphalt-Inst. e.V., Nachrichtenblatt d. European Asphalt Pavement Association
BUSINESS: CONSTRUCTION: Roads

ASR ANWALT/ANWÄLTIN IM SOZIALRECHT 721307G1A-3499
Editorial: Wachsbleiche 7, 53111 BONN
Tel: 228 919117 **Fax:** 228 9191123
Email: kontakt@anwaltverlag.de **Web site:** http://www.anwaltverlag.de
Freq: 6 issues yearly; **Annual Sub.:** EUR 93,40; **Circ:** 1,200
Editor: Gottfried Krutzki
Profile: Magazine from the social law workgroup in the German Lawyers' Association.
Language(s): German
ADVERTISING RATES:
Full Page Mono .... EUR 710
Full Page Colour .... EUR 1580
Mechanical Data: Type Area: 260 x 186 mm, No. of Columns (Display): 2, Col Widths (Display): 90 mm
Copy instructions: *Copy Date:* 21 days prior to publication

ASSCOMPACT 721309G1C-40
Editorial: Bindlacher Str. 4, 95448 BAYREUTH
Tel: 921 7575888 **Fax:** 921 7575820
Email: redaktion@asscompact.de **Web site:** http://www.asscompact.de
Freq: Monthly; **Cover Price:** EUR 3,80; **Circ:** 41,863
Editor: Brigitte Horn; **Advertising Manager:** Sven Jeron
Profile: AssCompact is the monthly magazine for managers and decision makers in the financial and insurance industry. The focus is on independent intermediaries such as brokerage, multiple agents, financial institutions, asset managers and financial advisers. With hands-on technical papers, Interviews, judgments and short messages AssCompact informed its readers and presented to the market concept and successful solutions for daily business.
Language(s): German
ADVERTISING RATES:
Full Page Colour .... EUR 7500
Mechanical Data: Type Area: 257 x 170 mm
Copy instructions: *Copy Date:* 30 days prior to publication
BUSINESS: FINANCE & ECONOMICS: Banking

ASSEKURANZ AKTUELL 721310G1D-40
Editorial: Schubertstr. 8, 65232 TAUNUSSTEIN
Tel: 6128 85604 **Fax:** 6128 84795
Freq: Weekly; **Circ:** 2,500
Editor: Wolfgang Horn
Profile: Information for insurance companies.
Language(s): German
ADVERTISING RATES:
Full Page Mono .... EUR 300
Mechanical Data: Type Area: 270 x 185 mm, No. of Columns (Display): 2, Col Widths (Display): 90 mm
Copy instructions: *Copy Date:* 2 days prior to publication

ASSEKURANZ AKTUELL 721310G1D-486
Editorial: Schubertstr. 8, 65232 TAUNUSSTEIN
Tel: 6128 85604 **Fax:** 6128 84795
Freq: Weekly; **Circ:** 2,500
Editor: Wolfgang Horn
Profile: Information for insurance companies.
Language(s): German
ADVERTISING RATES:
Full Page Mono .... EUR 300
Mechanical Data: Type Area: 270 x 185 mm, No. of Columns (Display): 2, Col Widths (Display): 90 mm
Copy instructions: *Copy Date:* 2 days prior to publication

ASTRO WOCHE 1749623A94X-1675
Editorial: Postfach 1026, 94152 NEUHAUS
Tel: 7712 358500 **Fax:** 7712 3585021
Email: service@astrowoche.de **Web site:** http://www.astrowoche.de
Freq: Daily; **Cover Price:** Paid; **Circ:** 535,677 Unique Users
Editor: Rudolf Kollböck
Profile: Ezine: Magazine on astrology and horoscopes.
Language(s): German
CONSUMER: OTHER CLASSIFICATIONS: Miscellaneous

ASTRONOMISCHE NACHRICHTEN 721324G55-320
Editorial: An der Sternwarte 16, 14482 POTSDAM
Tel: 331 7499232 **Fax:** 331 7499200
Email: an@aip.de **Web site:** http://www.an-journal.de
Freq: 10 issues yearly; **Annual Sub.:** EUR 1440,00; **Circ:** 300
Editor: K. G. Strassmeier; **Advertising Manager:** Patricia Filler
Profile: Magazine containing articles about astronomy and astrophysics.
Language(s): English
ADVERTISING RATES:
Full Page Mono .... EUR 800
Full Page Colour .... EUR 1400
Mechanical Data: Type Area: 249 x 171 mm
Copy instructions: *Copy Date:* 30 days prior to publication
BUSINESS: APPLIED SCIENCE & LABORATORIES

ASUPROTECT 1804774G56A-11478
Editorial: Forststr. 131, 70193 STUTTGART
Tel: 711 636720 **Fax:** 711 63672747
Email: asu@gentner.de **Web site:** http://www.gentner.de
Freq: Half-yearly; **Circ:** 7,500
Editor: Karl Landau; **Advertising Manager:** Angela Grüssner
Profile: Operational decision-makers and their staff are informed of the latest developments in occupational and health safety, the safety management and occupational hygiene.
Language(s): German
ADVERTISING RATES:
Full Page Mono .... EUR 1505
Full Page Colour .... EUR 1955
Mechanical Data: Type Area: 260 x 185 mm, No. of Columns (Display): 4, Col Widths (Display): 45 mm
Copy instructions: *Copy Date:* 14 days prior to publication
Supplement to: Arbeitsmedizin Sozialmedizin Umweltmedizin, Zeitschrift für Arbeitswissenschaft

ASZ DIE ALLGEMEINE SONNTAGSZEITUNG 720008G72-280
Editorial: Dominikanerplatz 8, 97070 WÜRZBURG
Tel: 931 308630 **Fax:** 931 3086333
Email: info@die-tagespost.de **Web site:** http://www.die-tagespost.de
Freq: Weekly; **Circ:** 11,658
Editor: Markus Reder; **News Editor:** Markus Reder; **Advertising Manager:** Anja Stichnoth
Profile: As a Catholic newspaper followed the ASZ Die Allgemeine Sonntagszeitung the current political events at home and abroad. We report on the centers of world politics and information about decisions and developments that are Christians are of particular importance. This applies to issues of bioethics and family policy as European policy or the international crisis and conflict regions alike. The focus of our reporting is on detailed analysis and expert background information. appreciate our readers to the "daily mail" to be informed that they are looking elsewhere, often in vain, or just about those topics and issues find at least not in this detail. One important aspect of our politics coverage is everywhere to be present where the dignity of the injured people, human rights violated or are threatened and persecuted minorities. This means: When choosing the theme to put special emphasis. And committed to further zuber layers, even when the lights of the world press have long since moved to a new venue. The scale of our political commentary is Catholic. As a Catholic newspaper notes the ASZ Die Allgemeine Sonntagszeitung the universal Church in the view. About the current religious situation in Germany, Austria and many other countries, we report to date, rich backgrounds and with competent partners. While others lament only and see the church in decline, we refer to the vitality of ancient traditions and young risers. In the Vatican correspondent of the newspaper is always on site. He reported and commented on Vatican news with proven competence. The Rome office of the ASZ Die Allgemeine Sonntagszeitung is situated near the Vatican. Faster than other papers documenting "the daily mail" teaching writing and speeches of the Holy Father and other important Vatican documents in full. The great travels of the Pope's support for our chosen and best "daily mail" writers. The major themes of Pope Benedict XVI. and after further inquiry, one of the exciting challenges of a Catholic daily newspaper. To take the Church to view the means for us but also to draw attention to the plight of the oppressed and suffering Christians in many countries around the world and let them speak for themselves. More to bring in information and background than others - and this always solidly researched - this is the right of churches reporting of the ASZ Die Allgemeine Sonntagszeitung In their love for the Church and the Successor of Peter, our authors can pay it no doubt.. As a Catholic newspaper stands for the ASZ Die Allgemeine Sonntagszeitung the person at the center on our page 8 also very practical. "Called by name" is a rubric that new and interesting lecture by prominent contemporaries. People make history, so on this page is a lot of space for humanity, for people and their stories. Entertaining, exciting, illuminating the historical background, but also anecdotes Empire is one of them. We concentrate on those topical issues of our time, which may be of interest to devout Christians who remain in other media may be under the perception threshold. As a Catholic newspaper, we are in the world with all its dazzling facets facing. What is always in the company of importance is also on the scale. Critical journalism is for us, social and time to be critical, sensitive to impending change and upheaval. The much-vaunted values and their change, the importance of change and loss of meaning of words, the abolition of old and the simultaneous construction of new taboos - all discussed our feature pages. Here in liberal circles is sometimes proclaimed longer maintained as practiced culture of debate. And so with a clear focus: All questions of medical ethics and bioethics, demographic shifts and their consequences, the collapse of any consensus on marriage and family, the right to life of the unborn as the sick very old, the rule of law and its exposure to which cross-cultural as the inter-religious dialogue for us but not fashion-duration issues. Profiled authors, renowned scholars and alert observer of political and social, regional or global developments pose the question: Where is the company? What will determine our lives and survival in the future? What goes and what stays? As a Catholic newspaper is the "daily mail" not to charlatan activism, but to education and culture in the breadth and depth of the Western tradition. This includes literary, like the great reader response to our series "The fifty best novels" proves, but also the tradition of thought our continent, we acknowledged in the series "Sixty major works of philosophy." Current exhibitions and performances are discussed in our culture page. But cultural philosophy, religious studies and intellectual themes found their proper place. In the confrontation with the spirit and demon of our time affects the "daily mail" in the original sense of the word enlightenment. Thoughtful and provocative contributions from social scientists of different faculties should encourage to further their own thinking and. As a Catholic newspaper, we know the power of the media, especially television and the Internet, but also about the power of the media agenda. What developments are welcome and helpful, which dangerous or unsafe? These and other media ethics issues, we do not spare us and others. In the information age to give reliable guidance to offer in the information overload a solid and diverse information, is our daily concern. For many years, the ASZ Die Allgemeine Sonntagszeitung quickly and on a solid foundation of values reviews the latest movies, recommended DVDs, television films and series, the new publications observed on the newspaper and magazine market. Many parents use this service already in the media education of their adolescent children. Others enjoy many a movie review before or instead of the movie, or decide by reading our media page, which film they see and buy what magazine they are. As a Catholic newspaper sees the ASZ Die

Allgemeine Sonntagszeitung man in the center of all political and economic as well all the bustle. Is not by chance that our economy side, which is every Saturday to find on page 7, "Man and the economy." We feel the Christian social teaching. Micro-and macro-economic developments, knocking the "daily mail" so from the principles of the common good, solidarity and subsidiarity. The focus of our reporting and commentary is always the question of how economic and global developments on the man and his dignity, to family and effects of social poverty in many countries, the rise of new emerging economies, the emerging crisis of traditional economies, price and currency fluctuations, international trade agreements and aid agreements, financial crises and their social impact -. finds all this under a Christian perspective on the economic side the "daily mail". Hours of leisure, recreation and leisure are important and are part of the rhythm of a healthy life. Our travel writers tell of the most beautiful spots in the world. But they travel a lot overseas, but also increasingly at home. Trips are on the subject is: often the good is much closer than you think. Each in the weekend edition appears the travel side of the ASZ Die Allgemeine Sonntagszeitung Whether a family vacation, educational travel, or cure.. Here you find reports, tips and suggestions The travel reporting, the ASZ Die Allgemeine Sonntagszeitung is complemented by our regular special publication "Travel & Well-Being." These special pages are devoted to specific topics. Our extensive coverage of the ecclesiastical affairs are in the department of "church date". There you will find daily news, exclusive correspondent reports and detailed background contributions. A team of translators ensures that the "daily mail" all important papal speeches and Vatican documents to document in full can. And faster than any other German-language print media. As "World Youth Day:" The daily mail has not only reported extensively from Sydney. As the only German-language newspaper, we have documented all papal speeches in full. In addition to this current reporting theological issues sometimes require a more detailed discussion. This is done on our special page, theology and history. "Historical issues can also be shown there in a larger context and discussed.
Language(s): German
ADVERTISING RATES:
SCC .... EUR 10,90
Mechanical Data: Type Area: 465 x 320 mm, No. of Columns (Display): 7, Col Widths (Display): 44 mm
Copy instructions: *Copy Date:* 6 days prior to publication
LOCAL NEWSPAPERS

AT INTERNATIONAL MINERAL PROCESSING
721392G30-1
Editorial: Avenwedder Str. 55, 33335 GÜTERSLOH
Tel: 5241 8090884 **Fax:** 5241 80690880
Email: petra.strunk@bauverlag.de **Web site:** http://www.at-online.info
Freq: 10 issues yearly; **Annual Sub.:** EUR 207,00; **Circ:** 5,573
Editor: Petra Strunk; **Advertising Manager:** Erdal Top
Profile: The journal AT International Mineral Processing (treatment technology for minerals) provides information for over 50 years of developments and issues in mechanical process technology in the fields of rocks and soils, coal, ores, secondary raw materials such as Construction waste and power plant byproducts. Topics include both technical-scientific and economic issues to the stages crushing and agglomeration, screening and sizing, grading, draining and drying, material handling and storage, homogenization, mixing and dosing, sampling and quality control. This monthly emphases come from the individual industry sectors, such as salt and potash or trends in coal preparation, as well as country-specific surveys.
Language(s): English; German
ADVERTISING RATES:
Full Page Mono .... EUR 2670
Full Page Colour .... EUR 4370
Mechanical Data: Type Area: 270 x 186 mm, No. of Columns (Display): 4, Col Widths (Display): 45 mm
Copy instructions: *Copy Date:* 15 days prior to publication
BUSINESS: MINING & QUARRYING

ATELIER
721341G84A-440
Editorial: Hospeltstr. 47, 50825 KÖLN
Tel: 221 9545858 **Fax:** 221 9545860
Email: fritzsche@atelier-verlag.de **Web site:** http://www.atelier-verlag.de
Freq: 6 issues yearly; **Annual Sub.:** EUR 22,75; **Circ:** 9,200
Editor: Bence Fritzsche; **Advertising Manager:** Viktor Tarnok
Profile: atelier is the information magazine for visual artists in Germany. The journal atelier is published each with the current art prize calendar, which publishes the current RFQs art. Information on exhibition opportunities, art and law, news about job-specific information for the visual artists as well as funding opportunities and tips will published in each issue.
Language(s): German
ADVERTISING RATES:
Full Page Mono .... EUR 765
Full Page Colour .... EUR 1400
Mechanical Data: Type Area: 242 x 180 mm, No. of Columns (Display): 3, Col Widths (Display): 57 mm
Copy instructions: *Copy Date:* 15 days prior to publication
CONSUMER: THE ARTS & LITERARY: Arts

ATEMWEGS- UND LUNGENKRANKHEITEN
721344G56A-1440
Editorial: Josef-Schneider-Str. 11, 97080 WÜRZBURG **Tel:** 931 20136556 **Fax:** 931 20136254
Email: schmidt_m1@medizin.uni-wuerzburg.de
Freq: Monthly; Free to qualifying individuals
Annual Sub.: EUR 193,00; **Circ:** 3,900
Editor: Michael Schmidt; **Advertising Manager:** Christian Graßl
Profile: Atemwegs- und Lungenkrankheiten publishes surveys, original researches, case reports, current comments, questions from practice / reader questions, Focus, Clinical Immunology - what's new?, letters to the editor, interviews, legal issues, professional policies, professional issues, announcements of relevant societies and also personal, conference announcements, book reviews, etc. from all areas of experimental and clinical pulmonology.
Language(s): German
ADVERTISING RATES:
Full Page Mono .... EUR 1900
Full Page Colour .... EUR 2890
Mechanical Data: Type Area: 242 x 167 mm, No. of Columns (Display): 3, Col Widths (Display): 56 mm
Copy instructions: *Copy Date:* 28 days prior to publication
Official Journal of: Organ d. Ges. f. Lungen- u. Atmungsforschung, d. Bad Reichenhaller Forschungsanstalt f. Krankheiten d. Atmungsorgane

THE ATLANTIC TIMES
1813142G73-630
Editorial: Tempelhofer Ufer 23, 10963 BERLIN
Tel: 30 21505422 **Fax:** 30 21505447
Email: info@atlantic-times.com **Web site:** http://www.atlantic-times.com
Freq: Monthly; **Annual Sub.:** EUR 45,00; **Circ:** 50,000
Editor: Rafael Seligmann; **Advertising Manager:** Janine Kulbrok
Profile: Journal of political leaders from government, industry and science in U.S. and Canada.
Language(s): English
ADVERTISING RATES:
Full Page Mono .... EUR 23000
Full Page Colour .... EUR 23000
Mechanical Data: Type Area: 530 x 290 mm

ATP EDITION
721357G5A-23
Editorial: Rosenheimer Str. 145, 81671 MÜNCHEN
Tel: 89 45051418 **Fax:** 89 45051323
Email: atp@oldenbourg.de **Web site:** http://www.oldenbourg-industrieverlag.de
Freq: 10 issues yearly; Free to qualifying individuals
Annual Sub.: EUR 490,00; **Circ:** 842
Editor: Anne Hütter; **Advertising Manager:** Helga Pelzer
Profile: The "atp edition" is the latest information and development of automation technology, the discussion of trends and experiences among practitioners. The topics treated in primary contributions. In reports from companies in ongoing series ("In practice"), in the introduction of new products and new literature as well as current news is reflected in the market place against the automation industry. This Journal of round market analysis and reports from Fair.
Language(s): German
Readership: Aimed at automatisation technicians.
ADVERTISING RATES:
Full Page Mono .... EUR 2990
Full Page Colour .... EUR 2990
Mechanical Data: Type Area: 256 x 189 mm, No. of Columns (Display): 2, Col Widths (Display): 82 mm
Copy instructions: *Copy Date:* 30 days prior to publication
Official Journal of: Organ d. NAMUR Interessengemeinschaft Automatisierung d. Prozessindustrie
BUSINESS: COMPUTERS & AUTOMATION: Automation & Instrumentation

ATZ AUTOMOBILTECHNISCHE ZEITSCHRIFT
721371G31A-313
Editorial: Abraham-Lincoln-Str. 46, 65189 WIESBADEN **Tel:** 611 7878342 **Fax:** 611 7878462
Email: johannes.winterhagen@springer.com **Web site:** http://www.atzonline.de
Freq: 11 issues yearly; **Annual Sub.:** EUR 229,00; **Circ:** 6,035
Editor: Johannes Winterhagen; **Advertising Manager:** Sabine Röck
Profile: The trade magazine for technology-oriented management in the automotive industry provides the very latest information from research and development. The ATZ Automobiltechnische Zeitschrift is the oldest surviving car magazine in the world. The focus of the report are results from research and development in the entire field of passenger cars and commercial vehicles. Authors from industry and academia to report on individual research projects, and production development of vehicles and their components. The ATZ Automobiltechnische Zeitschrift reports technically and scientifically sound and exclusively on advances in automotive technology and serves as an indispensable source of information for all engineers in the worldwide automotive industry. The "German trade press," recorded in May 2010 ATZ Automobiltechnische Zeitschrift as "trade magazine of the year 2010". Reason is the relaunch of ATZ, MTZ & Co. Finally, presenting the magazine since January 2010 in the new design. Reader-friendly, well structured and visually more appealing. The new and modern look clearly supports the technical and scientific orientation of the journals and are well-founded background information even more space.
Language(s): English; German
ADVERTISING RATES:
Full Page Mono .... EUR 3400
Full Page Colour .... EUR 5950
Mechanical Data: Type Area: 240 x 175 mm, No. of Columns (Display): 4, Col Widths (Display): 40 mm
Copy instructions: *Copy Date:* 28 days prior to publication
Official Journal of: Organ d. VDI-Ges. Fahrzeug- u. Verkehrstechnik, d. Forschungsvereinigung Automobiltechnik e.V., d. Dt. Inst. f. Normung e.V., Normenausschuß Kraftfahrzeuge, d. Wissenschaftl. Ges. f. Kraftfahrzeug- u. Motortechnik e.V.
BUSINESS: MOTOR TRADE: Motor Trade Accessories

AUDI MAGAZIN
721375G77E-50
Editorial: Auto-Union-Str., 85057 INGOLSTADT
Tel: 841 8936017 **Fax:** 841 8939919
Email: anja.weinhofer@audi.de **Web site:** http://www.audimagazin.de
Freq: Quarterly; **Cover Price:** EUR 5,50; **Circ:** 366,998
Editor: Ulrich Schwarze
Profile: Magazine for Audi owners.
Language(s): German
ADVERTISING RATES:
Full Page Mono .... EUR 11000
Full Page Colour .... EUR 13800
Mechanical Data: Type Area: 300 x 230 mm
CONSUMER: MOTORING & CYCLING: Club Cars

AUDI SCENE LIVE
721383G77A-100
Editorial: Hertener Mark 7, 45699 HERTEN
Tel: 2366 808100 **Fax:** 2366 808149
Email: red.audi@vest-netz.de
Freq: 6 issues yearly; **Annual Sub.:** EUR 38,00; **Circ:** 14,846
Editor: Arno Rudolf Welke
Profile: Audi car fanzine.
Language(s): German
ADVERTISING RATES:
Full Page Mono .... EUR 4100
Full Page Colour .... EUR 5900
Mechanical Data: Type Area: 255 x 185 mm, No. of Columns (Display): 4, Col Widths (Display): 42 mm
Copy instructions: *Copy Date:* 42 days prior to publication

AUDI SCENE LIVE
721383G77A-2924
Editorial: Hertener Mark 7, 45699 HERTEN
Tel: 2366 808100 **Fax:** 2366 808149
Email: red.audi@vest-netz.de
Freq: 6 issues yearly; **Annual Sub.:** EUR 38,00; **Circ:** 14,846
Editor: Arno Rudolf Welke
Profile: Audi car fanzine.
Language(s): German
ADVERTISING RATES:
Full Page Mono .... EUR 4100
Full Page Colour .... EUR 5900
Mechanical Data: Type Area: 255 x 185 mm, No. of Columns (Display): 4, Col Widths (Display): 42 mm
Copy instructions: *Copy Date:* 42 days prior to publication

AUDIO
721377G78A-20
Editorial: Leuschnerstr. 1, 70174 STUTTGART
Tel: 711 2070305500 **Fax:** 711 2070305501
Email: redaktion@audio.de **Web site:** http://www.audio.de
Freq: Monthly; **Cover Price:** EUR 5,30; **Circ:** 26,670
Editor: Dirk Waasen; **Advertising Manager:** Michael Hackenberg
Profile: The Magazine for HiFi, High End, music. Gives the fascinating worlds of experience HiFi Stereo, HiFi & Surround, High End and the thematic area of networking, the digital bridge between consumer electronics and computer technology in the living room. Audio indispensable guide before, during and after the purchase and as an early indicator of trends and tendencies in recognized in the industry.
Language(s): German
ADVERTISING RATES:
Full Page Mono .... EUR 6713
Full Page Colour .... EUR 8950
Mechanical Data: Type Area: 250 x 185 mm, No. of Columns (Display): 4, Col Widths (Display): 43 mm
Copy instructions: *Copy Date:* 31 days prior to publication
CONSUMER: CONSUMER ELECTRONICS: Hi-Fi & Recording

AUDIOPHIL
1923439G65A-263_101
Editorial: An der Frauenkirche 12, 01067 DRESDEN
Tel: 351 82129880
Email: info@audiophil.es **Web site:** http://www.audiophil.es
Freq: 6 issues yearly; **Annual Sub.:** EUR 24,00; **Circ:** 80,000
Editor: Ann Kathrin Bronner; **Advertising Manager:** Ann Kathrin Bronner
Profile: Magazine reports on music and music-related topics in the high culture. Facebook: http://www.facebook.com/audiophil.de Twitter: http://twitter.com/#!/audiophil_de This Outlet offers RSS (Really Simple Syndication).
Language(s): German
ADVERTISING RATES:
Full Page Colour .... EUR 7800
Mechanical Data: Type Area: 280 x 200 mm
Supplement to: Frankfurter Allgemeine, Süddeutsche Zeitung
NATIONAL DAILY & SUNDAY NEWSPAPERS: Unabhängiges konservatives MdEP

AUD!MAX DIE HOCHSCHULZEITSCHRIFT
721376G83-740
Editorial: Hauptmarkt 6, 90403 NÜRNBERG
Tel: 911 2377944 **Fax:** 911 204939
Email: leserbriefe@audimax.de **Web site:** http://www.audimax.de
Freq: 9 issues yearly; **Cover Price:** Free; **Circ:** 400,800
Editor: Julia Eggs; **Advertising Manager:** Josefine Lorenz
Profile: Magazine for students with a focus on job orientation.
Language(s): German
ADVERTISING RATES:
Full Page Mono .... EUR 12125
Full Page Colour .... EUR 17863
Mechanical Data: Type Area: 255 x 192 mm, No. of Columns (Display): 4, Col Widths (Display): 45 mm
Copy instructions: *Copy Date:* 25 days prior to publication
CONSUMER: STUDENT PUBLICATIONS

AUD!MAX ONLINE
1620763G62H-1172
Editorial: Hauptmarkt 6, 90403 NÜRNBERG
Tel: 911 2377944 **Fax:** 911 204939
Email: eggs@audimax.de **Web site:** http://www.audimax.de
Freq: Daily; **Cover Price:** Paid; **Circ:** 12,000 Unique Users
Editor: Julia Eggs; **Advertising Manager:** Josefine Lorenz
Profile: Ezine: Students' magazine.
Language(s): German
BUSINESS: CHURCH & SCHOOL EQUIPMENT & EDUCATION: Careers

AUF ATMEN
721390G87-880
Editorial: Catharinenstr. 2, 27472 CUXHAVEN
Tel: 4721 554755 **Fax:** 4721 33291
Email: info@aufatmen.de **Web site:** http://www.aufatmen.de
Freq: Quarterly; **Annual Sub.:** EUR 23,80; **Circ:** 28,500
Editor: Ulrich Eggers; **Advertising Manager:** Thilo Cunz
Profile: Christian magazine.
Language(s): German
ADVERTISING RATES:
Full Page Mono .... EUR 2179
Full Page Colour .... EUR 2421
Mechanical Data: Type Area: 258 x 188 mm, No. of Columns (Display): 4, Col Widths (Display): 44 mm
Copy instructions: *Copy Date:* 28 days prior to publication
CONSUMER: RELIGIOUS

AUF EINEN BLICK
721398G76C-20
Editorial: Burchardstr. 11, 20095 HAMBURG
Tel: 40 30192101 **Fax:** 40 30192148
Email: info@aufeinenblick.de **Web site:** http://www.bauerverlag.de
Freq: 26 issues yearly; **Annual Sub.:** EUR 70,20; **Circ:** 1,141,770
Editor: Michael Heun
Profile: The leisure and television magazine with the best mix of program guide, emotional conversation and competent guide! Week after week, has at a glance with the latest news from society, everyday life and the lives of stars. At a Glance provides authoritative, of course with the best tips on saving, home and garden, partnership, current judgments, fashion, travel, recipes and health. The TV program at a glance: each day is clearly presented on six pages. There are a large weekly review. The special feature: seven regional editions with the respective home stations in the region and the current radio program. Regularly starts to look great reader actions such as "Germany's most beautiful dog " or "Germany's dream garden ". There are competitions, quizzes, weekly romance.
Language(s): German
ADVERTISING RATES:
Full Page Mono .... EUR 34627
Full Page Colour .... EUR 34627
Mechanical Data: Type Area: 258 x 206 mm, No. of Columns (Display): 4, Col Widths (Display): 48 mm
CONSUMER: MUSIC & PERFORMING ARTS: TV & Radio

AUFGESCHLOSSEN
1923312G4E-7294
Editorial: Mettener Str. 33, 94469 DEGGENDORF
Tel: 991 370150 **Fax:** 991 33918
Email: mail@eigenschenk.de **Web site:** http://www.eigenschenk.de
Circ: 7,500
Editor: Tanja Belicic
Profile: Publication from the engineering company IFB Eigenschenk.
Language(s): German

DER AUFSICHTSRAT

1640337G14A-9584

Editorial: Grafenberger Allee 293, 40237 DÜSSELDORF **Tel:** 211 8871440 **Fax:** 211 887971440
Email: ar.redaktion@fachverlag.de **Web site:** http://www.aufsichtsrat.de
Freq: Monthly; **Annual Sub.:** EUR 258,00; **Circ:** 1,500
Editor: Annette Jünger-Fuhr; **Advertising Manager:** Ralf Pötzsch
Profile: The trade magazine "Der Aufsichtsrat" provides monthly business and legal professional journalistic information prepared and tailored to the needs of elected officials. "Der Aufsichtsrat" informed about new developments in corporate governance and its content includes all areas relevant to the elected officials for the proper exercise of its monitoring activities of importance.
Language(s): German
ADVERTISING RATES:
Full Page Mono .... EUR 3140
Full Page Colour .... EUR 3140
Mechanical Data: Type Area: 227 x 165 mm, No. of Columns (Display): 3
Copy instructions: *Copy Date:* 15 days prior to publication

AUFSTIEG UND FALL

1905213G73-667

Editorial: Prinzessinenstr. 19, 10969 BERLIN
Tel: 30 609824950 **Fax:** 30 609824959
Email: susann.kramer@aufstiegundfall.com
Freq: Quarterly; **Cover Price:** EUR 5,60; **Circ:** 10,000
Editor: Iván Aránega Tortosa
Profile: Genral interest magazine Facebook: http://www.facebook.com/AUFSTIEGUNDFALL Twitter: http://twitter.com/#!/aufstiegundfall.
Language(s): English; German

DER AUGENARZT

721417G56E-386

Editorial: Maaßstr. 32/1, 69123 HEIDELBERG
Tel: 6221 1377630 **Fax:** 6221 29910
Email: heusel@kaden-verlag.de **Web site:** http://www.kaden-verlag.de
Freq: 6 issues yearly; **Circ:** 8,500
Advertising Manager: Petra Hübler
Profile: der Augenarzt is the highest circulation in German-language journal of ophthalmology and reaches almost all eye doctors. As a newsmagazine for ophthalmology provides der Augenarzt professional politics first-hand news and information for optimal practice management - in an attractive, reader-friendly layout. der Augenarzt is well received: In a representative survey, 80% of the readers inside its association magazine notes 1 and 2.
Language(s): German
Readership: Read by members of the Association of German Ophthalmologists.
ADVERTISING RATES:
Full Page Mono .... EUR 2555
Full Page Colour .... EUR 3890
Mechanical Data: Type Area: 230 x 178 mm, No. of Columns (Display): 2, Col Widths (Display): 88 mm
Copy instructions: *Copy Date:* 30 days prior to publication
BUSINESS: HEALTH & MEDICAL: Optics

AUGENBLICK

721420G2A-240

Editorial: Wilhelm-Röpke-Str. 6a, 35039 MARBURG
Tel: 6421 2824634 **Fax:** 6421 2826989
Email: fauli@staff.uni-marburg.de **Web site:** http://www.uni-marburg.de/augenblick
Freq: 3 issues yearly; **Annual Sub.:** EUR 25,00; **Circ:** 600
Editor: Burkhard Röwekamp; **Advertising Manager:** Katrin Ahnemann
Profile: Magazine on media with critical focus on movies and tv.
Language(s): English; German
ADVERTISING RATES:
Full Page Mono .... EUR 180
Mechanical Data: Type Area: 185 x 115 mm

DER AUGENOPTIKER

721423G56E-20

Editorial: Ernst-Mey-Str. 8, 70771 LEINFELDEN-ECHTERDINGEN **Tel:** 711 7594240
Fax: 711 75941240
Email: ao.redaktion@konradin.de **Web site:** http://www.ao-online.de
Freq: Monthly; **Annual Sub.:** EUR 85,80; **Circ:** 9,760
Editor: Theo Mahr; **Advertising Manager:** Ines Scholz
Profile: Der Augenoptiker is a specialist in fashion, trends, marketing and communications, making self-employed and salaried optometrist, professionals in the industry, buyers and sellers in retail stores. Topics fidelity, high level of editorial expertise, market presence in all major trade and consumer shows, safe release dates, price loyalty, widespread distribution and reliability features of the magazine. Der Augenoptiker reported on key issues that are important in the daily work of the reader, such as: optical frames, sunglasses, fashion, sport optics, lenses, contact lenses and care products, shop construction, computers, workshop and machinery, the latest products, Audible acustic and low vision.
Language(s): German
ADVERTISING RATES:
Full Page Mono .... EUR 2960
Full Page Colour .... EUR 4520
Mechanical Data: Type Area: 270 x 188 mm, No. of Columns (Display): 4, Col Widths (Display): 44 mm
BUSINESS: HEALTH & MEDICAL: Optics

DER AUGENSPIEGEL

1609432G56A-11165

Editorial: Papiermühlenweg 74, 40882 RATINGEN
Tel: 2102 167817 **Fax:** 2102 167828
Email: redaktion@augenspiegel.com **Web site:** http://www.augenspiegel.com
Freq: 11 issues yearly; **Annual Sub.:** EUR 99,00; **Circ:** 6,082
Editor: Ulrike Lüdtke; **Advertising Manager:** Karin Lilge
Profile: Der Augenspiegel is an independent journal for ophthalmologists in clinics and practices. The current coverage of topics from the entire spectrum of ophthalmology has primarily the goal to inform the reader about the current practice developments, debates and challenges in the field of ophthalmology. Practical relevance, timeliness and expertise - this is substantive goals for the continued success of the venerable magazine Der Augenspiegel. For the conceptual implementation provide a dedicated editorial team of journalists and medical professionals in the publishing house, an active professional scientific advisory board of renowned ophthalmologists and renowned expert authors.
Language(s): German
ADVERTISING RATES:
Full Page Mono .... EUR 2387
Full Page Colour .... EUR 3950
Mechanical Data: Col Widths (Display): 82 mm, Type Area: 222 x 170 mm, No. of Columns (Display): 2
Copy instructions: *Copy Date:* 30 days prior to publication

AUGSBURGER ALLGEMEINE

721424G67B-2200

Editorial: Curt-Frenzel-Str. 2, 86167 AUGSBURG
Tel: 821 7770 **Fax:** 821 7772067
Email: redaktion@augsburger-allgemeine.de **Web site:** http://www.augsburger-allgemeine.de
Freq: 312 issues yearly; **Circ:** 100,161
Editor: Markus Günther; **News Editor:** Jörg Sigmund; **Advertising Manager:** Herbert Dachs
Profile: The Augsburger Allgemeine / Allgäuer Zeitung, the daily newspaper with the most subscribers in Bavaria (310 342 copies IVW fourth quarter of 2010). In conjunction with the Allgäuer Zeitung they reached a circulation of about 336,000 copies a day around 918 000 readers. In the main area of distribution, the government district Bavarian Swabia and parts of Upper Bavaria, 55.4% of the German population, the daily read with their total of 25 issues. Facebook: http://www.facebook.com/AugsburgerAllgemeine Twitter: http://twitter.com/AZ_Augsburg This Outlet offers RSS (Really Simple Syndication).
Language(s): German
ADVERTISING RATES:
SCC .... EUR 388,20
Mechanical Data: Type Area: 480 x 327 mm, No. of Columns (Display): 7, Col Widths (Display): 45 mm
Copy instructions: *Copy Date:* 1 day prior to publication
Supplement(s): Augsburg Direkt; CiA City News; City-Galerie aktuell; doppio
REGIONAL DAILY & SUNDAY NEWSPAPERS: Regional Daily Newspapers

AUGSBURGER ALLGEMEINE ONLINE

1620765G67B-16508

Editorial: Curt-Frenzel-Str. 2, 86167 AUGSBURG
Tel: 821 7773109 **Fax:** 821 7773122
Email: online-redaktion@augsburger-allgemeine.de
Web site: http://www.augsburger-allgemeine.de
Cover Price: Paid; **Circ:** 3,330,993 Unique Users
Editor: Sascha Borowski; **Advertising Manager:** Andreas Schmutterer
Profile: Ezine: augsburger-allgemeine.de is the news portal service and the Augsburger Allgemeine newspaper and his local newspapers. Your editors fill this constantly for the latest regional, national and international news. With approximately 24.4 million page impressions, about 3.6 million visits and 750,000 unique users augsburger-allgemeine.de is the highest reach of regional news portal for Bayerisch-Schwaben. Facebook: http://www.facebook.com/AugsburgerAllgemeine Twitter: http://twitter.com/AZ_Augsburg.
Language(s): German
REGIONAL DAILY & SUNDAY NEWSPAPERS: Regional Daily Newspapers

AUGUSTO

721431G89A-180

Editorial: Ostra-Allee 18, 01067 DRESDEN
Tel: 351 48642366 **Fax:** 351 48642563
Email: ufer.peter@dd-v.de **Web site:** http://www.sz-online.de/augusto
Freq: Annual; **Cover Price:** EUR 4,80; **Circ:** 20,000
Editor: Peter Ufer; **Advertising Manager:** Irene Schuster
Profile: Journal of gastronomy, and enjoyment of life in Dresden. The magazine provides Newspaper in the Saxon manner, not only of good suggestions for culinary expeditions through Dresden and surrounding area, but also high-class reviews to ratings for restaurants in the areas of Home cooking to gourmet. In addition to the testers, of course, the readers come to the word, which may in the action Augusto readers choose their favorites in the categories Gourmet Restaurant, Fine, elect Civic and International.
Language(s): German
ADVERTISING RATES:
Full Page Colour .... EUR 2750
Mechanical Data: Type Area: 255 x 205 mm
Copy instructions: *Copy Date:* 60 days prior to publication

AUMA_MESSEGUIDE DEUTSCHLAND

735363G14A-4700

Editorial: Littenstr. 9, 10179 BERLIN
Tel: 30 24000140 **Fax:** 30 24000340
Email: h.koetter@auma.de **Web site:** http://www.auma.de
Freq: Annual; **Cover Price:** Free; **Circ:** 2,100
Editor: Harald Kötter
Profile: Guide and preview for international fairs.
Language(s): German

AUR ARBEIT UND RECHT

721087G44-3087

Editorial: Mertonstr. 30, 60325 FRANKFURT
Tel: 69 24705720 **Fax:** 69 24705724
Email: rudolf.buschmann@dgb.de **Web site:** http://www.arbeitundrecht.eu
Freq: 11 issues yearly; **Annual Sub.:** EUR 148,80; **Circ:** 2,900
Editor: Rudolf Buschmann; **Advertising Manager:** Peter Beuther
Profile: Journal about the law relating to work.
Language(s): German
ADVERTISING RATES:
Full Page Mono .... EUR 1080
Full Page Colour .... EUR 1890
Mechanical Data: Type Area: 260 x 180 mm
Copy instructions: *Copy Date:* 20 days prior to publication
BUSINESS: LEGAL

AUSBAU + FASSADE

721452G4E-540

Editorial: Schubartstr. 21, 73312 GEISLINGEN
Tel: 7331 930158 **Fax:** 7331 930191
Email: andreas.gabriel@ausbauundfassade.de **Web site:** http://www.ausbauundfassade.de
Freq: Monthly; Free to qualifying individuals
Annual Sub.: EUR 110,21; **Circ:** 7,306
Editor: Andreas Gabriel; **Advertising Manager:** Sibylle Lutz
Profile: Magazine for interior walls and directed at the craft and business of plastering interior industry.
Language(s): German
ADVERTISING RATES:
Full Page Mono .... EUR 2500
Full Page Colour .... EUR 4240
Mechanical Data: Type Area: 262 x 185 mm, No. of Columns (Display): 4, Col Widths (Display): 43 mm
Copy instructions: *Copy Date:* 21 days prior to publication
BUSINESS: ARCHITECTURE & BUILDING: Building

AUSGABE TECHNIK

1639152G1C-1440

Editorial: Aschaffenburger Str. 19, 60599 FRANKFURT **Tel:** 69 97083335 **Fax:** 69 7078400
Email: red.technik@kreditwesen.de **Web site:** http://www.kreditwesen.de
Freq: Quarterly; **Annual Sub.:** EUR 62,20; **Circ:** 2,748
Editor: Berthold Morschhäuser; **Advertising Manager:** Ralf Werner
Profile: Magazine on IT for financial service providers.
Language(s): German
ADVERTISING RATES:
Full Page Mono .... EUR 2900
Full Page Colour .... EUR 4400
Mechanical Data: Type Area: 265 x 185 mm, No. of Columns (Display): 3, Col Widths (Display): 58 mm
Copy instructions: *Copy Date:* 15 days prior to publication
Supplement to: Zeitschrift für das gesamte Kreditwesen

AUSGEHEN IN HAMBURG

1893310G89A-12447

Editorial: Höherweg 287, 40231 DÜSSELDORF
Tel: 211 7357681 **Fax:** 211 7357680
Email: info@ueberblick.de **Web site:** http://www.ueberblick.de
Freq: Annual; **Cover Price:** EUR 7,80; **Circ:** 40,000
Editor: Peter Erik Hillenbach
Profile: Restaurant guide for Hamburg.
Language(s): German
ADVERTISING RATES:
Full Page Mono .... EUR 2390
Full Page Colour .... EUR 3490
Mechanical Data: Type Area: 260 x 190 mm, No. of Columns (Display): 4, Col Widths (Display): 44 mm

AUSGEWÄHLTE TAGUNGSHOTELS ZUM WOHLFÜHLEN

721468G89A-200

Editorial: Celsiusstr. 7, 86899 LANDSBERG
Tel: 8191 9471625 **Fax:** 8191 9471666
Email: schaffrath@tophotel.de **Web site:** http://www.tagungshotellerie.de
Freq: Annual; **Cover Price:** EUR 19,90; **Circ:** 10,950
Editor: Jacqueline Schaffrath; **Advertising Manager:** Martin Frey
Profile: Presentation of German conference hotels selected by feel-good criteria.
Language(s): German
ADVERTISING RATES:
Full Page Mono .... EUR 2080
Full Page Colour .... EUR 3160
Mechanical Data: Type Area: 210 x 90 mm
Copy instructions: *Copy Date:* 35 days prior to publication

AUSGEWÄHLTE WELLNESSHOTELS ZUM WOHLFÜHLEN

1606458G89A-11517

Editorial: Celsiusstr. 7, 86899 LANDSBERG
Tel: 8191 9471625 **Fax:** 8191 9471666
Email: schaffrath@tophotel.de **Web site:** http://www.wellnesshotellerie.de
Freq: Annual; **Cover Price:** EUR 19,90; **Circ:** 17,900
Editor: Jacqueline Schaffrath; **Advertising Manager:** Martin Frey
Profile: Presentation of approximately 160 wellness hotels, selected according to well-being criteria.
Language(s): German
ADVERTISING RATES:
Full Page Mono .... EUR 2080
Full Page Colour .... EUR 3160
Mechanical Data: Type Area: 210 x 90 mm
Copy instructions: *Copy Date:* 40 days prior to publication

AUSKUNFTS- UND VERZEICHNIS-MEDIEN

1829347G2A-5758

Editorial: Heerdter Sandberg 30, 40549 DÜSSELDORF **Tel:** 211 57799513
Fax: 211 57799544
Email: redaktion@vdav.org **Web site:** http://www.vdav.org
Freq: 7 issues yearly; **Circ:** 1,000
Editor: Rhett-Chr. Grammatik; **Advertising Manager:** Stephanie Hollstein
Profile: Magazine from the German Association of Information and Catalogue Media.
Language(s): German
ADVERTISING RATES:
Full Page Mono .... EUR 710
Full Page Colour .... EUR 710
Mechanical Data: Type Area: 297 x 210 mm
Copy instructions: *Copy Date:* 15 days prior to publication

AUSLANDSMESSEPROGRAMM DER BUNDESREPUBLIK DEUTSCHLAND UND DER BUNDESLÄNDER

1638161G14A-9565

Editorial: Littenstr. 9, 10179 BERLIN
Tel: 30 24000124 **Fax:** 30 24000320
Email: info@auma.de **Web site:** http://www.auma.de
Freq: Annual; **Cover Price:** Free; **Circ:** 10,000
Editor: Natalja Winges
Profile: Magazine with programmes of exhibitions.
Language(s): German

AUSSCHREIBUNGSANZEIGER SACHSEN-ANHALT

2051395G4E-7345

Editorial: Daniel-Vorländer-Str. 6, 06120 HALLE
Tel: 345 6932554 **Fax:** 345 6932555
Email: verlag@dvz-halle.de **Web site:** http://www.ausschreibungsanzeiger.com
Freq: Weekly; **Cover Price:** EUR 3,75; **Circ:** 4,000
Profile: Magazine containing features on new building products, technology and the latest developments in the construction industry.
Language(s): German

AUSSCHREIBUNGSBLATT BI

722776G4E-2760

Editorial: Faluner Weg 33, 24109 KIEL
Tel: 431 5359240 **Fax:** 431 5359226
Email: redaktion@bi-medien.de **Web site:** http://www.bi-medien.de
Freq: 260 issues yearly; **Annual Sub.:** EUR 528,36; **Circ:** 9,960
Editor: Rudi Grimm; **Advertising Manager:** Paul Fröhlich
Profile: Information on public invitations to bid for supplies, services and construction as well as private / commercial projects.
Language(s): German
ADVERTISING RATES:
Full Page Mono .... EUR 1404
Full Page Colour .... EUR 1908
Mechanical Data: Type Area: 286 x 204 mm, No. of Columns (Display): 2, Col Widths (Display): 100 mm
Copy instructions: *Copy Date:* 2 days prior to publication
BUSINESS: ARCHITECTURE & BUILDING: Building

AUSSENWIRTSCHAFT

721508G14C-160

Editorial: Am Wallgraben 115, 70565 STUTTGART
Tel: 711 7822048 **Fax:** 711 7821288
Email: johannes.buechs@dsv-gruppe.de **Web site:** http://www.dsv-gruppe.de
Freq: 6 issues yearly; **Circ:** 9,601
Editor: Johannes Büchs; **Advertising Manager:** Anneli Baumann
Profile: AussenWirtschaft appears now more consistent in content and visual style of modern business magazines: imaged a large area, rubricated clear, with emotional layout and headlines that pull in the story. This is always closely linked with the sales focus of the savings banks. The AussenWirtschaft has been expanded from 44 to 52 pages and is now bringing four countries portraits as a PDF download. Magazine focus is the international network of the world of savings banks with its contacts abroad and opportunities for the middle class. The paper profiled

thus the positioning of the savings banks in international business. This is also the Kreissparkasse Heilbronn: the magazine distributed to approximately 150 selected customers and evaluated it as a high quality instrument in the "toolbox of customer loyalty." The paper leaves much room for individualization by print service or on the editorial in the DSV: the AussenWirtschaft is with the Editorial and name of the institute in the title customizable. Thus, the magazine quality paid up to one brand. By DSV direct mail to reach customers the magazine, while the savings banks pay favorable postage rates and handling costs savings.
Language(s): German
ADVERTISING RATES:
Full Page Mono .... EUR 1440
Full Page Colour .... EUR 3000
Mechanical Data: Type Area: 229 x 176 mm, No. of Columns (Display): 3, Col Widths (Display): 56 mm
BUSINESS: COMMERCE, INDUSTRY & MANAGEMENT: International Commerce

AUSSENWIRTSCHAFT
1794467G14C-4768
Editorial: Mainzer Landstr. 199, 60326 FRANKFURT
Tel: 69 75912129 **Fax:** 69 75911966
Email: laender@faz-institut.de **Web site:** http://www.laenderdienste.de
Freq: Annual; **Cover Price:** EUR 38,00; **Circ:** 5,000
Advertising Manager: Karin Gangl
Profile: Economic data from Germany.Entrepreneurs Guide for exports and direct investment expertise to partners, markets, legal, personnel, logistics and finance.
Language(s): German
ADVERTISING RATES:
Full Page Mono .... EUR 1600
Full Page Colour .... EUR 1600
Mechanical Data: Type Area: 215 x 130 mm
Copy instructions: *Copy Date:* 60 days prior to publication

AUTO BILD
721567G77A-220
Editorial: Axel-Springer-Platz 1, 20350 HAMBURG
Tel: 40 34722142 **Fax:** 40 34726332
Email: redaktion@autobild.de **Web site:** http://www.autobild.de
Freq: Weekly; **Annual Sub.:** EUR 76,50; **Circ:** 541,369
Editor: Bernd Wieland; **News Editor:** Matthias Moetsch; **Advertising Manager:** Peter Hoffmann
Profile: AUTO BILD is the most popular and best-known German car magazine. Every Friday AUTO BILD is presented in full color: with tests and technical contributions, with extensive service issues. Great new and used car comparisons, workshops and tire tests, the latest news and reader tips, but also travel information and insurance issues are important parts of the editorial approach. By the very strong theme sections - Service / Technology / Features - AUTO BILD has a high competence for the mulilaterally interested readership. For millions of German drivers AUTO BILD is therefore a competent advisor and partner.
Language(s): German
Readership: Aimed at car enthusiasts.
ADVERTISING RATES:
Full Page Mono .... EUR 37900
Full Page Colour .... EUR 37900
Mechanical Data: Type Area: 296 x 209 mm, No. of Columns (Display): 4, Col Widths (Display): 50 mm
Copy instructions: *Copy Date:* 24 days prior to publication
Supplement(s): Auto Bild motorsport
CONSUMER: MOTORING & CYCLING: Motoring

AUTO BILD ALLRAD
755613G77D-1242
Editorial: Hansastr. 4a, 91126 SCHWABACH
Tel: 9122 985220 **Fax:** 9122 985222
Email: redaktion@autobildallrad.de **Web site:** http://www.autobild-allrad.de
Freq: Monthly; **Annual Sub.:** EUR 37,80; **Circ:** 66,810
Editor: Bernhard Weinbacher
Profile: AUTO BILD ALLRAD is Europe's largest Fourl-Wheel-Journal. Lifestyle associated with superior technology are the success factors of this glossy magazine. The monthly magazine with news, trends and inspiration from the new 4x4-world conveys security, optics and fun for all-wheel fans. The reader will find extensive tests and driving reports, accessory introductions in each issue. In addition to the 4x4 experience world the title focuses on the practical things of everyday 4x4 life on the road and off road. Facebook: http://www.facebook.com/autobild.
Language(s): German
ADVERTISING RATES:
Full Page Mono .... EUR 9800
Full Page Colour .... EUR 9800
Mechanical Data: No. of Columns (Display): 4, Col Widths (Display): 45 mm, Type Area: 266 x 196 mm
Copy instructions: *Copy Date:* 35 days prior to publication
CONSUMER: MOTORING & CYCLING: Motor Sports

AUTO BILD KLASSIK
1882074G77A-2866
Editorial: Axel-Springer-Platz 1, 20350 HAMBURG
Tel: 40 34722142 **Fax:** 40 34726332
Email: redaktion@autobild.de **Web site:** http://www.autobild.de
Freq: Monthly; **Annual Sub.:** EUR 27,40; **Circ:** 110,132
Editor: Bernd Wieland; **News Editor:** Matthias Moetsch
Profile: Magazine covering all aspects of vintage cars.
Language(s): German
ADVERTISING RATES:
Full Page Mono .... EUR 9100
Full Page Colour .... EUR 9100
Mechanical Data: Type Area: 266 x 196 mm, No. of Columns (Display): 4, Col Widths (Display): 48 mm
Copy instructions: *Copy Date:* 35 days prior to publication

AUTO BILD MOTORSPORT
721569G77D-120
Editorial: Hansastr. 4a, 91126 SCHWABACH
Tel: 9122 985220 **Fax:** 9122 985222
Email: redaktion@autobildmotorsport.de **Web site:** http://www.autobild-motorsport.de
Freq: 37 issues yearly; **Cover Price:** EUR 1,50; **Circ:** 500,094
Editor: Olaf Schilling
Profile: AUTO BILD MOTORSPORT offers the whole world of motor sport and also deals extensively with the grassroots. AUTO BILD MOTORSPORT offers the reader in each issue-date and weekly detailed information on Formula 1, the circuit racing and rally championships and an extensive coverage of popular sports including motorcycles - each with a results service and motor sports events. Further background information will be held, driver columns, news coverage, Test & Technology and classical categories.
Language(s): German
ADVERTISING RATES:
Full Page Mono .... EUR 30200
Full Page Colour .... EUR 30200
Mechanical Data: Type Area: 266 x 196 mm, No. of Columns (Display): 4, Col Widths (Display): 48 mm
Copy instructions: *Copy Date:* 35 days prior to publication
Supplement to: Auto Bild
CONSUMER: MOTORING & CYCLING: Motor Sports

AUTO BILD SPORTSCARS
755614G77D-1243
Editorial: Hansastr. 4a, 91126 SCHWABACH
Tel: 9122 985220 **Fax:** 9122 985222
Email: redaktion@autobildsportscars.de **Web site:** http://www.autobild-sportscars.de
Freq: Monthly; **Annual Sub.:** EUR 36,00; **Circ:** 63,672
Editor: Olaf Schilling
Profile: Magazine about car tuning. Facebook: http://www.facebook.com/autobild.
Language(s): German
ADVERTISING RATES:
Full Page Mono .... EUR 9800
Full Page Colour .... EUR 9800
Mechanical Data: Type Area: 266 x 196 mm, No. of Columns (Display): 4, Col Widths (Display): 48 mm
Copy instructions: *Copy Date:* 35 days prior to publication
CONSUMER: MOTORING & CYCLING: Motor Sports

AUTO CLASSIC
1745038G77A-2773
Editorial: Infanteriestr. 11a, 80797 MÜNCHEN
Tel: 89 130699720 **Fax:** 89 130699700
Email: redaktion@autoclassic.de **Web site:** http://www.autoclassic.de
Freq: 6 issues yearly; **Annual Sub.:** EUR 21,06; **Circ:** 35,358
Editor: Jörn Müller-Neuhaus; **Advertising Manager:** Helmut Krämer
Profile: Special-interest magazine for fans, drivers and collectors of historic international automobiles with a focus on the vehicles of the 50s, 60s and 70s. In every issue important types are presented in detail. The magazine provides comprehensive information on technology, historic motor sport, classic car events such as exhibitions, meetings and trips, but also for the proper maintenance and care of vintage and classic cars. Restoration stories and buying advice are also integral parts of the magazine.
Language(s): German
ADVERTISING RATES:
Full Page Colour .... EUR 3350
Mechanical Data: Type Area: 235 x 181 mm, No. of Columns (Display): 4, Col Widths (Display): 45 mm
Copy instructions: *Copy Date:* 40 days prior to publication

AUTO FACHMANN
721575G31A-315
Editorial: Max-Planck-Str. 7, 97082 WÜRZBURG
Tel: 931 4182466 **Fax:** 931 4182780
Email: werner.degen@vogel.de **Web site:** http://www.autofachmann.de
Freq: 11 issues yearly; **Annual Sub.:** EUR 119,40; **Circ:** 65,131
Editor: Werner Degen; **Advertising Manager:** Anna Gredel
Profile: Official Journal of Education for automotive mechatronics and mechanics for body maintenance technology.
Language(s): German
Readership: Aimed at mechanics within the Association.
ADVERTISING RATES:
Full Page Mono .... EUR 3730
Full Page Colour .... EUR 5410
Mechanical Data: Type Area: 270 x 190 mm, No. of Columns (Display): 4, Col Widths (Display): 46 mm
BUSINESS: MOTOR TRADE: Motor Trade Accessories

AUTO KATALOG
721588G77A-300
Editorial: Leuschnerstr. 1, 70174 STUTTGART
Tel: 711 1821241 **Fax:** 711 1821958
Email: redaktion_ams@motorpresse.de **Web site:** http://www.auto-motor-und-sport.de
Freq: Annual; **Cover Price:** EUR 7,90; **Circ:** 150,000
Editor: Bernd Ostmann; **Advertising Manager:** Jochen Bechtle
Profile: The Auto Katalog gives a comprehensive overview of the current model range and the new features of the car next year. Added to the test ratings from Auto Motor und Sport is the Auto Katalog a competent guide. Production cars and exotic cars from around the world form a detailed information pack about 3,000 cars. Technical data and a table of fees round out the car catalog as standard work and advice in the crucial orientation period before buying a car. Facebook: http://www.facebook.com/automotorundsport.
Language(s): German
ADVERTISING RATES:
Full Page Mono .... EUR 16900
Full Page Colour .... EUR 16900
Mechanical Data: Type Area: 248 x 185 mm, No. of Columns (Display): 4, Col Widths (Display): 43 mm
Copy instructions: *Copy Date:* 30 days prior to publication

AUTO MOTOR UND SPORT
721609G77A-55
Editorial: Leuschnerstr. 1, 70174 STUTTGART
Tel: 711 1821241 **Fax:** 711 1821958
Email: redaktion_ams@motorpresse.de **Web site:** http://www.auto-motor-und-sport.de
Freq: 26 issues yearly; **Annual Sub.:** EUR 83,20; **Circ:** 402,631
Editor: Bernd Ostmann; **Advertising Manager:** Jochen Bechtle
Profile: Not without reason is auto motor und sport an authority among automobile magazines. Particularly impressive is the broad topical spectrum that is unique in its journalistic quality and gives an up-to-date market summary every fortnight. True to the motto "Petrol in their blood", the magazine takes a topical, contemporary approach as it portrays and comments on the whole bandwidth of the automotive world. This is supported by critical analyses of the latest cars, manufacturers' secret plans, the latest trends in automotive construction and competent motorsports coverage. Regular tests probe and in-depth evaluate the cars performance. With its service tips and travel reports alongside traffic-related and environmental topics, the magazine sees far beyond the tip of its fine motoring nose. An absolute highlight of the year is the annual Best Cars reader survey. In this auto motor und sport has created an exclusive, international, consumer-based opinion barometer that has earned great respect right up to the boardrooms of the automotive industry: often copied, never matched. auto motor und sport remains the opinion leader among Germany's car magazines. auto motor und sport readers want not only to join in discussions on car-related issues, but also to be looked upon as opinion leaders. This attitude permeates many areas of their lives. With an above-average level of income and education, their interest in innovative products makes auto motor und sport readers keen consumers and a strongly brand-oriented target group.
Language(s): German
ADVERTISING RATES:
Full Page Mono .... EUR 35820
Full Page Colour .... EUR 35820
Mechanical Data: Type Area: 248 x 185 mm, No. of Columns (Display): 4, Col Widths (Display): 43 mm
CONSUMER: MOTORING & CYCLING: Motoring

AUTO MOTOR UND SPORT ECO DRIVE
1872999G77A-2864
Editorial: Leuschnerstr. 1, 70174 STUTTGART
Tel: 711 1821241 **Fax:** 711 1821958
Email: redaktion_ams@motorpresse.de **Web site:** http://www.auto-motor-und-sport.de
Freq: Half-yearly; **Cover Price:** EUR 4,20; **Circ:** 50,000
Editor: Bernd Ostmann; **Advertising Manager:** Jochen Bechtle
Profile: Car magazine with information about new models and technology Facebook: http://www.facebook.com/automotorundsport.
Language(s): German
ADVERTISING RATES:
Full Page Mono .... EUR 7700
Full Page Colour .... EUR 7700
Mechanical Data: Type Area: 248 x 185 mm, No. of Columns (Display): 4, Col Widths (Display): 43 mm
Copy instructions: *Copy Date:* 29 days prior to publication

AUTO NEWS
1660337G77A-2644
Editorial: Hans-Pinsel-Str. 10a, 85540 HAAR
Tel: 89 46237012 **Fax:** 89 466096
Email: redaktion@auto-news.de **Web site:** http://www.auto-news.de
Freq: 6 issues yearly; **Annual Sub.:** EUR 16,00; **Circ:** 15,001
Editor: Peter Hoffmann
Profile: Car drivers' magazine for drivers (news, reviews, technology, auto-catalog, video) Facebook: http://www.facebook.com/pages/Auto-News/274787673873.
Language(s): German
ADVERTISING RATES:
Full Page Mono .... EUR 5900
Full Page Colour .... EUR 5900
Mechanical Data: Type Area: 280 x 184 mm
CONSUMER: MOTORING & CYCLING: Motoring

AUTO STRASSENVERKEHR
721558G77A-120
Editorial: Leuschnerstr. 1, 70174 STUTTGART
Tel: 711 1821326 **Fax:** 711 1821834
Email: redaktion_auto@motorpresse.de **Web site:** http://www.autostrassenverkehr.de
Freq: 25 issues yearly; **Annual Sub.:** EUR 32,50; **Circ:** 157,522
Editor: Jens Katemann; **Advertising Manager:** Stephen Brand
Profile: Objectively and clearly "Auto Strassenverkehr" brings order into the dynamic automotive market, provides tranparency andrecommendates clearly. Compact and comprehensible the "Auto Strassenverkehr" shows important trends, offers views on new developments and provides updated product information in single, comparison and duration tests. The value for money relation is always central. In addition, cash-value tips are given on key service issues such as insurance, financing, maintenance and the used car market. The maximum utility for the general public has priority. The interests of "Auto Strassenverkehr" readers are widely spread. They see themselves as car users, less than a car enthusiast, and want to know what's on. The target audience of the magazine are mainly private car buyers. For their purchase decision a good value for money realation has top priority. The readers are open-minded about new products, their propensity is more controlled with the head than the belly.
Language(s): German
ADVERTISING RATES:
Full Page Mono .... EUR 15700
Full Page Colour .... EUR 15700
Mechanical Data: No. of Columns (Display): 4, Col Widths (Display): 51 mm, Type Area: 280 x 205 mm
Copy instructions: *Copy Date:* 30 days prior to publication
CONSUMER: MOTORING & CYCLING: Motoring

AUTO TEST
737090G77A-1760
Editorial: Hansastr. 4a, 91126 SCHWABACH
Tel: 9122 985220 **Fax:** 9122 985222
Email: autotests@autoverlag.de **Web site:** http://www.autobild.de/autotest
Freq: Monthly; **Annual Sub.:** EUR 24,00; **Circ:** 220,032
Editor: Olaf Schilling
Profile: AUTO TEST - the purchase of consultant AUTO BILD is the No. 3 in the market of car magazines. The title brings monthly tests, news, used cars and a comprehensive shopping guide. Strategic exclusive partnerships with the Institute JD POWER & Associates, EurotaxSchwacke, TÜV and DEKRA support the editorial expertise. AUTO TEST achieved primarily young and educated than the average reader, which are situated on the income her very well. AUTO TEST, and AUTO BILD form in the Display Combination "AUTO CONNEX" a unit that offers outstanding potential with exemplary efficiency. Facebook: http://www.facebook.com/autobild.
Language(s): German
Readership: Aimed at families.
ADVERTISING RATES:
Full Page Mono .... EUR 14800
Full Page Colour .... EUR 14800
Mechanical Data: Type Area: 245 x 190 mm, No. of Columns (Display): 4, Col Widths (Display): 45 mm
Copy instructions: *Copy Date:* 30 days prior to publication
CONSUMER: MOTORING & CYCLING: Motoring

AUTO TEST 4X4 EXTRA
1697640G77A-2740
Editorial: Hansastr. 4a, 91126 SCHWABACH
Tel: 9122 985220 **Fax:** 9122 985222
Email: autotests@autoverlag.de **Web site:** http://www.autobild.de
Freq: Half-yearly; **Cover Price:** EUR 3,90; **Circ:** 130,000
Editor: Olaf Schilling
Profile: Special publication of the monthly purchase consultant Autotest. The magazine offers a comprehensive look at the all-wheel industry with an outlook 2011 to 2012th A comprehensive overview of all model series, engine options and optical features (four-wheel-catalog). Facebook: http://www.facebook.com/autobild.
Language(s): German
ADVERTISING RATES:
Full Page Mono .... EUR 9800
Full Page Colour .... EUR 9800
Mechanical Data: Type Area: 266 x 196 mm, No. of Columns (Display): 3, Col Widths (Display): 65 mm
Copy instructions: *Copy Date:* 35 days prior to publication

AUTO TEST CABRIO
737091G77A-1780
Editorial: Hansastr. 4a, 91126 SCHWABACH
Tel: 9122 985220 **Fax:** 9122 985222
Email: autotests@autoverlag.de **Web site:** http://www.autobild.de/autotests
Freq: Annual; **Cover Price:** EUR 3,90; **Circ:** 130,000
Editor: Olaf Schilling
Profile: Annual about convertibles with tests and introduction of new cars. Facebook: http://www.facebook.com/autobild.
Language(s): German
ADVERTISING RATES:
Full Page Mono .... EUR 9100
Full Page Colour .... EUR 9100
Mechanical Data: Type Area: 266 x 196 mm, No. of Columns (Display): 3, Col Widths (Display): 65 mm
Copy instructions: *Copy Date:* 35 days prior to publication

AUTO TEST VAN-EXTRA
1793388G77A-2780
Editorial: Hansastr. 4a, 91126 SCHWABACH
Tel: 9122 985220 **Fax:** 9122 985222
Email: autotests@autoverlag.de **Web site:** http://www.autobild.de
Freq: Annual; **Cover Price:** EUR 3,90; **Circ:** 130,000
Editor: Olaf Schilling
Profile: Facebook: http://www.facebook.com/autobild.
Language(s): German
ADVERTISING RATES:
Full Page Mono .... EUR 8900
Full Page Colour .... EUR 8900
Mechanical Data: Type Area: 266 x 196 mm, No. of Columns (Display): 3, Col Widths (Display): 65 mm
Copy instructions: *Copy Date:* 35 days prior to publication

AUTO & REISE
721634G77E-100
Editorial: Oberntiefer Str. 20, 91438 BAD WINDSHEIM **Tel:** 9841 409182 **Fax:** 9841 409190
Email: redaktion@arcd.de **Web site:** http://www.autoundreise.de
Freq: 10 issues yearly; Free to qualifying individuals
Annual Sub.: EUR 25,00; **Circ:** 97,601
Editor: Josef Harrer
Profile: Official organ of the ARCD Auto und Reiseclub Deutschland with reports of cars, travel, tourism, road safety, policy, technology and leisure.
Language(s): German
Readership: Read by club members.
ADVERTISING RATES:
Full Page Mono .... EUR 7300
Full Page Colour .... EUR 7300
Mechanical Data: Type Area: 250 x 185 mm, No. of Columns (Display): 4, Col Widths (Display): 43 mm
Copy instructions: *Copy Date:* 30 days prior to publication
CONSUMER: MOTORING & CYCLING: Club Cars

AUTO ZEITUNG
721637G77A-2697
Editorial: Industriestr. 16, 50735 KÖLN
Tel: 221 7709102
Email: redaktion@autozeitung.de **Web site:** http://www.autozeitung.de
Freq: 26 issues yearly; **Cover Price:** EUR 2,00; **Circ:** 235,657
Editor: Volker Koerdt
Profile: Special interest magazine containing the latest news and views from the German motoring scene. Articles report from the traffic and motor sport everyday and uncover irregularities. What really has to offer new technology, like the cars of tomorrow look like, what about the safety of the vehicles.
Language(s): German
Readership: Aimed at people interested in cars, mostly men.
ADVERTISING RATES:
Full Page Mono .... EUR 20885
Full Page Colour .... EUR 20885
Mechanical Data: Type Area: 248 x 185 mm, No. of Columns (Display): 4, Col Widths (Display): 43 mm
Copy instructions: *Copy Date:* 30 days prior to publication
CONSUMER: MOTORING & CYCLING: Motoring

AUTOBAHN SERVICE
1795344G89A-12288
Editorial: Schloßbergstr. 61a, 77876 KAPPELRODECK **Tel:** 7842 948811
Email: fotopress-international@t-online.de
Freq: Quarterly; **Circ:** 750,000
Profile: Magazine on automobiles and traffic.
Language(s): German
ADVERTISING RATES:
Full Page Mono .... EUR 15032
Mechanical Data: Type Area: 210 x 200 mm, No. of Columns (Display): 4, Col Widths (Display): 45 mm
Copy instructions: *Copy Date:* 28 days prior to publication

AUTOCAD & INVENTOR MAGAZIN
721571G19J-1
Editorial: Johann-Sebastian-Bach-Str. 5, 85591 VATERSTETTEN **Tel:** 8106 350152 **Fax:** 8106 350190
Email: rt@win-verlag.de **Web site:** http://www.autocad-magazin.de
Freq: 8 issues yearly; **Annual Sub.:** EUR 118,40; **Circ:** 8,655
Editor: Rainer Trummer; **Advertising Manager:** Bernd Heilmeier
Profile: The exclusive targeting of Autodesk users is unique to the Autocad & Inventor Magazin and offers a unique opportunity, quality and quantity of this highly attractive to target potential customers with a professional medium. Focus not only IT-related topics in the center - we report on all aspects that are important for designers, architects and GIS professionals. We focus particularly on innovations in components and materials. The Autocad & Inventor Magazin is an independent trade magazine for all users and decision makers who work with software solutions from Autodesk. In addition to AutoCAD, these are among other things, AutoCAD LT, AutoCAD ecscad, AutoCAD Electrical, AutoCAD Mechanical, the Inventor product line, AutoCAD Architecture, AutoCAD Civil 3D, AutoCAD Map 3D, AutoCAD MEP, AutoCAD, Revit, 3ds Max Design, Autodesk MapGuide, Topobase, and Data management solutions to the family vault. The Inventor magazine, to account for the market development, as a separate line in the Autocad & Inventor Magazin published. In addition to the technical contributions from the Autodesk solutions, the Autocad & Inventor Magazin reported at a high level of applications for Autodesk software, additional software for designers, architects and GIS professionals. Autodesk's solutions in practice, hardware and peripherals for designers, architects and GIS professionals, materials and components for designers, engineers, architects, civil engineers and construction professionals. The Autocad & Inventor Magazin gives readers concrete problem-solving assistance with all matters relating to the use of design and planning solutions - from hardware selection to the choice of appropriate business solutions. New hardware and software products are not only presented and tested, but in practice examples described in detail. Thus the reader of the Autocad & Inventor Magazin comprehensive basis for decisions on its investments. Novelty in terms of CAD-/PLM-magazines is that we inform designers in each issue through technical articles and product news about innovations in drive technology, automation technology, technical, engineering components, fluid power and electrical engineering as well as innovative materials. Industries: • Architecture / Construction / Civil Engineering • mechanical engineering and plant engineering • Geographic Information Systems (GIS) and infrastructure • Building Services / Building techniques • Facility Management • Electrical and Electronics • consumer goods industry • Medical techniques • Tool and die industry • Plastics technology Categories Autocad Range: • Scene: News, events and exhibitions, interviews with key people in the industry, introduction of new products and solutions • Business: Commercial aspects within the design environment • Special: cross-industry topics, such as project management, Visualsierung, Collaboration, copy protection, IT security and outsourcing • Practice: Tips & Tricks for the everyday, case studies, workshops, AutoCAD LISP programming, and new tools • Mechanical: 2D Mechanical Principles, Best Practices and Applications • Architecture & Construction: AEC and Civil Engineering Principles, Best Practices and Applications • GIS & Infrastructure: Infrastructure and GIS basics, best practices and applications • Software: Short tests and presentation of software solutions • Hardware: Tests and performances of CAD-related hardware products • components for design engineers, drive technology, engineering components, connectivity, automation, fluid power engineering, electrical engineering • materials and materials for designers, architects, civil engineers and construction professionals Categories Inventor Range: • News: Business and personal messages, interviews, product news and events for Inventor users • Software: Solutions and Applications for Inventor, such as data management, FEA, CAM, sheet metal work, viewers, software design • Hardware: Presentation and tests the latest hardware products for Inventor users, such as workstations, graphics cards, monitors, printing solutions, 3D printers and storage solutions • Practice: Tips & Tricks for the everyday, case studies, workshops, AutoCAD programming, and new LISP tools.
Language(s): German
ADVERTISING RATES:
Full Page Mono .... EUR 6020
Full Page Colour .... EUR 7480
Mechanical Data: Type Area: 266 x 180 mm, No. of Columns (Display): 3, Col Widths (Display): 58 mm
Copy instructions: *Copy Date:* 24 days prior to publication
BUSINESS: ENGINEERING & MACHINERY: CAD & CIM (Computer Integrated Manufacture)

AUTODESK PARTNERLÖSUNGEN
1638130G2A-5532
Editorial: Johann-Sebastian-Bach-Str. 5, 85591 VATERSTETTEN **Tel:** 8106 3500 **Fax:** 8106 350190
Email: aak@win-verlag.de **Web site:** http://www.autodesk.de
Freq: Annual; **Cover Price:** EUR 24,90; **Circ:** 2,000
Advertising Manager: Bernd Heilmeier
Profile: Directory listing business addresses for CAD applications.
Language(s): German

AUTOFLOTTE
721577G49A-80
Editorial: Aschauer Str. 30, 81549 MÜNCHEN
Tel: 89 2030431172 **Fax:** 89 2030431254
Email: autoflotte@springer.com **Web site:** http://www.autoflotte.de
Freq: Monthly; **Annual Sub.:** EUR 57,90; **Circ:** 31,631
Editor: Andreas Dünkelmeyer; **Advertising Manager:** Peter Schätzko
Profile: Magazine for the efficient operation and management of company car-fleets. Twitter: http://twitter.com/#!/Autoflotte.
Language(s): German
ADVERTISING RATES:
Full Page Mono .... EUR 5090
Full Page Colour .... EUR 6410
Mechanical Data: Type Area: 240 x 175 mm
BUSINESS: TRANSPORT

AUTOFLOTTE ONLINE
1660925G49A-2382
Editorial: Aschauer Str. 30, 81549 MÜNCHEN
Tel: 89 2030431145
Email: presse.dienste@springer.com **Web site:** http://www.autoflotte.de
Freq: Daily; **Cover Price:** Paid; **Circ:** 56,853 Unique Users
Editor: Patrick Neumann; **Advertising Manager:** Peter Schätzko
Profile: Ezine: Magazine about the efficient operation and management of company car-fleets. Twitter: http://twitter.com/#!/Autoflotte.
Language(s): German
BUSINESS: TRANSPORT

DAS AUTOGAS JOURNAL
1995507G77A-2942
Editorial: Markgrafenstr. 3, 33602 BIELEFELD
Tel: 521 5251310 **Fax:** 521 5251311
Email: redaktion@autogas-journal.de **Web site:** http://www.autogas-journal.de
Freq: 6 issues yearly; **Annual Sub.:** EUR 21,00; **Circ:** 19,468
Editor: Martin Steffan; **Advertising Manager:** Sabine Meier
Profile: German consumer and popular magazine for the fuel LPG. It is particularly informative LPG drivers and interested parties, but also gas plant Umrüstbetriebe, gas plants, importers, associations, government agencies, car manufacturers and importers, also the technical research institutes and universities on all relevant topics of the leading German and European alternative fuel.
Language(s): German
ADVERTISING RATES:
Full Page Mono .... EUR 3434
Full Page Colour .... EUR 3434
Mechanical Data: Type Area: 255 x 182 mm
Copy instructions: *Copy Date:* 21 days prior to publication

AUTOHAUS
721584G31A-316
Editorial: Aschauer Str. 30, 81549 MÜNCHEN
Tel: 89 2030431136 **Fax:** 89 2030431205
Email: redaktion.autohaus@springer.com **Web site:** http://www.autohaus.de
Freq: 21 issues yearly; **Annual Sub.:** EUR 178,00; **Circ:** 19,683
Editor: Ralph M. Meunzel; **Advertising Manager:** Michael Harms
Profile: specialist magazine for company owners and managers of modern automotive operations. Focus: The whole automotive branch, vehicle trading and repair services (including vehicle electronics and brake services), spare parts, accessories and tyre Twitter: http://twitter.com/#!/autohausonline.
Language(s): German
ADVERTISING RATES:
Full Page Mono .... EUR 5830
Full Page Colour .... EUR 7900
Mechanical Data: Type Area: 240 x 175 mm
Supplement(s): Autohaus Spezial; DAT-Report
BUSINESS: MOTOR TRADE: Motor Trade Accessories

AUTOHAUS ONLINE
1622552G31A-327
Editorial: Aschauer Str. 30, 81549 MÜNCHEN
Tel: 89 2030431136 **Fax:** 89 2030431205
Email: redaktion.autohaus@springer.com **Web site:** http://www.autohaus.de
Freq: Daily; **Cover Price:** Paid; **Circ:** 556,893 Unique Users
Editor: Ralph M. Meunzel; **Advertising Manager:** Michael Harms
Profile: Ezine: portal for the automotive trade and industry. Twitter: http://twitter.com/#!/autohausonline.
Language(s): German
BUSINESS: MOTOR TRADE: Motor Trade Accessories

AUTOHIFI
721585G78A-60
Editorial: Leuschnerstr. 1, 70174 STUTTGART
Tel: 711 2070305500 **Fax:** 711 2070305501
Email: redaktion@autohifi-magazin.de **Web site:** http://www.autohifi-magazin.de
Freq: 6 issues yearly; **Cover Price:** EUR 5,00
Editor: Dirk Waasen; **Advertising Manager:** Michael Hackenberg
Profile: The magazine autohifi - the buying and practical guide for mobile media. Mediated enjoy good sound in the car and the fascination of mobile media. Checks mobile stereo, navigation, and a multimedia equipment in objective comparison tests on heart and kidney, is presenting the latest devices in trend reports, and market overviews. All tested devices are placed in a ranked list to autohifi most comprehensive purchasing guide makes. Mediated professional technical know-how in easily understandable way and gives specific instructions for optimum assembly of mobile media components in the car - for every need. In addition, before autohifi special vehicles of professionals and readers. For those who are facing choices, is autohifi advice-giving required reading. For dealers and manufacturers / distributors is autohifi indispensable source of information.
Language(s): German
Readership: Read by car enthusiasts.
ADVERTISING RATES:
Full Page Mono .... EUR 5213
Full Page Colour .... EUR 6950
Mechanical Data: Type Area: 250 x 185 mm, No. of Columns (Display): 3, Col Widths (Display): 58 mm
Copy instructions: *Copy Date:* 35 days prior to publication
CONSUMER: CONSUMER ELECTRONICS: Hi-Fi & Recording

AUTOHOF GUIDE LKW
721586G49A-100
Editorial: Schwarzwaldstr. 99, 71083 HERRENBERG
Tel: 7032 288205 **Fax:** 7032 288206
Email: e.goehrum@agentur-goehrum.de **Web site:** http://www.autohof-guide.de
Freq: Annual; **Cover Price:** EUR 2,50; **Circ:** 120,000
Editor: Eberhard Göhrum
Profile: Truck stops on the German Autobahn with current information, services and offers, especially for truck drivers.
Language(s): German
ADVERTISING RATES:
Full Page Mono .... EUR 5010
Full Page Colour .... EUR 5010
Mechanical Data: Type Area: 128 x 95 mm
Copy instructions: *Copy Date:* 18 days prior to publication
Supplement to: Fernfahrer

AUTOHOF GUIDE PKW
1606459G49A-2323
Editorial: Schwarzwaldstr. 99, 71083 HERRENBERG
Tel: 7032 288205 **Fax:** 7032 288206
Email: e.goehrum@agentur-goehrum.de **Web site:** http://www.autohof-guide.de
Freq: Annual; **Cover Price:** EUR 2,50; **Circ:** 120,000
Editor: Eberhard Göhrum
Profile: Truck stops on the German Autobahn with current information, services and offers, especially for car drivers.
Language(s): German
ADVERTISING RATES:
Full Page Mono .... EUR 5010
Full Page Colour .... EUR 5010
Mechanical Data: Type Area: 128 x 95 mm
Copy instructions: *Copy Date:* 34 days prior to publication

AUTOKAUF
1744904G77A-2772
Editorial: Leuschnerstr. 1, 70174 STUTTGART
Tel: 711 1821241 **Fax:** 711 1821958
Email: redaktion_ams@motorpresse.de **Web site:** http://www.automonat.de
Freq: Quarterly; **Cover Price:** EUR 6,00; **Circ:** 75,000
Editor: Bernd Ostmann; **Advertising Manager:** Jochen Bechtle
Profile: autokauf is the first complete and cross-media buying guide for the German car market. autokauf offers in print and online on auto-motor-und-sport.de in the section Car purchase the complete market overview of all available models and their equipment and all prices for new and used cars. Core of the printed magazine is model-catalog that lists all available series in Germany as a new car models. In the Internet and may be grouped with a multi-brand car configurator not only his desire peso model with all trim levels, but also compare different models with each other directly. Many additional relevant information for the purchase of automobiles complement the editorial content. Everything to know about buying a car like the latest news, travel reports, tests and more delivers auto sales four times a year. autokauf is an essential guide for all new and used cars buyers!.
Language(s): German
ADVERTISING RATES:
Full Page Mono .... EUR 8800
Full Page Colour .... EUR 8800
Mechanical Data: Type Area: 212 x 146 mm
Copy instructions: *Copy Date:* 27 days prior to publication

AUTOMAXX
725659G77A-940
Editorial: Rosenstr. 4, 84171 BAIERBACH
Tel: 8705 1503 **Fax:** 8705 9511
Email: automaxx-verlag@t-online.de **Web site:** http://www.automaxx.de
Freq: 16 issues yearly; **Annual Sub.:** EUR 25,00; **Circ:** 30,000
Profile: Car and motorcycle advertising magazine.
Language(s): German
ADVERTISING RATES:
Full Page Colour .... EUR 790
Mechanical Data: Type Area: 297 x 210 mm
Copy instructions: *Copy Date:* 5 days prior to publication

AUTOMOBIL INDUSTRIE
721603G31A-50
Editorial: Max-Planck-Str. 7, 97082 WÜRZBURG
Tel: 931 4182911 **Fax:** 931 4182779
Email: wilhelm.missler@vogel.de **Web site:** http://www.automobil-industrie.vogel.de
Freq: 10 issues yearly; **Annual Sub.:** EUR 117,00; **Circ:** 9,770
Editor: Wilhelm Mißler; **Advertising Manager:** Anna Gredel
Profile: "Automobil Industrie" informs managers in the technical and commercial management of the automotive business. For OEMs and leading suppliers, service providers and equipment suppliers along the entire product development process. In addition to the regular readers, the magazine is received by theme or issue specific selected target groups.
Language(s): German
Readership: Aimed at managers within the automotive industry.
ADVERTISING RATES:
Full Page Mono .... EUR 4140
Full Page Colour .... EUR 5760
Mechanical Data: Type Area: 270 x 190 mm, No. of Columns (Display): 4, Col Widths (Display): 46 mm

Copy instructions: *Copy Date:* 20 days prior to publication
BUSINESS: MOTOR TRADE: Motor Trade Accessories

AUTOMOBIL PRODUKTION
721604G31R-9
Editorial: Justus-von-Liebig-Str. 1, 86899 LANDSBERG **Tel:** 8191 125688 **Fax:** 8191 125279
Email: ap-red@mi-verlag.de **Web site:** http://www.automobil-produktion.de
Freq: Monthly; **Annual Sub.:** EUR 182,00; **Circ:** 15,757
Editor: Bettina Mayer; **Advertising Manager:** Michael Schollmeyer
Profile: Automobil Produktion is the industry magazine for the automotive and automotive supplier industry. The editorial program is consistently focused on the information needs of the target group - the automotive elite: With-decision-makers and decision makers in the technical areas (designers, developers, production) and top managers (directors, managers) and purchasing managers. The readers get exclusive information on OEM strategies, trends in the supplier market, procurement methods and market developments. The editorial focus is beyond human resources, finance and law. Automobil Produktion 'technology provides first-hand information on developments in technology, management know-how in processes and innovations. Contributions to research and science as well as future trends in development and design round off the editorial profile.
Language(s): German
ADVERTISING RATES:
Full Page Mono .... EUR 5950
Full Page Colour .... EUR 5950
Mechanical Data: Type Area: 257 x 178 mm, No. of Columns (Display): 4, Col Widths (Display): 41 mm
Copy instructions: *Copy Date:* 28 days prior to publication
BUSINESS: MOTOR TRADE: Motor Trade Related

AUTOMOBIL WIRTSCHAFT
721605G31A-1
Editorial: Neuturmstr. 10, 80331 MÜNCHEN
Tel: 89 2283929 **Fax:** 89 2283846
Email: automobilwirtschaft@t-online.de **Web site:** http://www.automobilwirtschaft-hofer.de
Freq: Quarterly; **Annual Sub.:** EUR 30,00; **Circ:** 20,960
Editor: Konrad Hofer; **Advertising Manager:** Klaus Peter Lang
Profile: Magazine containing information on supplement parts and accessories for vehicles.
Language(s): German
Readership: Aimed at car manufacturers.
ADVERTISING RATES:
Full Page Mono .... EUR 5220
Full Page Colour .... EUR 6945
Mechanical Data: Type Area: 270 x 187 mm, No. of Columns (Display): 4, Col Widths (Display): 43 mm
BUSINESS: MOTOR TRADE: Motor Trade Accessories

AUTOMOBIL-ELEKTRONIK
721599G31R-6
Editorial: Im Weiher 10, 69121 HEIDELBERG
Tel: 6221 489240 **Fax:** 6221 489482
Email: siegfried.best@huethig.de **Web site:** http://www.automobil-elektronik.de
Freq: 5 issues yearly; **Annual Sub.:** EUR 98,00; **Circ:** 11,366
Editor: Siegfried Best; **Advertising Manager:** Andreas Bausch
Profile: Automobil Elektronik is aimed at managers and engineers in the automotive electronics development and production along the entire value chain from the component of the animal to the OEM. Automobil Elektronik covers passenger car and commercial vehicle electronics.
Language(s): German
Readership: Read by managers in the car industry dealing with production, purchasing, quality and logistics.
ADVERTISING RATES:
Full Page Mono .... EUR 4319
Full Page Colour .... EUR 5394
Mechanical Data: Type Area: 257 x 178 mm, No. of Columns (Display): 4, Col Widths (Display): 41 mm
Copy instructions: *Copy Date:* 28 days prior to publication
BUSINESS: MOTOR TRADE: Motor Trade Related

AUTO-MOBILES TRÄUME WAGEN
721601G77A-360
Editorial: An der Strusbek 23, 22926 AHRENSBURG
Tel: 4102 47870 **Fax:** 4102 478794
Email: vertrieb@daz-verlag.de **Web site:** http://www.auto-mobiles.de
Freq: 13 issues yearly; **Annual Sub.:** EUR 29,00; **Circ:** 34,337
Editor: Marco Wendlandt; **Advertising Manager:** Marco Wendlandt
Profile: Advertising magazine for automobiles with focus on unusual cars.
Language(s): German
ADVERTISING RATES:
Full Page Mono .... EUR 1364
Full Page Colour .... EUR 1364
Mechanical Data: Type Area: 265 x 190 mm, No. of Columns (Display): 4, Col Widths (Display): 44 mm

Copy instructions: *Copy Date:* 14 days prior to publication
CONSUMER: MOTORING & CYCLING: Motoring

AUTOMOBILWOCHE
760203G31A-14
Editorial: Argelsrieder Feld 13, 82234 WESSLING
Tel: 8153 907420 **Fax:** 8153 907427
Email: greinking@craincom.de **Web site:** http://www.automobilwoche.de
Freq: 26 issues yearly; **Annual Sub.:** EUR 128,00; **Circ:** 29,278
Editor: Guido Reinking; **Advertising Manager:** Thomas Heringer
Profile: Automobilwoche is Germany's only B2B newspaper for the entire automotive industry. Whether management, development, production, sales or service, Automobilwoche is a must-read for anyone with a professional interest in automobiles. The editorial team provides critical and independent coverage of the automotive business. Automobilwoche delivers up-to-the-minute news and information, highly relevant to our readers' day-to-day work: around the clock at automobilwoche.de, daily in our newsletters and of course, every second Monday in print. Numerous leading media and news agencies regularly quote Automobilwoche exclusives. In fact, Automobilwoche is Germany's most-quoted industry publication. Automobilwoche's readership consists of movers and shakers at car manufacturers, suppliers and dealers.
Language(s): German
ADVERTISING RATES:
Full Page Mono .... EUR 7990
Full Page Colour .... EUR 9550
Mechanical Data: Type Area: 377 x 255 mm, No. of Columns (Display): 5, Col Widths (Display): 47 mm
Copy instructions: *Copy Date:* 17 days prior to publication
BUSINESS: MOTOR TRADE: Motor Trade Accessories

AUTO-MOTOR-UND-SPORT.DE
1704515G77D-1331
Editorial: Leuschnerstr. 1, 70174 STUTTGART
Tel: 711 1821416 **Fax:** 711 1822220
Email: redaktion_ams@motorpresse.de **Web site:** http://www.auto-motor-und-sport.de
Freq: Daily; **Cover Price:** Paid; **Circ:** 3,504,181 Unique Users
Profile: Ezine: Magazine covering all aspects of the car industry, with particular emphasis on the European market. Includes reviews, tests and profiles of new vehicles, motor sports news and articles on classic cars and travel. Facebook: http://www.facebook.com/automotorundsport.
Language(s): German
CONSUMER: MOTORING & CYCLING: Motor Sports

AUTONET
749080G77A-2500
Editorial: Am Treptower Park 75, 12435 BERLIN
Tel: 30 534320 **Fax:** 30 53432121
Email: info@ah-net.de **Web site:** http://www.ah-net.de
Freq: 6 issues yearly; **Cover Price:** EUR 1,90; **Circ:** 14,600
Profile: Auto-Photo Catalog of Berlin and Brandenburg, the 2-month in Berlin and Brandenburg appearing car-photo-catalog is the platform for professional automotive trade. The networking of print and online (www.zweitehand.de) guarantees your Success. Attractive new car ideas complete the offer.
Language(s): German
ADVERTISING RATES:
Full Page Mono .... EUR 770
Full Page Colour .... EUR 770
Mechanical Data: Type Area: 265 x 190 mm
Copy instructions: *Copy Date:* 9 days prior to publication

AUTORÄDERREIFEN - GUMMIBEREIFUNG
721615G39-6
Editorial: Im Mediapark 8, 50670 KÖLN
Tel: 221 2587343 **Fax:** 221 2587222
Email: olaf.tewes@bva-bielefeld.de **Web site:** http://www.gummibereifung.de
Freq: Monthly; **Annual Sub.:** EUR 129,60; **Circ:** 7,777
Editor: Olaf Tewes; **Advertising Manager:** Monika Grabe
Profile: Publication about car tyres.
Language(s): English; German
ADVERTISING RATES:
Full Page Mono .... EUR 2500
Full Page Colour .... EUR 3970
Mechanical Data: Type Area: 268 x 185 mm, No. of Columns (Display): 4, Col Widths (Display): 43 mm
Copy instructions: *Copy Date:* 22 days prior to publication
BUSINESS: PLASTICS & RUBBER

AUTOSALON AUTOPARADE
721620G77A-520
Editorial: Mehlemer Weg 25e, 53340 MECKENHEIM
Tel: 2225 945773 **Fax:** 2225 945774
Email: info@autodrom-online.de **Web site:** http://www.autodrom-online.de
Freq: Half-yearly; **Annual Sub.:** EUR 17,80; **Circ:** 45,000
Editor: Wolfram Nickel; **Advertising Manager:** Wolfram Nickel

Profile: Journal of buying a car with auto catalog, reviews, car prices and car costs.
Language(s): German
ADVERTISING RATES:
Full Page Mono .... EUR 1800
Full Page Colour .... EUR 2950
Mechanical Data: Type Area: 140 x 195 mm
Copy instructions: *Copy Date:* 30 days prior to publication

DIE AUTOWÄSCHE
721635G31R-15
Editorial: Stiftstr. 35, 32427 MINDEN
Tel: 571 886080 **Fax:** 571 8860820
Email: kramer@btg-minden.de **Web site:** http://www.btg-minden.de
Freq: 6 issues yearly; Free to qualifying individuals **Annual Sub.:** EUR 43,87; **Circ:** 3,400
Editor: Sigrid Pook; **Advertising Manager:** Cornelia Schu
Profile: Magazine about commercial car washes.
Language(s): German
ADVERTISING RATES:
Full Page Mono .... EUR 1290
Full Page Colour .... EUR 1290
Mechanical Data: Type Area: 260 x 180 mm
Copy instructions: *Copy Date:* 14 days prior to publication
BUSINESS: MOTOR TRADE: Motor Trade Related

AV SIGNAGE
1819036G2A-5738
Editorial: Pannesheider Str. 48, 52134 HERZOGENRATH **Tel:** 2407 918297
Fax: 2407 918298
Email: printzen@av-signage.de **Web site:** http://www.av-signage.de
Freq: Quarterly; **Annual Sub.:** EUR 18,00; **Circ:** 4,800
Editor: Max Printzen; **Advertising Manager:** Ralf Mrotzek
Profile: Information on technical possibilities and economic benefits Digital Information Systems.
Language(s): German
ADVERTISING RATES:
Full Page Mono .... EUR 1730
Full Page Colour .... EUR 1730
Mechanical Data: Type Area: 260 x 180 mm, No. of Columns (Display): 3
Copy instructions: *Copy Date:* 7 days prior to publication

AVANTI
721643G74A-440
Editorial: Karlsruher Str. 31, 76437 RASTATT
Tel: 7222 13389 **Fax:** 7222 13431
Email: edeltraut.bauer@vpm.de **Web site:** http://www.vpm.de
Freq: 17 issues yearly; **Cover Price:** EUR 0,59; **Circ:** 112,853
Editor: Susanne Webers
Profile: When women read a women's magazine, they want to relax - in the bus on the way home, cozy in bed or in the fragrant bubble bath. Avanti hit the real preferences of young, life-affirming women. Avanti is a brand new weekly women's magazine - a quick, colorful and happy. It combines mystery pleasure with joy of life and is the entertainment and puzzle magazine for the younger generation. Avanti is thus aimed at women between 20 and 39 years who are happy and move with the times. It wants to tell stories, evoke emotions and offer its readers a positive recreational experience.
Language(s): German
ADVERTISING RATES:
Full Page Mono .... EUR 3033
Full Page Colour .... EUR 3033
Mechanical Data: Type Area: 274 x 200 mm, No. of Columns (Display): 4, Col Widths (Display): 47 mm
CONSUMER: WOMEN'S INTEREST CONSUMER MAGAZINES: Women's Interest

AVN ALLGEMEINE VERMESSUNGS-NACHRICHTEN
721649G4C-1
Editorial: Marienstr. 9, 99423 WEIMAR
Tel: 3643 584531 **Fax:** 3643 584534
Email: willfried.schwarz@uni-weimar.de
Freq: 10 issues yearly; **Annual Sub.:** EUR 138,00; **Circ:** 1,895
Editor: Willfried Schwarz
Profile: Journal focusing on surveying and cartography.
Language(s): English; German
Readership: Read by surveyors.
ADVERTISING RATES:
Full Page Mono .... EUR 1060
Full Page Colour .... EUR 1980
Mechanical Data: Type Area: 257 x 178 mm, No. of Columns (Display): 4, Col Widths (Display): 41 mm
BUSINESS: ARCHITECTURE & BUILDING: Surveying

AVR ALLGEMEINER VLIESSTOFF-REPORT
721651G13-100
Editorial: Borsigstr. 1, 63150 HEUSENSTAMM
Tel: 6104 606309 **Fax:** 6104 606317
Email: a.hoerschelmann@kepplermediengruppe.de **Web site:** http://www.avronline.de
Freq: 6 issues yearly; **Annual Sub.:** EUR 98,00; **Circ:** 6,800
Editor: Angelika Hörschelmann; **Advertising Manager:** Jean-Pierre Ferreira

Profile: avr – "Allgemeiner Vliesstoff-Report" (General Nonwovens Report), the oldest trade magazine that is available on subscription in two languages, has been recognised as an authoritative publication throughout the industry for decades now. Its purpose is to provide manufacturers, converters, processors and users of nonwovens, technical textiles and geotextiles with information about international developments in the nonwoven fabrics field. The extensive nature of the magazine's reports is attributable both to internal research and to close contacts to the industry all over the world. avr is as a result a valuable link between producers and users. Company and economic policy in the industry is reflected in the different sections of the magazine, such as "Country Focus, Special, Technology & Machinery, R & D, Exhibitions/Events. The portraits of international companies and interviews with board chairmen provide an objective picture of sales and marketing strategy. avr keeps its readers informed about new developments in nonwovens production, processing and conversion, raw and auxiliary materials, technical textiles, machines and equipment. avr is aimed at professionals and/or decision-makers from nonwovens and technical textilesproduction, fibre production, processing and machine manufacturing for these areas. Due to the universal nature of the topics covered, our trade magazine is, however, also a valuable guide for users, research institutes and universities. avr is also read by purchasing and procurement departments. This Outlet offers RSS (Really Simple Syndication).
Language(s): English; German
ADVERTISING RATES:
Full Page Mono .... EUR 2775
Full Page Colour .... EUR 4135
Mechanical Data: Type Area: 255 x 184 mm, No. of Columns (Display): 4, Col Widths (Display): 43 mm
Copy instructions: *Copy Date:* 15 days prior to publication
BUSINESS: CHEMICALS

AV-VIEWS
721653G38-15
Editorial: Pannesheider Str. 48, 52134 HERZOGENRATH **Tel:** 2407 918295
Fax: 2407 572970
Email: printzen@av-views.com **Web site:** http://www.av-views.com
Freq: 6 issues yearly; **Annual Sub.:** EUR 25,00; **Circ:** 10,000
Editor: Max Printzen; **Advertising Manager:** Ralf Mrotzek
Profile: Magazine for audio-visual technologies and devices that are used at conferences, multimedia presentations, trade shows or events. Description and testing of new or current data and video projectors, Plasma-/LC-Displays, visualizer, audio systems, conference systems, presentation software, etc.
Language(s): German
Readership: Read by retailers and decision makers in schools and colleges.
ADVERTISING RATES:
Full Page Mono .... EUR 1922
Full Page Colour .... EUR 2995
Mechanical Data: Type Area: 263 x 180 mm, No. of Columns (Display): 4, Col Widths (Display): 41 mm
Copy instructions: *Copy Date:* 10 days prior to publication
BUSINESS: PHOTOGRAPHIC TRADE

AWA - AKTUELLER WIRTSCHAFTSDIENST FÜR APOTHEKER
721654G37-620
Editorial: Birkenwaldstr. 44, 70191 STUTTGART
Tel: 711 25820 **Fax:** 711 2582290
Email: awa@deutscher-apotheker-verlag.de **Web site:** http://www.dav-awa.de
Freq: 24 issues yearly; **Annual Sub.:** EUR 97,80; **Circ:** 6,311
Editor: Claudia Mittmeyer; **Advertising Manager:** Kornelia Wind
Profile: The AWA - Aktueller Wirtschaftsdienst für Apotheker provides carefully researched information and recommendations for the management of the pharmacy business and its future planning. The range of topics including contemporary pharmacy marketing, personnel management, insurance matters and current issues of the pharmacy, labor and antitrust law. A particular focus creates on the areas of taxes and tax savings. In addition, the service offers the pharmacists a wealth of information for their private financial management.
Language(s): German
ADVERTISING RATES:
Full Page Mono .... EUR 3400
Full Page Colour .... EUR 3400
Mechanical Data: Type Area: 261 x 180 mm
Copy instructions: *Copy Date:* 28 days prior to publication
BUSINESS: PHARMACEUTICAL & CHEMISTS

AWA ALLENSBACHER MARKT- UND WERBETRÄGERANALYSE AWA
721655G2A-260
Editorial: Radolfzeller Str. 8, 78476 ALLENSBACH
Tel: 7533 805272 **Fax:** 7533 805172
Email: awa@ifd-allensbach.de **Web site:** http://www.awa-online.de
Freq: Annual; **Cover Price:** EUR 700,00; **Circ:** 1,200
Editor: Renate Köcher
Profile: Magazine with information about media and market research.
Language(s): English; German

AW-PRAX
721664G14C-220
Editorial: Amsterdamer Str. 192, 50735 KÖLN
Tel: 221 97668181 **Fax:** 221 97668271
Email: wolffgang@aw-prax.de **Web site:** http://www.aw-portal.de
Freq: Monthly; **Annual Sub.:** EUR 259,20; **Circ:** 2,000
Editor: Hans-Michael Wolffgang; **Advertising Manager:** Melanie Saß
Profile: Magazine for the German export industry.
Language(s): German
ADVERTISING RATES:
Full Page Mono .... EUR 1089
Full Page Colour .... EUR 1749
Mechanical Data: Type Area: 260 x 186 mm, No. of Columns (Display): 3, Col Widths (Display): 57 mm
Copy instructions: *Copy Date:* 21 days prior to publication

AZ APOTHEKER ZEITUNG
721004G37-520
Editorial: Birkenwaldstr. 44, 70191 STUTTGART
Tel: 711 2582238 **Fax:** 711 2582291
Email: daz@deutscher-apotheker-verlag.de **Web site:** http://www.deutsche-apotheker-zeitung.de
Freq: Weekly; **Circ:** 27,067
Editor: Peter Ditzel; **Advertising Manager:** Kornelia Wind
Profile: The "Apotheker Zeitung (AZ)" is the latest information every week on Monday published by the Deutschen Apotheker Zeitung (DAZ). It complements the offerings of the DAZ and DAZ.online, the website of the DAZ. Main topics of the AZ are politics, economics, management and law. The AZ informs the pharmacist about all professional and health policy relevant issues. AZ supports him with information on management, operations management, to economic, financial and tax issues. The information is for the readers up to date, concise and easily readable processed. Important matters are discussed in comments and opinions. The Apotheker Zeitung is created by the editors of the Deutschen Apotheker Zeitung in collaboration with experts and professionals in the fields of economy, control, operation, management and law. This means sound information, competently prepared, matched to the right and interest of the pharmacist.
Language(s): German
ADVERTISING RATES:
Full Page Mono .... EUR 6100
Full Page Colour .... EUR 7700
Mechanical Data: Type Area: 375 x 271 mm, No. of Columns (Display): 5, Col Widths (Display): 51 mm
Copy instructions: *Copy Date:* 7 days prior to publication
BUSINESS: PHARMACEUTICAL & CHEMISTS

AZ NÜRNBERG
757997G67B-16369
Editorial: Winklerstr. 15, 90403 NÜRNBERG
Tel: 911 23310 **Fax:** 911 2331192
Email: info@abendzeitung-nuernberg.de **Web site:** http://www.abendzeitung-nuernberg.de
Freq: 312 issues yearly; **Circ:** 15,920
Editor: Andreas Hock; **News Editor:** Peter Groscurth; **Advertising Manager:** Hartmut Schmidt
Profile: The AZ Nürnberg does not have a local section along with many other departments. Nuremberg and Franconia will shape the entire page - including the political, economic, sports, and society reporting. Our editorial team looks at Nuremberg and Franconia in the whole world - dedicated, grassroots, entertaining, relevant. Facebook: http://www.facebook.com/abendzeitung Twitter: http://twitter.com/Abendzeitung This Outlet offers RSS (Really Simple Syndication).
Language(s): German
ADVERTISING RATES:
SCC .... EUR 48,70
Mechanical Data: Type Area: 485 x 325 mm, No. of Columns (Display): 7, Col Widths (Display): 45 mm
Copy instructions: *Copy Date:* 1 day prior to publication
Supplement(s): mehr Freude am Leben; TV-Woche
REGIONAL DAILY & SUNDAY NEWSPAPERS: Regional Daily Newspapers

AZ-WEB.DE
1620779G67B-16510
Editorial: Dresdener Str. 3, 52068 AACHEN
Tel: 241 5101357 **Fax:** 241 5101360
Email: u.kutsch@zva-digital.de **Web site:** http://www.az-web.de
Freq: Daily; **Cover Price:** Paid; **Circ:** 1,330,201 Unique Users
Editor: Ulrich Kutsch; **Advertising Manager:** Frank Mantler
Profile: News portal of the Aachener Zeitung: News on politics, economy, culture, sport, travel, technology, etc. Facebook: http://www.facebook.com/aachenerzeitung Twitter: http://twitter.com/#!/az_topnews This Outlet offers RSS (Really Simple Syndication).
Language(s): German
REGIONAL DAILY & SUNDAY NEWSPAPERS: Regional Daily Newspapers

B4B MITTELSTAND
1601545G14A-9347
Editorial: Kleine Grottenau 1, 86150 AUGSBURG
Tel: 821 4405454 **Fax:** 821 4405410
Email: astrid.schueler@b4bmittelstand.de **Web site:** http://www.b4bmittelstand.de
Freq: 6 issues yearly; **Circ:** 1,000,600
Advertising Manager: Wolfgang Hansel
Profile: Supplement to the Wirtschaftswoche and the Chamber of Commerce magazines. The focus is on regional economic reporting in the regions. Not only the big companies have their platform, but especially the hundreds of thousands of smaller companies, which are often not covered by the business coverage of existing media. Topics range from IT security, tax and legal issues concerning temporary employment and automotive testing to partner zones for the national advertising clients with objective focus of SMEs. Twitter: http://www.twitter.com/B4B_Mittelstand.
Language(s): German
ADVERTISING RATES:
Full Page Mono .... EUR 29790
Full Page Colour .... EUR 29790
Mechanical Data: No. of Columns (Display): 3, Col Widths (Display): 54 mm, Type Area: 230 x 172 mm
Copy instructions: *Copy Date:* 15 days prior to publication
Supplement to: Faktor Wirtschaft, Forum, hamburger wirtschaft, Hessische Wirtschaft, IHK Magazin Wirtschaft, quip, Wirtschaft ElbelWeser, wirtschaft zwischen Nord- und Ostsee
BUSINESS: COMMERCE, INDUSTRY & MANAGEMENT

B&B AGRAR
719740G21A-220
Editorial: Heilsbachstr. 16, 53123 BONN
Tel: 228 8499139 **Fax:** 228 84992139
Email: b.ziegler@aid-mail.de **Web site:** http://www.bub-agrar.de
Freq: 6 issues yearly; **Annual Sub.:** EUR 18,00; **Circ:** 1,500
Editor: Britta Ziegler
Profile: Journal for teachers in agricultural areas.
Language(s): German

B+B BAUEN IM BESTAND
722094G4F-20
Editorial: Stolberger Str. 84, 50933 KÖLN
Tel: 221 5497526 **Fax:** 221 54976273
Email: red.bauenimbestand@rudolf-mueller.de **Web site:** http://www.bauenimbestand24.de
Freq: 7 issues yearly; Free to qualifying individuals
Annual Sub.: EUR 139,00; **Circ:** 9,937
Editor: Gregor Reichle; **Advertising Manager:** Sabine Jahn
Profile: B+B Bauen im Bestand is the only trade magazine for the professional design and planning of qualified construction services in its stock. The focus of the reporting are procedures for the protection, maintenance and repair of build substance, for the energy efficiency of buildings and to maintain and increase the stock value. With object reports, practice-oriented technical papers, exclusive market overviews and product releases B+B provides decision support and practical assistance in solving the tasks in the building in stock. The consistent focus on the building in stock B+B is not only proven and indispensable source of information for contractors and consultants. Technical decision makers in the housing industry conveys B+B professional and sound basis for planning and implementing their building projects in its stock. This theme and target group-mix B+B makes for a unique advertising medium: As a provider you can get qualified with B+B and thus only a single journal your key target groups. Facebook: http://www.facebook.com/BauenimBestand24.de Twitter: https://twitter.com/#!/bauen_bestand.
Language(s): German
ADVERTISING RATES:
Full Page Mono .... EUR 3475
Full Page Colour .... EUR 5830
Mechanical Data: Type Area: 267 x 188 mm, No. of Columns (Display): 4, Col Widths (Display): 44 mm
Copy instructions: *Copy Date:* 15 days prior to publication
BUSINESS: ARCHITECTURE & BUILDING: Cleaning & Maintenance

B&I BETRIEBSTECHNIK INSTANDHALTUNG
1683908G14R-6109
Editorial: Herrenstr. 3, 58119 HAGEN
Tel: 8284 92990 **Fax:** 8284 92991
Email: redaktion@b-und-i.de **Web site:** http://www.b-und-i.de
Freq: 6 issues yearly; **Annual Sub.:** EUR 45,00; **Circ:** 15,026
Editor: Volker Zwick; **Advertising Manager:** Marcel Heller
Profile: Cross-industry newspaper for production and manufacturing professionals in the industry. With practical user reports and current reports, product information comprehensively on B & I production, material handling and maintenance. The focus of coverage is the goal of an economically meaningful and high quality production and an optimal availability and value of machinery, equipment and buildings.
Language(s): German
ADVERTISING RATES:
Full Page Mono .... EUR 5590
Full Page Colour .... EUR 5590
Mechanical Data: Type Area: 366 x 270 mm, No. of Columns (Display): 5, Col Widths (Display): 50 mm
Copy instructions: *Copy Date:* 21 days prior to publication
BUSINESS: COMMERCE, INDUSTRY & MANAGEMENT: Commerce Related

B+P. ZEITSCHRIFT FÜR BETRIEB UND PERSONAL
723920G14A-560
Editorial: Dechenstr. 7, 53115 BONN **Tel:** 228 7240
Fax: 228 72493081
Email: info@stollfuss.de **Web site:** http://www.stollfuss.de
Freq: Monthly; **Circ:** 5,000
Editor: Jürgen Schmidt-Troje; **Advertising Manager:** Carsten Priesel
Profile: The B+P. Zeitschrift für Betrieb und Personal is an established and successful for over 40 years professional journal for operations and personnel. It promptly informed about the latest developments in legislative, judicial, administrative and literature in the areas of employment law, human resources, the wage tax and social security law. Professionals and managers need to be always up to date, but have very little time to absorb new knowledge. The B+P is therefore understandable and designed to read quickly. Each issue brings you short articles on current issues, information on current decisions with explanatory notes and illustrated with examples of practice-relevant reports to key issues such as Outsourcing. In the magazine section is informed about important yet often not published judgments, administrative instructions and draft legislation. As a special subscription service is the "readers' questions / Current Cases" to matters of doubt from the operational staff work competently and reliably position taken.
Language(s): German
ADVERTISING RATES:
Full Page Mono .... EUR 2330
Full Page Colour .... EUR 3690
Mechanical Data: Type Area: 260 x 180 mm, No. of Columns (Display): 2, Col Widths (Display): 88 mm
Copy instructions: *Copy Date:* 21 days prior to publication

B&W BILDUNG UND WISSENSCHAFT
723925G62B-3186
Editorial: Silcherstr. 7, 70176 STUTTGART
Tel: 711 2103036 **Fax:** 711 2103055
Email: b+w@gew-bw.de **Web site:** http://www.gew-bw.de
Freq: 10 issues yearly; Free to qualifying individuals
Annual Sub.: EUR 40,00; **Circ:** 47,000
Editor: Manuela Hertweck; **Advertising Manager:** Rainer Dahlem
Profile: Member magazine of the Union for Education and Science in Baden-Württemberg.
Language(s): German
ADVERTISING RATES:
Full Page Mono .... EUR 1850
Mechanical Data: Type Area: 257 x 185 mm, No. of Columns (Display): 3, Col Widths (Display): 50 mm
Supplement(s): unterrichtspraxis
BUSINESS: CHURCH & SCHOOL EQUIPMENT & EDUCATION: Education Teachers

BA BERGSTRÄSSER ANZEIGER
721675G67B-2240
Editorial: Rodensteinstr. 6, 64625 BENSHEIM
Tel: 6251 10080 **Fax:** 6251 100841
Email: ba-redaktion@bergstraesser-anzeiger.de **Web site:** http://www.morgenweb.de
Freq: 312 issues yearly; **Circ:** 14,515
Editor: Karl-Josef Bänker; **Advertising Manager:** Werner Essinger
Profile: Regional daily newspaper with news on politics, economy, culture, sports, travel, technology, etc. BA Bergsträßer Anzeiger is a local edition of the Mannheimer Morgen. Facebook: http://www.facebook.com/pages/morgenweb/105113719526519 Twitter: http://twitter.com/morgenweb This Outlet offers RSS (Really Simple Syndication).
Language(s): German
ADVERTISING RATES:
SCC .... EUR 42,20
Mechanical Data: Type Area: 490 x 320 mm, No. of Columns (Display): 7, Col Widths (Display): 44 mm
Copy instructions: *Copy Date:* 1 day prior to publication
Supplement(s): Das will ich; essen & genießen in der Metropolregion; Mannheim im Weihnachtszauber; Natürlich; TV Morgen; 4 wände; Wirtschaftsmorgen; Wohlfühljournal
REGIONAL DAILY & SUNDAY NEWSPAPERS: Regional Daily Newspapers

BABY POST
721684G74D-30
Editorial: Yorckstr. 32, 50733 KÖLN
Tel: 221 9388597 **Fax:** 221 9388598
Email: aberger@ratgeber-eltern.de **Web site:** http://www.jazumbaby.de
Freq: 6 issues yearly; **Cover Price:** Free; **Circ:** 93,661
Editor: Antje Berger
Profile: Magazine covering baby care, health, nutrition and new products.
Language(s): German
Readership: Read by mothers with babies.
ADVERTISING RATES:
Full Page Mono .... EUR 7160
Full Page Colour .... EUR 7160
Mechanical Data: Type Area: 260 x 184 mm, No. of Columns (Display): 4, Col Widths (Display): 43 mm
Copy instructions: *Copy Date:* 42 days prior to publication
CONSUMER: WOMEN'S INTEREST CONSUMER MAGAZINES: Child Care

BABY UND FAMILIE
721685G74D-35
Editorial: Konradshöhe, 82065 BAIERBRUNN
Tel: 89 744330 **Fax:** 89 74433330
Email: baby@wortundbildverlag.de **Web site:** http://www.baby-und-familie.de
Freq: Monthly; **Cover Price:** Free; **Circ:** 802,719
Editor: Stefanie Becker; **Advertising Manager:** Brigitta Hackmann
Profile: Magazine focusing on health, education, pregnancy, birth, post-natal care and care of children.
Language(s): German
Readership: Aimed at parents in care of children from birth to 6 years.
ADVERTISING RATES:
Full Page Mono .... EUR 24800
Full Page Colour .... EUR 24800
Mechanical Data: Type Area: 256 x 184 mm, No. of Columns (Display): 3, Col Widths (Display): 56 mm
Copy instructions: *Copy Date:* 49 days prior to publication
CONSUMER: WOMEN'S INTEREST CONSUMER MAGAZINES: Child Care

BABY & GESUNDHEIT
732660G74D-118
Editorial: Breite Str. 40, 50667 KÖLN
Tel: 221 990330 **Fax:** 221 99033299
Email: juergens@medikom.de **Web site:** http://www.wireltern.de
Freq: 6 issues yearly; **Annual Sub.:** EUR 9,60; **Circ:** 295,217
Editor: Daniela Mutschler; **Advertising Manager:** Angelika Schöning
Profile: BABY HEALTH & Info is a magazine for expectant and new parents. The journal is devoted to all relevant topics from pregnancy, birth and babyhood, development, baby care and prevention. BABY & HEALTH distributed nationwide and is free to parents in pharmacies, available from midwives and gynecologists.
Language(s): German
Readership: Read by parents, members of the medical profession and those involved in childcare.
ADVERTISING RATES:
Full Page Mono .... EUR 10980
Full Page Colour .... EUR 10980
Mechanical Data: Type Area: 227 x 175 mm
CONSUMER: WOMEN'S INTEREST CONSUMER MAGAZINES: Child Care

BABY & JUNIOR
721686G47A-321
Editorial: Franz-Ludwig-Str. 7a, 96047 BAMBERG
Tel: 951 861188 **Fax:** 951 861158
Email: l.hebauer@meisenbach.de **Web site:** http://www.babyundjunior.de
Freq: 10 issues yearly; **Annual Sub.:** EUR 90,00; **Circ:** 4,884
Editor: Lioba Hebauer; **Advertising Manager:** Iris Lepach
Profile: Baby & Junior is the only trade magazine for children's and youth fashion and children's equipment in Germany, that is published 10 times a year. It is distributed in 25 countries. For 51 years, the sector's mouthpiece has focused on the exchange of information between trade and industry. Month by month, Baby & Junior informs its readers about current developments in trade and industry, the latest trends and new products, international trade fairs and other important trade events as well as news from both Germany and abroad. Baby & Junior reports about fashion for babies, children and young people, accessories and maternity wear, prams and children's furniture, car safety and hygiene products, textile equipment and toys for a child's first years - in brief: about everything needed for children. In a nutshell: Baby & Junior is aimed at the market for children's requirements - in a comprehensive, critical and competent way.
Language(s): German
ADVERTISING RATES:
Full Page Mono .... EUR 2538
Full Page Colour .... EUR 4069
Mechanical Data: Type Area: 263 x 192 mm
Official Journal of: Organ d. Industrieverb. f. Korbwaren u. -möbel, Kinderausstattung u. -wagen e.V.
BUSINESS: CLOTHING & TEXTILES

BACK JOURNAL
721698G8A-40
Editorial: Luisenstr. 1a, 49074 OSNABRÜCK
Tel: 541 58054451 **Fax:** 541 58054499
Email: waclawek@backjournal.de **Web site:** http://www.backjournal.de
Freq: 14 issues yearly; **Annual Sub.:** EUR 105,00; **Circ:** 16,000
Editor: Dirk Waclawek; **Advertising Manager:** Sonja Shirley
Profile: The target group of Back Journal are the state-oriented chain stores of the baking industry. With a circulation of over 17,000 copies per issue, it reaches the entrepreneurs and senior management in companies in Germany, Austria, Switzerland and South Tyrol. An integral part of the magazine dedicated to the foodservice market. With an interesting mix of topics we talk about the future operations and are looking even beyond the confines of the industry. Readers appreciate this orientation. Highlight: Marktkieker Awards. Since 1987, the Back Journal awards to the Marktkieker the most prestigious business award of the baking industry. Back Journal of the target group are the state-oriented chain stores of the baking industry. With a circulation of over 17,000 copies per issue, it reaches the entrepreneurs and senior management in companies in Germany, Austria, Switzerland and South Tyrol. An integral part of the magazine dedicated to the foodservice market. With an interesting mix of topics we talk about the future operations and are looking even beyond the confines of the industry. Readers appreciate this orientation. Highlight: Marktkieker Awards. Since 1987, the journal back to the awards Marktkieker the most prestigious business award of the baking industry.
Language(s): German
Readership: Aimed at independant bakers.

ADVERTISING RATES:
Full Page Mono .... EUR 4640
Full Page Colour .... EUR 6500
Mechanical Data: Type Area: 274 x 192 mm, No. of Columns (Display): 4, Col Widths (Display): 44 mm
Copy instructions: *Copy Date:* 21 days prior to publication
BUSINESS: BAKING & CONFECTIONERY: Baking

BACKBUSINESS 721689G8A-60
Editorial: Daudiecker Weg 18a, 21640 BLIEDERSDORF **Tel:** 4163 900891 **Fax:** 4163 900893
Email: mercado-verlag@t-online.de **Web site:** http://www.backbusiness.de
Freq: 18 issues yearly; **Annual Sub.:** EUR 180,50; **Circ:** 2,500
Editor: Günther Wohlers; **Advertising Manager:** Susanne Carstens
Profile: Newsletter covering all aspects of baking including retail and bakery markets.
Language(s): German
Readership: Aimed at those involved in the baking trade.
ADVERTISING RATES:
Full Page Mono .... EUR 1380
Full Page Colour .... EUR 2070
Mechanical Data: Type Area: 260 x 187 mm, No. of Columns (Display): 4, Col Widths (Display): 46 mm
Copy instructions: *Copy Date:* 7 days prior to publication
BUSINESS: BAKING & CONFECTIONERY: Baking

BACKEN LEICHT GEMACHT
721691G74P-989
Editorial: Römerstr. 90, 79618 RHEINFELDEN
Tel: 7623 9640 **Fax:** 7623 964200
Email: info@oz-verlag.de **Web site:** http://www.oz-verlag.de
Freq: 6 issues yearly; **Annual Sub.:** EUR 13,80; **Circ:** 65,000
Profile: Baking recipes from cake to cake up to Christmas cookies and Grandma's Bakery.
Language(s): German
ADVERTISING RATES:
Full Page Mono .... EUR 1360
Full Page Colour .... EUR 1680
Mechanical Data: Type Area: 226 x 159 mm, No. of Columns (Display): 4, Col Widths (Display): 35 mm

BACKEN NACH GROSSMUTTERS ART
721692G74P-100
Editorial: Rotweg 8, 76532 BADEN-BADEN
Tel: 7221 35010 **Fax:** 7221 3501288
Email: erika.poese@klambt.de **Web site:** http://www.media.klambt.de
Freq: Half-yearly; **Cover Price:** EUR 1,95; **Circ:** 72,800
Editor: Erika Poese
Profile: The home-baked cakes and pies of our grandmothers, the rolls from the cookie tins, the delicious pies and baked puddings, which are almost daily as dessert or with afternoon coffee were served, we all still from happier kids days in our memory. But why should these nostalgic baked goods remain just a memory? It ta bake is not difficult, and the ingredients of its they are also inexpensive. Want to bet that taste Grandma's pie for the whole family? Motto: baking like grandma's fun! In the old signature dishes included yeast from the plate, garnished with seasonal fruit (low-priced!), but also fine sponge cakes, also with fruits of the season is busy or full. Quick sponge cake with icing, sprinkles and poppy cake, sweet pies and delicate strudel conjured with fruity sauces our grandmothers from the inside out. And birthdays and other holidays were not missing butter cream and chocolate cakes, marzipan and nut cakes. Appetite get onto baking? We tested the recipes from grandma's bakery and the bakery from other European grandmothers and baked it - for our readers.
Language(s): German
ADVERTISING RATES:
Full Page Mono .... EUR 5370
Full Page Colour .... EUR 5370
Mechanical Data: Type Area: 250 x 195 mm, No. of Columns (Display): 4, Col Widths (Display): 45 mm
Copy instructions: *Copy Date:* 42 days prior to publication

BACKEN-AKTUELL 1626538G74P-1052
Editorial: Römerstr. 90, 79618 RHEINFELDEN
Tel: 7623 9640 **Fax:** 7623 964200
Email: info@oz-verlag.de **Web site:** http://www.oz-verlag.de
Freq: Quarterly; **Cover Price:** EUR 2,95; **Circ:** 60,000
Profile: Magazine with baking recipes.
Language(s): German
Mechanical Data: Type Area: 185 x 135 mm

BÄCKER BLUME 721770G94H-800
Editorial: Am Flugplatz 4, Haus 49, 23560 LÜBECK
Tel: 451 50405681 **Fax:** 451 50405688
Email: redaktion@hanse-medienkontor.de
Freq: Weekly; **Cover Price:** Free; **Circ:** 86,407
Editor: Björn Hansen
Profile: Customer magazine containing articles about baking and confectionery. Includes recipes, advice on ingredients and information on new products.
Language(s): German
Readership: Aimed at customers of bakeries in Germany.
ADVERTISING RATES:
Full Page Mono .... EUR 17000
Full Page Colour .... EUR 17000
Mechanical Data: Type Area: 260 x 189 mm, No. of Columns (Display): 4, Col Widths (Display): 45 mm
CONSUMER: OTHER CLASSIFICATIONS: Customer Magazines

BÄCKER ZEITUNG 721775G8A-100
Editorial: Vierhausstr. 112, 44807 BOCHUM
Tel: 234 9019942 **Fax:** 234 9019999
Email: arends@backmedia.info **Web site:** http://www.backmedia.info
Freq: 40 issues yearly; **Annual Sub.:** EUR 130,00; **Circ:** 4,646
Editor: Heike Arends; **Advertising Manager:** Katja Lofi
Profile: The coverage in the Bäcker Zeitung is focused on the corporate practice of small and medium-sized craft enterprises. The weekly publication ensures high relevance. 40 times a year, there is information about the baking industry, suggestions and tips for daily business practice especially in the bakery trade as well as outside the box. 1 x per month also brings the integrated in the journal regional edition BäckerWelt - which is also the traditional title „Bäcker und Konditor" includes - again reinforces the actions and events on site, from the North Sea to the Alps, with faces and stories into focus .
Language(s): German
Readership: Aimed at master bakers, bakers and sales managers.
ADVERTISING RATES:
Full Page Mono .... EUR 2485
Full Page Colour .... EUR 4100
Mechanical Data: Type Area: 270 x 189 mm, No. of Columns (Display): 4, Col Widths (Display): 45 mm
Copy instructions: *Copy Date:* 14 days prior to publication
BUSINESS: BAKING & CONFECTIONERY: Baking

DER BÄCKERMEISTER
721772G8A-120
Editorial: Lazarettstr. 4, 80636 MÜNCHEN
Tel: 89 12607228 **Fax:** 89 12607330
Email: fassmann@pflaum.de **Web site:** http://www.baeckermeister.de
Freq: Weekly; **Annual Sub.:** EUR 202,80
Editor: Gerhard Fassmann; **Advertising Manager:** Michael Dietl
Profile: Magazine containing news, facts, information and articles from the bakery trade.
Language(s): German
Readership: Aimed at independent master bakers and decision-makers within the trade.
Mechanical Data: Type Area: 270 x 187 mm, No. of Columns (Display): 4, Col Widths (Display): 43 mm
BUSINESS: BAKING & CONFECTIONERY: Baking

BÄCKER-WERK 721774G8A-80
Editorial: Ostendstr. 149, 90482 NÜRNBERG
Tel: 911 541949 **Fax:** 911 542828
Freq: 6 issues yearly; **Circ:** 750
Profile: Official journal of the Society of Professional Bakers in Nürnberg.
Language(s): German
Readership: Aimed at the members of the society in Nürnberg and surrounding areas.
ADVERTISING RATES:
Full Page Mono .... EUR 402
Mechanical Data: Type Area: 260 x 175 mm, No. of Columns (Display): 3, Col Widths (Display): 55 mm
Copy instructions: *Copy Date:* 11 days prior to publication
BUSINESS: BAKING & CONFECTIONERY: Baking

BACKNANGER KREISZEITUNG
721699G67B-2260
Editorial: Postgasse 7, 71522 BACKNANG
Tel: 7191 8080 **Fax:** 7191 808125
Email: redaktion@bkz.de **Web site:** http://www.bkz-online.de
Freq: 312 issues yearly; **Circ:** 16,867
Editor: Reinhard Fiedler; **Advertising Manager:** Bettina Reischl
Profile: Since 1832, a newspaper published in Backnang. From Caspar Hackh as „Intelligenzblatt" established organ moved in the first years of its existence several owners and was acquired in 1875 as a „Murrtal-Bote", together with the associated print shop of Friedrich Stroh. Newspapers and company developed in the following years, despite some setbacks with the time-dependent growth of the city as a major industrial site for the most widely read newspaper in the then Oberamt Backnang up to the war-related cancellation of the publication in 1945. Since 1951, the traditional home newspaper is published as a „Backnanger Kreiszeitung" and has its position as a voice for citizens and independent authority in the capacity as an official announcement page for the district capital of Backnang with their surroundings and what is now Rems-Murr-Kreis constantly expanded digital and strengthened.
Language(s): German
ADVERTISING RATES:
SCC .... EUR 42,00
Mechanical Data: Type Area: 485 x 327 mm, No. of Columns (Display): 7, Col Widths (Display): 45 mm
Copy instructions: *Copy Date:* 1 day prior to publication
Supplement(s): Fußball lokal; Handball lokal
REGIONAL DAILY & SUNDAY NEWSPAPERS: Regional Daily Newspapers

BAD DRIBURG AKTUELL
721707G72-1608
Editorial: Westerbachstr. 22, 37671 HÖXTER
Tel: 5271 972871 **Fax:** 5271 972872
Email: panorama@westfalen-blatt.de **Web site:** http://www.westfalen-blatt.de
Freq: Weekly; **Cover Price:** Free; **Circ:** 8,400
Editor: André Best; **Advertising Manager:** Gabriele Förster
Profile: Advertising journal (house-to-house) concentrating on local stories.
Language(s): German
ADVERTISING RATES:
Full Page Mono .... EUR 1408
Full Page Colour .... EUR 2048
Mechanical Data: Type Area: 320 x 228 mm, No. of Columns (Display): 5, Col Widths (Display): 44 mm
Copy instructions: *Copy Date:* 3 days prior to publication
LOCAL NEWSPAPERS

BAD KREUZNACHER WOCHENSPIEGEL 721738G72-1648
Editorial: Schlörgasse 4, 55543 BAD KREUZNACH
Tel: 671 8380622 **Fax:** 671 8380677
Email: red-badkreuznach@sw-verlag.de **Web site:** http://www.wochenspiegellive.de
Freq: Weekly; **Cover Price:** Free; **Circ:** 49,472
Editor: Kai Brückner
Profile: Advertising journal (house-to-house) concentrating on local stories.
Language(s): German
ADVERTISING RATES:
Full Page Mono .... EUR 3673
Full Page Colour .... EUR 5148
Mechanical Data: Type Area: 430 x 290 mm, No. of Columns (Display): 7, Col Widths (Display): 38 mm
Copy instructions: *Copy Date:* 2 days prior to publication
LOCAL NEWSPAPERS

BAD WILDUNGEN LIVE
1616164G89A-12147
Editorial: Brunnenallee 1, 34537 BAD WILDUNGEN
Tel: 5621 9656724 **Fax:** 5621 9656737
Email: nahler@badwildungen.net **Web site:** http://www.bad-wildungen.de
Freq: Quarterly; **Annual Sub.:** EUR 10,00; **Circ:** 6,000
Editor: Reckhard Pfeil; **Advertising Manager:** Regina Nahler
Profile: Magazine for visitors to the city Bad Wildungen.
Language(s): German
ADVERTISING RATES:
Full Page Mono .... EUR 650
Mechanical Data: Type Area: 270 x 207 mm

BAD WÖRISHOFEN KNEIPP & THERMAL IM ALLGÄU
721765G89A-240
Editorial: Grüntenseestr. 26, 87466 OY-MITTELBERG **Tel:** 8361 3330 **Fax:** 8361 3338
Email: info@titze-verlag.de
Freq: Annual; **Cover Price:** Free; **Circ:** 20,000
Profile: Map for tourists visiting the spa resort of Bad Wörrishofen.
Language(s): German
ADVERTISING RATES:
Full Page Mono .... EUR 1050
Full Page Colour .... EUR 1150
Mechanical Data: Type Area: 210 x 90 mm
Copy instructions: *Copy Date:* 60 days prior to publication

BADEN BADEN INTERNATIONALES OLDTIMER-MEETING
2098050G77A-2991
Editorial: Pariser Ring 37, 76532 BADEN-BADEN
Tel: 7221 971450 **Fax:** 7221 9714510
Email: buero@presse-baden.de **Web site:** http://www.aquensis-verlag.de
Freq: Annual; **Cover Price:** Free; **Circ:** 12,000
Editor: Manfred Söhner; **Advertising Manager:** Annette Dresel
Profile: Journal of the International Oldtimer Meeting in Baden-Baden.
Language(s): German
ADVERTISING RATES:
Full Page Mono .... EUR 1700
Full Page Colour .... EUR 2300
Mechanical Data: Type Area: 260 x 180 mm, No. of Columns (Display): 4, Col Widths (Display): 42 mm
Copy instructions: *Copy Date:* 60 days prior to publication

BADEN INTERN 733039G32A-294
Editorial: Unterwerkstr. 5, 79115 FREIBURG
Tel: 761 45153420 **Fax:** 761 45153421
Email: j.hemmerich@badische-zeitschriften.de **Web site:** http://www.badische-zeitschriften.de
Freq: Monthly; **Annual Sub.:** EUR 29,00; **Circ:** 6,000
Editor: Jörg Hemmerich; **Advertising Manager:** Herbert Beck
Profile: The regional business magazine Baden intern is read in particular decision-makers from the region's economy as well as representatives from government and municipal institutions. The magazine is the official journal of the economic regions of Freiburg and the Dreiländereck-Hochrhein and maintains an extensive economic background reports related to South Baden and reports on structural changes in the region. The editorial lays a hand on high value-date, on the other hand it is keen to portray complex issues understandable and detailed. This requires the abandonment of appetizers journalism - articles in Baden intern characterized are always characterized by profound facts presentation. The editorial is politically independent. Key points of our approach are: information on the economic development of the region, names, facts, background, presentation of examples of projects, background information from the regional policy, legal issues; Company Portrait, commentary and opinion.
Language(s): German
Readership: Read by administrators in town halls and offices.
ADVERTISING RATES:
Full Page Mono .... EUR 2300
Full Page Colour .... EUR 2300
Mechanical Data: Type Area: 256 x 184 mm
Official Journal of: Organ d. Wirtschaftsregionen Freiburg, Lörrach-Dreiländereck
BUSINESS: LOCAL GOVERNMENT, LEISURE & RECREATION: Local Government

BADEN ONLINE 1620783G67B-16511
Editorial: Marlener Str. 9, 77656 OFFENBURG
Tel: 781 5044300 **Fax:** 781 50484300
Email: info@baden-online.de **Web site:** http://www.baden-online.de
Freq: 313 times a year; **Cover Price:** Paid; **Circ:** 260,282 Unique Users
Advertising Manager: Sandra Göppert
Profile: Ezine: Regional daily newspaper with news on politics, economy, culture, sports, travel, technology, etc. Facebook: http://www.facebook.com/mittelbadische.presse.
Language(s): German
REGIONAL DAILY & SUNDAY NEWSPAPERS: Regional Daily Newspapers

BADISCHE NEUESTE NACHRICHTEN 721727G67B-2280
Editorial: Linkenheimer Landstr. 133, 76149 KARLSRUHE **Tel:** 721 7890 **Fax:** 721 789155
Email: redaktion@bnn.de **Web site:** http://www.bnn.de
Freq: 312 issues yearly; **Circ:** 131,363
Editor: Klaus Michael Baur; **News Editor:** Gerhard Windscheid; **Advertising Manager:** Jörg Stark
Profile: The Badische Neueste Nachrichten with a paid circulation of about 150,000 copies and 400,000 readers every day one of the major daily newspapers in the state of Baden-Wuerttemberg. This newspaper is understood in the concert of the leaves the country as a not to be hearing voices of Baden and the Palatinate region between and Ortenau, between the Black Forest and Rhine valley. Nine local editions in the distribution area in the Karlsruhe, Pforzheim and Bruchsal, Baden resources emphasize the character of this newspaper as Baden regional newspaper. On this image editing with a full working day with about 90 editors. Most of the editorial staff but provided in the local editors at ten locations in the distribution area the readers with local news. In addition to the BNN output Karlsruhe, Rastatt, Baden-Baden, Ettlingen arise then the Pforzheimer Kurier, the Bruchsaler Rundschau, the Brettener Nachrichten and not least the Acher- und Bühler Bote. Although the focus of reporting is very strong locally and regionally, the Badische Neueste Nachrichten offer their readers a broad and comprehensive news coverage. Here, the editors draw on the BNN parent company in Karlsruhe and the services of the news agency dpa German Press Agency and Associates Press AP. In Berlin, the BNN talk with other regional newspapers in a joint capital office. From the state capital Stuttgart reported its own correspondent for the BNN. In other well-known, West German newspapers have the Badische Neueste Nachrichten on a tightly knit network of correspondents in Europe and around the world. The fortunes of the newspaper company are held by the publishing family Baur. Hans Wilhelm Baur took over the early 70s the management of the company that developed after the war, Wilhelm Baur one of the leading media companies in the Karlsruhe area and the region between the Black Forest and Rhine valley. After the death of the publisher Bruno Baur in the fall of 2004 gave the publisher on some of the responsibility for the entire company to his adopted son, Klaus Michael Baur. He has since then not only, as has been since November 2000 as editor in chief, but now also the publisher of the major daily newspaper in the region around Karlsruhe the way the Badische Neueste Nachrichten between tradition and modernity, which in serious changes in the media landscape at the beginning of the 21. Century of increased journalistic flexibility as well as marked by adherence to the quality features of a reputable newspaper. Technically, the newspaper publisher is in the district of Karlsruhe Neureut at a very high level. Nationwide attention will be paid in recent forced introduction of digital production planning and control, which allows the simultaneous setting of the different color zones editorial contributions, such as elaborate displays together with all elements of the newspaper digital, fast and economical to bring to the press. They will be printed 150,000 copies of the Badische Neueste Nachrichten every night in full color on two parallel operating offset presses.
Language(s): German
ADVERTISING RATES:
SCC .... EUR 276,50
Mechanical Data: Type Area: 480 x 360 mm, No. of Columns (Display): 8, Col Widths (Display): 43 mm
Copy instructions: *Copy Date:* 1 day prior to publication

upplement(s): Kirchen Zeitung
EGIONAL DAILY & SUNDAY NEWSPAPERS: Regional Daily Newspapers

BADISCHE TURNZEITUNG

721731G75X-400
Editorial: Am Fächerbad 5, 76131 KARLSRUHE
Tel: 721 18150 **Fax:** 721 26176
Email: kurt.klumpp@badischer-turner-bund.de **Web site:** http://www.badischer-turner-bund.de
Freq: Monthly; **Annual Sub.:** EUR 30,00; **Circ:** 5,800
Editor: Kurt Klumpp; **Advertising Manager:** Henning Paul
Profile: May be the gymnastics and sports clubs want and need informed exercise leaders, department heads, directors, and club members to recognize new trends early and included in the association's program. But also to make traditional events and competition measures and known in their own association to offer. Both offer the Badische Turnzeitung. With valuable clues to the club's management, the reports from the fields and districts, official notices and tenders.
Language(s): German
ADVERTISING RATES:
Full Page Mono .... EUR 450
Full Page Colour .... EUR 800
Mechanical Data: Type Area: 248 x 175 mm
Copy instructions: *Copy Date:* 14 days prior to publication
CONSUMER: SPORT: Other Sport

DER BADISCHE WINZER

721732G21H-10
Editorial: Friedrichstr. 43, 79098 FREIBURG
Tel: 761 27133156 **Fax:** 761 2021887
Email: redaktion@blv-freiburg.de **Web site:** http://www.badischer-weinbauverband.de
Freq: Monthly; **Annual Sub.:** EUR 39,60; **Circ:** 7,566
Editor: Peter Wohlfahrth; **Advertising Manager:** Karin Wirbals-Langner
Profile: The Der Badische Winzer is an indispensable resource for every winery in Baden. Even beyond the region, the magazine has made a national responsibility in case of wine science, trade and marketing a name. It is for over 35 years, published by the Baden wine-growing association in close cooperation with the National Institute of Viticulture Freiburg. In Baden grow to around 15,500 hectares of vines, that will in modern cellars to mature wines. As a member of one of the approximately 100 winery or marketing cooperatives, as a winemaker or winery with its own independent Winery: In our magazine experience our readers a comprehensive, practical and competent with the latest trends in farming, winemaking technology and marketing. Complement the current industry information specialist part.
Language(s): German
ADVERTISING RATES:
Full Page Mono .... EUR 2905
Full Page Colour .... EUR 4800
Mechanical Data: Type Area: 270 x 185 mm, No. of Columns (Display): 4, Col Widths (Display): 45 mm
Copy instructions: *Copy Date:* 16 days prior to publication
BUSINESS: AGRICULTURE & FARMING: Vine Growing

BADISCHE ZEITUNG

721733G67B-2300
Editorial: Basler Str. 88, 79115 FREIBURG
Tel: 761 4960 **Fax:** 761 4965029
Email: redaktion@badische-zeitung.de **Web site:** http://www.badische-zeitung.de
Freq: 312 issues yearly; **Circ:** 162,979
Editor: Thomas Hauser; **News Editor:** Thomas Fricker; **Advertising Manager:** Ralph Strickler
Profile: Regional daily newspaper covering politics, economics, sports, travel and technology. Facebook: http://www.facebook.com/badischezeitung.de Twitter: http://twitter.com/#!/badischezeitung This Outlet offers RSS (Really Simple Syndication).
Language(s): German
ADVERTISING RATES:
SCC .... EUR 319,00
Mechanical Data: Col Widths (Display): 45 mm, No. of Columns (Display): 6
Copy instructions: *Copy Date:* 1 day prior to publication
Supplement(s): doppio; rtv
REGIONAL DAILY & SUNDAY NEWSPAPERS: Regional Daily Newspapers

BADISCHE ZEITUNG.DE

1620786G67B-16513
Editorial: Basler Str. 88, 79115 FREIBURG
Tel: 761 4960 **Fax:** 761 4965029
Email: redaktion@badische-zeitung.de **Web site:** http://www.badische-zeitung.de
Freq: Daily; **Cover Price:** Paid; **Circ:** 3,061,661 Unique Users
Editor: Thomas Hauser
Profile: Website of the Badische Zeitung and information platform for Südbaden and Freiburg, with news, local news, sports, opinion, leisure, advice, job & career, videos, photos, events and advertising markets. Facebook:http://www.facebook.com/badischezeitung.de Twitter: http://twitter.com/#!/badischezeitung This Outlet offers RSS (Really Simple Syndication).
Language(s): German
REGIONAL DAILY & SUNDAY NEWSPAPERS: Regional Daily Newspapers

BADISCHES TAGBLATT

721730G67B-2320
Editorial: Stephanienstr. 1, 76530 BADEN-BADEN
Tel: 7221 2150 **Fax:** 7221 2151440
Email: redaktion@badisches-tagblatt.de **Web site:** http://www.badisches-tagblatt.de
Freq: 312 issues yearly; **Circ:** 34,973
Editor: Markus Langer; **News Editor:** Markus Langer; **Advertising Manager:** Stefan Hörig
Profile: The Badische Tagblatt is the largest circulation daily newspaper in central Baden region it is created by a full production supplied approximately 90,000 readers with the latest information from government, business, sports and culture. Four local editions (Baden-Baden, Bühl, Rastatt and Murgtal).
Language(s): German
ADVERTISING RATES:
SCC .... EUR 106,40
Mechanical Data: Type Area: 435 x 282 mm, No. of Columns (Display): 6, Col Widths (Display): 45 mm
Copy instructions: *Copy Date:* 1 day prior to publication
Supplement(s): AusZeit
REGIONAL DAILY & SUNDAY NEWSPAPERS: Regional Daily Newspapers

BADISCHES WEIN MAGAZIN

1799421G74P-1229
Editorial: Unterwerkstr. 5, 79115 FREIBURG
Tel: 761 45153420 **Fax:** 761 45153421
Email: j.hemmrich@badische-zeitschriften.de **Web site:** http://www.badische-zeitschriften.de
Freq: Quarterly; **Annual Sub.:** EUR 12,90; **Circ:** 7,000
Editor: Jörg Hemmerich; **Advertising Manager:** Herbert Beck
Profile: The Badisches Wein Magazin reports quarterly on the wine scene in Baden with a wine focus. At the same time, the magazine understood but also as a forum of Baden lifestyle. Numerous articles and reports about wine are also part of editorial content. Baden is the southernmost German wine-growing region. The demands on the quality of the wine are higher than in other German wine provinces. It shows the complexity of the wine supply in the region between Tauberfranken, Badische Bergstrasse, Kraichgau, Ortenau, Breisgau, Kaiserstuhl, Tuniberg, Markgräflerland and Bodensee. But the wine's more: The uniqueness of the Baden region, which is of course also influenced by the neighboring countries of France and Switzerland and the uniqueness of the vineyards of Baden. The audience consists of mainly of people, those committed to a competent information on the Baden wine and joie de vivre. The readers are in generally upscale professionals and among consumers with exclusive rights. It reaches a readership with a strong interest in an upscale lifestyle. The magazine is sold nationally at selected top outlets (stations, airports, city kiosks, particularly in southwest Germany). Regional distribution is in large part on the newsstands and on the Baden wine cooperatives and wineries.
Language(s): German
ADVERTISING RATES:
Full Page Mono .... EUR 2350
Full Page Colour .... EUR 2350
Mechanical Data: Type Area: 256 x 184 mm

DIE BAGSO NACHRICHTEN

721793G74N-120
Editorial: Bonngasse 10, 53111 BONN
Tel: 228 24999313 **Fax:** 228 24999320
Email: klumpp@bagso.de **Web site:** http://www.bagso.de
Freq: Quarterly; **Annual Sub.:** EUR 16,00; **Circ:** 15,000
Editor: Guido Klumpp; **Advertising Manager:** Barbara Keck
Profile: The BAGSO Nachrichten treat in each issue a topical theme, such as "Internet makes possible," "fountain of health", "Financially, retirement planning" or "mobility at any age". It reports on projects, competitions, events and news on society, politics and science. On the pages "Seniors - Critical customers", the seniors are as expendable end at the center of more permanent categories are: "Health Care", "Finance and Investment" and "senior citizens worldwide". The BAGSO Nachrichten are nationwide in of assets of the seniors and senior policy read and used as a source of information and inspiration for their involvement.
Language(s): German
ADVERTISING RATES:
Full Page Mono .... EUR 1850
Full Page Colour .... EUR 1850
Mechanical Data: Type Area: 246 x 183 mm, Col Widths (Display): 58 mm
Copy instructions: *Copy Date:* 28 days prior to publication

BAHNSPORT AKTUELL

721809G77D-260
Editorial: Birkenweiherstr. 14, 63505 LANGENSELBOLD **Tel:** 6184 923330
Fax: 6184 923355
Email: redaktion@ziegler-verlag.de **Web site:** http://www.ziegler-verlag.de
Freq: Monthly; **Annual Sub.:** EUR 42,00; **Circ:** 50,000
Advertising Manager: Ralf Ziegler
Profile: Magazine about sand, grass and speedway racing.
Language(s): German
ADVERTISING RATES:
Full Page Mono .... EUR 1504
Full Page Colour .... EUR 2713
Mechanical Data: Type Area: 265 x 180 mm, No. of Columns (Display): 4, Col Widths (Display): 42 mm
Copy instructions: *Copy Date:* 21 days prior to publication
CONSUMER: MOTORING & CYCLING: Motor Sports

BÄKO MAGAZIN

721780G8A-140
Editorial: Marktplatz 13, 65183 WIESBADEN
Tel: 611 3609867 **Fax:** 611 301303
Email: falk.steins@baeko-magazin.de **Web site:** http://www.baeko-magazin.de
Freq: Monthly; **Annual Sub.:** EUR 62,00; **Circ:** 15,667
Editor: Falk Steins; **Advertising Manager:** Reinhard Volkmer
Profile: One of the leading journals in marketing and corporate management in the bakery and confectionery trades in Germany. The journal represents the business interests of BÄKO organization, informed the members and baking customers of BÄKO cooperatives, reaching around 16,000 Bakeries and confectioneries. News and expert reports on market activity, manufacturer and supplier industries and new products. The Bäko magazine provides assistance to Operations & Practice, Law & Taxes, training and product information. Other priorities are business equipment (production) and store equipment (sales). Recent reports on new markets and trade shows provide the baking industry decision support.
Language(s): German
ADVERTISING RATES:
Full Page Mono .... EUR 4000
Full Page Colour .... EUR 5890
Mechanical Data: Type Area: 265 x 185 mm, No. of Columns (Display): 4, Col Widths (Display): 43 mm
Copy instructions: *Copy Date:* 21 days prior to publication
Official Journal of: Organ d. Wirtschaftsorganisation d. Bäcker- u. Konditorenhandwerks
BUSINESS: BAKING & CONFECTIONERY: Baking

BALINT-JOURNAL

721815G56A-1480
Editorial: Faurndauer Str. 6, 73035 GÖPPINGEN
Web site: http://www.thieme.de/balint
Freq: Quarterly; **Annual Sub.:** EUR 126,80; **Circ:** 1,200
Editor: Günther Bergmann
Profile: Patients understand - Optimize Medical action. Conflicts and problems can be detected and solved prompt. Overview works of medicine and culture. The journal is devoted directly to the questions and results, reports and personal experiences from the practice of the Balint-group work. This is supplemented by research findings, theoretical developments related to Balint work as well as results from the medical, psychological, sociological and philosophical spheres.
Language(s): German
ADVERTISING RATES:
Full Page Mono .... EUR 1100
Full Page Colour .... EUR 2270
Mechanical Data: Type Area: 248 x 175 mm, No. of Columns (Display): 3, Col Widths (Display): 55 mm
Official Journal of: Organ d. Dt., d. Österr. u. d. Schweizer. Balint-Ges.

DAS BAND

721835G94F-220
Editorial: Brehmstr. 5, 40239 DÜSSELDORF
Tel: 211 6400414 **Fax:** 211 6400420
Email: dasband@bvkm.de **Web site:** http://www.bvkm.de
Freq: 6 issues yearly; Free to qualifying individuals
Annual Sub.: EUR 25,00; **Circ:** 20,000
Editor: Stephanie Wilken-Dapper
Profile: Publication for physically disabled people, their parents and professionals in the health care system.
Language(s): German
ADVERTISING RATES:
Full Page Mono .... EUR 2200
Full Page Colour .... EUR 2200
Mechanical Data: No. of Columns (Display): 4, Col Widths (Display): 42 mm, Type Area: 250 x 190 mm
Copy instructions: *Copy Date:* 30 days prior to publication
Supplement(s): info-bayern
CONSUMER: OTHER CLASSIFICATIONS: Disability

DIE BANK

721839G1C-80
Editorial: Burgstr. 28, 10178 BERLIN
Tel: 30 16631551 **Fax:** 30 16631552
Email: die-bank@bdb.de **Web site:** http://www.die-bank.de
Freq: 13 issues yearly; **Annual Sub.:** EUR 98,00; **Circ:** 7,766
Editor: Inge Niebergall
Profile: die bank is the Number 1 professional journal for bankers. Month by month we publish high-quality reports on current banking developments and perspectives. Our contributors include prominent directors and chairmen, top scientists, politicians and economists, decision-makers and leaders in the world of finance. Our regular sections on the financial markets, banking, business management, IT and communications and careers are required reading for any banker with a say in operating and business policy decisions.
Language(s): German
ADVERTISING RATES:
Full Page Mono .... EUR 3550
Full Page Colour .... EUR 3550
Mechanical Data: Type Area: 250 x 178 mm, No. of Columns (Display): 3, Col Widths (Display): 56 mm
Copy instructions: *Copy Date:* 40 days prior to publication
BUSINESS: FINANCE & ECONOMICS: Banking

BANKEN + PARTNER

1694605G1C-1461
Editorial: Otto-von-Guericke-Ring 3a, 65205 WIESBADEN **Tel:** 6122 705451 **Fax:** 6122 705470
Email: hamm@bankenundpartner.de **Web site:** http://www.bankenundpartner.de
Freq: 6 issues yearly; **Annual Sub.:** EUR 75,00; **Circ:** 10,355
Editor: Margaretha Hamm; **Advertising Manager:** Uwe Wagschal
Language(s): German
ADVERTISING RATES:
Full Page Mono .... EUR 2900
Full Page Colour .... EUR 4700
Mechanical Data: Type Area: 251 x 185 mm, No. of Columns (Display): 3, Col Widths (Display): 54 mm
Copy instructions: *Copy Date:* 20 days prior to publication
BUSINESS: FINANCE & ECONOMICS: Banking

BANKEN & SPARKASSEN

721844G1C-220
Editorial: Arabellastr. 4, 81925 MÜNCHEN
Tel: 89 92223176 **Fax:** 89 92223171
Email: h.sebald@av-finance.com **Web site:** http://www.av-finance.com
Freq: 6 issues yearly; **Annual Sub.:** EUR 56,00; **Circ:** 5,511
Editor: Herbert Sebald; **Advertising Manager:** Manuela Albutat
Profile: Banken & Sparkassen is the trade journal, which is aimed at executives, decision makers and IT managers in commercial banks, savings banks, credit unions and cooperative banks. The focus of Banken & Sparkassen located in the reporting on information technology and its strategic implication on business success. Banken & Sparkassen helps IT decision makers to understand technologies, to formulate strategies and select products. Banken & Sparkassen is the information platform for IT managers, IT manufacturers and IT service providers. The expert editorial team analyzes the latest developments and attaches great importance to readers benefit. For the strategic assessment of trends in banking institutions, the editorial staff collaborates with renowned experts from academia, practice and advice. Banken & Sparkassen rated exclusively, practice-oriented and use the relevant products, services and trends. Banken & Sparkassen divided clearly into the categories: strategy, marketing, technology and services. Well-researched topics and market summaries round off the trade publication.
Language(s): German
Readership: Aimed at managers in banks and saving banks.
ADVERTISING RATES:
Full Page Mono .... EUR 3735
Full Page Colour .... EUR 5195
Mechanical Data: Type Area: 260 x 185 mm, No. of Columns (Display): 3, Col Widths (Display): 57 mm
BUSINESS: FINANCE & ECONOMICS: Banking

BANKFACHKLASSE

721846G1C-100
Editorial: Abraham-Lincoln-Str. 46, 65189 WIESBADEN **Tel:** 611 7878205 **Fax:** 611 7878435
Email: bankfachklasse@gabler.de **Web site:** http://www.bankfachklasse.de
Freq: 10 issues yearly; **Annual Sub.:** EUR 136,00; **Circ:** 7,192
Editor: Peter Rensch; **Advertising Manager:** Annette Oberländer-Renner
Profile: Practice cases, test training and updates around the world of bank trainee. Fit for the exam - The BFK supports trainees with relevant knowledge for intermediate and final examinations, as well as information for school and work. The practice cases and the examination training to help trainees ideally prepared in the interim and final exam to go.
Language(s): German
ADVERTISING RATES:
Full Page Mono .... EUR 3350
Full Page Colour .... EUR 4850
Mechanical Data: Type Area: 240 x 175 mm, No. of Columns (Display): 4, Col Widths (Display): 40 mm
BUSINESS: FINANCE & ECONOMICS: Banking

BANKMAGAZIN

721853G1C-260
Editorial: Abraham-Lincoln-Str. 46, 65189 WIESBADEN **Tel:** 611 7878205 **Fax:** 611 7878435
Email: bankmagazin@gabler.de **Web site:** http://www.bankmagazin.de
Freq: Monthly; **Annual Sub.:** EUR 136,00; **Circ:** 10,880
Editor: Peter Rensch; **Advertising Manager:** Annette Oberländer-Renner
Profile: The banking industry first hand. Bankmagazin is the monthly, independent from associations, and leading trade magazine for the banking sector in the German speaking room. The editorial coverage is comprehensive and addresses all three pillars of the industry. Topics covered include: marketing, financial products, strategies, bank management, the latest news, law, education, careers, IT/telecommunications, case studies, interviews and job market. In addition, 6 issues a year appear "finance business" with topics related to investment advice, to financial products and sales training. Furthermore, there are 4 issues "IT Solutions" with topics for all relevant areas of the bank's IT.
Language(s): German
Readership: Aimed at qualified bank clerks.
ADVERTISING RATES:
Full Page Mono .... EUR 3800
Full Page Colour .... EUR 5630

Mechanical Data: Type Area: 240 x 175 mm, No. of Columns (Display): 4, Col Widths (Display): 40 mm
BUSINESS: FINANCE & ECONOMICS: Banking

BANKPRAKTIKER 1703510G1C-1465
Editorial: Plöck 32a, 69117 HEIDELBERG
Tel: 6221 998980 **Fax:** 6221 9989899
Email: bankpraktiker@fc-heidelberg.de **Web site:** http://www.bankpraktiker.de
Freq: 10 issues yearly; **Annual Sub.:** EUR 222,00; **Circ:** 2,000
Editor: Patrick Rösler; **Advertising Manager:** Stefanie Nauen
Profile: Magazine covering all aspects of corporate finance.
Language(s): German
ADVERTISING RATES:
Full Page Mono .... EUR 1000
Full Page Colour .... EUR 1000
Copy instructions: *Copy Date:* 30 days prior to publication

BAO DEPESCHE 2042237G56A-11708
Editorial: Essener Str. 4, 22419 HAMBURG
Tel: 40 32596116 **Fax:** 40 32596112
Email: antje@soleimanian.de **Web site:** http://www.operieren.de
Freq: 3 issues yearly; **Circ:** 1,500
Editor: Antje Soleimanian; **Advertising Manager:** Wolfgang Trede
Profile: Magazine with news, opinions and position from the Association for Ambulant Surgery.
Language(s): German

BARBIE 734094G91D-4880
Editorial: Wallstr. 59, 10179 BERLIN **Tel:** 30 240080 **Fax:** 30 24008455
Email: s.saydo@ehapa.de **Web site:** http://www.ehapa.de
Freq: Monthly; **Cover Price:** EUR 2,95; **Circ:** 34,397
Editor: Sanya Saydo
Profile: In the magazine girls place between 3 and 7 years everything that makes them fun: exciting photo stories with Barbie and her friends, great craft ideas, many puzzles and painting pages, interesting competitions and in each issue a super extra games, Dressing and dreams.
Language(s): German
ADVERTISING RATES:
Full Page Mono .... EUR 4400
Full Page Colour .... EUR 4400
Mechanical Data: Type Area: 280 x 210 mm, No. of Columns (Display): 4, Col Widths (Display): 52 mm
Copy instructions: *Copy Date:* 60 days prior to publication
CONSUMER: RECREATION & LEISURE: Children & Youth

BARMSTEDTER ZEITUNG 721875G67B-2340
Editorial: Damm 9, 25421 PINNEBERG
Tel: 4101 5356101 **Fax:** 4101 5356106
Email: redaktion@a-beig.de **Web site:** http://www.barmstedter-zeitung.de
Freq: 312 issues yearly; **Circ:** 2,521
Advertising Manager: Karsten Raasch
Profile: Daily newspaper with regional news and a local sports section. This Outlet offers RSS (Really Simple Syndication).
Language(s): German
ADVERTISING RATES:
SCC .... EUR 21,60
Mechanical Data: Type Area: 430 x 278 mm, No. of Columns (Display): 6, Col Widths (Display): 45 mm
Copy instructions: *Copy Date:* 1 day prior to publication
Supplement(s): nordisch gesund
REGIONAL DAILY & SUNDAY NEWSPAPERS: Regional Daily Newspapers

BARNSTORFER WOCHENBLATT 721877G72-1720
Editorial: Bahnhofstr. 9, 49356 DIEPHOLZ
Tel: 5441 908120 **Fax:** 5441 908150
Email: michael.duemer@aller-weser-verlag.de **Web site:** http://www.aller-weser-verlag.de
Cover Price: Free
Editor: Michael H. Dümer; **Advertising Manager:** Jürgen Bründer
Profile: Advertising journal (house-to-house) concentrating on local stories.
Language(s): German
LOCAL NEWSPAPERS

BASIC RESEARCH IN CARDIOLOGY 721893G56A-1500
Editorial: Hufelandstr. 55, 45147 ESSEN
Tel: 201 7234480 **Fax:** 201 7234481
Email: subscriptions@springer.com **Web site:** http://www.springerlink.com
Freq: 6 issues yearly; **Annual Sub.:** EUR 1779,00; **Circ:** 178
Editor: Gerd Heusch
Profile: Basic Research in Cardiology is an international journal for cardiovascular research. It provides a forum for original and review articles related to experimental cardiology that meet its stringent scientific standards. Thus, it comprises all aspects related to the physiology and pathology of the structure and function of the heart and the cardiovascular system, including their regulation by neuronal and humoral mechanisms. The journal regularly receives articles from the fields of - Molecular and Cellular Biology - Biochemistry - Biophysics - Pharmacology - Physiology and Pathology - Clinical Cardiology. Fields of interest: Cardiology, Physiology, Pathology.
Language(s): English
ADVERTISING RATES:
Full Page Mono .... EUR 740
Full Page Colour .... EUR 1780
Mechanical Data: Type Area: 240 x 175 mm
Official Journal of: Organ d. German Cardiac Society

BASKET 721898G75X-8859
Editorial: Schanzenstr. 36, 51063 KÖLN
Tel: 221 9608100 **Fax:** 221 9608550
Email: redaktion@basket.de **Web site:** http://www.basket.de
Freq: 10 issues yearly; **Annual Sub.:** EUR 35,00; **Circ:** 22,500
Editor: Fred Wipperfürth; **Advertising Manager:** Christoph Beyreiß
Profile: The magazine Basket is since 2006 the only officially licensed NBA German magazine. Focus in the magazine, the NBA superstars, the team with reports, analysis and current background information. Under the heading coaching it provides important tips for active players.
Language(s): German
ADVERTISING RATES:
Full Page Mono .... EUR 4000
Full Page Colour .... EUR 4000
Mechanical Data: Type Area: 252 x 184 mm
Copy instructions: *Copy Date:* 25 days prior to publication
CONSUMER: SPORT: Other Sport

BASTEI EXTRA RÄTSEL 726898G79F-580
Editorial: Münchener Str. 101/Geb. 09, 85737 ISMANING **Tel:** 89 272707811 **Fax:** 89 272707890
Email: info@raetsel.de **Web site:** http://www.raetsel.de
Freq: 6 issues yearly; **Annual Sub.:** EUR 13,20; **Circ:** 115,000
Editor: Bernd Koophamel
Profile: Magazine containing articles about problem-solving, including puzzles.
Language(s): German
Readership: Aimed at people interested in solving puzzles.
Mechanical Data: Type Area: 280 x 214 mm
CONSUMER: HOBBIES & DIY: Games & Puzzles

BASTEL-SPASS 1605058G79A-277
Editorial: Römerstr. 90, 79618 RHEINFELDEN
Tel: 7623 9640 **Fax:** 7623 964200
Email: info@oz-verlag.de **Web site:** http://www.oz-verlag.de
Profile: Magazine about building techniques.
Language(s): German
CONSUMER: HOBBIES & DIY

BAU 721947G4E-600
Editorial: Kaiserstr. 8, 13589 BERLIN
Tel: 30 3751515 **Fax:** 30 3754424
Email: peterknaak@aol.com **Web site:** http://www.bauindustrie-bb.de/baumagazin.htm
Freq: Monthly; Free to qualifying individuals
Annual Sub.: EUR 53,75; **Circ:** 4,900
Editor: Peter Knaak; **Advertising Manager:** Roger Ferch
Profile: Magazine focusing on the building industry.
Language(s): German
Readership: Read by independent building contractors, architects and engineers.
ADVERTISING RATES:
Full Page Mono .... EUR 1376
Full Page Colour .... EUR 2669
Mechanical Data: Type Area: 270 x 185 mm, No. of Columns (Display): 3, Col Widths (Display): 56 mm
Copy instructions: *Copy Date:* 14 days prior to publication
Official Journal of: Organ d. Bauindustrieverb. Bln.-Brandenburg e.V.
BUSINESS: ARCHITECTURE & BUILDING: Building

BAU AKTUELL 1601033G4E-6887
Editorial: Hopfenstr. 2e, 24114 KIEL **Tel:** 431 535470
Fax: 431 5354777
Email: info@bau-sh.de **Web site:** http://www.bau-sh.de
Freq: 6 issues yearly; **Circ:** 2,000
Editor: Georg Schareck
Profile: Magazine for Building Guild members.
Language(s): German
ADVERTISING RATES:
Full Page Colour .... EUR 550
Mechanical Data: Type Area: 275 x 187 mm
Copy instructions: *Copy Date:* 15 days prior to publication

BAU MAGAZIN 743902G4E-6120
Editorial: Hermann-von-Barth-Str. 2, 87435 KEMPTEN **Tel:** 831 522040 **Fax:** 831 5220450
Email: baumagazin@sbm-verlag.de **Web site:** http://www.baumagazin.eu
Freq: 11 issues yearly; **Annual Sub.:** EUR 50,50; **Circ:** 17,669
Editor: Michael Wulf; **Advertising Manager:** Manfred Zwick
Profile: Magazine covering all aspects of the building trade throughout Germany. Also covers some parts of Switzerland, Austria, the Netherlands, Belgium, Luxembourg, Denmark and France.
Language(s): German
ADVERTISING RATES:
Full Page Mono .... EUR 3180
Full Page Colour .... EUR 4770
Mechanical Data: Type Area: 265 x 185 mm, No. of Columns (Display): 4, Col Widths (Display): 42 mm
Copy instructions: *Copy Date:* 16 days prior to publication
BUSINESS: ARCHITECTURE & BUILDING: Building

BAU MARKT MANAGER 722100G25-5
Editorial: Stolberger Str. 84, 50933 KÖLN
Tel: 221 5497324 **Fax:** 221 5497278
Email: red.bauheimwerkermarkt@rohn.de **Web site:** http://www.baumarktmanager.de
Freq: Monthly; **Annual Sub.:** EUR 148,00; **Circ:** 6,936
Editor: Claus Albus; **Advertising Manager:** Verena Thiele
Profile: bau markt manager is the magazine of marketing of do-it-yourself sector. The magazine reaches the entire retail with do-it-yourself departments and the specialized forms of business with construction, home improvement and gardening needs. Focus of the editorial concept are reports from Germany and abroad, market surveys, presentation of marketing concepts and the latest news from the do-it-yourself sector. A large part of the editorial content will appear exclusively in bau markt manager.
Language(s): German
ADVERTISING RATES:
Full Page Mono .... EUR 3430
Full Page Colour .... EUR 6010
Mechanical Data: Type Area: 267 x 188 mm, No. of Columns (Display): 4, Col Widths (Display): 44 mm
Copy instructions: *Copy Date:* 14 days prior to publication
BUSINESS: HARDWARE

DER BAUBERATER 721946G4E-1820
Editorial: Ludwigstr. 23/Rgb., 80539 MÜNCHEN
Tel: 89 2866290 **Fax:** 89 282434
Email: info@heimat-bayern.de **Web site:** http://www.heimat-bayern.de
Freq: Quarterly; Free to qualifying individuals
Annual Sub.: EUR 11,00; **Circ:** 9,500
Editor: Helmut Gebhard
Profile: Magazine for building culture and architecture.
Language(s): German
Supplement to: Schönere Heimat

BAUBESCHLAG TASCHENBUCH 721950G4E-1840
Editorial: Stresemannstr. 20, 47051 DUISBURG
Tel: 203 3052728 **Fax:** 203 30527820
Email: n.schmitz@wohlfarth.de **Web site:** http://www.schloss-und-beschlagmarkt.de
Freq: Annual; **Cover Price:** EUR 18,90; **Circ:** 3,000
Editor: Norbert Schmitz; **Advertising Manager:** Stefan Hillebrand
Profile: Reference book for building hardware, hardware systems and security products, ideal for architects, engineers, planners and all who deal with fittings and safety.
Language(s): German
Mechanical Data: Type Area: 140 x 90 mm
Copy instructions: *Copy Date:* 60 days prior to publication

BAUDIREKT 721994G4E-2000
Editorial: Westfalendamm 229, 44141 DORTMUND
Tel: 231 9411580 **Fax:** 231 94115840
Email: grosser@bauverbaende.de **Web site:** http://www.bauverbaende.de
Freq: 11 issues yearly; **Circ:** 6,000
Editor: Hermann Schulte-Hiltrop; **Advertising Manager:** Nicole Großer
Profile: BAUDIREKT for the construction company is the leading scientific journal containing important information for the possession planning practice! The magazine is aimed at owners and managers in companies (construction, roofing, plastering, tile and floor layers, heat, cold, noise and fire protection establishments). The member companies of our guilds are regularly informed of the following current topics: work, pay and social rights, education and training, civil engineering, construction, construction, business, association work, business and tax law, literature and software.
Language(s): German
ADVERTISING RATES:
Full Page Mono .... EUR 1040
Full Page Colour .... EUR 1300
Mechanical Data: Type Area: 260 x 175 mm, No. of Columns (Display): 3, Col Widths (Display): 58 mm
Copy instructions: *Copy Date:* 15 days prior to publication
BUSINESS: ARCHITECTURE & BUILDING: Building

BAUDIREKT FORT- UND WEITERBILDUNG IN DER BAUWIRTSCHAFT 1866577G4E-724
Editorial: Westfalendamm 229, 44141 DORTMUND
Tel: 231 9411580 **Fax:** 231 94115840
Email: grosser@bauverbaende.de **Web site:** http://www.bauverbaende.de
Freq: Annual; **Cover Price:** EUR 10,00
Free to qualifying individuals ; **Circ:** 11,200
Editor: Hermann Schulte-Hiltrop; **Advertising Manager:** Nicole Großer
Profile: Journal of companies in the construction industry with seminar and tutorial proposals.
Language(s): German
ADVERTISING RATES:
Full Page Mono .... EUR 104
Full Page Colour .... EUR 130
Mechanical Data: Type Area: 260 x 175 mm
Copy instructions: *Copy Date:* 30 days prior to publication

BAUELEMENT + TECHNIK 721949G94H-104
Editorial: Stresemannstr. 20, 47051 DUISBURG
Tel: 203 3052726 **Fax:** 203 30527820
Email: t.schmidt@wohlfarth.de **Web site:** http://www.bauelement-und-technik.de
Freq: 6 issues yearly; **Annual Sub.:** EUR 30,82; **Circ:** 8,710
Editor: Thorsten Schmidt; **Advertising Manager:** Stefan Hillebrand
Profile: Customer magazine about locks, fittings and security.
Language(s): German
ADVERTISING RATES:
Full Page Mono .... EUR 225
Full Page Colour .... EUR 366
Mechanical Data: Type Area: 259 x 180 mm, No. of Columns (Display): 4, Col Widths (Display): 42 mm
CONSUMER: OTHER CLASSIFICATIONS: Customer Magazines

BAUELEMENTE BAU 721961G4E-188
Editorial: Mörikestr. 15, 70178 STUTTGART
Tel: 711 25855630 **Fax:** 711 6408972
Email: redaktion@bauelemente-bau.eu **Web site:** http://www.bauelemente-bau.eu
Freq: 11 issues yearly; **Annual Sub.:** EUR 66,90; **Circ:** 13,555
Editor: Hans U. Rohwer; **Advertising Manager:** Hans U. Rohwer
Profile: Bauelemente Bau is the information medium of choice for those working in the industry, window and door manufacturers, metal workers, carpenters, joiners and glaziers, the supplier of insulation and functional glass, as well as the companies in the rolle shutter and sun protection crafts and as well as the components and timber trade. As a reliable and objective source of information Bauelemente Bau not only in Germany but also in Europe and beyond will be appreciated. The range of topics includes the entire subcontracting all of the production of windows, doors and facades necessary components such as fittings, glazing, seals, adhesives, assembly items, etc. We report in detail on the entire spectrum of manufacturing technology and new production processes, provide new products and successful companies in form of reports before. Reports and information relating to issues of management, marketing / sales and legal as well as the monthly market overviews / documentaries on interior doors, sun protection systems, fittings, door panels, insulation and functional glass and aluminum and PVC profile systems from the editorial approach.
Language(s): German
ADVERTISING RATES:
Full Page Mono .... EUR 3890
Full Page Colour .... EUR 5613
Mechanical Data: Type Area: 265 x 185 mm, No. of Columns (Display): 4, Col Widths (Display): 45 mm
Copy instructions: *Copy Date:* 21 days prior to publication
BUSINESS: ARCHITECTURE & BUILDING: Building

BAUELEMENTE BAU INTERNATIONAL 721962G4E-1900
Editorial: Mörikestr. 15, 70178 STUTTGART
Tel: 711 25855630 **Fax:** 711 6408972
Email: redaktion@bauelemente-bau.eu **Web site:** http://www.bauelemente-bau.eu
Freq: Quarterly; **Annual Sub.:** EUR 27,50; **Circ:** 7,231
Editor: Stephan Engert
Profile: Bauelemente Bau is the information medium of choice for those working in the industry, window and door manufacturers, metal workers, carpenters, joiners and glaziers, the supplier of insulation and functional glass, as well as the companies in the roller shutter and sun protection crafts and as well as the components and timber trade. As a reliable and objective source of information Bauelemente Bau International will be appreciated. The range of topics includes the entire subcontracting all of the production of windows, doors and facades necessary components such as fittings, glazing, seals, adhesives, assembly items, etc. We report in detail on the entire spectrum of manufacturing technology and new production processes, provide new products and successful companies in form of reports before. Reports and information relating to issues of management, marketing / sales and legal as well as the monthly market overviews / documentaries on interior doors, sun protection systems, fittings, door panels, insulation and functional glass and aluminum and PVC profile systems from the editorial approach.
Language(s): Russian

ADVERTISING RATES:
Full Page Mono .... EUR 1970
Full Page Colour .... EUR 3441
Mechanical Data: Type Area: 265 x 185 mm, No. of Columns (Display): 4, Col Widths (Display): 45 mm
Copy instructions: *Copy Date:* 30 days prior to publication
BUSINESS: ARCHITECTURE & BUILDING: Building

BAUEN! 721963G4E-6905
Editorial: Höhenstr. 17, 70736 FELLBACH
Tel: 711 5206244 **Fax:** 711 5206300
Email: bauen@fachschriften.de **Web site:** http://www.fachschriften.de
Freq: 6 issues yearly; **Annual Sub.:** EUR 21,00; **Circ:** 37,535
Editor: Harald Fritsche; **Advertising Manager:** Wolfgang Loges
Profile: Magazine focusing on all aspects of building, especially with information on the fields of architecture, ecology and technology..
Language(s): German
Readership: Architects, planners, consumers and all aspects of the building trade.
ADVERTISING RATES:
Full Page Colour .... EUR 9850
Mechanical Data: Type Area: 247 x 187 mm, No. of Columns (Display): 4, Col Widths (Display): 43 mm
Copy instructions: *Copy Date:* 40 days prior to publication
Supplement(s): baugui.de; Energ!e Extra-Heft Lüftung und Klima; Energ!e Extra-Heft Pellets und Holz
BUSINESS: ARCHITECTURE & BUILDING: Building

BAUEN FÜR DIE LANDWIRTSCHAFT 721964G4E-1920
Editorial: Teltower Damm 155, 14167 BERLIN
Tel: 341 6010201 **Fax:** 341 6010290
Email: richter@bmo-leipzig.de
Freq: Annual; **Cover Price:** EUR 8,00; **Circ:** 8,000
Editor: Thomas Richter
Profile: Publication about agricultural building and architecture.
Language(s): German
BUSINESS: ARCHITECTURE & BUILDING: Building

BAUEN IN UND UM BREMEN 721966G4E-107
Editorial: Parkallee 14, 28209 BREMEN
Tel: 421 349394
Email: redaktion-schulz@t-online.de
Freq: Half-yearly; **Cover Price:** EUR 4,00
Free to qualifying individuals ; **Circ:** 6,000
Editor: Peter Schulz; **Advertising Manager:** Karin Wachendorf
Profile: Magazine containing articles about house building in the Bremen area, includes advice about finance.
Language(s): German
Readership: Read by private builders, tax consultants and lawyers.
ADVERTISING RATES:
Full Page Mono .... EUR 1000
Full Page Colour .... EUR 1000
Mechanical Data: Type Area: 260 x 185 mm, No. of Columns (Display): 4, Col Widths (Display): 45 mm
BUSINESS: ARCHITECTURE & BUILDING: Building

BAUEN MIT HOLZ 721967G4E-7050
Editorial: Stolberger Str. 84, 50993 KÖLN
Tel: 221 5497195 **Fax:** 221 54976195
Email: red.bauenmitholz@bruderverlag.de **Web site:** http://www.bauenmitholz.de
Freq: Monthly; **Annual Sub.:** EUR 143,00; **Circ:** 8,865
Editor: Markus Langenbach; **Advertising Manager:** Elke Herbst
Profile: Bauen Mit Holz, the magazine for designers and decision makers, deals with the timber construction, expansion, and the drywall. It combines these technical aspects with the concerns of the timber construction market and helps the wood constructioner way to operate successfully in the market. The editorial coverage informed about news of the entire spectrum of wood construction. News from the industry and the changing priorities at times technical issues are at the heart of every issue. Tendencies and trends in the timber construction market, such as sustainability, energy-efficient construction, compaction or foreign markets be backlit critical. Bauen Mit Holz accompanying the timber construcxtion out of an independent, critical and professionally competent recognized position among focus on technology and market, where the influences of politics and the economy are closely monitored on the timber construction. Construction, structural engineering, building physics and design are critically examined. Market considerations enter the wood building companies and planners with valuable information. Bauen Mit Holz is more than a century, the authoritative journal with the highest paid circulation.
Language(s): German
ADVERTISING RATES:
Full Page Mono .... EUR 2795
Full Page Colour .... EUR 4820
Mechanical Data: Type Area: 267 x 188 mm, No. of Columns (Display): 4, Col Widths (Display): 44 mm
Copy instructions: *Copy Date:* 22 days prior to publication
BUSINESS: ARCHITECTURE & BUILDING: Building

BAUEN & RENOVIEREN 721971G79A-20
Editorial: Höhenstr. 17, 70736 FELLBACH
Tel: 711 5206263 **Fax:** 711 5206300
Email: bauen+renovieren@fachschriften.de **Web site:** http://www.bautipps.de
Freq: 6 issues yearly; **Annual Sub.:** EUR 15,00; **Circ:** 33,733
Editor: Elmar Haag-Schwilk; **Advertising Manager:** Wolfgang Loges
Profile: The title offers practical knowledge on the subject construction and renovation, interior construction and housing, heating and building services, garden and tools. At the center are carefully documented work processes and lots of practical suggestions, tips and ideas.
Language(s): German
ADVERTISING RATES:
Full Page Colour .... EUR 9850
Mechanical Data: Type Area: 247 x 187 mm, No. of Columns (Display): 4, Col Widths (Display): 43 mm
Copy instructions: *Copy Date:* 40 days prior to publication
Supplement(s): baugui.de; Energ!e Extra-Heft dämmen + dichten; Energ!e Extra-Heft Pellets und Holz; Energ!e Extra-Heft Solar Energie
CONSUMER: HOBBIES & DIY

BAUERN ZEITUNG 721985G21A-460
Editorial: Wilhelmsaue 37, 10713 BERLIN
Tel: 30 46406301 **Fax:** 30 46406319
Email: bauernzeitung@bauernverlag.de **Web site:** http://www.bauernzeitung.de
Freq: Weekly; **Annual Sub.:** EUR 94,80; **Circ:** 23,310
Editor: Thomas Tanneberger; **Advertising Manager:** Frank Middendorf
Profile: BauernZeitung is the weekly newspaper for all who live in Mecklenburg-Vorpommern, Brandenburg, Saxony-Anhalt, Saxony and Thuringia and deal with agriculture. Expert writers and editors report every week on the European, national and regional agricultural policy in the five eastern German states. They keep you informed about all important developments in the agricultural and crop production, in animal keeping, agricultural engineering and management as well as the various agricultural markets. Integral part of BauernZeitung is also an extensive guide to country life. One in three acres of the German agricultural area is located in eastern Germany. There, The BauernZeitung is the most important trade magazine for the farmers.
Language(s): German
ADVERTISING RATES:
Full Page Mono .... EUR 5642
Full Page Colour .... EUR 8618
Mechanical Data: Type Area: 310 x 202 mm, No. of Columns (Display): 4, Col Widths (Display): 46 mm
Copy instructions: *Copy Date:* 8 days prior to publication
BUSINESS: AGRICULTURE & FARMING

BAUERNBLATT 721981G21J-16
Editorial: Am Kamp 19, 24768 RENDSBURG
Tel: 4331 127719 **Fax:** 4331 127762
Email: redaktion@bauernblatt.com **Web site:** http://www.bauernblatt.com
Freq: Weekly; **Annual Sub.:** EUR 77,00; **Circ:** 25,283
Editor: Ralph Judisch; **Advertising Manager:** Bernd Gerding
Profile: Journal of farmers in Schleswig-Holstein and Hamburg. Subject areas: agricultural policy, economics, family and leisure, health, horse and rider, country life and garden.
Language(s): German
Readership: Read by farmers living in Schleswig-Holstein and Hamburg.
ADVERTISING RATES:
Full Page Mono .... EUR 3066
Full Page Colour .... EUR 4412
Mechanical Data: Type Area: 270 x 198 mm, No. of Columns (Display): 4, Col Widths (Display): 48 mm
Copy instructions: *Copy Date:* 8 days prior to publication
Official Journal of: Organ d. Landwirtschaftskammer Schleswig-Holstein
BUSINESS: AGRICULTURE & FARMING: Agriculture & Farming - Regional

BAUERNKALENDER 721983G21A-580
Editorial: Bopserstr. 17, 70180 STUTTGART
Tel: 711 2140141 **Fax:** 711 2360232
Email: redaktion@bwagrar.de **Web site:** http://www.bwagrar.de
Freq: Annual; **Cover Price:** EUR 5,80; **Circ:** 70,000
Editor: Heiner Krehl; **Advertising Manager:** Gerhard Kretschmer
Profile: Calendar for farmers in the German federal state of Baden-Württemberg.
Language(s): German
ADVERTISING RATES:
Full Page Mono .... EUR 3024
Full Page Colour .... EUR 3714
Mechanical Data: Type Area: 205 x 142 mm, No. of Columns (Display): 3, Col Widths (Display): 45 mm

BAUFACHBLATT 721990G4E-1960
Editorial: Holbeinstr. 16, 79100 FREIBURG
Tel: 761 703020 **Fax:** 761 7030230
Email: service@bausuedbaden.de **Web site:** http://www.bausuedbaden.de
Freq: 6 issues yearly; Free to qualifying individuals
Annual Sub.: EUR 45,00; **Circ:** 1,550
Editor: Gregor Gierden; **Advertising Manager:** Petra Schramm
Profile: Magazine for farmers in the region of Südbaden.
Language(s): German
ADVERTISING RATES:
Full Page Mono .... EUR 860
Full Page Colour .... EUR 1400
Mechanical Data: Type Area: 267 x 189 mm, No. of Columns (Display): 2, Col Widths (Display): 92 mm
Copy instructions: *Copy Date:* 20 days prior to publication
Official Journal of: Organ d. Bauwirtschaft Südbaden

BAUGEWERBE 721993G42A-20
Editorial: Stolberger Str. 84, 50933 KÖLN
Tel: 221 5497257 **Fax:** 221 54976257
Email: red.baugewerbe@rudolf-mueller.de **Web site:** http://www.baugewerbe-magazin.de
Freq: 20 issues yearly; **Annual Sub.:** EUR 189,00; **Circ:** 19,959
Editor: Martin Mansel; **Advertising Manager:** Sabine Jahn
Profile: Journal for building contractors.
Language(s): German
ADVERTISING RATES:
Full Page Mono .... EUR 5100
Full Page Colour .... EUR 7530
Mechanical Data: Type Area: 267 x 188 mm, No. of Columns (Display): 4, Col Widths (Display): 44 mm
Copy instructions: *Copy Date:* 15 days prior to publication
Official Journal of: Organ d. Zentralverb. Dt. Baugewerbe
BUSINESS: CONSTRUCTION

BAUHANDWERK 721997G4E-2020
Editorial: Avenwedder Str. 55, 33335 GÜTERSLOH
Tel: 5241 8090884 **Fax:** 5241 80690880
Email: roland.herr@bauverlag.de **Web site:** http://www.bauhandwerk.de
Freq: 10 issues yearly; **Annual Sub.:** EUR 106,20; **Circ:** 23,850
Editor: Roland Herr; **Advertising Manager:** Axel Gase-Jochens
Profile: bauhandwerk is the execution-oriented professional magazine for owners of cottage industry, artisans and technicians who are in the craft comprehensive expansion and renovation work. Each issue is process-oriented prior to the construction site of the month, a prominent building. In the subject heading drywall, plaster + stucco, EIFS + color, insulation, building protection, bonding + densities and mounting technique with current news, construction reports, design + installation, practical tips and products the entire working range of shows in these areas make trades. These are supplemented by special sections parts such as windows + doors, flooring technology, renovation + restoration. This particular eye for the correct processing of the products and components will be sharpened, avoiding rework and costs for the company owner. The expertise of master craftsmen and technicians but will also open a view of the horizon of trade: Not only can knowledge of products and components are purchased from other trades, but their own work will also include more in the construction process. This not only saves time but also costs. In addition, a small company with a wide range of services will continue to remain competitive.
Language(s): German
ADVERTISING RATES:
Full Page Mono .... EUR 4800
Full Page Colour .... EUR 6870
Mechanical Data: Type Area: 270 x 186 mm, No. of Columns (Display): 4, Col Widths (Display): 41 mm
Copy instructions: *Copy Date:* 14 days prior to publication
Supplement(s): Brandschutz in öffentlichen und privatwirtschaftlichen Gebäuden; computer spezial
BUSINESS: ARCHITECTURE & BUILDING: Building

DER BAUHERR 721998G79A-30
Editorial: Hackerbrücke 6, 80335 MÜNCHEN
Tel: 89 89817204 **Fax:** 89 89817102
Email: info@derbauherr.de **Web site:** http://www.derbauherr.de
Freq: 6 issues yearly; **Annual Sub.:** EUR 20,00; **Circ:** 51,577
Editor: Stefanie Hutschenreuter; **Advertising Manager:** Peggy Hahn
Profile: Magazine for home construction with information on various topics of Concrete and prefabricated housing.
Language(s): German
Readership: Read by people who want to build their own house.
ADVERTISING RATES:
Full Page Mono .... EUR 7800
Full Page Colour .... EUR 11900
Mechanical Data: Type Area: 225 x 177 mm, No. of Columns (Display): 4, Col Widths (Display): 41 mm
CONSUMER: HOBBIES & DIY

BAUINDUSTRIE AKTUELL 722004G4E-2040
Editorial: Kurfürstenstr. 129, 10785 BERLIN
Tel: 30 212860 **Fax:** 30 21286189
Email: bauind@bauindustrie.de **Web site:** http://www.bauindustrie.de
Freq: 6 issues yearly; **Cover Price:** Free; **Circ:** 12,500
Editor: Heiko Stiepelmann
Profile: Magazine aimed at decision makers in the construction industry, inform practice and professionally based, provides space for convention and trade show reports and refers to the work of federal departments.
Language(s): German
ADVERTISING RATES:
Full Page Mono .... EUR 1534
Full Page Colour .... EUR 2454
Mechanical Data: Type Area: 248 x 180 mm

BAUINFO 1902903G4E-7269
Editorial: Graf-Recke-Str. 43, 40239 DÜSSELDORF
Tel: 211 914290 **Fax:** 211 9142931
Email: info@bgv-nrw.de **Web site:** http://www.bgv-nrw.de
Freq: 6 issues yearly; **Circ:** 4,779
Editor: Lutz Pollmann; **Advertising Manager:** Erwin Klein
Profile: Trade magazine for owners and senior managers of master and crafts enterprises of the building guilds in North Rhine-Westphalia.
Language(s): German
ADVERTISING RATES:
Full Page Mono .... EUR 1345
Full Page Colour .... EUR 1345
Mechanical Data: Type Area: 255 x 178 mm, No. of Columns (Display): 4, Col Widths (Display): 45 mm
Copy instructions: *Copy Date:* 21 days prior to publication

BAUINGENIEUR 722009G42A-22
Editorial: VDI-Platz 1, 40468 DÜSSELDORF
Tel: 211 6103484 **Fax:** 211 6103148
Email: veidl@technikwissen.de **Web site:** http://www.bauingenieur.de
Freq: 11 issues yearly; **Annual Sub.:** EUR 370,00; **Circ:** 4,850
Profile: Trade journal for the entire civil engineering. Civil brings essays on theory and practice of engineering designs, construction work and restored buildings of interest at home and abroad, machinery, equipment and their use on construction sites, building materials and construction informa questions, reports and articles on notable construction work and building products.
Language(s): German
Readership: Read by civil engineers.
ADVERTISING RATES:
Full Page Mono .... EUR 2712
Full Page Colour .... EUR 3867
Mechanical Data: Type Area: 270 x 185 mm, No. of Columns (Display): 4, Col Widths (Display): 45 mm
Official Journal of: Organ d. VDI-Ges. Bautechnik
BUSINESS: CONSTRUCTION

BAU-JOURNAL 1861874G4E-7239
Editorial: Max-Hufschmidt-Str. 11, 55130 MAINZ
Tel: 6131 983490 **Fax:** 6131 9834949
Email: bgv@bgvmz.de **Web site:** http://www.bgv-rheinland-pfalz.de
Freq: 10 issues yearly; **Circ:** 2,200
Editor: Harald Weber
Profile: Magazine for the building industry in the German federal state of Rheinland-Pfalz.
Language(s): German
ADVERTISING RATES:
Full Page Colour .... EUR 1300
Mechanical Data: Type Area: 245 x 183 mm, No. of Columns (Display): 2, Col Widths (Display): 86 mm
Copy instructions: *Copy Date:* 20 days prior to publication

BAUMA MOBILES INTERNATIONAL 724710G77A-860
Editorial: An der Strusbek 23, 22926 AHRENSBURG
Tel: 4102 47870 **Fax:** 4102 478794
Email: vertrieb@daz-verlag.de **Web site:** http://www.daz-verlag.de
Freq: 6 issues yearly; **Annual Sub.:** EUR 15,00; **Circ:** 11,432
Editor: Dorothea Aepler; **Advertising Manager:** Dirk Spars
Profile: Ad magazine about building machinery and equipment.
Language(s): German
ADVERTISING RATES:
Full Page Mono .... EUR 1232
Full Page Colour .... EUR 1232
Mechanical Data: Type Area: 275 x 190 mm, No. of Columns (Display): 4, Col Widths (Display): 44 mm
Copy instructions: *Copy Date:* 12 days prior to publication
CONSUMER: MOTORING & CYCLING: Motoring

BAUMARKT BAUWIRTSCHAFT 722017G4E-2100
Editorial: Avenwedder Str. 55, 33335 GÜTERSLOH
Tel: 5241 8090884 **Fax:** 5241 80690880
Email: roland.herr@bauverlag.de **Web site:** http://www.baumarkt-online.info
Freq: 10 issues yearly; **Annual Sub.:** EUR 192,60; **Circ:** 17,714
Editor: Roland Herr; **Advertising Manager:** Christian Reinke
Profile: The journal baumarkt bauwirtschaft informs the contractor objective, comprehensive and current.

For the construction industry part of our journal are available as priorities: • Regular news coverage including commentary, this practical legal tips + statutory interpretation • Several construction management items with a high draft editorial in every issue (controlling, human resources, marketing, IT, finance) • construction market data from 1 Hand (the Confederation of German Construction Industry) fast + topical For the daily work of a contractor, provides the practical part carefully edited professional contributions from the fields: • Problem-solving and application of new construction methods • The objective and competent presentation of new building materials and building systems • Clear and compact reports on new machinery and equipment In the Information part of our readers will find quick and reliable access to training, events and literature, news from the industry and current projects.
Language(s): German
ADVERTISING RATES:
Full Page Mono .... EUR 4225
Full Page Colour .... EUR 6070
Mechanical Data: Type Area: 270 x 186 mm, No. of Columns (Display): 4, Col Widths (Display): 45 mm
Copy instructions: *Copy Date:* 14 days prior to publication
Supplement(s): Brandschutz in öffentlichen und privatwirtschaftlichen Gebäuden
BUSINESS: ARCHITECTURE & BUILDING: Building

BAUMASCHINEN 722018G4E-2120
Editorial: Ritter-von-Schuh-Platz 3, 90459 NÜRNBERG **Tel:** 911 4308990 **Fax:** 911 43089920
Email: info@lectura.de **Web site:** http://www.lectura.de
Freq: Half-yearly; **Annual Sub.:** EUR 259,00; **Circ:** 6,000
Editor: Dieter Flach; **Advertising Manager:** Beatrice Lopez
Profile: Building industry magazine.
Language(s): English; French; German; Italian; Russian; Spanish
ADVERTISING RATES:
Full Page Mono .... EUR 950
Full Page Colour .... EUR 1360
Mechanical Data: Type Area: 140 x 95 mm
Copy instructions: *Copy Date:* 56 days prior to publication

BAUMEISTER 722020G4A-6
Editorial: Streitfeldstr. 35, 81673 MÜNCHEN
Tel: 89 436005118 **Fax:** 89 436005147
Email: a.gutzmer@baumeister.de **Web site:** http://www.baumeister.de
Freq: Monthly; **Annual Sub.:** EUR 159,00; **Circ:** 20,037
Editor: Alexander Gutzmer; **Advertising Manager:** Elmar Große
Profile: Magazine, provides information on architecture, planning, construction, sustainability, Green Energy offers, articles, photo galleries, detailed plans, interviews, architectural portraits, book reviews and architectural criticism.
Language(s): German
ADVERTISING RATES:
Full Page Mono .... EUR 5100
Full Page Colour .... EUR 7800
Mechanical Data: Type Area: 274 x 204 mm, No. of Columns (Display): 4, Col Widths (Display): 48 mm
Copy instructions: *Copy Date:* 27 days prior to publication
BUSINESS: ARCHITECTURE & BUILDING: Architecture

BAUMETALL 722021G4E-2160
Editorial: Schulstr. 3, 72218 WILDBERG
Tel: 7054 373170 **Fax:** 7054 373169
Email: redaktion@baumetall.de **Web site:** http://www.baumetall.de
Freq: 8 issues yearly; **Annual Sub.:** EUR 83,40; **Circ:** 5,310
Editor: Andreas Buck
Profile: The independent trade magazine for plumbing in building construction. The importance of Metals in building construction has continued to increase - despite the introduction of new building materials. Architects and builders recognize in increasing numbers the outstanding benefits of metallic materials for the durable design of roofs and facades, flashings and roof drainage systems, ornaments and weather vanes. This development is devoted to Baumetall and turns with a hands-on coverage of skilled artisans, architects, retailers and their suppliers. Baumetall also deals with the increasing potential for renovation of public buildings and private property. This Outlet offers RSS (Really Simple Syndication).
Language(s): German
ADVERTISING RATES:
Full Page Mono .... EUR 1980
Full Page Colour .... EUR 2730
Mechanical Data: Type Area: 265 x 187 mm, No. of Columns (Display): 4, Col Widths (Display): 43 mm
Copy instructions: *Copy Date:* 20 days prior to publication
BUSINESS: ARCHITECTURE & BUILDING: Building

BAUPHYSIK 722024G4E-2180
Editorial: Rotherstr. 21, 10245 BERLIN
Tel: 30 47031262 **Fax:** 30 47031270
Email: claudia.ozimek@wiley.com **Web site:** http://www.ernst-und-sohn.de
Freq: 6 issues yearly; **Annual Sub.:** EUR 309,23; **Circ:** 3,000
Editor: Claudia Ozimek; **Advertising Manager:** Sigrid Elgner
Profile: The journal Bauphysik includes contributions from the fields of heat, humidity, sound, fire, heating and ventilation systems and the rational use of energy. The close connection between building construction and building services are the Bauphysik an interdisciplinary character. The Bauphysik is concerned with both the new construction and the rehabilitation and modernization of the building stock with respect to the physical building protection goals. Readers of Bauphysik are advisory and consulting engineers for building physics, building acoustics and sound insulation and fire protection, planning for energy-saving building and architects in engineering and architectural firms, construction companies and public administrations. Facebook: http://www.facebook.com/ernstundsohn.
Language(s): German
ADVERTISING RATES:
Full Page Mono .... EUR 1350
Full Page Colour .... EUR 2220
Mechanical Data: Type Area: 260 x 181 mm, No. of Columns (Display): 2, Col Widths (Display): 88 mm
Copy instructions: *Copy Date:* 28 days prior to publication
BUSINESS: ARCHITECTURE & BUILDING: Building

BAUPORTAL 744726G42A-100
Editorial: Landsberger Str. 309, 80687 MÜNCHEN
Tel: 89 889702 **Fax:** 89 8897819
Email: bauportal@bgbau.de **Web site:** http://www.bgbau.de
Freq: Monthly; Free to qualifying individuals
Annual Sub.: EUR 52,40; **Circ:** 30,968
Editor: Klaus-Richard Bergmann; **Advertising Manager:** Böhler
Profile: Magazine covering building techniques, machinery and equipment, building practice and work-safety.
Language(s): German
Readership: Read by civil-engineers, building contractors and engineers.
ADVERTISING RATES:
Full Page Mono .... EUR 3350
Full Page Colour .... EUR 5330
Mechanical Data: Type Area: 262 x 184 mm, No. of Columns (Display): 3, Col Widths (Display): 59 mm
Copy instructions: *Copy Date:* 30 days prior to publication
BUSINESS: CONSTRUCTION

BAURECHT 722072G42A-30
Editorial: Goethestr. 8, 48341 ALTENBERGE
Email: redaktion@werner-baurecht.de **Web site:** http://www.werner-baurecht.de
Freq: Monthly; **Annual Sub.:** EUR 264,00; **Circ:** 5,900
Editor: Hans-Dieter Upmeier; **Advertising Manager:** Stefanie Szillat
Profile: baurecht is a comprehensive journal for the entire construction law with its many problems, both in public and civil law in the planning of construction projects, resulting in their creation and their use. baurecht appears on the practical work oriented technical papers and a judicial section, which is characterized by topicality. baurecht informes courts and zoning authorities what must apply the right of build or responsible for awarding and monitoring of works contracts are. With the same heavy weight baurecht is a constant source of information for lawyers and architects, for the construction industry and associated industries as well as for individuals and organizations that deal with the construction law. baurecht is thus entirely geared to the needs of the practice, informs and teaches fast, reliable and comprehensive information on legal developments in the field of construction law. Public construction law: construction planning law, building law, law of land tenure, expropriation law (including compensation), development rights (development contributions), pollution control laws, zoning procedure for the road laws. Civil construction Law: Construction contract law in great detail (construction contract between the builder and contractors to the Civil Code and the VOB, use contractor forms, construction contracts, etc.), public procurement, architectural contract law, Civilian Adjoining property, insurance law issues.
Language(s): German
ADVERTISING RATES:
Full Page Mono .... EUR 2193
Full Page Colour .... EUR 3300
Mechanical Data: Type Area: 200 x 140 mm
BUSINESS: CONSTRUCTION

DER BAUSACHVERSTÄNDIGE 755730G4E-6803
Editorial: Nobelstr. 12, 70569 STUTTGART
Tel: 711 9702709 **Fax:** 711 9702299
Email: thomas.altmann@irb.fraunhofer.de **Web site:** http://www.derbausv.de
Freq: 6 issues yearly; **Annual Sub.:** EUR 82,50; **Circ:** 3,420
Editor: Thomas Altmann; **Advertising Manager:** Melanie Saß
Profile: Magazine on all aspects of real estate evaluation.
Language(s): German
ADVERTISING RATES:
Full Page Mono .... EUR 1498
Full Page Colour .... EUR 1828
Mechanical Data: Type Area: 260 x 186 mm, No. of Columns (Display): 3, Col Widths (Display): 57 mm
Copy instructions: *Copy Date:* 28 days prior to publication

DIE BAUSTELLE 722082G4E-2280
Editorial: Baumschulenallee 12, 30625 HANNOVER
Tel: 511 957570 **Fax:** 511 9575740
Email: espel@bvn.de **Web site:** http://www.bvn.de
Freq: Monthly; **Circ:** 3,300
Editor: Hans Espel
Profile: The Construction Association of Lower Saxony - BVN - is the political interested home for all construction companies in Lower Saxony. The BVN represents as a trade association, employers association and association of technical interests of its members in legal, economic, social political and technical level. As the state Association for the construction of Lower Saxony BVN member guilds of the construction, masonry, carpentry, tiling, road builders, floor layers, plastering and concrete block manufacturers crafts assisted in fulfilling their duties. The BVN carries a voice to the construction companies in Lower Saxony to the fact that the common interests of supervising construction industry are considered in Lower Saxony - regionally, nationally, in Europe.
Language(s): German
ADVERTISING RATES:
Full Page Mono .... EUR 1200
Full Page Colour .... EUR 2175
Mechanical Data: Type Area: 244 x 175 mm, No. of Columns (Display): 3, Col Widths (Display): 55 mm
Copy instructions: *Copy Date:* 20 days prior to publication

BAUSTOFF MARKT 722084G4R-80
Editorial: Stresemannstr. 20, 47051 DUISBURG
Tel: 203 3052714 **Fax:** 203 30527820
Email: u.hennig@wohlfarth.de **Web site:** http://www.baustoffmarkt-online.de
Freq: Monthly; **Annual Sub.:** EUR 109,79; **Circ:** 4,643
Editor: Uwe Hennig; **Advertising Manager:** Mechthild Kaiser
Profile: The baustoff markt has a independent content profile with a clearly defined target group. It is a mediator of information between industry and trade, and: It is the business magazine for executives in the construction materials industry. The baustoff markt covers this target group each month from sustainable and reliable without wastage and almost completely. Each subscription will be used according to the current issue readership structure analysis of 4 with-readers. Executives familiar with the building materials sector read, use and appreciate "their industry magazine".
Language(s): German
ADVERTISING RATES:
Full Page Mono .... EUR 2460
Full Page Colour .... EUR 4170
Mechanical Data: Type Area: 259 x 180 mm, No. of Columns (Display): 4, Col Widths (Display): 42 mm
Copy instructions: *Copy Date:* 20 days prior to publication
Official Journal of: Organ d. Bundesverb. Dt. Baustoff-Fachhandel e.V.
BUSINESS: ARCHITECTURE & BUILDING: Building Related

BAUSTOFF PARTNER 722085G4E-2300
Editorial: Hermann-von-Barth-Str. 2, 87435 KEMPTEN **Tel:** 831 522040 **Fax:** 831 5220450
Email: baustoffpartner@sbm-verlag.de **Web site:** http://www.sbm-verlag.de
Freq: 11 issues yearly; **Annual Sub.:** EUR 51,00; **Circ:** 9,516
Editor: Gerd Rottstegge; **Advertising Manager:** Markus Holl
Profile: Magazine containing information about new products for the building industry. Includes reports on structural developments, technology, equipment and market trends.
Language(s): German
Readership: Aimed at builders, civil engineers, architects, manufacturers and distributors of building materials and equipment.
ADVERTISING RATES:
Full Page Mono .... EUR 2650
Full Page Colour .... EUR 3286
Mechanical Data: Type Area: 265 x 185 mm, No. of Columns (Display): 4, Col Widths (Display): 42 mm
Copy instructions: *Copy Date:* 20 days prior to publication
BUSINESS: ARCHITECTURE & BUILDING: Building

BAUSTOFFPRAXIS 722087G4R-201
Editorial: Stresemannstr. 20, 47051 DUISBURG
Tel: 203 3052721 **Fax:** 203 30527820
Email: r.grimm@wohlfarth.de **Web site:** http://www.baustoffmarkt-online.de
Freq: Monthly; **Annual Sub.:** EUR 46,22; **Circ:** 3,164
Editor: Roland Grimm; **Advertising Manager:** Mechthild Kaiser
Profile: "baustoffpraxis" is the magazine for the practice of building materials dealers and in the building trade and completed the business magazine "baustoff markt". The magazine reports monthly on new building products / systems and their processing, building materials and building physics technical expertise as well as news from the material development. The heading "The modernization Manager", refers specifically to the energy-technical consultants in construction materials dealers and focuses on current trends, products and legal framework surrounding the issue of the future building modernization. The heading "special knowledge" provides basic knowledge for future building professionals. In short: "baustoffpraxis" provides compact building knowledge for the case.
Language(s): German
ADVERTISING RATES:
Full Page Mono .... EUR 2310
Full Page Colour .... EUR 3900
Mechanical Data: Type Area: 259 x 180 mm, No. of Columns (Display): 4, Col Widths (Display): 42 mm
Copy instructions: *Copy Date:* 10 days prior to publication
BUSINESS: ARCHITECTURE & BUILDING: Building Related

BAUTECHNIK 722093G4E-2380
Editorial: Rotherstr. 21, 10245 BERLIN
Tel: 30 47031275 **Fax:** 30 47031270
Email: bautechnik@ernst-und-sohn.de **Web site:** http://www.ernst-und-sohn.de
Freq: Monthly; **Annual Sub.:** EUR 447,00; **Circ:** 1,866
Editor: Dirk Jesse; **Advertising Manager:** Sigrid Elgner
Profile: Journal focusing structural engineering containing information on building and construction techniques, geotechnics, environmental engineering, calculation and dimensioning. Facebook: http://www.facebook.com/ernstundsohn.
Language(s): German
ADVERTISING RATES:
Full Page Mono .... EUR 2740
Full Page Colour .... EUR 4285
Mechanical Data: Type Area: 260 x 181 mm, No. of Columns (Display): 4, Col Widths (Display): 42 mm
BUSINESS: ARCHITECTURE & BUILDING: Building

BAUTZNER WOCHENKURIER 722098G72-1752
Editorial: Wettiner Platz 10, 01067 DRESDEN
Tel: 351 491760 **Fax:** 351 4917674
Email: wochenkurier-dresden@dwk-verlag.de **Web site:** http://www.wochenkurier.info
Freq: Weekly; **Cover Price:** Free; **Circ:** 52,598
Editor: Regine Eberlein; **Advertising Manager:** Andreas Schönherr
Profile: Advertising journal (house-to-house) concentrating on local stories.
Language(s): German
ADVERTISING RATES:
Full Page Mono .... EUR 3131
Full Page Colour .... EUR 4383
Mechanical Data: Type Area: 430 x 290 mm, No. of Columns (Display): 7, Col Widths (Display): 38 mm
Copy instructions: *Copy Date:* 5 days prior to publication
LOCAL NEWSPAPERS

BAUVERLAG EINKAUFSFÜHRER BAU 722540G4E-2640
Editorial: Avenwedder Str. 55, 33335 GÜTERSLOH
Tel: 5241 8090884 **Fax:** 5241 80690880
Email: roland.herr@bauverlag.de **Web site:** http://www.einkaufsfuehrer-bau.de
Freq: Annual; **Cover Price:** EUR 33,90; **Circ:** 45,000
Editor: Roland Herr; **Advertising Manager:** Christiane Klose
Profile: The bauverlag Einkaufsführer Bau is the modern development of the Bertelsmann Baukatalog appearing for over 70 years. This new cross-media Business directory contains 3500 addresses of manufacturers. These are listed alphabetically in the corporate directory and the classified list sorted by product.
Language(s): German
ADVERTISING RATES:
Full Page Mono .... EUR 3060
Full Page Colour .... EUR 4590
Mechanical Data: Type Area: 210 x 140 mm
Copy instructions: *Copy Date:* 60 days prior to publication

BAUWELT 722106G4E-2460
Editorial: Schlüterstr. 42, 10707 BERLIN
Tel: 30 88410626 **Fax:** 30 8835167
Email: boris.schade-buensow@bauverlag.de **Web site:** http://www.bauwelt.de
Freq: 44 issues yearly; **Annual Sub.:** EUR 269,40; **Circ:** 11,172
Editor: Boris Schade-Bünsow; **Advertising Manager:** Christiane Klose
Profile: Bauwelt - weekly forum for involved critical analysis and commentary on current issues in architecture. Formulated positions, provides material for discussion, forms opinions on a competent readers with decision-making authority over high volume of orders in large architectural firms and building authorities. Each issue focusing on the key issues, e.g. to business and administrative buildings, renovations, residential, industrial and public construction.
Language(s): German
Readership: Read by architects and surveyors.
ADVERTISING RATES:
Full Page Mono .... EUR 4850
Full Page Colour .... EUR 7600
Mechanical Data: Type Area: 251 x 211 mm, No. of Columns (Display): 4, Col Widths (Display): 50 mm
Copy instructions: *Copy Date:* 14 days prior to publication
Supplement(s): computer spezial; Licht + Raum; Vorteile
BUSINESS: ARCHITECTURE & BUILDING: Building

BAV SPEZIAL 1971354G14A-10408
Editorial: Munzinger Str. 9, 79111 FREIBURG
Tel: 761 8983924 **Fax:** 761 8983112
Email: online@haufe-lexware.com **Web site:** http://www.haufe.de/mediacenter
Freq: Half-yearly; **Cover Price:** Free; **Circ:** 150,000
Editor: Katharina Schmitt
Profile: The supplement provides information on the key changes and trends in the company pension. There are specific recommendations for the safe and economic design of pension benefits by companies. Key target groups: business owners, managers, personnel managers, tax accountants.
Language(s): German
ADVERTISING RATES:
Full Page Mono .... EUR 13900
Full Page Colour .... EUR 13900
Mechanical Data: Type Area: 249 x 176 mm
Supplement(s): personalmagazin; ProFirma; SteuerConsultant

BAYARTZ NEWS & FACTS 722113G2B-34
Editorial: Bennostr. 6, 52134 HERZOGENRATH
Tel: 2406 669006
Email: info@bayartz.de **Web site:** http://www.bayartz.de
Freq: Half-yearly; **Circ:** 5,000
Editor: R. Smets; **Advertising Manager:** E. Bayartz
Profile: Magazine concerning the press industry.
Language(s): German
Readership: Aimed at reporters.
Mechanical Data: Type Area: 220 x 170 mm, No. of Columns (Display): 2
BUSINESS: COMMUNICATIONS, ADVERTISING & MARKETING: Press

BAYER REPORT 722173G37-1760
Editorial: 51368 LEVERKUSEN **Tel:** 214 3071485
Fax: 214 3071985
Web site: http://www.bayer.com
Freq: Half-yearly; **Cover Price:** Free; **Circ:** 180,000
Editor: Franz Rempe
Profile: Magazine of the Bayer company.
Language(s): German
ADVERTISING RATES:
Full Page Mono .... EUR 1000
Full Page Colour .... EUR 1000
Mechanical Data: Type Area: 245 x 190 mm
Copy instructions: *Copy Date:* 28 days prior to publication

BAYERISCH SCHWABEN MAGAZIN 1861435G89A-12418
Editorial: Schießgrabenstr. 14, 86150 AUGSBURG
Tel: 821 4504010 **Fax:** 821 45040120
Email: info@tvabs.de **Web site:** http://www.bayerisch-schwaben.de
Freq: Annual; **Cover Price:** Free; **Circ:** 40,000
Editor: Martin Kluger
Profile: Experience-Journal for the region between Augsburg, Danube and Ries.
Language(s): German

DER BAYERISCHE BÜRGERMEISTER 722119G32A-280
Editorial: Hultschiner Str. 8, 81677 MÜNCHEN
Tel: 89 21837940 **Fax:** 89 21837967940
Email: bay.buergermeister@hjr-verlag.de **Web site:** http://www.huethig-jehle-rehm.de
Freq: 11 issues yearly; **Annual Sub.:** EUR 159,95; **Circ:** 1,200
Editor: Katharina Hipp; **Advertising Manager:** Brigitte Höpfl
Profile: Publication for members of local government at all levels in Bavaria.
Language(s): German
Readership: Read by local government officials.
ADVERTISING RATES:
Full Page Mono .... EUR 722
Full Page Colour .... EUR 1382
Mechanical Data: Type Area: 260 x 180 mm, No. of Columns (Display): 3, Col Widths (Display): 56 mm
Copy instructions: *Copy Date:* 31 days prior to publication
Official Journal of: Organ d. kommunalen Spitzenverbände in Bayern
BUSINESS: LOCAL GOVERNMENT, LEISURE & RECREATION: Local Government

BAYERISCHE GEMEINDEZEITUNG 722120G32A-300
Editorial: Breslauer Weg 44, 82538 GERETSRIED
Tel: 8171 930711 **Fax:** 8171 80514
Email: info@gemeindezeitung.de **Web site:** http://www.gemeindezeitung.de
Freq: 22 issues yearly; **Annual Sub.:** EUR 81,43; **Circ:** 9,623
Editor: Anne-Marie von Hassel; **Advertising Manager:** Constanze von Hassel
Profile: Publication about municipal administration in Bavaria. Covers municipal policies, economic and business news, legal, technical and practical information.
Language(s): German
ADVERTISING RATES:
Full Page Mono .... EUR 5292
Full Page Colour .... EUR 6162
Mechanical Data: Type Area: 420 x 284 mm, No. of Columns (Display): 6, Col Widths (Display): 45 mm
Copy instructions: *Copy Date:* 10 days prior to publication
Official Journal of: Organ d. Kommunalpolit. Vereinigung d. CSU in Bayern
BUSINESS: LOCAL GOVERNMENT, LEISURE & RECREATION: Local Government

BAYERISCHE HAUSBESITZER-ZEITUNG 722121G74K-100
Editorial: Sonnenstr. 11, 80331 MÜNCHEN
Tel: 89 55141371 **Fax:** 89 540413355
Email: info@bayerische-hausbesitzer-zeitung.de **Web site:** http://www.bayerische-hausbesitzer-zeitung.de
Freq: Monthly; **Annual Sub.:** EUR 16,60; **Circ:** 33,728
Editor: Bernhard Stocker
Profile: The Bavarian Homeowners Association newspaper is the organ of Home Basic Bavaria. In our magazine information is provided around home base for our members, but also interested homeowners and property owners. The journal provides comprehensive and competent in all areas of home and housing industry. Priorities are, next to restored Latest from housing policy, finance, law and taxation, the issues and modernization, as well as services around the house.
Language(s): German
ADVERTISING RATES:
Full Page Mono .... EUR 1440
Full Page Colour .... EUR 1820
Mechanical Data: Type Area: 270 x 184 mm, No. of Columns (Display): 4, Col Widths (Display): 43 mm
Copy instructions: *Copy Date:* 25 days prior to publication
Official Journal of: Organ d. LV Bayer. Haus-, Wohnungs- u. Grundbesitzer e.V.
CONSUMER: WOMEN'S INTEREST CONSUMER MAGAZINES: Home Purchase

DAS BAYERISCHE KAMINKEHRERHANDWERK 722125G4F-1
Editorial: Lohweg 10b, 90537 FEUCHT
Tel: 9128 169999 **Fax:** 9128 169900
Email: post@flachenecker.info **Web site:** http://www.schlotfeger.info
Freq: Monthly; Free to qualifying individuals
Annual Sub.: EUR 29,26; **Circ:** 2,900
Editor: Stefan Flachenecker; **Advertising Manager:** Seigner
Profile: Official journal of the German Association of Chimney Sweeps.
Language(s): German
ADVERTISING RATES:
Full Page Mono .... EUR 530
Full Page Colour .... EUR 730
Mechanical Data: Type Area: 260 x 180 mm
Copy instructions: *Copy Date:* 30 days prior to publication
BUSINESS: ARCHITECTURE & BUILDING: Cleaning & Maintenance

BAYERISCHE RUNDSCHAU 722138G67B-2360
Editorial: Gutenbergstr. 1, 96050 BAMBERG
Tel: 951 1880 **Fax:** 951 188323
Email: redaktion.bamberg@infranken.de **Web site:** http://www.infranken.de
Freq: 312 issues yearly; **Circ:** 14,868
Advertising Manager: Bernd Seidel
Profile: Daily newspaper with regional news and a local sports section. Facebook: http://www.facebook.com/pages/inFrankende/209363937665 This Outlet offers RSS (Really Simple Syndication).
Language(s): German
ADVERTISING RATES:
SCC .... EUR 38,10
Mechanical Data: No. of Columns (Display): 6, Col Widths (Display): 45 mm, Type Area: 430 x 285 mm
Copy instructions: *Copy Date:* 1 day prior to publication
Supplement(s): doppio; Lebens Raum; rtv
REGIONAL DAILY & SUNDAY NEWSPAPERS: Regional Daily Newspapers

BAYERISCHE SCHULE 722142G62B-3184
Editorial: Heidwiesen 43, 97520 RÖTHLEIN
Tel: 9723 9370041 **Fax:** 9723 9370042
Email: redaktion@bayerische-schule.de **Web site:** http://www.bayerische-schule.de
Freq: 9 issues yearly; Free to qualifying individuals
Annual Sub.: EUR 51,13; **Circ:** 51,291
Editor: Tomi Neckov
Profile: Publication focusing on education and pedagogy. Journal of the Bavarian teachers and teachers' Association e.V.
Language(s): German
ADVERTISING RATES:
Full Page Mono .... EUR 1780
Full Page Colour .... EUR 2060
Mechanical Data: Type Area: 262 x 180 mm
Supplement(s): Begegnung & Gespräch
BUSINESS: CHURCH & SCHOOL EQUIPMENT & EDUCATION: Education Teachers

BAYERISCHE STAATSZEITUNG UND BAYERISCHER STAATSANZEIGER 722151G72-1756
Editorial: Herzog-Rudolf-Str. 1, 80539 MÜNCHEN
Tel: 89 2901420 **Fax:** 89 299562
Email: redaktion@bsz.de **Web site:** http://www.bsz.de
Freq: Weekly; **Circ:** 17,511
Editor: Ralph Schweinfurth; **Advertising Manager:** Marion Birkenmaier
Profile: The BSZ - Bayerische Staatszeitung und Bayerischer Staatsanzeiger - weekly informs on Bavaria's top issues in state and local government, business and culture. Expert Information for construction and related trades such as school - and kindergartenbuilding, ecological building, building with wood as regularly as renewable energy, alternative fuels or remediation of contaminated sites and services for SMEs in the editorial center. The BSZ reported on IT in management, e-government and the marketing of industrial estates. It researches on wastewater and canal rehabilitation, water supply and waste & recycling. The BSZ provides alerts on construction, supplies and services. A focus will be on state and local construction tenders. Information on tendering and procurement appear regularly in the BSZ.
Language(s): German
Readership: Aimed at local councils, but also planners, local government employees, schools and those interested in cultural events.
ADVERTISING RATES:
SCC .... EUR 39,50
Mechanical Data: Type Area: 474 x 324 mm, No. of Columns (Display): 7, Col Widths (Display): 45 mm
Copy instructions: *Copy Date:* 3 days prior to publication
Supplement(s): Bayerischer Staatsanzeiger; Unser Bayern
LOCAL NEWSPAPERS

DER BAYERISCHE WALDBESITZER 1861544G21A-4417
Editorial: Max-Joseph-Str. 9, 80333 MÜNCHEN
Tel: 89 5803089 **Fax:** 89 5807015
Email: bayer.waldbesitzerverband@t-online.de **Web site:** http://www.bayer-waldbesitzerverband.de
Freq: 6 issues yearly; Free to qualifying individuals
Annual Sub.: EUR 25,00; **Circ:** 10,000
Editor: Hans Baur
Profile: You want to be fully informed about the forest, wood and the environment. You want to be informed about the timber market. You want to be advised on tax and legal issues. You want to manage your forest operation profitably. You want to strengthen the community of forest owners, and thus defend the security of property. You want services to get taught. You need help and support.
Language(s): German
ADVERTISING RATES:
Full Page Mono .... EUR 585
Full Page Colour .... EUR 995
Mechanical Data: Type Area: 243 x 185 mm, No. of Columns (Display): 4, Col Widths (Display): 43 mm

BAYERISCHES ÄRZTEBLATT 722139G56A-1540
Editorial: Mühlbaurstr. 16, 81677 MÜNCHEN
Tel: 89 4147181 **Fax:** 89 4147202
Email: aerzteblatt@blaek.de **Web site:** http://www.blaek.de
Freq: Monthly; Free to qualifying individuals
Annual Sub.: EUR 40,00; **Circ:** 70,588
Editor: Dagmar Nedbal
Profile: Publication of the Bavarian Medical Association and the ministries for physical doctors in Bavaria.
Language(s): German
ADVERTISING RATES:
Full Page Mono .... EUR 3800
Full Page Colour .... EUR 5900
Mechanical Data: Type Area: 240 x 188 mm, No. of Columns (Display): 3, Col Widths (Display): 60 mm
Copy instructions: *Copy Date:* 30 days prior to publication
BUSINESS: HEALTH & MEDICAL

BAYERISCHES LANDWIRTSCHAFTLICHES WOCHENBLATT 722145G21J-17
Editorial: Bayerstr. 57, 80335 MÜNCHEN
Tel: 89 53098901 **Fax:** 89 5328537
Email: blw@dlv.de **Web site:** http://www.wochenblatt-dlv.de
Freq: Weekly; **Annual Sub.:** EUR 109,00; **Circ:** 102,515
Editor: Johannes Urban; **Advertising Manager:** Thomas Herrmann
Profile: Official publication of the Bavarian Farming Association. Covers farming techniques and equipment, animals, markets and prices and other aspects of life on the land.
Language(s): German
ADVERTISING RATES:
Full Page Mono .... EUR 10106
Full Page Colour .... EUR 16506
Mechanical Data: Type Area: 310 x 212 mm, No. of Columns (Display): 4, Col Widths (Display): 50 mm
Copy instructions: *Copy Date:* 10 days prior to publication
Official Journal of: Organ d. Bayer. Bauernverb.
Supplement(s): Unser Allgäu
BUSINESS: AGRICULTURE & FARMING: Agriculture & Farming - Regional

BAYERISCHES SONNTAGSBLATT 722147G87-1040
Editorial: Lange Str. 335, 59067 HAMM
Tel: 2381 940400 **Fax:** 2381 9404070
Email: redaktion@liborius.de **Web site:** http://www.bayerisches-sonntagsblatt.de
Freq: Weekly; **Cover Price:** EUR 1,60; **Circ:** 9,526
Editor: Andrea Groß-Schulte; **Advertising Manager:** Manfred Schmitz
Profile: Catholic magazine.
Language(s): German
ADVERTISING RATES:
Full Page Mono .... EUR 1260
Full Page Colour .... EUR 2016
Mechanical Data: Type Area: 315 x 216 mm, No. of Columns (Display): 5, Col Widths (Display): 40 mm
Copy instructions: *Copy Date:* 10 days prior to publication
CONSUMER: RELIGIOUS

BAYERN METALL 722161G27-3014
Editorial: Erhardtstr. 6, 80469 MÜNCHEN
Tel: 89 2025623 **Fax:** 89 20256250
Email: tauber@fachverband-metall-bayern.de **Web site:** http://www.fachverband-metall-bayern.de
Freq: Monthly; **Circ:** 4,600
Editor: Richard Tauber; **Advertising Manager:** Heidemarie Bolz
Profile: The bayern Metall is the official journal of the Association metal Bavaria for the craft of metal workers, precision mechanics, metal and bell-founders.
Language(s): German
Readership: Read by people in the metal industry.
ADVERTISING RATES:
Full Page Mono .... EUR 1050
Full Page Colour .... EUR 1545
Mechanical Data: Type Area: 250 x 185 mm, No. of Columns (Display): 4, Col Widths (Display): 43 mm
Copy instructions: *Copy Date:* 19 days prior to publication
Official Journal of: Organ d. Fachverb. Metall Bayern f. d. Handwerk d. Metallbauer, Feinwerkmechaniker sowie Metall- u. Glockengießer
BUSINESS: METAL, IRON & STEEL

BAYERN TURNER 722168G75X-460
Editorial: Georg-Brauchle-Ring 93, 80992 MÜNCHEN **Tel:** 89 15702318 **Fax:** 89 15702317
Email: heister@turnverband-bayern.de **Web site:** http://www.turnverband-bayern.de
Freq: 11 issues yearly; **Annual Sub.:** EUR 38,50,; **Circ:** 4,200
Editor: Ulrich Heister; **Advertising Manager:** Renate Trinkl
Profile: To technical information to gymnasts and to contact care with members the Bavarian Gymnastics Federation gives out its members newspaper.
Language(s): German
ADVERTISING RATES:
Full Page Mono .... EUR 400
Full Page Colour .... EUR 500
Mechanical Data: Type Area: 248 x 185 mm
CONSUMER: SPORT: Other Sport

BAYERNKURIER 722159G82-9480
Editorial: Nymphenburger Str. 64, 80335 MÜNCHEN
Tel: 89 120040 **Fax:** 89 1293050
Email: redaktion@bayernkurier.de **Web site:** http://www.bayernkurier.de
Freq: Weekly; **Annual Sub.:** EUR 75,00; **Circ:** 52,589
Editor: Peter Hausmann; **News Editor:** Wolfram Göll;
Advertising Manager: Karin Freese
Profile: Nationwide weekly newspaper: The Bayernkurier is not only a forum for politically motivated people. A detailed business and culture section offers an interesting and varied range of information on Bavaria for Bavaria.
Language(s): German
ADVERTISING RATES:
SCC .... EUR 43,00
Mechanical Data: Type Area: 480 x 325 mm, No. of Columns (Display): 7, Col Widths (Display): 42 mm
Copy instructions: *Copy Date:* 8 days prior to publication
CONSUMER: CURRENT AFFAIRS & POLITICS

BAYERNS PFERDE ZUCHT + SPORT 722163G81D-2
Editorial: Lothstr. 29, 80797 MÜNCHEN
Tel: 89 127051 **Fax:** 89 12705335
Email: annegret.strehle@dlv.de **Web site:** http://www.bayernspferde.de
Freq: Monthly; **Annual Sub.:** EUR 68,30; **Circ:** 11,880
Editor: Annegret Strehle; **Advertising Manager:** Thomas Herrmann
Profile: Dealing with the creature horse ranging from the first touch on the fence right up to the awards ceremony in the spotlight. In between are countless variations. This diversity has prescribed Bayerns Pferde Zucht + Sport as a forum for all horse people of the region. Here inform riders, drivers, vaulters and breeders about tournaments and other performance tests and their results. Seasonal topics on keeping, feeding, grooming, veterinary and legal issues find place alongside horsemanship, training, and numerous other posts. Here are the editorial team breeders, grooms, horse industry champions, tournament judges, veterinarians, lawyers, and of course recreational athletes and officials to the scene on the site. Photographers and graphic designers provide the current and appropriate background. Bayerns Pferde Zucht + Sport proves here that professionally competent reporting and reading

pleasure are not mutually exclusive. Bayerns Pferde Zucht + Sport published the tournament tenders exclusively for Bavaria. Bayerns Pferde Zucht + Sport is thus required reading for all active tournament participants.
Language(s): German
ADVERTISING RATES:
Full Page Mono .... EUR 1890
Full Page Colour .... EUR 3240
Mechanical Data: Type Area: 270 x 184 mm, No. of Columns (Display): 4, Col Widths (Display): 43 mm
Copy instructions: *Copy Date:* 28 days prior to publication
Official Journal of: Organ d. LV Bayer. Pferdezüchter u. d. Bayer. Reit- u. Fahrverb., d. Landeskommission f. Pferdeleistungsprüfung in Bayern, d. Förderkreises f. nationalen u. internat. Reitsport in Bayern u. d. Bayer. Westernpferde Sportverb.
CONSUMER: ANIMALS & PETS: Horses & Ponies

BAYERNSPORT 722165G75A-300
Editorial: Georg-Brauchle-Ring 93, 80992 MÜNCHEN **Tel:** 89 15702631 **Fax:** 89 15702565
Email: bayernsport@blsv.de **Web site:** http://www.blsv.de
Freq: Weekly; **Annual Sub.:** EUR 46,00; **Circ:** 22,300
Editor: Thomas Kern
Profile: Magazine about sport in Bavaria.
Language(s): German
ADVERTISING RATES:
Full Page Mono .... EUR 1990
Full Page Colour .... EUR 2690
Mechanical Data: Type Area: 262 x 183 mm, No. of Columns (Display): 3, Col Widths (Display): 58 mm
Copy instructions: *Copy Date:* 4 days prior to publication
CONSUMER: SPORT

BAYERWALD WOCHENBLATT 722181G72-1764
Editorial: Auwiesenweg 11, 94209 REGEN
Tel: 9921 882353 **Fax:** 9921 882355
Email: lothar.wandtner@wochenblatt.de **Web site:** http://www.wochenblatt.de
Freq: Weekly; **Cover Price:** Free; **Circ:** 33,500
Editor: Lothar Wandtner; **Advertising Manager:** Horst Zimmermann
Profile: Advertising journal (house-to-house) concentrating on local stories.
Language(s): German
ADVERTISING RATES:
Full Page Mono .... EUR 2705
Full Page Colour .... EUR 4030
Mechanical Data: Type Area: 460 x 280 mm, No. of Columns (Display): 6, Col Widths (Display): 43 mm
Copy instructions: *Copy Date:* 2 days prior to publication
LOCAL NEWSPAPERS

DER BAYERWALD-BOTE 722178G67B-2420
Editorial: Medienstr. 5, 94036 PASSAU
Tel: 851 8020 **Fax:** 851 802256
Email: pnp@vgp.de **Web site:** http://www.pnp.de
Freq: 312 issues yearly; **Circ:** 17,847
Advertising Manager: Gerhard Koller
Profile: Daily newspaper with regional news and a local sports section.
Language(s): German
ADVERTISING RATES:
SCC .... EUR 43,50
Mechanical Data: Type Area: 482 x 325 mm, No. of Columns (Display): 7, Col Widths (Display): 45 mm
Copy instructions: *Copy Date:* 2 days prior to publication
REGIONAL DAILY & SUNDAY NEWSPAPERS: Regional Daily Newspapers

BAYERWALD-ECHO 722179G67B-2440
Editorial: Margaretenstr. 4, 93047 REGENSBURG
Tel: 941 20765 **Fax:** 941 207142
Email: mz-redaktion@mittelbayerische.de **Web site:** http://www.mittelbayerische.de
Freq: 312 issues yearly; **Circ:** 15,538
Profile: Daily newspaper with regional news and a local sports section.
Language(s): German
ADVERTISING RATES:
SCC .... EUR 40,00
Mechanical Data: Type Area: 430 x 281 mm, No. of Columns (Display): 6, Col Widths (Display): 45 mm
Copy instructions: *Copy Date:* 1 day prior to publication
Supplement(s): Mittelbayerische jun.
REGIONAL DAILY & SUNDAY NEWSPAPERS: Regional Daily Newspapers

BAZ BADISCHE ANZEIGEN-ZEITUNG - AUSG. 2 721725G72-1692
Editorial: Dudenstr. 12, 68167 MANNHEIM
Tel: 621 39203 **Fax:** 621 3922810
Email: redaktion.baz@mamo.de
Freq: Weekly; **Cover Price:** Free; **Circ:** 25,423
Editor: Stefan Wagner; **Advertising Manager:** Michael Müller
Profile: Advertising journal (house-to-house) concentrating on local stories.
Language(s): German
ADVERTISING RATES:
Full Page Mono .... EUR 3190
Full Page Colour .... EUR 4151
Mechanical Data: Type Area: 490 x 319 mm, No. of Columns (Display): 7, Col Widths (Display): 45 mm
Copy instructions: *Copy Date:* 2 days prior to publication
LOCAL NEWSPAPERS

BAZ BADISCHE ANZEIGEN-ZEITUNG ZUM SONNTAG - AUSG. A 722188G72-1780
Editorial: Dudenstr. 12, 68167 MANNHEIM
Tel: 621 39203 **Fax:** 621 3922810
Email: redaktion.baz@mamo.de
Freq: Weekly; **Cover Price:** Free; **Circ:** 41,528
Editor: Stefan Wagner; **Advertising Manager:** Michael Müller
Profile: Advertising journal (house-to-house) concentrating on local stories.
Language(s): German
ADVERTISING RATES:
Full Page Mono .... EUR 5351
Full Page Colour .... EUR 6963
Mechanical Data: Type Area: 490 x 319 mm, No. of Columns (Display): 7, Col Widths (Display): 43 mm
Copy instructions: *Copy Date:* 2 days prior to publication
LOCAL NEWSPAPERS

BAZ BERGSTRÄSSER ANZEIGEN-ZEITUNG - AUSG. 21 722384G72-1880
Editorial: Dudenstr. 12, 68167 MANNHEIM
Tel: 621 39203 **Fax:** 621 3922810
Email: redaktion.baz@mamo.de
Freq: Weekly; **Cover Price:** Free; **Circ:** 27,830
Editor: Stefan Wagner; **Advertising Manager:** Michael Müller
Profile: Advertising journal (house-to-house) concentrating on local stories.
Language(s): German
ADVERTISING RATES:
Full Page Mono .... EUR 2847
Full Page Colour .... EUR 3705
Mechanical Data: Type Area: 490 x 319 mm, No. of Columns (Display): 7, Col Widths (Display): 43 mm
Copy instructions: *Copy Date:* 2 days prior to publication
LOCAL NEWSPAPERS

BBA BAU BERATUNG ARCHITEKTUR 722191G4E-2520
Editorial: Ernst-Mey-Str. 8, 70771 LEINFELDEN-ECHTERDINGEN **Tel:** 711 7594250
Fax: 711 7594397
Email: bba.redaktion@konradin.de **Web site:** http://www.bba-online.de
Freq: 10 issues yearly; **Annual Sub.:** EUR 85,00; **Circ:** 20,039
Editor: Jürgen Ostrowski; **Advertising Manager:** Bettina Mayer
Profile: bba is the modern periodical for architects and structural engineers which generates most response, providing unique service on trade information. Knowledge of products and systems needed every day in their practices, solving problems in construction, building facilities, building physics, and aesthetics in the business relations to clients, specialist planners and specialist craftspeople. The editorial aim is to focus the solutions to problems, regarding function as well as design aspects, for the benefits of the readers: For instance, in object reports problem complexes are commented on and relevant systems and products providing solutions are described in detail are described in detail. By this concept, bba gets in touch with persons in architectural and engineering practices who decide on systems or products or who take a leading role in finding decisions. The modified information service extends the previous reference number system and is completed by new consulting elements, relevant links, references to further reading, etc.. In regular intervals product manufacturers and providers of services are sent the contact details of readers who make use of the bba information service.
Language(s): German
Readership: Read by builders and planning engineers.
ADVERTISING RATES:
Full Page Mono .... EUR 5100
Full Page Colour .... EUR 6300
Mechanical Data: Type Area: 270 x 188 mm, No. of Columns (Display): 4, Col Widths (Display): 44 mm
BUSINESS: ARCHITECTURE & BUILDING: Building

BBE CHEF-TELEGRAMM 722194G14A-620
Editorial: Am Hammergraben 14, 56567 NEUWIED
Tel: 2631 879400 **Fax:** 2631 879403
Email: info@bbe-cheftelegramm.de **Web site:** http://www.bbe-cheftelegramm.de
Freq: 24 issues yearly; **Circ:** 1,100
Editor: Peter Rath
Profile: Magazine for employers in the retail trade.
Language(s): German

BBE CHEF-TELEGRAMM APOTHEKEN SPEZIAL 722195G37-640
Editorial: Am Hammergraben 14, 56567 NEUWIED
Tel: 2631 879400 **Fax:** 2631 879403
Email: info@bbe-cheftelegramm.de **Web site:** http://www.bbe-apotheken-spezial.de
Freq: 24 issues yearly; **Circ:** 500
Editor: Peter Rath
Profile: Magazine for pharmacists.
Language(s): German

BBE STEUERPRAXIS 722196G14A-640
Editorial: Am Hammergraben 14, 56567 NEUWIED
Tel: 2631 879400 **Fax:** 2631 879403
Email: info@bbe-steuerpraxis.de **Web site:** http://www.bbe-steuerpraxis.de
Freq: 24 issues yearly; **Circ:** 300
Editor: Peter Rath
Profile: Magazine on taxes.
Language(s): German

BBR 721781G27-300
Editorial: Talhofstr. 24b, 82205 GILCHING
Tel: 8105 385354 **Fax:** 8105 385311
Email: h.schaetzl@verlag-henrich.de **Web site:** http://www.bbr.de
Freq: 6 issues yearly; **Annual Sub.:** EUR 127,00; **Circ:** 13,527
Editor: Hans-Georg Schätzl; **Advertising Manager:** Thomas Schumann
Profile: Technical magazine about rolling mill engineering, sheet metal working, drawn and welded tubes and sections.
Language(s): German
ADVERTISING RATES:
Full Page Mono .... EUR 3035
Full Page Colour .... EUR 4115
Mechanical Data: Type Area: 282 x 200 mm, No. of Columns (Display): 4, Col Widths (Display): 47 mm
Copy instructions: *Copy Date:* 28 days prior to publication
Supplement(s): i Quadrat
BUSINESS: METAL, IRON & STEEL

BBR FACHMAGAZIN FÜR BRUNNEN- UND LEITUNGSBAU 722203G4E-2540
Editorial: Josef-Wirmer-Str. 3, 53123 BONN
Tel: 228 9191445 **Fax:** 228 9191499
Email: fuhl@wvgw.de **Web site:** http://www.bbr-online.de
Freq: 11 issues yearly; Free to qualifying individuals
Annual Sub.: EUR 129,00; **Circ:** 4,899
Editor: Stefan Fuhl
Profile: The bbr Fachmagazin für Brunnen- und Leitungsbau is the technical-scientific journal, in which all issues of water collection and treatment, the cross-media transmission line construction (drinking water, gas, district heating, buried data and high-voltage and highest-voltage transportation) are discussed. The focus is on areas of well drilling, geothermal drilling, foundation engineering, pipeline construction, sewer and cable lines constuction. Renowned authors present new technical techniques, procedures, systems and devices. Here the bbr proves that practicality and of course must not run counter to scientific accuracy. In this sense, bbr acts for over 60 years as a link between the sometimes highly specialized experts in science and research, development and planning, implementation and operation.
Language(s): German
ADVERTISING RATES:
Full Page Mono .... EUR 2496
Full Page Colour .... EUR 3620
Mechanical Data: Type Area: 255 x 172 mm, No. of Columns (Display): 3, Col Widths (Display): 54 mm
Copy instructions: *Copy Date:* 14 days prior to publication
Official Journal of: Organ d. Bundesfachabt. Leitungsbau im Hauptverb. d. Dt. Bauindustrie, Bundesfachgruppe Brunnenbau, Spezialtiefbau u. Geotechnik im Zentralverband Dt. Baugewerbe e.V., d. Bundesvereinigung d. Firmen im Gas- u. Wasserfach e.V., d. Rohrleitungsbauverb. e.V., d. Gütegemeinschaft Leitungstiefbau e.V. u. Österr. Vereinigung f. d. Gas- u. Wasserfach
BUSINESS: ARCHITECTURE & BUILDING: Building

BBV-NET 1620818G67B-16516
Editorial: Europaplatz 26, 46399 BOCHOLT
Tel: 2871 284140 **Fax:** 2871 284119
Email: redaktion@bbv-net.de **Web site:** http://www.bbv-net.de
Freq: Daily; **Cover Price:** Paid; **Circ:** 239,923 Unique Users
Editor: Rainer Kurlemann; **Advertising Manager:** Jürgen Angenent
Profile: Ezine: The Bocholter-Borkener Volksblatt online daily coverage of events in Bocholt, roadstead, Isselburg and Hamminkeln. Categories: News, Local, Sports, Local Sports, fotod, videos, events, ads and services. Facebook: http://www.facebook.com/bbvnet Twitter: http://twitter.com/#!/BBV_Bocholt This Outlet offers RSS (Really Simple Syndication).
Language(s): German
REGIONAL DAILY & SUNDAY NEWSPAPERS: Regional Daily Newspapers

BBZ BADISCHE BAUERN ZEITUNG 722210G21J-28
Editorial: Friedrichstr. 43, 79098 FREIBURG
Tel: 761 2713342 **Fax:** 761 2021887
Email: redaktion@blv-freiburg.de **Web site:** http://www.badische-bauern-zeitung.de
Freq: Weekly; **Annual Sub.:** EUR 101,40; **Circ:** 15,135
Editor: Richard Bruskowski; **Advertising Manager:** Karin Wirbals-Langner
Profile: Current news, agricultural politics and crops, are in addition to business management, animal husbandry and agricultural technology, the most commonly read sections. Market and price reports and classified advertisements are in the majority of respondents read regularly, even if no current intention to buy or sell.
Language(s): German
Readership: Aimed at members.
ADVERTISING RATES:
Full Page Mono .... EUR 3014
Full Page Colour .... EUR 4754
Mechanical Data: Type Area: 275 x 195 mm, No. of Columns (Display): 4, Col Widths (Display): 46 mm
Copy instructions: *Copy Date:* 6 days prior to publication
Supplement(s): wochenblatt Magazin
BUSINESS: AGRICULTURE & FARMING: Agriculture & Farming - Regional

BC ZEITSCHRIFT FÜR BILANZIERUNG, RECHNUNGSWESEN UND CONTROLLING 722866G1B-22
Editorial: Wilhelmstr. 9, 80801 MÜNCHEN
Tel: 89 38189530 **Fax:** 89 38189147
Email: redaktion.bc@beck.de **Web site:** http://www.bc-online.de
Freq: Monthly; **Annual Sub.:** EUR 129,90; **Circ:** 8,819
Editor: Ernst Maier-Siegert; **Advertising Manager:** Fritz Lebherz
Profile: The journal BC Zeitschrift für Bilanzierung, Rechnungswesen und Controlling informed currently and practically on all issues that are relevant for managers in finance, accounting and controlling. BC provides security in all matters relating to accounting and financial statements - for optimal response to current legislation, court decisions and administrative instructions. BC shows how the reporting is specifically designed and presented. BC provides new controlling concepts - to detect vulnerabilities and potential for success in business. BC are tips for effective financial management (eg to optimize the financial planning). BC provides orientation in the thicket of labor and business law regulations. The BC-range of topics also includes tax law, consulting practice and professional law. And very well established - the BC-certification program: The targeted training opportunities in print and online.
Language(s): German
Readership: Read by financial executives and accountants.
ADVERTISING RATES:
Full Page Mono .... EUR 2080
Full Page Colour .... EUR 2990
Mechanical Data: Type Area: 260 x 186 mm, No. of Columns (Display): 4, Col Widths (Display): 43 mm
Official Journal of: Organ d. Bundesverb. d. Bilanzbuchhalter u. Controller e.V.
BUSINESS: FINANCE & ECONOMICS: Accountancy

BD BAUMASCHINENDIENST 722213G4E-2560
Editorial: Walter-Schulz-Str. 1, 86825 BAD WÖRISHOFEN **Tel:** 8247 300743 **Fax:** 8247 300773
Email: harald.spaeth@krafthand.de **Web site:** http://www.bd-online.eu
Freq: Monthly; **Annual Sub.:** EUR 60,00; **Circ:** 15,907
Editor: Harald Späth; **Advertising Manager:** Romana Kennel
Profile: The bd baumaschinendienst is the magazine for the technology developers and managers in construction, civil engineering and road construction. Editorial Focus: Construction machinery, construction practices, machinery and equipment, utility vehicles, scaffolding and formwork, construction methods, business management.
Language(s): German
ADVERTISING RATES:
Full Page Mono .... EUR 3590
Full Page Colour .... EUR 5240
Mechanical Data: Type Area: 270 x 187 mm, No. of Columns (Display): 4, Col Widths (Display): 43 mm
Copy instructions: *Copy Date:* 15 days prior to publication
BUSINESS: ARCHITECTURE & BUILDING: Building

BDF AKTUELL 722217G46-2
Editorial: Silberborner Str. 1, 37586 DASSEL
Tel: 171 7612792 **Fax:** 5564 200869
Email: bdf.aktuell@t-online.de
Freq: Monthly; Free to qualifying individuals
Annual Sub.: EUR 31,50; **Circ:** 7,856
Editor: Armin Ristau
Profile: "BDF aktuell" informed with news and interviews, special reports on the activities of the association and on forest policy, forest economy, nature and environment.
Language(s): German
ADVERTISING RATES:
Full Page Mono .... EUR 1400
Full Page Colour .... EUR 2090
Mechanical Data: Type Area: 262 x 184 mm, No. of Columns (Display): 3, Col Widths (Display): 61 mm
Copy instructions: *Copy Date:* 20 days prior to publication
BUSINESS: TIMBER, WOOD & FORESTRY

BDI AKTUELL 722222G56A-1560
Editorial: Schöne Aussicht 5, 65193 WIESBADEN
Tel: 611 181330 **Fax:** 611 1813350
Email: info@bdi.de **Web site:** http://www.bdi.de
Freq: 11 issues yearly; **Circ:** 20,614
Editor: Hans-Friedrich Spies
Profile: BDI aktuell offers a unique form of a mixture of professional and health policy aspects as well as editorials on current medical topics. BDI aktuell is a modern, quick-read newspaper, which met all the requirements to a journal. Information and innovations in business, politics and law - all tailored to the specific information needs of internists. In addition, medical topics and a detailed service and event part.
Language(s): German
ADVERTISING RATES:
Full Page Mono .... EUR 2990
Full Page Colour .... EUR 4130
Mechanical Data: Type Area: 377 x 283 mm
Copy instructions: *Copy Date:* 28 days prior to publication
BUSINESS: HEALTH & MEDICAL

BDL 1654829G21A-4301
Editorial: Claire-Waldoff-Str. 7, 10117 BERLIN
Tel: 30 31904258 **Fax:** 30 31904206
Email: c.wandel-sucker@landjugend.de **Web site:** http://www.landjugend.de
Freq: Annual; **Circ:** 2,900
Editor: Christina Wandel-Sucker; **Advertising Manager:** Christina Wandel-Sucker
Profile: Calendar by Bund Deutscher Landjugend focusing on youth, education, agriculture, food.
Language(s): German
Mechanical Data: Type Area: 150 x 95 mm

BDL SPEZIAL 761428G21A-4209
Editorial: Claire-Waldoff-Str. 7, 10117 BERLIN
Tel: 30 31904258 **Fax:** 30 31904206
Email: c.wandel-sucker@landjugend.de **Web site:** http://www.landjugend.de
Freq: 3 issues yearly; **Circ:** 2,900
Editor: Christina Wandel-Sucker
Profile: Magazine for adolescents living in the country.
Language(s): German

BDM AKTUELL 1816165G21A-4372
Editorial: St. Georgen 15, 95448 BAYREUTH
Tel: 921 162717012 **Fax:** 921 162717020
Email: redaktion@bdm-aktuell.de **Web site:** http://www.bdm-verband.de
Freq: Monthly; Free to qualifying individuals
Annual Sub.: EUR 36,00; **Circ:** 38,500
Editor: Jutta Weiß
Profile: BDM aktuell is a national trade magazine for the dairy cattle herds in Germany. It has set itself the goal of compulsory reading for every dairy farmer to be, who is interested in current and independent information on the subject of milk and milk marketing. The magazine reaches without wastage the majority of active dairy farmers (through mail order, that is accurate!). With additional distribution at events and fairs achieved BDM aktuell the dairy farmers and also other agricultural policy and agricultural economic interested readers.
Language(s): German
ADVERTISING RATES:
Full Page Mono .... EUR 4060
Full Page Colour .... EUR 4460
Mechanical Data: Type Area: 272 x 176 mm, No. of Columns (Display): 4, Col Widths (Display): 41 mm

BDM AKTUELL 1816165G21A-4451
Editorial: St. Georgen 15, 95448 BAYREUTH
Tel: 921 162717012 **Fax:** 921 162717020
Email: redaktion@bdm-aktuell.de **Web site:** http://www.bdm-verband.de
Freq: Monthly; Free to qualifying individuals
Annual Sub.: EUR 36,00; **Circ:** 38,500
Editor: Jutta Weiß
Profile: BDM aktuell is a national trade magazine for the dairy cattle herds in Germany. It has set itself the goal of compulsory reading for every dairy farmer to be, who is interested in current and independent information on the subject of milk and milk marketing. The magazine reaches without wastage the majority of active dairy farmers (through mail order, that is accurate!). With additional distribution at events and fairs achieved BDM aktuell the dairy farmers and also other agricultural policy and agricultural economic interested readers.
Language(s): German
ADVERTISING RATES:
Full Page Mono .... EUR 4060
Full Page Colour .... EUR 4460
Mechanical Data: Type Area: 272 x 176 mm, No. of Columns (Display): 4, Col Widths (Display): 41 mm

BDVB AKTUELL 1605060G14A-9357
Editorial: Florastr. 29, 40217 DÜSSELDORF
Tel: 211 371022 **Fax:** 211 379468
Email: info@bdvb.de **Web site:** http://www.bdvb.de
Freq: Quarterly; **Cover Price:** EUR 7,50
Free to qualifying individuals ; **Circ:** 20,000
Editor: Cornelia Scott
Profile: bdvb aktuell is the member magazine of the Federal Association of German economics and business administration (bdvb). It reaches the decision makers in key positions and control centers in Germany and is published 4 times a year, always at the beginning of a calendar quarter.
Language(s): German
ADVERTISING RATES:
Full Page Mono .... EUR 1800
Full Page Colour .... EUR 2850
Mechanical Data: Type Area: 260 x 176 mm, No. of Columns (Display): 2, Col Widths (Display): 85 mm
Copy instructions: *Copy Date:* 33 days prior to publication

BDZ MAGAZIN 722233G1M-1
Editorial: Friedrichstr. 169, 10117 BERLIN
Tel: 30 40816600 **Fax:** 30 40816633
Email: post@bdz.eu **Web site:** http://www.bdz.dbb.de
Freq: 10 issues yearly; Free to qualifying individuals
Annual Sub.: EUR 28,12; **Circ:** 25,500
Editor: Klaus H. Leprich
Profile: Magazine for German tax inspectors. Each member of the BDZ free magazine. The ten times annual journal provides information on current professional and trade union issues.
Language(s): German
ADVERTISING RATES:
Full Page Mono .... EUR 2270
Full Page Colour .... EUR 3050
Mechanical Data: Type Area: 270 x 185 mm, No. of Columns (Display): 4, Col Widths (Display): 43 mm
BUSINESS: FINANCE & ECONOMICS: Taxation

BEAUTY FORUM 722239G15A-194
Editorial: Karl-Friedrich-Str. 14, 76133 KARLSRUHE
Tel: 721 165104 **Fax:** 721 165148
Email: yvonne.braun@health-and-beauty.com **Web site:** http://www.beauty-forum.com
Freq: Monthly; **Annual Sub.:** EUR 75,00; **Circ:** 23,040
Advertising Manager: Tobias Klumpp
Profile: Beauty Forum has been one of the leading beauty magazines in Germany. It is addressed to the decision makers in the industry and provides basic knowledge and current information from the fields of care and treatment apparatus, dermatology, color cosmetics, color, style and image consultancy, permanent make-up, Hand & Nail, foot care, wellness, nutrition and institution management and the Beauty Forum trade fairs. Facebook: http://www.facebook.com/beautyforum Twitter: http://www.twitter.com/BeautyForum.
Language(s): German
ADVERTISING RATES:
Full Page Mono .... EUR 3287
Full Page Colour .... EUR 4436
Mechanical Data: Type Area: 280 x 200 mm, No. of Columns (Display): 4, Col Widths (Display): 47 mm
Copy instructions: *Copy Date:* 25 days prior to publication
Official Journal of: Organ d. Beauty Forum München
Supplement(s): Beauty Forum Börse
BUSINESS: COSMETICS & HAIRDRESSING: Cosmetics

BEFUND KREBS 1683905G94F-1862
Editorial: Gezelinallee 37, 51375 LEVERKUSEN
Tel: 214 310570 **Fax:** 214 3105719
Email: info@gfmk.com **Web site:** http://www.gfmk.com
Freq: 5 issues yearly; **Cover Price:** Free; **Circ:** 29,384
Editor: Anke Tennemann; **Advertising Manager:** Kirsten Caspari
Profile: Magazine for cancer patients. Contains contributions from medical reports and patient experience issues. Psychology is also treated as Erhährung and health policy.
Language(s): German
ADVERTISING RATES:
Full Page Mono .... EUR 2540
Full Page Colour .... EUR 3810
Mechanical Data: Type Area: 240 x 178 mm, No. of Columns (Display): 3, Col Widths (Display): 48 mm
Copy instructions: *Copy Date:* 34 days prior to publication
CONSUMER: OTHER CLASSIFICATIONS: Disability

BEHINDERTENRECHT 722269G56L-2
Editorial: Jeilerstr. 6, 48147 MÜNSTER
Freq: 7 issues yearly; **Annual Sub.:** EUR 88,20; **Circ:** 2,150
Editor: Ulrich Adlhoch; **Advertising Manager:** Roland Schulz
Profile: Magazine about the laws relating to the physically disabled and handicapped.
Language(s): German
ADVERTISING RATES:
Full Page Mono .... EUR 892
Full Page Colour .... EUR 1822
Mechanical Data: Type Area: 260 x 180 mm, No. of Columns (Display): 2, Col Widths (Display): 88 mm
Copy instructions: *Copy Date:* 28 days prior to publication
BUSINESS: HEALTH & MEDICAL: Disability & Rehabilitation

BEHÖRDEN SPIEGEL 722271G32A-460
Editorial: Am Buschhof 8, 53227 BONN
Tel: 228 970970 **Fax:** 228 9709775
Email: redaktion@behoerdenspiegel.de **Web site:** http://www.behoerden-spiegel.de
Freq: Monthly; **Annual Sub.:** EUR 38,00; **Circ:** 98,960
Editor: R. Uwe Proll; **Advertising Manager:** Helga Woll
Profile: Newspaper with the latest information and reports from areas of the authorities of the municipality to the federal administration achieved the most important decision makers at local, state and federal levels, including elected representatives from all political decision-making areas. In the marketing part of the Behörden Spiegel current issues are discussed from the procurement law, simultaneously presented best practice examples and will be informed about new products and services. In addition, there is a monthly selected key issues related to the detailed topic list, which gives an overall view of the individual issues of January to December. Twitter: http://twitter.com/government2020.
Language(s): German
Readership: Aimed at the public service sector.
ADVERTISING RATES:
Full Page Mono .... EUR 7688
Full Page Colour .... EUR 10622
Mechanical Data: Type Area: 430 x 285 mm, No. of Columns (Display): 6, Col Widths (Display): 45 mm
Copy instructions: *Copy Date:* 7 days prior to publication
Supplement(s): Beschaffung special
BUSINESS: LOCAL GOVERNMENT, LEISURE & RECREATION: Local Government

BELLA 722323G74A-480
Editorial: Burchardstr. 11, 20095 HAMBURG
Tel: 40 30192555 **Fax:** 40 30195135
Email: bella@bauerredaktionen.de **Web site:** http://www.bauermedia.com
Freq: Weekly; **Annual Sub.:** EUR 65,00; **Circ:** 587,112
Editor: Sabine Ingwersen
Profile: bella offers everything that is good for body and soul, and reports each week on trends and news that make life more beautiful. bella is aimed at confident women who are living life and know exactly what they want. Bella knows what is best for body & soul: Slim and Fit programs, wellness, beauty and fashion are the basics in every issue. Whether wellness tips, styling, looks and the latest news from the beauty market - the bella-reader is well informed. A competent team of doctors and medical practitioners, psychologists and lawyers here are sound advice. Many reports offer plenty of reading material: sensitively told stories, supplemented by expert interviews and current information. Also, puzzles, short stories and travel reports provide variety and relaxation. The booklet is part of the food rounded: to seasonal food news as well as trendy recipe ideas stimulate the reader to enjoy the culinary side of life.
Language(s): German
ADVERTISING RATES:
Full Page Mono .... EUR 32989
Full Page Colour .... EUR 32989
Mechanical Data: Type Area: 258 x 206 mm, No. of Columns (Display): 4, Col Widths (Display): 49 mm
Copy instructions: *Copy Date:* 28 days prior to publication
CONSUMER: WOMEN'S INTEREST CONSUMER MAGAZINES: Women's Interest

BELLEVUE 1666551G1E-987
Editorial: Dorotheenstr. 64, 22301 HAMBURG
Tel: 40 6965950 **Fax:** 40 696595199
Email: leserbriefe@bellevue.de **Web site:** http://www.bellevue.de
Freq: 6 issues yearly; **Annual Sub.:** EUR 33,30; **Circ:** 22,281
Editor: Claus-Peter Haller; **Advertising Manager:** Sebastian Schurz
Profile: Bellevue – Europe's leading real-estate magazine Bellevue has showcased dream properties world wide each month since 1991. We present a wide selection of properties from around the world, within diverse price ranges – so our readers can find exactly what they're looking for. Bellevue offers a unique combination of high-quality editorial content and photographs, delivering indepth information and concrete advice on a variety of relevant subjects. What's more, we publish special supplements on specific themes – with articles researched and written locally by experts from our team. Our publications provide a highly attractive environment for advertising properties, with a strong focus on your target group.
Language(s): German
ADVERTISING RATES:
Full Page Mono .... EUR 3450
Full Page Colour .... EUR 3450
Mechanical Data: Type Area: 241 x 178 mm
Copy instructions: *Copy Date:* 35 days prior to publication
BUSINESS: FINANCE & ECONOMICS: Property

BELLEVUE 1620823G74K-1487
Editorial: Dorotheenstr. 64, 22301 HAMBURG
Tel: 40 696595350 **Fax:** 40 696595199
Email: leserbriefe@bellevue.de **Web site:** http://www.bellevue.de
Freq: Daily; **Cover Price:** Paid; **Circ:** 62,661 Unique Users
Editor: Thomas Kochhan
Profile: Ezine: Magazine on real estate.
Language(s): German
CONSUMER: WOMEN'S INTEREST CONSUMER MAGAZINES: Home Purchase

BENJAMIN 1640257G91D-9997
Editorial: Augustenstr. 124, 70197 STUTTGART
Tel: 711 6010021 **Fax:** 711 6010033
Email: redaktion@hallo-benjamin.de **Web site:** http://www.hallo-benjamin.de
Freq: Monthly; **Annual Sub.:** EUR 32,40; **Circ:** 7,427
Editor: Kathrin Kommerell
Profile: Benjamin offers every month children Christian support through the church year. Benjamin makes children laugh and brings children to learn, to reflect and to participate. Benjamin opens the door to the Bible and the Church. Benjamin makes the faith alive. Benjamin's Bible stories and knowledge pages, its suggestions for reflection and self-engaging and its many puzzles, games and crafts pages fell more and more children.
Language(s): German
ADVERTISING RATES:
Full Page Mono .... EUR 800
Full Page Colour .... EUR 800
Mechanical Data: Type Area: 280 x 210 mm
Copy instructions: *Copy Date:* 30 days prior to publication
CONSUMER: RECREATION & LEISURE: Children & Youth

BENJAMIN BLÜMCHEN 722337G91D-720
Editorial: Wallstr. 59, 10179 BERLIN **Tel:** 30 240080
Fax: 30 24008599
Email: s.saydo@ehapa.de **Web site:** http://www.benjaminbluemchen.de
Freq: Monthly; **Cover Price:** EUR 2,70; **Circ:** 65,456
Editor: Sanya Saydo
Profile: The stories of helpful Benjamin Blümchen are fun, informative and lovingly drawn. Benjamin's loud and world-famous "Torooo!" is a trademark of joyful and exciting adventure. The magazine also promote numerous Craft Tools and great sites to paint, play and learn the skill and creativity of children. For kids from 5-8 years!.
Language(s): German
ADVERTISING RATES:
Full Page Mono .... EUR 5400
Full Page Colour .... EUR 5400
Mechanical Data: Type Area: 280 x 210 mm, No. of Columns (Display): 4, Col Widths (Display): 52 mm
CONSUMER: RECREATION & LEISURE: Children & Youth

BENNI 722339G91D-740
Editorial: Lina-Ammon-Str. 30, 90471 NÜRNBERG
Tel: 911 6600172 **Fax:** 911 6600110
Email: kroemer@sailer-verlag.de **Web site:** http://www.sailer-verlag.de
Freq: Monthly; **Annual Sub.:** EUR 28,80; **Circ:** 41,930
Editor: Stefanie Krömer; **Advertising Manager:** Armin Baier
Profile: Benni - the interactive magazine for young explorers. Benni takes up topics and issues from the child's realm of experience, brings exciting reports from around the world and answered questions about nature and technology. Tricky puzzles, instructions for play and experimentation, a science poster and an eight-page paper model to Join an extra-strong paper to rain on. The concept of this magazine is also convincing experts: experienced teachers Benni recommended for children 6 to 10 years.
Language(s): German
ADVERTISING RATES:
Full Page Mono .... EUR 3250
Full Page Colour .... EUR 3250
Mechanical Data: Type Area: 252 x 188 mm
CONSUMER: RECREATION & LEISURE: Children & Youth

BEOBACHTER 722341G67B-2480
Editorial: Lautenthaler Str. 3, 38723 SEESEN
Tel: 5381 93650 **Fax:** 5381 936526
Email: webmaster@seesener-beobachter.de **Web site:** http://www.seesener-beobachter.de
Freq: 312 issues yearly; **Circ:** 5,364
Advertising Manager: Bernd Voß
Profile: Daily newspaper with regional news and a local sports section. Twitter: http://twitter.com/BeoOnline This Outlet offers RSS (Really Simple Syndication).
Language(s): German
ADVERTISING RATES:
SCC .... EUR 18,90
Mechanical Data: Type Area: 425 x 280 mm, No. of Columns (Display): 6, Col Widths (Display): 44 mm
Copy instructions: *Copy Date:* 1 day prior to publication
REGIONAL DAILY & SUNDAY NEWSPAPERS: Regional Daily Newspapers

BERATENDE INGENIEURE 1665770G19A-1095
Editorial: Budapester Str. 31, 10787 BERLIN
Tel: 30 26062230 **Fax:** 30 26062100
Email: bronowski@vbi.de **Web site:** http://www.vbi.de
Freq: 6 issues yearly; Free to qualifying individuals
Annual Sub.: EUR 120,00; **Circ:** 5,730
Editor: Ines Bronowski; **Advertising Manager:** Alke Schmeis
Profile: Beratende Ingenieure is the professional magazine of the independent planners and consultants in all fields of engineering around the building. The information and technical papers by engineers and journalists apply this innovative engineering services, solutions and working methods, eg through the use of modern information and communication technology, on duty of infrastructure, new construction and modernization of industrial, municipal and private buildings. The magazine informs planners and clients on the current building, new products and solutions from the industry for Structural Engineering, Technical equipment/building

services, lighting and electrical, water and waste management, surveying engineering and geotechnics. This regular industry-related laws, standards and guidelines, and recent court decisions are commented on. .
Language(s): German
ADVERTISING RATES:
Full Page Mono .... EUR 1468
Full Page Colour .... EUR 2241
Mechanical Data: Type Area: 257 x 185 mm, No. of Columns (Display): 3, Col Widths (Display): 56 mm
Copy instructions: *Copy Date:* 28 days prior to publication

BERCHTESGADENER ANZEIGER 722344G67B-2500
Editorial: Griesstätter Str. 1, 83471 BERCHTESGADEN **Tel:** 8652 958422
Fax: 8652 958429
Email: redaktion@berchtesgadener-anzeiger.de **Web site:** http://www.berchtesgadener-anzeiger.de
Freq: 312 issues yearly; **Circ:** 5,336
Editor: Iris Melcher; **Advertising Manager:** Josefine Pfnür
Profile: Daily newspaper with regional news and a local sports section.
Language(s): German
ADVERTISING RATES:
SCC .... EUR 13,00
Mechanical Data: Type Area: 420 x 280 mm, No. of Columns (Display): 6, Col Widths (Display): 45 mm
Copy instructions: *Copy Date:* 1 day prior to publication
Supplement(s): rtv
REGIONAL DAILY & SUNDAY NEWSPAPERS: Regional Daily Newspapers

BERGBAU 765190G58-1683
Editorial: Juliusstr. 9, 45128 ESSEN **Tel:** 201 232238
Fax: 201 234578
Email: bergbau@rdb-ev.de **Web site:** http://www.rdb-ev.de
Freq: Monthly; Free to qualifying individuals
Annual Sub.: EUR 72,00; **Circ:** 9,000
Editor: Konrad Hupfer; **Advertising Manager:** Herbert-K. Dwors
Profile: Journal of resource extraction, energy, environment for engineers, technicians and managers.
Language(s): German
ADVERTISING RATES:
Full Page Mono .... EUR 1520
Full Page Colour .... EUR 2500
Mechanical Data: Type Area: 270 x 186 mm
Copy instructions: *Copy Date:* 14 days prior to publication

BERGEDORFER ZEITUNG 722354G67B-2520
Editorial: Curslacker Neuer Deich 50, 21029 HAMBURG **Tel:** 40 725660 **Fax:** 40 72566219
Email: redaktion@bergedorfer-zeitung.de **Web site:** http://www.bergedorfer-zeitung.de
Freq: 312 issues yearly; **Circ:** 17,776
Editor: Wolfgang Rath; **Advertising Manager:** Ulf Kowitz
Profile: Daily newspaper with regional news and a local sports section. Facebook: http://www.facebook.com/bergedorferzeitung This Outlet offers RSS (Really Simple Syndication).
Language(s): German
ADVERTISING RATES:
SCC .... EUR 57,10
Mechanical Data: Type Area: 430 x 282 mm, No. of Columns (Display): 6, Col Widths (Display): 45 mm
Copy instructions: *Copy Date:* 1 day prior to publication
Supplement(s): doppio
REGIONAL DAILY & SUNDAY NEWSPAPERS: Regional Daily Newspapers

BERGISCHE LANDESZEITUNG 722371G67B-2540
Editorial: Stolkgasse 25, 50667 KÖLN
Tel: 221 1632558 **Fax:** 221 1632557
Email: print@kr-redaktion.de **Web site:** http://www.rundschau-online.de
Freq: 312 issues yearly; **Circ:** 233,008
Advertising Manager: Karsten Hundhausen
Profile: Daily newspaper with regional news and a local sports section. Facebook: http://www.facebook.com/pages/Kolnische-Rundschau/147616463739 This Outlet offers RSS (Really Simple Syndication).
Language(s): German
Mechanical Data: Type Area: 430 x 285 mm, No. of Columns (Display): 6, Col Widths (Display): 45 mm
Copy instructions: *Copy Date:* 2 days prior to publication
Supplement(s): prisma
REGIONAL DAILY & SUNDAY NEWSPAPERS: Regional Daily Newspapers

BERGISCHE MORGENPOST 722372G67B-2560
Editorial: Zülpicher Str. 10, 40549 DÜSSELDORF
Tel: 211 5050 **Fax:** 211 5047562
Email: redaktionssekretariat@rheinische-post.de
Web site: http://www.rp-online.de
Freq: 312 issues yearly; **Circ:** 13,432
Advertising Manager: Marc Arne Schümann
Profile: Daily newspaper with regional news and a local sports section. Facebook: http://www.facebook.com/rponline Twitter: http://www.rp-online.de/app/feed/twitter This Outlet offers RSS (Really Simple Syndication).
Language(s): German
ADVERTISING RATES:
SCC .... EUR 52,40
Mechanical Data: Type Area: 480 x 325 mm, No. of Columns (Display): 7, Col Widths (Display): 45 mm
Copy instructions: *Copy Date:* 2 days prior to publication
REGIONAL DAILY & SUNDAY NEWSPAPERS: Regional Daily Newspapers

BERGISCHE WIRTSCHAFT 722376G63-80
Editorial: Heinrich-Kamp-Platz 2, 42103 WUPPERTAL **Tel:** 202 2490110 **Fax:** 202 2490199
Email: c.novak@wuppertal.ihk.de **Web site:** http://www.wuppertal.ihk.de
Freq: Monthly; Free to qualifying individuals
Annual Sub.: EUR 26,26; **Circ:** 15,000
Editor: Claudia Novak; **Advertising Manager:** Katja Weinheimer
Profile: Journal of the Chamber of Trade and Industry for Wuppertal, Solingen and Remscheid.
Language(s): German
ADVERTISING RATES:
Full Page Mono .... EUR 1312
Full Page Colour .... EUR 2068
Mechanical Data: Type Area: 255 x 185 mm, No. of Columns (Display): 4, Col Widths (Display): 43 mm
Copy instructions: *Copy Date:* 20 days prior to publication
BUSINESS: REGIONAL BUSINESS

BERGISCHER ANZEIGER 722373G72-1864
Editorial: Konrad-Adenauer-Str. 2, 42853 REMSCHEID **Tel:** 2191 9090 **Fax:** 2191 909185
Email: redaktion@rga-online.de **Web site:** http://www.rga-online.de
Freq: Weekly; **Cover Price:** Free; **Circ:** 119,634
Editor: Horst-Michael Albrecht
Profile: Advertising journal (house-to-house) concentrating on local stories.
Language(s): German
ADVERTISING RATES:
Full Page Mono .... EUR 6889
Full Page Colour .... EUR 9288
Mechanical Data: Type Area: 430 x 282 mm, No. of Columns (Display): 6, Col Widths (Display): 45 mm
Copy instructions: *Copy Date:* 2 days prior to publication
LOCAL NEWSPAPERS

BERGISCHES HANDELSBLATT 722375G72-1868
Editorial: Hauptstr. 97, 51465 BERGISCH GLADBACH **Tel:** 2202 20080 **Fax:** 2202 200826
Email: redaktion@bergisches-handelsblatt.de **Web site:** http://www.rheinische-anzeigenblaetter.de
Freq: Weekly; **Cover Price:** Free; **Circ:** 94,770
Editor: Hans-Werner Klinkhammels; **Advertising Manager:** Jochen Asbeck
Profile: Advertising journal (house-to-house) concentrating on local stories.
Language(s): German
ADVERTISING RATES:
Full Page Mono .... EUR 3096
Full Page Colour .... EUR 4490
Mechanical Data: Type Area: 430 x 282 mm, No. of Columns (Display): 6, Col Widths (Display): 45 mm
Copy instructions: *Copy Date:* 2 days prior to publication
LOCAL NEWSPAPERS

BERGISCHES LAND GEHT AUS! 1893484G89A-12452
Editorial: Höherweg 287, 40231 DÜSSELDORF
Tel: 211 7357681 **Fax:** 211 7357680
Email: info@ueberblick.de **Web site:** http://www.ueberblick.de
Freq: Annual; **Cover Price:** EUR 3,80; **Circ:** 30,000
Editor: Konrad Schnabel
Profile: Gastronomy guide for Essen.
Language(s): German
ADVERTISING RATES:
Full Page Mono .... EUR 1790
Full Page Colour .... EUR 3133
Mechanical Data: Type Area: 260 x 190 mm, No. of Columns (Display): 4, Col Widths (Display): 44 mm
Copy instructions: *Copy Date:* 31 days prior to publication

BERGSTEIGER 722382G75L-240
Editorial: Infanteriestr. 11a, 80797 MÜNCHEN
Tel: 89 130699650 **Fax:** 89 130699690
Email: andreas.kubin@bruckmann.de **Web site:** http://www.bergsteiger.de
Freq: Monthly; **Annual Sub.:** EUR 59,40; **Circ:** 35,176
Editor: Andreas Kubin
Profile: Journal of climbers with reports and news about issues d. hiking, climbing walking, climbing, mountain biking, skiing and snow hiking. The mix of topics covering the full range of alpine sports. With high-quality images and text lines, the magazine raises aspirations and provides current information about single and multi-day tours with regional focuses, summarized in the removable Tour cards. In addition, the journal provides an extensive service section with market surveys and product testing expert in the equipment segment.
Language(s): German
ADVERTISING RATES:
Full Page Colour .... EUR 3650
Mechanical Data: Type Area: 235 x 181 mm, No. of Columns (Display): 4, Col Widths (Display): 45 mm
Copy instructions: *Copy Date:* 34 days prior to publication
CONSUMER: SPORT: Outdoor

BERICHTE 722394G4D-9
Editorial: Zimmerstr. 13, 10969 BERLIN
Tel: 30 39001209 **Fax:** 30 39001130
Email: wenke-thiem@difu.de **Web site:** http://www.difu.de/publikationen/difu-berichte-heftarchiv.html
Freq: Quarterly; **Cover Price:** Free; **Circ:** 12,000
Editor: Sybille Wenke-Thiem
Profile: The journal "Berichte" informed about news from the Difu project work, through publications and events as well as views of the German Institute of Urban Affairs.
Language(s): German

BERICHTE 722394G4D-116
Editorial: Zimmerstr. 13, 10969 BERLIN
Tel: 30 39001209 **Fax:** 30 39001130
Email: wenke-thiem@difu.de **Web site:** http://www.difu.de/publikationen/difu-bericte-heftarchiv.html
Freq: Quarterly; **Cover Price:** Free; **Circ:** 12,000
Editor: Sybille Wenke-Thiem
Profile: The journal "Berichte" informed about news from the Difu project work, through publications and events as well as views of the German Institute of Urban Affairs.
Language(s): German

BERICHTE ÜBER LANDWIRTSCHAFT 722403G21A-760
Editorial: Wilhelmstr. 54, 10117 BERLIN
Tel: 1888 5293229
Email: 511@bmelv.bund.de **Web site:** http://www.verbraucherministerium.de
Freq: 3 issues yearly; **Annual Sub.:** EUR 225,00; **Circ:** 1,200
Profile: Magazine for farmers.
Language(s): German

BERLIN PROGRAMM 722518G89C-220
Editorial: Karl-Hofer-Str. 11, 14163 BERLIN
Tel: 30 8021071 **Fax:** 30 8029988
Email: info@berlin-programm.de **Web site:** http://www.berlin-programm.de
Freq: Monthly; **Cover Price:** EUR 2,00; **Circ:** 25,154
Editor: Rainer Rimbach; **Advertising Manager:** Rainer Rimbach
Profile: Magazine containing listings of theatre, opera, museums, sports events and restaurants in Berlin.
Language(s): German
Readership: Aimed at tourists, visitors and local residents.
ADVERTISING RATES:
Full Page Mono .... EUR 1500
Full Page Colour .... EUR 2625
Mechanical Data: Type Area: 185 x 172 mm, No. of Columns (Display): 3, Col Widths (Display): 54 mm
Copy instructions: *Copy Date:* 23 days prior to publication
CONSUMER: HOLIDAYS & TRAVEL: Entertainment Guides

BERLIN STADTPLAN 742789G89A-8180
Editorial: Am Karlsbad 11, 10785 BERLIN
Tel: 30 2647480 **Fax:** 30 264748968
Email: susanna.weber@btm.de **Web site:** http://www.visitberlin.de
Freq: Annual; **Cover Price:** EUR 1,00; **Circ:** 220,000
Profile: City map of Berlin, including the tourist attractions, useful addresses and telephone numbers.
Language(s): German
Mechanical Data: Type Area: 210 x 100 mm
Copy instructions: *Copy Date:* 70 days prior to publication

BERLIN TO GO 724396G89A-480
Editorial: Am Karlsbad 11, 10785 BERLIN
Tel: 30 2647480 **Fax:** 30 264748968
Email: kulturinfo@btm.de **Web site:** http://www.visitberlin.de
Freq: Weekly; **Cover Price:** EUR 1,00; **Circ:** 5,000
Profile: Publication featuring a programme of events for Berlin.
Language(s): English; German
ADVERTISING RATES:
Full Page Mono .... EUR 950
Full Page Colour .... EUR 1380
Mechanical Data: Type Area: 216 x 156 mm
Copy instructions: *Copy Date:* 38 days prior to publication

BERLIN VIS-À-VIS EXTRATOUR 1897706G89A-12472
Editorial: Flottenstr. 4a, 13407 BERLIN
Tel: 30 41479120 **Fax:** 30 4145083
Email: redaktion@berlin-visavis.de **Web site:** http://www.berlin-visavis.de
Freq: Half-yearly; **Cover Price:** Free; **Circ:** 200,000
Editor: Ina Hegenberger; **Advertising Manager:** Jörg Schenk
Profile: City-Guide Berlin with district plan for City East, City West and Potsdamer Platz. Facebook: http://www.facebook.com/pages/Berlin-vis-a-vis-Das-Magazin-fur-StadtEntwicklung/144685348916732.
Language(s): English; German
ADVERTISING RATES:
Full Page Colour .... EUR 4500
Mechanical Data: Type Area: 135 x 91 mm

BERLIN-BRANDENBURGISCHES HANDWERK 722417G63-100
Editorial: Blücherstr. 68, 10961 BERLIN
Tel: 30 25903230 **Fax:** 30 25903235
Email: sarkandy@hwk-berlin.de **Web site:** http://www.hwk-berlin.de
Freq: 10 issues yearly; Free to qualifying individuals
Annual Sub.: EUR 47,00; **Circ:** 30,600
Editor: Elke Sarkandy
Profile: Communications from the Chamber of Berlin. The Chamber of Berlin informed once a month in her magazine Berlin-Brandenburgisches Handwerk from all member companies with headquarters in Berlin on news Political and economic changes in legislation, official announcements, updates from the finance, tax law and European law, but also on positions, as well as claims and demands against the policy. The journalistic medium "Berlin-Brandenburgisches Handwerk" position applies to all policy issues of registration and sees itself as an interface between member companies and politicians. Board and management also uses the journal to provide in the form of commentaries, editorials and reports to the demands of craft expression.
Language(s): German
ADVERTISING RATES:
Full Page Mono .... EUR 2950
Full Page Colour .... EUR 4580
Mechanical Data: Type Area: 257 x 170 mm, No. of Columns (Display): 3, Col Widths (Display): 54 mm
Copy instructions: *Copy Date:* 10 days prior to publication
BUSINESS: REGIONAL BUSINESS

BERLIN.DE 1661003G80-14300
Editorial: Karl-Liebknecht-Str. 29, 10178 BERLIN
Tel: 1805 807737 **Fax:** 1805 002897
Email: info@berlin.de **Web site:** http://www.berlin.de
Freq: Daily; **Cover Price:** Paid; **Circ:** 5,984,580 Unique Users
Advertising Manager: Sven Heller
Profile: Official website of the capital Berlin, the first point of contact for Berlin and Berlin-interested with information on e-Government, Tourism, Hotels, Entertainment & tickets and with extensive consumer service.
Language(s): German
CONSUMER: RURAL & REGIONAL INTEREST

BERLINER ABENDBLATT 722426G72-17407
Editorial: Karl-Liebknecht-Str. 29, 10178 BERLIN
Tel: 30 2938888 **Fax:** 30 29388773
Email: redaktion@abendblatt-berlin.de **Web site:** http://www.abendblatt-berlin.de
Freq: Weekly; **Cover Price:** Free; **Circ:** 101,850
Editor: Christine Meier; **Advertising Manager:** Johann Brunken
Profile: Advertising journal (house-to-house) concentrating on local stories.
Language(s): German
ADVERTISING RATES:
Full Page Mono .... EUR 7142
Full Page Colour .... EUR 9999
Mechanical Data: Type Area: 479 x 327 mm, No. of Columns (Display): 7, Col Widths (Display): 45 mm
Copy instructions: *Copy Date:* 4 days prior to publication
LOCAL NEWSPAPERS

BERLINER ABENDBLATT 722435G72-17847
Editorial: Karl-Liebknecht-Str. 29, 10178 BERLIN
Tel: 30 2938888 **Fax:** 30 29388773
Email: redaktion@abendblatt-berlin.de **Web site:** http://www.abendblatt-berlin.de
Freq: Weekly; **Cover Price:** Free; **Circ:** 39,160
Editor: Christine Meier; **Advertising Manager:** Johann Brunken
Profile: Advertising journal (house-to-house) concentrating on local stories.
Language(s): German
ADVERTISING RATES:
Full Page Mono .... EUR 3353
Full Page Colour .... EUR 4695
Mechanical Data: Type Area: 479 x 327 mm, No. of Columns (Display): 7, Col Widths (Display): 45 mm
Copy instructions: *Copy Date:* 4 days prior to publication
LOCAL NEWSPAPERS

BERLINER ANWALTSBLATT
722443G44-3090
Editorial: Littenstr. 11, 10179 BERLIN
Tel: 30 2513846 **Fax:** 30 2513263
Email: redaktion@berliner-anwaltsblatt.de **Web site:** http://www.berliner.anwaltsverein.de
Freq: Monthly; Free to qualifying individuals
Annual Sub.: EUR 75,00; **Circ:** 16,000
Editor: Eckart Yersin; **Advertising Manager:** Peter Gesellius
Profile: Magazine about the law and the legal system in Berlin.
Language(s): German
ADVERTISING RATES:
Full Page Mono .... EUR 1660
Full Page Colour .... EUR 2490
Mechanical Data: Type Area: 260 x 185 mm, No. of Columns (Display): 3, Col Widths (Display): 58 mm
Copy instructions: *Copy Date:* 20 days prior to publication
BUSINESS: LEGAL

BERLINER ÄRZTE
758067G56A-11096
Editorial: Friedrichstr. 16, 10969 BERLIN
Tel: 30 408064100 **Fax:** 30 408064199
Email: s.rudat@aekb.de **Web site:** http://www.aekb.de
Freq: Monthly; Free to qualifying individuals
Annual Sub.: EUR 78,00; **Circ:** 27,000
Editor: Sascha Rudat; **Advertising Manager:** Melanie Bölsdorff
Profile: Official Journal of the Medical Association of publications medical experts and professional bodies. The journal appears 12 times a year, on 1. of the month. The content of the magazine devoted addition to the current coverage of professional, health policy and the work of the Medical Association, in each month with a particular specialism.
Language(s): German
ADVERTISING RATES:
Full Page Mono .... EUR 1660
Full Page Colour .... EUR 2555
Mechanical Data: Type Area: 252 x 185 mm, No. of Columns (Display): 3, Col Widths (Display): 58 mm
Copy instructions: *Copy Date:* 20 days prior to publication

BERLINER ÄRZTEBLATT
722441G56A-4620
Editorial: Flemingstr. 12, 10557 BERLIN
Tel: 30 8336066 **Fax:** 30 84309677
Email: redaktion@berliner-aerzteverlag.de **Web site:** http://www.berliner-aerzteblatt.de
Freq: Monthly; **Annual Sub.:** EUR 60,00; **Circ:** 18,460
Editor: Christian Sachse; **Advertising Manager:** Torsten Sievers
Profile: The Berliner Ärzteblatt is an independent, chamber free and KV-free magazine for education, health and professional politics. The title is aimed primarily at the group of general practitioners, practitioners and internists, as well as the hospital doctors in Berlin and Brandenburg. Its special significance as "Doctors Journal of capital" is accordingly, sent the Berliner Ärzteblatt all members of the Bundestag and health politically active organizations. In the area of Berlin and Brandenburg, largest and free training calendar (mostly with CME points) in the Berliner Ärzteblatt guarantees a high reader loyalty. The section "Medicine compact" includes 20 to 25 the current news on medicine and research with more senior Internet links. Because of its broad spectrum, the training calendar, the diversity of issues and the independent status, combined with a high acceptance by the reader, the Berliner Ärzteblatt recommended as a powerful promotional partner for an effective response to their target audience.
Language(s): German
Readership: Aimed at people interested in healthcare.
ADVERTISING RATES:
Full Page Mono .... EUR 1650
Full Page Colour .... EUR 2850
Mechanical Data: Type Area: 268 x 180 mm
BUSINESS: HEALTH & MEDICAL

BERLINER BEHÖRDEN SPIEGEL
722445G32A-480
Editorial: Kaskelstr. 41, 10317 BERLIN
Tel: 30 55741220 **Fax:** 30 55741219
Email: redaktion@behoerdenspiegel.de **Web site:** http://www.behoerdenspiegel.de
Freq: Monthly; **Annual Sub.:** EUR 38,00; **Circ:** 35,920
Editor: R. Uwe Proll; **Advertising Manager:** Helga Woll
Profile: Newspaper with current information and reports from areas of the authorities in Berlin and Brandenburg, the local authority to the state government achieved the most important decision makers at local, state and federal levels, including elected representatives from all political decision-making areas. In the marketing part of the authorities mirror current issues are discussed from the procurement law, simultaneously presented best practice examples and will be informed about new products and services. In addition, there is a monthly selected key issues related to the detailed topic list, which gives an overall view of the individual issues of January to December.
Language(s): German
Readership: Read by government officials in Berlin and Brandenburg and those in the field of public procurement.
ADVERTISING RATES:
Full Page Mono .... EUR 7688
Full Page Colour .... EUR 10622
Mechanical Data: Type Area: 430 x 285 mm, No. of Columns (Display): 6, Col Widths (Display): 45 mm
Copy instructions: *Copy Date:* 30 days prior to publication
Supplement(s): Beschaffung special
BUSINESS: LOCAL GOVERNMENT, LEISURE & RECREATION: Local Government

BERLINER DEBATTE INITIAL
722450G1R-360
Editorial: Postfach 580254, 10412 BERLIN
Email: redaktion@berlinerdebatte.de **Web site:** http://www.berlinerdebatte.de
Freq: Quarterly; **Annual Sub.:** EUR 37,00
Editor: Jan Wielgohs
Profile: Magazine covering political and social debate.
Language(s): German
BUSINESS: FINANCE & ECONOMICS: Financial Related

BERLINER GARTENFREUND
722453G26C-360
Editorial: Bismarckstr. 108, 10625 BERLIN
Tel: 30 318690115 **Fax:** 30 31501066
Email: hauptmann@waechter.de **Web site:** http://www.gartenfreund.de
Freq: Monthly; Free to qualifying individuals
Annual Sub.: EUR 15,00; **Circ:** 71,597
Editor: Dieter Hauptmann; **Advertising Manager:** Gerd Schneider
Profile: Magazine for gardeners in Berlin. The Gartenfreund offers its readers about detailed topics posts around home and garden, with the national coat topics: Fruit, vegetables, ornamental gardens, soil care, fertilizers, pesticides, garden tools, garden art, garden design and maintenance. The extensive Berliner pages (idR64 inside pages) to bring the wide variety of topics of the hobby garden. Reports from Berlin allotment gardening, activities of municipalities and associations, garden guide, garden consultancy, Calendar and Events, Unterhaltsames.Der gardener consists of a cross-magazines-coat, and the nine different regional parts of the issuing state associations of the allotments, in which the regional and local Activities of clubs and associations are reported. Anhören Umschrift.
Language(s): German
Readership: Read by members of the Berlin Gardeners' Society and government officials.
ADVERTISING RATES:
Full Page Mono .... EUR 1899
Full Page Colour .... EUR 3036
Mechanical Data: Type Area: 260 x 181 mm, No. of Columns (Display): 4, Col Widths (Display): 43 mm
Copy instructions: *Copy Date:* 30 days prior to publication
BUSINESS: GARDEN TRADE

BERLINER HEILPRAKTIKER NACHRICHTEN
1830100G56A-11538
Editorial: Mommsenstr. 45, 10629 BERLIN
Tel: 30 3233050 **Fax:** 30 3249761
Email: homoeovet@t-online.de **Web site:** http://www.heilpraktiker-berlin.org
Freq: Annual; **Circ:** 2,500
Editor: Arne Krüger; **Advertising Manager:** Michael Aulbach
Profile: Magazine on naturopathy in the regions of Berlin and Brandenburg.
Language(s): German
ADVERTISING RATES:
Full Page Mono .... EUR 500
Full Page Colour .... EUR 980
Mechanical Data: No. of Columns (Display): 3

BERLINER KURIER
722456G67B-2580
Editorial: Karl-Liebknecht-Str. 29, 10178 BERLIN
Tel: 30 23275975 **Fax:** 30 23275254
Web site: http://www.berlinonline.de
Freq: 312 issues yearly; **Circ:** 174,579
Editor: Hans-Peter Buschheuer; **News Editor:** Katja Reim; **Advertising Manager:** Mathias Forkel
Profile: The "Berliner Kurier" was first published on 2 December 1990 on the pressure, "BZ am Abend. This was made clear that arose from a popular and widely read old sheet, a new newspaper for a new Berlin. The first issue of "BZ am Abend" was on 15 July 1949 in the Berlin Verlag GmbH, published initial print run: 200,000 copies, price 10 Pfennig in Berlin, 15 Pfennig away. With current affairs material, a colorful feature pages, detailed sports events, recreational counselors and a vibrant local section it became the darling of the East Berlin. In 1953 the Berlin publishing house and it was assumed that the "BZ am Abend" the Central Committee of the Socialist Unity Party of Germany. After the fall of the Berlin Wall in 1990 took over Gruner and Jahr with the publisher Robert Maxwell the Berlin publisher. Maxwell's share was 1992 at Gruner & Jahr. Gruner & Jahr, the forced conversion of the BZ am Abend "in the" Berliner Kurier ", signaling a determination to sign the renewal of Berlin set. A new newspaper to be created that builds a bridge for the integration of the city. You should inform dedicated to the life and the concerns of people who offer service and culture, sport and urban development. First came the "Berliner Kurier" as "Berliner Kurier am Abend" out and it was followed by the "Berliner Kurier am Morgen" and the Sonntagspost". For these three newspapers on 3 August 1992, today's "Berliner Kurier" emerged with its Sunday edition. In order to survive in competition with other Berlin newspapers can buy, had much to invest. A new editorial concept was developed, a modern editorial system was introduced, the jobs have been re-equipped and developed a new printing plant. On 20 February 1996 appeared the "Berliner Kurier" in its new format today, with new content. The Berliner Kurier is a critical but fair reporting from Berlin, Brandenburg and the world. His readers will appreciate the timeliness and reliability of the reports and the clear, clear presentation.
Language(s): German
ADVERTISING RATES:
SCC .... EUR 145,00
Mechanical Data: Type Area: 327 x 233 mm, No. of Columns (Display): 5, Col Widths (Display): 45 mm
Copy instructions: *Copy Date:* 1 day prior to publication
Supplement(s): rtv
REGIONAL DAILY & SUNDAY NEWSPAPERS: Regional Daily Newspapers

BERLINER KURIER AM SONNTAG
722457G67B-2600
Editorial: Karl-Liebknecht-Str. 29, 10178 BERLIN
Tel: 30 23275975 **Fax:** 30 23275254
Web site: http://www.berlinonline.de
Freq: Weekly; **Annual Sub.:** EUR 2,90; **Circ:** 174,579
Editor: Hans-Peter Buschheuer; **News Editor:** Katja Reim; **Advertising Manager:** Mathias Forkel
Profile: The "Berliner Kurier" was first published on 2 December 1990 on the pressure, "BZ am Abend. This was made clear that arose from a popular and widely read old sheet, a new newspaper for a new Berlin. The first issue of "BZ am Abend" was on 15 July 1949 in the Berlin Verlag GmbH, published initial print run: 200,000 copies, price 10 Pfennig in Berlin, 15 Pfennig away. With current affairs material, a colorful feature pages, detailed sports events, recreational counselors and a vibrant local section it became the darling of the East Berlin. In 1953 the Berlin publishing house and it was assumed that the "BZ am Abend" the Central Committee of the Socialist Unity Party of Germany. After the fall of the Berlin Wall in 1990 took over Gruner and Jahr with the publisher Robert Maxwell the Berlin publisher. Maxwell's share was 1992 at Gruner & Jahr. Gruner & Jahr, the forced conversion of the BZ am Abend "in the" Berliner Kurier ", signaling a determination to sign the renewal of Berlin set. A new newspaper to be created that builds a bridge for the integration of the city. You should inform dedicated to the life and the concerns of people who offer service and culture, sport and urban development. First came the "Berliner Kurier" as "Berliner Kurier am Abend" out and it was followed by the "Berliner Kurier am Morgen" and the Sonntagspost". For these three newspapers on 3 August 1992, today's "Berliner Kurier" emerged with its Sunday edition. In order to survive in competition with other Berlin newspapers can buy, had much to invest. A new editorial concept was developed, a modern editorial system was introduced, the jobs have been re-equipped and developed a new printing plant. On 20 February 1996 appeared the "Berliner Kurier" in its new format today, with new content. The Berliner Kurier is a critical but fair reporting from Berlin, Brandenburg and the world. His readers will appreciate the timeliness and reliability of the reports and the clear, clear presentation.
Language(s): German
ADVERTISING RATES:
SCC .... EUR 166,00
Mechanical Data: Type Area: 327 x 233 mm, No. of Columns (Display): 5, Col Widths (Display): 45 mm
Copy instructions: *Copy Date:* 1 day prior to publication
REGIONAL DAILY & SUNDAY NEWSPAPERS: Regional Daily Newspapers

BERLINER MERKUR
722464G63-1759
Editorial: Siegfriedstr. 204, 10365 BERLIN
Tel: 30 4725393 **Fax:** 30 4732251
Email: berliner-merkur@t-online.de **Web site:** http://www.berliner-merkur.de
Freq: 10 issues yearly; **Annual Sub.:** EUR 20,00; **Circ:** 29,950
Editor: Uwe Riemer; **Advertising Manager:** Liane Komoll
Profile: The Berliner Merkur is a regional, on the middle class-oriented business magazine, both the trade and services and trade and industry responsive. The distribution is one of the most dynamic and interesting regions of the new federal states - Berlin and Brandenburg. Published in February 1990 as the first private business magazine of the former East Germany, it has since informed reader-friendly, especially entrepreneurs and professionals, but also business-oriented decision-makers from politics and administration on the economic development in the capital Berlin and Brandenburg. In addition, technical articles appear regularly (including legal and tax, management, marketing).
Language(s): German
ADVERTISING RATES:
Full Page Mono .... EUR 2000
Full Page Colour .... EUR 3500
Mechanical Data: Type Area: 257 x 185 mm, No. of Columns (Display): 4, Col Widths (Display): 43 mm
BUSINESS: REGIONAL BUSINESS

BERLINER MORGENPOST
722465G67B-2620
Editorial: Axel-Springer-Str. 65, 10969 BERLIN
Tel: 30 259173636 **Fax:** 30 259173049
Email: redaktion@morgenpost.de **Web site:** http://www.morgenpost.de
Freq: 364 issues yearly; **Circ:** 163,533
Editor: Carsten Erdmann; **News Editor:** Alexander Uhl; **Advertising Manager:** Jan Schiller
Profile: The Berliner Morgenpost is created by the biggest local newsroom in Berlin and a network of 400 journalists and correspondents around the world. With high editorial quality the daily newspaper proves its great passion for Berlin, the proximity to the reader as well as its own and self-confident deal with the important and topical issues. In its national expertise the Berliner Morgenpost shows in the categories of politics and business, and by the knowledge page. In Berlin's largest regional section it includes not only all the important messages from the city with a strong culture and a large part of daily service to culture and leisure. The sports department of the newspaper provides a lot of recent information and detailed backgrounds. One of the great strengths of the Berliner Morgenpost is heading skills. The Berliner Morgenpost is among the Berlin broadsheets market leader in the job, real estate and travel market and has a strong car market. Facebook: http://www.facebook.com/morgenpost Twitter: http://twitter.com/bmonline This Outlet offers RSS (Really Simple Syndication).
Language(s): German
ADVERTISING RATES:
SCC .... EUR 169,50
Mechanical Data: Type Area: 528 x 374 mm, No. of Columns (Display): 8, Col Widths (Display): 45 mm
Copy instructions: *Copy Date:* 1 day prior to publication
Supplement(s): Berliner Bühnen; Berlin Live; doppio; Gesund; KarriereWelt; prisma
REGIONAL DAILY & SUNDAY NEWSPAPERS: Regional Daily Newspapers

BERLINER UND MÜNCHENER TIERÄRZTLICHE WOCHENSCHRIFT
722480G64H-60
Editorial: Postfach 040225, 10061 BERLIN
Tel: 30 80585412 **Fax:** 30 80585412
Email: bmtw-redaktion@schluetersche.de **Web site:** http://www.bmtw.de
Freq: 6 issues yearly; **Annual Sub.:** EUR 299,00; **Circ:** 300
Editor: Elke Vieler
Profile: Journal focusing on veterinary medicine.
Language(s): English; German
BUSINESS: OTHER CLASSIFICATIONS: Veterinary

BERLINER VERKEHRSBLÄTTER
722481G49A-2325
Editorial: Friedrichshaller Str. 31, 14199 BERLIN
Tel: 30 8223245 **Fax:** 30 3424855
Email: post@verkehrsblaetter.de **Web site:** http://www.verkehrsblaetter.de
Freq: Monthly; **Annual Sub.:** EUR 23,40; **Circ:** 3,000
Editor: Wolfgang Kramer
Profile: The Berliner Verkehrsblätter regularly report on the traffic situation in and around Berlin. This magazine is made of traffic friends in their spare time for on all current and even traffic on Berlin's historic interested readers. The report includes current and historical topics: Line Chronicle, Fleet, Industrial Relations, museum vehicles, technology, reviews and news flashes from the areas of train, subway, train, tram, bus and passenger shipping. Numerous photographs, title page is always colored, round out each issue.
Language(s): German
Mechanical Data: Type Area: 250 x 180 mm, No. of Columns (Display): 2, Col Widths (Display): 86 mm
Copy instructions: *Copy Date:* 14 days prior to publication

BERLINER WIRTSCHAFT
722483G63-120
Editorial: Fasanenstr. 85, 10623 BERLIN
Tel: 30 31510308 **Fax:** 30 31510344
Email: bw-redaktion@berlin.ihk.de **Web site:** http://www.berlin-ihk24.de
Freq: 11 issues yearly; Free to qualifying individuals
Annual Sub.: EUR 29,70; **Circ:** 49,000
Editor: Bernhard Schodrowski; **Advertising Manager:** Ulrike Beckers
Profile: Regional economic magazine from the Chamber of Trade and Industry of Berlin.
Language(s): German
ADVERTISING RATES:
Full Page Mono .... EUR 3675
Full Page Colour .... EUR 6200
Mechanical Data: Type Area: 250 x 188 mm, No. of Columns (Display): 3, Col Widths (Display): 54 mm
Supplement(s): Business in Berlin und Brandenburg
BUSINESS: REGIONAL BUSINESS

BERLINER ZEITUNG
722507G67B-2640
Editorial: Karl-Liebknecht-Str. 29, 10178 BERLIN
Tel: 30 23279 **Fax:** 30 23275533
Email: info@berliner-zeitung.de **Web site:** http://www.berliner-zeitung.de
Freq: 312 issues yearly; **Circ:** 185,825
Editor: Uwe Vorkötter; **News Editor:** Peter Riesbeck; **Advertising Manager:** Mathias Forkel
Profile: With the Berliner Zeitung to reach 427,000 readers in Berlin / Brandenburg. Meanwhile, a third of the readers comes from the western districts of Berlin. The Berliner Zeitung is the largest Abozeitung of Berlin. Facebook: http://www.facebook.com/pages/berliner-zeitungde/137267732953826 Twitter: http://twitter.com/BLZonline This Outlet offers RSS (Really Simple Syndication).
Language(s): German

ADVERTISING RATES:
SCC .... EUR 267,00
Mechanical Data: Type Area: 485 x 327 mm, No. of Columns (Display): 7
Supplement(s): doppio; rtv
REGIONAL DAILY & SUNDAY NEWSPAPERS: Regional Daily Newspapers

BERLINER ZUGPFERDE
1792700G65B-3_100
Editorial: Kantstr. 151, 10623 BERLIN
Tel: 30 2062673 **Fax:** 30 20626750
Email: antje.naumann@berliner-zugpferde.de **Web site:** http://www.berliner-zugpferde.de
Freq: Half-yearly; **Cover Price:** EUR 1,00; **Circ:** 450,000
Editor: Antje Naumann
Profile: The magazine Berliner Zugpferde shows the capital Berlin and their economic and cultural driving forces - a journal that communicates these facets of the capital in Germany. Renowned authors describe before the capital set, exciting, lovable, creative, dynamic and unknown sites and talk to people who have opted for Berlin. At the same time, the magazine shows the economic strengths of the city as an attractive location for investments between high-tech, science, entertainment, tourism and urban structures of a metropolis that is seen worldwide as a "first place " of the future.
Language(s): German
ADVERTISING RATES:
Full Page Mono .... EUR 10790
Full Page Colour .... EUR 10790
Mechanical Data: Type Area: 238 x 186 mm
Supplement to: Frankfurter Allgemeine Sonntagszeitung, Handelsblatt, Der Tagesspiegel, Die Zeit
NATIONAL DAILY & SUNDAY NEWSPAPERS: GB-Unabhängigkeits-MdEP

BERSENBRÜCKER KREISBLATT
722539G67B-2660
Editorial: Breiter Gang 10, 49074 OSNABRÜCK
Tel: 541 3100 **Fax:** 541 3100 485
Email: redaktion@noz.de **Web site:** http://www.noz.de
Freq: 312 issues yearly; **Circ:** 13,638
Profile: Daily newspaper with regional news and a local sports section. Facebook: http://www.facebook.com/pages/nozde/106261086094051 Twitter: http://twitter.com/noz_de This Outlet offers RSS (Really Simple Syndication).
Language(s): German
ADVERTISING RATES:
SCC .... EUR 44,60
Mechanical Data: Type Area: 487 x 318 mm, No. of Columns (Display): 7, Col Widths (Display): 43 mm
Copy instructions: *Copy Date:* 2 days prior to publication
Supplement(s): Berufswahl; Immo-Welt; Kfz-Welt; Natürlich Quakenbrück; TheaterZeitung; Toaster; Treffpunkt Bramsche
REGIONAL DAILY & SUNDAY NEWSPAPERS: Regional Daily Newspapers

BERUFS KRAFTFAHRER ZEITUNG
722555G49A-120
Editorial: Klinkumer Str. 40, 41844 WEGBERG
Tel: 2434 800827 **Fax:** 2434 800810
Email: info@hendrisch.de **Web site:** http://www.hendrisch.de
Freq: 10 issues yearly; Free to qualifying individuals
Annual Sub.: EUR 18,00; **Circ:** 23,578
Editor: Horst Hendrisch; **Advertising Manager:** Claire Hendrisch
Profile: Official journal of the Society of Professional Motorists.
Language(s): German
Readership: Aimed at professionals within the motor trade.
ADVERTISING RATES:
Full Page Mono .... EUR 1840
Full Page Colour .... EUR 2935
Mechanical Data: Type Area: 250 x 180 mm, No. of Columns (Display): 3, Col Widths (Display): 56 mm
Copy instructions: *Copy Date:* 20 days prior to publication
BUSINESS: TRANSPORT

DIE BERUFSBILDENDE SCHULE
722549G62H-120
Editorial: Lothstr. 17, 80335 MÜNCHEN
Tel: 89 28924277 **Fax:** 89 28924313
Email: schelten@tum.de **Web site:** http://www.blbs.de
Freq: 10 issues yearly; Free to qualifying individuals
Annual Sub.: EUR 42,72; **Circ:** 19,342
Editor: Andreas Schelten; **Advertising Manager:** Katy Netz
Profile: Magazine about careers and training in schools.
Language(s): German
ADVERTISING RATES:
Full Page Mono .... EUR 1170
Full Page Colour .... EUR 2330
Mechanical Data: Type Area: 257 x 187 mm, No. of Columns (Display): 2, Col Widths (Display): 91 mm
Copy instructions: *Copy Date:* 42 days prior to publication
BUSINESS: CHURCH & SCHOOL EQUIPMENT & EDUCATION: Careers

BERUFSKRAFTFAHRER UNTERWEGS
722556G49A-140
Editorial: Aschauer Str. 30, 81549 MÜNCHEN
Tel: 89 2030430 **Fax:** 89 2030432280
Email: ulf.sundermann@springer.com **Web site:** http://www.heinrich-vogel-shop.de
Freq: Annual; **Cover Price:** EUR 8,90; **Circ:** 23,500
Editor: Ulf Sundermann
Profile: Magazine for professional truck and bus drivers.
Language(s): German

BESCHAFFUNG AKTUELL
721676G10-20
Editorial: Ernst-Mey-Str. 8, 70771 LEINFELDEN-ECHTERDINGEN **Tel:** 711 7594431
Fax: 711 7594221
Email: ba.redaktion@konradin.de **Web site:** http://www.beschaffung-aktuell.de
Freq: Monthly; Free to qualifying individuals
Annual Sub.: EUR 122,20; **Circ:** 18,040
Editor: Daniel Zabota; **Advertising Manager:** Klaus-Dieter Mehnert
Profile: Beschaffung aktuell is the trade magazine for strategic buying and it covers the whole practice of modern supply management. The efficient supply chain draws ourcing, buying, logistics and materials management together to become a factor in overall company success. Beschaffung aktuell delivers monthly information, highlights the trends in today's and tomorrow's buying. The independent editorial team presents buying managers, managing directors and directors, innovative management methods, products, services and markets.
Language(s): German
ADVERTISING RATES:
Full Page Mono .... EUR 5170
Full Page Colour .... EUR 6460
Mechanical Data: Type Area: 270 x 188 mm, No. of Columns (Display): 4, Col Widths (Display): 44 mm
Official Journal of: Organ d. Bundesverb. Materialwirtschaft, Einkauf u. Logistik e.V.
Supplement(s): Supply
BUSINESS: MATERIALS HANDLING

BESCHAFFUNG SPECIAL
722567G32A-148
Editorial: Am Buschhof 8, 53227 BONN
Tel: 228 970970 **Fax:** 228 9709775
Email: redaktion@behoerdenspiegel.de **Web site:** http://www.behoerdenspiegel.de
Freq: Monthly; **Annual Sub.:** EUR 38,00; **Circ:** 104,000
Editor: R. Uwe Proll; **Advertising Manager:** Helga Woll
Profile: Journal containing municipal information.
Language(s): German
Readership: Aimed at the public service sector.
ADVERTISING RATES:
Full Page Mono .... EUR 7688
Full Page Colour .... EUR 10622
Mechanical Data: Type Area: 430 x 285 mm, No. of Columns (Display): 6, Col Widths (Display): 45 mm
Copy instructions: *Copy Date:* 10 days prior to publication
Supplement to: Behörden Spiegel, Berliner Behörden Spiegel
BUSINESS: LOCAL GOVERNMENT, LEISURE & RECREATION: Local Government

BESCHAFFUNGSDIENST GALABAU
722565G26C-343
Editorial: Kahden 17b, 22393 HAMBURG
Tel: 40 6068820 **Fax:** 40 60688288
Email: info@soll.de **Web site:** http://www.soll.de
Freq: 9 issues yearly; **Annual Sub.:** EUR 30,00; **Circ:** 14,477
Editor: Rolf Soll; **Advertising Manager:** Claudia-Regine Soll
Profile: For over 30 years reported Beschaffungsdienst Galabau (CC-journal) with practical articles on gardening and landscaping in Germany. A CC journal means that will be controlled circulation. The subscription is not prominent, but the quality of the addressee. He has to fit the defined target group. It is still essential, if it is a code number or password journal is, for here are requests generated, the signal of interest. This concept is adhered to when purchasing Beschaffungsdienst Galabau consistently. The coverage is extremely practical and is aimed at the middle and upper management including the business owner both in the private sector and the public sector. The free use of the password system, we are also very often a focal point in the search for specific products and services. Through this service package is a close reader-binding is achieved.
Language(s): German
ADVERTISING RATES:
Full Page Mono .... EUR 2620
Full Page Colour .... EUR 3934
Mechanical Data: Type Area: 280 x 190 mm, No. of Columns (Display): 4, Col Widths (Display): 45 mm
Copy instructions: *Copy Date:* 14 days prior to publication
BUSINESS: GARDEN TRADE

BESSER LACKIEREN!
722579G16B-151
Editorial: Plathnerstr. 4c, 30175 HANNOVER
Tel: 511 9910320 **Fax:** 511 9910339
Email: franziska.moennig@vincentz.net **Web site:** http://www.besserlackieren.de
Freq: 21 issues yearly; **Annual Sub.:** EUR 102,00; **Circ:** 11,602
Editor: Franziska Moennig; **Advertising Manager:** Frauke Hallwaß
Profile: Magazine about all aspects of surface refinement.
Language(s): German
ADVERTISING RATES:
Full Page Mono .... EUR 7622
Full Page Colour .... EUR 10232
Mechanical Data: Type Area: 365 x 277 mm, No. of Columns (Display): 6, Col Widths (Display): 42 mm
Copy instructions: *Copy Date:* 14 days prior to publication
Official Journal of: Organ d. European Coil Coating Association u. d. Europ. Ges. f. Lackiertechnik e.V.
BUSINESS: DECORATING & PAINT: Paint - Technical Manufacture

BEST PRACTICE ONKOLOGIE
1795081G56A-11451
Editorial: Tiergartenstr. 17, 69121 HEIDELBERG
Tel: 6221 4878533 **Fax:** 6221 48768533
Email: charlotte.leisse@springer.com **Web site:** http://www.springermedizin.de
Freq: 6 issues yearly; **Annual Sub.:** EUR 152,00; **Circ:** 9,800
Editor: Stephan Schmitz
Profile: best practice onkologie aimed at all doctors who work in oncology standard care - be it as a practitioner in private practice or in a clinic. The focus of the magazine, the topics with which the doctor comes into contact daily. In each issue, three issues will be dealt with practical and interdisciplinary. In an interview, an important figure in the field of oncology is presented with their work. Another article offers a look into the future of cancer medicine. A comprehensive service and information section to web addresses, current research and further reading rounds out each issue.
Language(s): German
ADVERTISING RATES:
Full Page Mono .... EUR 3700
Full Page Colour .... EUR 3700
Mechanical Data: Type Area: 240 x 174 mm

DAS BESTE AUS MEIN BEKENNTNIS
1833891G74A-3589
Editorial: Bäckerstr. 14, 25709 MARNE
Tel: 4851 964766 **Fax:** 4851 964767
Email: contact@conpart-verlag.de **Web site:** http://www.conpart-verlag.de
Freq: Annual; **Circ:** 80,000
Profile: Women report in the journal of formative experiences that have influenced her life. Of courageous decisions, bitter truths, dramatic developments, unexpected twists and devastating consequences. It's about disturbing and distressing events, unsparing confessions, tormenting guilt, bitter disappointments and sad memories. And also to fateful encounters that ended in love, suffering or one's life worth living made. In addition, see "Das Beste aus Mein Bekenntnis" different types of puzzles for a few relaxing minutes in between. The health tips and your own personal horoscope can help you through the day.
Language(s): German

DAS BESTE FÜR DIE FRAU
1825392G74A-3569
Editorial: Sieker Landstr. 126, 22143 HAMBURG
Tel: 40 6739780 **Fax:** 40 67397821
Email: wmb@cpvkg.de **Web site:** http://www.conpart-verlag.de
Freq: Monthly; **Cover Price:** EUR 0,70; **Circ:** 98,527
Editor: Wolfgang M. Biehler
Profile: The magazine contains the following categories: Love & Life | Beauty & Cosmetics | Cooking & Baking | Fashion & Chic | Rates & Win | Royals & Society | VIPs & Celebrities | Travel & Services | Ratings & more.
Language(s): German
ADVERTISING RATES:
Full Page Mono .... EUR 5000
Full Page Colour .... EUR 5000
Mechanical Data: Type Area: 283 x 212 mm, No. of Columns (Display): 4

DAS BESTE FÜR DIE FRAU REZEPTE & MEHR!
1800404G74P-1233
Editorial: Sieker Landstr. 126/II, 22143 HAMBURG
Tel: 40 6739780 **Fax:** 40 67397821
Email: wmb@cpvkg.de **Web site:** http://www.conpart-verlag.de
Freq: 3 issues yearly; **Cover Price:** EUR 1,95; **Circ:** 130,000
Editor: Wolfgang M. Biehler
Profile: Women's magazine with new cooking and baking ideas.
Language(s): German
ADVERTISING RATES:
Full Page Mono .... EUR 5000
Full Page Colour .... EUR 5000
Mechanical Data: Type Area: 300 x 220 mm, No. of Columns (Display): 4, Col Widths (Display): 55 mm

BESTE JAHRE
1837408G74N-951
Editorial: Augustenstr. 19, 93049 REGENSBURG
Tel: 941 20009970 **Fax:** 941 20009980
Email: info@beste-jahre.com **Web site:** http://www.beste-jahre.com
Freq: Monthly; **Annual Sub.:** EUR 19,80; **Circ:** 25,000
Editor: Elke Swoboda; **Advertising Manager:** Sandra Leitner
Profile: Journal for people in middle life. A particular and for the whole Eastern Bavaria unique feature of our city journal is to specialize in an active, life-affirming and joyful buying age group. The major topic of our magazine covers the entire range of interest of this generation.
Language(s): German
ADVERTISING RATES:
Full Page Mono .... EUR 1695
Full Page Colour .... EUR 1695
Mechanical Data: Type Area: 240 x 176 mm, No. of Columns (Display): 4, Col Widths (Display): 41 mm

DAS BESTE - SONDERAUSG. D. KE
722591G19B-102
Editorial: Justus-von-Liebig-Str. 1, 86899 LANDSBERG **Tel:** 8191 125401 **Fax:** 8191 125822
Email: franz.graf@mi-verlag.de **Web site:** http://www.konstruktion.de
Freq: Annual
Editor: Franz Graf; **Advertising Manager:** Stefan Pilz
Profile: Magazine focusing on engineering design, automation, steering and electro technology.
Language(s): German
Readership: Read by decision makers and designers.
BUSINESS: ENGINEERING & MACHINERY: Engineering - Design

DIE BESTEN OBSTKUCHEN
722593G74P-120
Editorial: Rotweg 8, 76532 BADEN-BADEN
Tel: 7221 3501841 **Fax:** 7221 3501133
Email: liliane.elomari@klambt.de **Web site:** http://www.klambt.de
Freq: Annual; **Cover Price:** EUR 1,95; **Circ:** 100,000
Editor: Liliane El Omari; **Advertising Manager:** Martin Fischer
Profile: Once does the summer entry. Nature spoiled us with delicious fruit - strawberries, plums, apples & Co. are the stars of colorful summer fruity cake or pie. Delicate compositions or a quick fruit cake for the spontaneous party. Treat yourself to the sweet fruits with delicious baking recipes, from classic to modern.
Language(s): German
ADVERTISING RATES:
Full Page Mono .... EUR 5369
Full Page Colour .... EUR 5369
Mechanical Data: Type Area: 250 x 195 mm
Copy instructions: *Copy Date:* 42 days prior to publication

BEST-MED-LINK
1681743G94F-1859
Editorial: Kaiserstr. 51, 63065 OFFENBACH
Tel: 69 8297140 **Fax:** 69 8004924
Email: info@bestmedlink.de **Web site:** http://www.bestmedlink.de
Cover Price: Paid; **Circ:** 76,318 Unique Users
Language(s): German
CONSUMER: OTHER CLASSIFICATIONS: Disability

BETEILIGUNGSIREPORT
1800763G1F-1702
Editorial: Altstadt 296, 84028 LANDSHUT
Tel: 871 4306330 **Fax:** 871 43063311
Email: info@beteiligungsreport.de **Web site:** http://www.beteiligungsreport.de
Freq: Quarterly; Free to qualifying individuals
Annual Sub.: EUR 30,00; **Circ:** 10,000
Editor: Edmund Pelikan
Profile: Magazine for closed funds. This Outlet offers RSS (Really Simple Syndication).
Language(s): German
ADVERTISING RATES:
Full Page Mono .... EUR 4200
Full Page Colour .... EUR 4200
Mechanical Data: Type Area: 277 x 190 mm, No. of Columns (Display): 3, Col Widths (Display): 60 mm

BETON
722606G42A-45
Editorial: Steinhof 39, 40699 ERKRATH
Tel: 211 9249951 **Fax:** 211 9249955
Email: deckers@verlagbt.de **Web site:** http://www.verlagbt.de
Freq: 10 issues yearly; **Annual Sub.:** EUR 245,00; **Circ:** 5,783
Editor: Stefan Deckers; **Advertising Manager:** Elmar Rump
Profile: The magazine beton delivers expert advice for your practice - current and clear. It secures construction companies, concrete and ready-mix concrete plants as well as engineering and design firms have an information advantage for daily work. The journal provides information for more than 50 years of concrete manufacturing, use, and maintenance. The articles always provide the latest knowledge from research and practice. There are presented examples of building projects from home and abroad. These are facts, figures and fundamentals delivered at a high level of concrete technology. In addition, beton offers current reports on construction activities and provides information on new machines and products as well as appointments, meetings and congresses of the concrete and cement industry.
Language(s): German
ADVERTISING RATES:
Full Page Mono .... EUR 2600
Full Page Colour .... EUR 4400

Mechanical Data: Type Area: 270 x 186 mm, No. of Columns (Display): 4, Col Widths (Display): 46 mm
Copy instructions: *Copy Date:* 15 days prior to publication
BUSINESS: CONSTRUCTION

BETON BAUTEILE 722610G4E-2700
Editorial: Avenwedder Str. 55, 33335 GÜTERSLOH
Tel: 5241 8090884 **Fax:** 5241 80690880
Email: andrea.janzen@bauverlag.de **Web site:** http://www.bft-online.info
Freq: Annual; **Cover Price:** EUR 36,00; **Circ:** 3,000
Editor: Andrea Janzen; **Advertising Manager:** Jens Maurus
Profile: Information about innovations in product offerings, planning requirements and precast and concrete industry.
Language(s): German
ADVERTISING RATES:
Full Page Mono .... EUR 1150
Full Page Colour .... EUR 1750
Mechanical Data: Type Area: 252 x 175 mm, No. of Columns (Display): 3, Col Widths (Display): 55 mm
Copy instructions: *Copy Date:* 32 days prior to publication

DER BETRIEB 722614G44-3091
Editorial: Grafenberger Allee 293, 40237 DÜSSELDORF **Tel:** 211 8871454 **Fax:** 211 8871450
Email: der-betrieb@fachverlag.de **Web site:** http://www.der-betrieb.de
Freq: Weekly; **Annual Sub.:** EUR 396,00; **Circ:** 20,539
Editor: Oliver Holzinger; **Advertising Manager:** Ralf Pötzsch
Profile: Journal about business law.
Language(s): German
Readership: Aimed at solicitors and those in the legal profession.
ADVERTISING RATES:
Full Page Mono .... EUR 3380
Full Page Colour .... EUR 4970
Mechanical Data: Type Area: 263 x 189 mm, No. of Columns (Display): 4, Col Widths (Display): 44 mm
Copy instructions: *Copy Date:* 8 days prior to publication
BUSINESS: LEGAL

BETRIEBS BERATER 722618G14A-840
Editorial: Mainzer Landstr. 251, 60326 FRANKFURT
Tel: 69 75952701 **Fax:** 69 75952730
Email: weber@betriebs-berater.de **Web site:** http://www.betriebs-berater.de
Freq: Weekly; **Annual Sub.:** EUR 429,00; **Circ:** 7,575
Editor: Martin Weber; **Advertising Manager:** Marion Gertzen
Profile: The Betriebs Berater (BB) is one of the leading journals in the field of law, economy, taxes. The BB provides week by week information quickly and competently in the four areas of economic, tax, accounting and employment law. There are divisions for all a four-part structure: 1st compact weekly overview of the key judgments, legislation and administrative instructions 2nd essays 3rd BB Comment: Full text judgment and comprehensive commentary by experts 4th Decision report: brief summaries and comments of judgments. The ad-free professional part is covered by the Roman pages to find where in addition to a guest commentary by renowned authors on the first page the following content: It is news to professional law, information and tips on office management, event listings and reports, and information on education and training. On the Roman pages all ads can be found. Twitter: http://twitter.com/BetriebsBerater.
Language(s): German
ADVERTISING RATES:
Full Page Mono .... EUR 3365
Full Page Colour .... EUR 4095
Mechanical Data: Type Area: 250 x 184 mm, No. of Columns (Display): 4, Col Widths (Display): 41 mm
Copy instructions: *Copy Date:* 7 days prior to publication
BUSINESS: COMMERCE, INDUSTRY & MANAGEMENT

DER BETRIEBSLEITER 722621G14D-20
Editorial: Lise-Meitner-Str. 2, 55129 MAINZ
Tel: 6131 992238 **Fax:** 6131 992100
Email: m.doeppert@vfmz.de **Web site:** http://www.industrie-service.de
Freq: 10 issues yearly; **Annual Sub.:** EUR 84,00; **Circ:** 16,690
Editor: Michael Döppert; **Advertising Manager:** Bernd Kostbade
Profile: The editorial concept is strongly application-oriented. It includes practical technical papers, reports and product information and give - function-orientated and spread over branches - prominence to reasonable technical solutions and the economic benefit for the readers. The field of application of the responsible persons for production is characterized as poly-technical. The central topics are production, manufacturing, assembly, handling, industrial robot, quality assurance, maintenance, material-flow, industrial safety and safety engineering, work place equipment as well as plant equipment.
Language(s): German
ADVERTISING RATES:
Full Page Mono .... EUR 4440
Full Page Colour .... EUR 5670
Mechanical Data: Type Area: 265 x 185 mm, No. of Columns (Display): 4, Col Widths (Display): 43 mm

Copy instructions: *Copy Date:* 14 days prior to publication
Supplement(s): kataloge orange
BUSINESS: COMMERCE, INDUSTRY & MANAGEMENT: Purchasing

DER BETRIEBSWIRT 722630G14A-860
Editorial: Bleichstr. 20, 76593 GERNSBACH
Tel: 7224 9397150 **Fax:** 7224 9397905
Email: info@betriebswirte-verlag.de **Web site:** http://www.betriebswirte-verlag.de
Freq: Quarterly; **Annual Sub.:** EUR 70,00; **Circ:** 1,700
Editor: Regina Meier; **Advertising Manager:** Matthias Liesch
Profile: Journal concerning theoretical and practical management.
Language(s): German
ADVERTISING RATES:
Full Page Mono .... EUR 600
Full Page Colour .... EUR 1500
Mechanical Data: Type Area: 260 x 175 mm
Copy instructions: *Copy Date:* 21 days prior to publication
BUSINESS: COMMERCE, INDUSTRY & MANAGEMENT

BETRIEBSWIRTSCHAFTLICHE BLÄTTER 722631G1C-280
Editorial: Charlottenstr. 47, 10117 BERLIN
Tel: 30 202255148 **Fax:** 30 202255152
Email: bbl@dsgv.de **Web site:** http://www.s-fachzeitschriften.de
Freq: Monthly; **Annual Sub.:** EUR 138,00; **Circ:** 2,876
Editor: Arnulf Sauter
Profile: Betriebswirtschaftliche Blätter is the magazine for corporate management in the savings bank financial group. It informes about everything professionals and managers need to know. Competent, informative, practical. It focuses on collaborative development, credit management, bank management, IT security and quality, product and sales management in the corporate and retail banking. Editorial line: Controlling / Treasury cost Management quality Management security Payments / business cards project Management.
Language(s): German
ADVERTISING RATES:
Full Page Mono .... EUR 2800
Full Page Colour .... EUR 4270
Mechanical Data: Type Area: 263 x 180 mm, No. of Columns (Display): 3, Col Widths (Display): 56 mm
Copy instructions: *Copy Date:* 17 days prior to publication
BUSINESS: FINANCE & ECONOMICS: Banking

BETRIEBSWIRTSCHAFTLICHE FORSCHUNG UND PRAXIS BFUP 722632G14A-880
Editorial: Universitätsstr. 11, 58097 HAGEN
Tel: 2331 9874366
Freq: 6 issues yearly; **Annual Sub.:** EUR 133,80; **Circ:** 656
Editor: Heiko Burchert; **Advertising Manager:** Andrea Reimann
Profile: Magazine for economists.
Language(s): German
ADVERTISING RATES:
Full Page Mono .... EUR 1090
Full Page Colour .... EUR 1690
Mechanical Data: Type Area: 208 x 125 mm

BETRIFFT: NATUR 1819808G57-2836
Editorial: Färberstr. 51, 24534 NEUMÜNSTER
Tel: 4321 53734 **Fax:** 4321 5981
Email: redaktion.bn@nabu-sh.de **Web site:** http://www.betrifft-natur.de
Freq: Quarterly; Free to qualifying individuals
Annual Sub.: EUR 40,00; **Circ:** 15,500
Editor: Hermann Schultz
Profile: Member magazine from the nature protection society NABU, section Schleswig-Holstein.
Language(s): German

BEWUSSTER LEBEN 722659G74G-1702
Editorial: Karlstr. 8, 79104 FREIBURG
Tel: 761 29280240 **Fax:** 761 29380348
Email: redaktion@bewusster-leben.de **Web site:** http://www.bewusster-leben.de
Freq: 6 issues yearly; **Annual Sub.:** EUR 24,00; **Circ:** 50,000
Editor: Winfried Hille; **Advertising Manager:** Inge Behrens
Profile: Magazine for the art of living, health and spirituality. The magazine is a pioneer and the leading popular magazine-spiritual space in the German-speaking. Interviews with people that are of interest, and a variety of information from health & spirituality to create awareness for new thinking and action. The built-conscious living? Books-Journal offers two times a year a unique range of accompanying appraisal tools.
Language(s): German
Readership: Read by people interested in maintaining a healthy lifestyle.
ADVERTISING RATES:
Full Page Mono .... EUR 1750
Full Page Colour .... EUR 2500
Mechanical Data: Type Area: 241 x 179 mm, No. of Columns (Display): 4, Col Widths (Display): 42 mm

Copy instructions: *Copy Date:* 14 days prior to publication
CONSUMER: WOMEN'S INTEREST CONSUMER MAGAZINES: Slimming & Health

BFF JAHRBUCH 722761G2A-400
Editorial: Tuttlinger Str. 95, 70619 STUTTGART
Tel: 711 473422 **Fax:** 711 475280
Email: info@bff.de **Web site:** http://www.bff.de
Freq: Annual; **Cover Price:** EUR 60,00; **Circ:** 5,000
Editor: Norbert Waning
Profile: Annual published by German Photo Designers.
Language(s): English; German
ADVERTISING RATES:
Full Page Mono .... EUR 1600
Full Page Colour .... EUR 3100
Mechanical Data: Type Area: 186 x 186 mm
Copy instructions: *Copy Date:* 150 days prior to publication

BFHE ENTSCHEIDUNGEN DES BUNDESFINANZHOFS 722763G1A-320
Editorial: Dechenstr. 7, 53115 BONN **Tel:** 228 7240
Fax: 228 72491181
Email: info@stollfuss.de **Web site:** http://www.stollfuss.de
Freq: 18 issues yearly; **Annual Sub.:** EUR 124,50; **Circ:** 1,250
Profile: Magazine with decisions of the German federal finance court.
Language(s): German

BFP FUHRPARK + MANAGEMENT 755716G49A-2301
Editorial: Rheinallee 193, 55120 MAINZ
Tel: 6131 6277611 **Fax:** 6131 6277620
Email: mag@fuhrpark.de **Web site:** http://www.fuhrpark.de
Freq: 10 issues yearly; **Annual Sub.:** EUR 30,00; **Circ:** 49,858
Editor: Hans-Joachim Mag; **Advertising Manager:** Marion Bäre
Profile: Magazine for car pool executives.
Language(s): German
ADVERTISING RATES:
Full Page Mono .... EUR 6000
Full Page Colour .... EUR 7800
Mechanical Data: Type Area: 272 x 188 mm, No. of Columns (Display): 3, Col Widths (Display): 60 mm
Copy instructions: *Copy Date:* 21 days prior to publication
BUSINESS: TRANSPORT

BFT INTERNATIONAL 722611G42A-52
Editorial: Avenwedder Str. 55, 33335 GÜTERSLOH
Tel: 5241 8090884 **Fax:** 5241 80690880
Email: andrea.janzen@bauverlag.de **Web site:** http://www.bft-online.info
Freq: Monthly; **Annual Sub.:** EUR 216,00; **Circ:** 7,804
Editor: Andrea Janzen; **Advertising Manager:** Jens Maurus
Profile: The BFT International is recognized for over seven decades of industry magazine for producers of concrete products and finished products and for companies specializing in precast. It is aimed primarily at managers of this important industry sector, the distribution is worldwide. The articles in BFT International include comprehensive information on mechanical equipment in the plants from the mixing process of actual production to transport the finished products. Continue to be in coverage in addition to scientific knowledge in concrete technology as well as the reinforcement and connection technology, questions of organization and rationalization. Using the example of modern concrete and precast concrete, the current technical status in the various branches of production is presented. In parallel, provide product and object representations suggestions for the design and construction. Also offer corporate, association and product news, the ability to track the latest industry happenings. BFT International, "mediator" between building material machinery industry and its suppliers and concrete plants as well as a platform for international exchange of experience, taking into account the latest scientific knowledge.
Language(s): English; German
Readership: Read by construction workers.
ADVERTISING RATES:
Full Page Mono .... EUR 2280
Full Page Colour .... EUR 3438
Mechanical Data: Type Area: 270 x 185 mm, No. of Columns (Display): 4, Col Widths (Display): 43 mm
Copy instructions: *Copy Date:* 14 days prior to publication
Official Journal of: Internat. Organ d. Beton- u. Fertigteilindustrie
BUSINESS: CONSTRUCTION

BG BAU AKTUELL 721952G4E-640
Editorial: Hildesheimer Str. 309, 30519 HANNOVER
Tel: 511 9872530 **Fax:** 511 9872545
Email: rolf.schaper@bgbau.de **Web site:** http://www.bgbau.de
Freq: Quarterly; **Circ:** 450,000
Editor: Rolf Schaper
Profile: Magazine of the Building Professional Cooperative.
Language(s): German

BGHM-AKTUELL 729396G27-800
Editorial: Seligmannallee 4, 30173 HANNOVER
Tel: 511 811816882 **Fax:** 180 3862470366
Email: klaus.taubitz@bghm.de **Web site:** http://www.bghm.de
Freq: 6 issues yearly; **Circ:** 310,000
Editor: Klaus Taubitz
Profile: Magazine of the trade association of wood and metal Twitter: http://twitter.com/BGHM_DE.
Language(s): German

BGL-INFODIENST 722770G49A-160
Editorial: Breitenbachstr. 1, 60487 FRANKFURT
Tel: 69 7919277 **Fax:** 69 7919227
Email: presse@bgl-ev.de **Web site:** http://www.bgl-ev.de
Freq: 6 issues yearly; **Circ:** 6,500
Editor: Karlheinz Schmidt
Profile: Magazine for the transport industry.
Language(s): German

BGRCI.MAGAZIN 741905G54B-5
Editorial: Hunscheidtstr. 18, 44789 BOCHUM
Tel: 234 316354 **Fax:** 234 316378
Email: redaktion@bgrci.de **Web site:** http://www.bgrci.de
Freq: 6 issues yearly; **Cover Price:** Free; **Circ:** 95,000
Editor: Ulrike Jansen
Profile: Journal of occupational health and safety of raw materials and chemical industry trade association.
Language(s): German
BUSINESS: SAFETY & SECURITY: Safety

BI BANKINFORMATION 721849G1C-120
Editorial: Schellingstr. 4, 10785 BERLIN
Tel: 30 20211341 **Fax:** 30 20211905
Email: bankinformation@bvr.de **Web site:** http://www.bankinformation.de
Freq: Monthly; **Circ:** 6,500
Editor: Markus Krüger
Profile: The magazine BI Bankinformation aimed at the leaders and decision makers in the cooperative banking group and the rest of the banking industry. As part of the BI - very practical problems of the banking business handled - with one main topic in every issue. The rapidly progressive mechanization in the banking industry, which are ever-intensifying competition between the groups of institutions and the ever-increasing business demands in the center of every issue.
Language(s): German
ADVERTISING RATES:
Full Page Mono .... EUR 4893
Full Page Colour .... EUR 4893
Mechanical Data: Type Area: 274 x 178 mm, No. of Columns (Display): 3, Col Widths (Display): 56 mm
Copy instructions: *Copy Date:* 21 days prior to publication
BUSINESS: FINANCE & ECONOMICS: Banking

BI BAUFAHRZEUGE 1703278G49C-89
Editorial: Faluner Weg 33, 24109 KIEL
Tel: 431 5359215 **Fax:** 431 5359226
Email: redaktion@bi-medien.de **Web site:** http://www.bi-medien.de
Freq: Half-yearly; **Circ:** 47,982
Editor: Wolfgang Tschakert; **Advertising Manager:** Benno Stahn
Profile: Journal for construction vehicles with competent and skilled exclusive articles on market trends and current technology.
Language(s): German
ADVERTISING RATES:
Full Page Mono .... EUR 3130
Full Page Colour .... EUR 4780
Mechanical Data: Type Area: 250 x 185 mm, No. of Columns (Display): 4, Col Widths (Display): 43 mm
Copy instructions: *Copy Date:* 21 days prior to publication
Supplement to: bi BauMagazin, bi GaLaBau, bi UmweltBau

BI BAUMAGAZIN 722933G4E-2820
Editorial: Faluner Weg 33, 24109 KIEL
Tel: 431 5359240 **Fax:** 431 5359225
Email: redaktion@bi-medien.de **Web site:** http://www.bi-medien.de
Freq: 9 issues yearly; **Annual Sub.:** EUR 64,00; **Circ:** 20,276
Editor: Rudi Grimm; **Advertising Manager:** Benno Stahn
Profile: The magazine provides decision-makers (business owner or manager), especially in medium-sized businesses are a big help. It provides information on construction equipment, construction materials and methods. Features, interviews and articles are processed fairly and professionally designed reading. Special profile given the journal by the heading "Management ". As an internal publication of the magazine devoted VSVI S-H intense in seven issues the issue of street road construction and road building.
Language(s): German
ADVERTISING RATES:
Full Page Mono .... EUR 2555
Full Page Colour .... EUR 3815
Mechanical Data: Type Area: 250 x 185 mm, No. of Columns (Display): 3, Col Widths (Display): 59 mm

Copy instructions: *Copy Date:* 15 days prior to publication
Official Journal of: Organ d. Straßenbau- u. Verkehrsingenieure S-H e.V.
Supplement(s): bi BauFahrzeuge
BUSINESS: ARCHITECTURE & BUILDING: Building

BI GALABAU 722777G26C-344
Editorial: Am Deich 43, 21723 HOLLERN-TWIELENFLETH **Tel:** 4141 776884 **Fax:** 4141 776885
Email: red.bauer@t-online.de **Web site:** http://www.bi-medien.de
Freq: 8 issues yearly; **Annual Sub.:** EUR 68,48; **Circ:** 13,822
Editor: Erwin Bauer; **Advertising Manager:** Nicole Schmidt
Profile: Magazine containing articles about gardens, landscaping and establishing sports fields.
Language(s): German
ADVERTISING RATES:
Full Page Mono .... EUR 2420
Full Page Colour .... EUR 3470
Mechanical Data: Type Area: 250 x 185 mm, No. of Columns (Display): 3, Col Widths (Display): 59 mm
Copy instructions: *Copy Date:* 15 days prior to publication
Supplement(s): bi BauFahrzeuge
BUSINESS: GARDEN TRADE

BI UMWELTBAU 722778G4E-2800
Editorial: Faluner Weg 33, 24109 KIEL
Tel: 431 5359243 **Fax:** 431 5359228
Email: redaktion@bi-medien.de **Web site:** http://www.bi-medien.de
Freq: 6 issues yearly; **Annual Sub.:** EUR 57,78; **Circ:** 14,817
Editor: Artur Graf zu Eulenburg; **Advertising Manager:** Benno Stahn
Profile: Building industry magazine with a focus on plumbing.
Language(s): German
ADVERTISING RATES:
Full Page Mono .... EUR 2490
Full Page Colour .... EUR 3690
Mechanical Data: Type Area: 250 x 185 mm, No. of Columns (Display): 3, Col Widths (Display): 59 mm
Copy instructions: *Copy Date:* 10 days prior to publication
Official Journal of: Organ d. Güterschutzverb. Horizontalbohrer e.V., d. Verb. zertifizierter Sanierungsberater f. Entwässerungssysteme e.V. u. d. Dt. Ges. f. grabenloses Bauen u. Instandhalten v. Leitungen e.V.
Supplement(s): bi BauFahrzeuge
BUSINESS: ARCHITECTURE & BUILDING: Building

BIBELSERVER.COM
1704614G87-14370
Editorial: Berliner Ring 62, 35576 WETZLAR
Tel: 6441 9572000 **Fax:** 6441 9572001
Email: info.de@bibelserver.com **Web site:** http://www.bibelserver.com
Cover Price: Paid; **Circ:** 54,374 Unique Users
Editor: Michael Gerster
Language(s): German
CONSUMER: RELIGIOUS

BIBI BLOCKSBERG 722797G91D-820
Editorial: Wallstr. 59, 10179 BERLIN **Tel:** 30 240080
Fax: 30 24008599
Email: s.saydo@ehapa.de **Web site:** http://www.bibiblocksberg.de
Freq: Monthly; **Cover Price:** EUR 2,95; **Circ:** 33,267
Editor: Sanya Saydo
Profile: Comic magazine offers its readers the most interesting conversation with haunted puzzles, great posters and fun games. Bibi Blocksberg has been for many years the favorite witch of the children. The magazine experienced the little witch fun and exciting adventure with their flying witches broom "mashed potatoes".
Language(s): German
ADVERTISING RATES:
Full Page Mono .... EUR 4200
Full Page Colour .... EUR 4200
Mechanical Data: Type Area: 280 x 210 mm, No. of Columns (Display): 4, Col Widths (Display): 52 mm
CONSUMER: RECREATION & LEISURE: Children & Youth

BIBI & TINA 763727G91D-9683
Editorial: Wallstr. 59, 10179 BERLIN **Tel:** 30 240080
Fax: 30 24008599
Email: s.saydo@ehapa.de **Web site:** http://www.ehapa.de
Freq: Monthly; **Cover Price:** EUR 2,95; **Circ:** 24,524
Editor: Sanya Saydo
Profile: Youth magazine for horse enthusiasts girls. Bibi Blocksberg and her friend Tina in her own magazine to do a lot of adventure: In addition to exciting comic adventures experienced the little horse lovers all about horses, horse care and other animals.
Language(s): German
ADVERTISING RATES:
Full Page Mono .... EUR 3500
Full Page Colour .... EUR 3500
Mechanical Data: Type Area: 280 x 210 mm, No. of Columns (Display): 4, Col Widths (Display): 52 mm
CONSUMER: RECREATION & LEISURE: Children & Youth

BIBLIOTHEK FORSCHUNG UND PRAXIS 722814G60B-160
Editorial: Platz der Göttinger Sieben 1, 37070 GÖTTINGEN **Tel:** 551 395212 **Fax:** 551 395222
Email: bfp@sub.uni-goettingen.de **Web site:** http://www.bibliothek-saur.de/index.html
Freq: 3 issues yearly; **Annual Sub.:** EUR 236,00; **Circ:** 1,800
Editor: Elmar Mittler; **Advertising Manager:** Dietlind Makswitat
Profile: Magazine about libraries.
Language(s): German
Readership: Read by librarians and librarian researchers.
ADVERTISING RATES:
Full Page Mono .... EUR 550
Full Page Colour .... EUR 1000
Mechanical Data: Type Area: 250 x 170 mm
Copy instructions: *Copy Date:* 45 days prior to publication
BUSINESS: PUBLISHING: Libraries

BIBLIOTHEKSDIENST
722815G60B-220
Editorial: Breite Str. 36, 10178 BERLIN
Tel: 30 90226456 **Fax:** 30 90226539
Email: redaktion.bibliotheksdienst@zlb.de **Web site:** http://www.zlb.de/aktivitaeten/bd_neu
Freq: Monthly; **Annual Sub.:** EUR 49,00; **Circ:** 2,600
Editor: Michael Dürr; **Advertising Manager:** Lutz Rehboldt
Profile: Official journal of the German Library Association.
Language(s): German
ADVERTISING RATES:
Full Page Mono .... EUR 395
Mechanical Data: Type Area: 160 x 110 mm
Copy instructions: *Copy Date:* 25 days prior to publication
Official Journal of: Organ d. Bibliothek & Information Deutschland
BUSINESS: PUBLISHING: Libraries

BIELEFELD GEHT AUS
722834G89A-340
Editorial: Goldstr. 16, 33602 BIELEFELD
Tel: 521 932560 **Fax:** 521 9325699
Email: redaktion@tips-verlag.de **Web site:** http://www.tips-verlag.de
Freq: Half-yearly; **Cover Price:** Free; **Circ:** 20,000
Editor: Friedrich Flöttmann
Profile: Magazine for city and region, concentrating on events, gastronomy, music, arts and events for the city of Bielefeld.
Language(s): German
ADVERTISING RATES:
Full Page Mono .... EUR 1156
Full Page Colour .... EUR 1847
Mechanical Data: Type Area: 190 x 130 mm, No. of Columns (Display): 3, Col Widths (Display): 40 mm
Copy instructions: *Copy Date:* 15 days prior to publication

BIELEFELD SPEZIAL SCHENKEN FEIERN LEBEN
765160G74A-3258
Editorial: Goldstr. 16, 33602 BIELEFELD
Tel: 521 932560 **Fax:** 521 9325699
Email: redaktion@tips-verlag.de **Web site:** http://www.tips-verlag.de
Freq: Annual; **Cover Price:** Free; **Circ:** 20,000
Editor: Friedrich Flöttmann
Profile: Gift guide for Bielefeld, the magazine to make the pleasure giving and Christmas in Bielefeld. With stories, reports and detailed gift tips Cathedral retail. Special service: The Gift Reviews are ordered by price groups and call the local sources of supply.
Language(s): German
ADVERTISING RATES:
Full Page Mono .... EUR 1490
Full Page Colour .... EUR 2357
Mechanical Data: Type Area: 260 x 190 mm, No. of Columns (Display): 4, Col Widths (Display): 43 mm
Copy instructions: *Copy Date:* 15 days prior to publication

BIELEFELDER 744974G80-13929
Editorial: Goldstr. 16, 33602 BIELEFELD
Tel: 521 9325640 **Fax:** 521 9325699
Email: redaktion@tips-verlag.de **Web site:** http://www.der-bielefelder.de
Freq: Monthly; **Cover Price:** Free; **Circ:** 24,802
Editor: Friedrich Flöttmann
Profile: City magazine for Bielefeld with information about the city and the people, culture, Life & Style, Shopping, going out and enjoying life. High-quality, informative, entertaining.
Language(s): German
ADVERTISING RATES:
Full Page Mono .... EUR 1346
Full Page Colour .... EUR 1953
Mechanical Data: Type Area: 260 x 190 mm, No. of Columns (Display): 4, Col Widths (Display): 44 mm
Copy instructions: *Copy Date:* 15 days prior to publication
CONSUMER: RURAL & REGIONAL INTEREST

DIE BIENE 722838G81G-3
Editorial: Weiherstr. 5, 79183 WALDKIRCH
Tel: 7681 409166 **Fax:** 7681 409165
Email: js-bienenredaktion@t-online.de **Web site:** http://www.dlv.de
Freq: Monthly; Free to qualifying individuals
Annual Sub.: EUR 37,50; **Circ:** 11,216
Editor: Jürgen Schwenkel; **Advertising Manager:** Thomas Herrmann
Profile: With the three journals, die biene, ADIZ Allgemeine Deutsche Imkerzeitung and Imkerfreund is the dlv Deutscher Landwirtschaftsverlag market leader in the field of regional and national beekeeping journals. Reaching over 33,100 copies distributed die biene, ADIZ and Imkerfreund a large part of the German beekeepers in major honey producing regions. In die biene and ADIZ are the oldest German regional bee newspapers and magazines Südwestdeutscher Imker, Westfälische Bienenzeitung and Deutsche Bienenwirtschaft united. Many large beekeeper organizations use the three beekeeping journals as their official organ: die biene: Hessian state association of beekeepers and beekeepers in the Saarland and the beekeepers associations of Rhineland and Nassau; ADIZ: State Association of Baden beekeepers and beekeepers association of Rhineland-Palatinate; Imkerfreund: State Association of Bavarian beekeepers. Association news, events, messages, personal data and other information from these organizations and the German Beekeepers' Association and from the state's beekeepers associations Saxony, Saxony-Anhalt, Thuringia and Mecklenburg-Western Pomerania are an integral part of every issue. The reader will find in their magazine also highly skilled technical contributions of high-qualified authors from academia and practice. The offer ranges from standard subjects such as beekeeping and farming, honey production and marketing, bee diseases and countermeasures about tips and tricks for beekeepers to information about honey bees, the history of beekeeping, special literature, nature protection and other beekeepers areas of interest. The journals die biene, ADIZ and Imkerfreund are read primarily by recreational and professional beekeepers, bee scientists at universities and bee institutes, consultants and employees in government agencies.
Language(s): German
ADVERTISING RATES:
Full Page Mono .... EUR 1539
Full Page Colour .... EUR 2579
Mechanical Data: Type Area: 270 x 184 mm, No. of Columns (Display): 4, Col Widths (Display): 43 mm
Copy instructions: *Copy Date:* 30 days prior to publication
Official Journal of: Organ d. Imkerverbände Hessen, Nassau, Rheinland u. Saarland
CONSUMER: ANIMALS & PETS: Bees

BIETIGHEIMER ZEITUNG
722849G67B-2700
Editorial: Kronenbergstr. 10, 74321 BIETIGHEIM-BISSINGEN **Tel:** 7142 403410 **Fax:** 7142 403128
Email: redaktion@bietigheimerzeitung.de **Web site:** http://www.bietigheimerzeitung.de
Freq: 312 issues yearly; **Circ:** 12,204
Editor: Andreas Lukesch; **Advertising Manager:** Johannes Schwiderowski
Profile: Daily newspaper with regional news and a local sports section.
Language(s): German
ADVERTISING RATES:
SCC .... EUR 42,60
Mechanical Data: Type Area: 485 x 320 mm, No. of Columns (Display): 7, Col Widths (Display): 44 mm
Copy instructions: *Copy Date:* 2 days prior to publication
Supplement(s): rtv
REGIONAL DAILY & SUNDAY NEWSPAPERS: Regional Daily Newspapers

BIKE 722857G77C-40
Editorial: Steinerstr. 15, 81369 MÜNCHEN
Tel: 89 7296020 **Fax:** 89 7296240
Email: redaktion@bike-magazin.de **Web site:** http://www.bike-magazin.de
Freq: Monthly; **Annual Sub.:** EUR 47,00; **Circ:** 84,204
Editor: Jochen Welz; **Advertising Manager:** Ingeborg Bockstette
Profile: European publication about mountain-biking.
Language(s): German
ADVERTISING RATES:
Full Page Mono .... EUR 5560
Full Page Colour .... EUR 9720
Mechanical Data: Type Area: 252 x 184 mm, No. of Columns (Display): 4, Col Widths (Display): 43 mm
Copy instructions: *Copy Date:* 42 days prior to publication
CONSUMER: MOTORING & CYCLING: Cycling

BIKE UND BUSINESS 721837G31B-4
Editorial: Max-Planck-Str. 7, 97082 WÜRZBURG
Tel: 931 4182918 **Fax:** 931 4182060
Email: stephan.maderner@vogel.de **Web site:** http://www.bikeundbusiness.de
Freq: 11 issues yearly; **Annual Sub.:** EUR 96,00; **Circ:** 7,433
Editor: Stephan Maderner; **Advertising Manager:** Anna Gredel
Profile: The business magazine »bike und business« is aimed at the two-wheeler industry in Germany, Austria and Switzerland. The mantle section of the magazine focuses on the motorcycle trade and service, workshops, dealers of accessories, techniques, clothing and helmets, manufacturers/ importers and associations. In addition, the editorial content includes a training section with topics at the level of European service technician.

Language(s): German
Readership: Read by mechanics and retailers.
ADVERTISING RATES:
Full Page Mono .... EUR 2030
Full Page Colour .... EUR 2990
Mechanical Data: Type Area: 270 x 190 mm, No. of Columns (Display): 4, Col Widths (Display): 46 mm
Copy instructions: *Copy Date:* 15 days prior to publication
Official Journal of: Organ d. Bundesinnungsverb. f. d. Dt. Zweiradmechaniker-Handwerk
BUSINESS: MOTOR TRADE: Motorcycle Trade

BIKER SZENE 722863G77B-1
Editorial: Friedrich-Lueg-Str. 10, 44867 BOCHUM
Tel: 2327 544590 **Fax:** 2327 5445999
Email: pbirnbreier@quoka.com **Web site:** http://www.bikerszene.de
Freq: Monthly; **Cover Price:** EUR 2,50; **Circ:** 50,000
Editor: Patric Birnbreier
Profile: Motorcycling journal.
Language(s): German
ADVERTISING RATES:
Full Page Mono .... EUR 3412
Full Page Colour .... EUR 3412
Mechanical Data: Type Area: 260 x 188 mm, No. of Columns (Display): 4, Col Widths (Display): 44 mm
Copy instructions: *Copy Date:* 14 days prior to publication

BIKER.DE 1661026G77A-2662
Editorial: Max-Planck-Str. 6, 50858 KÖLN
Tel: 221 91116 **Fax:** 221 911169
Email: henning@szene.de **Web site:** http://www.biker.de
Cover Price: Paid
Editor: Henning Rielinger
Language(s): German
CONSUMER: MOTORING & CYCLING: Motoring

BIKERS NEWS 722862G77A-640
Editorial: Markircher Str. 9a, 68229 MANNHEIM
Tel: 621 4836187 **Fax:** 621 4836115
Email: m.ahlsdorf@huber-verlag.de **Web site:** http://www.bikersnews.de
Freq: Monthly; **Annual Sub.:** EUR 52,00; **Circ:** 51,811
Editor: Michael Ahlsdorf; **Advertising Manager:** Nina Kropp
Profile: Magazine for bikers. Facebook: http://www.facebook.com/BikersNews.
Language(s): German
ADVERTISING RATES:
Full Page Colour .... EUR 3050
Mechanical Data: Type Area: 256 x 184 mm, No. of Columns (Display): 4, Col Widths (Display): 43 mm
Copy instructions: *Copy Date:* 34 days prior to publication
CONSUMER: MOTORING & CYCLING: Motoring

BILANZ + BUCHHALTUNG
1882033G14A-10263
Editorial: Munzinger Str. 9, 79111 FREIBURG
Tel: 761 8983032 **Fax:** 761 8983112
Email: online@haufe-lexware.com **Web site:** http://www.haufe.de/finance
Freq: 11 issues yearly; **Annual Sub.:** EUR 178,80; **Circ:** 3,500
Editor: Walter Strecker; **Advertising Manager:** Bernd Junker
Profile: The proven scientific journal "bilanz + buchhaltung" provides a quick and comprehensive overview of accounting and taxes. Is specially tailored to accountants' "bilanz + buchhaltung" with in-depth articles at your fingertips. Legal certainty and currently you can stay up to date and have all information you need as an accountant.
Language(s): German
ADVERTISING RATES:
Full Page Mono .... EUR 980
Full Page Colour .... EUR 1920
Mechanical Data: Type Area: 297 x 210 mm

BILANZEN IM MITTELSTAND
1866699G14A-10250
Editorial: Grafenberger Allee 293, 40237 DÜSSELDORF **Tel:** 211 8871435
Fax: 211 887971435
Email: bim.redaktion@fachverlag.de **Web site:** http://www.bilanzen-im-mittelstand.de
Freq: Quarterly; **Annual Sub.:** EUR 36,00; **Circ:** 26,000
Editor: Sebastian Boochs; **Advertising Manager:** Ralf Pötzsch
Profile: Magazine provides an update on the developments in the world of accounting from the perspective of SMEs. The emphasis is on naturally formulated professional contributions to both national HGB accounting as well as the most important developments in international accounting. Conference reports, reports, book reviews and events complement the editorial concept.
Language(s): German
ADVERTISING RATES:
Full Page Mono .... EUR 4290
Full Page Colour .... EUR 4290
Mechanical Data: Type Area: 265 x 165 mm
Copy instructions: *Copy Date:* 17 days prior to publication

BILD 722867G65A-40

Editorial: Axel-Springer-Str. 65, 10969 BERLIN
Tel: 30 25910
Web site: http://www.bild.de
Freq: 312 issues yearly; **Circ:** 2,917,454
Editor: Kai Diekmann; **News Editor:** Michel Rauch;
Advertising Manager: Peter Ludwig Müller
Profile: BILD is Europe's largest daily newspaper. With its direct and unmistakable style, they reached a daily audience, composed of all social classes. Through high relevance, commitment and unparalleled proximity to the reader understands BILD, get news, background information and entertainment from all areas of political and social life on a daily basis to the point. The successful concept of the image consists of five principles: * Information BILD moves people, BILD provides for reactions and discussions. Concise and provocative. * Personalization BILD combines concepts and minds. BILD works with characters - and itself has a distinctive character. * Entertainment Sometimes funny, sometimes serious - always original! * Visualization BILD is visually unique BILD news makes visible. BILD shows exclusive photos, which no other medium. * Orientation BILD informs its readers quickly and clearly. IMAGE is the medium for the essentials. Facebook: http://www.facebook.com/bild Twitter: http://twitter.com/BILD This Outlet offers RSS (Really Simple Syndication).
Language(s): German
Readership: Read by students, lower management, office staff and factory workers.
Mechanical Data: Type Area: 528 x 376 mm, No. of Columns (Display): 8, Col Widths (Display): 45 mm
Copy instructions: *Copy Date:* 3 days prior to publication
NATIONAL DAILY & SUNDAY NEWSPAPERS: National Daily Newspapers

BILD AM SONNTAG 722868G65B-1

Editorial: Axel-Springer-Str. 65, 10969 BERLIN
Tel: 30 259100 **Fax:** 30 259176535
Web site: http://www.bams.de
Freq: Weekly; **Cover Price:** EUR 1,70; **Circ:** 1,533,020
Editor: Walter Mayer; **News Editor:** Thomas Drechsler; **Advertising Manager:** Stefan Mölling
Profile: Largest Sunday newspaper in Germany. Germany talks about it! 10.39 million readers use Germany's largest Sunday paper to well informed in every Week. Because on Sunday image is on Sunday the issues of which Germany is speaking in the week. BILD am SONNTAG activated on Sunday reveals, enlightens. Is a critical observer, sports reporter and professional advice for all areas of life. News and exclusive. BILD am SONNTAG has the edge hot News, exclusive interviews from politics, business and sports. Versatile and informative. In Bild am Sonntag everyone finds his subject. Competently prepared and presented clearly segmented BILD am SONNTAG all relevant issues - including those from entertainment, advice and the world of VIP's. And up close and emotionally BILD am SONNTAG speaks the language of the reader, deals with their own best interests, the destiny. Twitter: http://twitter.com/BamSRatgeber RSS (Really Simple Syndication) is offered.
Language(s): German
Mechanical Data: Type Area: 369 x 257 mm, No. of Columns (Display): 4, Col Widths (Display): 60 mm
Copy instructions: *Copy Date:* 10 days prior to publication
Supplement(s): Bild am Sonntag Geschenke journal; Bild am Sonntag Reise Journal zur ITB Berlin; Bild am Sonntag Wohn Journal; Mensch Bleib Gesund
NATIONAL DAILY & SUNDAY NEWSPAPERS: National Sunday Newspapers

BILD BERLIN-BRANDENBURG 722869G67B-2720

Editorial: Axel-Springer-Str. 65, 10969 BERLIN
Tel: 30 259176300
Email: miriam.krekel@bild.de **Web site:** http://www.bild.de
Freq: 312 issues yearly; **Cover Price:** EUR 0,60; **Circ:** 103,163
Advertising Manager: Peter Ludwig Müller
Profile: BILD Berlin-Brandenburg is a regional newspaper. With its direct and unmistakable style, they reached a daily audience, composed of all social classes. Through high relevance, commitment and unparalleled proximity to the reader understands BILD get news, background information and entertainment from all areas of political and social life on a daily basis to the point. The successful concept of the image consists of five principles: * Information BILD moves people, IMAGE provides for reactions and discussions. Concise and provocative. * Personalization BILD combines concepts and minds. BILD works with characters - and itself has a distinctive character. * Entertainment Sometimes funny, sometimes serious - always original! * Visualization BILD is visually unique BILD news makes visible. BILD shows exclusive photos, which no other medium. * Orientation BILD informs its readers quickly and clearly. IMAGE is the medium for the essentials. Facebook: http://www.facebook.com/bild Twitter: http://twitter.com/BILD_Berlin This Outlet offers RSS (Really Simple Syndication).
Language(s): German
Mechanical Data: Type Area: 528 x 376 mm, No. of Columns (Display): 8, Col Widths (Display): 45 mm
Copy instructions: *Copy Date:* 1 day prior to publication
REGIONAL DAILY & SUNDAY NEWSPAPERS: Regional Daily Newspapers

BILD BREMEN 1639035G67B-16726

Editorial: Axel-Springer-Str. 65, 10969 BERLIN
Tel: 30 25910
Web site: http://www.bild.de
Freq: 312 issues yearly; **Cover Price:** EUR 0,60; **Circ:** 73,827
Advertising Manager: Alexander Sempf
Profile: BILD Bremen is a regional newspaper. With its direct and unmistakable style, they reached a daily audience, composed of all social classes. Through high relevance, commitment and unparalleled proximity to the reader understands BILD get news, background information and entertainment from all areas of political and social life on a daily basis to the point. The successful concept of the image consists of five principles: * Information BILD moves people, BILD provides for reactions and discussions. Concise and provocative. * Personalization BILD combines concepts and minds. BILD works with characters - and itself has a distinctive character. * Entertainment Sometimes funny, sometimes serious - always original! * Visualization BILD is visually unique BILD news makes visible. BILD shows exclusive photos, which no other medium. * Orientation BILD informs its readers quickly and clearly. IMAGE is the medium for the essentials. Facebook: http://www.facebook.com/bild Twitter: http://twitter.com/BILD_Berlin This Outlet offers RSS (Really Simple Syndication).
Language(s): German
Mechanical Data: Type Area: 528 x 376 mm, No. of Columns (Display): 8, Col Widths (Display): 45 mm
Copy instructions: *Copy Date:* 1 day prior to publication
REGIONAL DAILY & SUNDAY NEWSPAPERS: Regional Daily Newspapers

BILD CHEMNITZ 722870G67B-2740

Editorial: Axel-Springer-Str. 65, 10969 BERLIN
Tel: 30 25910
Web site: http://www.bild.de
Freq: 312 issues yearly; **Cover Price:** EUR 0,30; **Circ:** 41,673
Advertising Manager: Alexander Sempf
Profile: BILD Chemnitz is a regional newspaper. With its direct and unmistakable style, they reached a daily audience, composed of all social classes. Through high relevance, commitment and unparalleled proximity to the reader understands BILD get news, background information and entertainment from all areas of political and social life on a daily basis to the point. The successful concept of the image consists of five principles: * Information BILD moves people, BILD provides for reactions and discussions. Concise and provocative. * Personalization BILD combines concepts and minds. BILD works with characters - and itself has a distinctive character. * Entertainment Sometimes funny, sometimes serious - always original! * Visualization BILD is visually unique BILD news makes visible. BILD shows exclusive photos, which no other medium. * Orientation BILD informs its readers quickly and clearly. IMAGE is the medium for the essentials. Facebook: http://www.facebook.com/bild Twitter: http://twitter.com/BILD_Berlin This Outlet offers RSS (Really Simple Syndication).
Language(s): German
Mechanical Data: Type Area: 528 x 376 mm, No. of Columns (Display): 8, Col Widths (Display): 45 mm
Copy instructions: *Copy Date:* 1 day prior to publication
REGIONAL DAILY & SUNDAY NEWSPAPERS: Regional Daily Newspapers

BILD DER FRAU 722871G74A-500

Editorial: Axel-Springer-Platz 1, 20355 HAMBURG
Tel: 40 34700 **Fax:** 40 34723476
Email: service@bildderfrau.de **Web site:** http://www.bildderfrau.de
Freq: Weekly; **Cover Price:** EUR 0,95; **Circ:** 959,565
Editor: Sandra Immoor; **Advertising Manager:** Claudia Blumenberg
Profile: BILD der FRAU is Germany's largest women's magazine. Every week the latest information on all areas of life, but also of politics, economy and society. Facebook: http://www.facebook.com/bildderfrau.
Language(s): German
ADVERTISING RATES:
Full Page Mono .... EUR 43340
Full Page Colour .... EUR 43340
Mechanical Data: Type Area: 288 x 207 mm, No. of Columns (Display): 4, Col Widths (Display): 50 mm
Copy instructions: *Copy Date:* 25 days prior to publication
CONSUMER: WOMEN'S INTEREST CONSUMER MAGAZINES: Women's Interest

BILD DER FRAU GUT KOCHEN & BACKEN 722872G74P-160

Editorial: Axel-Springer-Platz 1, 20355 HAMBURG
Tel: 40 34700 **Fax:** 40 34723483
Email: service@bildderfrau.de **Web site:** http://www.bildderfrau.de
Freq: 6 issues yearly; **Cover Price:** EUR 1,80; **Circ:** 80,388
Editor: Sandra Immoor; **Advertising Manager:** Claudia Blumenberg
Profile: Magazine containing recipes and cookery tips. Facebook: http://www.facebook.com/bildderfrau.
Language(s): German
ADVERTISING RATES:
Full Page Mono .... EUR 12500
Full Page Colour .... EUR 12500
Mechanical Data: Type Area: 266 x 184 mm
Copy instructions: *Copy Date:* 49 days prior to publication
CONSUMER: WOMEN'S INTEREST CONSUMER MAGAZINES: Food & Cookery

BILD DER WISSENSCHAFT 722873G94J-60

Editorial: Ernst-Mey-Str. 8, 70771 LEINFELDEN-ECHTERDINGEN **Tel:** 711 7594447
Fax: 711 75945836
Email: wissenschaft@konradin.de **Web site:** http://www.wissenschaft.de
Freq: Monthly; **Annual Sub.:** EUR 83,40; **Circ:** 93,342
Editor: Wolfgang Hess; **Advertising Manager:** Julia Raudenbusch
Profile: The journal documented earlier than others, such as research and technology change our lives. All relevant topics are competently and critically illuminated. The best science journalists prepare for the reader-friendly magazine to complicated issues. A clear issue structure ensures that the innovations in science and technology at first sight striking. The magazine will be accompanied by contact information, web links, book reviews and event announcements.
Language(s): German
ADVERTISING RATES:
Full Page Mono .... EUR 7160
Full Page Colour .... EUR 11100
Mechanical Data: Type Area: 250 x 188 mm
Copy instructions: *Copy Date:* 35 days prior to publication
CONSUMER: OTHER CLASSIFICATIONS: Popular Science

BILD DER WISSENSCHAFT 1620850G94J-725

Editorial: Ernst-Mey-Str. 8, 70771 LEINFELDEN-ECHTERDINGEN **Tel:** 711 7594392
Fax: 711 75945835
Email: wissenschaft@konradin.de **Web site:** http://www.wissenschaft.de
Freq: Daily; **Cover Price:** Paid
Editor: Wolfgang Hess
Profile: Ezine: Journal publishing information about scientific developments.
Language(s): German
CONSUMER: OTHER CLASSIFICATIONS: Popular Science

BILD DRESDEN 722874G67B-2760

Editorial: Axel-Springer-Str. 65, 10969 BERLIN
Tel: 30 25910
Web site: http://www.bild.de
Freq: 312 issues yearly; **Cover Price:** EUR 0,40; **Circ:** 54,708
Advertising Manager: Alexander Sempf
Profile: BILD Dresden is a regional newspaper. With its direct and unmistakable style, they reached a daily audience, composed of all social classes. Through high relevance, commitment and unparalleled proximity to the reader understands BILD get news, background information and entertainment from all areas of political and social life on a daily basis to the point. The successful concept of the image consists of five principles: * Information BILD moves people, BILD provides for reactions and discussions. Concise and provocative. * Personalization BILD combines concepts and minds. BILD works with characters - and itself has a distinctive character. * Entertainment Sometimes funny, sometimes serious - always original! * Visualization BILD is visually unique BILD news makes visible. BILD shows exclusive photos, which no other medium. * Orientation BILD informs its readers quickly and clearly. IMAGE is the medium for the essentials. Facebook: http://www.facebook.com/bild Twitter: http://twitter.com/BILD_Berlin This Outlet offers RSS (Really Simple Syndication).
Language(s): German
Mechanical Data: Type Area: 528 x 376 mm, No. of Columns (Display): 8, Col Widths (Display): 45 mm
Copy instructions: *Copy Date:* 1 day prior to publication
REGIONAL DAILY & SUNDAY NEWSPAPERS: Regional Daily Newspapers

BILD DÜSSELDORF 722875G67B-2780

Editorial: Axel-Springer-Str. 65, 10969 BERLIN
Tel: 30 25910
Web site: http://www.bild.de
Freq: 312 issues yearly; **Cover Price:** EUR 0,60; **Circ:** 74,388
Advertising Manager: Alexander Sempf
Profile: BILD Düsseldorf is a regional newspaper. With its direct and unmistakable style, they reached a daily audience, composed of all social classes. Through high relevance, commitment and unparalleled proximity to the reader understands BILD get news, background information and entertainment from all areas of political and social life on a daily basis to the point. The successful concept of the image consists of five principles: * Information BILD moves people, BILD provides for reactions and discussions. Concise and provocative. * Personalization BILD combines concepts and minds. BILD works with characters - and itself has a distinctive character. * Entertainment Sometimes funny, sometimes serious - always original! * Visualization BILD is visually unique BILD news makes visible. BILD shows exclusive photos, which no other medium. * Orientation BILD informs its readers quickly and clearly. IMAGE is the medium for the essentials. Facebook: http://www.facebook.com/bild Twitter: http://twitter.com/BILD_Berlin This Outlet offers RSS (Really Simple Syndication).
Language(s): German
Mechanical Data: Type Area: 528 x 376 mm, No. of Columns (Display): 8, Col Widths (Display): 45 mm
Copy instructions: *Copy Date:* 1 day prior to publication
REGIONAL DAILY & SUNDAY NEWSPAPERS: Regional Daily Newspapers

BILD HALLE 722879G67B-2820

Editorial: Axel-Springer-Str. 65, 10969 BERLIN
Tel: 30 25910
Web site: http://www.bild.de
Freq: 312 issues yearly; **Cover Price:** EUR 0,40; **Circ:** 69,551
Advertising Manager: Alexander Sempf
Profile: BILD Halle is a regional newspaper. With its direct and unmistakable style, they reached a daily audience, composed of all social classes. Through high relevance, commitment and unparalleled proximity to the reader understands BILD get news, background information and entertainment from all areas of political and social life on a daily basis to the point. The successful concept of the image consists of five principles: * Information BILD moves people, BILD provides for reactions and discussions. Concise and provocative. * Personalization BILD combines concepts and minds. BILD works with characters - and itself has a distinctive character. * Entertainment Sometimes funny, sometimes serious - always original! * Visualization BILD is visually unique BILD news makes visible. BILD shows exclusive photos, which no other medium. * Orientation BILD informs its readers quickly and clearly. BILD is the medium for the essentials. Facebook: http://www.facebook.com/bild Twitter: http://twitter.com/BILD_Berlin This Outlet offers RSS (Really Simple Syndication).
Language(s): German
Mechanical Data: Type Area: 528 x 376 mm, No. of Columns (Display): 8, Col Widths (Display): 45 mm
Copy instructions: *Copy Date:* 1 day prior to publication
REGIONAL DAILY & SUNDAY NEWSPAPERS: Regional Daily Newspapers

BILD HAMBURG 722880G67B-2840

Editorial: Axel-Springer-Str. 65, 10969 BERLIN
Tel: 30 25910
Web site: http://www.bild.de
Freq: 312 issues yearly; **Cover Price:** EUR 0,50; **Circ:** 223,369
Advertising Manager: Alexander Sempf
Profile: BILD Hamburg is a regional newspaper. With its direct and unmistakable style, they reached a daily audience, composed of all social classes. Through high relevance, commitment and unparalleled proximity to the reader understands BILD get news, background information and entertainment from all areas of political and social life on a daily basis to the point. The successful concept of the image consists of five principles: * Information BILD moves people, BILD provides for reactions and discussions. Concise and provocative. * Personalization BILD combines concepts and minds. BILD works with characters - and itself has a distinctive character. * Entertainment Sometimes funny, sometimes serious - always original! * Visualization BILD is visually unique BILD news makes visible. BILD shows exclusive photos, which no other medium. * Orientation BILD informs its readers quickly and clearly. BILD is the medium for the essentials. Facebook: http://www.facebook.com/bild Twitter: http://twitter.com/BILD_Berlin This Outlet offers RSS (Really Simple Syndication).
Language(s): German
Mechanical Data: Type Area: 528 x 376 mm, No. of Columns (Display): 8, Col Widths (Display): 45 mm
Copy instructions: *Copy Date:* 1 day prior to publication
REGIONAL DAILY & SUNDAY NEWSPAPERS: Regional Daily Newspapers

BILD HANNOVER 722881G67B-2860

Editorial: Axel-Springer-Str. 65, 10969 BERLIN
Tel: 30 25910
Web site: http://www.bild.de
Freq: 312 issues yearly; **Cover Price:** EUR 0,50; **Circ:** 86,714
Advertising Manager: Alexander Sempf
Profile: BILD Hannover is a regional newspaper. With its direct and unmistakable style, they reached a daily audience, composed of all social classes. Through high relevance, commitment and unparalleled proximity to the reader understands BILD get news, background information and entertainment from all areas of political and social life on a daily basis to the point. The successful concept of the image consists of five principles: * Information BILD moves people, BILD provides for reactions and discussions. Concise and provocative. * Personalization BILD combines concepts and minds. BILD works with characters - and itself has a distinctive character. * Entertainment Sometimes funny, sometimes serious - always original! * Visualization BILD is visually unique BILD news makes visible. BILD shows exclusive photos, which no other medium. * Orientation BILD informs its readers quickly and clearly. BILD is the medium for the essentials. Facebook: http://www.facebook.com/bild Twitter: http://twitter.com/BILD_Berlin This Outlet offers RSS (Really Simple Syndication).
Language(s): German
Mechanical Data: Type Area: 528 x 376 mm, No. of Columns (Display): 8, Col Widths (Display): 45 mm
Copy instructions: *Copy Date:* 1 day prior to publication
REGIONAL DAILY & SUNDAY NEWSPAPERS: Regional Daily Newspapers

BILD KÖLN 722883G67B-2880

Editorial: Axel-Springer-Str. 65, 10969 BERLIN
Tel: 30 25910
Web site: http://www.bild.de
Freq: 312 issues yearly; **Cover Price:** EUR 0,50; **Circ:** 62,563
Advertising Manager: Alexander Sempf
Profile: BILD Köln is a regional newspaper. With its direct and unmistakable style, they reached a daily audience, composed of all social classes. Through

high relevance, commitment and unparalleled proximity to the reader understands BILD get news, background information and entertainment from all areas of political and social life on a daily basis to the point. The successful concept of the image consists of five principles: * Information BILD moves people, BILD provides for reactions and discussions. Concise and provocative. * Personalization BILD combines concepts and minds. BILD works with characters - and itself has a distinctive character. * Entertainment Sometimes funny, sometimes serious - always original! * Visualization BILD is visually unique BILD news makes visible. BILD shows exclusive photos, which no other medium. * Orientation BILD informs its readers quickly and clearly. BILD is the medium for the essentials. Facebook: http://www.facebook.com/ bild Twitter: http://twitter.com/BILD_Berlin This Outlet offers RSS (Really Simple Syndication).
Language(s): German
Mechanical Data: Type Area: 528 x 376 mm, No. of Columns (Display): 8, Col Widths (Display): 45 mm
Copy instructions: *Copy Date:* 1 day prior to publication
REGIONAL DAILY & SUNDAY NEWSPAPERS: Regional Daily Newspapers

BILD LEIPZIG 722884G67B-2900
Editorial: Axel-Springer-Str. 65, 10969 BERLIN
Tel: 30 25910
Web site: http://www.bild.de
Freq: 312 issues yearly; **Cover Price:** EUR 0,40;
Circ: 66,778
Advertising Manager: Alexander Sempf
Profile: BILD Leipzig is a regional newspaper. With its direct and unmistakable style, they reached a daily audience, composed of all social classes. Through high relevance, commitment and unparalleled proximity to the reader understands BILD get news, background information and entertainment from all areas of political and social life on a daily basis to the point. The successful concept of the image consists of five principles: * Information BILD moves people, BILD provides for reactions and discussions. Concise and provocative. * Personalization BILD combines concepts and minds. BILD works with characters - and itself has a distinctive character. * Entertainment Sometimes funny, sometimes serious - always original! * Visualization BILD is visually unique BILD news makes visible. BILD shows exclusive photos, which no other medium. * Orientation BILD informs its readers quickly and clearly. BILD is the medium for the essentials. Facebook: http://www.facebook.com/ bild Twitter: http://twitter.com/BILD_Berlin This Outlet offers RSS (Really Simple Syndication).
Language(s): German
Mechanical Data: Type Area: 528 x 376 mm, No. of Columns (Display): 8, Col Widths (Display): 45 mm
Copy instructions: *Copy Date:* 1 day prior to publication
REGIONAL DAILY & SUNDAY NEWSPAPERS: Regional Daily Newspapers

BILD MAGDEBURG 722885G67B-2920
Editorial: Axel-Springer-Str. 65, 10969 BERLIN
Tel: 30 25910
Web site: http://www.bild.de
Freq: 312 issues yearly; **Cover Price:** EUR 0,40;
Circ: 43,278
Advertising Manager: Alexander Sempf
Profile: BILD Magdeburg is a regional newspaper. With its direct and unmistakable style, they reached a daily audience, composed of all social classes. Through high relevance, commitment and unparalleled proximity to the reader understands BILD get news, background information and entertainment from all areas of political and social life on a daily basis to the point. The successful concept of the image consists of five principles: * Information BILD moves people, BILD provides for reactions and discussions. Concise and provocative. * Personalization BILD combines concepts and minds. BILD works with characters - and itself has a distinctive character. * Entertainment Sometimes funny, sometimes serious - always original! * Visualization BILD is visually unique BILD news makes visible. BILD shows exclusive photos, which no other medium. * Orientation BILD informs its readers quickly and clearly. BILD is the medium for the essentials. Facebook: http://www.facebook.com/ bild Twitter: http://twitter.com/BILD_Berlin This Outlet offers RSS (Really Simple Syndication).
Language(s): German
Mechanical Data: Type Area: 528 x 376 mm, No. of Columns (Display): 8, Col Widths (Display): 45 mm
Copy instructions: *Copy Date:* 1 day prior to publication
REGIONAL DAILY & SUNDAY NEWSPAPERS: Regional Daily Newspapers

BILD MAINZ-WIESBADEN
1638475G67B-16723
Editorial: Axel-Springer-Str. 65, 10969 BERLIN
Tel: 30 25910
Web site: http://www.bild.de
Freq: 312 issues yearly; **Cover Price:** EUR 0,60;
Circ: 40,992
Advertising Manager: Peter Ludwig Müller
Profile: BILD Mainz-Wiesbaden is a regional newspaper. With its direct and unmistakable style, they reached a daily audience, composed of all social classes. Through high relevance, commitment and unparalleled proximity to the reader understands BILD get news, background information and entertainment from all areas of political and social life on a daily basis to the point. The successful concept of the image consists of five principles: * Information BILD moves people, BILD provides for reactions and discussions. Concise and provocative. * Personalization BILD combines concepts and minds. BILD works with characters - and itself has a distinctive character. * Entertainment Sometimes funny, sometimes serious - always original! * Visualization BILD is visually unique BILD news makes visible. BILD shows exclusive photos, which no other medium. * Orientation BILD informs its readers quickly and clearly. BILD is the medium for the essentials. Facebook: http://www.facebook.com/ bild Twitter: http://twitter.com/BILD_Berlin This Outlet offers RSS (Really Simple Syndication).
Language(s): German
Mechanical Data: Type Area: 528 x 376 mm, No. of Columns (Display): 8, Col Widths (Display): 45 mm
Copy instructions: *Copy Date:* 1 day prior to publication
REGIONAL DAILY & SUNDAY NEWSPAPERS: Regional Daily Newspapers

BILD MECKLENBURG-VORPOMMERN 722886G67B-2940
Editorial: Axel-Springer-Str. 65, 10969 BERLIN
Tel: 30 25910
Web site: http://www.bild.de
Freq: 312 issues yearly; **Cover Price:** EUR 0,40;
Circ: 82,753
Advertising Manager: Alexander Sempf
Profile: BILD Mecklenburg-Vorpommern is a regional newspaper. With its direct and unmistakable style, they reached a daily audience, composed of all social classes. Through high relevance, commitment and unparalleled proximity to the reader understands BILD get news, background information and entertainment from all areas of political and social life on a daily basis to the point. The successful concept of the image consists of five principles: * Information BILD moves people, BILD provides for reactions and discussions. Concise and provocative. * Personalization BILD combines concepts and minds. BILD works with characters - and itself has a distinctive character. * Entertainment Sometimes funny, sometimes serious - always original! * Visualization BILD is visually unique BILD news makes visible. BILD shows exclusive photos, which no other medium. * Orientation BILD informs its readers quickly and clearly. BILD is the medium for the essentials. Facebook: http://www.facebook.com/ bild Twitter: http://twitter.com/BILD_Berlin This Outlet offers RSS (Really Simple Syndication).
Language(s): German
Mechanical Data: Type Area: 528 x 376 mm, No. of Columns (Display): 8, Col Widths (Display): 45 mm
Copy instructions: *Copy Date:* 1 day prior to publication
REGIONAL DAILY & SUNDAY NEWSPAPERS: Regional Daily Newspapers

BILD MÜNCHEN 722887G67B-2960
Editorial: Axel-Springer-Str. 65, 10969 BERLIN
Tel: 30 25910
Web site: http://www.bild.de
Freq: 312 issues yearly; **Cover Price:** EUR 0,50;
Circ: 107,684
Advertising Manager: Alexander Sempf
Profile: BILD München is a regional newspaper. With its direct and unmistakable style, they reached a daily audience, composed of all social classes. Through high relevance, commitment and unparalleled proximity to the reader understands BILD get news, background information and entertainment from all areas of political and social life on a daily basis to the point. The successful concept of the image consists of five principles: * Information BILD moves people, BILD provides for reactions and discussions. Concise and provocative. * Personalization BILD combines concepts and minds. BILD works with characters - and itself has a distinctive character. * Entertainment Sometimes funny, sometimes serious - always original! * Visualization BILD is visually unique BILD news makes visible. BILD shows exclusive photos, which no other medium. * Orientation BILD informs its readers quickly and clearly. BILD is the medium for the essentials. Facebook: http://www.facebook.com/ bild Twitter: http://twitter.com/BILD_Berlin This Outlet offers RSS (Really Simple Syndication).
Language(s): German
Mechanical Data: Type Area: 528 x 376 mm, No. of Columns (Display): 8, Col Widths (Display): 45 mm
Copy instructions: *Copy Date:* 1 day prior to publication
REGIONAL DAILY & SUNDAY NEWSPAPERS: Regional Daily Newspapers

BILD NÜRNBERG 722888G67B-2980
Editorial: Axel-Springer-Str. 65, 10969 BERLIN
Tel: 30 25910
Web site: http://www.bild.de
Freq: 312 issues yearly; **Cover Price:** EUR 0,50;
Circ: 64,556
Advertising Manager: Alexander Sempf
Profile: BILD Nürnberg is a regional newspaper. With its direct and unmistakable style, they reached a daily audience, composed of all social classes. Through high relevance, commitment and unparalleled proximity to the reader understands BILD get news, background information and entertainment from all areas of political and social life on a daily basis to the point. The successful concept of the image consists of five principles: * Information BILD moves people, BILD provides for reactions and discussions. Concise and provocative. * Personalization BILD combines concepts and minds. BILD works with characters - and itself has a distinctive character. * Entertainment Sometimes funny, sometimes serious - always original! * Visualization BILD is visually unique BILD news makes visible. BILD shows exclusive photos, which no other medium. * Orientation BILD informs its readers quickly and clearly. BILD is the medium for the essentials. Facebook: http://www.facebook.com/ bild Twitter: http://twitter.com/BILD_Berlin This Outlet offers RSS (Really Simple Syndication).
Language(s): German
Mechanical Data: Type Area: 528 x 376 mm, No. of Columns (Display): 8, Col Widths (Display): 45 mm
Copy instructions: *Copy Date:* 1 day prior to publication
REGIONAL DAILY & SUNDAY NEWSPAPERS: Regional Daily Newspapers

BILD RHEIN-NECKAR
722889G67B-3000
Editorial: Axel-Springer-Str. 65, 10969 BERLIN
Tel: 30 25910
Web site: http://www.bild.de
Freq: 312 issues yearly; **Cover Price:** EUR 0,60;
Circ: 63,071
Advertising Manager: Peter Ludwig Müller
Profile: BILD Rhein-Neckar is a regional newspaper. With its direct and unmistakable style, they reached a daily audience, composed of all social classes. Through high relevance, commitment and unparalleled proximity to the reader understands BILD get news, background information and entertainment from all areas of political and social life on a daily basis to the point. The successful concept of the image consists of five principles: * Information BILD moves people, BILD provides for reactions and discussions. Concise and provocative. * Personalization BILD combines concepts and minds. BILD works with characters - and itself has a distinctive character. * Entertainment Sometimes funny, sometimes serious - always original! * Visualization BILD is visually unique BILD news makes visible. BILD shows exclusive photos, which no other medium. * Orientation BILD informs its readers quickly and clearly. BILD is the medium for the essentials. Facebook: http://www.facebook.com/ bild Twitter: http://twitter.com/BILD_Berlin This Outlet offers RSS (Really Simple Syndication).
Language(s): German
Mechanical Data: Type Area: 528 x 376 mm, No. of Columns (Display): 8, Col Widths (Display): 45 mm
Copy instructions: *Copy Date:* 1 day prior to publication
REGIONAL DAILY & SUNDAY NEWSPAPERS: Regional Daily Newspapers

BILD SAARLAND 1696431G67B-16751
Editorial: Axel-Springer-Str. 65, 10969 BERLIN
Tel: 30 25910
Web site: http://www.bild.de
Freq: 312 issues yearly; **Cover Price:** EUR 0,50;
Circ: 58,384
Advertising Manager: Alexander Sempf
Profile: BILD Saarland is a regional newspaper. With its direct and unmistakable style, they reached a daily audience, composed of all social classes. Through high relevance, commitment and unparalleled proximity to the reader understands BILD get news, background information and entertainment from all areas of political and social life on a daily basis to the point. The successful concept of the image consists of five principles: * Information BILD moves people, BILD provides for reactions and discussions. Concise and provocative. * Personalization BILD combines concepts and minds. BILD works with characters - and itself has a distinctive character. * Entertainment Sometimes funny, sometimes serious - always original! * Visualization BILD is visually unique BILD news makes visible. BILD shows exclusive photos, which no other medium. * Orientation BILD informs its readers quickly and clearly. BILD is the medium for the essentials. Facebook: http://www.facebook.com/ bild Twitter: http://twitter.com/BILD_Berlin This Outlet offers RSS (Really Simple Syndication).
Language(s): German
Mechanical Data: Type Area: 528 x 376 mm, No. of Columns (Display): 8, Col Widths (Display): 45 mm
Copy instructions: *Copy Date:* 1 day prior to publication
REGIONAL DAILY & SUNDAY NEWSPAPERS: Regional Daily Newspapers

BILD STUTTGART 722890G67B-3020
Editorial: Axel-Springer-Str. 65, 10969 BERLIN
Tel: 30 25910
Web site: http://www.bild.de
Freq: 312 issues yearly; **Cover Price:** EUR 0,50;
Circ: 94,746
Advertising Manager: Alexander Sempf
Profile: BILD Stuttgart is a regional newspaper. With its direct and unmistakable style, they reached a daily audience, composed of all social classes. Through high relevance, commitment and unparalleled proximity to the reader understands BILD get news, background information and entertainment from all areas of political and social life on a daily basis to the point. The successful concept of the image consists of five principles: * Information BILD moves people, BILD provides for reactions and discussions. Concise and provocative. * Personalization BILD combines concepts and minds. BILD works with characters - and itself has a distinctive character. * Entertainment Sometimes funny, sometimes serious - always original! * Visualization BILD is visually unique BILD news makes visible. BILD shows exclusive photos, which no other medium. * Orientation BILD informs its readers quickly and clearly. BILD is the medium for the essentials. Facebook: http://www.facebook.com/ bild Twitter: http://twitter.com/BILD_Berlin This Outlet offers RSS (Really Simple Syndication).
Language(s): German
Mechanical Data: Type Area: 528 x 376 mm, No. of Columns (Display): 8, Col Widths (Display): 45 mm
Copy instructions: *Copy Date:* 1 day prior to publication
REGIONAL DAILY & SUNDAY NEWSPAPERS: Regional Daily Newspapers

BILD THÜRINGEN 722891G67B-3040
Editorial: Axel-Springer-Str. 65, 10969 BERLIN
Tel: 30 25910
Web site: http://www.bild.de
Freq: 312 issues yearly; **Cover Price:** EUR 0,40;
Circ: 70,852
Advertising Manager: Alexander Sempf
Profile: BILD Thüringen is a regional newspaper. With its direct and unmistakable style, they reached a daily audience, composed of all social classes. Through high relevance, commitment and unparalleled proximity to the reader understands BILD get news, background information and entertainment from all areas of political and social life on a daily basis to the point. The successful concept of the image consists of five principles: * Information BILD moves people, BILD provides for reactions and discussions. Concise and provocative. * Personalization BILD combines concepts and minds. BILD works with characters - and itself has a distinctive character. * Entertainment Sometimes funny, sometimes serious - always original! * Visualization BILD is visually unique BILD news makes visible. BILD shows exclusive photos, which no other medium. * Orientation BILD informs its readers quickly and clearly. BILD is the medium for the essentials. Facebook: http://www.facebook.com/ bild Twitter: http://twitter.com/BILD_Berlin This Outlet offers RSS (Really Simple Syndication).
Language(s): German
Mechanical Data: Type Area: 528 x 376 mm, No. of Columns (Display): 8, Col Widths (Display): 45 mm
Copy instructions: *Copy Date:* 1 day prior to publication
REGIONAL DAILY & SUNDAY NEWSPAPERS: Regional Daily Newspapers

BILD + FUNK 722892G76C-40
Editorial: Münchener Str. 101, 85737 ISMANING
Tel: 89 272700 **Fax:** 89 272707490
Email: kontakt@gongverlag.de **Web site:** http://www.gong-verlag.de
Freq: Weekly; **Annual Sub.:** EUR 78,00; **Circ:** 644,574
Editor: Carsten Pfefferkorn
Profile: Journal with the highest utility by a large part of service: From Money / right on health, science / nature, travel, community / family, car, sports, art to cinema / culture, the reader current and critical issues value and easily packed consumable. Complementing the jacket part by a big radio and puzzle-magazine.
Language(s): German
ADVERTISING RATES:
Full Page Mono .... EUR 13920
Full Page Colour .... EUR 17300
Mechanical Data: Type Area: 260 x 196 mm, No. of Columns (Display): 4, Col Widths (Display): 46 mm
Copy instructions: *Copy Date:* 25 days prior to publication
CONSUMER: MUSIC & PERFORMING ARTS: TV & Radio

BILD.DE 1623473G65A-271
Editorial: Axel-Springer-Str. 65, 10888 BERLIN
Tel: 30 25910
Email: info@bild.de **Web site:** http://www.bild.de
Freq: Daily; **Cover Price:** Paid; **Circ:** 167,139,583 Unique Users
Editor: Manfred Hart; **News Editor:** Jörg Hansen
Profile: Bild.de is the leading print-based general-interest portal and is available for passionate Bild-journalism on the net. The most important and latest news and entertainment portal offers exciting content around the Clock: top news, local content in the regional editions, sports events, lifestyle reports, news from the world of celebrities, modern video portal with daily videos and video archive Facebook: http://www.facebook.com/bild Twitter: http:// twitter.com/BILD This Outlet offers RSS (Really Simple Syndication).
Language(s): German
NATIONAL DAILY & SUNDAY NEWSPAPERS: National Daily Newspapers

DER BILDERMARKT 722877G2A-460
Editorial: Sächsische Str. 63, 10707 BERLIN
Tel: 30 3249917 **Fax:** 30 3247001
Email: info@bvpa.org **Web site:** http://www.bvpa.org
Freq: Annual; Free to qualifying individuals
Annual Sub.: EUR 33,00; **Circ:** 5,000
Profile: Each year, up to date: The standard work for those who have a professional to do with photography. A comprehensive overview of the German market pictures. Current and fundamental information on the business of photos and use rights. BVPA all member agencies, focusing on topics, index and address. Extensive address register with important addresses in the industry. Facebook: http://www.facebook.com/bvpaorg.
Language(s): German
ADVERTISING RATES:
Full Page Mono .... EUR 680
Full Page Colour .... EUR 1190
Mechanical Data: Type Area: 190 x 125 mm
Copy instructions: *Copy Date:* 61 days prior to publication

BILDHONORARE 722882G2A-480
Editorial: Sächsische Str. 63, 10707 BERLIN
Tel: 30 3249917 **Fax:** 30 3247001
Email: info@bvpa.org **Web site:** http://www.foto-marketing.org
Freq: Annual; **Annual Sub.:** EUR 33,00; **Circ:** 5,000
Profile: The overview of the market remuneration for use of image rights, compiled by the MFM. A must for

anyone who wants to sell in Germany photos. Updated annually, summarizes all the possible uses of photos clearly according to usage, image size and circulation.
Language(s): German
ADVERTISING RATES:
Full Page Mono .... EUR 680
Full Page Colour .... EUR 1190
Mechanical Data: Type Area: 190 x 125 mm
Copy instructions: *Copy Date:* 61 days prior to publication

BILDSCHIRMSCHONER.DE
1661028G78D-917
Editorial: Raiffeisenstr. 10, 63225 LANGEN
Tel: 6103 59730 **Fax:** 6103 597318
Email: office@andersundseim.de **Web site:** http://www.bildschirmschoner.de
Freq: Weekly; **Cover Price:** Paid; **Circ:** 195,557 Unique Users
Editor: Markus Seim
Language(s): German
CONSUMER: CONSUMER ELECTRONICS: Games

BILDWOCHE
722923G76C-60
Editorial: Axel-Springer-Platz 1, 20355 HAMBURG
Tel: 40 34700 **Fax:** 40 34722601
Email: bildwoche-service@axelspringer.de **Web site:** http://www.axelspringer.de
Freq: Weekly; **Annual Sub.:** EUR 70,20; **Circ:** 152,462
Editor: Jan von Frenckell; **Advertising Manager:** Arne Bergmann
Profile: Magazine containing TV listings. Also includes lifestyle articles and general interest features.
Language(s): German
ADVERTISING RATES:
Full Page Mono .... EUR 7400
Full Page Colour .... EUR 7400
Mechanical Data: Type Area: 270 x 206 mm, No. of Columns (Display): 4, Col Widths (Display): 50 mm
Copy instructions: *Copy Date:* 17 days prior to publication
CONSUMER: MUSIC & PERFORMING ARTS: TV & Radio

BILFINGER BERGER MAGAZIN
753705G4E-2830
Editorial: Carl-Reiß-Platz 1, 68165 MANNHEIM
Tel: 621 4590 **Fax:** 621 4592366
Email: dsim@bilfinger.de **Web site:** http://www.magazin.bilfinger.de
Freq: Half-yearly; **Cover Price:** Free; **Circ:** 25,000
Editor: Daniela Simpson
Profile: Magazine for customers of the Bilfinger Berger company.
Language(s): German

BILLE WOCHENBLATT
722929G72-2124
Editorial: Curslacker Neuer Deich 50, 21029 HAMBURG **Tel:** 40 725660 **Fax:** 40 72566249
Web site: http://www.bergedorfer-zeitung.de
Freq: Weekly; **Cover Price:** Free; **Circ:** 82,125
Editor: M. Stachow; **Advertising Manager:** Michael Stehr
Profile: Advertising journal (house-to-house) concentrating on local stories.
Language(s): German
ADVERTISING RATES:
Full Page Mono .... EUR 4232
Full Page Colour .... EUR 4352
Mechanical Data: Type Area: 430 x 282 mm, No. of Columns (Display): 6, Col Widths (Display): 45 mm
Copy instructions: *Copy Date:* 2 days prior to publication
LOCAL NEWSPAPERS

BILLERBECKER ANZEIGER
722928G67B-3060
Editorial: Rosenstr. 2, 48653 COESFELD
Tel: 2541 921151 **Fax:** 2541 921155
Email: redaktion@azonline.de **Web site:** http://www.azonline.de
Freq: 312 issues yearly; **Circ:** 17,950
Advertising Manager: Ralf Bohlje
Profile: Daily newspaper with regional news and a local sports section.
Language(s): German
ADVERTISING RATES:
SCC .... EUR 38,50
Mechanical Data: Type Area: 488 x 324 mm, No. of Columns (Display): 7, Col Widths (Display): 44 mm
Copy instructions: *Copy Date:* 1 day prior to publication
Supplement(s): prisma
REGIONAL DAILY & SUNDAY NEWSPAPERS: Regional Daily Newspapers

BINDEREPORT
722937G60A-35
Editorial: Brühl 21, 04109 LEIPZIG **Tel:** 341 2251472
Fax: 341 2251871
Email: matthias.will@schluetersche.de **Web site:** http://www.bindereport.de
Freq: Monthly; **Annual Sub.:** EUR 101,00; **Circ:** 4,779
Editor: Matthias Will; **Advertising Manager:** Susann Buglass
Profile: bindereport is the only technical magazine for bookbinding and finishing in Germany and Switzerland. bindereport regularly informs about technical innovations in the fields of machines and devices for bookbinders, machines for digital printing and duplicating, machines for print finishing, management of craftsmen's trade and industry, professional improvement, new processes and technique, questions of law, news from special organizations, latest reports on economy, politics and supplying industry.
Language(s): German
ADVERTISING RATES:
Full Page Mono .... EUR 2271
Full Page Colour .... EUR 3510
Mechanical Data: Type Area: 272 x 188 mm, No. of Columns (Display): 4, Col Widths (Display): 44 mm
Copy instructions: *Copy Date:* 25 days prior to publication
BUSINESS: PUBLISHING: Publishing & Book Trade

BINGER WOCHENBLATT
722940G72-2132
Editorial: Hasengasse 1, 55411 BINGEN
Tel: 6721 990684 **Fax:** 6721 2739
Email: redaktion@binger-wochenblatt.de **Web site:** http://www.binger-wochenblatt.de
Freq: Weekly; **Cover Price:** Free; **Circ:** 37,351
Editor: Rüdiger Benda; **Advertising Manager:** Rainer Baumann
Profile: Advertising journal (house-to-house) concentrating on local stories.
Language(s): German
ADVERTISING RATES:
Full Page Mono .... EUR 3461
Full Page Colour .... EUR 4704
Mechanical Data: Type Area: 480 x 325 mm, No. of Columns (Display): 7, Col Widths (Display): 45 mm
Copy instructions: *Copy Date:* 2 days prior to publication
LOCAL NEWSPAPERS

BINNENSCHIFFFAHRT
722947G45C-20
Editorial: Georgsplatz 1, 20099 HAMBURG
Tel: 8138 6976360 **Fax:** 8138 6976359
Email: f_oehlerking@hansa-online.de **Web site:** http://www.zeitschrift-binnenschifffahrt.de
Freq: Monthly; **Annual Sub.:** EUR 81,60; **Circ:** 3,464
Editor: Friedrich Oehlerking; **Advertising Manager:** Christian Döpp
Profile: The magazine Binnenschifffahrt for ship technology, waterways, ports and logistics is one of the leading magazines for this complex. It informs the decision-makers in the industry. Shipbuilding and marine engineering, shipping and logistics, legal and insurance, by industry experts said, markets, trends and potentials, sound analyzing industry news and important personal data will be presented compactly.
Language(s): German
ADVERTISING RATES:
Full Page Mono .... EUR 1500
Full Page Colour .... EUR 2262
Mechanical Data: Type Area: 266 x 180 mm, No. of Columns (Display): 3, Col Widths (Display): 57 mm
Copy instructions: *Copy Date:* 14 days prior to publication
Official Journal of: Organ d. Binnenschiffahrts-Berufsgenossenschaft
BUSINESS: MARINE & SHIPPING: Maritime Freight

BIO
722951G74G-17
Editorial: Monatshauser Str. 8, 82327 TUTZING
Tel: 8158 8022 **Fax:** 8158 7142
Email: biomagazin@aol.com **Web site:** http://www.biomagazin.de
Freq: 6 issues yearly; **Annual Sub.:** EUR 24,90; **Circ:** 120,000
Editor: Monica Ritter; **Advertising Manager:** Edith von Hafenbrädl
Profile: European magazine concerned with health in body, mind and soul, along with general well-being.
Language(s): German
Readership: Aimed at people interested in natural healing, nutrition, medicine, the environment and spirituality.
ADVERTISING RATES:
Full Page Mono .... EUR 2450
Full Page Colour .... EUR 3650
Mechanical Data: Type Area: 250 x 184 mm, No. of Columns (Display): 3, Col Widths (Display): 58 mm
Copy instructions: *Copy Date:* 30 days prior to publication
CONSUMER: WOMEN'S INTEREST CONSUMER MAGAZINES: Slimming & Health

BIO LIFE
2086404G57-2965
Editorial: Nordfelder Reihe 20, 30159 HANNOVER
Tel: 511 2625399 **Fax:** 511 2625399
Email: presse@biolife-magazin.de **Web site:** http://www.biolife-magazin.de
Freq: Quarterly; **Cover Price:** EUR 4,95; **Circ:** 37,500
Profile: Bio Life is the biological-ecological lifestyle magazine for a healthy and sustainable living. It deals not only with basic topics such as nutrition and health. Even highly topical content as the future of nuclear energy in the light of Fukushima disaster are discussed. This magazine focuses primarily on matters relevant to everyday areas that will delight newcomers to the so-called LOHAS (Lifestyle of Health and Sustainability). It provides information on organically grown products, services and innovations. The aim is to inform consumers comprehensive and well researched. Target audience: consumers age 30 and older, with an environmentally-conscious organic lifestyle. Facebook: http://www.facebook.com/BioLifeMagazin This Outlet offers RSS (Really Simple Syndication).
Language(s): German
ADVERTISING RATES:
Full Page Mono .... EUR 2688
Full Page Colour .... EUR 2688
Mechanical Data: Type Area: 280 x 193 mm

BIO MATERIALIEN
722967G56A-1600
Editorial: Paul-Gerhardt-Allee 46, 81245 MÜNCHEN
Tel: 89 31890557 **Fax:** 89 31890553
Email: angelika.schaller@vnmonline.de **Web site:** http://www.biomaterialien.com
Freq: Quarterly; **Annual Sub.:** EUR 358,00; **Circ:** 1,280
Editor: Angelika Schaller; **Advertising Manager:** Elke Zimmermann
Profile: Magazine about bio materials for the human body.
Language(s): English; German
ADVERTISING RATES:
Full Page Mono .... EUR 869
Full Page Colour .... EUR 1521
Mechanical Data: Type Area: 260 x 175 mm, No. of Columns (Display): 2, Col Widths (Display): 85 mm
Official Journal of: Organ d. Dt. Ges. f. Biomaterialien e.V.

BIOFORUM
1613752G56A-11167
Editorial: Rößlerstr. 90, 64293 DARMSTADT
Tel: 6151 8090211 **Fax:** 6151 8090179
Email: jutta.jessen@wiley.com **Web site:** http://www.bioforum.de
Freq: Half-yearly; **Cover Price:** EUR 14,50; **Circ:** 29,494
Editor: Jutta Jessen; **Advertising Manager:** Katja Habermüller
Profile: Bioforum reported for over 30 years on current trends and technologies the F & E in biotechnology and pharmaceuticals. Genomics, proteomics and cell biology are also part of the constant themes of Bioforum as the latest developments in analytics, microscopy, bioinformatics and bioprocessing. Latest news, interviews and selected business issues in the industries round out the spectrum. Bioforum published twice a year and each issue reaches 30,000 persons receiver in industrial research and development and in science.
Language(s): German
ADVERTISING RATES:
Full Page Mono .... EUR 4820
Full Page Colour .... EUR 6300
Mechanical Data: Type Area: 260 x 185 mm, No. of Columns (Display): 4, Col Widths (Display): 43 mm
Copy instructions: *Copy Date:* 14 days prior to publication
BUSINESS: HEALTH & MEDICAL

BIOGRAPH
722954G80-1480
Editorial: Citadellstr. 14, 40213 DÜSSELDORF
Tel: 211 8668212 **Fax:** 211 8668222
Email: info@biograph-online.de **Web site:** http://www.biograph-online.de
Freq: Monthly; **Cover Price:** Free; **Circ:** 29,915
Editor: Peter Liese
Profile: Magazine for city and region, concentrating on gastronomy, music, arts and events.
Language(s): German
ADVERTISING RATES:
Full Page Mono .... EUR 1700
Full Page Colour .... EUR 3300
Mechanical Data: Type Area: 265 x 190 mm, No. of Columns (Display): 4, Col Widths (Display): 44 mm
CONSUMER: RURAL & REGIONAL INTEREST

BIOLAND
722957G21A-820
Editorial: Kaiserstr. 18, 55116 MAINZ
Tel: 6131 1408693 **Fax:** 6131 1408697
Email: redaktion@bioland.de **Web site:** http://www.bioland-verlag.de
Freq: Monthly; Free to qualifying individuals
Annual Sub.: EUR 46,00; **Circ:** 8,000
Editor: Annegret Grafen-Engert
Profile: The bioland trade magazine is the leading trade journal for organic farming. Besides a political focus, the bioland magazine brings solid technical information from the ecological livestock, from biological farming and crop production, from business administration and marketing.
Language(s): German
Readership: Read by farmers, processors, advisors and researchers.
ADVERTISING RATES:
Full Page Mono .... EUR 1100
Full Page Colour .... EUR 2060
Mechanical Data: Type Area: 240 x 180 mm, No. of Columns (Display): 4, Col Widths (Display): 42 mm
Copy instructions: *Copy Date:* 28 days prior to publication
Official Journal of: Organ d. Bioland-Verb. f. organ.-biolog. Landbau e.V.
BUSINESS: AGRICULTURE & FARMING

BIOLOGICAL CHEMISTRY
722958G64F-280
Editorial: Genthiner Str. 13, 10785 BERLIN
Tel: 30 26005176 **Fax:** 30 26005298
Email: biol.chem.editorial@degruyter.com **Web site:** http://www.degruyter.de/journals/bc
Freq: Monthly; **Annual Sub.:** EUR 1364,00; **Circ:** 700
Editor: Helmut Sies
Profile: Journal about all aspects of biological chemistry.
Language(s): English
ADVERTISING RATES:
Full Page Mono .... EUR 745
Full Page Colour .... EUR 1590
Mechanical Data: Type Area: 250 x 170 mm
Copy instructions: *Copy Date:* 28 days prior to publication
Official Journal of: Associated with the Ges. f. Biochemie u. Molekularbiologie
BUSINESS: OTHER CLASSIFICATIONS: Biology

BIOLOGIE IN UNSERER ZEIT
722960G64F-320
Editorial: Föhrenweg 6, 68305 MANNHEIM
Tel: 621 7897448 **Fax:** 621 7897449
Email: c.vonsee@t-online.de **Web site:** http://www.biuz.de
Freq: 6 issues yearly; **Annual Sub.:** EUR 245,00; **Circ:** 8,459
Editor: Claudia von See; **Advertising Manager:** Nicole Schramm
Profile: Biologie in unserer Zeit gives insights into the entire spectrum of biology and information about exciting research results from biotechnology, molecular biology, animal and plant physiology, ecology and many other biological disciplines. Renowned authors bring you the latest issues in more detail - in a comprehensible way and color illustrations. Biologie in unserer Zeit provides news of research, business, university and school, a glossary of technical terms, practical excursion tips, background information for working in the laboratory and interesting experiments for the classroom.
Language(s): German
ADVERTISING RATES:
Full Page Mono .... EUR 2950
Full Page Colour .... EUR 4370
Mechanical Data: Type Area: 260 x 180 mm, No. of Columns (Display): 3, Col Widths (Display): 57 mm
Copy instructions: *Copy Date:* 36 days prior to publication
Official Journal of: Organ d. Verb. Biologie, Biowissenschaften u. Biomedizin in Deutschland e.V.
BUSINESS: OTHER CLASSIFICATIONS: Biology

BIOMEDIZINISCHE TECHNIK / BIOMEDICAL ENGINEERING
1663462G56A-11333
Editorial: Genthiner Str. 13, 10785 BERLIN
Tel: 30 26005279 **Fax:** 30 26005325
Email: bmt.editorial@degruyter.com **Web site:** http://www.degruyter.de/journals/bmt
Freq: 6 issues yearly; **Annual Sub.:** EUR 440,00; **Circ:** 2,500
Editor: Olaf Dössel
Profile: Interdisciplinary journal with scientific contributions from mechnaical engineering, electrical engineering, physic and medicine.
Language(s): English; German
ADVERTISING RATES:
Full Page Mono .... EUR 2300
Full Page Colour .... EUR 3145
Mechanical Data: Type Area: 250 x 170 mm, No. of Columns (Display): 2, Col Widths (Display): 81 mm
Copy instructions: *Copy Date:* 28 days prior to publication
Official Journal of: Organ d. Dt. Ges. f. Biomedizin. Technik im VDE, d. Österr. u. d. Schweizer. Ges. f. Biomedizin. Technik

BIONACHRICHTEN
722969G21A-840
Editorial: Stelzlhof 1, 94034 PASSAU
Tel: 851 7565016 **Fax:** 851 7565025
Email: kuhnt@biokreis.de **Web site:** http://www.bionachrichten.de
Freq: 6 issues yearly; **Circ:** 4,000
Editor: Simone Kuhnt; **Advertising Manager:** Heidi Scheitza
Profile: Magazine on biological farming and nutrition. In the category "News" to find interesting news and events from the organic sector. In addition, relevant developments in agricultural policy and on the food market are highlighted and commented. Interesting and worth knowing about is the work of our association and its producers rings in the category "Biokreis". There also appear regularly technical articles with helpful hints for farmers and processors. Each issue has a thematic focus: This once treated a group of products, such as Organic milk or honey, sometimes a topical issue such as biodiversity or bio in the hospitality industry. In the fourth section "Biowelt" interesting personalities from the industry are presented, it can be found here, delicious recipes, exciting things about health and references. An extensive exchange of goods for farmers, processors and consumers rounds from the magazine.
Language(s): German
ADVERTISING RATES:
Full Page Colour .... EUR 495
Mechanical Data: Type Area: 254 x 180 mm, No. of Columns (Display): 3, Col Widths (Display): 56 mm
Copy instructions: *Copy Date:* 21 days prior to publication

BIOPLASTICS MAGAZINE.COM
1994466G35-179
Editorial: Dammer Str. 112, 41066 MÖNCHENGLADBACH **Tel:** 2161 6884469
Fax: 2161 6884468

Email: mt@bioplasticsmagazine.com **Web site:** http://www.bioplasticsmagazine.com
Freq: 6 issues yearly; **Annual Sub.:** EUR 149,00; **Circ:** 5,000
Editor: Michael Thielen; **Advertising Manager:** Elke Hoffmann
Profile: Journal of bioplastics from industry, commerce and science.
Language(s): English
ADVERTISING RATES:
Full Page Mono .... EUR 3350
Full Page Colour .... EUR 3350
Mechanical Data: Type Area: 277 x 190 mm, No. of Columns (Display): 3, Col Widths (Display): 60 mm
Copy instructions: *Copy Date:* 24 days prior to publication

BIOPRESS 722971G22R-50
Editorial: Schulstr. 10, 74927 ESCHELBRONN
Tel: 6226 951110 **Fax:** 6226 40047
Email: presse@biopress.de **Web site:** http://www.biopress.de
Freq: Quarterly; **Annual Sub.:** EUR 30,00
Editor: Erich Margrander; **Advertising Manager:** Marita Sentz
Profile: Magazine containing information on organic products.
Language(s): German
Mechanical Data: Type Area: 242 x 171 mm
Copy instructions: *Copy Date:* 30 days prior to publication
BUSINESS: FOOD: Food Related

BIOPROCESS AND BIOSYSTEMS ENGINEERING
722972G64F-340
Editorial: Boltzmannstr. 15, 85748 GARCHING
Email: bpbse@lrz.tum.de **Web site:** http://www.springerlink.com
Freq: 9 issues yearly; **Annual Sub.:** EUR 2022,00; **Circ:** 211
Editor: Dirk Weuster-Botz
Profile: Publication concerning bioreactors, upstream and downstream processes, measurement and control.
Language(s): English
ADVERTISING RATES:
Full Page Mono .... EUR 740
Full Page Colour .... EUR 1780
Mechanical Data: Type Area: 240 x 175 mm
BUSINESS: OTHER CLASSIFICATIONS: Biology

BIOSPEKTRUM 722975G64F-260
Editorial: Tiergartenstr. 17, 69121 HEIDELBERG
Tel: 6221 4878043 **Fax:** 6221 48768043
Email: biospektrum@springer.com **Web site:** http://www.biospektrum.de
Freq: 7 issues yearly; Free to qualifying individuals
Annual Sub.: EUR 79,00; **Circ:** 14,985
Editor: Christine Schreiber
Profile: BIOspektrum is the leading journal of the publisher Spektrum Akademischer Verlag, which is a part of Springer Verlag Heidelberg since October 2009. Since foundation BIOspektrum expanded increasingly. This positive development was even enhanced by its relaunch in 2006. The magazine BIOspektrum reflects an intensive exchange of the active scientific disciplines as a collective publication of the leading professional societies in molecular biological research (GBM, VAAM, GfG, GfE and DGPT) and of the partner organizations in the field of biotechnology (VBU & Dechema) as well as of the umbrella organization VBIO. Due to this fruitful partnership BIOspektrum shows a high reader acceptance and recognition of the journal. Right from the start and increasing, the authors are outstanding scientists. Positive trends of BIOspektrum: Increasing readers - In 2009, we obtained a new group of readers: the German biotechnologists. Since the beginning of 2009, BIOspektrum gained thereby 1.800 new readers and is now partner of the German biotechnological organizations Dechema and VBU. New contents - We have launched a new category: the section "Biotechnology". Since our co-operation with the German biotechnologists you will find 8 pages of background information and comments out of the branch. New editorial department biotechnology - With our biotechnology crew, we received all requirements for a competent and professional presentation of our new subject area. Thus BIOspektrum opens its horizons for potential new alliances. New paths of publication - With the database SpringerLink and online first, beside our website www.biospektrum.de, we gained new online publication paths which underline the status of BIOspektrum as a highly scientific journal. For our authors, online publication provides a higher accessibility, presence of their papers and feedback to their work. Honored twice with the prize Business medium of the year „And the winner is....BIOspektrum !" BIOspektrum has already been twice awarded for being one of the best German business publications in the category "Science" with a silver medal in 2007 and a gold medal in 2009. Since 2005, the German Business Media decorates the best German business media. The aim of the prize is to direct the intention of the branch to excellent information tools for professional stakeholders. Extract from the statement of the jury: "BIOspektrum combines contents and aesthetics. It is clearly structured and arouses the reader's curiosity. Every section contains detailed scientific articles with excellent illustrations, shorter essays and news. The attractive layout and the typography are exemplary. This is science wrote by scientist for scientists, their institutions and companies, here scrolling is fun, even for non-scientists.".
Language(s): German
ADVERTISING RATES:
Full Page Mono .... EUR 4360
Full Page Colour .... EUR 5460
Mechanical Data: Type Area: 260 x 180 mm, No. of Columns (Display): 3, Col Widths (Display): 58 mm
Copy instructions: *Copy Date:* 28 days prior to publication
BUSINESS: OTHER CLASSIFICATIONS: Biology

BIOWELT 1698983G22A-3266
Editorial: Luisenstr. 1a, 49074 OSNABRÜCK
Tel: 541 58054443 **Fax:** 541 58054499
Email: info@biowelt-online.de **Web site:** http://www.biowelt-online.de
Freq: Monthly; **Annual Sub.:** EUR 78,00; **Circ:** 10,000
Editor: Karsten Runge; **Advertising Manager:** Sonja Shirley
Profile: Magazine for entrepreneurs and decision makers of the organic industry, which rely on tradition, excellence and innovation. For entrepreneurs who want to get and keep the overview and working to conviction for a healthy nutrition and sustainable development. For all the creative minds who want to always bring the latest knowledge. The BIOwelt informed innovative small firms as well as the successful middle class, but also the conventional food retailers with an attractive range of organic products. The topics are aimed at entrepreneurs with experience and competence for the business thinking and acting, and excellent organic quality of their products are natural.
Language(s): German
ADVERTISING RATES:
Full Page Mono .... EUR 2800
Full Page Colour .... EUR 4000
Mechanical Data: Type Area: 297 x 189 mm, No. of Columns (Display): 4, Col Widths (Display): 45 mm
Copy instructions: *Copy Date:* 14 days prior to publication
BUSINESS: FOOD

BISCHOFSWERDAER WOCHENKURIER 722994G72-2152
Editorial: Wettiner Platz 10, 01067 DRESDEN
Tel: 351 491760 **Fax:** 351 4917674
Email: wochenkurier-dresden@dwk-verlag.de **Web site:** http://www.wochenkurier.info
Freq: Weekly; **Cover Price:** Free; **Circ:** 16,783
Editor: Regine Eberlein; **Advertising Manager:** Andreas Schönherr
Profile: Advertising journal (house-to-house) concentrating on local stories.
Language(s): German
ADVERTISING RATES:
Full Page Mono .... EUR 2258
Full Page Colour .... EUR 3161
Mechanical Data: Type Area: 430 x 290 mm, No. of Columns (Display): 7, Col Widths (Display): 38 mm
Copy instructions: *Copy Date:* 5 days prior to publication
LOCAL NEWSPAPERS

BIT 723004G34-60
Editorial: Fasanenweg 18, 70771 LEINFELDEN-ECHTERDINGEN **Tel:** 711 7591316
Fax: 711 7591336
Email: jziegler@bitverlag.de **Web site:** http://www.bitverlag.de/bit
Freq: 7 issues yearly; **Annual Sub.:** EUR 78,00; **Circ:** 9,751
Editor: Jacques Ziegler; **Advertising Manager:** Joachim Ahnfeldt
Profile: Magazine for efficient business processes. The journal reports on document management and enterprise content management in all facets. Bit provides valuable information for planning, selecting and implementing systems and solutions for business processes. It shows how to document processes from input to delivery and archiving can be made more efficient. Bit provides a solid foundation of knowledge in all aspects of a modern electronic document organization, and productivity enhancing processes. Bit-readers: IT Manager, responsible for process management, heads of departments with high document throughput, purchasers of hardware and software, responsible for printing and mailing, consultants, and data center managers. Twitter: http://twitter.com/#!/bit_news This Outlet offers RSS (Really Simple Syndication).
Language(s): German
ADVERTISING RATES:
Full Page Mono .... EUR 3960
Full Page Colour .... EUR 5580
Mechanical Data: Type Area: 264 x 180 mm, No. of Columns (Display): 4, Col Widths (Display): 40 mm
Copy instructions: *Copy Date:* 22 days prior to publication
BUSINESS: OFFICE EQUIPMENT

B.I.T. ONLINE 723008G60B-12
Editorial: 93042 REGENSBURG **Tel:** 941 9433900
Fax: 941 9431646
Email: info@b-i-t-online.de **Web site:** http://www.b-i-t-online.de
Freq: 5 issues yearly; **Annual Sub.:** EUR 148,00; **Circ:** 3,350
Editor: Rafael Ball; **Advertising Manager:** Erwin König
Profile: B.I.T. online - The source of bibliographic information in print and online - www.bit online.de. In the field of library journals trod the journal „B.I.T. online" from their first appearance of new paths. In designing and implementation of the medium was as an innovative approach, the combination of print and electronic publication in the foreground. Thus, "B.I.T. online" is still at a quarterly publication at any time meet the demands of actuality. Interested parties will find "B.I.T. online" in full text at www.bit-online.de in the Internet. The subtitle, "Journal of Library, Information and Technology" refers to all the important aspects of librarianship. The main focus of the journal included in the information topics in computing, digital, telecommunications, multimedia and Internet and technology issues in the field of building design and interior furnishings and equipment over to data processing in multimedia form. Increasingly devoted to „B.I.T. online" also the subject of library management as well as an extensive report of the numerous events taking place in the library field.
Language(s): German
Readership: Aimed at librarians and the information sector.
ADVERTISING RATES:
Full Page Mono .... EUR 1300
Full Page Colour .... EUR 1900
Mechanical Data: Type Area: 257 x 180 mm, No. of Columns (Display): 3, Col Widths (Display): 55 mm
Copy instructions: *Copy Date:* 14 days prior to publication
BUSINESS: PUBLISHING: Libraries

BIZTRAVEL 1800768G89A-12310
Editorial: Wandsbeker Allee 1, 22041 HAMBURG
Tel: 40 41448288 **Fax:** 40 41448299
Email: redaktion@biztravel.de **Web site:** http://www.biztravel.de
Freq: 6 issues yearly; **Annual Sub.:** EUR 28,80; **Circ:** 27,831
Editor: Oliver Graue; **Advertising Manager:** Michael Körner
Profile: BizTravel is the magazine for all those business trips and events Plan (MICE) and shopping.BizTravel provides guidance on the best deal for business and conferences. Practical Article ensure maximum benefit and direct applicability to the reader. The magazine features articles with many casual and entertaining overview graphics, photos and useful tips. BizTravel aimed primarily at medium-sized enterprises - the board or travel managers and meeting planners as well as to chief secretaries, assistants and buyers. This Outlet offers RSS (Really Simple Syndication).
Language(s): German
ADVERTISING RATES:
Full Page Mono .... EUR 8500
Full Page Colour .... EUR 8500
Mechanical Data: Type Area: 241 x 205 mm, No. of Columns (Display): 4, Col Widths (Display): 47 mm
Copy instructions: *Copy Date:* 28 days prior to publication

BJV REPORT 723018G2B-60
Editorial: Wächterstr. 2, 90489 NÜRNBERG
Tel: 911 22814 **Fax:** 911 22815
Email: redaktion@bjv-report.de **Web site:** http://www.bjv.de
Freq: 6 issues yearly; Free to qualifying individuals
Annual Sub.: EUR 52,00; **Circ:** 9,600
Editor: Michael Anger; **Advertising Manager:** Lydia Kastenhuber
Profile: Magazine for members of the Bavarian Journalists Association with news, commentaries, reports, features and glosses on media and professional specific aspects of journalists in Bavaria.
Language(s): German
ADVERTISING RATES:
Full Page Mono .... EUR 1400
Full Page Colour .... EUR 1500
Mechanical Data: Type Area: 260 x 176 mm, No. of Columns (Display): 3, Col Widths (Display): 55 mm
Copy instructions: *Copy Date:* 15 days prior to publication
BUSINESS: COMMUNICATIONS, ADVERTISING & MARKETING: Press

BK BAUKAMMER BERLIN
723020G4E-6908
Editorial: Gutsmuthsstr. 24, 12163 BERLIN
Tel: 30 7974430 **Fax:** 30 79744329
Email: info@baukammerberlin.de **Web site:** http://www.baukammerberlin.de
Freq: Quarterly; Free to qualifying individuals
Annual Sub.: EUR 50,00; **Circ:** 3,943
Editor: Joachim Wanjura; **Advertising Manager:** Peter Gesellius
Profile: Bulletin of the engineers working in construction.
Language(s): German
ADVERTISING RATES:
Full Page Mono .... EUR 1100
Full Page Colour .... EUR 1650
Mechanical Data: Type Area: 260 x 185 mm
BUSINESS: ARCHITECTURE & BUILDING: Building

BKH BAUMASCHINEN | KRANE | HEBETECHNIK 1996264G4E-7331
Editorial: Wilhelm-Giese-Str. 26, 27616 BEVERSTEDT **Tel:** 4747 8741301 **Fax:** 4747 8741222
Email: hpeimann@kran-und-hebetechnik.de **Web site:** http://www.kran-und-hebetechnik.de
Freq: Quarterly; **Cover Price:** EUR 4,00; **Circ:** 12,175
Editor: Herbert Peimann; **Advertising Manager:** Frank Stüven
Profile: Magazine on the optimal usage of crane and elevation technology.
Language(s): German
ADVERTISING RATES:
Full Page Mono .... EUR 3000
Full Page Colour .... EUR 3000
Mechanical Data: Type Area: 250 x 184 mm, No. of Columns (Display): 4, Col Widths (Display): 43 mm
Copy instructions: *Copy Date:* 21 days prior to publication

DIE BKK 723024G1D-15
Editorial: Kronprinzenstr. 6, 45128 ESSEN
Tel: 201 1791140 **Fax:** 201 1791003
Email: diebkk@bkk-bv.de **Web site:** http://www.bkk.de
Freq: Monthly; **Annual Sub.:** EUR 39,60; **Circ:** 3,800
Profile: Contributions for "Die BKK" written by renowned authors from the company health insurance and their thematic context. "Die BKK" is practical, provides technical and background knowledge, and provides know-how. She brings management information, it is a discussion forum. "Die BKK" informed currently and continuously. Who "Die BKK" subscribed remains technically at the height and gets fit for leadership roles in healthcare. Even managers offer "BKK" the view of the whole. Facebook: http://www.facebook.com/BKKlive2010.
Language(s): German
Readership: Aimed at health insurers.
ADVERTISING RATES:
Full Page Colour .... EUR 1420
Mechanical Data: Type Area: 264 x 180 mm
Copy instructions: *Copy Date:* 20 days prior to publication
BUSINESS: FINANCE & ECONOMICS: Insurance

BKK GESUNDHEITSREPORT
1696532G74M-771
Editorial: Spittelmarkt 12, 10117 BERLIN
Tel: 30 212336242 **Fax:** 30 212336499
Email: erika.zoike@spectrumk.de **Web site:** http://www.spectrumk.de
Freq: Annual; **Cover Price:** Free; **Circ:** 2,500
Editor: Erika Zoike
Profile: Facebook: http://www.facebook.com/BKKlive2010.
Language(s): German

BKR ZEITSCHRIFT FÜR BANK- UND KAPITALMARKTRECHT
1635468G1A-3538
Editorial: Rheinwerkallee 6, 53227 BONN
Tel: 228 9459450 **Fax:** 228 94594555
Email: bkr@beck.de **Web site:** http://www.bkr.beck.de
Freq: Monthly; **Annual Sub.:** EUR 346,30; **Circ:** 1,200
Editor: Volker Lang; **Advertising Manager:** Fritz Lebherz
Profile: Juristic magazine about bank and capital market law.
Language(s): German
ADVERTISING RATES:
Full Page Mono .... EUR 1460
Full Page Colour .... EUR 2960
Mechanical Data: Type Area: 260 x 186 mm, No. of Columns (Display): 4, Col Widths (Display): 43 mm

BKU JOURNAL 1664592G14A-9727
Editorial: Georgstr. 18, 50676 KÖLN **Tel:** 221 272370
Fax: 221 2723727
Email: unterberg@bku.de **Web site:** http://www.bku.de
Freq: Quarterly; Free to qualifying individuals
Annual Sub.: EUR 20,00; **Circ:** 4,500
Editor: Peter Unterberg; **Advertising Manager:** Peter Unterberg
Profile: Magazine for church executives.
Language(s): German
ADVERTISING RATES:
Full Page Mono .... EUR 1800
Full Page Colour .... EUR 1800
Mechanical Data: Type Area: 250 x 160 mm, No. of Columns (Display): 3, Col Widths (Display): 50 mm
Copy instructions: *Copy Date:* 20 days prior to publication

BLACHREPORT 723026G2A-540
Editorial: Hopfenfeld 5, 31311 UETZE
Tel: 5173 98270 **Fax:** 5173 982739
Email: pblach@blachreport.de **Web site:** http://www.blachreport.de
Freq: 25 issues yearly; **Annual Sub.:** EUR 183,50; **Circ:** 1,000
Editor: Peter Blach; **Advertising Manager:** Stefan Winterfeldt
Profile: Current and sound information for management in the live communication with marketing events, sponsorship and sales promotions. At the forefront of reporting are people and markets. Permanent interlocutor editorial director and marketing director of companies, agencies and event services. Competently researched main topics complement the current coverage for our readers in the communications departments and agencies.
Language(s): German
Readership: Aimed at marketing and media companies.
ADVERTISING RATES:
Full Page Mono .... EUR 1050
Full Page Colour .... EUR 1550
Mechanical Data: Type Area: 253 x 175 mm, No. of Columns (Display): 3, Col Widths (Display): 55 mm
Copy instructions: *Copy Date:* 7 days prior to publication

Supplement(s): PocketEvent
BUSINESS: COMMUNICATIONS, ADVERTISING & MARKETING

BLACHREPORT AUTOMOBIL EVENTS
1936381G2A-5882
Editorial: Hopfenfeld 5, 31311 UETZE
Tel: 5173 98270 **Fax:** 5173 982739
Email: info@automobil-events.de **Web site:** http://www.automobil-events.de
Freq: Half-yearly; **Annual Sub.:** EUR 20,00; **Circ:** 5,000
Editor: Peter Blach; **Advertising Manager:** Stefan Winterfeldt
Profile: Magazine about the planning of marketing and communication media events, in particular sponsoring, incentives and promotions.
Language(s): German
ADVERTISING RATES:
Full Page Mono .... EUR 2400
Full Page Colour .... EUR 3600
Mechanical Data: Type Area: 253 x 175 mm, No. of Columns (Display): 3, Col Widths (Display): 50 mm
Copy instructions: *Copy Date:* 14 days prior to publication

BLACHREPORT MESSE + MARKETING
1799494G2A-5704
Editorial: Hopfenfeld 5, 31311 UETZE
Tel: 5173 98270 **Fax:** 5173 982739
Email: pblach@blachreport.de **Web site:** http://www.messeundmarketing.de
Freq: 6 issues yearly; **Annual Sub.:** EUR 36,00; **Circ:** 2,000
Editor: Peter Blach; **Advertising Manager:** Stefan Winterfeldt
Profile: Information on fairs, exhibitions and design of brand architectures.
Language(s): German
ADVERTISING RATES:
Full Page Mono .... EUR 1320
Full Page Colour .... EUR 1980
Mechanical Data: Type Area: 253 x 175 mm, No. of Columns (Display): 3, Col Widths (Display): 50 mm
Copy instructions: *Copy Date:* 6 days prior to publication
Supplement(s): PocketEvent

BLACHREPORT MUSEUM
1739393G2A-5682
Editorial: Hopfenfeld 5, 31311 UETZE
Tel: 5173 98270 **Fax:** 5173 982739
Email: info@museumsreport.de **Web site:** http://www.museumsreport.de
Freq: 3 issues yearly; **Annual Sub.:** EUR 30,00; **Circ:** 2,000
Editor: Peter Blach; **Advertising Manager:** Stefan Winterfeldt
Profile: Magazine about the planning of marketing and communication media events, in particular sponsoring, incentives and promotions.
Language(s): German
ADVERTISING RATES:
Full Page Mono .... EUR 1200
Full Page Colour .... EUR 1800
Mechanical Data: Type Area: 253 x 175 mm, No. of Columns (Display): 3, Col Widths (Display): 50 mm
Copy instructions: *Copy Date:* 7 days prior to publication

BLACHREPORT MUSEUM
1739393G2A-5884
Editorial: Hopfenfeld 5, 31311 UETZE
Tel: 5173 98270 **Fax:** 5173 982739
Email: info@museumsreport.de **Web site:** http://www.museumsreport.de
Freq: 3 issues yearly; **Annual Sub.:** EUR 30,00; **Circ:** 2,000
Editor: Peter Blach; **Advertising Manager:** Stefan Winterfeldt
Profile: Magazine about the planning of marketing and communication media events, in particular sponsoring, incentives and promotions.
Language(s): German
ADVERTISING RATES:
Full Page Mono .... EUR 1200
Full Page Colour .... EUR 1800
Mechanical Data: Type Area: 253 x 175 mm, No. of Columns (Display): 3, Col Widths (Display): 50 mm
Copy instructions: *Copy Date:* 7 days prior to publication

DIE BLASMUSIK
723060G61-23
Editorial: Olgastr. 140, 70180 STUTTGART
Tel: 711 1259502
Email: redaktion@die-blasmusik.de
Freq: Monthly; Free to qualifying individuals
Annual Sub.: EUR 19,90; **Circ:** 6,450
Editor: Georg Bruder; **Advertising Manager:** Alexander Knam
Profile: Magazine about wind and brass instruments.
Language(s): German
ADVERTISING RATES:
Full Page Mono .... EUR 676
Full Page Colour .... EUR 800
Mechanical Data: Type Area: 260 x 185 mm, No. of Columns (Display): 4, Col Widths (Display): 45 mm
Copy instructions: *Copy Date:* 15 days prior to publication
BUSINESS: MUSIC TRADE

BLÄTTER DER WOHLFAHRTSPFLEGE
723038G32G-520
Editorial: Eichwaldstr. 45, 60385 FRANKFURT
Tel: 69 447401
Email: gerhard.pfannendoerfer@t-online.de **Web site:** http://www.blaetter-der-wohlfahrtspflege.de
Freq: 6 issues yearly; **Annual Sub.:** EUR 79,84; **Circ:** 2,800
Editor: Gerhard Pfannendörfer
Profile: Magazine for German social workers.
Language(s): German
ADVERTISING RATES:
Full Page Mono .... EUR 790
Full Page Colour .... EUR 2140
Mechanical Data: Type Area: 270 x 179 mm, No. of Columns (Display): 3, Col Widths (Display): 57 mm
Copy instructions: *Copy Date:* 30 days prior to publication
BUSINESS: LOCAL GOVERNMENT, LEISURE & RECREATION: Community Care & Social Services

BLÄTTER FÜR DEUTSCHE UND INTERNATIONALE POLITIK
723043G82-900
Editorial: Torstr. 178, 10115 BERLIN
Tel: 30 30883640 **Fax:** 30 30883645
Email: redaktion@blaetter.de **Web site:** http://www.blaetter.de
Freq: Monthly; **Annual Sub.:** EUR 75,60; **Circ:** 7,900
Editor: Albrecht von Lucke; **Advertising Manager:** Daniel Leisegang
Profile: Not Springer. Not Burda. Not Murdoch. In times of growing media concentration guarantee „Blätter für deutsche und internationale Politik" continues to be a lively coverage - regardless of corporations, political parties, associations and churches. The Blätter are as a forum for current scientific and political discussions. On 128 pages it each provide critical commentaries, analysis and alternatives beyond technocratic constraints and neoliberal unemployment alternatives. The subscribers secure the editorial and economic independence of the Blätter - and thus an independent format for unconventional opinions and political interventions. The editorial team is supported by an editorial board that shares our goal of an emancipatory analysis of political debates. In his personal continuity, he makes sure that the "Blätter" should remain in the future what they have for over 50 years: "an island of sanity in a sea of nonsense".
Language(s): German
ADVERTISING RATES:
Full Page Mono .... EUR 1025
Mechanical Data: Type Area: 195 x 118 mm
Copy instructions: *Copy Date:* 21 days prior to publication
CONSUMER: CURRENT AFFAIRS & POLITICS

BLATTGOLD
723067G74A-520
Editorial: Monumentenstr. 26, 10965 BERLIN
Tel: 30 7868547 **Fax:** 30 7866215
Email: blattgold.berlin@snafu.de **Web site:** http://www.blattgold-berlin.de
Freq: 10 issues yearly; **Annual Sub.:** EUR 30,00; **Circ:** 3,000
Editor: Christa Müller; **Advertising Manager:** Adele Meyer
Profile: Magazine for women with news from culture and politics and events in the city of Berlin.
Language(s): German
ADVERTISING RATES:
Full Page Mono .... EUR 400
Mechanical Data: Type Area: 248 x 152 mm, No. of Columns (Display): 3, Col Widths (Display): 48 mm
Copy instructions: *Copy Date:* 17 days prior to publication

BLB.NRW
1923385G4E-7295
Editorial: Mercedesstr. 12, 40470 DÜSSELDORF
Tel: 211 61700180 **Fax:** 211 61700182
Email: info@blb.nrw.de **Web site:** http://www.blb.nrw.de
Freq: Quarterly; **Cover Price:** Free; **Circ:** 6,300
Editor: Dietmar Zeleny
Profile: Magazine about real estate investments in Northrhine-Westfalia.
Language(s): German

BLECH
723105G27-320
Editorial: Göggingerstr. 105a, 86199 AUGSBURG
Tel: 821 31988017 **Fax:** 821 31988080
Email: koegel@schluetersche.de **Web site:** http://www.blechonline.de
Freq: 7 issues yearly; **Annual Sub.:** EUR 56,00; **Circ:** 13,235
Editor: Günter Kögel; **Advertising Manager:** Manfred Rosin
Profile: Blech is a trade magazine (specifically and exclusively) for sheet metal working companies and departments. Because of the ambitious-journalistic working way (nearly all contributions are self-researched), focused editorial content to the form of descriptive reports and reports on new developments and its practical application, on critical interviews, industry analysis, and offer overviews.Blech informed then, are decision support and expressing an opinion. Thematically dealing Blech containing all the sheet metal machining used manufacturing equipment: in particular, with mechanical and hydraulic presses as well as all the components for the Automation, with Punching and Nibbling machines, plasma and laser cutting machines, bending-shaping machines, linking different (CNC) machines to flexible manufacturing cells or flexible manufacturing system, as well as CNC controllers and computer integration, and all relevant tools for shaping, cutting and clamping.
Language(s): German
ADVERTISING RATES:
Full Page Mono .... EUR 2820
Full Page Colour .... EUR 3900
Mechanical Data: Type Area: 272 x 188 mm, No. of Columns (Display): 4, Col Widths (Display): 44 mm
Copy instructions: *Copy Date:* 14 days prior to publication
BUSINESS: METAL, IRON & STEEL

BLECH ROHRE PROFILE
758074G27-2945
Editorial: Franz-Ludwig-Str. 7a, 96047 BAMBERG
Tel: 951 861117 **Fax:** 951 861170
Email: blechrohreprofile@meisenbach.de **Web site:** http://www.blechrohreprofile.de
Freq: 9 issues yearly; **Annual Sub.:** EUR 120,00; **Circ:** 11,768
Editor: Volker Albrecht; **Advertising Manager:** Georg Meisenbach
Profile: Blech Rohre Profile is a recognised technical journal for the manufacture, processing and finishing of strip, sheet metal, tubes and sections, embracing all related areas. Blech Rohre Profile addresses all companies within the sheet metal working industry. This encompasses iron, sheet metal and metal manufacturers, the electrics industry as well as producers of machinery, apparatus, tools, plant, vehicles, ships and aeroplanes. Content Blech Rohre Profile features original reports by competent authors focusing on the latest technological and economic developments. Information provided by economic associations covering new developments in technology and management round off the scope of the publication's quality editorial section. Blech Rohre Profile importance for the sector is confirmed by the fact that it is the mouthpiece of the international institution for Production engineering Research (CiRP-related magazine).
Language(s): German
ADVERTISING RATES:
Full Page Mono .... EUR 3029
Full Page Colour .... EUR 4313
Mechanical Data: Type Area: 260 x 184 mm, No. of Columns (Display): 3, Col Widths (Display): 59 mm
Copy instructions: *Copy Date:* 20 days prior to publication
Supplement(s): kataloge orange
BUSINESS: METAL, IRON & STEEL

BLECHNET
1806090G27-3048
Editorial: Max-Planck-Str. 7, 97082 WÜRZBURG
Tel: 931 4182449 **Fax:** 931 4182770
Email: dietmar.kuhn@vogel.de **Web site:** http://www.blechnet.com
Freq: 6 issues yearly; **Cover Price:** EUR 9,00; **Circ:** 10,240
Editor: Dietmar Kuhn; **Advertising Manager:** Renate Zehnter
Profile: The industry magazine blechnet presents the complete process chain of economic sheet metal processing: from product development through the use of CAD / CAM systems, tooling and production to assembly. Markets, movers and opinions give a deep insight into the events of industry. The demand creation topics of blechnet in the online space is compressed on www.blechnet.com and accompanied by a weekly newsletter. The business platform blechnet.com attended to the information needs of users for current job functions. Precise, structured, and above all quickly.
Language(s): German
ADVERTISING RATES:
Full Page Mono .... EUR 2820
Full Page Colour .... EUR 3879
Mechanical Data: Type Area: 257 x 185 mm, No. of Columns (Display): 3, Col Widths (Display): 59 mm
Supplement(s): kataloge orange

BLEIBGESUND
723109G94H-1380
Editorial: Siemensstr. 6, 61352 BAD HOMBURG
Tel: 6172 6700 **Fax:** 6172 670166
Email: bleibgesund@wdv.de **Web site:** http://www.wdv.de
Freq: 6 issues yearly; **Circ:** 6,720,097
Editor: Kai Stiehl; **Advertising Manager:** Walter Krey
Profile: Magazine for members of the health insurance company AOK.
Language(s): German
ADVERTISING RATES:
Full Page Mono .... EUR 47400
Full Page Colour .... EUR 47400
Mechanical Data: Type Area: 250 x 189 mm
CONSUMER: OTHER CLASSIFICATIONS: Customer Magazines

BLICK
723114G72-2200
Editorial: Dransfelder Str. 1, 37079 GÖTTINGEN
Tel: 551 901224 **Fax:** 551 901216
Email: goebel@blick-goettingen.de **Web site:** http://www.blick-goettingen.de
Freq: Weekly; **Cover Price:** Free; **Circ:** 109,000
Editor: Gerd Goebel; **Advertising Manager:** Oliver Moll
Profile: Advertising journal (house-to-house) concentrating on local stories.
Language(s): German
ADVERTISING RATES:
Full Page Mono .... EUR 5264
Full Page Colour .... EUR 6605
Mechanical Data: Type Area: 430 x 277 mm, No. of Columns (Display): 6, Col Widths (Display): 45 mm
Copy instructions: *Copy Date:* 2 days prior to publication
LOCAL NEWSPAPERS

BLICK
724258G72-2952
Editorial: Brückenstr. 15, 09111 CHEMNITZ
Tel: 371 65622140 **Fax:** 371 65627210
Email: bernd.seidel@blick.de **Web site:** http://www.blick.de
Freq: Weekly; **Cover Price:** Free; **Circ:** 114,373
Editor: Bernd Seidel; **Advertising Manager:** Uwe Arlt
Profile: Advertising journal (house-to-house) concentrating on local stories.
Language(s): German
ADVERTISING RATES:
Full Page Mono .... EUR 6383
Full Page Colour .... EUR 8949
Mechanical Data: Type Area: 470 x 314 mm, No. of Columns (Display): 7, Col Widths (Display): 43 mm
Copy instructions: *Copy Date:* 2 days prior to publication
Supplement(s): Willkommen aktuell
LOCAL NEWSPAPERS

BLICK
726508G72-3600
Editorial: Brückenstr. 15, 09111 CHEMNITZ
Tel: 371 65622140 **Fax:** 371 65627210
Email: bernd.seidel@blick.de **Web site:** http://www.blick.de
Freq: Weekly; **Cover Price:** Free; **Circ:** 38,950
Editor: Bernd Seidel; **Advertising Manager:** Jutta Kolmorgen
Profile: Advertising journal (house-to-house) concentrating on local stories.
Language(s): German
ADVERTISING RATES:
Full Page Mono .... EUR 3159
Full Page Colour .... EUR 4409
Mechanical Data: Type Area: 470 x 314 mm, No. of Columns (Display): 7, Col Widths (Display): 43 mm
Copy instructions: *Copy Date:* 5 days prior to publication
Supplement(s): Willkommen aktuell
LOCAL NEWSPAPERS

BLICK
727487G72-3892
Editorial: Brückenstr. 15, 09111 CHEMNITZ
Tel: 371 65622140 **Fax:** 371 65627210
Email: bernd.seidel@blick.de **Web site:** http://www.blick.de
Freq: Weekly; **Cover Price:** Free; **Circ:** 26,435
Editor: Bernd Seidel; **Advertising Manager:** Marion Schreiber
Profile: Advertising journal (house-to-house) concentrating on local stories.
Language(s): German
ADVERTISING RATES:
Full Page Mono .... EUR 2797
Full Page Colour .... EUR 3916
Mechanical Data: Type Area: 470 x 314 mm, No. of Columns (Display): 7, Col Widths (Display): 43 mm
Copy instructions: *Copy Date:* 5 days prior to publication
Supplement(s): Willkommen aktuell
LOCAL NEWSPAPERS

BLICK
727889G72-4000
Editorial: Brückenstr. 15, 09111 CHEMNITZ
Tel: 371 65622140 **Fax:** 371 65627210
Email: bernd.seidel@blick.de **Web site:** http://www.blick.de
Freq: Weekly; **Cover Price:** Free; **Circ:** 49,853
Editor: Bernd Seidel; **Advertising Manager:** Marion Schreiber
Profile: Advertising journal (house-to-house) concentrating on local stories.
Language(s): German
ADVERTISING RATES:
Full Page Mono .... EUR 3784
Full Page Colour .... EUR 5396
Mechanical Data: Type Area: 470 x 314 mm, No. of Columns (Display): 7, Col Widths (Display): 43 mm
Copy instructions: *Copy Date:* 5 days prior to publication
Supplement(s): Willkommen aktuell
LOCAL NEWSPAPERS

BLICK
729983G72-5332
Editorial: Brückenstr. 15, 09111 CHEMNITZ
Tel: 371 65622140 **Fax:** 371 65627210
Email: bernd.seidel@blick.de **Web site:** http://www.blick.de
Freq: Weekly; **Cover Price:** Free; **Circ:** 33,081
Editor: Bernd Seidel; **Advertising Manager:** Hartmut Meyer
Profile: Advertising journal (house-to-house) concentrating on local stories.
Language(s): German
ADVERTISING RATES:
Full Page Mono .... EUR 2929
Full Page Colour .... EUR 4113
Mechanical Data: Type Area: 470 x 314 mm, No. of Columns (Display): 7, Col Widths (Display): 43 mm
Copy instructions: *Copy Date:* 5 days prior to publication
Supplement(s): Willkommen aktuell
LOCAL NEWSPAPERS

Germany

BLICK
736280G72-8988

Editorial: Brückenstr. 15, 09111 CHEMNITZ
Tel: 371 656222140 **Fax:** 371 65627211
Email: bernd.seidel@blick.de **Web site:** http://www.blick.de
Freq: Weekly; **Cover Price:** Free; **Circ:** 34,257
Editor: Bernd Seidel; **Advertising Manager:** Hartmut Meyer
Profile: Advertising journal (house-to-house) concentrating on local stories.
Language(s): German
ADVERTISING RATES:
Full Page Mono .... EUR 2929
Full Page Colour .... EUR 4113
Mechanical Data: Type Area: 470 x 314 mm, No. of Columns (Display): 7, Col Widths (Display): 43 mm
Copy instructions: *Copy Date:* 5 days prior to publication
Supplement(s): Willkommen aktuell
LOCAL NEWSPAPERS

BLICK
739100G72-10508

Editorial: Brückenstr. 15, 09111 CHEMNITZ
Tel: 371 656222140 **Fax:** 371 65627210
Email: bernd.seidel@blick.de **Web site:** http://www.blick.de
Freq: Weekly; **Cover Price:** Free; **Circ:** 28,336
Editor: Bernd Seidel; **Advertising Manager:** Christfried Schäfer
Profile: Advertising journal (house-to-house) concentrating on local stories.
Language(s): German
ADVERTISING RATES:
Full Page Mono .... EUR 2929
Full Page Colour .... EUR 4113
Mechanical Data: Type Area: 470 x 314 mm, No. of Columns (Display): 7, Col Widths (Display): 43 mm
Copy instructions: *Copy Date:* 5 days prior to publication
Supplement(s): Willkommen aktuell
LOCAL NEWSPAPERS

BLICK
740929G72-11440

Editorial: Brückenstr. 15, 09111 CHEMNITZ
Tel: 371 656222140 **Fax:** 371 65627210
Email: bernd.seidel@blick.de **Web site:** http://www.blick.de
Freq: Weekly; **Cover Price:** Free; **Circ:** 45,443
Editor: Bernd Seidel; **Advertising Manager:** Hartmut Meyer
Profile: Advertising journal (house-to-house) concentrating on local stories.
Language(s): German
ADVERTISING RATES:
Full Page Mono .... EUR 3290
Full Page Colour .... EUR 4606
Mechanical Data: Type Area: 470 x 314 mm, No. of Columns (Display): 7, Col Widths (Display): 43 mm
Copy instructions: *Copy Date:* 5 days prior to publication
Supplement(s): Willkommen aktuell
LOCAL NEWSPAPERS

BLICK
742187G72-12128

Editorial: Brückenstr. 15, 09111 CHEMNITZ
Tel: 371 656222140 **Fax:** 371 65627210
Email: bernd.seidel@blick.de **Web site:** http://www.blick.de
Freq: Weekly; **Cover Price:** Free; **Circ:** 84,596
Editor: Bernd Seidel; **Advertising Manager:** Christfried Schäfer
Profile: Advertising journal (house-to-house) concentrating on local stories.
Language(s): German
ADVERTISING RATES:
Full Page Mono .... EUR 4705
Full Page Colour .... EUR 6580
Mechanical Data: Type Area: 470 x 314 mm, No. of Columns (Display): 7, Col Widths (Display): 43 mm
Copy instructions: *Copy Date:* 2 days prior to publication
LOCAL NEWSPAPERS

BLICK
749090G72-16716

Editorial: Brückenstr. 15, 09111 CHEMNITZ
Tel: 371 656222140 **Fax:** 371 65627210
Email: bernd.seidel@blick.de **Web site:** http://www.blick.de
Freq: Weekly; **Cover Price:** Free; **Circ:** 76,846
Editor: Bernd Seidel; **Advertising Manager:** Christfried Schäfer
Profile: Advertising journal (house-to-house) concentrating on local stories.
Language(s): German
ADVERTISING RATES:
Full Page Mono .... EUR 4113
Full Page Colour .... EUR 5758
Mechanical Data: Type Area: 470 x 314 mm, No. of Columns (Display): 7, Col Widths (Display): 43 mm
Copy instructions: *Copy Date:* 5 days prior to publication
Supplement(s): Willkommen aktuell
LOCAL NEWSPAPERS

BLICK AM SONNTAG
742188G72-12132

Editorial: Brückenstr. 15, 09111 CHEMNITZ
Tel: 371 656222140 **Fax:** 371 65627210
Email: bernd.seidel@blick.de **Web site:** http://www.blick.de
Freq: Weekly; **Cover Price:** Free; **Circ:** 110,421
Editor: Bernd Seidel; **Advertising Manager:** Jens-Peter Zschach
Profile: Advertising journal (house-to-house) concentrating on local stories.
Language(s): German
ADVERTISING RATES:
Full Page Mono .... EUR 5396
Full Page Colour .... EUR 7699
Mechanical Data: Type Area: 470 x 314 mm, No. of Columns (Display): 7, Col Widths (Display): 43 mm
Copy instructions: *Copy Date:* 2 days prior to publication
LOCAL NEWSPAPERS

BLICK FF DELIKAT
723118G22D-60

Editorial: Rheintalstr. 6, 53498 BAD BREISIG
Tel: 2633 454027 **Fax:** 2633 97415
Email: m.jakobi@blmedien.de **Web site:** http://www.fleischnet.de
Freq: 10 issues yearly; **Annual Sub.:** EUR 10,00; **Circ:** 9,832
Editor: Michael Jakobi; **Advertising Manager:** Johann B. Rosenbaum
Profile: Trade magazine for production and sale of meat, sausage and deli. Emphasis will be heading ranges, production and technology, marketing and operations management, butcher-specialist as well as trends and news.
Language(s): German
ADVERTISING RATES:
Full Page Mono .... EUR 5500
Full Page Colour .... EUR 5500
Mechanical Data: Type Area: 260 x 190 mm, No. of Columns (Display): 4, Col Widths (Display): 45 mm
Copy instructions: *Copy Date:* 29 days prior to publication
BUSINESS: FOOD: Meat Trade

BLICK - LOKALANZEIGER F. D. VOGTLAND, AUSG. AUERBACH, REICHENBACH
746638G72-14748

Editorial: Brückenstr. 15, 09111 CHEMNITZ
Tel: 371 656222140 **Fax:** 371 65627210
Email: bernd.seidel@blick.de **Web site:** http://www.blick.de
Freq: Weekly; **Cover Price:** Free; **Circ:** 53,704
Editor: Bernd Seidel; **Advertising Manager:** Jens-Peter Zschach
Profile: Advertising journal (house-to-house) concentrating on local stories.
Language(s): German
ADVERTISING RATES:
Full Page Mono .... EUR 3784
Full Page Colour .... EUR 5297
Mechanical Data: Type Area: 470 x 314 mm, No. of Columns (Display): 7, Col Widths (Display): 43 mm
Copy instructions: *Copy Date:* 5 days prior to publication
Supplement(s): Willkommen aktuell
LOCAL NEWSPAPERS

BLICK - LOKALANZEIGER F. D. VOGTLAND, AUSG. PLAUEN
746637G72-14744

Editorial: Brückenstr. 15, 09111 CHEMNITZ
Tel: 371 656222140 **Fax:** 371 65627210
Email: bernd.seidel@blick.de **Web site:** http://www.blick.de
Freq: Weekly; **Cover Price:** Free; **Circ:** 64,046
Editor: Bernd Seidel; **Advertising Manager:** Jens-Peter Zschach
Profile: Advertising journal (house-to-house) concentrating on local stories.
Language(s): German
ADVERTISING RATES:
Full Page Mono .... EUR 4310
Full Page Colour .... EUR 6021
Mechanical Data: Type Area: 470 x 314 mm, No. of Columns (Display): 7, Col Widths (Display): 43 mm
Copy instructions: *Copy Date:* 5 days prior to publication
Supplement(s): Willkommen aktuell
LOCAL NEWSPAPERS

BLICK PUNKT BALVE
1828388G2A-5756

Editorial: Hönnestr. 45, 58809 NEUENRADE
Tel: 2394 61690 **Fax:** 2394 61691
Email: redaktion@plakart.de **Web site:** http://www.plakart.de
Freq: 6 issues yearly; **Cover Price:** Free; **Circ:** 6,000
Editor: Karin Braukhaus-Becker
Profile: Company publication.
Language(s): German
ADVERTISING RATES:
Full Page Mono .... EUR 900
Full Page Colour .... EUR 900
Mechanical Data: Type Area: 297 x 210 mm
Copy instructions: *Copy Date:* 15 days prior to publication

BLICKPUNKT DSTG
1659605G1M-16

Editorial: Elisabethstr. 40, 40217 DÜSSELDORF
Tel: 211 906950 **Fax:** 211 9069522
Email: dstg.nrw@t-online.de **Web site:** http://www.dstg-nrw.de
Freq: 9 issues yearly; **Circ:** 22,000
Editor: Rainer Hengst
Profile: Magazine for members of the German Tax Union Association, for tax advisors and politicians.
Language(s): German

BLICKPUNKT WEDEL
723210G72-2416

Editorial: Großer Sand 3, 25436 UETERSEN
Tel: 4103 6362 **Fax:** 4103 17678
Email: redaktion@blickpunkt-wedel.com **Web site:** http://www.blickpunkt-wedel.com
Freq: 26 issues yearly; **Cover Price:** Free; **Circ:** 26,000
Editor: Klaus Plath; **Advertising Manager:** Claudia Einkopf
Profile: Advertising journal (house-to-house) concentrating on local stories.
Language(s): German
ADVERTISING RATES:
Full Page Mono .... EUR 1089
Full Page Colour .... EUR 1239
Mechanical Data: Type Area: 275 x 187 mm, No. of Columns (Display): 4, Col Widths (Display): 45 mm
Copy instructions: *Copy Date:* 7 days prior to publication
LOCAL NEWSPAPERS

BLICKPUNKT WIRTSCHAFT
723211G14A-960

Editorial: Konrad-Adenauer-Ufer 21, 50668 KÖLN
Tel: 221 4981251 **Fax:** 221 4981258
Email: redaktion@blickpunkt-wirtschaft.de **Web site:** http://www.div-blickpunkt.de
Freq: Monthly; **Annual Sub.:** EUR 19,00; **Circ:** 45,000
Editor: Ulrich von Lampe
Profile: Business magazine.
Language(s): German

BLINKER
723222G92-40

Editorial: Troplowitzstr. 5, 22529 HAMBURG
Tel: 40 38906222 **Fax:** 40 38906303
Email: henning.stilke@blinker.de **Web site:** http://www.blinker.de
Freq: Monthly; **Annual Sub.:** EUR 51,00; **Circ:** 77,134
Editor: Henning Stilke; **Advertising Manager:** Sandra Böthin
Profile: Blinker is Europe's largest fishing magazine - and groundbreaking on the fishing sector through exciting written contributions of a high utility value and a clear layout. Indicator offers practical, reports on travel and news from the world of water and fishing.
Language(s): German
Readership: Read mainly by people with a high disposable income aged between 20 and 49 years.
ADVERTISING RATES:
Full Page Mono .... EUR 5976
Full Page Colour .... EUR 6972
Mechanical Data: Type Area: 248 x 185 mm, No. of Columns (Display): 4, Col Widths (Display): 45 mm
Supplement(s): Angeln und Fischen
CONSUMER: ANGLING & FISHING

BLITZ! - AUSG. CHEMNITZ
724256G80-2000

Editorial: Lindenthaler Hauptstr. 98, 04158 LEIPZIG
Tel: 341 4618213 **Fax:** 341 4618214
Email: info@blitz-world.de **Web site:** http://www.blitz-world.de
Freq: 11 issues yearly; **Cover Price:** Free; **Circ:** 22,813
Editor: Bert Hähne; **Advertising Manager:** Torsten Reineck
Profile: With the city magazines Blitz! reach the active young adults, in Saxony, Saxony-Anhalt and Thuringia. Blitz! appears in the metropolitan areas of Leipzig, Dresden, Chemnitz, Halle and Thuringia (Erfurt, Jena and Weimar). In the middle of urban life - where will meet your target group! Blitz! there since January 1990 in Leipzig, Dresden, Chemnitz and Halle. As of 1999, in Erfurt, Weimar and Jena. The circulation grew steadily since then to today's 145,000 copies. Blitz! produces five magazines a month for seven East German cities and university towns. We have editorial offices in Chemnitz, Dresden, Erfurt, Halle and Leipzig and move every day within our target group we believe to know well about. Local actors are also known to us - in person to a large extent. The focal points are in the areas of catering, cinema, music, fashion and lifestyle. All our city magazines are made of a specific local and a national part. Street party with the highlights of the month and views of the major events throughout the region. Cinema: monthly tips and short film shows, music: interviews, concert dates, seasonal music specials, presentation of young bands and musicians as "Local Heroes", CD reviews. Photo: a monthly double-page spread (erotic) photographs of a newcomer in the region. Travel: own trip reports and exclusive travel and readers about this: seasonal and theme ideas, columns, portraits of local actors, classifieds, crossword puzzles and games, and ticket raffles. stadt-mag: New interesting people and events, theater, vaudeville and cabaret reviews; diary: concert, dance, party, stage and other events for the next four weeks; lifestyle: fashion, photo reportage and entertainment tips (new bars, new shops, new people, new drinks).
Language(s): German
ADVERTISING RATES:
Full Page Colour .... EUR 2250
Mechanical Data: Type Area: 260 x 190 mm, No. of Columns (Display): 4, Col Widths (Display): 44 mm
Copy instructions: *Copy Date:* 15 days prior to publication
CONSUMER: RURAL & REGIONAL INTEREST

BLITZ! - AUSG. DRESDEN
725637G80-2780

Editorial: Lindenthaler Hauptstr. 98, 04158 LEIPZIG
Tel: 341 4618213 **Fax:** 341 4618214
Email: info@blitz-world.de **Web site:** http://www.blitz-world.de
Freq: 11 issues yearly; **Cover Price:** Free; **Circ:** 30,792
Editor: Bert Hähne; **Advertising Manager:** Torsten Reineck
Profile: With the city magazines Blitz! reach the active young adults, in Saxony, Saxony-Anhalt and Thuringia. Blitz! appears in the metropolitan areas of Leipzig, Dresden, Chemnitz, Halle and Thuringia (Erfurt, Jena and Weimar). In the middle of urban life - where will meet your target group! Blitz! there since January 1990 in Leipzig, Dresden, Chemnitz and Halle. As of 1999, in Erfurt, Weimar and Jena. The circulation grew steadily since then to today's 145,000 copies. Blitz! produces five magazines a month for seven East German cities and university towns. We have editorial offices in Chemnitz, Dresden, Erfurt, Halle and Leipzig and move every day within our target group we believe to know well about. Local actors are also known to us - in person to a large extent. The focal points are in the areas of catering, cinema, music, fashion and lifestyle. All our city magazines are made of a specific local and a national part. Street party with the highlights of the month and views of the major events throughout the region. Cinema: monthly tips and short film shows, music: interviews, concert dates, seasonal music specials, presentation of young bands and musicians as "Local Heroes", CD reviews. Photo: a monthly double-page spread (erotic) photographs of a newcomer in the region. Travel: own trip reports and exclusive travel and readers about this: seasonal and theme ideas, columns, portraits of local actors, classifieds, crossword puzzles and games, and ticket raffles. stadt-mag: New interesting people and events, theater, vaudeville and cabaret reviews; diary: concert, dance, party, stage and other events for the next four weeks; lifestyle: fashion, photo reportage and entertainment tips (new bars, new shops, new people, new drinks).
Language(s): German
ADVERTISING RATES:
Full Page Colour .... EUR 2780
Mechanical Data: Type Area: 260 x 190 mm, No. of Columns (Display): 4, Col Widths (Display): 44 mm
Copy instructions: *Copy Date:* 15 days prior to publication
CONSUMER: RURAL & REGIONAL INTEREST

BLITZ! - AUSG. HALLE
729509G80-4420

Editorial: Lindenthaler Hauptstr. 98, 04158 LEIPZIG
Tel: 341 4618213 **Fax:** 341 4618214
Email: info@blitz-world.de **Web site:** http://www.blitz-world.de
Freq: 11 issues yearly; **Cover Price:** Free; **Circ:** 25,777
Editor: Bert Hähne; **Advertising Manager:** Torsten Reineck
Profile: With the city magazines Blitz! reach the active young adults, in Saxony, Saxony-Anhalt and Thuringia. Blitz! appears in the metropolitan areas of Leipzig, Dresden, Chemnitz, Halle and Thuringia (Erfurt, Jena and Weimar). In the middle of urban life - where will meet your target group! Blitz! there since January 1990 in Leipzig, Dresden, Chemnitz and Halle. As of 1999, in Erfurt, Weimar and Jena. The circulation grew steadily since then to today's 145,000 copies. Blitz! produces five magazines a month for seven East German cities and university towns. We have editorial offices in Chemnitz, Dresden, Erfurt, Halle and Leipzig and move every day within our target group we believe to know well about. Local actors are also known to us - in person to a large extent. The focal points are in the areas of catering, cinema, music, fashion and lifestyle. All our city magazines are made of a specific local and a national part. Street party with the highlights of the month and views of the major events throughout the region. Cinema: monthly tips and short film shows, music: interviews, concert dates, seasonal music specials, presentation of young bands and musicians as "Local Heroes", CD reviews. Photo: a monthly double-page spread (erotic) photographs of a newcomer in the region. Travel: own trip reports and exclusive travel and readers about this: seasonal and theme ideas, columns, portraits of local actors, classifieds, crossword puzzles and games, and ticket raffles. stadt-mag: New interesting people and events, theater, vaudeville and cabaret reviews; diary: concert, dance, party, stage and other events for the next four weeks; lifestyle: fashion, photo reportage and entertainment tips (new bars, new shops, new people, new drinks).
Language(s): German
ADVERTISING RATES:
Full Page Colour .... EUR 2420
Mechanical Data: Type Area: 260 x 190 mm, No. of Columns (Display): 4, Col Widths (Display): 44 mm
Copy instructions: *Copy Date:* 15 days prior to publication
CONSUMER: RURAL & REGIONAL INTEREST

BLITZ! - AUSG. LEIPZIG
734044G80-7060

Editorial: Lindenthaler Hauptstr. 98, 04158 LEIPZIG
Tel: 341 4618213 **Fax:** 341 4618214
Email: info@blitz-world.de **Web site:** http://www.blitz-world.de
Freq: 11 issues yearly; **Cover Price:** Free; **Circ:** 38,806
Editor: Bert Hähne; **Advertising Manager:** Torsten Reineck
Profile: With the city magazines Blitz! reach the active young adults, in Saxony, Saxony-Anhalt and

Thuringia. Blitz! appears in the metropolitan areas of Leipzig, Dresden, Chemnitz, Halle and Thuringia (Erfurt, Jena and Weimar). In the middle of urban life - where will meet your target group! Blitz! there since January 1990 in Leipzig, Dresden, Chemnitz and Halle. As of 1999, in Erfurt, Weimar and Jena. The circulation grew steadily since then to today's 145,000 copies. Blitz! produces five magazines a month for seven East German cities and university towns. We have editorial offices in Chemnitz, Dresden, Erfurt, Halle and Leipzig and move every day within our target group we believe to know well about. Local actors are also known to us - in person to a large extent. The focal points are in the areas of catering, cinema, music, fashion and lifestyle. All our city magazines are made of a specific local and a national part. Street party with the highlights of the month and views of the major events throughout the region. Cinema: monthly tips and short film shows, music: interviews, concert dates, seasonal music specials, presentation of young bands and musicians as "Local Heroes", CD reviews. Photo: a monthly double-page spread (erotic) photographs of a newcomer in the region. Travel: own trip reports and exclusive travel and readers about this: seasonal and theme ideas, columns, portraits of local actors, classifieds, crossword puzzles and games, and ticket raffles. stadt-mag: New interesting people and events, theater, vaudeville and cabaret reviews; diary: concert, dance, party, stage and other events for the next four weeks; lifestyle: fashion, photo reportage and entertainment tips (new bars, new shops, new people, new drinks).
Language(s): German
ADVERTISING RATES:
Full Page Colour .... EUR 3490
Mechanical Data: Type Area: 260 x 190 mm, No. of Columns (Display): 4, Col Widths (Display): 44 mm
Copy instructions: *Copy Date:* 15 days prior to publication
CONSUMER: RURAL & REGIONAL INTEREST

BLITZ! - AUSG. THÜRINGEN
744678G80-11360
Editorial: Lindenthaler Hauptstr. 98, 04158 LEIPZIG
Tel: 341 4618213 **Fax:** 341 4618214
Email: info@blitz-world.de **Web site:** http://www.blitz-world.de
Freq: 11 issues yearly; **Cover Price:** Free; **Circ:** 25,788
Editor: Bert Hähne; **Advertising Manager:** Torsten Reineck
Profile: With the city magazines Blitz! reach the active young adults, in Saxony, Saxony-Anhalt and Thuringia. Blitz! appears in the metropolitan areas of Leipzig, Dresden, Chemnitz, Halle and Thuringia (Erfurt, Jena and Weimar). In the middle of urban life - where will meet your target group! Blitz! there since January 1990 in Leipzig, Dresden, Chemnitz and Halle. As of 1999, in Erfurt, Weimar and Jena. The circulation grew steadily since then to today's 145,000 copies. Blitz! produces five magazines a month for seven East German cities and university towns. We have editorial offices in Chemnitz, Dresden, Erfurt, Halle and Leipzig and move every day within our target group we believe to know well about. Local actors are also known to us - in person to a large extent. The focal points are in the areas of catering, cinema, music, fashion and lifestyle. All our city magazines are made of a specific local and a national part. Street party with the highlights of the month and views of the major events throughout the region. Cinema: monthly tips and short film shows, music: interviews, concert dates, seasonal music specials, presentation of young bands and musicians as "Local Heroes", CD reviews. Photo: a monthly double-page spread (erotic) photographs of a newcomer in the region. Travel: own trip reports and exclusive travel and readers about this: seasonal and theme ideas, columns, portraits of local actors, classifieds, crossword puzzles and games, and ticket raffles. stadt-mag: New interesting people and events, theater, vaudeville and cabaret reviews; diary: concert, dance, party, stage and other events for the next four weeks; lifestyle: fashion, photo reportage and entertainment tips (new bars, new shops, new people, new drinks).
Language(s): German
ADVERTISING RATES:
Full Page Colour .... EUR 2420
Mechanical Data: Type Area: 260 x 190 mm, No. of Columns (Display): 4, Col Widths (Display): 44 mm
Copy instructions: *Copy Date:* 15 days prior to publication
CONSUMER: RURAL & REGIONAL INTEREST

BLITZ ILLU.DE
1661053G86A-1398
Editorial: Harburger Schloßstr. 28, 21079 HAMBURG
Tel: 40 7679601792 **Fax:** 40 7679601791
Email: online@imckg.de **Web site:** http://www.blitz-illu.de
Freq: Weekly; **Cover Price:** Paid; **Circ:** 749,395 Unique Users
Editor: Stefan Schellenberg
Profile: Ezine: General interest magazine.
Language(s): German
CONSUMER: ADULT & GAY MAGAZINES: Adult Magazines

BLIX
1683913G80-14529
Editorial: Hauptstr. 93/1, 88326 AULENDORF
Tel: 7525 92120 **Fax:** 7525 921222
Email: redaktion@blix.info **Web site:** http://www.blix.info
Freq: 11 issues yearly; **Cover Price:** Free; **Circ:** 14,854
Editor: Roland Reck; **Advertising Manager:** Roland Reck
Profile: Blix - the magazine for Oberschwaben - month after month provides interesting content from politics to culture and leisure to education and health.
Language(s): German
ADVERTISING RATES:
Full Page Mono .... EUR 1150
Full Page Colour .... EUR 1350
Mechanical Data: Type Area: 273 x 186 mm
Copy instructions: *Copy Date:* 15 days prior to publication
CONSUMER: RURAL & REGIONAL INTEREST

BLONDE
723242G74F-40
Editorial: Offakamp 9a, 22529 HAMBURG
Tel: 40 570026720 **Fax:** 40 570026718
Email: bettina.bergmann@blonde.de **Web site:** http://www.blonde.de
Freq: Quarterly; **Cover Price:** EUR 5,00; **Circ:** 30,000
Editor: Bettina Bergmann; **Advertising Manager:** Conny Niemann
Profile: Magazine containing short stories and articles on fashion, sport, music and lifestyle.
Language(s): German
Readership: Read by teenagers and young adults.
ADVERTISING RATES:
Full Page Mono .... EUR 6090
Full Page Colour .... EUR 6090
Mechanical Data: Type Area: 340 x 240 mm
CONSUMER: WOMEN'S INTEREST CONSUMER MAGAZINES: Teenage

BLUTALKOHOL
723260G56A-1680
Editorial: Grapengießerstr. 30, 23556 LÜBECK
Tel: 335 55342463 **Fax:** 335 55342456
Email: info@steintor-verlag.de **Web site:** http://www.bads.de
Freq: 6 issues yearly; Free to qualifying individuals
Annual Sub.: EUR 46,00; **Circ:** 3,000
Editor: Uwe Scheffler
Profile: In the scientific journal Blutalkohol will be published for legal and medical practice transport policy, legal and medical posts and the latest research results on the effectiveness of alcohol and drugs on driving ability.
Language(s): English; German
ADVERTISING RATES:
Full Page Mono .... EUR 1023
Full Page Colour .... EUR 1841
Mechanical Data: Type Area: 210 x 126 mm
Copy instructions: *Copy Date:* 20 days prior to publication

BLZ
723266G62B-3185
Editorial: Löningstr. 35, 28195 BREMEN
Tel: 421 71153 **Fax:** 421 3376430
Email: burger@gew-hb.de **Web site:** http://www.gew-bremen.de
Freq: 9 issues yearly; Free to qualifying individuals
Annual Sub.: EUR 15,00; **Circ:** 4,500
Editor: Jürgen Burger
Profile: The acronym BLZ comes from the times when the GEW was a teachers' association: Bremer LehrerZeitung. As education union GEW organized as well as social and educational professionals and scientists, from the historic name only the acronym has remained. The editorial work is voluntary and for suggestions and letters to the GEW-members always welcome. The GEW-boards use the BLZ to inform the current policy.
Language(s): German
Readership: Aimed at teachers in the Bremen, Bremerhaven and Umland regions.
ADVERTISING RATES:
Full Page Mono .... EUR 505
Mechanical Data: Type Area: 262 x 184 mm, No. of Columns (Display): 3, Col Widths (Display): 58 mm
Copy instructions: *Copy Date:* 20 days prior to publication
BUSINESS: CHURCH & SCHOOL EQUIPMENT & EDUCATION: Education Teachers

BM
723267G23A-60
Editorial: Ernst-Mey-Str. 8, 70771 LEINFELDEN-ECHTERDINGEN **Tel:** 711 7594256
Fax: 711 7594397
Email: bm.redaktion@konradin.de **Web site:** http://www.bm-online.de
Freq: Monthly; **Annual Sub.:** EUR 148,85; **Circ:** 21,630
Editor: Manfred Maier; **Advertising Manager:** Claudia Weygang
Profile: Leading trade magazine for international distribution for wood, plastic and light metal working in interior design, furniture manufacturing and components manufacturing, sales and installation.
Language(s): German
ADVERTISING RATES:
Full Page Mono .... EUR 5670
Full Page Colour .... EUR 7470
Mechanical Data: Type Area: 270 x 188 mm, No. of Columns (Display): 4, Col Widths (Display): 44 mm
Official Journal of: Organ d. Tischlerinnung Berlin u. d. Landesfachverbände d. holz-, kunststoff- u. aluminiumverarbeitenden Handwerks in Baden-Württemberg, Brandenburg, Hessen, Niedersachsen/ Bremen, Nordrhein-Westfalen, Rheinland-Pfalz, Saar, Sachsen, Sachsen-Anhalt, Schleswig-Holstein, Thüringen
BUSINESS: FURNISHINGS & FURNITURE

BM BANK UND MARKT
723268G1C-300
Editorial: Aschaffenburger Str. 19, 60599 FRANKFURT **Tel:** 69 97083348 **Fax:** 69 7078400
Email: red.bum@kreditwesen.de **Web site:** http://www.kreditwesen.de
Freq: Monthly; **Annual Sub.:** EUR 386,56; **Circ:** 1,286
Editor: Swantje Benkelberg; **Advertising Manager:** Ralf Werner
Profile: Journal about bank management, technology, marketing and organisation.
Language(s): German
Readership: Read by professionals in the banking and finance sector.
ADVERTISING RATES:
Full Page Mono .... EUR 4120
Full Page Colour .... EUR 6220
Mechanical Data: Type Area: 265 x 185 mm, No. of Columns (Display): 3, Col Widths (Display): 58 mm
Copy instructions: *Copy Date:* 14 days prior to publication
Supplement(s): cards Karten cartes
BUSINESS: FINANCE & ECONOMICS: Banking

BMW MAGAZIN - AUSG. DEUTSCHLAND
723283G94H-1580
Editorial: Grillparzerstr. 12, 81675 MÜNCHEN
Tel: 89 41981356 **Fax:** 89 41981345
Email: redaktion@bmw-magazin.de **Web site:** http://www.hoffmann-und-campe.de
Freq: 3 issues yearly; **Circ:** 659,431
Editor: Bernd Zerelles
Profile: Magazine for customers of the German BMW car company, edition: Germany.
Language(s): German
ADVERTISING RATES:
Full Page Mono .... EUR 12670
Full Page Colour .... EUR 14900
Mechanical Data: Type Area: 244 x 183 mm, No. of Columns (Display): 3, Col Widths (Display): 58 mm
Copy instructions: *Copy Date:* 53 days prior to publication
CONSUMER: OTHER CLASSIFICATIONS: Customer Magazines

BMW MOTORRÄDER
723303G77A-660
Editorial: Schrempfstr. 8, 70597 STUTTGART
Tel: 711 24897600 **Fax:** 711 24897628
Email: redaktion@mo-web.de **Web site:** http://www.mo-web.de
Freq: Quarterly; **Cover Price:** EUR 6,20; **Circ:** 55,000
Editor: Jochen Soppa; **Advertising Manager:** Sabine Schermer
Profile: BMW special edition for all friends and friends of the white-blue mark. Review of the current machines, many scenes, even more background and especially portraits of the people who bring life into the whole story.
Language(s): German
ADVERTISING RATES:
Full Page Mono .... EUR 3655
Full Page Colour .... EUR 6140
Mechanical Data: Type Area: 262 x 187 mm, No. of Columns (Display): 4, Col Widths (Display): 43 mm
Copy instructions: *Copy Date:* 28 days prior to publication

BN BETRIEBSWIRTSCHAFTLICHE NACHRICHTEN FÜR DIE LANDWIRTSCHAFT
1928825G21A-4445
Editorial: Gut Albshausen, 34302 GUXHAGEN
Tel: 5665 30962 **Fax:** 5665 1759
Freq: Monthly; **Annual Sub.:** EUR 45,00; **Circ:** 700
Editor: Volker Wolfram
Profile: Journal containing business management news for farmers.
Language(s): German
ADVERTISING RATES:
Full Page Mono .... EUR 260
Mechanical Data: Type Area: 180 x 110 mm
Copy instructions: *Copy Date:* 12 days prior to publication

BOB DER BAUMEISTER
755740G91D-9586
Editorial: Rotebühlstr. 87, 70178 STUTTGART
Tel: 711 94768780 **Fax:** 711 94768830
Email: info@panini.de **Web site:** http://www.panini.de
Freq: 13 issues yearly; **Cover Price:** EUR 2,70; **Circ:** 80,361
Editor: Gabriele El Hag
Profile: For the cult TV series on Super RTL is published by Panini, the successful magazine "Bob the Builder. Bob is painted, and crafted a mystery. These are strong's extras - great fun for the kids! Additionally, Panini runs 4 times a year with Bob ideas especially lots of puzzles, coloring pages and super extras out.
Language(s): German
ADVERTISING RATES:
Full Page Mono .... EUR 4900
Full Page Colour .... EUR 4900
Mechanical Data: Type Area: 265 x 197 mm
CONSUMER: RECREATION & LEISURE: Children & Youth

BOCHOLTER BORKENER VOLKSBLATT
723311G67B-3120
Editorial: Europaplatz 26, 46399 BOCHOLT
Tel: 2871 2840 **Fax:** 2871 284240
Email: redaktion@bbv-net.de **Web site:** http://www.bbv-net.de
Freq: 312 issues yearly; **Circ:** 22,977
Advertising Manager: Jürgen Angenent
Profile: Daily newspaper with regional news and a local sports section. Facebook: http://www.facebook.com/bbvnet Twitter: http://twitter.com/#!/BBV_Bocholt This Outlet offers RSS (Really Simple Syndication).
Language(s): German
ADVERTISING RATES:
SCC .... EUR 63,60
Mechanical Data: Type Area: 480 x 325 mm, No. of Columns (Display): 7, Col Widths (Display): 45 mm
Copy instructions: *Copy Date:* 1 day prior to publication
Supplement(s): prisma
REGIONAL DAILY & SUNDAY NEWSPAPERS: Regional Daily Newspapers

BOCHOLTER REPORT
723312G72-2504
Editorial: Jägerstr. 1, 46395 BOCHOLT
Tel: 2871 259812 **Fax:** 2871 6963
Email: redaktion@bocholter-report.de **Web site:** http://www.bocholter-report.de
Freq: 104 issues yearly; **Cover Price:** Free; **Circ:** 45,850
Editor: Gabi Frentzen; **Advertising Manager:** Heiner Wolters
Profile: Advertising journal (house-to-house) concentrating on local stories.
Language(s): German
ADVERTISING RATES:
Full Page Mono .... EUR 1353
Full Page Colour .... EUR 1805
Mechanical Data: Type Area: 480 x 320 mm, No. of Columns (Display): 7, Col Widths (Display): 44 mm
Copy instructions: *Copy Date:* 2 days prior to publication
Supplement(s): Inside; Report extra
LOCAL NEWSPAPERS

BODDEN BLITZ AM SONNTAG
723318G72-2520
Editorial: Tribseer Damm 2, 18437 STRALSUND
Tel: 3831 2677451 **Fax:** 3831 2677402
Email: wilfried.stabenow@blitzverlag.de **Web site:** http://www.blitzverlag.de
Freq: Weekly; **Cover Price:** Free; **Circ:** 25,430
Editor: Wilfried Stabenow; **Advertising Manager:** André Holfert
Profile: Advertising journal (house-to-house) concentrating on local stories.
Language(s): German
ADVERTISING RATES:
Full Page Mono .... EUR 2319
Full Page Colour .... EUR 2709
Mechanical Data: Type Area: 420 x 285 mm, No. of Columns (Display): 6, Col Widths (Display): 45 mm
Copy instructions: *Copy Date:* 2 days prior to publication
LOCAL NEWSPAPERS

BODEN WAND DECKE
723327G4B-704
Editorial: Gewerbestr. 2, 86825 BAD WÖRISHOFEN
Tel: 8247 354215 **Fax:** 8247 3544215
Email: redbwd@holzmann-medien.de **Web site:** http://www.boden-wand-decke.de
Freq: 11 issues yearly; **Annual Sub.:** EUR 124,00; **Circ:** 7,832
Editor: Stefan Heinze; **Advertising Manager:** Michaela Sammer
Profile: 'boden wand decke' is the magazine for the floor laying craft, its associated specialist retail and wholesale as well as the floor covering industry. As a generalist offers 'boden wand decke' all important information for the entire industry under one roof. 'boden wand decke' is every month a comprehensive overview of the World of Flooring (textile and resilient floor coverings, parquet, cork, laminate, flooring screeds and industry). 'boden wand decke' describes the latest developments in flooring technology. In regular technical papers provides 'boden wand decke' to the floor, parquet and floor layers, the interior decorator and painter working in multidisciplinary field-tested tools of materials science techniques to work on business advice and tips. News, reports, analysis and commentary to give each issue of 'boden wand decke' important guidance and thus make the diversely structured industry transparent. Additional special parts to help users to gain fast and accurate a thorough overview of the current market in certain segments. Regular interviews and discussions with experts to make burning issues 'boden wand decke' for a discussion forum for the industry. Twitter: http://twitter.com/#!/bodenwanddecke.
Language(s): German
ADVERTISING RATES:
Full Page Mono .... EUR 2350
Full Page Colour .... EUR 4240
Mechanical Data: Type Area: 266 x 185 mm, No. of Columns (Display): 4, Col Widths (Display): 43 mm
Copy instructions: *Copy Date:* 20 days prior to publication
Official Journal of: Organ d. Bundesinnung d. Bodenleger Österr.
BUSINESS: ARCHITECTURE & BUILDING: Interior Design & Flooring

BODENSCHUTZ 723322G57-240
Editorial: Adelheidisstr. 16, 53757 ST. AUGUSTIN
Tel: 2241 3971905
Email: r.schmidt@bvboden.de **Web site:** http://www.bodenschutzdigital.de
Freq: Quarterly; Free to qualifying individuals
Annual Sub.: EUR 62,45; **Circ:** 1,200
Editor: Rainer Schmidt; **Advertising Manager:** Peter Taprogge
Profile: Key issues: contaminated sites, landscaping, land reclamation, soil evaluation, soil protection, spatial planning, etc. Target group: Managers in soil conservation authorities, engineers, surveyors, lawyers, scientists, and research. But also agriculture and their organizations, industry and insurance companies like to fall back on reliable information.
Language(s): German
ADVERTISING RATES:
Full Page Mono .... EUR 960
Full Page Colour .... EUR 1860
Mechanical Data: Type Area: 254 x 185 mm, No. of Columns (Display): 2, Col Widths (Display): 84 mm
BUSINESS: ENVIRONMENT & POLLUTION

BODENSEE MAGAZIN 723324G89A-360
Editorial: Max-Stromeyer-Str. 116, 78467 KONSTANZ **Tel:** 7531 907125 **Fax:** 7531 907131
Email: redaktion@labhard.de **Web site:** http://www.labhard.de
Freq: Annual; **Cover Price:** EUR 6,00; **Circ:** 120,000
Editor: Sigi Gentner; **Advertising Manager:** Claudia Manz
Profile: Travel and Leisure magazine for the international Lake Constance region and informed about the German part of Lake Constance in eastern Switzerland, Liechtenstein and Vorarlberg, and in addition to the Allgäu, Oberschwaben. The Magazine provides all the tourist relevant information on attractions, cities, towns and regions, museums, restaurants, health, water, history and family tips, complemented by an international calendar of events and a comprehensive museum guide, maps, timetables and addresses.
Language(s): German
ADVERTISING RATES:
Full Page Colour .... EUR 7300
Mechanical Data: Type Area: 263 x 188 mm
Copy instructions: *Copy Date:* 30 days prior to publication
CONSUMER: HOLIDAYS & TRAVEL: Travel

BODENSEE MAGAZIN AKTUELL 1648477G89A-11860
Editorial: Max-Stromeyer-Str. 116, 78467 KONSTANZ **Tel:** 7531 907115 **Fax:** 7531 907131
Email: ukoch@labhard.de **Web site:** http://www.labhard.de
Freq: 5 issues yearly; **Cover Price:** Free; **Circ:** 20,000
Editor: Carola Buchwald; **Advertising Manager:** Beate Laub
Profile: Bodensee magazine currently is the free newspaper for the international Lake Constance region. The publication of the Lake magazine informed of updates from culture, tourism, economy and society.
Language(s): German
ADVERTISING RATES:
Full Page Colour .... EUR 1200
Mechanical Data: No. of Columns (Display): 4, Col Widths (Display): 50 mm, Type Area: 276 x 209 mm

BODO'S POWER SYSTEMS 1773233G58-1763
Editorial: Katzbek 17a, 24235 LABOE
Tel: 4343 421790 **Fax:** 4343 421789
Email: editor@bodospower.com **Web site:** http://www.bodospower.com
Freq: Monthly; **Annual Sub.:** EUR 150,00; **Circ:** 18,289
Editor: Bodo Arlt
Profile: Magazine focusing on power system design including power quality, communication, energy distribution and power supplies.
Language(s): English
ADVERTISING RATES:
Full Page Mono .... EUR 5100
Full Page Colour .... EUR 5100
Mechanical Data: Type Area: 270 x 180 mm

BODY LIFE 723331G32H-7
Editorial: Karl-Friedrich-Str. 14, 76133 KARLSRUHE
Tel: 721 165132 **Fax:** 721 165150
Email: max.barth@health-and-beauty.com **Web site:** http://www.bodylife.com
Freq: Monthly; **Annual Sub.:** EUR 79,00; **Circ:** 7,100
Editor: Max Barth; **Advertising Manager:** Isabell Prokscha
Profile: body Life Germany is Europe's No. 1 of the fitness magazines and appears as the only industry magazine on a monthly basis. The modern design, high benefit for readers and the innovative concept of body Life have made body Life to the market leader in the German market. By the equally successful foreign issues body Life is also in the international market leading. Industry currently, products & concepts, business & Best Practice, Medical fitness, wellness & spa and diet are the main points of the body Life.
Language(s): German
Readership: Aimed at owners and managers of sports facilities, sports doctors and physiotherapists.
ADVERTISING RATES:
Full Page Mono .... EUR 2150
Full Page Colour .... EUR 2750
Mechanical Data: Type Area: 250 x 194 mm, No. of Columns (Display): 3, Col Widths (Display): 62 mm
BUSINESS: LOCAL GOVERNMENT, LEISURE & RECREATION: Leisure, Recreation & Entertainment

BODY & MIND 1938692G74A-3734
Editorial: Rudolfstr. 22, 60327 FRANKFURT
Tel: 69 6656320 **Fax:** 69 66563222
Email: redaktion@dasistwellness.de **Web site:** http://www.dasistwellness.de
Freq: Quarterly; **Annual Sub.:** EUR 8,90; **Circ:** 60,000
Editor: Martin Brückner; **Advertising Manager:** Dagmar Hummel
Profile: Wellness magazine.
Language(s): German
ADVERTISING RATES:
Full Page Mono .... CHF 1689
Full Page Colour .... CHF 2194
Mechanical Data: Type Area: 257 x 170 mm, No. of Columns (Display): 3, Col Widths (Display): 54 mm

BOGENER ZEITUNG - HEIMATAUSG. D. STRAUBINGER TAGBLATTS 723357G67B-3140
Editorial: Ludwigsplatz 30, 94315 STRAUBING
Tel: 9421 9404601 **Fax:** 9421 9404609
Email: landkreis@straubinger-tagblatt.de **Web site:** http://www.idowa.de
Freq: 312 issues yearly; **Circ:** 26,804
Advertising Manager: Klaus Huber
Profile: Regional daily newspaper with news on politics, economy, culture, sports, travel, technology, etc. It is a local issue by Straubinger Tagblatt for the old County Bogen. Twitter: http://twitter.com/idowa This Outlet offers RSS (Really Simple Syndication).
Language(s): German
ADVERTISING RATES:
SCC .... EUR 62,90
Mechanical Data: Type Area: 430 x 282 mm, No. of Columns (Display): 6, Col Widths (Display): 45 mm
Copy instructions: *Copy Date:* 1 day prior to publication
Supplement(s): Zuhause
REGIONAL DAILY & SUNDAY NEWSPAPERS: Regional Daily Newspapers

BOGENSPORT MAGAZIN 723359G75X-17_30
Editorial: Bert-Brecht-Str. 15, 78054 VILLINGEN-SCHWENNINGEN **Tel:** 7720 394212
Fax: 7720 394294
Email: magazin@bogensport.de **Web site:** http://www.bogensport.de
Freq: 6 issues yearly; **Annual Sub.:** EUR 22,80; **Circ:** 10,000
Editor: Günther Baumann; **Advertising Manager:** André M. Gegg
Profile: Magazine for archers, reports on training, competitions etc.
Language(s): German
ADVERTISING RATES:
Full Page Mono .... EUR 1585
Full Page Colour .... EUR 2085
Mechanical Data: Type Area: 235 x 170 mm, No. of Columns (Display): 4, Col Widths (Display): 40 mm
Copy instructions: *Copy Date:* 21 days prior to publication
CONSUMER: SPORT: Other Sport

BÖHME-ZEITUNG 723336G67B-3160
Editorial: Harburger Str. 63, 29614 SOLTAU
Tel: 5191 808135 **Fax:** 5191 808146
Email: redaktion@boehme-zeitung.de **Web site:** http://www.boehme-zeitung.de
Freq: 312 issues yearly; **Circ:** 11,434
Profile: The editorial staff gathers information and offers readers the most important and interesting to them - whether in the print edition of Böhme-Zeitung or in the online edition BZ-Online. Its core tasks is to control the leaders in politics and governance at the local and district level by reports on their actions and intentions and concerns as needed, in the form of a commentary. This is to the readers to be able to give impressions of the political actors in the region. To fulfill this task must have the editors staff, work organization, technical equipment and facilities. Twitter: http://twitter.com/BZRedaktion This Outlet offers RSS (Really Simple Syndication).
Language(s): German
ADVERTISING RATES:
SCC .... EUR 43,60
Mechanical Data: Type Area: 435 x 282 mm, No. of Columns (Display): 6, Col Widths (Display): 45 mm
Copy instructions: *Copy Date:* 1 day prior to publication
Supplement(s): Arena
REGIONAL DAILY & SUNDAY NEWSPAPERS: Regional Daily Newspapers

BOLD 2038824G74A-3767
Editorial: Chausseestr. 104, 10115 BERLIN
Tel: 30 40005668
Email: info@bold-magazine.eu **Web site:** http://www.bold-magazine.eu
Freq: 6 issues yearly; **Annual Sub.:** EUR 25,50; **Circ:** 110,000
Editor: Mike Kuhlmey
Profile: Lifestyle Magazine: fashion, art and culture. Facebook: http://www.facebook.com/FACEMAGAZIN.
Language(s): German
ADVERTISING RATES:
Full Page Colour .... EUR 5990
Copy instructions: *Copy Date:* 14 days prior to publication

BONIFATIUSBOTE 723373G87-1640
Editorial: Liebfrauenplatz 10, 55116 MAINZ
Tel: 6131 2875525 **Fax:** 6131 2875522
Email: j-becher@kirchenzeitung.de **Web site:** http://www.kirchenzeitung.de
Freq: Weekly; **Annual Sub.:** EUR 73,20; **Circ:** 9,472
Editor: Johannes Becher; **Advertising Manager:** Sylvia Ehrengard
Profile: Catholic magazine.
Language(s): German
ADVERTISING RATES:
Full Page Mono .... EUR 3206
Mechanical Data: Type Area: 458 x 325 mm, No. of Columns (Display): 7, Col Widths (Display): 45 mm
Copy instructions: *Copy Date:* 14 days prior to publication
CONSUMER: RELIGIOUS

BONJOUR 723374G33-40
Editorial: Schützenstr. 25, 10117 BERLIN
Tel: 30 20276237 **Fax:** 30 2027796237
Email: cornelia.schulze@total.de **Web site:** http://www.total.de
Freq: 5 issues yearly; **Cover Price:** Free; **Circ:** 5,000
Editor: Cornelia Schulze
Profile: Company publication published by Total Deutschland.
Language(s): German
ADVERTISING RATES:
Full Page Mono .... EUR 2600
Full Page Colour .... EUR 2600
Mechanical Data: Type Area: 270 x 198 mm

BONN EXPRESS 723387G67B-3180
Editorial: Amsterdamer Str. 192, 50735 KÖLN
Tel: 221 2240 **Fax:** 221 2243403
Email: redaktion@express.de **Web site:** http://www.express.de
Freq: 312 issues yearly; **Circ:** 16,047
Advertising Manager: Karsten Hundhausen
Profile: The local-based tabloid newspaper from the publisher M. DuMont Schauberg is the currently-cheeky voice of the region and the lawyer of his readers. Six times a week, the editors demonstrate their competence, for the Express, there are more than just sensational headline. Exciting coverage is combined with in-depth background information and critical comments. The Express is the leading newspaper purchase of the Rhineland with the highest competence in the region. He appears in the circulation area with three issues: in Cologne, Dusseldorf and Bonn, from the Eifel to the Oberbergische Land. The Express is characterized by recent, strong acceptance themes, series and service elements. His style is like the people on the Rhine: tolerant, cosmopolitan, humorous with a touch of emotion. One of the very strong points of the Express: sport. Facebook: http://www.facebook.com/express.de.
Language(s): German
ADVERTISING RATES:
SCC .... EUR 33,10
Mechanical Data: Type Area: 430 x 285 mm, No. of Columns (Display): 6, Col Widths (Display): 45 mm
Copy instructions: *Copy Date:* 1 day prior to publication
REGIONAL DAILY & SUNDAY NEWSPAPERS: Regional Daily Newspapers

BONNER RUNDSCHAU 723382G67B-3200
Editorial: Martinsplatz 2a, 53113 BONN
Tel: 228 98420 **Fax:** 228 9842230
Email: bonner.rundschau@kr-redaktion.de **Web site:** http://www.rundschau-online.de
Freq: 312 issues yearly; **Circ:** 84,346
Advertising Manager: Karsten Hundhausen
Profile: Regional daily newspaper covering politics, economics, sport, travel and technology. Facebook: http://www.facebook.com/pages/Kolnische-Rundschau/147616463739.
Language(s): German
ADVERTISING RATES:
SCC .... EUR 150,00
Mechanical Data: Type Area: 430 x 285 mm, No. of Columns (Display): 6, Col Widths (Display): 45 mm
Copy instructions: *Copy Date:* 2 days prior to publication
Supplement(s): prisma
REGIONAL DAILY & SUNDAY NEWSPAPERS: Regional Daily Newspapers

BONNER UMWELT ZEITUNG 1836834G57-2868
Editorial: Hatschiergasse 2, 53111 BONN
Tel: 228 692220 **Fax:** 228 9768615
Email: umwelt@oez-bonn.de **Web site:** http://www.oez-bonn.de
Freq: 6 issues yearly; **Circ:** 6,000
Profile: The Bonner Umwelt Zeitung informed on current environmental issues newspaper in Bonn and the region, reports on the local agenda process and operations of the various environmental initiatives. The Bonner Umwelt Zeitung provides an overview of important dates, addresses and contacts for environmental issues (the environment addresses). It is the voice of the Bonn environmental groups and members' magazine of the Eco-Centre Bonn, VCD Circle Group Bonn / Rhein-Sieg / Ahr eV, the Bund district group in Bonn, the Association of Sustainable Bonn and the Association Livable Seven Mountains region eV is available free in many public facilities, health food stores, bookstores, bars, etc. from.
Language(s): German
ADVERTISING RATES:
Full Page Mono .... EUR 913
Full Page Colour .... EUR 1063
Mechanical Data: Type Area: 430 x 282 mm, No. of Columns (Display): 4, Col Widths (Display): 66 mm
Copy instructions: *Copy Date:* 14 days prior to publication

BONNES VACANCES 755745G89A-12129
Editorial: Dernburgstr. 47, 14057 BERLIN
Tel: 30 3213615 **Fax:** 30 3216558
Email: info@bonnesvacances.de **Web site:** http://www.bonnesvacances.de
Freq: Half-yearly; **Annual Sub.:** EUR 15,00; **Circ:** 30,000
Editor: Sigrun Lüddecke; **Advertising Manager:** Sigrun Lüddecke
Profile: Magazine about exclusive holiday destinations.
Language(s): German
ADVERTISING RATES:
Full Page Mono .... EUR 3510
Full Page Colour .... EUR 3900
Mechanical Data: Type Area: 265 x 185 mm, No. of Columns (Display): 3
Copy instructions: *Copy Date:* 42 days prior to publication

BÖNNIGHEIMER ZEITUNG 723339G67B-3220
Editorial: Kronenbergstr. 10, 74321 BIETIGHEIM-BISSINGEN **Tel:** 7142 403410 **Fax:** 7142 403128
Email: redaktion@bietigheimerzeitung.de **Web site:** http://www.bietigheimerzeitung.de
Freq: 312 issues yearly; **Circ:** 12,204
Advertising Manager: Johannes Schwiderowski
Profile: Daily newspaper with regional news and a local sports section.
Language(s): German
ADVERTISING RATES:
SCC .... EUR 42,60
Mechanical Data: Type Area: 485 x 320 mm, No. of Columns (Display): 7, Col Widths (Display): 44 mm
Copy instructions: *Copy Date:* 2 days prior to publication
Supplement(s): rtv
REGIONAL DAILY & SUNDAY NEWSPAPERS: Regional Daily Newspapers

BONUS 723391G94H-1980
Editorial: Leipziger Str. 35, 65191 WIESBADEN
Tel: 611 50661388 **Fax:** 611 50661500
Email: bonus@dgverlag.de **Web site:** http://www.vr-bonus.net
Freq: Monthly; **Circ:** 89,763
Profile: Magazine concerning investment and personal finance.
Language(s): German
Readership: Aimed at customers of the Volksbank and Raiffeisenbank.
ADVERTISING RATES:
Full Page Colour .... EUR 9424
Mechanical Data: Type Area: 245 x 175 mm
CONSUMER: OTHER CLASSIFICATIONS: Customer Magazines

BOOTE 723394G91A-40
Editorial: Raboisen 8, 20095 HAMBURG
Tel: 40 3396680 **Fax:** 40 33966888
Email: redaktion@boote-magazin.de **Web site:** http://www.boote-magazin.de
Freq: Monthly; **Annual Sub.:** EUR 49,50; **Circ:** 33,542
Editor: Torsten Moench; **Advertising Manager:** Ingo van Holt
Profile: Magazine about yachts and motorboats.
Language(s): German
Readership: Aimed at boating and maritime enthusiasts.
ADVERTISING RATES:
Full Page Mono .... EUR 5810
Full Page Colour .... EUR 8690
Mechanical Data: Type Area: 254 x 192 mm, No. of Columns (Display): 4, Col Widths (Display): 45 mm
Copy instructions: *Copy Date:* 40 days prior to publication
CONSUMER: RECREATION & LEISURE: Boating & Yachting

BOOTE EXCLUSIV 723395G91A-41
Editorial: Raboisen 8, 20095 HAMBURG
Tel: 40 3396680 **Fax:** 40 33966888
Email: exclusiv@boote-exclusiv.com **Web site:** http://www.boote-exclusiv.com
Freq: 6 issues yearly; **Annual Sub.:** EUR 41,00; **Circ:** 40,000
Editor: Marcus Krall; **Advertising Manager:** Ingo van Holt
Profile: The magazine shows what is possible today on the water: Expensive Yacht-technology, luxurious interiors. The spacious layout granted by boote

Exclusiv extraordinary insights. boote Exclusiv provides detailed and knowledgeable sensitive about this scene.
Language(s): English; German
Readership: Aimed at owners of luxury yachts.
ADVERTISING RATES:
Full Page Mono .... EUR 3160
Full Page Colour .... EUR 5900
Mechanical Data: Type Area: 252 x 192 mm, No. of Columns (Display): 4, Col Widths (Display): 45 mm
Copy instructions: *Copy Date:* 49 days prior to publication
CONSUMER: RECREATION & LEISURE: Boating & Yachting

BOOTSHANDEL 749082G91A-320

Editorial: Am Treptower Park 75, 12435 BERLIN
Tel: 30 53432129 **Fax:** 30 53433132
Email: stefan.gerhard@bootshandel-magazin.de
Web site: http://www.bootshandel-magazin.de
Freq: Monthly; **Cover Price:** EUR 4,20; **Circ:** 14,128
Editor: Stefan Gerhard
Profile: The Bootshandel-Magazin is the most successful magazine start-up of the last thirteen years in the boat and water sport magazine. The boat trade magazine one of the leading German magazines in its market segment. The Bootshandel-Magazin published every month nationwide and, via the portal boot trade-magazin.de one of the largest online boat markets in Germany. The Bootshandel-Magazin speaks determined and consistent boat owners, of water sports, boat dealers and interested newcomers. The reader will find displays of sailing and motor boats, solar boats, canoes, boat charter and rental, moorings, transportation, marine engines and accessories. The Bootshandel-Magazin published in großen entrants mainly color photo packages, which provide an attractive advertising environment.
Language(s): German
ADVERTISING RATES:
Full Page Colour .... EUR 2200
Mechanical Data: Type Area: 270 x 190 mm, No. of Columns (Display): 4, Col Widths (Display): 45 mm
Copy instructions: *Copy Date:* 10 days prior to publication
CONSUMER: RECREATION & LEISURE: Boating & Yachting

BORBECK KURIER 723401G72-2532

Editorial: Bert-Brecht-Str. 29, 45128 ESSEN
Tel: 201 8041715 **Fax:** 201 8041716
Email: redaktion@borbeckkurier-essen.de **Web site:** http://www.lokalkompass.de/essen-borbeck
Freq: 104 issues yearly; **Cover Price:** Free; **Circ:** 43,400
Editor: Christa Herlinger; **Advertising Manager:** Lars Staehler
Profile: Advertising journal (house-to-house) concentrating on local stories.
Language(s): German
ADVERTISING RATES:
Full Page Mono .... EUR 3396
Full Page Colour .... EUR 4584
Mechanical Data: Type Area: 445 x 315 mm, No. of Columns (Display): 7, Col Widths (Display): 42 mm
Copy instructions: *Copy Date:* 2 days prior to publication
LOCAL NEWSPAPERS

BORBECKER NACHRICHTEN 723400G72-2536

Editorial: Vinckestr. 2, 45355 ESSEN
Tel: 201 8670011 **Fax:** 201 678360
Email: redaktion@borbecker-nachrichten.de
Freq: Weekly; **Cover Price:** EUR 1,00; **Circ:** 5,814
Editor: Susanne Hölter; **News Editor:** Jörg Weiner
Profile: Regional weekly covering politics, economics, sport, travel, technology and the arts.
Language(s): German
ADVERTISING RATES:
SCC .... EUR 39,20
Mechanical Data: Type Area: 445 x 325 mm, No. of Columns (Display): 7, Col Widths (Display): 45 mm
Copy instructions: *Copy Date:* 1 day prior to publication
LOCAL NEWSPAPERS

BÖRDE VOLKSSTIMME 723343G67B-3240

Editorial: Bahnhofstr. 17, 39104 MAGDEBURG
Tel: 391 59990 **Fax:** 391 5999210
Email: chefredaktion@volksstimme.de **Web site:** http://www.volksstimme.de
Freq: 312 issues yearly; **Circ:** 12,327
Advertising Manager: Rainer Pfeil
Profile: As the largest daily newspaper in northern Saxony-Anhalt, the Volksstimme reaches 536,000 readers a day* (MA 2010). From Monday to Saturday a team of highly qualified editors put together the latest information and news from the region and around the world. Thanks the 18 local editions is the Volksstimme always close to the action. Twitter: http://twitter.com/volksstimme This Outlet offers RSS (Really Simple Syndication).
Language(s): German
ADVERTISING RATES:
SCC .... EUR 51,20
Mechanical Data: Type Area: 480 x 327 mm, No. of Columns (Display): 7, Col Widths (Display): 45 mm
Copy instructions: *Copy Date:* 2 days prior to publication
Supplement(s): Anstoss in Oschersleben und Wanzleben; bauRatgeber; Biber; Leser-Reisen; prisma; Standort Bördekreis
REGIONAL DAILY & SUNDAY NEWSPAPERS: Regional Daily Newspapers

BORKENER ZEITUNG 723408G67B-3260

Editorial: Bahnhofstr. 6, 46325 BORKEN
Tel: 2861 9440 **Fax:** 2861 944179
Email: redaktion@borkenerzeitung.de **Web site:** http://www.borkenerzeitung.de
Freq: 312 issues yearly; **Circ:** 17,576
Editor: Gregor Wenzel; **Advertising Manager:** Wolfgang Rickert
Profile: News from the neighborhood, from the region and around the world: the Borkener Zeitung is the modern daily newspaper for the people in the Münsterland. The Borkener Zeitung is indispensable resource for anyone who wants to know what's going on in their city, their neighborhood, in Westphalia, in the Republic and all over the globe. With a circulation of about 20,000 copies in conjunction with the Zeitungsgruppe Münsterland (ZGM) is Borkener Zeitung the leading daily newspaper and the largest advertising medium in Borken and surrounding areas. Facebook: http://www.facebook.com/borkenerzeitung Twitter: http://twitter.com/BorkenerZeitung This Outlet offers RSS (Really Simple Syndication).
Language(s): German
ADVERTISING RATES:
SCC .... EUR 52,40
Mechanical Data: Type Area: 488 x 322 mm, No. of Columns (Display): 7, Col Widths (Display): 43 mm
Copy instructions: *Copy Date:* 1 day prior to publication
Supplement(s): prisma
REGIONAL DAILY & SUNDAY NEWSPAPERS: Regional Daily Newspapers

BÖRSE ONLINE 1622272G1F-1518

Editorial: Am Baumwall 11, 20459 HAMBURG
Tel: 40 37030 **Fax:** 40 37038310
Email: naskrent.joergen@guj.de **Web site:** http://www.boerse-online.de
Freq: Daily; **Cover Price:** Paid; **Circ:** 1,325,896 Unique Users
Editor: Stefanie Burgmaier; **News Editor:** Philipp Jaklin
Profile: Ezine: Boerse-online.de comments for private and institutional investors promptly, competently and independently of developments in the stock markets and makes concrete recommendations. It also includes valuable tools boerseonline.de like stocks, funds, certificates analyzer and a Glossary. For users prefer the moving images, has also Boerse-online.de Video Format: Each week, be prepared concisely current stocks, funds and other investment news. Even more, the mobile site of the investor magazine a wide range of topics in high-Boerse online quality, with a focus on stocks, technical analysis, certificates and mutual funds. Twitter: http://www.facebook.com/boerseonline This Outlet offers RSS (Really Simple Syndication).
Language(s): German
BUSINESS: FINANCE & ECONOMICS: Investment

BÖRSE ONLINE 1860163G1F-1746

Editorial: Nibelungenplatz 3, 60318 FRANKFURT
Tel: 69 1530970 **Fax:** 69 15309750
Email: chefredaktion@boerse-online.de **Web site:** http://www.boerse-online.de
Freq: 16 issues yearly; **Annual Sub.:** EUR 175,00; **Circ:** 75,273
Editor: Stefanie Burgmaier; **News Editor:** Philipp Jaklin; **Advertising Manager:** Jens Kauerauf
Profile: Magazine focusing on the German stock market.
Language(s): German
ADVERTISING RATES:
Full Page Mono .... EUR 12000
Full Page Colour .... EUR 12000
Mechanical Data: Type Area: 246 x 178 mm, No. of Columns (Display): 3, Col Widths (Display): 56 mm
Copy instructions: *Copy Date:* 14 days prior to publication

BÖRSE-AKTUELL 723345G1F-200

Editorial: Fritz-Elsas-Str. 49, 70174 STUTTGART
Tel: 711 61414111 **Fax:** 711 61414333
Email: beck.dieter@boerse-aktuell.de **Web site:** http://www.boerse-aktuell.de
Freq: 26 issues yearly; **Annual Sub.:** EUR 146,00; **Circ:** 50,000
Editor: Dieter Beck
Profile: Magazine focusing on the stockmarket.
Language(s): German
Readership: Aimed at investors.
BUSINESS: FINANCE & ECONOMICS: Investment

BÖRSENBLATT 723348G60A-160

Editorial: Großer Hirschgraben 17, 60311 FRANKFURT **Tel:** 69 1306339 **Fax:** 69 1306424
Email: info@mvb-online.de **Web site:** http://www.mvb-boersenblatt.de
Freq: Weekly; Free to qualifying individuals
Annual Sub.: EUR 450,00; **Circ:** 9,529
Editor: Torsten Casimir; **Advertising Manager:** Jörg Gerschlauer
Profile: The Börsenblatt is the most widely read magazine in the industry and offers weekly news alongside a diverse range of topics. Portraits and interviews, comments and personalities are included as well as interesting background information and practical examples. As the market leader in the industry magazines each issue is an indispensable resource for booksellers, publishers, between booksellers, librarians, writers, journalists and other cultural workers. Of the readers will look in particular appreciated the professional quality of the content and the high credibility of the editors. Twitter: http://twitter.com/bbl_news.
Language(s): German
ADVERTISING RATES:
Full Page Mono .... EUR 1470
Full Page Colour .... EUR 2410
Mechanical Data: Type Area: 260 x 180 mm, No. of Columns (Display): 4, Col Widths (Display): 41 mm
Copy instructions: *Copy Date:* 6 days prior to publication
BUSINESS: PUBLISHING: Publishing & Book Trade

BÖRSEN-ZEITUNG 723354G14A-1000

Editorial: Düsseldorfer Str. 16, 60329 FRANKFURT
Tel: 69 27320 **Fax:** 69 232264
Email: redaktion@boersen-zeitung.de **Web site:** http://www.boersen-zeitung.com
Freq: 260 issues yearly
Editor: Claus Döring; **Advertising Manager:** Jens Zinke
Profile: The Börsen-Zeitung is the only exclusively on the financial sector-oriented newspaper. The stock exchange gazette is published daily Tuesday through Saturday, and reports on the latest developments on the German and international financial centers. The focus of coverage in the form of news, analysis, commentary and background reports for publicly listed companies on credit and insurance industry, international financing institutions, German and international capital markets to the monetary policy, economic and financial policy. The course and table part is an essential part of daily output. Courses and prices are available online for subscribers from October 1998 in the securities information system "WPI" free searchable. Twitter: http://twitter.com/boersenzeitung This Outlet offers RSS (Really Simple Syndication).
Language(s): German
Readership: Aimed at leaders in industry, banking and finance.
ADVERTISING RATES:
SCC .... EUR 191,00
Mechanical Data: Type Area: 460 x 315 mm, No. of Columns (Display): 7, Col Widths (Display): 45 mm
Copy instructions: *Copy Date:* 1 day prior to publication
Supplement(s): rendite
BUSINESS: COMMERCE, INDUSTRY & MANAGEMENT

BOSS 723419G34-529

Editorial: Fasanenweg 18, 70771 LEINFELDEN-ECHTERDINGEN **Tel:** 711 7591313
Fax: 711 75913775
Email: selsass@bitverlag.de **Web site:** http://www.boss-magazin.de
Freq: 11 issues yearly; **Annual Sub.:** EUR 89,50; **Circ:** 6,721
Editor: Siegfried Elsaß; **Advertising Manager:** Joachim Ahnfeldt
Profile: Trade magazine for the office supplies industry. Core target group are the high-volume office supply dealers, and the upstream industry levels of wholesale, distributors and industry. The Globals, as well as the vast majority of office cooperated retailer (Soennecken, Büroring, Prisma etc.) are also resistant to readers such as marketing groups, and a full-line distributor route. But also the distribution channels such as PBS and purchasing departments of department stores, specialty stores, chain stores, discounters and supermarkets, the magazine reaches a monthly basis. The magazine section this neutral and independent information about the current development of the PBS sector. Background reports, features and interviews from the manufacturer's retail scene as well as provide a concise overview of what's driving the industry and what one is talking. A recent special issue is the lead story in every issue. As the only industry magazine the magazine also provides a test report from the purchase trade. Current topics such as seasonal focus on a core range of PBS and add trade complete the monthly reporting industry to find new and interesting products PBS. Facebook: http://www.facebook.com/pages/Bossticker/149890035061413 Twitter: http://twitter.com/#!/bossticker This Outlet offers RSS (Really Simple Syndication).
Language(s): German
Readership: Read by purchasers of office, stationery and school equipment.
ADVERTISING RATES:
Full Page Mono .... EUR 2860
Full Page Colour .... EUR 4180
Mechanical Data: Type Area: 262 x 180 mm, No. of Columns (Display): 3, Col Widths (Display): 55 mm
Copy instructions: *Copy Date:* 24 days prior to publication
BUSINESS: OFFICE EQUIPMENT

DER BOTE FÜR NÜRNBERG-LAND 723436G67B-3300

Editorial: Nürnberger Str. 5, 90537 FEUCHT
Tel: 9128 707232 **Fax:** 9128 707272
Email: redaktion@der-bote.de **Web site:** http://www.der-bote.de
Freq: 312 issues yearly; **Circ:** 10,511
Profile: Daily newspaper with regional news and a local sports section. This Outlet offers RSS (Really Simple Syndication).
Language(s): German
ADVERTISING RATES:
SCC .... EUR 29,30
Mechanical Data: Type Area: 430 x 280 mm, No. of Columns (Display): 6, Col Widths (Display): 45 mm
Copy instructions: *Copy Date:* 2 days prior to publication
Supplement(s): Amtsblatt für den Landkreis Nürnberger Land; sechs+sechzig
REGIONAL DAILY & SUNDAY NEWSPAPERS: Regional Daily Newspapers

BOTE VOM HASSGAU 723439G67B-3340

Editorial: Berner Str. 2, 97084 WÜRZBURG
Tel: 931 60010 **Fax:** 931 6001242
Web site: http://www.mainpost.de
Freq: 312 issues yearly; **Circ:** 2,910
Advertising Manager: Matthias Faller
Profile: Daily newspaper with regional news and a local sports section. Twitter: http://twitter.com/mainpost This Outlet offers RSS (Really Simple Syndication).
Language(s): German
ADVERTISING RATES:
SCC .... EUR 21,30
Mechanical Data: Type Area: 466 x 310 mm, No. of Columns (Display): 7, Col Widths (Display): 43 mm
Copy instructions: *Copy Date:* 1 day prior to publication
Supplement(s): 4 Wände
REGIONAL DAILY & SUNDAY NEWSPAPERS: Regional Daily Newspapers

BOTE VOM UNTER=MAIN 723440G67B-3360

Editorial: Weichertstr. 20, 63741 ASCHAFFENBURG
Tel: 6021 396229 **Fax:** 6021 396499
Email: redaktion@main-echo.de **Web site:** http://www.main-netz.de
Freq: 312 issues yearly; **Circ:** 9,509
Advertising Manager: Reinhard Fresow
Profile: Daily newspaper with regional news and a local sports section. Facebook: http://www.facebook.com/mainnetz?v=wall Twitter: http://twitter.com/mainnetz This Outlet offers RSS (Really Simple Syndication).
Language(s): German
ADVERTISING RATES:
SCC .... EUR 30,50
Mechanical Data: Type Area: 480 x 366 mm, No. of Columns (Display): 8, Col Widths (Display): 44 mm
Copy instructions: *Copy Date:* 1 day prior to publication
Supplement(s): Gesundheit!
REGIONAL DAILY & SUNDAY NEWSPAPERS: Regional Daily Newspapers

BOX 723456G86B-140

Editorial: Christianstr. 52, 50825 KÖLN
Tel: 221 95433335 **Fax:** 221 3553387259
Email: box@box-medien.de **Web site:** http://www.box-online.de
Freq: Monthly; **Annual Sub.:** EUR 36,00; **Circ:** 43,900
Editor: Michael Zgonjanin; **Advertising Manager:** Ingo Toenges
Profile: National free of charge magazine for gays.
Language(s): German
ADVERTISING RATES:
Full Page Mono .... EUR 3920
Full Page Colour .... EUR 3920
Mechanical Data: Type Area: 260 x 190 mm
Copy instructions: *Copy Date:* 7 days prior to publication
CONSUMER: ADULT & GAY MAGAZINES: Gay & Lesbian Magazines

BOX SPORT 723457G75Q-60

Editorial: Im Mediapark 8, 50670 KÖLN
Tel: 221 2587260 **Fax:** 221 2587212
Email: reski@sportverlag.de **Web site:** http://www.box-sport.de
Freq: Monthly; **Annual Sub.:** EUR 45,60; **Circ:** 30,000
Editor: Hans Reski
Profile: Official journal of the German Amateur Boxing Association.
Language(s): German
ADVERTISING RATES:
Full Page Mono .... EUR 3000
Full Page Colour .... EUR 3000
Mechanical Data: Type Area: 265 x 185 mm, No. of Columns (Display): 4, Col Widths (Display): 43 mm
Copy instructions: *Copy Date:* 8 days prior to publication
CONSUMER: SPORT: Combat Sports

BPZ BAUPRAXIS ZEITUNG 723463G42A-25

Editorial: Ernst-Mey-Str. 8, 70771 LEINFELDEN-ECHTERDINGEN **Tel:** 711 7594251
Fax: 711 7594397
Email: bpz.redaktion@konradin.de **Web site:** http://www.bpz-online.de
Freq: 10 issues yearly; **Annual Sub.:** EUR 61,50; **Circ:** 20,039
Editor: Paul Deder; **Advertising Manager:** Bettina Mayer
Profile: The bpz baupraxis zeitung offers contractors in construction, civil engineering and road

construction as well as equipment dealers valuable impulses, practical experience and decision support for their business success. As a generalist, the bpz reported month after month holistically about efficient building site management, the economic use of construction machinery and equipment as well as the potential of modern building materials. This balanced mix of topics covering the entire professional practice of decision-makers from the construction. The reporting of bpz focused on the essential and contributes to the information needs and the limited time resources of the target group equally into account. bpz has its ear to the pulse of the industry - building site reports, field reports, system comparison reports, trend and product reports, and interviews provide impetus to the current topics, answer questions and demonstrate solutions to problems. Of course, reason the bpz local presence - whether at the building site, the factory or the dealer. bpz that are must-have, not nice-to-have information for successful contractors and distributors.
Language(s): German
ADVERTISING RATES:
Full Page Mono .... EUR 4410
Full Page Colour .... EUR 5610
Mechanical Data: Type Area: 270 x 188 mm, No. of Columns (Display): 4, Col Widths (Display): 44 mm
BUSINESS: CONSTRUCTION

BR BAURECHTS-REPORT
723545G4E-2880
Editorial: Kalvarienbergstr. 22, 93491 STAMSRIED
Tel: 9466 94000 **Fax:** 9466 1276
Email: voegel@voegel.com **Web site:** http://www.verlag-voegel.de
Freq: Monthly; **Annual Sub.:** EUR 40,64; **Circ:** 12,000
Editor: Olaf Hofmann
Profile: The VOB-Verlag Ernst Vögel OHG has focused entirely on practical publications on private construction law. Contractors, construction managers, architects, engineers, public and private clients and their advisors will find here lots of valuable information to building law. And in ways that it can be used immediately for daily practice. By the VOB-Verlag Ernst Vögel OHG monthly published fact sheets "BR Baurechts-Report", "Vergaberechts-Report" and "Planerrechts-Report" informed of all significant new choices for construction, procurement and planning law and enjoy a wide acceptance among readers. Thanks to the high circulations can ensure the VOB-Verlag Ernst Vögel OHG for his works a very favorable price-performance ratio.
Language(s): German

BRAIN STRUCTURE AND FUNCTION
1832484G56A-11544
Editorial: 52425 JÜLICH **Tel:** 2461 613015
Fax: 2461 612990
Email: k.zilles@fz-juelich.de
Freq: Quarterly; **Annual Sub.:** EUR 1759,00; **Circ:** 143
Editor: Karl Zilles
Profile: This journal provides a forum for the discussion of structure-function relationship in the mammalian brain.
Language(s): English
ADVERTISING RATES:
Full Page Mono .... EUR 740
Full Page Colour .... EUR 1780
Mechanical Data: Type Area: 240 x 175 mm

BRAKEL ERLEBEN
723472G72-2612
Editorial: Am Markt 3, 33034 BRAKEL
Tel: 5272 374117
Email: extra_brakel@westfalen-blatt.de **Web site:** http://www.westfalen-blatt.de
Freq: Weekly; **Cover Price:** Free; **Circ:** 8,000
Editor: André Best; **Advertising Manager:** Gabriele Förster
Profile: Advertising journal (house-to-house) concentrating on local stories.
Language(s): German
ADVERTISING RATES:
Full Page Mono .... EUR 1408
Full Page Colour .... EUR 2048
Mechanical Data: Type Area: 320 x 228 mm, No. of Columns (Display): 5, Col Widths (Display): 44 mm
Copy instructions: *Copy Date:* 2 days prior to publication
LOCAL NEWSPAPERS

BRAK-MITTEILUNGEN
723473G44-3096
Editorial: Littenstr. 9, 10179 BERLIN **Tel:** 30 2849390
Fax: 30 28493911
Email: zentrale@brak.de **Web site:** http://www.brak-mitteilungen.de
Freq: 6 issues yearly; Free to qualifying individuals
Annual Sub.: EUR 116,90; **Circ:** 158,960
Editor: Christian Dahns; **Advertising Manager:** Thorsten Deuse
Profile: Magazine from the federal chamber of lawyers.
Language(s): German
ADVERTISING RATES:
Full Page Mono .... EUR 4075
Full Page Colour .... EUR 6991
Mechanical Data: Type Area: 260 x 180 mm, No. of Columns (Display): 2, Col Widths (Display): 88 mm
Supplement(s): BRAK Magazin
BUSINESS: LEGAL

BRAMSCHER NACHRICHTEN
723474G67B-3380
Editorial: Breiter Gang 10, 49074 OSNABRÜCK
Tel: 541 3100 **Fax:** 541 310485
Email: redaktion@noz.de **Web site:** http://www.n-oz.de
Freq: 312 issues yearly; **Circ:** 6,397
Profile: Daily newspaper with regional news and a local sports section. Facebook: http://www.facebook.com/pages/nozde/106261086094051 Twitter: http://twitter.com/noz_de This Outlet offers RSS (Really Simple Syndication).
Language(s): German
ADVERTISING RATES:
SCC .... EUR 36,90
Mechanical Data: Type Area: 487 x 318 mm, No. of Columns (Display): 7, Col Widths (Display): 43 mm
Copy instructions: *Copy Date:* 2 days prior to publication
Supplement(s): Berufswahl; Immo-Welt; Kfz-Welt; TheaterZeitung; Toaster; Treffpunkt Bramsche; wir für wallenhorst
REGIONAL DAILY & SUNDAY NEWSPAPERS: Regional Daily Newspapers

BRANCHEN INDEX GALVANOTECHNIK DÜNNE SCHICHTEN
753711G27-370
Editorial: Abraham-Lincoln-Str. 46, 65189 WIESBADEN **Tel:** 611 7878154 **Fax:** 611 7878407
Email: christiane.imhof@gwv-media.de **Web site:** http://www.branchenindex.de
Freq: Annual; **Cover Price:** EUR 15,00; **Circ:** 4,800
Editor: Christiane Imhof; **Advertising Manager:** Petra Neumann
Profile: Directory for the plating industry, equipment and service suppliers, methods and materials, environment techniques.
Language(s): German
ADVERTISING RATES:
Full Page Mono .... EUR 2760
Full Page Colour .... EUR 3510
Mechanical Data: Type Area: 240 x 175 mm, No. of Columns (Display): 3, Col Widths (Display): 55 mm
Copy instructions: *Copy Date:* 41 days prior to publication

BRANCHENBRIEF INTERNATIONAL
723476G48A-20
Editorial: Bahnhofstr. 22, 96117 MEMMELSDORF
Tel: 951 4066622 **Fax:** 951 4066649
Email: nostheide@nostheide.de **Web site:** http://www.toyscene.de
Freq: 24 issues yearly; **Annual Sub.:** EUR 144,45; **Circ:** 1,450
Editor: Thorsten Heinermann; **Advertising Manager:** Barbara Nostheide
Profile: Magazine with general information and new product news for the toys and games trade.
Language(s): German
Readership: Read by owners and workers of retail outlets, also buyers for the toy industry.
ADVERTISING RATES:
Full Page Mono .... EUR 1020
Full Page Colour .... EUR 1400
Mechanical Data: Type Area: 265 x 180 mm, No. of Columns (Display): 2, Col Widths (Display): 85 mm
Copy instructions: *Copy Date:* 4 days prior to publication
BUSINESS: TOY TRADE & SPORTS GOODS: Toy Trade

BRAND EINS
723485G14A-1020
Editorial: Speersort 1, 20095 HAMBURG
Tel: 40 3233160 **Fax:** 40 32331620
Email: gabriele_fischer@brandeins.de **Web site:** http://www.brandeins.de
Freq: Monthly; **Annual Sub.:** EUR 79,80; **Circ:** 98,702
Editor: Gabriele Fischer; **Advertising Manager:** Eva-Maria Büttner
Profile: brand eins is the business magazine that makes change its theme. The status quo does not interest us. We are interested in coming trends. We are on the lookout for signs of a new era in business, society and culture, and for people and companies who face up to the future. We are not looking for eople to blame. We seek causes, circumstances, backgrounds. Our editorial staff was formed from within our own company and views business and business people, their successes and failures, from a different angle. Not with tables and checklists, but with stories that give them ideas or explain backgrounds and trends. And show that what makes people move. Facebook: http://www.facebook.com/brand.eins.
Language(s): German
Readership: Aimed at people interested in management and the economy.
ADVERTISING RATES:
Full Page Mono .... EUR 13900
Full Page Colour .... EUR 13900
Mechanical Data: No. of Columns (Display): 3, Col Widths (Display): 59 mm, Type Area: 258 x 189 mm
Copy instructions: *Copy Date:* 28 days prior to publication
BUSINESS: COMMERCE, INDUSTRY & MANAGEMENT

BRAND EINS NEULAND
1826019G14A-10075
Editorial: Speersort 1, 20095 HAMBURG
Tel: 40 80805890 **Fax:** 40 808058989
Email: susanne_risch@brandeinswissen.de **Web site:** http://www.brandeins-neuland.de
Freq: Quarterly; **Cover Price:** EUR 10,00; **Circ:** 40,000
Editor: Susanne Risch; **Advertising Manager:** Eva-Maria Büttner
Profile: brand eins Neuland is the business magazine that provides your location in the heart - and sets out to find the differences. In a world whose borders are more permeable, the nation-state becomes less important. Its decisions may limit the success of a country only . influence The scale of successful economy by the global development defined - and from the networks and regions of a country. Already they compete globally for investment and resources, they forge transnational alliances and market themselves and their specific capital: human, Knowledge, projects and ideas.
Language(s): German
ADVERTISING RATES:
Full Page Mono .... EUR 12500
Full Page Colour .... EUR 12500
Mechanical Data: Type Area: 240 x 170 mm

BRANDENBURGISCHE FORSTNACHRICHTEN
1828389G21A-4380
Editorial: Karl-Marx-Str. 73, 14612 FALKENSEE
Tel: 3322 243749 **Fax:** 3322 243750
Email: christian.naffin@affrup.brandenburg.de **Web site:** http://www.mil.brandenburg.de
Freq: 6 issues yearly; **Circ:** 3,300
Editor: Christian Naffin
Profile: Magazine for employees and all interested from the Federal Forest Administration of Brandenburg.
Language(s): German

BRANDENBURGISCHES ÄRZTEBLATT
1648583G56A-11300
Editorial: Friedrich-List-Platz 2, 04103 LEIPZIG
Tel: 341 8709840 **Fax:** 341 87098414
Email: laekb@4imedia.com **Web site:** http://www.4imedia.com
Freq: 11 issues yearly; Free to qualifying individuals
Annual Sub.: EUR 35,00; **Circ:** 107,000
Editor: Kay A. Schönewerk
Profile: Magazine of the Medical Board of Brandenburg.
Language(s): German
ADVERTISING RATES:
Full Page Mono .... EUR 1560
Full Page Colour .... EUR 2506
Mechanical Data: Type Area: 260 x 186 mm, No. of Columns (Display): 4, Col Widths (Display): 46 mm
Copy instructions: *Copy Date:* 28 days prior to publication

BRANDHILFE - AUSG. BADEN-WÜRTTEMBERG
723493G54A-80
Editorial: Klosterring 1, 78050 VILLINGEN-SCHWENNINGEN **Tel:** 7721 89870 **Fax:** 7721 898750
Email: frey@neckar-verlag.de **Web site:** http://www.neckar-verlag.de
Freq: Monthly; **Annual Sub.:** EUR 44,80; **Circ:** 7,667
Editor: Harry Frey; **Advertising Manager:** Uwe Stockburger
Profile: Magazine for firefighters from the German federal state of Baden-Württemberg.
Language(s): German
BUSINESS: SAFETY & SECURITY: Fire Fighting

BRANDSCHUTZ / DEUTSCHE FEUERWEHR-ZEITUNG
723494G54A-100
Editorial: Heßbrühlstr. 69, 70565 STUTTGART
Tel: 711 78637231 **Fax:** 711 78638454
Email: brandschutz.dfz@kohlhammer.de **Web site:** http://www.brandschutz-zeitschrift.de
Freq: Monthly; **Annual Sub.:** EUR 98,00; **Circ:** 12,768
Editor: Jochen Thorns; **Advertising Manager:** Sabine Zinke
Profile: Brandschutz / Deutsche Feuerwehr-Zeitung is by far the leading trade magazine for the fire department practice and is aimed at emergency services, professional, work and volunteer fire departments and industrial fire protection. They all achieved in Germany and in German-speaking countries, many executives and decision makers responsible for procurement. Brandschutz / Deutsche Feuerwehr-Zeitung is a magazine that reaches as required reading in circulation of nearly 80,000 readers.
Language(s): German
ADVERTISING RATES:
Full Page Mono .... EUR 2140
Full Page Colour .... EUR 3520
Mechanical Data: Type Area: 238 x 185 mm
Copy instructions: *Copy Date:* 15 days prior to publication
Official Journal of: Organ d. Dt. Feuerwehrverb.
BUSINESS: SAFETY & SECURITY: Fire Fighting

BRANDSCHUTZ IN ÖFFENTLICHEN UND PRIVATWIRTSCHAFTLICHEN GEBÄUDEN
723495G54A-38
Editorial: Avenwedder Str. 55, 33335 GÜTERSLOH
Tel: 5241 8090884 **Fax:** 5241 8067958
Email: christoph.brauneis@bauverlag.de **Web site:** http://www.bauverlag.de
Freq: Half-yearly; **Cover Price:** EUR 20,00; **Circ:** 83,760
Editor: Christoph Brauneis; **Advertising Manager:** Herbert Walhorn
Profile: Magazine focusing on protection against fire in the building industry.
Language(s): German
ADVERTISING RATES:
Full Page Mono .... EUR 6975
Full Page Colour .... EUR 9855
Mechanical Data: Type Area: 270 x 186 mm, No. of Columns (Display): 4, Col Widths (Display): 45 mm
Copy instructions: *Copy Date:* 14 days prior to publication
Supplement to: bauhandwerk, baumarkt bauwirtschaft, Bauwelt, BundesBauBlatt, DBZ Deutsche BauZeitschrift, Facility Management, TAB Technik am Bau
BUSINESS: SAFETY & SECURITY: Fire Fighting

BRANDWACHT
723497G54A-120
Editorial: Odeonsplatz 3, 80539 MÜNCHEN
Tel: 89 21922653 **Fax:** 89 21922655
Email: brandwacht@stmi.bayern.de **Web site:** http://www.diefeuerwehr.com
Freq: 6 issues yearly; **Annual Sub.:** EUR 17,00; **Circ:** 16,993
Editor: Helmut Graf; **Advertising Manager:** Heidi Grund-Thorpe
Profile: The brandwacht informed in the form of technical papers on current issues reliably and continuously for fire and civil protection. Reports on specific fire events, fire and disaster operations, and firefighting equipment rentals are included as well as current events and dates. In addition, the readers about technology (eg equipment, DIN standards, telecommunications matters) as well as legal and insurance issues will be kept up to date.
Language(s): German
Readership: Aimed at people in the fire service, police, planning departments and safety officers.
ADVERTISING RATES:
Full Page Mono .... EUR 1838
Full Page Colour .... EUR 2888
Mechanical Data: Type Area: 265 x 185 mm
BUSINESS: SAFETY & SECURITY: Fire Fighting

BRAUINDUSTRIE
723503G9B-2
Editorial: Schloss Mindelburg, 87719 MINDELHEIM
Tel: 8261 999311 **Fax:** 8261 999395
Email: hofbauer@sachon.de **Web site:** http://www.brauindustrie.de
Freq: Monthly; Free to qualifying individuals
Annual Sub.: EUR 70,62; **Circ:** 7,074
Editor: Andreas Hofbauer; **Advertising Manager:** Anita Elsäßer
Profile: Technology- and marketing-oriented monthly trade magazine for the successful brewery, with a strong international distribution. The monthly trade magazine provides information with journalistic flair and expertise about new technology and techniques, draws on current market and marketing issues and reports extensively on industry policy and economic contexts. Reports and contributions from around the world, and flashbacks to historical developments are not too short. A qualified staff guarantees the placement of nutzungsorientiertem firsthand knowledge, primary research and journalistic treatment make the Brauindustrie to a modern trade publication.
Language(s): German
ADVERTISING RATES:
Full Page Mono .... EUR 4555
Full Page Colour .... EUR 5935
Mechanical Data: Type Area: 270 x 185 mm, No. of Columns (Display): 4, Col Widths (Display): 45 mm
Copy instructions: *Copy Date:* 30 days prior to publication
BUSINESS: DRINKS & LICENSED TRADE: Brewing

BRAUNSCHWEIG REPORT
723517G72-2620
Editorial: Kreuztor 8, 38126 BRAUNSCHWEIG
Tel: 531 3800025 **Fax:** 531 3800020
Email: redaktion@braunschweigreport.de **Web site:** http://www.braunschweigreport.de
Freq: Weekly; **Cover Price:** Free; **Circ:** 164,700
Editor: Klaus Knodt; **Advertising Manager:** Ursula Manegold
Profile: Advertising journal (house-to-house) concentrating on local stories.
Language(s): German
ADVERTISING RATES:
Full Page Mono .... EUR 8514
Full Page Colour .... EUR 12345
Mechanical Data: Type Area: 430 x 280 mm, No. of Columns (Display): 6, Col Widths (Display): 45 mm
Copy instructions: *Copy Date:* 2 days prior to publication
LOCAL NEWSPAPERS

BRAUNSCHWEIGER ZEITUNG
723512G67B-3400
Editorial: Hamburger Str. 277, 38114 BRAUNSCHWEIG **Tel:** 531 39000 **Fax:** 531 3900610
Email: redaktion@bzv.de **Web site:** http://www.newsclick.de
Freq: 312 issues yearly; **Circ:** 177,413
Editor: Armin Maus; **News Editor:** Hans-Dieter Schlawis; **Advertising Manager:** Raphael Feldmann
Profile: Regional daily newspaper covering politics, economics, culture, sports, travel and technology. Almost half a million readers between resin and the Lüneburg Heath and regularly access to the Braunschweiger Zeitung (BZ), the second largest

newspaper in Lower Saxony. The BZ appears weekdays and has an average paid circulation of 150,000 copies. With the main titles Braunschweiger Zeitung, Salzgitter-Zeitung and Wolfsburger Nachrichten news and the seven local editions of the Braunschweiger Zeitung profiled as a strong regional newspaper in a historically significant landscape, the Brunswick Country. The Braunschweiger Zeitung considers itself not only as an information medium but also as a forum. Twitter: http://twitter.com/ os_zeitung This Outlet offers RSS (Really Simple Syndication).
Language(s): German
ADVERTISING RATES:
SCC .... EUR 348,40
Mechanical Data: Type Area: 435 x mm, No. of Columns (Display): 6, Col Widths (Display): 45 mm
Copy instructions: *Copy Date:* 1 day prior to publication
Official Journal of: Organ d. Niedersächsischen Börse zu Hannover
Supplement(s): prisma
REGIONAL DAILY & SUNDAY NEWSPAPERS: Regional Daily Newspapers

BRAUT & BRÄUTIGAM
723520G74L-20
Editorial: Hörsterplatz 2b, 48147 MÜNSTER
Tel: 251 5390219 **Fax:** 251 5390230
Email: s.lippe@brautmedia.de **Web site:** http://das.braut.net
Freq: 6 issues yearly; **Cover Price:** EUR 5,90; **Circ:** 82,500
Editor: Susan Lippe-Bernard; **Advertising Manager:** Eike Gunnar Schröder
Profile: Wedding magazine.
Language(s): German
ADVERTISING RATES:
Full Page Colour .... EUR 7530
Mechanical Data: Type Area: 258 x 202 mm, No. of Columns (Display): 4, Col Widths (Display): 48 mm
Supplement(s): Fashion-News
CONSUMER: WOMEN'S INTEREST CONSUMER MAGAZINES: Brides

BRAUWELT
723522G9B-12
Editorial: Andernacher Str. 33a, 90411 NÜRNBERG
Tel: 911 9528558 **Fax:** 911 952858160
Email: winkelmann@hanscarl.com **Web site:** http://www.brauwelt.de
Freq: 36 issues yearly; **Annual Sub.:** EUR 173,90; **Circ:** 3,555
Editor: Lydia Winkelmann; **Advertising Manager:** Wolf-Dieter Schoyerer
Profile: Magazine for the entire brewing and beverage industry. Worldwide, qualified capture all the economic and technological developments in this sector.
Language(s): German
ADVERTISING RATES:
Full Page Mono .... EUR 3680
Full Page Colour .... EUR 5138
Mechanical Data: Type Area: 275 x 185 mm, No. of Columns (Display): 4, Col Widths (Display): 43 mm
Copy instructions: *Copy Date:* 10 days prior to publication
BUSINESS: DRINKS & LICENSED TRADE: Brewing

BRAUWELT INTERNATIONAL
723526G9B-3
Editorial: Andernacher Str. 33a, 90411 NÜRNBERG
Tel: 911 9528558 **Fax:** 911 952858160
Email: winkelmann@hanscarl.com **Web site:** http://www.brauwelt-international.com
Freq: 6 issues yearly; **Annual Sub.:** EUR 97,00; **Circ:** 11,327
Editor: Lydia Winkelmann; **Advertising Manager:** Wolf-Dieter Schoyerer
Profile: Journal for the International brewing and beverage industry.
Language(s): English
Readership: Aimed at managers and decision makers in this industry.
ADVERTISING RATES:
Full Page Mono .... EUR 3669
Full Page Colour .... EUR 5127
Mechanical Data: Type Area: 275 x 185 mm, No. of Columns (Display): 4, Col Widths (Display): 43 mm
Copy instructions: *Copy Date:* 28 days prior to publication
BUSINESS: DRINKS & LICENSED TRADE: Brewing

BRAVO
723530G91D-1020
Editorial: Charles-de-Gaulle-Str. 8, 81737 MÜNCHEN **Tel:** 89 67867503 **Fax:** 89 6702033
Email: aschnarrenberger@bravo.de **Web site:** http://www.bravo.de
Freq: Weekly; **Cover Price:** EUR 1,40; **Circ:** 419,763
Editor: Philipp Jessen
Profile: BRAVO is the original among the youth magazines and the undisputed market leader. For the core readership 12-17 years BRAVO is the ain entertainment and information magazine. BRAVO appears weekly as the only youth magazine. The themes of stars, Dr. Sommer and Real Life are the three core areas of the booklet and through extensive service issues in the areas of styling, Beauty, Fun, Movie & TV rounded. BRAVO brings together national and international stars up close. Home Stories, exclusive reports and interviews provide readers with a high entertainment Faktor.Mit the Dr. Sommer team provides clarification on the main brand. Germany's competent youth counseling and creates unique trust Facebook: http://www.facebook.com/BRAVO.
Language(s): German
ADVERTISING RATES:
Full Page Mono .... EUR 40564
Full Page Colour .... EUR 40564
Mechanical Data: Type Area: 262 x 194 mm, No. of Columns (Display): 4, Col Widths (Display): 45 mm
Copy instructions: *Copy Date:* 21 days prior to publication
CONSUMER: RECREATION & LEISURE: Children & Youth

BRAVO GIRL!
723533G74F-50
Editorial: Charles-de-Gaulle-Str. 8, 81737 MÜNCHEN **Tel:** 89 67867302 **Fax:** 89 6732922
Email: sabrina.berges@bravogirl.de **Web site:** http://www.bravo.de
Freq: 26 issues yearly; **Cover Price:** EUR 1,70; **Circ:** 160,918
Editor: Iris Woehrle
Profile: BRAVO GiRL! is the most successful magazine for girls on the German market. With the core areas of celebrities, fashion, beauty and boys provides BRAVO GiRL! all that interested in girls. Fashion & Beauty: BRAVO GiRL! shows not just the latest trend parts or make-up products, but offers readers a unique service. Our fashion and beauty stories cater to the daily lives and needs of the target group. In the large distances it comes to questions like: What is the coolest school outfit? What styles like boys? What should I wear to get in to the disco? How can I reapplication the hottest Star Looks? IN & OUT: BRAVO GiRL! is trendy. BRAVO GiRL! In each issue, a trend barometer. New products, cool trends - all the girls have to have now said they BRAVO GiRL!. After-and imitation factor: 100%! Guys: In BRAVO GiRL! get the readers all the answers to their questions from real guys. So as to achieve our columnists NICK every week hundreds of emails from women who want to understand the boys better, or need advice for the conquering of their flock. Stories in large real guys play the main roles - make-comb, style and girls, tell them the best flirting tactics, etc. LOVE & SEX: BRAVO GiRL! discussed sex, love, flirting, friendship, self-awareness, and more. Only here the girls get the answers that gives them no one else. processed open, natural, high quality makes the girls! reconnaissance no fear, but fun. FIGURE: Since 2009, we explain to our readers with the successful issue campaign "Well, as you are," why kilos on the scales say nothing about the figure. BRAVO GiRL! corrects the obvious weird ideas of the girl of figure and weight and makes them realize that normal weight is not a dirty word. REAL-LIFE All our readers are "Bravo Girl," and part of a friendly group of girls. Other girls magazines write about girls. In BRAVO GiRL! get the girls to speak for themselves! This is also reflected in our fashion and beauty stories: because rather than relying on professional models, works BRAVO GiRL! as a single title for years exclusively with reader models who come every Friday to the casting to the office. Facebook: http://www.facebook.com/BRAVOGirl.
Language(s): German
Readership: Aimed at teenage girls.
ADVERTISING RATES:
Full Page Mono .... EUR 18231
Full Page Colour .... EUR 18231
Mechanical Data: Type Area: 239 x 188 mm, No. of Columns (Display): 4, Col Widths (Display): 44 mm
Copy instructions: *Copy Date:* 23 days prior to publication
CONSUMER: WOMEN'S INTEREST CONSUMER MAGAZINES: Teenage

BRAVO.DE
1620900G74F-2
Editorial: Burchardstr. 11, 20095 HAMBURG
Tel: 40 30190 **Fax:** 40 30191991
Email: online@bravo.de **Web site:** http://www.bravo.de
Freq: Daily; **Cover Price:** Paid; **Circ:** 2,372,070 Unique Users
Editor: Tina Sabalat
Profile: Ezine: Magazine about cinema, TV, computer culture, video and computer games. Facebook: http://www.facebook.com/BRAVO.
Language(s): German
CONSUMER: WOMEN'S INTEREST CONSUMER MAGAZINES: Teenage

BREMEN 4U
1638311G80-13977
Editorial: Martinistr. 43, 28195 BREMEN
Tel: 421 36710 **Fax:** 421 36711000
Email: redaktion@weser-kurier.de **Web site:** http://www.bremen4u.de
Freq: Monthly; **Annual Sub.:** EUR 12,00; **Circ:** 31,360
Editor: Lars Haider
Profile: Magazine for city and region, concentrating on gastronomy, music, arts and events. Facebook: http://www.facebook.com/bremen4u.
Language(s): German
ADVERTISING RATES:
Full Page Mono .... EUR 2236
Full Page Colour .... EUR 2236
Mechanical Data: Type Area: 334 x 230 mm
CONSUMER: RURAL & REGIONAL INTEREST

BREMEN MAGAZIN
723559G80-1660
Editorial: Contrescarpe 56, 28195 BREMEN
Tel: 421 330350 **Fax:** 421 3303529
Email: redaktion@bremen-magazin.de **Web site:** http://www.bremen-magazin.de
Freq: Monthly; **Cover Price:** Free; **Circ:** 120,000
Advertising Manager: Hermann Bruckmann
Profile: News magazine for Bremen.
Language(s): German
ADVERTISING RATES:
Full Page Colour .... EUR 3990
Mechanical Data: Type Area: 272 x 189 mm, No. of Columns (Display): 4, Col Widths (Display): 45 mm
Copy instructions: *Copy Date:* 7 days prior to publication
CONSUMER: RURAL & REGIONAL INTEREST

BREMER
723561G89C-4784
Editorial: Altenwall 9, 28195 BREMEN
Tel: 421 7900711 **Fax:** 421 7900777
Email: redaktion@bremer.de **Web site:** http://www.bremer.de
Freq: Monthly; **Annual Sub.:** EUR 15,30; **Circ:** 15,075
Editor: Lothar Bienkowski; **Advertising Manager:** Thomas Jacob-Rüdiger
Profile: Founded back in 1976 as a Bremer Blatt, Metropolis Magazine is now an integral part of the local media landscape. Monthly reports the Bremer on cultural, political and entertaining topics of the Hanseatic city. The rubrics music, party, film, theater, art, gastronomy and literature with detailed information about cultural and leisure activities in Bremen. Gripping stories and portraits of interesting people are as much to the Bremer as fashion features and news from the Hanseatic city. The great program calendar and pages of classified ads to make the Bremer indispensable companion throughout the whole month.
Language(s): German
Readership: Aimed at visitors and local residents.
ADVERTISING RATES:
Full Page Mono .... EUR 1890
Full Page Colour .... EUR 2890
Mechanical Data: Type Area: 260 x 190 mm, No. of Columns (Display): 4, Col Widths (Display): 44 mm
CONSUMER: HOLIDAYS & TRAVEL: Entertainment Guides

BREMER ANZEIGER - AUSG. WEST
723564G72-17446
Editorial: Martinistr. 33, 28195 BREMEN
Tel: 421 518045900 **Fax:** 421 518045901
Email: redaktion@bremer-anzeiger.de **Web site:** http://www.bremer-anzeiger.de
Freq: 104 issues yearly; **Cover Price:** Free; **Circ:** 35,517
Editor: Peter Tänzer; **Advertising Manager:** Marc Bode
Profile: Advertising journal (house-to-house) concentrating on local stories.
Language(s): German
ADVERTISING RATES:
Full Page Mono .... EUR 1921
Full Page Colour .... EUR 2672
Mechanical Data: Type Area: 334 x 237 mm, No. of Columns (Display): 5, Col Widths (Display): 45 mm
Copy instructions: *Copy Date:* 3 days prior to publication
LOCAL NEWSPAPERS

BREMER ÄRZTE JOURNAL
1861599G56A-11573
Editorial: Schwachhauser Heerstr. 30, 28209 BREMEN **Tel:** 421 34040 **Fax:** 421 3404209
Web site: http://www.bremer-aerztejournal.de
Freq: 10 issues yearly; **Circ:** 5,100
Editor: Franz-Josef Blömer; **Advertising Manager:** Sarah Hennig
Profile: The Bremer Ärzte Journal is the official medium of the Medical Association of Bremen and the Bremen physicians' association. It is intended as a single title of medical specialist and professional press in Bremen at more than 4,500 physicians, including more than 1,300 "permanent residents". The monthly journal provides a wide range of information. These include professional political contributions, scientific articles, interesting facts from the region, information on training, conferences and congresses and official notices.
Language(s): German
ADVERTISING RATES:
Full Page Mono .... EUR 980
Full Page Colour .... EUR 1950
Mechanical Data: Type Area: 271 x 175 mm, No. of Columns (Display): 3, Col Widths (Display): 55 mm
Copy instructions: *Copy Date:* 30 days prior to publication

BREMER KIRCHENZEITUNG
723572G67B-3420_500
Editorial: Franziuseck 2, 28199 BREMEN
Tel: 421 5597221 **Fax:** 421 5597206
Email: redaktion@kirche-bremen.de **Web site:** http://www.kirche-bremen.de
Freq: Quarterly; **Circ:** 150,000
Editor: Sabine Hatscher
Profile: Christian magazine for Bremen.
Language(s): German
Supplement to: Bremer Nachrichten, Weser-Kurier
REGIONAL DAILY & SUNDAY NEWSPAPERS: Regional Daily Newspapers

BREMER NACHRICHTEN
723573G67B-3420
Editorial: Martinistr. 43, 28195 BREMEN
Tel: 421 36710 **Fax:** 421 36711000
Email: redaktion@bremer-nachrichten.de **Web site:** http://www.bremer-nachrichten.de
Freq: 312 issues yearly; **Circ:** 169,335
Editor: Helge Matthiesen
Profile: Regional daily newspaper covering politics, economics, sport, travel and technology. Facebook: http://www.facebook.com/pages/weser-kurierde/48412147711 Twitter: http://twitter.com/#!/WESER_KURIER.
Language(s): German
ADVERTISING RATES:
SCC .... EUR 284,50
Mechanical Data: Type Area: 490 x 334 mm, No. of Columns (Display): 7, Col Widths (Display): 46 mm
Copy instructions: *Copy Date:* 1 day prior to publication
Supplement(s): bremer kirchenzeitung; Ferienjournal; wochen Journal
REGIONAL DAILY & SUNDAY NEWSPAPERS: Regional Daily Newspapers

BREMER SPECIAL
723575G89A-400
Editorial: Altenwall 9, 28195 BREMEN
Tel: 421 7900712 **Fax:** 421 7900777
Email: bienkowski@bremer.de **Web site:** http://www.bremer.de
Freq: Annual; **Cover Price:** EUR 4,50; **Circ:** 25,000
Editor: Lothar Bienkowski; **Advertising Manager:** Thomas Jacob-Rüdiger
Profile: Shopping guide for the city of Bremen.
Language(s): German
ADVERTISING RATES:
Full Page Mono .... EUR 1890
Full Page Colour .... EUR 3030
Mechanical Data: Type Area: 260 x 190 mm, No. of Columns (Display): 4, Col Widths (Display): 44 mm
Copy instructions: *Copy Date:* 15 days prior to publication

BREMER SPECIAL
723576G89A-420
Editorial: Altenwall 9, 28195 BREMEN
Tel: 421 7900712 **Fax:** 421 7900777
Email: bienkowski@bremer.de **Web site:** http://www.bremer.de
Freq: Annual; **Cover Price:** EUR 4,50; **Circ:** 25,000
Editor: Lothar Bienkowski; **Advertising Manager:** Thomas Jacob-Rüdiger
Profile: Restaurant and pub guide for the city of Bremen.
Language(s): German
ADVERTISING RATES:
Full Page Mono .... EUR 1890
Full Page Colour .... EUR 3030
Mechanical Data: Type Area: 260 x 190 mm, No. of Columns (Display): 4, Col Widths (Display): 44 mm
Copy instructions: *Copy Date:* 15 days prior to publication

BREMERVÖRDER ANZEIGER
723580G72-2696
Editorial: Alte Str. 73, 27432 BREMERVÖRDE
Tel: 4761 977515 **Fax:** 4761 977555
Email: redaktion@anzeiger-verlag.de **Web site:** http://www.marktplatz-bremervoerde.de
Freq: Weekly; **Cover Price:** Free; **Circ:** 24,600
Editor: Stefanie Kettler; **Advertising Manager:** Birgit Wrissenberg
Profile: Advertising journal (house-to-house) concentrating on local stories.
Language(s): German
ADVERTISING RATES:
Full Page Mono .... EUR 3705
Full Page Colour .... EUR 4035
Mechanical Data: Type Area: 490 x 330 mm, No. of Columns (Display): 7, Col Widths (Display): 45 mm
Copy instructions: *Copy Date:* 2 days prior to publication
LOCAL NEWSPAPERS

BREMERVÖRDER ZEITUNG
723581G67B-3440
Editorial: Marktstr. 30, 27432 BREMERVÖRDE
Tel: 4761 9970 **Fax:** 4761 99737
Email: redaktion@brv-zeitung.de **Web site:** http://www.brv-zeitung.de
Freq: 312 issues yearly; **Circ:** 7,146
Editor: Rolf Borgardt; **Advertising Manager:** Norbert Ullrich
Profile: Daily newspaper with regional news and a local sports section.
Language(s): German
ADVERTISING RATES:
SCC .... EUR 21,20
Mechanical Data: Type Area: 487 x 325 mm, No. of Columns (Display): 7, Col Widths (Display): 45 mm
Copy instructions: *Copy Date:* 1 day prior to publication
Supplement(s): Ferienjournal
REGIONAL DAILY & SUNDAY NEWSPAPERS: Regional Daily Newspapers

BRENNESSEL MAGAZIN
723588G80-1720
Editorial: Blumenstr. 271b, 86633 NEUBURG
Tel: 8431 42836 **Fax:** 8431 42853
Email: info@brennessel.com **Web site:** http://www.brennessel.com
Freq: Monthly; **Cover Price:** Free; **Circ:** 9,980
Editor: Cristian Dumitru; **Advertising Manager:** Cristian Dumitru
Profile: Magazine for city and region, concentrating on gastronomy, music, arts and events.
Language(s): German
ADVERTISING RATES:
Full Page Mono .... EUR 693
Full Page Colour .... EUR 861
Mechanical Data: Type Area: 272 x 190 mm, No. of Columns (Display): 4, Col Widths (Display): 43 mm

Copy instructions: *Copy Date:* 6 days prior to publication
CONSUMER: RURAL & REGIONAL INTEREST

BRENNSTOFFSPIEGEL UND MINERALÖLRUNDSCHAU
723598G58-1701
Editorial: Industriestr. 85, 04229 LEIPZIG
Tel: 341 4924011 **Fax:** 341 4924012
Email: redaktion@brennstoffspiegel.de **Web site:** http://www.brennstoffspiegel.de
Freq: Monthly; **Annual Sub.:** EUR 64,20; **Circ:** 3,489
Editor: Hans-Henning Manz; **Advertising Manager:** Ricky Pasch
Profile: Numerous companies in the industry as well as partners from the heating, the chimney sweep trade, construction planners, architects and related professionals to use the monthly German Energy Magazine "Brennstoffspiegel und mineralölrundschau" for their current and varied information. Here they get a broad overview of market and companies, trends and developments, products and services.
Language(s): German
ADVERTISING RATES:
Full Page Mono .... EUR 1496
Full Page Colour .... EUR 2305
Mechanical Data: Type Area: 267 x 190 mm, No. of Columns (Display): 4, Col Widths (Display): 45 mm
Copy instructions: *Copy Date:* 20 days prior to publication
BUSINESS: ENERGY, FUEL & NUCLEAR

BRENZTAL-BOTE
723601G67B-3460
Editorial: Olgastr. 15, 89518 HEIDENHEIM
Tel: 7321 347153 **Fax:** 7321 347102
Email: redaktion@hz-online.de **Web site:** http://www.hz-online.de
Freq: 312 issues yearly; **Circ:** 1,587
Advertising Manager: Eberhardt Looser
Profile: Daily newspaper with regional news and a local sports section.
Language(s): German
ADVERTISING RATES:
SCC .... EUR 36,50
Mechanical Data: Type Area: 480 x 320 mm, No. of Columns (Display): 7, Col Widths (Display): 44 mm
Copy instructions: *Copy Date:* 1 day prior to publication
Supplement(s): da heim; Das Magazin; Noise
REGIONAL DAILY & SUNDAY NEWSPAPERS: Regional Daily Newspapers

BRETTENER NACHRICHTEN
723604G67B-3480
Editorial: Linkenheimer Landstr. 133, 76149 KARLSRUHE **Tel:** 721 7890 **Fax:** 721 789155
Email: redaktion@bnn.de **Web site:** http://www.bnn.de
Freq: 312 issues yearly; **Circ:** 19,707
Advertising Manager: Jörg Stark
Profile: The Badische Neueste Nachrichten with a paid circulation of about 150,000 copies and 400,000 readers every day one of the major daily newspapers in the state of Baden-Wuerttemberg. This newspaper is understood in the concert of the leaves the country as a not to be hearing voices of Baden and the Palatinate region between and Ortenau, between the Black Forest and Rhine valley. Nine local editions in the distribution area in the Karlsruhe, Pforzheim and Bruchsal, Baden resources emphasize the character of this newspaper as Baden regional newspaper. On this image editing with a full working day with about 90 editors. Most of the editorial staff but provided in the local editors at ten locations in the distribution area the readers with local news. In addition to the BNN output Karlsruhe, Rastatt, Baden-Baden, Ettlingen arise then the Pforzheimer Kurier, the Bruchsaler Rundschau, the Brettener Nachrichten and not least the Acher- und Bühler Bote. Although the focus of reporting is very strong locally and regionally, the Badische Neueste Nachrichten offer their readers a broad and comprehensive news coverage.
Language(s): German
ADVERTISING RATES:
SCC .... EUR 36,50
Mechanical Data: Type Area: 480 x 360 mm, No. of Columns (Display): 8, Col Widths (Display): 43 mm
Copy instructions: *Copy Date:* 1 day prior to publication
REGIONAL DAILY & SUNDAY NEWSPAPERS: Regional Daily Newspapers

BREWING AND BEVERAGE INDUSTRY INTERNATIONAL
723609G9B-4
Editorial: Schloss Mindelburg, 87719 MINDELHEIM
Tel: 8261 999317 **Fax:** 8261 999395
Email: gabler@sachon.de **Web site:** http://www.sachon.de
Freq: 6 issues yearly
Editor: Fabian Gabler; **Advertising Manager:** Sabine Berchtenbreiter
Profile: Marketing-and technology-oriented, English-language trade magazine for the international brewing and beverage industry. The attractively designed magazine covers specific industry issues, which are also beyond the borders of interest. With the known trade journals Brauindustrie and Getränkeindustrie, the publisher Sachon has a solid base for top information. Well-known authors in the industry talk about current issues in the field of technics, technology, packaging, logistics, marketing and management. This information is supplemented by research by the editorial team on site, particularly at international fairs and events.
Language(s): English
ADVERTISING RATES:
Full Page Mono .... EUR 3720
Full Page Colour .... EUR 5100
Mechanical Data: Type Area: 270 x 185 mm, No. of Columns (Display): 4, Col Widths (Display): 45 mm
BUSINESS: DRINKS & LICENSED TRADE: Brewing

BRIEFMARKEN SPIEGEL
723621G79C-1
Editorial: Benzstr. 1c, 37083 GÖTTINGEN
Tel: 551 4990540 **Fax:** 551 4990530
Email: redaktion@philapress.de **Web site:** http://www.philapress.de
Freq: Monthly; **Annual Sub.:** EUR 36,00; **Circ:** 36,000
Editor: Markus Riese; **Advertising Manager:** Werner P. Rühling
Profile: Magazine containing articles on stamps.
Language(s): German
Readership: Read by collectors.
ADVERTISING RATES:
Full Page Mono .... EUR 1350
Full Page Colour .... EUR 2030
Mechanical Data: Type Area: 261 x 185 mm, No. of Columns (Display): 4, Col Widths (Display): 45 mm
Copy instructions: *Copy Date:* 17 days prior to publication
CONSUMER: HOBBIES & DIY: Philately

BRIEFMARKENPOST MIT MÜNZENPOST
723620G79C-50
Editorial: Benzstr. 1c, 37083 GÖTTINGEN
Tel: 551 4990540 **Fax:** 551 4990530
Email: info@philapress.de **Web site:** http://www.philapress.de
Freq: Monthly; **Cover Price:** Free; **Circ:** 16,800
Editor: Werner P. Rühling; **Advertising Manager:** Werner P. Rühling
Profile: Magazine about stamp collecting. Also covers numismatics.
Language(s): German
ADVERTISING RATES:
Full Page Mono .... EUR 670
Full Page Colour .... EUR 972
Mechanical Data: Type Area: 176 x 122 mm, No. of Columns (Display): 2, Col Widths (Display): 58 mm
Copy instructions: *Copy Date:* 20 days prior to publication
CONSUMER: HOBBIES & DIY: Philately

BRIGITTE
723628G74A-560
Editorial: Am Baumwall 11, 20459 HAMBURG
Tel: 40 37030 **Fax:** 40 37035679
Email: infoline@brigitte.de **Web site:** http://www.brigitte.de
Freq: 26 issues yearly; **Annual Sub.:** EUR 67,60; **Circ:** 660,840
Editor: Andreas Lebert; **Advertising Manager:** Anja Dreßler
Profile: Germany's most-read "classic" women's magazine. The most important thing for the BRIGITTE editorial: the reader. Women who read BRIGITTE have high standards. Theydo not only expect excellent entertainment and reliable information, but above all, a strong benefit. Issue for issue. In fashion and cosmetics, cultural and social issues as well as in the psychology dossier. BRIGITTE allows the reader to experience feelings of others and learn, they remind themselves just to do something good, it inspires women to grab things - and encourages them to succeed. With the initiative "Without Models" BRIGITTE was the first women's magazine, that stepped on a new contemporary way, to show fashion and beauty. It responds to changes in society and moves once more the personality of the woman into focus - for the overwhelming enthusiasm of the readers. A reader service, which answers up to 500 questions per day, the leading women's website in Germany and least but not last more than 50 years of experience and tradition: that is the strength of BRIGITTE. Facebook: http://www.facebook.com/ Brigitte Twitter: http://twitter.com/brigitteonline This Outlet offers RSS (Really Simple Syndication).
Language(s): German
Readership: Aimed at women.
ADVERTISING RATES:
Full Page Mono .... EUR 49900
Full Page Colour .... EUR 49900
Mechanical Data: Type Area: 231 x 180 mm, No. of Columns (Display): 3, Col Widths (Display): 57 mm
Copy instructions: *Copy Date:* 50 days prior to publication
CONSUMER: WOMEN'S INTEREST CONSUMER MAGAZINES: Women's Interest

BRIGITTE BALANCE
1643721G74A-3413
Editorial: Am Baumwall 11, 20459 HAMBURG
Tel: 40 37030 **Fax:** 40 37035679
Email: lebert.andreas@brigitte.de **Web site:** http://www.balance-brigitte.de
Freq: 6 issues yearly; **Cover Price:** EUR 3,50; **Circ:** 200,000
Editor: Andreas Lebert; **Advertising Manager:** Anja Dreßler
Profile: Brigitte Balance moves between the poles of our everyday life: between work and leisure time, body and soul, sports and relaxation, love and freedom. For women who like to run along up front, feel well, to find the middle for a moment. The major focus of Brigitte Balance: - Fitness and Wellness for every day - beauty that is right for us because it meets our needs - Food that makes fit and suits everyday life - health, seen holistically - from modern medicine to natural remedies - feelings because we can not live without them, but sometimes would like to switch them off - job so it fulfillst us, but does not devour us - trips that inspire us, move and give strength.
Language(s): German
ADVERTISING RATES:
Full Page Mono .... EUR 11750
Full Page Colour .... EUR 11750
Mechanical Data: Type Area: 227 x 183 mm

BRIGITTE KALENDER
723631G74A-3312
Editorial: Am Baumwall 11, 20459 HAMBURG
Tel: 40 37032146 **Fax:** 40 37035799
Email: tsolodimos.christine@brigitte.de **Web site:** http://www.brigitte.de
Freq: Annual; **Cover Price:** EUR 6,50; **Circ:** 110,000
Editor: Christine Tsolodimos
Profile: Annual Calendar with quotes, poems, illustrations and space for personal notes. This detailed information and address section, fold-year summary and Telephone Directory. Facebook: http://www.facebook.com/Brigitte.
Language(s): German

BRIGITTE WOMAN
723633G74A-600
Editorial: Am Baumwall 11, 20459 HAMBURG
Tel: 40 37030 **Fax:** 40 37035679
Email: infoline@brigitte.de **Web site:** http://www.brigitte-woman.de
Freq: Monthly; **Annual Sub.:** EUR 42,00; **Circ:** 232,918
Editor: Andreas Lebert; **Advertising Manager:** Anja Dreßler
Profile: BRIGITTE WOMAN readers are enjoyers, take pleasure in beautiful things, exceptional travels and perceive time for yourself as pure luxury. Luxury they not only grant for themselves but can also afford. They have a high demand on information and services, visual design and choice of topics. The readers are living life and know what they want. They have high standards of beauty and fashion set sound priorities when it comes to finance or insurance. And they can easily afford more, no matter whether it is about cars, travel or fashion. So you not only have a first class environment for your brand communication, but also the unique opportunity to reach this challenging target group without coverage loss. BRIGITTE WOMAN dispenses women's issues such as diets, recipes, housekeeping. Twitter: http://twitter.com/BRIGITTEwoman This Outlet offers RSS (Really Simple Syndication).
Language(s): German
ADVERTISING RATES:
Full Page Mono .... EUR 20900
Full Page Colour .... EUR 20900
Mechanical Data: Type Area: 257 x 185 mm, No. of Columns (Display): 3, Col Widths (Display): 59 mm
Copy instructions: *Copy Date:* 43 days prior to publication
CONSUMER: WOMEN'S INTEREST CONSUMER MAGAZINES: Women's Interest

BRIGITTE.DE
1620911G74A-3363
Editorial: Stubbenhuk 5, 20459 HAMBURG
Tel: 40 37034679 **Fax:** 40 37035845
Email: service@brigitte.de **Web site:** http://www.brigitte.de
Freq: Daily; **Cover Price:** Paid; **Circ:** 5,591,404 Unique Users
Editor: Brigitte Huber
Profile: Ezine: Internet portal and community for women, fashion, beauty, luxury, recipes, figure, health, society, culture, travel, housing, jobs, horoscope, service issues, photo galleries, videos and shop. Facebook: http://www.facebook.com/ Brigitte Twitter: http://twitter.com/brigitteonline This Outlet offers RSS (Really Simple Syndication).
Language(s): German
CONSUMER: WOMEN'S INTEREST CONSUMER MAGAZINES: Women's Interest

BRITISH CLASSICS
723642G77A-680
Editorial: Lise-Meitner-Str. 2, 55129 MAINZ
Tel: 6131 9920 **Fax:** 6131 992100
Email: redaktion@british-classics.de **Web site:** http://www.british-classics.de
Freq: 6 issues yearly; **Annual Sub.:** EUR 21,00; **Circ:** 25,000
Editor: Martin Brüggemann
Profile: Magazine about British oldtimers.
Language(s): German
ADVERTISING RATES:
Full Page Mono .... EUR 2100
Full Page Colour .... EUR 2500
Mechanical Data: Type Area: 260 x 185 mm

BROT + BACKWAREN
723658G8A-160
Editorial: Behnstr. 61, 22767 HAMBURG
Tel: 40 39901227 **Fax:** 40 39901229
Email: keil@foodmultimedia.de **Web site:** http://www.foodmultimedia.de
Freq: 6 issues yearly; **Annual Sub.:** EUR 75,00; **Circ:** 6,500
Editor: Hildegard Maria Keil; **Advertising Manager:** Dirk Dixon
Profile: The magazine brot + backwaren tailored precisely to the needs of industry practitioners. In this journal you will find current reports on the technical and technological new developments for the industry and expert analysis of the German and European bakery market and its environment. Concentration is called for in the baking industry. Therefore addresses the journal brot + backwaren with operating reports, product testing and technical articles on the leading German bakery companies. The baking industry in Germany, Austria and Switzerland show the same characteristics: the number of companies falls persistently, the market share of the sales size categories are shifting in a rush in favor of medium and large enterprises, the larger the company, the higher the productivity and willingness to innovate and to invest. Therefore, the information concept is aimed at decision makers in the industry to be well informed about the market.
Language(s): German
Readership: Aimed at big commercial bakeries of cakes but also at the bread bakeries producing ready wrapped and sliced bread.
ADVERTISING RATES:
Full Page Mono .... EUR 2400
Full Page Colour .... EUR 3600
Mechanical Data: Type Area: 265 x 184 mm, No. of Columns (Display): 4, Col Widths (Display): 43 mm
Copy instructions: *Copy Date:* 27 days prior to publication
Official Journal of: Organ d. Vereinigung d. Backbranche e.V. u. d. Association de la Boulangerie Industrielle
BUSINESS: BAKING & CONFECTIONERY: Baking

BROT & SPIELE
723659G89C-40
Editorial: Treibgasse 19, 63739 ASCHAFFENBURG
Tel: 6021 4448823 **Fax:** 6021 4448844
Email: b.bogner@morgen-welt.de **Web site:** http://www.kultmag.de
Freq: 11 issues yearly; **Cover Price:** Free; **Circ:** 15,000
Editor: Bettina Bogner; **Advertising Manager:** Dirk Bogner
Profile: The cultural magazine for the region Aschaffenburg. The entire cultural program of the month: Colos-Saal, Aschaffenburg Cultural Office, City Hall at the castle, museums, cabaret Hofgarten, county of Miltenberg, JUKUZ & other operators.
Language(s): German
ADVERTISING RATES:
Full Page Mono .... EUR 1875
Full Page Colour .... EUR 1875
Mechanical Data: No. of Columns (Display): 4, Col Widths (Display): 44 mm, Type Area: 270 x 190 mm
Copy instructions: *Copy Date:* 7 days prior to publication
CONSUMER: HOLIDAYS & TRAVEL: Entertainment Guides

BRUCHSALER RUNDSCHAU
723662G67B-3500
Editorial: Linkenheimer Landstr. 133, 76149 KARLSRUHE **Tel:** 721 7890 **Fax:** 721 789155
Email: redaktion@bnn.de **Web site:** http://www.bnn.de
Freq: 312 issues yearly; **Circ:** 22,196
Advertising Manager: Jörg Stark
Profile: The Badische Neueste Nachrichten with a paid circulation of about 150,000 copies and 400,000 readers every day one of the major daily newspapers in the state of Baden-Wuerttemberg. This newspaper is understood in the concert of the leaves the country as a not to be hearing voices of Baden and the Palatinate region between and Ortenau, between the Black Forest and Rhine valley. Nine local editions in the distribution area in the Karlsruhe, Pforzheim and Bruchsal, Baden resources emphasize the character of this newspaper as Baden regional newspaper. On this image editing with a full working day with about 90 editors. Most of the editorial staff but provided in the local editors at ten locations in the distribution area the readers with local news. In addition to the BNN output Karlsruhe, Rastatt, Baden-Baden, Ettlingen arise then the Pforzheimer Kurier, the Bruchsaler Rundschau, the Brettener Nachrichten and not least the Acher- und Bühler Bote. Although the focus of reporting is very strong locally and regionally, the Badische Neueste Nachrichten offer their readers a broad and comprehensive news coverage.
Language(s): German
ADVERTISING RATES:
SCC .... EUR 51,00
Mechanical Data: Type Area: 480 x 360 mm, No. of Columns (Display): 8, Col Widths (Display): 43 mm
Copy instructions: *Copy Date:* 1 day prior to publication
REGIONAL DAILY & SUNDAY NEWSPAPERS: Regional Daily Newspapers

BRÜCKE
1664442G74A-3459
Editorial: Magdeburger Allee 116, 99086 ERFURT
Tel: 361 74981134 **Fax:** 361 74981139
Email: strassenzeitung@kontaktinkrisen.de **Web site:** http://www.kontaktinkrisen.de
Freq: 3 issues yearly; **Annual Sub.:** EUR 10,00; **Circ:** 4,500
Editor: Birgit Vogt; **Advertising Manager:** Dagmar Fleischmann
Profile: Brücke, the street magazine is created by an editorial team and people in difficult social situations sold it on the street. The Brücke offers a cross-section of the region with social, cultural and local priorities.
Language(s): German
ADVERTISING RATES:
Full Page Mono .... EUR 307
Full Page Colour .... EUR 499
Copy instructions: *Copy Date:* 14 days prior to publication

BRÜCKE - INFORMATIONEN F. ARBEITSSICHERHEIT U. GESUNDHEITSSCHUTZ, AUSG. ELEKTRO FEINMECHANIK
723676G17-20
Editorial: Gustav-Heinemann-Ufer 130, 50968 KÖLN
Tel: 221 37781010 **Fax:** 221 37781011
Email: presse@bgetem.de **Web site:** http://www.bgetem.de
Freq: 6 issues yearly; Free to qualifying individuals
Annual Sub.: EUR 6,38; **Circ:** 216,000
Editor: Christoph Nocker
Profile: Member magazine of the Professional Association ETEM energy electric textile media outlets, electrical output Subcontracting small.
Language(s): German

BRUNSBÜTTELER ZEITUNG
723708G67B-3560
Editorial: Wulf-Isebrand-Platz 1, 25746 HEIDE
Tel: 481 6886200 **Fax:** 481 688690200
Email: redaktion@boyens-medien.de **Web site:** http://www.boyens-medien.de
Freq: 312 issues yearly; **Circ:** 9,151
Profile: Daily newspaper with reports on politics, economy, stock market, entertainment, events, culture and sport, are available from the Dithmarscher Landeszeitung with a large regional news and sports pages.
Language(s): German
ADVERTISING RATES:
SCC .... EUR 24,10
Mechanical Data: Type Area: 430 x 285 mm, No. of Columns (Display): 6, Col Widths (Display): 45 mm
Copy instructions: *Copy Date:* 1 day prior to publication
REGIONAL DAILY & SUNDAY NEWSPAPERS: Regional Daily Newspapers

BSH NVN NATUR SPECIAL REPORT
723713G57-2656
Editorial: Gartenweg 5, 26203 WARDENBURG
Tel: 4407 5111 **Fax:** 4407 6760
Email: info@bsh-natur.de **Web site:** http://www.bsh-natur.de
Freq: Annual; **Cover Price:** EUR 2,56; **Circ:** 1,200
Editor: Remmer Akkermann
Profile: Magazine on nature conservancy and ecologic research.
Language(s): German

BTB MAGAZIN
723722G19A-1053
Editorial: Maximinerweg 10, 54318 MERTESDORF
Tel: 651 9950077 **Fax:** 651 9950078
Email: btb.berndniesen@t-online.de **Web site:** http://www.btb-online.org
Freq: 10 issues yearly; **Cover Price:** EUR 3,70
Free to qualifying individuals ; **Circ:** 12,500
Editor: Bernd Niesen; **Advertising Manager:** Katy Netz
Profile: Journal for engineers and technicians in the public sector.
Language(s): German
ADVERTISING RATES:
Full Page Mono .... EUR 1410
Full Page Colour .... EUR 2350
Mechanical Data: Type Area: 270 x 185 mm, No. of Columns (Display): 4, Col Widths (Display): 43 mm
Copy instructions: *Copy Date:* 42 days prior to publication
BUSINESS: ENGINEERING & MACHINERY

BTH HEIMTEX
730059G23B-40
Editorial: An der Alster 21, 20099 HAMBURG
Tel: 40 2484540 **Fax:** 40 2803788
Email: bth@snfachpresse.de **Web site:** http://www.raumausstattung.de
Freq: 11 issues yearly; **Annual Sub.:** EUR 128,00; **Circ:** 8,369
Editor: Claudia Weidt; **Advertising Manager:** Rene S. Spiegelberger
Profile: Magazine about carpets, floor coverings, curtains and textiles.
Language(s): German
Readership: Aimed at people in schools, associations, organisations, trade and industry.
ADVERTISING RATES:
Full Page Mono .... EUR 3340
Full Page Colour .... EUR 6130
Mechanical Data: Type Area: 252 x 184 mm, No. of Columns (Display): 4, Col Widths (Display): 43 mm
Copy instructions: *Copy Date:* 13 days prior to publication
Official Journal of: Organ d. Verb. d. dt. Heimtextilienindustrie u. d. Zentralverb. Gewerbl. Verbundgruppen
BUSINESS: FURNISHINGS & FURNITURE: Furnishings, Carpets & Flooring

BTI BETON TEKNIK INTERNATIONAL
2053204G4E-7346
Editorial: Industriestr. 180, 50999 KÖLN
Tel: 2236 962390 **Fax:** 2236 962396
Email: editor@cpi-worldwide.com **Web site:** http://www.cpi-worldwide.com
Freq: 6 issues yearly; Free to qualifying individuals
Annual Sub.: EUR 120,00; **Circ:** 2,000
Editor: Holger Karutz; **Advertising Manager:** Gerhard Klöckner
Profile: Magazine for concrete producers.
Language(s): Turkish
Mechanical Data: Type Area: 260 x 180 mm, No. of Columns (Display): 3, Col Widths (Display): 56 mm
Copy instructions: *Copy Date:* 30 days prior to publication

BUB FORUM BIBLIOTHEK UND INFORMATION
723732G60B-280
Editorial: Gartenstr. 18, 72764 REUTLINGEN
Tel: 7121 34910 **Fax:** 7121 300433
Email: bub@bib-info.de **Web site:** http://www.b-u-b.de
Freq: 10 issues yearly; Free to qualifying individuals
Annual Sub.: EUR 100,00; **Circ:** 8,351
Editor: Bernd Schleh; **Advertising Manager:** Gabi Bott
Profile: »BuB Forum Bibliothek und Information« is the most common, interdisciplinary trade journal for the library and information sector in the German-speaking area. It includes essays, commentaries, discussions, interviews, reports and news on the topics of public and academic libraries and the educational and cultural policy. Among the authors of the paper include - in addition to librarians and information professionals at home and abroad - university professors, politicians, writers and journalists, too.
Language(s): German
ADVERTISING RATES:
Full Page Mono .... EUR 1350
Full Page Colour .... EUR 1680
Mechanical Data: Type Area: 263 x 183 mm, No. of Columns (Display): 4, Col Widths (Display): 43 mm
Copy instructions: *Copy Date:* 30 days prior to publication
BUSINESS: PUBLISHING: Libraries

BÜCHENER ANZEIGER
723763G72-2772
Editorial: Schefestr. 11, 21493 SCHWARZENBEK
Tel: 4151 88900 **Fax:** 4151 889044
Email: redaktion@buechener-anzeiger.de **Web site:** http://www.viebranz.de
Freq: Weekly; **Cover Price:** Free; **Circ:** 7,000
Editor: Christina Kriegs-Schmidt
Profile: Advertising journal (house-to-house) concentrating on local stories.
Language(s): German
ADVERTISING RATES:
Full Page Mono .... EUR 1961
Full Page Colour .... EUR 19952021
Mechanical Data: Type Area: 430 x 282 mm, No. of Columns (Display): 6, Col Widths (Display): 45 mm
Copy instructions: *Copy Date:* 1 day prior to publication
LOCAL NEWSPAPERS

BUCHJOURNAL
723741G65A-180_105
Editorial: Großer Hirschgraben 17, 60311 FRANKFURT **Tel:** 69 1306373 **Fax:** 69 289986
Email: e.baier@buchjournal.de **Web site:** http://www.buchjournal.de
Freq: 6 issues yearly; **Annual Sub.:** EUR 30,00; **Circ:** 267,502
Editor: Eckart Baier; **Advertising Manager:** Katrin Willwater
Profile: Magazine containing book reviews and general information concerning literature. Distributed via book shops in Germany.
Language(s): German
Readership: Aimed at people interested in literature.
ADVERTISING RATES:
Full Page Mono .... EUR 5900
Full Page Colour .... EUR 5900
Mechanical Data: Type Area: 248 x 188 mm, No. of Columns (Display): 3, Col Widths (Display): 60 mm
Copy instructions: *Copy Date:* 49 days prior to publication
Supplement to: Süddeutsche Zeitung
Supplement(s): buchjournal extra Hörbuch & DVD
NATIONAL DAILY & SUNDAY NEWSPAPERS: National Daily Newspapers

BUCHLOER ZEITUNG
723748G67B-3580
Editorial: Heisinger Str. 14, 87437 KEMPTEN
Tel: 831 206439 **Fax:** 831 206123
Email: redaktion@azv.de **Web site:** http://www.all-in.de
Freq: 312 issues yearly; **Circ:** 4,059
Advertising Manager: Reinhard Melder
Profile: Daily newspaper with regional news and a local sports section. Facebook: http://www.facebook.com/allin.de.dasallgaeuonline.
Language(s): German
ADVERTISING RATES:
SCC .... EUR 39,80
Mechanical Data: Type Area: 480 x 327 mm, No. of Columns (Display): 7, Col Widths (Display): 45 mm
Copy instructions: *Copy Date:* 2 days prior to publication
Supplement(s): Allgäu-Dribbler; allgäu weit; allgäu weit Allgäuer Kultursommer; allgäu weit Gesundheit; allgäu weit Sommer; allgäu weit Winter; Golfregion Allgäu; rtv; Die Schwäbische Bäderstrasse Kraft-Quellen
REGIONAL DAILY & SUNDAY NEWSPAPERS: Regional Daily Newspapers

BUCHMARKT
723749G60A-340
Editorial: Sperberweg 4a, 40668 MEERBUSCH
Tel: 2150 91910 **Fax:** 2150 919191
Email: redaktion@buchmarkt.de **Web site:** http://www.buchmarkt.de
Freq: Monthly; **Annual Sub.:** EUR 246,00; **Circ:** 4,200
Editor: Christian von Zittwitz; **Advertising Manager:** Kirsten Peters
Profile: Marketing and idea magazine for the book trade. Twitter: http://twitter.com/cvz1.
Language(s): German
ADVERTISING RATES:
Full Page Mono .... EUR 1145
Full Page Colour .... EUR 1565
Mechanical Data: Type Area: 260 x 180 mm, No. of Columns (Display): 3, Col Widths (Display): 60 mm
Copy instructions: *Copy Date:* 14 days prior to publication
BUSINESS: PUBLISHING: Publishing & Book Trade

BUCHREPORT EXPRESS
723752G60A-360
Editorial: Königswall 21, 44137 DORTMUND
Tel: 231 9056200 **Fax:** 231 9056111
Email: wilking@buchreport.de **Web site:** http://www.buchreport.de
Freq: Weekly; **Annual Sub.:** EUR 491,86; **Circ:** 4,500
Editor: Thomas Wilking; **Advertising Manager:** Michael Janscheidt
Profile: Publication containing background reports, events, commentaries, bestseller lists and new publications. Facebook: http://www.facebook.com/buchreport.
Language(s): German
Readership: Aimed at booksellers.
ADVERTISING RATES:
Full Page Mono .... EUR 620
Full Page Colour .... EUR 1000
Mechanical Data: Type Area: 258 x 180 mm
Copy instructions: *Copy Date:* 2 days prior to publication
BUSINESS: PUBLISHING: Publishing & Book Trade

BUCHREPORT MAGAZIN
723753G60A-380
Editorial: Königswall 21, 44137 DORTMUND
Tel: 231 9056200 **Fax:** 231 9056111
Email: wilking@buchreport.de **Web site:** http://www.buchreport.de
Freq: Monthly; **Annual Sub.:** EUR 77,80; **Circ:** 4,500
Editor: Thomas Wilking; **Advertising Manager:** Michael Janscheidt
Profile: Magazine for the book industry, opinion-forming magazine of the German book industry, the information medium for publishers and booksellers in Germany, Austria and Switzerland and their service providers. Even international media companies, publishers and distributors are a permanent branch subscriber base. buchreport divided news, analysis, background reports and opinion pieces in various media formats and functional appearance fanned rhythms. Facebook: http://www.facebook.com/buchreport.
Language(s): German
Readership: Aimed at booksellers.
ADVERTISING RATES:
Full Page Mono .... EUR 700
Full Page Colour .... EUR 1025
Mechanical Data: Type Area: 258 x 180 mm, No. of Columns (Display): 3, Col Widths (Display): 58 mm
Copy instructions: *Copy Date:* 7 days prior to publication
Supplement(s): buchreport.spezial
BUSINESS: PUBLISHING: Publishing & Book Trade

BÜCHSENMACHER MESSER & SCHERE
723772G27-380
Editorial: Pastorenberg 4, 31167 BOCKENEM
Tel: 5067 247150 **Fax:** 5067 247153
Email: redaktion@buechsenmacherverlag.de **Web site:** http://www.buechsenmacherverlag.de
Freq: Monthly; **Annual Sub.:** EUR 44,90; **Circ:** 3,500
Editor: Carsten Bothe; **Advertising Manager:** Jo Groß
Profile: For over 100 years, Büchsenmacher Messer & Schere, is the mouthpiece of the industry. It is primarily targeted at retailers and resellers in the industries of hunting, outdoor and knives. For readers but of course also include the producers in these sectors. Büchsenmacher Messer & Schere has a worldwide distribution. The focus is on Germany, Austria and Switzerland.
Language(s): German
Readership: Aimed at retailers.
ADVERTISING RATES:
Full Page Mono .... EUR 2300
Full Page Colour .... EUR 2300
Mechanical Data: Type Area: 265 x 185 mm, No. of Columns (Display): 3, Col Widths (Display): 58 mm
Copy instructions: *Copy Date:* 15 days prior to publication
BUSINESS: METAL, IRON & STEEL

BUCHUNGSKATALOG THÜRINGEN
767935G50-1196
Editorial: Willy-Brandt-Platz 1, 99084 ERFURT
Tel: 361 3742216 **Fax:** 361 3742299
Email: fauss@thueringen-tourismus.de **Web site:** http://www.thueringen-tourismus.de
Freq: Annual; **Cover Price:** Free; **Circ:** 35,000
Editor: Peggy Fauß
Profile: Directory listing accommodation facilities for direct booking in Thüringen.
Language(s): German
Copy instructions: *Copy Date:* 90 days prior to publication

BUDO KARATE BUDOWORLD
723762G75Q-80
Editorial: Bergstr. 18, 47906 KEMPEN
Tel: 2845 80593 **Fax:** 2845 80392
Email: satori@budoworld.net **Web site:** http://www.budoworld.net
Freq: 6 issues yearly; **Annual Sub.:** EUR 39,60; **Circ:** 36,900
Editor: Norbert Schiffer
Profile: Magazine containing information about karate, budo, kung fu, taekwondo and kickboxing.
Language(s): German
ADVERTISING RATES:
Full Page Colour .... EUR 4280
Mechanical Data: Type Area: 285 x 210 mm, No. of Columns (Display): 4, Col Widths (Display): 44 mm
CONSUMER: SPORT: Combat Sports

BÜHNEN MAGAZIN
1609477G4E-6903
Editorial: Ringstr. 7, 67808 STAHLBERG
Tel: 6361 929685 **Fax:** 6361 929686
Email: nsbuschmeyer@kmverlag.de **Web site:** http://www.kranmagazin.de
Freq: 6 issues yearly; **Annual Sub.:** EUR 38,00; **Circ:** 12,000
Editor: Sven Buschmeyer
Profile: Magazine about elevatable work platforms of all kinds.
Language(s): German
ADVERTISING RATES:
Full Page Mono .... EUR 2800
Full Page Colour .... EUR 3500
Mechanical Data: Type Area: 274 x 188 mm

BÜHNENGENOSSENSCHAFT
723785G64K-28
Editorial: Feldbrunnenstr. 74, 20148 HAMBURG
Tel: 40 445185 **Fax:** 40 456002
Email: redaktion@buehnengenossenschaft.de **Web site:** http://www.buehnengenossenschaft.de
Freq: 10 issues yearly; Free to qualifying individuals
Annual Sub.: EUR 26,10; **Circ:** 5,500
Editor: Hans Herdlein; **Advertising Manager:** Jörg Rowohlt
Profile: Trade journal of the cooperative of German stage members.
Language(s): German
ADVERTISING RATES:
Full Page Colour .... EUR 1600
Mechanical Data: Type Area: 255 x 188 mm
Copy instructions: *Copy Date:* 25 days prior to publication
BUSINESS: OTHER CLASSIFICATIONS: Cinema Entertainment

BUILD
1656724G4E-7013
Editorial: Hofaue 63, 42103 WUPPERTAL
Tel: 202 248360 **Fax:** 202 2483610
Email: build@build-magazin.com **Web site:** http://www.build-magazin.de
Freq: 6 issues yearly; **Annual Sub.:** EUR 50,00; **Circ:** 8,545
Editor: Ralf Ferdinand Broekman; **Advertising Manager:** Leif Hallerbach
Profile: Magazine for architects.
Language(s): German
ADVERTISING RATES:
Full Page Mono .... EUR 3646
Full Page Colour .... EUR 5417
Mechanical Data: Type Area: 250 x 186 mm, No. of Columns (Display): 4, Col Widths (Display): 43 mm
Copy instructions: *Copy Date:* 19 days prior to publication
BUSINESS: ARCHITECTURE & BUILDING: Building

BUILDING & AUTOMATION
723837G17-40
Editorial: Merianstr. 29, 63069 OFFENBACH
Tel: 69 8400061331 **Fax:** 69 8400061399
Email: building-automation@vde-verlag.de **Web site:** http://www.building-and-automation.de
Freq: 6 issues yearly; **Annual Sub.:** EUR 39,60; **Circ:** 35,872
Editor: Ronald Heinze; **Advertising Manager:** Markus Lehnert
Profile: The building & automation leads electricians and electrical planners a comprehensive overview of all new products for their work areas. Can explain in detailed statements professionals to new technologies and systems, which expand with the electricians and greatly facilitate its work. A special section is the cross-functional building automation, building control and networking technologies allowed. But the traditional focus of electrical installation is in each issue. Recipients are the electricians in craft and industry, planners and the electrical wholesale trade.
Language(s): German
ADVERTISING RATES:
Full Page Mono .... EUR 5255
Full Page Colour .... EUR 6785
Mechanical Data: Type Area: 270 x 189 mm, No. of Columns (Display): 4, Col Widths (Display): 44 mm
BUSINESS: ELECTRICAL

Germany

BULA
723839G32A-640

Editorial: Kahden 17b, 22393 HAMBURG
Tel: 40 6068820 **Fax:** 40 60688288
Email: info@soll.de **Web site:** http://www.soll.de
Freq: 6 issues yearly; **Annual Sub.:** EUR 22,00; **Circ:** 10,160
Editor: Rolf Soll; **Advertising Manager:** Claudia-Regine Soll
Profile: The designation Bula is based on a abbreviation of the earlier title called „Beschaffungsdienst für Bundes- und Landesbehörden". The audience has now but considerably improved at the targets municipalities and municipal associations. Bula is aimed at executives and decision makers in the participating units, departments, etc. With the practice-oriented reporting Bula is an important adviser on the way to the "modern and efficient state". One focus is in the segment "procurement". According to the BDI, the state purchased the time for more than 254 billion euros in kind. New are the accessorie parts: The clean city and building management. For better orientation, these topics represented in the various editions focused and offer the reader a quicker finding of practical information.
Language(s): German
Readership: Aimed at decision makers within local government.
ADVERTISING RATES:
Full Page Mono .... EUR 2680
Full Page Colour .... EUR 3760
Mechanical Data: Type Area: 280 x 190 mm, No. of Columns (Display): 4, Col Widths (Display): 45 mm
Copy instructions: *Copy Date:* 14 days prior to publication
BUSINESS: LOCAL GOVERNMENT, LEISURE & RECREATION: Local Government

BULK SOLIDS HANDLING
723841G10-5

Editorial: Max-Planck-Str. 7, 97082 WÜRZBURG
Tel: 931 4182301 **Fax:** 931 4182090
Email: marcel.droettboom@vogel.de **Web site:** http://www.bulk-solids-handling.com
Freq: 8 issues yearly; **Annual Sub.:** EUR 310,00; **Circ:** 9,987
Editor: Marcel Dröttboom; **Advertising Manager:** Klaus-Michael Göhler
Profile: bulk solids handling - the sole truly international technical journal. For all aspects of bulk materials handling provides all those involved in the mining, cement, metallurgical, chemical, and power generation industry as well as in the transport logistics area with up-to-date application oriented technical information. Business news, management topics and market trends complete the range of information. Via cross-media channels as the technical journal bulk solids handling, events and the website www.bulk-solids-handling.com experts and managers are supplied with beneficial content that offers solutions for their day-to-day challenges. Leading technical magazine and unique source of information for professionals in the fields of transportation, storage and handling of bulk solids.
Language(s): English
Readership: Read by technical managers, consultants, manufacturers and suppliers.
ADVERTISING RATES:
Full Page Mono .... EUR 3005
Full Page Colour .... EUR 3905
Mechanical Data: Type Area: 270 x 180 mm, No. of Columns (Display): 3, Col Widths (Display): 56 mm
Copy instructions: *Copy Date:* 21 days prior to publication
BUSINESS: MATERIALS HANDLING

BUND NATURSCHUTZ IN BAYERN E.V. KREISGRUPPE BAYREUTH-RUNDBRIEF
1659863G57-2731

Editorial: Alexanderstr. 9, 95444 BAYREUTH
Tel: 921 27230 **Fax:** 921 851497
Email: bayreuth@bund-naturschutz.de **Web site:** http://www.bayreuth.bund-naturschutz.de
Freq: Annual; **Cover Price:** Free; **Circ:** 2,450
Editor: Helmut Korn
Profile: Information from the Association for Environmental Protection in Bavaria for Bayreuth.
Language(s): German
ADVERTISING RATES:
Full Page Mono .... EUR 180
Mechanical Data: No. of Columns (Display): 2, Col Widths (Display): 55 mm
Copy instructions: *Copy Date:* 60 days prior to publication

BUND+BERUF
723924G40-15

Editorial: Unter dem Schöneberg 1, 34212 MELSUNGEN **Tel:** 5661 7310 **Fax:** 5661 731400
Email: juergen.hoppe@bernecker.de **Web site:** http://www.bernecker.de
Freq: Quarterly; **Annual Sub.:** EUR 16,00; **Circ:** 20,000
Editor: Jürgen Hoppe; **Advertising Manager:** Ralf Spohr
Profile: Journal of soldiers on time just before they leaving the army. Bund + Beruf forms a bridge between the Bundeswehr and the economy. With a solid overview of the market and the right strategy and training of entry into professional life easier for the military service. The magazine clarifies the risks and opportunities for service end. There are current, comprehensive information on promising occupations to training and career opportunities. Rounding out the Bund + Beruf literature with recommendations and a job board.
Language(s): German
ADVERTISING RATES:
Full Page Mono .... EUR 1700
Full Page Colour .... EUR 2360
Mechanical Data: Type Area: 270 x 185 mm, No. of Columns (Display): 4, Col Widths (Display): 45 mm
Copy instructions: *Copy Date:* 30 days prior to publication
BUSINESS: DEFENCE

BUNDESBAUBLATT
723899G4D-115

Editorial: Avenwedder Str. 55, 33335 GÜTERSLOH
Tel: 5241 8090884 **Fax:** 5241 80690880
Email: burkhard.froehlich@bauverlag.de **Web site:** http://www.bundesbaublatt.de
Freq: 10 issues yearly; **Annual Sub.:** EUR 186,60; **Circ:** 11,793
Editor: Burkhard Fröhlich; **Advertising Manager:** Herbert Walhorn
Profile: Journal about town, building and environmental planning.
Language(s): German
ADVERTISING RATES:
Full Page Mono .... EUR 3480
Full Page Colour .... EUR 4815
Mechanical Data: Type Area: 270 x 186 mm, No. of Columns (Display): 4, Col Widths (Display): 45 mm
Copy instructions: *Copy Date:* 14 days prior to publication
Supplement(s): Brandschutz in öffentlichen und privatwirtschaftlichen Gebäuden
BUSINESS: ARCHITECTURE & BUILDING: Planning & Housing

BUNDESGESUNDHEITSBLATT GESUNDHEITSFORSCHUNG GESUNDHEITSSCHUTZ
723909G56A-1780

Editorial: Nordufer 20, 13353 BERLIN
Tel: 30 187542328
Email: rohdewohldh@rki.de **Web site:** http://www.springerlink.com
Freq: Monthly; **Annual Sub.:** EUR 142,00; **Circ:** 2,339
Editor: Heidemarie Rohdewohld
Profile: The monthly publication Bundesgesundheitsblatt Gesundheitsforschung Gesundheitsschutz covers all areas that are addressed in public health and public health policy. The aim is firstly to keep informed of relevant developments in bio-medical research to date and informed as on specific policies on health, on approaches to prevention, risk prevention and health promotion. Important topics are the epidemiology of communicable diseases, environmental health and health economics, medical ethics and legal issues. A Section - Bekanntmachungen/Amtliche Mitteilungen - at the end of each issue contains an official statement published by the Institutes.
Language(s): German
ADVERTISING RATES:
Full Page Mono .... EUR 1390
Full Page Colour .... EUR 2430
Mechanical Data: Type Area: 240 x 175 mm
BUSINESS: HEALTH & MEDICAL

BUNDESSTEUERBLATT
723915G1A-400

Editorial: Dechenstr. 7, 53115 BONN **Tel:** 228 7240
Fax: 228 72491181
Email: info@stollfuss.de **Web site:** http://www.stollfuss.de
Freq: 25 issues yearly; **Annual Sub.:** EUR 52,00; **Circ:** 60,000
Profile: National official paper.
Language(s): German

DIE BUNDESWEHR
723917G40-120

Editorial: Südstr. 123, 53175 BONN
Tel: 228 3823212 **Fax:** 228 3823219
Email: presse@dbwv.de **Web site:** http://www.dbwv.de
Freq: Monthly; Free to qualifying individuals
Annual Sub.: EUR 42,00; **Circ:** 170,504
Editor: Frank Henning
Profile: Die Bundeswehr is the monthly membership magazine of the German Armed Forces Association (DBwV). It is the largest German military magazine and reached as far institutions specialized body of the association's members, numerous readers in the political sphere, in government and society. Increasing interest in women, they found: Both the soldiers in the armed forces as well as the wives of the soldiers. The magazine publishes social and societal contributions, and the combined political demands. Moreover there are security issues, military and civil clerical vocational education and training as well as reports and stories "around the collar" and from sports and motor world as attractive offers to readers inside and outside the DBwV.
Language(s): German
ADVERTISING RATES:
Full Page Mono .... EUR 4110
Full Page Colour .... EUR 5343
Mechanical Data: Type Area: 285 x 198 mm, No. of Columns (Display): 4, Col Widths (Display): 47 mm
Copy instructions: *Copy Date:* 26 days prior to publication
BUSINESS: DEFENCE

BUNDMAGAZIN
723919G57-320

Editorial: Am Köllnischen Park 1, 10179 BERLIN
Tel: 30 2758640 **Fax:** 30 27586440
Email: redaktion@bund.net **Web site:** http://www.bund.net
Freq: Quarterly; Free to qualifying individuals
Annual Sub.: EUR 15,00; **Circ:** 154,649
Editor: Severin Zillich
Profile: Journal of the German Environment and Nature Protection Association. The magazine of the Association for the Environment and nature conservation, Germany informed on key issues of environmental protection and nature conservation, reports on the work of the association and are Ökotipps for everyday life. The magazine provides information about healthy food, efficient electrical appliances and interesting books: The BUNDmagazin recommends new publications on nature conservation, environmental policy and sustainable living. The Association for Environment and nature conservation Germany is part of the global environmental network Friends of the Earth. The BUNDmagazin reported on international nature conservation and environmental protection. Facebook: http://www.facebook.com/BUND.Bundesverband.
Language(s): German
Readership: Read by members.
ADVERTISING RATES:
Full Page Mono .... EUR 6450
Full Page Colour .... EUR 7100
Mechanical Data: Type Area: 242 x 188 mm, No. of Columns (Display): 4, Col Widths (Display): 43 mm
Copy instructions: *Copy Date:* 29 days prior to publication
Supplement(s): BUNDzeit; Rundbrief Mecklenburg-Vorpommern
BUSINESS: ENVIRONMENT & POLLUTION

BUNDZEIT
1834267G57-2865

Editorial: Crellestr. 35, 10827 BERLIN
Tel: 30 78790016 **Fax:** 30 78790018
Email: redaktion@bundzeit.de **Web site:** http://www.bundzeit.de
Freq: Quarterly; Free to qualifying individuals
Annual Sub.: EUR 5,00; **Circ:** 30,000
Editor: Carmen Schultze; **Advertising Manager:** Thorsten Edler
Profile: Quarterly environmental magazine for Berlin and Brandenburg, with information and background reports.
Language(s): German
ADVERTISING RATES:
Full Page Mono .... EUR 1500
Full Page Colour .... EUR 1500
Mechanical Data: Type Area: 380 x 185 mm, No. of Columns (Display): 3, Col Widths (Display): 60 mm
Copy instructions: *Copy Date:* 30 days prior to publication
Supplement to: BUNDmagazin

BUNSENMAGAZIN
1861921G37-1856

Editorial: Petersenstr. 20, 64287 DARMSTADT
Tel: 6151 162707 **Fax:** 6151 166015
Email: bunsenmagazin@bunsen.de
Freq: 6 issues yearly; Free to qualifying individuals ; **Circ:** 1,600
Editor: Rolf Schäfer
Profile: Journal about physical chemistry.
Language(s): German
ADVERTISING RATES:
Full Page Mono .... EUR 700
Mechanical Data: Type Area: 243 x 175 mm
Copy instructions: *Copy Date:* 30 days prior to publication

BUNTE
723926G73-80

Editorial: Arabellastr. 23, 81925 MÜNCHEN
Tel: 89 92500 **Fax:** 89 92503427
Email: bunte@burda.com **Web site:** http://www.bunte.de
Freq: Weekly; **Annual Sub.:** EUR 156,00; **Circ:** 638,870
Editor: Patricia Riekel; **News Editor:** Annette Dörrfuß
Profile: Nothing interests people as much as men. For more than 60 years Bunte is the guarantor of highly professional news reporting on the key events in German society. Editor and editor in chief Patricia Riekel: "We are the barometer of the German company Community and its sensitivities. "Colorful embodies the absolute passion for people like no other medium and is therefore undisputed number 1 in the German media market, or - as the Süddeutsche Zeitung - "the dominant medium of the Berlin Republic. Bunte is pure emotion. Advertisers benefit from this clear positioning. With emotions makes colorful products with trademarks and brands Stars. It connects Bunte media attention with the possibilities of individual and interactive communication. And love helping people achieve the lifestyle and luxury. Bunte is an integral part of a growing cultural event in Germany: print, online and IP-TV formats, the current brand Bunte making it the largest media platform, people in Germany. Facebook: http://www.facebook.com/Bunte.de Twitter: http://twitter.com/bunteonline.
Language(s): German
ADVERTISING RATES:
Full Page Mono .... EUR 32300
Full Page Colour .... EUR 32300
Mechanical Data: Type Area: 251 x 192 mm, No. of Columns (Display): 3, Col Widths (Display): 64 mm
Copy instructions: *Copy Date:* 21 days prior to publication
CONSUMER: NATIONAL & INTERNATIONAL PERIODICALS

BUNTE ONLINE
1620934G74A-3378

Editorial: Arabellastr. 23, 81925 MÜNCHEN
Tel: 89 92500 **Fax:** 89 92502340
Email: online-redaktion@bunte.de **Web site:** http://www.bunte.de
Freq: Daily; **Cover Price:** Paid; **Circ:** 10,309,054 Unique Users
Editor: Jürgen Bruckmeier
Profile: Ezine: Bunte.de - younger, female, modern, current and faster - information on all of the latest People-top themes. People and Lifestyle Portal. Facebook: http://www.facebook.com/Bunte.de Twitter: http://twitter.com/bunteonline.
Language(s): German
CONSUMER: WOMEN'S INTEREST CONSUMER MAGAZINES: Women's Interest

BUONGIORNO ITALIA
1644137G11A-1592

Editorial: Bechsteinstr. 27, 99423 WEIMAR
Tel: 3643 41580 **Fax:** 3643 415819
Email: redazione@chefmedia.de **Web site:** http://www.chefmedia.de
Freq: 10 issues yearly; **Annual Sub.:** EUR 44,95; **Circ:** 7,294
Editor: Elena Guglielmin; **Advertising Manager:** Sandra Schelonke
Profile: Magazine for Italian restaurant owners in Germany.
Language(s): Italian
ADVERTISING RATES:
Full Page Mono .... EUR 3790
Full Page Colour .... EUR 3790
Mechanical Data: Type Area: 267 x 182 mm
Copy instructions: *Copy Date:* 20 days prior to publication
BUSINESS: CATERING: Catering, Hotels & Restaurants

BURDA EASY FASHION
1938693G74A-3735

Editorial: Arabellastr. 23, 81925 MÜNCHEN
Tel: 89 92502879 **Fax:** 89 92503935
Email: burdastyle@burda.com **Web site:** http://www.burdastyle.de
Freq: Half-yearly; **Cover Price:** EUR 4,50; **Circ:** 50,000
Editor: Dagmar Bily
Profile: Magazine features women's fashion, news, ideas and styles for beginner for home sewing. Facebook: http://www.facebook.com/event.php.
Language(s): German
ADVERTISING RATES:
Full Page Mono .... EUR 5800
Full Page Colour .... EUR 5800
Mechanical Data: Type Area: 229 x 175 mm, No. of Columns (Display): 4, Col Widths (Display): 40 mm
Copy instructions: *Copy Date:* 63 days prior to publication

BURDA PLUS FASHION
1938694G74A-3736

Editorial: Arabellastr. 23, 81925 MÜNCHEN
Tel: 89 92502879 **Fax:** 89 92503935
Email: burdastyle@burda.com **Web site:** http://www.burdastyle.de
Freq: Half-yearly; **Cover Price:** EUR 5,00; **Circ:** 50,000
Editor: Dagmar Bily
Profile: Magazine providing women's fashion news and ideas in larger sizes for sewing Facebook: http://www.facebook.com/event.php.
Language(s): German
ADVERTISING RATES:
Full Page Mono .... EUR 5800
Full Page Colour .... EUR 5800
Mechanical Data: Type Area: 229 x 175 mm, No. of Columns (Display): 4, Col Widths (Display): 40 mm
Copy instructions: *Copy Date:* 60 days prior to publication

BURDA STYLE
723941G74B-30

Editorial: Arabellastr. 23, 81925 MÜNCHEN
Tel: 89 92502879 **Fax:** 89 92503935
Email: burdastyle@burda.com **Web site:** http://www.burdastyle.de
Freq: Monthly; **Annual Sub.:** EUR 54,00; **Circ:** 142,860
Editor: Dagmar Bily
Profile: burda style is the world's largest fashion magazine. In 17 different languages it has become a synonymous with fashion and style in more than 90 countries. The magazine inspires creativity in various areas of life: fashion, accessories, lifestyle, beauty and home decoration - and thus offers more than just fashion for self-stitching. burda style translates the vision of its founder Aenne Burda into the present day and into the future - in the magazine and worldwide on the web. burda style inspires and encourages modern and creative women of all ages to realize themselves and live their desire for individuality. For the readers of burda style have one thing in common: the creative potential and pleasure in particular.
Language(s): German
Readership: Aimed at women.
ADVERTISING RATES:
Full Page Mono .... EUR 13900
Full Page Colour .... EUR 13900
Mechanical Data: Type Area: 229 x 175 mm, No. of Columns (Display): 4, Col Widths (Display): 40 mm
Copy instructions: *Copy Date:* 59 days prior to publication
CONSUMER: WOMEN'S INTEREST CONSUMER MAGAZINES: Women's Interest - Fashion

BURGHAUSER ANZEIGER

723965G67B-3680

Editorial: Medienstr. 5, 94036 PASSAU
Tel: 851 8020 **Fax:** 851 802256
Email: pnp@vgp.de **Web site:** http://www.pnp.de
Freq: 312 issues yearly; **Circ:** 20,257
Advertising Manager: Gerhard Koller
Profile: Daily newspaper with regional news and a local sports section. Twitter: http://twitter.com/pnp_online This Outlet offers RSS (Really Simple Syndication).
Language(s): German
ADVERTISING RATES:
SCC .... EUR 55,50
Mechanical Data: Type Area: 482 x 325 mm, No. of Columns (Display): 7, Col Widths (Display): 45 mm
Copy instructions: *Copy Date:* 2 days prior to publication
REGIONAL DAILY & SUNDAY NEWSPAPERS: Regional Daily Newspapers

BURGWEDELER NACHRICHTEN

723972G72-2888

Editorial: Marktstr. 16, 31303 BURGDORF
Tel: 5136 89940 **Fax:** 5136 899430
Email: redaktion.burgwedel@marktspiegel-verlag.de
Web site: http://www.marktspiegel-verlag.de
Freq: Weekly; **Cover Price:** Free; **Circ:** 21,700
Editor: Birgit Schröder; **Advertising Manager:** Klaus Hoffmann
Profile: Advertising journal (house-to-house) concentrating on local stories.
Language(s): German
ADVERTISING RATES:
Full Page Mono .... EUR 3122
Full Page Colour .... EUR 3612
Mechanical Data: Type Area: 430 x 277 mm, No. of Columns (Display): 6, Col Widths (Display): 45 mm
Copy instructions: *Copy Date:* 2 days prior to publication
LOCAL NEWSPAPERS

DAS BÜRO

723823G34-120

Editorial: Zimmerstr. 56, 10117 BERLIN
Tel: 30 47907118 **Fax:** 30 47907120
Email: rn@officeabc.de **Web site:** http://www.das-buero-magazin.de
Freq: 6 issues yearly; **Annual Sub.:** EUR 27,00; **Circ:** 24,590
Editor: Robert Nehring; **Advertising Manager:** Bärbel Skrzypczak
Profile: Magazine for the entire office: office culture - Offices - Office Supplies - Office Supplies. The magazine is aimed at medium-sized entrepreneurs, buyers and Office Professionals. It is aimed at consumers, but also achieved many professional traders. The journal das büro informed the Office decision-makers knowledgeable and practical solutions in the areas of outstanding office culture, office space, office equipment and office supplies. A particular focus of the magazine for Office Excellence is the linking of ergonomics, design, quality, innovation, economy and ecology. The office is competent, compact, complete. das büro is an organ of I.O.E. Excellence Initiative Office.
Language(s): German
ADVERTISING RATES:
Full Page Mono .... EUR 5795
Full Page Colour .... EUR 5795
Mechanical Data: Type Area: 228 x 185 mm, No. of Columns (Display): 3, Col Widths (Display): 56 mm
Copy instructions: *Copy Date:* 30 days prior to publication
Official Journal of: Organ d. I.O.E. Initiative Office-Excellence

DIE BÜROBERUFE

723822G14F-4

Editorial: Eschstr. 22, 44629 HERNE
Tel: 2323 141900 **Fax:** 2323 141123
Email: u.hoelzer@kiehl.de **Web site:** http://www.kiehl.de
Freq: Monthly; **Annual Sub.:** EUR 61,80; **Circ:** 3,792
Editor: Ulrike Hölzer; **Advertising Manager:** Andreas Reimann
Profile: The magazine „Die Büroberufe" includes not only current issues primarily audit related contributions from the areas of office management, accounting, economics and social science and information processing. Numerous case examples and diagrams provide a graphic processing of complex facts and the testing tasks provide the opportunity for self-control has been learned.
Language(s): German
ADVERTISING RATES:
Full Page Mono .... EUR 930
Full Page Colour .... EUR 1300
Mechanical Data: Type Area: 260 x 186 mm
Copy instructions: *Copy Date:* 30 days prior to publication
BUSINESS: COMMERCE, INDUSTRY & MANAGEMENT: Training & Recruitment

BÜROWIRTSCHAFT

732899G34-142_50

Editorial: Georg-Westermann-Allee 66, 38104 BRAUNSCHWEIG **Tel:** 531 7080 **Fax:** 531 708343
Email: service@winklers.de **Web site:** http://www.winklers.de
Freq: Quarterly; **Cover Price:** EUR 6,95
Free to qualifying individuals ; **Circ:** 1,500
Editor: Peter Flühr
Profile: Magazine about equipment for shorthand, typewriting and information processing.
Language(s): German
ADVERTISING RATES:
Full Page Mono .... EUR 250
Mechanical Data: Type Area: 194 x 126 mm
Copy instructions: *Copy Date:* 28 days prior to publication
BUSINESS: OFFICE EQUIPMENT

BÜRSTÄDTER ZEITUNG

723828G67B-3700

Editorial: Erich-Dombrowski-Str. 2, 55127 MAINZ
Tel: 6131 485805 **Fax:** 6131 485833
Web site: http://www.allgemeine-zeitung.de
Freq: 312 issues yearly; **Circ:** 5,377
Advertising Manager: Gerhard Müller
Profile: Daily newspaper with regional news and a local sports section. Facebook: http://www.facebook.com/pages/Allgemeine-Zeitung/255951758912 Twitter: http://twitter.com/aznachrichten This Outlet offers RSS (Really Simple Syndication).
Language(s): German
ADVERTISING RATES:
SCC .... EUR 38,50
Mechanical Data: Type Area: 480 x 325 mm, No. of Columns (Display): 7, Col Widths (Display): 45 mm
Copy instructions: *Copy Date:* 1 day prior to publication
Supplement(s): pepper
REGIONAL DAILY & SUNDAY NEWSPAPERS: Regional Daily Newspapers

BUS BLICKPUNKT

723975G49B-1

Editorial: Darmstädter Str. 121, 64625 BENSHEIM
Tel: 6251 93490 **Fax:** 6251 934949
Email: juergen.weidlich@busblickpunkt.de **Web site:** http://www.busnetz.de
Freq: Monthly; **Annual Sub.:** EUR 48,00; **Circ:** 10,036
Editor: Jürgen Weidlich; **Advertising Manager:** Katja Dehn
Profile: The bus blickpunkt is a trade journal with information for bus operators. The bus blickpunkt sees itself as independent and critical guide to the bus industry. In news, reports, commentaries and interviews coach tour, bus technology, general destination-based traffic and policy-relevant information is reflected.
Language(s): German
Readership: Read by owners and drivers of bus and coaches, travel agents and hotel couriers.
ADVERTISING RATES:
Full Page Mono .... EUR 4248
Full Page Colour .... EUR 4930
Mechanical Data: Type Area: 378 x 265 mm, No. of Columns (Display): 6, Col Widths (Display): 40 mm
Copy instructions: *Copy Date:* 14 days prior to publication
BUSINESS: TRANSPORT: Bus & Coach Transport

BUS FAHRT

723986G49B-10

Editorial: Dießemer Bruch 167, 47805 KREFELD
Tel: 2151 5100118 **Fax:** 2151 5100105
Email: lutz.gerritzen@stuenings.de **Web site:** http://www.busfahrt.com
Freq: Monthly; Free to qualifying individuals
Annual Sub.: EUR 68,00; **Circ:** 7,947
Editor: Lutz Gerritzen; **Advertising Manager:** Ulrich Miggel
Profile: Comprehensive magazine for bus ride with monthly updated news from the areas of technology, business, Traffic, Politics & Organizations, Laws & Regulations, a large archive, extensive collection of test and driving reports, private coach tourism section with news from the tourism industry, Events and large tour planners. Facebook: http://www.facebook.com/pages/Bus-Fahrt/135872319795281.
Language(s): German
ADVERTISING RATES:
Full Page Mono .... EUR 2480
Full Page Colour .... EUR 3890
Mechanical Data: Type Area: 255 x 185 mm, No. of Columns (Display): 3, Col Widths (Display): 59 mm
Copy instructions: *Copy Date:* 20 days prior to publication
Supplement(s): NFZ Werkstatt
BUSINESS: TRANSPORT: Bus & Coach Transport

BUS MAGAZIN

724001G49B-11

Editorial: Siegfriedstr. 28, 53179 BONN
Tel: 228 9545344 **Fax:** 228 9545327
Email: busmagazin@kirschbaum.de **Web site:** http://www.kirschbaum.de
Freq: 10 issues yearly; **Annual Sub.:** EUR 75,00; **Circ:** 7,920
Editor: Dirk Sanne; **Advertising Manager:** Volker Rutkowski
Profile: Bus Magazin is a trade magazine on corporate governance for private bus operators, they make travel and / or regular service. The magazine's editorial focus as automotive engineering and coach tourism. In the Technology section will be presented including the results of vehicle tests. In the tourism section is reported on worthwhile goals for trip planning and travel organization. Business and trade policy issues and current information on cross-border traffic complete the reading and readers offer.
Language(s): German
ADVERTISING RATES:
Full Page Mono .... EUR 2660
Full Page Colour .... EUR 3650
Mechanical Data: Type Area: 248 x 185 mm, No. of Columns (Display): 4, Col Widths (Display): 44 mm
BUSINESS: TRANSPORT: Bus & Coach Transport

BUS SYSTEME

724006G4E-6909

Editorial: Friedrich-Wolf-Str. 16a, 12527 BERLIN
Tel: 30 67489289 **Fax:** 30 6744508
Email: redaktion@bussysteme.de **Web site:** http://www.bussysteme.de
Freq: Quarterly; **Annual Sub.:** EUR 30,00; **Circ:** 7,938
Editor: Ursula Maria Lange; **Advertising Manager:** Ursula Maria Lange
Profile: Journal of modern building technology. Conveys knowledge of systems, products and solutions to modern and innovative building technology and information on theoretical principles, technology / innovation (product in the application), practice (examples), system concepts, business ideas, product information, information (trade show reports, short reports, book reviews), training and developments.
Language(s): German
Readership: Read by planners and designers.
ADVERTISING RATES:
Full Page Mono .... EUR 1840
Full Page Colour .... EUR 3070
Mechanical Data: Type Area: 267 x 166 mm, No. of Columns (Display): 3, Col Widths (Display): 50 mm
Copy instructions: *Copy Date:* 30 days prior to publication
BUSINESS: ARCHITECTURE & BUILDING: Building

BUS SYSTEMS

1820250G17-1592

Editorial: Friedrich-Wolf-Str. 16a, 12527 BERLIN
Tel: 30 67489289 **Fax:** 30 6744508
Email: redaktion@bussysteme.de **Web site:** http://www.bussysteme.de
Freq: Annual; **Cover Price:** EUR 7,50; **Circ:** 8,000
Editor: Ursula Maria Lange; **Advertising Manager:** Ursula Maria Lange
Profile: Magazine focusing on building systems technology.
Language(s): English
ADVERTISING RATES:
Full Page Mono .... EUR 1840
Full Page Colour .... EUR 3070
Mechanical Data: Type Area: 257 x 166 mm, No. of Columns (Display): 3, Col Widths (Display): 51 mm
Copy instructions: *Copy Date:* 30 days prior to publication

BUS TOURIST

724007G50-180

Editorial: In der Bannhalde 30, 74343 SACHSENHEIM **Tel:** 7147 270128 **Fax:** 7147 270129
Email: info@bustourist.com **Web site:** http://www.bustourist.com
Freq: Quarterly; **Annual Sub.:** EUR 20,00; **Circ:** 11,657
Editor: Rainer Rex; **Advertising Manager:** Thomas Tritschler
Profile: Bus Tourist - The magazine for travel by bus - with an average circulation of approximately 11,450 copies is one of the leading and the largest circulation magazine in the coach tourism sector. Services, such as catalog and coupon service round out the sound and independent editorial preparation from the magazine.
Language(s): German
ADVERTISING RATES:
Full Page Mono .... EUR 2135
Full Page Colour .... EUR 3185
Mechanical Data: Type Area: 270 x 185 mm, No. of Columns (Display): 4, Col Widths (Display): 43 mm
Copy instructions: *Copy Date:* 30 days prior to publication
BUSINESS: TRAVEL & TOURISM

BUS ZIELE

1743731G89A-12240

Editorial: Dießemer Bruch 167, 47805 KREFELD
Tel: 2151 5100118 **Fax:** 2151 5100105
Email: lutz.gerritzen@stuenings.de **Web site:** http://www.busziele.com
Freq: Annual; **Cover Price:** EUR 5,00; **Circ:** 50,000
Editor: Lutz Gerritzen; **Advertising Manager:** Ulrich Miggel
Profile: Bus-Ziele, has proven to be a planning guide for bus tours and group tours by bus companies and tour operators. The extensive information on hotels, guesthouses, restaurants, attractions, excursions and tourist attractions make the planning and execution of group tours and bus tours.
Language(s): German
ADVERTISING RATES:
Full Page Mono .... EUR 3860
Full Page Colour .... EUR 3860
Mechanical Data: Type Area: 260 x 185 mm, No. of Columns (Display): 3, Col Widths (Display): 58 mm

BUSCHE HOTELS & RESTAURANTS

1740098G89A-12223

Editorial: Schleefstr. 1, 44287 DORTMUND
Tel: 231 444770 **Fax:** 231 4447777
Email: hauptredaktion@busche.de **Web site:** http://www.deutschland-reisen.de
Freq: Annual; **Cover Price:** EUR 19,80; **Circ:** 23,444
Advertising Manager: Jörg Leu
Profile: Hotel and restaurant guide for Germany. 6,600 Hotels and Restaurants in Germany - the Guide "Hotels & Restaurants" keeps the cozy inn ready to fine luxury hotel the whole range and is one of the largest hotel and restaurant guides in Germany. It is an essential companion for travelers is to use and require high information content.
Language(s): German
ADVERTISING RATES:
Full Page Mono .... EUR 2300
Full Page Colour .... EUR 2300
Mechanical Data: Type Area: 184 x 118 mm

BUSCHE WINZER & WEINGÜTER

1740099G89A-12224

Editorial: Schleefstr. 1, 44287 DORTMUND
Tel: 231 444770 **Fax:** 231 4447777
Email: hauptredaktion@busche.de **Web site:** http://www.wein-ziele.com
Freq: Annual; **Cover Price:** EUR 19,80; **Circ:** 23,771
Advertising Manager: Jörg Leu
Profile: Wine Guide, which presents about 1,200 wineries, winegrowers and wineries in Germany, Alsace, Luxembourg, Austria and South Tyrol clearly and vividly. In addition, the book contains much information about wine from the interesting history of the many wine growing areas to possible combination of wines with certain foods. Other content: Mapping the wine-growing regions, wine encyclopedia, local register.
Language(s): German
ADVERTISING RATES:
Full Page Mono .... EUR 2300
Full Page Colour .... EUR 2300
Mechanical Data: Type Area: 184 x 118 mm

BUSINESS GEOMATICS

763208G55-3851

Editorial: Pasteurstr. 1a, 50735 KÖLN
Tel: 221 92182552 **Fax:** 221 92182516
Email: grebe@business-geomatics.com **Web site:** http://www.business-geomatics.com
Freq: 11 issues yearly; **Annual Sub.:** EUR 60,00; **Circ:** 14,542
Editor: Stefan Grebe; **Advertising Manager:** Felix Vieth
Profile: Business magazine about geodinformatics.
Language(s): German
ADVERTISING RATES:
Full Page Colour .... EUR 5490
Mechanical Data: Type Area: 405 x 270 mm
Supplement(s): Business Geomatics Fokus
BUSINESS: APPLIED SCIENCE & LABORATORIES

BUSINESS GEOMATICS FOKUS

1925487G14A-10346

Editorial: Pasteurstr. 1a, 50735 KÖLN
Tel: 221 92182552 **Fax:** 221 92182516
Email: grebe@business-geomatics.com **Web site:** http://www.business-geomatics.com
Freq: Quarterly; **Circ:** 15,000
Editor: Stefan Grebe; **Advertising Manager:** Regina Longerich
Profile: Business magazine about geodinformatics.
Language(s): German
Mechanical Data: Type Area: 258 x 175 mm
Supplement to: Business Geomatics

BUSINESS INTELLIGENCE MAGAZINE

1852308G14A-10199

Editorial: Augustinusstr. 11d, 50226 FRECHEN
Tel: 2234 202581 **Fax:** 2234 659694
Email: wms@bi-magazine.net **Web site:** http://www.bi-magazine.net
Freq: Quarterly; **Annual Sub.:** EUR 29,00; **Circ:** 18,796
Editor: Wolf K. Müller Scholz
Profile: The BUSINESS INTELLIGENCE MAGAZINE is the business magazine for successful business management based on analytical methods and IT systems. It serves top decision makers in German-speaking as a central source of information for topics such as performance control and customer relations, compliance and controlling. The magazine is published four times a year. Total Circulation, IVW-audited: 20,000 pieces per issue. The BUSINESS INTELLIGENCE MAGAZINE is aimed at top decision makers (C level) as senior executives and directors, financial managers and controllers, marketing and sales leaders and IT senior managers from all sectors. The BUSINESS INTELLIGENCE MAGAZINE will be sent personally to decision makers at companies with more than 100 employees in Switzerland and Germany.
Language(s): German
ADVERTISING RATES:
Full Page Mono .... EUR 5800
Full Page Colour .... EUR 5800
Mechanical Data: Type Area: 244 x 182 mm, No. of Columns (Display): 3, Col Widths (Display): 70 mm

BUSINESS INTELLIGENCE MAGAZINE

1936219G14A-10401

Editorial: Augustinusstr. 11d, 50226 FRECHEN
Tel: 2234 202581 **Fax:** 2234 659694
Email: wms@bi-magazine.net **Web site:** http://www.bi-magazine.net
Freq: Quarterly; **Annual Sub.:** CHF 45,00; **Circ:** 6,004
Editor: Wolf K. Müller Scholz
Profile: Business magazine.
Language(s): German
ADVERTISING RATES:
Full Page Mono .... CHF 6900
Full Page Colour .... CHF 6900
Mechanical Data: Type Area: 244 x 182 mm, No. of Columns (Display): 3, Col Widths (Display): 70 mm

BUSINESS LIVE

1831481G14A-10124

Editorial: Grüner Weg 13, 52070 AACHEN
Tel: 241 9183011 **Fax:** 241 9183050
Email: info@businessclub-aachen.com **Web site:** http://www.businessclub-aachen.com
Freq: Quarterly; **Circ:** 1,500

Profile: Member magazine from the Business Club Aachen Maastricht with internal information.
Language(s): German

BUSINESS NEWS 1863831G33-348
Editorial: Wittener Str. 45, 44789 BOCHUM
Tel: 234 3153625
Email: beate.muellmann@aral.com **Web site:** http://www.aral.de
Freq: Quarterly; **Cover Price:** Free; **Circ:** 4,100
Editor: Beate Müllmann
Profile: Information for filling station managers.
Language(s): German
ADVERTISING RATES:
Full Page Mono .... EUR 1227
Full Page Colour .... EUR 2045
Mechanical Data: Type Area: 219 x 170 mm

BUSINESS PER TOPKONTAKT
745159G14A-7500
Editorial: Landsberger Str. 77, 82205 GILCHING
Tel: 8105 376390 **Fax:** 8105 376392
Email: info@top-kontakt.de **Web site:** http://www.top-kontakt.de
Freq: Half-yearly; **Cover Price:** Free; **Circ:** 100,000
Editor: Martina Lontzek; **Advertising Manager:** Harald Walther
Profile: Selected product information for decision makers in the German economy. For 20 years, the most famous and successful Verbundmailingmagzin in Germany. The balanced Adressenmix the partial address of 6-7 suppliers (no big list broker) is guaranteed, high response. Per company only a decision is written down. All addresses are personalized and most of them are post buyer. The magazines are not only collectible but also of ideas at the same time.
Language(s): German
ADVERTISING RATES:
Full Page Mono .... EUR 3100
Full Page Colour .... EUR 3100
Copy instructions: *Copy Date:* 47 days prior to publication

BUSINESS PUNK 1928732G14A-10377
Editorial: Am Baumwall 11, 20459 HAMBURG
Tel: 40 37030 **Fax:** 40 37038310
Email: redaktion@business-punk.com **Web site:** http://www.business-punk.com
Freq: 3 issues yearly; **Cover Price:** EUR 6,00; **Circ:** 80,000
Editor: Steffen Klusmann; **Advertising Manager:** Martina Hoss
Profile: Business Punks is a business lifestyle magazine for men who make a difference and want to succeed. For a job more than a job, because it defines their lives and drives them. Men who are willing to reinzuknien for a project. For the times only one type of target velocity, and sleep is a necessary evil, because they celebrate after work with colleagues and dear friends. Sometimes into the early morning. Who knows this attitude is the right choice for business punk. This is about business beyond sales figures and profit forecasts. It's about the loud, fast life that is raging behind the business. And to types that do business in anything.
Language(s): German
ADVERTISING RATES:
Full Page Mono .... EUR 9000
Full Page Colour .... EUR 9000
Mechanical Data: Type Area: 245 x 185 mm

BUSINESS SPOTLIGHT
723998G88B-260
Editorial: Fraunhoferstr. 22, 82152 PLANEGG
Tel: 89 856810 **Fax:** 89 85681210
Email: business@spotlight-verlag.de **Web site:** http://www.business-spotlight.de
Freq: 6 issues yearly; **Annual Sub.:** EUR 87,90; **Circ:** 46,684
Editor: Ian McMaster; **Advertising Manager:** Axel Zettler
Profile: Business Spotlight is the business English magazine for German-speaking readers: staff in internationally operating companies, from managers to assistants, who need English in their jobs. Our editors and language experts – all of them native speakers – cover a great range of cross-industry topics such as intercultural communication on the job and while travelling, business and management skills, technical developments, career planning, etc. Business Spotlight's unique editorial concept assists readers in effectively expanding their vocabulary while learning new and exciting facts from the international world of business and finance.
Language(s): English; German
ADVERTISING RATES:
Full Page Mono .... EUR 5203
Full Page Colour .... EUR 8670
Mechanical Data: Type Area: 246 x 186 mm, No. of Columns (Display): 4, Col Widths (Display): 43 mm
Copy instructions: *Copy Date:* 35 days prior to publication
CONSUMER: EDUCATION: Adult Education

BUSINESS TRAVELLER
723999G50-1221
Editorial: Schulstr. 34, 80634 MÜNCHEN
Tel: 89 130143210 **Fax:** 89 130143222
Email: tuegel@businesstraveller.de **Web site:** http://www.businesstraveller.de
Freq: 6 issues yearly; **Cover Price:** EUR 3,50; **Circ:** 51,957
Editor: Marc Tügel
Profile: The business magazine aimed directly to the traveler as a decision maker and provides comprehensive information on all areas that are associated with missions of importance. Fly, hotel, train, car, travel electronics and lifestyle are among the regular columns every issue.
Language(s): German
Readership: Aimed at frequent international business travellers.
ADVERTISING RATES:
Full Page Mono .... EUR 8520
Full Page Colour .... EUR 9550
Mechanical Data: Type Area: 236 x 176 mm, No. of Columns (Display): 3, Col Widths (Display): 58 mm
Copy instructions: *Copy Date:* 30 days prior to publication
Official Journal of: Organ f. VDR, HSMA
BUSINESS: TRAVEL & TOURISM

BUSINESS&IT 1641852G5C-51
Editorial: Richard-Reitzner-Allee 2, 85540 HAAR
Tel: 89 255561124 **Fax:** 89 255561621
Email: aeichelsdoerfer@wekanet.de **Web site:** http://www.businessportal.de
Freq: Monthly; **Annual Sub.:** EUR 71,00; **Circ:** 30,512
Editor: Andreas Eichelsdörfer; **Advertising Manager:** Karin Kienberger
Profile: Business & IT is the indispensable source of information regarding investment and management decisions. The smooth flow of business processes is the basis for business success. Business & IT is the business-critical processes into the editorial issues and shows a practical coverage of how these processes themselves, or by using external service providers optimally controlled.
Language(s): German
ADVERTISING RATES:
Full Page Mono .... EUR 7050
Full Page Colour .... EUR 9400
Mechanical Data: Type Area: 250 x 185 mm, No. of Columns (Display): 4, Col Widths (Display): 43 mm
Copy instructions: *Copy Date:* 26 days prior to publication
BUSINESS: COMPUTERS & AUTOMATION: Professional Personal Computers

BUSINESS & LAW 1696606G1A-3614
Editorial: Bergheimer Str. 104, 69115 HEIDELBERG
Tel: 6221 653060 **Fax:** 6221 6530630
Email: redaktion@businessandlaw.de **Web site:** http://www.businessandlaw.de
Freq: Annual; **Cover Price:** EUR 7,80; **Circ:** 15,000
Advertising Manager: Barbara Claußen
Language(s): German
ADVERTISING RATES:
Full Page Mono .... EUR 4210
Full Page Colour .... EUR 4210
Mechanical Data: Type Area: 240 x 184 mm
BUSINESS: FINANCE & ECONOMICS

BUSINESS & LAW 1696607G14R-6126
Editorial: Bergheimer Str. 104, 69115 HEIDELBERG
Tel: 6221 653060 **Fax:** 6221 6530630
Email: redaktion@businessandlaw.de **Web site:** http://www.businessandlaw.de
Freq: Annual; **Cover Price:** EUR 7,80; **Circ:** 15,000
Advertising Manager: Barbara Claußen
Language(s): German
ADVERTISING RATES:
Full Page Mono .... EUR 4210
Full Page Colour .... EUR 4210
Mechanical Data: Type Area: 240 x 184 mm
BUSINESS: COMMERCE, INDUSTRY & MANAGEMENT: Commerce Related

BUSINESS & LAW 1696608G14R-6127
Editorial: Bergheimer Str. 104, 69115 HEIDELBERG
Tel: 6221 653060 **Fax:** 6221 6530630
Email: redaktion@businessandlaw.de **Web site:** http://www.businessandlaw.de
Freq: Annual; **Cover Price:** EUR 7,80; **Circ:** 15,000
Advertising Manager: Barbara Claußen
Language(s): German
ADVERTISING RATES:
Full Page Mono .... EUR 4210
Full Page Colour .... EUR 4210
Mechanical Data: Type Area: 240 x 184 mm
BUSINESS: COMMERCE, INDUSTRY & MANAGEMENT: Commerce Related

BUSINESS & LAW 1703779G14R-6139
Editorial: Bergheimer Str. 104, 69115 HEIDELBERG
Tel: 6221 653060 **Fax:** 6221 6530630
Email: redaktion@businessandlaw.de **Web site:** http://www.businessandlaw.de
Freq: Annual; **Cover Price:** EUR 7,80; **Circ:** 13,500
Advertising Manager: Barbara Claußen
Language(s): German
ADVERTISING RATES:
Full Page Mono .... EUR 4210
Full Page Colour .... EUR 4210
Mechanical Data: Type Area: 240 x 184 mm
BUSINESS: COMMERCE, INDUSTRY & MANAGEMENT: Commerce Related

BUSINESS & LAW 1739821G14R-6169
Editorial: Bergheimer Str. 104, 69115 HEIDELBERG
Tel: 6221 653060 **Fax:** 6221 6530630
Email: redaktion@businessandlaw.de **Web site:** http://www.businessandlaw.de
Freq: Annual; **Cover Price:** EUR 7,80; **Circ:** 15,000
Advertising Manager: Barbara Claußen
Language(s): German
ADVERTISING RATES:
Full Page Mono .... EUR 4210
Full Page Colour .... EUR 4210
Mechanical Data: Type Area: 240 x 184 mm
BUSINESS: COMMERCE, INDUSTRY & MANAGEMENT: Commerce Related

BUSPLANER INTERNATIONAL
1830867G50-1253
Editorial: Joseph-Dollinger-Bogen 5, 80807 MÜNCHEN **Tel:** 89 32391450 **Fax:** 89 32391163
Email: redaktion@busplaner.de **Web site:** http://www.busplaner.de
Freq: 10 issues yearly; **Annual Sub.:** EUR 90,80; **Circ:** 7,205
Editor: Thomas Burgert; **Advertising Manager:** Ulrike Schauf
Profile: The journal is one of the leading journals in the bus industry and provides ideas and information in travel planning, group travel, technology, transport and vehicles as well as corporate and association policy. The magazine received bus companies and tour operators in German speaking countries (D, A, CH).
Language(s): German
ADVERTISING RATES:
Full Page Colour .... EUR 4160
Mechanical Data: Type Area: 270 x 185 mm, No. of Columns (Display): 4, Col Widths (Display): 43 mm
Supplement(s): Die Profi Werkstatt

BUSSTOP 724005G50-220
Editorial: Am Karlsbad 11, 10785 BERLIN
Tel: 30 2647480 **Fax:** 30 264748968
Email: susanna.weber@btm.de **Web site:** http://www.visitberlin.de
Freq: Annual; **Cover Price:** Free; **Circ:** 12,000
Profile: City map for bus travel agents.
Language(s): English; German
ADVERTISING RATES:
Full Page Mono .... EUR 4050
Full Page Colour .... EUR 4050
Mechanical Data: Type Area: 210 x 100 mm
Copy instructions: *Copy Date:* 63 days prior to publication

BUTZBACHER ZEITUNG
724012G67B-3720
Editorial: Langgasse 16, 35510 BUTZBACH
Tel: 6033 96060 **Fax:** 6033 960649
Email: mail@butzbacher-zeitung.de **Web site:** http://www.butzbacher-zeitung.de
Freq: 312 issues yearly; **Annual Sub.:** EUR 20,10; **Circ:** 6,349
Editor: Christel Gratzfeld
Profile: Daily newspaper with regional news and a local sports section.
Language(s): German
ADVERTISING RATES:
SCC .... EUR 21,60
Mechanical Data: Type Area: 430 x 282 mm, No. of Columns (Display): 6, Col Widths (Display): 45 mm
Copy instructions: *Copy Date:* 1 day prior to publication
REGIONAL DAILY & SUNDAY NEWSPAPERS: Regional Daily Newspapers

BUXTEHUDER TAGEBLATT
724013G67B-3740
Editorial: Glückstädter Str. 10, 21682 STADE
Tel: 4141 9360 **Fax:** 4141 936294
Email: redaktion-std@tageblatt.de **Web site:** http://www.tageblatt.de
Freq: 312 issues yearly; **Circ:** 8,969
Advertising Manager: Georg Lempke
Profile: Daily newspaper with regional news and a local sports section. This Outlet offers RSS (Really Simple Syndication).
Language(s): German
ADVERTISING RATES:
SCC .... EUR 41,80
Mechanical Data: Type Area: 487 x 324 mm, No. of Columns (Display): 7, Col Widths (Display): 45 mm
Copy instructions: *Copy Date:* 1 day prior to publication
Supplement(s): Ferienjournal; Stader Buxtehuder Altländer Tageblatt Freizeit Magazin; Stader Buxtehuder Altländer Tageblatt Steilpass
REGIONAL DAILY & SUNDAY NEWSPAPERS: Regional Daily Newspapers

BUZAKTUELL 1789747G1D-478
Editorial: Theodor-Heuss-Ring 11, 50668 KÖLN
Tel: 221 9738678 **Fax:** 221 9738824
Email: marianne.kutzner@genre.com **Web site:** http://www.genre.com/business-school
Freq: Half-yearly; **Circ:** 1,500
Editor: Marianne Kutzner
Profile: Newsletter from the insurance company General Reinsurance Corporation about occupational disability.
Language(s): German

BVGD INFO 1794307G56A-11445
Editorial: Rüdigerstr. 14, 70469 STUTTGART
Tel: 711 89310 **Fax:** 711 8931298
Email: kundenservice@thieme.de **Web site:** http://www.thieme.de
Freq: 3 issues yearly; **Cover Price:** Free; **Circ:** 6,160
Profile: Communications on Gastroenterology.
Language(s): German
ADVERTISING RATES:
Full Page Mono .... EUR 2630
Full Page Colour .... EUR 3890
Mechanical Data: Type Area: 256 x 180 mm
Supplement to: Zeitschrift für Gastroenterologie German Journal of Gastroenterology

BVM INBRIEF 1663598G2A-5613
Editorial: Friedrichstr. 187, 10117 BERLIN
Tel: 30 49907420 **Fax:** 30 49907421
Email: info@bvm.org **Web site:** http://www.bvm.org
Freq: 3 issues yearly; **Cover Price:** Free; **Circ:** 3,000
Editor: Ulrike Schöneberg
Profile: Directory on market research companies.
Language(s): German
ADVERTISING RATES:
Full Page Mono .... EUR 710
Mechanical Data: Type Area: 265 x 176 mm

BW AGRAR LANDWIRTSCHAFTLICHES WOCHENBLATT 724019G21J-27
Editorial: Bopserstr. 17, 70180 STUTTGART
Tel: 711 2140141 **Fax:** 711 2360232
Email: redaktion-lw@bwagrar.de **Web site:** http://www.bwagrar.de
Freq: Weekly; **Annual Sub.:** EUR 101,40; **Circ:** 28,869
Editor: Heiner Krehl; **Advertising Manager:** Gerhard Kretschmer
Profile: BW agrar Landwirtschaftliches Wochenblatt is the weekly trade magazine for agriculture and rural life. BW agrar reaches on average 3.7 further readers per household and business, which amounts to some 225,000 people: agricultural entrepreneurs in the main and part-time farmes with their families. BW agrar is at home on the farms for generations and for farmers and rural families, it is the important medium of information in their daily work but also in many issues of life. These strong ties and its focus on the region are reporting the particular strength of BW agrar. The result is the almost complete coverage of the target group and a special closeness to the people who face the many challenges in their businesses today and in future . BWagrar reports on political events, topics and life in the country. The Economic and Market section informs with extensive market tables. The regional supplements additionally cover the reports with local, regional contributions and the indispensable smallads market.
Language(s): German
Readership: Aimed at members of the farming community in Baden-Württemberg.
ADVERTISING RATES:
Full Page Mono .... EUR 5192
Full Page Colour .... EUR 7472
Mechanical Data: Type Area: 275 x 195 mm, No. of Columns (Display): 4, Col Widths (Display): 47 mm
Copy instructions: *Copy Date:* 6 days prior to publication
Supplement(s): wochenblatt Magazin
BUSINESS: AGRICULTURE & FARMING: Agriculture & Farming - Regional

BW AGRAR SCHWÄBISCHER BAUER 1665771G21J-46
Editorial: Gartenstr. 63, 88212 RAVENSBURG
Tel: 751 3615921 **Fax:** 751 14284
Email: redaktion-sb@bwagrar.de **Web site:** http://www.bwagrar.de
Freq: Weekly; **Annual Sub.:** EUR 101,40; **Circ:** 15,165
Editor: Eberhard Stümpfle; **Advertising Manager:** Klaus-Dieter Schmidt
Profile: BWagrar is a weekly agricultural magazine for agriculture and rural life. BWagrar reports on political events, topics and life in the country. The Economic and Market section informs with extensive market tables. The regional supplements additionally cover the reports with local, regional contributions and the indispensable smallads market.
Language(s): German
ADVERTISING RATES:
Full Page Mono .... EUR 3014
Full Page Colour .... EUR 4754
Mechanical Data: Type Area: 275 x 195 mm, No. of Columns (Display): 4, Col Widths (Display): 47 mm
Copy instructions: *Copy Date:* 5 days prior to publication
Supplement(s): wochenblatt Magazin
BUSINESS: AGRICULTURE & FARMING: Agriculture & Farming - Regional

BWI BETONWERK INTERNATIONAL 724022G4E-2980
Editorial: Industriestr. 180, 50999 KÖLN
Tel: 2236 962390 **Fax:** 2236 962396
Email: h.karutz@cpi-worldwide.com **Web site:** http://www.cpi-worldwide.com
Freq: 6 issues yearly; Free to qualifying individuals
Annual Sub.: EUR 120,00; **Circ:** 3,000
Editor: Holger Karutz; **Advertising Manager:** Gerhard Klöckner
Profile: The journals of "CPI-Worldwide" are the only source for cutting-edge technical data, news and information for the concrete industry - from around

the world. This information processed editorially and professional - are aimed directly regardless of location to business owners, decision makers and managers. The articles are well-written by world-renowned and in their field well-known experts. Each topic is presented in a way that the audience important information available, it brings on the cutting edge of technology and so to increase productivity and operational performance contributes.
Language(s): German
Mechanical Data: Type Area: 260 x 180 mm, No. of Columns (Display): 3, Col Widths (Display): 56 mm
Copy instructions: *Copy Date:* 30 days prior to publication
BUSINESS: ARCHITECTURE & BUILDING: Building

BWK 724024G58-160

Editorial: VDI-Platz 1, 40468 DÜSSELDORF
Tel: 211 6103526 **Fax:** 211 6103148
Email: bwk@technikwissen.de **Web site:** http://www.ebwk.de
Freq: 10 issues yearly; **Annual Sub.:** EUR 252,00; **Circ:** 15,709
Editor: Peter v. Hindte
Profile: BWK is the energy trade magazine for decision makers in the energy sector and energy technology. It reports practical and competent on all relevant issues in the energy industry. BWK is consistently and distributors on the information needs of decision makers in energy companies, manufacturers and service providers, with plant managers and energy users aligned. It is characterized by the combination of broad overview and in-depth reporting, and the practical relevance is paramount. Whether generation, supply or distribution, energy trading or buying, whether energy policy, energy sources and energy management - BWK covers the entire spectrum around the topic of energy.
Language(s): German
ADVERTISING RATES:
Full Page Mono .... EUR 4080
Full Page Colour .... EUR 5280
Mechanical Data: Type Area: 270 x 185 mm, No. of Columns (Display): 4, Col Widths (Display): 45 mm
Copy instructions: *Copy Date:* 21 days prior to publication
Official Journal of: Organ d. VDI-Ges. Energietechnik, Fachverb. Dampfkessel-, Behälter- u. Rohrleitungsbau e.V., Forschungsstelle f. Energiewirtschaft u. d. Dt. Dampfkesselausschusses
BUSINESS: ENERGY, FUEL & NUCLEAR

BWNOTZ ZEITSCHRIFT FÜR DAS NOTARIAT IN BADEN-WÜRTTEMBERG 1914726G1A-3779

Editorial: Kronenstr. 34, 70174 STUTTGART
Tel: 711 2237951 **Fax:** 711 2237956
Email: schaal@notarakademie.justiz.bwl.de **Web site:** http://www.notare-wuerttemberg.de
Freq: 6 issues yearly; **Annual Sub.:** EUR 45,00; **Circ:** 1,800
Editor: Daniel Schaal
Profile: Magazine for notaries in Baden-Wuerttemberg.
Language(s): German

BWP BERUFSBILDUNG IN WISSENSCHAFT UND PRAXIS 724025G62H-280

Editorial: Robert-Schuman-Platz 3, 53175 BONN
Tel: 228 1071722 **Fax:** 228 1072967
Email: bwp@bibb.de **Web site:** http://www.bibb.de
Freq: 6 issues yearly; **Annual Sub.:** EUR 45,70; **Circ:** 2,500
Editor: Christiane Jäger
Profile: Scientific magazine about vocational and educational training.
Language(s): German
ADVERTISING RATES:
Full Page Mono .... EUR 760
Mechanical Data: Type Area: 246 x 172 mm
Copy instructions: *Copy Date:* 30 days prior to publication
Supplement(s): BWP plus
BUSINESS: CHURCH & SCHOOL EQUIPMENT & EDUCATION: Careers

B.Z. 724032G67B-2220

Editorial: Kurfürstendamm 21, 10719 BERLIN
Tel: 30 259173715 **Fax:** 30 259173131
Email: redaktion@bz-berlin.de **Web site:** http://www.bz-berlin.de
Freq: 312 issues yearly; **Circ:** 160,056
Editor: Peter Huth; **News Editor:** Mathias Heller; **Advertising Manager:** Stephan Madel
Profile: The B.Z. is the largest and longest established newspaper in Berlin, and for over 130 years, a distinctive hallmark of the city. The B.Z. reflects the soul of Berlin every day. As a modern tabloid newspaper it knows the emotions of the people of the metropolis. It presents news from Berlin and Brandenburg, reports, sports, culture, puzzles and scene - quick and to the point. The B.Z. stands out editorially: - with expert authors on politics and world events - with a lavish double-page photo in the news section that presents the images of the day with short texts - with its own culture section - with a large, competent reporting sports section - practical tips for every day, delivered by two service pages, - Friday with a 4-page puzzle special Regional daily newspaper covering politics, economics, sport, travel and technology. Facebook: http://www.facebook.com/pages/BZ/57187632436 Twitter: http://twitter.com/BLZonline This Outlet offers RSS (Really Simple Syndication).
Language(s): German
ADVERTISING RATES:
SCC .... EUR 390,50
Mechanical Data: Type Area: 370 x 248 mm, No. of Columns (Display): 5, Col Widths (Display): 45 mm
Copy instructions: *Copy Date:* 1 day prior to publication
Supplement(s): prisma
REGIONAL DAILY & SUNDAY NEWSPAPERS: Regional Daily Newspapers

B.Z. AM SONNTAG 724033G72-1568

Editorial: Kurfürstendamm 21, 10719 BERLIN
Tel: 30 259173715 **Fax:** 30 259173131
Email: redaktion@bz-berlin.de **Web site:** http://www.bz-berlin.de
Freq: Weekly; **Cover Price:** EUR 0,75; **Circ:** 92,011
Editor: Peter Huth; **News Editor:** Mathias Heller; **Advertising Manager:** Stephan Madel
Profile: The B.Z. am Sonntag is a newspaper for the whole family with a varied mix of information, entertainment, exciting reports and an extensive sports section. Twitter: http://twitter.com/BLZonline This Outlet offers RSS (Really Simple Syndication).
Language(s): German
ADVERTISING RATES:
SCC .... EUR 165,50
Mechanical Data: Type Area: 370 x 248 mm, No. of Columns (Display): 5, Col Widths (Display): 45 mm
Copy instructions: *Copy Date:* 3 days prior to publication
LOCAL NEWSPAPERS

BZM BRENNSTOFFZELLEN MAGAZIN 1626897G58-1723

Editorial: Talhofstr. 24b, 82205 GILCHING
Tel: 8105 385336 **Fax:** 8105 385311
Email: v.tisken@verlag-henrich.de **Web site:** http://www.b-z-m.de
Freq: Quarterly; **Annual Sub.:** EUR 32,00; **Circ:** 17,500
Editor: Volker Tisken; **Advertising Manager:** Diana Beatrice Schmidt
Profile: bzm Brennstoffzellen Magazin is the magazine for fuel cell technology, hydrogen economy and electro-mobility. bzm reports four times a year on research and development of stationary, portable and mobile fuel cells. In addition to trends and concepts in the mass production and practical applications of this technology of the future are in the foreground. To growing synergies of fuel cell technology and electric vehicles meet, was the range of topics of bzm around the area of Electric Mobility expands. bzm reading today for the technology of tomorrow and is achieved with this combination, the decision makers in industry and energy economy.
Language(s): German
ADVERTISING RATES:
Full Page Mono .... EUR 3400
Full Page Colour .... EUR 4780
Mechanical Data: Type Area: 255 x 184 mm, No. of Columns (Display): 4, Col Widths (Display): 42 mm
Copy instructions: *Copy Date:* 28 days prior to publication

C&PI CALCESTRUZZO & PREFABBRICAZIONE INTERNATIONAL 1790289G4E-7117

Editorial: Industriestr. 180, 50999 KÖLN
Tel: 2236 962390 **Fax:** 2236 962396
Email: h.karutz@cpi-worldwide.com **Web site:** http://www.cpi-worldwide.com
Freq: 6 issues yearly; **Annual Sub.:** EUR 120,00; **Circ:** 2,000
Editor: Holger Karutz; **Advertising Manager:** Gerhard Klöckner
Profile: Magazine for concrete producers.
Language(s): Italian
Mechanical Data: Type Area: 260 x 180 mm, No. of Columns (Display): 3, Col Widths (Display): 56 mm
Copy instructions: *Copy Date:* 30 days prior to publication

CAD NEWS 724042G19J-90

Editorial: Quellenstr. 32, 67433 NEUSTADT
Tel: 6321 89980 **Fax:** 6321 899899
Email: hagenbucher@up2media.de **Web site:** http://www.cad-news.de
Freq: Monthly; **Annual Sub.:** EUR 62,00; **Circ:** 20,500
Editor: Silvia Hagenbucher; **Advertising Manager:** Peter Marbe
Profile: Magazine focusing on technology, architecture, electronics, trade fairs, mechanical engineering and the building trade for professional CAD users.
Language(s): German
Readership: Aimed at engineers and architects.
Mechanical Data: Type Area: 270 x 191 mm, No. of Columns (Display): 3, Col Widths (Display): 60 mm
BUSINESS: ENGINEERING & MACHINERY: CAD & CIM (Computer Integrated Manufacture)

CAD-CAM REPORT 724040G19J-80

Editorial: Havelstr. 9, 64295 DARMSTADT
Tel: 6151 380173 **Fax:** 6151 38099173
Email: corban@hoppenstedt.de **Web site:** http://www.hoppenstedt-zeitschriften.de
Freq: 8 issues yearly; **Annual Sub.:** EUR 180,00; **Circ:** 15,950
Editor: Michael Corban; **Advertising Manager:** Nadine Prieur
Profile: CAD-CAM Report provides information as a recognized professional journal of the latest trends and developments in the PLM area (product lifecycle management), taking into account CAD/CAM-, CAE, and PDM technologies for all industrial applications areas in production technology. Particular attention is given to applications in industrial companies within the automotive aerospace construction, machine tools and special machinery construction, mechanical engineering, chemical engineering, molds and tools construction, electrical and control engineering. CAD-CAM Report at a glance: on-site research in manufacturing firms and boardrooms, among users and providers, research and academic institutions, the latest firsthand information and opinions and observations on the emerging trends. Collaboration with recognized experts from research and practice. Practice-oriented features, interviews and reports - competent, industry needs, across applications, process optimization and forward looking.
Language(s): German
ADVERTISING RATES:
Full Page Mono .... EUR 5808
Full Page Colour .... EUR 7728
Mechanical Data: Type Area: 252 x 175 mm, No. of Columns (Display): 3, Col Widths (Display): 55 mm
Copy instructions: *Copy Date:* 17 days prior to publication
BUSINESS: ENGINEERING & MACHINERY: CAD & CIM (Computer Integrated Manufacture)

CALIBER 1639575G75F-1060

Editorial: Sachsenring 73, 50677 KÖLN
Tel: 221 91287613 **Fax:** 221 9128766
Email: caliber@vsmedien.de **Web site:** http://www.caliber.de
Freq: 10 issues yearly; **Annual Sub.:** EUR 43,50; **Circ:** 8,463
Editor: Stefan Perey; **Advertising Manager:** Peter Hoffmann
Profile: caliber is the magazine for practical shooting. Choice for serious shooters and professionals find weapons carrier here the latest news from the world of weaponry and shooting practice. International Master reveal here their own special tricks. The tests of the current rifles are always practical and brutally honest: By professionals for professionals.
Language(s): German
ADVERTISING RATES:
Full Page Mono .... EUR 2300
Full Page Colour .... EUR 2900
Mechanical Data: Type Area: 253 x 186 mm, No. of Columns (Display): 4, Col Widths (Display): 43 mm
CONSUMER: SPORT: Shooting

CALLCENTER PROFI 724054G18B-2140

Editorial: Abraham-Lincoln-Str. 46, 65189 WIESBADEN **Tel:** 611 7878336 **Fax:** 611 7878450
Email: simone.fojut@gabler.de **Web site:** http://www.callcenterprofi.de
Freq: 8 issues yearly; **Annual Sub.:** EUR 95,00; **Circ:** 11,358
Editor: Simone Fojut
Profile: CallCenter Profi is the specialist magazine for all questions around the topics customer service and communication. All channels - whether inbound or outbound - is reported in the call or communication centers. CallCenter Profi reported to date and comprehensive on technical, organizational and corporate insider knowledge on the topics of call center and tele-marketing and CRM. The editorial board sees itself as a knowledge manager, the industry is not only about the print product CallCenter Profi, but also online (www.callcenterprofi.de), informed by e-mail newsletters, trade shows, meetings and through an expanding book program.
Language(s): German
ADVERTISING RATES:
Full Page Mono .... EUR 3720
Full Page Colour .... EUR 5370
Mechanical Data: No. of Columns (Display): 3, Col Widths (Display): 55 mm, Type Area: 240 x 175 mm
BUSINESS: ELECTRONICS: Telecommunications

CAMPING 724068G91B-420

Editorial: Mandlstr. 28, 80802 MÜNCHEN
Tel: 89 38014225 **Fax:** 89 38014242
Email: info@campingpresse.de **Web site:** http://www.camping-club.de
Freq: Monthly; Free to qualifying individuals
Annual Sub.: EUR 39,90; **Circ:** 32,156
Editor: Viktoria Groß; **Advertising Manager:** Rosmarie Swoboda
Profile: The club magazine of the Deutscher Camping-Club eV is published monthly and reported around the camping recreation on tents, caravans, motor homes, news, car tests, new safety systems and picturesque tourist destinations. You get first hand information about the "Arts" on our way.
Language(s): German
Readership: Read by members of the Deutscher Camping-Club.
ADVERTISING RATES:
Full Page Mono .... EUR 3210
Full Page Colour .... EUR 6095
Mechanical Data: Type Area: 251 x 192 mm, No. of Columns (Display): 4, Col Widths (Display): 45 mm
Copy instructions: *Copy Date:* 35 days prior to publication
CONSUMER: RECREATION & LEISURE: Camping & Caravanning

CAMPING CARS & CARAVANS 724069G91B-440

Editorial: Postwiesenstr. 5a, 70327 STUTTGART
Tel: 711 1346654 **Fax:** 711 1346668
Email: info@camping-cars-caravans.de **Web site:** http://www.camping-cars-caravans.de
Freq: Monthly; **Annual Sub.:** EUR 39,60; **Circ:** 55,000
Editor: Raymond Eckl; **Advertising Manager:** Sylke Wohlschiess
Profile: "CAMPING CARS & Caravans" is the current monthly magazine for caravan and camping fun and can also be seen as a competent caravan magazine throughout Europe. Every four weeks, there's the full range. "CAMPING CARS & Caravans", the great German monthly magazine for campers: thorough testing, the latest news, great travel features - so you are informed in a competent way and entertained. New every month: "CAMPING CARS & Caravans" takes care of everything of interest to caravanners. For example, in hard and objective tests. The core is the professional test, where four technology professionals and a housewife examine a caravan in detail. In addition to the tests there are tips for self-installation of accessories, current reports on new trends and special travel stories for caravanners, of course, with extensive service at camp sites and other excursions. Facebook: http://www.facebook.com/camping.cars.caravans.
Language(s): German
ADVERTISING RATES:
Full Page Mono .... EUR 3090
Full Page Colour .... EUR 5040
Mechanical Data: Type Area: 252 x 184 mm, No. of Columns (Display): 4, Col Widths (Display): 43 mm
Copy instructions: *Copy Date:* 20 days prior to publication
CONSUMER: RECREATION & LEISURE: Camping & Caravanning

CAMPINGIMPULSE 724070G50-260

Editorial: Postwiesenstr. 5a, 70327 STUTTGART
Tel: 711 1346654 **Fax:** 711 1346668
Email: eckl@doldemedien.de **Web site:** http://www.campingimpulse.de
Freq: 6 issues yearly; **Annual Sub.:** EUR 59,40; **Circ:** 1,700
Editor: Raymond Eckl; **Advertising Manager:** Sylke Wohlschiess
Profile: Magazine for innovative camping entrepreneurs. Editorial Focus: business management, space optimization, tax, legal and financial advice, targeted marketing, product news, interviews, panorama etc.
Language(s): German
ADVERTISING RATES:
Full Page Mono .... EUR 1410
Full Page Colour .... EUR 2115
Mechanical Data: Type Area: 270 x 186 mm, No. of Columns (Display): 4, Col Widths (Display): 43 mm
Copy instructions: *Copy Date:* 30 days prior to publication

CAMPOS 724074G4E-3000

Editorial: Wollgrasweg 41, 70599 STUTTGART
Tel: 711 4507184 **Fax:** 711 4507207
Email: cvonfreyberg@ulmer.de **Web site:** http://www.campos-net.de
Freq: Monthly; **Annual Sub.:** EUR 47,40; **Circ:** 10,316
Editor: Claudia von Freyberg; **Advertising Manager:** Marc Alber
Profile: campos practical everyday work supported in gardening and landscaping businesses with information on new developments and products, actionable tips for work and training, news from the industry. Here are utility and decision support in the first place. With a collegial approach, compact, yet carefully prepared text, vivid images and a dash of entertainment and humor provides campos information about work processes - whether earth and stone work, planting, care and more, presentations of plants, plant and auxiliary materials, technology, computer, helps to operate in everyday life, especially at the operational and personnel management, communication, education and training, legal, portraits of exemplary companies, suppliers, projects and people in the industry, news and reports from shows and other events. The constant themes are News, events and trends of the industry, company organization, personnel, marketing, education and training, technology and materials for construction, lawn maintenance, perennials, shrubs, plantings, building greening, water engineering and irrigation, plant protection, fertilization and substrates, Health tips.
Language(s): German
ADVERTISING RATES:
Full Page Mono .... EUR 2178
Full Page Colour .... EUR 3678
Mechanical Data: Type Area: 284 x 205 mm, No. of Columns (Display): 4, Col Widths (Display): 48 mm
Copy instructions: *Copy Date:* 25 days prior to publication
BUSINESS: ARCHITECTURE & BUILDING: Building

CANCER CHEMOTHERAPY AND PHARMACOLOGY 724082G56A-1800

Editorial: Tiergartenstr. 17, 69121 HEIDELBERG
Tel: 6221 4870 **Fax:** 6221 4878366
Email: subscriptions@springer.com **Web site:** http://www.springerlink.com
Freq: 6 issues yearly; **Annual Sub.:** EUR 4744,00; **Circ:** 269
Editor: D. R. Newell
Profile: Magazine on cancer chemotherapy and pharmacology.
Language(s): English

ADVERTISING RATES:
Full Page Mono .... EUR 740
Full Page Colour .... EUR 1780
Mechanical Data: Type Area: 240 x 175 mm

CANNSTATTER ZEITUNG
724086G67B-3760
Editorial: Wilhelmstr. 18, 70372 STUTTGART
Tel: 711 955680 **Fax:** 711 9556833
Email: lokales@caze-online.de **Web site:** http://www.cannstatter-zeitung.de
Freq: 312 issues yearly; **Circ:** 8,719
Editor: Sigfried Baumann; **Advertising Manager:** Sigfried Baumann
Profile: Regional daily newspaper with news on politics, economy, culture, sports, travel, technology, etc. Facebook: http://www.facebook.com/pages/Esslinger-Zeitung/332067873971.
Language(s): German
ADVERTISING RATES:
SCC .... EUR 40,80
Mechanical Data: Type Area: 485 x 324 mm, No. of Columns (Display): 7, Col Widths (Display): 45 mm
Copy instructions: *Copy Date:* 1 day prior to publication
REGIONAL DAILY & SUNDAY NEWSPAPERS: Regional Daily Newspapers

CAPITAL
724089G14A-1240
Editorial: Am Baumwall 11, 20459 HAMBURG
Tel: 40 37030 **Fax:** 40 37038310
Email: leserbriefe@capital.de **Web site:** http://www.capital.de
Freq: Monthly; **Annual Sub.:** EUR 68,40; **Circ:** 173,335
Editor: Steffen Klusmann; **News Editor:** Philipp Jaklin; **Advertising Manager:** Jens Kauerauf
Profile: German business magazine for decision makers. CAPITAL is for more than four decades, one of the leading business magazines for decision makers in Germany - independent, reliable, confident and vital. CAPITAL combines valuable information and analysis on personal finance with investigative business stories and surprising portraits, economic and political classification trenchant comments. The range of topics is selected from the perspective of investors and operators in the capital markets. CAPITAL succeeds with relevant content that is presented in an understandable way to set the tone. With a modern and reader-friendly layout and a picture language that conveys proximity and arouses curiosity, the title creates a high level of reading pleasure.
Language(s): German
Readership: Aimed at decision makers within the field.
ADVERTISING RATES:
Full Page Mono .... EUR 27900
Full Page Colour .... EUR 27900
Mechanical Data: Type Area: 245 x 185 mm, No. of Columns (Display): 3, Col Widths (Display): 65 mm
BUSINESS: COMMERCE, INDUSTRY & MANAGEMENT

CAPITAL.DE
1661124G14A-9671
Editorial: Am Baumwall 11, 20459 HAMBURG
Tel: 40 37030 **Fax:** 40 37038310
Email: online@capital.de **Web site:** http://www.capital.de
Cover Price: Paid; **Circ:** 532,151 Unique Users
Editor: Joachim Dreykluft; **News Editor:** Joachim Dreykluft
Profile: The interactive marketing platform Capital.de provides decision aids that would help users to manage their finances optimally. Bids are both current topics in-depth information - based around the headings: policy, finance, real estate, Business, Tax & Law, Auto & Technology. The core competencies of the Capital is reporting about real estate. The interactive properties Compass (www.capital.de / or real estate www.real-kompass.de) offers users the opportunity to give thanks to interactive maps with a quick overview of price levels in different cities and regions - by criteria such as purchase or Rent, apartment or house, detached or terraced house. In addition to other utility-grade tools Capital.de also offers mobile services on the go. To "Capital Mobil" the user finds the most important news of the day and also has its own portfolio at a glance. Other services that can be used mobile, the news ticker and the day and time deposit calculator. Capital Mobil is the non-needed and forward-looking media channel to reach decision makers in their daily lives: at any time, anywhere. Facebook: http://de-de.facebook.com/capital This Outlet offers RSS (Really Simple Syndication).
Language(s): German
BUSINESS: COMMERCE, INDUSTRY & MANAGEMENT

CAPRI POST
724092G77A-700
Editorial: Berliner Str. 7, 64409 MESSEL
Tel: 6159 1292 **Fax:** 6159 913838
Email: info@capripost.de **Web site:** http://www.capripost.de
Freq: 3 issues yearly; **Annual Sub.:** EUR 24,00; **Circ:** 500
Editor: Andrea Mandl
Profile: Magazine for Ford Capri fans.
Language(s): German

CAR & HIFI
724094G78A-120
Editorial: Gartroper Str. 42, 47138 DUISBURG
Tel: 203 4292274 **Fax:** 203 4292249
Email: michels@brieden.de **Web site:** http://www.carhifi-magazin.de
Freq: 6 issues yearly; **Annual Sub.:** EUR 20,40; **Circ:** 8,403
Editor: Elmar Michels
Profile: Car hi-fi magazine.
Language(s): German
ADVERTISING RATES:
Full Page Mono .... EUR 4581
Full Page Colour .... EUR 7384
Mechanical Data: Type Area: 284 x 197 mm
Official Journal of: Organ d. European Car Audio Press
CONSUMER: CONSUMER ELECTRONICS: Hi-Fi & Recording

CARAVANING
724096G91B-480
Editorial: Leuschnerstr. 1, 70174 STUTTGART
Tel: 711 1822472 **Fax:** 711 1822479
Email: redaktion@caravaning.de **Web site:** http://www.caravaning.de
Freq: Monthly; **Annual Sub.:** EUR 33,50; **Circ:** 32,598
Editor: Kai Feyerabend; **Advertising Manager:** Peter Steinbach
Profile: Caravaning is Europe's largest camping-magazine. Click to learn driving and camping all you need to know. Two key points characterize each issue: First, does the magazine always present and often exclusive tests, presentations and market overviews of caravans, cars and camping and leisure accessories. On the other takes up the subject of "Camping" wide space, with all the travel and leisure features tailored specifically to the interests of the campers and the user is in focus. A large part of news, expert tips, and the camp archive to gather round the issue mix. Caravaning aimed primarily at active caravan and tourist campers, but also offers home owners, particularly in the camping and travel reporting great benefits. The magazine advertises in the era of mass tourism and package for a nature-loving, sustainable and individual type of holiday.
Language(s): German
ADVERTISING RATES:
Full Page Mono .... EUR 3270
Full Page Colour .... EUR 5200
Mechanical Data: Type Area: 248 x 185 mm, No. of Columns (Display): 4, Col Widths (Display): 43 mm
Copy instructions: *Copy Date:* 28 days prior to publication
CONSUMER: RECREATION & LEISURE: Camping & Caravaning

CARAVANING
1692992G91B-2509
Editorial: Leuschnerstr. 1, 70174 STUTTGART
Tel: 7152 941575 **Fax:** 7152 941597
Email: msteinheil@motorpresse.de **Web site:** http://www.caravaning.de
Freq: Daily; **Cover Price:** Paid; **Circ:** 36,732 Unique Users
Editor: Mario Steinheil; **Advertising Manager:** Peter Steinbach
Profile: Ezine: Magazine covering all aspects of leisure caravanning.
Language(s): German
CONSUMER: RECREATION & LEISURE: Camping & Caravanning

CARD
726728G49A-420
Editorial: Herzogstr. 3, 92637 WEIDEN
Tel: 961 38818190 **Fax:** 961 388181940
Email: info@pp-m.net **Web site:** http://www.pp-m.net
Freq: Quarterly; **Cover Price:** Free; **Circ:** 20,150
Profile: Magazine for executives of car fleets.
Language(s): German
ADVERTISING RATES:
Full Page Colour .... EUR 4800
Mechanical Data: Type Area: 250 x 190 mm
BUSINESS: TRANSPORT

CARD COLLECTOR
1639779G91D-9967
Editorial: Karlsruher Str. 31, 76437 RASTATT
Tel: 7222 130 **Fax:** 7222 13284
Email: info@vpm-youngmedia.de **Web site:** http://www.vpm.de
Freq: Monthly; **Cover Price:** EUR 2,99; **Circ:** 24,280
Advertising Manager: Rainer Groß
Profile: The trend of trading card games - mainly from the Japanese anime and manga area - the target group of the 8-12-year-old boys in full control. This is where Card Collector and provides its readers every month with 52 pages exciting reports, news and information about the currently most popular trading card games. Whether collectors or players at the launch of new card editions, strong decks, combos, tips and strategies about trends such as Yu-Gi-Oh! and Pokémon is, everybody gets their costs. In addition, readers gain the opportunity to participate in surveys, sweepstakes, barter exchange and letters themselves and participate actively the content of the magazine. Is accompanied each issue of trading-card-game posters, a Price Guide, in the card collectors can learn the value of their treasures and a high-quality extra from the area of the collectible cards.
Language(s): German
ADVERTISING RATES:
Full Page Mono .... EUR 4200
Full Page Colour .... EUR 4200
Mechanical Data: Type Area: 280 x 210 mm, No. of Columns (Display): 4, Col Widths (Display): 50 mm
Copy instructions: *Copy Date:* 42 days prior to publication
CONSUMER: RECREATION & LEISURE: Children & Youth

CARD MASTER
1642018G91D-10018
Editorial: Rotebühlstr. 87, 70178 STUTTGART
Tel: 711 947680 **Fax:** 711 9476830
Email: info@panini.de **Web site:** http://www.panini.de
Freq: Monthly; **Cover Price:** EUR 2,99; **Circ:** 18,323
Editor: Jo Löffler
Profile: Card Master - the magazine to all the hot collectible card games. All information about the sought-for Kids trading card game Yu-Gi-Oh, Pokemon and Naruto. Each issue is packed with tips and strategies. Cards galleries, Price Guides, the tournaments round out the magazine. Every real player's trading card Master Card indispensable. Candy on top of it: an extra per issue!.
Language(s): German
ADVERTISING RATES:
Full Page Mono .... EUR 4900
Full Page Colour .... EUR 4900
Mechanical Data: Type Area: 250 x 180 mm
CONSUMER: RECREATION & LEISURE: Children & Youth

CARDIO NEWS
724100G56A-1820
Editorial: Aschauer Str. 30, 81549 MÜNCHEN
Tel: 89 2030431329 **Fax:** 89 2030431399
Email: rainer.klawki@springer.com **Web site:** http://www.springermedizin.de
Freq: 9 issues yearly; Free to qualifying individuals
Annual Sub.: EUR 99,00; **Circ:** 30,060
Editor: Rainer Klawki; **Advertising Manager:** Ines Spankau
Profile: "Cardio News" provides competent and up to date information from all areas of cardiology and in the adjacent fields of internal medicine. The paper is divided into three parts: News - News from the national and international congresses of cardiology, relevant issues from health policy, and news from the literature, medicine - general review for all relevant indications, scene - Personal and news from the clinics or comments about cardiovascular issues in the public media. "Cardio News" provides a bridge between science and practice, and sees itself as a forum for discussion and communication - with letter to the editor pages and comments of opinion leaders.
Language(s): German
ADVERTISING RATES:
Full Page Mono .... EUR 3980
Full Page Colour .... EUR 5740
Mechanical Data: Type Area: 390 x 286 mm
Official Journal of: Organ d. Dt. Ges. f. Kardiologie - Herz- u. Kreislaufforschung
Supplement(s): Cardio Compact

CARDIOVASC
724101G56A-1840
Editorial: Aschauer Str. 30, 81549 MÜNCHEN
Tel: 89 2030431300 **Fax:** 89 2030431399
Email: dirk.einecke@springer.com **Web site:** http://www.cardiovasc.de
Freq: 6 issues yearly; Free to qualifying individuals
Annual Sub.: EUR 83,10; **Circ:** 18,823
Editor: Dirk Einecke; **Advertising Manager:** Ines Spankau
Profile: "Cardiovasc" is an interdisciplinary training journal for cardiovascular medicine. It concentrates on those issues, which require prevention, diagnosis and therapy, a combination of several disciplines. The magazine offers a current supply with extensive conference and symposium reports from the major cardiovascular conferences, background reports, expert opinion and professional controversies of all the current topics in cardiovascular medicine, a CME part of a interdisciplinary topic in the form of peer-reviewed overview and original articles, an overview of the cardiovascular specialist literature in the form of practice-related papers that are written by the editors and commented on. Cardiovasc cooperates with the following scientific societies: •Hochdruckliga •Deutsche Gesellschaft zur Bekämpfung von Fettstoffwechselstörungen und ihren Folgeerkrankungen •Fachkommission Diabetes in Bayern •Nordrhein-Westfälische Gesellschaft für Endokrinologie & Diabetologie •Deutsche Adipositas-Gesellschaft •Deutsche Arbeitsgemeinschaft für Klinische Nephrologie •Stiftung „Der herzkranke Diabetiker" •Deutsche Liga zur Bekämpfung von Gefäßerkrankungen •Stiftung Deutsche Schlaganfall-Hilfe •Stiftung zur Prävention der Arteriosklerose •Deutsche Gesellschaft für Sportmedizin und Prävention.
Language(s): German
ADVERTISING RATES:
Full Page Mono .... EUR 3000
Full Page Colour .... EUR 4750
Mechanical Data: Type Area: 240 x 174 mm
Official Journal of: Organ d. Dt. Hochdruckliga-Dt. Hypertonie Ges., d. Stiftung z. Prävention d. Arteriosklerose, Dt. Liga z. Bekämpfung v. Gefäßerkrankungen, d. Stiftung "Der herzkranke Diabetiker", Stiftung Dt. Schlaganfallhilfe, d. Dt. ArGe f. klin. Nephrologie e.V., d. Dt. Adipositas-Ges., d. Nordrhein-Westfäl. Ges. f. Endokrinologie u. Diabetologie u. d. Fachkommission Diabetes in Bayern, d. Dt. Ges. z. Bekämpfung v. Fettstoffwechselstörungen u. ihrer Folgeerkrankungen (Lipid-Liga)
BUSINESS: HEALTH & MEDICAL

CARDS KARTEN CARTES
724103G14A-1320
Editorial: Aschaffenburger Str. 19, 60599 FRANKFURT **Tel:** 69 97083348 **Fax:** 69 7078400
Email: red.karten@kreditwesen.de **Web site:** http://www.kreditwesen.de
Freq: Quarterly; **Annual Sub.:** EUR 117,40; **Circ:** 2,755
Editor: Swantje Benkelberg; **Advertising Manager:** Ralf Werner
Profile: cards Karten cartes accompanied the diverse market across all industries around the plastic cards, of national and international perspective. Pricing policies and product design, marketing and customer loyalty, acquiring and processing, security and cards law - these are the core issues.
Language(s): German
ADVERTISING RATES:
Full Page Mono .... EUR 4120
Full Page Colour .... EUR 6220
Mechanical Data: Type Area: 265 x 185 mm, No. of Columns (Display): 3, Col Widths (Display): 58 mm
Copy instructions: *Copy Date:* 15 days prior to publication
Supplement to: bm bank und markt
BUSINESS: COMMERCE, INDUSTRY & MANAGEMENT

CARE KONKRET
724109G56B-18
Editorial: Plathnerstr. 4c, 30175 HANNOVER
Tel: 511 9910107 **Fax:** 511 9910196
Email: stefan.neumann@vincentz.net **Web site:** http://www.carekonkret.vincentz.net
Freq: Weekly; **Annual Sub.:** EUR 145,00; **Circ:** 5,536
Editor: Stefan Neumann; **Advertising Manager:** Thomas Veitschegger
Profile: Care konkret is a weekly newspaper with the crucial information about the entire care market. As an outpatient and hospital. It combines a compact and competent, what need to know time-poor managers of each level.
Language(s): German
Readership: Aimed at managers and staff of nursing homes.
ADVERTISING RATES:
Full Page Mono .... EUR 4520
Full Page Colour .... EUR 6830
Mechanical Data: Type Area: 323 x 250 mm, No. of Columns (Display): 5, Col Widths (Display): 46 mm
Copy instructions: *Copy Date:* 14 days prior to publication
BUSINESS: HEALTH & MEDICAL: Nursing

CARITAS IN NRW
724117G32G-57
Editorial: Lindenstr. 178, 40233 DÜSSELDORF
Tel: 211 51606620 **Fax:** 211 51606625
Email: redaktion@caritas-nrw.de **Web site:** http://www.caritas-nrw.de
Freq: Quarterly; **Circ:** 14,000
Editor: Markus Lahrmann
Profile: Magazine focusing on social and welfare work in the Nordrhein-Westfalen area.
Language(s): German
Readership: Aimed at councillors and social workers.
ADVERTISING RATES:
Full Page Mono .... EUR 1815
Full Page Colour .... EUR 1905
Mechanical Data: Type Area: 260 x 200 mm, Col Widths (Display): 80 mm, No. of Columns (Display): 2
Copy instructions: *Copy Date:* 16 days prior to publication
BUSINESS: LOCAL GOVERNMENT, LEISURE & RECREATION: Community Care & Social Services

CARO
724125G12A-8
Editorial: Stolberger Str. 84, 50933 KÖLN
Tel: 221 5497205 **Fax:** 221 54976205
Email: red.caro@rudolf-mueller.de **Web site:** http://www.rudolf-mueller.de
Freq: 6 issues yearly; **Annual Sub.:** EUR 96,00; **Circ:** 7,374
Editor: Sabina Grafen; **Advertising Manager:** Volker Kunz
Profile: Caro informed yearly now available in 6 print editions, 12 online editions and 6 e-mail newsletters the tile and plumbing trade on current market and trade issues, innovative bathroom equipment and products, customizable design of the exhibition rooms and gives sound tips for the sales advice around the bath. Caro selectively filters the information for the daily operations with tile and bath. Own contributions, solid research and the use of reliable sources assure the quality of reporting in print as well as online. The combination of fast knowledge, complex topics, opinion-forming comments and high-quality trade journal Caro makes a unique companion for the professional practice in trade and an eye-catching cross-media advertising carrier.
Language(s): German
Readership: Aimed at tile retailers, wholesalers and people in the building and DIY trade.
ADVERTISING RATES:
Full Page Mono .... EUR 3200
Full Page Colour .... EUR 5870
Mechanical Data: Type Area: 267 x 188 mm, No. of Columns (Display): 4, Col Widths (Display): 44 mm
BUSINESS: CERAMICS, POTTERY & GLASS: Ceramics & Pottery

CASA DECO
724133G74C-440
Editorial: Rosenkavalierplatz 14, 81925 MÜNCHEN
Tel: 89 9100930 **Fax:** 89 91009353
Email: a.schwarz@ipm-verlag.de **Web site:** http://www.ipm-verlag.de

Freq: 6 issues yearly; **Annual Sub.:** EUR 29,00
Editor: Anke Schwarz; **Advertising Manager:** Lidija Crncic
Profile: Magazine covering a specialised range of subjects for the home and garden, including fabrics, glass and porcelain design.
Language(s): German
ADVERTISING RATES:
Full Page Mono .... EUR 7100
Full Page Colour .... EUR 7100
Mechanical Data: Type Area: 260 x 186 mm
CONSUMER: WOMEN'S INTEREST CONSUMER MAGAZINES: Home & Family

CASH. 724137G1F-280
Editorial: Stresemannstr. 163, 22769 HAMBURG
Tel: 40 514440 **Fax:** 40 51444120
Email: info@cash-online.de **Web site:** http://www.cash-online.de
Freq: Monthly; Free to qualifying individuals
Annual Sub.: EUR 50,90; **Circ:** 51,543
Editor: Frank Milewski; **News Editor:** Hannes Breustedt; **Advertising Manager:** Helge Schaubode
Profile: Cash. is the monthly trade magazine for the long-term investment and asset accumulation, and the must-read for free agents, brokers and banking consultants. Cash. has been published since the last 27 years and is the leading special-interest title for the financial services industry in Germany. With Cash. magazine the decision makers in the industry are reached without wastage. Independent media studies have shown this leadership position in an impressive manner. Since 2005, Cash. reached the first place at the yearly HBS-media study in unbroken succession. For the media agency analysis of MRTK Research, published in June 2010 for the first time, Cash. also achieved very good results in the reader and display analysis of journals in the broker market. Bank managers are in accordance with innovative editorial topics, another important target group of Cash. No other print media dedicated to investment and, in particular the distribution of the different products so comprehensively. Cash. offers - on the basis of mutual funds, insurance, real estate, closed-end funds to alternative investments and certificates - the whole range of issues for the long-term wealth accumulation. For each department professional editors are in close contact to the players in the industry to prepare the latest trends and developments with the high journalistic quality of the magazine. In addition to the 12 regular issues a year published in 2011 there will be four special editions, from the mono thematic areas of the closed-end funds, mutual funds, real estate and insurance.
Language(s): German
ADVERTISING RATES:
Full Page Colour .... EUR 7600
Mechanical Data: Type Area: 252 x 178 mm, No. of Columns (Display): 3, Col Widths (Display): 54 mm
Copy instructions: *Copy Date:* 21 days prior to publication
BUSINESS: FINANCE & ECONOMICS: Investment

CASTELLER NACHRICHTEN 724144G14A-1360
Editorial: Rathausplatz 1, 97355 CASTELL
Tel: 9325 60136 **Fax:** 9325 60126
Email: pr@castell-bank.de **Web site:** http://www.castell-bank.de
Freq: Annual; **Cover Price:** Free; **Circ:** 25,000
Editor: Maria Fürstin zu Castell-Rüdenhausen
Profile: Magazine for employees of Castell.
Language(s): German

CATERING INSIDE 724151G11A-120
Editorial: Am Hammergraben 14, 56567 NEUWIED
Tel: 2631 879154 **Fax:** 2631 879213
Email: h.krone@lpv-verlag.de **Web site:** http://www.cateringinside.de
Freq: 7 issues yearly; **Annual Sub.:** EUR 45,60; **Circ:** 16,159
Editor: Hans Jürgen Krone; **Advertising Manager:** Rachid Attaoua
Profile: Magazine for the German catering sector.
Language(s): German
ADVERTISING RATES:
Full Page Mono .... EUR 4684
Full Page Colour .... EUR 6455
Mechanical Data: Type Area: 256 x 186 mm, No. of Columns (Display): 4, Col Widths (Display): 43 mm
Copy instructions: *Copy Date:* 28 days prior to publication
BUSINESS: CATERING: Catering, Hotels & Restaurants

CATERING MANAGEMENT 724152G11A-140
Editorial: Mandichostr. 18, 86504 MERCHING
Tel: 8233 381128 **Fax:** 8233 381212
Email: redaktion@catering.de **Web site:** http://www.catering.de
Freq: 10 issues yearly; **Annual Sub.:** EUR 77,30; **Circ:** 16,447
Editor: Daniela Müller; **Advertising Manager:** Thomas Hodermann
Profile: Catering Management is of the opinion-leading stocks with a high reach among executives of the GM industry in Germany. Thoroughly researched facts and hands-on background reports to make the magazine an indispensable, current source of information for top decision makers in the field of large meals. Catering Management reception issues related items, answers and discuss perspectives.
Language(s): German
Readership: Aimed at decision-makers in all areas of the catering industry.
ADVERTISING RATES:
Full Page Mono .... EUR 8950
Full Page Colour .... EUR 8950
Mechanical Data: Type Area: 480 x 320 mm, No. of Columns (Display): 3, Col Widths (Display): 100 mm
Copy instructions: *Copy Date:* 25 days prior to publication
Supplement(s): Vending Management
BUSINESS: CATERING: Catering, Hotels & Restaurants

CATHOLICA 724153G87-65
Editorial: Leostr. 19a, 33098 PADERBORN
Email: jam@moehlerinstitut.de **Web site:** http://www.moehlerinstitut.de
Freq: Quarterly; **Annual Sub.:** EUR 49,90; **Circ:** 550
Editor: Johannes Oeldemann
Profile: Magazine for ecumenical theology.
Language(s): German
ADVERTISING RATES:
Full Page Mono .... EUR 256
Mechanical Data: Type Area: 190 x 127 mm
Copy instructions: *Copy Date:* 28 days prior to publication
CONSUMER: RELIGIOUS

CAV CHEMIE-ANLAGEN + VERFAHREN 724159G13-200
Editorial: Ernst-Mey-Str. 8, 70771 LEINFELDEN-ECHTERDINGEN **Tel:** 711 7594291
Fax: 711 7594397
Email: cav.redaktion@konradin.de **Web site:** http://www.prozesstechnik-online.de/cav
Freq: Monthly; **Annual Sub.:** EUR 82,80; **Circ:** 21,833
Editor: Günter Eckhardt; **Advertising Manager:** Manuela Bumler
Profile: cav chemie anlagen + verfahren is a magazine that application and practice-related articles, reports, interviews and product information on procedures, systems, devices and components for the chemical and pharmaceutical Industries provides. The magazine also provides information on IT, instrumentation, control and automation technology, analytical techniques, packaging, storage, materials. Current economic and business reports along with the reports from research and science complete the offer of information.
Language(s): German
Readership: Read by people in the chemical industry.
ADVERTISING RATES:
Full Page Mono .... EUR 5410
Full Page Colour .... EUR 6480
Mechanical Data: Type Area: 270 x 188 mm, No. of Columns (Display): 4, Col Widths (Display): 44 mm
BUSINESS: CHEMICALS

CAVALLO 724158G81D-40
Editorial: Leuschnerstr. 1, 70174 STUTTGART
Tel: 711 1822101 **Fax:** 711 1822102
Email: redaktion@cavallo.de **Web site:** http://www.cavallo.de
Freq: Monthly; **Annual Sub.:** EUR 42,50; **Circ:** 72,640
Editor: Christine Felsinger; **Advertising Manager:** Michael G. Müller
Profile: Best Selling Riding and Equestrian Sport magazine in Germany. Each issue offers several consumer-oriented products by high professional competence. A great editorial team researched and reported independently, engaged and critical. Cavallo is known for its wide variety of topics with a strong utility character. The journal is sound advice for all styles and methods of riding and horse training. Product testing, the critical test of riding schools, reports of equine medicine, behavioral science and feeding provide the latest findings and developments. News from the breeding, training the horse and carriage driving and generous race portraits and reports round out the spectrum. Cavallo is open to any horse riding and every race. Facebook: http://www.facebook.com/cavallo.magazin.
Language(s): German
ADVERTISING RATES:
Full Page Mono .... EUR 4285
Full Page Colour .... EUR 6500
Mechanical Data: Type Area: 248 x 195 mm, No. of Columns (Display): 4, Col Widths (Display): 45 mm
Copy instructions: *Copy Date:* 30 days prior to publication
CONSUMER: ANIMALS & PETS: Horses & Ponies

CBBC-INFO 1826883G77A-2828
Editorial: Berrenrather Str. 315b, 50937 KÖLN
Tel: 221 33451370
Email: redaktion@cbbc.de
Freq: 6 issues yearly; **Cover Price:** EUR 5,00
Free to qualifying individuals ; **Circ:** 1,000
Editor: Wolfgang Wagner; **Advertising Manager:** Wolfgang Wagner
Profile: Magazine from the Classic British Bike Club with internal information.
Language(s): German

CCI 724167G3D-41
Editorial: Borsigstr. 3, 76185 KARLSRUHE
Tel: 721 5651427 **Fax:** 721 5651435
Email: redaktion@cci-promotor.de **Web site:** http://www.cci-promotor.de
Freq: 14 issues yearly; **Annual Sub.:** EUR 159,00; **Circ:** 5,007
Editor: Thomas Mietzker; **Advertising Manager:** Mirja Becker
Profile: CCI is one of the leading and best-read German publications in the field of ventilation, air-conditioning, refrigeration, building automation and controls. Since more than 45 years CCI provides information to its targeted audience of hvac/r contractors, consulting engineers, wholesalers, distributors, manufacturers, sales representatives, equipment users and additional professionals employed in the field. CCI researches, analyses and reports on topics and events which concern and affect the hvac/r industry. As the only independent newspaper serving this field, CCI is relied on by the hvac/r industry to provide timely, accurate, helpful and unbiased information and features within its pages. Exclusive survey results, company transactions and personal changes help make the CCI the best-read publication in the industry.
Language(s): German
ADVERTISING RATES:
Full Page Mono .... EUR 5080
Full Page Colour .... EUR 5080
Mechanical Data: Type Area: 400 x 270 mm, No. of Columns (Display): 5, Col Widths (Display): 50 mm
Copy instructions: *Copy Date:* 25 days prior to publication
BUSINESS: HEATING & VENTILATION: Heating & Plumbing

CCLM CLINICAL CHEMISTRY AND LABORATORY MEDICINE 724168G56A-1880
Editorial: Genthiner Str. 13, 10785 BERLIN
Tel: 30 26005220 **Fax:** 30 26005325
Email: cclm.editorial@degruyter.com **Web site:** http://www.degruyter.de/journals/cclm
Freq: Monthly; **Annual Sub.:** EUR 1322,00; **Circ:** 1,500
Editor: Mario Plebani
Profile: Magazine on clinical chemistry and laboratory medicine.
Language(s): English
ADVERTISING RATES:
Full Page Mono .... EUR 695
Full Page Colour .... EUR 1540
Mechanical Data: Type Area: 250 x 170 mm, No. of Columns (Display): 2, Col Widths (Display): 81 mm
Copy instructions: *Copy Date:* 28 days prior to publication
Official Journal of: Organ d. Internat. Federation of Clinical Chemistry and Laboratory Medicine u. d. Forum of the European Societies of Clinical Chemistry

CCLR CARBON & CLIMATE LAW REVIEW 1828399G1A-3695
Editorial: Güntzelstr. 63, 10717 BERLIN
Tel: 30 81450615 **Fax:** 30 81450622
Email: kickum@lexxion.de **Web site:** http://www.lexxion.de
Freq: Quarterly; **Annual Sub.:** EUR 372,36; **Circ:** 500
Editor: Christina Kickum
Profile: Provides news on rapidly evolving carbon market, legal policy recommendations with articles on legal aspects of carbon trading and other dimensions of greenhouse gas regulation.
Language(s): English
ADVERTISING RATES:
Full Page Colour .... EUR 500
Mechanical Data: Type Area: 220 x 157 mm
Copy instructions: *Copy Date:* 21 days prior to publication

CD SICHERHEITS-MANAGEMENT 724178G54C-2
Editorial: Barbarossastr. 21, 63517 RODENBACH
Tel: 6184 95080 **Fax:** 6184 54524
Email: redaktion@security-service.com **Web site:** http://www.security-service.com
Freq: 6 issues yearly; **Annual Sub.:** EUR 54,00; **Circ:** 9,927
Editor: Helmut Brückmann; **Advertising Manager:** Inge Schuch
Profile: CD Sicherheits-Management is one of the leading journals of the German-speaking security industry. The magazine contains valuable information on the development of crime and terrorism in the economy and society. Analysis, trends and consequences will be prepared and described by journalists and leading authors in their field. In addition, the latest security techniques, technologies and concepts are introduced. The focus is security solutions available from practice for practice as well as overarching technical papers on selected topics of security. Co-editors and editorial team stand for competence and professionalism. To give our readers an in-depth reporting, writing exclusively for our selected authors who are experts in their field. They use different ways of journalistic representation - whether in the form of case studies, interviews or essays.
Language(s): German
Readership: Aimed at security managers and members of the police force.
ADVERTISING RATES:
Full Page Mono .... EUR 1915
Full Page Colour .... EUR 3145
Mechanical Data: Type Area: 180 x 125 mm, No. of Columns (Display): 2, Col Widths (Display): 50 mm
Copy instructions: *Copy Date:* 21 days prior to publication
BUSINESS: SAFETY & SECURITY: Security

CE MARKT 724190G43A-60
Editorial: Schmiedberg 2a, 86415 MERING
Tel: 8233 4117 **Fax:** 8233 30206
Email: verlag@ce-markt.de **Web site:** http://www.ce-markt.de
Freq: 11 issues yearly; **Annual Sub.:** EUR 44,00; **Circ:** 22,330
Editor: Jan Uebe; **Advertising Manager:** Annette Pfänder-Coleman
Profile: Insider Bulletin d. consumer electronics market: consumer electronics, digital photo & video, telecommunications, multimedia, PC, car and infotainment, games, home nets, accessories. Readers of the magazine's owner/managers and other managers, buyers, sales managers and sellers in the trading companies of all sizes, including branches, manager of the cotion center, the departments of department stores and wholesale distribution companies and their trade outlets, mail order business and the professional wholesale trade.
Language(s): German
Readership: Aimed at store managers and personnel.
ADVERTISING RATES:
Full Page Mono .... EUR 5210
Full Page Colour .... EUR 6180
Mechanical Data: Type Area: 279 x 185 mm, No. of Columns (Display): 4, Col Widths (Display): 43 mm
Copy instructions: *Copy Date:* 21 days prior to publication
Official Journal of: Organ d. Informationsgemeinschaft Consumer Electronics e.V.
Supplement(s): electro
BUSINESS: ELECTRICAL RETAIL TRADE

CEB AKTUELL 1609351G89A-12139
Editorial: Leipartstr. 22, 81369 MÜNCHEN
Tel: 89 7242573 **Fax:** 89 72400595
Email: campingerholungsverein@arcor.de
Freq: Half-yearly; **Circ:** 3,000
Editor: Hans-Georg Heidger; **Advertising Manager:** Hans-Georg Heidger
Profile: Promoting the idea of ??camping in Bavaria.
Language(s): German
Mechanical Data: Type Area: 265 x 185 mm, No. of Columns (Display): 4, Col Widths (Display): 43 mm
Copy instructions: *Copy Date:* 28 days prior to publication

C.EBRA 1850121G34-560
Editorial: Marktplatz 13, 65183 WIESBADEN
Tel: 611 3609824 **Fax:** 611 3609877
Email: elke.sondermann@cebra.biz **Web site:** http://www.cebra.biz
Freq: 6 issues yearly; **Annual Sub.:** EUR 45,00; **Circ:** 9,747
Editor: Elke Sondermann; **Advertising Manager:** Torsten Wessel
Profile: "C.ebra" (Journal of efficient procurement around the office and workplace) provides background, context, and gives guidance for the efficient procurement of office supplies industrial (C-products), office furniture and technology products. The journal is aimed at buyers and decision makers in companies, authorities and institutions with at least fifty office workstations. "C.ebra" sees itself as a central information and communication platform for the relevant market participants. The aim is to establish a network between producers/suppliers, dealers and the purchasing companies and authorities to support a qualitative benchmarking process sustainable. In view of the competent and timely reports are prepared on the brand, the importance of retailers for the shopping, the representation of the market environment and the situation of the buyer in the procurement process. On the issues social acceptability in production, "green procurement" and the important segment "Public Procurement", particular attention is placed.
Language(s): German
ADVERTISING RATES:
Full Page Mono .... EUR 3200
Full Page Colour .... EUR 4550
Mechanical Data: Type Area: 256 x 175 mm
Copy instructions: *Copy Date:* 13 days prior to publication

CELL NEWS 1819076G56A-11516
Editorial: Im Neuenheimer Feld 280, 69120 HEIDELBERG **Tel:** 6221 423451 **Fax:** 6221 423452
Email: dgz@dkfz.de **Web site:** http://www.zellbiologie.de
Freq: Quarterly; **Circ:** 1,800
Editor: Sabine Reichel-Klingmann; **Advertising Manager:** Sabine Reichel-Klingmann
Profile: Information from the German Society for Cell Biology.
Language(s): German

CELLER BLICKPUNKT 724184G80-1900
Editorial: Bahnhofstr. 30, 29221 CELLE
Tel: 5141 92920 **Fax:** 5141 929292
Email: info@celler-blickpunkt.de **Web site:** http://www.celler-blickpunkt.de
Freq: Monthly; **Cover Price:** Free; **Circ:** 19,815
Editor: Andrea Hoffmann; **Advertising Manager:** M. Fritze
Profile: Magazine with information on recreation, sports, health, culture and art in Celle and environment with classified ads.
Language(s): German
ADVERTISING RATES:
Full Page Mono .... EUR 2259
Full Page Colour .... EUR 2659

Mechanical Data: No. of Columns (Display): 4, Col Widths (Display): 45 mm, Type Area: 260 x 189 mm
Copy instructions: *Copy Date:* 12 days prior to publication
CONSUMER: RURAL & REGIONAL INTEREST

CELLER KURIER
724185G72-2932
Editorial: Mühlenstr. 8a, 29221 CELLE
Tel: 5141 92430 **Fax:** 5141 6469
Email: redaktion@celler-kurier.de **Web site:** http://www.celler-kurier.de
Freq: 104 issues yearly; **Cover Price:** Free; **Circ:** 62,100
Editor: Ralf Müller; **Advertising Manager:** Rüdiger Kirsch
Profile: Advertising journal (house-to-house) concentrating on local stories.
Language(s): German
ADVERTISING RATES:
Full Page Mono .... EUR 5341
Full Page Colour .... EUR 5731
Mechanical Data: Type Area: 430 x 282 mm, No. of Columns (Display): 6, Col Widths (Display): 45 mm
Copy instructions: *Copy Date:* 3 days prior to publication
LOCAL NEWSPAPERS

CELLER MARKT
724186G72-2936
Editorial: Bahnhofstr. 1, 29221 CELLE
Tel: 5141 990331 **Fax:** 5141 990335
Email: celler-markt@cellesche-zeitung.de **Web site:** http://www.cellesche-zeitung.de
Freq: Weekly; **Cover Price:** Free; **Circ:** 53,500
Editor: Katja Müller; **Advertising Manager:** Carsten Wießner
Profile: Advertising journal (house-to-house) concentrating on local stories.
Language(s): German
ADVERTISING RATES:
Full Page Mono .... EUR 3767
Full Page Colour .... EUR 5083
Mechanical Data: Type Area: 430 x 277 mm, No. of Columns (Display): 6, Col Widths (Display): 45 mm
Copy instructions: *Copy Date:* 2 days prior to publication
LOCAL NEWSPAPERS

CELLESCHE ZEITUNG
724188G67B-3780
Editorial: Bahnhofstr. 1, 29221 CELLE
Tel: 5141 990110 **Fax:** 5141 990112
Email: redaktion@cellesche-zeitung.de **Web site:** http://www.cellesche-zeitung.de
Freq: 312 issues yearly; **Circ:** 30,817
Editor: Ralf Leineweber; **News Editor:** Andreas Babel; **Advertising Manager:** Carsten Wießner
Profile: The Cellesche Zeitung is a medium sized local newspaper. It appears in the town and district of Celle. Except for the peripheral areas of Hanover region, where the Hannover Allgemeine Zeitung is related to, the Celle newspaper a monopoly in the local reporting. The newspaper, despite their small size or their own executive editor, that is, it produces not only the local section, but also the national political, economic and sports pages themselves Twitter: http://twitter.com/cezett This Outlet offers RSS (Really Simple Syndication).
Language(s): German
ADVERTISING RATES:
SCC .... EUR 51,90
Mechanical Data: Type Area: 430 x 277 mm, No. of Columns (Display): 6, Col Widths (Display): 45 mm
Copy instructions: *Copy Date:* 1 day prior to publication
Supplement(s): rtv
REGIONAL DAILY & SUNDAY NEWSPAPERS: Regional Daily Newspapers

CEMENT INTERNATIONAL
1606023G4E-6899
Editorial: Steinhof 39, 40699 ERKRATH
Tel: 211 9249951 **Fax:** 211 9249955
Email: deckers@verlagbt.de **Web site:** http://www.verlagbt.de
Freq: 6 issues yearly; **Annual Sub.:** EUR 198,00; **Circ:** 3,679
Editor: Stefan Deckers; **Advertising Manager:** Günther Jung
Profile: Technical scientific magazine on processing, performing and applying cement and similar materials.
Language(s): English; German
ADVERTISING RATES:
Full Page Mono .... EUR 1550
Full Page Colour .... EUR 2570
Mechanical Data: Type Area: 265 x 172 mm
Copy instructions: *Copy Date:* 14 days prior to publication
Official Journal of: Organ d. Vereins Dt. Zementwerke u. d. Bundesverb. d. Dt. Zementindustrie e.V. u. d. Ungar. Zementverb.
BUSINESS: ARCHITECTURE & BUILDING: Building

CENTRAL EUROPEAN NEUROSURGERY
748821G56A-11020
Editorial: Rüdigerstr. 14, 70469 STUTTGART
Tel: 711 8931314 **Fax:** 711 8931393
Email: renate.luz@thieme.de **Web site:** http://www.thieme.de/fz/neurosurgery.html
Freq: Quarterly; Free to qualifying individuals
Annual Sub.: EUR 298,60; **Circ:** 1,720
Editor: Veit Rohde
Profile: This journal provides comprehensive information on all clinical, research and practical aspects of Neurosurgery. An esteemed and international advisory board guarantees the highest quality information. In addition to this Zentralblatt für Neurochirurgie - Central European Neurosurgery is the organ of the most important German societies in neurosurgery. Relevant original papers and case reports, technical innovations, book reviews, congress announcements.
Language(s): English; German
ADVERTISING RATES:
Full Page Mono .... EUR 1220
Full Page Colour .... EUR 2420
Mechanical Data: Type Area: 248 x 175 mm, No. of Columns (Display): 4, Col Widths (Display): 40 mm
Official Journal of: Organ d. Dt. Ges. f. Neurochirurgie u. d. Berufsverb. Dt. Neurochirurgen
BUSINESS: HEALTH & MEDICAL

CFI CERAMIC FORUM INTERNATIONAL
724209G12A-1
Editorial: Aschmattstr. 8, 76532 BADEN-BADEN
Tel: 7221 502241 **Fax:** 7221 502222
Email: scharrer@cfi.de **Web site:** http://www.cfi.de
Freq: 10 issues yearly; Free to qualifying individuals
Annual Sub.: EUR 126,50; **Circ:** 4,439
Editor: Karin Scharrer; **Advertising Manager:** Corinna Zepter
Profile: cfi ceramic forum international is a technical-scientific journal, which covers topics concerned mainly with wall and floor tiles, tableware, sanitaryware, refractories as well as heavy clay and advanced ceramics (incl. carbon) and powder metallurgy worldwide. In the English-language scientific section great importance is given to the interaction between theory and practice. The latest findings of the supplying industry (raw materials, equipment) are evaluated. In addition, information on all management questions is included: market analysis, reports, economic questions, product developments.
Language(s): English; German
ADVERTISING RATES:
Full Page Mono .... EUR 2465
Full Page Colour .... EUR 2950
Mechanical Data: Type Area: 270 x 186 mm, No. of Columns (Display): 4, Col Widths (Display): 45 mm
Copy instructions: *Copy Date:* 15 days prior to publication
BUSINESS: CERAMICS, POTTERY & GLASS: Ceramics & Pottery

CHAMER ZEITUNG
724216G67B-3800
Editorial: Ludwigsplatz 30, 94315 STRAUBING
Tel: 9421 9404601 **Fax:** 9421 9404609
Email: landkreis@straubinger-tagblatt.de **Web site:** http://www.idowa.de
Freq: 312 issues yearly; **Circ:** 11,935
Advertising Manager: Klaus Huber
Profile: Regional daily newspaper with news on politics, economy, culture, sports, travel, technology, etc. She is a local edition of Straubinger Tagblatt for the county Cham Twitter: http://twitter.com/idowa This Outlet offers RSS (Really Simple Syndication).
Language(s): German
ADVERTISING RATES:
SCC .... EUR 13,50
Mechanical Data: Type Area: 430 x 282 mm, No. of Columns (Display): 6, Col Widths (Display): 45 mm
Copy instructions: *Copy Date:* 1 day prior to publication
Supplement(s): Zuhause
REGIONAL DAILY & SUNDAY NEWSPAPERS: Regional Daily Newspapers

CHAMLAND AKTUELL
724217G72-2940
Editorial: Rindermarkt 9, 93413 CHAM
Tel: 9971 85440 **Fax:** 9971 854444
Email: anzeigen.cham@chamer-zeitung.de
Freq: Weekly; **Cover Price:** Free; **Circ:** 42,316
Profile: Advertising journal (house-to-house) concentrating on local stories.
Language(s): German
ADVERTISING RATES:
Full Page Mono .... EUR 2219
Full Page Colour .... EUR 3096
Mechanical Data: Type Area: 430 x 280 mm, No. of Columns (Display): 6, Col Widths (Display): 45 mm
Copy instructions: *Copy Date:* 2 days prior to publication
LOCAL NEWSPAPERS

CHANCEN
1911157G1C-1495
Editorial: Kasernenstr. 69, 40213 DÜSSELDORF
Tel: 211 54227651 **Fax:** 211 54227603
Email: florian.flicke@corps-verlag.de **Web site:** http://www.corps-verlag.de
Freq: 3 issues yearly; **Circ:** 35,000
Editor: Florian Flicke
Profile: Bank customer magazine.
Language(s): German

CHANNELPARTNER
724553G5E-1
Editorial: Lyonel-Feininger-Str. 26, 80807 MÜNCHEN
Tel: 89 36086396 **Fax:** 89 36086389
Email: redaktion@channelpartner.de **Web site:** http://www.channelpartner.de
Freq: 24 issues yearly; **Circ:** 19,090
Editor: Christian Meyer; **Advertising Manager:** Sascha Neubacher
Profile: Channel Partner (CP) is one of the leading information sources for dealers, systems integrators and service providers from the fields of information technology (IT), telecommunications (TC) and consumer electronics (CE). Channel partner support significantly desProduktsortiments dealer in the strategic orientation of companies, the selection of suppliers and the composition. CP provides current, practical and independent. Through regular reader surveys identified channel partners the information needs of the target group. In selecting the topics relevant and business benefits of the highest priority. In many exclusive products by channel partners rely newspapers, online media and broadcasters.
Language(s): German
ADVERTISING RATES:
Full Page Mono .... EUR 11000
Full Page Colour .... EUR 11000
Mechanical Data: Type Area: 263 x 195 mm, No. of Columns (Display): 4, Col Widths (Display): 45 mm
Copy instructions: *Copy Date:* 8 days prior to publication
Supplement(s): Focus Reseller Magazin
BUSINESS: COMPUTERS & AUTOMATION: Data Transmission

CHANNELPARTNER
1621002G43A-1497
Editorial: Lyonel-Feininger-Str. 26, 80807 MÜNCHEN
Tel: 89 36086388 **Fax:** 89 36086389
Email: redaktion@channelpartner.de **Web site:** http://www.channelpartner.de
Freq: Daily; **Cover Price:** Paid; **Circ:** 701,349 Unique Users
Editor: Christian Meyer; **Advertising Manager:** Sascha Neubacher
Profile: Ezine: Magazine providing information about IT, including the latest news and background history.
Language(s): German
BUSINESS: ELECTRICAL RETAIL TRADE

CHARLOTTENBURG KOMPAKT
1898565G74M-887
Editorial: Bundesallee 23, 10717 BERLIN
Tel: 30 863030 **Fax:** 30 86303200
Email: info@bfb.de **Web site:** http://www.bfb.de
Freq: Annual; **Cover Price:** Free; **Circ:** 105,000
Profile: Industry district magazine. The core of this handy reference book is neatly sorted according to different themes of industry. Here you will find a plethora of vendors from the neighborhood. In preparation to the respective subject area raises a company, in an interview. To know your environment better, we present in the district windows, etc. beautiful places, monuments, museums, etc. For better orientation in the neighborhood also an integrated neighborhood with street plan is register. Furthermore, the county information you provide an overview of important phone numbers and agencies in your neighborhood.
Language(s): German
ADVERTISING RATES:
Full Page Mono .... EUR 990
Full Page Colour .... EUR 990
Mechanical Data: Type Area: 185 x 126 mm

CHEFBÜRO
724234G14A-9394
Editorial: Oberer Eisbergweg 7, 73734 ESSLINGEN
Tel: 711 3482070 **Fax:** 711 3482071
Email: sb@chefbuero.de **Web site:** http://www.chefbuero.de
Freq: 8 issues yearly; Free to qualifying individuals
Annual Sub.: EUR 40,00; **Circ:** 39,704
Editor: Stefan Beuchel
Profile: IT & Business magazine for managers - is aimed at owners, managers and management in industrial and service companies. Chefbüro offers the investment decision makers in the industry for over three decades, competently researched and prepared information on the topics of information and communication technology, organization and office organization and management and leadership issues. Chefbüro reported on the basis of interviews, news, practice examples, product, system and solution presentations, and critical technical papers. In each edition will be Chefbüro-solution offerings to current problems comprehensively and deepened shown. The environment of national and international IT and office furniture fairs will be accompanied by Chefbüro editorial. Chefbüro has the motto "No side too much and too little is no line for "a clear categorization with color code to quickly and easily access specific areas of interest can. Employed by-product and solution presentations to Chefbüro with questions about motivation at work, there is room for neutral articles on current, general interest topics and allows insiders and trend analysis views to speak. This is the reference range far beyond the traditional IT and office journal. Twitter: http://twitter.com/#!/chefbuero.
Language(s): German
Readership: Aimed at business executives.
ADVERTISING RATES:
Full Page Mono .... EUR 5400
Full Page Colour .... EUR 7200
Mechanical Data: Type Area: 259 x 178 mm, No. of Columns (Display): 4, Col Widths (Display): 43 mm
Copy instructions: *Copy Date:* 10 days prior to publication
Official Journal of: Organ d. VOI-Verb. f. Organisations- u. Informationssysteme e.V. u. d. Export-Club Bayern e.V.
BUSINESS: COMMERCE, INDUSTRY & MANAGEMENT

CHEMANAGER
724238G13-240
Editorial: Rößlerstr. 90, 64293 DARMSTADT
Tel: 6151 8090165 **Fax:** 6151 8090133
Email: michael.reubold@wiley.com **Web site:** http://www.chemanager-online.com
Freq: 16 issues yearly; **Annual Sub.:** EUR 89,88; **Circ:** 42,017
Editor: Michael Reubold; **Advertising Manager:** Claudia Vogel
Profile: CHEManager is the leading newspaper for the management of chemical and pharmaceutical industry. Latest news, interviews and opinion-depth market and technical reports CHEManager give readers a decisive information advantage! The quarterly survey conducted by top managers in the chemical and pharmaceutical industry - CHEMonitor - is a trend barometer for the industry. So has CHEManager - now in the 20th Born - as an information platform and image makers for the chemical and pharmaceutical industries established. Facebook: http://www.facebook.com/CHEManager This Outlet offers RSS (Really Simple Syndication).
Language(s): German
Readership: Aimed at managers in the chemical and pharmaceutical industries.
ADVERTISING RATES:
Full Page Mono .... EUR 7140
Full Page Colour .... EUR 8970
Mechanical Data: Type Area: 260 x 185 mm, No. of Columns (Display): 4, Col Widths (Display): 43 mm
BUSINESS: CHEMICALS

CHEMICAL ENGINEERING & TECHNOLOGY
724240G13-2359
Editorial: Boschstr. 12, 69469 WEINHEIM
Tel: 6201 606520 **Fax:** 6201 606525
Email: cet@wiley.com **Web site:** http://www.cet-journal.de
Freq: Monthly; **Annual Sub.:** EUR 3701,00; **Circ:** 1,000
Editor: Barbara Böck; **Advertising Manager:** Marion Schulz
Profile: Magazine covering industrial chemistry, plant equipment, process engineering and biotechnology.
Language(s): English
Readership: Aimed at chemical and mechanical engineers.
ADVERTISING RATES:
Full Page Mono .... EUR 1200
Full Page Colour .... EUR 2200
Mechanical Data: Type Area: 260 x 180 mm, No. of Columns (Display): 2, Col Widths (Display): 90 mm
Copy instructions: *Copy Date:* 40 days prior to publication
BUSINESS: CHEMICALS

CHEMICAL FIBERS INTERNATIONAL
724241G47A-160
Editorial: Mainzer Landstr. 251, 60326 FRANKFURT
Tel: 69 75951393 **Fax:** 69 75951390
Email: edi-cfi@dfv.de **Web site:** http://www.chemical-fibers.com
Freq: Quarterly; **Annual Sub.:** EUR 169,40; **Circ:** 5,019
Editor: Claudia van Bonn; **Advertising Manager:** Dagmar Henning
Profile: Chemical Fibers International is the English language technical publication for purchasing decision-makers and all areas of management in chemical fiber production facilities, and their suppliers (chemical fiber machinery and accessories manufacturers, dyestuff and auxiliary manufacturers) throughout the world. Special topics are: Fiber Raw Materials, Fibers/Yarns, Fiber Production, Texturing and Nonwovens as well as International Fiber Industry News, Management and Patents.
Language(s): English
ADVERTISING RATES:
Full Page Mono .... EUR 3265
Full Page Colour .... EUR 4630
Mechanical Data: Type Area: 256 x 185 mm, No. of Columns (Display): 4, Col Widths (Display): 42 mm
Copy instructions: *Copy Date:* 21 days prior to publication
BUSINESS: CLOTHING & TEXTILES

CHEMIE DER ERDE GEOCHEMISTRY
724243G55-500
Editorial: Burgweg 11, 07749 JENA
Tel: 3641 948600 **Fax:** 3641 948602
Email: ckh@rz.uni-jena.de
Freq: Quarterly; **Annual Sub.:** EUR 141,00
Editor: Klaus Heide
Profile: Aimed at mineralogists, petrologists, pedologists, geochemists, meteoritic studies experts, mineral deposit experts, geologists, miners, limnologists, marine research experts and environmental scientists.
Language(s): English; German
Readership: Aimed at mineralogists, petrologists, pedologists, geochemists, meteoritic studies experts, mineraldeposit experts, geologists, miners, limnologists, marine research experts and environmental scientists.
BUSINESS: APPLIED SCIENCE & LABORATORIES

CHEMIE IN UNSERER ZEIT
724246G13-280
Editorial: Boschstr. 12, 69469 WEINHEIM
Tel: 6201 606317 **Fax:** 6201 606328
Email: chiuz@wiley-vch.de **Web site:** http://www.chiuz.de
Freq: 6 issues yearly; **Annual Sub.:** EUR 120,00; **Circ:** 4,960

Editor: Doris Fischer-Henningsen; **Advertising Manager:** Nicole Schramm
Profile: Chemie in unserer Zeit reliably informed about current developments in chemistry and its related disciplines. The reader gets a fascinating insight into all aspects of this promising science, it is also prepared to understand complex issues. Leading experts bring new developments of great significance in more detail - presented color illustrated and reader-friendly. From scientific surveys, course-related materials, traceable experiments to controversial issues of environmental chemistry and current social discussion. Review articles and varied categories convey knowledge in an entertaining way and give some help in orientation in the field.
Language(s): German
ADVERTISING RATES:
Full Page Mono .... EUR 2950
Full Page Colour .... EUR 4370
Mechanical Data: Type Area: 260 x 180 mm, No. of Columns (Display): 3, Col Widths (Display): 57 mm
Copy instructions: *Copy Date:* 37 days prior to publication
BUSINESS: CHEMICALS

CHEMIE INGENIEUR TECHNIK
724245G13-300
Editorial: Boschstr. 12, 69469 WEINHEIM
Tel: 6201 606520 **Fax:** 6201 606203
Email: cit@wiley-vch.de **Web site:** http://www.cit-journal.com
Freq: 11 issues yearly; **Annual Sub.:** EUR 2376,00; **Circ:** 5,390
Editor: Barbara Böck; **Advertising Manager:** Marion Schulz
Profile: The scientific and technical journal Chemical Engineering Technology (CIT) is in the German-speaking area premier source for original papers in the field of chemical engineering. In a reader survey, readers are certified highest level of editorial expertise and CIT designated as ideal for information. The leading experts from academia and industry describe in practical overview of the current state of knowledge contributions from research and development, design and production. Research articles about more mature areas, text messages, make sure that the CIT readers are always informed about the latest state of the art. Special Issues examine the state of the art of selected areas. With issues of process engineering, instrumentation, control and process control techniques, and laboratory practice, the CIT has a high reputation in process engineering and chemical engineers, biotechnologists and equipment manufacturers and is read by decision makers in the industry. This Outlet offers RSS (Really Simple Syndication).
Language(s): German
ADVERTISING RATES:
Full Page Mono .... EUR 4200
Full Page Colour .... EUR 5640
Mechanical Data: Type Area: 256 x 170 mm, No. of Columns (Display): 4, Col Widths (Display): 45 mm
Copy instructions: *Copy Date:* 42 days prior to publication
Official Journal of: Organ d. Ges. Dt. Chemiker, d. Dechema u. d. VDI-GVC Ges. Verfahrenstechnik u. Chemieingenieurwesen
BUSINESS: CHEMICALS

CHEMIE TECHNIK
724249G13-360
Editorial: Im Weiher 10, 69121 HEIDELBERG
Tel: 6221 489388 **Fax:** 6221 489490
Email: redaktion@chemietechnik.de **Web site:** http://www.chemietechnik.de
Freq: 11 issues yearly; **Annual Sub.:** EUR 162,80; **Circ:** 29,879
Editor: Armin Scheuermann; **Advertising Manager:** Sabine Wegmann
Profile: Magazine for decision makers: chemical engineering is the process technology magazine for managers and investment decision-makers in chemical plant. The journal provides a monthly practical technical articles and short reports on current issues of selected authors from more than 20 areas. Themes are all procedures, planning, construction, operation and maintenance of chemical plants relevant offers the industry. In addition, all new and further development are represented in these areas.
Language(s): German
Readership: Aimed at those involved in the chemical industry.
ADVERTISING RATES:
Full Page Mono .... EUR 5190
Full Page Colour .... EUR 6290
Mechanical Data: Type Area: 257 x 178 mm, No. of Columns (Display): 4, Col Widths (Display): 41 mm
Copy instructions: *Copy Date:* 28 days prior to publication
BUSINESS: CHEMICALS

CHEMMEDCHEM
1732115G37-1832
Editorial: Boschstr. 12, 69469 WEINHEIM
Tel: 6201 606142 **Fax:** 6201 606328
Email: chemmedchem@wiley-vch.de **Web site:** http://www.wiley-vch.de
Freq: Monthly; **Circ:** 1,000
Editor: Natalia Ortúzar; **Advertising Manager:** Marion Schulz
Profile: Journal at the interface of chemistry, biology and medicine.
Language(s): English
ADVERTISING RATES:
Full Page Mono .... EUR 2450
Full Page Colour .... EUR 3400
Mechanical Data: Type Area: 260 x 180 mm
Supplement to: Angewandte Chemie, Angewandte Chemie

CHEMNITZER MORGENPOST
724260G67B-3820
Editorial: Ostra-Allee 20, 01067 DRESDEN
Tel: 351 48642626 **Fax:** 351 48642467
Email: mopo.cmp@dd-v.de
Freq: 312 issues yearly; **Circ:** 28,061
Advertising Manager: Tobias Spitzhorn
Profile: Regional daily newspaper magazine with news on politics, economy, culture, sports, travel, technology, etc. The Morgenpost is a regional daily newspaper published in the cities of Dresden and Chemnitz and the surrounding areas. It is after the Sächsische Zeitung second largest newspaper in the region.
Language(s): German
ADVERTISING RATES:
SCC .... EUR 52,80
Mechanical Data: Type Area: 327 x 233 mm, No. of Columns (Display): 5, Col Widths (Display): 45 mm
Copy instructions: *Copy Date:* 1 day prior to publication
REGIONAL DAILY & SUNDAY NEWSPAPERS: Regional Daily Newspapers

CHEMOTHERAPIE JOURNAL
724262G56A-1940
Editorial: Birkenwaldstr. 44, 70191 STUTTGART
Tel: 711 2582234 **Fax:** 711 2582283
Email: ctj@wissenschaftliche-verlagsgesellschaft.de **Web site:** http://www.wissenschaftliche-verlagsgesellschaft.de/ctj
Freq: 6 issues yearly; Free to qualifying individuals
Annual Sub.: EUR 185,50; **Circ:** 4,000
Editor: Annemarie Musch; **Advertising Manager:** Kornelia Wind
Profile: The Chemotherapie Journal contains works from all areas, especially the anti-infective, antineoplastic chemotherapy, and also to the pathophysiology, diagnosis and treatment of infectious diseases. The journal reflects the activities of the PEG, which represents in its sections following areas: Antibacterial, antiviral, antiparasitic and antifungal chemotherapy, infections in hematology, immunology and basic research.
Language(s): German
ADVERTISING RATES:
Full Page Mono .... EUR 2132
Full Page Colour .... EUR 3512
Mechanical Data: Type Area: 262 x 182 mm, No. of Columns (Display): 3, Col Widths (Display): 56 mm
Copy instructions: *Copy Date:* 20 days prior to publication
BUSINESS: HEALTH & MEDICAL

CHEMSUSCHEM
1873456G37-1862
Editorial: Boschstr. 12, 69469 WEINHEIM
Tel: 6201 606324 **Fax:** 6201 606331
Email: chemsuschem@wiley-vch.de **Web site:** http://www.chemsuschem.org
Freq: Monthly; **Annual Sub.:** EUR 1980,00; **Circ:** 1,000
Editor: Peter Gölitz; **Advertising Manager:** Marion Schulz
Profile: Journal of aChemistry & Sustainability, Energy & Materials.
Language(s): English
ADVERTISING RATES:
Full Page Mono .... EUR 2450
Full Page Colour .... EUR 3400
Mechanical Data: Type Area: 260 x 180 mm

CHIEMGAU-ZEITUNG
724271G67B-3840
Editorial: Hafnerstr. 5, 83022 ROSENHEIM
Tel: 8031 213201 **Fax:** 8031 213216
Email: redaktion@ovb.net **Web site:** http://www.ovb-online.de
Freq: 312 issues yearly; **Circ:** 7,111
Advertising Manager: Max Breu
Profile: Regional daily newspaper with news on politics, economy, culture, sports, travel, technology, etc. The Chiemgau-Zeitung is a regional edition of the newspaper "Oberbayerisches Volksblatt". This Outlet offers RSS (Really Simple Syndication).
Language(s): German
ADVERTISING RATES:
SCC .... EUR 45,10
Mechanical Data: Type Area: 474 x 324 mm, No. of Columns (Display): 7, Col Widths (Display): 45 mm
Copy instructions: *Copy Date:* 1 day prior to publication
Supplement(s): rtv
REGIONAL DAILY & SUNDAY NEWSPAPERS: Regional Daily Newspapers

CHILD'S NERVOUS SYSTEM CHNS
724274G56A-1960
Editorial: Tiergartenstr. 17, 69121 HEIDELBERG
Tel: 6221 4870 **Fax:** 6221 4878366
Email: subscriptions@springer.com **Web site:** http://www.springerlink.com
Freq: Monthly; **Annual Sub.:** EUR 3060,00; **Circ:** 406
Editor: C. di Rocco
Profile: Magazine about children's nervous systems.
Language(s): English
ADVERTISING RATES:
Full Page Mono .... EUR 740
Full Page Colour .... EUR 1780
Mechanical Data: Type Area: 240 x 175 mm
Official Journal of: Organ d. Internat., d. European, d. Brazilian, d. Chinese, d. Japanese u. d. Korean Societies for Pediatric Neurosurgery

CHINA CONTACT
1799529G14C-4769
Editorial: Ritterstr. 2b, 10969 BERLIN
Tel: 30 61508926 **Fax:** 30 61508927
Email: pt@owc.de **Web site:** http://www.owc.de
Freq: Monthly; **Annual Sub.:** EUR 127,33; **Circ:** 8,330
Editor: Peter Tichauer; **Advertising Manager:** Norbert Mayer
Profile: Magazine focusing on future business negotiations with China. Also contains market analyses and trends.
Language(s): German
ADVERTISING RATES:
Full Page Mono .... EUR 2500
Full Page Colour .... EUR 3200
Mechanical Data: Type Area: 265 x 175 mm
Supplement(s): Taiwan Contact

CHINESISCHE MEDIZIN
724288G56A-1980
Editorial: Aschauer Str. 30, 81549 MÜNCHEN
Tel: 89 2030431300 **Fax:** 89 2030431399
Email: heidrun.guthoehrlein@springer.com **Web site:** http://www.springermedizin.de
Freq: Quarterly; Free to qualifying individuals
Annual Sub.: EUR 139,00; **Circ:** 1,700
Editor: Heidrun Guthörlein; **Advertising Manager:** Barbara Kanters
Profile: Chinese medicine is the first German-language TCM magazine, which gives the reader with factual research and educational articles on all aspects of traditional Chinese medicine - written by leading Chinese doctors. Selected articles from Chinese journals are translated directly. In addition, the magazine deals with issues such as drug therapies, movement therapies (Taiji, qigong), Chinese Manual Therapy (Tuina), dietetics. Since 1986, the prestigious magazine is published by the SMS. The Society promotes the appreciation and dissemination of TCM, is their education standards and is respected and important contact for medical associations, funds, authorities and universities in Germany and Switzerland.
Language(s): German
ADVERTISING RATES:
Full Page Mono .... EUR 1100
Full Page Colour .... EUR 2100
Mechanical Data: Type Area: 240 x 174 mm
Official Journal of: Organ d. Societas Medicinae Sinensis, Internat. Ges. f. chin. Medizinu. u. d. Schweizer. Ärzteges. f. Akupunktur-Chin. Medizin-Aurikulomedizin

CHIP
724289G5R-630
Editorial: Poccistr. 11, 80336 MÜNCHEN
Tel: 89 74642141 **Fax:** 89 74642274
Email: redaktion@chip.de **Web site:** http://www.chip.de
Freq: Monthly; **Annual Sub.:** EUR 59,88; **Circ:** 296,955
Editor: Thomas Pyczak; **Advertising Manager:** Jochen Lutz
Profile: Chip is testing facility, technical advice and trend barometer. With extensive sales advice and smart solutions we offer our readers value and orientation. Chip is committed to quality and independence: to the most stringent international standards free editors and engineers test, more than 2,000 products of the digital world - from flat screen TV up for online banking every year. Chip is the No. 1 media brand for digital technology. With 350,000 copies sold, the magazine is at the top of the monthly technology titles. Chip and Chip Online are the leading cross-media offerings for men in Germany.
Language(s): German
Readership: Aimed at the IT departments of companies.
ADVERTISING RATES:
Full Page Mono .... EUR 16600
Full Page Colour .... EUR 16600
Mechanical Data: Type Area: 265 x 195 mm
Copy instructions: *Copy Date:* 21 days prior to publication
BUSINESS: COMPUTERS & AUTOMATION: Computers Related

CHIP FOTO-VIDEO
1616026G85A-778
Editorial: Poccistr. 11, 80336 MÜNCHEN
Tel: 89 746420 **Fax:** 89 7466560
Email: florian.schuster@chip-fotowelt.de **Web site:** http://www.fotowelt.chip.de
Freq: Monthly; **Annual Sub.:** EUR 73,80; **Circ:** 61,781
Editor: Florian Schuster; **Advertising Manager:** Jochen Lutz
Profile: The magazine informs each month comprising the entire spectrum of photography, practical tests, tips for better photos and stunning visuals. Chip Foto-Video Digital reported to date and regardless of everything that interests the serious photographer. With its own test lab and a private studio.
Language(s): German
ADVERTISING RATES:
Full Page Mono .... EUR 10600
Full Page Colour .... EUR 10600
Mechanical Data: Type Area: 280 x 210 mm
Copy instructions: *Copy Date:* 23 days prior to publication
CONSUMER: PHOTOGRAPHY & FILM MAKING: Photography

CHIP ONLINE.DE
1620977G5C-21
Editorial: Poccistr. 11, 80336 MÜNCHEN
Tel: 89 74642382 **Fax:** 89 74642357
Email: presse@chip.de **Web site:** http://www.chip.de
Freq: Daily; **Cover Price:** Paid; **Circ:** 62,985,811 Unique Users
Editor: Christian Riedel
Profile: Ezine: Magazine with information about hard- and software. Includes test results. Facebook: http://www.facebook.com/CHIPde.
Language(s): German
BUSINESS: COMPUTERS & AUTOMATION: Professional Personal Computers

CHIP TEST & KAUF
1732222G5-11399
Editorial: Poccistr. 11, 80336 MÜNCHEN
Tel: 89 74642141 **Fax:** 89 74642274
Email: testundkauf@chip.de **Web site:** http://www.chip.de
Freq: Monthly; **Annual Sub.:** EUR 18,00; **Circ:** 37,298
Editor: Ingo Kuss; **Advertising Manager:** Jochen Lutz
Profile: The areas of consumer electronics, computers and telecommunications are seemingly endless possibilities - and are always in need of explanation! No other industry is so many technical innovations and new products in such a short time. This is where Chip Test & Kauf provide compact and cutting-edge consumer magazine for digital technology. With tests, background and support. With information, inform people, rather than hinders. Chip Test & Kauf is available for purchase bookers who want to be advised shortly, competent, clear and right on the point of purchase.
Language(s): German
ADVERTISING RATES:
Full Page Mono .... EUR 7500
Full Page Colour .... EUR 7500
Mechanical Data: Type Area: 265 x 195 mm
BUSINESS: COMPUTERS & AUTOMATION

CHIQUE
1663334G73-573
Editorial: Brühl 54, 04109 LEIPZIG **Tel:** 341 2698020
Fax: 341 2698088
Email: chefredaktion@kreuzer-leipzig.de **Web site:** http://www.chique-online.com
Freq: Annual; **Cover Price:** EUR 2,80; **Circ:** 20,000
Editor: Jens Wollweber; **Advertising Manager:** Egbert Pietsch
Profile: Buying for Leipzig with insider knowledge from Leipzig's lifestyle and fashion world. With exceptional fashion spreads as well as ambitious photographer many product and shopping tips, the magazine is the perfect companion for every shopping trip.
Language(s): German
ADVERTISING RATES:
Full Page Mono .... EUR 1990
Full Page Colour .... EUR 1990
Mechanical Data: Type Area: 235 x 190 mm, No. of Columns (Display): 3, Col Widths (Display): 60 mm
Copy instructions: *Copy Date:* 22 days prior to publication

DER CHIRURG
724291G56A-2000
Editorial: Tiergartenstr. 17, 69121 HEIDELBERG
Tel: 6221 4878210 **Fax:** 6221 48768210
Email: christiane.jurek@springer.com **Web site:** http://www.springermdizin.de
Freq: Monthly; **Annual Sub.:** EUR 345,00; **Circ:** 5,700
Editor: Jörg Rüdiger Siewert; **Advertising Manager:** Noëla Krischer-Janka
Profile: The aim of this specialist journal is the representation of secured results of scientific research as well as surgical and general medical recommendations for daily practice to give. In each issue recognized authors take in review articles on a current theme position. Further solid editorial components are original, certified training, review papers on special topics, case reports, clinical studies, book reviews and conference announcements.
Language(s): German
ADVERTISING RATES:
Full Page Mono .... EUR 2880
Full Page Colour .... EUR 4180
Mechanical Data: Type Area: 240 x 174 mm
Official Journal of: Organ d. Berufsverb. d. Dt. Chirurgen e.V., d. Dt. Ges. f. Chirurgie u. d. Dt. Ges. f. Allg.- u. Viszeralchirurgie
BUSINESS: HEALTH & MEDICAL

DER CHIRURG BDC
724292G56A-2020
Editorial: Tiergartenstr. 17, 69121 HEIDELBERG
Tel: 6221 4870 **Fax:** 6221 4878366
Email: subscriptions@springer.com **Web site:** http://www.springerlink.com
Freq: Monthly; **Circ:** 20,300
Editor: Michael Polonius; **Advertising Manager:** Noëla Krischer-Janka
Profile: Magazine from the association of German surgeons.
Language(s): German
ADVERTISING RATES:
Full Page Mono .... EUR 2440
Full Page Colour .... EUR 4180
Mechanical Data: Type Area: 240 x 174 mm

CHIRURGISCHE ALLGEMEINE
724294G56A-2040
Editorial: Maaßstr. 32/1, 69123 HEIDELBERG
Tel: 6221 1377610 **Fax:** 6221 6599590
Email: kraemer@kaden-verlag.de **Web site:** http://www.kaden-verlag.de
Freq: 10 issues yearly; **Annual Sub.:** EUR 96,00; **Circ:** 7,200

Editor: Norbert Krämer; **Advertising Manager:** Ingo Rosenstock
Profile: Magazine with news and reports on further education for surgeons.
Language(s): German
ADVERTISING RATES:
Full Page Mono .... EUR 2050
Full Page Colour .... EUR 3295
Mechanical Data: Type Area: 250 x 198 mm, No. of Columns (Display): 3, Col Widths (Display): 56 mm
Copy instructions: *Copy Date:* 15 days prior to publication

CHOICES 724300G89C-4786
Editorial: Maastrichter Str. 6, 50672 KÖLN
Tel: 221 2725260 **Fax:** 221 2725288
Email: info@choices.de **Web site:** http://www.choices.de
Freq: Monthly; **Annual Sub.:** EUR 30,00; **Circ:** 34,767
Editor: Christian Meyer
Profile: Events and listings magazine for the Cologne region. Facebook: http://www.facebook.com/choicescologne.
Language(s): German
ADVERTISING RATES:
Full Page Mono .... EUR 2500
Full Page Colour .... EUR 3300
Mechanical Data: Type Area: 265 x 190 mm, No. of Columns (Display): 4, Col Widths (Display): 44 mm
Copy instructions: *Copy Date:* 15 days prior to publication
CONSUMER: HOLIDAYS & TRAVEL: Entertainment Guides

CHRISMON PLUS 724309G87-13489
Editorial: Emil-von-Behring-Str. 3, 60439 FRANKFURT **Tel:** 69 58098003 **Fax:** 69 58098286
Email: redaktion@chrismon.de **Web site:** http://www.chrismon.de
Freq: Monthly; **Annual Sub.:** EUR 48,00; **Circ:** 15,785
Editor: Arnd Brummer
Profile: Local magazine focusing on Christian issues such as life, truth, freedom, solidarity and peace.
Language(s): German
Readership: Read by members of the Bavarian Christian community.
ADVERTISING RATES:
Full Page Mono .... EUR 2250
Full Page Colour .... EUR 2700
Mechanical Data: Type Area: 248 x 185 mm
Copy instructions: *Copy Date:* 40 days prior to publication
CONSUMER: RELIGIOUS

CHRISMON PLUS RHEINLAND 1639547G87-13651
Editorial: Kaiserswerther Str. 450, 40474 DÜSSELDORF **Tel:** 211 43690150
Fax: 211 43690100
Email: redaktion@chrismon-rheinland.de **Web site:** http://www.chrismon-rheinland.de
Freq: Monthly; **Annual Sub.:** EUR 30,00; **Circ:** 19,612
Editor: Volker Göttsche; **Advertising Manager:** Ulrich Fluck
Profile: Evangelical magazine.
Language(s): German
ADVERTISING RATES:
Full Page Mono .... EUR 1900
Full Page Colour .... EUR 2280
Mechanical Data: Type Area: 248 x 185 mm, No. of Columns (Display): 3, Col Widths (Display): 59 mm
Copy instructions: *Copy Date:* 30 days prior to publication
CONSUMER: RELIGIOUS

CHRIST IN DER GEGENWART 724317G87-2320
Editorial: Hermann-Herder-Str. 4, 79104 FREIBURG
Tel: 761 2717276 **Fax:** 761 2717518
Email: cig@herder.de **Web site:** http://www.christ-in-der-gegenwart.de
Freq: Weekly; **Circ:** 32,240
Editor: Johannes Röser; **Advertising Manager:** Friederike Ward
Profile: Magazine containing Christian news in Germany and worldwide.
Language(s): German
ADVERTISING RATES:
Full Page Mono .... EUR 1530
Full Page Colour .... EUR 2065
Mechanical Data: Type Area: 312 x 228 mm
Copy instructions: *Copy Date:* 21 days prior to publication
CONSUMER: RELIGIOUS

CHRISTOPHORUS 724325G77A-720
Editorial: Porscheplatz 1, 70435 STUTTGART
Tel: 711 91125278 **Fax:** 711 91125208
Email: cpm@porsche.de **Web site:** http://www.porsche.com/christophorus
Freq: 6 issues yearly; **Annual Sub.:** EUR 24,00; **Circ:** 335,000
Editor: Karen Schulze
Profile: The Porsche Magazine Christophorus informed about the activities of the Group and its products. In addition, there are lifestyle stories, sports and cultural features. "Christophorus" has been around since 1952 and was one of the first customer magazines at all. In September 1997, Christophorus internationalized and subjected to a graphic and editorial re-launch, as well 2007th Audiences / readers: Target customers, friends of the house and are prospective. In Germany, the Porsche driver, the magazine receives over his Porsche Centre in the other countries on the Porsche subsidiaries or the importer. The target group is not exclusively men, many women are enthusiastic about more and more for Porsche.
Language(s): German
ADVERTISING RATES:
Full Page Mono .... EUR 7300
Full Page Colour .... EUR 10500
Mechanical Data: Type Area: 247 x 187 mm, No. of Columns (Display): 3, Col Widths (Display): 44 mm
Copy instructions: *Copy Date:* 21 days prior to publication

CHRISTSEIN HEUTE 724331G87-2480
Editorial: Bodenborn 43, 58452 WITTEN
Tel: 2302 93093811 **Fax:** 2302 93093899
Email: schnepper@bundes-verlag.de **Web site:** http://www.christsein-heute.de
Freq: Monthly; **Annual Sub.:** EUR 61,80; **Circ:** 5,500
Editor: Arndt E. Schnepper; **Advertising Manager:** Thilo Cunz
Profile: Christian family magazine.
Language(s): German
ADVERTISING RATES:
Full Page Mono .... EUR 815
Full Page Colour .... EUR 1088
Mechanical Data: Type Area: 258 x 188 mm, No. of Columns (Display): 4, Col Widths (Display): 44 mm
Copy instructions: *Copy Date:* 20 days prior to publication
Supplement(s): FeG Forum
CONSUMER: RELIGIOUS

DIE CHRISTUS-POST 1833480G18B-2180
Editorial: Kölner Str. 15, 58553 HALVER
Tel: 2353 661455
Email: k.e.behling@cptv-online.de **Web site:** http://www.cptv-online.de
Freq: 5 issues yearly; **Cover Price:** Free; **Circ:** 3,500
Editor: Ernst Behling
Profile: To awaken, encourage and strengthen the faith and strengthening of community and connectedness we publish "Die Christus-Post". It brings the good news that Jesus Christ will be Lord of our lives. Appear in the magazine articles, some of which are written by colleagues. In addition, our journal brings information about our work and our meetings.
Language(s): German

CHROM & FLAMMEN 724337G77A-820
Editorial: Hertener Mark 7, 45699 HERTEN
Tel: 2366 808104 **Fax:** 2366 808149
Email: red.cuf@vest-netz.de
Freq: Monthly; **Annual Sub.:** EUR 44,00; **Circ:** 37,597
Editor: Michael Stein
Profile: Magazine about customised cars.
Language(s): Dutch; Flemish; German
Mechanical Data: Type Area: 260 x 184 mm, No. of Columns (Display): 3, Col Widths (Display): 48 mm
Copy instructions: *Copy Date:* 28 days prior to publication
CONSUMER: MOTORING & CYCLING: Motoring

CHROMATOGRAPHIA 724335G37-740
Editorial: Abraham-Lincoln-Str. 46, 65189 WIESBADEN **Tel:** 611 7878380 **Fax:** 611 7878439
Email: chromatographia@springer.com **Web site:** http://www.chromatographia.de
Freq: Monthly; **Annual Sub.:** EUR 2040,19
Editor: Petra Russkamp; **Advertising Manager:** Bianca Matzek
Profile: Journal about chromatography, electrophoresis and associated techniques.
Language(s): English
Mechanical Data: Type Area: 240 x 175 mm, No. of Columns (Display): 3
BUSINESS: PHARMACEUTICAL & CHEMISTS

CHRONOS 724343G79K-320
Editorial: Karlstr. 41, 89073 ULM **Tel:** 731 152002
Fax: 731 1520171
Email: chronos@ebnerverlag.de **Web site:** http://www.watchtime.net
Freq: 6 issues yearly; **Annual Sub.:** EUR 60,00; **Circ:** 20,031
Editor: Rüdiger Bucher; **Advertising Manager:** Andrea Scheungrab
Profile: Chronos writes for readers and buyers with an eye for technical quality, design, brand and luxury watches. As a clear market leader in supporting the Chronos watch magazines is years since first in the popularity of the reader the clear No. Objective is to provide watch and product at the highest level. Editorial content of watches are testing new products and market overviews and watch classics and brand-portraits. With understandable texts, so watch technology is clear and understandable. With depth, which underscores the claim of the competence issue. And with a fascinating product aesthetics, which arouses the reader's enthusiasm for the world of luxury brands Facebook: http://www.facebook.com/watchtime.net.
Language(s): German
Readership: Aimed at watch collectors.
ADVERTISING RATES:
Full Page Mono .... EUR 4450
Full Page Colour .... EUR 6250
Mechanical Data: Type Area: 245 x 175 mm, No. of Columns (Display): 3, Col Widths (Display): 55 mm
Copy instructions: *Copy Date:* 30 days prior to publication
CONSUMER: HOBBIES & DIY: Collectors Magazines

CICERO 1642128G82-9691
Editorial: Lennéstr. 1, 10785 BERLIN
Tel: 30 981941200 **Fax:** 30 981941299
Email: redaktion@cicero.de **Web site:** http://www.cicero.de
Freq: Monthly; **Annual Sub.:** EUR 84,00; **Circ:** 90,142
Editor: Michael Naumann
Profile: Sophisticated and opinion-writer for the magazine first-class journalism, a writing elite. Influential personalities of contemporary history and renowned journalists belong here monthly position on relevant issues of politics, economy and culture. Facebook: http://www.facebook.com/CiceroMagazin Twitter: http://twitter.com/#!/cicero_online This Outlet offers RSS (Really Simple Syndication).
Language(s): German
ADVERTISING RATES:
Full Page Mono .... EUR 14500
Full Page Colour .... EUR 14500
Mechanical Data: No. of Columns (Display): 3, Col Widths (Display): 53 mm, Type Area: 268 x 177 mm
Copy instructions: *Copy Date:* 17 days prior to publication
CONSUMER: CURRENT AFFAIRS & POLITICS

CII CANCER IMMUNOLOGY IMMUNOTHERAPY 724347G56A-2100
Editorial: Tiergartenstr. 17, 69121 HEIDELBERG
Tel: 6221 4870 **Fax:** 6221 4878366
Email: subscriptions@springer.com **Web site:** http://www.springerlink.com
Freq: Monthly; **Annual Sub.:** EUR 4337,00; **Circ:** 296
Editor: G. Pawelec
Profile: Magazine on cancer immunology immunotherapy.
Language(s): English
ADVERTISING RATES:
Full Page Mono .... EUR 740
Full Page Colour .... EUR 1780
Mechanical Data: Type Area: 240 x 175 mm
Official Journal of: Organ d. Association for Cancer Immunotherapy

CIM CONFERENCE & INCENTIVE MANAGEMENT 724348G2C-10
Editorial: Hilpertstr. 3, 64295 DARMSTADT
Tel: 6151 39070 **Fax:** 6151 3907959
Email: k.hoffmann@cimunity.com **Web site:** http://www.cimunity.com
Freq: 6 issues yearly; **Annual Sub.:** EUR 42,80; **Circ:** 20,472
Editor: Kerstin Hoffmann; **Advertising Manager:** Ellen Hellbusch
Profile: cim Conference & Incentive Management is the business magazine for the convention, incentive and event happenings. Focus on current issues, trends and techniques of the meetings and incentive industry and are targeted event marketing - both globally and locally. Committed researched and published by a competent team of journalists. cim is independent and guarantees a free, unbound association coverage.
Language(s): English; German
ADVERTISING RATES:
Full Page Mono .... EUR 5100
Full Page Colour .... EUR 6200
Mechanical Data: Type Area: 255 x 181 mm, No. of Columns (Display): 4, Col Widths (Display): 42 mm
Copy instructions: *Copy Date:* 30 days prior to publication
BUSINESS: COMMUNICATIONS, ADVERTISING & MARKETING: Conferences & Exhibitions

CIM ONLINE 1704282G14A-9824
Editorial: Hilpertstr. 3, 64295 DARMSTADT
Tel: 6151 3907951 **Fax:** 6151 3907959
Email: k.hoffmann@cimunity.com **Web site:** http://www.cimunity.com
Freq: Daily; **Cover Price:** Paid; **Circ:** 28,098 Unique Users
Editor: Kerstin Hoffmann; **Advertising Manager:** Ellen Hellbusch
Profile: Internet Media: www.cimnuity.com is not only the updated daily supplement to the print editions, but also offers the CIMunity, the online community in the meetings industry, the ultimate networking platform. In addition, CIM includes an online job market, calendar with all important industry events, the database professional partner agency, et cetera. Twitter: http://twitter.com/#!/cim_kerstin This Outlet offers RSS (Really Simple Syndication).
Language(s): German
BUSINESS: COMMERCE, INDUSTRY & MANAGEMENT

CINEMA 724354G76A-220
Editorial: Christoph-Probst-Weg 1, 20251 HAMBURG **Tel:** 40 41312201 **Fax:** 40 41312024
Email: ajung@cinema.de **Web site:** http://www.cinema.de
Freq: Monthly; **Annual Sub.:** EUR 46,80; **Circ:** 79,549
Editor: Artur Jung
Profile: The young, digital film and lifestyle magazine - gives readers all the latest exclusive information and pictures about the world of film and film stars! With their expertise in the fields of cinema, digital lifestyle, celebrities, DVD and technology, cinema every month. Cinema is film and lifestyle. No other magazine combines the relevance and breadth of topic movie with the exclusivity of the young, digital lifestyle. Facebook: http://www.facebook.com/cinema.de.
Language(s): German
ADVERTISING RATES:
Full Page Mono .... EUR 14100
Full Page Colour .... EUR 14100
Mechanical Data: Type Area: 236 x 173 mm
Copy instructions: *Copy Date:* 28 days prior to publication
CONSUMER: MUSIC & PERFORMING ARTS: Cinema

CINEMA ONLINE 1620984G76A-1487
Editorial: Steinhauser Str. 1, 81677 MÜNCHEN
Tel: 89 92502404
Email: cinema@tomorrow-focus.de **Web site:** http://www.cinema.de
Freq: Daily; **Cover Price:** Paid; **Circ:** 1,056,495 Unique Users
Editor: Thomas Mende
Profile: Ezine: Cinema Online is current movie reviews, movie news and an archive of over 56,000 films, 24,000 DVDs and 98,000 actors the No. 1 site for all film fans in Germany. Facebook: http://www.facebook.com/cinema.de.
Language(s): German
CONSUMER: MUSIC & PERFORMING ARTS: Cinema

CIO 755776G14A-9222
Editorial: Lyonel-Feininger-Str. 26, 80807 MÜNCHEN
Tel: 89 36086517 **Fax:** 89 36086511
Email: redaktion@cio.de **Web site:** http://www.cio.de
Freq: 10 issues yearly; **Annual Sub.:** EUR 96,00; **Circ:** 9,489
Editor: Horst Ellermann; **Advertising Manager:** Sebastian Wörle
Profile: CIO Magazin provides eight times a year CIOs and business decision-makers of the top management level, the information base necessary to meet the increasing demands on strategic IT decisions and to understand and to realise the effective use of IT in business. With best practice the editors show the successful implementation of IT, preferably in globally established companies and multinational players. The strategic and economic aspects of IT are always in the foreground. In addition, CIO compactly provides the major technology trends and management techniques. Twitter: http://twitter.com/CIOredaktion.
Language(s): German
ADVERTISING RATES:
Full Page Mono .... EUR 11580
Full Page Colour .... EUR 11580
Mechanical Data: Type Area: 254 x 200 mm
BUSINESS: COMMERCE, INDUSTRY & MANAGEMENT

CIO 1622496G14A-9501
Editorial: Lyonel-Feininger-Str. 26, 80807 MÜNCHEN
Tel: 89 36086517 **Fax:** 89 36086511
Email: info@cio.de **Web site:** http://www.cio.de
Cover Price: Paid; **Circ:** 491,079 Unique Users
Editor: Horst Ellermann; **Advertising Manager:** Sebastian Wörle
Profile: Online IT-business magazine for business executives and senior management.
Language(s): German
BUSINESS: COMMERCE, INDUSTRY & MANAGEMENT

CIT PLUS 724366G55-32
Editorial: Rößlerstr. 90, 64293 DARMSTADT
Tel: 6151 8090240 **Fax:** 6151 8090184
Email: wolfgang.siess@wiley.com **Web site:** http://www.citplus.de
Freq: 9 issues yearly; Free to qualifying individuals
Annual Sub.: EUR 174,41; **Circ:** 25,795
Editor: Wolfgang Sieß; **Advertising Manager:** Roland Thomé
Profile: The procedural journal CITplus is in the German room one of the top destinations for comprehensive application-and practice-oriented articles, reports, interviews and product launches in the areas of process engineering, instrumentation and control technology and automation technology. As the official organ of ProcessNet, the merger of two trade associations and co-editor of VDI-GVC and DECHEMA, CITplus provides its readers the crucial and often exclusive (background) information for daily work. The editorial bandwidth ranges from pumps, compressors and compressed air for filter and separation technology, mechanical process and bulk solids technology and software to processes and procedures to instrumentation and automation.
Language(s): German
ADVERTISING RATES:
Full Page Mono .... EUR 5720
Full Page Colour .... EUR 7200
Mechanical Data: Type Area: 260 x 185 mm, No. of Columns (Display): 4, Col Widths (Display): 43 mm
Copy instructions: *Copy Date:* 14 days prior to publication
BUSINESS: APPLIED SCIENCE & LABORATORIES

CITY 724372G80-2060
Editorial: Alstädter Kirchenweg 43, 75175 PFORZHEIM **Tel:** 7231 313102 **Fax:** 7231 314394

Email: city-stadtmagazin@regiomarkt.de **Web site:** http://www.city-stadtmagazin.de
Freq: Monthly; **Annual Sub.:** EUR 24,00; **Circ:** 6,350
Editor: Claudius Fingberg; **Advertising Manager:** Claudius Fingberg
Profile: For over 22 years, there is the town magazine of Pforzheim City. Since then, we accompany the culture and events scene with the most comprehensive calendar of the region and provide information about music, beauty, jewelry, bands or catering events - anything that is in the region of interest.
Language(s): German
ADVERTISING RATES:
Full Page Mono .... EUR 894
Full Page Colour .... EUR 1571
Mechanical Data: Type Area: 250 x 190 mm
Copy instructions: *Copy Date:* 15 days prior to publication
CONSUMER: RURAL & REGIONAL INTEREST

CITY FASZINATIONEN
1898760G89A-12473
Editorial: Emil-Hoffmann-Str. 55, 50999 KÖLN
Tel: 2236 848814 **Fax:** 2236 848824
Email: es@ella-verlag.de **Web site:** http://www.city-faszinationen.de
Freq: Half-yearly; **Cover Price:** EUR 3,90; **Circ:** 28,500
Advertising Manager: Elke Latupersia
Profile: The magazine for Germany discoverer researched the best events, with information from neighboring countries and a guide for the whole family with the following topics: Active & Wellness - are walking and relaxation, excursions and holiday ideas, constant Categories: Cities portraits, child-friendly events, food, Cultural life, the best museums.
Language(s): German
ADVERTISING RATES:
Full Page Mono .... EUR 2660
Full Page Colour .... EUR 2660
Mechanical Data: Type Area: 249 x 178 mm

CITY FASZINATIONEN WEIHNACHTSMARKT
1898761G89A-12474
Editorial: Emil-Hoffmann-Str. 55, 50999 KÖLN
Tel: 2236 848814 **Fax:** 2236 848824
Email: es@ella-verlag.de **Web site:** http://www.city-faszinationen.de
Freq: Annual; **Cover Price:** EUR 6,00; **Circ:** 39,000
Advertising Manager: Elke Latuperisa
Profile: The groundbreaking magazine for Christmas lovers with large reports with atmospheric images and clear presentations by region with the following topics: the most beautiful Christmas markets, delicious recipes for the festival, exquisite gift ideas and Christmas stories worldwide.
Language(s): German
ADVERTISING RATES:
Full Page Mono .... EUR 2660
Full Page Colour .... EUR 2660
Mechanical Data: Type Area: 249 x 178 mm

CITY GUIDE
1665680G89A-11962
Editorial: Am Karlsbad 11, 10785 BERLIN
Tel: 30 2647480 **Fax:** 30 264748509
Email: susanna.weber@btm.de **Web site:** http://www.visitberlin.de
Freq: Annual; **Circ:** 100,000
Profile: Directory of hotels in the city of Berlin and the German federal state of Brandenburg.
Language(s): English; German
ADVERTISING RATES:
Full Page Mono .... EUR 3050
Full Page Colour .... EUR 3050
Mechanical Data: Type Area: 183 x 133 mm
Copy instructions: *Copy Date:* 74 days prior to publication

CITY GUIDE BOCHUM TOP TIPPS
1866767G89A-12437
Editorial: Kornharpener Str. 118, 44791 BOCHUM
Tel: 234 8102297 **Fax:** 234 8102296
Email: info@top-tipps.org **Web site:** http://www.top-tipps.org
Freq: Monthly; **Cover Price:** Free; **Circ:** 20,000
Profile: City Guide for Bochum, it presents the various dining establishments.
Language(s): German
Copy instructions: *Copy Date:* 21 days prior to publication

CITY GUIDE DORTMUND TOP TIPPS
1866768G89A-12438
Editorial: Kemnader Str. 13a, 44797 BOCHUM
Tel: 234 8102297 **Fax:** 234 8102296
Email: info@top-tipps.org **Web site:** http://www.top-tipps.org
Freq: Monthly; **Cover Price:** Free; **Circ:** 20,000
Profile: City Guide for Dortmund, it presents the various dining establishments.
Language(s): German

CITY GUIDE DRESDEN
1830181G89A-12405
Editorial: Prager Str. 2b, 01069 DRESDEN
Tel: 351 8007030 **Fax:** 351 8007070
Email: redaktion@maxity.de **Web site:** http://www.maxity.de
Freq: Annual; **Cover Price:** Free; **Circ:** 20,000
Editor: Christine Herzog; **Advertising Manager:** Cathleen Moosche
Profile: City Guide Dresden serves international overnight visitors to the city as well as foreign citizens to better focus on opportunities in the areas of dining, shopping, culture & education, and excursions and mobility, thereby contributing significantly to an even better tourism marketing Dresden.
Language(s): English
Mechanical Data: Type Area: 126 x 85 mm

CITY GUIDE DÜSSELDORF TOP TIPPS
1866769G89A-12439
Editorial: Kemnader Str. 13a, 44797 BOCHUM
Tel: 234 8102297 **Fax:** 234 8102296
Email: info@top-tipps.org **Web site:** http://www.top-tipps.org
Freq: Monthly; **Cover Price:** Free; **Circ:** 30,000
Profile: City Guide for Düsseldorf, it presents the various dining establishments.
Language(s): German

CITY GUIDE ESSEN TOP TIPPS
1866770G89A-12440
Editorial: Kemnader Str. 13a, 44797 BOCHUM
Tel: 234 8102297 **Fax:** 234 8102296
Email: info@top-tipps.org **Web site:** http://www.top-tipps.org
Freq: Monthly; **Cover Price:** Free; **Circ:** 30,000
Profile: City Guide for Essen, it presents the various dining establishments.
Language(s): German

CITY GUIDE WUPPERTAL TOP TIPPS
1866582G89A-12435
Editorial: Kemnader Str. 13a, 44797 BOCHUM
Tel: 234 8102297 **Fax:** 234 8102296
Email: info@top-tipps.org **Web site:** http://www.top-tipps.org
Freq: Monthly; **Cover Price:** Free; **Circ:** 20,000
Profile: City Guide for Wuppertal, it presents the various dining establishments.
Language(s): German

DER CITY-FÜHRER FÜR GASTRONOMIE UND FREIZEIT
724381G89A-440
Editorial: Markt 1, 41460 NEUSS **Tel:** 2131 21293
Fax: 2131 275760
Email: info@kuepping.de **Web site:** http://www.kuepping.de
Freq: Half-yearly; **Cover Price:** Free; **Circ:** 10,000
Editor: Frank Küpping; **Advertising Manager:** Frank Küpping
Profile: Gastronomy and leisure guide for Neuss.
Language(s): German
ADVERTISING RATES:
Full Page Mono .... EUR 565
Full Page Colour .... EUR 723
Mechanical Data: Type Area: 225 x 145 mm, No. of Columns (Display): 2, Col Widths (Display): 45 mm
Copy instructions: *Copy Date:* 10 days prior to publication

CLASSIC DRIVER
1661162G77A-2665
Editorial: Mittelweg 158b, 20148 HAMBURG
Tel: 40 28008320 **Fax:** 40 28008350
Email: jcr@classicdriver.de **Web site:** http://www.classicdriver.de
Cover Price: Paid; **Circ:** 312,983 Unique Users
Editor: Jan-Christian Richter
Profile: Classicdriver.com is the leading international website for classic and prestige cars. With articles published regularly in English/French/German it is seen by discerning car enthusiasts from all over the world as the website for the premium car sector, not only for information on News and Events, but also as a car marketplace without equal on the Internet. The Classic Driver website stands out with its sophisticated automobile database showing a wide range of very rare and expensive cars. High-quality editorial content features a broad range of stories about new cars, events and auctions. Facebook: http://www.facebook.com/classicdriver.de Twitter: http://twitter.com/#!/ClassicDriverDE.
Language(s): German
CONSUMER: MOTORING & CYCLING: Motoring

CLEVER REISEN!
727476G89A-11527
Editorial: Am Büschchen 2a, 47179 DUISBURG
Tel: 203 554248 **Fax:** 203 547970
Email: redaktion@fliegen-sparen.de **Web site:** http://www.clever-reisen-magazin.de
Freq: Quarterly; **Annual Sub.:** EUR 20,40; **Circ:** 29,445
Editor: Jürgen Zupancic
Profile: Magazine containing details about bargain holidays and the cheapest places for food and entertainment. Contains information and advice about money-saving tips and price comparisons.
Language(s): German
Readership: Aimed at holiday makers and travellers.
ADVERTISING RATES:
Full Page Mono .... EUR 1880
Full Page Colour .... EUR 3110
Mechanical Data: Type Area: 270 x 190 mm, No. of Columns (Display): 4, Col Widths (Display): 44 mm
Copy instructions: *Copy Date:* 30 days prior to publication
CONSUMER: HOLIDAYS & TRAVEL: Travel

CLICK
1626964G49C-84
Editorial: Dießemer Bruch 167, 47805 KREFELD
Tel: 2151 5100118 **Fax:** 2151 5100215
Email: click@stuenings.de **Web site:** http://www.click-a-truck.com
Freq: Annual; **Cover Price:** EUR 2,50; **Circ:** 45,000
Editor: Lutz Gerritzen; **Advertising Manager:** Cornelia Assen
Profile: Business directory of Internet addresses around the truck around. At 182 pages, over 400 categories has an answer Click on all of your questions about commercial vehicle. To move more quickly to their destination, the main groups TRUCK, BUS, CONSTRUCTION WORKSHOP and are divided into four sectors, the headings - each in German and English - are arranged alphabetically.
Language(s): English; German
ADVERTISING RATES:
Full Page Mono .... EUR 1980
Full Page Colour .... EUR 1980
Mechanical Data: Type Area: 185 x 85 mm
Copy instructions: *Copy Date:* 60 days prior to publication

CLINICAL AUTONOMIC RESEARCH CAR
765228G56A-11110
Editorial: Tiergartenstr. 17, 69121 HEIDELBERG
Tel: 6221 4870 **Fax:** 6221 4878366
Email: subscriptions@springer.com **Web site:** http://www.springer.com
Freq: 6 issues yearly; **Annual Sub.:** EUR 1472,00; **Circ:** 500
Editor: Horacio Kaufmann
Profile: Clinical Autonomic Research car aims to draw together and disseminate research work from various disciplines and specialties dealing with clinical problems resulting from autonomic dysfunction. Areas to be covered include: cardiovascular system, neurology, diabetes, endocrinology, urology, pain disorders, ophthalmology, gastroenterology, toxicology and clinical pharmacology, skin infectious diseases, renal disease. This journal is an essential source of new information for everyone working in areas involving the autonomic nervous system. A major feature of Clinical Autonomic Research car is its speed of publication coupled with the highest refereeing standards.
Language(s): English
Copy instructions: *Copy Date:* 21 days prior to publication
Official Journal of: Organ d. American Autonomic Society, d. Clinical Autonomic Research Society u. d. European Federation of Autonomic Societies

CLINICAL NEURORADIOLOGY
732881G56A-6000
Editorial: Josef-Schneider-Str. 11, 97080 WÜRZBURG
Email: solymosi@neuroradiologie.uni-wuerzburg.de
Web site: http://www.clinical-neuroradiology.org
Freq: Quarterly; **Annual Sub.:** EUR 219,00; **Circ:** 1,000
Editor: László Solymosi
Profile: Clinical Neuroradiology provides current information, original contributions, and reviews in the field of neuroradiology. An interdisciplinary approach is accomplished by diagnostic and therapeutic contributions related to associated subjects. The international coverage and relevance of the journal is underlined by its being the official journal of the German, Swiss, and Austrian Societies of Neuroradiology.
Language(s): English; German
ADVERTISING RATES:
Full Page Mono .... EUR 1300
Full Page Colour .... EUR 2400
Mechanical Data: Type Area: 240 x 174 mm
Official Journal of: Organ d. Dt., Österr. u. Schweizer. Ges. f. Neuroradiologie

CLINICAL ORAL INVESTIGATIONS
724429G56D-140
Editorial: Tiergartenstr. 17, 69121 HEIDELBERG
Tel: 6221 4870 **Fax:** 6221 4878366
Email: subscriptions@springer.com **Web site:** http://www.springerlink.com
Freq: 6 issues yearly; **Annual Sub.:** EUR 464,00; **Circ:** 175
Editor: G. Schmalz
Profile: International journal focusing on all aspects of dentistry, includes oral and maxillofacial science, orthodontics, dental materials, epidemiology, preventive dentistry and related issues.
Language(s): English
ADVERTISING RATES:
Full Page Mono .... EUR 740
Full Page Colour .... EUR 1780
Mechanical Data: Type Area: 240 x 175 mm
Official Journal of: Organ d. Dt. Ges. f. Zahn-, Mund- u. Kieferheilkunde
BUSINESS: HEALTH & MEDICAL: Dental

CLINICAL RESEARCH IN CARDIOLOGY
748682G56A-10680
Editorial: Tiergartenstr. 17, 69121 HEIDELBERG
Tel: 6221 4878819 **Fax:** 6221 48768819
Email: denskus.steinkopff@springer.com **Web site:** http://www.springermedizin.de
Freq: Monthly; **Annual Sub.:** EUR 263,90; **Circ:** 2,700
Profile: Clinical Research in Cardiology is an international journal for clinical cardiovascular research. It provides a forum for original and review articles as well as critical perspective articles. The journal regularly receives articles from the field of clinical cardiology, angiology, as well as heart and vascular surgery. As the official journal of the German Cardiac Society, it gives a current and competent survey on the diagnosis and therapy of heart and vascular diseases.
Language(s): English; German
ADVERTISING RATES:
Full Page Mono .... EUR 1460
Full Page Colour .... EUR 2780
Mechanical Data: Type Area: 240 x 174 mm
Official Journal of: Organ d. Dt. Ges. f. Kardiologie - Herz- u. Kreislaufforschung e.V. in Kooperation m. d. ArGe Leitender Kardiolog. Krankenhausärzte, d. Dt. Ges. f. Pädiatr. Kardiologie, d. Dt. Ges. f. Prävention u. Rehabilitation v. Herz-Kreislauferkrankungen e.V. u. d. Sektion Kardiologie im Berufsverb. Dt. Internisten e.V.
BUSINESS: HEALTH & MEDICAL

CLIO
724432G74G-19
Editorial: Bamberger Str. 51, 10777 BERLIN
Tel: 30 2139597 **Fax:** 30 2141927
Email: ffgzberlin@snafu.de **Web site:** http://www.ffgz.de
Freq: Half-yearly; **Annual Sub.:** EUR 20,40; **Circ:** 3,000
Editor: Petra Bentz; **Advertising Manager:** Cornelia Burgert
Profile: clio - The Journal of Women's Health - includes feminist assessments of health policy and women's health-related topics as well as extensive information on diseases and their treatment options. Noteworthy is the simple and understandable language of clio. The special is also that it is written by women from the health sector as well as from the perspective of those affected. Basic items can be looked up for years.
Language(s): German
Readership: Aimed at women between 20 and 60 years of age.
ADVERTISING RATES:
Full Page Mono .... EUR 456
Mechanical Data: Type Area: 270 x 180 mm, No. of Columns (Display): 2, Col Widths (Display): 82 mm
Copy instructions: *Copy Date:* 60 days prior to publication
CONSUMER: WOMEN'S INTEREST CONSUMER MAGAZINES: Slimming & Health

CLIPS
755780G15B-401
Editorial: Wilhelm-Backhaus-Str. 2, 50931 KÖLN
Tel: 221 9440670 **Fax:** 221 94406710
Email: redaktion@clips-verlag.de **Web site:** http://www.clips-verlag.de
Freq: Monthly; **Annual Sub.:** EUR 78,00; **Circ:** 10,238
Editor: Heidrun Barbie; **Advertising Manager:** Christine Berthold
Profile: Clips For the stylist: The magazine with a young look, fresh ideas, bold, simple, practical, critical and open-minded. Clips says, where it's in fashion and consumer trends. We make concepts for success clear and give you tips for a successful salon marketing and information on the latest products. Clips CHeF-inFO: The monthly booklet of ideas for chefs and managers. In the CHeF-inFO are information necessary to business and marketing technical control of a hairdressing company required. A compass for market success in terms of associations, tax, legal and personnel policy. Clips JuniOr: pure motivation for the next generation. Because of the success of tomorrow starts with the enthusiasm and knowledge to the job today.
Language(s): German
ADVERTISING RATES:
Full Page Mono .... EUR 2340
Full Page Colour .... EUR 4095
Mechanical Data: Type Area: 270 x 190 mm, No. of Columns (Display): 4, Col Widths (Display): 42 mm
Copy instructions: *Copy Date:* 40 days prior to publication
BUSINESS: COSMETICS & HAIRDRESSING: Hairdressing

CLIVIA
724433G94H-2280
Editorial: Breslauer Str. 300, 90471 NÜRNBERG
Tel: 911 8920195 **Fax:** 911 8920232
Email: vertrieb@clivia.de **Web site:** http://www.clivia-magazin.de
Freq: Monthly; **Cover Price:** Free; **Circ:** 158,607
Editor: Kristine Fiedler
Profile: Magazine containing articles about hair and cosmetics distributed via barber shops.
Language(s): German
ADVERTISING RATES:
Full Page Mono .... EUR 10650
Full Page Colour .... EUR 10650
Mechanical Data: Type Area: 240 x 193 mm, No. of Columns (Display): 4, Col Widths (Display): 43 mm
Copy instructions: *Copy Date:* 47 days prior to publication
CONSUMER: OTHER CLASSIFICATIONS: Customer Magazines

CLOPPENBURGER WOCHENBLATT
724435G72-2984
Editorial: Emsteker Str. 14, 49661 CLOPPENBURG
Tel: 4471 922544 **Fax:** 4471 922542
Email: redaktion@mev-online.de **Web site:** http://www.mev-online.de
Freq: Weekly; **Cover Price:** Free; **Circ:** 60,019
Editor: Gaby Westerkamp; **Advertising Manager:** Andreas Ludmann
Profile: Advertising journal (house-to-house) concentrating on local stories.
Language(s): German
ADVERTISING RATES:
Full Page Mono .... EUR 3125
Full Page Colour .... EUR 4007
Mechanical Data: Type Area: 420 x 280 mm, No. of Columns (Display): 6, Col Widths (Display): 44 mm
Copy instructions: *Copy Date:* 2 days prior to publication
LOCAL NEWSPAPERS

CME
1663526G56A-11334
Editorial: Tiergartenstr. 17, 69121 HEIDELBERG
Tel: 6221 4878322 **Fax:** 6221 48768322
Email: sonja.kempinski@springer.com **Web site:** http://cme.springer.de
Freq: Monthly; **Annual Sub.:** EUR 219,00; **Circ:** 61,441
Editor: Sonja Kempinski; **Advertising Manager:** Michaela Schmitz
Profile: "CME" offers the practitioner premium training for medical practice. The heart of each issue are three special didactic specially prepared contributions, which are the main themes from daily practice comprehensive and easy to understand present. For documentation of the gained knowledge, participants can answer questions of certification. Presentations of current clinical trials, interesting interviews and case studies round out the journal for the family doctor.
Language(s): German
ADVERTISING RATES:
Full Page Mono .... EUR 5050
Full Page Colour .... EUR 6600
Mechanical Data: Type Area: 240 x 174 mm
BUSINESS: HEALTH & MEDICAL

CN BMW VETERANEN-CLUB NACHRICHTEN
1826439G77A-2825
Editorial: Bahnhofstr. 17, 35745 HERBORN
Tel: 2772 41665 **Fax:** 2772 41666
Email: info@bmw-veteranenclub.de **Web site:** http://www.bmw-veteranenclub.de
Freq: Quarterly; **Circ:** 1,800
Editor: Rüdiger Jopp
Profile: Club magazine, oldtimer cars.
Language(s): German
ADVERTISING RATES:
Full Page Mono .... EUR 464
Full Page Colour .... EUR 464
Copy instructions: *Copy Date:* 15 days prior to publication

COACH MEN'S HEALTH
1911553G86C-242
Editorial: Leverkusenstr. 54, 22761 HAMBURG
Tel: 40 8533030 **Fax:** 40 853303933
Email: leserbriefe@menshealth.de **Web site:** http://www.menshealth.de
Freq: Quarterly; **Cover Price:** EUR 5,00; **Circ:** 100,000
Editor: Wolfgang Melcher; **Advertising Manager:** Sascha Gröschel
Profile: Magazine covering health and fashion. Facebook: http://www.facebook.com/MensHealth.de Twitter: http://twitter.com/#!/menshealth_de.
Language(s): German
ADVERTISING RATES:
Full Page Mono .... EUR 6000
Full Page Colour .... EUR 6000
Mechanical Data: Type Area: 250 x 210 mm
Copy instructions: *Copy Date:* 46 days prior to publication

COBRA NEWS
2056911G77A-2978
Editorial: Alfons-Härtel-Weg 8, 70567 STUTTGART
Tel: 711 6339335
Email: dietmar.mettke@cobra-ig.de **Web site:** http://www.cobra-ig.de
Freq: 3 issues yearly; **Cover Price:** EUR 10,00; **Circ:** 500
Editor: Dietmar Mettke; **Advertising Manager:** Dietmar Mettke
Profile: Car magazine.
Language(s): German
ADVERTISING RATES:
Full Page Mono .... EUR 100
Full Page Colour .... EUR 175

COBURGER TAGEBLATT
724468G67B-3860
Editorial: Hindenburgstr. 3a, 96450 COBURG
Tel: 9561 888100 **Fax:** 9561 888102
Email: info@infranken.de **Web site:** http://www.infranken.de
Freq: 312 issues yearly; **Circ:** 14,170
Editor: Oliver Schmidt; **Advertising Manager:** Stefan Apfel
Profile: Daily newspaper with regional news and a local sports section. Facebook: http://www.facebook.com/pages/inFrankende/209363937665.
Language(s): German
ADVERTISING RATES:
SCC .... EUR 42,70
Mechanical Data: No. of Columns (Display): 6, Col Widths (Display): 45 mm, Type Area: 430 x 285 mm
Copy instructions: *Copy Date:* 1 day prior to publication
Supplement(s): doppio; Lebens Raum; rtv
REGIONAL DAILY & SUNDAY NEWSPAPERS: Regional Daily Newspapers

COCHEMER WOCHENSPIEGEL
724470G72-2992
Editorial: Rosengasse, 56727 MAYEN
Tel: 2651 981800 **Fax:** 2651 981814
Email: red-cochem@wvm-verlag.de **Web site:** http://www.wochenspiegellive.de
Freq: Weekly; **Cover Price:** Free; **Circ:** 21,081
Editor: Mario Zender; **Advertising Manager:** Frank Günther
Profile: Advertising journal (house-to-house) concentrating on local stories.
Language(s): German
ADVERTISING RATES:
Full Page Mono .... EUR 2740
Full Page Colour .... EUR 3823
Mechanical Data: Type Area: 430 x 290 mm, No. of Columns (Display): 7, Col Widths (Display): 38 mm
Copy instructions: *Copy Date:* 2 days prior to publication
LOCAL NEWSPAPERS

COFFEE
1995168G74P-1333
Editorial: Leuschnerstr. 1, 70174 STUTTGART
Tel: 711 2070305500 **Fax:** 711 2070305501
Email: redaktion@magnus.de **Web site:** http://www.coffee-magazin.de
Freq: Quarterly; **Cover Price:** EUR 4,90; **Circ:** 60,000
Editor: Dirk Waasen; **Advertising Manager:** Vasili Tsialos
Profile: Magazine for technology enthusiasts and coffee lovers interested in the purchase decision for the right machine is this new Special Edition is the ideal companion. Consumer-oriented product testing be added to topics from A to accessories and aroma with plenty of information, background knowledge and reading fun rounded. Coffee is for coffee lovers and fans of high-quality machines for the coffee, cappuccino or latte macchiato not only drinks, but are a piece of the spirit of the age.
Language(s): German
ADVERTISING RATES:
Full Page Mono .... EUR 5900
Full Page Colour .... EUR 5900
Mechanical Data: Type Area: 250 x 185 mm, No. of Columns (Display): 4, Col Widths (Display): 43 mm

COFFEE & MORE
1898762G74P-1287
Editorial: Postfach 102126, 42765 HAAN
Tel: 2104 173681 **Fax:** 2104 177589
Email: coffeeundmore@meisenbach.de **Web site:** http://www.coffeeandmoremagazin.de
Freq: Half-yearly; **Circ:** 97,000
Editor: Matthias M. Machan; **Advertising Manager:** Dominik Lippold
Profile: The special interest publisher in the coffee cult sees itself as a stimulant for stimulating trade and consumers. With information on the latest equipment (fully automatic capsule-and-pad systems, filter presses) on the market, a lot of trends and coffee knowledge, interviews, recipes and accessories associated with the brown bean. Germany lives and staged the coffee. Coffee lifestyle, the expression of a distinctive ambience. "Coffee & more" conveys this feeling of "Generation Coffee.
Language(s): German
ADVERTISING RATES:
Full Page Mono .... EUR 6599
Full Page Colour .... EUR 8160
Mechanical Data: Type Area: 253 x 185 mm
Supplement to: Elektromarkt

COLLOID AND POLYMER SCIENCE
724492G37-760
Editorial: Linnéstr. 5, 04103 LEIPZIG
Tel: 341 9732550 **Fax:** 341 9732599
Email: kremer@physik.uni-leipzig.de **Web site:** http://www.springerlink.com
Freq: 18 issues yearly; **Annual Sub.:** EUR 4325,00; **Circ:** 188
Editor: F. Kremer
Profile: Magazine on colloid and polymer sciences.
Language(s): English
ADVERTISING RATES:
Full Page Mono .... EUR 740
Full Page Colour .... EUR 1780
Mechanical Data: Type Area: 240 x 175 mm
Official Journal of: Organ d. Kolloid-Ges.

COLOPROCTOLOGY
724496G56A-2160
Editorial: Aschauer Str. 30, 81549 MÜNCHEN
Tel: 89 2030431300 **Fax:** 89 2030431399
Email: th.hager@web.de **Web site:** http://www.springermedizin.de
Freq: 6 issues yearly; Free to qualifying individuals
Annual Sub.: EUR 230,00; **Circ:** 3,800
Editor: Thorolf Hager; **Advertising Manager:** Renate Senfft
Profile: Coloproctologists find current, interdisciplinary and practice-relevant original papers and educational contributions. The Journal Club is a critical overview of the major international publications from the pen of the leading Coloproctologists of Germany. All the important news and personalities from the field of coloproctological societies are published here.
Language(s): English; German
Readership: Aimed at doctors and dermatologists.
ADVERTISING RATES:
Full Page Mono .... EUR 2400
Full Page Colour .... EUR 3650
Mechanical Data: Type Area: 240 x 174 mm
Official Journal of: Organ d. Dt. Ges. f. Koloproktologie, d. Bundesverb. d. Coloproktologen Deutschlands, d. ArGe f. Coloproctologie d. Österr. Ges. f. Chirurgie u. d. Schweizer. AG f. Koloproktologie
BUSINESS: HEALTH & MEDICAL

COLORFOTO
724497G85A-140
Editorial: Richard-Reitzner-Allee 2, 85540 HAAR
Tel: 89 255561731 **Fax:** 89 255561186
Email: redaktion@colorfoto.de **Web site:** http://www.colorfoto.de
Freq: Monthly; **Cover Price:** EUR 5,50; **Circ:** 39,374
Editor: Werner Lüttgens; **Advertising Manager:** Michael Hackenberg
Profile: ColorFoto is serious and competent buyers guide guide for beginners, advanced amateur photographers and semi-professionals. The editorial focus is on the field of digital photography. Magazine Content: practical tips, tests, buying advice and outstanding works of renowned photographers for beginners, amateurs, semi-professionals and professionals of the analog and digital photography.
Language(s): German
ADVERTISING RATES:
Full Page Mono .... EUR 8213
Full Page Colour .... EUR 10950
Mechanical Data: Type Area: 250 x 185 mm, No. of Columns (Display): 4, Col Widths (Display): 43 mm
Copy instructions: *Copy Date:* 29 days prior to publication
CONSUMER: PHOTOGRAPHY & FILM MAKING: Photography

COM!
724531G5E-29
Editorial: Bayerstr. 16a, 80335 MÜNCHEN
Tel: 89 74117302 **Fax:** 89 74117132
Email: redaktion@com-magazin.de **Web site:** http://www.com-magazin.de
Freq: Monthly; **Annual Sub.:** EUR 39,90; **Circ:** 199,693
Editor: Roland Bischoff; **Advertising Manager:** Bettina Günther
Profile: Germany's high-circulation monthly PC-title writes about technical innovations in computing and the internet. Readers of com! are highly motivated, applications-oriented with a strong buying potential. The editorial contents of com! is news-oriented with background information and test reports and is as well a guidebook with a high benefit for ambitious computer users. News up to date information, more than just the news Computing PC-applications Internet everything around the technical side of the internet Test Reports test reports to help to find the most suitable products Tips & Tricks solutions for difficult PC problems CD/DVD all programmes and data that the reader needs in addition to the magazine.
Language(s): German
ADVERTISING RATES:
Full Page Mono .... EUR 12360
Full Page Colour .... EUR 12360
Mechanical Data: Type Area: 231 x 175 mm
Copy instructions: *Copy Date:* 25 days prior to publication
BUSINESS: COMPUTERS & AUTOMATION: Data Transmission

CO'MED
724501G56A-2180
Editorial: Rüdesheimer Str. 40, 65239 HOCHHEIM
Tel: 6146 907412 **Fax:** 6146 907444
Email: redaktion@comedverlag.de **Web site:** http://www.comedverlag.de
Freq: Monthly; Free to qualifying individuals
Annual Sub.: EUR 90,00; **Circ:** 12,098
Editor: Manfred Maiworm; **Advertising Manager:** Manfred Maiworm
Profile: Magazine for Complementary Medicine. Platform to get regular updates on developments in the field of Complementary Medicine replace and expand existing concepts. Whether traditional or natural healing energy regulatory proceedings, whether in addition or as an alternative to conventional medicine used - only the connection in diagnosis and therapy can capture the complex human system in its individuality and provide appropriate solutions. Co'Med thus makes a decisive contribution to the shift in consciousness in medicine and the changing health care system are new landmarks.
Language(s): German
ADVERTISING RATES:
Full Page Mono .... EUR 2400
Full Page Colour .... EUR 3105
Mechanical Data: Type Area: 260 x 185 mm, No. of Columns (Display): 4, Col Widths (Display): 44 mm
Copy instructions: *Copy Date:* 25 days prior to publication
Official Journal of: Organ d. B.I.T.-Ärzte-Ges., d. Freien Verb. Dt. Heilpraktiker, d. Ges. f. therapeut. Hypnose, d. Arbeitgebervereinigung d. Heilberufler, d. Europ. Verb. f. Kinesiologie, d. Dt. Ges. f. Energet. u. Informationsmedizin u. d. Bund DT. Heilpraktiker u. Naturheilkundiger
BUSINESS: HEALTH & MEDICAL

COMMUNICATIO SOCIALIS
724529G2A-740
Editorial: Ostenstr. 26, 85072 EICHSTÄTT
Tel: 8421 931562 **Fax:** 8421 931786
Email: walter.hoemberg@ku-eichstaett.de **Web site:** http://www.communicatio-socialis.de
Freq: Quarterly; **Annual Sub.:** EUR 43,20; **Circ:** 500
Editor: Walter Hömberg; **Advertising Manager:** Sabrina Reusch
Profile: Magazine on theology and the sciences of communication.
Language(s): English; German
ADVERTISING RATES:
Full Page Mono .... EUR 350
Full Page Colour .... EUR 350
Mechanical Data: Type Area: 195 x 115 mm
Copy instructions: *Copy Date:* 28 days prior to publication

COMPACT
724532G27-400
Editorial: Kaiser-Wilhelm-Str. 100, 47166 DUISBURG
Tel: 203 5224515 **Fax:** 203 5225707
Email: christiane.hoch-baumann@thyssenkrupp.com
Web site: http://www.thyssenkrupp-steel-europe.com
Freq: 3 issues yearly; **Circ:** 6,000
Editor: Christiane Hoch-Baumann
Profile: Company publication published by ThyssenKrupp Steel AG.
Language(s): English; German

COMPUTATIONAL MECHANICS
768414G19A-1050
Editorial: Appelstr. 11, 30167 HANNOVER
Email: wriggers@ikm.uni-hannover.de **Web site:** http://www.springerlink.com
Freq: Monthly; **Annual Sub.:** EUR 3506,00; **Circ:** 106
Editor: P. Wriggers
Profile: Magazine on computer based mechanics.
Language(s): English
ADVERTISING RATES:
Full Page Mono .... EUR 740
Full Page Colour .... EUR 1780
Mechanical Data: Type Area: 240 x 175 mm

COMPUTER BILD
724543G78E-10
Editorial: Axel-Springer-Platz 1, 20355 HAMBURG
Tel: 40 34724300 **Fax:** 40 34724683
Email: presse@computerbild.de **Web site:** http://www.computerbild.de
Freq: 26 issues yearly; **Annual Sub.:** EUR 96,20; **Circ:** 537,202
Editor: Hans-Martin Burr; **Advertising Manager:** Holger Braack
Profile: Since its launch in September 1996 COMPUTER BILD accompanies technical progress objectively and professionally. Over 4 million readers benefit from the numerous tests, courses and reports. Offered will be profound know-how for the safe and efficient use of PC and Internet, application guides and buying advice on the areas of telecommunications and consumer electronics round out the profile. All easy to understand and with a lot of reading fun. COMPUTER BILD readers are familiar with the latest technical achievements. For it is no longer just the PC that is in focus. They are interested in the entire world of multimedia. Facebook: http://www.facebook.com/COMPUTERBILD.
Language(s): German
Readership: Aimed at the professional personal end user.
ADVERTISING RATES:
Full Page Mono .... EUR 24900
Full Page Colour .... EUR 24900
Mechanical Data: Type Area: 299 x 207 mm, No. of Columns (Display): 4, Col Widths (Display): 50 mm
CONSUMER: CONSUMER ELECTRONICS: Home Computing

COMPUTER RESELLER NEWS
724556G5C-1
Editorial: Gruber Str. 46a, 85586 POING
Tel: 8121 951559 **Fax:** 8121 951597
Email: markus.reuter@cmp-weka.de **Web site:** http://www.crn.de
Freq: Weekly; **Cover Price:** Free; **Circ:** 25,332
Editor: Markus Reuter; **Advertising Manager:** Sandra Hanel
Profile: Computer Reseller News, the trade publication for professional dealers, integrators and system vendors will, in the IT / TK used-successfully and in the UE-Channel as the main medium for years. Exclusive information from the upper echelons of German manufacturers, distributors and systems houses are also part of the core elements of Computer Reseller News as solid background reports, thoroughly researched facts and rigorous analysis. Facebook: http://www.facebook.com/crn.de.
Language(s): German
ADVERTISING RATES:
Full Page Colour .... EUR 12950
Mechanical Data: Type Area: 360 x 260 mm, No. of Columns (Display): 5, Col Widths (Display): 48 mm
Copy instructions: *Copy Date:* 10 days prior to publication
Supplement(s): Distribution Extra; IT-Solutions; Solution Extra
BUSINESS: COMPUTERS & AUTOMATION: Professional Personal Computers

COMPUTER SCIENCE - RESEARCH AND DEVELOPMENT
731107G5B-78_30
Editorial: Tiergartenstr. 17, 69121 HEIDELBERG
Tel: 6221 4870 **Fax:** 6221 4878366
Email: subscriptions@springer.com **Web site:** http://www.springerlink.com
Freq: Quarterly; **Annual Sub.:** EUR 512,00; **Circ:** 1,000
Editor: Sabine Glesner
Profile: Journal concerned with research and development in information studies.
Language(s): German
ADVERTISING RATES:
Full Page Mono .... EUR 920
Full Page Colour .... EUR 1960
Mechanical Data: Type Area: 240 x 175 mm
Official Journal of: Organ d. Ges. f. Informatik e.V.
BUSINESS: COMPUTERS & AUTOMATION: Data Processing

COMPUTER SPEZIAL
724559G4A-7
Editorial: Avenwedder Str. 55, 33335 GÜTERSLOH
Tel: 5241 8090884 **Fax:** 5241 80690880
Email: burkhard.froehlich@bauverlag.de **Web site:** http://www.bauverlag.de
Freq: Half-yearly; **Cover Price:** EUR 20,00; **Circ:** 49,107
Editor: Burkhard Fröhlich; **Advertising Manager:** Andreas Kirchgessner
Profile: computer spezial with treatment in addition to the issues of CAD and AVA / configuration software for architects, engineers and builders and the area of hardware and accessories. As a supplement to the journals DBZ Deutsche Bauzeitschrift, Bauwelt, TAB Technik am Bau, Bauhandwerk, Baumarkt + Bauwirtschaft and tis Tiefbau Ingenieurbau Straßenbau, the issue achieved virtually all of a construction project stakeholders such as architects, engineers, companies and institutions. By working closely with the developers of the editors and distributors of construction software reflects the magazine reflects the current state of this market. Success stories give the reader valuable tips for the everyday use of the computer and the Internet. On the hardware and accessories side are printers, plotters, video and data entry technology, the focus of the article, is also sporadic reports of peripheral areas of the relevant products for building computer applications (eg, photogrammetry, facility management). This concept makes computer spezial to an important information, not just for architects and engineers, but also for craftsmen of various trades.
Language(s): German
Readership: Aimed at architects and the building trade.
ADVERTISING RATES:
Full Page Mono .... EUR 5550
Full Page Colour .... EUR 7540
Mechanical Data: Type Area: 270 x 186 mm, No. of Columns (Display): 4, Col Widths (Display): 45 mm
Copy instructions: *Copy Date:* 16 days prior to publication
Supplement to: bauhandwerk, Bauwelt, DBZ Deutsche BauZeitschrift, Facility Management, TAB Technik am Bau
BUSINESS: ARCHITECTURE & BUILDING: Architecture

COMPUTER UND ARBEIT
724548G5R-632
Editorial: Heddernheimer Landstr. 144, 60439 FRANKFURT **Tel:** 69 79501030 **Fax:** 69 133077665
Email: redaktion@cua-web.de **Web site:** http://www.cua-web.de
Freq: 11 issues yearly; **Annual Sub.:** EUR 87,60; **Circ:** 3,875
Editor: Olaf Lutz; **Advertising Manager:** Peter Beuther
Profile: »Computer und Arbeit« is a specialty magazine for works councils. For 20 years it taught knowledge, need the works councils to cope with the spread of information and communication technology (ICT), associated tasks. Experienced authors analyze carefully ICT systems under technical, legal and data protection issues. Numerous practical examples and sample-operation and servicing agreements to help the works councils in developing their own solutions in operations and administrations. A comprehensive magazine section offers the latest news. Permanent themes: participation practice, ICT use in enterprises and government agencies, technology trends, data protection, ICT Law, PC use in the works councils office.
Language(s): German
ADVERTISING RATES:
Full Page Mono .... EUR 1080
Full Page Colour .... EUR 1350
Mechanical Data: Type Area: 247 x 180 mm
Copy instructions: *Copy Date:* 20 days prior to publication
BUSINESS: COMPUTERS & AUTOMATION: Computers Related

COMPUTER & AUTOMATION
724562G5-800
Editorial: Parkweg 11, 87719 MINDELHEIM
Tel: 8261 737603 **Fax:** 8261 70183
Email: redaktion@computer-automation.de **Web site:** http://www.computer-automation.de
Freq: Monthly; **Annual Sub.:** EUR 78,40; **Circ:** 26,874
Editor: Meinrad Happacher; **Advertising Manager:** Peter Eberhard
Profile: Benefit from Computer & Automation for your advertising success. The media brand Computer & Automation provides high quality editorial, targeted circulation and a high credibility amongst decision makers in manufacturing and processing industries. Monthly automation magazine Computer & Automation reports about all topics from the complete automation pyramid of the manufacturing and processing industries. Successful crossmedia campaigns are based on advertising in the monthly technical journal Computer & Automation, the web service www.computer-automation.de and the weekly automation newsletter.Tailor made and 24 hours a day www.computer-automation.de reports about all topics from the complete automation pyramid of the manufacturing and processing industries. Plus, your ad in the automation newsletter reaches decision makers in manufacturing and processing industries each week offering tailor made news, products and expert knowledge. The media brand Computer & Automation supports suppliers in automation to increase their communications success.
Language(s): German
Readership: Aimed at electrotechnical engineers, company management and designers of automated machinery.
ADVERTISING RATES:
Full Page Mono .... EUR 5290
Full Page Colour .... EUR 7380
Mechanical Data: Type Area: 262 x 195 mm, No. of Columns (Display): 4, Col Widths (Display): 43 mm
BUSINESS: COMPUTERS & AUTOMATION

COMPUTER UND RECHT
724564G5R-690
Editorial: Gustav-Heinemann-Ufer 58, 50968 KÖLN
Tel: 221 93738180 **Fax:** 221 93738903
Email: computerundrecht@otto-schmidt.de **Web site:** http://www.computerundrecht.de
Freq: Monthly; **Annual Sub.:** EUR 375,90; **Circ:** 1,510
Editor: Ulrich Gasper; **Advertising Manager:** Thorsten Deuse
Profile: Magazine focusing on the law relating to data processing, computer information, automation and communication.
Language(s): German
ADVERTISING RATES:
Full Page Mono .... EUR 1550
Full Page Colour .... EUR 2713
Mechanical Data: Type Area: 260 x 180 mm, No. of Columns (Display): 2, Col Widths (Display): 88 mm
BUSINESS: COMPUTERS & AUTOMATION: Computers Related

COMPUTER + UNTERRICHT
724566G62B-420
Editorial: Im Brande 17, 30926 SEELZE
Tel: 511 40004112 **Fax:** 511 40004975
Email: lichtenstern@friedrich-verlag.de **Web site:** http://www.friedrich-verlag.de
Freq: Quarterly; **Annual Sub.:** EUR 67,00; **Circ:** 3,500
Editor: Hedi Lichtenstern; **Advertising Manager:** Bernd Schrader
Profile: Discover the many basic reports of practice learning opportunities and pathways that open up computers in all subjects and grade levels. Take advantage of the teaching models and innovative projects and give your students a creative and critical approach to media! Ideological and practical materials to help you prepare for lessons. In each issue you will receive instructions on user-oriented software, compact backgrounds and useful tips.
Language(s): German
ADVERTISING RATES:
Full Page Mono .... EUR 1160
Full Page Colour .... EUR 1740
Mechanical Data: Type Area: 258 x 183 mm, No. of Columns (Display): 3, Col Widths (Display): 58 mm
Copy instructions: *Copy Date:* 49 days prior to publication
Supplement(s): bildung+medien; bildung+reisen; bildung+science
BUSINESS: CHURCH & SCHOOL EQUIPMENT & EDUCATION: Education Teachers

COMPUTER VIDEO
724568G43D-30
Editorial: Baumschulenweg 12a, 48159 MÜNSTER
Tel: 251 2652744 **Fax:** 251 2652745
Email: info@computervideo.de **Web site:** http://www.computervideo.de
Freq: 6 issues yearly; **Annual Sub.:** EUR 36,50; **Circ:** 28,000
Editor: Roland Schäfer; **Advertising Manager:** Roland Schäfer
Profile: The magazine provides the decision makers in creative business - editing studios, agencies, producers of industrial, commercial, training and music videos - as well as private power users with all relevant information about the video section at the Computer: Tips and tricks, new hardware and software products, market surveys, tests, trends and backgrounds.
Language(s): German
Readership: Aimed at purchasers in videostudios, producers of music videos, manufacturers, post artists and editors.
ADVERTISING RATES:
Full Page Mono .... EUR 2350
Full Page Colour .... EUR 3350
Mechanical Data: Type Area: 270 x 185 mm, No. of Columns (Display): 3, Col Widths (Display): 59 mm
Copy instructions: *Copy Date:* 17 days prior to publication
BUSINESS: ELECTRICAL RETAIL TRADE: Video

COMPUTERN IM H@NDWERK
724552G5B-61
Editorial: Beethovenplatz 2, 80336 MÜNCHEN
Tel: 89 5446560 **Fax:** 89 531327
Email: redaktion@cv-verlag.de **Web site:** http://www.handwerke.de
Freq: 10 issues yearly; **Annual Sub.:** EUR 39,00; **Circ:** 72,083
Editor: Horst Neureuther; **Advertising Manager:** Heide Tschinkel-Neureuther
Profile: Magazine for modern communication with the computer and telecommunications technologies to optimize office, workshop and site work in the construction of farms and by-trade.
Language(s): German
ADVERTISING RATES:
Full Page Mono .... EUR 7644
Full Page Colour .... EUR 9876
Mechanical Data: Type Area: 250 x 185 mm, No. of Columns (Display): 4, Col Widths (Display): 41 mm
Copy instructions: *Copy Date:* 14 days prior to publication
BUSINESS: COMPUTERS & AUTOMATION: Data Processing

COMPUTERWOCHE
724571G5R-635
Editorial: Lyonel-Feininger-Str. 26, 80807 MÜNCHEN
Tel: 89 36086170 **Fax:** 89 36086109
Email: cw@computerwoche.de **Web site:** http://www.computerwoche.de
Freq: Weekly; **Annual Sub.:** EUR 239,20; **Circ:** 17,702
Editor: Heinrich Vaske; **News Editor:** Jan-Bernd Meyer; **Advertising Manager:** Sebastian Wörle
Profile: COMPUTERWOCHE is the leading German-language weekly newspaper for IT managers and professionals in companies. Every Monday it provides reliable and application-oriented information about the markets of information and communications technology, provides strategic information and provides in-depth analysis. The content is optimally-cut to the specific information needs of IT decision makers and professionals in business and provides a reliable basis for decisions on corporate IT investments. In each issue, the editors dedicate the cover story in detail to a current topic. Besides the regular sections, the magazine reports on trends & analysis, products and practices, IT strategies and job & career. Special topics, such as CW TOPICS, the CW series middle class or the special supplement CW plus complete the range of topics.
Language(s): German
Readership: Read mainly by IT managers in large and medium-sized organisations.
ADVERTISING RATES:
Full Page Mono .... EUR 23400
Full Page Colour .... EUR 23400
Mechanical Data: Type Area: 267 x 205 mm, No. of Columns (Display): 4, Col Widths (Display): 47 mm
Copy instructions: *Copy Date:* 7 days prior to publication
BUSINESS: COMPUTERS & AUTOMATION: Computers Related

COMPUTERWOCHE.DE
1621007G5C-19
Editorial: Lyonel-Feininger-Str. 26, 80807 MÜNCHEN
Tel: 89 36086170 **Fax:** 89 36086109
Email: tcloer@computerwoche.de **Web site:** http://www.computerwoche.de
Freq: Daily; **Cover Price:** Paid; **Circ:** 965,294 Unique Users
Editor: Thomas Cloer
Profile: Ezine: Magazine covering the latest developments in hardware, software, peripherals and supply products.
Language(s): German
BUSINESS: COMPUTERS & AUTOMATION: Professional Personal Computers

CONCEPT OPHTHALMOLOGIE
2055528G56A-11713
Editorial: Lange Gasse 19, 88239 WANGEN
Tel: 7522 931073 **Fax:** 7522 7079832
Email: redaktion@concept-ophthalmologie.de **Web site:** http://www.concept-ophthalmologie.de
Freq: 6 issues yearly; **Circ:** 5,828
Editor: Christiane Schumacher
Profile: Magazine for ophthalmologists.
Language(s): German
ADVERTISING RATES:
Full Page Mono .... EUR 2652
Full Page Colour .... EUR 4122
Mechanical Data: Type Area: 242 x 173 mm, No. of Columns (Display): 4, Col Widths (Display): 39 mm
Copy instructions: *Copy Date:* 24 days prior to publication

CONCEPTS BY HOCHTIEF
1882162G4E-7252
Editorial: Harvestehuder Weg 42, 20149 HAMBURG
Tel: 40 44188457 **Fax:** 40 44188236
Email: cp@hoca.de **Web site:** http://cp.hoca.de
Freq: Half-yearly; **Cover Price:** Free; **Circ:** 22,000
Editor: Oliver Driesen
Profile: Magazine for building companies.
Language(s): English; German

CONDITION
724589G75J-100
Editorial: Von-Coels-Str. 390, 52080 AACHEN
Tel: 241 9581024 **Fax:** 241 9581010
Email: redaktion@m-m-sports.com **Web site:** http://www.dersportverlag.de
Freq: 10 issues yearly; **Annual Sub.:** EUR 38,00; **Circ:** 15,000
Editor: Jörg Valentin; **Advertising Manager:** Kirsten Schiffer
Profile: For more than 25 years, "condition" the German magazine guide for the running and endurance sports. The detailed training plans, nutrition tips, product testing, support etc. endurance athletes of all ages and abilities to implement their training goals.
Language(s): German
ADVERTISING RATES:
Full Page Mono .... EUR 1200
Full Page Colour .... EUR 1980
Mechanical Data: Type Area: 254 x 175 mm
Copy instructions: *Copy Date:* 20 days prior to publication
CONSUMER: SPORT: Athletics

CONDOR
724591G89D-3
Editorial: Stralauer Allee 2a, 10245 BERLIN
Tel: 30 364440950 **Fax:** 30 364440999
Email: postamt@freshmilk.de **Web site:** http://www.freshmilk.de/creativemedia
Freq: 3 issues yearly; **Cover Price:** Free; **Circ:** 120,710
Editor: Kai Werner; **Advertising Manager:** Tina Schäfer
Profile: Magazine containing articles about holidays and travel, fitness and health, flying, aircraft technology and inflight entertainment.
Language(s): German
Readership: Read by people travelling on Lufthansa charter flights.
ADVERTISING RATES:
Full Page Mono .... EUR 9900
Full Page Colour .... EUR 9900
Mechanical Data: Type Area: 260 x 205 mm
CONSUMER: HOLIDAYS & TRAVEL: In-Flight Magazines

CONNECT
724595G18B-300
Editorial: Leuschnerstr. 1, 70174 STUTTGART
Tel: 711 1821696 **Fax:** 711 1821832
Email: redaktion@connect.de **Web site:** http://www.connect.de
Freq: Monthly; **Cover Price:** EUR 4,30; **Circ:** 77,269
Editor: Dirk Waasen; **Advertising Manager:** Vasili Tsialos
Profile: Europe's largest magazine for telecommunications. From his special point of view investigated and analyzed connect the adjacent border areas such as notebooks, PDAs, (mobile) internet and in particular the possibilities of networking devices, whether indoors (home connect) or outdoor. Specially designed for use in mobile vehicle specific media such as navigation systems, infotainment and mobile office complete the range of topics in the Navigation category.
Language(s): German
ADVERTISING RATES:
Full Page Mono .... EUR 7463
Full Page Colour .... EUR 9950
Mechanical Data: Type Area: 250 x 185 mm, No. of Columns (Display): 4, Col Widths (Display): 43 mm
Copy instructions: *Copy Date:* 28 days prior to publication
BUSINESS: ELECTRONICS: Telecommunications

CONSENS MAINZ
2055529G74N-1028
Editorial: An der Oberpforte 1, 55128 MAINZ
Tel: 6131 364579 **Fax:** 6131 369740
Email: info@consens-seniorenmagazin.de **Web site:** http://www.consens-seniorenmagazin.de
Freq: Quarterly; **Cover Price:** Free; **Circ:** 20,000
Profile: Magazine for the elderly.
Language(s): German
Copy instructions: *Copy Date:* 14 days prior to publication

CONSENS WIESBADEN
2055530G74N-1029
Editorial: An der Oberpforte 1, 55128 MAINZ
Tel: 6131 364579 **Fax:** 6131 369740
Email: info@consens-seniorenmagazin.de **Web site:** http://www.consens-seniorenmagazin.de
Freq: Quarterly; **Cover Price:** Free; **Circ:** 20,000
Profile: Magazine for the elderly.
Language(s): German
Copy instructions: *Copy Date:* 14 days prior to publication

CONTITECH INITIATIV
1862042G14A-10222
Editorial: Vahrenwalder Str. 9, 30165 HANNOVER
Tel: 511 93801 **Fax:** 511 93881770
Email: service@contitech.de **Web site:** http://www.contitech.de
Freq: Quarterly; **Circ:** 9,000
Editor: Anja Graf
Profile: Company publication published by ContiTech Holding.
Language(s): German
ADVERTISING RATES:
Full Page Colour .... EUR 4000
Mechanical Data: Type Area: 300 x 240 mm

Copy instructions: *Copy Date:* 45 days prior to publication

CONTITECH INITIATIV
1862043G14A-10223
Editorial: Vahrenwalder Str. 9, 30165 HANNOVER
Tel: 511 93801 **Fax:** 511 93881770
Email: service@contitech.de **Web site:** http://www.contitech.de
Freq: Quarterly; **Circ:** 3,500
Editor: Anja Graf
Profile: Company publication published by ContiTech Holding.
Language(s): English
ADVERTISING RATES:
Full Page Colour .... EUR 4000
Mechanical Data: Type Area: 300 x 240 mm
Copy instructions: *Copy Date:* 45 days prior to publication

CONTRASTE
724629G14A-1560
Editorial: Postfach 104520, 69035 HEIDELBERG
Tel: 6221 162467
Email: contraste@online.de **Web site:** http://www.contraste.org
Freq: 11 issues yearly; **Annual Sub.:** EUR 45,00; **Circ:** 4,000
Editor: Dieter Poschen; **Advertising Manager:** Dieter Poschen
Profile: Contraste is the only national monthly newspaper for self-organization and serves as a mouthpiece and discussion forum for the alternative movements. Activists from different movements with the publication of the newspaper track the target, the shaped by globalization, welfare cuts, mass unemployment and environmental degradation discuss alternatives to existing conditions, identify trends, to develop their own utopias and to test them. Regular reports provide information on start-up and activities of projects, self-help initiatives, self-managed enterprises and cooperatives, alternative and solidarity economy, alternative media, new media, environmental crafts, culture "from below" and much more. When there is a service projects and job market, useful information about self-government associations, seminars, events and new publications on the book market. Contraste is as colorful mixed as the movement itself and a reflection of this diversity. The choice of monthly reports, discussions and documentaries are independent and non-dogmatic.
Language(s): German
ADVERTISING RATES:
Full Page Mono .... EUR 1738
Mechanical Data: Type Area: 420 x 284 mm, No. of Columns (Display): 4, Col Widths (Display): 68 mm
Copy instructions: *Copy Date:* 20 days prior to publication

CONTROLLER MAGAZIN
724632G14A-1580
Editorial: Münchner Str. 10, 82237 WÖRTHSEE
Tel: 8153 8041 **Fax:** 8153 8043
Email: silvia.froehlich@vcw.de **Web site:** http://www.controllermagazin.de
Freq: 6 issues yearly; Free to qualifying individuals
Annual Sub.: EUR 157,20; **Circ:** 8,410
Editor: Klaus Eiselmayer
Profile: The "Controller Magazin" is the largest circulation magazine for controllers in Germany. Controlling experts and all the who want to be there here read, as the growing needs in controlling current and future do justice to. Dr. Albrecht Deyhle, Chairman of the Supervisory Board of the Controller Akademie AG and a member of the Board of Trustees of the International Controller Association (ICV): "Take advantage of the expertise and look forward to specialist posts, with which you work the whole controlling and accounting more efficient." As readers of the Controller Magazin, you benefit from a comprehensive network. The Controller Magazin is produced in close collaboration with the trainers of the controller Academy.
Language(s): German
ADVERTISING RATES:
Full Page Mono .... EUR 2100
Full Page Colour .... EUR 2950
Mechanical Data: Type Area: 253 x 178 mm
Official Journal of: Organ d. Internat. Controller Verein

CONTROLLING & MANAGEMENT
733199G1B-30
Editorial: Abraham-Lincoln-Str. 46, 65189 WIESBADEN **Tel:** 611 7878235 **Fax:** 611 7878411
Email: zfcm@whu.edu **Web site:** http://www.zfcm.de
Freq: 6 issues yearly; **Annual Sub.:** EUR 155,00; **Circ:** 3,100
Editor: Heiko Icks; **Advertising Manager:** Annette Oberländer-Renner
Profile: Magazine about auditing methods.
Language(s): German
Readership: Aimed at accountants.
ADVERTISING RATES:
Full Page Mono .... EUR 2080
Full Page Colour .... EUR 3080
Mechanical Data: No. of Columns (Display): 3, Col Widths (Display): 53 mm, Type Area: 250 x 175 mm
Copy instructions: *Copy Date:* 28 days prior to publication
BUSINESS: FINANCE & ECONOMICS: Accountancy

CONVENIENCE SHOP
724637G53-20
Editorial: Am Hammergraben 14, 56567 NEUWIED
Tel: 2631 879154 **Fax:** 2631 879204
Email: h.krone@lpv-verlag.de **Web site:** http://www.convenienceshop.de
Freq: 10 issues yearly; **Annual Sub.:** EUR 27,70; **Circ:** 29,748
Editor: Hans Jürgen Krone; **Advertising Manager:** Torsten Zelleröhr
Profile: Magazine about convenience stores and retail garage outlets.
Language(s): German
ADVERTISING RATES:
Full Page Mono .... EUR 5650
Full Page Colour .... EUR 9888
Mechanical Data: Type Area: 256 x 185 mm, No. of Columns (Display): 4, Col Widths (Display): 42 mm
Copy instructions: *Copy Date:* 15 days prior to publication
BUSINESS: RETAILING & WHOLESALING

CONVENTION INTERNATIONAL
724638G2C-12
Editorial: Wiedbachstr. 50, 56567 NEUWIED
Tel: 2631 964639 **Fax:** 2631 964640
Email: t.scholz@convention-net.de **Web site:** http://www.convention-net.de
Freq: 6 issues yearly; **Annual Sub.:** EUR 51,00; **Circ:** 11,125
Editor: Thomas P. Scholz; **Advertising Manager:** Oliver-W. Glaser-Gallion
Profile: Convention International is an independent, regularly bimonthly magazine for event planners and service providers. The report covers the entire spectrum of congress, conference, event and incentive market and the entire year of events. Special interest in the topics of destinations, venues, conference hotels, social programs and infrastructure / services. Our readers are event planners and decision makers from all areas of industry, associations, public institutions and other organizations with appropriate information needs in terms of convention and event capacity, program opportunities, organizational and technical logistics, and general location profiles. We are working together with numerous local and regional convention bureaus. International Convention was established in 1982 and is published in advance of important industry trade shows such as ITB, IMEX, SuisseEMEX, access and EIBTM.
Language(s): German
Readership: Aimed at businessmen.
ADVERTISING RATES:
Full Page Mono .... EUR 3900
Full Page Colour .... EUR 3900
Mechanical Data: Type Area: 297 x 210 mm, No. of Columns (Display): 3, Col Widths (Display): 55 mm
Copy instructions: *Copy Date:* 20 days prior to publication
BUSINESS: COMMUNICATIONS, ADVERTISING & MARKETING: Conferences & Exhibitions

COOLIBRI - AUSG. DÜSSELDORF, NEUSS U. KREIS ME
724640G80-2340
Editorial: Graf-Adolf-Str. 80, 40210 DÜSSELDORF
Tel: 211 384660 **Fax:** 211 3846616
Email: redaktion.duesseldorf@coolibri.de **Web site:** http://www.coolibri.de
Freq: Monthly; **Cover Price:** Free; **Circ:** 71,736
Editor: Alexandra Wehrmann; **Advertising Manager:** Holger Ziefuß
Profile: City magazines for Düsseldorf, Neuss and Mettmann. The editorial team provides the (almost) complete event overview, elaborately researched and updated. For more tips on leisure activities and nightlife complete the content: the current cinema program to new CDs, from food shopping, do a lot of personal ads and raffles - coolibri the leisure guide. The magazine speaks specifically to the leisure assets, the event and interested in culture and with it the joyous entertainment, reaching especially the key demographic core target audience of 14 - to 49-year-old urbanites. Facebook: http://www.facebook.com/coolibrimagazin Twitter: http://twitter.com/#!/coolibri.
Language(s): German
ADVERTISING RATES:
Full Page Mono .... EUR 3985
Full Page Colour .... EUR 5730
Mechanical Data: Type Area: 260 x 194 mm, No. of Columns (Display): 7, Col Widths (Display): 26 mm
CONSUMER: RURAL & REGIONAL INTEREST

COOLIBRI - AUSG. RUHRSTADT
724639G80-2320
Editorial: Ehrenfeldstr. 34, 44789 BOCHUM
Tel: 234 9373770 **Fax:** 234 9373797
Email: redaktion.bochum@coolibri.de **Web site:** http://www.coolibri.de
Freq: Monthly; **Cover Price:** Free; **Circ:** 122,641
Editor: Werner Dickob; **Advertising Manager:** Udo Wagner
Profile: City magazines for Ruhrgebiet. The editorial team provides the (almost) complete event overview, elaborately researched and updated. For more tips on leisure activities and nightlife complete the content: the current cinema program to new CDs, from food shopping, do a lot of personal ads and raffles - coolibri the leisure guide. The magazine speaks specifically to the leisure assets, the event and interested in culture and with it the joyous entertainment, reaching especially the key demographic core target audience of 14 - to 49-year-old urbanites. Facebook: http://www.facebook.com/coolibrimagazin Twitter: http://twitter.com/#!/coolibri.
Language(s): German
Readership: Aimed at residents of the Ruhrgebiet.
ADVERTISING RATES:
Full Page Mono .... EUR 5730
Full Page Colour .... EUR 8240
Mechanical Data: Type Area: 260 x 194 mm, No. of Columns (Display): 7, Col Widths (Display): 26 mm
CONSUMER: RURAL & REGIONAL INTEREST

CORPORATE AV
724657G2A-840
Editorial: Hegnacher Str. 30, 71336 WAIBLINGEN
Tel: 7151 23331 **Fax:** 7151 23338
Email: medienreport@yahoo.de **Web site:** http://www.medienreport.de
Freq: Annual; **Cover Price:** EUR 15,00; **Circ:** 4,300
Editor: Rolf G. Lehmann; **Advertising Manager:** Isa Lehmann
Profile: Magazine on media trends in marketing and education.
Language(s): German
ADVERTISING RATES:
Full Page Mono .... EUR 2180
Full Page Colour .... EUR 2878
Mechanical Data: Type Area: 244 x 175 mm
Copy instructions: *Copy Date:* 30 days prior to publication

CORPORATE AV
724657G2A-5867
Editorial: Hegnacher Str. 30, 71336 WAIBLINGEN
Tel: 7151 23331 **Fax:** 7151 23338
Email: medienreport@yahoo.de **Web site:** http://www.medienreport.de
Freq: Annual; **Cover Price:** EUR 15,00; **Circ:** 4,300
Editor: Rolf G. Lehmann; **Advertising Manager:** Isa Lehmann
Profile: Magazine on media trends in marketing and education.
Language(s): German
ADVERTISING RATES:
Full Page Mono .... EUR 2180
Full Page Colour .... EUR 2878
Mechanical Data: Type Area: 244 x 175 mm
Copy instructions: *Copy Date:* 30 days prior to publication

CORPORATE FINANCE BIZ
727331G1A-33
Editorial: Grafenberger Allee 293, 40237 DÜSSELDORF **Tel:** 211 8871435
Fax: 211 887971435
Email: cf.redaktion@fachverlag.de **Web site:** http://www.cf-biz.de
Freq: 8 issues yearly; **Annual Sub.:** EUR 456,00; **Circ:** 1,522
Editor: Elke Hartmann; **Advertising Manager:** Ralf Pötzsch
Profile: Journal of the issues of financial management, business valuation and capital markets and business start-up.
Language(s): German
Readership: Aimed at bankers and accountants.
ADVERTISING RATES:
Full Page Mono .... EUR 1300
Full Page Colour .... EUR 1450
Mechanical Data: Type Area: 260 x 175 mm
Copy instructions: *Copy Date:* 13 days prior to publication
BUSINESS: FINANCE & ECONOMICS

CORPORATE FINANCE LAW
1983071G1A-3822
Editorial: Grafenberger Allee 293, 40237 DÜSSELDORF **Tel:** 211 8871470
Fax: 211 887971470
Email: cf.redaktion@fachverlag.de **Web site:** http://www.cf-law.de
Freq: 8 issues yearly; **Annual Sub.:** EUR 456,00; **Circ:** 1,542
Editor: Elke Hartmann; **Advertising Manager:** Ralf Pötzsch
Profile: Corporate Finance law provides a bridge between law and economics. Economics topics that are necessary for an understanding of legal contexts, is prepared for the target audience is primarily legal. Renowned experts provide corporate and securities law and tax and accounting law issues in their economic and financial context dar. Corporate Finance law contains articles in English and German contributions in order to illuminate current issues and trends from other countries.
Language(s): German
ADVERTISING RATES:
Full Page Mono .... EUR 1300
Full Page Colour .... EUR 1450
Mechanical Data: Type Area: 260 x 175 mm
Copy instructions: *Copy Date:* 14 days prior to publication

CORREO
724660G21A-1020
Editorial: Alfred-Nobel-Str. 50, 40789 MONHEIM
Tel: 2173 383540 **Fax:** 2173 383454
Email: bernhard.grupp@bayercropscience.com **Web site:** http://www.agrocourier.com
Freq: Half-yearly; **Cover Price:** Free; **Circ:** 12,000
Editor: Bernhard Grupp
Profile: Magazine on agriculture from the Bayer chemical company.
Language(s): Spanish

COSMOPOLITAN
724667G74A-880
Editorial: Arabellastr. 33, 81925 MÜNCHEN
Tel: 89 92340 **Fax:** 89 9234202
Email: cosmo.redaktion@mvg.de **Web site:** http://www.cosmopolitan.de
Freq: Monthly; **Annual Sub.:** EUR 29,00; **Circ:** 313,609
Editor: Carolin Schuhler; **Advertising Manager:** Lisa Habermayer
Profile: Cosmopolitan is a personal coach for all areas of life: Relationship & Sex, Work & Career, Beauty & Fashion, Culture & Lifestyle. Cosmopolitan motivates to developown potentials to lead a happy and fulfilled life. For even the most successful women love to be encouraged in who and how they really are: ".. very smart sexy. " Cosmopolitan appears in over 100 countries and has about 77 million readers is the largest international women's magazine in the world.
Language(s): German
Readership: Aimed at young women.
ADVERTISING RATES:
Full Page Mono .... EUR 31000
Full Page Colour .... EUR 31000
Mechanical Data: Type Area: 250 x 178 mm, No. of Columns (Display): 3, Col Widths (Display): 57 mm
Copy instructions: *Copy Date:* 44 days prior to publication
CONSUMER: WOMEN'S INTEREST CONSUMER MAGAZINES: Women's Interest

COSMOPOLITAN
1773237G74A-3506
Editorial: Arabellastr. 33, 81925 MÜNCHEN
Tel: 89 92340 **Fax:** 89 9234202
Email: cosmo.redaktion@mvg.de **Web site:** http://www.cosmopolitan.de
Freq: Monthly; **Annual Sub.:** CHF 58,00; **Circ:** 313,609
Editor: Carolin Schuhler; **Advertising Manager:** Lisa Habermayer
Profile: Cosmopolitan is a personal coach for all areas of life: Relationship & Sex, Work & Career, Beauty & Fashion, Culture & Lifestyle. Cosmopolitan motivates to developown potentials to lead a happy and fulfilled life. For even the most successful women love to be encouraged in who and how they really are: ".. very smart sexy. " Cosmopolitan appears in over 100 countries and has about 77 million readers is the largest international women's magazine in the world.
Language(s): German
ADVERTISING RATES:
Full Page Mono .... CHF 30000
Full Page Colour .... CHF 30000
Mechanical Data: Type Area: 250 x 178 mm, No. of Columns (Display): 3, Col Widths (Display): 57 mm
Copy instructions: *Copy Date:* 44 days prior to publication

COSSMA
724669G15A-183
Editorial: Karl-Friedrich-Str. 14, 76133 KARLSRUHE
Tel: 721 165169 **Fax:** 721 165150
Email: angelika.meiss@health-and-beauty.com **Web site:** http://www.cossma.com
Freq: 10 issues yearly; **Annual Sub.:** EUR 192,00; **Circ:** 4,156
Editor: Angelika Meiss; **Advertising Manager:** Dorothea Michaelis
Profile: COSSMA aimes at the international cosmetic producing industry and to manufacturers of detergents and cleaning agents. It reports on ingredients and their applications, research and development, packaging and design, aerosol and spray technology, machinery and equipment and services for the cosmetics industry. Reports continue to appear regularly on important industry events and trade shows. The editorial approach of COSSMA reduces complex information to the essentials, making the magazine a "must" for all decision makers in the industry.
Language(s): English; German
ADVERTISING RATES:
Full Page Mono .... EUR 2350
Full Page Colour .... EUR 3350
Mechanical Data: Type Area: 265 x 182 mm, No. of Columns (Display): 4, Col Widths (Display): 43 mm
Copy instructions: *Copy Date:* 42 days prior to publication
BUSINESS: COSMETICS & HAIRDRESSING: Cosmetics

COST & LOGIS
724670G11A-160
Editorial: Friedensallee 43, 22765 HAMBURG
Tel: 40 30685212 **Fax:** 40 30685210
Email: j.riemann@mercado-verlag.de **Web site:** http://www.cost-logis.de
Freq: 18 issues yearly; **Annual Sub.:** EUR 153,75; **Circ:** 2,500
Editor: Jens Riemann; **Advertising Manager:** Susanne Carstens
Profile: Magazine providing facts, news and analyses on a wide range of issues concerning the hotel and catering industry.
Language(s): German
ADVERTISING RATES:
Full Page Mono .... EUR 726
Full Page Colour .... EUR 1360
Mechanical Data: Type Area: 260 x 187 mm, No. of Columns (Display): 4, Col Widths (Display): 46 mm
Copy instructions: *Copy Date:* 7 days prior to publication
BUSINESS: CATERING: Catering, Hotels & Restaurants

COTTBUSER WOCHENKURIER
724674G72-3000
Editorial: Karl-Marx-Str. 68, 03044 COTTBUS
Tel: 355 4312381 **Fax:** 355 472910

Email: kerstintwarok@cwk-verlag.de **Web site:** http://www.wochenkurier.info
Freq: Weekly; **Cover Price:** Free; **Circ:** 68,130
Editor: Kerstin Twarok; **Advertising Manager:** Uwe Peschel
Profile: Advertising journal (house-to-house) concentrating on local stories.
Language(s): German
ADVERTISING RATES:
Full Page Mono .... EUR 3883
Full Page Colour .... EUR 5437
Mechanical Data: Type Area: 430 x 290 mm, No. of Columns (Display): 7, Col Widths (Display): 38 mm
Copy instructions: *Copy Date:* 5 days prior to publication
LOCAL NEWSPAPERS

COUNTRY 724678G74C-460
Editorial: Rindermarkt 6, 80331 MÜNCHEN
Tel: 89 242099941 **Fax:** 89 242099959
Email: redaktion@country-online.de **Web site:** http://www.country-online.de
Freq: 6 issues yearly; **Annual Sub.:** EUR 30,00; **Circ:** 81,051
Editor: Barbara Friedrich; **Advertising Manager:** Roberto Sprengel
Profile: COUNTRY displays all facets of the lived rural housing and reports on most beautiful, authentic, high-quality facilities. COUNTRY conveys warmth and intimacy, quenches the desire for an enjoyable and fulfilling life in harmony with nature and takes its readers on trips to beautiful places. COUNTRY is realistic and enjoyable and bases the selection of topics on the seasons.
Language(s): German
Readership: Read by those with a high disposable income.
ADVERTISING RATES:
Full Page Mono .... EUR 10220
Full Page Colour .... EUR 10220
Mechanical Data: Type Area: 258 x 188 mm, No. of Columns (Display): 4, Col Widths (Display): 44 mm
Copy instructions: *Copy Date:* 49 days prior to publication
CONSUMER: WOMEN'S INTEREST CONSUMER MAGAZINES: Home & Family

COUNTRY HOMES 730497G74C-1620
Editorial: Rosenkavalierplatz 14, 81925 MÜNCHEN
Tel: 89 9100930 **Fax:** 89 91009353
Email: s.berger@ipm-verlag.de **Web site:** http://www.ipm-verlag.de
Freq: 6 issues yearly; **Annual Sub.:** EUR 29,00; **Circ:** 70,150
Editor: Sabine Berger; **Advertising Manager:** Rüdiger Knapp
Profile: Country Homes: The high-end magazine in the field of English country style, which offers to its readers a high usage value. The magazine presents exquisite country homes in extensive features. Moreover, the reader finds advice on home decoration as well as the latest trends in furniture, home accessories, decoration, kitchen and bathroom. Target group: well-established persons with a very high income.
Language(s): German
Readership: Read by home owners.
ADVERTISING RATES:
Full Page Mono .... EUR 7100
Full Page Colour .... EUR 7100
Mechanical Data: Type Area: 260 x 186 mm
CONSUMER: WOMEN'S INTEREST CONSUMER MAGAZINES: Home & Family

COUNTRY STYLE 724681G74C-480
Editorial: Höfeweg 40, 33619 BIELEFELD
Tel: 521 911110 **Fax:** 521 9111112
Email: info@klocke-verlag.de **Web site:** http://www.country-style.de
Freq: Quarterly; **Annual Sub.:** EUR 28,00; **Circ:** 30,180
Editor: Martina Klocke; **Advertising Manager:** Wolfgang Pohl
Profile: Magazine for home decor and lifestyle in a country style. It grants four times a year an insight into the most beautiful houses in the country, presents extraordinary objects and people that have met with the restoration of a villa is often a lifelong dream. Not only houses in Germany are shown, but also in Austria, Tuscany, Provence and of course in Mallorca. In addition to the home stories, the magazine also provides information about table and dining culture, home accessories, products of organic farmers, are recipes and travel tips and much more.
Language(s): German
Readership: Aimed at people living in the countryside.
ADVERTISING RATES:
Full Page Mono .... EUR 4750
Full Page Colour .... EUR 8400
Copy instructions: *Copy Date:* 42 days prior to publication
CONSUMER: WOMEN'S INTEREST CONSUMER MAGAZINES: Home & Family

COUPÉ 1661206G73-524
Editorial: Harburger Schlosstr. 28, 21079 HAMBURG
Tel: 1805 558345
Email: online@imckg.de **Web site:** http://www.coupe.de
Cover Price: Paid
Editor: Rudolf Koslowski
Profile: Ezine: Magazine containing adult photography.
Language(s): German
CONSUMER: NATIONAL & INTERNATIONAL PERIODICALS

COURAGE 724685G74A-900
Editorial: Holsteiner Str. 28, 42107 WUPPERTAL
Tel: 202 4969749
Email: frauenverband-courage@t-online.de **Web site:** http://www.fvcourage.de
Freq: 6 issues yearly; **Annual Sub.:** EUR 11,00; **Circ:** 2,000
Editor: Linda Weißgerber
Profile: Magazine of the women's Club Courage.
Language(s): German

CP MONITOR 1895927G2A-5802
Editorial: Nebendahlstr. 16, 22041 HAMBURG
Tel: 40 60847445 **Fax:** 40 60900977
Email: monington@cp-monitor.de **Web site:** http://www.cp-monitor.de
Freq: Quarterly; **Annual Sub.:** EUR 60,00; **Circ:** 3,500
Editor: Beatrice Monington West; **Advertising Manager:** Jörg Luttkau
Profile: Magazine about corporate publishing media.
Language(s): German
ADVERTISING RATES:
Full Page Mono .... EUR 2475
Full Page Colour .... EUR 2475
Mechanical Data: Type Area: 255 x 180 mm
Copy instructions: *Copy Date:* 20 days prior to publication

CP + T CASTING PLANT AND TECHNOLOGY INTERNATIONAL 724701G27-420
Editorial: Sohnstr. 70, 40237 DÜSSELDORF
Tel: 211 6871107 **Fax:** 211 6871365
Email: redaktion@bdguss.de **Web site:** http://www.bdguss.de
Freq: Quarterly; **Annual Sub.:** EUR 110,00; **Circ:** 8,170
Editor: Michael Franken; **Advertising Manager:** Sigrid Klinge
Profile: CP + T is an industry-oriented international code-magazine. It treats the entire foundry technology for iron and steel castings, including diecast and non-ferrous metal casting. It includes both raw and auxiliary materials as well as issues of quality control and environmental protection. The focus is on plant and process engineering technical papers from the practice of plant manufacturers, suppliers and foundries. Short messages about new equipment and processes, and important events of the foundry industry complement the editorial content. These short messages are marked with identifying numbers.
Language(s): English
Readership: Aimed at foundry owners and managers.
ADVERTISING RATES:
Full Page Mono .... EUR 2362
Full Page Colour .... EUR 3160
Mechanical Data: Type Area: 260 x 174 mm
BUSINESS: METAL, IRON & STEEL

CPI CONCRETE PLANT INTERNATIONAL 1863394G4E-7240
Editorial: Industriestr. 180, 50999 KÖLN
Tel: 2236 962390 **Fax:** 2236 962396
Email: editor@cpi-worldwide.com **Web site:** http://www.cpi-worldwide.com
Freq: Annual; **Circ:** 3,000
Editor: Holger Karutz; **Advertising Manager:** Gerhard Klöckner
Profile: The journals of "CPI-Worldwide" are the only source for cutting-edge technical data, news and information for the concrete industry - from around the world. This information processed editorially and professional - are aimed directly regardless of location to business owners, decision makers and managers. The articles are well-written by world-renowned and in their field well-known experts. Each topic is presented in a way that the audience important information available, it brings on the cutting edge of technology and so to increase productivity and operational performance contributes.
Language(s): Arabic
Mechanical Data: Type Area: 260 x 180 mm, No. of Columns (Display): 3, Col Widths (Display): 56 mm
Copy instructions: *Copy Date:* 30 days prior to publication

CPI CONCRETE PLANT INTERNATIONAL 1863463G4E-7241
Editorial: Industriestr. 180, 50999 KÖLN
Tel: 2236 962390 **Fax:** 2236 962396
Email: h.karutz@cpi-worldwide.com **Web site:** http://www.cpi-worldwide.com
Freq: 6 issues yearly; Free to qualifying individuals
Annual Sub.: EUR 120,00; **Circ:** 4,500
Editor: Holger Karutz; **Advertising Manager:** Gerhard Klöckner
Profile: The journals of "CPI-Worldwide" are the only source for cutting-edge technical data, news and information for the concrete industry - from around the world. This information processed editorially and professional - are aimed directly regardless of location to business owners, decision makers and managers. The articles are well-written by world-renowned and in their field well-known experts. Each topic is presented in a way that the audience important information available, it brings on the cutting edge of technology and so to increase productivity and operational performance contributes.
Language(s): Russian
Mechanical Data: Type Area: 260 x 180 mm, No. of Columns (Display): 3, Col Widths (Display): 56 mm
Copy instructions: *Copy Date:* 30 days prior to publication

CQ DL 724705G79D-80
Editorial: Lindenallee 4, 34225 BAUNATAL
Tel: 561 9498894 **Fax:** 561 9498855
Email: redaktion@darcverlag.de **Web site:** http://www.cqdl.de
Freq: Monthly; **Circ:** 41,000
Editor: Alexander Strutzke; **Advertising Manager:** Petra Rothe
Profile: Amateur radio magazine of the Deutschen Amateur-Radio-Club (DARC). True to the motto "from radio amateurs for radio amateurs", each issue is filled with a selection of current events in the amateur radio world, technical articles and radio operating instructions and experiences.
Language(s): German
ADVERTISING RATES:
Full Page Mono .... EUR 1660
Full Page Colour .... EUR 2581
Mechanical Data: Type Area: 260 x 185 mm, No. of Columns (Display): 3, Col Widths (Display): 59 mm
CONSUMER: HOBBIES & DIY: Radio Electronics

CREATIV VERPACKEN 724713G35-40
Editorial: Wilmersdorfer Str. 6, 16278 ANGERMÜNDE **Tel:** 33334 85200 **Fax:** 33334 852029
Email: redaktion@creativverpacken.de **Web site:** http://www.creativverpacken.de
Freq: 8 issues yearly; **Annual Sub.:** EUR 114,00; **Circ:** 10,000
Editor: Ute von Buch; **Advertising Manager:** Dietrich von Buch
Profile: creativ verpacken is the first and only packaging magazine in the German-speaking area for all budget managers of product-to-market chain, which want to market successfully using the package. The aim of the editorial staff of creativ verpacken is the readers through high-quality and stimulating editorial content a pilot to their facilities of successful marketing with packaging to be and have to encourage them to contact. This offers creativ verpacken its advertisers a platform to cultivate interest, technically oriented as well as new customers to address and win. Compared to other media offers this journal cross-border information and suggestions for the reader - an essential factor for the promotion of creative solutions in every respect.
Language(s): English; German
ADVERTISING RATES:
Full Page Colour .... EUR 4270
Mechanical Data: Type Area: 250 x 186 mm
Copy instructions: *Copy Date:* 28 days prior to publication
BUSINESS: PACKAGING & BOTTLING

CREATIV-IDEE 1605062G79A-279
Editorial: Römerstr. 90, 79618 RHEINFELDEN
Tel: 7623 964421 **Fax:** 7623 96464421
Email: info@oz-verlag.de **Web site:** http://www.oz-verlag.de
Freq: Quarterly; **Annual Sub.:** EUR 15,00; **Circ:** 90,000
Editor: Irmgard Veith
Profile: Creativ-Idee - the popular, handy craft magazine with the most beautiful models and window frames made of paper and cardboard. Each of the four issues containing motifs and ideas on a specific topic from spring to winter and Easter and Christmas.
Language(s): German
ADVERTISING RATES:
Full Page Mono .... EUR 3460
Full Page Colour .... EUR 4480
Mechanical Data: Type Area: 226 x 159 mm
CONSUMER: HOBBIES & DIY

CREDITREFORM 724715G14A-1640
Editorial: Grafenberger Allee 293, 40237 DÜSSELDORF **Tel:** 211 8871464 **Fax:** 211 8871463
Email: creditreform-service@fachverlag.de **Web site:** http://www.creditreform-magazin.de
Freq: Monthly; Free to qualifying individuals
Annual Sub.: EUR 54,00; **Circ:** 123,892
Editor: Ingo Schenk; **Advertising Manager:** Anne Forst
Profile: Creditreform is the business magazine for entrepreneurs. This high demand, the business magazine from the publishing group Handelsblatt by its high quality and reliable reporting requirements. Creditreform provides more than basic know-how from the fields of finance, tax, legal, IT and communications, fleet or e-business. Always up to date, focused on the vital interests of the middle class. The competence of this information service is highly valued by managers and used active - both for operations and for the strategic development of their enterprises. Creditreform readers are entrepreneurs, managers and executives, both technically and commercially, in medium-sized enterprises. This represent a high investment potential and make a relevant audience for your business-to-business communication.
Language(s): German
ADVERTISING RATES:
Full Page Mono .... EUR 11950
Full Page Colour .... EUR 11950
Mechanical Data: Type Area: 250 x 180 mm, No. of Columns (Display): 3, Col Widths (Display): 54 mm
Copy instructions: *Copy Date:* 21 days prior to publication
BUSINESS: COMMERCE, INDUSTRY & MANAGEMENT

CRESCENDO 724719G76F-160
Editorial: Senefelderstr. 14, 80336 MÜNCHEN
Tel: 89 7415090 **Fax:** 89 74150911
Email: redaktion@crescendo.de **Web site:** http://www.crescendo.de
Freq: 7 issues yearly; **Annual Sub.:** EUR 34,00; **Circ:** 70,191
Editor: Robert Kittel; **Advertising Manager:** Liselotte Richter-Lux
Profile: Magazine for classical music. crescendo brings the world of music from the ivory tower into the center of society. crescendo of opinion makers among the music media. Exciting for amateurs and those interested, a must for professionals. In crescendo write prominent music journalists, the stars of the classical, literary figures and politicians. Seven times a year brings the music crescendo in the discussion, looks behind the scenes and hear the best in CDs. Stars such as Jonas Kaufmann, Rolando Villazon and Lang Lang enthusiasm for classical music. Opera and concert to celebrate a renaissance. This trend reflects the successful crescendo-Concept. With the selection of topics, editorial input and contemporary look crescendo reached cultured people of all ages. The distribution takes place nationwide through distributors, direct purchasers / subscribers and the special delivery service in cultural centers such as München, Berlin, Hamburg and Nordrhein-Westfalen / Ruhrgebiet. About 50% of the edition will be personally and exclusively delivered to the driver of the publisher.
Language(s): German
Readership: Aimed at people who enjoy classical music and opera.
ADVERTISING RATES:
Full Page Mono .... EUR 8500
Full Page Colour .... EUR 8500
Mechanical Data: Type Area: 263 x 190 mm, No. of Columns (Display): 3, Col Widths (Display): 60 mm
Supplement(s): crescendo festspiel-guide
CONSUMER: MUSIC & PERFORMING ARTS: Opera

CRM-HANDBUCH REISEMEDIZIN 1794346G56A-11446
Editorial: Hansaallee 321, 40549 DÜSSELDORF
Tel: 211 904290 **Fax:** 211 9042999
Email: info@crm.de **Web site:** http://www.crm.de
Freq: Half-yearly; **Annual Sub.:** EUR 75,95; **Circ:** 14,800
Editor: Tomas Jelinek
Profile: The CRM-Handbuch Reisemedizin provides solid, medical travel information for more than 200 countries. The structured division into five themes: Country information from A-Z, travel vaccinations, measures for malaria prevention, an extensive service section and maps of global spread of selected diseases are the physicians and pharmacies, a proven and efficient tool for the qualified travel medical advice on the hand.
Language(s): German
ADVERTISING RATES:
Full Page Mono .... EUR 2940
Full Page Colour .... EUR 2940
Mechanical Data: Type Area: 297 x 210 mm

CRM-HANDBUCH REISEN MIT VORERKRANKUNGEN 1931956G56A-11651
Editorial: Hansaallee 321, 40549 DÜSSELDORF
Tel: 211 904290 **Fax:** 211 9042999
Email: info@crm.de **Web site:** http://www.crm.de
Freq: Annual; **Annual Sub.:** EUR 36,90; **Circ:** 4,900
Profile: The CRM-Handbuch Reisen mit Vorerkrankungen is based on the CRM-Handbuch Reisemedizin and provides in-depth information on travel medicine advice to patients with health problems. For some 50 diseases receive the travel medicine advisory physician or pharmacist comprehensive information to assess and evaluate the ability to travel, the transport of medications, health insurance questions and information about medical infrastructure abroad.
Language(s): German
ADVERTISING RATES:
Full Page Mono .... EUR 1160
Full Page Colour .... EUR 1160
Mechanical Data: Type Area: 297 x 210 mm

CROSS-ROAD AUTO MOTOR UND SPORT 1606924G77A-2554
Editorial: Leuschnerstr. 1, 70174 STUTTGART
Tel: 711 1821241 **Fax:** 711 1821958
Email: redaktion_ams@motorpresse.de **Web site:** http://www.auto-motor-und-sport.de
Freq: Annual; **Cover Price:** EUR 4,20; **Circ:** 40,000
Editor: Bernd Ostmann; **Advertising Manager:** Andrea Bantle
Profile: Car magazine. Facebook: http://www.facebook.com/automotorundsport.
Language(s): German
ADVERTISING RATES:
Full Page Mono .... EUR 6900
Full Page Colour .... EUR 6900
Mechanical Data: Type Area: 248 x 185 mm, No. of Columns (Display): 4, Col Widths (Display): 43 mm
Copy instructions: *Copy Date:* 30 days prior to publication

CSR MAGAZIN 2073693G14A-10508

Editorial: Unterscheideweg 13, 42499 HÜCKESWAGEN **Tel:** 2192 8770000
Fax: 6039 937538403
Email: redaktion@csr-news.net **Web site:** http://www.csr-news.net
Freq: Quarterly; **Circ:** 1,500
Editor: Achim Halfmann
Profile: CSR Magazine, the magazine for social nternehmensverantwortung answers to questions on corporate social responsibility in corporate governance in independent and cross-industry reports. The magazine takes into account the perspective of companies, NGOs and science and is the ideal tool for optimizing the B2B communications between firms and supports the professional CSR work The CSR Magazine combines professional and journalistic professionalism of CSR NEWS with the powers of the multimedia Full Service Partner for B2B communication Vogel Business Media.
Language(s): German
ADVERTISING RATES:
Full Page Mono .... EUR 1480
Full Page Colour .... EUR 1480
Mechanical Data: Type Area: 250 x 178 mm

C'T MAGAZIN FÜR COMPUTERTECHNIK 724730G5B-35

Editorial: Karl-Wiechert-Allee 10, 30625 HANNOVER
Tel: 511 5352300 **Fax:** 511 5352417
Email: ct@ctmagazin.de **Web site:** http://www.ctmagazin.de
Freq: 26 issues yearly; **Annual Sub.:** EUR 84,00; **Circ:** 317,568
Editor: Christian Persson; **Advertising Manager:** Udo Elsner
Profile: Founded in 1983, is one of the best-selling c't computer magazine in Europe and one of the most respected sources of information for the computer professional and the demanding user. Our readers appreciate the unique character of the magazine, which is characterized by thematic diversity, technical expertise, journalistic independence and thoroughness. The focus of the principle-vendor and multi-platform reporting in addition to networks, communications, operating systems and hardware technology is above all the contemporary applications of the computer. Whether e-mail or web design, mobile computing and wireless LANs - c't all the exciting developments have firmly in mind: as well as digital audio and video applications, from digital cameras to MP3 or DVD player, video-Recording, multichannel audio to DVB reception. c't published 14 daily and ensure a dynamic market for both readers and advertisers the appropriate timeliness and responsiveness. For the professional decision-makers c't is the irreplaceable basis of information.
Language(s): German
Readership: Aimed at the professional end user.
ADVERTISING RATES:
Full Page Mono .... EUR 10400
Full Page Colour .... EUR 12900
Mechanical Data: Type Area: 260 x 185 mm
Copy instructions: *Copy Date:* 19 days prior to publication
BUSINESS: COMPUTERS & AUTOMATION: Data Processing

LA CUCINA ITALIANA 1800299G74P-1232

Editorial: Bayerstr. 38, 53332 BORNHEIM
Tel: 2222 952213 **Fax:** 2222 952111
Email: redaktion@lacucinaitaliana.de **Web site:** http://www.lacucinaitaliana.de
Freq: 6 issues yearly; **Annual Sub.:** EUR 29,80; **Circ:** 33,243
Editor: Stefan Hermes; **Advertising Manager:** Stefan Hermes
Profile: The readers of the LA CUCINA ITALIANA are the real gourmet: Versatile and educated. Inquisitive and purchasing power. From the "Toscana Faction " the opinion of everyday life have become. You enjoy the finer things in life. If you are interested in all that is precious and good: Innovative technics of Household is as much about how to travel or interesting products for pleasure and lifestyle. The LA CUCINA ITALIANA is collected.
Language(s): German
ADVERTISING RATES:
Full Page Mono .... EUR 5900
Full Page Colour .... EUR 5900
Mechanical Data: Type Area: 252 x 185 mm, No. of Columns (Display): 3, Col Widths (Display): 60 mm
Copy instructions: *Copy Date:* 21 days prior to publication

CURARE 1626547G56A-11258

Editorial: Spindelstr. 3, 14482 POTSDAM
Tel: 331 7044681 **Fax:** 331 7044682
Freq: 3 issues yearly; Free to qualifying individuals
Annual Sub.: EUR 57,00; **Circ:** 700
Editor: Ekkehard Schröder
Profile: Journal of Medical Anthropology and Transcultural Psychiatry, is a forum of exchange and discussion between those who are interested in traditional medical systems, medical aid programmes, health planning, and related issues. It thereby promotes the interdisciplinary discourse between those disciplines of social and cultural sciences dealing with health, disease, health prevention and healing on the one side and various fields of practical and theoretical medicine on the other.
Language(s): English; French; German
Mechanical Data: Type Area: 210 x 140 mm
Copy instructions: *Copy Date:* 30 days prior to publication

CURIERUL 1633048G21A-4280

Editorial: Alfred-Nobel-Str. 50, 40789 MONHEIM
Tel: 2173 383540 **Fax:** 2173 383454
Email: bernhard.grupp@bayercropscience.com **Web site:** http://www.bayercropscience.com
Cover Price: Free; **Circ:** 4,000
Editor: Bernhard Grupp
Profile: Company publication published by Bayer CropScience.
Language(s): Romanian

CUSTOMBIKE 722861G77A-620

Editorial: Markircher Str. 9a, 68229 MANNHEIM
Tel: 621 4836184 **Fax:** 621 4836153
Email: d.mangartz@huber-verlag.de **Web site:** http://www.custombike.de
Freq: 6 issues yearly; **Annual Sub.:** EUR 27,00; **Circ:** 30,231
Editor: Dirk Mangartz; **Advertising Manager:** Björn Meißner
Profile: Magazine on exclusive bikes.
Language(s): German
ADVERTISING RATES:
Full Page Colour .... EUR 2100
Mechanical Data: Type Area: 256 x 184 mm, No. of Columns (Display): 4, Col Widths (Display): 43 mm
Copy instructions: *Copy Date:* 31 days prior to publication
CONSUMER: MOTORING & CYCLING: Motoring

CUT 1896770G74A-3671

Editorial: Widenmayerstr. 16, 80538 MÜNCHEN
Tel: 89 29001529 **Fax:** 89 29001515
Email: lucie.schmid@cut-magazine.com **Web site:** http://www.cut-magazine.com
Freq: Half-yearly; **Cover Price:** EUR 9,50; **Circ:** 20,000
Editor: Lucie Schmid
Profile: The unconventional fashion-oriented and do-it-yourself magazine for young women and men between 16 and 40 of the world with strong interest in individual Mode.Jungdesigner and young talents will be presented with their careers, creations and the shootings to their collections, expensive fashion spreads staged and derived from this style inspiration. Cut provides guidance for funny creations scene and interviewed personalities with that special something to her wardrobe contents. The magazine researched in the middle of the creative scene and tracks fashion trends. The Urban Special trendy Creative venues are presented with their moods, stores, designers and trendy bars.
Language(s): German
ADVERTISING RATES:
Full Page Mono .... EUR 4800
Full Page Colour .... EUR 5000
Mechanical Data: Type Area: 270 x 210 mm

CUXHAVENER NACHRICHTEN 724741G67B-3880

Editorial: Kaemmererplatz 2, 27472 CUXHAVEN
Tel: 4721 585360 **Fax:** 4721 585369
Email: redaktion@cuxonline.de **Web site:** http://www.cn-online.de
Freq: 312 issues yearly; **Circ:** 25,289
Editor: Hans-Christian Winters; **Advertising Manager:** Ralf Drossner
Profile: Daily newspaper with regional news and a local sports section. Facebook: http://www.facebook.com/pages/Cuxhavener-Nachrichten/117590404925183?ref=search Twitter: http://twitter.com/CN_Online This Outlet offers RSS (Really Simple Syndication).
Language(s): German
Mechanical Data: Type Area: 487 x 324 mm, No. of Columns (Display): 7, Col Widths (Display): 45 mm
Copy instructions: *Copy Date:* 1 day prior to publication
Supplement(s): Cuxjournal; Cuxtipps; Ferienjournal
REGIONAL DAILY & SUNDAY NEWSPAPERS: Regional Daily Newspapers

CYTO-INFO 724753G56A-2320

Editorial: Zur Wasserburg 40, 31228 PEINE
Tel: 5171 292065 **Fax:** 5171 292065
Email: t.barbaric@vdca.de **Web site:** http://www.vdca.de
Freq: Quarterly; Free to qualifying individuals
Annual Sub.: EUR 52,00; **Circ:** 1,800
Editor: Tatjana Barbaric
Profile: Magazine on zytology.
Language(s): German
ADVERTISING RATES:
Full Page Mono .... EUR 370
Full Page Colour .... EUR 592
Mechanical Data: Type Area: 255 x 185 mm, No. of Columns (Display): 2, Col Widths (Display): 90 mm

DA CAPO 724762G89C-4788

Editorial: Ebertallee 45a, 38104 BRAUNSCHWEIG
Tel: 531 798347 **Fax:** 531 798343
Email: da-capo@t-online.de
Freq: Monthly; **Annual Sub.:** EUR 24,00; **Circ:** 10,132
Editor: Birgit Schmied; **Advertising Manager:** Holger Wehrenberg
Profile: Entertainment guide to Braunschweig.
Language(s): German
ADVERTISING RATES:
Full Page Colour .... EUR 950
Mechanical Data: Type Area: 260 x 190 mm, No. of Columns (Display): 4, Col Widths (Display): 44 mm
Copy instructions: *Copy Date:* 15 days prior to publication
CONSUMER: HOLIDAYS & TRAVEL: Entertainment Guides

DA WAIDLER 746832G89A-12119

Editorial: Sachsenring 26, 94481 GRAFENAU
Tel: 8552 3680 **Fax:** 8552 3668
Email: prasser@t-online.de **Web site:** http://www.waidler.com
Freq: 6 issues yearly; **Cover Price:** Free; **Circ:** 15,000
Editor: Roswitha Prasser
Profile: Magazine for tourists including a programme of events for the Grafenau-Schönberg region.
Language(s): German
ADVERTISING RATES:
Full Page Colour .... EUR 490
Mechanical Data: Type Area: 260 x 184 mm, No. of Columns (Display): 4
Copy instructions: *Copy Date:* 21 days prior to publication

DACH + GRÜN 724773G26D-35

Editorial: Reinsburgstr. 82, 70178 STUTTGART
Tel: 711 238860 **Fax:** 711 2388625
Email: joerg.bleyhl@pressecompany.de
Freq: Quarterly; **Annual Sub.:** EUR 24,00; **Circ:** 11,000
Editor: Jörg Bleyhl; **Advertising Manager:** Karin Navaei
Profile: Dach + Grün is supported by three European green roof associations - Germany (FBB), Switzerland (SfG) and Austria (VfB) supported. Dach + Grün is the only German-language journal that deals exclusively with the subjects of the roof, facade and interior greening at a high professional level. For some time now, there a stronger upward movement from the roof greening market.
Language(s): German
Readership: Aimed at professional gardeners within the industry.
ADVERTISING RATES:
Full Page Mono .... EUR 2290
Full Page Colour .... EUR 3550
Mechanical Data: Type Area: 265 x 183 mm, No. of Columns (Display): 4, Col Widths (Display): 42 mm
Copy instructions: *Copy Date:* 21 days prior to publication
BUSINESS: GARDEN TRADE: Garden Trade Horticulture

DACH + HOLZBAU 1986143G4E-7328

Editorial: Avenwedder Str. 55, 33335 GÜTERSLOH
Tel: 5241 8090884 **Fax:** 5241 80690880
Email: roland.herr@bauverlag.de **Web site:** http://www.bauhandwerk.de
Freq: Quarterly; **Annual Sub.:** EUR 29,40; **Circ:** 17,877
Editor: Roland Herr; **Advertising Manager:** Axel Gase-Jochens
Profile: dach + holzbau - the professional magazine for roofers and carpenters - reported four times a year on construction projects, current trends and new products in the roof and timber construction. The special issue of the magazine bauhandwerk is aimed at roofers, carpenters and roof-building materials trade and achieved additional subscribers of bauhandwerk.
Language(s): German
ADVERTISING RATES:
Full Page Mono .... EUR 3320
Full Page Colour .... EUR 4835
Mechanical Data: Type Area: 270 x 186 mm, No. of Columns (Display): 4, Col Widths (Display): 45 mm
Copy instructions: *Copy Date:* 14 days prior to publication

DACH, WAND & BODEN 756541G4E-6912

Editorial: Schwanthalerstr. 10, 80336 MÜNCHEN
Tel: 89 59908122 **Fax:** 89 59908133
Email: claudia.mannschott@cpz.de **Web site:** http://www.bau-welt.de
Freq: Annual; **Cover Price:** Free; **Circ:** 265,000
Editor: Claudia Mannschott; **Advertising Manager:** Sebastian Schmidt
Profile: Magazine containing information for house builders and renovators edition roof, walls and floor.
Language(s): German
ADVERTISING RATES:
Full Page Mono .... EUR 10850
Full Page Colour .... EUR 15500
Mechanical Data: No. of Columns (Display): 4, Col Widths (Display): 42 mm, Type Area: 285 x 175 mm
Copy instructions: *Copy Date:* 40 days prior to publication
Supplement to: Das Einfamilien Haus, Umbauen & Modernisieren, Unser Haus für die ganze Familie

DACHAUER NACHRICHTEN 724767G67B-3900

Editorial: Pfaffenrieder Str. 9, 82515 WOLFRATSHAUSEN **Tel:** 8171 2690
Fax: 8171 269240
Email: fsav@merkur-online.de **Web site:** http://www.merkur-online.de
Freq: 312 issues yearly; **Circ:** 13,681
Advertising Manager: Hans-Georg Bechthold
Profile: The Münchner Merkur with its own local newspapers, of which the Dachauer Nachrichten is one that, the leading regional newspaper brand in the Munich area - the most affluent area of Germany. The combination of newspaper and region is the foundation on which to build the success of the title. This is the newspaper not only the factual news agency, but forms a community of solidarity with its readers and the local community. The clear focus on local reporting creates a high regard to human reader loyalty. She presses one hand in the very high number of close to 180,000 subscribers. Also for the high reader-commitment is the loyalty of the total current 827 000 daily readers, the Münchner Merkur or one of its local newspapers usually read over many years. The Münchner Merkur with its own local newspapers is a newspaper for the whole family, tradition and modern life for one of the most beautiful regions of Germany unites. Reliable, informative, critical: the Münchner Merkur is the indispensable daily newspaper for the region. This Outlet offers RSS (Really Simple Syndication).
Language(s): German
ADVERTISING RATES:
SCC .... EUR 43,60
Mechanical Data: Type Area: 474 x 324 mm, No. of Columns (Display): 7, Col Widths (Display): 45 mm
Copy instructions: *Copy Date:* 1 day prior to publication
REGIONAL DAILY & SUNDAY NEWSPAPERS: Regional Daily Newspapers

DACHAUER RUNDSCHAU 724768G72-3028

Editorial: Konrad-Adenauer-Str. 27, 85221 DACHAU
Tel: 8131 51810 **Fax:** 8131 518130
Email: redaktion@dachauer-rundschau.de **Web site:** http://www.dachauer-rundschau.de
Freq: Weekly; **Cover Price:** Free; **Circ:** 60,200
Editor: Ilona Hahnel-Stienen; **Advertising Manager:** Michael Eisenreich
Profile: Advertising journal (house-to-house) concentrating on local stories.
Language(s): German
ADVERTISING RATES:
Full Page Mono .... EUR 2430
Full Page Colour .... EUR 3159
Mechanical Data: Type Area: 324 x 231 mm, No. of Columns (Display): 5, Col Widths (Display): 45 mm
Copy instructions: *Copy Date:* 1 day prior to publication
LOCAL NEWSPAPERS

DACHBAU MAGAZIN 724770G4E-3100

Editorial: Römerstr. 4, 86438 KISSING
Tel: 8233 237135 **Fax:** 8233 237111
Email: christoph.dauner@weka.de **Web site:** http://www.dachbau-magazin.de
Freq: 9 issues yearly; **Annual Sub.:** EUR 98,00; **Circ:** 9,456
Editor: Christoph Maria Dauner; **Advertising Manager:** C. M. Dauner
Profile: Practice-based reporting techniques in the areas of roof, wall, facade and waterproofing for roofers, architects, wholesale and retail, government, Wohnungsbauges. 's, colleges and industry. The magazine reported: roof téchnology, roofs, green roofs, solar and photovoltaic technology, insulation, waterproofing / roofing of pitched and flat roofs, skylights, Bauklempnerarbeiten, roof windows, skylights, chimney head coverings, roof architecture, current roof design, integrated solar roofing solutions, accurate restoration of historic Roof structures, Reetbedachung, installation of prefabricated dormers, operations management, successful, results-oriented methods for sales, advertising, operating and personnel management, budgeting and computer applications, information on employment, tax and construction law, future-oriented training opportunities for farmers and staff, effective marketing, business equipment, efficient use of assembly techniques, hand machinery, vehicles, cranes, scaffolding, installation aids, office equipment, software for Roofing contractors, industrial safety.
Language(s): German
Readership: Aimed at those in the building and DIY trade, architects and designers.
ADVERTISING RATES:
Full Page Mono .... EUR 2360
Full Page Colour .... EUR 4040
Mechanical Data: Type Area: 258 x 178 mm, No. of Columns (Display): 4, Col Widths (Display): 43 mm
BUSINESS: ARCHITECTURE & BUILDING: Building

DER DACHSHUND 724772G81X-460

Editorial: Prinzenstr. 38, 47058 DUISBURG
Tel: 203 330005 **Fax:** 203 330007
Email: dachshund@dtk1888.de **Web site:** http://www.dtk1888.de
Freq: 10 issues yearly; **Circ:** 17,646
Editor: Margitta Trogisch
Profile: Magazine from the association of basset keepers.
Language(s): German
ADVERTISING RATES:
Full Page Mono .... EUR 1490
Full Page Colour .... EUR 2500
Mechanical Data: Type Area: 260 x 184 mm, No. of Columns (Display): 3, Col Widths (Display): 57 mm
Copy instructions: *Copy Date:* 25 days prior to publication
CONSUMER: ANIMALS & PETS

DAHEIM IN DEUTSCHLAND

1793054G73-615

Editorial: Vordernbergstr. 6, 70191 STUTTGART
Tel: 711 6602559 **Fax:** 711 6602858
Email: redaktion@daheim-in-deutschland.de **Web site:** http://www.daheim-in-deutschland.de
Freq: 7 issues yearly; **Annual Sub.:** EUR 26,90; **Circ:** 39,212
Editor: Michael Kallinger; **Advertising Manager:** Anett Groch
Profile: Daheim in Deutschland is the only national magazine that puts Germany in all its facets into the center of interest and lets the readers come to word in the form of submitted contributions. It is for active people who enjoy being in nature or with friends, who live in the city or the country.
Language(s): German
ADVERTISING RATES:
Full Page Mono .... EUR 9950
Full Page Colour .... EUR 9950
Mechanical Data: Type Area: 297 x 210 mm
Copy instructions: *Copy Date:* 48 days prior to publication
BUSINESS: COMPUTERS & AUTOMATION: Computers Related

DAMALS

724795G94J-80

Editorial: Ernst-Mey-Str. 8, 70771 LEINFELDEN-ECHTERDINGEN **Tel:** 711 7594418
Fax: 711 75945836
Email: damals@konradin.de **Web site:** http://www.damals.de
Freq: Monthly; **Annual Sub.:** EUR 88,80; **Circ:** 25,316
Editor: Marlene P. Hiller; **Advertising Manager:** Gabriele S. Brand
Profile: The magazine makes history and is dedicated to different areas, cultures and eras. Each issue has a thematic focus, often on topics that are currently in the historical and cultural discussion. Reports, information blocks, and interviews illuminate the subject from different sides. Numerous reports on culture and art history, technology and economic history, science and religion complement the classical political and historical events. Exciting, understandable and entertaining write-known scholars, accompanied by an expert editorial board. The magazine offers readers reliable information on the current state of historical research. The texts are complemented by a rich illustrations. Therefore only fitting that the magazine of knowledge with an appealing visual concept. Target groups: people with a strong interest in history, art and culture, politics and social issues. The readership lives in upscale conditions and belong to the socio-economically most powerful layer. RSS (Really Simple Syndication) wird angeboten.
Language(s): German
ADVERTISING RATES:
Full Page Mono .... EUR 3250
Full Page Colour .... EUR 4320
Mechanical Data: Type Area: 250 x 188 mm
Supplement(s): ecco
CONSUMER: OTHER CLASSIFICATIONS: Popular Science

DARMSTÄDTER ECHO

724808G67B-3920

Editorial: Holzhofallee 25, 64295 DARMSTADT
Tel: 6151 3871 **Fax:** 6151 387307
Email: redaktion@darmstaedter-echo.de **Web site:** http://www.echo-online.de
Freq: 312 issues yearly; **Circ:** 50,618
Editor: Jörg Riebartsch; **News Editor:** Rainer H. Schlender; **Advertising Manager:** Andreas Wohlfart
Profile: Regional daily newspaper covering politics, economics, sports, travel and technology. Facebook: http://www.facebook.com/echoonline This Outlet offers RSS (Really Simple Syndication).
Language(s): German
ADVERTISING RATES:
SCC .... EUR 59,70
Mechanical Data: Type Area: 491 x 339 mm, No. of Columns (Display): 7, Col Widths (Display): 45 mm
Copy instructions: *Copy Date:* 1 day prior to publication
Supplement(s): Generation; Gesund leben heute; handwerk aktuell; Die Hupe; i2 immobilien; Kinder Echo; Odenwälder Kartoffelsupp; Sonntags Echo; Start frei; theaterlzeitung
REGIONAL DAILY & SUNDAY NEWSPAPERS: Regional Daily Newspapers

DATENSCHUTZ-BERATER

724828G5R-637

Editorial: Pattweg 8, 50259 PULHEIM
Tel: 2234 927827 **Fax:** 2234 927962
Email: datenschutz-berater@fachverlag.de **Web site:** http://www.datenschutz-berater.de
Freq: 11 issues yearly; **Annual Sub.:** EUR 252,00; **Circ:** 2,800
Editor: Hans Gliss; **Advertising Manager:** Ralf Pötzsch
Profile: The Datenschutz-Berater is a monthly information service of the Handelsblatt publishing group and offers practical reports and organization solutions for corporate and public data protection officials. It provides information on current data protection legislation and new developments in the field of data protection. Decision-makers in companies and government agencies that are responsible for the data protection obtained so a full overview.
Language(s): German
ADVERTISING RATES:
Full Page Mono .... EUR 1355
Full Page Colour .... EUR 2470
Mechanical Data: Type Area: 253 x 176 mm
Copy instructions: *Copy Date:* 22 days prior to publication
BUSINESS: COMPUTERS & AUTOMATION: Computers Related

DATES

1660085G80-14280

Editorial: Fischmarkt 6, 99084 ERFURT
Tel: 361 2417710 **Fax:** 361 2417719
Email: spfeufer@dates-online.de **Web site:** http://www.bewegungsmelder.de/erfurt
Freq: Monthly; **Cover Price:** Free; **Circ:** 24,795
Editor: Stefanie Pfeufer; **Advertising Manager:** Jennifer Habelitz
Profile: City magazine for Erfurt.
Language(s): German
ADVERTISING RATES:
Full Page Mono .... EUR 1090
Full Page Colour .... EUR 1850
Mechanical Data: Type Area: 270 x 190 mm, No. of Columns (Display): 4, Col Widths (Display): 44 mm
CONSUMER: RURAL & REGIONAL INTEREST

DATES

724833G89C-4789

Editorial: Zum Handelshof 7, 39108 MAGDEBURG
Tel: 391 7325230 **Fax:** 391 7325231
Email: redaktion@dates-online.de **Web site:** http://www.bewegungsmelder.de/dates
Freq: Monthly; **Cover Price:** Free; **Circ:** 30,356
Editor: Conrad Engelhardt; **Advertising Manager:** Jörg Segler
Profile: Magazine for Magdeburg and surrounding area (Haldensleben, Schönebeck, Wolmirstedt). Dates reported on local issues as well as events (music shows, exhibitions, films, etc.). It targets aimed at young urbanites that are trendy and culturally active. Self-distributed in clubs, trendy shops, restaurants, pubs, cinemas, bookstores, gas stations and other public venues.
Language(s): German
ADVERTISING RATES:
Full Page Mono .... EUR 1290
Full Page Colour .... EUR 2200
Mechanical Data: Type Area: 270 x 190 mm, No. of Columns (Display): 6, Col Widths (Display): 30 mm
CONSUMER: HOLIDAYS & TRAVEL: Entertainment Guides

DATEV MAGAZIN

1605886G1A-3479

Editorial: Paumgartnerstr. 6, 90429 NÜRNBERG
Tel: 911 3190 **Fax:** 911 3193196
Email: magazin@datev.de **Web site:** http://www.datev.de
Freq: 6 issues yearly; **Circ:** 42,000
Profile: Company publication published by DATEV.
Language(s): German
ADVERTISING RATES:
Full Page Mono .... EUR 3290
Full Page Colour .... EUR 5750
Mechanical Data: No. of Columns (Display): 3, Col Widths (Display): 55 mm, Type Area: 263 x 192 mm

DATEV MAGAZIN

1605886G1A-3837

Editorial: Paumgartnerstr. 6, 90429 NÜRNBERG
Tel: 911 3190 **Fax:** 911 3193196
Email: magazin@datev.de **Web site:** http://www.datev.de
Freq: 6 issues yearly; **Circ:** 42,000
Profile: Company publication published by DATEV.
Language(s): German
ADVERTISING RATES:
Full Page Mono .... EUR 3290
Full Page Colour .... EUR 5750
Mechanical Data: No. of Columns (Display): 3, Col Widths (Display): 55 mm, Type Area: 263 x 192 mm

DATTELNER MORGENPOST

724839G67B-3940

Editorial: Kampstr. 84b, 45772 MARL **Tel:** 2365 1070
Fax: 2365 1071490
Email: info@medienhaus-bauer.de **Web site:** http://www.medienhaus-bauer.de
Freq: 312 issues yearly; **Circ:** 6,332
Advertising Manager: Carsten Dingerkuss
Profile: Regional daily newspaper with news on politics, economy, culture, sports, travel, technology, etc. The newspaper offers a mix of local, regional and international News from all areas. Fun and interactive content such as forums, polls or betting games are also part of the program. Local out of the city and the neighborhood is the focus of attention. Facebook: http://www.facebook.com/medienhbauer This Outlet offers RSS (Really Simple Syndication).
Language(s): German
ADVERTISING RATES:
SCC .... EUR 26,30
Mechanical Data: Type Area: 487 x 325 mm, No. of Columns (Display): 7, Col Widths (Display): 43 mm
Copy instructions: *Copy Date:* 1 day prior to publication
Supplement(s): prisma
REGIONAL DAILY & SUNDAY NEWSPAPERS: Regional Daily Newspapers

DATZ

724840G81E-4

Editorial: Skagerrakstr. 36, 45888 GELSENKIRCHEN
Tel: 209 1474301 **Fax:** 209 1474302
Email: stawikowski@ms-verlag.de **Web site:** http://www.datz.de
Freq: Monthly; **Annual Sub.:** EUR 68,80; **Circ:** 10,500
Editor: Rainer Stawikowski; **Advertising Manager:** Alexandra Rooke
Profile: The Datz-content concept: As a generalist Datz covers every month three areas: fresh water, sea water, pond. Datz is thus required reading for all aquarists who operate their hobby with particular enthusiasm. The constant themes: • keeping and breeding of aquarium animals • Plants and Design • Techniques and Water Sciences • nutrition and animal health • Newly imported animals and plants • Habitat descriptions • Behavioral observations • habitat and species protection • Systematics and faunistic • Destinations • Public aquaria • garden pond technology, animals, and plants.
Language(s): German
ADVERTISING RATES:
Full Page Mono .... EUR 1860
Full Page Colour .... EUR 2640
Mechanical Data: Type Area: 254 x 185 mm, No. of Columns (Display): 4, Col Widths (Display): 42 mm
Copy instructions: *Copy Date:* 35 days prior to publication
Official Journal of: Organ d. Verb. Dt. Vereine f. Aquarien- u. Terrarienkunde u. d. Verb. d. österr. Aquarien- u. Terrarienvereine
Supplement to: Aquarien-Praxis
CONSUMER: ANIMALS & PETS: Fish

DAUN-GEROLSTEINER WOCHENSPIEGEL

724842G72-3044

Editorial: Gartenstr. 6, 54550 DAUN
Tel: 6592 985601 **Fax:** 6592 985602
Email: red-daun@weiss-verlag.de **Web site:** http://www.wochenspiegellive.de
Freq: Weekly; **Cover Price:** Free; **Circ:** 28,294
Editor: Alexander Lenders
Profile: Advertising journal (house-to-house) concentrating on local stories.
Language(s): German
ADVERTISING RATES:
Full Page Mono .... EUR 2890
Full Page Colour .... EUR 4034
Mechanical Data: Type Area: 430 x 290 mm, No. of Columns (Display): 7, Col Widths (Display): 38 mm
Copy instructions: *Copy Date:* 2 days prior to publication
LOCAL NEWSPAPERS

DAV PANORAMA

724848G75L-320

Editorial: Von-Kahr-Str. 2, 80997 MÜNCHEN
Tel: 89 140030 **Fax:** 89 14000398
Email: dav-panorama@alpenverein.de **Web site:** http://www.dav-panorama.de
Freq: 6 issues yearly; **Circ:** 557,823
Editor: Georg Hohenester
Profile: DAV Panorama is the traditional and service-oriented leisure magazine of the German Alpine Club. It is aimed at those who spend their time actively in the Alps: hiking, mountaineering, climbing, trekking, traveling, mountain bikers, cyclists, skiers, etc. - all-round sportsman 290 000 8 sports practice, everything from Twitter: http://twitter.com/DAV_Alpenverein.
Language(s): German
Readership: Aimed at mountain climbers.
ADVERTISING RATES:
Full Page Mono .... EUR 14800
Full Page Colour .... EUR 19400
Mechanical Data: Type Area: 244 x 185 mm, No. of Columns (Display): 4, Col Widths (Display): 43 mm
Copy instructions: *Copy Date:* 57 days prior to publication
Supplement(s): Winter Journal
CONSUMER: SPORT: Outdoor

DAZ AUTO TOTAL

724850G77A-880

Editorial: An der Strusbek 23, 22926 AHRENSBURG
Tel: 4102 47870 **Fax:** 4102 478795
Email: info@daz-verlag.de **Web site:** http://www.daz24.de
Freq: 13 issues yearly; **Annual Sub.:** EUR 29,00; **Circ:** 24,664
Editor: Matthias Rose; **Advertising Manager:** Marco Wendlandt
Profile: Magazine with advertisements of exclusive cars. The magazine has an interesting selection of many thousands of vehicles with images. The focus is on the offers from the car trade.
Language(s): German
ADVERTISING RATES:
Full Page Mono .... EUR 2468
Full Page Colour .... EUR 2468
Mechanical Data: Type Area: 355 x 250 mm, No. of Columns (Display): 5, Col Widths (Display): 46 mm
Copy instructions: *Copy Date:* 5 days prior to publication
CONSUMER: MOTORING & CYCLING: Motoring

DAZ CARS!

1799755G77A-2783

Editorial: An der Strusbek 23, 22926 AHRENSBURG
Tel: 4102 47870 **Fax:** 4102 478795
Email: info@daz-verlag.de **Web site:** http://www.daz24.de
Freq: 13 issues yearly; **Cover Price:** Free; **Circ:** 35,000
Advertising Manager: Marco Wendlandt
Profile: Offer magazine around the small and medium-sized car.
Language(s): German
ADVERTISING RATES:
Full Page Mono .... EUR 650
Full Page Colour .... EUR 650
Mechanical Data: Type Area: 275 x 190 mm

DAZ DEUTSCHE APOTHEKERZEITUNG

725001G37-820

Editorial: Birkenwaldstr. 44, 70191 STUTTGART
Tel: 711 2582238 **Fax:** 711 2582291
Email: daz@deutscher-apotheker-verlag.de **Web site:** http://www.deutsche-apotheker-zeitung.de
Freq: Weekly; **Annual Sub.:** EUR 261,80; **Circ:** 29,026
Editor: Peter Ditzel; **Advertising Manager:** Kornelia Wind
Profile: The "Deutsche Apotheker Zeitung" (DAZ) is the pharmaceutical trade magazine for all pharmacists and all other pharmaceutical professionals. The DAZ is the only pharmaceutical trade magazine that has about 20,000 (IVW) personally paying subscribers (the closest reader-bound). Focus of the editorial program is to provide all information and news from the fields of science, drug therapy, surgery, occupational and health policy and law and order, which are of interest for pharmaceutical professionals. This includes current releases and information about medicines, review articles by recognized professional authors from science and practice, meeting and conference reports, news about drugs and drug therapies, comments and opinions. The DAZ also has four regularly published editorial supplements: Neue Arzneimittel - Student und Praktikant - Geschichte der Pharmazie - PKaktiv. The annual subscription also includes the weekly supply of Apotheker Zeitung (DAZ-Monday edition) and full access to DAZ.online. Six times a year the Apotheken Praxis is in the DAZ, with current contributions to communications and marketing. One focus of the Apotheken Praxis, the customer contact and client meetings. Marketing know-how, pharmacy operations, pharmacy design and pharmacy needs are the other foci. The contributions are distinguished by particular practical relevance. The DAZ is indispensable for every pharmacist in the pharmacy, hospital pharmacy, academia, government agencies and industry.
Language(s): German
Readership: Aimed at pharmacy owners.
ADVERTISING RATES:
Full Page Mono .... EUR 3650
Full Page Colour .... EUR 5330
Mechanical Data: Type Area: 250 x 182 mm, No. of Columns (Display): 3, Col Widths (Display): 48 mm
Copy instructions: *Copy Date:* 7 days prior to publication
Supplement(s): AP Apotheken Praxis; Geschichte der Pharmazie; Neue Arzneimittel; PKA aktiv; Student und Praktikant
BUSINESS: PHARMACEUTICAL & CHEMISTS

DAZ TRANSPORTER

1665398G49A-2389

Editorial: An der Strusbek 23, 22926 AHRENSBURG
Tel: 4102 47870 **Fax:** 4102 478795
Email: a.aepler@daz-verlag.de **Web site:** http://www.daz-transporter.de
Freq: 13 issues yearly; **Annual Sub.:** EUR 39,00; **Circ:** 8,618
Editor: Andreas Aepler; **Advertising Manager:** Marco Wendlandt
Profile: Offer magaziner for transporters, busses, pickups and vans.
Language(s): German
ADVERTISING RATES:
Full Page Mono .... EUR 1705
Full Page Colour .... EUR 1705
Mechanical Data: Type Area: 275 x 190 mm, No. of Columns (Display): 4, Col Widths (Display): 45 mm

DB DEUTSCHE BAUZEITUNG

724862G4E-3120

Editorial: Ernst-Mey-Str. 8, 70771 LEINFELDEN-ECHTERDINGEN **Tel:** 711 7594560
Fax: 711 7594211
Email: db.redaktion@konradin.de **Web site:** http://db.bauzeitung.de
Freq: Monthly; Free to qualifying individuals
Annual Sub.: EUR 144,00; **Circ:** 31,034
Editor: Ulrike Kunkel; **Advertising Manager:** Bettina Mayer
Profile: Comprehensive architectural criticism, building culture, and technical innovations and developments are the central themes of the db deutsche bauzeitung, the oldest and most famous German architectural journal. The db filters the relevant issues of construction processes, classifying, questioning them critically, provides background knowledge, takes a stand and makes an active contribution to the architectural debate. The monthly focal point for exemplary projects from home and abroad, urban planning, architectural, construction, civil engineering, energy and economic point of view are presented critically and are accompanied by additional technical articles on the topic. In the column technology news, new technical developments, reflecting their importance to the construction activities and their future applications. Because of the particular relevance of the topic of energy, energy-efficient building is dedicated to the db with all aspects of the past four years, an entire section.
Language(s): German
ADVERTISING RATES:
Full Page Mono .... EUR 7580
Full Page Colour .... EUR 10550
Mechanical Data: Type Area: 270 x 188 mm, No. of Columns (Display): 4, Col Widths (Display): 44 mm
Official Journal of: Organ d. Bundes Dt. Baumeister, Architekten u. Ingenieure e.V.
BUSINESS: ARCHITECTURE & BUILDING: Building

Germany

DBB MAGAZIN 724854G32A-680
Editorial: Friedrichstr. 169, 10117 BERLIN
Tel: 30 408140 **Fax:** 30 40815598
Email: magazin@dbb.de **Web site:** http://www.dbb.de
Freq: 10 issues yearly; Free to qualifying individuals
Annual Sub.: EUR 32,90; **Circ:** 584,281
Editor: Walter Schmitz; **Advertising Manager:** Katy Netz
Profile: The magazine is the journal of the dbb officers nationwide, collective union for civil servants, employees and workers in public services and rail and mail. The dbb magazin information about job and wage policy and presents association activities. Entertaining features, interviews, information on training, travel tips and online news round off the editorial content.
Language(s): German
ADVERTISING RATES:
Full Page Mono .... EUR 12180
Full Page Colour .... EUR 18770
Mechanical Data: Type Area: 270 x 185 mm, No. of Columns (Display): 4, Col Widths (Display): 43 mm
Copy instructions: *Copy Date:* 42 days prior to publication
BUSINESS: LOCAL GOVERNMENT, LEISURE & RECREATION: Local Government

DBI DER BAYERISCHE INTERNIST 722123G56A-1520
Editorial: E.-C.-Baumann-Str. 5, 95326 KULMBACH
Tel: 9221 949393 **Fax:** 9221 949377
Email: bfv@mg-oberfranken.de **Web site:** http://www.der-bayerische-internist.de
Freq: 6 issues yearly; **Annual Sub.:** EUR 48,00; **Circ:** 12,641
Editor: E. Hiller; **Advertising Manager:** Gabriele Lenhard
Profile: Publication focusing on internal medicine.
Language(s): German
ADVERTISING RATES:
Full Page Mono .... EUR 2100
Full Page Colour .... EUR 3100
Mechanical Data: Type Area: 237 x 174 mm, No. of Columns (Display): 4, Col Widths (Display): 40 mm
BUSINESS: HEALTH & MEDICAL

DBK DEUTSCHE BAUERN KORRESPONDENZ 1861195G21A-4413
Editorial: Claire-Waldoff-Str. 7, 10117 BERLIN
Tel: 30 31904242 **Fax:** 30 31904431
Email: presse@bauernverband.net **Web site:** http://www.bauernverband.de
Freq: Monthly; **Annual Sub.:** EUR 33,50; **Circ:** 5,000
Editor: Anni Neu
Profile: The dbk Deutsche Bauern Korrespondenz is the monthly journal of the German Farmers' Association. dbk analyzed current and national agricultural policy issues for the honor and full-time elected officials of the DBV. Facebook: http://www.facebook.com/pages/Deutschlands-Bauern/116869994990037.
Language(s): German

DBU AKTUELL 1903317G57-2906
Editorial: An der Bornau 2, 49090 OSNABRÜCK
Tel: 541 9633962 **Fax:** 541 9633990
Email: zuk-info@dbu.de **Web site:** http://www.dbu.de
Freq: 11 issues yearly; **Cover Price:** Free; **Circ:** 9,000
Editor: Stefan Rümmele
Profile: Information from the activity of the German Federal Environmental Foundation.
Language(s): German

DBW DIE BETRIEBSWIRTSCHAFT 724867G14A-1660
Editorial: Werastr. 21, 70182 STUTTGART
Tel: 711 21940 **Fax:** 711 2194218
Email: dbw@schaeffer-poeschel.de **Web site:** http://www.dbwnet.de
Freq: 6 issues yearly; **Annual Sub.:** EUR 89,00; **Circ:** 1,500
Editor: Marita Rollnik-Mollenhauer; **Advertising Manager:** Petra Bourscheid
Profile: Magazine on business economies for managers, scientists and students.
Language(s): German
ADVERTISING RATES:
Full Page Mono .... EUR 537
Mechanical Data: Type Area: 215 x 144 mm, No. of Columns (Display): 2, Col Widths (Display): 70 mm
Copy instructions: *Copy Date:* 30 days prior to publication

DBZ DEUTSCHE BAUZEITSCHRIFT 724870G4E-3140
Editorial: Avenwedder Str. 55, 33335 GÜTERSLOH
Tel: 5241 802111 **Fax:** 5241 80690880
Email: burkhard.froehlich@bauverlag.de **Web site:** http://www.dbz.de
Freq: Monthly; **Annual Sub.:** EUR 165,00; **Circ:** 30,766
Editor: Burkhard Fröhlich; **Advertising Manager:** Andreas Kirchgessner
Profile: Since its founding in 1953, the DBZ Deutsche BauZeitschrift one of the most respected and independent architectural magazines has developed. With the priority fields of architecture, construction technology and products it is every month the desire of architects and civil engineers for practical assistance in solving the daily work tasks. A comprehensive range of topics covers all relevant segments of the construction planning.
Language(s): German
ADVERTISING RATES:
Full Page Mono .... EUR 6990
Full Page Colour .... EUR 10730
Mechanical Data: Type Area: 259 x 200 mm, No. of Columns (Display): 4, Col Widths (Display): 47 mm
Copy instructions: *Copy Date:* 14 days prior to publication
Official Journal of: Organ d. BDB Bund Dt. Baumeister, Architekten u. Ingenieure e.V.
Supplement(s): Brandschutz in öffentlichen und privatwirtschaftlichen Gebäuden; computer spezial; Licht + Raum
BUSINESS: ARCHITECTURE & BUILDING: Building

DBZ LICHT+RAUM 723824G4E-2960
Editorial: Avenwedder Str. 55, 33335 GÜTERSLOH
Tel: 5241 8090884 **Fax:** 5241 80690880
Email: burkhard.froehlich@bauverlag.de **Web site:** http://www.bauverlag-media.de
Freq: Quarterly; **Annual Sub.:** EUR 69,00; **Circ:** 18,000
Editor: Burkhard Fröhlich; **Advertising Manager:** Andreas Kirchgessner
Profile: Magazine on office design and planning, light design, control and communications technologies and air conditioning technology.
Language(s): German
ADVERTISING RATES:
Full Page Mono .... EUR 5230
Full Page Colour .... EUR 8310
Mechanical Data: Type Area: 259 x 200 mm, No. of Columns (Display): 4, Col Widths (Display): 45 mm

D.B.Z MAGAZIN 724872G8A-220
Editorial: Vierhausstr. 112, 44807 BOCHUM
Tel: 234 9019932 **Fax:** 234 9019949
Email: kleinemeier@backmedia.info **Web site:** http://www.backmedia.info
Freq: 13 issues yearly; **Annual Sub.:** EUR 130,00; **Circ:** 11,935
Editor: Hermann Kleinemeier; **Advertising Manager:** Katja Lofi
Profile: The monthly D.B.Z magazin is the successful user title for the baking industry and achieved both the craft and the branch offices in Germany, Austria and Switzerland. D.B.Z magazin offers the highest levels of professional technology titles in all professional baker trade magazines. Detailed technical issues with practical examples present solutions for production and sales. In addition, the D.B.Z magazin latest news, interviews, recipes, management reports of German and international top companies as well as articles on business and legal issues. With the heading special location raises the D.B.Z magazin also look beyond the typical bakery and shows extraordinary places in which is also baked. This diversity is augmented by the themes of snacks, coffee, computers and cars - suitable to meet the increased customer demands at bakeries. Demonstrated the qualities of D.B.Z magazin in a survey by the prestigious EMNID Institute (published 2007) with peaks among readers in the areas of competence and acceptance.
Language(s): German
ADVERTISING RATES:
Full Page Mono .... EUR 4222
Full Page Colour .... EUR 6000
Mechanical Data: Type Area: 270 x 189 mm, No. of Columns (Display): 4, Col Widths (Display): 45 mm
Copy instructions: *Copy Date:* 7 days prior to publication
BUSINESS: BAKING & CONFECTIONERY: Baking

D.B.Z WECKRUF 724868G8A-180
Editorial: Vierhausstr. 112, 44807 BOCHUM
Tel: 234 9019942 **Fax:** 234 9019999
Email: arends@backmedia.info **Web site:** http://www.backmedia.info
Freq: 40 issues yearly; **Annual Sub.:** EUR 130,00; **Circ:** 5,328
Editor: Heike Arends; **Advertising Manager:** Katja Lofi
Profile: The D.B.Z Weckruf is firmly rooted in craft bakeries. The traditional title with nearly a hundred years of history has a very high level of reader loyalty. The high proportion of subscription by more than half the total circulation proves the importance of the D.B.Z Weckruf from the readers. In particular, the regional reference binds to a large number of readers. It is also interesting for advertisers, enabling them to accurately reach their target audience. As an organ of the Bakers' Associations Westfalen-Lippe, Rhineland and Bavaria is the D.B.Z Weckruf particularly strong in western and southern Germany.
Language(s): German
ADVERTISING RATES:
Full Page Mono .... EUR 2485
Full Page Colour .... EUR 4100
Mechanical Data: Type Area: 270 x 189 mm, No. of Columns (Display): 4, Col Widths (Display): 45 mm
Copy instructions: *Copy Date:* 7 days prior to publication
Official Journal of: Organ d. Bäckerinnungs-Verbände Rheinland, Westfalen-Lippe u. Bayern
BUSINESS: BAKING & CONFECTIONERY: Baking

DCC-CAMPINGFÜHRER EUROPA 724873G89A-520
Editorial: Mandlstr. 28, 80802 MÜNCHEN
Tel: 89 3801420 **Fax:** 89 38014242
Email: info@camping-club.de **Web site:** http://www.camping-club.de
Freq: Annual; **Cover Price:** EUR 19,90; **Circ:** 80,000
Editor: Karl Zahlmann
Profile: The camping guide informed over 6000 campsites in Europe, more than 1,400 campsites in Germany, clear 5-star classification, detailed information on individual sites, with e-mail addresses, available with GPS data as far as general maps of the transit countries, the sSeparate Map Germany "rote Punkt" for motor caravan service stations, mobile homes and tents, rental information to caravan, bungalow, Alpine passes and passports, Winter Sports Camps. Additional Information: specially marked DCC contract places and natural places.
Language(s): German
ADVERTISING RATES:
Full Page Mono .... EUR 2655
Full Page Colour .... EUR 4800
Mechanical Data: Type Area: 212 x 144 mm, No. of Columns (Display): 2, Col Widths (Display): 67 mm
Copy instructions: *Copy Date:* 135 days prior to publication

DDH DAS DACHDECKER-HANDWERK 724877G4E-3160
Editorial: Stolberger Str. 84, 50933 KÖLN
Tel: 221 5497201 **Fax:** 221 5496201
Email: red.ddh@rudolf-mueller.de **Web site:** http://www.ddh.de
Freq: 23 issues yearly; **Annual Sub.:** EUR 201,00; **Circ:** 10,426
Editor: Elke Herbst; **Advertising Manager:** Elke Herbst
Profile: DDH Das Dachdecker-Handwerk is Germany's leading magazine for roof, wall and insulation technology. In 23 issues per year receive roof specialists trade information for their profession. The diverse range of topics geared to the needs of the market, the individual contributions and categories - technology, products, ZVDH, roof + Timber, company and industry - are tailored to the everyday work of a roofer. Market surveys, economic barometers, market levels and detailed reporting on fairs to help roof specialists to compete in the marketplace. The hand on the pulse of the industry, DDH Das Dachdecker-Handwerk also provides information about new markets and helps the roofer, to attract new business.
Language(s): German
ADVERTISING RATES:
Full Page Mono .... EUR 3850
Full Page Colour .... EUR 6355
Mechanical Data: Type Area: 267 x 188 mm, No. of Columns (Display): 4, Col Widths (Display): 44 mm
Copy instructions: *Copy Date:* 21 days prior to publication
Official Journal of: Organ d. Zentralverb. d. Dt. Dachdeckerhandwerks e.V.
BUSINESS: ARCHITECTURE & BUILDING: Building

DDH EDITION 724878G4E-3180
Editorial: Stolberger Str. 84, 50933 KÖLN
Tel: 221 5497201 **Fax:** 221 5496201
Email: red.ddh@rudolf-mueller.de **Web site:** http://www.ddh.de
Freq: Half-yearly; **Cover Price:** EUR 20,00; **Circ:** 8,000
Advertising Manager: Elke Herbst
Profile: The DDH Editionen each focusing on a subject of Roofers.
Language(s): German
ADVERTISING RATES:
Full Page Mono .... EUR 3215
Full Page Colour .... EUR 5720
Mechanical Data: Type Area: 267 x 188 mm, No. of Columns (Display): 3, Col Widths (Display): 58 mm
Copy instructions: *Copy Date:* 32 days prior to publication

DDS 724882G23A-140
Editorial: Ernst-Mey-Str. 8, 70771 LEINFELDEN-ECHTERDINGEN **Tel:** 711 7594455
Fax: 711 7594397
Email: hans-joerg.graffe@konradin.de **Web site:** http://www.dds-online.de
Freq: Monthly; **Annual Sub.:** EUR 136,80; **Circ:** 21,208
Editor: Hans-Jörg Graffé; **Advertising Manager:** Andreas Schweizer
Profile: dds the leading trade magazine for carpenters and joiners, interior designers and window builder. dds reported in each issue comprehensively on the issues of design, technology, marketing and training. With monthly title issues, specific priorities are set. The editorial preparation of the information is concise and focused on solutions. The Meinungsfreudigkeit the editors provide the reader with the classification and assessment of industry events and facilitating his orientation. Regular testing of tools and machinery, market surveys, CAD workshops, trade show reports and interviews provide background knowledge and support investment decisions. With dds WINDOOR, a quarterly "Special section, " the magazine offers a forum for the components industry. Manufacturers, distributors and installers of windows and doors made of wood, plastic and aluminum found much information carefully on the subject components.
Language(s): German
ADVERTISING RATES:
Full Page Mono .... EUR 5580
Full Page Colour .... EUR 8040
Mechanical Data: Type Area: 270 x 188 mm, No. of Columns (Display): 4, Col Widths (Display): 44 mm
Official Journal of: Organ d. Fach- bzw. Wirtschaftsverbände Holz u. Kunststoff in Baden, Baden-Württemberg, Bayern, Berlin, Brandenburg, Hamburg, Hessen, Mecklenburg-Vorpommern, Nordrhein-Westfalen u. Rheinland-Pfalz
BUSINESS: FURNISHINGS & FURNITURE

DE DER ELEKTRO- UND GEBÄUDETECHNIKER 724894G17-1537
Editorial: Lazarettstr. 4, 80636 MÜNCHEN
Tel: 89 12607248 **Fax:** 89 12607111
Email: redaktion@de-online.info **Web site:** http://www.de-online.info
Freq: 20 issues yearly; **Annual Sub.:** EUR 120,00; **Circ:** 43,691
Editor: Andreas Stöcklhuber; **Advertising Manager:** Michael Dietl
Profile: The journal provides electrical engineering expertise in the full range of electrical installation and building technology and renewable energies (photovoltaic, solar thermal, heat pumps, wind power), but also from the fields of information and automation technology. In-depth technical articles modern technologies, systems and applications are explained. Practical application examples produce the reference to the professional life of the reader. Target audience: owners, managers and senior staff from the electrical trade, planners, engineers and technicians, electrician, electricians in industrial, energy companies and the public sector, employees in the electrical wholesale trade.
Language(s): German
ADVERTISING RATES:
Full Page Mono .... EUR 6420
Full Page Colour .... EUR 9645
Mechanical Data: Type Area: 256 x 185 mm, No. of Columns (Display): 4, Col Widths (Display): 46 mm
Copy instructions: *Copy Date:* 19 days prior to publication
Official Journal of: Organ d. Zentralverb. d. Dt. Elektro- u. Informationstechn. Handwerke ZVEH u. d. angeschlossenen Landesinnungs-Verbände
Supplement(s): Bayern Live; E.Punkt NRW
BUSINESS: ELECTRICAL

DE UTKIEKER 1864719G89A-12427
Editorial: Marienkamper Str. 1, 26427 ESENS
Tel: 4971 91050 **Fax:** 4971 910550
Email: info@soeker-druck.de **Web site:** http://www.de-utkieker.de
Freq: 8 issues yearly; **Annual Sub.:** EUR 27,30; **Circ:** 6,500
Profile: Publication featuring information about the spa resort Langehoog, including programme of events.
Language(s): German
Mechanical Data: Type Area: 180 x 86 mm

DE VOOR 746701G21A-1080
Editorial: John-Deere-Str. 70, 68163 MANNHEIM
Tel: 621 8298418 **Fax:** 621 8298300
Email: hironjeanclaude@johndeere.com **Web site:** http://www.johndeere.com
Freq: Quarterly; **Cover Price:** Free; **Circ:** 49,000
Editor: Jean-Claude Hiron
Profile: Company publication published by Deere & Company.
Language(s): Dutch

DEAL MAGAZIN 1705258G14A-9832
Editorial: Promenadeplatz 12, 80333 MÜNCHEN
Tel: 89 244488810 **Fax:** 89 244488829
Email: pr@deal-magazin.com **Web site:** http://www.deal-magazin.com
Freq: Quarterly; **Annual Sub.:** EUR 27,20; **Circ:** 25,000
Editor: Bernd Eger; **Advertising Manager:** Bernd Eger
Profile: Business magazine for real estate, investment and financial topics. Twitter: http://twitter.com/#!/DealMagazin.
Language(s): German
ADVERTISING RATES:
Full Page Mono .... EUR 5880
Full Page Colour .... EUR 5880
Mechanical Data: Type Area: 297 x 210 mm

DECO 724892G23A-765
Editorial: Nymphenburger Str. 1, 80335 MÜNCHEN
Tel: 89 29001188 **Fax:** 89 29001190
Email: friederike.sauter@winkler-online.de **Web site:** http://www.deco.de
Freq: 5 issues yearly; **Annual Sub.:** EUR 32,00; **Circ:** 69,290
Editor: Friederike Sauter; **Advertising Manager:** Gunnar Reckstat
Profile: The Living magazine dedicated to the only German-language media entirely of the textile, high-quality and exclusive interior. Nowhere else will readers find more ideas for the toile de Jouy, jacquard or Vichy-Karo effectively set the scene. Seduce extravagant residential and hotel reports from the most beautiful locations in the world of dreams. In diverse portraits of young designers, artisans and businesses, the magazine also raises a look behind the scenes of the interior design scene. Compact and clearly presents an extra share tips and news on special topics such as kitchen, bathroom, garden & Co. The target group are the higher end of a

et household income have to be informed and a rowing number of professional interior designers who appreciate about innovations in the field of nterior textiles and furniture quickly and selected.
Language(s): German
Readership: Aimed at interior designers.
ADVERTISING RATES:
Full Page Colour .... EUR 7460
Mechanical Data: Type Area: 266 x 185 mm, No. of Columns (Display): 4, Col Widths (Display): 42 mm
Copy instructions: *Copy Date:* 75 days prior to publication
BUSINESS: FURNISHINGS & FURNITURE

DEDICA 724895G2A-900
Editorial: Blumenstr. 15, 90402 NÜRNBERG
Tel: 911 2018240 **Fax:** 911 2018100
Email: dedica@harnisch.com **Web site:** http://www.dedica.de
Freq: Quarterly; **Annual Sub.:** EUR 42,00; **Circ:** 10,341
Editor: Yvonne Weiß; **Advertising Manager:** Yvonne Weiß
Profile: dedica is a trade magazine that reports independent of distribution channels, through advertising media, incentives and promotions. Four times a year you will find information on selected topics as well as Company and Product news, Fair reports, association news and much more. dedica the goal of the wide range of objective advertising is to present detailed and transparent. The reader will find strategies for effective use of advertising media, coupled with information on topics from marketing and business management. dedica serves all areas can be tackled effectively through existing sales organization. The reader will successful benefit from this wealth of ideas and suggestions. The advertiser is here to make its products and new solutions for discussion and to convince the market of products and services.
Language(s): German
Readership: Read by marketing managers.
ADVERTISING RATES:
Full Page Mono .... EUR 2500
Full Page Colour .... EUR 3700
Mechanical Data: Type Area: 256 x 175 mm, No. of Columns (Display): 4, Col Widths (Display): 40 mm
Copy instructions: *Copy Date:* 28 days prior to publication
BUSINESS: COMMUNICATIONS, ADVERTISING & MARKETING

DEGA GALABAU 1827410G21A-4379
Editorial: Wollgrasweg 41, 70599 STUTTGART
Tel: 711 4507218 **Fax:** 711 4507207
Email: dega@ulmer.de **Web site:** http://www.dega-galabau.de
Freq: Monthly; **Annual Sub.:** EUR 128,60; **Circ:** 7,039
Editor: Tjards Wendebourg; **Advertising Manager:** Marc Alber
Profile: Dega Galabau is the magazine for horticulture and landscaping. The horticulture and landscaping contractor gets in tight and entertaining way everything that is important for the successful management: recent developments in terms of business and construction law, current knowledge of construction technology, standardization and product development, tips for successful marketing, current trends in the design and planting of open spaces (gardens, commercial complexes, public spaces), new products (building materials, plants, machinery, vehicles), dates, tax tips, job and used machinery market, tips for personal and business everyday-life, current overview of the industry. Taut journalistic texts edited it possible for businesses to get information fast and thereby to learn more than comparable properties. Dega Galabau keeps an eye on the overall market and is a reliable partner in business everyday-life. The constant themes are horticulture and landscaping news, business administration / management, construction management and IT, landscaping and horticulture Marketing, Construction machines & techniques, working methods and construction technology, design and use of plants, landscaping and open space management, turf / golf / sports field, tree care, education.
Language(s): German
ADVERTISING RATES:
Full Page Mono .... EUR 2700
Full Page Colour .... EUR 3810
Mechanical Data: Type Area: 270 x 175 mm, No. of Columns (Display): 4, Col Widths (Display): 40 mm
Copy instructions: *Copy Date:* 22 days prior to publication

DEGA GRÜNER MARKT 729307G26B-30
Editorial: Wollgrasweg 41, 70599 STUTTGART
Tel: 711 4507215 **Fax:** 711 4507207
Email: redaktion-gm@ulmer.de **Web site:** http://www.gruener-markt-online.de
Freq: 6 issues yearly; **Annual Sub.:** EUR 108,00; **Circ:** 3,959
Editor: Doris Ganninger-Hauck; **Advertising Manager:** Yasmin Heyer
Profile: Dega Grüner Markt is - for over 50 years - a comprehensive knowledge source for decision makers in the garden market industry. Dega Grüner Markt - The Magazine for success in the garden retail deals current issues on exclusive, is close to the people, gives guidance for planning and everyday life. Dega Grüner Markt is not only editorially credible, but also fresh, entertaining and high quality features. All topics and texts are journalistic processed and allow the reader to get information fast and fun. The topics cover the full range of market and companies. Developments in the industry are commented on and rated. Product examples and suggestions for modern management of companies are in addition to opinions from industry experts and leading industry participants - A mix for maximum benefit. The constant themes including industry news, business and management, plants and product lines, markets and fairs. Facebook: http://www.facebook.com/pages/DEGA-Gartenbau-Produktion-Handel/120523167985050.
Language(s): German
Readership: Aimed at purchasers of horticultural supplies.
ADVERTISING RATES:
Full Page Mono .... EUR 2444
Full Page Colour .... EUR 3509
Mechanical Data: Type Area: 260 x 185 mm, No. of Columns (Display): 4, Col Widths (Display): 45 mm
Copy instructions: *Copy Date:* 31 days prior to publication
BUSINESS: GARDEN TRADE: Garden Trade Supplies

DEGA PRODUKTION & HANDEL 724897G26D-1
Editorial: Wollgrasweg 41, 70599 STUTTGART
Tel: 711 4507181 **Fax:** 711 4507207
Email: ckillgus@ulmer.de **Web site:** http://www.dega-gartenbau.de
Freq: Monthly; **Annual Sub.:** EUR 132,00; **Circ:** 4,057
Editor: Christoph Killgus; **Advertising Manager:** Marc Alber
Profile: The magazine, which has been known and valued in the horticulture industry for more than 60 years, is aimed at management in the horticulture industry. It provides beneficial knowledge in an up-to-date and easy-to-understand way and reports about all the fundamental developments in horticulture in Germany and internationally. Up-to-date news and reports from the horticulture industry in Germany and worldwide. Provision of specialist information, as concentrated as possible and as in-depth as necessary. The articles provide decision-making support and are oriented to the benefits. In every edition, there are reports from opinion leaders and entrepreneurs. The focus is on successful practical examples which encourage initiative. The Regular Themes are Developments in the horticulture industry in Germany and worldwide, Trends on the market, Successful company concepts, Employee and operations management, Training, Top cultures and plant innovations, Culture methods, Pest management, Services in the retail trade, Graveyard culture, Technical systems and solutions, Exhibitions and markets, Dates and events, Legal and fiscal questions. Facebook: http://www.facebook.com/pages/DEGA-Gartenbau-Produktion-Handel/120523167985050.
Language(s): German
Readership: Aimed at professionals in the horticultural trade.
ADVERTISING RATES:
Full Page Mono .... EUR 2700
Full Page Colour .... EUR 3810
Mechanical Data: Type Area: 270 x 175 mm, No. of Columns (Display): 4, Col Widths (Display): 40 mm
Copy instructions: *Copy Date:* 23 days prior to publication
BUSINESS: GARDEN TRADE: Garden Trade Horticulture

DEGGENDORF AKTUELL 724900G72-3064
Editorial: Westlicher Stadtgraben 19a, 94469 DEGGENDORF **Tel:** 991 3701752 **Fax:** 991 3701790
Email: anzeigen@donau-anzeiger.de
Freq: Weekly; **Cover Price:** Free; **Circ:** 44,203
Advertising Manager: Klaus Huber
Profile: Advertising journal (house-to-house) concentrating on local stories.
Language(s): German
ADVERTISING RATES:
Full Page Mono .... EUR 2013
Full Page Colour .... EUR 2787
Mechanical Data: Type Area: 430 x 280 mm, No. of Columns (Display): 6, Col Widths (Display): 45 mm
Copy instructions: *Copy Date:* 3 days prior to publication
LOCAL NEWSPAPERS

DEGGENDORFER WOCHENBLATT 724901G72-3068
Editorial: Graflinger Str. 19, 94469 DEGGENDORF
Tel: 991 3721315 **Fax:** 991 3721320
Email: hannes.lehner@wochenblatt.de **Web site:** http://www.wochenblatt.de
Freq: Weekly; **Cover Price:** Free; **Circ:** 46,000
Editor: Hannes Lehner; **Advertising Manager:** Edwin Ebner
Profile: Advertising journal (house-to-house) concentrating on local stories.
Language(s): German
ADVERTISING RATES:
Full Page Mono .... EUR 3147
Full Page Colour .... EUR 4720
Mechanical Data: Type Area: 460 x 280 mm, No. of Columns (Display): 6, Col Widths (Display): 43 mm
Copy instructions: *Copy Date:* 2 days prior to publication
LOCAL NEWSPAPERS

DEGGENDORFER ZEITUNG 724902G67B-3960
Editorial: Medienstr. 5, 94036 PASSAU
Tel: 851 8020 **Fax:** 851 802256
Email: pnp@vgp.de **Web site:** http://www.pnp.de
Freq: 312 issues yearly; **Circ:** 22,743
Advertising Manager: Gerhard Koller
Profile: Daily newspaper with regional news and a local sports section. Twitter: http://twitter.com/pnp_online This Outlet offers RSS (Really Simple Syndication).
Language(s): German
ADVERTISING RATES:
SCC .... EUR 62,50
Mechanical Data: Type Area: 482 x 325 mm, No. of Columns (Display): 7, Col Widths (Display): 45 mm
Copy instructions: *Copy Date:* 2 days prior to publication
REGIONAL DAILY & SUNDAY NEWSPAPERS: Regional Daily Newspapers

DEHOGA MAGAZIN 1654939G11A-1594
Editorial: Augustenstr. 6, 70178 STUTTGART
Tel: 711 619880 **Fax:** 711 6198846
Email: ohl@dehogabw.de **Web site:** http://www.dehogabw.de
Freq: Monthly; **Circ:** 10,639
Editor: Daniel Ohl; **Advertising Manager:** Karin Weber
Profile: Magazine for members of the Association of Hotels and Gastronomy in the region of Baden-Württemberg.
Language(s): German
ADVERTISING RATES:
Full Page Mono .... EUR 2395
Full Page Colour .... EUR 3162
Mechanical Data: Type Area: 262 x 187 mm, No. of Columns (Display): 3, Col Widths (Display): 62 mm
Copy instructions: *Copy Date:* 28 days prior to publication
BUSINESS: CATERING: Catering, Hotels & Restaurants

DEI DIE ERNÄHRUNGSINDUSTRIE 724906G22C-35
Editorial: Ernst-Mey-Str. 8, 70771 LEINFELDEN-ECHTERDINGEN **Tel:** 711 7594291
Fax: 711 7594221
Email: dei.redaktion@konradin.de **Web site:** http://www.prozesstechnik-online.de/dei
Freq: 10 issues yearly; **Annual Sub.:** EUR 63,50; **Circ:** 9,040
Editor: Günter Eckhardt; **Advertising Manager:** Manuela Bumler
Profile: Leading trade journal for the entire food and beverage processing industry. It reports in the form of practical application and technical papers, reports, interviews and product information on procedures, equipment, apparatus and components for the food handling and processing. Other topics include basic materials and additives, packaging, material handling and logistics, and the entire measurement and automation technology and IT technologies for this industry. Current economic and corporate news round off the program.
Language(s): German
ADVERTISING RATES:
Full Page Mono .... EUR 3770
Full Page Colour .... EUR 4785
Mechanical Data: Type Area: 270 x 188 mm, No. of Columns (Display): 4, Col Widths (Display): 44 mm
BUSINESS: FOOD: Food Processing & Packaging

DEINE BAHN 724909G49E-200
Editorial: Linienstr. 214, 10119 BERLIN
Tel: 30 20095220 **Fax:** 30 200952229
Email: redaktion@bahn-fachverlag.de **Web site:** http://www.deine-bahn.de
Freq: Monthly; **Annual Sub.:** EUR 64,80; **Circ:** 4,403
Editor: Hans-Peter Schonert; **Advertising Manager:** Marion Clevers
Profile: Deine Bahn is over 35 years one of the leading magazines for the vocational education and training in the rail industry. It gives monthly knowledge in the fields of railway engineering, operational safety and human resources. The overall context of rail transport as well as current developments in the industry and individual business units is Deine Bahn in the context. Deine Bahn promotes the smooth cooperation in the system network. Well-known editors and writers from the DB Group, the railway industry as well as education and policy guarantee a high professional standard of quality and practicality.
Language(s): German
ADVERTISING RATES:
Full Page Mono .... EUR 1800
Full Page Colour .... EUR 2300
Mechanical Data: Type Area: 279 x 190 mm, No. of Columns (Display): 3, Col Widths (Display): 56 mm
Copy instructions: *Copy Date:* 14 days prior to publication
Official Journal of: Organ d. DB Training, Learning & Consulting u. d. Verb. Dt. Eisenbahnfachschulen
BUSINESS: TRANSPORT: Railways

DEISTER-LEINE-ZEITUNG 724913G67B-3980
Editorial: Bahnhofstr. 5, 30890 BARSINGHAUSEN
Tel: 5105 770720 **Fax:** 5105 770733
Email: redaktion@deister-leine-zeitung.de **Web site:** http://www.deister-leine-zeitung.de
Freq: 312 issues yearly; **Circ:** 4,961
Advertising Manager: Emke Hillrichs
Profile: Daily newspaper with regional news and a local sports section. This Outlet offers RSS (Really Simple Syndication).
Language(s): German
ADVERTISING RATES:
SCC .... EUR 19,00
Mechanical Data: Type Area: 430 x 281 mm, No. of Columns (Display): 6, Col Widths (Display): 45 mm
Copy instructions: *Copy Date:* 1 day prior to publication
REGIONAL DAILY & SUNDAY NEWSPAPERS: Regional Daily Newspapers

DEKORATIVES HÄKELN 1614241G74A-3321
Editorial: Römerstr. 90, 79618 RHEINFELDEN
Tel: 7623 9640 **Fax:** 7623 964200
Email: info@oz-verlag.de **Web site:** http://www.oz-verlag.de
Freq: 6 issues yearly; **Annual Sub.:** EUR 13,20; **Circ:** 65,000
Profile: Magic crochet magazine with models for reworking - curtains, rugs, tablecloths and doilies in different shapes and sizes, and more to beautify the home or at Easter / Christmas.
Language(s): German
ADVERTISING RATES:
Full Page Mono .... EUR 2480
Full Page Colour .... EUR 2960
Mechanical Data: No. of Columns (Display): 4, Col Widths (Display): 35 mm, Type Area: 226 x 159 mm

DELIKATESSEN 724922G89A-540
Editorial: Giselastr. 4/Rgb., 80802 MÜNCHEN
Tel: 89 3061000 **Fax:** 89 30610012
Email: delikatessen@muenchner.de **Web site:** http://www.muenchner.de
Freq: Annual; **Cover Price:** EUR 7,80; **Circ:** 30,000
Editor: Jossi Loibl; **Advertising Manager:** Evelyn Geyer
Profile: Gastronomy guide for the city of Munich. The spectrum ranges from traditional pub up to the current hot spot, from star restaurant to the Italian con grazia e amore. All tested premises divided into divisions. Any strategy needs to be catering facilities such as (precious) restaurants, taverns, bars, cafes, discussed pubs, clubs and beer gardens. In addition to the restaurant reviews, there are features, interviews, stories about eating, drinking and going out. The surrounding part makes you want to discover old farms, tourist cafes, young, imaginative cuisine or regional brewery inns and invites you to a trip to the region.
Language(s): German
ADVERTISING RATES:
Full Page Mono .... EUR 2460
Full Page Colour .... EUR 3060
Mechanical Data: Type Area: 260 x 190 mm
Copy instructions: *Copy Date:* 27 days prior to publication

DELIKATESSEN 724922G89A-12535
Editorial: Giselastr. 4/Rgb., 80802 MÜNCHEN
Tel: 89 3061000 **Fax:** 89 30610012
Email: delikatessen@muenchner.de **Web site:** http://www.muenchner.de
Freq: Annual; **Cover Price:** EUR 7,80; **Circ:** 30,000
Editor: Jossi Loibl; **Advertising Manager:** Evelyn Geyer
Profile: Gastronomy guide for the city of Munich. The spectrum ranges from traditional pub up to the current hot spot, from star restaurant to the Italian con grazia e amore. All tested premises divided into divisions. Any strategy needs to be catering facilities such as (precious) restaurants, taverns, bars, cafes, discussed pubs, clubs and beer gardens. In addition to the restaurant reviews, there are features, interviews, stories about eating, drinking and going out. The surrounding part makes you want to discover old farms, tourist cafes, young, imaginative cuisine or regional brewery inns and invites you to a trip to the region.
Language(s): German
ADVERTISING RATES:
Full Page Mono .... EUR 2460
Full Page Colour .... EUR 3060
Mechanical Data: Type Area: 260 x 190 mm
Copy instructions: *Copy Date:* 27 days prior to publication

DELMENHORSTER KREISBLATT 724926G67B-4020
Editorial: Lange Str. 122, 27749 DELMENHORST
Tel: 4221 156220 **Fax:** 4221 156290
Email: redaktion@dk-online.de **Web site:** http://www.dk-online.de
Freq: 312 issues yearly; **Circ:** 18,585
Editor: Ralf Freitag; **News Editor:** Michael Korn;
Advertising Manager: Achim Matzat
Profile: Daily newspaper with regional news and a local sports section. Facebook: http://www.facebook.com/delmenhorster.kreisblatt This Outlet offers RSS (Really Simple Syndication).
Language(s): German
ADVERTISING RATES:
SCC .... EUR 36,90
Mechanical Data: Type Area: 432 x 285 mm, No. of Columns (Display): 6, Col Widths (Display): 45 mm
Copy instructions: *Copy Date:* 1 day prior to publication
REGIONAL DAILY & SUNDAY NEWSPAPERS: Regional Daily Newspapers

DELMENHORSTER KREISBLATT ONLINE
1621098G67B-16533
Editorial: Lange Str. 122, 27749 DELMENHORST
Tel: 4221 156220 **Fax:** 4221 156290
Email: redaktion@dk-online.de **Web site:** http://www.dk-online.de
Freq: Daily; **Cover Price:** Paid; **Circ:** 104,592 Unique Users
Editor: Ralf Freitag; **Advertising Manager:** Achim Matzat
Profile: Ezine: Regional daily newspaper covering politics, economics, sports, travel and technology. Facebook: http://www.facebook.com/delmenhorster.kreisblatt.
Language(s): German
REGIONAL DAILY & SUNDAY NEWSPAPERS: Regional Daily Newspapers

DELTA P
724929G19D-12
Editorial: Uhlandstr. 1, 72631 AICHTAL
Tel: 7127 56609 **Fax:** 7127 56649
Email: ruediger.nagel@pumps-directory.com **Web site:** http://www.pumpeninfo.de
Freq: 5 issues yearly; **Annual Sub.:** EUR 70,00; **Circ:** 8,850
Editor: Rüdiger Nagel
Profile: delta p is concentrated on the pump technology, techniques in use for pumping and metering of liquids, fluids and gases and their applications in business practice. delta p informs users, developers and practitioners in all industries where liquids transported, dispensed or handled. Technical and application fees, current product information and news from and for these industries form the editorial framework.
Language(s): German
ADVERTISING RATES:
Full Page Mono .... EUR 3420
Full Page Colour .... EUR 4340
Mechanical Data: Type Area: 270 x 190 mm, No. of Columns (Display): 4, Col Widths (Display): 46 mm
Copy instructions: *Copy Date:* 20 days prior to publication
BUSINESS: ENGINEERING & MACHINERY: Hydraulic Power

DEMETER GARTENRUNDBRIEF
724931G21A-1100
Editorial: Reinsbürg 10, 74585 ROT
Tel: 7958 926391 **Fax:** 7958 926393
Email: redaktion@gartenrundbrief.de **Web site:** http://www.gartenrundbrief.de
Freq: 6 issues yearly; **Annual Sub.:** EUR 12,00; **Circ:** 3,000
Editor: Iris Mühlberger
Profile: In demeter Gartenrundbrief there as application tips for the biodynamic herbal preparations and experiences • a bi-monthly work calendar with sowing and planting time table • Tips for an insect-friendly natural garden • Information about biological plant protection and organic fertilizer and of course recipes • profiles of old fruit and vegetable varoeties • information on organic herb production • a page on the ecological beekeeping • events of Demeter house garden Groups • introduction courses in the Biodynamic method of cultivation • book tips. As a special feature in the Gartenrundbrief will published current references from professional organic gardeners, which also affect the hobby gardener.
Language(s): German

DEMMINER BLITZ AM SONNTAG
724933G72-3104
Editorial: Markt 3, 17489 GREIFSWALD
Tel: 3834 7737741 **Fax:** 3834 7737730
Email: mathias.kerber@blitzverlag.de **Web site:** http://www.blitzverlag.de
Freq: Weekly; **Cover Price:** Free; **Circ:** 32,840
Editor: Mathias Kerber; **Advertising Manager:** Frank Rohde
Profile: Advertising journal (house-to-house) concentrating on local stories.
Language(s): German
ADVERTISING RATES:
Full Page Mono .... EUR 2546
Full Page Colour .... EUR 2936
Mechanical Data: Type Area: 420 x 285 mm, No. of Columns (Display): 6, Col Widths (Display): 45 mm
Copy instructions: *Copy Date:* 2 days prior to publication
LOCAL NEWSPAPERS

DEMO
724936G32A-7140
Editorial: Stresemannstr. 30, 10963 BERLIN
Tel: 30 25594200 **Fax:** 30 25594290
Email: redaktion@demo-online.de **Web site:** http://www.demo-online.de
Freq: 6 issues yearly; Free to qualifying individuals
Annual Sub.: EUR 42,00; **Circ:** 28,560
Editor: Barbara Behrends; **Advertising Manager:** Michael Blum
Profile: Municipal communications made easy: You seek the dialogue with mayors, city councilors and local government in cities, towns and counties, with the political decision makers and opinion leaders in communities and municipal economy. The Berliner vorwärts Verlagsgesellschaft offers you this forward with its products to targeted solutions. • Democratic community - Demo: For over 60 years, the leading monthly magazine for decision makers in municipal politics, administration and economy. • With regional editions are targeted contacts for eleven possible states. • Demo Newsletter: Always on the pulse of local politics - once a month are sent out the latest community developments and trends via e-mail. • Demo Events: Demo municipal congress, demo trade forums, party evenings and exhibition tours with local politicians.
Language(s): German
Readership: Read by local government officials.
ADVERTISING RATES:
Full Page Mono .... EUR 3880
Full Page Colour .... EUR 4480
Mechanical Data: Type Area: 260 x 185 mm, No. of Columns (Display): 4, Col Widths (Display): 43 mm
Copy instructions: *Copy Date:* 30 days prior to publication
Official Journal of: Fachorgan d. Sozialdemokrat. Gemeinschaft f. Kommunalpolitik
BUSINESS: LOCAL GOVERNMENT, LEISURE & RECREATION: Local Government

DENTAL DIALOGUE
1615486G56D-1270
Editorial: Hauptstr. 1, 86925 FUCHSTAL
Tel: 8243 969233 **Fax:** 8243 969239
Email: redaktion.dd@teamwork-media.de **Web site:** http://www.teamwork-media.de
Freq: 10 issues yearly; **Annual Sub.:** EUR 90,00; **Circ:** 14,023
Editor: Ralf Suckert; **Advertising Manager:** Waltraud Hernandez
Profile: Magazine for the dental technicians sector, German / Austrian edition.
Language(s): German
ADVERTISING RATES:
Full Page Mono .... EUR 3680
Full Page Colour .... EUR 3680
Mechanical Data: Type Area: 260 x 185 mm
Copy instructions: *Copy Date:* 28 days prior to publication
BUSINESS: HEALTH & MEDICAL: Dental

DAS DENTAL LABOR
724956G56D-220
Editorial: Paul-Gerhardt-Allee 46, 81245 MÜNCHEN
Tel: 89 31890557 **Fax:** 89 31890553
Email: dl.redaktion@vnmonline.de **Web site:** http://www.dlonline.de
Freq: Monthly; **Annual Sub.:** EUR 127,50; **Circ:** 7,935
Editor: Angelika Schaller
Profile: The magazine „das dental labor" is THE medium when it comes to topics related to dentistry. The magazine's editorial concept is applied broadly unrivaled. It includes primary dental specialist articles and informative about the industry.
Language(s): German
Readership: Read by dental and prosthetic technicians.
ADVERTISING RATES:
Full Page Mono .... EUR 2580
Full Page Colour .... EUR 4457
Mechanical Data: Type Area: 260 x 185 mm, No. of Columns (Display): 3, Col Widths (Display): 59 mm
Copy instructions: *Copy Date:* 28 days prior to publication
BUSINESS: HEALTH & MEDICAL: Dental

DENTAL MAGAZIN
724957G56D-240
Editorial: Dieselstr. 2, 50859 KÖLN
Tel: 2234 7011244 **Fax:** 2234 70116244
Email: pecanov-schroeder@aerzteverlag.de **Web site:** http://www.zahnheilkunde.de
Freq: 6 issues yearly; **Annual Sub.:** EUR 60,00; **Circ:** 19,121
Editor: Anne Barfuß; **Advertising Manager:** Marga Pinsdorf
Profile: Dental Magazin is the dental journal with a practical focus for practicing dentists. Its editorial mission is to stimulate dialogue between clinical practice, academic research and training and the dental industry. Dental expertise is defined by a triangle delineated by practice, university and industry – and the views of all three are represented in Dental Magazin. It helps dentists form well-founded opinions about important current topics in the dental world and successfully incorporate new ideas in their daily practice. A unique and integrated part of the overall concept of Dental Magazin is its visual appearance: exclusive photography and a clearly structured, modern design.
Language(s): German
ADVERTISING RATES:
Full Page Mono .... EUR 3060
Full Page Colour .... EUR 4230
Mechanical Data: Type Area: 260 x 185 mm, No. of Columns (Display): 4, Col Widths (Display): 45 mm
BUSINESS: HEALTH & MEDICAL: Dental

DENTAL TRIBUNE
1684554G56D-1301
Editorial: Holbeinstr. 29, 04229 LEIPZIG
Tel: 341 48474133 **Fax:** 341 48474173
Email: j.enders@dental-tribune.com **Web site:** http://www.dental-tribune.com
Freq: 10 issues yearly; **Cover Price:** EUR 5,00; **Circ:** 19,642
Editor: Jeannette Enders; **Advertising Manager:** Peter Witteczek
Profile: Specialist information for dentists-date information on training courses.
Language(s): German
ADVERTISING RATES:
Full Page Mono .... EUR 4350
Full Page Colour .... EUR 4350
Mechanical Data: Type Area: 400 x 280 mm
Copy instructions: *Copy Date:* 14 days prior to publication
BUSINESS: HEALTH & MEDICAL: Dental

DENTAL:SPIEGEL
724958G56D-260
Editorial: Im Ikaruspark/Lilienthalstr. 3, 82178 PUCHHEIM **Tel:** 89 8299470 **Fax:** 89 82994716
Email: redaktion@franzmedien.com **Web site:** http://www.franzmedien.com
Freq: 8 issues yearly; **Annual Sub.:** EUR 21,94; **Circ:** 37,863
Editor: Eckhard Franz; **Advertising Manager:** Philipp D. Franz
Profile: Dentist magazine for the successful practice team. The magazine is devoted to each issue on a current topic. Focus: Economics & Law, case studies and PR.
Language(s): German
ADVERTISING RATES:
Full Page Mono .... EUR 5300
Full Page Colour .... EUR 5300
Mechanical Data: Type Area: 260 x 186 mm
Copy instructions: *Copy Date:* 14 days prior to publication
BUSINESS: HEALTH & MEDICAL: Dental

DENTALZEITUNG
724959G56D-280
Editorial: Holbeinstr. 29, 04229 LEIPZIG
Tel: 341 48474110 **Fax:** 341 48474290
Email: dz-redaktion@oemus-media.de **Web site:** http://www.oemus-media.de
Freq: 6 issues yearly; **Annual Sub.:** EUR 34,00; **Circ:** 49,527
Editor: Torsten Hartmann; **Advertising Manager:** Stefan Thieme
Profile: Interregional communication organ of the AAD, source of the dental specialist trade on the Dental Specialists. The magazine for dentists, dental laboratories and dental depots is guide for product decisions in practice.
Language(s): German
ADVERTISING RATES:
Full Page Mono .... EUR 4950
Full Page Colour .... EUR 5850
Mechanical Data: Type Area: 249 x 174 mm, No. of Columns (Display): 3, Col Widths (Display): 52 mm
BUSINESS: HEALTH & MEDICAL: Dental

DERM
724967G56A-2340
Editorial: Borsteler Chaussee 85, Haus 16, 22453 HAMBURG **Tel:** 40 232334 **Fax:** 40 230292
Email: info@omnimedonline.de **Web site:** http://www.omnimedonline.de
Freq: 6 issues yearly; **Annual Sub.:** EUR 53,50; **Circ:** 10,913
Editor: Dieter Reinel; **Advertising Manager:** Vanessa Baack
Profile: Journal concerning the developments and new treatments in dermatology.
Language(s): German
ADVERTISING RATES:
Full Page Mono .... EUR 1800
Full Page Colour .... EUR 3360
Mechanical Data: Type Area: 250 x 180 mm, No. of Columns (Display): 3, Col Widths (Display): 56 mm
Copy instructions: *Copy Date:* 42 days prior to publication
BUSINESS: HEALTH & MEDICAL

DERMATOLOGIE IN BERUF UND UMWELT
1646163G56A-11296
Editorial: Thibautstr. 3, 69115 HEIDELBERG
Tel: 6221 568751 **Fax:** 6221 565584
Email: thomas.diepgen@med.uni-heidelberg.de
Freq: Quarterly; **Annual Sub.:** EUR 82,50; **Circ:** 2,700
Editor: T. L. Diepgen; **Advertising Manager:** Christian Graßl
Profile: Magazine about occupational and environmental dermatology.
Language(s): German
ADVERTISING RATES:
Full Page Mono .... EUR 1435
Full Page Colour .... EUR 2425
Mechanical Data: Type Area: 242 x 167 mm, No. of Columns (Display): 3, Col Widths (Display): 56 mm
Copy instructions: *Copy Date:* 28 days prior to publication
Official Journal of: Organ d. ArGe f. Berufs- u. Umweltdermatologie in d. DDG

DESCH AKTUELL
1663602G19E-1886
Editorial: Kleinbahnstr. 21, 59759 ARNSBERG
Tel: 2932 3000 **Fax:** 2932 300899
Email: birgitt.cordes@desch.de **Web site:** http://www.desch.de
Freq: 3 issues yearly; **Circ:** 3,000
Editor: Alexa Desch-Gerber
Profile: Magazine from the Desch-Antriebstechnik company for business partners, customers and employees.
Language(s): English; German

DESIGN IN ACRYLICS
739104G4B-560
Editorial: Rheinstr. 99.3, 64295 DARMSTADT
Tel: 6151 599020 **Fax:** 6151 5990279
Email: info@profilwerkstatt.de **Web site:** http://www.profilwerkstatt.de
Freq: 3 issues yearly; **Cover Price:** Free; **Circ:** 50,000
Editor: Martina Keller
Profile: Company publication published by Röhm.
Language(s): German

DESIGN REPORT
724978G14J-1
Editorial: Ernst-Mey-Str. 8, 70771 LEINFELDEN-ECHTERDINGEN **Tel:** 711 7594514
Fax: 711 7594397
Email: lars.quadejacob@konradin.de **Web site:** http://www.design-report.de
Freq: 6 issues yearly; **Annual Sub.:** EUR 73,50; **Circ:** 6,101
Editor: Lars Quadejacob; **Advertising Manager:** Bettina Mayer
Profile: design report - work equipment and a source of inspiration for all who create, in design invest and decide on design. The design report sees design as a discipline, which moves in the field of technology, business and arts / culture - and that reflect the theme of this issue. The thematic focus is on product design - from furniture, to capital goods - but the links are always considered to neighboring disciplines such as branding, communication design and architecture. The focus of reporting is on concepts, contexts and processes of product development. The full interview "visit to ...", exhibition shows, personal data, comments and a gloss round off the issue and make the design report to an important organ of the design scene. The aim of the book design and structure is a high density of information: There are almost no white space to give the text and image information as much space as possible.
Language(s): German
ADVERTISING RATES:
Full Page Mono .... EUR 4350
Full Page Colour .... EUR 5400
Mechanical Data: Type Area: 250 x 188 mm, No. of Columns (Display): 4, Col Widths (Display): 44 mm
BUSINESS: COMMERCE, INDUSTRY & MANAGEMENT: Commercial Design

DESIGN + BESCHLAG MAGAZIN
722568G4R-120
Editorial: Fasanenweg 18, 70771 LEINFELDEN-ECHTERDINGEN **Tel:** 711 7591289
Fax: 711 7591440
Email: info@drw-verlag.de **Web site:** http://www.drw-verlag.de
Freq: Annual; **Cover Price:** EUR 5,00; **Circ:** 13,000
Editor: Wolfgang Rüter; **Advertising Manager:** Oliver Heinz
Profile: Magazine covering interior building and ornamental mountings.
Language(s): English; German
ADVERTISING RATES:
Full Page Mono .... EUR 5000
Full Page Colour .... EUR 6680
Mechanical Data: Type Area: 270 x 175 mm, No. of Columns (Display): 4, Col Widths (Display): 40 mm
Copy instructions: *Copy Date:* 30 days prior to publication
Supplement to: HK Holz- und Kunststoffverarbeitung, Holz-Zentralblatt
BUSINESS: ARCHITECTURE & BUILDING: Building Related

DESIGN+DESIGN
724979G19B-60
Editorial: Körnerstr. 5, 22301 HAMBURG
Tel: 40 2792223 **Fax:** 40 2798132
Email: joklatt@design-und-design.de **Web site:** http://www.design-und-design.de
Freq: Quarterly; **Annual Sub.:** EUR 24,00; **Circ:** 1,000
Editor: Jo Klatt; **Advertising Manager:** Jo Klatt
Profile: Magazine for industrial design and design collectors.
Language(s): English; German
ADVERTISING RATES:
Full Page Mono .... EUR 675
Full Page Colour .... EUR 1378
Mechanical Data: Type Area: 267 x 197 mm, No. of Columns (Display): 3, Col Widths (Display): 62 mm
Copy instructions: *Copy Date:* 8 days prior to publication
BUSINESS: ENGINEERING & MACHINERY: Engineering - Design

DESIGN&ELEKTRONIK
724980G18A-22
Editorial: Gruber Str. 46a, 85586 POING
Tel: 8121 951340 **Fax:** 8121 951654
Email: cgrote@design-elektronik.de **Web site:** http://www.elektroniknet.de
Freq: Monthly; **Annual Sub.:** EUR 68,40; **Circ:** 21,213
Editor: Caspar Grote; **Advertising Manager:** Christian Stadler
Profile: Magazine offers information about products and know-how for the electronic field. Twelve issues published annually, in which the editors find current coverage of each of a particular topic, the current state of technology, new developments and trends, especially solutions to current pressing problems, and presents. To gather together without the relevant information as individual pieces from various sources, even to an overall image to have to get the developers of electronic circuits and components fast, focused and thorough insight into the subject. Facebook: http://www.facebook.com/pages/elektroniknetde/121306857884722.
Language(s): German
Readership: Aimed at designers of electronic devices and systems and electronic engineers.
ADVERTISING RATES:
Full Page Mono .... EUR 5170
Full Page Colour .... EUR 7240
Mechanical Data: Type Area: 260 x 186 mm, No. of Columns (Display): 4, Col Widths (Display): 43 mm
Copy instructions: *Copy Date:* 24 days prior to publication
BUSINESS: ELECTRONICS

DESIGN + LICHT
724981G17-120
Editorial: Ohmstr. 50, 83301 TRAUNREUT
Tel: 8669 33237 **Fax:** 8669 33710
Email: designundlicht@siteco.de **Web site:** http://www.siteco.de
Freq: Annual; **Cover Price:** EUR 7,50; **Circ:** 17,000
Editor: Claudia Vokinger
Profile: Magazine on design with focus on light and architecture.
Language(s): German
ADVERTISING RATES:
Full Page Colour .... EUR 2500

DESIGN + LICHT
724981G17-1637
Editorial: Ohmstr. 50, 83301 TRAUNREUT
Tel: 8669 33237 **Fax:** 8669 33710
Email: designundlicht@siteco.de **Web site:** http://www.siteco.de
Freq: Annual; **Cover Price:** EUR 7,50; **Circ:** 17,000
Editor: Claudia Vokinger
Profile: Magazine on design with focus on light and architecture.
Language(s): German
ADVERTISING RATES:
Full Page Colour .... EUR 2500

DESIGNERS DIGEST
724975G14J-100
Editorial: Trenknerweg 64, 22765 HAMBURG
Tel: 40 39906267 **Fax:** 40 39906968
Email: klaus.tiedge@bkt-network.de **Web site:** http://www.designers-digest.de
Freq: 5 issues yearly; **Annual Sub.:** EUR 55,00; **Circ:** 10,000
Editor: Klaus Tiedge; **Advertising Manager:** Werner Deisenroth
Profile: Magazine covering graphics and industrial design.
Language(s): English; German
Readership: Read by graphic designers, advertising agencies and architectural firms.
ADVERTISING RATES:
Full Page Mono .... EUR 3600
Full Page Colour .... EUR 5400
Mechanical Data: Type Area: 300 x 230 mm
BUSINESS: COMMERCE, INDUSTRY & MANAGEMENT: Commercial Design

DETAIL
724988G4A-8
Editorial: Hackerbrücke 6, 80335 MÜNCHEN
Tel: 89 38162057 **Fax:** 89 338761
Email: redaktion@detail.de **Web site:** http://www.detail.de
Freq: 10 issues yearly; **Annual Sub.:** EUR 139,90; **Circ:** 30,455
Editor: Christian Schittich; **Advertising Manager:** Edith Arnold
Profile: Trade magazine for architects, civil engineers, building authorities and developers. The title of the magazine characterizes the goal set at the outset: documentation and information on building projects in all categories. Focus: The detail in the design and architec tonic context. Detail is a unique source of information for planning and architectural firms and increases with this editorial concept and a very high quality a special position in one market.
Language(s): English; French; German; Italian; Russian; Spanish
ADVERTISING RATES:
Full Page Mono .... EUR 5965
Full Page Colour .... EUR 9100
Mechanical Data: Type Area: 271 x 189 mm, No. of Columns (Display): 4, Col Widths (Display): 45 mm
Copy instructions: *Copy Date:* 30 days prior to publication
BUSINESS: ARCHITECTURE & BUILDING: Architecture

DETAIL
2028145G4E-7337
Editorial: Hackerbrücke 6, 80335 MÜNCHEN
Tel: 89 38162057 **Fax:** 89 338761
Email: redaktion@detail.de **Web site:** http://www.detail.de
Freq: 6 issues yearly; **Cover Price:** EUR 15,50; **Circ:** 12,500
Editor: Christian Schittich; **Advertising Manager:** Edith Arnold
Profile: Trade magazine for architects, civil engineers, building authorities and developers. The title of the magazine characterizes the goal set at the outset: documentation and information on building projects in all categories. Focus: The detail in the design and architec tonic context. Detail is a unique source of information for planning and architectural firms and increases with this editorial concept and a very high quality a special position in one market.
Language(s): English
ADVERTISING RATES:
Full Page Mono .... EUR 3110
Full Page Colour .... EUR 4110
Mechanical Data: Type Area: 271 x 189 mm, No. of Columns (Display): 4, Col Widths (Display): 45 mm
Copy instructions: *Copy Date:* 35 days prior to publication

DETAIL GREEN
1903949G4E-7271
Editorial: Hackerbrücke 6, 80335 MÜNCHEN
Tel: 89 38162081 **Fax:** 89 338761
Email: jakob.schoof@detail.de **Web site:** http://www.detail.de
Freq: Half-yearly; **Cover Price:** EUR 15,50; **Circ:** 31,346
Editor: Christian Schittich; **Advertising Manager:** Edith Arnold
Profile: Magazine providing articles and information about all aspects of architecture.
Language(s): English; French; German; Italian; Russian
ADVERTISING RATES:
Full Page Mono .... EUR 5880
Full Page Colour .... EUR 8970
Mechanical Data: Type Area: 271 x 189 mm, No. of Columns (Display): 3, Col Widths (Display): 63 mm
Copy instructions: *Copy Date:* 30 days prior to publication

DETAIL.DE
1704285G4A-245
Editorial: Hackerbrücke 6, 80335 MÜNCHEN
Tel: 89 38162049 **Fax:** 89 338761
Email: online@detail.de **Web site:** http://www.detail.de
Freq: Annual; **Cover Price:** Paid; **Circ:** 614,609 Unique Users
Editor: Nina Fiolka; **Advertising Manager:** Edith Arnold
Profile: Internet Media: Detail.de is the international architecture of the portal home Detail. In various sections shows Detail.de current developments in architecture, in-depth content and expertise to the hilt for the architect. The aspects of sustainable design are the focus of the rubric of "Green". Additional content related to latest developments in research and technology through programs and legislation relevant to projects / products. The column "issue" is more detailed content as it is enigmatic articles, films, image galleries, projects and other details of the latest Detail Print publications are available. New materials and product development, selectable by trade shows under the heading "Products". The heading "Archive" provides content from books and the online segment is completed and available by download possibilities of professional articles and detailed drawings.
Language(s): German
BUSINESS: ARCHITECTURE & BUILDING: Architecture

DEUTSCH
1641528G74A-3408
Editorial: Neuer Zollhof 2, 40221 DÜSSELDORF
Tel: 211 22950500 **Fax:** 211 229505013
Email: redaktion@deutschmagazine.org **Web site:** http://www.deutschmagazine.org
Freq: 5 issues yearly; **Annual Sub.:** EUR 25,00; **Circ:** 100,000
Editor: Lydia Koeppel; **Advertising Manager:** Julia Neuhaus
Profile: The magazine is an international lifestyle magazine, issues and trends in art, photography, design, architecture, music, entertainment, fashion, beauty and society highlights and links. The editors researched quality content, correspondents and scouts report from the metropolises of the world from New York to Paris to Shanghai. Intelligent and diverse content, excellent and inspiring photography of modernists determine the issues of the magazine world.
Language(s): German
ADVERTISING RATES:
Full Page Mono .... EUR 9950
Full Page Colour .... EUR 9950
Mechanical Data: Type Area: 240 x 174 mm

DEUTSCH PERFEKT
1703016G88B-1492
Editorial: Fraunhoferstr. 22, 82152 PLANEGG
Tel: 89 856810 **Fax:** 89 85681105
Email: redaktion@deutsch-perfekt.com **Web site:** http://www.deutsch-perfekt.com
Freq: Monthly; **Annual Sub.:** EUR 69,60; **Circ:** 19,388
Editor: Jörg Walser; **Advertising Manager:** Axel Zettler
Profile: Deutsch perfekt is the language magazine for readers around the world who wish to improve their German. Current-affairs reporting and top-quality language training are professionally interwoven, month by month, in the magazine's broad selection of stories on business, society, politics and lifestyle in Germany, Austria and Switzerland. Short news items alternate with long features, interviews and travel stories, as well as valuable advice for improving your career, education and conversation skills. Regular sections on cuisine, literature, cultural events and travel destinations are also part of each issue.
Language(s): German
ADVERTISING RATES:
Full Page Mono .... EUR 2686
Full Page Colour .... EUR 4476
Mechanical Data: Type Area: 246 x 186 mm, No. of Columns (Display): 4, Col Widths (Display): 43 mm
CONSUMER: EDUCATION: Adult Education

DEUTSCHE AKADEMIE DER NATURFORSCHER LEOPOLDINA JAHRBUCH
724995G56A-2420
Editorial: Emil-Abderhalden-Str. 37, 06108 HALLE
Tel: 345 4723934 **Fax:** 345 4723939
Email: kaasch@leopoldina.uni-halle.de
Freq: Annual; **Cover Price:** EUR 30,00; **Circ:** 1,800
Editor: J. Kaasch
Profile: Annual from the German academy of nature studies Leopoldina.
Language(s): English; German

DEUTSCHE ANGESTELLTEN ZEITUNG DHV
724997G14A-1680
Editorial: Droopweg 31, 20537 HAMBURG
Tel: 40 6328020 **Fax:** 40 63280218
Email: daz@dhv-cgb.de **Web site:** http://www.dhv-cgb.de
Freq: 6 issues yearly; Free to qualifying individuals
Annual Sub.: EUR 12,00; **Circ:** 70,000
Editor: Henning Röders; **Advertising Manager:** Henning Röders
Profile: Trade newspaper of DHV - Die Berufsgenossenschaft. The union represents the interests of 80,000 members in the commercial and administrative professions who work in the private sector and public service. Topics: labor and social policy, tariff policy and education.
Language(s): German
Readership: Read by employment agencies, employers, local authorities and members of the public seeking employment.
ADVERTISING RATES:
Full Page Mono .... EUR 2900
Full Page Colour .... EUR 5800
Mechanical Data: Type Area: 267 x 178 mm, No. of Columns (Display): 3, Col Widths (Display): 56 mm
Copy instructions: *Copy Date:* 22 days prior to publication
BUSINESS: COMMERCE, INDUSTRY & MANAGEMENT

DEUTSCHE BAUMSCHULE
725003G46-3
Editorial: Frankfurter Str. 3d, 38122 BRAUNSCHWEIG **Tel:** 531 3800415
Fax: 531 3800440
Email: red.dt.baumschule@haymarket.de **Web site:** http://www.deutschebaumschule.de
Freq: Monthly; **Annual Sub.:** EUR 159,60; **Circ:** 2,658
Editor: Sabine Müller; **Advertising Manager:** Christian Rueß
Profile: Journal of the tree nursery, tree nursery management, production and trade. Topics: trees and shrubs, substrate / fertilizer / crop protection, engineering, sales / marketing, use of plants, fruit, and tax law, IT / business administration, new products / books, faires, reports from companies.
Language(s): German
Readership: Aimed at professionals within the industry.
ADVERTISING RATES:
Full Page Mono .... EUR 2557
Full Page Colour .... EUR 3775
Mechanical Data: Type Area: 272 x 186 mm, No. of Columns (Display): 4, Col Widths (Display): 45 mm
BUSINESS: TIMBER, WOOD & FORESTRY

DEUTSCHE BEHINDERTEN-ZEITSCHRIFT
725004G94F-1833
Editorial: Baumschulenweg 11, 53424 REMAGEN
Tel: 2642 992696 **Fax:** 2642 992652
Email: reha-verlag@online.de **Web site:** http://www.reha-verlag.com
Freq: 6 issues yearly; **Annual Sub.:** EUR 19,90; **Circ:** 10,000
Editor: Andrea Berreßem
Profile: The "Deutsche Behinderten-Zeitschrift" is a politically, religiously and independent of associations magazine and has earned a good reputation since its founding, the best source of information to be in all areas of health, social services and rehabilitation. The "DBZ" is mainly used for target group parents, educators, families, facilities for handicapped written and deals with all aspects of life of these populations. The experience, combined with real advice and job aids is at the center of "DBZ". The "DBZ" is the constant column: Holidays for disabled people - everyday problems - News - Events calendar - Contact requests - look over the fence - Disabled children in kindergarten - Disabled children in school - The workshop for the handicapped - Law and legislation, incentives, tax benefits - our Health - rehabilitation Technology at home and abroad - young, disabled adults - contributions.
Language(s): German
ADVERTISING RATES:
Full Page Mono .... EUR 980
Full Page Colour .... EUR 1310
Mechanical Data: Type Area: 242 x 176 mm, No. of Columns (Display): 4, Col Widths (Display): 41 mm
Copy instructions: *Copy Date:* 31 days prior to publication
CONSUMER: OTHER CLASSIFICATIONS: Disability

DEUTSCHE BRIEFMARKEN-REVUE
725006G79C-2
Editorial: Eisenhüttenstr. 4, 40882 RATINGEN
Tel: 2102 2046830 **Fax:** 2102 895825
Email: billion@deutsche-briefmarken-revue.de **Web site:** http://www.deutsche-briefmarken-revue.de
Freq: Monthly; **Annual Sub.:** EUR 31,00; **Circ:** 26,000
Editor: Jan Billion; **Advertising Manager:** Jan Billion
Profile: Philatelic background reporting for stamp collectors and dealers. The journal provides comprehensive and up to date - of new issues from around the world ranging from the industry. Analysis and background reports provide an overview that the reader needs for his hobby.
Language(s): German
Readership: Aimed at stamp collectors.
ADVERTISING RATES:
Full Page Mono .... EUR 750
Full Page Colour .... EUR 1400
Mechanical Data: Type Area: 263 x 188 mm, No. of Columns (Display): 3, Col Widths (Display): 58 mm
Copy instructions: *Copy Date:* 28 days prior to publication
CONSUMER: HOBBIES & DIY: Philately

DIE DEUTSCHE BÜHNE
725007G76B-980
Editorial: St.-Apern-Str. 17, 50667 KÖLN
Tel: 221 2081218 **Fax:** 221 2081229
Email: brandenburg@die-deutsche-buehne.de **Web site:** http://www.die-deutsche-buehne.de
Freq: Monthly; **Annual Sub.:** EUR 74,00; **Circ:** 6,000
Editor: Detlef Brandenburg
Profile: The theater magazine, die deutsche bühne is the oldest theater magazine in German language. die deutsche bühne reports monthly on all theater genres (musical, dance, drama, children's and youth theater), brings interviews, reviews, reports, essays on everything that makes theater exciting. There are both the results of artistic work, so the performances, as well as structural and cultural-political issues of theater operations in the spotlight. die deutsche bühne reaches all decision makers in the German-speaking theater area, and interested persons of superior education in Germany, in German-speaking countries and in other foreign countries. Among the regular recipients are many opinion leaders, as a significant proportion of the subscribed copies going into theaters, editorial offices, institutions and associations from hand to hand.
Language(s): German
Readership: Aimed at producers, production people and those interested in stage productions.
ADVERTISING RATES:
Full Page Mono .... EUR 1700
Full Page Colour .... EUR 2600
Mechanical Data: No. of Columns (Display): 3, Col Widths (Display): 52 mm, Type Area: 245 x 192 mm
Copy instructions: *Copy Date:* 25 days prior to publication
CONSUMER: MUSIC & PERFORMING ARTS: Theatre

DER DEUTSCHE DERMATOLOGE
725011G56A-2440
Editorial: Aschauer Str. 30, 81549 MÜNCHEN
Tel: 89 2030431300 **Fax:** 89 2030431399
Email: robert.bublak@springer.com **Web site:** http://www.urban-vogel.de
Freq: Monthly; Free to qualifying individuals
Annual Sub.: EUR 204,00; **Circ:** 4,525
Editor: Robert Bublak
Profile: In the official organ of the Professional Association of German Dermatologists professional political developments are controversial. The "required reading" for the dermatologist also offers first-hand training that is certified under the guidelines of the German Academy of Dermatology. There are also interviews and reports on important issues in dermatology and related fields. Services, for example on the right and practice management, complete the spectrum.
Language(s): German
ADVERTISING RATES:
Full Page Mono .... EUR 2350
Full Page Colour .... EUR 4100
Mechanical Data: Type Area: 240 x 174 mm
Official Journal of: Organ d. Berufsverb. d. Dt. Dermatologen e.V.

DER DEUTSCHE FALLSCHIRMJÄGER
1862090G40-993
Editorial: Im Klein Feld 19, 76689 KARLSDORF-NEUTHARD **Tel:** 7251 348120 **Fax:** 7251 348121
Email: oehlerddf@gmx.de **Web site:** http://www.fschjgbund.de
Freq: 6 issues yearly; **Annual Sub.:** EUR 25,00; **Circ:** 3,000
Editor: Hans-Joachim Oehler
Profile: Der Deutsche Fallschirmjäger reported e.g. three major areas - Current / News / Opinion - Basics / History - Reports from the camaraderie overall, a range of topics for all members and from the structure generation and the use generation of active force.
Language(s): German

DEUTSCHE GESELLSCHAFT FÜR CHIRURGIE MITTEILUNGEN
725015G56A-2460
Editorial: Luisenstr. 58, 10117 BERLIN
Tel: 30 28876290 **Fax:** 30 28876299
Email: dgchirurgie@t-online.de **Web site:** http://www.dgch.de
Freq: Quarterly; **Annual Sub.:** EUR 111,80; **Circ:** 6,740
Editor: Hartwig Bauer
Profile: Current releases of the German Surgical Society, information on career policy, training, conferences, awards ceremonies and personalities as well as extensive convention preview.
Language(s): German
ADVERTISING RATES:
Full Page Mono .... EUR 2760
Full Page Colour .... EUR 3960
Mechanical Data: Type Area: 256 x 180 mm, No. of Columns (Display): 4, Col Widths (Display): 42 mm
BUSINESS: HEALTH & MEDICAL

Germany

DEUTSCHE GESELLSCHAFT FÜR UNFALLCHIRURGIE E.V. MITTEILUNGEN UND NACHRICHTEN 1614866G56A-11197

Editorial: Luisenstr. 58, 10117 BERLIN
Tel: 30 2800430 **Fax:** 30 28004306
Email: gdunfallchirurgie@dgu-online.de **Web site:** http://www.thieme.de/fz/dgunfall
Freq: Half-yearly; Free to qualifying individuals
Annual Sub.: EUR 68,80; **Circ:** 4,820
Editor: Hartmut Siebert
Profile: Releases of the German Society of Trauma Surgery, information about conferences, training, awards, appointments, honors, and a comprehensive convention preview.
Language(s): German
ADVERTISING RATES:
Full Page Mono .... EUR 2140
Full Page Colour .... EUR 3310
Mechanical Data: Type Area: 256 x 180 mm, No. of Columns (Display): 4, Col Widths (Display): 42 mm

DEUTSCHE GETRÄNKE WIRTSCHAFT 725018G9A-18

Editorial: Nansenstr. 11, 58300 WETTER
Tel: 2335 739801 **Fax:** 2335 739802
Email: red@deutschegetraenkewirtschaft.de **Web site:** http://www.deutschegetraenkewirtschaft.de
Freq: 10 issues yearly; **Annual Sub.:** EUR 56,00; **Circ:** 12,000
Editor: Monika Busch
Profile: The economic and news magazine for beverage professionals in trade and gastronomy as well as for manufacturers and importers. The deutsche getränke wirtschaft reports on market data, facts with background from politics and economy. Continuous basic informations are of course naturally. Current market and product information, as well as foresighted central topics of interest for the development of the versatile market segments are a part of every issue - a founded orientation over the current happening for the beverage professional. The deutsche getränke wirtschaft determines contents with the Special and title topics for the respective output at very short notice and after the topicality. Background reports, analyses and the necessary evaluation of the current happenings are the editorial emphasis. Our team sets on investigative journalism, in order to represent the dynamics of the globalized market with all their facets.
Language(s): German
Readership: Aimed at managers of pubs and restaurants.
ADVERTISING RATES:
Full Page Mono .... EUR 3138
Full Page Colour .... EUR 5215
Mechanical Data: Type Area: 236 x 188 mm
BUSINESS: DRINKS & LICENSED TRADE: Drinks, Licensed Trade, Wines & Spirits

DEUTSCHE HANDWERKS ZEITUNG 725019G63-1723

Editorial: Gewerbestr. 2, 86825 BAD WÖRISHOFEN
Tel: 8247 354117 **Fax:** 8247 354180
Email: reddhz@holzmann-medien.de **Web site:** http://www.deutsche-handwerks-zeitung.de
Freq: 21 issues yearly; Free to qualifying individuals
Annual Sub.: EUR 39,00; **Circ:** 479,653
Editor: Burkhard Riering; **Advertising Manager:** Eva Maria Hammer
Profile: The 'Deutsche Handwerks Zeitung' is Germany's biggest publication covering medium-sized enterprises in the crafts industry. It is the official voice of 23 trade chambers and the Baden-Württembergischen Handwerkstag (Baden-Württemberg Crafts Association). It informs more than 470,000 crafts businesses and small and medium-sized companies in Germany on all current business, financial and socio-political developments. Entrepreneurs in Bavaria, Baden-Württemberg, Hessen, Saxony, Thuringia and Saxony-Anhalt are competently informed in detail in the "Business Management" section on laws and taxes, business administration, technology and contemporary crafts. Correspondents and editors in Brussels and Berlin increase the area of activity of the newspaper and inform their readers on important development relevant to medium-sized enterprises. Decision-makers from the world of politics and the economy feature regularly in interviews and analyses. With specials on economic and financial policy focal points, the editorial staff highlight background and documentation. The focus of the DHZ is on the beneficial value of the information for the reader and entrepreneur. Additional editorial services are the business cycle analysis for the crafts indus try appearing quarterly and exclusively for the DHZ, DHZ focuses on business management and technical areas and editorial inserts on practical special topics. The 'Deutsche Handwerks Zeitung' is also the official announcer of the International Crafts Trade Fair, i. e. the GHM (Gesellschaft für Handwerksausstellungen und –messen mbH, Munich).
Language(s): German
ADVERTISING RATES:
Full Page Mono .... EUR 29972
Full Page Colour .... EUR 51644
Mechanical Data: Type Area: 480 x 325 mm, No. of Columns (Display): 7, Col Widths (Display): 45 mm
Copy instructions: *Copy Date:* 10 days prior to publication
BUSINESS: REGIONAL BUSINESS

DEUTSCHE HEBAMMEN ZEITSCHRIFT 725020G56B-1695

Editorial: Fuchsrain 18a, 30657 HANNOVER
Tel: 511 65100305 **Fax:** 511 651788
Email: info@staudeverlag.de **Web site:** http://www.deutschehebammenzeitschrift.de
Freq: Monthly; **Annual Sub.:** EUR 70,00; **Circ:** 7,426
Editor: Elisabeth Niederstucke
Profile: The Deutsche Hebammen Zeitschrift is the independent trade magazine for professional skills training and training for midwives. Central themes include obstetrics, prenatal care, postpartum care, the newborn child, and professional practice as legal issues. In addition, the special role of midwives as the contact person and advisor for the mother and family is taken into account. Here, the magazine informs about health, social and health policy issues.
Language(s): German
ADVERTISING RATES:
Full Page Mono .... EUR 1550
Full Page Colour .... EUR 2350
Mechanical Data: Type Area: 265 x 185 mm, No. of Columns (Display): 3, Col Widths (Display): 58 mm
Supplement(s): Eltern-info
BUSINESS: HEALTH & MEDICAL: Nursing

DEUTSCHE JAGD ZEITUNG 725024G75F-120

Editorial: Erich-Kästner-Str. 2, 56379 SINGHOFEN
Tel: 2604 978801 **Fax:** 2604 978802
Email: djz@paulparey.de **Web site:** http://www.djz.de
Freq: Monthly; **Annual Sub.:** EUR 46,00; **Circ:** 38,102
Editor: Frank Rakow; **Advertising Manager:** Sylvia Lühert
Profile: The hunting magazine offers a mix of hunting practices, wildlife biology, recent reports, reports with hunting "exciting" and the famous Klavinius cartoon. The publication includes the first game magazine world, the gap between print and TV. The DVD also provides the monthly magazine 45 minutes to their regular readers exclusive reports from the hunting practice. Your own camera crew is on its way in all interesting districts of Germany with real professionals and hunters hunting from next door.
Language(s): German
ADVERTISING RATES:
Full Page Mono .... EUR 2892
Full Page Colour .... EUR 4865
Mechanical Data: Type Area: 253 x 186 mm, No. of Columns (Display): 4, Col Widths (Display): 43 mm
Copy instructions: *Copy Date:* 28 days prior to publication
CONSUMER: SPORT: Shooting

DEUTSCHE JUGEND ZEITSCHRIFT FÜR DIE JUGENDARBEIT 725026G32G-620

Editorial: Haierbäumchen 88, 41169 MÖNCHENGLADBACH **Tel:** 2161 551535
Fax: 2161 558376
Email: brenner-mg@gmx.de
Freq: 11 issues yearly; **Annual Sub.:** EUR 63,00; **Circ:** 2,500
Editor: Gerd Brenner; **Advertising Manager:** Karola Weiss
Profile: deutsche jugend Zeitschrift für die Jugendarbeit is the only not to an institution-bound trade journal for the practice field of youth work. deutsche jugend informed about events and developments in youth policy, youth work and youth services, offers suggestions for the practice of youth work and youth education, discussed theories and concepts and comments on current problems. deutsche jugend are engaged in the discussion of new concepts in youth work.
Language(s): German
Readership: Aimed at youth and social workers.
ADVERTISING RATES:
Full Page Mono .... EUR 620
Mechanical Data: Type Area: 198 x 149 mm, No. of Columns (Display): 2, Col Widths (Display): 72 mm
Copy instructions: *Copy Date:* 30 days prior to publication
BUSINESS: LOCAL GOVERNMENT, LEISURE & RECREATION: Community Care & Social Services

DEUTSCHE NOTAR-ZEITSCHRIFT 725036G44-3102

Editorial: Burgmauer 53, 50667 KÖLN
Tel: 221 27793590 **Fax:** 221 256808
Email: dnotz@dnotz.de **Web site:** http://www.dnotz.de
Freq: Monthly; **Annual Sub.:** EUR 105,70; **Circ:** 6,686
Editor: Gregor Rieger; **Advertising Manager:** Fritz Lebherz
Profile: The Deutsche Notar-Zeitschrift is the Gazette of the Federal Chamber of Notaries, and thus the leading trade magazine for notaries in Germany. According to federal notary regulations it is legal required reading for all notaries in Germany. It covers the target group of notaries completely. The Deutsche Notar-Zeitschrift brings monthly articles and current decisions from all of the notary relevant jurisdictions and informed about important legislative changes, training events and the work of the Federal Chamber of Notaries, aimed primarily at notaries, lawyers and judges who deal with notary law questions, informed about the latest case law on general civil law, real estate law, family law, inheritance law, corporate and commercial law, legal costs and notary law. In their contributions of outstanding experts from academia and notarial practice will be published.
Language(s): German
ADVERTISING RATES:
Full Page Mono .... EUR 1660
Full Page Colour .... EUR 2390
Mechanical Data: Type Area: 194 x 120 mm, No. of Columns (Display): 2, Col Widths (Display): 58 mm
Copy instructions: *Copy Date:* 27 days prior to publication
BUSINESS: LEGAL

DEUTSCHE POLIZEI 725039G32F-180

Editorial: Stromstr. 4, 10555 BERLIN
Tel: 30 399921114 **Fax:** 30 399921190
Email: gdp-redaktion@gdp-online.de **Web site:** http://www.gdp.de
Freq: Monthly; Free to qualifying individuals
Annual Sub.: EUR 38,80; **Circ:** 175,171
Editor: Marion Tetzner; **Advertising Manager:** Antje Kleuker
Profile: Magazine containing information about the German police force. Topics: Police law, civil service law, traffic law, criminal and criminal procedural law, criminal investigation, criminology, leadership and commitment, police technology, environmental protection. Target group: You can reach the decision makers and staff councils in terms of procurement. Readers are police officers (civil servants and public employees) and have a secure income. The readers are very interested in the subject facilities / equipment, financial products, insurance, travel and recreation, sports and entertainment electronics.
Language(s): German
ADVERTISING RATES:
Full Page Mono .... EUR 8600
Full Page Colour .... EUR 12500
Mechanical Data: Type Area: 251 x 176 mm, No. of Columns (Display): 3, Col Widths (Display): 56 mm
Copy instructions: *Copy Date:* 28 days prior to publication
Supplement(s): Bayern LandesJournal; Berlin LandesJournal; Hessen LandesJournal; Mecklenburg-Vorpommern LandesJournal; Nordrhein-Westfalen LandesJournal; Rheinland-Pfalz LandesJournal
BUSINESS: LOCAL GOVERNMENT, LEISURE & RECREATION: Police

DER DEUTSCHE RECHTSPFLEGER RPFLEGER 725049G1A-540

Editorial: Ernst-Wessel-Str. 9, 15366 HOPPEGARTEN **Tel:** 3342 309881 **Fax:** 3342 309882
Email: hintzenudo@aol.com **Web site:** http://www.rpfleger.de
Freq: 11 issues yearly; **Annual Sub.:** EUR 132,00; **Circ:** 8,300
Editor: Udo Hintzen; **Advertising Manager:** Barbara Brante
Profile: The Deutsche Rechtspfleger Rpfleger is the legal trade magazine for property and land registry law, family and inheritance law, commercial and registration law, civil process, foreclosure, bankruptcy law, criminal procedure and criminal enforcement and taxation of costs and expenses.
Language(s): German
ADVERTISING RATES:
Full Page Mono .... EUR 1850
Full Page Colour .... EUR 3170
Mechanical Data: Type Area: 260 x 185 mm
Copy instructions: *Copy Date:* 18 days prior to publication

DEUTSCHE RICHTERZEITUNG 725053G44-3103

Editorial: Kronenstr. 73, 10117 BERLIN
Tel: 30 2061250 **Fax:** 30 20612525
Email: info@drb.de **Web site:** http://www.driz.de
Freq: 11 issues yearly; **Annual Sub.:** EUR 68,00; **Circ:** 11,000
Editor: Lothar Jünemann
Profile: The Deutsche RichterZeitung informed than trade magazine with a clear structure and a modern layout of current and fundamental issues of justice, legal policy and legal development. It is divided into sections reports, information, commentary, case law and articles.
Language(s): German
ADVERTISING RATES:
Full Page Mono .... EUR 2250
Full Page Colour .... EUR 3954
Mechanical Data: Type Area: 270 x 186 mm, No. of Columns (Display): 4, Col Widths (Display): 45 mm
Official Journal of: Organ d. Dt. Richterbundes, Bund d. Richterinnen u. Richter, Staatsanwältinnen u. Staatsanwälte
BUSINESS: LEGAL

DIE DEUTSCHE SCHULE 725077G62A-640

Editorial: Schlosswender Str. 1, 30159 HANNOVER
Tel: 511 76217325
Email: redaktion@dds-home.de **Web site:** http://www.dds.uni-hannover.de
Freq: Quarterly; **Annual Sub.:** EUR 53,00; **Circ:** 1,000
Editor: Martin Heinrich; **Advertising Manager:** Martina Kaluza
Profile: Magazine focusing on educational science, educational policy and educational practice.
Language(s): German
Readership: Aimed at people in education.
BUSINESS: CHURCH & SCHOOL EQUIPMENT & EDUCATION: Education

DEUTSCHE SCHÜTZENZEITUNG 725076G75F-140

Editorial: Otto-Volger-Str. 15, 65843 SULZBACH
Tel: 6196 7667241 **Fax:** 6196 7667269
Email: s.paulini@uzv.de **Web site:** http://www.dsb.de/aktuelles/schuetzenzeitung
Freq: Monthly; **Annual Sub.:** EUR 46,20; **Circ:** 9,721
Profile: The Deutsche SchützenZeitung is the official newsletter of the DSB. There are not only all the important dates and invitations to the various competitions and events of the association, the Deutsche SchützenZeitung also reported extensively and intensively about the events from the entire sports program of the fourth largest German sports association. In addition, provide professional writers - such as the national coach and her assistants - also a club member useful tips he can implement at home on the range for themselves. And current contributions to the weapons and environmental law as well as construction of shooting ranges are naturally found in the DSZ.
Language(s): German
ADVERTISING RATES:
Full Page Mono .... EUR 1600
Full Page Colour .... EUR 2330
Mechanical Data: No. of Columns (Display): 4, Col Widths (Display): 42 mm, Type Area: 250 x 184 mm
Copy instructions: *Copy Date:* 11 days prior to publication
CONSUMER: SPORT: Shooting

DEUTSCHE SEESCHIFFFAHRT 725081G45A-140

Editorial: Esplanade 6, 20354 HAMBURG
Tel: 40 35097238 **Fax:** 40 35097211
Email: johns@reederverband.de **Web site:** http://www.reederverband.de
Freq: 11 issues yearly; Free to qualifying individuals
Annual Sub.: EUR 58,50; **Circ:** 7,500
Editor: Dirk Max Johns; **Advertising Manager:** Hedwig Lyko-Wiese
Profile: The maritime industry combines the world - and German companies have a significant share of it. Open-minded and technologically adept: So presents itself the Deutsche Seeschifffahrt. Shipbuilding, power transmission, navigation, communication, increased efficiency, fleet management, insurance, financing: report on technical innovation, economic development and political debates are accompanied by entertaining topics - from the documentary about life on board, the large cruise route to the historic digression. A attractive design with generous images and clear graphics makes the reading of the magazine at a special pleasure. At Best of Corporate Publishing, the world's most important competition for corporate magazines and annual reports, was the Deutsche Seeschifffahrt three times with a silver medal and once a gold medal (category "environmental management" and "Transport and Logistics") awarded. The magazine is also for the "Design Award of the Federal Republic of Germany" nominated. Regular topics: Software and electronics (navigation, communications, marine operations, etc.), marine technology (engines, accessories), coatings (coating, anti-fouling, corrosion protection, etc.), environment (new standards, innovations, research vessels), Travel/Culture: Cruises (attractive itineraries, new ships), ports (German and international ports), logistics (linking land, loading equipment, terminals), heavy loading equipment (cranes & Co.), ballast water, containers (types, technology, market), special vessels (FPSO, wind farm installation vessels etc.), financing and insurance (funds, ship insurance, secondary market), are: interviews with initiators, history: historic ships, books, portraits: Reeder personalities, maritime originals and new ships: tankers, ferries, bulk carriers, passenger ships, container ships.
Language(s): German
ADVERTISING RATES:
Full Page Mono .... EUR 1700
Full Page Colour .... EUR 2800
Mechanical Data: Type Area: 250 x 185 mm
Copy instructions: *Copy Date:* 20 days prior to publication
BUSINESS: MARINE & SHIPPING

DER DEUTSCHE SPITZ 725093G81B-17

Editorial: Angerstr. 5, 86179 AUGSBURG
Tel: 821 812943 **Fax:** 821 812943
Email: peter.machetanz@freenet.de **Web site:** http://www.deutsche-spitze.de
Freq: Quarterly; **Cover Price:** EUR 5,00
Free to qualifying individuals ; **Circ:** 3,000
Editor: Peter Machetanz; **Advertising Manager:** Peter Machetanz
Profile: The magazine informs about current club events in the groups, at the exhibitions and other activities of the club. In addition to the dates for dog shows, the judges' reports of recent months are reprinted in full. As an advertising medium for our breeders and stud dog owner is "Der Deutsche Spitz" often used.
Language(s): German
Readership: Aimed at dog lovers in general and Spitz owners in particular.
Mechanical Data: Type Area: 185 x 120 mm, No. of Columns (Display): 2, Col Widths (Display): 57 mm
Copy instructions: *Copy Date:* 30 days prior to publication
CONSUMER: ANIMALS & PETS: Dogs

DEUTSCHE TENNIS ZEITUNG 725110G75H-120

Editorial: Böblinger Str. 68/1, 71065 SINDELFINGEN
Tel: 7031 862800 **Fax:** 7031 862801

mail: sekretariat@deutsche-tennis-zeitung.de **Web ite:** http://www.deutsche-tennis-zeitung.de
req: 11 issues yearly; **Annual Sub.:** EUR 55,00; **irc:** 19,848
ditor: Brigitte Schurr; **Advertising Manager:** Timo Vagenblast
rofile: Tennis newspaper published by German ennis Association: Scene - Youth - Training - Medicine - Tips - Travel - Events - Ranking. Target roup: Tennis players, coaches, officials and opinion eaders in over 10,000 clubs in the DTB and perators of commercial sport and leisure facilities.
anguage(s): German
ADVERTISING RATES:
ull Page Mono .... EUR 1900
ull Page Colour .... EUR 2950
Mechanical Data: Type Area: 247 x 180 mm, No. of Columns (Display): 4, Col Widths (Display): 42 mm
Copy instructions: *Copy Date:* 35 days prior to ublication
Official Journal of: Organ d. Dt. Tennis Bund
CONSUMER: SPORT: Racquet Sports

DEUTSCHE WACHTELHUND ZEITUNG
725114G81B-18
Editorial: Boizenburger Str. 14, 92670 WINDISCHESCHENBACH **Tel:** 9681 688
Fax: 9681 688
Web site: http://www.wachtelhund.de
Freq: Monthly; **Circ:** 4,000
Editor: Sven Halletz
Profile: Magazine about guard dogs.
Language(s): German
ADVERTISING RATES:
Full Page Mono .... EUR 264
Mechanical Data: Type Area: 203 x 140 mm, No. of Columns (Display): 2, Col Widths (Display): 67 mm
Copy instructions: *Copy Date:* 21 days prior to publication
CONSUMER: ANIMALS & PETS: Dogs

DER DEUTSCHE WEINBAU
725115G21H-1
Editorial: Maximilianstr. 7, 67433 NEUSTADT
Tel: 6321 890854 **Fax:** 6321 890821
Email: bader@meininger.de **Web site:** http://www.der-deutsche-weinbau.de
Freq: 24 issues yearly; **Annual Sub.:** EUR 81,60; **Circ:** 7,902
Editor: Rudolf Nickenig; **Advertising Manager:** Ralf Clemens
Profile: Der Deutsche Weinbau is the official publication of the German Viniculture Association and its member associations and a source of information on all wine-growing policy topics as well as being a guide to marketing and to wine-growing and winery technology. As the information leaflet of the German Working Team for Viniculture Technology (Arbeitsgemeinschaft für Technik im Weinbau, ATW), Der Deutsche Weinbau leads the way in all areas of research and development. What is more, every second issue of Der Deutsche Weinbau includes "Der Oenologe", the newsletter for the Federation of German Oenologists and graduates from the Geisenheim Faculty of Viniculture and Beverages Technology. So Der Deutsche Weinbau magazine is undisputedly the leading information medium - for practicians as well as all executive personnel in viniculture, oenology and beverages technology. Facebook: http://www.facebook.com/pages/Der-Deutsche-Weinbau/125396110831131.
Language(s): German
ADVERTISING RATES:
Full Page Mono .... EUR 2725
Full Page Colour .... EUR 4160
Mechanical Data: Type Area: 260 x 185 mm, No. of Columns (Display): 4, Col Widths (Display): 43 mm
Copy instructions: *Copy Date:* 11 days prior to publication
Supplement(s): Der Oenologe
BUSINESS: AGRICULTURE & FARMING: Vine Growing

DAS DEUTSCHE WEINMAGAZIN
725116G21H-2
Editorial: Weberstr. 9, 55130 MAINZ
Tel: 6131 620530 **Fax:** 6131 620544
Email: h.seibert@fraund.de **Web site:** http://www.fraund.de
Freq: 26 issues yearly; **Annual Sub.:** EUR 79,80; **Circ:** 6,810
Editor: Henning Seibert; **Advertising Manager:** Manfred Schulz
Profile: Magazine covering developments in methods of vine growing.
Language(s): German
ADVERTISING RATES:
Full Page Mono .... EUR 2760
Full Page Colour .... EUR 4140
Mechanical Data: Type Area: 270 x 185 mm, No. of Columns (Display): 4, Col Widths (Display): 43 mm
Copy instructions: *Copy Date:* 12 days prior to publication
BUSINESS: AGRICULTURE & FARMING: Vine Growing

DER DEUTSCHE WIRTSCHAFTSANWALT
1740193G1A-3635
Editorial: Güntzelstr. 63, 10717 BERLIN
Tel: 30 8145060 **Fax:** 30 81450622
Email: mail@lexxion.de **Web site:** http://www.lexxion.de
Freq: Annual; **Cover Price:** EUR 48,00; **Circ:** 10,000
Advertising Manager: Nils Olhorn
Profile: Handbook for jurists.
Language(s): German
ADVERTISING RATES:
Full Page Mono .... EUR 3800
Full Page Colour .... EUR 3800
Mechanical Data: Type Area: 210 x 148 mm
Copy instructions: *Copy Date:* 60 days prior to publication

DEUTSCHE ZEITSCHRIFT FÜR ONKOLOGIE
1606461G56A-11157
Editorial: Oswald-Hesse-Str. 50, 70469 STUTTGART
Tel: 711 8931737 **Fax:** 711 8931705
Email: cornelius.grumbkow@medizinverlage.de **Web site:** http://www.medizinverlage.de
Freq: Quarterly; Free to qualifying individuals
Annual Sub.: EUR 79,40; **Circ:** 4,800
Editor: Cornelius von Grumbkow; **Advertising Manager:** Nancy Ruhland
Profile: Magazine about oncology.
Language(s): English; German
ADVERTISING RATES:
Full Page Mono .... EUR 1810
Full Page Colour .... EUR 2985
Mechanical Data: Type Area: 230 x 176 mm
Copy instructions: *Copy Date:* 40 days prior to publication

DEUTSCHE ZEITSCHRIFT FÜR SPORTMEDIZIN
725122G56A-2520
Editorial: 89070 ULM **Tel:** 731 50045322
Fax: 731 50045303
Email: juergen.steinacker@uni-ulm.de **Web site:** http://www.zeitschrift-sportmedizin.de
Freq: 11 issues yearly; Free to qualifying individuals
Annual Sub.: EUR 64,90; **Circ:** 11,500
Editor: Jürgen M. Steinacker
Profile: The Deutsche Zeitschrift für Sportmedizin is the leading and most widely read German-language magazine for the entire sports medicine. It is aimed at all physicians working in sports medicine, general practitioners, internists, cardiologists, orthopedists, surgeons and others, as well as other sports medicine/sports science researchers interested in all disciplines as well as physical therapists, trainers, practitioners and athletes.
Language(s): German
Readership: Aimed at German and Austrian doctors specialising in sports injuries.
ADVERTISING RATES:
Full Page Mono .... EUR 2200
Full Page Colour .... EUR 3525
Mechanical Data: Type Area: 240 x 175 mm
Copy instructions: *Copy Date:* 20 days prior to publication
Official Journal of: Organ d. Dt. Ges. f. Sportmedizin u. Prävention e.V. u. d. Österr. Ges. d. Sportmedizin u. Prävention
BUSINESS: HEALTH & MEDICAL

DEUTSCHEANWALTAKADEMIE SEMINARVERZEICHNIS
1647540G1A-3560
Editorial: Littenstr. 11, 10179 BERLIN
Tel: 30 726153142 **Fax:** 30 726153144
Email: daa@anwaltakademie.de **Web site:** http://www.anwaltakademie.de
Freq: Half-yearly; **Circ:** 60,000
Advertising Manager: Tilmann Pusch
Profile: Seminar programme from the German Lawyer's Academy.
Language(s): German
ADVERTISING RATES:
Full Page Mono .... EUR 1750
Mechanical Data: Type Area: 180 x 85 mm

DEUTSCHER DRUCKER
725048G41A-200
Editorial: Riedstr. 25, 73760 OSTFILDERN
Tel: 711 4481720 **Fax:** 711 4481782
Email: b.niemela@print.de **Web site:** http://www.print.de
Freq: 38 issues yearly; Free to qualifying individuals
Annual Sub.: EUR 145,15; **Circ:** 8,321
Editor: Bernhard Niemela; **Advertising Manager:** Michael Bieber
Profile: "Deutscher Drucker" is the No. 1 of all the trade magazines for the printing and media industry. "Deutscher Drucker" reaches like no other medium specific industry professionals and executives, professionals and the technical and commercial management in the entire print and media industry. Readers of "Deutscher Drucker"s due to their leadership positions have extremely high demands on their magazine - and are highly satisfied for it is no coincidence that the vast majority of listed subscribers within the printing press are "Deutscher Drucker" readers. The 38 volumes of the almost weekly magazine are a must read in the print industry. The current weekly information section provides the most important product, economic and company news and reports directly from the most interesting industry events. In-depth technical articles, reports, interviews, application examples and an analysis arefound by the readers in the categories Products & Technology, Operation & Management and customers and markets. Numerous exciting series and a weekly round up the main topic of information. For over 25 years, "Deutscher Drucker" is official information organ of the prestigious "Fachverband Führungskräfte der Druckindustrie und Informationsverarbeitung e.V. (FDI). "Deutscher Drucker" has an international weight and is the sole German member of the international information pools EUROGRAPHIC PRESS (EP), a collaboration of the leading print trade magazines from 16 European countries.
Language(s): German
ADVERTISING RATES:
Full Page Mono .... EUR 4250
Full Page Colour .... EUR 6200
Mechanical Data: Type Area: 269 x 206 mm, No. of Columns (Display): 4, Col Widths (Display): 49 mm
Copy instructions: *Copy Date:* 7 days prior to publication
Official Journal of: Organ d. Fachverb. Führungskräfte d. Druckindustrie u. Informationsverarbeitung e.V.
BUSINESS: PRINTING & STATIONERY: Printing

DEUTSCHER HOTELFÜHRER
1881514G89A-12444
Editorial: Silberburgstr. 122, 70176 STUTTGART
Tel: 711 2133334 **Fax:** 711 2133377
Email: hotelguide@matthaes.de **Web site:** http://www.hotelguide.de
Freq: Annual; **Cover Price:** EUR 24,90; **Circ:** 50,000
Profile: Der Deutsche Hotehlführer provides the reader with more than 5,000 overnight stays in Germany. The combination of book and Internet versions www.hotelguide.de the hotel guide to an essential assistant for your trip planning. His four-color layout and the photos of the registered hotels round out the book and simplify the search for a suitable place to stay. Whether pleasant place, an idyllic country inn or exclusive hotel - whatever your budget to find the right offer. The clear structure and clear imagery to convince by means of pictograms. At a Glance price, accessibility, amenities and services of the house are covered.
Language(s): German

DEUTSCHER PRESSERAT JAHRBUCH
725058G2A-940
Editorial: Fritzschestr. 27, 10585 BERLIN
Tel: 30 3670070 **Fax:** 30 36700799
Email: info@presserat.de **Web site:** http://www.presserat.de
Freq: Annual; **Cover Price:** EUR 29,00; **Circ:** 2,000
Editor: Lutz Tillmanns
Profile: Magazine with decisions of the German Press Council.
Language(s): German
ADVERTISING RATES:
Full Page Mono .... EUR 880
Full Page Colour .... EUR 1420
Mechanical Data: Type Area: 170 x 112 mm, No. of Columns (Display): 2, Col Widths (Display): 55 mm
Copy instructions: *Copy Date:* 40 days prior to publication

DEUTSCHER SPARKASSENKALENDER
725059G1C-380
Editorial: Am Wallgraben 115, 70565 STUTTGART
Tel: 711 7821582 **Fax:** 711 7821709
Email: wilfried.sehm@dsv-gruppe.de **Web site:** http://www.sparkassenverlag.de
Freq: Annual; **Cover Price:** EUR 18,08; **Circ:** 10,000
Profile: The Savings Bank calendar next to the calendar contains detailed address lists of associations and institutes of the Savings Banks Financial Group. The part of savings bank practice includes table collections for the credit business and the customer and investment advice. Recent compilations of the labor and social law round out the range of information.
Language(s): German

DEUTSCHER WALDBESITZER
1616267G46-14
Editorial: Kabelkamp 6, 30179 HANNOVER
Tel: 511 67806117 **Fax:** 511 67806910
Email: tanja.freytag@dlv.de **Web site:** http://www.forstpraxis.de
Freq: 6 issues yearly; **Annual Sub.:** EUR 32,00; **Circ:** 12,000
Editor: Tanja Freytag; **Advertising Manager:** Jens Riegamer
Profile: The publication "Deutscher Waldbesitzer" is directed with the latest association news and background reports on timber market, silviculture, forestry and forestry policy to private forest owners, decision makers in forestry associations, service foresters of Chambers of Agriculture and state forest managers and to managers in the municipalities. In the regions of Lower Saxony, Hesse, Saxony-Anhalt, Brandenburg and Mecklenburg-Vorpommern this forestry title represents as an attractive regional advertising for the forestry sector in total around 40,000 forest owners with a total area of 1/2 million acres of forest.
Language(s): German
ADVERTISING RATES:
Full Page Mono .... EUR 825
Full Page Colour .... EUR 1305
Mechanical Data: Type Area: 270 x 184 mm, No. of Columns (Display): 4, Col Widths (Display): 43 mm
Copy instructions: *Copy Date:* 12 days prior to publication
Official Journal of: Organ d. Hess. Waldbesitzerverb. e.V., d. Waldbesitzerverbände Brandenburg e.V., Mecklenburg-Vorpommern e.V., Hannover in Niedersachsen e.V., Sachsen-Anhalt e.V. u. Weser-Ems e.V.
Supplement(s): Hessischer Waldbesitzerverband

DEUTSCHES ARCHITEKTENBLATT
725068G4A-9
Editorial: Askanischer Platz 4, 10963 BERLIN
Tel: 30 26394451 **Fax:** 30 26394452
Email: roland.stimpel@corps-verlag.de **Web site:** http://www.dabonline.de
Freq: 10 issues yearly; Free to qualifying individuals
Annual Sub.: EUR 61,00; **Circ:** 126,150
Editor: Roland Stimpel; **Advertising Manager:** Dagmar Schaafs
Profile: The journal with the largest distribution and the longest range of subjects for architects and for designers / engineers. As the official organ of the German Federal Chamber of Architects and the 16 regional Chambers of Architects, appears in a print run of approximately 126,000 copies. The Deutsche Architektenblatt provides information on issues of architecture and planning, office management and organization, civil and training. Not the finished building is at the center, but the work of those who design and manage it. They are advised practicalyl, competently and timely. Important topics are marketing and management, office equipment and software, legal and professional policies, building materials and materials, but also building processes and logistics. For architects and planners the Deutsche Architektenblatt is speaker for their professional organization. The legal and policy issues and decisions are the proper foundation for solving the many problems in building construction, expansion, landscaping and urban planning projects. Furthermore, the Deutsche Architektenblatt offers assistance to many business decisions. Here, the journal emphasizes human, emotional aspects: reports, sensitive portraits and interviews, social issues and private leisure facilities put the architects and planners in the center.
Language(s): German
ADVERTISING RATES:
Full Page Mono .... EUR 7900
Full Page Colour .... EUR 12100
Mechanical Data: Type Area: 259 x 185 mm, No. of Columns (Display): 4, Col Widths (Display): 43 mm
Copy instructions: *Copy Date:* 21 days prior to publication
Official Journal of: Organ d. Bundesarchitektenkammer u. d. Architektenkammern d. Bundesländer
BUSINESS: ARCHITECTURE & BUILDING: Architecture

DEUTSCHES ÄRZTEBLATT
725067G56A-2540
Editorial: Ottostr. 12, 50859 KÖLN
Tel: 2234 7011120 **Fax:** 2234 7011142
Email: aerzteblatt@aerzteblatt.de **Web site:** http://www.aerzteblatt.de
Freq: Weekly; Free to qualifying individuals
Annual Sub.: EUR 291,20; **Circ:** 410,705
Editor: Heinz Stüwe; **Advertising Manager:** Petra Pahlke-Schäfers
Profile: The German Medical Journal is the official publication of the Federal Medical Association and the National Association of Statutory Health Insurance Physicians. It is intended as the only title of the medical trade press to all doctors in the Federal Republic of Germany. These are addressed in three issues: Issue A: Hands-output (general practitioners) Issue B: Hospital Edition (Clinician) 'C: All other physicians The aim of the editorial staff is competent, objective information the physician. The editorial content features in particular: • Current reports from the occupational, health and social policy • Practice-related, current medical education • Scientific contributions to medicine • Communication to the Editor • Current, practical reports from industry and pharmaceutical research • Further contributions in respect of matters of interest to the medical profession and private: Praxis-IT/Organisation, economic, financial, insurance and legal issues, professional and career planning, art, music, literature, film and media, travel • Supplement and special pages on various topics. Facebook: http://www.facebook.com/aerzteblatt.
Language(s): German
ADVERTISING RATES:
Full Page Mono .... EUR 12960
Full Page Colour .... EUR 17100
Mechanical Data: Type Area: 260 x 185 mm, No. of Columns (Display): 4, Col Widths (Display): 45 mm
Supplement(s): Praxis; ReiseMagazin; Vitamedici
BUSINESS: HEALTH & MEDICAL

DEUTSCHES AUSSCHREIBUNGSBLATT
723897G14A-1100
Editorial: Höherweg 278, 40231 DÜSSELDORF
Tel: 211 370848 **Fax:** 211 381607
Email: service@deutsches-ausschreibungsblatt.de
Web site: http://www.deutsches-ausschreibungsblatt.de
Freq: 150 issues yearly; **Annual Sub.:** EUR 194,00; **Circ:** 20,000
Advertising Manager: Erwin Filippi
Profile: National official paper.
Language(s): German
ADVERTISING RATES:
Full Page Mono .... EUR 1030
Mechanical Data: Type Area: 312 x 220 mm, No. of Columns (Display): 3, Col Widths (Display): 70 mm
Copy instructions: *Copy Date:* 2 days prior to publication

DEUTSCHES BAUBLATT
725071G4E-3300
Editorial: Graf-Zeppelin-Platz 1, 85748 GARCHING
Tel: 89 32000636 **Fax:** 89 32000646
Email: redaktion@baublatt.de **Web site:** http://www.baublatt.de
Freq: 6 issues yearly; **Cover Price:** Free; **Circ:** 21,000
Editor: Sonja Reimann
Profile: The magazine is widely read trade magazine for contractors, managers and decision makers in the construction industry, mining industry and building authorities. The newspaper is to these individuals personally delivered addressed so that decision-makers and managers certainly be achieved. The magazine is the supplement "Construction equipment market trader" in, with offers of used construction machinery in Germany.
Language(s): German
Mechanical Data: Type Area: 446 x 281 mm, No. of Columns (Display): 5, Col Widths (Display): 53 mm
BUSINESS: ARCHITECTURE & BUILDING: Building

DEUTSCHES BIENEN JOURNAL
725072G81G-5
Editorial: Wilhelmsaue 37, 10713 BERLIN
Tel: 30 46406245 **Fax:** 30 46406450
Email: bienenjournal@bauernverlag.de **Web site:** http://www.bienenjournal.de
Freq: Monthly; **Annual Sub.:** EUR 39,50; **Circ:** 18,047
Editor: Silke Beckedorf; **Advertising Manager:** Frank Middendorf
Profile: The "Deutsche Bienen-Journal" is a guide for both leisure and professional beekeepers and equips its readers with the necessary expertise for the care and keeping of bees. In close cooperation with renowned scientists of the German Institute for Bee Research, the "Deutsche Bienen-Journal" month after month is a current and lively forum for science and practice. With a circulation of about 17,000, the "Deutsche Bienen-Journal" is the most subscribed and most widely used magazine on regional beekeeping in Germany. The "Deutsche Bienen-Journal " is organ of thelmkerlandesverbände of Berlin, Brandenburg, Hamburg, Hannover, Mecklenburg-Vorpommern, Sachsen, Sachsen-Anhalt, Thüringen, Weser-Ems, Westfalen-Lippe and of "Deutscher Berufs- und Erwerbsimkerbundes e. V.".
Language(s): German
ADVERTISING RATES:
Full Page Mono .... EUR 1961
Full Page Colour .... EUR 3021
Mechanical Data: Type Area: 265 x 188 mm, No. of Columns (Display): 4, Col Widths (Display): 44 mm
Copy instructions: *Copy Date:* 25 days prior to publication
Official Journal of: Organ d. Imkerlandesverbände Berlin, Brandenburg, Hamburg, Hannover, Mecklenburg u. Vorpommern, Sachsen, Sachsen-Anhalt, Thüringen, Weser-Ems, Westfalen-Lippe, d. Dt. Berufs- u. Erwerbsimkerverbundes e.V., d. Ges. d. Freunde d. Niedersächs. Landesinst. f. Bienenkunde, m. Mttl. d. Dt. Imkerbundes e.V. u. d. ArGe d. Inst. f. Bienenforschung e.V.
CONSUMER: ANIMALS & PETS: Bees

DEUTSCHES HANDWERKSBLATT
725087G63-1724
Editorial: Auf'm Tetelberg 7, 40221 DÜSSELDORF
Tel: 211 3909847 **Fax:** 211 3909839
Email: gottschalk@handwerksblatt.de **Web site:** http://www.handwerksblatt.de
Free to qualifying individuals
Annual Sub.: EUR 30,00; **Circ:** 309,803
Editor: Rüdiger Gottschalk
Profile: For decades, the DHB is a medium for entrepreneurs in the craft. As the market leader in the distribution area, it informs with its total circulation almost every third workshop in Germany. Owners, managers and executives in the workshop industry learn important information they need for their everyday business from their trade paper. The reader can rely on a competent editorial team and are informed about all important issues around the trade: economic policy, business management, technology, education and training. Facebook: http://www.facebook.com/handwerksblatt Twitter: http://twitter.com/Handwerksblatt This Outlet offers RSS (Really Simple Syndication).
Language(s): German
ADVERTISING RATES:
Full Page Mono .... EUR 19278
Full Page Colour .... EUR 38338
Mechanical Data: Col Widths (Display): 44 mm
Copy instructions: *Copy Date:* 14 days prior to publication
Official Journal of: Organ d. Handwerkskammern Cottbus, Dortmund, Düsseldorf, Frankfurt (Oder), Koblenz, Köln, Leipzig, Rheinhessen (Mainz), Münster, Ostmecklenburg-Vorpommern, Ostwestfalen-Lippe zu Bielefeld, d. Pfalz (Kaiserslautern), Potsdam, Südwestfalen, Saarland, Trier
Supplement(s): Handwerkskammer Trier; Südwestfälisches Handwerk
BUSINESS: REGIONAL BUSINESS

DEUTSCHES INGENIEURBLATT
725089G14R-1460
Editorial: Lahrring 36, 53639 KÖNIGSWINTER
Tel: 2223 9098000 **Fax:** 2223 9098001
Email: redaktion@deutsches-ingenieurblatt.de **Web site:** http://www.deutsches-ingenieurblatt.de
Freq: 10 issues yearly; Free to qualifying individuals
Annual Sub.: EUR 118,00; **Circ:** 48,192
Editor: Klaus Werwath; **Advertising Manager:** Lutz Diesbach
Profile: Journal of the current technical and professional information to the engineers on the construction. Documenting the state of the art in relevant areas of activity and object of construction planning and project management as well as the building inspection / construction management activities. Information for the daily management tasks, market outlook, trade shows, conventions and meetings.
Language(s): German
ADVERTISING RATES:
Full Page Mono .... EUR 5625
Full Page Colour .... EUR 7833
Mechanical Data: Type Area: 268 x 183 mm, No. of Columns (Display): 4, Col Widths (Display): 43 mm
Copy instructions: *Copy Date:* 21 days prior to publication
Official Journal of: Organ d. dt. Ingenieurkammern
Supplement(s): Ingenieurkammer Hessen Offizielle Kammer-Nachrichten und Informationen; ingkamm; Kammer Report; Kammer-Spiegel; Nachrichten und Informationen; Sachsen.Land der ingenieure
BUSINESS: COMMERCE, INDUSTRY & MANAGEMENT: Commerce Related

DEUTSCHES POLIZEIBLATT FÜR DIE AUS- UND FORTBILDUNG DPOLBL
725094G32F-220
Editorial: Scharrstr. 2, 70563 STUTTGART
Tel: 711 73850 **Fax:** 711 7385100
Email: mail@boorberg.de **Web site:** http://www.boorberg.de
Freq: 6 issues yearly; **Annual Sub.:** EUR 58,20; **Circ:** 2,070
Editor: Bernd Walter; **Advertising Manager:** Roland Schulz
Profile: Magazine about career development within the German police force.
Language(s): German
Readership: Aimed at senior officers.
ADVERTISING RATES:
Full Page Mono .... EUR 1040
Full Page Colour .... EUR 1950
Mechanical Data: Type Area: 260 x 180 mm
Copy instructions: *Copy Date:* 28 days prior to publication
BUSINESS: LOCAL GOVERNMENT, LEISURE & RECREATION: Police

DEUTSCHES STEUERRECHT DSTR
725099G1M-2
Editorial: Wilhelmstr. 9, 80801 MÜNCHEN
Tel: 89 38189334 **Fax:** 89 38189468
Email: dstr@beck.de **Web site:** http://www.beck.de
Freq: Weekly; **Circ:** 25,687
Editor: Karl-Heinz Sporer; **Advertising Manager:** Fritz Lebherz
Profile: The magazine weekly information up to date and practical information on all relevant issues to tax: tax law, corporate and commercial law, Business administration and accounting. Target groups: accountants, tax agents, accountants, certified accountants, lawyers specializing in tax law, tax experts in companies, managers in business enterprises.
Language(s): German
ADVERTISING RATES:
Full Page Mono .... EUR 3490
Full Page Colour .... EUR 4990
Mechanical Data: Type Area: 260 x 186 mm, No. of Columns (Display): 4, Col Widths (Display): 43 mm
Copy instructions: *Copy Date:* 9 days prior to publication
Official Journal of: Organ d. Bundessteuerberaterkammer
Supplement(s): DStR Entscheidungs-Dienst DStRE
BUSINESS: FINANCE & ECONOMICS: Taxation

DEUTSCHES TIERÄRZTEBLATT BTK
725101G64H-120
Editorial: Französische Str. 53, 10117 BERLIN
Tel: 30 201433880 **Fax:** 30 201433888
Email: geschaeftsstelle@btkberlin.de **Web site:** http://www.bundestieraerztekammer.de
Freq: Monthly; **Annual Sub.:** EUR 122,00; **Circ:** 37,710
Editor: Susanne L. Platt; **Advertising Manager:** Bettina Kruse
Profile: Publication with legal regulations regarding the protection of animals from the Veterinarian Board.
Language(s): German
Readership: Read by veterinary surgeons.
ADVERTISING RATES:
Full Page Mono .... EUR 2399
Full Page Colour .... EUR 3695
Mechanical Data: Type Area: 272 x 188 mm, No. of Columns (Display): 4, Col Widths (Display): 44 mm
Copy instructions: *Copy Date:* 20 days prior to publication
BUSINESS: OTHER CLASSIFICATIONS: Veterinary

DEUTSCHES TURNEN
725103G75X-1260
Editorial: Otto-Fleck-Schneise 8, 60528 FRANKFURT
Tel: 69 67801129 **Fax:** 69 67801111
Freq: Monthly; Free to qualifying individuals
Annual Sub.: EUR 34,00; **Circ:** 18,350
Editor: Kirsten Kleinert; **Advertising Manager:** Kirsten Schiffer
Profile: The club magazine of the German Gymnastics Federation. As varied as the range of the DTB settled Associations also the thematic range of Deutsches Turnen is: Article on major sporting events can be found here as well as dates for training events.
Language(s): German
ADVERTISING RATES:
Full Page Mono .... EUR 1280
Full Page Colour .... EUR 2480
Mechanical Data: Type Area: 255 x 180 mm
Copy instructions: *Copy Date:* 33 days prior to publication
CONSUMER: SPORT: Other Sport

DEUTSCHES VERWALTUNGSBLATT DVBL MIT VERWALTUNGSARCHIV
725105G32A-840
Editorial: Falkenhagener Str. 35, 14612 FALKENSEE
Tel: 3322 42477974 **Fax:** 332 42477974
Email: khoewekamp@wolterskluwer.de
Freq: 24 issues yearly; **Annual Sub.:** EUR 329,00; **Circ:** 2,300
Editor: Klaus H. Höwekamp
Profile: Publication about public administration in Germany with legal emphasis.
Language(s): German
ADVERTISING RATES:
Full Page Mono .... EUR 1564
Full Page Colour .... EUR 2440
Mechanical Data: Type Area: 270 x 186 mm, No. of Columns (Display): 4, Col Widths (Display): 45 mm
Copy instructions: *Copy Date:* 21 days prior to publication
BUSINESS: LOCAL GOVERNMENT, LEISURE & RECREATION: Local Government

DEVDORADO.DE
1660343G5C-56
Editorial: Blomenburg, 24238 SELENT
Tel: 4384 593490 **Fax:** 4384 5934999
Email: info@zoschke.com **Web site:** http://www.zoschke.com
Freq: Quarterly; **Cover Price:** Free; **Circ:** 25,000
Editor: Cordula Lochmann
Profile: Magazine for professional software developers.
Language(s): German

DEWEZET
724914G67B-4000
Editorial: Osterstr. 15, 31785 HAMELN
Tel: 5151 2000 **Fax:** 5151 200429
Email: redaktion@dewezet.de **Web site:** http://www.dewezet.de
Freq: 312 issues yearly; **Circ:** 28,812
Editor: Frank Werner; **News Editor:** Thomas Thimm; **Advertising Manager:** Michael Steuer
Profile: The Deister- und Weserzeitung (Dewezet) from Hameln one of the middle-sized local newspapers in Lower Saxony with regional news and sports pages. The main distribution area, the district Hameln-Pyrmont, and the northern part of the district of Holzminden. It first appeared in 1848 and is since 1884 a daily newspaper. Facebook: http://www.facebook.com/pages/Dewezet/145221692200220 Twitter: http://twitter.com/#!/DewezetRSS This Outlet offers RSS (Really Simple Syndication).
Language(s): German
ADVERTISING RATES:
SCC .... EUR 102,00
Mechanical Data: Type Area: 430 x mm, No. of Columns (Display): 6
Copy instructions: *Copy Date:* 2 days prior to publication
REGIONAL DAILY & SUNDAY NEWSPAPERS: Regional Daily Newspapers

DEWEZET.DE
1621075G67B-16531
Editorial: Osterstr. 15, 31785 HAMELN
Tel: 5151 200400 **Fax:** 5151 200429
Email: redaktion@dewezet.de **Web site:** http://www.dewezet.de
Freq: Daily; **Cover Price:** Paid; **Circ:** 249,114 Unique Users
Editor: Julia Niemeyer; **Advertising Manager:** Rolf Grummel
Profile: Ezine: The Deister- und Weserzeitung (Dewezet) from Hameln one of the middle-sized local newspapers in Lower Saxony with regional news and sports pages. Facebook: http://www.facebook.com/pages/Dewezet/145221692200220 Twitter: http://twitter.com/#!/Dewezet This Outlet offers RSS (Really Simple Syndication).
Language(s): German
REGIONAL DAILY & SUNDAY NEWSPAPERS: Regional Daily Newspapers

DEWI MAGAZIN
1659922G58-1739
Editorial: Ebertstr. 96, 26382 WILHELMSHAVEN
Tel: 4421 48080 **Fax:** 4421 4808843
Email: dewi@dewi.de **Web site:** http://www.dewi.de
Freq: Half-yearly; **Cover Price:** Free; **Circ:** 4,200
Editor: Jens Peter Molly; **Advertising Manager:** Carsten Ender
Profile: Magazine from the German institution of wind energy.
Language(s): English; German; Spanish
ADVERTISING RATES:
Full Page Mono .... EUR 750
Full Page Colour .... EUR 1600
Mechanical Data: Type Area: 258 x 176 mm

DFM
1739824G15B-41
Editorial: Piechlerstr. 18, 86356 NEUSÄSS
Tel: 821 44471300 **Fax:** 821 44471390
Email: r.bodingbauer@dfm.de **Web site:** http://www.dfm.eu
Freq: 6 issues yearly; **Cover Price:** EUR 6,00; **Circ:** 76,766
Editor: Roswitha Bodingbauer; **Advertising Manager:** Markus Schoo
Profile: Hairdressers magazine with articles and information on lifestyle, beauty and fashion. Facebook: http://www.facebook.com/pages/dfm-das-friseur-magazin/257061550911.
Language(s): German
ADVERTISING RATES:
Full Page Mono .... EUR 6800
Full Page Colour .... EUR 6800
Mechanical Data: Type Area: 256 x 174 mm, No. of Columns (Display): 4, Col Widths (Display): 40 mm
Copy instructions: *Copy Date:* 30 days prior to publication
BUSINESS: COSMETICS & HAIRDRESSING: Hairdressing

DFV-FAMILIE
725175G74C-3501
Editorial: Luisenstr. 48, 10117 BERLIN
Tel: 30 30882960 **Fax:** 30 30882961
Email: redaktion@deutscher-familienverband.de **Web site:** http://www.deutscher-familienverband.de
Freq: 6 issues yearly; Free to qualifying individuals
Annual Sub.: EUR 12,30; **Circ:** 94,002
Editor: Sintje Sander-Peuker
Profile: Family magazine with tips, information, discussion and articles concerning politics.
Language(s): German
ADVERTISING RATES:
Full Page Mono .... EUR 3170
Full Page Colour .... EUR 4755
Mechanical Data: Type Area: 255 x 175 mm
Copy instructions: *Copy Date:* 20 days prior to publication
CONSUMER: WOMEN'S INTEREST CONSUMER MAGAZINES: Home & Family

DFZ DER FREIE ZAHNARZT
727925G56D-480
Editorial: Auguststr. 28, 10117 BERLIN
Tel: 30 24342711 **Fax:** 30 24342767
Email: dfz@fvdz.de **Web site:** http://www.fvdz.de
Freq: 11 issues yearly; Free to qualifying individuals
Annual Sub.: EUR 170,00; **Circ:** 48,842
Editor: Peter Kind
Profile: The magazine "DFZ Der Freie Zahnarzt" is tailored to freelance of the established dentist. The latest information and background on the association's policies and to important professional political events in the health and social policy are as much issues such as the practice of creation, business management practices, taxation and finance, pensions, legal and personnel matters. Another important pillar are CME articles by renowned scholars in the field of dental education, offering the reader the possibility of individual online learning success and the acquisition of CME credits. The category "young dentists" is aimed specifically at the target group of students, assistants and newly established dentists as well as practical assistance.
Language(s): German
ADVERTISING RATES:
Full Page Mono .... EUR 5950
Full Page Colour .... EUR 5950
Mechanical Data: Type Area: 240 x 174 mm, No. of Columns (Display): 3, Col Widths (Display): 54 mm
Supplement(s): wissen kompakt
BUSINESS: HEALTH & MEDICAL: Dental

DGS
725186G21D-3
Editorial: Claire-Waldoff-Str. 7, 10117 BERLIN
Tel: 30 81450397 **Fax:** 30 81450438
Email: dgs-magazin@ulmer.de **Web site:** http://www.dgs-magazin.de
Freq: Monthly; **Annual Sub.:** EUR 209,40; **Circ:** 4,871
Editor: Cordula Möbius; **Advertising Manager:** Gerhard Kretschmer
Profile: DGS is aimed at professional poultry and pig farmers. It is an important source of information for those who have directly or indirectly involved in poultry farming and pig production, such as Supplier of livestock equipment and feed, etc., agencies and organizations. With a circulation of 5,300 copies DGS achieved any professional in the field of poultry. At the beginning of the month will appear the colorful and extensive DGS magazine, on the other Saturdays in a compact form DGS-Intern with date information, schedules and market data. DGS bridges the gap between science and practice in the Poultry farming and pig production. Recent research results are presented for granted in this journal for practitioners. The exchange of experiences among colleagues used detailed operating reports. In addition, DGS provides for the industry news from politics, industry and associations. Regular topics include breeding, husbandry, feeding, health and hygiene of poultry (hens, chickens, turkeys, water and specialty poultry) and pigs, market and prices, operating economy, quality of products of poultry and pig, reporting on trade fairs and seminars, ostriches.
Language(s): German
ADVERTISING RATES:
Full Page Mono .... EUR 2862
Full Page Colour .... EUR 4002
Mechanical Data: Type Area: 270 x 184 mm, No. of Columns (Display): 4, Col Widths (Display): 43 mm
Copy instructions: *Copy Date:* 8 days prior to publication

fficial Journal of: Organ d. Zentralverb. d. Dt. eflügelwirtschaft e.V.
upplement(s): DGS intern
USINESS: AGRICULTURE & FARMING: Livestock

DGUV ARBEIT & GESUNDHEIT

721083G14R-200
ditorial: Mittelstr. 51, 10117 BERLIN
el: 30 288763800 **Fax:** 30 288763808
mail: dagmar.schittly@dguv.de **Web site:** http://ww.arbeit-und-gesundheit.de
req: Monthly; **Annual Sub.:** EUR 10,80; **Circ:** 26,326
ditor: Dagmar Schittly; **Advertising Manager:** Anne rautsch
rofile: Magazine on labour security, traffic security nd environment protection. Twitter: http://witter.com/arbeitundgesund.
anguage(s): German
DVERTISING RATES:
ull Page Mono .... EUR 8950
ull Page Colour .... EUR 8950
echanical Data: Type Area: 259 x 176 mm
USINESS: COMMERCE, INDUSTRY & ANAGEMENT: Commerce Related

DGUV FAKTOR ARBEITSSCHUTZ

727040G54B-7_50
ditorial: Mittelstr. 51, 10117 BERLIN
el: 30 288763768 **Fax:** 30 288763808
mail: presse@dguv.de **Web site:** http://www.aktor-arbeitsschutz.de
req: 6 issues yearly; **Annual Sub.:** EUR 11,40; **Circ:** 0,000
ditor: Gregor Doepke
rofile: Journal about safety in the public service ector.
anguage(s): German
eadership: Read by managers.
DVERTISING RATES:
ull Page Mono .... EUR 2440
ull Page Colour .... EUR 2440
echanical Data: Type Area: 270 x 176 mm, No. of olumns (Display): 3, Col Widths (Display): 56 mm
USINESS: SAFETY & SECURITY: Safety

DGUV PLUSPUNKT

739121G54B-31
ditorial: Mittelstr. 51, 10117 BERLIN
el: 2241 2311206 **Fax:** 30 288763 70
mail: andreas.baader@dguv.de **Web site:** http://www.pluspunkt-online.de
req: Quarterly; **Annual Sub.:** EUR 11,60; **Circ:** 7,332
ditor: Andreas Baader; **Advertising Manager:** Anne rautsch
rofile: Journal for accident prevention, safety and oad safety education in public schools. For teachers nd school principals and for all security officers.
anguage(s): German
eadership: Read by teachers and members of local uthorities responsible for school safety.
DVERTISING RATES:
ull Page Mono .... EUR 2480
ull Page Colour .... EUR 2480
echanical Data: Type Area: 266 x 180 mm
USINESS: SAFETY & SECURITY: Safety

DHB MAGAZIN

729809G74C-155
ditorial: Auguststr. 29, 53229 BONN
el: 228 9096619 **Fax:** 228 9096655
mail: magazin@mediacompany.com **Web site:** ttp://www.mediacompany.com
req: 6 issues yearly; Free to qualifying individuals
Annual Sub.: EUR 20,00; **Circ:** 32,000
Editor: Armin Senger; **Advertising Manager:** Renate Arenz
Profile: Magazine of the Association of German Housewives. In reports, news and reporting it addresses the wide range of issues concerning management, locating information in the career field of financial sponsor and is the communication platform of DHB members. Readership: The magazine reaches over Germany in the household working women and men who are members of the DHB. The partners of the association, referring the magazine regularly, are the German Nutrition Society (dgh), evaluation and information service of the Ministry of Agriculture, Food and Forestry (aid), Advisory Council money and financial (Sparkassenverband), German Women, industry association for body care and Detergent e. V., Southwest Radio, Federal Family Forum, German Family Association, Women's Group of the CDU / CSU.
Language(s): German
ADVERTISING RATES:
Full Page Mono .... EUR 1850
Full Page Colour .... EUR 3348
Mechanical Data: Type Area: 250 x 188 mm, No. of Columns (Display): 3, Col Widths (Display): 60 mm
Copy instructions: *Copy Date:* 20 days prior to publication
CONSUMER: WOMEN'S INTEREST CONSUMER MAGAZINES: Home & Family

DHD24 FRIENDS

1662703G86A-1408
Editorial: Drostestr. 14, 30161 HANNOVER
Tel: 511 39091320 **Fax:** 511 39091387
Email: f.schultheiss@dhd.de **Web site:** http://friends.dhd24.com
Cover Price: Paid; **Circ:** 498,500 Unique Users
Advertising Manager: Curd Kitzelmann
Language(s): German
CONSUMER: ADULT & GAY MAGAZINES: Adult Magazines

DHF INTRALOGISTIK

725195G49A-280
Editorial: Dr.-Türk-Str. 2, 45476 MÜLHEIM
Tel: 205 6267526
Email: sabine.barde@pr-solution.de **Web site:** http://www.dhf-magazin.com
Freq: 10 issues yearly; **Annual Sub.:** EUR 99,00; **Circ:** 12,252
Editor: Sabine Barde; **Advertising Manager:** Simone Hildenbrand
Profile: The international journal dhf Intralogistik deals with the entire field of intralogistics, conveyor, storage and transport technology, with rationalization of conveyor and storage processes, also mechanization and automation of the internal flow of materials and also design, operational method, equipment, planning, installations and systems of all types of conveyors. It provides special information and allows an exchange between the specialists of planning, production, organization and design.
Language(s): German
ADVERTISING RATES:
Full Page Mono .... EUR 3350
Full Page Colour .... EUR 4580
Mechanical Data: Type Area: 270 x 185 mm, No. of Columns (Display): 4, Col Widths (Display): 43 mm
Copy instructions: *Copy Date:* 18 days prior to publication
Supplement(s): kataloge orange
BUSINESS: TRANSPORT

DHZ DER HESSISCHE ZAHNARZT

725200G56D-360
Editorial: Lyoner Str. 21, 60528 FRANKFURT
Tel: 69 6607421 **Fax:** 69 6607388
Email: j.pompetzki@kzvh.de
Freq: 11 issues yearly; Free to qualifying individuals
Annual Sub.: EUR 28,60; **Circ:** 6,750
Editor: Jörg Pompetzki; **Advertising Manager:** Franz Stypa
Profile: Magazine about dentistry in Hessen.
Language(s): German
ADVERTISING RATES:
Full Page Mono .... EUR 1420
Full Page Colour .... EUR 2370
Mechanical Data: Type Area: 268 x 184 mm
Copy instructions: *Copy Date:* 60 days prior to publication
BUSINESS: HEALTH & MEDICAL: Dental

DI DIGITAL IMAGING

1665831G85A-831
Editorial: Fasanenweg 18, 70771 LEINFELDEN-ECHTERDINGEN **Tel:** 711 7591314
Fax: 711 75913775
Email: hortner@bitverlag.de **Web site:** http://www.bitverlag.de
Freq: 6 issues yearly; **Cover Price:** Free; **Circ:** 5,745
Editor: Hubert Ortner; **Advertising Manager:** Christa Winkler
Language(s): German
ADVERTISING RATES:
Full Page Mono .... EUR 2860
Full Page Colour .... EUR 4180
Mechanical Data: Type Area: 242 x 172 mm, No. of Columns (Display): 3, Col Widths (Display): 55 mm
Copy instructions: *Copy Date:* 25 days prior to publication
CONSUMER: PHOTOGRAPHY & FILM MAKING: Photography

DIABETES AKTUELL FÜR DIE HAUSARZTPRAXIS

724210G56A-1900
Editorial: Rüdigerstr. 14, 70469 STUTTGART
Tel: 711 8931440 **Fax:** 711 8931322
Email: guenther.buck@thieme.de **Web site:** http://www.thieme.de/fz/diabetesaktuell.html
Freq: 8 issues yearly; **Annual Sub.:** EUR 64,00; **Circ:** 22,450
Editor: Günther Buck
Profile: The diabetes is a growing epidemic, not only in Germany but also worldwide. Therefore, prevention, guidelines-recommended treatment and prevention of secondary damage are top priority. Diabetes aktuell is the medium for the information and training of general practitioners and diabetologists and the cooperation between GPs and diabetologists. A focus is the imparting of latest research results and their implementation in everyday practice.
Language(s): German
ADVERTISING RATES:
Full Page Mono .... EUR 2800
Full Page Colour .... EUR 4405
Mechanical Data: Type Area: 245 x 175 mm

DIABETES FORUM

725203G56A-2700
Editorial: Josefstr. 41, 48703 STADTLOHN
Tel: 2563 20740 **Fax:** 2563 207420
Email: dr.lederle@freenet.de **Web site:** http://www.diabetesforum-online.de
Freq: 10 issues yearly; Free to qualifying individuals
Annual Sub.: EUR 27,60; **Circ:** 10,708
Editor: Martin Lederle; **Advertising Manager:** Björn Lindenau
Profile: The current journal for all health care professionals such as diabetes consultants, diabetologists and general practitioners. And the forum for professional diabetes care: Topics include: Quality management in clinic and practice and of course the interdisciplinary work between diabetologists and experts from other disciplines, eg Psychologists, politicians and representatives of health insurers and industry etc. Also: Medical key issues, hotlines and many useful tips.
Language(s): German
ADVERTISING RATES:
Full Page Mono .... EUR 3590
Full Page Colour .... EUR 3590
Mechanical Data: Type Area: 245 x 178 mm, No. of Columns (Display): 4, Col Widths (Display): 40 mm
Copy instructions: *Copy Date:* 28 days prior to publication
Official Journal of: Organ d. Verb. d. Diabetesberatungs- u. Schulungsberufe in Deutschland e.V., d. Berufsverb. Dt. Diabetologen, d. Verb. d. Dipl.-Oecotrophologen e.V., d. D. A. CH.-Verb.: Zusammenschluss d. Diabetes BeraterInnen Deutschland, Österr. u. Schweiz Bundesverb. Kln. Diabeteseinrichtungen e.V.
BUSINESS: HEALTH & MEDICAL

DIABETES JOURNAL

725202G94F-420
Editorial: Kaiserstr. 41, 55116 MAINZ
Tel: 6131 9607030 **Fax:** 6131 9607090
Email: nuber@kirchheim-verlag.de **Web site:** http://www.diabetes-journal.de
Freq: Monthly; Free to qualifying individuals
Annual Sub.: EUR 39,00; **Circ:** 60,331
Editor: Günter Nuber; **Advertising Manager:** Björn Lindenau
Profile: Magazine for people with diabetes. In the journal, the affected people to speak for themselves - each issue contains in addition to medical contributions of the leading experts reviews, letters and patient issues. Psychology is the same way as food and health policy. Given a lot of valuable tips, recipes and useful telephone numbers. Target group: diabetes, their family members, friends and carers.
Language(s): German
ADVERTISING RATES:
Full Page Mono .... EUR 6930
Full Page Colour .... EUR 6930
Mechanical Data: Type Area: 245 x 178 mm, No. of Columns (Display): 4, Col Widths (Display): 40 mm
Copy instructions: *Copy Date:* 7 days prior to publication
Official Journal of: Organ d. Dt. Diabetiker-Bundes e.V. u. d. Dt. Diabetes-Union e.V.
CONSUMER: OTHER CLASSIFICATIONS: Disability

DIABETES RATGEBER

725209G94H-2700
Editorial: Konradshöhe, 82065 BAIERBRUNN
Tel: 89 744330 **Fax:** 89 74433460
Email: dr@wortundbildverlag.de **Web site:** http://www.diabetes-ratgeber.net
Freq: Monthly; **Cover Price:** Free; **Circ:** 1,266,474
Editor: Andreas Baum; **Advertising Manager:** Brigitta Hackmann
Profile: Magazine with advice and products for diabetics.
Language(s): German
ADVERTISING RATES:
Full Page Mono .... EUR 23500
Full Page Colour .... EUR 23500
Mechanical Data: Type Area: 177 x 133 mm
Copy instructions: *Copy Date:* 54 days prior to publication
CONSUMER: OTHER CLASSIFICATIONS: Customer Magazines

DIABETES, STOFFWECHSEL UND HERZ

1739485G56A-11397
Editorial: Kölner Platz 1, 80804 MÜNCHEN
Tel: 89 38380700 **Fax:** 89 38380701
Email: oliver.schnell@lrz.uni-muenchen.de **Web site:** http://www.ds-herz.de
Freq: 6 issues yearly; Free to qualifying individuals
Annual Sub.: EUR 105,60; **Circ:** 10,577
Editor: Oliver Schnell; **Advertising Manager:** Björn Lindenau
Profile: Publication about research and developments in diabetes and metabolic diseases.
Language(s): German
ADVERTISING RATES:
Full Page Mono .... EUR 4300
Full Page Colour .... EUR 4300
Mechanical Data: Type Area: 245 x 178 mm, No. of Columns (Display): 4, Col Widths (Display): 40 mm
Copy instructions: *Copy Date:* 28 days prior to publication
BUSINESS: HEALTH & MEDICAL

DIABETES-CONGRESS-REPORT

766659G94F-1722
Editorial: Postfach 1475, 37424 BAD LAUTERBERG
Tel: 5524 999101
Email: info@kirchheim-verlag.de **Web site:** http://www.diabetes-congress-report.de
Freq: 6 issues yearly; **Annual Sub.:** EUR 31,50; **Circ:** 10,707
Editor: Berend Willms; **Advertising Manager:** Björn Lindenau
Profile: Magazine on national and international diabetes congresses.
Language(s): German
ADVERTISING RATES:
Full Page Mono .... EUR 4300
Full Page Colour .... EUR 4300
Mechanical Data: Type Area: 245 x 178 mm, No. of Columns (Display): 4, Col Widths (Display): 40 mm
Copy instructions: *Copy Date:* 28 days prior to publication
CONSUMER: OTHER CLASSIFICATIONS: Disability

DIABETESIDE KONKRET

1932696G56A-11653
Editorial: Rüdigerstr. 14, 70469 STUTTGART
Tel: 711 89310 **Fax:** 711 8931298
Email: kundenservice@thieme.de **Web site:** http://www.thieme.de
Freq: 6 issues yearly; **Circ:** 10,950
Profile: diabetes|DE konkret is a magazine specifically for patients, doctors, scientists, diabetes educators and other professionals in Diabetes Care.
Language(s): German
ADVERTISING RATES:
Full Page Mono .... EUR 3120
Full Page Colour .... EUR 4590
Mechanical Data: Type Area: 248 x 175 mm, No. of Columns (Display): 3, Col Widths (Display): 55 mm
Supplement to: Diabetologie und Stoffwechsel, Experimental and Clinical Endocrinology & Diabetes

DER DIABETOLOGE

1696791G56A-11375
Editorial: Tiergartenstr. 17, 69121 HEIDELBERG
Tel: 6221 4878533 **Fax:** 6221 48768533
Email: charlotte.leisse@springer.com **Web site:** http://www.springermedizin.de
Freq: 8 issues yearly; **Annual Sub.:** EUR 174,00; **Circ:** 5,800
Profile: Der Diabetologe offers up-to-date information for all diabetologists working in practical and clinical environments and scientists who are particularly interested in issues of diabetology. The focus is on current developments regarding prevention, diagnostic approaches, management of complications and current therapy strategies. Comprehensive reviews on a specific topical issue provide evidenced based information on diagnostics and therapy. Review articles under the rubric "Continuing Medical Education" present verified results of scientific research and their integration into daily practice.
Language(s): German
ADVERTISING RATES:
Full Page Mono .... EUR 4290
Full Page Colour .... EUR 4290
Mechanical Data: Type Area: 240 x 174 mm
Official Journal of: Organ d. Dt. Ges. f. Innere Medizin, d. Berufsverb. Dt. Internisten, d. Berufsverb. Dt. Endokrinologen, d. Berufsverb. d. Diabetologen in Kliniken u. d. ArGe. niedergelassener Diabetologen

DIABETOLOGIA

725210G56A-2720
Editorial: Tiergartenstr. 17, 69121 HEIDELBERG
Tel: 6221 487 0 **Fax:** 6221 4878366
Email: subscriptions@springer.com **Web site:** http://www.springerlink.de
Freq: Monthly; **Annual Sub.:** EUR 2079,00; **Circ:** 6,800
Editor: Edwin Gale; **Advertising Manager:** Noëla Krischer
Profile: Diabetologia publishes original clinical and experimental research within the field of diabetes. We are interested in papers that convey new information or insight into any aspect of the condition, ranging from basic science to clinical applications. These are judged in terms of their scientific quality, novelty, relevance and interest to our broadly based readership. Diabetologia also hosts editorials, commentaries, debates and reviews, relating to any aspect of diabetes and related conditions, and welcomes submissions from any part of the world.
Language(s): English
ADVERTISING RATES:
Full Page Mono .... EUR 2020
Full Page Colour .... EUR 3210
Mechanical Data: Type Area: 240 x 175 mm
Official Journal of: Organ d. European Association for the Study of Diabetes

DIABETOLOGIE UND STOFFWECHSEL

725205G56A-2620
Editorial: Rüdigerstr. 14, 70469 STUTTGART
Tel: 711 8931429 **Fax:** 711 8931408
Email: christiane.weseloh@thieme.de **Web site:** http://www.thieme.de/fz/dus.html
Freq: 6 issues yearly; Free to qualifying individuals
Annual Sub.: EUR 180,90; **Circ:** 8,570
Editor: Dirk Müller-Wieland
Profile: As the official organ of the German Diabetes Society, the journal is the date reference medium for diabetology in Germany. In addition to research articles, the magazine regularly contains an expanded training and information section. With the newly annual published practice guidelines of the DDG, the enclosed platform of DDG and VDBD „DiabetesDE konkret" the magazine stands in the center of attention of all doctors working diabetologic. With the Refresher offers in each issue CME-certified training.
Language(s): German
ADVERTISING RATES:
Full Page Mono .... EUR 3120
Full Page Colour .... EUR 4590
Mechanical Data: Type Area: 248 x 175 mm, No. of Columns (Display): 3, Col Widths (Display): 55 mm
Official Journal of: Organ d. Dt. Diabetes-Ges.
Supplement(s): diabetes|DE konkret
BUSINESS: HEALTH & MEDICAL

Germany

DIABOLO
725212G80-2620
Editorial: Wallstr. 11, 26122 OLDENBURG
Tel: 441 218350 **Fax:** 441 2183520
Email: info@diabolo-mox.de **Web site:** http://www.diabolo-mox.de
Freq: Weekly; **Cover Price:** Free; **Circ:** 37,000
Editor: Rosemarie Reichert; **Advertising Manager:** Rüdiger Schön
Profile: Magazine for the Oldenburg area.
Language(s): German
ADVERTISING RATES:
Full Page Mono .... EUR 1846
Full Page Colour .... EUR 2416
Mechanical Data: Type Area: 285 x 208 mm, No. of Columns (Display): 4, Col Widths (Display): 49 mm
Copy instructions: *Copy Date:* 6 days prior to publication
CONSUMER: RURAL & REGIONAL INTEREST

DIAGNOSTICA
725216G56N-35
Editorial: Rohnsweg 25, 37085 GÖTTINGEN
Tel: 551 496090 **Fax:** 551 4960988
Email: verlag@hogrefe.de **Web site:** http://www.hogrefe.de/zeitschriften/diagnostica
Freq: Quarterly; **Annual Sub.:** EUR 86,95; **Circ:** 1,200
Editor: Olaf Köller; **Advertising Manager:** Nadine Teichert
Profile: Publication about the diagnosis and practice of psychotherapy.
Language(s): German
Readership: Aimed at psychologists.
ADVERTISING RATES:
Full Page Mono .... EUR 475
Mechanical Data: Type Area: 250 x 170 mm, No. of Columns (Display): 2, Col Widths (Display): 85 mm
Copy instructions: *Copy Date:* 42 days prior to publication
BUSINESS: HEALTH & MEDICAL: Mental Health

DIAKONIE MAGAZIN
725222G87-2800
Editorial: Stafflenbergstr. 76, 70184 STUTTGART
Tel: 711 2159455 **Fax:** 711 2159566
Email: redaktion@diakonie.de **Web site:** http://www.diakonie.de
Freq: Quarterly; **Circ:** 48,941
Editor: Andreas Wagner
Profile: Magazine concerning social welfare issues. Emphasis is placed on workers' rights and conditions.
Language(s): German
Readership: Aimed at those employed in the social welfare sector.
ADVERTISING RATES:
Full Page Colour .... EUR 4500
Mechanical Data: Type Area: 259 x 193 mm
Supplement(s): in der Tat
CONSUMER: RELIGIOUS

DIALOG
1697560G2A-5665
Editorial: Hasengartenstr. 14, 65189 WIESBADEN
Tel: 611 9779316 **Fax:** 611 9779399
Email: n.schulze@ddv.de **Web site:** http://www.ddv.de
Freq: Quarterly; **Circ:** 18,000
Editor: Nanah Schulze; **Advertising Manager:** Rudolf Panek
Profile: dialog is a trade publication of the German Dialogue Marketing Association (DDV). The magazine is aimed at marketing managers to run the 360-degrees of communication, as well as experts from the fields of one-to-one, dialogue, online and permission marketing. The DDV is the largest national association of dialogue marketing companies in Europe and one of the leading associations of the communications industry in Germany. It represents the interests of advertising making companies, using the dialogue marketing, and service providers, they offers relevant benefits and services. The magazine presents the pioneering developments in on- and offline dialogue marketing, delivers the latest relevant findings from practice and science, offers extensive know-how for the targeted and efficient use of dialogue marketing tools, bridging the gap between dialogue marketing and other in the marketing-related disciplines. Editorial Focus: Background knowledge on current trends and developments: technology, planning, implementation, integration, cost, efficiency, controlling; Profiles, guest articles, interviews with personalities from the industry; Successful case studies from practice; Studies, diploma works, academic projects; Legal issues: innovation, examples, explanations; Activities and projects of the Association; Overview of important events and seminars.
Language(s): German
ADVERTISING RATES:
Full Page Mono .... EUR 5750
Full Page Colour .... EUR 5750
Mechanical Data: Type Area: 280 x 210 mm
Supplement to: Horizont

DIALOGMARKETING-TRENDS
1633131G2A-5521
Editorial: Bei den Mühren 91, 20457 HAMBURG
Tel: 40 3698320 **Fax:** 40 36983236
Email: redaktion@fischers-archiv.de **Web site:** http://www.dialogmarketing-trends.info
Freq: Annual; **Cover Price:** EUR 49,00; **Circ:** 6,100
Editor: Johannes Jagusch; **Advertising Manager:** Birgit Haß
Profile: Documentation of recent dialogue marketing campaigns for dialogue marketing services providers and users.
Language(s): German

DIALYSE AKTUELL
725246G56A-2740
Editorial: Rüdigerstr. 14, 70469 STUTTGART
Tel: 711 8931440 **Fax:** 711 8931322
Email: guenther.buck@thieme.de **Web site:** http://www.thieme.de/fz/dialyseaktuell.html
Freq: 10 issues yearly; **Annual Sub.:** EUR 46,00; **Circ:** 7,770
Editor: Günther Buck
Profile: The magazine is the undisputed German magazine on dialysis. Contents: current and practical issues that arise in the treatment of dialysis patients current information on all innovations in the field Reports of the relevant conventions latest news from industry and research Case reports.
Language(s): German
ADVERTISING RATES:
Full Page Mono .... EUR 1750
Full Page Colour .... EUR 2575
Mechanical Data: No. of Columns (Display): 3, Col Widths (Display): 50 mm, Type Area: 245 x 175 mm

DIANA MODEN
1614248G74A-3328
Editorial: Römerstr. 90, 79618 RHEINFELDEN
Tel: 7623 9640 **Fax:** 7623 964200
Email: info@oz-verlag.de **Web site:** http://www.oz-verlag.de
Freq: Quarterly; **Annual Sub.:** EUR 20,00; **Circ:** 75,000
Profile: Magazine with sewing instructions for Ladies Large Sizes - sporty, lively and witty fashion for the home sewing nähbegeisterte "seamstresses".
Language(s): German
ADVERTISING RATES:
Full Page Mono .... EUR 2480
Full Page Colour .... EUR 2960
Mechanical Data: Type Area: 251 x 183 mm

DIATRA JOURNAL
725254G56A-2780
Editorial: Kiedricher Str. 25, 65343 ELTVILLE
Tel: 6123 73478 **Fax:** 6123 73287
Email: dj@diatra-verlag.de **Web site:** http://www.diatra-verlag.de
Freq: Quarterly; **Annual Sub.:** EUR 19,00; **Circ:** 18,000
Editor: Robert Laube
Profile: Information for doctors, patients and staff in internal medicine-nephrology area with the subjects of medicine, organ donation and transplantation, travel for dialysis patients, nutrition for chronic kidney diseases and patient experiences.
Language(s): German
ADVERTISING RATES:
Full Page Mono .... EUR 1620
Full Page Colour .... EUR 2850
Mechanical Data: Type Area: 265 x 174 mm, No. of Columns (Display): 2, Col Widths (Display): 82 mm
Copy instructions: *Copy Date:* 30 days prior to publication

DIBT MITTEILUNGEN
735725G4E-5400
Editorial: Kolonnenstr. 30L, 10829 BERLIN
Tel: 30 78730244 **Fax:** 30 78730320
Email: rsm@dibt.de **Web site:** http://www.dibt.de
Freq: 6 issues yearly; **Annual Sub.:** EUR 144,45; **Circ:** 3,750
Editor: Renate Schmidt-Staudinger; **Advertising Manager:** Jost Lüddecke
Profile: Magazine reporting on the activities of the German Institution of Building Techniques.
Language(s): German
ADVERTISING RATES:
Full Page Mono .... EUR 2740
Full Page Colour .... EUR 4285
Mechanical Data: Type Area: 260 x 181 mm, No. of Columns (Display): 4, Col Widths (Display): 42 mm
Copy instructions: *Copy Date:* 21 days prior to publication

DICHT!
1799165G19E-1911
Editorial: Am Exerzierplatz 1a, 68167 MANNHEIM
Tel: 621 71768880 **Fax:** 621 71768888
Email: hbest@isgatec.com **Web site:** http://www.isgatec.com
Freq: Quarterly; **Annual Sub.:** EUR 43,30; **Circ:** 9,206
Editor: Holger Best; **Advertising Manager:** Bärbel Schäfer
Profile: Company publication with information about products, developments, trends and technical solutions concerning seal technology and adhesives technology.
Language(s): German
ADVERTISING RATES:
Full Page Mono .... EUR 3240
Full Page Colour .... EUR 3240
Mechanical Data: Type Area: 247 x 183 mm, No. of Columns (Display): 3, Col Widths (Display): 57 mm
Copy instructions: *Copy Date:* 25 days prior to publication

DICHTUNGSTECHNIK
725258G19E-220
Editorial: Huyssenallee 52, 45128 ESSEN
Tel: 201 8200225 **Fax:** 201 8200240
Email: w.moenning@vulkan-verlag.de **Web site:** http://www.vulkan-verlag.de
Freq: Half-yearly; **Annual Sub.:** EUR 55,00; **Circ:** 2,214
Editor: Wolfgang Mönning; **Advertising Manager:** Helga Pelzer
Profile: Contents of „Dichtungstechnik" are practice-related articles from all areas of sealing technology, such as seals for containers and piping flanges, stuffing gland packagings for pumps and valves, mechanical seals and rotary shaft seals, rod seals for hydraulic and pneumatic systems as well as non-contact seals.
Language(s): German
Readership: Aimed at those involved in the engineering sector.
ADVERTISING RATES:
Full Page Mono .... EUR 2550
Full Page Colour .... EUR 3840
Mechanical Data: Type Area: 250 x 182 mm, No. of Columns (Display): 3, Col Widths (Display): 58 mm
Copy instructions: *Copy Date:* 21 days prior to publication
BUSINESS: ENGINEERING & MACHINERY: Machinery, Machine Tools & Metalworking

DIE ZEITSCHRIFT FÜR ERWACHSENENBILDUNG
725269G88B-300
Editorial: Friedrich-Ebert-Allee 38, 53113 BONN
Tel: 228 3294203 **Fax:** 228 32944203
Email: brandt@die-bonn.de **Web site:** http://www.diezeitschrift.de
Freq: Quarterly; **Annual Sub.:** EUR 37,00; **Circ:** 1,400
Editor: Peter Brandt
Profile: Magazine containing articles about further education.
Language(s): German
Readership: Aimed at teachers, mature students and researchers.
ADVERTISING RATES:
Full Page Mono .... EUR 560
Mechanical Data: Type Area: 235 x 190 mm
Copy instructions: *Copy Date:* 30 days prior to publication
CONSUMER: EDUCATION: Adult Education

DIEBURGER ANZEIGER
725273G67B-4040
Editorial: Schlossergasse 4, 64807 DIEBURG
Tel: 6071 25005 **Fax:** 6071 81358
Email: red.dieburg@op-online.de **Web site:** http://www.op-online.de
Freq: 104 issues yearly; **Circ:** 3,930
Advertising Manager: Helmut Moser
Profile: Daily newspaper with regional news and a local sports section. This Outlet offers RSS (Really Simple Syndication).
Language(s): German
ADVERTISING RATES:
SCC .... EUR 19,60
Mechanical Data: Type Area: 470 x 322 mm, No. of Columns (Display): 7, Col Widths (Display): 43 mm
Copy instructions: *Copy Date:* 3 days prior to publication
REGIONAL DAILY & SUNDAY NEWSPAPERS: Regional Daily Newspapers

DIEDERICH FACHKALENDER
725276G18B-360
Editorial: Berner Str. 2, 97084 WÜRZBURG
Tel: 931 6001324 **Fax:** 931 6001252
Email: gert.diederich@t-online.de **Web site:** http://www.diederich-fachkalender.de
Freq: Annual; **Cover Price:** EUR 12,00; **Circ:** 28,000
Editor: Gert Diederich; **Advertising Manager:** Rainer Schlereth
Profile: Annual for the personnel of the German Mail, Telekom, Postbank and Federal authorities.
Language(s): German
ADVERTISING RATES:
Full Page Mono .... EUR 869
Mechanical Data: Type Area: 128 x 81 mm
Copy instructions: *Copy Date:* 92 days prior to publication

DIEPHOLZER KREISBLATT
725282G67B-4060
Editorial: Am Ristedter Weg 17, 28857 SYKE
Tel: 4242 58300 **Fax:** 4242 58332
Email: redaktion@kreiszeitung.de **Web site:** http://www.kreiszeitung.de
Freq: 312 issues yearly; **Circ:** 16,282
Advertising Manager: Axel Berghoff
Profile: The Kreiszeitung publishing group is the fifth largest newspaper in Niedersachsen, with a daily circulation of over 82,000 copies. Regional daily newspaper covering politics, economics, sport, travel and technology. Facebook: http://www.facebook.com/pages/Kreiszeitung This Outlet offers RSS (Really Simple Syndication).
Language(s): German
ADVERTISING RATES:
SCC .... EUR 53,60
Mechanical Data: Type Area: 472 x 325 mm, No. of Columns (Display): 7, Col Widths (Display): 45 mm
Copy instructions: *Copy Date:* 1 day prior to publication
REGIONAL DAILY & SUNDAY NEWSPAPERS: Regional Daily Newspapers

DIEPHOLZER WOCHENBLATT
725283G72-3128
Editorial: Bahnhofstr. 9, 49356 DIEPHOLZ
Tel: 5441 908120 **Fax:** 5441 908139
Email: michael.duemer@aller-weser-verlag.de **Web site:** http://www.aller-weser-verlag.de
Freq: Weekly; **Cover Price:** Free; **Circ:** 28,400
Editor: Michael H. Dümer; **Advertising Manager:** Sabine Düßmann
Profile: Advertising journal (house-to-house) concentrating on local stories.
Language(s): German
ADVERTISING RATES:
Full Page Mono .... EUR 363
Full Page Colour .... EUR 527
Mechanical Data: Type Area: 472 x 325 mm, No. of Columns (Display): 7, Col Widths (Display): 45 mm
Copy instructions: *Copy Date:* 5 days prior to publication
LOCAL NEWSPAPERS

DIGEST
725292G74C-350
Editorial: Ernst-Mey-Str. 8, 70771 LEINFELDEN-ECHTERDINGEN **Tel:** 711 75940
Email: redaktion.digest@konradin.de **Web site:** http://www.digest-online.de
Freq: 6 issues yearly; **Annual Sub.:** EUR 56,10; **Circ:** 8,126
Editor: Ingrid Horn; **Advertising Manager:** Anna Waskala
Profile: Digest is the magazine for trade-oriented lifestyle, decorating, home, outdoors, cooking and eating. It moves sovereign on the territory between manufacturers and dealers. The magazine offers wid range of information from the above areas. Digest reports on the industry events, shows new developments and trends, conveyed news from the industry to the trade and provides solutions to questions about the trade.
Language(s): German
Readership: Aimed at people shopping for gifts.
ADVERTISING RATES:
Full Page Mono .... EUR 260
Full Page Colour .... EUR 416
Mechanical Data: Type Area: 260 x 184 mm, No. of Columns (Display): 4, Col Widths (Display): 45 mm
CONSUMER: WOMEN'S INTEREST CONSUMER MAGAZINES: Home & Family

DIGITAL HOME
1683937G76A-159
Editorial: Gartroper Str. 42, 47138 DUISBURG
Tel: 203 4292166 **Fax:** 203 4292149
Email: weyel@brieden.de **Web site:** http://www.digitalhome-magazin.de
Freq: Quarterly; **Cover Price:** EUR 1,80; **Circ:** 50,000
Editor: Dirk Weyel
Profile: The magazine deals with the digitization of al media and presents current, tangible and solutions available that make the digital home a reality today. The focus of the tests in digital home are the applicability and usefulness of the presented products. All information is processed so that they remain understandable even for the novice with no technical background. Regular basic stories, encompassing service lines and numerous single-simple explanations of common terminology to assis readers of digital home to find their way in new technologies and create acceptance for the theme.
Language(s): German
ADVERTISING RATES:
Full Page Mono .... EUR 531
Full Page Colour .... EUR 779
Mechanical Data: Type Area: 284 x 197 mm, No. of Columns (Display): 4, Col Widths (Display): 49 mm
CONSUMER: MUSIC & PERFORMING ARTS: Cinema

DIGITAL PRODUCTION
725301G18A-80
Editorial: Hackerbrücke 6, 80335 MÜNCHEN
Tel: 89 89817367 **Fax:** 89 89817350
Email: jb@digitalproduction.com **Web site:** http://www.digitalproduction.com
Freq: 6 issues yearly; **Annual Sub.:** EUR 89,00; **Circ:** 5,437
Editor: Jan Bruhnke; **Advertising Manager:** Maik Euscher
Profile: Digital Production is the leading German-language magazine in the area of digital content creation (DCC). As the only professional journal, it covers the entire spectrum of digital media production, and reports on the topics CG, VFX, Compositing, film, video and broadcast as well as through interactive media such as DVD or Web.
Language(s): German
ADVERTISING RATES:
Full Page Mono .... EUR 4800
Full Page Colour .... EUR 4800
Mechanical Data: Type Area: 270 x 180 mm, No. of Columns (Display): 4, Col Widths (Display): 45 mm
Copy instructions: *Copy Date:* 35 days prior to publication
BUSINESS: ELECTRONICS

DIGITALBUSINESS
737664G5E-330
Editorial: Johann-Sebastian-Bach-Str. 5, 85591 VATERSTETTEN **Tel:** 8106 350183 **Fax:** 8106 350190
Email: sg@win-verlag.de **Web site:** http://www.digital-business-magazin.de
Freq: 8 issues yearly; **Annual Sub.:** EUR 90,00; **Circ:** 11,932
Editor: Stefan Girschner; **Advertising Manager:** Bernd Heilmeier
Profile: Magazine as a counselor, a supplier of ideas and advice on all aspects and Domaine v. Notes and composite applications to d. Categories: 1st Product Focus - This is where new products are introduced with a short code. The detailed version in Form of an article (advertorial) is published on the website. 2nd Management of Information - Below are all the solutions, services and products are subsumed, having to do with data, information and content

nanagement solutions. Primarily it is intended here to o to strategic information management with the aim o show how information of any kind integrated into usiness processes and can be deployed across ectors as a service. 3rd Flexibility of business rocesses - here, all solutions, services and products re presented, that the Management and allow omplete control over the core business processes in rder to create the perfect combination between usiness and IT. This includes the monitoring, djustment, protection and management of all esources that enable it to make the flexible nfrastructure. The presentation of tools such as equirements management, quality and change nanagement, but also complement the project and ortfolio management, this view concludes. 4th mployee productivity - Here are all the solutions, ervices and products are grouped together, the staff elp you competently on new requirements, to espond flexibly and quickly. It is both a dynamic nnovative communication and to exchange nowledge with the use of key technologies such as nessaging, collaboration, instant messaging and Knowledge Discovery. 5th Competency-side - where xperts come to the main topic to speak. 6th SME-riented - Increasing customer demands, high ompetitive pressure and increasing globalization - to eal with these challenges, the middle class now. Here, efficient and easy to use IT solution packages ncluding hardware, software and services are eeded that are tailored and industry-specific to the eeds of SMEs. 7th Looking to the future - here are ne topics to be subsumed, which have to deal with ompanies to align themselves future-oriented nanner. They will also address the requirements iscussed at the next executive be.
.anguage(s): German
ADVERTISING RATES:
ull Page Mono .... EUR 4340
ull Page Colour .... EUR 5400
Mechanical Data: No. of Columns (Display): 3, Col Widths (Display): 58 mm, Type Area: 266 x 180 mm
Copy instructions: *Copy Date:* 30 days prior to ublication
BUSINESS: COMPUTERS & AUTOMATION: Data Transmission

DIGITAL.WORLD 1684562G18B-2098
Editorial: Lyonel-Feininger-Str. 26, 80807 MÜNCHEN
Tel: 89 36086222 **Fax:** 89 36086459
Email: redaktion@digital-world.de **Web site:** http://www.digital-world.de
Freq: Daily; **Cover Price:** Paid; **Circ:** 194,277 Unique Users
Editor: Andreas Perband
Language(s): German
BUSINESS: ELECTRONICS: Telecommunications

DILLINGER EXTRA 748203G72-16440
Editorial: Große Allee 47, 89407 DILLINGEN
Tel: 9071 794980 **Fax:** 9071 794989
Email: brigitta.ernst@donau-zeitung.de
Freq: Weekly; **Cover Price:** Free; **Circ:** 31,094
Editor: Brigitta Ernst; **Advertising Manager:** Ursula Slavicek
Profile: Advertising journal (house-to-house) concentrating on local stories.
Language(s): German
ADVERTISING RATES:
Full Page Mono .... EUR 3528
Full Page Colour .... EUR 5343
Mechanical Data: Type Area: 480 x 327 mm, No. of Columns (Display): 7, Col Widths (Display): 45 mm
Copy instructions: *Copy Date:* 2 days prior to publication
LOCAL NEWSPAPERS

DILL-POST 725305G67B-4080
Editorial: Elsa-Brandström-Str. 18, 35578 WETZLAR
Tel: 6441 9590 **Fax:** 6441 959292
Email: redaktion.wnz@mittelhessen.de **Web site:** http://www.mittelhessen.de
Freq: 312 issues yearly; **Circ:** 21,471
Advertising Manager: Peter Rother
Profile: Daily newspaper with regional news and a local sports section. This Outlet offers RSS (Really Simple Syndication).
Language(s): German
ADVERTISING RATES:
SCC .... EUR 66,50
Mechanical Data: Type Area: 490 x 328 mm, No. of Columns (Display): 7, Col Widths (Display): 44 mm
Copy instructions: *Copy Date:* 1 day prior to publication
Supplement(s): Anpfiff; [f]amilie& freizeit; [g]esundl; rtv
REGIONAL DAILY & SUNDAY NEWSPAPERS: Regional Daily Newspapers

DILL-POST AM SONNTAG
1606878G72-17861
Editorial: Elsa-Brandström-Str. 18, 35578 WETZLAR
Tel: 6441 9590 **Fax:** 6441 959292
Email: redaktion.wnz@mittelhessen.de **Web site:** http://www.mittelhessen.de
Freq: Weekly; **Cover Price:** EUR 1,00; **Circ:** 21,471
Advertising Manager: Peter Rother
Profile: Regional weekly covering politics, economics, sport, travel, technology and the arts.
Language(s): German
ADVERTISING RATES:
SCC .... EUR 66,50
Mechanical Data: Type Area: 490 x 328 mm, No. of Columns (Display): 7, Col Widths (Display): 44 mm

Copy instructions: *Copy Date:* 2 days prior to publication
LOCAL NEWSPAPERS

DILL-ZEITUNG 725306G67B-4100
Editorial: Rathausstr. 1, 35683 DILLENBURG
Tel: 2771 874260 **Fax:** 2771 874261
Email: redaktion@dill.de **Web site:** http://www.dill.de
Freq: 312 issues yearly; **Annual Sub.:** EUR 27,30; **Circ:** 7,559
Editor: Friedhelm Sohn
Profile: Daily newspaper with regional news and a local sports section.
Language(s): German
ADVERTISING RATES:
SCC .... EUR 27,80
Mechanical Data: Type Area: 467 x 327 mm, No. of Columns (Display): 7, Col Widths (Display): 44 mm
Copy instructions: *Copy Date:* 1 day prior to publication
Supplement(s): Anpfiff; [g]esund!
REGIONAL DAILY & SUNDAY NEWSPAPERS: Regional Daily Newspapers

DILL-ZEITUNG AM SONNTAG
1609301G72-17866
Editorial: Rathausstr. 1, 35683 DILLENBURG
Tel: 2771 874260 **Fax:** 2771 874261
Email: redaktion@dill.de **Web site:** http://www.dill.de
Freq: Weekly; **Cover Price:** EUR 1,20; **Circ:** 7,559
Editor: Friedhelm Sohn
Profile: Regional weekly covering politics, economics, sport, travel, technology and the arts.
Language(s): German
ADVERTISING RATES:
SCC .... EUR 27,80
Mechanical Data: Type Area: 490 x 328 mm, No. of Columns (Display): 7, Col Widths (Display): 44 mm
Copy instructions: *Copy Date:* 2 days prior to publication
LOCAL NEWSPAPERS

DIMA 725307G19E-1855
Editorial: Teinacher Str. 34, 71634 LUDWIGSBURG
Tel: 7141 223133 **Fax:** 7141 223131
Email: fahry@agt-verlag.de **Web site:** http://www.dima-magazin.com
Freq: 6 issues yearly; **Annual Sub.:** EUR 66,00; **Circ:** 13,764
Editor: Gerd Fahry; **Advertising Manager:** Simone Hildenbrand
Profile: dima offers as a technical periodical the communication platform for production and manufacturing responsible persons of the processing industry with the emphasis on metalworking. It takes up problem definitions in line with standard usage and informs about solutions and realized projects. In the focus of the reportingstands the opinions, concepts and solutions for more efficient working and production runs in enterprises. Enclosed is the rational employment of machine tools and tools, the material and workpiece handling, the quality control, the handling and rational handling and/or use of manufacturing auxiliary materials as well as operational funds.
Language(s): German
Readership: Aimed at mechanical engineers, tool makers and metal workers.
ADVERTISING RATES:
Full Page Mono .... EUR 3050
Full Page Colour .... EUR 4280
Mechanical Data: Type Area: 270 x 185 mm, No. of Columns (Display): 4, Col Widths (Display): 43 mm
Copy instructions: *Copy Date:* 14 days prior to publication
BUSINESS: ENGINEERING & MACHINERY: Machinery, Machine Tools & Metalworking

DIN MITTEILUNGEN 725314G19R-20
Editorial: Burggrafenstr. 6, 10787 BERLIN
Tel: 30 26012403 **Fax:** 30 2601142750
Email: renate.schulz@beuth.de **Web site:** http://www.din-mitteilungen.de
Freq: Monthly; **Annual Sub.:** EUR 415,40; **Circ:** 2,856
Editor: Ulrike Bohnsack
Profile: The DIN Mitteilungen reports on 100 individual fields of national, European and international standardization. They shall include all of the DIN standardization projects and activities of other legislators, domestic and foreign one. In addition to basic standardization issues are the subject of the current standardization trends relevant posts.
Language(s): German
ADVERTISING RATES:
Full Page Mono .... EUR 1530
Full Page Colour .... EUR 1989
Mechanical Data: Type Area: 251 x 176 mm
Copy instructions: *Copy Date:* 20 days prior to publication
BUSINESS: ENGINEERING & MACHINERY: Engineering Related

DINERS CLUB MAGAZIN
1655685G73-510
Editorial: Hanns-Seidel-Platz 5, 81737 MÜNCHEN
Tel: 89 6427970 **Fax:** 89 64279777
Email: info@journal-international.de **Web site:** http://www.pmi-publishing.de
Freq: Monthly; **Annual Sub.:** EUR 49,20,; **Circ:** 50,000
Editor: Gerd Giesler; **Advertising Manager:** Regina Bouga
Profile: Credit card customer magazine reporting on culture, travel, cuisine, portrait, art and gastronomy. Information on travel destinations and interviews. 2005 and 2008, the magazine with the silver medal of the BCP Award.
Language(s): German
ADVERTISING RATES:
Full Page Mono .... EUR 9900
Full Page Colour .... EUR 9900
Mechanical Data: Type Area: 238 x 185 mm

DINGOLFINGER ANZEIGER
725312G67B-4120
Editorial: Ludwigsplatz 30, 94315 STRAUBING
Tel: 9421 9400 **Fax:** 9421 940140
Email: service@idowa.de **Web site:** http://www.idowa.de
Freq: 312 issues yearly; **Circ:** 9,917
Advertising Manager: Max Wälischmiller
Profile: Regional daily newspaper with news on politics, economy, culture, sports, travel, technology, etc. Its a local issue by Straubinger Tagblatt for the old County Dingolfing. Twitter: http://twitter.com/idowa This Outlet offers RSS (Really Simple Syndication).
Language(s): German
ADVERTISING RATES:
SCC .... EUR 20,90
Mechanical Data: Type Area: 430 x 282 mm, No. of Columns (Display): 6, Col Widths (Display): 45 mm
Copy instructions: *Copy Date:* 1 day prior to publication
Supplement(s): Zuhause
REGIONAL DAILY & SUNDAY NEWSPAPERS: Regional Daily Newspapers

DIPPOLDISWALDER WOCHENKURIER 725320G72-3144
Editorial: Wettiner Platz 10, 01067 DRESDEN
Tel: 351 491760 **Fax:** 351 4917674
Email: wochenkurier-dresden@dwk-verlag.de **Web site:** http://www.wochenkurier.info
Freq: Weekly; **Cover Price:** Free; **Circ:** 17,188
Editor: Regine Eberlein; **Advertising Manager:** Andreas Schönherr
Profile: Advertising journal (house-to-house) concentrating on local stories.
Language(s): German
ADVERTISING RATES:
Full Page Mono .... EUR 2258
Full Page Colour .... EUR 3161
Mechanical Data: Type Area: 430 x 290 mm, No. of Columns (Display): 7, Col Widths (Display): 38 mm
Copy instructions: *Copy Date:* 5 days prior to publication
LOCAL NEWSPAPERS

DIREKT! 1694806G2A-5657
Editorial: Bundesallee 221, 10719 BERLIN
Tel: 30 23635680 **Fax:** 30 23635688
Email: info@bundesverband-direktvertrieb.de **Web site:** http://www.bundesverband-direktvertrieb.de
Freq: 6 issues yearly; **Cover Price:** Free; **Circ:** 2,200
Editor: Wolfgang Bohle
Profile: Magazine on direct marketing.
Language(s): German

DIREKT 1657083G4E-7018
Editorial: Kronenstr. 55, 10117 BERLIN
Tel: 30 20314408 **Fax:** 30 20314420
Email: presse@zdb.de **Web site:** http://www.zdb.de
Freq: 6 issues yearly; **Cover Price:** Free; **Circ:** 5,800
Editor: Ilona K. Klein
Profile: Magazine from the Association of the German Building Business.
Language(s): German
ADVERTISING RATES:
Full Page Mono .... EUR 1395
Full Page Colour .... EUR 1395
Mechanical Data: Type Area: 269 x 180 mm, No. of Columns (Display): 3, Col Widths (Display): 50 mm
Copy instructions: *Copy Date:* 21 days prior to publication

DIREKT 766153G14A-9319
Editorial: Solmsstr. 4, 60486 FRANKFURT
Tel: 69 79220 **Fax:** 69 79224500
Web site: http://www.concardis.com
Freq: 3 issues yearly; **Cover Price:** Free; **Circ:** 36,000
Editor: Berit Temmeyer
Profile: Magazine for dealers accepting credit cards.
Language(s): German

DIREKT AUS BERLIN
1860306G14A-10217
Editorial: Am Weidendamm 1a, 10117 BERLIN
Tel: 30 59009950 **Fax:** 30 590099519
Email: info@bga.de **Web site:** http://www.bga.de
Freq: Weekly; **Circ:** 600
Editor: André Schwarz
Profile: Economics magazine about taxes and politics.
Language(s): German

DIREKT MARKETING
725341G2A-1060
Editorial: Munzinger Str. 9, 79111 FREIBURG
Tel: 761 8983031 **Fax:** 761 8983112
Email: redaktion@acquisa.de **Web site:** http://www.acquisa.de
Freq: Quarterly; **Cover Price:** Free; **Circ:** 24,055
Editor: Christoph Pause
Profile: direkt marketing reports in the form of technical papers on topics of direct marketing, printing, letter shop and CRM and delivers everything worth knowing about the mailing days. Includes address book for service and technology providers of Dialog Marketing and Sales.
Language(s): German
ADVERTISING RATES:
Full Page Mono .... EUR 4080
Full Page Colour .... EUR 4080
Mechanical Data: Type Area: 249 x 176 mm
Supplement to: acquisa
BUSINESS: COMMUNICATIONS, ADVERTISING & MARKETING

DIRK JASPER FILMLEXIKON
1661240G76A-1601
Editorial: Aulergasse 9, 55496 ARGENTHAL
Tel: 170 5514210
Email: redaktion@djfl.de **Web site:** http://www.djfl.de
Freq: Weekly; **Cover Price:** Paid; **Circ:** 466,193 Unique Users
Editor: Dirk Jasper
Language(s): German
CONSUMER: MUSIC & PERFORMING ARTS: Cinema

DISCO MAGAZIN 725348G64C-24
Editorial: Grotemeyerstr. 38, 48159 MÜNSTER
Tel: 251 213232 **Fax:** 251 213594
Email: discomagazin@t-online.de **Web site:** http://www.disco-magazin.de
Freq: 10 issues yearly; **Annual Sub.:** EUR 69,00; **Circ:** 3,482
Editor: Klaus Niester; **Advertising Manager:** Christian H. Rosenberg
Profile: Magazine focusing on lighting, music, hi-fi and party entertainment.
Language(s): German
Readership: Aimed at managers of discotheques and clubs, also diskjockeys.
ADVERTISING RATES:
Full Page Mono .... CHF 1849
Full Page Colour .... CHF 2914
Mechanical Data: Type Area: 235 x 185 mm, No. of Columns (Display): 3, Col Widths (Display): 59 mm
Copy instructions: *Copy Date:* 14 days prior to publication
BUSINESS: OTHER CLASSIFICATIONS: Clubs

DISNEY EINFACH TIERISCH
1615158G91D-9807
Editorial: Wallstr. 59, 10179 BERLIN **Tel:** 30 240080
Fax: 30 24008599
Email: p.hoepfner@ehapa.de **Web site:** http://www.ehapa.de
Freq: 6 issues yearly; **Cover Price:** EUR 2,95; **Circ:** 38,406
Editor: Peter Höpfner
Profile: Animal magazine for children aged 4 to 11 years. Readers of comics expect from the Disney World, funny animal pictures, animal jokes and interesting records. In reports, the animal quiz and the pet page useful information about animals is presented in a way that makes it fun for children.
Language(s): German
ADVERTISING RATES:
Full Page Mono .... EUR 3600
Full Page Colour .... EUR 3600
Mechanical Data: Type Area: 280 x 210 mm
CONSUMER: RECREATION & LEISURE: Children & Youth

DISNEY PRINZESSIN
725363G91D-1840
Editorial: Wallstr. 59, 10179 BERLIN **Tel:** 30 240080
Fax: 30 24008599
Email: p.hoepfner@ehapa.de **Web site:** http://www.ehapa.de
Freq: 13 issues yearly; **Cover Price:** EUR 3,20; **Circ:** 61,852
Editor: Peter Höpfner
Profile: Magazine for little princesses. Romantic stories with the popular Disney Princesses Cinderella, Sleeping Beauty, Belle, Snow White and Ariel invite young girls aged 3 to 8 years old to dream. Games, puzzles, and nice layout! coloring pages round out the magazine concept and ensure royal fun. There is also a wonderful gift: Charming rings, a great make-up cell phone or a gorgeous tiara - all things dream of little princesses.
Language(s): German
ADVERTISING RATES:
Full Page Mono .... EUR 4900
Full Page Colour .... EUR 4900
Mechanical Data: Type Area: 280 x 210 mm, No. of Columns (Display): 4, Col Widths (Display): 52 mm
CONSUMER: RECREATION & LEISURE: Children & Youth

DISNEY WINNIE PUUH

725364G91D-1860

Editorial: Wallstr. 59, 10179 BERLIN **Tel:** 30 240080 **Fax:** 30 24008599
Email: p.hoepfner@ehapa.de **Web site:** http://www.winnie-puuh.de
Freq: 13 issues yearly; **Cover Price:** EUR 2,95; **Circ:** 65,283
Editor: Peter Höpfner
Profile: Winnie the Pooh has a diverse mix of puzzles, reading stories and a lovely poster. A holistic approach that encourages children already in preschool through stimulating play and edutainment to delight even the parents. Target group: 3 - to 7-year-old girls and boys.
Language(s): German
ADVERTISING RATES:
Full Page Mono .... EUR 5900
Full Page Colour .... EUR 5900
Mechanical Data: Type Area: 280 x 210 mm, No. of Columns (Display): 4, Col Widths (Display): 52 mm
CONSUMER: RECREATION & LEISURE: Children & Youth

DISPLAY

725365G2A-1100

Editorial: Am Neumarkt 30, 22041 HAMBURG
Tel: 40 30060560 **Fax:** 40 300605622
Email: m.waage@display.de **Web site:** http://www.display.de
Freq: 6 issues yearly; **Annual Sub.:** EUR 45,00; **Circ:** 12,500
Editor: Matthias Waage; **Advertising Manager:** Thomas Bohnhof
Profile: International magazine about developments in sales and marketing.
Language(s): German
ADVERTISING RATES:
Full Page Mono .... EUR 3420
Full Page Colour .... EUR 4360
Mechanical Data: Type Area: 255 x 187 mm, No. of Columns (Display): 4, Col Widths (Display): 43 mm
BUSINESS: COMMUNICATIONS, ADVERTISING & MARKETING

DISTANZ AKTUELL

725372G75E-100

Editorial: Zum Ludwigstal 17, 45527 HATTINGEN
Tel: 2324 23841 **Fax:** 2324 951048
Email: gsvdd@online.de **Web site:** http://www.vdd-distanz.de
Freq: 6 issues yearly; Free to qualifying individuals
Annual Sub.: EUR 18,00; **Circ:** 2,600
Editor: Ilka Fichtel
Profile: Magazine for endurance riders.
Language(s): German
ADVERTISING RATES:
Full Page Mono .... EUR 441
Full Page Colour .... EUR 661
Mechanical Data: Type Area: 271 x 185 mm, No. of Columns (Display): 3, Col Widths (Display): 59 mm
Copy instructions: *Copy Date:* 15 days prior to publication
Official Journal of: Organ d. VDD, DRAV, ZSAA
CONSUMER: SPORT: Horse Racing

DITHMARSCHER BAUERNBRIEF

725377G21A-1240

Editorial: Waldschlößchenstr. 39, 25746 HEIDE
Tel: 481 850420 **Fax:** 481 8504220
Email: kbv@bauernverbandsh.de **Web site:** http://www.bauernverbandsh.de
Freq: 7 issues yearly; **Circ:** 3,000
Editor: Hans-Jürgen Henßen
Profile: Journal of agricultural enterprises in Dithmarschen.
Language(s): German
ADVERTISING RATES:
Full Page Mono .... EUR 562
Full Page Colour .... EUR 1023
Mechanical Data: Type Area: 275 x 186 mm, No. of Columns (Display): 4, Col Widths (Display): 45 mm
Copy instructions: *Copy Date:* 10 days prior to publication

DITHMARSCHER LANDESZEITUNG

725379G67B-4140

Editorial: Wulf-Isebrand-Platz 1, 25746 HEIDE
Tel: 481 6886200 **Fax:** 481 688690200
Email: redaktion@boyens-medien.de **Web site:** http://www.boyens-medien.de
Freq: 312 issues yearly; **Circ:** 28,483
Editor: Gerhard Wagner; **News Editor:** Christiane Sengebusch; **Advertising Manager:** Klaus Böhlke
Profile: Regional daily newspaper with reports on politics, economy, stock market, entertainment, events, culture and sport, with its local editions Brunsbütteler Zeitung, Dithmarscher Kurier and Marner Zeitung and its own large regional news and sports section on the west coast of Schleswig-Holstein.
Language(s): German
ADVERTISING RATES:
SCC .... EUR 60,00
Mechanical Data: Type Area: 430 x 285 mm, No. of Columns (Display): 6, Col Widths (Display): 45 mm
Copy instructions: *Copy Date:* 1 day prior to publication
REGIONAL DAILY & SUNDAY NEWSPAPERS: Regional Daily Newspapers

DIVI

2059535G56A-11715

Editorial: Dieselstr. 2, 50859 KÖLN
Tel: 2234 7011241 **Fax:** 2234 7011515
Email: schubert@aerzteverlag.de **Web site:** http://www.online-divi.de
Freq: Quarterly; Free to qualifying individuals
Annual Sub.: EUR 118,00; **Circ:** 1,530
Editor: Hilmar Burchardi
Profile: The magazine DIVI, founded in 2010, is the member magazine of the German Interdisciplinary Association for Intensive Care and Emergency Medicine (DIVI). The challenge DIVI employer organization is a coalition of scientific societies, trade associations and professional characteristics of individual members. The magazine is to serve the members as an integration and object of dentification, with the The aim of the promotion of intensive care and emergency medicine. The DIVI members' magazine is a training track and provides scientific based information relevant to the intensive care practice. Besides Review articles, studies, case reports and conference papers, texts for Training, continuing education and training in the Intensive Care and Emergency Medicine, user-Reports te from the industry and company news published. The highquality contributions reflect the current state of intensive care and enable a practical application of acquired knowledge to their work. The DIVI is thus aimed at anesthesiologists, internists, surgeons, pediatricians, emergency physicians and neurologists, eurosurgeons and non-medical staff (specialist care, physical therapists, paramedics, firefighters) in the intensity sive care and emergency medicine. The contributions of the "CME: Continuing Education - Education "present" assured results of scientific search and their medical experience tion for the daily practice. The manuscripts are subject to a scientific and editorial machining tion by the editor / co-editor.
Language(s): German
ADVERTISING RATES:
Full Page Mono .... EUR 1300
Full Page Colour .... EUR 2440
Mechanical Data: Type Area: 268 x 168 mm, No. of Columns (Display): 4, Col Widths (Display): 37 mm
Official Journal of: Organ d. Dt. Interdisziplinären Vereinigung f. Intensiv- u. Notfallmedizin e.V.

DIY

725388G25-7

Editorial: Am Erlengraben 8, 76275 ETTLINGEN
Tel: 7243 575208 **Fax:** 7243 575200
Email: j.bengelsdorf@daehne.de **Web site:** http://www.diyonline.de
Freq: 11 issues yearly; **Annual Sub.:** EUR 126,00; **Circ:** 6,253
Editor: Jochim Bengelsdorf; **Advertising Manager:** Thomas Heinen
Profile: diy is the specialist magazine for the DIY sector. Every issue contains current news on developments in both trade and industry, personnel announcements, company profiles, reports on new openings, previews and reviews of trade fairs, plus product news and analysis of industry events and statistics. Supplementary contributions on the subject of marketing, logistics and services also appear on a regular basis. A changing series of keynote topics concentrates on trends in the product ranges relevant to the DIY market. Each issue contains a "Gartenmarkt" section specially geared to garden centres and DIY stores with garden sections.
Language(s): German
ADVERTISING RATES:
Full Page Mono .... EUR 3110
Full Page Colour .... EUR 5672
Mechanical Data: Type Area: 270 x 187 mm, No. of Columns (Display): 4, Col Widths (Display): 43 mm
Copy instructions: *Copy Date:* 30 days prior to publication
BUSINESS: HARDWARE

DIY INTERNATIONAL

725391G25-8

Editorial: Am Erlengraben 8, 76275 ETTLINGEN
Tel: 7243 575207 **Fax:** 7243 575200
Email: r.strnad@daehne.de **Web site:** http://www.diyglobal.com
Freq: Quarterly; **Annual Sub.:** EUR 50,00; **Circ:** 11,298
Editor: Rainer Strnad; **Advertising Manager:** Thomas Heinen
Profile: DIY International is the specialist magazine for the international do-it-yourself and garden sector. The magazine is read by DIY retailers, as well as by suppliers and service providers all over the world. Every issue contains reports on developments in the international DIY trade, current news, previews and reviews of signifiant trade fairs, detailed country reports complete with statistics and analysis, profiles of manufacturers of DIY and garden products, plus new product announcements. Correspondents on the spot provide their analysis of regional market events. Keynote topics shed light on individual product areas.
Language(s): English; German
ADVERTISING RATES:
Full Page Mono .... EUR 2270
Full Page Colour .... EUR 3815
Mechanical Data: Type Area: 270 x 187 mm, No. of Columns (Display): 4, Col Widths (Display): 43 mm
Copy instructions: *Copy Date:* 30 days prior to publication
BUSINESS: HARDWARE

DKA DEUTSCHES KRANKENHAUS ADRESSBUCH MIT ÖSTERREICH UND SCHWEIZ MIT "EUROHOSPITAL" BEZUGSQUELLENNACHWEIS

1620626G56A-11213

Editorial: Unterwerkstr. 5, 79115 FREIBURG
Tel: 761 45000 **Fax:** 761 45002124
Email: info@dka.de **Web site:** http://www.dka.de
Freq: Annual; **Cover Price:** EUR 79,00; **Circ:** 4,800
Advertising Manager: Brigitte Kemle
Profile: Directory with addresses of hospitals in Germany, Austria and Switzerland including supply addresses.
Language(s): German
ADVERTISING RATES:
Full Page Mono .... EUR 2007
Mechanical Data: Type Area: 265 x 180 mm
Copy instructions: *Copy Date:* 90 days prior to publication

DLG MITTEILUNGEN

725416G21A-1260

Editorial: Eschborner Landstr. 122, 60489 FRANKFURT **Tel:** 69 24788460 **Fax:** 69 24788481
Email: dlg-mitteilungen@dlg.org **Web site:** http://www.dlg-mitteilungen.de
Freq: Monthly; Free to qualifying individuals
Annual Sub.: EUR 84,60; **Circ:** 20,406
Editor: Thomas Preuße
Profile: The DLG-Mitteilungen offer farmers comprehensive and thoroughly researched articles on the production, management, marketing and technology in agriculture. The readers are highly educated and guided on average large farm units. As an entrepreneur-farmers appreciate intense and expertise are among the opinion leaders in the agricultural economy.
Language(s): German
ADVERTISING RATES:
Full Page Mono .... EUR 3680
Full Page Colour .... EUR 6072
Mechanical Data: Type Area: 270 x 190 mm, No. of Columns (Display): 4, Col Widths (Display): 46 mm
Copy instructions: *Copy Date:* 21 days prior to publication
BUSINESS: AGRICULTURE & FARMING

DLG TEST LANDWIRTSCHAFT

1828410G21A-4381

Editorial: Eschborner Landstr. 122, 60489 FRANKFURT **Tel:** 69 24788212 **Fax:** 69 24788480
Email: r.winter@dlg.org **Web site:** http://www.dlg.org
Freq: Quarterly; **Annual Sub.:** EUR 33,00; **Circ:** 20,000
Editor: Rainer Winter
Profile: Magazine for farmers, reports of test results in the technology and resources.
Language(s): German

DLH INFO

725417G56A-11174

Editorial: Thomas-Mann-Str. 40, 53111 BONN
Tel: 228 33889200 **Fax:** 228 33889222
Email: info@leukaemie-hilfe.de **Web site:** http://www.leukaemie-hilfe.de
Freq: 3 issues yearly; Free to qualifying individuals
Annual Sub.: EUR 25,00; **Circ:** 8,000
Editor: Ulrike Holtkamp
Profile: Magazine from the German Leukaemia and Lymphoma Association.
Language(s): German

DLZ AGRARMAGAZIN

725421G21A-1300

Editorial: Lothstr. 29, 80797 MÜNCHEN
Tel: 89 12705277 **Fax:** 89 12705546
Email: reddlz@dlv.de **Web site:** http://www.dlz-agrarmagazin.de
Freq: Monthly; **Annual Sub.:** EUR 76,50; **Circ:** 79,034
Editor: Detlef Steinert; **Advertising Manager:** Thomas Herrmann
Profile: Agricultural trade magazine with about 60 years of expertise for entrepreneurial farmers and practitioners. As the magazine is designed for performance-dlz farmers in all farm structures and production sectors of agriculture in the German-speaking countries and for agricultural youth. The new concept is aimed at the target-group specific information needs of agriculture. The base magazine contains an average of more than 160 pages per issue, the scope of core subject areas: - Practice: production in all agricultural areas with a focus Planzenbau, farming, market crop, the latest practical technology, success-oriented and market-oriented management. - Future: Trends and analysis dernationalen / international markets, agribusiness, agricultural policy, prospects, opportunities, visions, future factors for agriculture in the future. The monthly focus topic, current information and news from agriculture, industry, upstream and downstream areas of science and research, complete the information concept. Life: The guide for people at work or home environment in agriculture. The monthly focus topic, current information and news from agriculture, industry, upstream and downstream areas of science and research, complete the information concept. Facebook: http://www.facebook.com/pages/agrarheutecom/152897127443 This Outlet offers RSS (Really Simple Syndication).
Language(s): German

Readership: Aimed at landowners, agricultural and forestry managers and workers.
ADVERTISING RATES:
Full Page Mono .... EUR 645
Full Page Colour .... EUR 999
Mechanical Data: Type Area: 270 x 184 mm, No. of Columns (Display): 4, Col Widths (Display): 43 mm
Copy instructions: *Copy Date:* 24 days prior to publication
Supplement(s): dlz Biogas spezial; dlz next; primus Rind; primus Schwein
BUSINESS: AGRICULTURE & FARMING

D.M.K DIE MODERNE KÜCHE

725426G23C-48

Editorial: Holzhofallee 25, 64295 DARMSTADT
Tel: 6151 387250 **Fax:** 6151 387678
Email: redaktion@echo-kp.de **Web site:** http://www.kuecheninfo.net
Freq: 6 issues yearly; **Annual Sub.:** EUR 53,00; **Circ:** 10,300
Editor: Yvonne Davy
Profile: International trade journal with specialist product information for kitchen retailers, specialists and planners in kitchen studios, kitchen stores, furniture stores with kitchen departments, architects, joiners and interior fitters as well as the electrical and plumbing trade. It reports on business trends and technical developments, standards, guidelines for planners and architects, presents new products and provides news from the industry to the retail trade. From 1 January 2011 will find our newly structured website to be relaunched. Editorially and visually connected closely with the DMK, there are industry-relevant news headlines in the news section, display the trade partners, corporate videos, a forum for the exchange of views and the reference book "Who offers what" ready. Lounge members have exclusive access to facts and figures, studies and articles from the DMK.
Language(s): German
ADVERTISING RATES:
Full Page Mono .... EUR 2881
Full Page Colour .... EUR 4177
Mechanical Data: Type Area: 250 x 176 mm, No. of Columns (Display): 5, Col Widths (Display): 32 mm
Copy instructions: *Copy Date:* 20 days prior to publication
Official Journal of: Organ d. ArGe Die Moderne Küche
BUSINESS: FURNISHINGS & FURNITURE: Furnishings & Furniture - Kitchens & Bathrooms

DMM DER MOBILITÄTSMANAGER

1748912G14A-9895

Editorial: Buchbrunner Str. 21, 97318 KITZINGEN
Tel: 9321 388511 **Fax:** 9321 388510
Email: gz@vfm.travel **Web site:** http://dmm.travel
Freq: 6 issues yearly; **Annual Sub.:** EUR 36,00; **Circ:** 24,630
Editor: Gernot Zielonka; **Advertising Manager:** Mathias Herbig
Profile: Industry, trade and business magazine for business travel, global communication and meeting business. Target audience: decision makers in the travel, event and fleet management, directors and officers of the tour operators, airlines and airport Bert collectors, railway companies, event agencies, car rental and leasing industry, hotels, wholesale departments in the automotive industry. This Outlet offers RSS (Really Simple Syndication).
Language(s): German
ADVERTISING RATES:
Full Page Mono .... EUR 7500
Full Page Colour .... EUR 7500
Mechanical Data: Type Area: 259 x 183 mm, No. of Columns (Display): 4, Col Widths (Display): 43 mm
Copy instructions: *Copy Date:* 10 days prior to publication
BUSINESS: COMMERCE, INDUSTRY & MANAGEMENT

DMW DEUTSCHE MEDIZINISCHE WOCHENSCHRIFT

725430G56A-2820

Editorial: Rüdigerstr. 14, 70469 STUTTGART
Tel: 711 8931232 **Fax:** 711 8931235
Email: martin.middeke@thieme.de **Web site:** http://www.thieme.de/dmw
Freq: 46 issues yearly; **Annual Sub.:** EUR 279,00; **Circ:** 9,709
Editor: Martin Middeke
Profile: As a renowned and most cited German-speaking internal medicine scientific journal, the DMW Deutsche Medizinische Wochenschrift in the medical profession is recognized nationwide. DMW-subscribers have high expectations of themselves and their profession. The DMW provides its readers training at a high level, but also entertainment and the latest scientific findings. The DMW offers a high efficiency and a large multi-reader potential.
Language(s): German
ADVERTISING RATES:
Full Page Mono .... EUR 2450
Full Page Colour .... EUR 3650
Mechanical Data: Type Area: 248 x 175 mm, No. of Columns (Display): 4, Col Widths (Display): 40 mm
Copy instructions: *Copy Date:* 21 days prior to publication
Official Journal of: Organ d. Dt. Ges. f. Innere Medizin u. d. Ges. Dt. Naturforscher u. Ärzte
Supplement(s): Current congress
BUSINESS: HEALTH & MEDICAL

DMW DIE MILCHWIRTSCHAFT

725030G21G-6

ditorial: Maxstr. 64, 45127 ESSEN
el: 201 89425572 **Fax:** 201 89425573
mail: edm-dmw@th-mann.de **Web site:** http://www.h-mann.de
req: 25 issues yearly; **Annual Sub.:** EUR 312,00; **irc:** 3,602
ditor: Sabine Tykfer-Büssing; **Advertising lanager:** Claudia Röllke-Skiebe
rofile: The trade magazine for the dairy - cheese - airy industries. "DMW Die Milchwirtschaft" reports n all the action in the white sector: milk collection, andling and processing of milk, butter and cheese naking, production of milk and whey powder and ondensed milk, cream, yogurt and cream cheese, evelopments in the international dairy processing nd packaging of milk and dairy products and rinking milk, UHT milk, sterile milk with all the ecessary machinery, auxiliary substances and dditives, milk Economic analysis, the latest market nformation and market analysis for retail, wholesale nd foreign trade with milk and milk products, the atest findings of the dairy Research and agricultural nd dairy policy. Moreover, even special ontributions: Current Market (14 days) Austrian dairy nd food industry (in any edition) Swiss dairy industry n any edition) Commodity value of milk and ommentary - monthly. Übersetzung von Deutsch ach Englisch The trade magazine for the dairy - heese - dairy industries. "DMW The dairy industry" ercihtet on all the action in the white sector: milk ollection, handling and processing of milk, butter nd cheese making, production of milk and whey owder and condensed milk, cream, yogurt and ream cheese, developments in the international airy processing and packaging of milk and dairy roducts and drinking milk, UHT milk, sterile milk with ll the necessary machinery, auxiliary substances and dditives, milk Economic analysis, the latest market nformation and market analysis for retail, wholesale nd foreign trade with milk and milk products, the atest findings of the dairy Research and agricultural nd dairy policy. Moreover, even special ontributions: Current Market (14 days) Austrian dairy nd food industry (in any edition) Swiss dairy industry n any edition) Commodity value of milk and ommentary - monthly. Neu! Halten Sie die Jmschalttaste gedrückt, klicken Sie und ziehen Sie lann die oben stehenden Wörter, um sie neu zu ortieren. Schließen Google Übersetzer Jr:SuchenVideosE-MailTelefonChatUnternehmen Jber Google ÜbersetzerSofortübersetzung leaktivierenDatenschutzHilfe.
anguage(s): German
DVERTISING RATES:
ull Page Mono .... EUR 1680
ull Page Colour .... EUR 2640
lechanical Data: Type Area: 270 x 186 mm, No. of Columns (Display): 3, Col Widths (Display): 58 mm
opy instructions: *Copy Date:* 8 days prior to ublication
BUSINESS: AGRICULTURE & FARMING: Milk

DNP DER NEUROLOGE & PSYCHIATER

725434G56A-2840

ditorial: Aschauer Str. 30, 81549 MÜNCHEN
el: 89 2030431435 **Fax:** 89 2030431399
mail: dnp.redaktion@springer.com **Web site:** http://www.derneurologe-psychiater.de
req: 11 issues yearly; Free to qualifying individuals **Annual Sub.:** EUR 79,00; **Circ:** 9,834
Editor: Gunter Freese; **Advertising Manager:** Peter Jrban
Profile: DNP Der Neurologe & Psychiater, the CME ournal for neurologists, psychiatrists, child and adolescent psychiatrist in practice and clinic. DNP is compact and clearly structured, practical overviews of the state of the art in diagnosis and therapy as well as an outlook on future treatment options on the main ssues in neurology and psychiatry. Each issue of DNP offers two modules "Certified Education".
Language(s): German
ADVERTISING RATES:
Full Page Mono .... EUR 2160
Full Page Colour .... EUR 3340
Mechanical Data: No. of Columns (Display): 3, Col Widths (Display): 55 mm, Type Area: 230 x 174 mm
Official Journal of: Organ d. Dt. Ges. f. Neurogenetik u. d. ArGe f. Neuropsychopharmakologie u. Pharmakopsychiatrie

DNV DER NEUE VERTRIEB

725435G25-11

Editorial: Nebendahlstr. 16, 22041 HAMBURG
Tel: 40 60900980 **Fax:** 40 60900988
Email: ralf.deppe@presse-fachverlag.de **Web site:** http://www.dnv-online.net
Freq: 21 issues yearly; **Annual Sub.:** EUR 220,00; **Circ:** 173
Editor: Ralf Deppe; **Advertising Manager:** Lars Lücke
Profile: Magazine reporting about the press distribution service.
Language(s): German
ADVERTISING RATES:
Full Page Mono .... EUR 2620
Full Page Colour .... EUR 3220
Mechanical Data: Type Area: 262 x 175 mm, No. of Columns (Display): 3, Col Widths (Display): 55 mm
Copy instructions: *Copy Date:* 20 days prior to publication
Official Journal of: Organ d. Bundesverb. Presse-Grosso e.V., d. Bundesverb. d. Werbenden Buch- u. Zs.-Handels e.V., d. Verb. Dt. Bahnhofsbuchhändler e.V. u. d. Verb. Dt. Lesezirkel e.V.
BUSINESS: HARDWARE

DN-WOCHE

725436G72-3152

Editorial: Ferdinand-Clasen-Str. 21, 41812 ERKELENZ **Tel:** 2431 968618 **Fax:** 2431 81651
Email: redaktion@dn-woche.de **Web site:** http://www.dn-woche.de
Freq: Weekly; **Cover Price:** Free; **Circ:** 77,750
Editor: Ulrich C. Kronenberg; **Advertising Manager:** Günter Paffen
Profile: Advertising journal (house-to-house) concentrating on local stories.
Language(s): German
ADVERTISING RATES:
Full Page Mono .... EUR 5298
Full Page Colour .... EUR 6068
Mechanical Data: Type Area: 430 x 292 mm, No. of Columns (Display): 7, Col Widths (Display): 40 mm
Copy instructions: *Copy Date:* 2 days prior to publication
LOCAL NEWSPAPERS

DO DEUTSCHE ZEITSCHRIFT FÜR OSTEOPATHIE

1606560G56A-11159

Editorial: Oswald-Hesse-Str. 50, 70469 STUTTGART
Tel: 711 8931952 **Fax:** 711 8931705
Email: redaktion.do@medizinverlage.de **Web site:** http://www.medizinverlage.de
Freq: Quarterly; Free to qualifying individuals
Annual Sub.: EUR 90,40; **Circ:** 4,500
Editor: Christiane Thomas; **Advertising Manager:** Kathrin Thomas
Profile: Magazine on osteopathy.
Language(s): German
ADVERTISING RATES:
Full Page Mono .... EUR 1180
Full Page Colour .... EUR 2080
Mechanical Data: No. of Columns (Display): 3, Col Widths (Display): 60 mm, Type Area: 251 x 186 mm
Copy instructions: *Copy Date:* 40 days prior to publication
Official Journal of: Organ d. Osteopathen Deutschland e.V., d. Dt. Akademie f. Osteopath. Medizin u. d. Assóciation Luxembourgeoise des Ostéopathes

DÖBELNER ALLGEMEINE ZEITUNG

725443G67B-4180

Editorial: Peterssteinweg 19, 04107 LEIPZIG
Tel: 341 21810 **Fax:** 341 21811543
Email: chefredaktion@lvz.de **Web site:** http://www.lvz.de
Freq: 312 issues yearly; **Circ:** 8,832
Advertising Manager: Harald Weiß
Profile: Daily newspaper with regional news and a local sports section. Facebook: http://www.facebook.com/lvzonline Twitter: http://twitter.com/lvzonline This Outlet offers RSS (Really Simple Syndication).
Language(s): German
ADVERTISING RATES:
SCC .... EUR 36,80
Mechanical Data: Type Area: 528 x 371 mm, No. of Columns (Display): 8, Col Widths (Display): 45 mm
Copy instructions: *Copy Date:* 2 days prior to publication
Supplement(s): prisma
REGIONAL DAILY & SUNDAY NEWSPAPERS: Regional Daily Newspapers

DÖBELNER ANZEIGER

725444G67B-4200

Editorial: Rosa-Luxemburg-Str. 5, 04720 DÖBELN
Tel: 3431 71940 **Fax:** 3431 719499
Email: da.redaktion@dd-v.de **Web site:** http://www.doebelneranzeiger.de
Freq: 312 issues yearly; **Circ:** 10,753
Advertising Manager: Matthias T. Poch
Profile: Daily newspaper with regional news and a local sports section. Facebook: http://www.facebook.com/szonline This Outlet offers RSS (Really Simple Syndication).
Language(s): German
ADVERTISING RATES:
SCC .... EUR 38,00
Mechanical Data: Type Area: 485 x 327 mm, No. of Columns (Display): 7, Col Widths (Display): 45 mm
Copy instructions: *Copy Date:* 2 days prior to publication
REGIONAL DAILY & SUNDAY NEWSPAPERS: Regional Daily Newspapers

DÖBELNER WOCHENKURIER

725446G72-3160

Editorial: Bäckerstr. 2, 04720 DÖBELN
Tel: 3431 574517 **Fax:** 3431 574518
Email: marliesdaeberitz@lwk-verlag.de **Web site:** http://www.sachsenlive.de
Freq: Weekly; **Cover Price:** Free; **Circ:** 33,941
Editor: Marlies Däberitz; **Advertising Manager:** Sina Häse
Profile: Advertising journal (house-to-house) concentrating on local stories.
Language(s): German
ADVERTISING RATES:
Full Page Mono .... EUR 2980
Full Page Colour .... EUR 4172
Mechanical Data: Type Area: 430 x 290 mm, No. of Columns (Display): 7, Col Widths (Display): 38 mm
Copy instructions: *Copy Date:* 2 days prior to publication
LOCAL NEWSPAPERS

DOCMA

1638266G5F-36

Editorial: Am Rain 1, 35466 RABENAU
Tel: 6407 400777
Email: doc@docma.info **Web site:** http://www.docma.info
Freq: 6 issues yearly; **Annual Sub.:** EUR 51,60; **Circ:** 15,107
Editor: Hans D. Baumann
Profile: Docma is the great magazine for all those creative image editing with Photoshop, Lightroom and other image editing software want to learn or improve their knowledge. The publishers are the renowned Photoshop expert Doc Baumann and Christopher Künne. In detailed tutorials, readers learn step-by-step, such as photos are perfected, fascinating montages and illustrations created. In addition, control expert technical writers at exclusive contributions in their specialized knowledge. Guarantee for a diverse and comprehensive treatment of the subject. Perfectly complements the editorial approach with tips and tricks, current information, instructions for their own projects and in-depth knowledge. Docma is required reading for all who are serious about image editing at a professional level. That's why the title is already on the market since 2002.
Language(s): German
ADVERTISING RATES:
Full Page Mono .... EUR 2460
Full Page Colour .... EUR 3245
Mechanical Data: Type Area: 260 x 180 mm
Copy instructions: *Copy Date:* 42 days prior to publication

DOCUMENTS

2077898G18B-2248

Editorial: Wieblinger Weg 17, 69123 HEIDELBERG
Tel: 6621 3310203 **Fax:** 6621 3310299
Email: info@haymarket.de **Web site:** http://www.haymarket.de
Freq: Annual; **Circ:** 17,500
Editor: Thomas Fasold; **Advertising Manager:** Michael Bradke
Profile: Supplement to the magazine print and media with information on new products in multi-dimensional communication.
Language(s): German
ADVERTISING RATES:
Full Page Mono .... EUR 6500
Full Page Colour .... EUR 6500
Mechanical Data: Type Area: 297 x 210 mm
Copy instructions: *Copy Date:* 30 days prior to publication
Supplement to: Druck & Medien

DER DOEMENSIANER

725448G9B-5

Editorial: Schloss Mindelburg, 87719 MINDELHEIM
Tel: 8261 999311 **Fax:** 8261 999395
Email: hofbauer@sachon.de **Web site:** http://www.sachon.de
Freq: Annual; **Cover Price:** EUR 11,00
Free to qualifying individuals ; **Circ:** 3,013
Editor: Andreas Hofbauer; **Advertising Manager:** Anita Elsäßer
Profile: Doemens, the familiar, traditional training and consulting company for the brewing and beverage industry operates worldwide. Der Doemensianer is the trade organ for the brewing, malting and beverage management at home and abroad. Because of its affiliation Der Doemensianer enjoys his readers - who the most part studied at the Academy Doemens - high acceptance. The coverage includes brewing and marketing and technical sales-oriented professional topics. Ads that are placed in this specific editorial environment to enjoy so that a high attention value. Der Doemensianer is excellent bridge between theory and practice, between industry and education. The proximity of the reader to Doemensianer is thus strong.
Language(s): German
ADVERTISING RATES:
Full Page Mono .... EUR 2080
Full Page Colour .... EUR 3460
Mechanical Data: Type Area: 270 x 185 mm, No. of Columns (Display): 2, Col Widths (Display): 90 mm
Copy instructions: *Copy Date:* 41 days prior to publication
Official Journal of: Nachrichtenorgan v. Doemens m. Akademie, Seminare u. Technikum
BUSINESS: DRINKS & LICENSED TRADE: Brewing

DOKUMENTE DOCUMENTS

725484G82-2300

Editorial: Dottendorfer Str. 86, 53129 BONN
Tel: 228 9239805 **Fax:** 228 690385
Email: redaktion@dokumente-documents.info **Web site:** http://www.dokumente-documents.info
Freq: Quarterly; **Annual Sub.:** EUR 18,90; **Circ:** 1,300
Editor: Gérard Foussier; **Advertising Manager:** Kerstin Harnisch
Profile: Magazine focusing on French culture and society. Provides articles on politics and current affairs.
Language(s): French; German
Readership: Aimed at students, those with an interest in France and the French language, journalists and authors.
ADVERTISING RATES:
Full Page Mono .... EUR 540
Full Page Colour .... EUR 1500
Mechanical Data: Type Area: 195 x 125 mm
Copy instructions: *Copy Date:* 30 days prior to publication
CONSUMER: CURRENT AFFAIRS & POLITICS

DER DOM

725489G87-3060

Editorial: Karl-Schurz-Str. 26, 33100 PADERBORN
Tel: 5251 153241 **Fax:** 5251 153133
Email: redaktion@derdom.de **Web site:** http://www.derdom.de
Freq: Weekly; **Annual Sub.:** EUR 78,00; **Circ:** 38,625
Editor: Matthias Nückel; **Advertising Manager:** Karl Wegener
Profile: Catholic magazine.
Language(s): German
Readership: Aimed at Catholic people aged 45 and over.
ADVERTISING RATES:
Full Page Mono .... EUR 2296
Full Page Colour .... EUR 2576
Mechanical Data: Type Area: 280 x 204 mm, No. of Columns (Display): 4, Col Widths (Display): 48 mm
Copy instructions: *Copy Date:* 12 days prior to publication
Supplement(s): Kirche in unserer Stadt; PfarrBrief
CONSUMER: RELIGIOUS

DONAU ZEITUNG

725506G67B-4240

Editorial: Curt-Frenzel-Str. 2, 86167 AUGSBURG
Tel: 821 7770 **Fax:** 821 7772067
Web site: http://www.augsburger-allgemeine.de
Freq: 312 issues yearly; **Circ:** 14,506
Advertising Manager: Herbert Dachs
Profile: Daily newspaper with regional news and a local sports section. Facebook: http://www.facebook.com/AugsburgerAllgemeine Twitter: http://twitter.com/AZ_Augsburg This Outlet offers RSS (Really Simple Syndication).
Language(s): German
ADVERTISING RATES:
SCC .... EUR 45,20
Mechanical Data: Type Area: 480 x 327 mm, No. of Columns (Display): 7, Col Widths (Display): 45 mm
Copy instructions: *Copy Date:* 1 day prior to publication
REGIONAL DAILY & SUNDAY NEWSPAPERS: Regional Daily Newspapers

DONAUKURIER

725497G67B-4260

Editorial: Stauffenbergstr. 2a, 85051 INGOLSTADT
Tel: 841 9666251 **Fax:** 841 9666255
Email: redaktion@donaukurier.de **Web site:** http://www.donaukurier.de
Freq: 312 issues yearly; **Circ:** 96,585
Editor: Gerd Schneider; **News Editor:** Angela Wermter; **Advertising Manager:** Hermann Fetsch
Profile: Regional daily newspaper covering politics, economics, sports, travel and technology. Facebook: http://www.facebook.com/donaukurier.online Twitter: http://twitter.com/donaukurier This Outlet offers RSS (Really Simple Syndication).
Language(s): German
ADVERTISING RATES:
SCC .... EUR 106,50
Mechanical Data: No. of Columns (Display): 6
Copy instructions: *Copy Date:* 1 day prior to publication
REGIONAL DAILY & SUNDAY NEWSPAPERS: Regional Daily Newspapers

DONAUKURIER.DE

1621106G67B-16536

Editorial: Stauffenbergstr. 2a, 85051 INGOLSTADT
Tel: 841 9666270 **Fax:** 841 9666255
Email: online@donaukurier.de **Web site:** http://www.donaukurier.de
Freq: Daily; **Cover Price:** Paid; **Circ:** 766,850 Unique Users
Editor: Gerd Schneider; **Advertising Manager:** Thomas Bauer
Profile: Internet portal of the newspaper Donaukurier in Ingolstadt and the region with local news from politics, business, Bavaria and the world, sports, culture and technology. donaukurier.de is an independent media that sees its task in the high-quality information to its readers (users). Here are the imparting of knowledge, the critical involvement of society and the commitment to the interests of the people a top priority. The quality standards for the registered apply the Donaukurier reasons, thus the work of online editors. Facebook: http://www.facebook.com/donaukurier.online Twitter: http://twitter.com/donaukurier RSS (Really Simple Syndication) wird angeboten.
Language(s): German
REGIONAL DAILY & SUNDAY NEWSPAPERS: Regional Daily Newspapers

DONAU-POST

725499G67B-4220

Editorial: Ludwigsplatz 30, 94315 STRAUBING
Tel: 9421 9404601 **Fax:** 9421 9404609
Email: landkreis@straubinger-tagblatt.de **Web site:** http://www.idowa.de
Freq: 312 issues yearly; **Circ:** 4,921
Advertising Manager: Klaus Huber
Profile: Regional daily newspaper with news on politics, economy, culture, sports, travel, technology, etc. She is a local issue by Straubinger Tagblatt for the northern part of County Regensburg Twitter: http://twitter.com/idowa This Outlet offers RSS (Really Simple Syndication).
Language(s): German
ADVERTISING RATES:
SCC .... EUR 14,70
Mechanical Data: Type Area: 430 x 282 mm, No. of Columns (Display): 6, Col Widths (Display): 45 mm
Copy instructions: *Copy Date:* 1 day prior to publication

Supplement(s): Zuhause
REGIONAL DAILY & SUNDAY NEWSPAPERS: Regional Daily Newspapers

DONAUWÖRTHER ZEITUNG
725505G67B-4280
Editorial: Curt-Frenzel-Str. 2, 86167 AUGSBURG
Tel: 821 7770 **Fax:** 821 7772067
Web site: http://www.augsburger-allgemeine.de
Freq: 312 issues yearly; **Circ:** 15,238
Advertising Manager: Herbert Dachs
Profile: Daily newspaper with regional news and a local sports section. Facebook: http://www.facebook.com/AugsburgerAllgemeine Twitter: http://twitter.com/AZ_Augsburg This Outlet offers RSS (Really Simple Syndication).
Language(s): German
ADVERTISING RATES:
SCC .... EUR 45,30
Mechanical Data: Type Area: 480 x 327 mm, No. of Columns (Display): 7, Col Widths (Display): 45 mm
Copy instructions: *Copy Date:* 1 day prior to publication
REGIONAL DAILY & SUNDAY NEWSPAPERS: Regional Daily Newspapers

DOPPELPUNKT
725528G80-2720
Editorial: Am Haag 10, 97234 REICHENBERG
Tel: 931 69469 **Fax:** 931 69470
Email: info@doppelpunkt.de **Web site:** http://www.doppelpunkt.de
Freq: 11 issues yearly; **Annual Sub.:** EUR 22,00; **Circ:** 44,746
Editor: Werner Schmitt
Profile: The treatment has made clear the Doppelpunkt, freed of trends, a no-nonsense information carrier with a very good image. The very size A 5 has a remarkable spread effect, coupled with a high advertising value and benefits. Targeted distribution ensures us an exclusive readership. The Doppelpunkt is in the Nuremberg, Fürth and Erlangen, a reliable and effective dissemination of information, both at the events, as well as the advertising claims. The Doppelpunkt is almost the only medium in the Nuremberg area with a readership with an age band of 18 to 50 years - and achieved with minimal losses of both a trendy clientele, such as in the field of techno / house and the dignified jazz and theater audiences. Especially the ads do not necessarily reflect trends and intertwine so with the information. In many distribution points, the designed amount of Doppelpunkt is sold out in no time.
Language(s): German
ADVERTISING RATES:
Full Page Mono .... EUR 1340
Full Page Colour .... EUR 2365
Mechanical Data: No. of Columns (Display): 2, Col Widths (Display): 58 mm, Type Area: 175 x 123 mm
Copy instructions: *Copy Date:* 12 days prior to publication
CONSUMER: RURAL & REGIONAL INTEREST

DORFENER ANZEIGER
725534G67B-4300
Editorial: Pfaffenrieder Str. 9, 82515 WOLFRATSHAUSEN **Tel:** 8171 2690
Fax: 8171 269240
Email: fsav@merkur-online.de **Web site:** http://www.merkur-online.de
Freq: 312 issues yearly; **Circ:** 15,958
Advertising Manager: Hans-Georg Bechthold
Profile: Daily newspaper with regional news and a local sports section. Facebook: http://www.facebook.com/pages/merkur-online.de/190176143327 This Outlet offers RSS (Really Simple Syndication).
Language(s): German
ADVERTISING RATES:
SCC .... EUR 43,60
Mechanical Data: Type Area: 474 x 324 mm, No. of Columns (Display): 7, Col Widths (Display): 45 mm
Copy instructions: *Copy Date:* 1 day prior to publication
REGIONAL DAILY & SUNDAY NEWSPAPERS: Regional Daily Newspapers

DORSTENER ZEITUNG
725574G67B-4320
Editorial: Westenhellweg 86, 44137 DORTMUND
Tel: 231 90590 **Fax:** 231 90598402
Email: redaktion.rn@mdhl.de **Web site:** http://www.dorstenerzeitung.de
Freq: 312 issues yearly; **Circ:** 16,443
Profile: Daily newspaper with regional news and a local sports section. This Outlet offers RSS (Really Simple Syndication).
Language(s): German
ADVERTISING RATES:
SCC .... EUR 46,40
Mechanical Data: Type Area: 450 x 315 mm, No. of Columns (Display): 7, Col Widths (Display): 42 mm
Copy instructions: *Copy Date:* 2 days prior to publication
Supplement(s): Freizeit; prisma
REGIONAL DAILY & SUNDAY NEWSPAPERS: Regional Daily Newspapers

DORTMUND GEHT AUS!
1927057G89A-12531
Editorial: Höherweg 287, 40231 DÜSSELDORF
Tel: 211 7357681 **Fax:** 211 7357680
Email: info@ueberblick.de **Web site:** http://www.ueberblick.de
Freq: Annual; **Cover Price:** EUR 6,80; **Circ:** 40,000
Editor: Peter Erik Hillenbach; **Advertising Manager:** Andreas Huber
Profile: Gastronomy guide for Dortmund.
Language(s): German
ADVERTISING RATES:
Full Page Mono .... EUR 2390
Full Page Colour .... EUR 3490
Mechanical Data: Type Area: 260 x 190 mm, No. of Columns (Display): 4, Col Widths (Display): 44 mm
Copy instructions: *Copy Date:* 25 days prior to publication

DOTNETPRO
744171G5B-132
Editorial: Bayerstr. 16a, 80335 MÜNCHEN
Tel: 89 74117803 **Fax:** 89 74117183
Email: redaktion@dotnetpro.de **Web site:** http://www.dotnetpro.de
Freq: Monthly; **Circ:** 8,844
Editor: Tilman Börner; **Advertising Manager:** Angelika Hochmuth
Profile: dotnetpro aims at professional system and application developers in companies, system houses or self-employed people as well as decision makers that deal with the selection of technologies, platforms, database and development environments.
Language(s): German
Readership: Read by software developers.
ADVERTISING RATES:
Full Page Mono .... EUR 5270
Full Page Colour .... EUR 5270
Mechanical Data: Type Area: 270 x 175 mm, No. of Columns (Display): 3, Col Widths (Display): 55 mm
Copy instructions: *Copy Date:* 26 days prior to publication
BUSINESS: COMPUTERS & AUTOMATION: Data Processing

DOW JONES ENERGY WEEKLY
1657418G58-1737
Editorial: Wilhelm-Leuschner-Str. 78, 60329 FRANKFURT **Tel:** 69 29725400 **Fax:** 69 29725440
Email: energy.de@dowjones.com **Web site:** http://www.djnewsletters.de
Freq: Weekly; **Circ:** 600
Editor: Armin Kalbfleisch; **Advertising Manager:** Nadine Voiß-Wolf
Profile: Weekly reports on all relevant issues and developments of the German energy market and its impact on the industry. "Dow Jones Energy Weekly" once a week provides you with a comprehensive coverage of the major themes of the energy industry such as: energy policy, energy regulation law Renewable Energies guest contributions from energy law expert studies and business strategies for longer-term market development.
Language(s): German
ADVERTISING RATES:
Full Page Mono .... EUR 850
Full Page Colour .... EUR 850
Mechanical Data: Type Area: 297 x 210 mm
Copy instructions: *Copy Date:* 7 days prior to publication

DOZ OPTOMETRIE & FASHION
725590G56E-80
Editorial: Luisenstr. 14, 69115 HEIDELBERG
Tel: 6221 905175 **Fax:** 6221 905171
Email: hoeckmann@doz-verlag.de **Web site:** http://www.doz-verlag.de
Freq: Monthly; **Annual Sub.:** EUR 82,10; **Circ:** 8,326
Editor: Christine Höckmann; **Advertising Manager:** Carina Currie
Profile: DOZ Optometrie & Fashion (formerly "Deutsche Optikerzeitung") is the oldest German specialist magazine for the ocular optics industry. Subscriptions to DOZ are taken out by the industry's decision makers, independent and non-independent opticians and management personnel in the ocular optics industry and in the retail trade in Germany, Austria and Switzerland. DOZ is read not just by many purchasing and sales people in companies dealing with ocular optics and their sales forces, but is also recognised specialist reading material in many vocational and specialist colleges. With its high quality editorial policy, with up to date reporting on, for example, new products, technology, design, marketing and management, DOZ provides critical information on all aspects of the ocular optics market. The latest fashion trends are presented in DOZ and in the biannual Brille & Mode magazine. Facebook: http://www.facebook.com/pages/edit/pages/DOZ-Verlag-optische-Fachveroffentlichung-GmbH/317740342850.
Language(s): German
ADVERTISING RATES:
Full Page Mono .... EUR 4315
Full Page Colour .... EUR 4315
Mechanical Data: Type Area: 248 x 185 mm, No. of Columns (Display): 4, Col Widths (Display): 41 mm
Copy instructions: *Copy Date:* 12 days prior to publication
Supplement(s): Brille & Mode; DOZ Kleinanzeiger
BUSINESS: HEALTH & MEDICAL: Optics

DPN
1740060G1F-1679
Editorial: Nibelungenplatz 3, 60318 FRANKFURT
Tel: 69 15685115 **Fax:** 69 5975528
Email: maik.rodewald@ft.com **Web site:** http://www.dpn-online.com
Freq: 6 issues yearly; **Cover Price:** Free; **Circ:** 11,075
Editor: Pascal Bazzazi
Language(s): German
ADVERTISING RATES:
Full Page Mono .... EUR 8800
Full Page Colour .... EUR 8800
Mechanical Data: Type Area: 266 x 178 mm
BUSINESS: FINANCE & ECONOMICS: Investment

DER DPRG-INDEX PR-BERATER
725591G2A-1160
Editorial: Marienstr. 24, 10117 BERLIN
Tel: 30 80409733 **Fax:** 30 80409734
Email: info@dprg.de **Web site:** http://www.dprg.de
Freq: Annual; **Cover Price:** EUR 15,00
Free to qualifying individuals ; **Circ:** 2,000
Profile: Index from 2003 listing public relations agencies and public relations agents in Germany, edited by the German Public Relations Society.
Language(s): German
Mechanical Data: Type Area: 210 x 148 mm
Copy instructions: *Copy Date:* 23 days prior to publication

DPS
725595G14R-1520
Editorial: Heidecker Weg 112, 31275 LEHRTE
Tel: 5132 859140 **Fax:** 5132 8599940
Email: redaktion@beckmann-verlag.de **Web site:** http://www.schaedlings.net
Freq: 11 issues yearly; Free to qualifying individuals
Annual Sub.: EUR 134,00; **Circ:** 1,213
Editor: Hans-Günter Dörpmund; **Advertising Manager:** Edward Kurdzielewicz
Profile: Journal containing information for the Society of German Pest Controllers.
Language(s): German
Readership: Aimed at members.
ADVERTISING RATES:
Full Page Colour .... EUR 1542
Mechanical Data: Type Area: 270 x 190 mm, No. of Columns (Display): 4, Col Widths (Display): 45 mm
Official Journal of: Organ d. DSV Dt. Schädlingsbekämpfer Verb. e.V.
BUSINESS: COMMERCE, INDUSTRY & MANAGEMENT: Commerce Related

DPVKOM MAGAZIN
725596G18B-380
Editorial: Postfach 1431, 53004 BONN
Tel: 228 9114020 **Fax:** 228 9114098
Email: maik.brandenburger@dpvkom.de **Web site:** http://www.dpvkom.de
Freq: 10 issues yearly; Free to qualifying individuals
Annual Sub.: EUR 25,00; **Circ:** 26,500
Editor: Maik Brandenburger
Profile: Who is a member of a union would be well informed about things that affect his job and if possible have a knowledge advantage over non-union workers. Finally, today information is essential when it comes to improving their own professional situation or react to certain rules and announcements to the employer. Only someone who knows about such as innovations in their professional environment, on current developments in its operation and only those who know their rights, in the case of the cases have a say and to defend themselves if necessary against corporate decisions. This is especially true when the company restructuring has negative effects on their own jobs. Against this background, the DPVKOM a duty to their members. And that it comes back regularly, either by their members is published ten times a year magazine "DPVKOM Magazin", through posters, leaflets and pamphlets on current issues or brochures with numerous current and background information.
Language(s): German
Readership: Read by staff working for the German postal service and those in the telecommunications and broadcasting fields.
ADVERTISING RATES:
Full Page Mono .... EUR 1825
Full Page Colour .... EUR 2695
Mechanical Data: Type Area: 270 x 185 mm, No. of Columns (Display): 4, Col Widths (Display): 43 mm
Copy instructions: *Copy Date:* 42 days prior to publication
BUSINESS: ELECTRONICS: Telecommunications

DR. MED. MABUSE
725464G56A-2860_50
Editorial: Kasseler Str. 1a, 60486 FRANKFURT
Tel: 69 70799615 **Fax:** 69 704152
Email: redaktion@mabuse-verlag.de **Web site:** http://www.mabuse-verlag.de
Freq: 6 issues yearly; **Annual Sub.:** EUR 42,00; **Circ:** 28,700
Editor: Hermann Löffler; **Advertising Manager:** Fee Braunsdorf
Profile: Critical Health Policy, Update on developments in the health professions, armed like it to medical and nursing care, ethical and social, to practical and theoretical issues, Authentic from training and professional life, visionary to a human and inclusive health system of tomorrow.
Language(s): German
ADVERTISING RATES:
Full Page Mono .... EUR 2300
Full Page Colour .... EUR 2300
Mechanical Data: Type Area: 248 x 178 mm, No. of Columns (Display): 4, Col Widths (Display): 42 mm
Copy instructions: *Copy Date:* 21 days prior to publication
BUSINESS: HEALTH & MEDICAL

DRAHT
758112G27-2946
Editorial: Franz-Ludwig-Str. 7a, 96047 BAMBERG
Tel: 951 861118 **Fax:** 951 861170
Email: draht@meisenbach.de **Web site:** http://www.umformtechnik.net
Freq: 6 issues yearly; **Annual Sub.:** EUR 95,00; **Circ:** 6,291
Editor: Wolfgang Fili; **Advertising Manager:** Georg Meisenbach
Profile: Magazine for producers and processors of wires and cables.
Language(s): German
ADVERTISING RATES:
Full Page Mono .... EUR 2468
Full Page Colour .... EUR 3722
Mechanical Data: Type Area: 260 x 184 mm
Copy instructions: *Copy Date:* 10 days prior to publication
Official Journal of: Organ d. VDKM, VDFI, IWMA
BUSINESS: METAL, IRON & STEEL

DRAN
725608G91D-1920
Editorial: Bodenborn 43, 58452 WITTEN
Tel: 2302 93093820 **Fax:** 2302 93093899
Email: info@dran.de **Web site:** http://www.dran.de
Freq: 9 issues yearly; **Annual Sub.:** EUR 37,80; **Circ:** 13,000
Editor: Pascal Görtz; **Advertising Manager:** Thilo Cunz
Profile: dran is the magazine for same faith. It offers the reader the opportunity to inform themselves about certain issues, cultural events, personalities and trends in the Christian scene and to form their own opinion. Facebook: http://www.facebook.com/dranbleiben.
Language(s): German
ADVERTISING RATES:
Full Page Mono .... EUR 1110
Full Page Colour .... EUR 1407
Mechanical Data: Type Area: 258 x 188 mm, No. of Columns (Display): 4, Col Widths (Display): 44 mm
CONSUMER: RECREATION & LEISURE: Children & Youth

DREAM-MACHINES
725612G77B-2
Editorial: Markircher Str. 9a, 68229 MANNHEIM
Tel: 621 4836185 **Fax:** 621 4836153
Email: h.christmann@huber-verlag.de **Web site:** http://www.dream-machines.de
Freq: 6 issues yearly; **Annual Sub.:** EUR 27,00; **Circ:** 18,695
Editor: Heinrich Christmann; **Advertising Manager:** Karin Besser
Profile: Magazine focusing on dream motorcycles particularly Harley Davidsons.
Language(s): German
Readership: Read by motorcycle owners and enthusiasts.
ADVERTISING RATES:
Full Page Colour .... EUR 2010
Mechanical Data: Type Area: 256 x 184 mm, No. of Columns (Display): 4, Col Widths (Display): 43 mm
Copy instructions: *Copy Date:* 29 days prior to publication
CONSUMER: MOTORING & CYCLING: Motorcycling

DREHTEIL + DREHMASCHINE
725618G19E-240
Editorial: Neustr. 163, 42553 VELBERT
Tel: 2053 981251 **Fax:** 2053 981256
Email: redaktion@fachverlag-moeller.de **Web site:** http://www.fachverlag-moeller.de
Freq: 6 issues yearly; **Annual Sub.:** EUR 30,00; **Circ:** 2,816
Editor: Erik Möller; **Advertising Manager:** Erik Möller
Profile: Drehteil + Drehmaschine is the best advertising medium for CNC lathe machines, lathe tools, controls, feeders, clamping systems, cleaning equipment, measuring equipment, used equipment, job ads, services in the area of lathe techniques, etc.
Language(s): German
ADVERTISING RATES:
Full Page Mono .... EUR 640
Full Page Colour .... EUR 1120
Mechanical Data: Type Area: 260 x 180 mm, No. of Columns (Display): 4, Col Widths (Display): 44 mm
Copy instructions: *Copy Date:* 14 days prior to publication
Supplement(s): kataloge orange
BUSINESS: ENGINEERING & MACHINERY: Machinery, Machine Tools & Metalworking

DREIEICH-ZEITUNG
725621G72-3264
Editorial: Dreieichstr. 4, 64546 MÖRFELDEN-WALLDORF **Tel:** 6105 9802300 **Fax:** 6105 9802327
Email: marc.stornfels@dreieich-zeitung.de **Web site:** http://www.dreieich-zeitung.de
Freq: Weekly; **Cover Price:** Free; **Circ:** 144,970
Editor: Marc Stornfels
Profile: Advertising journal (house-to-house) concentrating on local stories.
Language(s): German
ADVERTISING RATES:
Full Page Mono .... EUR 4050
Mechanical Data: Type Area: 345 x 250 mm, No. of Columns (Display): 6, Col Widths (Display): 41 mm
Copy instructions: *Copy Date:* 2 days prior to publication
LOCAL NEWSPAPERS

DRESDNER
725640G89C-4790

Editorial: Schweriner Str. 48, 01067 DRESDEN **Tel:** 351 807210 **Fax:** 351 8072133
Email: redaktion@dresdner.nu **Web site:** http://www.dresdner.nu
Freq: Monthly; **Cover Price:** Free; **Circ:** 35,740
Editor: Heinz Koschinske; **Advertising Manager:** Jana Betscher
Profile: In the categories film, stage, art, literature and music expert authors provide information about the highlights of the month. Also specials, features and news from the youth scene of Dresden to find their place. What is not here, there is not! The timer is the indispensable compass through the cultural life of Dresden. The cultural diversity of Dresden for a whole month, is clearly and fully represented. The extensive background: concert preview, party zone, film-ABC, prompter, live literature, art galleries and museums as well as addresses. By the timer curious, here brings the reader the basic background information.
Language(s): German
Readership: Aimed at people between 16 and 35 years.
ADVERTISING RATES:
Full Page Mono .... EUR 1740
Full Page Colour .... EUR 3355
Mechanical Data: Type Area: 260 x 190 mm, No. of Columns (Display): 4, Col Widths (Display): 44 mm
Copy instructions: *Copy Date:* 19 days prior to publication
CONSUMER: HOLIDAYS & TRAVEL: Entertainment Guides

DRESDNER KINOKALENDER
725643G76A-320

Editorial: Görlitzer Str. 16, 01099 DRESDEN
Tel: 351 8118421 **Fax:** 351 8029950
Email: info@kinokalender.com **Web site:** http://www.kinokalender.com
Freq: Monthly; **Cover Price:** Free; **Circ:** 17,965
Editor: Andrej Krabbe; **Advertising Manager:** Reinhard Lichtenhahn
Profile: Magazine about movies and cinemas in Dresden.
Language(s): German
ADVERTISING RATES:
Full Page Mono .... EUR 799
Full Page Colour .... EUR 940
Mechanical Data: Type Area: 320 x 230 mm
Copy instructions: *Copy Date:* 10 days prior to publication
CONSUMER: MUSIC & PERFORMING ARTS: Cinema

DRESDNER MORGENPOST
725645G67B-4340

Editorial: Ostra-Allee 20, 01067 DRESDEN
Tel: 351 48642626 **Fax:** 351 48642467
Email: mopodd.chefredaktion@dd-v.de **Web site:** http://www.sz-online.de
Freq: 312 issues yearly; **Circ:** 61,361
Editor: Peter Rzepus; **Advertising Manager:** Tobias Spitzhorn
Profile: Regional daily newspaper magazine with news on politics, economy, culture, sports, travel, technology, etc. The Morgenpost is a regional daily newspaper published in the cities of Dresden and Chemnitz and the surrounding areas. It is after the Sächsische Zeitung second largest newspaper in the region Facebook: http://www.facebook.com/szonline.
Language(s): German
ADVERTISING RATES:
SCC .... EUR 70,20
Mechanical Data: Type Area: 327 x 233 mm, No. of Columns (Display): 5, Col Widths (Display): 45 mm
Copy instructions: *Copy Date:* 1 day prior to publication
Supplement(s): rtv
REGIONAL DAILY & SUNDAY NEWSPAPERS: Regional Daily Newspapers

DRESDNER NEUESTE NACHRICHTEN
725647G67B-4360

Editorial: Hauptstr. 21, 01097 DRESDEN
Tel: 351 8075211 **Fax:** 351 8075221
Email: lokales@dnn.de **Web site:** http://www.dnn-online.de
Freq: 312 issues yearly; **Circ:** 26,136
Editor: Dirk Birgel; **Advertising Manager:** Armin Stroeve
Profile: Daily newspaper with regional news and a local sports section. Facebook: http://www.facebook.com/dnnonline Twitter: http://twitter.com/dnn_online This Outlet offers RSS (Really Simple Syndication).
Language(s): German
ADVERTISING RATES:
SCC .... EUR 58,50
Mechanical Data: Type Area: 528 x 371 mm, No. of Columns (Display): 8, Col Widths (Display): 45 mm
Copy instructions: *Copy Date:* 2 days prior to publication
Supplement(s): Gesund; prisma
REGIONAL DAILY & SUNDAY NEWSPAPERS: Regional Daily Newspapers

DRINK TECHNOLOGY & MARKETING
725653G9A-1

Editorial: Blumenstr. 15, 90402 NÜRNBERG
Tel: 911 2018215 **Fax:** 911 2018100
Email: drink@harnisch.com **Web site:** http://www.harnisch.com/drink
Freq: Quarterly; **Annual Sub.:** EUR 55,00; **Circ:** 13,100
Editor: Ian D. Healey; **Advertising Manager:** Benno Keller
Profile: drink Technology & Marketing is the first magazine for the entire beverage industry worldwide. Author contributions, original articles and short information covers the entire spectrum of beverage production and bottling, the raw materials, logistics, packaging and marketing. We also report on issues of regional interest and on trends in the beverage industry. As an advertising medium for the entire beverage industry provides drink Technology & Marketing comprehensive coverage, on average, in particular currently developing regions like South America and Asia. You can reach with only one journal world-wide all aspects of the beverage industry.
Language(s): English
ADVERTISING RATES:
Full Page Mono .... EUR 3590
Full Page Colour .... EUR 4940
Mechanical Data: No. of Columns (Display): 3, Col Widths (Display): 57 mm, Type Area: 244 x 184 mm
Copy instructions: *Copy Date:* 30 days prior to publication
BUSINESS: DRINKS & LICENSED TRADE: Drinks, Licensed Trade, Wines & Spirits

DRIVE
725660G77A-960

Editorial: Hertener Mark 7, 45699 HERTEN
Tel: 2366 808104 **Fax:** 2366 808149
Email: red.drive@vest-netz.de **Web site:** http://www.fordscene.de
Freq: Quarterly; **Annual Sub.:** EUR 42,00; **Circ:** 35,000
Editor: Michael Stein
Profile: Car magazine featuring Ford vehicles.
Language(s): German
Mechanical Data: Type Area: 252 x 184 mm, No. of Columns (Display): 3, Col Widths (Display): 55 mm
Copy instructions: *Copy Date:* 28 days prior to publication

DRIVE & CONTROL
740516G19A-820

Editorial: Maria-Theresien-Str. 23, 97816 LOHR
Tel: 9352 181091 **Fax:** 9352 181190
Email: karin.rosenkranz@boschrexroth.de **Web site:** http://www.boschrexroth.com
Freq: 3 issues yearly; **Cover Price:** Free; **Circ:** 60,000
Editor: Karin Rosenkranz
Profile: Company publication published by Bosch Rexroth.
Language(s): German
Supplement(s): drive & control local

DRUCK & MEDIEN
725686G41A-280

Editorial: Weidestr. 122a, 22083 HAMBURG
Tel: 40 69206252 **Fax:** 40 69206333
Email: red.druck-medien@haymarket.de **Web site:** http://www.druck-medien.net
Freq: Monthly; **Annual Sub.:** EUR 92,00; **Circ:** 10,730
Editor: Clemens von Frentz; **Advertising Manager:** Michael Bradke
Profile: International publication covering the whole graphics industry.
Language(s): German
ADVERTISING RATES:
Full Page Mono .... EUR 5150
Full Page Colour .... EUR 5150
Mechanical Data: Type Area: 272 x 184 mm, No. of Columns (Display): 4, Col Widths (Display): 43 mm
Supplement(s): documents
BUSINESS: PRINTING & STATIONERY: Printing

DRUCKERCHANNEL
1704680G41A-2188

Editorial: Landsberger Str. 18, 86932 PÜRGEN
Tel: 8196 998167 **Fax:** 8196 998169
Email: info@druckerchannel.de **Web site:** http://www.druckerchannel.de
Freq: Daily; **Cover Price:** Paid; **Circ:** 270,653 Unique Users
Editor: Florian Heise
Language(s): German
BUSINESS: PRINTING & STATIONERY: Printing

DRUCKLUFT KOMMENTARE
1664811G19E-1888

Editorial: Jägerstr. 5, 53639 KÖNIGSWINTER
Tel: 2244 871247 **Fax:** 2244 871518
Email: thomas.preuss@de.atlascopco.com **Web site:** http://www.atlascopco.de
Freq: Half-yearly; **Circ:** 40,000
Editor: Thomas Preuß
Profile: Magazine about compressed air.
Language(s): German
ADVERTISING RATES:
Full Page Colour .... EUR 3500
Copy instructions: *Copy Date:* 30 days prior to publication

DRUCKLUFTTECHNIK
725679G19D-15

Editorial: Lise-Meitner-Str. 2, 55129 MAINZ
Tel: 6131 992352 **Fax:** 6131 992100
Email: m.pfister@vfmz.de **Web site:** http://www.industrie-service.de
Freq: 6 issues yearly; **Annual Sub.:** EUR 94,00; **Circ:** 9,662
Editor: Michael Pfister; **Advertising Manager:** Andreas Zepig
Profile: Drucklufttechnik treats with the use of compressed air in all areas of industry. As the only magazine of its kind in German speaking countries, Drucklufttechnik covers this topic exclusively: from generation, processing and distribution to the control and use of compressed air in equipment, machinery and plants. Examples of design, technical essays, user reports, market surveys and an assortment of product reports provide comprehensive information on the compressed air market.
Language(s): German
ADVERTISING RATES:
Full Page Mono .... EUR 3900
Full Page Colour .... EUR 5130
Mechanical Data: Type Area: 265 x 185 mm, No. of Columns (Display): 4, Col Widths (Display): 43 mm
Copy instructions: *Copy Date:* 14 days prior to publication
BUSINESS: ENGINEERING & MACHINERY: Hydraulic Power

DER DRUCKSPIEGEL
725683G41A-300

Editorial: Borsigstr. 1, 63150 HEUSENSTAMM
Tel: 6104 606305 **Fax:** 6104 606444
Email: druckspiegel@kepplermediengruppe.de **Web site:** http://www.druckspiegel.de
Freq: Monthly; Free to qualifying individuals
Annual Sub.: EUR 85,00; **Circ:** 11,200
Editor: Johann Sajdowski; **Advertising Manager:** Kai-Uwe Busch
Profile: Der Druckspiegel is one of the leading journals for decision-makers in the printing and media industry in the German-speaking area. Der Druckspiegel provides exclusive, practical and user-oriented information in its monthly reports on the most important technological and economic information in the industry. Exclusive industry reports, exciting articles, the presentation of successful business models, personnel updates, product descriptions, comments and interviews round off the high quality reports by the editorial staff. The modern and extremely high quality layout of the Druckspiegel is impressive not just because of the significantly improved guidance for readers.The permanent columns such as One Year Later, 100 Days, Legal Tips and Benchmarking set a new standard for quality among graphics journals. This Outlet offers RSS (Really Simple Syndication).
Language(s): German
ADVERTISING RATES:
Full Page Colour .... EUR 5970
Mechanical Data: Type Area: 270 x 185 mm, No. of Columns (Display): 4
Copy instructions: *Copy Date:* 14 days prior to publication
Official Journal of: Organ d. Lehrer-ArGe Medien e.V. u. Verein dt. Druckingenieure
BUSINESS: PRINTING & STATIONERY: Printing

DRUMS & PERCUSSION
725692G76D-1080

Editorial: Eifelring 28, 53879 EUSKIRCHEN
Tel: 2251 650460 **Fax:** 2251 6504699
Email: dp@nitschke-verlag.de **Web site:** http://www.drumsundpercussion.de
Freq: 6 issues yearly; **Annual Sub.:** EUR 25,80; **Circ:** 21,000
Editor: Manfred v. Bohr
Profile: drums & percussion for every drummer is the most important thing next to his instrument. Here he learns everything worth knowing from the scene, both nationally and internationally. Tests and support the training workshops, new and proven competence is mediated. Interviews and portraits offer practice-oriented reporting. Tips for the upcoming CD and book purchase complete the picture.
Language(s): German
Readership: Aimed at amateur musicians.
ADVERTISING RATES:
Full Page Mono .... EUR 1435
Full Page Colour .... EUR 2460
Mechanical Data: Type Area: 254 x 185 mm, No. of Columns (Display): 4, Col Widths (Display): 40 mm
Copy instructions: *Copy Date:* 44 days prior to publication
CONSUMER: MUSIC & PERFORMING ARTS: Music

DSTG MAGAZIN
743474G1M-8

Editorial: Friedrichstr. 169, 10117 BERLIN
Tel: 30 206256600 **Fax:** 30 206256601
Email: stgv@dstg-verlag.de **Web site:** http://www.dstg-verlag.de
Freq: 10 issues yearly; **Circ:** 72,000
Editor: Dieter Ondracek; **Advertising Manager:** Elke Schmidt
Profile: Magazine for the tax inspectors' trade union, tax advisors and those involved in the financial services industry.
Language(s): German
Readership: Read by tax inspectors and tax advisors and those involved in bookkeeping and economy.
ADVERTISING RATES:
Full Page Mono .... EUR 2550
Full Page Colour .... EUR 4239
Mechanical Data: Type Area: 270 x 185 mm, No. of Columns (Display): 4, Col Widths (Display): 43 mm
Copy instructions: *Copy Date:* 30 days prior to publication
Supplement(s): Die Steuer-Warte
BUSINESS: FINANCE & ECONOMICS: Taxation

DSTZ DEUTSCHE STEUER-ZEITUNG
725704G1A-680

Editorial: Dechenstr. 7, 53115 BONN **Tel:** 228 7240
Fax: 228 72491181
Email: j.schiffers@jschiffers.de **Web site:** http://www.stollfuss.de
Freq: 24 issues yearly; **Circ:** 2,500
Editor: Joachim Schiffers; **Advertising Manager:** Carsten Priesel
Profile: Magazine about tax law, company law and about the professional law for tax advisors.
Language(s): German
ADVERTISING RATES:
Full Page Mono .... EUR 1455
Full Page Colour .... EUR 2290
Mechanical Data: Type Area: 260 x 180 mm, No. of Columns (Display): 2, Col Widths (Display): 88 mm
Copy instructions: *Copy Date:* 21 days prior to publication

DSV AKTIV SKI & SPORTMAGAZIN
719821G75A-60

Editorial: Hubertusstr. 1, 82152 PLANEGG
Tel: 89 85790235 **Fax:** 89 85790229
Email: redaktion@ski-online.de **Web site:** http://www.ski-online.de
Freq: 6 issues yearly; Free to qualifying individuals
Annual Sub.: EUR 27,50; **Circ:** 203,422
Editor: Florian Schmidt; **Advertising Manager:** Bernd Holzhauer
Profile: DSV aktiv Ski & Sportmagazin is the magazine of the German Ski Federation and the Friends of Winter Sports. Over the whole year, it impressed physically active winter sports fans with cutting-edge news, in-depth tests, an array of services and packing travel issues and not just during the winter season. DSV aktiv Ski & Sportmagazin-readers are outside of the cold season, very active. On average, each reader carries from more than five different sports. Ski, snowboard, cycling, mountain biking, hiking, nordic walking, inline skating, tennis and golf are just some of the activities of it. In all sports and leisure segment informed DSV aktiv Ski & Sportmagazin competent beginners and professionals about the latest trends and developments. Features: DSV aktiv Ski & Sportmagazin is consistently on the year-round recreational interests of active winter sports oriented. Good and sound testing of sports equipment and accessories, such as the only ski test according to DIN standard, and a diverse range of topics provide a multitude of services and provide orientation. These experts give profound fitness and nutrition tips and make even in summer the right accessories, from mountain bike on Heart Rate Monitor to the clothing. The fascinating DSV aktiv Ski & Sportmagazin-trip reports offer and explore the tourist destinations of the world in summer and winter. Individuals and families come here of their costs. In short, DSV aktiv Ski & Sportmagazin is opinion leader and department advisor and has rendered by its high level of competence a large acceptance.
Language(s): German
ADVERTISING RATES:
Full Page Mono .... EUR 9930
Full Page Colour .... EUR 13950
Mechanical Data: Type Area: 248 x 180 mm, No. of Columns (Display): 4, Col Widths (Display): 43 mm
Copy instructions: *Copy Date:* 28 days prior to publication
CONSUMER: SPORT

DSV SKI-ATLAS
738138G89A-3540

Editorial: Loisach-Ufer 26, 82515 WOLFRATSHAUSEN **Tel:** 8171 41866
Fax: 8171 16967
Email: info@srt-redaktion.de **Web site:** http://www.srt-redaktion.de
Freq: Annual; **Cover Price:** EUR 24,90; **Circ:** 40,000
Editor: Rainer Krause
Profile: The DSV SKI-ATLAS presents the most beautiful 550 ski regions of the world. From the Alps, the German Mittelgebirge mountains, Eastern Europe and Scandinavia via the USA and Canada to the rest of the world: the standard reference work of the German Ski Association provides every winter-sports enthusiast with over 900 pages of condensed winter sport enjoyment. Also snowboarders, Nordic walkers, families and fans of unusual kinds of winter sports can depend on the wealth of soundly researched, expert information it contains.
Language(s): German
ADVERTISING RATES:
Full Page Colour .... EUR 7500
Mechanical Data: Type Area: 274 x 192 mm, No. of Columns (Display): 4, Col Widths (Display): 45 mm
Copy instructions: *Copy Date:* 123 days prior to publication

DTZ DIE TABAK ZEITUNG
744201G8C-200

Editorial: Erich-Dombrowski-Str. 2, 55127 MAINZ
Tel: 6131 58410 **Fax:** 6131 5841101
Email: folker.kling@konradin.de **Web site:** http://www.tabakzeitung.de
Freq: Weekly; **Annual Sub.:** EUR 163,80; **Circ:** 10,217
Editor: Folker Kling; **Advertising Manager:** Michael Günther
Profile: Publication for the tobacconist trade.
Language(s): German
Readership: Aimed at the wholesale and retail trade of tobacconists.
ADVERTISING RATES:
Full Page Mono .... EUR 7550
Full Page Colour .... EUR 9130

Mechanical Data: Type Area: 480 x 325 mm, No. of Columns (Display): 6, Col Widths (Display): 51 mm
Copy instructions: *Copy Date:* 7 days prior to publication
Supplement(s): DTZ Shop
BUSINESS: BAKING & CONFECTIONERY: Confectioners & Tobacconists

DU UND DAS TIER 725757G81A-100

Editorial: Baumschulallee 15, 53115 BONN
Tel: 228 604960 **Fax:** 228 6049640
Email: bg@tierschutzbund.de **Web site:** http://www.tierschutzbund.de
Freq: 6 issues yearly; Free to qualifying individuals
Annual Sub.: EUR 17,40; **Circ:** 30,000
Profile: The magazine du und das tier information on all important developments in the field of animal and nature protection in Germany and Europe. It describes the abuses that lead to animal suffering, identifying those responsible and shows what can be done to remove the animal to suffer. du und das tier is the magazine for all who want to improve animal welfare. Animal rights activists find it important arguments. du und das tier describes how you can become active and it is read, what do the Deutscher Tierschutzbund and its local animal protection groups for the welfare of animals. The report of the successful mediation of a shelter protege has in du und das tier as its place as the discussion of agricultural policy issues, or to information about current scientific issues of the alternative methods of research. du und das tier also varies in the decision-makers from business and industry, science and politics, and the representatives of authorities and consistently takes sides with the animals. Facebook: http://www.facebook.com/tierschutzbund.
Language(s): German
ADVERTISING RATES:
Full Page Mono .... EUR 1500
Full Page Colour .... EUR 2400
Mechanical Data: Type Area: 224 x 184 mm, No. of Columns (Display): 3, Col Widths (Display): 58 mm
CONSUMER: ANIMALS & PETS: Animals & Pets Protection

DER DUISBURGER 1601140G89C-4767

Editorial: Uhlenbroicher Weg 30a, 47269 DUISBURG
Tel: 203 729207 **Fax:** 203 719378
Email: curran@derduisburger.de **Web site:** http://www.derduisburger.de
Freq: Monthly; **Annual Sub.:** EUR 22,00; **Circ:** 20,577
Editor: Ralph Curran
Profile: Programme of events in Duisburg.
Language(s): German
ADVERTISING RATES:
Full Page Mono .... EUR 586
Full Page Colour .... EUR 586
Mechanical Data: No. of Columns (Display): 3, Col Widths (Display): 31 mm, Type Area: 136 x 98 mm
Copy instructions: *Copy Date:* 15 days prior to publication
CONSUMER: HOLIDAYS & TRAVEL: Entertainment Guides

DÜKER NACHRICHTEN

1660279G27-3001
Editorial: Hauptstr. 39, 63846 LAUFACH
Tel: 6093 870 **Fax:** 6093 87246
Email: info@dueker.de **Web site:** http://www.dueker.de
Freq: Half-yearly; **Circ:** 3,000
Editor: Kerstin Markgraf
Profile: Magazine for customers and employees of the Düker company.
Language(s): German

DÜLMENER ZEITUNG

725713G67B-4380
Editorial: Marktstr. 25, 48249 DÜLMEN
Tel: 2594 9560 **Fax:** 2594 95649
Email: redaktion@dzonline.de **Web site:** http://www.dzonline.de
Freq: 312 issues yearly; **Circ:** 8,772
Advertising Manager: P. Kersen
Profile: Daily newspaper with regional news and a local sports section. Facebook: http://www.facebook.com/pages/Dulmener-Zeitung/145231442179920?v=wall Twitter: http://twitter.com/DZ_Duelmen This Outlet offers RSS (Really Simple Syndication).
Language(s): German
ADVERTISING RATES:
SCC .... EUR 39,60
Mechanical Data: Type Area: 488 x 324 mm, No. of Columns (Display): 7, Col Widths (Display): 44 mm
Copy instructions: *Copy Date:* 1 day prior to publication
Supplement(s): prisma
REGIONAL DAILY & SUNDAY NEWSPAPERS: Regional Daily Newspapers

DUMMY 1799068G73-618

Editorial: Torstr. 109, 10119 BERLIN
Tel: 30 300230233 **Fax:** 30 300230231
Email: redaktion@dummy-magazin.de **Web site:** http://www.dummy-magazin.de
Freq: Quarterly; **Annual Sub.:** EUR 20,00; **Circ:** 45,000
Advertising Manager: Frieder Schmid
Profile: The society magazine devoted to each issue in a particular subject. The content of the title itself as an alternative to the routine of established professional magazines such as the eccentric emptiness of popular lifestyle and fashion pages.
Language(s): German
ADVERTISING RATES:
Full Page Mono .... EUR 2350
Full Page Colour .... EUR 4350
Mechanical Data: Type Area: 287 x 222 mm
Copy instructions: *Copy Date:* 28 days prior to publication

DUMONT BILDATLAS

729883G89A-12098
Editorial: Marco-Polo-Str. 1, 73760 OSTFILDERN
Tel: 711 4502343 **Fax:** 711 4502135
Email: info@dumontreise.de **Web site:** http://www.dumontreise.de
Freq: Monthly; **Annual Sub.:** EUR 88,80; **Circ:** 10,000
Editor: Birgit Borowski
Profile: Travel magazine. Facebook: http://www.facebook.com/dumont.reise.
Language(s): German
ADVERTISING RATES:
Full Page Mono .... EUR 4900
Full Page Colour .... EUR 4900
Mechanical Data: Type Area: 282 x 208 mm
Copy instructions: *Copy Date:* 92 days prior to publication

DURCHBLICK 725748G32A-7141

Editorial: Adam-Karrillon-Str. 62, 55118 MAINZ
Tel: 6131 611356 **Fax:** 6131 679995
Email: malte.hestermann@dbb-rlp.de **Web site:** http://www.dbb-rlp.de
Freq: 10 issues yearly; **Circ:** 30,000
Editor: Malte Hestermann; **Advertising Manager:** Katy Netz
Profile: Publication about public service and local government in Rheinland-Pfalz.
Language(s): German
ADVERTISING RATES:
Full Page Mono .... EUR 1085
Full Page Colour .... EUR 2105
Mechanical Data: Type Area: 270 x 185 mm, No. of Columns (Display): 4, Col Widths (Display): 43 mm
BUSINESS: LOCAL GOVERNMENT, LEISURE & RECREATION: Local Government

DURCHBLICK 2003028G74N-1015

Editorial: Marienborner Str. 151, 57074 SIEGEN
Tel: 271 61647
Email: redaktion@durchblick-siegen.de **Web site:** http://www.durchblick-siegen.de
Freq: Quarterly; **Cover Price:** Free; **Circ:** 12,000
Editor: Friedhelm Eickhoff
Profile: Seniors information.
Language(s): German
ADVERTISING RATES:
Full Page Mono .... EUR 1000
Full Page Colour .... EUR 1000
Mechanical Data: Type Area: 260 x 185 mm, No. of Columns (Display): 2, Col Widths (Display): 90 mm

DÜRENER NACHRICHTEN

725716G67B-4400
Editorial: Dresdener Str. 3, 52068 AACHEN
Tel: 241 5101310 **Fax:** 241 5101360
Email: redaktion@zeitungsverlag-aachen.de **Web site:** http://www.an-online.de
Freq: 312 issues yearly; **Circ:** 23,350
Advertising Manager: Christian Kretschmer
Profile: Daily newspaper with regional news and a local sports section. Facebook: http://facebook.com/aachenernachrichten Twitter: http://twitter.com/an_topnews This Outlet offers RSS (Really Simple Syndication).
Language(s): German
ADVERTISING RATES:
SCC .... EUR 65,20
Mechanical Data: Type Area: 480 x 324 mm, No. of Columns (Display): 7, Col Widths (Display): 44 mm
Copy instructions: *Copy Date:* 1 day prior to publication
Supplement(s): prisma
REGIONAL DAILY & SUNDAY NEWSPAPERS: Regional Daily Newspapers

DÜRENER ZEITUNG 725717G67B-4420

Editorial: Dresdener Str. 3, 52068 AACHEN
Tel: 241 5101310 **Fax:** 241 5101360
Email: redaktion@zeitungsverlag-aachen.de **Web site:** http://www.aachener-zeitung.de
Freq: 312 issues yearly; **Circ:** 23,350
Advertising Manager: Christian Kretschmer
Profile: Daily newspaper with regional news and a local sports section. Facebook: http://facebook.com/aachenerzeitung This Outlet offers RSS (Really Simple Syndication).
Language(s): German
ADVERTISING RATES:
SCC .... EUR 65,20
Mechanical Data: Type Area: 480 x 324 mm, No. of Columns (Display): 7, Col Widths (Display): 44 mm
Copy instructions: *Copy Date:* 1 day prior to publication
Supplement(s): prisma
REGIONAL DAILY & SUNDAY NEWSPAPERS: Regional Daily Newspapers

DÜSSELDORF EXPRESS

725726G67B-4440
Editorial: Königsallee 27, 40212 DÜSSELDORF
Tel: 211 13930 **Fax:** 211 324835
Email: duesseldorf@express.de **Web site:** http://www.express.de
Freq: 312 issues yearly; **Circ:** 43,629
Advertising Manager: Karsten Hundhausen
Profile: The local-based tabloid newspaper from the publisher M. DuMont Schauberg is the currently-cheeky voice of the region and the lawyer of his readers. Six times a week, the editors demonstrate their competence, for the Express, there are more than just sensational headline. Exciting coverage is combined with in-depth background information and critical comments. The Express is the leading newspaper purchase of the Rhineland with the highest competence in the region. He appears in the circulation area with three issues: in Cologne, Dusseldorf and Bonn, from the Eifel to the Oberbergische Land. The Express is characterized by recent, strong acceptance themes, series and service elements. His style is like the people on the Rhine: tolerant, cosmopolitan, humorous with a touch of emotion. One of the very strong points of the Express: sport. Facebook: http://www.facebook.com/express.de.
Language(s): German
ADVERTISING RATES:
SCC .... EUR 100,80
Mechanical Data: Type Area: 430 x 285 mm, No. of Columns (Display): 6, Col Widths (Display): 45 mm
Copy instructions: *Copy Date:* 1 day prior to publication
REGIONAL DAILY & SUNDAY NEWSPAPERS: Regional Daily Newspapers

DÜSSELDORF FÜR KINDER!

1893315G89A-12448
Editorial: Höherweg 287, 40231 DÜSSELDORF
Tel: 211 7357681 **Fax:** 211 7357680
Email: info@ueberblick.de **Web site:** http://www.ueberblick.de
Freq: Annual; **Cover Price:** EUR 6,00; **Circ:** 30,000
Editor: Konrad Schnabel
Profile: Düsseldorf family guide with over 300 active tips for leisure time with children.
Language(s): German
ADVERTISING RATES:
Full Page Mono .... EUR 2060
Full Page Colour .... EUR 3070
Mechanical Data: Type Area: 260 x 190 mm, No. of Columns (Display): 4, Col Widths (Display): 44 mm
Copy instructions: *Copy Date:* 31 days prior to publication

DÜSSELDORF GEHT AUS!

1893316G89A-12449
Editorial: Emanuel-Leutze-Str. 17, 40547 DÜSSELDORF **Tel:** 211 52801822
Fax: 211 52801820
Email: martina.vogt@rheinland-presse.de
Freq: Annual; **Cover Price:** EUR 8,80; **Circ:** 50,000
Editor: Martina Vogt; **Advertising Manager:** Andreas Huber
Profile: Restaurant guide for the city of Düsseldorf.
Language(s): German
ADVERTISING RATES:
Full Page Mono .... EUR 2990
Full Page Colour .... EUR 4375
Mechanical Data: Type Area: 260 x 190 mm, No. of Columns (Display): 4, Col Widths (Display): 44 mm
Copy instructions: *Copy Date:* 30 days prior to publication

DÜSSELDORF GUIDE>

725727G89A-660
Editorial: Markenstr. 21, 40227 DÜSSELDORF
Tel: 211 7773131 **Fax:** 211 7883325
Email: info@duesseldorf-guide.de **Web site:** http://www.duesseldorf-guide.de
Freq: Monthly; **Cover Price:** Free; **Circ:** 20,000
Editor: Michael Nelle; **Advertising Manager:** Michael Nelle
Profile: Programme of events for Düsseldorf.
Language(s): German
ADVERTISING RATES:
Full Page Mono .... EUR 600
Full Page Colour .... EUR 600

DÜSSELDORF IM ÜBERBLICK!

1893317G89A-12450
Editorial: Höherweg 287, 40231 DÜSSELDORF
Tel: 211 7357681 **Fax:** 211 7357680
Email: info@ueberblick.de **Web site:** http://www.ueberblick.de
Freq: Annual; **Cover Price:** EUR 6,80; **Circ:** 30,000
Editor: Martina Vogt
Profile: Guides for Dusseldorf with information about the districts.
Language(s): German
ADVERTISING RATES:
Full Page Mono .... EUR 2060
Full Page Colour .... EUR 3070
Mechanical Data: Type Area: 260 x 190 mm, No. of Columns (Display): 4, Col Widths (Display): 44 mm
Copy instructions: *Copy Date:* 28 days prior to publication

DÜSSELDORF KAUFT EIN!

1893318G89A-12451
Editorial: Höherweg 287, 40231 DÜSSELDORF
Tel: 211 7357681 **Fax:** 211 7357680
Email: info@ueberblick.de **Web site:** http://www.ueberblick.de
Freq: Annual; **Cover Price:** EUR 6,80; **Circ:** 30,000
Editor: Martina Vogt
Profile: Buying guide for the city of Düsseldorf.
Language(s): German
ADVERTISING RATES:
Full Page Mono .... EUR 2060
Full Page Colour .... EUR 3070
Mechanical Data: Type Area: 260 x 190 mm, No. of Columns (Display): 4, Col Widths (Display): 44 mm
Copy instructions: *Copy Date:* 31 days prior to publication

DÜSSELDORFER AMTSBLATT

725721G72-3296
Editorial: Marktplatz 2, 40213 DÜSSELDORF
Tel: 211 8993134 **Fax:** 211 8994179
Email: amtsblatt@duesseldorf.de **Web site:** http://www.duesseldorf.de
Freq: Weekly; **Annual Sub.:** EUR 30,60; **Circ:** 2,500
Editor: Gregor Andreas Geiger; **Advertising Manager:** Petra Grübl
Profile: Magazine covering documentation of planning permission and building sites in Düsseldorf.
Language(s): German
Readership: Aimed at builders and prospective home-buyers.
ADVERTISING RATES:
Full Page Mono .... EUR 795
Mechanical Data: Type Area: 265 x 182 mm, No. of Columns (Display): 3, Col Widths (Display): 58 mm
Copy instructions: *Copy Date:* 5 days prior to publication
LOCAL NEWSPAPERS

DÜSSELDORFER ANZEIGER

725722G72-3300
Editorial: Karl-Geusen-Str. 185, 40231 DÜSSELDORF **Tel:** 211 9030641 **Fax:** 211 9030649
Email: kontakt@duesseldorfer-anzeiger.de **Web site:** http://www.duesseldorfer-anzeiger.de
Freq: Weekly; **Cover Price:** Free; **Circ:** 291,155
Editor: Yvonne Hofer; **Advertising Manager:** Edmund Weigerding
Profile: Advertising journal (house-to-house) concentrating on local stories.
Language(s): German
ADVERTISING RATES:
Full Page Mono .... EUR 11288
Full Page Colour .... EUR 15803
Mechanical Data: Type Area: 430 x 291 mm, No. of Columns (Display): 7, Col Widths (Display): 39 mm
Copy instructions: *Copy Date:* 1 day prior to publication
LOCAL NEWSPAPERS

DÜSSELDORFER BRANCHEN

1641599G14R-6036
Editorial: Wielandstr. 24, 40699 ERKRATH
Tel: 211 5203091 **Fax:** 211 5203092
Email: info@branchen-duesseldorf.de **Web site:** http://www.branchen-duesseldorf.de
Freq: Annual; **Cover Price:** Free; **Circ:** 272,700
Profile: Mercantile and telephone directory.
Language(s): German
Mechanical Data: Type Area: 283 x 189 mm, No. of Columns (Display): 4, Col Widths (Display): 45 mm
Copy instructions: *Copy Date:* 60 days prior to publication
BUSINESS: COMMERCE, INDUSTRY & MANAGEMENT: Commerce Related

DV-DIALOG 725763G5R-639

Editorial: Bertram-Blank-Str. 8, 51427 BERGISCH GLADBACH **Tel:** 2204 92140 **Fax:** 2204 921430
Email: redaktion@dv-dialog.de **Web site:** http://www.dv-dialog.de
Freq: 10 issues yearly; **Annual Sub.:** EUR 75,00; **Circ:** 14,680
Editor: Berthold Wesseler; **Advertising Manager:** Thomas Büchel
Profile: DV-Dialog is the leading German-speaking trade journal for the management of IBM Business Systems as well as its precursors System i and AS/400. DV-Dialog monthly reports on new products, market developments and trends in the field of hardware, software, communication and services. Focus on topics around the development and operation of IT systems as well as the optimisation of internal business processes. Practical tips and ideas given by masterminds within the industry. Geared towards the requirements of decision makers who are responsible for investments in commercial IT systems.
Language(s): German
ADVERTISING RATES:
Full Page Mono .... EUR 9800
Full Page Colour .... EUR 11450
Mechanical Data: Type Area: 400 x 285 mm, No. of Columns (Display): 5, Col Widths (Display): 53 mm
Copy instructions: *Copy Date:* 14 days prior to publication
BUSINESS: COMPUTERS & AUTOMATION: Computers Related

DVGW ENERGIE|WASSER-PRAXIS 726294G3D-100
Editorial: Josef-Wirmer-Str. 3, 53123 BONN
Tel: 228 9191433 **Fax:** 228 9191494
Email: maul@wvgw.de **Web site:** http://www.energie-wasser-praxis.de
Freq: 10 issues yearly; Free to qualifying individuals
Annual Sub.: EUR 59,00; **Circ:** 14,977
Editor: Stephan Maul
Profile: The journal informed with breaking news, practice-oriented technical papers and an extensive information sectionabout the the development in the gas - and water industry. It is official organ of the Association of the German Technical and Scientific Association for Gas and Water Industry Association / Technical and Scientific Association and report to readers about the latest club work and new developments. The content will be considered in addition to regular specials on various topics following categories: News, Technology, Organization and Management, Technical Regulations & Standards, DVGW-News, Events, law I eck, information and services, research and development (at irregular intervals) . Target group: core audiences are technical managers, supervisors and skilled workers in public and private utility companies (such as public utilities) of the gas and water sector. More than 90 percent of these companies are members of the DVGW. As a multi-utility companies, these are essential in the supply of gas, water and energy. Over 12,000 subscribers in these utilities get the magazine in person. In addition, among the regular readers of large market partners (in the range of the HVAC industry), institutes and research organizations and manufacturers and service of gas and water sectors.
Language(s): German
Readership: Aimed at plumbers and electric and heating engineers.
ADVERTISING RATES:
Full Page Mono .... EUR 3408
Full Page Colour .... EUR 5112
Mechanical Data: Type Area: 255 x 172 mm, No. of Columns (Display): 3, Col Widths (Display): 54 mm
Copy instructions: *Copy Date:* 28 days prior to publication
BUSINESS: HEATING & VENTILATION: Heating & Plumbing

DVR REPORT 725771G49A-340
Editorial: Auguststr. 29, 53229 BONN
Tel: 228 4000172 **Fax:** 228 4000167
Email: srademacher@dvr.de **Web site:** http://www.dvr-report.de
Freq: Quarterly; **Cover Price:** Free; **Circ:** 27,000
Editor: Sven Rademacher
Profile: Information about different aspects of road safety, trends and new research results.
Language(s): German
BUSINESS: TRANSPORT

DVW BAYERN E.V. 735777G19A-640
Editorial: Alexandrastr. 4, 80538 MÜNCHEN
Tel: 89 21291527 **Fax:** 89 212921527
Email: dvw-bayern@lvg.bayern.de **Web site:** http://www.dvw-bayern.de
Freq: Quarterly; Free to qualifying individuals
Annual Sub.: EUR 25,00; **Circ:** 1,700
Editor: Robert Roschlaub
Profile: Magazine from the German Association for Surveying and Mapping.
Language(s): German
ADVERTISING RATES:
Full Page Mono .... EUR 150
Full Page Colour .... EUR 200
Mechanical Data: Type Area: 166 x 107 mm

DVW MITTEILUNGEN HESSEN-THÜRINGEN 1655151G19A-1090
Editorial: Schaperstr. 16, 65195 WIESBADEN
Tel: 611 5355345 **Fax:** 611 5355490
Email: bernhard.heckmann@hvbg.hessen.de **Web site:** http://www.dvwhessen.de
Freq: Half-yearly; Free to qualifying individuals
Annual Sub.: EUR 4,00; **Circ:** 1,100
Editor: Bernhard Heckmann
Profile: Information about surveying and mapping, geoinformatics, cartography, land division and the evaluation of real estate.
Language(s): German

DVZ BRIEF 1665399G49A-2388
Editorial: Nordkanalstr. 36, 20097 HAMBURG
Tel: 40 23714254 **Fax:** 40 23714226
Email: redaktion@dvz.de **Web site:** http://www.dvz.de
Freq: Weekly; **Annual Sub.:** EUR 455,82; **Circ:** 2,090
Editor: Björn Helmke
Profile: Weekly newsletter for executives of the transport business.
Language(s): German

DVZ BRIEF 1665399G49A-2468
Editorial: Nordkanalstr. 36, 20097 HAMBURG
Tel: 40 23714254 **Fax:** 40 23714226
Email: redaktion@dvz.de **Web site:** http://www.dvz.de
Freq: Weekly; **Annual Sub.:** EUR 455,82; **Circ:** 2,090
Editor: Björn Helmke
Profile: Weekly newsletter for executives of the transport business.
Language(s): German

DVZ DEUTSCHE LOGISTIK-ZEITUNG 725778G49A-380
Editorial: Nordkanalstr. 36, 20097 HAMBURG
Tel: 40 23714254 **Fax:** 40 23714226
Email: redaktion@dvz.de **Web site:** http://www.dvz.de
Freq: 156 issues yearly; **Annual Sub.:** EUR 359,52;
Circ: 12,533
Editor: Björn Helmke; **Advertising Manager:** Oliver Detje
Profile: topics: Every edition: German and international transport policy and economy, company news, politics & economy, businesses and markets, logistics and shippers, carriers and freight forwarding, International, Final. Every week: business links, job listings, rental / lease, purchase and sale, real estate (Thursday), Bremen ship list (Tue), Hamburg Ship List (Sat.). 14-day: real estate, personnel / seminar calendar. Monthly: Verladeplan the forwarder's groupage shipments (domestic and foreign). Regular pages: Management & Law, hazardous materials, Technology & Innovation.
Language(s): German
ADVERTISING RATES:
Full Page Mono .... EUR 9300
Full Page Colour .... EUR 16275
Mechanical Data: Type Area: 430 x 281 mm, No. of Columns (Display): 6, Col Widths (Display): 45 mm
Copy instructions: *Copy Date:* 4 days prior to publication
Supplement(s): Bremer Schiffsliste; Hamburger Schiffsliste
BUSINESS: TRANSPORT

DW DIE WOHNUNGSWIRTSCHAFT 748277G1E-420
Editorial: Tangstedter Landstr. 83, 22415 HAMBURG
Tel: 40 52010320 **Fax:** 40 52010312
Email: redaktion@hammonia.de **Web site:** http://www.dw-web.info
Freq: Monthly; Free to qualifying individuals
Annual Sub.: EUR 102,00; **Circ:** 3,776
Editor: Ulrike Silberberg; **Advertising Manager:** Heike Tiedemann
Profile: Journal focusing on the management and sale of flats.
Language(s): German
ADVERTISING RATES:
Full Page Mono .... EUR 1980
Full Page Colour .... EUR 3420
Mechanical Data: Type Area: 264 x 185 mm
Copy instructions: *Copy Date:* 22 days prior to publication
Supplement(s): Betriebskosten aktuell
BUSINESS: FINANCE & ECONOMICS: Property

DWJ DEUTSCHES WAFFEN-JOURNAL 725780G75F-180
Editorial: Rudolf-Diesel-Str. 46, 74572 BLAUFELDEN
Tel: 7953 9787100 **Fax:** 7953 9787880
Email: walter.schulz@dwj-verlag.de **Web site:** http://www.dwj.de
Freq: Monthly; **Annual Sub.:** EUR 56,00; **Circ:** 23,900
Editor: Walter Schulz; **Advertising Manager:** Jürgen Hofmann
Profile: The DWJ Deutsches Waffen-Journal is one of the world's most renowned German language journals, which deals with the topics of sports, hunting and service weapons, historical firearms, ammunition, weapons law, optics and accessories. For 40 years, reports the DWJ Deutsches Waffen-Journal sound and reliable information on weapons technology developments, market innovations, trade shows, unique weapons collectors, auction results and shooting sports competitions as well as weapons-legal and legal policy topics. Aspects such as the retention of weapons or the protection of the values are also part of the spectrum. The editorial content is clearly structured, table of contents and color coding system guide the reader through the magazine and make the discovery sought topics and posts easily. The journalistic styles range from the message of the technical report to the feature and commentary, is a mixture of facts and personal opinion, not teaching it. Timeliness and the provision of sound facts in journalism and design of high-quality form of the game.
Language(s): German
Readership: Read by hunters, marksmen and collectors.
ADVERTISING RATES:
Full Page Mono .... EUR 2226
Full Page Colour .... EUR 2968
Mechanical Data: Type Area: 265 x 197 mm, No. of Columns (Display): 4, Col Widths (Display): 47 mm
Copy instructions: *Copy Date:* 21 days prior to publication
CONSUMER: SPORT: Shooting

DWZ 724883G15A-40
Editorial: Bergsonstr. 29a, 81245 MÜNCHEN
Tel: 89 12768801 **Fax:** 89 12768803
Email: info@wintherburg.de **Web site:** http://www.drogeriewarenzeitung.de
Freq: 6 issues yearly; Free to qualifying individuals
Annual Sub.: EUR 50,00; **Circ:** 7,766
Editor: Alexander Schwaab; **Advertising Manager:** Alexander Schwaab
Profile: The DWZ is an independent trade magazine for decision makers in the purchase and sale of drug stores, beauty shops, department stores and industry. The DWZ is an independent information base for the commercial staff. Which items are "in" what is "out"? What we must conduct in trade, which is interesting for Erstplazierungen? As the industry is structured? Who has something to say? Which shows are interesting for the industry? What partnerships are available? Who will rise and who from? Whose Trade marketing is successful? How is the brand industry against cheap commercial brands? Where control the associations? What new laws affecting the industry? What are the new market figures? The DWZ provides answers for the target group product manager and managing director of brand industry as well as managers and sales staff of the industry trade.
Language(s): German
Readership: Aimed at owners and managers of chemists shops, pharmacies and perfumeries.
ADVERTISING RATES:
Full Page Mono .... EUR 4600
Full Page Colour .... EUR 4600
Mechanical Data: Type Area: 297 x 210 mm
Copy instructions: *Copy Date:* 20 days prior to publication
Official Journal of: Organ d. Verb. Dt. Drogisten VDD
BUSINESS: COSMETICS & HAIRDRESSING: Cosmetics

DWZ DIE WINZER-ZEITSCHRIFT 725788G21H-4
Editorial: Karl-Tesche-Str. 3, 56073 KOBLENZ
Tel: 261 304220 **Fax:** 261 304221000
Email: knebel@bwv-net.de **Web site:** http://www.lv-net.de
Freq: Monthly; **Annual Sub.:** EUR 33,30; **Circ:** 4,370
Editor: Josef Derstappen; **Advertising Manager:** Michael Nau
Profile: Magazine about vine growing in the North Rheinland and Saarland regions of Germany.
Language(s): German
ADVERTISING RATES:
Full Page Mono .... EUR 2900
Full Page Colour .... EUR 4060
Mechanical Data: Type Area: 290 x 205 mm, No. of Columns (Display): 4, Col Widths (Display): 50 mm
Copy instructions: *Copy Date:* 10 days prior to publication
Official Journal of: Organ d. Bauern- u. Winzerverb. Rheinland-Nassau u. d. Landwirtschaftskammer Rheinland-Pfalz
BUSINESS: AGRICULTURE & FARMING: Vine Growing

DYNAMIT 1660529G86C-218
Editorial: Grüner Weg 60a, 50321 BRÜHL
Tel: 2232 9499281 **Fax:** 2232 9499282
Email: dynamit@atoz-scripts.de **Web site:** http://www.dynamit-magazin.de
Freq: 11 issues yearly; **Annual Sub.:** EUR 55,00;
Circ: 24,300
Editor: Ulrike Heuser
Profile: Men Magazine.
Language(s): German
ADVERTISING RATES:
Full Page Mono .... EUR 780
Full Page Colour .... EUR 1550
Mechanical Data: Type Area: 262 x 180 mm, No. of Columns (Display): 3, Col Widths (Display): 61 mm

DZW KOMPAKT 725799G56D-400
Editorial: Kurt-Schumacher-Str. 6, 53113 BONN
Tel: 228 2892160 **Fax:** 228 28921620
Email: redaktion@dzw.de **Web site:** http://www.dzw.de
Freq: 6 issues yearly; **Circ:** 45,960
Editor: Marion Marschall; **Advertising Manager:** Heike Müller-Wüstenfeld
Profile: DZW Kompakt is published 6 times a year as a supplement to Die Zahnarzt Woche DZW and provides dental emphases. Current and comprehensive user and background reports, scientific articles and conference articles, the dentist informed of developments such as endodontics, restorative Dentistry or hygiene in the dental office. Current issues are taken promptly.
Language(s): German
ADVERTISING RATES:
Full Page Mono .... EUR 3400
Full Page Colour .... EUR 4870
Mechanical Data: Type Area: 245 x 183 mm, No. of Columns (Display): 3, Col Widths (Display): 55 mm
Copy instructions: *Copy Date:* 21 days prior to publication
Supplement to: Die Zahnarzt Woche DZW
BUSINESS: HEALTH & MEDICAL: Dental

DZW ZAHNTECHNIK 725801G56D-440
Editorial: Kurt-Schumacher-Str. 6, 53113 BONN
Tel: 228 2892160 **Fax:** 228 28921620
Email: redaktion@dzw.de **Web site:** http://www.dzw.de
Freq: 9 issues yearly; **Circ:** 45,967
Editor: Marion Marschall; **Advertising Manager:** Heike Müller-Wüstenfeld
Profile: Supplement to the weekly newspaper "Die Zahnarzt Woche", focuses on the dental side of dentistry and is thus not only the technician, but the dentist who wants to keep in dentistry to date. Current dental key issues with regard to technological developments and innovative solutions to inform readers about developments in the market.
Language(s): German
ADVERTISING RATES:
Full Page Mono .... EUR 3400
Full Page Colour .... EUR 4870
Mechanical Data: Type Area: 245 x 176 mm, No. of Columns (Display): 3, Col Widths (Display): 55 mm
Copy instructions: *Copy Date:* 21 days prior to publication
Supplement to: Die Zahnarzt Woche DZW
BUSINESS: HEALTH & MEDICAL: Dental

DZZ DIE ZUCKER RÜBENZEITUNG 725802G21A-1360
Editorial: Marktbreiter Str. 74, 97199 OCHSENFURT
Tel: 9331 91875 **Fax:** 9331 91874
Email: dzz@vsz.de **Web site:** http://www.vsz.de
Freq: 6 issues yearly; Free to qualifying individuals
Annual Sub.: EUR 15,00; **Circ:** 21,643
Editor: Fred Zeller
Profile: The dzz Die Zucker Rübenzeitung fully informed on all topics related to sugar beet. Editorial focus: Agriculture, seeding, irrigation, biogas, bioethanol, tillage, harvesting, by-products for animal consumption, renewable raw materials, plant protection, land clearing, beet prices, beet transportation, first aid being, world sugar market, sugar regime, sugar in the diet, sugar industry, breeding.
Language(s): German
ADVERTISING RATES:
Full Page Mono .... EUR 7200
Full Page Colour .... EUR 8200
Mechanical Data: Type Area: 455 x 310 mm, No. of Columns (Display): 5, Col Widths (Display): 58 mm
Copy instructions: *Copy Date:* 30 days prior to publication
Supplement(s): Zuckerrüben-Magazin
BUSINESS: AGRICULTURE & FARMING

E COMMERCE MAGAZIN 725896G14A-9720
Editorial: Johann-Sebastian-Bach-Str. 5, 85591 VATERSTETTEN **Tel:** 8106 350150 **Fax:** 8106 350190
Email: dk@win-verlag.de **Web site:** http://www.e-commerce-magazin.de
Freq: 8 issues yearly; **Annual Sub.:** EUR 66,00; **Circ:** 11,428
Editor: Dunja Koelwel; **Advertising Manager:** Bernd Heilmeier
Profile: An intermediary between sellers and market reports and independent, competent and critical of current trends, strategies, applications and solutions of e-commerce - both in the local, national and even global context. The e-commerce magazine provides practical assistance in the selection, implementation, operation, and in the advancement of E-Commerce-Lösungen/Systemen to help in the settlement of the action and with services and products via the Internet. Important aspects are the costs and profit orientation in the context of the current market environment. Technology issues are handled by the e-commerce magazine on a comprehensible level and serve the communication and understanding between the IT department, whether internally or externally, and promote business decision-makers.
Language(s): German
Readership: Aimed at directors and marketing managers seeking to expand the effectiveness of their businesses with Internet-technology applications.
ADVERTISING RATES:
Full Page Mono .... EUR 5620
Full Page Colour .... EUR 6990
Mechanical Data: Type Area: 266 x 180 mm, No. of Columns (Display): 3, Col Widths (Display): 58 mm
Copy instructions: *Copy Date:* 27 days prior to publication
BUSINESS: COMMERCE, INDUSTRY & MANAGEMENT

E EXPERTEN REPORT 1898568G1C-1494
Editorial: Pelkovenstr. 81b, 80992 MÜNCHEN
Tel: 89 21961220 **Fax:** 89 219612220
Email: info@experten.de **Web site:** http://www.experten.de
Freq: Quarterly; **Cover Price:** Free; **Circ:** 50,035
Editor: Brigitte Hicker
Profile: The trade magazine of the financial and insurance industry communicates with in-depth quarterly contributions neutral institutions and product providers on various insurance topics. The focus is on current market offerings, trends and developments are in all sectors of the insurance industry.
Language(s): German
ADVERTISING RATES:
Full Page Mono .... EUR 2500
Full Page Colour .... EUR 2500
Mechanical Data: Type Area: 256 x 177 mm, No. of Columns (Display): 3
Copy instructions: *Copy Date:* 43 days prior to publication

E&E FASZINATION ELEKTRONIK 724982G18A-222
Editorial: Nymphenburger Str. 86, 80636 MÜNCHEN
Tel: 89 50038317 **Fax:** 89 50038310
Email: eue.redaktion@publish-industry.net **Web site:** http://www.eue24.net
Freq: 8 issues yearly; **Circ:** 16,480
Editor: Michael Brunn; **Advertising Manager:** Saskia Albert
Profile: Magazine focusing on electronics, includes tests, components, systems, software, EMC and related issues.
Language(s): German
Readership: Read by engineers and designers.
ADVERTISING RATES:
Full Page Mono .... EUR 4675
Full Page Colour .... EUR 5500

Mechanical Data: Type Area: 232 x 178 mm, No. of Columns (Display): 4, Col Widths (Display): 42 mm
BUSINESS: ELECTRONICS

E & W ERZIEHUNG UND WISSENSCHAFT 726603G62A-700

Editorial: Berliner Allee 16, 30175 HANNOVER
Tel: 511 338040 **Fax:** 511 3380421
Email: j.tiemer@gew-nds.de **Web site:** http://www.gew-nds.de
Freq: 10 issues yearly; Free to qualifying individuals
Annual Sub.: EUR 18,50; **Circ:** 29,653
Editor: Joachim Tiemer; **Advertising Manager:** Mathias Müller
Profile: Publication focusing on education and pedagogy, published by teacher trade union GEW Niedersachsen.
Language(s): German
Mechanical Data: Type Area: 265 x 195 mm, No. of Columns (Display): 4, Col Widths (Display): 45 mm
Copy instructions: *Copy Date:* 31 days prior to publication
BUSINESS: CHURCH & SCHOOL EQUIPMENT & EDUCATION: Education

EASTGATE 1855772G74M-873

Editorial: Marzahner Promenade 1a, 12679 BERLIN
Tel: 30 9114590 **Fax:** 30 911459111
Email: info@eastgate-berlin.de **Web site:** http://www.eastgate-berlin.de
Freq: Monthly; **Cover Price:** Free; **Circ:** 150,000
Editor: Bianka Käppler
Profile: Shopping centre publication.
Language(s): German

EASYLINUX! 1616387G5C-16

Editorial: Putzbrunner Str. 71, 81739 MÜNCHEN
Tel: 89 9934110 **Fax:** 89 99341199
Email: redaktion@easylinux.de **Web site:** http://www.easylinux.de
Freq: Quarterly; **Annual Sub.:** EUR 33,30; **Circ:** 35,000
Editor: Hans-Georg Eßer; **Advertising Manager:** Hubert Wiest
Profile: EasyLinux aimed at connecting passengers coming from other operating systems and there have sound experience. EasyLinux treated Linux as a desktop operating system and in practice comprehensible step-by-step instructions. Readers of linux are easy on new technologies far above average interest.
Language(s): German
ADVERTISING RATES:
Full Page Mono .... EUR 1680
Full Page Colour .... EUR 2300
Mechanical Data: Type Area: 248 x 181 mm
Copy instructions: *Copy Date:* 24 days prior to publication

EASYRIDERS 725810G77A-980

Editorial: Hertener Mark 7, 45699 HERTEN
Tel: 2366 808104 **Fax:** 2366 808149
Email: red.easy@vest-netz.de
Freq: Monthly; **Annual Sub.:** EUR 50,00; **Circ:** 14,389
Editor: Michael Stein
Profile: Magazine for fans of the brand Harley Davidson.
Language(s): German
ADVERTISING RATES:
Full Page Mono .... EUR 1800
Full Page Colour .... EUR 3000
Mechanical Data: Type Area: 259 x 184 mm, No. of Columns (Display): 3, Col Widths (Display): 57 mm
CONSUMER: MOTORING & CYCLING: Motoring

EAT MAGAZINE 1861924G89A-12419

Editorial: Waldhofer Str. 19, 69123 HEIDELBERG
Tel: 6221 75704100 **Fax:** 6221 75704109
Email: juergen.franke@eat-magazine.de **Web site:** http://www.eat-magazine.de
Freq: Half-yearly; **Annual Sub.:** EUR 20,00; **Circ:** 25,000
Editor: Jürgen Franke; **Advertising Manager:** Thea Maria Rachel
Profile: eat magazine looks into the bubbling pots of the hottest cities around the world. It speaks to travelers who do not wish to consciously walk the beaten paths of the packages and look at the good food and drink as an essential component of a successful journey. Each issue contains 160 pages of graphically rich reports and put up reading stories that are all exclusively researched locally and exclusively for private, unpublished images is used. Eat the magazine can also be used directly as city guides: A 40-page guide and recipe section presents in concise form all the major wine and food, culinary and cultural figures as well as selected hotel recommendations and tips and tricks from the metropolis. Whether Bangkok, Barcelona or Shanghai ... eat magazine moves where normality ends and the extraordinary begins.
Language(s): German
ADVERTISING RATES:
Full Page Mono .... EUR 5500
Full Page Colour .... EUR 5500
Mechanical Data: Type Area: 300 x 230 mm

EATSMARTER! 2035898G74P-1370

Editorial: Schulterblatt 58, 20357 HAMBURG
Email: info@eatsmarter.de **Web site:** http://www.eatsmarter.de
Freq: 6 issues yearly; **Annual Sub.:** EUR 15,00; **Circ:** 150,000
Profile: EAT SMARTER clears up in a very popular way of healthy eating and shows readers how they can live more consciously without sacrificing enjoyment. Editorial contributions and extensive recipes dispel the misconception that healthy food can not taste good.
Language(s): German
ADVERTISING RATES:
Full Page Mono .... EUR 9000
Full Page Colour .... EUR 9000
Mechanical Data: Type Area: 232 x 178 mm

EB ELEKTRISCHE BAHNEN 725815G49E-240

Editorial: Rosenheimer Str. 145, 81671 MÜNCHEN
Tel: 89 45051206 **Fax:** 89 45051207
Email: eb-redaktion@t-online.de **Web site:** http://www.eb-info.eu
Freq: 10 issues yearly; **Annual Sub.:** EUR 289,00; **Circ:** 983
Editor: Eberhard Buhl
Profile: Journal of development, construction, operation and repair of electric railways and new transport systems with a focus on energy supply and electric power units.
Language(s): German
ADVERTISING RATES:
Full Page Mono .... EUR 2920
Full Page Colour .... EUR 4060
Mechanical Data: Type Area: 250 x 176 mm, No. of Columns (Display): 4, Col Widths (Display): 41 mm
BUSINESS: TRANSPORT: Railways

EBERBACHER ZEITUNG 725819G67B-4460

Editorial: Frauenstr. 77, 89073 ULM **Tel:** 731 1560
Fax: 731 156308
Email: redaktion@swp.de **Web site:** http://www.swp.de
Freq: 312 issues yearly; **Circ:** 2,636
Advertising Manager: Inge Höltzcke
Profile: Daily newspaper with regional news and a local sports section. Twitter: http://twitter.com/swpde.
Language(s): German
ADVERTISING RATES:
SCC .... EUR 14,70
Mechanical Data: Type Area: 420 x 280 mm, No. of Columns (Display): 6, Col Widths (Display): 45 mm
Copy instructions: *Copy Date:* 3 days prior to publication
REGIONAL DAILY & SUNDAY NEWSPAPERS: Regional Daily Newspapers

EBERSBERGER ZEITUNG 725823G67B-4480

Editorial: Pfaffenrieder Str. 9, 82515 WOLFRATSHAUSEN **Tel:** 8171 2690
Fax: 8171 269240
Email: fsav@merkur-online.de **Web site:** http://www.merkur-online.de
Freq: 312 issues yearly; **Circ:** 11,753
Advertising Manager: Hans-Georg Bechthold
Profile: The Münchner Merkur with its own local newspapers, of which the Ebersberger Zeitung is one that, the leading regional newspaper brand in the Munich area - the most affluent area of Germany. The combination of newspaper and region is the foundation on which to build the success of the title. This is the newspaper not only the factual news agency, but forms a community of solidarity with its readers and the local community. The clear focus on local reporting creates a high regard to human reader loyalty. She presses one hand in the very high number of close to 180,000 subscribers. Also for the high reader-commitment is the loyalty of the total current 827 000 daily readers, the Münchner Merkur or one of its local newspapers usually read over many years. The Münchner Merkur with its own local newspapers is a newspaper for the whole family, tradition and modern life for one of the most beautiful regions of Germany unites. Reliable, informative, critical: the Münchner Merkur is the indispensable daily newspaper for the region. Facebook: http://www.facebook.com/pages/merkur-online.de/190176143327 This Outlet offers RSS (Really Simple Syndication).
Language(s): German
ADVERTISING RATES:
SCC .... EUR 43,60
Mechanical Data: Type Area: 474 x 324 mm, No. of Columns (Display): 7, Col Widths (Display): 45 mm
Copy instructions: *Copy Date:* 1 day prior to publication
REGIONAL DAILY & SUNDAY NEWSPAPERS: Regional Daily Newspapers

EC EUROPEAN COATINGS JOURNAL 725882G16B-15

Editorial: Plathnerstr. 4c, 30175 HANNOVER
Tel: 511 9910211 **Fax:** 511 9910299
Email: miriam.von.bardeleben@vincentz.net **Web site:** http://www.european-coatings.com
Freq: 10 issues yearly; **Annual Sub.:** EUR 179,76; **Circ:** 8,205
Editor: Miriam von Bardeleben; **Advertising Manager:** Anette Pennartz
Profile: EC European Coatings Journal is eitorial leader in the provision of information for the European English language coatings industry: highly developed reader acceptance and the publication's high reputation provide an outstanding editorial environment for advertising. EC is covering the European market with a third-party audited circulation and an extremely high proportion of personally addressed copies: an average of three additional readers per copy provides a unique reach of around 32,000 professionals with every issue. EC is read in all operational areas of the European English language coatings industry: your advertising will reach the decision-makers and leading opinions in laboratory, production and management throughout Europe.
Language(s): English
ADVERTISING RATES:
Full Page Mono .... EUR 3000
Full Page Colour .... EUR 4500
Mechanical Data: Type Area: 250 x 175 mm, No. of Columns (Display): 4, Col Widths (Display): 42 mm
Copy instructions: *Copy Date:* 17 days prior to publication
BUSINESS: DECORATING & PAINT: Paint - Technical Manufacture

ECC EUROPA CAMPING + CARAVANING 726645G89A-780

Editorial: Heusee 19, 73655 PLÜDERHAUSEN
Tel: 7181 86020 **Fax:** 7181 860229
Email: mail@drei-brunnen-verlag.de **Web site:** http://www.ecc-campingfuehrer.de
Freq: Annual; **Cover Price:** EUR 14,90; **Circ:** 80,000
Editor: Ursel Wunder-Gessler; **Advertising Manager:** Thomas Müller
Profile: Camping guide. Facebook: http://www.facebook.com/pages/ECC-Campingfuhrer/150858898278583.
Language(s): English; French; German
ADVERTISING RATES:
Full Page Mono .... EUR 2420
Full Page Colour .... EUR 4480
Mechanical Data: Type Area: 252 x 140 mm, No. of Columns (Display): 2, Col Widths (Display): 68 mm
Copy instructions: *Copy Date:* 90 days prior to publication

ECHAZ-BOTE 725840G67B-4500

Editorial: Burgstr. 1, 72764 REUTLINGEN
Tel: 7121 3020 **Fax:** 7121 302677
Email: redaktion@gea.de **Web site:** http://www.gea.de
Freq: 312 issues yearly; **Circ:** 41,687
Advertising Manager: Stephan Körting
Profile: Daily newspaper with regional news and a local sports section. Twitter: http://twitter.com/geaonline.
Language(s): German
ADVERTISING RATES:
SCC .... EUR 91,90
Mechanical Data: Type Area: 480 x 320 mm, No. of Columns (Display): 7, Col Widths (Display): 44 mm
Copy instructions: *Copy Date:* 1 day prior to publication
Supplement(s): GEA Sport Magazin
REGIONAL DAILY & SUNDAY NEWSPAPERS: Regional Daily Newspapers

ECHO 725870G53-1

Editorial: Domstr. 20, 50668 KÖLN **Tel:** 221 1491070
Fax: 221 1499108
Email: presse@rewe-group.com
Freq: Monthly; **Annual Sub.:** EUR 14,76; **Circ:** 51,258
Editor: Pierre de la Motte
Profile: Magazine about all aspects of the modern retail trade.
Language(s): German
ADVERTISING RATES:
Full Page Mono .... EUR 5266
Full Page Colour .... EUR 8952
Mechanical Data: Type Area: 241 x 178 mm, No. of Columns (Display): 3, Col Widths (Display): 56 mm
Copy instructions: *Copy Date:* 28 days prior to publication
BUSINESS: RETAILING & WHOLESALING

ECHO DER FRAU 725864G74A-920

Editorial: Münchener Str. 101/09, 85737 ISMANING
Tel: 89 272700 **Fax:** 89 272703290
Email: echoderfrau@waz-zeitschriften.de
Freq: Weekly; **Cover Price:** EUR 1,50; **Circ:** 224,422
Editor: Christiane Ams
Profile: Exciting reports from the world of the aristocracy, the celebrities, pop, folk music and society and the great service section with fashion, beauty, recipes and expert guide ECHO DER Frau shape as well as their great medicine part., entertaining women's magazine with great puzzle part.
Language(s): German
ADVERTISING RATES:
Full Page Mono .... EUR 5710
Full Page Colour .... EUR 5710
Mechanical Data: Type Area: 260 x 195 mm, No. of Columns (Display): 4, Col Widths (Display): 45 mm
Copy instructions: *Copy Date:* 30 days prior to publication
CONSUMER: WOMEN'S INTEREST CONSUMER MAGAZINES: Women's Interest

ECHO ZUM SONNTAG 725879G72-3364

Editorial: Gipsmühlenweg 2, 37520 OSTERODE
Tel: 5522 31700 **Fax:** 5522 3170390
Email: redaktion@harzkurier.de **Web site:** http://www.harzkurier.de
Freq: Weekly; **Cover Price:** Free; **Circ:** 53,400
Editor: Peter Bischof; **Advertising Manager:** Bernd Spieß
Profile: Advertising journal (house-to-house) concentrating on local stories.
Language(s): German
ADVERTISING RATES:
Full Page Mono .... EUR 3159
Full Page Colour .... EUR 4751
Mechanical Data: Type Area: 435 x 282 mm, No. of Columns (Display): 6, Col Widths (Display): 45 mm
Copy instructions: *Copy Date:* 2 days prior to publication
LOCAL NEWSPAPERS

ECHT KABELEINS 1704301G73-607

Editorial: Medienallee 6, 85774 UNTERFÖHRING
Tel: 89 950710 **Fax:** 89 95078901
Email: onlinefeedback@kabeleins.de **Web site:** http://www.kabeleins.de
Freq: Daily; **Cover Price:** Paid; **Circ:** 1,082,136 Unique Users
Editor: Robin Seckler
Profile: Ezine: Cable and satellite station broadcasting entertainment.
Language(s): German
CONSUMER: NATIONAL & INTERNATIONAL PERIODICALS

ECKERNFÖRDER RUNDSCHAU 736383G72-9036

Editorial: Fleethörn 1, 24103 KIEL **Tel:** 431 9032925
Fax: 431 9032929
Email: exp.red@kieler-nachrichten.de **Web site:** http://www.kn-online.de
Freq: Weekly; **Cover Price:** Free; **Circ:** 28,000
Editor: Jürgen Heinemann; **Advertising Manager:** Marc Paris
Profile: Advertising journal (house-to-house) concentrating on local stories.
Language(s): German
ADVERTISING RATES:
Full Page Mono .... EUR 1864
Full Page Colour .... EUR 2731
Mechanical Data: Type Area: 430 x 281 mm, No. of Columns (Display): 6, Col Widths (Display): 45 mm
Copy instructions: *Copy Date:* 2 days prior to publication
LOCAL NEWSPAPERS

ECKERNFÖRDER ZEITUNG 725886G67B-4520

Editorial: Schulweg 7, 24340 ECKERNFÖRDE
Tel: 4351 900844 **Fax:** 4351 900891
Email: redaktion.eckernfoerde@shz.de **Web site:** http://www.eckernfoerder-zeitung.de
Freq: 312 issues yearly; **Circ:** 8,884
Advertising Manager: Ingeborg Schwarz
Profile: The Eckernförder Zeitung was first published in 1851 and is since 1 October 2004 sh:z Schleswig-Holsteinischer Zeitungsverlag. The distribution of the newspaper is the city of Eckernförde and the surrounding area. Twitter: http://twitter.com/shz_de This Outlet offers RSS (Really Simple Syndication).
Language(s): German
ADVERTISING RATES:
SCC .... EUR 50,80
Mechanical Data: Type Area: 480 x 325 mm, No. of Columns (Display): 7, Col Widths (Display): 45 mm
Copy instructions: *Copy Date:* 1 day prior to publication
Supplement(s): nordisch gesund; Schleswig-Holstein Journal; tv magazin
REGIONAL DAILY & SUNDAY NEWSPAPERS: Regional Daily Newspapers

ECO WORLD 1601549G57-2642

Editorial: Gotzinger Str. 48, 81371 MÜNCHEN
Tel: 89 7466110 **Fax:** 89 74661160
Email: info@eco-world.de **Web site:** http://www.eco-world.de
Freq: Annual; **Cover Price:** EUR 7,50; **Circ:** 50,000
Advertising Manager: Petra Siftar
Profile: Directory for supply for ecological products.
Language(s): German
ADVERTISING RATES:
Full Page Mono .... EUR 4520
Full Page Colour .... EUR 4800
Mechanical Data: Type Area: 257 x 189 mm, No. of Columns (Display): 4, Col Widths (Display): 45 mm

ECONOMIC ENGINEERING 724043G19J-4

Editorial: Aschmattstr. 8, 76532 BADEN-BADEN
Tel: 7221 502210 **Fax:** 7221 502222
Email: valnion@economic-engineering.de **Web site:** http://www.economic-engineering.de
Freq: 6 issues yearly; **Annual Sub.:** EUR 74,90; **Circ:** 8,414
Editor: Bernhard D. Valnion; **Advertising Manager:** Silja Aretz
Profile: Economic Engineering reported on technological and economic aspects of product development. Economic processes and methods in engineering and manufacturing, are shown to use emerging technologies and methodological expertise of suppliers. CAx techniques and supporting hardware are an important part of reporting. Economic Engineering is thus required reading for all innovative engineers. Each issue of Economic

ngineering presents an industry special with echnology trends and future markets in the mobility ndustry or the machinery and equipment onstruction - broken down by various industries. igitalPlant is the English-language magazine in the ssue on IT strategies for the large plant construction nd operation of facilities.
anguage(s): English; German
eadership: Read by design engineers.
DVERTISING RATES:
ull Page Mono .... EUR 4125
ull Page Colour .... EUR 5595
Aechanical Data: Type Area: 265 x 185 mm
opy instructions: *Copy Date:* 21 days prior to ublication
USINESS: ENGINEERING & MACHINERY: CAD & IM (Computer Integrated Manufacture)

ECONOMY TRIBUNE 725903G1A-3494
Editorial: Timmerhellstr. 39, 45478 MÜLHEIM
el: 208 377080 **Fax:** 208 380077
mail: info@iwn-verlag.de **Web site:** http://www. wn-verlag.de
req: 6 issues yearly; **Annual Sub.:** EUR 28,00; **Circ:** 1,000
ditor: Stephen Smith
rofile: Magazine with information about companies, markets, technologies and innovations from industry, ade and services in Europe, the Far East and North merica.
anguage(s): English
Aechanical Data: Type Area: 266 x 184 mm, No. of olumns (Display): 4, Col Widths (Display): 43 mm

---

ECOREPORTER 2091391G1F-1870
Editorial: Weidenbohrerweg 15, 44269 DORTMUND
el: 231 47735960 **Fax:** 231 47735961
mail: info@ecoreporter.de **Web site:** http://www. coreporter.de
req: 3 issues yearly; **Cover Price:** EUR 6,80; **Circ:** 5,000
ditor: Jörg Weber; **Advertising Manager:** Hans-ürgen Fengler
rofile: The magazine offers current information bout stocks, mutual funds, certificates and other nvestment products with sustainable focus. acebook: http://www.facebook.com/ecoreporter.de witter: http://twitter.com/#!/ECOreporter.
anguage(s): German
DVERTISING RATES:
ull Page Mono .... EUR 2538
ull Page Colour .... EUR 2877
Mechanical Data: Type Area: 297 x 210 mm

ÉCOUTE 725908G88B-380
Editorial: Fraunhoferstr. 22, 82152 PLANEGG
el: 89 856810 **Fax:** 89 85681230
Email: ecoute@spotlight-verlag.de **Web site:** http:// www.ecoute.de
req: Monthly; **Annual Sub.:** EUR 107,40; **Circ:** 6,683
ditor: Karl Jetter; **Advertising Manager:** Axel Zettler
Profile: écoute, the magazine for lovers of France reported, exciting and full of variety of current issues and developments in France and the French-speaking world. With voltage, the Francophile readers expect every month the compelling features of the local correspondents on the latest news from politics, culture, music, literature and film as well as on atmospheric destinations such as Paris, the castles of the Loire, the Atlantic coast, Provence and the Cote d 'Azur. Finally, these are interesting portraits of personalities of the Grande Nation, and insights into the culinary delights of French cuisine - all mixed with a strong dash of savoir-vivre.
Language(s): French; German
ADVERTISING RATES:
Full Page Mono .... EUR 3429
Full Page Colour .... EUR 5715
Mechanical Data: Type Area: 246 x 186 mm, No. of Columns (Display): 4, Col Widths (Display): 43 mm
Copy instructions: *Copy Date:* 35 days prior to publication
CONSUMER: EDUCATION: Adult Education

ECO@WORK 737933G57-1620
Editorial: Merzhauser Str. 173, 79100 FREIBURG
Tel: 761 452950 **Fax:** 761 4529588
Email: redaktion@oeko.de **Web site:** http://www. oeko.de
Freq: Quarterly; **Circ:** 3,000
Editor: Mandy Schoßig; **Advertising Manager:** Romy Klupsch
Profile: Information from the Institute for Applied Ecology.
Language(s): German
Mechanical Data: Type Area: 260 x 180 mm
Copy instructions: *Copy Date:* 26 days prior to publication
BUSINESS: ENVIRONMENT & POLLUTION

EDITION PROFESSIONELL - AUSG. BAU 746014G4E-6894
Editorial: Im Ried 4, 79429 MALSBURG
Tel: 7626 977413 **Fax:** 7626 977419
Email: rolf.albrecht@ed-pro.de **Web site:** http:// www.ed-pro.de
Freq: Quarterly; **Annual Sub.:** EUR 19,00; **Circ:** 12,000
Editor: Rolf Albrecht; **Advertising Manager:** Chantal Albrecht
Profile: Magazine on external and internal house building.
Language(s): German
ADVERTISING RATES:
Full Page Mono .... EUR 2000
Full Page Colour .... EUR 3200
Mechanical Data: Type Area: 270 x 184 mm, No. of Columns (Display): 4, Col Widths (Display): 43 mm
Copy instructions: *Copy Date:* 10 days prior to publication

EDITION ÜBERBLICK NIEDERRHEIN GEHT AUS!
1927058G89A-12532
Editorial: Höherweg 287, 40231 DÜSSELDORF
Tel: 211 7357681 **Fax:** 211 7357680
Email: info@ueberblick.de **Web site:** http://www. ueberblick.de
Freq: Annual; **Cover Price:** EUR 6,80; **Circ:** 30,000
Editor: Konrad Schnabel; **Advertising Manager:** Andreas Huber
Profile: Gastronomy guide for the Lower Rhine region.
Language(s): German
ADVERTISING RATES:
Full Page Mono .... EUR 1790
Full Page Colour .... EUR 2630
Mechanical Data: Type Area: 260 x 190 mm, No. of Columns (Display): 4, Col Widths (Display): 44 mm

---

EDM EUROPEAN DAIRY MAGAZINE 725927G21G-2
Editorial: Maxstr. 64, 45127 ESSEN
Tel: 201 89425572 **Fax:** 209 89425573
Email: edm-dmw@th-mann.de **Web site:** http://www. th-mann.de
Freq: 6 issues yearly; **Annual Sub.:** EUR 70,00; **Circ:** 6,230
Editor: Sabine Tykfer-Büssing; **Advertising Manager:** Claudia Röllke-Skiebe
Profile: English-language trade journal for the areas of technology, product innovations, ice cream manufacturing, milk and agricultural policy, market trends, marketing and import and export in dairy and liquid food manufacturing industry.
Language(s): English
Readership: Aimed at milk processors, cheesemakers and ice-cream manufacturers in the European Union.
ADVERTISING RATES:
Full Page Mono .... EUR 2160
Full Page Colour .... EUR 3120
Mechanical Data: Type Area: 270 x 186 mm, No. of Columns (Display): 3, Col Widths (Display): 58 mm
Copy instructions: *Copy Date:* 22 days prior to publication
BUSINESS: AGRICULTURE & FARMING: Milk

EDM REPORT 1613991G14A-9421
Editorial: Havelstr. 9, 64295 DARMSTADT
Tel: 6151 380174 **Fax:** 6151 38099174
Email: graf@hoppenstedt.de **Web site:** http://www. hoppenstedt-zeitschriften.de
Freq: Quarterly; **Annual Sub.:** EUR 60,00; **Circ:** 14,470
Editor: Stefan Graf; **Advertising Manager:** Nadine Prieur
Profile: Magazine containing information about developments and trends of electronic data and documents management.
Language(s): German
ADVERTISING RATES:
Full Page Mono .... EUR 5808
Full Page Colour .... EUR 7728
Mechanical Data: Type Area: 252 x 175 mm, No. of Columns (Display): 3, Col Widths (Display): 55 mm
Copy instructions: *Copy Date:* 17 days prior to publication

EFA FORUM 1651737G14A-9610
Editorial: Mülheimer Str. 100, 47057 DUISBURG
Tel: 203 3787930 **Fax:** 203 3787944
Email: efa@efanrw.de **Web site:** http://www.efanrw. de
Freq: Quarterly; **Cover Price:** Free; **Circ:** 12,500
Editor: Ingo Menssen
Profile: Magazine about production integrated environmental protection.
Language(s): German

EFFECTEN SPIEGEL 1865502G1F-1750
Editorial: Tiergartenstr. 17, 40237 DÜSSELDORF
Tel: 211 683022
Web site: http://www.effecten-spiegel.de
Freq: Weekly; **Annual Sub.:** EUR 99,00; **Circ:** 80,000
Editor: Marion Czaja
Profile: Magazine about stocks and bonds.
Language(s): German

EFFILEE 1860307G74P-1267
Editorial: Rothenbaumchaussee 73, 20148 HAMBURG **Tel:** 40 80905380 **Fax:** 40 809053822
Email: info@effilee.de **Web site:** http://www.effilee. de
Freq: 6 issues yearly; **Annual Sub.:** EUR 39,90; **Circ:** 100,000
Editor: Peter Lau
Profile: Magazine for pleasure and food culture with recipes, book recommendations, profiles, interviews and competitions. Effilee deals on high quality and sensual way with the themes of food, nutrition, pleasure and sophisticated cuisine. It is a magazine for those who is for the good food more than a fashion: a valuable part of their lives. So you see the issue in-depth interviews with top chefs in addition to reports from foreign countries and complex gourmet recipes in addition to our fast dishes, simple but sophisticated dishes for everyday life. In Effilee Learn why it pays to eat in Iceland cakes, why Ouzo in Greece at best, tastes like you cooked at low temperature, which a shepherd feels when his sheep to the slaughter brings, and why not all bad, what the EU decides. Facebook: http://www.facebook.com/ pages/Effilee/65616880399.
Language(s): German
ADVERTISING RATES:
Full Page Mono .... EUR 8900
Full Page Colour .... EUR 8900
Mechanical Data: Type Area: 255 x 174 mm

EFFL EUROPEAN FOOD AND FEED LAW REVIEW 1828415G1A-3696
Editorial: Güntzelstr. 63, 10717 BERLIN
Tel: 30 8145060 **Fax:** 30 81450622
Email: effl@lexxion.de **Web site:** http://www.lexxion. de
Freq: 6 issues yearly; **Annual Sub.:** EUR 421,58; **Circ:** 500
Editor: Vivian Keßels
Profile: Journal offers a forum for jurisprudence led by experts in the field of food and feed law.
Language(s): English
ADVERTISING RATES:
Full Page Mono .... EUR 500
Mechanical Data: Type Area: 220 x 157 mm
Copy instructions: *Copy Date:* 21 days prior to publication

EFG ENTSCHEIDUNGEN DER FINANZGERICHTE 1976413G1A-3814
Editorial: Dechenstr. 7, 53115 BONN **Tel:** 228 7240
Fax: 228 72493033
Email: info@stollfuss.de **Web site:** http://www. efg-hfr.de
Freq: 24 issues yearly; **Circ:** 9,000
Editor: Jürgen Schmidt-Troje; **Advertising Manager:** Carsten Priesel
Profile: Jurisdiction collection to the entire tax law and tax advice law. Main topics: decisions of judges in financial courts are analyzed and commented.
Language(s): German
ADVERTISING RATES:
Full Page Mono .... EUR 1455
Full Page Colour .... EUR 2625
Mechanical Data: Type Area: 260 x 180 mm, No. of Columns (Display): 2, Col Widths (Display): 88 mm
Copy instructions: *Copy Date:* 21 days prior to publication

EGOVERNMENT COMPUTING
764177G5-4429
Editorial: August-Wessels-Str. 27, 86156 AUGSBURG **Tel:** 821 2177296 **Fax:** 821 217735296
Email: gerald.viola@vogel-it.de **Web site:** http:// www.egovernment-computing.de
Freq: 10 issues yearly; **Annual Sub.:** EUR 64,20; **Circ:** 17,120
Editor: Gerald Viola; **Advertising Manager:** Harald Czelnai
Profile: Information for IT decision makers in federal, state, municipal and public institutions on all relevant technical areas of digital information processing in the Public Sector Facebook: http:// www.facebook.com/pages/eGovernment-Computing/302304285014 Twitter: http://twitter.com/ #!/egovcomde This Outlet offers RSS (Really Simple Syndication).
Language(s): German
ADVERTISING RATES:
Full Page Colour .... EUR 8900
Mechanical Data: Type Area: 480 x 320 mm
Copy instructions: *Copy Date:* 14 days prior to publication
Supplement(s): eGovernment Computing Sources
BUSINESS: COMPUTERS & AUTOMATION

EHEMALIGENBRIEF ROTTHALMÜNSTER
725954G21A-1400
Editorial: 94094 ROTTHALMÜNSTER
Tel: 8533 960702 **Fax:** 8533 9607130
Freq: 3 issues yearly; **Circ:** 1,300
Editor: Georg Dietl
Profile: Magazine for members of the Association of Former Students from the Faculty of Agriculture.
Language(s): German

EHEMALIGENVERBAND SCHÖNBRUNN-WEIHENSTEPHAN MITTEILUNGEN 1614107G21A-4231
Editorial: Am Lurzenhof 3, 84036 LANDSHUT
Tel: 871 9521100 **Fax:** 871 9521102
Email: ehemaligenverb.scheller@freenet.de **Web site:** http://www.ehemaligenverband.de
Freq: Half-yearly; **Circ:** 2,000
Editor: Hans-Joachim Frey; **Advertising Manager:** Michaela Scheller
Profile: Magazine for former students from the faculties of agriculture and forestry, horticulture and ecological cultivation.
Language(s): German

EI DER EISENBAHNINGENIEUR
725971G49E-260
Editorial: Nordkanalstr. 36, 20097 HAMBURG
Tel: 40 23714281 **Fax:** 40 23714205
Email: jennifer.schykowski@dvvmedia.com **Web site:** http://www.eurailpress.de
Freq: Monthly; Free to qualifying individuals
Annual Sub.: EUR 132,00; **Circ:** 7,094
Editor: Jürgen Marx; **Advertising Manager:** Silke Härtel
Profile: Founded as a "Monatsschrift für deutsche Bahnmeister" is EI Der Eisenbahningenieur now one of the leading international journals for railways and railway engineering in German language. Above all, engineers, professionals and managers from transport companies, rail industry and engineering offices are here "from practice for practice" across the entire spectrum of modern railway technology (from the road to the vehicle) as well as innovative business management in long-distance and short-distance informed. With its regular sections, such as promotions, train-news and Industry Report, the magazine in addition to their readers is always a current overview of key industry events, on significant developments in European rail companies, as well as future-oriented products and services to the international railway industry. Information about activities of VDEI and news from the European Association UEEIV round off the comprehensive range of this journal.
Language(s): German
ADVERTISING RATES:
Full Page Mono .... EUR 3150
Full Page Colour .... EUR 4140
Mechanical Data: Type Area: 265 x 182 mm, No. of Columns (Display): 4, Col Widths (Display): 42 mm
Copy instructions: *Copy Date:* 20 days prior to publication
BUSINESS: TRANSPORT: Railways

EICHSTÄTTER KURIER
725968G67B-4540
Editorial: Stauffenbergstr. 2a, 85051 INGOLSTADT
Tel: 841 96660 **Fax:** 841 9666255
Email: redaktion@donaukurier.de **Web site:** http:// www.donaukurier.de
Freq: 312 issues yearly; **Circ:** 11,154
Advertising Manager: Hermann Fetsch
Profile: Daily newspaper with regional news and a local sports section. Facebook: http:// www.facebook.com/donaukurier.online Twitter: http://twitter.com/donaukurier This Outlet offers RSS (Really Simple Syndication).
Language(s): German
ADVERTISING RATES:
SCC .... EUR 29,70
Mechanical Data: Type Area: 435 x 282 mm, No. of Columns (Display): 6, Col Widths (Display): 45 mm
Copy instructions: *Copy Date:* 1 day prior to publication
REGIONAL DAILY & SUNDAY NEWSPAPERS: Regional Daily Newspapers

---

EID ENERGIE INFORMATIONSDIENST
726428G33-15
Editorial: Neue Burg 2, 20457 HAMBURG
Tel: 40 3037350 **Fax:** 40 30373535
Email: redaktion@eid.de **Web site:** http://www. eid-aktuell.de
Freq: Weekly; **Annual Sub.:** EUR 980,00; **Circ:** 992
Editor: Rainer Wiek; **Advertising Manager:** Heike Sauer
Profile: Energy information service for business and politics about mineral oil and natural gas. Independent information service for the energy industry. Always close to the market, he shows early on developments in the energy market. With its comprehensive, critical reporting and reliable pricing information it is essential for decision-makers from the energy sector, industry, government and politics. Highly appreciated by the readers is the range of topics of EID, which includes all energy sources.
Language(s): German
ADVERTISING RATES:
Full Page Colour .... EUR 2338
Mechanical Data: Type Area: 271 x 186 mm, No. of Columns (Display): 3, Col Widths (Display): 56 mm
Copy instructions: *Copy Date:* 7 days prior to publication
BUSINESS: OIL & PETROLEUM

EIDELSTEDTER WOCHENBLATT 725970G72-3404
Editorial: Harburger Rathausstr. 40, 21073 HAMBURG **Tel:** 40 85322933 **Fax:** 40 85322939
Email: post@wochenblatt-redaktion.de **Web site:** http://www.eidelstedter-wochenblatt.de
Freq: Weekly; **Cover Price:** Free; **Circ:** 45,876
Editor: Olaf Zimmermann; **Advertising Manager:** Jürgen Müller
Profile: Advertising journal (house-to-house) concentrating on local stories.
Language(s): German
ADVERTISING RATES:
Full Page Mono .... EUR 4257
Full Page Colour .... EUR 4377
Mechanical Data: Type Area: 430 x 282 mm, No. of Columns (Display): 6, Col Widths (Display): 45 mm

Germany

Copy instructions: *Copy Date:* 2 days prior to publication
Supplement(s): Elbe-Einkaufszentrum Aktuell
LOCAL NEWSPAPERS

EIER WILD GEFLÜGEL MARKT
725974G21F-2
Editorial: Am Flugplatz 7, 31137 HILDESHEIM
Tel: 5121 9187035 **Fax:** 5121 9187059
Email: info@wemcard.de **Web site:** http://www.wemcard.de
Freq: 102 issues yearly; **Annual Sub.:** EUR 372,00; **Circ:** 1,780
Editor: Daniela Zidek-Clages; **Advertising Manager:** Sven Böttcher
Profile: Magazine containing information about chicken, hens and egg-production.
Language(s): German
ADVERTISING RATES:
Full Page Mono .... EUR 1309
Full Page Colour .... EUR 1309
Mechanical Data: Type Area: 255 x 190 mm, No. of Columns (Display): 3, Col Widths (Display): 60 mm
Copy instructions: *Copy Date:* 7 days prior to publication
BUSINESS: AGRICULTURE & FARMING: Poultry

EIFELER NACHRICHTEN
725977G67B-4560
Editorial: Dresdener Str. 3, 52068 AACHEN
Tel: 241 5101310 **Fax:** 241 5101360
Email: redaktion@zeitungsverlag-aachen.de **Web site:** http://www.an-online.de
Freq: 312 issues yearly; **Circ:** 45,364
Advertising Manager: Christian Kretschmer
Profile: Daily newspaper with regional news and a local sports section. Facebook: http://facebook.com/aachenernachrichten This Outlet offers RSS (Really Simple Syndication).
Language(s): German
ADVERTISING RATES:
SCC .... EUR 118,80
Mechanical Data: Type Area: 480 x 324 mm, No. of Columns (Display): 7, Col Widths (Display): 44 mm
Copy instructions: *Copy Date:* 1 day prior to publication
Supplement(s): prisma
REGIONAL DAILY & SUNDAY NEWSPAPERS: Regional Daily Newspapers

EIFELER ZEITUNG
725978G67B-4580
Editorial: Dresdener Str. 3, 52068 AACHEN
Tel: 241 5101310 **Fax:** 241 5101360
Email: redaktion@zeitungsverlag-aachen.de **Web site:** http://www.aachener-zeitung.de
Freq: 312 issues yearly; **Circ:** 45,364
Advertising Manager: Christian Kretschmer
Profile: Daily newspaper with regional news and a local sports section. Facebook: http://facebook.com/aachenerzeitung This Outlet offers RSS (Really Simple Syndication).
Language(s): German
ADVERTISING RATES:
SCC .... EUR 118,80
Mechanical Data: Type Area: 480 x 324 mm, No. of Columns (Display): 7, Col Widths (Display): 44 mm
Copy instructions: *Copy Date:* 1 day prior to publication
Supplement(s): prisma
REGIONAL DAILY & SUNDAY NEWSPAPERS: Regional Daily Newspapers

EIK EISENBAHN INGENIEUR KALENDER
726066G49E-280
Editorial: Nordkanalstr. 36, 20097 HAMBURG
Tel: 40 23714152 **Fax:** 40 23714205
Email: christoph.mueller@dvvmedia.com **Web site:** http://www.eurailpress.de
Freq: Annual; **Cover Price:** EUR 39,00; **Circ:** 6,189
Editor: Peter Schill; **Advertising Manager:** Silke Härtel
Profile: Annual on railway transport and technology.
Language(s): German
ADVERTISING RATES:
Full Page Mono .... EUR 1510
Full Page Colour .... EUR 2500
Mechanical Data: Type Area: 176 x 122 mm
Copy instructions: *Copy Date:* 60 days prior to publication
BUSINESS: TRANSPORT: Railways

EILBOTE
725985G21E-2
Editorial: Winsener Landstr. 7, 21423 WINSEN
Tel: 4171 78350 **Fax:** 4171 783535
Email: redaktion@eilbote-online.de **Web site:** http://www.eilbote-online.de
Freq: Weekly; **Annual Sub.:** EUR 93,73; **Circ:** 6,594
Editor: Jürgen Boomgaarden; **Advertising Manager:** Dagmar Michel
Profile: The only weekly magazine for agricultural machinery trade and handicraft, machinery departments of the cooperatives, agricultural engineering forging plants, garden, municipal and forestry trade and motorists as well as agricultural machinery manufacturers and their factory representatives, agricultural machinery wholesale, agricultural machinery importers and agricultural engineering contractors. The Eilbote is rightly known as the fastest medium in its industry. News on the agricultural machinery sector, the reader experiences within a short period. Problems of the craft are also brought to the language, such as tax and economic issues.
Language(s): German
Readership: Aimed at manufacturers, importers, wholesalers and retailers of agricultural machinery and engineers.
ADVERTISING RATES:
Full Page Mono .... EUR 2819
Full Page Colour .... EUR 3479
Mechanical Data: Type Area: 270 x 192 mm, No. of Columns (Display): 4, Col Widths (Display): 45 mm
Copy instructions: *Copy Date:* 7 days prior to publication
BUSINESS: AGRICULTURE & FARMING: Agriculture - Machinery & Plant

EIN HERZ FÜR TIERE
730177G81A-50
Editorial: Münchener Str. 101, 85737 ISMANING
Tel: 89 272707511 **Fax:** 89 272707590
Email: redaktion@herz-fuer-tiere.de **Web site:** http://www.herz-fuer-tiere.de
Freq: Monthly; **Annual Sub.:** EUR 25,80; **Circ:** 73,005
Editor: Ursula Birr
Profile: In "EIN HERZ FÜR TIERE" everything revolves around the animal. "EIN HERZ FÜR TIERE" is number 1 when it comes to questions and answers about the pet and animal keeping. With the highest expertise, quite critical, never negative, "EIN HERZ FÜR TIERE" makes desire for animals, is determined to animals and accompanies the pet owner through his "animal" life. EIN HERZ FÜR TIERE is made for all large and small pet owners and pet friends. With a modern, clean appearance, which presents the information professional, and a balanced mix of topics, the magazine appeals to the whole family. "EIN HERZ FÜR TIERE" informs about news from the animal world, from pet research, science and veterinary medicine. Practical tips on handling, housing, education, health and care of the most popular housemates are to be found in the service section. Travel Tips, trips to zoos and wildlife parks, events and information from the wildlife scene and TV highlights of the month, complete the service section. Facebook: http://www.facebook.com/EinHerzfuerTiere.
Language(s): German
Readership: Mainly read by families with children.
ADVERTISING RATES:
Full Page Mono .... EUR 7000
Full Page Colour .... EUR 10800
Mechanical Data: Type Area: 267 x 180 mm, No. of Columns (Display): 4, Col Widths (Display): 42 mm
Copy instructions: *Copy Date:* 35 days prior to publication
CONSUMER: ANIMALS & PETS: Animals & Pets Protection

EINBECKER MORGENPOST
725993G67B-4600
Editorial: Marktplatz 12, 37574 EINBECK
Tel: 5561 4002 **Fax:** 5561 73383
Email: redaktion@einbecker-morgenpost.de **Web site:** http://www.einbecker-morgenpost.de
Freq: 312 issues yearly; **Annual Sub.:** EUR 13,25; **Circ:** 9,320
Editor: Edith Kondziella; **Advertising Manager:** Jürgen Rüttgerodt
Profile: For a well informed start to make your day, that is the goal of Einbecker Morgenpost, the newspaper for the area Einbeck/Dassel. Founded in 1810, has headed the family Rüttgerodt half the time the publishing house with the readers close principle Morgenpost read - been there! Twitter: http://twitter.com/einmorgenpost This Outlet offers RSS (Really Simple Syndication).
Language(s): German
ADVERTISING RATES:
SCC .... EUR 22,80
Mechanical Data: Type Area: 425 x 281 mm, No. of Columns (Display): 6, Col Widths (Display): 45 mm
Copy instructions: *Copy Date:* 1 day prior to publication
REGIONAL DAILY & SUNDAY NEWSPAPERS: Regional Daily Newspapers

EINBLICK
725996G14L-1700
Editorial: Wallstr. 60, 10179 BERLIN **Tel:** 30 3088240
Fax: 30 30882420
Email: redaktion@einblick.info **Web site:** http://www.einblick.dgb.de
Freq: 24 issues yearly; **Cover Price:** Free; **Circ:** 12,153
Editor: Anne Graef
Profile: einblick provides information on trade union-related policy issues and introduces services and offers from trade unions and trade union facilities.
Language(s): German
Readership: Read by active trade union members and officials of local authorities.
ADVERTISING RATES:
Full Page Mono .... EUR 2547
Full Page Colour .... EUR 3081
Mechanical Data: Type Area: 277 x 190 mm
BUSINESS: COMMERCE, INDUSTRY & MANAGEMENT: Trade Unions

EINFACH GUT GRILLEN
1935309G74P-1317
Editorial: Ruhrtalstr. 67, 45239 ESSEN
Tel: 201 24688222 **Fax:** 201 24688140
Email: k.franz@stegenwaller.de **Web site:** http://www.stegenwaller.de
Freq: Annual; **Cover Price:** EUR 2,30; **Circ:** 210,000
Editor: Kerstin Franz; **Advertising Manager:** Oliver Schulte
Profile: Einfach Gut Grillen in a practical pocket format offers great recipes, tips and tricks for the summer barbecue and make for an unforgettable experience. Not only salads and delicious meat dishes are the focus here, even dips, appetizers, desserts, cocktails and ice do not miss out.
Language(s): German
ADVERTISING RATES:
Full Page Mono .... EUR 4500
Full Page Colour .... EUR 4500
Mechanical Data: Type Area: 237 x 196 mm

EINFACH GUT KOCHEN
1935310G74P-1318
Editorial: Ruhrtalstr. 67, 45239 ESSEN
Tel: 201 24688222 **Fax:** 201 24688140
Email: k.franz@stegenwaller.de **Web site:** http://www.stegenwaller.de
Freq: Quarterly; **Cover Price:** EUR 1,99; **Circ:** 28,713
Editor: Kerstin Franz; **Advertising Manager:** Oliver Schulte
Profile: Magazine with recipes. The 144 pages include classic dishes with lots of tips, tricks and information about cooking topic. A simple system explains the difficulty levels of the respective recipes. But enthusiasm is not just recipes, and detailed product knowledge, advice and product round the friendly food magazine from skillfully. In addition to delicious meat, pasta and fish dishes and seasonal culinary highlights in detail. Finally, even sweet desserts are presented.
Language(s): German
ADVERTISING RATES:
Full Page Mono .... EUR 4500
Full Page Colour .... EUR 4500
Mechanical Data: Type Area: 237 x 196 mm
Copy instructions: *Copy Date:* 21 days prior to publication

DAS EINFAMILIEN HAUS
1609481G74C-3498
Editorial: Schwanthalerstr. 10, 80336 MÜNCHEN
Tel: 89 59908111 **Fax:** 89 59908133
Email: redaktion@cpz.de **Web site:** http://www.bau-welt.de
Freq: 6 issues yearly; **Annual Sub.:** EUR 17,40; **Circ:** 56,975
Editor: Claudia Mannschott; **Advertising Manager:** Sebastian Schmidt
Profile: Magazine containing information for private house builders.
Language(s): German
ADVERTISING RATES:
Full Page Mono .... EUR 6440
Full Page Colour .... EUR 9200
Mechanical Data: Type Area: 270 x 180 mm, No. of Columns (Display): 4, Col Widths (Display): 42 mm
Copy instructions: *Copy Date:* 40 days prior to publication
Supplement(s): Bäder & Küchen; Dach, Wand & Boden; Erneuerbare Energien; Fenster, Türen & Garagentore; Heizung & Energiesparen; Smart Wohnen: Haustechnik & Sicherheit
CONSUMER: WOMEN'S INTEREST CONSUMER MAGAZINES: Home & Family

EINIGKEIT
726024G47A-1617
Editorial: Haubachstr. 76, 22765 HAMBURG
Tel: 40 38013155 **Fax:** 40 38013220
Email: hv.redaktion@ngg.net **Web site:** http://www.ngg.net
Freq: 6 issues yearly; **Circ:** 202,000
Editor: Silvia Tewes
Profile: For our members six times a year the publication of „einigkeit". In einigkeit we find out about our projects, our positions on current issues, the situation in the NGG-industries, etc.
Language(s): German
BUSINESS: CLOTHING & TEXTILES

E-INSTALLATION
726041G17-160
Editorial: Nägelsbachstr. 33, 91052 ERLANGEN
Tel: 9131 9192501 **Fax:** 9131 9192594
Email: publishing-magazines@publicis-erlangen.de
Web site: http://www.publicis-erlangen.de
Freq: 3 issues yearly; **Cover Price:** Free; **Circ:** 21,000
Editor: Robert Engelhardt
Profile: Magazine about innovative products and systems about electro installation technologies.
Language(s): German

EINSTEIGER
1638930G14A-9573
Editorial: Universitätsallee 18, 28359 BREMEN
Tel: 421 94990120 **Fax:** 421 94991019
Email: einsteiger@bvl-campus.de **Web site:** http://www.dav-einsteiger.de
Freq: Annual; **Circ:** 1,500
Profile: Students' magazine.
Language(s): German

EISENBAHN JOURNAL
726067G79J-50
Editorial: Am Fohlenhof 9a, 82256 FÜRSTENFELDBRUCK **Tel:** 8141 5348118
Fax: 8141 5348133
Email: redaktion@eisenbahn-journal.de **Web site:** http://www.eisenbahn-journal.de
Freq: Monthly; **Annual Sub.:** EUR 78,00; **Circ:** 10,847
Editor: Gerhard Zimmermann; **Advertising Manager:** Elke Albrecht
Profile: The Eisenbahn Journal ... has enjoyed three decades of the excellent reputation of a high-profile special-interest-sheet for railway enthusiasts and model railroaders; ... convinces with first class researched, technically sound contributions from renowned experts and experienced model model train professionals, ... has traditionally fostered strong ties with a sophisticated and affluent audience, ... combines informative articles in a sophisticated language with excellent illustrations in recognition of high quality; ... applies in the high-profile retailers as an image carrier with a very sales-and revenue-enhancing effect, ... sees itself as a continuously updated reference work of all the new items in the model train and accessories industry, ... wants to impart knowledge, inspire, and help maintain, if it involved one of the most interesting hobby you go.
Language(s): German
ADVERTISING RATES:
Full Page Mono .... EUR 1500
Full Page Colour .... EUR 1990
Mechanical Data: Type Area: 268 x 180 mm
Copy instructions: *Copy Date:* 28 days prior to publication
CONSUMER: HOBBIES & DIY: Rail Enthusiasts

EISENBAHN KURIER
726070G49E-990
Editorial: Lörracher Str. 16, 79115 FREIBURG
Tel: 761 703100 **Fax:** 761 7031053
Email: redaktion@eisenbahn-kurier.de **Web site:** http://www.eisenbahn-kurier.de
Freq: Monthly; **Annual Sub.:** EUR 84,00; **Circ:** 40,080
Editor: Thomas Frister; **Advertising Manager:** Waltraud Gänßmantel
Profile: For over 40 years is Eisenbahn Kurier one of Germany's leading special-interest magazines about railway. In the EK model part transport policy concepts, vehicles and systems as well as critical articles will published. So the Eisenbahn Kurier comes as a mediator between the decision makers from government, industry and railway the general public a long-recognized importance. In the model part news, innovations, technology and design with high-quality recordings will be presented at a demanding level.
Language(s): German
ADVERTISING RATES:
Full Page Mono .... EUR 1890
Full Page Colour .... EUR 2550
Mechanical Data: Type Area: 249 x 187 mm, No. of Columns (Display): 4, Col Widths (Display): 44 mm
Copy instructions: *Copy Date:* 28 days prior to publication
BUSINESS: TRANSPORT: Railways

EISENBAHN MODELLBAHN MAGAZIN
726074G49E-995
Editorial: Willstätterstr. 9, 40549 DÜSSELDORF
Tel: 211 5201334 **Fax:** 211 5201328
Email: em@alba-verlag.de **Web site:** http://www.alba-verlag.de
Freq: Monthly; **Annual Sub.:** EUR 72,00; **Circ:** 21,201
Editor: Jan Asshauer; **Advertising Manager:** Robert A. Braun
Profile: Publication for all railway and model railway enthusiasts.
Language(s): German
ADVERTISING RATES:
Full Page Mono .... EUR 2700
Full Page Colour .... EUR 3610
Mechanical Data: Type Area: 255 x 191 mm, No. of Columns (Display): 4, Col Widths (Display): 45 mm
Copy instructions: *Copy Date:* 18 days prior to publication
Official Journal of: Organ d. Bundesverb. Dt. Eisenbahn-Freunde e.V. u. d. Verb. Dt. Museums- u. Touristikbahnen e.V.
BUSINESS: TRANSPORT: Railways

EISENBAHN-LANDWIRT
726073G93-160
Editorial: Kurt-Georg-Kiesinger-Allee 2, 53175 BONN
Tel: 228 3077225 **Fax:** 228 30775225
Email: hauptverband@blw-aktuell.de **Web site:** http://www.blw-aktuell.de
Freq: Monthly; Free to qualifying individuals
Annual Sub.: EUR 8,20; **Circ:** 76,802
Editor: Andree Runne; **Advertising Manager:** Christine Krückl
Profile: The journal "Eisenbahn-Landwirt" is the official journal of the Hauptverband der Bahn-Landwirtschaft. It is the oldest German gardening magazine and is published once a month.
Language(s): German
ADVERTISING RATES:
Full Page Mono .... EUR 3643
Full Page Colour .... EUR 6922
Mechanical Data: Type Area: 253 x 190 mm, No. of Columns (Display): 4, Col Widths (Display): 45 mm
Copy instructions: *Copy Date:* 21 days prior to publication
CONSUMER: GARDENING

EKO AKTUELL
726097G27-620
Editorial: Werkstr. 1, 15890 EISENHÜTTENSTADT
Tel: 3364 372460 **Fax:** 3364 37652460
Email: ramona.behrend@arcelormittal.com **Web site:** http://www.arcelormittal.com/eisenhuettenstadt
Freq: Quarterly; **Circ:** 5,000
Editor: Ramona Behrend
Profile: Magazine for employees of Arcelor Eisenhüttenstadt GmbH.
Language(s): German

EL INFO ELEKTRONIK INFORMATIONEN 726144G18A-226

Editorial: Eversbuschstr. 134, 80999 MÜNCHEN
Tel: 89 54884291 **Fax:** 89 54884299
Email: laasch@at-fachverlag.de **Web site:** http://www.el-info.de
Freq: Monthly; **Annual Sub.:** EUR 62,00; **Circ:** 27,679
Editor: Matthias Laasch; **Advertising Manager:** Norbert Schöne
Profile: EL info Elektronik Informationen is a monthly journal for the development, design-in, design and application of electronic products used in industrial environments. The target group is the developer and all in the development and marketing of a product people involved primarily with technical background. About 75% of the consistently unnamed readers work in the electronics, electrical engineering, telecommunications, automotive and mechanical engineering. According to the information needs of modern industrial society and the understanding of EL info Elektronik Informationen, the magazine, the reader able to obtain information quickly and comprehensively to the relevant news from the world of hardware and software in an intelligible form.
Language(s): German
ADVERTISING RATES:
Full Page Mono .... EUR 5310
Full Page Colour .... EUR 6510
Mechanical Data: Type Area: 264 x 185 mm, No. of Columns (Display): 4, Col Widths (Display): 43 mm
BUSINESS: ELECTRONICS

ELBE-ELSTER WOCHENKURIER - AUSG. BAD LIEBENWERDA 721744G72-1656

Editorial: Markt 16, 04924 BAD LIEBENWERDA
Tel: 35341 64212 **Fax:** 35341 9385
Email: kerstintwarok@cwk-verlag.de **Web site:** http://www.wochenkurier.info
Freq: Weekly; **Cover Price:** Free; **Circ:** 21,130
Editor: Kerstin Twarok; **Advertising Manager:** Uwe Peschel
Profile: Advertising journal (house-to-house) concentrating on local stories.
Language(s): German
ADVERTISING RATES:
Full Page Mono .... EUR 2439
Full Page Colour .... EUR 3414
Mechanical Data: Type Area: 430 x 290 mm, No. of Columns (Display): 7, Col Widths (Display): 38 mm
Copy instructions: *Copy Date:* 3 days prior to publication
LOCAL NEWSPAPERS

ELBE-ELSTER WOCHENKURIER - AUSG. FINSTERWALDE 727385G72-3868

Editorial: Leipziger Str. 52, 03238 FINSTERWALDE
Tel: 3531 717812 **Fax:** 3531 717820
Email: kerstintwarok@cwk-verlag.de **Web site:** http://www.wochenkurier.info
Freq: Weekly; **Cover Price:** Free; **Circ:** 21,297
Editor: Kerstin Twarok; **Advertising Manager:** Uwe Peschel
Profile: Advertising journal (house-to-house) concentrating on local stories.
Language(s): German
ADVERTISING RATES:
Full Page Mono .... EUR 2439
Full Page Colour .... EUR 3414
Mechanical Data: Type Area: 430 x 290 mm, No. of Columns (Display): 7, Col Widths (Display): 38 mm
Copy instructions: *Copy Date:* 6 days prior to publication
LOCAL NEWSPAPERS

ELBE-ELSTER WOCHENKURIER - AUSG. HERZBERG 730172G72-5472

Editorial: Markt 16, 04924 BAD LIEBENWERDA
Tel: 35341 64212 **Fax:** 35341 9385
Email: kerstintwarok@cwk-verlag.de **Web site:** http://www.wochenkurier.info
Freq: Weekly; **Cover Price:** Free; **Circ:** 14,318
Editor: Kerstin Twarok; **Advertising Manager:** Uwe Peschel
Profile: Advertising journal (house-to-house) concentrating on local stories.
Language(s): German
ADVERTISING RATES:
Full Page Mono .... EUR 2077
Full Page Colour .... EUR 2908
Mechanical Data: Type Area: 430 x 290 mm, No. of Columns (Display): 7, Col Widths (Display): 38 mm
Copy instructions: *Copy Date:* 6 days prior to publication
LOCAL NEWSPAPERS

ELBE-ELSTER-LAND REISEJOURNAL 1795350G89A-12289

Editorial: Markt 20, 04924 BAD LIEBENWERDA
Tel: 35341 30652 **Fax:** 35341 12672
Email: info@elbe-elster-land.de **Web site:** http://www.elbe-elster-land.de
Freq: Annual; **Cover Price:** Free; **Circ:** 30,000
Profile: Lots of tips for the holiday and leisure time are the new "Elbe-Elster-Land Reisejournal". Cycling, Industrial Heritage, Culture & History, Land & Natural and Fit & Active are the issues over which the brochure important contact information and information for vacation planning holds locally.
Language(s): German

ELBE-JEETZEL-ZEITUNG 726107G67B-4640

Editorial: Wallstr. 22, 29439 LÜCHOW
Tel: 5841 1270 **Fax:** 5841 127380
Email: redaktion@ejz.de **Web site:** http://www.ejz.de
Freq: 312 issues yearly; **Circ:** 12,264
Editor: Hans-Hermann Müller; **Advertising Manager:** Thorsten-Eik Schrader
Profile: Daily newspaper with regional news and a local sports section. This Outlet offers RSS (Really Simple Syndication).
Language(s): German
ADVERTISING RATES:
SCC .... EUR 41,20
Mechanical Data: Type Area: 435 x 282 mm, No. of Columns (Display): 6, Col Widths (Display): 45 mm
Copy instructions: *Copy Date:* 1 day prior to publication
REGIONAL DAILY & SUNDAY NEWSPAPERS: Regional Daily Newspapers

ELBVORORTE WOCHENBLATT 726118G72-3488

Editorial: Harburger Rathausstr. 40, 21073 HAMBURG **Tel:** 40 85322933 **Fax:** 40 85322939
Email: post@wochenblatt-redaktion.de **Web site:** http://www.elbvororte-wochenblatt.de
Freq: Weekly; **Cover Price:** Free; **Circ:** 46,294
Editor: Olaf Zimmermann; **Advertising Manager:** Jürgen Müller
Profile: Advertising journal (house-to-house) concentrating on local stories.
Language(s): German
ADVERTISING RATES:
Full Page Mono .... EUR 4412
Full Page Colour .... EUR 4532
Mechanical Data: Type Area: 430 x 282 mm, No. of Columns (Display): 6, Col Widths (Display): 45 mm
Copy instructions: *Copy Date:* 2 days prior to publication
Supplement(s): Elbe-Einkaufszentrum Aktuell
LOCAL NEWSPAPERS

ELDE EXPRESS 726120G72-3492

Editorial: Ziegenmarkt 10a, 19370 PARCHIM
Tel: 3871 622081818 **Fax:** 3871 62208185
Email: illa@svz.de
Freq: Weekly; **Cover Price:** Free; **Circ:** 28,292
Editor: Ilona Langer; **Advertising Manager:** Dagmar Albertsen
Profile: Advertising journal (house-to-house) concentrating on local stories.
Language(s): German
ADVERTISING RATES:
Full Page Mono .... EUR 2386
Full Page Colour .... EUR 3092
Mechanical Data: Type Area: 480 x 325 mm, No. of Columns (Display): 7, Col Widths (Display): 45 mm
Copy instructions: *Copy Date:* 3 days prior to publication
LOCAL NEWSPAPERS

ELECTROANALYSIS 1655857G37-1803

Editorial: Boschstr. 12, 69469 WEINHEIM
Tel: 6201 6060 **Fax:** 6201 606203
Email: stm-journals@wiley-vch.de **Web site:** http://www.wiley-vch.de
Freq: Monthly; **Annual Sub.:** EUR 3445,00; **Circ:** 1,000
Editor: Joseph Wang; **Advertising Manager:** Marion Schulz
Profile: International journal covering all branches of electroanalytical chemistry.
Language(s): English
ADVERTISING RATES:
Full Page Mono .... EUR 1200
Full Page Colour .... EUR 2200
Mechanical Data: Type Area: 260 x 180 mm
Copy instructions: *Copy Date:* 28 days prior to publication

ELEKTOR 726129G18A-223

Editorial: Süsterfeldstr. 25, 52072 AACHEN
Tel: 241 889090 **Fax:** 241 8890977
Email: redaktion@elektor.de **Web site:** http://www.elektor.de
Freq: 11 issues yearly; **Annual Sub.:** EUR 77,50; **Circ:** 22,590
Editor: Ernst Krempelsauer
Profile: The international electronics magazine Elektor aimed at the target group of electronics and computers interested reader with qualified expertise in the field of electronics and computer technology and the need for sound scientific information for both the professional and the private electronic application. The magazine provides modern electronics and technical computer science through the publication replica safe, professionally-designed circuits and provides information on technological and market-related developments as well as of other products and techniques.
Language(s): German
ADVERTISING RATES:
Full Page Mono .... EUR 3325
Full Page Colour .... EUR 4516
Mechanical Data: Type Area: 265 x 185 mm, No. of Columns (Display): 4, Col Widths (Display): 43 mm
Copy instructions: *Copy Date:* 28 days prior to publication
BUSINESS: ELECTRONICS

ELEKTRO AUTOMATION 726130G17-220

Editorial: Ernst-Mey-Str. 8, 70771 LEINFELDEN-ECHTERDINGEN **Tel:** 711 7594417
Fax: 711 7594221
Email: ea.redaktion@konradin.de **Web site:** http://www.wir-automatisierer.de
Freq: 10 issues yearly; **Annual Sub.:** EUR 69,50; **Circ:** 18,036
Editor: Stefan Ziegler; **Advertising Manager:** Andreas Hugel
Profile: Reader benefits: The maximum information concerning products and processes for electrical automation technology. Needs based - for strategic investment decisions and solutions to technical production problems - divided into clear editorial sections for market, trends, news and practice. Supplemented by informative online activities (eg. expert forum) and events (including the Automation Award). Expert reporting on the following themes: Drive systems, automation software, image processing, data communication, industrial computing (software and hardware), interface technology and systems components, measurement technology and sensors, safety systems as well as control technology. Targets readers who are specialists and managers across industry divisions in positions such as design/development, systems planning, production management in addition to senior technical management. Twitter: http://twitter.com/elektroAUTOMATI.
Language(s): German
Readership: Read by managers and engineers in the electronics and auto electrics industry.
ADVERTISING RATES:
Full Page Mono .... EUR 4790
Full Page Colour .... EUR 5880
Mechanical Data: Type Area: 270 x 188 mm, No. of Columns (Display): 4, Col Widths (Display): 44 mm
BUSINESS: ELECTRICAL

DER ELEKTRO FACHMANN 726134G17-260

Editorial: Wilhelminenhofstr. 75, 12459 BERLIN
Tel: 30 8595580 **Fax:** 30 85955888
Email: mail@eh-bb.de
Freq: 9 issues yearly; Free to qualifying individuals
Annual Sub.: EUR 70,50; **Circ:** 2,933
Editor: Constantin Rehlinger; **Advertising Manager:** Michael Dietl
Profile: Journal of the Guild of Electricians in Berlin.
Language(s): German
ADVERTISING RATES:
Full Page Mono .... EUR 1320
Full Page Colour .... EUR 2055
Mechanical Data: Type Area: 256 x 184 mm, No. of Columns (Display): 4, Col Widths (Display): 43 mm
Official Journal of: Organ d. Elektro-Innung Berlin u. d. Landesinnungsverb. Elektrotechn. Handwerke Berlin/Brandenburg
BUSINESS: ELECTRICAL

ELEKTRO MODELL 726139G79B-440

Editorial: Klosterring 1, 78050 VILLINGEN-SCHWENNINGEN **Tel:** 7721 89870 **Fax:** 7721 898750
Email: mueller@neckar-verlag.de **Web site:** http://www.neckar-verlag.de
Freq: Quarterly; **Annual Sub.:** EUR 35,00; **Circ:** 16,900
Editor: Ralph Müller; **Advertising Manager:** Klaus Pechmann
Profile: Magazine about electronic, radio-controlled models of aeroplanes.
Language(s): German
Readership: Aimed at people interested in electro flying.
CONSUMER: HOBBIES & DIY: Models & Modelling

ELEKTRO WIRTSCHAFT 726152G43A-400

Editorial: Siegburgstr. 5, 44359 DORTMUND
Tel: 231 33690 **Fax:** 231 336920
Email: redaktion@elektrowirtschaft.de **Web site:** http://www.elektrowirtschaft.de
Freq: Monthly; **Annual Sub.:** EUR 62,00; **Circ:** 5,886
Editor: Gudrun Arnold-Schoenen; **Advertising Manager:** Silke Triebsch
Profile: The entrepreneurs and executives in the electrical wholesalers read their association magazine understandably very hard and dedicate their time more than they can afford the large number of journals in general. The editorial objective of her turns, the „Elektro Wirtschaft" more aware of the merchant as to the technicians in the factories. It thus differs from the majority of the remaining, mostly technically oriented journals in the industry. The „Elektro Wirtschaft", so to speak especially to those persons who seek to reach the seller, because he is largely responsible for the important business deals. Favorite subjects are therefore strong economic accented reports on new equipment, products and processes, detailed reports on trade fairs and exhibitions, short reports and annual reports from the electrical industry, white papers, insightful statistics, history, etc. In almost every issue forward board and management of associations referred to the electrical wholesalers useful suggestions, comments and opinions on current market issues, the situation in specific subject areas or even individual devices and products.
Language(s): German
Readership: Aimed at professionals in the electrical industry.
ADVERTISING RATES:
Full Page Mono .... EUR 2015
Full Page Colour .... EUR 2690
Mechanical Data: Type Area: 262 x 184 mm
Copy instructions: *Copy Date:* 14 days prior to publication
Official Journal of: Organ d. Bundesverb. d. Elektro-Grosshandels e.V.
BUSINESS: ELECTRICAL RETAIL TRADE

ELEKTROBÖRSE HANDEL 726132G43A-420

Editorial: Hinterer Floßanger 10, 96450 COBURG
Tel: 9561 649128 **Fax:** 9561 6180
Email: thess@wekanet.de **Web site:** http://www.elektroboerse-online.de
Freq: Monthly; **Annual Sub.:** EUR 50,00; **Circ:** 16,544
Editor: Tanja Heß; **Advertising Manager:** Fred Friedrich
Profile: elektrobörse Handel provides the electrical retailers with a comprehensive overview on all relevant issues. Review articles on electrical small and large appliances are complemented by interviews and company reports useful. Information on fairs and events co-found as well as practical advice on trends and activities in and for the retailers. Light and many special topics, such as batteries, rechargeable batteries, chargers, round out the magazine. Background and knowledge base across our high quality service contributions to the legal and tax issues, advertising, marketing and organization.
Language(s): German
ADVERTISING RATES:
Full Page Mono .... EUR 3970
Full Page Colour .... EUR 5730
Mechanical Data: Type Area: 260 x 184 mm, No. of Columns (Display): 4, Col Widths (Display): 43 mm
Copy instructions: *Copy Date:* 21 days prior to publication
BUSINESS: ELECTRICAL RETAIL TRADE

ELEKTROBÖRSE SMARTHOUSE 1638973G17-1555

Editorial: Hinterer Floßanger 10, 96450 COBURG
Tel: 9561 649128 **Fax:** 9561 6180
Email: tjungmann@wekanet.de **Web site:** http://www.elektroboerse-online.de
Freq: Monthly; **Annual Sub.:** EUR 50,00; **Circ:** 25,467
Editor: Thomas Jungmann; **Advertising Manager:** Fred Friedrich
Profile: Industry news for the electrical trade. With extensive information and expert coverage of all facets of the (electrical) building services, electrical installation, light technical and renewable energy sources (solar and heat pumps).
Language(s): German
ADVERTISING RATES:
Full Page Mono .... EUR 4260
Full Page Colour .... EUR 6325
Mechanical Data: Type Area: 260 x 184 mm, No. of Columns (Display): 4, Col Widths (Display): 43 mm
Copy instructions: *Copy Date:* 21 days prior to publication
BUSINESS: ELECTRICAL

ELEKTROFACHKRAFT.DE 1833125G17-1611

Editorial: Römerstr. 4, 86438 KISSING
Tel: 8233 237088 **Fax:** 8233 2357088
Email: oliver.bresch@weka.de **Web site:** http://www.elektrofachkraft.de
Freq: Quarterly; **Annual Sub.:** EUR 24,90; **Circ:** 20,120
Editor: Oliver Bresch; **Advertising Manager:** Stephan-Andreas Schaefer
Profile: Magazine for professionals and executives in the fields of electrical engineering and electrical maintenance. elektrofachkraft.de is the magazine for all professional occupations on electrical engineering and electrical safety. The Journal provides extensive information on the subject audit, regulations, liability, installation work, hazards / risk, skills, EMI / EMC and organization.
Language(s): German
ADVERTISING RATES:
Full Page Mono .... EUR 2600
Full Page Colour .... EUR 3380
Mechanical Data: Type Area: 325 x 230 mm, No. of Columns (Display): 4, Col Widths (Display): 54 mm
Copy instructions: *Copy Date:* 20 days prior to publication

ELEKTROMARKT 726138G43A-380

Editorial: Franz-Ludwig-Str. 7a, 96047 BAMBERG
Tel: 951 861115 **Fax:** 951 861158
Email: elektromarkt@meisenbach.de **Web site:** http://www.elektromarkt.de
Freq: 10 issues yearly; **Annual Sub.:** EUR 52,00; **Circ:** 16,339
Editor: Matthias M. Machan; **Advertising Manager:** Dominik Lippold
Profile: Elektromarkt, the trade magazine for electrical goods, is the business motor for trade and industry. Appearing for over 90 years, this publication features the top issues that move the electrical goods sector. With the concentrated power of electrical goods and kitchenware, it is the ideal companion for anyone trading in electrical goods. It is professional, opinion-forming and informative. Three main sections help our readers to find their bearings quickly and easily, providing them with a rounded insight into this dynamic sector: „Handel & Praxis" spotlights the sector's bestselling products, whilst shedding light on international concepts and original marketing ideas presented by the specialist retail trade. The focus also falls on industry-related politics and strategies, the activities of buying groups and trade partnerships as well as plenty of intelligent ideas for retailers. „Sortiment & Tiefe" takes an in-depth look at a broad

spectrum of household appliances, enabling retailers to pepper their product ranges with exciting and attention-grabbing highlights, be it to create a feeling of luxury with exquisite coffee machines, to evoke pure enjoyment in the kitchen, or to redefine the world of haircare, well-being or even floor care. „Industrie & Marketing" is Elektromarkt's marketplace. This is where new products are presented along with accompanying marketing campaigns and PoS promotions. Elektromarkt creates a line of communication between trade and industry, providing retailers with valuable sales advice and ideas. The trade magazine that bridges the gap between haircare and household appliances, enjoyment and health, kitchens and coffee-making, energy efficiency and lifestyle products.
Language(s): German
ADVERTISING RATES:
Full Page Colour .... EUR 5301
Mechanical Data: Type Area: 260 x 190 mm
Copy instructions: *Copy Date:* 20 days prior to publication
Supplement(s): Coffee & more
BUSINESS: ELECTRICAL RETAIL TRADE

ELEKTROMASCHINEN UND ANTRIEBE
724917G19E-160
Editorial: Lazarettstr. 4, 80636 MÜNCHEN
Tel: 89 12607299 **Fax:** 89 12607310
Email: buch@de-online.info **Web site:** http://www.de-jahrbuch.info
Freq: Annual; **Cover Price:** EUR 21,80; **Circ:** 5,200
Advertising Manager: Michael Dietl
Profile: The yearbook provides - for professionals in the industry and the craft - a comprehensive overview of current happenings in the field of electrical machines and drive systems, to development trends and the current state of standards and regulations. Important basic knowledge for daily practice complements the technical papers.
Language(s): German
ADVERTISING RATES:
Full Page Mono .... EUR 1040
Mechanical Data: Type Area: 156 x 98 mm
Copy instructions: *Copy Date:* 70 days prior to publication

ELEKTRONIK
726141G18A-224
Editorial: Gruber Str. 46a, 85586 POING
Tel: 8121 951337 **Fax:** 8121 951652
Email: redaktion@elektronik.de **Web site:** http://www.elektroniknet.de
Freq: 26 issues yearly; **Annual Sub.:** EUR 149,00; **Circ:** 30,608
Editor: Gerhard Stelzer; **Advertising Manager:** Peter Eberhard
Profile: Elektronik is the media brand for design engineers and technical management. The bi-weekly technical journal Elektronik, the web service elektroniknet.de as well as the elektroniknet.de newsletter report about all aspects of industrial electronics. The editorial content ranges from components and devices to test & measurement and automation. It also covers communications technologies, hard- and software and computer aided design engineering, as well as manufacturing and testing. The cross media brand Elektronik organizes sophisticated events, such as wireless congress, ecodesign congress and automotive congress. Elektronik provides reliable and highly technical information which is why Elektronik has the highest paid-for circulation of all professional electronics titles in Europe today (IVW audited). Advertisments in Elektronik are regarded as useful information by Elektronik's recipients. Facebook: http://www.facebook.com/pages/elektroniknetde/121306857884722.
Language(s): German
Readership: Aimed at electronics engineers working in the IT and communications industries.
ADVERTISING RATES:
Full Page Mono .... EUR 5470
Full Page Colour .... EUR 8130
Mechanical Data: Type Area: 260 x 185 mm, No. of Columns (Display): 4, Col Widths (Display): 44 mm
Copy instructions: *Copy Date:* 28 days prior to publication
BUSINESS: ELECTRONICS

ELEKTRONIK AUTOMOTIVE
1639977G5A-21
Editorial: Gruber Str. 46a, 85586 POING
Tel: 8121 951369 **Fax:** 8121 951652
Email: sjanouch@elektronik.de **Web site:** http://www.elektroniknet.de
Freq: 10 issues yearly; **Annual Sub.:** EUR 72,00; **Circ:** 20,116
Editor: Stephan Janouch; **Advertising Manager:** Peter Eberhard
Profile: Monthly Elektronik automotive informs in-depth about solutions, concepts and products in automotive electronics. A large variety of positive readers reactions prove elektronik automotive's importance as a reliable and credible information source for the decision makers in automotive electronics – design engineers and managers in vehicle construction and its subcontracting industries. elektroniknet.de's competence center „automotive" is running high speed. 9.5 million IVW-Online audited page impressions per year (August 08 - July 09) make elektroniknet.de the most frequented media site for professional electronics. Plus: the weekly Automotive-newsletter provides latest trends, products and experts' knowledge to more than 48,000 recipients which make it the ideal advertising medium. Elektronik automotive congress presents the strengths of innovative exhibitors and sponsors. Highly qualified speakers create a technically sophisticated programme for all attendees. Facebook: http://www.facebook.com/pages/elektroniknetde/121306857884722.
Language(s): German
ADVERTISING RATES:
Full Page Mono .... EUR 5580
Full Page Colour .... EUR 8290
Mechanical Data: Type Area: 260 x 185 mm, No. of Columns (Display): 4, Col Widths (Display): 44 mm
Copy instructions: *Copy Date:* 15 days prior to publication
BUSINESS: COMPUTERS & AUTOMATION: Automation & Instrumentation

ELEKTRONIK INDUSTRIE
726143G18A-225
Editorial: Im Weiher 10, 69121 HEIDELBERG
Tel: 6221 489240 **Fax:** 6221 489482
Email: siegfried.best@huethig.de **Web site:** http://www.all-electronics.de
Freq: 10 issues yearly; **Annual Sub.:** EUR 167,80; **Circ:** 29,839
Editor: Siegfried Best; **Advertising Manager:** Andreas Bausch
Profile: elektronik industrie defines itself as the leading technical trade publications for electronics designers in Germany. This claim is supported with a circulation increase of 50% to 30,000 copies. The focus of the editorial offers are practical, application-oriented contributions and trends for all relevant sectors.
Language(s): German
Readership: Aimed at design and electronics engineers.
ADVERTISING RATES:
Full Page Mono .... EUR 5566
Full Page Colour .... EUR 6641
Mechanical Data: Type Area: 257 x 178 mm, No. of Columns (Display): 4, Col Widths (Display): 41 mm
Copy instructions: *Copy Date:* 27 days prior to publication
BUSINESS: ELECTRONICS

ELEKTRONIK JOURNAL - DEUTSCHLAND-AUSG.
1749484G18A-262
Editorial: Justus-von-Liebig-Str. 1, 86899 LANDSBERG **Tel:** 8191 125403 **Fax:** 8191 125141
Email: achim.leitner@huethig.de **Web site:** http://www.elektronikjournal.de
Freq: Monthly; **Annual Sub.:** EUR 60,00; **Circ:** 40,303
Editor: Achim Leitner; **Advertising Manager:** Andreas Bausch
Profile: electronics Journal, the magazine issues for decision-makers around the electronics development. Focus of the editorial articles and short reports, the technical and economic benefits of products and solutions. Journalists bring the relevant issues in a fresh magazine-style course and get oriented to the point. Every magazine focus is preparing them for comprehensive and sustainable, from the basics and technologies to the application and the components to the system.
Language(s): German
ADVERTISING RATES:
Full Page Mono .... EUR 6900
Full Page Colour .... EUR 6900
Mechanical Data: Type Area: 257 x 178 mm, No. of Columns (Display): 4, Col Widths (Display): 41 mm
BUSINESS: ELECTRONICS

ELEKTRONIK PRAXIS
726146G18A-228
Editorial: Max-Planck-Str. 7, 97082 WÜRZBURG
Tel: 931 4183081 **Fax:** 931 4183093
Email: johann.wiesboeck@vogel.de **Web site:** http://www.elektronikpraxis.de
Freq: 24 issues yearly; **Annual Sub.:** EUR 203,00; **Circ:** 39,967
Editor: Johann Wiesböck; **Advertising Manager:** Franziska Harfy
Profile: Elektronik Praxis is a competent provider of application-oriented technical and industry information with the greatest benefit forf electronic design engineers, buyers, technical management and production experts. Every four days Elektronik Praxis reports on current events in the electronics industry as well as products, technologies and development processes. Elektronik Praxis informs hardware and software developers, buyers, specialists in construction and related engineering and assembly manufacturing and decision makers in the electronics industry in Germany. In addition to the contents of the 24 main issues Elektronik Praxis compresses most important topics in 5 special issues. Facebook: http://www.facebook.com/elektronikpraxis Twitter: http://twitter.com/#!/RedaktionEP This Outlet offers RSS (Really Simple Syndication).
Language(s): German
ADVERTISING RATES:
Full Page Mono .... EUR 6780
Full Page Colour .... EUR 8640
Mechanical Data: Type Area: 270 x 190 mm, No. of Columns (Display): 4, Col Widths (Display): 46 mm
Copy instructions: *Copy Date:* 25 days prior to publication
BUSINESS: ELECTRONICS

ELEKTRONIK PRAXIS
1621154G18A-261
Editorial: Max-Planck-Str. 7, 97082 WÜRZBURG
Tel: 931 4183081 **Fax:** 931 4182843
Email: elektronikpraxis@vogel.de **Web site:** http://www.elektronikpraxis.de
Freq: Daily; **Cover Price:** Paid; **Circ:** 246,401 Unique Users
Editor: Johann Wiesböck; **Advertising Manager:** Franziska Harfy
Profile: Ezine: Internet portal for the hardware and software developers, buyers, specialists in construction and connection technology, and assembly manufacturing and decision makers in the electronics industry. Facebook: http://www.facebook.com/elektronikpraxis Twitter: http://twitter.com/#!/RedaktionEP This Outlet offers RSS (Really Simple Syndication).
Language(s): German
BUSINESS: ELECTRONICS

ELEKTROTECHNIK
726149G17-380
Editorial: Max-Planck-Str. 7, 97082 WÜRZBURG
Tel: 931 4182260 **Fax:** 931 4182766
Email: wolfgang.leppert@vogel.de **Web site:** http://www.elektrotechnik.de
Freq: Monthly; **Annual Sub.:** EUR 99,00; **Circ:** 20,034
Editor: Wolfgang Leppert; **Advertising Manager:** Silvia Zeiner
Profile: elektrotechnik, the automation magazine, reports on the entire value chain of automation technology for engineers, planners, operating and production engineers, buyers and service providers and technical management in the factory, process and building automation, and mobile automation. The focus is on the practical application of automation products and systems, technologies and services, their use, and potential for improvement as well as their usefulness for business practice. In addition, electrical current background information on technical trends and industry developments. Facebook: http://www.facebook.com/elektrotechnik.automation Twitter: http://twitter.com/#!/elektrotechnik1 This Outlet offers RSS (Really Simple Syndication).
Language(s): German
ADVERTISING RATES:
Full Page Mono .... EUR 4895
Full Page Colour .... EUR 6060
Mechanical Data: Type Area: 270 x 190 mm, No. of Columns (Display): 4, Col Widths (Display): 46 mm
Copy instructions: *Copy Date:* 26 days prior to publication
BUSINESS: ELECTRICAL

ELEKTROTECHNIK
1621155G17-1548
Editorial: Max-Planck-Str. 7, 97082 WÜRZBURG
Tel: 931 4182754 **Fax:** 931 4182014
Email: elektrotechnik@vogel.de **Web site:** http://www.elektrotechnik.de
Freq: Daily; **Cover Price:** Paid; **Circ:** 50,453 Unique Users
Editor: Wolfgang Leppert; **Advertising Manager:** Silvia Zeiner
Profile: Web site for electrical engineers and automation professionals in development, design, planning and engineering. Facebook: http://www.facebook.com/elektrotechnik.automation Twitter: http://twitter.com/#!/elektrotechnik1 This Outlet offers RSS (Really Simple Syndication).
Language(s): German
BUSINESS: ELECTRICAL

ELEKTROTECHNIK FÜR HANDWERK UND INDUSTRIE
724918G17-100
Editorial: Lazarettstr. 4, 80636 MÜNCHEN
Tel: 89 12607299 **Fax:** 89 12607310
Email: buch@de-online.info **Web site:** http://www.de-jahrbuch.info
Freq: Annual; **Cover Price:** EUR 21,80
Annual Sub.: EUR 18,80; **Circ:** 27,000
Advertising Manager: Michael Dietl
Profile: For more than three decades, the annual electrical engineering from the reliable and informative companion for the daily work force for all professionals working in the electronics practice. The more than 50 technical papers are based primarily on current changes in standards and regulations, and on new techniques and technologies. Are supplemented by the statements important basic and referencing information. The focus of the current issue are on the following topics: * Photovoltaic systems * minimum requirements of DIN 18015-2, * Rooms with bath and shower, * Electrical equipment for TRBS, * small cogeneration plants, * BGI electrician - EuP, * Supplement for TAB 2007 * Operation of electrical installations to VDE 0105-100, * Protective measures in Formula I cars, * Smart Metering * Generic cabling systems.
Language(s): German
ADVERTISING RATES:
Full Page Mono .... EUR 2195
Mechanical Data: Type Area: 156 x 98 mm
Copy instructions: *Copy Date:* 70 days prior to publication

ELEMENT + BAU
726156G4E-3360
Editorial: Blumenstr. 15, 90402 NÜRNBERG
Tel: 911 2018230 **Fax:** 911 2018100
Email: koenig@harnisch.com **Web site:** http://www.harnisch.com
Freq: 6 issues yearly; **Annual Sub.:** EUR 54,00; **Circ:** 6,548
Editor: Armin König; **Advertising Manager:** Armin König
Profile: element + Bau treated the total area of the object construction. The construction of public buildings such as schools, kindergartens and administration buildings has its place, as well as the large-scale of residential and industrial construction. The focus here is on the design implementation as well as reporting on details, the used products and applied systems. Special consideration also economically and environmentally progressive solutions, pre-fabrication and cost reduction, mixed construction and use of prefabricated systems. Property coverage, products, information technology, news, events and literature are among the regular sections. In various editions available - depending on the trend in the construction industry - Specials on the editorial calendar, in which each topic is covered in detail.
Language(s): German
ADVERTISING RATES:
Full Page Mono .... EUR 2635
Full Page Colour .... EUR 3985
Mechanical Data: Type Area: 256 x 171 mm, No. of Columns (Display): 3, Col Widths (Display): 57 mm
Copy instructions: *Copy Date:* 30 days prior to publication
BUSINESS: ARCHITECTURE & BUILDING: Building

ELITE
1639036G21A-4295
Editorial: Hülsebrockstr. 2, 48165 MÜNSTER
Tel: 2501 801685 **Fax:** 2501 801204
Email: redaktion@elite-magazin.de **Web site:** http://www.elite-magazin.de
Freq: 6 issues yearly; **Annual Sub.:** EUR 43,80; **Circ:** 20,411
Editor: Gregor Veauthier; **Advertising Manager:** Peter Wiggers
Profile: Elite is the specialist magazine for successful milk production with independent, critical race and cross-reporting. Internationally renowned authors from practice, consultancy and research, and the editorial team provide a high level of information. This is to remove a key supplier of know-how for innovative dairy producers, consultants and veterinarians with the forward vision. The topics range from Elite extends from field reports and analysis of successful dairy farms from around the world about recent research results to extension recommendations. Pay particular attention to contributions from major milk producing regions such as Germany, USA, Canada, Netherlands, New Zealand, France and Scandinavia. Elite is read mainly by the forward-looking dairy farmers.
Language(s): German
ADVERTISING RATES:
Full Page Mono .... EUR 2664
Full Page Colour .... EUR 4263
Mechanical Data: Type Area: 270 x 190 mm, No. of Columns (Display): 4, Col Widths (Display): 46 mm

ELLE
726164G74A-960
Editorial: Arabellastr. 23, 81925 MÜNCHEN
Tel: 89 92500 **Fax:** 89 92503332
Web site: http://www.elle.de
Freq: Monthly; **Annual Sub.:** EUR 66,00; **Circ:** 216,586
Editor: Sabine Nedelchev; **Advertising Manager:** Sabine Adleff
Profile: Fashion, Beauty, Wellness, Culture & Lifestyle: Elle's style consultant, not a style dictator, Elle has style, but not a snob; Elle enjoys luxury without airs, Elle's character and not afraid; Elle immerses where others shut down, Elle is a trendsetter Instead of copying Facebook: http://www.facebook.com/ElleGermany.
Language(s): German
ADVERTISING RATES:
Full Page Mono .... EUR 25200
Full Page Colour .... EUR 25200
Mechanical Data: Type Area: 255 x 180 mm, No. of Columns (Display): 3, Col Widths (Display): 55 mm
Copy instructions: *Copy Date:* 48 days prior to publication
CONSUMER: WOMEN'S INTEREST CONSUMER MAGAZINES: Women's Interest

ELLE DECORATION
726166G74C-640
Editorial: Arabellastr. 23, 81925 MÜNCHEN
Tel: 89 92500 **Fax:** 89 92503761
Web site: http://www.elle.de/decoration
Freq: 6 issues yearly; **Annual Sub.:** EUR 33,00; **Circ:** 128,967
Editor: Sabine Nedelchev; **Advertising Manager:** Sabine Adleff
Profile: Elle Decoration is a sophisticated interior and luxury magazine. Elle Decoration is elegant, modern, style-conscious. Set to true values, remain at the same time open to new ideas. Elle Decoration shows the most interesting and beautiful interior design styles around the globe. Thus, the Interiors are experienced and lived out. Elle Decoration informed about current trends in design, art, architecture. Imparts knowledge in a sophisticated and attractive manner. Elle Decoration staged products inspiring and imaginative. And makes you want to, get creative to change his life-world. Elle Decoration is going on tour. Portrayed cities, shows hot spots, finds the most beautiful hotels, discovered parks and gardens. Elle Decoration design trends associated with trends in other lifestyle areas such as fashion, jewelry and beauty. Elle Decoration is international, with 23 editions worldwide.
Language(s): German
Readership: Aimed at financially independent home owners.
ADVERTISING RATES:
Full Page Mono .... EUR 17200
Full Page Colour .... EUR 17200
Mechanical Data: Type Area: 252 x 190 mm, No. of Columns (Display): 3, Col Widths (Display): 60 mm
Copy instructions: *Copy Date:* 56 days prior to publication
CONSUMER: WOMEN'S INTEREST CONSUMER MAGAZINES: Home & Family

ELMSHORNER NACHRICHTEN
726171G67B-4660
Editorial: Nikolaistr. 7, 24937 FLENSBURG
Tel: 461 8080 **Fax:** 461 8081058
Email: redaktion@shz.de **Web site:** http://www.shz.de
Freq: 312 issues yearly; **Circ:** 11,749
Editor: Rainer Strandmann; **Advertising Manager:** Ingeborg Schwarz
Profile: Daily newspaper with regional news and a local sports section. Facebook: http://www.facebook.com/shzonline Twitter: http://twitter.com/shz_de This Outlet offers RSS (Really Simple Syndication).
Language(s): German
ADVERTISING RATES:
SCC .... EUR 51,80
Mechanical Data: Type Area: 430 x 282 mm, No. of Columns (Display): 6, Col Widths (Display): 45 mm
Copy instructions: *Copy Date:* 1 day prior to publication
Supplement(s): EMTV-Nachrichten; Hainholzer Bote; nordisch gesund; Watt Löppt bei den Stadtwerken Elmshorn und im Badepark
REGIONAL DAILY & SUNDAY NEWSPAPERS: Regional Daily Newspapers

ELTERN
726180G74C-660
Editorial: Weihenstephaner Str. 7, 81673 MÜNCHEN
Tel: 89 4152703 **Fax:** 89 4152651
Email: redaktion@eltern.de **Web site:** http://www.eltern.de
Freq: 5 issues yearly; **Annual Sub.:** EUR 30,60; **Circ:** 297,403
Editor: Marie-Luise Lewicki; **Advertising Manager:** Andrea Wörsdörfer
Profile: Behind the varied topics of Eltern is an editorial team that knows what it writes, for Eltern und Eltern family are written by parents! By mothers and fathers with a lot of personal experience and excellent contacts to those who also know much - doctors, midwives, lactation consultants, educators, psychologists and researchers. Eltern is a special women's magazine - a magazine for women who live it all: a life with children and a life as a woman! Eltern inspires these women to a fulfilled and happy life - from pregnancy to childhood, from job to beauty. Eltern defines topics, whether it comes to kindergarten fees or the mood of young parents is in Germany. Facebook: http://www.facebook.com/eltern.de This Outlet offers RSS (Really Simple Syndication).
Language(s): German
ADVERTISING RATES:
Full Page Mono .... EUR 29900
Full Page Colour .... EUR 29900
Mechanical Data: Type Area: 245 x 185 mm, No. of Columns (Display): 3, Col Widths (Display): 59 mm
Copy instructions: *Copy Date:* 48 days prior to publication
CONSUMER: WOMEN'S INTEREST CONSUMER MAGAZINES: Home & Family

ELTERN FAMILY
726192G74D-55
Editorial: Weihenstephaner Str. 7, 81673 MÜNCHEN
Tel: 89 4152703 **Fax:** 89 4152651
Email: redaktion@eltern.de **Web site:** http://www.elternforfamily.de
Freq: Monthly; **Annual Sub.:** EUR 33,60; **Circ:** 133,009
Editor: Marie-Luise Lewicki; **Advertising Manager:** Andrea Wörsdörfer
Profile: Eltern family is a family magazine for young families with children from four years of age on. Every daily life with the young person is exciting and challenging. Eltern family discussed family issues from different point of view concerning education, development, school education and health, and gives suggestions for the balancing act between career and family. Facebook: http://www.facebook.com/eltern.de.
Language(s): German
ADVERTISING RATES:
Full Page Mono .... EUR 14700
Full Page Colour .... EUR 14700
Mechanical Data: Type Area: 245 x 185 mm, No. of Columns (Display): 3, Col Widths (Display): 59 mm
Copy instructions: *Copy Date:* 40 days prior to publication
Supplement(s): Quix!
CONSUMER: WOMEN'S INTEREST CONSUMER MAGAZINES: Child Care

ELTERN RATGEBER ARZT UND SCHWANGERSCHAFT
726184G74C-740
Editorial: Weihenstephaner Str. 7, 81673 MÜNCHEN
Tel: 89 415200 **Fax:** 89 4152627
Web site: http://www.gujmedia.de
Freq: 3 issues yearly; **Cover Price:** Free; **Circ:** 299,970
Editor: Marie-Luise Lewicki; **Advertising Manager:** Hans-Joachim Weber
Profile: ARZT UND SCHWANGERSCHAF is the medical attendant in the 40 most exciting weeks of each woman. It offers all the important information, understand and medically sound, as gynecologists provide professional input and give him your pregnant for reading all the pregnancy issues. PLUS: All medical terms for pregnancy from A to Z PLUS: All technical terms relating to pregnancy and birth in Turkish.
Language(s): German
ADVERTISING RATES:
Full Page Mono .... EUR 25200
Full Page Colour .... EUR 25200
Mechanical Data: Type Area: 230 x 170 mm, No. of Columns (Display): 3, Col Widths (Display): 54 mm
CONSUMER: WOMEN'S INTEREST CONSUMER MAGAZINES: Home & Family

ELTERN RATGEBER DAS GESUNDE KIND
1640017G74C-3582
Editorial: Weihenstephaner Str. 7, 81673 MÜNCHEN
Tel: 89 415200 **Fax:** 89 4152627
Web site: http://www.gujmedia.de
Freq: Half-yearly; **Cover Price:** Free; **Circ:** 299,975
Editor: Marie-Luise Lewicki; **Advertising Manager:** Hans-Joachim Weber
Profile: The health of their children is particularly important to parents. Therefore the parents-provides up along with the Child Health Foundation, researchers and pediatricians to all the important information and news. DAS GESUNDE KIND is a pleasure to read for everything that makes a happy and relaxed family life: the common meal and recreation as well as advice on legal matters and insurance coverage. PLUS: Great overview of the health care of the free tests U1 - J1 for all children from birth to adolescence.
Language(s): German
ADVERTISING RATES:
Full Page Mono .... EUR 19200
Full Page Colour .... EUR 19200
Mechanical Data: Type Area: 230 x 170 mm
CONSUMER: WOMEN'S INTEREST CONSUMER MAGAZINES: Home & Family

ELTERN RATGEBER KLINIKFÜHRER GEBURT
726194G74D-78
Editorial: Weihenstephaner Str. 7, 81673 MÜNCHEN
Tel: 89 415200 **Fax:** 89 4152627
Web site: http://www.gujmedia.de
Freq: Half-yearly; **Cover Price:** Free; **Circ:** 345,140
Editor: Marie-Luise Lewicki; **Advertising Manager:** Hans-Joachim Weber
Profile: Everything ready for the big moment: KLINIKFÜHRER GEBURT provides expectant parents with all the information they need to birth. Perfect for the anticipation and preparation for the delivery room. In addition, all important for pregnancy and the first time with the baby, from pregnancy care to the financial security of the family. PLUS: Regional inner part of all maternity hospitals and birthing centers illuminates in detail so that each woman her best place to find childbearing.
Language(s): German
Readership: Aimed at expectant mothers and parents of babies.
ADVERTISING RATES:
Full Page Mono .... EUR 23000
Full Page Colour .... EUR 23000
Mechanical Data: Type Area: 250 x 185 mm, No. of Columns (Display): 3, Col Widths (Display): 59 mm
Copy instructions: *Copy Date:* 70 days prior to publication
CONSUMER: WOMEN'S INTEREST CONSUMER MAGAZINES: Child Care

ELTERN RATGEBER - (PRAXIS-RATGEBER) AUSG. KINDERARZT
726195G74D-56
Editorial: Weihenstephaner Str. 7, 81673 MÜNCHEN
Tel: 89 415200 **Fax:** 89 4152627
Web site: http://www.gujmedia.de
Freq: Quarterly; **Cover Price:** Free; **Circ:** 140,000
Editor: Marie-Luise Lewicki; **Advertising Manager:** Hans-Joachim Weber
Profile: Magazine containing articles about pregnancy and birth.
Language(s): German
Readership: Aimed at expectant mothers and new parents.
ADVERTISING RATES:
Full Page Mono .... EUR 9200
Full Page Colour .... EUR 9200
Mechanical Data: Type Area: 165 x 125 mm
Copy instructions: *Copy Date:* 60 days prior to publication
CONSUMER: WOMEN'S INTEREST CONSUMER MAGAZINES: Child Care

ELTERN.DE
1621157G74C-3542
Editorial: Weihenstephaner Str. 7, 81673 MÜNCHEN
Tel: 89 415200 **Fax:** 89 4152651
Web site: http://www.eltern.de
Freq: Daily; **Cover Price:** Paid; **Circ:** 2,661,699 Unique Users
Editor: Rosemarie Wetscher
Profile: Family portal on the Internet connects you with the exchange of editorial content in over 1200 forums and a social network. the Abo & Shop area completes the offer with subscriptions and parents merchandising products. Facebook: http://www.facebook.com/eltern.de.
Language(s): German
CONSUMER: WOMEN'S INTEREST CONSUMER MAGAZINES: Home & Family

EMA ELEKTRISCHE MASCHINEN
726203G18A-229
Editorial: Lazarettstr. 4, 80636 MÜNCHEN
Tel: 89 12607248 **Fax:** 89 12607111
Email: stoecklhuber@de-online.info **Web site:** http://www.de-online.info
Freq: 9 issues yearly; **Annual Sub.:** EUR 81,40; **Circ:** 1,943
Editor: Andreas Stöcklhuber; **Advertising Manager:** Michael Dietl
Profile: Journal covering all aspects of the electronics industry.
Language(s): German
ADVERTISING RATES:
Full Page Mono .... EUR 1100
Full Page Colour .... EUR 1805
Mechanical Data: Type Area: 198 x 145 mm, No. of Columns (Display): 3, Col Widths (Display): 45 mm
Copy instructions: *Copy Date:* 28 days prior to publication
Official Journal of: Organ d. Bundesfachgruppe Elektromaschinenbau im Zentralverb. d. Dt. Elektrohandwerke
BUSINESS: ELECTRONICS

EMAIL
735695G19C-65
Editorial: Dölauer Str. 60, 06120 HALLE
Tel: 345 5507368 **Fax:** 345 6830654
Email: peter.hellmold@t-online.de
Freq: 6 issues yearly; Free to qualifying individuals
Annual Sub.: EUR 75,00; **Circ:** 450
Editor: Peter Hellmold; **Advertising Manager:** Claus Thielmann
Profile: International journal containing news from the Society of Enamelling Specialists.
Language(s): German
ADVERTISING RATES:
Full Page Mono .... EUR 510
Full Page Colour .... EUR 923
Mechanical Data: Type Area: 260 x 180 mm, No. of Columns (Display): 3, Col Widths (Display): 55 mm
Copy instructions: *Copy Date:* 14 days prior to publication
BUSINESS: ENGINEERING & MACHINERY: Finishing

EMDER ZEITUNG
726213G67B-4680
Editorial: Zwischen beiden Märkten 2, 26721 EMDEN
Tel: 4921 890040 **Fax:** 4921 8900489
Email: redaktion@emderzeitung.de **Web site:** http://www.emderzeitung.de
Freq: 312 issues yearly; **Circ:** 11,060
Editor: Klaus Fackert; **News Editor:** Christian Schollbach; **Advertising Manager:** Gert Janßen
Profile: Regional daily newspaper with news on politics, economy, culture, sports, travel, technology, etc. The Emder Zeitung is a daily newspaper published in the East Frisian Emden. The Emder Zeitung is the smallest full-Emden newspaper in Germany, that it produces all sides (including the so-called shell, that is the most supplied by news agencies nationwide part) itself This Outlet offers RSS (Really Simple Syndication).
Language(s): German
ADVERTISING RATES:
SCC .... EUR 51,50
Mechanical Data: Type Area: 426 x 280 mm, No. of Columns (Display): 6, Col Widths (Display): 45 mm
Copy instructions: *Copy Date:* 2 days prior to publication
REGIONAL DAILY & SUNDAY NEWSPAPERS: Regional Daily Newspapers

EMERGENCY RADIOLOGY
1638478G56A-11275
Editorial: Tiergartenstr. 17, 69121 HEIDELBERG
Tel: 6221 4870 **Fax:** 6221 4878366
Email: subscriptions@springer.com **Web site:** http://www.springerlink.com
Freq: 6 issues yearly; **Annual Sub.:** EUR 495,00; **Circ:** 454
Editor: Ronald J. Zagoria
Profile: Information about emergency radiology.
Language(s): English
ADVERTISING RATES:
Full Page Mono .... EUR 740
Full Page Colour .... EUR 1780
Mechanical Data: Type Area: 240 x 175 mm
Official Journal of: Organ d. American Society of Emergency Radiology

EMMA
726217G74A-1020
Editorial: Bayenturm, 50678 KÖLN
Tel: 221 60606011 **Fax:** 221 60606029
Email: redaktion@emma.de **Web site:** http://www.emma.de
Freq: Quarterly; **Annual Sub.:** EUR 42,00; **Circ:** 43,181
Editor: Alice Schwarzer
Profile: Feminist magazine. Facebook: http://www.facebook.com/pages/EMMA/158003690895324.
Language(s): German
ADVERTISING RATES:
Full Page Mono .... EUR 6000
Full Page Colour .... EUR 6000
Mechanical Data: Type Area: 240 x 179 mm
Copy instructions: *Copy Date:* 28 days prior to publication
CONSUMER: WOMEN'S INTEREST CONSUMER MAGAZINES: Women's Interest

EMOBILE PLUS SOLAR
742109G77A-2120
Editorial: Reifenberg 85, 91365 WEILERSBACH
Tel: 9194 8985 **Fax:** 9194 4262
Email: reichel@solarmobil.net **Web site:** http://www.solarmobil.de/zeitschrift
Freq: Quarterly; Free to qualifying individuals
Annual Sub.: EUR 24,00; **Circ:** 1,600
Editor: Roland Reichel; **Advertising Manager:** Roland Reichel
Profile: Magazine for electric vehicles and solar mobility.
Language(s): German
ADVERTISING RATES:
Full Page Colour .... EUR 400
Mechanical Data: Type Area: 275 x 190 mm, No. of Columns (Display): 2, Col Widths (Display): 92 mm
Copy instructions: *Copy Date:* 14 days prior to publication
Official Journal of: Organ d. Bundesverb. Solare Mobilität e.V. u. d. Solarmobil Vereins Erlangen

EMSDETTENER VOLKSZEITUNG
726226G67B-4740
Editorial: Im Hagenkamp 4, 48282 EMSDETTEN
Tel: 2572 956010 **Fax:** 2572 956019
Email: redaktion@emsdettener-volkszeitung.de **Web site:** http://www.emsdettener-volkszeitung.de
Freq: 312 issues yearly; **Circ:** 8,169
Profile: Daily newspaper with regional news and a local sports section.
Language(s): German
ADVERTISING RATES:
SCC .... EUR 35,60
Mechanical Data: Type Area: 478 x 315 mm, No. of Columns (Display): 7, Col Widths (Display): 42 mm
Copy instructions: *Copy Date:* 2 days prior to publication
Supplement(s): prisma
REGIONAL DAILY & SUNDAY NEWSPAPERS: Regional Daily Newspapers

EMS-ZEITUNG
726231G67B-4700
Editorial: Breiter Gang 10, 49074 OSNABRÜCK
Tel: 541 3100 **Fax:** 541 310485
Email: redaktion@noz.de **Web site:** http://www.noz.de
Freq: 312 issues yearly; **Circ:** 17,307
Profile: Daily newspaper with regional news and a local sports section. Facebook: http://www.facebook.com/pages/nozde/106261086094051 Twitter: http://twitter.com/noz_de This Outlet offers RSS (Really Simple Syndication).
Language(s): German
ADVERTISING RATES:
SCC .... EUR 45,90
Mechanical Data: Type Area: 487 x 318 mm, No. of Columns (Display): 7, Col Widths (Display): 43 mm
Copy instructions: *Copy Date:* 2 days prior to publication
Supplement(s): Immo-Welt; Kfz-Welt
REGIONAL DAILY & SUNDAY NEWSPAPERS: Regional Daily Newspapers

EMV-ESD ELEKTROMAGNETISCHE VERTRÄGLICHKEIT
726232G18A-26_75
Editorial: Oberer Schenkgarten 4, 55218 INGELHEIM
Tel: 6132 431647 **Fax:** 6132 431649
Email: ullrichw@smt-verlag.de **Web site:** http://www.smt-verlag.de
Freq: Quarterly; **Annual Sub.:** EUR 28,00; **Circ:** 9,580
Editor: Ullrich Wachs; **Advertising Manager:** Vera Neumann
Profile: Magazine focusing on electronics and electromagnetics, contains details of new developments and research, also applications within industry.
Language(s): German
Readership: Read by professionals in construction, safety, quality control and related sectors.
ADVERTISING RATES:
Full Page Mono .... EUR 3450
Full Page Colour .... EUR 4400
Mechanical Data: Type Area: 260 x 185 mm, No. of Columns (Display): 4, Col Widths (Display): 42 mm
BUSINESS: ELECTRONICS

ENDOKRINOLOGIE INFORMATIONEN
726244G56A-2960
Editorial: Rüdigerstr. 14, 70469 STUTTGART
Tel: 711 8931430 **Fax:** 711 8931392
Email: kundenservice@thieme.de **Web site:** http://www.thieme-connect.de
Freq: 5 issues yearly; **Circ:** 1,650
Profile: Current releases of the German Society of Endocrinology, information about conferences, training, awards, appointments, honors, and a comprehensive convention preview.
Language(s): German
ADVERTISING RATES:
Full Page Mono .... EUR 1360
Full Page Colour .... EUR 2510
Mechanical Data: Type Area: 250 x 180 mm, No. of Columns (Display): 4, Col Widths (Display): 42 mm
Official Journal of: Organ d. Dt. Ges. f. Endokrinologie u. d. Dt. Diabetesges.
Supplement to: Experimental and Clinical Endocrinology & Diabetes

ENDO-PRAXIS
726245G56A-2940
Editorial: Ferdinand-Sauerbruch-Weg 16, 89075 ULM
Email: uk-beilenhoff@t-online.de **Web site:** http://www.thieme.de/endopraxis
Freq: Quarterly; **Annual Sub.:** EUR 41,80; **Circ:** 2,400

Profile: The Endo-Praxis offers its readers practical information, especially to the important technical and medical innovations. Political career news, society announcements, conference reports and a current calendar of events will keep you up to date with what's happening in your field. For over 20 years, the only and leading trade magazine for endoscopy personnel. Hands-on expertise in primary and review articles. Terms, Tips & Tricks, hygiene, management & human resources management, the special case. Standards for the coat pocket. Industry News.
Language(s): German
ADVERTISING RATES:
Full Page Mono .... EUR 1390
Full Page Colour .... EUR 2290
Mechanical Data: Type Area: 245 x 175 mm
Official Journal of: Organ d. Dt. Ges. f. Endoskopie-Assistenzpersonal, d. Schweizer. Vereinigung Endoskopiepersonal SVEP/ASPE u. d. European Society of Gastroenterology and Endoscopy Nurses and Associates ESGENA

ENDOSCOPY
726246G56A-2980
Editorial: Rüdigerstr. 14, 70469 STUTTGART
Tel: 711 89310 **Fax:** 711 8931298
Email: kundenservice@thieme.de **Web site:** http://www.thieme.de/endoscopy
Freq: Monthly; Free to qualifying individuals
Annual Sub.: EUR 325,80; **Circ:** 5,870
Editor: Thomas Rösch
Profile: Keep up to date in Gastrointestinal Endoscopy. Excellent original papers. Outstanding reviews. Evidence-Based Endoscopy. An international team of editors provides all benefits of a worldwide information network.
Language(s): English
ADVERTISING RATES:
Full Page Mono .... EUR 2040
Full Page Colour .... EUR 3270
Mechanical Data: Type Area: 248 x 175 mm, No. of Columns (Display): 4, Col Widths (Display): 40 mm
Official Journal of: Organ d. European Society of Gastrointestinal Endoscopy u. a.
BUSINESS: HEALTH & MEDICAL

ENDOSKOPIE HEUTE
726247G56A-3000
Editorial: Rüdigerstr. 14, 70469 STUTTGART
Tel: 711 8931430 **Fax:** 711 8931392
Email: hj.schulz@sana-kl.de **Web site:** http://www.thieme.de/endoheute
Freq: Quarterly; Free to qualifying individuals
Annual Sub.: EUR 142,80; **Circ:** 1,400
Editor: Hans-Joachim Schulz
Profile: Thinking outside the box! - The full spectrum of endoscopic and related fields. Recent developments in gastroenterology, surgery, pathology, urology, radiology, nuclear medicine and gynecology. Overview of the entire endoscopy. Developments in related fields. Interdisciplinary original articles, case studies, overviews. Latest developments referenced and evaluated by specialists. Results of scientific research and technological development. Calendar of Events.
Language(s): German
ADVERTISING RATES:
Full Page Mono .... EUR 2080
Full Page Colour .... EUR 3190
Mechanical Data: Type Area: 248 x 175 mm, No. of Columns (Display): 3, Col Widths (Display): 55 mm
Official Journal of: Organ d. Dt. Ges. f. Endoskopie u. bildgebende Verfahren e.V.

ENDURO
726248G77B-50
Editorial: Adlerstr. 6, 73540 HEUBACH
Tel: 7173 714500 **Fax:** 7173 7145020
Email: redaktion@enduro-press.de **Web site:** http://www.enduro-press.de
Freq: Monthly; **Annual Sub.:** EUR 38,00; **Circ:** 6,703
Editor: Norbert Bauer; **Advertising Manager:** Ute Werner
Profile: Magazine for motorcyclists; test and driving records of all in the market existing trail bikes, accessories and clothing tests, technical articles, practical tips, sports and travel reports.
Language(s): German
ADVERTISING RATES:
Full Page Mono .... EUR 1940
Full Page Colour .... EUR 3435
Mechanical Data: Type Area: 248 x 185 mm, No. of Columns (Display): 4, Col Widths (Display): 43 mm
Copy instructions: *Copy Date:* 24 days prior to publication
CONSUMER: MOTORING & CYCLING: Motorcycling

ENERGIE PFLANZEN
1622777G58-1715
Editorial: Moorhofweg 11, 27383 SCHEESSEL
Tel: 4263 93950 **Fax:** 4263 939521
Email: info@forstfachverlag.de **Web site:** http://www.energie-pflanzen.de
Freq: 6 issues yearly; **Annual Sub.:** EUR 34,50; **Circ:** 4,500
Editor: Dieter Biernath; **Advertising Manager:** Jörg Rösch
Profile: Magazine for renewable resources, renewable energy, biogas, wood energy, oil and fiber plants, solar energy, hydropower, wind energy Audiences: producers, processors, users, consumers of renewable materials and bioenergy, decision makers from the fields of agriculture, municipal, forestry, services, craft, trade, industry, politics and teaching / research.
Language(s): German
ADVERTISING RATES:
Full Page Mono .... EUR 995
Full Page Colour .... EUR 1820
Mechanical Data: Type Area: 262 x 185 mm, No. of Columns (Display): 3, Col Widths (Display): 59 mm

ENERGIE & MANAGEMENT
726277G58-280
Editorial: Schloss Mühlfeld 20, 82211 HERRSCHING
Tel: 8152 93110 **Fax:** 8152 931122
Email: t.kraegenow@energiemarkt-medien.de **Web site:** http://www.energiemarkt-medien.de
Freq: 21 issues yearly; **Annual Sub.:** EUR 166,00; **Circ:** 6,020
Editor: Timm Krägenow
Profile: Newspaper for energy management and policy, power generation and distribution, energy technology and management, energy services and services, decentralized and renewable energies, energy and emission trading.
Language(s): German
ADVERTISING RATES:
Full Page Mono .... EUR 3950
Full Page Colour .... EUR 5705
Mechanical Data: Type Area: 385 x 270 mm, No. of Columns (Display): 5, Col Widths (Display): 51 mm
Copy instructions: *Copy Date:* 12 days prior to publication
BUSINESS: ENERGY, FUEL & NUCLEAR

ENERGIE & TECHNIK
1932698G58-1826
Editorial: Gruber Str. 46a, 85586 POING
Tel: 8121 951253 **Fax:** 8121 951652
Email: harnold@energie-und-technik.de **Web site:** http://www.energie-und-technik.de
Freq: 6 issues yearly; **Annual Sub.:** EUR 58,80; **Circ:** 26,456
Editor: Heinz Arnold; **Advertising Manager:** Christian Stadler
Profile: How to find one's way through the jungle of energy efficiency. We are continously dealing with keywords about energy saving, renewable energies, energy saving facility management and electric cars. "Energie & Technik" supports its readers in finding their way through the jungle of green technologies. "Energie & Technik" structures the complex issue of energy efficiency. The segregated consideration of individual aspects does not show how close those aspects are linked and how they enable the efficient generation and use only in interaction with one another. "Energie & Technik" presents individual aspects indepth, such as photovoltaics in their whole value-added chain – from materials to manufacturing of cells and effective assembly of modules. Further examples are batteries, fuel cells, energy harvesting, wireless sensor networks for building automation, electric mobility, effective motor controls and power supplies. We always report about more than just those individual aspects. We combine all the aspects dealing with energy efficiency to create an expedient coherence. Readers get to know about trends and products to use energy efficiently.
Language(s): German
ADVERTISING RATES:
Full Page Mono .... EUR 4200
Full Page Colour .... EUR 5880
Mechanical Data: Type Area: 260 x 186 mm, No. of Columns (Display): 4, Col Widths (Display): 43 mm

ENERGIEDEPESCHE
726255G58-1702
Editorial: Frankfurter Str. 1, 53572 UNKEL
Tel: 2224 9603436 **Fax:** 2224 10321
Email: redaktion@energiedepesche.de **Web site:** http://www.energieverbraucher.de
Freq: Quarterly; Free to qualifying individuals
Annual Sub.: EUR 22,00; **Circ:** 16,811
Editor: Aribert Peters
Profile: Publication of the Energy Users Association. Covers all energy themes, including energy saving, and alternative energy sources.
Language(s): German
ADVERTISING RATES:
Full Page Mono .... EUR 1250
Full Page Colour .... EUR 2500
Mechanical Data: Type Area: 252 x 175 mm, No. of Columns (Display): 4, Col Widths (Display): 40 mm
Copy instructions: *Copy Date:* 15 days prior to publication
BUSINESS: ENERGY, FUEL & NUCLEAR

ENERGIEWIRTSCHAFTLICHE TAGESFRAGEN ET
726296G58-320
Editorial: Montebruchstr. 2, 45219 ESSEN
Tel: 2054 953211 **Fax:** 2054 953260
Email: franz.lamprecht@etvessen.de **Web site:** http://www.et-energie-online.de
Freq: 11 issues yearly; **Annual Sub.:** EUR 171,60; **Circ:** 2,821
Editor: Martin Czakainski
Profile: Magazine about energy and associated environmental issues.
Language(s): German
ADVERTISING RATES:
Full Page Mono .... EUR 2420
Full Page Colour .... EUR 3545
Mechanical Data: Type Area: 237 x 180 mm, No. of Columns (Display): 3, Col Widths (Display): 56 mm
Copy instructions: *Copy Date:* 25 days prior to publication
BUSINESS: ENERGY, FUEL & NUCLEAR

E.NEWS
768553G14A-9332
Editorial: Berliner Str. 260, 33330 GÜTERSLOH
Tel: 5241 822521 **Fax:** 5241 8242521
Email: e.news@stadtwerke-gt.de **Web site:** http://www.stadtwerke-gt.de
Freq: Quarterly; **Cover Price:** Free; **Circ:** 3,000
Editor: Roland Stüwe
Profile: Magazine with information for business partners of the Stadtwerke Gütersloh.
Language(s): German

ENGELS
724353G76A-200
Editorial: Maastrichter Str. 6, 50672 KÖLN
Tel: 221 2725260 **Fax:** 221 2725288
Email: info@engels-kinokultur.de **Web site:** http://www.engels-kinokultur.de
Freq: Monthly; **Cover Price:** Free; **Circ:** 14,915
Editor: Linda Hoemberg
Profile: Magazine about cinema, culture and movies. Facebook: http://www.facebook.com/pages/engels-Wuppertal/367759372373.
Language(s): German
ADVERTISING RATES:
Full Page Mono .... EUR 700
Full Page Colour .... EUR 1200
Mechanical Data: Type Area: 265 x 190 mm, No. of Columns (Display): 4, Col Widths (Display): 44 mm
Copy instructions: *Copy Date:* 15 days prior to publication
CONSUMER: MUSIC & PERFORMING ARTS: Cinema

ENGLISH@OFFICE
1615632G34-535
Editorial: Abraham-Lincoln-Str. 46, 65189 WIESBADEN **Tel:** 611 7878246 **Fax:** 611 7878490
Email: workingoffice@gabler.de **Web site:** http://www.workingoffice.de
Freq: Quarterly; **Circ:** 30,079
Editor: Maria Akhavan-Hezavei; **Advertising Manager:** Eva Hanenberg
Profile: Supplement: English-special part of the magazine working@office.
Language(s): English; German
Mechanical Data: Type Area: 250 x 175 mm, No. of Columns (Display): 3, Col Widths (Display): 59 mm
Supplement to: working@office

ENORM
1983703G14A-10416
Editorial: Planckstr. 13, 22765 HAMBURG
Tel: 40 88885772 **Fax:** 40 88885781
Email: redaktion@enorm-magazin.de **Web site:** http://www.enorm-magazin.de
Freq: Quarterly; **Annual Sub.:** EUR 30,00; **Circ:** 35,000
Editor: Thomas Friemel; **Advertising Manager:** Martina Sander
Profile: The magazine highlights the economic models, companies and individuals who respond to the growing local and global challenges in society and the environment, and consider writing contribute new ideas and valuable contributions to a positive shaping our future.
Language(s): German
ADVERTISING RATES:
Full Page Mono .... EUR 6900
Full Page Colour .... EUR 6900
Mechanical Data: Type Area: 256 x 190 mm

DIE ENTSCHEIDUNG
726337G91D-2140
Editorial: Inselstr. 1b, 10179 BERLIN
Tel: 30 2787870 **Fax:** 30 27878720
Email: redaktion@entscheidung.de **Web site:** http://www.entscheidung.de
Freq: 6 issues yearly; **Annual Sub.:** EUR 15,34; **Circ:** 11,450
Editor: Sidney Pfannstiel; **Advertising Manager:** Alexander Lenders
Profile: Magazine of the political party Junge Union Deutschland.
Language(s): German
ADVERTISING RATES:
Full Page Mono .... EUR 2200
Full Page Colour .... EUR 2200
Mechanical Data: Type Area: 239 x 182 mm, No. of Columns (Display): 3, Col Widths (Display): 58 mm
Copy instructions: *Copy Date:* 14 days prior to publication
Supplement(s): Black
CONSUMER: RECREATION & LEISURE: Children & Youth

ENTSCHEIDUNGEN ZUM WIRTSCHAFTSRECHT EWIR
726344G44-840
Editorial: Aachener Str. 222, 50931 KÖLN
Tel: 221 4008812 **Fax:** 221 4008877
Email: redaktion-ewir@rws-verlag.de **Web site:** http://www.ewir-online.de
Freq: 24 issues yearly; **Annual Sub.:** EUR 378,60; **Circ:** 4,700
Editor: Katherine Knauth; **Advertising Manager:** Karl-Heinz Schneider
Profile: Magazine containing details of rulings in commercial and business law.
Language(s): German
ADVERTISING RATES:
Full Page Mono .... EUR 550
Full Page Colour .... EUR 963
Mechanical Data: Type Area: 210 x 135 mm, No. of Columns (Display): 2, Col Widths (Display): 65 mm
Copy instructions: *Copy Date:* 7 days prior to publication
Supplement to: Zeitschrift für Wirtschaftsrecht ZIP
BUSINESS: LEGAL

ENTSORGA
726345G57-2657
Editorial: Mainzer Landstr. 251, 60326 FRANKFURT
Tel: 69 75951541 **Fax:** 69 75952550
Email: redaktion@entsorga-magazin.de **Web site:** http://www.entsorga-magazin.de
Freq: 8 issues yearly; **Annual Sub.:** EUR 102,60; **Circ:** 10,433
Editor: Martin Boeckh; **Advertising Manager:** Heidrun Dangl
Profile: Magazine about the recycling and disposal of waste and sewage.
Language(s): German
ADVERTISING RATES:
Full Page Mono .... EUR 4010
Full Page Colour .... EUR 4890
Mechanical Data: Type Area: 268 x 185 mm, No. of Columns (Display): 4, Col Widths (Display): 43 mm
Copy instructions: *Copy Date:* 21 days prior to publication
BUSINESS: ENVIRONMENT & POLLUTION

ENTSPANNUNGSVERFAHREN
755876G56A-11086
Editorial: Blanckstr. 3, 23564 LÜBECK
Email: geschaeftsstelle@dg-e.de **Web site:** http://www.dg-e.de
Freq: Annual; **Cover Price:** EUR 12,50
Free to qualifying individuals ; **Circ:** 1,400
Advertising Manager: Wolfgang Pabst
Profile: Magazine about psychotherapy by relaxation methods.
Language(s): English; German
Mechanical Data: Type Area: 176 x 124 mm

ENTWICKLER MAGAZIN
726347G5R-642
Editorial: Geleitsstr. 14, 60599 FRANKFURT
Tel: 69 6300890 **Fax:** 69 63008989
Email: info@entwickler-magazin.de **Web site:** http://www.entwickler-magazin.de
Freq: 6 issues yearly; **Annual Sub.:** EUR 27,60; **Circ:** 5,173
Editor: Robert Lippert
Profile: Magazine focusing on Pascal and C++ programming. Includes technical information concerning database programming and mediaware technology.
Language(s): German
Readership: Aimed at IT managers, programmers and project managers.
ADVERTISING RATES:
Full Page Mono .... EUR 3150
Full Page Colour .... EUR 4350
Mechanical Data: Type Area: 231 x 184 mm, No. of Columns (Display): 4, Col Widths (Display): 46 mm
BUSINESS: COMPUTERS & AUTOMATION: Computers Related

ENVIRONMENTAL CHEMISTRY LETTERS
1638630G37-1793
Editorial: Tiergartenstr. 17, 69121 HEIDELBERG
Tel: 6221 4870 **Fax:** 6221 4878177
Email: subscriptions@springer.com **Web site:** http://www.springerlink.com
Freq: Quarterly; **Annual Sub.:** EUR 332,00; **Circ:** 55
Editor: Jan Schwarzbauer; **Advertising Manager:** Sabine Weidner
Profile: Information about environmental chemistry.
Language(s): English
ADVERTISING RATES:
Full Page Mono .... EUR 740
Full Page Colour .... EUR 1780
Mechanical Data: Type Area: 240 x 175 mm

ENVIRONMENTAL SCIENCE AND POLLUTION RESEARCH
726353G57-440
Editorial: Tiergartenstr. 17, 69121 HEIDELBERG
Tel: 6221 4870 **Fax:** 6221 4878177
Email: subscriptions@springer.com **Web site:** http://www.springer.com
Freq: 9 issues yearly; **Annual Sub.:** EUR 299,00; **Circ:** 272
Editor: Alvin L. Young
Profile: International journal about environmental science and pollution research.
Language(s): English
ADVERTISING RATES:
Full Page Mono .... EUR 740
Full Page Colour .... EUR 1780
Mechanical Data: Type Area: 270 x 200 mm
Copy instructions: *Copy Date:* 42 days prior to publication
Official Journal of: Organ d. EuCheMS Division of Chemistry and the Environment
BUSINESS: ENVIRONMENT & POLLUTION

ENZTAL
1640289G89A-11822
Editorial: Baetznerstr. 85, 75323 BAD WILDBAD
Tel: 7081 3030 **Fax:** 7081 303100
Email: info@staatsbad-wildbad.de **Web site:** http://www.enztal.de
Freq: Annual; **Cover Price:** Free; **Circ:** 30,000

Profile: Catalogue of thermal springs in the Schwarzwald.
Language(s): English; French; German

EP ELEKTROPRAKTIKER
726365G17-420
Editorial: Am Friedrichshain 22, 10407 BERLIN
Tel: 30 42151304 **Fax:** 30 42151251
Email: redaktion@elektropraktiker.de **Web site:** http://www.elektropraktiker.de
Freq: Monthly; **Annual Sub.:** EUR 73,80; **Circ:** 43,268
Editor: Rüdiger Tuzinski; **Advertising Manager:** Torsten Ernst
Profile: Range of topics: electrical installation, home automation, electrical equipment, switchgear, power electronics, lighting equipment, standardization issues, electrical safety, education and training, management in the trades, master of knowledge, technical and business skills, software and literature recommendations, updates from the industry, guilds and associations. Constant feature of the magazine is "Lernen & Können" - a special 16-page section for the electrical engineering education and training. Quarterly published the "Arbeitsschutzbrief" with instructions to direct health and safety instructions in various areas of electrical work.
Language(s): German
ADVERTISING RATES:
Full Page Mono .... EUR 6600
Full Page Colour .... EUR 9750
Mechanical Data: Type Area: 266 x 185 mm, No. of Columns (Display): 4, Col Widths (Display): 43 mm
Copy instructions: *Copy Date:* 21 days prior to publication
BUSINESS: ELECTRICAL

EP ELEKTROPRAKTIKER PHOTOVOLTAIK
1898570G17-1626
Editorial: Am Friedrichshain 22, 10407 BERLIN
Tel: 30 42151304 **Fax:** 30 42151251
Email: redaktion@elektropraktiker.de **Web site:** http://www.ep-photovoltaik.de
Freq: 8 issues yearly; **Circ:** 14,817
Editor: Rüdiger Tuzinski; **Advertising Manager:** Torsten Ernst
Profile: ep Elektropraktiker Photovoltaik is a magazine for electricians in the trade and industry as well as planning and engineering firms. The magazine was published in February 2008, initially under the title "ep Photovoltaik aktuell" as a supplement of the trade title ep Elektropraktiker and was sent only to the latter. Since issue 1/2-2009 the ep Elektropraktiker Photovoltaik is independent. It can thus be obtained independently from a ep-subscription.
Language(s): German
ADVERTISING RATES:
Full Page Mono .... EUR 2480
Full Page Colour .... EUR 3140
Mechanical Data: Type Area: 266 x 185 mm, No. of Columns (Display): 4, Col Widths (Display): 43 mm
Copy instructions: *Copy Date:* 33 days prior to publication

EPD FILM
726361G76A-440
Editorial: Emil-von-Behring-Str. 3, 60439 FRANKFURT **Tel:** 69 58098205 **Fax:** 69 58098445
Email: film@epd.de **Web site:** http://www.epd-film.de
Freq: Monthly; **Annual Sub.:** EUR 59,40; **Circ:** 7,230
Profile: Magazine for film enthusiasts.
Language(s): German
ADVERTISING RATES:
Full Page Mono .... EUR 810
Full Page Colour .... EUR 990
Mechanical Data: Type Area: 263 x 182 mm
Copy instructions: *Copy Date:* 15 days prior to publication
CONSUMER: MUSIC & PERFORMING ARTS: Cinema

EPD MEDIEN
726362G76A-460
Editorial: Emil-von-Behring-Str. 3, 60439 FRANKFURT **Tel:** 69 58098202 **Fax:** 69 58098261
Email: medien@epd.de **Web site:** http://www.epd.de
Freq: Weekly; **Annual Sub.:** EUR 792,00; **Circ:** 981
Editor: Thomas Schiller
Profile: Current information service for decision makers, program planners, and media observers. The readers get weekly updates on the whole world of media: television, radio, press and Internet, media policy, program analysis, staff members, new broadcasting legislation, the advertising market and media ethics.
Language(s): German
ADVERTISING RATES:
Full Page Mono .... EUR 730
Full Page Colour .... EUR 1380
Mechanical Data: Type Area: 230 x 158 mm
Copy instructions: *Copy Date:* 8 days prior to publication
CONSUMER: MUSIC & PERFORMING ARTS: Cinema

EPD SOZIAL
755878G32G-2942
Editorial: Emil-von-Behring-Str. 3, 60439 FRANKFURT **Tel:** 69 58098133 **Fax:** 69 58098294
Email: sozial@epd.de **Web site:** http://www.epd.de
Freq: Weekly; **Annual Sub.:** EUR 237,60; **Circ:** 802
Editor: Thomas Schiller
Profile: Magazine reporting about recent developments in social policy and social economy in nursing, health, family, migration, labour, habitation, pension and law sectors.
Language(s): German
ADVERTISING RATES:
Full Page Mono .... EUR 580
Full Page Colour .... EUR 1230
Mechanical Data: Type Area: 255 x 165 mm
Copy instructions: *Copy Date:* 10 days prior to publication
BUSINESS: LOCAL GOVERNMENT, LEISURE & RECREATION: Community Care & Social Services

EPP ELEKTRONIK PRODUKTION & PRÜFTECHNIK
726375G18A-230
Editorial: Ernst-Mey-Str. 8, 70771 LEINFELDEN-ECHTERDINGEN **Tel:** 711 7594417
Fax: 711 7594221
Email: stefan.ziegler@konradin.de **Web site:** http://www.epp-online.de
Freq: 7 issues yearly; **Annual Sub.:** EUR 85,60; **Circ:** 9,040
Editor: Stefan Ziegler; **Advertising Manager:** Andreas Hugel
Profile: High level expertise through practical and application oriented reporting on all aspects of electronics production. Interviews with leading figures in the market are a distinctive feature. EPP is the highest print run German language trade magazine in the field of electronics manufacturing and testing. The regular issues of EPP focus on practical topics relating to assembly & PCB production, chip packaging & mounting and testing & quality assurance.
Language(s): German
ADVERTISING RATES:
Full Page Mono .... EUR 3800
Full Page Colour .... EUR 4770
Mechanical Data: Type Area: 270 x 188 mm, No. of Columns (Display): 4, Col Widths (Display): 44 mm
BUSINESS: ELECTRONICS

EPP EUROPE
726380G18A-231
Editorial: Ernst-Mey-Str. 8, 70771 LEINFELDEN-ECHTERDINGEN **Tel:** 711 7594417
Fax: 711 7594221
Email: stefan.ziegler@konradin.de **Web site:** http://www.epp-online.de
Freq: Quarterly; **Annual Sub.:** EUR 85,60; **Circ:** 19,937
Editor: Stefan Ziegler; **Advertising Manager:** Andreas Hugel
Profile: Launched in 1975, EPP was the very first trade publication in Germany to exclusively cover all aspects of the electronics manufacture and test industry. Since then our readers have been working with more than 300 issues featuring countless in-depth Articles, Interviews, Product Reports and Industry News, built upon our reputation for informative, qualified and in? uential editorial with leading industry experts from around the world. EPP predominantly meets the needs of the influential German speaking industry. Anticipating the rapidly developing European market, in 1995 we launched the sister publication EPP Europe. We are proud to see EPP Europe now established as the leading independent magazine for European electronics manufacture. EPP Europe is only delivered to qualified specialists (Company, Technical, Production and Quality Management) within Companies that include in-house electronics manufacturing. EPP Europe is subject to an independent circulation audit. No competitor does the same.
Language(s): English
ADVERTISING RATES:
Full Page Mono .... EUR 4460
Full Page Colour .... EUR 5495
Mechanical Data: Type Area: 270 x 188 mm, No. of Columns (Display): 4, Col Widths (Display): 44 mm
BUSINESS: ELECTRONICS

EPPI
726381G2A-1260
Editorial: Waltherstr. 49, 51069 KÖLN
Tel: 221 689110 **Fax:** 221 6891110
Email: barth@waorg.com **Web site:** http://www.eppi-magazine.com
Freq: 6 issues yearly; **Annual Sub.:** EUR 26,00; **Circ:** 10,000
Editor: Till Barth; **Advertising Manager:** Sarah Vieten
Profile: Publication containing information about advertising articles and promotional gifts for English-speaking resellers in Europe.
Language(s): English
ADVERTISING RATES:
Full Page Mono .... EUR 1480
Full Page Colour .... EUR 2350
Mechanical Data: Type Area: 260 x 182 mm, No. of Columns (Display): 3, Col Widths (Display): 60 mm
Copy instructions: *Copy Date:* 21 days prior to publication
BUSINESS: COMMUNICATIONS, ADVERTISING & MARKETING

EPPPL EUROPEAN PUBLIC PRIVATE PARTNERSHIP LAW REVIEW
1828417G1A-3697
Editorial: Güntzelstr. 63, 10717 BERLIN
Tel: 30 81450621 **Fax:** 30 8145062952
Email: hellmuth@lexxion.de **Web site:** http://www.lexxion.de
Freq: Quarterly; **Annual Sub.:** EUR 372,36; **Circ:** 500
Editor: Patricia Hellmuth
Profile: Journal provides detailed coverage of all significant developments in the phenomenon of public private partnerships area across the European Union and beyond.
Language(s): English
ADVERTISING RATES:
Full Page Mono .... EUR 500
Mechanical Data: Type Area: 220 x 157 mm
Copy instructions: *Copy Date:* 21 days prior to publication

E.PUNKT NRW
1864582G17-1614
Editorial: Hannöversche Str. 22, 44143 DORTMUND
Tel: 231 519850 **Fax:** 231 5198544
Email: info@feh-nrw.de **Web site:** http://www.feh-nrw.de
Freq: Monthly; Free to qualifying individuals
Annual Sub.: EUR 19,00; **Circ:** 7,200
Editor: Simone Merkel
Profile: Magazine for craftsmen in electro and information technology in the region of Nordrhein-Westfalen.
Language(s): German
ADVERTISING RATES:
Full Page Mono .... EUR 1450
Full Page Colour .... EUR 1762
Mechanical Data: Type Area: 252 x 172 mm, No. of Columns (Display): 3, Col Widths (Display): 54 mm
Copy instructions: *Copy Date:* 29 days prior to publication
Supplement to: de Der Elektro- und Gebäudetechniker

ERBE UND AUFTRAG
726393G87-3520
Editorial: Abteistr. 2, 88631 BEURON
Tel: 7466 17247 **Fax:** 7466 17248
Email: redaktion@erbeundauftrag.de **Web site:** http://www.erbeundauftrag.de
Freq: Quarterly; **Annual Sub.:** EUR 36,00; **Circ:** 1,200
Editor: Albert Schmidt; **Advertising Manager:** Joachim Schlude
Profile: Religious magazine.
Language(s): German
ADVERTISING RATES:
Full Page Mono .... EUR 400
Mechanical Data: Type Area: 185 x 125 mm
CONSUMER: RELIGIOUS

ERBEN + VERMÖGEN
1646358G1A-3555
Editorial: Eschstr. 22, 44629 HERNE
Tel: 2323 141373 **Fax:** 2323 141205
Web site: http://www.nwb.de/go/modul9
Freq: Monthly; **Annual Sub.:** EUR 231,60; **Circ:** 1,500
Editor: Annette Kubiak; **Advertising Manager:** Andreas Reimann
Profile: Magazine containing information about all aspects of tax oriented investment counselling.
Language(s): German
ADVERTISING RATES:
Full Page Mono .... EUR 1260
Full Page Colour .... EUR 2280
Mechanical Data: Type Area: 260 x 186 mm
Copy instructions: *Copy Date:* 14 days prior to publication

DER ERBSCHAFT-STEUER-BERATER
1626356G1A-3524
Editorial: Gustav-Heinemann-Ufer 58, 50968 KÖLN
Tel: 221 93738151 **Fax:** 221 93738902
Email: verlag@otto-schmidt.de **Web site:** http://www.erbstb.de
Freq: Monthly; **Annual Sub.:** EUR 160,90; **Circ:** 1,440
Editor: Annette Stuhldreier; **Advertising Manager:** Thorsten Deuse
Profile: Magazine for tax advisors and tax lawyers.
Language(s): German
ADVERTISING RATES:
Full Page Mono .... EUR 595
Full Page Colour .... EUR 1042
Mechanical Data: Type Area: 260 x 180 mm, No. of Columns (Display): 2, Col Widths (Display): 88 mm

ERDINGER ANZEIGER
726423G67B-4840
Editorial: Pfaffenrieder Str. 9, 82515 WOLFRATSHAUSEN **Tel:** 8171 2690
Fax: 8171 269240
Email: fsav@merkur-online.de **Web site:** http://www.merkur-online.de
Freq: 312 issues yearly; **Circ:** 15,958
Advertising Manager: Hans-Georg Bechthold
Profile: The Münchner Merkur with its own local newspapers, of which the Erdinger Anzeiger is one that, the leading regional newspaper brand in the Munich area - the most affluent area of Germany. The combination of newspaper and region is the foundation on which to build the success of the title. This is the newspaper not only the factual news agency, but forms a community of solidarity with its readers and the local community. The clear focus on local reporting creates a high regard to human reader loyalty. She presses one hand in the very high number of close to 180,000 subscribers. Also for the high reader-commitment is the loyalty of the total current 827 000 daily readers, the Münchner Merkur or one of its local newspapers usually read over many years. The Münchner Merkur with its own local newspapers is a newspaper for the whole family, tradition and modern life for one of the most beautiful regions of Germany unites. Reliable, informative, critical: the Münchner Merkur is the indispensable daily newspaper for the region. Facebook: http://www.facebook.com/pages/merkur-online.de/190176143327 This Outlet offers RSS (Really Simple Syndication).
Language(s): German
ADVERTISING RATES:
SCC .... EUR 43,60
Mechanical Data: Type Area: 474 x 324 mm, No. of Columns (Display): 7, Col Widths (Display): 45 mm
Copy instructions: *Copy Date:* 1 day prior to publication
REGIONAL DAILY & SUNDAY NEWSPAPERS: Regional Daily Newspapers

ERDÖL ERDGAS KOHLE
726429G58-380
Editorial: Neumann-Reichardt-Str. 34, 22041 HAMBURG **Tel:** 40 65694540 **Fax:** 40 65694550
Email: h.j.mager@oilgaspublisher.de **Web site:** http://www.oilgaspublisher.de
Freq: 11 issues yearly; **Annual Sub.:** EUR 325,71; **Circ:** 2,632
Editor: Hans Jörg Mager; **Advertising Manager:** Harald Jordan
Profile: Journal about the oil, gas and coal upgrading industries.
Language(s): German
ADVERTISING RATES:
Full Page Mono .... EUR 2350
Full Page Colour .... EUR 3400
Mechanical Data: Type Area: 260 x 185 mm, No. of Columns (Display): 3, Col Widths (Display): 60 mm
Copy instructions: *Copy Date:* 10 days prior to publication
Official Journal of: Organ d. DGMK-Dt. Wissenschaftl. Ges. f. Erdöl, Erdgas u. Kohle, d. ÖGEW-Österr. Ges. f. Erdölwissenschaften
BUSINESS: ENERGY, FUEL & NUCLEAR

ERFAHRUNGSHEILKUNDE
726431G56A-3060
Editorial: Oswald-Hesse-Str. 50, 70469 STUTTGART
Tel: 711 8931732 **Fax:** 711 8931748
Email: daniela.elsasser@medizinverlage.de **Web site:** http://www.medizinverlage.de
Freq: 6 issues yearly; Free to qualifying individuals
Annual Sub.: EUR 84,95; **Circ:** 8,300
Editor: Daniela Elsasser; **Advertising Manager:** Markus Stehle
Profile: Magazine about all aspects of holistic medicine.
Language(s): German
ADVERTISING RATES:
Full Page Mono .... EUR 1920
Full Page Colour .... EUR 2800
Mechanical Data: No. of Columns (Display): 3, Col Widths (Display): 54 mm, Type Area: 240 x 170 mm
Official Journal of: Organ d. Ärzteges. f. Erfahrungsheilkunde e.V., d. Hufelandges. f. Gesamtmedizin u. d. Europ. Vereinigung d. Ärzteverbände d. besonderen Therapierichtungen
BUSINESS: HEALTH & MEDICAL

ERF.DE
1691355G87-13975
Editorial: Berliner Ring 62, 35576 WETZLAR
Tel: 6441 9572000 **Fax:** 6441 9572001
Email: online@erf.de **Web site:** http://www.erf.de
Freq: Daily; **Cover Price:** Paid; **Circ:** 84,278 Unique Users
Editor: Michael Gerster
Language(s): German
CONSUMER: RELIGIOUS

ERFOLGREICH SELBSTÄNDIG
1862712G14A-10229
Editorial: Schloß Bergfeld, 54533 EISENSCHMITT
Tel: 6567 960820 **Fax:** 6567 960819
Freq: 6 issues yearly; Free to qualifying individuals
Annual Sub.: EUR 22,00; **Circ:** 15,245
Editor: Maria E. Krämer
Profile: Magazine containing information about maintaining a successful business.
Language(s): German
Mechanical Data: Type Area: 240 x 188 mm, No. of Columns (Display): 3, Col Widths (Display): 60 mm

ERGO
1791363G56A-11435
Editorial: Keßlerstr. 1, 76185 KARLSRUHE
Tel: 721 59610 **Fax:** 721 59611188
Email: eva.frien@kvbawue.de
Freq: Quarterly; **Cover Price:** Free; **Circ:** 22,000
Editor: Eva Frien
Profile: "ergo" is published four times a year as a free newsletter for members of the physicians' association of Baden-Wuerttemberg and information on current developments in Baden-Württemberg, on policy choices in the health system, on specific topics of daily routines, official notices and ongoing training.
Language(s): German

ERGO-MED
726453G56A-3080
Editorial: Dischingerstr. 8, 69123 HEIDELBERG
Tel: 6221 64460 **Fax:** 6221 644640
Email: ergomed@konradin.de **Web site:** http://www.ergo-med.de
Freq: 6 issues yearly; **Annual Sub.:** EUR 60,00; **Circ:** 1,000
Editor: Detlev Jung; **Advertising Manager:** Sandra Rink

Profile: Periodical focusing on work-related medical practice.
Language(s): German
ADVERTISING RATES:
Full Page Mono .... EUR 720
Full Page Colour .... EUR 1044
Mechanical Data: Type Area: 250 x 172 mm, No. of Columns (Display): 4, Col Widths (Display): 44 mm
Copy instructions: *Copy Date:* 30 days prior to publication
Supplement(s): baua: Aktuell
BUSINESS: HEALTH & MEDICAL

ERGOTHERAPIE UND REHABILITATION 726456G56L-37
Editorial: Drostestr. 8, 30161 HANNOVER
Tel: 511 3941008
Email: c.berting@et-reha.dve.info **Web site:** http://www.schulz-kirchner.de/ergotherapie
Freq: Monthly; Free to qualifying individuals
Annual Sub.: EUR 82,95; **Circ:** 13,107
Editor: Christa Berting-Hüneke; **Advertising Manager:** Tanja Kern
Profile: Magazine covering physiotherapy for health problems caused by the working environment.
Language(s): German
ADVERTISING RATES:
Full Page Mono .... EUR 1271
Full Page Colour .... EUR 1631
Mechanical Data: Type Area: 260 x 180 mm, No. of Columns (Display): 2, Col Widths (Display): 87 mm
Copy instructions: *Copy Date:* 31 days prior to publication
BUSINESS: HEALTH & MEDICAL: Disability & Rehabilitation

ERHALTEN & GESTALTEN 726457G4E-3380
Editorial: Döllgaststr. 7, 86199 AUGSBURG
Tel: 821 344570 **Fax:** 821 3445719
Email: info@mkpublishing.de **Web site:** http://www.mkpublishing.de
Freq: Half-yearly; **Cover Price:** Free; **Circ:** 20,000
Profile: Magazine of customers of the Keimfarben company.
Language(s): German

ERLANGER NACHRICHTEN 726469G67B-4920
Editorial: Marienstr. 9, 90402 NÜRNBERG
Tel: 911 2160 **Fax:** 911 2162432
Web site: http://www.nuernberger-nachrichten.de
Freq: 312 issues yearly; **Circ:** 35,203
Profile: Daily newspaper with regional news and a local sports section.
Language(s): German
ADVERTISING RATES:
SCC .... EUR 94,00
Mechanical Data: Type Area: 430 x 280 mm, No. of Columns (Display): 6, Col Widths (Display): 45 mm
Copy instructions: *Copy Date:* 1 day prior to publication
Supplement(s): sechs+sechzig
REGIONAL DAILY & SUNDAY NEWSPAPERS: Regional Daily Newspapers

ERNÄHRUNGS UMSCHAU 726482G56R-540
Editorial: Otto-Volger-Str. 15, 65843 SULZBACH
Tel: 6196 7667240 **Fax:** 6196 7676269
Email: h.recktenwald@uzv.de **Web site:** http://www.ernaehrungs-umschau.de
Freq: Monthly; **Annual Sub.:** EUR 91,80; **Circ:** 10,270
Editor: Heike Recktenwald; **Advertising Manager:** Tanja Kilbert
Profile: Aimed at caterers and dietitians in big institutions.
Language(s): German
Readership: Aimed at caterers and dietitians in big institutions.
ADVERTISING RATES:
Full Page Mono .... EUR 2907
Full Page Colour .... EUR 4545
Mechanical Data: Type Area: 240 x 179 mm, No. of Columns (Display): 3, Col Widths (Display): 57 mm
Copy instructions: *Copy Date:* 22 days prior to publication
Official Journal of: Organ d. Dt. Ges. f. Ernährung e.V., d. Verb. d. Diätassistenten-Dt. Bundesverb. e.V., d. RAL Gütegemeinschaft Ernährungskompetenz e.V., d. Verb. d. Diplom-Oecotrophologen e.V. u. Bundesverb. Dt. Ernährungsmediziner e.V.
Supplement(s): DGE info; ernährungslehre & -praxis
BUSINESS: HEALTH & MEDICAL: Health Medical Related

ERNEUERBARE ENERGIEN 726485G58-400
Editorial: Hans-Böckler-Allee 7, 30173 HANNOVER
Tel: 511 85502563 **Fax:** 511 85502560
Email: redaktion@sunmediaverlag.de **Web site:** http://www.erneuerbareenergien.de
Freq: Monthly; **Annual Sub.:** EUR 68,00; **Circ:** 12,793
Editor: Karsten Schäfer; **Advertising Manager:** Patrick Krumbach
Profile: Magazine about regenerative energy.
Language(s): German
ADVERTISING RATES:
Full Page Mono .... EUR 1010
Full Page Colour .... EUR 2180
Mechanical Data: Type Area: 261 x 195 mm, No. of Columns (Display): 4, Col Widths (Display): 45 mm
Copy instructions: *Copy Date:* 21 days prior to publication
Supplement(s): Wind Turbine Market

DER ERTRAG-STEUER-BERATER 726500G1A-860
Editorial: Gustav-Heinemann-Ufer 58, 50968 KÖLN
Tel: 221 93738151 **Fax:** 221 93738902
Email: verlag@otto-schmidt.de **Web site:** http://www.estb.de
Freq: Monthly; **Annual Sub.:** EUR 166,90; **Circ:** 2,313
Editor: Annette Stuhldreier; **Advertising Manager:** Thorsten Deuse
Profile: Magazine about profits tax law.
Language(s): German
ADVERTISING RATES:
Full Page Mono .... EUR 875
Full Page Colour .... EUR 1532
Mechanical Data: Type Area: 260 x 180 mm, No. of Columns (Display): 2, Col Widths (Display): 88 mm
BUSINESS: FINANCE & ECONOMICS

ERWERBS-OBSTBAU 726504G26C-25
Editorial: Tiergartenstr. 17, 69121 HEIDELBERG
Tel: 6221 4870 **Fax:** 6221 4878366
Email: subscriptions@springer.com **Web site:** http://www.springerlink.com
Freq: Quarterly; **Annual Sub.:** EUR 446,00; **Circ:** 194
Profile: Journal about professional fruit growing.
Language(s): German
ADVERTISING RATES:
Full Page Mono .... EUR 740
Full Page Colour .... EUR 1780
Mechanical Data: Type Area: 240 x 175 mm
BUSINESS: GARDEN TRADE

ERZHÄUSER ANZEIGER 726512G72-3612
Editorial: Eulerweg 11, 64291 DARMSTADT
Tel: 6151 9515247 **Fax:** 6151 9515249
Email: info@printdesign24.de **Web site:** http://www.arheilger-post.de
Freq: Weekly; **Cover Price:** Free; **Circ:** 3,400
Profile: Advertising journal (house-to-house) concentrating on local stories.
Language(s): German
Mechanical Data: Type Area: 420 x 280 mm, No. of Columns (Display): 6, Col Widths (Display): 45 mm
Copy instructions: *Copy Date:* 2 days prior to publication
LOCAL NEWSPAPERS

ERZIEHUNG UND WISSENSCHAFT - ZS. D. BILDUNGSGEWERKSCHAFT GEW (BUNDESAUSG.) 726520G62A-800
Editorial: Reifenberger Str. 21, 60489 FRANKFURT
Tel: 69 789730 **Fax:** 69 78973202
Email: ulf.roedde@gew.de **Web site:** http://www.gew.de
Freq: 11 issues yearly; Free to qualifying individuals
Annual Sub.: EUR 18,50; **Circ:** 254,913
Editor: Ulf Rödde; **Advertising Manager:** Mathias Müller
Profile: Publication focusing on nationwide education and science, published by teacher trade union GEW Germany. The nationally distributed magazine "Erziehung und Wissenschaft" - by the way by far - the largest circulation magazine for educators.
Language(s): German
Readership: Read by teachers.
ADVERTISING RATES:
Full Page Mono .... EUR 5440
Full Page Colour .... EUR 7168
Mechanical Data: Type Area: 270 x 202 mm, No. of Columns (Display): 4, Col Widths (Display): 45 mm
Copy instructions: *Copy Date:* 31 days prior to publication
Supplement(s): blz; DDS; Erziehung und Wissenschaft im Saarland; Erziehung und Wissenschaft plus; E & W plus; E & W Sachsen; GEW news; GEW-Zeitung Rheinland-Pfalz; HLZ; tz. thüringer zeitschrift für bildung, erziehung und wissenschaft; Zeitschrift für Erziehung und Wissenschaft in Schleswig-Holstein
BUSINESS: CHURCH & SCHOOL EQUIPMENT & EDUCATION: Education

ESCHWEILER NACHRICHTEN 726537G67B-4940
Editorial: Dresdener Str. 3, 52068 AACHEN
Tel: 241 5101310 **Fax:** 241 5101360
Email: redaktion@zeitungsverlag-aachen.de **Web site:** http://www.an-online.de
Freq: 312 issues yearly; **Circ:** 29,821
Advertising Manager: Christian Kretschmer
Profile: Daily newspaper with regional news and a local sports section. Facebook: http://facebook.com/aachenernachrichten This Outlet offers RSS (Really Simple Syndication).
Language(s): German
ADVERTISING RATES:
SCC .... EUR 62,80
Mechanical Data: Type Area: 480 x 324 mm, No. of Columns (Display): 7, Col Widths (Display): 44 mm
Copy instructions: *Copy Date:* 1 day prior to publication
Supplement(s): prisma
REGIONAL DAILY & SUNDAY NEWSPAPERS: Regional Daily Newspapers

ESCHWEILER ZEITUNG 726538G67B-4960
Editorial: Dresdener Str. 3, 52068 AACHEN
Tel: 241 5101310 **Fax:** 241 5101360
Email: redaktion@zeitungsverlag-aachen.de **Web site:** http://www.aachener-zeitung.de
Freq: 312 issues yearly; **Circ:** 29,821
Advertising Manager: Christian Kretschmer
Profile: Daily newspaper with regional news and a local sports section. Facebook: http://facebook.com/aachenerzeitung This Outlet offers RSS (Really Simple Syndication).
Language(s): German
ADVERTISING RATES:
SCC .... EUR 62,80
Mechanical Data: Type Area: 480 x 324 mm, No. of Columns (Display): 7, Col Widths (Display): 44 mm
Copy instructions: *Copy Date:* 1 day prior to publication
Supplement(s): prisma
REGIONAL DAILY & SUNDAY NEWSPAPERS: Regional Daily Newspapers

ESOX 726544G92-60
Editorial: Troplowitzstr. 5, 22529 HAMBURG
Tel: 40 38906227 **Fax:** 40 38906303
Email: sven.halletz@jahr-tsv.de **Web site:** http://www.esox.de
Freq: Monthly; **Annual Sub.:** EUR 24,00; **Circ:** 49,510
Editor: Sven Halletz; **Advertising Manager:** Sandra Böthin
Profile: Esox is the Latin term for Germany's most popular predator, the pike. And like a pike Esox is pushed into the market of the German fishing magazines.
Language(s): German
Readership: Aimed at angling enthusiasts.
ADVERTISING RATES:
Full Page Mono .... EUR 1966
Full Page Colour .... EUR 2092
Mechanical Data: Type Area: 248 x 185 mm, No. of Columns (Display): 4, Col Widths (Display): 45 mm
Copy instructions: *Copy Date:* 27 days prior to publication
CONSUMER: ANGLING & FISHING

ESPELKAMPER ZEITUNG 726546G67B-4980
Editorial: Sudbrackstr. 14, 33611 BIELEFELD
Tel: 521 5850 **Fax:** 521 585489
Email: wb@westfalen-blatt.de **Web site:** http://www.westfalen-blatt.de
Freq: 312 issues yearly; **Circ:** 9,122
Advertising Manager: Gabriele Förster
Profile: Daily newspaper with regional news and a local sports section.
Language(s): German
Mechanical Data: Type Area: 490 x 320 mm, No. of Columns (Display): 7, Col Widths (Display): 44 mm
Copy instructions: *Copy Date:* 1 day prior to publication
Supplement(s): Mein Garten; www.wb-immo.net
REGIONAL DAILY & SUNDAY NEWSPAPERS: Regional Daily Newspapers

ESSEN GEHT AUS! 1893491G89A-12453
Editorial: Höherweg 287, 40231 DÜSSELDORF
Tel: 211 7357681 **Fax:** 211 7357680
Email: info@ueberblick.de **Web site:** http://www.ueberblick.de
Freq: Annual; **Cover Price:** EUR 6,80; **Circ:** 40,000
Editor: Peter Erik Hillenbach
Profile: Restaurant guide for the city of Essen.
Language(s): German
ADVERTISING RATES:
Full Page Mono .... EUR 2390
Full Page Colour .... EUR 3490
Mechanical Data: Type Area: 260 x 190 mm, No. of Columns (Display): 4, Col Widths (Display): 44 mm
Copy instructions: *Copy Date:* 40 days prior to publication

ESSEN & TRINKEN 726559G74P-300
Editorial: Am Baumwall 11, 20459 HAMBURG
Tel: 40 37032724 **Fax:** 40 37035677
Email: buchelt.martina@guj.de **Web site:** http://www.essen-und-trinken.de
Freq: Monthly; **Annual Sub.:** EUR 45,60; **Circ:** 175,236
Editor: Stephan Schäfer; **Advertising Manager:** Nicole Schostak
Profile: Culinary magazine including recipes, restaurant and travel reviews from around the world. Also includes interviews, product reports and descriptions of new directions in cookery.
Language(s): German
ADVERTISING RATES:
Full Page Mono .... EUR 20900
Full Page Colour .... EUR 20900
Mechanical Data: Type Area: 236 x 179 mm, No. of Columns (Display): 3, Col Widths (Display): 57 mm
CONSUMER: WOMEN'S INTEREST CONSUMER MAGAZINES: Food & Cookery

ESSEN & TRINKEN FÜR JEDEN TAG 1623541G74P-1047
Editorial: Am Baumwall 11, 20459 HAMBURG
Tel: 40 37032724 **Fax:** 40 37035677
Email: buchelt.martina@guj.de **Web site:** http://www.essen-und-trinken.de
Freq: Monthly; **Annual Sub.:** EUR 31,20; **Circ:** 165,456
Editor: Wolfgang-Robert Zahner; **Advertising Manager:** Nicole Schostak
Profile: For over 35 years, "essen & trinken" is Germany's most successful premium magazine for connoisseurs. With passion and reliability "essen & trinken" in its categories provides delicious recipes, seasonal market tips, live reports and insider news from the latest culinary world as well as travel tips with the best restaurant and hotel recommendations in the most beautiful regions of the world, interesting stories about wines and spirits and lots of practical advice on how to cook.
Language(s): German
ADVERTISING RATES:
Full Page Mono .... EUR 13700
Full Page Colour .... EUR 13700
Mechanical Data: Type Area: 190 x 128 mm, No. of Columns (Display): 3, Col Widths (Display): 39 mm
CONSUMER: WOMEN'S INTEREST CONSUMER MAGAZINES: Food & Cookery

ESSEN UND TRINKEN IN MECKLENBURG-VORPOMMERN 1866433G89A-12434
Editorial: Am Campus 25, 18182 BENTWISCH
Tel: 381 2066811 **Fax:** 381 2066812
Email: info@klatschmohn.de **Web site:** http://www.klatschmohn.de
Freq: Annual; **Cover Price:** Free; **Circ:** 50,000
Editor: Angelika Kleinfeld; **Advertising Manager:** Angelika Kleinfeld
Profile: Hotel and restaurant guide for Mecklenburg-Vorpommern.
Language(s): German
ADVERTISING RATES:
Full Page Mono .... EUR 900
Full Page Colour .... EUR 900
Mechanical Data: Type Area: 170 x 80 mm
Copy instructions: *Copy Date:* 60 days prior to publication

ESSEN UND TRINKEN IN TÜBINGEN 1785806G89A-12265
Editorial: An der Neckarbrücke 1, 72072 TÜBINGEN
Tel: 7071 91360
Email: mail@tuebingen-info.de **Web site:** http://www.tuebingen-info.de
Freq: Annual; **Cover Price:** Free; **Circ:** 30,000
Advertising Manager: Barbara Honner
Profile: Restaurant guide for Tübingen with recommendations and tips.
Language(s): German

DIE ESSENER 1622478G14R-5973
Editorial: Dahlhauser Str. 106, 45279 ESSEN
Tel: 201 2799646 **Fax:** 201 2799452
Email: info@dieessener.com **Web site:** http://www.essener-branchenbuch.de
Freq: Annual; **Cover Price:** Free; **Circ:** 281,220
Profile: Regional mercantile and telephone directory.
Language(s): German
ADVERTISING RATES:
Full Page Mono .... EUR 8150
Full Page Colour .... EUR 11410
Mechanical Data: Type Area: 283 x 186 mm, No. of Columns (Display): 3, Col Widths (Display): 60 mm
BUSINESS: COMMERCE, INDUSTRY & MANAGEMENT: Commerce Related

ESSLINGER ECHO 726562G72-3648
Editorial: Zeppelinstr. 116, 73730 ESSLINGEN
Tel: 711 758700160 **Fax:** 711 758700148
Email: redaktion@ihr-wochenblatt-echo.de **Web site:** http://www.ihr-wochenblatt-echo.de
Freq: Weekly; **Cover Price:** Free; **Circ:** 43,500
Editor: Barbara Scherer; **Advertising Manager:** Oliver Vollmer
Profile: Advertising journal (house-to-house) concentrating on local stories.
Language(s): German
ADVERTISING RATES:
Full Page Mono .... EUR 1684
Full Page Colour .... EUR 2220
Mechanical Data: Type Area: 370 x 255 mm, No. of Columns (Display): 5, Col Widths (Display): 45 mm
Copy instructions: *Copy Date:* 2 days prior to publication
LOCAL NEWSPAPERS

ESSLINGER ZEITUNG 726563G67B-5000
Editorial: Zeppelinstr. 116, 73730 ESSLINGEN
Tel: 711 9310205 **Fax:** 711 3169124
Email: redaktion@ez-online.de **Web site:** http://www.esslinger-zeitung.de
Freq: 312 issues yearly; **Circ:** 44,047
Editor: Markus Bleistein; **News Editor:** Markus Bleistein; **Advertising Manager:** Natalie Bankston
Profile: Regional daily newspaper with news on politics, economy, culture, sports, travel, technology, etc. It is spread schwerpunktmäig in the district of Esslingen. Facebook: http://www.facebook.com/

esslinger.zeitung Twitter: http://twitter.com/Ez_online This Outlet offers RSS (Really Simple Syndication).
Language(s): German
ADVERTISING RATES:
SCC .... EUR 101,80
Mechanical Data: Type Area: 485 x 324 mm, No. of Columns (Display): 7, Col Widths (Display): 45 mm
Copy instructions: *Copy Date:* 1 day prior to publication
Supplement(s): Bei uns in Plochingen Aichwald Deizisau Altbach; Bei uns in Reichenbach Baltmannsweiler Hochdorf Lichtenwald; Neckar Journal
REGIONAL DAILY & SUNDAY NEWSPAPERS: Regional Daily Newspapers

ESTHETIC PURE 1819064G74A-3565
Editorial: Uhlemeyerstr. 16, 30175 HANNOVER
Tel: 511 3882639 **Fax:** 511 9904430
Email: info@holimed-verlag.de **Web site:** http://www.estheticpure.de
Cover Price: EUR 3,50; **Circ:** 25,000
Editor: Sigrid Tille; **Advertising Manager:** Claus Deiters
Profile: Pure Esthetic presented since the first edition in 2002 layout for the regions Hanover, Brunswick, Hamburg and Berlin in the high-quality glossy. The Lifestyle Journal informed about the latest findings of the health & medicine, beauty, wellness and lifestyle worlds, cuisine, sports and special destinations.
Language(s): German
ADVERTISING RATES:
Full Page Mono .... EUR 1190
Full Page Colour .... EUR 1590
Mechanical Data: Type Area: 240 x 176 mm, No. of Columns (Display): 3, Col Widths (Display): 56 mm

ESTRICHTECHNIK & FUSSBODENBAU 726566G4E-3400
Editorial: Gewerbestr. 2, 86825 BAD WÖRISHOFEN
Tel: 8247 35401 **Fax:** 8247 354170
Email: info@fussbodenbau.de **Web site:** http://www.fussbodenbau.de
Freq: 6 issues yearly; **Circ:** 1,613
Editor: Stefan Heinze
Profile: Magazine focusing on industrial floorings.
Language(s): German
ADVERTISING RATES:
Full Page Mono .... EUR 1220
Full Page Colour .... EUR 2240
Mechanical Data: Type Area: 260 x 185 mm, No. of Columns (Display): 4, Col Widths (Display): 43 mm
Copy instructions: *Copy Date:* 30 days prior to publication
BUSINESS: ARCHITECTURE & BUILDING: Building

ETTENHEIMER STADTANZEIGER 726591G72-3664
Editorial: Denzlinger Str. 42, 79312 EMMENDINGEN
Tel: 7641 938011 **Fax:** 7641 938010
Email: redaktion@ettenheimer-stadtanzeiger.de **Web site:** http://www.wzo.de
Freq: Weekly; **Cover Price:** Free; **Circ:** 12,850
Editor: Herbert Birkle; **Advertising Manager:** Clemens Merkle
Profile: Advertising journal (house-to-house) concentrating on local stories.
Language(s): German
ADVERTISING RATES:
Full Page Mono .... EUR 1840
Full Page Colour .... EUR 2520
Mechanical Data: Type Area: 420 x 285 mm, No. of Columns (Display): 6, Col Widths (Display): 45 mm
Copy instructions: *Copy Date:* 2 days prior to publication
LOCAL NEWSPAPERS

ETZ 726595G18A-232
Editorial: Merianstr. 29, 63069 OFFENBACH
Tel: 69 8400061331 **Fax:** 69 8400061399
Email: etz-redaktion@vde-verlag.de **Web site:** http://www.etz.de
Freq: Monthly; **Annual Sub.:** EUR 166,00; **Circ:** 22,724
Editor: Ronald Heinze; **Advertising Manager:** Markus Lehnert
Profile: The etz is published monthly plus 5 special editions and offers important technical information on electrical automation, electric power, test and inspection techniques as well as industrial electronics in order to act as a mainstay for engineers from a number of fields, such as electrical engineering, mechanical and industrial engineering as well as power systems. The etz has a high subscription rate.
Language(s): German
Readership: Read by electrical engineers.
ADVERTISING RATES:
Full Page Mono .... EUR 4365
Full Page Colour .... EUR 5865
Mechanical Data: Type Area: 270 x 189 mm, No. of Columns (Display): 4, Col Widths (Display): 44 mm
Copy instructions: *Copy Date:* 18 days prior to publication
Official Journal of: Organ d. VDE u. d. ETG
Supplement(s): Profibus & Profinet Journal
BUSINESS: ELECTRONICS

EULENSPIEGEL 726599G82-2720
Editorial: Gubener Str. 47, 10243 BERLIN
Tel: 30 29346311 **Fax:** 30 29346321
Email: redaktion@eulenspiegel-zeitschrift.de **Web site:** http://www.eulenspiegel-zeitschrift.de
Freq: Monthly; **Annual Sub.:** EUR 28,00; **Circ:** 119,700
Editor: Mathias Wedel; **Advertising Manager:** Peter Keller
Profile: Journal of satire and humor with a high proportion cartoon for politically interested and critical reader. Facebook: http://www.facebook.com/pages/Eulenspiegel-Satiremagazin/112820228746532 Twitter: http://twitter.com/#!/superfunzel.
Language(s): German
Readership: Aimed at the younger generation.
ADVERTISING RATES:
Full Page Mono .... EUR 3553
Full Page Colour .... EUR 6187
Mechanical Data: Type Area: 272 x 190 mm, No. of Columns (Display): 4, Col Widths (Display): 47 mm
Copy instructions: *Copy Date:* 34 days prior to publication
CONSUMER: CURRENT AFFAIRS & POLITICS

€URO 727335G1F-520
Editorial: Bayerstr. 71, 80335 MÜNCHEN
Tel: 89 27264300 **Fax:** 89 27264199
Email: redaktion@finanzen.net **Web site:** http://www.euro-magazin.de
Freq: Monthly; **Annual Sub.:** EUR 59,40; **Circ:** 105,197
Editor: Frank Bernhard Werner; **Advertising Manager:** Belinda Lohse
Profile: €uro is the monthly magazine for business, stock market and private finance. And the largest in Germany, new economic trends, investment recommendations, balanced and smart money saving tips are equally highly weighted. €uro is not a classic investor booklet, but a business magazine with a unique variety of topics and depth of information. So readers experience in the input unit "Opinions & Movers, " what haunts economic decision-makers - as in the large-€uro-Interview with Federal Minister Brüderle, Metro chief Cordes, the private banker Friedrich von Metzler and others. Even the "dossier" put readers in the exciting world of economy, whether in the nightmare factory Hollywood, African mining towns or in the transmission of the money machine folk music. After that the department "Politics & Company ", where in particular the European economic policy and the future prospects of the DAX and other companies are looked at. In the largest resort "Exchange & Investments" funds, stocks, bonds, ETFs, certificates, warrants, commodities, precious metals and real estate of all stripes are explained and analyzed. In addition, the editors examine investment strategies of renowned fund managers and asset managers such as Klaus Kaldemorgen, Edouard Carmignac and Jens Ehrhardt. In our division, "Taxes and Saving", readers learn how they conduct their personal finances and what tax-optimal pension products are the best for them. Rounding out the offering with strong product testing and rankings, from the best insurance companies, banks and asset managers to finding the cheapest electricity suppliers.
Language(s): German
Readership: Aimed at sophisticated private investors as well as institutional investors.
ADVERTISING RATES:
Full Page Mono .... EUR 15800
Full Page Colour .... EUR 15800
Mechanical Data: Type Area: 241 x 171 mm, No. of Columns (Display): 4, Col Widths (Display): 36 mm
Copy instructions: *Copy Date:* 22 days prior to publication
Supplement(s): €uro best-buy; €uro spezial
BUSINESS: FINANCE & ECONOMICS: Investment

€URO AM SONNTAG 726612G74M-687
Editorial: Bayerstr. 71, 80335 MÜNCHEN
Tel: 89 272640 **Fax:** 89 27264189
Email: redaktion@eurams.de **Web site:** http://www.eurams.de
Freq: Weekly; **Annual Sub.:** EUR 161,20; **Circ:** 76,929
Editor: Frank Bernhard Werner; **Advertising Manager:** Nikos Koloutsos
Profile: €uro am Sonntag is a weekly economic and financial newspaper and is a specialist in cutting-edge financial information in the German language area. What opportunities do the markets offer, which plants are suitable for economic developments in the capital market to implement? To assess this, investors need reliable background information and thoroughly researched reports on companies, comparisons with competitors, analysts comments and ratings. First hand. €uro am Sonntag each week analyzes new developments and provides independent and sustainable information for a successful investment strategy. €uro am Sonntag offers detailed information on German and international stocks and funds, ETFs, certificates, warrants, bonds and alternative financial products. An important role is play the "Private Finances", with important references to pensions, insurance companies, closed-end funds, real estate and taxes. €uro am Sonntag combines modern news journalism with a sophisticated magazine journalism and provides the background, exclusive interviews and a collaboration with The Wall Street Journal, the leading business and financial paper in the U.S.. Twitter: http://twitter.com/EuroamSonntag.
Language(s): German
Readership: Read by private investors.
ADVERTISING RATES:
Full Page Mono .... EUR 11016
Full Page Colour .... EUR 11016
Mechanical Data: Type Area: 340 x 235 mm, No. of Columns (Display): 4, Col Widths (Display): 47 mm
Copy instructions: *Copy Date:* 9 days prior to publication
Supplement(s): €uro spezial
CONSUMER: WOMEN'S INTEREST CONSUMER MAGAZINES: Personal Finance

€URO BEST-BUY 1896777G1F-1756
Editorial: Bayerstr. 71, 80335 MÜNCHEN
Tel: 89 27264300 **Fax:** 89 27264199
Email: redaktion@finanzen.net **Web site:** http://www.finanzen.net
Freq: Monthly; **Circ:** 213,157
Editor: Frank-B. Werner; **Advertising Manager:** Belina Lohse
Profile: Business magazine with a focus on medium-to long-term investments for private and institutional investors.
Language(s): German
Mechanical Data: Type Area: 251 x 180 mm, No. of Columns (Display): 4, Col Widths (Display): 43 mm
Supplement to: €uro

EURO COSMETICS 726620G15A-184
Editorial: Eisenacher Str. 10, 80804 MÜNCHEN
Tel: 89 36037427 **Fax:** 89 32667553
Email: info@eurocosmetics-magazine.com **Web site:** http://www.eurocosmetics-magazine.com
Freq: 10 issues yearly; **Annual Sub.:** EUR 135,00; **Circ:** 2,660
Editor: Gerhard Buchbauer; **Advertising Manager:** Dagmar Melcher
Profile: Magazine focusing on the cosmetic and perfume industry in Europe. It deals with all aspects relating to the development, production, technical processes and testing of cosmetics, it also includes company profiles, interviews and trade news.
Language(s): English; German
Readership: Read by chemists, technicians, manufacturers and suppliers in the cosmetic and perfume industry.
ADVERTISING RATES:
Full Page Mono .... EUR 1840
Full Page Colour .... EUR 3070
Mechanical Data: Type Area: 256 x 183 mm, No. of Columns (Display): 2, Col Widths (Display): 89 mm
Official Journal of: Organ d. Ges. f. Dermopharmazie (e.V.)
BUSINESS: COSMETICS & HAIRDRESSING: Cosmetics

€URO EXTRA 1732119G1F-1674
Editorial: Bayerstr. 71, 80335 MÜNCHEN
Tel: 89 27264300 **Fax:** 89 27264199
Email: redaktion@finanzen.net **Web site:** http://www.finanzen.net
Freq: Half-yearly; **Cover Price:** EUR 6,90; **Circ:** 120,000
Editor: Ronny Kohl; **Advertising Manager:** Belinda Lohse
Profile: Business magazine with a focus on medium-to long-term investments for private and institutional investors.
Language(s): German
ADVERTISING RATES:
Full Page Mono .... EUR 12900
Full Page Colour .... EUR 12900
Mechanical Data: Type Area: 241 x 171 mm

EURO JOURNAL PRO MANAGEMENT 764089G14A-9276
Editorial: Lanzenweg 2a, 90455 NÜRNBERG
Tel: 911 880087 **Fax:** 911 880087
Email: r.p@fek-eurojournal.de **Web site:** http://www.eurojournal.info
Freq: Quarterly; Free to qualifying individuals
Annual Sub.: EUR 42,50; **Circ:** 20,000
Editor: Peter Verbata
Profile: Documentation and information about European economies, politics, sciences and cultures. Target audience: decision makers in the business, trade and economic institutions, and in the selected industrial and trade chambers in the EU member states, national parliaments in the EU area as well as members of the EU Parliament, diplomatic representatives in Brussels, educational institutions, such as European academies and European houses, university libraries connected with the world and members of the Society for the Promotion of European communication (FEK) e.V.
Language(s): Czech; English; French; German; Hungarian; Italian; Polish; Slovak
Mechanical Data: Type Area: 250 x 184 mm, No. of Columns (Display): 3, Col Widths (Display): 58 mm
Copy instructions: *Copy Date:* 10 days prior to publication

EURO LASER 726635G55-3992
Editorial: Göggingerstr. 105a, 86199 AUGSBURG
Tel: 821 31988017 **Fax:** 821 31988080
Email: koegel@schluetersche.de **Web site:** http://www.eurolaser.de
Freq: Quarterly; **Annual Sub.:** EUR 52,00; **Circ:** 9,890
Editor: Günter Kögel; **Advertising Manager:** Gabriele Maier
Profile: European forum for the concerns of industrial laser technology. As a user journal with international aspirations Euro laser reports from industry, universities and institutes. The laser materials processing in its full width and the laser-based measuring technique thereby form thematic priorities. The focus of the information offered are self-researched articles and reports and market analysis, company profiles and background reports from the industry. Technical articles competent authors complete the picture. Intended audience is the production and management development across all sectors.
Language(s): German
ADVERTISING RATES:
Full Page Mono .... EUR 3280
Full Page Colour .... EUR 4360
Mechanical Data: No. of Columns (Display): 4, Col Widths (Display): 44 mm, Type Area: 272 x 188 mm
Copy instructions: *Copy Date:* 14 days prior to publication
BUSINESS: APPLIED SCIENCE & LABORATORIES

EURO MOTORHOME 726639G77A-1040
Editorial: Schloßhof 2, 85283 WOLNZACH
Tel: 8442 925335 **Fax:** 8442 4426
Email: euromotorhome@kastner.de **Web site:** http://www.kastner.de
Freq: Quarterly; Free to qualifying individuals
Annual Sub.: EUR 30,00; **Circ:** 5,000
Editor: Gerd Kreusch; **Advertising Manager:** Gertrud Arnold
Profile: Car club magazine from the Euro Motorhome Club.
Language(s): German
ADVERTISING RATES:
Full Page Mono .... EUR 700
Full Page Colour .... EUR 1200
Mechanical Data: Type Area: 261 x 184 mm, No. of Columns (Display): 4, Col Widths (Display): 43 mm
Copy instructions: *Copy Date:* 30 days prior to publication

EURO SAAR 1664157G73-575
Editorial: Zum Letten 26, 66450 BEXBACH
Tel: 6826 2348 **Fax:** 6826 510559
Email: g.bayer@eurosaar.info **Web site:** http://www.eurosaar.info
Freq: 6 issues yearly; **Annual Sub.:** EUR 30,00; **Circ:** 9,765
Editor: Gabriele Bayer; **Advertising Manager:** Gabriele Bayer
Language(s): German
ADVERTISING RATES:
Full Page Mono .... EUR 1560
Full Page Colour .... EUR 1560
Copy instructions: *Copy Date:* 10 days prior to publication
CONSUMER: NATIONAL & INTERNATIONAL PERIODICALS

EURO SECURITY 1832660G14A-10131
Editorial: Peckhauser Str. 29, 40822 METTMANN
Tel: 2104 958972 **Fax:** 2104 5728
Email: redaktion@euro-security.de **Web site:** http://www.euro-security.de
Freq: 9 issues yearly; **Annual Sub.:** EUR 150,00; **Circ:** 10,465
Editor: Claudia Mrozek-Nassreddine; **Advertising Manager:** T.-J. Materre
Profile: Magazine for the security industry in Germany and Europe.
Language(s): German
ADVERTISING RATES:
Full Page Mono .... EUR 2200
Full Page Colour .... EUR 3730
Mechanical Data: Type Area: 255 x 186 mm, No. of Columns (Display): 4, Col Widths (Display): 44 mm
Copy instructions: *Copy Date:* 7 days prior to publication

EURO TUNER 726738G77A-1060
Editorial: Paffrather Str. 80, 51465 BERGISCH GLADBACH **Tel:** 2202 41857 **Fax:** 2202 41877
Email: info@eurotuner.de **Web site:** http://www.tuning2go.de
Freq: 6 issues yearly; **Annual Sub.:** EUR 18,00; **Circ:** 34,850
Editor: Olivier Fourcade; **Advertising Manager:** Olivier Fourcade
Profile: European magazine focusing on automobile technology and tuned vehicles.
Language(s): German
Readership: Aimed at car enthusiasts aged between 18 and 50.
ADVERTISING RATES:
Full Page Mono .... EUR 4100
Full Page Colour .... EUR 4990
Mechanical Data: Type Area: 267 x 181 mm, No. of Columns (Display): 4, Col Widths (Display): 42 mm
Copy instructions: *Copy Date:* 28 days prior to publication
CONSUMER: MOTORING & CYCLING: Motoring

EUROBUS 726615G49B-15
Editorial: Rosenweg 11, 68623 LAMPERTHEIM
Tel: 6256 6511 **Fax:** 6256 6512
Email: redaktion@eurobus.de **Web site:** http://www.eurobus.de
Freq: Monthly; **Annual Sub.:** EUR 46,00; **Circ:** 10,153
Editor: Heinz Lopuszansky; **Advertising Manager:** Irene Kleefeld
Profile: Publication containing technical and travel news, also information about driving regulations in Europe.
Language(s): German
Readership: Aimed at bus and coach drivers and owners, also tour operators.
ADVERTISING RATES:
Full Page Mono .... EUR 3890
Full Page Colour .... EUR 4980

Mechanical Data: Type Area: 378 x 265 mm, No. of Columns (Display): 3, Col Widths (Display): 85 mm
Copy instructions: *Copy Date:* 10 days prior to publication
BUSINESS: TRANSPORT: Bus & Coach Transport

EURODECOR 726621G16A-1
Editorial: Maximilianstr. 7, 67433 NEUSTADT
Tel: 6321 890842 **Fax:** 6321 890873
Email: eurodecor@meininger.de **Web site:** http://www.eurodecor.de
Freq: 10 issues yearly; **Annual Sub.:** EUR 89,40; **Circ:** 7,430
Editor: Birgit Jünger; **Advertising Manager:** Ralf Clemens
Profile: eurodecor is a specialist magazine for all those trading with products for the interior decoration industry. This includes floor and wall coverings, paints, sun shades, wall coverings, decorative fabrics, furnishing coverings and accessories. The designated eurodecor target group operates in retailing and wholesaling, in the interior decoration industry and crafts and trades. The content and design of the editorial section meet the exact information requirements of the target group, offering brief, compact and clear professional information. They are presented in an optimum visual and contemporary style and give dealers the extra information and knowledge that they need for their successful daily work. The editorial programme covers information from and about the trade, news and comments on the whole industrial sector, market trends and product infos on new collections, together with lots of interviews, portraits and trade fair reports.
Language(s): German
Readership: Read by retailers, suppliers and manufacturers.
ADVERTISING RATES:
Full Page Mono .... EUR 4550
Full Page Colour .... EUR 4550
Mechanical Data: Type Area: 286 x 199 mm, No. of Columns (Display): 4, Col Widths (Display): 46 mm
Copy instructions: *Copy Date:* 28 days prior to publication
BUSINESS: DECORATING & PAINT

EUROFISH MAGAZINE 1605471G22A-3195
Editorial: An der Alster 21, 20099 HAMBURG
Tel: 40 2484540 **Fax:** 40 24845425
Email: fischmagazin@snfachpresse.de **Web site:** http://www.snfachpresse.de
Freq: 6 issues yearly; **Annual Sub.:** EUR 106,00; **Circ:** 3,000
Editor: Aina Afanasjeva
Profile: European magazine for the fishing industry.
Language(s): English; Russian
ADVERTISING RATES:
Full Page Mono .... EUR 1620
Full Page Colour .... EUR 2580
Mechanical Data: Type Area: 252 x 184 mm, No. of Columns (Display): 4, Col Widths (Display): 43 mm
BUSINESS: FOOD

EUROGUIDE 726626G89A-760
Editorial: Alsterdorfer Str. 262, 22297 HAMBURG
Tel: 40 4908043 **Fax:** 40 499034
Email: info@euroguide.de **Web site:** http://www.euroguide.de
Freq: Annual; **Cover Price:** EUR 12,27
Free to qualifying individuals ; **Circ:** 5,000
Profile: Hotel and travel guide.
Language(s): English; French; German

EUROHEAT & POWER 726628G58-440
Editorial: Kleyerstr. 88, 60326 FRANKFURT
Tel: 69 7104687321 **Fax:** 69 7104687451
Email: silke.laufkoetter@ew-online.de **Web site:** http://www.ew-online.de
Freq: 10 issues yearly; **Annual Sub.:** EUR 203,00; **Circ:** 1,273
Editor: Silke Laufkötter
Profile: European journal for the combined heat and power industry, heat supply stations and waste heat utilisation.
Language(s): German
ADVERTISING RATES:
Full Page Mono .... EUR 1795
Full Page Colour .... EUR 2725
Mechanical Data: Type Area: 268 x 185 mm, No. of Columns (Display): 4, Col Widths (Display): 45 mm
Copy instructions: *Copy Date:* 15 days prior to publication
BUSINESS: ENERGY, FUEL & NUCLEAR

EUROHEAT & POWER 1638164G58-1727
Editorial: Kleyerstr. 88, 60326 FRANKFURT
Tel: 69 7104687478 **Fax:** 69 7104687451
Email: manfred.heinrichs@ew-online.de **Web site:** http://www.ew-online.de
Freq: Quarterly; **Annual Sub.:** EUR 101,00; **Circ:** 4,000
Editor: Martin Heinrichs
Profile: Magazine about short and long distance heating technology.
Language(s): English
ADVERTISING RATES:
Full Page Mono .... EUR 1795
Full Page Colour .... EUR 2725
Mechanical Data: Type Area: 268 x 185 mm, No. of Columns (Display): 4, Col Widths (Display): 45 mm

EUROKUNST 726633G89A-11526
Editorial: Am Salzpfad 26, 35633 LAHNAU
Tel: 6441 5673787
Email: eurokunst@web.de **Web site:** http://www.eurokunst.com
Freq: Quarterly; Free to qualifying individuals
Annual Sub.: EUR 18,00; **Circ:** 16,100
Editor: Anton R. Purtauf; **Advertising Manager:** H. E. Bender
Profile: Travel magazine providing information and opinions on resorts, entertainment and airlines worldwide.
Language(s): German
Readership: Aimed at regular travellers.
ADVERTISING RATES:
Full Page Mono .... EUR 1900
Full Page Colour .... EUR 2300
Mechanical Data: Type Area: 270 x 190 mm, No. of Columns (Display): 3, Col Widths (Display): 60 mm
Copy instructions: *Copy Date:* 20 days prior to publication
Official Journal of: Organ d. Eurokunst-Reise-Club
CONSUMER: HOLIDAYS & TRAVEL: Travel

EUROPA EXPRESS 1605084G72-17786
Editorial: Großbeerenstr. 186, 12277 BERLIN
Tel: 30 26947501 **Fax:** 30 26947500
Email: info@wernermedia.de **Web site:** http://www.euxpress.de
Freq: Weekly; **Annual Sub.:** EUR 45,00; **Circ:** 73,668
Editor: Michail Goldberg; **News Editor:** Vitalij Kropman; **Advertising Manager:** Olga Bellin
Profile: Russian national weekly national daily covering politics, economics, sport, travel and the arts.
Language(s): Russian
ADVERTISING RATES:
SCC .... EUR 91,50
Mechanical Data: Type Area: 370 x 247 mm, No. of Columns (Display): 5, Col Widths (Display): 46 mm
Copy instructions: *Copy Date:* 8 days prior to publication
Supplement(s): TV arena
LOCAL NEWSPAPERS

EUROPÄISCHE SICHERHEIT 726655G40-200
Editorial: Hochkreuzallee 1, 53175 BONN
Tel: 228 3078911 **Fax:** 228 3078915
Email: henningbartels@europaeische-sicherheit.de
Web site: http://www.europaeische-sicherheit.de
Freq: Monthly; Free to qualifying individuals
Annual Sub.: EUR 63,50; **Circ:** 18,591
Editor: Henning Bartels
Profile: Publication about European security. Covers politics, economy, technology and the armed forces.
Language(s): German
ADVERTISING RATES:
Full Page Mono .... EUR 3130
Full Page Colour .... EUR 4270
Mechanical Data: Type Area: 247 x 185 mm
Copy instructions: *Copy Date:* 30 days prior to publication
Official Journal of: Organ d. Ges. f. Wehr- u. Sicherheitspolitik e.V., d. Clausewitzges. e.V., d. Internat. Sicherheitspolit. Tagung München, d. Bundesakademie f. Sicherheitspolitik u. d. Führungsakademie d. Bundeswehr
BUSINESS: DEFENCE

EUROPÄISCHER LASER MARKT 726650G19E-320
Editorial: Kolpingstr. 46, 86916 KAUFERING
Tel: 8191 964111 **Fax:** 8191 964141
Email: klinker@b-quadrat.de **Web site:** http://www.b-quadrat.de
Freq: Annual; **Cover Price:** EUR 13,00; **Circ:** 11,631
Editor: Wolfgang Klinker; **Advertising Manager:** Werner Duda
Profile: Directory about products, systems and other supply for laser technology.
Language(s): German
ADVERTISING RATES:
Full Page Mono .... EUR 3400
Full Page Colour .... EUR 4550
Mechanical Data: Type Area: 250 x 175 mm, No. of Columns (Display): 4, Col Widths (Display): 40 mm
Copy instructions: *Copy Date:* 28 days prior to publication

EUROPAKURIER 726636G14A-2180
Editorial: Landersumer Weg 40, 48431 RHEINE
Tel: 5971 921630 **Fax:** 5971 921163896
Email: info@europa-kurier.com **Web site:** http://www.europa-kurier.com
Freq: 6 issues yearly; **Annual Sub.:** EUR 82,00; **Circ:** 40,000
Editor: Manfred Brinkmann; **Advertising Manager:** Anette Janssen
Profile: Magazine about European products and companies.
Language(s): German
BUSINESS: COMMERCE, INDUSTRY & MANAGEMENT

EUROPEAN ARCHIVES OF OTO-RHINO-LARYNGOLOGY 726678G56A-3160
Editorial: Tiergartenstr. 17, 69121 HEIDELBERG
Tel: 6221 4870 **Fax:** 6221 4878366
Email: subscriptions@springer.com **Web site:** http://www.springerlink.com
Freq: Monthly; **Annual Sub.:** EUR 4315,00; **Circ:** 438
Editor: Jochen A. Werner
Profile: European archives of oto-rhino-laryngology.
Language(s): English
ADVERTISING RATES:
Full Page Mono .... EUR 740
Full Page Colour .... EUR 1780
Mechanical Data: Type Area: 240 x 175 mm
Official Journal of: Organ d. European Federation of Oto-Rhino-Laryngological Societies, d. European Laryngological Society, d. European Academy of ORL-Head and Neck Surgery u. d. European Head and Neck Society

EUROPEAN ARCHIVES OF PSYCHIATRY AND CLINICAL NEUROSCIENCE 726679G56A-3180
Editorial: Nussbaumstr. 7, 80336 MÜNCHEN
Tel: 89 51605501 **Fax:** 89 51605522
Email: christine.hauer@med.uni-muenchen.de **Web site:** http://www.springerlink.com
Freq: 8 issues yearly; **Annual Sub.:** EUR 1960,00; **Circ:** 423
Editor: Hans-Jürgen Möller
Profile: The original papers published in the European Archives of Psychiatry and Clinical Neuroscience deal with all aspects of psychiatry and related clinical neuroscience. Clinical psychiatry, psychopathology, epidemiology as well as brain imaging, neuropathological, neurophysiological, neurochemical and moleculargenetic studies of psychiatric disorders are among the topics covered. Thus both the clinician and the neuroscientist are provided with a handy source of information on important scientific developments. Fields of interest: Psychiatry (psychopathology, clinical psychiatry, epidemiology, genetics), neurological sciences (neuropathology, neurophysiology, neurochemistry, neuropsychology, neurology, neurosurgery).
Language(s): English
ADVERTISING RATES:
Full Page Mono .... EUR 840
Full Page Colour .... EUR 1880
Mechanical Data: Type Area: 240 x 175 mm
Official Journal of: Organ d. German Society for Biological Psychiatry

EUROPEAN BUSINESS JOURNAL 1881552G14A-10262
Editorial: Landersumer Weg 40, 48431 RHEINE
Tel: 5971 92160 **Fax:** 5971 92161854
Email: ibv@international-business.de **Web site:** http://www.european-business-journal.com
Freq: Monthly; **Circ:** 10,512
Editor: Manfred Brinkmann
Profile: European Business Journal is one of Europe's most international business magazines providing its readers world-wide with a global business perspective on people, companies and ideas that are shaping the economic development in Europe. For more than 20 years now, our publication has been set books for general managers and decision makers, for sales people, buyers and marketing professionals and representatives of international and export-oriented enterprises with their mind set on future expansion. Travelling around Europe, the editors of European Business Journal provide cutting-edge research and exclusive insight into leading European companies.
Language(s): English
ADVERTISING RATES:
Full Page Mono .... EUR 3050
Full Page Colour .... EUR 4450
Mechanical Data: Type Area: 257 x 200 mm, No. of Columns (Display): 4, Col Widths (Display): 47 mm
Copy instructions: *Copy Date:* 7 days prior to publication

EUROPEAN FOOD RESEARCH AND TECHNOLOGY 726682G22A-3261
Editorial: Lise-Meitner-Str. 34, 85354 FREISING
Email: subscriptions@springer.com **Web site:** http://www.springerlink.com
Freq: Monthly; **Annual Sub.:** EUR 2491,00; **Circ:** 206
Editor: T. Hofmann
Profile: European journal focusing on food research and technology.
Language(s): English
ADVERTISING RATES:
Full Page Mono .... EUR 740
Full Page Colour .... EUR 1780
Mechanical Data: Type Area: 240 x 175 mm
Official Journal of: Organ d. FECS/Division of Food Chemistry
BUSINESS: FOOD

EUROPEAN JOURNAL OF APPLIED PHYSIOLOGY 726684G56A-3200
Editorial: Tiergartenstr. 17, 69121 HEIDELBERG
Tel: 6221 4870 **Fax:** 6221 4878366
Email: subscriptions@springer.com **Web site:** http://www.springerlink.com
Freq: Monthly; **Annual Sub.:** EUR 5730,00; **Circ:** 211
Editor: Susan A. Ward
Profile: European journal of applied physiology.
Language(s): English
ADVERTISING RATES:
Full Page Mono .... EUR 740
Full Page Colour .... EUR 1780
Mechanical Data: Type Area: 240 x 175 mm

EUROPEAN JOURNAL OF CELL BIOLOGY 726685G64F-80
Editorial: Hugo-Eckener-Str. 49, 55122 MAINZ
Tel: 6131 372064 **Fax:** 6131 5539577
Email: d.gebauer@elsevier.com **Web site:** http://www.elsevier.de
Freq: Monthly; **Annual Sub.:** EUR 431,00
Editor: Dagmar Gebauer
Profile: European journal concerning experimental cell investigation. Includes information on the structure, function and macro-molecular organisation of cells and cell components.
Language(s): English
Readership: Aimed at cell biologists, molecular biologists, microscopists, biochemists, anatomists and histologists.
Official Journal of: Organ d. Dt. Ges. f. Elektronenmikroskopie, d. Dt. Ges. f. Zellbiologie u. d. European Cell Biology Organization
BUSINESS: OTHER CLASSIFICATIONS: Biology

EUROPEAN JOURNAL OF CLINICAL PHARMACOLOGY 726687G56A-3240
Editorial: Tiergartenstr. 17, 69121 HEIDELBERG
Tel: 6221 4870 **Fax:** 6221 4878366
Email: subscriptions@springer.com **Web site:** http://www.springerlink.com
Freq: Monthly; **Annual Sub.:** EUR 3225,00; **Circ:** 439
Editor: Rune Dahlqvist
Profile: European journal of clinical pharmacology.
Language(s): English
ADVERTISING RATES:
Full Page Mono .... EUR 830
Full Page Colour .... EUR 1870
Mechanical Data: Type Area: 240 x 175 mm

EUROPEAN JOURNAL OF FOREST RESEARCH 727664G46-5
Editorial: Am Hochanger 13, 85354 FREISING
Tel: 8161 714710 **Fax:** 8161 714721
Email: ejfor@lrz.tu-muenchen.de **Web site:** http://www.springerlink.com
Freq: 6 issues yearly; **Annual Sub.:** EUR 615,00; **Circ:** 147
Editor: Hans Pretzsch
Profile: Magazine about all aspects of forestry and timber.
Language(s): English; German
ADVERTISING RATES:
Full Page Mono .... EUR 740
Full Page Colour .... EUR 1780
Mechanical Data: Type Area: 240 x 175 mm
BUSINESS: TIMBER, WOOD & FORESTRY

EUROPEAN JOURNAL OF HORTICULTURAL SCIENCE 728313G26D-3
Editorial: Emil-Wolff-Str. 25, 70599 STUTTGART
Tel: 711 45922368 **Fax:** 711 45922351
Email: ejhs@uni-hohenheim.de **Web site:** http://www.ejhs.de
Freq: 6 issues yearly; **Annual Sub.:** EUR 571,50; **Circ:** 590
Editor: Jens Wünsche
Profile: Magazine focusing on the techniques and economics of horticulture.
Language(s): English
Readership: Aimed at professionals within the sector.
ADVERTISING RATES:
Full Page Mono .... EUR 948
Mechanical Data: Type Area: 260 x 185 mm, No. of Columns (Display): 2, Col Widths (Display): 90 mm
Copy instructions: *Copy Date:* 21 days prior to publication
Official Journal of: Organ d. Dt. Gartenbauwissenschaftl. Ges. e.V.
BUSINESS: GARDEN TRADE: Garden Trade Horticulture

EUROPEAN JOURNAL OF IMMUNOLOGY 726690G56A-3260
Editorial: Boschstr. 12, 69469 WEINHEIM
Tel: 6201 606382 **Fax:** 6201 606172
Email: ejied@wiley.com **Web site:** http://www.eji.de
Freq: Monthly; **Annual Sub.:** EUR 1548,00; **Circ:** 1,330
Editor: Cate Livingstone; **Advertising Manager:** Marion Schulz
Profile: European journal of immunology.
Language(s): English
ADVERTISING RATES:
Full Page Mono .... EUR 2300
Full Page Colour .... EUR 3200
Mechanical Data: Type Area: 260 x 180 mm
Copy instructions: *Copy Date:* 25 days prior to publication
Official Journal of: Organ d. European Federation of Immunologicial Societies

EUROPEAN JOURNAL OF INORGANIC CHEMISTRY 726691G55-3885
Editorial: Boschstr. 12, 69469 WEINHEIM
Tel: 6201 606255 **Fax:** 6201 606203
Email: eurjic@wiley-vch.de **Web site:** http://www.eurjic.org

Freq: 36 issues yearly; **Annual Sub.:** EUR 4526,00; **Circ:** 1,000
Editor: Karen J. Hindson; **Advertising Manager:** Marion Schulz
Profile: European journal about inorganic and organometallic chemistry.
Language(s): English
Readership: Read by university graduates and industrial chemists.
ADVERTISING RATES:
Full Page Mono .... EUR 2450
Full Page Colour .... EUR 3400
Mechanical Data: Type Area: 260 x 180 mm, No. of Columns (Display): 4, Col Widths (Display): 42 mm
BUSINESS: APPLIED SCIENCE & LABORATORIES

EUROPEAN JOURNAL OF LIPID SCIENCE AND TECHNOLOGY
726692G13-740
Editorial: Boschstr. 12, 69469 WEINHEIM
Tel: 6201 606231 **Fax:** 6201 606525
Email: ejlst@wiley-vch.de **Web site:** http://www.ejlst.de
Freq: Monthly; **Annual Sub.:** EUR 1390,00; **Circ:** 952
Editor: Ines Chyla; **Advertising Manager:** Patricia Filler
Profile: European magazine about science and technology concerning fats, oils and waxes.
Language(s): English
ADVERTISING RATES:
Full Page Mono .... EUR 1300
Full Page Colour .... EUR 2560
Mechanical Data: Type Area: 260 x 180 mm, No. of Columns (Display): 4, Col Widths (Display): 42 mm
Copy instructions: *Copy Date:* 28 days prior to publication
Official Journal of: Organ d. European Federation for the Science and Technology of Lipids
BUSINESS: CHEMICALS

EUROPEAN JOURNAL OF NUCLEAR MEDICINE AND MOLECULAR IMAGING
726693G56A-3280
Editorial: Tiergartenstr. 17, 69121 HEIDELBERG
Tel: 6221 4870 **Fax:** 6221 4878366
Email: ute.heilmann@springer.com **Web site:** http://www.springerlink.com
Freq: Monthly; **Annual Sub.:** EUR 2181,00; **Circ:** 3,300
Editor: Ignasi Carrio; **Advertising Manager:** Noëla Krischer
Profile: European journal of nuclear medicine and molecular imaging.
Language(s): English
ADVERTISING RATES:
Full Page Mono .... EUR 1600
Full Page Colour .... EUR 2640
Mechanical Data: Type Area: 240 x 175 mm
Official Journal of: Organ d. European Association of Nuclear Medicine

EUROPEAN JOURNAL OF NUTRITION
726694G56R-67
Editorial: Haid-und-Neu-Str. 9, 76131 KARLSRUHE
Tel: 721 6625200 **Fax:** 721 6625111
Email: ejn@mri.bund.de **Web site:** http://www.ejn.springer.de
Freq: 8 issues yearly; **Annual Sub.:** EUR 742,00; **Circ:** 300
Editor: Gerhard Rechkemmer
Profile: The European Journal of Nutrition publishes original papers, reviews, and short communications in the nutritional sciences. The manuscripts submitted to the European Journal of Nutrition should have their major focus on the impact of nutrients and non-nutrients on •immunology and inflammation, •gene expression, •metabolism, •chronic diseases, or •carcinogenesis, or a major focus on •epidemiology, including intervention studies with healthy subjects and with patients, •food safety, or •biofunctionality of food and food components.
Language(s): English
Readership: Read by scientists and members of the medical profession specialising in nutrition.
ADVERTISING RATES:
Full Page Mono .... EUR 740
Full Page Colour .... EUR 1780
Mechanical Data: Type Area: 240 x 175 mm
Official Journal of: Organ d. European Academy of Nutritional Sciences
BUSINESS: HEALTH & MEDICAL: Health Medical Related

EUROPEAN JOURNAL OF PEDIATRIC SURGERY
726696G56A-3320
Editorial: Carl-Neuberg-Str. 1, 30625 HANNOVER
Tel: 511 5329060 **Fax:** 511 5329059
Email: ure.benno@mh-hannover.de **Web site:** http://www.thieme.de/ejps
Freq: 6 issues yearly; Free to qualifying individuals
Annual Sub.: EUR 279,80; **Circ:** 1,280
Editor: Benno M. Ure
Profile: This broad-based international journal updates you on vital developments in pediatric surgery through original articles, reviews, case reports, meeting announcements and society news. You will find state-of-the-art information on abdominal and thoracic surgery, neurosurgery, urology, gynecology, oncology, orthopedics, traumatology, anesthesiology, child pathology, embryology, morphology. Written by surgeons, physicians, anesthesiologists, radiologists, and others involved in the surgical care of neonates, infants, and children, the European Journal of Pediatric Surgery is an indispensable resource for all specialists. EJPS maintains the high quality of its content through the expert guidance of a truly international editorial board. Their experience, knowledge and hard work ensure that the EJPS addresses the needs of surgeons, doctors and researchers across the globe.
Language(s): English
ADVERTISING RATES:
Full Page Mono .... EUR 1010
Full Page Colour .... EUR 2120
Mechanical Data: Type Area: 248 x 175 mm, No. of Columns (Display): 4, Col Widths (Display): 40 mm
BUSINESS: HEALTH & MEDICAL

EUROPEAN JOURNAL OF PLASTIC SURGERY
726697G56A-3340
Editorial: Tiergartenstr. 17, 69121 HEIDELBERG
Tel: 6221 4870 **Fax:** 6221 4878366
Email: subscriptions@springer.com **Web site:** http://www.springerlink.com
Freq: 6 issues yearly; **Annual Sub.:** EUR 901,00; **Circ:** 961
Editor: Ian T. Jackson
Profile: Official journal of the Association of Plastic Surgeons in Germany, Austria, Belgium, Turkey and the Netherlands.
Language(s): English
ADVERTISING RATES:
Full Page Mono .... EUR 920
Full Page Colour .... EUR 1960
Mechanical Data: Type Area: 240 x 175 mm
Official Journal of: Organ d. European Association of Plastic Surgeons u. d. European Burns Association
BUSINESS: HEALTH & MEDICAL

EUROPEAN JOURNAL OF TRAUMA AND EMERGENCY SURGERY
726701G56P-60
Editorial: Aschauer Str. 30, 81549 MÜNCHEN
Tel: 89 2030431308 **Fax:** 89 2030431399
Email: daniela.oesterle@springer.com **Web site:** http://www.europeantrauma.net
Freq: 6 issues yearly; **Annual Sub.:** EUR 278,50; **Circ:** 3,300
Editor: Daniela Oesterle
Profile: This international English-language journal offers an interdisciplinary forum for the scientific exchange between research and hospital. Coverage includes surveys and original papers on diagnostics and therapy. In addition to classic orthopedic traumatology all related fields are considered: critical care medicine, neurotraumatology, new materials, tissue engineering, and more. The European Journal of Trauma and Emergency Surgery is the official publication of the European Trauma Society.
Language(s): English
ADVERTISING RATES:
Full Page Mono .... EUR 1800
Full Page Colour .... EUR 3050
Mechanical Data: Type Area: 240 x 174 mm
Official Journal of: Organ d. European Trauma Society for Trauma and Emergency Surgery
BUSINESS: HEALTH & MEDICAL: Casualty & Emergency

EUROPEAN JOURNAL OF WILDLIFE RESEARCH
748681G64F-2560
Editorial: Pützchens Chaussee 228, 53229 BONN
Tel: 228 9775525 **Fax:** 228 432023
Email: walburga.lutz@wald-und-holz.nrw.de **Web site:** http://www.springerlink.com
Freq: 6 issues yearly; **Annual Sub.:** EUR 475,00; **Circ:** 125
Editor: Walburga Lutz
Profile: Journal containing information about wildlife. Covers biological and ecological aspects, as well as diseases.
Language(s): English; German
Readership: Aimed at those who have a professional and general interest in wildlife.
ADVERTISING RATES:
Full Page Mono .... EUR 740
Full Page Colour .... EUR 1780
Mechanical Data: Type Area: 240 x 175 mm
BUSINESS: OTHER CLASSIFICATIONS: Biology

EUROPEAN RADIOLOGY
726710G56J-20
Editorial: Tiergartenstr. 17, 69121 HEIDELBERG
Tel: 6221 4870 **Fax:** 6221 4878366
Email: ute.heilmann@springer.com **Web site:** http://www.springerlink.com
Freq: Monthly; **Annual Sub.:** EUR 1332,00; **Circ:** 2,000
Editor: Adrian K. Dixon; **Advertising Manager:** Noëla Krischer
Profile: International journal of the European Society of Radiology.
Language(s): English
Readership: Aimed at radiologists.
ADVERTISING RATES:
Full Page Mono .... EUR 1900
Full Page Colour .... EUR 3200
Mechanical Data: Type Area: 240 x 175 mm
Official Journal of: Organ d. European Society of Radiology
BUSINESS: HEALTH & MEDICAL: Radiography

EUROPEAN SECURITY AND DEFENCE
1637504G40-959
Editorial: Hochkreuzallee 1, 53175 BONN
Tel: 228 3078911 **Fax:** 228 3078915
Email: henningbartels@europaeische-sicherheit.de **Web site:** http://www.europaeische-sicherheit.de
Freq: Half-yearly; **Circ:** 6,000
Editor: Henning Bartels
Profile: Magazine about European security and defence.
Language(s): English
ADVERTISING RATES:
Full Page Mono .... EUR 3130
Full Page Colour .... EUR 4270
Mechanical Data: Type Area: 247 x 185 mm

EUROPEAN SPINE JOURNAL
726712G56A-3400
Editorial: Tiergartenstr. 17, 69121 HEIDELBERG
Tel: 6221 4878212 **Fax:** 6221 4878634
Email: gabriele.schroeder@springer.com **Web site:** http://www.springerlink.com
Freq: Monthly; **Annual Sub.:** EUR 2091,00; **Circ:** 1,100
Editor: Max Aebi; **Advertising Manager:** Noëla Krischer
Profile: Magazine about spinal surgery.
Language(s): English
ADVERTISING RATES:
Full Page Mono .... EUR 1090
Full Page Colour .... EUR 2130
Mechanical Data: Type Area: 240 x 175 mm
Official Journal of: Organ d. EuroSpine, The Spine Society of Europe

EUROPEAN STATE AID LAW QUARTERLY
1828419G1A-3698
Editorial: Güntzelstr. 63, 10717 BERLIN
Tel: 30 81450615 **Fax:** 30 81450622
Email: kickum@lexxion.de **Web site:** http://www.lexxion.de
Freq: Quarterly; **Annual Sub.:** EUR 472,94; **Circ:** 500
Editor: Christina Kickum
Profile: Magazine for jurists.
Language(s): English
ADVERTISING RATES:
Full Page Mono .... EUR 500
Mechanical Data: Type Area: 220 x 158 mm
Copy instructions: *Copy Date:* 21 days prior to publication

EUSKIRCHENER WOCHENSPIEGEL
726743G72-3676
Editorial: Gerberstr. 41, 53879 EUSKIRCHEN
Tel: 2251 942430 **Fax:** 2251 942499
Email: red-euskirchen@weiss-verlag.de **Web site:** http://www.wochenspiegellive.de
Freq: Weekly; **Cover Price:** Free; **Circ:** 55,707
Editor: Alexander Lenders
Profile: Advertising journal (house-to-house) concentrating on local stories.
Language(s): German
ADVERTISING RATES:
Full Page Mono .... EUR 3251
Full Page Colour .... EUR 4546
Mechanical Data: Type Area: 430 x 290 mm, No. of Columns (Display): 7, Col Widths (Display): 38 mm
Copy instructions: *Copy Date:* 2 days prior to publication
LOCAL NEWSPAPERS

EUWID EUROPÄISCHER WIRTSCHAFTSDIENST KUNSTSTOFF
726747G39-15
Editorial: Bleichstr. 20, 76593 GERNSBACH
Tel: 7224 9397140 **Fax:** 7224 9397903
Email: kunststoff@euwid.de **Web site:** http://www.euwid-kunststoff.de
Freq: Weekly; **Annual Sub.:** EUR 495,00; **Circ:** 890
Editor: Monika Bender; **Advertising Manager:** Florian Mai
Profile: EUWID Kunststoff is the news service for the German-speaking plastics industry. Its readers are specialists and executives in the industry who use the printed EUWID Kunststoff every week for up-to-the-minute information on the latest developments on the German and European plastics market.EUWID Kunststoff examines the market developments and provides weekly news, analyses, and background information on price developments, politics, and the economy – researched, given in-depth coverage, and presented in a compact form by expert editors. As a unique information package tailored precisely to serve the needs of its readers as a sound basis for routine managerial decisions.
Language(s): German
Readership: Aimed at producers and converters.
ADVERTISING RATES:
Full Page Mono .... EUR 570
Full Page Colour .... EUR 1470
Mechanical Data: Type Area: 256 x 187 mm, No. of Columns (Display): 3, Col Widths (Display): 59 mm
Copy instructions: *Copy Date:* 7 days prior to publication
BUSINESS: PLASTICS & RUBBER

EUWID EUROPÄISCHER WIRTSCHAFTSDIENST LAUBHOLZ
726748G46-29
Editorial: Bleichstr. 20, 76593 GERNSBACH
Tel: 7224 9397120 **Fax:** 7224 9397910
Email: holz@euwid.de **Web site:** http://www.euwid-holz.de
Freq: 25 issues yearly; **Annual Sub.:** EUR 230,00; **Circ:** 380
Editor: Andreas Ruf; **Advertising Manager:** Florian Mai
Profile: EUWID Laubholz is the central source of news for the wood and wood-based panel industry and the timber trade. The publication provides coverage of the latest developments on the timber markets in Germany and Europe and on overseas markets. Its readers are specialists and executives in the industry who use the printed EUWID Laubholz fortnightly and visit the website at www.euwid-holz.de for up-to-the-minute information on the latest market developments. EUWID Laubholz appears every fortnight and provides news, analyses and background information in market developments and the economy – researched, given in-depth coverage, and presented in a compact form by expert editors. A unique information package tailored precisely to serve the needs of its readers as a reliable basis for routine managerial decisions.
Language(s): German
ADVERTISING RATES:
Full Page Mono .... EUR 570
Full Page Colour .... EUR 1470
Mechanical Data: Type Area: 260 x 189 mm, No. of Columns (Display): 3, Col Widths (Display): 59 mm
Copy instructions: *Copy Date:* 14 days prior to publication
BUSINESS: TIMBER, WOOD & FORESTRY

EUWID EUROPÄISCHER WIRTSCHAFTSDIENST MÖBEL
726750G23A-30
Editorial: Bleichstr. 20, 76593 GERNSBACH
Tel: 7224 9397120 **Fax:** 7224 9397910
Email: moebel@euwid.de **Web site:** http://www.euwid-moebel.de
Freq: Weekly; **Annual Sub.:** EUR 325,00; **Circ:** 920
Editor: Andreas Ruf; **Advertising Manager:** Florian Mai
Profile: EUWID Möbel is the news service for the furniture industry in German-speaking Europe. Its readers are the specialists and executives in the furniture industry, the furniture trade, the machine manufacturing sector, component suppliers, the chemical industry, and the paper industry. EUWID Möbel examines the trends and developments on the international furniture markets and supplies weekly news, analyses, and background information on market developments and the economy – researched, given in-depth coverage, and presented in a compact form by expert editors. A unique information package tailored precisely to serve the needs of its readers as a sound basis for routine managerial decisions. The information service is rounded by the website at www.euwid-moebel.de. Daily news updates, charts and analyses, upcoming events and an extensive news archive are available here for your use.
Language(s): German
ADVERTISING RATES:
Full Page Mono .... EUR 1220
Full Page Colour .... EUR 2120
Mechanical Data: Type Area: 256 x 187 mm, No. of Columns (Display): 3, Col Widths (Display): 59 mm
Copy instructions: *Copy Date:* 14 days prior to publication
BUSINESS: FURNISHINGS & FURNITURE

EUWID EUROPÄISCHER WIRTSCHAFTSDIENST NEUE ENERGIEN
2095142G58-1848
Editorial: Bleichstr. 20, 76593 GERNSBACH
Tel: 7224 9397341 **Fax:** 7224 9397907
Email: energie@euwid.de **Web site:** http://www.euwid-energie.de
Freq: 26 issues yearly; **Annual Sub.:** EUR 210,00; **Circ:** 1,820
Editor: Stefan Preiß; **Advertising Manager:** Florian Mai
Profile: Appearing every fortnight, EUWID Neue Energien provides an overview of the latest developments on the markets for renewable energies and innovative energy concepts. The focus of the news coverage is placed on the use of biomass for energy, developments on the markets for energy products from the solar, wind, and geothermal power-generation sectors. The publication's editorial spectrum is augmented by the ? elds of cogeneration of heat and power, electric mobility, and low-CO2 power generation from coal. The EUWID Neue Energien Internet portal at www.euwid-energie.de o? ers another dimension in individual procurement of information. In addition to daily news updates, an extensive database of events equipped with a research function and sector-speci? c commercial-register entries, the website also features a range of other online services.
Language(s): German
ADVERTISING RATES:
Full Page Mono .... EUR 1220
Full Page Colour .... EUR 2120
Mechanical Data: Type Area: 256 x 187 mm, No. of Columns (Display): 3, Col Widths (Display): 59 mm
Copy instructions: *Copy Date:* 14 days prior to publication

EUWID EUROPÄISCHER WIRTSCHAFTSDIENST PAPIER UND ZELLSTOFF 726752G36-16

Editorial: Bleichstr. 20, 76593 GERNSBACH
Tel: 7224 9397300 **Fax:** 7224 9397903
Email: papier@euwid.de **Web site:** http://www.euwid-papier.de
Freq: Weekly; **Annual Sub.:** EUR 545,00; **Circ:** 2,830
Editor: Ellen Streckel; **Advertising Manager:** Florian Mai
Profile: EUWID Papier und Zellstoff is the news service for the pulp and paper industry. Its readers are specialists and executives in the industry who use the printed EUWID Papier und Zellstoff every week and visit the website at www.euwid-papier.de for up-to-the-minute information on the latest developments on the German and European pulp and paper market. EUWID Papier und Zellstoff examines the market developments in Germany, France, and the UK and provides weekly news, analyses, and background information on price developments, politics, and the economy – researched, given in-depth coverage, and presented in a compact form by expert editors. As a unique information package tailored precisely to serve the needs of its readers as a sound basis for routine managerial decisions, EUWID Papier und Zellstoff is an ideal environment for your advertising without wastage. The EUWID information package is rounded off by the website at www.euwid-papier.de. Besides daily news updates, a variety of other services are also available to users. Subscribers have direct access to market reports and analyses, price developments, an extensive news archive, and a calendar of the main upcoming events in the industry.
Language(s): German
ADVERTISING RATES:
Full Page Mono .... EUR 1490
Full Page Colour .... EUR 2390
Mechanical Data: Type Area: 256 x 187 mm, No. of Columns (Display): 3, Col Widths (Display): 59 mm
Copy instructions: *Copy Date:* 14 days prior to publication

EUWID EUROPÄISCHER WIRTSCHAFTSDIENST RECYCLING UND ENTSORGUNG 726755G57-500

Editorial: Bleichstr. 20, 76593 GERNSBACH
Tel: 7224 9397330 **Fax:** 7224 9397904
Email: recycling@euwid.de **Web site:** http://www.euwid-recycling.de
Freq: Weekly; **Annual Sub.:** EUR 485,00; **Circ:** 4,360
Editor: Jürgen Zachmann
Profile: EUWID Recycling und Entsorgung is the leading information service for and on the recycling and waste disposal industry. Its readers are specialists and executives in the industry as well as those in a variety of other industrial sectors. EUWID Recycling und Entsorgung examines the state of the market and prices relating to the most important secondary raw materials (recovered paper, scrap metal, steel scrap, electronic scrap, recovered plastic, wood scrap) and supplies weekly news, analyses, and backgrounds on market developments, politics, and the economy – researched, given in-depth coverage, and presented in a compact form by expert editors. A unique information package tailored precisely to serve the needs of its readers as a sound basis for routine managerial decisions. EUWID Recycling und Entsorgung is thus an ideal environment for your press advertising.The information service is rounded off by the website at www.euwid.recycling.de. Daily news updates, charts and analyses, upcoming events and an archive with more than 50,000 articles is available here for your use. With 20,000 readers every week and an average of 40,000 visits per month you can be sure to communicate your message to the qualified circle of readers responsible for budgetary decisions.
Language(s): German
Readership: Aimed at public and private companies in the recycling and waste management sector, local and national authorities and administration, national and international traders and consumers of recycled materials (paper, metals and plastics), hazardous waste management companies, consulting companies, specialised law firms, executives and environment managers from other sectors who need to stay up to date on recycling and waste-related issues, industry associations, universities, scientific and research institutes.
ADVERTISING RATES:
Full Page Mono .... EUR 2050
Full Page Colour .... EUR 2950
Mechanical Data: Type Area: 260 x 189 mm, No. of Columns (Display): 3, Col Widths (Display): 59 mm
Copy instructions: *Copy Date:* 14 days prior to publication
BUSINESS: ENVIRONMENT & POLLUTION

EUWID EUROPÄISCHER WIRTSCHAFTSDIENST VERPACKUNG 726756G35-60

Editorial: Bleichstr. 20, 76593 GERNSBACH
Tel: 7224 9397300 **Fax:** 7224 9397903
Email: verpackung@euwid.de **Web site:** http://www.euwid-verpackung.de
Freq: Weekly; **Annual Sub.:** EUR 495,00; **Circ:** 1,940
Editor: Ellen Streckel; **Advertising Manager:** Florian Mai
Profile: EUWID Verpackung examines the state of the market and prices for the relevant packaging materials and packing such as paper and board, standard plastics, pallets, tin packaging, glass packaging, and aluminium packaging - researched, given in-depth coverage, and presented in a compact form by expert editors. Specialists and executives in the industry use the printed version of EUWID Verpackung every week and visit the website at www.euwid-verpackung.de for up-to-the-minute information on the latest developments in the German and European packaging sector. As a unique information package tailored precisely to serve the needs of its readers as a sound basis for routine managerial decisions, EUWID Verpackung is an ideal environment for your advertising without wastage. The EUWID information package is rounded off by the www.euwid-verpackung.de. website, featuring daily news updates, market reports, charts and analyses, a calendar of the main upcoming events in the industry, and an extensive news archive.
Language(s): German
ADVERTISING RATES:
Full Page Mono .... EUR 1220
Full Page Colour .... EUR 2120
Mechanical Data: Type Area: 256 x 187 mm, No. of Columns (Display): 3, Col Widths (Display): 59 mm
Copy instructions: *Copy Date:* 14 days prior to publication
BUSINESS: PACKAGING & BOTTLING

EUWID WASSER SPECIAL 2095147G58-1850

Editorial: Bleichstr. 20, 76593 GERNSBACH
Tel: 7224 9397131 **Fax:** 7224 9397231
Email: sbroeker@euwid.de **Web site:** http://www.euwid-wasser.de
Freq: Half-yearly; **Circ:** 5,500
Editor: Stefan Bröker; **Advertising Manager:** Sascha Wenz
Profile: EUWID WASSER SPECIAL is a single theme special edition of the weekly information service dedicated to EUWID Wasser und Abwasser. At least two issues are published annually. It provides a comprehensive overview of the respective sub-markets and also serves as a forum for new products and innovative processes and technologies. EUWID WASSER SPECIALl continues with its editorial approach that is focused on the objective and comprehensive presentation of market and industry information.
Language(s): German
ADVERTISING RATES:
Full Page Mono .... EUR 2350
Full Page Colour .... EUR 3250
Mechanical Data: Type Area: 256 x 187 mm, No. of Columns (Display): 3, Col Widths (Display): 59 mm

EUWID WASSER UND ABWASSER 726757G57-2658

Editorial: Bleichstr. 20, 76593 GERNSBACH
Tel: 7224 9397131 **Fax:** 7224 9397912
Email: wasser@euwid.de **Web site:** http://www.euwid-wasser.de
Freq: Weekly; **Annual Sub.:** EUR 420,00; **Circ:** 1,270
Editor: Stefan Bröker; **Advertising Manager:** Sascha Wenz
Profile: EUWID Wasser und Abwasser is the news service for the water resources management sector in German-speaking Europe. Specialists and executives in business, politics, and administration use the printed version of EUWID Wasser und Abwasser every week and visit the website at www.euwid-wasser.de to bring them- selves up to date on the latest developments on the German and European water market. EUWID Wasser und Abwasser provides information on companies and markets, political developments at a European, a national and regional level in all the fields relevant to water resources management, the latest jurisdiction, and on new technologies and products. As a unique information package tailored precisely to serve the needs of its readers as a sound basis for routine managerial decisions, EUWID Wasser und Abwasser is an ideal environment for your advertising without wastage. The EUWID information package is rounded off by the website www.euwid-wasser.de. Daily news updates, policy documents, current verdicts, a calendar of the sector's main current upcoming events, and an extensive archive are available to subscribers at no extra charge.
Language(s): German
Readership: Read by operators of cleaning facilities for drains, sewers and canals, consultant engineers, town cleaning, refuse collection and recycling facilities, also chemical, wood, paper, printing and metal processing industries.
ADVERTISING RATES:
Full Page Mono .... EUR 1220
Full Page Colour .... EUR 2120
Mechanical Data: Type Area: 260 x 189 mm, No. of Columns (Display): 3, Col Widths (Display): 59 mm
Copy instructions: *Copy Date:* 14 days prior to publication
BUSINESS: ENVIRONMENT & POLLUTION

EVANGELISCHE SONNTAGS-ZEITUNG 726767G87-3720

Editorial: Rechneigrabenstr. 10, 60311 FRANKFURT
Tel: 69 92107442 **Fax:** 69 92107466
Email: sonntagszeitung@ev-medienhaus.de **Web site:** http://www.evangelische-sonntagszeitung.de
Freq: Weekly; **Annual Sub.:** EUR 57,60; **Circ:** 14,910
Editor: Wolfgang Weissgerber; **Advertising Manager:** Erika E. Richter
Profile: Christian magazine for Hessen and Nassau.
Language(s): German
Readership: Read by members of the church and those with an interest in religion.
ADVERTISING RATES:
Full Page Mono .... EUR 2004
Full Page Colour .... EUR 3674
Mechanical Data: Type Area: 334 x 250 mm, No. of Columns (Display): 5, Col Widths (Display): 46 mm
Copy instructions: *Copy Date:* 10 days prior to publication
CONSUMER: RELIGIOUS

EVANGELISCHE ZEITUNG FÜR HAMBURG & SCHLESWIG-HOLSTEIN 737608G87-9900

Editorial: Gartenstr. 20, 24103 KIEL
Tel: 431 55779246 **Fax:** 431 55779297
Email: redaktion@evangelische-zeitung.de
Freq: Weekly; **Annual Sub.:** EUR 72,00; **Circ:** 9,465
Editor: Carsten Splitt; **News Editor:** Jochen Rudolphsen-Brandenburg; **Advertising Manager:** Bodo Elsner
Profile: Protestant magazine for the areas of Schleswig-Holstein, Hamburg and Nordschleswig/Dänemark.
Language(s): German
ADVERTISING RATES:
Full Page Mono .... EUR 3300
Full Page Colour .... EUR 5100
Mechanical Data: Type Area: 485 x 325 mm
Copy instructions: *Copy Date:* 13 days prior to publication
CONSUMER: RELIGIOUS

EVANGELISCHER KIRCHENBOTE 726771G87-3780

Editorial: Beethovenstr. 4, 67346 SPEYER
Tel: 6232 132321 **Fax:** 6232 132324
Email: redaktion@evpfalz.de **Web site:** http://www.evangelischer-kirchenbote.de
Freq: Weekly; **Annual Sub.:** EUR 43,20; **Circ:** 21,992
Editor: Hartmut Metzger; **Advertising Manager:** Bärbel Hardt
Profile: Publication for the Evangelical Church of Pfalz.
Language(s): German
ADVERTISING RATES:
Full Page Mono .... EUR 2015
Full Page Colour .... EUR 2821
Mechanical Data: Type Area: 310 x 226 mm, No. of Columns (Display): 5, Col Widths (Display): 45 mm
Copy instructions: *Copy Date:* 14 days prior to publication
CONSUMER: RELIGIOUS

EVANGELISCHES GEMEINDEBLATT FÜR WÜRTTEMBERG UND STUTTGARTER EVANGELISCHES SONNTAGSBLATT 1616463G87-13513

Editorial: Augustenstr. 124, 70197 STUTTGART
Tel: 711 6010074 **Fax:** 711 6010070
Email: redaktion@evanggemeindeblatt.de **Web site:** http://www.evangelisches-gemeindeblatt.de
Freq: Weekly; **Annual Sub.:** EUR 63,60; **Circ:** 72,614
Editor: Petra Ziegler
Profile: Evangelical Christian magazine.
Language(s): German
ADVERTISING RATES:
Full Page Mono .... EUR 4200
Full Page Colour .... EUR 7728
Mechanical Data: Type Area: 280 x 200 mm, No. of Columns (Display): 4, Col Widths (Display): 45 mm
Copy instructions: *Copy Date:* 12 days prior to publication
CONSUMER: RELIGIOUS

EVANGELISCHES SONNTAGSBLATT AUS BAYERN 726777G87-3840

Editorial: Erlbacher Str. 104, 91541 ROTHENBURG
Tel: 9861 400400 **Fax:** 9861 40079
Email: sonntagsblatt@rotabene.de **Web site:** http://www.evangelisches-sonntagsblatt.de
Freq: Weekly; **Annual Sub.:** EUR 58,00; **Circ:** 20,166
Editor: Helmut Frank; **Advertising Manager:** Wolfgang Schneider
Profile: Evangelical magazine for the Bavarian region.
Language(s): German
ADVERTISING RATES:
Full Page Mono .... EUR 1824
Full Page Colour .... EUR 3192
Mechanical Data: Type Area: 285 x 212 mm, No. of Columns (Display): 4, Col Widths (Display): 45 mm
Copy instructions: *Copy Date:* 14 days prior to publication
CONSUMER: RELIGIOUS

EVENT. 1605394G94H-14061

Editorial: Dingolfinger Str. 6, 81369 MÜNCHEN
Tel: 89 41600457 **Fax:** 89 41600455
Email: joke.jordan@kps.de **Web site:** http://www.eventmagazin.info
Freq: 11 issues yearly; **Annual Sub.:** EUR 18,00; **Circ:** 181,298
Editor: Joke Jordan; **Advertising Manager:** Fabio Maxia
Profile: Programme of events.
Language(s): German
ADVERTISING RATES:
Full Page Mono .... EUR 6696
Full Page Colour .... EUR 8420
Mechanical Data: Type Area: 263 x 190 mm
Copy instructions: *Copy Date:* 13 days prior to publication
CONSUMER: OTHER CLASSIFICATIONS: Customer Magazines

EVENT PARTNER 726784G2A-1300

Editorial: Emil-Hoffmann-Str. 13, 50996 KÖLN
Tel: 2236 9621745 **Fax:** 2236 962175
Email: redaktion@event-partner.de **Web site:** http://www.event-partner.de
Freq: 6 issues yearly; **Annual Sub.:** EUR 52,15; **Circ:** 13,808
Editor: Walter Wehrhan; **Advertising Manager:** Angelika Müller
Profile: EVENT PARTNER is the specialist magazine for event marketing in German. The magazine is published six times a year, supplemented by special exhibitions and publications for special interest topics in the event business. She reports competently about facts and trends, basics and updates from the entire spectrum of integrated marketing communications and is the recognized source of information in the industry, current reading and Nachschlagetool for agencies, service providers, operators and marketing decision-makers from corporations and businesses. EVENT PARTNER has the highest priority as a trade publication in courses or degree programs such as marketing and communication at all "education and training facilities and is committed to increased transparency and quality in education and training as a positive option for the long-term development of the industry. The magazine covers the sections magazine, report, location, portrait, business, column, forum and trade fair event, the entire theme of the events market ab.und offers an extensive service section space for company displays, Jobs, image campaigns and representation of businesses. EVENT PARTNER is thus an established and indispensable communications tool for the industry. The magazine reaches all key segments of the event business. Excellent contacts with the Heads and decision makers to ensure timely and sound information for both sides, the principal events of their clients.
Language(s): German
ADVERTISING RATES:
Full Page Mono .... EUR 2230
Full Page Colour .... EUR 4110
Mechanical Data: Type Area: 254 x 185 mm, No. of Columns (Display): 4, Col Widths (Display): 43 mm
BUSINESS: COMMUNICATIONS, ADVERTISING & MARKETING

EVENTLOCATIONS 1864905G50-1260

Editorial: Geranienweg 1, 85598 BALDHAM
Tel: 8106 379480 **Fax:** 8106 306804
Email: info@eventlocations.info **Web site:** http://www.eventlocations.info
Freq: Annual; **Cover Price:** Free; **Circ:** 39,050
Editor: Peter Baldur; **Advertising Manager:** Manfred Bauriedl
Profile: Magazine on event locations. The annually published handbook is sent free of charge to companies, agencies and event organizers. The nearly 300-page manual EVENTLOCATIONS offers a wide selection of professionally managed venues and event service providers in the Germany, Austria and Sitzerland. Itis well organized by region and contains detailed descriptions of the locations - many of which are new to the market or are among the secrets of expert . The location portraits convince large, continuous 4-color photo spreads. In addition, all specifications listed, such as ceiling heights, capacities and seating arrangements. Reliable contact information, up to enhance contact, in addition your pace.
Language(s): German
Mechanical Data: Type Area: 278 x 200 mm
Copy instructions: *Copy Date:* 60 days prior to publication

EVENTS 1663666G2C-359

Editorial: Emil-Hoffmann-Str. 13, 50996 KÖLN
Tel: 2236 3366113 **Fax:** 2236 3366118
Email: heinrich@events-magazine.de **Web site:** http://www.events-magazine.com
Freq: 5 issues yearly; **Annual Sub.:** EUR 51,63; **Circ:** 13,475
Editor: Hans-Jürgen Heinrich; **Advertising Manager:** Inga Schade
Profile: The International Management Magazine for Meetings, Incentives, Congresses, Events.
Language(s): English; German
ADVERTISING RATES:
Full Page Mono .... EUR 4795
Full Page Colour .... EUR 5760
Mechanical Data: Type Area: 263 x 179 mm, No. of Columns (Display): 4, Col Widths (Display): 43 mm
BUSINESS: COMMUNICATIONS, ADVERTISING & MARKETING: Conferences & Exhibitions

EVENTS 726785G89C-4791

Editorial: Friedrich-Ebert-Str. 29, 14467 POTSDAM
Tel: 331 2006060 **Fax:** 331 9678027
Email: info@seipt-media.de **Web site:** http://www.seipt-media.de
Freq: Monthly; **Cover Price:** Free; **Circ:** 35,055
Editor: Thomas Seipt; **Advertising Manager:** Thomas Seipt
Profile: Magazine providing details of events in Potsdam and the surrounding area. Includes interviews, news about music, culture, gastronomy and film. Distributed free in bars, restaurants, fitness centres, hotels, banks and public institutions. Facebook: http://www.facebook.com/pages/

EVENTS-Das-Potsdamer-Stadtmagazin/
133920579952137.
Language(s): German
Readership: Aimed at people between 16 and 36 years.
ADVERTISING RATES:
Full Page Mono .... EUR 2290
Full Page Colour .... EUR 2290
Mechanical Data: No. of Columns (Display): 4, Col Widths (Display): 44 mm, Type Area: 270 x 190 mm
Copy instructions: *Copy Date:* 15 days prior to publication
CONSUMER: HOLIDAYS & TRAVEL: Entertainment Guides

EVG IMTAKT
745287G49E-840
Editorial: Chausseestr. 84, 10115 BERLIN
Tel: 30 42439075 **Fax:** 30 42439071
Email: redaktion@evg-online.org **Web site:** http://www.evg-online.org
Freq: 10 issues yearly
Editor: Oliver Kaufhold
Profile: Magazine for members of the Railway and Transport union EVG.
Language(s): German
Readership: Read by member of the union and officials of the railway.
BUSINESS: TRANSPORT: Railways

EVIKO BANKENEINKAUFSFÜHRER
1664060G1C-1455
Editorial: Arabellastr. 4, 81925 MÜNCHEN
Tel: 89 92223176 **Fax:** 89 92223171
Email: h.sebald@av-finance.com **Web site:** http://www.eviko.de
Freq: Annual; **Cover Price:** EUR 49,00; **Circ:** 14,500
Editor: Herbert Sebald; **Advertising Manager:** Manuela Albutat
Profile: Directory listing suppliers and service companies for banks and savings banks.
Language(s): German
Mechanical Data: Type Area: 260 x 185 mm

EVIKO BANKENEINKAUFSFÜHRER
1664060G1C-1468
Editorial: Arabellastr. 4, 81925 MÜNCHEN
Tel: 89 92223176 **Fax:** 89 92223171
Email: h.sebald@av-finance.com **Web site:** http://www.eviko.de
Freq: Annual; **Cover Price:** EUR 49,00; **Circ:** 14,500
Editor: Herbert Sebald; **Advertising Manager:** Manuela Albutat
Profile: Directory listing suppliers and service companies for banks and savings banks.
Language(s): German
Mechanical Data: Type Area: 260 x 185 mm

EW - DAS MAGAZIN FÜR DIE ENERGIE WIRTSCHAFT
726793G58-480
Editorial: Kleyerstr. 88, 60326 FRANKFURT
Tel: 69 7104687320 **Fax:** 69 7104687451
Email: wolfgang.boehmer@ew-online.de **Web site:** http://www.ew-online.de
Freq: 23 issues yearly; **Annual Sub.:** EUR 370,00; **Circ:** 3,549
Editor: Wolfgang Böhmer; **Advertising Manager:** Thorsten Lukas
Profile: The ew - das magazin für die energie wirtschaft is the most traditional energy magazine in the German-language area. It combines the power industry with industry-related sectors of the economy and the politics. Topics range from power generation and power transmission to the services into the areas of electricity, gas and renewable energy. Timeliness and competence, they stand out. Here, the ew as an information and advertising medium is equally interesting. Main topics: Energy industry, energy technology, energy policy and energy law in the areas of electricity, gas and renewable energy. Economical and technical aspects have been retained.
Language(s): English; German
ADVERTISING RATES:
Full Page Mono .... EUR 1945
Full Page Colour .... EUR 2875
Mechanical Data: Type Area: 268 x 185 mm, No. of Columns (Display): 4, Col Widths (Display): 42 mm
Copy instructions: *Copy Date:* 18 days prior to publication
BUSINESS: ENERGY, FUEL & NUCLEAR

EXAKT
726804G46-30
Editorial: Fasanenweg 18, 70771 LEINFELDEN-ECHTERDINGEN **Tel:** 711 7591215
Fax: 711 7591267
Email: cgahle@drw-verlag.de **Web site:** http://www.drw-verlag.de
Freq: 9 issues yearly; **Annual Sub.:** EUR 27,00; **Circ:** 12,597
Editor: Christian Gahle; **Advertising Manager:** Ralf Arnold
Profile: Journal about carpentry focusing on the making of tables, chests, drawers and wardrobes.
Language(s): German
ADVERTISING RATES:
Full Page Mono .... EUR 4200
Full Page Colour .... EUR 5850
Mechanical Data: Type Area: 270 x 175 mm, No. of Columns (Display): 4, Col Widths (Display): 40 mm
Copy instructions: *Copy Date:* 15 days prior to publication
BUSINESS: TIMBER, WOOD & FORESTRY

EXECUTIVE EXCELLENCE
726808G14A-9342
Editorial: Schanzenstsr. 23, 51063 KÖLN
Tel: 221 95649057
Email: redaktion@text-ur.de **Web site:** http://www.text-ur.de
Freq: Quarterly; **Cover Price:** EUR 14,80; **Circ:** 1,000
Profile: Facebook: http://www.facebook.com/people/Christiane-Gierke/100000116373352.
Language(s): German

EXIT
1615428G86B-645
Editorial: Sternstr. 49, 40479 DÜSSELDORF
Tel: 211 41667440 **Fax:** 211 41667441
Email: redaktion@exit-magazin.de **Web site:** http://www.exit-magazin.de
Freq: Monthly; **Cover Price:** Free; **Circ:** 19,870
Editor: Lars Lienen; **Advertising Manager:** Simon Blaeser
Profile: Scene magazine for gay men in North Rhine-Westphalia. Facebook: http://www.facebook.com/pages/inqueeryde-deine-news-deine-szene-dein-stil/115382608494011.
Language(s): German
ADVERTISING RATES:
Full Page Mono .... EUR 2090
Full Page Colour .... EUR 2090
Mechanical Data: Type Area: 260 x 190 mm, No. of Columns (Display): 4, Col Widths (Display): 45 mm
Copy instructions: *Copy Date:* 14 days prior to publication
CONSUMER: ADULT & GAY MAGAZINES: Gay & Lesbian Magazines

EXPERIMENTAL AND CLINICAL ENDOCRINOLOGY & DIABETES
726817G56A-3420
Editorial: Rüdigerstr. 14, 70469 STUTTGART
Tel: 711 8931430 **Fax:** 711 8931392
Email: kundenservice@thieme.de **Web site:** http://www.thieme.de/eced
Freq: 10 issues yearly; **Cover Price:** Free to qualifying individuals
Annual Sub.: EUR 488,80; **Circ:** 1,900
Profile: Publishing outstanding articles from all fields of endocrinology and diabetology, from molecular biology to clinical research, this journal is an outstanding resource. Since being published in 1983, both the impact factor and popularity of this journal have grown steadily, reflecting the importance of this publication within its field. From molecular biology to clinical research, Experimental and Clinical Endocrinology & Diabetes covers all aspects of these fields. Case reports, original contributions and short communications appear in each issue along with reviews addressing current topics. In addition, supplementary issues are published each year presenting abstract or proceedings of national and international scientific meetings.
Language(s): English
ADVERTISING RATES:
Full Page Mono .... EUR 1450
Full Page Colour .... EUR 2550
Mechanical Data: Type Area: 248 x 175 mm, No. of Columns (Display): 3, Col Widths (Display): 55 mm
Official Journal of: Organ d. Dt. Ges. f. Endokrinologie u. d. Dt. Diabetesges.
Supplement(s): diabetesIDE konkret; Endokrinologie Informationen
BUSINESS: HEALTH & MEDICAL

EXPERIMENTAL BRAIN RESEARCH
726819G56A-3460
Editorial: Tiergartenstr. 17, 69121 HEIDELBERG
Tel: 6221 4870 **Fax:** 6221 4878366
Email: andrea.pillmann@springer.com **Web site:** http://www.springerlink.com
Freq: Quarterly; **Annual Sub.:** EUR 9778,00; **Circ:** 168
Editor: J. C. Rothwell
Profile: Magazine about experimental brain research.
Language(s): English
ADVERTISING RATES:
Full Page Mono .... EUR 740
Full Page Colour .... EUR 1780
Mechanical Data: Type Area: 240 x 175 mm

EXPRESS
726827G67B-5020
Editorial: Amsterdamer Str. 192, 50735 KÖLN
Tel: 221 2240 **Fax:** 221 2243403
Email: redaktion@express.de **Web site:** http://www.express.de
Freq: 312 issues yearly; **Circ:** 153,993
Editor: Rudolf Kreitz; **News Editor:** Dirk Amarell;
Advertising Manager: Karsten Hundhausen
Profile: The local-based tabloid newspaper from the publisher M. DuMont Schauberg is the currently-cheeky voice of the region and the lawyer of his readers. Six times a week, the editors demonstrate their competence, for the Express, there are more than just sensational headline. Exciting coverage is combined with in-depth background information and critical comments. The Express is the leading newspaper purchase of the Rhineland with the highest competence in the region. He appears in the circulation area with three issues: in Cologne, Dusseldorf and Bonn, from the Eifel to the Oberbergische Land. The Express is characterized by recent, strong acceptance themes, series and service elements. His style is like the people on the Rhine: tolerant, cosmopolitan, humorous with a touch of emotion. One of the very strong points of the Express: sport. Facebook: http://www.facebook.com/express.de Twitter: http://twitter.com/Express24 This Outlet offers RSS (Really Simple Syndication).
Language(s): German
ADVERTISING RATES:
SCC .... EUR 136,70
Mechanical Data: Type Area: 430 x 285 mm, No. of Columns (Display): 6, Col Widths (Display): 45 mm
Copy instructions: *Copy Date:* 1 day prior to publication
REGIONAL DAILY & SUNDAY NEWSPAPERS: Regional Daily Newspapers

---

EXPRESSCHEN ANGEBOTSKALENDER
1925957G74A-3699
Editorial: Köpenicker Str. 187, 10997 BERLIN
Tel: 30 6110023 **Fax:** 30 6110021
Email: kontakt@hydra-ev.org **Web site:** http://www.hydra-ev.org
Freq: Quarterly; **Circ:** 300
Profile: Magazine containing information for prostitutes.
Language(s): German
Copy instructions: *Copy Date:* 14 days prior to publication

EXPRESS.DE
1621204G67B-16545
Editorial: Amsterdamer Str. 192, 50735 KÖLN
Tel: 221 2243070 **Fax:** 221 2243080
Email: post@express.de **Web site:** http://www.express.de
Freq: Daily; **Cover Price:** Paid; **Circ:** 1,709,283 Unique Users
Editor: Thomas Kemmerer; **Advertising Manager:** Karsten Hundhausen
Profile: Online newspaper for the Rheinland: with strong local and national content from the fields of politics, opinion, business, local news, sports, panorama, culture, travel, campus, health and magazine for the region is Express.de essential. Express.de shines with above-average range for men, professionals, young and middle age groups, and better educated. Facebook: http://www.facebook.com/express.de Twitter: http://twitter.com/Express24 This Outlet offers RSS (Really Simple Syndication).
Language(s): German
REGIONAL DAILY & SUNDAY NEWSPAPERS: Regional Daily Newspapers

---

EXPULS
726846G80-3220
Editorial: Hochstr. 8, 92637 WEIDEN
Tel: 961 390820 **Fax:** 961 3908226
Email: redaktion@expuls.de **Web site:** http://www.expuls.de
Freq: 6 issues yearly; **Cover Price:** Free; **Circ:** 8,000
Editor: Brigitte Lindner; **Advertising Manager:** Brigitte Lindner
Profile: News and events magazine for Oberpfalz. Covers theatre, cinema, concerts, book reviews, music and interviews.
Language(s): German
Readership: Read by local residents with an interest in culture.
ADVERTISING RATES:
Full Page Mono .... EUR 1220
Full Page Colour .... EUR 1270
Mechanical Data: No. of Columns (Display): 4, Col Widths (Display): 43 mm, Type Area: 270 x 190 mm
Copy instructions: *Copy Date:* 15 days prior to publication
CONSUMER: RURAL & REGIONAL INTEREST

EXTRA AM MITTWOCH
726910G72-3764
Editorial: Bäckerstr. 31, 38640 GOSLAR
Tel: 5321 333152 **Fax:** 5321 333199
Email: kontakt@extra-am-mittwoch.de **Web site:** http://www.extra-am-mittwoch.de
Freq: Weekly; **Cover Price:** Free; **Circ:** 90,580
Advertising Manager: Gerd Niehus
Profile: Advertising journal (house-to-house) concentrating on local stories.
Language(s): German
ADVERTISING RATES:
Full Page Mono .... EUR 5038
Full Page Colour .... EUR 7152
Mechanical Data: Type Area: 435 x 282 mm, No. of Columns (Display): 6, Col Widths (Display): 45 mm
Copy instructions: *Copy Date:* 3 days prior to publication
LOCAL NEWSPAPERS

EXTRA TIP
726900G72-3736
Editorial: Prinzenstr. 10, 37073 GÖTTINGEN
Tel: 551 3838651 **Fax:** 551 3838650
Email: conrad@extratip-goettingen.de **Web site:** http://www.extratip-goettingen.de
Freq: Weekly; **Cover Price:** Free; **Circ:** 90,769
Editor: Lutz Conrad; **Advertising Manager:** Martin Benderoth
Profile: Advertising journal (house-to-house) concentrating on local stories.
Language(s): German
ADVERTISING RATES:
Full Page Mono .... EUR 5708
Full Page Colour .... EUR 7050
Mechanical Data: Type Area: 430 x 284 mm, No. of Columns (Display): 6, Col Widths (Display): 45 mm
Copy instructions: *Copy Date:* 2 days prior to publication
LOCAL NEWSPAPERS

EXTRA TIP
726901G72-3740
Editorial: Kölnische Str. 16, 34117 KASSEL
Tel: 561 7070200 **Fax:** 561 7070111
Email: redaktion@ks.extratip.de **Web site:** http://www.extratip.de
Freq: 104 issues yearly; **Cover Price:** Free
Editor: Rainer Hahne; **Advertising Manager:** Petra Goßmann
Profile: Advertising journal (house-to-house) concentrating on local stories.
Language(s): German
Mechanical Data: Type Area: 430 x 285 mm, No. of Columns (Display): 6, Col Widths (Display): 45 mm
Copy instructions: *Copy Date:* 2 days prior to publication
LOCAL NEWSPAPERS

EXTRAKTE
726897G22A-3198
Editorial: Wolfgang-Döring-Str. 2, 40595 DÜSSELDORF **Tel:** 211 701011 **Fax:** 211 701013
Freq: Weekly; **Circ:** 3,935
Editor: Richard Leroch
Profile: Journal focusing on food, nutrition and health.
Language(s): German
ADVERTISING RATES:
Full Page Mono .... EUR 1688
Full Page Colour .... EUR 2608
Mechanical Data: Type Area: 260 x 180 mm
Copy instructions: *Copy Date:* 14 days prior to publication
BUSINESS: FOOD

EXTRA-RAN
726899G72-3732
Editorial: Deininger Str. 8, 86720 NÖRDLINGEN
Tel: 9081 83257 **Fax:** 9081 83228
Email: richard.lechner@rieser-nachrichten.de
Freq: Weekly; **Cover Price:** Free; **Circ:** 41,693
Editor: Richard Lechner; **Advertising Manager:** Martin Eigenrauch
Profile: Advertising journal (house-to-house) concentrating on local stories.
Language(s): German
ADVERTISING RATES:
Full Page Mono .... EUR 3662
Full Page Colour .... EUR 5549
Mechanical Data: Type Area: 480 x 327 mm, No. of Columns (Display): 7, Col Widths (Display): 45 mm
Copy instructions: *Copy Date:* 2 days prior to publication
LOCAL NEWSPAPERS

EXTRATOUR
726907G91C-100
Editorial: Leonardo-da-Vinci-Weg 1, 32760 DETMOLD **Tel:** 5231 993655 **Fax:** 5231 993666
Email: service@djh.org **Web site:** http://www.extratour-online.de
Freq: 6 issues yearly; **Circ:** 702,700
Editor: Bernd Dohn; **Advertising Manager:** Ralf Sugland
Profile: 2 million members of the German Youth Hostel Association to use the benefits of membership for their intensive travel and leisure activities in Germany and internationally. Most are between 18 - 49 years old, very good (off) educated and have higher than average net income. They are loves to travel and leisure interests-active and strong on all social issues. extratour offers an attractive mix of travel, sports and leisure-time reports from Germany, Europe and overseas, information on youth hostels, and extensive catalog inserts to travel and shop facilities.
Language(s): German
Readership: Aimed at youth leaders and back packers planning trips though Germany.
ADVERTISING RATES:
Full Page Mono .... EUR 11500
Full Page Colour .... EUR 16500
Mechanical Data: Type Area: 268 x 186 mm, No. of Columns (Display): 4, Col Widths (Display): 42 mm
CONSUMER: RECREATION & LEISURE: Hostelling

EXTRUSION
739075G39-109
Editorial: Gleueler Str. 373, 50935 KÖLN
Tel: 221 439256 **Fax:** 221 438121
Email: f.vollmer@vm-verlag.com **Web site:** http://www.extrusion-info.com
Freq: 8 issues yearly; **Annual Sub.:** EUR 168,00; **Circ:** 3,960
Editor: Fritz Vollmer; **Advertising Manager:** Inge Böhle
Profile: Magazine focusing on plastics, includes articles about preparation, compounding, extrusion, extrusion blow moulding, thermoforming and downstream technology.
Language(s): English; German
ADVERTISING RATES:
Full Page Mono .... EUR 3000
Full Page Colour .... EUR 3000
Mechanical Data: Type Area: 250 x 185 mm, No. of Columns (Display): 3, Col Widths (Display): 58 mm
Copy instructions: *Copy Date:* 14 days prior to publication
Official Journal of: Organ d. Masterbatch-Verb.
BUSINESS: PLASTICS & RUBBER

EXZELLENT 1665052G4E-7057

Editorial: Im Krummen Ort 6, 28870 FISCHERHUDE
Tel: 4293 7894890 **Fax:** 4293 7894891
Email: info@teubert-kommunikation.de **Web site:** http://www.teubert-kommunikation.de
Freq: Quarterly; **Annual Sub.:** EUR 32,00; **Circ:** 9,800
Editor: Joachim Teubert; **Advertising Manager:** Andrea Böker
Profile: Magazine for entrepreneurs, managers and executives of the construction industry, construction, component and equipment manufacturers, distributors, architects, planners, government agencies, associations, experts, banks, policy makers, investors.
Language(s): German
ADVERTISING RATES:
Full Page Mono .... EUR 2200
Full Page Colour .... EUR 3200
Mechanical Data: Type Area: 250 x 182 mm, No. of Columns (Display): 2, Col Widths (Display): 89 mm
Copy instructions: *Copy Date:* 14 days prior to publication
Official Journal of: Organ d. Bauindustrieverb. Niedersachsen-Bremen e.V. u. d. Ingenieurverb. d. Wasser- u. Schiffahrtsstraßenverwaltung e.V.

EYEBIZZ 1644189G56E-396

Editorial: Steiner Str. 31, 78337 ÖHNINGEN
Tel: 7735 9191957 **Fax:** 7735 9191960
Email: graf@eyebizz.de **Web site:** http://www.eyebizz.de
Freq: 6 issues yearly; **Annual Sub.:** EUR 24,00; **Circ:** 12,012
Editor: Martin Graf
Profile: Magazine for opticians.
Language(s): German
ADVERTISING RATES:
Full Page Mono .... EUR 4450
Full Page Colour .... EUR 4450
Mechanical Data: Type Area: 272 x 178 mm, No. of Columns (Display): 4, Col Widths (Display): 44 mm
BUSINESS: HEALTH & MEDICAL: Optics

EZ EVANGELISCHE ZEITUNG - CHRISTL. WOCHENZTG. F. NIEDERSACHSEN, AUSG. LANDESKIRCHE BRAUNSCHWEIG 726926G87-3980

Editorial: Knochenhauerstr. 38, 30159 HANNOVER
Tel: 511 1241713 **Fax:** 511 329730
Email: ez@lvh.de **Web site:** http://www.evangelische-zeitung.de
Freq: Weekly; **Circ:** 18,963
Editor: Michael Eberstein; **Advertising Manager:** Christine Smolin
Profile: Christian weekly for Lower Saxony, edition national church of Braunschweig.
Language(s): German
ADVERTISING RATES:
Full Page Mono .... EUR 3600
Full Page Colour .... EUR 6400
Mechanical Data: Type Area: 400 x 280 mm, No. of Columns (Display): 6, Col Widths (Display): 42 mm
Copy instructions: *Copy Date:* 10 days prior to publication
CONSUMER: RELIGIOUS

EZ TOOLS & TRADE EISENWAREN-ZEITUNG 726082G25-35

Editorial: Eichendorffstr. 3, 40474 DÜSSELDORF
Tel: 211 4705066 **Fax:** 211 4705064
Email: ez.hz@gmx.de **Web site:** http://www.ez-hz.de
Freq: 10 issues yearly; **Annual Sub.:** EUR 57,00; **Circ.:** 4,063
Editor: Achim Mecklenbeck; **Advertising Manager:** Ulrich Wrobel
Profile: The EZ Tools & Trade Eisenwaren-Zeitung serves the entire market hardware, tools, fittings and garden products. Recipients: The decision makers about the store in the areas of PVH (production-associated trade) hardware trade / wholesale, tools, locks and fittings market, fixing techniques, motorists and garden needs. Members of purchasing cooperatives ede and northwest, DIY markets, SB stores. Topics: news and trends, sales promotion, marketing, personal, Economic developments, market data, trade fairs, etc.
Language(s): German
ADVERTISING RATES:
Full Page Mono .... EUR 2350
Full Page Colour .... EUR 4047
Mechanical Data: Type Area: 259 x 175 mm, No. of Columns (Display): 3, Col Widths (Display): 55 mm
Copy instructions: *Copy Date:* 12 days prior to publication
Official Journal of: Organ d. Zentralverb. Hartwarenhandel e.V.
BUSINESS: HARDWARE

F+H FÖRDERN UND HEBEN 728160G10-25

Editorial: Lise-Meitner-Str. 2, 55129 MAINZ
Tel: 6131 992322 **Fax:** 6131 992340
Email: r.wesselowski@vfmz.de **Web site:** http://www.industrie-service.de
Freq: 10 issues yearly; **Annual Sub.:** EUR 157,00; **Circ.:** 11,602
Editor: Reiner Wesselowski; **Advertising Manager:** Gundula Unverzagt
Profile: The focus of the f+h-topics are technical and science oriented information and reports on the possibilities of innovative technologies and products for intralogistics. Reports in f+h are inspiration and pulse for the daily logistics business and provide practical value. The large proportion of exclusive reports, published from the point: the problem, alternative solutions and ultimately implemented system solutions, characterize the high-quality journalism. For 60 years readers of f+h truts this professional, journalistic authority. Since 1998 the monthly published independent fork-lift truck test underlines the editorial innovation and provides important impetus for investment decision-makers. Topics include: material handling, warehousing, logistics software, cranes and hoists, material handling equipment, conveyors, logistics management.
Language(s): German
Readership: Aimed at managers of enterprises, construction, purchase, products, logistics and sales.
ADVERTISING RATES:
Full Page Mono .... EUR 4200
Full Page Colour .... EUR 5430
Mechanical Data: Type Area: 265 x 185 mm, No. of Columns (Display): 4, Col Widths (Display): 43 mm
Copy instructions: *Copy Date:* 14 days prior to publication
BUSINESS: MATERIALS HANDLING

F+H PROJEKTGUIDE INTRALOGISTIK 734852G49A-940

Editorial: Lise-Meitner-Str. 2, 55129 MAINZ
Tel: 6131 992322 **Fax:** 6131 992100
Email: r.wesselowski@vfmz.de **Web site:** http://www.industrie-service.de
Freq: Annual; **Cover Price:** EUR 38,00; **Circ:** 15,000
Editor: Reiner Wesselowski; **Advertising Manager:** Gundula Unverzagt
Profile: The special issue f+h Projektguide Intralogistik provides important basic knowledge, useful information and practical tips for planning, designing, Modernization and the efficient operation of intra-logistics systems and equipment. Current table works from the fields of warehousing and material handling equipment round off the profile from and provide information about the product portfolio of manufacturers and suppliers.
Language(s): German
ADVERTISING RATES:
Full Page Mono .... EUR 5290
Full Page Colour .... EUR 6520
Mechanical Data: Type Area: 265 x 185 mm, No. of Columns (Display): 4, Col Widths (Display): 43 mm
Copy instructions: *Copy Date:* 25 days prior to publication

F+H REPORT 728161G49A-480

Editorial: Lise-Meitner-Str. 2, 55129 MAINZ
Tel: 6131 992322 **Fax:** 6131 992340
Email: r.wesselowski@vfmz.de **Web site:** http://www.industrie-service.de
Freq: Annual; **Annual Sub.:** EUR 157,00; **Circ:** 11,635
Editor: Reiner Wesselowski; **Advertising Manager:** Gundula Unverzagt
Profile: The f+h Report provides decision makers an overview of the current range of products from the entire field of logistics. This annual special issue of the f+h allows with online service links a rapid contact between the interested readers and potential customers, the manufacturers and advertisers.
Language(s): German
ADVERTISING RATES:
Full Page Mono .... EUR 4200
Full Page Colour .... EUR 5430
Mechanical Data: Type Area: 265 x 185 mm, No. of Columns (Display): 4, Col Widths (Display): 43 mm
Copy instructions: *Copy Date:* 15 days prior to publication

F+I-BAU BAUEN MIT SYSTEMEN 728162G4A-246

Editorial: Ernst-Heinkel-Str. 4/2, 70734 FELLBACH
Tel: 711 5057165 **Fax:** 711 5057166
Email: element-verlag@t-online.de **Web site:** http://www.elementverlag.de
Freq: Quarterly; **Annual Sub.:** EUR 22,50; **Circ:** 5,000
Editor: Hans Schmid
Profile: Journal about planning and organisation in building.
Language(s): German
Readership: Read by architects, designers and managers of building companies.
ADVERTISING RATES:
Full Page Mono .... EUR 1755
Full Page Colour .... EUR 2783
Mechanical Data: Type Area: 272 x 185 mm, No. of Columns (Display): 4, Col Widths (Display): 42 mm
Copy instructions: *Copy Date:* 12 days prior to publication
BUSINESS: ARCHITECTURE & BUILDING: Architecture

F+K FAHRZEUG + KAROSSERIE 727032G31A-100

Editorial: Forststr. 131, 70193 STUTTGART
Tel: 5137 128394 **Fax:** 5137 128395
Email: ingo.roever@t-online.de **Web site:** http://www.fahrzeug-und-karosserie.de
Freq: Monthly; **Annual Sub.:** EUR 132,60; **Circ:** 6,077
Editor: Ingo Röver; **Advertising Manager:** Mareike Zander
Profile: Journal about the repair and respraying of cars.
Language(s): German
Readership: Aimed at mechanics.
ADVERTISING RATES:
Full Page Mono .... EUR 2080
Full Page Colour .... EUR 3340
Mechanical Data: Type Area: 268 x 187 mm, No. of Columns (Display): 4, Col Widths (Display): 43 mm
Official Journal of: Organ d. Zentralverb. Karosserie- u. Fahrzeugtechnik
BUSINESS: MOTOR TRADE: Motor Trade Accessories

F & S FILTRIEREN UND SEPARIEREN 728166G19R-40

Editorial: Birkenstr. 1a, 67724 GONBACH
Tel: 6302 5707 **Fax:** 6302 5708
Email: sripperger@t-online.de **Web site:** http://www.fs-journal.de
Freq: 7 issues yearly; **Annual Sub.:** EUR 61,00; **Circ:** 6,360
Editor: Siegfried Ripperger; **Advertising Manager:** Eckhard von der Lühe
Profile: Journal containing information about filtration and separation.
Language(s): German
Readership: Aimed at engineers, development managers and technicians.
ADVERTISING RATES:
Full Page Mono .... EUR 3355
Full Page Colour .... EUR 4515
Mechanical Data: Type Area: 260 x 177 mm, No. of Columns (Display): 3, Col Widths (Display): 55 mm
BUSINESS: ENGINEERING & MACHINERY: Engineering Related

F & W FÜHREN UND WIRTSCHAFTEN IM KRANKENHAUS 728171G56C-1

Editorial: Stadtwaldpark 10, 34212 MELSUNGEN
Tel: 5661 734482 **Fax:** 5661 734444
Email: uta.meurer@bibliomed.de **Web site:** http://www.bibliomed.de
Freq: 6 issues yearly; **Annual Sub.:** EUR 93,00; **Circ:** 5,195
Editor: Uta Meurer
Profile: Hospital administration journal.
Language(s): German
ADVERTISING RATES:
Full Page Mono .... EUR 3200
Full Page Colour .... EUR 3200
Mechanical Data: No. of Columns (Display): 3, Col Widths (Display): 52 mm, Type Area: 241 x 170 mm
Copy instructions: *Copy Date:* 14 days prior to publication
Official Journal of: Organ d. Bundesverb. Dt. Privatkliniken e.V.
BUSINESS: HEALTH & MEDICAL: Hospitals

FABRIKVERKAUF IN DEUTSCHLAND 726932G74M-180

Editorial: Janningsstr. 5, 70563 STUTTGART
Tel: 711 733010 **Fax:** 711 733015
Email: info@zeppelin-verlag.de **Web site:** http://www.zeppelin-verlag.de
Freq: Annual; **Cover Price:** EUR 9,95; **Circ:** 75,000
Profile: Shopping guide with addresses of all the factory outlets in Germany.
Language(s): German
ADVERTISING RATES:
Full Page Mono .... EUR 995
Mechanical Data: Type Area: 154 x 96 mm
Copy instructions: *Copy Date:* 90 days prior to publication

FACHANWALT ARBEITSRECHT 753756G1A-885

Editorial: Luxemburger Str. 449, 50939 KÖLN
Tel: 221 943737223 **Fax:** 221 943737201
Email: hkuennemann@wolterskluwer.de **Web site:** http://www.fa-fachanwalt-arbeitsrecht.de
Freq: Monthly; **Annual Sub.:** EUR 170,60; **Circ:** 1,800
Editor: Heike Künnemann
Profile: Magazine for lawyers and judges of labour law.
Language(s): German
ADVERTISING RATES:
Full Page Mono .... EUR 855
Full Page Colour .... EUR 1962
Mechanical Data: Type Area: 255 x 184 mm, No. of Columns (Display): 2, Col Widths (Display): 90 mm

FACHARZT.DE 1661537G56A-11381

Editorial: Kattjahren 4, 22359 HAMBURG
Tel: 40 6091540 **Fax:** 40 60915444
Email: j.scholz@aend.de **Web site:** http://www.facharzt.de
Freq: Daily; **Cover Price:** Paid; **Circ:** 282,502 Unique Users
Editor: Jan Scholz; **Advertising Manager:** Benjamin Häusser
Language(s): German
BUSINESS: HEALTH & MEDICAL

DER FACHBERATER 726938G93-180

Editorial: Elsasser Str. 41, 28211 BREMEN
Tel: 421 3484218 **Fax:** 421 3484228
Email: pleiner@waechter.de **Web site:** http://www.waechter.de
Freq: Quarterly; **Annual Sub.:** EUR 12,00; **Circ:** 19,292
Editor: Jutta Pleiner; **Advertising Manager:** Rita Kropp
Profile: Magazine about gardening and green issues.
Language(s): German
ADVERTISING RATES:
Full Page Mono .... EUR 3429
Full Page Colour .... EUR 3429
Mechanical Data: Type Area: 260 x 180 mm, No. of Columns (Display): 4, Col Widths (Display): 43 mm
Copy instructions: *Copy Date:* 34 days prior to publication
CONSUMER: GARDENING

FACHBLATT DER NEBENBERUFLICHEN LANDWIRTSCHAFT 731171G21A-2240

Editorial: Saarloiuser Str. 54, 66346 PÜTTLINGEN
Tel: 171 2632635 **Fax:** 6806 920661
Email: info@vln-saar.de **Web site:** http://www.vln-saar.de
Freq: Quarterly; Free to qualifying individuals
Annual Sub.: EUR 36,00; **Circ:** 1,500
Editor: Hans-Werner Wagner
Profile: Magazine for part-time farmers.
Language(s): German
ADVERTISING RATES:
Full Page Mono .... EUR 350
Full Page Colour .... EUR 350
Mechanical Data: Type Area: 260 x 180 mm, No. of Columns (Display): 4, Col Widths (Display): 42 mm
Copy instructions: *Copy Date:* 20 days prior to publication

FACHZEITSCHRIFTEN-PORTAL 1661539G2A-5577

Editorial: Südstr. 18, 58644 ISERLOHN
Tel: 2371 77270 **Fax:** 2371 772720
Email: info@fachzeitschriften-portal.de **Web site:** http://www.fachzeitschriften-portal.de
Cover Price: Paid
Language(s): German
BUSINESS: COMMUNICATIONS, ADVERTISING & MARKETING

FACILITY MANAGEMENT 726968G4F-21

Editorial: Avenwedder Str. 55, 33335 GÜTERSLOH
Tel: 5241 8090884 **Fax:** 5241 80690880
Email: burkhard.froehlich@bauverlag.de **Web site:** http://www.facility-management.de
Freq: 6 issues yearly; **Annual Sub.:** EUR 84,00; **Circ:** 9,884
Editor: Burkhard Fröhlich; **Advertising Manager:** Herbert Walhorn
Profile: The trade magazine Facility Management appeals to the economically responsible for real estate and property that are used commercially, in public or industrial. Technical papers cover the need for information from all interested parties to FM. The latest information, product news, Legal, and news from the industry add the editorial section. Important editorial focuses are the integrated planning, the technical, the commercial and infrastructural building management. A special position occupied by the object analysis. Here an already-realized building with special features in facility management and / or building management is presented as an example.
Language(s): German
ADVERTISING RATES:
Full Page Mono .... EUR 4190
Full Page Colour .... EUR 5735
Mechanical Data: Type Area: 270 x 186 mm, No. of Columns (Display): 4, Col Widths (Display): 45 mm
Copy instructions: *Copy Date:* 14 days prior to publication
Supplement(s): Brandschutz in öffentlichen und privatwirtschaftlichen Gebäuden; computer spezial; Licht + Raum
BUSINESS: ARCHITECTURE & BUILDING: Cleaning & Maintenance

DER FACILITY MANAGER 726970G4F-22

Editorial: Mandichostr. 18, 86504 MERCHING
Tel: 8233 381120 **Fax:** 8233 381212
Email: martin.graeber@facility-manager.de **Web site:** http://www.facility-manager.de
Freq: 10 issues yearly; **Annual Sub.:** EUR 100,50; **Circ:** 9,650
Editor: Martin Gräber; **Advertising Manager:** Helmut Junginger
Profile: Magazine for facilities managers or those responsible for facility management and building services in real estate companies and administrations.
Language(s): German
ADVERTISING RATES:
Full Page Mono .... EUR 5460
Full Page Colour .... EUR 5460
Mechanical Data: Type Area: 264 x 190 mm, No. of Columns (Display): 4, Col Widths (Display): 44 mm
Copy instructions: *Copy Date:* 23 days prior to publication
BUSINESS: ARCHITECTURE & BUILDING: Cleaning & Maintenance

FACTORY 745982G14A-9399

Editorial: Heinrich-Heine-Str. 9, 35039 MARBURG
Tel: 6421 15233 **Fax:** 6421 166815
Email: gk@factory-magazin.de **Web site:** http://www.factory-magazin.de

Freq: Quarterly; Free to qualifying individuals
Annual Sub.: EUR 23,50; **Circ:** 2,000
Editor: Gerhard Kaminski; **Advertising Manager:** Ralf Bindel
Profile: Magazine focusing on the impact of business and trade on the environment.
Language(s): German
Readership: Read by managers.
ADVERTISING RATES:
Full Page Mono .... EUR 614
Full Page Colour .... EUR 1278
Mechanical Data: Type Area: 250 x 182 mm, No. of Columns (Display): 3, Col Widths (Display): 57 mm
Copy instructions: *Copy Date:* 28 days prior to publication

FACTS 726971G34-160
Editorial: Theodor-Althoff-Str. 45, 45133 ESSEN
Tel: 201 87126800 **Fax:** 201 87126810
Email: redaktion@factsverlag.de **Web site:** http://www.factsverlag.de
Freq: Monthly; **Annual Sub.:** EUR 49,50; **Circ:** 50,000
Advertising Manager: Sabine Schnitzler
Profile: Magazine about business and industry.
Language(s): German
ADVERTISING RATES:
Full Page Mono .... EUR 6160
Full Page Colour .... EUR 6160
Mechanical Data: Type Area: 266 x 182 mm, No. of Columns (Display): 4, Col Widths (Display): 53 mm
Copy instructions: *Copy Date:* 20 days prior to publication
Supplement(s): Facts office
BUSINESS: OFFICE EQUIPMENT

FAHRER-JAHRBUCH 1863708G49A-2454
Editorial: Joseph-Dollinger-Bogen 5, 80807 MÜNCHEN **Tel:** 89 323910 **Fax:** 89 32391417
Email: management@huss-verlag.de **Web site:** http://www.huss-verlag.de
Freq: Annual; **Cover Price:** EUR 8,45; **Circ:** 35,000
Profile: Magazine containing specific information for truckers.
Language(s): German
ADVERTISING RATES:
Full Page Mono .... EUR 2880
Full Page Colour .... EUR 2880
Mechanical Data: Type Area: 148 x 105 mm
Copy instructions: *Copy Date:* 50 days prior to publication

FAHRLEHRER-BRIEF 726990G49A-520
Editorial: Aschauer Str. 30, 81549 MÜNCHEN
Tel: 89 2030432275 **Fax:** 89 2030432207
Email: dietmar.fund@springer.com **Web site:** http://www.springer-transport-media.de
Freq: 10 issues yearly; **Annual Sub.:** EUR 82,90; **Circ:** 5,800
Editor: Dietmar Fund
Profile: Magazine for driving instructors with professional, economic and pedagogical issues.
Language(s): German

FAHRSCHULE 727029G31D-1
Editorial: Aschauer Str. 30, 81549 MÜNCHEN
Tel: 89 2030432269 **Fax:** 89 2030432207
Email: dietmar.fund@springer.com **Web site:** http://www.fahrschule-online.de
Freq: Monthly; **Annual Sub.:** EUR 89,90; **Circ:** 16,009
Editor: Dietmar Fund; **Advertising Manager:** Marisa d'Arbonneau
Profile: Magazine for driving instructors and schools.
Language(s): German
Readership: Aimed at members.
ADVERTISING RATES:
Full Page Mono .... EUR 4200
Full Page Colour .... EUR 6025
Mechanical Data: Type Area: 250 x 185 mm, No. of Columns (Display): 4, Col Widths (Display): 43 mm
Copy instructions: *Copy Date:* 30 days prior to publication
BUSINESS: MOTOR TRADE: Driving Schools

FAHRZEUGE 749079G77A-2480
Editorial: Am Treptower Park 75, 12435 BERLIN
Tel: 30 53432109 **Fax:** 30 53432121
Email: gensrich@zweitehand.de **Web site:** http://www.zweitehand.de
Freq: Weekly; **Cover Price:** EUR 2,50; **Circ:** 15,600
Editor: Kay Gensrich
Profile: Private and commercial classifieds for cars, a popular and successful marketplace for customers with specific intent to purchase and every week for more than 25,000 copies circulated, the market leader in Berlin and Brandenburg.
Language(s): German
Readership: Aimed at people interested in buying and selling second hand cars.
ADVERTISING RATES:
Full Page Mono .... EUR 2408
Full Page Colour .... EUR 2408
Mechanical Data: Type Area: 280 x 190 mm, No. of Columns (Display): 4, Col Widths (Display): 45 mm
Copy instructions: *Copy Date:* 3 days prior to publication
CONSUMER: MOTORING & CYCLING: Motoring

FAIRKEHR 727035G77A-2698
Editorial: Niebuhrstr. 16b, 53113 BONN
Tel: 228 9858545 **Fax:** 228 9858550
Email: redaktion@fairkehr.de **Web site:** http://www.fairkehr-magazin.de
Freq: 6 issues yearly; Free to qualifying individuals
Annual Sub.: EUR 23,00; **Circ:** 65,000
Editor: Michael Adler; **Advertising Manager:** Dorothee Schenzielorz
Profile: Members magazine of the Drivers Club of Germany covering environmental issues, as well as driving, travel and leisure.
Language(s): German
ADVERTISING RATES:
Full Page Colour .... EUR 3950
Mechanical Data: No. of Columns (Display): 4, Col Widths (Display): 45 mm, Type Area: 260 x 185 mm
Copy instructions: *Copy Date:* 28 days prior to publication
CONSUMER: MOTORING & CYCLING: Motoring

FAKTOR C 724332G14A-1460
Editorial: Nikolausstr. 86, 50937 KÖLN
Tel: 221 43092180 **Fax:** 221 43092183
Email: redaktion@faktor-c-magazin.de **Web site:** http://www.faktor-c-magazin.de
Freq: Quarterly; Free to qualifying individuals
Annual Sub.: EUR 16,00; **Circ:** 5,000
Editor: Stephan Pesch; **Advertising Manager:** Heike Striemer
Profile: Economy from a Christian perspective. Faktor C is the quarterly magazine for a business audience interested in values. The focus is on information, analysis, reports and opinions about the economy from a Christian perspective. Faktor C consists of two distinct parts: 1) the magazine, that relevant economic and ethical issues for a broad audience prepared and 2) CiW Internally, a range of services around the association, the members also receive all. Faktor C reported on issues and trends in the economy that require or encourage Christian business ethics. The critical discussion sensitized, motivated the Christian perspective. Faktor C provides specific outlooks and insights, hints, tips, best-practice examples and ideas. Faktor C is positioning itself as a modern, contemporary print magazine, that breaks down barriers, arouses curiosity, is thought-provoking, stimulates the "imitation", will gladly read and passed.
Language(s): German
ADVERTISING RATES:
Full Page Mono .... EUR 850
Full Page Colour .... EUR 850
Mechanical Data: Type Area: 256 x 185 mm, No. of Columns (Display): 3, Col Widths (Display): 58 mm
Copy instructions: *Copy Date:* 30 days prior to publication

FAKTOR WIRTSCHAFT 727041G63-240
Editorial: Katharinenstr. 48, 17033 NEUBRANDENBURG **Tel:** 395 5597104
Fax: 395 5665046
Email: lubensky@neubrandenburg.ihk.de **Web site:** http://www.neubrandenburg.ihk.de
Freq: 10 issues yearly; **Circ:** 19,039
Editor: Bodo Lubensky
Profile: Regional business newspaper, the official organ of the Commerce and Industry Chamber of Neubrandenburg.
Language(s): German
ADVERTISING RATES:
Full Page Mono .... EUR 1190
Full Page Colour .... EUR 1900
Mechanical Data: Type Area: 318 x 220 mm, No. of Columns (Display): 4, Col Widths (Display): 52 mm
Copy instructions: *Copy Date:* 14 days prior to publication
Supplement(s): B4B Mittelstand
BUSINESS: REGIONAL BUSINESS

FALK GASTRO REVIEW JOURNAL 728348G56A-11163
Editorial: Hugstetter Str. 55, 79106 FREIBURG
Freq: Quarterly; **Cover Price:** Free; **Circ:** 35,000
Editor: Wolfgang Kreisel
Profile: Magazine containing abstracts of the latest publications on gastroenterology and hepatology.
Language(s): German

DER FALKE 727043G81F-3
Editorial: Industriepark 3, 56291 WIEBELSHEIM
Tel: 6766 903141 **Fax:** 6766 903320
Email: falke@aula-verlag.de **Web site:** http://www.falke-journal.de
Freq: Monthly; **Annual Sub.:** EUR 58,75; **Circ:** 8,000
Editor: Norbert Schäffer
Profile: Read by ornithologists and birdwatchers.
Language(s): German
Readership: Read by ornithologists and birdwatchers.
ADVERTISING RATES:
Full Page Colour .... EUR 1140
Mechanical Data: Type Area: 247 x 169 mm, No. of Columns (Display): 3, Col Widths (Display): 53 mm
Copy instructions: *Copy Date:* 30 days prior to publication
CONSUMER: ANIMALS & PETS: Birds

FAMILIE & CO 727075G74D-60
Editorial: Schnewlinstr. 6, 79098 FREIBURG
Tel: 761 70578559 **Fax:** 761 70578656
Email: redaktion@familymedia.de **Web site:** http://www.familie.de
Freq: Monthly; **Annual Sub.:** EUR 32,40; **Circ:** 171,724
Editor: Dirk Müller; **Advertising Manager:** Sabine Mecklenburg
Profile: Magazine concerning child development, education and development.
Language(s): German
Readership: Aimed at parents with young children.
ADVERTISING RATES:
Full Page Mono .... EUR 15900
Full Page Colour .... EUR 15900
Mechanical Data: Type Area: 234 x 184 mm, No. of Columns (Display): 4, Col Widths (Display): 40 mm
Copy instructions: *Copy Date:* 42 days prior to publication
Supplement(s): Urlaub
CONSUMER: WOMEN'S INTEREST CONSUMER MAGAZINES: Child Care

FAMILIE.DE 1621215G74C-3544
Editorial: Leonrodstr. 52, 80633 MÜNCHEN
Tel: 761 705780 **Fax:** 761 70578651
Email: online@familymedia.de **Web site:** http://www.familie.de
Freq: Daily; **Cover Price:** Paid; **Circ:** 750,358 Unique Users
Editor: Fabian Knecht
Profile: The website familie.de offers families all relevant and current topics, presents the magazine range. Promotions and competitions to increase the attractiveness of the pages and invite to join the user to stay. familie.de includes all families relevant and current issues, is very popular among the target group of young families, has a high percentage of repeat users, offers a variety of interactive content (such as contests, baby photo contests, promotions), stands out for its attractiveness, relevance and interaction, is editorially strong: 5 editors research and inform professional and competent our users, has a strong cross-media integration. Facebook:http://de-de.facebook.com/familie.de.
Language(s): German
CONSUMER: WOMEN'S INTEREST CONSUMER MAGAZINES: Home & Family

FAMILIENHEIM UND GARTEN 727065G74C-920
Editorial: Oberer Lindweg 2, 53129 BONN
Tel: 228 604680 **Fax:** 228 6046830
Email: redaktion@fug-verlag.de **Web site:** http://www.fug-verlag.de
Freq: Monthly; Free to qualifying individuals
Annual Sub.: EUR 13,20; **Circ:** 367,892
Editor: Gerd Böker; **Advertising Manager:** Gerd Böker
Profile: "Familienheim und Garten" - Guide for Home, Garden and Family is positioned in the segment of the home and garden magazines. All subscribers are homeowners and have larger than average gardens. "Familienheim und Garten" is cut to the interests of its readers: All issues affecting the maintenance, modernization and renovation of the house, maintenance of utility and decorative garden and leisure activities are a regular part of the journal. The reader is characterized by specific modernization and renovation plans and supplementary and replacement purchases in garden tools. In addition, "Familienheim und Garten" has a strong reader loyalty. This Outlet offers RSS (Really Simple Syndication).
Language(s): German
ADVERTISING RATES:
Full Page Mono .... EUR 5950
Full Page Colour .... EUR 9330
Mechanical Data: Type Area: 265 x 187 mm, No. of Columns (Display): 4, Col Widths (Display): 43 mm
Copy instructions: *Copy Date:* 39 days prior to publication
CONSUMER: WOMEN'S INTEREST CONSUMER MAGAZINES: Home & Family

FAMILY 727078G74C-65
Editorial: Bodenborn 43, 58452 WITTEN
Tel: 2302 93093840 **Fax:** 2302 93093899
Email: info@family.de **Web site:** http://www.family.de
Freq: 6 issues yearly; **Annual Sub.:** EUR 25,80; **Circ:** 34,141
Editor: Martin Gundlach; **Advertising Manager:** Thilo Cunz
Profile: Magazine with the themes: communication in the partnership, conflict and family life, sexuality, and educational issues.
Language(s): German
Readership: Aimed at Christians.
ADVERTISING RATES:
Full Page Mono .... EUR 2537
Full Page Colour .... EUR 3329
Mechanical Data: Type Area: 258 x 188 mm, No. of Columns (Display): 4, Col Widths (Display): 44 mm
Copy instructions: *Copy Date:* 35 days prior to publication
CONSUMER: WOMEN'S INTEREST CONSUMER MAGAZINES: Home & Family

FAMILY HOME 726015G4E-6910
Editorial: Mörikestr. 67, 70199 STUTTGART
Tel: 711 96666995 **Fax:** 711 96666980
Email: katja.manitz@familyhome.de **Web site:** http://www.hurra-wir-bauen.de
Freq: 6 issues yearly; **Annual Sub.:** EUR 6,00; **Circ:** 44,134
Editor: Katja Manitz; **Advertising Manager:** Ute Cramer
Profile: Already in the eighth year appears in the Family Home, the successful magazine publishing family home. Thanks to his emotional speech reader and its comprehensive editorial concept (Subtitles - building, housing, renovation), the magazine enjoys not only the readers but also in the hoise/construction industry of the highest reputation. The periodical is published bimonthly, six times a year. Families with children need not only space but also enough space to develop - be it to the lively band to better under control, or to escape the restrictions of life tenant. Where could be better achieved than in the house? Family home is in each issue about 15 authentic building histories, talking to the families and interviewed them about their experience during adventure construction. Building families 15 - 15 houses - 15 concepts presented in detail and most important, including the information on this house. The desire for protection and ordered structures, security and continuity of providing the family, the private retreat, the topic of building and living a new meaning. Conservative investments, such as investment in their own property and investment in the personal retirement, enjoying again the highest regard. Family home advising future owners with a lot of planning tips and funding examples. Fantastic live up new trends and to link the structural and energetic as well as financial opportunities in an individual mix for a personal style of living, that is the special attraction of a new building. Technology building blocks and residential ingredients in it's rich variety in each issue of the family home.
Language(s): German
Readership: Aimed at builders.
ADVERTISING RATES:
Full Page Mono .... EUR 5775
Full Page Colour .... EUR 7700
Mechanical Data: Type Area: 248 x 185 mm, No. of Columns (Display): 4, Col Widths (Display): 43 mm
Copy instructions: *Copy Date:* 28 days prior to publication
BUSINESS: ARCHITECTURE & BUILDING: Building

FÅRA 727089G21A-1480
Editorial: John-Deere-Str. 70, 68163 MANNHEIM
Tel: 621 8298416 **Fax:** 621 8298300
Email: hironjeanclaude@johndeere.com **Web site:** http://www.johndeere.com
Freq: Quarterly; **Cover Price:** Free; **Circ:** 33,000
Editor: Jean-Claude Hiron
Profile: Company publication published by Deere & Company.
Language(s): Norwegian

FÅRAN 727090G21A-1500
Editorial: John-Deere-Str. 70, 68163 MANNHEIM
Tel: 621 8298416 **Fax:** 621 8298300
Email: hironjeanclaude@johndeere.com **Web site:** http://www.johndeere.com
Freq: Quarterly; **Cover Price:** Free; **Circ:** 27,000
Editor: Jean-Claude Hiron
Profile: Company publication published by Deere & Company.
Language(s): Swedish

FARBE UND LACK 727095G16B-20
Editorial: Plathnerstr. 4c, 30175 HANNOVER
Tel: 511 9910211 **Fax:** 511 9910299
Email: miriam.von.bardeleben@vincentz.net **Web site:** http://www.farbeundlack.de
Freq: Monthly; **Annual Sub.:** EUR 117,00; **Circ:** 4,329
Editor: Miriam von Bardeleben; **Advertising Manager:** Anette Pennartz
Profile: Journal containing information on the formulation, production and marketing of paints and coatings.
Language(s): German
Readership: Aimed at chemists.
ADVERTISING RATES:
Full Page Mono .... EUR 2760
Full Page Colour .... EUR 4260
Mechanical Data: Type Area: 250 x 175 mm, No. of Columns (Display): 4, Col Widths (Display): 42 mm
Copy instructions: *Copy Date:* 15 days prior to publication
Official Journal of: Organ d. Ges. Dt. Chemiker, Fachgruppe Lackchemie, d. Schweizer. Vereinigung d. Lack- u. Farbenchemiker u. d. Verb. d. Ingenieure d. Lack- u. Farbenfaches
BUSINESS: DECORATING & PAINT: Paint - Technical Manufacture

FASSADE 727103G4E-3440
Editorial: Herner Str. 299, 44809 BOCHUM
Tel: 234 9539126 **Fax:** 234 9539130
Email: jens.meyerling@kleffmann-verlag.de **Web site:** http://www.die-fassade.de
Freq: 6 issues yearly; **Annual Sub.:** EUR 47,60; **Circ:** 11,758
Editor: Jens Meyerling
Profile: Publication about the planning and construction of building facades.
Language(s): German
Readership: Read by architects, town planners, building and construction engineers.
ADVERTISING RATES:
Full Page Mono .... EUR 2090
Full Page Colour .... EUR 3350
Mechanical Data: Type Area: 258 x 178 mm, No. of Columns (Display): 4, Col Widths (Display): 42 mm
Supplement to: RTS Magazin
BUSINESS: ARCHITECTURE & BUILDING: Building

FASSADENTECHNIK 727106G4E-3460
Editorial: Knauerstr. 1, 20249 HAMBURG
Tel: 40 28096750 **Fax:** 40 28096752
Email: redaktion@fassadentechnik.de **Web site:** http://www.fassadentechnik.de
Freq: 6 issues yearly; **Annual Sub.:** EUR 80,00; **Circ:** 6,960
Editor: Martin Jung; **Advertising Manager:** Kirsten Jung
Profile: Technical journal about curtain wall systems and their components. Also covers statics, building physics, scaffolding and tools.
Language(s): English; German
ADVERTISING RATES:
Full Page Mono .... EUR 2260
Full Page Colour .... EUR 3790
Mechanical Data: Type Area: 259 x 190 mm, No. of Columns (Display): 4, Col Widths (Display): 30 mm
BUSINESS: ARCHITECTURE & BUILDING: Building

FASZINATION STAHL 1705271G27-3030
Editorial: Hohe Str. 8, 40213 DÜSSELDORF
Tel: 211 3116300 **Fax:** 211 31163024
Email: info@lankenfeld.com **Web site:** http://www.lankenfeld.com
Freq: Half-yearly; **Cover Price:** Free; **Circ:** 1,500,000
Editor: Horst Woeckner
Profile: The „Faszination Stahl" was planned as a one time cost. By the great success and the inexhaustible variety of topics, it was developed as a magazine series and published annually since 2000, twice now with a circulation of 1.8 million copies. It has established itself as a research tool for the media to pick up on the website regularly in TV reports and newspaper articles. As a PR tool ensures the „Faszination Stahl" the long term the positive image of steel.
Language(s): German

FAZ.NET 1621217G65A-266
Editorial: Hellerhofstr. 2, 60327 FRANKFURT
Tel: 69 75910 **Fax:** 69 75912323
Email: info@faz.de **Web site:** http://www.faz.net
Freq: Daily; **Cover Price:** Paid; **Circ:** 23,214,521 Unique Users
Editor: Kai N. Pritzsche; **Advertising Manager:** Florian Pütz
Profile: News on politics, economy, culture, sports, travel, medicine among others. Online presence of the Frankfurter Allgemeine Zeitung and one of the leading news portals in the German Internet - with a focus on politics, economics, finance and cultural magazine. The close integration of print and online newsrooms and the global network of correspondents will enable the Frankfurter Allgemeine Zeitung, provide users on the Internet high-quality journalism and an exceptional background reporting. Facebook: http://www.facebook.com/faz Twitter: https://twitter.com/FAZ_NET This Outlet offers RSS (Really Simple Syndication).
Language(s): German
NATIONAL DAILY & SUNDAY NEWSPAPERS: National Daily Newspapers

FBR-WASSERSPIEGEL 1832342G4E-7216
Editorial: Havelstr. 7a, 64295 DARMSTADT
Tel: 6151 339257 **Fax:** 6151 339258
Email: info@fbr.de **Web site:** http://www.fbr.de
Freq: Quarterly; Free to qualifying individuals
Annual Sub.: EUR 20,00; **Circ:** 5,000
Editor: Andrea Hofstaetter; **Advertising Manager:** Andrea Hofstaetter
Profile: Information about water recycling and rainwater utilization.
Language(s): German
ADVERTISING RATES:
Full Page Mono .... EUR 1499
Full Page Colour .... EUR 1874
Mechanical Data: Type Area: 252 x 176 mm, No. of Columns (Display): 2, Col Widths (Display): 86 mm
Copy instructions: *Copy Date:* 28 days prior to publication

FCI FABRICA DE CONCRETO INTERNACIONAL 2053208G4E-7348
Editorial: Industriestr. 180, 50999 KÖLN
Tel: 2236 962390 **Fax:** 2236 962396
Email: editor@cpi-worldwide.com **Web site:** http://www.cpi-worldwide.com
Freq: 6 issues yearly; Free to qualifying individuals
Annual Sub.: EUR 120,00; **Circ:** 2,500
Editor: Holger Karutz; **Advertising Manager:** Gerhard Klöckner
Profile: The journals of "CPI-Worldwide" are the only source for cutting-edge technical data, news and information for the concrete industry - from around the world. This information processed editorially and professional - are aimed directly regardless of location to business owners, decision makers and managers. The articles are well-written by world-renowned and in their field well-known experts. Each topic is presented in a way that the audience important information available, it brings on the cutting edge of technology and so to increase productivity and operational performance contributes.
Language(s): Portuguese
Mechanical Data: Type Area: 260 x 180 mm, No. of Columns (Display): 3, Col Widths (Display): 56 mm
Copy instructions: *Copy Date:* 30 days prior to publication

FECHENHEIMER ANZEIGER 727129G72-3800
Editorial: Kennedystr. 44, 63477 MAINTAL
Tel: 6181 40900 **Fax:** 6181 409030
Email: redaktion@maintaltagesanzeiger.de **Web site:** http://www.maintaltagesanzeiger.de
Freq: Weekly; **Circ:** 6,450
Advertising Manager: Richard Brandl
Profile: Regional weekly covering politics, economics, sport, travel, technology and the arts.
Language(s): German
ADVERTISING RATES:
SCC .... EUR 21,00
Mechanical Data: Type Area: 480 x 325 mm, No. of Columns (Display): 7, Col Widths (Display): 44 mm
Copy instructions: *Copy Date:* 1 day prior to publication
LOCAL NEWSPAPERS

FECHTSPORT 727132G75X-1680
Editorial: Hans-Sachs-Str. 55, 40237 DÜSSELDORF
Tel: 211 2396170 **Fax:** 211 2396171
Email: rimesse@aol.com **Web site:** http://www.fechten.org
Freq: 6 issues yearly; Free to qualifying individuals
Annual Sub.: EUR 20,00; **Circ:** 15,000
Editor: Andreas Schirmer; **Advertising Manager:** Kirsten Schiffer
Profile: The official organ of the German Fencing Federation. "Fechtsport" has many tournament reports on major national and international events, contributions to fencing history, a comprehensive schedule and much more.
Language(s): German
ADVERTISING RATES:
Full Page Mono .... EUR 1280
Full Page Colour .... EUR 2480
Mechanical Data: No. of Columns (Display): 3, Col Widths (Display): 58 mm, Type Area: 240 x 182 mm
Copy instructions: *Copy Date:* 40 days prior to publication
CONSUMER: SPORT: Other Sport

FEEDMAGAZINE KRAFTFUTTER 733225G21B-30
Editorial: Mainzer Landstr. 251, 60326 FRANKFURT
Tel: 69 75951587 **Fax:** 69 75951580
Email: bernd.springer@dfv.de **Web site:** http://www.feedmagazine.net
Freq: 6 issues yearly; **Annual Sub.:** EUR 187,00; **Circ:** 2,182
Editor: Bernd Springer; **Advertising Manager:** Dirk Armbruster
Profile: Journal about animal feed and grain.
Language(s): English; German
ADVERTISING RATES:
Full Page Mono .... EUR 1850
Full Page Colour .... EUR 2790
Mechanical Data: Type Area: 270 x 190 mm, No. of Columns (Display): 4, Col Widths (Display): 44 mm
Copy instructions: *Copy Date:* 21 days prior to publication
BUSINESS: AGRICULTURE & FARMING: Agriculture - Supplies & Services

FEIERN IM BERGISCHEN LAND 1819689G89A-12364
Editorial: Stammheimer Str. 47a, 50735 KÖLN
Tel: 221 76802710 **Fax:** 221 76802713
Email: torsten.schlosser@agentur-janke.de **Web site:** http://www.agentur-janke.de
Freq: Quarterly; **Circ:** 30,000
Editor: Anke Kerp; **Advertising Manager:** Stefanie Urban
Profile: It is published four times a year our magazine "celebrations in the Bergisch Land" with detailed descriptions of the cuisine and the specialties of the region.
Language(s): German
ADVERTISING RATES:
Full Page Mono .... EUR 1055
Full Page Colour .... EUR 1055
Mechanical Data: Type Area: 303 x 213 mm
Supplement to: hera Hochzeit

FEIERN & TAGEN DRESDEN 1830183G89A-12406
Editorial: Prager Str. 2b, 01069 DRESDEN
Tel: 351 8007030 **Fax:** 351 8007070
Email: redaktion@maxity.de **Web site:** http://www.feiernundtagen.com
Freq: Annual; **Cover Price:** Free; **Circ:** 15,000
Editor: Christine Herzog
Profile: Directory listing event and seminar accomodations in Dresden.
Language(s): German
Mechanical Data: Type Area: 126 x 85 mm

FEINE WELT 1799502G65B-2_104
Editorial: Adersstr. 12, 40215 DÜSSELDORF
Tel: 211 96488161 **Fax:** 211 96488171
Email: nrw@wams.de **Web site:** http://www.feinewelt-ruhrgebiet.de
Freq: Half-yearly; **Circ:** 47,000
Editor: Willi Keinhorst; **Advertising Manager:** Karl-Heinz Zechner
Profile: Premium magazine in the Welt am Sonntag for the Ruhrgebiet. In the magazine, the special attractions of the region are characteristic and suggest a link between luxury and lifestyle, culture, original and pleasure and aesthetics.
Language(s): German
ADVERTISING RATES:
Full Page Mono .... EUR 2348
Full Page Colour .... EUR 2348
Mechanical Data: Type Area: 260 x 210 mm
Supplement to: Welt am Sonntag
NATIONAL DAILY & SUNDAY NEWSPAPERS: GB-Unabhängigkeits-MdEP

FEINE WELT 1799500G65B-2_105
Editorial: Adersstr. 12, 40215 DÜSSELDORF
Tel: 211 96488161 **Fax:** 211 96488171
Email: nrw@wams.de **Web site:** http://www.feinewelt-duesseldorf.de
Freq: Half-yearly; **Circ:** 32,000
Editor: Willi Keinhorst; **Advertising Manager:** Karl-Heinz Zechner
Profile: Premium magazine in the Welt am Sonntag for Düsseldorf. In the magazine, the special attractions of the region are characteristic and suggest a link between luxury and lifestyle, culture, original and pleasure and aesthetics.
Language(s): German
ADVERTISING RATES:
Full Page Mono .... EUR 2348
Full Page Colour .... EUR 2348
Mechanical Data: Type Area: 260 x 210 mm
Supplement to: Welt am Sonntag
NATIONAL DAILY & SUNDAY NEWSPAPERS: GB-Unabhängigkeits-MdEP

FEINE WELT 1799501G65B-2_106
Editorial: Aderssstr. 12, 40215 DÜSSELDORF
Tel: 211 96488161 **Fax:** 211 96488171
Email: nrw@wams.de **Web site:** http://www.feinewelt-koeln.de
Freq: Half-yearly; **Circ:** 35,000
Editor: Willi Keinhorst; **Advertising Manager:** Karl-Heinz Zechner
Profile: Premium magazine in the Welt am Sonntag for Cologne. In the magazine, the special attractions of the region are characteristic and suggest a link between luxury and lifestyle, culture, original and pleasure and aesthetics.
Language(s): German
ADVERTISING RATES:
Full Page Mono .... EUR 2348
Full Page Colour .... EUR 2348
Mechanical Data: Type Area: 260 x 210 mm
Supplement to: Welt am Sonntag
NATIONAL DAILY & SUNDAY NEWSPAPERS: GB-Unabhängigkeits-MdEP

FEINE WELT 1799503G65B-2_107
Editorial: Aderssstr. 12, 40215 DÜSSELDORF
Tel: 211 96488161 **Fax:** 211 96488171
Email: nrw@wams.de **Web site:** http://www.feinewelt-westfalen.de
Freq: Half-yearly; **Circ:** 32,000
Editor: Willi Keinhorst; **Advertising Manager:** Karl-Heinz Zechner
Profile: Premium magazine in the Welt am Sonntag for the Westfalen region. In the magazine, the special attractions of the region are characteristic and suggest a link between luxury and lifestyle, culture, original and pleasure and aesthetics.
Language(s): German
ADVERTISING RATES:
Full Page Mono .... EUR 2348
Full Page Colour .... EUR 2348
Mechanical Data: Type Area: 260 x 210 mm
Supplement to: Welt am Sonntag
NATIONAL DAILY & SUNDAY NEWSPAPERS: GB-Unabhängigkeits-MdEP

DER FEINSCHMECKER 727166G74P-340
Editorial: Poßmoorweg 2, 22301 HAMBURG
Tel: 40 27173722 **Fax:** 40 27172062
Email: redaktion@der-feinschmecker.de **Web site:** http://www.der-feinschmecker-club.de
Freq: Monthly; **Annual Sub.:** EUR 72,00; **Circ:** 92,600
Editor: Madeleine Jakits; **Advertising Manager:** Sabine Rethmeier
Profile: New trends, new locations, new recipes, new wines - every page in DER FEINSCHMECKER animates all sense of sensualists. With ist culinary expertise in all matters at home and abroad, it is an indispensable guide for discerning individuals. The opulent look will provide both tangible information and will make each trip a culinary event.
Language(s): German
ADVERTISING RATES:
Full Page Mono .... EUR 17900
Full Page Colour .... EUR 17900
Mechanical Data: Type Area: 258 x 188 mm, No. of Columns (Display): 4, Col Widths (Display): 44 mm
Copy instructions: *Copy Date:* 50 days prior to publication
Supplement(s): Der Feinschmecker Gourmet-Shop
CONSUMER: WOMEN'S INTEREST CONSUMER MAGAZINES: Food & Cookery

DER FEINSCHMECKER BOOKAZINE 1743254G74P-1218
Editorial: Poßmoorweg 2, 22301 HAMBURG
Tel: 40 27173722 **Fax:** 40 27172062
Email: redaktion@der-feinschmecker.de **Web site:** http://www.der-feinschmecker-club.de
Freq: Quarterly; **Annual Sub.:** EUR 39,80; **Circ:** 100,000
Editor: Madeleine Jakits; **Advertising Manager:** Sabine Rethmeier
Profile: International Gourmet Magazine; topics shear points: Recipes, Wine, Travel.
Language(s): German
ADVERTISING RATES:
Full Page Mono .... EUR 11500
Full Page Colour .... EUR 11500
Mechanical Data: Type Area: 258 x 188 mm

DER FEINSCHMECKER GOURMET-SHOP 1643553G74P-1138
Editorial: Poßmoorweg 2, 22301 HAMBURG
Tel: 40 27170 **Fax:** 40 27172121
Email: info@der-feinschmecker-shop.de **Web site:** http://www.der-feinschmecker-shop.de
Freq: Half-yearly; **Cover Price:** Free; **Circ:** 500,000
Editor: Justus Hertle
Profile: DER FEINSCHMECKER GOURMET-SHOP is the culinary international mail order gourmet Journals DER FEINSCHMECKER. The range of shops includes the areas of wine and delicacies, cooking enjoyment & Lifestyle, Travel & Life Style. All offers will be tested by the FEINSCHMECKERr editorial. Started 25 years ago as a service to readers under the name THE FEINSCHMECKER-CLUB initially only a small number of high quality products and travel in the premium magazine GOURMET was offered. Meanwhile, the range to over 2,000 exclusive offers has increased, all of which are found online at www.the-gourmet-shop.de. Since 2004, twice the annual premium catalog DER FEINSCHMECKER GOURME- SHOP MAGAZIN is published each spring and fall.
Language(s): German
ADVERTISING RATES:
Full Page Mono .... EUR 7000
Full Page Colour .... EUR 7000
Mechanical Data: Type Area: 285 x 215 mm
Supplement to: Der Feinschmecker

FELDSALAT 727177G2A-1340
Editorial: Stühmeyerstr. 16, 44787 BOCHUM
Tel: 234 50740 **Fax:** 234 5074199
Email: info@ftmafo.de **Web site:** http://www.ftmafo.de
Freq: Quarterly; **Cover Price:** Free; **Circ:** 4,500
Editor: Susanne Stein
Profile: Magazine for employees of foerster & thelen Marktforschung-Feldservice GmbH.
Language(s): German

FELLBACHER WOCHENBLATT 727180G72-3820
Editorial: Plieninger Str. 150, 70567 STUTTGART
Tel: 711 72083321 **Fax:** 711 72083340
Email: redaktion@stw.zgs.de
Freq: Weekly; **Cover Price:** Free; **Circ:** 28,350
Editor: Bernd Ruof; **Advertising Manager:** Sven Gernhardt
Profile: Advertising journal (house-to-house) concentrating on local stories.
Language(s): German
ADVERTISING RATES:
Full Page Mono .... EUR 3031
Full Page Colour .... EUR 4478
Mechanical Data: Type Area: 492 x 320 mm, No. of Columns (Display): 7, Col Widths (Display): 45 mm
Copy instructions: *Copy Date:* 2 days prior to publication
LOCAL NEWSPAPERS

FELLBACHER ZEITUNG 727181G67B-5060
Editorial: Plieninger Str. 150, 70567 STUTTGART
Tel: 711 72050 **Fax:** 711 72057138
Email: cvd@stn.zgs.de **Web site:** http://www.stuttgarter-nachrichten.de
Freq: 312 issues yearly; **Circ:** 204,304
Profile: Daily newspaper with regional news and a local sports section. Facebook: http://www.facebook.com/stuttgarternachrichten Twitter: http://twitter.com/StN_News This Outlet offers RSS (Really Simple Syndication).
Language(s): German
ADVERTISING RATES:
SCC .... EUR 358,00
Mechanical Data: Type Area: 492 x 321 mm, No. of Columns (Display): 7, Col Widths (Display): 44 mm
Copy instructions: *Copy Date:* 1 day prior to publication
REGIONAL DAILY & SUNDAY NEWSPAPERS: Regional Daily Newspapers

FELSBAU MAGAZIN 727182G30-43
Editorial: Montebruchstr. 2, 45219 ESSEN
Tel: 2054 924112 **Fax:** 2054 924149
Email: info@moduscom.de **Web site:** http://www.vge.de
Freq: 6 issues yearly; **Annual Sub.:** EUR 72,50; **Circ:** 2,500
Editor: Manfred König; **Advertising Manager:** Monika Motzfeld
Profile: Independent trade magazine for the construction in rock and soil. It reports to date, independent, competent and practical than in rock engineering projects, tunnel and rock engineering Kavernenbau. The magazine treats the entire spectrum of topics: - Project management and

quality management - Planning, analysis and design, construction, monitoring, security, operation and liability - New construction, repair, claims - Energy (hydro and geothermal) - Natural Hazards - Building Products / Processes - Innovation, Research and Development - Training people teaching languages, knowledge management.
Language(s): English; German
ADVERTISING RATES:
Full Page Mono .... EUR 2390
Full Page Colour .... EUR 3440
Mechanical Data: Type Area: 269 x 182 mm
Copy instructions: *Copy Date:* 24 days prior to publication
BUSINESS: MINING & QUARRYING

DAS FENSTER
727190G74N-180
Editorial: Sachsenweg 6, 59073 HAMM
Tel: 2381 176761 **Fax:** 2381 176730
Email: pieper@stadt.hamm.de **Web site:** http://www.hamm.de
Freq: Quarterly; **Cover Price:** Free; **Circ:** 7,000
Editor: Andreas Pieper
Profile: Magazine for the elderly from the region of Hamm.
Language(s): German

FENSTER, TÜREN & GARAGENTORE
756542G4E-6913
Editorial: Schwanthalerstr. 10, 80336 MÜNCHEN
Tel: 89 59908122 **Fax:** 89 59908133
Email: claudia.mannschott@cpz.de **Web site:** http://www.bau-welt.de
Freq: Annual; **Cover Price:** Free; **Circ:** 265,000
Editor: Claudia Mannschott; **Advertising Manager:** Sebastian Schmidt
Profile: Magazine containing information for house builders and renovators, edition windows, doors and garage doors.
Language(s): German
ADVERTISING RATES:
Full Page Mono .... EUR 10850
Full Page Colour .... EUR 15500
Mechanical Data: No. of Columns (Display): 4, Col Widths (Display): 42 mm, Type Area: 285 x 175 mm
Copy instructions: *Copy Date:* 40 days prior to publication
Supplement to: Das Einfamilien Haus, Umbauen & Modernisieren, Unser Haus für die ganze Familie

FERIEN-BUNGALOW-FÜHRER
1616169G89A-12091
Editorial: Heusee 19, 73655 PLÜDERHAUSEN
Tel: 7181 86020 **Fax:** 7181 860229
Email: mail@drei-brunnen-verlag.de **Web site:** http://www.drei-brunnen-verlag.de
Freq: Annual; **Cover Price:** EUR 9,90; **Circ:** 40,000
Editor: Jochen Müller; **Advertising Manager:** Thomas Müller
Profile: International guide with information about some 600 holiday parks, chalets, mobile homes and holiday villages in France, Italy, Spain, Croatia and Germany. Detailed information about the different accommodations, information about travel, location, opening times, sports, entertainment, and services at the resort, wide range of leisure and entertainment, detailed floor plans, many plans and sketches, many color illustrations and detailed map section, additional Services: GPS coordinates.
Language(s): English; French; German
ADVERTISING RATES:
Full Page Colour .... EUR 2990
Mechanical Data: Type Area: 205 x 95 mm, No. of Columns (Display): 1, Col Widths (Display): 95 mm
Copy instructions: *Copy Date:* 90 days prior to publication

FERIENKALENDER
1686184G89A-12087
Editorial: Goethestr. 73, 19053 SCHWERIN
Tel: 385 760760 **Fax:** 385 7607620
Email: ljr@inmv.de **Web site:** http://www.jugend.inmv.de
Freq: Annual; **Cover Price:** Free; **Circ:** 20,000
Editor: Claudia Heibrock
Profile: Calendar of Landesjugendring Mecklenburg-Vorpommern e.V. contains advertisements, regardless of whether active vacation or beach lazing in the sun, whether in other states or in Mecklenburg-Vorpommern and abroad. From the scout camp on holiday, riding up to the media camp.
Language(s): German

FERNFAHRER
727207G49D-20
Editorial: Handwerkstr. 15, 70565 STUTTGART
Tel: 711 7849843 **Fax:** 711 7849826
Email: fernfahrer@etm-verlag.de **Web site:** http://www.fernfahrer.de
Freq: Monthly; **Annual Sub.:** EUR 39,90; **Circ:** 43,091
Editor: Andreas Techel; **Advertising Manager:** Norbert Blucke
Profile: Magazine for the professional driver, carrier and decision makers in the commercial vehicle industry. Editorial balance between sound vehicle tests, driving tests and informative and entertaining features have made the truck drivers in recent years to a recognized qualification for drivers and management. The drivers speak for themselves and see the truck driver as a voice for their concerns. Reports on technical innovations and current developments in the commercial and transport sector round out the editorial spectrum. Facebook: http://www.facebook.com/pages/FERNFAHRER/116900631668385.
Language(s): German
ADVERTISING RATES:
Full Page Mono .... EUR 7820
Full Page Colour .... EUR 7820
Mechanical Data: Type Area: 263 x 196 mm, No. of Columns (Display): 4, Col Widths (Display): 45 mm
Supplement(s): Autohof Guide LKW; Truck Sport Guide; Truck Sport Magazin
BUSINESS: TRANSPORT: Commercial Vehicles

FERRARI WORLD
727215G77A-1120
Editorial: Friesenheimer Str. 18, 68169 MANNHEIM
Tel: 621 712202 **Fax:** 621 3214459
Email: p.braun@heel-verlag.de
Freq: Quarterly; **Annual Sub.:** EUR 24,00; **Circ:** 17,800
Editor: Peter Braun; **Advertising Manager:** Sabine Blüm
Profile: Magazine about the myth of Ferrari for the high income, brand-conscious and luxury-oriented men's market. Reports on current models and classic Formula 1 racing and historical reports.
Language(s): German
ADVERTISING RATES:
Full Page Mono .... EUR 3270
Full Page Colour .... EUR 4660
Mechanical Data: Type Area: 256 x 175 mm, No. of Columns (Display): 4, Col Widths (Display): 43 mm
Copy instructions: *Copy Date:* 35 days prior to publication
Official Journal of: Organ d. Ferrari Club Deutschland

FERRUM
727219G27-680
Editorial: Hindenburgstr. 32, 55118 MAINZ
Tel: 6131 557531 **Fax:** 6131 557539
Email: ferrum@pfalzmetall.de **Web site:** http://www.pfalzmetall.de
Freq: Monthly; **Circ:** 14,800
Editor: Marcel Speker
Profile: Journal of the Association of Metal and Electrical Industries.
Language(s): German
Readership: Aimed at people in the metal and electrical industries.
BUSINESS: METAL, IRON & STEEL

FERTIGHÄUSER
727220G4E-371_75
Editorial: Höhenstr. 17, 70736 FELLBACH
Tel: 711 5206244 **Fax:** 711 5206300
Email: fritsche@fachschriften.de **Web site:** http://www.bautipps.de
Freq: Annual; **Cover Price:** EUR 7,80; **Circ:** 75,000
Editor: Harald Fritsche; **Advertising Manager:** Barbara Hoof
Profile: Publication about all aspects of home building.
Language(s): German
ADVERTISING RATES:
Full Page Colour .... EUR 11000
Mechanical Data: Type Area: 247 x 187 mm, No. of Columns (Display): 4, Col Widths (Display): 43 mm
Copy instructions: *Copy Date:* 40 days prior to publication
Supplement(s): baugui.de
BUSINESS: ARCHITECTURE & BUILDING: Building

FERTIGUNG
727225G19F-20
Editorial: Justus-von-Liebig-Str. 1, 86899 LANDSBERG **Tel:** 8191 125343 **Fax:** 8191 125822
Email: wolfgang.pittrich@mi-verlag.de **Web site:** http://www.fertigung.de
Freq: 9 issues yearly; **Annual Sub.:** EUR 118,00; **Circ:** 16,211
Editor: Wolfgang Pittrich; **Advertising Manager:** Helmut Schempp
Profile: Magazine for the production level in the metal industry the process - from production manager to become a skilled worker at the machine. The focus of coverage is the question: What can increase machinery, tools and processes of metal-working operation at the present time its productivity to remain competitive? The main reason is the holistic view of manufacturing process - from engineering technology through to workflow management and industrial engineering. Practice-based reports with utility boxes, product reviews, background articles as well as machine comparisons take on current trends and developments and evaluate them in the direction of practicality. The magazine is therefore an essential decision making tool when it comes to means of production investments for metalworking.
Language(s): German
Readership: Aimed at those involved in the engineering sector.
ADVERTISING RATES:
Full Page Mono .... EUR 4120
Full Page Colour .... EUR 5680
Mechanical Data: Type Area: 257 x 178 mm, No. of Columns (Display): 4, Col Widths (Display): 41 mm
Copy instructions: *Copy Date:* 28 days prior to publication
BUSINESS: ENGINEERING & MACHINERY: Production & Mechanical Engineering

FESTIVAL CHRISTMAS
727227G52C-10
Editorial: Bahnhofstr. 22, 96117 MEMMELSDORF
Tel: 951 406660 **Fax:** 951 4066649
Email: jens@nostheide.de **Web site:** http://www.nostheide.de
Freq: Annual; **Annual Sub.:** EUR 14,00; **Circ:** 6,300
Editor: Jens Nostheide; **Advertising Manager:** Judith Stahlberg
Profile: International trade journal about goods specifically made for Christmas.
Language(s): English; German
ADVERTISING RATES:
Full Page Mono .... EUR 1250
Full Page Colour .... EUR 1910
Mechanical Data: Type Area: 265 x 185 mm
BUSINESS: GIFT TRADE: Fancy Goods

FESTIVAL GIFTS SOUVENIRS TROPHIES
727228G52C-14
Editorial: Bahnhofstr. 22, 96117 MEMMELSDORF
Tel: 951 406660 **Fax:** 951 4066649
Email: jens@nostheide.de **Web site:** http://www.nostheide.de
Freq: 3 issues yearly; Free to qualifying individuals
Annual Sub.: EUR 18,00; **Circ:** 4,200
Editor: Jens Nostheide; **Advertising Manager:** Judith Stahlberg
Profile: International trade journal for fan and fun, trophies and promotion, festive and party items and licensing is the official organ of the German Association of the Souvenir, Gift and Trophy Branch, BSGE.
Language(s): English; German
ADVERTISING RATES:
Full Page Mono .... EUR 1250
Full Page Colour .... EUR 1910
Mechanical Data: Type Area: 265 x 185 mm, No. of Columns (Display): 3, Col Widths (Display): 57 mm
Official Journal of: Organ d. Bundesverb. Souvenir-Geschenke-Ehrenpreise e.V.
BUSINESS: GIFT TRADE: Fancy Goods

FESTIVAL SEASONS
727231G52C-15
Editorial: Bahnhofstr. 22, 96117 MEMMELSDORF
Tel: 951 406660 **Fax:** 951 4066649
Email: jens@nostheide.de **Web site:** http://www.nostheide.de
Freq: Annual; **Annual Sub.:** EUR 14,00; **Circ:** 5,900
Editor: Jens Nostheide; **Advertising Manager:** Judith Stahlberg
Profile: International trade journal for festive occasions.
Language(s): English; German
ADVERTISING RATES:
Full Page Mono .... EUR 1250
Full Page Colour .... EUR 1910
Mechanical Data: Type Area: 265 x 185 mm
BUSINESS: GIFT TRADE: Fancy Goods

FESTIVALPLANER
755915G89C-4663
Editorial: Heiliger Weg 1, 44135 DORTMUND
Tel: 231 5571310 **Fax:** 231 55713131
Email: redaktion@festivalplaner.de **Web site:** http://www.festivalplaner.de
Freq: Annual; **Cover Price:** Free; **Circ:** 283,810
Editor: Hauke Hackstein; **Advertising Manager:** Katja Ross
Profile: Schedule for music festivals Twitter: http://twitter.com/Festivalplaner.
Language(s): German
Mechanical Data: Type Area: 146 x 105 mm
Copy instructions: *Copy Date:* 28 days prior to publication
CONSUMER: HOLIDAYS & TRAVEL: Entertainment Guides

FEUERBACHER WOCHE
727238G72-3836
Editorial: Bessemerstr. 7, 70435 STUTTGART
Tel: 711 8200050 **Fax:** 711 8200059
Email: redaktion@eheinz.de **Web site:** http://www.eheinz.de
Cover Price: Free
Editor: Peter Heinz; **Advertising Manager:** Peter Heinz
Profile: Advertising journal (house-to-house) concentrating on local stories.
Language(s): German
LOCAL NEWSPAPERS

FEUERTRUTZ
1841650G4E-7226
Editorial: Stolberger Str. 84, 50933 KÖLN
Tel: 221 5497136 **Fax:** 221 54976136
Email: g.ruhe@feuertrutz.de **Web site:** http://www.feuertrutz.de
Freq: 6 issues yearly; **Annual Sub.:** EUR 82,00; **Circ:** 6,859
Editor: Günter Ruhe; **Advertising Manager:** Thomas Füngerlings
Profile: Fire protection magazine for planners give practical knowledge on all areas of construction and building services Brandschutzes.Es informed of planning tools, solutions and insider knowledge.
Language(s): German
ADVERTISING RATES:
Full Page Mono .... EUR 3155
Full Page Colour .... EUR 5105
Mechanical Data: Type Area: 267 x 188 mm, No. of Columns (Display): 4, Col Widths (Display): 44 mm
Copy instructions: *Copy Date:* 28 days prior to publication
Official Journal of: Organ d. Bundesvereinigung Fachplaner u. Sachverständige f. d. vorbeugenden Brandschutz e.V. u. Vereinigung Brandschutzplaner e.V.

FEUERVERZINKEN
755918G27-2943
Editorial: Sohnstr. 66, 40237 DÜSSELDORF
Tel: 211 6907650 **Fax:** 211 689599
Email: holger.glinde@feuerverzinken.com **Web site:** http://www.feuerverzinken.com
Freq: Quarterly; **Cover Price:** Free; **Circ:** 33,500
Editor: Holger Glinde
Profile: Magazine about hot galvanisation for architects, planners, steel builders, lock and blacksmiths, engineers, technicians and builders.
Language(s): Dutch; English; German; Spanish

FEUERWEHR
745619G54A-620
Editorial: Am Friedrichshain 22, 10407 BERLIN
Tel: 30 42151445 **Fax:** 30 42151234
Email: feuerwehr.redaktion@hussberlin.de **Web site:** http://www.feuerwehr-ub.de
Freq: 10 issues yearly; **Annual Sub.:** EUR 48,00; **Circ:** 25,490
Editor: Mathias Obst; **Advertising Manager:** Ulrich Leps
Profile: Official magazin of the country fire brigade associations Schleswig-Holstein, Mecklenburg-Vorpommern, Bremen, Brandenburg, Thuringia and Saxony. Feuerwehr reaches persons who are responsible and experts in fire brigades, rescue crews, disaster control organizations, offices, associations, engineering office, industry and insurances. The magazine supports the readers at the orientation on new technology and equipment.
Language(s): German
ADVERTISING RATES:
Full Page Mono .... EUR 2405
Full Page Colour .... EUR 3605
Mechanical Data: Type Area: 265 x 185 mm, No. of Columns (Display): 3, Col Widths (Display): 59 mm
Copy instructions: *Copy Date:* 28 days prior to publication
Official Journal of: Organ d. Landesfeuerwehrverb. Brandenburg, Bremen, Mecklenburg-Vorpommern, Sachsen, Schleswig-Holstein u. Thüringen
BUSINESS: SAFETY & SECURITY: Fire Fighting

FEUERWEHR MAGAZIN
727245G54A-280
Editorial: Kurt-Schumacher-Allee 2, 28329 BREMEN
Tel: 421 468860 **Fax:** 421 4688630
Email: redaktion@feuerwehrmagazin.de **Web site:** http://www.feuerwehrmagazin.de
Freq: Monthly; **Annual Sub.:** EUR 50,00; **Circ:** 55,032
Editor: Jan-Erik Hegemann
Profile: Magazine about firefighting techniques, equipment and rescue services.
Language(s): German
ADVERTISING RATES:
Full Page Mono .... EUR 2620
Full Page Colour .... EUR 4115
Mechanical Data: Type Area: 243 x 188 mm, No. of Columns (Display): 4, Col Widths (Display): 45 mm
BUSINESS: SAFETY & SECURITY: Fire Fighting

FEWO-DIREKT.DE
1704286G89A-12190
Editorial: Ludwig-Erhard-Str. 4, 34131 KASSEL
Tel: 561 92095010 **Fax:** 561 920950150
Email: presse@fewo-direkt.de **Web site:** http://www.fewo-direkt.de
Freq: Daily; **Cover Price:** Paid; **Circ:** 3,287,559 Unique Users
Language(s): German
CONSUMER: HOLIDAYS & TRAVEL: Travel

FIFTY
1859599G74N-960
Editorial: Weihenstephaner Str. 7, 81673 MÜNCHEN
Tel: 89 415200 **Fax:** 89 4152627
Email: fifty@guj.de **Web site:** http://www.gujmedia.de
Freq: Half-yearly; **Cover Price:** Free; **Circ:** 299,400
Editor: Doro Kammerer; **Advertising Manager:** Hans-Joachim Weber
Profile: Free publication for 50 to 69 years. Is to a specialist, spa and wellness hotels, fitness clubs and selected trade shows. fifty shows that in later years, edibility, enterprise, sociability, desire and knowledge are as important as health care, and as refreshing as anti-aging Strategien. Das booklet provides in-depth information, opulent look and feature writers reading pleasure for well-off people.
Language(s): German
ADVERTISING RATES:
Full Page Mono .... EUR 18900
Full Page Colour .... EUR 18900
Mechanical Data: Type Area: 230 x 170 mm

FILEMAKER MAGAZIN
727300G5C-33_20
Editorial: Mörkenstr. 12, 22767 HAMBURG
Tel: 40 589657970 **Fax:** 40 589657977
Email: redaktion@filemaker-magazin.de **Web site:** http://www.filemaker-magazin.de
Freq: 6 issues yearly; **Annual Sub.:** EUR 60,00; **Circ:** 1,400
Editor: Klemens Kegebein; **Advertising Manager:** Gabriela Rajski-Gerigk
Profile: Magazine providing information about FileMaker programming in Crossplatform, Windows and MacOS environments.
Language(s): German
Readership: Aimed at all users of FileMaker Pro, both end users and IT professionals.
ADVERTISING RATES:
Full Page Mono .... EUR 1180
Full Page Colour .... EUR 2200

Mechanical Data: Type Area: 265 x 180 mm
Copy instructions: *Copy Date:* 15 days prior to publication
BUSINESS: COMPUTERS & AUTOMATION: Professional Personal Computers

FILETHÄKELN LEICHT GEMACHT
1614337G74A-3350
Editorial: Römerstr. 90, 79618 RHEINFELDEN
Tel: 7623 9640 **Fax:** 7623 964200
Email: info@oz-verlag.de **Web site:** http://www.oz-verlag.de
Freq: 6 issues yearly; **Annual Sub.:** EUR 13,20; **Circ:** 80,000
Profile: Magic crochet magazine with models for reworking - curtains, rugs, tablecloths and doilies in different shapes and sizes, and more to beautify the home or at Easter / Christmas.
Language(s): German
ADVERTISING RATES:
Full Page Mono .... EUR 2480
Full Page Colour .... EUR 2960
Mechanical Data: No. of Columns (Display): 4, Col Widths (Display): 35 mm, Type Area: 226 x 159 mm

FILM & TV KAMERAMANN
727320G64K-70
Editorial: Ohmstr. 15, 80802 MÜNCHEN
Tel: 89 38308688 **Fax:** 89 38308683
Email: redaktion@kameramann.de **Web site:** http://www.kameramann.de
Freq: Monthly; **Annual Sub.:** EUR 64,90; **Circ:** 8,213
Editor: Evelyn Voigt-Müller
Profile: Journal about film, sound and television technology.
Language(s): German
ADVERTISING RATES:
Full Page Mono .... EUR 1290
Full Page Colour .... EUR 2340
Mechanical Data: Type Area: 199 x 131 mm, No. of Columns (Display): 2, Col Widths (Display): 63 mm
Copy instructions: *Copy Date:* 20 days prior to publication
BUSINESS: OTHER CLASSIFICATIONS: Cinema Entertainment

FILMECHO FILMWOCHE
727306G64K-80
Editorial: Marktplatz 13, 65183 WIESBADEN
Tel: 611 3609847 **Fax:** 611 372878
Email: ralf.boegner@filmecho.de **Web site:** http://www.filmecho.de
Freq: Weekly; **Annual Sub.:** EUR 290,00; **Circ:** 2,651
Editor: Ralf Bögner; **Advertising Manager:** Marc Stille
Profile: Journal for the entire film and cinema industry. In addition to a comprehensive, weekly statistical reports and market research each issue contains reports on the current film industry events: Article for film premieres and festivals, and film reviews in addition to economic technical papers on topics such as film production, financing or the capital market. Extensive coverage of filming, cinema and film technical innovations, the latest multimedia developments and business portraits also appear regularly. This Outlet offers RSS (Really Simple Syndication).
Language(s): German
ADVERTISING RATES:
Full Page Mono .... EUR 1790
Full Page Colour .... EUR 2765
Mechanical Data: Type Area: 274 x 205 mm, No. of Columns (Display): 4, Col Widths (Display): 48 mm
Copy instructions: *Copy Date:* 7 days prior to publication
Official Journal of: Organ d. HDF-Kino e.V.
BUSINESS: OTHER CLASSIFICATIONS: Cinema Entertainment

FILTER
1739828G80-14928
Editorial: Am Brixener Hof 12, 93047 REGENSBURG
Tel: 941 5956080 **Fax:** 941 59560810
Email: redaktion@filter-magazin.com **Web site:** http://www.filter-magazin.com
Freq: Monthly; **Cover Price:** Free; **Circ:** 17,853
Editor: Constantin Weber; **Advertising Manager:** Peter Gnilka
Profile: Regional magazine for Regensburg and Eastern Bavaria.
Language(s): German
ADVERTISING RATES:
Full Page Mono .... EUR 1725
Full Page Colour .... EUR 1725
Mechanical Data: Type Area: 264 x 182 mm
Copy instructions: *Copy Date:* 14 days prior to publication
CONSUMER: RURAL & REGIONAL INTEREST

FINANCE
1978756G1A-3821
Editorial: Mainzer Landstr. 199, 60326 FRANKFURT
Tel: 69 75912490 **Fax:** 69 75913224
Email: editor@finance-magazine.eu **Web site:** http://www.finance-magazine.eu
Freq: Quarterly; **Annual Sub.:** EUR 48,00; **Circ:** 16,000
Editor: Bastian Frien; **Advertising Manager:** Stefanie Kieslich
Profile: Economy magazine.
Language(s): English
ADVERTISING RATES:
Full Page Mono .... EUR 10000
Full Page Colour .... EUR 10000
Mechanical Data: Type Area: 240 x 176 mm
Copy instructions: *Copy Date:* 18 days prior to publication

FINANCE
727325G14A-2360
Editorial: Mainzer Landstr. 199, 60326 FRANKFURT
Tel: 69 75912579 **Fax:** 69 75913224
Email: redaktion@finance-magazin.de **Web site:** http://www.finance-magazin.de
Freq: 10 issues yearly; Free to qualifying individuals
Annual Sub.: EUR 54,00; **Circ:** 21,056
Editor: Bastian Frien; **Advertising Manager:** Sylvia Daun
Profile: Magazine provides chief financial officers of innovative financing models and ways of the balance sheet optimization. The magazine provides a monthly insight into the exciting world of finance of large companies, and useful tips for daily work in their finance departments. In close and critical dialogue with CFOs, banks and the rest of the financial community is the Finance Editor for entertaining and informative financial journalism of the highest quality.
Language(s): German
ADVERTISING RATES:
Full Page Mono .... EUR 7600
Full Page Colour .... EUR 7600
Mechanical Data: Type Area: 240 x 176 mm
Copy instructions: *Copy Date:* 21 days prior to publication
Supplement(s): Der Treasurer

FINANCIAL TIMES DEUTSCHLAND
727327G65A-27
Editorial: Am Baumwall 11, 20459 HAMBURG
Tel: 40 37030 **Fax:** 40 37038310
Email: leserservice@ftd.de **Web site:** http://www.ftd.de
Freq: 260 issues yearly; **Circ:** 102,188
Editor: Steffen Klusmann; **News Editor:** Sven-Oliver Clausen; **Advertising Manager:** Jens Kauerauf
Profile: The FINANCIAL TIMES GERMANY, published every trading day, is a daily economic and financial newspaper. It combines modern news journalism with the sophisticated forms of magazine journalism: In a clear structure and a direct, uncomplicated style it selects the most important information, classifys and comments on it. Besides the main product the FTD regularly publishes premium supplements in magazine format, such as the luxury magazine "how to spend it" and the business magazine "enable".
Language(s): German
Readership: Read by decision makers, senior executives, managers, office personnel and students.
ADVERTISING RATES:
SCC .... EUR 626,70
Mechanical Data: Type Area: 445 x 314 mm, No. of Columns (Display): 6, Col Widths (Display): 49 mm
Copy instructions: *Copy Date:* 1 day prior to publication
Supplement(s): enable; how to spend it; visAvis Economy; visAvis Finanzmagazin.Info; visAvis Global Management; visAvis Web-Business
NATIONAL DAILY & SUNDAY NEWSPAPERS: National Daily Newspapers

FINANZ TEST JAHRBUCH
1655808G74M-689
Editorial: Lützowplatz 11, 10785 BERLIN
Tel: 30 26312303 **Fax:** 30 26312395
Email: finanztest@stiftung-warentest.de **Web site:** http://www.test.de
Freq: Annual; **Cover Price:** EUR 9,50; **Circ:** 25,000
Editor: Hermann-Josef Tenhagen
Profile: Magazine presenting the findings of independent surveys of financial products.
Language(s): German

FINANZ TEST SPEZIAL
727369G74M-670
Editorial: Lützowplatz 11, 10785 BERLIN
Tel: 30 26310 **Fax:** 30 26312395
Email: h.landwehr@stiftung-warentest.de **Web site:** http://www.test.de
Freq: 5 issues yearly; **Cover Price:** EUR 7,80; **Circ:** 100,000
Editor: Hermann-Josef Tenhagen
Profile: For particularly large and complex topics appear special folders. Consumers special issues devoted to topics such as "taxes ", "retirement" or "tenancy".
Language(s): German

DER FINANZBERATER
727330G1F-500
Editorial: Hauptstr. 8b, 82319 STARNBERG
Tel: 8151 65650 **Fax:** 8151 656529
Email: info@der-finanzberater.de **Web site:** http://www.der-finanzberater.de
Freq: Monthly; **Annual Sub.:** EUR 51,00; **Circ:** 2,200
Editor: F. J. Wunderle
Profile: Magazine for financial advisers who are members of the Bundesverband.
Language(s): German
BUSINESS: FINANCE & ECONOMICS: Investment

DER FINANZDIENSTLEISTER
753695G1C-1435
Editorial: Oststr. 10, 40211 DÜSSELDORF
Tel: 211 3694558 **Fax:** 211 369679
Email: popp@dbv-gewerkschaft.de **Web site:** http://www.dbv-gewerkschaft.de
Freq: Half-yearly; **Cover Price:** EUR 1,25
Free to qualifying individuals ; **Circ:** 20,000
Editor: Oliver Popp
Profile: Union paper for bank and insurance employees.
Language(s): German

FINANZEN.NET
1621234G1A-3520
Editorial: Hirschstr. 2, 76133 KARLSRUHE
Tel: 721 1617660
Web site: http://www.finanzen.net
Freq: Daily; **Cover Price:** Paid; **Circ:** 14,304,356 Unique Users
Profile: Ezine: Magazine covering international financial markets.
Language(s): German
BUSINESS: FINANCE & ECONOMICS

FINANZPLATZ
1668527G1C-1457
Editorial: Niedenau 13, 60325 FRANKFURT
Tel: 69 9291547 **Fax:** 69 9291512
Email: altenbockum@dai.de **Web site:** http://www.dai.de
Freq: 6 issues yearly; **Cover Price:** Free; **Circ:** 10,000
Editor: Uta-Bettina von Altenbockum
Profile: The report provides readers with an interest in the German and European capital markets, a critical discussion forum with information and analysis on financial markets in Germany and Europe.
Language(s): English; German
ADVERTISING RATES:
Full Page Mono .... EUR 2900
Full Page Colour .... EUR 2900
Mechanical Data: Type Area: 257 x 186 mm
Copy instructions: *Copy Date:* 18 days prior to publication

FINANZTEST
727368G74M-200
Editorial: Lützowplatz 11, 10785 BERLIN
Tel: 30 26312303 **Fax:** 30 26312395
Email: finanztest@stiftung-warentest.de **Web site:** http://www.test.de
Freq: Monthly; **Annual Sub.:** EUR 47,50; **Circ:** 275,000
Editor: Hermann-Josef Tenhagen
Profile: Magazine presenting the findings of independent surveys of financial products.
Language(s): German
Readership: Aimed at the general public.
CONSUMER: WOMEN'S INTEREST CONSUMER MAGAZINES: Personal Finance

FINANZTREFF.DE
1661581G14A-9680
Editorial: Krausenstr. 8, 10117 BERLIN
Tel: 30 2005980
Email: ccc@finanztreff.de **Web site:** http://www.finanztreff.de
Freq: Daily; **Cover Price:** Paid; **Circ:** 3,475,918 Unique Users
Language(s): German
BUSINESS: COMMERCE, INDUSTRY & MANAGEMENT

FINANZWELT
1616217G1C-1421
Editorial: Söhnleinstr. 17, 65201 WIESBADEN
Tel: 611 2676626 **Fax:** 611 2676618
Email: m.oehme@finanzwelt.de **Web site:** http://www.finanzwelt.de
Freq: 6 issues yearly; **Annual Sub.:** EUR 25,00; **Circ:** 48,000
Editor: Marc Oehme; **Advertising Manager:** Maria Roberto
Profile: Magazine on financial services.
Language(s): German
ADVERTISING RATES:
Full Page Mono .... EUR 5550
Full Page Colour .... EUR 6225
Mechanical Data: Type Area: 270 x 177 mm, No. of Columns (Display): 3, Col Widths (Display): 53 mm

FINE DAS WEINMAGAZIN
1846574G74P-1262
Editorial: Sonnenberger Str. 43, 65191 WIESBADEN
Tel: 611 5055840 **Fax:** 611 5055842
Email: thomas.schroeder@fine-magazines.de **Web site:** http://www.fine-magazines.de
Freq: Quarterly; **Annual Sub.:** EUR 60,00; **Circ:** 20,000
Editor: Thomas Schröder; **Advertising Manager:** Ann-Kathrin Grauel
Profile: Reports, background stories and updates about the finest wines in the world.
Language(s): German
ADVERTISING RATES:
Full Page Mono .... EUR 7900
Full Page Colour .... EUR 7900
Mechanical Data: Type Area: 287 x 230 mm
Copy instructions: *Copy Date:* 28 days prior to publication

FINEST.FINANCE!
1705926G73-610
Editorial: Wilhelm-Keim-Str. 3, 82031 GRÜNWALD
Tel: 89 6938806
Email: redaktion@finestfinance.com **Web site:** http://www.finestfinance.com
Freq: 6 issues yearly; **Annual Sub.:** EUR 25,00; **Circ:** 40,000
Editor: Elke Bauer
Profile: Magazine for assets, values, and luxury.
Language(s): English; German
ADVERTISING RATES:
Full Page Mono .... EUR 10800
Full Page Colour .... EUR 10800
Mechanical Data: Type Area: 215 x 170 mm
Copy instructions: *Copy Date:* 28 days prior to publication

FIPPS
728163G80-3240
Editorial: Dorfstr. 28, 79249 MERZHAUSEN
Tel: 761 1307702 **Fax:** 761 405341
Email: redaktion@fipps-freiburg.de **Web site:** http://www.fipps-freiburg.de
Freq: Monthly; **Cover Price:** Free; **Circ:** 15,080
Editor: Günter Lorenz; **Advertising Manager:** Brigitte Hrabé-Lorenz
Profile: Magazine for city and region, concentrating on gastronomy, music, arts and events.
Language(s): German
ADVERTISING RATES:
Full Page Mono .... EUR 2200
Full Page Colour .... EUR 2200
Mechanical Data: Type Area: 270 x 195 mm, No. of Columns (Display): 4, Col Widths (Display): 45 mm
Copy instructions: *Copy Date:* 16 days prior to publication
CONSUMER: RURAL & REGIONAL INTEREST

FIRE&FOOD
1605555G74P-993
Editorial: Waldseer Str. 3, 88250 WEINGARTEN
Tel: 751 56177518 **Fax:** 751 56177559
Email: redaktion@fire-food.com **Web site:** http://www.fire-food.com
Freq: 3 issues yearly; Free to qualifying individuals
Annual Sub.: EUR 10,00; **Circ:** 45,000
Editor: Klaus Winter; **Advertising Manager:** Elmar Fetscher
Profile: Fire&Food is the lifestyle magazine for people with enjoyment of life, who spend their spare time with family and friends outside. The joy of grilling is inextricably linked with this life. Fire&Food shows the very finest on the "outside life " and reported twice a year on the latest trends in European grill and barbecue scene. Background information, practical tips and service issues round out the editorial and graphics from sophisticated magazine. The editorial approach is comprised of various sections such as Basics - learn here, "Beginner" everything worth knowing about - and Classics, in which the archaic side is questioned. Regular special parts in eating and drinking information about the best meat and vegetables for grilling and provide exceptional recipes with step-by-step instructions.
Language(s): German
ADVERTISING RATES:
Full Page Mono .... EUR 4100
Full Page Colour .... EUR 4100
Mechanical Data: Type Area: 262 x 182 mm, No. of Columns (Display): 3, Col Widths (Display): 58 mm
Copy instructions: *Copy Date:* 20 days prior to publication
Official Journal of: Organ d. WBQA, d. GBA, d. SBA u. d. Grillverb. e.V. BIAG

FIRMENAUTO
727388G49A-620
Editorial: Handwerkstr. 15, 70565 STUTTGART
Tel: 711 7849836 **Fax:** 711 7849888
Email: hanno.boblenz@etm-verlag.de **Web site:** http://www.firmenauto.de
Freq: 10 issues yearly; **Annual Sub.:** EUR 36,00; **Circ:** 50,442
Editor: Hanno Boblenz; **Advertising Manager:** Thomas Beck
Profile: For Firmenauto is all about the vehicle used for business. Practical tests with accurate cost estimates are the basis for the buy recommendations of the editors. There are also extensive market surveys, which represent not only the range of vehicles in each segment, but above all, make statements on residual value and maintenance costs. The management review to help fleet managers to reduce their costs and manage their fleet better. The range covers all the specific topics of company car tax, insurance, leasing, financing and law through to Fuel card - and tires Management. Another key focus owner liability and accident prevention. Travel tips are also available. This is the magazine for decision makers the right tool for fleet management and mobility.
Language(s): German
ADVERTISING RATES:
Full Page Mono .... EUR 10320
Full Page Colour .... EUR 10320
Mechanical Data: Type Area: 248 x 183 mm, No. of Columns (Display): 3, Col Widths (Display): 58 mm
Supplement(s): ecoFleet; Who Is Who im Flottenmarkt
BUSINESS: TRANSPORT

FIRST CLASS
727397G11A-380
Editorial: Augustenstr. 10, 80333 MÜNCHEN
Tel: 89 370600 **Fax:** 89 37060111
Email: muc@blmedien.de **Web site:** http://www.firstclass-online.com
Freq: 10 issues yearly; Free to qualifying individuals
Annual Sub.: EUR 55,00; **Circ:** 20,995

Editor: Annemarie Heinrichsdobler; **Advertising Manager:** Bernd Moeser
Profile: "First Class" is a management magazine for successful hotel and restaurant concepts. ... offers a very extensive market coverage of German hotels and top restaurants. ... is successful in the market since 1983. ... tailored to the specific communication needs of top executives in the industry. ... offers updated information on the structural change in the hotel and restaurant, investigates the trends in travel habits. ... reports on the expectations of business and private hotel users. ... offers expert decision support for the food & beverage sector. ... gives suggestions for modernization, renovation, equipment and facilities in hotels, restaurants and kitchens. ... researches thoroughly and informs deeply, comprehensive, clear and legible. ... information up to date about innovations in the segment of IT, communications technology and the Internet. ... shows in well defined supplements (such as coffee & Co., Technical Update) cross-industry trends. ... the official organ and partner to key industry associations.
Language(s): German
ADVERTISING RATES:
Full Page Mono .... EUR 5580
Full Page Colour .... EUR 7840
Mechanical Data: Type Area: 254 x 185 mm, No. of Columns (Display): 4, Col Widths (Display): 43 mm
Copy instructions: *Copy Date:* 15 days prior to publication
Official Journal of: Organ d. Verb. d. Serviermeister, Restaurant- u. Hotelfachkräfte e.V.
Supplement(s): Kaffee & Co.; Trinktime
BUSINESS: CATERING: Catering, Hotels & Restaurants

FISCH & FANG 727405G92-307
Editorial: Erich-Kästner-Str. 2, 56379 SINGHOFEN
Tel: 2604 978350 **Fax:** 2604 978360
Email: fuf@paulparey.de **Web site:** http://www.fischundfang.de
Freq: Monthly; **Annual Sub.:** EUR 45,50; **Circ:** 77,188
Editor: Henning Stühring; **Advertising Manager:** Sylvia Lühert
Profile: Magazine focusing on angling with new techniques and products.
Language(s): German
Readership: Aimed at anglers.
ADVERTISING RATES:
Full Page Mono .... EUR 2913
Full Page Colour .... EUR 5727
Mechanical Data: Type Area: 253 x 186 mm, No. of Columns (Display): 4, Col Widths (Display): 43 mm
Copy instructions: *Copy Date:* 30 days prior to publication
CONSUMER: ANGLING & FISHING

FISCHER & TEICHWIRT 727403G92-306
Editorial: Königstorgraben 11, 90402 NÜRNBERG
Tel: 911 223910 **Fax:** 911 241453
Email: redaktion@fischer-teichwirt.de **Web site:** http://www.fischer-teichwirt.de
Freq: Monthly; **Annual Sub.:** EUR 34,00; **Circ:** 7,500
Editor: Dieter Piwernetz
Profile: Magazine for the Inland Fisheries.
Language(s): German
ADVERTISING RATES:
Full Page Mono .... EUR 1000
Full Page Colour .... EUR 1400
Mechanical Data: Type Area: 270 x 185 mm
Copy instructions: *Copy Date:* 17 days prior to publication
CONSUMER: ANGLING & FISHING

FISCHER'S ARCHIV 727401G2A-1400
Editorial: Bei den Mühren 91, 20457 HAMBURG
Tel: 40 36983224 **Fax:** 40 36983236
Email: redaktion@fischers-archiv.de **Web site:** http://www.fischers-archiv.de
Freq: Monthly; **Annual Sub.:** EUR 319,00; **Circ:** 1,500
Editor: Claudia Bayer; **Advertising Manager:** Birgit Haß
Profile: Documentation of recent dialogue marketing campaigns for dialogue marketing service providers and users.
Language(s): German
ADVERTISING RATES:
Full Page Mono .... EUR 660
Full Page Colour .... EUR 660
Mechanical Data: Type Area: 273 x 201 mm

FISCHMAGAZIN 753769G22G-1
Editorial: An der Alster 21, 20099 HAMBURG
Tel: 40 24845417 **Fax:** 40 2803788
Email: fischmagazin@snfachpresse.de **Web site:** http://www.snfachpresse.de
Freq: 11 issues yearly; **Annual Sub.:** EUR 115,00; **Circ:** 4,036
Editor: Michael Steinert
Profile: Magazine for the fish trade.
Language(s): German
ADVERTISING RATES:
Full Page Mono .... EUR 1620
Full Page Colour .... EUR 2580
Mechanical Data: Type Area: 252 x 184 mm, No. of Columns (Display): 4, Col Widths (Display): 43 mm
BUSINESS: FOOD: Fish Trade

FIT FOR FUN 727415G74G-520
Editorial: Christoph-Probst-Weg 1, 20251 HAMBURG **Tel:** 40 41313401 **Fax:** 40 41312040
Email: service@fitforfun.de **Web site:** http://www.fitforfun.de
Freq: Monthly; **Annual Sub.:** EUR 35,40; **Circ:** 168,791
Editor: Alexander Steudel; **Advertising Manager:** Lutz Nierhoff
Profile: Germany's most coverage lifestyle magazine aimed at all people who have an active and healthy lifestyle is important to achieve inner balance and outer attractiveness. Fit For Fun boosts self-confidence, the appeal of self to take in hand and develop. The triad of journalistic exercise, nutrition and relaxation offers readers the best possibilities to achieve their individual goals. Fit For Fun is a positive and optimistic editorial environment creates for an audience that wants to make her life and is the only complete package for true appeal.
Language(s): German
ADVERTISING RATES:
Full Page Mono .... EUR 25630
Full Page Colour .... EUR 25630
Mechanical Data: Type Area: 240 x 174 mm, No. of Columns (Display): 4, Col Widths (Display): 38 mm
Copy instructions: *Copy Date:* 35 days prior to publication
CONSUMER: WOMEN'S INTEREST CONSUMER MAGAZINES: Slimming & Health

FIT FOR FUN 1621241G74G-1742
Editorial: Steinhauser Str. 1, 81677 MÜNCHEN
Tel: 89 92502404
Email: fitforfun@tomorrow-focus.de **Web site:** http://www.fittorfun.de
Freq: Daily; **Cover Price:** Paid; **Circ:** 1,106,377 Unique Users
Editor: Thomas Mende
Profile: Ezine: Journal about fitness, free time and travel. Facebook: http://www.facebook.com/FitForFun.de.
Language(s): German
CONSUMER: WOMEN'S INTEREST CONSUMER MAGAZINES: Slimming & Health

FIT + 50 727428G94H-14570
Editorial: Hansaring 97, 50670 KÖLN
Tel: 221 9574270 **Fax:** 221 95742777
Email: marken-info@markenverlag.de **Web site:** http://www.markenverlag.de
Freq: 6 issues yearly; **Cover Price:** Free; **Circ:** 65,768
Advertising Manager: Frank Krauthäuser
Profile: Health and fitness magazine for the elderly.
Language(s): German
Readership: Aimed at people over fifty.
ADVERTISING RATES:
Full Page Mono .... EUR 2900
Full Page Colour .... EUR 2900
Mechanical Data: Type Area: 180 x 133 mm, No. of Columns (Display): 3, Col Widths (Display): 40 mm
Copy instructions: *Copy Date:* 42 days prior to publication
CONSUMER: OTHER CLASSIFICATIONS: Customer Magazines

FIZZZ 727430G11A-400
Editorial: Maximilianstr. 7, 67433 NEUSTADT
Tel: 6321 890875 **Fax:** 6321 890873
Email: fizzz@meininger.de **Web site:** http://www.fizzz.de
Freq: Monthly; **Annual Sub.:** EUR 74,40; **Circ:** 6,903
Editor: Barbara Becker; **Advertising Manager:** Ralf Clemens
Profile: Magazin with information on innovative dining concepts are at home and abroad Fizzz at the center. This will be complemented by providing service issues that restaurateurs implementable practical tips on business management, engineering, food choices, design trends and product knowledge. Sales figures, background knowledge and product know-how of providing all beverages readers an insight into the beverage industry. Information on consumer trends, industry news and events make Fizzz to comprehensive trade journal. Facebook: http://facebook.com/pages/fizzz.
Language(s): German
ADVERTISING RATES:
Full Page Mono .... EUR 4570
Full Page Colour .... EUR 4570
Mechanical Data: Type Area: 303 x 204 mm, No. of Columns (Display): 4, Col Widths (Display): 48 mm
Copy instructions: *Copy Date:* 28 days prior to publication
BUSINESS: CATERING: Catering, Hotels & Restaurants

FKT 727435G2D-240
Editorial: Wilhelm-Backhaus-Str. 21, 50931 KÖLN
Tel: 221 2762830 **Fax:** 221 2762831
Email: wagner@schiele-schoen.de **Web site:** http://www.fkt.schiele-schoen.de
Freq: 10 issues yearly; Free to qualifying individuals **Annual Sub.:** EUR 161,00; **Circ:** 2,880
Editor: Reinhard E. Wagner; **Advertising Manager:** Stefan Nepita
Profile: International journal containing information about video, film and TV production, technology and new media.
Language(s): German
Readership: Aimed at professionals in the entertainment production field, broadcasting engineers and film engineers.
ADVERTISING RATES:
Full Page Mono .... EUR 1692
Full Page Colour .... EUR 2835
Mechanical Data: Type Area: 257 x 178 mm, No. of Columns (Display): 4, Col Widths (Display): 41 mm
Official Journal of: Organ d. Fernseh- u. Kinotechn. Ges. in Verbindung m. d. FB 3 d. ITG, d. Normenausschusses Bild u. Film, Arbeitsausschuss NBF 6 "Laufbildtechnik - Bild- u. Tonbearbeitung", d. Verb. d. Techn. Betriebe f. Film u. Fernsehen, in Zusammenarbeit m. d. Verb. Dt. Tonmeister, vereinigt m. "fernseh + filmTechnikum"
BUSINESS: COMMUNICATIONS, ADVERTISING & MARKETING: Broadcasting

FLASH 727443G77E-200
Editorial: Hertener Mark 7, 45699 HERTEN
Tel: 2366 808400
Email: flash.opel@vest-netz.de **Web site:** http://www.flash.de
Freq: Monthly; **Annual Sub.:** EUR 42,00; **Circ:** 24,231
Editor: Arno Rudolf Welke
Profile: Magazine for owners and drivers of Opel cars.
Language(s): Dutch; German
ADVERTISING RATES:
Full Page Mono .... EUR 3800
Full Page Colour .... EUR 4900
Mechanical Data: Type Area: 250 x 184 mm, No. of Columns (Display): 3, Col Widths (Display): 58 mm
Copy instructions: *Copy Date:* 28 days prior to publication
CONSUMER: MOTORING & CYCLING: Club Cars

FLEET MAGAZINE 1976972G49A-2481
Editorial: Schloß Reichenberg, 97234 REICHENBERG **Tel:** 931 660660 **Fax:** 931 6606690
Email: post@lattkeundlattke.de **Web site:** http://www.volkswagen-fleet.de
Freq: Quarterly; **Circ:** 20,000
Profile: Magazine for customers of the Volkswagen AG with information on economy, management techniques, environmental protection and transports.
Language(s): German
ADVERTISING RATES:
Full Page Mono .... EUR 4850
Full Page Colour .... EUR 4850
Mechanical Data: Type Area: 290 x 220 mm

FLEISCH MAGAZIN 753773G22D-90
Editorial: An der Alster 21, 20099 HAMBURG
Tel: 40 2484540 **Fax:** 40 24845425
Email: fleischmagazin@snfachpresse.de **Web site:** http://www.snfachpresse.de
Freq: 10 issues yearly; **Annual Sub.:** EUR 92,00; **Circ:** 6,250
Editor: Michael Steinert
Profile: Magazine for the meat processing industry.
Language(s): German
ADVERTISING RATES:
Full Page Mono .... EUR 1840
Full Page Colour .... EUR 2838
Mechanical Data: Type Area: 252 x 184 mm, No. of Columns (Display): 4, Col Widths (Display): 43 mm
Copy instructions: *Copy Date:* 14 days prior to publication
Official Journal of: Organ d. Bundesfachverb. Fleisch e.V.
BUSINESS: FOOD: Meat Trade

DIE FLEISCHEREI 727454G22D-120
Editorial: Gewerbestr. 2, 86825 BAD WÖRISHOFEN
Tel: 8247 354111 **Fax:** 8247 354170
Email: redfl@holzmann-medien.de **Web site:** http://www.fleischerei.de
Freq: 10 issues yearly; **Annual Sub.:** EUR 119,00,; **Circ:** 6,025
Editor: Thomas Röhr; **Advertising Manager:** Cristine Keller
Profile: Magazine providing information about the meat-processing industry.
Language(s): English; German
ADVERTISING RATES:
Full Page Mono .... EUR 3027
Full Page Colour .... EUR 4677
Mechanical Data: Type Area: 265 x 184 mm, No. of Columns (Display): 4, Col Widths (Display): 43 mm
Copy instructions: *Copy Date:* 22 days prior to publication
BUSINESS: FOOD: Meat Trade

FLEISCHRINDER JOURNAL 727457G21D-4
Editorial: Hülsebrockstr. 2, 48165 MÜNSTER
Tel: 2501 801202 **Fax:** 2501 801204
Email: friedhoff@lv.de **Web site:** http://www.frj.de
Freq: Quarterly; **Annual Sub.:** EUR 31,80; **Circ:** 10,815
Editor: Friedrich Friedhoff; **Advertising Manager:** Reinhard Geissel
Profile: Magazine about the breeding, rearing and care of cows for the production of beef.
Language(s): German
ADVERTISING RATES:
Full Page Mono .... EUR 1440
Full Page Colour .... EUR 2458
Mechanical Data: Type Area: 270 x 190 mm, No. of Columns (Display): 4, Col Widths (Display): 46 mm
Official Journal of: Organ d. Bundesverb. Dt. Fleischrindzüchter u. -halter e.V.
BUSINESS: AGRICULTURE & FARMING: Livestock

FLEISCHWIRTSCHAFT 727459G22D-140
Editorial: Mainzer Landstr. 251, 60326 FRANKFURT
Tel: 69 75951571 **Fax:** 69 75951570
Email: red-flw@dfv.de **Web site:** http://www.fleischwirtschaft.de
Freq: Monthly; **Annual Sub.:** EUR 326,00; **Circ:** 6,110
Editor: Gerd Abeln; **Advertising Manager:** Claudia Besand-Groth
Profile: Journal about meat manufacturing and abattoirs.
Language(s): English; German
ADVERTISING RATES:
Full Page Mono .... EUR 5215
Full Page Colour .... EUR 6000
Mechanical Data: Type Area: 265 x 189 mm, No. of Columns (Display): 4, Col Widths (Display): 45 mm
Copy instructions: *Copy Date:* 28 days prior to publication
Official Journal of: Organ d. Bundesverb. d. Dt. Fleischwarenindustrie e.V.
BUSINESS: FOOD: Meat Trade

FLEISCHWIRTSCHAFT INTERNATIONAL 727460G22D-160
Editorial: Mainzer Landstr. 251, 60326 FRANKFURT
Tel: 69 75951571 **Fax:** 69 75951570
Email: red-flw@dfv.de **Web site:** http://www.fleischwirtschaft.com
Freq: 6 issues yearly; **Annual Sub.:** EUR 110,63; **Circ:** 9,161
Editor: Gerd Abeln; **Advertising Manager:** Claudia Besand-Groth
Profile: Magazine for the meat processing industry.
Language(s): English
ADVERTISING RATES:
Full Page Mono .... EUR 5215
Full Page Colour .... EUR 6000
Mechanical Data: Type Area: 265 x 189 mm, No. of Columns (Display): 4, Col Widths (Display): 45 mm
Copy instructions: *Copy Date:* 28 days prior to publication
BUSINESS: FOOD: Meat Trade

FLEISCHWIRTSCHAFT.DE 1696870G22D-227
Editorial: Mainzer Landstr. 251, 60326 FRANKFURT
Tel: 69 75951551 **Fax:** 69 75951250
Email: renate.kuehlcke@dfv.de **Web site:** http://www.fleischwirtschaft.de
Freq: Daily; **Cover Price:** Paid; **Circ:** 20,716 Unique Users
Editor: Renate Kühlcke
Language(s): German
BUSINESS: FOOD: Meat Trade

FLENSBURGER TAGEBLATT 727465G67B-5100
Editorial: Nikolaistr. 7, 24937 FLENSBURG
Tel: 461 8080 **Fax:** 461 8081058
Email: redaktion@shz.de **Web site:** http://www.shz.de
Freq: 312 issues yearly; **Circ:** 36,504
Editor: Stephan Richter; **News Editor:** Frank Albrecht; **Advertising Manager:** Ingeborg Schwarz
Profile: The "Flensburger Tageblatt is the largest and most important newspaper of the sh:z. With this newspaper in 1865, the foundation stone for the Schleswig-Holstein newspaper publisher has been paid. Facebook: http://www.facebook.com/shzonline Twitter: http://twitter.com/shz_de This Outlet offers RSS (Really Simple Syndication).
Language(s): German
ADVERTISING RATES:
SCC .... EUR 116,80
Mechanical Data: Type Area: 480 x 325 mm, No. of Columns (Display): 7, Col Widths (Display): 45 mm
Copy instructions: *Copy Date:* 1 day prior to publication
Supplement(s): nordisch gesund; Schleswig-Holstein Journal; tv magazin
REGIONAL DAILY & SUNDAY NEWSPAPERS: Regional Daily Newspapers

FLEXO&GRAVURE INTERNATIONAL 727470G36-3
Editorial: Am Stollen 6/1, 79261 GUTACH
Tel: 7685 918110 **Fax:** 7685 909011
Email: klos-geiger@flexo.de **Web site:** http://www.flexo.de
Freq: Quarterly; **Annual Sub.:** EUR 79,00; **Circ:** 9,800
Editor: Wolfgang Klos-Geiger; **Advertising Manager:** Sven Mittermaier
Profile: Magazine focusing on the world's paper, film and foil converting industries.
Language(s): English
Readership: Read by printers.
ADVERTISING RATES:
Full Page Mono .... EUR 2600
Full Page Colour .... EUR 4000
Mechanical Data: Type Area: 262 x 178 mm, No. of Columns (Display): 4, Col Widths (Display): 42 mm
Copy instructions: *Copy Date:* 18 days prior to publication
BUSINESS: PAPER

FLEXO+TIEF-DRUCK 727472G41A-680
Editorial: Am Stollen 6/1, 79261 GUTACH
Tel: 7685 918110 **Fax:** 7685 909011

Email: klos-geiger@flexo.de **Web site:** http://www.flexo.de
Freq: 6 issues yearly; **Annual Sub.:** EUR 85,60; **Circ:** 4,800
Editor: Ansgar Wessendorf; **Advertising Manager:** Sven Mittermaier
Profile: Magazine about modern printing and typeface.
Language(s): German
ADVERTISING RATES:
Full Page Mono .... EUR 1760
Full Page Colour .... EUR 2760
Mechanical Data: Type Area: 262 x 178 mm, No. of Columns (Display): 4, Col Widths (Display): 42 mm
Copy instructions: *Copy Date:* 28 days prior to publication
Official Journal of: Organ d. DFTA e.V.
BUSINESS: PRINTING & STATIONERY: Printing

FLF FINANZIERUNG LEASING FACTORING 727473G1K-10
Editorial: Antoniusstr. 6, 40215 DÜSSELDORF
Tel: 211 3850052 **Fax:** 211 3850017
Email: redaktion@flf.de **Web site:** http://www.flf.de
Freq: 6 issues yearly; **Annual Sub.:** EUR 80,60; **Circ:** 1,400
Editor: Marianne M. Schmidt; **Advertising Manager:** Marianne M. Schmidt
Profile: Magazine covering finance, factoring and leasing.
Language(s): German
ADVERTISING RATES:
Full Page Mono .... EUR 945
Full Page Colour .... EUR 1796
Mechanical Data: Type Area: 241 x 176 mm, No. of Columns (Display): 3, Col Widths (Display): 55 mm
Copy instructions: *Copy Date:* 30 days prior to publication
BUSINESS: FINANCE & ECONOMICS: Rental Leasing

FLIEGE. 1645062G32G-3052
Editorial: Aschmattstr. 8, 76532 BADEN-BADEN
Tel: 7221 502450 **Fax:** 7221 502459
Email: fliege@readytoshow.biz **Web site:** http://www.fliege.de
Freq: Monthly; **Annual Sub.:** EUR 39,90; **Circ:** 21,601
Editor: Jürgen Stollberg
Profile: Magazine for women in their mid 40 with the main themes: natural medicines, healthy eating, natural medicine, natural cosmetics, wellness, self-help, spiritual journeys, expert tips, well-being of body, mind and soul, happy family life, environmental awareness and do not last: faith.
Language(s): German
ADVERTISING RATES:
Full Page Mono .... EUR 2750
Full Page Colour .... EUR 2750
Mechanical Data: Type Area: 265 x 190 mm, No. of Columns (Display): 3, Col Widths (Display): 60 mm
BUSINESS: LOCAL GOVERNMENT, LEISURE & RECREATION: Community Care & Social Services

FLIEGENFISCHEN 727475G92-100
Editorial: Troplowitzstr. 5, 22529 HAMBURG
Tel: 40 38906128 **Fax:** 40 38906550
Email: michael.werner@fliegenfischen.de **Web site:** http://www.fliegenfischen.de
Freq: 6 issues yearly; **Annual Sub.:** EUR 51,00; **Circ:** 12,104
Editor: Michael Werner; **Advertising Manager:** Sandra Böthin
Profile: The Fly-only magazine for the active angler. Created by internationally renowned practitioners, led by chief editor and author Michael Werner. Practice that offers readers practical use. Travel. News from the world of exclusive fly fishing.
Language(s): German
Readership: Read by fly fishermen.
ADVERTISING RATES:
Full Page Mono .... EUR 3520
Full Page Colour .... EUR 4120
Mechanical Data: Type Area: 248 x 185 mm, No. of Columns (Display): 4, Col Widths (Display): 45 mm
CONSUMER: ANGLING & FISHING

FLIEGER MAGAZIN 727478G75N-190
Editorial: Troplowitzstr. 5, 22529 HAMBURG
Tel: 40 38906520 **Fax:** 40 38906529
Email: thomas.borchert@fliegermagazin.de **Web site:** http://www.fliegermagazin.de
Freq: Monthly; **Annual Sub.:** EUR 58,80; **Circ:** 21,118
Editor: Thomas Borchert; **Advertising Manager:** Klaus Macholz
Profile: flieger magazin is the magazine for active pilots of single- and twin-engine aircraft. News: Products (avionics, aircraft and pilot accessories), pilot reports, Industry and International aviation policy. Practice: practical tips for beginners and advanced pilot in navigation, weather, air band, flying techniques for visual and instrument flying, flight safety. Facebook: http://www.facebook.com/pages/fliegermagazin/251643829764.
Language(s): German
Readership: Aimed at pilots and those involved in aviation.
ADVERTISING RATES:
Full Page Mono .... EUR 3794
Full Page Colour .... EUR 6641
Mechanical Data: Type Area: 248 x 185 mm, No. of Columns (Display): 4, Col Widths (Display): 45 mm
CONSUMER: SPORT: Flight

FLIEGER REVUE 727479G6A-540
Editorial: Ehrig-Hahn-Str. 4, 16356 AHRENSFELDE
Tel: 30 41909516 **Fax:** 30 41909599
Email: redaktion@fliegerrevue.de **Web site:** http://www.fliegerrevue.de
Freq: Monthly; **Annual Sub.:** EUR 51,00; **Circ:** 9,631
Editor: Lutz Buchmann; **Advertising Manager:** Reinhard Villwock
Profile: The magazine every month brings news, reports and background information on current issues in international aviation and aerospace. Other sections: History, series, series collection, model-News.
Language(s): German
Readership: Aimed at pilots and those interested in air- and spacecraft.
ADVERTISING RATES:
Full Page Mono .... EUR 2720
Full Page Colour .... EUR 3940
Mechanical Data: Type Area: 264 x 183 mm, No. of Columns (Display): 4, Col Widths (Display): 42 mm
Copy instructions: *Copy Date:* 23 days prior to publication
BUSINESS: AVIATION & AERONAUTICS

FLIEGERBLATT 1929720G40-1004
Editorial: Julius-Leber-Str. 16, 53340 MECKENHEIM
Tel: 2225 6649 **Fax:** 2225 6649
Email: fliegerblatt@aol.com **Web site:** http://www.fliegergemeinschaft.de
Freq: 6 issues yearly; Free to qualifying individuals
Annual Sub.: EUR 40,00; **Circ:** 2,500
Profile: Magazine for former and active pilots/crews of the domestic and foreign air force.
Language(s): German

FLIESEN & PLATTEN 727480G4B-10
Editorial: Stolberger Str. 84, 50933 KÖLN
Tel: 221 5497205 **Fax:** 221 54976205
Email: red.fliesen@rudolf-mueller.de **Web site:** http://www.fliesenundplatten.de
Freq: Monthly; **Annual Sub.:** EUR 187,00; **Circ:** 11,434
Editor: Sabina Grafen; **Advertising Manager:** Volker Kunz
Profile: Journal for the tile industry with reports on market developments.
Language(s): German
ADVERTISING RATES:
Full Page Mono .... EUR 4020
Full Page Colour .... EUR 6960
Mechanical Data: Type Area: 267 x 188 mm, No. of Columns (Display): 4, Col Widths (Display): 44 mm
Official Journal of: Organ d. Fachverb. Fliesen u. Naturstein im ZDB e.V.
BUSINESS: ARCHITECTURE & BUILDING: Interior Design & Flooring

FLORA 727500G64F-940
Editorial: Neuwerk 21, 06108 HALLE
Tel: 345 5526210 **Fax:** 345 5527094
Email: jaeger@botanik.uni-halle.de
Freq: Monthly; **Annual Sub.:** EUR 271,00
Editor: Eckehart J. Jäger
Profile: Journal covering botany, ecology and morphology.
Language(s): English
BUSINESS: OTHER CLASSIFICATIONS: Biology

FLORA GARTEN 727499G93-200
Editorial: Stubbenhuk 10, 20459 HAMBURG
Tel: 40 37033771 **Fax:** 40 37035682
Email: redaktion@flora-garten.de **Web site:** http://www.flora-garten.de
Freq: Monthly; **Annual Sub.:** EUR 36,00; **Circ:** 106,914
Editor: Holger Radloff; **Advertising Manager:** Heiko Hager
Profile: Magazine for amateur gardeners.
Language(s): German
ADVERTISING RATES:
Full Page Mono .... EUR 11500
Full Page Colour .... EUR 11500
Mechanical Data: Type Area: 254 x 184 mm, No. of Columns (Display): 3, Col Widths (Display): 58 mm
Copy instructions: *Copy Date:* 42 days prior to publication
CONSUMER: GARDENING

FLORIAN HESSEN 727502G54A-300
Editorial: Friedrich-Ebert-Allee 12, 65185 WIESBADEN **Tel:** 611 3531612 **Fax:** 611 3531608
Email: pressestelle@hmdis.hessen.de **Web site:** http://www.feuerwehr.hessen.de
Freq: 10 issues yearly; **Annual Sub.:** EUR 28,12; **Circ:** 24,000
Editor: Michael Bußer
Profile: Journal for the fire brigade in Hessen.
Language(s): German
ADVERTISING RATES:
Full Page Mono .... EUR 1585
Full Page Colour .... EUR 2775
Mechanical Data: Type Area: 248 x 184 mm, No. of Columns (Display): 4, Col Widths (Display): 43 mm
BUSINESS: SAFETY & SECURITY: Fire Fighting

FLORIEREN! 727505G26C-100
Editorial: Wollgrasweg 41, 70599 STUTTGART
Tel: 711 4507133 **Fax:** 711 4507207
Email: estrupf@ulmer.de **Web site:** http://www.florieren-online.de
Freq: Monthly; **Annual Sub.:** EUR 108,00; **Circ:** 8,003
Editor: Edith Strupf; **Advertising Manager:** Anna Greiner
Profile: florieren! is an independent monthly magazine which supports the flower retail on the way to a successful future. florieren! is also a ideal medium for your professional B-to-B communication - and thus also for your success! Success in the floral retail is based on two pillars: good, challenging floristry in combination with a business management and sales-oriented thinking. The consistent combination of inspiration and marketing is therefore a central theme in florieren! and comes in monthly to focus on expression. The constant themes: floristry, Range / shopping sources, trends and new markets, plant, operations management, marketing, services, new ways and concepts, training, trade shows and exhibitions.
Language(s): German
ADVERTISING RATES:
Full Page Mono .... EUR 2267
Full Page Colour .... EUR 3332
Mechanical Data: Type Area: 260 x 176 mm, No. of Columns (Display): 4, Col Widths (Display): 41 mm
Copy instructions: *Copy Date:* 26 days prior to publication
BUSINESS: GARDEN TRADE

FLORIST 727504G26C-80
Editorial: Am Friedrichshain 22, 10407 BERLIN
Tel: 30 27894315 **Fax:** 30 27894313
Email: red.florist@haymarket.de **Web site:** http://www.florist.de
Freq: Monthly; **Annual Sub.:** EUR 105,60; **Circ:** 6,115
Editor: Christine Meyn; **Advertising Manager:** Christian Rueß
Profile: Trade magazine for florists, flower shops and retail nurseries. The range of subjects is specifically for those target groups and assists the companies to cut their daily work. The reader will find understandable tips, suggestions and a lot of seasonal business ideas. The magazine points to his readers to new business areas and reports on the latest trends in floristry.
Language(s): German
ADVERTISING RATES:
Full Page Mono .... EUR 2720
Full Page Colour .... EUR 4022
Mechanical Data: Type Area: 272 x 186 mm, No. of Columns (Display): 4, Col Widths (Display): 43 mm
Copy instructions: *Copy Date:* 31 days prior to publication
BUSINESS: GARDEN TRADE

FLÖTE AKTUELL 727489G76D-1400
Editorial: Strubbergstr. 80, 60489 FRANKFURT
Tel: 69 5962446
Email: floete@floete.net **Web site:** http://www.floete.net
Freq: Quarterly; Free to qualifying individuals
Annual Sub.: EUR 51,10; **Circ:** 2,200
Advertising Manager: Cordula Hacke
Profile: Official journal of the German Flute Society.
Language(s): German
ADVERTISING RATES:
Full Page Mono .... EUR 640
Full Page Colour .... EUR 832
Mechanical Data: Type Area: 252 x 180 mm, No. of Columns (Display): 3, Col Widths (Display): 57 mm
Copy instructions: *Copy Date:* 62 days prior to publication
CONSUMER: MUSIC & PERFORMING ARTS: Music

FLOTTEN MANAGEMENT 1644067G49A-2371
Editorial: Rudolf-Diesel-Str. 14, 53859 NIEDERKASSEL **Tel:** 228 4595470 **Fax:** 228 4595479
Email: rw@flotte.de **Web site:** http://www.flotte.de
Freq: 6 issues yearly; **Annual Sub.:** EUR 20,00; **Circ:** 28,500
Editor: Ralph Wuttke; **Advertising Manager:** Bernd Franke
Profile: Flottenmanagement is the independent magazine for fleet management. A competent guide with professional decision-making by utility tables, practice reports, cost comparisons, market surveys, with tips on management, leasing, tax, insurance, tires, alternative power, communications and law. Car tests with critical and relevant facts.
Language(s): German
ADVERTISING RATES:
Full Page Mono .... EUR 4889
Full Page Colour .... EUR 5294
Mechanical Data: Type Area: 300 x 215 mm, No. of Columns (Display): 4, Col Widths (Display): 52 mm
BUSINESS: TRANSPORT

FLUG REVUE 727533G6A-560
Editorial: Ubierstr. 83, 53173 BONN
Tel: 228 9565100 **Fax:** 228 9565247
Email: redaktion@flugrevue.de **Web site:** http://www.flugrevue.de
Freq: Monthly; **Annual Sub.:** EUR 54,90; **Circ:** 33,362
Editor: Volker K. Thomalla
Profile: Flug Revue is Europe's best selling aerospace magazine in German. Flug Revue focuses on: current news from industry and politics, the international air transport scene including the regional airline industry and business aviation, space, and military aviation as well as aerospace technology. Flug Revue intensifies the discussion on all issues concerning air transport, space and military aviation. For this reason, Flug Revue is at the same time an important forum for public discussions on high-explosive topics and of great importance regarding the formation of opinion. As a partner of the aerospace and airline industries, Flug Revue plays a significant role in the acceptance of aerospace and aviation by the public. Flug Revue is targeted at people who are interested in aerospace industry, but especially at those who work in the aerospace industry, at decision makers in authorities, politicians and Air Force commanders and, moreover, to the management in airline and aerospace industry. Twitter: http://twitter.com/flugrevue.
Language(s): English; German
Readership: Read by management in business and the aerospace industry.
ADVERTISING RATES:
Full Page Mono .... EUR 5280
Full Page Colour .... EUR 9770
Mechanical Data: Type Area: 248 x 185 mm, No. of Columns (Display): 4, Col Widths (Display): 43 mm
Copy instructions: *Copy Date:* 35 days prior to publication
BUSINESS: AVIATION & AERONAUTICS

FLUGMEDIZIN TROPENMEDIZIN REISEMEDIZIN 1809979G56A-11500
Editorial: Rüdigerstr. 14, 70469 STUTTGART
Tel: 711 8931440 **Fax:** 711 8931322
Email: guenther.buck@thieme.de **Web site:** http://www.thieme.de/fz/flug-reisemedizin.html
Freq: Quarterly; **Annual Sub.:** EUR 48,00; **Circ:** 4,580
Editor: Günther Buck
Profile: Competence and safety in travel medicine advice. Technical information from the field for the field to travel medical advice before travel and for the diagnosis and treatment of diseases that travelers 'bring'. Recent reports from the mountain and expedition medicine, maritime medicine and diving medicine. Plus in each issue: travel feature with general articles and photo spreads about interesting destinations and communications of the societies.
Language(s): German
ADVERTISING RATES:
Full Page Mono .... EUR 2010
Full Page Colour .... EUR 3150
Mechanical Data: Type Area: 245 x 175 mm, No. of Columns (Display): 3, Col Widths (Display): 50 mm

FLUGSICHERHEIT 1703792G40-978
Editorial: Postfach 906110, 51127 KÖLN
Tel: 2203 9083124 **Fax:** 2203 9084092
Email: klemensloeb@bundeswehr.org
Freq: Quarterly; **Cover Price:** Free; **Circ:** 2,000
Editor: Klemens Löb
Profile: Magazine on military air traffic safety.
Language(s): German

FLUGZEUG CLASSIC 727541G79B-1652
Editorial: Infanteriestr. 11a, 80797 MÜNCHEN
Tel: 89 130699720 **Fax:** 89 130699700
Email: redaktion@flugzeugclassic.de **Web site:** http://www.flugzeugclassic.de
Freq: Monthly; **Annual Sub.:** EUR 59,40; **Circ:** 17,222
Editor: Markus Wunderlich; **Advertising Manager:** Helmut Kramer
Profile: Historical aviation magazine, reported extensively on the civil and military aviation of past eras and establishes in the classic car scene of today. The focus of the book are vintage planes along with their history and technology.
Language(s): German
ADVERTISING RATES:
Full Page Mono .... EUR 2940
Full Page Colour .... EUR 2940
Mechanical Data: Type Area: 250 x 181 mm
Copy instructions: *Copy Date:* 21 days prior to publication
CONSUMER: HOBBIES & DIY: Models & Modelling

FLUID 727547G19D-2
Editorial: Justus-von-Liebig-Str. 1, 86899 LANDSBERG **Tel:** 8191 125401 **Fax:** 8191 125822
Email: franz.graf@mi-verlag.de **Web site:** http://www.fluid.de
Freq: 11 issues yearly; **Annual Sub.:** EUR 118,00; **Circ:** 10,879
Editor: Franz Graf; **Advertising Manager:** Gabi Claus
Profile: Journal focusing on hydraulics, pneumatics and electronics.
Language(s): German
ADVERTISING RATES:
Full Page Mono .... EUR 4640
Full Page Colour .... EUR 5490
Mechanical Data: Type Area: 257 x 178 mm, No. of Columns (Display): 4, Col Widths (Display): 41 mm
Copy instructions: *Copy Date:* 28 days prior to publication
BUSINESS: ENGINEERING & MACHINERY: Hydraulic Power

FLUID MARKT 1651738G19E-1875
Editorial: Justus-von-Liebig-Str. 1, 86899 LANDSBERG **Tel:** 8191 125347 **Fax:** 8191 125211
Email: franz.graf@mi-verlag.de **Web site:** http://www.fluid.de
Freq: Annual; **Circ:** 20,000
Editor: Franz Graf; **Advertising Manager:** Gabi Claus

Profile: Magazine for hydraulic, pneumatic and accessories, with 20,000 copies gives the designers and developers with a comprehensive overview fluid power products and their suppliers.
Language(s): German
ADVERTISING RATES:
Full Page Mono .... EUR 4640
Full Page Colour .... EUR 5490
Mechanical Data: Type Area: 257 x 178 mm, No. of Columns (Display): 4, Col Widths (Display): 41 mm

FLUR UND FURCHE 727549G21A-1540
Editorial: John-Deere-Str. 70, 68163 MANNHEIM
Tel: 621 8298416 **Fax:** 621 8298300
Email: macherainer@johndeere.com **Web site:** http://www.johndeere.de
Freq: Quarterly; **Cover Price:** Free; **Circ:** 163,000
Editor: Steven Roller
Profile: Company publication published by Deere & Company.
Language(s): German

FLÜSSIGES OBST 727515G9A-87
Editorial: Raiffeisenstr. 27, 56587 STRASSENHAUS
Tel: 2634 923511 **Fax:** 2634 923535
Email: redaktion@fluessiges-obst.de **Web site:** http://www.fluessiges-obst.de
Freq: Monthly; **Annual Sub.:** EUR 144,00; **Circ:** 1,191
Editor: Evi Brennich; **Advertising Manager:** Kerstin Schoop
Profile: Journal about fruit processing and fruit juice from the raw material to the marketing of the final product.
Language(s): German
ADVERTISING RATES:
Full Page Mono .... EUR 1810
Full Page Colour .... EUR 2620
Mechanical Data: Type Area: 250 x 175 mm, No. of Columns (Display): 2, Col Widths (Display): 85 mm
Copy instructions: *Copy Date:* 27 days prior to publication
Official Journal of: Organ d. Baumann-Gonser-Stiftung, d. Verb. d. dt. Fruchtsaft-Industrie e.V. u. d. Verb. d. dt. Fruchtwein- u. Fruchtschaumwein-Industrie e.V.
BUSINESS: DRINKS & LICENSED TRADE: Drinks, Licensed Trade, Wines & Spirits

FLÜSSIGGAS 727516G24-1
Editorial: Zur Feldmühle 9, 59821 ARNSBERG
Tel: 89 21111206 **Fax:** 2931 890038
Email: a.ring@strobel-verlag.de **Web site:** http://www.fluessiggas-magazin.de
Freq: 6 issues yearly; **Annual Sub.:** EUR 61,00; **Circ:** 4,560
Editor: Anne-Marie Ring; **Advertising Manager:** Stefan Schütte
Profile: Journal focusing on liquid gas.
Language(s): German
ADVERTISING RATES:
Full Page Mono .... EUR 1601
Full Page Colour .... EUR 2511
Mechanical Data: Type Area: 265 x 184 mm, No. of Columns (Display): 4, Col Widths (Display): 43 mm
BUSINESS: GAS

FML DER FAHRZEUG- UND METALL-LACKIERER/DAS LACKIERHANDWERK 727562G31R-17
Editorial: Westenriederstr. 49, 80331 MÜNCHEN
Tel: 89 2422830 **Fax:** 89 24228319
Email: fml@audin.de **Web site:** http://www.audin.de
Freq: 10 issues yearly; **Annual Sub.:** EUR 49,50; **Circ:** 5,500
Editor: Wolfgang Auer; **Advertising Manager:** Gabriele Dinnendahl
Profile: Journal about car spraying and painting.
Language(s): German
Readership: Aimed at those involved in the vehicle repair trade.
ADVERTISING RATES:
Full Page Mono .... EUR 2200
Full Page Colour .... EUR 4190
Mechanical Data: Type Area: 260 x 185 mm, No. of Columns (Display): 2, Col Widths (Display): 90 mm
Copy instructions: *Copy Date:* 26 days prior to publication
BUSINESS: MOTOR TRADE: Motor Trade Related

(FN WEB 1621261G67B-16546
Editorial: Schmiederstr. 19, 97941 TAUBERBISCHOFSHEIM **Tel:** 9341 83200
Fax: 9341 83161
Email: red.tbb@fraenkische-nachrichten.de **Web site:** http://www.fnweb.de
Freq: Daily; **Cover Price:** Paid; **Circ:** 110,018 Unique Users
Editor: Dieter Schwab
Profile: Ezine: Daily newspaper with regional news and a local sports section.
Language(s): German
REGIONAL DAILY & SUNDAY NEWSPAPERS: Regional Daily Newspapers

FNG-MAGAZIN 727603G22A-920
Editorial: Blumenstr. 15, 90402 NÜRNBERG
Tel: 911 2018250 **Fax:** 911 2018100
Email: fng@harnisch.com **Web site:** http://www.fng-info.de
Freq: 6 issues yearly; **Annual Sub.:** EUR 52,00; **Circ:** 22,306
Editor: Philipp Hirt-Reger; **Advertising Manager:** Thomas Mlynarik
Profile: Magazine about the food, non-food and beverages trade as well as retailing management.
Language(s): German
ADVERTISING RATES:
Full Page Mono .... EUR 4620
Full Page Colour .... EUR 6300
Mechanical Data: Type Area: 260 x 185 mm
Copy instructions: *Copy Date:* 14 days prior to publication
BUSINESS: FOOD

FOCUS 727566G56E-120
Editorial: Papiermühlenweg 74, 40882 RATINGEN
Tel: 2102 167810 **Fax:** 2102 167828
Email: s.sage@euro-focus.de **Web site:** http://www.euro-focus.de
Freq: 11 issues yearly; **Annual Sub.:** EUR 67,30; **Circ:** 10,001
Editor: Silke Sage; **Advertising Manager:** Heike Bergfeld
Profile: Magazine for optometrists, dispensing opticians and the optical industry.
Language(s): German
ADVERTISING RATES:
Full Page Mono .... EUR 2604
Full Page Colour .... EUR 4164
Mechanical Data: Type Area: 270 x 190 mm
Copy instructions: *Copy Date:* 28 days prior to publication
BUSINESS: HEALTH & MEDICAL: Optics

FOCUS 727565G82-2900
Editorial: Arabellastr. 23, 81925 MÜNCHEN
Tel: 89 92500 **Fax:** 89 92502026
Web site: http://www.focus.de
Freq: Weekly; **Annual Sub.:** EUR 166,40; **Circ:** 588,745
Editor: Uli Baur; **News Editor:** Annette Dörrfuß;
Advertising Manager: Ingo Müller
Profile: Focus is one with a pointed position on the media in Germany to determine the agenda of politics, economy and cultural scene. Focus has carried its claim of leadership among the top relevant quality media. The news magazine is clearly future-oriented, socially relevant, gives room to controversially discussed sociallrelevant topics and sees itself as a journalistic informed voice beyond the mainstream. Iin clearly defined departments Focus offers its readers a comprehensive orientation, makes backgrounds transparent and has a clear attitude. Focus has both the courage of own thoughts and is open for an exciting, controversial debate culture. Focus is the basic medium for a cosmopolitan, future-oriented elite in Germany. This target group has a powerful potential to public opinion in the German society like no other. The attitude of this elite is marked by achievement and competition, social responsibility and public spirit, of great interest in culture and in future-oriented science. Their high creative drive and their communication skills make them the "cluster" of modern German society. Twitter: http://twitter.com/focusonline This Outlet offers RSS (Really Simple Syndication).
Language(s): German
ADVERTISING RATES:
Full Page Mono .... EUR 46410
Full Page Colour .... EUR 46410
Mechanical Data: Type Area: 238 x 186 mm, No. of Columns (Display): 3, Col Widths (Display): 55 mm
Copy instructions: *Copy Date:* 24 days prior to publication
CONSUMER: CURRENT AFFAIRS & POLITICS

FOCUS MONEY 727567G74M-685
Editorial: Arabellastr. 23, 81925 MÜNCHEN
Tel: 89 92502565 **Fax:** 89 92502602
Email: leserservice@focus-money.de **Web site:** http://www.focus-money.de
Freq: Weekly; **Annual Sub.:** EUR 171,60; **Circ:** 138,491
Editor: Frank Pöpsel; **News Editor:** Annette Dörrfuß;
Advertising Manager: Manuela Löffler
Profile: Focus Money is the modern business magazine. It offers its readers a broad spectrum of business, politics, business, finance, tax, legal, investment and insurance companies. This unique mix of topics and the concept of the current economic facts are accurate to the high demands of economic interest information elite cut. This elite required date, reliable information. To this attractive potential include top decision makers and opinion leaders who actively shape the economy and society. This Outlet offers RSS (Really Simple Syndication).
Language(s): German
Readership: Aimed at investors, economists and insurance policy holders.
ADVERTISING RATES:
Full Page Mono .... EUR 14780
Full Page Colour .... EUR 14780
Mechanical Data: Type Area: 238 x 186 mm, No. of Columns (Display): 3, Col Widths (Display): 55 mm
Copy instructions: *Copy Date:* 17 days prior to publication
CONSUMER: WOMEN'S INTEREST CONSUMER MAGAZINES: Personal Finance

FOCUS MONEY ONLINE 1621262G74M-668
Editorial: Steinhauser Str. 1, 81677 MÜNCHEN
Tel: 89 92503895 **Fax:** 89 92501389
Email: redaktion@focus.de **Web site:** http://www.focus-money.de
Cover Price: Paid
Profile: Ezine: Magazine covering the economy, taxes, insurance and investments. This Outlet offers RSS (Really Simple Syndication).
Language(s): German
CONSUMER: WOMEN'S INTEREST CONSUMER MAGAZINES: Personal Finance

FOCUS NEREZ 1849382G27-3082
Editorial: Sonsbecker Str. 40, 46509 XANTEN
Tel: 2801 98260 **Fax:** 2801 982611
Email: info@focus-rostfrei.com **Web site:** http://www.focus-rostfrei.de
Annual Sub.: EUR 245,00; **Circ:** 3,000
Editor: Rüdiger Beckmann
Profile: Magazine about stainless steels.
Language(s): Czech
Mechanical Data: Type Area: 275 x 190 mm, No. of Columns (Display): 4, Col Widths (Display): 38 mm
Copy instructions: *Copy Date:* 10 days prior to publication

FOCUS NIERDZEWNE 1849383G27-3083
Editorial: Sonsbecker Str. 40, 46509 XANTEN
Tel: 2801 98260 **Fax:** 2801 982611
Email: info@focus-rostfrei.com **Web site:** http://www.focus-rostfrei.de
Annual Sub.: EUR 245,00; **Circ:** 4,000
Editor: Rüdiger Beckmann
Profile: Magazine about stainless steels.
Language(s): Polish
Mechanical Data: Type Area: 275 x 190 mm, No. of Columns (Display): 4, Col Widths (Display): 38 mm
Copy instructions: *Copy Date:* 10 days prior to publication

FOCUS ONLINE 1621264G82-9545
Editorial: Steinhauser Str. 1, 81677 MÜNCHEN
Tel: 89 92503895 **Fax:** 89 92501389
Email: redaktion@focus.de **Web site:** http://www.focus.de
Freq: Daily; **Cover Price:** Paid; **Circ:** 32,526,744 Unique Users
Editor: Daniel Steil; **News Editor:** Iris Mayer
Profile: Ezine: International news and current affairs magazine. Twitter: http://twitter.com/focusonline.
Language(s): German
CONSUMER: CURRENT AFFAIRS & POLITICS

FOCUS SCHULE 1665101G74C-3653
Editorial: Arabellastr. 23, 81925 MÜNCHEN
Tel: 89 92503609 **Fax:** 89 92501739
Email: sekretariat@focus-schule.de **Web site:** http://www.focus-schule.de
Freq: 6 issues yearly; **Annual Sub.:** EUR 29,70; **Circ:** 124,657
Editor: Mathias Brüggemeier; **News Editor:** Annette Dörrfuß; **Advertising Manager:** Vanessa Schneider
Profile: Focus Schule stands for the topics school, learning and family. The education magazine convinces dedicated parents. Those are over averagely educated, on high income, successful and want to off the best possible education to their children. They use Focus Schule as a competent navigator through the educational jungle. Focus Schule offers advice on high journalistic standards. The editorial presents important background information, facts about current developments, fundamental discussions and practical tips. The range of topics including school, education, training, education politics, science, technology, health and psychology.
Language(s): German
ADVERTISING RATES:
Full Page Mono .... EUR 16470
Full Page Colour .... EUR 16470
Mechanical Data: Type Area: 223 x 177 mm, No. of Columns (Display): 3, Col Widths (Display): 48 mm
Copy instructions: *Copy Date:* 35 days prior to publication
Supplement(s): Focus Schule Lernatlas
CONSUMER: WOMEN'S INTEREST CONSUMER MAGAZINES: Home & Family

FOCUS UNI-LUEBECK 727568G56A-3600
Editorial: Ratzeburger Allee 160, 23562 LÜBECK
Tel: 451 5003004 **Fax:** 451 5005718
Email: labahn@zuv.uni-luebeck.de **Web site:** http://www.uni-luebeck.de/aktuelles/focus.php
Freq: Half-yearly; **Circ:** 2,362
Editor: H. P. Bruch
Profile: Magazine about sciences, research and teaching at the medical university of Lübeck.
Language(s): German

FOLIO 1881705G58-1806
Editorial: Rellinghauser Str. 1, 45128 ESSEN
Tel: 201 1773340 **Fax:** 201 1773181
Email: folio@evonik.com **Web site:** http://www.evonik.com
Freq: Monthly; **Circ:** 80,000
Editor: Sven Scharnhorst
Profile: Magazine for employees of Evonik Industries AG.
Language(s): English; German

FONDS MAGAZIN 727595G1F-640
Editorial: Mainzer Landstr. 16, 60325 FRANKFURT
Tel: 69 71471556 **Fax:** 69 71472718
Email: fondsmagazin@dekabank.de **Web site:** http://www.dekabank.de
Freq: Quarterly; **Circ:** 629,925
Editor: Thomas Stoll; **Advertising Manager:** Annelie Baumann
Profile: Magazine focusing on savings and pension funds.
Language(s): German
Readership: Aimed at investors of the Deka-Gruppe and savings banks.
ADVERTISING RATES:
Full Page Mono .... EUR 9900
Full Page Colour .... EUR 9900
Mechanical Data: Type Area: 237 x 182 mm, No. of Columns (Display): 3, Col Widths (Display): 54 mm
Copy instructions: *Copy Date:* 21 days prior to publication
BUSINESS: FINANCE & ECONOMICS: Investment

FONDS PROFESSIONELL 1872972G1C-1491
Editorial: Neuenhöfer Allee 153, 50935 KÖLN
Tel: 221 9411345 **Fax:** 221 9411346
Email: heuser@fondsprofessionell.com **Web site:** http://www.fondsprofessionell.de
Freq: Quarterly; **Cover Price:** EUR 5,80; **Circ:** 85,100
Editor: Hans Heuser
Profile: Magazine sees itself as a basis for independent financial service providers as well as bank consultants, fund picker and other professional market participants.
Language(s): German
ADVERTISING RATES:
Full Page Mono .... EUR 6620
Full Page Colour .... EUR 6620
Mechanical Data: Type Area: 250 x 182 mm

FONDS & CO. 1657623G1F-1565
Editorial: Südliche Hauptstr. 21, 83700 ROTTACH-EGERN **Tel:** 89 80928050 **Fax:** 89 27264333
Email: redaktion@fondsundco.de **Web site:** http://www.fondsundco.de
Freq: Quarterly; **Cover Price:** EUR 6,90; **Circ:** 17,819
Editor: Ludwig Riepl; **Advertising Manager:** Maria Schmid
Profile: The Journal provides market reports, product reviews, primary market research, Background information, articles on taxation and law, expert interviews, and selected sales-relevant topics. The magazine is published in cooperation with experienced journalists and industry analysts created.
Language(s): German
ADVERTISING RATES:
Full Page Mono .... EUR 8400
Full Page Colour .... EUR 8400
Mechanical Data: Type Area: 241 x 171 mm
Copy instructions: *Copy Date:* 21 days prior to publication
Supplement(s): €uro spezial
BUSINESS: FINANCE & ECONOMICS: Investment

FONDSZEITUNG 763032G14A-9262
Editorial: Uhlandstr. 1, 10623 BERLIN
Tel: 30 40006820 **Fax:** 30 40006829
Email: redaktion@fondszeitung.de **Web site:** http://www.fondszeitung.de
Freq: 25 issues yearly; **Annual Sub.:** EUR 420,55; **Circ:** 1,200
Editor: Tilman Welther; **Advertising Manager:** Nadine Dost
Profile: Magazine on the closed-funds market with information on products, providers and brokers.
Language(s): German
ADVERTISING RATES:
Full Page Mono .... EUR 1100
Mechanical Data: Type Area: 224 x 179 mm

FONDSZEITUNG DAS MAGAZIN 1866160G14A-10239
Editorial: Uhlandstr. 1, 10623 BERLIN
Tel: 30 40006820 **Fax:** 30 40006829
Email: redaktion@fondszeitung.de **Web site:** http://www.fondszeitung.de
Freq: 6 issues yearly; **Annual Sub.:** EUR 420,55; **Circ:** 10,040
Editor: Tilman Welther; **Advertising Manager:** Nadine Dost
Profile: Magazine on the closed-funds market with information on products, providers and brokers.
Language(s): German
ADVERTISING RATES:
Full Page Mono .... EUR 5500
Full Page Colour .... EUR 5500
Mechanical Data: Type Area: 224 x 179 mm

FONO FORUM 727598G76D-5976
Editorial: Eifelring 28, 53879 EUSKIRCHEN
Tel: 2251 650460 **Fax:** 2251 6504699
Email: fonoforum@nitschke-verlag.de **Web site:** http://www.fonoforum.de
Freq: Monthly; **Annual Sub.:** EUR 69,60; **Circ:** 10,490
Editor: Björn Woll; **Advertising Manager:** Franz Pilz
Profile: Fono Forum is the leading magazine for classical music and jazz and in 2006 celebrated its 50th anniversary. A competent editorial team month after month decision-making in the purchase of CDs, DVDs, SACDs, and the course of experts formulated hi-session provides the combination of good music

and good sound. In the full service section provides the music magazine an annotated list of concerts and festivals and encourages cultural tours.
Language(s): German
ADVERTISING RATES:
Full Page Mono .... EUR 2552
Full Page Colour .... EUR 4100
Mechanical Data: Type Area: 248 x 185 mm, No. of Columns (Display): 4, Col Widths (Display): 44 mm
Copy instructions: *Copy Date:* 33 days prior to publication
CONSUMER: MUSIC & PERFORMING ARTS: Music

FOOD AND TRAVEL 2002365G74P-1343
Editorial: Gasstr. 14, 22761 HAMBURG
Tel: 40 38904016 **Fax:** 40 38904020
Email: redaktion@foodandtravel.de **Web site:** http://www.foodandtravel.de
Freq: 6 issues yearly; **Cover Price:** EUR 5,90; **Circ:** 65,000
Editor: Anne Coppenrath
Profile: Food and Travel offers seasonal recipes from the regional and international cuisine, kitchen secrets by professional cooks, specialties to order, the world's best restaurants, new hotels, the most beautiful spas, cruises on sea and in the air, feast tours, exciting travel accounts and a lot more. Presented are worldwide travel destinations from the North to the South Pole, but also regional destinations, short breaks, weekend trips, adventure tours and gourmet trips. "Cooking for friends", "flavours of the world", "hotel newcomer", "gourmet traveller" as well as "active traveller" and a "wine series" are constant columns of the magazine. For each topic there are "news" pages. The section containing food images is not interrupted by text. The recipes are to find in a clear collection at the end of each issue under the heading "collection". Facebook: http://www.facebook.com/pages/Food-and-Travel/129721913725798.
Language(s): German
ADVERTISING RATES:
Full Page Mono .... EUR 8900
Full Page Colour .... EUR 8900
Mechanical Data: Type Area: 265 x 200 mm

FOOD SERVICE 727608G11A-420
Editorial: Mainzer Landstr. 251, 60326 FRANKFURT
Tel: 69 75951511 **Fax:** 69 75951510
Email: foodservice@dfv.de **Web site:** http://www.food-service.de
Freq: 11 issues yearly; **Annual Sub.:** EUR 132,00; **Circ:** 10,620
Editor: Gretel Weiss; **Advertising Manager:** Friederike Smuda
Profile: Magazine covering all aspects of modern gastronomy, including fast food, snack food and restaurant chains in Germany, Austria and Switzerland.
Language(s): German
ADVERTISING RATES:
Full Page Mono .... EUR 5082
Full Page Colour .... EUR 6555
Mechanical Data: Type Area: 260 x 190 mm, No. of Columns (Display): 4, Col Widths (Display): 45 mm
BUSINESS: CATERING: Catering, Hotels & Restaurants

FOOD TECHNOLOGIE
727610G22A-960
Editorial: Blumenstr. 15, 90402 NÜRNBERG
Tel: 911 2018235 **Fax:** 911 2018100
Email: martinek@harnisch.com **Web site:** http://www.harnisch.com/fmtg
Freq: 5 issues yearly; **Annual Sub.:** EUR 60,00; **Circ:** 11,612
Editor: Sebastian Martinek; **Advertising Manager:** Ursula-Susanna Simon
Profile: Magazine about food technology. Includes information on additives, quality control, production technology, packaging and equipment.
Language(s): German
ADVERTISING RATES:
Full Page Mono .... EUR 3640
Full Page Colour .... EUR 4990
Mechanical Data: Type Area: 250 x 184 mm, No. of Columns (Display): 4, Col Widths (Display): 42 mm
Copy instructions: *Copy Date:* 30 days prior to publication
BUSINESS: FOOD

FÖRDER MAGAZIN 727579G62R-2388
Editorial: Rosenheimer Str. 145, 81671 MÜNCHEN
Tel: 89 45051371 **Fax:** 89 45051310
Email: holler@oldenbourg.de **Web site:** http://www.oldenbourg-bsv.de
Freq: 6 issues yearly; **Annual Sub.:** EUR 95,40; **Circ:** 3,485
Editor: Stefan Holler; **Advertising Manager:** Christian Schwarzbauer
Profile: Magazine about further education.
Language(s): German
Readership: Aimed at teachers.
ADVERTISING RATES:
Full Page Mono .... EUR 720
Full Page Colour .... EUR 1150
Mechanical Data: Type Area: 257 x 177 mm, No. of Columns (Display): 3, Col Widths (Display): 56 mm
Copy instructions: *Copy Date:* 49 days prior to publication
Supplement(s): Eine Welt in der Schule
BUSINESS: CHURCH & SCHOOL EQUIPMENT & EDUCATION: Education Related

FORENSISCHE PSYCHIATRIE, PSYCHOLOGIE, KRIMINOLOGIE
1806039G56A-11490
Editorial: Tiergartenstr. 17, 69121 HEIDELBERG
Tel: 6221 4870 **Fax:** 6221 4878366
Email: subscriptions@springer.com **Web site:** http://www.springer.com
Freq: Quarterly; **Annual Sub.:** EUR 199,00; **Circ:** 280
Profile: The Forensische Psychiatrie, Psychologie, Kriminologie is a forum for scientific discussion of the causes and consequences of offending. The focus is on the question how the relationship is between people, social factors and delinquency. It is about law enforcement, assessment, intervention and prevention. The Forensische Psychiatrie, Psychologie, Kriminologie would call for an interdisciplinary dialogue between the law on the one hand and the psychiatric-psychotherapeutic and psychological make-criminological disciplines on the other side. This involves the development and discussion of new concepts, to promote and ensure the quality of forensic assessment, treatment of offenders and the criminal law dealing with delinquent become human.
Language(s): German
ADVERTISING RATES:
Full Page Mono .... EUR 740
Full Page Colour .... EUR 1780
Mechanical Data: Type Area: 240 x 175 mm

FORENSISCHE PSYCHIATRIE UND PSYCHOTHERAPIE
727618G56A-3620
Editorial: Eichengrund 28, 49525 LENGERICH
Tel: 5484 308 **Fax:** 5484 550
Email: wp@pabst-publishers.com **Web site:** http://www.psychologie-aktuell.com/fpp
Freq: Half-yearly; **Annual Sub.:** EUR 30,00; **Circ:** 600
Editor: Wolfgang Pabst; **Advertising Manager:** Wolfgang Pabst
Profile: Magazine relevant for all those working within the field of forensic psychiatry, in detention centres, and also for related areas of work, for all those who are interested in keeping abreast with developments in dealing with the psycically ill offender, his confinement and his treatment.
Language(s): English; German
ADVERTISING RATES:
Full Page Mono .... EUR 256
Mechanical Data: Type Area: 165 x 110 mm

FORM+WERKZEUG 727630G19E-380
Editorial: Kolbergerstr. 22, 81679 MÜNCHEN
Tel: 89 99830611 **Fax:** 89 99830623
Email: fachtan@hanser.de **Web site:** http://www.form-werkzeug.de
Freq: 6 issues yearly; **Annual Sub.:** EUR 79,00; **Circ:** 10,900
Editor: Richard Fachtan; **Advertising Manager:** Dietmar von der Au
Profile: Subcontractors engaged in tool and mold making play a key role in the production chain. Increasingly demanding requirements in the development and manufacture of molds and tools necessitate the use of modern technology by tool and mold manufacturers. Form+Werkzeug is aimed at the decision makers in this innovative industrial sector. It contains the information they need on subjects relating to machine tools, HSC, tool technologies, CAD/CAM, the use of software and rapid prototyping/rapid tooling. Reports on new developments and current matters relating to operational processes complete the editorial coverage, which is derived from practical situations and is orientated towards the needs of the industry.
Language(s): German
ADVERTISING RATES:
Full Page Mono .... EUR 3180
Full Page Colour .... EUR 4980
Mechanical Data: Type Area: 250 x 175 mm, No. of Columns (Display): 4, Col Widths (Display): 41 mm
Official Journal of: Organ d. VDMA Werkzeugbau
Supplement(s): kataloge orange
BUSINESS: ENGINEERING & MACHINERY: Machinery, Machine Tools & Metalworking

FORM+ZWECK 1895087G19B-117
Editorial: Dorotheenstr. 4, 12557 BERLIN
Tel: 30 6555722 **Fax:** 30 65880653
Email: info@formundzweck.com **Web site:** http://www.formundzweck.com
Freq: Annual; **Circ:** 2,000
Profile: Magazine focused on design.
Language(s): English; German

FORSCHENDE KOMPLEMENTÄRMEDIZIN RESEARCH IN COMPLEMENTARY MEDICINE
1614883G56A-11198
Editorial: Wilhelmstr. 20a, 79098 FREIBURG
Tel: 761 452070 **Fax:** 761 4520714
Email: information@karger.de **Web site:** http://www.karger.com/fok
Freq: 6 issues yearly; Free to qualifying individuals
Annual Sub.: EUR 173,00; **Circ:** 3,450
Editor: H. Walach; **Advertising Manager:** Verena Hering
Profile: Research in complementary and classical natural medicine.
Language(s): English; German
ADVERTISING RATES:
Full Page Mono .... EUR 2370
Full Page Colour .... EUR 3990
Mechanical Data: Type Area: 242 x 180 mm, No. of Columns (Display): 2, Col Widths (Display): 90 mm
Copy instructions: *Copy Date:* 42 days prior to publication
Official Journal of: Organ d. Schweizer. Medizin. Ges. f. Phytotherapie u. d. European Society for Complementary and Natural Medicine

FORSCHUNG IM INGENIEURWESEN 727640G19A-260
Editorial: 22039 HAMBURG **Tel:** 40 65412735
Fax: 40 65412005
Email: kabelac@hsu-hh.de **Web site:** http://www.springerlink.com
Freq: Quarterly; **Annual Sub.:** EUR 889,00; **Circ:** 58
Editor: Stephan Kabelac
Profile: Magazine about engineering sciences.
Language(s): English; German
ADVERTISING RATES:
Full Page Mono .... EUR 740
Full Page Colour .... EUR 1780
Mechanical Data: Type Area: 240 x 175 mm

FORSCHUNG & LEHRE
727653G62A-980
Editorial: Rheinallee 18, 53173 BONN
Tel: 228 9026615 **Fax:** 228 9026690
Email: redaktion@forschung-und-lehre.de **Web site:** http://www.forschung-und-lehre.de
Freq: Monthly; Free to qualifying individuals
Annual Sub.: EUR 76,50; **Circ:** 29,458
Editor: Felix Grigat; **Advertising Manager:** Angelika Miebach
Profile: Magazine about German universities and cultural issues.Readers: university professors, young scientists, journalists and decision makers in politics and business.
Language(s): German
ADVERTISING RATES:
Full Page Mono .... EUR 2246
Full Page Colour .... EUR 3146
Mechanical Data: Type Area: 256 x 182 mm, No. of Columns (Display): 3, Col Widths (Display): 57 mm
Copy instructions: *Copy Date:* 20 days prior to publication
BUSINESS: CHURCH & SCHOOL EQUIPMENT & EDUCATION: Education

FORSCHUNG UND PRAXIS
727654G56A-3640
Editorial: Am Forsthaus Gravenbruch 5, 63263 NEU-ISENBURG **Tel:** 6102 5060 **Fax:** 6102 58870
Email: info@aerztezeitung.de **Web site:** http://www.aerztezeitung.de
Freq: Monthly; **Circ:** 59,823
Editor: Wolfgang van den Bergh; **Advertising Manager:** Ute Krille
Profile: Magazine on medicine, therapy and medical congresses.
Language(s): German
ADVERTISING RATES:
Full Page Mono .... EUR 6720
Full Page Colour .... EUR 8440
Mechanical Data: Type Area: 260 x 171 mm, No. of Columns (Display): 3, Col Widths (Display): 54 mm
Copy instructions: *Copy Date:* 7 days prior to publication
Supplement to: Ärzte Zeitung

FORST & TECHNIK 727663G46-4
Editorial: Berliner Str. 112a, 13189 BERLIN
Tel: 30 29397426 **Fax:** 30 29397459
Email: oliver.gabriel@dlv.de **Web site:** http://www.forstpraxis.de
Freq: Monthly; **Annual Sub.:** EUR 69,50; **Circ:** 9,981
Editor: Oliver Gabriel; **Advertising Manager:** Thomas Herrmann
Profile: Magazine about forestry, techniques and timber transportation.
Language(s): German
Readership: Read by owners of forests, forestry workers and suppliers of machinery.
ADVERTISING RATES:
Full Page Mono .... EUR 1685
Full Page Colour .... EUR 2592
Mechanical Data: Type Area: 270 x 184 mm, No. of Columns (Display): 4, Col Widths (Display): 43 mm
Copy instructions: *Copy Date:* 30 days prior to publication
Official Journal of: Organ d. Bundesvereinigung d. Holztransport-Gewerbes, d. Dt. Forstunternehmer-Verb., d. Forstunternehmerverb. Brandenburg e.V., d. ArGe forstwirtschaftl. Lohnunternehmer Hessen, Mecklenburg-Vorpommern, Niedersachsen, Nordrhein-Westfalen, Sachsen-Anhalt, Thüringen, d. Fachgruppe Bayer. Forstunternehmer im VdAW e.V., d. Fachgruppe Baden-Württemberg. Forstunternehmer im VdAW e.V., d. Lohnunternehmer in Land- u. Forstwirtschaft Rheinland-Pfalz-Saarland, d. Lohnunternehmer in Land- u. Forstwirtschaft Schleswig-Holstein u. d. Sächs. Forstunternehmer Verb.
BUSINESS: TIMBER, WOOD & FORESTRY

FORSTMASCHINEN PROFI
1622781G46-16
Editorial: Moorhofweg 11, 27383 SCHEESSEL
Tel: 4263 93950 **Fax:** 4263 939521
Email: info@forstfachverlag.de **Web site:** http://www.forstmaschinen-profi.de
Freq: Monthly; **Annual Sub.:** EUR 62,00; **Circ:** 7,000
Editor: Dieter Biernath; **Advertising Manager:** Jörg Rösch
Profile: Journal of Forest Engineering, timber transport, timber logistics, forest policy, machinery shows, cable crane technology, silviculture, wood current prices. Audiences: Forest managers, forest owners, machine operators, foresters, forestry officials, etc.
Language(s): German
ADVERTISING RATES:
Full Page Mono .... EUR 1080
Full Page Colour .... EUR 1801
Mechanical Data: Type Area: 262 x 185 mm, No. of Columns (Display): 3, Col Widths (Display): 59 mm
Copy instructions: *Copy Date:* 20 days prior to publication

FORSTTECHNISCHE INFORMATIONEN 727661G21A-1620
Editorial: Spremberger Str. 1, 64823 GROSS-UMSTADT **Tel:** 6078 78522 **Fax:** 6078 78550
Email: fti@kwf-online.de **Web site:** http://www.kwf-online.de
Freq: 6 issues yearly; Free to qualifying individuals
Annual Sub.: EUR 18,50; **Circ:** 2,800
Editor: Andreas Forbrig
Profile: Magazine with information about forestry.
Language(s): German

FORTSCHRITTE DER NEUROLOGIE - PSYCHIATRIE
727670G56N-13
Editorial: Rüdigerstr. 14, 70469 STUTTGART
Tel: 711 8931281 **Fax:** 711 8931408
Email: grit.vollmer@thieme.de **Web site:** http://www.thieme.de/fz/fdnp.html
Freq: Monthly; **Annual Sub.:** EUR 274,40; **Circ:** 2,362
Editor: Grit Vollmer
Profile: Information about the entire field of neurology, with a bridge between neurology and psychiatry. Comprehensive and critical papers, overview presentations on the advances in the diagnosis and therapy.
Language(s): German
ADVERTISING RATES:
Full Page Mono .... EUR 1970
Full Page Colour .... EUR 3080
Mechanical Data: Type Area: 248 x 175 mm, No. of Columns (Display): 4, Col Widths (Display): 40 mm
Official Journal of: Organ d. Berufsverb. Dt. Nervenärzte, d. Viktor v. Weizsäcker Ges. u. d. Dt. Ges. f. Gerontopsychiatrie u. -psychotherapie
Supplement(s): Current congress
BUSINESS: HEALTH & MEDICAL: Mental Health

FORUM 1895128G4E-7255
Editorial: Frankfurter Landstr. 2, 61440 OBERURSEL
Tel: 6171 614320 **Fax:** 6171 614689
Email: jutta.bringazi@lafarge.com **Web site:** http://www.lafarge.de
Freq: 3 issues yearly; **Circ:** 2,500
Editor: Jutta Bringazi
Profile: Magazine for employees and customers of the 'Lafarge Zement' and 'Lafarge Beton' companies.
Language(s): German

FORUM 755932G56A-11084
Editorial: Tiergartenstr. 17, 69121 HEIDELBERG
Tel: 6221 4878225 **Fax:** 6221 48768225
Email: gabriele.staab@springer.com **Web site:** http://www.springermedizin.de
Freq: 6 issues yearly; Free to qualifying individuals
Annual Sub.: EUR 119,00; **Circ:** 7,500
Editor: Gabriele Staab
Profile: The oncology journal Forum is the official magazine of the German Cancer Society. Each issue of the journal is devoted to an interdisciplinary focus and light it from a medical, professional and social policy aspect. Renowned experts reports on their work and take a stand on major issues in oncology. News from the national companies, scientific associations, the supporting members and the office of the German Cancer Society complete the picture. In addition, the magazine informs about current events and presents the results in the form of conference proceedings.
Language(s): German
ADVERTISING RATES:
Full Page Mono .... EUR 3300
Full Page Colour .... EUR 3300
Mechanical Data: Type Area: 240 x 174 mm
Official Journal of: Organ d. Dt. Krebsges.
BUSINESS: HEALTH & MEDICAL

FORUM 755933G56A-11085
Editorial: Borsteler Chaussee 85, Haus 16, 22453 HAMBURG **Tel:** 40 232334 **Fax:** 40 230292
Email: info@omnimedonline.de **Web site:** http://www.omnimedonline.de
Freq: 6 issues yearly; Free to qualifying individuals
Annual Sub.: EUR 53,50; **Circ:** 6,116
Editor: Thomas Grundmann; **Advertising Manager:** Vanessa Baack
Profile: Magazine for ear, nose and throat practitioners.
Language(s): German
ADVERTISING RATES:
Full Page Mono .... EUR 1600
Full Page Colour .... EUR 3160

Mechanical Data: Type Area: 250 x 180 mm, No. of Columns (Display): 3, Col Widths (Display): 56 mm
Copy instructions: *Copy Date:* 42 days prior to publication
BUSINESS: HEALTH & MEDICAL

FORUM 1681754G57-2758
Editorial: Am Coulombwall, 85748 GARCHING
Tel: 89 28913700 **Fax:** 89 28913718
Freq: Quarterly; **Circ:** 300
Editor: Brigitte Helmreich
Profile: Journal for authorities, consulting engineers area water management.
Language(s): German

FORUM 727694G63-260
Editorial: Breite Str. 2a, 14467 POTSDAM
Tel: 331 2786152 **Fax:** 331 2842990
Email: gottschling@potsdam.ihk.de **Web site:** http://www.potsdam.ihk24.de
Freq: 11 issues yearly; Free to qualifying individuals
Annual Sub.: EUR 42,80; **Circ:** 49,562
Editor: Detlef Gottschling; **Advertising Manager:** Caridad Nyári
Profile: "FORUM" - the Brandenburg business magazine - is a regional business magazine, the official journal from the Chambers of Commerce and industry of the state of Brandenburg. "FORUM" is aimed at companies in the Chamber of Commerce districts Potsdam, East Brandenburg, and Cottbus, and also at numerous companies and authorities in the neighboring counties. With a monthly circulation of 51,000 copies in this area "FORUM" reaches nationwide enterprises, medium-sized enterprises, individual entrepreneurs and self-employed without any wastage. The number of readers is made ??up of owners, mangers, board members and executives. The readers represent a high investment potential and are an important target group for the business-to-business communication. They are involved in decision processes covering all competence area,.
Language(s): German
ADVERTISING RATES:
Full Page Mono .... EUR 4365
Full Page Colour .... EUR 5685
Mechanical Data: Type Area: 260 x 185 mm, No. of Columns (Display): 4, Col Widths (Display): 45 mm
Copy instructions: *Copy Date:* 10 days prior to publication
Supplement(s): B4B Mittelstand; Business in Berlin und Brandenburg
BUSINESS: REGIONAL BUSINESS

FORUM DER PSYCHOANALYSE 727705G56N-15_50
Editorial: Klugstr. 39, 80638 MÜNCHEN
Email: regine.karcher-reiners@springer.com **Web site:** http://www.springer.com
Freq: Quarterly; **Annual Sub.:** EUR 189,00; **Circ:** 2,350
Editor: Regine Karcher-Reiners
Profile: The Forum der Psychoanalyse is a forum for discussion of topics of psychoanalytic clinical theory and technique from the perspective of various trends at home and abroad. It also covers related subjects, for example the connection between psychoanalysis and allied disciplines, issues of training, psychoanalysis as a profession, and basic issues of psychoanalysis as a science. The magazine was founded in 1985 by psychoanalysts of different societies.
Language(s): German
ADVERTISING RATES:
Full Page Mono .... EUR 1390
Full Page Colour .... EUR 2430
Mechanical Data: Type Area: 200 x 130 mm
BUSINESS: HEALTH & MEDICAL: Mental Health

FORUM FAMILIENRECHT 727715G1A-3500
Editorial: Kölner Str. 73, 53879 EUSKIRCHEN
Tel: 2251 777740 **Fax:** 2251 7777420
Email: schnitzler@kanzlei-schnitzler.de **Web site:** http://www.forum-familienrecht.de
Freq: 11 issues yearly; Free to qualifying individuals
Annual Sub.: EUR 162,90; **Circ:** 7,600
Editor: Klaus Schnitzler
Profile: Magazine for lawyers in family law.
Language(s): German
ADVERTISING RATES:
Full Page Mono .... EUR 1700
Full Page Colour .... EUR 2570
Mechanical Data: Type Area: 260 x 186 mm, No. of Columns (Display): 2, Col Widths (Display): 90 mm
Copy instructions: *Copy Date:* 20 days prior to publication
Official Journal of: Organ d. Dt. Anwaltverein, ArGe Familienrecht

FORUM LOGOPÄDIE 727735G56R-620
Editorial: Glockenblumenweg 15, 21360 VÖGELSEN
Tel: 4131 921181 **Fax:** 4131 921182
Email: redaktion.wilhelm@t-online.de **Web site:** http://www.schulz-kirchner.de/logopaedie
Freq: 6 issues yearly; Free to qualifying individuals
Annual Sub.: EUR 62,95; **Circ:** 12,633
Editor: Michael Wilhelm; **Advertising Manager:** Andrea Rau
Profile: Journal covering speech therapy.
Language(s): German
ADVERTISING RATES:
Full Page Mono .... EUR 1071
Full Page Colour .... EUR 1431
Mechanical Data: Type Area: 260 x 180 mm, No. of Columns (Display): 2, Col Widths (Display): 87 mm
Copy instructions: *Copy Date:* 31 days prior to publication
BUSINESS: HEALTH & MEDICAL: Health Medical Related

FORUM MLP - WIRTSCHAFTSAUSG. 727684G14A-2440
Editorial: Alte Ziegelei 43, 53474 BAD NEUENAHR-AHRWEILER **Tel:** 221 34803811 **Fax:** 221 34803841
Email: info@redaktionforum.de **Web site:** http://www.mlp-forum.de
Freq: Half-yearly; **Cover Price:** EUR 4,00; **Circ:** 345,000
Editor: Melanie Contoli
Profile: Company publication published by MLP Finanzdienstleistung.
Language(s): German
ADVERTISING RATES:
Full Page Mono .... EUR 8957
Full Page Colour .... EUR 10610
Mechanical Data: Type Area: 285 x 183 mm, No. of Columns (Display): 3, Col Widths (Display): 67 mm
Copy instructions: *Copy Date:* 61 days prior to publication
BUSINESS: COMMERCE, INDUSTRY & MANAGEMENT

FORUM NACHHALTIG WIRTSCHAFTEN 1898998G14A-10296
Editorial: Gotzingerstr. 48, 81371 MÜNCHEN
Tel: 89 74661123 **Fax:** 89 74661160
Email: redaktion@forum-csr.net **Web site:** http://www.forum-csr.net
Freq: Quarterly; **Annual Sub.:** EUR 25,00; **Circ:** 21,237
Editor: Fritz Lietsch; **Advertising Manager:** Tina Teucher
Profile: The magazine reported to date and reliable information on new developments, trends and success stories on sustainability and corporate responsibility in business, politics and society. With news, literature and surfing tips, and events on sustainability.
Language(s): German
ADVERTISING RATES:
Full Page Mono .... EUR 3600
Full Page Colour .... EUR 3600
Mechanical Data: Type Area: 240 x 165 mm, No. of Columns (Display): 3, Col Widths (Display): 53 mm

FORUM VERKEHR NEWSLETTER 731072G49A-740
Editorial: Klingelhöferstr. 7, 10785 BERLIN
Tel: 30 26395470 **Fax:** 30 26395422
Email: kreyenborg@verkehrsforum.de **Web site:** http://www.verkehrsforum.de
Freq: 6 issues yearly; **Circ:** 4,000
Editor: Ingrid Kudirka
Profile: Magazine with information about the activities of the German Verkehrsforum.
Language(s): German

FORUM WOHNEN UND STADTENTWICKLUNG 746471G4E-6480
Editorial: Fritschestr. 27, 10585 BERLIN
Tel: 30 390473230 **Fax:** 30 390473190
Email: redaktion@forum-ws.de **Web site:** http://www.forum-ws.de
Freq: 6 issues yearly; Free to qualifying individuals
Annual Sub.: EUR 68,80; **Circ:** 2,600
Editor: Peter Rohland
Profile: Magazine on property formation and city development for communes, real estate economists, planners and architects, credit economy.
Language(s): German
Mechanical Data: Type Area: 270 x 190 mm

FOTO DIGITAL 727757G85A-776
Editorial: Postfach 400852, 80708 MÜNCHEN
Tel: 89 33035149
Email: patrick.henninges@foto-digital.org **Web site:** http://www.digital.eu
Freq: 6 issues yearly; **Annual Sub.:** EUR 41,40; **Circ:** 13,400
Editor: Patrick Hennings; **Advertising Manager:** Stefanie Richter
Profile: Magazine for amateur photographers and semi-professionals with tests, photo news and manufacturer practice. This Outlet offers RSS (Really Simple Syndication).
Language(s): German
ADVERTISING RATES:
Full Page Mono .... EUR 3700
Full Page Colour .... EUR 5000
Mechanical Data: Type Area: 263 x 185 mm, No. of Columns (Display): 3, Col Widths (Display): 54 mm
Copy instructions: *Copy Date:* 15 days prior to publication
CONSUMER: PHOTOGRAPHY & FILM MAKING: Photography

FOTO HITS EINKAUFSFÜHRER 727759G85A-200
Editorial: Holzstr. 2, 40221 DÜSSELDORF
Tel: 211 3900944 **Fax:** 211 3900955
Email: j.janke@gfw.de **Web site:** http://www.fotohits.de
Freq: Annual; **Cover Price:** EUR 7,90; **Circ:** 43,967
Editor: Jutta Janke; **Advertising Manager:** Walter Hauck
Profile: Publication focusing on photographic and video products.
Language(s): German
Readership: Aimed at amateur photographers.
ADVERTISING RATES:
Full Page Mono .... EUR 4000
Full Page Colour .... EUR 5900
Mechanical Data: Type Area: 272 x 185 mm, No. of Columns (Display): 4, Col Widths (Display): 43 mm
Copy instructions: *Copy Date:* 46 days prior to publication
CONSUMER: PHOTOGRAPHY & FILM MAKING: Photography

FOTO MAGAZIN 727762G85A-220
Editorial: Troplowitzstr. 5, 22529 HAMBURG
Tel: 40 38906170 **Fax:** 40 38906185
Email: franz.raith@fotomagazin.de **Web site:** http://www.fotomagazin.de
Freq: Monthly; **Annual Sub.:** EUR 62,40; **Circ:** 38,907
Editor: Franz Raith; **Advertising Manager:** Jutta Friedrichsen-Devakar
Profile: Magazine for Photography and Imaging. Professionals tell the reader valuable practical tips. In-depth reports on the latest technology developments and expert product tests provide essential support with clear criteria for new acquisitions. A particular focus is on high-quality interactive services such as test events, competitions and workshops.
Language(s): German
ADVERTISING RATES:
Full Page Mono .... EUR 7956
Full Page Colour .... EUR 10600
Mechanical Data: Type Area: 248 x 185 mm, No. of Columns (Display): 4, Col Widths (Display): 45 mm
Copy instructions: *Copy Date:* 24 days prior to publication
CONSUMER: PHOTOGRAPHY & FILM MAKING: Photography

FOTO WIRTSCHAFT 727765G38-1
Editorial: Troplowitzstr. 5, 22529 HAMBURG
Tel: 40 38906170 **Fax:** 40 38906185
Email: raith@jahr-tsv.de **Web site:** http://www.jahr-tsv.de
Freq: Monthly; **Annual Sub.:** EUR 70,20; **Circ:** 3,763
Editor: Franz Raith; **Advertising Manager:** Jutta Friedrichsen-Devakar
Profile: Foto wirtschaft is the business magazine for the photo industry with effective advisory functions in matters photographic industry, commerce and trade. The main themes of Foto wirtschaft are in addition to new ideas and background stories from the photo and video section, also strongly sales-oriented contributions that support the dealers effectively in their daily work. Reports on the professional applications of digital image communication give the dealer outlook on future developments in this increasingly important field of image processing. Foto wirtschaft gives the decision makers in photo and computer stores the necessary information and background reports, which are important for the daily work.
Language(s): German
Readership: Aimed at photographers.
ADVERTISING RATES:
Full Page Mono .... EUR 2392
Full Page Colour .... EUR 3952
Mechanical Data: Type Area: 248 x 185 mm, No. of Columns (Display): 4, Col Widths (Display): 45 mm
Copy instructions: *Copy Date:* 20 days prior to publication
BUSINESS: PHOTOGRAPHIC TRADE

FOTOFORUM 725251G2A-980
Editorial: Ludwig-Wolker-Str. 37, 48157 MÜNSTER
Tel: 251 143930 **Fax:** 251 143939
Email: redaktion@fotoforum.de **Web site:** http://www.fotoforum.de
Freq: 6 issues yearly; **Annual Sub.:** EUR 42,00; **Circ:** 12,105
Editor: Martin Breutmann; **Advertising Manager:** Martin Breutmann
Profile: fotoforum is the magazine for amateurs, enthusiasts and semi-professionals who deal in complex ways with photography and presentation. In the fotoforum, the photo, the road to successful photography and the presentation in the center of the information concept. Therefore waived fotoforum aware of the attempt to map the photo market in tests and chart lists. Instead, choose from fotoforum specifically for the reader from the flood of information, provides guidance and gives practical solutions to everyday issues of photographs. In each issue presents the fotoforum outstanding photographers and reports on current trends in the photography scene. Experienced practitioners provide competent, objective and understandable information, around high-class photography and photo equipment - digital and analog. With bi-monthly publication and high depth of information that is used intensively fotoforum. The high demanding quality of the fotoforum-editing is the key to the remarkable and continually growing base of currently more than 7,000 subscribers. The distinctive demanding quality of our readers documented a number of very clear: 96% of our readers take pictures with SLR cameras.
Language(s): German
ADVERTISING RATES:
Full Page Mono .... EUR 2820
Full Page Colour .... EUR 3320
Mechanical Data: Type Area: 262 x 185 mm, No. of Columns (Display): 4, Col Widths (Display): 42 mm
Copy instructions: *Copy Date:* 45 days prior to publication

FOVO FORDERUNG & VOLLSTRECKUNG 731566G1A-3474
Editorial: Wachsbleiche 7, 53111 BONN
Tel: 228 9191125 **Fax:** 228 9191123
Email: schwabe@anwaltverlag.de **Web site:** http://www.anwaltverlag.de
Freq: Monthly; **Annual Sub.:** EUR 184,80; **Circ:** 2,500
Editor: Sabine Jungbauer
Profile: Magazine about insolvency law.
Language(s): German
ADVERTISING RATES:
Full Page Mono .... EUR 1210
Full Page Colour .... EUR 2080
Mechanical Data: Type Area: 260 x 186 mm, No. of Columns (Display): 2, Col Widths (Display): 90 mm

FR FINANZ-RUNDSCHAU ERTRAGSTEUERRECHT 728001G1M-3
Editorial: Gustav-Heinemann-Ufer 58, 50968 KÖLN
Tel: 221 93738151 **Fax:** 221 93738902
Email: lingemann@otto-schmidt.de **Web site:** http://www.finanzrundschau.de
Freq: 24 issues yearly; **Annual Sub.:** EUR 316,90; **Circ:** 2,120
Editor: Wolfgang Lingemann; **Advertising Manager:** Thosten Deuse
Profile: Review of income tax and corporation tax.
Language(s): German
ADVERTISING RATES:
Full Page Mono .... EUR 1195
Full Page Colour .... EUR 2091
Mechanical Data: Type Area: 260 x 180 mm, No. of Columns (Display): 2, Col Widths (Display): 88 mm
BUSINESS: FINANCE & ECONOMICS: Taxation

FRACHT DIENST 727773G49C-73
Editorial: Jasperallee 82, 38102 BRAUNSCHWEIG
Tel: 531 2346197 **Fax:** 531 2347101
Email: o.kortegast@frachtdienst-online.de **Web site:** http://www.frachtdienst-online.de
Freq: 6 issues yearly; **Annual Sub.:** EUR 18,00; **Circ:** 8,117
Editor: Olaf Kortegast; **Advertising Manager:** J. R. Lodiga
Profile: Publication about freight. Includes information on storage, logistics, transport and driving.
Language(s): German
ADVERTISING RATES:
Full Page Mono .... EUR 2000
Full Page Colour .... EUR 3200
Mechanical Data: Type Area: 270 x 185 mm, No. of Columns (Display): 4, Col Widths (Display): 43 mm

FRACHT DIENST 727773G49C-91
Editorial: Jasperallee 82, 38102 BRAUNSCHWEIG
Tel: 531 2346197 **Fax:** 531 2347101
Email: o.kortegast@frachtdienst-online.de **Web site:** http://www.frachtdienst-online.de
Freq: 6 issues yearly; **Annual Sub.:** EUR 18,00; **Circ:** 8,117
Editor: Olaf Kortegast; **Advertising Manager:** J. R. Lodiga
Profile: Publication about freight. Includes information on storage, logistics, transport and driving.
Language(s): German
ADVERTISING RATES:
Full Page Mono .... EUR 2000
Full Page Colour .... EUR 3200
Mechanical Data: Type Area: 270 x 185 mm, No. of Columns (Display): 4, Col Widths (Display): 43 mm

FRAG DOCH MAL DIE MAUS 734987G91D-9656
Editorial: Breitscheidstr. 10, 70174 STUTTGART
Tel: 711 2202990 **Fax:** 711 22029919
Email: peter@blue-ocean-ag.de **Web site:** http://www.blue-ocean-ag.de
Freq: 6 issues yearly; **Annual Sub.:** EUR 17,70; **Circ:** 57,856
Editor: Simon Peter; **Advertising Manager:** Jennifer Kilian
Profile: What's in the air? How did the dinosaurs? And as the letters come in a book? These and similar questions from the everyday world of the 6 - to 9-year-olds answered the main character of the popular for decades, ,,Sendung mit der Maus" to 36 exciting pages. It encourages experimentation with fascinating and tricky puzzles to join in awe and, introduces incredible phenomena of animal life and experiences with their friends, the duck and the elephant, great adventure. In keeping with the topic of the bimonthly magazine Frag doch mal die Maus is opening a startling charge extra and a fascinating knowledge poster to wonder.
Language(s): German
ADVERTISING RATES:
Full Page Mono .... EUR 4900
Full Page Colour .... EUR 4900

Mechanical Data: Type Area: 260 x 190 mm
CONSUMER: RECREATION & LEISURE: Children & Youth

FRANCHISE €RFOLGE
1850129G14A-10183
Editorial: Im Wingert 13, 53424 REMAGEN
Tel: 2228 9129120
Email: martin.schaefer@unternehmerverlag.de **Web site:** http://www.franchise-erfolge.de
Freq: 6 issues yearly; **Annual Sub.:** EUR 23,40; **Circ:** 20,000
Editor: Martin Schäfer; **Advertising Manager:** Susanne Schäfer
Profile: FFranchising is a successful path to independence. The magazine is aimed at interested in franchise founder and potential franchisees. This magazine is the important role of franchising for business creation and enterprise safety requirements. Franchising encourages independence and provides new opportunities for the middle class. Well-known experts in treating the sections franchiseRecht, franchiseExperten and franchiseWissen special issues in the industry as the legal aspects of a franchise agreement or franchise opportunities in foreign markets and provide important information about starting and running a business. Also have our renowned attorneys also point to the dark side of franchising and tell where and when to be careful. In franchiseInterviews we talk to successful franchise owner or well-known personalities from politics and society. Here the reader gets an insight into practice and benefit from the tips, the experience and advice. In franchiseHistory, there are the exciting stories from well-known franchise systems and franchise our special editorial describes entertaining, economies in which business fields and industries franchise owner successful and what new opportunities arise here. Entrepreneurs in the franchise industry, their ideas, their history and their success makes the special charm of franchise from successes.
Language(s): German
ADVERTISING RATES:
Full Page Mono .... EUR 2400
Full Page Colour .... EUR 2400
Mechanical Data: Type Area: 269 x 178 mm
Copy instructions: *Copy Date:* 28 days prior to publication

FRANKEN REPORT
727810G72-3948
Editorial: Winklerstr. 15, 90403 NÜRNBERG
Tel: 911 2331130 **Fax:** 911 2331192
Email: info@frankenreport.info **Web site:** http://www.frankenreport.info
Freq: Weekly; **Cover Price:** Free; **Circ:** 375,000
Editor: Andreas Hock; **Advertising Manager:** Roland Finn
Profile: Advertising journal (house-to-house) concentrating on local stories.
Language(s): German
ADVERTISING RATES:
Full Page Mono .... EUR 16093
Full Page Colour .... EUR 21593
Mechanical Data: Type Area: 485 x 325 mm, No. of Columns (Display): 7, Col Widths (Display): 45 mm
Copy instructions: *Copy Date:* 2 days prior to publication
LOCAL NEWSPAPERS

FRANKENBERGER ALLGEMEINE
730350G67B-7080
Editorial: Frankfurter Str. 168, 34121 KASSEL
Tel: 561 20300 **Fax:** 561 2032406
Email: info@hna.de **Web site:** http://www.hna.de
Freq: 312 issues yearly; **Circ:** 6,847
Advertising Manager: Andrea Schaller-Öller
Profile: Regional daily newspaper with news on politics, economy, culture, sports, travel, technology, etc. The Frankenberger Allgemeine is a local issue of HNA Hessische/Niedersächsische Allgemeine. Twitter: http://twitter.com/hna_online This Outlet offers RSS (Really Simple Syndication).
Language(s): German
ADVERTISING RATES:
SCC .... EUR 29,30
Mechanical Data: Type Area: 430 x 285 mm, No. of Columns (Display): 6, Col Widths (Display): 45 mm
Copy instructions: *Copy Date:* 2 days prior to publication
REGIONAL DAILY & SUNDAY NEWSPAPERS: Regional Daily Newspapers

FRANKENBERGER ZEITUNG
727801G67B-5140
Editorial: Lengefelder Str. 6, 34497 KORBACH
Tel: 5631 560150 **Fax:** 5631 560159
Email: info@wlz-fz.de **Web site:** http://www.wlz-fz.de
Freq: 312 issues yearly; **Circ:** 6,014
Advertising Manager: Marina Kieweg
Profile: Daily newspaper with regional news and a local sports section. This Outlet offers RSS (Really Simple Syndication).
Language(s): German
ADVERTISING RATES:
SCC .... EUR 24,70
Mechanical Data: Type Area: 430 x 277 mm, No. of Columns (Display): 6, Col Widths (Display): 45 mm
Copy instructions: *Copy Date:* 2 days prior to publication
REGIONAL DAILY & SUNDAY NEWSPAPERS: Regional Daily Newspapers

FRANKENPOST
727807G67B-5160
Editorial: Poststr. 9, 95028 HOF **Tel:** 9281 8160
Fax: 9281 816283
Email: redaktion@frankenpost.de **Web site:** http://www.frankenpost.de
Freq: 312 issues yearly; **Circ:** 62,293
Editor: Johann Pirthauer; **News Editor:** Max Busl; **Advertising Manager:** Stefan Sailer
Profile: Regional daily newspaper with news on politics, economy, culture, sports, travel, technology, etc. The Frankenpost is the major local newspaper in the northeast of Upper Franconia. It appears among the seven Namn weterer newspapers in the region: Frankenpost Sechsämterbote, Frankenpost Sechsämter Neues Nachrichten, Hofer Anzeiger, Marktredwitzer Tagblatt Frankenpost, Nünchberg-Helmbrechtser Tageszeitung, Rehauer Tagblatt Frankenpost, Selber Tagblatt Frankenpost. Facebook: http://www.facebook.com/Frankenpost Twitter: http://twitter.com/frankenpost This Outlet offers RSS (Really Simple Syndication).
Language(s): German
ADVERTISING RATES:
SCC .... EUR 173,10
Mechanical Data: Col Widths (Display): 44 mm, Type Area: 485 x 325 mm, No. of Columns (Display): 7
Copy instructions: *Copy Date:* 1 day prior to publication
Supplement(s): Ferienland Fichtelgebirge; rtv
REGIONAL DAILY & SUNDAY NEWSPAPERS: Regional Daily Newspapers

FRANKENPOST SECHSÄMTER NEUESTE NACHRICHTEN
727809G67B-5180
Editorial: Poststr. 9, 95028 HOF **Tel:** 9281 8160
Fax: 9281 816283
Email: redaktion@frankenpost.de **Web site:** http://www.frankenpost.de
Freq: 312 issues yearly; **Circ:** 2,415
Advertising Manager: Stefan Sailer
Profile: Regional daily newspaper with news on politics, economy, culture, sports, travel, technology, etc. Frankenpost Sechsämterbote Neueste Nachrichten is a local edition of the newspaper Frankenpost. Facebook: http://www.facebook.com/pages/Frankenpost/330862476314 Twitter: http://twitter.com/frankenpost This Outlet offers RSS (Really Simple Syndication).
Language(s): German
ADVERTISING RATES:
SCC .... EUR 27,60
Mechanical Data: Type Area: 485 x 325 mm, No. of Columns (Display): 7, Col Widths (Display): 44 mm
Copy instructions: *Copy Date:* 1 day prior to publication
Supplement(s): rtv
REGIONAL DAILY & SUNDAY NEWSPAPERS: Regional Daily Newspapers

FRANKENPOST SECHSÄMTERBOTE
727808G67B-5200
Editorial: Poststr. 9, 95028 HOF **Tel:** 9281 8160
Fax: 9281 816283
Email: redaktion@frankenpost.de **Web site:** http://www.frankenpost.de
Freq: 312 issues yearly; **Circ:** 6,194
Advertising Manager: Stefan Sailer
Profile: Regional daily newspaper with news on politics, economy, culture, sports, travel, technology, etc. Frankenpost Sechsämterbote is a local edition of the newspaper Frankenpost. Facebook: http://www.facebook.com/pages/Frankenpost/330862476314 Twitter: http://twitter.com/frankenpost This Outlet offers RSS (Really Simple Syndication).
Language(s): German
ADVERTISING RATES:
SCC .... EUR 39,40
Mechanical Data: Type Area: 485 x 325 mm, No. of Columns (Display): 7, Col Widths (Display): 44 mm
Copy instructions: *Copy Date:* 1 day prior to publication
Supplement(s): rtv
REGIONAL DAILY & SUNDAY NEWSPAPERS: Regional Daily Newspapers

FRANKFURT KAUFT EIN!
1828427G89A-12396
Editorial: Ludwigstr. 37, 60327 FRANKFURT
Tel: 69 974600 **Fax:** 69 97460400
Email: journal@mmg.de
Freq: Annual; **Cover Price:** EUR 5,80; **Circ:** 28,000
Editor: Anja Ruppel; **Advertising Manager:** Melanie Hennemann
Profile: Shopping guide for the Rhein-Main region.
Language(s): German
ADVERTISING RATES:
Full Page Mono .... EUR 2650
Full Page Colour .... EUR 3960
Mechanical Data: Type Area: 270 x 195 mm, No. of Columns (Display): 4, Col Widths (Display): 45 mm
Copy instructions: *Copy Date:* 28 days prior to publication

FRANKFURT KAUFT EIN!
1828427G89A-12542
Editorial: Ludwigstr. 37, 60327 FRANKFURT
Tel: 69 974600 **Fax:** 69 97460400
Email: journal@mmg.de
Freq: Annual; **Cover Price:** EUR 5,80; **Circ:** 28,000
Editor: Anja Ruppel; **Advertising Manager:** Melanie Hennemann
Profile: Shopping guide for the Rhein-Main region.
Language(s): German
ADVERTISING RATES:
Full Page Mono .... EUR 2650
Full Page Colour .... EUR 3960
Mechanical Data: Type Area: 270 x 195 mm, No. of Columns (Display): 4, Col Widths (Display): 45 mm
Copy instructions: *Copy Date:* 28 days prior to publication

FRANKFURTER ALLGEMEINE
10787G65A-263
Editorial: Hellerhofstr. 2, 60327 FRANKFURT
Tel: 69 75910 **Fax:** 69 75911743
Email: redaktion@faz.de **Web site:** http://www.faz.net
Freq: 312 issues yearly; **Circ:** 396,793
Editor: Holger Steltzner; **News Editor:** Jasper von Altenbockum; **Advertising Manager:** Andreas Formen
Profile: Who takes his morning newspaper Frankfurter Allgemeine out of the mailbox has at least four newspaper books in hand. Policy: Opinion at the beginning and think in the end, that is the emblem of the first book of the newspaper. Editorial gloss and editorial commentary on the front page ever since the outer image that the newspaper has its own opinion - separate from the news. Review a decision on the last page with glosses and analyzes the policy book. In between, the reader will find news, background reports and reports from Germany and abroad. Economy: The F.A.Z. as a leading business newspaper in Germany. The second Book of newspaper reports on national and international economic policy and the domestic and global business world and from all industries and markets. Economic concerns everyone. For without knowledge of the relationships in the economy, it is hardly possible to understand political events or to interpret. Financial market (and Sport): This is most evident in the third book of a financial market. All major capital market will be analyzed with high technical understanding and worked up. The F.A.Z.-Share Index and the F.A.Z.-term indicator for decision-makers and readers are real classics. Accompany the variety of sport and its events from around the world with reports and commentaries, the strengths of the sports editors. On Monday, the sport receives a book, devoted primarily to King Football. Feature: to artistic or intellectual positions daily to acquire and to describe developments in culture and science is the objective of the cultural section. This goes beyond the discussion of literature, theater and opera also, for the reader to share in discussions dealing with the future of our and other societies. The feature editorial concern and obligation is the same time. Rhein-Main-Zeitung: In and around Frankfurt, the reader gets, in principle, two newspapers: the newspaper for Germany and the Rhein-Main-Zeitung, a landmark in the German newspaper today. The RMZ also deals with politics, economy, culture, science and sport - with a clear view of the city and the region. Special pages: On different days of the week appear additional supplements and special pages such as Tuesdays "Technology and engine," on Wednesday it is "Nature and Science" and the "humanities", on Thursday the "Travel Journal", on Friday the "real estate market." On Saturday there is "Images and times" and the "art market". Careers are on Saturdays in major German job market and in the "Career and Opportunity". Facebook: http://www.facebook.com/faz Twitter: https://twitter.com/FAZ_NET This Outlet offers RSS (Really Simple Syndication).
Language(s): German
Readership: Readership includes civil servants, company directors, senior and middle managers, university students and academics.
ADVERTISING RATES:
SCC .... EUR 770,00
Mechanical Data: No. of Columns (Display): 8, Col Widths (Display): 45 mm, Type Area: 528 x 371 mm
Copy instructions: *Copy Date:* 1 day prior to publication
Supplement(s): audiophil; chrismon; Frankfurter Allgemeine Piazza; The Red Bulletin; Start frei; taktvoll; Z Die Schönen Seiten
NATIONAL DAILY & SUNDAY NEWSPAPERS: National Daily Newspapers

FRANKFURTER ALLGEMEINE HOCHSCHULANZEIGER
730380G83-5220
Editorial: Hellerhofstr. 2, 60327 FRANKFURT
Tel: 69 75911359 **Fax:** 69 75911360
Email: j.krieg@faz.de **Web site:** http://www.hochschulanzeiger.de
Freq: 6 issues yearly; **Annual Sub.:** EUR 8,40; **Circ:** 234,358
Editor: Josef Krieg
Profile: Students' magazine.
Language(s): German
ADVERTISING RATES:
Full Page Mono .... EUR 13052
Full Page Colour .... EUR 16316
Mechanical Data: Type Area: 272 x 200 mm, No. of Columns (Display): 4, Col Widths (Display): 47 mm
Copy instructions: *Copy Date:* 28 days prior to publication
CONSUMER: STUDENT PUBLICATIONS

FRANKFURTER ALLGEMEINE HOCHSCHULANZEIGER.DE
1621285G62H-1180
Editorial: Hellerhofstr. 2, 60327 FRANKFURT
Tel: 69 75911639 **Fax:** 69 75912330
Email: gabriele.sonntag@faz.de **Web site:** http://www.hochschulanzeiger.de
Freq: Weekly; **Cover Price:** Paid; **Circ:** 200,000 Unique Users
Editor: Gabriele Sonntag
Profile: Ezine: Students' magazine.
Language(s): German
BUSINESS: CHURCH & SCHOOL EQUIPMENT & EDUCATION: Careers

FRANKFURTER ALLGEMEINE SONNTAGSZEITUNG
727818G65B-3
Editorial: Hellerhofstr. 2, 60327 FRANKFURT
Tel: 69 75910 **Fax:** 69 75911743
Email: sonntagszeitung@faz.de **Web site:** http://www.faz.net
Freq: Weekly; **Circ:** 385,970
Editor: Holger Steltzner; **Advertising Manager:** Andreas Formen
Profile: People like to take things at a more leisurely pace on a Sunday, be it the process of actually getting up, having breakfast or reading the paper. People also like to indulge themselves a little on Sundays, perhaps with a third cup of coffee or another croissant. So if their Sunday paper is also a little out of the ordinary, for example with an unusual front page design, a large photo or an unexpected illustration, then so much the better. People are encouraged to read on when the inside pages offer even more: background reports, bold opinions, eye-opening interviews, well-informed portraits, delicious gossip and useful tips. This neatly sums up the Frankfurter Allgemeine Sonntagszeitung, which has been giving readers an informative and entertaining reading experience on the day of rest since autumn 2001. And it has been so successful that it has become an integral part of the perfect Sunday for more than a million readers. The F.A.S. is not merely a Sunday paper, nor is it the seventh edition of the F.A.Z. in the week. It is a weekly paper that appears on a Sunday, addressing issues of the past week and of the week to come. Its tone is light and lively. But there is nevertheless no shortage of news, including any Saturday evening events – the last pieces of news are incorporated into the F.A.S. at 10:00 p.m.. How else can the F.A.S.be distinguished from the F.A.Z.. It has a seven-column rather than a six-column layout. It also uses a different typeface, its name appears in blue, and is put together by a different team. It is a team of around 50 editors who are supported by the F.A..Z. correspondents around the world. As is the case with the F.A.Z., journalistic responsibility for the F.A.S. lies in the hands of the five editors? As the readers of the Sunday paper are people who like to indulge themselves, the paper is full of nothing but the remarkable. The comprehensive paper features: Politics-The stories behind the news of the day and the stories set to hit the front page further down the line. Sport-All the latest from the world of football, tennis or Formula 1. And who is the talk of the town in the seasonal sports. Features section-What literary figures are up to, what film-makers' dreams are made of, where musicians go wrong, and why the TV schedule is the way it is. Business-All the big and not so big business deals, the state of pensions and healthcare contributions, and what is next in line to be reformed. Money and more-Which way the stocks and shares are going, how best to invest your portfolio, and why avarice is not a sin. Society-What governs our social coexistence, what top chefs and designers have up their sleeves, and what celebrities really get up to. Science-What doctors hope to be able to achieve, what scientists believe in, and how magnificent the world is. Additionally Travel, technology and cars, property, careers and recruitment. Facebook: http://www.facebook.com/faz Twitter: https://twitter.com/FAZ_NET This Outlet offers RSS (Really Simple Syndication).
Language(s): German
ADVERTISING RATES:
SCC .... EUR 652,00
Mechanical Data: Type Area: 528 x 371 mm, No. of Columns (Display): 8, Col Widths (Display): 45 mm
Copy instructions: *Copy Date:* 3 days prior to publication
Supplement(s): Berliner Zugpferde; Hamburg: Das Magazin aus der Metropole; Main feeling
NATIONAL DAILY & SUNDAY NEWSPAPERS: National Sunday Newspapers

DIE FRANKFURTER FAMILIENSEITEN
1842742G74N-956
Editorial: Hellweg 1, 15234 FRANKFURT
Tel: 335 2288794 **Fax:** 335 2288794
Email: red@frankfurterfamilienseiten.de **Web site:** http://www.frankfurterfamilienseiten.de
Freq: Monthly; **Cover Price:** Free; **Circ:** 10,000
Editor: Katja Gehring
Profile: Family event magazine for Frankfurt.
Language(s): German
Mechanical Data: Type Area: x 230 mm, No. of Columns (Display): 5, Col Widths (Display): 44 mm
Copy instructions: *Copy Date:* 7 days prior to publication

FRANKFURTER NEUE PRESSE
727825G67B-5220
Editorial: Frankenallee 71, 60327 FRANKFURT
Tel: 69 75010 **Fax:** 69 75014232
Email: redaktion@fnp.de **Web site:** http://www.fnp.de
Freq: 312 issues yearly; **Circ:** 92,182
Editor: Rainer M. Gefeller; **News Editor:** Dieter Sattler
Profile: The Frankfurter Neue Presse is inside major regional daily newspaper. Together with its regional editions Höchster Kreisblatt, Nassauische Neue

Presse and Taunus Zeitung it stands for regionality and journalistic skills. The Frankfurter Neue Presse, the regional newspaper for the people in and around Frankfurt. The proximity to her readers is the FNP of particular concern - that is why the local and regional base their essential core competency. The editors of the newspaper site research and report on all those issues that concern people, without neglecting the national and international events. The Frankfurter Neue Presse will provide guidance to people - by background reports, interviews with experts and engaged comments. This will not only founded the FNP report, but also be entertaining and exciting. This results in a newspaper that arrives from the readers. Facebook: http://www.facebook.com/pages/FNP/115994585097103 Twitter: http://twitter.com/fnp_zeitung This Outlet offers RSS (Really Simple Syndication).
Language(s): German
ADVERTISING RATES:
SCC .... EUR 129,60
Mechanical Data: Type Area: 528 x 371 mm, No. of Columns (Display): 8, Col Widths (Display): 45 mm
Copy instructions: *Copy Date:* 1 day prior to publication
REGIONAL DAILY & SUNDAY NEWSPAPERS: Regional Daily Newspapers

FRANKFURTER RUNDSCHAU

727826G65A-120
Editorial: Karl-Gerold-Platz 1, 60594 FRANKFURT
Tel: 69 21991 **Fax:** 69 21993666
Email: chefredaktion@fr-online.de **Web site:** http://www.fr-online.de
Freq: 312 issues yearly; **Circ:** 145,691
Editor: Joachim Frank; **Advertising Manager:** Oliver Moll
Profile: Opinion leaders and innovators, responsible and politically interested people, cosmopolitan and regionally rooted, trendsetters and advertising savvy. This draws heavily from the readers of the Frankfurter Rundschau. This high quality of readers and users is the result of a progressive and dynamic product development on all channels and the adherence to the typical FR-quality journalism. For this, the Frankfurter Rundschau with numerous awards at the European Newspaper Award and also the Wächterpreis of the German daily press, 2009, the Hessian Journalist Award 2009 or the future price of the German travel journalists in 2010 rewarded. Effective for the advertising industry, it is then, if not only the quality of true-to-reach potential customers, but also in the abundant number available. According to media analysis achieved in 2010 dailies, the Frankfurter Rundschau 365 000 readers, according to the Allensbach market analysis and advertising 494 000 2010 even readers. In the AWA represents an increase of 86,000 readers over the previous year. Twitter: http://twitter.com/fronline This Outlet offers RSS (Really Simple Syndication).
Language(s): German
Readership: Readership includes the business community, academics, teachers, university students and civil servants.
ADVERTISING RATES:
SCC .... EUR 310,00
Mechanical Data: Type Area: 370 x 245 mm, No. of Columns (Display): 5, Col Widths (Display): 45 mm
Copy instructions: *Copy Date:* 1 day prior to publication
Supplement(s): chrismon; doppio; FR Reisen Magazin; Heimspiel; journalplaner Rhein-Main; Start frei; Urlaub
NATIONAL DAILY & SUNDAY NEWSPAPERS: National Daily Newspapers

FRANKFURTER RUNDSCHAU AM FREITAG MITTAG

727827G72-3964
Editorial: Karl-Gerold-Platz 1, 60594 FRANKFURT
Tel: 69 21991 **Fax:** 69 21993521
Web site: http://www.fr-online.de
Freq: Weekly; **Cover Price:** EUR 1,80; **Circ:** 125,360
Editor: Joachim Frank; **News Editor:** Edgar Auth; **Advertising Manager:** Alexander Neetzow
Profile: Regional weekly covering politics, culture, economics, sports, travel, technology and the arts.
Language(s): German
ADVERTISING RATES:
SCC .... EUR 304,00
Mechanical Data: Type Area: 370 x 245 mm, No. of Columns (Display): 5, Col Widths (Display): 45 mm
Copy instructions: *Copy Date:* 1 day prior to publication
LOCAL NEWSPAPERS

FRÄNKISCHE LANDESZEITUNG

727774G67B-5240
Editorial: Nürnberger Str. 9, 91522 ANSBACH
Tel: 981 95000 **Fax:** 981 13961
Email: redaktion@flz.de **Web site:** http://www.flz.de
Freq: 312 issues yearly; **Circ:** 47,470
Editor: Peter M. Szymanowski; **Advertising Manager:** Jürgen Lang
Profile: Daily newspaper with regional news and a local sports section.
Language(s): German
ADVERTISING RATES:
SCC .... EUR 104,40
Mechanical Data: Type Area: 430 x 280 mm, No. of Columns (Display): 6, Col Widths (Display): 45 mm
Copy instructions: *Copy Date:* 1 day prior to publication
REGIONAL DAILY & SUNDAY NEWSPAPERS: Regional Daily Newspapers

FRÄNKISCHE NACHRICHTEN

727775G67B-5260
Editorial: Schmiederstr. 19, 97941 TAUBERBISCHOFSHEIM **Tel:** 9341 830
Fax: 9341 83122
Email: red.tbb@fraenkische-nachrichten.de **Web site:** http://www.fnweb.de
Freq: 312 issues yearly; **Circ:** 27,211
Advertising Manager: Michael Hollfelder
Profile: Daily newspaper with regional news and a local sports section. Facebook: http://www.facebook.com/pages/morgenweb/105113719526519?ref=search&sid=1469388759.1280026596..1 This Outlet offers RSS (Really Simple Syndication).
Language(s): German
ADVERTISING RATES:
SCC .... EUR 69,10
Mechanical Data: Type Area: 490 x 320 mm, No. of Columns (Display): 7, Col Widths (Display): 44 mm
Copy instructions: *Copy Date:* 2 days prior to publication
REGIONAL DAILY & SUNDAY NEWSPAPERS: Regional Daily Newspapers

FRÄNKISCHE WOCHENPOST - AUSG. A TAUBERBISCHOFSHEIM

727787G72-3988
Editorial: Schmiederstr. 19, 97941 TAUBERBISCHOFSHEIM **Tel:** 9341 83105
Fax: 9341 83122
Email: red.tbb@fraenkische-nachrichten.de **Web site:** http://www.fnweb.de
Freq: Weekly; **Cover Price:** Free; **Circ:** 39,888
Editor: Paul von Brandenstein; **Advertising Manager:** Michael Hollfelder
Profile: Advertising journal (house-to-house) concentrating on local stories.
Language(s): German
ADVERTISING RATES:
Full Page Mono .... EUR 4048
Full Page Colour .... EUR 5248
Mechanical Data: Type Area: 490 x 320 mm, No. of Columns (Display): 7, Col Widths (Display): 44 mm
Copy instructions: *Copy Date:* 3 days prior to publication
LOCAL NEWSPAPERS

FRÄNKISCHER ANZEIGER

727776G67B-5280
Editorial: Erlbacher Str. 102, 91541 ROTHENBURG
Tel: 9861 400120 **Fax:** 9861 40016
Email: info@rotabene.de **Web site:** http://www.fraenkischer-anzeiger.de
Freq: 312 issues yearly; **Circ:** 5,490
Profile: Daily newspaper with regional news and a local sports section.
Language(s): German
ADVERTISING RATES:
SCC .... EUR 32,80
Mechanical Data: Type Area: 430 x 280 mm, No. of Columns (Display): 6, Col Widths (Display): 45 mm
Copy instructions: *Copy Date:* 1 day prior to publication
Supplement(s): Die Linde
REGIONAL DAILY & SUNDAY NEWSPAPERS: Regional Daily Newspapers

FRÄNKISCHER TAG

727779G67B-5300
Editorial: Gutenbergstr. 1, 96050 BAMBERG
Tel: 951 1880 **Fax:** 951 188323
Email: redaktion@infranken.de **Web site:** http://www.infranken.de
Freq: 312 issues yearly; **Circ:** 82,859
Editor: Joachim Widmann; **Advertising Manager:** Philipp Gatz
Profile: Regional daily newspaper covering politics, economics, sports, travel and technology. Facebook: http://www.facebook.com/inFranken http://twitter.com/#!/infranken This Outlet offers RSS (Really Simple Syndication).
Language(s): German
ADVERTISING RATES:
SCC .... EUR 91,40
Mechanical Data: Type Area: 430 x 285 mm, No. of Columns (Display): 6, Col Widths (Display): 45 mm
Copy instructions: *Copy Date:* 1 day prior to publication
Supplement(s): doppio; Lebens Raum; Lebens Raum; Lebens Raum; Rathaus Journal; rtv
REGIONAL DAILY & SUNDAY NEWSPAPERS: Regional Daily Newspapers

FRANKREICH ERLEBEN

1732355G89A-12214
Editorial: Erich-Weinert-Str. 22, 10439 BERLIN
Tel: 30 50178145 **Fax:** 30 920372065
Email: info@frankreicherleben.de **Web site:** http://www.frankreicherleben.de
Freq: 6 issues yearly; **Annual Sub.:** EUR 25,20; **Circ:** 30,000
Advertising Manager: Stefan Wrage
Profile: German-language magazine that exclusively presents France as a holiday destination, while offering fascinating insights into the everyday life of the French. Every two months, the editors of this together to 100 pages a colorful variety of topics, from the travel, culture, lifestyle, luxury, wine, politics, economy and society.
Language(s): German
ADVERTISING RATES:
Full Page Colour .... EUR 3500
Mechanical Data: Type Area: 247 x 180 mm
Copy instructions: *Copy Date:* 40 days prior to publication

FRANZZ

727841G89C-780
Editorial: Johann-Wilhelm-Lindlar-Str. 9, 51465 BERGISCH GLADBACH **Tel:** 2202 9369010
Fax: 2202 9369022
Email: redaktion@franzz.de **Web site:** http://www.franzz.de
Freq: Monthly; **Cover Price:** Free; **Circ:** 19,847
Editor: Klaus Pehle; **Advertising Manager:** Klaus Schell
Profile: Guide to events in Bergisch-Gladbach.
Language(s): German
Readership: Read by local residents.
ADVERTISING RATES:
Full Page Mono .... EUR 1457
Full Page Colour .... EUR 1457
Mechanical Data: Type Area: 270 x 190 mm, No. of Columns (Display): 4, Col Widths (Display): 44 mm
Copy instructions: *Copy Date:* 15 days prior to publication
CONSUMER: HOLIDAYS & TRAVEL: Entertainment Guides

FRÄSEN + BOHREN

2053227G19E-1973
Editorial: Neustr. 163, 42553 VELBERT
Tel: 2053 981251 **Fax:** 2053 981256
Email: redaktion@fachverlag-moeller.de **Web site:** http://www.fachverlag-moeller.de
Freq: 6 issues yearly; **Annual Sub.:** EUR 30,00; **Circ:** 10,000
Editor: Erik Möller; **Advertising Manager:** Erik Möller
Profile: Magazine providing information about using conventional and automatic machinery.
Language(s): German
ADVERTISING RATES:
Full Page Mono .... EUR 1900
Full Page Colour .... EUR 3100
Mechanical Data: Type Area: 260 x 180 mm, No. of Columns (Display): 4, Col Widths (Display): 44 mm
Copy instructions: *Copy Date:* 14 days prior to publication

FRAU AKTUELL

727844G74A-1100
Editorial: Münchener Str. 101/09, 85737 ISMANING
Tel: 89 272700 **Fax:** 89 272707290
Email: frauaktuell@waz-zeitschriften.de
Freq: Weekly; **Cover Price:** EUR 1,50; **Circ:** 193,801
Editor: Anne Hoffmann
Profile: Always top of the events - with exciting and entertaining features on celebrities from society, film, show and nobility. Woman currently move through themes from the world of fashion, beauty, cooking, finance and law. The great health magazine including interviews with experts and professors rounds out the editorial profile.
Language(s): German
ADVERTISING RATES:
Full Page Mono .... EUR 5890
Full Page Colour .... EUR 5890
Mechanical Data: Type Area: 260 x 195 mm, No. of Columns (Display): 4, Col Widths (Display): 45 mm
Copy instructions: *Copy Date:* 30 days prior to publication
CONSUMER: WOMEN'S INTEREST CONSUMER MAGAZINES: Women's Interest

FRAU IM BLICK

1828429G74A-3579
Editorial: Sieker Landstr. 126, 22143 HAMBURG
Tel: 40 6739780 **Fax:** 40 673991020
Email: wmb@cpvkg.de **Web site:** http://www.conpart-verlag.de
Freq: Monthly; **Cover Price:** EUR 0,75; **Circ:** 77,574
Editor: Wolfgang M. Biehler
Profile: The magazine contains the following categories: Love & Life | Beauty & Cosmetics | Cooking & Baking | Fashion & Chic | Rates & Win | Royals & Society | VIPs & Celebrities | Travel & Services | Ratings & more.
Language(s): German
ADVERTISING RATES:
Full Page Mono .... EUR 5000
Full Page Colour .... EUR 5000
Mechanical Data: Type Area: 272 x 209 mm, No. of Columns (Display): 4

FRAU IM LEBEN

727869G87-4280
Editorial: Lindenstr. 20, 50674 KÖLN
Tel: 221 277570 **Fax:** 221 2775710
Email: frauimleben@bayard-media.de **Web site:** http://www.f-i-l.de
Freq: Monthly; **Annual Sub.:** EUR 28,80; **Circ:** 135,488
Editor: Jürgen Sinn; **Advertising Manager:** Armin Baier
Profile: High Quality Advisor magazine provides practical answers to all questions that interest people in the second phase of life really. Frau im Leben will help readers to enjoy this phase of life as rich and valuable. This high level of consulting expertise, the magazine has led to an unusually high proportion of subscribers. The high level of quality is also expressed in a long time reader of Frau im Leben of the reader. With five major subject areas, the magazine covers all important aspects of life of people off in the second half of life: health and fitness, beauty and fashion, food, drink, enjoyment, Food & Wine and Travel & Culture.
Language(s): German
ADVERTISING RATES:
Full Page Mono .... EUR 8280
Full Page Colour .... EUR 8280
Mechanical Data: Type Area: 217 x 175 mm, No. of Columns (Display): 4, Col Widths (Display): 39 mm
CONSUMER: RELIGIOUS

FRAU IM SPIEGEL

727870G74A-1120
Editorial: Münchener Str. 101/09, 85737 ISMANING
Tel: 89 272700 **Fax:** 89 272708993
Email: redaktion@frau-im-spiegel.de **Web site:** http://www.frau-im-spiegel.de
Freq: Weekly; **Annual Sub.:** EUR 83,20; **Circ:** 292,096
Editor: Claudia Cieslarczyk
Profile: Genus founder of People magazine in Germany with the best mix of entertainment and service: Outstanding needle skills, serious and credible Star reporting that visually brilliant service world "Beautiful Life " and an informed medical part of the woman in the mirror coverage convinced by their high. Consulting competence and integrity and thus belongs to the premium people magazines.
Language(s): German
ADVERTISING RATES:
Full Page Mono .... EUR 12600
Full Page Colour .... EUR 12600
Mechanical Data: Type Area: 260 x 196 mm, No. of Columns (Display): 4, Col Widths (Display): 46 mm
Copy instructions: *Copy Date:* 22 days prior to publication
CONSUMER: WOMEN'S INTEREST CONSUMER MAGAZINES: Women's Interest

FRAU IM TREND

1616134G74A-3356
Editorial: Hubert-Burda-Platz 1, 77652 OFFENBURG
Tel: 781 843117 **Fax:** 781 843227
Email: margot.nikolic@burda.com
Freq: Weekly; **Annual Sub.:** EUR 49,40; **Circ:** 333,304
Editor: Thomas Otto; **Advertising Manager:** Antje Damer
Profile: Woman in the trend is the latest info-magazine for women who take their lives actively in the hand and make timely do. A utilitarian magazine that her emotional response more than dry facts and gives readers the inside in such a pleasant way through their world accompanied.
Language(s): German
ADVERTISING RATES:
Full Page Mono .... EUR 16500
Full Page Colour .... EUR 16500
Mechanical Data: Type Area: 264 x 209 mm
CONSUMER: WOMEN'S INTEREST CONSUMER MAGAZINES: Women's Interest

FRAU MIT HERZ

727871G74A-1140
Editorial: Rotweg 8, 76532 BADEN-BADEN
Tel: 7221 3501132 **Fax:** 7221 3501133
Email: fraumitherz@klambt.de **Web site:** http://www.klambt.de
Freq: Weekly; **Annual Sub.:** EUR 91,00; **Circ:** 90,268
Editor: Barbara Jung
Profile: Frau mit Herz is a recent colorful tabloid magazine with modern graphics and fully colored. As a classic in the segment of the weekly entertaining women's magazines is Frau mit Herz for over 50 years in the world of European nobility at home and informed since generations in the course of time length on the enigmatic life of crowned heads, the Life-Style of attractive princesses and princes, of fateful events in the shadow of the crown. The current approach takes into account not reports from the royal and nobility houses equivalent to the whole world of showbiz with stories about film and television stars and the world of international society, with detailed reports on the glamorous life of high society. Frau mit Herz shall in all current issues particular attention to the "story behind the story". Frau mit Herz-readers are about the background moving events always well informed. In the service and advice part takes Frau mit Herz all the important subjects of interest to women: When new and helpful information from the medical as well as a large advice section on housing, nutrition and recipes, fashion and beauty, travel and nature, law and advice. At all subjects is the name of Frau mit Herz program: the readers, will be in addition to the high utility value, and emotionally attuned to the issues - just with the heart. Rounding out the issue mix with thrilling stories of fate, life coaching and a puzzle part with attractive prizes, a short TV program for the week, horoscopes and humor.
Language(s): German
Readership: Aimed at women aged 40 plus.
ADVERTISING RATES:
Full Page Mono .... EUR 4560
Full Page Colour .... EUR 4560
Mechanical Data: Type Area: 260 x 195 mm, No. of Columns (Display): 4, Col Widths (Display): 45 mm
Copy instructions: *Copy Date:* 28 days prior to publication
CONSUMER: WOMEN'S INTEREST CONSUMER MAGAZINES: Women's Interest

FRAU MIT HERZ EINMACHEN & EINKOCHEN

2086896G74P-1395
Editorial: Rotweg 8, 76532 BADEN-BADEN
Tel: 7221 3501132 **Fax:** 7221 3501133
Email: fraumitherz@klambt.de **Web site:** http://www.klambt.de
Freq: Annual; **Circ:** 80,000
Profile: Canning is absolutely a trend. It's fun, tastes good and you know what's inside. Homemade treats are always a very special gift. There is something for every taste: Fruity jams, spicy chutney, spicy pickles, fine syrup recipes, sophisticated jellies - just everything is delicious!.

Language(s): German
ADVERTISING RATES:
Full Page Mono .... EUR 5370
Full Page Colour .... EUR 5370
Mechanical Data: Type Area: 250 x 195 mm, No. of Columns (Display): 4, Col Widths (Display): 45 mm
Copy instructions: *Copy Date:* 28 days prior to publication

FRAU MIT HERZ MUFFINS & CUPCAKES
2086897G74P-1396
Editorial: Rotweg 8, 76532 BADEN-BADEN
Tel: 7221 3501132 **Fax:** 7221 3501133
Email: fraumitherz@klambt.de **Web site:** http://www.klambt.de
Freq: Annual; **Circ:** 80,000
Profile: Cupcakes are the new stars of heaven of baking: Quickly done and decorated with delicious creams, they are always a sin worth. Under the motto "small is beautiful" can be found here, sweet and savory temptations: Cupcakes - trendy Minis with sweet hood, savory tartlets: Hearty on the fine art, Macarons - it melts on the tongue.
Language(s): German
ADVERTISING RATES:
Full Page Mono .... EUR 5370
Full Page Colour .... EUR 5370
Mechanical Data: Type Area: 250 x 195 mm, No. of Columns (Display): 4, Col Widths (Display): 45 mm
Copy instructions: *Copy Date:* 28 days prior to publication

FRAU MIT HERZ OFENHITS
2086898G74P-1397
Editorial: Rotweg 8, 76532 BADEN-BADEN
Tel: 7221 3501132 **Fax:** 7221 3501133
Email: fraumitherz@klambt.de **Web site:** http://www.klambt.de
Freq: Annual; **Circ:** 80,000
Profile: Lots of oven-Stars await you in this issue. Whether sweet pies, creamy gratin, spicy meatloaf, delicious with potatoes or international cuisine - all meals are so delicious that you definitely do not make only once! Incidentally, the recipes are still low-priced to - no dish costs more than 1.50 € per person ...
Language(s): German
ADVERTISING RATES:
Full Page Mono .... EUR 5370
Full Page Colour .... EUR 5370
Mechanical Data: Type Area: 250 x 195 mm, No. of Columns (Display): 4, Col Widths (Display): 45 mm
Copy instructions: *Copy Date:* 28 days prior to publication

FRAU MIT HERZ SÜSSES AUS OMAS BACKBUCH
2086899G74P-1398
Editorial: Rotweg 8, 76532 BADEN-BADEN
Tel: 7221 3501132 **Fax:** 7221 3501133
Email: fraumitherz@klambt.de **Web site:** http://www.klambt.de
Freq: Annual; **Circ:** 80,000
Profile: These recipes will be a warm-hearted. The tempting smell of sweet semolina dumplings, cherry Michel or a juicy sponge cake with sunken fruit awakens memories of Grandma's goodies: waffles, baking with fruit, heavenly dumplings, delicate dessert ideas.
Language(s): German
ADVERTISING RATES:
Full Page Mono .... EUR 5370
Full Page Colour .... EUR 5370
Mechanical Data: Type Area: 250 x 195 mm, No. of Columns (Display): 4, Col Widths (Display): 45 mm
Copy instructions: *Copy Date:* 28 days prior to publication

FRAU + MUTTER
727875G87-4300
Editorial: Prinz-Georg-Str. 44, 40477 DÜSSELDORF
Tel: 211 4499240 **Fax:** 211 4499275
Email: redaktion@kfdfum.de **Web site:** http://www.frauundmutter.de
Freq: 11 issues yearly; **Circ:** 556,150
Editor: Barbara Leckel
Profile: Magazine for Catholic women.
Language(s): German
CONSUMER: RELIGIOUS

FRAU & POLITIK
727877G82-3000
Editorial: Klingelhöferstr. 8, 10785 BERLIN
Tel: 30 22070451 **Fax:** 30 22070439
Email: fu@cdu.de
Freq: 6 issues yearly; **Annual Sub.:** EUR 15,00; **Circ:** 3,000
Editor: Silke Adam
Profile: Magazine concerning the involvement of women in politics.
Language(s): German
CONSUMER: CURRENT AFFAIRS & POLITICS

FRAU VON HEUTE
1616135G74A-3357
Editorial: Axel-Springer-Platz 1, 20355 HAMBURG
Tel: 40 34725494 **Fax:** 40 34728860
Email: redaktion@frauvonheute.de **Web site:** http://www.frauvonheute.de
Freq: Weekly; **Annual Sub.:** EUR 44,20; **Circ:** 167,376
Editor: Sandra Immoor; **Advertising Manager:** Claudia Blumenberg
Profile: FRAU von HEUTE offers relaxing entertainment with exciting celebrity interviews, exclusive reports, moving stories, puzzles and knowledge sites. FRAU von HEUTE offers real everyday help with an extensive guide part. From medicine to partnership from money to law. A special highlight: the 5-minutes guide for the week - all important dates, current judgments and recommendations at a glance. Service to all areas of everyday life: From beauty to diet advice, from DIY tips to decorating ideas.
Language(s): German
ADVERTISING RATES:
Full Page Mono .... EUR 14060
Full Page Colour .... EUR 14060
Mechanical Data: Type Area: 255 x 207 mm, No. of Columns (Display): 4, Col Widths (Display): 49 mm
CONSUMER: WOMEN'S INTEREST CONSUMER MAGAZINES: Women's Interest

FRAUEN KALENDER
1657002G74A-3422
Editorial: Fliethstr. 86, 41061 MÖNCHENGLADBACH
Tel: 2161 253611 **Fax:** 2161 253619
Email: gleichstellungsstelle@moenchengladbach.de
Web site: http://www.moenchengladbach.de
Freq: Half-yearly; **Cover Price:** Free; **Circ:** 8,000
Editor: Brinkmann
Profile: Calendar for women.
Language(s): German

FRAUENARZT
727848G56A-3740
Editorial: Paul-Heyse-Str. 28, 80336 MÜNCHEN
Tel: 89 51616175 **Fax:** 89 51616199
Email: frauenarzt@publimed.de **Web site:** http://www.publimed.de
Freq: Monthly; Free to qualifying individuals
Annual Sub.: EUR 155,60; **Circ:** 19,358
Editor: Christina Usbeck; **Advertising Manager:** Monika Fürst-Ladner
Profile: Official magazine of the Professional Association of Gynaecologists and the German Society for Gynaecology and Midwifery.
Language(s): German
ADVERTISING RATES:
Full Page Mono .... EUR 4040
Full Page Colour .... EUR 5600
Mechanical Data: Type Area: 236 x 174 mm, No. of Columns (Display): 3, Col Widths (Display): 54 mm
Copy instructions: *Copy Date:* 30 days prior to publication
Supplement(s): Gynäkologie aktuell
BUSINESS: HEALTH & MEDICAL

FRAUENHEILKUNDE UP2DATE
1799758G56A-11466
Editorial: Universitätsstr. 21, 91054 ERLANGEN
Email: fk-direktion@uk-erlangen.de **Web site:** http://www.thieme.de/fz/frauenheilkunde-u2d.html
Freq: 6 issues yearly; **Annual Sub.:** EUR 194,40; **Circ:** 2,300
Editor: Matthias W. Beckmann
Profile: 6 issues per year, each with four completed continuing education units to bring you on the latest state of knowledge: Brush up on your specialist knowledge: The state-of-the-art understandable recycled into science-based review articles. Perfect accompaniment by the training: In three years, covers all mandatory subjects of further education regulations. Guaranteed Functional: Maximum practical benefits through real case studies and consistent focus on clinical practice. Every edition with 12 CME points per year, you can earn up to 72 CME points. You can put together your personal Textbook: The training units are separately bound to refer individually and can be included in up2date-ring binder to archive individually.
Language(s): German
ADVERTISING RATES:
Full Page Mono .... EUR 1890
Full Page Colour .... EUR 3030
Mechanical Data: Type Area: 256 x 180 mm

FRAUENRAT
1609397G74A-3313
Editorial: Axel-Springer-Str. 54a, 10117 BERLIN
Tel: 30 20456917 **Fax:** 30 20456944
Email: u.helwerth@frauenrat.de **Web site:** http://www.frauenrat.de
Freq: 6 issues yearly; **Annual Sub.:** EUR 23,52; **Circ:** 2,000
Editor: Ulrike Helwerth
Profile: Magazine containing information for women.
Language(s): German

FREEDOMBMX
727883G77C-100
Editorial: An der Linde 11, 50668 KÖLN
Tel: 221 9140010 **Fax:** 221 9140099
Email: kay@freedombmx.de **Web site:** http://www.freedombmx.de
Freq: 6 issues yearly; **Annual Sub.:** EUR 18,00; **Circ:** 25,500
Editor: Kay Clauberg; **Advertising Manager:** Ingo Kraus
Profile: Magazine about BMX bikes and cycling. All editors know - sometimes decades - the BMX scene, driving himself and BMX are represented in all relevant german and international events. Trends and innovations in the market to be addressed so not only early, but the active part in shaping and shaped. Facebook: http://www.facebook.com/freedombmx This Outlet offers RSS (Really Simple Syndication).
Language(s): German
ADVERTISING RATES:
Full Page Mono .... EUR 2400
Full Page Colour .... EUR 3200
Mechanical Data: Type Area: 300 x 230 mm
CONSUMER: MOTORING & CYCLING: Cycling

FREI KÖRPER KULTUR
727431G91R-30
Editorial: Finkenbecke 31, 44894 BOCHUM
Tel: 234 9233770 **Fax:** 234 9244770
Email: redaktion@dfk.org **Web site:** http://www.dfk.org
Freq: 6 issues yearly; Free to qualifying individuals
Annual Sub.: EUR 18,00; **Circ:** 16,000
Editor: Michaela Toepper; **Advertising Manager:** Michaela Toepper
Profile: Magazine for naturists.
Language(s): German
ADVERTISING RATES:
Full Page Mono .... EUR 1500
Full Page Colour .... EUR 1500
Mechanical Data: Type Area: 230 x 180 mm
Copy instructions: *Copy Date:* 30 days prior to publication
CONSUMER: RECREATION & LEISURE: Recreation & Leisure Related

FREIBERG AKTUELL
747450G89A-12159
Editorial: Kirchgässchen 1, 09599 FREIBERG
Tel: 3731 37624100 **Fax:** 3731 65627410
Email: marion.schreiber@blick.de **Web site:** http://www.blick.de
Freq: Annual; **Cover Price:** EUR 3,90; **Circ:** 5,000
Editor: Marion Schreiber; **Advertising Manager:** Cornelia Wirbeleit
Profile: Magazine for city and region, concentrating on gastronomy, music, arts and events.
Language(s): German
ADVERTISING RATES:
Full Page Mono .... EUR 1058
Full Page Colour .... EUR 1058
Mechanical Data: Type Area: 265 x 195 mm

FREIBURGER HAUSBESITZER-ZEITUNG
727895G74K-220
Editorial: Erbprinzenstr. 7, 79098 FREIBURG
Tel: 761 380560 **Fax:** 761 3805660
Email: verband@haus-grund-freiburg.de **Web site:** http://www.haus-grund-freiburg.de
Freq: 10 issues yearly; **Circ:** 5,500
Editor: Manfred Harner
Profile: Newspaper focusing on the financial implications of home ownership.
Language(s): German
Readership: Aimed particularly at property owners living in the Freiburg area of Germany.
ADVERTISING RATES:
Full Page Mono .... EUR 920
Full Page Colour .... EUR 1242
Mechanical Data: Type Area: 270 x 189 mm, No. of Columns (Display): 4, Col Widths (Display): 45 mm
Copy instructions: *Copy Date:* 25 days prior to publication
CONSUMER: WOMEN'S INTEREST CONSUMER MAGAZINES: Home Purchase

FREIBURGER UNI-MAGAZIN
727901G83-4000
Editorial: Fahnenbergplatz, 79085 FREIBURG
Tel: 761 2034301 **Fax:** 761 2034285
Email: eva.opitz@pr.uni-freiburg.de
Freq: 6 issues yearly; **Annual Sub.:** EUR 13,00; **Circ:** 15,000
Editor: Eva Opitz; **Advertising Manager:** Mona Stegmaier
Profile: Magazine of the University of Freiburg.
Language(s): German
Readership: Read by University members.
ADVERTISING RATES:
Full Page Mono .... EUR 1585
Full Page Colour .... EUR 1957
Mechanical Data: Type Area: 262 x 190 mm, No. of Columns (Display): 3, Col Widths (Display): 60 mm
Copy instructions: *Copy Date:* 28 days prior to publication
CONSUMER: STUDENT PUBLICATIONS

FREIBURGER WOCHENBERICHT
727903G72-4012
Editorial: Basler Str. 88, 79115 FREIBURG
Tel: 761 45153545 **Fax:** 761 45153502
Email: redaktion@freiburger-wochenbericht.de **Web site:** http://www.freiburger-wochenbericht.de
Freq: Weekly; **Cover Price:** Free; **Circ:** 113,500
Editor: Sven Meyer; **Advertising Manager:** Martin Zenke
Profile: Advertising journal (house-to-house) concentrating on local stories.
Language(s): German
ADVERTISING RATES:
Full Page Mono .... EUR 6215
Full Page Colour .... EUR 8526
Mechanical Data: Type Area: 428 x 285 mm, No. of Columns (Display): 6, Col Widths (Display): 45 mm
Copy instructions: *Copy Date:* 1 day prior to publication
LOCAL NEWSPAPERS

DER FREIE ARZT
1615073G56A-11204
Editorial: Zur Tannenburg 43, 66280 SULZBACH
Tel: 6897 983886 **Fax:** 6897 983686
Email: carsten.kroeger@m-m-verlag.de **Web site:** http://www.m-m-verlag.de
Freq: 6 issues yearly; **Annual Sub.:** EUR 70,00; **Circ:** 4,306
Editor: Carsten Kröger; **Advertising Manager:** Renate Graf
Profile: Magazine for the medical profession.
Language(s): German
ADVERTISING RATES:
Full Page Mono .... EUR 1620
Full Page Colour .... EUR 2700
Mechanical Data: Type Area: 260 x 185 mm, No. of Columns (Display): 3, Col Widths (Display): 59 mm
Copy instructions: *Copy Date:* 18 days prior to publication
Official Journal of: Organ d. Zentrum z. Dokumentation f. Naturheilverfahren u. d. Akademie Mondiale
BUSINESS: HEALTH & MEDICAL

DER FREIE BERATER
1622676G1F-1533
Editorial: Seligenstädter Str. 71, 63322 RÖDERMARK **Tel:** 6074 3709872
Fax: 721 151349115
Email: redaktion@derfreieberater.de **Web site:** http://www.derfreieberater.de
Freq: Quarterly; **Annual Sub.:** EUR 12,00; **Circ:** 160,000
Editor: Andreas Müller-Alwart; **Advertising Manager:** Kerstin Shahin
Profile: Magazine containing information about the protection for financial investors.
Language(s): German
ADVERTISING RATES:
Full Page Mono .... EUR 3000
Full Page Colour .... EUR 3000
Mechanical Data: Type Area: 280 x 210 mm

DER FREIE BERATER
1622676G1F-1836
Editorial: Seligenstädter Str. 71, 63322 RÖDERMARK **Tel:** 6074 3709872
Fax: 721 151349115
Email: redaktion@derfreieberater.de **Web site:** http://www.derfreieberater.de
Freq: Quarterly; **Annual Sub.:** EUR 12,00; **Circ:** 160,000
Editor: Andreas Müller-Alwart; **Advertising Manager:** Kerstin Shahin
Profile: Magazine containing information about the protection for financial investors.
Language(s): German
ADVERTISING RATES:
Full Page Mono .... EUR 3000
Full Page Colour .... EUR 3000
Mechanical Data: Type Area: 280 x 210 mm

DER FREIE BERUF
727908G14A-2540
Editorial: Reinhardtstr. 34, 10117 BERLIN
Tel: 30 28444438 **Fax:** 30 28444479
Email: redaktion@der-freie-beruf.de **Web site:** http://www.der-freie-beruf.de
Freq: 9 issues yearly; Free to qualifying individuals
Annual Sub.: EUR 25,56; **Circ:** 5,000
Editor: Arno Metzler; **Advertising Manager:** Claudia Dittberner
Profile: Magazine about employment and business.
Language(s): German
Readership: Aimed at managers in commerce and local government.
ADVERTISING RATES:
Full Page Mono .... EUR 2020
Full Page Colour .... EUR 2800
Mechanical Data: Type Area: 247 x 188 mm, No. of Columns (Display): 4, Col Widths (Display): 44 mm
Copy instructions: *Copy Date:* 14 days prior to publication
BUSINESS: COMMERCE, INDUSTRY & MANAGEMENT

DAS FREIE FORUM
727911G2A-1480
Editorial: Postfach 1216, 72641 OBERBOIHINGEN
Tel: 7022 39941
Web site: http://www.gfp-netz.de
Freq: Quarterly; Free to qualifying individuals
Annual Sub.: EUR 16,00; **Circ:** 3,000
Editor: R. Kosiek
Profile: Official publication from the Society for Free Journalism.
Language(s): German

DAS FREIE MEDIKAMENT
1882117G37-1863
Editorial: Ubierstr. 71, 53173 BONN
Tel: 228 9574522 **Fax:** 228 9574590
Email: bah@bah-bonn.de **Web site:** http://www.bah-bonn.de
Freq: 8 issues yearly; **Annual Sub.:** EUR 15,00; **Circ:** 2,234
Editor: Heinz-Gert Schmickler
Profile: Magazine about all aspects of the medical profession.
Language(s): German

FREIE PRESSE 727918G67B-5320

Editorial: Brückenstr. 15, 09111 CHEMNITZ
Tel: 371 6560 **Fax:** 371 643042
Email: die.tageszeitung@freiepresse.de **Web site:** http://www.freiepresse.de
Freq: 312 issues yearly; **Circ:** 279,213
Editor: Torsten Kleditzsch; **News Editor:** Sascha Aurich; **Advertising Manager:** Sven Manske
Profile: Regional daily newspaper covering politics, economics, sports, travel and technology. http://www.facebook.com/freiepresse Twitter: http://twitter.com/freie_presse This Outlet offers RSS (Really Simple Syndication).
Language(s): German
ADVERTISING RATES:
SCC .... EUR 633,30
Mechanical Data: Type Area: 474 x 314 mm, No. of Columns (Display): 7, Col Widths (Display): 43 mm
Copy instructions: *Copy Date:* 2 days prior to publication
Supplement(s): capriccio; colori; rtv
REGIONAL DAILY & SUNDAY NEWSPAPERS: Regional Daily Newspapers

FREIE WERKSTATT 721618G31A-314

Editorial: Philipp-Nicolai-Weg 3, 58313 HERDECKE
Tel: 2330 91830 **Fax:** 2330 13570
Email: info@verlag-kaufhold.de **Web site:** http://www.verlag-kaufhold.de
Freq: 10 issues yearly; **Annual Sub.:** EUR 35,70; **Circ:** 13,495
Editor: Claudia Pfleging; **Advertising Manager:** Selina Wannke
Profile: Freie Werkstatt is intended as an independent, critical and strategic trade journal primarily to holders of qualified internal and masterful multi-brand shops in the car repair and service market. In addition, decision makers are the parts industry, wholesaling, and recently more and more car dealerships to readers. Uninfluenced by political memberships Freie Werkstatt shows the readers and leaders in their reporting on ways and means to secure the future of your company in the fiercely competitive market. In close cooperation with the parts industry, the wholesale and the workshop systems and partnerships, readers are given a practical overview of the current market. At the same ways for the utilization of our workshop are presented. The Freie Werkstatt is one of the clearly established journals in the market and is of medium-sized businesses a master mechanic in addition to technical journals regularly used for the alignment of daily business.
Language(s): German
Readership: Aimed at owners and managers of vehicle repair centres and those involved in the automotive industry.
ADVERTISING RATES:
Full Page Mono .... EUR 2473
Full Page Colour .... EUR 4551
Mechanical Data: Type Area: 257 x 184 mm, No. of Columns (Display): 3, Col Widths (Display): 57 mm
Copy instructions: *Copy Date:* 21 days prior to publication
BUSINESS: MOTOR TRADE: Motor Trade Accessories

FREIEPRESSE.DE 1621289G67B-16548

Editorial: Brückenstr. 15, 09111 CHEMNITZ
Tel: 371 6560 **Fax:** 371 643042
Email: thomas.boy@freiepresse.de **Web site:** http://www.freiepresse.de
Freq: Daily; **Cover Price:** Paid; **Circ:** 1,030,691 Unique Users
Editor: Thomas Boy
Profile: Internet portal of the regional daily newspaper Freie Presse. Here are the most important topics in Chemnitz, Zwickau, Vogtland, Erzgebirge, Germany and the world. The website covers the areas of Saxony, Germany, world, sport, business, stock market, guide, panorama, culture, multimedia, video, image galleries, events and weather Twitter: http://twitter.com/freie_presse This Outlet offers RSS (Really Simple Syndication).
Language(s): German
REGIONAL DAILY & SUNDAY NEWSPAPERS: Regional Daily Newspapers

FREIES WORT 727924G67B-5360

Editorial: Schützenstr. 2, 98527 SUHL
Tel: 3681 851200 **Fax:** 3681 851211
Email: redaktion@freies-wort.de **Web site:** http://www.freies-wort.de
Freq: 312 issues yearly; **Circ:** 81,629
Editor: Herbert Wessels; **Advertising Manager:** Thomas Graul
Profile: Regional daily newspaper with news on politics, economy, culture, sports, travel, technology, etc. As a regional newspaper is Freies Wort an important voice in Thuringia. The reports from our distribution area is of special importance. Freies Wort publishes eight local editions in South Thuringia. Editors and freelancers are always on hand to keep the reader on the latest news from their hometown and its region to date. Freies Wort represents journalistic interests in the region and is also involved socially. The recognized non-profit organization "Freies Wort hilft eV", which was founded in 1998, it has taken on the task with the help of donations through no fault of helping bureaucracy in need of people from the region or social institutions to support their work financially. About the activities of the club is informed. Twitter: http://twitter.com/freieswort This Outlet offers RSS (Really Simple Syndication).
Language(s): German
ADVERTISING RATES:
SCC .... EUR 283,60
Mechanical Data: No. of Columns (Display): 7, Type Area: 487 x 325 mm, Col Widths (Display): 44 mm
Copy instructions: *Copy Date:* 2 days prior to publication
Supplement(s): Amtsblatt des Landkreises Sonneberg; Anpfiff; Bikers Guide; Kinderzeitung; rtv; Wir Heiraten
REGIONAL DAILY & SUNDAY NEWSPAPERS: Regional Daily Newspapers

FREILASSINGER ANZEIGER 727932G67B-5380

Editorial: Schachtstr. 4, 83435 BAD REICHENHALL
Tel: 8651 9810 **Fax:** 8651 981160
Email: info@bgl-medien.de **Web site:** http://www.bgl-medien.de
Freq: 312 issues yearly; **Circ:** 10,058
Advertising Manager: Hans Straniak
Profile: The Freilassinger Anzeiger has its range in the city of Freilassing (14,500 inhabitants) and surrounding the Freilassing economic territory belonging to communities that have to exhibit their industries, an active business life. As a border town close to the gates of Salzburg and of district Berchtesgadener Land Freilassing in Berchtesgadener Land has a large traffic engineering importance, particularly since the city on the international route from Munich - Salzburg - Vienna, with branches to Bad Reichenhall - Berchtesgaden.
Language(s): German
ADVERTISING RATES:
SCC .... EUR 24,00
Mechanical Data: Type Area: 420 x 280 mm, No. of Columns (Display): 6, Col Widths (Display): 44 mm
Copy instructions: *Copy Date:* 1 day prior to publication
REGIONAL DAILY & SUNDAY NEWSPAPERS: Regional Daily Newspapers

FREISINGER TAGBLATT 727940G67B-5400

Editorial: Pfaffenrieder Str. 9, 82515 WOLFRATSHAUSEN **Tel:** 8171 2690
Fax: 8171 269240
Email: fsav@merkur-online.de **Web site:** http://www.merkur-online.de
Freq: 312 issues yearly; **Circ:** 13,615
Advertising Manager: Hans-Georg Bechthold
Profile: The Münchner Merkur with its own local newspapers, of which the Freisinger Tagblatt is one that, the leading regional newspaper brand in the Munich area - the most affluent area of Germany. The combination of newspaper and region is the foundation on which to build the success of the title. This is the newspaper not only the factual news agency, but forms a community of solidarity with its readers and the local community. The clear focus on local reporting creates a high regard to human reader loyalty. She presses one hand in the very high number of close to 180,000 subscribers. Also for the high reader-commitment is the loyalty of the total current 827 000 daily readers, the Münchner Merkur or one of its local newspapers usually read over many years. The Münchner Merkur with its own local newspapers is a newspaper for the whole family, tradition and modern life for one of the most beautiful regions of Germany unites. Reliable, informative, critical: the Münchner Merkur is the indispensable daily newspaper for the region. Facebook: http://www.facebook.com/pages/merkur-online.de/190176143327.
Language(s): German
ADVERTISING RATES:
SCC .... EUR 43,60
Mechanical Data: Type Area: 474 x 324 mm, No. of Columns (Display): 7, Col Widths (Display): 45 mm
Copy instructions: *Copy Date:* 1 day prior to publication
REGIONAL DAILY & SUNDAY NEWSPAPERS: Regional Daily Newspapers

DER FREITAG 727946G72-4024

Editorial: Hegelplatz 1, 10117 BERLIN
Tel: 30 2500870 **Fax:** 30 25008799
Email: info@freitag.de **Web site:** http://www.freitag.de
Freq: Weekly; **Annual Sub.:** EUR 145,60; **Circ:** 19,890
Editor: Philip Grassmann; **News Editor:** Ulrike Winkelmann; **Advertising Manager:** Johann Plank
Profile: der Freitag define quality journalism in the digital age for the German speaking again. Confident, ambitious and smart calls on der Freitag for social dialogue and discussion. And carries himself with critical and constructive opinions to this. der Freitag offers readers much more than breaking news, pointing to background information, international networking and information from all media channels. It allowed a relevant perspective on today's world - online and offline alike. der Freitag takes advantage of all the various online tools that keeps the Internet. He uses innovative strategies to news, issues and ideas better link. They are prepared to understand and actively participated in media and social debates. The topics to be addressed and illuminated are easier to retrieve, analyze and disseminate information. This makes der Freitag to a real pioneer in the German media market. Strong international syndication as "The Guardian" and networking with other voices from around the world der Freitag to make a medium with a truly global perspective. Would like for people in Germany who understand world events, discuss and help shape - it is the platform for dialogue and exchange of views. Up to this point has no German media offer managed to inspire the young, active thinkers and the media: core audience for der Freitag are highly educated personalities between 20 and 49 who live in urban areas and engage in society. This group of people know that there is any history of more than one perspective. It uses media, preferably the Internet to learn new things, form an opinion and even to develop further. Knowledge and attitude are values that are maintained by it - beyond political borders. der Freitag does give the group the necessary content and inspiration. It combines an optimistic and consumer-friendly entertainment with quality journalism. Networked content, using a variety of innovative tools of the Internet and a modern and dynamic visuals to fill this position with life. Through a clear journalistic line and brand message of der Freitag, the first choice among the media for Germany's sovereign sense viewfinder will be. If something is being given to the world media oscar, the opinion of the media der Freitag is almost always part: Grimme Online Award 2009: shortly after the launch nominated in two categories, awarded a total of 10 awards at the 11th and 12th European Newspaper Award, the largest design competition of European newspapers, elected at the Lead Awards 2010 as the web magazine of the year award for "World's Best Designed Newspaper" -. International accolade was der Freitag by the American Society for News Design "for excellence in design, graphics and photo, 2010 bronze nail for the online offering in the category" Online Editorial". Award from the German Art Directors Club. For all awards, the judges agree: The decisive criterion is the winner of courage to break new ground. Like no other German media interlocked "der Freitag - the opinion media" traditional journalism with blogs, print to online. Whether social justice, or power structures in business and in politics: key issues in the network every day and Thursday at the kiosk for discussion. Facebook: http://www.facebook.com/derfreitag Twitter: http://twitter.com/derfreitag This Outlet offers RSS (Really Simple Syndication).
Language(s): German
ADVERTISING RATES:
SCC .... EUR 170,00
Mechanical Data: Type Area: 468 x 320 mm, No. of Columns (Display): 5, Col Widths (Display): 60 mm
Copy instructions: *Copy Date:* 15 days prior to publication
LOCAL NEWSPAPERS

FREITAGS-ANZEIGER FÜR MÖRFELDEN-WALLDORF, KELSTERBACH UND ZEPPELINHEIM 727949G72-4032

Editorial: Tizianplatz 35, 64546 MÖRFELDEN-WALLDORF **Tel:** 6105 22001 **Fax:** 6105 25486
Email: redaktion@freitags-anzeiger.de **Web site:** http://www.freitags-anzeiger.de
Freq: Weekly; **Circ:** 5,078
Editor: Werner Nies; **Advertising Manager:** Waltraud Kunz
Profile: Regional weekly covering politics, economics, sport, travel, technology and the arts.
Language(s): German
ADVERTISING RATES:
SCC .... EUR 19,50
Mechanical Data: Type Area: 487 x 333 mm, No. of Columns (Display): 7, Col Widths (Display): 45 mm
Copy instructions: *Copy Date:* 2 days prior to publication
Supplement(s): rtv; Start frei
LOCAL NEWSPAPERS

FREITALER WOCHENKURIER 727951G72-4036

Editorial: Wettiner Platz 10, 01067 DRESDEN
Tel: 351 491760 **Fax:** 351 4917674
Email: wochenkurier-dresden@dwk-verlag.de **Web site:** http://www.wochenkurier.info
Freq: Weekly; **Cover Price:** Free; **Circ:** 36,867
Editor: Regine Eberlein; **Advertising Manager:** Andreas Schönherr
Profile: Advertising journal (house-to-house) concentrating on local stories.
Language(s): German
ADVERTISING RATES:
Full Page Mono .... EUR 2740
Full Page Colour .... EUR 3835
Mechanical Data: Type Area: 430 x 290 mm, No. of Columns (Display): 7, Col Widths (Display): 38 mm
Copy instructions: *Copy Date:* 5 days prior to publication
LOCAL NEWSPAPERS

FREIZEIT EXKLUSIV 2043667G74A-3773

Editorial: Münchener Str. 101/09, 85737 ISMANING
Tel: 89 272700
Freq: Monthly; **Cover Price:** EUR 0,55; **Circ:** 383,000
Editor: Christiane Ams; **Advertising Manager:** Benita Ahsendorf
Profile: Magazine containing articles of topical interest, including fashion, cosmetics, cooking, recipes, news and profiles of royalty and rich and famous people.
Language(s): German
ADVERTISING RATES:
Full Page Mono .... EUR 5000
Full Page Colour .... EUR 5000
Mechanical Data: Type Area: 260 x 195 mm

FREIZEIT EXTRA 1913859G74A-3688

Editorial: Sieker Landstr. 126, 22143 HAMBURG
Tel: 40 6739780 **Fax:** 40 67397821
Email: wmb@cpvkg.de **Web site:** http://www.conpart-verlag.de
Freq: Monthly; **Cover Price:** EUR 0,80; **Circ:** 90,627
Editor: Wolfgang M. Biehler
Profile: The journal contains the following headings: Royals & Society | International Scene | Stars from TV and film | Cooking & Baking | Health Care | Fashion & Chic | Rates & Win | Travel & Services | Tips, Tricks & more.
Language(s): German
ADVERTISING RATES:
Full Page Mono .... EUR 5000
Full Page Colour .... EUR 5000
Mechanical Data: Type Area: 291 x 212 mm, No. of Columns (Display): 4

FREIZEIT ILLUSTRIERTE 1825396G74A-3570

Editorial: Sieker Landstr. 126, 22143 HAMBURG
Tel: 40 6739780 **Fax:** 40 67397821
Email: wmb@cpvkg.de **Web site:** http://www.conpart-verlag.de
Freq: Monthly; **Cover Price:** EUR 0,59; **Circ:** 98,147
Editor: Wolfgang M. Biehler
Profile: The journal contains the following headings: Royals & Society | VIPs & Celebrities | Love & Life | House & Home | Healthy & Fit | Fashion & Chic | Rates & Win | Travel & Services | Tips, Tricks & more.
Language(s): German
ADVERTISING RATES:
Full Page Mono .... EUR 5000
Full Page Colour .... EUR 5000
Mechanical Data: Type Area: 291 x 212 mm, No. of Columns (Display): 4

FREIZEIT REVUE 727963G74A-1200

Editorial: Am Kestendamm 1, 77652 OFFENBURG
Tel: 781 842264 **Fax:** 781 842034
Email: doris.schlichte@burda.com **Web site:** http://www.freizeitrevue.de
Freq: Weekly; **Circ:** 911,170
Editor: Robert Pölzer
Profile: Freizeit Revue informs, advises and relaxes - but also to stimulate discussion and active employment. Recent reports, travel and luxury, many puzzles as well as "Better Living" with tips and information that make everyday life easier. A large part of health, great recipes, beauty and fashion trends, "Plants and Animals ", "Finance and law" characterize the editorial content. As of severe extra-large inserts: Germany's best cookbook for collecting. Freizeit Revue is a content-rich, deliberately mixed with interactive elements read cocktail.
Language(s): German
Readership: Aimed at women.
ADVERTISING RATES:
Full Page Mono .... EUR 18400
Full Page Colour .... EUR 18400
Mechanical Data: Type Area: 268 x 204 mm, No. of Columns (Display): 4, Col Widths (Display): 48 mm
Copy instructions: *Copy Date:* 22 days prior to publication
CONSUMER: WOMEN'S INTEREST CONSUMER MAGAZINES: Women's Interest

FREIZEIT SPASS 1663336G74A-3453

Editorial: Am Kestendamm 1, 77652 OFFENBURG
Tel: 781 842264 **Fax:** 781 842034
Email: doris.schlichte@burda.com
Freq: Weekly; **Cover Price:** EUR 0,80; **Circ:** 422,850
Editor: Robert Pölzer
Profile: Freizeit Spass relies on emotional appeal, actionable advice and professional advice on all aspects of everyday life. Entertaining, diverse and as varied as life itself. Exciting and entertaining stories about celebrities, current affairs, and many service pages on topics such as health, wellness, fashion, plants and decoration, career, money and law characterize the editorial Freizeit Spass-offering. Rounding out this mix of topics from a great trip report and lots of puzzles.
Language(s): German
ADVERTISING RATES:
Full Page Mono .... EUR 6600
Full Page Colour .... EUR 6600
Mechanical Data: Type Area: 268 x 204 mm, No. of Columns (Display): 4, Col Widths (Display): 48 mm
CONSUMER: WOMEN'S INTEREST CONSUMER MAGAZINES: Women's Interest

FREIZEIT SPIEGEL 727968G80-3780

Editorial: Plochinger Str. 102, 73730 ESSLINGEN
Tel: 711 9318350 **Fax:** 711 93183535
Email: freizeitspiegel@fzsinfo.de **Web site:** http://www.freizeitspiegel-home.de
Freq: Monthly; **Cover Price:** Free; **Circ:** 16,373
Editor: Hans-Martin Seitz; **Advertising Manager:** Hans-Martin Seitz
Profile: Culture and events magazine for Stuttgart, Esslingen, Fildern and Neckarraum. The Freizeit Spiegel offers active recreational readers many possibilities for spending your leisure varied and interesting. Every month, over a thousand events and free-time attractions. Reports on regional issues of sport and culture, new movies, books, CDs, travel, trends, etc. The specimens are about 800 shops, restaurants and hotels, banks, savings banks, theater and distributed music centers, government agencies and schools, doctors' waiting rooms, etc., with strong customer and visitors.
Language(s): German
ADVERTISING RATES:
Full Page Mono .... EUR 2400
Full Page Colour .... EUR 2400
Mechanical Data: Type Area: 276 x 192 mm, No. of Columns (Display): 4, Col Widths (Display): 45 mm

Copy instructions: *Copy Date:* 10 days prior to publication
CONSUMER: RURAL & REGIONAL INTEREST

FREIZEIT TOTAL 1895125G74A-3661

Editorial: Ruhrtalstr. 67, 45239 ESSEN
Tel: 201 246880 **Fax:** 201 24688140
Email: b.matten@stegenwaller.de **Web site:** http://www.stegenwaller.de
Freq: Monthly; **Cover Price:** EUR 0,49; **Circ:** 350,000
Editor: Britta Matten; **Advertising Manager:** Oliver Schulte
Profile: Women's magazine with thrilling stories from the world of celebrities, lots of puzzles with great profits. This guide's interesting themes and tasty recipe ideas to try at home. This mix ensures a wide target audience: entertainment around stars and starlets in the foreground. Ratings and health care sites with numerous experts for advice with real information. Fashion, travel and decor complement the portfolio of the Issue from skillfully.
Language(s): German
ADVERTISING RATES:
Full Page Mono .... EUR 4500
Full Page Colour .... EUR 4500
Mechanical Data: Type Area: 260 x 199 mm
Copy instructions: *Copy Date:* 47 days prior to publication

FREIZEIT VERGNÜGEN

1843580G74A-3619
Editorial: Bärheide 1, 38442 WOLFSBURG
Tel: 5362 949733
Email: redaktion@allesguteverlag.de **Web site:** http://www.allesguteverlag.de
Freq: 10 issues yearly; **Cover Price:** EUR 0,59; **Circ:** 145,370
Editor: Bodo Scharffetter
Profile: Women's magazine with celebrity stories, travel tips and puzzles as well as service part.
Language(s): German
ADVERTISING RATES:
Full Page Mono .... EUR 6350
Full Page Colour .... EUR 6350
Mechanical Data: Type Area: 261 x 207 mm

FREIZEIT WOCHE 1643724G74A-3414

Editorial: Rotweg 8, 76532 BADEN-BADEN
Tel: 7221 3501722 **Fax:** 7221 3501799
Email: manuela.hirn@freizeit-woche.de **Web site:** http://www.freizeitwoche-online.de
Freq: Weekly; **Cover Price:** EUR 0,80; **Circ:** 503,130
Editor: Herbert Martin
Profile: Freizeit Woche is aimed at women aged 35 to 59 who are life- and consumer experience and who enjoy with Freizeit Woche their own personal time off from work and family. The weekly track information in current news and interviews on national and international celebrities from the fields of show, music, film and television, and presents interesting stories and background reports from the European nobility. Particularly comprehensive is the professional service and consulting unit with a focus on health, travel (with a generous look) and cooking - with recipes for the connoisseur. Informative and to the point are also advice pages on the topics of fashion, home, law in everyday life and life coaching. The 20-page puzzle part rounds out the editorial approach. It is impressive by variety puzzle fun and offers many hours of relaxation. In addition, week after week giving away attractive cash prizes and prizes.
Language(s): German
ADVERTISING RATES:
Full Page Mono .... EUR 8498
Full Page Colour .... EUR 8498
Mechanical Data: Type Area: 265 x 207 mm, No. of Columns (Display): 4, Col Widths (Display): 49 mm
Copy instructions: *Copy Date:* 28 days prior to publication
CONSUMER: WOMEN'S INTEREST CONSUMER MAGAZINES: Women's Interest

FREIZEITBERATER

1826389G89A-12389
Editorial: Stiftsplatz 4, 88131 LINDAU
Tel: 8382 270155 **Fax:** 8382 27077155
Email: tourismus@landkreis-lindau.de **Web site:** http://www.landkreis-lindau.de
Freq: Annual; **Cover Price:** Free; **Circ:** 11,000
Profile: Travel and leisure time guide for the international Bodensee region.
Language(s): German

FREIZEITBERATER

1826389G89A-12534
Editorial: Stiftsplatz 4, 88131 LINDAU
Tel: 8382 270155 **Fax:** 8382 27077155
Email: tourismus@landkreis-lindau.de **Web site:** http://www.landkreis-lindau.de
Freq: Annual; **Cover Price:** Free; **Circ:** 11,000
Profile: Travel and leisure time guide for the international Bodensee region.
Language(s): German

FREUNDIN 727993G74A-1220

Editorial: Arabellastr. 23, 81925 MÜNCHEN
Tel: 89 92500 **Fax:** 89 92503991
Email: freundin@freundin.de **Web site:** http://www.freundin.de
Freq: 27 issues yearly; **Annual Sub.:** EUR 62,40; **Circ:** 514,924
Editor: Ulrike Zeitlinger; **Advertising Manager:** Meike Göttsch
Profile: Friendship is one of the few constants in life. Friends to accompany and support over decades, coach each other and try new things together. For fashion, beauty, food, travel, recreation or entertainment - together make Find more fun! girlfriend stands for Lifestyle with value. Under the direction of Ulrike Zeitlinger and her editorial team, the magazine every two weeks to a rich source of inspiration and a compeissuer for life. girlfriend wants to leave their reader "life easier" and identifies solutions that make life better and easier. girlfriend informed, involved, inspired and integrated. Their emotional editorial concept gives a unique positive and optimistic attitude to life - from the first to the last page. Facebook: http://www.facebook.com/freundin.de This Outlet offers RSS (Really Simple Syndication).
Language(s): German
Readership: Aimed at young women.
ADVERTISING RATES:
Full Page Mono .... EUR 35200
Full Page Colour .... EUR 35200
Mechanical Data: Type Area: 229 x 175 mm, No. of Columns (Display): 4, Col Widths (Display): 40 mm
Copy instructions: *Copy Date:* 42 days prior to publication
CONSUMER: WOMEN'S INTEREST CONSUMER MAGAZINES: Women's Interest

FREUNDIN DONNA 1999443G74A-3749

Editorial: Arabellastr. 23, 81925 MÜNCHEN
Tel: 89 92500 **Fax:** 89 92503991
Email: freundin@freundin.de **Web site:** http://www.freundin.de
Freq: Monthly; **Cover Price:** EUR 3,00; **Circ:** 300,000
Editor: Ulrike Zeitlinger; **Advertising Manager:** Hannelore Grüning
Profile: freundin Donna - the magazine for adult and sophisticated women. It is about the particular wishes, dreams, needs, issues and claims that women over 40 years. For women in this age segment again entering a time of new beginnings and an exciting new phase of life in which almost anything is possible and the freundin Donna, readers accompany will.Von friend Donna can expect the readers everything that makes a good women's magazine: Fashion, beauty, lifestyle, interviews, psychology, partnership, health, culture, travel and services. Facebook: http://www.facebook.com/freundin.de This Outlet offers RSS (Really Simple Syndication).
Language(s): German
Copy instructions: *Copy Date:* a.A

FREUNDIN KALENDER

1865833G74A-3652
Editorial: Arabellastr. 23, 81925 MÜNCHEN
Tel: 89 92500 **Fax:** 89 92503021
Email: freundin@burda.com **Web site:** http://www.freundin.de
Freq: Annual; **Cover Price:** EUR 6,95; **Circ:** 30,000
Profile: Calendar from freundin magazine. Facebook: http://www.facebook.com/freundin.de.
Language(s): German

FREUNDIN WELLFIT

747107G74G-1640
Editorial: Arabellastr. 23, 81925 MÜNCHEN
Tel: 89 92503549 **Fax:** 89 92503935
Web site: http://www.freundin.de
Freq: Quarterly; **Annual Sub.:** EUR 9,20; **Circ:** 192,372
Editor: Ulrike Zeitlinger; **Advertising Manager:** Meike Göttsch
Profile: "All that is good for me", means pleasure, exercise, new food concepts, relaxation and vitality. freundin wellfit takes a holistic health claim for body, mind and soul. And provides inspiration for all aspects of a contented life. freundin wellfit is published quarterly - focused on the season. With the trends, tricks and tips to make the spring, summer, autumn or winter better. Facebook: http://www.facebook.com/freundin.de.
Language(s): German
ADVERTISING RATES:
Full Page Mono .... EUR 14900
Full Page Colour .... EUR 14900
Mechanical Data: Type Area: 229 x 175 mm, No. of Columns (Display): 3, Col Widths (Display): 55 mm
Copy instructions: *Copy Date:* 42 days prior to publication
CONSUMER: WOMEN'S INTEREST CONSUMER MAGAZINES: Slimming & Health

FREUNDIN.DE 1621293G74A-3367

Editorial: Steinhauser Str. 1, 81677 MÜNCHEN
Tel: 89 92503872 **Fax:** 89 92501390
Email: freundin@freundin.de **Web site:** http://www.freundin.de
Cover Price: Paid; **Circ:** 939,941 Unique Users
Editor: Miriam Thomas
Profile: Ezine: Magazine covering fashion, beauty, work, relationships and travel. Facebook: http://www.facebook.com/freundin.de.
Language(s): German
CONSUMER: WOMEN'S INTEREST CONSUMER MAGAZINES: Women's Interest

FRIDA 2020557G74P-1367

Editorial: Tharandter Str. 69, 01187 DRESDEN
Tel: 351 4136180 **Fax:** 351 4136291
Email: frida@konsum-dresden.de **Web site:** http://www.konsum.de
Freq: 5 issues yearly; **Cover Price:** Free; **Circ:** 288,000
Editor: Roger Ulke; **Advertising Manager:** Ulrich Pold
Profile: Gourmet magazine with recipes and suggestions on products in the Konsum markets. Facebook: www.facebook.de/konsumdresden.
Language(s): German

FRIEDBERGER ALLGEMEINE

728012G67B-5420
Editorial: Curt-Frenzel-Str. 2, 86167 AUGSBURG
Tel: 821 7770 **Fax:** 821 7772067
Email: redaktion@augsburger-allgemeine.de **Web site:** http://www.augsburger-allgemeine.de
Freq: 312 issues yearly; **Circ:** 13,185
Advertising Manager: Herbert Dachs
Profile: Daily newspaper with regional news and a local sports section. Facebook: http://www.facebook.com/AugsburgerAllgemeine Twitter: http://twitter.com/AZ_Augsburg This Outlet offers RSS (Really Simple Syndication).
Language(s): German
ADVERTISING RATES:
SCC .... EUR 46,80
Mechanical Data: Type Area: 480 x 327 mm, No. of Columns (Display): 7, Col Widths (Display): 45 mm
Copy instructions: *Copy Date:* 1 day prior to publication
Supplement(s): CiA City News
REGIONAL DAILY & SUNDAY NEWSPAPERS: Regional Daily Newspapers

FRIEDHOFSKULTUR 728023G64L-3

Editorial: Frankfurter Str. 3d, 38122 BRAUNSCHWEIG **Tel:** 531 3800413
Fax: 531 3800440
Email: red.friedhofskultur@haymarket.de **Web site:** http://www.friedhofskultur.de
Freq: Monthly; **Annual Sub.:** EUR 142,20; **Circ:** 2,933
Editor: Evelin Scheibe
Profile: Magazine about the funeral trade. Target audience: managers and cemetery sexton.
Language(s): German
ADVERTISING RATES:
Full Page Mono .... EUR 2557
Full Page Colour .... EUR 3817
Mechanical Data: Type Area: 272 x 186 mm, No. of Columns (Display): 4, Col Widths (Display): 45 mm
BUSINESS: OTHER CLASSIFICATIONS: Funeral Directors, Cemeteries & Crematoria

FRIENDS THE GAYMAP - AUSG. ALICANTE 1638106G89A-11740

Editorial: Max-Eyth-Str. 22, 71686 REMSECK
Tel: 7146 286330 **Fax:** 7146 286332
Email: mail@gaymap.info **Web site:** http://www.gaymap.info
Freq: Annual; **Cover Price:** Free; **Circ:** 25,000
Editor: Claus Lemanczyk; **Advertising Manager:** Claus Lemanczyk
Profile: City maps, Tourist information, index and ads for the gay and lesbian audience. The most common travel information of the scene, Alicante edition.
Language(s): English
ADVERTISING RATES:
Full Page Mono .... EUR 980
Full Page Colour .... EUR 980
Mechanical Data: Type Area: 190 x 74 mm

FRIENDS THE GAYMAP - AUSG. AMSTERDAM 728034G89A-1780

Editorial: Max-Eyth-Str. 22, 71686 REMSECK
Tel: 7146 286330 **Fax:** 7146 286332
Email: mail@gaymap.info **Web site:** http://www.gaymap.info
Freq: Half-yearly; **Cover Price:** Free; **Circ:** 50,000
Editor: Claus Lemanczyk; **Advertising Manager:** Claus Lemanczyk
Profile: City maps, Tourist information, index and ads for the gay and lesbian audience. The most common travel information of the scene, edition Amsterdam.
Language(s): English
ADVERTISING RATES:
Full Page Mono .... EUR 980
Full Page Colour .... EUR 980
Mechanical Data: Type Area: 190 x 74 mm

FRIENDS THE GAYMAP - AUSG. ANTWERPEN 728047G89A-2040

Editorial: Max-Eyth-Str. 22, 71686 REMSECK
Tel: 7146 286330 **Fax:** 7146 286332
Email: mail@gaymap.info **Web site:** http://www.gaymap.info
Freq: Annual; **Cover Price:** Free; **Circ:** 25,000
Editor: Claus Lemanczyk; **Advertising Manager:** Claus Lemanczyk
Profile: City maps, Tourist information, index and ads for the gay and lesbian audience. The most common travel information of the scene, Antwerp edition.
Language(s): English; German
ADVERTISING RATES:
Full Page Mono .... EUR 980
Full Page Colour .... EUR 980
Mechanical Data: Type Area: 190 x 74 mm

FRIENDS THE GAYMAP - AUSG. BARCELONA 728045G89A-2000

Editorial: Max-Eyth-Str. 22, 71686 REMSECK
Tel: 7146 286330 **Fax:** 7146 286332
Email: mail@gaymap.info **Web site:** http://www.gaymap.info
Freq: Half-yearly; **Cover Price:** Free; **Circ:** 25,000
Editor: Claus Lemanczyk; **Advertising Manager:** Claus Lemanczyk
Profile: City maps, Tourist information, index and ads for the gay and lesbian audience. The most common travel information of the scene, Barcelona edition.
Language(s): English; Spanish
ADVERTISING RATES:
Full Page Mono .... EUR 980
Full Page Colour .... EUR 980
Mechanical Data: Type Area: 190 x 74 mm

FRIENDS THE GAYMAP - AUSG. BENIDORM 728044G89A-1980

Editorial: Max-Eyth-Str. 22, 71686 REMSECK
Tel: 7146 286330 **Fax:** 7146 286332
Email: mail@gaymap.info **Web site:** http://www.gaymap.info
Freq: Annual; **Cover Price:** Free; **Circ:** 25,000
Editor: Claus Lemanczyk; **Advertising Manager:** Claus Lemanczyk
Profile: City maps, Tourist information, index and ads for the gay and lesbian audience. The most common travel information of the scene, Benidorm edition.
Language(s): English; Spanish
ADVERTISING RATES:
Full Page Mono .... EUR 980
Full Page Colour .... EUR 980
Mechanical Data: Type Area: 190 x 74 mm

FRIENDS THE GAYMAP - AUSG. BERLIN 728037G89A-1840

Editorial: Max-Eyth-Str. 22, 71686 REMSECK
Tel: 7146 286330 **Fax:** 7146 286332
Email: mail@gaymap.info **Web site:** http://www.gaymap.info
Freq: Half-yearly; **Cover Price:** Free; **Circ:** 50,000
Editor: Claus Lemanczyk; **Advertising Manager:** Claus Lemanczyk
Profile: City maps, Tourist information, index and ads for the gay and lesbian audience. The most common travel information of the scene, Berlin edition.
Language(s): English; German
ADVERTISING RATES:
Full Page Mono .... EUR 980
Full Page Colour .... EUR 980
Mechanical Data: Type Area: 190 x 74 mm

FRIENDS THE GAYMAP - AUSG. BRÜSSEL 728043G89A-1960

Editorial: Max-Eyth-Str. 22, 71686 REMSECK
Tel: 7146 286330 **Fax:** 7146 286332
Email: mail@gaymap.info **Web site:** http://www.gaymap.info
Freq: Half-yearly; **Cover Price:** Free; **Circ:** 25,000
Editor: Claus Lemanczyk; **Advertising Manager:** Claus Lemanczyk
Profile: City maps, Tourist information, index and ads for the gay and lesbian audience. The most common travel information of the scene, Brussels edition.
Language(s): English; French
ADVERTISING RATES:
Full Page Mono .... EUR 980
Full Page Colour .... EUR 980
Mechanical Data: Type Area: 190 x 74 mm

FRIENDS THE GAYMAP - AUSG. BUDAPEST 728042G89A-1940

Editorial: Max-Eyth-Str. 22, 71686 REMSECK
Tel: 7146 286330 **Fax:** 7146 286332
Email: mail@gaymap.info **Web site:** http://www.gaymap.info
Freq: Annual; **Cover Price:** Free; **Circ:** 25,000
Editor: Claus Lemanczyk; **Advertising Manager:** Claus Lemanczyk
Profile: City maps, Tourist information, index and ads for the gay and lesbian audience. The most common travel information of the scene, Budapest edition.
Language(s): English; German; Hungarian
ADVERTISING RATES:
Full Page Mono .... EUR 980
Full Page Colour .... EUR 980
Mechanical Data: Type Area: 190 x 74 mm

FRIENDS THE GAYMAP - AUSG. CITTÀ DEL VATICANO

1638104G89A-11738
Editorial: Max-Eyth-Str. 22, 71686 REMSECK
Tel: 7146 286330 **Fax:** 7146 286332
Email: mail@gaymap.info **Web site:** http://www.gaymap.info
Freq: Annual; **Cover Price:** Free; **Circ:** 25,000
Editor: Claus Lemanczyk; **Advertising Manager:** Claus Lemanczyk
Profile: City maps, Tourist information, index and ads for the gay and lesbian audience. The most common travel information of the scene, Vatican edition.
Language(s): English
ADVERTISING RATES:
Full Page Mono .... EUR 980
Full Page Colour .... EUR 980
Mechanical Data: Type Area: 190 x 74 mm

FRIENDS THE GAYMAP - AUSG. COLOGNE
728040G89A-1900
Editorial: Max-Eyth-Str. 22, 71686 REMSECK
Tel: 7146 286330 **Fax:** 7146 286332
Email: mail@gaymap.info **Web site:** http://www.gaymap.info
Freq: Half-yearly; **Cover Price:** Free; **Circ:** 25,000
Editor: Claus Lemanczyk; **Advertising Manager:** Claus Lemanczyk
Profile: City maps, Tourist information, index and ads for the gay and lesbian audience. The most common travel information of the scene, Cologne edition.
Language(s): English; German
ADVERTISING RATES:
Full Page Mono .... EUR 840
Full Page Colour .... EUR 840
Mechanical Data: Type Area: 190 x 74 mm

FRIENDS THE GAYMAP - AUSG. COPENHAGEN
753780G89A-2070
Editorial: Max-Eyth-Str. 22, 71686 REMSECK
Tel: 7146 286330 **Fax:** 7146 286332
Email: mail@gaymap.info **Web site:** http://www.gaymap.info
Freq: Annual; **Cover Price:** Free; **Circ:** 25,000
Editor: Claus Lemanczyk; **Advertising Manager:** Claus Lemanczyk
Profile: City maps, Tourist information, index and ads for the gay and lesbian audience. The most common travel information of the scene, Copenhagen edition.
Language(s): English
ADVERTISING RATES:
Full Page Mono .... EUR 980
Full Page Colour .... EUR 980
Mechanical Data: Type Area: 190 x 74 mm

FRIENDS THE GAYMAP - AUSG. DÜSSELDORF
1601192G89A-11462
Editorial: Max-Eyth-Str. 22, 71686 REMSECK
Tel: 7146 286330 **Fax:** 7146 286332
Email: mail@gaymap.info **Web site:** http://www.gaymap.info
Freq: Annual; **Cover Price:** Free; **Circ:** 25,000
Editor: Claus Lemanczyk; **Advertising Manager:** Claus Lemanczyk
Profile: City maps, Tourist information, index and ads for the gay and lesbian audience. The most common travel information of the scene. Düsseldorf edition.
Language(s): English; German
ADVERTISING RATES:
Full Page Mono .... EUR 840
Full Page Colour .... EUR 840
Mechanical Data: Type Area: 190 x 74 mm

FRIENDS THE GAYMAP - AUSG. FORT LAUDERDALE
1638110G89A-11744
Editorial: Max-Eyth-Str. 22, 71686 REMSECK
Tel: 7146 286330 **Fax:** 7146 286332
Email: mail@gaymap.info **Web site:** http://www.gaymap.info
Freq: Half-yearly; **Cover Price:** Free; **Circ:** 25,000
Editor: Claus Lemanczyk; **Advertising Manager:** Claus Lemanczyk
Profile: City maps, Tourist information, index and ads for the gay and lesbian audience. The most common travel information of the scene, Fort Lauderdale edition.
Language(s): English
ADVERTISING RATES:
Full Page Mono .... EUR 1280
Full Page Colour .... EUR 1280
Mechanical Data: Type Area: 190 x 74 mm

FRIENDS THE GAYMAP - AUSG. FRANKFURT/MAIN
728036G89A-1820
Editorial: Max-Eyth-Str. 22, 71686 REMSECK
Tel: 7146 286330 **Fax:** 7146 286332
Email: mail@gaymap.info **Web site:** http://www.gaymap.info
Freq: Half-yearly; **Cover Price:** Free; **Circ:** 25,000
Editor: Claus Lemanczyk; **Advertising Manager:** Claus Lemanczyk
Profile: City maps, Tourist information, index and ads for the gay and lesbian audience. The most common travel information of the scene, Frankfurt on the Main edition.
Language(s): English; German
ADVERTISING RATES:
Full Page Mono .... EUR 840
Full Page Colour .... EUR 840
Mechanical Data: Type Area: 190 x 74 mm

FRIENDS THE GAYMAP - AUSG. HAMBURG
728038G89A-1860
Editorial: Max-Eyth-Str. 22, 71686 REMSECK
Tel: 7146 286330 **Fax:** 7146 286332
Email: mail@gaymap.info **Web site:** http://www.gaymap.info
Freq: Half-yearly; **Cover Price:** Free; **Circ:** 25,000
Editor: Claus Lemanczyk; **Advertising Manager:** Claus Lemanczyk
Profile: City maps, Tourist information, index and ads for the gay and lesbian audience. The most common travel information of the scene, Hamburg edition.
Language(s): English; German
ADVERTISING RATES:
Full Page Mono .... EUR 840
Full Page Colour .... EUR 840
Mechanical Data: Type Area: 190 x 74 mm

FRIENDS THE GAYMAP - AUSG. HANNOVER
728035G89A-1800
Editorial: Max-Eyth-Str. 22, 71686 REMSECK
Tel: 7146 286330 **Fax:** 7146 286332
Email: mail@gaymap.info **Web site:** http://www.gaymap.info
Freq: Annual; **Cover Price:** Free; **Circ:** 25,000
Editor: Claus Lemanczyk; **Advertising Manager:** Claus Lemanczyk
Profile: City maps, Tourist information, index and ads for the gay and lesbian audience. The most common travel information of the scene, Hannover edition.
Language(s): English; German
ADVERTISING RATES:
Full Page Mono .... EUR 840
Full Page Colour .... EUR 840
Mechanical Data: Type Area: 190 x 74 mm

FRIENDS THE GAYMAP - AUSG. IBIZA EIVISSA
1601196G89A-11466
Editorial: Max-Eyth-Str. 22, 71686 REMSECK
Tel: 7146 286330 **Fax:** 7146 286332
Email: mail@gaymap.info **Web site:** http://www.gaymap.info
Freq: Annual; **Cover Price:** Free; **Circ:** 25,000
Editor: Claus Lemanczyk; **Advertising Manager:** Claus Lemanczyk
Profile: City maps, Tourist information, index and ads for the gay and lesbian audience. The most common travel information of the scene, Ibiza Eivissa edition.
Language(s): English; Spanish
ADVERTISING RATES:
Full Page Mono .... EUR 980
Full Page Colour .... EUR 980
Mechanical Data: Type Area: 190 x 74 mm

FRIENDS THE GAYMAP - AUSG. KEY WEST
1638108G89A-11742
Editorial: Max-Eyth-Str. 22, 71686 REMSECK
Tel: 7146 286330 **Fax:** 7146 286332
Email: mail@gaymap.info **Web site:** http://www.gaymap.info
Freq: Annual; **Cover Price:** Free; **Circ:** 25,000
Editor: Claus Lemanczyk; **Advertising Manager:** Claus Lemanczyk
Profile: City maps, Tourist information, index and ads for the gay and lesbian audience. The most common travel information of the scene, Key West edition.
Language(s): English
ADVERTISING RATES:
Full Page Mono .... EUR 1280
Full Page Colour .... EUR 1280
Mechanical Data: Type Area: 190 x 74 mm

FRIENDS THE GAYMAP - AUSG. LISSABON
1601191G89A-11461
Editorial: Max-Eyth-Str. 22, 71686 REMSECK
Tel: 7146 286330 **Fax:** 7146 286332
Email: mail@gaymap.info **Web site:** http://www.gaymap.info
Freq: Annual; **Cover Price:** Free; **Circ:** 25,000
Editor: Claus Lemanczyk; **Advertising Manager:** Claus Lemanczyk
Profile: City maps, Tourist information, index and ads for the gay and lesbian audience. The most common travel information of the scene, Lissabon edition.
Language(s): English
ADVERTISING RATES:
Full Page Mono .... EUR 980
Full Page Colour .... EUR 980
Mechanical Data: Type Area: 190 x 74 mm

FRIENDS THE GAYMAP - AUSG. LONDON
724498G89A-500
Editorial: Max-Eyth-Str. 22, 71686 REMSECK
Tel: 7146 286330 **Fax:** 7146 286332
Email: mail@gaymap.info **Web site:** http://www.gaymap.info
Freq: Annual; **Cover Price:** Free; **Circ:** 25,000
Editor: Claus Lemanczyk; **Advertising Manager:** Claus Lemanczyk
Profile: City maps, Tourist information, index and ads for the gay and lesbian audience. The most common travel information of the scene, London edition.
Language(s): English
ADVERTISING RATES:
Full Page Mono .... EUR 980
Full Page Colour .... EUR 980
Mechanical Data: Type Area: 190 x 74 mm

FRIENDS THE GAYMAP - AUSG. MADRID
1601195G89A-11465
Editorial: Max-Eyth-Str. 22, 71686 REMSECK
Tel: 7146 286330 **Fax:** 7146 286332
Email: mail@gaymap.info **Web site:** http://www.gaymap.info
Freq: Half-yearly; **Cover Price:** Free; **Circ:** 25,000
Editor: Claus Lemanczyk; **Advertising Manager:** Claus Lemanczyk
Profile: City maps, Tourist information, index and ads for the gay and lesbian audience. The most common travel information of the scene, Madrid edition.
Language(s): English; Spanish
ADVERTISING RATES:
Full Page Mono .... EUR 980
Full Page Colour .... EUR 980
Mechanical Data: Type Area: 190 x 74 mm

FRIENDS THE GAYMAP - AUSG. MANNHEIM
1638439G89A-11775
Editorial: Max-Eyth-Str. 22, 71686 REMSECK
Tel: 7146 286330 **Fax:** 7146 286332
Email: mail@gaymap.info **Web site:** http://www.gaymap.info
Freq: Annual; **Cover Price:** Free; **Circ:** 25,000
Editor: Claus Lemanczyk; **Advertising Manager:** Claus Lemanczyk
Profile: City maps, Tourist information, index and ads for the gay and lesbian audience. The most common travel information of the scene, Mannheim edition.
Language(s): English; German
ADVERTISING RATES:
Full Page Mono .... EUR 840
Full Page Colour .... EUR 840
Mechanical Data: Type Area: 190 x 74 mm

FRIENDS THE GAYMAP - AUSG. MIAMI
1638109G89A-11743
Editorial: Max-Eyth-Str. 22, 71686 REMSECK
Tel: 7146 286330 **Fax:** 7146 286332
Email: mail@gaymap.info **Web site:** http://www.gaymap.info
Freq: Annual; **Cover Price:** Free; **Circ:** 25,000
Editor: Claus Lemanczyk; **Advertising Manager:** Claus Lemanczyk
Profile: City maps, Tourist information, index and ads for the gay and lesbian audience. The most common travel information of the scene, Miami edition.
Language(s): English
ADVERTISING RATES:
Full Page Mono .... EUR 1280
Full Page Colour .... EUR 1280
Mechanical Data: Type Area: 190 x 74 mm

FRIENDS THE GAYMAP - AUSG. MONTRÉAL
1793687G89A-12278
Editorial: Max-Eyth-Str. 22, 71686 REMSECK
Tel: 7146 286330 **Fax:** 7146 286332
Email: mail@gaymap.info **Web site:** http://www.gaymap.info
Freq: Annual; **Cover Price:** Free; **Circ:** 25,000
Editor: Claus Lemanczyk; **Advertising Manager:** Claus Lemanczyk
Profile: City maps, Tourist information, index and ads for the gay and lesbian audience. The most common travel information of the scene, Montréal edition.
Language(s): English
ADVERTISING RATES:
Full Page Mono .... EUR 1280
Full Page Colour .... EUR 1280
Mechanical Data: Type Area: 190 x 74 mm

FRIENDS THE GAYMAP - AUSG. MÜNCHEN-MUNICH
728031G89A-1720
Editorial: Max-Eyth-Str. 22, 71686 REMSECK
Tel: 7146 286330 **Fax:** 7146 286332
Email: mail@gaymap.info **Web site:** http://www.gaymap.info
Freq: Half-yearly; **Cover Price:** Free; **Circ:** 25,000
Editor: Claus Lemanczyk; **Advertising Manager:** Claus Lemanczyk
Profile: City maps, Tourist information, index and ads for the gay and lesbian audience. The most common travel information of the scene, Munich edition.
Language(s): English; German
ADVERTISING RATES:
Full Page Mono .... EUR 840
Full Page Colour .... EUR 840
Mechanical Data: Type Area: 190 x 74 mm

FRIENDS THE GAYMAP - AUSG. NEW YORK CITY
1977614G89A-12561
Editorial: Max-Eyth-Str. 22, 71686 REMSECK
Tel: 7146 286330 **Fax:** 7146 286332
Email: mail@gaymap.info **Web site:** http://www.gaymap.info
Freq: Annual; **Cover Price:** Free; **Circ:** 25,000
Editor: Claus Lemanczyk; **Advertising Manager:** Claus Lemanczyk
Profile: City maps, Tourist information, index and ads for the gay and lesbian audience. The most common travel information of the scene, New York City edition.
Language(s): English
ADVERTISING RATES:
Full Page Mono .... EUR 1280
Full Page Colour .... EUR 1280
Mechanical Data: Type Area: 190 x 74 mm

FRIENDS THE GAYMAP - AUSG. NÜRNBERG
728041G89A-1920
Editorial: Max-Eyth-Str. 22, 71686 REMSECK
Tel: 7146 286330 **Fax:** 7146 286332
Email: mail@gaymap.info **Web site:** http://www.gaymap.info
Freq: Annual; **Cover Price:** Free; **Circ:** 25,000
Editor: Claus Lemanczyk; **Advertising Manager:** Claus Lemanczyk
Profile: City maps, Tourist information, index and ads for the gay and lesbian audience. The most common travel information of the scene, Nuremberg edition.
Language(s): English; German
ADVERTISING RATES:
Full Page Mono .... EUR 840
Full Page Colour .... EUR 840
Mechanical Data: Type Area: 190 x 74 mm

FRIENDS THE GAYMAP - AUSG. ORLANDO
1977613G89A-12560
Editorial: Max-Eyth-Str. 22, 71686 REMSECK
Tel: 7146 286330 **Fax:** 7146 286332
Email: mail@gaymap.info **Web site:** http://www.gaymap.info
Freq: Annual; **Cover Price:** Free; **Circ:** 25,000
Editor: Claus Lemanczyk; **Advertising Manager:** Claus Lemanczyk
Profile: City maps, Tourist information, index and ads for the gay and lesbian audience. The most common travel information of the scene, Orlando edition.
Language(s): English
ADVERTISING RATES:
Full Page Mono .... EUR 1280
Full Page Colour .... EUR 1280
Mechanical Data: Type Area: 190 x 74 mm

FRIENDS THE GAYMAP - AUSG. PARIS
1601194G89A-11464
Editorial: Max-Eyth-Str. 22, 71686 REMSECK
Tel: 7146 286330 **Fax:** 7146 286332
Email: mail@gaymap.info **Web site:** http://www.gaymap.info
Freq: Annual; **Cover Price:** Free; **Circ:** 25,000
Editor: Claus Lemanczyk; **Advertising Manager:** Claus Lemanczyk
Profile: City maps, Tourist information, index and ads for the gay and lesbian audience. The most common travel information of the scene, Paris edition.
Language(s): English; French
ADVERTISING RATES:
Full Page Mono .... EUR 980
Full Page Colour .... EUR 980
Mechanical Data: Type Area: 190 x 74 mm

FRIENDS THE GAYMAP - AUSG. PLAYA DEL INGLES
1825305G89A-12375
Editorial: Max-Eyth-Str. 22, 71686 REMSECK
Tel: 7146 286330 **Fax:** 7146 286332
Email: mail@gaymap.info **Web site:** http://www.gaymap.info
Freq: Half-yearly; **Cover Price:** Free; **Circ:** 25,000
Editor: Claus Lemanczyk; **Advertising Manager:** Claus Lemanczyk
Profile: City maps, Tourist information, index and ads for the gay and lesbian audience. The most common travel information of the scene, Playa del Ingles edition.
Language(s): English
ADVERTISING RATES:
Full Page Mono .... EUR 980
Full Page Colour .... EUR 980
Mechanical Data: Type Area: 190 x 74 mm

FRIENDS THE GAYMAP - AUSG. PRAG
1793685G89A-12276
Editorial: Max-Eyth-Str. 22, 71686 REMSECK
Tel: 7146 286330 **Fax:** 7146 286332
Email: mail@gaymap.info **Web site:** http://www.gaymap.info
Freq: Annual; **Cover Price:** Free; **Circ:** 25,000
Editor: Claus Lemanczyk; **Advertising Manager:** Claus Lemanczyk
Profile: City maps, Tourist information, index and ads for the gay and lesbian audience. The most common travel information of the scene, Prag edition.
Language(s): English
ADVERTISING RATES:
Full Page Mono .... EUR 980
Full Page Colour .... EUR 980
Mechanical Data: Type Area: 190 x 74 mm

FRIENDS THE GAYMAP - AUSG. ROMA
753782G89A-2077
Editorial: Max-Eyth-Str. 22, 71686 REMSECK
Tel: 7146 286330 **Fax:** 7146 286332
Email: mail@gaymap.info **Web site:** http://www.gaymap.info
Freq: Annual; **Cover Price:** Free; **Circ:** 25,000
Editor: Claus Lemanczyk; **Advertising Manager:** Claus Lemanczyk
Profile: City maps, Tourist information, index and ads for the gay and lesbian audience. The most common travel information of the scene, Rome edition.
Language(s): English
ADVERTISING RATES:
Full Page Mono .... EUR 980
Full Page Colour .... EUR 980
Mechanical Data: Type Area: 190 x 74 mm

FRIENDS THE GAYMAP - AUSG. ROTTERDAM
1601193G89A-11463
Editorial: Max-Eyth-Str. 22, 71686 REMSECK
Tel: 7146 286330 **Fax:** 7146 286332
Email: mail@gaymap.info **Web site:** http://www.gaymap.info
Freq: Annual; **Cover Price:** Free; **Circ:** 25,000
Editor: Claus Lemanczyk; **Advertising Manager:** Claus Lemanczyk
Profile: City maps, Tourist information, index and ads for the gay and lesbian audience. The most common travel information of the scene., Rotterdam edition.
Language(s): English
ADVERTISING RATES:
Full Page Mono .... EUR 980
Full Page Colour .... EUR 980
Mechanical Data: Type Area: 190 x 74 mm

FRIENDS THE GAYMAP - AUSG. RUHR
1977611G89A-12559

Editorial: Max-Eyth-Str. 22, 71686 REMSECK
Tel: 7146 286330 **Fax:** 7146 286332
Email: mail@gaymap.info **Web site:** http://www.gaymap.info
Freq: Annual; **Cover Price:** Free; **Circ:** 25,000
Editor: Claus Lemanczyk; **Advertising Manager:** Claus Lemanczyk
Profile: City maps, Tourist information, index and ads for the gay and lesbian audience. The most common travel information of the scene, Ruhrgebiet edition.
Language(s): English; German
ADVERTISING RATES:
Full Page Mono .... EUR 840
Full Page Colour .... EUR 840
Mechanical Data: Type Area: 190 x 74 mm

FRIENDS THE GAYMAP - AUSG. SITGES
728046G89A-2020

Editorial: Max-Eyth-Str. 22, 71686 REMSECK
Tel: 7146 286330 **Fax:** 7146 286332
Email: mail@gaymap.info **Web site:** http://www.gaymap.info
Freq: Annual; **Cover Price:** Free; **Circ:** 25,000
Editor: Claus Lemanczyk; **Advertising Manager:** Claus Lemanczyk
Profile: City maps, Tourist information, index and ads for the gay and lesbian audience. The most common travel information of the scene, Sitges edition.
Language(s): English; Spanish
ADVERTISING RATES:
Full Page Mono .... EUR 980
Full Page Colour .... EUR 980
Mechanical Data: Type Area: 190 x 74 mm

FRIENDS THE GAYMAP - AUSG. STUTTGART
728032G89A-1740

Editorial: Max-Eyth-Str. 22, 71686 REMSECK
Tel: 7146 286330 **Fax:** 7146 286332
Email: mail@gaymap.info **Web site:** http://www.gaymap.info
Freq: Annual; **Cover Price:** Free; **Circ:** 25,000
Editor: Claus Lemanczyk; **Advertising Manager:** Claus Lemanczyk
Profile: City maps, Tourist information, index and ads for the gay and lesbian audience. The most common travel information of the scene, Stuttgart edition.
Language(s): English; German
ADVERTISING RATES:
Full Page Mono .... EUR 840
Full Page Colour .... EUR 840
Mechanical Data: Type Area: 190 x 74 mm

FRIENDS THE GAYMAP - AUSG. TEL AVIV
1825304G89A-12374

Editorial: Max-Eyth-Str. 22, 71686 REMSECK
Tel: 7146 286330 **Fax:** 7146 286332
Email: mail@gaymap.info **Web site:** http://www.gaymap.info
Freq: Half-yearly; **Cover Price:** Free; **Circ:** 25,000
Editor: Claus Lemanczyk; **Advertising Manager:** Claus Lemanczyk
Profile: City maps, Tourist information, index and ads for the gay and lesbian audience. The most common travel information of the scene, Tel Aviv edition.
Language(s): English
ADVERTISING RATES:
Full Page Mono .... EUR 1280
Full Page Colour .... EUR 1280
Mechanical Data: Type Area: 190 x 74 mm

FRIENDS THE GAYMAP - AUSG. VIAREGGIO & TORRE DEL LAGO
1793686G89A-12277

Editorial: Max-Eyth-Str. 22, 71686 REMSECK
Tel: 7146 286330 **Fax:** 7146 286332
Email: mail@gaymap.info **Web site:** http://www.gaymap.info
Freq: Annual; **Cover Price:** Free; **Circ:** 25,000
Editor: Claus Lemanczyk; **Advertising Manager:** Claus Lemanczyk
Profile: City maps, Tourist information, index and ads for the gay and lesbian audience. The most common travel information of the scene, Viareggio & Torre del Lago edition.
Language(s): English
ADVERTISING RATES:
Full Page Mono .... EUR 980
Full Page Colour .... EUR 980
Mechanical Data: Type Area: 190 x 74 mm

FRIENDS THE GAYMAP - AUSG. WIEN
728048G89A-2060

Editorial: Max-Eyth-Str. 22, 71686 REMSECK
Tel: 7146 286330 **Fax:** 7146 286332
Email: mail@gaymap.info **Web site:** http://www.gaymap.info
Freq: Annual; **Cover Price:** Free; **Circ:** 25,000
Editor: Claus Lemanczyk; **Advertising Manager:** Claus Lemanczyk
Profile: City maps, Tourist information, index and ads for the gay and lesbian audience. The most common travel information of the scene, Vienna edition.
Language(s): English; German
ADVERTISING RATES:
Full Page Mono .... EUR 980
Full Page Colour .... EUR 980
Mechanical Data: Type Area: 190 x 74 mm

FRIENDS THE GAYMAP - AUSG. ZÜRICH
728033G89A-1760

Editorial: Max-Eyth-Str. 22, 71686 REMSECK
Tel: 7146 286330 **Fax:** 7146 286332
Email: mail@gaymap.info **Web site:** http://www.gaymap.info
Freq: Annual; **Cover Price:** Free; **Circ:** 25,000
Editor: Claus Lemanczyk; **Advertising Manager:** Claus Lemanczyk
Profile: City maps, Tourist information, index and ads for the gay and lesbian audience. The most common travel information of the scene, Zurich edition.
Language(s): English; German
ADVERTISING RATES:
Full Page Mono .... EUR 980
Full Page Colour .... EUR 980
Mechanical Data: Type Area: 190 x 74 mm

FRISCH VOM BAUERN
1799227G74M-831

Editorial: Creutzfelderstr. 29, 74629 PFEDELBACH
Tel: 7941 984166 **Fax:** 7941 984165
Email: reinhold.bruetting@mediabuero-sued.de **Web site:** http://www.frischvombauern.info
Freq: Annual; **Cover Price:** Free; **Circ:** 30,000
Profile: Direct Market Directory: Direct marketer in Hohenlohe and Unterland.
Language(s): German
Mechanical Data: Type Area: 240 x 175 mm

FRISCHELOGISTIK
1639748G10-523

Editorial: Am Eichenwald 2, 21335 LÜNEBURG
Tel: 4131 265522
Email: marcus.sefrin@agrimedia.com **Web site:** http://www.frischelogistik.com
Freq: 6 issues yearly; **Annual Sub.:** EUR 66,60; **Circ:** 5,000
Editor: Marcus Sefrin; **Advertising Manager:** Ute Friedrich
Profile: Magazine on food logistics.
Language(s): German
ADVERTISING RATES:
Full Page Mono .... EUR 1820
Full Page Colour .... EUR 2750
Mechanical Data: Type Area: 267 x 188 mm, No. of Columns (Display): 4, Col Widths (Display): 47 mm
Copy instructions: *Copy Date:* 14 days prior to publication
Official Journal of: Organ d. Verb. dt. Kühlhäuser u. Kühllogistikunternehmen e.V. u. d. Transfrigoroute Deutschland e.V.

FRISEUR DIRECT
728056G15B-140

Editorial: Deggingstr. 16, 44141 DORTMUND
Tel: 231 527615 **Fax:** 231 575175
Email: info@friseure-nrw.de **Web site:** http://www.friseure-nrw.de
Freq: Quarterly; Free to qualifying individuals
Annual Sub.: EUR 10,00; **Circ:** 7,780
Editor: Olaf Kraußlach
Profile: Official magazine of the Hairdressers' Association in NRW, containing articles on hair-styling and cutting.
Language(s): German
ADVERTISING RATES:
Full Page Mono .... EUR 1989
Full Page Colour .... EUR 1989
Mechanical Data: Type Area: 255 x 178 mm, No. of Columns (Display): 4, Col Widths (Display): 45 mm
Copy instructions: *Copy Date:* 28 days prior to publication
BUSINESS: COSMETICS & HAIRDRESSING: Hairdressing

FRISEUR WELT
728057G15B-160

Editorial: Neuhauser Str. 21, 78464 KONSTANZ
Tel: 7531 812221 **Fax:** 7531 812299
Email: stolz@friseurwelt-online.de **Web site:** http://www.friseurwelt.net
Freq: Monthly; Free to qualifying individuals
Annual Sub.: EUR 78,00; **Circ:** 34,409
Editor: Heidi Stolz; **Advertising Manager:** Ulrike Buchta
Profile: FRISEUR WELT has over 60 years, the magazine for hairdressers in Germany.FRISEUR WELT reached a monthly circulation of over 35,000 copies all relevant market participants. As official media partner of the German Confederation of Hairdressing are all organized guild of hairdressers and their employees reader salon businesses. Other readers are salon owners in the self-guided or master hairdresser salon in the local branches to their employees as well as industry, trade and service providers of the hair cosmetic industry and educational institutions. FRISEUR WELT up to date on the happenings in the industry, as the hairstyle trends and techniques. Other topics are new and existing products, interviews, portraits salon, business management, etc.
Language(s): German
Readership: Aimed at hairdressers.
ADVERTISING RATES:
Full Page Mono .... EUR 3000
Full Page Colour .... EUR 4800
Mechanical Data: Type Area: 284 x 199 mm, No. of Columns (Display): 4, Col Widths (Display): 48 mm
Copy instructions: *Copy Date:* 35 days prior to publication
Official Journal of: Organ d. Zentralverb. d. Dt. Friseurhandwerks
BUSINESS: COSMETICS & HAIRDRESSING: Hairdressing

FRISUREN
1606880G74A-3310

Editorial: Rotweg 8, 76532 BADEN-BADEN
Tel: 7221 3501130 **Fax:** 7221 3501133
Email: andrea.muesel@klambt.de **Web site:** http://www.media.klambt.de
Freq: Half-yearly; **Cover Price:** EUR 1,95; **Circ:** 90,000
Editor: Andrea Müsel
Profile: Magazine for women focusing on hair dressing.
Language(s): German
ADVERTISING RATES:
Full Page Mono .... EUR 3985
Full Page Colour .... EUR 4322
Mechanical Data: Type Area: 250 x 195 mm, No. of Columns (Display): 4, Col Widths (Display): 45 mm
Copy instructions: *Copy Date:* 42 days prior to publication

FRISUREN WELT DER FRAU SPEZIAL
728059G74A-1260

Editorial: Rotweg 8, 76530 BADEN-BADEN
Tel: 7221 3501131 **Fax:** 7221 3501304
Email: meike.adler@klambt.de **Web site:** http://www.media.klambt.de
Freq: Quarterly; **Cover Price:** EUR 1,95; **Circ:** 100,000
Profile: Special issue of the magazine Welt der Frau with trends and tips for hairstyles for women between 18 and 58 years.
Language(s): German
ADVERTISING RATES:
Full Page Mono .... EUR 3985
Full Page Colour .... EUR 4322
Mechanical Data: Type Area: 250 x 195 mm, No. of Columns (Display): 4, Col Widths (Display): 45 mm

FRITZLAR-HOMBERGER ALLGEMEINE
730351G67B-7100

Editorial: Frankfurter Str. 168, 34121 KASSEL
Tel: 561 20300 **Fax:** 561 2032406
Email: info@hna.de **Web site:** http://www.hna.de
Freq: 312 issues yearly; **Circ:** 14,681
Advertising Manager: Andrea Schaller-Öller
Profile: Regional daily newspaper with news on politics, economy, culture, sports, travel, technology, etc. The Fritzlar-Homberger Allgemeine is a local issue of HNA Hessische/Niedersächsische Allgemeine. Twitter: http://twitter.com/hna_online This Outlet offers RSS (Really Simple Syndication).
Language(s): German
ADVERTISING RATES:
SCC .... EUR 37,10
Mechanical Data: Type Area: 430 x 285 mm, No. of Columns (Display): 6, Col Widths (Display): 45 mm
Copy instructions: *Copy Date:* 2 days prior to publication
REGIONAL DAILY & SUNDAY NEWSPAPERS: Regional Daily Newspapers

FRIZZ
728065G80-3900

Editorial: Postfach 110570, 35350 GIESSEN
Tel: 641 932610 **Fax:** 641 9326161
Email: redaktion@frizz-mittelhessen.net **Web site:** http://www.frizz-online.de
Freq: Monthly; **Cover Price:** Free; **Circ:** 16,680
Editor: Peter Hoffmann
Profile: Magazine for the cities of Gießen, Marburg, Wetzlar and the region, with a focus on food, music, art and events. Facebook: http://www.facebook.com/frizz.magazin.
Language(s): German
ADVERTISING RATES:
Full Page Colour .... EUR 2500
Mechanical Data: Type Area: 270 x 195 mm, No. of Columns (Display): 4, Col Widths (Display): 44 mm
CONSUMER: RURAL & REGIONAL INTEREST

FRIZZ
728070G80-3980

Editorial: Katharinenstr. 21, 04109 LEIPZIG
Tel: 341 1494046 **Fax:** 341 1494047
Email: redaktion@leipzig-frizz.de **Web site:** http://www.frizz-magazin.de
Freq: Monthly; **Cover Price:** Free; **Circ:** 25,000
Editor: Eike Käubler; **Advertising Manager:** Alexander Koning
Profile: Magazine for the city of Leipzig and the region, with a focus on food, music, art and events. Facebook: http://www.facebook.com/frizz.magazin.
Language(s): German
ADVERTISING RATES:
Full Page Colour .... EUR 2880
Mechanical Data: Type Area: 270 x 195 mm, No. of Columns (Display): 4, Col Widths (Display): 45 mm
CONSUMER: RURAL & REGIONAL INTEREST

FRIZZ
728074G80-4060

Editorial: Wilhelminenstr. 7A, 64283 DARMSTADT
Tel: 6151 915814 **Fax:** 6151 915858
Email: achim.gliem@frizz-darmstadt.de **Web site:** http://www.frizz-darmstadt.de
Freq: Monthly; **Cover Price:** Free; **Circ:** 14,800
Editor: Achim Gliem; **Advertising Manager:** Birgit Adler
Profile: Magazine for the city of Darmstadt and the region, with a focus on food, music, art and events. Facebook: http://www.facebook.com/frizz.magazin.
Language(s): German
Readership: Aimed at young people between 15 and 35 years of age who enjoy experiences and socialising.
ADVERTISING RATES:
Full Page Colour .... EUR 3200
Mechanical Data: Type Area: 270 x 190 mm, No. of Columns (Display): 4, Col Widths (Display): 44 mm
Copy instructions: *Copy Date:* 15 days prior to publication
CONSUMER: RURAL & REGIONAL INTEREST

FRIZZ
739163G80-9100

Editorial: Hans-Bunte-Str. 8, 69123 HEIDELBERG
Tel: 6221 7500270 **Fax:** 6221 7500273
Email: landau@smv-medien.de **Web site:** http://www.frizz-magazin.de
Freq: Monthly; **Cover Price:** Free; **Circ:** 8,994
Editor: Jürgen Bruch; **Advertising Manager:** Jürgen Bruch
Profile: Magazine for the city of Landau and the region Palatinate, with a focus on food, music, art and events. Facebook: http://www.facebook.com/frizz.magazin.
Language(s): German
Readership: Aimed at people from 16 to 40 years of age.
ADVERTISING RATES:
Full Page Mono .... EUR 1760
Full Page Colour .... EUR 2200
Mechanical Data: No. of Columns (Display): 4, Col Widths (Display): 45 mm, Type Area: 270 x 195 mm
Copy instructions: *Copy Date:* 12 days prior to publication
CONSUMER: RURAL & REGIONAL INTEREST

FRIZZ
1622679G80-13902

Editorial: Gerberstr. 7, 97070 WÜRZBURG
Tel: 931 3299916 **Fax:** 931 3299922
Email: schmitt@frizz-wuerzburg.de **Web site:** http://www.frizz-wuerzburg.de
Freq: Monthly; **Cover Price:** Free; **Circ:** 24,523
Editor: Max Schmitt; **Advertising Manager:** Stefan Luz
Profile: City magazine for Würzburg and the region reported on music, party, film, culture and entertainment events on the ground. It is from 30 the previous month in more than 500 cafes, bars, clubs, pubs, restaurants, cinemas and retail in Würzburg and environment. Facebook: http://www.facebook.com/pages/FRIZZ-W%C3%9CRZBURG/501315135471.
Language(s): German
ADVERTISING RATES:
Full Page Mono .... EUR 1450
Full Page Colour .... EUR 2500
Mechanical Data: Type Area: 270 x 190 mm, No. of Columns (Display): 4, Col Widths (Display): 44 mm
Copy instructions: *Copy Date:* 8 days prior to publication
CONSUMER: RURAL & REGIONAL INTEREST

FRIZZ
1659655G80-14269

Editorial: Barbarossaplatz 6, 76137 KARLSRUHE
Tel: 721 9378682 **Fax:** 721 9378696
Email: breveglieri@smv-medien.de **Web site:** http://www.frizz-magazin.de
Freq: Monthly; **Cover Price:** Free; **Circ:** 16,885
Editor: Daniele Breveglieri; **Advertising Manager:** Daniele Breveglieri
Profile: Magazine for the cities of Karlsruhe, Pforzheim, Offenburg and the region, with a focus on food, music, art and events. Facebook: http://www.facebook.com/frizz.magazin.
Language(s): German
ADVERTISING RATES:
Full Page Colour .... EUR 3000
Mechanical Data: Type Area: 270 x 195 mm, No. of Columns (Display): 4, Col Widths (Display): 45 mm
Copy instructions: *Copy Date:* 12 days prior to publication
CONSUMER: RURAL & REGIONAL INTEREST

FRIZZ
1659656G80-14270

Editorial: Hans-Bunte-Str. 8, 69123 HEIDELBERG
Tel: 6221 7500270 **Fax:** 6221 7500273
Email: heidelberg@smv-medien.de **Web site:** http://www.frizz-magazin.de
Freq: Monthly; **Cover Price:** Free; **Circ:** 7,406
Editor: Jürgen Bruch; **Advertising Manager:** Jürgen Bruch
Profile: Magazine for the city of Heidelberg and the region, with a focus on food, music, art and events. Facebook: http://www.facebook.com/frizz.magazin.
Language(s): German
ADVERTISING RATES:
Full Page Colour .... EUR 2200
Mechanical Data: Type Area: 270 x 195 mm, No. of Columns (Display): 4, Col Widths (Display): 45 mm
Copy instructions: *Copy Date:* 12 days prior to publication
CONSUMER: RURAL & REGIONAL INTEREST

FRIZZ
728061G89C-4794

Editorial: Treibgasse 19, 63739 ASCHAFFENBURG
Tel: 6021 4448823 **Fax:** 6021 4448844
Email: b.bogner@frizz-ab.de **Web site:** http://www.frizz-ab.de
Freq: Monthly; **Cover Price:** Free; **Circ:** 17,834
Editor: Bettina Bogner; **Advertising Manager:** Rainer Koehl
Profile: Magazine for the city of Aschaffenburg and the region, with a focus on food, music, art and events.
Language(s): German
Readership: Aimed at young people between 15 and 35 years of age.

ADVERTISING RATES:
Full Page Mono .... EUR 2500
Full Page Colour .... EUR 2500
Mechanical Data: Type Area: 270 x 190 mm, No. of Columns (Display): 4, Col Widths (Display): 44 mm
Copy instructions: *Copy Date:* 10 days prior to publication
CONSUMER: HOLIDAYS & TRAVEL: Entertainment Guides

FRIZZ 728062G89C-4795
Editorial: Varrentrappstr. 53, 60486 FRANKFURT
Tel: 69 97951731 **Fax:** 69 97951729
Email: zehentner@frizz-frankfurt.de **Web site:** http://www.frizz-magazin.de
Freq: Monthly; **Cover Price:** Free; **Circ:** 39,403
Editor: Heidi Zehentner; **Advertising Manager:** Erk Walter
Profile: Magazine for the city of Frankfurt and the region Vordertaunus, with a focus on food, music, art and events. Facebook: http://www.facebook.com/frizz.magazin.
Language(s): German
Readership: Aimed at people between 15 and 35 years.
ADVERTISING RATES:
Full Page Mono .... EUR 2200
Full Page Colour .... EUR 3800
Mechanical Data: Type Area: 270 x 195 mm, No. of Columns (Display): 4, Col Widths (Display): 45 mm
CONSUMER: HOLIDAYS & TRAVEL: Entertainment Guides

FRIZZ 728064G89C-4796
Editorial: Waldstr. 226, 63071 OFFENBACH
Tel: 69 80106782 **Fax:** 69 80106784
Email: info@frizz-offenbach.de **Web site:** http://www.frizz-offenbach.de
Freq: Monthly; **Cover Price:** Free; **Circ:** 9,962
Profile: Magazine for the cities of Offenbach, Hanau and the region, with a focus on food, music, art and events. Facebook: http://www.facebook.com/frizz.magazin.
Language(s): German
Readership: Aimed at young people between 15 and 35 years of age.
ADVERTISING RATES:
Full Page Mono .... EUR 2400
Full Page Colour .... EUR 2400
Mechanical Data: Type Area: 270 x 195 mm, No. of Columns (Display): 4, Col Widths (Display): 44 mm
Copy instructions: *Copy Date:* 17 days prior to publication
CONSUMER: HOLIDAYS & TRAVEL: Entertainment Guides

FRIZZ 728067G89C-4797
Editorial: Sophienstr. 34, 34117 KASSEL
Tel: 561 720900 **Fax:** 561 7209045
Email: info@frizz-kassel.de **Web site:** http://www.frizz-kassel.de
Freq: Monthly; **Cover Price:** Free; **Circ:** 19,817
Editor: Alexander Röder; **Advertising Manager:** Melanie Lange
Profile: Magazine for the city of Kassel and the region, with a focus on food, music, art and events. Facebook: http://www.facebook.com/frizz.magazin.
Language(s): German
Readership: Aimed at young people between 15 and 35 years of age.
ADVERTISING RATES:
Full Page Colour .... EUR 2550
Mechanical Data: Type Area: 270 x 195 mm, No. of Columns (Display): 4, Col Widths (Display): 44 mm
CONSUMER: HOLIDAYS & TRAVEL: Entertainment Guides

FRIZZ 728068G89C-4798
Editorial: Görlitzer Str. 43, 01099 DRESDEN
Tel: 351 42696430 **Fax:** 351 79664612
Email: redaktion@dresden-frizz.de **Web site:** http://www.frizz-magazin.de
Freq: Monthly; **Cover Price:** Free; **Circ:** 17,800
Editor: Eike Käubler; **Advertising Manager:** Frank Lotzmann
Profile: Magazine for the city of Dresden and the region, with a focus on food, music, art and events. Facebook: http://www.facebook.com/frizz.magazin.
Language(s): German
Readership: Aimed at young people between 15 and 35 years of age.
ADVERTISING RATES:
Full Page Mono .... EUR 1640
Full Page Colour .... EUR 2880
Mechanical Data: Type Area: 270 x 195 mm, No. of Columns (Display): 4, Col Widths (Display): 45 mm
Copy instructions: *Copy Date:* 15 days prior to publication
CONSUMER: HOLIDAYS & TRAVEL: Entertainment Guides

FRIZZ 728069G89C-4799
Editorial: Barfüßer Str. 7, 06108 HALLE
Tel: 345 2080452 **Fax:** 345 2080452
Email: redaktion@halle-frizz.de **Web site:** http://www.halle-frizz.de
Freq: Monthly; **Cover Price:** Free; **Circ:** 25,000
Editor: Eike Käubler; **Advertising Manager:** Gerd Behrendt
Profile: Magazine for the city of Halle and the region, with a focus on food, music, art and events. Facebook: http://www.facebook.com/frizz.magazin.
Language(s): German
Readership: Aimed at young people between 15 and 35 years of age.
ADVERTISING RATES:
Full Page Colour .... EUR 2880
Mechanical Data: Type Area: 270 x 195 mm, No. of Columns (Display): 4, Col Widths (Display): 45 mm
CONSUMER: HOLIDAYS & TRAVEL: Entertainment Guides

FRIZZ 728072G89C-4800
Editorial: Weberstr. 17, 55130 MAINZ
Tel: 6131 9651131 **Fax:** 6131 9651190
Email: beaterappold@frizzgehtaus.de **Web site:** http://www.frizz-magazin.de
Freq: Monthly; **Cover Price:** Free; **Circ:** 17,706
Editor: Beate Rappold; **Advertising Manager:** Michael Rappold
Profile: Magazine for the cities of Mainz, Wiesbaden and the region, with a focus on food, music, art and events. Facebook: http://www.facebook.com/frizz.magazin.
Language(s): German
Readership: Aimed at young people between 15 and 35 years of age.
ADVERTISING RATES:
Full Page Colour .... EUR 3300
Mechanical Data: Type Area: 270 x 195 mm, No. of Columns (Display): 4, Col Widths (Display): 44 mm
Copy instructions: *Copy Date:* 15 days prior to publication
CONSUMER: HOLIDAYS & TRAVEL: Entertainment Guides

FRIZZ - AUSG. ULM 728075G80-4080
Editorial: Henkersgraben 41, 89073 ULM
Tel: 731 8000918 **Fax:** 731 8000910
Email: lea.baader@frizz-ulm.de **Web site:** http://www.frizz-ulm.de
Freq: Monthly; **Cover Price:** Free; **Circ:** 15,297
Editor: Lea Baader; **Advertising Manager:** Yasmin Tan
Profile: Magazine for the cities of Ulm, Neu-Ulm and the region, with a focus on food, music, art and events. Facebook: http://www.facebook.com/frizz.magazin.
Language(s): German
ADVERTISING RATES:
Full Page Mono .... EUR 2000
Full Page Colour .... EUR 2500
Mechanical Data: Type Area: 270 x 190 mm, No. of Columns (Display): 4, Col Widths (Display): 44 mm
CONSUMER: RURAL & REGIONAL INTEREST

FRUCHTHANDEL MAGAZIN 728086G26C-40_50
Editorial: Lindemannstr. 12, 40237 DÜSSELDORF
Tel: 211 9910435 **Fax:** 211 663162
Email: redaktion@fruchthandel.de **Web site:** http://www.fruchthandel.de
Freq: Weekly; **Annual Sub.:** EUR 237,00; **Circ:** 4,213
Editor: Gabriele Bastian; **Advertising Manager:** Hans-J. Fuhrmann
Profile: Magazine about all aspects of the fruit trade.
Language(s): German
ADVERTISING RATES:
Full Page Mono .... EUR 1640
Full Page Colour .... EUR 2765
Mechanical Data: Type Area: 281 x 186 mm, No. of Columns (Display): 3, Col Widths (Display): 58 mm
Copy instructions: *Copy Date:* 10 days prior to publication
Supplement(s): fresh convenience
BUSINESS: GARDEN TRADE

FRÜHFÖRDERUNG INTERDISZIPLINÄR 728089G62G-60
Editorial: Seidlstr. 4/II, 80335 MÜNCHEN
Tel: 89 54589820 **Fax:** 89 54589829
Email: thurmair@astffby.de
Freq: Quarterly; **Annual Sub.:** EUR 49,90; **Circ:** 1,800
Editor: Martin Thurmair
Profile: Medical journal about the theory and practice of child care. Focuses on the care and development of children with learning and physical disabilities.
Language(s): German
ADVERTISING RATES:
Full Page Mono .... EUR 625
Full Page Colour .... EUR 1555
Mechanical Data: Type Area: 200 x 130 mm, No. of Columns (Display): 2, Col Widths (Display): 63 mm
Copy instructions: *Copy Date:* 31 days prior to publication
Official Journal of: Organ d. Vereinigung f. interdisziplinäre Frühförderung e.V.
BUSINESS: CHURCH & SCHOOL EQUIPMENT & EDUCATION: Special Needs Education

---

FRUIT PROCESSING 728092G22A-1020
Editorial: Raiffeisenstr. 27, 56587 STRASSENHAUS
Tel: 2634 92350 **Fax:** 2634 923535
Email: editorial@fruit-processing.com **Web site:** http://www.fruit-processing.com
Freq: 6 issues yearly; **Annual Sub.:** EUR 115,00; **Circ:** 3,784
Editor: Evi Brennich; **Advertising Manager:** Cornelia Hebbe
Profile: Technical journal about fruit processing and fruit juice.
Language(s): English
Readership: Aimed at technical and commercial managers, beverage and food technologists, marketing managers and scientists.
ADVERTISING RATES:
Full Page Mono .... EUR 2030
Full Page Colour .... EUR 2840
Mechanical Data: Type Area: 250 x 175 mm, No. of Columns (Display): 3, Col Widths (Display): 55 mm
Copy instructions: *Copy Date:* 25 days prior to publication
BUSINESS: FOOD

FRUNCH 2004323G74P-1344
Editorial: Walter-Oertel-Str. 50, 09112 CHEMNITZ
Tel: 371 3550312 **Fax:** 371 3550314
Email: info@371stadtmagazin.de **Web site:** http://www.371stadtmagazin.de
Freq: Annual; **Cover Price:** Free; **Circ:** 15,000
Editor: Lars Neuenfeld
Profile: Facebook: http://www.facebook.com/pages/371-Stadtmagazin/111663338878072.
Language(s): German

FT FLEISCHEREI TECHNIK MEAT TECHNOLOGY 728108G22D-180
Editorial: Augustenstr. 10, 80333 MÜNCHEN
Tel: 89 370600 **Fax:** 89 37060111
Email: muc@blmedien.de **Web site:** http://www.fleischerei-technik.de
Freq: 6 issues yearly; **Annual Sub.:** EUR 81,00; **Circ:** 7,188
Editor: Annemarie Heinrichsdobler; **Advertising Manager:** Bernd Moeser
Profile: Magazine for managers of the meat processing industry, craftsmen in the meat processing industry and producers and sellers of meat processing machinery.
Language(s): English; German; Spanish
ADVERTISING RATES:
Full Page Mono .... EUR 3550
Full Page Colour .... EUR 6030
Mechanical Data: Type Area: 254 x 185 mm, No. of Columns (Display): 4, Col Widths (Display): 43 mm
Copy instructions: *Copy Date:* 15 days prior to publication
BUSINESS: FOOD: Meat Trade

FUB FLÄCHENMANAGEMENT UND BODENORDNUNG 1829855G4C-19
Editorial: Marktplatz 13, 65183 WIESBADEN
Tel: 611 360980 **Fax:** 611 301303
Email: info@chmielorz.de **Web site:** http://www.chmielorz.de
Freq: 6 issues yearly; **Annual Sub.:** EUR 119,00; **Circ:** 1,300
Editor: Theo Kötter; **Advertising Manager:** Franz Stypa
Profile: Journal of Real Estate, Planning and Surveying. The fub Flächenmanagement und Bodenordnung published practice-relevant contributions from the following areas: land management, land planning, urban and regional planning, land transactions, land valuation, land registry and surveying.
Language(s): German
ADVERTISING RATES:
Full Page Mono .... EUR 800
Full Page Colour .... EUR 1700
Mechanical Data: Type Area: 244 x 175 mm, No. of Columns (Display): 2, Col Widths (Display): 84 mm
Copy instructions: *Copy Date:* 21 days prior to publication

FUCHSBAU 728111G27-780
Editorial: Derschlager Str. 26, 58540 MEINERZHAGEN **Tel:** 2354 73580 **Fax:** 2354 73201
Email: fuchsbau@otto-fuchs.com **Web site:** http://www.otto-fuchs.com
Freq: Annual; **Cover Price:** Free; **Circ:** 5,000
Editor: Holger Müller
Profile: Magazine for employees of Otto Fuchs Metallwerke.
Language(s): German

FULDAER ZEITUNG 728149G67B-5460
Editorial: Frankfurter Str. 8, 36043 FULDA
Tel: 661 280304 **Fax:** 661 280279
Email: redaktion@fuldaerzeitung.de **Web site:** http://www.fuldaerzeitung.de
Freq: 312 issues yearly; **Circ:** 106,031
Editor: Hermann-Josef Seggewiß; **News Editor:** Michael Tillmann; **Advertising Manager:** Rudolf Lechner
Profile: Regional daily newspaper covering politics, economics, sports, travel and technology. Facebook: http://www.facebook.com/pages/Fuldaer-Zeitung/162547827109989 Twitter: http://twitter.com/fuldaerzeitung This Outlet offers RSS (Really Simple Syndication).
Language(s): German
ADVERTISING RATES:
SCC .... EUR 254,40
Copy instructions: *Copy Date:* 3 days prior to publication
REGIONAL DAILY & SUNDAY NEWSPAPERS: Regional Daily Newspapers

---

FUNK UHR 728181G76C-180
Editorial: Axel-Springer-Platz 1, 20355 HAMBURG
Tel: 40 34700 **Fax:** 40 34722601
Email: funkuhr@axelspringer.de **Web site:** http://www.axelspringer.de
Freq: Weekly; **Annual Sub.:** EUR 70,20; **Circ:** 556,472
Editor: Jan von Frenckell; **Advertising Manager:** Arne Bergmann
Profile: FUNK UHR is the magazine that appeals to a competent reporting and the thematic focus primarily women and is still used by men like and intense. Around the detailed TV program provides part of the mantle FUNK UHR key issues such as health and wellness, background information and current news on nutrition, fashion, beauty, partnership and family, tips on money, legal and budget. In addition, reports on special people, stories of emotion and each month a specific topic. FUNK UHR is like a girlfriend. It shows the reader that she knows them and gives you the feeling so it is just I think too.
Language(s): German
ADVERTISING RATES:
Full Page Mono .... EUR 16000
Full Page Colour .... EUR 24200
Mechanical Data: Type Area: 270 x 206 mm, No. of Columns (Display): 4, Col Widths (Display): 50 mm
Copy instructions: *Copy Date:* 21 days prior to publication
CONSUMER: MUSIC & PERFORMING ARTS: TV & Radio

FUNKSCHAU 1661690G2D-769
Editorial: Gruber Str. 46a, 85586 POING
Tel: 8121 951351 **Fax:** 8121 951656
Email: mkien@funkschau.de **Web site:** http://www.funkschau.de
Cover Price: Paid; **Circ:** 65,794 Unique Users
Editor: Ernst Lehmhofer; **Advertising Manager:** Michael Nerke
Profile: Ezine: Magazine containing information about electronic communications.
Language(s): German
BUSINESS: COMMUNICATIONS, ADVERTISING & MARKETING: Broadcasting

---

FUNKSCHAU 728176G18B-95
Editorial: Gruber Str. 46a, 85586 POING
Tel: 8121 951352 **Fax:** 8121 951656
Email: rladner@funkschau.de **Web site:** http://www.funkschau.de
Freq: 23 issues yearly; **Annual Sub.:** EUR 109,00; **Circ:** 39,102
Editor: Ralf Ladner; **Advertising Manager:** Michael Nerke
Profile: funkschau is the medium for professional communication technologies. funkschau's editorial value and its credibility are confirmed by the high level of subscription circulation. Influential ITC decision makers rely on their funkschau when they gather information about new products, solutions and services in professional elecommunication and IT. They benefit from bi-weekly funkschau as intensely as from the up-to-date web service funkschau.de and the funkschau.de newsletter.
Language(s): German
ADVERTISING RATES:
Full Page Colour .... EUR 8995
Mechanical Data: Type Area: 262 x 195 mm, No. of Columns (Display): 3, Col Widths (Display): 56 mm
Copy instructions: *Copy Date:* 21 days prior to publication
BUSINESS: ELECTRONICS: Telecommunications

FUNKSCHAU HANDEL 728177G43A-500
Editorial: Gruber Str. 46a, 85586 POING
Tel: 8121 951352 **Fax:** 8121 951656
Email: rladner@funkschau.de **Web site:** http://www.funkschau.de
Freq: Monthly; **Annual Sub.:** EUR 89,00; **Circ:** 10,678
Editor: Ralf Ladner; **Advertising Manager:** Michael Nerke
Profile: Magazine covering aspects of distribution, carrier, provider, telecommunications, consumer electronics, satellite techniques, IT and network engineering.
Language(s): German
ADVERTISING RATES:
Full Page Colour .... EUR 4385
Mechanical Data: Type Area: 260 x 185 mm, No. of Columns (Display): 3, Col Widths (Display): 56 mm
Copy instructions: *Copy Date:* 21 days prior to publication
BUSINESS: ELECTRICAL RETAIL TRADE

FUR FAMILIE UND RECHT 728189G44-3110
Editorial: Luxemburger Str. 449, 50939 KÖLN
Tel: 221 943737000 **Fax:** 221 943737201
Email: info@wolterskluwer.de **Web site:** http://www.wolterskluwer.de
Freq: Monthly; **Annual Sub.:** EUR 160,90; **Circ:** 2,100
Editor: Michael Klein
Profile: Journal covering family law.
Language(s): German
Readership: Aimed at members of the legal profession.
ADVERTISING RATES:
Full Page Mono .... EUR 890
Full Page Colour .... EUR 1955
Mechanical Data: Type Area: 255 x 184 mm
Copy instructions: *Copy Date:* 35 days prior to publication
BUSINESS: LEGAL

FÜR SIE 728134G74A-1280

Editorial: Poßmoorweg 2, 22301 HAMBURG
Tel: 40 27173574 **Fax:** 40 27172059
Email: redaktion@fuer-sie.de **Web site:** http://www.fuer-sie.de
Freq: 26 issues yearly; **Annual Sub.:** EUR 57,20; **Circ:** 426,248
Editor: Susanne Walsleben; **Advertising Manager:** Tobias van Duynen
Profile: FÜR SIE - is the modern classic in the segment of the 14-day women's magazines. Diverse, pragmatic and close to everyday life, it stands for a modern mix of topics for women from 35 onwards. FÜR SIE lives a close and trusting relationship with its readers, which is based on a comprehensive understanding of the needs of modern women. FÜR SIE stands for sound and involved journalism in implementation of appropriate topics - from fashion and beauty about fitness and health up to cooking and culture. Facebook: http://www.facebook.com/Kreativkommando.
Language(s): German
Readership: Aimed at women.
ADVERTISING RATES:
Full Page Mono .... EUR 28200
Full Page Colour .... EUR 28200
Mechanical Data: Type Area: 243 x 174 mm, No. of Columns (Display): 4, Col Widths (Display): 41 mm
Copy instructions: *Copy Date:* 49 days prior to publication
CONSUMER: WOMEN'S INTEREST CONSUMER MAGAZINES: Women's Interest

FUREN 728188G21A-1680

Editorial: John-Deere-Str. 70, 68163 MANNHEIM
Tel: 621 8298416 **Fax:** 621 8298300
Email: hironjeanclaude@johndeere.com **Web site:** http://www.johndeere.com
Freq: Quarterly; **Cover Price:** Free; **Circ:** 28,000
Editor: Jean-Claude Hiron
Profile: Company publication published by Deere & Company.
Language(s): Danish

FURNIER MAGAZIN 728190G23A-753

Editorial: Fasanenweg 18, 70771 LEINFELDEN-ECHTERDINGEN **Tel:** 711 7591306
Fax: 711 7591440
Email: info@drw-verlag.de **Web site:** http://www.drw-verlag.de
Freq: Annual; **Cover Price:** EUR 5,00; **Circ:** 13,000
Editor: Karsten Koch; **Advertising Manager:** Oliver Heinz
Profile: Magazine covering distribution and production of veneer furniture.
Language(s): English; German
ADVERTISING RATES:
Full Page Mono .... EUR 5000
Full Page Colour .... EUR 6680
Mechanical Data: Type Area: 270 x 175 mm, No. of Columns (Display): 4, Col Widths (Display): 40 mm
Copy instructions: *Copy Date:* 30 days prior to publication
Supplement to: HK Holz- und Kunststoffverarbeitung, Holz-Zentralblatt
BUSINESS: FURNISHINGS & FURNITURE

THE FURROW 728191G21A-1700

Editorial: John-Deere-Str. 70, 68163 MANNHEIM
Tel: 621 8298416 **Fax:** 621 8298300
Email: hironjeanclaude@johndeere.com **Web site:** http://www.johndeere.com
Freq: 5 issues yearly; **Cover Price:** Free; **Circ:** 56,000
Editor: Jean-Claude Hiron
Profile: Company publication published by Deere & Company.
Language(s): English

FÜRSTENFELDBRUCKER TAGBLATT 728138G67B-5480

Editorial: Pfaffenrieder Str. 9, 82515 WOLFRATSHAUSEN **Tel:** 8171 2690
Fax: 8171 269240
Email: fsav@merkur-online.de **Web site:** http://www.merkur-online.de
Freq: 312 issues yearly; **Circ:** 17,081
Advertising Manager: Hans-Georg Bechthold
Profile: The Münchner Merkur with its own local newspapers, of which the Fürstenfeldbrucker Tagblatt is one that, the leading regional newspaper brand in the Munich area - the most affluent area of Germany. The combination of newspaper and region is the foundation on which to build the success of the title. This is the newspaper not only the factual news agency, but forms a community of solidarity with its readers and the local community. The clear focus on local reporting creates a high regard to human reader loyalty. She presses one hand in the very high number of close to 180,000 subscribers. Also for the high reader-commitment is the loyalty of the total current 827 000 daily readers, the Münchner Merkur or one of its local newspapers usually read over many years. The Münchner Merkur with its own local newspapers is a newspaper for the whole family, tradition and modern life for one of the most beautiful regions of Germany unites. Reliable, informative, critical: the Münchner Merkur is the indispensable daily newspaper for the region. Facebook: http://www.facebook.com/pages/merkur-online.de/190176143327.
Language(s): German
ADVERTISING RATES:
SCC .... EUR 43,60
Mechanical Data: Type Area: 474 x 324 mm, No. of Columns (Display): 7, Col Widths (Display): 45 mm
Copy instructions: *Copy Date:* 1 day prior to publication
Supplement(s): Gröbenzell im Blick
REGIONAL DAILY & SUNDAY NEWSPAPERS: Regional Daily Newspapers

FÜRTHER NACHRICHTEN 728139G67B-5500

Editorial: Marienstr. 9, 90402 NÜRNBERG
Tel: 911 2160 **Fax:** 911 2162432
Email: emr@nn-online.de **Web site:** http://www.nuernberger-nachrichten.de
Freq: 312 issues yearly; **Circ:** 31,096
Profile: Daily newspaper with regional news and a local sports section.
Language(s): German
ADVERTISING RATES:
SCC .... EUR 87,20
Mechanical Data: Type Area: 430 x 280 mm, No. of Columns (Display): 6, Col Widths (Display): 45 mm
Copy instructions: *Copy Date:* 2 days prior to publication
Supplement(s): sechs+sechzig
REGIONAL DAILY & SUNDAY NEWSPAPERS: Regional Daily Newspapers

DER FUSS 742636G52D-120

Editorial: Schubartstr. 21, 73312 GEISLINGEN
Tel: 7331 930153 **Fax:** 7331 930191
Email: thomas.schmidt@der-fuss.de **Web site:** http://www.der-fuss.de
Freq: 7 issues yearly; Free to qualifying individuals
Annual Sub.: EUR 45,15; **Circ:** 8,329
Editor: Thomas Schmidt; **Advertising Manager:** Sibylle Lutz
Profile: Magazine on podology and chiropody.
Language(s): German
ADVERTISING RATES:
Full Page Mono .... EUR 1785
Full Page Colour .... EUR 2985
Mechanical Data: Type Area: 262 x 185 mm, No. of Columns (Display): 4, Col Widths (Display): 43 mm
Copy instructions: *Copy Date:* 21 days prior to publication
BUSINESS: GIFT TRADE: Leather

FUSS & SPRUNGGELENK 1616262G56A-11211

Editorial: Salzburger Leite 1, 97616 BAD NEUSTADT
Tel: 3669 662320 **Fax:** 36691 81013
Email: raefuhrmann@aol.com
Freq: Quarterly; **Annual Sub.:** EUR 187,00; **Circ:** 2,630
Editor: Renée Fuhrmann
Profile: Journal of foot and ankle surgery.
Language(s): German
ADVERTISING RATES:
Full Page Mono .... EUR 1600
Full Page Colour .... EUR 2920
Mechanical Data: Type Area: 240 x 175 mm
Official Journal of: Organ d. Dt. Assoziation f. Orthopäd. Fußchirurgie

FUSSBALL TRAINING 728203G75B-70

Editorial: Rektoratsweg 36, 48159 MÜNSTER
Tel: 251 2300571 **Fax:** 251 2300589
Email: ft@philippka.de **Web site:** http://www.fussballtraining.com
Freq: 10 issues yearly; **Annual Sub.:** EUR 46,20; **Circ:** 23,837
Editor: Dietrich Späte; **Advertising Manager:** Peter Möllers
Profile: "fussballtraining" provides reviews from practice for practice: every month trainer and recognized experts give tips on training and the supervision of teams from district league and Bundesliga. With methodical play and exercise series and systematic training sessions the reader is supported with the work with his team. Practical essays on topics from the fields of tactics, training, psychology, sports medicine, sports nutrition and technology also provide comprehensive background knowledge.
Language(s): German
Readership: Aimed at football trainers and coaches.
ADVERTISING RATES:
Full Page Mono .... EUR 2015
Full Page Colour .... EUR 2630
Mechanical Data: Type Area: 267 x 180 mm, No. of Columns (Display): 3, Col Widths (Display): 55 mm
Copy instructions: *Copy Date:* 28 days prior to publication
CONSUMER: SPORT: Football

FUSSBODEN TECHNIK 728206G3D-828

Editorial: An der Alster 21, 20099 HAMBURG
Tel: 40 2484540 **Fax:** 40 2803788
Email: fussbodentechnik@snfachpresse.de **Web site:** http://www.raumausstattung.de
Freq: 6 issues yearly; **Annual Sub.:** EUR 92,00; **Circ:** 7,848
Editor: Michael Steinert; **Advertising Manager:** Rene S. Spiegelberger
Profile: Magazine covering floor heating, radiator installation and sanitation.
Language(s): German
Readership: Read by heating installation engineers.
ADVERTISING RATES:
Full Page Mono .... EUR 2270
Full Page Colour .... EUR 3960
Mechanical Data: Type Area: 252 x 184 mm, No. of Columns (Display): 4, Col Widths (Display): 43 mm
BUSINESS: HEATING & VENTILATION: Heating & Plumbing

FÜSSEN IM ALLGÄU 1931310G89A-12536

Editorial: Kaiser-Maximilian-Platz 1, 87629 FÜSSEN
Tel: 8362 93850 **Fax:** 8362 938520
Email: tourismus@fuessen.de **Web site:** http://www.tourismus-fuessen.de
Freq: Annual; **Cover Price:** Free; **Circ:** 90,000
Profile: Tourist magazine about the spa and holiday resort Füssen with a directory listing accommodation facilities in Füssen, Bad Faulenbach, Hopfen am See and Weissensee.
Language(s): German

FÜSSEN IM ALLGÄU 1931311G89A-12537

Editorial: Kaiser-Maximilian-Platz 1, 87629 FÜSSEN
Tel: 8362 93850 **Fax:** 8362 938520
Email: tourismus@fuessen.de **Web site:** http://www.tourismus-fuessen.de
Freq: Annual; **Cover Price:** Free; **Circ:** 30,000
Profile: Description of the tourist offer of the spa and Holiday resort Füssen, surrounding Allgäuer Königswinkels with Accommodation Directory feet, Füssen, Bad Faulenbach, Hopfen am See and Weissensee.
Language(s): Japanese

FÜSSEN IM ALLGÄU 1931312G89A-12538

Editorial: Kaiser-Maximilian-Platz 1, 87629 FÜSSEN
Tel: 8362 93850 **Fax:** 8362 938520
Email: tourismus@fuessen.de **Web site:** http://www.tourismus-fuessen.de
Freq: Annual; **Cover Price:** Free; **Circ:** 30,000
Profile: Description of the tourist offer of the spa and Holiday resort Füssen, surrounding Allgäuer Königswinkels with Accommodation Directory feet, Füssen, Bad Faulenbach, Hopfen am See and Weissensee.
Language(s): Chinese

FÜSSEN IN THE KING'S NOOK 1931313G89A-12539

Editorial: Kaiser-Maximilian-Platz 1, 87629 FÜSSEN
Tel: 8362 93850 **Fax:** 8362 938520
Email: tourismus@fuessen.de **Web site:** http://www.tourismus-fuessen.de
Freq: Annual; **Cover Price:** Free; **Circ:** 30,000
Profile: Description of the tourist offer of the spa and Holiday resort Füssen, surrounding Allgäuer Königswinkels with Accommodation Directory feet, Füssen, Bad Faulenbach, Hopfen am See and Weissensee.
Language(s): English

FÜSSEN NELLA TERRA DEL RE 1931314G89A-12540

Editorial: Kaiser-Maximilian-Platz 1, 87629 FÜSSEN
Tel: 8362 93850 **Fax:** 8362 938520
Email: tourismus@fuessen.de **Web site:** http://www.tourismus-fuessen.de
Freq: Annual; **Cover Price:** Free; **Circ:** 30,000
Profile: Description of the tourist offer of the spa and Holiday resort Füssen, surrounding Allgäuer Königswinkels with Accommodation Directory feet, Füssen, Bad Faulenbach, Hopfen am See and Weissensee.
Language(s): Italian

FUTUR 728209G19A-300

Editorial: Pascalstr. 8, 10587 BERLIN
Tel: 30 39006140 **Fax:** 30 39006392
Email: info@ipk.fraunhofer.de **Web site:** http://www.ipk.fraunhofer.de
Freq: 3 issues yearly; **Circ:** 10,000
Editor: Steffen Pospischil
Profile: Releases of the Production Technology Centre (PTZ) Berlin. The magazine is aimed at our partners, to executives in companies and interested parties from business, academia and politics.
Language(s): German

FVW 728217G50-380

Editorial: Wandsbeker Allee 1, 22041 HAMBURG
Tel: 40 41448288 **Fax:** 40 41448299
Email: redaktion@fvw.de **Web site:** http://www.fvw.de
Freq: 26 issues yearly; **Annual Sub.:** EUR 126,80; **Circ:** 30,892
Editor: Klaus Hildebrandt; **Advertising Manager:** Michael Körner
Profile: The bi-weekly trade magazine for tourism and business travel provides independent and objective information about the latest trends and urrent developments in the market. fvw is known as a synonym for reliable and objective journalism with a maximum of in-depth information and great variety of topics. Its analysis and background reports serve as basis for decision-making. And last but not least, fvw also offers practical support for day-to-day business while features, commentaries, and a modern magazine-style design ensure reading fun. Anyone who wants to know what is happening in the travel industry reads fvw. This Outlet offers RSS (Really Simple Syndication).
Language(s): German
Readership: Aimed at professionals in the tourism and business travel industry.
ADVERTISING RATES:
Full Page Mono .... EUR 9500
Full Page Colour .... EUR 9500
Mechanical Data: Type Area: 241 x 195 mm
BUSINESS: TRAVEL & TOURISM

FW MEININGER TAGEBLATT 735241G67B-9440

Editorial: Neu-Ulmer Str. 8a, 98617 MEININGEN
Tel: 3693 440331 **Fax:** 3693 440335
Email: redaktion@fw-mt.de **Web site:** http://www.insuedthueringen.de
Freq: 312 issues yearly; **Circ:** 11,838
Editor: Herbert Wessels
Profile: Daily newspaper with regional news and a local sports section.
Language(s): German
ADVERTISING RATES:
SCC .... EUR 65,60
Mechanical Data: Type Area: 487 x 325 mm, No. of Columns (Display): 7, Col Widths (Display): 44 mm
Copy instructions: *Copy Date:* 2 days prior to publication
Supplement(s): Anpfiff; Bikers Guide; rtv; Wir Heiraten
REGIONAL DAILY & SUNDAY NEWSPAPERS: Regional Daily Newspapers

FZ EUROPAS TREND-MAGAZIN FÜR UHREN, SCHMUCK & ACCESSOIRES 728219G52A-41

Editorial: Walther-Rathenau-Str. 13, 75203 KÖNIGSBACH-STEIN **Tel:** 7232 400720
Fax: 7232 400799
Email: info@verlag-schoener.de **Web site:** http://www.verlag-schoener.de
Freq: 8 issues yearly; Free to qualifying individuals
Annual Sub.: EUR 70,00; **Circ:** 22,444
Editor: Elke Schöner; **Advertising Manager:** Elke Seitz
Profile: Information and reports from the industry, as an intermediary between supply and demand. Receivers are jewelers, jewelry and watches stores, goldsmiths. Watchmaker, jewelry and watches wholesalers, importers, exporters, rocktrade. Jewelry, watches and silverware manufacturers and suppliers.
Language(s): German
Readership: Read by buyers, owners of retail outlets of fancy goods and jewellers.
ADVERTISING RATES:
Full Page Mono .... EUR 2870
Full Page Colour .... EUR 4310
Mechanical Data: Type Area: 307 x 203 mm, No. of Columns (Display): 4, Col Widths (Display): 54 mm
Copy instructions: *Copy Date:* 14 days prior to publication
Official Journal of: Organ d. Bundesverb. d. Schmuck- u. Uhren-Großhandels e.V.
BUSINESS: GIFT TRADE: Jewellery

G+G GESUNDHEIT UND GESELLSCHAFT 729389G1D-444

Editorial: Rosenthaler Str. 31, 10178 BERLIN
Tel: 30 22011102 **Fax:** 30 22011105
Email: gug-redaktion@kompart.de **Web site:** http://www.kompart.de
Freq: 11 issues yearly; **Annual Sub.:** EUR 69,70; **Circ:** 9,135
Editor: Hans-Bernhard Henkel-Hoving; **Advertising Manager:** Werner Mahlau
Profile: Magazine containing political information regarding the AOK medical insurance company in Germany.
Language(s): German
Readership: Aimed at politicians, civil servants and doctors.
ADVERTISING RATES:
Full Page Mono .... EUR 3650
Full Page Colour .... EUR 3650
Mechanical Data: Type Area: 237 x 180 mm
Copy instructions: *Copy Date:* 21 days prior to publication
BUSINESS: FINANCE & ECONOMICS: Insurance

G+H GEBÄUDETECHNIK UND HANDWERK 729390G4E-371_90

Editorial: Talhofstr. 24b, 82205 GILCHING
Tel: 8105 385379 **Fax:** 8105 385311
Email: e.schwandke@verlag-henrich.de **Web site:** http://www.guh-elektro.de
Freq: 7 issues yearly; **Annual Sub.:** EUR 82,00; **Circ:** 15,736
Editor: Elmo Schwandke; **Advertising Manager:** Martin Brey
Profile: Magazine focusing on building construction and planning.
Language(s): German
ADVERTISING RATES:
Full Page Mono .... EUR 4150
Full Page Colour .... EUR 5530
Mechanical Data: Type Area: 282 x 200 mm, No. of Columns (Display): 4, Col Widths (Display): 47 mm
Copy instructions: *Copy Date:* 28 days prior to publication
BUSINESS: ARCHITECTURE & BUILDING: Building

G+J EMS NEWSLETTER
1925971G2A-5856
Editorial: Stubbenhuk 5, 20459 HAMBURG
Tel: 40 37037338 **Fax:** 40 3703177388
Email: jasperneite.michaela@ems.guj.de **Web site:** http://www.ems.guj.de
Freq: Quarterly; **Cover Price:** Free; **Circ:** 2,800
Editor: Michaela Jasperneite
Profile: Company publication published by G + J Electronic Media Sales.
Language(s): German

G & V GESTALTEN UND VERKAUFEN
729397G26C-120
Editorial: Am Friedrichshain 22, 10407 BERLIN
Tel: 30 27894315 **Fax:** 30 27894313
Email: red.gundv@haymarket.de **Web site:** http://www.gundv.de
Freq: Monthly; **Annual Sub.:** EUR 106,20; **Circ:** 6,514
Editor: Christine Meyn; **Advertising Manager:** Christian Rueß
Profile: Trade magazine for florists and retail gardener. It reports on current trends, practical calculation examples, ideas for product presentation and design of the range. Regular Specials information on topics such as grief and trade shows.
Language(s): German
Readership: Aimed at gardeners and florists.
ADVERTISING RATES:
Full Page Mono .... EUR 2775
Full Page Colour .... EUR 4077
Mechanical Data: Type Area: 272 x 186 mm, No. of Columns (Display): 4, Col Widths (Display): 45 mm
Copy instructions: *Copy Date:* 30 days prior to publication
BUSINESS: GARDEN TRADE

GAB
762898G86B-625
Editorial: Kaiserstr. 72, 60329 FRANKFURT
Tel: 69 27404220 **Fax:** 69 27404222
Email: redaktion@gab-magazin.de **Web site:** http://www.gab-magazin.de
Freq: Monthly; **Circ:** 28,153
Editor: Björn Berndt; **Advertising Manager:** Gaby Wanzke
Profile: City magazine for gays about Frankfurt and the Rhine-Main-Neckar region.
Language(s): German
ADVERTISING RATES:
Full Page Mono .... EUR 2640
Full Page Colour .... EUR 2640
Mechanical Data: Type Area: 260 x 190 mm, No. of Columns (Display): 6, Col Widths (Display): 29 mm
Copy instructions: *Copy Date:* 14 days prior to publication
CONSUMER: ADULT & GAY MAGAZINES: Gay & Lesbian Magazines

GAIA
1660346G57-2734
Editorial: Waltherstr. 29, 80337 MÜNCHEN
Tel: 89 54418445 **Fax:** 89 54418449
Email: mickler@oekom.de **Web site:** http://www.oekom.de
Freq: Quarterly; **Annual Sub.:** EUR 102,75; **Circ:** 1,600
Editor: Tobias Mickler; **Advertising Manager:** Stefanie Ott
Profile: Magazine about ecological perspectives in natural sciences, humanities and economies.
Language(s): German
ADVERTISING RATES:
Full Page Mono .... EUR 1330
Full Page Colour .... EUR 2410
Mechanical Data: Type Area: 225 x 175 mm, No. of Columns (Display): 3, Col Widths (Display): 55 mm

GAK GUMMI-FASERN-KUNSTSTOFFE
728263G39-20
Editorial: Am Stadion 3b, 40878 RATINGEN
Tel: 2102 93450 **Fax:** 2102 934520
Email: info@gupta-verlag.de **Web site:** http://www.gupta-verlag.de
Freq: Monthly; **Annual Sub.:** EUR 280,00; **Circ:** 1,800
Editor: Heinz Gupta; **Advertising Manager:** Heinz Gupta
Profile: International magazine for professionals in the plastics and rubber manufacturing and processing industry. Application-oriented and scientific contributions highlight new developments in raw materials, Processing technology, measuring and testing methods, machines and equipment, organization and quality assurance. Current economic developments in the industry as well as conference and exhibition reports add to the extensive informationtion offered.
Language(s): German
Readership: Aimed at those who work in the synthetic materials and rubber industries.
ADVERTISING RATES:
Full Page Mono .... EUR 3000
Full Page Colour .... EUR 3500
Mechanical Data: Type Area: 265 x 185 mm, No. of Columns (Display): 4, Col Widths (Display): 45 mm
Copy instructions: *Copy Date:* 20 days prior to publication
BUSINESS: PLASTICS & RUBBER

GALA
728265G74A-1320
Editorial: Schaarsteinweg 14, 20459 HAMBURG
Tel: 40 37034163 **Fax:** 40 37035744
Email: redaktion@gala.de **Web site:** http://www.gala.de
Freq: Weekly; **Annual Sub.:** EUR 135,20; **Circ:** 343,248
Editor: Peter Lewandowski
Profile: GALA, the premium people and lifestyle magazine, reports every Thursday on current stars from around the world. GALA presents well-researched background information on the stories behind the message. With exclusive pictures, insightful stories, honest interviews and brilliant photo spreads GALA creates an intimate, but always respectful closeness to the stars and sets standards week after week for stylistic, glamorous journalism. GALA is a class of its own - this claim is confirmed by the premium people and lifestyle magazine over and over again. In the Style section on over 20 opulently designed pages all the important news and trends from the fashion and beauty world are shown, fashion and beauty at its best. Exceptional photo series, a sense of optics, style and modernity: the service-oriented trend pages about the latest fashion and beauty trends. The rich put up heading style is a unique presentation platform for high fashion and cosmetic lines. With the mix of people and trends, from opulent presentation and generous booklet format, GALA has developed a premium target group who does not only read luxury but also wants to experience it. It is cosmopolitan, consumer-minded, brand-oriented and has a high income. Every week, GALA reports about current celebrities from around the world. Facebook: http://www.facebook.com/galade Twitter: http://twitter.com/galalive.
Language(s): German
Readership: Aimed at women.
ADVERTISING RATES:
Full Page Mono .... EUR 22200
Full Page Colour .... EUR 22200
Mechanical Data: Type Area: 270 x 197 mm
Copy instructions: *Copy Date:* 17 days prior to publication
CONSUMER: WOMEN'S INTEREST CONSUMER MAGAZINES: Women's Interest

GALA MEN
1929640G86C-245
Editorial: Schaarsteinweg 14, 20459 HAMBURG
Tel: 40 37034163 **Fax:** 40 37035744
Email: redaktion@gala.de **Web site:** http://www.gala.de
Freq: Half-yearly; **Cover Price:** EUR 5,00; **Circ:** 100,000
Editor: Peter Lewandowski
Profile: Facebook: http://www.facebook.com/galade.
Language(s): German
ADVERTISING RATES:
Full Page Mono .... EUR 15000
Full Page Colour .... EUR 15000
Mechanical Data: Type Area: 235 x 194 mm

GALA STYLE
1793688G74A-3523
Editorial: Schaarsteinweg 14, 20459 HAMBURG
Tel: 40 37034163 **Fax:** 40 37035744
Email: redaktion@gala.de **Web site:** http://www.gala.de
Freq: Half-yearly; **Cover Price:** EUR 3,30; **Circ:** 150,000
Editor: Peter Lewandowski
Profile: People and lifestyle magazine. The magazine is a comprehensive guide to the trends in Fashion, Jewellery, wellness, lifestyle and beauty. Clearly and thoroughly researched, close to the VIPs and high utility and pleasure factor in the cosmopolitan and trendy affine reader. Facebook: http://www.facebook.com/galade.
Language(s): German
ADVERTISING RATES:
Full Page Mono .... EUR 15000
Full Page Colour .... EUR 15000
Mechanical Data: Type Area: 237 x 166 mm

GALVANOTECHNIK
728277G19C-30
Editorial: Karlstr. 4, 88348 BAD SAULGAU
Tel: 7581 480116 **Fax:** 7581 480110
Email: herbert.kaeszmann@leuze-verlag.de **Web site:** http://www.galvanotechnik.com
Freq: Monthly; **Annual Sub.:** EUR 72,55; **Circ:** 3,474
Editor: Herbert Käszmann; **Advertising Manager:** Katja Praegla
Profile: Extensive essays and scientific articles on the latest technological developments, practical information and reviews about businesses, events, patents, etc. Target group: Professionals in the metalworking industry, dealing with electroplating and surface treatment of metals and plastics and companies in the supply industry.
Language(s): English; German
Readership: Read by managers, designers and engineers.
ADVERTISING RATES:
Full Page Mono .... EUR 1020
Full Page Colour .... EUR 1500
Mechanical Data: Type Area: 200 x 135 mm, No. of Columns (Display): 2, Col Widths (Display): 65 mm
Copy instructions: *Copy Date:* 31 days prior to publication
BUSINESS: ENGINEERING & MACHINERY: Finishing

GAMBERO ROSSO VINI D'ITALIA
1641302G74P-1135
Editorial: Grillparzerstr. 12, 81675 MÜNCHEN
Tel: 89 41981453 **Fax:** 89 41981123
Web site: http://www.graefe-und-unzer.de
Freq: Annual; **Cover Price:** EUR 29,90; **Circ:** 20,000
Profile: Publication about Italian wines.
Language(s): German
Mechanical Data: Type Area: 257 x 116 mm
Copy instructions: *Copy Date:* 77 days prior to publication

GAMEPRO
768311G78D-885
Editorial: Lyonel-Feininger-Str. 26, 80807 MÜNCHEN
Tel: 89 36086679 **Fax:** 89 360869306
Email: post@gamepro.de **Web site:** http://www.gamepro.de
Freq: Monthly; **Annual Sub.:** EUR 60,00; **Circ:** 23,987
Editor: Markus Schwerdtel; **Advertising Manager:** Ralf Sattelberger
Profile: Magazine about computer games, including shopping advice for Playstation2, Xbox, GameCube and Gameboy.
Language(s): German
ADVERTISING RATES:
Full Page Mono .... EUR 8260
Full Page Colour .... EUR 8260
Mechanical Data: Type Area: 250 x 162 mm
CONSUMER: CONSUMER ELECTRONICS: Games

GAMEPRO.DE
1621319G78D-898
Editorial: Lyonel-Feininger-Str. 26, 80807 MÜNCHEN
Tel: 89 36086679 **Fax:** 89 360869306
Email: post@gamepro.de **Web site:** http://www.gamepro.de
Freq: Daily; **Cover Price:** Paid; **Circ:** 1,970,832 Unique Users
Editor: Markus Schwerdtel; **Advertising Manager:** Dirk Heib
Language(s): German
CONSUMER: CONSUMER ELECTRONICS: Games

GAMES AKTUELL
1616305G78D-895
Editorial: Dr.-Mack-Str. 83, 90762 FÜRTH
Tel: 911 2872100 **Fax:** 911 2872200
Email: thomas.szedlak@computec.de **Web site:** http://www.gamesaktuell.de
Freq: Monthly; **Annual Sub.:** EUR 39,90; **Circ:** 29,650
Editor: Thomas Szedlak
Profile: Games Aktuell is one of the most successful multi-format gaming magazines. With comprehensive news, previews, tests and reports, Games Aktuell covers the entire gaming market. The magazine concept features straightforward language and avoids confusing jargon. Games Aktuell comes with a double DVD loaded with demos and videos as a special bonus.
Language(s): German
ADVERTISING RATES:
Full Page Mono .... EUR 7590
Full Page Colour .... EUR 7590
Mechanical Data: Type Area: 270 x 190 mm, No. of Columns (Display): 4, Col Widths (Display): 46 mm
Copy instructions: *Copy Date:* 26 days prior to publication
CONSUMER: CONSUMER ELECTRONICS: Games

GAMESHOP
728282G78D-44
Editorial: Weihenstephaner Str. 7, 81673 MÜNCHEN
Tel: 89 45114280 **Fax:** 89 45114444
Email: h.hesse@e-media.de **Web site:** http://www.e-media.de
Freq: 6 issues yearly; **Cover Price:** Free; **Circ:** 251,983
Editor: Harald Hesse; **Advertising Manager:** Susanne Hübner
Profile: Magazine containing articles about computer games and equipment.
Language(s): German
Readership: Aimed at teenagers.
ADVERTISING RATES:
Full Page Mono .... EUR 7980
Full Page Colour .... EUR 7980
Mechanical Data: Type Area: 250 x 185 mm, No. of Columns (Display): 4, Col Widths (Display): 45 mm
CONSUMER: CONSUMER ELECTRONICS: Games

GAMESTAR
728284G78D-260
Editorial: Lyonel-Feininger-Str. 26, 80807 MÜNCHEN
Tel: 89 36086660 **Fax:** 89 36086652
Email: brief@gamestar.de **Web site:** http://www.gamestar.de
Freq: Monthly; **Annual Sub.:** EUR 55,00; **Circ:** 113,610
Editor: Michael Trier; **Advertising Manager:** Ralf Sattelberger
Profile: GameStar is the leading monthly pure PC Games magazine in Europe and therefore the number one source of information for all the dedicated PC gamer. GameStar offers the most reliable buying advice for games and hardware. Recent reports and trends, interviews and on-site reporting round off gamestar.de. Facebook: http://www.facebook.com/gamestar.de.
Language(s): German
ADVERTISING RATES:
Full Page Mono .... EUR 11860
Full Page Colour .... EUR 11860
Mechanical Data: Type Area: 250 x 162 mm, No. of Columns (Display): 4, Col Widths (Display): 37 mm
CONSUMER: CONSUMER ELECTRONICS: Games

GAMESTAR.DE
1621321G78D-984
Editorial: Lyonel-Feininger-Str. 26, 80807 MÜNCHEN
Tel: 89 36086660 **Fax:** 89 36086652
Email: brief@gamestar.de **Web site:** http://www.gamestar.de
Freq: Daily; **Cover Price:** Paid; **Circ:** 10,921,403 Unique Users
Editor: Michael Trier; **Advertising Manager:** Ralf Sattelberger
Profile: Ezine: Magazine focusing on computer games. Provides previews, tips, advice and tests, information on current hard- and software and relevant product news. Facebook: http://www.facebook.com/gamestar.de.
Language(s): German
CONSUMER: CONSUMER ELECTRONICS: Games

GAMIGO
1621322G78D-899
Editorial: Behringstr. 16b, 22765 HAMBURG
Tel: 40 226305260 **Fax:** 40 226305255
Email: support@gamigo.de **Web site:** http://www.gamigo.de
Freq: Daily; **Cover Price:** Paid; **Circ:** 2,968,586 Unique Users
Editor: Sven Ossenbrüggen
Language(s): German
CONSUMER: CONSUMER ELECTRONICS: Games

GANDERSHEIMER KREISBLATT
728287G67B-5520
Editorial: Alte Gasse 19, 37581 BAD GANDERSHEIM
Tel: 5382 981130 **Fax:** 5382 6356
Email: kreisblatt@t-online.de **Web site:** http://www.gandersheimer-kreisblatt.de
Freq: 312 issues yearly; **Circ:** 4,850
Profile: Daily newspaper with regional news and a local sports section.
Language(s): German
ADVERTISING RATES:
SCC .... EUR 16,80
Mechanical Data: Type Area: 425 x 285 mm, No. of Columns (Display): 6, Col Widths (Display): 45 mm
Copy instructions: *Copy Date:* 2 days prior to publication
REGIONAL DAILY & SUNDAY NEWSPAPERS: Regional Daily Newspapers

GANZ-MUENCHEN.DE
1704288G89A-12191
Editorial: Rossmarkt 6, 80331 MÜNCHEN
Tel: 89 23077611 **Fax:** 89 24223508
Email: schmitz@ganz-muenchen.de **Web site:** http://www.ganz-muenchen.de
Freq: Daily; **Cover Price:** Paid; **Circ:** 292,948 Unique Users
Editor: Martin Schmitz; **Advertising Manager:** Martin Schmitz
Language(s): German
CONSUMER: HOLIDAYS & TRAVEL: Travel

GARMISCH-PARTENKIRCHNER TAGBLATT
728302G67B-5560
Editorial: Pfaffenrieder Str. 9, 82515 WOLFRATSHAUSEN **Tel:** 8171 2690
Fax: 8171 269240
Email: fsav@merkur-online.de **Web site:** http://www.merkur-online.de
Freq: 312 issues yearly; **Circ:** 15,089
Advertising Manager: Hans-Georg Bechthold
Profile: The Münchner Merkur with its own local newspapers, of which the Garmisch-Partenkirchner Tagblatt is one that, the leading regional newspaper brand in the Munich area - the most affluent area of Germany. The combination of newspaper and region is the foundation on which to build the success of the title. This is the newspaper not only the factual news agency, but forms a community of solidarity with its readers and the local community. The clear focus on local reporting creates a high regard to human reader loyalty. She presses one hand in the very high number of close to 180,000 subscribers. Also for the high reader-commitment is the loyalty of the total current 827 000 daily readers, the Münchner Merkur or one of its local newspapers usually read over many years. The Münchner Merkur with its own local newspapers is a newspaper for the whole family, tradition and modern life for one of the most beautiful regions of Germany unites. Reliable, informative, critical: the Münchner Merkur is the indispensable daily newspaper for the region. Facebook: http://www.facebook.com/pages/merkur-online.de/190176143327.
Language(s): German
ADVERTISING RATES:
SCC .... EUR 43,60
Mechanical Data: Type Area: 474 x 324 mm, No. of Columns (Display): 7, Col Widths (Display): 45 mm
Copy instructions: *Copy Date:* 1 day prior to publication
REGIONAL DAILY & SUNDAY NEWSPAPERS: Regional Daily Newspapers

GARTEN EDEN
725917G93-990
Editorial: Carl-Bertelsmann-Str. 33, 33311 GÜTERSLOH **Tel:** 5241 2348072 **Fax:** 5241 2348022
Email: redaktion@garten-eden.de **Web site:** http://www.garten-eden.de
Freq: 6 issues yearly; **Annual Sub.:** EUR 22,00; **Circ:** 24,397
Editor: Oliver Kipp; **Advertising Manager:** Nicole Dürdoth
Profile: Garden of Eden is the only high-quality premium garden magazine. It offers high added value by many practical suggestions and tips for everyday gardeners on a high journalistic standards and an

opulent look. Garden of Eden inspired passionate garden and plant lovers who are interested in challenging, active leisure, income and a versatile, high value on aesthetic representation, but equally practical advice. Garden of Eden suggests stylish and passionate lyrics and opulent photo spreads to dream and goes at the same time a step further: from the planning idea of the right machine for the garden practice, to portraits of exceptional plant and horticulture, from the design ideas for specific garden situations of matching furniture to for stylish decorating ideas, the reader finds everything worth knowing about bundled Garden - Gardening presented by passionate experts.
Language(s): German
Readership: Aimed at people who enjoy visiting famous gardens and gardening enthusiasts.
ADVERTISING RATES:
Full Page Mono .... EUR 4900
Full Page Colour .... EUR 4900
Mechanical Data: No. of Columns (Display): 3, Col Widths (Display): 63 mm, Type Area: 277 x 195 mm
CONSUMER: GARDENING

GARTEN SPASS
728322G93-240
Editorial: Hubert-Burda-Platz 1, 77652 OFFENBURG
Tel: 781 842592 **Fax:** 781 842254
Email: garten@burda.com **Web site:** http://www.gartenspass.com
Freq: Monthly; **Annual Sub.:** EUR 26,40; **Circ:** 67,050
Editor: Andrea Kögel; **Advertising Manager:** Malte Schwerdtfeger
Profile: The monthly magazine garten spaß shows home gardeners how low-maintenance plants, simple design tips and lots of creative ideas lead to the own dream garden - and still have enough time to enjoy and celebrate in the garden. garten spaß can provide solutions that are also understood and put into practice by beginners. Numerous step-by-step sequences demonstrate how to properly maintain plants, the lawn, shrubs and hedges are cut or a garden pond is created. Integral parts of every garten spaß issue are creative indoor and outdoor decorating ideas for as well as delicious recipes with ingredients from the garden.
Language(s): German
ADVERTISING RATES:
Full Page Mono .... EUR 7400
Full Page Colour .... EUR 7400
Mechanical Data: Type Area: 250 x 196 mm, No. of Columns (Display): 4, Col Widths (Display): 46 mm
Copy instructions: *Copy Date:* 42 days prior to publication
CONSUMER: GARDENING

GARTEN & FREIZEITMARKT
728325G26B-15
Editorial: Alter Flughafen 15, 30179 HANNOVER
Tel: 511 6740864 **Fax:** 511 6740853
Email: westermann@patzer-verlag.de **Web site:** http://www.patzerverlag.de
Freq: Monthly; **Annual Sub.:** EUR 55,20; **Circ:** 3,930
Editor: Alexandra Westermann; **Advertising Manager:** Bodo Ulbricht
Profile: Journal about supplies for the gardening industry.
Language(s): German
ADVERTISING RATES:
Full Page Mono .... EUR 1965
Full Page Colour .... EUR 3438
Mechanical Data: Type Area: 261 x 184 mm, No. of Columns (Display): 4, Col Widths (Display): 43 mm
Copy instructions: *Copy Date:* 21 days prior to publication
BUSINESS: GARDEN TRADE: Garden Trade Supplies

GARTEN + LANDSCHAFT
728326G26D-95
Editorial: Streitfeldstr. 35, 81673 MÜNCHEN
Tel: 89 436005150 **Fax:** 89 436005147
Email: r.schaefer@topos.de **Web site:** http://www.garten-landschaft.de
Freq: Monthly; **Annual Sub.:** EUR 132,00; **Circ:** 5,133
Editor: Robert Schäfer; **Advertising Manager:** Elmar Große
Profile: Journal concerning landscape architecture. Focuses on planting, planning, building and the preservation of nature.
Language(s): German
Readership: Aimed at professional gardeners and landscaping companies.
ADVERTISING RATES:
Full Page Mono .... EUR 3050
Full Page Colour .... EUR 4790
Mechanical Data: Type Area: 268 x 185 mm, No. of Columns (Display): 4, Col Widths (Display): 43 mm
Copy instructions: *Copy Date:* 28 days prior to publication
BUSINESS: GARDEN TRADE: Garden Trade Horticulture

GARTEN ZEITUNG
728327G93-280
Editorial: Wilhelmsaue 37, 10713 BERLIN
Tel: 30 46406208 **Fax:** 30 46406313
Email: gartenzeitung@bauernverlag.de **Web site:** http://www.gartenzeitung.de
Freq: Monthly; **Annual Sub.:** EUR 33,00; **Circ:** 115,103
Editor: Christian Gehler; **Advertising Manager:** Frank Middendorf
Profile: Practice and competence for successful gardening - that's the recipe for the success of the GARTEN ZEITUNG for over 60 years. The magazine gives tips and suggestions to follow suit and enjoys a readership for which the preoccupation with the green oasis of its own has become expression of life. Besides the presentation of visually beautiful private gardens from all over Germany, the editorial approach is understood as a counselor in the design of useful and ornamental gardens. In addition, GARTEN ZEITUNG informs regularly about news in the industry and reports on interesting practical tests and comparisons of different products.
Language(s): German
Readership: Aimed at gardening enthusiasts.
ADVERTISING RATES:
Full Page Mono .... EUR 6988
Full Page Colour .... EUR 10368
Mechanical Data: Type Area: 245 x 195 mm, No. of Columns (Display): 4, Col Widths (Display): 45 mm
Copy instructions: *Copy Date:* 30 days prior to publication
CONSUMER: GARDENING

GARTENBAU AKTUELL
728308G21A-1800
Editorial: Hirschgartenallee 19, 80639 MÜNCHEN
Tel: 89 178670 **Fax:** 89 1786799
Email: service@bgv-muenchen.de **Web site:** http://www.bgv-muenchen.de
Freq: 11 issues yearly; Free to qualifying individuals
Annual Sub.: EUR 45,75; **Circ:** 1,800
Profile: Magazine for members of the Bavarian Association for Tree Nursery, Public Authority Horticulture, Research, Teaching and Experimental Institutes.
Language(s): German
ADVERTISING RATES:
Full Page Mono .... EUR 840
Mechanical Data: Type Area: 250 x 170 mm, No. of Columns (Display): 3, Col Widths (Display): 54 mm
Copy instructions: *Copy Date:* 13 days prior to publication

GARTENBAU IN BADEN-WÜRTTEMBERG
728309G21A-1820
Editorial: Alte Karlsruher Str. 8, 76227 KARLSRUHE
Tel: 721 944807 **Fax:** 721 9448080
Email: reiss@hortus.de
Freq: Monthly; **Circ:** 2,200
Editor: Jochen Reiss Fey; **Advertising Manager:** Carmen Balier
Profile: Magazine about horticulture in the region of Baden.
Language(s): German
ADVERTISING RATES:
Full Page Mono .... EUR 1404
Full Page Colour .... EUR 1612
Mechanical Data: Type Area: 260 x 195 mm, No. of Columns (Display): 4, Col Widths (Display): 45 mm

GARTENBAU IN NIEDERSACHSEN UND BREMEN
728310G26D-2
Editorial: Johann-Neudörffer-Str. 2, 28355 BREMEN
Tel: 421 536410 **Fax:** 421 552182
Email: ngv@hdgbremen.de **Web site:** http://www.hdgbremen.de
Freq: 11 issues yearly; Free to qualifying individuals
Annual Sub.: EUR 12,00; **Circ:** 1,550
Editor: Axel Boese; **Advertising Manager:** Joachim Meyer-Rehberg
Profile: Official publication of the Horticultural Association of North West Germany. Includes production of vegetables and young tree plantations.
Language(s): German
Readership: Read by market gardeners and foresters.
ADVERTISING RATES:
Full Page Mono .... EUR 529
Full Page Colour .... EUR 919
Mechanical Data: Type Area: 275 x 190 mm, No. of Columns (Display): 4, Col Widths (Display): 45 mm
Copy instructions: *Copy Date:* 20 days prior to publication
BUSINESS: GARDEN TRADE: Garden Trade Horticulture

GARTENFREUND
732845G93-560
Editorial: Elsasser Str. 41, 28211 BREMEN
Tel: 421 3484218 **Fax:** 421 3484228
Email: pleiner@waechter.de **Web site:** http://www.gartenfreunde.de
Freq: Monthly; Free to qualifying individuals
Annual Sub.: EUR 15,00; **Circ:** 16,964
Editor: Jutta Pleiner; **Advertising Manager:** Rita Kropp
Profile: Gardening magazine with regional section of Saxony. The gardener offers its readers about detailed topics posts around home and garden, with the national coat topics: Fruit, vegetables, ornamental gardens, soil care, fertilizers, pesticides, garden tools, garden art, garden design and maintenance. The gardener is composed of a cross-magazines-coat, and the nine different regional parts of the issuing state associations of the allotments, which report on the regional and local activities of clubs and associations.
Language(s): German
ADVERTISING RATES:
Full Page Mono .... EUR 968
Full Page Colour .... EUR 1549
Mechanical Data: Type Area: 260 x 181 mm, No. of Columns (Display): 4, Col Widths (Display): 43 mm
Copy instructions: *Copy Date:* 30 days prior to publication
CONSUMER: GARDENING

GARTENFREUND
732846G93-580
Editorial: Elsasser Str. 41, 28211 BREMEN
Tel: 421 3484218 **Fax:** 421 3484228
Email: pleiner@waechter.de **Web site:** http://www.gartenfreunde.de
Freq: Monthly; Free to qualifying individuals
Annual Sub.: EUR 15,00; **Circ:** 16,128
Editor: Jutta Pleiner; **Advertising Manager:** James Hübner
Profile: Gardening magazine with regional section Bremen. The Gartenfreund offers its readers about detailed topics posts around home and garden, with the national coat topics: Fruit, vegetables, ornamental gardens, soil care, fertilizers, pesticides, garden tools, garden art, garden design and maintenance. The gardener is composed of a cross-magazines-coat, and the nine different regional parts of the issuing state associations of the allotments, which report on the regional and local activities of clubs and associations.
Language(s): German
ADVERTISING RATES:
Full Page Mono .... EUR 792
Full Page Colour .... EUR 1267
Mechanical Data: Type Area: 260 x 181 mm, No. of Columns (Display): 4, Col Widths (Display): 43 mm
Copy instructions: *Copy Date:* 30 days prior to publication
CONSUMER: GARDENING

GARTENFREUND
732848G93-620
Editorial: Elsasser Str. 41, 28211 BREMEN
Tel: 421 3484218 **Fax:** 421 3484228
Email: pleiner@waechter.de **Web site:** http://www.gartenfreunde.de
Freq: Monthly; Free to qualifying individuals
Annual Sub.: EUR 15,00; **Circ:** 15,279
Editor: Jutta Pleiner; **Advertising Manager:** Rita Kropp
Profile: Gardening magazine with regional regional section of Schleswig-Holstein. The Gartenfreund offers its readers about detailed topics posts around home and garden, with the national coat topics: Fruit, vegetables, ornamental gardens, soil care, fertilizers, pesticides, garden tools, garden art, garden design and maintenance. The gardener is composed of a cross-magazines-coat, and the nine different regional parts of the issuing state associations of the allotments, which report on the regional and local activities of clubs and associations.
Language(s): German
ADVERTISING RATES:
Full Page Mono .... EUR 1134
Full Page Colour .... EUR 1814
Mechanical Data: Type Area: 260 x 181 mm, No. of Columns (Display): 4, Col Widths (Display): 43 mm
Copy instructions: *Copy Date:* 30 days prior to publication
CONSUMER: GARDENING

GARTENFREUND
732849G93-640
Editorial: Elsasser Str. 41, 28211 BREMEN
Tel: 421 3484218 **Fax:** 421 3484228
Email: pleiner@waechter.de **Web site:** http://www.gartenfreunde.de
Freq: Monthly; Free to qualifying individuals
Annual Sub.: EUR 15,00; **Circ:** 23,405
Editor: Jutta Pleiner; **Advertising Manager:** James Hübner
Profile: Gardening magazine with regional section of Lower Saxony. The Gartenfreund offers its readers about issues detailed reviews around home and garden, with the national coat topics: Fruit, vegetables, ornamental gardens, soil care, fertilizers, pesticides, garden tools, garden art, garden design and maintenance. The gardener is composed of a cross-magazines-coat, and the nine different regional parts of the issuing state associations of the allotments, which report on the regional and local activities of clubs and associations.
Language(s): German
ADVERTISING RATES:
Full Page Mono .... EUR 1219
Full Page Colour .... EUR 1950
Mechanical Data: Type Area: 260 x 181 mm, No. of Columns (Display): 4, Col Widths (Display): 43 mm
Copy instructions: *Copy Date:* 30 days prior to publication
CONSUMER: GARDENING

GARTENPRAXIS
728321G26C-347
Editorial: Wollgrasweg 41, 70599 STUTTGART
Tel: 711 4507128 **Fax:** 711 4507207
Email: kruecker@ulmer.de **Web site:** http://www.gartenpraxis.de
Freq: Monthly; **Annual Sub.:** EUR 98,60; **Circ:** 11,976
Editor: Karlheinz Rücker; **Advertising Manager:** Marc Alber
Profile: Gartenpraxis is the magazine for sophisticated garden and landscape architects, civil engineers garden, garden and landscape designers, master gardeners and garden owners that make their environment actively and individually and who value the stylish ambience in the garden. The entire range of garden plants, including new varieties and the use of plants and garden design are the focus. Excellently illustrated examples from the garden at home and abroad provide the garden and landscape architects as well as the garden lover practical examples for own implementation. Recent reviews of new plants and knowledge of plant use round out this picture. Regular topics include pond, professional irrigation, stones (natural stones, concrete blocks and bricks), light in the garden, plants (perennials, shrubs, water plants, vines, bulbs and tubers), landscaping (design and installation of contemporary gardens), lawns (riding mower, lawn mowers, turf, grass seed, etc.). Greenspace (saws, scissors, etc.), pesticides (Everything for healthy plants), materials for the perfect garden (fencing, wooden garden - terraces and wooden floors, balcony panels, etc.), indoor planting, fertilizers, soils and substrates.
Language(s): German
ADVERTISING RATES:
Full Page Mono .... EUR 195
Full Page Colour .... EUR 250
Mechanical Data: Type Area: 235 x 183 mm, No. of Columns (Display): 4, Col Widths (Display): 43 mm
Copy instructions: *Copy Date:* 52 days prior to publication
BUSINESS: GARDEN TRADE

GARTENTEICH
728323G93-30
Editorial: Dompfaffweg 53, 42659 SOLINGEN
Tel: 212 819878 **Fax:** 212 816216
Email: redaktion@gartenteich.com **Web site:** http://www.gartenteich.com
Freq: Quarterly; **Annual Sub.:** EUR 22,50; **Circ:** 21,358
Editor: Harro Hieronimus; **Advertising Manager:** Thomas Heinen
Profile: Magazine about garden technology, building and arrangements of ponds. Contents: - All about plants and animals at the pond - Design, maintenance and engineering - Illustrative reports, beautiful photos - Useful tips for your own garden pond.
Language(s): German
Readership: Aimed at people interested in garden and ponds.
ADVERTISING RATES:
Full Page Mono .... EUR 2695
Full Page Colour .... EUR 4915
Mechanical Data: Type Area: 250 x 189 mm, No. of Columns (Display): 4, Col Widths (Display): 43 mm
Copy instructions: *Copy Date:* 40 days prior to publication
CONSUMER: GARDENING

GARTENTOUR
1814392G89A-12348
Editorial: Max-Stromeyer-Str. 116, 78467 KONSTANZ **Tel:** 7531 907110 **Fax:** 7531 907131
Email: gschindler@labhard.de **Web site:** http://www.labhard.de
Freq: Annual; **Cover Price:** EUR 5,00; **Circ:** 39,500
Editor: Gabriele Schindler; **Advertising Manager:** Gabriele Schindler
Profile: Year-round current travel and leisure guide in magazine format. The magazine leads to the most beautiful castles, parks and gardens in Germany, contains lots of interesting and entertaining. A calendar of events and service addresses, provide great benefits. The magazine Gartentour is a high quality lavishly produced purchase object with collection character.
Language(s): German
ADVERTISING RATES:
Full Page Colour .... EUR 2795
Copy instructions: *Copy Date:* 31 days prior to publication

GÄRTNERN LEICHT GEMACHT
728223G93-320
Editorial: Lindenstr. 20, 50674 KÖLN
Tel: 221 3980160 **Fax:** 221 39801610
Email: kroll@l-m-verlag.de **Web site:** http://www.livingandmore.de
Freq: 11 issues yearly; **Annual Sub.:** EUR 34,80; **Circ:** 71,691
Editor: Erhard Held
Profile: Gärtnern leicht gemacht is a magazine made easy concept for garden beginners, the experienced amateur gardeners also offers great benefits. Gardening is made easy just by its product promises a practical treatment of the themes and content specifications. Gardening knowledge and garden practice are the focus. Linked to pictures, drawings and concise text with image sequences and processes mediated "green" knowledge step by step.
Language(s): German
Readership: Read by people interested in gardens and gardening.
ADVERTISING RATES:
Full Page Mono .... EUR 6500
Full Page Colour .... EUR 6500
Mechanical Data: Type Area: 244 x 190 mm
Copy instructions: *Copy Date:* 32 days prior to publication
CONSUMER: GARDENING

GAS
728328G24-2
Editorial: Rosenheimer Str. 145, 81671 MÜNCHEN
Tel: 2336 473164 **Fax:** 2336 4705970
Email: postbox@calovini.net **Web site:** http://www.oldenbourg-industrieverlag.de
Freq: Quarterly; **Annual Sub.:** EUR 49,00; **Circ:** 2,703
Editor: Martin Calovini; **Advertising Manager:** Claudia Fuchs
Profile: Magazine containing information about the gas industry.
Language(s): German
ADVERTISING RATES:
Full Page Mono .... EUR 2750
Full Page Colour .... EUR 3920
Mechanical Data: Type Area: 250 x 176 mm, No. of Columns (Display): 3, Col Widths (Display): 56 mm
Official Journal of: Organ d. ArGe f. sparsamen u. umweltfreundl. Energieverbrauch e.V., d. Bundesverb. d. Energie- u. Wasserwirtschaft e.V., d. Bundesvereinigung d. Firmen im Gas u. Wasserfach e.V., d. Dt. Vereinigung d. Gas- u. Wasserfaches e.V., d. Industrieverb. Haus-, Heiz- u. Küchentechnik e.V., d. Österr. Vereinigung f. d. Gas- u. Wasserfach, d.

/erb. d. Schweizer. Gasindustrie u. d. Zentralverb. Sanitär Heizung Klima
BUSINESS: GAS

GAST FREUNDSCHAFT
1748994G11A-1617
Editorial: Albert-Einstein-Str. 18, 50226 FRECHEN
Tel: 2234 1834171 **Fax:** 2234 1834179
Email: haake@geva.com **Web site:** http://www.geva.com
Freq: Quarterly; **Annual Sub.:** EUR 16,00; **Circ:** 10,007
Editor: Britta Haake
Language(s): German
ADVERTISING RATES:
Full Page Mono .... EUR 3250
Full Page Colour .... EUR 4300
Mechanical Data: Type Area: 257 x 180 mm
Copy instructions: *Copy Date:* 31 days prior to publication
BUSINESS: CATERING: Catering, Hotels & Restaurants

GASTEIG KULTUR FÜR MÜNCHEN
728336G89C-900
Editorial: Rosenheimer Str. 5, 81667 MÜNCHEN
Tel: 89 48098133 **Fax:** 89 480981830
Email: r.wirth@gasteig.de **Web site:** http://www.gasteig.de
Freq: 11 issues yearly; **Cover Price:** Free; **Circ:** 70,000
Editor: Rainer A. Wirth
Profile: Guide containing events-listings for Munich.
Language(s): German
Mechanical Data: Type Area: 193 x 132 mm
Copy instructions: *Copy Date:* 48 days prior to publication
CONSUMER: HOLIDAYS & TRAVEL: Entertainment Guides

GASTGEBERKATALOG BRANDENBURG
1927764G50-1282
Editorial: Linienstr. 214, 10119 BERLIN
Tel: 30 28018149 **Fax:** 30 28018400
Email: info@runze-casper.de **Web site:** http://www.reiseland-brandenburg.de
Freq: Annual; **Cover Price:** Free; **Circ:** 100,000
Profile: Magazine on travel and holiday facilities in Brandenburg.
Language(s): English; German

GASTGEBERVERZEICHNIS
741346G89A-3940
Editorial: Weinbergweg 1, 91154 ROTH
Tel: 9171 81329 **Fax:** 9171 81399
Email: tourismus@landratsamt-roth.de **Web site:** http://www.urlaub-roth.de
Freq: Annual; **Cover Price:** Free; **Circ:** 26,000
Profile: Accommodation directory for the Franconian seas, Rothsee / Brombachsee.
Language(s): German

GASTGEBERVERZEICHNIS HOHENLOHE+SCHWÄBISCH HALL
1799229G89A-12301
Editorial: Münzstr. 1, 74523 SCHWÄBISCH HALL
Tel: 791 7557444 **Fax:** 791 7557447
Email: info@hs-tourismus.de **Web site:** http://www.hs-tourismus.de
Freq: Annual; **Cover Price:** Free; **Circ:** 20,000
Profile: Directory listing accomodations for guests and tourists of Hohenlohe and Schwaebisch Hall. Facebook: http://www.facebook.com/pages/Hohenlohe-Schw%C3%A4bisch-Hall-Tourismus-eV/145377418857212.
Language(s): German

GASTGEWERBE
1666050G11A-1608
Editorial: Ahornblick 10, 40629 DÜSSELDORF
Tel: 211 699909112 **Fax:** 211 699909119
Email: kawohl@gastgewerbe.us **Web site:** http://www.gastgewerbe-magazin.de
Freq: 10 issues yearly; Free to qualifying individuals
Annual Sub.: EUR 50,00; **Circ:** 32,562
Editor: Anja Kawohl
Profile: gastgewerbe informs gastronomy and hotellery in Germany and is aimed primarily at owners and managers. gastgewerbe provides the information required by a hotelier and restaurateur, to successfully carry out operations. There is a range from industry and business news to current trends, products and services, and vocational-oriented subjects. Facebook: http://www.facebook.com/pages/gastgewerbe-Magazin/100370176677164.
Language(s): German
ADVERTISING RATES:
Full Page Mono .... EUR 4120
Full Page Colour .... EUR 6150
Mechanical Data: Type Area: 270 x 184 mm, No. of Columns (Display): 4, Col Widths (Display): 43 mm
Official Journal of: Organ d. Bayer. Hotel- u. Gaststättenverb., d. Dehoga Gastgewerbe NRW, d. Hotel- u. Gaststättenverb. Brandenburg u. d. Dehoga Saarland, Dehoga Thüringen
BUSINESS: CATERING: Catering, Hotels & Restaurants

GASTRHOTEL
728345G11A-500
Editorial: Theodor-Althoff-Str. 39, 45133 ESSEN
Tel: 201 87126949 **Fax:** 201 87126941
Email: h.seng@gastrotel.de **Web site:** http://www.gastrotel.de
Freq: 6 issues yearly; **Annual Sub.:** EUR 12,00; **Circ:** 100,266
Editor: Hans Herbert Seng; **Advertising Manager:** Fabian Meutsch
Profile: Gastrotel is as a national, independent trade magazine for entrepreneurs and managers of hotels and restaurants, the largest circulation publication in the industry. With a circulation of over 100,000 copies almost reached Gastrotel every other catering outlets in Germany. The focus of the editorial credits include the ideas and successes oriented practice reports from the width of the target group (bistros, cafes, restaurants, pubs, restaurants, Trendy restaurants, guest houses, family hotels, etc.) as well as freshly researched and innovations of the market-oriented issues from the segments • Equipment & Ambience • Features & Specifications • Food • Drinks supplemented by focused on the operating profit management and marketing issues. Also accompanied the editorial relevant to the sector of social, economic and political developments, combined with news, comments, opinions and statements. Behind all the issues are competent technical editors and technical writers. But that's not all: with a dynamic layout and numerous facts and profile information boxes, readers are concentrated by the relevant content or information held in short form.
Language(s): German
Readership: Aimed at entrepreneurs and managers in the hotel and gastronomy trade.
ADVERTISING RATES:
Full Page Mono .... EUR 9110
Full Page Colour .... EUR 15250
Mechanical Data: Type Area: 274 x 184 mm, No. of Columns (Display): 4, Col Widths (Display): 43 mm
Copy instructions: *Copy Date:* 14 days prior to publication
Official Journal of: Organ d. Dehoga Westfalen e.V., d. Verb. Gaststätten- u. Hotelgewerbe Lippe e.V., d. LV Bremen e.V. u. d. IHV Internat. Hotellerie-Vereinigung Europ. Fachverb. f. Hotellerie u. Gastronomie
BUSINESS: CATERING: Catering, Hotels & Restaurants

DER GASTROENTEROLOGE
1752569G56A-11408
Editorial: Tiergartenstr. 17, 69121 HEIDELBERG
Tel: 6221 4878820 **Fax:** 6221 48768820
Email: annette.gasser@springer.com **Web site:** http://www.springermedizin.de
Freq: 6 issues yearly; **Annual Sub.:** EUR 174,00; **Circ:** 2,800
Advertising Manager: Sigrid Christ
Profile: Der Gastroenterologe offers up-to-date information for all gastroenterologists and hepatologists working in practical and clinical environments and scientists who are interested in issues of gastroenterology and hepatology. The focus is on current developments regarding prevention, diagnostic approaches, management of complications and current therapy strategies. Comprehensive reviews on a specific topical issue provide evidenced based information on diagnostics and therapy. Review articles under the rubric "Continuing Medical Education" present verified results of scientific research and their integration into daily practice.
Language(s): German
ADVERTISING RATES:
Full Page Mono .... EUR 4280
Full Page Colour .... EUR 4280
Mechanical Data: Type Area: 240 x 174 mm
Official Journal of: Organ d. Dt. Ges. f. Innere Medizin, d. Berufsverb. Dt. Internisten, d. Mitteldt. Ges. f. Gastroenterologie, d. Gastroenterolog. ArGe Rheinland-Pfalz/Saarland u. d. Ges. f. Gastroenterologie in Nordrhein-Westfalen

GASTROENTEROLOGIE UP2DATE
1703023G56A-11388
Editorial: Ernst-Grube-Str. 40, 06120 HALLE
Email: thomas.seufferlein@medizin.uni-halle.de **Web site:** http://www.thieme.de/fz/gastroenterologie-u2d.html
Freq: Quarterly; **Annual Sub.:** EUR 155,40; **Circ:** 2,000
Editor: Thomas Seufferlein
Profile: Gastroenterology up2date is the hands-on comprehensive course for the CME-certified training in gastroenterology. Each issue contains four high-quality color designed CME Individual contributions, which are bound separately and stored individually by the subscribers in a ring binder.
Language(s): German
ADVERTISING RATES:
Full Page Mono .... EUR 1890
Full Page Colour .... EUR 3030
Mechanical Data: Type Area: 256 x 180 mm
Official Journal of: Organ d. Dt. Ges. f. Verdauungs- u. Stoffwechselkrankheiten u. d. Bundesverb. Gastroenterologie in Deutschland

GASTRONEWS
2037973G56A-11700
Editorial: Aschauer Str. 30, 81549 MÜNCHEN
Tel: 89 2030431300 **Fax:** 89 2030431399
Email: thomas.riedel@springer.com **Web site:** http://www.springermedizin.de
Freq: 6 issues yearly; **Annual Sub.:** EUR 93,50; **Circ:** 3,300
Editor: Thomas Riedel
Profile: The journal „GastroNews" is an independent and practical continuing education magazine with all the relevant issues from all fields of gastroenterology. „GastroNews" is a solid overview of the current state of diagnosis, treatment and research. The focus is of experts commented papers of the international trade literature. Each issue contains two certifiable training posts. Gastroenterologists provide updated information on professional policy and practice management.
Language(s): German
ADVERTISING RATES:
Full Page Mono .... EUR 3800
Full Page Colour .... EUR 3800
Mechanical Data: Type Area: 240 x 174 mm

GASTRONOMIE REPORT
728354G11A-560
Editorial: Weißenburger Str. 19, 81667 MÜNCHEN
Tel: 89 3241810 **Fax:** 89 4807514
Email: stadler@gastronomie-report.de **Web site:** http://www.gastronomie-report.de
Freq: 10 issues yearly; **Annual Sub.:** EUR 43,00; **Circ:** 6,066
Editor: Josef Stadler; **Advertising Manager:** Willy Faber
Profile: Naughty, aggressive, critical - Gastronomie report appear as a trade magazine for the catering and hotel industry in Bavaria: The latest industry news, top concepts from all over the world, new products and innovations, trends and news reports from the most important fairs in the world, revenue-generating ideas and practical Tips & Tricks, key issues - from the IFA market to interior design, rubrics such as "Wine of the month" and "beer-News" specials such as "Kitchen of the future" and "Outdoor Dining" and much more. In short, the Gastronomie report provides everything you need to know successful catering entrepreneur. Tough but fair in the matter, concise style and always directed to focus on adding value to the reader. Basis of success is the regional concept, the high value of every single issue and the close reader loyalty. Out of the kitchen of ideas of Gastronomie report are also contests of ideas for the restaurant of the future that will be organized in close cooperation with technical colleges and universities every two years. In a time of radical change and great challenges the Gastronomie report is convinced that only a close dialogue between all parties - restaurateurs, industry and trade journals - to create prerequisites for a successful future- and market-oriented catering trade. Exploit the regional power of the Gastronomie report for a strong presence in Bavaria - the most important tourism and catering site in Germany! Facebook: http://www.facebook.com/gastronomie.report.
Language(s): German
Readership: Aimed at those involved in the catering industry including hotel and restaurant owners.
ADVERTISING RATES:
Full Page Mono .... EUR 1460
Full Page Colour .... EUR 2440
Mechanical Data: Type Area: 261 x 184 mm, No. of Columns (Display): 4, Col Widths (Display): 43 mm
Copy instructions: *Copy Date:* 22 days prior to publication
BUSINESS: CATERING: Catering, Hotels & Restaurants

GASTRONOMIE & HOTELLERIE
728352G11A-540
Editorial: Am Friedrichshain 22, 10407 BERLIN
Tel: 30 42151464 **Fax:** 30 42151214
Email: gastro.redaktion@hussberlin.de **Web site:** http://www.gastronomie-hotellerie.com
Freq: 10 issues yearly; **Annual Sub.:** EUR 72,00; **Circ:** 20,848
Editor: Barbara Böhme; **Advertising Manager:** Ines Neumann
Profile: Magazine focusing on hotels, restaurants and gastronomy.
Language(s): German
Readership: Aimed at managers of hotels and restaurants.
ADVERTISING RATES:
Full Page Mono .... EUR 5080
Full Page Colour .... EUR 7030
Mechanical Data: Type Area: 266 x 182 mm, No. of Columns (Display): 3, Col Widths (Display): 58 mm
Copy instructions: *Copy Date:* 15 days prior to publication
BUSINESS: CATERING: Catering, Hotels & Restaurants

GASTRONOMIE-PRAXIS
722077G4E-2260
Editorial: Danziger Str. 20, 74321 BIETIGHEIM-BISSINGEN **Tel:** 7142 63782 **Fax:** 7142 61298
Freq: Monthly; **Annual Sub.:** EUR 86,40; **Circ:** 3,300
Editor: Maria Justen
Profile: The Gastronomie-Praxis is a magazine for the education and training in the restaurant industry. It is the first monthly magazine that deals exclusively with professional matters, namely with the curricular content of training. It is important to cover a wide range: hotel, kitchen, restaurant, food, beverages, etc. And also important are the many tips about training, which appear regularly in the Gastronomie-Praxis. With this much content, the magazine accompanied by the reliable training and professional development.
Language(s): German
ADVERTISING RATES:
Full Page Mono .... EUR 580
Full Page Colour .... EUR 1107
Mechanical Data: Type Area: 265 x 185 mm, No. of Columns (Display): 4, Col Widths (Display): 42 mm
Copy instructions: *Copy Date:* 30 days prior to publication
BUSINESS: ARCHITECTURE & BUILDING: Building

GASWÄRME INTERNATIONAL
728362G3B-2
Editorial: Huyssenallee 52, 45128 ESSEN
Tel: 201 8200212 **Fax:** 201 8200240
Email: s.schalm@vulkan-verlag.de **Web site:** http://www.gaswaerme-markt.de
Freq: 6 issues yearly; **Annual Sub.:** EUR 266,00; **Circ:** 2,130
Editor: Stephan Schalm; **Advertising Manager:** Jutta Zierold
Profile: Magazine for industrial and commercial gas application technology. The magazine gives readers inland and abroad, a current and comprehensive reporting on issues of energy-efficient gas application technology, the efficient and environmentally friendly energy use in industry and the current state of technology in industrial furnaces. Important themes here are the optimization of energy consumption in combustion processes, reduction of pollutant emissions, the use of waste heat to improve the overall efficiency, the energetically favorable heating of large spaces, as well as the technical security and energy management systems of industrial thermal process technology. Specifically, the areas of industrial furnaces and heat treatment equipment, gas burners and firing systems, measurement, control and safety devices, treated automation of thermal processes, standard work, FOGI projects, equipment and building materials from industrial furnaces, energy efficiency, emissions trading and contracting solutions for industrial applications.
Language(s): English; German
ADVERTISING RATES:
Full Page Mono .... EUR 1940
Full Page Colour .... EUR 3125
Mechanical Data: Type Area: 255 x 182 mm, No. of Columns (Display): 3, Col Widths (Display): 58 mm
Copy instructions: *Copy Date:* 15 days prior to publication
Official Journal of: Organ d. Gas-Wärme-Inst. Esn., d. Univ. Karlsruhe, Engler-Bunte-Inst., Bereich Feuerungstechnik, d. Rhein.-Westfäl. Techn. Hochschule Aachen, Inst. f. Industrieofenbau u. Wärmetechnik im Hüttenwesen, d. Inst. f. Energieverfahrenstechnik d. Lehrstuhls Hochtemperaturanlagen, d. Inst. f. Wärmetechnik u. Thermodynamik d. Techn. Univ. Bergakademie Freiberg u. d. Fachverb. Thermoprozess- u. Abfalltechnik im VDMA
BUSINESS: HEATING & VENTILATION: Industrial Heating & Ventilation

GÄUBODEN AKTUELL
728255G72-4112
Editorial: Ludwigsplatz 30, 94315 STRAUBING
Tel: 9421 9403141 **Fax:** 9421 9404139
Email: redaktion@gaeuboden-aktuell.de **Web site:** http://www.idowa.de
Freq: Weekly; **Cover Price:** Free; **Circ:** 71,728
Editor: Rosi Thoma; **Advertising Manager:** Klaus Huber
Profile: Advertising journal (house-to-house) concentrating on local stories.
Language(s): German
ADVERTISING RATES:
Full Page Mono .... EUR 2813
Full Page Colour .... EUR 3948
Mechanical Data: Type Area: 430 x 280 mm, No. of Columns (Display): 6, Col Widths (Display): 45 mm
Copy instructions: *Copy Date:* 2 days prior to publication
LOCAL NEWSPAPERS

GÄUBOTE
728256G67B-5580
Editorial: Horber Str. 42, 71083 HERRENBERG
Tel: 7032 9525200 **Fax:** 7032 9525109
Email: redaktion@gaeubote.de **Web site:** http://www.gaeubote.de
Freq: 312 issues yearly; **Circ:** 12,073
Advertising Manager: Christina Samel
Profile: Daily newspaper with regional news and a local sports section. Facebook: http://www.facebook.com/pages/Gaubote/128212357224404.
Language(s): German
ADVERTISING RATES:
SCC .... EUR 39,40
Mechanical Data: Type Area: 485 x 321 mm, No. of Columns (Display): 7, Col Widths (Display): 44 mm
Copy instructions: *Copy Date:* 1 day prior to publication
Supplement(s): Kinder-Gäubote
REGIONAL DAILY & SUNDAY NEWSPAPERS: Regional Daily Newspapers

GAULT MILLAU DEUTSCHLAND
1792762G89A-12273
Editorial: Infanteriestr. 11, 80797 MÜNCHEN
Tel: 89 1306990 **Fax:** 89 13069911
Email: gault-millau@christian-verlag.de **Web site:** http://www.gaultmillau.de
Freq: Annual; **Cover Price:** EUR 29,95; **Circ:** 50,000
Editor: Bianca Turtur
Profile: Guide for gourmets on assessment of 1060 restaurants and 365 hotels in Germany.
Language(s): German
ADVERTISING RATES:
Full Page Mono .... EUR 7700
Full Page Colour .... EUR 7700

Mechanical Data: Type Area: 185 x 117 mm, No. of Columns (Display): 2, Col Widths (Display): 56 mm
Copy instructions: *Copy Date:* 65 days prior to publication

GAULT MILLAU WEINGUIDE DEUTSCHLAND 1792764G89A-12274

Editorial: Infanteriestr. 11, 80797 MÜNCHEN
Tel: 89 1306990 **Fax:** 89 13069911
Email: gault-millau@christian-verlag.de **Web site:** http://www.gaultmillau.de
Freq: Annual; **Cover Price:** EUR 29,95; **Circ:** 25,000
Editor: Claudia Eilus
Profile: A dozen journalists wine tasted and evaluated for this guide more than 12,000 wines, visiting wineries and discover new talents. A logistic major project in which each step is well thought out.
Language(s): German
ADVERTISING RATES:
Full Page Mono .... EUR 4100
Full Page Colour .... EUR 4100
Mechanical Data: Type Area: 185 x 117 mm, No. of Columns (Display): 2, Col Widths (Display): 56 mm
Copy instructions: *Copy Date:* 65 days prior to publication

GAYFRIENDLY CANADA 1657308G89A-11885

Editorial: Birkenleiten 11, 81543 MÜNCHEN
Tel: 89 62439772 **Fax:** 89 62439771
Email: fs@tomontour.de **Web site:** http://www.tomontour.de
Freq: Annual; **Cover Price:** Free; **Circ:** 40,000
Editor: Frank Störbrauck; **Advertising Manager:** Tom Dedek
Profile: Extensively researched gay guide to Kanada. Facebook: http://www.facebook.com/pages/TOM-ON-TOUR/80220127132 Twitter: http://twitter.com/#!/tomontour.
Language(s): English; German
ADVERTISING RATES:
Full Page Mono .... EUR 3250
Full Page Colour .... EUR 3250
Mechanical Data: Type Area: 280 x 216 mm

GAYFRIENDLY FLANDERN 1800075G89A-12308

Editorial: Birkenleiten 11, 81543 MÜNCHEN
Tel: 89 62439772 **Fax:** 89 62439771
Email: fs@tomontour.de **Web site:** http://www.tomontour.de
Freq: Annual; **Cover Price:** Free; **Circ:** 70,000
Editor: Frank Störbrauck; **Advertising Manager:** Tom Dedek
Profile: Extensively researched gay guide to Flandern. Facebook: http://www.facebook.com/pages/TOM-ON-TOUR/80220127132 Twitter: http://twitter.com/#!/tomontour.
Language(s): English; German
ADVERTISING RATES:
Full Page Mono .... EUR 3250
Full Page Colour .... EUR 3250
Mechanical Data: Type Area: 280 x 216 mm

GAYFRIENDLY SPAIN 1860167G89A-12416

Editorial: Birkenleiten 11, 81543 MÜNCHEN
Tel: 89 62439772 **Fax:** 89 62439771
Email: fs@tomontour.de **Web site:** http://www.tomontour.de
Freq: Annual; **Cover Price:** Free; **Circ:** 60,000
Editor: Frank Störbrauck; **Advertising Manager:** Tom Dedek
Profile: Extensively researched gay guide to Spain. Facebook: http://www.facebook.com/pages/TOM-ON-TOUR/80220127132 Twitter: http://twitter.com/#!/tomontour.
Language(s): English; German
Mechanical Data: Type Area: 280 x 216 mm

GAYFRIENDLY USA 1800076G89A-12309

Editorial: Birkenleiten 11, 81543 MÜNCHEN
Tel: 89 62439772 **Fax:** 89 62439771
Email: fs@tomontour.de **Web site:** http://www.tomontour.de
Freq: Annual; **Cover Price:** Free; **Circ:** 60,000
Editor: Frank Störbrauck; **Advertising Manager:** Tom Dedek
Profile: Extensively researched gay guide to USA. Facebook: http://www.facebook.com/pages/TOM-ON-TOUR/80220127132 Twitter: http://twitter.com/#!/tomontour.
Language(s): English; German
ADVERTISING RATES:
Full Page Mono .... EUR 3950
Full Page Colour .... EUR 3950
Mechanical Data: Type Area: 280 x 216 mm

DIE GAZETTE 1643600G73-506

Editorial: Kunigundenstr. 42, 80805 MÜNCHEN
Tel: 89 36039666 **Fax:** 89 36039667
Email: redaktion@gazette.de **Web site:** http://www.gazette.de
Freq: Quarterly; **Annual Sub.:** EUR 32,00; **Circ:** 4,500
Profile: Political culture magazine.
Language(s): German
ADVERTISING RATES:
Full Page Mono .... EUR 480
Full Page Colour .... EUR 520
Mechanical Data: Type Area: 258 x 175 mm, No. of Columns (Display): 2, Col Widths (Display): 85 mm

GAZETTE - AUSG. CHARLOTTENBURG 728375G72-17450

Editorial: Badensche Str. 44, 10715 BERLIN
Tel: 30 8449330 **Fax:** 30 84493313
Email: redaktion@gazette-berlin.de **Web site:** http://www.gazette-berlin.de
Freq: Monthly; **Cover Price:** Free; **Circ:** 40,200
Editor: Karl-Heinz Christ; **Advertising Manager:** Karl-Heinz Christ
Profile: Advertising journal (house-to-house) concentrating on local stories.
Language(s): German
ADVERTISING RATES:
Full Page Mono .... EUR 1500
Full Page Colour .... EUR 1950
Mechanical Data: Type Area: 325 x 231 mm, No. of Columns (Display): 5, Col Widths (Display): 43 mm
Copy instructions: *Copy Date:* 18 days prior to publication
LOCAL NEWSPAPERS

GB GÄRTNERBÖRSE 1605106G93-991

Editorial: Bendstr. 3, 52066 AACHEN
Tel: 241 4095611 **Fax:** 241 4095619
Email: red.gb-zierpflanzenbau@haymarket.de **Web site:** http://www.gaertnerboerse.de
Freq: Monthly; **Annual Sub.:** EUR 142,80; **Circ:** 2,703
Editor: Heinrich Dreßler; **Advertising Manager:** Christian Rueß
Profile: Magazine about ornamental plant growing. Every month the magazine delivers cutting-edge data and facts around the issues of production and marketing of bedding and patio plants, potted plants and cut flowers. Contributions to the most important fairs in ornamental horticulture complete the range of topics. Target group: Entrepreneurs and executives in ornamental horticulture.
Language(s): German
ADVERTISING RATES:
Full Page Mono .... EUR 2557
Full Page Colour .... EUR 3775
Mechanical Data: Type Area: 272 x 186 mm, No. of Columns (Display): 4, Col Widths (Display): 45 mm
CONSUMER: GARDENING

GDL MAGAZIN VORAUS 728392G14L-43

Editorial: Baumweg 45, 60316 FRANKFURT
Tel: 69 405709111 **Fax:** 69 405709119
Email: presse@gdl.de **Web site:** http://www.gdl.de
Freq: 10 issues yearly; Free to qualifying individuals
Annual Sub.: EUR 10,00; **Circ:** 37,000
Editor: Gerda Seibert
Profile: Magazine of the Trade Union of Engine Drivers. Features articles on trade union policy and train technology. Also includes news on government train policy.
Language(s): German
Readership: Read by members.
ADVERTISING RATES:
Full Page Mono .... EUR 1305
Full Page Colour .... EUR 2150
Mechanical Data: Type Area: 270 x 185 mm, No. of Columns (Display): 4, Col Widths (Display): 43 mm
BUSINESS: COMMERCE, INDUSTRY & MANAGEMENT: Trade Unions

GEA.DE REUTLINGER GENERAL-ANZEIGER 1621931G80-13872

Editorial: Burgstr. 1, 72764 REUTLINGEN
Tel: 7121 302338 **Fax:** 7121 302677
Email: zen@gea.de **Web site:** http://www.gea.de
Freq: Daily; **Cover Price:** Paid; **Circ:** 216,008 Unique Users
Editor: Hartmut Troebs
Profile: Ezine: Regional daily newspaper covering politics, economics, sport, travel and technology. Twitter: http://twitter.com/geaonline This Outlet offers RSS (Really Simple Syndication).
Language(s): German
CONSUMER: RURAL & REGIONAL INTEREST

GEBÄUDE ENERGIEBERATER 1703347G3D-856

Editorial: Forststr. 131, 70193 STUTTGART
Tel: 711 63672823 **Fax:** 711 63672723
Email: grossmann@geb-info.de **Web site:** http://www.geb-info.de
Freq: 10 issues yearly; **Annual Sub.:** EUR 164,60; **Circ:** 11,173
Editor: Britta Großmann; **Advertising Manager:** Bettina Landwehr
Language(s): German
ADVERTISING RATES:
Full Page Mono .... EUR 2840
Full Page Colour .... EUR 3890
Mechanical Data: Type Area: 265 x 187 mm, No. of Columns (Display): 4, Col Widths (Display): 43 mm
BUSINESS: HEATING & VENTILATION: Heating & Plumbing

GEBÄUDETECHNIK 1601694G17-1534

Editorial: Lazarettstr. 4, 80636 MÜNCHEN
Tel: 89 12607299 **Fax:** 89 12607310
Email: buch@de-online.info **Web site:** http://www.de-jahrbuch.info
Freq: Annual; **Cover Price:** EUR 21,80; **Circ:** 6,800
Advertising Manager: Michael Dietl
Profile: Magazine on building services engineering.
Language(s): German
ADVERTISING RATES:
Full Page Mono .... EUR 1575
Mechanical Data: Type Area: 156 x 98 mm
Copy instructions: *Copy Date:* 70 days prior to publication

GEBRAUCHTWAGEN AUTO MOTOR UND SPORT 721611G77A-380

Editorial: Leuschnerstr. 1, 70174 STUTTGART
Tel: 711 1821241 **Fax:** 711 1821958
Email: redaktion_ams@motorpresse.de **Web site:** http://www.auto-motor-und-sport.de
Freq: Annual; **Cover Price:** EUR 4,50; **Circ:** 100,000
Editor: Bernd Ostmann; **Advertising Manager:** Jochen Bechtle
Profile: Magazine for used car buyers. Facebook: http://www.facebook.com/automotorundsport.
Language(s): German
ADVERTISING RATES:
Full Page Mono .... EUR 12900
Full Page Colour .... EUR 12900
Mechanical Data: Type Area: 248 x 185 mm, No. of Columns (Display): 4, Col Widths (Display): 43 mm
Copy instructions: *Copy Date:* 32 days prior to publication

GEBRAUCHTWAGEN PRAXIS 728405G31-7

Editorial: Max-Planck-Str. 7, 97082 WÜRZBURG
Tel: 931 4182645 **Fax:** 931 4182150
Email: silvia.lulei@vogel.de **Web site:** http://www.kfz-betrieb.vogel.de
Freq: Monthly; **Annual Sub.:** EUR 180,00; **Circ:** 4,631
Editor: Silvia Lulei; **Advertising Manager:** Anna Gredel
Profile: Magazine on the used car trade business.
Language(s): German
ADVERTISING RATES:
Full Page Mono .... EUR 1805
Full Page Colour .... EUR 1805
Copy instructions: *Copy Date:* 14 days prior to publication

GEBURTSHILFE UND FRAUENHEILKUNDE 728407G56A-3880

Editorial: Theodor-Stern-Kai 7, 60590 FRANKFURT
Web site: http://www.thieme.de/gebfra
Freq: Monthly; Free to qualifying individuals
Annual Sub.: EUR 319,90; **Circ:** 2,700
Editor: M. Kaufmann
Profile: The Geburtshilfe und Frauenheilkunde you informed about the latest scientific findings and developments in obstetrics and gynecology. With every other issue you will also earn CME points for your regular training. GebFra-Science: scientific papers and summaries, commentaries on international studies, compact overviews and selected original research, case reports provide current findings are related to practice, a discussion forum on controversial topics and current developments. GebFra-Training: The GebFra Refresher gather regularly 3 CME points for your further education. GebFra-Refresher treated challenging clinical issues and selected specialty areas in a detailed, separately stitched CME article.
Language(s): German
Readership: Read by gynaecologists.
ADVERTISING RATES:
Full Page Mono .... EUR 2160
Full Page Colour .... EUR 3510
Mechanical Data: Type Area: 248 x 175 mm, No. of Columns (Display): 3, Col Widths (Display): 55 mm
Official Journal of: Organ d. Dt. Ges. f. Gynäkologie u. Geburtshilfe
BUSINESS: HEALTH & MEDICAL

GEE 1638672G78D-906

Editorial: Hongkongstr. 7, 20457 HAMBURG
Tel: 40 226335958 **Fax:** 40 226335959
Email: grohe@geemag.de **Web site:** http://www.geemag.de
Freq: Quarterly; **Annual Sub.:** EUR 20,00; **Circ:** 18,035
Editor: Moses Grohé; **Advertising Manager:** Volker Hansch
Profile: Video game magazine with photo stories, reports, product news in the field of entertainment electronics, games and news from the branch.
Language(s): German
ADVERTISING RATES:
Full Page Mono .... EUR 4900
Full Page Colour .... EUR 4900
Mechanical Data: Type Area: 180 x 230 mm
Copy instructions: *Copy Date:* 18 days prior to publication
CONSUMER: CONSUMER ELECTRONICS: Games

GEESTHACHTER ANZEIGER 728410G72-4148

Editorial: Schefestr. 11, 21493 SCHWARZENBEK
Tel: 4151 88900 **Fax:** 4151 889044
Email: redaktion@geesthachter-anzeiger.de **Web site:** http://www.viebranz.de
Freq: Weekly; **Cover Price:** Free; **Circ:** 22,545
Editor: Olaf Kührmann; **Advertising Manager:** Andreas Runge
Profile: Advertising journal (house-to-house) concentrating on local stories.
Language(s): German
ADVERTISING RATES:
Full Page Mono .... EUR 2813
Full Page Colour .... EUR 2873
Mechanical Data: Type Area: 430 x 282 mm, No. of Columns (Display): 6, Col Widths (Display): 45 mm
Copy instructions: *Copy Date:* 1 day prior to publication
LOCAL NEWSPAPERS

GEFAHR/GUT 728415G49C-23

Editorial: Aschauer Str. 30, 81549 MÜNCHEN
Tel: 89 2030432521 **Fax:** 89 2030432384
Email: birgit.bauer@springer.com **Web site:** http://www.gefahrgut-online.de
Freq: Monthly; **Annual Sub.:** EUR 189,00; **Circ:** 4,848
Editor: Birgit Bauer; **Advertising Manager:** Matthias Pioro
Profile: Publication about storage, handling and transport by road of hazardous goods.
Language(s): German
ADVERTISING RATES:
Full Page Colour .... EUR 3245
Mechanical Data: Type Area: 250 x 185 mm, No. of Columns (Display): 4, Col Widths (Display): 43 mm
BUSINESS: TRANSPORT: Freight

GEFAHRGUT AKTUELL 1660094G10-527

Editorial: Striepenweg 31, 21147 HAMBURG
Tel: 40 79713133 **Fax:** 40 79713101
Email: ak@storck-verlag.de
Freq: 26 issues yearly; **Annual Sub.:** EUR 169,00; **Circ:** 600
Editor: Uwe Heins
Profile: Technical information from hazardous and dangerous practice of law for entrepreneurs, managers, hazardous materials officer, commissioned people (transport, chemical, pharmaceutical, mineral economics, army, government, hazardous materials instructor).
Language(s): German

GEFAHRGUT PROFI 728418G49C-75

Editorial: Am Grauen Stein, 51105 KÖLN
Tel: 221 8063517 **Fax:** 221 8063510
Email: angelika.heinze@de.tuv.com **Web site:** http://www.tuev-media.de
Freq: 6 issues yearly; **Annual Sub.:** EUR 63,70; **Circ:** 2,600
Editor: Angelika Heinze; **Advertising Manager:** Gudrun Karafiol
Profile: Publication about the transport of hazardous goods.
Language(s): German
ADVERTISING RATES:
Full Page Mono .... EUR 1140
Full Page Colour .... EUR 1725
Mechanical Data: Type Area: 250 x 183 mm, No. of Columns (Display): 3, Col Widths (Display): 58 mm
Copy instructions: *Copy Date:* 54 days prior to publication

DER GEFAHRGUTBEAUFTRAGTE 728417G49C-24

Editorial: Striepenweg 31, 21147 HAMBURG
Tel: 40 79713135 **Fax:** 40 79713101
Email: ur@storck-verlag.de **Web site:** http://www.dergefahrgutbeauftragte.de
Freq: Monthly; **Annual Sub.:** EUR 132,95; **Circ:** 3,671
Editor: Uwe Rainer
Profile: Publication about the transport of hazardous goods.
Language(s): German
Readership: Aimed at safety advisors, transport companies and ADR licence holders.
ADVERTISING RATES:
Full Page Mono .... EUR 1560
Full Page Colour .... EUR 2400
Mechanical Data: Type Area: 260 x 185 mm
Copy instructions: *Copy Date:* 21 days prior to publication
BUSINESS: TRANSPORT: Freight

GEFÄHRLICHE LADUNG 728412G49C-30

Editorial: Striepenweg 31, 21147 HAMBURG
Tel: 40 79713130 **Fax:** 40 79713101
Email: uh@storck-verlag.de **Web site:** http://www.gelaweb.de
Freq: Monthly; **Annual Sub.:** EUR 139,95; **Circ:** 5,263
Editor: Uwe Heins; **Advertising Manager:** Horst Hamann
Profile: Publication about the storage, handling and transportation of hazardous goods.
Language(s): German
ADVERTISING RATES:
Full Page Mono .... EUR 2030
Full Page Colour .... EUR 3100
Mechanical Data: Type Area: 260 x 185 mm
Copy instructions: *Copy Date:* 21 days prior to publication
BUSINESS: TRANSPORT: Freight

GEFAHRSTOFFE REINHALTUNG DER LUFT
728420G57-540
Editorial: VDI-Platz 1, 40468 DÜSSELDORF
Tel: 211 6103343 **Fax:** 211 6103148
Email: gefahrstoffe@technikwissen.de **Web site:** http://www.technikwissen.de/gest
Freq: 9 issues yearly; Free to qualifying individuals
Annual Sub.: EUR 337,50; **Circ:** 1,888
Editor: Elisabeth Zimmermann
Profile: Gefahrstoffe – Reinhaltung der Luft is the magazine for the whole area of air pollution. It reports on pollutant formation, propagation, detection and separation, sampling and measurement techniques, effects of air pollution, safety engineering, about the dangers of dust and smoke at work, including the discussion of limits from a technical and occupational health perspective as well as technical and personal protective measures and medical surveillance.
Language(s): German
ADVERTISING RATES:
Full Page Mono .... EUR 1872
Full Page Colour .... EUR 2952
Mechanical Data: Type Area: 270 x 185 mm, No. of Columns (Display): 4, Col Widths (Display): 45 mm
Copy instructions: *Copy Date:* 21 days prior to publication
BUSINESS: ENVIRONMENT & POLLUTION

GEFÄSSCHIRURGIE 728414G56A-3900
Editorial: Tiergartenstr. 17, 69121 HEIDELBERG
Tel: 6221 4878178 **Fax:** 6221 48768178
Email: tina.suhai@springer.com **Web site:** http://www.springermedizin.de
Freq: 8 issues yearly; **Annual Sub.:** EUR 280,00; **Circ:** 2,450
Advertising Manager: Noëla Krischer-Janka
Profile: The magazine „Gefässchirurgie" provides information on current developments in the vascular and endovascular surgery. Original papers presenting relevant clinical research. Review articles on selected topics and engage in case reports are interesting cases presented. Other sections discuss not only scientific content and practical and professional issues. The training and continuing education offers the opportunity for certification. Regular communications between companies will be published.
Language(s): German
ADVERTISING RATES:
Full Page Mono .... EUR 1488
Full Page Colour .... EUR 2528
Mechanical Data: Type Area: 240 x 174 mm
Official Journal of: Organ d. Dt., d. Österr. u. d. Schweizer. Ges. f. Gefäßchirurgie
BUSINESS: HEALTH & MEDICAL

GEFÄSSREPORT AKTUELL
1793844G56A-11444
Editorial: Postfach 4038, 69254 MALSCH
Tel: 7253 26228 **Fax:** 7253 278160
Email: heike.ruck@t-online.de **Web site:** http://www.deutsche-gefaessliga.de
Freq: Half-yearly; **Cover Price:** EUR 1,50
Free to qualifying individuals ; **Circ:** 15,000
Editor: Curt Diehm
Profile: Magazine informs about the prevention from vascular diseases.
Language(s): German
Mechanical Data: Type Area: 303 x 213 mm, No. of Columns (Display): 2, Col Widths (Display): 85 mm

GEFIEDERTE WELT 728422G81F-4
Editorial: Aspacher Str. 15, 71522 BACKNANG
Tel: 7191 4950222 **Fax:** 7191 4950223
Email: gefiedertewelt@arcor.de **Web site:** http://www.gefiederte-welt.de
Freq: Monthly; **Annual Sub.:** EUR 84,60; **Circ:** 7,800
Editor: Dietmar Schmidt; **Advertising Manager:** Anna Greiner
Profile: Gefiederte Welt has been published since 1872 and is the world's oldest and most prestigious special-interest publication for all aspects of keeping and breeding birds. With 6,750 subscribers, the Gefiederte Welt is industry leader in all non-union-bound journals. The constant themes: keeping and breeding of birds of all kinds, feeding issues, animal health, aviary construction and equipment, product innovations from industry and trade, breeders portraits, behavior observations, bird parks and zoos, faunistic and systematic, travel, field observations, bird photography, laws and regulations, bird and species protection, ringing, scientific research results, trade fairs and exhibitions.
Language(s): German
ADVERTISING RATES:
Full Page Mono .... EUR 992
Full Page Colour .... EUR 1342
Mechanical Data: Type Area: 266 x 176 mm, No. of Columns (Display): 4, Col Widths (Display): 41 mm
Copy instructions: *Copy Date:* 22 days prior to publication
CONSUMER: ANIMALS & PETS: Birds

GEFLÜGEL ZEITUNG 725013G81F-2
Editorial: Wilhelmsaue 37, 10713 BERLIN
Tel: 30 897454541 **Fax:** 30 897454555
Email: gefluegelzeitung@hk-verlag.de **Web site:** http://www.gefluegelzeitung.de
Freq: 24 issues yearly; **Annual Sub.:** EUR 61,50; **Circ:** 23,000
Editor: Uwe Oehm; **Advertising Manager:** Frank Middendorf
Profile: The newspaper as a leading magazine for poultry breeders and owners of Poultry in Germany is indispensable magazine for all lovers of poultry. As the official organ of the Federation of German breed poultry (BDRG) the poultry newspaper reported on current events from the national associations and organizations. The always cutting-edge event calendar rounds out the association's coverage. In addition to the poultry farmers, the title race is also directed to breeders and friends of ornamental birds, exotics and canaries. The broad range of issues is the diversity of farming, breeding and feeding, up to diseases and heredity. Another focus of the poultry is on the newspaper publication of race reports and the presentation of interesting portraits breeders. In addition, extensive reports provide important information about exhibitions and events for interested growers.
Language(s): German
Readership: Aimed at bird breeders and enthusiasts.
ADVERTISING RATES:
Full Page Mono .... EUR 1700
Full Page Colour .... EUR 2754
Mechanical Data: Type Area: 262 x 184 mm, No. of Columns (Display): 4, Col Widths (Display): 43 mm
Copy instructions: *Copy Date:* 14 days prior to publication
Official Journal of: Organ d. Bundes Dt. Rassegeflügelzüchter
CONSUMER: ANIMALS & PETS: Birds

GEFLÜGEL-BÖRSE 728423G81X-1060
Editorial: Gabriele-Münter-Str. 5, 82110 GERMERING **Tel:** 89 894184307 **Fax:** 89 894184320
Email: redaktion@gefluegel-boerse.de **Web site:** http://www.gefluegel-boerse.de
Freq: 24 issues yearly; **Annual Sub.:** EUR 75,60; **Circ:** 17,000
Editor: Michael von Lüttwitz
Profile: Magazine informs about race poultry, ornamental fowl, pigeons and small animals.
Language(s): German
ADVERTISING RATES:
Full Page Mono .... EUR 1508
Full Page Colour .... EUR 2150
Mechanical Data: Type Area: 260 x 185 mm, No. of Columns (Display): 4, Col Widths (Display): 45 mm
Copy instructions: *Copy Date:* 11 days prior to publication
Official Journal of: Organ d. Bundes Dt. Rassegeflügelzüchter e.V.
CONSUMER: ANIMALS & PETS

GEISLINGER ZEITUNG
728440G67B-5620
Editorial: Hauptstr. 38, 73312 GEISLINGEN
Tel: 7331 20242 **Fax:** 7331 20250
Email: geislinger-zeitung.redaktion@swp.de **Web site:** http://www.geislinger-zeitung.de
Freq: 312 issues yearly; **Circ:** 12,670
Editor: Roderich Schmauz; **Advertising Manager:** Bettina Holzwarth
Profile: Daily newspaper with regional news and a local sports section.
Language(s): German
ADVERTISING RATES:
SCC .... EUR 60,80
Mechanical Data: Type Area: 480 x 320 mm, No. of Columns (Display): 7, Col Widths (Display): 44 mm
Copy instructions: *Copy Date:* 1 day prior to publication
Supplement(s): Das Magazin
REGIONAL DAILY & SUNDAY NEWSPAPERS: Regional Daily Newspapers

GELBE LISTE IDENTA
728459G56A-3920
Editorial: Am Forsthaus Gravenbruch 7, 63263 NEU-ISENBURG **Tel:** 6102 502249 **Fax:** 6102 502220
Email: m.kaemmer@mmi.de **Web site:** http://www.gelbe-liste.de
Freq: Annual; **Cover Price:** EUR 29,00; **Circ:** 20,000
Editor: Marianne Kämmer-Reusch; **Advertising Manager:** Thomas Lang
Profile: Directory listing pharmaceutical products.
Language(s): German
Mechanical Data: Type Area: 195 x 128 mm
Copy instructions: *Copy Date:* 42 days prior to publication

GELBE LISTE PHARMINDEX
728460G56A-3940
Editorial: Am Forsthaus Gravenbruch 7, 63263 NEU-ISENBURG **Tel:** 6102 502249 **Fax:** 6102 502220
Email: m.kaemmer@mmi.de **Web site:** http://www.gelbe-liste.de
Freq: Annual; **Cover Price:** EUR 21,00; **Circ:** 2,700
Editor: Marianne Kämmer-Reusch; **Advertising Manager:** Thomas Lang
Profile: Index of pharmaceutical products for urologists.
Language(s): German
ADVERTISING RATES:
Full Page Mono .... EUR 5550
Full Page Colour .... EUR 6840
Mechanical Data: Type Area: 206 x 152 mm
Copy instructions: *Copy Date:* 63 days prior to publication

GELBE LISTE PHARMINDEX
728461G56A-3960
Editorial: Am Forsthaus Gravenbruch 7, 63263 NEU-ISENBURG **Tel:** 6102 502249 **Fax:** 6102 502220
Email: m.kaemmer@mmi.de **Web site:** http://www.gelbe-liste.de
Freq: Annual; **Cover Price:** EUR 21,00; **Circ:** 6,000
Editor: Marianne Kämmer-Reusch; **Advertising Manager:** Thomas Lang
Profile: Index of pharmaceutical products for paediatry.
Language(s): German
ADVERTISING RATES:
Full Page Mono .... EUR 5800
Full Page Colour .... EUR 7090
Mechanical Data: Type Area: 206 x 152 mm
Copy instructions: *Copy Date:* 63 days prior to publication

GELBE LISTE PHARMINDEX
728462G56A-3980
Editorial: Am Forsthaus Gravenbruch 7, 63263 NEU-ISENBURG **Tel:** 6102 502249 **Fax:** 6102 502220
Email: m.kaemmer@mmi.de **Web site:** http://www.gelbe-liste.de
Freq: Annual; **Cover Price:** EUR 24,50; **Circ:** 15,000
Editor: Marianne Kämmer-Reusch; **Advertising Manager:** Thomas Lang
Profile: Magazine on pharmaceutical products for homeopathy.
Language(s): German
ADVERTISING RATES:
Full Page Mono .... EUR 6300
Full Page Colour .... EUR 7590
Mechanical Data: Type Area: 206 x 152 mm
Copy instructions: *Copy Date:* 63 days prior to publication

GELBE LISTE PHARMINDEX
728463G56A-4000
Editorial: Am Forsthaus Gravenbruch 7, 63263 NEU-ISENBURG **Tel:** 6102 502249 **Fax:** 6102 502220
Email: m.kaemmer@mmi.de **Web site:** http://www.gelbe-liste.de
Freq: Annual; **Cover Price:** EUR 21,00; **Circ:** 5,800
Editor: Marianne Kämmer-Reusch; **Advertising Manager:** Thomas Lang
Profile: Index of pharmaceutical products for ophthalmologists.
Language(s): German
ADVERTISING RATES:
Full Page Mono .... EUR 5800
Full Page Colour .... EUR 7090
Mechanical Data: Type Area: 206 x 152 mm
Copy instructions: *Copy Date:* 63 days prior to publication

GELBE LISTE PHARMINDEX
728464G56A-4020
Editorial: Am Forsthaus Gravenbruch 7, 63263 NEU-ISENBURG **Tel:** 6102 502249 **Fax:** 6102 502220
Email: m.kaemmer@mmi.de **Web site:** http://www.gelbe-liste.de
Freq: Half-yearly; **Annual Sub.:** EUR 36,00; **Circ:** 5,000
Editor: Marianne Kämmer-Reusch; **Advertising Manager:** Thomas Lang
Profile: Index of pharmaceutical products for neurologists and psyciatrists.
Language(s): German
ADVERTISING RATES:
Full Page Mono .... EUR 5800
Full Page Colour .... EUR 7090
Mechanical Data: Type Area: 206 x 152 mm
Copy instructions: *Copy Date:* 63 days prior to publication

GELBE LISTE PHARMINDEX
728465G56A-4040
Editorial: Am Forsthaus Gravenbruch 7, 63263 NEU-ISENBURG **Tel:** 6102 502249 **Fax:** 6102 502220
Email: m.kaemmer@mmi.de **Web site:** http://www.gelbe-liste.de
Freq: Annual; **Cover Price:** EUR 32,00; **Circ:** 14,000
Editor: Marianne Kämmer-Reusch; **Advertising Manager:** Thomas Lang
Profile: Index of pharmaceutical products for internists.
Language(s): German
Mechanical Data: Type Area: 206 x 152 mm
Copy instructions: *Copy Date:* 63 days prior to publication

GELBE LISTE PHARMINDEX
728466G56A-4060
Editorial: Am Forsthaus Gravenbruch 7, 63263 NEU-ISENBURG **Tel:** 6102 502249 **Fax:** 6102 502220
Email: m.kaemmer@mmi.de **Web site:** http://www.gelbe-liste.de
Freq: Annual; **Cover Price:** EUR 21,00; **Circ:** 3,600
Editor: Marianne Kämmer-Reusch; **Advertising Manager:** Thomas Lang
Profile: Index of pharmaceutical products for ENT.
Language(s): German
ADVERTISING RATES:
Full Page Mono .... EUR 5550
Full Page Colour .... EUR 6840
Mechanical Data: Type Area: 206 x 152 mm
Copy instructions: *Copy Date:* 63 days prior to publication

GELBE LISTE PHARMINDEX
728467G56A-4080
Editorial: Am Forsthaus Gravenbruch 7, 63263 NEU-ISENBURG **Tel:** 6102 502249 **Fax:** 6102 502220
Email: m.kaemmer@mmi.de **Web site:** http://www.gelbe-liste.de
Freq: Annual; **Cover Price:** EUR 21,00; **Circ:** 5,000
Editor: Marianne Kämmer-Reusch; **Advertising Manager:** Thomas Lang
Profile: Index of pharmaceutical products for orthopaedists.
Language(s): German
ADVERTISING RATES:
Full Page Mono .... EUR 5800
Full Page Colour .... EUR 7090
Mechanical Data: Type Area: 206 x 152 mm
Copy instructions: *Copy Date:* 63 days prior to publication

GELBE LISTE PHARMINDEX
728468G56A-4100
Editorial: Am Forsthaus Gravenbruch 7, 63263 NEU-ISENBURG **Tel:** 6102 502249 **Fax:** 6102 502220
Email: m.kaemmer@mmi.de **Web site:** http://www.gelbe-liste.de
Freq: Half-yearly; **Annual Sub.:** EUR 36,00; **Circ:** 3,200
Editor: Marianne Kämmer-Reusch; **Advertising Manager:** Thomas Lang
Profile: Index of pharmaceutical products for dermatologists.
Language(s): German
ADVERTISING RATES:
Full Page Mono .... EUR 5550
Full Page Colour .... EUR 6840
Mechanical Data: Type Area: 206 x 152 mm
Copy instructions: *Copy Date:* 63 days prior to publication

GELBE LISTE PHARMINDEX
728469G56A-4120
Editorial: Am Forsthaus Gravenbruch 7, 63263 NEU-ISENBURG **Tel:** 6102 502249 **Fax:** 6102 502220
Email: m.kaemmer@mmi.de **Web site:** http://www.gelbe-liste.de
Freq: Half-yearly; **Annual Sub.:** EUR 58,80; **Circ:** 43,000
Editor: Marianne Kämmer-Reusch; **Advertising Manager:** Thomas Lang
Profile: Index of pharmaceutical products for general practitioners.
Language(s): German
ADVERTISING RATES:
Full Page Mono .... EUR 11200
Full Page Colour .... EUR 13480
Mechanical Data: Type Area: 206 x 152 mm
Copy instructions: *Copy Date:* 63 days prior to publication

GELBE LISTE PHARMINDEX
728470G56A-4140
Editorial: Am Forsthaus Gravenbruch 7, 63263 NEU-ISENBURG **Tel:** 6102 502249 **Fax:** 6102 502220
Email: m.kaemmer@mmi.de **Web site:** http://www.gelbe-liste.de
Freq: Annual; **Cover Price:** EUR 21,00; **Circ:** 9,000
Editor: Marianne Kämmer-Reusch; **Advertising Manager:** Thomas Lang
Profile: Index of pharmaceutical products for gynaecologists.
Language(s): German
ADVERTISING RATES:
Full Page Mono .... EUR 6300
Full Page Colour .... EUR 7590
Mechanical Data: Type Area: 206 x 152 mm
Copy instructions: *Copy Date:* 63 days prior to publication

GELBESEITEN 1704532G14R-6143
Editorial: Wiesenhüttenstr. 18, 60329 FRANKFURT
Tel: 69 26827818 **Fax:** 69 26827890
Email: info@detemedien.de **Web site:** http://www.gelbeseiten.de
Freq: Daily; **Cover Price:** Paid; **Circ:** 8,093,529 Unique Users
Profile: Mercantile telefon directory.
Language(s): German
BUSINESS: COMMERCE, INDUSTRY & MANAGEMENT: Commerce Related

GELD UND KAPITAL 755964G1C-1401
Editorial: Detmolder Str. 133, 33604 BIELEFELD
Web site: http://www.steiner-verlag.de/GuK
Freq: Annual; **Annual Sub.:** EUR 43,70; **Circ:** 500
Editor: Harald Wixforth
Profile: Annual of the Association for Middle European Bank and Savings Bank History.
Language(s): German

GELDPROFI 728480G1G-1
Editorial: Am Wallgraben 115, 70565 STUTTGART
Tel: 711 7821301 **Fax:** 711 7822880
Email: pamela.klink@dsv-gruppe.de **Web site:** http://www.s-fachzeitschriften.de
Freq: 6 issues yearly; **Annual Sub.:** EUR 31,90; **Circ:** 6,640
Editor: Heinz-Wilbrandt Knüppel

Profile: Magazine covering all aspects of credit trading.
Language(s): German
ADVERTISING RATES:
Full Page Mono .... EUR 2350
Full Page Colour .... EUR 3910
Mechanical Data: Type Area: 247 x 184 mm, No. of Columns (Display): 3, Col Widths (Display): 49 mm
Copy instructions: *Copy Date:* 35 days prior to publication
BUSINESS: FINANCE & ECONOMICS: Credit Trading

GELIEBTE KATZE 728486G81C-3
Editorial: Münchener Str. 101, 85737 ISMANING
Tel: 89 272707511 **Fax:** 89 272707590
Email: redaktion@herz-fuer-tiere.de **Web site:** http://www.geliebte-katze.de
Freq: Monthly; **Annual Sub.:** EUR 25,80; **Circ:** 40,285
Editor: Ursula Birr
Profile: Geliebte KATZE is Europe's largest cat magazine Geliebte KATZE is not limited to purebred cats, cat owners, but also provides all information, service issues, news reports and entertainment around the theme of "cat". Editorial expertise and high utility pays: For over 16 years of successful market reaches 0.47 Mio. Readers. • Geliebte KATZE is the magazine for all cat lovers. The cat - whether noble breed cat or house cat - and the fascinating lives are with her in the center. • focus of the book is the extensive service and practical component. All questions and requests that occur in the attitude of a cat to be answered. Experts provide readers with advice and tips on nutrition, health, education, behavior and character of the cat. In each issue of beloved cat a cat breed is presented in detail with posters. • For beats the entertainment section. Reports about cats from all over the world and prominent cat owners, tricky puzzles and games to maintain a high level and invite you to join in and relax. Facebook: http://www.facebook.com/GeliebteKatze.
Language(s): German
Readership: Read by cat lovers.
ADVERTISING RATES:
Full Page Mono .... EUR 3000
Full Page Colour .... EUR 4300
Mechanical Data: Type Area: 267 x 180 mm, No. of Columns (Display): 4, Col Widths (Display): 42 mm
Copy instructions: *Copy Date:* 35 days prior to publication
CONSUMER: ANIMALS & PETS: Cats

GELNHÄUSER NEUE ZEITUNG 728490G67B-5640
Editorial: Gutenbergstr. 1, 63571 GELNHAUSEN
Tel: 6051 833210 **Fax:** 6051 833230
Email: redaktion@gnz.de **Web site:** http://www.gnz.de
Freq: 312 issues yearly; **Circ:** 8,862
Editor: Thomas Welz; **Advertising Manager:** Nicolai Rhein
Profile: Daily newspaper with regional news and a local sports section.
Language(s): German
ADVERTISING RATES:
SCC .... EUR 29,00
Mechanical Data: Type Area: 488 x 326 mm, No. of Columns (Display): 7, Col Widths (Display): 44 mm
Copy instructions: *Copy Date:* 1 day prior to publication
Supplement(s): rtv
REGIONAL DAILY & SUNDAY NEWSPAPERS: Regional Daily Newspapers

GELNHÄUSER TAGEBLATT 728491G67B-5660
Editorial: Barbarossastr. 5, 63571 GELNHAUSEN
Tel: 6051 824248 **Fax:** 6051 824259
Email: redaktion@gelnhaeuser-tageblatt.de **Web site:** http://www.gelnhaeuser-tageblatt.de
Freq: 312 issues yearly; **Circ:** 6,447
Advertising Manager: Lutz Bernhard
Profile: Daily newspaper with regional news and a local sports section.
Language(s): German
ADVERTISING RATES:
SCC .... EUR 30,30
Mechanical Data: Type Area: 430 x 278 mm, No. of Columns (Display): 6, Col Widths (Display): 45 mm
Copy instructions: *Copy Date:* 1 day prior to publication
REGIONAL DAILY & SUNDAY NEWSPAPERS: Regional Daily Newspapers

DIE GEMEINDE 728498G32A-1140
Editorial: Panoramastr. 33, 70174 STUTTGART
Tel: 711 2257245 **Fax:** 711 2257247
Email: silke.gerboth-sahm@gemeindetag-bw.de **Web site:** http://www.gemeindetag-bw.de
Freq: 23 issues yearly; **Annual Sub.:** EUR 125,00; **Circ:** 5,000
Editor: Silke Gerboth-Sahm
Profile: Journal about public administration in Baden-Württemberg.
Language(s): German
ADVERTISING RATES:
Full Page Mono .... EUR 1100
Full Page Colour .... EUR 1940
Mechanical Data: Type Area: 265 x 185 mm, No. of Columns (Display): 3, Col Widths (Display): 60 mm
Copy instructions: *Copy Date:* 14 days prior to publication
BUSINESS: LOCAL GOVERNMENT, LEISURE & RECREATION: Local Government

GEMEINDE ANZEIGER 728505G72-4212
Editorial: Benzstr. 24, 76316 MALSCH
Tel: 7246 922828 **Fax:** 7246 922879
Email: anzeiger@druckerei-stark.de **Web site:** http://www.druckerei-stark.de
Freq: Weekly; **Cover Price:** EUR 0,65; **Circ:** 3,900
Profile: Local official paper.
Language(s): German
ADVERTISING RATES:
Full Page Mono .... EUR 517
Full Page Colour .... EUR 1132
Mechanical Data: Type Area: 275 x 185 mm, No. of Columns (Display): 4, Col Widths (Display): 45 mm
Copy instructions: *Copy Date:* 2 days prior to publication
LOCAL NEWSPAPERS

GEMEINDEBRIEF 728554G2A-1580
Editorial: Emil-von-Behring-Str. 3, 60439 FRANKFURT **Tel:** 69 58098164 **Fax:** 69 58098271
Email: redaktion@gemeindebrief.de **Web site:** http://www.gemeindebrief.de
Freq: 6 issues yearly; **Annual Sub.:** EUR 43,20; **Circ:** 6,350
Editor: Stefan Lotz
Profile: Magazine with information about church affairs.
Language(s): German
ADVERTISING RATES:
Full Page Mono .... EUR 980
Full Page Colour .... EUR 1190
Mechanical Data: Type Area: 257 x 190 mm
Copy instructions: *Copy Date:* 40 days prior to publication
BUSINESS: COMMUNICATIONS, ADVERTISING & MARKETING

DER GEMEINDEHAUSHALT 728561G32A-1200
Editorial: Wilhelm-Nieswandt-Allee 133, 45326 ESSEN **Tel:** 201 3195748 **Fax:** 201 3195911
Email: jw.schmidt@t-online.de **Web site:** http://www.gemeindehaushalt.de
Freq: Monthly; **Annual Sub.:** EUR 149,50; **Circ:** 1,800
Editor: J. W. Schmidt
Profile: Magazine about municipal government, finance and business in Cologne.
Language(s): German
Readership: Read by local government officials.
ADVERTISING RATES:
Full Page Mono .... EUR 850
Full Page Colour .... EUR 2320
Mechanical Data: Type Area: 260 x 185 mm
Copy instructions: *Copy Date:* 30 days prior to publication
BUSINESS: LOCAL GOVERNMENT, LEISURE & RECREATION: Local Government

DIE GEMEINDEKASSE BAYERN 728568G32C-17
Editorial: Levelingstr. 6a, 81673 MÜNCHEN
Tel: 89 43600020 **Fax:** 89 4361564
Email: mail@boorberg.de **Web site:** http://www.boorberg.de
Freq: 24 issues yearly; **Annual Sub.:** EUR 308,40; **Circ:** 1,890
Editor: Franz Königsperger; **Advertising Manager:** Roland Schulz
Profile: Magazine about public finance in Bavaria.
Language(s): German
Readership: Read by local government officials.
ADVERTISING RATES:
Full Page Mono .... EUR 777
Full Page Colour .... EUR 1707
Mechanical Data: Type Area: 172 x 117 mm
Copy instructions: *Copy Date:* 28 days prior to publication
BUSINESS: LOCAL GOVERNMENT, LEISURE & RECREATION: Local Government Finance

DER GEMEINDERAT 728604G32A-1300
Editorial: Stauffenbergstr. 18, 74523 SCHWÄBISCH HALL **Tel:** 791 9506116 **Fax:** 791 9506141
Email: w.markus@eppinger-verlag.de **Web site:** http://www.gemeinderat-online.de
Freq: 11 issues yearly; **Annual Sub.:** EUR 87,19; **Circ:** 12,000
Editor: Wolfram Markus; **Advertising Manager:** Gertrud Gärtig
Profile: Independent magazine covering municipal politics.
Language(s): German
Readership: Aimed at official representatives.
ADVERTISING RATES:
Full Page Mono .... EUR 3600
Full Page Colour .... EUR 4700
Mechanical Data: Type Area: 270 x 185 mm, No. of Columns (Display): 4, Col Widths (Display): 43 mm
Copy instructions: *Copy Date:* 20 days prior to publication
BUSINESS: LOCAL GOVERNMENT, LEISURE & RECREATION: Local Government

GEMEINSAM LEBEN 728631G62G-80
Editorial: Alte Dorfstr. 3, 23860 KLEIN WESENBERG
Email: klaus-rainer.martin@gmx.net **Web site:** http://www.juventa.de
Freq: Quarterly; **Annual Sub.:** EUR 52,50; **Circ:** 500
Editor: Klaus-Rainer Martin; **Advertising Manager:** Annette Hopp
Profile: Gemeinsam leben is the magazine for theory and practice of co-education of disabled and non disabled children and young people in nurseries, mainstream schools, homes and public youth organizations. Gemeinsam leben is professional discussion forum, workshop sheets, educational and socio-political bulletin and counselor in the integration landscape. Gemeinsam leben contains the BAG information of the federal study group "live together - learn together, parents against segregation".
Language(s): German
ADVERTISING RATES:
Full Page Mono .... EUR 310
Mechanical Data: Type Area: 202 x 134 mm, No. of Columns (Display): 3, Col Widths (Display): 44 mm
BUSINESS: CHURCH & SCHOOL EQUIPMENT & EDUCATION: Special Needs Education

GEMÜSE 728643G26C-50
Editorial: Weinbergstr. 7, 64665 ALSBACH-HÄHNLEIN **Tel:** 6257 903133 **Fax:** 6257 903134
Email: gemuese@t-online.de **Web site:** http://www.gemuese-online.de
Freq: Monthly; **Annual Sub.:** EUR 85,20; **Circ:** 5,762
Editor: Elke Hormes
Profile: Gemüse is the only monthly magazine for the vegetable growing industry in Germany with high prevalence in the entire German-speaking countries, including Austria and Switzerland. The magazine Gemüse has the highest number of sold copies in this target group. Use the journal Gemüse for your professional B-to-B communication, if you want to reach decision-makers and opinion leaders in the vegetable growing industry. The editorial approach reflects current, critical and independent resist the constant changes in vegetable growing. Gemüse depth coverage of market trends, economic cultivation techniques, technology and automation, machinery and equipment, operating and personnel management. Practical operating reports from Germany and abroad round out the spectrum. The constant themes are cultivation, plant protection, fertilizer, seeds and varieties, special asparagus, machinery & equipment, marketing, processing, events, training, business management, operational reports from Germany and abroad.
Language(s): German
Readership: Aimed at professional gardeners.
ADVERTISING RATES:
Full Page Mono .... EUR 2926
Full Page Colour .... EUR 4036
Mechanical Data: Type Area: 270 x 186 mm, No. of Columns (Display): 4, Col Widths (Display): 45 mm
Copy instructions: *Copy Date:* 21 days prior to publication
Official Journal of: Organ d. Fachgruppe Gemüsebau im Bundesausschuss Obst u. Gemüse
BUSINESS: GARDEN TRADE

GENAU 1665774G23A-766
Editorial: Hans-Böckler-Allee 7, 30173 HANNOVER
Tel: 511 85502455 **Fax:** 511 85502403
Email: genau.redaktion@schluetersche.de **Web site:** http://www.schluetersche.de
Freq: 10 issues yearly; Free to qualifying individuals
Annual Sub.: EUR 18,50; **Circ:** 19,940
Editor: Irmke Frömling; **Advertising Manager:** Andreas Dirschauer
Profile: Magazine for contractors in the cabinetmaker's trade.
Language(s): German
ADVERTISING RATES:
Full Page Mono .... EUR 3770
Full Page Colour .... EUR 4520
Mechanical Data: Type Area: 284 x 200 mm, No. of Columns (Display): 4, Col Widths (Display): 47 mm
Copy instructions: *Copy Date:* 21 days prior to publication
BUSINESS: FURNISHINGS & FURNITURE

GENERAL-ANZEIGER 728651G67B-5700
Editorial: Justus-von-Liebig-Str. 15, 53121 BONN
Tel: 228 6688444 **Fax:** 228 6688605
Email: redaktion@ga-bonn.de **Web site:** http://www.general-anzeiger-bonn.de
Freq: 312 issues yearly; **Annual Sub.:** EUR 25,40; **Circ:** 81,129
Editor: Andreas Tyrock; **News Editor:** Wolfgang Wentsch; **Advertising Manager:** Martin Busch
Profile: Regional daily newspaper covering politics, economics, sports, travel and technology. Facebook: http://de-de.facebook.com/generalanzeigerbonn Twitter: http://twitter.com/gabonn This Outlet offers RSS (Really Simple Syndication).
Language(s): German
ADVERTISING RATES:
SCC .... EUR 145,50
Mechanical Data: Type Area: 480 x 325 mm, No. of Columns (Display): 7, Col Widths (Display): 45 mm
Copy instructions: *Copy Date:* 1 day prior to publication
Supplement(s): prisma
REGIONAL DAILY & SUNDAY NEWSPAPERS: Regional Daily Newspapers

GENERAL-ANZEIGER 728653G67B-5720
Editorial: Untenende 21, 26817 RHAUDERFEHN
Tel: 4952 927450 **Fax:** 4952 927422
Email: redaktion@ga-online.de **Web site:** http://www.ga-online.de
Freq: 312 issues yearly; **Circ:** 9,501
Advertising Manager: Uwe Boden
Profile: Daily newspaper with regional news and a local sports section. This Outlet offers RSS (Really Simple Syndication).
Language(s): German
ADVERTISING RATES:
SCC .... EUR 43,6
Mechanical Data: Type Area: 420 x 282 mm, No. of Columns (Display): 6, Col Widths (Display): 43 mm
Copy instructions: *Copy Date:* 2 days prior to publication
REGIONAL DAILY & SUNDAY NEWSPAPERS: Regional Daily Newspapers

GENERAL-ANZEIGER BURG 723962G72-281
Editorial: Bahnhofstr. 17, 39104 MAGDEBURG
Tel: 391 5999439 **Fax:** 391 5999430
Email: uwe.bade@generalanzeiger.de **Web site:** http://www.generalanzeiger.de
Freq: Weekly; **Cover Price:** Free; **Circ:** 30,066
Editor: Uwe Bade; **Advertising Manager:** Jörg Mansch
Profile: Advertising journal (house-to-house) concentrating on local stories.
Language(s): German
ADVERTISING RATES:
Full Page Mono .... EUR 329
Full Page Colour .... EUR 480
Mechanical Data: Type Area: 480 x 327 mm, No. of Columns (Display): 7, Col Widths (Display): 45 mm
Copy instructions: *Copy Date:* 5 days prior to publication
LOCAL NEWSPAPERS

GENERAL-ANZEIGER GENTHIN 728681G72-4576
Editorial: Bahnhofstr. 17, 39104 MAGDEBURG
Tel: 391 5999439 **Fax:** 391 5999430
Email: uwe.bade@generalanzeiger.de **Web site:** http://www.generalanzeiger.de
Freq: Weekly; **Cover Price:** Free; **Circ:** 15,770
Editor: Uwe Bade; **Advertising Manager:** Jörg Mansch
Profile: Advertising journal (house-to-house) concentrating on local stories.
Language(s): German
ADVERTISING RATES:
Full Page Mono .... EUR 2588
Full Page Colour .... EUR 3764
Mechanical Data: Type Area: 480 x 327 mm, No. of Columns (Display): 7, Col Widths (Display): 45 mm
Copy instructions: *Copy Date:* 5 days prior to publication
LOCAL NEWSPAPERS

GENERAL-ANZEIGER HALBERSTADT 729504G72-4908
Editorial: Bahnhofstr. 17, 39104 MAGDEBURG
Tel: 391 5999439 **Fax:** 391 5999430
Email: uwe.bade@generalanzeiger.de **Web site:** http://www.generalanzeiger.de
Freq: 104 issues yearly; **Cover Price:** Free
Editor: Uwe Bade; **Advertising Manager:** Jörg Mansch
Profile: Advertising journal (house-to-house) concentrating on local stories.
Language(s): German
Mechanical Data: Type Area: 480 x 327 mm, No. of Columns (Display): 7, Col Widths (Display): 45 mm
LOCAL NEWSPAPERS

GENERAL-ANZEIGER HALDENSLEBEN/ WOLMIRSTEDT 738159G72-10200
Editorial: Bahnhofstr. 17, 39104 MAGDEBURG
Tel: 391 5999430 **Fax:** 391 5999439
Email: uwe.bade@generalanzeiger.de **Web site:** http://www.generalanzeiger.de
Freq: 104 issues yearly; **Cover Price:** Free
Editor: Uwe Bade; **Advertising Manager:** Jörg Mansch
Profile: Advertising journal (house-to-house) concentrating on local stories.
Language(s): German
Mechanical Data: Type Area: 480 x 327 mm, No. of Columns (Display): 7, Col Widths (Display): 45 mm
Supplement(s): Amtsblatt für den Landkreis Börde
LOCAL NEWSPAPERS

GENERAL-ANZEIGER LÜCHOW-DANNENBERG 734499G72-7056
Editorial: Bahnhofstr. 17, 39104 MAGDEBURG
Tel: 391 5999439 **Fax:** 391 5999430
Email: uwe.bade@generalanzeiger.de **Web site:** http://www.generalanzeiger.de
Freq: Weekly; **Cover Price:** Free; **Circ:** 22,066
Editor: Uwe Bade; **Advertising Manager:** Jörg Mansch
Profile: Advertising journal (house-to-house) concentrating on local stories.
Language(s): German
ADVERTISING RATES:
Full Page Mono .... EUR 2957
Full Page Colour .... EUR 4301
Mechanical Data: Type Area: 480 x 327 mm, No. of Columns (Display): 7, Col Widths (Display): 45 mm

opy instructions: *Copy Date:* 5 days prior to
blication
OCAL NEWSPAPERS

ENERAL-ANZEIGER IAGDEBURG 734676G72-7116

litorial: Bahnhofstr. 17, 39104 MAGDEBURG
l: 391 5999439 **Fax:** 391 5999430
nail: uwe.bade@generalanzeiger.de **Web site:**
p://www.generalanzeiger.de
eq: 104 issues yearly; **Cover Price:** Free
litor: Uwe Bade; **Advertising Manager:** Jörg
ansch
ofile: Advertising journal (house-to-house)
ncentrating on local stories.
nguage(s): German
echanical Data: Type Area: 480 x 327 mm, No. of
olumns (Display): 7, Col Widths (Display): 45 mm
OCAL NEWSPAPERS

ENERAL-ANZEIGER ONLINE 1621348G67B-16557

litorial: Justus-von-Liebig-Str. 15, 53121 BONN
l: 228 66880 **Fax:** 228 6688391
nail: w.schmitz-vianden@ga-bonn.de **Web site:**
tp://www.general-anzeiger-bonn.de
eq: Daily; **Cover Price:** Paid; **Circ:** 1,894,819
nique Users
litor: Wolfgang Schmitz-Vianden
ofile: Ezine: Online Service of the Bonner General-
nzeiger. Information and services around the region
Bonn, Rhein-Sieg-Kreis, Neuwied and district
rweiler. Facebook: http://de-de.facebook.com/
eneralanzeigerbonn Twitter: http://twitter.com/#!/
abonn This Outlet offers RSS (Really Simple
yndication).
anguage(s): German
EGIONAL DAILY & SUNDAY NEWSPAPERS:
egional Daily Newspapers

ENERAL-ANZEIGER SCHÖNEBECK 741338G72-11732

litorial: Bahnhofstr. 17, 39104 MAGDEBURG
el: 391 5999439 **Fax:** 391 5999430
nail: uwe.bade@generalanzeiger.de **Web site:**
tp://www.generalanzeiger.de
req: 104 issues yearly; **Cover Price:** Free
litor: Uwe Bade; **Advertising Manager:** Jötg
ansch
rofile: Advertising journal (house-to-house)
oncentrating on local stories.
anguage(s): German
lechanical Data: Type Area: 480 x 327 mm, No. of
olumns (Display): 7, Col Widths (Display): 45 mm
OCAL NEWSPAPERS

ENERAL-ANZEIGER UELZEN 745646G72-14456

ditorial: Bahnhofstr. 17, 39104 MAGDEBURG
el: 391 5999439 **Fax:** 391 5999430
mail: uwe.bade@generalanzeiger.de **Web site:**
ttp://www.generalanzeiger.de
req: Weekly; **Cover Price:** Free; **Circ:** 45,967
ditor: Uwe Bade; **Advertising Manager:** Jörg
lansch
rofile: Advertising journal (house-to-house)
oncentrating on local stories.
anguage(s): German
DVERTISING RATES:
ull Page Mono .... EUR 5208
ull Page Colour .... EUR 7527
lechanical Data: Type Area: 480 x 327 mm, No. of
olumns (Display): 7, Col Widths (Display): 45 mm
opy instructions: *Copy Date:* 5 days prior to
ublication
OCAL NEWSPAPERS

GENERAL-ANZEIGER WERNIGERODE 747211G72-15112

Editorial: Bahnhofstr. 17, 39104 MAGDEBURG
Tel: 391 5999439 **Fax:** 391 5999430
Email: uwe.bade@generalanzeiger.de **Web site:**
http://www.generalanzeiger.de
Freq: 104 issues yearly; **Cover Price:** Free
Editor: Uwe Bade; **Advertising Manager:** Jörg
Mansch
Profile: Advertising journal (house-to-house)
concentrating on local stories.
Language(s): German
Mechanical Data: Type Area: 480 x 327 mm, No. of
Columns (Display): 7, Col Widths (Display): 45 mm
LOCAL NEWSPAPERS

GENERAL-ANZEIGER ZERBST 748829G72-16668

Editorial: Bahnhofstr. 17, 39104 MAGDEBURG
Tel: 391 5999439 **Fax:** 391 5999430
Email: uwe.bade@generalanzeiger.de **Web site:**
http://www.generalanzeiger.de
Freq: Weekly; **Cover Price:** Free; **Circ:** 13,968
Editor: Uwe Bade; **Advertising Manager:** Jörg
Mansch
Profile: Advertising journal (house-to-house)
concentrating on local stories.
Language(s): German
ADVERTISING RATES:
Full Page Mono .... EUR 2621
Full Page Colour .... EUR 3831

Mechanical Data: Type Area: 480 x 327 mm, No. of
Columns (Display): 7, Col Widths (Display): 45 mm
Copy instructions: *Copy Date:* 5 days prior to
publication
LOCAL NEWSPAPERS

GENERATION 55PLUS 743821G74N-700

Editorial: Uhlandstr. 104, 73614 SCHORNDORF
Tel: 7181 253231 **Fax:** 7181 258878
Email: redaktion@seniorenzeitung-bw.de **Web site:**
http://www.seniorenzeitung-bw.de
Freq: Monthly; **Annual Sub.:** EUR 27,50; **Circ:** 15,000
Editor: Werner Stoll; **Advertising Manager:** Beate
Heibel
Profile: Magazine for the elderly containing articles
about politics and social issues, culture, society, new
books, entertainment, puzzles and events.
Language(s): German
Readership: Aimed at people aged 55 years and
over.
ADVERTISING RATES:
Full Page Mono .... EUR 2960
Full Page Colour .... EUR 3700
Mechanical Data: Type Area: 320 x 230 mm, No. of
Columns (Display): 5, Col Widths (Display): 45 mm
**CONSUMER: WOMEN'S INTEREST CONSUMER
MAGAZINES: Retirement**

GENERATION 55PLUS 1638051G74N-837

Editorial: Uhlandstr. 104, 73614 SCHORNDORF
Tel: 7181 253231 **Fax:** 7181 258878
Email: redaktion@seniorenzeitung-bw.de **Web site:**
http://www.seniorenzeitung-bw.de
Freq: Monthly; **Annual Sub.:** EUR 27,50; **Circ:** 15,000
Editor: Werner Stoll; **Advertising Manager:** Beate
Heibel
Profile: Magazine for the elderly from the region of
Freiburg.
Language(s): German
ADVERTISING RATES:
Full Page Mono .... EUR 2960
Full Page Colour .... EUR 3700
Mechanical Data: Type Area: 320 x 230 mm, No. of
Columns (Display): 5, Col Widths (Display): 45 mm

GENERATION 55PLUS 1655461G74N-848

Editorial: Uhlandstr. 104, 73614 SCHORNDORF
Tel: 7181 253231 **Fax:** 7181 258878
Email: redaktion@seniorenzeitung-bw.de **Web site:**
http://www.seniorenzeitung-bw.de
Freq: Monthly; **Annual Sub.:** EUR 27,50; **Circ:** 25,000
Editor: Werner Stoll; **Advertising Manager:** Beate
Heibel
Profile: Seniors magazine for the 50 plus. Best-Ager-
Magazine for Baden-Baden and Offenburg offers
reviews, interviews and reports on the topics of
fitness, travel, art, culture, health, housing, portraits
of prominent personalities.
Language(s): German
ADVERTISING RATES:
Full Page Mono .... EUR 2960
Full Page Colour .... EUR 3700
Mechanical Data: Type Area: 320 x 230 mm, No. of
Columns (Display): 5, Col Widths (Display): 45 mm

GENERATION 55PLUS 1708914G74N-892

Editorial: Uhlandstr. 104, 73614 SCHORNDORF
Tel: 7181 253231 **Fax:** 7181 258878
Email: redaktion@seniorenzeitung-bw.de **Web site:**
http://www.seniorenzeitung-bw.de
Freq: Monthly; **Annual Sub.:** EUR 27,50; **Circ:** 25,000
Editor: Werner Stoll; **Advertising Manager:** Beate
Heibel
Profile: Magazine for the elderly containing articles
about politics and social issues, culture, society, new
books, entertainment, puzzles and events.
Language(s): German
ADVERTISING RATES:
Full Page Mono .... EUR 3760
Full Page Colour .... EUR 4700
Mechanical Data: Type Area: 320 x 230 mm, No. of
Columns (Display): 5, Col Widths (Display): 45 mm

GENERATION 55PLUS 1882081G74N-978

Editorial: Uhlandstr. 104, 73614 SCHORNDORF
Tel: 7181 253231 **Fax:** 7181 258878
Email: redaktion@seniorenzeitung-bw.de **Web site:**
http://www.seniorenzeitung-bw.de
Freq: Quarterly; **Annual Sub.:** EUR 27,50; **Circ:**
50,000
Editor: Werner Stoll; **Advertising Manager:** Beate
Heibel
Profile: Magazine for the elderly from the region of
Freiburg.
Language(s): German
ADVERTISING RATES:
Full Page Mono .... EUR 2960
Full Page Colour .... EUR 3700
Mechanical Data: Type Area: 320 x 230 mm, No. of
Columns (Display): 5, Col Widths (Display): 45 mm

GENIESSEN & MEHR 1862048G89A-12420

Editorial: Augustenstr. 10, 80333 MÜNCHEN
Tel: 89 370600 **Fax:** 89 37060111
Email: muc@blmedien.de **Web site:** http://www.
geniessen-mehr.com
Freq: Quarterly; **Annual Sub.:** EUR 13,00; **Circ:**
118,493
Editor: Annemarie Heinrichsdobler; **Advertising
Manager:** Bernd Moeser
Profile: Travel and Gourmet magazine on the bright
side of life, designed for high-income target group
from 35, which has found its way to better quality of
life already. Content: Travel, Gourmet Trips and tips,
culinary recipes to try, table and dining culture,
hospitality and gourmet potential for themselves, in
pairs and the Friends, sophisticated hotels and
restaurants around the world, spa treatments and
much more. Prominent chefs known from the media,
TV, etc., present to the readers their exclusive
recipes and menu suggestions to try at home.
Language(s): German
ADVERTISING RATES:
Full Page Mono .... EUR 7395
Full Page Colour .... EUR 9250
Mechanical Data: Type Area: 254 x 185 mm, No. of
Columns (Display): 4, Col Widths (Display): 43 mm

GENIOS GERMAN BUSINESS INFORMATION 1704531G14R-6142

Editorial: Freischützstr. 96, 81927 MÜNCHEN
Tel: 89 9928790 **Fax:** 89 99287999
Email: info@genios.de **Web site:** http://www.genios.
de
Freq: Daily; **Cover Price:** Paid; **Circ:** 823,352 Unique
Users
Profile: Online information on economics, press,
management and science.
Language(s): German
**BUSINESS: COMMERCE, INDUSTRY &
MANAGEMENT: Commerce Related**

GENOGRAPH 1866379G21A-4426

Editorial: Heilbronner Str. 41, 70191 STUTTGART
Tel: 711 222132772 **Fax:** 711 222137377
Email: verbandszeitschrift@geno-stuttgart.de **Web
site:** http://www.bwgv-info.de
Freq: Monthly; **Circ:** 3,700
Editor: Reinhard Bock-Müller; **Advertising Manager:**
Kora Cygan
Profile: Magazine for managers and executives of
cooperatives.
Language(s): German
ADVERTISING RATES:
Full Page Mono .... EUR 2010
Full Page Colour .... EUR 2680
Mechanical Data: Type Area: 257 x 179 mm
Copy instructions: *Copy Date:* 21 days prior to
publication

GENOSSENSCHAFTS-MAGAZIN WESER-EMS 728676G59-1

Editorial: Raiffeisenstr. 26, 26122 OLDENBURG
Tel: 441 2100559 **Fax:** 441 2100529
Email: harald.lesch@gvweser-ems.de **Web site:**
http://www.gvweser-ems.de
Freq: Monthly; **Annual Sub.:** EUR 46,00; **Circ:** 1,800
Editor: Harald Lesch
Profile: Magazine covering cooperatives in the
Weser-Ems region.
Language(s): German
ADVERTISING RATES:
Full Page Mono .... EUR 829
Full Page Colour .... EUR 1700
Mechanical Data: Type Area: 272 x 182 mm, No. of
Columns (Display): 3, Col Widths (Display): 58 mm
Copy instructions: *Copy Date:* 18 days prior to
publication
BUSINESS: CO-OPERATIVES

GENUSS MAGAZIN 1932033G89A-12544

Editorial: Ludwigstr. 37, 60327 FRANKFURT
Tel: 69 974600 **Fax:** 69 97460400 ,
Email: essenundtrinken@journalportal.de **Web site:**
http://www.journalportal.de
Freq: Quarterly; **Circ:** 28,000
Editor: Bastian Fiebig; **Advertising Manager:**
Melanie Hennemann
Profile: Gastronomy guide for the Rhein-Main region.
Facebook: http://www.facebook.com/
journalfrankfurt.
Language(s): German
ADVERTISING RATES:
Full Page Mono .... EUR 2100
Full Page Colour .... EUR 3040
Mechanical Data: Type Area: 246 x 177 mm
Supplement to: Journal Edition, Journal Frankfurt
Führer

GENUSS PUR PROFESSIONAL 739756G23C-400

Editorial: Neuenbaumer Str. 5, 41470 NEUSS
Tel: 2131 936970 **Fax:** 2131 9369720
Email: schauwecker@wws-verlag.de **Web site:**
http://www.wws-verlag.de
Freq: 5 issues yearly; **Annual Sub.:** EUR 46,00; **Circ:**
7,200
Editor: Regina Schauwecker; **Advertising Manager:**
Gudrun van Leyen
Profile: In five issues per year reported in the industry
magazine Genuss pur Professional for Industry and
Trade, industry-related events, concepts, products.
Insights into trading concepts, overview of sales
promotion novelty items, views on important order
dates for our industry. Genuss pur Professional
researched for exciting interviews, innovative retail
concepts, promising products for Tableware, trendy
products for the kitchen, high speed Verschenk ideas
and marketing strategies that will ensure at the point
of sale for more frequency.
Language(s): German
Readership: Read by suppliers and wholesalers.
ADVERTISING RATES:
Full Page Mono .... EUR 2580
Full Page Colour .... EUR 3870
Mechanical Data: Type Area: 260 x 184 mm
Copy instructions: *Copy Date:* 30 days prior to
publication
**BUSINESS: FURNISHINGS & FURNITURE:
Furnishings & Furniture - Kitchens & Bathrooms**

GEO 728683G94J-160

Editorial: Am Baumwall 11, 20459 HAMBURG
Tel: 40 37032073 **Fax:** 40 37035648
Email: briefe@geo.de **Web site:** http://www.geo.de
Freq: Monthly; **Cover Price:** EUR 6,30; **Circ:** 310,383
Editor: Peter-Matthias Gaede; **Advertising
Manager:** Martina Hoss
Profile: More about research and science on climate
change and biodiversity. More on the brain,
emotions, thoughts. More on education and training,
we have to offer to secure economic prosperity and
cultural richness. More about the most beautiful
regions of the earth and the greatest adventure on it.
The basic idea of GEO is still valid: GEO is equivalent
to a "yes" to sustainability and stands for the idea of
reconciliation of different cultures, economic activity
and social and environmental responsibility. GEO
makes ??each month a sld circulation of over
310,000 copies, is read by 3.24 million people,
making it the best-selling and highest reach OTC
monthly magazine.
Language(s): German
ADVERTISING RATES:
Full Page Mono .... EUR 37000
Full Page Colour .... EUR 37000
Mechanical Data: Type Area: 229 x 178 mm, No. of
Columns (Display): 4, Col Widths (Display): 40 mm
Official Journal of: Organ d. Geo schützt d.
Regenwald e.V.
**CONSUMER: OTHER CLASSIFICATIONS: Popular
Science**

GEO EPOCHE 728688G94J-180

Editorial: Am Baumwall 11, 20459 HAMBURG
Tel: 40 37032080 **Fax:** 40 37035648
Email: briefe@geo.de **Web site:** http://www.
geo-epoche.de
Freq: 6 issues yearly; **Cover Price:** EUR 9,00; **Circ:**
135,100
Editor: Michael Schaper; **Advertising Manager:**
Sabine Plath
Profile: GEO EPOCHE is the history magazine of
GEO. Each issue is devoted to a historical theme -
such as the Industrial Revolution eras, countries such
as the Weimar Republic, powers like Egypt under the
Pharaohs. People are telling stories about important
and dramatic events of everyday life and culture,
politics, society and science. In precise historical
reconstruction and opulent picture essays, with maps
and information boxes that each era is brought to life.
Language(s): German
ADVERTISING RATES:
Full Page Mono .... EUR 11100
Full Page Colour .... EUR 11100
Mechanical Data: Type Area: 229 x 178 mm, No. of
Columns (Display): 4, Col Widths (Display): 40 mm
**CONSUMER: OTHER CLASSIFICATIONS: Popular
Science**

GEO SAISON 728715G89A-11529

Editorial: Am Baumwall 11, 20459 HAMBURG
Tel: 40 37033712 **Fax:** 40 37035680
Email: swiderek.judith@geo.de **Web site:** http://
www.geo-saison.de
Freq: Monthly; **Cover Price:** EUR 5,00; **Circ:** 95,811
Editor: Lars Nielsen; **Advertising Manager:** Martina
Hoss
Profile: GEO SAISON is a monthly travel magazine
GEO. GEO SAISON reporters and photographers
research on the spot report, critical, comprehensive
and carefully, the credibility and quality - guarantee -
the trademark of GEO. GEO SAISON submitted travel
as way of life. GEO SAISON is a travel magazine,
travel with pleasure, and reading about it combines
with pleasure. It shows in an entertaining way
towards a new culture of travel, to tourism, which
does not destroy what he discovered, but met people
from other cultures with sensitivity and respect. GEO
SAISON provides ideas and guidance - before, during
and after the trip. GEO SAISON offers a wide variety
of tourist destinations and themes, and fills it with
many important and utility information: Each book
contains around 700 tips and hints. GEO SAISON
fascinated, inspired, informed, appropriate and ideal
for self-discovery. Readers of GEO SAISON are
frequent travelers, opinion and enjoy life and
therefore a very attractive target group. Facebook:
http://www.facebook.com/geomagazin.
Language(s): German
ADVERTISING RATES:
Full Page Mono .... EUR 16700
Full Page Colour .... EUR 16700
Mechanical Data: Type Area: 229 x 178 mm, No. of
Columns (Display): 4, Col Widths (Display): 40 mm
CONSUMER: HOLIDAYS & TRAVEL: Travel

GEO SPECIAL
728716G89A-11530
Editorial: Am Baumwall 11, 20459 HAMBURG
Tel: 40 37032768 **Fax:** 40 37035648
Email: briefe@geo.de **Web site:** http://www.geo.de
Freq: 6 issues yearly; **Annual Sub.:** EUR 41,70; **Circ:** 88,012
Editor: Peter-Matthias Gaede; **Advertising Manager:** Martina Hoss
Profile: For over 30 years, the GEO SPECIALS can rely on a large number of readers, who have special requirements for travel. The claim, above all, to be able to explain what happened to them at the destination. The GEO SPECIALS transform this curiosity into knowledge. They are dedicated to a country, region, city or a special topic. Targets, which are spoken about - just as unknown and yet to be discovered destinations. Their magic formula is: In about three-quarters of the whole issue, the reader gets great report meals offered instead of snacks, extensive research, authentic and legitimate. With all the journalistic skills of GEO. As a reading enjoyment and visual experience. Facebook: http://www.facebook.com/geomagazin.
Language(s): German
Readership: Aimed at travellers and readers.
ADVERTISING RATES:
Full Page Mono .... EUR 16900
Full Page Colour .... EUR 16900
Mechanical Data: Type Area: 229 x 178 mm, No. of Columns (Display): 4, Col Widths (Display): 40 mm
CONSUMER: HOLIDAYS & TRAVEL: Travel

GEO.DE
1621352G94J-728
Editorial: Am Baumwall 11, 20459 HAMBURG
Tel: 40 37032768 **Fax:** 40 37035648
Email: dehne.ulrich@geo.de **Web site:** http://www.geo.de
Cover Price: Paid; **Circ:** 1,117,670 Unique Users
Editor: Ulrich Dehne
Profile: Facebook: http://www.facebook.com/geomagazin.
Language(s): German
CONSUMER: OTHER CLASSIFICATIONS: Popular Science

GEOGRAPHISCHE ZEITSCHRIFT
728695G62B-247
Editorial: 54286 TRIER
Email: sailer@uni-trier.de **Web site:** http://www.steiner-verlag.de/GZ
Freq: Quarterly; **Annual Sub.:** EUR 152,60; **Circ:** 700
Editor: Ulrike Sailer; **Advertising Manager:** Susanne Szoradi
Profile: Magazine providing technical and scientific articles about geography.
Language(s): English; German
Readership: Read by geography teachers, specialists within the field and university professors.
ADVERTISING RATES:
Full Page Mono .... EUR 750
Mechanical Data: Type Area: 190 x 120 mm
BUSINESS: CHURCH & SCHOOL EQUIPMENT & EDUCATION: Education Teachers

GEOLINO
728697G91D-2820
Editorial: Am Baumwall 11, 20459 HAMBURG
Tel: 40 37032761 **Fax:** 40 37035647
Email: geolino@geo.de **Web site:** http://www.geolino.de
Freq: Monthly; **Annual Sub.:** EUR 36,60; **Circ:** 212,422
Editor: Martin Verg; **Advertising Manager:** Lars Niemann
Profile: This innovative children's magazine from GEO Experience of GEO magazine GEOlino is the development of the GEO-concept for young audiences. GEOlino presents itself as a logical precursor to adult GEO. General Interest Magazine in cooperation with UNICEF The range of topics virtually no limitations from the nucleus to the universe of Indian children in the Amazon Jungle to polar explorers in the eternal ice of Antarctica. The GEO-known quality in appearance and soundness of the issues is essential determination. The child-oriented implementation in text and layout exemplary. Unique concept of pure fun, broadening horizons and values education With each story GEOlino knowledge conveyed in playful and friendly school in this way his readers in conscious contact with people, animals and the world in which we live. As the largest children's magazine in a class by itself GEOlino sold nearly 230,000 copies per month (IVW Ø I 2010 - IV/ 2010) with over 170,000 subscribers, making it the largest children's magazine in Germany. GEOlino achieved confident opinion-leading school children between 8 and 14 years and their parents in high education budgets.
Language(s): German
Readership: Aimed at children aged between 8 and 12 years.
ADVERTISING RATES:
Full Page Mono .... EUR 16300
Full Page Colour .... EUR 16300
Mechanical Data: Type Area: 229 x 178 mm, No. of Columns (Display): 3, Col Widths (Display): 57 mm
CONSUMER: RECREATION & LEISURE: Children & Youth

GEOMECHANIK UND TUNNELBAU
1873506G4E-7250
Editorial: Rotherstr. 21, 10245 BERLIN
Tel: 30 47031265 **Fax:** 30 47031277
Email: helmut.richter@wiley.com **Web site:** http://www.ernst-und-sohn.de
Freq: 6 issues yearly; Free to qualifying individuals
Annual Sub.: EUR 115,00; **Circ:** 3,000
Editor: Helmut Richter; **Advertising Manager:** Fred Doischer
Profile: Journal publishes articles on practical aspects of applied engineering geology, rock and soil mechanics, and especially of the tunnel. The individual issues are special issues that are devoted to a current topic or a specific project. Short messages, and conference reports Baureportagen round out the contents. An international advisory board represents an interesting choice of topics and ensures the high quality of the contributions.
Language(s): English; German
ADVERTISING RATES:
Full Page Mono .... EUR 2280
Full Page Colour .... EUR 3570
Mechanical Data: Type Area: 260 x 181 mm, No. of Columns (Display): 4, Col Widths (Display): 42 mm
Copy instructions: *Copy Date:* 20 days prior to publication

GEOTECHNIK
728717G42A-54
Editorial: Montebruchstr. 2, 45219 ESSEN
Tel: 2054 924114 **Fax:** 2054 924119
Email: kb@vge.de **Web site:** http://www.vge.de
Freq: Quarterly; Free to qualifying individuals
Annual Sub.: EUR 43,00
Editor: Katrin Brummermann; **Advertising Manager:** Ute Perkovic
Profile: Publication about geotechnical engineering.
Language(s): German
BUSINESS: CONSTRUCTION

GEOTHERMISCHE ENERGIE
728719G58-600
Editorial: Gartenstr. 36, 49744 GEESTE
Tel: 5907 545 **Fax:** 5907 7379
Email: info@mediafrac.de **Web site:** http://www.mediafrac.de
Freq: 6 issues yearly; Free to qualifying individuals
Annual Sub.: EUR 32,50; **Circ:** 2,700
Editor: Werner Bußmann
Profile: Magazine covering all aspects of the use of geothermal energy.
Language(s): English; German
ADVERTISING RATES:
Full Page Mono .... EUR 1000
Mechanical Data: Type Area: 268 x 189 mm, No. of Columns (Display): 2, Col Widths (Display): 89 mm
Copy instructions: *Copy Date:* 20 days prior to publication

GERETSRIEDER MERKUR
728723G67B-5760
Editorial: Pfaffenrieder Str. 9, 82515 WOLFRATSHAUSEN **Tel:** 8171 269235
Fax: 8171 269240
Email: ger.il-bote@merkur-online.de **Web site:** http://www.merkur-online.de
Freq: 312 issues yearly; **Circ:** 8,342
Advertising Manager: Hans-Georg Bechthold
Profile: The Münchner Merkur with its own local newspapers, of which the Geretsrieder Merkur is one that, the leading regional newspaper brand in the Munich area - the most affluent area of Germany. The combination of newspaper and region is the foundation on which to build the success of the title. This is the newspaper not only the factual news agency, but forms a community of solidarity with its readers and the local community. The clear focus on local reporting creates a high regard to human reader loyalty. She presses one hand in the very high number of close to 180,000 subscribers. Also for the high reader-commitment is the loyalty of the total current 827 000 daily readers, the Münchner Merkur or one of its local newspapers usually read over many years. The Münchner Merkur with its own local newspapers is a newspaper for the whole family, tradition and modern life for one of the most beautiful regions of Germany unites. Reliable, informative, critical: the Münchner Merkur is the indispensable daily newspaper for the region. Facebook: http://www.facebook.com/pages/merkur-online.de/190176143327.
Language(s): German
ADVERTISING RATES:
SCC .... EUR 43,60
Mechanical Data: Type Area: 474 x 324 mm, No. of Columns (Display): 7, Col Widths (Display): 45 mm
Copy instructions: *Copy Date:* 1 day prior to publication
REGIONAL DAILY & SUNDAY NEWSPAPERS: Regional Daily Newspapers

THE GERMAN TIMES FOR EUROPE
1813150G14A-10026
Editorial: Tempelhofer Ufer 23, 10963 BERLIN
Tel: 30 21505422 **Fax:** 30 21505447
Email: info@german-times.com **Web site:** http://www.german-times.com
Freq: Monthly; **Annual Sub.:** EUR 45,00; **Circ:** 50,000
Editor: Bruno Waltert; **Advertising Manager:** Janine Kulbrok
Profile: Provides information for business executives on the world of politics, economy and science in Europe.
Language(s): English
ADVERTISING RATES:
Full Page Mono .... EUR 23000
Full Page Colour .... EUR 23000
Mechanical Data: Type Area: 530 x 290 mm
Copy instructions: *Copy Date:* 5 days prior to publication

GERMANY PARTNER OF THE WORLD
738595G14C-1160
Editorial: Malvenweg 4, 51061 KÖLN
Tel: 221 9635640 **Fax:** 221 96356427
Email: redaktion@orschel-verlag.de **Web site:** http://www.orschel-verlag.de
Freq: Annual; **Cover Price:** EUR 7,00; **Circ:** 20,000
Editor: Hans-Peter Wagner
Profile: Business English documentation provides overview of the capabilities of German industry and its position as a partner in world economic relations.
Language(s): English
ADVERTISING RATES:
Full Page Mono .... EUR 3900
Full Page Colour .... EUR 6800
Mechanical Data: Type Area: 260 x 190 mm

GERMANYCONTACT INDIA
2047456G14C-4792
Editorial: Ritterstr. 2b, 10969 BERLIN
Tel: 30 6150890 **Fax:** 30 61508929
Email: redaktion@owc.de **Web site:** http://www.owc.de
Freq: 6 issues yearly; **Circ:** 25,000
Editor: Achim Rodewald; **Advertising Manager:** Norbert Mayer
Profile: Magazine focusing on future business negotiations with India. Also contains market analyses and trends.
Language(s): English
ADVERTISING RATES:
Full Page Mono .... EUR 3950
Full Page Colour .... EUR 5400
Mechanical Data: Type Area: 265 x 175 mm

GESCHERER ZEITUNG
728770G67B-5780
Editorial: Rosenstr. 2, 48653 COESFELD
Tel: 2541 921151 **Fax:** 2541 921155
Email: redaktion@azonline.de **Web site:** http://www.azonline.de
Freq: 312 issues yearly; **Circ:** 17,950
Advertising Manager: Ralf Bohlje
Profile: Daily newspaper with regional news and a local sports section.
Language(s): German
ADVERTISING RATES:
SCC .... EUR 38,50
Mechanical Data: Type Area: 488 x 324 mm, No. of Columns (Display): 7, Col Widths (Display): 44 mm
Copy instructions: *Copy Date:* 1 day prior to publication
Supplement(s): prisma
REGIONAL DAILY & SUNDAY NEWSPAPERS: Regional Daily Newspapers

GESCHICHTE DER PHARMAZIE
728772G37-940
Editorial: Birkenwaldstr. 44, 70191 STUTTGART
Tel: 711 25820 **Fax:** 711 2582290
Email: daz@deutscher-apotheker-verlag.de **Web site:** http://www.deutscher-apotheker-verlag.de
Freq: Quarterly; **Annual Sub.:** EUR 46,00; **Circ:** 30,262
Editor: Wolf-Dieter Müller-Jahncke
Profile: Organ of the Deutschen Gesellschaft für Geschichte der Pharmazie e.V. is the Geschichte der Pharmazie. This original research papers, essays and bio-bibliographical articles are published. Also contains the history of pharmacy and the news of the DGGP and IGGP. She appears regularly as a quarterly supplement of the Deutsche Apotheker Zeitung,.
Language(s): German
Readership: Aimed at professionals within the pharmaceutical sector.
Supplement to: DAZ Deutsche ApothekerZeitung
BUSINESS: PHARMACEUTICAL & CHEMISTS

GESEKER ZEITUNG
728790G67B-5800
Editorial: Hansastr. 2, 59557 LIPPSTADT
Tel: 2941 20100 **Fax:** 2941 201297
Email: redaktion@derpatriot.de **Web site:** http://www.derpatriot.de
Freq: 312 issues yearly; **Circ:** 25,377
Advertising Manager: Andreas Grunig
Profile: The proximity to the reader is the guideline. And the events in the region, our big issue. Day after day. Informative to be, entertaining, critical and helpful - as understood by the Patriot's role that he perceives already since 1848. From the small beginnings of the newspaper's founder has become a modern media house, which looks back with pride on the past and at the same time introduces the new challenges of present and future. Through the diverse coverage - about local politics, community life, sport, culture and the local economy - the Patriot will raise awareness of home and origin, and simultaneously direct our attention to the country and the wide world. The Geseker Zeitung is a regional edition of the Patriot.
Language(s): German
ADVERTISING RATES:
SCC .... EUR 64,80
Mechanical Data: Type Area: 466 x 316 mm, No. of Columns (Display): 7, Col Widths (Display): 43 mm
Copy instructions: *Copy Date:* 1 day prior to publication
Supplement(s): prisma
REGIONAL DAILY & SUNDAY NEWSPAPERS: Regional Daily Newspapers

DAS GESPRÄCH AUS DER FERNE
728808G73-14
Editorial: Dorfstr. 10, 23883 KLEIN ZECHER
Email: gueges@t-online.de **Web site:** http://www.gadf.de
Freq: Quarterly; **Annual Sub.:** EUR 26,00; **Circ:** 650
Editor: Günter Geschke; **Advertising Manager:** Günter Geschke
Profile: Publication about political, social and cultur subjects.
Language(s): German
Mechanical Data: Type Area: 262 x 180 mm, No. of Columns (Display): 3, Col Widths (Display): 57 mm
Copy instructions: *Copy Date:* 10 days prior to publication

GESPRÄCHSPSYCHO-THERAPIE UND PERSONZENTRIERTE BERATUNG
763580G56A-1110
Editorial: Melatengürtel 125a, 50825 KÖLN
Tel: 221 92590851 **Fax:** 221 92590819
Email: reinsch@gwg-ev.org **Web site:** http://www.gwg-ev.org
Freq: Quarterly; Free to qualifying individuals
Annual Sub.: EUR 40,00; **Circ:** 3,600
Editor: Ursula Reinsch; **Advertising Manager:** Michael Barg
Profile: Magazine for psychotherapists, psychologists and pedagogues.
Language(s): German
ADVERTISING RATES:
Full Page Mono .... EUR 80
Mechanical Data: Type Area: 260 x 190 mm
Copy instructions: *Copy Date:* 42 days prior to publication

GESPRÄCHSPSYCHO-THERAPIE UND PERSONZENTRIERTE BERATUNG
763580G56A-1161
Editorial: Melatengürtel 125a, 50825 KÖLN
Tel: 221 92590851 **Fax:** 221 92590819
Email: reinsch@gwg-ev.org **Web site:** http://www.gwg-ev.org
Freq: Quarterly; Free to qualifying individuals
Annual Sub.: EUR 40,00; **Circ:** 3,600
Editor: Ursula Reinsch; **Advertising Manager:** Michael Barg
Profile: Magazine for psychotherapists, psychologists and pedagogues.
Language(s): German
ADVERTISING RATES:
Full Page Mono .... EUR 80
Mechanical Data: Type Area: 260 x 190 mm
Copy instructions: *Copy Date:* 42 days prior to publication

GESR GESUNDHEITSRECHT
1647152G1A-3557
Editorial: Gustav-Heinemann-Ufer 58, 50968 KÖLN
Tel: 221 93738108 **Fax:** 221 93738906
Email: gesr@otto-schmidt.de **Web site:** http://www.gesr.de
Freq: Monthly; **Annual Sub.:** EUR 305,90; **Circ:** 980
Editor: Stefanie Fuchs-Galilea; **Advertising Manager:** Thorsten Deuse
Profile: Magazine about health law.
Language(s): German
ADVERTISING RATES:
Full Page Mono .... EUR 695
Full Page Colour .... EUR 1217
Mechanical Data: Type Area: 260 x 180 mm, No. of Columns (Display): 2, Col Widths (Display): 88 mm

GESTALT KRITIK
1606364G56A-11156
Editorial: Rurstr. 9, 50937 KÖLN **Tel:** 221 416163
Fax: 221 447652
Email: gik-gestalttherapie@gmx.de **Web site:** http://www.gestalt.de
Freq: Half-yearly; **Cover Price:** EUR 4,80
Free to qualifying individuals ; **Circ:** 16,500
Editor: Erhard Doubrawa
Profile: Main topics: Gestalt Therapy and its development, Gestalt therapy as spiritual search, Gestalt therapy as a political practice. Gestalt Kritk combines the announcement of current events and continuing education program with the impression of original articles: Texts from our "workshops" and those of our friends.
Language(s): German
ADVERTISING RATES:
Full Page Mono .... EUR 1400
Mechanical Data: Type Area: 246 x 180 mm
Copy instructions: *Copy Date:* 60 days prior to publication
Supplement(s): Gestalttherapie; Programm

GESTERN HEUTE + MORGEN
728812G74N-280
Editorial: Carl-Miele-Str. 214, 33335 GÜTERSLOH
Tel: 5241 740533 **Fax:** 5241 740548
Email: monika.hovell@gtvh.de **Web site:** http://www.gtvh.de
Freq: 8 issues yearly; **Annual Sub.:** EUR 16,80; **Circ:** 13,000
Editor: Monika Hovell

Profile: Magazine for the elderly from the parishes.
Facebook: http://www.facebook.com/
GueterslоherVerlagshaus.
Language(s): German

GESUNDE MEDIZIN 728815G74G-680
Editorial: Untere Burghalde 51, 71229 LEONBERG
Tel: 7152 356211 **Fax:** 7633 982060
Email: redaktion@gesundemedizin.de **Web site:** http://www.gesundemedizin.de
Freq: Monthly; **Annual Sub.:** EUR 22,80; **Circ:** 36,230
Editor: Nicole Franke-Griksch; **Advertising Manager:** Thomas Tritschler
Profile: One of the oldest health title on the German market: "Gesunde Medizin" is aimed at readers with positive and health-conscious lifestyle. The magazine is supposed to awaken interest in the own well-being. In addition to many health information the magazine offers every month, a focus and a titlestory and a variety of other contributions. Addressed are the areas of body care from head to toe, in the spiritual life balance, healthy living, travel destinations for body, mind and soul and a balanced diet with lots of recipes to try out. Service pages in all sections provide entertaining information and provide an overview of new products on the market. The test and expert club in each issue is a close dialogue conducted with the readers.
Language(s): German
ADVERTISING RATES:
Full Page Mono .... EUR 8295
Full Page Colour .... EUR 8295
Mechanical Data: Type Area: 254 x 195 mm, No. of Columns (Display): 4, Col Widths (Display): 45 mm
Copy instructions: *Copy Date:* 42 days prior to publication
Supplement to: Medical Tribune
CONSUMER: WOMEN'S INTEREST CONSUMER MAGAZINES: Slimming & Health

GESUNDE PFLANZEN
728816G26D-148
Editorial: Postfach 140270, 52107 BONN
Email: 517@bmelv.bund.de **Web site:** http://www.springerlink.com
Freq: Quarterly; **Annual Sub.:** EUR 183,00; **Circ:** 153
Editor: Karola Schorn
Profile: Magazine containing information about plants, including articles on environmental issues.
Language(s): German
Readership: Aimed at professionals within the horticultural industry.
ADVERTISING RATES:
Full Page Mono .... EUR 740
Full Page Colour .... EUR 1780
Mechanical Data: Type Area: 240 x 175 mm
BUSINESS: GARDEN TRADE: Garden Trade Horticulture

GESUNDHEIT HEUTE
728826G74G-700
Editorial: Weidenstr. 15, 46499 HAMMINKELN
Tel: 2852 968631 **Fax:** 2852 968632
Email: info@gesundheitheute.com **Web site:** http://www.gesundheitheute.com
Freq: 6 issues yearly; **Annual Sub.:** EUR 15,00; **Circ:** 120,000
Editor: Ulrike Ernsten; **Advertising Manager:** Ulrike Ernsten
Profile: Current trends and innovations in the fields all around healthy food and beverage, natural medicine, travel, news from the medical, family and Co., advice and assistance, wellness and beauty.
Language(s): German
Readership: Read by health enthusiasts.
ADVERTISING RATES:
Full Page Mono .... EUR 2975
Full Page Colour .... EUR 4075
Mechanical Data: No. of Columns (Display): 4, Col Widths (Display): 43 mm, Type Area: 242 x 184 mm
Copy instructions: *Copy Date:* 30 days prior to publication
CONSUMER: WOMEN'S INTEREST CONSUMER MAGAZINES: Slimming & Health

GESUNDHEIT KONKRET
721871G94H-1000
Editorial: Lichtscheider Str. 89, 42285 WUPPERTAL
Tel: 18 500990 **Fax:** 18 500991459
Email: redaktion@barmer-gek.de **Web site:** http://www.barmer-gek.de
Freq: Quarterly; **Circ:** 5,800,000
Editor: Doris Goedecke-Vorberg
Profile: Magazine focusing on health.
Language(s): German
Readership: Read by customers of the Barmer, a German health insurance company.
ADVERTISING RATES:
Full Page Colour .... EUR 47000
Copy instructions: *Copy Date:* 30 days prior to publication
CONSUMER: OTHER CLASSIFICATIONS: Customer Magazines

GESUNDHEITS JOURNAL
1639175G74M-674
Editorial: Winterstr. 49, 33649 BIELEFELD
Tel: 8000.255255 **Fax:** 521 5228700
Email: journal@bkkgs.de **Web site:** http://www.bkkgs.de
Freq: 6 issues yearly; **Circ:** 106,500
Editor: Marita Schapeit
Profile: Magazine for members oft the BKK health insurance company.
Language(s): German

GESUNDHEITS PROFI 728839G56C-3
Editorial: Oberkasseler Str. 100, 40545 DÜSSELDORF **Tel:** 211 5770822 **Fax:** 211 5770812
Email: gp.redaktion@sternefeld.de **Web site:** http://www.gesundheitsprofi.de
Freq: Monthly; **Annual Sub.:** EUR 112,00; **Circ:** 4,800
Editor: Tobias Kurtz; **Advertising Manager:** Dagmar Brumme
Profile: Magazine providing a complete overview of hospitals and healthcare management.
Language(s): German
Readership: Aimed at health and medical equipment shops, also medical specialists, in fields such as Orthopaedics and Rehabilitation.
ADVERTISING RATES:
Full Page Mono .... EUR 1630
Full Page Colour .... EUR 2710
Mechanical Data: Type Area: 265 x 173 mm, No. of Columns (Display): 4, Col Widths (Display): 38 mm
Copy instructions: *Copy Date:* 14 days prior to publication
BUSINESS: HEALTH & MEDICAL: Hospitals

GESUNDHEITS- UND SOZIALPOLITIK 721088G82-420_50
Editorial: Waldseestr. 3, 76530 BADEN-BADEN
Tel: 7221 21040 **Fax:** 7221 210427
Email: erwin.dehlinger@dpbln.aok.de **Web site:** http://www.nomos.de
Freq: 6 issues yearly; **Annual Sub.:** EUR 150,13; **Circ:** 1,300
Editor: Erwin Dehlinger
Profile: Journal about socio-political problems and solutions in Germany and overseas. Topics covered include benefits and pensions, health care, unemployment and care of the elderly.
Language(s): German
ADVERTISING RATES:
Full Page Mono .... EUR 1290
Full Page Colour .... EUR 2415
Mechanical Data: No. of Columns (Display): 3, Col Widths (Display): 56 mm, Type Area: 233 x 178 mm
CONSUMER: CURRENT AFFAIRS & POLITICS

GESUNDHEITSÖKONOMIE & QUALITÄTSMANAGEMENT
728835G56C-2
Editorial: Rüdigerstr. 14, 70469 STUTTGART
Tel: 711 8931593 **Fax:** 711 8931408
Email: silvia.geuenich@thieme.de **Web site:** http://www.thieme.de/gesqm
Freq: 6 issues yearly; Free to qualifying individuals
Annual Sub.: EUR 415,90; **Circ:** 1,100
Editor: Silvia Geuenich
Profile: The Forum for Health Economics and Quality of Health Care Management. Economic evaluation of therapies. Successful ways to systematic quality improvement. Practical solutions and future scenarios: cut costs, maintain quality standards. Light into the thicket of data: Methodological studies on economic approaches. Issue of patient satisfaction: concepts and surveys.
Language(s): German
ADVERTISING RATES:
Full Page Mono .... EUR 1310
Full Page Colour .... EUR 2450
Mechanical Data: Type Area: 248 x 175 mm, No. of Columns (Display): 3, Col Widths (Display): 55 mm
Official Journal of: Organ d. Ges. f. Qualitätsmanagement in d. Gesundheitsversorgung u. d. Bundesverb. Managed Care e.V
BUSINESS: HEALTH & MEDICAL: Hospitals

DER GESUNDHEITSPARTNER
1668319G74M-738
Editorial: Äppelallee 27, 65203 WIESBADEN
Tel: 611 186860 **Fax:** 611 1868610
Email: info@bkk-ihv.de **Web site:** http://www.bkk-ihv.de
Freq: Quarterly; **Circ:** 11,650
Editor: Nicole Lemmer
Profile: Health insurance member magazine.
Language(s): German

DAS GESUNDHEITSWESEN
728843G32B-20
Editorial: Veterinärstr. 2, 85764 OBERSCHLEISSHEIM
Email: manfred.wildner@lgl.bayern.de **Web site:** http://www.thieme.de/gesu
Freq: 11 issues yearly; **Annual Sub.:** EUR 249,90; **Circ:** 1,260
Editor: Manfred Wildner
Profile: The German-language forum for all areas of healthcare - for over 70 years! The main themes of health services comprehensive - to date - well-founded, guidelines, overviews, commentaries, latest research results, scientific information, CME-certified education and training, announcements of professional societies.
Language(s): German
ADVERTISING RATES:
Full Page Mono .... EUR 1360
Full Page Colour .... EUR 2470
Mechanical Data: Type Area: 248 x 175 mm, No. of Columns (Display): 4, Col Widths (Display): 40 mm
Official Journal of: Organ d. Bundesverb. d. Ärzte d. Öffentl. Gesundheitsdienstes e.V., d. Bundesverb. d. Sozialversicherungsärzte e.V., d. Dt. Ges. f. Sozialmedizin u. Prävention e.V., d. Medizin. Dienst d. Spitzenverbände d. Krankenkassen, d. Dt. Ges. f. Public Health e.V.
BUSINESS: LOCAL GOVERNMENT, LEISURE & RECREATION: Public Health & Cleaning

GETRÄNKE! 728862G9A-6
Editorial: Blumenstr. 15, 90402 NÜRNBERG
Tel: 911 2018160 **Fax:** 911 2018100
Email: gtm@harnisch.com **Web site:** http://www.harnisch.com/gtm
Freq: 5 issues yearly; **Annual Sub.:** EUR 58,00; **Circ:** 8,906
Editor: Gertrude Schöneberg; **Advertising Manager:** Gertrude Schöneberg
Profile: Magazine covering technical and marketing issues related to the drinks industry in Germany.
Language(s): German
ADVERTISING RATES:
Full Page Mono .... EUR 3620
Full Page Colour .... EUR 4970
Mechanical Data: Type Area: 250 x 189 mm, No. of Columns (Display): 3, Col Widths (Display): 57 mm
Copy instructions: *Copy Date:* 28 days prior to publication
BUSINESS: DRINKS & LICENSED TRADE: Drinks, Licensed Trade, Wines & Spirits

GETRÄNKE FACHGROSSHANDEL 728857G9A-2
Editorial: Schloss Mindelburg, 87719 MINDELHEIM
Tel: 8261 999313 **Fax:** 8261 999395
Email: eisler@sachon.de **Web site:** http://www.getraenkefachgrosshandel.de
Freq: Monthly; **Annual Sub.:** EUR 59,92; **Circ:** 15,014
Editor: Thomas Eisler; **Advertising Manager:** Helga Reß
Profile: Magazine covering wholesaling through specialist shops.
Language(s): German
Readership: Aimed at managers and decision makers in the drinks industry.
ADVERTISING RATES:
Full Page Mono .... EUR 5502
Full Page Colour .... EUR 7182
Mechanical Data: Type Area: 270 x 185 mm, No. of Columns (Display): 4, Col Widths (Display): 45 mm
Official Journal of: Organ d. Bundesverb. d. Dt. Getränkefachgroßhandels e.V.
BUSINESS: DRINKS & LICENSED TRADE: Drinks, Licensed Trade, Wines & Spirits

GETRÄNKE ZEITUNG 728863G9A-7
Editorial: Maximilianstr. 7, 67433 NEUSTADT
Tel: 6321 890868 **Fax:** 6321 890873
Email: gz@meininger.de **Web site:** http://www.getraenke-zeitung.de
Freq: 26 issues yearly; Free to qualifying individuals
Annual Sub.: EUR 99,60; **Circ:** 9,843
Editor: Angelika Thielen; **Advertising Manager:** Ralf Clemens
Profile: The Getränke Zeitung is the trade publication of choice for all decision-makers involved in buying and selling beverages in the beverages and food retail sector. GZ's readership includes managers from beverage wholesaling, food retailing, the beverage sector and beverage importers. As well as offering an up-to-date section with concise information, news and accounts of current events in the market, GZ focuses on extensive background reports on developments in the individual beverage segments and on shop reports, research findings and individual company portraits. Other established features of GZ are its special issues dealing with major sector events and panel discussions with leading figures from industry and trade. Jobs section geared specifically towards the beverages sector. GZ is compulsory reading for all managers in the beverages sector and is an essential source of information for the industry as a whole.
Language(s): German
Readership: Aimed at wholesalers and retailers within the food and drink industry.
ADVERTISING RATES:
Full Page Mono .... EUR 5950
Full Page Colour .... EUR 5950
Mechanical Data: Type Area: 440 x 310 mm, No. of Columns (Display): 6, Col Widths (Display): 48 mm
Copy instructions: *Copy Date:* 15 days prior to publication
BUSINESS: DRINKS & LICENSED TRADE: Drinks, Licensed Trade, Wines & Spirits

GETRÄNKEHERSTELLUNG DEUTSCHLAND 728858G22A-1120
Editorial: Bert-Brecht-Str. 15, 78054 VILLINGEN-SCHWENNINGEN **Tel:** 7720 394118
Fax: 7720 394175
Email: findeisen@kuhnverlag.de **Web site:** http://www.kuhn-kataloge.de
Freq: Annual; **Cover Price:** EUR 17,00; **Circ:** 6,097
Editor: Steffi Findeisen; **Advertising Manager:** Konrad Baumann
Profile: Magazine for the beverage producing industry.
Language(s): German
ADVERTISING RATES:
Full Page Mono .... EUR 2240
Full Page Colour .... EUR 3055
Mechanical Data: Type Area: 254 x 180 mm
BUSINESS: FOOD

GETRÄNKEINDUSTRIE 728859G9A-3
Editorial: Schloss Mindelburg, 87719 MINDELHEIM
Tel: 8261 999317 **Fax:** 8261 999395
Email: gabler@sachon.de **Web site:** http://www.sachon.de
Freq: Monthly; Free to qualifying individuals
Annual Sub.: EUR 59,92; **Circ:** 9,344
Editor: Fabian Gabler; **Advertising Manager:** Sabine Berchtenbreiter
Profile: Magazine dealing with all aspects of the drinks industry.
Language(s): German
ADVERTISING RATES:
Full Page Mono .... EUR 4965
Full Page Colour .... EUR 6345
Mechanical Data: Type Area: 270 x 185 mm, No. of Columns (Display): 4, Col Widths (Display): 45 mm
Official Journal of: Organ d. Wirtschaftsvereinigung alkoholfreie Getränke e.V.
BUSINESS: DRINKS & LICENSED TRADE: Drinks, Licensed Trade, Wines & Spirits

GETREIDE MAGAZIN
728865G21A-2080
Editorial: Clemens-August-Str. 12, 53115 BONN
Tel: 228 9694230 **Fax:** 228 630311
Email: redaktion@dlg-agrofoodmedien.de **Web site:** http://www.dlg-agrofoodmedien.de
Freq: Quarterly; **Annual Sub.:** EUR 29,00; **Circ:** 48,175
Editor: Heinz-Peter Pütz; **Advertising Manager:** Rainer Schluck
Profile: Magazine about cereal and grain cultivation.
Language(s): German
Readership: Read by arable farmers.
ADVERTISING RATES:
Full Page Mono .... EUR 3990
Full Page Colour .... EUR 6025
Mechanical Data: Type Area: 270 x 186 mm, No. of Columns (Display): 4, Col Widths (Display): 42 mm
BUSINESS: AGRICULTURE & FARMING

GETREIDETECHNOLOGIE [CEREAL TECHNOLOGY]
728866G8A-240
Editorial: Schützenberg 10, 32756 DETMOLD
Tel: 5231 6166419 **Fax:** 5231 20505
Email: info@agf-detmold.de **Web site:** http://www.agfdt.de
Freq: Quarterly; **Annual Sub.:** EUR 259,00; **Circ:** 1,906
Editor: Jochen Bode; **Advertising Manager:** Charles Green
Profile: Journal covering grain cultivation, milling, baking and cereal based foods.
Language(s): English; German
Readership: Aimed at the baking and food industry.
ADVERTISING RATES:
Full Page Mono .... EUR 920
Full Page Colour .... EUR 1690
Mechanical Data: Type Area: 270 x 189 mm, No. of Columns (Display): 4, Col Widths (Display): 45 mm
Copy instructions: *Copy Date:* 21 days prior to publication
BUSINESS: BAKING & CONFECTIONERY: Baking

GEWÄSSER-INFO 728868G4C-18
Editorial: Theodor-Heuss-Allee 17, 53773 HENNEF
Tel: 2242 872210 **Fax:** 2242 872135
Email: schrenk@dwa.de **Web site:** http://www.dwa.de
Freq: 3 issues yearly; Free to qualifying individuals
Annual Sub.: EUR 21,00; **Circ:** 3,500
Editor: Georg Schrenk; **Advertising Manager:** Andrea Vogel
Profile: The latest information, practical reports and legal aspects of water management and water development are published in the gewässer-info. The magazine serves as a platform for the presentation of methodological approaches and practical experience in the biotope equitable water management. In addition to articles on professional work on the water is reported on the results of local inspections and debates (site visits) and on the current work and publications of the waters neighborhoods.
Language(s): German
Readership: Aimed at geographers.
ADVERTISING RATES:
Full Page Mono .... EUR 760
Full Page Colour .... EUR 760
Mechanical Data: Type Area: 253 x 186 mm, No. of Columns (Display): 3, Col Widths (Display): 58 mm
Copy instructions: *Copy Date:* 40 days prior to publication
Supplement to: KA Korrespondenz Abwasser Abfall, KW Korrespondenz Wasserwirtschaft
BUSINESS: ARCHITECTURE & BUILDING: Surveying

GEWERBE REPORT 728871G14H-25
Editorial: Hüttenbergstr. 38, 66538 NEUNKIRCHEN
Tel: 6821 306251 **Fax:** 6821 306241
Email: redaktion@gewerbereport.com **Web site:** http://www.gewerbereport.com
Freq: Quarterly; Free to qualifying individuals
Annual Sub.: EUR 12,00; **Circ:** 13,286
Editor: Margit Berger
Profile: Journal containing information for the self-employed and small businesses in Germany and the European Union.
Language(s): German
ADVERTISING RATES:
Full Page Mono .... EUR 1875
Full Page Colour .... EUR 1875

Mechanical Data: Type Area: 267 x 180 mm, No. of Columns (Display): 3, Col Widths (Display): 55 mm
Copy instructions: *Copy Date:* 28 days prior to publication
BUSINESS: COMMERCE, INDUSTRY & MANAGEMENT: Small Business

GEWERBE & ENERGIE

728872G14A-2800
Editorial: Putzbrunner Str. 38, 85521 OTTOBRUNN
Tel: 89 6080010 **Fax:** 89 60800130
Email: info@trumit.de **Web site:** http://www.trumit.de
Freq: Quarterly; **Cover Price:** Free; **Circ:** 2,200
Profile: Company publication published by Stadtwerke Fellbach.
Language(s): German

GFF

728915G12B-1
Editorial: Gewerbestr. 2, 86825 BAD WÖRISHOFEN
Tel: 8247 354231 **Fax:** 8247 3544231
Email: reinhold.kober@holzmann-medien.de **Web site:** http://www.gff-magazin.de
Freq: 11 issues yearly; **Annual Sub.:** EUR 112,20; **Circ:** 7,876
Editor: Reinhold Kober; **Advertising Manager:** Michaela Sammer
Profile: Magazine about the glass and frame industry.
Language(s): German
Readership: Read by glaziers, carpenters, insulating and glass industry workers, window and metal manufacturers.
ADVERTISING RATES:
Full Page Mono .... EUR 1795
Full Page Colour .... EUR 2770
Mechanical Data: Type Area: 270 x 179 mm, No. of Columns (Display): 4, Col Widths (Display): 44 mm
Copy instructions: *Copy Date:* 30 days prior to publication
Official Journal of: Organ f. d. Landesinnungsverbände d. Glaserhandwerks v. Baden-Württemberg, Brandenburg, Rheinland-Pfalz, Sachsen, Sachsen-Anhalt u. Thüringen sowie f. d. Glaserinnungen Düsseldorf u. Oldenburg
BUSINESS: CERAMICS, POTTERY & GLASS: Glass

GFK INSITE

755982G14A-9534
Editorial: Nordwestring 101, 90419 NÜRNBERG
Tel: 911 3954440 **Fax:** 911 3954041
Email: public.relations@gfk.com **Web site:** http://www.gfk.com
Freq: Quarterly; **Cover Price:** Free; **Circ:** 13,500
Editor: Natalie Bajon; **Advertising Manager:** Diana Kleinöder
Profile: Customer and employee magazine of gfk.
Language(s): English; German
ADVERTISING RATES:
Full Page Mono .... EUR 570
Full Page Colour .... EUR 1120
Mechanical Data: Type Area: 265 x 176 mm
Copy instructions: *Copy Date:* 21 days prior to publication

GI GELDINSTITUTE

728939G1C-640
Editorial: Gewerbestr. 2, 86825 BAD WÖRISHOFEN
Tel: 8247 354106 **Fax:** 8247 354108
Email: redaktion@geldinstitute.de **Web site:** http://www.geldinstitute.de
Freq: 6 issues yearly; **Annual Sub.:** EUR 109,00; **Circ:** 5,692
Editor: Erwin Ströbele; **Advertising Manager:** Thomas Pohl
Profile: The trade magazine for IT, organization and communication, is considered required reading for executives in banks, private banks, specialized banks, savings banks, Cash clearing houses, credit unions, credit institutions on a cooperative basis and building society, post office savings bank and post office. Editors, Scientific Advisory Board and a staff of experts in all areas to ensure that any information is equipped with an additional benefit. For example, reports in words and pictures on Bank-IT, banking technology and organization, systems and resources for modern planning, establishment and organization of financial institutions by comparison, cost studies and recommended to be extended to applications, thus paving usefully to the skilled reader.
Independent experts from home and abroad rain with reports, case studies, analysis and opinions in discussions. monetary institute takes up the problems of IT decision makers in financial institutions, offers solutions and serves as a bridge from the manufacturer to the user.
Language(s): German
ADVERTISING RATES:
Full Page Mono .... EUR 3825
Full Page Colour .... EUR 4995
Mechanical Data: Type Area: 255 x 185 mm, No. of Columns (Display): 4, Col Widths (Display): 43 mm
Copy instructions: *Copy Date:* 22 days prior to publication
BUSINESS: FINANCE & ECONOMICS: Banking

GI GESUNDHEITS INGENIEUR

728940G3D-180
Editorial: Pfaffenbergstr. 95, 67663 KAISERSLAUTERN **Tel:** 631 2052295
Fax: 631 2054510
Email: balzereit@oiv.de
Freq: 6 issues yearly; **Annual Sub.:** EUR 200,00; **Circ:** 437
Editor: Klaus W. Usemann; **Advertising Manager:** Inge Matos Feliz
Profile: The magazine for home technology, building physics and environmental engineering with the fields of heating and air conditioning systems, technical installations, water and wastewater.
Language(s): German
Readership: Read by heating and ventilation engineers.
ADVERTISING RATES:
Full Page Mono .... EUR 2090
Full Page Colour .... EUR 3260
Mechanical Data: Type Area: 250 x 176 mm, No. of Columns (Display): 4, Col Widths (Display): 41 mm
Copy instructions: *Copy Date:* 26 days prior to publication
BUSINESS: HEATING & VENTILATION: Heating & Plumbing

GIESSENER ALLGEMEINE

728925G67B-5960
Editorial: Marburger Str. 18, 35390 GIESSEN
Tel: 641 30030 **Fax:** 641 3003305
Email: redaktion@giessener-allgemeine.de **Web site:** http://www.giessener-allgemeine.de
Freq: 312 issues yearly; **Circ:** 30,075
Editor: Christian Rempel; **News Editor:** Burkhard Bräuning; **Advertising Manager:** Wilfried Kämpf
Profile: Regional daily newspaper with news on politics, economy, culture, sports, travel, technology, etc. The Giessener Allgemeine is the leading daily newspaper is pouring in the district. With its local edition Alsfelder Allgemeine is also represented in the district Vogelsberg. Facebook: http://www.facebook.com/GiessenerAllgemeine Twitter: http://twitter.com/allgemeine This Outlet offers RSS (Really Simple Syndication).
Language(s): German
ADVERTISING RATES:
SCC .... EUR 101,10
Mechanical Data: Type Area: 430 x 282 mm, No. of Columns (Display): 6, Col Widths (Display): 45 mm
Copy instructions: *Copy Date:* 1 day prior to publication
Supplement(s): streifzug
REGIONAL DAILY & SUNDAY NEWSPAPERS: Regional Daily Newspapers

GIESSENER ANZEIGER

728926G67B-5980
Editorial: Am Urnenfeld 12, 35396 GIESSEN
Tel: 641 95043405 **Fax:** 641 95043411
Email: redaktion@giessener-anzeiger.de **Web site:** http://www.giessener-anzeiger.de
Freq: 312 issues yearly; **Circ:** 29,257
Editor: Wolfgang Maaß; **News Editor:** Astrid Knöß; **Advertising Manager:** Harald Lappessen
Profile: Regional daily newspaper covering politics, economics, sports, travel and technology. This Outlet offers RSS (Really Simple Syndication). This Outlet offers RSS (Really Simple Syndication).
Language(s): German
ADVERTISING RATES:
SCC .... EUR 55,20
Mechanical Data: Type Area: 430 x 278 mm, No. of Columns (Display): 6, Col Widths (Display): 45 mm
Copy instructions: *Copy Date:* 1 day prior to publication
REGIONAL DAILY & SUNDAY NEWSPAPERS: Regional Daily Newspapers

GIESSENER MAGAZIN EXPRESS

728927G80-4240
Editorial: Ernst-Giller-Str. 20a, 35039 MARBURG
Tel: 6421 68440 **Fax:** 6421 684444
Email: redaktion@marbuch-verlag.de **Web site:** http://www.marbuch-verlag.de
Freq: Weekly; **Cover Price:** Free; **Circ:** 14,108
Editor: Georg Kronenberg
Profile: Magazine for the Gießen area.
Language(s): German
ADVERTISING RATES:
Full Page Mono .... EUR 1352
Full Page Colour .... EUR 1790
Mechanical Data: Type Area: 260 x 190 mm, No. of Columns (Display): 4, Col Widths (Display): 45 mm
Copy instructions: *Copy Date:* 3 days prior to publication
CONSUMER: RURAL & REGIONAL INTEREST

GIESSEREI

728930G27-860
Editorial: Sohnstr. 70, 40237 DÜSSELDORF
Tel: 211 6871107 **Fax:** 211 6871365
Email: redaktion@bdguss.de **Web site:** http://www.bdguss.de
Freq: Monthly; **Annual Sub.:** EUR 159,00; **Circ:** 4,396
Editor: Michael Franken; **Advertising Manager:** Dagmar Dieterle-Witte
Profile: Publication about foundries and technology.
Language(s): German
Readership: Aimed at foundry and technology managers in the industry.
ADVERTISING RATES:
Full Page Mono .... EUR 1750
Full Page Colour .... EUR 2548
Mechanical Data: Type Area: 260 x 174 mm, No. of Columns (Display): 3, Col Widths (Display): 54 mm
Copy instructions: *Copy Date:* 19 days prior to publication
Official Journal of: Organ d. Bundesverb. d. Dt. Gießerei-Industrie
BUSINESS: METAL, IRON & STEEL

GIESSEREI-ERFAHRUNGSAUSTAUSCH

728931G27-880
Editorial: Sohnstr. 70, 40237 DÜSSELDORF
Tel: 211 6871107 **Fax:** 211 6871365
Email: redaktion@bdguss.de **Web site:** http://www.bdguss.de
Freq: 10 issues yearly; **Annual Sub.:** EUR 59,00; **Circ:** 5,449
Editor: Michael Franken; **Advertising Manager:** Dagmar Dieterle-Witte
Profile: Journal about the theory and practice of the foundry industry.
Language(s): German
Readership: Aimed at foundry workers.
ADVERTISING RATES:
Full Page Mono .... EUR 1200
Full Page Colour .... EUR 1950
Mechanical Data: Type Area: 260 x 174 mm, No. of Columns (Display): 3, Col Widths (Display): 55 mm
Copy instructions: *Copy Date:* 14 days prior to publication
Official Journal of: Organ d. Bundesverb. d. Dt. Gießerei-Industrie
BUSINESS: METAL, IRON & STEEL

GIESSEREIFORSCHUNG INTERNATIONAL FOUNDRY RESEARCH

728932G19A-320
Editorial: Sohnstr. 70, 40237 DÜSSELDORF
Tel: 211 6871107 **Fax:** 211 6871365
Email: redaktion@bdguss.de **Web site:** http://www.bdguss.de
Freq: Quarterly; **Annual Sub.:** EUR 249,00; **Circ:** 400
Editor: Michael Franken; **Advertising Manager:** Dagmar Dieterle-Witte
Profile: Scientific supplement to the 'Giesserei' magazine.
Language(s): English; German
ADVERTISING RATES:
Full Page Mono .... EUR 348
Mechanical Data: Type Area: 250 x 171 mm
Copy instructions: *Copy Date:* 26 days prior to publication
Official Journal of: Organ d. Bundesverb. d. Dt. Gießerei-Industrie

GIFHORNER RUNDBLICK AM SONNTAG

728936G72-4644
Editorial: Steinweg 73, 38518 GIFHORN
Tel: 5371 808102 **Fax:** 5371 808147
Email: redaktion@rundblick-gif.de **Web site:** http://www.rundblick-gif.de
Freq: Weekly; **Cover Price:** Free; **Circ:** 47,452
Editor: Frank Hitzschke; **Advertising Manager:** Horst Schubert
Profile: Advertising journal (house-to-house) concentrating on local stories.
Language(s): German
ADVERTISING RATES:
Full Page Mono .... EUR 3458
Full Page Colour .... EUR 4257
Mechanical Data: Type Area: 430 x 277 mm, No. of Columns (Display): 6, Col Widths (Display): 45 mm
Copy instructions: *Copy Date:* 3 days prior to publication
LOCAL NEWSPAPERS

GIG

728938G89C-4801
Editorial: Sauerländer Weg 2a, 48145 MÜNSTER
Tel: 251 987230 **Fax:** 251 9872350
Email: office@gig-online.de **Web site:** http://www.gig-online.de
Freq: Monthly; **Cover Price:** Free; **Circ:** 31,440
Editor: Hubert Steinert; **Advertising Manager:** Martin Lückemeier
Profile: By Culture & Event Magazine GIG to reach over 65,000 young and young at heart and mobile people between 20 and 49, students and the target group of professionals who spend their free time on an active Entertainment and consumer behavior Define, direct and without wastage. The GIG has a place where our readers are at work: at the point of entertainment. Here defined scene expertise that the traditional media are difficult or even not reached.
Language(s): German
ADVERTISING RATES:
Full Page Mono .... EUR 1720
Full Page Colour .... EUR 2810
Mechanical Data: Type Area: 250 x 180 mm, No. of Columns (Display): 6, Col Widths (Display): 27 mm
Copy instructions: *Copy Date:* 9 days prior to publication
CONSUMER: HOLIDAYS & TRAVEL: Entertainment Guides

GIGA.DE

1704625G78D-1023
Editorial: Chausseestr. 8, 10115 BERLIN
Tel: 30 9210640 **Fax:** 30 92106431
Email: info@econa.com **Web site:** http://www.giga.de
Cover Price: Paid; **Circ:** 1,770,170 Unique Users
Editor: David Hain
Profile: Ezine: Giga.de is the unique combination of gaming, lifestyle and community. In addition to editorial content on the fields of games, fun, technology/gadgets and movies DVD, users have the opportunity to participate actively in the site and its contents and send in your own news, articles, reviews, and video. In addition, there is a daily live-on-tape in the video highlights of the website and current issues of the community are addressed. Facebook: http://www.facebook.com/GIGA.DE Twitter: http://twitter.com/#!/Follow_The_G This Outlet offers RSS (Really Simple Syndication).
Language(s): German
CONSUMER: CONSUMER ELECTRONICS: Games

GIS.BUSINESS

728686G5B-77_5
Editorial: Schanzenstr. 36, 51063 KÖLN
Tel: 221 93119286 **Fax:** 221 9608550
Email: redaktion@gis-business.de **Web site:** http://www.gis-biz.de
Freq: 6 issues yearly; **Annual Sub.:** EUR 158,00; **Circ:** 4,874
Editor: Monika Rech; **Advertising Manager:** Christoph Beyreiss
Profile: Journal focusing on spatial information technology, includes planning, telecommunications, new products, industry trends and the development of the GIS (Geographical Information Systems) market.
Language(s): German
Readership: Read by users of GIS systems.
ADVERTISING RATES:
Full Page Mono .... EUR 2900
Full Page Colour .... EUR 2900
Mechanical Data: Type Area: 262 x 185 mm, No. of Columns (Display): 3, Col Widths (Display): 59 mm
Copy instructions: *Copy Date:* 21 days prior to publication
Official Journal of: Organ d. dt. Dachverb. f. Geoinformation e.V.
BUSINESS: COMPUTERS & AUTOMATION: Data Processing

GIS.TRENDS+MARKETS

1863724G19A-1133
Editorial: Schanzenstr. 36, 51063 KÖLN
Tel: 221 93119286 **Fax:** 221 9608550
Email: redaktion@gis-business.de **Web site:** http://www.gis-biz.de
Freq: Half-yearly; **Circ:** 12,000
Editor: Monika Rech; **Advertising Manager:** Christoph Beyreiss
Profile: Journal focusing on spatial information technology, includes planning, telecommunications, new products, industry trends and the development of the GIS (Geographical Information Systems) market.
Language(s): English; German
ADVERTISING RATES:
Full Page Mono .... EUR 1950
Full Page Colour .... EUR 1950
Mechanical Data: Type Area: 262 x 185 mm, No. of Columns (Display): 3, Col Widths (Display): 59 mm
Copy instructions: *Copy Date:* 21 days prior to publication

G.I.T. LABORATORY JOURNAL EUROPE

728962G55-3893
Editorial: Rößlerstr. 90, 64293 DARMSTADT
Tel: 6151 8090139 **Fax:** 6151 8090144
Email: arne.kusserow@wiley.com **Web site:** http://www.gitverlag.com
Freq: 6 issues yearly; **Annual Sub.:** EUR 77,04; **Circ:** 27,000
Editor: Arne Kusserow; **Advertising Manager:** Katja-Carola Habermüller
Profile: G.I.T. Laboratory Journal Europe consists of three parts. • In the "Research and Development" section we publish up-to-date scientific research articles from highly reputated authors • The "Screening inside" section reports on recent developments in the drug discovery and pharmaceutical industry, contract research and clinical testing • The "Technology & Instrumentation" section reports on new developments in laboratory instrumentation and application Reflecting the increasing overlap of the chemistry and biology business and academia we strongly increased the editorial coverage on life sciences. Who are the readers of the G.I.T. Laboratory Journal Europe? G.I.T. Laboratory Journal Europe is published bimonthly and reaches 27.000 personalized addressees in industrial R&D and scientific institutions throughout Europe. Decision makers from R&D departments of universities, chemical, pharmaceutical and biotechnological corporations rely on the articles and news provided by the G.I.T. Laboratory Journal Europe. Our readership spread all across Europe; the G.I.T. Laboratory Journal Europe is read mainly the UK, Germany, Switzer- land, Austria, Scandinavia and the Netherlands.
Language(s): English
ADVERTISING RATES:
Full Page Mono .... EUR 5640
Full Page Colour .... EUR 7120
Mechanical Data: Type Area: 260 x 185 mm, No. of Columns (Display): 4, Col Widths (Display): 43 mm
BUSINESS: APPLIED SCIENCE & LABORATORIES

GIT LABOR-FACHZEITSCHRIFT

728963G55-3894
Editorial: Rößlerstr. 90, 64293 DARMSTADT
Tel: 6151 8090136 **Fax:** 6151 8090176
Email: margareta.dellert-ritter@wiley.com **Web site:** http://www.pro-4-pro.com
Freq: Monthly; **Annual Sub.:** EUR 135,89; **Circ:** 28,942
Editor: Margareta Dellert-Ritter; **Advertising Manager:** Katja- Carola Habermüller
Profile: The GIT Labor-Fachzeitschrift reported in detail, current and application based on all topics related to industrial and scientific laboratories. Among the main topics of the GIT spectroscopy, chromatography, microscopy, and software are just as laboratory equipment, technology and automation

all applications. A special part of regular life cience eepens the range of topics in bioanalysis, 'Omics, ioprocess engineering, biotechnology, ioinformatics, microarrays and molecular iagnostics. The GIT Labor-Fachzeitschrift covers all reas of the laboratory. With 30,000 individual ecipients has GIT laboratory journal, the largest rculation in German-speaking!.
anguage(s): German
DVERTISING RATES:
ull Page Mono .... EUR 7220
ull Page Colour .... EUR 8700
lechanical Data: Type Area: 260 x 185 mm, No. of olumns (Display): 4, Col Widths (Display): 43 mm
USINESS: APPLIED SCIENCE & LABORATORIES

GIT SICHERHEIT + MANAGEMENT 728964G54B-7_75
ditorial: Rößlerstr. 90, 64293 DARMSTADT
el: 6151 8090130 Fax: 6151 8090179
mail: steffen.ebert@wiley.com Web site: http://ww.gitsicherheit.de
req: 10 issues yearly; Free to qualifying individuals
nnual Sub.: EUR 112,35; Circ: 29,040
ditor: Steffen Ebert; Advertising Manager: Heiko aumgartner
rofile: GIT SICHERHEIT + MANAGEMENT agazine reaches all decision makers involved in vestment – in purchasing, through specialist epartments and up to management level, in the rivate as well as in the public sector. This ublication speaks to the whole distribution channel, om the manufacturer and all kinds of distributors long to the end-users. The magazine deals with the iversity and complexity of safety and security topics nd covers them in regular sections: Management, ecurity, IT and IT-Security, Fire Protection and afety. Decision makers and opinion leaders inform hemselves with GIT SICHERHEIT + MANAGEMENT bout market news, products, companies, pplications and trends. With 30,000 printed copies nd a qualified circulation of 28,200 copies per issue VW-audited, Q2 10) GIT SICHERHEIT + IANAGEMENT is the magazine with the highest rculation in the target markets of Germany, Austria nd Switzerland. The outstanding high market enetration and the exceptional editorial quality is ombined with a big variety of online information ervices: The GIT Business Web GIT-SICHERHEIT.de nd the product platform PRO-4-PRO.com make GIT ICHERHEIT + MANAGEMENT the #1 publication.
anguage(s): German
eadership: Aimed at decision-makers.
DVERTISING RATES:
ull Page Mono .... EUR 6810
ull Page Colour .... EUR 8290
lechanical Data: Type Area: 260 x 185 mm, No. of olumns (Display): 4, Col Widths (Display): 43 mm
opy instructions: *Copy Date:* 14 days prior to ublication
USINESS: SAFETY & SECURITY: Safety

GITARRE & BASS 728960G76D-1660
ditorial: Emil-Hoffmann-Str. 13, 50996 KÖLN
el: 2236 9621730 Fax: 2236 96217930
mail: redaktion@gitarrebass.de Web site: http://ww.gitarrebass.de
req: Monthly; Annual Sub.: EUR 50,00; Circ: 29,426
ditor: Dieter Roesberg; Advertising Manager: Christiane Weyres
rofile: Gitarre & Bass is the monthly magazine for uitarists and bass players, the amateur musicians nd professionals alike respond. For years, it is the est-selling music magazine in Germany. A survey of e University of Munich found has it a readership eveloped with a uniform age structure: the G & B-eaders is accordingly in equal groups of "13 to 20", 20 to 30", "30 to 40" and " about 40 years. Gitarre & ass offers four main subject areas: first are the etailed and professionally written reviews of new nstruments, amplifiers, effects units and accessories. here are also stories and features on current topics s well as historical musical, detailed interviews with nter-national musicians of all styles, and exhibition eports and portraits of instrument manufacturers. lusical practice is covered with workshops and ranscription competent authors and famous nusicians. Completing the editorial content of the omprehensive and current news & service section vith technical information, CD, DVD and book eviews as well as tour dates and TV shows etc. As urvey results, the reviews in Gitarre & Bass haracterized by high credibility and competence and ave a proven major role in purchasing decisions of eaders. For many years, Guitar & Bass also resented extensively on the web. G & B Online ffers additional information, tips, links and search acilities and access to back issues lying article itations, examples and a comprehensive range of earing about the workshops and transcriptions. There are also high quality of studio musicians ecorded live by Jam Playalongs. The editors of Guitar & Bass is a monthly analysis on average two to hree thousand letters from depth, so that a constant, irect contact and relation to the needs and uggestions for topics the reader is warrants. acebook: http://www.facebook.com/restglut.
anguage(s): German
eadership: Aimed at amateur musicians.
lechanical Data: Type Area: 254 x 185 mm, No. of olumns (Display): 4, Col Widths (Display): 43 mm
CONSUMER: MUSIC & PERFORMING ARTS: Music

GLAMOUR 728967G74A-1360
ditorial: Karlstr. 23, 80333 MÜNCHEN
el: 89 381040 Fax: 89 38104307
mail: glamour@glamour.de Web site: http://www.lamour.de
Freq: Monthly; **Annual Sub.:** EUR 24,60; **Circ:** 490,735
Editor: Andrea Ketterer; **Advertising Manager:** Susanne Förg-Randazzo
Profile: Trend and style guide for the young, open-minded and communicative woman takes on the complex needs of the fashion-conscious, mobile, educated and self-conscious target group and becomes a trend-setting brand in the network. The variety consists Fashion & Style, Beauty & Lifestyle, Life: and the currently accessible. Facebook: http://www.facebook.com/glamour.de.
Language(s): German
Readership: Aimed at women aged between 18 and 60 years.
ADVERTISING RATES:
Full Page Mono .... EUR 27900
Full Page Colour .... EUR 27900
Mechanical Data: Type Area: 190 x 138 mm, No. of Columns (Display): 2, Col Widths (Display): 64 mm
Copy instructions: *Copy Date:* 32 days prior to publication
CONSUMER: WOMEN'S INTEREST CONSUMER MAGAZINES: Women's Interest

GLAS 728971G4E-3760
Editorial: Ernst-Mey-Str. 8, 70771 LEINFELDEN-ECHTERDINGEN **Tel:** 711 7594519
Fax: 711 7594397
Email: juergen.braun@konradin.de **Web site:** http://www.glas-online.de
Freq: 6 issues yearly; **Annual Sub.:** EUR 52,80; **Circ:** 6,931
Editor: Jürgen Braun; **Advertising Manager:** Bettina Mayer
Profile: The magazine shows exemplary solutions for a transparent architecture and its background. In connection with design and construction details of energy concepts for the use of glass and other transparent and translucent materials in various fields such as textile, plastic or metal mesh are shown. Major component is the building envelope, whose areas of glazing, window profile systems and facade structures are the focus of the editorial work. The journal provides current knowledge on transparent and translucent materials, as well as new applications of materials in architecture in detail for the daily practice of planning and designing. The chief editor Prof. Dipl.-Ing. Jürgen Braun is through his experience in teaching and as an architect for many years familiar with the material glass and its applications.
Language(s): German
ADVERTISING RATES:
Full Page Mono .... EUR 2280
Full Page Colour .... EUR 4050
Mechanical Data: Type Area: 270 x 188 mm, No. of Columns (Display): 4, Col Widths (Display): 44 mm
BUSINESS: ARCHITECTURE & BUILDING: Building

GLAS + RAHMEN 728979G12B-3
Editorial: Auf'm Tetelberg 7, 40221 DÜSSELDORF
Tel: 211 3909853 **Fax:** 211 3909839
Email: fier@glas-rahmen.de **Web site:** http://www.verlagsanstalt-handwerk.de
Freq: Monthly; Free to qualifying individuals
Annual Sub.: EUR 94,00; **Circ:** 8,210
Editor: Stefan Fier
Profile: Glas+Rahmen reports twelve times a year up to date and most technically competent on technical, economic and legal innovations and product innovations from the glass, window and facade industry. Glas+Rahmen is the specialist magazine for entrepreneurs and executives. Receivers are trade and industry, suppliers, retailers, architects and planners as well as research institutions and professional institutions in Germany, Austria and Switzerland. Glas+Rahmen is the sole organ of the German Federal Association for the Glazier, the Association of Young Glass and Window Manufacturers, and many Guilds.
Language(s): German
Readership: Read by architects, designers, manufacturers, suppliers and glaziers.
ADVERTISING RATES:
Full Page Mono .... EUR 1529
Full Page Colour .... EUR 2732
Mechanical Data: Type Area: 270 x 185 mm, No. of Columns (Display): 4, Col Widths (Display): 44 mm
Copy instructions: *Copy Date:* 21 days prior to publication
Official Journal of: Organ d. Bundesinnungsverb. d. Glaserhandwerkes, d. Bundesverb. d. Jungglaser u. Fensterbauer u. d. Landesverbände Nordrhein-Westfalen, Bayern, Bremen, Niedersachsen, Hamburg, Mecklenburg-Vorpommern, Hessen, Berlin, Schleswig-Holstein, Sachsen u. Thüringen
BUSINESS: CERAMICS, POTTERY & GLASS: Glass

GLASWELT 728981G12B-5
Editorial: Forststr. 131, 70193 STUTTGART
Tel: 711 63672843 **Fax:** 711 63672743
Email: glaswelt@glaswelt.de **Web site:** http://www.glaswelt.de
Freq: Monthly; **Annual Sub.:** EUR 154,60; **Circ:** 9,112
Editor: Matthias Rehberger; **Advertising Manager:** Walter Karl Eder
Profile: Magazine focusing on the glass and window trade. Containing articles about production, processing, use and finishing of glass.
Language(s): German
ADVERTISING RATES:
Full Page Mono .... EUR 1975
Full Page Colour .... EUR 2795
Mechanical Data: Type Area: 265 x 187 mm, No. of Columns (Display): 4, Col Widths (Display): 43 mm
Copy instructions: *Copy Date:* 15 days prior to publication
BUSINESS: CERAMICS, POTTERY & GLASS: Glass

GLAUBE+HEIMAT - MITTELDT. KIRCHENZTG., AUSG. SACHSEN-ANHALT PLUS 732679G87-7100
Editorial: Hegelstr. 1, 39104 MAGDEBURG
Tel: 391 5346414 **Fax:** 391 5346419
Email: magdeburg@glaube-und-heimat.de **Web site:** http://www.glaube-und-heimat.de
Freq: Weekly; **Annual Sub.:** EUR 42,00; **Circ:** 3,423
Editor: Martin Hanusch; **Advertising Manager:** Stefanie Rost
Profile: Evangelical weekly for Christians in Anhalt and Saxony.
Language(s): German
ADVERTISING RATES:
Full Page Mono .... EUR 2193
Full Page Colour .... EUR 4020
Mechanical Data: Type Area: 406 x 282 mm, No. of Columns (Display): 6, Col Widths (Display): 45 mm
Copy instructions: *Copy Date:* 13 days prior to publication
CONSUMER: RELIGIOUS

GLAUBE+HEIMAT - MITTELDT. KIRCHENZTG., AUSG. THÜRINGEN 728988G87-4960
Editorial: Lisztstr. 2a, 99423 WEIMAR
Tel: 3643 246120 **Fax:** 3643 246112
Email: redaktion@glaube-und-heimat.de **Web site:** http://www.glaube-und-heimat.de
Freq: Weekly; **Annual Sub.:** EUR 42,00; **Circ:** 11,642
Editor: Martin Hanusch; **Advertising Manager:** Stefanie Rost
Profile: Evangelical magazine for the Thüringen region.
Language(s): German
ADVERTISING RATES:
Full Page Mono .... EUR 2436
Full Page Colour .... EUR 3411
Mechanical Data: Type Area: 406 x 282 mm, No. of Columns (Display): 6, Col Widths (Display): 45 mm
Copy instructions: *Copy Date:* 13 days prior to publication
CONSUMER: RELIGIOUS

GLAUBE UND LEBEN 728990G87-4980
Editorial: Liebfrauenplatz 10, 55116 MAINZ
Tel: 6131 2875525 **Fax:** 6131 2875522
Email: j-becher@kirchenzeitung.de **Web site:** http://www.kirchenzeitung.de
Freq: Weekly; **Annual Sub.:** EUR 73,20; **Circ:** 17,731
Editor: Johannes Becher; **Advertising Manager:** Sylvia Ehrengard
Profile: Catholic magazine.
Language(s): German
ADVERTISING RATES:
Full Page Mono .... EUR 3847
Mechanical Data: Type Area: 458 x 325 mm, No. of Columns (Display): 7, Col Widths (Display): 45 mm
Copy instructions: *Copy Date:* 14 days prior to publication
CONSUMER: RELIGIOUS

GLEICHHEIT. 728994G82-3280
Editorial: Postfach 040144, 10061 BERLIN
Tel: 30 30872440 **Fax:** 30 30872620
Email: info@gleichheit.de **Web site:** http://www.gleichheit.de
Freq: 5 issues yearly; **Annual Sub.:** EUR 17,50
Editor: Peter Schwarz
Profile: Magazine covering culture and Socialist politics.
Language(s): German
CONSUMER: CURRENT AFFAIRS & POLITICS

GLINDER ZEITUNG 728998G72-4660
Editorial: Beim Zeugamt 4, 21509 GLINDE
Tel: 40 71090820 **Fax:** 40 71090888
Email: info@glinder-zeitung.de **Web site:** http://www.glinder-zeitung.de
Freq: Weekly; **Cover Price:** Free; **Circ:** 41,100
Editor: Gabriele Hiersekorn; **Advertising Manager:** Roderich Körte
Profile: Advertising journal (house-to-house) concentrating on local stories.
Language(s): German
ADVERTISING RATES:
Full Page Mono .... EUR 3125
Full Page Colour .... EUR 4562
Mechanical Data: Type Area: 420 x 282 mm, No. of Columns (Display): 6, Col Widths (Display): 45 mm
Copy instructions: *Copy Date:* 4 days prior to publication
LOCAL NEWSPAPERS

DIE GLOCKE 729006G67B-6000
Editorial: Engelbert-Holterdorf-Str. 4, 59302 OELDE
Tel: 2522 730 **Fax:** 2522 73166
Email: redaktion@die-glocke.de **Web site:** http://www.die-glocke.de
Freq: 312 issues yearly; **Circ:** 56,687
Editor: Fried Gehring; **News Editor:** Ralf Ostermann; **Advertising Manager:** Hans-Georg Hippel
Profile: Regional daily newspaper covering politics, economics, sports, travel and technology. http://www.facebook.com/GlockeOnline Twitter: http://twitter.com/DieGlocke This Outlet offers RSS (Really Simple Syndication).
Language(s): German
ADVERTISING RATES:
SCC .... EUR 112,40
Mechanical Data: Type Area: 480 x 320 mm, No. of Columns (Display): 7, Col Widths (Display): 44 mm
Copy instructions: *Copy Date:* 1 day prior to publication
Supplement(s): prisma
REGIONAL DAILY & SUNDAY NEWSPAPERS: Regional Daily Newspapers

GLOSS 1824124G18B-2172
Editorial: Hanns-Seidel-Platz 5, 81737 MÜNCHEN
Tel: 89 64279743 **Fax:** 89 64279777
Email: schaeffel@journal-international.de **Web site:** http://www.journal-international.de
Freq: Quarterly; **Cover Price:** Free; **Circ:** 88,000
Editor: Anna Schäffel
Profile: Styling, emotion, trend-feeling - the Wella-magazine gloss is a "trendsetter", an innovative, emotional guiding medium where the past is not a client visit to the hairdresser. Each issue contains fascinating stories, features, interviews and advice about beauty and styling themes. So, the Wella magazine carried an attractive styling and trend-feeling about hairstyles, styling, beauty and lifestyle.
Language(s): German

GLOSS 1824124G18B-2251
Editorial: Hanns-Seidel-Platz 5, 81737 MÜNCHEN
Tel: 89 64279743 **Fax:** 89 64279777
Email: schaeffel@journal-international.de **Web site:** http://www.journal-international.de
Freq: Quarterly; **Cover Price:** Free; **Circ:** 88,000
Editor: Anna Schäffel
Profile: Styling, emotion, trend-feeling - the Wella-magazine gloss is a "trendsetter", an innovative, emotional guiding medium where the past is not a client visit to the hairdresser. Each issue contains fascinating stories, features, interviews and advice about beauty and styling themes. So, the Wella magazine carried an attractive styling and trend-feeling about hairstyles, styling, beauty and lifestyle.
Language(s): German

GLÜCK 729010G79F-10
Editorial: Weseler Str. 108, 48151 MÜNSTER
Tel: 251 70061181 **Fax:** 221 70061637
Email: glueckzeitung@westlotto.com **Web site:** http://www.westdeutsche-lotterie.de
Freq: Weekly; **Cover Price:** Free; **Circ:** 550,000
Editor: Siegfried Drach
Profile: Magazine focusing on the lottery.
Language(s): German
Readership: Read by people participating in the lottery.
CONSUMER: HOBBIES & DIY: Games & Puzzles

GLÜCKAUF 729012G58-640
Editorial: Montebruchstr. 2, 45219 ESSEN
Tel: 2054 924110 **Fax:** 2054 924119
Email: kg@vge.de **Web site:** http://www.vge.de
Freq: 8 issues yearly; **Annual Sub.:** EUR 243,00; **Circ:** 2,000
Editor: Karsten Gutberlet; **Advertising Manager:** Ute Perkovic
Profile: Technical scientific magazine on mining technology, equipment, planning, safety as well as processing and refinement of raw materials.
Language(s): English; German
ADVERTISING RATES:
Full Page Mono .... EUR 2215
Full Page Colour .... EUR 3265
Mechanical Data: Type Area: 269 x 182 mm
Copy instructions: *Copy Date:* 24 days prior to publication
Official Journal of: Organ d. DMT Dt. Montan Technologie f. Rohstoff, Energie, Umwelt e.V. u. d. Gesamtverb. Steinkohle e.V.

GLÜCKAUF MINING REPORTER 729016G30-2
Editorial: Montebruchstr. 2, 45219 ESSEN
Tel: 2054 924110 **Fax:** 2054 924119
Email: kg@vge.de **Web site:** http://www.mining-reporter.com
Freq: Half-yearly; **Cover Price:** Free; **Circ:** 3,000
Editor: Karsten Gutberlet; **Advertising Manager:** Ute Perkovic
Profile: Export journal focusing on mining equipment.
Language(s): English
ADVERTISING RATES:
Full Page Mono .... EUR 2425
Full Page Colour .... EUR 3475
Mechanical Data: Type Area: 269 x 182 mm
BUSINESS: MINING & QUARRYING

GLÜCKS REVUE 729022G79F-840
Editorial: Ruhrtalstr. 67, 45239 ESSEN
Tel: 201 246880 **Fax:** 201 24688100
Email: gluecksrevue@stegenwaller.de **Web site:** http://www.freizeitfreunde.de
Freq: Weekly; **Cover Price:** EUR 1,30; **Circ:** 135,889
Editor: Brigitta Heyer

Profile: Glücks Revue - the name says it all. For Glücks Revue is the popular puzzle and competition magazine with great prizes and lots of varied puzzles. Sun giving away the only Glücks Revue magazine in Germany every week a car. In addition to this huge bunch of good entertainment, the magazine still offers service at its best: comprehensive guide and inform health segments factual, fascinating travelogues invite you to dream, and attractive fashion decoration suggest that emotional reports tell of the midst of life. This successful mix not only provides a varied reading fun, would also guarantee a reliable everyday help. A successful mix also because it is associated with intensive use and high magazine editorial response.
Language(s): German
ADVERTISING RATES:
Full Page Mono .... EUR 5300
Full Page Colour .... EUR 5300
Mechanical Data: Type Area: 258 x 196 mm, No. of Columns (Display): 4, Col Widths (Display): 46 mm
Copy instructions: *Copy Date:* 21 days prior to publication
CONSUMER: HOBBIES & DIY: Games & Puzzles

GMBH CHEF. 1837441G14A-10160
Editorial: Rolandstr. 48, 53179 BONN
Tel: 228 951240 **Fax:** 228 9512490
Email: redaktion@gmbhchef.de **Web site:** http://www.gmbhchef.de
Freq: 6 issues yearly; **Annual Sub.:** EUR 27,00; **Circ:** 11,500
Editor: Hagen Prühs; **Advertising Manager:** Hans Stender
Profile: Ezine: Current information on taxes, law and economics for managing directors.
Language(s): German
ADVERTISING RATES:
Full Page Mono .... EUR 1650
Full Page Colour .... EUR 1650
Mechanical Data: Type Area: 245 x 176 mm
Copy instructions: *Copy Date:* 15 days prior to publication

GMBH CHEF. 1837442G14A-10161
Editorial: Rolandstr. 48, 53179 BONN
Tel: 228 951240 **Fax:** 228 9512490
Email: redaktion@gmbhchef.de **Web site:** http://www.gmbhchef.de
Freq: 6 issues yearly; **Annual Sub.:** EUR 24,00; **Circ:** 11,500
Editor: Hagen Prühs; **Advertising Manager:** Hans Stender
Profile: Magazine for GmbH managing director in companies in all industries.
Language(s): German
ADVERTISING RATES:
Full Page Mono .... EUR 1650
Full Page Colour .... EUR 1650
Mechanical Data: Type Area: 245 x 176 mm
Copy instructions: *Copy Date:* 15 days prior to publication

GMBHRUNDSCHAU 729032G44-1100
Editorial: Gustav-Heinemann-Ufer 58, 50968 KÖLN
Tel: 221 93738561 **Fax:** 221 93738952
Email: gmbhr@otto-schmidt.de **Web site:** http://www.gmbhr.de
Freq: 24 issues yearly; **Annual Sub.:** EUR 291,90; **Circ:** 6,440
Editor: Brigitta Peters; **Advertising Manager:** Thorsten Deuse
Profile: Review of limited companies.
Language(s): German
ADVERTISING RATES:
Full Page Mono .... EUR 1750
Full Page Colour .... EUR 3063
Mechanical Data: Type Area: 260 x 180 mm, No. of Columns (Display): 2, Col Widths (Display): 88 mm
BUSINESS: LEGAL

DER GMBH-STEUER-BERATER 729033G1A-1180
Editorial: Gustav-Heinemann-Ufer 58, 50968 KÖLN
Tel: 221 93738151 **Fax:** 221 93738902
Email: verlag@otto-schmidt.de **Web site:** http://www.gmbhstb.de
Freq: Monthly; **Annual Sub.:** EUR 156,90; **Circ:** 3,312
Editor: Annette Stuhldreier; **Advertising Manager:** Thorsten Deuse
Profile: Magazine for tax advisors of limited corporations.
Language(s): German
ADVERTISING RATES:
Full Page Mono .... EUR 1095
Full Page Colour .... EUR 1917
Mechanical Data: Type Area: 260 x 180 mm, No. of Columns (Display): 2, Col Widths (Display): 88 mm
BUSINESS: FINANCE & ECONOMICS

GMBH-STEUERPRAXIS 1654901G14A-9613
Editorial: Rolandstr. 48, 53179 BONN
Tel: 228 951240 **Fax:** 228 9512490
Email: vsrw@vsrw.de **Web site:** http://www.vsrw.de
Freq: Monthly; **Annual Sub.:** EUR 171,26; **Circ:** 5,500
Editor: Dietmar Zimmers; **Advertising Manager:** Eva Hilger
Profile: Magazine for managers, associates and advisors of limited companies.
Language(s): German
ADVERTISING RATES:
Full Page Mono .... EUR 1200
Full Page Colour .... EUR 1575
Mechanical Data: Type Area: 260 x 180 mm, No. of Columns (Display): 2
Supplement(s): Steuerzahler-Tip

GMÜNDER TAGESPOST 729039G67B-6020
Editorial: Vordere Schmiedgasse 18, 73525 SCHWÄBISCH GMÜND **Tel:** 7171 6001711
Fax: 7171 6001724
Email: redaktion@gmuender-tagespost.de **Web site:** http://www.gmuender-tagespost.de
Freq: 312 issues yearly; **Circ:** 10,370
Editor: Michael Länge; **Advertising Manager:** Falko Pütz
Profile: Daily newspaper with regional news and a local sports section. This Outlet offers RSS (Really Simple Syndication).
Language(s): German
ADVERTISING RATES:
SCC .... EUR 60,60
Mechanical Data: Type Area: 430 x 283 mm, No. of Columns (Display): 6, Col Widths (Display): 45 mm
Copy instructions: *Copy Date:* 1 day prior to publication
Supplement(s): Das Magazin
REGIONAL DAILY & SUNDAY NEWSPAPERS: Regional Daily Newspapers

GN GRAFSCHAFTER NACHRICHTEN 729044G67B-6040
Editorial: Coesfelder Hof 2, 48527 NORDHORN
Tel: 5921 707300 **Fax:** 5921 707350
Email: redaktion@gn-online.de **Web site:** http://www.gn-online.de
Freq: 312 issues yearly; **Circ:** 24,810
Editor: Guntram Dörr
Profile: About the area, in the newspaper readers and newspaper editors live, report in all its diversity every day, is the basis, presenting, explaining and clear up any issues that affect everyone's daily life will continue to gain in importance. The newspaper reports with care and a sense of what is happening in the county, in the surrounding region, in Lower Saxony, Germany and the world. Around the core, the local section with reports, commentaries and interviews, grouped in words and pictures the sporting and cultural events, politics and business, service and leisure.
Language(s): German
ADVERTISING RATES:
SCC .... EUR 59,10
Mechanical Data: Type Area: 487 x 318 mm, No. of Columns (Display): 7, Col Widths (Display): 43 mm
Copy instructions: *Copy Date:* 2 days prior to publication
Supplement(s): Szene Magazin
REGIONAL DAILY & SUNDAY NEWSPAPERS: Regional Daily Newspapers

GO! 729046G17-540
Editorial: Nägelsbachstr. 33, 91052 ERLANGEN
Tel: 9131 9192501 **Fax:** 9131 9192594
Email: publishing-magazines@publicis-erlangen.de
Web site: http://www.publicis-erlangen.de
Freq: Half-yearly; **Cover Price:** Free; **Circ:** 32,000
Editor: Robert Engelhardt
Profile: Journal about products and trends how to use them for electricians, fitters and engineers.
Language(s): German

GO GIRL 1647110G91D-10033
Editorial: Wallstr. 59, 10179 BERLIN **Tel:** 30 240080
Fax: 30 24008599
Email: s.saydo@ehapa.de **Web site:** http://www.gogirl-blog.de
Freq: Monthly; **Cover Price:** EUR 2,60; **Circ:** 25,481
Editor: Sanya Saydo
Profile: GO girl is the cool girl, sassy magazine for young girls aged 10 to 15 years. GO girl is best friend and big sister at the same time. The magazine is fun, but can also provide orientation and all that gossip about what is the best friend.
Language(s): German
ADVERTISING RATES:
Full Page Mono .... EUR 5900
Full Page Colour .... EUR 5900
Mechanical Data: Type Area: 280 x 210 mm, No. of Columns (Display): 4, Col Widths (Display): 52 mm
Copy instructions: *Copy Date:* 50 days prior to publication
CONSUMER: RECREATION & LEISURE: Children & Youth

GO GLOBAL BIZ 2080655G14A-10510
Editorial: Rheinallee 193, 55120 MAINZ
Tel: 6131 6277626 **Fax:** 6131 6277620
Email: langrock@goglobalbiz.de **Web site:** http://wwwgoglobalbiz.de
Freq: 6 issues yearly; **Annual Sub.:** EUR 20,00; **Circ:** 35,412
Editor: Ralph Langrock; **Advertising Manager:** christian Welc
Profile: GO GLOBAL BIZ is the independent magazine for travel and event manager. It helps planners and buyers of business travel and events with current trends, studies and benchmarks, product and price lists, information on tax and statutory regulations, particulars and further education. GO GLOBAL BIZ, together with its sister magazine bfp fuhrpark + management information base for mobility.
Language(s): German
ADVERTISING RATES:
Full Page Mono .... EUR 8000
Full Page Colour .... EUR 7800
Mechanical Data: Type Area: 272 x 188 mm, No. of Columns (Display): 4, Col Widths (Display): 44 mm
Copy instructions: *Copy Date:* 21 days prior to publication

GO LONGLIFE! 762823G74N-806
Editorial: Rudolf-Diesel-Str. 5, 86470 THANNHAUSEN **Tel:** 8281 799660
Fax: 8281 7996650
Email: golonglife@made.de **Web site:** http://www.golonglife.de
Freq: 6 issues yearly; **Annual Sub.:** EUR 18,30; **Circ:** 55,926
Editor: Eva Schmid-Baumeister; **Advertising Manager:** Elisabeth Greck
Profile: The lifestyle magazine for the elderly. With news, current trends and events, everything important about your health, how to live a long, happy life and how an optimal diet keeps your body fit and active. We also offer interesting travel tips and inform you about the latest being - trends. Likewise, news from the lifestyle, garden, home computer, finance and automobiles.
Language(s): German
ADVERTISING RATES:
Full Page Mono .... EUR 9108
Full Page Colour .... EUR 10120
Mechanical Data: Type Area: 240 x 175 mm, No. of Columns (Display): 2, Col Widths (Display): 85 mm
Copy instructions: *Copy Date:* 28 days prior to publication

GO LONGLIFE! 1926827G74N-993
Editorial: Rudolf-Diesel-Str. 5, 86470 THANNHAUSEN **Tel:** 8281 799660
Fax: 8281 7996650
Email: hans.georg.schmid@golonglife.de **Web site:** http://www.golonglife.de
Circ: 256,000
Editor: Hans Georg Schmid; **Advertising Manager:** Elisabeth Greck
Profile: Ezine: Magazine for the elderly containing information on health, nutrition, fitness, wellness, travelling, beauty, lifestyle, computing, insurance and finances.
Language(s): German

GOINGPUBLIC 729075G1F-820
Editorial: Hofmannstr. 7a, 81379 MÜNCHEN
Tel: 89 200033910 **Fax:** 89 200033933
Email: fb@goingpublic.de **Web site:** http://www.goingpublic.de
Freq: 11 issues yearly; **Annual Sub.:** EUR 58,20; **Circ:** 3,800
Editor: Falko Bozicevic; **Advertising Manager:** Johanna Wagner
Profile: Journal focusing on IPO market, contains profiles of new IPOs, reports of recently completed IPOs, profiles and interviews.
Language(s): German
Readership: Read by IPO professionals, institutional and sophisticated private investors.
ADVERTISING RATES:
Full Page Mono .... EUR 2900
Full Page Colour .... EUR 2900
Mechanical Data: Type Area: 246 x 164 mm, No. of Columns (Display): 2, Col Widths (Display): 80 mm
Copy instructions: *Copy Date:* 12 days prior to publication
BUSINESS: FINANCE & ECONOMICS: Investment

DAS GOLDENE BLATT 729081G74A-1380
Editorial: Münchener Str. 101/09, 85737 ISMANING
Tel: 89 272703337 **Fax:** 89 272703390
Email: dasgoldeneblatt@waz-zeitschriften.de
Freq: Weekly; **Cover Price:** EUR 1,50; **Circ:** 231,459
Editor: Claudia Groß-Alioui; **Advertising Manager:** Benita Ahsendorf
Profile: Optimistic, positive, really: the exciting reports from the world of the nobility and the stars, reports, interviews and photos in the leaf are always authentic, exclusive and emotional. Compelling Guide pages, a competent medical professional part, recipes to cook for collecting cards, travel reports and draw a lot of puzzles in the title.
Language(s): German
ADVERTISING RATES:
Full Page Mono .... EUR 6070
Full Page Colour .... EUR 6070
Mechanical Data: Type Area: 260 x 195 mm, No. of Columns (Display): 4, Col Widths (Display): 45 mm
Copy instructions: *Copy Date:* 30 days prior to publication
CONSUMER: WOMEN'S INTEREST CONSUMER MAGAZINES: Women's Interest

GOLF AKTUELL 729113G75D-60
Editorial: Konrad-Zuse-Platz 10, 81829 MÜNCHEN
Tel: 89 5468540 **Fax:** 89 5804439
Email: redaktion@golfaktuell.com **Web site:** http://www.golfaktuell.com
Freq: 6 issues yearly; **Annual Sub.:** EUR 18,00; **Circ:** 71,200
Editor: Fred König; **Advertising Manager:** Markus Graf von Bentzel-Sternau
Profile: GOLFaktuell currently covers topics relevant to the attractive target group of active and potential golfers and their standard of living of interest: News from the world of golf, from major international events including regional tournaments, plus Background reports and profiles of top players and news from the areas of hardware and equipment, and training tips. Reports of attractive destinations: from traditional golf destinations to tips in near and far, to fine hotels and restaurants. Lifestyle trends in fashion, art, accessories and jewelry, plus financial tips, art sites and book presentations. Comprehensive health and wellness tips for the golfer. Extensive testing in the car heading golf mobile. The main focus is on the subject equipment (25%), scene (20%), travel (20%) and lifestyle (15%).
Language(s): German
ADVERTISING RATES:
Full Page Mono .... EUR 560
Full Page Colour .... EUR 730
Mechanical Data: Type Area: 284 x 210 mm, No. of Columns (Display): 3, Col Widths (Display): 67 mm
Copy instructions: *Copy Date:* 23 days prior to publication
CONSUMER: SPORT: Golf

GOLF GENUSS 1753097LI75D-
Editorial: Steinstr. 44, 81667 MÜNCHEN
Tel: 89 99548460 **Fax:** 89 99548466
Email: golf@clef.de **Web site:** http://www.golf-genuss.de
Freq: Quarterly; **Cover Price:** EUR 5,80; **Circ:** 30,500
Editor: Ulrich Clef; **Advertising Manager:** Ulrich Clef
Profile: golfgenuss is the successful Special-Interest Medium for golfers in the German speaking countries The idea behind this innovative magazine is to provide a medium for all golfers interested in the sport with the personal focus on pleasure, enjoyment and lifestyle of this wonderful game. The magazine is not only targeting golf in terms of sport, but provides the readers information, reports and illustrated stories about the pleasure, the relaxation and entertainment golf brings along. golfgenuss readers are educated, have abo- ve average disposable incomes, feature a distinct consumer behaviour and can usually be found in high-end positions, when it comes to their occupation. These high-end readers provide a large number of opinion leaders and deciders. golfgenuss provides competence, high quality reports with premium class pictures, especially about the most beautiful and fascinating destinations for golfers. The magazine reports competent, informative, entertaining, emotional but certainly serious about topics, events and results from all around and about the golf-globe. Tips and trends of the golf market, behind the scenes reports, as well as articles about innovations, equipment, newest fashion trends, exclusive interviews and much more are the top stories of golfgenuss. The magazine provides the most crucial information for readers for their buying decisions, when it comes to new equipment, accessories and golf vacations. Modern, up-to-date and highest quality in terms of editing, photographs and printing is a must for golfgenuss. The print run fo Germany, Austria and Switzerland is 30.500 units per edition by four editions per year. Companies benefit from this high end magazine through its quality, the reliability in planning and by its stable communication platform, that reaches premium readers most efficiently and most effective. Every golfgenuss edition provides an exclusive supplement for a specific target group: ladygolf, golfvital, younggolf and golflernen.
Language(s): German
ADVERTISING RATES:
Full Page Mono .... EUR 5950
Full Page Colour .... EUR 590
Mechanical Data: Type Area: 264 x 194 mm
CONSUMER: SPORT: Golf

GOLF IN BERLIN UND BRANDENBURG 729120G75D-120
Editorial: Forststr. 34, 12163 BERLIN
Tel: 30 8236502 **Fax:** 30 8234098
Email: info@golf-masters.de **Web site:** http://www.golf-masters.de
Freq: 9 issues yearly; **Annual Sub.:** EUR 27,00; **Circ:** 9,000
Editor: Roderich Wegener-Wenzel; **Advertising Manager:** Roderich Wegener-Wenzel
Profile: Magazine about playing golf in Berlin and Brandenburg.
Language(s): German
ADVERTISING RATES:
Full Page Mono .... EUR 1044
Full Page Colour .... EUR 1878
Mechanical Data: Type Area: 274 x 182 mm
Copy instructions: *Copy Date:* 22 days prior to publication
Official Journal of: Organ d. Landesgolfverb. Bln. Brandenburg
CONSUMER: SPORT: Golf

GOLF IN HAMBURG 729121G75D-140
Editorial: Mattentwiete 5, 20457 HAMBURG
Tel: 40 3698040 **Fax:** 40 36980460
Email: info@lachschulz.de **Web site:** http://www.lachschulz.de
Freq: 6 issues yearly; **Circ:** 12,931
Editor: Erhard Heine; **Advertising Manager:** Michael Witte
Profile: Magazine containing tips, trends, details of tournaments, golfing news and reports.
Language(s): German
Readership: Read by members of the Hamburg Golf Association.
ADVERTISING RATES:
Full Page Mono .... EUR 2140

Full Page Colour .... EUR 2440
Mechanical Data: Type Area: 265 x 190 mm, No. of Columns (Display): 3, Col Widths (Display): 60 mm
CONSUMER: SPORT: Golf

GOLF JOURNAL 729123G75D-180

Editorial: Brienner Str. 41, 80333 MÜNCHEN
Tel: 89 552410 **Fax:** 89 55241121
Email: info@golfjournal.de **Web site:** http://www.golf.de/journal
Freq: Monthly; **Annual Sub.:** EUR 52,80; **Circ:** 37,398
Editor: Stefan Engert; **Advertising Manager:** Benedikt Aidelsburger
Profile: With reports from around the world, appealing image and stretch many utility issues shows the GOLF JOURNAL All the fascination of sport and accompanied the golfers competent counselor. The journalistic quality documents in the high proportion of own productions, carefully researched background stories and columns from renowned Authors. This high-quality blend of sports, travel and life style, which finds the Web at golfjournal.de continued, GOLF JOURNAL makes unique and one of the leading Golf magazines in Germany. The opinion-leader of the brand shows GOLF JOURNAL further by organizing one of the largest Amateur golf tournament series, "MLP GOLF JOURNAL Trophy, " which throughout Germany in over 35 golf clubs.
Language(s): German
ADVERTISING RATES:
Full Page Mono .... EUR 5400
Full Page Colour .... EUR 8850
Mechanical Data: Type Area: 260 x 190 mm, No. of Columns (Display): 4, Col Widths (Display): 42 mm
CONSUMER: SPORT: Golf

GOLF MANAGER 729126G32H-100

Editorial: Ernst-Robert-Curtius-Str. 14, 53117 BONN
Tel: 228 9898223 **Fax:** 228 9898299
Email: redaktion@koellen.de **Web site:** http://www.koellen.de
Freq: 6 issues yearly; Free to qualifying individuals
Annual Sub.: EUR 60,00; **Circ:** 4,200
Editor: Franz Josef Ungerechts; **Advertising Manager:** Monika Tischler-Möbius
Profile: Official Magazine of the German Golf-Management Association.
Language(s): German
Readership: Read by managers of golf clubs.
ADVERTISING RATES:
Full Page Mono .... EUR 2300
Full Page Colour .... EUR 2300
Mechanical Data: Type Area: 260 x 178 mm, No. of Columns (Display): 4, Col Widths (Display): 41 mm
Copy instructions: *Copy Date:* 20 days prior to publication
Official Journal of: Organ d. GMVD e.V. u. d. BVGA e.V.
BUSINESS: LOCAL GOVERNMENT, LEISURE & RECREATION: Leisure, Recreation & Entertainment

GOLF TIME 729129G75D-20

Editorial: Oskar-von-Miller-Str. 11, 82008 UNTERHACHING **Tel:** 89 42718181
Fax: 89 42718171
Email: redaktion@golftime.de **Web site:** http://www.golftime.de
Freq: 8 issues yearly; **Annual Sub.:** EUR 32,50; **Circ:** 63,632
Editor: Oskar Brunnthaler; **Advertising Manager:** Evelyn Grund
Profile: Objective sports journalism supplemented by reports about golf, lifestyle, travel, fitness and wellness. Comprehensive and expert information for golfers and golf enthusiasts on the latest golf news and events of today. Professional golf at the national and international level. Comprehensive and expert information for golfers and golf enthusiasts on the latest golf news and events of today. Professional golf at the national and international level.
Language(s): German
ADVERTISING RATES:
Full Page Mono .... EUR 10000
Full Page Colour .... EUR 10000
Mechanical Data: Type Area: 238 x 199 mm, No. of Columns (Display): 4, Col Widths (Display): 44 mm
Copy instructions: *Copy Date:* 30 days prior to publication
CONSUMER: SPORT: Golf

GOLFMAGAZIN 729124G75D-200

Editorial: Troplowitzstr. 5, 22529 HAMBURG
Tel: 40 38906230 **Fax:** 40 38906304
Email: dieter.genske@golfmagazin.de **Web site:** http://www.golfmagazin.de
Freq: Monthly; **Annual Sub.:** EUR 64,80; **Circ:** 45,706
Editor: Dieter Genske; **Advertising Manager:** Wolfgang Vogler
Profile: The Golfmagazin, one of the most widely read golf magazines in Germany reported to date and detailed information on all the major events in the Gulf. Brilliant photographs and exciting reports reflect the fascinating atmosphere. Golfmagazin conducts independent club testing, shows new trends in the equipment sector on, reports independently and objectively about German courses, visits the big stars of the Gulf, says the most beautiful destinations near and far and the successful tips and tricks of the best players in the world. Even beginners found an adequate forum for their hobby.
Language(s): German
Readership: Read by golfing enthusiasts.
ADVERTISING RATES:
Full Page Mono .... EUR 5514
Full Page Colour .... EUR 8970
Mechanical Data: Type Area: 248 x 185 mm, No. of Columns (Display): 4, Col Widths (Display): 45 mm
Copy instructions: *Copy Date:* 27 days prior to publication
CONSUMER: SPORT: Golf

GOLIVING.DE IN BERLIN

2100881G74N-1034
Editorial: Zweibrückenstr. 1, 80331 MÜNCHEN
Tel: 89 80038063
Email: info@goliving.de **Web site:** http://www.goliving.de
Cover Price: Free; **Circ:** 34,500
Editor: Ursula Kronenberger; **Advertising Manager:** Sabine Krämer
Profile: Magazine for individuals they in the second half of life to keep their good taste. They are interested in culture, design, quality finishes, types of housing in the second half of life, barrier-free homes, lifestyle, sports, travel, health.
Language(s): German
ADVERTISING RATES:
Full Page Mono .... EUR 2760
Full Page Colour .... EUR 2760
Mechanical Data: Type Area: 280 x 215 mm
Copy instructions: *Copy Date:* 4 days prior to publication

GOLIVING.DE IN HAMBURG

2100882G74N-1035
Editorial: Zweibrückenstr. 1, 80331 MÜNCHEN
Tel: 89 80038063
Email: info@goliving.de **Web site:** http://www.goliving.de
Cover Price: Free; **Circ:** 34,500
Editor: Ursula Kronenberger; **Advertising Manager:** Sabine Krämer
Profile: Magazine for individuals they in the second half of life to keep their good taste. They are interested in culture, design, quality finishes, types of housing in the second half of life, barrier-free homes, lifestyle, sports, travel, health.
Language(s): German
ADVERTISING RATES:
Full Page Mono .... EUR 2760
Full Page Colour .... EUR 2760
Mechanical Data: Type Area: 280 x 215 mm
Copy instructions: *Copy Date:* 4 days prior to publication

GOLIVING.DE IN KÖLN/BONN

2065533G74N-1031
Editorial: Zweibrückenstr. 1, 80331 MÜNCHEN
Tel: 89 80038063
Email: info@goliving.de **Web site:** http://www.goliving.de
Cover Price: Free; **Circ:** 34,500
Editor: Ursula Kronenberger; **Advertising Manager:** Sabine Krämer
Profile: Magazine for individuals they in the second half of life to keep their good taste. They are interested in culture, design, quality finishes, types of housing in the second half of life, barrier-free homes, lifestyle, sports, travel, health.
Language(s): German
ADVERTISING RATES:
Full Page Mono .... EUR 2760
Full Page Colour .... EUR 2760
Mechanical Data: Type Area: 280 x 215 mm
Copy instructions: *Copy Date:* 4 days prior to publication

GOLIVING.DE IN MÜNCHEN

2100883G74N-1036
Editorial: Zweibrückenstr. 1, 80331 MÜNCHEN
Tel: 89 80038063
Email: info@goliving.de **Web site:** http://www.goliving.de
Cover Price: Free; **Circ:** 34,500
Editor: Ursula Kronenberger; **Advertising Manager:** Sabine Krämer
Profile: Magazine for individuals they in the second half of life to keep their good taste. They are interested in culture, design, quality finishes, types of housing in the second half of life, barrier-free homes, lifestyle, sports, travel, health.
Language(s): German
ADVERTISING RATES:
Full Page Mono .... EUR 2760
Full Page Colour .... EUR 2760
Mechanical Data: Type Area: 280 x 215 mm
Copy instructions: *Copy Date:* 4 days prior to publication

GÖRLITZER WOCHENKURIER

729060G72-4712
Editorial: Wettiner Platz 10, 01067 DRESDEN
Tel: 351 491760 **Fax:** 351 4917674
Email: wochenkurier-dresden@dwk-verlag.de **Web site:** http://www.wochenkurier.info
Freq: Weekly; **Cover Price:** Free; **Circ:** 37,527
Editor: Regine Eberlein; **Advertising Manager:** Andreas Schönherr
Profile: Advertising journal (house-to-house) concentrating on local stories.
Language(s): German
ADVERTISING RATES:
Full Page Mono .... EUR 3161
Full Page Colour .... EUR 4425
Mechanical Data: Type Area: 430 x 290 mm, No. of Columns (Display): 7, Col Widths (Display): 38 mm
Copy instructions: *Copy Date:* 5 days prior to publication
LOCAL NEWSPAPERS

GOSLARSCHE ZEITUNG

729147G67B-6060
Editorial: Bäckerstr. 31, 38640 GOSLAR
Tel: 5321 333222 **Fax:** 5321 333299
Email: redaktion@goslarsche-zeitung.de **Web site:** http://www.goslarsche.de
Freq: 312 issues yearly; **Circ:** 26,148
Editor: Andreas Rietschel; **Advertising Manager:** Gerd Niehus
Profile: Regional daily newspaper with news on politics, economy, culture, sports, travel, technology, etc. Nearly 80,000 readers a day to give the information and advertising medium No. 1 in the district of Goslar, trust and attention. This is the reward for continuity, timeliness, independence and impartiality of the elftältesten daily newspaper in Germany - founded 1783rd Twitter: http://twitter.com/goslarsche This Outlet offers RSS (Really Simple Syndication).
Language(s): German
ADVERTISING RATES:
SCC .... EUR 84,30
Mechanical Data: Type Area: 435 x 283 mm, No. of Columns (Display): 6, Col Widths (Display): 45 mm
Copy instructions: *Copy Date:* 1 day prior to publication
Supplement(s): prisma
REGIONAL DAILY & SUNDAY NEWSPAPERS: Regional Daily Newspapers

GOSLARSCHE.DE 1621403G67B-16564

Editorial: Bäckerstr. 31, 38640 GOSLAR
Tel: 5321 333300 **Fax:** 5321 333309
Email: lars.grollmisch@goslarsche-zeitung.de **Web site:** http://www.goslarsche.de
Freq: Daily; **Cover Price:** Paid; **Circ:** 287,142 Unique Users
Editor: Lars Grollmisch; **Advertising Manager:** Lars Grollmisch
Profile: Ezine: Web news magazine of Goslarschen Zeitung with daily news from the Harz and from around the world. You will find daily updated news from the resin and from around the world, a great service as part event with tips and links, important information about professionals in the Harz and an easily searchable display market. Twitter: http://twitter.com/#!/goslarsche This Outlet offers RSS (Really Simple Syndication).
Language(s): German
REGIONAL DAILY & SUNDAY NEWSPAPERS: Regional Daily Newspapers

GÖTTINGER TAGEBLATT

729070G67B-6080
Editorial: Dransfelder Str. 1, 37079 GÖTTINGEN
Tel: 551 901766 **Fax:** 551 901760
Email: redaktion@goettinger-tageblatt.de **Web site:** http://www.goettinger-tageblatt.de
Freq: 312 issues yearly; **Circ:** 40,556
Editor: Ilse Stein; **News Editor:** Markus Scharf; **Advertising Manager:** Jens Kreye
Profile: Regional daily newspaper with news on politics, economy, culture, sports, travel, technology, etc. The Göttinger Tageblatt reports daily from all over the world, informed about politics, economy, culture and sports. Above all, the Göttinger Tageblatt deals with topics from the region. The daily newspaper, the contents of more than 30 editors and many freelance writers will create, the many readers needs to be justified by well-researched and interesting contributions. "We're up to date and intensive background reporting, " says editor in chief Ilse Stein the demands of the newspaper, the six times weekly has a circulation of 43 000. Apart from the recent news from the city and county, business and politics, culture, higher education and sports, can be found in the daily newspaper, a daily science page, weekly children's and health pages, special pages about computer news as well as excursions and holiday tips. Also published the Göttinger Tageblatt local shows and special publications on the villages of the district, the regional business potential or reported rates for students. Podcasts, local video on current issues and supervised by the editors "Wiki Göttingen" are also available in the online environment and emphasize in this way the cross-media alignment of a modern newspaper. Facebook: http://www.facebook.com/goettingertageblatt This Outlet offers RSS (Really Simple Syndication).
Language(s): German
ADVERTISING RATES:
SCC .... EUR 100,80
Mechanical Data: Type Area: 430 x 277 mm, No. of Columns (Display): 6, Col Widths (Display): 45 mm
Copy instructions: *Copy Date:* 1 day prior to publication
Supplement(s): Bauen & Wohnen
REGIONAL DAILY & SUNDAY NEWSPAPERS: Regional Daily Newspapers

GOURMET KOMPASS

1696543G89A-12169
Editorial: Emil-Hoffmann-Str. 55, 50999 KÖLN
Tel: 2236 848813 **Fax:** 2236 848824
Email: jl@ella-verlag.de **Web site:** http://www.reisenexclusiv.com
Freq: Annual; **Cover Price:** EUR 5,50; **Circ:** 55,500
Editor: Jennifer Latuperisa; **Advertising Manager:** Susanne Gorny
Profile: Special issue of reisen Exclusiv, combines stylishly on travel topics food and drink for pleasure-loving and demanding readership. Specialties from distant countries and the best destinations complete the rally this Gourmet magazine.
Language(s): German
ADVERTISING RATES:
Full Page Colour .... EUR 5190
Mechanical Data: Type Area: 240 x 175 mm
Copy instructions: *Copy Date:* 30 days prior to publication

GP GESTEINS-PERSPEKTIVEN

732591G4E-5000
Editorial: Josef-Herrmann-Str. 1, 76473 IFFEZHEIM
Tel: 7229 6060 **Fax:** 7229 60610
Email: redaktion@stein-verlaggmbh.de **Web site:** http://www.stein-verlaggmbh.de
Freq: 8 issues yearly; **Annual Sub.:** EUR 48,00; **Circ:** 7,000
Editor: Friedhelm Rese
Profile: Building business magazine.
Language(s): German
ADVERTISING RATES:
Full Page Mono .... EUR 1765
Full Page Colour .... EUR 2640
Mechanical Data: Type Area: 255 x 175 mm, No. of Columns (Display): 3, Col Widths (Display): 55 mm
Copy instructions: *Copy Date:* 14 days prior to publication
Official Journal of: Organ d. Bundesverb. d. Dt. Kies- u. Sandindustrie, d. Bundesverb. Mineral. Rohstoffe u. ihrer Landesverbände

GPS SOLUTIONS 1638673G5E-22

Editorial: Tiergartenstr. 17, 69121 HEIDELBERG
Tel: 6221 4870 **Fax:** 6221 4878177
Email: subscription@springer.com **Web site:** http://www.springerlink.com
Freq: Quarterly; **Annual Sub.:** EUR 451,00; **Circ:** 157
Editor: Alfred Leick
Profile: GPS magazine.
Language(s): English
ADVERTISING RATES:
Full Page Mono .... EUR 740
Full Page Colour .... EUR 1780
Mechanical Data: Type Area: 240 x 175 mm

GQ 729163G86C-80

Editorial: Karlstr. 23, 80333 MÜNCHEN
Tel: 89 381040 **Fax:** 89 38104260
Email: gqpost@gqnet.de **Web site:** http://www.gq.com
Freq: Monthly; **Annual Sub.:** EUR 51,00; **Circ:** 142,871
Editor: José Redondo-Vega; **Advertising Manager:** Anja Grewe
Profile: Lifestyle men's magazine. GQ lifestyle for men who are entitled. With intellect, charm, journalistic expertise, a definite attitude and always stylish GQ through the male worlds - from business to relationships, from fashion to mobility. The ministries and issues of GQ are as varied as the lives of its sophisticated and cosmopolitan readers. GQ informed, operates at a high level, inspired amused, discovers trends, advice, and opens new perspectives. Opulent photo galleries, exclusive interviews with people who make the world a gentlemen and a strong opinion columns make the only GQ magazine in Germany, are for men more than the sum of their stereotypes. Facebook: http://www.facebook.com/gqmagazin.de.
Language(s): German
Readership: Aimed at men.
ADVERTISING RATES:
Full Page Mono .... EUR 19200
Full Page Colour .... EUR 19200
Mechanical Data: Type Area: 251 x 183 mm, No. of Columns (Display): 4, Col Widths (Display): 40 mm
Copy instructions: *Copy Date:* 31 days prior to publication
Supplement(s): GQ Care; GQ Uhren
CONSUMER: ADULT & GAY MAGAZINES: Men's Lifestyle Magazines

GQ CARE 2078845G86C-258

Editorial: Karlstr. 23, 80333 MÜNCHEN
Tel: 89 381040 **Fax:** 89 38104260
Email: gqpost@gqnet.de **Web site:** http://www.gq.com
Freq: Annual; **Circ:** 206,412
Editor: José Redondo-Vega; **Advertising Manager:** Anja Grewe
Profile: GQ Care - Extra Beauty Supplement of GQ - published annually by GQ May issue and offers a panoramic advice for the care-conscious men, no matter whether it is the right scent is, the right hair styling, dental care and also about what beard what type of guy fits. At a high level of journalistic GQ Care takes in interviews, essays and expensive photo shoots the modern man and his beauty Idea under the microscope. The four departments Face, Hair, Body and scent, which are very entertaining and informative Leitlektüre for body-conscious men. GQ Care is a demanding complete guide to theme and provides care for the GQ reader guidance and inspiration on issues such as how much care is necessary? or How much care should be?. Facebook: http://www.facebook.com/gqmagazin.de.
Language(s): German
ADVERTISING RATES:
Full Page Mono .... EUR 19200
Full Page Colour .... EUR 19200
Mechanical Data: Type Area: 251 x 183 mm, No. of Columns (Display): 4, Col Widths (Display): 40 mm

Copy instructions: *Copy Date:* 31 days prior to publication
Supplement to: GQ

GQ STYLE 1638937G86C-215
Editorial: Karlstr. 23, 80333 MÜNCHEN
Tel: 89 381040 **Fax:** 89 38104260
Email: gqpost@gqnet.de **Web site:** http://www.gq.com
Freq: Half-yearly; **Cover Price:** EUR 6,80; **Circ:** 90,000
Editor: José Redondo-Vega; **Advertising Manager:** Christina Linder
Profile: GQ style is the leading fashion magazine for men. With a comprehensive editorial topics offer the latest fashion trends, accessories and must-haves of the season will be staged and implemented. GQ style it has reached a quality and significance that goes far beyond Germany and enjoys international recognition. GQ style appears twice a year as a fashion special issue of GQ. At about 350 pages of current trends and collections are shown for the man: the key designers, the new looks, the news from the catwalks of Paris, Milan and New York and in general everything that is important in terms of men's fashion and fashionable. Facebook: http://www.facebook.com/gqmagazin.de.
Language(s): German
ADVERTISING RATES:
Full Page Mono .... EUR 14100
Full Page Colour .... EUR 14100
Mechanical Data: Type Area: 258 x 196 mm, No. of Columns (Display): 2, Col Widths (Display): 95 mm

---

GQ STYLE 1638937G86C-236
Editorial: Karlstr. 23, 80333 MÜNCHEN
Tel: 89 381040 **Fax:** 89 38104260
Email: gqpost@gqnet.de **Web site:** http://www.gq.com
Freq: Half-yearly; **Cover Price:** EUR 6,80; **Circ:** 90,000
Editor: José Redondo-Vega; **Advertising Manager:** Christina Linder
Profile: GQ style is the leading fashion magazine for men. With a comprehensive editorial topics offer the latest fashion trends, accessories and must-haves of the season will be staged and implemented. GQ style it has reached a quality and significance that goes far beyond Germany and enjoys international recognition. GQ style appears twice a year as a fashion special issue of GQ. At about 350 pages of current trends and collections are shown for the man: the key designers, the new looks, the news from the catwalks of Paris, Milan and New York and in general everything that is important in terms of men's fashion and fashionable. Facebook: http://www.facebook.com/gqmagazin.de.
Language(s): German
ADVERTISING RATES:
Full Page Mono .... EUR 14100
Full Page Colour .... EUR 14100
Mechanical Data: Type Area: 258 x 196 mm, No. of Columns (Display): 2, Col Widths (Display): 95 mm

---

GQ UHREN 2078846G86C-259
Editorial: Karlstr. 23, 80333 MÜNCHEN
Tel: 89 381040 **Fax:** 89 38104260
Email: gqpost@gqnet.de **Web site:** http://www.gq.com
Freq: Annual; **Circ:** 206,412
Editor: José Redondo-Vega; **Advertising Manager:** Anja Grewe
Profile: GQ Uhren magazine has stood for years expertise in the watch segment and offers the ideal combination of optical quality and long-term experience. The magazine reports on some 150 pages about the most important accessory of the man who shows the interesting innovations of the year and the most beautiful fashion models and provides interesting background information and portraits. The photo galleries are by the editors with experience and attention to detail directed, wrote the lyrics of renowned watches journalists. In addition, a watch dealer guide with the most important addresses of specialist dealers from Germany, Austria and Switzerland, the GQ readers a service. The magazine is the guide for watch connoisseurs and those who want to become an important decision and thus help in buying. Facebook: http://www.facebook.com/gqmagazin.de.
Language(s): German
ADVERTISING RATES:
Full Page Mono .... EUR 19200
Full Page Colour .... EUR 19200
Mechanical Data: Type Area: 251 x 183 mm, No. of Columns (Display): 4, Col Widths (Display): 40 mm
Copy instructions: *Copy Date:* 31 days prior to publication
Supplement to: GQ

GRAEFE'S ARCHIVE FOR CLINICAL AND EXPERIMENTAL OPHTHALMOLOGY 729168G56A-4220
Editorial: Tiergartenstr. 17, 69121 HEIDELBERG
Tel: 6221 4870 **Fax:** 6221 4878366
Email: subscriptions@springer.com **Web site:** http://www.springerlink.com
Freq: Monthly; **Annual Sub.:** EUR 2401,00; **Circ:** 848
Editor: B. Kirchhof
Profile: Archive for clinical and experimental ophthalmology.
Language(s): English
ADVERTISING RATES:
Full Page Mono .... EUR 920
Full Page Colour .... EUR 1960
Mechanical Data: Type Area: 240 x 175 mm
Official Journal of: Organ d. Clubs Jules Krieglstein

GRAFENAUER ANZEIGER 729170G67B-6100
Editorial: Medienstr. 5, 94036 PASSAU
Tel: 851 8020 **Fax:** 851 802256
Email: pnp@vgp.de **Web site:** http://www.pnp.de
Freq: 312 issues yearly; **Circ:** 15,056
Advertising Manager: Gerhard Koller
Profile: Daily newspaper with regional news and a local sports section. Twitter: http://twitter.com/pnp_online This Outlet offers RSS (Really Simple Syndication).
Language(s): German
ADVERTISING RATES:
SCC .... EUR 43,00
Mechanical Data: Type Area: 482 x 325 mm, No. of Columns (Display): 7, Col Widths (Display): 45 mm
Copy instructions: *Copy Date:* 2 days prior to publication
REGIONAL DAILY & SUNDAY NEWSPAPERS: Regional Daily Newspapers

---

GRAFISCHE PALETTE - AUSG. BADEN-WÜRTTEMBERG 1656896G41A-2169
Editorial: Riedstr. 25, 73760 OSTFILDERN
Tel: 711 4481727 **Fax:** 711 442099
Email: m.schuele@print.de **Web site:** http://www.print.de
Freq: Quarterly; **Cover Price:** Free; **Circ:** 3,008
Profile: Magazine with the highest total circulation within the printing and media industry. The target group are all small and medium enterprises in the graphics industry, including the printing house. Editorial topics include the sheetfed offset and digital printing production areas. Divided the magazine is published four times a year in a total of six regional and parts.
Language(s): German
ADVERTISING RATES:
Full Page Mono .... EUR 1850
Full Page Colour .... EUR 1850
Mechanical Data: Type Area: 202 x 145 mm, No. of Columns (Display): 3, Col Widths (Display): 45 mm
Copy instructions: *Copy Date:* 30 days prior to publication
BUSINESS: PRINTING & STATIONERY: Printing

GRAFISCHE PALETTE - AUSG. BAYERN 1656893G41A-2166
Editorial: Riedstr. 25, 73760 OSTFILDERN
Tel: 711 4481727 **Fax:** 711 442099
Email: m.schuele@print.de **Web site:** http://www.print.de
Freq: Quarterly; **Cover Price:** Free; **Circ:** 3,396
Profile: Magazine with the highest total circulation within the printing and media industry. The target group are all small and medium enterprises in the graphics industry, including the printing house. Editorial topics include the sheetfed offset and digital printing production areas. Divided the magazine is published four times a year in a total of six regional and parts.
Language(s): German
ADVERTISING RATES:
Full Page Mono .... EUR 1850
Full Page Colour .... EUR 1850
Mechanical Data: Type Area: 205 x 145 mm, No. of Columns (Display): 3, Col Widths (Display): 45 mm
Copy instructions: *Copy Date:* 30 days prior to publication
BUSINESS: PRINTING & STATIONERY: Printing

GRAFISCHE PALETTE - AUSG. NORD 1656892G41A-2165
Editorial: Riedstr. 25, 73760 OSTFILDERN
Tel: 711 4481727 **Fax:** 711 442099
Email: m.schuele@print.de **Web site:** http://www.print.de
Freq: Quarterly; **Cover Price:** Free; **Circ:** 3,275
Profile: Magazine with the highest total circulation within the printing and media industry. The target group are all small and medium enterprises in the graphics industry, including the printing house. Editorial topics include the sheetfed offset and digital printing production areas. Divided the magazine is published four times a year in a total of six regional and parts.
Language(s): German
ADVERTISING RATES:
Full Page Mono .... EUR 1850
Full Page Colour .... EUR 1850
Mechanical Data: Type Area: 205 x 145 mm, No. of Columns (Display): 3, Col Widths (Display): 45 mm
Copy instructions: *Copy Date:* 30 days prior to publication
BUSINESS: PRINTING & STATIONERY: Printing

GRAFISCHE PALETTE - AUSG. NORDRHEIN-WESTFALEN 1656891G41A-2164
Editorial: Riedstr. 25, 73760 OSTFILDERN
Tel: 711 4481727 **Fax:** 711 442099
Email: m.schuele@print.de **Web site:** http://www.print.de
Freq: Quarterly; **Cover Price:** Free; **Circ:** 4,594
Profile: Magazine with the highest total circulation within the printing and media industry. The target group are all small and medium enterprises in the graphics industry, including the printing house. Editorial topics include the sheetfed offset and digital printing production areas. Divided the magazine is published four times a year in a total of six regional and parts.
Language(s): German
ADVERTISING RATES:
Full Page Mono .... EUR 1850
Full Page Colour .... EUR 1850
Mechanical Data: Type Area: 205 x 145 mm, No. of Columns (Display): 3, Col Widths (Display): 45 mm
Copy instructions: *Copy Date:* 30 days prior to publication
BUSINESS: PRINTING & STATIONERY: Printing

GRAFISCHE PALETTE - AUSG. OST 1656895G41A-2168
Editorial: Riedstr. 25, 73760 OSTFILDERN
Tel: 711 4481727 **Fax:** 711 442099
Email: m.schuele@print.de **Web site:** http://www.print.de
Freq: Quarterly; **Cover Price:** Free; **Circ:** 2,948
Profile: Magazine with the highest total circulation within the printing and media industry. The target group are all small and medium enterprises in the graphics industry, including the printing house. Editorial topics include the sheetfed offset and digital printing production areas. Divided the magazine is published four times a year in a total of six regional and parts.
Language(s): German
ADVERTISING RATES:
Full Page Mono .... EUR 1850
Full Page Colour .... EUR 1850
Mechanical Data: Type Area: 202 x 145 mm, No. of Columns (Display): 3, Col Widths (Display): 45 mm
Copy instructions: *Copy Date:* 30 days prior to publication
BUSINESS: PRINTING & STATIONERY: Printing

GRAFISCHE PALETTE - AUSG. SÜDWEST 1656894G41A-2167
Editorial: Riedstr. 25, 73760 OSTFILDERN
Tel: 711 4481727 **Fax:** 711 442099
Email: m.schuele@print.de **Web site:** http://www.print.de
Freq: Quarterly; **Cover Price:** Free; **Circ:** 2,948
Profile: Magazine with the highest total circulation within the printing and media industry. The target group are all small and medium enterprises in the graphics industry, including the printing house. Editorial topics include the sheetfed offset and digital printing production areas. Divided the magazine is published four times a year in a total of six regional and parts.
Language(s): German
ADVERTISING RATES:
Full Page Mono .... EUR 1850
Full Page Colour .... EUR 1850
Mechanical Data: Type Area: 205 x 145 mm, No. of Columns (Display): 3, Col Widths (Display): 45 mm
Copy instructions: *Copy Date:* 30 days prior to publication
BUSINESS: PRINTING & STATIONERY: Printing

GRAFSCHAFTER WOCHENBLATT AM MITTWOCH 729175G72-4744
Editorial: Max-Planck-Str. 4, 48529 NORDHORN
Tel: 5921 5055 **Fax:** 5921 77297
Email: andreas.meistermann@grafschafter-wochenblatt.de **Web site:** http://www.grafschafter-wochenblatt.de
Freq: Weekly; **Cover Price:** Free; **Circ:** 51,500
Editor: Andreas Meistermann
Profile: Advertising journal (house-to-house) concentrating on local stories.
Language(s): German
ADVERTISING RATES:
Full Page Mono .... EUR 3205
Full Page Colour .... EUR 3451
Mechanical Data: Type Area: 487 x 317 mm, No. of Columns (Display): 7, Col Widths (Display): 43 mm
Copy instructions: *Copy Date:* 2 days prior to publication
LOCAL NEWSPAPERS

GRANSEE-ZEITUNG 729183G67B-6120
Editorial: Lehnitzstr. 13, 16515 ORANIENBURG
Tel: 3301 59630 **Fax:** 3301 596350
Email: lokales@oranienburger-generalanzeiger.de **Web site:** http://www.die-mark-online.de
Freq: 312 issues yearly; **Circ:** 4,717
Advertising Manager: Tibor Szabo
Profile: Daily newspaper with regional news and a local sports section.
Language(s): German
ADVERTISING RATES:
SCC .... EUR 22,00
Mechanical Data: Type Area: 485 x 327 mm, No. of Columns (Display): 7, Col Widths (Display): 43 mm
Copy instructions: *Copy Date:* 3 days prior to publication
Supplement(s): rtv
REGIONAL DAILY & SUNDAY NEWSPAPERS: Regional Daily Newspapers

---

GRÄNZBOTE 729169G67B-6140
Editorial: Jägerhofstr. 4, 78532 TUTTLINGEN
Tel: 7461 70150 **Fax:** 7461 701547
Web site: http://www.schwaebische.de
Freq: 312 issues yearly; **Circ:** 22,517
Advertising Manager: Tarkan Tekin
Profile: In its edition provides the "Gränzbote" its readers daily with the latest information from government, business, sports, culture and food from the local environment. Twitter: http://twitter.com/Schwaebische This Outlet offers RSS (Really Simple Syndication).
Language(s): German
ADVERTISING RATES:
SCC .... EUR 77,20
Mechanical Data: Type Area: 480 x 320 mm, No. of Columns (Display): 7, Col Widths (Display): 44 mm
Copy instructions: *Copy Date:* 1 day prior to publication
Supplement(s): rtv
REGIONAL DAILY & SUNDAY NEWSPAPERS: Regional Daily Newspapers

---

GRAZIA 1976414G74A-3737
Editorial: Gänsemarkt 21, 20354 HAMBURG
Tel: 40 4118825301 **Fax:** 40 4118825302
Email: michaela.hinck@grazia-magazin.de **Web site:** http://www.grazia-magazin.de
Freq: Weekly; **Cover Price:** EUR 1,00; **Circ:** 181,627
Editor: Claudia ten Hoevel; **Advertising Manager:** Ulrike Geisert
Profile: The fashion and People magazine Grazia is the first female glossy crossover, the week, after week, the most interesting topics Highlights of Style, People & News summarizes current and entertaining. It is a style magazine with a heavy dose people and current events, which is based in the upper mainstream market a new magazine genre for female audiences. Fashionable but not elitist, style-oriented but not superficial, intelligent but still entertaining, it covers the whole thematic range of fast, cosmopolitan weekly magazine. Facebook: http://www.facebook.com/GraziaMagazin.
Language(s): German
ADVERTISING RATES:
Full Page Mono .... EUR 13000
Full Page Colour .... EUR 13000
Mechanical Data: Type Area: 270 x 210 mm

GREENBUILDING 1852947G4E-7231
Editorial: Langhansstr. 8, 13086 BERLIN
Tel: 30 4724918 **Fax:** 30 47303561
Email: kopf@schiele-schoen.de **Web site:** http://www.greenbuilding-planning.de
Freq: 10 issues yearly; **Annual Sub.:** EUR 124,00; **Circ:** 5,735
Editor: Iris Kopf; **Advertising Manager:** Lutz Diesbach
Profile: Magazine about enduring house building.
Language(s): German
ADVERTISING RATES:
Full Page Mono .... EUR 2500
Full Page Colour .... EUR 3640
Mechanical Data: Type Area: 259 x 182 mm, No. of Columns (Display): 3, Col Widths (Display): 58 mm

---

GREENKEEPERS JOURNAL 739950G64D-1
Editorial: Ernst-Robert-Curtius-Str. 14, 53117 BONN
Tel: 228 9898223 **Fax:** 228 9898299
Email: redaktion@koellen.de **Web site:** http://www.koellen.de
Freq: Quarterly; Free to qualifying individuals
Annual Sub.: EUR 40,00; **Circ:** 3,800
Editor: Franz Josef Ungerechts; **Advertising Manager:** Monika Tischler-Möbius
Profile: Magazine for Vegetation technology in horticulture, landscaping and sports facilities as well as for research and practice.
Language(s): English; French; German
Readership: Aimed at gardeners and professionals within the trade.
ADVERTISING RATES:
Full Page Mono .... EUR 1850
Full Page Colour .... EUR 1850
Mechanical Data: Type Area: 260 x 178 mm, No. of Columns (Display): 4, Col Widths (Display): 41 mm
Copy instructions: *Copy Date:* 31 days prior to publication
Official Journal of: Organ d. Federation of European Golf Greenkeepers Associations, d. Greenkeeper Verb. Deutschland, d. Swiss Greenkeepers' Association u. d. Interessengemeinschaft d. Greenkeeper Österr.
BUSINESS: OTHER CLASSIFICATIONS: Course Maintenance

GREENPEACE 729207G57-580
Editorial: Große Elbstr. 145d, 22767 HAMBURG
Tel: 40 808128080 **Fax:** 40 808128099
Email: gpm@greenpeace-magazin.de **Web site:** http://www.greenpeace-magazin.de
Freq: Quarterly; **Circ:** 512,000
Editor: Jochen Schildt
Profile: News for Sponsors of the environmental organization Greenpeace with emphases on climate and environment Facebook: http://facebook.com/greenpeacemagazin Twitter: http://twitter.com/greenpeacemag.
Language(s): German

GREENPEACE MAGAZIN. 729210G57-600
Editorial: Große Elbstr. 145d, 22767 HAMBURG
Tel: 40 808128080 **Fax:** 40 808128099
Email: gpm@greenpeace-magazin.de **Web site:** http://www.greenpeace-magazin.de

Freq: 6 issues yearly; **Annual Sub.:** EUR 28,50; **Circ:** 105,000
Editor: Jochen Schildt
Profile: Magazine concerning the activities of the German branch of Greenpeace and general environmental news. Facebook: http://facebook.com/greenpeacemagazin.
Language(s): German
Readership: Read by members of Greenpeace.
BUSINESS: ENVIRONMENT & POLLUTION

GREVENER ZEITUNG
729235G67B-6160
Editorial: Neubrückenstr. 8, 48143 MÜNSTER
Tel: 251 5924051 **Fax:** 251 5928457
Email: redaktion.newsdesk@mdhl.de **Web site:** http://www.grevenerzeitung.de
Freq: 312 issues yearly; **Annual Sub.:** EUR 26,00; **Circ:** 4,041
Profile: Daily newspaper with regional news and a local sports section.
Language(s): German
ADVERTISING RATES:
SCC .... EUR 26,40
Mechanical Data: Type Area: 478 x 315 mm, No. of Columns (Display): 7, Col Widths (Display): 42 mm
Copy instructions: *Copy Date:* 2 days prior to publication
Supplement(s): Freizeit; Theaterzeitung
REGIONAL DAILY & SUNDAY NEWSPAPERS: Regional Daily Newspapers

GREVESMÜHLENER BLITZ AM SONNTAG
729236G72-4796
Editorial: Lübsche Str. 21, 23966 WISMAR
Tel: 3841 6280843 **Fax:** 3841 6280830
Email: kerstin.vogt@blitzverlag.de **Web site:** http://www.blitzverlag.de
Freq: Weekly; **Cover Price:** Free; **Circ:** 28,780
Editor: Kerstin Vogt; **Advertising Manager:** Georg Brandt
Profile: Advertising journal (house-to-house) concentrating on local stories.
Language(s): German
ADVERTISING RATES:
Full Page Mono .... EUR 2193
Full Page Colour .... EUR 2583
Mechanical Data: Type Area: 420 x 285 mm, No. of Columns (Display): 6, Col Widths (Display): 45 mm
Copy instructions: *Copy Date:* 2 days prior to publication
LOCAL NEWSPAPERS

GRILL MAGAZIN
2004326G74P-1345
Editorial: Merowingerstr. 30, 40223 DÜSSELDORF
Tel: 211 933470 **Fax:** 211 9334710
Email: mdolny@databecker.de **Web site:** http://www.grill-praxis.de
Freq: Quarterly; **Cover Price:** EUR 7,99; **Circ:** 60,000
Editor: Michael Dolny; **Advertising Manager:** Jörg Hausch
Profile: The magazine for barbecue grill and more. All that grilling, eating and enjoying even more enjoyable is the topic of Magazins.Themenbereiche accessories Barbecue equipment, prepare grill food properly and marinate, now recognize and quality. The best recipes, the best sauces and marinades.
Language(s): German
ADVERTISING RATES:
Full Page Mono .... EUR 4200
Full Page Colour .... EUR 4200
Mechanical Data: Type Area: 274 x 180 mm

DER GROSSE KNIGGE
743507G74Q-2
Editorial: Theodor-Heuss-Str. 2, 53177 BONN
Tel: 228 82050 **Fax:** 228 3696122
Email: info@stil.de **Web site:** http://www.stil.de
Freq: 8 issues yearly; **Annual Sub.:** EUR 259,60; **Circ:** 5,000
Editor: Agnes Anna Jarosch
Profile: Magazine about style and etiquette.
Language(s): German

GROSSENHAINER WOCHENKURIER
729262G72-4832
Editorial: Wettiner Platz 10, 01067 DRESDEN
Tel: 351 491760 **Fax:** 351 4917674
Email: wochenkurier-dresden@dwk-verlag.de **Web site:** http://www.wochenkurier.info
Freq: Weekly; **Cover Price:** Free; **Circ:** 16,813
Editor: Regine Eberlein; **Advertising Manager:** Andreas Schönherr
Profile: Advertising journal (house-to-house) concentrating on local stories.
Language(s): German
ADVERTISING RATES:
Full Page Mono .... EUR 2228
Full Page Colour .... EUR 3119
Mechanical Data: Type Area: 430 x 290 mm, No. of Columns (Display): 7, Col Widths (Display): 38 mm
Copy instructions: *Copy Date:* 5 days prior to publication
LOCAL NEWSPAPERS

GROSS-GERAUER ECHO
730051G67B-6800
Editorial: Holzhofallee 25, 64295 DARMSTADT
Tel: 6151 3871 **Fax:** 6151 387307
Email: redaktion@darmstaedter-echo.de **Web site:** http://www.echo-online.de
Freq: 312 issues yearly; **Circ:** 17,165
Advertising Manager: Andreas Wohlfart
Profile: Daily newspaper with regional news and a local sports section.
Language(s): German
ADVERTISING RATES:
SCC .... EUR 26,70
Mechanical Data: Type Area: 491 x 339 mm, No. of Columns (Display): 7, Col Widths (Display): 45 mm
Copy instructions: *Copy Date:* 1 day prior to publication
Supplement(s): Generation; Gesund leben heute; Die Hupe; i2 immobilien; Kinder Echo; Odenwälder Kartoffelsupp; Sonntags Echo; Start frei
REGIONAL DAILY & SUNDAY NEWSPAPERS: Regional Daily Newspapers

DIE GROSSHANDELSKAUFLEUTE
729273G62H-520
Editorial: Eschstr. 22, 44629 HERNE
Tel: 2323 141900 **Fax:** 2323 141123
Email: l.kurz@kiehl.de **Web site:** http://www.kiehl.de
Freq: Monthly; **Annual Sub.:** EUR 61,80; **Circ:** 2,056
Editor: Lothar Kurz; **Advertising Manager:** Andreas Reimann
Profile: „Die Großhandelskaufleute" takes a clear and understandable themes from the fields of business, economics and accounting at. Numerous examples and cases to facilitate learning. Photos, charts and graphs to illustrate the issues from the practice of wholesale trade. Regular examination trainings offer readers the chance to fest their current knowledge.
Language(s): German
ADVERTISING RATES:
Full Page Mono .... EUR 750
Full Page Colour .... EUR 1050
Mechanical Data: Type Area: 260 x 186 mm
Copy instructions: *Copy Date:* 30 days prior to publication
BUSINESS: CHURCH & SCHOOL EQUIPMENT & EDUCATION: Careers

GROSSHANDELSMARKT
1978876G53-215
Editorial: Koblenzer Str. 97, 32584 LÖHNE
Tel: 5731 981040 **Fax:** 5731 6641009
Email: post@bem-media.de **Web site:** http://www.predprinimatel.de
Freq: Monthly; **Circ:** 2,980
Profile: Russian language newspaper for Germany.
Language(s): Russian

GROSS-ZIMMERNER LOKAL-ANZEIGER
729282G67B-6220
Editorial: Schlossergasse 4, 64807 DIEBURG
Tel: 6071 25005 **Fax:** 6071 81358
Email: red.dieburg@op-online.de **Web site:** http://www.op-online.de
Freq: 156 issues yearly; **Circ:** 3,930
Advertising Manager: Helmut Moser
Profile: Regional daily newspaper covering politics, economics, sport, travel and technology.
Language(s): German
ADVERTISING RATES:
SCC .... EUR 19,60
Mechanical Data: Type Area: 470 x 322 mm, No. of Columns (Display): 7, Col Widths (Display): 43 mm
Copy instructions: *Copy Date:* 3 days prior to publication
REGIONAL DAILY & SUNDAY NEWSPAPERS: Regional Daily Newspapers

GROW!
1632921G73-499
Editorial: Liebenauer Str. 19a, 34396 LIEBENAU
Tel: 5676 920920 **Fax:** 5676 921340
Email: redaktion@grow.de **Web site:** http://www.grow.de
Freq: 6 issues yearly; **Annual Sub.:** EUR 16,50; **Circ:** 35,500
Editor: Winni Fleckner
Profile: Lifestyle and cultural magazine.
Language(s): German
ADVERTISING RATES:
Full Page Mono .... EUR 1950
Full Page Colour .... EUR 1950
Mechanical Data: Type Area: 297 x 210 mm, No. of Columns (Display): 4, Col Widths (Display): 46 mm
Copy instructions: *Copy Date:* 30 days prior to publication

GRÜN
729289G74C-1060
Editorial: Lindenstr. 20, 50674 KÖLN
Tel: 221 3980160 **Fax:** 221 39801610
Email: kroll@l-m-verlag.de **Web site:** http://www.livingandmore.de
Freq: 10 issues yearly; **Annual Sub.:** EUR 11,60; **Circ:** 40,833
Editor: Erhard Held
Profile: Grün - 1000 Ideen für Haus und Garten is a creative magazine show "Inside and Outside". In addition to the classical garden-theme, combined with valuable practice tips, Grün offers a number of design proposals for balcony and terrace, decorative items for home and garden and ideas for living with flowers. The magazin is his product promises justified by issues of diversity and their imaginative, hands-on treatment. Through a variety of tips and suggestions "1000 Ideas for the design of the personal environment in the garden, balcony and terrace, in the home will be taught.
Language(s): German
ADVERTISING RATES:
Full Page Mono .... EUR 5600
Full Page Colour .... EUR 5600
Mechanical Data: Type Area: 267 x 195 mm, No. of Columns (Display): 4, Col Widths (Display): 45 mm
Copy instructions: *Copy Date:* 30 days prior to publication
CONSUMER: WOMEN'S INTEREST CONSUMER MAGAZINES: Home & Family

GRÜN IST LEBEN
1837085G21A-4394
Editorial: Bismarckstr. 49, 25421 PINNEBERG
Tel: 4101 20590 **Fax:** 4101 205931
Email: schwarz@bund-deutscher-baumschulen.de **Web site:** http://www.bund-deutscher-baumschulen.de
Freq: 6 issues yearly; Free to qualifying individuals
Annual Sub.: EUR 24,00; **Circ:** 2,550
Editor: Helmuth G. Schwarz; **Advertising Manager:** Jörg Hengster
Profile: Association journal of the Association of German nurseries. Informed of updates from the association events, the latest BdB activities, latest trends and developments in the nursery industry, in business and politics.
Language(s): German
ADVERTISING RATES:
Full Page Mono .... EUR 1295
Full Page Colour .... EUR 1695
Mechanical Data: Type Area: 275 x 180 mm
Copy instructions: *Copy Date:* 30 days prior to publication

DAS GRUNDEIGENTUM
729323G1E-180
Editorial: Potsdamer Str. 143, 10783 BERLIN
Tel: 30 4147690 **Fax:** 30 41476943
Email: bluemmel@grundeigentum-verlag.de **Web site:** http://www.grundeigentum-verlag.de
Freq: 24 issues yearly; Free to qualifying individuals
Annual Sub.: EUR 145,00; **Circ:** 7,250
Advertising Manager: Gabriele Stöckel
Profile: Magazine covering building laws, planning regulations, taxation and tenants rights.
Language(s): German
ADVERTISING RATES:
Full Page Mono .... EUR 1770
Full Page Colour .... EUR 2790
Mechanical Data: Type Area: 260 x 175 mm, No. of Columns (Display): 3, Col Widths (Display): 55 mm
Copy instructions: *Copy Date:* 18 days prior to publication
Official Journal of: Organ d. Bundes d. Berliner Haus- u. Grundbesitzervereine e.V. u. d. Ring Dt. Makler, LV Bln. u. Brandenburg e.V.
BUSINESS: FINANCE & ECONOMICS: Property

GRÜNDERZEIT
1616327G14A-9442
Editorial: Am Baumwall 11, 20459 HAMBURG
Tel: 40 37038584 **Fax:** 40 37038595
Email: chefredaktion@impulse.de **Web site:** http://www.impulse.de/gruenderzeit
Freq: Half-yearly; **Cover Price:** EUR 7,50; **Circ:** 80,000
Editor: Nikolaus Förster; **Advertising Manager:** Helma Spieker
Profile: Magazine for enterprise promoters.
Language(s): German
ADVERTISING RATES:
Full Page Mono .... EUR 5500
Full Page Colour .... EUR 5500

GRÜNDERZEITEN
1749898G14A-9898
Editorial: Spessartstr. 11, 14197 BERLIN
Tel: 30 32601420 **Fax:** 30 32601421
Email: hebestreit@pid-net.de
Freq: 56 issues yearly; **Cover Price:** Free; **Circ:** 30,000
Profile: The publication series for entrepreneurs and young companies is based on known problems and provides tips and tries to identify possible solutions for the practice.
Language(s): German

GRUNDSCHULE
729326G62C-60
Editorial: Georg-Westermann-Allee 66, 38104 BRAUNSCHWEIG **Tel:** 531 708391 **Fax:** 531 708374
Email: gru@westermann.de **Web site:** http://www.die-grundschule.de
Freq: 11 issues yearly; **Annual Sub.:** EUR 94,60; **Circ:** 8,000
Editor: Ursula Flemmer; **Advertising Manager:** Peter Kniep
Profile: Magazine for primary school teachers, students, and trainees in teacher training and employment.
Language(s): German
ADVERTISING RATES:
Full Page Mono .... EUR 2200
Full Page Colour .... EUR 3520
Mechanical Data: No. of Columns (Display): 4, Col Widths (Display): 43 mm, Type Area: 264 x 185 mm
Copy instructions: *Copy Date:* 35 days prior to publication
BUSINESS: CHURCH & SCHOOL EQUIPMENT & EDUCATION: Junior Education

GRUNDSCHULE MUSIK
729327G62C-65
Editorial: Im Brande 17, 30926 SEELZE
Tel: 511 40004128 **Fax:** 511 40004975
Email: lux@friedrich-verlag.de **Web site:** http://www.grundschulemusik.de
Freq: Quarterly; **Annual Sub.:** EUR 82,00; **Circ:** 7,500
Editor: Janina Lux; **Advertising Manager:** Bernd Schrader
Profile: Discover music together with children in class 1 to 6. Grundschule Musik - the magazine for strange times teachers, trained music professionals and seminar leader in the education and training. Grundschule Musik offers: a wealth of proven ideas for a creative and challenging music lessons in grades 1-6. Grundschule Musik comes from the world of children and provides space for individual and community music making and music that appeal to children varied: classical music, traditional songs and modern pop songs and nursery rhymes. The CD booklet contains the complete recordings of all songs and pieces; stylish contemporary instrumental backing tracks for all songs, plays and animation on the CD-ROM portion of motion video sequences or contributions to illustrate techniques, etc. With the index cards, transparencies, posters, games or pictures you can go directly and without much preparation time in the classroom. Professionals and strange times teachers will also receive didactic and methodological repertoire, techniques and information in trade publications and workshops.
Language(s): German
Readership: Aimed at music teachers in primary schools.
ADVERTISING RATES:
Full Page Mono .... EUR 1540
Full Page Colour .... EUR 1540
Mechanical Data: Type Area: 243 x 185 mm
Copy instructions: *Copy Date:* 28 days prior to publication
Supplement(s): bildung+Lernen; bildung+medien; bildung+reisen; bildung+science
BUSINESS: CHURCH & SCHOOL EQUIPMENT & EDUCATION: Junior Education

GRUNDSCHULMAGAZIN
729330G62C-2
Editorial: Rosenheimer Str. 145, 81671 MÜNCHEN
Tel: 89 45051371 **Fax:** 89 45051310
Email: holler@oldenbourg.de **Web site:** http://www.grundschulmagazin.de
Freq: 6 issues yearly; **Annual Sub.:** EUR 75,90; **Circ:** 5,950
Editor: Stefan Holler; **Advertising Manager:** Christian Schwarzbauer
Profile: Magazine focusing on teaching in primary schools.
Language(s): German
ADVERTISING RATES:
Full Page Mono .... EUR 1305
Full Page Colour .... EUR 2090
Mechanical Data: Type Area: 250 x 180 mm, No. of Columns (Display): 3, Col Widths (Display): 56 mm
Copy instructions: *Copy Date:* 35 days prior to publication
Supplement(s): Eine Welt in der Schule
BUSINESS: CHURCH & SCHOOL EQUIPMENT & EDUCATION: Junior Education

GRUNDSCHULUNTERRICHT
729331G62C-3
Editorial: Rosenheimer Str. 145, 81671 MÜNCHEN
Tel: 89 450510 **Fax:** 89 45051310
Email: holler@oldenbourg.de **Web site:** http://www.grundschulunterricht.de
Freq: Monthly; **Annual Sub.:** EUR 86,90; **Circ:** 5,350
Editor: Stefan Holler; **Advertising Manager:** Christian Schwarzbauer
Profile: Magazine about primary school education.
Language(s): German
ADVERTISING RATES:
Full Page Mono .... EUR 1740
Full Page Colour .... EUR 1740
Mechanical Data: Type Area: 260 x 184 mm
Supplement(s): Eine Welt in der Schule
BUSINESS: CHURCH & SCHOOL EQUIPMENT & EDUCATION: Junior Education

DIE GRUNDSCHULZEITSCHRIFT
729332G62C-4
Editorial: Im Brande 17, 30926 SEELZE
Tel: 511 40004231 **Fax:** 511 40004219
Email: redaktion.gsz@friedrich-verlag.de **Web site:** http://www.grundschulzeitschrift.de
Freq: 10 issues yearly; **Annual Sub.:** EUR 109,00; **Circ:** 5,361
Editor: Janina Lux; **Advertising Manager:** Bernd Schrader
Profile: Good school - good teaching. Teaching, school life, learning level surveys, team work and work with parents, educational policy changes - these are just some of the requirements that make your professional life as a teacher. So feel good all in elementary school, happy and successful learning and work, like Die Grundschulzeitschrift: You strengthen your professional life, to support you in the development of school and classroom culture, give you guidance in educational policy changing times, provide you diverse, stimulating and innovative teaching ideas! Die Grundschulzeitschrift is divided into two parts: "Making good school" with themes that go beyond your everyday teaching, such as Health of teachers, AD(H)S, school inspections and latest educational developments, "Good teaching" with a variety of methods, teaching methods and

materials for the different subjects a priority issue. Twice a year, you receive a package of materials for direct use in your classroom.
Language(s): German
ADVERTISING RATES:
Full Page Mono .... EUR 2130
Full Page Colour .... EUR 2130
Mechanical Data: Type Area: 258 x 183 mm
Copy instructions: *Copy Date:* 49 days prior to publication
Supplement(s): bildung+Lernen; bildung+medien; bildung+reisen; bildung+science
BUSINESS: CHURCH & SCHOOL EQUIPMENT & EDUCATION: Junior Education

DER GRUNDSTEIN 729333G4E-3780
Editorial: Olof-Palme-Str. 19, 60439 FRANKFURT
Tel: 69 95737126 **Fax:** 69 95737139
Email: grundstein@igbau.de **Web site:** http://www.igbau.de
Freq: 10 issues yearly; **Circ:** 340,000
Editor: Jörg Herpich
Profile: Magazine for Members of the Industriegewerkschaft Bauen-Agrar-Umwelt.
Language(s): German
ADVERTISING RATES:
Full Page Colour .... EUR 12350
Mechanical Data: No. of Columns (Display): 3, Col Widths (Display): 60 mm, Type Area: 248 x 191 mm
Copy instructions: *Copy Date:* 30 days prior to publication
BUSINESS: ARCHITECTURE & BUILDING: Building

GRÜNSTIFT 1605086G57-2646
Editorial: Hans-Sachs-Str. 26, 40237 DÜSSELDORF
Tel: 211 663582
Email: likaweingarten@gmx.de
Freq: 3 issues yearly; **Circ:** 3,995
Editor: Lika Weingarten; **Advertising Manager:** Helwig v. Lieben
Profile: Environment magazine for Düsseldorf.
Language(s): German
ADVERTISING RATES:
Full Page Mono .... EUR 315
Mechanical Data: Type Area: 253 x 180 mm, No. of Columns (Display): 3, Col Widths (Display): 56 mm
Copy instructions: *Copy Date:* 30 days prior to publication

GRUPPENPSYCHOTHERAPIE UND GRUPPENDYNAMIK 729340G56A-11147
Editorial: Hartwigstr. 2c, 28209 BREMEN
Tel: 421 21868607
Email: kniebank@uni-bremen.de
Freq: Quarterly; **Annual Sub.:** EUR 82,00; **Circ:** 800
Editor: Kay Niebank; **Advertising Manager:** Anja Kütemeyer
Profile: Contributions to social psychology and therapeutic practice.
Language(s): German
ADVERTISING RATES:
Full Page Mono .... EUR 450
Mechanical Data: Type Area: 190 x 120 mm
Official Journal of: Organ d. Dt. Arbeitskreis f. Gruppenpsychotherapie u. Gruppendynamik

GUG GRUNDSTÜCKSMARKT UND GRUNDSTÜCKSWERT 729372G1E-220
Editorial: Luxemburger Str. 449, 50939 KÖLN
Tel: 221 943737237 **Fax:** 221 943737281
Email: equardon-winkler@wolterskluwer.de **Web site:** http://www.gug-aktuell.de
Freq: 6 issues yearly; Free to qualifying individuals
Annual Sub.: EUR 189,00; **Circ:** 3,900
Editor: Wolfgang Kleiber; **Advertising Manager:** Markus Kipp
Profile: Journal providing news about the property market, including land and property values.
Language(s): German
ADVERTISING RATES:
Full Page Mono .... EUR 895
Full Page Colour .... EUR 1960
Mechanical Data: Type Area: 260 x 170 mm
Copy instructions: *Copy Date:* 28 days prior to publication
Official Journal of: Organ d. Bundesverb. Dt. Grundstückssachverständiger
BUSINESS: FINANCE & ECONOMICS: Property

GUITAR 729381G76D-1740
Editorial: Dachauer Str. 37b, 85232 BERGKIRCHEN
Tel: 8131 565547 **Fax:** 8131 565510
Email: juergen.ehness@guitar.de **Web site:** http://www.guitar.de
Freq: Monthly; **Annual Sub.:** EUR 61,20; **Circ:** 18,331
Editor: Jürgen Ehness; **Advertising Manager:** Sabine Frischmuth
Profile: The magazine for guitarists and bass players will appear with an extensive notes section and a play-along CD and thus stimulates in the active music making. Facebook: http://www.facebook.com/pages/Guitar-Magazin/114802794183 myspace: http://www.myspace.com/guitarmagazin.
Language(s): German
ADVERTISING RATES:
Full Page Mono .... EUR 2890
Full Page Colour .... EUR 4850
Mechanical Data: Type Area: 254 x 185 mm, No. of Columns (Display): 4, Col Widths (Display): 43 mm
Copy instructions: *Copy Date:* 30 days prior to publication
CONSUMER: MUSIC & PERFORMING ARTS: Music

DER GULLER - AUSG. ACHERN/ OBERKIRCH 729382G72-4872
Editorial: Scheffelstr. 21, 77654 OFFENBURG
Tel: 781 9340144 **Fax:** 781 9340153
Email: redaktion@staz-online.de **Web site:** http://www.stadtanzeiger-ortenau.de
Freq: Weekly; **Cover Price:** Free; **Circ:** 35,300
Editor: Rembert Graf Kerssenbrock; **Advertising Manager:** Klaus Pusch
Profile: Advertising journal (house-to-house) concentrating on local stories.
Language(s): German
ADVERTISING RATES:
Full Page Mono .... EUR 3402
Full Page Colour .... EUR 3652
Mechanical Data: Type Area: 420 x 284 mm, No. of Columns (Display): 6, Col Widths (Display): 45 mm
Copy instructions: *Copy Date:* 2 days prior to publication
LOCAL NEWSPAPERS

GÜNZBURGER EXTRA 726850G72-3680
Editorial: Hofgasse 9, 89312 GÜNZBURG
Tel: 8221 91739 **Fax:** 8221 91718
Email: extra-redaktion@guenzburger-zeitung.de
Freq: Weekly; **Cover Price:** Free; **Circ:** 40,368
Editor: Petra Kruhl; **Advertising Manager:** Markus Seitz
Profile: Advertising journal (house-to-house) concentrating on local stories.
Language(s): German
ADVERTISING RATES:
Full Page Mono .... EUR 3629
Full Page Colour .... EUR 5511
Mechanical Data: Type Area: 480 x 327 mm, No. of Columns (Display): 7, Col Widths (Display): 45 mm
Copy instructions: *Copy Date:* 2 days prior to publication
LOCAL NEWSPAPERS

GÜNZBURGER ZEITUNG 729364G67B-6240
Editorial: Curt-Frenzel-Str. 2, 86167 AUGSBURG
Tel: 821 7770 **Fax:** 821 7772067
Web site: http://www.augsburger-allgemeine.de
Freq: 312 issues yearly; **Circ:** 15,390
Advertising Manager: Herbert Dachs
Profile: Daily newspaper with regional news and a local sports section. Facebook: http://www.facebook.com/AugsburgerAllgemeine Twitter: http://twitter.com/AZ_Augsburg This Outlet offers RSS (Really Simple Syndication).
Language(s): German
ADVERTISING RATES:
SCC .... EUR 45,30
Mechanical Data: Type Area: 480 x 327 mm, No. of Columns (Display): 7, Col Widths (Display): 45 mm
Copy instructions: *Copy Date:* 1 day prior to publication
Supplement(s): Freizeit journal
REGIONAL DAILY & SUNDAY NEWSPAPERS: Regional Daily Newspapers

GUSS I ASPHALT MAGAZIN 729401G4E-3800
Editorial: Dottendorfer Str. 86, 53129 BONN
Tel: 228 239899 **Fax:** 228 239399
Email: info@gussasphalt.de **Web site:** http://www.gussasphalt.de
Freq: Annual; **Circ:** 35,000
Editor: Peter Rode
Profile: Magazine for planners, architects and communes.
Language(s): German

GUT & PREISWERT BED & BREAKFAST FRANKREICH 1740103G89A-12226
Editorial: Schleefstr. 1, 44287 DORTMUND
Tel: 231 444770 **Fax:** 231 4447777
Email: hauptredaktion@busche.de **Web site:** http://www.lowprix.com
Freq: Annual; **Cover Price:** EUR 9,90; **Circ:** 20,000
Advertising Manager: Jörg Leu
Profile: Information for those traveling with reference to the French way of life. Let all France's friends in the right direction in our neighboring country. The huge choice of private rooms, which puts together the paperback, offers a variety of activities ranging from farm to the Château. All houses have clearly structured information on facilities, directions and destinations. Almost every house is illustrated. In a few sentences each features of the house or the host are presented.
Language(s): German
ADVERTISING RATES:
Full Page Mono .... EUR 1400
Full Page Colour .... EUR 1400
Mechanical Data: Type Area: 176 x 104 mm

GUT & PREISWERT BETT MIT BAD BIS 50 EURO 1740104G89A-12227
Editorial: Schleefstr. 1, 44287 DORTMUND
Tel: 231 444770 **Fax:** 231 4447777
Email: hauptredaktion@busche.de **Web site:** http://www.lowprix.com
Freq: Annual; **Cover Price:** EUR 9,90; **Circ:** 26,896
Advertising Manager: Jörg Leu
Profile: Good and inexpensive stay: Under this motto, the Guide presents cheap accommodation throughout Germany. Carefully researched and selected extends the range of around 3,500 hotels and inns in Germany. The inexpensive yet comfortable rooms have bath or shower and toilet. In the hotel guide the traveler finds a convenient base guarantees a balanced price-performance ratio.
Language(s): German
ADVERTISING RATES:
Full Page Mono .... EUR 1400
Full Page Colour .... EUR 1400
Mechanical Data: Type Area: 176 x 104 mm

GUT & PREISWERT MIT DEM BIKE ÜBERNACHTEN 1740105G89A-12228
Editorial: Schleefstr. 1, 44287 DORTMUND
Tel: 231 444770 **Fax:** 231 4447777
Email: hauptredaktion@busche.de **Web site:** http://www.lowprix.de
Freq: Annual; **Cover Price:** EUR 9,90; **Circ:** 15,000
Advertising Manager: Jörg Leu
Profile: Anyone on two wheels - whether motorcycle or bicycle - is on tour in Germany will find this guide of hotels around 2,700 hotels and guest houses, that is to its special needs taken into consideration. Bikers know above all, a storage for their vehicle to appreciate. In assembling the houses was taken to an excellent price-performance ratio.
Language(s): German
ADVERTISING RATES:
Full Page Mono .... EUR 1100
Full Page Colour .... EUR 1100
Mechanical Data: Type Area: 192 x 120 mm

GUT & PREISWERT MIT KINDERN ÜBERNACHTEN 1740106G89A-12229
Editorial: Schleefstr. 1, 44287 DORTMUND
Tel: 231 444770 **Fax:** 231 4447777
Email: hauptredaktion@busche.de **Web site:** http://www.lowprix.com
Freq: Annual; **Cover Price:** EUR 9,90; **Circ:** 15,000
Advertising Manager: Jörg Leu
Profile: Who's going with the whole family on the go, often must pay for his budget. A good value for money is in the choice of accommodation is crucial. This hotel guide presents around 2,500 hotels and inns in Germany and South Tyrol that meet this criterion and distinguish themselves by providing child-friendly.
Language(s): German
ADVERTISING RATES:
Full Page Mono .... EUR 1100
Full Page Colour .... EUR 1100
Mechanical Data: Type Area: 176 x 104 mm

GUT & PREISWERT MIT TIEREN ÜBERNACHTEN 1740107G89A-12230
Editorial: Schleefstr. 1, 44287 DORTMUND
Tel: 231 444770 **Fax:** 231 4447777
Email: hauptredaktion@busche.de **Web site:** http://www.lowprix.com
Freq: Annual; **Cover Price:** EUR 9,90; **Circ:** 15,000
Advertising Manager: Jörg Leu
Profile: Many hotels pets are welcome, many have even set up specifically to them. This pet-friendly hotel guide presents houses where the "little darling " is welcome. The more than 2,500 hotels and guesthouses, which are here for you to give, not only to animals, but also affordable. No one needs more to his "dearest" to give support on vacation.
Language(s): German
ADVERTISING RATES:
Full Page Mono .... EUR 1100
Full Page Colour .... EUR 1100
Mechanical Data: Type Area: 176 x 104 mm

GUTE ARBEIT. 1739428G14A-9850
Editorial: Heddernheimer Landstr. 144, 60439 FRANKFURT **Tel:** 69 133077635 **Fax:** 69 133077615
Email: gutearbeit@bund-verlag.de **Web site:** http://www.gutearbeit-online.de
Freq: 11 issues yearly; **Annual Sub.:** EUR 162,00; **Circ:** 1,800
Editor: Jürgen Reusch; **Advertising Manager:** Peter Beuther
Profile: Magazine about health and safety at work. Also includes information about ecology in business.
Language(s): German
ADVERTISING RATES:
Full Page Mono .... EUR 490
Full Page Colour .... EUR 613
Mechanical Data: Type Area: 256 x 164 mm
Copy instructions: *Copy Date:* 20 days prior to publication

GUTE FAHRT 729411G77E-220
Editorial: Am Sandfeld 15a, 76149 KARLSRUHE
Tel: 721 627380 **Fax:** 721 6273811
Email: redaktion@gute-fahrt.de **Web site:** http://www.gute-fahrt.de
Freq: Monthly; **Annual Sub.:** EUR 36,30; **Circ:** 68,563
Editor: Joachim Fischer; **Advertising Manager:** Sigrid Pinke
Profile: The magazine is one of the very first car titles, and also one of the very first special-interest magazines in the German market at all. Competence and credibility are in more than 50 years have become the hallmark of the magazine. Topic is not the bargains, but quality for which we happily paid. The magazine creates a favorable environment for deliberately chosen good products. This corresponds with the optical quality of the leaf and his journalistic professionalism. The magazine counts as a special target group, the most loyal customers of both brands to your readers, which put the vehicle purchase if shown above-average brand loyalty to the day that are nonetheless maintained want.the Focus is concentrated on high-class, non-cash goods and services related to its Volkswagen and Audi.
Language(s): German
ADVERTISING RATES:
Full Page Mono .... EUR 7820
Full Page Colour .... EUR 13950
Mechanical Data: Type Area: 260 x 190 mm, No. of Columns (Display): 4, Col Widths (Display): 43 mm
Copy instructions: *Copy Date:* 40 days prior to publication
CONSUMER: MOTORING & CYCLING: Club Cars

GUTE LAUNE 1615795G74A-3354
Editorial: Ruhrtalstr. 67, 45239 ESSEN
Tel: 201 246880 **Fax:** 201 24688100
Email: b.heyer@stegenwaller.de **Web site:** http://www.stegenwaller.de
Freq: 26 issues yearly; **Annual Sub.:** EUR 35,00; **Circ:** 123,938
Editor: Brigitta Heyer; **Advertising Manager:** Kerstin Franz
Profile: The target group of the +40-year-old women estimate the extensive range. Information from the fields of health, money, family life and partnership are treated as attractively as the season-oriented cooking and baking recipes that awaken the desire to cook and taste them by simply looking at them.
Language(s): German
ADVERTISING RATES:
Full Page Mono .... EUR 4500
Full Page Colour .... EUR 4500
Mechanical Data: Type Area: 260 x 196 mm
Copy instructions: *Copy Date:* 35 days prior to publication
CONSUMER: WOMEN'S INTEREST CONSUMER MAGAZINES: Women's Interest

GUTE ZEITEN SCHLECHTE ZEITEN 1621401G91D-10030
Editorial: Picassoplatz 1, 50679 KÖLN
Tel: 221 45660 **Fax:** 221 45669999
Email: frank.mueller@rtl.de **Web site:** http://gzsz.rtl.de
Freq: Daily; **Cover Price:** Paid; **Circ:** 21,660,000 Unique Users
Editor: Frank Müller
Language(s): German
CONSUMER: RECREATION & LEISURE: Children & Youth

GUTER RAT 729423G74M-260
Editorial: Zimmerstr. 28, 10969 BERLIN
Tel: 30 23876600 **Fax:** 30 23876395
Email: redaktion@guter-rat.de **Web site:** http://www.guter-rat.de
Freq: Monthly; **Annual Sub.:** EUR 27,60; **Circ:** 221,575
Editor: Werner Zedler; **Advertising Manager:** Christian Schmidt
Profile: "Guter Rat" provides guidance and decision support for all aspects of household management. Guter Rat covers a diverse range of topics: - Money and Insurance - Legal and Tax - Products and Tests - Car - Health & Nutrition - Home and Family - Travel and Leisure Facebook: http://www.facebook.com/guter.rat This Outlet offers RSS (Really Simple Syndication).
Language(s): German
Readership: Aimed at women.
ADVERTISING RATES:
Full Page Mono .... EUR 15100
Full Page Colour .... EUR 15100
Mechanical Data: Type Area: 248 x 187 mm, No. of Columns (Display): 4, Col Widths (Display): 43 mm
Copy instructions: *Copy Date:* 27 days prior to publication
CONSUMER: WOMEN'S INTEREST CONSUMER MAGAZINES: Personal Finance

GÜTERBAHNEN 1609400G49C-68
Editorial: Willstätterstr. 9, 40549 DÜSSELDORF
Tel: 211 5201372 **Fax:** 211 5201378
Email: dnv@alba-verlag.de **Web site:** http://www.alba-verlag.de
Freq: Quarterly; **Annual Sub.:** EUR 40,00; **Circ:** 1,150
Editor: Lothar Kuttig; **Advertising Manager:** Beatrice van Dijk
Profile: Magazine for the transport business.
Language(s): German
ADVERTISING RATES:
Full Page Mono .... EUR 1800
Full Page Colour .... EUR 2480
Mechanical Data: No. of Columns (Display): 4, Type Area: 272 x 198 mm, Col Widths (Display): 46 mm
Copy instructions: *Copy Date:* 20 days prior to publication

fficial Journal of: Organ d. Verb. Dt. erkehrsunternehmen e.V.

GUTERRAT.DE
1621400G74M-662

Editorial: Zimmerstr. 28, 10969 BERLIN
Tel: 30 23876600 **Fax:** 30 23876395
Email: post@guter-rat.de **Web site:** http://www.uter-rat.de
Freq: Daily; **Cover Price:** Paid; **Circ:** 174,010 Unique Jsers
Editor: Steffen Beck
Profile: Ezine: Magazine providing information on ashion, money matters, the law, health and beauty, ravel and motoring.
Language(s): German
CONSUMER: WOMEN'S INTEREST CONSUMER MAGAZINES: Personal Finance

GÜTERSLOH GEHT AUS
765168G89A-11433

Editorial: Goldstr. 16, 33602 BIELEFELD
Tel: 521 932560 **Fax:** 521 9325699
Email: redaktion@tips-verlag.de **Web site:** http://www.guetersloh-geht-aus.de
Freq: Half-yearly; **Cover Price:** Free; **Circ:** 20,000
Editor: Friedrich Flöttmann
Profile: In the half-year intervals informed "Gütersloh geht aus" to local gastronomy and cultural andscape. Gütersloh, Rheda-Wiedenbrück, Rietberg and the surrounding area offer a diverse culinary scene. Since its first edition in 1992, this compact restaurant guide has developed into a unique, professional local guide. The heart of the magazine handy in the DIN-A-5 format is the great service with well-researched part addresses of restaurants, pubs, cafes, hotels and nightclubs. Stories, recipes, news and recommendations of local celebrities around going out and enjoying. The dining guide is free in the good food, available in selected stores of the retail and tourist information.
Language(s): German
ADVERTISING RATES:
Full Page Mono .... EUR 1156
Full Page Colour .... EUR 1847
Mechanical Data: Type Area: 190 x 130 mm, No. of Columns (Display): 3, Col Widths (Display): 40 mm
Copy instructions: *Copy Date:* 15 days prior to publication

GÜTERVERKEHR
729370G49C-76

Editorial: Siegfriedstr. 28, 53179 BONN
Tel: 228 9545344 **Fax:** 228 9545327
Email: gueterverkehr@kirschbaum.de **Web site:** http://www.kirschbaum.de
Freq: 9 issues yearly; **Annual Sub.:** EUR 70,00; **Circ:** 24,862
Editor: Dirk Sanne; **Advertising Manager:** Volker Rutkowski
Profile: "güterverkehr" is a trade magazine on corporate governance for business and fleet management in the company of commercial road transport, both for short-distance traffic and long-distance traffic goods as well as for. The journal has an editorial focus on vehicle technology, transport, handling and storage techniques. Business and trade policy issues as well as current information on international transport, logistics, law and road safety round out the reading range.
Language(s): German
Readership: Aimed at managers, engineers and technologists.
ADVERTISING RATES:
Full Page Mono .... EUR 5020
Full Page Colour .... EUR 6720
Mechanical Data: Type Area: 260 x 185 mm, No. of Columns (Display): 4, Col Widths (Display): 44 mm
BUSINESS: TRANSPORT: Freight

GV KOMPAKT
729438G11A-640

Editorial: Am Friedrichshain 22, 10407 BERLIN
Tel: 30 42151427 **Fax:** 30 42151214
Email: gv-kompakt.redaktion@hussberlin.de **Web site:** http://www.gv-kompakt.de
Freq: 10 issues yearly; **Annual Sub.:** EUR 60,00; **Circ:** 10,844
Editor: Asim Loncaric; **Advertising Manager:** Ines Neumann
Profile: Magazine for the catering and gastronomy trade.
Language(s): German
ADVERTISING RATES:
Full Page Mono .... EUR 3820
Full Page Colour .... EUR 4600
Mechanical Data: Type Area: 266 x 184 mm, No. of Columns (Display): 4, Col Widths (Display): 43 mm
Copy instructions: *Copy Date:* 15 days prior to publication
Official Journal of: Organ d. Verb. d. Küchenleiter/-innen in Krankenhäusern + Pflegeeinrichtungen e.V.
BUSINESS: CATERING: Catering, Hotels & Restaurants

GVMANAGER
729439G11A-680

Editorial: Augustenstr. 10, 80333 MÜNCHEN
Tel: 89 370600 **Fax:** 89 37060111
Email: muc@blmedien.de **Web site:** http://www.gvmanager.de
Freq: 10 issues yearly; **Annual Sub.:** EUR 81,00; **Circ:** 13,979
Editor: Annemarie Heinrichsdobler; **Advertising Manager:** Bernd Moeser
Profile: "Gvmanager", as one of the leading industry trade journals offers executives in large restaurants and catering services training information. "Gvmanager" gives precise and easily comprehensible product and industry information to sales-intensive groups, provides an overview of developments and trends in the out-of-home catering, focused on the manager. Embedded in journalistic forms (report, declaration, report, comment) the exclusive scientific article is in the center of the editorial approach. "Gvmanager" focuses in clear outlined structure the main highlights of the industry, gives practical marketing recommendations, provides customers with product category overviews and product profiles, industry knowledge deepened by recent interviews, news and business reports. "Gvmanager" provides a unique overview of the current program of seminar providers and management institutions in the form of a seminar and event calendar, presents expansive markets like catering, take-away-business and e-commerce in detail through case studies and market surveys. Target groups: managers in large restaurants and catering, exclusively decision makers for example, providers of large dining facilities, company cafeterias, hospitals, nursing homes, cafeterias, wholesale and contract catering.
Language(s): German
Readership: Aimed at caterers and managers of large catering facilities.
ADVERTISING RATES:
Full Page Mono .... EUR 4975
Full Page Colour .... EUR 6860
Mechanical Data: Type Area: 260 x 185 mm, No. of Columns (Display): 4, Col Widths (Display): 43 mm
Copy instructions: *Copy Date:* 15 days prior to publication
Supplement(s): Kaffee & Co.; Trinktime
BUSINESS: CATERING: Catering, Hotels & Restaurants

GV-PRAXIS
729441G11A-660

Editorial: Mainzer Landstr. 251, 60326 FRANKFURT
Tel: 69 75951226 **Fax:** 69 75951507
Email: red.gv-p@dfv.de **Web site:** http://www.gv-praxis.de
Freq: 11 issues yearly; **Annual Sub.:** EUR 143,00; **Circ:** 11,148
Editor: Burkart Schmid; **Advertising Manager:** Christiane Pretz
Profile: Magazine focusing on catering on a large-scale for the institutional food service.
Language(s): German
Readership: Aimed at managers and cooks of large food-serving facilities.
ADVERTISING RATES:
Full Page Mono .... EUR 5082
Full Page Colour .... EUR 6555
Mechanical Data: Type Area: 260 x 190 mm, No. of Columns (Display): 4, Col Widths (Display): 45 mm
BUSINESS: CATERING: Catering, Hotels & Restaurants

GWF GAS ERDGAS
729443G24-70

Editorial: Rosenheimer Str. 145, 81671 MÜNCHEN
Tel: 89 45051388 **Fax:** 89 45051323
Email: trenkle@oldenbourg.de **Web site:** http://www.oldenbourg-industrieverlag.de
Freq: Monthly; **Annual Sub.:** EUR 319,00; **Circ:** 1,898
Editor: Volker Trenkle; **Advertising Manager:** Helga Pelzer
Profile: Magazine covering production, distribution and use of gas.
Language(s): German
Readership: Aimed at professionals in the gas supply industry.
ADVERTISING RATES:
Full Page Mono .... EUR 2840
Full Page Colour .... EUR 4010
Mechanical Data: Type Area: 252 x 188 mm, No. of Columns (Display): 7, Col Widths (Display): 23 mm
Copy instructions: *Copy Date:* 25 days prior to publication
Official Journal of: Organ d. Dt. Vereinigung d. Gas- u. Wasserfaches e.V., d. Bundesverb. d. Energie- u. Wasserwirtschaft e.V., d. Bundesvereinigung d. Firmen im Gas- u. Wasserfach e.V., d. Österr. Vereinigung f. d. Gas- u. Wasserfach u. d. Fachverb. d. Gas- u. Wärmeversorgungsunternehmen Österr., d. Fachverb. Kathod. Korrosionsschutz
Supplement(s): R + S Recht und Steuern im Gas- und Wasserfach
BUSINESS: GAS

GWF WASSER ABWASSER
729444G42C-25

Editorial: Rosenheimer Str. 145, 81671 MÜNCHEN
Tel: 89 45051318 **Fax:** 89 45051207
Email: ziegler@oiv.de **Web site:** http://www.gwf-wasser-abwasser.de
Freq: Monthly; **Annual Sub.:** EUR 318,00; **Circ:** 2,581
Editor: Christine Ziegler; **Advertising Manager:** Inge Matos Feliz
Profile: gwf Wasser Abwasser is the leading technical and scientific journal for qualitative and quantitative water management, hydrogeological principles of water management, catchment, storage or distribution of water as well as wastewater collection or drainage. gwf-Wasser|Abwasser reports on the process engineering for water treatment, wastewater purification and sludge treatment, on developments in analysis, metrology and control technology, on hygiene and microbiology and operational experiences, common concerns of water protection from the perspective of water use and wastewater disposal as well as on judical subjects and economic concerns.
Language(s): German
Readership: Read by managers of utility companies, engineers, members of local authorities, manufacturers and suppliers of plant and equipment.
ADVERTISING RATES:
Full Page Mono .... EUR 2990
Full Page Colour .... EUR 4160
Mechanical Data: Type Area: 250 x 176 mm, No. of Columns (Display): 4, Col Widths (Display): 41 mm
Official Journal of: Organ d. Dt. Vereinigung d. Gas- u. Wasserfaches e.V., d. Bundesverb. d. Energie- u. Wasserwirtschaft e.V., d. Bundesvereinigung d. Firmen im Gas- u. Wasserfach e.V., d. Dt. Vereinigung f. Wasserwirtschaft, Abwasser u. Abfall, d. Österr. Vereinigung f. d. Gas- u. Wasserfach, d. Fachverb. d. Gas- u. Wärmeversorgungsunternehmen Österr., d. ArGe Wasserwerke Bodensee-Rhein, d. ArGe Rhein-Wasserwerke e.V., d. ArGe d. Wasserwerke an d. Ruhr u. d. ArGe Trinkwassertalsperren e.V.
Supplement(s): R + S Recht und Steuern im Gas- und Wasserfach
BUSINESS: CONSTRUCTION: Water Engineering

GW-TRENDS
1792623G27-3034

Editorial: Aschauer Str. 30, 81549 MÜNCHEN
Tel: 89 2030432440 **Fax:** 89 20304362440
Email: gwtrends@springer.com **Web site:** http://www.gw-trends.de
Freq: 6 issues yearly; **Annual Sub.:** EUR 124,00; **Circ:** 13,705
Editor: Martin Endlein; **Advertising Manager:** Michael Harms
Profile: Twitter: http://twitter.com/#!/gwtrends.
Language(s): German
ADVERTISING RATES:
Full Page Colour .... EUR 6470
Mechanical Data: Type Area: 240 x 175 mm

GYMNASIUM
729448G62D-2330

Editorial: Unter den Linden 6, 10099 BERLIN
Email: ulrich.schmitzer@staff.hu-berlin.de
Freq: 6 issues yearly; **Annual Sub.:** EUR 83,40; **Circ:** 950
Editor: Ulrich Schmitzer; **Advertising Manager:** Rotraud Hohlbein
Profile: Magazine about education within German grammar schools.
Language(s): English; German
ADVERTISING RATES:
Full Page Mono .... EUR 558
Mechanical Data: Type Area: 190 x 113 mm
Official Journal of: Organ d. Dt. Altphilologen-Verb.
BUSINESS: CHURCH & SCHOOL EQUIPMENT & EDUCATION: Secondary Education

GYN
729454G56A-4260

Editorial: Borsteler Chaussee 85, Haus 16, 22453 HAMBURG **Tel:** 40 232334 **Fax:** 40 230292
Email: info@omnimedonline.de **Web site:** http://www.omnimedonline.de
Freq: 6 issues yearly; **Annual Sub.:** EUR 53,50; **Circ:** 16,553
Editor: Andreas Salfelder; **Advertising Manager:** Vanessa Baack
Profile: Medical journal focusing on gynaecology.
Language(s): German
ADVERTISING RATES:
Full Page Mono .... EUR 2370
Full Page Colour .... EUR 3930
Mechanical Data: Type Area: 250 x 180 mm, No. of Columns (Display): 3, Col Widths (Display): 56 mm
Copy instructions: *Copy Date:* 42 days prior to publication
BUSINESS: HEALTH & MEDICAL

DER GYNÄKOLOGE
729455G56A-4300

Editorial: Tiergartenstr. 17, 69121 HEIDELBERG
Tel: 6221 4878891 **Fax:** 6221 48768891
Email: katharina.bernsmeier@springer.com **Web site:** http://www.dergynaekologe.de
Freq: Monthly; **Annual Sub.:** EUR 285,00; **Circ:** 4,105
Advertising Manager: Odette Thomßen
Profile: Der Gynäkologe is a respected publication organ for all gynecologists working in practical and clinical environments and scientists who are particularly interested in issues of gynecology. The journal offers up-to-date information from all fields of gynecology and obstetrics including topics from the fields of endocrinology and reproductive medicine. The bandwidth of the journal?s content is complemented by interdisciplinary and related topics from oncology, surgery, internal medicine, and legal medicine. Comprehensive reviews on a specific topical issue provide evidenced based information on diagnostics and therapy. Review articles under the rubric "Continuing Medical Education" present verified results of scientific research and their integration into daily practice.
Language(s): German
ADVERTISING RATES:
Full Page Mono .... EUR 2940
Full Page Colour .... EUR 4130
Mechanical Data: Type Area: 240 x 174 mm
Official Journal of: Organ d. Dt. Ges. f. Gynäkologie u. Geburtshilfe
BUSINESS: HEALTH & MEDICAL

GYNÄKOLOGIE + GEBURTSHILFE
729457G56A-4320

Editorial: Aschauer Str. 30, 81549 MÜNCHEN
Tel: 89 2030431403 **Fax:** 89 2030431399
Email: claudia.maeck@springer.com **Web site:** http://www.gynundgeburtshilfe.de
Freq: 11 issues yearly; **Annual Sub.:** EUR 143,00; **Circ:** 11,126
Editor: Claudia Mäck
Profile: The journal gynäkologie + geburtshilfe offers profound and practical training with the latest results from research and clinic of the department and neighboring areas. The training is based on three pillars: Short presentations by experienced gynecologists commented international studies, i.a. from oncology, well-structured review articles and conference proceedings. In addition, controversial issues in the pros and cons discussed and innovative practice concepts presented. The contents of the journal are accepted by the Bavarian Medical Council for certified training.
Language(s): German
ADVERTISING RATES:
Full Page Mono .... EUR 2820
Full Page Colour .... EUR 4320
Mechanical Data: Type Area: 240 x 174 mm
Official Journal of: Organ d. ArGe Naturheilkunde, Akupunktur u. Umweltmedizin in d. Dt. Ges. f. Gynäkologie u. Geburtshilfe e.V. u. d. Ärztl. Genossenschaft GenoGyn e.G.
BUSINESS: HEALTH & MEDICAL

GYNÄKOLOGISCHE ENDOKRINOLOGIE
1609356G56A-11164

Editorial: Tiergartenstr. 17, 69121 HEIDELBERG
Tel: 6221 4870 **Fax:** 6221 4878366
Email: subscriptions@springer.com **Web site:** http://www.springerlink.com
Freq: Quarterly; **Annual Sub.:** EUR 125,00; **Circ:** 1,300
Editor: Thomas Strowitzki; **Advertising Manager:** Kathrin Müller-Kölling
Profile: Gynäkologische Endokrinologie offers up-to-date review articles and original papers for all gynaecologists working in practical and clinical environments and scientists who are particularly interested in issues of endocrinology. The content covers all areas of gynaecological endocrinology and reproduction medicine. The focus is on current developments regarding prevention, diagnostic approaches, management of complications and current therapy strategies. Freely submitted original papers allow the presentation of important clinical studies and serve scientific exchange. Comprehensive reviews on a specific topical issue focus on providing evidenced based information on diagnostics and therapy. Review articles under the rubric "Continuing Medical Education" present verified results of scientific research and their integration into daily practice.
Language(s): German
ADVERTISING RATES:
Full Page Mono .... EUR 1180
Full Page Colour .... EUR 2220
Mechanical Data: No. of Columns (Display): 3, Col Widths (Display): 54 mm, Type Area: 240 x 175 mm
Official Journal of: Organ d. Dt. Ges. f. Gynäkol. Endokrinologie u. Fortpflanzungsmedizin u. d. Dt. Menopause Ges.

GYN-DEPESCHE
729462G56A-4280

Editorial: Paul-Wassermann-Str. 15, 81829 MÜNCHEN **Tel:** 89 436630230 **Fax:** 89 436630211
Email: ehnert@gfi-online.de **Web site:** http://www.gfi-medien.de
Freq: 6 issues yearly; **Annual Sub.:** EUR 36,00; **Circ:** 10,595
Editor: Wilfried Ehnert; **Advertising Manager:** Klaus Bombös
Profile: Medical journal containing information and research for the field of gynaecology.
Language(s): German
ADVERTISING RATES:
Full Page Mono .... EUR 2395
Full Page Colour .... EUR 3635
Mechanical Data: Type Area: 258 x 185 mm, No. of Columns (Display): 3, Col Widths (Display): 59 mm
Copy instructions: *Copy Date:* 21 days prior to publication
BUSINESS: HEALTH & MEDICAL

GYNE
1665817G56A-11342

Editorial: Postfach 440265, 80751 MÜNCHEN
Email: redaktion@gyne.de **Web site:** http://www.gyne.de
Freq: Monthly; Free to qualifying individuals
Annual Sub.: EUR 30,00; **Circ:** 9,752
Editor: Christian J. Thaler
Profile: Magazine for gynaecologists.
Language(s): German
ADVERTISING RATES:
Full Page Mono .... EUR 2880
Full Page Colour .... EUR 4130
Mechanical Data: Type Area: 283 x 212 mm, No. of Columns (Display): 3, Col Widths (Display): 67 mm
Copy instructions: *Copy Date:* 28 days prior to publication
BUSINESS: HEALTH & MEDICAL

GYNECOLOGICAL SURGERY
1832426G56A-11542

Editorial: Heidelberger Platz 3, 14197 BERLIN
Tel: 30 827870 **Fax:** 30 8214091
Email: subscriptions@springer.com **Web site:** http://www.springer.com
Freq: Quarterly; **Annual Sub.:** EUR 676,00; **Circ:** 1,142
Editor: Ivo Brosens
Profile: Gynecological Surgery presents the surgical aspects of endoscopic imaging and allied techniques.

Language(s): English
ADVERTISING RATES:
Full Page Mono .... EUR 920
Full Page Colour .... EUR 1960
Mechanical Data: Type Area: 240 x 175 mm
Official Journal of: Organ d. European Society for Gynaecological Endoscopy

GZ GOLDSCHMIEDE ZEITUNG
729466G52A-42
Editorial: Innocentiastr. 33, 20144 HAMBURG
Tel: 40 189881140 Fax: 40 189881111
Email: info@gz-online.de Web site: http://www.gz-online.de
Freq: Monthly; Annual Sub.: EUR 118,15; Circ: 9,933
Editor: Christian Jürgens; Advertising Manager: Rolf Bendel
Profile: International trade magazine containing information on the jewellery, clock and watch trade.
Language(s): German
Readership: Aimed at retailers.
ADVERTISING RATES:
Full Page Mono .... EUR 2650
Full Page Colour .... EUR 3880
Mechanical Data: Type Area: 268 x 193 mm, No. of Columns (Display): 4, Col Widths (Display): 45 mm
Copy instructions: Copy Date: 20 days prior to publication
Official Journal of: Organ d. Landesinnungsverb. d. Juweliere, Gold- u. Silberschmiede Niedersachsen/Bremen, d. LV d. Gold- u. Silberschmiede sowie Juweliere Nordrhein-Westfalen, d. LV Bayern f. d. Gold- u. Silberschmiedehandwerk u. d. Ges. f. Goldschmiedekunst e.V. f. d. Saarland, Mttl. d. Zentralverb. d. Dt. Gold-, Silberschmiede u. Juweliere e.V., Mttbl. d. Verbände u. Innungen sowie d. Bundesverb. d. Schmuck-Großhandels e.V., d. Bundesgroßhandelsverb. f. Uhren u. uhrentechn. Bedarf e.V. u. d. Fachvereinigung Edelmetalle e.V.
BUSINESS: GIFT TRADE: Jewellery

GZ LIVE
2084939G74A-3825
Editorial: Innocentiastr. 33, 20144 HAMBURG
Tel: 40 1898810 Fax: 40 189881111
Email: s.juergens@untitled-verlag.de Web site: http://www.gzlive.de
Freq: Half-yearly; Cover Price: EUR 7,50; Circ: 24,000
Editor: Sigrid Jürgens; Advertising Manager: Sabine Schwerg
Profile: Fashion, Jewellery and Watches Magazine.
Language(s): German
ADVERTISING RATES:
Full Page Colour .... EUR 4200
Mechanical Data: Type Area: 280 x 210 mm

H & E
730637G25-1
Editorial: Rabenkopfweg 32, 65931 FRANKFURT
Tel: 69 363560 Fax: 69 362654
Email: hwq@hehandelszeitung.com Web site: http://www.hehandelszeitung.com
Freq: 6 issues yearly; Annual Sub.: EUR 18,60; Circ: 5,870
Editor: Helmut W. Quast; Advertising Manager: Jutta Quast
Profile: Magazine about new products and marketing techniques within the hardware trade. Covers tools and equipment, ironmongery, electronic appliances and garden requisites.
Language(s): German
ADVERTISING RATES:
Full Page Mono .... EUR 5480
Full Page Colour .... EUR 7550
Mechanical Data: Type Area: 390 x 285 mm, No. of Columns (Display): 6, Col Widths (Display): 45 mm
Copy instructions: Copy Date: 21 days prior to publication
BUSINESS: HARDWARE

H & E HAUS & ELEKTRONIK
756024G17-1522
Editorial: Krummbogen 14, 35039 MARBURG
Tel: 6421 96140 Fax: 6421 961423
Email: redaktion@beam-verlag.de Web site: http://www.beam-verlag.de
Freq: Quarterly; Circ: 5,000
Editor: Frank Sichla; Advertising Manager: Frank Wege
Profile: Magazine about building services engineering and security technology.
Language(s): German
ADVERTISING RATES:
Full Page Mono .... EUR 1600
Full Page Colour .... EUR 2000
Mechanical Data: Type Area: 264 x 185 mm, No. of Columns (Display): 4, Col Widths (Display): 43 mm

H & V JOURNAL
730664G14A-3140
Editorial: Am Weidendamm 1a, 10117 BERLIN
Tel: 30 72625600 Fax: 30 72625699
Email: mischon@cdh.de Web site: http://www.cdh.de
Freq: 10 issues yearly; Free to qualifying individuals
Annual Sub.: EUR 85,00; Circ: 11,046
Editor: Hermann Hubert Pfeil; Advertising Manager: Eva Hanenberg
Profile: Official journal of the Central Association of Trade Representatives.
Language(s): German
ADVERTISING RATES:
Full Page Mono .... EUR 3330
Full Page Colour .... EUR 4854
Mechanical Data: Type Area: 240 x 175 mm, No. of Columns (Display): 4, Col Widths (Display): 40 mm
BUSINESS: COMMERCE, INDUSTRY & MANAGEMENT

HABEN & SEIN
1865601G89A-12430
Editorial: Arcisstr. 68, 80801 MÜNCHEN
Tel: 89 5505660 Fax: 89 55056612
Email: redaktion@gomuenchen.com Web site: http://www.gomuenchen.de
Freq: Annual; Cover Price: EUR 7,80; Circ: 20,000
Editor: Daniel Wiechmann; Advertising Manager: Susanne Staßer
Profile: Shopping guide for Munich. Detailed descriptions and illustrations of the 300 Top Shops Munich, with maps and many other service information.
Language(s): English; German
ADVERTISING RATES:
Full Page Mono .... EUR 2260
Full Page Colour .... EUR 3580
Mechanical Data: Type Area: 265 x 188 mm, No. of Columns (Display): 4, Col Widths (Display): 44 mm
Copy instructions: Copy Date: 21 days prior to publication

HAIGERER KURIER
729497G67B-6280
Editorial: Rathausstr. 1, 35683 DILLENBURG
Tel: 2771 8740 Fax: 2771 874261
Email: redaktion@dill.de Web site: http://www.dill.de
Freq: 312 issues yearly; Circ: 7,559
Profile: Daily newspaper with regional news and a local sports section.
Language(s): German
ADVERTISING RATES:
SCC .... EUR 27,80
Mechanical Data: Type Area: 467 x 327 mm, No. of Columns (Display): 7, Col Widths (Display): 44 mm
Copy instructions: Copy Date: 1 day prior to publication
Supplement(s): Anpfiff; [g]esund!
REGIONAL DAILY & SUNDAY NEWSPAPERS: Regional Daily Newspapers

HAIGERER KURIER AM SONNTAG
1609305G72-17867
Editorial: Rathausstr. 1, 35683 DILLENBURG
Tel: 2771 8740 Fax: 2771 874261
Email: redaktion@dill.de Web site: http://www.dill.de
Freq: Weekly; Cover Price: EUR 1,20; Circ: 7,559
Profile: Regional weekly covering politics, economics, sport, travel, technology and the arts.
Language(s): German
ADVERTISING RATES:
SCC .... EUR 27,80
Mechanical Data: Type Area: 490 x 328 mm, No. of Columns (Display): 7, Col Widths (Display): 44 mm
Copy instructions: Copy Date: 2 days prior to publication
LOCAL NEWSPAPERS

HAIGERER ZEITUNG
729498G67B-6300
Editorial: Elsa-Brandström-Str. 18, 35578 WETZLAR
Tel: 6441 9590 Fax: 6441 959292
Email: redaktion.wnz@mittelhessen.de Web site: http://www.mittelhessen.de
Freq: 312 issues yearly; Circ: 21,471
Advertising Manager: Peter Rother
Profile: Daily newspaper with regional news and a local sports section.
Language(s): German
ADVERTISING RATES:
SCC .... EUR 66,50
Mechanical Data: Type Area: 490 x 328 mm, No. of Columns (Display): 7, Col Widths (Display): 44 mm
Copy instructions: Copy Date: 1 day prior to publication
Supplement(s): Anpfiff; [f]amilie& freizeit; [g]esund!; rtv
REGIONAL DAILY & SUNDAY NEWSPAPERS: Regional Daily Newspapers

HAI-LIGHTS
729499G89C-4802
Editorial: Max-Planck-Ring 45, 65205 WIESBADEN
Tel: 6122 70740 Fax: 6122 707410
Email: info@hailights.de Web site: http://www.hailights.de
Freq: Quarterly; Cover Price: Free; Circ: 20,000
Advertising Manager: Mathias Vogel
Profile: The city magazine of Wiesbaden and Mainz with dates and events of the region.
Language(s): German
ADVERTISING RATES:
Full Page Mono .... EUR 1600
Full Page Colour .... EUR 1600
Mechanical Data: Type Area: 180 x 118 mm, No. of Columns (Display): 4, Col Widths (Display): 28 mm
Copy instructions: Copy Date: 15 days prior to publication
CONSUMER: HOLIDAYS & TRAVEL: Entertainment Guides

HAIR UND BEAUTY
729502G74H-45
Editorial: Rosenkavalierplatz 14, 81925 MÜNCHEN
Tel: 89 9100930 Fax: 89 91009353
Email: p.kerler@ipm-verlag.de Web site: http://www.ipm-verlag.de
Freq: 6 issues yearly; Annual Sub.: EUR 17,00; Circ: 50,000
Editor: Pamela Kerler; Advertising Manager: Rüdiger Knapp
Profile: International magazine focusing on hair and beauty.
Language(s): German
ADVERTISING RATES:
Full Page Mono .... EUR 8400
Full Page Colour .... EUR 8400
Mechanical Data: Type Area: 260 x 185 mm
CONSUMER: WOMEN'S INTEREST CONSUMER MAGAZINES: Hair & Beauty

HAIRSTYLE!
729501G74H-47
Editorial: Rosenkavalierplatz 14, 81925 MÜNCHEN
Tel: 89 9100930 Fax: 89 91009353
Email: p.kerler@ipm-verlag.de Web site: http://www.ipm-verlag.de
Freq: Annual; Cover Price: EUR 3,50; Circ: 50,000
Editor: Pamela Kerler; Advertising Manager: Rüdiger Knapp
Profile: Magazine containing information about hairstyles, haircolouring and trends.
Language(s): German
Readership: Read by teenagers and women up to 25 years.
ADVERTISING RATES:
Full Page Mono .... EUR 4500
Full Page Colour .... EUR 4500
Mechanical Data: Type Area: 206 x 148 mm
CONSUMER: WOMEN'S INTEREST CONSUMER MAGAZINES: Hair & Beauty

HALBERSTÄDTER VOLKSSTIMME
729505G67B-6320
Editorial: Bahnhofstr. 17, 39104 MAGDEBURG
Tel: 391 59990 Fax: 391 5999210
Email: chefredaktion@volksstimme.de Web site: http://www.volksstimme.de
Freq: 312 issues yearly; Circ: 13,689
Advertising Manager: Rainer Pfeil
Profile: As the largest daily newspaper in northern Saxony-Anhalt, the Volksstimme reaches 536,000 readers a day* (MA 2010). From Monday to Saturday a team of highly qualified editors put together the latest information and news from the region and around the world. Thanks the 18 local editions is the Volksstimme always close to the action. Twitter: http://twitter.com/volksstimme This Outlet offers RSS (Really Simple Syndication).
Language(s): German
ADVERTISING RATES:
SCC .... EUR 56,00
Mechanical Data: Type Area: 480 x 327 mm, No. of Columns (Display): 7, Col Widths (Display): 45 mm
Copy instructions: Copy Date: 2 days prior to publication
Supplement(s): Anstoss in Halberstadt; bauRatgeber; Biber; Leser-Reisen; prisma; Standort Landkreis Halberstadt
REGIONAL DAILY & SUNDAY NEWSPAPERS: Regional Daily Newspapers

HALBSTARK
1978877G65A-220_101
Editorial: Allende-Platz 1, 20146 HAMBURG
Tel: 40 41429881
Email: redaktion@halbstark-online.de Web site: http://www.halbstark-online.de
Freq: Quarterly; Circ: 90,000
Editor: Dominik Betz
Profile: In the magazine young authors write about young subjects. Each issue presents heads and issues of our generation, represents a variety of lifestyles - and shows similarities where none are expected. Published by journalism students, the work of young writers, graphic designers and photographers. Target group: 20 - to 35-year-old with high education.
Language(s): German
ADVERTISING RATES:
Full Page Mono .... EUR 3869
Full Page Colour .... EUR 5507
Mechanical Data: Type Area: 427 x 282 mm, No. of Columns (Display): 4, Col Widths (Display): 70 mm
Supplement to: taz.die tageszeitung
NATIONAL DAILY & SUNDAY NEWSPAPERS: Unabhängiges konservatives MdEP

HALDENSLEBER VOLKSSTIMME
738160G67B-11280
Editorial: Bahnhofstr. 17, 39104 MAGDEBURG
Tel: 391 59990 Fax: 391 5999210
Email: chefredaktion@volksstimme.de Web site: http://www.volksstimme.de
Freq: 312 issues yearly; Circ: 7,247
Advertising Manager: Rolf Grummel
Profile: As the largest daily newspaper in northern Saxony-Anhalt, the Volksstimme reaches 536,000 readers a day* (MA 2010). From Monday to Saturday a team of highly qualified editors put together the latest information and news from the region and around the world. Thanks the 18 local editions is the Volksstimme always close to the action. Twitter: http://twitter.com/volksstimme This Outlet offers RSS (Really Simple Syndication).
Language(s): German
ADVERTISING RATES:
SCC .... EUR 60,40
Mechanical Data: Type Area: 480 x 327 mm, No. of Columns (Display): 7, Col Widths (Display): 45 mm
Copy instructions: Copy Date: 2 days prior to publication
Supplement(s): Anstoss in Haldensleben und Wolmirstedt; bauRatgeber; Biber; Leser-Reisen; prisma; Standort Ohrekreis
REGIONAL DAILY & SUNDAY NEWSPAPERS: Regional Daily Newspapers

HALLER KREISBLATT
729512G67B-634
Editorial: Gutenbergstr. 2, 33790 HALLE
Tel: 5201 1501 Fax: 5201 15166
Email: redaktion@haller-kreisblatt.de Web site: http://www.haller-kreisblatt.de
Freq: 312 issues yearly; Circ: 12,287
Advertising Manager: Thomas Deppe
Profile: Daily newspaper with regional news and a local sports section. Facebook: http://de-de.facebook.com/people/Haller-Kreisblatt/100001117955759 Twitter: http://twitter.com/KreisblattHalle This Outlet offers RSS (Really Simple Syndication).
Language(s): German
ADVERTISING RATES:
SCC .... EUR 54,40
Mechanical Data: Type Area: 490 x 324 mm, No. of Columns (Display): 7, Col Widths (Display): 45 mm
Copy instructions: Copy Date: 1 day prior to publication
REGIONAL DAILY & SUNDAY NEWSPAPERS: Regional Daily Newspapers

HALLER TAGBLATT
729514G67B-6360
Editorial: Haalstr. 5, 74523 SCHWÄBISCH HALL
Tel: 791 404410 Fax: 791 404480
Email: redaktion@hallertagblatt.de Web site: http://www.hallertagblatt.de
Freq: 312 issues yearly; Circ: 17,643
Editor: Tanja Kurz; Advertising Manager: Josef Jasper
Profile: Daily newspaper with regional news and a local sports section.
Language(s): German
ADVERTISING RATES:
SCC .... EUR 32,80
Mechanical Data: Type Area: 420 x 274 mm, No. of Columns (Display): 6, Col Widths (Display): 44 mm
Copy instructions: Copy Date: 1 day prior to publication
Supplement(s): Fußball lokal; Leben plus; Das Magazin
REGIONAL DAILY & SUNDAY NEWSPAPERS: Regional Daily Newspapers

HALLERTAUER ZEITUNG
729515G67B-6380
Editorial: Altstadt 89, 84028 LANDSHUT
Tel: 871 8500 Fax: 871 850132
Email: redaktion@landshuter-zeitung.de Web site: http://www.idowa.de
Freq: 312 issues yearly; Circ: 5,632
Advertising Manager: Irmgard Haberger
Profile: Regional daily newspaper with news on politics, economy, culture, sports, travel, technology, etc. She is a Local issue of the Landshuter Zeitung for the old County Mainburg. Twitter: http://twitter.com/idowa.
Language(s): German
ADVERTISING RATES:
SCC .... EUR 20,90
Mechanical Data: Type Area: 430 x 282 mm, No. of Columns (Display): 6, Col Widths (Display): 45 mm
Copy instructions: Copy Date: 1 day prior to publication
Supplement(s): Zuhause
REGIONAL DAILY & SUNDAY NEWSPAPERS: Regional Daily Newspapers

HALLO ANZEIGER
720879G72-1436
Editorial: August-Madsack-Str. 1, 30559 HANNOVER Tel: 511 5182034 Fax: 511 5182023
Email: hans.joerg.fiedler@wochenblaetter.de Web site: http://www.wochenblaetter.de
Freq: Weekly; Cover Price: Free; Circ: 18,900
Editor: Thomas Oberdorfer; Advertising Manager: Wolfgang Schiemann
Profile: Advertising journal (house-to-house) concentrating on local stories.
Language(s): German
ADVERTISING RATES:
Full Page Mono .... EUR 2322
Full Page Colour .... EUR 2632
Mechanical Data: Type Area: 430 x 277 mm, No. of Columns (Display): 6, Col Widths (Display): 45 mm
Copy instructions: Copy Date: 2 days prior to publication
LOCAL NEWSPAPERS

HALLO BERG AM LAIM
729523G72-4924
Editorial: Hans-Pinsel-Str. 9a, 85540 HAAR
Tel: 89 462335620 Fax: 89 462335699
Email: muenchen@hallo-verlag.de Web site: http://www.hallo-verlag.de
Freq: Weekly; Cover Price: Free; Circ: 20,155
Editor: Thomas Fischer; Advertising Manager: Monika Boguth
Profile: Advertising journal (house-to-house) concentrating on local stories.
Language(s): German
ADVERTISING RATES:
Full Page Mono .... EUR 1523
Full Page Colour .... EUR 1980

Mechanical Data: Type Area: 324 x 231 mm, No. of Columns (Display): 5, Col Widths (Display): 45 mm
Copy instructions: *Copy Date:* 2 days prior to publication
LOCAL NEWSPAPERS

HALLO HAAR/VATERSTETTEN
729543G72-5000
Editorial: Hans-Pinsel-Str. 9a, 85540 HAAR
Tel: 89 462335610 **Fax:** 89 462335699
Email: ost@hallo-verlag.de **Web site:** http://www.hallo-verlag.de
Freq: Weekly; **Cover Price:** Free; **Circ:** 22,220
Editor: Alfred Schwaiger; **Advertising Manager:** Monika Boguth
Profile: Advertising journal (house-to-house) concentrating on local stories.
Language(s): German
ADVERTISING RATES:
Full Page Mono .... EUR 1652
Full Page Colour .... EUR 2148
Mechanical Data: Type Area: 324 x 231 mm, No. of Columns (Display): 5, Col Widths (Display): 45 mm
Copy instructions: *Copy Date:* 2 days prior to publication
Supplement(s): Hallo Kultur
LOCAL NEWSPAPERS

HALLO HANNOVERSCHES WOCHENBLATT - AUSG. NORD
729732G72-5196
Editorial: August-Madsack-Str. 1, 30559 HANNOVER **Tel:** 511 5182070 **Fax:** 511 5182079
Email: gesamtredaktion@wochenblaetter.de **Web site:** http://www.wochenblaetter.de
Freq: Weekly; **Cover Price:** Free; **Circ:** 45,930
Editor: Thomas Oberdorfer; **Advertising Manager:** Wolfgang Schiemann
Profile: Advertising journal (house-to-house) concentrating on local stories.
Language(s): German
ADVERTISING RATES:
Full Page Mono .... EUR 4128
Full Page Colour .... EUR 4722
Mechanical Data: Type Area: 430 x 277 mm, No. of Columns (Display): 6, Col Widths (Display): 45 mm
Copy instructions: *Copy Date:* 2 days prior to publication
LOCAL NEWSPAPERS

HALLO LAATZENER WOCHE
733683G72-6556
Editorial: Albert-Schweitzer-Str. 1, 30880 LAATZEN
Tel: 511 824051 **Fax:** 511 824616
Email: laatzener.woche@wochenblaetter.de **Web site:** http://www.wochenblaetter.de
Freq: Weekly; **Cover Price:** Free; **Circ:** 36,230
Editor: Thomas Oberdorfer; **Advertising Manager:** Wolfgang Schiemann
Profile: Advertising journal (house-to-house) concentrating on local stories.
Language(s): German
ADVERTISING RATES:
Full Page Mono .... EUR 2967
Full Page Colour .... EUR 3406
Mechanical Data: Type Area: 430 x 277 mm, No. of Columns (Display): 6, Col Widths (Display): 45 mm
Copy instructions: *Copy Date:* 2 days prior to publication
LOCAL NEWSPAPERS

HALLO! LEIPZIG
729545G72-5008
Editorial: Gerberstr. 15, 04105 LEIPZIG
Tel: 341 9881433 **Fax:** 341 9800541
Email: redhallo@lwk-verlag.de **Web site:** http://www.hallo-leipzig.de
Freq: Weekly; **Cover Price:** Free; **Circ:** 233,340
Editor: Marlies Däberitz; **Advertising Manager:** Sina Häse
Profile: Advertising journal (house-to-house) concentrating on local stories.
Language(s): German
ADVERTISING RATES:
Full Page Mono .... EUR 4358
Full Page Colour .... EUR 6529
Mechanical Data: Type Area: 324 x 232 mm, No. of Columns (Display): 5, Col Widths (Display): 44 mm
Copy instructions: *Copy Date:* 3 days prior to publication
LOCAL NEWSPAPERS

HALLO MÜNCHNER NORDOSTEN
729542G72-4996
Editorial: Hans-Pinsel-Str. 9a, 85540 HAAR
Tel: 89 462335610 **Fax:** 89 462335699
Email: ost@hallo-verlag.de **Web site:** http://www.hallo-verlag.de
Freq: Weekly; **Cover Price:** Free; **Circ:** 24,160
Editor: Alfred Schwaiger; **Advertising Manager:** Monika Boguth
Profile: Advertising journal (house-to-house) concentrating on local stories.
Language(s): German
ADVERTISING RATES:
Full Page Mono .... EUR 1555
Full Page Colour .... EUR 2022
Mechanical Data: Type Area: 324 x 231 mm, No. of Columns (Display): 5, Col Widths (Display): 45 mm
Copy instructions: *Copy Date:* 2 days prior to publication
Supplement(s): Hallo Kultur
LOCAL NEWSPAPERS

HALLO RUNDBLICK GARBSEN/ SEELZE
740753G72-11224
Editorial: Rathausplatz 11, 30823 GARBSEN
Tel: 5131 462820
Email: redaktion.garbsen@wochenblaetter.de **Web site:** http://www.wochenblaetter.de
Freq: Weekly; **Cover Price:** Free; **Circ:** 48,240
Editor: Thomas Oberdorfer; **Advertising Manager:** Wolfgang Schiemann
Profile: Advertising journal (house-to-house) concentrating on local stories.
Language(s): German
ADVERTISING RATES:
Full Page Mono .... EUR 2967
Full Page Colour .... EUR 3408
Mechanical Data: Type Area: 430 x 277 mm, No. of Columns (Display): 6, Col Widths (Display): 45 mm
Copy instructions: *Copy Date:* 2 days prior to publication
LOCAL NEWSPAPERS

HALLO SONNTAG IM EICHSFELD
729575G72-5116
Editorial: In der Worth 16, 37077 GÖTTINGEN
Tel: 551 5220215 **Fax:** 551 484682
Email: red@ast-medien.de
Freq: Weekly; **Cover Price:** Free; **Circ:** 61,600
Editor: Andreas Stephainski; **Advertising Manager:** Martin Benderoth
Profile: Advertising journal (house-to-house) concentrating on local stories.
Language(s): German
ADVERTISING RATES:
Full Page Mono .... EUR 4386
Full Page Colour .... EUR 5754
Mechanical Data: Type Area: 430 x 277 mm, No. of Columns (Display): 6, Col Widths (Display): 45 mm
Copy instructions: *Copy Date:* 3 days prior to publication
LOCAL NEWSPAPERS

HALLO TAXI
1708253G49A-2411
Editorial: Jakobistr. 20, 28195 BREMEN
Tel: 421 170470 **Fax:** 421 170473
Email: redaktion@hallo-taxi.de **Web site:** http://www.hallo-taxi.de
Freq: 10 issues yearly; **Annual Sub.:** EUR 19,00; **Circ:** 25,000
Editor: Jan Cassalette
Profile: Magazine for the taxi business.
Language(s): German
ADVERTISING RATES:
Full Page Mono .... EUR 7824
Full Page Colour .... EUR 7824
Mechanical Data: Type Area: 270 x 185 mm, No. of Columns (Display): 3, Col Widths (Display): 58 mm
Copy instructions: *Copy Date:* 14 days prior to publication

HALLO TOURIST!
1813548G89A-12340
Editorial: Hauptstr. 28, 32457 PORTA WESTFALICA
Tel: 571 9752950 **Fax:** 571 9752915
Email: mag@hallo-tourist.eu **Web site:** http://www.hallo-tourist.eu
Freq: Annual; **Cover Price:** Free; **Circ:** 100,000
Editor: Marlene Gerber; **Advertising Manager:** Marlene Gerber
Profile: Tourist guide with interesting trips for families, groups and singles, including map of the area. If tourists and local day-trippers in the region in tourist information offices, palaces, castles, spas, museums, play, leisure and wildlife parks, hotels, camping, gardens, parks and passenger cruises offered free for the taking.
Language(s): German

HALLO TOURIST!
1813549G89A-12341
Editorial: Max-Samson-Str. 24, 33165 LICHTENAU
Tel: 5292 930640 **Fax:** 5292 930641
Email: info@hallo-tourist.eu **Web site:** http://www.hallo-tourist.eu
Freq: Annual; **Cover Price:** Free; **Circ:** 100,000
Profile: Tourist guide with interesting trips for families, groups and singles, including map of the area. If tourists and local day-trippers in the region in tourist information offices, palaces, castles, spas, museums, play, leisure and wildlife parks, hotels, camping, gardens, parks and passenger cruises offered free for the taking.
Language(s): German

HALLO TOURIST!
1813550G89A-12342
Editorial: Hauptstr. 28, 32457 PORTA WESTFALICA
Tel: 571 9752950 **Fax:** 571 9752915
Email: mag@hallo-tourist.de **Web site:** http://www.hallo-tourist.eu
Freq: Annual; **Cover Price:** Free; **Circ:** 100,000
Editor: Marlene Gerber; **Advertising Manager:** Marlene Gerber
Profile: Tourist guide with interesting trips for families, groups and singles, including map of the area. If tourists and local day-trippers in the region in tourist information offices, palaces, castles, spas, museums, play, leisure and wildlife parks, hotels, camping, gardens, parks and passenger cruises offered free for the taking.
Language(s): German
Mechanical Data: No. of Columns (Display): 2
Copy instructions: *Copy Date:* 60 days prior to publication

HALLO TOURIST!
1813551G89A-12343
Editorial: Hauptstr. 28, 32457 PORTA WESTFALICA
Tel: 571 9752950 **Fax:** 571 9752915
Email: mag@hallo-tourist.de **Web site:** http://www.hallo-tourist.eu
Freq: Annual; **Cover Price:** Free; **Circ:** 100,000
Editor: Marlene Gerber; **Advertising Manager:** Marlene Gerber
Profile: Tourist guide with interesting trips for families, groups and singles, including map of the area. If tourists and local day-trippers in the region in tourist information offices, palaces, castles, spas, museums, play, leisure and wildlife parks, hotels, camping, gardens, parks and passenger cruises offered free for the taking.
Language(s): German
Mechanical Data: No. of Columns (Display): 2
Copy instructions: *Copy Date:* 60 days prior to publication

HALLO TOURIST!
1813552G89A-12344
Editorial: Hauptstr. 28, 32457 PORTA WESTFALICA
Tel: 571 9752950 **Fax:** 571 9752915
Email: mag@hallo-tourist.de **Web site:** http://www.hallo-tourist.eu
Freq: Annual; **Cover Price:** Free; **Circ:** 100,000
Editor: Marlene Gerber; **Advertising Manager:** Marlene Gerber
Profile: Tourist guide with interesting trips for families, groups and singles, including map of the area. If tourists and local day-trippers in the region in tourist information offices, palaces, castles, spas, museums, play, leisure and wildlife parks, hotels, camping, gardens, parks and passenger cruises offered free for the taking.
Language(s): German
Mechanical Data: No. of Columns (Display): 2
Copy instructions: *Copy Date:* 60 days prior to publication

HALLO TOURIST!
1813553G89A-12345
Editorial: Hauptstr. 28, 32457 PORTA WESTFALICA
Tel: 571 9752950 **Fax:** 571 9752915
Email: mag@hallo-tourist.de **Web site:** http://www.hallo-tourist.eu
Freq: Annual; **Cover Price:** Free; **Circ:** 100,000
Editor: Marlene Gerber; **Advertising Manager:** Marlene Gerber
Profile: Tourist guide with interesting trips for families, groups and singles, including a map. If tourists and local day-trippers in the region in tourist information offices, palaces, castles, spas, museums, play, leisure and wildlife parks, hotels, camping, gardens, parks and passenger cruises offered free for the taking.
Language(s): German
Mechanical Data: No. of Columns (Display): 2
Copy instructions: *Copy Date:* 60 days prior to publication

HALTERNER ZEITUNG
729595G67B-6400
Editorial: Westenhellweg 86, 44137 DORTMUND
Tel: 231 90590 **Fax:** 231 90598402
Email: redaktion.rn@mdhl.de **Web site:** http://www.ruhrnachrichten.de
Freq: 312 issues yearly; **Circ:** 9,774
Profile: Daily newspaper with regional news and a local sports section. Twitter: http://twitter.com/ruhrnachrichten This Outlet offers RSS (Really Simple Syndication).
Language(s): German
ADVERTISING RATES:
SCC .... EUR 36,80
Mechanical Data: Type Area: 450 x 315 mm, No. of Columns (Display): 7, Col Widths (Display): 42 mm
Copy instructions: *Copy Date:* 2 days prior to publication
Supplement(s): Freizeit; prisma
REGIONAL DAILY & SUNDAY NEWSPAPERS: Regional Daily Newspapers

HAMBURG FÜHRER
729628G89A-2480
Editorial: Alter Wall 65, 20457 HAMBURG
Tel: 40 448185 **Fax:** 40 452368
Email: info@hamburg-fuehrer.de **Web site:** http://www.hamburg-fuehrer.de
Freq: Monthly; **Annual Sub.:** EUR 18,20; **Circ:** 44,432
Editor: Kerstin Golla; **Advertising Manager:** Karin Hahne
Profile: Hamburg Guide for residents and visitors with tips on events, restaurants and hotels, culture, shopping and sports.
Language(s): German
ADVERTISING RATES:
Full Page Mono .... EUR 2165
Full Page Colour .... EUR 3235
Mechanical Data: Type Area: 185 x 90 mm, No. of Columns (Display): 2, Col Widths (Display): 40 mm
Copy instructions: *Copy Date:* 19 days prior to publication
CONSUMER: HOLIDAYS & TRAVEL: Travel

HAMBURG GUIDE
729602G89C-165
Editorial: Alter Wall 65, 20457 HAMBURG
Tel: 40 448185 **Fax:** 40 452368
Email: info@hamburg-fuehrer.de **Web site:** http://www.hamburg-guide.de
Freq: Monthly; **Annual Sub.:** EUR 18,20; **Circ:** 30,000
Editor: Heike Schulte
Profile: Hamburg Guide for residents and visitors with tips on events, restaurants and hotels, culture, shopping and sports.
Language(s): English
Readership: Aimed at English-speaking visitors.
ADVERTISING RATES:
Full Page Mono .... EUR 2165
Full Page Colour .... EUR 3235
Mechanical Data: Type Area: 185 x 90 mm
Copy instructions: *Copy Date:* 19 days prior to publication
CONSUMER: HOLIDAYS & TRAVEL: Entertainment Guides

HAMBURGER ABENDBLATT
729603G67B-6420
Editorial: Axel-Springer-Platz 1, 20355 HAMBURG
Tel: 40 34700 **Fax:** 40 34726110
Email: briefe@abendblatt.de **Web site:** http://www.abendblatt.de
Freq: 312 issues yearly; **Circ:** 209,246
Editor: Lars Haider; **News Editor:** Matthias Pützstück; **Advertising Manager:** Dirk Seidel
Profile: As the largest subscription newspaper in the metropolitan region of Hamburg the Abendblatt is as attractive as never before. For our 701 000 readers as well as for your advertising. Place your offer in a highly attractive environment and benefit from unmatched appeal! - competent, reputable and opinion-forming - all important news from politics, local, culture, business and sports - exciting Features - numerous tips and deadlines in LIVE täglich and every Thursday in the city magazine Hamburg LIVE - various special topics - regular service-oriented supplements to sports events, cultural issues, further education and much more. Facebook: http://www.facebook.com/abendblatt/ Twitter: http://twitter.com/abendblatt_hh This Outlet offers RSS (Really Simple Syndication).
Language(s): German
Mechanical Data: Col Widths (Display): 45 mm
Copy instructions: *Copy Date:* 1 day prior to publication
Supplement(s): doppio; Gesund; Hamburger Abendblatt Alstertal Walddörfer; Hamburger Abendblatt Auto; Hamburger Abendblatt Elbvororte; Hamburger Abendblatt Hafencity live; Hamburger Abendblatt Wohnen; Himmel & Elbe; Live Hamburger Abendblatt
REGIONAL DAILY & SUNDAY NEWSPAPERS: Regional Daily Newspapers

HAMBURGER ÄRZTEBLATT
729604G56A-4440
Editorial: Humboldtstr. 56, 22083 HAMBURG
Tel: 40 202299205 **Fax:** 40 202299400
Email: verlag@aekhh.de
Freq: 11 issues yearly; **Annual Sub.:** EUR 69,98; **Circ:** 15,400
Editor: Hanno Scherf
Profile: Journal of the Hamburg medical profession and duty of each leaf Hamburg physician. The magazine published the messages of the Hamburg Chamber of Physicians, the Kassenärzlichen Vereinigung Hamburg, the Hamburg Medical Fund, and the authority, in particular the health authority. The Hamburger Ärzteblatt informed the doctor about the problems of professional policies, with special consideration of current issues from the Hamburg area. In addition, the Hamburger Ärzteblatt of dedicated training by publishing medical and scientific articles, reports of the evenings of the Medical Association and the references to training events, conferences and congresses and personal messages, such as birthdays and deaths, medical specialist awards, appointments and awards.
Language(s): German
ADVERTISING RATES:
Full Page Mono .... EUR 1608
Full Page Colour .... EUR 2573
Mechanical Data: Type Area: 260 x 188 mm, No. of Columns (Display): 4, Col Widths (Display): 44 mm
BUSINESS: HEALTH & MEDICAL

HAMBURGER MORGENPOST
729615G67B-6440
Editorial: Griegstr. 75, 22763 HAMBURG
Tel: 40 809057341 **Fax:** 40 809057349
Email: chefredaktion@mopo.de **Web site:** http://www.mopo.de
Freq: 312 issues yearly; **Circ:** 107,693
Editor: Frank Niggemeier; **News Editor:** Joachim Ortmann; **Advertising Manager:** Matthias Rahnfeld
Profile: For over 60 years shows the Hamburger Morgenpost, since 1986 in a handy tabloid format. She invites her readers a day, quickly over the news of the day, to inform most of the metropolitan region of Hamburg. Tapered and curious she writes with great passion about what moves Hamburg. Keeps you young. It is the professional magazine for the underground, the pubs and vibrant places in the city. The Hamburger Morgenpost, is read by an attractive target group: opinion leaders, innovators, regionally based, cosmopolitan Hanseatic, trend setters and creative people. The Hamburger Morgenpost has the youngest audience in Hamburg with a share of 68 percent of readers in its commercial target group between 14 and 49 years. Readers of the Hamburger Morgenpost are formed. 33 percent of readers have university-entrance diploma. Morning Post readers have a job and earn well. Sun 69 per cent of readers in a job and 57 percent have net monthly on more than 2,000 €. The Hamburger Morgenpost is a

medium for communicative people. The Morgenpost offers many opportunities to place the advertising message effectively and purposefully. Advertisers receive a customized advertising plan for their needs, as required, including the creative design. About the Hamburger Morgenpost daily advertising message reaches 360 000 readers. Since 2006, the Morgenpost published on Sunday. The Morgenpost am Sonntag is indispensable in Hamburg since then. Every Sunday informed the newspaper proved the point about Hamburg and the world. Especially the sport is the focus of reporting. Facebook: http://www.facebook.com/hamburgermorgenpost Twitter: http://twitter.com/mopo This Outlet offers RSS (Really Simple Syndication).
Language(s): German
ADVERTISING RATES:
SCC .... EUR 133,30
Mechanical Data: Type Area: 285 x 210 mm, No. of Columns (Display): 5, Col Widths (Display): 38 mm
Copy instructions: *Copy Date:* 1 day prior to publication
Supplement(s): plan7; rtv
REGIONAL DAILY & SUNDAY NEWSPAPERS: Regional Daily Newspapers

HAMBURGER MORGENPOST WWW.MOPO.DE
1621413G67B-16567
Editorial: Griegstr. 75, 22763 HAMBURG
Tel: 40 809057334 **Fax:** 4 809057349
Web site: http://www.mopo.de
Freq: Daily; **Cover Price:** Paid; **Circ:** 5,253,179 Unique Users
Editor: Frank Niggemeier; **News Editor:** Joachim Ortmann; **Advertising Manager:** Christian Bruhn
Profile: Ezine: Regional daily newspaper covering politics, economics, culture, sport, travel and technology. Facebook: http://www.facebook.com/hamburgermorgenpost.
Language(s): German
REGIONAL DAILY & SUNDAY NEWSPAPERS: Regional Daily Newspapers

HAMBURGER UNTERNEHMENSPORTRAITS
1833081G14A-10140
Editorial: Doormannsweg 22, 20259 HAMBURG
Tel: 40 414333830 **Fax:** 40 414333818
Email: info@hbzv.com **Web site:** http://www.hamburger-unternehmensportraits.de
Freq: Half-yearly; **Cover Price:** Free; **Circ:** 30,000
Editor: Henner Schulz-Karstens; **Advertising Manager:** Henner Schulz-Karstens
Profile: The publication Hamburger Unternehmensportraits is a forum that successful companies provides the opportunity to customers, presenting partners, suppliers and institutions in an editorial context. The magazine is read by entrepreneurs and executives from industry, trade and services. Supplement to the hamburger industry.
Language(s): German
ADVERTISING RATES:
Full Page Mono .... EUR 2499
Full Page Colour .... EUR 2499
Mechanical Data: Type Area: 280 x 210 mm
Copy instructions: *Copy Date:* 30 days prior to publication
Supplement to: hamburger wirtschaft

HAMBURGER UNTERNEHMENSPORTRAITS
1833081G14A-10529
Editorial: Doormannsweg 22, 20259 HAMBURG
Tel: 40 414333830 **Fax:** 40 414333818
Email: info@hbzv.com **Web site:** http://www.hamburger-unternehmensportraits.de
Freq: Half-yearly; **Cover Price:** Free; **Circ:** 30,000
Editor: Henner Schulz-Karstens; **Advertising Manager:** Henner Schulz-Karstens
Profile: The publication Hamburger Unternehmensportraits is a forum that successful companies provides the opportunity to customers, presenting partners, suppliers and institutions in an editorial context. The magazine is read by entrepreneurs and executives from industry, trade and services. Supplement to the hamburger industry.
Language(s): German
ADVERTISING RATES:
Full Page Mono .... EUR 2499
Full Page Colour .... EUR 2499
Mechanical Data: Type Area: 280 x 210 mm
Copy instructions: *Copy Date:* 30 days prior to publication
Supplement to: hamburger wirtschaft

HAMBURGER WIRTSCHAFT
729624G63-280
Editorial: Adolphsplatz 1, 20457 HAMBURG
Tel: 40 36138305 **Fax:** 40 36138460
Email: redaktion@hamburger-wirtschaft.de **Web site:** http://www.hamburger-wirtschaft.de
Freq: Monthly; Free to qualifying individuals
Annual Sub.: EUR 30,00; **Circ:** 62,630
Editor: Wolfgang Ehemann; **Advertising Manager:** Henner Schulz-Karstens
Profile: The journal hamburger wirtschaft is the official publication of the Hamburg Chamber of Commerce. The regional business magazine reaches all the registered full members of the Chamber of Commerce in the fields of industry, commerce, services and transport at the strong economy in Hamburg. Many small business owners like to read the magazine. The recipients decide on the investments in their businesses and are affluent consumers. The magazine highlighted the economy and economic policy from a regional perspective, comments on regional policy decisions from the perspective of the economy, gives tips for the daily management practice, provides information on tax, finance, law, foreign trade, sales, trade, transport, vocational training or further education and help, new markets to open up.
Language(s): German
ADVERTISING RATES:
Full Page Mono .... EUR 3722
Full Page Colour .... EUR 6146
Mechanical Data: Type Area: 260 x 185 mm, No. of Columns (Display): 3, Col Widths (Display): 58 mm
Copy instructions: *Copy Date:* 21 days prior to publication
Supplement(s): B4B Mittelstand; Hamburger Unternehmensportraits
BUSINESS: REGIONAL BUSINESS

HAMBURGER ZAHNÄRZTEBLATT
729625G56D-500
Editorial: Möllner Landstr. 31, 22111 HAMBURG
Tel: 40 73340517 **Fax:** 40 7334059917
Email: gerd.eisentraut@zahnaerzte-hh.de **Web site:** http://www.zahnaerzte-hh.de
Freq: 11 issues yearly; Free to qualifying individuals
Annual Sub.: EUR 42,00; **Circ:** 3,349
Editor: Gerd Eisentraut; **Advertising Manager:** Horst Benad
Profile: Official newsletter of the Dental Association of Hamburg and the physicians' association in Hamburg. Target group: Practicing dentists, and in retirement.
Language(s): German
ADVERTISING RATES:
Full Page Mono .... EUR 1014
Full Page Colour .... EUR 1605
Mechanical Data: Type Area: 265 x 183 mm, No. of Columns (Display): 3, Col Widths (Display): 58 mm
Copy instructions: *Copy Date:* 20 days prior to publication
BUSINESS: HEALTH & MEDICAL: Dental

HAMBURG:PUR
729635G80-4460
Editorial: Behringstr. 14, 22765 HAMBURG
Tel: 40 4328420 **Fax:** 40 4328230
Email: musik@hamburg-pur.de **Web site:** http://www.hamburg-pur.de
Freq: Monthly; **Cover Price:** Free; **Circ:** 42,261
Editor: Michael Weiland; **Advertising Manager:** Christian Kröger
Profile: Magazine with details of the arts in Hamburg.
Language(s): German
Readership: Aimed at the young people in Hamburg.
ADVERTISING RATES:
Full Page Mono .... EUR 2280
Full Page Colour .... EUR 3880
Mechanical Data: No. of Columns (Display): 3, Col Widths (Display): 61 mm, Type Area: 260 x 190 mm
Copy instructions: *Copy Date:* 14 days prior to publication
CONSUMER: RURAL & REGIONAL INTEREST

HAMELNER MARKT
729637G72-5176
Editorial: Baustr. 44, 31785 HAMELN
Tel: 5151 578814 **Fax:** 5151 578816
Email: e.hesse@wrw-hameln.de **Web site:** http://www.wrw-hameln.de
Freq: Weekly; **Cover Price:** Free; **Circ:** 75,000
Editor: Guido-Erol Hesse-Öztanil; **Advertising Manager:** Claudia Reisch
Profile: Advertising journal (house-to-house) concentrating on local stories.
Language(s): German
ADVERTISING RATES:
Full Page Mono .... EUR 3499
Full Page Colour .... EUR 4199
Mechanical Data: Type Area: 430 x 281 mm, No. of Columns (Display): 6, Col Widths (Display): 44 mm
Copy instructions: *Copy Date:* 2 days prior to publication
LOCAL NEWSPAPERS

HÄMOSTASEOLOGIE
729476G56A-4460
Editorial: Hölderlinstr. 3, 70174 STUTTGART
Tel: 711 2298733 **Fax:** 711 2298765
Email: barbara.tshisuaka@schattauer.de **Web site:** http://www.haemostaseologie-online.de
Freq: Quarterly; **Annual Sub.:** EUR 140,00; **Circ:** 3,100
Editor: Barbara Tshisuaka; **Advertising Manager:** Christian Matthe
Profile: The interdisciplinary, CME-certified specialist scientific organ on the topics of hemorrhage and thromboembolism is aimed at specialists in Hemostasis and clinically and practice active physicians of many areas of expertise. The audience finds itself in accordance with the curative internal medicine as well as in the surgical specialties. Each issue is devoted to a topic. The overview articles provide the state of the art of diagnosis and therapy in Hemostasis contrary to a training focus. In addition, information papers and short communications on topical issues.
Language(s): English; German
ADVERTISING RATES:
Full Page Mono .... EUR 2115
Full Page Colour .... EUR 3255
Mechanical Data: Type Area: 243 x 179 mm, No. of Columns (Display): 3, Col Widths (Display): 57 mm
Copy instructions: *Copy Date:* 40 days prior to publication
Official Journal of: Organ d. Ges. f. Thrombose- u. Hämostaseforschung e.V.
BUSINESS: HEALTH & MEDICAL

HANAUER ANZEIGER
729646G67B-6500
Editorial: Donaustr. 5, 63452 HANAU
Tel: 6181 2903333 **Fax:** 6181 2903300
Email: redaktion@hanauer.de **Web site:** http://www.hanauer.de
Freq: 312 issues yearly; **Circ:** 17,275
Editor: Dieter Schreier; **News Editor:** Robert Göbel; **Advertising Manager:** Klaus-Peter Reinert
Profile: Regional daily newspaper covering politics, economics, sport, travel and technology.
Language(s): German
ADVERTISING RATES:
SCC .... EUR 43,50
Mechanical Data: Type Area: 480 x 323 mm, No. of Columns (Display): 7, Col Widths (Display): 44 mm
Copy instructions: *Copy Date:* 1 day prior to publication
REGIONAL DAILY & SUNDAY NEWSPAPERS: Regional Daily Newspapers

HANAUER WOCHENPOST
729648G72-5192
Editorial: Donaustr. 5, 63452 HANAU
Tel: 6181 29030 **Fax:** 6181 2903500
Email: redaktion@hanauer.de **Web site:** http://www.hanauer.de
Freq: Weekly; **Cover Price:** Free; **Circ:** 91,835
Editor: Dieter Schreier; **Advertising Manager:** Klaus-Peter Reinert
Profile: Advertising journal (house-to-house) concentrating on local stories.
Language(s): German
ADVERTISING RATES:
Full Page Mono .... EUR 6116
Full Page Colour .... EUR 7325
Mechanical Data: Type Area: 480 x 323 mm, No. of Columns (Display): 7, Col Widths (Display): 44 mm
Copy instructions: *Copy Date:* 2 days prior to publication
LOCAL NEWSPAPERS

HANDBALL TRAINING
729654G32H-251
Editorial: Rektoratsweg 36, 48159 MÜNSTER
Tel: 251 2300570 **Fax:** 251 2300599
Email: ht@philippka.de **Web site:** http://www.philippka.de
Freq: Monthly; **Annual Sub.:** EUR 45,00; **Circ:** 10,269
Editor: Dietrich Späte; **Advertising Manager:** Peter Möllers
Profile: Practical approach is the first concern, "handball training" does not float in the clouds of theory, but gives the reader practical suggestions and tips for training, provides examples of performance-oriented preparation of a team and enlarges background knowledge in an understandable way, such as tactics, training theory and sports psychology. This concept is well accepted: meanwhile four handball coaches in the Federal Republic work - purely statistical - with this magazine. This coverage is unparalleled. It is obvious that "handball training" also has an excellent reputation abroad. The editorial includes under the editorship of Dietrich Late the top-coaches Martin Heuberger, Jens Pledges and Klaus-Dieter Petersen.
Language(s): German
Readership: Aimed at teachers of physical education.
ADVERTISING RATES:
Full Page Mono .... EUR 1155
Full Page Colour .... EUR 1870
Mechanical Data: Type Area: 267 x 180 mm, No. of Columns (Display): 3, Col Widths (Display): 55 mm
Copy instructions: *Copy Date:* 28 days prior to publication
BUSINESS: LOCAL GOVERNMENT, LEISURE & RECREATION: Leisure, Recreation & Entertainment

HANDBALL WOCHE
729655G75X-55_40
Editorial: Im Mediapark 8, 50670 KÖLN
Tel: 221 2587307 **Fax:** 221 58919504
Email: redaktion@handballwoche.de **Web site:** http://www.handballwoche.de
Freq: Weekly; **Annual Sub.:** EUR 93,60; **Circ:** 14,172
Editor: Olaf Bruchmann; **Advertising Manager:** Ingeborg Schwarz
Profile: Europe's largest handball-journal. Click to see handball fans the latest news, results and tables of their favorite teams from the national team to the Champions League until the league. Reporting, background information and analysis on the palm Facebook: http://www.facebook.com/handballwoche.
Language(s): German
ADVERTISING RATES:
Full Page Mono .... EUR 2650
Full Page Colour .... EUR 2650
Mechanical Data: Type Area: 325 x 231 mm, No. of Columns (Display): 5, Col Widths (Display): 45 mm
Copy instructions: *Copy Date:* 7 days prior to publication
CONSUMER: SPORT: Other Sport

HANDBUCH FÜR DAS GESUNDHEITSWESEN IN HAMBURG
729667G56A-4480
Editorial: Humboldtstr. 56, 22083 HAMBURG
Tel: 40 228020 **Fax:** 40 22099400
Email: post@aekhh.de **Web site:** http://www.aerztekammer-hamburg.de
Freq: Annual; **Cover Price:** EUR 36,90; **Circ:** 5,000
Profile: Directory for physical doctors, dentists, pharmacists and organisations dealing with health care.
Language(s): German
ADVERTISING RATES:
Full Page Mono .... EUR 875
Mechanical Data: Type Area: 180 x 116 mm

HANDBUCH MEMO-MEDIA
1685592G2A-5636
Editorial: Rölefeld 31, 51545 WALDBRÖL
Tel: 2296 900946 **Fax:** 2296 900947
Email: info@memo-media.de **Web site:** http://www.memo-media.de
Freq: Annual; **Cover Price:** EUR 24,90; **Circ:** 9,000
Editor: Kerstin Meisner; **Advertising Manager:** Jens Kahnert
Profile: Guide for event planners and conceptionists.
Language(s): German
ADVERTISING RATES:
Full Page Mono .... EUR 1999
Full Page Colour .... EUR 1999
Mechanical Data: Type Area: 260 x 190 mm, No. of Columns (Display): 4, Col Widths (Display): 45 mm
Copy instructions: *Copy Date:* 50 days prior to publication
BUSINESS: COMMUNICATIONS, ADVERTISING & MARKETING

HANDBUCH REHA- UND VORSORGE-EINRICHTUNGEN
729682G56A-4520
Editorial: Am Forsthaus Gravenbruch 7, 63263 NEU-ISENBURG **Tel:** 6102 502249 **Fax:** 6102 502220
Email: m.kaemmer@mmi.de **Web site:** http://www.mmi.de
Freq: Annual; **Cover Price:** EUR 36,00; **Circ:** 30,000
Editor: Marianne Kämmer-Reusch; **Advertising Manager:** Thomas Lang
Profile: Directory listing rehabilitation and precautionary institutions. Target groupr: General practitioners, specialists and hospital doctors, medical services, social services, addiction counseling centers, health insurers and service centers of the social security office.
Language(s): German
ADVERTISING RATES:
Full Page Colour .... EUR 5200
Mechanical Data: Type Area: 205 x 130 mm

HANDCHIRURGIE MIKROCHIRURGIE PLASTISCHE CHIRURGIE
729683G56A-4540
Editorial: Rüdigerstr. 14, 70469 STUTTGART
Tel: 711 89310 **Fax:** 711 8931298
Email: kundenservice@thieme.de **Web site:** http://www.thieme.de/hamipla
Freq: 6 issues yearly; Free to qualifying individuals
Annual Sub.: EUR 312,40; **Circ:** 1,600
Editor: Riccardo E. Giunta
Profile: The magazine is aimed at professionals and training doctors in the fields of plastic surgery: • Hand Surgery, • Reconstructive Plastic Surgery, • Burn Surgery and • Aesthetic Surgery. There are discussed the treatment of injuries, diseases and congenital malformations. In original articles and case reports can be found on the latest information: • diagnosis • selection process • state of the art / latest techniques • Reconstructive procedures • treatment as a result of trauma or surgery • Evaluation of results • Clinical Research.
Language(s): English; German
ADVERTISING RATES:
Full Page Mono .... EUR 1270
Full Page Colour .... EUR 2440
Mechanical Data: No. of Columns (Display): 4, Col Widths (Display): 40 mm, Type Area: 248 x 175 mm
Official Journal of: Organ d. Dt.-sprachigen ArGe f. Handchirurgie, d. Dt. u. d. Österr. Ges. f. Handchirurgie, d. Dt.-sprachigen ArGe f. Mikrochirurgie d. peripheren Nerven u. Gefäße u. d. Dt. Ges. d. Plast., Rekonstruktiven u. Ästhet. Chirurgen

DER HANDEL.
729684G14A-2980
Editorial: Mainzer Landstr. 251, 60326 FRANKFURT
Tel: 69 75951691 **Fax:** 69 75951690
Email: chefredaktion@derhandel.de **Web site:** http://www.derhandel.de
Freq: 11 issues yearly; **Annual Sub.:** EUR 47,00; **Circ:** 84,146
Editor: Marcelo Crescenti; **Advertising Manager:** Ernst-Ludwig Schneider
Profile: The magazine reports every month on comprehensive and current political and economic issues from the trade. His medium-sized readership, the magazine also serves as a practical guide to the business areas of IT, finance, fleet and personnel. In each issue, the magazine provides detailed background information on specific key issues - from marketing to sales shop up to the financial security of the company. Thus, the magazine offers top decision-makers (owners, company directors and

managers) a comprehensive information base for the successful management of medium-sized enterprises.
Language(s): German
ADVERTISING RATES:
Full Page Mono .... EUR 14500
Full Page Colour .... EUR 14500
Mechanical Data: Type Area: 264 x 181 mm, No. of Columns (Display): 3, Col Widths (Display): 49 mm
Supplement to: Lebensmittel Zeitung
BUSINESS: COMMERCE, INDUSTRY & MANAGEMENT

HANDELS MAGAZIN 729699G14A-3020
Editorial: Alter Flughafen 15, 30179 HANNOVER
Tel: 511 6740864 **Fax:** 511 6740853
Email: westermann@patzer-verlag.de **Web site:** http://www.handelsmagazin.de
Freq: 26 issues yearly; **Annual Sub.:** EUR 68,12; **Circ:** 25,550
Editor: Alexandra Westermann
Profile: Purchasing magazine for all retail, wholesale and retail with extensive advertising section.
Language(s): German
ADVERTISING RATES:
Full Page Mono .... EUR 1250
Full Page Colour .... EUR 2800
Mechanical Data: Type Area: 280 x 202 mm, No. of Columns (Display): 5, Col Widths (Display): 38 mm
Copy instructions: *Copy Date:* 2 days prior to publication
BUSINESS: COMMERCE, INDUSTRY & MANAGEMENT

HANDELSAUSKUNFT
729690G14A-9543
Editorial: Grafenberger Allee 39, 40237 DÜSSELDORF **Tel:** 211 686766 **Fax:** 211 6798605
Email: n.tsamourtzis@handelsauskunft.de **Web site:** http://www.handelsauskunft.de
Freq: Monthly; Free to qualifying individuals
Annual Sub.: EUR 175,00; **Circ:** 3,700
Editor: Nikolas Tsamourtzis; **Advertising Manager:** Holger S. Kirkman
Profile: Magazine covering business and management information.
Language(s): German
ADVERTISING RATES:
Full Page Mono .... EUR 1010
Full Page Colour .... EUR 1336
Mechanical Data: Type Area: 270 x 185 mm, No. of Columns (Display): 2, Col Widths (Display): 90 mm
Copy instructions: *Copy Date:* 10 days prior to publication

HANDELSBLATT 729691G65A-264
Editorial: Kasernenstr. 67, 40213 DÜSSELDORF
Tel: 211 8870 **Fax:** 211 887971240
Email: handelsblatt@vhb.de **Web site:** http://www.handelsblatt.com
Freq: 260 issues yearly; **Circ:** 140,765
Editor: Gabor Steingart; **News Editor:** Peter Brors
Profile: Handelsblatt is the largest economic and financial newspaper in German. About 150 editors and correspondents around the world are a critical and analytical journalism, national and global reports exclusively and currently researched and analyzed. It operates with about 30 correspondents worldwide is one of the largest networks in the German daily newspapers. As the main medium of the economic elite, it reaches the top decision-makers (managers 298 000 / 12.4%, according LAE 2009) in Germany. Like no other medium, the Handelsblatt takes the No.1 position with a long range, disproportionate target affinities and best economy in the speech of arbiter target groups. It is according to Media Tenor 2010, the by far most frequently cited economic medium and thus most relevant in the opinion. The Handelsblatt is synonymous with high relevance, reliability, substance and objectivity. Messages are researched, analyzed and categorized in the complex context. The lighting of the background, commentary, analysis has particular weight. Whether the global development of financial markets and economies, international trade agreements or national tax regime - the decision maker needs to know a lot of external factors. With in-depth reports on future trends and new technologies provided by the Handelsblatt important insights for a successful work in ever changing industries and markets. The modern business format meets the so-called Quick Reader functionality highest demands for mobility and fast information. The title page, the novelty of a complete table of contents and cross-departmental "Daily News", the reader is the first compact overview. The decider thus securing the first information advantage of the day. Entry into the deeper reporting and opinion, the theme of the day and the pages "opinion & analysis". The three great departments, "Economics & Politics", "Companies & Markets" and "Finance & exchanges" offer extensive reporting background. The Friday edition also includes the following departments: "Real Estate" - the latest market developments and analysis of the property market at home and abroad for private and institutional investors. "Career" - All about career topics, executive education and MBA for top decision makers, professionals and executives and young professionals. "Literature" - with a focus on economic literature, equipment and textbooks, but also entertaining news for decision makers. "Art market" - with current market reports and background analysis for art collectors. Art is one of the best ways to invest his money. Handelsblatt is published in a modern, convenient and very reader-friendly business format. The layout follows the consistent double-sided principle, combining imagery and content to a clearly structured unit. The magazine-like appearance is also supported by a stitching and provides more reading comfort. The editorial concept combines actuality and enigmatic reporting. By business format is the trade newspaper is no longer the classic structure of the paper bound books. Thus, the editorial staff can better respond to current situations and to expand the coverage, according to news situation. In-depth, exclusive and networked mobile receives the decision of the relevant economic and financial information as a basis for its decisions. All media channels of the trade mark Handelsblatt are linked consistently and optimally access a consistent look and feel of each other. They are adapted to the usage behavior of the medium and provide the decision makers with all relevant information around the clock. Thus, the commercial sheet fits to changing usage patterns of its target group, setting a new cross-media information standard. Facebook: http://www.facebook.com/handelsblatt Twitter: http://twitter.com/handelsblatt This Outlet offers RSS (Really Simple Syndication).
Language(s): German
Readership: Aimed at senior managers and executives, financial directors and economics students.
Mechanical Data: Type Area: 371 x 249 mm, No. of Columns (Display): 5, Col Widths (Display): 47 mm
Copy instructions: *Copy Date:* 2 days prior to publication
Official Journal of: Organ aller dt. Wertpapierbörsen u. d. Warenterminbörse Hannover
Supplement(s): Berliner Zugpferde; Initiativbanking; Legal success
NATIONAL DAILY & SUNDAY NEWSPAPERS: National Daily Newspapers

HANDELSBLATT ONLINE
1621416G14A-9467
Editorial: Kasernenstr. 67, 40213 DÜSSELDORF
Tel: 211 8870 **Fax:** 211 8872980
Email: economy.one.pm@vhb.de **Web site:** http://www.handelsblatt.com
Freq: Daily; **Cover Price:** Paid; **Circ:** 10,057,130 Unique Users
Editor: Oliver Stock; **News Editor:** Martin Tofern
Profile: Ezine: National daily specialising in economy and finance. Twitter: http://twitter.com/handelsblatt This Outlet offers RSS (Really Simple Syndication).
Language(s): German
BUSINESS: COMMERCE, INDUSTRY & MANAGEMENT

HANDELSFORUM 1986028G14A-10422
Editorial: Buschfenne 14, 26789 LEER
Tel: 491 96070151 **Fax:** 491 96070120
Email: hans-peter.heikens@gerhard-verlag.de **Web site:** http://www.gerhard-verlag.de
Freq: Monthly; **Annual Sub.:** EUR 12,00; **Circ:** 20,300
Editor: Hans-Peter Heikens; **Advertising Manager:** Günter Wiegmann
Profile: Associated with economic competence and grip in the region, the regional business magazine information from the fields of finance, tax and legal as well as interviews with current affairs in the economic area, supplemented by useful tips for the daily management tasks. The business magazine focused target group-oriented and market-maker. The recipients decide on investing in their businesses. They and their employees contribute significantly to consumer demand, demand for the region.
Language(s): German
ADVERTISING RATES:
Full Page Mono .... EUR 3578
Mechanical Data: Type Area: 420 x 280 mm, No. of Columns (Display): 6, Col Widths (Display): 45 mm
Copy instructions: *Copy Date:* 5 days prior to publication

HANDELSJOURNAL 729698G53-2
Editorial: Am Weidendamm 1a, 10117 BERLIN
Tel: 30 72625111 **Fax:** 30 72625144
Email: handelsjournal@lpv-verlag.de **Web site:** http://www.handelsjournal.de
Freq: Monthly; Free to qualifying individuals
Annual Sub.: EUR 34,00; **Circ:** 47,824
Editor: Andrea Kurtz; **Advertising Manager:** Ingo Melson
Profile: As a business magazine for the German retail handelsjournal, the background reports, features and interviews from all branches of trade. Currently, practical and utilitarian, the technical papers in the areas of marketing, controlling, finance, economy, competition, investment, labor and tax law. The handelsjournal reaches the entrepreneurs and managers in all sectors, types and sales size categories of the German retail trade. The journal covers all areas in need retail business professional and management-related information and offer a forum for retailers great value with regard to the specific interests of readers.
Language(s): German
Readership: Read by managers of retail outlets.
ADVERTISING RATES:
Full Page Mono .... EUR 10800
Full Page Colour .... EUR 10800
Mechanical Data: Type Area: 250 x 185 mm, No. of Columns (Display): 3, Col Widths (Display): 59 mm
Copy instructions: *Copy Date:* 31 days prior to publication
BUSINESS: RETAILING & WHOLESALING

HANDELSRUNDSCHAU 729700G53-3
Editorial: New-York-Ring 6, 22297 HAMBURG
Tel: 40 63772469 **Fax:** 40 63772478
Email: verlag@edeka.de **Web site:** http://www.edeka-handelsrundschau.de
Freq: 24 issues yearly; **Cover Price:** EUR 2,10; **Circ:** 11,168
Editor: Michaela Fischer-Zernien; **Advertising Manager:** Marina Haarhaus
Profile: Magazine containing news and information about the German retail trade.
Language(s): German
ADVERTISING RATES:
Full Page Mono .... EUR 6200
Full Page Colour .... EUR 6200
Mechanical Data: Type Area: 251 x 180 mm
Copy instructions: *Copy Date:* 19 days prior to publication
BUSINESS: RETAILING & WHOLESALING

HANDFEST 1641602G14R-6038
Editorial: Sternwartstr. 27, 40223 DÜSSELDORF
Tel: 211 3007700 **Fax:** 211 3007900
Email: rolf.goebels@handwerk-nrw.de **Web site:** http://www.handfest-online.de
Freq: 6 issues yearly; **Annual Sub.:** EUR 14,75; **Circ:** 102,213
Editor: Rolf Göbels
Profile: Youth magazine of the German Confederation of Skilled Crafts and Trades Facebook: http://www.facebook.com/pages/handfest/218761308151831.
Language(s): German
ADVERTISING RATES:
Full Page Mono .... EUR 3950
Full Page Colour .... EUR 3950
Mechanical Data: Type Area: 262 x 192 mm
Copy instructions: *Copy Date:* 31 days prior to publication
BUSINESS: COMMERCE, INDUSTRY & MANAGEMENT: Commerce Related

HÄNDLER-VERZEICHNIS FOCUS ROSTFREI 1849387G27-3084
Editorial: Sonsbecker Str. 40, 46509 XANTEN
Tel: 2801 98260 **Fax:** 2801 982611
Email: info@focus-rostfrei.com **Web site:** http://www.focus-rostfrei.de
Freq: Half-yearly; **Cover Price:** EUR 21,35; **Circ:** 12,000
Editor: Rüdiger Beckmann; **Advertising Manager:** Christine Schmidt
Profile: Directory listing addresses of traders of stainless metal.
Language(s): German
ADVERTISING RATES:
Full Page Mono .... EUR 1100
Full Page Colour .... EUR 1550
Mechanical Data: Type Area: 275 x 190 mm, No. of Columns (Display): 4, Col Widths (Display): 38 mm
Copy instructions: *Copy Date:* 10 days prior to publication
Supplement to: Focus Rostfrei

HANDLING 729707G10-180
Editorial: Havelstr. 9, 64295 DARMSTADT
Tel: 6151 380320 **Fax:** 6151 38099320
Email: handling-redaktion@hoppenstedt.de **Web site:** http://www.handling.de
Freq: 10 issues yearly; **Annual Sub.:** EUR 68,00; **Circ:** 27,794
Editor: Petra Born; **Advertising Manager:** Robert Horn
Profile: handling is the independent magazine for automation, handling systems and internal logistics. With its user-oriented reporting is one of the leading brands in the automation industry and provides its readers with important decision-making and guidance for future investments. The magazine is aimed at executives across all industries, decision makers and practitioners in the manufacturing and processing industry. The recipients are known by name to the publisher. The magazine covers the full range of mechanical, electrical and mechatronic solutions for factory automation and optimization of internal processes. The range of topics: handling systems, assembly and linear systems, lifting equipment, material handling equipment, transport and conveying systems, storage systems, intra-logistics, logistics software, warehouse logistics, identification systems / RFID and automation components.
Language(s): German
Readership: Aimed at managers of trade and industry.
ADVERTISING RATES:
Full Page Mono .... EUR 5600
Full Page Colour .... EUR 7220
Mechanical Data: Type Area: 252 x 180 mm, No. of Columns (Display): 4, Col Widths (Display): 42 mm
Copy instructions: *Copy Date:* 14 days prior to publication
Supplement(s): kataloge orange
BUSINESS: MATERIALS HANDLING

HANDWERK MAGAZIN
729713G14R-2560
Editorial: Rudolf-Diesel-Str. 1, 82166 GRÄFELFING
Tel: 89 8982610 **Fax:** 89 89826133
Email: redaktion@handwerk-magazin.de **Web site:** http://www.handwerk-magazin.de
Freq: Monthly; **Annual Sub.:** EUR 75,00; **Circ:** 73,521
Editor: Holger Externbrink; **Advertising Manager:** Eva Maria Hammer
Profile: Business magazine for crafts entrepreneurs who make a difference. The focus of reporting by the contractor consistent with its values, performance, strategies. With the departments policy, management, taxes and finances, it must provide relevant information to guide its operation successfully. These include new developments in the labor and tax law, classical, and alternative methods of corporate finance to marketing and innovation management. One focus is on issues where the business is investing large sums of money and therefore need high decision confidence: fleet management, IT and telecommunications equipment and the acquisition and financing of machinery. Considerable attention is also in craft magazine reporting on insurance and pensions for entrepreneurs as well as personal investment.
Language(s): German
Readership: Aimed at professional craftsmen.
ADVERTISING RATES:
Full Page Mono .... EUR 13600
Full Page Colour .... EUR 13600
Mechanical Data: Type Area: 228 x 173 mm, No. of Columns (Display): 4, Col Widths (Display): 42 mm
Copy instructions: *Copy Date:* 28 days prior to publication
BUSINESS: COMMERCE, INDUSTRY & MANAGEMENT: Commerce Related

HANNOVER GEHT AUS!
729723G89A-2520
Editorial: Hallerstr. 27, 30161 HANNOVER
Tel: 511 3402445 **Fax:** 511 3402464
Email: hga@schaedelspalter.de **Web site:** http://www.schaedelspalter.de
Freq: Half-yearly; **Cover Price:** EUR 5,00; **Circ:** 15,000
Editor: Thomas Steinhausen; **Advertising Manager:** Reinhard Mahl
Profile: Hotel and restaurant guide for Hanover.
Language(s): German
ADVERTISING RATES:
Full Page Mono .... EUR 1480
Full Page Colour .... EUR 2700
Mechanical Data: Type Area: 260 x 190 mm, No. of Columns (Display): 4, Col Widths (Display): 44 mm

HANNOVER HOTELS
1925438G89A-12524
Editorial: Bahnhofstr. 6, 30159 HANNOVER
Tel: 511 12345111 **Fax:** 511 12345112
Email: info@hannover-tourismus.de **Web site:** http://www.hannover-tourismus.de
Freq: Annual; **Cover Price:** Free; **Circ:** 20,000
Editor: Lars Gerhardts
Profile: Hotel Guide Hannover, with detailed maps of neighboring municipalities and regions. Facebook: http://www.facebook.com/tourismus.hannover.de.
Language(s): English; German

HANNOVER KAUFT EIN
1866775G89A-12441
Editorial: Hallerstr. 27, 30161 HANNOVER
Tel: 511 3402445 **Fax:** 511 3402464
Email: hke@schaedelspalter.de **Web site:** http://www.schaedelspalter.de
Freq: Half-yearly; **Circ:** 15,000
Editor: Thomas Steinhausen; **Advertising Manager:** Reinhard Mahl
Profile: Sales guide for the Hanover region.
Language(s): German
ADVERTISING RATES:
Full Page Mono .... EUR 700
Full Page Colour .... EUR 700
Mechanical Data: Type Area: 185 x 135 mm
Supplement to: Schädelspalter

HANNOVER LIVE 729726G89C-1080
Editorial: Lange Laube 22, 30159 HANNOVER
Tel: 511 15551 **Fax:** 511 1316169
Email: redaktion@stroetmann-verlag.de **Web site:** http://www.stroetmann-verlag.de
Freq: Monthly; **Cover Price:** Free; **Circ:** 19,518
Editor: Reinhard Stroetmann; **Advertising Manager:** Reinhard Stroetmann
Profile: City and regional magazine with tips, trends and events for Hannover.
Language(s): German
ADVERTISING RATES:
Full Page Mono .... EUR 1480
Full Page Colour .... EUR 2470
Mechanical Data: Type Area: 270 x 190 mm, No. of Columns (Display): 4, Col Widths (Display): 42 mm
Copy instructions: *Copy Date:* 10 days prior to publication
CONSUMER: HOLIDAYS & TRAVEL: Entertainment Guides

HANNOVER ... SCHÖNSTE SEITEN! 756019G50-1182
Editorial: Bahnhofstr. 6, 30159 HANNOVER
Tel: 511 12345111 **Fax:** 511 12345112
Email: info@hannover-tourismus.de **Web site:** http://www.hannover-tourismus.de
Freq: Annual; **Cover Price:** Free; **Circ:** 18,000
Editor: Lars Gerhardts; **Advertising Manager:** Lars Gerhardts
Profile: Facebook: http://www.facebook.com/tourismus.hannover.de.
Language(s): English; German
ADVERTISING RATES:
Full Page Mono .... EUR 1500
Full Page Colour .... EUR 1500
Mechanical Data: Type Area: 297 x 210 mm
Copy instructions: *Copy Date:* 30 days prior to publication

DER HANNOVERANER 729722G81D-4
Editorial: Lindhooper Str. 92, 27283 VERDEN
Tel: 4231 6730 **Fax:** 4231 67312
Email: redaktion@hannoveraner.com **Web site:** http://www.hannoveraner.com
Freq: Monthly; Free to qualifying individuals
Annual Sub.: EUR 50,00; **Circ:** 18,364
Editor: Britta Züngel
Profile: News from the regional and international association events and information about the auction life. Recent reports from sport and breeding with the results of tournaments, but also the broodmare tests and mare shows are among the other contents of the periodical. You will also find regular informative reports from the various subject areas of feeding, housing, health reports, etc. For the young, the young breeder site about the latest events. The pages of "Pony and Pony" and the "cold-blooded animals in Lower Saxony are another part of the periodical. The conclusion of each issue is the extensive advertising section with different offers in the areas of sales, training, real estate, etc. For foreign members, we publish an English translation of the summary of the most interesting articles and news. Anhören Umschrift.
Language(s): German
Readership: Read by breeders, trainers and those interested in Hanoverian horses.
ADVERTISING RATES:
Full Page Mono .... EUR 1700
Full Page Colour .... EUR 2880
Mechanical Data: Type Area: 257 x 186 mm, No. of Columns (Display): 4, Col Widths (Display): 45 mm
Copy instructions: *Copy Date:* 20 days prior to publication
Official Journal of: Organ d. Hannoveraner Verb. e.V., d. Hannover. Reit- u. Fahrschule Ve. e.V., d. Verb. d. Pony- u. Kleinpferdezüchter e.V., d. Stammbuches f. Kaltblutpferde Niedersachsen u. d. niedersächs. Landgestüts Celle
CONSUMER: ANIMALS & PETS: Horses & Ponies

HANNOVERSCHE ALLGEMEINE ZEITUNG 729727G67B-6520
Editorial: August-Madsack-Str. 1, 30559 HANNOVER **Tel:** 511 5180 **Fax:** 511 5182899
Email: haz@madsack.de **Web site:** http://www.haz.de
Freq: 312 issues yearly; **Circ:** 590,819
Editor: Hendrik Brandt; **News Editor:** Jörg Kallmeyer; **Advertising Manager:** Olaf Kuhlwein
Profile: The Hannover Allgemeine Zeitung is a leader in Lower Saxony. The success is based on a simple yet sophisticated approach: the HAZ combines the proximity of a local newspaper with the foresight of a national news media. That's how we read today - the slogan of the new press is programme. As a modern newspaper for Hanover, the HAZ profiles as a competent city newspaper, always close to the pulse of the city and the reader. Fast and cheeky but also true and credible. Twitter: http://twitter.com/haz This Outlet offers RSS (Really Simple Syndication).
Language(s): German
ADVERTISING RATES:
SCC .... EUR 1131,80
Copy instructions: *Copy Date:* 3 days prior to publication
Supplement(s): Anzeiger Burgdorf & Uetze; Anzeiger Lehrte & Sehnde; Calenberger Zeitung; Deister-Anzeiger Springe Bad Münder; Ernst-August-Galerie Aktuell; Gesund; Leine-Nachrichten; Leine-Zeitung Garbsen Seelze; Leine-Zeitung Neustadt Wunstorf; Nordhannoversche Zeitung; RegionsJournal; Spielzeit; Zuhause in Hannover und der Region
REGIONAL DAILY & SUNDAY NEWSPAPERS: Regional Daily Newspapers

HANSA 729737G45A-420
Editorial: Georgsplatz 1, 20099 HAMBURG
Tel: 40 707080216 **Fax:** 40 707080214
Email: r_hinrichs@hansa-online.de **Web site:** http://www.hansa-online.de
Freq: Monthly; **Annual Sub.:** EUR 162,00; **Circ:** 6,266
Editor: Ralf Hinrichs; **Advertising Manager:** Christian Döpp
Profile: Magazine about ship building and voyages from the port of Hamburg.
Language(s): English; German
ADVERTISING RATES:
Full Page Mono .... EUR 3400
Full Page Colour .... EUR 3400
Mechanical Data: Type Area: 266 x 180 mm, No. of Columns (Display): 3, Col Widths (Display): 57 mm
Copy instructions: *Copy Date:* 20 days prior to publication
Official Journal of: Organ d. Verb. f. Schiffbau u. Meerestechnik e.V., d. ArGe Schiffbau- u. Offshore-Zulieferindustrie im VDMA, d. German. Lloyd, d. See-Berufsgenossenschaft, d. Seeverkehrsbeirates d. Bundesverkehrsministeriums, d. Dt. Ges. f. Ortung u. Navigation, d. Hafenbautechn. Ges. e.V., d. Naut. Vereine, d. Hafentechn. Ges., d. Pianc u. d. Zentralverb. d. dt. Seehafenbetriebe
BUSINESS: MARINE & SHIPPING

HANSE-ART 1785459G73-613
Editorial: Waidmannstr. 35, 22769 HAMBURG
Tel: 40 8500607 **Fax:** 40 8512808
Email: info@hanse-art.net **Web site:** http://www.hanse-art.net
Freq: 6 issues yearly; **Annual Sub.:** EUR 15,50; **Circ:** 24,000
Editor: Dieter Zwörner
Profile: Journal of Hanseatic way of life, economy and culture, the magazine presents a vivid and lively picture of the Hanseatic city and its activities. Lens, but also critically accompany the journal and current reports exclusively about art, culture, business, port, events, sports and much more in and around Hamburg. The performance of companies in Hamburg and Hamburg personalities are highlighted.
Language(s): German
ADVERTISING RATES:
Full Page Mono .... EUR 1790
Full Page Colour .... EUR 2790
Mechanical Data: Type Area: 250 x 190 mm
Copy instructions: *Copy Date:* 28 days prior to publication

HANSER AUTOMOTIVE 735436G31A-29
Editorial: Kolbergerstr. 22, 81679 MÜNCHEN
Tel: 89 99830425 **Fax:** 89 99830152
Email: oertel@hanser.de **Web site:** http://www.hanser-automotive.de
Freq: 8 issues yearly; **Annual Sub.:** EUR 79,00; **Circ:** 13,878
Editor: Klaus Oertel; **Advertising Manager:** Annemarie Scharl-Send
Profile: Hanser automotive is a practice-based source of information covering every application of automobile electronics. Its readers, who are known by name, are buyers and development, project and applications engineers with a direct interest in products and procurement, and management staff wishing to obtain an overview of products, components and systems. The magazine accordingly contains reports in the form of specialised articles, interviews and brief contributions on products, systems, trends and the latest developments in vehicle electronics, as well as on consumer and industrial products and solutions from industries such as telecoms/datacoms, which are suitable for use in cars. In addition articles about e-mobility and electronics in mobile machines complete the information portfolio.
Language(s): German
ADVERTISING RATES:
Full Page Mono .... EUR 4520
Full Page Colour .... EUR 5580
Mechanical Data: Type Area: 250 x 175 mm, No. of Columns (Display): 4, Col Widths (Display): 40 mm
BUSINESS: MOTOR TRADE: Motor Trade Accessories

HAPPINEZ 2002058G74A-3753
Editorial: Burchardstr. 11, 20095 HAMBURG
Tel: 40 30194277 **Fax:** 40 30191043
Email: happinez@bauerredaktionen.de **Web site:** http://www.bauermedia.com
Freq: 6 issues yearly; **Annual Sub.:** EUR 29,70; **Circ:** 150,000
Editor: Uwe Bokelmann
Profile: Family Style magazine for women who value a conscious lifestyle and emontionale development set. Magazine with interviews, features and columns written by popular authors for clearer access to a wide range of topics with a focus on wisdom, psychology and spirituality. The themes of life, job, health, nutrition, living, travel and nature, art and culture are treated versatile and added a new dimension. Facebook: http://www.facebook.com/pages/Happinez/126175924069168.
Language(s): German
ADVERTISING RATES:
Full Page Mono .... EUR 12000
Full Page Colour .... EUR 12000

HAPPY INFO 729743G89A-12096
Editorial: Lengefelder Str. 6, 34497 KORBACH
Tel: 5631 56000 **Fax:** 5631 560159
Email: gaestejournal@wlz-fz.de **Web site:** http://www.wlz-fz.de
Freq: 8 issues yearly; **Cover Price:** Free; **Circ:** 20,000
Editor: Jörg Kleine; **Advertising Manager:** Marina Kieweg
Profile: The Happy Info Guest Journal informed of events and recreational opportunities in the Waldecker Land.
Language(s): German
ADVERTISING RATES:
Full Page Mono .... EUR 818
Full Page Colour .... EUR 1053
Mechanical Data: Type Area: 280 x 184 mm, No. of Columns (Display): 4, Col Widths (Display): 45 mm
Copy instructions: *Copy Date:* 20 days prior to publication

HARBURGER ANZEIGEN UND NACHRICHTEN 729747G67B-6540
Editorial: Harburger Rathausstr. 40, 21073 HAMBURG **Tel:** 40 77177199 **Fax:** 40 7650262
Email: lokales@han-online.de **Web site:** http://www.han-online.de
Freq: 312 issues yearly; **Circ:** 15,175
Editor: Thomas Oldach; **News Editor:** Wolfgang Becker; **Advertising Manager:** Jens Kalkowski
Profile: Regional daily newspaper covering politics, economics, sport, travel and technology. Facebook: http://www.facebook.com/HarburgerZeitung Twitter: http://twitter.com/harburger.
Language(s): German
ADVERTISING RATES:
SCC .... EUR 56,20
Mechanical Data: Type Area: 430 x 282 mm, No. of Columns (Display): 6, Col Widths (Display): 45 mm
Copy instructions: *Copy Date:* 1 day prior to publication
Supplement(s): doppio
REGIONAL DAILY & SUNDAY NEWSPAPERS: Regional Daily Newspapers

HARBURGER ANZEIGEN UND NACHRICHTEN 1621422G67B-16570
Editorial: Harburger Rathausstr. 40, 21073 HAMBURG **Tel:** 40 77177199 **Fax:** 40 7650262
Email: lokales@han-online.de **Web site:** http://www.han-online.de
Freq: Daily; **Cover Price:** Paid; **Circ:** 71,751 Unique Users
Editor: Thomas Oldach; **Advertising Manager:** Jens Kalkowski
Profile: Ezine: Regional daily newspaper covering politics, economics, culture, sport, travel and technology. Facebook: http://www.facebook.com/HarburgerZeitung Twitter: http://twitter.com/#!/harburger.
Language(s): German
REGIONAL DAILY & SUNDAY NEWSPAPERS: Regional Daily Newspapers

HARBURGER WOCHENBLATT 729748G72-5204
Editorial: Harburger Rathausstr. 40, 21073 HAMBURG **Tel:** 40 85322933 **Fax:** 40 85322939
Email: post@wochenblatt-redaktion.de **Web site:** http://www.harburger-wochenblatt.de
Freq: Weekly; **Cover Price:** Free; **Circ:** 58,824
Editor: Olaf Zimmermann; **Advertising Manager:** Jürgen Müller
Profile: Advertising journal (house-to-house) concentrating on local stories.
Language(s): German
ADVERTISING RATES:
Full Page Mono .... EUR 4696
Full Page Colour .... EUR 4816
Mechanical Data: Type Area: 430 x 282 mm, No. of Columns (Display): 6, Col Widths (Display): 45 mm
Copy instructions: *Copy Date:* 2 days prior to publication
LOCAL NEWSPAPERS

HARDTHÖHEN-KURIER 729753G40-320
Editorial: Karthäuserstr. 38, 53332 BORNHEIM
Tel: 2222 9915404 **Fax:** 2222 9915405
Email: karteusch@hardthoehenkurier.de **Web site:** http://www.hardthoehenkurier.de
Freq: 6 issues yearly; Free to qualifying individuals
Annual Sub.: EUR 28,00; **Circ:** 15,000
Editor: Klaus Karteusch; **Advertising Manager:** Stefan Jendrusch
Profile: Magazine for members of the German army.
Language(s): English; German
ADVERTISING RATES:
Full Page Mono .... EUR 1900
Full Page Colour .... EUR 3200
Mechanical Data: No. of Columns (Display): 3, Type Area: 259 x 186 mm, Col Widths (Display): 60 mm
Copy instructions: *Copy Date:* 15 days prior to publication

HARDWARE LUXX 1739830G5-11400
Editorial: Zum Wiehegraben 5, 30519 HANNOVER
Tel: 511 4756963 **Fax:** 511 4756491
Email: dbode@hardwareluxx.com **Web site:** http://www.hardwareluxx.de
Freq: 6 issues yearly; **Annual Sub.:** EUR 17,90; **Circ:** 11,086
Editor: Dennis Bode
Profile: Magazine for luxury hardware testing and detailed reports on current topics for advanced PC-PC users and gamers.
Language(s): German
ADVERTISING RATES:
Full Page Mono .... EUR 2200
Full Page Colour .... EUR 2200
Copy instructions: *Copy Date:* 31 days prior to publication
BUSINESS: COMPUTERS & AUTOMATION

DIE HARKE 729755G67B-6560
Editorial: An der Stadtgrenze 2, 31582 NIENBURG
Tel: 5021 966200 **Fax:** 5021 966113
Email: m.thielking-rumpeltin@dieharke.de **Web site:** http://www.dieharke.de
Freq: 312 issues yearly; **Circ:** 19,485
Editor: Martina Thielking-Rumpeltin; **Advertising Manager:** Jürgen Folk
Profile: Daily newspaper with regional news and a local sports section. Twitter: http://twitter.com/die_harke This Outlet offers RSS (Really Simple Syndication).
Language(s): German
ADVERTISING RATES:
SCC .... EUR 54,70
Mechanical Data: Type Area: 430 x 277 mm, No. of Columns (Display): 6, Col Widths (Display): 45 mm
Copy instructions: *Copy Date:* 1 day prior to publication
REGIONAL DAILY & SUNDAY NEWSPAPERS: Regional Daily Newspapers

DIE HARNBLASE 1983360G56A-11675
Editorial: Tulpenstr. 13, 44289 DORTMUND
Tel: 231 403676 **Fax:** 32222 479547
Email: bockelbrink@selbsthilfe-bund-blasenkrebs.de **Web site:** http://www.harnblasenkrebs.de
Freq: Half-yearly; **Cover Price:** Free; **Circ:** 2,500
Editor: Karl-Heinz Bockelbrink
Profile: Information from the self aid organization for bladder cancer.
Language(s): German

HARTMANNBUND MAGAZIN 729763G56A-4560
Editorial: Schützenstr. 6a, 10117 BERLIN
Tel: 30 2062080 **Fax:** 30 20620829
Email: hb-info@hartmannbund.de **Web site:** http://www.hartmannbund.de
Freq: 6 issues yearly; **Circ:** 40,000
Editor: Katja Krahmer; **Advertising Manager:** Christa Bellert
Profile: The Hartmann Bund Magazin is the magazine for members of the Association of German Physicians. In addition to internal information linking current health policy issues are the focus, such as information about prior medical, social and health policy, medical and dental research, hospital management and practice leadership.
Language(s): German
ADVERTISING RATES:
Full Page Mono .... EUR 3560
Full Page Colour .... EUR 3560
Mechanical Data: Type Area: 257 x 183 mm, No. of Columns (Display): 4, Col Widths (Display): 42 mm
Copy instructions: *Copy Date:* 28 days prior to publication
BUSINESS: HEALTH & MEDICAL

HARTMANNBUND VERBAND DER ÄRZTE DEUTSCHLANDS 1666719G56A-11343
Editorial: Tersteegenstr. 12, 40474 DÜSSELDORF
Tel: 211 2005450 **Fax:** 211 20054529
Email: lv.wl@hartmannbund.de
Freq: Quarterly; **Circ:** 34,000
Editor: Klaus Reinhardt; **Advertising Manager:** André Mielitz
Profile: Magazine for GPs.
Language(s): German
ADVERTISING RATES:
Full Page Mono .... EUR 3165
Full Page Colour .... EUR 4400
Mechanical Data: Type Area: 273 x 186 mm
Copy instructions: *Copy Date:* 14 days prior to publication

HARVARD BUSINESS MANAGER 729767G14A-3080
Editorial: Dovenfleet 5, 20457 HAMBURG
Tel: 40 3080050 **Fax:** 40 30800549
Email: info@harvardbusinessmanager.de **Web site:** http://www.harvardbusinessmanager.de
Freq: Monthly; **Annual Sub.:** EUR 149,40; **Circ:** 26,938
Editor: Christoph Seeger; **Advertising Manager:** Norbert Facklam
Profile: The best articles from the Harvard Business Review and selected articles of German-speaking experts from academia and practice. Innovative approaches to management, trends in management, advanced business concepts and their implementation. Harvard Business Manager is the most widely read and best-known German-language management magazine. The magazine reports monthly on the latest approaches to business and people management, presents trends and presents proven strategies for management.
Language(s): German
Readership: Read by managers.
ADVERTISING RATES:
Full Page Mono .... EUR 7114
Full Page Colour .... EUR 7114
Mechanical Data: Type Area: 252 x 178 mm, No. of Columns (Display): 3, Col Widths (Display): 56 mm
Copy instructions: *Copy Date:* 22 days prior to publication
Supplement(s): Initiativbanking
BUSINESS: COMMERCE, INDUSTRY & MANAGEMENT

HARZ KURIER 729772G67B-6580
Editorial: Gipsmühlenweg 2, 37520 OSTERODE
Tel: 5522 31700 **Fax:** 5522 3170390
Email: redaktion@harzkurier.de **Web site:** http://www.harzkurier.de
Freq: 312 issues yearly; **Circ:** 16,402
Editor: Peter Bischof; **Advertising Manager:** Bernd Spieß
Profile: Daily newspaper with regional news and a local sports section.
Language(s): German
ADVERTISING RATES:
SCC .... EUR 50,60
Mechanical Data: Type Area: 435 x 282 mm, No. of Columns (Display): 6, Col Widths (Display): 45 mm
Copy instructions: *Copy Date:* 1 day prior to publication
REGIONAL DAILY & SUNDAY NEWSPAPERS: Regional Daily Newspapers

HARZER HIGHLIGHTS 1912783G89A-12495
Editorial: Goetheweg 1, 06502 THALE
Email: info@harzer-highlights.de **Web site:** http://www.harzer-highlights.de
Freq: Annual; **Cover Price:** Free; **Circ:** 300,000
Profile: Experience of the Harz.
Language(s): German

HARZER VOLKSSTIMME
729771G67B-6600
Editorial: Bahnhofstr. 17, 39104 MAGDEBURG
Tel: 391 59990 **Fax:** 391 5999210
Email: chefredaktion@volksstimme.de **Web site:** http://www.volksstimme.de
Freq: 312 issues yearly; **Circ:** 18,472
Advertising Manager: Rainer Pfeil
Profile: As the largest daily newspaper in northern Saxony-Anhalt, the Volksstimme reaches 536,000 readers a day* (MA 2010). From Monday to Saturday a team of highly qualified editors put together the latest information and news from the region and around the world. Thanks the 18 local editions is the Volksstimme always close to the action. Twitter: http://twitter.com/volksstimme This Outlet offers RSS (Really Simple Syndication).
Language(s): German
ADVERTISING RATES:
SCC .... EUR 62,40
Mechanical Data: Type Area: 480 x 327 mm, No. of Columns (Display): 7, Col Widths (Display): 45 mm
Copy instructions: *Copy Date:* 2 days prior to publication
Supplement(s): Anstoss in Wernigerode; bauRatgeber; Biber; Leser-Reisen; prisma; Standort Landkreis Wernigerode
REGIONAL DAILY & SUNDAY NEWSPAPERS: Regional Daily Newspapers

HARZER WOCHENSPIEGEL
729769G72-5224
Editorial: Gipsmühlenweg 2, 37520 OSTERODE
Tel: 5522 31700 **Fax:** 5522 3170390
Email: redaktion@harzkurier.de **Web site:** http://www.harzkurier.de
Freq: Weekly; **Cover Price:** Free; **Circ:** 52,600
Editor: Peter Bischof; **Advertising Manager:** Bernd Spieß
Profile: Advertising journal (house-to-house) concentrating on local stories.
Language(s): German
ADVERTISING RATES:
Full Page Mono .... EUR 2845
Full Page Colour .... EUR 4281
Mechanical Data: Type Area: 435 x 282 mm, No. of Columns (Display): 6, Col Widths (Display): 45 mm
Copy instructions: *Copy Date:* 2 days prior to publication
LOCAL NEWSPAPERS

HASSFURTER TAGBLATT
729781G67B-6620
Editorial: Augsfelder Str. 19, 97437 HASSFURT
Tel: 9521 69923 **Fax:** 9521 69911
Email: redaktion@hassfurter-tagblatt.de **Web site:** http://www.hassfurter-tagblatt.de
Freq: 312 issues yearly; **Circ:** 5,910
Editor: Wolfgang Sandler; **Advertising Manager:** Roland Thein
Profile: Daily newspaper with regional news and a local sports section.
Language(s): German
ADVERTISING RATES:
SCC .... EUR 32,10
Mechanical Data: Type Area: 466 x 310 mm, No. of Columns (Display): 7, Col Widths (Display): 43 mm
Copy instructions: *Copy Date:* 1 day prior to publication
REGIONAL DAILY & SUNDAY NEWSPAPERS: Regional Daily Newspapers

DAS HAUS
729788G74C-1120
Editorial: Arabellastr. 23, 81925 MÜNCHEN
Tel: 89 92500 **Fax:** 89 92503055
Email: userservice@haus.de **Web site:** http://www.haus.de
Freq: 10 issues yearly; **Annual Sub.:** EUR 12,00; **Circ:** 1,824,775
Editor: Gaby Miketta
Profile: "Das Haus" - a guide on the topics building, housing, better living is published 10 times a year. The magazine has a high reader-binding and so dramatically increases advertising exposure opportunities. "DAS HAUS" is to 99% related on a subscription basis. An independent editorial provides credible researched and much-quoted articles with information leading to practical tips and creative ideas that transforms dreams to reality. "Das Haus" is read by over 75% by people who are down to earth and also very well situated property owners. Facebook: http://www.facebook.com/DasHaus.de.
Language(s): German
Readership: Aimed at people seeking to improve their home environment.
ADVERTISING RATES:
Full Page Mono .... EUR 26300
Full Page Colour .... EUR 39980
Mechanical Data: Type Area: 246 x 192 mm, No. of Columns (Display): 4, Col Widths (Display): 45 mm
Copy instructions: *Copy Date:* 42 days prior to publication
CONSUMER: WOMEN'S INTEREST CONSUMER MAGAZINES: Home & Family

DAS HAUS
1621425G74C-3546
Editorial: Arabellastr. 23, 81925 MÜNCHEN
Tel: 89 92500 **Fax:** 89 92502350
Email: info@haus.de **Web site:** http://www.haus.de
Cover Price: Paid; **Circ:** 298,865 Unique Users
Editor: Ursula Gräfin Lambsdorff
Profile: Ezine: Magazine covering building, conversions, interior fittings and furnishings, garden layout and design.
Language(s): German
CONSUMER: WOMEN'S INTEREST CONSUMER MAGAZINES: Home & Family

HAUS TEST
729817G4E-375
Editorial: Höhenstr. 17, 70736 FELLBACH
Tel: 711 5206244 **Fax:** 711 5206300
Email: fritsche@fachschriften.de **Web site:** http://www.bautipps.de
Freq: Annual; **Cover Price:** EUR 6,80; **Circ:** 60,000
Editor: Harald Fritsche; **Advertising Manager:** Barbara Hoof
Profile: The magazine compares prefabricated houses on objective, transparent criteria, such as wall construction, insulation and equipment features. This book combines the elaborate and carefully researched, test-oriented reviews of "Hausbau" and „pro fertighaus".
Language(s): German
Readership: For architects, heating engineers and all aspects of the building trade.
ADVERTISING RATES:
Full Page Colour .... EUR 9550
Mechanical Data: Type Area: 247 x 187 mm, No. of Columns (Display): 4, Col Widths (Display): 43 mm
Copy instructions: *Copy Date:* 40 days prior to publication
BUSINESS: ARCHITECTURE & BUILDING: Building

HAUS UND GARTEN
729821G93-360
Editorial: Heigelinstr. 15, 70567 STUTTGART
Tel: 711 7155307 **Fax:** 711 724066
Email: gensicke@landesverband-bw.de **Web site:** http://www.landesverband-bw.de
Freq: 11 issues yearly; Free to qualifying individuals ; **Circ:** 68,566
Editor: Jörg Gensicke; **Advertising Manager:** Christine Krückl
Profile: Journal of the National Association of Baden-Württemberg the allotment holders. The magazine informs members about the full range of garden area. The editorial focus is the description of the monthly recurring gardening complemented by a wealth of tips and advice. The publications are tailored to the needs of gardeners, but also the home garden owners. For the settlers, homeowners and homeowners of our association, we report on current tax and legal matters.
Language(s): German
Readership: Aimed at members of regional home-owning associations.
ADVERTISING RATES:
Full Page Mono .... EUR 3036
Full Page Colour .... EUR 5769
Mechanical Data: Type Area: 253 x 190 mm, No. of Columns (Display): 4, Col Widths (Display): 45 mm
Copy instructions: *Copy Date:* 21 days prior to publication
CONSUMER: GARDENING

HAUS & GRUND
756023G74K-1443
Editorial: Huyssenallee 50, 45128 ESSEN
Tel: 201 810660 **Fax:** 201 8106644
Email: eissing@hug-essen.de **Web site:** http://www.hug-essen.de
Freq: Monthly; Free to qualifying individuals
Annual Sub.: EUR 48,00; **Circ:** 31,802
Editor: Christian Eissing; **Advertising Manager:** Thomas Walter
Profile: Magazine for real estate owners, architects, building companies and agents occupied in law and tax counselling.
Language(s): German
ADVERTISING RATES:
Full Page Mono .... EUR 1845
Full Page Colour .... EUR 2985
Mechanical Data: Type Area: 270 x 184 mm, No. of Columns (Display): 4, Col Widths (Display): 43 mm
Copy instructions: *Copy Date:* 30 days prior to publication
Official Journal of: Organ d. Haus-, Wohnungs- u. Grundeigentümerverb. Ruhr e.V.
CONSUMER: WOMEN'S INTEREST CONSUMER MAGAZINES: Home Purchase

HAUS & GRUND
743903G74K-1469
Editorial: Mittelgewannweg 15, 69123 HEIDELBERG
Tel: 6221 145114 **Fax:** 6221 145119
Email: sww@jedermann.de **Web site:** http://www.hem-baden.de
Freq: Monthly; Free to qualifying individuals
Annual Sub.: EUR 36,00; **Circ:** 62,440
Editor: Gerhard Hotz; **Advertising Manager:** Anita Eulenbach
Profile: Journal of house, land and property owners in Baden. You fully informed and knowledgeable about all aspects of home and housing industry. Priorities are, in addition to renovation of current housing policy, finance, law and taxation, the issues and modernization, as well as services around the house.
Language(s): German
ADVERTISING RATES:
Full Page Mono .... EUR 2700
Full Page Colour .... EUR 3320
Mechanical Data: Type Area: 270 x 184 mm, No. of Columns (Display): 4, Col Widths (Display): 43 mm
Copy instructions: *Copy Date:* 25 days prior to publication
Official Journal of: Organ d. LV Bad. Haus-, Wohnungs- u. Grundeigentümer e.V.
CONSUMER: WOMEN'S INTEREST CONSUMER MAGAZINES: Home Purchase

HAUS & GRUND
1660293G74K-1500
Editorial: Grüneburgweg 64, 60322 FRANKFURT
Tel: 69 729458 **Fax:** 69 172635
Email: hughessen@arcor.de **Web site:** http://www.hausundgrundhessen.de
Freq: Monthly; Free to qualifying individuals
Annual Sub.: EUR 18,00; **Circ:** 21,117
Editor: Günther Belz; **Advertising Manager:** Christa Neidhöfer
Profile: Journal of house, land and property owners in Hessen with information on leases, WE-law, tax law and general around the property.
Language(s): German
ADVERTISING RATES:
Full Page Mono .... EUR 1381
Full Page Colour .... EUR 1993
Mechanical Data: Type Area: 254 x 184 mm, No. of Columns (Display): 4, Col Widths (Display): 43 mm
Copy instructions: *Copy Date:* 15 days prior to publication
CONSUMER: WOMEN'S INTEREST CONSUMER MAGAZINES: Home Purchase

HAUS UND GRUND JOURNAL - AUSG. STADT U. REGION AACHEN
729833G74K-540
Editorial: Martinistr. 5, 45701 HERTEN
Tel: 209 16218555 **Fax:** 209 16218557
Email: gerhard.modrow@av-westerholt.de **Web site:** http://www.av-westerholt.de
Freq: Monthly; Free to qualifying individuals
Annual Sub.: EUR 18,00; **Circ:** 6,500
Editor: Gerhard Modrow
Profile: Magazine for house and land owners in the Aachen region.
Language(s): German
ADVERTISING RATES:
Full Page Mono .... EUR 1360
Full Page Colour .... EUR 1460
Mechanical Data: Type Area: 260 x 185 mm, No. of Columns (Display): 4, Col Widths (Display): 45 mm
Copy instructions: *Copy Date:* 7 days prior to publication
CONSUMER: WOMEN'S INTEREST CONSUMER MAGAZINES: Home Purchase

HAUS UND GRUND NIEDERSACHSEN
729851G1E-197
Editorial: Schulze-Delitzsch-Str. 35, 30938 BURGWEDEL **Tel:** 5139 899936 **Fax:** 5139 899950
Email: redaktion.hug@winkler-stenzel.de **Web site:** http://www.winkler-stenzel.de
Freq: 10 issues yearly; Free to qualifying individuals
Annual Sub.: EUR 13,00; **Circ:** 39,800
Editor: Andreas Winkler; **Advertising Manager:** Kerstin Schökel
Profile: Journal of house, land and property owners in Lower Saxony with information about leases, WE-law, tax law and general around the property.
Language(s): German
ADVERTISING RATES:
Full Page Mono .... EUR 5290
Full Page Colour .... EUR 6640
Mechanical Data: Type Area: 414 x 280 mm, No. of Columns (Display): 6, Col Widths (Display): 45 mm
Copy instructions: *Copy Date:* 25 days prior to publication
Official Journal of: Organ d. LV Niedersächs. Haus-, Wohnungs- u. Grundeigentümer e.V.
BUSINESS: FINANCE & ECONOMICS: Property

HAUS & GRUND SAARLAND
729831G74K-520
Editorial: Bismarckstr. 52, 66121 SAARBRÜCKEN
Tel: 681 668370 **Fax:** 681 68035
Email: info@haus-und-grund-saarland.de **Web site:** http://www.haus-und-grund-saarland.de
Freq: Monthly; **Cover Price:** EUR 1,00
Free to qualifying individuals ; **Circ:** 15,000
Editor: Michael Weiskopf; **Advertising Manager:** Birgit Bruch
Profile: Magazine about homes and property in the Saarland region.
Language(s): German
ADVERTISING RATES:
Full Page Mono .... EUR 1404
Full Page Colour .... EUR 1545
Mechanical Data: Type Area: 270 x 180 mm, No. of Columns (Display): 4, Col Widths (Display): 45 mm
Copy instructions: *Copy Date:* 21 days prior to publication
CONSUMER: WOMEN'S INTEREST CONSUMER MAGAZINES: Home Purchase

HAUS & GRUND WÜRTTEMBERG
729852G74K-880
Editorial: Reinsburgstr. 82, 70178 STUTTGART
Tel: 711 238860 **Fax:** 711 2388619
Email: j.bleyhl@verlagsmarketing.de
Freq: 13 issues yearly; Free to qualifying individuals
Annual Sub.: EUR 16,00; **Circ:** 84,053
Editor: Dieter A. Kuberski
Profile: Journal of house, land and property owners in Baden-Württemberg with information on leases, WE-law, tax law and general around the property.
Language(s): German
Readership: Aimed at home owners and prospective purchasers.
ADVERTISING RATES:
Full Page Mono .... EUR 4760
Full Page Colour .... EUR 6110
Mechanical Data: Type Area: 280 x 195 mm, No. of Columns (Display): 4, Col Widths (Display): 45 mm
Copy instructions: *Copy Date:* 20 days prior to publication
CONSUMER: WOMEN'S INTEREST CONSUMER MAGAZINES: Home Purchase

HAUS UND GRUND-MAGAZIN WUPPERTAL
729850G1E-198
Editorial: An der Clefbrücke 2a, 42275 WUPPERTAL
Tel: 202 255950 **Fax:** 202 255954
Email: hausundgrundwpt@t-online.de **Web site:** http://www.hausundgrundwpt.de
Freq: Monthly; Free to qualifying individuals
Annual Sub.: EUR 18,50; **Circ:** 4,600
Editor: Wolfgang Friedrich; **Advertising Manager:** Claudia Gellhorn
Profile: Journal giving advice on land purchase, property construction, renovation and insurance.
Language(s): German
Readership: Aimed at property and land developers in and around Wuppertal.
ADVERTISING RATES:
Full Page Mono .... EUR 940
Full Page Colour .... EUR 1316
Mechanical Data: Type Area: 270 x 185 mm, No. of Columns (Display): 4, Col Widths (Display): 45 mm
Copy instructions: *Copy Date:* 30 days prior to publication
BUSINESS: FINANCE & ECONOMICS: Property

HAUS & MARKT - AUSG. DRESDEN
729858G74C-1220
Editorial: Zschortauer Str. 71, 04129 LEIPZIG
Tel: 341 6010017 **Fax:** 341 6010023
Email: dresden@hausundmarkt.de **Web site:** http://www.hausundmarkt-mitteldeutschland.de
Freq: Monthly; **Cover Price:** Free; **Circ:** 35,850
Editor: Michael Krause; **Advertising Manager:** Michael Krause
Profile: Magazine for house and property owners in Dresden. Magazine with the theme: bath and plumbing, construction and renovation, furnishing and housing, energy and heating, garden, winter garden, green building, security, economic and capital. Home market is understood as a counselor of real estate. The magazine is one of the best and most innovative news services for homeowners and those who wish to be. Our aim is to report on all aspects currently affecting the property. At a glance, the reader can recognize what is important and what is important. "Home", "Renovation", "energy" and "Extra" with different focal points are called the pillars on which our website.
Language(s): German
ADVERTISING RATES:
Full Page Colour .... EUR 3760
Mechanical Data: Type Area: 272 x 188 mm, No. of Columns (Display): 4, Col Widths (Display): 44 mm
Copy instructions: *Copy Date:* 14 days prior to publication
CONSUMER: WOMEN'S INTEREST CONSUMER MAGAZINES: Home & Family

HAUS & MARKT - AUSG. DÜSSELDORF
729856G74C-1180
Editorial: Ruhrallee 185, 45136 ESSEN
Tel: 201 8945270 **Fax:** 201 894545
Email: consens@cityweb.de **Web site:** http://www.hausundmarkt.de
Freq: 6 issues yearly; **Cover Price:** Free; **Circ:** 40,000
Advertising Manager: Andreas Wimmers
Profile: Magazine for home and property owners in Düsseldorf. Magazine with the theme: bath and plumbing, construction and renovation, furnishing and housing, energy and heating, garden, winter garden, green building, security, economic and capital. Home market is understood as a counselor of real estate. The magazine is one of the best and most innovative news services for homeowners and those who wish to be. Our aim is to report on all aspects currently affecting the property. At a glance, the reader can recognize what is important and what is important. "Home", "Renovation", "energy" and "Extra" with different focal points are called the pillars on which our website.
Language(s): German
ADVERTISING RATES:
Full Page Mono .... EUR 3705
Full Page Colour .... EUR 3705
Mechanical Data: Type Area: 265 x 185 mm, No. of Columns (Display): 4, Col Widths (Display): 42 mm
CONSUMER: WOMEN'S INTEREST CONSUMER MAGAZINES: Home & Family

HAUS & MARKT - AUSG. HANNOVER/HILDESHEIM
729864G74C-1340
Editorial: Hans-Böckler-Allee 7, 30173 HANNOVER
Tel: 511 85502652 **Fax:** 511 85502420
Email: junge@hausundmarkt.de **Web site:** http://www.hausundmarkt.de
Freq: Monthly; **Annual Sub.:** EUR 15,00; **Circ:** 76,500
Editor: Jutta Junge
Profile: Magazine for home and property owners in Hannover/Hildesheim. Magazine with the theme: bath and plumbing, construction and renovation, furnishing and housing, energy and heating, garden, winter garden, green building, security, economic and capital. Home market is understood as a counselor of real estate. The magazine is one of the best and most innovative news services for homeowners and those who wish to be. Our aim is to report on all aspects currently affecting the property. At a glance, the reader can recognize what is important and what is

important. "Home", "Renovation", "energy" and "Extra" with different focal points are called the pillars on which our website.
Language(s): German
ADVERTISING RATES:
Full Page Mono .... EUR 3412
Full Page Colour .... EUR 4606
Mechanical Data: Type Area: 272 x 188 mm, No. of Columns (Display): 4, Col Widths (Display): 44 mm
Copy instructions: *Copy Date:* 29 days prior to publication
CONSUMER: WOMEN'S INTEREST CONSUMER MAGAZINES: Home & Family

HAUS&WELLNESS 1640306G74C-3583
Editorial: Rosenheimer Str. 145i, 81671 MÜNCHEN
Tel: 89 45709625 **Fax:** 89 45709610
Email: fh@bt.de **Web site:** http://www.bt.de
Freq: 6 issues yearly; **Annual Sub.:** EUR 17,00; **Circ:** 21,287
Editor: Florian Hahn; **Advertising Manager:** Nicole Jancke
Profile: Germany's leading magazine for pool & spa. haus&wellness brings the spa-trend at home. If you want to purchase a swimming pool, a Jacuzzi, a sauna and a spa room, you will find in the magazine guarantees important ideas and examples.
Language(s): German
ADVERTISING RATES:
Full Page Mono .... EUR 4960
Full Page Colour .... EUR 4960
Mechanical Data: Type Area: 283 x 196 mm, No. of Columns (Display): 3, Col Widths (Display): 58 mm
Copy instructions: *Copy Date:* 21 days prior to publication
Supplement(s): Bad Design
CONSUMER: WOMEN'S INTEREST CONSUMER MAGAZINES: Home & Family

HAUSARBEITEN.DE
1661834G91D-10142
Editorial: Marienstr. 17, 80331 MÜNCHEN
Tel: 89 5505590 **Fax:** 89 55055910
Email: info@grin.com **Web site:** http://www.hausarbeiten.de
Freq: Daily; **Cover Price:** Paid; **Circ:** 693,944 Unique Users
Language(s): German
CONSUMER: RECREATION & LEISURE: Children & Youth

DER HAUSARZT 729791G56A-4600
Editorial: Aschauer Str. 30, 81549 MÜNCHEN
Tel: 89 2030431361 **Fax:** 89 2030431399
Email: hausarzt.redaktion@springer.com **Web site:** http://www.hausarzt-online.de
Freq: 20 issues yearly; Free to qualifying individuals
Annual Sub.: EUR 95,00; **Circ:** 53,378
Editor: Monika von Berg; **Advertising Manager:** Barbara Kanters
Profile: The journal is the official organ of the German Association of General Practitioners, the most important association in outpatient care in Germany. Who wants to know, therefore, the future looks like the family doctor who reads the association organ! In addition to professional and health policy at first hand each issue also shows the realities of everyday general practice. A focus on all aspects of practice management, for example, fees and billing tips from experts and connoisseurs KV. The focus of medicine provides practical training and GP-CME-related preparation of medical topics - from general practitioners for practitioners. Latest convention coverage is the family doctor a good overview of the current scientific standards. Contentious issues are addressed in pro-and contra-discussions, practical issues resolved in the "consultation".
Language(s): German
ADVERTISING RATES:
Full Page Mono .... EUR 3560
Full Page Colour .... EUR 5310
Mechanical Data: Type Area: 240 x 174 mm
Official Journal of: Organ d. Dt. Hausärzteverb. e.V.
BUSINESS: HEALTH & MEDICAL

DER HAUSARZT IN WESTFALEN
1863732G56A-11578
Editorial: Wilhelm-Brand-Str. 1a, 44141 DORTMUND
Tel: 231 821175 **Fax:** 231 825364
Email: bda-westfalen-lippe@t-online.de **Web site:** http://www.hausaerzteverband-wl.de
Freq: Quarterly; **Circ:** 3,500
Editor: Horst A. Massing; **Advertising Manager:** Doris Lippe-Kuchheuser
Profile: Magazine from the Association of General Practitioners for the region of Westfalen-Lippe.
Language(s): German
ADVERTISING RATES:
Full Page Mono .... EUR 800
Full Page Colour .... EUR 1100
Copy instructions: *Copy Date:* 20 days prior to publication

HAUSBAU 729794G74C-1500
Editorial: Höhenstr. 17, 70736 FELLBACH
Tel: 711 5206244 **Fax:** 711 5206300
Email: hausbau@fachschriften.de **Web site:** http://www.bautipps.de
Freq: 6 issues yearly; **Annual Sub.:** EUR 21,00; **Circ:** 39,404
Editor: Harald Fritsche; **Advertising Manager:** Barbara Hoof
Profile: Magazine about building, renovating and decorating the home.
Language(s): German
Readership: For homebuilders, architects and those in the construction industry.
ADVERTISING RATES:
Full Page Mono .... EUR 9130
Full Page Colour .... EUR 11000
Mechanical Data: Type Area: 247 x 187 mm, No. of Columns (Display): 4, Col Widths (Display): 43 mm
Copy instructions: *Copy Date:* 40 days prior to publication
CONSUMER: WOMEN'S INTEREST CONSUMER MAGAZINES: Home & Family

DAS HAUSEIGENTUM
729801G1E-227_50
Editorial: Potsdamer Str. 143, 10783 BERLIN
Tel: 30 41476917 **Fax:** 30 4113025
Email: ritter@grundeigentum-verlag.de **Web site:** http://www.das-hauseigentum.de
Freq: Monthly; Free to qualifying individuals
Annual Sub.: EUR 31,00; **Circ:** 2,500
Editor: Marlies Ritter; **Advertising Manager:** Gabriele Stöckel
Profile: Magazine about building laws, planning regulations, taxation and tenants' rights in the former DDR.
Language(s): German
ADVERTISING RATES:
Full Page Mono .... EUR 780
Full Page Colour .... EUR 1580
Mechanical Data: Type Area: 260 x 175 mm, No. of Columns (Display): 3, Col Widths (Display): 55 mm
Copy instructions: *Copy Date:* 18 days prior to publication
Official Journal of: Organ d. LV d. Haus- u. Grundeigentümervereine Brandenburg
BUSINESS: FINANCE & ECONOMICS: Property

HÄUSER 729482G74C-1520
Editorial: Am Baumwall 11, 20459 HAMBURG
Tel: 40 37032258 **Fax:** 40 37035676
Email: haeuser@guj.de **Web site:** http://www.schoener-wohnen.de
Freq: 6 issues yearly; **Annual Sub.:** EUR 54,00; **Circ:** 50,700
Editor: Wolfgang Nagel; **Advertising Manager:** Nicole Schostak
Profile: The premium magazine, with a clear, unmistakable profile. For architects, builders, design enthusiasts and those who want to beautify their living situation. The magazine is a competent companion of the architectural community and to provide entertaining and at length about international architecture, its protagonists and trends. The focus always successful single-family homes, alterations and renovations - all national borders. Complemented by the best interior, lifestyle and cultural highlights. Given in each issue of the Design class for kitchen, bathroom and the living room. The magazine which offers freshness, actuality and real value. And underlines its competence with the Häuser Award, which has become in ten years one of the most important German architectural awards. Facebook: http://www.facebook.com/schoenerwohnen.
Language(s): German
Readership: Aimed at home owners aged between 30 and 59 years.
ADVERTISING RATES:
Full Page Mono .... EUR 12400
Full Page Colour .... EUR 12400
Mechanical Data: No. of Columns (Display): 3, Col Widths (Display): 64 mm, Type Area: 268 x 200 mm
Supplement(s): blue kompakt.
CONSUMER: WOMEN'S INTEREST CONSUMER MAGAZINES: Home & Family

HÄUSER BAUEN & SPAREN
732211G74C-1720
Editorial: Höhenstr. 17, 70736 FELLBACH
Tel: 711 5206244 **Fax:** 711 5206300
Email: haeuser-billiger-bauen@fachschriften.de **Web site:** http://www.bautipps.de
Freq: Half-yearly; **Cover Price:** EUR 3,80; **Circ:** 31,583
Editor: Harald Fritsche; **Advertising Manager:** Barbara Hoof
Profile: The starter booklet has been dedicated to the budget-conscious building and support to owners in achieving their dream house. Compact and of course, the reader, where much can save the bottom line.
Language(s): German
Readership: Aimed at young people seeking to improve their home environment.
ADVERTISING RATES:
Full Page Colour .... EUR 9550
Mechanical Data: No. of Columns (Display): 4, Col Widths (Display): 43 mm, Type Area: 247 x 187 mm
Copy instructions: *Copy Date:* 40 days prior to publication
CONSUMER: WOMEN'S INTEREST CONSUMER MAGAZINES: Home & Family

HÄUSLICHE PFLEGE 729485G56B-660
Editorial: Plathnerstr. 4c, 30175 HANNOVER
Tel: 511 9910135 **Fax:** 511 9910196
Email: stefan.neumann@vincentz.net **Web site:** http://www.haeusliche-pflege.vincentz.net
Freq: Monthly; **Annual Sub.:** EUR 96,00; **Circ:** 6,511
Editor: Stefan Neumann; **Advertising Manager:** Thomas Veitschegger
Profile: The only monthly magazine for the management in the professional outpatient nursing and elderly care. Exclusive technical articles by renowned authors make the market-leading publication for executives in home care indispensable. From practice to practice will reports on effective methods of managing patient care services, the latest in case law and on relevant developments in the market for home care. Häusliche Pflege is the value problem solver for the management of outpatient services. The additional supplement PDL practice is the magazine for nursing services in outpatient services and reported practice of all that the leaders need to know to care. In the special part of homecare every three months, major trends in intensive care at home are presented.
Language(s): German
ADVERTISING RATES:
Full Page Mono .... EUR 1550
Full Page Colour .... EUR 2730
Mechanical Data: Type Area: 250 x 175 mm, No. of Columns (Display): 4, Col Widths (Display): 42 mm
Copy instructions: *Copy Date:* 17 days prior to publication
BUSINESS: HEALTH & MEDICAL: Nursing

HAUSTEX 729818G47A-110
Editorial: Ahmser Str. 190, 32052 HERFORD
Tel: 5221 1748886 **Fax:** 5221 1748889
Email: dietram.neuper@snfachpresse.de **Web site:** http://www.raumausstattung.de
Freq: 11 issues yearly; **Annual Sub.:** EUR 63,50; **Circ:** 5,453
Editor: Dietram Neuper
Profile: Haustex is Europe's leading trade magazine and the only of its kind in Germany for beds, bedding, blankets, mattresses / sleep systems, bed, table and kitchen linen. The readers are executives and sales of household textiles in the beds retail, furniture stores and bed wards in the industry. Haustex offers its readers more than universal journals: Reports from retailers and bedding departments, extensive range of focal points, supply portraits.
Language(s): German
ADVERTISING RATES:
Full Page Mono .... EUR 3020
Full Page Colour .... EUR 5220
Mechanical Data: Type Area: 252 x 184 mm, No. of Columns (Display): 4, Col Widths (Display): 44 mm
Official Journal of: Organ d. Fachverb. Matratzen-Industrie e.V. u. d. Verb. d. Dt. Daunen- u. Federindustrie e.V.
BUSINESS: CLOTHING & TEXTILES

HAUT 729875G56A-4640
Editorial: Otto-Hahn-Str. 7, 50997 KÖLN
Tel: 2236 3760 **Fax:** 2236 376999
Email: sde@biermann.net **Web site:** http://www.viavital.net
Freq: 6 issues yearly; **Annual Sub.:** EUR 84,00; **Circ:** 4,986
Editor: Maria Zabel; **Advertising Manager:** Bettina Thiermeyer
Profile: Haut Dermatologist keeps up to date. The journal publishes articles from current dermatology, allergy, aesthetics and cosmetology. Dermatologists also speaks from around the world in Haut over their work - by competent medical editors translated into German. In each issue, noted experts give tips on billing to EBM, GOÄ and IGeL. Also legal and economic aspects as well as important issues to insurance be discussed. News from the pharmaceutical industry and medical technology round off the program.
Language(s): German
ADVERTISING RATES:
Full Page Mono .... EUR 1915
Full Page Colour .... EUR 3265
Mechanical Data: Type Area: 240 x 188 mm
Copy instructions: *Copy Date:* 21 days prior to publication
BUSINESS: HEALTH & MEDICAL

HAUT & ALLERGIE AKTUELL
729880G56A-4660
Editorial: René-Schickele-Str. 10, 53123 BONN
Tel: 228 367910 **Fax:** 228 3679190
Email: info@dha-allergien.de **Web site:** http://www.dha-allergien.de
Freq: Quarterly; **Circ:** 15,000
Editor: Dorit Harms; **Advertising Manager:** Dorit Harms
Profile: Magazine on neurodermatitis, psoriasis, asthma, allergies and dermal diseases.
Language(s): German
ADVERTISING RATES:
Full Page Mono .... EUR 1800
Full Page Colour .... EUR 3045
Mechanical Data: No. of Columns (Display): 3, Col Widths (Display): 58 mm, Type Area: 245 x 185 mm
Copy instructions: *Copy Date:* 15 days prior to publication

DER HAUTARZT 729876G56A-4680
Editorial: Tiergartenstr. 17, 69121 HEIDELBERG
Tel: 6221 4878724 **Fax:** 6221 48768724
Email: julie.kind@springer.com **Web site:** http://www.springermedizin.de
Freq: Monthly; **Annual Sub.:** EUR 322,00; **Circ:** 2,168
Advertising Manager: Sabine Weidner
Profile: Der Hautarzt is an internationally recognized journal informing all dermatologists working in practical or clinical environments about important developments in the field of dermatology including allergology, venereology and related areas. Comprehensive reviews on a specific topical issue focus on providing evidenced based information on diagnostics and therapy. Freely submitted original papers allow the presentation of important clinical studies and serve the scientific exchange. Case reports feature interesting cases and aim at optimizing diagnostic and therapeutic strategies. Review articles under the rubric "Continuing Medical Education" present verified results of scientific research and their integration into daily practice.
Language(s): German
Readership: Aimed at doctors and dermatologists.
ADVERTISING RATES:
Full Page Mono .... EUR 1880
Full Page Colour .... EUR 2920
Mechanical Data: Type Area: 240 x 174 mm
Official Journal of: Organ d. Dt. STD (Sexually Transmitted Disease) Ges., Dt. Dermatolog. Ges. u. d. Dt. Dermatolog. Laserges.
BUSINESS: HEALTH & MEDICAL

HAUTNAH DERMATOLOGIE
729879G56A-4700
Editorial: Aschauer Str. 30, 81549 MÜNCHEN
Tel: 89 2030431407 **Fax:** 89 2030431399
Email: ulrich.schneider@springer.com **Web site:** http://www.hautnah-dermatologie.de
Freq: 6 issues yearly; **Annual Sub.:** EUR 105,50; **Circ:** 4,581
Editor: Ulrich Schneider
Profile: hautnah dermatologie provides clear and practical training from the broad occupational field of dermatologically active doctors. Focus is packed with pictures overviews and case reports and current conference reports. Summaries of international studies and contributions to legal questions. The contents of the journal are accepted by the Bavarian Medical Council for certified training.
Language(s): German
ADVERTISING RATES:
Full Page Mono .... EUR 2250
Full Page Colour .... EUR 4000
Mechanical Data: Type Area: 240 x 174 mm
BUSINESS: HEALTH & MEDICAL

HAV INFO 1772559G1A-3648
Editorial: Sievekingplatz 1, 20355 HAMBURG
Tel: 40 6116350 **Fax:** 40 354231
Email: info@hav.de **Web site:** http://www.hav.de
Freq: Quarterly; **Cover Price:** EUR 2,50
Free to qualifying individuals ; **Circ:** 3,150
Editor: Carolin Müller-Dieckert; **Advertising Manager:** Claudia Leicht
Profile: Information from the Hamburg Lawyer's board.
Language(s): German
ADVERTISING RATES:
Full Page Mono .... EUR 550
Full Page Colour .... EUR 950
Copy instructions: *Copy Date:* 35 days prior to publication

HCP JOURNAL 2042052G56A-11707
Editorial: Besenbinderhof 60, 20097 HAMBURG
Email: v.ravenhorst@hcp-journal.de **Web site:** http://www.hcp-journal.de
Cover Price: EUR 3,00
Free to qualifying individuals ; **Circ:** 30,000
Editor: Volker Ravenhorst
Profile: The magazine provides practical information on the topic "working with disabilities" or preventive measures for people at risk of disability. The spokespersons of the severely disabled, the directors, the staff of the HR departments and all staff members experienced in the Hamburger establishments find out more about opportunities for consultation and training (some free). The journal represents an important link that is to encourage dialogue with all stakeholders and support the work of the trust people.
Language(s): German
ADVERTISING RATES:
Full Page Mono .... EUR 1900
Full Page Colour .... EUR 2620
Mechanical Data: Type Area: 255 x 187 mm

HEALTH TECHNOLOGIES
1824352G56A-11521
Editorial: Callinstr. 36, 30167 HANNOVER
Tel: 511 7623827
Email: besdo@ifv.uni-hannover.de
Freq: 5 issues yearly; **Circ:** 2,400
Editor: Silke Besdo
Profile: Magazine of the German Association for bio-medical techniques.
Language(s): German

HEAT AND MASS TRANSFER
729895G58-95
Editorial: Kurt-Wolters-Str. 3, 34109 KASSEL
Email: subscriptions@springer.com **Web site:** http://www.springerlink.com
Freq: Monthly; **Annual Sub.:** EUR 3308,00; **Circ:** 83
Editor: Andrea Luke
Profile: International journal about energy and heat transfer.
Language(s): English
ADVERTISING RATES:
Full Page Mono .... EUR 740
Full Page Colour .... EUR 1780
Mechanical Data: Type Area: 240 x 175 mm
BUSINESS: ENERGY, FUEL & NUCLEAR

HEAT PROCESSING

1626578G19E-1872
Editorial: Huyssenallee 52, 45128 ESSEN
Tel: 201 8200212 **Fax:** 201 8200240
Email: s.schalm@vulkan-verlag.de **Web site:** http://www.heatprocessing-online.com
Freq: Quarterly; **Annual Sub.:** EUR 132,00; **Circ:** 3,146
Editor: Stephan Schalm; **Advertising Manager:** Bettina Schwarzer-Hahn
Profile: "Heat Processing" is the technical journal for the entire field of industrial furnace, heat treatment plants, the efficient use of energy in thermoprocessing systems, as well as being the international forum for interchange of knowledge and experience between heat-process industry suppliers and users.
Language(s): English
ADVERTISING RATES:
Full Page Mono .... EUR 1955
Full Page Colour .... EUR 3155
Mechanical Data: Type Area: 255 x 182 mm, No. of Columns (Display): 3, Col Widths (Display): 58 mm
Official Journal of: Organ d. European Committee of Industrial Furnace and Heating Equipment Associations
BUSINESS: ENGINEERING & MACHINERY: Machinery, Machine Tools & Metalworking

DIE HEBAMME

729896G56B-95
Editorial: Oswald-Hesse-Str. 50, 70469 STUTTGART
Tel: 711 89310 **Fax:** 711 8931706
Web site: http://www.medizinverlage.de
Freq: Quarterly; **Annual Sub.:** EUR 61,50; **Circ:** 4,400
Editor: Renate Reutter; **Advertising Manager:** Nancy Ruhland
Profile: Magazine about midwifery.
Language(s): German
ADVERTISING RATES:
Full Page Mono .... EUR 1250
Full Page Colour .... EUR 2290
Mechanical Data: Type Area: 240 x 176 mm, No. of Columns (Display): 3, Col Widths (Display): 55 mm
Copy instructions: *Copy Date:* 30 days prior to publication
BUSINESS: HEALTH & MEDICAL: Nursing

HEBAMMEN FORUM

1638975G56R-11272
Editorial: Hornstr. 10, 10963 BERLIN
Tel: 30 61675225 **Fax:** 30 69598229
Email: redaktion@hebammenverband.de
Freq: Monthly; **Annual Sub.:** EUR 67,00; **Circ:** 8,872
Editor: Marion Ebeling
Profile: Magazine of the German Midwives' Association.
Language(s): German
ADVERTISING RATES:
Full Page Mono .... EUR 1300
Full Page Colour .... EUR 2150
Mechanical Data: Type Area: 269 x 184 mm, No. of Columns (Display): 4, Col Widths (Display): 43 mm
Copy instructions: *Copy Date:* 22 days prior to publication
BUSINESS: HEALTH & MEDICAL: Health Medical Related

HEBEZEUGE FÖRDERMITTEL

729899G19D-25
Editorial: Am Friedrichshain 22, 10407 BERLIN
Tel: 30 42151475 **Fax:** 30 42151207
Email: hf.redaktion@hussberlin.de **Web site:** http://www.hebezeuge-foerdermittel.de
Freq: 10 issues yearly; **Annual Sub.:** EUR 155,00; **Circ:** 11,861
Editor: Norbert Hamke; **Advertising Manager:** Marco Fiolka
Profile: Technical journal about research and development into conveyance, materials handling, logistics and lifting technology application. Hebezeuge Fördermittel is a value-orientated technical magazine for conveyor technics and series lifting equipment across all branches of industry, trade and services. The editorial concept of Hebezeuge Fördermittel is focused on system solutions and components in warehousing, handling and conveying, information management, transport and transhipment, cranes and cranes technologies, hoisting equipment and fork lift trucks. Hebezeuge Fördermittel covers all parts of conveyor technique and hoisting devices that are relevant for company logistics manager and buying departments. Our readers are producers as well as users of the techno logies and products above.Hebezeuge Fördermittel has developed to one of the leading and most acknowledged magazines of the branch with an excellent standing.
Language(s): German
ADVERTISING RATES:
Full Page Mono .... EUR 3980
Full Page Colour .... EUR 5180
Mechanical Data: Type Area: 266 x 185 mm, No. of Columns (Display): 4, Col Widths (Display): 43 mm
Copy instructions: *Copy Date:* 26 days prior to publication
BUSINESS: ENGINEERING & MACHINERY: Hydraulic Power

DAS HEFT

729904G80-4600
Editorial: Haarener Str. 32, 33178 BORCHEN
Tel: 5251 62624 **Fax:** 5251 62628
Email: mail@heft.de **Web site:** http://www.heft.de
Freq: 11 issues yearly; **Annual Sub.:** EUR 20,00; **Circ:** 10,000
Editor: Harald Morsch; **Advertising Manager:** Harald Morsch
Profile: Magazine for the Paderborn area.
Language(s): German
Readership: Read by local residents.
ADVERTISING RATES:
Full Page Mono .... EUR 590
Full Page Colour .... EUR 708
Mechanical Data: Type Area: 178 x 123 mm, No. of Columns (Display): 2, Col Widths (Display): 59 mm
Copy instructions: *Copy Date:* 15 days prior to publication
CONSUMER: RURAL & REGIONAL INTEREST

HEIDELBERG

1978772G89A-12565
Editorial: Hauptstr. 25, 69117 HEIDELBERG
Tel: 6221 6594877 **Fax:** 6221 6594879
Email: info@heidelberg-aktuell.de **Web site:** http://www.heidelberg-aktuell.de
Freq: Annual; **Cover Price:** EUR 1,00; **Circ:** 80,000
Editor: Richard Merges
Profile: The annual magazine presents Heidelberg as a city of romance, science, business, culture and hospitality. Distribution: sending as initial information to companies and visitors to the city of Heidelberg, to tour operators, hotels, Heidelberg interested in Germany and abroad, at international tourism fairs as well as domestic airports and train stations, and the sale of the magazine retail and selected outlets.
Language(s): English; German
ADVERTISING RATES:
Full Page Mono .... EUR 2347
Full Page Colour .... EUR 2761
Mechanical Data: Type Area: 230 x 184 mm, No. of Columns (Display): 3, Col Widths (Display): 58 mm

HEIDENHEIMER NEUE PRESSE

729941G67B-6680
Editorial: Marienstr. 9, 89518 HEIDENHEIM
Tel: 7321 347201 **Fax:** 7321 347200
Email: redaktion@hnp-online.de **Web site:** http://www.hnp-online.de
Freq: 312 issues yearly; **Circ:** 27,906
Editor: Manfred Allenhöfer; **Advertising Manager:** Eberhardt Looser
Profile: Daily newspaper with regional news and a local sports section.
Language(s): German
ADVERTISING RATES:
SCC .... EUR 105,30
Mechanical Data: Type Area: 480 x 320 mm, No. of Columns (Display): 7, Col Widths (Display): 44 mm
Copy instructions: *Copy Date:* 1 day prior to publication
Supplement(s): da heim; Noise; Schlossblick
REGIONAL DAILY & SUNDAY NEWSPAPERS: Regional Daily Newspapers

HEIDENHEIMER ZEITUNG

729943G67B-6700
Editorial: Olgastr. 15, 89518 HEIDENHEIM
Tel: 7321 347153 **Fax:** 7321 347102
Email: redaktion@hz-online.de **Web site:** http://www.hz-online.de
Freq: 312 issues yearly; **Circ:** 27,906
Editor: Hendrik Rupp; **Advertising Manager:** Eberhardt Looser
Profile: Daily newspaper with regional news and a local sports section.
Language(s): German
ADVERTISING RATES:
SCC .... EUR 105,30
Mechanical Data: Type Area: 480 x 320 mm, No. of Columns (Display): 7, Col Widths (Display): 44 mm
Copy instructions: *Copy Date:* 1 day prior to publication
Supplement(s): da heim; Das Magazin; Noise; Schlossblick
REGIONAL DAILY & SUNDAY NEWSPAPERS: Regional Daily Newspapers

HEILBERUFE

729950G56B-1646
Editorial: Heidelberger Platz 3, 14197 BERLIN
Tel: 30 827875500 **Fax:** 30 827875505
Email: heilberufe@springer.com **Web site:** http://www.heilberufe-online.de
Freq: Monthly; **Annual Sub.:** EUR 49,90; **Circ:** 18,723
Editor: Katja Kupfer-Geißler; **Advertising Manager:** Paul Berger
Profile: The nursing magazine is aimed at carers of all service areas and linking the various disciplines of health and pediatric nursing, the nursing care to the elderly in hospitals, nursing homes and in outpatient care. In the three major categories-care practice, care routines, care perspectives nurses find interesting, practical training posts, as well as tips for everyday life at work and on the station. With the medical profession care program offers the magazine to a regular long-distance training, will get the readers to successfully completing an approved training certificate as proof. The magazine is also the official newsletter of the German Nursing Council - with the latest information on health policy for nurses - PflegePositionen. Special issues on selected topics and the scientific supplement online supplement the supply of health professionals Sience magazine.
Language(s): German
ADVERTISING RATES:
Full Page Mono .... EUR 2350
Full Page Colour .... EUR 3800
Mechanical Data: Type Area: 240 x 174 mm
Official Journal of: Organ d. Dt. Pflegeverb. u. Anbieterverb. Qualitätsorientierte Gesundheitspflegeeinrichtungen e.V.
Supplement(s): Pflege Positionen
BUSINESS: HEALTH & MEDICAL: Nursing

HEILBRONNER STIMME

729954G67B-6720
Editorial: Allee 2, 74072 HEILBRONN **Tel:** 7131 6150
Fax: 7131 615373
Email: redaktion@stimme.de **Web site:** http://www.stimme.de
Freq: 312 issues yearly; **Circ:** 92,477
Editor: Uwe Ralf Heer; **News Editor:** Siegfried Lambert; **Advertising Manager:** Martin Küfner
Profile: Regional daily newspaper covering politics, economics, sport, travel and technology. Once again, the Heilbronner Stimme included in the International Color Quality Club, which puts them among the 50 daily newspapers with the world's best image and print quality. Twitter: http://twitter.com/stimmeonline This Outlet offers RSS (Really Simple Syndication).
Language(s): German
ADVERTISING RATES:
SCC .... EUR 138,80
Mechanical Data: Type Area: 490 x 327 mm, No. of Columns (Display): 7, Col Widths (Display): 45 mm
Copy instructions: *Copy Date:* 1 day prior to publication
Supplement(s): autoStimme; Lokalanzeiger für Bad Friedrichshall, Gundelsheim, Neudenau, Oedheim und Offenau; Neckarsulmer Stimme für Neckarsulm, Erlenbach, Untereisesheim; sole; Stadtgalerie aktuell; WirtschaftsStimme
REGIONAL DAILY & SUNDAY NEWSPAPERS: Regional Daily Newspapers

HEILPFLANZEN-WELT

1704292G74G-1857
Editorial: Lützowstr. 47, 10785 BERLIN
Tel: 30 80613679 **Fax:** 30 80613680
Email: info@heilpflanzen-welt.de **Web site:** http://www.heilpflanzen-welt.de
Cover Price: Paid; **Circ:** 900,000 Unique Users
Editor: Rainer H. Bubenzer; **Advertising Manager:** Marion Kaden
Profile: Information about medical palnts.
Language(s): German
CONSUMER: WOMEN'S INTEREST CONSUMER MAGAZINES: Slimming & Health

HEIM UND WELT

730062G74A-1480
Editorial: Rotweg 8, 76532 BADEN-BADEN
Tel: 7221 3501300 **Fax:** 7221 3501133
Email: barbara.jung@klambt.de **Web site:** http://www.heimundwelt.de
Freq: Weekly; **Cover Price:** EUR 1,50; **Circ:** 41,780
Editor: Barbara Jung
Profile: Heim und Welt is a magazine with tradition. With recent reports and reports on celebrities from the nobility, the TV and pop industry as well as film, society and sport reflects and commented Heim und Welt the events of the week. A comprehensive service section provides practical advice and timely tips for everyday life: fashion suggestions and trend-Telegram, travel reports and holiday information, decorating ideas and gardening tips, home and shopping advice, recipes and the latest market information, with answers to questions of health and general well-being, a side to the current medical education "health for the family", with a section on "domestic animals" as well as a horoscope and an Astro-reader service. Heim und Welt is one of the oldest magazines for entertainment, current affairs, partnership and life coaching.
Language(s): German
ADVERTISING RATES:
Full Page Mono .... EUR 2580
Full Page Colour .... EUR 2580
Mechanical Data: Type Area: 260 x 195 mm, No. of Columns (Display): 4, Col Widths (Display): 45 mm
Copy instructions: *Copy Date:* 28 days prior to publication
CONSUMER: WOMEN'S INTEREST CONSUMER MAGAZINES: Women's Interest

HEIMAT ECHO

730006G72-5340
Editorial: Rheinstr. 41, 56203 HÖHR-GRENZHAUSEN **Tel:** 2624 9110 **Fax:** 2624 911115
Email: info@wittich-hoehr.de **Web site:** http://www.wittich.de
Freq: Weekly; **Cover Price:** Free; **Circ:** 8,800
Editor-in-Chief: Franz-Peter Eudenbach;
Advertising Manager: Annette Steil
Profile: Local official paper.
Language(s): German
ADVERTISING RATES:
Full Page Mono .... EUR 572
Full Page Colour .... EUR 642
Mechanical Data: Type Area: 275 x 185 mm, No. of Columns (Display): 2, Col Widths (Display): 90 mm
Copy instructions: *Copy Date:* 1 day prior to publication
LOCAL NEWSPAPERS

HEIMATANZEIGER FÜR RADEVORMWALD MIT WUPPERORTSCHAFTEN

729972G72-5364
Editorial: Kaiserstr. 75, 42477 RADEVORMWALD
Tel: 2195 5035 **Fax:** 2195 5039
Email: heimatanzeiger@rga-online.de
Freq: Weekly; **Cover Price:** Free; **Circ:** 13,025
Editor: Frank Michalczak
Profile: Advertising journal (house-to-house) concentrating on local stories.
Language(s): German
ADVERTISING RATES:
Full Page Mono .... EUR 2064
Full Page Colour .... EUR 2580
Mechanical Data: Type Area: 430 x 282 mm, No. of Columns (Display): 6, Col Widths (Display): 45 mm
Copy instructions: *Copy Date:* 2 days prior to publication
LOCAL NEWSPAPERS

DER HEIMATBOTE

729989G67B-16747
Editorial: Laudenbacher Str. 4, 63825 SCHÖLLKRIPPEN **Tel:** 6024 67210 **Fax:** 6024 7763
Email: peter.ostheimerheimatbote@t-online.de
Freq: 156 issues yearly; **Circ:** 3,000
Editor: Peter Ostheimer
Profile: Regional daily newspaper covering politics, economics, sport, travel and technology.
Language(s): German
ADVERTISING RATES:
SCC .... EUR 8,00
Mechanical Data: Type Area: 420 x 280 mm, No. of Columns (Display): 6, Col Widths (Display): 45 mm
Copy instructions: *Copy Date:* 1 day prior to publication
REGIONAL DAILY & SUNDAY NEWSPAPERS: Regional Daily Newspapers

HEIMATBOTE

729988G72-5376
Editorial: Waldstr. 226, 63071 OFFENBACH
Tel: 69 85008270 **Fax:** 69 85008296
Email: red.heimatpost@stadtpost.de **Web site:** http://www.stadtpost.de
Freq: Weekly; **Cover Price:** Free; **Circ:** 13,150
Editor: Wolfgang Janz; **Advertising Manager:** Helmut Moser
Profile: Advertising journal (house-to-house) concentrating on local stories.
Language(s): German
ADVERTISING RATES:
Full Page Mono .... EUR 3060
Full Page Colour .... EUR 4284
Mechanical Data: Type Area: 470 x 322 mm, No. of Columns (Display): 7, Col Widths (Display): 43 mm
Copy instructions: *Copy Date:* 2 days prior to publication
LOCAL NEWSPAPERS

HEIMATSPIEGEL

730042G72-5396
Editorial: Rugenbarg 53a, 22848 NORDERSTEDT
Tel: 40 523080 **Fax:** 40 52308130
Email: info@verlagshaus-meincke.de **Web site:** http://www.verlagshaus-meincke.de
Freq: Weekly; **Cover Price:** Free; **Circ:** 69,919
Editor: Bert Langbehn; **Advertising Manager:** Inga Rabehl
Profile: Advertising journal (house-to-house) concentrating on local stories.
Language(s): German
ADVERTISING RATES:
Full Page Mono .... EUR 3545
Full Page Colour .... EUR 3757
Mechanical Data: Type Area: 425 x 280 mm, No. of Columns (Display): 6, Col Widths (Display): 45 mm
Copy instructions: *Copy Date:* 5 days prior to publication
LOCAL NEWSPAPERS

HEIMATSPIEGEL EXTRA

730044G72-5404
Editorial: Rugenbarg 53a, 22848 NORDERSTEDT
Tel: 40 523080 **Fax:** 40 52308130
Email: info@verlagshaus-meincke.de **Web site:** http://www.verlagshaus-meincke.de
Freq: Weekly; **Cover Price:** Free; **Circ:** 60,807
Editor: Bert Langbehn; **Advertising Manager:** Inga Rabehl
Profile: Advertising journal (house-to-house) concentrating on local stories.
Language(s): German
ADVERTISING RATES:
Full Page Mono .... EUR 3545
Full Page Colour .... EUR 3757
Mechanical Data: Type Area: 425 x 280 mm, No. of Columns (Display): 6, Col Widths (Display): 45 mm
Copy instructions: *Copy Date:* 3 days prior to publication
LOCAL NEWSPAPERS

HEIMKINO

730056G76B-120_50
Editorial: Gartroper Str. 42, 47138 DUISBURG
Tel: 203 4292231 **Fax:** 203 4292136
Email: koehler@brieden.de **Web site:** http://www.heimkino-magazin.de
Freq: Monthly; **Annual Sub.:** EUR 39,60; **Circ:** 50,000
Editor: Heinz Köhler
Profile: Television has recently acquired a new dimension: Large Format Picture and sound like in the movies bring the movie experience into the living room. The magazine tests the associated technology and presents the latest DVDs. The journal is devoted to the topic in a competent, yet understandable way.
Language(s): German
ADVERTISING RATES:
Full Page Mono .... EUR 5182
Full Page Colour .... EUR 7603

Mechanical Data: Type Area: 248 x 185 mm, No. of Columns (Display): 4, Col Widths (Display): 45 mm
CONSUMER: MUSIC & PERFORMING ARTS: Theatre

HEIMSPIEL
1925857G65A-120_102
Editorial: Karl-Gerold-Platz 1, 60594 FRANKFURT
Tel: 69 21993504 **Fax:** 69 21993681
Email: sport@fr-online.de **Web site:** http://www.fr-online.de
Freq: 17 issues yearly; **Circ:** 81,285
Profile: Football magazine for home matches of Eintracht Frankfurt.
Language(s): German
ADVERTISING RATES:
Full Page Mono .... EUR 3080
Full Page Colour .... EUR 3915
Mechanical Data: Type Area: 370 x 245 mm
Copy instructions: *Copy Date:* 10 days prior to publication
Supplement to: Frankfurter Rundschau
NATIONAL DAILY & SUNDAY NEWSPAPERS: Unabhängiges konservatives MdEP

HEIMVORTEIL
745810G83-13260
Editorial: Maastrichter Str. 49, 50672 KÖLN
Tel: 221 9515410 **Fax:** 221 95154111
Email: gesellschaft@stadtrevue.de **Web site:** http://www.stadtrevue.de
Freq: Half-yearly; **Cover Price:** Free; **Circ:** 20,000
Profile: Cologne University magazine.
Language(s): German
ADVERTISING RATES:
Full Page Mono .... EUR 1750
Full Page Colour .... EUR 2510
Mechanical Data: Type Area: 262 x 190 mm, No. of Columns (Display): 4, Col Widths (Display): 44 mm
CONSUMER: STUDENT PUBLICATIONS

HEINRICHSBLATT
730073G87-5500
Editorial: Heinrichsdamm 32, 96047 BAMBERG
Tel: 951 51920 **Fax:** 951 519225
Email: kuschbert@heinrichs-verlag.de **Web site:** http://www.heinrichsblatt.de
Freq: Weekly; **Annual Sub.:** EUR 66,00; **Circ:** 30,233
Editor: Andreas Kuschbert; **Advertising Manager:** Hans Ramer
Profile: Catholic magazine.
Language(s): German
ADVERTISING RATES:
Full Page Mono .... EUR 1848
Full Page Colour .... EUR 2632
Mechanical Data: Type Area: 280 x 210 mm, No. of Columns (Display): 4, Col Widths (Display): 48 mm
Copy instructions: *Copy Date:* 9 days prior to publication
CONSUMER: RELIGIOUS

HEINZ
730076G80-5340
Editorial: Tannenbergstr. 35, 42103 WUPPERTAL
Tel: 202 371700 **Fax:** 202 3717023
Email: redaktion@heinz-magazin.de **Web site:** http://www.heinz-magazin.de
Freq: Monthly; **Cover Price:** Free; **Circ:** 24,514
Editor: Gerhard Roßmann; **Advertising Manager:** Susanne Claas
Profile: Culture and entertainment magazine for Dortmund. In the film categories, offer stage, art, literature and music specialist writers information about the highlights of the month. Also features, specials, features and news from the youth scenes find their place. What is not here, does not exist! The timer is the indispensable compass through the cultural program. The cultural diversity for a whole month is presented in a clear and complete with extensive background information: concert preview, party zone, film-ABC, prompter, live literature, art galleries and museums and addresses.
Language(s): German
ADVERTISING RATES:
Full Page Mono .... EUR 1500
Full Page Colour .... EUR 2400
Mechanical Data: Type Area: 260 x 190 mm, No. of Columns (Display): 4, Col Widths (Display): 44 mm
Copy instructions: *Copy Date:* 15 days prior to publication
CONSUMER: RURAL & REGIONAL INTEREST

HEINZ
730077G80-5360
Editorial: Brasserstr. 6, 45130 ESSEN
Tel: 201 7988663 **Fax:** 201 7988664
Email: redaktion@heinz-magazin.de **Web site:** http://www.heinz-magazin.de
Freq: Monthly; **Cover Price:** Free; **Circ:** 22,990
Editor: Gerhard Roßmann; **Advertising Manager:** Boris Langen
Profile: Culture and entertainment magazine for Essen. In the film categories, offer stage, art, literature and music specialist writers information about the highlights of the month. Also features, specials, features and news from the youth scenes find their place. What is not here, does not exist! The timer is the indispensable compass through the cultural program. Cultural diversity for a whole month is presented in a clear and complete with extensive background information: concert preview, party zone, film-ABC, prompter, live literature, art galleries and museums and addresses. Anhören Umschrift.
Language(s): German
ADVERTISING RATES:
Full Page Mono .... EUR 1500
Full Page Colour .... EUR 2400
Mechanical Data: Type Area: 260 x 190 mm, No. of Columns (Display): 4, Col Widths (Display): 44 mm
Copy instructions: *Copy Date:* 15 days prior to publication
CONSUMER: RURAL & REGIONAL INTEREST

HEINZ
730078G80-5380
Editorial: Tannenbergstr. 35, 42103 WUPPERTAL
Tel: 202 371700 **Fax:** 202 3717023
Email: redaktion@heinz-magazin.de **Web site:** http://www.heinz-magazin.de
Freq: Monthly; **Cover Price:** Free; **Circ:** 23,492
Editor: Gerhard Roßmann; **Advertising Manager:** Ute Herzog
Profile: Culture and entertainment magazine for Wuppertal, Solingen and Remscheid. In the film categories, offer stage, art, literature and music specialist writers information about the highlights of the month. Also features, specials, features and news from the youth scenes find their place. What is not here, does not exist! The timer is the indispensable compass through the cultural program. Cultural diversity for a whole month is presented in a clear and complete with extensive background information: concert preview, party zone, film-ABC, prompter, live literature, art galleries and museums and addresses. Anhören Umschrift.
Language(s): German
ADVERTISING RATES:
Full Page Mono .... EUR 1500
Full Page Colour .... EUR 2400
Mechanical Data: Type Area: 270 x 190 mm, No. of Columns (Display): 4, Col Widths (Display): 44 mm
Copy instructions: *Copy Date:* 15 days prior to publication
CONSUMER: RURAL & REGIONAL INTEREST

HEINZ
753821G80-5390
Editorial: Tannenbergstr. 35, 42103 WUPPERTAL
Tel: 202 371700 **Fax:** 202 3717023
Email: redaktion@heinz-magazin.de **Web site:** http://www.heinz-magazin.de
Freq: Monthly; **Cover Price:** Free; **Circ:** 21,012
Editor: Gerhard Roßmann; **Advertising Manager:** Barbara Scharf
Profile: Culture and entertainment magazine for Duisburg, Oberhausen and Mülheim. In the film categories, offer stage, art, literature and music specialist writers information about the highlights of the month. Also features, specials, features and news from the youth scenes find their place. What is not here, does not exist! The timer is the indispensable compass through the cultural program. The cultural diversity for a whole month is presented in a clear and complete with extensive background information: concert preview, party zone, film-ABC, prompter, live literature, art galleries and museums and addresses.
Language(s): German
ADVERTISING RATES:
Full Page Mono .... EUR 1120
Full Page Colour .... EUR 1950
Mechanical Data: Type Area: 270 x 190 mm, No. of Columns (Display): 4, Col Widths (Display): 44 mm
Copy instructions: *Copy Date:* 15 days prior to publication
CONSUMER: RURAL & REGIONAL INTEREST

HEINZ
1666723G80-14496
Editorial: Brassertstr. 6, 45130 ESSEN
Tel: 201 7988663 **Fax:** 201 7988664
Email: redaktion@heinz-magazin.de **Web site:** http://www.heinz-magazin.de
Freq: Monthly; **Cover Price:** Free; **Circ:** 20,508
Editor: Gerhard Roßmann; **Advertising Manager:** Barbara Scharf
Profile: Culture and entertainment magazine for Bochum, Herne and Witten. In the film categories, offer stage, art, literature and music specialist writers information about the highlights of the month. Also features, specials, features and news from the youth scenes find their place. What is not here, does not exist! The timer is the indispensable compass through the cultural program. The cultural diversity for a whole month is presented in a clear and complete with extensive background information: concert preview, party zone, film-ABC, prompter, live literature, art galleries and museums and addresses.
Language(s): German
ADVERTISING RATES:
Full Page Mono .... EUR 1000
Full Page Colour .... EUR 1700
Mechanical Data: Type Area: 260 x 190 mm, No. of Columns (Display): 4, Col Widths (Display): 44 mm
Copy instructions: *Copy Date:* 15 days prior to publication
CONSUMER: RURAL & REGIONAL INTEREST

HEIRATEN - IHR HOCHZEITSPLANER FÜR CHEMNITZ UND UMGEBUNG
2090091G74A-3827
Editorial: Heinrich-Lorenz-Str. 2, 09120 CHEMNITZ
Tel: 371 5289358 **Fax:** 371 5289391
Email: j.flachowsky@wochenspiegel-sachsen.de
Web site: http://www.wochenspiegel-sachsen.de
Freq: Quarterly; **Cover Price:** Free; **Circ:** 10,000
Editor: Ingolf Müller; **Advertising Manager:** Jennifer Flachowsky
Profile: One of the most exciting and most important days in a couple's life is his own wedding day. So the wedding party but also really unforgotten, the adviser is "Heiraten - Ihr Hochzeitsplaner für Chemnitz und Umgebung" valuable tips and suggestions to all points of wedding planning.
Language(s): German

ADVERTISING RATES:
Full Page Mono .... EUR 850
Full Page Colour .... EUR 850
Mechanical Data: Type Area: 190 x 190 mm

HEISE ONLINE
1623193G5F-30
Editorial: Karl-Wiechert-Allee 10, 30625 HANNOVER
Tel: 511 5352300 **Fax:** 511 5352417
Email: presse@ct.heise.de **Web site:** http://www.heise.de
Freq: Daily; **Cover Price:** Paid; **Circ:** 24,123,809 Unique Users
Editor: Christian Persson; **Advertising Manager:** Thomas Goldmann
Profile: Ezine: European magazine about networks, the Internet, Windows NT and Unix. Includes results of tests of new software.
Language(s): German
BUSINESS: COMPUTERS & AUTOMATION: Multimedia

HEIZUNG & ENERGIESPAREN
760150G4B-682
Editorial: Schwanthalerstr. 10, 80336 MÜNCHEN
Tel: 89 59908122 **Fax:** 89 59908133
Email: claudia.mannschott@cpz.de **Web site:** http://www.bau-welt.de
Freq: Annual; **Cover Price:** Free; **Circ:** 265,000
Editor: Lutz Mannschott; **Advertising Manager:** Sebastian Schmidt
Profile: Magazine with information for builders and renovators. Proven and innovative heating systems for new and old buildings, water heating, fuel alternatives. Comfort, convenience and reliability as a decision support. Energy-saving techniques are introduced. Extensive market surveys with detailed information, expert guide posts and numerous examples from everyday practice.
Language(s): German
ADVERTISING RATES:
Full Page Mono .... EUR 10850
Full Page Colour .... EUR 15500
Mechanical Data: No. of Columns (Display): 4, Col Widths (Display): 42 mm, Type Area: 285 x 175 mm
Copy instructions: *Copy Date:* 34 days prior to publication
Supplement to: Das Einfamilien Haus, Umbauen & Modernisieren, Unser Haus für die ganze Familie

HEIZUNGSJOURNAL
730096G3A-70
Editorial: Eibenweg 20, 71364 WINNENDEN
Tel: 6223 74009 **Fax:** 6223 74148
Email: redaktion@heizungsjournal.de **Web site:** http://www.heizungsjournal.de
Freq: 9 issues yearly; **Annual Sub.:** EUR 73,30; **Circ:** 37,053
Editor: Dieter-Martin Funk; **Advertising Manager:** Elke Oechsner-Jung
Profile: The journal has distinguished itself in the more than 40 years of existence, into a nationally and internationally recognized information and advertising to the general field of heating. The high quality of the reports and the practical view of market developments in the industry with particular focus on innovative heating and ventilation technology have given this journal acceptance in industry, craft, design professionals and trade. Forward-heating technology and energy concepts - with the collaboration of renowned authors and experts - are the focus of the rich information spectrum. Target groups: heating and installers, energy consultants, service and maintenance company / customer services, building services planners, engineers and project offices / TGA, dealers heating and plumbing.
Language(s): German
ADVERTISING RATES:
Full Page Mono .... EUR 6170
Full Page Colour .... EUR 6170
Mechanical Data: Type Area: 260 x 184 mm, No. of Columns (Display): 4, Col Widths (Display): 43 mm
Copy instructions: *Copy Date:* 21 days prior to publication
BUSINESS: HEATING & VENTILATION: Domestic Heating & Ventilation

HEKATRON TREND
764095G14A-9277
Editorial: Döllgaststr. 7, 86199 AUGSBURG
Tel: 821 344570 **Fax:** 821 3445719
Email: info@mkpublishing.de **Web site:** http://www.mkpublishing.de
Freq: Quarterly; **Circ:** 600
Profile: Magazine for employees of Hekatron GmbH.
Language(s): German

HELFRECHT METHODIK
1601710G14A-9350
Editorial: Markgrafenstr. 32, 95680 BAD ALEXANDERSBAD **Tel:** 9232 601255
Fax: 9232 601282
Email: redaktion@helfrecht.de **Web site:** http://www.helfrecht.de
Freq: 6 issues yearly; **Annual Sub.:** EUR 57,00; **Circ:** 3,000
Editor: Christoph Beck
Profile: Magazine about management in small business companies.
Language(s): German

HELLWEGER ANZEIGER
730118G67B-6860
Editorial: Ostring 17a, 59423 UNNA
Tel: 2303 202114 **Fax:** 2303 202211
Email: vl@hellwegeranzeiger.de **Web site:** http://www.hellwegeranzeiger.de
Freq: 312 issues yearly; **Circ:** 26,145
Editor: Volker Stennei; **Advertising Manager:** Ursula Brauner
Profile: The Hellweger Anzeiger as the leading local newspaper in the room Unna, Kamen, Bergkamen, Fröndenberg and Holzwickede is traditionally especially a partner in the local trade. In the clearly structured display part uses the local dealers the opportunity to present their achievements. After all, most newspaper readers read their newspaper while having breakfast - best opportunity so for the advertising industry, to provide an impetus for purchasing. In addition, the Hellweger Anzeiger in recent years worked with hundreds of special publications an excellent reputation: whether issues relating to house and garden, the senior magazine, location portraits, or the auto-inserts - in an editorial attractively designed environment, the advertising still works intense. This Outlet offers RSS (Really Simple Syndication).
Language(s): German
ADVERTISING RATES:
SCC .... EUR 82,00
Mechanical Data: Type Area: 470 x 320 mm, No. of Columns (Display): 7, Col Widths (Display): 43 mm
Copy instructions: *Copy Date:* 1 day prior to publication
Supplement(s): prisma
REGIONAL DAILY & SUNDAY NEWSPAPERS: Regional Daily Newspapers

HELLWEGER ANZEIGER
1621421G67B-16569
Editorial: Ostring 17a, 59423 UNNA
Tel: 2303 202114 **Fax:** 2303 202211
Email: vl@hellwegeranzeiger.de **Web site:** http://www.hellwegeranzeiger.de
Freq: Daily; **Cover Price:** Paid; **Circ:** 89,327 Unique Users
Editor: Volker Stennei; **Advertising Manager:** Ursula Brauner
Profile: Ezine: Regional daily newspaper covering politics, economics, sport, travel and technology.
Language(s): German
REGIONAL DAILY & SUNDAY NEWSPAPERS: Regional Daily Newspapers

HELMSTEDTER BLITZ
730121G72-5432
Editorial: Papenberg 1, 38350 HELMSTEDT
Tel: 5351 58980 **Fax:** 5351 42963
Email: redaktion@helmstedter-blitz.de **Web site:** http://www.helmstedter-blitz.de
Freq: Weekly; **Cover Price:** Free; **Circ:** 47,000
Editor: Nico Jäckel; **Advertising Manager:** Jutta Höll
Profile: Advertising journal (house-to-house) concentrating on local stories.
Language(s): German
ADVERTISING RATES:
Full Page Mono .... EUR 4257
Full Page Colour .... EUR 4647
Mechanical Data: Type Area: 430 x 282 mm, No. of Columns (Display): 6, Col Widths (Display): 45 mm
Copy instructions: *Copy Date:* 2 days prior to publication
LOCAL NEWSPAPERS

HEPHAISTOS
730130G27-2957
Editorial: Gnadenberger Weg 4, 87509 IMMENSTADT **Tel:** 8379 728016 **Fax:** 8379 728018
Email: tobias.schumacher@metall-aktiv.de **Web site:** http://www.metall-aktiv.de
Freq: 6 issues yearly; **Annual Sub.:** EUR 99,00; **Circ:** 3,465
Editor: Tobias Schumacher; **Advertising Manager:** Sven Christian Abend
Profile: Hephaestus accompanying the metal designers in their work. While the art was forged major component of the magazine in its first decade of the work, now come to a greater extent modern techniques and interesting new sales areas. As metallic design today means all designed metal work in and on public and private buildings (doors, gates, fences, fittings, stair and balcony railings, building art, etc.), interior design, shop fitting, well, boom, company signs and emblems, sculptures, wind chimes, or sound objects. Designer metal handicrafts are also equipped with small objects on the market - drawing from individually designed fireplace tool over copper or stainless steel bowls to cork, hand-forged knives and key chains. All these works are presented in Hephaestus. The editorial staff seeks out new trends and developments, market and technology analysis and examined changes. Hephaestus is read throughout the German-speaking countries and in other 43 countries and is the world's largest and most respected journal in the field of metal design.
Language(s): German
ADVERTISING RATES:
Full Page Mono .... EUR 710
Full Page Colour .... EUR 1260
Mechanical Data: Type Area: 272 x 218 mm, No. of Columns (Display): 4, Col Widths (Display): 49 mm
Copy instructions: *Copy Date:* 30 days prior to publication
Official Journal of: Organ d. Europ. Zentrums f. zeitgemäße Metallgestaltung in Kolbermoor e.V. u. d. Ringes europ. Schmiedestädte e.V.

HERA HOCHZEIT - REG.-AUSG. F. NORDRHEIN-WESTFALEN/ RHEINLAND-PFALZ/HESSEN

762824G74A-3253

Editorial: Stammheimer Str. 47a, 50735 KÖLN
Tel: 221 76802710 **Fax:** 221 76802713
Email: anke.kerp@agentur-janke.de **Web site:** http://www.agentur-janke.de
Freq: 6 issues yearly; **Annual Sub.:** EUR 28,00; **Circ:** 15,000
Editor: Anke Kerp; **Advertising Manager:** Stefanie Urban
Profile: Regional magazine about wedding services.
Language(s): German
ADVERTISING RATES:
Full Page Mono .... EUR 1450
Full Page Colour .... EUR 1450
Mechanical Data: Type Area: 277 x 182 mm, No. of Columns (Display): 4, Col Widths (Display): 44 mm
Copy instructions: *Copy Date:* 18 days prior to publication
Supplement(s): Feiern im Bergischen Land

HERBORNER ECHO

730135G67B-6880

Editorial: Rathausstr. 1, 35683 DILLENBURG
Tel: 2771 8740 **Fax:** 2771 874261
Email: redaktion@dill.de **Web site:** http://www.dill.de
Freq: 312 issues yearly; **Circ:** 7,559
Profile: Daily newspaper with regional news and a local sports section.
Language(s): German
ADVERTISING RATES:
SCC .... EUR 27,80
Mechanical Data: Type Area: 467 x 327 mm, No. of Columns (Display): 7, Col Widths (Display): 44 mm
Copy instructions: *Copy Date:* 1 day prior to publication
Supplement(s): Anpfiff; [g]esund!; Wetzlarer Hefte Das Stadtmagazin
REGIONAL DAILY & SUNDAY NEWSPAPERS: Regional Daily Newspapers

HERBORNER ECHO AM SONNTAG

1609306G72-17868

Editorial: Rathausstr. 1, 35683 DILLENBURG
Tel: 2771 8740 **Fax:** 2771 874261
Email: redaktion@dill.de **Web site:** http://www.dill.de
Freq: Weekly; **Cover Price:** EUR 1,20; **Circ:** 7,559
Profile: Regional weekly covering politics, economics, sport, travel, technology and the arts.
Language(s): German
ADVERTISING RATES:
SCC .... EUR 27,80
Mechanical Data: Type Area: 490 x 328 mm, No. of Columns (Display): 7, Col Widths (Display): 44 mm
Copy instructions: *Copy Date:* 2 days prior to publication
LOCAL NEWSPAPERS

HERBORNER TAGEBLATT

730136G67B-6900

Editorial: Elsa-Brandström-Str. 18, 35578 WETZLAR
Tel: 6441 9590 **Fax:** 6441 959292
Email: redaktion.wnz@mittelhessen.de **Web site:** http://www.mittelhessen.de
Freq: 312 issues yearly; **Circ:** 21,471
Advertising Manager: Peter Rother
Profile: Daily newspaper with regional news and a local sports section.
Language(s): German
ADVERTISING RATES:
SCC .... EUR 66,50
Mechanical Data: Type Area: 490 x 328 mm, No. of Columns (Display): 7, Col Widths (Display): 44 mm
Copy instructions: *Copy Date:* 1 day prior to publication
Supplement(s): Anpfiff; [f]amilie& freizeit; [g]esund!; rtv; Wetzlarer Hefte Das Stadtmagazin
REGIONAL DAILY & SUNDAY NEWSPAPERS: Regional Daily Newspapers

HERBST-BLATT

1615829G74N-812

Editorial: Hertinger Str. 12, 59423 UNNA
Tel: 2303 256903 **Fax:** 2303 256905
Email: herbstblattredaktion@gmx.de **Web site:** http://www.unna.de
Freq: Quarterly; **Cover Price:** Free; **Circ:** 3,000
Editor: Brigitte Paschedag
Profile: Magazine for the elderly from the region of Unna.
Language(s): German

HERDER KORRESPONDENZ

730140G87-5620

Editorial: Hermann-Herder-Str. 4, 79104 FREIBURG
Tel: 761 27170 **Fax:** 761 2717426
Email: herderkorrespondenz@herder.de **Web site:** http://www.herderkorrespondenz.de
Freq: Monthly; **Circ:** 7,300
Editor: Ulrich Ruh; **Advertising Manager:** Friederike Ward
Profile: Catholic magazine.
Language(s): German
ADVERTISING RATES:
Full Page Mono .... EUR 1490
Mechanical Data: Type Area: 254 x 181 mm
CONSUMER: RELIGIOUS

HERFORDER KREISBLATT

730141G67B-6920

Editorial: Brüderstr. 30, 32052 HERFORD
Tel: 5221 59080 **Fax:** 5221 590816
Freq: 312 issues yearly; **Circ:** 19,206
Profile: Daily newspaper with regional news and a local sports section.
Language(s): German
Mechanical Data: Type Area: 490 x 320 mm, No. of Columns (Display): 7, Col Widths (Display): 44 mm
Copy instructions: *Copy Date:* 1 day prior to publication
REGIONAL DAILY & SUNDAY NEWSPAPERS: Regional Daily Newspapers

HERMANN

730143G89C-4804

Editorial: Friedrich-Ebert-Str. 36, 03044 COTTBUS
Tel: 355 431240 **Fax:** 355 4312424
Email: hermann@lausitz.net **Web site:** http://www.hermannimnetz.de
Freq: 11 issues yearly; **Cover Price:** Free; **Circ:** 11,845
Editor: Thomas Richert; **Advertising Manager:** Thomas Richert
Profile: Magazine containing listings of events in Cottbus.
Language(s): German
ADVERTISING RATES:
Full Page Mono .... EUR 1399
Full Page Colour .... EUR 1399
Mechanical Data: Type Area: 275 x 190 mm, No. of Columns (Display): 4, Col Widths (Display): 44 mm
Copy instructions: *Copy Date:* 10 days prior to publication
CONSUMER: HOLIDAYS & TRAVEL: Entertainment Guides

HERSBRUCKER ZEITUNG

730164G67B-6940

Editorial: Nürnberger Str. 7, 91217 HERSBRUCK
Tel: 9151 73070 **Fax:** 9151 730799
Email: lokales@hersbrucker-zeitung.de **Web site:** http://www.hersbrucker-zeitung.de
Freq: 312 issues yearly; **Circ:** 7,780
Profile: Daily newspaper with regional news and a local sports section.
Language(s): German
ADVERTISING RATES:
SCC .... EUR 28,70
Mechanical Data: Type Area: 430 x 280 mm, No. of Columns (Display): 6, Col Widths (Display): 45 mm
Copy instructions: *Copy Date:* 2 days prior to publication
Supplement(s): Amtsblatt für den Landkreis Nürnberger Land; sechs+sechzig
REGIONAL DAILY & SUNDAY NEWSPAPERS: Regional Daily Newspapers

HERTENER ALLGEMEINE

730166G67B-6960

Editorial: Kampstr. 84b, 45772 MARL **Tel:** 2365 1070 **Fax:** 2365 1071490
Email: info@medienhaus-bauer.de **Web site:** http://www.medienhaus-bauer.de
Freq: 312 issues yearly; **Circ:** 10,020
Advertising Manager: Carsten Dingerkuss
Profile: Regional daily newspaper with news on politics, economy, culture, sports, travel, technology, etc. The newspaper offers a mix of local, regional and international News from all areas. Fun and interactive content such as forums, polls or betting games are also part of the program. Local out of the city and the neighborhood is the focus of attention. Facebook: http://www.facebook.com/medienhbauer This Outlet offers RSS (Really Simple Syndication). This Outlet offers RSS (Really Simple Syndication).
Language(s): German
ADVERTISING RATES:
SCC .... EUR 30,10
Mechanical Data: Type Area: 487 x 325 mm, No. of Columns (Display): 7, Col Widths (Display): 43 mm
Copy instructions: *Copy Date:* 1 day prior to publication
Supplement(s): prisma
REGIONAL DAILY & SUNDAY NEWSPAPERS: Regional Daily Newspapers

HERZ

730171G56A-4740

Editorial: Aschauer Str. 30, 81549 MÜNCHEN
Tel: 89 2030431300 **Fax:** 89 2030431399
Email: brigitta.schneider@springer.com **Web site:** http://www.herz-cardiovascular-diseases.de
Freq: 8 issues yearly; Free to qualifying individuals
Annual Sub.: EUR 268,00; **Circ:** 3,800
Editor: Brigitta Schneider; **Advertising Manager:** Ines Spankau
Profile: Peer-reviewed educational journal for clinicians and practicing cardiologists. It provides in-depth primary and review articles on current cardiac emphases in German and English. The renowned authors eighth at both high scientific level and to understand and practical relevance. "Heart" offers Originalia, current conference reports, new studies from the interventional cardiology (Cathlab Hotline) and the official communications of the Association established cardiologists.
Language(s): English; German
ADVERTISING RATES:
Full Page Mono .... EUR 2500
Full Page Colour .... EUR 3770
Mechanical Data: Type Area: 240 x 174 mm
Official Journal of: Organ d. Bundesverb. Niedergelassener Kardiologen u. d. ArGe Leitender Kardiolog. Krankenhausärzte
BUSINESS: HEALTH & MEDICAL

HERZ HEUTE

730179G56A-11177

Editorial: Vogtstr. 50, 60322 FRANKFURT
Tel: 69 9551280 **Fax:** 69 955128345
Email: redaktion@herzstiftung.de **Web site:** http://www.herzstiftung.de
Freq: Quarterly; **Circ:** 150,000
Editor: Irene Oswalt
Profile: Magazine of the German Heart Foundation.
Language(s): German

HERZ MEDIZIN

758166G56A-11098

Editorial: Seefeld 18, 91093 HESSDORF
Tel: 9135 71230 **Fax:** 9135 712340
Email: markus.hartmann@hartmann-verlag.de **Web site:** http://www.hartmann-verlag.de
Freq: Quarterly; **Annual Sub.:** EUR 36,00; **Circ:** 4,900
Editor: Markus Hartmann; **Advertising Manager:** Jürgen Hartmann
Profile: Magazine about cardiology.
Language(s): German
ADVERTISING RATES:
Full Page Mono .... EUR 1675
Full Page Colour .... EUR 2442
Mechanical Data: Type Area: 264 x 185 mm, No. of Columns (Display): 3, Col Widths (Display): 50 mm

HERZBLATT

730174G56A-11176

Editorial: Vogtstr. 50, 60322 FRANKFURT
Tel: 69 9551280 **Fax:** 69 955128345
Email: redaktion@herzstiftung.de **Web site:** http://www.herzstiftung.de
Freq: Quarterly; **Circ:** 5,000
Editor: Irene Oswalt
Profile: Magazine of the Children's Heart Foundation.
Language(s): German

HERZ-ECHO

730176G56A-4760

Editorial: Friedrich-Ebert-Ring 38, 56068 KOBLENZ
Tel: 261 309233 **Fax:** 261 309232
Email: info@rheinland-pfalz.dgpr.de **Web site:** http://www.rheinland-pfalz.dgpr.de
Freq: Quarterly; **Circ:** 1,500
Editor: Peter Ritter
Profile: Magazine for physical doctors and trainers, psychologists and nutrition specialists.
Language(s): German
ADVERTISING RATES:
Full Page Colour .... EUR 629

HERZSCHRITTMACHER-THERAPIE + ELEKTROPHYSIOLOGIE

730182G56A-4780

Editorial: Tiergartenstr. 17, 69121 HEIDELBERG
Tel: 6221 4878819 **Fax:** 6221 48768819
Email: denskus.steinkopff@springer.com **Web site:** http://www.springermedizin.de
Freq: Quarterly; **Annual Sub.:** EUR 169,00; **Circ:** 700
Profile: With scientific original and review articles, reports on modern surgical techniques and experimental methods is the journal Herzschrittmachertherapie + Elektrophysiologie a forum to discuss topics such as: - Cellular Electrophysiology - Theoretical Electrophysiology - Clinical Electrophysiology - Applied pacing - bradycardia and tachycardia arrhythmias - Sudden cardiac death and risk stratification - Electrocardiography - Electro-medical Technology - Experimental and Clinical Pharmacology - Heart Surgery for Cardiac Arrhythmias Communications from the working groups of pacemakers and arrhythmia of the German Society of Cardiology - Heart and Circulatory Research and opinions and practical advice round out the wide spectrum of this journal. Interests: cardiology, cardiac pacing, pacemaker technology, clinical electrophysiology.
Language(s): English; German
ADVERTISING RATES:
Full Page Mono .... EUR 1128
Full Page Colour .... EUR 2168
Mechanical Data: Type Area: 240 x 174 mm
Official Journal of: Organ d. Dt. Ges. f. Kardiologie - Herz- u. Kreislaufforschung

HESSENJÄGER

730186G75F-300

Editorial: Am Römerkastell 9, 61231 BAD NAUHEIM
Tel: 6032 2008 **Fax:** 6032 4255
Email: info@ljv-hessen.de **Web site:** http://www.ljv-hessen.de
Freq: Monthly; Free to qualifying individuals
Annual Sub.: EUR 42,00; **Circ:** 19,489
Editor: Alexander Michel
Profile: Journal of the Hunting Association of Hessen.
Language(s): German
ADVERTISING RATES:
Full Page Mono .... EUR 2344
Full Page Colour .... EUR 3910
Mechanical Data: Type Area: 270 x 185 mm, No. of Columns (Display): 4, Col Widths (Display): 45 mm
Copy instructions: *Copy Date:* 15 days prior to publication
CONSUMER: SPORT: Shooting

HESSISCHE ALLGEMEINE HNA

730352G67B-7120

Editorial: Frankfurter Str. 168, 34121 KASSEL
Tel: 561 20300 **Fax:** 561 2032406
Email: info@hna.de **Web site:** http://www.hna.de
Freq: 312 issues yearly; **Circ:** 183,877
Advertising Manager: Andrea Schaller-Öller
Profile: Regional daily newspaper with news on politics, economy, culture, sports, travel, technology, etc. The Hessische Allgemeine HN a local edition of the HNA Hessische/Niedersächsische Allgemeine. . Facebook: http://www.facebook.com/HNA Twitter: http://twitter.com/HNA_online This Outlet offers RSS (Really Simple Syndication).
Language(s): German
ADVERTISING RATES:
SCC .... EUR 105,50
Mechanical Data: Type Area: 430 x 285 mm, No. of Columns (Display): 6, Col Widths (Display): 45 mm
Copy instructions: *Copy Date:* 2 days prior to publication
Supplement(s): dez Aktuell
REGIONAL DAILY & SUNDAY NEWSPAPERS: Regional Daily Newspapers

HESSISCHE GASTRONOMIE

730196G11A-740

Editorial: Robert-Bosch-Str. 10, 63477 MAINTAL
Tel: 6181 94340 **Fax:** 6181 45719
Email: kramer@seitensatz.de **Web site:** http://www.hessengastro.de
Freq: 10 issues yearly; Free to qualifying individuals
Annual Sub.: EUR 55,00; **Circ:** 6,800
Editor: Ursula Mühlens; **Advertising Manager:** Ulrike Minnich
Profile: Magazine about gastronomy and catering in the province of Hessen.
Language(s): German
ADVERTISING RATES:
Full Page Mono .... EUR 1355
Full Page Colour .... EUR 2370
Mechanical Data: Type Area: 265 x 184 mm, No. of Columns (Display): 4, Col Widths (Display): 43 mm
Copy instructions: *Copy Date:* 21 days prior to publication
Official Journal of: Organ d. Dehoga-Verb. Hessen
BUSINESS: CATERING: Catering, Hotels & Restaurants

DER HESSISCHE OBST- U. GARTENBAU

730200G26D-5

Editorial: Hüttersdorfer Str. 29, 66839 SCHMELZ
Tel: 6887 9032999 **Fax:** 6887 9032998
Email: info@unsergarten-verlag.de **Web site:** http://www.unsergarten-verlag.de
Freq: Monthly; **Annual Sub.:** EUR 16,80; **Circ:** 5,025
Editor: Monika Lambert-Debong; **Advertising Manager:** Monika Lambert-Debong
Profile: Magazine about horticulture and fruit growing in Hessen.
Language(s): German
ADVERTISING RATES:
Full Page Mono .... EUR 615
Full Page Colour .... EUR 1490
Mechanical Data: Type Area: 264 x 189 mm, No. of Columns (Display): 4, Col Widths (Display): 45 mm
Copy instructions: *Copy Date:* 20 days prior to publication
BUSINESS: GARDEN TRADE: Garden Trade Horticulture

HESSISCHE SENIOREN BLÄTTER

756041G74N-803

Editorial: Dostojewskistr. 4, 65187 WIESBADEN
Tel: 611 8173584 **Fax:** 611 8173566
Email: susanne.andriessens@hsm.hessen.de **Web site:** http://www.hsm.hessen.de
Freq: Quarterly; **Cover Price:** Free; **Circ:** 100,000
Editor: Susanne Andriessens
Profile: For the target group of senior citizens in Hesse, the Ministry of the quarterly journal, "hessische senioren blätter' out. In the city of Frankfurt am Main, she is out in shops in many towns, cities and counties in the district town halls.
Language(s): German
ADVERTISING RATES:
Full Page Mono .... EUR 3040
Full Page Colour .... EUR 3930
Mechanical Data: Type Area: 260 x 174 mm

HESSISCHER KLEINGÄRTNER

730204G93-400

Editorial: Feldscheidenstr. 2, 60435 FRANKFURT
Tel: 69 5482552 **Fax:** 69 5400871
Email: info@kleingarten-hessen.de **Web site:** http://www.kleingarten-hessen.de
Freq: 11 issues yearly; Free to qualifying individuals
Annual Sub.: EUR 17,60; **Circ:** 34,904
Profile: The journal is the organ of the Association of allotment of Hessen. Content: News from the local and national association events and everything that has to do with the small garden.
Language(s): German
ADVERTISING RATES:
Full Page Mono .... EUR 1367
Full Page Colour .... EUR 2596
Mechanical Data: Type Area: 253 x 190 mm, No. of Columns (Display): 4, Col Widths (Display): 45 mm
Copy instructions: *Copy Date:* 21 days prior to publication
CONSUMER: GARDENING

HESSISCHES ÄRZTEBLATT

730207G56A-4800

Editorial: Im Vogelsgesang 3, 60488 FRANKFURT
Tel: 69 97672147 **Fax:** 69 97672247
Email: angelika.kob@laekh.de **Web site:** http://www.laekh.de
Freq: Monthly; Free to qualifying individuals
Annual Sub.: EUR 121,00; **Circ:** 31,200
Editor: Toni Graf-Baumann; **Advertising Manager:** Livia Kummer
Profile: Newsletter of the Medical Council to prevention, environmental health, ethics, health policy, business tips, treatment recommendations and personalities.
Language(s): German
ADVERTISING RATES:
Full Page Mono .... EUR 3090
Full Page Colour .... EUR 4320
Mechanical Data: Type Area: 252 x 185 mm, No. of Columns (Display): 3, Col Widths (Display): 58 mm
Copy instructions: *Copy Date:* 20 days prior to publication
BUSINESS: HEALTH & MEDICAL

HEUBERGER BOTE

730214G67B-6980

Editorial: Jägerhofstr. 4, 78532 TUTTLINGEN
Tel: 7461 70150 **Fax:** 7461 701547
Web site: http://www.schwaebische.de
Freq: 312 issues yearly; **Circ:** 22,517
Advertising Manager: Tarkan Tekin
Profile: In its edition provides the "Heuberger Bote" its readers daily with the latest information from government, business, sports, culture and food from the local environment. Twitter: http://twitter.com/Schwaebische This Outlet offers RSS (Really Simple Syndication).
Language(s): German
ADVERTISING RATES:
SCC .... EUR 77,20
Mechanical Data: Type Area: 480 x 320 mm, No. of Columns (Display): 7, Col Widths (Display): 44 mm
Copy instructions: *Copy Date:* 1 day prior to publication
Supplement(s): rtv
REGIONAL DAILY & SUNDAY NEWSPAPERS: Regional Daily Newspapers

HEY!

1657725G91D-10066

Editorial: Rotebühlstr. 87, 70178 STUTTGART
Tel: 711 947680 **Fax:** 711 9476830
Email: info@panini.de **Web site:** http://www.panini.de
Freq: 18 issues yearly; **Cover Price:** EUR 1,99; **Circ:** 145,883
Editor: Martin Klingseisen
Profile: hey! The Star Magazine of Panini infected, a total of 100 pages packed with all that interested in trendy teens: exclusive star interviews, news from the music scene, from film and television and lots of fun, Star-Jokes, Celebrity style and celebrity beauty. Found in the large category Love is all around the themes of love, flirtation and eroticism. In addition there is a great photo-love story, great competitions and the highlight: 18 very cool poster.
Language(s): German
ADVERTISING RATES:
Full Page Mono .... EUR 11500
Full Page Colour .... EUR 11500
Mechanical Data: Type Area: 255 x 190 mm
CONSUMER: RECREATION & LEISURE: Children & Youth

HF-PRAXIS

730231G18A-125

Editorial: Krummbogen 14, 35039 MARBURG
Tel: 6421 96140 **Fax:** 6421 961423
Email: redaktion@beam-verlag.de **Web site:** http://www.beam-verlag.de
Freq: Monthly; **Circ:** 3,500
Editor: Frank Sichla; **Advertising Manager:** Frank Wege
Profile: Magazine containing news and information about microwave technology.
Language(s): German
Readership: Aimed at engineers and technicians.
ADVERTISING RATES:
Full Page Mono .... EUR 2000
Full Page Colour .... EUR 2400
Mechanical Data: Type Area: 264 x 185 mm, No. of Columns (Display): 4, Col Widths (Display): 43 mm
BUSINESS: ELECTRONICS

HI TEC ELEKTROFACH

726133G43A-440

Editorial: Obergplatz 14, 47804 KREFELD
Tel: 2151 1525610 **Fax:** 2151 1525628
Email: info@sok-verlag.de **Web site:** http://www.hitec-elektrofach.de
Freq: 10 issues yearly; Free to qualifying individuals
Annual Sub.: EUR 60,00; **Circ:** 20,000
Editor: Jo Clahsen
Profile: The magazine hi tec elektrofach is an information platform for manufacturers, distributors and retailers. As the official organ of the Bundesverband Technik des Einzelhandels, it provides information for about 50 years, the decision makers, owners, managers, sales managers and dealers, as all senior staff from manufacturers and distributors about the latest developments in the electrical, kitchen and lighting trade, and in the electrical installation trade. Here, hi tec elektrofach presented as an information and idea exchange for trading in the areas of electrical household appliances, installation and lighting and building control. Sessions will cover new products and marketing strategies, background reports and trend reports, personal and corporate portraits. Special issues and special reports examined in several subject areas. Write for hi tec elektrofach only experienced journalists, Journal makers and industry experts who will shape the distinctive style of the magazine.
Language(s): German
ADVERTISING RATES:
Full Page Mono .... EUR 3130
Full Page Colour .... EUR 5400
Mechanical Data: Type Area: 270 x 187 mm, No. of Columns (Display): 4, Col Widths (Display): 43 mm
Copy instructions: *Copy Date:* 20 days prior to publication
Official Journal of: Organ d. Bundesverb. Technik d. Einzelhandels e.V.
BUSINESS: ELECTRICAL RETAIL TRADE

HI TEC HANDEL

730331G43A-53

Editorial: Obergplatz 14, 47804 KREFELD
Tel: 2151 1525615 **Fax:** 2151 1525628
Email: info@sok-verlag.de **Web site:** http://www.hitec-handel.de
Freq: 10 issues yearly; Free to qualifying individuals
Annual Sub.: EUR 55,00; **Circ:** 19,500
Editor: Jo Clahsen
Profile: Journal of the German Radio and Television Traders' Association.
Language(s): German
Readership: Aimed at radio and TV traders.
ADVERTISING RATES:
Full Page Mono .... EUR 3130
Full Page Colour .... EUR 5400
Mechanical Data: No. of Columns (Display): 4, Col Widths (Display): 43 mm, Type Area: 270 x 187 mm
Copy instructions: *Copy Date:* 20 days prior to publication
Official Journal of: Organ d. Bundesverb. Technik d. Einzelhandels e.V.
BUSINESS: ELECTRICAL RETAIL TRADE

HI TEC HOME

1745553G18B-2136

Editorial: Obergplatz 14, 47804 KREFELD
Tel: 2151 1525610 **Fax:** 2151 1525628
Email: info@sok-verlag.de **Web site:** http://www.hitec-handel.de
Freq: 3 issues yearly; **Cover Price:** Free; **Circ:** 100,000
Editor: Jo Clahsen
Profile: Magazine for consumer electronics, domestic appliances, photo, cell phones and more. With news about trends, tips, techniques, products, services and competitions.
Language(s): German
ADVERTISING RATES:
Full Page Mono .... EUR 4450
Full Page Colour .... EUR 4450
Mechanical Data: Type Area: 297 x 210 mm, No. of Columns (Display): 4, Col Widths (Display): 43 mm
Copy instructions: *Copy Date:* 31 days prior to publication

HIDDEN-CHAMPIONS

1664568G14A-9726

Editorial: Marlener Str. 2, 77656 OFFENBURG
Tel: 781 955070 **Fax:** 781 955063
Email: redaktion@econo.de **Web site:** http://www.econo.de
Freq: Annual; **Cover Price:** EUR 6,00; **Circ:** 34,000
Editor: Robert Schwarz; **Advertising Manager:** Christian Hügerich
Profile: Yearbook of the middle class, examples of successful companies.
Language(s): German
ADVERTISING RATES:
Full Page Mono .... EUR 3200
Full Page Colour .... EUR 3200
Mechanical Data: Type Area: 150 x 225 mm, No. of Columns (Display): 3, Col Widths (Display): 62 mm
Copy instructions: *Copy Date:* 21 days prior to publication

HIDEAWAYS

730238G89A-11532

Editorial: Höfeweg 40, 33619 BIELEFELD
Tel: 521 911110 **Fax:** 521 9111112
Email: info@klocke-verlag.de **Web site:** http://www.hideaways.de
Freq: Half-yearly; **Annual Sub.:** EUR 30,00; **Circ:** 50,000
Editor: Thomas Klocke; **Advertising Manager:** Wolfgang Pohl
Profile: Since its launch in 1996, Hideaways has established itself as one of the most exclusive travel magazines in the world. The "classic" edition, appearing twice a year in March and September, has become "the" magazine for all connoisseurs and premium travellers in Germany, Austria, Luxembourg and Switzerland. First class photography, a superb layout and the highest quality in printing sets the standards among all premiummagazines. Every hotel featured in Hideaways has been visited personally and researched on the spot, all articles are produced exclusively for Klocke Publishing Company. The circulation of each issue is 60,000 copies, from which a third is supplied to First Class of Lufthansa on international flights, to all Senator Lounges worldwide, Business Classes of other airlines and a lot of VIP-lounges and business-clubs. Hideaways is also available for its sophisticated readership at the suites of all featured hotels, at exclusive newsstands and at a selected number of the best travel agents. The list of the 10.000 private subscribers, among which are a lot of celebrities, reads like a "who is who" from show-business, politics and industry.
Language(s): English; German
ADVERTISING RATES:
Full Page Colour .... EUR 10600
Mechanical Data: Type Area: 252 x 172 mm
Copy instructions: *Copy Date:* 56 days prior to publication
CONSUMER: HOLIDAYS & TRAVEL: Travel

HIFI TEST

730247G78A-240

Editorial: Gartroper Str. 42, 47138 DUISBURG
Tel: 203 4292222 **Fax:** 203 4292136
Email: voigt@brieden.de **Web site:** http://www.hifitest-magazin.de
Freq: 6 issues yearly; **Annual Sub.:** EUR 15,00; **Circ:** 59,374
Editor: Michael Voigt
Profile: The magazine shows test-oriented and has in-depth comparison and individual test equipment from all areas of consumer electronics, with easy to understand reporting, it conveys the fun of the devices and provides visibility in complicated technology. Service issues help in dealing with the equipment and provide expert consultation. Target groupe: Interested in buying consumer electronics.
Language(s): German
ADVERTISING RATES:
Full Page Mono .... EUR 5804
Full Page Colour .... EUR 9339
Mechanical Data: Type Area: 284 x 197 mm, No. of Columns (Display): 4, Col Widths (Display): 50 mm
CONSUMER: CONSUMER ELECTRONICS: Hi-Fi & Recording

HIGH LIFE

1606928G86C-206

Editorial: Höfeweg 40, 33619 BIELEFELD
Tel: 521 911110 **Fax:** 521 9111112
Email: info@klocke-verlag.de **Web site:** http://www.klocke-verlag.de
Freq: 3 issues yearly; **Annual Sub.:** EUR 18,00; **Circ:** 100,000
Editor: Thomas Klocke; **Advertising Manager:** Wolfgang Pohl
Profile: High Life has established itself after the successful launch as the ultimate magazine for international, exclusive lifestyle. The editorial concept is based on all the issues for which men with the highest standards are interested. As with all other titles from Klocke, are also in this premium magazine produces almost all of the features exclusive to high life. Readers of High Life to appreciate the serious approach they prefer more of a good bottle of Bordeaux than to castigate the washboard stomach, instead of bare skin, we talk to competently researched exclusive stories from all walks of life.
Language(s): English; German
ADVERTISING RATES:
Full Page Mono .... EUR 9500
Full Page Colour .... EUR 12500
Mechanical Data: Type Area: 252 x 172 mm

HIGH POTENTIAL

730260G83-5160

Editorial: Dillwächterstr. 4, 80686 MÜNCHEN
Tel: 89 76900371 **Fax:** 89 76900339
Email: redaktion@high-potential.com **Web site:** http://www.academicworld.net
Freq: Quarterly; **Cover Price:** Free; **Circ:** 77,000
Editor: Nicolai Haase; **Advertising Manager:** Nicolai Haase
Profile: Students' magazine.
Language(s): German
ADVERTISING RATES:
Full Page Mono .... EUR 7780
Full Page Colour .... EUR 7780
Mechanical Data: Type Area: 267 x 186 mm, No. of Columns (Display): 4, Col Widths (Display): 45 mm
Copy instructions: *Copy Date:* 7 days prior to publication
CONSUMER: STUDENT PUBLICATIONS

HIGHLIGHT

730250G17-175

Editorial: Braugasse 2, 59602 RÜTHEN
Tel: 2952 9759200 **Fax:** 2952 9759201
Email: info@highlight-verlag.de **Web site:** http://www.highlight-web.de
Freq: 6 issues yearly; **Annual Sub.:** EUR 53,00; **Circ:** 9,349
Editor: Markus Helle; **Advertising Manager:** Jutta Füser
Profile: Journal containing information about the lighting trade.
Language(s): German
ADVERTISING RATES:
Full Page Mono .... EUR 2375
Full Page Colour .... EUR 4025
Mechanical Data: Type Area: 275 x 196 mm, No. of Columns (Display): 4, Col Widths (Display): 46 mm
Supplement(s): Highlight Kompakt
BUSINESS: ELECTRICAL

HILDESHEIMER ALLGEMEINE ZEITUNG

730272G67B-7000

Editorial: Rathausstr. 18, 31134 HILDESHEIM
Tel: 5121 106301 **Fax:** 5121 106241
Email: redaktion@hildesheimer-allgemeine.de **Web site:** http://www.hildesheimer-allgemeine.de
Freq: 312 issues yearly; **Circ:** 41,088
Editor: Hartmut Reichardt; **Advertising Manager:** Kai Wagener
Profile: Daily newspaper with regional news and a local sports section. Facebook: http://www.facebook.com/hinews Twitter: http://twitter.com/#!/hinews This Outlet offers RSS (Really Simple Syndication).
Language(s): German
ADVERTISING RATES:
SCC .... EUR 116,70
Mechanical Data: Col Widths (Display): 45 mm
REGIONAL DAILY & SUNDAY NEWSPAPERS: Regional Daily Newspapers

HILPOLTSTEINER KURIER

730282G67B-7020

Editorial: Stauffenbergstr. 2a, 85051 INGOLSTADT
Tel: 841 96660 **Fax:** 841 9666255
Email: redaktion@donaukurier.de **Web site:** http://www.donaukurier.de
Freq: 312 issues yearly; **Circ:** 3,676
Advertising Manager: Hermann Fetsch
Profile: Daily newspaper with regional news and a local sports section. Facebook: http://www.facebook.com/donaukurier.online.
Language(s): German
ADVERTISING RATES:
SCC .... EUR 17,40
Mechanical Data: Type Area: 435 x 282 mm, No. of Columns (Display): 6, Col Widths (Display): 45 mm
Copy instructions: *Copy Date:* 1 day prior to publication
REGIONAL DAILY & SUNDAY NEWSPAPERS: Regional Daily Newspapers

HILPOLTSTEINER ZEITUNG

730283G67B-7040

Editorial: Allee 2, 91154 ROTH **Tel:** 9171 970311
Fax: 9171 970326
Email: verlag@roth-hilpoltsteiner-volkszeitung.de
Web site: http://www.roth-hilpoltsteiner-volkszeitung.de
Freq: 312 issues yearly; **Circ:** 11,116
Profile: Daily newspaper with regional news and a local sports section.
Language(s): German
ADVERTISING RATES:
SCC .... EUR 31,00
Mechanical Data: Type Area: 430 x 280 mm, No. of Columns (Display): 6, Col Widths (Display): 45 mm
Copy instructions: *Copy Date:* 2 days prior to publication
REGIONAL DAILY & SUNDAY NEWSPAPERS: Regional Daily Newspapers

HINNERK

730299G86B-260

Editorial: Steindamm 11, 20099 HAMBURG
Tel: 40 28411522 **Fax:** 40 28411580
Email: redaktion@hinnerk.de **Web site:** http://www.hinnerk.de
Freq: Monthly; **Annual Sub.:** EUR 45,00; **Circ:** 24,336
Editor: Stefan Mielchen; **Advertising Manager:** Christian Kranz
Profile: Gay city magazine for Hamburg. It reports on current issues in Hamburg and the world. This provides hinnerk both in print and online (www.hinnerk.de) the extensive calendar of gay events in Hamburg. New Releases and trends in the fields of culture, politics, travel and fashion complete the website. facebook: http://www.facebook.com/pages/hinnerk-Hamburgs-schwules-Stadtmagazin/183692058286.
Language(s): German
Readership: Read by gay men living in Hamburg and North Germany.
ADVERTISING RATES:
Full Page Mono .... EUR 2440
Full Page Colour .... EUR 2440
Mechanical Data: Type Area: 260 x 190 mm, No. of Columns (Display): 4, Col Widths (Display): 45 mm
Copy instructions: *Copy Date:* 15 days prior to publication
CONSUMER: ADULT & GAY MAGAZINES: Gay & Lesbian Magazines

HINTERLÄNDER ANZEIGER

730301G67B-7060

Editorial: Elsa-Brandström-Str. 18, 35578 WETZLAR
Tel: 6441 9590 **Fax:** 6441 959292
Email: redaktion.wnz@mittelhessen.de **Web site:** http://www.mittelhessen.de
Freq: 312 issues yearly; **Circ:** 11,006
Advertising Manager: Peter Rother
Profile: Daily newspaper with regional news and a local sports section.
Language(s): German
ADVERTISING RATES:
SCC .... EUR 35,00
Mechanical Data: Type Area: 490 x 328 mm, No. of Columns (Display): 7, Col Widths (Display): 44 mm
Copy instructions: *Copy Date:* 1 day prior to publication
Supplement(s): [f]amilie& freizeit; Fußball-Kalender; [g]esund!; rtv
REGIONAL DAILY & SUNDAY NEWSPAPERS: Regional Daily Newspapers

HINTERLÄNDER ANZEIGER AM SONNTAG

1606884G72-17862

Editorial: Elsa-Brandström-Str. 18, 35578 WETZLAR
Tel: 6441 9590 **Fax:** 6441 959292
Email: redaktion.wnz@mittelhessen.de **Web site:** http://www.mittelhessen.de
Freq: Weekly; **Cover Price:** EUR 1,00; **Circ:** 11,006
Advertising Manager: Peter Rother

Profile: Regional weekly covering politics, economics, sport, travel, technology and the arts.
Language(s): German
ADVERTISING RATES:
SCC .... EUR 35,00
Mechanical Data: Type Area: 490 x 328 mm, No. of Columns (Display): 7, Col Widths (Display): 44 mm
Copy instructions: *Copy Date:* 2 days prior to publication
LOCAL NEWSPAPERS

HINZ&KUNZT 730305G32G-1060
Editorial: Altstädter Twiete 1, 20095 HAMBURG
Tel: 40 32108311 Fax: 40 30399638
Email: redaktion@hinzundkunzt.de Web site: http://www.hinzundkunzt.de
Freq: Monthly; Annual Sub.: EUR 39,00; Circ: 56,677
Editor: Birgit Müller; Advertising Manager: Isabel Schwartau
Profile: Street magazine for Hamburg.
Language(s): German
ADVERTISING RATES:
Full Page Mono .... EUR 1768
Full Page Colour .... EUR 2854
Mechanical Data: Type Area: 280 x 197 mm, No. of Columns (Display): 4, Col Widths (Display): 50 mm
Copy instructions: *Copy Date:* 15 days prior to publication
BUSINESS: LOCAL GOVERNMENT, LEISURE & RECREATION: Community Care & Social Services

HIRADÓ 737572G21A-3000
Editorial: Alfred-Nobel-Str. 50, 40789 MONHEIM
Tel: 2173 383540 Fax: 2173 383454
Email: bernhard.grupp@bayercropscience.com Web site: http://www.bayercropscience.com
Freq: Half-yearly; Cover Price: Free; Circ: 10,000
Editor: Bernhard Grupp
Profile: Company publication published by Bayer CropScience.
Language(s): Hungarian

HISTORIA 730310G94X-3540
Editorial: 99105 ERFURT Tel: 361 375000
Fax: 361 7375009
Email: historia@uni-erfurt.de Web site: http://www.steiner-verlag.de/Historia
Freq: Quarterly; Annual Sub.: EUR 263,80; Circ: 900
Editor: Kai Brodersen; Advertising Manager: Susanne Szoradi
Profile: Journal covering ancient history.
Language(s): English; French; German; Italian
ADVERTISING RATES:
Full Page Mono .... EUR 750
Mechanical Data: Type Area: 190 x 120 mm
CONSUMER: OTHER CLASSIFICATIONS: Miscellaneous

HK HOLZ- UND KUNSTSTOFFVERARBEITUNG 730338G23A-280
Editorial: Fasanenweg 18, 70771 LEINFELDEN-ECHTERDINGEN Tel: 711 7591273
Fax: 711 7591440
Email: hk-red@drw-verlag.de Web site: http://www.hk-magazin.com
Freq: 6 issues yearly; Annual Sub.: EUR 123,00; Circ: 6,080
Editor: Markus Schmalz; Advertising Manager: Oliver Heinz
Profile: Magazine containing information about furniture and wood products.
Language(s): English; German
ADVERTISING RATES:
Full Page Mono .... EUR 3840
Full Page Colour .... EUR 5490
Mechanical Data: Type Area: 270 x 175 mm, No. of Columns (Display): 4, Col Widths (Display): 40 mm
Copy instructions: *Copy Date:* 30 days prior to publication
Supplement(s): Design + Beschlag Magazin; Furnier Magazin; Holzbau Magazin; Laminat Magazin; MDF Magazin; Surface Magazin; Türen Magazin
BUSINESS: FURNISHINGS & FURNITURE

HLBS REPORT 730342G1A-1280
Editorial: Kölnstr. 202, 53757 ST. AUGUSTIN
Tel: 2241 8661710 Fax: 2241 8661729
Email: verband@hlbs.de Web site: http://www.hlbs.de
Freq: 6 issues yearly; Free to qualifying individuals
Annual Sub.: EUR 50,00; Circ: 1,700
Editor: Peter Meinhardt
Profile: Magazine containing information for tax advisors and officials in charge.
Language(s): German
ADVERTISING RATES:
Full Page Mono .... EUR 400
Full Page Colour .... EUR 1000
Mechanical Data: Type Area: 260 x 180 mm, No. of Columns (Display): 2, Col Widths (Display): 88 mm
Copy instructions: *Copy Date:* 21 days prior to publication

HLH LÜFTUNG/KLIMA HEIZUNG/SANITÄR GEBÄUDETECHNIK 730343G3B-40
Editorial: VDI-Platz 1, 40468 DÜSSELDORF
Tel: 211 6103462 Fax: 211 6103148
Email: hlh@technikwissen.de Web site: http://www.hlh-online.de
Freq: Monthly; Annual Sub.: EUR 184,50; Circ: 11,790
Editor: Hermann Bliesener
Profile: HLH is an organ of the Department of Building Services (VDI-TGA) of the VDI Society for Building and Construction. HLH informed all the engineers in the fields of planning, design and application, and thus the key professionals in the HVAC systems on the overall technical events in the areas of ventilation / air conditioning, heating / plumbing, building. The technical and scientific contributions of the author or practically-oriented journal HLH are supplemented by brief reports on current developments, news from business and industry, information from institutions, associations and publications on exhibitions and conferences.
Language(s): German
Readership: Aimed at engineers, architects and those involved in heating and ventilation.
ADVERTISING RATES:
Full Page Mono .... EUR 4008
Full Page Colour .... EUR 5163
Mechanical Data: Type Area: 270 x 185 mm, No. of Columns (Display): 4, Col Widths (Display): 45 mm
Copy instructions: *Copy Date:* 21 days prior to publication
BUSINESS: HEATING & VENTILATION: Industrial Heating & Ventilation

HLZ 730347G62A-1740
Editorial: Klingenberger Str. 13, 60599 FRANKFURT
Tel: 69 636269 Fax: 69 6313775
Email: freiling.hlz@t-online.de
Freq: 9 issues yearly; Free to qualifying individuals
Annual Sub.: EUR 12,90; Circ: 25,500
Editor: Harald Freiling
Profile: The HLZ is the member magazine of the Union for Education and Science National Association of Hessen.
Language(s): German
ADVERTISING RATES:
Full Page Mono .... EUR 1280
Full Page Colour .... EUR 1800
Mechanical Data: Type Area: 250 x 172 mm, No. of Columns (Display): 3, Col Widths (Display): 54 mm
Copy instructions: *Copy Date:* 25 days prior to publication
Supplement to: Erziehung und Wissenschaft
BUSINESS: CHURCH & SCHOOL EQUIPMENT & EDUCATION: Education

HLZ 730346G62B-3187
Editorial: Rothenbaumchaussee 15, 20148 HAMBURG Tel: 40 493607 Fax: 40 440877
Email: hlz@gew-hamburg.de Web site: http://www.gew-hamburg.de
Freq: 7 issues yearly; Circ: 10,000
Editor: Joachim Geffers
Profile: Journal focusing on teaching in Hamburg.
Language(s): German
BUSINESS: CHURCH & SCHOOL EQUIPMENT & EDUCATION: Education Teachers

HM 729653G75X-55
Editorial: Rektoratsweg 36, 48159 MÜNSTER
Tel: 251 2300569 Fax: 251 2300599
Email: beckmann@handball-magazin.com Web site: http://www.handball-magazin.com
Freq: Monthly; Annual Sub.: EUR 45,60; Circ: 12,165
Editor: Arnulf Beckmann; Advertising Manager: Peter Möllers
Profile: HM is the magazine for the premium sport handball in Germany. HM offers its readers high quality stories that illuminate Handball, its stars and its influential personalities from various poinzs of view and with a variety of journalistic forms.Repots, features, profiles, interviews, commentaries, satires, but also home stories and great reading stories about clubs, fans, players, coaches or managers, garnished with high-quality photos, allow a new, intense, entertaining, knowledgeable and exciting look behind the scene, beyond the usual 1-0 coverage of the daily media.
Language(s): German
ADVERTISING RATES:
Full Page Mono .... EUR 1455
Full Page Colour .... EUR 1990
Mechanical Data: Type Area: 267 x 180 mm, No. of Columns (Display): 3, Col Widths (Display): 55 mm
Copy instructions: *Copy Date:* 28 days prior to publication
CONSUMER: SPORT: Other Sport

HMRG HISTORISCHE MITTEILUNGEN 730315G62B-250
Editorial: Gronewaldstr. 2, 50931 KÖLN
Tel: 221 4702100
Email: juergen.elvert@uni-koeln.de Web site: http://www.steiner-verlag.de/HMRG
Freq: Annual; Annual Sub.: EUR 76,20; Circ: 400
Editor: Jürgen Elvert
Profile: Historical journal presenting new scientific findings including Contributions from the field of Modern and Contemporary History.
Language(s): English; German
Readership: Aimed at history teachers, professors and students.
ADVERTISING RATES:
Full Page Mono .... EUR 750
Mechanical Data: Type Area: 190 x 120 mm
Official Journal of: Organ d. Ranke-Ges., Vereinigung f. Geschichte im öffentl. Leben e.V.
BUSINESS: CHURCH & SCHOOL EQUIPMENT & EDUCATION: Education Teachers

HNA HESSISCHE/ NIEDERSÄCHSISCHE ALLGEMEINE 1660624G67B-16736
Editorial: Frankfurter Str. 168, 34121 KASSEL
Tel: 561 20300 Fax: 561 2032406
Email: info@hna.de Web site: http://www.hna.de
Freq: 260 issues yearly; Circ: 221,551
Editor: Horst Seidenfaden; News Editor: Tibor Pézsa; Advertising Manager: Andrea Schaller-Öller
Profile: Regional daily newspaper with news on politics, economy, culture, sports, travel, technology, etc. The Hessische/Niedersächsische Allgemeine (HNA) is one of a daily newspaper published Monday to Saturday for northern Hesse and southern Lower Saxony. The HNA also serves the areas surrounding the city of Kassel, more precisely the circles Waldeck-Frankenberg, Schwalm-Eder, Werra-Meißner and Hersfeld-Rotenburg. In Lower Saxony has the HNA editorial in Göttingen, Hann. Lead, Northeim and Solling (Uslar). In total there are 16 different local editions of the HNA, ranging from Northeim the north and Schwalmstadt in to the south. Facebook: http://www.facebook.com/HNA?ref=search&sid=1469388759.4008253159..1 Twitter: http://twitter.com/hna_online This Outlet offers RSS (Really Simple Syndication).
Language(s): German
ADVERTISING RATES:
SCC .... EUR 323,70
Mechanical Data: Type Area: 430 x mm, No. of Columns (Display): 6, Col Widths (Display): 45 mm
Copy instructions: *Copy Date:* 2 days prior to publication
REGIONAL DAILY & SUNDAY NEWSPAPERS: Regional Daily Newspapers

HNA.DE 1621446G67B-16576
Editorial: Frankfurter Str. 168, 34121 KASSEL
Tel: 561 2031379 Fax: 561 2032334
Email: jna@hna.de Web site: http://www.hna.de
Freq: Daily; Cover Price: Paid; Circ: 2,382,465 Unique Users
Editor: Jens Nähler; Advertising Manager: Andrea Schaller-Öller
Profile: Ezine: Regional daily newspaper covering politics, economics, culture, sports, travel and technology. Facebook: http://de-de.facebook.com/HNA Twitter: http://twitter.com/#!/HNA_online This Outlet offers RSS (Really Simple Syndication).
Language(s): German
REGIONAL DAILY & SUNDAY NEWSPAPERS: Regional Daily Newspapers

HNO 730365G56A-4820
Editorial: Tiergartenstr. 17, 69121 HEIDELBERG
Tel: 6221 4878167 Fax: 6221 48768167
Email: dagmar.lorenz@springer.com Web site: http://www.springermedizin.de
Freq: Monthly; Annual Sub.: EUR 317,00; Circ: 1,597
Editor: Peter K. Plinkert; Advertising Manager: Odette Thomßen
Profile: HNO is an internationally recognized journal and addresses all ENT specialists in practices and clinics dealing with all aspects of ENT medicine, e.g. prevention, diagnostic methods, complication management, modern therapy strategies and surgical procedures. Review articles provide an overview on selected topics and offer the reader a summary of current findings from all fields of ENT medicine. Freely submitted original papers allow the presentation of important clinical studies and serve the scientific exchange. Case reports feature interesting cases and aim at optimizing diagnostic and therapeutic strategies. Review articles under the rubric "Continuing Medical Education" present verified results of scientific research and their integration into daily practice.
Language(s): German
Readership: Aimed at doctors in hospitals and clinics.
ADVERTISING RATES:
Full Page Mono .... EUR 1630
Full Page Colour .... EUR 2670
Mechanical Data: Type Area: 240 x 174 mm
Official Journal of: Organ d. Dt. Ges. f. HNO-Heilkunde, Kopf- u. Hals-Chirurgie, d. Vereinigungen Westdt., Nordwestdt. u. Schleswig-Holstein. HNO-Ärzte, d. Oto-Laryngolog. Ges.'en zu Berlin, d. oto-Rhino-Laryngolog. Ges. zu München, d. Ges. d. HNO-Ärzte in Hamburg, d. Dt. Ges. f. Phoniatrie u. Pädaudiologie, d. Österr. Ges. f. Hals-, Nasen- u. Ohrenheilkunde, Kopf- u. Halschirurgie u. d. Schweizer. Ges. f. Oto-Rhino-Laryngologie, Hals- u. Gesichtschirurgie
BUSINESS: HEALTH & MEDICAL

HNO INFORMATIONEN 1605475G56A-11153
Editorial: Fleischmannstr. 8, 17475 GREIFSWALD
Tel: 3834 866202 Fax: 3834 866201
Email: hosemann@uni-greifswald.de
Freq: Quarterly; Free to qualifying individuals
Annual Sub.: EUR 87,00; Circ: 4,212
Editor: W. G. Hosemann; Advertising Manager: Nicole Ohmann
Profile: The magazine HNO Informationen is the official journal of the German Society of Oto-Rhino-Laryngology, Head and Neck Surgery. The target group includes more than 4680 members of the German Society of Oto-Rhino-Laryngology, Head and Neck Surgery, additional subscribers and participants of congresses, which are addressed with four issues a year. The magazine reported HNO Informationen on developments in the field of ear, nose and throat medicine, in particular also with regard to the history. Other priorities are to: Current releases of the Bureau and from among the members of the Company, statements and issues related to jurisdiction of the Counsel, reports from associations and groups, information about conferences, training, awards, appointments, honors. Each issue is complemented by a comprehensive calendar of events, which the reader is to assist in scheduling.
Language(s): German
ADVERTISING RATES:
Full Page Mono .... EUR 1650
Full Page Colour .... EUR 2650
Mechanical Data: Type Area: 260 x 185 mm, No. of Columns (Display): 2, Col Widths (Display): 85 mm
Copy instructions: *Copy Date:* 30 days prior to publication

HNO KOMPAKT 730366G56A-4840
Editorial: Maaßstr. 32/1, 69123 HEIDELBERG
Tel: 6221 1377700 Fax: 6221 29910
Email: karcher@kaden-verlag.de Web site: http://www.kaden-verlag.de
Freq: 6 issues yearly; Annual Sub.: EUR 86,00; Circ: 3,322
Editor: Detlef Brehmer; Advertising Manager: Susanne Koeberich
Profile: Journal discussing political issues within the medical world.
Language(s): German
ADVERTISING RATES:
Full Page Mono .... EUR 1415
Full Page Colour .... EUR 2330
Mechanical Data: Type Area: 241 x 190 mm, No. of Columns (Display): 3, Col Widths (Display): 45 mm
Copy instructions: *Copy Date:* 27 days prior to publication
BUSINESS: HEALTH & MEDICAL

HNO MITTEILUNGEN 730367G56A-4860
Editorial: Haart 221, 24539 NEUMÜNSTER
Tel: 4321 97250 Fax: 4321 972611
Email: bv@hno-aerzte.de Web site: http://www.hno-aerzte.de
Freq: 6 issues yearly; Annual Sub.: EUR 28,80; Circ: 4,994
Editor: Detlef Walter; Advertising Manager: Marga Pinsdorf
Profile: The HNO-Mitteilungen releases are is the official organ of the German Professional Association of Ear, Nose and Throat Specialists. The readers of this journal from the members of the Professional Association - he has been so exclusively composed of physicians men who work in the field of ear, nose and throat medicine. The magazine reports on the work of the professional association of professional and political, economic and technical-scientific questions of this specialist group. With LpA-a range of 82.7% (according to reader analysis of medical journals - LA-MED) to read as HNO-Mitteilungen messages from most established Ear, Nose and Throat Specialists physicians.
Language(s): German
ADVERTISING RATES:
Full Page Mono .... EUR 1700
Full Page Colour .... EUR 2700
Mechanical Data: Type Area: 260 x 185 mm, No. of Columns (Display): 4, Col Widths (Display): 45 mm
BUSINESS: HEALTH & MEDICAL

HNO NACHRICHTEN 730368G56A-4880
Editorial: Aschauer Str. 30, 81549 MÜNCHEN
Tel: 89 2030431415 Fax: 89 2030431399
Email: gabriele.zoerrgiebel@springer.com Web site: http://www.hno-nachrichten.de
Freq: 6 issues yearly; Annual Sub.: EUR 69,50; Circ: 4,672
Editor: Gabriele Zörrgiebel
Profile: HNO Nachrichten report from the field for practice on issues that are directly tailored to the interest area of the target group. Experienced ENT doctors from hospitals and practice editorial responsibility and writers as the contents. The training section offers practical articles on current developments in diagnosis, therapy and surgical techniques in the ENT, the specialist oncology as well as allergy and the environment. Recent international studies on the selection referenced and commented by a team of experts. And approved by the Bavarian Medical Association training module allows each issue to the acquisition of three CME credits. The practice management section provides information on billing issues, business law and professional / political issues. Reports on scientific congresses, pharmacological and technical innovations complete the range of editorial.
Language(s): German
ADVERTISING RATES:
Full Page Mono .... EUR 1840
Full Page Colour .... EUR 3090
Mechanical Data: Type Area: 240 x 174 mm
BUSINESS: HEALTH & MEDICAL

HOB DIE HOLZBEARBEITUNG 730372G46-6
Editorial: Teinacher Str. 34, 71634 LUDWIGSBURG
Tel: 7141 223134 Fax: 7141 223131
Email: bucki@agt-verlag.de Web site: http://www.hob-magazin.com

Freq: 10 issues yearly; **Annual Sub.:** EUR 110,00; **Circ:** 11,416
Editor: Carsten Bucki; **Advertising Manager:** Simone Hildenbrand
Profile: HOB Die Holzbearbeitung is an international journal which deals with the design and the use of machines, installations and tools for processing wood, wood materials and materials which are worked in the same way as wood. Every issue provides information on the latest knowledge and discoveries in the field of surface, glue and control technology, measurement techniques, also the fields of warehousing, material handling, assembling, rationalization and automation.
Language(s): German
ADVERTISING RATES:
Full Page Mono .... EUR 3140
Full Page Colour .... EUR 4370
Mechanical Data: Type Area: 270 x 185 mm, No. of Columns (Display): 4, Col Widths (Display): 43 mm
Copy instructions: *Copy Date:* 14 days prior to publication
BUSINESS: TIMBER, WOOD & FORESTRY

HOBBYART 730370G52C-30

Editorial: Fasanenweg 18, 70771 LEINFELDEN-ECHTERDINGEN **Tel:** 711 75913773
Fax: 711 75913775
Email: mbrandenburger@bitverlag.de **Web site:** http://www.hobbyart-online.de
Freq: 6 issues yearly; **Annual Sub.:** EUR 58,50; **Circ:** 3,679
Editor: Manuela Brandenburger; **Advertising Manager:** Joachim Ahnfeldt
Profile: Journal for the trading hobby, artist and supplies. The focus is on trade related issues in these industries: current events, industry news and background information, news and interviews, portraits of specialist retailers, companies and artists and Authors, Hobby techniques, technical or material science, products, hobby and craft books and videos, store concepts, product display, showcase and shop design, event calendar and additional peripheral issues. Topics: paper and cardboard, painting and drawing, silk painting and textile design, modeling, floral, design of glass, wood, ceramic, porcelain, wax dolls, stuffed animals and teddy bears, jewelry, airbrushing, books, handicrafts and others in the market current hot topics. Target or beneficiary group: hobby and art supply industry, handicraft industry and its allied sectors, specialist retailers, specialist retailers and manufacturers and their sales representatives, creative freelance, hobby and craft work including teachers.
Language(s): German
Readership: Aimed at retailers of hobby goods.
ADVERTISING RATES:
Full Page Mono .... EUR 1920
Full Page Colour .... EUR 2790
Mechanical Data: Type Area: 262 x 180 mm, No. of Columns (Display): 3, Col Widths (Display): 55 mm
Copy instructions: *Copy Date:* 27 days prior to publication
BUSINESS: GIFT TRADE: Fancy Goods

HÖCHSTER KREISBLATT

730405G67B-7360
Editorial: Frankenallee 71, 60327 FRANKFURT
Tel: 69 75010 **Fax:** 69 75014232
Email: redaktion@fnp.de **Web site:** http://www.fnp.de
Freq: 312 issues yearly; **Circ:** 36,976
Profile: The Höchster Kreisblatt is opinion-forming daily newspaper in the western part of Frankfurt and the Main-Taunus-Kreis. In this area, it has most of their readers. With editorial offices in Höchst and Hofheim the Höchster Kreisblatt is always very close to the action. It accompanies life in the circulation area, uncovers wrongdoing, highlights positive and discovered something new. With their own events such as the Höchster Kreisstadt-run it is the driving force in the region. The Höchster Kreisblatt is a regional edition of the Frankfurter Neue Presse. Facebook: http://www.facebook.com/pages/FNP/115994585097103 This Outlet offers RSS (Really Simple Syndication).
Language(s): German
ADVERTISING RATES:
SCC .... EUR 68,00
Mechanical Data: Type Area: 528 x 371 mm, No. of Columns (Display): 8, Col Widths (Display): 45 mm
Copy instructions: *Copy Date:* 1 day prior to publication
REGIONAL DAILY & SUNDAY NEWSPAPERS: Regional Daily Newspapers

HOCHWÄLDER WOCHENSPIEGEL 730392G72-5564

Editorial: Max-Planck-Str. 10, 54296 TRIER
Tel: 651 716565 **Fax:** 651 7165669
Email: red-hochwald@tw-verlag.de **Web site:** http://www.wochenspiegellive.de
Freq: Weekly; **Cover Price:** Free; **Circ:** 13,728
Editor: Arnt Finkenberg; **Advertising Manager:** Andreas Noll
Profile: Advertising journal (house-to-house) concentrating on local stories.
Language(s): German
ADVERTISING RATES:
Full Page Mono .... EUR 2047
Full Page Colour .... EUR 2860
Mechanical Data: Type Area: 430 x 290 mm, No. of Columns (Display): 7, Col Widths (Display): 38 mm
Copy instructions: *Copy Date:* 2 days prior to publication
Supplement(s): Frauen 'xtra
LOCAL NEWSPAPERS

HOCHZEIT - DEUTSCHLAND AUSG. 730395G74L-50

Editorial: Neuhauser Str. 21, 78464 KONSTANZ
Tel: 7531 812231 **Fax:** 7531 812299
Email: litterscheidt@hochzeit-magazin.de **Web site:** http://www.hochzeit-magazin.de
Freq: 6 issues yearly; **Annual Sub.:** EUR 40,00; **Circ:** 82,000
Editor: Marina Litterscheidt; **Advertising Manager:** Michaela Groß
Profile: Magazine for bridal couples in Germany, Austria and Switzerland. It covers all topics that are of interest to couples in preparation for this important event: elegant outfits, shiny wedding rings, beautiful honeymoon destinations and great social ideas.
Language(s): German
Readership: Aimed at brides-to-be.
ADVERTISING RATES:
Full Page Mono .... EUR 4068
Full Page Colour .... EUR 6492
Mechanical Data: Type Area: 266 x 185 mm, No. of Columns (Display): 4, Col Widths (Display): 45 mm
Copy instructions: *Copy Date:* 47 days prior to publication
CONSUMER: WOMEN'S INTEREST CONSUMER MAGAZINES: Brides

HOCHZEITSPLANER

1661864G74A-3443
Editorial: Weltenburger Str. 4, 81677 MÜNCHEN
Tel: 89 41969424 **Fax:** 89 4705364
Email: info@avr-werbeagentur.de **Web site:** http://www.hochzeitsplaner.de
Freq: Quarterly; **Cover Price:** EUR 5,50; **Circ:** 17,307
Editor: Bettina Klocke; **Advertising Manager:** Füsin Lindner
Profile: Magazine containing information about wedding preparations. Categories: fashion, beauty, planning, venues, palpitations, parties, jewelry, stores, sequins and fair. Facebook: http://www.facebook.com/pages/Hochzeitsplaner/127418177294284.
Language(s): German
ADVERTISING RATES:
Full Page Mono .... EUR 3770
Full Page Colour .... EUR 4200
Mechanical Data: Type Area: 222 x 163 mm
CONSUMER: WOMEN'S INTEREST CONSUMER MAGAZINES: Women's Interest

HOCKENHEIMER TAGESZEITUNG 730397G67B-7380

Editorial: Carl-Theodor-Str. 1, 68723 SCHWETZINGEN **Tel:** 6202 2050 **Fax:** 6202 205392
Email: sz-redaktion@schwetzinger-zeitung.de **Web site:** http://www.schwetzinger-zeitung.de
Freq: 312 issues yearly; **Annual Sub.:** EUR 27,10; **Circ:** 16,218
Advertising Manager: Heiner Hugo
Profile: Daily newspaper with regional news and a local sports section. This Outlet offers RSS (Really Simple Syndication).
Language(s): German
ADVERTISING RATES:
SCC .... EUR 52,50
Mechanical Data: Type Area: 490 x 320 mm, No. of Columns (Display): 7, Col Widths (Display): 44 mm
Copy instructions: *Copy Date:* 2 days prior to publication
Supplement(s): Morgen Magazin; TV Morgen; Wirtschaftsmorgen
REGIONAL DAILY & SUNDAY NEWSPAPERS: Regional Daily Newspapers

HOF DIREKT 730427G21A-2160

Editorial: Hülsebrockstr. 2, 48165 MÜNSTER
Tel: 251 801822 **Fax:** 251 801872
Email: hofdirektredaktion@wochenblatt.com **Web site:** http://www.hofdirekt.com
Freq: 6 issues yearly; **Annual Sub.:** EUR 49,50; **Circ:** 11,000
Editor: Ute Heimann; **Advertising Manager:** Nicole Neubauer
Profile: Magazine for farmers, selling their products directly.
Language(s): German
ADVERTISING RATES:
Full Page Mono .... EUR 1584
Full Page Colour .... EUR 2036
Mechanical Data: Type Area: 270 x 190 mm, No. of Columns (Display): 4, Col Widths (Display): 46 mm

HOFER ANZEIGER 730428G67B-7400

Editorial: Poststr. 9, 95028 HOF **Tel:** 9281 8160
Fax: 9281 816283
Email: redaktion@frankenpost.de **Web site:** http://www.frankenpost.de
Freq: 312 issues yearly; **Circ:** 19,807
Advertising Manager: Stefan Sailer
Profile: Regional daily newspaper with news on politics, economy, culture, sports, travel, technology, etc. Hofer Anzeiger is a local edition of the newspaper Frankenpost. Facebook: http://www.facebook.com/pages/Frankenpost/330862476314 Twitter: http://twitter.com/frankenpost This Outlet offers RSS (Really Simple Syndication).
Language(s): German
ADVERTISING RATES:
SCC .... EUR 109,60
Mechanical Data: Type Area: 485 x 325 mm, No. of Columns (Display): 7, Col Widths (Display): 44 mm
Copy instructions: *Copy Date:* 1 day prior to publication

Supplement(s): rtv
REGIONAL DAILY & SUNDAY NEWSPAPERS: Regional Daily Newspapers

HOFGEISMARER ALLGEMEINE

730353G67B-7140
Editorial: Frankfurter Str. 168, 34121 KASSEL
Tel: 561 20300 **Fax:** 561 2032406
Email: info@hna.de **Web site:** http://www.hna.de
Freq: 312 issues yearly; **Circ:** 15,903
Advertising Manager: Andrea Schaller-Öller
Profile: Regional daily newspaper with news on politics, economy, culture, sports, travel, technology, etc. The Hofgeismarer Allgemeine a local edition of theHNA Hessische/Niedersächsische Allgemeine Twitter: http://twitter.com/hna_online This Outlet offers RSS (Really Simple Syndication).
Language(s): German
ADVERTISING RATES:
SCC .... EUR 37,10
Mechanical Data: Type Area: 430 x 285 mm, No. of Columns (Display): 6, Col Widths (Display): 45 mm
Copy instructions: *Copy Date:* 2 days prior to publication
REGIONAL DAILY & SUNDAY NEWSPAPERS: Regional Daily Newspapers

HOHENLOHER TAGBLATT

730442G67B-7440
Editorial: Ludwigstr. 6, 74564 CRAILSHEIM
Tel: 7951 409321 **Fax:** 7951 409329
Email: redaktion.ht@swp.de **Web site:** http://www.hohenloher-tagblatt.de
Freq: 312 issues yearly; **Circ:** 14,472
Editor: Andreas Harthan; **Advertising Manager:** Herbert Huber
Profile: Daily newspaper with regional news and a local sports section. Twitter: http://twitter.com/SWPde This Outlet offers RSS (Really Simple Syndication).
Language(s): German
ADVERTISING RATES:
SCC .... EUR 32,90
Mechanical Data: Type Area: 420 x 274 mm, No. of Columns (Display): 6, Col Widths (Display): 44 mm
Copy instructions: *Copy Date:* 1 day prior to publication
Supplement(s): Das Magazin; Regio Business; rtv
REGIONAL DAILY & SUNDAY NEWSPAPERS: Regional Daily Newspapers

HOHENLOHER ZEITUNG

730445G67B-7460
Editorial: Allee 2, 74072 HEILBRONN **Tel:** 7131 6150
Fax: 7131 615200
Email: redaktion@stimme.de **Web site:** http://www.stimme.de
Freq: 312 issues yearly; **Circ:** 19,902
Advertising Manager: Martin Kufner
Profile: Daily newspaper with regional news and a local sports section. Once again, the Hohenloher Zeitung included in the International Color Quality Club, which puts them among the 50 daily newspapers with the world's best image and print quality. Twitter: http://twitter.com/stimmeonline This Outlet offers RSS (Really Simple Syndication).
Language(s): German
ADVERTISING RATES:
SCC .... EUR 53,20
Mechanical Data: Type Area: 490 x 327 mm, No. of Columns (Display): 7, Col Widths (Display): 45 mm
Copy instructions: *Copy Date:* 1 day prior to publication
Supplement(s): autoStimme; Hohenlohekreis direkt; WirtschaftsStimme
REGIONAL DAILY & SUNDAY NEWSPAPERS: Regional Daily Newspapers

HOHENZOLLERISCHE ZEITUNG 730452G67B-7480

Editorial: Obertorplatz 19, 72379 HECHINGEN
Tel: 7471 931527 **Fax:** 7471 931550
Email: hoz.redaktion@swp.de **Web site:** http://www.suedwest-aktiv.de
Freq: 312 issues yearly; **Circ:** 6,955
Advertising Manager: Dietmar Merz
Profile: Daily newspaper with regional news and a local sports section. Twitter: http://twitter.com/SWPde This Outlet offers RSS (Really Simple Syndication).
Language(s): German
ADVERTISING RATES:
SCC .... EUR 24,40
Mechanical Data: Type Area: 480 x 320 mm, No. of Columns (Display): 7, Col Widths (Display): 44 mm
Copy instructions: *Copy Date:* 1 day prior to publication
REGIONAL DAILY & SUNDAY NEWSPAPERS: Regional Daily Newspapers

HOLSTEINER ALLGEMEINE

730463G72-5628
Editorial: Schulstr. 20, 25335 ELMSHORN
Tel: 4121 26730 **Fax:** 4121 267355
Email: anzeigen@holsteiner-allgemeine.de **Web site:** http://www.holsteiner-allgemeine.de
Freq: Weekly; **Cover Price:** Free; **Circ:** 67,590
Editor: Bert C. Biehl; **Advertising Manager:** Constanze Neumann
Profile: Advertising journal (house-to-house) concentrating on local stories.

Language(s): German
ADVERTISING RATES:
Full Page Mono .... EUR 3478
Full Page Colour .... EUR 3637
Mechanical Data: Type Area: 430 x 287 mm, No. of Columns (Display): 6, Col Widths (Display): 45 mm
Copy instructions: *Copy Date:* 5 days prior to publication
LOCAL NEWSPAPERS

HOLSTEINISCHER COURIER

730464G67B-7500
Editorial: Nikolaistr. 7, 24937 FLENSBURG
Tel: 461 8080 **Fax:** 461 8081058
Email: redaktion@shz.de **Web site:** http://www.shz.de
Freq: 312 issues yearly; **Circ:** 17,812
Advertising Manager: Ingeborg Schwarz
Profile: The "Holsteinischer Courier" was founded in 1872 by a printer and Breslauer. It has been one since 1.1.2001 to the Schleswig-Holsteinischer Zeitungsverlag. The distribution area is the city of Neumünster, and the corresponding surrounding region. Facebook: http://www.facebook.com/shzonline Twitter: http://twitter.com/shz_de This Outlet offers RSS (Really Simple Syndication).
Language(s): German
ADVERTISING RATES:
SCC .... EUR 56,00
Mechanical Data: Type Area: 480 x 325 mm, No. of Columns (Display): 7, Col Widths (Display): 45 mm
Copy instructions: *Copy Date:* 1 day prior to publication
Supplement(s): nordisch gesund; Schleswig-Holstein Journal; tv magazin
REGIONAL DAILY & SUNDAY NEWSPAPERS: Regional Daily Newspapers

HOLZ FORUM MIT FENSTER- UND TÜRENMARKT 730474G46-9

Editorial: Am Erlengraben 8, 76275 ETTLINGEN
Tel: 7243 575203 **Fax:** 7243 575200
Email: h.ziegler@daehne.de **Web site:** http://www.holzonline.de
Freq: 6 issues yearly; **Annual Sub.:** EUR 49,00; **Circ:** 4,757
Editor: Hans-Ludwig Ziegler; **Advertising Manager:** Thomas Heinen
Profile: Holz Forum mit Fenster- und Türenmarkt is the specialist magazine for the timber trade in German-speaking countries. Specialist articles on the different product areas, market analyses, company profiles and trade fair reports provide authoritative information about developments in both industry and commerce. Market overviews geared to the different keynote topics are complemented by reporting on new products. A special section of each issue provides regular information from the "Windows and Doors" market. Constant coverage is also given to the sector's other core product areas, "Floors, Walls and Ceilings", "Wood in the Garden" and "Wood as a Building Material". The magazine sees itself as a medium of information for specialist timber merchants and builders' merchants, both wholesale and retail, for the timber departments of DIY superstores, for parquet and door studios, and for all suppliers of core or peripheral product ranges.
Language(s): German
Readership: Aimed at those working in the timber trade.
ADVERTISING RATES:
Full Page Mono .... EUR 1762
Full Page Colour .... EUR 3427
Mechanical Data: Type Area: 270 x 187 mm, No. of Columns (Display): 4, Col Widths (Display): 43 mm
Copy instructions: *Copy Date:* 25 days prior to publication
BUSINESS: TIMBER, WOOD & FORESTRY

HOLZ PLUS 730482G4E-3880

Editorial: Döllgaststr. 7, 86199 AUGSBURG
Tel: 821 344570 **Fax:** 821 3445719
Email: info@mkpublishing.de **Web site:** http://www.mkpublishing.de
Freq: Half-yearly; **Cover Price:** Free; **Circ:** 40,000
Profile: Company publication published by Hekatron GmbH.
Language(s): German

HOLZ- UND MÖBELINDUSTRIE DEUTSCHLAND 730475G23A-400

Editorial: Bert-Brecht-Str. 15, 78054 VILLINGEN-SCHWENNINGEN **Tel:** 7720 394118
Fax: 7720 394175
Email: findeisen@kuhnverlag.de **Web site:** http://www.kuhn-kataloge.de
Freq: Annual; **Cover Price:** EUR 17,00; **Circ:** 5,478
Editor: Steffi Findeisen; **Advertising Manager:** Konrad Baumann
Profile: Magazine for the furniture and wood processing industries. Includes a special on furniture accessories.
Language(s): German
ADVERTISING RATES:
Full Page Mono .... EUR 2405
Full Page Colour .... EUR 3020
Mechanical Data: Type Area: 254 x 180 mm, No. of Columns (Display): 3
BUSINESS: FURNISHINGS & FURNITURE

HOLZBAU DIE NEUE QUADRIGA
1663320G4E-7051
Editorial: Schloßhof 2, 85283 WOLNZACH
Tel: 8442 925330 **Fax:** 8442 4426
Email: info@quadriga-news.de **Web site:** http://www.dieneuequadriga.de
Freq: 6 issues yearly; **Annual Sub.:** EUR 60,00; **Circ:** 12,192
Editor: Eduard Kastner
Profile: Magazine about building with wood.
Language(s): German
ADVERTISING RATES:
Full Page Mono .... EUR 2100
Full Page Colour .... EUR 3650
Mechanical Data: Type Area: 261 x 184 mm, No. of Columns (Display): 4, Col Widths (Display): 43 mm
BUSINESS: ARCHITECTURE & BUILDING: Building

HOLZBAU MAGAZIN
730468G46-8
Editorial: Fasanenweg 18, 70771 LEINFELDEN-ECHTERDINGEN **Tel:** 711 7591306
Fax: 711 7591440
Email: info@drw-verlag.de **Web site:** http://www.drw-verlag.de
Freq: Annual; **Cover Price:** EUR 5,00; **Circ:** 13,000
Editor: Karsten Koch; **Advertising Manager:** Oliver Heinz
Profile: Magazine focusing on the timber industry.
Language(s): English; German
Readership: Read by managers in the timber trade.
ADVERTISING RATES:
Full Page Mono .... EUR 5000
Full Page Colour .... EUR 6680
Mechanical Data: Type Area: 270 x 175 mm, No. of Columns (Display): 4, Col Widths (Display): 40 mm
Copy instructions: *Copy Date:* 33 days prior to publication
Supplement to: HK Holz- und Kunststoffverarbeitung, Holz-Zentralblatt
BUSINESS: TIMBER, WOOD & FORESTRY

HOLZFORSCHUNG
730472G55-3895
Editorial: Genthiner Str. 13, 10785 BERLIN
Tel: 30 26005245 **Fax:** 30 26005298
Email: holzforschung.editorial@degruyter.com **Web site:** http://www.degruyter.de/journals/holz
Freq: 6 issues yearly; **Annual Sub.:** EUR 1498,00; **Circ:** 400
Editor: Oskar Faix
Profile: Holzforschung is an international scholarly journal that publishes cutting-edge research on the biology, chemistry, physics and technology of wood and wood components. Rated year after year as the number one scientific journal in the category of Pulp and Paper (ISI Journal Citation Index), Holzforschung represents innovative, high quality basic and applied research.
Language(s): English
ADVERTISING RATES:
Full Page Mono .... EUR 500
Full Page Colour .... EUR 900
Mechanical Data: Type Area: 250 x 170 mm
Copy instructions: *Copy Date:* 28 days prior to publication
BUSINESS: APPLIED SCIENCE & LABORATORIES

DER HOLZFUCHS
1848167G21A-4403
Editorial: Regensburger Str. 148, 93309 KELHEIM
Tel: 9441 175029 **Fax:** 9441 174916
Email: gs@wbv-kelheim-thaldorf.de **Web site:** http://www.wbv-kelheim-thaldorf.de
Free to qualifying individuals
Annual Sub.: EUR 5,00; **Circ:** 1,150
Editor: Rupert Gruber
Profile: Regional magazine with information for forest owners.
Language(s): German

HOLZKIRCHNER MERKUR
730479G67B-7520
Editorial: Pfaffenrieder Str. 9, 82515 WOLFRATSHAUSEN **Tel:** 8171 2690
Fax: 8171 269240
Email: fsav@merkur-online.de **Web site:** http://www.merkur-online.de
Freq: 312 issues yearly; **Circ:** 16,666
Advertising Manager: Hans-Georg Bechthold
Profile: The Münchner Merkur with its own local newspapers, of which the Holzkirchner Merkur is one that, the leading regional newspaper brand in the Munich area - the most affluent area of Germany. The combination of newspaper and region is the foundation on which to build the success of the title. This is the newspaper not only the factual news agency, but forms a community of solidarity with its readers and the local community. The clear focus on local reporting creates a high regard to human reader loyalty. She presses one hand in the very high number of close to 180,000 subscribers. Also for the high reader-commitment is the loyalty of the total current 827 000 daily readers, the Münchner Merkur or one of its local newspapers usually read over many years. The Münchner Merkur with its own local newspapers is a newspaper for the whole family, tradition and modern life for one of the most beautiful regions of Germany unites. Reliable, informative, critical: the Münchner Merkur is the indispensable daily newspaper for the region. Facebook: http://www.facebook.com/pages/merkur-online.de/190176143327.
Language(s): German
ADVERTISING RATES:
SCC .... EUR 43,60
Mechanical Data: Type Area: 474 x 324 mm, No. of Columns (Display): 7, Col Widths (Display): 45 mm
Copy instructions: *Copy Date:* 1 day prior to publication
REGIONAL DAILY & SUNDAY NEWSPAPERS: Regional Daily Newspapers

HOLZ-ZENTRALBLATT
730488G46-10
Editorial: Fasanenweg 18, 70771 LEINFELDEN-ECHTERDINGEN **Tel:** 711 7591275
Fax: 711 7591267
Email: hz-red@holz-zentralblatt.com **Web site:** http://www.holz-zentralblatt.com
Freq: Weekly; **Annual Sub.:** EUR 254,80; **Circ:** 13,981
Advertising Manager: Peter Beerhalter
Profile: Magazine for the German and international wood industry.
Language(s): German
ADVERTISING RATES:
Full Page Mono .... EUR 9348
Full Page Colour .... EUR 10473
Mechanical Data: Type Area: 380 x 285 mm, No. of Columns (Display): 6, Col Widths (Display): 45 mm
Copy instructions: *Copy Date:* 3 days prior to publication
Supplement(s): B + H Bauen + Holz; Design + Beschlag Magazin; Furnier Magazin; Holzbau Magazin; Laminat Magazin; MDF Magazin; Surface Magazin; Türen Magazin
BUSINESS: TIMBER, WOOD & FORESTRY

H.O.M.E.
730493A74C-400
Editorial: Schlesische Str. 29, 10997 BERLIN
Tel: 30 6113080 **Fax:** 30 6113088
Email: home@aheadmedia.com **Web site:** http://www.home-mag.com
Freq: 10 issues yearly; **Annual Sub.:** EUR 40,00; **Circ:** 24,442
Editor: Gerhard Amann
Profile: Magazine about homes and decorating, architecture and lifestyle.
Language(s): German
ADVERTISING RATES:
Full Page Mono .... EUR 4750
Full Page Colour .... EUR 6250
Mechanical Data: Type Area: 272 x 202 mm, No. of Columns (Display): 3, Col Widths (Display): 60 mm
Copy instructions: *Copy Date:* 20 days prior to publication
CONSUMER: WOMEN'S INTEREST CONSUMER MAGAZINES: Home & Family

H.O.M.E.
730492G74C-1100
Editorial: Schlesische Str. 29, 10997 BERLIN
Tel: 30 6113080 **Fax:** 30 6113088
Email: home@aheadmedia.com **Web site:** http://www.home-mag.com
Freq: 9 issues yearly; **Annual Sub.:** EUR 40,00; **Circ:** 70,668
Editor: Alexander Geringer; **Advertising Manager:** Thomas M. Biegerl
Profile: Lifestyle Magazine about homes, interior design, architecture and lifestyle.
Language(s): German
ADVERTISING RATES:
Full Page Mono .... EUR 7250
Full Page Colour .... EUR 9810
Mechanical Data: Type Area: 272 x 202 mm, No. of Columns (Display): 3, Col Widths (Display): 60 mm
Copy instructions: *Copy Date:* 20 days prior to publication
Supplement(s): stilwerk Magazin
CONSUMER: WOMEN'S INTEREST CONSUMER MAGAZINES: Home & Family

HOMES & GARDENS
730496G74C-1600
Editorial: Rosenkavalierplatz 14, 81925 MÜNCHEN
Tel: 89 9100930 **Fax:** 89 91009353
Email: u.passoth@ipm-verlag.de **Web site:** http://www.ipm-verlag.de
Freq: 6 issues yearly; **Annual Sub.:** EUR 29,00; **Circ:** 68,176
Editor: Ulrike Passoth; **Advertising Manager:** Rüdiger Knapp
Profile: For more than 10 years this magazine has been setting the trend for a classic and British-inspired style of living of highest standards. The title stands for a demanding target group and attracts readers with an income well above average who are excessively free-spending, consumption-oriented and have a huge purchasing potential.
Language(s): German
ADVERTISING RATES:
Full Page Mono .... EUR 15500
Full Page Colour .... EUR 15500
Mechanical Data: Type Area: 260 x 186 mm
Copy instructions: *Copy Date:* 40 days prior to publication
CONSUMER: WOMEN'S INTEREST CONSUMER MAGAZINES: Home & Family

HOMILETISCHE MONATSHEFTE
730501G87-5840
Editorial: Theaterstr. 13, 37073 GÖTTINGEN
Tel: 551 508440 **Fax:** 551 5084422
Email: info@v-r.de **Web site:** http://www.v-r.de
Freq: Monthly; **Annual Sub.:** EUR 69,00; **Circ:** 1,900
Advertising Manager: Sylvia Göthel
Profile: Religious magazine.
Language(s): German
ADVERTISING RATES:
Full Page Mono .... EUR 580
Mechanical Data: Type Area: 190 x 117 mm
CONSUMER: RELIGIOUS

HOMÖOPATHIE
1832351G56A-11540
Editorial: Reinhardtstr. 37, 10117 BERLIN
Tel: 30 325973411 **Fax:** 30 325973419
Email: presse@dzvhae.de **Web site:** http://www.welt-der-homoeopathie.de
Freq: Quarterly; **Annual Sub.:** EUR 5,00; **Circ:** 40,000
Editor: Christoph Trapp
Profile: Magazine about homoepathy.
Language(s): German
ADVERTISING RATES:
Full Page Mono .... EUR 2550
Full Page Colour .... EUR 2550
Mechanical Data: Type Area: 252 x 180 mm

HOMÖOPATHIE ZEITSCHRIFT
730504G56A-4920
Editorial: Grubmühlerfeldstr. 14a, 82131 GAUTING
Tel: 89 89999626 **Fax:** 89 89999610
Email: redaktion@homoeopathie-zeitschrift.de **Web site:** http://www.homoeopathie-zeitschrift.de
Freq: 3 issues yearly; **Annual Sub.:** EUR 44,40; **Circ:** 6,000
Editor: Eva Kolbinger
Profile: Magazine on classical homeopathy.
Language(s): German
ADVERTISING RATES:
Full Page Mono .... EUR 890
Full Page Colour .... EUR 1113
Mechanical Data: Type Area: 240 x 190 mm

HÖRAKUSTIK
730413G56R-85
Editorial: Im Breitspiel 11a, 69126 HEIDELBERG
Tel: 6221 905090 **Fax:** 6221 9050920
Email: info@median-verlag.de **Web site:** http://www.median-verlag.de
Freq: Monthly; **Annual Sub.:** EUR 133,90; **Circ:** 3,000
Editor: Björn Kerzmann; **Advertising Manager:** Kyra Schiffke
Profile: Publication about hearing aids.
Language(s): German
ADVERTISING RATES:
Full Page Mono .... EUR 1455
Full Page Colour .... EUR 2370
Mechanical Data: Type Area: 250 x 188 mm, No. of Columns (Display): 3, Col Widths (Display): 60 mm
Copy instructions: *Copy Date:* 25 days prior to publication
BUSINESS: HEALTH & MEDICAL: Health Medical Related

HORIZONT
730525G2A-1640
Editorial: Mainzer Landstr. 251, 60326 FRANKFURT
Tel: 69 75951602 **Fax:** 69 75951600
Email: chefredaktion@horizont.net **Web site:** http://www.horizont.net
Freq: Weekly; **Annual Sub.:** EUR 254,00; **Circ:** 17,706
Editor: Volker Schütz; **Advertising Manager:** Petra Linke
Profile: Magazine about marketing, advertising and media.
Language(s): German
ADVERTISING RATES:
Full Page Colour .... EUR 9700
Mechanical Data: Type Area: 390 x 286 mm, No. of Columns (Display): 5, Col Widths (Display): 54 mm
Copy instructions: *Copy Date:* 7 days prior to publication
Supplement(s): dialog; Horizont Media Guide; Die Zeitungen
BUSINESS: COMMUNICATIONS, ADVERTISING & MARKETING

HORIZONT.NET
1621461G2A-5454
Editorial: Mainzer Landstr. 251, 60326 FRANKFURT
Tel: 69 75951617 **Fax:** 69 75951600
Email: schuetz@horizont.net **Web site:** http://www.horizont.net
Freq: Daily; **Cover Price:** Paid; **Circ:** 972,404 Unique Users
Editor: Volker Schütz; **Advertising Manager:** Petra Linke
Profile: Ezine: Magazine about marketing, advertising and media. Twitter: http://twitter.com/HorizontNet.
Language(s): German
BUSINESS: COMMUNICATIONS, ADVERTISING & MARKETING

HORMONE AND METABOLIC RESEARCH
730532G56A-4960
Editorial: Rüdigerstr. 14, 70469 STUTTGART
Tel: 711 89310 **Fax:** 711 8931298
Email: kundenservice@thieme.de **Web site:** http://www.thieme.de/hmr
Freq: Monthly; **Circ:** 450
Editor: W. A. Scherbaum
Profile: Covering the fields of endocrinology and metabolism from both a clinical and basic science perspective, this well regarded monthly journal publishes original articles, and short communications on cutting edge topics. Speedy publication time is given high priority, ensuring that endocrinologists worldwide get timely, fast-breaking information as it happens. Hormone and Metabolic Research presents reviews, original papers, and short communications, and includes a section on Innovative Methods. With a preference for experimental over observational studies, this journal disseminates new and reliable experimental data from across the field of endocrinology and metabolism to researchers, scientists and doctors world-wide.
Language(s): English
ADVERTISING RATES:
Full Page Mono .... EUR 1050
Full Page Colour .... EUR 2220
Mechanical Data: Type Area: 248 x 175 mm, No. of Columns (Display): 3, Col Widths (Display): 55 mm
BUSINESS: HEALTH & MEDICAL

HORTIVISION
1978889G21A-4458
Editorial: Azaleenstr. 87, 26639 WIESMOOR
Tel: 4944 920486 **Fax:** 4944 919416
Email: info@dehne.de **Web site:** http://www.dehne-internet.de
Freq: Annual; **Cover Price:** Free; **Circ:** 40,000
Editor: Lars Dehne; **Advertising Manager:** Lars Dehne
Profile: Reference and supplier directory for the german market gardening.
Language(s): German
ADVERTISING RATES:
Full Page Mono .... EUR 480
Full Page Colour .... EUR 480
Mechanical Data: Type Area: 122 x 90 mm
Copy instructions: *Copy Date:* 30 days prior to publication

HÖRZU
730421G76C-240
Editorial: Axel-Springer-Platz 1, 20355 HAMBURG
Tel: 40 34700 **Fax:** 40 34722628
Email: leserbriefe@hoerzu.de **Web site:** http://www.hoerzu.de
Freq: Weekly; **Annual Sub.:** EUR 91,00; **Circ:** 1,351,519
Editor: Christian Hellmann; **Advertising Manager:** Arne Bergmann
Profile: HÖRZU is the leading weekly magazine program with the highest coverage in the "winning generation"- the better educated generation of adults, in the professions of high average income reached, thus achieving a higher social status. HÖRZU stands for quality and excellent value. Editorial focuses on the shell part, which presents a target group-affine mix of topics are popular topics from the fields of knowledge, research, history and science. This exclusivity is very important. A large number of prominent authors and experts are the core competence of HÖRZU. Recognized experts in health, medicine, environment, nature, psychology, travel, cooking and finances strengthen credibility and exclusivity. Service and Nutzthemen are consistently provided with prominent sponsors. The issue is overall rich look. The positive, emotional art form has premium quality. Twitter: http://www.twitter.com/HOERZUnews.
Language(s): German
ADVERTISING RATES:
Full Page Mono .... EUR 35500
Full Page Colour .... EUR 43900
Mechanical Data: Type Area: 265 x 202 mm, No. of Columns (Display): 4, Col Widths (Display): 49 mm
Copy instructions: *Copy Date:* 24 days prior to publication
CONSUMER: MUSIC & PERFORMING ARTS: TV & Radio

HÖRZU WISSEN
1932591G74A-3719
Editorial: Axel-Springer-Platz 1, 20355 HAMBURG
Tel: 40 34700 **Fax:** 40 34722628
Email: leserbriefe@hoerzu.de **Web site:** http://www.hoerzu.de
Freq: 6 issues yearly; **Cover Price:** EUR 3,50; **Circ:** 143,010
Editor: Christian Hellmann; **Advertising Manager:** Arne Bergmann
Profile: HÖRZU WISSEN presents various popular, mainstream-ready knowledge topics that are entertaining and worked up in an opulent look. Prominent experts and competent TV-heads are on the way as authors of HÖRZU WISSEN and report on their experiences. Twitter: http://www.twitter.com/HOERZUnews.
Language(s): German
ADVERTISING RATES:
Full Page Mono .... EUR 9950
Full Page Colour .... EUR 9950
Mechanical Data: Type Area: 285 x 225 mm, No. of Columns (Display): 3, Col Widths (Display): 70 mm
Copy instructions: *Copy Date:* 26 days prior to publication

HOTEL GUIDE BERLIN
1799870G89A-12307
Editorial: Am Karlsbad 11, 10785 BERLIN
Tel: 30 2647480 **Fax:** 30 264748968
Email: susanna.weber@btm.de **Web site:** http://www.visitberlin.de
Freq: Annual; **Cover Price:** Free; **Circ:** 50,000
Profile: Directory of hotels in the city of Berlin and the German federal state of Brandenburg.
Language(s): English; French; German; Italian; Russian; Spanish
ADVERTISING RATES:
Full Page Mono .... EUR 1500
Full Page Colour .... EUR 2900
Mechanical Data: Type Area: 187 x 130 mm
Copy instructions: *Copy Date:* 101 days prior to publication

HOTEL- UND GASTSTÄTTEN-KURIER 730562G11A-840
Editorial: Günterstalstr. 78, 79100 FREIBURG
Tel: 761 73400 **Fax:** 761 700963
Email: althoff@dehogabw.de
Freq: Monthly; Free to qualifying individuals
Annual Sub.: EUR 35,00; **Circ:** 3,800
Editor: Klaus Althoff
Profile: Publication about the hotel and restaurant business. Contains news, information and articles.
Language(s): German
ADVERTISING RATES:
Full Page Mono .... EUR 748
Full Page Colour .... EUR 999
Mechanical Data: Type Area: 260 x 185 mm, No. of Columns (Display): 4, Col Widths (Display): 45 mm
Copy instructions: *Copy Date:* 21 days prior to publication
BUSINESS: CATERING: Catering, Hotels & Restaurants

HOTEL & TECHNIK 730565G11A-1567
Editorial: Saarlandstr. 28, 70734 FELLBACH
Tel: 711 95295134 **Fax:** 711 95295199
Email: hettrich@at-fachverlag.de **Web site:** http://www.hotel-und-technik.de
Freq: 6 issues yearly; **Annual Sub.:** EUR 40,00; **Circ:** 20,796
Editor: Arnulf Hettrich; **Advertising Manager:** Barbara Hahn
Profile: Investment magazine for the hospitality industry. The main target group are hotel owners, hotel developers, architects, interior designers and investors in self- constantly run companies and in chains and corporations. The magazine deals with topics related to new construction, existing buildings and operation of Hotels in the area of equipment, facilities, health, energy conservation and communication. The technical aspects are an understandable even for non technician. By focusing on technical content, the target is achieved without any wastage. Facebook: http://www.facebook.com/hotelundtechnik.
Language(s): German
ADVERTISING RATES:
Full Page Mono .... EUR 5610
Full Page Colour .... EUR 6990
Mechanical Data: Type Area: 264 x 185 mm, No. of Columns (Display): 4, Col Widths (Display): 43 mm
Copy instructions: *Copy Date:* 28 days prior to publication
BUSINESS: CATERING: Catering, Hotels & Restaurants

HOTELGUIDE FRANKFURT RHEIN MAIN 1789681G89A-12266
Editorial: Ludwig-Erhard-Anlage 1, 60327 FRANKFURT **Tel:** 69 75756083 **Fax:** 69 75756802
Email: bettina.ivers-tiffee@messefrankfurt.com **Web site:** http://www.hotelguide-frankfurt.de
Freq: Annual; **Cover Price:** EUR 4,40; **Circ:** 27,000
Editor: Bettina Ivers-Tiffée
Profile: Regional Hotel Guide for Frankfurt Rhein Main.
Language(s): English; German
ADVERTISING RATES:
Full Page Mono .... EUR 2310
Full Page Colour .... EUR 2310
Mechanical Data: Type Area: 246 x 182 mm

HOTELS UND PENSIONEN 1826183G89A-12381
Editorial: Kardinal-Höffner-Platz 1, 50667 KÖLN
Tel: 221 22130400 **Fax:** 221 22130410
Email: info@koelntourismus.de **Web site:** http://www.koelntourismus.de
Freq: Annual; **Cover Price:** Free; **Circ:** 40,000
Profile: Accommodation in and around Cologne.
Language(s): English; German
ADVERTISING RATES:
Full Page Mono .... EUR 3498
Full Page Colour .... EUR 3498
Mechanical Data: Type Area: 277 x 190 mm

HOUSE AND MORE 736461G94H-9240
Editorial: Dorotheenstr. 64, 22301 HAMBURG
Tel: 40 6965950 **Fax:** 40 696595199
Email: leserbrief@houseandmore.de **Web site:** http://www.houseandmore.de
Freq: Quarterly; **Cover Price:** EUR 0,95; **Circ:** 2,070,409
Editor: Claus-Peter Haller; **Advertising Manager:** Sebastian Schurz
Profile: Magazine containing information about purchasing a home.
Language(s): German
ADVERTISING RATES:
Full Page Mono .... EUR 27760
Full Page Colour .... EUR 50100
Mechanical Data: Type Area: 220 x 174 mm, No. of Columns (Display): 4, Col Widths (Display): 45 mm
Copy instructions: *Copy Date:* 42 days prior to publication
CONSUMER: OTHER CLASSIFICATIONS: Customer Magazines

HOYERSWERDAER WOCHENKURIER 730571G72-5668
Editorial: Karl-Marx-Str. 68, 03044 COTTBUS
Tel: 355 4312381 **Fax:** 355 472910
Email: kerstintwarok@cwk-verlag.de **Web site:** http://www.wochenkurier.info
Freq: Weekly; **Cover Price:** Free; **Circ:** 36,854
Editor: Kerstin Twarok; **Advertising Manager:** Uwe Peschel
Profile: Advertising journal (house-to-house) concentrating on local stories.
Language(s): German
ADVERTISING RATES:
Full Page Mono .... EUR 3372
Full Page Colour .... EUR 4720
Mechanical Data: Type Area: 430 x 290 mm, No. of Columns (Display): 7, Col Widths (Display): 38 mm
Copy instructions: *Copy Date:* 5 days prior to publication
LOCAL NEWSPAPERS

HP NATUR-HEILKUNDE 1615225G56A-11208
Editorial: Zur Tannenburg 43, 66280 SULZBACH
Tel: 6897 983886 **Fax:** 6897 983686
Email: carsten.kroeger@m-m-verlag.de **Web site:** http://www.m-m-verlag.de
Freq: 6 issues yearly; Free to qualifying individuals
Annual Sub.: EUR 70,00; **Circ:** 8,074
Editor: Carsten Kröger; **Advertising Manager:** Renate Graf
Profile: Magazine on naturopathy.
Language(s): German
ADVERTISING RATES:
Full Page Mono .... EUR 1620
Full Page Colour .... EUR 2700
Mechanical Data: Type Area: 260 x 185 mm, No. of Columns (Display): 3, Col Widths (Display): 59 mm
Copy instructions: *Copy Date:* 18 days prior to publication
Official Journal of: Organ d. Union biolog. Krebstherapie (UBK) e.V.
BUSINESS: HEALTH & MEDICAL

HPR HESSISCHE POLIZEIRUNDSCHAU 730201G32F-280
Editorial: Friedrich-Ebert-Allee 12, 65185 WIESBADEN **Tel:** 611 3531546 **Fax:** 611 3531608
Email: b.heib@hmdi.hessen.de **Web site:** http://www.hmdi.hessen.de
Freq: 10 issues yearly; Free to qualifying individuals
Annual Sub.: EUR 13,50; **Circ:** 9,400
Editor: Michael Bußer
Profile: Magazine for the police force in Hessen.
Language(s): German
ADVERTISING RATES:
Full Page Mono .... EUR 1410
Full Page Colour .... EUR 2400
Mechanical Data: Type Area: 242 x 174 mm
BUSINESS: LOCAL GOVERNMENT, LEISURE & RECREATION: Police

HR PERFORMANCE 1626546G14A-9527
Editorial: Augustinusstr. 9d, 50226 FRECHEN
Tel: 2234 9661013 **Fax:** 2234 966109
Email: langecker@datakontext.com **Web site:** http://www.datakontext.com
Freq: 8 issues yearly; **Annual Sub.:** EUR 104,00; **Circ:** 4,000
Editor: Franz Langecker; **Advertising Manager:** Caroline Esser
Profile: HR Performance supports and assists staff and managment responsibles for the organization and optimization of human resources work. HR Performance is the magazine for (eHR) HR software, HR information and communication solutions, HR portals, e-learning, job boards, HR tools and HR interfaces. HR Performance offers practical examples and market overviews, provides help in investment decisions and provides information on the role and impact of IT and communication technologies on the human resources work. HR Performance reports current and most practical on applications, methods, techniques and solutions of the staff work and the computerized personnel management. HR Performance provides an overview of new developments and the current state of HR software and HR-IT developments. HR Performance introduces Web 2.0 applications, solutions and practical examples.
Language(s): German
ADVERTISING RATES:
Full Page Mono .... EUR 1575
Full Page Colour .... EUR 2757
Mechanical Data: Type Area: 244 x 186 mm, No. of Columns (Display): 3, Col Widths (Display): 58 mm
Copy instructions: *Copy Date:* 21 days prior to publication

HR SERVICES 730576G14F-18
Editorial: Augustinusstr. 9d, 50226 FRECHEN
Tel: 2234 9661013 **Fax:** 2234 966109
Email: langecker@datakontext.com **Web site:** http://www.datakontext.com/hrservices
Freq: 6 issues yearly; **Annual Sub.:** EUR 98,00; **Circ:** 9,000
Editor: Franz Langecker; **Advertising Manager:** Caroline Esser
Profile: Magazine focusing on human resources for business, contains information about market trends.
Language(s): German
Readership: Read by managers dealing with recruitment.
ADVERTISING RATES:
Full Page Mono .... EUR 2410
Full Page Colour .... EUR 4218
Mechanical Data: Type Area: 232 x 178 mm, No. of Columns (Display): 3, Col Widths (Display): 56 mm
Copy instructions: *Copy Date:* 30 days prior to publication
BUSINESS: COMMERCE, INDUSTRY & MANAGEMENT: Training & Recruitment

HS-WOCHE - AUSG. HEINSBERG 730588G72-5672
Editorial: Ferdinand-Clasen-Str. 21, 41812 ERKELENZ **Tel:** 2431 968618 **Fax:** 2431 81651
Email: redaktion@hs-woche.de **Web site:** http://www.hs-woche.de
Freq: Weekly; **Cover Price:** Free; **Circ:** 38,150
Editor: Ulrich C. Kronenberg; **Advertising Manager:** Günter Paffen
Profile: Advertising journal (house-to-house) concentrating on local stories.
Language(s): German
ADVERTISING RATES:
Full Page Mono .... EUR 3733
Full Page Colour .... EUR 4503
Mechanical Data: Type Area: 430 x 292 mm, No. of Columns (Display): 7, Col Widths (Display): 40 mm
Copy instructions: *Copy Date:* 2 days prior to publication
LOCAL NEWSPAPERS

HTM JOURNAL OF HEAT TREATMENT AND MATERIALS 730592G13-2360
Editorial: Badgasteiner Str. 3, 28359 BREMEN
Tel: 421 2185336 **Fax:** 421 2185333
Email: hohnloser@iwt-bremen.de **Web site:** http://www.htm-journal.de
Freq: 6 issues yearly; **Annual Sub.:** EUR 394,00; **Circ:** 1,556
Editor: Hans-Werner Zoch; **Advertising Manager:** Dietmar von der Au
Profile: HTM Journal of Heat Treatment and Materials is the periodical definitive standard publication for materials, heat treatment and manufacturing. Thanks to the publication of practical field reports and pioneering research contributions the HTM serves equally industrial manufacturing and the solution of scientific problems. Readers of HTM are experts dealing questions surrounding heat treatment, hardening technology and material science. For this target group HTM publishes, in every edition, pioneering research results and practical contributions about heat treatment facilities and methods, heat treatment process technology, structures and properties, material and component strength as well as coating technologies.
Language(s): German
ADVERTISING RATES:
Full Page Mono .... EUR 1860
Full Page Colour .... EUR 29400
Mechanical Data: Type Area: 250 x 175 mm, No. of Columns (Display): 4, Col Widths (Display): 41 mm
Official Journal of: Organ d. ArGe Wärmebehandlung u. Werkstofftechnik e.V.
BUSINESS: CHEMICALS

HUBERTUS VON HOHENLOHES 500 VERY SPECIAL HOTELS 1696612G89A-12170
Editorial: Knesebeckstr. 11, 10623 BERLIN
Tel: 30 30641410 **Fax:** 30 30641411
Email: office@guidesandmore.com **Web site:** http://www.veryspecialhotels.com
Freq: Annual; **Cover Price:** EUR 8,90; **Circ:** 132,000
Profile: Reviews of travel journalists, industry professionals and celebrities, and the Top 500 Hotels in the German speaking countries.The reader will find the best homes with innovative service and pampering ideas, evaluated according to the categories of Future, wellness, environment, Friendship and Gourmet. Facebook: http://www.facebook.com/HvH500Hotels Twitter. http://twitter.com/#!/HvH500Hotels.
Language(s): English; German; Russian
ADVERTISING RATES:
Full Page Mono .... EUR 4800
Full Page Colour .... EUR 4800
Mechanical Data: Type Area: 280 x 210 mm

HUDDLE 730603G75X-65
Editorial: Laubacher Str. 10, 14197 BERLIN
Tel: 30 82009339 **Fax:** 30 82009353
Email: huddle@huddle-verlag.de **Web site:** http://www.huddle-verlag.de
Freq: Weekly; **Annual Sub.:** EUR 110,00; **Circ:** 16,500
Editor: Michael Auerbach; **Advertising Manager:** Gregor Wittig
Profile: Magazine about American football in Germany and Europe, as well as reports from the U.S. over the NFL and college football.
Language(s): German
ADVERTISING RATES:
Full Page Mono .... EUR 990
Full Page Colour .... EUR 1490
Mechanical Data: Type Area: 274 x 190 mm, No. of Columns (Display): 4, Col Widths (Display): 43 mm
Copy instructions: *Copy Date:* 8 days prior to publication
CONSUMER: SPORT: Other Sport

DER HUND 730636G81B-5
Editorial: Wilhelmsaue 37, 10713 BERLIN
Tel: 30 46406210 **Fax:** 30 46406313
Email: derhund@bauernverlag.de **Web site:** http://www.derhund.de
Freq: Monthly; **Annual Sub.:** EUR 33,00; **Circ:** 30,237
Editor: Jördis Götz; **Advertising Manager:** Frank Middendorf
Profile: DER HUND is one of the oldest German-language magazines for dog lovers and is addressed to all lovers, breeders, exhibitors and dog athletes looking for useful first hand information and who want to be entertained on a high standard. Practical and scientifically sound DER HUND covers all fields of Canine knowledge: diet and nutrition, veterinary science, breeding, behavior research and education. In addition to the races and race dogs, the animal welfare and the human-dog relationship are thematically in the foreground. DER HUND is the dog magazine for those who want to be informed and want to be on the cutting edge of knowledge. DER HUND is alsodesired because of its extensive display part in which breeders and dog school addresses, holiday offers, products and services are published. In addition to the high professional standard, the level of entertainment and the wide range of topics and the service character of the journal will be particularly appreciated by the readers.
Language(s): German
ADVERTISING RATES:
Full Page Mono .... EUR 3074
Full Page Colour .... EUR 4929
Mechanical Data: Type Area: 265 x 188 mm, No. of Columns (Display): 4, Col Widths (Display): 44 mm
Copy instructions: *Copy Date:* 30 days prior to publication
CONSUMER: ANIMALS & PETS: Dogs

HUNDEWELT 730647G81B-7
Editorial: Monschauer Str. 2, 41068 MÖNCHENGLADBACH **Tel:** 2161 9463820
Fax: 2161 9463840
Email: redaktion@minervaverlag.de **Web site:** http://www.hunde-welt.de
Freq: Monthly; **Annual Sub.:** EUR 28,80; **Circ:** 81,500
Editor: Frank de la Motte
Profile: Magazine for dog owners, dog breeders and dog lovers. Every month, it informed all in color and modern design, on the absolute top issues around the dog. Well-known authors and recognized experts are a permanent base and provide the author readers of the magazine with a brand new insider information on a broad base of knowledge and discuss the latest pet medical and behavioral research approaches, as well as the optimal training methods. Target groups: dog owners in general, breeders, dog lovers.
Language(s): German
ADVERTISING RATES:
Full Page Mono .... EUR 2548
Full Page Colour .... EUR 4332
Mechanical Data: Type Area: 260 x 192 mm, No. of Columns (Display): 4, Col Widths (Display): 45 mm
CONSUMER: ANIMALS & PETS: Dogs

HUNDEWELT SPORT 719688G81B-1
Editorial: Monschauer Str. 2, 41068 MÖNCHENGLADBACH **Tel:** 2161 9463820
Fax: 2161 9463840
Email: redaktion@minervaverlag.de **Web site:** http://www.hundewelt-sport.de
Freq: 6 issues yearly; **Annual Sub.:** EUR 24,00; **Circ:** 12,500
Editor: Frank de la Motte
Profile: HundeWelt Sport is the only German-language periodical magazine for dog sports. The declared aim is to dog lovers the joy of sport with the dog to bring closer and get them excited about this. HundeWelt Sport is concerned with the agility sport but also with other dog sports such as flyball, obedience, DiscDogging, dog dancing, dog sports tournaments, dog sled sports, etc. Hence the HundeWelt Sport is the modern magazine for the dog sport. Even sports medicine topics are not neglected.
Language(s): German
Readership: Read by dog-owners.
ADVERTISING RATES:
Full Page Mono .... EUR 1456
Full Page Colour .... EUR 2476
Mechanical Data: Type Area: 260 x 192 mm
CONSUMER: ANIMALS & PETS: Dogs

HÜNFELDER ZEITUNG 730610G67B-7580
Editorial: Frankfurter Str. 8, 36043 FULDA
Tel: 661 280304 **Fax:** 661 280279
Email: redaktion@fuldaerzeitung.de **Web site:** http://www.fuldaerzeitung.de
Freq: 312 issues yearly; **Circ:** 7,556
Advertising Manager: Rudolf Lechner
Profile: Daily newspaper with regional news and a local sports section. Facebook: http://www.facebook.com/pages/Fuldaer-Zeitung/162547827109989.
Language(s): German
ADVERTISING RATES:
SCC .... EUR 34,40
Mechanical Data: Type Area: 432 x 280 mm, No. of Columns (Display): 6, Col Widths (Display): 45 mm
Copy instructions: *Copy Date:* 1 day prior to publication
REGIONAL DAILY & SUNDAY NEWSPAPERS: Regional Daily Newspapers

HUNSRÜCKER WOCHENSPIEGEL 730651G72-5692

Editorial: Johann-Trarbach-Str. 16, 55469 SIMMERN
Tel: 6761 950116 **Fax:** 6761 950120
Email: red-hunsrueck@sw-verlag.de **Web site:** http://www.wochenspiegellive.de
Freq: Weekly; **Cover Price:** Free; **Circ:** 28,544
Editor: Kai Brückner
Profile: Advertising journal (house-to-house) concentrating on local stories.
Language(s): German
ADVERTISING RATES:
Full Page Mono .... EUR 2860
Full Page Colour .... EUR 4004
Mechanical Data: Type Area: 430 x 290 mm, No. of Columns (Display): 7, Col Widths (Display): 38 mm
Copy instructions: *Copy Date:* 2 days prior to publication
LOCAL NEWSPAPERS

HÜRRIYET - DEUTSCHLANDAUSG. D. TÜRK. TAGESZTG. 1638944G90-4

Editorial: An der Brücke 20, 64546 MÖRFELDEN-WALLDORF **Tel:** 6105 327900 **Fax:** 6105 327999
Email: info@dogan-media.com **Web site:** http://www.hurriyet.de
Freq: 364 issues yearly; **Cover Price:** EUR 1,00; **Circ:** 39,231
Editor: Turgay Rasit
Profile: The Turkish daily newspaper Hürriyet has been in existence since 1965 and is an important component of the European media landscape. Its appears seven days a week and reaches the Turkish community in all over Europe with news from home and the region they live and work in. Democracy and laicism are core values of Hürriyet. Its independent journalism reflects the complete opinions of the Turkish community. The Turkish culture has been an integral component of the European culture for centuries and Hürriyet supports the full membership of Turkey in the EU. It therefore its supports for the rights of the Turkish community in Europe and encourages their integration. The newspaper consists of 28-30 pages with around 220 news articles and 120 visuals. It covers economy, politics, sports and culture in Turkish and caters to the needs of the Turkish first, second and the younger third generation in Germany and other parts of Europ. This Outlet offers RSS (Really Simple Syndication).
Language(s): Turkish
Mechanical Data: Type Area: 525 x 324 mm, No. of Columns (Display): 9, Col Widths (Display): 33 mm
Copy instructions: *Copy Date:* 4 days prior to publication
Supplement(s): Lezzet Dünyasi; Seninle
CONSUMER: ETHNIC

HUSUMER NACHRICHTEN 730659G67B-7600

Editorial: Nikolaistr. 7, 24937 FLENSBURG
Tel: 461 8080 **Fax:** 461 8081058
Email: redaktion@shz.de **Web site:** http://www.shz.de
Freq: 312 issues yearly; **Circ:** 21,688
Advertising Manager: Ingeborg Schwarz
Profile: The "Husumer Nachrichten" were founded in 1873 by two book printers and in 1970 by Flensburger Zeitungsverlag accepted. The support is mainly in the southern part of the North Friesland, which also includes many islets and Pellworm disseminated. Facebook: http://www.facebook.com/shzonline Twitter: http://twitter.com/shz_de This Outlet offers RSS (Really Simple Syndication).
Language(s): German
ADVERTISING RATES:
SCC .... EUR 73,20
Mechanical Data: Type Area: 480 x 325 mm, No. of Columns (Display): 7, Col Widths (Display): 45 mm
Copy instructions: *Copy Date:* 1 day prior to publication
Supplement(s): nordisch gesund; Schleswig-Holstein Journal; tv magazin
REGIONAL DAILY & SUNDAY NEWSPAPERS: Regional Daily Newspapers

HUXARIA EXTRA 730663G72-5724

Editorial: Westerbachstr. 22, 37671 HÖXTER
Tel: 5271 972871 **Fax:** 5271 972872
Email: panorama@westfalen-blatt.de **Web site:** http://www.westfalen-blatt.de
Freq: Weekly; **Cover Price:** Free; **Circ:** 30,900
Editor: André Best; **Advertising Manager:** Gabriele Förster
Profile: Advertising journal (house-to-house) concentrating on local stories.
Language(s): German
ADVERTISING RATES:
Full Page Mono .... EUR 1696
Full Page Colour .... EUR 2464
Mechanical Data: Type Area: 320 x 228 mm, No. of Columns (Display): 5, Col Widths (Display): 44 mm
Copy instructions: *Copy Date:* 2 days prior to publication
LOCAL NEWSPAPERS

HV MAGAZIN 1837450G14A-10163

Editorial: Hofmannstr. 7a, 81379 MÜNCHEN
Tel: 89 200033913 **Fax:** 89 200033939
Email: redaktion@hv-magazin.de **Web site:** http://www.hv-magazin.de
Freq: 6 issues yearly; **Annual Sub.:** EUR 48,00; **Circ:** 2,500
Editor: Daniela Gebauer
Profile: Issues and trends around the Annual General Meeting.
Language(s): German
ADVERTISING RATES:
Full Page Mono .... EUR 2200
Full Page Colour .... EUR 2200
Mechanical Data: Type Area: 272 x 185 mm, No. of Columns (Display): 3, Col Widths (Display): 59 mm
Copy instructions: *Copy Date:* 11 days prior to publication

HYGIENE REPORT 738448G22R-53

Editorial: Blumenstr. 15, 90402 NÜRNBERG
Tel: 911 2018230 **Fax:** 911 2018100
Email: koenig@harnisch.com **Web site:** http://www.harnisch.com
Freq: 5 issues yearly; **Annual Sub.:** EUR 32,10; **Circ:** 17,712
Editor: Armin König; **Advertising Manager:** Armin König
Profile: Magazine focusing on quality protection in the food and drink industry.
Language(s): German
ADVERTISING RATES:
Full Page Mono .... EUR 3345
Full Page Colour .... EUR 4695
Mechanical Data: Type Area: 256 x 190 mm, No. of Columns (Display): 3, Col Widths (Display): 60 mm
Copy instructions: *Copy Date:* 30 days prior to publication
BUSINESS: FOOD: Food Related

HYGIENE + MEDIZIN 730676G56C-25_50

Editorial: Marktplatz 13, 65183 WIESBADEN
Tel: 611 5059333 **Fax:** 611 5059311
Email: hygmed@mhp-verlag.de **Web site:** http://www.mhp-verlag.de
Freq: 10 issues yearly; Free to qualifying individuals
Annual Sub.: EUR 89,90; **Circ:** 3,895
Editor: Petra Plößer; **Advertising Manager:** Walter Bockemühl
Profile: Hygiene & Medizin is the leading scientific journal in the field of hospital hygiene and infection prevention in Germany. For more than 30 years it has been a standard reference for all who are responsible for the organization and implementation of hygiene measures to protect patients, staff and the environment. The wide variety of articles to professional hygiene management promoted, facilitated the dialogue between science and industry practice and quality assurance will become more transparent. Also, current health policy issues are handled. The focal points - Clinical and technical hygiene - Prevention of nosocomial infections - Management of multi-resistant pathogens - Surveillance - Efficacy testing of disinfectants and antiseptics - Hygienic safety of medical devices - Public health services.
Language(s): English; German
Readership: Read by hospital anaesthetists, intensive care staff, pharmacists and general practitioners.
ADVERTISING RATES:
Full Page Mono .... EUR 1975
Full Page Colour .... EUR 3090
Mechanical Data: Type Area: 273 x 179 mm, No. of Columns (Display): 3, Col Widths (Display): 57 mm
Copy instructions: *Copy Date:* 14 days prior to publication
Official Journal of: Organ d. Arbeitskreises Krankenhaus- u. Praxishygiene d. AWMF, d. Dt. Ges. f. Krankenhaushygiene u. d. Verbundes f. Angewandte Hygiene e.V.
BUSINESS: HEALTH & MEDICAL: Hospitals

HZ HAUSRAT-ZEITUNG HAUSHALT & ELEKTRO 729814G52C-20

Editorial: Eichendorffstr. 3, 40474 DÜSSELDORF
Tel: 211 4705066 **Fax:** 211 4705064
Email: ez.hz@gmx.de **Web site:** http://www.ez-hz.de
Freq: 6 issues yearly; **Annual Sub.:** EUR 36,00; **Circ:** 4,065
Editor: Achim Mecklenbeck; **Advertising Manager:** Ulrich Wrobel
Profile: Newspaper for the housewares trade including glass, porcelain and cutlery.
Language(s): German
ADVERTISING RATES:
Full Page Mono .... EUR 2350
Full Page Colour .... EUR 4047
Mechanical Data: Type Area: 259 x 175 mm, No. of Columns (Display): 3, Col Widths (Display): 55 mm
Copy instructions: *Copy Date:* 12 days prior to publication
Official Journal of: Organ d. Zentralverb. Hartwarenhandel e.V.
BUSINESS: GIFT TRADE: Fancy Goods

HZ HERSFELDER ZEITUNG 730684G67B-7640

Editorial: Gutenbergstr. 1, 36251 BAD HERSFELD
Tel: 6621 1610 **Fax:** 6621 161148
Email: redaktion@hersfelder-zeitung.de **Web site:** http://www.hersfelder-zeitung.de
Freq: 312 issues yearly; **Circ:** 14,559
Editor: Kai A. Struthoff; **Advertising Manager:** Markus Pfromm
Profile: Daily newspaper with regional news and a local sports section. This Outlet offers RSS (Really Simple Syndication).
Language(s): German
ADVERTISING RATES:
SCC .... EUR 32,80
Mechanical Data: Type Area: 430 x 285 mm, No. of Columns (Display): 6, Col Widths (Display): 45 mm
Copy instructions: *Copy Date:* 1 day prior to publication
REGIONAL DAILY & SUNDAY NEWSPAPERS: Regional Daily Newspapers

HZWEI 730685G58-760

Editorial: Gartenweg 5, 16727 OBERKRÄMER
Tel: 33055 21322 **Fax:** 33055 21320
Email: geitmann@hydrogeit.de **Web site:** http://www.hzwei.info
Freq: Quarterly; **Annual Sub.:** EUR 25,00; **Circ:** 4,200
Editor: Sven Geitmann; **Advertising Manager:** Barbara Makowka
Profile: Magazine about hydrogen and fuel cells.
Language(s): German
ADVERTISING RATES:
Full Page Mono .... EUR 2290
Full Page Colour .... EUR 2790
Mechanical Data: Type Area: 265 x 175 mm, No. of Columns (Display): 3, Col Widths (Display): 55 mm
Copy instructions: *Copy Date:* 30 days prior to publication

I. PROGRAMM FÜR MÜNCHEN & BAYERN 733163G76D-2880

Editorial: Agnes-Bernauer-Str. 129, 80687 MÜNCHEN **Tel:** 89 69365657 **Fax:** 89 69365656
Email: info@ipunkt.net **Web site:** http://www.ipunkt.net
Freq: Monthly; **Cover Price:** Free; **Circ:** 28,165
Editor: Gernot Schnedlitz; **Advertising Manager:** Gernot Schnedlitz
Profile: Monthly program for Munich and Bavaria, with all the major events in the region.
Language(s): German
Readership: Aimed at music enthusiasts.
ADVERTISING RATES:
Full Page Colour .... EUR 950
Mechanical Data: No. of Columns (Display): 2, Col Widths (Display): 43 mm
Copy instructions: *Copy Date:* 20 days prior to publication
Supplement to: Applaus
CONSUMER: MUSIC & PERFORMING ARTS: Music

IAB FORUM 1752882G14A-9904

Editorial: Regensburger Str. 104, 90478 NÜRNBERG
Tel: 911 1790 **Fax:** 911 1798418
Email: iab.wmk@iab.de **Web site:** http://www.iab.de
Freq: Half-yearly; **Annual Sub.:** EUR 10,90; **Circ:** 5,000
Editor: Andrea Kargus
Profile: Magazine about the employment market and occupational research.
Language(s): German

IAS IMPULSE 1895223G14A-10278

Editorial: Steinhäuserstr. 19, 76135 KARLSRUHE
Tel: 721 82040 **Fax:** 721 8204400
Email: service@ias-stiftung.de **Web site:** http://www.ias-stiftung.de
Freq: Quarterly; Free to qualifying individuals
Annual Sub.: EUR 10,00; **Circ:** 10,000
Editor: Dirk-Matthias Rose
Profile: Magazine for company doctors and company security guards.
Language(s): German

IBBENBÜRENER VOLKSZEITUNG 730729G67B-7660

Editorial: Wilhelmstr. 240, 49475 IBBENBÜREN
Tel: 5451 933242 **Fax:** 5451 933192
Email: redaktion@ivz-online.de **Web site:** http://www.ivz-online.de
Freq: 312 issues yearly; **Circ:** 20,717
Advertising Manager: Ralf Eickenbusch
Profile: Daily newspaper with regional news and a local sports section. Facebook: http://de-de.facebook.com/people/Ibbenburener-Volkszeitung/100000415063949 Twitter: http://twitter.com/ivzonline This Outlet offers RSS (Really Simple Syndication).
Language(s): German
ADVERTISING RATES:
SCC .... EUR 49,80
Mechanical Data: Type Area: 488 x 323 mm, No. of Columns (Display): 7, Col Widths (Display): 43 mm
Copy instructions: *Copy Date:* 1 day prior to publication
Supplement(s): prisma
REGIONAL DAILY & SUNDAY NEWSPAPERS: Regional Daily Newspapers

IBN 730734G91A-50

Editorial: Malvine-Schiesser-Weg 3, 78315 RADOLFZELL **Tel:** 7732 96061 **Fax:** 7732 96062
Email: ibn@ibn-online.de **Web site:** http://www.ibn-online.de
Freq: Monthly; **Annual Sub.:** EUR 58,00; **Circ:** 7,500
Editor: Hans-Dieter Möhlhenrich; **Advertising Manager:** Klaus Jetter
Profile: Journal covering charter and power cruisers, sailing dinghies, yachts and sportsboats. Also features products for boats.
Language(s): German
Readership: Aimed at people who sail on Lake Constance.
ADVERTISING RATES:
Full Page Mono .... EUR 1341
Full Page Colour .... EUR 1641
Mechanical Data: Type Area: 265 x 190 mm, No. of Columns (Display): 4, Col Widths (Display): 43 mm
Copy instructions: *Copy Date:* 21 days prior to publication
CONSUMER: RECREATION & LEISURE: Boating & Yachting

IBUSINESS EXECUTIVE SUMMARY 730740G5F-5

Editorial: Wilhelm-Riehl-Str. 13, 80687 MÜNCHEN
Tel: 89 5783870 **Fax:** 89 57838799
Email: redaktion@ibusiness.de **Web site:** http://www.ibusiness.de
Freq: 20 issues yearly; Free to qualifying individuals
Annual Sub.: EUR 290,00; **Circ:** 4,300
Editor: Joachim Graf; **Advertising Manager:** Daniel Treplin
Profile: Magazine providing information about the Internet.
Language(s): German
ADVERTISING RATES:
Full Page Colour .... EUR 1690
Mechanical Data: Type Area: 240 x 195 mm, No. of Columns (Display): 2
Copy instructions: *Copy Date:* 7 days prior to publication
Supplement(s): iBusiness Dossier
BUSINESS: COMPUTERS & AUTOMATION: Multimedia

ICJ MICE MAGAZINE 730984G2A-122

Editorial: Keltenring 22, 85658 EGMATING
Tel: 8095 87260 **Fax:** 8095 872629
Email: ec@icj-mm.de **Web site:** http://www.icj-mm.de
Freq: Quarterly; **Annual Sub.:** EUR 26,75; **Circ:** 16,504
Editor: Gerald W. Huft; **Advertising Manager:** Ivo Baumann
Profile: Magazine about motivation-meetings, incentives, meetings, congresses and events.
Language(s): German
ADVERTISING RATES:
Full Page Colour .... EUR 5590
Mechanical Data: Type Area: 265 x 190 mm, No. of Columns (Display): 3, Col Widths (Display): 60 mm
Copy instructions: *Copy Date:* 30 days prior to publication
BUSINESS: COMMUNICATIONS, ADVERTISING & MARKETING

ICON 1793886G65B-2_102

Editorial: Axel-Springer-Str. 65, 10888 BERLIN
Tel: 30 259171903 **Fax:** 30 259171910
Email: icon@wams.de **Web site:** http://www.welt.de
Freq: 6 issues yearly; **Circ:** 550,000
Editor: Inga Griese; **Advertising Manager:** Philipp Zwez
Profile: ICON is the award-winning style magazine of "Welt am Sonntag", that bi-monthly transfers the competence of the international Sunday newspaper in a magazine format. ICON offers its readers the best of both worlds: the great look of an oversize page layout and the quality of journalistic opinion-leading authors of the WELT- group. ICON provides a selection of topics from fashion, jewelry, beauty, travel and changing further subjects. Distinctive the journalistic style, elegance and humor in the word again and again combined with bold and surprising optics. Fashion shoots are presented with detailed travel experiences, prominent authors provide insights into their personal lifestyle world and international illustrators appreciate the large stage of the magazine. Exclusivity and extravagance at its best form the basis for the inspirational reading experience. Facebook: http://www.facebook.com/weltonline Twitter: http://twitter.com/weltonline This Outlet offers RSS (Really Simple Syndication).
Language(s): German
ADVERTISING RATES:
Full Page Mono .... EUR 20960
Full Page Colour .... EUR 20960
Mechanical Data: Type Area: 365 x 260 mm, No. of Columns (Display): 5, Col Widths (Display): 52 mm
Copy instructions: *Copy Date:* 30 days prior to publication
Supplement to: Welt am Sonntag
NATIONAL DAILY & SUNDAY NEWSPAPERS: GB-Unabhängigkeits-MdEP

IDAR-OBERSTEINER WOCHENSPIEGEL 730756G72-5748

Editorial: Hauptstr. 61, 55743 IDAR-OBERSTEIN
Tel: 6781 947719 **Fax:** 6781 947777
Email: red-idaroberstein@sw-verlag.de **Web site:** http://www.wochenspiegellive.de
Freq: Weekly; **Cover Price:** Free; **Circ:** 39,052
Editor: Kai Brückner
Profile: Advertising journal (house-to-house) concentrating on local stories.
Language(s): German
ADVERTISING RATES:
Full Page Mono .... EUR 3612
Full Page Colour .... EUR 5057
Mechanical Data: Type Area: 430 x 290 mm, No. of Columns (Display): 7, Col Widths (Display): 38 mm
Copy instructions: *Copy Date:* 2 days prior to publication
LOCAL NEWSPAPERS

IDEA ONLINE
1621486G87-13534
Editorial: Steinbühlstr. 3, 35578 WETZLAR
Tel: 6441 9150 **Fax:** 6441 915118
Email: idea@idea.de **Web site:** http://www.idea.de
Freq: Daily; **Cover Price:** Paid; **Circ:** 117,512 Unique Users
Editor: Helmut Matthies
Language(s): German
CONSUMER: RELIGIOUS

IDEA SPEKTRUM
730762G87-5900
Editorial: Steinbühlstr. 3, 35578 WETZLAR
Tel: 6441 9150 **Fax:** 6441 915118
Email: idea@idea.de **Web site:** http://www.idea.de
Freq: Weekly; **Annual Sub.:** EUR 99,60; **Circ:** 31,649
Editor: Helmut Matthies
Profile: Evangelical magazine.
Language(s): German
ADVERTISING RATES:
Full Page Mono .... EUR 1760
Full Page Colour .... EUR 2543
Mechanical Data: Type Area: 259 x 194 mm, No. of Columns (Display): 4, Col Widths (Display): 45 mm
Copy instructions: *Copy Date:* 6 days prior to publication
Supplement(s): idea Spektrum Spezial
CONSUMER: RELIGIOUS

IDEENMANAGEMENT
730770G14A-3220
Editorial: Friedrichstr. 10, 60327 FRANKFURT
Tel: 69 9716523 **Fax:** 69 9716525
Email: sarah.dittrich@dib.de **Web site:** http://www.ideenmanagementdigital.info
Freq: Quarterly; **Annual Sub.:** EUR 42,45; **Circ:** 1,200
Editor: Sarah Dittrich; **Advertising Manager:** Peter Taprogge
Profile: Magazine on employee suggestions in business and administration.
Language(s): German
ADVERTISING RATES:
Full Page Mono .... EUR 1260
Full Page Colour .... EUR 2160
Mechanical Data: Type Area: 254 x 185 mm

IDSTEINER ZEITUNG
730783G67B-7680
Editorial: Langgasse 21, 65183 WIESBADEN
Tel: 611 3490 **Fax:** 611 3492233
Freq: 260 issues yearly; **Circ:** 63,127
Advertising Manager: Gerhard Müller
Profile: Regional daily newspaper with news on politics, economy, culture, sports, travel, technology, etc. The Idsteiner Zeitung is a local issue of the Wiesbadener Tagblatt.
Language(s): German
ADVERTISING RATES:
SCC .... EUR 143,20
Mechanical Data: Type Area: 480 x 325 mm, No. of Columns (Display): 7, Col Widths (Display): 45 mm
Copy instructions: *Copy Date:* 1 day prior to publication
Supplement(s): Idsteiner anzeiger
REGIONAL DAILY & SUNDAY NEWSPAPERS: Regional Daily Newspapers

IDW FACHNACHRICHTEN
730784G1A-1300
Editorial: Tersteegenstr. 14, 40474 DÜSSELDORF
Tel: 211 4561105 **Fax:** 211 4561204
Email: schrage@idw.de **Web site:** http://www.idw.de
Freq: Monthly; **Circ:** 22,000
Editor: Cornelia Schrage
Profile: Content: results of work of professional bodies national and international (statements or entries). Reporting on further discussion by the statute-making bodies. Current, for the daily work of the auditor important business law, tax, legal and professional developments and decisions from outside sources (legislation / law / administrative instructions). Education and training and other services. Audience: IDW members and at the request of their employees and CPA exam candidates (limited).
Language(s): German
Copy instructions: *Copy Date:* 14 days prior to publication

IEE
730785G18A-127_60
Editorial: Im Weiher 10, 69121 HEIDELBERG
Tel: 6221 489308 **Fax:** 6221 489482
Email: harald.wollstadt@huethig.de **Web site:** http://www.all-electronics.de
Freq: 10 issues yearly; **Annual Sub.:** EUR 179,00; **Circ:** 26,170
Editor: Harald Wollstadt; **Advertising Manager:** Anja Breuer
Profile: IEE is the practical and solution-oriented magazine for the electrical automation and drive technology. The editorial of topics covering the entire automation pyramid from the guidance and control to the field level off. Independently researched and thorough article make the IEE to the information source for automation professionals in all industries. Thus speaks the modern and attractive magazine at just the investment decision-makers in the machine and plant construction, and project and departmental management in automation.
Language(s): German
Readership: Read by engineers and professionals in the electronics sector.
ADVERTISING RATES:
Full Page Mono .... EUR 4958
Full Page Colour .... EUR 6033
Mechanical Data: Type Area: 257 x 178 mm, No. of Columns (Display): 4, Col Widths (Display): 41 mm
Copy instructions: *Copy Date:* 28 days prior to publication
BUSINESS: ELECTRONICS

IF
1660097G40-972
Editorial: Kurt-Schumacher-Damm 41, 13405 BERLIN **Tel:** 30 49813523 **Fax:** 30 49813525
Email: norbertstaeblein@bundeswehr.org **Web site:** http://www.if-zeitschrift.de
Freq: Quarterly; **Circ:** 53,000
Editor: Norbert Stäblein
Profile: Magazine informs on behalf of the Inspector General of the Bundeswehr on principles of leadership development and its applications. At the same time if provide insights into fundamental questions of military service in a changing world. The Bundeswehr is in a permanent process of transformation. This also leads to increased placement and debate was needed on issues of leadership development. The journal aims to provide with as discursive content, but the officers orientations to profile for their professional self-understanding and strengthen their ethical discernment can. The focus of the editorial program, the basic questions of military service are in the context of the transformation of societies in an era of globalization.
Language(s): German

IFFOCUS
1837551G19E-1945
Editorial: Sandtorstr. 22, 39106 MAGDEBURG
Tel: 391 4090446 **Fax:** 391 4090596
Email: presse@iff.fraunhofer.de **Web site:** http://www.iff.fraunhofer.de
Freq: Half-yearly; **Cover Price:** Free; **Circ:** 4,500
Editor: Anna-Kristina Wassilew
Profile: Magazine with news and articles about research and current events at the Fraunhofer IFF.
Language(s): English; German

IG BCE KOMPAKT
734634G14L-6830
Editorial: Königsworther Platz 6, 30167 HANNOVER
Tel: 511 7631329 **Fax:** 511 7000891
Email: kompakt@igbce.de **Web site:** http://www.igbce.de
Freq: 11 issues yearly; Free to qualifying individuals
Annual Sub.: EUR 10,00; **Circ:** 664,247
Editor: Christian Hülsmeier
Profile: Magazine of the trade union for mining, chemistry and energy. Twitter: http://twitter.com/igbce This Outlet offers RSS (Really Simple Syndication).
Language(s): German
ADVERTISING RATES:
Full Page Mono .... EUR 10000
Full Page Colour .... EUR 10000
Mechanical Data: Type Area: 268 x 185 mm, No. of Columns (Display): 4, Col Widths (Display): 45 mm
Copy instructions: *Copy Date:* 28 days prior to publication
BUSINESS: COMMERCE, INDUSTRY & MANAGEMENT: Trade Unions

IGM DIREKT
1799874G27-3038
Editorial: Wilhelm-Leuschner-Str. 79, 60329 FRANKFURT **Tel:** 69 66932633 **Fax:** 69 66932002
Email: direkt@igmetall.de **Web site:** http://www.igmetall.de
Freq: 22 issues yearly; **Circ:** 150,000
Editor: Susanne Rohmund
Profile: Facebook: http://de-de.facebook.com/pages/IG-Metall/249296718436.
Language(s): German
ADVERTISING RATES:
Full Page Mono .... EUR 6390
Full Page Colour .... EUR 6390
Mechanical Data: No. of Columns (Display): 4, Col Widths (Display): 40 mm, Type Area: 260 x 185 mm
Copy instructions: *Copy Date:* 30 days prior to publication

IGM DIREKT
1799874G27-3118
Editorial: Wilhelm-Leuschner-Str. 79, 60329 FRANKFURT **Tel:** 69 66932633 **Fax:** 69 66932002
Email: direkt@igmetall.de **Web site:** http://www.igmetall.de
Freq: 22 issues yearly; **Circ:** 150,000
Editor: Susanne Rohmund
Profile: Facebook: http://de-de.facebook.com/pages/IG-Metall/249296718436.
Language(s): German
ADVERTISING RATES:
Full Page Mono .... EUR 6390
Full Page Colour .... EUR 6390
Mechanical Data: No. of Columns (Display): 4, Col Widths (Display): 40 mm, Type Area: 260 x 185 mm
Copy instructions: *Copy Date:* 30 days prior to publication

IHK JOURNAL KOBLENZ
730814G63-320
Editorial: Schlossstr. 2, 56068 KOBLENZ
Tel: 261 106217 **Fax:** 261 106105
Email: sauerborn@koblenz.ihk.de **Web site:** http://www.ihk-koblenz.de
Freq: 11 issues yearly; Free to qualifying individuals
Annual Sub.: EUR 25,50; **Circ:** 47,791
Editor: Judith Sauerborn; **Advertising Manager:** Jürgen Schirra
Profile: Regional business magazine published by the Chamber of Trade and Industry in Koblenz.
Language(s): German
ADVERTISING RATES:
Full Page Mono .... EUR 4099
Full Page Colour .... EUR 5335
Mechanical Data: Type Area: 265 x 185 mm, No. of Columns (Display): 4, Col Widths (Display): 43 mm
Copy instructions: *Copy Date:* 20 days prior to publication
BUSINESS: REGIONAL BUSINESS

IHK MAGAZIN
732364G63-520
Editorial: Nordwall 39, 47798 KREFELD
Tel: 2151 635355 **Fax:** 2151 635319
Email: ludewig@krefeld.ihk.de **Web site:** http://www.mittlerer-niederrhein.ihk.de
Freq: Monthly; Free to qualifying individuals
Annual Sub.: EUR 23,00; **Circ:** 59,393
Editor: Joachim Ludewig; **Advertising Manager:** Iris Domann
Profile: The ,,IHK magazin'' is the official journal of Chamber of Industry and Commerce for Krefeld, Viersen, Neuss and Mönchengladbach. The official notice of institution is designed as a regional business magazine and contains valuable information and tips, and news and reports, especially from medium-sized enterprises. The ,,IHK magazin'' is aimed at all commercial enterprises of the District of the Chamber of Commerce (with the exception of the traditional crafts) and also by subscription to companies in the neighboring regions. The ,,IHK magazin'' achieved in this area everywhere large enterprises, medium-sized enterprises and individual entrepreneurs, and without any wastage. The number of such readers is made up of owners, managers and board members and executives. This readership is characterized by high living and education standard and entrepreneurial interest.
Language(s): German
Readership: Read by entrepreneurs and decision makers in economics.
ADVERTISING RATES:
Full Page Mono .... EUR 2976
Full Page Colour .... EUR 3984
Mechanical Data: Type Area: 253 x 188 mm, No. of Columns (Display): 4, Col Widths (Display): 44 mm
Copy instructions: *Copy Date:* 28 days prior to publication
BUSINESS: REGIONAL BUSINESS

IHK MAGAZIN NORDSCHWARZWALD
731147G63-460
Editorial: Dr.-Brandenburg-Str. 6, 75173 PFORZHEIM **Tel:** 7231 201151 **Fax:** 7231 201158
Email: service@pforzheim.ihk.de **Web site:** http://www.nordschwarzwald.ihk24.de
Freq: 10 issues yearly; Free to qualifying individuals
Annual Sub.: EUR 24,54; **Circ:** 23,106
Editor: Jens Mühleisen; **Advertising Manager:** Barbara Rosenberger
Profile: Publication of the Chamber of Trade and Industry for Nordschwarzwald Pforzheim.
Language(s): German
ADVERTISING RATES:
Full Page Mono .... EUR 2368
Full Page Colour .... EUR 2960
Mechanical Data: Type Area: 250 x 185 mm, No. of Columns (Display): 4, Col Widths (Display): 43 mm
Copy instructions: *Copy Date:* 28 days prior to publication
BUSINESS: REGIONAL BUSINESS

IHK MAGAZIN RHEIN-NECKAR
747745G63-1640
Editorial: L 1, 2, 68161 MANNHEIM
Tel: 621 1709210 **Fax:** 621 1709102
Email: andrea.kiefer@rhein-neckar.ihk24.de **Web site:** http://www.rhein-neckar.ihk24.de
Freq: 11 issues yearly; Free to qualifying individuals
Annual Sub.: EUR 30,00; **Circ:** 22,710
Editor: Andrea Kiefer; **Advertising Manager:** Achim Hartkopf
Profile: The IHK magazin Rhein-Neckar is a regional business magazine for the cities of Mannheim and Heidelberg and the Rhein-Neckar-Kreis and the Neckar Odenwald-Kreis and informed about taxes, finance, law, foreign trade, transport, industry / innovation, education and training, employment and social affairs, environment, trade shows and business and industries in the region. Because of its regional editorial focus is the IHK Rhein-Neckar-magazine the obvious reading for the middle class from the region with high reader loyalty Journal. Target group: The readers are entrepreneurs and executives from industry, trade, services and transport. They are owners, officers, directors and executives - that the first and second Management level in companies.
Language(s): German
ADVERTISING RATES:
Full Page Mono .... EUR 3088
Full Page Colour .... EUR 3440
Mechanical Data: Type Area: 250 x 185 mm, No. of Columns (Display): 4, Col Widths (Display): 43 mm
Copy instructions: *Copy Date:* 27 days prior to publication
BUSINESS: REGIONAL BUSINESS

IHK MAGAZIN WIRTSCHAFT
756060G63-1702
Editorial: Jägerstr. 30, 70174 STUTTGART
Tel: 711 2005273 **Fax:** 711 2005327
Email: bernd.engelhardt@stuttgart.ihk.de **Web site:** http://www.stuttgart.ihk.de
Freq: 11 issues yearly; Free to qualifying individuals
Annual Sub.: EUR 25,00; **Circ:** 81,459
Editor: Bernd Engelhardt
Profile: The magazine of the Chamber of Commerce and Industry Region Stuttgart editorial positions itself as a regional business magazine, the reader responds with corporate responsibility. In addition to a journalist prepared message part and a cover story with a regional edition contains any comprehensive, specific, clearly structured, non-cash property, information for business practice. The topics cover the full spectrum of CCI's work.
Language(s): German
ADVERTISING RATES:
Full Page Mono .... EUR 5200
Full Page Colour .... EUR 7900
Mechanical Data: Type Area: 245 x 184 mm, No. of Columns (Display): 3, Col Widths (Display): 58 mm
Copy instructions: *Copy Date:* 25 days prior to publication
Supplement(s): B4B Mittelstand
BUSINESS: REGIONAL BUSINESS

IHK PLUS
734923G63-560
Editorial: Unter Sachsenhausen 10, 50667 KÖLN
Tel: 221 1640161 **Fax:** 221 1640169
Email: presse@koeln.ihk.de **Web site:** http://www.ihk-koeln.de
Freq: 10 issues yearly; Free to qualifying individuals
Annual Sub.: EUR 15,00; **Circ:** 136,780
Editor: Arnd Klein-Zirbes; **Advertising Manager:** Lars Lehmanski
Profile: Publication featuring economics news from the Chamber of Trade and Industry for the region of Cologne. Facebook: http://www.facebook.com/pages/IHK-Köln/119872641404344 Xing: http://www.xing.com/net/ihkkoeln/ This Outlet offers RSS (Really Simple Syndication).
Language(s): German
Readership: Read by economics and marketing managers.
ADVERTISING RATES:
Full Page Mono .... EUR 5365
Full Page Colour .... EUR 9340
Mechanical Data: Type Area: 274 x 185 mm, No. of Columns (Display): 4, Col Widths (Display): 43 mm
Copy instructions: *Copy Date:* 34 days prior to publication
BUSINESS: REGIONAL BUSINESS

IHK WIRTSCHAFT
730811G63-300
Editorial: Brabandtstr. 11, 38100 BRAUNSCHWEIG
Tel: 531 4715209 **Fax:** 531 4715298
Email: jochen.hotop@braunschweig.ihk.de **Web site:** http://www.braunschweig.ihk.de
Freq: Monthly; Free to qualifying individuals
Annual Sub.: EUR 19,00; **Circ:** 18,097
Editor: Jochen Hotop; **Advertising Manager:** Marianne Schack
Profile: Publication of the Chamber of Trade and Industry in Braunschweig.
Language(s): German
ADVERTISING RATES:
Full Page Mono .... EUR 2650
Full Page Colour .... EUR 3850
Mechanical Data: Type Area: 260 x 185 mm, No. of Columns (Display): 3, Col Widths (Display): 58 mm
Supplement(s): kulturmagazin transparent
BUSINESS: REGIONAL BUSINESS

IHK WIRTSCHAFT AN STROM UND MEER
747579G63-1080
Editorial: Friedrich-Ebert-Str. 6, 27570 BREMERHAVEN **Tel:** 471 9246027 **Fax:** 471 9246090
Email: kaden@bremerhaven.ihk.de **Web site:** http://www.bremerhaven.ihk.de
Freq: 10 issues yearly; Free to qualifying individuals
Annual Sub.: EUR 17,00; **Circ:** 4,637
Editor: Michael Stark; **Advertising Manager:** Gabriele Husmann
Profile: Journal of the Bremerhaven Chamber of Trade and Industry.
Language(s): German
ADVERTISING RATES:
Full Page Mono .... EUR 1035
Full Page Colour .... EUR 1812
Mechanical Data: Type Area: 252 x 184 mm, No. of Columns (Display): 3, Col Widths (Display): 58 mm
Copy instructions: *Copy Date:* 30 days prior to publication
Supplement(s): bls aktuell
BUSINESS: REGIONAL BUSINESS

IHK WIRTSCHAFT IM REVIER
747584G63-1140
Editorial: Ostring 30, 44787 BOCHUM
Tel: 234 91130 **Fax:** 234 9113110
Email: ihk@bochum.ihk.de **Web site:** http://www.bochum.ihk.de
Freq: 11 issues yearly; Free to qualifying individuals
Annual Sub.: EUR 24,50; **Circ:** 22,000
Editor: Christoph Burghaus; **Advertising Manager:** Monika Droege
Profile: Publication of the Bochum Chamber of Trade and Industry. It publishes the only economic and corporate reports from the region, informing them about environmental protection, new technology, transport, foreign trade, law, taxation and finance,

vocational education and training. Readership: 33,000 decision makers (owners, managers, executives) from industry, trade, services and transport.
Language(s): German
ADVERTISING RATES:
Full Page Mono .... EUR 2114
Full Page Colour .... EUR 3461
Mechanical Data: Type Area: 257 x 186 mm, No. of Columns (Display): 4, Col Widths (Display): 42 mm
BUSINESS: REGIONAL BUSINESS

IHK WIRTSCHAFT IN DER TECHNOLOGIEREGION KARLSRUHE 730818G63-380
Editorial: Lammstr. 13, 76133 KARLSRUHE
Tel: 721 174126 **Fax:** 721 174115
Email: pressestelle@karlsruhe.ihk.de **Web site:** http://www.karlsruhe.ihk.de
Freq: 11 issues yearly; Free to qualifying individuals
Annual Sub.: EUR 15,34; **Circ:** 25,036
Editor: Michael Hölle; **Advertising Manager:** Barbara Rosenberger
Profile: Local business magazine from the Chamber of Trade and Industry for the region of Karlsruhe. It provides information on current topics and trends of regional economic activities and news from the corporate world, provides practical tips for everyday business and communications from the Chamber of Commerce released to their members. Because of its regional editorial line is the show the obvious must-read for the middle class with high leaf reader loyalty. The readers are entrepreneurs and executives from industry, trade, tourism, services and transport. They are owners, officers, directors and executives - that the first and second Management level in companies.
Language(s): German
Readership: Read by members of the local business community.
ADVERTISING RATES:
Full Page Mono .... EUR 2848
Full Page Colour .... EUR 3584
Mechanical Data: Type Area: 250 x 185 mm, No. of Columns (Display): 4, Col Widths (Display): 43 mm
Copy instructions: *Copy Date:* 27 days prior to publication
BUSINESS: REGIONAL BUSINESS

IHK WIRTSCHAFTSFORUM 730819G63-400
Editorial: Börsenplatz 4, 60313 FRANKFURT
Tel: 69 21971203 **Fax:** 69 21971488
Email: wirtschaftsforum@frankfurt-main.ihk.de **Web site:** http://www.frankfurt-main.ihk.de
Freq: 10 issues yearly; Free to qualifying individuals
Annual Sub.: EUR 30,00; **Circ:** 76,150
Editor: Petra Menke; **Advertising Manager:** Alexandra Lueg
Profile: Journal of the Frankfurt Chamber of Trade and Industry. The business magazine for the Region Frankfurt am Main inform the member companies of the Industry and Commerce of the regional economic activity.
Language(s): German
ADVERTISING RATES:
Full Page Mono .... EUR 4822
Full Page Colour .... EUR 7093
Mechanical Data: Type Area: 255 x 185 mm, No. of Columns (Display): 3, Col Widths (Display): 55 mm
Copy instructions: *Copy Date:* 20 days prior to publication
BUSINESS: REGIONAL BUSINESS

IHK-REPORT DARMSTADT RHEIN MAIN NECKAR 730816G63-340
Editorial: Rheinstr. 89, 64295 DARMSTADT
Tel: 6151 871280 **Fax:** 6151 871100280
Email: redaktion@darmstadt.ihk.de **Web site:** http://www.darmstadt.ihk24.de
Freq: 10 issues yearly; Free to qualifying individuals
Annual Sub.: EUR 32,00; **Circ:** 51,573
Editor: Uwe Vetterlein; **Advertising Manager:** Achim Hartkopf
Profile: The IHK Report is the regional business magazine of Industry and Commerce for the Darmstadt Darmstadt Rhein Main Neckar. The magazine is aimed at the management teams of companies in the districts of Darmstadt-Dieburg, Groß-Gerau, Bergstrasse, Odenwald and the city of Darmstadt. The economically strong metropolitan regions Rhein-Main and Rhein-Neckar partly belong to the area of distribution. The readers are CEOs of small and medium enterprises, medium-sized enterprises in industry, commerce and services as well as the management teams of international groups. There are also important political actors and research institutions. The IHK Report provides current information on legal and taxation, training, training market, industries and markets, innovation, technology, transport, promotion and support programs. The main topics indicate the economic of the future, analyze the central economic issues of the region and explain what creates all the CCI for its members. In addition to policy statements and recent opinions of the CCI, the magazine offers a summary of all important dates. at the Chamber.
Language(s): German
ADVERTISING RATES:
Full Page Mono .... EUR 4810
Full Page Colour .... EUR 4810
Mechanical Data: Type Area: 260 x 185 mm, No. of Columns (Display): 4, Col Widths (Display): 43 mm
Copy instructions: *Copy Date:* 20 days prior to publication
BUSINESS: REGIONAL BUSINESS

IHR INTERNATIONALES HANDELSRECHT 1640374G1A-3548
Editorial: Schaarsteinwegsbrücke 2, 20459 HAMBURG **Tel:** 40 37858811 **Fax:** 40 37858899
Email: herber@internationales-handelsrecht.net **Web site:** http://www.internationales-handelsrecht.net
Freq: 6 issues yearly; **Annual Sub.:** EUR 132,00; **Circ:** 1,000
Editor: Rolf Herber; **Advertising Manager:** Anja Urbanek
Profile: Magazine about international business law.
Language(s): English; German
ADVERTISING RATES:
Full Page Mono .... EUR 600
Full Page Colour .... EUR 1500
Mechanical Data: Type Area: 256 x 176 mm

IKEA FAMILY LIVE 1697212G94H-14932
Editorial: Am Wandersmann 2, 65719 HOFHEIM
Email: redaktion@ikeafamilylive.de **Web site:** http://www.ikeafamilylive.de
Freq: Quarterly; Free to qualifying individuals
Annual Sub.: EUR 6,00; **Circ:** 489,168
Editor: Patrick Mann
Language(s): German
ADVERTISING RATES:
Full Page Mono .... EUR 13250
Full Page Colour .... EUR 13250
Mechanical Data: Type Area: 240 x 195 mm
CONSUMER: OTHER CLASSIFICATIONS: Customer Magazines

IKZ HAUSTECHNIK 730854G3A-80
Editorial: Zur Feldmühle 9, 59821 ARNSBERG
Tel: 2931 890041 **Fax:** 2931 890048
Email: redaktion@strobel-verlag.de **Web site:** http://www.ikz.de
Freq: 22 issues yearly; Free to qualifying individuals
Annual Sub.: EUR 137,00; **Circ:** 33,640
Editor: Markus Sironi; **Advertising Manager:** Uwe Derr
Profile: The official journal of the Association of Plumbing Heating and Air HVAC informed of the exporting country's trade associations Professional in the same way as the master company imSHK buyers-wholesalers, architects and the HVAC industry. The IKZ-Haustechnik reaches the decision makers for plumbing, heating, ventilation, air conditioning, control, plumbing, solar and electrical engineering at all levels. Facebook: http://www.facebook.com/pages/IKZ-HAUSTECHNIK/371650650791 Twitter: http://twitter.com/#!/ikz_haustechnik This Outlet offers RSS (Really Simple Syndication).
Language(s): German
ADVERTISING RATES:
Full Page Mono .... EUR 5715
Full Page Colour .... EUR 6390
Mechanical Data: No. of Columns (Display): 4, Col Widths (Display): 43 mm, Type Area: 265 x 184 mm
Official Journal of: Organ d. Zentralverb. Sanitär, Heizung, Klima u. v. Fachverbänden Sanitär, Heizung, Klima u. Klempnerei
BUSINESS: HEATING & VENTILATION: Domestic Heating & Ventilation

IKZ PRAXIS 730855G3A-82
Editorial: Zur Feldmühle 9, 59821 ARNSBERG
Tel: 2931 890040 **Fax:** 2931 890048
Email: redaktion@strobel-verlag.de **Web site:** http://www.ikz-praxis.de
Freq: Monthly; **Annual Sub.:** EUR 36,50; **Circ:** 12,500
Editor: Detlev Knecht; **Advertising Manager:** Uwe Derr
Profile: Journal focusing on heating, air treatment and plumbing. Facebook: http://www.facebook.com/pages/IKZ-HAUSTECHNIK/371650650791.
Language(s): German
Readership: Aimed at apprentices in these fields.
BUSINESS: HEATING & VENTILATION: Domestic Heating & Ventilation

ILLERTISSER ZEITUNG 730861G67B-7700
Editorial: Curt-Frenzel-Str. 2, 86167 AUGSBURG
Tel: 821 7770 **Fax:** 821 7772067
Web site: http://www.augsburger-allgemeine.de
Freq: 312 issues yearly; **Circ:** 9,844
Advertising Manager: Herbert Dachs
Profile: Daily newspaper with regional news and a local sports section. Facebook: http://www.facebook.com/AugsburgerAllgemeine Twitter: http://twitter.com/AZ_Augsburg This Outlet offers RSS (Really Simple Syndication).
Language(s): German
ADVERTISING RATES:
SCC .... EUR 45,30
Mechanical Data: Type Area: 480 x 327 mm, No. of Columns (Display): 7, Col Widths (Display): 45 mm
Copy instructions: *Copy Date:* 1 day prior to publication
REGIONAL DAILY & SUNDAY NEWSPAPERS: Regional Daily Newspapers

IM BLICK 730889G74N-834
Editorial: Wolfgang-Stock-Str. 17, 72076 TÜBINGEN
Tel: 7071 369095 **Fax:** 7071 369093
Email: pass-wort@t-online.de **Web site:** http://www.verlag-schuh.de
Freq: Quarterly; **Annual Sub.:** EUR 14,50; **Circ:** 25,000
Profile: Official journal of the National Seniors Council Baden-Württemberg: issues from all walks of life. Target group: 55 plus generation.
Language(s): German
ADVERTISING RATES:
Full Page Mono .... EUR 2756
Full Page Colour .... EUR 2756
Mechanical Data: Type Area: 260 x 185 mm, No. of Columns (Display): 4, Col Widths (Display): 45 mm

IM FOCUS ONKOLOGIE 730897G56A-5060
Editorial: Aschauer Str. 30, 81549 MÜNCHEN
Tel: 89 2030431300 **Fax:** 89 2030431399
Email: sabrina.grass@springer.com **Web site:** http://www.im-focus-onkologie.de
Freq: 10 issues yearly; **Annual Sub.:** EUR 126,00; **Circ:** 11,204
Editor: Sabrina Graß; **Advertising Manager:** Renate Senfft
Profile: Im Focus Onkologie, the journalistic quality format and renowned educational magazine for oncology practitioners, provides the selective target group news and information on all relevant facets of oncology and hematology-oncology. Clearly, factually and utilitarian to the point. On the latest international standard to all tumor entities. Contents: Concise, practical training, study units currently important publications in international journals (focus) - with expert commentary outstanding studies, CME-training, selected training series of diagnostic, therapeutic and supportive strategies in oncology, as well as cutting-edge reports pointed highlights of the international congresses .
Language(s): German
Readership: Read by members of the medical profession.
ADVERTISING RATES:
Full Page Mono .... EUR 2900
Full Page Colour .... EUR 4400
Mechanical Data: Type Area: 240 x 174 mm
Official Journal of: Organ d. ArGe Supportive Maßnahmen in d. Onkologie, Rehabilitation u. Sozialmedizin d. Dt. Krebsges.
BUSINESS: HEALTH & MEDICAL

IM GARTEN 730898G94H-6900
Editorial: An Menses Mühle 4, 59387 ASCHEBERG
Tel: 2599 1715 **Fax:** 251 5101236
Web site: http://www.garten-magazin.de
Freq: 6 issues yearly; **Cover Price:** Free; **Circ:** 95,000
Editor: Edith Budde; **Advertising Manager:** Gabriele Wittkowski
Profile: Magazine covering all aspects of gardening as a hobby.
Language(s): German
ADVERTISING RATES:
Full Page Mono .... EUR 2848
Full Page Colour .... EUR 4672
Mechanical Data: Type Area: 270 x 190 mm, No. of Columns (Display): 4, Col Widths (Display): 46 mm
CONSUMER: OTHER CLASSIFICATIONS: Customer Magazines

IM INFORMATION MANAGEMENT & CONSULTING 730877G62D-1040
Editorial: Altenkesseler Str. 17, 66115 SAARBRÜCKEN **Tel:** 681 94760 **Fax:** 681 9476530
Email: info@im-c.de **Web site:** http://www.im-fachzeitschrift.de
Freq: Quarterly; **Annual Sub.:** EUR 99,00; **Circ:** 1,300
Editor: Tamara Hausmann; **Advertising Manager:** Tamara Hausmann
Profile: Magazine about information management and consulting.
Language(s): English; German
ADVERTISING RATES:
Full Page Mono .... EUR 1400
Full Page Colour .... EUR 1850
Mechanical Data: Type Area: 230 x 170 mm, No. of Columns (Display): 3, Col Widths (Display): 53 mm
Copy instructions: *Copy Date:* 40 days prior to publication
BUSINESS: CHURCH & SCHOOL EQUIPMENT & EDUCATION: Secondary Education

IM INSTITUTIONAL MONEY 1846364G1F-1741
Editorial: Neuenhöfer Allee 153, 50935 KÖLN
Tel: 221 4759797 **Fax:** 221 4759798
Email: heuser@institutional-money.com **Web site:** http://www.institutional-money.com
Freq: Quarterly; **Cover Price:** EUR 9,00; **Circ:** 23,000
Editor: Hans Heuser
Profile: Institutional Money informed institutional investors from Germany, Austria, Switzerland, Liechtenstein and Luxembourg four times a year on the latest trends and developments affecting their work. Topics range from analysis of new and popular product solutions through the presentation of interesting asset classes and the current financial and scientific knowledge and its relevance to practice, to the myriad of national and international standards in terms of legal and tax environment.
Language(s): German
ADVERTISING RATES:
Full Page Mono .... EUR 8390
Full Page Colour .... EUR 8390
Mechanical Data: Type Area: 250 x 182 mm

IMAGE HIFI 730880G78A-260
Editorial: Alois-Harbeck-Platz 3, 82178 PUCHHEIM
Tel: 89 894184510 **Fax:** 89 894184512
Email: cai.brockmann@image-magazine.de **Web site:** http://www.image-hifi.com
Freq: 6 issues yearly; **Annual Sub.:** EUR 65,00; **Circ:** 20,000
Editor: Cai Brockmann; **Advertising Manager:** Susanne Zausinger
Profile: HiFi-high-end magazine for high-quality consumer electronics and music playback.
Language(s): German
Readership: Aimed at musicians and amateurs with an interest in recording music.
ADVERTISING RATES:
Full Page Mono .... EUR 1860
Full Page Colour .... EUR 2680
Mechanical Data: Type Area: 224 x 186 mm, No. of Columns (Display): 3, Col Widths (Display): 59 mm
CONSUMER: CONSUMER ELECTRONICS: Hi-Fi & Recording

IMAGING DECISIONS MRI 1639478G56A-11282
Editorial: Rotherstr. 21, 10245 BERLIN
Tel: 30 47031450 **Fax:** 30 47031410
Email: klaus.mickus@wiley.com **Web site:** http://www.wiley.com
Freq: Quarterly; **Annual Sub.:** EUR 75,00; **Circ:** 8,800
Editor: Matthijs Oudkerk
Profile: Optimising diagnosis and treatment with MRI.
Language(s): English

IMAGING + FOTO CONTACT 1654831G43A-1514
Editorial: Freiligrathring 18, 40878 RATINGEN
Tel: 2102 20270 **Fax:** 2102 202790
Email: t.bloemer@cat-verlag.de **Web site:** http://www.worldofphoto.de
Freq: 11 issues yearly; **Annual Sub.:** EUR 39,90; **Circ:** 7,293
Editor: Thomas Blömer; **Advertising Manager:** Thomas Blömer
Profile: Magazine for the photo and imaging branch.
Language(s): German
ADVERTISING RATES:
Full Page Mono .... EUR 2580
Full Page Colour .... EUR 4386
Mechanical Data: Type Area: 267 x 180 mm, No. of Columns (Display): 4, Col Widths (Display): 41 mm
Copy instructions: *Copy Date:* 14 days prior to publication
BUSINESS: ELECTRICAL RETAIL TRADE

IMKERFREUND 730900G81G-6
Editorial: Weiherstr. 5, 79183 WALDKIRCH
Tel: 7681 409166 **Fax:** 7681 409165
Email: js-bienenredaktion@t-online.de **Web site:** http://www.imkerfreund.de
Freq: Monthly; **Annual Sub.:** EUR 37,50; **Circ:** 13,302
Editor: Jürgen Schwenkel; **Advertising Manager:** Thomas Herrmann
Profile: With the three journals, die biene, ADIZ Allgemeine Deutsche Imkerzeitung and Imkerfreund is the dlv Deutscher Landwirtschaftsverlag market leader in the field of regional and national beekeeping journals. Reaching over 33,100 copies distributed die biene, ADIZ and Imkerfreund a large part of the German beekeepers in major honey producing regions. In die biene and ADIZ are the oldest German regional bee newspapers and magazines Südwestdeutscher Imker, Westfälische Bienenzeitung and Deutsche Bienenwirtschaft united. Many large beekeeper organizations use the three beekeeping journals as their official organ: die biene: Hessian state association of beekeepers and beekeepers in the Saarland and the beekeepers associations of Rhineland and Nassau; ADIZ: State Association of Baden beekeepers and beekeepers association of Rhineland-Palatinate; Imkerfreund: State Association of Bavarian beekeepers. Association news, events, messages, personal data and other information from these organizations and the German Beekeepers' Association and from the state's beekeepers associations Saxony, Saxony-Anhalt, Thuringia and Mecklenburg-Western Pomerania are an integral part of every issue. The reader will find in their magazine also highly skilled technical contributions of high-qualified authors from academia and practice. The offer ranges from standard subjects such as beekeeping and farming, honey production and marketing, bee diseases and countermeasures about tips and tricks for beekeepers to information about honey bees, the history of beekeeping, special literature, nature protection and other beekeepers areas of interest. The journals die biene, ADIZ and Imkerfreund are read primarily by recreational and professional beekeepers, bee scientists at universities and bee institutes, consultants and employees in government agencies.
Language(s): German
ADVERTISING RATES:
Full Page Mono .... EUR 967
Full Page Colour .... EUR 1664
Mechanical Data: Type Area: 270 x 184 mm, No. of Columns (Display): 4, Col Widths (Display): 43 mm
Official Journal of: Organ d. LV Bayer. Imker e.V., Mttl. d. Dt. Imkerbundes, d. Landesimkerverbände Sachsen, Sachsen-Anhalt, Mecklenburg-Vorpommern u. Thüringen
CONSUMER: ANIMALS & PETS: Bees

IMMERGRÜN
1827776G57-2847
Editorial: Maastrichter Str. 49, 50672 KÖLN
Tel: 221 95154126 **Fax:** 221 95154111
Email: bernd.wilberg@stadtrevue.de **Web site:** http://www.stadtrevue.de
Freq: Annual; **Cover Price:** Free; **Circ:** 30,000
Editor: Bernd Wilberg
Profile: Cologne eco-guide. The provider commented directory of more than 200 addresses each year, new research. Distribution: Free distribution of targeted and supplement in the December issue of StadtRevue.
Language(s): German
ADVERTISING RATES:
Full Page Mono .... EUR 1390
Full Page Colour .... EUR 1920
Mechanical Data: Type Area: 184 x 124 mm
Copy instructions: *Copy Date:* 40 days prior to publication
Supplement to: StadtRevue

IMMISSIONSSCHUTZ
730908G57-720
Editorial: Schwanstr. 3, 40476 DÜSSELDORF
Tel: 211 4566571 **Fax:** 211 4566949
Email: eckehard.koch@munlv.nrw.de **Web site:** http://www.immissionsschutzdigital.de
Freq: Quarterly; **Annual Sub.:** EUR 73,65; **Circ:** 1,000
Editor: Eckehard Koch; **Advertising Manager:** Peter Taprogge
Profile: Specialist journal on air pollution control, covering the prevention of air pollution, noise prevention, building security, recycling and use of energy.
Language(s): German
Readership: Aimed at those involved in industry, economics and engineering.
ADVERTISING RATES:
Full Page Mono .... EUR 1100
Full Page Colour .... EUR 2010
Mechanical Data: Type Area: 254 x 185 mm, No. of Columns (Display): 2, Col Widths (Display): 84 mm
Copy instructions: *Copy Date:* 21 days prior to publication
BUSINESS: ENVIRONMENT & POLLUTION

IMMOBILIEN MANAGER
730923G1E-340
Editorial: Stolberger Str. 84, 50933 KÖLN
Tel: 221 5497131 **Fax:** 221 54976131
Email: imv@immobilienmanager.de **Web site:** http://www.immobilienmanager.de
Freq: 10 issues yearly; **Annual Sub.:** EUR 136,50; **Circ:** 16,722
Editor: Christof Hardebusch; **Advertising Manager:** Thomas Ceppok
Profile: Journal covering professional property management. Twitter: http://twitter.com/#!/immomanager.
Language(s): English; German
ADVERTISING RATES:
Full Page Mono .... EUR 6120
Full Page Colour .... EUR 7995
Mechanical Data: Type Area: 252 x 175 mm, No. of Columns (Display): 3, Col Widths (Display): 55 mm
Copy instructions: *Copy Date:* 30 days prior to publication
Supplement(s): im immobilien manager edition; im immobilien manager special
BUSINESS: FINANCE & ECONOMICS: Property

IMMOBILIEN UND FINANZIERUNG
733884G1G-40
Editorial: Aschaffenburger Str. 19, 60599 FRANKFURT **Tel:** 69 97083340 **Fax:** 69 7078400
Email: red.immofinanz@kreditwesen.de **Web site:** http://www.kreditwesen.de
Freq: 24 issues yearly; **Annual Sub.:** EUR 447,60; **Circ:** 1,095
Editor: Philipp Otto; **Advertising Manager:** Uwe Cappel
Profile: Journal specialising in long-term credit.
Language(s): German
ADVERTISING RATES:
Full Page Mono .... EUR 3120
Full Page Colour .... EUR 4620
Mechanical Data: Type Area: 265 x 185 mm, No. of Columns (Display): 3, Col Widths (Display): 58 mm
Copy instructions: *Copy Date:* 9 days prior to publication
BUSINESS: FINANCE & ECONOMICS: Credit Trading

IMMOBILIEN VERMIETEN & VERWALTEN
746316G74K-1320
Editorial: Am Friedrichshain 22, 10407 BERLIN
Tel: 30 42151221 **Fax:** 30 42151332
Email: peter-michael.fritsch@hussberlin.de **Web site:** http://www.vermieter-ratgeber.de
Freq: 10 issues yearly; Free to qualifying individuals
Annual Sub.: EUR 88,00; **Circ:** 9,870
Editor: Peter-Michael Fritsch; **Advertising Manager:** Torsten Hanke
Profile: Magazine containing information about homes and property.
Language(s): German
Readership: Aimed at home owners.
ADVERTISING RATES:
Full Page Mono .... EUR 4300
Full Page Colour .... EUR 6250
Mechanical Data: No. of Columns (Display): 4, Col Widths (Display): 43 mm, Type Area: 266 x 185 mm
Copy instructions: *Copy Date:* 16 days prior to publication
CONSUMER: WOMEN'S INTEREST CONSUMER MAGAZINES: Home Purchase

IMMOBILIEN ZEITUNG
730933G1E-460
Editorial: Luisenstr. 24, 65185 WIESBADEN
Tel: 611 973260 **Fax:** 611 9732632
Email: redaktion@iz.de **Web site:** http://www.immobilien-zeitung.de
Freq: Weekly; **Annual Sub.:** EUR 235,00; **Circ:** 11,073
Editor: Thomas Porten; **News Editor:** Monika Leykam; **Advertising Manager:** Markus Schmidtke
Profile: Journal covering all aspects of the property trade.
Language(s): German
ADVERTISING RATES:
Full Page Mono .... EUR 12360
Full Page Colour .... EUR 16800
Mechanical Data: Type Area: 480 x 325 mm, No. of Columns (Display): 5, Col Widths (Display): 61 mm
Copy instructions: *Copy Date:* 8 days prior to publication
BUSINESS: FINANCE & ECONOMICS: Property

DER IMMOBILIENVERWALTER
730932G1E-500
Editorial: Reinsburgstr. 82, 70178 STUTTGART
Tel: 711 238860 **Fax:** 711 2388625
Email: joerg.bleyhl@pressecompany.de **Web site:** http://www.immoclick24.de
Freq: 7 issues yearly; **Annual Sub.:** EUR 29,00; **Circ:** 9,794
Editor: Jörg Bleyhl; **Advertising Manager:** Karin Navaei
Profile: Magazine about building techniques, regulations, practice and association news.
Language(s): German
Readership: Aimed at property managers.
ADVERTISING RATES:
Full Page Mono .... EUR 4120
Full Page Colour .... EUR 5560
Mechanical Data: Type Area: 270 x 185 mm, No. of Columns (Display): 3, Col Widths (Display): 59 mm
Copy instructions: *Copy Date:* 15 days prior to publication
Official Journal of: Organ d. Dachverb. Dt. Immobilienverwalter e.V.
BUSINESS: FINANCE & ECONOMICS: Property

IMMOBILIENWIRTSCHAFT
730925G1E-360
Editorial: Munzinger Str. 9, 79111 FREIBURG
Tel: 761 8983507 **Fax:** 761 8983112
Email: redaktion@immobilienwirtschaft.de **Web site:** http://www.immobilienwirtschaft.de
Freq: 10 issues yearly; **Annual Sub.:** EUR 128,00; **Circ:** 17,977
Editor: Dirk Labusch
Profile: Immobilienwirtschaft is the most common and best-selling magazine for real estate professionals in Germany. The unique combination of management and legal topics will be given top managers a sound basis for their decisions. Audience: CEO of real estate companies, brokers, developers, asset managers, project developers, managers and investors. Twitter: http://twitter.com/#!/haufeimmobilien.
Language(s): German
ADVERTISING RATES:
Full Page Mono .... EUR 7000
Full Page Colour .... EUR 7750
Mechanical Data: Type Area: 249 x 176 mm, No. of Columns (Display): 3, Col Widths (Display): 56 mm
Copy instructions: *Copy Date:* 21 days prior to publication
BUSINESS: FINANCE & ECONOMICS: Property

IMPFDIALOG
756067G56A-11087
Editorial: Justus-von-Liebig-Str. 1, 86899 LANDSBERG **Tel:** 8191 125500 **Fax:** 8191 125492
Email: susanne.fischer@hjr-verlag.de **Web site:** http://www.ecomed-medizin.de/impfdialog
Freq: Quarterly; **Annual Sub.:** EUR 55,20; **Circ:** 3,500
Editor: Susanne Fischer; **Advertising Manager:** Reingard Herbst
Profile: Magazine about immunology.
Language(s): German

IMPULS
730959G17-580
Editorial: Gustav-Heinemann-Ufer 130, 50968 KÖLN
Tel: 221 37781010 **Fax:** 221 37781011
Email: presse@bgetem.de **Web site:** http://www.bgetem.de
Freq: 6 issues yearly; Free to qualifying individuals
Annual Sub.: EUR 4,07; **Circ:** 580,000
Editor: Christoph Nocker
Profile: Magazine from the Professional Association of Fine Mechanics and Electro Technics.
Language(s): German

IMPULSE
730966G14A-3300
Editorial: Am Baumwall 11, 20459 HAMBURG
Tel: 40 37030 **Fax:** 40 37038310
Email: chefredaktion@impulse.de **Web site:** http://www.impulse.de
Freq: Monthly; **Annual Sub.:** EUR 82,80; **Circ:** 100,954
Editor: Nikolaus Förster; **News Editor:** Philipp Jaklin; **Advertising Manager:** Martina Hoss
Profile: The magazine for business owners. For more nearly 30 years, hundreds of thousands of company managers, self-employed business owners and freelancers have depended, month after month, on the valuable advice IMPULSE provides. IMPULSE offers expert tips and information designed to give company owners added confidence when making important decisions every day. In addition to serving as a modern business consultant for experienced company managers, IMPULSE also addresses the needs of budding entrepreneurs and company founders through regular reports in the magazine. Readership: 156 000 every month, IMPULSE reaches decision-makers (LAE 2009). IMPULSE readers are mainly entrepreneurs and top decision makers in medium-sized businesses. They represent an enormous investment potential and are an important target group for the business-to-business communications. Facebook: http://www.facebook.com/impulse This Outlez offers RSS (Really Simple Syndication).
Language(s): German
Readership: Read by business employers, high and middle management.
ADVERTISING RATES:
Full Page Mono .... EUR 16900
Full Page Colour .... EUR 16900
Mechanical Data: Type Area: 244 x 175 mm, No. of Columns (Display): 3, Col Widths (Display): 55 mm
Copy instructions: *Copy Date:* 30 days prior to publication
Supplement(s): impulse wissen
BUSINESS: COMMERCE, INDUSTRY & MANAGEMENT

IMPULSE
722962G56A-11171
Editorial: Voßstr. 3, 69115 HEIDELBERG
Tel: 6221 138020 **Fax:** 6221 1380220
Email: presse@biokrebs.de **Web site:** http://www.biokrebs.de
Freq: Quarterly; **Cover Price:** Free; **Circ:** 20,000
Editor: György Irmey
Profile: Magazine containing information about biological cancer treatment and about the activities of the Society for biological Cancer Blocking.
Language(s): German
Supplement to: Signal

IMPULSE ONLINE
1621508G14A-9469
Editorial: Am Baumwall 11, 20459 HAMBURG
Tel: 40 37030 **Fax:** 40 37038310
Email: online@impulse.de **Web site:** http://www.impulse.de
Freq: Daily; **Cover Price:** Paid; **Circ:** 298,003 Unique Users
Editor: Joachim Dreykluft; **News Editor:** Philipp Jaklin
Profile: Ezine: Information platform for entrepreneurs in the German network. Impulse responses online are there, where entrepreneurship faces particular challenges. As the mouthpiece of the innovative SME provides useful information for entrepreneurs in management, finance, pensions, tax and IT solutions. A variety of interactive tools are also available with a specific value. Facebook: http://www.facebook.com/impulse This Outlet offers RSS (Really Simple Syndication).
Language(s): German
BUSINESS: COMMERCE, INDUSTRY & MANAGEMENT

IN ASIEN!
1615538G89A-12145
Editorial: Rudolfstr. 22, 60327 FRANKFURT
Tel: 69 6656320 **Fax:** 69 66563222
Email: redaktion@inasien.de **Web site:** http://www.inasien.de
Freq: 6 issues yearly; **Annual Sub.:** EUR 27,50; **Circ:** 30,000
Editor: Martin Brückner
Profile: Magazine for fans of Asia-Pacific region in Germany, Austria and Switzerland. Every two months, we bring them all the charm of the region close - through reports and photo reports from authors who are really at home there. Articles about cultural and economic backgrounds will help to understand foreign cultures better. The magazine "inAsien" is much more than interesting reading. A comprehensive range of services easier for our readers their travel decision. Increase In addition to detailed country information and Vacation offers a list of cheap flight tickets the usefulness of the magazine. Facebook: http://www.facebook.com/pages/wwwinasiende/101698066542562.
Language(s): German
ADVERTISING RATES:
Full Page Mono .... EUR 2575
Full Page Colour .... EUR 3347
Mechanical Data: Type Area: 250 x 157 mm, No. of Columns (Display): 4, Col Widths (Display): 48 mm

IN DAS STAR & STYLE MAGAZIN
1693410G74A-3475
Editorial: Rosenthaler Str. 40, 10178 BERLIN
Tel: 30 319914100 **Fax:** 30 319914400
Email: in@in-verlag.de **Web site:** http://www.in-starmagazin.de
Freq: Weekly; **Cover Price:** EUR 1,80; **Circ:** 215,287
Editor: Oliver Opitz
Profile: Young German stars and rising stars who are in conversation or want to get to, in Das Star & Style Magazin is not over. Bunte is what the generation 60, in Das Star & Style Magazin for the 30th generation Exclusive shoots, weddings, baby pictures and trendy German VIPs are also found in in Das Star & Style Magazin and critical reporting on the life of the Society. From the heart of Berlin out of small charming aberrations, we cover up embarrassing scandals add anything to what's happening in the Society. The new friend of Sarah Connor will also be found first of all in in Das Star & Style Magazin as the private Christmas dinner by Heidi Klum. And now, we will investigate and reveal even more, always fair and respectful, never offensive, but genuine and critical. The truth is not like any celebrity. But our readers - and are our first priority. in Das Star & Style Magazin is the people and lifestyle magazine, which reports every week from the trend capital of Berlin to life, entertaining and emotionally on German and international stars, and offers style guidance for young fashion-conscious women. Trendy and hip is not a question of age. Therefore, the celebrities are chosen in Das Star & Style Magazin is not on their age, but by its nature Trendy. Many exclusive interviews with both international as well as with German stars give the reader a very intimate look into the everyday life of their favorite stars. Exceptional and exclusive photo shoots, the readers themselves feel "live" there. Beauty and fashion are based in in Das Star & Style Magazin accessible to the hottest celebrities. Stars make trends, trends make stars. in Das Star & Style Magazin shows both. The favorite looks of the stars will be presented to the reader every week to date. In-depth tips to stimulate the Nachstylen. In exclusive "Beauty Talks" betray their own personal celebrity beauty secrets beauty in exclusive photo shootings in unusual venues they perform in front of the latest fashions and matching accessories. Therefore, especially the young and fashion-conscious women put on the beauty and fashion tips in Das Star & Style Magazin. Facebook: http://www.facebook.com/pages/in-Das-STAR-STYLE-Magazin/113282938691822.
Language(s): German
ADVERTISING RATES:
Full Page Mono .... EUR 13700
Full Page Colour .... EUR 13700
Mechanical Data: Type Area: 268 x 191 mm
Copy instructions: *Copy Date:* 28 days prior to publication
CONSUMER: WOMEN'S INTEREST CONSUMER MAGAZINES: Women's Interest

IN KUERZE
731339G5F-7
Editorial: Ostenstr. 24, 85072 EICHSTÄTT
Tel: 8421 931214 **Fax:** 8421 932745
Email: inkuerze@ku-eichstaett.de **Web site:** http://www.ku-eichstaett.de/Rechenzentrum/dienstleist/schriften/inkuerze
Freq: Half-yearly; **Cover Price:** Free; **Circ:** 800
Editor: Wolfgang A. Slaby
Profile: Journal of the Catholic University of Eichstätt-Ingolstadt reports on IT development for members of the university and director of data centers in German universities.
Language(s): German

IN MÜNCHEN
731343G89C-4805
Editorial: Hohenstaufenstr. 1, 80801 MÜNCHEN
Tel: 89 38997114 **Fax:** 89 390351
Email: redaktion@in-muenchen.de **Web site:** http://www.in-muenchen.de
Freq: 26 issues yearly; **Cover Price:** Free; **Circ:** 83,907
Editor: Uwe Feigl; **Advertising Manager:** Rupert Klostermeier
Profile: City magazine in Munich. It includes all dates in competently annotated form: cinema - concerts - parties - classical - theatre - cabaret - exhibitions - literature - lectures - tours - markets - sports - kids - television and of course all the special events and festivals in and around Munich. The magazine obviously supports all editorial sections and also offers gossip, local, Internet, CD and DVD reviews. It offers thematic display special pages such as dancing - housing - jobs - sport - awareness of life - sound check, supported by editorial content and information boxes. Facebook: http://www.facebook.com/InMuenchen.
Language(s): German
Readership: Aimed at tourists, visitors and local residents.
ADVERTISING RATES:
Full Page Mono .... EUR 3425
Full Page Colour .... EUR 3975
Mechanical Data: Type Area: 285 x 205 mm, No. of Columns (Display): 5, Col Widths (Display): 39 mm
Copy instructions: *Copy Date:* 8 days prior to publication
CONSUMER: HOLIDAYS & TRAVEL: Entertainment Guides

IN SHOES
1984058G74A-3743
Editorial: Neuer Kamp 25, 20359 HAMBURG
Tel: 40 8797659 **Fax:** 40 879765920
Email: meckert@inshoes-online.de **Web site:** http://www.inshoes-online.de
Freq: 6 issues yearly; **Annual Sub.:** EUR 25,00; **Circ:** 100,000
Editor: Michael Eckert; **Advertising Manager:** Sanja Schröder
Profile: Magazine reports on people and their shoes from manufacturers, Stars and bag carrier.
Language(s): German
ADVERTISING RATES:
Full Page Colour .... EUR 9200
Mechanical Data: Type Area: 260 x 185 mm
Copy instructions: *Copy Date:* 9200 days prior to publication

INDAT-REPORT 730986G1A-1320

Editorial: Aachener Str. 222, 50931 KÖLN
Tel: 221 88821156 **Fax:** 221 88821138
Email: reuter@indat-report.de **Web site:** http://www.indat-report.de
Freq: 10 issues yearly; **Annual Sub.:** EUR 198,00; **Circ:** 1,300
Editor: Peter Reuter; **Advertising Manager:** Thomas Fuhrmann
Profile: Database with recent company insolvencies.
Language(s): German
ADVERTISING RATES:
Full Page Mono .... EUR 1750
Full Page Colour .... EUR 1750
Mechanical Data: Type Area: 277 x 180 mm
Copy instructions: *Copy Date:* 10 days prior to publication

INDEX FÜR DIE GESUNDHEITSWIRTSCHAFT 720723G56A-540

Editorial: Heidelberger Platz 3, 14197 BERLIN
Tel: 30 827870 **Fax:** 30 8214091
Email: subscriptions@springer.com **Web site:** http://www.springer.com
Freq: Monthly; **Circ:** 7,000
Editor: Uwe K. Preusker
Profile: A renowned, together with the economic research institute RWI Essen (Rhine-Westphalia Institute for Economic Research) project developed, which collects the current and future assessment of the players in the healthcare industry to earnings, growth in demand and price trends and development fee and published.
Language(s): English; German
ADVERTISING RATES:
Full Page Mono .... EUR 3500

INDEX FÜR DIE GESUNDHEITSWIRTSCHAFT 720723G56A-11678

Editorial: Heidelberger Platz 3, 14197 BERLIN
Tel: 30 827870 **Fax:** 30 8214091
Email: subscriptions@springer.com **Web site:** http://www.springer.com
Freq: Monthly; **Circ:** 7,000
Editor: Uwe K. Preusker
Profile: A renowned, together with the economic research institute RWI Essen (Rhine-Westphalia Institute for Economic Research) project developed, which collects the current and future assessment of the players in the healthcare industry to earnings, growth in demand and price trends and development fee and published.
Language(s): English; German
ADVERTISING RATES:
Full Page Mono .... EUR 3500

INDIANSUMMER MAGAZIN 1861928G74N-968

Editorial: Aegidii-Markt 7, 48143 MÜNSTER
Tel: 251 7036430 **Fax:** 251 7036435
Email: info@indiansummer-magazin.de **Web site:** http://www.indiansummer-magazin.de
Freq: Monthly; **Annual Sub.:** EUR 58,80; **Circ:** 30,000
Editor: Andreas Höner; **Advertising Manager:** Wilma Bratke
Profile: Monthly magazine for the 50 + - information on all aspects of travel, culture and lifestyle. In each issue published indian summer a special holiday of a reader and can report on it in a report. The magazine brings the current cultural top events in Germany and Europe. These are the highlights of Music, Theatre & Cinema, Musicals & Circus. There are, of course, detailed background reports. From cars to computers to test for amateur photography, beauty of literature to astrology - reports on everything.
Language(s): German
ADVERTISING RATES:
Full Page Mono .... EUR 4500
Full Page Colour .... EUR 4500
Mechanical Data: Type Area: 280 x 210 mm

INDIENCONTACT 1799532G14C-4770

Editorial: Ritterstr. 2b, 10969 BERLIN
Tel: 30 6150890 **Fax:** 30 61508929
Email: redaktion@owc.de **Web site:** http://www.owc.de
Freq: 6 issues yearly; **Annual Sub.:** EUR 52,43; **Circ:** 9,000
Editor: Achim Rodewald; **Advertising Manager:** Norbert Mayer
Profile: Magazine focusing on future business negotiations with India. Also contains market analyses and trends.
Language(s): German
ADVERTISING RATES:
Full Page Mono .... EUR 2500
Full Page Colour .... EUR 3200
Mechanical Data: Type Area: 265 x 175 mm

INDIGO 1660534G80-14288

Editorial: Lessingstr. 66, 38440 WOLFSBURG
Tel: 5361 8484881 **Fax:** 5361 8484888
Email: redaktion@indigo.cc **Web site:** http://www.indigo.cc
Freq: Monthly; **Cover Price:** Free; **Circ:** 7,980
Editor: Sebastian Heise; **Advertising Manager:** Michael Hoffmann
Profile: City Magazine for Wolfsburg & Gifhorn. It provides information on cultural activities and events. Topics: theater, film, music, exhibitions, sports, lifestyle and party. Facebook: http://www.facebook.com/indigoMagazin This Outlet offres RSS (Really Simple Syndication).
Language(s): German
ADVERTISING RATES:
Full Page Mono .... EUR 1025
Full Page Colour .... EUR 1559
Mechanical Data: Type Area: 260 x 190 mm, No. of Columns (Display): 4, Col Widths (Display): 45 mm
Copy instructions: *Copy Date:* 15 days prior to publication
CONSUMER: RURAL & REGIONAL INTEREST

INDUSTRIAL ENGINEERING 740097G14E-120

Editorial: Wittichstr. 2, 64295 DARMSTADT
Tel: 6151 8801180 **Fax:** 6151 8801260
Email: presse@refa.de **Web site:** http://www.refa.de
Freq: Quarterly; Free to qualifying individuals
Annual Sub.: EUR 42,80; **Circ:** 14,000
Editor: Manfred Stroh; **Advertising Manager:** Alexandra Gambs
Profile: Journal containing information on work study and business administration.
Language(s): German
ADVERTISING RATES:
Full Page Mono .... EUR 2450
Full Page Colour .... EUR 2940
Mechanical Data: Type Area: 250 x 175 mm, No. of Columns (Display): 4, Col Widths (Display): 40 mm
Copy instructions: *Copy Date:* 20 days prior to publication
BUSINESS: COMMERCE, INDUSTRY & MANAGEMENT: Work Study

INDUSTRIALVISION 1807346G17-1588

Editorial: Lise-Meitner-Str. 2, 55129 MAINZ
Tel: 6131 992345 **Fax:** 6131 992340
Email: d.schaar@vfmz.de **Web site:** http://www.industrie-service.de
Freq: Quarterly; **Annual Sub.:** EUR 36,00; **Circ:** 14,704
Editor: Dirk Schaar; **Advertising Manager:** Oliver Jennen
Profile: IndustrialVision deals with the entire spectrum of image processing and optical technologies in industrial automation. That magazine informs technically competent of the current trends and the status of research and development primarily by the practical use of machine vision systems and components as well as cameras, optosensors, identification systems, quality assurance and microscopy. These sections ensure that users have in development, production, design and quality assurance, always the industries happen currently in view.
Language(s): German
ADVERTISING RATES:
Full Page Mono .... EUR 3560
Full Page Colour .... EUR 4790
Mechanical Data: Type Area: 265 x 185 mm, No. of Columns (Display): 4, Col Widths (Display): 43 mm

INDUSTRIE ANZEIGER 730999G14B-24

Editorial: Ernst-Mey-Str. 8, 70771 LEINFELDEN-ECHTERDINGEN **Tel:** 711 7594451
Fax: 711 7594398
Email: werner.goetz@konradin.de **Web site:** http://www.industrieanzeiger.de
Freq: 30 issues yearly; **Annual Sub.:** EUR 196,50; **Circ:** 40,039
Editor: Werner Götz; **Advertising Manager:** Klaus-Dieter Mehnert
Profile: As a high quality professional journal Industrieanzeiger reaches top decision makers in the manufacturing industry in German-speaking countries. These are predominantly owners, managing directors and technical directors in medium-sized companies, and the technical management in facilities of large companies. The up-to-date and exclusive reporting relating to practice is proof of the journalistic approach and is tailored to the requirements of modern management. The interdisciplinary technical articles provide a comprehensive survey of technical interrelations. In addition to mechanical engineering, metal-working and metal processing, plastics manufacturing and processing, automotive and electrical engineering the focus is also on service companies working with and for the industry. Twitter: http://twitter.com/industrieanzeig.
Language(s): German
ADVERTISING RATES:
Full Page Mono .... EUR 6380
Full Page Colour .... EUR 7890
Mechanical Data: Type Area: 270 x 188 mm, No. of Columns (Display): 4, Col Widths (Display): 44 mm
Official Journal of: Organ d. Wirtschaftsverb. Stahl- u. Metallverarbeitung e.V.
BUSINESS: COMMERCE, INDUSTRY & MANAGEMENT: Industry & Factories

INDUSTRIE MANAGEMENT 731011G14B-24_75

Editorial: Hochschulring 20, 28359 BREMEN
Tel: 421 2189787 **Fax:** 421 2185640
Email: himstedt@industrie-management.de **Web site:** http://www.industrie-management.de
Freq: 6 issues yearly; **Annual Sub.:** EUR 211,00; **Circ:** 2,639
Editor: Alexsandra Himstedt; **Advertising Manager:** Martina Braun
Profile: Journal focusing on innovative strategies for organisation and computer usage in manufacturing.
Language(s): German
Readership: Read by managers.
ADVERTISING RATES:
Full Page Colour .... EUR 2160
Mechanical Data: Type Area: 234 x 175 mm, No. of Columns (Display): 3, Col Widths (Display): 55 mm
Official Journal of: Organ d. Fachgruppe Informationssysteme in Industrie u. Handel d. Ges. f. Informatik e.V.
BUSINESS: COMMERCE, INDUSTRY & MANAGEMENT: Industry & Factories

INDUSTRIEARMATUREN 731001G19G-75

Editorial: Huyssenallee 52, 45128 ESSEN
Tel: 201 8200225 **Fax:** 201 8200240
Email: w.moenning@vulkan-verlag.de **Web site:** http://www.industriearmaturen.de
Freq: Quarterly; **Annual Sub.:** EUR 128,00; **Circ:** 5,883
Editor: Wolfgang Mönning; **Advertising Manager:** Helga Pelzer
Profile: The journal is the forum for the exchange of knowledge and experience between industrial valves suppliers and users. It reports quarterly comprehensive and technically detailed information on developments and solutions of the valve technology in industrial applications. Focus of this current form of each issue, practice-oriented technical papers competent authors. In addition, corporate and product news as well as editorial market levels over valves, valve actuators / positioners, sealing systems, etc. published. The magazine provides information on fixtures and their components in chemical and process engineering in the power generation and heating technology, in general Industry, water management, waste water technology, in sterile applications and in large HVAC systems.
Language(s): English; German
Readership: Read by engineers.
ADVERTISING RATES:
Full Page Mono .... EUR 2670
Full Page Colour .... EUR 3990
Mechanical Data: Type Area: 255 x 182 mm, No. of Columns (Display): 3, Col Widths (Display): 58 mm
Copy instructions: *Copy Date:* 15 days prior to publication
BUSINESS: ENGINEERING & MACHINERY: Pipelines

INDUSTRIEBAU 731002G4E-4740

Editorial: Mandichostr. 18, 86504 MERCHING
Tel: 8233 381155 **Fax:** 8233 381212
Email: melanie.meinig@forum-zeitschriften.de **Web site:** http://www.industriebau-online.de
Freq: 6 issues yearly; Free to qualifying individuals
Annual Sub.: EUR 138,00; **Circ:** 3,201
Editor: Melanie Meinig; **Advertising Manager:** Helmut Junginger
Profile: Trade magazine for professional design, construction and operation of the permanent buildings for industry, commerce and trade. She turns to the client in building design, FM and Real Estate departments, as well as to architects and planners.
Language(s): German
ADVERTISING RATES:
Full Page Mono .... EUR 3460
Full Page Colour .... EUR 3460
Mechanical Data: Type Area: 264 x 190 mm, No. of Columns (Display): 4, Col Widths (Display): 44 mm
Official Journal of: Organ d. ArGe Industriebau e.V.
BUSINESS: ARCHITECTURE & BUILDING: Building

INDUSTRIEBEDARF 731003G14B-27

Editorial: Schloss Mindelburg, 87719 MINDELHEIM
Tel: 8261 999336 **Fax:** 8261 999391
Email: pietzke@sachon.de **Web site:** http://www.sachon.de
Freq: 9 issues yearly; Free to qualifying individuals
Annual Sub.: EUR 34,24; **Circ:** 5,985
Editor: Margit Pietzke; **Advertising Manager:** Helga Reß
Profile: Magazine focusing on industrial purchases, machine and plant trade.
Language(s): German
ADVERTISING RATES:
Full Page Mono .... EUR 3130
Full Page Colour .... EUR 4633
Mechanical Data: Type Area: 270 x 185 mm, No. of Columns (Display): 4, Col Widths (Display): 45 mm
Official Journal of: Organ d. Fachverb. d. dt. Maschinen- u. Werkzeug-Großhandels e.V.
Supplement(s): kataloge orange
BUSINESS: COMMERCE, INDUSTRY & MANAGEMENT: Industry & Factories

DIE INDUSTRIEKAUFLEUTE 765584G14A-9292

Editorial: Eschstr. 22, 44629 HERNE
Tel: 2323 141900 **Fax:** 2323 141123
Email: l.kurz@kiehl.de **Web site:** http://www.kiehl.de
Freq: Monthly; **Annual Sub.:** EUR 61,80; **Circ:** 4,323
Editor: Lothar Kurz; **Advertising Manager:** Andreas Reimann
Profile: „Die Industriekaufleute", mainly contains information, articles and practice cases from the test areas business processes, commercial management and control and economic and social studies. An education-oriented language and many examples provide a high degree of intelligibility. Charts and graphs to illustrate more complex issues. Test and exam questions offer readers the ability to control their knowledge.
Language(s): German
ADVERTISING RATES:
Full Page Mono .... EUR 930
Full Page Colour .... EUR 1300
Mechanical Data: Type Area: 260 x 186 mm
Copy instructions: *Copy Date:* 30 days prior to publication
BUSINESS: COMMERCE, INDUSTRY & MANAGEMENT

INDUSTRIEPUMPEN + KOMPRESSOREN 731012G19D-27

Editorial: Huyssenallee 52, 45128 ESSEN
Tel: 201 8200225 **Fax:** 201 8200240
Email: w.moenning@vulkan-verlag.de **Web site:** http://www.industriepumpen-online.de
Freq: Quarterly; **Annual Sub.:** EUR 128,00; **Circ:** 1,690
Editor: Wolfgang Mönning; **Advertising Manager:** Jutta Zierold
Profile: The forum for the exchange of knowledge and experience between the pump and compressor providers and users. Information about pumps and their components in chemical and process engineering in the power generation and heating technology, in large HVAC systems, water management, waste water technology, and sterile applications in general industry. Quarterly comprehensive and technically detailed, practical technical articles on developments and solutions to problems of pumps and compressor technology in industrial applications. Target group: responsible technicians and engineers, decision makers and technical management of industrial pump / compressor users, producers and Provider of industrial pumps and compressors.
Language(s): German
ADVERTISING RATES:
Full Page Mono .... EUR 2350
Full Page Colour .... EUR 3550
Mechanical Data: Type Area: 250 x 182 mm, No. of Columns (Display): 3, Col Widths (Display): 58 mm
Copy instructions: *Copy Date:* 15 days prior to publication
BUSINESS: ENGINEERING & MACHINERY: Hydraulic Power

INFO 731033G56A-11180

Editorial: Falltorweg 6, 65428 RÜSSELSHEIM
Tel: 6142 32240 **Fax:** 6142 175642
Email: buero@lhrm.de **Web site:** http://www.lhrm.de
Freq: 3 issues yearly; **Circ:** 500
Profile: Magazine for doctors, patients and relatives focused on leukaemia.
Language(s): German

INFO DIABETOLOGIE 1934248G56A-11655

Editorial: Aschauer Str. 30, 81549 MÜNCHEN
Tel: 89 2030431300 **Fax:** 89 2030431399
Email: dirk.einecke@springer.com **Web site:** http://www.info-diabetologie.de
Freq: 6 issues yearly; **Annual Sub.:** EUR 94,50; **Circ:** 8,300
Editor: Dirk Einecke; **Advertising Manager:** Renate Senfft
Profile: „Info Diabetologie" is an interdisciplinary journal for scientific and practical diabetology with focus on prevention, diagnosis and therapy. Recent research results, data and trends from the Diabetes are reported and commented by experts from practice, clinical and science. Focus is the journal screen with interdisciplinary contributions from all relevant departments. In each issue will also be offered one or two CME-training of high practical relevance. In other sections the reader will find the latest reports of international congresses, instructive case reports, public health messages and tips for practical guidance. In the field of health policy is cooperation with the professional association of practicing diabetologists in Bavaria.
Language(s): German
ADVERTISING RATES:
Full Page Mono .... EUR 2690
Full Page Colour .... EUR 3990
Mechanical Data: Type Area: 240 x 174 mm

INFO EHINGEN 731051G72-5820

Editorial: Marktplatz 9, 89584 EHINGEN
Tel: 7391 500426 **Fax:** 7391 52292
Email: redaktion.ehi@info-wochenzeitung.de **Web site:** http://www.info-wochenzeitung.de
Freq: Weekly; **Cover Price:** Free; **Circ:** 27,300
Editor: Dietmar Burgmaier; **Advertising Manager:** Peter Groß
Profile: Advertising journal (house-to-house) concentrating on local stories.
Language(s): German
ADVERTISING RATES:
Full Page Mono .... EUR 5108
Full Page Colour .... EUR 7661
Mechanical Data: Type Area: 480 x 320 mm, No. of Columns (Display): 7, Col Widths (Display): 44 mm
Copy instructions: *Copy Date:* 1 day prior to publication
LOCAL NEWSPAPERS

INFO NEUROLOGIE & PSYCHIATRIE 731086G56A-5160
Editorial: Aschauer Str. 30, 81549 MÜNCHEN
Tel: 89 2030431300 **Fax:** 89 2030431399
Email: brigitte.moreano@springer.com **Web site:** http://www.info-neurologie-psychiatrie.de
Freq: 11 issues yearly; **Annual Sub.:** EUR 111,00; **Circ:** 13,052
Editor: Brigitte Müller-Moreano; **Advertising Manager:** Peter Urban
Profile: The goal of InFo Neurologie & Psychiatrie is to encourage interdisciplinary dialogue between these disciplines and other fields of medicine. The journal is the following substantive areas: • Overview of the scientific quality and practical international literature selected, reported, and critical comments by the high-caliber advisory board. • Established certified training (CME) • Recent reports of neurological and psychiatric training events, pro and contra controversy, interdisciplinary case discussions, interviews, editorials, and image diagnosis in the recent news.
Language(s): German
Readership: Read by specialists and practitioners in the field.
ADVERTISING RATES:
Full Page Mono .... EUR 2160
Full Page Colour .... EUR 3460
Mechanical Data: Type Area: 240 x 174 mm
Official Journal of: Organ d. Dt. Ges. f. Neurologie
BUSINESS: HEALTH & MEDICAL

INFO OASE 1786314G74N-902
Editorial: Homburger Str. 7, 51674 WIEHL
Tel: 2262 797123 **Fax:** 22362 797121
Email: oase@wiehl.de **Web site:** http://www.wiehl.de
Freq: Quarterly; **Cover Price:** Free; **Circ:** 800
Editor: Elke Neuburg
Profile: Magazine for the elderly living in Wiehl.
Language(s): German

INFO ONKOLOGIE 731089G56A-5180
Editorial: Aschauer Str. 30, 81549 MÜNCHEN
Tel: 89 2030431404 **Fax:** 89 2030431399
Email: doris.berger@springer.com **Web site:** http://www.info-onko.de
Freq: 8 issues yearly; Free to qualifying individuals
Annual Sub.: EUR 154,50; **Circ:** 3,800
Editor: Doris Berger; **Advertising Manager:** Renate Senfft
Profile: InFo Onkologie - Interdisciplinary training in oncology is the forum for all aspects of oncology and hematology-oncology, gynecological, urological, pediatric, dermatology and radiation oncology. Also contribute to tumor biology, pathology, and individualized cancer therapy can be considered. With in-depth articles with analytical and critical commentary by expert oncologists / hematologists processed to date, the magazine sets the standard in oncology. Experts and opinion-select-date, speak and comment - even from the point of the Evidence-Based Medicine - the most important in the international literature (Journal Club). The reader gets a thorough overview of the current state of research, diagnosis and therapy. The training section offers a high quality, practice relevant CME-training with AIO-credits. With this, the journal is positioned as a sophisticated training journal with high quality content and opinion-value for the highly specialized audience.
Language(s): German
ADVERTISING RATES:
Full Page Mono .... EUR 2350
Full Page Colour .... EUR 3650
Mechanical Data: Type Area: 240 x 174 mm
Official Journal of: Organ d. Berufsverb. d. niedergelassenen Hämatologen u. Onkologen in Deutschland

INFO-ATLAS 731039G62A-1760
Editorial: Helmlinger Str. 1, 77839 LICHTENAU
Tel: 7227 505010 **Fax:** 7227 505050
Email: martina.wollmer@b-b-v.de **Web site:** http://www.b-b-v.de
Freq: Annual; **Cover Price:** Free; **Circ:** 35,000
Profile: The practice-oriented magazine - especially for school trips and school trips, city trips, after-school learning sites, zoos, museums, amusement parks, adventure education, study abroad, student exchange and service part: • Internet travel destination. Here the reader finds interesting URLs with brief comment • InfoPoint school trip. Sorted by postal code addresses the teacher facilitate the search for the ideal destination. And not only magazine but also for a whole year www.bbv.de on our high traffic website • The new voucher section makes one curious about your offers and agrees to readers positively to your business. Your voucher is available for immediate use - or it remains a whole year in mind and consciousness of the reader.
Language(s): German
ADVERTISING RATES:
Full Page Mono .... EUR 2575
Full Page Colour .... EUR 2575
Mechanical Data: Type Area: 260 x 180 mm, No. of Columns (Display): 3, Col Widths (Display): 55 mm
Copy instructions: *Copy Date:* 72 days prior to publication
BUSINESS: CHURCH & SCHOOL EQUIPMENT & EDUCATION: Education

INFOMARKT 731076G14A-3380
Editorial: Fischerstr. 49, 40477 DÜSSELDORF
Tel: 211 6878550 **Fax:** 211 68785525
Email: redaktion@infomarkt.de **Web site:** http://www.infomarkt.de
Freq: 24 issues yearly; **Annual Sub.:** EUR 208,65; **Circ:** 3,500
Editor: Frank Grünberg; **Advertising Manager:** Kim Liisa Schneider
Profile: Magazine containing information about office and information technology.
Language(s): German
ADVERTISING RATES:
Full Page Mono .... EUR 1850
Full Page Colour .... EUR 2450
Mechanical Data: Type Area: 270 x 180 mm, No. of Columns (Display): 3, Col Widths (Display): 57 mm
Copy instructions: *Copy Date:* 30 days prior to publication

INFOMARKT 731081G34-240
Editorial: Fischerstr. 49, 40477 DÜSSELDORF
Tel: 211 6878550 **Fax:** 211 68785525
Email: kontakt@infomarkt.de **Web site:** http://www.infomarkt.de
Freq: Half-yearly; **Annual Sub.:** EUR 107,40; **Circ:** 1,500
Profile: Guide to multi functional systems.
Language(s): German

INFOPOST 731090G40-360
Editorial: Alte Heerstr. 90, 53757 ST. AUGUSTIN
Tel: 2241 152181 **Fax:** 2241 152960
Email: infopost@nw-w.de
Freq: Quarterly; **Cover Price:** Free; **Circ:** 250,000
Editor: Franz-Theo Reiß
Profile: Youth magazine of the Bundeswehr.
Language(s): German

INFOPRINT 1623412G14A-9520
Editorial: Alte Heerstr. 111, 53757 ST. AUGUSTIN
Tel: 2241 2316030 **Fax:** 2241 2316111
Email: rau@basi.de **Web site:** http://www.basi.de
Freq: Quarterly; **Circ:** 25,000
Editor: Wolfgang Rau
Profile: Journal of Occupational and health protection for members of the Bundesarbeitsgemeinschaft für Sicherheit und Gesundheit bei der Arbeit (Basi) e.V.
Language(s): German

INFORM 731096G4E-4760
Editorial: Siegburger Str. 241, 50679 KÖLN
Tel: 221 8242480 **Fax:** 221 8242385
Web site: http://www.strabag.de
Freq: 3 issues yearly; **Circ:** 55,000
Editor: Bernd Hinrichs
Profile: Magazine for employees of Strabag AG.
Language(s): Czech; English; German; Hungarian; Polish; Russian

INFORMATIK SPEKTRUM 731110G5B-78_33
Editorial: Tiergartenstr. 17, 69121 HEIDELBERG
Tel: 6221 4870 **Fax:** 6221 4878366
Email: hermann.engesser@springer.com **Web site:** http://www.springerlink.de
Freq: 6 issues yearly; Free to qualifying individuals
Annual Sub.: EUR 648,00; **Circ:** 23,800
Editor: Hermann Engesser; **Advertising Manager:** Jens Dessin
Profile: Official journal of the Association of Information Studies.
Language(s): German
ADVERTISING RATES:
Full Page Mono .... EUR 2830
Full Page Colour .... EUR 4460
Mechanical Data: No. of Columns (Display): 3, Col Widths (Display): 54 mm, Type Area: 240 x 175 mm
Official Journal of: Organ d. Ges. f. Informatik e.V. u. d. Schweizer Informatiker Ges.
BUSINESS: COMPUTERS & AUTOMATION: Data Processing

INFORMATION WISSENSCHAFT & PRAXIS 737416G5F-157
Editorial: Viktoriaplatz 8, 64293 DARMSTADT
Tel: 6151 869812 **Fax:** 6151 869818
Email: ockenfeld@dgi-info.de **Web site:** http://www.dgi-info.de
Freq: 7 issues yearly; Free to qualifying individuals
Annual Sub.: EUR 208,00; **Circ:** 3,250
Editor: Marlies Ockenfeld; **Advertising Manager:** Erwin König
Profile: Magazine containing information and practical advice on information management, database management systems, technical documentation, library systems and multimedia.
Language(s): English; German
ADVERTISING RATES:
Full Page Mono .... EUR 1000
Full Page Colour .... EUR 1600
Mechanical Data: Type Area: 257 x 180 mm, No. of Columns (Display): 3, Col Widths (Display): 56 mm
Copy instructions: *Copy Date:* 14 days prior to publication
BUSINESS: COMPUTERS & AUTOMATION: Multimedia

INFORMATIONEN AUS DER FORSCHUNG DES BBSR 731131G4D-10
Editorial: Deichmanns Aue 31, 53179 BONN
Tel: 22899 4012277 **Fax:** 22899 4012315
Email: hans-peter.gatzweiler@bbr.bund.de **Web site:** http://www.bbsr.bund.de
Freq: 6 issues yearly; **Cover Price:** Free; **Circ:** 1,800
Editor: Hans-Peter Gatzweiler
Profile: Reports about the work of the scientific section of the Bundeszentrale für Bauwesen und Raumordung.
Language(s): German

INFORMATIONEN AUS ERSTER HAND 1852812G21A-4409
Editorial: Asham 9, 83123 AMERANG **Tel:** 8075 9390
Fax: 8075 9391
Email: wbv-wshaag@gmx.de **Web site:** http://www.wbv-wasserburg.de
Circ: 2,400
Editor: Rupert Mayer
Profile: Member magazine from the Forest Owners Association Wasserburg/Haag.
Language(s): German

INFORMATIONEN DES KREISBAUERNVERBANDES SCHLESWIG 2098702G21A-4480
Editorial: Lise-Meitner Str. 2, 24837 SCHLESWIG
Tel: 4621 3057010 **Fax:** 4621 30570155
Email: kbv.schleswig@bauernverbandsh.de
Freq: Quarterly; **Circ:** 2,600
Profile: Information from the Kreisbauernverband Schleswig.
Language(s): German

INFORMATIONEN FÜR DEN BETRIEBSARZT 731138G56A-5220
Editorial: Gustav-Heinemann-Ufer 130, 50968 KÖLN
Tel: 221 37781010 **Fax:** 221 37781011
Email: info@bgetem.de **Web site:** http://www.bgetem.de
Circ: 3,000
Editor: Corinna Kowald
Profile: Magazine for company physicians.
Language(s): German

INFORMATIONEN FÜR DEN SICHERHEITSBEAUFTRAGTEN 731141G17-600
Editorial: Gustav-Heinemann-Ufer 130, 50968 KÖLN
Tel: 221 37781010 **Fax:** 221 37781011
Email: info@bgetem.de **Web site:** http://www.bgetem.de
Freq: 3 issues yearly; **Circ:** 35,000
Editor: Corinna Kowald
Profile: Journal of Vocational Cooperative Electric Energy textile media products for safety inspector.
Language(s): German

INFORMATIONEN FÜR DIE SICHERHEITSFACHKRAFT 731146G17-620
Editorial: Gustav-Heinemann-Ufer 130, 50968 KÖLN
Tel: 221 37781010 **Fax:** 221 37781011
Email: info@bgetem.de **Web site:** http://www.bgetem.de
Freq: 6 issues yearly; **Circ:** 13,000
Editor: Corinna Kowald
Profile: Magazine from the Professional Association of Fine Mechanics and Electro Technics.
Language(s): German

INFORMATIONEN ZUR RAUMENTWICKLUNG 731159G4D-11
Editorial: Deichmanns Aue 31, 53179 BONN
Tel: 22899 4012277 **Fax:** 22899 4012315
Email: hans-peter.gatzweiler@bbr.bund.de **Web site:** http://www.bbsr.bund.de
Freq: Monthly; **Annual Sub.:** EUR 62,00; **Circ:** 1,500
Editor: Hans-Peter Gatzweiler
Profile: Information about regional developments.
Language(s): English; German

INFORMATIONSBRIEF AUSLÄNDERRECHT 731178G44-1180
Editorial: Holstenwall 7, 20355 HAMBURG
Tel: 40 4502160 **Fax:** 40 4502166
Email: infauslr@web.de **Web site:** http://www.infauslr.de
Freq: 10 issues yearly; **Annual Sub.:** EUR 145,00; **Circ:** 2,100
Editor: Gerhard Strate; **Advertising Manager:** Markus Kipp
Profile: Magazine informs about the most important case law on the problem areas of the residence law, refugee law and nationality law and European law and on social issues.
Language(s): German
Mechanical Data: Type Area: 255 x 184 mm
BUSINESS: LEGAL

INFORMATIONSDIENST GROSS- UND AUSSENHANDEL 731292G14A-3460
Editorial: Sonninstr. 28, 20097 HAMBURG
Tel: 40 2360160 **Fax:** 40 23601610
Email: contact@wga-hh.de **Web site:** http://www.wga-hh.de
Freq: 25 issues yearly; Free to qualifying individuals
Annual Sub.: EUR 476,00; **Circ:** 750
Editor: Rodger Wegner; **Advertising Manager:** Daniela Suhrbier
Profile: Magazine from the Business Association of Wholesale and Export Trades.
Language(s): German
ADVERTISING RATES:
Full Page Mono .... EUR 928
Copy instructions: *Copy Date:* 1 day prior to publication

INFORMATIONSDIENST NATURSCHUTZ NIEDERSACHSEN 1836843G57-2869
Editorial: Göttinger Chaussee 76a, 30453 HANNOVER **Tel:** 511 30343309 **Fax:** 511 30343501
Email: manfred.rasper@nlwkn-h.niedersachsen.de
Web site: http://www.nlwkn.niedersachsen.de
Freq: Quarterly; **Annual Sub.:** EUR 15,00; **Circ:** 3,000
Editor: Manfred Rasper
Profile: Contributions to issues of conservation in Lower Saxony.
Language(s): German

INFORMATIONSTECHNOLOGIE 741787G5C-44
Editorial: Zettachring 4, 70567 STUTTGART
Tel: 711 72846112 **Fax:** 711 72846108
Email: brigitte.krcmar@integrata.de **Web site:** http://www.integrata.de
Freq: Annual; **Cover Price:** Free; **Circ:** 65,000
Profile: Programme featuring seminars for computer users.
Language(s): German

INFORMATIONSTECHNOLOGIE 741787G5C-69
Editorial: Zettachring 4, 70567 STUTTGART
Tel: 711 72846112 **Fax:** 711 72846108
Email: brigitte.krcmar@integrata.de **Web site:** http://www.integrata.de
Freq: Annual; **Cover Price:** Free; **Circ:** 65,000
Profile: Programme featuring seminars for computer users.
Language(s): German

INFRANKEN.DE 1621281G67B-16547
Editorial: Gutenbergstr. 1, 96050 BAMBERG
Tel: 951 1880 **Fax:** 951 188335
Email: redaktion@infranken.de **Web site:** http://www.infranken.de
Freq: Daily; **Cover Price:** Paid
Annual Sub.: EUR 17,50; **Circ:** 1,374,460 Unique Users
Editor: Walter Schweinsberg; **Advertising Manager:** Klaus Dünisch
Profile: Ezine: Regional daily newspaper covering politics, economics, sport, travel and technology. Facebook: http://www.facebook.com/pages/inFrankende/209363937665.
Language(s): German
REGIONAL DAILY & SUNDAY NEWSPAPERS: Regional Daily Newspapers

INGELHEIMER WOCHENBLATT 731329G72-5888
Editorial: Lärchenweg 4, 55218 INGELHEIM
Tel: 6132 896203 **Fax:** 6132 896204
Email: redaktion@ingelheimer-wochenblatt.de **Web site:** http://www.ingelheimer-wochenblatt.de
Freq: Weekly; **Cover Price:** Free; **Circ:** 26,287
Editor: Rüdiger Benda; **Advertising Manager:** Rainer Baumann
Profile: Advertising journal (house-to-house) concentrating on local stories.
Language(s): German
ADVERTISING RATES:
Full Page Mono .... EUR 3125
Full Page Colour .... EUR 4234
Mechanical Data: Type Area: 480 x 325 mm, No. of Columns (Display): 7, Col Widths (Display): 45 mm
Copy instructions: *Copy Date:* 2 days prior to publication
LOCAL NEWSPAPERS

INGENIEURBLATT FÜR BADEN-WÜRTTEMBERG 731330G4E-4840
Editorial: Aulberstr. 25, 72764 REUTLINGEN
Tel: 7121 946411 **Fax:** 7121 946430
Email: redaktion@ingenieurblatt.de **Web site:** http://www.ingenieurblatt.de
Freq: 6 issues yearly; **Cover Price:** EUR 3,00
Free to qualifying individuals ; **Circ:** 5,000
Editor: Dieter Baral; **Advertising Manager:** Dieter Baral
Profile: Magazine on architecture, building and surveying.
Language(s): German

ADVERTISING RATES:
Full Page Mono .... EUR 675
Full Page Colour .... EUR 1440
Mechanical Data: Type Area: 256 x 185 mm, Col Widths (Display): 90 mm, No. of Columns (Display): 2
Copy instructions: *Copy Date:* 14 days prior to publication

INGENIEUR-NACHRICHTEN
1830238G19A-1121
Editorial: Augsburger Str. 75a, 01309 DRESDEN
Tel: 351 8361990 **Fax:** 351 8361992
Email: dresden@vitw-sachsen.de **Web site:** http://www.vitw-sachsen.de
Freq: 6 issues yearly; **Annual Sub.:** EUR 10,20; **Circ:** 5,000
Profile: Magazine for engineers, technicians and scientists, teachers and students.
Language(s): German
ADVERTISING RATES:
Full Page Mono .... EUR 1455
Full Page Colour .... EUR 2030
Mechanical Data: Type Area: 260 x 186 mm, No. of Columns (Display): 3, Col Widths (Display): 58 mm

INITIATIV - DAS WIRTSCHAFTSMAGAZIN
731332G14A-3480
Editorial: Bleichstr. 25, 55543 BAD KREUZNACH
Tel: 671 839930 **Fax:** 671 8399339
Email: initiativ@ess.de **Web site:** http://www.ess.de
Freq: Quarterly; **Annual Sub.:** EUR 20,00; **Circ:** 8,000
Editor: Torsten Strauß; **Advertising Manager:** Michael Wies
Profile: Business magazine.
Language(s): German
ADVERTISING RATES:
Full Page Colour .... EUR 1530
Mechanical Data: Type Area: 275 x 185 mm, No. of Columns (Display): 4, Col Widths (Display): 45 mm

INITIATIVBANKING
731333G65A-264_106
Editorial: Kasernenstr. 69, 40213 DÜSSELDORF
Tel: 211 54227603 **Fax:** 211 54227722
Email: florian.flicke@corps-verlag.de **Web site:** http://www.corps-verlag.de
Freq: Quarterly; **Cover Price:** Free; **Circ:** 185,800
Editor: Wilfried Lülsdorf
Profile: Customer magazine from the Westdeutsche Genossenschafts-Zentralbank.
Language(s): German
ADVERTISING RATES:
Full Page Mono .... EUR 6500
Full Page Colour .... EUR 6500
Mechanical Data: Type Area: 233 x 171 mm
Supplement to: Handelsblatt, Harvard Business manager
NATIONAL DAILY & SUNDAY NEWSPAPERS: National Daily Newspapers

INNOVATION UND TECHNIK
731358G41A-1280
Editorial: Auf dem Brink 6, 58762 ALTENA
Tel: 2352 71366 **Fax:** 2352 71913
Email: u.bachmann@t-online.de **Web site:** http://www.innovationundtechnik.de
Freq: Monthly; **Annual Sub.:** EUR 85,00; **Circ:** 3,440
Editor: Ulrich Bachmann
Profile: Magazine about engraving.
Language(s): German
Readership: Read by people interested in the engraving of metals.
ADVERTISING RATES:
Full Page Mono .... EUR 1166
Full Page Colour .... EUR 2108
Mechanical Data: Type Area: 255 x 190 mm, No. of Columns (Display): 4, Col Widths (Display): 42 mm
Official Journal of: Organ d. Bundesinnung f. d. Flexografen-Handwerk, d. Association Européenne des Graveurs et des Flexographes u. d. Bundesinnungsverb. d. Galvaniseure, Graveure u. Metallbildner
BUSINESS: PRINTING & STATIONERY: Printing

INNOVATIVE VERWALTUNG
746702G34-198
Editorial: Hinterm Berg 87a, 27726 WORPSWEDE
Tel: 4792 955277 **Fax:** 4792 955279
Email: innovative-verwaltung@kloeker.com **Web site:** http://www.innovative-verwaltung.de
Freq: 10 issues yearly; **Annual Sub.:** EUR 155,00; **Circ:** 6,111
Editor: Michael Klöker; **Advertising Manager:** Eva Hanenberg
Profile: Journal focusing on successful office and administrative management, including details on supplies and equipment.
Language(s): German
Readership: Aimed at people working within the public sector.
ADVERTISING RATES:
Full Page Mono .... EUR 2340
Full Page Colour .... EUR 3990
Mechanical Data: Type Area: 240 x 175 mm, No. of Columns (Display): 4, Col Widths (Display): 40 mm
BUSINESS: OFFICE EQUIPMENT

INNSIDE
731369G89C-4806
Editorial: Wiener Str. 37, 94032 PASSAU
Tel: 851 32001 **Fax:** 851 32004
Email: innside@t-online.de **Web site:** http://www.innside-passau.de
Freq: 10 issues yearly; **Cover Price:** Free; **Circ:** 19,727
Editor: Gerd Jakobi; **Advertising Manager:** Gerd Jakobi
Profile: Regional magazine for Ostbayern and Upper Austria. As a free program and culture magazine is published monthly with interesting features on current topics related to the cultural industry, but also treated Lifstyle issues, interviews, and economic issues. With the probably most complete cultural calendar of Niederbayern, the magazine is a must for anyone interested in live culture. The ARTS-section of the magazine also offers a nearly complete picture of the galleries and museums of our region and, with his portrait artist every month from a regional artist. But the hottest clubs and pubs of the region can be found in the regional magazine. Movie show times, book, CD, health and fitness tips complete the service section of the magazine.
Language(s): German
ADVERTISING RATES:
Full Page Mono .... EUR 2950
Full Page Colour .... EUR 2950
Mechanical Data: Type Area: 260 x 180 mm
Copy instructions: *Copy Date:* 14 days prior to publication
CONSUMER: HOLIDAYS & TRAVEL: Entertainment Guides

INPHO IMAGING & BUSINESS
731371G38-4
Editorial: Kreuzbergstr. 12, 40489 DÜSSELDORF
Tel: 211 41558866 **Fax:** 211 41558867
Email: f.isphording@gfw.de **Web site:** http://www.inphonews.de
Freq: 11 issues yearly; **Annual Sub.:** EUR 92,00; **Circ:** 9,122
Editor: Frank Isphording; **Advertising Manager:** Stephan Rattunde
Profile: Journal providing information concerning the photographic and video trade.
Language(s): German
ADVERTISING RATES:
Full Page Mono .... EUR 2500
Full Page Colour .... EUR 4300
Mechanical Data: Type Area: 274 x 187 mm, No. of Columns (Display): 4, Col Widths (Display): 43 mm
Copy instructions: *Copy Date:* 20 days prior to publication
BUSINESS: PHOTOGRAPHIC TRADE

INSBÜRO
1687386G1A-3607
Editorial: Feldstiege 100, 48161 MÜNSTER
Tel: 2533 9300672 **Fax:** 2533 930050
Email: regina.dick@lexisnexis.de **Web site:** http://www.lexisnexis.de/insbuero-zeitschrift
Freq: Monthly; **Annual Sub.:** EUR 252,20; **Circ:** 1,100
Editor: Hans Haarmeyer; **Advertising Manager:** Anja Christensen
Profile: Magazine for lawyers specialised in law of obligations.
Language(s): German
ADVERTISING RATES:
Full Page Mono .... EUR 678
Full Page Colour .... EUR 1044
Mechanical Data: Type Area: 239 x 174 mm
Copy instructions: *Copy Date:* 14 days prior to publication

DIE INSEL
731376G89A-12102
Editorial: Gärtnerkoppel 3, 24259 WESTENSEE
Tel: 4305 992992 **Fax:** 4305 992993
Email: gkprkiel@t-online.de **Web site:** http://www.syltmagazin.de
Freq: Annual; **Cover Price:** EUR 6,50; **Circ:** 35,000
Editor: Günter Kohl
Profile: Travel Information on Sylt, reports, tips, culinary advice, catering guide, events, trends.
Language(s): German
ADVERTISING RATES:
Full Page Colour .... EUR 3230
Mechanical Data: Type Area: 270 x 185 mm

DER INSEL-BOTE
731378G67B-7740
Editorial: Nikolaistr. 7, 24937 FLENSBURG
Tel: 461 8080 **Fax:** 461 8081058
Email: redaktion@shz.de **Web site:** http://www.shz.de
Freq: 312 issues yearly; **Circ:** 3,249
Advertising Manager: Ingeborg Schwarz
Profile: Predecessor of the "Insel-Bote" were the "Westsee Inseln", which first appeared 1870. 1880, the "Insel-Bote" was founded, and in 1954 in the Flensburger Zeitungsverlag integrated. Every day the specimens are transported by sea to the readers of Foehr and Amrum as well as some islets. Facebook: http://www.facebook.com/shzonline Twitter: http://twitter.com/shz_de This Outlet offers RSS (Really Simple Syndication).
Language(s): German
ADVERTISING RATES:
SCC .... EUR 40,00
Mechanical Data: Type Area: 480 x 325 mm, No. of Columns (Display): 7, Col Widths (Display): 45 mm
Copy instructions: *Copy Date:* 1 day prior to publication
Supplement(s): nordisch gesund; Schleswig-Holstein Journal; tv magazin
REGIONAL DAILY & SUNDAY NEWSPAPERS: Regional Daily Newspapers

INSIDE
731384G22A-1220
Editorial: St.-Jakobs-Platz 12, 80331 MÜNCHEN
Tel: 89 232490611 **Fax:** 89 232490610
Email: redaktion@inside-getraenke.de **Web site:** http://www.inside-getraenke.de
Freq: 24 issues yearly; **Annual Sub.:** EUR 341,80; **Circ:** 2,263
Editor: Niklas Other; **Advertising Manager:** Adele Westphal
Profile: Inside Getränke-Markt-Magazin is an independent, not only relatable on a subscription news service for the beverage industry group. The magazine published no drinks advertising, only bodies, representation and service ads.
Language(s): German
ADVERTISING RATES:
Full Page Mono .... EUR 1820
Full Page Colour .... EUR 2650
Mechanical Data: Type Area: 255 x 180 mm, No. of Columns (Display): 2, Col Widths (Display): 85 mm
Copy instructions: *Copy Date:* 4 days prior to publication
BUSINESS: FOOD

INSIDE
731385G23A-67
Editorial: Destouchesstr. 6, 80803 MÜNCHEN
Tel: 89 3835670 **Fax:** 89 342124
Email: info@inside-wohnen.de **Web site:** http://www.inside-wohnen.de
Freq: 24 issues yearly; **Annual Sub.:** EUR 288,04; **Circ:** 2,089
Editor: Simon Feldmer; **Advertising Manager:** Ulrike Lechtenfeld
Profile: Magazine focusing on design and production of furniture.
Language(s): German
Readership: Read by manufacturers.
ADVERTISING RATES:
Full Page Mono .... EUR 2470
Full Page Colour .... EUR 2470
Mechanical Data: Type Area: 255 x 180 mm, No. of Columns (Display): 2, Col Widths (Display): 85 mm
Copy instructions: *Copy Date:* 4 days prior to publication
BUSINESS: FURNISHINGS & FURNITURE

INSIDE B
723993G14A-1140
Editorial: Marlener Str. 9, 77656 OFFENBURG
Tel: 781 5045620 **Fax:** 781 5045609
Email: redaktion@inside-b.de **Web site:** http://www.inside-b.de
Freq: Monthly; **Annual Sub.:** EUR 39,00; **Circ:** 14,437
Editor: Sabine Schwendemann; **Advertising Manager:** Daniela Sturm
Language(s): German
ADVERTISING RATES:
Full Page Colour .... EUR 2824
Mechanical Data: Type Area: 252 x 186 mm, No. of Columns (Display): 3, Col Widths (Display): 58 mm
Copy instructions: *Copy Date:* 21 days prior to publication
BUSINESS: COMMERCE, INDUSTRY & MANAGEMENT

INSIDE-DIGITAL.DE
1704295G2D-776
Editorial: Bahnhofstr. 11, 50321 BRÜHL
Tel: 2232 5044600 **Fax:** 2232 5044609
Email: presse@inside-digital.de **Web site:** http://www.inside-digital.de
Cover Price: Paid; **Circ:** 161,034 Unique Users
Editor: Jan Freynick
Profile: Portal around the topic of "Digital Entertainment ". It provides next-to-date news from the world of technology around TV, receiver and BluRay player one of the most extensive device databases.The attendees are predominantly male, well educated and with a high income. Facebook: http://www.facebook.com/insidedigital Twitter: http://twitter.com/inside_red.
Language(s): German
BUSINESS: COMMUNICATIONS, ADVERTISING & MARKETING: Broadcasting

INSIDE-HANDY.DE
1704296G74M-789
Editorial: Bahnhofstr. 11, 50321 BRÜHL
Tel: 2232 5044600 **Fax:** 2232 5044609
Email: presse@inside-handy.de **Web site:** http://www.inside-handy.de
Cover Price: Paid; **Circ:** 1,346,112 Unique Users
Editor: Jan Freynick
Profile: Online portal with news Mobile phone services. Current trends, testing, data to mobile phones, tariffs, and Tablet PCs Facebook: http://www.facebook.com/insidehandy Twitter: http://twitter.com/inside_red.
Language(s): German
CONSUMER: WOMEN'S INTEREST CONSUMER MAGAZINES: Personal Finance

INSIGHT
753839G14A-3150
Editorial: Rellinger Str. 64a, 20257 HAMBURG
Tel: 40 8531330 **Fax:** 40 85313322
Email: mail@stroomer-pr.de **Web site:** http://www.stroomer-pr.de
Freq: 3 issues yearly; **Circ:** 7,500
Profile: Magazine for employees of General Logistics Systems Germany.
Language(s): German

INSPECT
1615857G17-1542
Editorial: Rößlerstr. 90, 64293 DARMSTADT
Tel: 6151 8090153 **Fax:** 6151 8090154
Email: gabriele.jansen@wiley.com **Web site:** http://www.inspect-online.com
Freq: 8 issues yearly; **Annual Sub.:** EUR 48,15; **Circ:** 19,295
Editor: Gabriele Jansen; **Advertising Manager:** Oliver Scheel
Profile: INSPECT (circulation: 20,000) is the leading European magazine for machine vision and optical metrology. It is read across all industries by direct and indirect decision-makers involved in the application and procurement of these components, products and technologies. The three regular sections of Vision, Automation and Control structure the contents into the fields of components and technologies, turn-key systems and applications, and material testing and measuring instruments. Up-to-date reports, hot topics, trade show previews and reviews, as well as interviews with the industry leaders complement the expert topics, application reports and product information. INSPECT is published 7 times per year, including PRO-4-PRO (issue 4–5/2011) as well as the international Buyers Guide (issue 6/2011). Furthermore the INSPECT portal (www.inspect-online.com) gives you an additional possibility to reach your target group.
Language(s): German
ADVERTISING RATES:
Full Page Mono .... EUR 4500
Full Page Colour .... EUR 5980
Mechanical Data: Type Area: 260 x 185 mm, No. of Columns (Display): 4, Col Widths (Display): 43 mm

INSTANDHALTUNG
731408G19E-70
Editorial: Justus-von-Liebig-Str. 1, 86899 LANDSBERG **Tel:** 8191 125376 **Fax:** 8191 125483
Email: ingo.busch@mi-verlag.de **Web site:** http://www.instandhaltung.de
Freq: 9 issues yearly; **Annual Sub.:** EUR 74,80; **Circ:** 13,991
Editor: Ingo Busch; **Advertising Manager:** Helmut Schempp
Profile: The trade magazine "maintenance" is concerned with the inspection, maintenance and repair of machinery, industrial equipment and in all industries. Besides the presentation of new technical procedures, equipment and tools and solutions for the organization and integration of maintenance activities in the operational processes are introduced in practice. This makes identifying the latest trends in the use of modern techniques and organizational forms of this journal an indispensable guide for operation and maintenance managers.
Language(s): German
ADVERTISING RATES:
Full Page Mono .... EUR 4400
Full Page Colour .... EUR 5200
Mechanical Data: Type Area: 257 x 178 mm, No. of Columns (Display): 4, Col Widths (Display): 41 mm
Copy instructions: *Copy Date:* 28 days prior to publication
BUSINESS: ENGINEERING & MACHINERY: Machinery, Machine Tools & Metalworking

INSTANDHALTUNGSJOURNAL & GEBÄUDEMANAGEMENT
731409G4F-4
Editorial: Arnikaweg 8, 85521 OTTOBRUNN
Tel: 89 604075 **Fax:** 89 6016135
Email: redaktion@instandhaltungsjournal.de **Web site:** http://www.instandhaltungsjournal.de
Freq: 10 issues yearly; **Annual Sub.:** EUR 96,00; **Circ:** 11,678
Editor: Adolf Raschendorfer; **Advertising Manager:** Margarete Tajnai
Profile: Magazine about maintenance and building management. Covers heating, sanitation and renovation in industrial buildings and factories, hotels and hospitals.
Language(s): German
ADVERTISING RATES:
Full Page Mono .... EUR 3395
Full Page Colour .... EUR 4730
Mechanical Data: Type Area: 260 x 184 mm, No. of Columns (Display): 3, Col Widths (Display): 51 mm
Copy instructions: *Copy Date:* 28 days prior to publication
BUSINESS: ARCHITECTURE & BUILDING: Cleaning & Maintenance

INSTANT
1818834G2A-5736
Editorial: Leerbachstr. 57, 60322 FRANKFURT
Tel: 69 79588780 **Fax:** 69 795887818
Email: g.schecker@e-instant.de **Web site:** http://www.e-instant.de
Cover Price: EUR 15,00; **Circ:** 2,000
Editor: Thomas Feicht; **Advertising Manager:** Gitta Schecker
Profile: Company publication.
Language(s): German
ADVERTISING RATES:
Full Page Mono .... EUR 5000
Full Page Colour .... EUR 7500

INSTANT DDC
1818835G2A-5737
Editorial: Leerbachstr. 57, 60322 FRANKFURT
Tel: 69 79588780 **Fax:** 69 795887818
Email: office@e-instant.de **Web site:** http://www.e-instant.de
Cover Price: EUR 15,00; **Circ:** 2,000
Editor: Gitta Schecker; **Advertising Manager:** Gitta Schecker
Profile: Company publication.

Language(s): German
ADVERTISING RATES:
Full Page Mono .... EUR 2500
Full Page Colour .... EUR 5000

INSTYLE
731413G74A-1580
Editorial: Arabellastr. 23, 81925 MÜNCHEN
Tel: 89 92501754 **Fax:** 89 92502583
Email: info@instyle.burda.com **Web site:** http://www.instyle.de
Freq: Monthly; **Annual Sub.:** EUR 35,40; **Circ:** 450,703
Editor: Patricia Riekel
Profile: InStyle is the original concept of all star fashion magazines. Often imitated but never duplicated. For over 10 years on the German market, InStyle where it owns a leading position. InStyle's fashion, beauty and lifestyle - always with a direct connection to celebrities. InStyle is current, inspiring and versatile. InStyle presents the latest trends - the style of the stars - and delivers the ultimate shopping service with the same. Over 1 million InStyle readers use the valuable momentum. Because they are oriented like the current trends. InStyle why they read and be inspired by the style icons of our time. Facebook: http://www.facebook.com/InStyleGermany Twitter: https://twitter.com/InStyleGermany.
Language(s): German
Readership: Read by women of all ages.
ADVERTISING RATES:
Full Page Mono .... EUR 27100
Full Page Colour .... EUR 27100
Mechanical Data: Type Area: 258 x 212 mm
Copy instructions: *Copy Date:* 37 days prior to publication
Supplement(s): InStyle Men
CONSUMER: WOMEN'S INTEREST CONSUMER MAGAZINES: Women's Interest

INTENSIV
730844G56C-26_50
Editorial: Schneddingstr. 56, 48129 MÜNSTER
Email: lothar.ullrich@mednet.uni-muenster.de **Web site:** http://www.thieme.de/intensiv
Freq: 6 issues yearly; **Annual Sub.:** EUR 99,50; **Circ:** 3,420
Editor: Lothar Ullrich
Profile: Specialist nurses from intensive care and anesthesiology make this magazine, which contributes with articles on education, training and continuing education for the professionalisation and training of specialist care. Content: News in brief Original works Professional Policy and Law Calendar of events.
Language(s): German
ADVERTISING RATES:
Full Page Mono .... EUR 1330
Full Page Colour .... EUR 2120
Mechanical Data: Type Area: 248 x 175 mm
Official Journal of: Organ d. Dt. Ges. f. Fachkrankenpflege u. Funktionsdienste e.V.
BUSINESS: HEALTH & MEDICAL: Hospitals

INTENSIV- UND NOTFALLBEHANDLUNG
731425G56P-61
Editorial: Ernst-Grube-Str. 40, 06120 HALLE
Tel: 345 5572601 **Fax:** 345 5572072
Email: karl.werdan@medizin.uni-halle.de
Freq: Quarterly; **Annual Sub.:** EUR 82,50; **Circ:** 1,500
Editor: K. Werdan; **Advertising Manager:** Christian Graßl
Profile: Journal of internal medicine, cardiology, nephrology, anesthesiology, surgery, neurology, pediatrics, intensive care and guard stations.
Language(s): German
ADVERTISING RATES:
Full Page Mono .... EUR 1150
Full Page Colour .... EUR 2140
Mechanical Data: Type Area: 242 x 167 mm, No. of Columns (Display): 3, Col Widths (Display): 56 mm
Copy instructions: *Copy Date:* 28 days prior to publication
BUSINESS: HEALTH & MEDICAL: Casualty & Emergency

INTENSIVE CARE MEDICINE
731422G56C-28
Editorial: Tiergartenstr. 17, 69121 HEIDELBERG
Tel: 6221 4870 **Fax:** 6221 4878366
Email: ute.heilmann@springer.com **Web site:** http://www.springerlink.com
Freq: Monthly; **Annual Sub.:** EUR 1148,00; **Circ:** 4,300
Editor: Massimo Antonelli; **Advertising Manager:** Kathrin Müller-Kölling
Profile: Official journal of the European Society of Intensive Care Medicine. Includes trade news, case reports, new methods and equipment.
Language(s): English
Readership: Read by doctors, anaesthetists and surgeons.
ADVERTISING RATES:
Full Page Mono .... EUR 1710
Full Page Colour .... EUR 2750
Mechanical Data: Type Area: 240 x 175 mm
Official Journal of: Organ d. European Society of Intensive Care Medicine u. d. European Society of Pediatric and Neonatal Intensive Care
BUSINESS: HEALTH & MEDICAL: Hospitals

INTENSIVMEDIZIN UND NOTFALLMEDIZIN
731423G56P-62
Editorial: Tiergartenstr. 17, 69121 HEIDELBERG
Tel: 6221 4878178 **Fax:** 6221 48768178
Email: tina.suhai@springer.com **Web site:** http://www.springermedizin.de
Freq: 8 issues yearly; Free to qualifying individuals
Annual Sub.: EUR 223,00; **Circ:** 2,800
Advertising Manager: Odette Thomßen
Profile: The Journal Intensivmedizin und Notfallmedizin is the essence of the field created according to an interdisciplinary: in addition to questions from the Internal Intensive Care the reader is also regularly issues in anesthesiology, surgery, neurology and pediatrics, as well as issues of cross-curricular relevance. The magazine is aimed primarily at medical staff in intensive care units and emergency rooms, it offers - for example, under the headings of care and physiotherapy - but also contributions for non-medical professionals in intensive care. Each issue has a main point addressed in the recognized experts in several reviews current issues in intensive care and emergency medicine. The sum of the individual issues are here an overview in terms of a "State of the Art" and reflects the progress of the area. High relevance for the daily work is the focus of this review. Free submitted original papers presenting important studies of the field and promote scientific exchange. Case reports show interesting cases and unusual diseases or courses of treatment. In the rubric Journal Club commenting Experts outstanding publications in the international literature Other sections deal with specific aspects of intensive care and issues affecting the profession policy. Another concern is the continuing education. The Magazine offers 8 CME education units per year.
Language(s): German
ADVERTISING RATES:
Full Page Mono .... EUR 1380
Full Page Colour .... EUR 2420
Mechanical Data: Type Area: 240 x 174 mm
Official Journal of: Organ d. Dt. Ges. f. Internist. Intensivmedizin u. Notfallmedizin, d. Österr. Ges. f. Internist. u. Allg. Intensivmedizin, d. ArGe Intensivmedizin im Berufsverb. Dt. Internisten, d. Dt. Ges. f. Neurointensiv- & Notfallmedizin, d. Dt. Interdisziplinären Vereinigung f. Intensivmedizin & Notfallmedizin u. d. Dt. Ges. f. Innere Medizin
BUSINESS: HEALTH & MEDICAL: Casualty & Emergency

INTERAKTIV
1683997G19A-1098
Editorial: Nobelstr. 12, 70569 STUTTGART
Tel: 711 9701177 **Fax:** 711 9701400
Email: grosser@ipa.fraunhofer.de **Web site:** http://www.ipa.fraunhofer.de
Freq: 3 issues yearly; **Cover Price:** Free; **Circ:** 8,000
Editor: Hubert Grosser
Profile: Magazine about research and development work in the fields of corporate organization, surface engineering, automation.
Language(s): German

INTERCERAM
731430G12A-30
Editorial: Aachener Str. 172, 40223 DÜSSELDORF
Tel: 211 1591230 **Fax:** 211 1591150
Email: redaktion-keramik@dvs-hg.de **Web site:** http://www.interceram-review.info
Freq: 6 issues yearly; **Annual Sub.:** EUR 248,50; **Circ:** 5,000
Editor: Hubert Pelc; **Advertising Manager:** Iris Jansen
Profile: International ceramic review, focuses on research, new technology and developments, new products, market analyses, company reports and trade fairs.
Language(s): English
Readership: Aimed at manufacturers, suppliers of fine technical ceramics and refractories.
ADVERTISING RATES:
Full Page Mono .... EUR 1720
Full Page Colour .... EUR 2290
Mechanical Data: Type Area: 261 x 191 mm, No. of Columns (Display): 3, Col Widths (Display): 59 mm
BUSINESS: CERAMICS, POTTERY & GLASS: Ceramics & Pottery

INTERGERMA HOTELS UND TAGUNGSSTÄTTEN
1864906G50-1261
Editorial: Alfred-Fischer-Weg 12, 59073 HAMM
Tel: 2381 307090 **Fax:** 2381 3070919
Email: info@intergerma.de **Web site:** http://www.intergerma.de
Freq: Annual; **Cover Price:** Free; **Circ:** 35,000
Editor: Markus Schmidt; **Advertising Manager:** Silke Offermann
Profile: Magazine on hotels and seminar places.
Language(s): German
Mechanical Data: Type Area: 267 x 194 mm
Copy instructions: *Copy Date:* 90 days prior to publication

INTERMEZZO
1829912G14A-10106
Editorial: Großen Str. 37, 27356 ROTENBURG
Tel: 4261 819990 **Fax:** 4261 8199999
Email: kontakt@intermezzo-magazin.de **Web site:** http://www.intermezzo-magazin.de
Freq: Half-yearly; **Circ:** 40,000
Advertising Manager: Bernd Braumüller
Profile: Lifestyle magazine for entrepreneurs and managers in industry, commerce and trade. It is distributed via the Chamber of Commerce magazines space 50 kilometers around Bremen.
Language(s): German

ADVERTISING RATES:
Full Page Colour .... EUR 6400
Mechanical Data: Type Area: 260 x 185 mm
Supplement to: Wirtschaft ElbelWeser

INTERN
721980G60R-50
Editorial: Burchardstr. 11, 20095 HAMBURG
Tel: 40 30191037 **Fax:** 40 30191043
Email: astrid.heissen@bauermedia.com **Web site:** http://www.bauermedia.com
Freq: 11 issues yearly; **Cover Price:** Free; **Circ:** 3,000
Editor: Astrid Heissen
Profile: Employee Newsletter of the Bauer Media Group and the Bauer group.
Language(s): German
Readership: Read by employees of the publisher.
BUSINESS: PUBLISHING: Publishing Related

INTERNATIONAL ARCHIVES OF OCCUPATIONAL AND ENVIRONMENTAL HEALTH
731461G56A-5340
Editorial: Schillerstr. 25, 91054 ERLANGEN
Tel: 9131 8522312 **Fax:** 9131 8522317
Email: hans.drexler@rzmail.uni-erlangen.de **Web site:** http://www.springerlink.com
Freq: 8 issues yearly; **Annual Sub.:** EUR 3329,00; **Circ:** 162
Editor: Hans Drexler
Profile: International archives of occupational and environmental health.
Language(s): English
ADVERTISING RATES:
Full Page Mono .... EUR 740
Full Page Colour .... EUR 1780
Mechanical Data: Type Area: 240 x 175 mm

INTERNATIONAL CONTACT
731463G38-5
Editorial: Freiligrathring 18, 40878 RATINGEN
Tel: 2102 20270 **Fax:** 2102 202790
Email: thb@cat-verlag.de **Web site:** http://www.worldofphoto.com
Freq: 6 issues yearly; **Annual Sub.:** EUR 30,00; **Circ:** 11,876
Editor: Thomas Blömer; **Advertising Manager:** Ralf Gruna
Profile: Independent magazine for the international imaging market.
Language(s): English
ADVERTISING RATES:
Full Page Colour .... EUR 3960
Mechanical Data: Type Area: 294 x 230 mm, No. of Columns (Display): 3, Col Widths (Display): 72 mm
Copy instructions: *Copy Date:* 30 days prior to publication
BUSINESS: PHOTOGRAPHIC TRADE

INTERNATIONAL HERALD TRIBUNE - FRANKFURT
1937394G65G-1
Editorial: Friedrichstrasse 52, 60323 FRANKFURT
Tel: 69 7167 7911
Email: jewing@iht.com **Web site:** http://global.nytimes.com/?iht
Freq: Daily; **Circ:** 21,416
Advertising Director: Christoph Bajjaly
Profile: German bureau of The International Herald Tribune, the global edition of The New York Times.
Language(s): English
NATIONAL DAILY & SUNDAY NEWSPAPERS: Plaid-Cymru-MdEP

INTERNATIONAL JOURNAL OF CLINICAL PHARMACOLOGY AND THERAPEUTICS
756086G56A-11088
Editorial: Postfach 200232, 63308 RÖDERMARK
Email: woodcock@clinpharmacol.com
Freq: Monthly; **Annual Sub.:** EUR 268,00; **Circ:** 4,000
Editor: B. G. Woodcock; **Advertising Manager:** Jörg Feistle
Profile: International journal of clinical pharmacology and therapeutics.
Language(s): English
Mechanical Data: Type Area: 242 x 167 mm, No. of Columns (Display): 3, Col Widths (Display): 52 mm
Copy instructions: *Copy Date:* 28 days prior to publication

INTERNATIONAL JOURNAL OF COLORECTAL DISEASE
731507G56A-5360
Editorial: Tiergartenstr. 17, 69121 HEIDELBERG
Tel: 6221 4870 **Fax:** 6221 4878366
Email: subscriptions@springer.com **Web site:** http://www.springerlink.com
Freq: Monthly; **Annual Sub.:** EUR 2115,00; **Circ:** 263
Editor: Heinz J. Buhr
Profile: International Journal of colorectal disease.
Language(s): English
ADVERTISING RATES:
Full Page Mono .... EUR 740
Full Page Colour .... EUR 1780
Mechanical Data: Type Area: 240 x 175 mm
Official Journal of: Organ d. Association of Coloproctology of Great Britain and Ireland

INTERNATIONAL JOURNAL OF LEGAL MEDICINE
731512G56A-5400
Editorial: Röntgenstr. 23, 48129 MÜNSTER
Fax: 251 8355158
Email: pfeiffh@uni-muenster.de **Web site:** http://www.springerlink.com
Freq: 6 issues yearly; **Annual Sub.:** EUR 1829,00; **Circ:** 323
Editor: H. Pfeiffer
Profile: International journal of legal medicine.
Language(s): English
ADVERTISING RATES:
Full Page Mono .... EUR 740
Full Page Colour .... EUR 1780
Mechanical Data: Type Area: 240 x 175 mm
Official Journal of: Organ d. Internat. Academy of Legal Medicine

THE INTERNATIONAL JOURNAL OF LIFE CYCLE ASSESSMENT
731513G57-900
Editorial: Kirschgartenstr. 91, 69126 HEIDELBERG
Tel: 6221 4334545
Email: abh.scientificjournals@googlemail.com **Web site:** http://www.springer.com
Freq: 9 issues yearly; **Annual Sub.:** EUR 512,50; **Circ:** 720
Editor: Walter Klöpffer
Profile: Journal dealing with ecological burdens and impacts connected with products, systems and human activities.
Language(s): English
ADVERTISING RATES:
Full Page Mono .... EUR 830
Full Page Colour .... EUR 1870
Mechanical Data: Type Area: 240 x 175 mm
Official Journal of: Organ d. Life Cycle Assessment Society of Japan, d. Indian, d. Korean u. d. Australian Society for Life Cycle Assessment

INTERNATIONAL JOURNAL OF MATERIALS RESEARCH
748703G27-2880
Editorial: Heisenbergstr. 5, 70569 STUTTGART
Tel: 711 6893520 **Fax:** 711 6893522
Email: ijmr@mf.mpg.de **Web site:** http://www.ijmr.de
Freq: Monthly; **Annual Sub.:** EUR 698,00; **Circ:** 800
Editor: Manfred Rühle; **Advertising Manager:** Hermann J. Kleiner
Profile: The International Journal of Materials Research is one of the most internationally recognized journals, which deals with research, development, structure and properties of metallic materials and their production, processing and application. IJMR is a reflection of the scientific and technical development in this area. The authors of the original papers are leading experts from home and abroad. Thus the magazine offers an excellent forum for scientific and technical information exchange. An international advisory board guarantees a high level. Contributions published in German or English. The IJMR also publishes the news of DGM, the reports of events, bodies and persons, including an events calendar.
Language(s): English; German
Readership: Read by people within the metal industry.
ADVERTISING RATES:
Full Page Mono .... EUR 1800
Full Page Colour .... EUR 2880
Mechanical Data: Type Area: 245 x 175 mm
BUSINESS: METAL, IRON & STEEL

INTERNATIONAL JOURNAL OF PHYSICAL EDUCATION
731515G62B-260_50
Editorial: Steinwasenstr. 6, 73614 SCHORNDORF
Tel: 7181 4020 **Fax:** 7181 402111
Email: info@hofmann-verlag.de **Web site:** http://www.hofman-verlag.de
Freq: Quarterly; **Annual Sub.:** EUR 45,00; **Circ:** 1,400
Editor: Herbert Haag; **Advertising Manager:** Julia Hechler
Profile: Magazine focusing on the teaching of PE in schools and further education colleges.
Language(s): English; French; German; Spanish
ADVERTISING RATES:
Full Page Mono .... EUR 360
Full Page Colour .... EUR 1230
Mechanical Data: Type Area: 207 x 140 mm, No. of Columns (Display): 2, Col Widths (Display): 68 mm
Copy instructions: *Copy Date:* 30 days prior to publication
BUSINESS: CHURCH & SCHOOL EQUIPMENT & EDUCATION: Education Teachers

INTERNATIONAL JOURNAL OF SPORTS MEDICINE
731519G56A-5420
Editorial: Rüdigerstr. 14, 70469 STUTTGART
Tel: 711 89310 **Fax:** 711 8931298
Email: kundenservice@thieme.de **Web site:** http://www.thieme.de/fz/sportsmedicine.html
Freq: Monthly; **Annual Sub.:** EUR 340,80; **Circ:** 1,090
Editor: Hans-Joachim Appell
Profile: The magazine informs about current scientific results from the sports physiology, biochemistry, biomechanics and sports medicine experiences in

disciplines such as internal medicine, cardiology and orthopedics. As the first international sports medical journal, it promotes a global communications in this field that has in recent years not only for competitive sports, but also for prevention and rehabilitation gained considerable importance.
Language(s): English
ADVERTISING RATES:
Full Page Mono .... EUR 1270
Full Page Colour .... EUR 2440
Mechanical Data: Type Area: 248 x 175 mm, No. of Columns (Display): 4, Col Widths (Display): 40 mm
BUSINESS: HEALTH & MEDICAL

INTERNATIONAL ORTHOPAEDICS 731523G56A-5440
Editorial: Tiergartenstr. 17, 69121 HEIDELBERG
Tel: 6221 4870 **Fax:** 6221 4878366
Email: gabriele.schroeder@springer.com **Web site:** http://www.springerlink.com
Freq: Monthly; **Annual Sub.:** EUR 1779,00; **Circ:** 2,100
Editor: M. Pecina; **Advertising Manager:** Noëla Krischer
Profile: International orthopaedics and traumatology.
Language(s): English; French
ADVERTISING RATES:
Full Page Mono .... EUR 1760
Full Page Colour .... EUR 2800
Mechanical Data: Type Area: 240 x 175 mm
Official Journal of: Organ d. Internat. Society of Orthopaedic Surgery and Traumatology

INTERNATIONALES HOTELVERZEICHNIS INTERNATIONAL HOTEL GUIDE GUIDE INTERNATIONAL DES HÔTELS IHV 1614685G89A-11551
Editorial: Alsterdorfer Str. 262, 22297 HAMBURG
Tel: 40 4908043 **Fax:** 40 499034
Email: international-hotelguide@t-online.de **Web site:** http://www.international-hotel-guide.com
Freq: Annual; **Cover Price:** EUR 12,27; **Circ:** 5,000
Profile: International hotel guide.
Language(s): English; French; German

INTERNATIONALES VERKEHRSWESEN 731496G49A-800
Editorial: Nordkanalstr. 36, 20097 HAMBURG
Tel: 40 23714230 **Fax:** 40 23714205
Email: bettina.guiot@dvvmedia.com **Web site:** http://www.eurailpress.de
Freq: 10 issues yearly; Free to qualifying individuals
Annual Sub.: EUR 146,00; **Circ:** 4,326
Editor: Frank Straube; **Advertising Manager:** Silke Härtel
Profile: Publication giving scientific and practical information for the international transport and communications industry.
Language(s): English; German
ADVERTISING RATES:
Full Page Mono .... EUR 2940
Full Page Colour .... EUR 3930
Mechanical Data: Type Area: 257 x 180 mm, No. of Columns (Display): 3, Col Widths (Display): 58 mm
Copy instructions: *Copy Date:* 25 days prior to publication
Official Journal of: Organ d. Dt. Verkehrswissenschaftl. Ges. e.V.
BUSINESS: TRANSPORT

INTERNET INTERN 731536G18B-840
Editorial: Merowingerstr. 30, 40223 DÜSSELDORF
Tel: 211 933470 **Fax:** 211 9334710
Email: mdolny@databecker.de **Web site:** http://www.pcpraxis.de
Freq: Quarterly; **Cover Price:** EUR 7,99; **Circ:** 22,350
Editor: Michael Dolny; **Advertising Manager:** Jörg Hausch
Profile: Magazine for web designers and developers. Internet Intern offers detailed and thorough articles for professional web applications and professional web design. The focus is on basic items and workshops on topics such as web server administration, Flash animation, HTML editors, web tools, web page design and web graphics. In addition, Internet Intern professional know-how in the areas of Internet providers, e-commerce and content management systems.
Language(s): German
ADVERTISING RATES:
Full Page Mono .... EUR 4200
Full Page Colour .... EUR 4200
Mechanical Data: Type Area: 274 x 180 mm, No. of Columns (Display): 4, Col Widths (Display): 42 mm
Copy instructions: *Copy Date:* 20 days prior to publication

INTERNET MAGAZIN 731537G5F-8
Editorial: Richard-Reitzner-Allee 2, 85540 HAAR
Tel: 89 255561118 **Fax:** 89 255560118
Email: redaktion@internet-magazin.de **Web site:** http://www.internet-magazin.de
Freq: Monthly; **Cover Price:** EUR 4,50; **Circ:** 7,684
Editor: Wolfgang Koser; **Advertising Manager:** Gisela Nerke
Profile: Magazine about developments on the Internet.
Language(s): German
ADVERTISING RATES:
Full Page Mono .... EUR 4425
Full Page Colour .... EUR 5900
Mechanical Data: Type Area: 250 x 185 mm, No. of Columns (Display): 4, Col Widths (Display): 43 mm
Copy instructions: *Copy Date:* 26 days prior to publication
BUSINESS: COMPUTERS & AUTOMATION: Multimedia

INTERNET WORLD BUSINESS 1626157G5E-21
Editorial: Bayerstr. 16a, 80335 MÜNCHEN
Tel: 89 74117381 **Fax:** 89 74117385
Email: mail@internetworld.de **Web site:** http://www.internetworld.de
Freq: 26 issues yearly; **Annual Sub.:** EUR 107,00; **Circ:** 16,821
Editor: Dominik Grollmann; **Advertising Manager:** Angelika Hochmuth
Profile: Magazine for Internet professionals, investment decision-makers and active web users.The platform comprises of bi-weekly issues of the trade magazine for Internet professionals. Under the headings Online advertising, E-Commerce and Technology, Internet professionals can discover all they need to know for more success on the Internet.
Language(s): German
ADVERTISING RATES:
Full Page Mono .... EUR 8450
Full Page Colour .... EUR 8450
Mechanical Data: Type Area: 350 x 250 mm, No. of Columns (Display): 4, Col Widths (Display): 59 mm
Supplement(s): Internet World Business Guide Ad Networks; Internet World Business Guide E-Payment/E-Shop; Internet World Business Guide Mobile Internet; Internet World Business Guide Online-Mediaplaner; Internet World Business Guide Online Werbeplanung; Internet World Business Guide Webagenturen; PHP Journal + Internet World Business Guide Webhosting
BUSINESS: COMPUTERS & AUTOMATION: Data Transmission

INTERNET WORLD BUSINESS GUIDE ONLINE WERBEPLANUNG 1626639G2A-5509
Editorial: Bayerstr. 16a, 80335 MÜNCHEN
Tel: 89 74117338 **Fax:** 89 74117101
Email: gerda.uhl@nmg.de **Web site:** http://www.nmg.de
Freq: Quarterly; **Circ:** 18,000
Editor: Gerda Uhl; **Advertising Manager:** Gerda Uhl
Profile: Magazine for internet professionals.
Language(s): German
ADVERTISING RATES:
Full Page Mono .... EUR 1900
Full Page Colour .... EUR 1900
Mechanical Data: Type Area: 210 x 148 mm
Supplement to: internet World Business

INTERNETCOLOGNE 1704297G18B-2126
Editorial: Am Coloneum 9, 50829 KÖLN
Tel: 221 2222880 **Fax:** 221 2222988
Email: onlineredaktion@netcologne.de **Web site:** http://www.internetcologne.de
Freq: Daily; **Cover Price:** Paid; **Circ:** 1,477,669 Unique Users
Editor: Edgar Franzmann; **Advertising Manager:** Jörg Severin
Language(s): German
BUSINESS: ELECTRONICS: Telecommunications

DER INTERNIST 731542G56A-5460
Editorial: Tiergartenstr. 17, 69121 HEIDELBERG
Tel: 6221 4878960 **Fax:** 6221 4878690
Email: juergen.meyerzutittingdorf@springer.com **Web site:** http://www.springermedizin.de
Freq: Monthly; **Annual Sub.:** EUR 346,00; **Circ:** 40,096
Advertising Manager: Sigrid Christ
Profile: "Der Internist" informed of all relevant diagnostic and therapeutic developments in internal medicine. Each issue is under a theme that is represented by experts in systematic reviews. Additional headings and the release pages of BDI and DGIM provide a current practical experience and professional political orientation. Articles in the section "CME: Continuing Education - Certified Education "present assured results of scientific research and their medical experience for the daily practice. After reading the articles the reader can verify the gained knowledge. The section is based on the training procedure of the field Internal medicine.
Language(s): German
Readership: Aimed at internists.
ADVERTISING RATES:
Full Page Mono .... EUR 4080
Full Page Colour .... EUR 5580
Mechanical Data: Type Area: 240 x 174 mm
Official Journal of: Organ d. Berufsverb. Dt. Internisten e.V. u. d. Dt. Ges. f. Innere Medizin
BUSINESS: HEALTH & MEDICAL

INTERSECTION 1896513G74A-3670
Editorial: Strelitzer Str. 2, 10115 BERLIN
Tel: 30 28884043 **Fax:** 30 28884044
Email: redaktion@intersection-magazin.de **Web site:** http://www.intersection-magazin.de
Freq: Quarterly; **Cover Price:** EUR 2,00; **Circ:** 50,000
Editor: Götz Offergeld
Profile: magazine for men: fashion, design, mobility, car.
Language(s): German
ADVERTISING RATES:
Full Page Mono .... EUR 9500
Full Page Colour .... EUR 9500
Mechanical Data: Type Area: 277 x 230 mm, No. of Columns (Display): 3, Col Widths (Display): 76 mm

INTOUCH 1703724G74A-3491
Editorial: Burchardstr. 19, 20095 HAMBURG
Tel: 40 30192523 **Fax:** 40 30192525
Email: kirsten.neumann@bauermedia.com **Web site:** http://www.intouch-magazin.de
Freq: Weekly; **Annual Sub.:** EUR 106,60; **Circ:** 267,752
Editor: Tim Affeld
Profile: InTouch is Germany's latest and boldest people magazine (starting 20 October 2005). InTouch is printed weekly show from the world of stars. Full delight packed with all the news that young urban women between 16 and 39 years. Our reader is ready to consume and trendy. InTouch provides fun mainly, but also informative fashion, beauty and lifestyle stories. InTouch is pure entertainment. With the unique concept enthusiastically InTouch more readers. Facebook: http://www.facebook.com/pages/InTouch/114830035347.
Language(s): German
ADVERTISING RATES:
Full Page Mono .... EUR 19610
Full Page Colour .... EUR 19610
Mechanical Data: Type Area: 226 x 180 mm
Copy instructions: *Copy Date:* 27 days prior to publication
CONSUMER: WOMEN'S INTEREST CONSUMER MAGAZINES: Women's Interest

INTRAS 1749650A4E-1305
Editorial: Thomasstr. 27, 12053 BERLIN
Tel: 30 6889080 **Fax:** 30 68890832
Email: info@intrakustik.de **Web site:** http://www.intrakustik.de
Freq: 3 issues yearly; **Cover Price:** Free; **Circ:** 6,400
Profile: Company publication published by Intrakustik Baustoffhandel.
Language(s): German

!INTRO 731553G76D-401
Editorial: Venloer Str. 241, 50823 KÖLN
Tel: 221 949930 **Fax:** 221 9499399
Email: thomas.venker@intro.de **Web site:** http://www.intro.de
Freq: 10 issues yearly; **Cover Price:** Free; **Circ:** 117,448
Editor: Thomas Venker; **Advertising Manager:** Oliver Bresch
Profile: Music Magazine. Intro is not just media, but a living part of the scene. Each month the magazine informs competent and reliable aon current bands, trends and products. This applies to all facets of pop culture: music, movies, games, fashion, art and technology. Facebook: http://www.facebook.com/introredaktion Twitter: http://twitter.com/#!/intromagazin This Outlet offers RSS (Really Simple Syndication).
Language(s): German
ADVERTISING RATES:
Full Page Colour .... EUR 6700
Mechanical Data: Type Area: 256 x 182 mm
Supplement(s): projektor
CONSUMER: MUSIC & PERFORMING ARTS: Music

DAS INVESTMENT 727593G1F-620
Editorial: Goldbekplatz 3, 22303 HAMBURG
Tel: 40 40199950 **Fax:** 40 40199960
Email: info@dasinvestment.com **Web site:** http://www.dasinvestment.com
Freq: Monthly; **Annual Sub.:** EUR 49,00; **Circ:** 43,871
Editor: Malte Dreher
Profile: DAS INVESTMENT is one of Germany's leading independent trade magazines for corporate investment and financial advice. Core competence in investment funds, derivatives, insurances and occupational pension schemes, closed-end funds and alternative investments, portfolio (asset allocation) as well as financial adviser and broker themes (education and training, regulation, legal & tax). DAS INVESTMENT researches innovations in the financial sector at an early stage, gives expert opinion to all asset classes and provides orientation on the diversity of financial products and trends in the financial advisory services - in the print magazine and online at DAS INVESTMENT.com. The investment faund statistics section of DAS INVESTMENT is one of the most comprehensive of its kind and takes into account all relevant ratings. The experienced team of editors, the neutrality of the publisher and its economic independence ensure a high level of journalistic niveau and position DAS INVESTMENT as a quality title.
Language(s): German
ADVERTISING RATES:
Full Page Mono .... EUR 5913
Full Page Colour .... EUR 7153
Mechanical Data: Type Area: 267 x 180 mm, No. of Columns (Display): 3, Col Widths (Display): 55 mm
Copy instructions: *Copy Date:* 29 days prior to publication
Official Journal of: Organ d. maz. e.V.
BUSINESS: FINANCE & ECONOMICS: Investment

DAS INVESTMENT.COM 1622780G1F-1534
Editorial: Goldbekplatz 3, 22303 HAMBURG
Tel: 40 40199942 **Fax:** 40 40199960
Email: hannemann@dasinvestment.com **Web site:** http://www.dasinvestment.com
Freq: 260 times a year; **Cover Price:** Paid; **Circ:** 140,969 Unique Users
Editor: Felix Hannemann; **Advertising Manager:** Hero Harder
Profile: Internet Media: financial professionals and experienced private investors see the Investment.com Financial News, background information and product analysis they need for their regular investment decisions. Twitter: http://twitter.com/#!/dasinvestment/ This Outlet offers RSS (Really Simple Syndication).
Language(s): German
BUSINESS: FINANCE & ECONOMICS: Investment

INWOHNEN 735246G74C-2380
Editorial: Schillstr. 51, 33330 GÜTERSLOH
Tel: 5241 2239813 **Fax:** 5241 337762
Email: s.hilgert@strobel-verlag.de **Web site:** http://www.in-wohnen.de
Freq: 5 issues yearly; **Annual Sub.:** EUR 20,75; **Circ:** 75,000
Editor: Sybille Hilgert; **Advertising Manager:** Stefan Schütte
Profile: Guide for house, home and design with the latest news, tips and tricks to modern life and living style. The focus is on expert reports, practical information and a high utility value for the reader. Thus, indwelling innovative counselor and co-planning assistance around the home, housing and design.
Language(s): German
ADVERTISING RATES:
Full Page Mono .... EUR 7900
Full Page Colour .... EUR 7900
Mechanical Data: Type Area: 252 x 190 mm, No. of Columns (Display): 4, Col Widths (Display): 44 mm
Copy instructions: *Copy Date:* 28 days prior to publication
CONSUMER: WOMEN'S INTEREST CONSUMER MAGAZINES: Home & Family

IPF- UND JAGST-ZEITUNG 731569G67B-7760
Editorial: Rudolf-Roth-Str. 18, 88299 LEUTKIRCH
Tel: 7561 800 **Fax:** 7561 80134
Email: redaktion@schwaebische-zeitung.de **Web site:** http://www.schwaebische.de
Freq: 312 issues yearly; **Circ:** 10,690
Profile: In its edition provides the "Ipf- und Jagst-Zeitung" its readers daily with the latest information from government, business, sports, culture and food from the local environment.
Language(s): German
ADVERTISING RATES:
SCC .... EUR 63,20
Mechanical Data: Type Area: 480 x 320 mm, No. of Columns (Display): 7, Col Widths (Display): 44 mm
Copy instructions: *Copy Date:* 1 day prior to publication
REGIONAL DAILY & SUNDAY NEWSPAPERS: Regional Daily Newspapers

IPW 731581G36-4
Editorial: Rüsterstr. 11, 60325 FRANKFURT
Tel: 30 29309515 **Fax:** 69 20737584
Email: sha@ipwonline.de **Web site:** http://www.ipwonline.de
Freq: 8 issues yearly; Free to qualifying individuals
Annual Sub.: EUR 150,00; **Circ:** 7,463
Editor: Susanne Haase; **Advertising Manager:** Roswitha Keppler Junius
Profile: International magazine covering the paper industry, includes forestry management, pulp and paper technology, economic trends, market reviews, packaging and printing.
Language(s): English; German
Readership: Read by senior executives, mill managers, marketing and engineering managers, research specialists and scientists.
ADVERTISING RATES:
Full Page Mono .... EUR 2995
Full Page Colour .... EUR 4585
Mechanical Data: No. of Columns (Display): 3, Col Widths (Display): 58 mm, Type Area: 248 x 186 mm
Copy instructions: *Copy Date:* 30 days prior to publication
Official Journal of: Organ d. Vereins d. Zellstoff- u. Papierchemiker u. -ingenieure
BUSINESS: PAPER

IS REPORT 763419G14A-9270
Editorial: Albert-Schweitzer-Str. 66, 81735 MÜNCHEN **Tel:** 89 9048620 **Fax:** 89 90486255
Email: eheins@isreport.de **Web site:** http://www.isreport.de
Freq: 10 issues yearly; **Annual Sub.:** EUR 85,00; **Circ:** 17,628
Editor: Eberhard Heins; **Advertising Manager:** Stefan Raupach
Language(s): German
ADVERTISING RATES:
Full Page Mono .... EUR 5500
Full Page Colour .... EUR 5500
Mechanical Data: Type Area: 266 x 180 mm
Copy instructions: *Copy Date:* 12 days prior to publication
BUSINESS: COMMERCE, INDUSTRY & MANAGEMENT

Germany

ISAR AKTUELL 731594G72-5916
Editorial: Brumather Str., 84130 DINGOLFING
Tel: 8731 7030 **Fax:** 8731 70333
Email: anzeigen@dingolfinger-anzeiger.de
Freq: Weekly; **Cover Price:** Free; **Circ:** 33,281
Editor: Petra Elle
Profile: Advertising journal (house-to-house) concentrating on local stories.
Language(s): German
ADVERTISING RATES:
Full Page Mono .... EUR 2297
Full Page Colour .... EUR 3225
Mechanical Data: Type Area: 430 x 280 mm, No. of Columns (Display): 6, Col Widths (Display): 45 mm
Copy instructions: *Copy Date:* 2 days prior to publication
LOCAL NEWSPAPERS

ISAR-LOISACHBOTE 731597G67B-7780
Editorial: Pfaffenrieder Str. 9, 82515 WOLFRATSHAUSEN **Tel:** 8171 269232
Fax: 8171 269240
Email: il-bote@merkur-online.de **Web site:** http://www.merkur-online.de
Freq: 312 issues yearly; **Circ:** 8,342
Advertising Manager: Hans-Georg Bechthold
Profile: The Münchner Merkur with its own local newspapers, of which the Isar-Loisachbote is one that, the leading regional newspaper brand in the Munich area - the most affluent area of Germany. The combination of newspaper and region is the foundation on which to build the success of the title. This is the newspaper not only the factual news agency, but forms a community of solidarity with its readers and the local community. The clear focus on local reporting creates a high regard to human reader loyalty. She presses one hand in the very high number of close to 180,000 subscribers. Also for the high reader-commitment is the loyalty of the total current 827 000 daily readers, the Münchner Merkur or one of its local newspapers usually read over many years. The Münchner Merkur with its own local newspapers is a newspaper for the whole family, tradition and modern life for one of the most beautiful regions of Germany unites. Reliable, informative, critical: the Münchner Merkur is the indispensable daily newspaper for the region. Facebook: http://www.facebook.com/pages/merkur-online.de/190176143327 This Outlet offers RSS (Really Simple Syndication).
Language(s): German
ADVERTISING RATES:
SCC .... EUR 43,60
Mechanical Data: Type Area: 474 x 324 mm, No. of Columns (Display): 7, Col Widths (Display): 45 mm
Copy instructions: *Copy Date:* 1 day prior to publication
REGIONAL DAILY & SUNDAY NEWSPAPERS: Regional Daily Newspapers

ISENHAGENER KREISBLATT 731600G67B-7820
Editorial: Gr. Liederner Str. 45, 29525 UELZEN
Tel: 581 80891202 **Fax:** 581 80891290
Email: redaktion.az@cbeckers.de **Web site:** http://www.az-online.de
Freq: 312 issues yearly; **Circ:** 5,812
Advertising Manager: Heike Köhn
Profile: Daily newspaper with regional news and a local sports section. Facebook: http://www.facebook.com/pages/az-online/428840365229.
Language(s): German
ADVERTISING RATES:
SCC .... EUR 40,90
Mechanical Data: Type Area: 435 x 285 mm, No. of Columns (Display): 6, Col Widths (Display): 45 mm
Copy instructions: *Copy Date:* 1 day prior to publication
Supplement(s): IK-Anpfiff
REGIONAL DAILY & SUNDAY NEWSPAPERS: Regional Daily Newspapers

ISERLOHNER KREISANZEIGER UND ZEITUNG 731603G67B-7840
Editorial: Theodor-Heuss-Ring 4, 58636 ISERLOHN
Tel: 2371 822221 **Fax:** 2371 822220
Email: ikz@ikz-online.de **Web site:** http://www.ikz-online.de
Freq: 312 issues yearly; **Circ:** 23,456
Editor: Thomas Reunert; **News Editor:** Thomas Reunert; **Advertising Manager:** Leo Plattes
Profile: Regional daily newspaper with news on politics, economy, culture, sports, travel, technology, etc. The newspaper is the largest in room Iserlohn and Hemer. The newspaper sees itself as a local paper in the best sense, closely linked to the local people and always live for the good of the citizens.
Language(s): German
ADVERTISING RATES:
SCC .... EUR 70,00
Mechanical Data: Type Area: 445 x 320 mm, No. of Columns (Display): 7, Col Widths (Display): 44 mm
Copy instructions: *Copy Date:* 2 days prior to publication
Supplement(s): Mein Auto; Mein Beruf; Meine besten Jahre; Meine Familie; Meine Freizeit; Mein neues Jahr!; Mein Shopping; Mein Stil; Mein Team; Mein Urlaub; Mein Zuhause; :Programm; rtv
REGIONAL DAILY & SUNDAY NEWSPAPERS: Regional Daily Newspapers

ISOLIER TECHNIK 731616G4E-4880
Editorial: Hauptstr. 6, 83536 GARS **Tel:** 8073 2550
Fax: 8073 2535
Email: info@isolier-technik.de **Web site:** http://www.isolier-technik.de
Freq: Quarterly; **Annual Sub.:** EUR 28,00; **Circ:** 11,700
Editor: Lutz Koophamel; **Advertising Manager:** Sigrid Spieß
Profile: Magazine focusing on all aspects of the insulation industry, including technical advice about new insulation materials.
Language(s): German
Readership: Aimed at contractors, suppliers and manufacturers of insulation materials, architects and designers, also students and teachers in technical schools.
ADVERTISING RATES:
Full Page Mono .... EUR 2000
Full Page Colour .... EUR 3500
Mechanical Data: Type Area: 260 x 176 mm, No. of Columns (Display): 3, Col Widths (Display): 54 mm
Copy instructions: *Copy Date:* 30 days prior to publication
Official Journal of: Organ d. ZDB, d. HDB, d. VÖDU u. d. IsolSuisse
BUSINESS: ARCHITECTURE & BUILDING: Building

IT BANKEN & VERSICHERUNGEN 731636G1C-900
Editorial: Arabellastr. 4, 81925 MÜNCHEN
Tel: 89 92223176 **Fax:** 89 92223171
Email: h.sebald@av-finance.com **Web site:** http://www.av-finance.com
Freq: 6 issues yearly; **Annual Sub.:** EUR 56,00; **Circ:** 11,156
Editor: Herbert Sebald; **Advertising Manager:** Manuela Albutat
Profile: Magazine for IT specialists and users in banks, savings banks and insurances.
Language(s): German
ADVERTISING RATES:
Full Page Mono .... EUR 3345
Full Page Colour .... EUR 4885
Mechanical Data: Type Area: 260 x 185 mm, No. of Columns (Display): 3, Col Widths (Display): 57 mm
BUSINESS: FINANCE & ECONOMICS: Banking

IT FREELANCER MAGAZIN 1659883G5E-27
Editorial: Wallstr. 39, 10179 BERLIN
Tel: 30 28886496
Email: redaktion@it-free.info **Web site:** http://www.it-freelancer-magazin.info
Freq: 6 issues yearly; **Annual Sub.:** EUR 60,00; **Circ:** 5,000
Editor: Wolf-Dietrich Lorenz; **Advertising Manager:** Ulrich Bode
Profile: Magazine for IT experts in the German speaking regions.
Language(s): German
ADVERTISING RATES:
Full Page Mono .... EUR 700
Full Page Colour .... EUR 700
Mechanical Data: Type Area: 297 x 210 mm
Copy instructions: *Copy Date:* 35 days prior to publication

IT INFORMATION TECHNOLOGY 731656G5R-647
Editorial: Rosenheimer Str. 145, 81671 MÜNCHEN
Tel: 89 45051221 **Fax:** 89 45051292
Email: julia.multerer@oldenbourg.de **Web site:** http://www.it-information-technology.de
Freq: 6 issues yearly; **Annual Sub.:** EUR 367,00; **Circ:** 1,750
Editor: Julia Multerer; **Advertising Manager:** Julia Multerer
Profile: Magazine focusing on information technology and technical computer science. Featuring all the latest research, procedures and technology.
Language(s): English; German
ADVERTISING RATES:
Full Page Mono .... EUR 2175
Full Page Colour .... EUR 3315
Mechanical Data: Type Area: 240 x 165 mm, No. of Columns (Display): 3, Col Widths (Display): 51 mm
Copy instructions: *Copy Date:* 30 days prior to publication
Official Journal of: Organ d. Fachbereichs Techn. Informatik u. Fachbereich Informatik in d. Lebenswissenschaften d. GI e.V. unter Mitwirkung d. Fachbereich 6 d. Informationstechn. Ges. im VDE
BUSINESS: COMPUTERS & AUTOMATION: Computers Related

IT MANAGEMENT 731646G5E-10
Editorial: Rudolf-Diesel-Ring 32, 82054 SAUERLACH
Tel: 8104 649414 **Fax:** 8104 649422
Email: u.parthier@it-verlag.de **Web site:** http://www.it-verlag.de
Freq: 10 issues yearly; **Annual Sub.:** EUR 100,00; **Circ:** 9,772
Editor: Ulrich Parthier; **Advertising Manager:** Carmen Keller-Maiwald
Profile: Magazine about management and data communications.
Language(s): German
ADVERTISING RATES:
Full Page Mono .... EUR 4050
Full Page Colour .... EUR 6340
Mechanical Data: Type Area: 248 x 178 mm, No. of Columns (Display): 3, Col Widths (Display): 56 mm
Copy instructions: *Copy Date:* 14 days prior to publication
BUSINESS: COMPUTERS & AUTOMATION: Data Transmission

IT MITTELSTAND 1605006G18B-1968
Editorial: Bertram-Blank-Str. 8, 51427 BERGISCH GLADBACH **Tel:** 2204 92140 **Fax:** 2204 921430
Email: redaktion@itmittelstand.de **Web site:** http://www.itmittelstand.de
Freq: 10 issues yearly; **Annual Sub.:** EUR 75,00; **Circ:** 33,625
Editor: Guido Piech; **Advertising Manager:** Thomas Büchel
Profile: Magazine provides the IT investment decision-makers: CEOs, IT chiefs and division managers in small or midsize to large companies, banks, insurance companies, government agencies or within the IT industry and in software, hardware and telecommunications companies.
Language(s): German
ADVERTISING RATES:
Full Page Mono .... EUR 9400
Full Page Colour .... EUR 11050
Mechanical Data: Type Area: 248 x 176 mm, No. of Columns (Display): 3, Col Widths (Display): 56 mm
Copy instructions: *Copy Date:* 14 days prior to publication
BUSINESS: ELECTRONICS: Telecommunications

IT SECURITY 731652G5R-645
Editorial: Rudolf-Diesel-Ring 32, 82054 SAUERLACH
Tel: 8104 649414 **Fax:** 8104 649422
Email: it-security@it-verlag.de **Web site:** http://www.it-verlag.de
Freq: 6 issues yearly; **Annual Sub.:** EUR 100,00; **Circ:** 9,336
Editor: Ulrich Parthier; **Advertising Manager:** Ulrich Parthier
Profile: Magazine containing articles and advice about system security, includes firewalls, intrusion detection, digital signatures, smart cards and data protection.
Language(s): German
Readership: Read by IT managers.
ADVERTISING RATES:
Full Page Mono .... EUR 3700
Full Page Colour .... EUR 5260
Mechanical Data: Type Area: 248 x 178 mm
Copy instructions: *Copy Date:* 21 days prior to publication
BUSINESS: COMPUTERS & AUTOMATION: Computers Related

IT & PRODUCTION 731634G14A-172_50
Editorial: Zu den Sandbeeten 2, 35043 MARBURG
Tel: 6421 308625 **Fax:** 6421 308618
Email: redaktion@it-production.com **Web site:** http://www.it-production.com
Freq: 10 issues yearly; **Annual Sub.:** EUR 60,00; **Circ:** 14,044
Editor: Michael Eckl; **Advertising Manager:** Christoph Kirschenmann
Profile: Magazine focusing on the use of IT in production; includes trends, technology, applications, market overview, interviews and information on hard- and software.
Language(s): German
Readership: Read by development managers.
ADVERTISING RATES:
Full Page Mono .... EUR 3410
Full Page Colour .... EUR 3980
Mechanical Data: No. of Columns (Display): 4, Col Widths (Display): 40 mm, Type Area: 270 x 185 mm
Supplement(s): IT & Production; IT & Production; IT & Production
BUSINESS: COMMERCE, INDUSTRY & MANAGEMENT

IT-BUSINESS 731637G5B-82_25
Editorial: August-Wessels-Str. 27, 86156 AUGSBURG **Tel:** 821 2177206 **Fax:** 821 2177150
Email: harry.jacob@vogel-it.de **Web site:** http://www.it-business.de
Freq: 25 issues yearly; **Cover Price:** EUR 6,00; **Circ:** 25,267
Editor: Harry Jacob; **Advertising Manager:** Ljiljana Kos
Profile: Magazine with reliable researched background information in the IT market and strategically relevant business and technology knowledge. Informs the last 20 years of IT trading partners quickly, competently and accurately. In-depth background reports, well-researched facts, practical case studies, which together make the GfK published "ITC Channel Index"and the exclusive online research area with IDC them to a top source of information for decision makers in the IT market. Facebook: http://www.facebook.com/itbusinessde.
Language(s): German
Readership: Aimed at wholesalers, owners of small businesses resellers, VARs, integrators and PC-retailers.
ADVERTISING RATES:
Full Page Mono .... EUR 10000
Full Page Colour .... EUR 10000
Mechanical Data: Type Area: 281 x 200 mm
Copy instructions: *Copy Date:* 7 days prior to publication
BUSINESS: COMPUTERS & AUTOMATION: Data Processing

IT-DIRECTOR 731641G5B-82_30
Editorial: Bertram-Blank-Str. 8, 51427 BERGISCH GLADBACH **Tel:** 2204 92140 **Fax:** 2204 921430
Email: redaktion@it-director.de **Web site:** http://www.it-director.de
Freq: 10 issues yearly; **Annual Sub.:** EUR 75,00; **Circ:** 20,657
Editor: Ina Schlücker; **Advertising Manager:** Thomas Büchel
Profile: Magazine with background reports, market surveys of Infomationstechnologie, use of modern information and communication technology and methodology for IT investment decision makers in small or midsize to large companies, banks, insurance companies, government agencies or within the IT industry and in software, hardware and telecommunications providers .
Language(s): German
ADVERTISING RATES:
Full Page Mono .... EUR 8400
Full Page Colour .... EUR 10050
Mechanical Data: Type Area: 225 x 169 mm, No. of Columns (Display): 3, Col Widths (Display): 53 mm
Copy instructions: *Copy Date:* 14 days prior to publication
BUSINESS: COMPUTERS & AUTOMATION: Data Processing

ITESPRESSO.DE 1662845G5-4621
Editorial: Karl-Theodor-Str. 55, 80803 MÜNCHEN
Tel: 89 309045300 **Fax:** 89 309045555
Email: redaktion@netmediaeurope.com **Web site:** http://www.itespresso.de
Freq: Daily; **Cover Price:** Paid; **Circ:** 965,629 Unique Users
Editor: Manfred Kohlen; **Advertising Manager:** Michael Petry
Language(s): German
BUSINESS: COMPUTERS & AUTOMATION

DER IT-RECHTS-BERATER 731648G1A-1380
Editorial: Gustav-Heinemann-Ufer 58, 50968 KÖLN
Tel: 221 93738186 **Fax:** 221 93738903
Email: fuchs-galilea@otto-schmidt.de **Web site:** http://www.itrb.de
Freq: Monthly; **Annual Sub.:** EUR 206,90; **Circ:** 990
Editor: Stefanie Fuchs-Galilea; **Advertising Manager:** Thorsten Deuse
Profile: Magazine with information for legal advisors in computer systems, multimedia and telecommunications.
Language(s): German
ADVERTISING RATES:
Full Page Mono .... EUR 800
Full Page Colour .... EUR 1400
Mechanical Data: Type Area: 260 x 180 mm, No. of Columns (Display): 2, Col Widths (Display): 88 mm

IT-SICHERHEIT 731655G5R-646
Editorial: Augustinusstr. 9d, 50226 FRECHEN
Tel: 2234 9661018 **Fax:** 2234 966109
Email: knop@datakontext.com **Web site:** http://www.datakontext.com/it-sicherheit
Freq: 6 issues yearly; **Annual Sub.:** EUR 85,00; **Circ:** 4,100
Editor: Jan von Knop; **Advertising Manager:** Thomas Reinhard
Profile: The magazine provides information security and data protection supervisor with cutting-edge information on the topics of latest IT security technology, IT, data protection and compliance, has a separate practical section with introductory and.
Language(s): German
Readership: Read by IT and security managers.
ADVERTISING RATES:
Full Page Mono .... EUR 1400
Full Page Colour .... EUR 2450
Mechanical Data: Type Area: 260 x 181 mm, No. of Columns (Display): 3, Col Widths (Display): 57 mm
Copy instructions: *Copy Date:* 21 days prior to publication
BUSINESS: COMPUTERS & AUTOMATION: Computers Related

IX 731668G5E-100
Editorial: Karl-Wiechert-Allee 10, 30625 HANNOVER
Tel: 511 5352387 **Fax:** 511 5352361
Email: post@ix.de **Web site:** http://www.ix.de
Freq: Monthly; **Annual Sub.:** EUR 65,00; **Circ:** 43,135
Editor: Jürgen Seeger; **Advertising Manager:** Michael Hanke
Profile: With focus of the IT professional, magazine iX is the enterprise-wide deployment of networked computers, focusing on the areas of: - Internet / Intranet - Security - Operating Systems - Networks - Servers - Software Development - Mobility - Storage - Embedded Systems - Data Center It also covers all groundbreaking developments in the IT field, from the personal communicator to virtual reality. iX informs on products - from the announcement of the latest tests to review, over the companies behind them - financial strength, support, future plans, products. iX writes for the practice - with reports on cutting-edge solutions, systems administration, programming, practical tips. iX reports theories and concepts from science, research and development - to be able to understand today the products of tomorrow. iX brings transparency in the market - so that the reader keeps track in an increasingly confusing world of IT. Twitter: http://twitter.com/iXmagazin.
Language(s): German
Readership: Read by IT professionals.
ADVERTISING RATES:
Full Page Mono .... EUR 4470

Full Page Colour .... EUR 5700
Mechanical Data: Type Area: 260 x 185 mm, No. of Columns (Display): 4, Col Widths (Display): 43 mm
Copy instructions: *Copy Date:* 30 days prior to publication
BUSINESS: COMPUTERS & AUTOMATION: Data Transmission

IZ REGIONAL PFAFFENHOFENER ANZEIGER
731672G72-5940
Editorial: Hauptplatz 19, 85276 PFAFFENHOFEN
Tel: 8441 499120 **Fax:** 8441 499125
Email: petra.frye-weber@iz-regional.de **Web site:** http://www.iz-regional.de
Freq: Weekly; **Cover Price:** Free; **Circ:** 27,816
Editor: Petra Frye-Weber
Profile: Advertising journal (house-to-house) concentrating on local stories.
Language(s): German
ADVERTISING RATES:
Full Page Mono .... EUR 2036
Full Page Colour .... EUR 3289
Mechanical Data: Type Area: 435 x 282 mm, No. of Columns (Display): 6, Col Widths (Display): 45 mm
Copy instructions: *Copy Date:* 2 days prior to publication
LOCAL NEWSPAPERS

JA ZUM BABY
731929G74D-95
Editorial: Yorkstr. 32, 50733 KÖLN **Tel:** 221 9388597
Fax: 221 9388598
Email: aberger@ratgeber-eltern.de **Web site:** http://www.jazumbaby.de
Freq: Half-yearly; **Cover Price:** Free; **Circ:** 350,600
Editor: Antje Berger
Profile: As a competent guide JA zum Baby young mothers to baby's first year of their baby. Questions about baby's health and development. Pediatrics, nutrition and development experts provide sound information for the Lebenmit the baby. Here young parents also compe- tente help when it comes to furniture, equipment and the purchase of toys.
Language(s): German
Readership: Aimed at parents-to-be and parents with young babies.
ADVERTISING RATES:
Full Page Mono .... EUR 27500
Full Page Colour .... EUR 27500
Mechanical Data: Type Area: 260 x 184 mm, No. of Columns (Display): 4, Col Widths (Display): 43 mm
Copy instructions: *Copy Date:* 42 days prior to publication
CONSUMER: WOMEN'S INTEREST CONSUMER MAGAZINES: Child Care

JAG MAG
1895229G77A-2869
Editorial: Hainkopfstr. 26, 65779 KELKHEIM
Tel: 6198 579800 **Fax:** 6198 579801
Email: jagmag@jaguar-association.de **Web site:** http://www.jagmag.de
Freq: 6 issues yearly; **Circ:** 2,500
Editor: Mike Riedner
Profile: Magazine for Jaguar drivers.
Language(s): German
ADVERTISING RATES:
Full Page Mono .... EUR 800
Full Page Colour .... EUR 1300
Mechanical Data: Type Area: 280 x 190 mm

JAGD IN BAYERN
731692G75F-340
Editorial: Hohenlindner Str. 12, 85622 FELDKIRCHEN **Tel:** 89 99023419 **Fax:** 89 99023435
Email: jib@jagd-bayern.de **Web site:** http://www.jagd-bayern.de
Freq: Monthly; Free to qualifying individuals
Annual Sub.: EUR 45,00; **Circ:** 45,277
Advertising Manager: Heidi Grund-Thorpe
Profile: Journal of the Hunting Association of Bavaria.
Language(s): German
ADVERTISING RATES:
Full Page Mono .... EUR 2299
Full Page Colour .... EUR 3975
Mechanical Data: Type Area: 258 x 184 mm, No. of Columns (Display): 4, Col Widths (Display): 43 mm
Copy instructions: *Copy Date:* 30 days prior to publication
CONSUMER: SPORT: Shooting

JAGD.DE
1661980G75F-1071
Editorial: Max-Planck-Str. 6, 50858 KÖLN
Tel: 221 91116 **Fax:** 221 911169
Email: info@jagd.de **Web site:** http://www.jagd.de
Cover Price: Paid
Language(s): German
CONSUMER: SPORT: Shooting

DER JAGDGEBRAUCHSHUND
731691G81B-80
Editorial: Kernerstr. 12, 74193 SCHWAIGERN
Tel: 7138 3654 **Fax:** 7138 3653
Email: redaktion.jagdgebrauchshund@dlv.de **Web site:** http://www.jagderleben.de/jgh
Freq: Monthly; **Annual Sub.:** EUR 44,80; **Circ:** 6,798
Editor: Karl Walch; **Advertising Manager:** Thomas Herrmann
Profile: Magazine containing information, news and articles about gun dogs.
Language(s): German
Readership: Aimed at hunters and dog owners.
ADVERTISING RATES:
Full Page Mono .... EUR 1296
Full Page Colour .... EUR 2592
Mechanical Data: Type Area: 270 x 184 mm, No. of Columns (Display): 4, Col Widths (Display): 43 mm
Official Journal of: Organ d. Jagdgebrauchshundverb. e.V.
CONSUMER: ANIMALS & PETS: Dogs

DER JAGDSPANIEL
731694G81B-20
Editorial: Schillerstr. 10, 26160 BAD ZWISCHENAHN
Tel: 4403 984987
Email: schriftleitung@jagdspaniel-klub.de **Web site:** http://www.jagdspaniel-klub.de
Freq: 6 issues yearly; Free to qualifying individuals
Annual Sub.: EUR 25,00; **Circ:** 2,000
Editor: Heribert Ballhause
Profile: Publication about hunting with spaniels.
Language(s): German
Readership: Aimed at members of hunting dog clubs.
ADVERTISING RATES:
Full Page Mono .... EUR 60
Full Page Colour .... EUR 60
Mechanical Data: Type Area: 180 x 120 mm, No. of Columns (Display): 2, Col Widths (Display): 60 mm
Copy instructions: *Copy Date:* 45 days prior to publication
Official Journal of: Organ d. Österr. Jagdspaniel-Klubs u. d. Spaniel-Clubs d. Schweiz, VDH, IGHV, FCI
CONSUMER: ANIMALS & PETS: Dogs

JAGEN WELTWEIT
731697G75F-380
Editorial: Erich-Kästner-Str. 2, 56379 SINGHOFEN
Tel: 2604 978801 **Fax:** 2604 978802
Email: jww@paulparey.de **Web site:** http://www.jagen-weltweit.de
Freq: 6 issues yearly; **Annual Sub.:** EUR 47,00; **Circ:** 12,877
Editor: Frank Rakow; **Advertising Manager:** Sylvia Lühert
Profile: Jagen Weltweit is the only magazine in Europe, which exclusively reports on hunting and related travels in foreign lands. Every two months our Jagen Weltweit magazine provides our readers with a view to international hunting exotica; to unbridled excitement and adventure: from the Outback of Australia to the Anden of Chile; Greenland to the dry desserts of Namibia or deep in the Karpaten; our high quality and well researched articles coupled with practical participation. Every issue comprehensively reports on the latest equipment and tests. Jagen Weltweit is simply a must for the professional hunter and aspiring amateur alike.
Language(s): German
ADVERTISING RATES:
Full Page Mono .... EUR 2358
Full Page Colour .... EUR 3383
Mechanical Data: Type Area: 253 x 186 mm, No. of Columns (Display): 4, Col Widths (Display): 43 mm
Copy instructions: *Copy Date:* 37 days prior to publication
CONSUMER: SPORT: Shooting

JÄGER
731685G75F-400
Editorial: Troplowitzstr. 5, 22529 HAMBURG
Tel: 40 389061110 **Fax:** 40 38906305
Email: roland.korioth@jaegermagazin.de **Web site:** http://www.jaegermagazin.de
Freq: Monthly; **Annual Sub.:** EUR 62,40; **Circ:** 29,528
Editor: Roland Korioth; **Advertising Manager:** Rainer Propp
Profile: The Jäger is one of the leading hunting magazines in Germany. Since 1974, the title is clearly excluded from the competition. The Jäger is the magazine for the active sportsman - for the territory owners as well as for the ambitious young hunters. Therefore, the district practice is clearly the focus of reporting. The Jäger helps, advises and informs its readers - like a true hunting enthusiast. Facebook: http://www.facebook.com/pages/jaegermagazin/293503062502.
Language(s): German
ADVERTISING RATES:
Full Page Mono .... EUR 2900
Full Page Colour .... EUR 4790
Mechanical Data: Type Area: 248 x 185 mm, No. of Columns (Display): 4, Col Widths (Display): 45 mm
CONSUMER: SPORT: Shooting

DER JÄGER IN BADEN-WÜRTTEMBERG
731687G75F-420
Editorial: Felix-Dahn-Str. 41, 70597 STUTTGART
Tel: 711 2684360 **Fax:** 711 26843629
Email: baade@landesjagdverband.de **Web site:** http://www.landesjagdverband.de
Freq: Monthly; **Circ:** 29,538
Editor: Ulrich Baade; **Advertising Manager:** Ruth Reschke
Profile: The journal is the official and sole organ of the National Hunting Association of Baden-Wuerttemberg. It is read as the mirror of hunting and hunting political events in the country. Subscribers to the journal are all members of this Association together closed hunting clubs and hunting groups. The magazine is delivered to about 29,000 fighters in Baden-Württemberg through the mail. 95% of hunting license holders in Baden-Württemberg can be achieved.
Language(s): German
ADVERTISING RATES:
Full Page Mono .... EUR 2400
Full Page Colour .... EUR 3360
Mechanical Data: Type Area: 270 x 187 mm, No. of Columns (Display): 4, Col Widths (Display): 45 mm
Copy instructions: *Copy Date:* 21 days prior to publication
CONSUMER: SPORT: Shooting

JÄGER IN SCHLESWIG-HOLSTEIN
731689G75F-440
Editorial: Böhnhusener Weg 6, 24220 FLINTBEK
Tel: 4347 90870
Email: jaeger-in-sh@ljv-sh.de **Web site:** http://www.ljv-sh.de
Freq: 10 issues yearly; Free to qualifying individuals
Annual Sub.: EUR 7,80; **Circ:** 16,563
Editor: Holger Behrens; **Advertising Manager:** Bernd Dürrmeier
Profile: Magazine about hunting and fishing in Schleswig-Holstein.
Language(s): German
ADVERTISING RATES:
Full Page Mono .... EUR 1765
Full Page Colour .... EUR 2580
Mechanical Data: Type Area: 265 x 185 mm, No. of Columns (Display): 4, Col Widths (Display): 43 mm
Copy instructions: *Copy Date:* 28 days prior to publication
CONSUMER: SPORT: Shooting

JAHRBUCH
731710G2A-2080
Editorial: ZDF-Str. 1, 55127 MAINZ **Tel:** 6131 702625
Fax: 6131 708532
Email: walter.b@zdf.de **Web site:** http://www.zdf.de
Freq: Half-yearly; **Cover Price:** EUR 13,00; **Circ:** 8,000
Editor: Barbara Walter
Profile: Annual of ZDF for journalists, university scientists and managers from politics and economy.
Language(s): German

JAHRBUCH DER BAUMPFLEGE
731722G21A-2260
Editorial: Frankfurter Str. 3d, 38122 BRAUNSCHWEIG **Tel:** 531 380040 **Fax:** 531 3800425
Email: info@haymarket.de **Web site:** http://www.haymarket.de
Freq: Annual; **Cover Price:** EUR 39,80; **Circ:** 2,000
Editor: Martina Borowski; **Advertising Manager:** Christian Rueß
Profile: Directory listing addresses and supply contacts concerning tree maintenance.
Language(s): German
ADVERTISING RATES:
Full Page Mono .... EUR 920
Full Page Colour .... EUR 1185
Mechanical Data: Type Area: 185 x 135 mm
Copy instructions: *Copy Date:* 60 days prior to publication
Official Journal of: Organ d. Dt. Baumpflegetage

JAHRBUCH DER WERBUNG
731752G2A-2100
Editorial: Friedrichstr. 126, 10117 BERLIN
Tel: 30 23456413 **Fax:** 30 23456515
Email: nadine.staedtner@econ.de **Web site:** http://www.jdw.de
Freq: Annual; **Cover Price:** EUR 98,00; **Circ:** 3,000
Editor: Peter Strahlendorf; **Advertising Manager:** Nadine Städtner
Profile: Annual for the advertising and communications branches. Facebook: http://www.facebook.com/jahrbuch.
Language(s): German
ADVERTISING RATES:
Full Page Mono .... EUR 3470
Full Page Colour .... EUR 3470
Mechanical Data: Type Area: 248 x 161 mm

JAHRBUCH FERNSEHEN
731778G2A-2140
Editorial: Fasanenstr. 73, 10719 BERLIN
Tel: 30 8800139014 **Fax:** 30 8800139030
Email: info@institut-medienpolitik.de **Web site:** http://www.jahrbuch-fernsehen.de
Freq: Annual; **Cover Price:** EUR 34,90; **Circ:** 3,000
Editor: Sabine Sasse
Profile: Annual about the German TV and media branch.
Language(s): German
Mechanical Data: Type Area: 190 x 123 mm

JAHRBUCH FÜR KRITISCHE MEDIZIN UND GESUNDHEITSWISSEN-SCHAFTEN
731807G56A-11151
Editorial: Theodor-Stern-Kai 7, 60590 FRANKFURT
Email: jkmg.redaktion@googlemail.com
Freq: Half-yearly; **Annual Sub.:** EUR 26,00; **Circ:** 600
Editor: Thomas Gerlinger
Profile: Annual about critical medicine dealing with the social interaction with health and illness.
Language(s): German
ADVERTISING RATES:
Full Page Mono .... EUR 480
Mechanical Data: Type Area: 172 x 95 mm

JAHRBUCH GARTEN- UND LANDSCHAFTSBAU
1696086G21A-4330
Editorial: Koenigsallee 65, 14193 BERLIN
Tel: 30 8959030 **Fax:** 30 89590317
Email: info@patzerverlag.de **Web site:** http://www.patzerverlag.de
Freq: Annual; **Cover Price:** EUR 10,10; **Circ:** 14,500
Editor: Jürgen Prigge; **Advertising Manager:** Bodo Ulbricht
Profile: Annual about horticulture and landscaping.
Language(s): German
Mechanical Data: Type Area: 129 x 90 mm, No. of Columns (Display): 2, Col Widths (Display): 43 mm

JAHRBUCH GARTENBAU
731829G21A-2300
Editorial: Frankfurter Str. 3d, 38122 BRAUNSCHWEIG **Tel:** 531 380040 **Fax:** 531 3800425
Email: renate.veth@haymarket.de **Web site:** http://www.haymarket.de
Freq: Annual; **Cover Price:** EUR 19,80; **Circ:** 3,000
Editor: Renate Veth; **Advertising Manager:** Christian Rueß
Profile: Annual calendar for the horticulture and florist trade listing all relevant dates.
Language(s): German
ADVERTISING RATES:
Full Page Mono .... EUR 984
Full Page Colour .... EUR 2172
Mechanical Data: No. of Columns (Display): 2, Col Widths (Display): 55 mm, Type Area: 186 x 115 mm
Copy instructions: *Copy Date:* 60 days prior to publication

JAHRBUCH LÄDEN
731836G4B-280
Editorial: Mainzer Landstr. 251, 60326 FRANKFURT
Tel: 69 75952128 **Fax:** 69 75952110
Email: buchverlag@dfv-fachbuch.de **Web site:** http://www.dfv-fachbuch.de
Freq: Annual; **Cover Price:** EUR 98,00; **Circ:** 2,200
Editor: Caroline Schauwienold; **Advertising Manager:** Eva Triantafillidou
Profile: Magazine about new shops and new interior design for the textile retail trade.
Language(s): German
ADVERTISING RATES:
Full Page Mono .... EUR 1580
Full Page Colour .... EUR 2460
Mechanical Data: Type Area: 250 x 221 mm
Copy instructions: *Copy Date:* 70 days prior to publication

JAHRBUCH LÄDEN
731836G4B-712
Editorial: Mainzer Landstr. 251, 60326 FRANKFURT
Tel: 69 75952128 **Fax:** 69 75952110
Email: buchverlag@dfv-fachbuch.de **Web site:** http://www.dfv-fachbuch.de
Freq: Annual; **Cover Price:** EUR 98,00; **Circ:** 2,200
Editor: Caroline Schauwienold; **Advertising Manager:** Eva Triantafillidou
Profile: Magazine about new shops and new interior design for the textile retail trade.
Language(s): German
ADVERTISING RATES:
Full Page Mono .... EUR 1580
Full Page Colour .... EUR 2460
Mechanical Data: Type Area: 250 x 221 mm
Copy instructions: *Copy Date:* 70 days prior to publication

JAHRBUCH OBERFLÄCHENTECHNIK
1655018G27-2999
Editorial: Karlstr. 4, 88348 BAD SAULGAU
Tel: 7581 48010 **Fax:** 7581 480110
Email: info@leuze-verlag.de **Web site:** http://www.leuze-verlag.de
Freq: Annual; **Cover Price:** EUR 58,00; **Circ:** 1,200
Editor: Richard Suchentrunk; **Advertising Manager:** Katja Praegla
Profile: Reference book: coating method, pre-and post-treatment process, surface treatment of light metals, coating characterization, quality assurance / process management, environmental engineering / operations management, electrical engineering and microsystems technology, medical technology.
Language(s): English; German
ADVERTISING RATES:
Full Page Mono .... EUR 1020
Full Page Colour .... EUR 1500
Mechanical Data: Type Area: 200 x 135 mm, No. of Columns (Display): 2, Col Widths (Display): 65 mm

JAHRBUCH ÖKOLOGIE
731841G57-920
Editorial: Reichpietschufer 50, 10785 BERLIN
Tel: 30 25491245 **Fax:** 30 25491247
Email: simonis@wzb.eu **Web site:** http://www.jahrbuch-oekologie.de
Freq: Annual; **Cover Price:** EUR 19,80; **Circ:** 2,000
Editor: Udo E. Simonis
Profile: Ecology annual.
Language(s): German

JAHRBUCH SCHWEISSTECHNIK 731845G27-1480
Editorial: Aachener Str. 172, 40223 DÜSSELDORF
Tel: 211 1591276 **Fax:** 211 1591350
Email: media@dvs-hg.de **Web site:** http://www.dvs-media.info
Freq: Annual; **Cover Price:** EUR 44,80; **Circ:** 5,000
Advertising Manager: Iris Jansen
Profile: Annual about covering all aspects of welding technology.
Language(s): German
ADVERTISING RATES:
Full Page Mono .... EUR 2000
Full Page Colour .... EUR 3200
Mechanical Data: Type Area: 172 x 117 mm, No. of Columns (Display): 2, Col Widths (Display): 58 mm
Copy instructions: *Copy Date:* 62 days prior to publication

JAHRBUCH STAHL 731848G27-1500
Editorial: Sohnstr. 65, 40237 DÜSSELDORF
Tel: 211 6707551 **Fax:** 211 6707517
Email: barbara.keisker@stahleisen.de **Web site:** http://www.stahleisen.de
Freq: Annual; **Cover Price:** EUR 40,00; **Circ:** 4,900
Advertising Manager: Barbara Keisker
Profile: Annual about steel.
Language(s): German
ADVERTISING RATES:
Full Page Mono .... EUR 828
Full Page Colour .... EUR 1398
Mechanical Data: Type Area: 170 x 120 mm
Copy instructions: *Copy Date:* 30 days prior to publication

JAHRBUCH VERWALTUNGS-MODERNISIERUNG 1739832G32A-7257
Editorial: Novalisstr. 7, 10115 BERLIN
Tel: 30 2848810 **Fax:** 30 28488111
Email: info@wegweiser.de **Web site:** http://www.wegweiser.de
Freq: Annual; **Cover Price:** EUR 99,00
Language(s): German
Copy instructions: *Copy Date:* 20 days prior to publication
BUSINESS: LOCAL GOVERNMENT, LEISURE & RECREATION: Local Government

JAHRESWIRTSCHAFTS-BERICHT 1781166G14A-9950
Editorial: Scharnhorststr. 34, 10115 BERLIN
Fax: 30 186157010
Email: oeffentlichkeitsarbeit@bmwi.bund.de **Web site:** http://www.bmwi.de
Freq: Annual; **Cover Price:** Free; **Circ:** 6,000
Profile: Information from the Federal Office for Economy and Technology.
Language(s): English; German

JAMIE 2068177G74P-1382
Editorial: Am Baumwall 11, 20459 HAMBURG
Tel: 40 37032724 **Fax:** 40 37035677
Email: buchelt.martina@guj.de **Web site:** http://www.jamiemagazin.de
Freq: 6 issues yearly; **Cover Price:** EUR 4,90; **Circ:** 100,000
Editor: Wolfgang-Robert Zahner; **Advertising Manager:** André Pollmann
Profile: Food magazine.
Language(s): German
ADVERTISING RATES:
Full Page Mono .... EUR 12500
Full Page Colour .... EUR 12500
Mechanical Data: Type Area: 265 x 210 mm

JAPAN CONTACT 1799534G14C-4771
Editorial: Ritterstr. 2b, 10969 BERLIN
Tel: 30 61508926 **Fax:** 30 61508927
Email: pt@owc.de **Web site:** http://www.owc.de
Freq: Annual; **Cover Price:** EUR 7,00; **Circ:** 9,000
Editor: Peter Tichauer; **Advertising Manager:** Norbert Mayert
Profile: Magazine focusing on future business negotiations with Japan. Also contains market analyses and trends.
Language(s): German
ADVERTISING RATES:
Full Page Mono .... EUR 2500
Full Page Colour .... EUR 3200
Mechanical Data: Type Area: 265 x 175 mm

JAVAMAGAZIN 731926G5B-83
Editorial: Geleitsstr. 14, 60599 FRANKFURT
Tel: 69 6300890 **Fax:** 69 63008989
Email: redaktion@javamagazin.de **Web site:** http://www.javamagazin.de
Freq: Monthly; **Annual Sub.:** EUR 84,00; **Circ:** 11,880
Editor: Sebastian Meyen; **Advertising Manager:** Patrik Baumann
Profile: Magazine focusing on Java programming. Includes technical information and articles on database development.
Language(s): German
Readership: Aimed at IT managers, programmers and project managers.
ADVERTISING RATES:
Full Page Mono .... EUR 3150
Full Page Colour .... EUR 4350
Mechanical Data: Type Area: 231 x 184 mm, No. of Columns (Display): 4, Col Widths (Display): 46 mm
Copy instructions: *Copy Date:* 26 days prior to publication
BUSINESS: COMPUTERS & AUTOMATION: Data Processing

JAVASPEKTRUM 731927G5E-140
Editorial: Auenstr. 34, 80469 MÜNCHEN
Tel: 2241 2341100 **Fax:** 2241 2341199
Email: javaspektrum@sigs-datacom.de **Web site:** http://www.javaspektrum.de
Freq: 6 issues yearly; **Annual Sub.:** EUR 34,20; **Circ:** 16,000
Editor: Michael Stal
Profile: Magazine containing articles and information about java and Internet technology.
Language(s): German
ADVERTISING RATES:
Full Page Mono .... EUR 3005
Full Page Colour .... EUR 4365
Mechanical Data: Type Area: 250 x 180 mm
Copy instructions: *Copy Date:* 25 days prior to publication
BUSINESS: COMPUTERS & AUTOMATION: Data Transmission

JAZZ THING & BLUE RHYTHM 731939G76D-2160
Editorial: Sülzburgstr. 74, 50937 KÖLN
Tel: 221 9414888 **Fax:** 221 413166
Email: redaktion@jazzthing.de **Web site:** http://www.jazzthing.de
Freq: 5 issues yearly; **Annual Sub.:** EUR 27,00; **Circ:** 26,000
Editor: Axel Stinshoff; **Advertising Manager:** Axel Stinshoff
Profile: Magazine for cosmopolitan music lovers. It should be understood not as a socially inclusive jazz style concept, but as a potentially limitless spirit of openness. The authors appreciate the tradition and look forward at the same time happy. Purposeful they feel jazz vibes on music in styles that do not run in the classic sense in jazz: for example in hip-hop, in soul, in the Club or the Music of us not so-called "world music ". More than ten years, Salsa, Flamenco, Son, Sahara blues, Balkan Brass, Samba, Afro Beat, Fado, Bossa Nova & Co. in the Supplement "Blue Rhythm" theme. Meanwhile, these and many other styles such a natural part of our musical reality has become that they are held equal in the home folder. Filigree folklorists come here just to words and pictures as ikonenstürzende sound revolutionary, the old with the new mix and East with West. Also in visual aesthetics and graphic design is treading new paths Jazz thing. After all, music and especially jazz, has always been more than just an acoustic phenomenon. Facebook: http://www.facebook.com/pages/Jazz-thing/216758205658.
Language(s): German
ADVERTISING RATES:
Full Page Mono .... EUR 1600
Full Page Colour .... EUR 2605
Mechanical Data: Type Area: 268 x 180 mm, No. of Columns (Display): 4, Col Widths (Display): 40 mm
Copy instructions: *Copy Date:* 21 days prior to publication
CONSUMER: MUSIC & PERFORMING ARTS: Music

JDDG JOURNAL DER DEUTSCHEN DERMATOLOGISCHEN GESELLSCHAFT JOURNAL OF THE GERMAN SOCIETY OF DERMATOLOGY 730648G56A-4420
Editorial: Robert-Koch-Platz 7, 10115 BERLIN
Tel: 30 2462530 **Fax:** 30 24625329
Email: jddg@derma.de **Web site:** http://www.jddg.de
Freq: Monthly; Free to qualifying individuals
Annual Sub.: EUR 617,00; **Circ:** 3,904
Editor: Wolfram Sterry; **Advertising Manager:** Tobias Trinkl
Profile: Journal on clinical dermatology, focusing on diagnosis and treatment of diseases.
Language(s): English; German
Mechanical Data: No. of Columns (Display): 3, Col Widths (Display): 52 mm, Type Area: 242 x 167 mm
Copy instructions: *Copy Date:* 21 days prior to publication
BUSINESS: HEALTH & MEDICAL

JESSY 1647556G91D-10038
Editorial: Rotebühlstr. 87, 70178 STUTTGART
Tel: 711 947680 **Fax:** 711 9476830
Email: info@panini.de **Web site:** http://www.panini.de
Freq: 6 issues yearly; **Cover Price:** EUR 2,70; **Circ:** 36,092
Editor: Martin Klingseisen
Profile: Jessy is the modern horse comic. Experience with horses, exciting adventure, discover the secrets of first love and friends have lots of fun - of girls dream of 9-14 years. Jessy In these dreams reality. Each issue offers two comic stories, a lot of information about horses, a photo novel and two great posters. And as a gift on top of it there is an extra.
Language(s): German
ADVERTISING RATES:
Full Page Mono .... EUR 3900
Full Page Colour .... EUR 3900
Mechanical Data: Type Area: 250 x 180 mm
CONSUMER: RECREATION & LEISURE: Children & Youth

JESUS.DE 1661988G87-13744
Editorial: Bodenborn 43, 58452 WITTEN
Tel: 2302 93093651 **Fax:** 2302 93093709
Email: info@jesus.de **Web site:** http://www.jesus.de
Cover Price: Paid; **Circ:** 703,924 Unique Users
Editor: Rolf Krüger; **Advertising Manager:** Thilo Cunz
Language(s): German
CONSUMER: RELIGIOUS

JET KONTAKT 1695557G33-346
Editorial: Überseering 27, 22297 HAMBURG
Tel: 40 638010
Freq: 3 issues yearly; **Circ:** 1,500
Profile: Aeronautical club magazine with internal information.
Language(s): German
Copy instructions: *Copy Date:* 60 days prior to publication

JEVERSCHES WOCHENBLATT 731960G67B-7860
Editorial: Wangerstr. 14, 26441 JEVER
Tel: 4461 944280 **Fax:** 4461 944299
Email: redaktion@jeversches-wochenblatt.de **Web site:** http://www.jeversches-wochenblatt.de
Freq: 312 issues yearly; **Circ:** 8,563
Editor: Helmut Burlager; **Advertising Manager:** Horst-Wilhelm Lamberti
Profile: Daily newspaper with regional news and a local sports section. Facebook: http://de-de.facebook.com/jeversches.wochenblatt This Outlet offers RSS (Really Simple Syndication).
Language(s): German
ADVERTISING RATES:
SCC .... EUR 30,30
Mechanical Data: Type Area: 420 x 282 mm, No. of Columns (Display): 6, Col Widths (Display): 45 mm
Copy instructions: *Copy Date:* 1 day prior to publication
Supplement(s): Kinderblatt; küstenanzeiger
REGIONAL DAILY & SUNDAY NEWSPAPERS: Regional Daily Newspapers

J:O EXTRA 731970G74G-63_50
Editorial: Siemensstr. 6, 61352 BAD HOMBURG
Tel: 6172 670128 **Fax:** 6172 670519
Email: jomail@wdv.de **Web site:** http://www.aok4you.de/jo
Freq: Annual; **Cover Price:** Free; **Circ:** 710,000
Editor: Anja Stamm
Profile: Journal containing information, news and articles about health, sports, diet and nutrition.
Language(s): German
Readership: Aimed at young people.
Supplement to: J:O
CONSUMER: WOMEN'S INTEREST CONSUMER MAGAZINES: Slimming & Health

JOEMAX.DE 1662003G91D-10153
Editorial: Berliner Ring 62, 35576 WETZLAR
Tel: 6441 9572000 **Fax:** 6441 9572001
Email: redaktion@joemax.de **Web site:** http://www.joemax.de
Cover Price: Paid; **Circ:** 6,713 Unique Users
Editor: Michael Gerster
Profile: Christliches portal for children from 9 to 14 years.
Language(s): German
CONSUMER: RECREATION & LEISURE: Children & Youth

JOHANNITER 731975G56P-100
Editorial: Lützowstr. 94, 10785 BERLIN
Tel: 30 26997353 **Fax:** 30 26997359
Email: frak.markowski@juh.de **Web site:** http://www.juh.de
Freq: Quarterly; **Circ:** 1,226,321
Editor: Wolfgang Brenner
Profile: Journal of the Friends of St John's Ambulance. It documents how the funds are used in the assigned areas. It focuses on topics such as health, aging and leisure tips Facebook: http://www.facebook.com/DieJohanniter Twitter: http://twitter.com/juh_helfen.
Language(s): German
ADVERTISING RATES:
Full Page Mono .... EUR 12500
Full Page Colour .... EUR 14000
Mechanical Data: Type Area: 255 x 185 mm, No. of Columns (Display): 2, Col Widths (Display): 90 mm
Copy instructions: *Copy Date:* 48 days prior to publication
Supplement(s): b.punkt; In Stadt & Land Harburg; In & um Hamburg; Mecklenburg-Vorpommern Regional; Schleswig-Holstein Nord/West Regional; Schleswig-Holstein Süd/Ost Regional; Wir Die Johanniter; Wir in der Region
BUSINESS: HEALTH & MEDICAL: Casualty & Emergency

JOLIE 1635480G74A-3397
Editorial: Leonrodstr. 52, 80636 MÜNCHEN
Tel: 89 69749453 **Fax:** 89 69749450
Email: jolie.redaktion@vision-media.de **Web site:** http://www.jolie.de
Freq: Monthly; **Annual Sub.:** EUR 21,60; **Circ:** 362,058
Editor: Anja Müller-Lochner; **Advertising Manager:** Marit Böhmer
Profile: Everything that makes life better - that's Jolie. Whether glamorous fashion shoots, authentic portraits and interviews, opulent beauty lines, exciting features, service issues, moving stories of real people or exclusive photo shoots with celebrities.
Language(s): German
ADVERTISING RATES:
Full Page Mono .... EUR 19800
Full Page Colour .... EUR 19800
Mechanical Data: Type Area: 234 x 175 mm, No. of Columns (Display): 4, Col Widths (Display): 32 mm
CONSUMER: WOMEN'S INTEREST CONSUMER MAGAZINES: Women's Interest

JOT JOURNAL FÜR OBERFLÄCHENTECHNIK 731985G19C-54
Editorial: Aschauer Str. 30, 81549 MÜNCHEN
Tel: 89 2030432305 **Fax:** 89 2030432265
Email: jochen.kecht@springer.com **Web site:** http://www.jot-oberflaeche.de
Freq: Monthly; Free to qualifying individuals
Annual Sub.: EUR 159,00; **Circ:** 9,342
Editor: Jochen Kecht; **Advertising Manager:** Petra Neumann
Profile: Journal containing information about surface technology.
Language(s): German
ADVERTISING RATES:
Full Page Mono .... EUR 3280
Full Page Colour .... EUR 5110
Mechanical Data: Type Area: 233 x 175 mm, No. of Columns (Display): 3, Col Widths (Display): 50 mm
Copy instructions: *Copy Date:* 20 days prior to publication
Official Journal of: Organ d. Europ. Ges. f. Lackiertechnik
BUSINESS: ENGINEERING & MACHINERY: Finishing

JOULE 1794799G58-1833
Editorial: Lothstr. 29, 80797 MÜNCHEN
Tel: 89 12705332 **Fax:** 89 12705335
Email: johann.woerle@dlv.de **Web site:** http://www.joule-dlv.de
Freq: 6 issues yearly; **Annual Sub.:** EUR 36,50; **Circ:** 15,000
Editor: Johann Wörle; **Advertising Manager:** Thomas Herrmann
Profile: Agricultural journal covering management production and technology.
Language(s): German
ADVERTISING RATES:
Full Page Mono .... EUR 2892
Full Page Colour .... EUR 2892
Mechanical Data: Type Area: 270 x 184 mm, No. of Columns (Display): 4, Col Widths (Display): 43 mm
Copy instructions: *Copy Date:* 39 days prior to publication

JOURNAL 1913831G4E-7288
Editorial: Bremer Weg 184, 29223 CELLE
Tel: 5141 50192 **Fax:** 5141 50104
Email: ulrich.schmidt-kuhl@heinze.de **Web site:** http://www.heinze.de
Freq: Quarterly; **Circ:** 38,441
Editor: Ulrich Schmidt-Kuhl
Profile: The journal is 4 times a year to 43 000 architecture and planning firms in Germany sent and read by an average of 3 employees per office. In a sophisticated design of this target group will be presented primarily in the construction application. This includes both the latest innovations and proven solutions include the construction industry.
Language(s): German
ADVERTISING RATES:
Full Page Mono .... EUR 3880
Full Page Colour .... EUR 3880
Mechanical Data: Type Area: 245 x 180 mm

JOURNAL 1773240G56A-11413
Editorial: Postfach 160145, 19091 SCHWERIN
Tel: 385 7431213 **Fax:** 385 7431386
Email: presse@kvmv.de **Web site:** http://www.kvmv.de
Freq: Monthly; Free to qualifying individuals
Annual Sub.: EUR 37,20; **Circ:** 3,300
Editor: Eveline Schott
Profile: Magazine from the Doctor's Association in Mecklenburg-Vorpommern.
Language(s): German
ADVERTISING RATES:
Full Page Mono .... EUR 800
Mechanical Data: Type Area: 297 x 210 mm, No. of Columns (Display): 2, Col Widths (Display): 82 mm
Copy instructions: *Copy Date:* 27 days prior to publication

JOURNAL AM MITTWOCH 732000G72-5984
Editorial: Große Str. 37, 27356 ROTENBURG
Tel: 4261 720 **Fax:** 4261 72200

Email: redaktion@rotenburger-kreiszeitung.de **Web site:** http://www.rotenburger-journal.de
Freq: Weekly; **Cover Price:** Free; **Circ:** 32,760
Editor: Siegfried Franke
Profile: Advertising journal (house-to-house) concentrating on local stories.
Language(s): German
ADVERTISING RATES:
Full Page Mono .... EUR 2586
Full Page Colour .... EUR 3750
Mechanical Data: Type Area: 431 x 276 mm, No. of Columns (Display): 6, Col Widths (Display): 44 mm
Copy instructions: *Copy Date:* 2 days prior to publication
LOCAL NEWSPAPERS

JOURNAL AM SONNTAG
732005G72-6004
Editorial: Große Str. 37, 27356 ROTENBURG
Tel: 4261 720 **Fax:** 4261 72200
Email: redaktion@rotenburger-kreiszeitung.de **Web site:** http://www.rotenburger-journal.de
Freq: Weekly; **Cover Price:** Free; **Circ:** 32,550
Editor: Siegfried Franke
Profile: Advertising journal (house-to-house) concentrating on local stories.
Language(s): German
ADVERTISING RATES:
Full Page Mono .... EUR 2586
Full Page Colour .... EUR 3750
Mechanical Data: Type Area: 431 x 276 mm, No. of Columns (Display): 6, Col Widths (Display): 44 mm
Copy instructions: *Copy Date:* 3 days prior to publication
LOCAL NEWSPAPERS

JOURNAL DER DEUTSCHEN GESELLSCHAFT FÜR PLASTISCHE UND WIEDERHERSTELLUNG-SCHIRURGIE E.V.
1659884G56A-11314
Editorial: Elise-Averdieck-Str. 17, 27356 ROTENBURG **Tel:** 4261 772127 **Fax:** 4261 772128
Email: info@dgpw.de **Web site:** http://www.dgpw.de
Freq: Half-yearly; Free to qualifying individuals
Annual Sub.: EUR 39,00; **Circ:** 1,095
Editor: Peter M. Vogt
Profile: Magazine about plastic surgery and anaplasty.
Language(s): English; German
ADVERTISING RATES:
Full Page Mono .... EUR 890
Full Page Colour .... EUR 1610
Mechanical Data: Type Area: 200 x 130 mm
Copy instructions: *Copy Date:* 31 days prior to publication

JOURNAL EDITION
1932036G89A-12545
Editorial: Ludwigstr. 37, 60327 FRANKFURT
Tel: 69 974600 **Fax:** 69 97460400
Email: essenundtrinken@journalportal.de **Web site:** http://www.journalportal.de
Freq: Annual; **Circ:** 40,000
Editor: Bastian Fiebig; **Advertising Manager:** Melanie Hennemann
Profile: Gastronomy guide for the Rhein-Main region. Facebook: http://www.facebook.com/journalfrankfurt.
Language(s): German
ADVERTISING RATES:
Full Page Mono .... EUR 2530
Full Page Colour .... EUR 3780
Mechanical Data: Type Area: 270 x 195 mm, No. of Columns (Display): 4, Col Widths (Display): 45 mm
Copy instructions: *Copy Date:* 34 days prior to publication
Supplement(s): Genuss Magazin

JOURNAL FRANKFURT
732046G80-6040
Editorial: Ludwigstr. 37, 60327 FRANKFURT
Tel: 69 97460285 **Fax:** 69 97460400
Email: chefredaktion@mmg.de **Web site:** http://www.journal-frankfurt.de
Freq: 24 issues yearly; **Annual Sub.:** EUR 39,80; **Circ:** 25,185
Editor: Nils Bremer; **Advertising Manager:** Melanie Hennemann
Profile: Every 14 days about 100,000 people in and around Frankfurt, read the JOURNAL FRANKFURT. Certainly the reason for this is the extensive magazine section of interesting stories of the city as well as the unique culture section. Exciting reports, interesting stories and exclusive interviews are just as typical for the JOURNAL FRANKFURT as the crisp calendar of events and the TV program. The JOURNAL FRANKFURT business directory is the marketplace for Frankfurt. Here direct and low-cost communication with interested customers in the different sections is possible. The editorial gastronomy line with restaurant reviews, useful tips, book recommendations and recipes is one of the "prime" in the booklet. Facebook: http://www.facebook.com/journalfrankfurt.
Language(s): German
ADVERTISING RATES:
Full Page Mono .... EUR 3030
Full Page Colour .... EUR 4390
Mechanical Data: Type Area: 270 x 195 mm, No. of Columns (Display): 4, Col Widths (Display): 45 mm
Copy instructions: *Copy Date:* 8 days prior to publication
CONSUMER: RURAL & REGIONAL INTEREST

JOURNAL FRANKFURT FÜHRER
1828425G89A-12394
Editorial: Ludwigstr. 37, 60327 FRANKFURT
Tel: 69 974600 **Fax:** 69 97460400
Email: journal@mmg.de
Freq: Annual; **Cover Price:** EUR 5,80; **Circ:** 30,000
Editor: Bastian Fiebig; **Advertising Manager:** Melanie Hennemann
Profile: Gastronomy guide for the Rhein-Main region.
Language(s): German
ADVERTISING RATES:
Full Page Mono .... EUR 2650
Full Page Colour .... EUR 3960
Mechanical Data: Type Area: 270 x 195 mm, No. of Columns (Display): 4, Col Widths (Display): 45 mm
Copy instructions: *Copy Date:* 31 days prior to publication
Supplement(s): Genuss Magazin

JOURNAL FRANKFURT FÜHRER
1828425G89A-12541
Editorial: Ludwigstr. 37, 60327 FRANKFURT
Tel: 69 974600 **Fax:** 69 97460400
Email: journal@mmg.de
Freq: Annual; **Cover Price:** EUR 5,80; **Circ:** 30,000
Editor: Bastian Fiebig; **Advertising Manager:** Melanie Hennemann
Profile: Gastronomy guide for the Rhein-Main region.
Language(s): German
ADVERTISING RATES:
Full Page Mono .... EUR 2650
Full Page Colour .... EUR 3960
Mechanical Data: Type Area: 270 x 195 mm, No. of Columns (Display): 4, Col Widths (Display): 45 mm
Copy instructions: *Copy Date:* 31 days prior to publication
Supplement(s): Genuss Magazin

JOURNAL FÜR ANÄSTHESIE UND INTENSIVBEHANDLUNG
732049G56A-5660
Editorial: Eichengrund 28, 49525 LENGERICH
Tel: 5484 308 **Fax:** 5484 550
Email: pabst.publishers@t-online.de **Web site:** http://www.pabst-publishers.de/jai
Freq: Quarterly; **Annual Sub.:** EUR 30,00; **Circ:** 11,800
Advertising Manager: Wolfgang Pabst
Profile: Magazine about anaesthesia and intensive care: practical, critical, independent, with a broad spectrum of current background information.
Language(s): English; German
ADVERTISING RATES:
Full Page Mono .... EUR 1253
Full Page Colour .... EUR 2045
Mechanical Data: Type Area: 235 x 140 mm
Copy instructions: *Copy Date:* 20 days prior to publication

JOURNAL FÜR ÄSTHETISCHE CHIRURGIE
1934682G56A-11659
Editorial: Tiergartenstr. 17, 69121 HEIDELBERG
Tel: 6221 48768178 **Fax:** 6221 48768178
Email: tina.suhai@springer.com **Web site:** http://www.springermedizin.de
Freq: Quarterly; **Annual Sub.:** EUR 133,00; **Circ:** 900
Advertising Manager: Sabine Weidner
Profile: The journal für ästhetische chirurgie (Journal of Aesthetic Surgery) provides state-of-the-art further education for all practitioners working in the field of Surgery, Dermatology, Gynecologists, ENT, OMS, Ophthalmology and Plastic Surgery in both practical and clinical environments. The contents cover all areas of applied Aesthetic Surgery from a practical point of view. The focus is on topics relevant to the safe and effective practice of aesthetic surgery, descriptions of clinical techniques, case reports and operation management. The journal includes important research and techniques in reconstructive surgical procedures having a significant aesthetic component. It also provides a forum for original articles advancing the art of aesthetic surgery. The core of each issue is made up by extensive works that provide an overview on a current focus subject. In this, the focus is on solid knowledge about current scientific and clinical advances with a high relevance for the practitioners everyday work.
Language(s): German
ADVERTISING RATES:
Full Page Mono .... EUR 1670
Full Page Colour .... EUR 2710
Mechanical Data: Type Area: 240 x 174 mm
Official Journal of: Organ d. Ges. f. Ästhet. Chirurgie Deutschland e.V.

JOURNAL FÜR DIE APOTHEKE
1641610G94H-14372
Editorial: Gewerbestr. 9, 79219 STAUFEN
Tel: 7633 9332018 **Fax:** 7633 9332020
Email: journal-apotheke@pacs-online.com **Web site:** http://www.pacs-online.com
Freq: 6 issues yearly; **Cover Price:** Free; **Circ:** 20,334
Editor: Claudia Pfeil-Zander; **Advertising Manager:** Thomas Tritschler
Profile: Magazine for pharmacists and pharmacy staff with a focus on owner education and counseling at the pharmacy, as well as travel reports and travel medical issues.
Language(s): German
ADVERTISING RATES:
Full Page Mono .... EUR 2275
Full Page Colour .... EUR 4550
Mechanical Data: Type Area: 252 x 175 mm, No. of Columns (Display): 3, Col Widths (Display): 55 mm
Copy instructions: *Copy Date:* 30 days prior to publication
CONSUMER: OTHER CLASSIFICATIONS: Customer Magazines

JOURNAL FÜR GENERATIONENGERECH-TIGKEIT
728666G57-2711
Editorial: Ludwig-Erhard-Str. 16a, 61440 OBERURSEL **Tel:** 6171 982367 **Fax:** 6171 952566
Email: kontakt@srzg.de **Web site:** http://www.srzg.de
Freq: Quarterly; Free to qualifying individuals
Annual Sub.: EUR 25,00; **Circ:** 7,500
Editor: Jörg Tremmel; **Advertising Manager:** Urs Wahl
Profile: Magazine of the Foundation for the Rights of Future Generations.
Language(s): English; German
ADVERTISING RATES:
Full Page Mono .... EUR 2000
Full Page Colour .... EUR 2000
Mechanical Data: No. of Columns (Display): 3
Copy instructions: *Copy Date:* 14 days prior to publication

JOURNAL FÜR GENERATIONENGERECH-TIGKEIT
728666G57-2939
Editorial: Ludwig-Erhard-Str. 16a, 61440 OBERURSEL **Tel:** 6171 982367 **Fax:** 6171 952566
Email: kontakt@srzg.de **Web site:** http://www.srzg.de
Freq: Quarterly; Free to qualifying individuals
Annual Sub.: EUR 25,00; **Circ:** 7,500
Editor: Jörg Tremmel; **Advertising Manager:** Urs Wahl
Profile: Magazine of the Foundation for the Rights of Future Generations.
Language(s): English; German
ADVERTISING RATES:
Full Page Mono .... EUR 2000
Full Page Colour .... EUR 2000
Mechanical Data: No. of Columns (Display): 3
Copy instructions: *Copy Date:* 14 days prior to publication

JOURNAL FÜR KUNSTGESCHICHTE
732060G84A-1360
Editorial: Universitätsstr. 1, 56070 KOBLENZ
Tel: 261 2872120 **Fax:** 261 2872121
Email: tavernier@uni-koblenz.de
Freq: Quarterly; **Annual Sub.:** EUR 39,00; **Circ:** 1,050
Editor: Ludwig Tavernier; **Advertising Manager:** Astrid Hoffmann
Profile: Journal covering European art history, providing surveys, reports and book reviews of literature from the past and present.
Language(s): German
Readership: Aimed at research and museum librarians, people involved in conserving historical monuments, teachers, art students and enthusiasts.
ADVERTISING RATES:
Full Page Mono .... EUR 265
Mechanical Data: Type Area: 186 x 125 mm
Copy instructions: *Copy Date:* 20 days prior to publication
CONSUMER: THE ARTS & LITERARY: Arts

JOURNAL FÜR PERFEKTES HAUSHALTEN
732066G94H-7140
Editorial: Am Flugplatz 4, Haus 49, 23560 LÜBECK
Tel: 451 50405681 **Fax:** 451 50405688
Email: redaktion@hanse-medienkontor.de
Freq: Weekly; **Cover Price:** Free; **Circ:** 9,908
Editor: Björn Hansen
Profile: Magazine covering family fitness, health, cookery, finance, travel and the environment.
Language(s): German
Readership: Aimed at customers of Edeka grocery stores.
ADVERTISING RATES:
Full Page Mono .... EUR 17000
Full Page Colour .... EUR 17000
Mechanical Data: Type Area: 260 x 189 mm, No. of Columns (Display): 4, Col Widths (Display): 45 mm
Copy instructions: *Copy Date:* 58 days prior to publication
CONSUMER: OTHER CLASSIFICATIONS: Customer Magazines

JOURNAL MED
1926854G56A-11630
Editorial: Watmarkt 1, 93047 REGENSBURG
Tel: 941 584030 **Fax:** 941 5840379
Email: antje.blum@rsmedia-verlag.de **Web site:** http://www.journalmed.de
Circ: 2,300,000
Editor: Antje Blum; **Advertising Manager:** Adi Rixner
Profile: Ezine: Magazine for general practitioners.
Language(s): German

JOURNAL OF CANCER RESEARCH AND CLINICAL ONCOLOGY
732095G56A-5720
Editorial: Tiergartenstr. 17, 69121 HEIDELBERG
Tel: 6221 4870 **Fax:** 6221 4878366
Email: subscriptions@springer.com **Web site:** http://www.springerlink.com
Freq: Monthly; **Annual Sub.:** EUR 3989,00; **Circ:** 273
Editor: Klaus Höffken
Profile: Journal of cancer research and clinical oncology.
Language(s): English
ADVERTISING RATES:
Full Page Mono .... EUR 740
Full Page Colour .... EUR 1780
Mechanical Data: Type Area: 240 x 175 mm
Official Journal of: Organ d. Dt. Krebsges. e.V.

JOURNAL OF COMPARATIVE PHYSIOLOGY B
732098G56A-5740
Editorial: Karl-von-Frisch-Str., 35043 MARBURG
Fax: 6421 288937
Email: heldmaier@staff.uni-marburg.de **Web site:** http://www.springerlink.com
Freq: 8 issues yearly; **Annual Sub.:** EUR 2961,00; **Circ:** 126
Editor: Gerhard Heldmaier
Profile: Journal of comparative physiology.
Language(s): English
ADVERTISING RATES:
Full Page Mono .... EUR 740
Full Page Colour .... EUR 1780
Mechanical Data: Type Area: 240 x 175 mm

JOURNAL OF INSTITUTIONAL AND THEORETICAL ECONOMICS JITE
732110G1A-3495
Editorial: Wilhelmstr. 18, 72074 TÜBINGEN
Tel: 7071 9230 **Fax:** 7071 51104
Email: info@mohr.de **Web site:** http://www.mohr.de
Freq: Quarterly; **Annual Sub.:** EUR 180,80; **Circ:** 1,000
Profile: Journal of institutional and theoretical economics.
Language(s): English; German
ADVERTISING RATES:
Full Page Mono .... EUR 800
Mechanical Data: Type Area: 180 x 108 mm

JOURNAL OF MOLECULAR MEDICINE
732118G56A-5760
Editorial: Tiergartenstr. 17, 69121 HEIDELBERG
Tel: 6221 4870 **Fax:** 6221 4878366
Email: subscriptions@springer.com **Web site:** http://www.springerlink.de
Freq: Monthly; **Annual Sub.:** EUR 1257,00; **Circ:** 176
Editor: Detlev Ganten
Profile: Journal of molecular medicine.
Language(s): English
ADVERTISING RATES:
Full Page Mono .... EUR 740
Full Page Colour .... EUR 1780
Mechanical Data: Type Area: 240 x 175 mm

JOURNAL OF MOLECULAR MODELING
1638676G37-1794
Editorial: Nägelsbachstr. 25, 91052 ERLANGEN
Fax: 9131 8526565
Email: jmolmod@chemie.uni-erlangen.de **Web site:** http://www.springerlink.com
Freq: Monthly; **Annual Sub.:** EUR 1229,00; **Circ:** 55
Editor: Tim Clark
Profile: Journal of molecular modelling.
Language(s): English
ADVERTISING RATES:
Full Page Mono .... EUR 740
Full Page Colour .... EUR 1780
Mechanical Data: Type Area: 240 x 175 mm

JOURNAL OF NEUROLOGY
756113G56A-11089
Editorial: Tiergartenstr. 17, 69121 HEIDELBERG
Tel: 6221 4870 **Fax:** 6221 4878366
Email: subscriptions@springer.com **Web site:** http://www.springer.com
Freq: Monthly; **Annual Sub.:** EUR 3114,00; **Circ:** 2,436
Profile: The Journal of Neurology is an international peer-reviewed journal which officially represents the European Neurological Society and provides a source for publishing original communications on clinical neurology and related basic research in neuroscience. Commentaries on new developments in clinical neuroscience, which may be commissioned or submitted, are published as editorials. Letters to the Editors serve as a forum for the exchange of ideas or clinical cases which highlight important new findings. A section on Medical progress serves to summarise the major findings in certain fields of neurology, as illustrated by recent articles published in the Journal. News sections provide information on the development of neurological medicine, society news, and reports on recent congresses. Every neurologist interested in the field of organic neurological disease needs access to the information contained in this valuable journal.
Language(s): English
ADVERTISING RATES:
Full Page Mono .... EUR 1390
Full Page Colour .... EUR 2430

Mechanical Data: Type Area: 240 x 175 mm
Copy instructions: *Copy Date:* 28 days prior to publication
Official Journal of: Organ d. European Neurological Society

JOURNAL OF ORNITHOLOGY
732065G81F-75
Editorial: An der Vogelwarte 21, 26386 WILHELMSHAVEN **Tel:** 4421 96890
Fax: 4421 968955
Email: franz.bairlein@ifv-vogelwarte.de **Web site:** http://www.springerlink.com
Freq: Quarterly; Free to qualifying individuals
Annual Sub.: EUR 644,00; **Circ:** 2,071
Editor: Franz Bairlein
Profile: Journal for the German Ornithology Society.
Language(s): English; German
ADVERTISING RATES:
Full Page Mono .... EUR 1390
Full Page Colour .... EUR 2430
Mechanical Data: Type Area: 240 x 175 mm
CONSUMER: ANIMALS & PETS: Birds

JOURNAL OF PERINATAL MEDICINE
732124G56A-5780
Editorial: Genthiner Str. 13, 10785 BERLIN
Tel: 30 26005245 **Fax:** 30 26005298
Email: jpm.editorial@degruyter.com **Web site:** http://www.degruyter.de/journals/jpm
Freq: 6 issues yearly; **Annual Sub.:** EUR 649,00; **Circ:** 1,000
Editor: Joachim W. Dudenhausen
Profile: Journal of perinatal medicine.
Language(s): English
ADVERTISING RATES:
Full Page Mono .... EUR 645
Full Page Colour .... EUR 1395
Mechanical Data: Type Area: 250 x 170 mm
Copy instructions: *Copy Date:* 28 days prior to publication
Official Journal of: Organ of the World Association of Perinatal Medicine

JOURNAL OF PLANNING AND CONTROL
748732G14A-9000
Editorial: Reichenhainer Str. 39, 09107 CHEMNITZ
Email: zp@wirtschaft.tu-chemnitz.de **Web site:** http://www.springerlink.com
Freq: Quarterly; **Annual Sub.:** EUR 376,50; **Circ:** 180
Editor: Uwe Götze
Profile: Journal focusing on business planning and control.
Language(s): English; German
ADVERTISING RATES:
Full Page Mono .... EUR 740
Full Page Colour .... EUR 1780
Mechanical Data: Type Area: 200 x 130 mm

JOURNAL OF PLANNING AND CONTROL
748732G14A-10103
Editorial: Reichenhainer Str. 39, 09107 CHEMNITZ
Email: zp@wirtschaft.tu-chemnitz.de **Web site:** http://www.springerlink.com
Freq: Quarterly; **Annual Sub.:** EUR 376,50; **Circ:** 180
Editor: Uwe Götze
Profile: Journal focusing on business planning and control.
Language(s): English; German
ADVERTISING RATES:
Full Page Mono .... EUR 740
Full Page Colour .... EUR 1780
Mechanical Data: Type Area: 200 x 130 mm

JOURNAL OF PLANT DISEASES AND PROTECTION
748728G26D-310
Editorial: Hermann-Rodewald-Str. 9, 24118 KIEL
Tel: 431 8802996 **Fax:** 431 8801583
Email: javerreet@phytomed.uni-kiel.de **Web site:** http://www.zfpflkr.de
Freq: 6 issues yearly; **Annual Sub.:** EUR 564,30; **Circ:** 400
Editor: Joseph-Alexander Verreet; **Advertising Manager:** Maria Scheurenbrand
Profile: Magazine about plant care and the treatment of diseased plants.
Language(s): English; German
ADVERTISING RATES:
Full Page Mono .... EUR 580
Mechanical Data: Type Area: 210 x 130 mm, No. of Columns (Display): 2, Col Widths (Display): 63 mm
Copy instructions: *Copy Date:* 21 days prior to publication
Official Journal of: Organ d. Dt. Phytomedizin. Ges. e.V.
Supplement(s): DPG Phytomedizin
BUSINESS: GARDEN TRADE: Garden Trade Horticulture

JOURNAL OF PUBLIC HEALTH
748670G56A-10620
Editorial: Fiedlerstr. 27, 01307 DRESDEN
Tel: 351 4582815 **Fax:** 351 4584341
Email: subscriptions@springer.com **Web site:** http://www.springerlink.com
Freq: 6 issues yearly; **Annual Sub.:** EUR 202,00; **Circ:** 359
Editor: Wilhelm Kirch
Profile: Magazine about public health.
Language(s): English; German
ADVERTISING RATES:
Full Page Mono .... EUR 830
Full Page Colour .... EUR 1870
Mechanical Data: Type Area: 240 x 175 mm

JOURNAL OF SEPARATION SCIENCE
732131G37-1040
Editorial: Boschstr. 12, 69469 WEINHEIM
Tel: 6201 6060 **Fax:** 6201 606328
Email: fsvec@lbl.gov **Web site:** http://www.jss-journal.de
Freq: 22 issues yearly; **Annual Sub.:** EUR 2372,00; **Circ:** 1,000
Editor: Frantisek Svec; **Advertising Manager:** Marion Schulz
Profile: Journal of separation science.
Language(s): English
ADVERTISING RATES:
Full Page Mono .... EUR 1150
Full Page Colour .... EUR 2150
Mechanical Data: Type Area: 260 x 180 mm
Official Journal of: Organ d. European Society for Separation Science u. d. California Separation Science Society

JOURNAL ONKOLOGIE
1684001G56A-11355
Editorial: Watmarkt 1, 93047 REGENSBURG
Tel: 941 584030 **Fax:** 941 5840379
Email: redaktion@rsmedia-verlag.de **Web site:** http://www.journalonko.de
Freq: 9 issues yearly; **Annual Sub.:** EUR 43,50; **Circ:** 13,089
Editor: Barbara Schmalfeldt; **Advertising Manager:** Birgit Weigerstorfer
Profile: Journal for physicians with medical-scientific and practice-relevant information.
Language(s): German
ADVERTISING RATES:
Full Page Colour .... EUR 4170
Mechanical Data: Type Area: 249 x 181 mm
Copy instructions: *Copy Date:* 28 days prior to publication
BUSINESS: HEALTH & MEDICAL

JOURNALISMUS.COM
1662009G2B-1035
Editorial: Holzgasse 29, 91781 WEISSENBURG
Tel: 9141 873949 **Fax:** 9141 874067
Email: pdiesler@journalismus.com **Web site:** http://www.journalismus.com
Freq: Daily; **Cover Price:** Paid; **Circ:** 600,000 Unique Users
Editor: Peter Diesler
Language(s): German
BUSINESS: COMMUNICATIONS, ADVERTISING & MARKETING: Press

JOURNALIST
732076G2B-400
Editorial: Bennauerstr. 60, 53115 BONN
Tel: 228 2017224 **Fax:** 228 2017233
Email: journalist@journalist.de **Web site:** http://www.journalist.de
Freq: Monthly; Free to qualifying individuals
Annual Sub.: EUR 149,00; **Circ:** 45,893
Editor: Matthias Daniel
Profile: The magazine reported nonpartisan and objective from the media (press, TV and radio). New media projects, economic and mediapolitical background as job development and working conditions of journalists are currently displayed and critical. Media trends, research tools, techniques and forms of representation are analyzed. News about people and developments as well as tips on journalistic practice and further round out the editorial spectrum. The interviews are the people behind the headlines. Round-table discussions open eye for new arguments. Target group: Members of the German Journalists Association. In addition, the journal of editors and employees of all media, public relations, press offices and news agencies and publishing lines and media managers, based mostly on subscription or retail sale, when they received the trade magazine is not already by the DJV membership. Facebook: http://www.facebook.com/derjournalist Twitter: http://twitter.com/#!/journ_online This Outlet offers RSS (Really Simple Syndication).
Language(s): German
Readership: Aimed at journalists and political and media scientists.
ADVERTISING RATES:
Full Page Mono .... EUR 5700
Full Page Colour .... EUR 7950
Mechanical Data: Type Area: 260 x 185 mm, No. of Columns (Display): 4, Col Widths (Display): 43 mm
Copy instructions: *Copy Date:* 15 days prior to publication
Supplement(s): Fakten; Themen; ViaVision
BUSINESS: COMMUNICATIONS, ADVERTISING & MARKETING: Press

JOY
732155G74A-1660
Editorial: Arabellastr. 33, 81925 MÜNCHEN
Tel: 89 9234540 **Fax:** 89 9234534
Email: redaktion@joy-mag.de **Web site:** http://www.joy.de
Freq: Monthly; **Annual Sub.:** EUR 21,50; **Circ:** 416,409
Editor: Gerald Büchelmaier
Profile: JOY is the trend magazine, that offers modern and dynamic women a fashionable topic mix with subtle beauty looks, the hippest fashion trends, the most original people-stories and the most insolent men's Tricks and guarantees the JOY-readers that they really belong to the trendsetters. With this unique magazine concept, JOY is very specific to the needs of women. With a circulation of over 450,000 sold copies on newsstands JOY is the leading monthly women's magazine. The great success of JOY in Germany is the basis for the internationalization of the Trend magazine. JOY has 13 editions in 19 countries and has started to take a leading position internationally in the monthly women's magazine segment. Facebook: http://www.facebook.com/joymagazin Twitter: http://twitter.com/onlinejoy.
Language(s): German
Readership: Aimed at young women.
ADVERTISING RATES:
Full Page Mono .... EUR 25000
Full Page Colour .... EUR 25000
Mechanical Data: Type Area: 190 x 138 mm, No. of Columns (Display): 3, Col Widths (Display): 46 mm
Copy instructions: *Copy Date:* 42 days prior to publication
CONSUMER: WOMEN'S INTEREST CONSUMER MAGAZINES: Women's Interest

JOY
1773241G74A-3507
Editorial: Araballastr. 33, 81925 MÜNCHEN
Tel: 89 9234540 **Fax:** 89 9234534
Email: redaktion@joy-mag.de **Web site:** http://www.joy.de
Freq: Monthly; **Annual Sub.:** CHF 40,00; **Circ:** 416,409
Editor: Gerald Büchelmaier; **Advertising Manager:** Christine Malecki
Profile: Magazine for women Facebook: http://www.facebook.com/pages/JOY-Magazin/109681622383971.
Language(s): German
ADVERTISING RATES:
Full Page Mono .... CHF 24200
Full Page Colour .... CHF 24200
Mechanical Data: Type Area: 190 x 138 mm, No. of Columns (Display): 3, Col Widths (Display): 46 mm
Copy instructions: *Copy Date:* 38 days prior to publication

JOYCE
756117G74A-3243
Editorial: Wellingsbütteler Landstr. 200m, 22337 HAMBURG **Tel:** 40 27808466
Email: joyce@bundes-verlag.de **Web site:** http://www.joycenet.de
Freq: Quarterly; **Annual Sub.:** EUR 16,80; **Circ:** 18,000
Editor: Melanie Carstens; **Advertising Manager:** Thilo Cunz
Profile: Magazine for women from churches and free churches of all denominations.
Language(s): German
ADVERTISING RATES:
Full Page Mono .... EUR 1340
Full Page Colour .... EUR 1842
Mechanical Data: Type Area: 258 x 188 mm, No. of Columns (Display): 4, Col Widths (Display): 44 mm

JS MAGAZIN
732161G40-400
Editorial: Emil-von-Behring-Str. 3, 60439 FRANKFURT **Tel:** 69 58098170 **Fax:** 69 58098163
Email: info@js-magazin.de **Web site:** http://www.js-magazin.de
Freq: Monthly; **Cover Price:** Free; **Circ:** 22,800
Editor: Dorothea Siegle
Profile: Magazine concerning military and defence issues.
Language(s): German
Readership: Aimed at soldiers between 18 and 28 years of age.
BUSINESS: DEFENCE

JS MAGAZIN
1621555G40-951
Editorial: Normannenweg 17, 20537 HAMBURG
Tel: 40 251150 **Fax:** 40 257466
Email: info@js-redaktion.de **Web site:** http://www.militaerseelsorge.de
Circ: 115,000
Editor: Dorothea Siegle; **Advertising Manager:** Burkhard Rodmann
Profile: Ezine: Magazine concerning military and defence issues.
Language(s): German

JÜDISCHE ALLGEMEINE
720000G87-260
Editorial: Hausvogteiplatz 12, 10117 BERLIN
Tel: 30 4998880 **Fax:** 30 49988899
Email: buero@juedische-allgemeine.de **Web site:** http://www.juedische-allgemeine.de
Freq: Weekly; **Annual Sub.:** EUR 99,90; **Circ:** 7,145
Editor: Detlef David Kauschke; **Advertising Manager:** Bettina Menke
Profile: The Jüdische Allgemeine is one of the most important Jewish media in Germany. The traditional leaf was launched in 1946 and is journalistically in the tradition of the »Allgemeine Zeitung des Judenthums«. In 2009, the Jüdische Allgemeine won an Oscar for a relaunch of Newspaper Design: As part of the European Newspaper Award she won in the category of 'front page weekly newspaper. Back in 2003 the paper received an Award of Excellence in the category typography. Facebook: http://www.facebook.com/pages/Judische-Allgemeine/362784088409 This Outlet offers RSS (Really Simple Syndication).
Language(s): German
Mechanical Data: Type Area: 474 x 321 mm, No. of Columns (Display): 5, Col Widths (Display): 61 mm
Copy instructions: *Copy Date:* 7 days prior to publication
Supplement(s): Jüdische Illustrierte; Jüdische Literatur
CONSUMER: RELIGIOUS

JUDO MAGAZIN
732166G75Q-120
Editorial: Lindenstr. 18, 63571 GELNHAUSEN
Email: kauer-berk@ecos.net
Freq: 11 issues yearly; **Annual Sub.:** EUR 29,00; **Circ:** 12,000
Editor: Oliver Kauer-Berk; **Advertising Manager:** Kirsten Schiffer
Profile: Official journal of the German Judo Association for tournaments and techniques.
Language(s): German
ADVERTISING RATES:
Full Page Mono .... EUR 980
Full Page Colour .... EUR 1780
Mechanical Data: Type Area: 236 x 170 mm, No. of Columns (Display): 4, Col Widths (Display): 43 mm
Copy instructions: *Copy Date:* 30 days prior to publication
CONSUMER: SPORT: Combat Sports

JUGEND & BUNDESWEHR
732193G40-420
Editorial: Carl-Mosterts-Platz 1, 40477 DÜSSELDORF **Tel:** 211 4693184 **Fax:** 211 4693120
Email: aktion.kaserne@bdkj.de **Web site:** http://www.jugendhaus-duesseldorf.de
Freq: Quarterly; **Circ:** 4,000
Editor: Stefan Dengel
Profile: Magazine about young people and the army.
Language(s): German

JUGENDHILFE
732181G32G-1300
Editorial: Luxemburger Str. 449, 50939 KÖLN
Tel: 221 943737202 **Fax:** 221 943737206
Email: redaktion@jugendhilfe-netz.de **Web site:** http://www.jugendhilfe-netz.de
Freq: 6 issues yearly; **Annual Sub.:** EUR 66,00; **Circ:** 1,900
Editor: Ann-Kathrin Schrepfer
Profile: Publication about the care and guidance of children and young people in the community.
Language(s): German
ADVERTISING RATES:
Full Page Mono .... EUR 595
Full Page Colour .... EUR 1660
Mechanical Data: Type Area: 205 x 135 mm
Copy instructions: *Copy Date:* 28 days prior to publication
BUSINESS: LOCAL GOVERNMENT, LEISURE & RECREATION: Community Care & Social Services

JUICE
1639480G76D-6109
Editorial: Sandstr. 3, 80335 MÜNCHEN
Tel: 89 30774212 **Fax:** 89 30774233
Email: juice@piranha-media.de **Web site:** http://www.juice.de
Freq: 6 issues yearly; **Annual Sub.:** EUR 45,00; **Circ:** 17,924
Editor: Stephan Szillus
Profile: Magazine about HipHop music. JUICE illuminates the scene in all its aspects and to the highest journalistic standards. Detailed and personal interviews with the biggest stars of the scene. Critical background reports. A comprehensive and timely service part that is without equal worldwide. This the latest in fashion, graffiti, Beats'n'Rhymes, underground, street, games and lifestyle. This results in every month an impressive picture of hip-hop culture in all its diversity. Beats'n'Rhymes, underground and mainstream, Berlin and New York, the history and stories. Facebook: http://www.facebook.com/juicemagazin Twitter: http://twitter.com/#!/juicemagazin This Outlet offers RSS (Really Simple Syndication).
Language(s): German
ADVERTISING RATES:
Full Page Mono .... EUR 3950
Full Page Colour .... EUR 3950
Mechanical Data: Type Area: 295 x 230 mm
CONSUMER: MUSIC & PERFORMING ARTS: Music

JÜLICHER NACHRICHTEN
732171G67B-7880
Editorial: Dresdener Str. 3, 52068 AACHEN
Tel: 241 5101310 **Fax:** 241 5101360
Email: redaktion@zeitungsverlag-aachen.de **Web site:** http://www.an-online.de
Freq: 312 issues yearly; **Circ:** 10,056
Advertising Manager: Christian Kretschmer
Profile: Daily newspaper with regional news and a local sports section. Facebook: http://facebook.com/aachenernachrichten This Outlet offers RSS (Really Simple Syndication).
Language(s): German
ADVERTISING RATES:
SCC .... EUR 38,80
Mechanical Data: Type Area: 480 x 324 mm, No. of Columns (Display): 7, Col Widths (Display): 44 mm
Copy instructions: *Copy Date:* 1 day prior to publication

Supplement(s): prisma
REGIONAL DAILY & SUNDAY NEWSPAPERS:
Regional Daily Newspapers

JÜLICHER WOCHE 732172G72-6012
Editorial: Ferdinand-Clasen-Str. 21, 41812 ERKELENZ **Tel:** 2431 968618 **Fax:** 2431 81651
Email: redaktion@hs-woche.de **Web site:** http://www.juelicher-woche.de
Freq: Weekly; **Cover Price:** Free; **Circ:** 33,150
Editor: Ulrich C. Kronenberg; **Advertising Manager:** Günter Paffen
Profile: Advertising journal (house-to-house) concentrating on local stories.
Language(s): German
ADVERTISING RATES:
Full Page Mono .... EUR 3582
Full Page Colour .... EUR 4352
Mechanical Data: Type Area: 430 x 292 mm, No. of Columns (Display): 7, Col Widths (Display): 40 mm
Copy instructions: *Copy Date:* 2 days prior to publication
LOCAL NEWSPAPERS

JÜLICHER ZEITUNG 732173G67B-7900
Editorial: Dresdener Str. 3, 52068 AACHEN
Tel: 241 5101310 **Fax:** 241 5101360
Email: redaktion@zeitungsverlag-aachen.de **Web site:** http://www.aachener-zeitung.de
Freq: 312 issues yearly; **Circ:** 10,056
Advertising Manager: Christian Kretschmer
Profile: Daily newspaper with regional news and a local sports section. Facebook: http://facebook.com/aachenerzeitung This Outlet offers RSS (Really Simple Syndication).
Language(s): German
ADVERTISING RATES:
SCC .... EUR 38,80
Mechanical Data: Type Area: 480 x 324 mm, No. of Columns (Display): 7, Col Widths (Display): 44 mm
Copy instructions: *Copy Date:* 1 day prior to publication
Supplement(s): prisma
REGIONAL DAILY & SUNDAY NEWSPAPERS: Regional Daily Newspapers

JUNGE FAMILIE 732206G74D-110
Editorial: Raboisen 30, 20095 HAMBURG
Tel: 40 344434 **Fax:** 40 352540
Email: info@junior-verlag.de **Web site:** http://www.wireltern.de
Freq: 6 issues yearly; **Annual Sub.:** EUR 9,00; **Circ:** 269,528
Editor: Elena Rudolph; **Advertising Manager:** Birgit König
Profile: "Junge Familie" established itself within the parents press firmly as a basic medium and in 2009 celebrated its 40th anniversary. The magazine supported the young family from pregnancy through baby's first months of life until about the second year of age. The young mother is addressed by topics as "Beauty & Health ", "Pregnancy & Birth" or "motherhood" and important tips and information are obtained in each issue. Through a highly efficient distribution channel you will reach the young mother on a direct path. Therefor the "Junge Familie" is an effective advertising medium of products for pregnancy and baby area for many industries beyond . "Junge Familie " reaches expectant mothers and young parents directly.
Language(s): German
Readership: Aimed at parents of young children.
ADVERTISING RATES:
Full Page Mono .... EUR 18900
Full Page Colour .... EUR 18900
Mechanical Data: Type Area: 260 x 183 mm
Copy instructions: *Copy Date:* 42 days prior to publication
CONSUMER: WOMEN'S INTEREST CONSUMER MAGAZINES: Child Care

JUNGE KUNST 732214G84A-1400
Editorial: Bachstr. 28, 53115 BONN
Tel: 228 9652896
Email: a.wendorf@jungekunst-magazin.de **Web site:** http://www.kunstwelt-online.de
Freq: Quarterly; **Annual Sub.:** EUR 29,00; **Circ:** 3,000
Editor: Alexandra Wendorf; **Advertising Manager:** Vanessa Karacuha
Profile: Information and communications magazine for the visual arts.
Language(s): German
Readership: Aimed at people interested in art.
ADVERTISING RATES:
Full Page Mono .... EUR 742
Full Page Colour .... EUR 1187
Mechanical Data: Type Area: 226 x 177 mm, No. of Columns (Display): 3, Col Widths (Display): 56 mm
Copy instructions: *Copy Date:* 30 days prior to publication
CONSUMER: THE ARTS & LITERARY: Arts

JUNGE SAMMLER 732216G79C-230
Editorial: Im vorderen Pfeiler 8e, 55291 SAULHEIM
Tel: 6732 938512 **Fax:** 6732 9356466
Email: redaktion@dphj.de
Freq: Quarterly; Free to qualifying individuals
Annual Sub.: EUR 10,00; **Circ:** 10,000
Editor: Markus Bachen
Profile: Magazine for young stamp collectors.
Language(s): German
ADVERTISING RATES:
Full Page Mono .... EUR 398
Full Page Colour .... EUR 398
Mechanical Data: Type Area: 210 x 148 mm, No. of Columns (Display): 2, Col Widths (Display): 70 mm
Copy instructions: *Copy Date:* 40 days prior to publication
CONSUMER: HOBBIES & DIY: Philately

JUNGE WELT 732219G65A-140
Editorial: Torstr. 6, 10119 BERLIN **Tel:** 30 5363550
Fax: 30 53635544
Email: redaktion@jungewelt.de **Web site:** http://www.jungewelt.de
Freq: 312 issues yearly; **Circ:** 18,500
Editor: Arnold Schölzel; **Advertising Manager:** Silke Schubert
Profile: The junge Welt is a leftist, Marxist-oriented, national daily newspaper with a high proportion of background information and comprehensive analysis. The print edition is published every working day with at least 16 pages, on weekends in addition to the eight-page insert "laziness and labor," she is by subscription and at the kiosk. The online edition is published the day before. The daily newspaper junge Welt is published 8. Mai GmbH, the majority of the cooperative of its readers and the staff is (LPG junge Welt eG). Neither political parties and organizations have large publishing houses, churches and banks have shares in publishing or cooperative. Each member of the cooperative has one vote, no matter how many shares were subscribed by him. The junge Welt is financed almost exclusively from the revenues the print and online editions. The cooperative LPG junge Welt eG assumes the financial security (cash, investments). Other major sources of funding do not exist. Herein is the economic independence of the junge Welt founded. The online edition can be viewed largely free of charge. Some specials and the archive are available only to online subscribers unlimited access. The junge Welt also offers a free sample of the print edition of the reference period of three weeks. Ultimately, the daily newspaper junge Welt exist only if they participate in the Users of the product at the expense of about a quarter of a million € per month. At the center of journalistic activity are social issues and war. This focus is directed them that capitalism after 1990 in a period of worsening economic and social contradictions occurred. Expression of this are the reduction of the welfare state and parliamentary democracy, increased repression and social demagoguery - including the revival of fascism and the use of force, violence and war in violation of international law at the international level. The junge Welt promotes all forms of political protest and resistance against these tendencies. It supports the struggle for alternatives, dialogue and networking between the different currents of the left. About the history of the socialist countries is critical, but reported no anti-communism. In view of the evolution of bourgeois states to authoritarian forms of rule development, young world for the respect and the preservation of liberal rights standards and respect for international law as a first condition for peace. It stands on an enlightened position without condescension, and acts by arguments, high quality, entertainment value and bite. For the junge Welt, it is relevant, what is happening in other parts of the world. She puts such great emphasis on a comprehensive and inclusive coverage of the progressive developments in Latin America. Solidarity is understood the junge Welt not as a one-way street: The experience left movements and organizations from around the world will also be used for fighting in the country. This approach highlights the young world, with the International Rosa-Luxembourg-conference that they organized annually on the second Saturday in January, along with others in Berlin. The junge Welt was founded in 1947 in the anti-fascist spirit as a weekly newspaper in Berlin. Since 1952, daily newspaper, it developed until 1989 for the largest circulation in the GDR. Critical and informative than other media, reaching the young world, a high popularity. Even at this time, the originally conceived as a youth newspaper junge Welt ("the central organ of the FDJ") read in all age groups. After the privatization of the junge Welt by selling a cord at a West Berlin-based media group, the edition quickly dropped, partly because the newspaper did not differ enough from others and went left no clear course. An attempt in 1994 to profile the newspaper clearly was stopped prematurely: the former owner stopped the production of the daily newspaper junge Welt early April 1995. Staff went on to the publisher 8. Mai GmbH (and later the junge Welt eG Cooperative LPG) and were able to realize the further release of the world as a young Marxist newspaper - until today. This was possible by clarity of content, multiple actions of publishers and editors, the strong support of the readers and the work of the cooperative - and not least through the dedicated work of employees of publishers and editors as well as many freelance writers. Twitter: http://twitter.com/jungeweltde This Outlet offers RSS (Really Simple Syndication).
Language(s): German
Readership: Read by students and predominantly the younger generation.
ADVERTISING RATES:
SCC .... EUR 50,00
Mechanical Data: Type Area: 432 x 285 mm, No. of Columns (Display): 5, Col Widths (Display): 53 mm
Copy instructions: *Copy Date:* 2 days prior to publication
NATIONAL DAILY & SUNDAY NEWSPAPERS: National Daily Newspapers

JUNGLE WORLD 732224G72-19074
Editorial: Bergmannstr. 68, 10961 BERLIN
Tel: 30 61282730 **Fax:** 30 6182055
Email: redaktion@jungle-world.com **Web site:** http://www.jungle-world.com
Freq: Weekly; **Circ:** 16,250
Editor: Bernd Beier; **News Editor:** Ivo Bozic
Profile: National weekly covering politics, economics, sports, travel and the arts. Facebook: http://www.facebook.com/JungleWorld Twitter: http://twitter.com/#!/Jungle_World.
Language(s): German
Mechanical Data: Type Area: 437 x 282 mm, No. of Columns (Display): 4, Col Widths (Display): 66 mm
Copy instructions: *Copy Date:* 10 days prior to publication
LOCAL NEWSPAPERS

JUNIOR - AUSG. DEUTSCHLAND U. ÖSTERREICH 732228G91D-4040
Editorial: Dieselstr. 16, 89160 DORNSTADT
Tel: 7348 928139 **Fax:** 7348 928114
Email: h.rothermel@junior.ch **Web site:** http://www.hallojunior.de
Freq: Monthly; **Cover Price:** Free; **Circ:** 1,020,022
Editor: Harald Rothermel
Profile: Magazine for children.
Language(s): German
ADVERTISING RATES:
Full Page Mono .... CHF 19500
Full Page Colour .... CHF 19500
Mechanical Data: Type Area: 175 x 128 mm
Copy instructions: *Copy Date:* 30 days prior to publication
CONSUMER: RECREATION & LEISURE: Children & Youth

JURA JURISTISCHE AUSBILDUNG 732233G44-1300
Editorial: Genthiner Str. 13, 10785 BERLIN
Tel: 30 26005175 **Fax:** 30 26005329
Email: jura@degruyter.com **Web site:** http://www.jura-zeitschrift.de
Freq: Monthly; **Annual Sub.:** EUR 162,80; **Circ:** 4,300
Advertising Manager: Dietlind Makswitat
Profile: Magazine containing news and information for the German legal profession, especially German legal students. Facebook: http://www.facebook.com/degruyter.publishers.
Language(s): German
Readership: Read mainly by students and teachers of law.
Mechanical Data: Type Area: 250 x 170 mm
Copy instructions: *Copy Date:* 27 days prior to publication
BUSINESS: LEGAL

JURISTISCHE ARBEITSBLÄTTER JA 732242G44-1320
Editorial: Wilhelmstr. 9, 80801 MÜNCHEN
Tel: 89 381890 **Fax:** 89 38189398
Email: jaredaktion@vahlen.de **Web site:** http://www.ja-aktuell.de
Freq: 11 issues yearly; **Circ:** 5,900
Advertising Manager: Fritz Lebherz
Profile: Journal containing news, information and articles about the study of law and the work situation for law students and graduates.
Language(s): German
Readership: Aimed at law students and young lawyers.
ADVERTISING RATES:
Full Page Mono .... EUR 1240
Full Page Colour .... EUR 1850
Mechanical Data: Type Area: 260 x 186 mm
BUSINESS: LEGAL

DAS JURISTISCHE BÜRO 732244G44-3115
Editorial: Luxemburger Str. 449, 50939 KÖLN
Tel: 221 943737161 **Fax:** 221 943737203
Email: gmathias@wolterskluwer.de **Web site:** http://www.wolterskluwer.de
Freq: Monthly; **Annual Sub.:** EUR 209,00; **Circ:** 2,600
Editor: Gisela Mathias
Profile: Magazine containing articles about all aspects of the law.
Language(s): German
ADVERTISING RATES:
Full Page Mono .... EUR 1100
Full Page Colour .... EUR 2207
Mechanical Data: Type Area: 255 x 184 mm
Copy instructions: *Copy Date:* 21 days prior to publication
BUSINESS: LEGAL

JURMEDIA 1928664G1A-3801
Editorial: Wachsbleiche 7, 53111 BONN
Tel: 228 9191172 **Fax:** 228 9191123
Email: jurmedia@soldan.de **Web site:** http://www.soldan.de
Freq: 6 issues yearly; **Annual Sub.:** EUR 30,00; **Circ:** 40,000
Profile: The magazine JURMEDIA is published six times a year and offers a free overview of current releases, reissues, best-selling and introduces each issue interesting textbooks, journals or databases.
Language(s): German
ADVERTISING RATES:
Full Page Colour .... EUR 2750
Mechanical Data: Type Area: 255 x 190 mm, No. of Columns (Display): 3, Col Widths (Display): 60 mm

JUROPE 732247G74F-110
Editorial: Am Schlag 1, 82223 EICHENAU
Tel: 8141 82458
Freq: Quarterly; **Cover Price:** Free; **Circ:** 10,000
Editor: Ruprecht Kertscher; **Advertising Manager:** Ruprecht Kertscher
Profile: Magazine of interest to teenagers.
Language(s): German
ADVERTISING RATES:
Full Page Mono .... EUR 345
Copy instructions: *Copy Date:* 28 days prior to publication
CONSUMER: WOMEN'S INTEREST CONSUMER MAGAZINES: Teenage

JUS JURISTISCHE SCHULUNG 732250G44-3117
Editorial: Beethovenstr. 7b, 60325 FRANKFURT
Tel: 69 7560910 **Fax:** 69 75609149
Email: redaktion@jus.de **Web site:** http://www.jus.beck.de
Freq: Monthly; **Circ:** 12,326
Editor: Georg Neureither; **Advertising Manager:** Fritz Lebherz
Profile: Magazine containing information about legal practice and legislation.
Language(s): German
Readership: Read by people training to become lawyers.
ADVERTISING RATES:
Full Page Mono .... EUR 2620
Full Page Colour .... EUR 3730
Mechanical Data: Type Area: 260 x 186 mm, No. of Columns (Display): 4, Col Widths (Display): 43 mm
Copy instructions: *Copy Date:* 24 days prior to publication
BUSINESS: LEGAL

JUST KICK-IT! 1667773G91D-10289
Editorial: Rotebühlstr. 87, 70178 STUTTGART
Tel: 711 947680 **Fax:** 711 9476830
Email: justkickit@panini.de **Web site:** http://www.panini.de
Freq: Monthly; **Cover Price:** EUR 2,99; **Circ:** 40,841
Profile: Whistle for Just kick-it!, the magazine for avid football fans! It puts the brim with great extras, the football-obsessed boys aged between 8 and 13 years are: posters, 3D and other extras, attractive competitions and football insider knowledge to collect. Given all the news and background information, hot stories about the soccer stars, top games nationally and internationally as well as the best newcomer.
Language(s): German
ADVERTISING RATES:
Full Page Mono .... EUR 5500
Full Page Colour .... EUR 5500
Mechanical Data: Type Area: 250 x 180 mm
CONSUMER: RECREATION & LEISURE: Children & Youth

JUSTAMENT 732251G44-3118
Editorial: Güntzelstr. 63, 10717 BERLIN
Tel: 30 81450623 **Fax:** 30 81450622
Email: justament@lexxion.de **Web site:** http://www.justament.de
Freq: 6 issues yearly; **Annual Sub.:** EUR 23,46; **Circ:** 20,640
Editor: Thomas Claer
Profile: The magazine focuses on substantive and organizational questions of legal education and careers. It incorporates current socio-political issues in order to assess the legal labor market better by tomorrow. For example, in the developments in media law or in the area of insolvency law created new fields of work for lawyers. With interviews and contributions are demanding such new areas of activity highlighted and developed information Statement, which was among the first steps after graduation, it will help towards a market-oriented additional qualifications or independence. Especially at the legal market, the business idea to the most important factor for the success of the firm foundation has become. In the service of the Justament practical guidance on the legal education and training is offered in tax tips for lawyers, about dealing with health insurance, to exercise regularly published exams for the 2nd State Exam. In addition, the magazine serves as a medium of communication and discussion forum. justament addresses topics that are of interest throughout the country. Audience: The magazine is aimed at the legal offspring, especially clerks, clerk candidates, young qualified lawyers and advanced law students. The magazine reaches readers but also within the judiciary, administration and lawyers associated with legal training in the compound. The distribution of justament is targeted and monitored at over 400 controlled output, which always frequented by the target group of legal training bodies, law schools, libraries, bookstores, etc.).
Language(s): German
ADVERTISING RATES:
Full Page Mono .... EUR 1720
Full Page Colour .... EUR 2494
Mechanical Data: Type Area: 248 x 176 mm
Copy instructions: *Copy Date:* 21 days prior to publication
BUSINESS: LEGAL

JUVE HANDBUCH WIRTSCHAFTSKANZLEIEN
732258G14A-3740

Editorial: Sachsenring 6, 50677 KÖLN
Tel: 221 91388011 **Fax:** 221 91388018
Email: handbuch@juve.de **Web site:** http://www.juve.de
Freq: Annual; **Cover Price:** EUR 59,00; **Circ:** 20,000
Editor: Aled Griffiths; **Advertising Manager:** Christopher Savill
Profile: In Juve Handbuch Wirtschaftskanzleien you can read in detail, recommended that law firms for a specific set of legal solutions to problems. Lawyers and clients are the main sources of information for the Juve-editors. The firms are sorted by city or region and by areas of law. With information about specific strengths and handled with instructions on personnel strength and the individual sites.
Language(s): German
ADVERTISING RATES:
Full Page Mono .... EUR 6890
Full Page Colour .... EUR 6890
Mechanical Data: Type Area: 235 x 160 mm

JUVE RECHTSMARKT
732260G1A-1480

Editorial: Sachsenring 6, 50677 KÖLN
Tel: 221 91388011 **Fax:** 221 91388018
Email: redaktion@juve.de **Web site:** http://www.juve.de
Freq: Monthly; **Cover Price:** EUR 12,50; **Circ:** 13,000
Editor: Aled Griffiths; **Advertising Manager:** Christopher Savill
Profile: The magazine analyzed the potentials in various fields of law, provides information on nationwide and regional particularities and trends abroad. Another focus is on reports from and about corporate legal departments.
Language(s): German
ADVERTISING RATES:
Full Page Mono .... EUR 3950
Full Page Colour .... EUR 3950
Mechanical Data: Type Area: 257 x 186 mm
Copy instructions: *Copy Date:* 16 days prior to publication

JVB-PRESSE
732265G32F-340

Editorial: Deinfelderstr. 11, 92224 AMBERG
Tel: 9621 13727 **Fax:** 9621 22524
Freq: 6 issues yearly; **Circ:** 3,000
Editor: Johann Lautenschlager; **Advertising Manager:** Johann Lautenschlager
Profile: Journal for employees of the German penal system.
Language(s): German
ADVERTISING RATES:
Full Page Mono .... EUR 210
Mechanical Data: Type Area: 250 x 180 mm, No. of Columns (Display): 2, Col Widths (Display): 85 mm
BUSINESS: LOCAL GOVERNMENT, LEISURE & RECREATION: Police

K KUNSTSTOFF-BERATER
732757G39-75

Editorial: Hans-Böckler-Allee 9, 30173 HANNOVER
Tel: 511 7304136 **Fax:** 511 7304157
Email: a.graevemeyer@giesel.de **Web site:** http://www.kunststoffberater.de
Freq: 10 issues yearly; **Annual Sub.:** EUR 133,00; **Circ:** 5,943
Editor: Arne Grävemeyer; **Advertising Manager:** Gero Trinkaus
Profile: Magazine covering the man-made materials industry. Contains news and information about machinery and process technology.
Language(s): German
Readership: Read by engineers and technical personnel within the field.
ADVERTISING RATES:
Full Page Mono .... EUR 2540
Full Page Colour .... EUR 4020
Mechanical Data: Type Area: 263 x 160 mm, No. of Columns (Display): 3, Col Widths (Display): 50 mm
Copy instructions: *Copy Date:* 25 days prior to publication
BUSINESS: PLASTICS & RUBBER

K & L-MAGAZIN
733521G3B-41

Editorial: Friedrichstr. 22, 70736 FELLBACH
Tel: 711 54041910 **Fax:** 711 54041912
Email: lorenz@gentner.de
Freq: 8 issues yearly; **Annual Sub.:** EUR 59,00; **Circ:** 2,829
Editor: Jutta Lorenz; **Advertising Manager:** Bettina Landwehr
Profile: Official journal of the Society of Sanitation, Heating and Air Conditioning. Also provides information on stoves.
Language(s): German
ADVERTISING RATES:
Full Page Mono .... EUR 1180
Full Page Colour .... EUR 1855
Mechanical Data: Type Area: 265 x 187 mm, No. of Columns (Display): 4, Col Widths (Display): 43 mm
Copy instructions: *Copy Date:* 29 days prior to publication
Official Journal of: Organ d. ZVSHK - Zentralverb. Sanitär, Heizung, Klima, d. AdK - ArGe d. dt. Kachelofenwirtschaft u. d. GGK - Gütegemeinschaft Kachelofen
BUSINESS: HEATING & VENTILATION: Industrial Heating & Ventilation

K+S INFORMATION
1637723G58-1726

Editorial: Bertha-von-Suttner-Str. 7, 34131 KASSEL
Tel: 561 93011043 **Fax:** 561 93011666
Email: uwe.handke@k-plus-s.com **Web site:** http://www.k-plus-s.com
Freq: 6 issues yearly; **Cover Price:** Free; **Circ:** 16,500
Editor: Uwe Handke
Profile: Magazine for employees of K+S Gruppe.
Language(s): German

K ZEITUNG
733681G39-30

Editorial: Hans-Böckler-Allee 9, 30173 HANNOVER
Tel: 511 7304136 **Fax:** 511 7304157
Email: k-redaktion@giesel.de **Web site:** http://www.k-zeitung.de
Freq: 23 issues yearly; **Annual Sub.:** EUR 158,00; **Circ:** 15,952
Editor: Joachim Rönisch; **Advertising Manager:** Gero Trinkaus
Profile: Newspaper covering all aspects of the plastic and rubber trade. Includes news items and articles on trends and tendencies.
Language(s): German
Readership: Read by senior and middle managers.
ADVERTISING RATES:
Full Page Mono .... EUR 3945
Full Page Colour .... EUR 5370
Mechanical Data: Type Area: 385 x 265 mm, No. of Columns (Display): 6, Col Widths (Display): 40 mm
Copy instructions: *Copy Date:* 16 days prior to publication
BUSINESS: PLASTICS & RUBBER

KA KORRESPONDENZ ABWASSER ABFALL
732469G42C-3

Editorial: Theodor-Heuss-Allee 17, 53773 HENNEF
Tel: 2242 872190 **Fax:** 2242 872151
Email: bringewski@dwa.de **Web site:** http://www.dwa.de
Freq: Monthly; **Circ:** 12,725
Editor: Frank Bringewski; **Advertising Manager:** Andrea Vogel
Profile: The editorial focus is on the drainage systems, municipal and industrial wastewater treatment, disposal and recycling of waste materials, such as sewage sludge, screenings, fat separator.
Language(s): German
ADVERTISING RATES:
Full Page Mono .... EUR 2080
Full Page Colour .... EUR 3430
Mechanical Data: Type Area: 256 x 176 mm, No. of Columns (Display): 3, Col Widths (Display): 56 mm
Copy instructions: *Copy Date:* 32 days prior to publication
Official Journal of: Organ d. DWA Dt. Vereinigung f. Wasserwirtschaft, Abwasser u. Abfall u. d. Güteschutz Kanalbau e.V.
Supplement(s): gewässer-info; KA-Betriebs-Info
BUSINESS: CONSTRUCTION: Water Engineering

KAB IMPULS
732275G14R-6098

Editorial: Bernhard-Letterhaus-Str. 26, 50670 KÖLN
Tel: 221 7722131 **Fax:** 221 7722135
Email: matthias.rabbe@ketteler-verlag.de **Web site:** http://www.kab.de
Freq: 10 issues yearly; Free to qualifying individuals
Annual Sub.: EUR 19,40; **Circ:** 135,000
Editor: Matthias Rabbe
Profile: Newspaper for Catholic employees.
Language(s): German
Mechanical Data: Type Area: 262 x 188 mm, No. of Columns (Display): 4
Copy instructions: *Copy Date:* 18 days prior to publication
BUSINESS: COMMERCE, INDUSTRY & MANAGEMENT: Commerce Related

KA-BETRIEBS-INFO
732274G4E-4920

Editorial: Theodor-Heuss-Allee 17, 53773 HENNEF
Tel: 2242 872190 **Fax:** 2242 872151
Email: bringewski@dwa.de **Web site:** http://www.dwa.de
Freq: Quarterly; **Circ:** 22,500
Editor: Frank Bringewski; **Advertising Manager:** Andrea Vogel
Profile: Information, comments, facts and figures for the operating staff of sewage systems containing the KA-Betriebs-Info. Here, for example practical experiences exchanged and presented its own technical developments, but also the health and safety is a particular focus.
Language(s): German
ADVERTISING RATES:
Full Page Mono .... EUR 963
Full Page Colour .... EUR 2133
Mechanical Data: Type Area: 253 x 176 mm, No. of Columns (Display): 3, Col Widths (Display): 56 mm
Copy instructions: *Copy Date:* 40 days prior to publication
Supplement to: KA Korrespondenz Abwasser Abfall

KACHELOFEN & KAMIN
732279G3B-50

Editorial: Haldenweg 18, 71336 WAIBLINGEN
Tel: 7146 87650 **Fax:** 7146 876565
Email: redaktion@dierote.de **Web site:** http://www.dierote.de
Freq: Monthly; **Annual Sub.:** EUR 63,00; **Circ:** 3,834
Editor: Gustav Kopf; **Advertising Manager:** Jens Fischer
Profile: Magazine containing articles about chimneys, fireplaces, stoves and hot-air heating.
Language(s): German
Readership: Read by heating specialists.
ADVERTISING RATES:
Full Page Mono .... EUR 1300
Full Page Colour .... EUR 1990
Mechanical Data: Type Area: 255 x 185 mm, No. of Columns (Display): 4, Col Widths (Display): 45 mm
Copy instructions: *Copy Date:* 30 days prior to publication
BUSINESS: HEATING & VENTILATION: Industrial Heating & Ventilation

KÄFER REVUE
1814340G77A-2814

Editorial: Am Sandfeld 15a, 76149 KARLSRUHE
Tel: 721 6273820 **Fax:** 721 6273811
Email: redaktion@kr-magazin.de **Web site:** http://www.kr-magazin.de
Freq: Annual; **Cover Price:** EUR 4,90; **Circ:** 23,000
Editor: Arne Olerth; **Advertising Manager:** Sigrid Pinke
Profile: Käfer Revue includes everything that makes the friends of air-cooled Volkswagen fun. Original vehicles can be found here alongside souped Wolfsburgers, features renowned motor journalists create excitement and detailed reports to improve care and help to guarantee the old treasures of longevity.
Language(s): German
ADVERTISING RATES:
Full Page Colour .... EUR 3360
Mechanical Data: Type Area: 260 x 190 mm
Copy instructions: *Copy Date:* 46 days prior to publication

KAISERSTÜHLER WOCHENBERICHT
732311G72-6044

Editorial: Denzlinger Str. 42, 79312 EMMENDINGEN
Tel: 7641 938015 **Fax:** 7641 938010
Email: redaktion@kaiserstuehler-wochenbericht.de
Web site: http://www.wzo.de
Freq: Weekly; **Cover Price:** Free; **Circ:** 18,950
Editor: Hubert Fetterer; **Advertising Manager:** Clemens Merkle
Profile: Advertising journal (house-to-house) concentrating on local stories.
Language(s): German
ADVERTISING RATES:
Full Page Mono .... EUR 2142
Full Page Colour .... EUR 2924
Mechanical Data: Type Area: 420 x 285 mm, No. of Columns (Display): 6, Col Widths (Display): 45 mm
Copy instructions: *Copy Date:* 2 days prior to publication
LOCAL NEWSPAPERS

KALLIPYGOS-BRIEFE
1698993G74A-3487

Editorial: Finkenstr. 56, 47057 DUISBURG
Email: situationspresse@gmx.de **Web site:** http://www.buchhandlung-weltbuehne.de
Freq: 6 issues yearly; **Annual Sub.:** EUR 26,00; **Circ:** 300
Profile: Magazine containing erotic literature.
Language(s): German
ADVERTISING RATES:
Full Page Mono .... EUR 15
Mechanical Data: Type Area: 180 x 110 mm, No. of Columns (Display): 2, Col Widths (Display): 50 mm

DIE KÄLTE- UND KLIMATECHNIK
732753G3C-10

Editorial: Forststr. 131, 70193 STUTTGART
Tel: 711 63672807 **Fax:** 711 63672707
Email: schmitt@diekaelte.de **Web site:** http://www.diekaelte.de
Freq: Monthly; **Annual Sub.:** EUR 169,60; **Circ:** 5,094
Editor: Matthias Schmitt; **Advertising Manager:** Sandra Bayer
Profile: Magazine about cooling, deep-freezing and air-conditioning.
Language(s): German
ADVERTISING RATES:
Full Page Mono .... EUR 1960
Full Page Colour .... EUR 2660
Mechanical Data: Type Area: 265 x 187 mm, No. of Columns (Display): 4, Col Widths (Display): 43 mm
Copy instructions: *Copy Date:* 20 days prior to publication
Official Journal of: Organ d. Bundesinnungsverb. d. Dt. Kälteanlagenbauerhandwerks
BUSINESS: HEATING & VENTILATION: Refrigeration & Ventilation

KAMENZER WOCHENKURIER
732356G72-6056

Editorial: Karl-Marx-Str. 68, 03044 COTTBUS
Tel: 355 4312381 **Fax:** 355 472910
Email: kerstintwarok@cwk-verlag.de **Web site:** http://www.wochenkurier.info
Freq: Weekly; **Cover Price:** Free; **Circ:** 32,703
Editor: Kerstin Twarok; **Advertising Manager:** Uwe Peschel
Profile: Advertising journal (house-to-house) concentrating on local stories.
Language(s): German
ADVERTISING RATES:
Full Page Mono .... EUR 3010
Full Page Colour .... EUR 4214
Mechanical Data: Type Area: 430 x 290 mm, No. of Columns (Display): 7, Col Widths (Display): 38 mm
Copy instructions: *Copy Date:* 5 days prior to publication
LOCAL NEWSPAPERS

KAMINE & KACHELÖFEN
732362G3A-83

Editorial: Höhenstr. 17, 70736 FELLBACH
Tel: 711 5206274 **Fax:** 711 5206300
Email: jeni@fachschriften.de **Web site:** http://www.ofenwelten.de
Freq: Annual; **Cover Price:** EUR 7,80; **Circ:** 60,000
Editor: Kurt Jeni; **Advertising Manager:** Marc Kurowski
Profile: "Kamine & Kachelöfen" domestic oven enthusiastic fans as a competent source of information about the fire spell. The magazine presents the most important technical news and also provides a fascinating slide show about the hot ovens. The furnace worlds present a wide range of furnaces including prices. Not to be neglected: the right chimney and a rational approach to the fuels wood & pellets, coal, oil and gas. Of course there are design innovations that are shown in "Kamine & Kachelöfen" for the first time. Who wants to look at the best and most beautiful stoves and fireplaces may look forward to a diversity of models that is unique. Then the reader can take immediate contact with an efficient stove makers, these are listed in the yellow pages by zip code. Special experiences mean the visits in oven and ceramic workshops, the editorial presents businesses. And beautiful house reports allow the reader to feel the effects already installed stoves or fireplaces on the atmosphere of a residential area.
Language(s): German
Readership: Aimed at architects, planners and housebuilders.
ADVERTISING RATES:
Full Page Colour .... EUR 5180
Mechanical Data: Type Area: 247 x 187 mm
Copy instructions: *Copy Date:* 64 days prior to publication
BUSINESS: HEATING & VENTILATION: Domestic Heating & Ventilation

KAMMER FORUM
740045G44-3142

Editorial: Riehler Str. 30, 50668 KÖLN
Tel: 221 9730100 **Fax:** 221 97301050
Email: kontakt@rak-koeln.de **Web site:** http://www.rak-koeln.de
Freq: 6 issues yearly; **Circ:** 12,600
Editor: Martin W. Huff; **Advertising Manager:** Fritz Lebherz
Profile: Publication from the Chamber of Lawyers in Cologne.
Language(s): German
ADVERTISING RATES:
Full Page Mono .... EUR 1700
Full Page Colour .... EUR 2400
Mechanical Data: Type Area: 260 x 186 mm, No. of Columns (Display): 4, Col Widths (Display): 43 mm
BUSINESS: LEGAL

KAMMER IM GESPRÄCH
756131G37-1721

Editorial: Postfach 200839, 41236 MÖNCHENGLADBACH **Tel:** 2166 62820
Fax: 2166 628233
Email: info@muebri.de **Web site:** http://www.muebri.de
Freq: Quarterly; **Circ:** 10,500
Profile: magazine for pharmacists.
Language(s): German

KAMMERRUNDSCHREIBEN
1861449G1A-3718

Editorial: Gutleutstr. 175, 60327 FRANKFURT
Tel: 69 1530020 **Fax:** 69 15300260
Email: geschaeftsstelle@stbk-hessen.de **Web site:** http://www.stbk-hessen.de
Freq: Quarterly; **Circ:** 30,000
Editor: Thomas Ehry
Profile: Magazine for members.
Language(s): German

KANINCHEN ZEITUNG
732376G81X-1560

Editorial: Wilhelmsaue 37, 10713 BERLIN
Tel: 30 897454539 **Fax:** 30 897454555
Email: kaninchenzeitung@hk-verlag.de **Web site:** http://www.kaninchenzeitung.de
Freq: 24 issues yearly; **Annual Sub.:** EUR 59,50; **Circ:** 19,000
Editor: Gisela Becker; **Advertising Manager:** Frank Middendorf
Profile: The Kaninchenzeitung is the only German trade magazine for race rabbit breeders and all friends of the rabbit breeding. It is also in this segment the leading trade title in Europe. The title which offers a modern look as well as informative photographs. The reader is offered a wealth of technical information about the rabbit breeding with a correspondingly wide range of topics - from breeding, keeping and feeding on Race and breeders portraits to diseases and heredity. In addition, provide comprehensive reports on exhibitions and events important information for the proposed breeding friend. The organization part is complemented by an ever-cutting-edge event calendar.

Language(s): German
ADVERTISING RATES:
Full Page Mono .... EUR 1520
Full Page Colour .... EUR 2463
Mechanical Data: Type Area: 262 x 184 mm, No. of Columns (Display): 4, Col Widths (Display): 43 mm
Official Journal of: Organ d. Zentralverb. Dt. Rasse-Kaninchenzüchter e.V.
CONSUMER: ANIMALS & PETS

KANU MAGAZIN 732387G75M-320
Editorial: Mittlerer Lech 44, 86150 AUGSBURG
Tel: 821 42078411 Fax: 821 42078420
Email: glocker@red-gun.com Web site: http://www.kanumagazin.de
Freq: 8 issues yearly; Annual Sub.: EUR 46,50; Circ: 12,639
Editor: Stephan Glocker; Advertising Manager: Sandra Wilderer
Profile: For over 15 years, is the Kanu Magazin required reading for all canoeists. Whether in salt water, on the Central European inland waters and the wild water of any difficulty - Kanu Magazin paddle appear to be anywhere. The editors, all self-confessed canoeists for decades spanned the gamut from content-day trip for everyone to multi-week holiday overseas. Priority area are and remain easily accessible destinations in Germany and neighboring countries. With concrete proposals route takes you Kanu Magazin easily on the water or make with exciting reading stories like for their next own small or great adventure of outside the front door. The second pillar of the editorial approach are competent and honest product launches and tests that bring light into the darkness of the canoe market. Workshops complement this "technology part", give the nuts and bolts of the paddle art and ensure that security remains on the water is not a closed book. Rounding out Kanu Magazin from a kind of "sports section", will reported in the paddler sized about excellence, whether in the extreme wildwater, over long distances or there, "where the pepper grows. " Here, the subtle portraits of outstanding personalities of canoeing are located. Twitter: http://twitter.com/KANUmagazin.
Language(s): German
ADVERTISING RATES:
Full Page Mono .... EUR 2360
Full Page Colour .... EUR 3540
Mechanical Data: No. of Columns (Display): 3, Col Widths (Display): 58 mm, Type Area: 248 x 185 mm
CONSUMER: SPORT: Water Sports

KANU MAGAZIN 1704303G75M-1079
Editorial: Mittlerer Lech 44, 86150 AUGSBURG
Tel: 821 42078411 Fax: 821 42078420
Email: neumann@kanumagazin.com Web site: http://www.kanumagazin.de
Freq: Daily; Cover Price: Paid
Editor: Michael Neumann; Advertising Manager: Sandra Wilderer
Profile: Ezine: In close cooperation with KANU MAGAZIN, which is published eight times a year, we are supplying the growing number of online fans at www.kanumagazin.de with current information on a daily basis. There you can access different sections of the magazine, like the equipment tests of the past few years, extended descriptions of the terrain at different destinations and extra-long interviews, as well as topical news from the canoeing scene, competitions, coverage of events and torus, photo galleries and videos. Last but not least the service section, currently updated by our editorial staff: in the canoe second hand market you can find almost anything that still floats in a half-decent way. The paddling and travel companion section helps you find like-minded people as well as information regarding lost and found pieces of equipment, accompanied by hazard alerts and job offers. Our KANU MAGAZIN newsletter informs on the latest news in regular intervals, these are also passed on via the social networks of facebook and twitter.
Language(s): German
CONSUMER: SPORT: Water Sports

KANU SPORT 732388G75M-340
Editorial: Bertaallee 8, 47055 DUISBURG
Tel: 203 9975954 Fax: 203 9975961
Email: dieter.reinmuth@kanu.de Web site: http://www.kanu-sport.com
Freq: Monthly; Annual Sub.: EUR 30,00; Circ: 7,965
Editor: Dieter Reinmuth; Advertising Manager: Sabine Egermann
Profile: Official journal of the German Canoe Association.
Language(s): German
Readership: Aimed at canoe and kayaking enthusiasts.
ADVERTISING RATES:
Full Page Mono .... EUR 990
Full Page Colour .... EUR 1490
Mechanical Data: Type Area: 251 x 178 mm, No. of Columns (Display): 4, Col Widths (Display): 40 mm
Copy instructions: *Copy Date:* 20 days prior to publication
Official Journal of: Organ d. Dt. Kanu-Verb. e.V.
CONSUMER: SPORT: Water Sports

KAPITALFORUM 1794910G1F-1700
Editorial: Hopfenrain 1, 35114 HAINA
Tel: 6456 81200 Fax: 6456 81205
Email: red@kapitalforum.info Web site: http://www.kapitalforum.info
Freq: 10 issues yearly; Annual Sub.: EUR 22,00; Circ: 6,400
Editor: Georg H. L. Geiss; Advertising Manager: Jürgen von Bomsdorff
Profile: International magazine focusing on economics and finance.
Language(s): German
ADVERTISING RATES:
Full Page Mono .... EUR 1420
Full Page Colour .... EUR 1680
Mechanical Data: Type Area: 240 x 175 mm, No. of Columns (Display): 3, Col Widths (Display): 55 mm
Copy instructions: *Copy Date:* 10 days prior to publication

KAPITAL-MARKT INTERN 732394G1A-57
Editorial: Grafenberger Allee 30, 40237 DÜSSELDORF Tel: 211 6698164 Fax: 211 6912440
Email: kmi@markt-intern.de Web site: http://www.markt-intern.de
Freq: Weekly; Annual Sub.: EUR 383,53
Editor: Uwe Kremer
Profile: Magazine containing articles about finance and marketing.
Language(s): German
Readership: Aimed at financial advisors and marketing managers.
BUSINESS: FINANCE & ECONOMICS

DER KARDIOLOGE 1828689G56A-11536
Editorial: Tiergartenstr. 17, 69121 HEIDELBERG
Tel: 6221 4878519 Fax: 6221 48768519
Email: claudia.zappe@springer.com Web site: http://www.springermedizin.de
Freq: 6 issues yearly; Annual Sub.: EUR 180,00; Circ: 4,800
Editor: Eckart Fleck
Profile: Der Kardiologe offers up-to-date information for all cardiologists working in practical and clinical environments and scientists who are particularly interested in issues of cardiology. The focus is on current developments regarding prevention, diagnostic approaches, management of complications and current therapy strategies. Current guidelines and recommendations of the German Cardiac Society complement each issue. Case reports feature interesting cases and aim at optimizing diagnostic and therapeutic strategies. Review articles under the rubric ?Continuing Medical Education? present verified results of scientific research and their integration into daily practice.
Language(s): German
ADVERTISING RATES:
Full Page Mono .... EUR 1932
Full Page Colour .... EUR 2972
Mechanical Data: Type Area: 240 x 174 mm
Official Journal of: Organ d. Dt. Ges. f. Kardiologie - Herz-Kreislaufforschung

KARDIOLOGIE UP2DATE 1667775G56A-11350
Editorial: Fetscherstr. 76, 01307 DRESDEN
Email: ruth.strasser@mailbox.tu-dresden.de Web site: http://www.thieme.de/fz/kardiologie-u2d.html
Freq: Quarterly; Free to qualifying individuals
Annual Sub.: EUR 155,40; Circ: 2,050
Editor: Ruth Strasser
Profile: Kardiologie up2date is the comprehensive practical course for the CME-certified training in cardiology. Each issue contains four high-quality color designed individual contributions per issue, which are bound separately and stored individually by the subscribers in a ring binder.
Language(s): German
ADVERTISING RATES:
Full Page Mono .... EUR 1860
Full Page Colour .... EUR 3000
Mechanical Data: Type Area: 256 x 180 mm

KARLSRUHER KIND 732409G74D-115
Editorial: Gritznerstr. 3, 76227 KARLSRUHE
Tel: 721 5966990 Fax: 721 59669959
Email: info@karlsruher-kind.de Web site: http://www.karlsruher-kind.de
Freq: Monthly; Annual Sub.: EUR 20,00; Circ: 35,000
Editor: Karl Goerner; Advertising Manager: Karl Goerner
Profile: Magazine for parents in and around Karlsruhe.
Language(s): German
ADVERTISING RATES:
Full Page Mono .... EUR 1805
Full Page Colour .... EUR 2350
Mechanical Data: Type Area: 298 x 223 mm, No. of Columns (Display): 5, Col Widths (Display): 43 mm
Copy instructions: *Copy Date:* 14 days prior to publication
CONSUMER: WOMEN'S INTEREST CONSUMER MAGAZINES: Child Care

KARLSRUHER WIRTSCHAFTSSPIEGEL 732411G14A-3760
Editorial: Zähringerstr. 65a, 76133 KARLSRUHE
Tel: 721 1337311 Fax: 721 1337309
Email: sabine.rapp@wifoe.karlsruhe.de Web site: http://www.karlsruhe.de/wirtschaft
Freq: Annual; Cover Price: Free; Circ: 20,000
Editor: Sabine Rapp
Profile: Magazine about business activities in Karlsruhe.
Language(s): German
ADVERTISING RATES:
Full Page Mono .... EUR 2410
Full Page Colour .... EUR 3400
Mechanical Data: Type Area: 265 x 181 mm
Copy instructions: *Copy Date:* 90 days prior to publication

KARRIERE.DE 1625967G94K-756
Editorial: Kasernenstr. 67, 40213 DÜSSELDORF
Tel: 211 8872760 Fax: 211 887972760
Email: karriere@vhb.de Web site: http://www.karriere.de
Freq: Weekly; Cover Price: Paid; Circ: 495,738 Unique Users
Editor: Tanja Kewes
Profile: Online information platform for students, graduates, elder and young professionals. Comprehensive and up to date reports in categories of career, business, service and money, on professional and career issues for target group from 20 - to 40 years of age.
Language(s): German
CONSUMER: OTHER CLASSIFICATIONS: Job Seekers

KARRIEREFÜHRER BAUINGENIEURE 1739911G4E-7102
Editorial: Weyertal 59, 50937 KÖLN
Tel: 221 4722330 Fax: 221 4722370
Email: info@karrierefuehrer.de Web site: http://www.karrierefuehrer.de
Freq: Annual; Cover Price: Free; Circ: 10,000
Profile: Students' magazine.
Language(s): German
ADVERTISING RATES:
Full Page Mono .... EUR 4444
Full Page Colour .... EUR 4444
Mechanical Data: Type Area: 270 x 191 mm
Copy instructions: *Copy Date:* 30 days prior to publication

KARRIEREFÜHRER FINANZDIENSTLEISTUNGEN 1739912G1C-1470
Editorial: Weyertal 59, 50937 KÖLN
Tel: 221 4722330 Fax: 221 4722370
Email: info@karrierefuehrer.de Web site: http://www.karrierefuehrer.de
Freq: Annual; Cover Price: Free; Circ: 15,000
Profile: Students' magazine.
Language(s): German
ADVERTISING RATES:
Full Page Mono .... EUR 4444
Full Page Colour .... EUR 4444
Mechanical Data: Type Area: 270 x 191 mm
Copy instructions: *Copy Date:* 40 days prior to publication

KARTOFFELBAU 732427G21A-2380
Editorial: Clemens-August-Str. 12, 53115 BONN
Tel: 228 9694230 Fax: 228 630311
Email: redaktion@dlg-agrofoodmedien.de Web site: http://www.dlg-agrofoodmedien.de
Freq: 10 issues yearly; Annual Sub.: EUR 70,00; Circ: 4,975
Editor: Heinz-Peter Pütz; Advertising Manager: Rainer Schluck
Profile: Journal about potato growing.
Language(s): German
Readership: Read by arable farmers.
ADVERTISING RATES:
Full Page Mono .... EUR 1710
Full Page Colour .... EUR 2880
Mechanical Data: Type Area: 270 x 186 mm, No. of Columns (Display): 3, Col Widths (Display): 58 mm
Official Journal of: Organ d. Förderungsgemeinschaft d. Kartoffelwirtschaft e.V., d. Bundesvereinigung d. Dt. Kartoffelwirtschaft e.V., d. KTBL-Versuchsstation Dethlingen u. d. Verb. d. Kartoffel-, Lager-, Abpack- u. Schälbetriebe e.V.
BUSINESS: AGRICULTURE & FARMING

KÄSE-THEKE 732304G22A-1280
Editorial: Rheintalstr. 6, 53498 BAD BREISIG
Tel: 2633 454020 Fax: 2633 97415
Email: witteriede@milch-marketing.de Web site: http://www.moproweb.de
Freq: 6 issues yearly; Annual Sub.: EUR 29,96; Circ: 6,999
Editor: Thorsten Witteriede; Advertising Manager: Carola Seiwert
Profile: Magazine about the production and retail of cheese.
Language(s): German
ADVERTISING RATES:
Full Page Mono .... EUR 4810
Full Page Colour .... EUR 4810
Mechanical Data: Type Area: 250 x 184 mm, No. of Columns (Display): 4, Col Widths (Display): 43 mm
Copy instructions: *Copy Date:* 21 days prior to publication
BUSINESS: FOOD

KASSELER SONNTAGSBLATT 732435G87-6740
Editorial: Werner-Heisenberg-Str. 7, 34123 KASSEL
Tel: 561 9583010 Fax: 561 9583013
Email: info@kasseler-sonntagsblatt.de Web site: http://www.kasseler-sonntagsblatt.de
Freq: Weekly; Annual Sub.: EUR 94,80; Circ: 12,524
Editor: Reinhard Heubner; Advertising Manager: Silke Dippel
Profile: Christian family magazine.
Language(s): German
ADVERTISING RATES:
Full Page Mono .... EUR 1882
Full Page Colour .... EUR 3293
Mechanical Data: Type Area: 280 x 205 mm, No. of Columns (Display): 4, Col Widths (Display): 49 mm
Copy instructions: *Copy Date:* 14 days prior to publication
CONSUMER: RELIGIOUS

KATECHETISCHE BLÄTTER 732440G87-203
Editorial: Flüggenstr. 2, 80639 MÜNCHEN
Tel: 89 17801137 Fax: 89 17801111
Email: katbl@koesel.de Web site: http://www.katbl.de
Freq: 6 issues yearly; Annual Sub.: EUR 55,50; Circ: 4,500
Editor: Helga Kohler-Spiegel
Profile: Publication about religious instruction, church youth groups and Sunday schools.
Language(s): German
ADVERTISING RATES:
Full Page Mono .... EUR 850
Mechanical Data: Type Area: 210 x 139 mm, No. of Columns (Display): 2, Col Widths (Display): 67 mm
Supplement(s): Materialbrief Gemeindekatechese; Materialbrief RU Sekundarstufe
CONSUMER: RELIGIOUS

DER KATHOLISCHE MESNER 732442G87-6780
Editorial: Albert-Greiner-Str. 50, 86151 AUGSBURG
Tel: 821 5677923 Fax: 821 5677923
Email: anton.claudia.fuchs@t-online.de
Freq: 6 issues yearly; Annual Sub.: EUR 6,75; Circ: 3,260
Editor: Anton Fuchs; Advertising Manager: Edeltraud Hüttmann
Profile: Publication for Catholic vergers.
Language(s): German
ADVERTISING RATES:
Full Page Mono .... EUR 235
Mechanical Data: Type Area: 190 x 135 mm, No. of Columns (Display): 2, Col Widths (Display): 65 mm
Copy instructions: *Copy Date:* 35 days prior to publication
Official Journal of: Standesorgan d. kath. Mesnerverb. d. Diözese Aug. u. d. ArGe'en d. Süddt. Mesnerverbände
CONSUMER: RELIGIOUS

KATHOLISCHE SONNTAGSZEITUNG FÜR DAS BISTUM AUGSBURG 732448G87-6800
Editorial: Hafnerberg 2, 86152 AUGSBURG
Tel: 821 5024260 Fax: 821 5024281
Email: redaktion@suv.de Web site: http://www.katholische-sonntagszeitung.de
Freq: Weekly; Annual Sub.: EUR 96,60; Circ: 27,725
Editor: Johannes Müller; Advertising Manager: Edeltraud Hüttmann
Profile: Catholic magazine for the Augsburg diocese.
Language(s): German
ADVERTISING RATES:
Full Page Mono .... EUR 1885
Full Page Colour .... EUR 3045
Mechanical Data: Type Area: 290 x 230 mm, No. of Columns (Display): 5, Col Widths (Display): 45 mm
Copy instructions: *Copy Date:* 10 days prior to publication
CONSUMER: RELIGIOUS

KATHOLISCHE SONNTAGSZEITUNG FÜR DAS BISTUM REGENSBURG 740116G87-11140
Editorial: Königsstr. 2, 93047 REGENSBURG
Tel: 941 5867620 Fax: 941 5867666
Email: sonntagszeitung-regensburg@suv.de
Freq: Weekly; Annual Sub.: EUR 78,00; Circ: 23,262
Editor: Stefan Mohr; Advertising Manager: Karin Schlicker
Profile: Catholic Sunday paper for the diocese of Regensburg.
Language(s): German
ADVERTISING RATES:
Full Page Mono .... EUR 1885
Full Page Colour .... EUR 3045
Mechanical Data: Type Area: 320 x 230 mm, No. of Columns (Display): 5, Col Widths (Display): 45 mm
Copy instructions: *Copy Date:* 10 days prior to publication
CONSUMER: RELIGIOUS

KATHOLISCHE SONNTAGSZEITUNG FÜR DEUTSCHLAND 724320G87-2420
Editorial: Komödienstr. 48, 50667 KÖLN
Tel: 221 1300790 Fax: 201 1301857
Email: sonntagszeitung-deutschland@suv.de Web site: http://www.katholische-sonntagszeitung.de
Freq: Weekly; Annual Sub.: EUR 69,60; Circ: 62,193
Editor: Johannes Müller
Profile: Magazine for the Catholic family.

Language(s): German
ADVERTISING RATES:
Full Page Mono .... EUR 4205
Full Page Colour .... EUR 5510
Mechanical Data: Type Area: 290 x 230 mm, No. of Columns (Display): 5, Col Widths (Display): 45 mm
Copy instructions: *Copy Date:* 9 days prior to publication
CONSUMER: RELIGIOUS

KATHOLISCHES SONNTAGSBLATT 732449G87-6900
Editorial: Senefelderstr. 12, 73760 OSTFILDERN
Tel: 711 4406121 **Fax:** 711 4406170
Email: redaktion@kathsonntagsblatt.de **Web site:** http://www.kathsonntagsblatt.de
Freq: Weekly; **Annual Sub.:** EUR 74,40; **Circ:** 49,222
Editor: Reiner Schlotthauer
Profile: Catholic newspaper containing religious news, along with information on culture and international affairs.
Language(s): German
ADVERTISING RATES:
Full Page Mono .... EUR 2912
Full Page Colour .... EUR 5376
Mechanical Data: Type Area: 280 x 200 mm, No. of Columns (Display): 4, Col Widths (Display): 45 mm
Copy instructions: *Copy Date:* 12 days prior to publication
CONSUMER: RELIGIOUS

KAUFMACHER DRESDEN
1830240G89A-12407
Editorial: Prager Str. 2b, 01069 DRESDEN
Tel: 351 8007030 **Fax:** 351 8007070
Email: redaktion@maxity.de **Web site:** http://www.maxity.de
Freq: Annual; **Cover Price:** Free; **Circ:** 15,000
Editor: Christine Herzog; **Advertising Manager:** Cathleen Moosche
Profile: Shopping guide for Dresden.
Language(s): German
ADVERTISING RATES:
Full Page Mono .... EUR 395
Full Page Colour .... EUR 395
Mechanical Data: Type Area: 126 x 85 mm

KAUPERTS STRASSENFÜHRER DURCH BERLIN MIT GEMEINDEVERZEICHNIS LAND BRANDENBURG 1825528G89A-12379
Editorial: Spandauer Damm 89, 14059 BERLIN
Tel: 30 30301404 **Fax:** 30 30301482
Email: c.moewe@kaupertmedia.de **Web site:** http://www.kaupertmedia.de
Freq: Annual; **Cover Price:** EUR 19,45; **Circ:** 10,000
Editor: Cornelia Möwe
Profile: Road map of Berlin and directory listing the communities of Brandenburg Facebook: http://www.facebook.com/pages/KAUPERTS-Strassenfuhrer-durch-Berlin/156657379256.
Language(s): German
ADVERTISING RATES:
Full Page Mono .... EUR 1450
Full Page Colour .... EUR 1450
Mechanical Data: Type Area: 150 x 100 mm
Copy instructions: *Copy Date:* 40 days prior to publication

KBD KOMMUNALER BESCHAFFUNGS-DIENST
733036G32A-1800
Editorial: Junge Weinberge 17, 71334 WAIBLINGEN
Tel: 7151 987771 **Fax:** 7151 987772
Email: niels.buhrke@t-online.de **Web site:** http://www.kbd.de
Freq: 10 issues yearly; **Annual Sub.:** EUR 34,24; **Circ:** 10,255
Editor: Niels W. Buhrke; **Advertising Manager:** Norbert Müller
Profile: Journal focusing on municipal purchasing, containing business and technical information.
Language(s): German
Readership: Aimed at personnel in municipal administration and public works departments.
ADVERTISING RATES:
Full Page Mono .... EUR 3080
Full Page Colour .... EUR 4280
Mechanical Data: Type Area: 280 x 185 mm, No. of Columns (Display): 4, Col Widths (Display): 43 mm
Copy instructions: *Copy Date:* 20 days prior to publication
BUSINESS: LOCAL GOVERNMENT, LEISURE & RECREATION: Local Government

KE KONSTRUKTION & ENGINEERING 732488G42A-3
Editorial: Justus-von-Liebig-Str. 1, 86899 LANDSBERG **Tel:** 8191 125401 **Fax:** 8191 125209
Email: redaktion@mi-verlag.de **Web site:** http://www.konstruktion.de
Freq: Monthly; **Annual Sub.:** EUR 89,00; **Circ:** 22,664
Editor: Franz Graf; **Advertising Manager:** Stefan Pilz
Profile: ke Konstruktion & Engineering is a trade magazine targeted at designers and developers in the field of machine and plant engineering. The trade journal conveys compact trade knowledge against the background of changes in the work environment and the information requirements. It offers information comprising current product developments and market trends, applications and experience in the use of components and systems, as well as successful implementation of organizational concepts in design management. The editorial concept's extensive content of rapidly consumable information and Internet tools makes ke Konstruktion & Engineering a magazine that satisfies the technological and market needs of decision-making designers and developers. For distribution of press releases please use redaktion@konstruktion.de. For personal contact with regards invitations and meetings, please use joachim.vogl@mi-verlag.de.
Language(s): German
ADVERTISING RATES:
Full Page Mono .... EUR 5530
Full Page Colour .... EUR 6380
Mechanical Data: Type Area: 257 x 178 mm, No. of Columns (Display): 4, Col Widths (Display): 41 mm
BUSINESS: CONSTRUCTION

KEHLER ZEITUNG 732483G67B-7980
Editorial: Marlener Str. 9, 77656 OFFENBURG
Tel: 781 5040 **Fax:** 781 5047002
Email: leserservice@reiff.de **Web site:** http://www.baden-online.de
Freq: 312 issues yearly; **Circ:** 8,775
Advertising Manager: Kurt Michelfelder
Profile: Regional daily newspaper with news on politics, economy, culture, sports, travel, technology, etc. The Mittelbadische Presse are Offenburger Tageblatt, Kehler Zeitung, Lahrer Zeitung and Acher-Rench-Zeitung. With a total circulation of about 60,000 specimens come from the media company Reiff, "the" home of the newspapers Ortenau. Partly for nearly 200 years we have * Absolute readers around because the reader is with us in the self-Journal * Regional expertise * Information Platform of the events and life in the region * instrument of human communication, commerce, economics and politics in the Ortenau and therefore ideal promotional tool. Newspapers are, six days a week: * News * Independent * unique - they are always subject.
Language(s): German
ADVERTISING RATES:
SCC .... EUR 27,80
Mechanical Data: Type Area: 420 x 284 mm, No. of Columns (Display): 6, Col Widths (Display): 44 mm
Copy instructions: *Copy Date:* 1 day prior to publication
REGIONAL DAILY & SUNDAY NEWSPAPERS: Regional Daily Newspapers

KELKHEIMER ZEITUNG
732492G72-6112
Editorial: Theresenstr. 2, 61462 KÖNIGSTEIN
Tel: 6174 93850 **Fax:** 6174 938550
Email: kw@hochtaunus.de **Web site:** http://www.hochtaunus.de/kw
Freq: Annual; **Cover Price:** Free; **Circ:** 17,700
Editor: Peter Hillebrecht
Profile: Advertising journal (house-to-house) concentrating on local stories.
Language(s): German
ADVERTISING RATES:
Full Page Mono .... EUR 2168
Full Page Colour .... EUR 2288
Mechanical Data: Type Area: 430 x 282 mm, No. of Columns (Display): 6, Col Widths (Display): 45 mm
Copy instructions: *Copy Date:* 3 days prior to publication
LOCAL NEWSPAPERS

KEM 732501G19E-820
Editorial: Ernst-Mey-Str. 8, 70771 LEINFELDEN-ECHTERDINGEN **Tel:** 711 7594281
Fax: 711 7594398
Email: kem.redaktion@konradin.de **Web site:** http://www.kem.de
Freq: Monthly; **Annual Sub.:** EUR 85,20; **Circ:** 22,539
Editor: Herbert Neumann; **Advertising Manager:** Walter Schwager
Profile: Leading trade magazine for design and development engineers and engineering design managers, primarily in the fields of machinery construction, electrical engineering and electronics. Current and practical information and useful tips ensure that readers stay ahead of the pack every month. KEM has an extensive readership in medium-sized and large companies in particular, where design engineers make decisions about substantial investments. First in the market of information: 90% of the articles dealing with market launches are exclusive and only appear in KEM or appear there first.
Language(s): German
ADVERTISING RATES:
Full Page Mono .... EUR 5650
Full Page Colour .... EUR 6740
Mechanical Data: Type Area: 270 x 188 mm, No. of Columns (Display): 4, Col Widths (Display): 44 mm
BUSINESS: ENGINEERING & MACHINERY: Machinery, Machine Tools & Metalworking

KEP AKTUELL 732503G49A-820
Editorial: Handwerkstr. 15, 70565 STUTTGART
Tel: 711 7849837 **Fax:** 711 7849888
Email: transaktuell@etm-verlag.de **Web site:** http://www.etm-verlag.de
Freq: Quarterly; **Annual Sub.:** EUR 17,90; **Circ:** 61,696
Editor: Nicole de Jong; **Advertising Manager:** Werner Faas
Profile: KEP is currently reporting regularly on the latest trends, identifies practical solutions to everyday corporate life, and portrays their business activities and provides decision support with current market overviews. Tests of KEP services, as well as vehicle testing round out the editorial content. The experts from the fields of courier, express and postal services KEP currently certified for years a high level of competence. Here, seasoned professionals that moves the industry. Supplement to the magazine trans aktuell.
Language(s): German
ADVERTISING RATES:
Full Page Mono .... EUR 15420
Full Page Colour .... EUR 15420
Mechanical Data: Type Area: 420 x 288 mm, No. of Columns (Display): 6, Col Widths (Display): 43 mm
Supplement to: trans aktuell

KEP SPEZIAL 1684581G49C-87
Editorial: Aschauer Str. 30, 81549 MÜNCHEN
Tel: 89 2030432273 **Fax:** 89 2030432384
Email: birgit.bauer@springer.com **Web site:** http://www.verkehrsrundschau.de
Freq: Half-yearly; **Circ:** 36,000
Editor: Birgit Bauer; **Advertising Manager:** Matthias Pioro
Profile: Supplement to the verkehrs Rundschau, issue C: magazine by and about the CEP industry with exclusive interviews with top decision makers in CEP, Commerce and Industry, comprehensive service section and best-practice solutions, and the relevant trends in the CEP sector.
Language(s): German
ADVERTISING RATES:
Full Page Colour .... EUR 8000
Mechanical Data: Type Area: 250 x 185 mm
Supplement to: verkehrs Rundschau

KERAMISCHE ZEITSCHRIFT
732509G12A-2
Editorial: Aachener Str. 172, 40223 DÜSSELDORF
Tel: 211 1591230 **Fax:** 211 1591150
Email: redaktion-keramik@dvs-hg.de **Web site:** http://www.expert-fachmedien.de
Freq: 6 issues yearly; **Annual Sub.:** EUR 178,50; **Circ:** 4,719
Editor: Hubert Pelc; **Advertising Manager:** Iris Jansen
Profile: Magazine about ceramics. Covers technology, employees, raw materials, management and business.
Language(s): German
Readership: Aimed at suppliers of machinery, raw materials, scientists, researchers and manufacturers of ceramics.
ADVERTISING RATES:
Full Page Mono .... EUR 1720
Full Page Colour .... EUR 2290
Mechanical Data: Type Area: 269 x 191 mm, No. of Columns (Display): 3, Col Widths (Display): 61 mm
BUSINESS: CERAMICS, POTTERY & GLASS: Ceramics & Pottery

KERBE 732510G56N-3
Editorial: Saalstr. 12, 70825 KORNTAL-MÜNCHINGEN **Tel:** 711 8386308
Email: cclass@gmx.de
Freq: Quarterly; **Annual Sub.:** EUR 22,80; **Circ:** 1,368
Editor: Cornelie Class-Hähnel
Profile: Journal about the latest developments in psychiatry and mental health.
Language(s): German
ADVERTISING RATES:
Full Page Mono .... EUR 804
Mechanical Data: Type Area: 268 x 159 mm, No. of Columns (Display): 3, Col Widths (Display): 51 mm
Copy instructions: *Copy Date:* 30 days prior to publication
BUSINESS: HEALTH & MEDICAL: Mental Health

KERNTECHNIK 732511G58-960
Editorial: Ingolstädter Landstr. 1, 85764 OBERSCHLEISSHEIM **Tel:** 1888 332110
Fax: 1888 3332115
Email: schmitt@bfs.de **Web site:** http://www.nuclear-engineering-journal.com
Freq: Quarterly; **Annual Sub.:** EUR 835,80; **Circ:** 500
Editor: Annemarie Schmitt-Hanning; **Advertising Manager:** Dietmar von der Au
Profile: The scope of the journal is research and development in nuclear engineering, energy systems, radiation, and radiological protection. Topics in nuclear engineering include the design, operation, safety and economics of nuclear power stations, research reactors, simulators and their components as well as the complete fuel cycle. Radiation means the application of ionizing radiation in industry, medicine and research. Topics in radiological protection cover biological effects of ionizing radiation, the system of protection for occupational, medical and public exposures, the assessment of doses, operational protection and safety programmes, management of radioactive wastes, decommissioning and regulatory requirements. The articles are published almost exclusively in English.
Language(s): English; German
Mechanical Data: Type Area: 250 x 170 mm
BUSINESS: ENERGY, FUEL & NUCLEAR

KETTWIG KURIER 732519G72-6140
Editorial: Hauptstr. 48, 45219 ESSEN
Tel: 2054 92370 **Fax:** 2054 85545
Email: redaktion@kettwigkurier-essen.de **Web site:** http://www.lokalkompass.de/essen-kettwig
Freq: 104 issues yearly; **Cover Price:** Free; **Circ:** 11,800
Editor: Silke Heidenblut; **Advertising Manager:** Lars Staehler
Profile: Advertising journal (house-to-house) concentrating on local stories.
Language(s): German
ADVERTISING RATES:
Full Page Mono .... EUR 2368
Full Page Colour .... EUR 3196
Mechanical Data: Type Area: 445 x 315 mm, No. of Columns (Display): 7, Col Widths (Display): 42 mm
Copy instructions: *Copy Date:* 2 days prior to publication
LOCAL NEWSPAPERS

KEYBOARDS 732525G76D-2320
Editorial: Emil-Hoffmann-Str. 13, 50996 KÖLN
Tel: 2236 9621733 **Fax:** 2236 96217933
Email: redaktion@keyboards.de **Web site:** http://www.keyboards.de
Freq: 6 issues yearly; **Annual Sub.:** EUR 29,00; **Circ:** 7,284
Editor: Gerald Dellmann; **Advertising Manager:** Christiane Weyres
Profile: KEYBOARDS - the magazine for musicians dealing with keyboard instruments of all kinds. From the digital stage piano and keyboards on portable to workstations and synthesizers KEYBOARDS covers the complete range of keyboard instruments. Here are a few software solutions rather than the hardware keyboard in the foreground. With lots of reviews, interviews, practice reports, workshops and musical transcriptions KEYBOARDS informed every two months on the happenings around the black and white keys. In parallel, there is the complex KEYBOARDS online portal to more information, downloads and movie reviews in KEYBOARDS TV.
Language(s): German
Mechanical Data: Type Area: 254 x 185 mm, No. of Columns (Display): 4, Col Widths (Display): 43 mm
CONSUMER: MUSIC & PERFORMING ARTS: Music

KEYS 732528G78A-105
Editorial: Dachauer Str. 37b, 85232 BERGKIRCHEN
Tel: 8131 565545 **Fax:** 8131 565510
Email: udo.weyers@keys.de **Web site:** http://www.keys.de
Freq: Monthly; **Annual Sub.:** EUR 58,80; **Circ:** 8,321
Editor: Udo Weyers; **Advertising Manager:** Mario di Meola
Profile: Magazine about keyboards, computers and recording. Includes reviews of new instruments and gives background information on a wide range of music news.
Language(s): German
ADVERTISING RATES:
Full Page Mono .... EUR 2980
Full Page Colour .... EUR 5070
Mechanical Data: Type Area: 254 x 185 mm, No. of Columns (Display): 4, Col Widths (Display): 43 mm
Copy instructions: *Copy Date:* 25 days prior to publication
CONSUMER: CONSUMER ELECTRONICS: Hi-Fi & Recording

KFZ ANZEIGER 732531G49D-45
Editorial: Dießemer Bruch 167, 47805 KREFELD
Tel: 2151 5100118 **Fax:** 2151 5100215
Email: kfz-anzeiger@stuenings.de **Web site:** http://www.kfz-anzeiger.com
Freq: 24 issues yearly; **Annual Sub.:** EUR 78,00; **Circ:** 34,895
Editor: Lutz Gerritzen; **Advertising Manager:** Cornelia Assem
Profile: Independent of the editorial priorities and according to its task as a high-volume commercial vehicle trade journal extensive coverage by the entire transport and commercial vehicles instead of in each issue of the KFZ anzeiger. Constant reports in the areas of Automotive Engineering (with actual driving tests and reports) and from the commercial vehicle workshop, reports and comments on political and economic issues, and traffic updates from the industry. News and information from home and abroad, personal and anniversaries, spectrum, company news and new products, legal practice, literature, workshop equipment, loading and storage, periodic market surveys, eg Trailers and bodies, tail lifts, cranes, car washes, wheels and tires, CEP vehicles, LVN and city logistics, light construction, safety for driver and load, Mitnehmgabelstapler, brakes and axles, combined transport, refrigeration units, refrigerated trucks, tank trucks, tanker vehicles, retarder, beverage vehicles, towing and recovery vehicles, cab equipment, ski equipment, IT transportation, vehicle graphics, truck tarpaulins, sales vehicles, dangerous goods, load security, vehicle rental / leasing, telematics, building and furnishing etc. Facebook: http://www.facebook.com/pages/KFZ-Anzeiger/154822384554755.
Language(s): German
ADVERTISING RATES:
Full Page Mono .... EUR 5100
Full Page Colour .... EUR 7650
Mechanical Data: Type Area: 255 x 185 mm, No. of Columns (Display): 4, Col Widths (Display): 45 mm
Copy instructions: *Copy Date:* 12 days prior to publication
Supplement(s): NFZ Werkstatt
BUSINESS: TRANSPORT: Commercial Vehicles

KFZ-BETRIEB 732532G31A-125
Editorial: Max-Planck-Str. 7, 97082 WÜRZBURG
Tel: 931 4182561 **Fax:** 931 4182060

Email: wolfgang.michel@vogel.de **Web site:** http://www.kfz-betrieb.vogel.de
Freq: Weekly; **Annual Sub.:** EUR 166,40; **Circ:** 26,570
Editor: Wolfgang Michel; **News Editor:** Jens Rehberg; **Advertising Manager:** Anna Gredel
Profile: For 100 years now, the "kfz-betrieb" accompanies the market of the automotive industry, making it the oldest and most traditional trade magazine of this important industry. It approaches the owners, managers and executives in the retail and service and provides all relevant information for this target group. "kfz-betrieb" reports each week from various sub-segments of the industry e.g. organizational and personnel management, IT, market development, automotive technology, workshop technology, names and companies. "kfz-betrieb" followes in its comprehensive coverage the aim of maximum relevance and high editorial competence. The weekly magazine provides background information, analysis and first-aid information and support with the monthly continuing education sement "service technician" in completing the readers knowledge.
Language(s): German
Readership: Aimed at members.
ADVERTISING RATES:
Full Page Mono .... EUR 5490
Full Page Colour .... EUR 7350
Mechanical Data: Type Area: 270 x 190 mm, No. of Columns (Display): 4, Col Widths (Display): 46 mm
Copy instructions: *Copy Date:* 20 days prior to publication
Official Journal of: Organ d. Dt. Kraftfahrzeuggewerbes
BUSINESS: MOTOR TRADE: Motor Trade Accessories

KFZ-INSERAT
732535G77A-1300
Editorial: Frankfurter Str. 39, 63303 DREIEICH
Tel: 6103 48400 **Fax:** 6103 4840440
Email: info@das-inserat.de **Web site:** http://www.das-inserat.de
Freq: Weekly; **Cover Price:** EUR 2,80; **Circ:** 6,630
Advertising Manager: Thorsten Klemt
Profile: Magazine containing car offers.
Language(s): German
ADVERTISING RATES:
Full Page Colour .... EUR 1885
Mechanical Data: Type Area: 275 x 210 mm, No. of Columns (Display): 5, Col Widths (Display): 40 mm
Copy instructions: *Copy Date:* 2 days prior to publication

KFZ-SH.DE
732534G27-1560
Editorial: Faluner Weg 28, 24109 KIEL
Tel: 431 533310 **Fax:** 431 525067
Email: info@kfz-sh.de **Web site:** http://www.kfz-sh.de
Freq: 5 issues yearly; **Cover Price:** EUR 2,50
Free to qualifying individuals ; **Circ:** 3,000
Editor: Bernd Schweitzer; **Advertising Manager:** Martin Seydell
Profile: Magazine providing information for garage and gas station owners in the region of Schleswig-Holstein.
Language(s): German
Official Journal of: Organ d. Verb. d. Kfz-Gewerbes Schleswig-Holstein e.V. u. d. Landesinnungsverb. d. Kraftfahrzeughandwerks Schleswig-Holstein

KGK KAUTSCHUK GUMMI KUNSTSTOFFE
732539G39-35
Editorial: Im Weiher 10, 69121 HEIDELBERG
Tel: 6221 489246 **Fax:** 6221 489481
Email: etwina.gandert@huethig.de **Web site:** http://www.kgk-rubberpoint.de
Freq: 10 issues yearly; **Annual Sub.:** EUR 269,00; **Circ:** 2,235
Editor: Etwina Gandert; **Advertising Manager:** Ludger Aulich
Profile: KGK Kautschuk Gummi Kunststoffe is the world's only bilingual magazine for development, processing and application in the rubber and plastics industry. Unique: Authors from around the world have their know-how and their latest findings included in the editorial program. Technical articles on issues and trends in structural analysis, material composition, recycling, quality management and product reports on raw materials and additives, machines and newly developed instruments shape the editorial concept. Readers are primarily decision-makers: senior and middle management as well as in the departments of research, development and production.
Language(s): English; German
ADVERTISING RATES:
Full Page Mono .... EUR 2060
Full Page Colour .... EUR 3130
Mechanical Data: Type Area: 257 x 178 mm, No. of Columns (Display): 4, Col Widths (Display): 41 mm
Copy instructions: *Copy Date:* 27 days prior to publication
Official Journal of: Organ d. Dt. Kautschuk-Ges. e.V. u. d. Normenausschuss Kautschuktechnik m. DIN
BUSINESS: PLASTICS & RUBBER

KHS COMPETENCE
732550G19E-880
Editorial: Juchostr. 20, 44143 DORTMUND
Tel: 231 5691339 **Fax:** 231 5691226
Email: manfred.rueckstein@khs.com **Web site:** http://www.khs.com
Freq: Quarterly; **Cover Price:** Free; **Circ:** 6,000
Editor: Manfred Rückstein
Profile: Company publication published by KHS AG.
Language(s): German

KI KÄLTE LUFT KLIMATECHNIK
732597G3B-60
Editorial: Im Weiher 10, 69121 HEIDELBERG
Tel: 6221 489492 **Fax:** 6221 489490
Email: mrosk.huethig@email.de **Web site:** http://www.ki-portal.de
Freq: 9 issues yearly; **Annual Sub.:** EUR 199,00; **Circ:** 3,388
Editor: Cornelia Mrosk; **Advertising Manager:** Ludger Aulich
Profile: KI Kälte Luft Klimatechnik is the trade and technical journal for all specialists from the fields of refrigeration, ventilation and air conditioning technology. Bridging the gap between science and practice, KI publishes specialist articles by high-profile writers from science, research and technology in its academic section, along with thoroughly researched user reports for planning and development, practical reports, forums and product information in its practical section. It also contains current information relating to the industry such as personnel and company news, information from associations and institutes, specialist literature and dates of forthcoming industry events. Readers of KI work primarily in industry, in sectors using refrigeration and air conditioning technology, in planning or engineering offices, for plant manufacturers, large refrigeration and air conditioning companies or for associations or institutions. KI is an interdisciplinary publication for the entire refrigeration and air conditioning industry.
Language(s): German
ADVERTISING RATES:
Full Page Mono .... EUR 1840
Full Page Colour .... EUR 2735
Mechanical Data: Type Area: 257 x 178 mm, No. of Columns (Display): 4, Col Widths (Display): 41 mm
Copy instructions: *Copy Date:* 21 days prior to publication
BUSINESS: HEATING & VENTILATION: Industrial Heating & Ventilation

KI SOZIALPOLITISCHE KURZINFORMATIONEN
1655254G1D-466
Editorial: Arabellastr. 29, 81925 MÜNCHEN
Tel: 89 9220010 **Fax:** 89 92200151
Email: agvvers@agv-vers.de **Web site:** http://www.agv-vers.de
Freq: Monthly; **Circ:** 7,500
Editor: Michael Niebler
Profile: Magazine on economic and social politics especially for the private insurance business.
Language(s): German

KICKER ONLINE
1622919G75A-3588
Editorial: Badstr. 4, 90402 NÜRNBERG
Tel: 911 2162131 **Fax:** 911 2161586
Email: info@kicker.de **Web site:** http://www.kicker.de
Freq: Daily; **Cover Price:** Paid; **Circ:** 33,109,896 Unique Users
Editor: Alexander Wagner
Profile: Internet portal for topics related to soccer and highlights from the world of sport. Facebook: http://www.facebook.com/kickeronline Twitter: http://twitter.com/kicker_live Twitter: http://twitter.com/kicker_bl_li Twitter: http://twitter.com/kicker_2bl_li Twitter: http://twitter.com/kicker_3liga_li Twitter: http://twitter.com/kicker_cl_li Twitter: http://twitter.com/kicker_uefa_li Twitter: http://twitter.com/kicker_nat_li This Outlet offers RSS (Really Simple Syndication).
Language(s): German
CONSUMER: SPORT

KICKER SPORTMAGAZIN
732558G75B-5
Editorial: Badstr. 4, 90402 NÜRNBERG
Tel: 911 2162242 **Fax:** 911 9922420
Email: redaktion@kicker.de **Web site:** http://www.kicker.de
Freq: 104 issues yearly; **Annual Sub.:** EUR 189,60; **Circ:** 200,402
Editor: Klaus Smentek; **Advertising Manager:** Axel Nieber
Profile: kicker - this stands for 90 years for pure soccerl. World Championships, European Championships, Champions League or the Bundesliga as well as the top leagues of England, Spain or Italy. kicker, this are over three million young, high-income men who are professionally successful and not only consume the sport happily, but also exert active. kicker-men live in households with three or more people.
Language(s): German
ADVERTISING RATES:
Full Page Mono .... EUR 23300
Full Page Colour .... EUR 23300
Mechanical Data: Type Area: 282 x 203 mm, No. of Columns (Display): 4, Col Widths (Display): 47 mm
Copy instructions: *Copy Date:* 28 days prior to publication
CONSUMER: SPORT: Football

KIDS ZONE
732572G91D-4260
Editorial: Dr.-Mack-Str. 83, 90762 FÜRTH
Tel: 911 2872100 **Fax:** 911 2872235
Email: redaktion@kidszone.de **Web site:** http://www.kidszone.de
Freq: 13 issues yearly; **Annual Sub.:** EUR 33,90
Editor: Silke Menne; **Advertising Manager:** Gunnar Obermeier
Profile: The magazine for kids with animes, games, puzzles and lots more. Kids Zone satisfies young readers thirst for knowledge and gives them the scoop on all the latest trends from anime, manga and cards, TV, music, movies and electronic gaming. The target audience comprises boys and girls between 6 and 15 who want the low-down on the latest anime series, PC and video games and fun sports.
Language(s): German
ADVERTISING RATES:
Full Page Mono .... EUR 4990
Full Page Colour .... EUR 4990
Mechanical Data: Type Area: 280 x 210 mm, No. of Columns (Display): 4, Col Widths (Display): 52 mm
Copy instructions: *Copy Date:* 29 days prior to publication
CONSUMER: RECREATION & LEISURE: Children & Youth

KIELER EXPRESS AM WOCHENENDE - AUSG. OST
732582G72-6160
Editorial: Fleethörn 1, 24103 KIEL **Tel:** 431 9032925
Fax: 431 9032929
Email: exp.red@kieler-nachrichten.de
Freq: Weekly; **Cover Price:** Free; **Circ:** 92,300
Editor: Claudia Beylage-Haarmann; **Advertising Manager:** Michael Sulenski
Profile: Advertising journal (house-to-house) concentrating on local stories.
Language(s): German
ADVERTISING RATES:
Full Page Mono .... EUR 3509
Full Page Colour .... EUR 5088
Mechanical Data: Type Area: 430 x 281 mm, No. of Columns (Display): 6, Col Widths (Display): 45 mm
Copy instructions: *Copy Date:* 2 days prior to publication
LOCAL NEWSPAPERS

KIELER EXPRESS - AUSG. NORD
732581G72-6156
Editorial: Fleethörn 1, 24103 KIEL **Tel:** 431 9032925
Fax: 431 9032929
Email: exp.red@kieler-nachrichten.de **Web site:** http://www.kn-online.de
Freq: Weekly; **Cover Price:** Free; **Circ:** 25,200
Editor: Jürgen Heinemann; **Advertising Manager:** Marc Paris
Profile: Advertising journal (house-to-house) concentrating on local stories.
Language(s): German
ADVERTISING RATES:
Full Page Mono .... EUR 1864
Full Page Colour .... EUR 2731
Mechanical Data: Type Area: 430 x 281 mm, No. of Columns (Display): 6, Col Widths (Display): 45 mm
Copy instructions: *Copy Date:* 2 days prior to publication
LOCAL NEWSPAPERS

KIELER NACHRICHTEN
732584G67B-8000
Editorial: Fleethörn 1, 24103 KIEL **Tel:** 431 9032801
Fax: 431 9032935
Email: redaktion@kieler-nachrichten.de **Web site:** http://www.kn-online.de
Freq: 312 issues yearly; **Circ:** 103,778
Editor: Jürgen Heinemann; **News Editor:** Klaus Kramer; **Advertising Manager:** Marc Paris
Profile: The Kieler Nachrichten are traditionally the highest reach of newspaper in the state capital Kiel: the region closely connected, valued by its readers. The Kieler Nachrichten stand for quality journalism. The competent national and international playback issues and events is still the necessary complement to a comprehensive local coverage from the state capital and adjoining counties. The various regions of the Distribution area dedicate the Kieler Nachrichten daily regional edition with its own dedicated local reporting and our own editorial offices. These are real local variables: Eckernförde Nachrichten, Ostholsteiner Zeitung, Holsteiner Zeitung and Kiel Lokal. The balanced mix of news, background, commentary, entertainment and service issues due to the excellent reputation of the KN subscription newspaper in Kiel and in whole Schleswig-Holstein. Facebook: http://www.facebook.com/pages/KN-onlinede/243523866537 Twitter: http://twitter.com/Fleethoern This Outlet offers RSS (Really Simple Syndication).
Language(s): German
ADVERTISING RATES:
SCC .... EUR 399,20
Mechanical Data: Type Area: 430 x 281 mm, No. of Columns (Display): 7, Col Widths (Display): 45 mm
Copy instructions: *Copy Date:* 2 days prior to publication
Supplement(s): Inkiel; theaterZeit*; unizeit
REGIONAL DAILY & SUNDAY NEWSPAPERS: Regional Daily Newspapers

KIEN TIED ... KIEN TIED
1616486G74N-821
Editorial: Im Sack 12, 49716 MEPPEN
Tel: 5931 929333
Email: seniorenzeitung.kientied@ewetel.net
Freq: Half-yearly; **Circ:** 5,000
Editor: Hermann Stroot
Profile: The Meppen seniors newspaper with the relationship-full title "Kien Tied ... Kien Tied" has become an integral part of the seniors working in Meppen. The senior newspaper contains news, reports and information on senior-specific issues. For entertainment provide descriptions from the past and "Dönkes".
Language(s): German

KIND IM RHEIN-MAIN-GEBIET
1606032G89A-11490
Editorial: Rödingsmarkt 9, 20459 HAMBURG
Tel: 40 30604636 **Fax:** 40 30604690
Email: braun@companions.de **Web site:** http://www.companions.de
Freq: Annual; **Cover Price:** EUR 10,50; **Circ:** 15,000
Editor: Marta Braun; **Advertising Manager:** Natalie Domagalski
Profile: Travel magazine about the Rhein-Main region focusing on children.
Language(s): German
ADVERTISING RATES:
Full Page Mono .... EUR 2040
Full Page Colour .... EUR 2040
Mechanical Data: Type Area: 156 x 93 mm

KIND IM RHEIN-MAIN-GEBIET
1606032G89A-12548
Editorial: Rödingsmarkt 9, 20459 HAMBURG
Tel: 40 30604636 **Fax:** 40 30604690
Email: braun@companions.de **Web site:** http://www.companions.de
Freq: Annual; **Cover Price:** EUR 10,50; **Circ:** 15,000
Editor: Marta Braun; **Advertising Manager:** Natalie Domagalski
Profile: Travel magazine about the Rhein-Main region focusing on children.
Language(s): German
ADVERTISING RATES:
Full Page Mono .... EUR 2040
Full Page Colour .... EUR 2040
Mechanical Data: Type Area: 156 x 93 mm

KIND IM RUHRGEBIET
1606033G89A-11491
Editorial: Rödingsmarkt 9, 20459 HAMBURG
Tel: 40 30604636 **Fax:** 40 30604690
Email: braun@companions.de **Web site:** http://www.companions.de
Freq: Annual; **Cover Price:** EUR 10,50; **Circ:** 15,000
Editor: Marta Braun; **Advertising Manager:** Natalie Domagalski
Profile: Travel magazine about the Ruhr Basin region focusing on children.
Language(s): German
ADVERTISING RATES:
Full Page Mono .... EUR 2040
Full Page Colour .... EUR 2040
Mechanical Data: Type Area: 156 x 93 mm

KIND IM RUHRGEBIET
1606033G89A-12549
Editorial: Rödingsmarkt 9, 20459 HAMBURG
Tel: 40 30604636 **Fax:** 40 30604690
Email: braun@companions.de **Web site:** http://www.companions.de
Freq: Annual; **Cover Price:** EUR 10,50; **Circ:** 15,000
Editor: Marta Braun; **Advertising Manager:** Natalie Domagalski
Profile: Travel magazine about the Ruhr Basin region focusing on children.
Language(s): German
ADVERTISING RATES:
Full Page Mono .... EUR 2040
Full Page Colour .... EUR 2040
Mechanical Data: Type Area: 156 x 93 mm

KIND IN BERLIN MIT POTSDAM UND BERLINER UMLAND
1605993G89A-11477
Editorial: Rödingsmarkt 9, 20459 HAMBURG
Tel: 40 30604636 **Fax:** 40 30604690
Email: braun@companions.de **Web site:** http://www.companions.de
Freq: Annual; **Cover Price:** EUR 10,50; **Circ:** 15,000
Editor: Marta Braun; **Advertising Manager:** Natalie Domagalski
Profile: Travel magazine about the Potsdam and Berlin regions focusing on children.
Language(s): German
ADVERTISING RATES:
Full Page Mono .... EUR 2040
Full Page Colour .... EUR 2040
Mechanical Data: Type Area: 156 x 93 mm

KIND IN BERLIN MIT POTSDAM UND BERLINER UMLAND
1605993G89A-12550
Editorial: Rödingsmarkt 9, 20459 HAMBURG
Tel: 40 30604636 **Fax:** 40 30604690
Email: braun@companions.de **Web site:** http://www.companions.de
Freq: Annual; **Cover Price:** EUR 10,50; **Circ:** 15,000
Editor: Marta Braun; **Advertising Manager:** Natalie Domagalski
Profile: Travel magazine about the Potsdam and Berlin regions focusing on children.
Language(s): German

ADVERTISING RATES:
Full Page Mono .... EUR 2040
Full Page Colour .... EUR 2040
Mechanical Data: Type Area: 156 x 93 mm

KIND IN DÜSSELDORF
1606034G89A-11492
Editorial: Rödingsmarkt 9, 20459 HAMBURG
Tel: 40 30604636 **Fax:** 40 30604690
Email: braun@companions.de **Web site:** http://www.companions.de
Freq: Annual; **Cover Price:** EUR 10,50; **Circ:** 15,000
Editor: Marta Braun; **Advertising Manager:** Natalie Domagalski
Profile: Travel magazine about Düsseldorf focusing on children.
Language(s): German
ADVERTISING RATES:
Full Page Mono .... EUR 2040
Full Page Colour .... EUR 2040
Mechanical Data: Type Area: 156 x 93 mm

KIND IN DÜSSELDORF
1606034G89A-12551
Editorial: Rödingsmarkt 9, 20459 HAMBURG
Tel: 40 30604636 **Fax:** 40 30604690
Email: braun@companions.de **Web site:** http://www.companions.de
Freq: Annual; **Cover Price:** EUR 10,50; **Circ:** 15,000
Editor: Marta Braun; **Advertising Manager:** Natalie Domagalski
Profile: Travel magazine about Düsseldorf focusing on children.
Language(s): German
ADVERTISING RATES:
Full Page Mono .... EUR 2040
Full Page Colour .... EUR 2040
Mechanical Data: Type Area: 156 x 93 mm

KIND IN HAMBURG
1606036G89A-11494
Editorial: Rödingsmarkt 9, 20459 HAMBURG
Tel: 40 30604636 **Fax:** 40 30604690
Email: braun@companions.de **Web site:** http://www.companions.de
Freq: Annual; **Cover Price:** EUR 10,50; **Circ:** 15,000
Editor: Marta Braun; **Advertising Manager:** Natalie Domagalski
Profile: Travel magazine about Hamburg focusing on children.
Language(s): German
ADVERTISING RATES:
Full Page Mono .... EUR 2040
Full Page Colour .... EUR 2040
Mechanical Data: Type Area: 156 x 93 mm

KIND IN HAMBURG
1606036G89A-12553
Editorial: Rödingsmarkt 9, 20459 HAMBURG
Tel: 40 30604636 **Fax:** 40 30604690
Email: braun@companions.de **Web site:** http://www.companions.de
Freq: Annual; **Cover Price:** EUR 10,50; **Circ:** 15,000
Editor: Marta Braun; **Advertising Manager:** Natalie Domagalski
Profile: Travel magazine about Hamburg focusing on children.
Language(s): German
ADVERTISING RATES:
Full Page Mono .... EUR 2040
Full Page Colour .... EUR 2040
Mechanical Data: Type Area: 156 x 93 mm

KIND IN KÖLN/BONN
1606038G89A-11496
Editorial: Rödingsmarkt 9, 20459 HAMBURG
Tel: 40 30604636 **Fax:** 40 30604690
Email: braun@companions.de **Web site:** http://www.companions.de
Freq: Annual; **Cover Price:** EUR 10,50; **Circ:** 15,000
Editor: Marta Braun; **Advertising Manager:** Natalie Domagalski
Profile: Travel magazine about the Cologne/Bonn region focusing on children.
Language(s): German
ADVERTISING RATES:
Full Page Mono .... EUR 2040
Full Page Colour .... EUR 2040
Mechanical Data: Type Area: 156 x 93 mm

KIND IN KÖLN/BONN
1606038G89A-12554
Editorial: Rödingsmarkt 9, 20459 HAMBURG
Tel: 40 30604636 **Fax:** 40 30604690
Email: braun@companions.de **Web site:** http://www.companions.de
Freq: Annual; **Cover Price:** EUR 10,50; **Circ:** 15,000
Editor: Marta Braun; **Advertising Manager:** Natalie Domagalski
Profile: Travel magazine about the Cologne/Bonn region focusing on children.
Language(s): German
ADVERTISING RATES:
Full Page Mono .... EUR 2040
Full Page Colour .... EUR 2040
Mechanical Data: Type Area: 156 x 93 mm

KIND IN MÜNCHEN
1606039G89A-11497
Editorial: Rödingsmarkt 9, 20459 HAMBURG
Tel: 40 30604636 **Fax:** 40 30604690
Email: braun@companions.de **Web site:** http://www.companions.de
Freq: Annual; **Cover Price:** EUR 10,50; **Circ:** 15,000
Editor: Marta Braun; **Advertising Manager:** Natalie Domagalski
Profile: Travel magazine about Munich focusing on children.
Language(s): German
ADVERTISING RATES:
Full Page Mono .... EUR 2040
Full Page Colour .... EUR 2040
Mechanical Data: Type Area: 156 x 93 mm

KIND IN MÜNCHEN
1606039G89A-12555
Editorial: Rödingsmarkt 9, 20459 HAMBURG
Tel: 40 30604636 **Fax:** 40 30604690
Email: braun@companions.de **Web site:** http://www.companions.de
Freq: Annual; **Cover Price:** EUR 10,50; **Circ:** 15,000
Editor: Marta Braun; **Advertising Manager:** Natalie Domagalski
Profile: Travel magazine about Munich focusing on children.
Language(s): German
ADVERTISING RATES:
Full Page Mono .... EUR 2040
Full Page Colour .... EUR 2040
Mechanical Data: Type Area: 156 x 93 mm

KIND IN STUTTGART
1606042G89A-11500
Editorial: Rödingsmarkt 9, 20459 HAMBURG
Tel: 40 30604636 **Fax:** 40 30604690
Email: braun@companions.de **Web site:** http://www.companions.de
Freq: Annual; **Cover Price:** EUR 10,50; **Circ:** 15,000
Editor: Marta Braun; **Advertising Manager:** Natalie Domagalski
Profile: Travel magazine about Stuttgart focusing on children.
Language(s): German
ADVERTISING RATES:
Full Page Mono .... EUR 2040
Full Page Colour .... EUR 2040
Mechanical Data: Type Area: 156 x 93 mm

KIND IN STUTTGART
1606042G89A-12557
Editorial: Rödingsmarkt 9, 20459 HAMBURG
Tel: 40 30604636 **Fax:** 40 30604690
Email: braun@companions.de **Web site:** http://www.companions.de
Freq: Annual; **Cover Price:** EUR 10,50; **Circ:** 15,000
Editor: Marta Braun; **Advertising Manager:** Natalie Domagalski
Profile: Travel magazine about Stuttgart focusing on children.
Language(s): German
ADVERTISING RATES:
Full Page Mono .... EUR 2040
Full Page Colour .... EUR 2040
Mechanical Data: Type Area: 156 x 93 mm

KINDER
732601G74C-1820
Editorial: Raboisen 30, 20095 HAMBURG
Tel: 40 344434 **Fax:** 40 352540
Email: info@junior-verlag.de **Web site:** http://www.wireltern.de
Freq: Monthly; **Annual Sub.:** EUR 15,60; **Circ:** 287,720
Editor: Daniela Mutschler; **Advertising Manager:** Birgit König
Profile: KiNDER reaches families with children in the nuclear age from 3 to 8 years precisely through selected distribution channels such as kindergartens and childrenclinics - mostly through group subscriptions and bulk orders. For 40 years, KiNDER supports the educational work of parents and educators, and offers accuracy and competence.
Language(s): German
ADVERTISING RATES:
Full Page Mono .... EUR 16200
Full Page Colour .... EUR 16200
Mechanical Data: Type Area: 260 x 183 mm, No. of Columns (Display): 4, Col Widths (Display): 42 mm
Copy instructions: *Copy Date:* 41 days prior to publication
CONSUMER: WOMEN'S INTEREST CONSUMER MAGAZINES: Home & Family

KINDER BRANCHENBUCH
1694820G74C-3688
Editorial: Fuhrberger Weg 10, 30900 WEDEMARK
Tel: 5130 928190 **Fax:** 5130 9281929
Email: verlag@kibra-hamburg.de **Web site:** http://www.kibra-hamburg.de
Freq: Annual; **Cover Price:** Free; **Circ:** 182,525
Editor: Anissa Hruby; **Advertising Manager:** Anissa Hruby
Profile: Regional Business Directory as a reference for the target groups of parents, educators and those who have personally done to work or during leisure time with children and in the field have an information need.
Language(s): German
ADVERTISING RATES:
Full Page Mono .... EUR 4050
Full Page Colour .... EUR 4050
Mechanical Data: Type Area: 180 x 143 mm, No. of Columns (Display): 3, Col Widths (Display): 45 mm
CONSUMER: WOMEN'S INTEREST CONSUMER MAGAZINES: Home & Family

KINDER KRANKENSCHWESTER
732631G56B-1647
Editorial: Lutherplatz 25, 47805 KREFELD
Tel: 2151 500081 **Fax:** 2151 500567
Email: kinderkrankenschwester@t-online.de
Freq: Monthly; Free to qualifying individuals
Annual Sub.: EUR 33,60; **Circ:** 8,751
Editor: Hermann Schulte-Wissermann; **Advertising Manager:** Bernd Dürrmeier
Profile: Publication for nurses looking after children.
Language(s): German
ADVERTISING RATES:
Full Page Mono .... EUR 1980
Full Page Colour .... EUR 3465
Mechanical Data: No. of Columns (Display): 4, Col Widths (Display): 43 mm, Type Area: 265 x 185 mm
Copy instructions: *Copy Date:* 28 days prior to publication
Official Journal of: Organ d. Fachausschusses Kinderkrankenpflege d. Dt. Ges. f. Sozialpädiatrie u. Jugendmedizin e.V., d. Berufsverb. Kinderkrankenpflege Deutschlands e.V. u. d. Berufsverb. Kinderkrankenpflege Österr.
BUSINESS: HEALTH & MEDICAL: Nursing

KINDER- UND JUGENDARZT
732648G56A-5860
Editorial: Janusz-Korczak-Allee 12, 30173 HANNOVER **Tel:** 511 81153320
Freq: Monthly; Free to qualifying individuals
Annual Sub.: EUR 106,70; **Circ:** 12,085
Editor: Hans-Jürgen Christen; **Advertising Manager:** Christiane Kermel
Profile: Publication of the Association of German Paediatricians.
Language(s): German
ADVERTISING RATES:
Full Page Mono .... EUR 2635
Full Page Colour .... EUR 4705
Mechanical Data: Type Area: 297 x 210 mm, No. of Columns (Display): 3, Col Widths (Display): 57 mm
Copy instructions: *Copy Date:* 30 days prior to publication
BUSINESS: HEALTH & MEDICAL

KINDER- UND JUGENDMEDIZIN
732651G56A-5880
Editorial: Liebigstr. 20a, 04103 LEIPZIG
Tel: 341 9726003 **Fax:** 341 9720139
Email: gesine.nagl@medizin.uni-leipzig.de **Web site:** http://www.kinder-und-jugendmedizin-online.de
Freq: 6 issues yearly; **Annual Sub.:** EUR 140,00; **Circ:** 9,544
Advertising Manager: Jasmin Thurner
Profile: The Kinder- und Jugendmedizin is a recognized training and further education magazine for pediatricians. Because pediatricians are in addition to the family doctors the first point of contact in pediatric problems often and which paved the way for a competent specialist treatment in their hands, which the magazine will also apply to them. It is one of the most widely pediatric journals in Germany. Original and review articles, observational studies, case reports and conference reports from all disciplines, are the basis for a scientifically sound and practical at the same time continuing education. Of course, with the magazine can also continuing education credits under the "continuing medical education (CME) collected.
Language(s): German
ADVERTISING RATES:
Full Page Mono .... EUR 2695
Full Page Colour .... EUR 3835
Mechanical Data: Type Area: 243 x 179 mm, No. of Columns (Display): 3, Col Widths (Display): 57 mm
Copy instructions: *Copy Date:* 40 days prior to publication
Official Journal of: Organ d. Dt. Akademie f. Entwicklungsförderung u. Gesundheit d. Kindes u. Jugendl. e.V., d. Sächs.-Thüring. Ges. f. Kinder- u. Jugendmedizin u. Kinderchirurgie u. d. Dt. Ges. f. d. Neugeborenenscreening
BUSINESS: HEALTH & MEDICAL

KINDERANALYSE
732603G56N-28
Editorial: Am Weilersbach 6, 72070 TÜBINGEN
Tel: 7071 551226 **Fax:** 7071 2536840
Email: kinderanalyse@t-online.de **Web site:** http://www.kinderanalyse.de
Freq: Quarterly; **Annual Sub.:** EUR 68,00; **Circ:** 1,300
Editor: Heidi Zimmermann-Günter; **Advertising Manager:** Friederike Kamann
Profile: Publication about psychotherapy for children and young people.
Language(s): German
Readership: Aimed at psychologists, psychoanalysts, child and youth psychotherapists, paediatricians and social workers.
ADVERTISING RATES:
Full Page Mono .... EUR 540
Mechanical Data: Type Area: 180 x 113 mm, No. of Columns (Display): 2, Col Widths (Display): 54 mm
Copy instructions: *Copy Date:* 30 days prior to publication
BUSINESS: HEALTH & MEDICAL: Mental Health

KINDERÄRZTLICHE PRAXIS
732602G56A-5900
Editorial: Heiglhofstr. 63, 81377 MÜNCHEN
Fax: 89 71009315
Email: alex@hachmeister.de **Web site:** http://www.kinderaerztliche-praxis.de
Freq: 6 issues yearly; Free to qualifying individuals
Annual Sub.: EUR 47,40; **Circ:** 9,424
Editor: Knut Brockmann; **Advertising Manager:** Björn Lindenau
Profile: Official journal of the German Association of Social Paediatricians.
Language(s): German
ADVERTISING RATES:
Full Page Mono .... EUR 3670
Full Page Colour .... EUR 3670
Mechanical Data: Type Area: 245 x 178 mm, No. of Columns (Display): 4, Col Widths (Display): 40 mm
Copy instructions: *Copy Date:* 28 days prior to publication
BUSINESS: HEALTH & MEDICAL

KINDERGARTEN HEUTE
732609G62C-8
Editorial: Hermann-Herder-Str. 4, 79104 FREIBURG
Tel: 761 2717250 **Fax:** 761 2717240
Email: redaktion@kindergarten-heute.de **Web site:** http://www.kindergarten-heute.de
Freq: 10 issues yearly; **Annual Sub.:** EUR 57,30; **Circ:** 35,529
Editor: Christine Merz-Foschepoth; **Advertising Manager:** Bettina Schillinger-Wegmann
Profile: kindergarten heute is the largest independent magazine of Germany, education is. It deals with fundamental questions of psychology and pedagogy, as well as job-specific topics. In addition, the magazine about current political and social changes with a view contains all types of non-home care for children.
Language(s): German
Readership: Aimed at teachers and all those who work with children.
ADVERTISING RATES:
Full Page Mono .... EUR 8600
Full Page Colour .... EUR 8600
Mechanical Data: Type Area: 260 x 185 mm
Copy instructions: *Copy Date:* 41 days prior to publication
BUSINESS: CHURCH & SCHOOL EQUIPMENT & EDUCATION: Junior Education

KINDERZEIT
732653G62C-13
Editorial: Schnewlinstr. 6, 79098 FREIBURG
Tel: 761 70578558 **Fax:** 761 70578657
Email: kinderzeit@familymedia.de **Web site:** http://www.kinderzeit.de
Freq: Quarterly; **Annual Sub.:** EUR 18,40; **Circ:** 52,000
Editor: Stephan Wessolek; **Advertising Manager:** Sabine Mecklenburg
Profile: Magazine for preschool teachers in preschool, teachers in primary schools and parents.
Language(s): German
ADVERTISING RATES:
Full Page Mono .... EUR 2640
Full Page Colour .... EUR 4400
Mechanical Data: No. of Columns (Display): 4, Type Area: 250 x 185 mm
Copy instructions: *Copy Date:* 28 days prior to publication
BUSINESS: CHURCH & SCHOOL EQUIPMENT & EDUCATION: Junior Education

KINDHEIT UND ENTWICKLUNG
732658G56A-5920
Editorial: Rohnsweg 25, 37085 GÖTTINGEN
Tel: 551 496090 **Fax:** 551 4960988
Email: verlag@hogrefe.de **Web site:** http://www.hogrefe.de/zeitschriften/ke
Freq: Quarterly; **Annual Sub.:** EUR 86,95; **Circ:** 2,200
Editor: Ulrike Petermann; **Advertising Manager:** Nadine Teichert
Profile: Magazine about clinical psychology with relation to children and young people.
Language(s): German
ADVERTISING RATES:
Full Page Mono .... EUR 600
Mechanical Data: Type Area: 250 x 170 mm, No. of Columns (Display): 2, Col Widths (Display): 85 mm
Copy instructions: *Copy Date:* 42 days prior to publication

KING MAGAZINE
732663G91D-9774
Editorial: Sandstr. 3, 80335 MÜNCHEN
Tel: 89 30774215 **Fax:** 89 30774233
Email: petra.lengnick@piranha-media.de **Web site:** http://www.piranha-media.de
Freq: Monthly; **Cover Price:** Free; **Circ:** 500,000
Editor: Petra Lengnick; **Advertising Manager:** Jörg Sauer
Profile: Burger King youth magazine about music, cinema, games, sport and fashion.
Language(s): German
ADVERTISING RATES:
Full Page Mono .... EUR 9000
Full Page Colour .... EUR 9000
Mechanical Data: Type Area: 280 x 210 mm
CONSUMER: RECREATION & LEISURE: Children & Youth

KINO JOURNAL FRANKFURT
732664G76A-900

Editorial: Ludwigstr. 37, 60327 FRANKFURT
Tel: 69 974600 **Fax:** 69 97460400
Web site: http://www.kinojournal-frankfurt.de
Freq: Weekly; **Cover Price:** Free; **Circ:** 29,925
Editor: Andreas Dosch; **Advertising Manager:** Melanie Hennemann
Profile: Journal featuring cinema programmes in Frankfurt.
Language(s): German
ADVERTISING RATES:
Full Page Mono .... EUR 1670
Full Page Colour .... EUR 2680
Mechanical Data: Type Area: 270 x 195 mm, No. of Columns (Display): 4, Col Widths (Display): 45 mm
Copy instructions: *Copy Date:* 7 days prior to publication
CONSUMER: MUSIC & PERFORMING ARTS: Cinema

KINO.DE
1662058G76A-1538

Editorial: Weihenstephaner Str. 7, 81673 MÜNCHEN
Tel: 89 45114271 **Fax:** 89 45114444
Email: b.sunjic@e-media.de **Web site:** http://www.kino.de
Freq: Daily; **Cover Price:** Paid; **Circ:** 3,096,053 Unique Users
Editor: Ulrich Höcherl; **Advertising Manager:** Susanne Hübner
Profile: Online portal for movie, DVD-/Video-, music and games.
Language(s): German
CONSUMER: MUSIC & PERFORMING ARTS: Cinema

KINZIGTAL-NACHRICHTEN
732671G67B-8020

Editorial: Frankfurter Str. 8, 36043 FULDA
Tel: 661 280304 **Fax:** 661 280279
Email: redaktion@fuldaerzeitung.de **Web site:** http://www.fuldaerzeitung.de
Freq: 312 issues yearly; **Circ:** 7,413
Advertising Manager: Rudolf Lechner
Profile: Daily newspaper with regional news and a local sports section. Facebook: http://www.facebook.com/pages/Fuldaer-Zeitung/162547627109989 This Outlet offers RSS (Really Simple Syndication).
Language(s): German
ADVERTISING RATES:
SCC .... EUR 34,40
Mechanical Data: Type Area: 432 x 280 mm, No. of Columns (Display): 6, Col Widths (Display): 45 mm
Copy instructions: *Copy Date:* 1 day prior to publication
REGIONAL DAILY & SUNDAY NEWSPAPERS: Regional Daily Newspapers

KIR ROYAL
1852821G74P-1266

Editorial: Hafnerstr. 13, 83043 BAD AIBLING
Tel: 8061 392788 **Fax:** 8061 392790
Email: office@kirroyal.eu **Web site:** http://www.kirroyal-geniesserjournal.de
Freq: Half-yearly; **Annual Sub.:** EUR 9,60; **Circ:** 19,500
Editor: Peter Weilacher; **Advertising Manager:** Gabriela Weilacher
Profile: Regional food and gourmet magazine and for Bavaria. This Outlet offers RSS (Really Simple Syndication).
Language(s): German
ADVERTISING RATES:
Full Page Mono .... EUR 1650
Full Page Colour .... EUR 1650
Mechanical Data: Type Area: 265 x 185 mm, No. of Columns (Display): 3, Col Widths (Display): 58 mm

DIE KIRCHE
732675G87-7040

Editorial: Georgenkirchstr. 69, 10249 BERLIN
Tel: 30 28874821 **Fax:** 30 28874820
Email: info@wichern.de **Web site:** http://www.die-kirche.de
Freq: Weekly; **Annual Sub.:** EUR 54,00; **Circ:** 8,285
Editor: Sybille Sterzik
Profile: Magazine for evangelical Christians in the regions of Berlin and Brandenburg.
Language(s): German
ADVERTISING RATES:
Full Page Mono .... EUR 2160
Mechanical Data: Type Area: 400 x 285 mm, No. of Columns (Display): 6, Col Widths (Display): 45 mm
Copy instructions: *Copy Date:* 10 days prior to publication
CONSUMER: RELIGIOUS

KIRCHE HEUTE
732683G87-7140

Editorial: Postfach 1406, 84498 ALTÖTTING
Tel: 8671 880430 **Fax:** 8671 880431
Email: info@kirche-heute.de **Web site:** http://www.kirche-heute.de
Freq: 11 issues yearly; **Annual Sub.:** EUR 30,00; **Circ:** 10,098
Editor: Thomas Maria Rimmel; **Advertising Manager:** Maria Kugler
Profile: Magazine about the Catholic Church of the present and the future.
Language(s): German
Readership: Aimed at the Catholic community.
ADVERTISING RATES:
Full Page Mono .... EUR 1195
Full Page Colour .... EUR 1585
Mechanical Data: Type Area: 269 x 184 mm, No. of Columns (Display): 4, Col Widths (Display): 42 mm
Copy instructions: *Copy Date:* 20 days prior to publication
CONSUMER: RELIGIOUS

KIRCHE + LEBEN
732704G87-7200

Editorial: Cheruskerring 19, 48147 MÜNSTER
Tel: 251 48390 **Fax:** 251 4839111
Email: redaktion@dialogverlag.de **Web site:** http://www.kircheundleben.de
Freq: Weekly; **Circ:** 97,967
Editor: Hans-Josef Joest
Profile: Weekly from the diocese of Münster.
Language(s): German
ADVERTISING RATES:
Full Page Mono .... EUR 9531
Full Page Colour .... EUR 14776
Mechanical Data: Type Area: 470 x 310 mm, No. of Columns (Display): 6, Col Widths (Display): 45 mm
Copy instructions: *Copy Date:* 12 days prior to publication
CONSUMER: RELIGIOUS

KIRCHENBOTE
732692G87-7220

Editorial: Kleine Domsfreiheit 23, 49074 OSNABRÜCK **Tel:** 541 318540 **Fax:** 541 318529
Email: redaktion@kirchenbote.de **Web site:** http://www.kirchenbote.de
Freq: Weekly; **Annual Sub.:** EUR 62,40; **Circ:** 27,318
Editor: Ulrich Waschki
Profile: Parish magazine for Osnabrück.
Language(s): German
ADVERTISING RATES:
Full Page Mono .... EUR 4032
Full Page Colour .... EUR 5376
Mechanical Data: Type Area: 480 x 325 mm, No. of Columns (Display): 7, Col Widths (Display): 43 mm
Copy instructions: *Copy Date:* 12 days prior to publication
CONSUMER: RELIGIOUS

KIRCHENZEITUNG FÜR DAS BISTUM EICHSTÄTT
732702G87-7340

Editorial: Sollnau 2, 85072 EICHSTÄTT
Tel: 8421 97810 **Fax:** 8421 978120
Email: redaktion@kirchenzeitung-eichstaett.de **Web site:** http://www.kirchenzeitung-eichstaett.de
Freq: Weekly; **Circ:** 20,691
Profile: Catholic magazine.
Language(s): German
Readership: Aimed at people with Catholic belief.
ADVERTISING RATES:
Full Page Mono .... EUR 1188
Mechanical Data: Type Area: 270 x 210 mm, No. of Columns (Display): 4, Col Widths (Display): 48 mm
Copy instructions: *Copy Date:* 13 days prior to publication
CONSUMER: RELIGIOUS

KIRCHENZEITUNG FÜR DAS ERZBISTUM KÖLN
732699G87-7300

Editorial: Ursulaplatz 1, 50668 KÖLN
Tel: 221 1619131 **Fax:** 221 1619216
Email: redaktion@kirchenzeitung-koeln.de **Web site:** http://www.kirchenzeitung-koeln.de
Freq: Weekly; **Annual Sub.:** EUR 70,20; **Circ:** 47,313
Editor: Stephan Georg Schmidt; **Advertising Manager:** Klaus Boscanin
Profile: Catholic newspaper for the archdiocese of Cologne.
Language(s): German
ADVERTISING RATES:
Full Page Mono .... EUR 3405
Full Page Colour .... EUR 5448
Mechanical Data: Type Area: 280 x 198 mm, No. of Columns (Display): 4, Col Widths (Display): 45 mm
Copy instructions: *Copy Date:* 10 days prior to publication
CONSUMER: RELIGIOUS

KIRNER ZEITUNG
732728G67B-8040

Editorial: August-Horch-Str. 28, 56070 KOBLENZ
Tel: 261 892240 **Fax:** 261 892770
Email: redaktion@rhein-zeitung.net **Web site:** http://www.rhein-zeitung.de
Freq: 312 issues yearly; **Circ:** 18,650
Profile: Regional daily newspaper with news on politics, economy, culture, sports, travel, technology, etc. The Kirner Zeitung is a local issue the in koblenz appearing Rhein-Zeitung. Facebook: http://www.facebook.com/rheinzeitung Twitter: http://www.rhein-zeitung.de/twitter.html This Outlet offers RSS (Really Simple Syndication).
Language(s): German
ADVERTISING RATES:
SCC .... EUR 69,80
Mechanical Data: Type Area: 480 x 325 mm, No. of Columns (Display): 7, Col Widths (Display): 45 mm
Copy instructions: *Copy Date:* 1 day prior to publication
REGIONAL DAILY & SUNDAY NEWSPAPERS: Regional Daily Newspapers

DIE KITZINGER
732747G67B-8060

Editorial: Herrnstr. 10, 97318 KITZINGEN
Tel: 9321 700911 **Fax:** 9321 700944
Email: redaktion.kitzingen@infranken.de **Web site:** http://www.infranken.de/diekitzinger
Freq: 312 issues yearly; **Circ:** 5,441
Advertising Manager: Barbara Haßfurter
Profile: Regional daily newspaper covering politics, economics, sport, travel and technology. Facebook: http://de-de.facebook.com/pages/Mediengruppe-Oberfranken/145490768797885?v=wall Twitter: http://twitter.com/infranken This Outlet offers RSS (Really Simple Syndication).
Language(s): German
ADVERTISING RATES:
SCC .... EUR 24,70
Mechanical Data: Type Area: 430 x 285 mm, No. of Columns (Display): 6, Col Widths (Display): 45 mm
Copy instructions: *Copy Date:* 1 day prior to publication
Supplement(s): doppio; rtv
REGIONAL DAILY & SUNDAY NEWSPAPERS: Regional Daily Newspapers

KKA KÄLTE KLIMA AKTUELL
732283G3C-1

Editorial: Avenwedder Str. 55, 33335 GÜTERSLOH
Tel: 5241 8090884 **Fax:** 5241 80690880
Email: christoph.brauneis@bauverlag.de **Web site:** http://www.kka-online.info
Freq: 6 issues yearly; **Annual Sub.:** EUR 81,60; **Circ:** 3,783
Editor: Christoph Brauneis; **Advertising Manager:** Ariane Ewers
Profile: The trade magazine KKA Kälte Klima Aktuell offers new information for the Current key target groups of the market: executing refrigeration and air-conditioning manufacturers, manufacturers of equipment and operators involved in industrial and commercial companies and HVAC companies. The topics of "Climate Engineering ", "Commercial refrigeration" and "Industrial refrigeration", "heat pump", "refrigerators / cold rooms", "control technology", "Electrical Engineering " and "insulation", "mobile refrigeration equipment" and "transport refrigeration" are carefully researched technical papers of competent authors discussed in detail. Also economic and fiscal problems from daily practice are discussed. Latest news, products, specials, application and contract reviews, reports on trade shows, market trends and developments of education and association information draw KKA Kälte Klima Aktuell as a particularly important source of information for professional decision makers.
Language(s): German
ADVERTISING RATES:
Full Page Mono .... EUR 1230
Full Page Colour .... EUR 1860
Mechanical Data: Type Area: 270 x 186 mm, No. of Columns (Display): 4, Col Widths (Display): 45 mm
Copy instructions: *Copy Date:* 15 days prior to publication
Official Journal of: Organ d. Überwachungsgemeinschaft Kälte-Klimatechnik e.V., d. Innung f. Kälte- u. Klimatechnik f. d. Handwerkskammerbezirk Dortmund, d. Innung f. Kältetechnik im Kammerbezirk Bremen-Oldenburg, d. Landesinnung f. d. Kälteanlagenbauerhandwerk Baden-Württemberg, d. Kälteanlagenbauer-Innung Nordrhein u. d. Kälteanlagenbauer-Innung Berlin-Brandenburg
BUSINESS: HEATING & VENTILATION: Refrigeration & Ventilation

KKV INFORMATION
732759G14A-3840

Editorial: Paul-Klee-Weg 52, 48165 MÜNSTER
Tel: 2501 922435
Email: dietersp@t-online.de **Web site:** http://www.kkv-muenster.de
Freq: Quarterly; **Circ:** 200
Editor: Dieter Spevak
Profile: Magazine from the Catholic Commercial Club Hansa.
Language(s): German
ADVERTISING RATES:
Full Page Mono .... EUR 116
Mechanical Data: Type Area: 180 x 130 mm
Copy instructions: *Copy Date:* 15 days prior to publication

KLANG + TON
732766G78A-463

Editorial: Gartroper Str. 42, 47138 DUISBURG
Tel: 203 4292139 **Fax:** 203 4292215
Email: barske@brieden.de **Web site:** http://www.klangundton-magazin.de
Freq: 6 issues yearly; **Annual Sub.:** EUR 23,10; **Circ:** 25,000
Editor: Holger Barske
Profile: Klang + Ton is the magazine for all who deal creatively with the theme music playback. The focus of Klang + Ton is in the DIY loudspeakers. Each issue presents in his own laboratory-developed loudspeaker-building instructions. Craft processes, such as wood processing, electrical wiring and Gehäusebedämpfung learn a detailed treatment. Also, the construction of amplifiers with tube and transistor is a regular item.
Language(s): German
ADVERTISING RATES:
Full Page Mono .... EUR 2512
Full Page Colour .... EUR 3702
Mechanical Data: Type Area: 248 x 185 mm
CONSUMER: CONSUMER ELECTRONICS: Hi-Fi & Recording

KLAPPE AUF
732767G80-6180

Editorial: Kreuzstr. 3, 76133 KARLSRUHE
Tel: 721 380893 **Fax:** 721 380121
Email: info@klappeauf.de **Web site:** http://www.klappeauf.de
Freq: Monthly; **Annual Sub.:** EUR 30,00; **Circ:** 21,318
Editor: Alfred Godulla
Profile: Cultural interest magazine for Karlsruhe, Bruchsal and Rastatt, including an entertainment guide.
Language(s): German
Readership: Aimed at people aged between 18 and 30 years old.
ADVERTISING RATES:
Full Page Mono .... EUR 1480
Full Page Colour .... EUR 2200
Mechanical Data: Type Area: 260 x 190 mm, No. of Columns (Display): 4, Col Widths (Display): 44 mm
Copy instructions: *Copy Date:* 14 days prior to publication
CONSUMER: RURAL & REGIONAL INTEREST

KLASSIK MOTORRAD
1639224G77A-2609

Editorial: Schrempfstr. 8, 70597 STUTTGART
Tel: 711 24897600 **Fax:** 711 24897628
Web site: http://www.mo-web.de
Freq: 6 issues yearly; **Annual Sub.:** EUR 30,00; **Circ:** 50,000
Editor: Frank-Albert Illg; **Advertising Manager:** Sabine Schermer
Profile: Motorcycles, which can no longer get out of my head. They are classics. Motorcycles, which we would always like to buy. These are classic cars. That is what this issue. Promotional material for true connoisseurs. Fascinating background-tories. Technical aesthetics to perfection. Reports from the international classical scene. Each issue is a collector's item. And the audience is getting younger.
Language(s): German
ADVERTISING RATES:
Full Page Mono .... EUR 3655
Full Page Colour .... EUR 6140
Mechanical Data: No. of Columns (Display): 4, Col Widths (Display): 43 mm, Type Area: 262 x 187 mm
Copy instructions: *Copy Date:* 30 days prior to publication

KLASSIK UHREN
732778G79K-800

Editorial: Karlstr. 41, 89073 ULM **Tel:** 731 1520148
Fax: 731 1520171
Email: klassik-uhren@ebnerverlag.de **Web site:** http://www.ebnerverlag.de
Freq: 6 issues yearly; **Annual Sub.:** EUR 79,80; **Circ:** 1,842
Editor: Christian Pfeiffer-Belli; **Advertising Manager:** Andrea Scheungrab
Profile: Klassik Uhren reports on the true originals. About wristwatches that still really represent the traditional classical art of watchmaking in front of the machine age. Klassik Uhren go into detail afraid to not be afraid, difficult technical designs clearly and generally understand. The fascination of antique clocks listened to Klassik Uhren at the watch on not, clocks and large clocks and pocket watches above all, take a large space in the variety of topics. Competent auction reports reflect the trends in the collectors' market. Brilliant, large-format photographs and written contributions can be a great exciting era of watchmaking in front of your eyes back to life. Anhören Umschrift.
Language(s): German
Readership: Aimed at collectors of clocks.
ADVERTISING RATES:
Full Page Mono .... EUR 990
Full Page Colour .... EUR 1990
Mechanical Data: Type Area: 245 x 175 mm, No. of Columns (Display): 4, Col Widths (Display): 40 mm
Copy instructions: *Copy Date:* 30 days prior to publication
CONSUMER: HOBBIES & DIY: Collectors Magazines

KLASSIKER DER LUFTFAHRT
1609396G6A-1514

Editorial: Ubierstr. 83, 53173 BONN
Tel: 228 9565100 **Fax:** 228 9565247
Email: redaktion@klassiker-der-luftfahrt.de **Web site:** http://www.klassiker-der-luftfahrt.de
Freq: 8 issues yearly; **Annual Sub.:** EUR 36,90; **Circ:** 16,734
Editor: Volker K. Thomalla
Profile: The magazine Klassiker der Luftfahrt brings news from the classic car scene. Detailed descriptions of historical aircraft, background reports on the still flying witnesses in aviation history and museum tips form the backbone of the magazine.
Language(s): German
ADVERTISING RATES:
Full Page Mono .... EUR 4150
Full Page Colour .... EUR 4150
Mechanical Data: Type Area: 248 x 185 mm, No. of Columns (Display): 4, Col Widths (Display): 43 mm
Copy instructions: *Copy Date:* 28 days prior to publication
BUSINESS: AVIATION & AERONAUTICS

KLÄX
732761G91D-4560

Editorial: Bodenborn 43, 58452 WITTEN
Tel: 2302 93093850 **Fax:** 2302 93093899
Email: info@klaex.de **Web site:** http://www.klaex.de
Freq: 10 issues yearly; **Annual Sub.:** EUR 34,00; **Circ:** 12,500
Editor: Christiane Henrich; **Advertising Manager:** Thilo Cunz
Profile: Magazine with a Christian emphasis.
Language(s): German
Readership: Aimed at children between 7 and 13 years.

ADVERTISING RATES:
Full Page Mono .... EUR 1519
Full Page Colour .... EUR 1519
Mechanical Data: Type Area: 258 x 188 mm, No. of Columns (Display): 4, Col Widths (Display): 44 mm
Copy instructions: *Copy Date:* 17 days prior to publication
CONSUMER: RECREATION & LEISURE: Children & Youth

KLEIN & GROSS 732855G62C-21
Editorial: Rosenheimer Str. 145, 81671 MÜNCHEN
Tel: 89 45051371 **Fax:** 89 45051310
Email: holler@oldenbourg.de **Web site:** http://www.oldenbourg-bsv.de
Freq: 10 issues yearly; **Annual Sub.:** EUR 54,90; **Circ:** 7,825
Editor: Stefan Holler; **Advertising Manager:** Christian Schwarzbauer
Profile: Magazine about pre-school education.
Language(s): German
ADVERTISING RATES:
Full Page Mono .... EUR 1780
Full Page Colour .... EUR 1780
Mechanical Data: Type Area: 256 x 185 mm, No. of Columns (Display): 3, Col Widths (Display): 56 mm
Copy instructions: *Copy Date:* 35 days prior to publication
BUSINESS: CHURCH & SCHOOL EQUIPMENT & EDUCATION: Junior Education

KLEINBRENNEREI 732792G9C-3
Editorial: Am Talfeld 5, 82380 PEISSENBERG
Tel: 8803 489266 **Fax:** 8803 489265
Email: brigitte.gassner@t-online.de **Web site:** http://www.kleinbrennerei.de
Freq: Monthly; **Annual Sub.:** EUR 45,60; **Circ:** 8,107
Editor: Brigitte Gassner; **Advertising Manager:** Anna Greiner
Profile: Kleinbrennerei is the leading and largest circulation trade magazine for the production of alcohol in small and medium enterprises. It is an important source of information for those who have directly or indirectly related to the alcohol industry. With a circulation of 8,000 copies the Kleinbrennerei offers in the closed and settlement distillery a high range. Successful bridge between tradition-conscious manufacturing and latest quality-oriented practices. Description of old and new fruit varieties. Care and harvesting of fruit trees and shrubs. From the mash until distillate - procedures at the distillery. Advice and tips to improve quality. Presentation and marketing. The legal framework at a glance. Expansion of product range for direct marketers (jams, vinegar, juice, etc.). History of alcohol production. The constant themes are raw fruits: which varieties are suitable for the distillery?, process engineering and safety, operations management, (direct) marketing, latest research results, practical tips: mashing, fermentation, burning, removal, filtration, lowering, filling and labeling, awards, legal issues, reporting on exhibitions, educational events, field trips, as well as the current Association news, business reports: successful distiller looked over his shoulder.
Language(s): German
ADVERTISING RATES:
Full Page Mono .... EUR 2204
Full Page Colour .... EUR 2744
Mechanical Data: Type Area: 260 x 185 mm, No. of Columns (Display): 4, Col Widths (Display): 45 mm
Copy instructions: *Copy Date:* 22 days prior to publication
BUSINESS: DRINKS & LICENSED TRADE: Licensed Trade, Wines & Spirits

DIE KLEINE 1930998G74N-996
Editorial: Hegwiesen 10, 72764 REUTLINGEN
Tel: 7121 240459 **Fax:** 7121 210542
Email: info@heyd-pr.de **Web site:** http://www.die-kleine-zeitschrift.de
Freq: 6 issues yearly; **Cover Price:** Free; **Circ:** 15,000
Editor: Gabriele Heyd; **Advertising Manager:** Gabriele Heyd
Profile: Magazine for people who think of the future.
Language(s): German
ADVERTISING RATES:
Full Page Mono .... EUR 1400
Full Page Colour .... EUR 1460
Mechanical Data: Type Area: 277 x 192 mm, No. of Columns (Display): 4, Col Widths (Display): 45 mm
Copy instructions: *Copy Date:* 23 days prior to publication

DER KLEINE BUSINESS KOMPASS 1882042G14A-10266
Editorial: Fraunhoferstr. 5, 82152 PLANEGG
Tel: 89 895170 **Fax:** 89 89517250
Email: online@haufe.de **Web site:** http://www.haufe.de
Freq: Annual; **Cover Price:** EUR 4,95; **Circ:** 100,000
Profile: Overview of all important issues around the topic of economics, law and taxes. "Der kleine Business Kompass" can be made of 500 copies with your own envelope from a run.
Language(s): German

DIE KLEINE DIANA 732830G74A-3272
Editorial: Römerstr. 90, 79618 RHEINFELDEN
Tel: 7623 964164 **Fax:** 7623 964459
Email: info@oz-verlag.de **Web site:** http://www.oz-verlag.de

Freq: 10 issues yearly; **Annual Sub.:** EUR 16,50; **Circ:** 60,000
Editor: Jutta Götz
Profile: Needlework magazine with Häkelmodellen for every occasion and every season with instructions for reworking.
Language(s): German
ADVERTISING RATES:
Full Page Mono .... EUR 2000
Full Page Colour .... EUR 2560
Mechanical Data: Type Area: 226 x 159 mm, No. of Columns (Display): 4, Col Widths (Display): 35 mm

DER KLEINE JOHNSON 1657216G74P-1142
Editorial: Grillparzerstr. 12, 81675 MÜNCHEN
Tel: 89 41981453 **Fax:** 89 41981123
Web site: http://www.graefe-und-unzer.de
Freq: Annual; **Cover Price:** EUR 19,90; **Circ:** 100,000
Profile: Magazine about exclusive wine.
Language(s): German
Mechanical Data: Type Area: 168 x 75 mm

KLEINER INTERN 1894767G27-3099
Editorial: Göppinger Str. 2, 75179 PFORZHEIM
Tel: 7231 60720 **Fax:** 7231 60721039
Email: marketing@kleiner-gmbh.de **Web site:** http://www.kleiner-gmbh.de
Freq: Half-yearly; **Circ:** 400
Editor: Martina Kleiner
Profile: Company publication.
Language(s): German

KLEINES TABELLENBUCH FÜR STEUERLICHE BERATER 1627045G1A-3532
Editorial: Werastr. 21, 70182 STUTTGART
Tel: 711 2194203 **Fax:** 711 2194219
Email: katzenmayer@schaeffer-poeschel.de **Web site:** http://www.schaeffer-poeschel.de
Freq: Annual; **Cover Price:** EUR 9,95; **Circ:** 11,000
Editor: Katharina Jenak
Profile: Charts about tax law and social insurances for tax advisors and officials in charge. Facebook: http://www.facebook.com/schaefferpoeschel.
Language(s): German

KLEINES TABELLENBUCH FÜR STEUERLICHE BERATER 1627045G1A-3820
Editorial: Werastr. 21, 70182 STUTTGART
Tel: 711 2194203 **Fax:** 711 2194219
Email: katzenmayer@schaeffer-poeschel.de **Web site:** http://www.schaeffer-poeschel.de
Freq: Annual; **Cover Price:** EUR 9,95; **Circ:** 11,000
Editor: Katharina Jenak
Profile: Charts about tax law and social insurances for tax advisors and officials in charge. Facebook: http://www.facebook.com/schaefferpoeschel.
Language(s): German

KLEINTIERMEDIZIN 732853G64H-200
Editorial: Jurastr. 23, 72072 TÜBINGEN
Tel: 7473 21292
Email: bptbawue@telebinder.net
Freq: 6 issues yearly; **Annual Sub.:** EUR 57,00; **Circ:** 7,429
Editor: Thomas Steidl; **Advertising Manager:** Berndt H. Holthaus
Profile: Journal about the veterinary care of small animals.
Language(s): German
Readership: Aimed at vets caring for small animals.
ADVERTISING RATES:
Full Page Mono .... EUR 1740
Full Page Colour .... EUR 2880
Mechanical Data: Type Area: 248 x 180 mm, No. of Columns (Display): 3, Col Widths (Display): 56 mm
Copy instructions: *Copy Date:* 21 days prior to publication
BUSINESS: OTHER CLASSIFICATIONS: Veterinary

KLEINTIERPRAXIS 732854G64H-220
Editorial: Oertzenweg 19b, 14163 BERLIN
Tel: 30 81082394
Freq: Monthly; **Annual Sub.:** EUR 136,80; **Circ:** 3,245
Editor: Leo Brunnberg
Profile: Magazine for veterinarians focusing on small animals. Practical articles and case studies for practical veterinarians, animal hospitals, laboratories and medical schools for training and education.
Language(s): German
Readership: Aimed at veterinary surgeons.
ADVERTISING RATES:
Full Page Mono .... EUR 1143
Full Page Colour .... EUR 1939
Mechanical Data: Type Area: 297 x 210 mm, No. of Columns (Display): 4, Col Widths (Display): 44 mm
Copy instructions: *Copy Date:* 21 days prior to publication
Official Journal of: Organ d. Dt. Ges. f. Kleintiermedizin u. d. Fachgruppe Chirurgie d. DVG
BUSINESS: OTHER CLASSIFICATIONS: Veterinary

KLENKES 732860G80-6200
Editorial: Oranienstr. 9, 52066 AACHEN
Tel: 241 9450111 **Fax:** 241 9450180
Email: lb@klenkes.de **Web site:** http://www.klenkes.de
Freq: Monthly; **Cover Price:** Free; **Circ:** 33,655
Editor: Lutz Bernhardt; **Advertising Manager:** Josef Heinrichs
Profile: Cinema, art, culture - for more than 35 years, the Klenkes for its readers the most important advice in matters film, concerts, theater, exhibitions, readings, and nightlife. City magazine reflects all areas of life in Aachen and the Euregio every month in all its diversity: issues in society and politics, the regional economy and the hospitality industry. Facebook: http://www.facebook.com/klenkes.de.
Language(s): German
ADVERTISING RATES:
Full Page Colour .... EUR 2300
Mechanical Data: Type Area: 260 x 190 mm, No. of Columns (Display): 4, Col Widths (Display): 45 mm
Copy instructions: *Copy Date:* 21 days prior to publication
CONSUMER: RURAL & REGIONAL INTEREST

KLERUSBLATT 732861G87-7640
Editorial: Stephansplatz 3, 80337 MÜNCHEN
Tel: 89 265464 **Fax:** 89 266671
Email: klerusverband@t-online.de
Freq: Monthly; **Annual Sub.:** EUR 18,40; **Circ:** 3,000
Editor: Florian Trenner; **Advertising Manager:** Susanne Hagendorn
Profile: Publication for the Catholic community in the Bayern and Pfalz regions.
Language(s): German
ADVERTISING RATES:
Full Page Mono .... EUR 647
Mechanical Data: Type Area: 285 x 210 mm, No. of Columns (Display): 4, Col Widths (Display): 50 mm
Copy instructions: *Copy Date:* 15 days prior to publication
CONSUMER: RELIGIOUS

KLETTERN 732862G75L-600
Editorial: Rosentalstr. 28, 70563 STUTTGART
Tel: 711 9547926 **Fax:** 711 9547928
Email: redaktion@klettern-magazin.de **Web site:** http://www.klettern.de
Freq: 8 issues yearly; **Annual Sub.:** EUR 43,50; **Circ:** 18,946
Editor: Volker Leuchsner; **Advertising Manager:** Bernd Holzhauer
Profile: klettern is the modern German-speaking magazine for all active climbers and mountaineers. The magazine covers all mountain sports disciplines: pure rock-climbing - whether boulder, sports or big wall climbing -, classic mountaineering in rock and ice, ice climbing, and expeditions to the mountains of the world. klettern is also keenly devoted to the rapidly growing target group of indoor climbers. klettern presents the most beautiful climbing destinations, is a reliable product and equipment guide and fascinates the reader with enthralling images from the world of the vertical. klettern is made by climbers fpr climbers. Alongside up-to-date coverage of the booming climbing scene, background articles and imterviews as well as in-depth local and regional information and route tips, klettern provides a comprehensive service on mountain sports products and all aspects of climbing-related safety. klettern feels just as much at home in the climbing hall: the annual maxi-special "halls & walls", for example, caters to the steadily rising numbers of indoor climbers.
Language(s): German
ADVERTISING RATES:
Full Page Mono .... EUR 2395
Full Page Colour .... EUR 3590
Mechanical Data: No. of Columns (Display): 4, Col Widths (Display): 43 mm, Type Area: 248 x 185 mm
Copy instructions: *Copy Date:* 24 days prior to publication
CONSUMER: SPORT: Outdoor

KLIMAINFOS 1785524G57-2803
Editorial: Prinzenstr. 12, 30159 HANNOVER
Tel: 511 61623973 **Fax:** 511 61623975
Email: info@klimaschutzagentur.de **Web site:** http://www.klimaschutz-hannover.de
Freq: 3 issues yearly; **Cover Price:** Free; **Circ:** 3,500
Editor: Monika Dening-Müller
Profile: Magazine about climate protection in the Hanover region.
Language(s): German

KLINIKARZT 732874G56A-5940
Editorial: Rüdigerstr. 14, 70469 STUTTGART
Tel: 711 8931433 **Fax:** 711 8931322
Email: tanja.stumpp@thieme.de **Web site:** http://www.klinikarzt.info
Freq: 11 issues yearly; Free to qualifying individuals
Annual Sub.: EUR 110,00; **Circ:** 22,074
Editor: Tanja Stumpp
Profile: Expert interdisciplinary training for every dedicated doctor in the hospital and for all chief and senior physicians. 11 times a year informs the klinikarzt in its CME-certified key issues in collaboration with renowned opinion leaders. Review articles of practical advances in medicine. Originalia, case studies, interviews and conference reports complement and deepen the practice relevant focus.
Language(s): German
Readership: Aimed at doctors, senior physicians and senior consultants practising at the clinic.

ADVERTISING RATES:
Full Page Mono .... EUR 513
Full Page Colour .... EUR 657
Mechanical Data: Type Area: 245 x 175 mm, No. of Columns (Display): 3, Col Widths (Display): 50 mm
Official Journal of: Organ d. Medica Dt. Ges. f. interdisziplinäre Medizin e.V.
Supplement(s): Current congress
BUSINESS: HEALTH & MEDICAL

KLINIKUMMEDICUS 1851496G56A-1156
Editorial: Krumenauerstr. 25, 85049 INGOLSTADT
Tel: 841 8801060 **Fax:** 841 880661060
Email: presse@klinikum-ingolstadt.de **Web site:** http://www.klinikum-ingolstadt.de
Freq: 3 issues yearly; **Circ:** 2,500
Editor: Joschi Haunsperger
Profile: Hospital magazine Facebook: http://www.facebook.com/pages/Klini-Maskottchen/139808256047254.
Language(s): German

KLINISCHE MONATSBLÄTTER FÜR AUGENHEILKUNDE 732879G56E-66_50
Editorial: Rüdigerstr. 14, 70469 STUTTGART
Tel: 711 8931630 **Fax:** 711 8931499
Email: anna.hecker@thieme.de **Web site:** http://www.thieme.de/klimo
Freq: Monthly; **Annual Sub.:** EUR 380,80; **Circ:** 1,240
Editor: Anna Hecker
Profile: Klinische Monatsblätter für Augenheilkunde is a pure subscription magazine and published in original papers, surveys and case reports the latest results of clinical research in all areas of ophthalmology. In a magazine-like layout editorial part KliMo provides an overview of new and practical developments, the most important in the international literature as well as diagnostic and therapeutic indications.
Language(s): German
ADVERTISING RATES:
Full Page Mono .... EUR 1540
Full Page Colour .... EUR 2650
Mechanical Data: Type Area: 248 x 175 mm, No. of Columns (Display): 4, Col Widths (Display): 40 mm
BUSINESS: HEALTH & MEDICAL: Optics

KLINISCHE NEUROPHYSIOLOGIE 732880G56N-29
Editorial: Carl-Neuberg-Str. 1, 30625 HANNOVER
Email: kundenservice@thieme.de **Web site:** http://www.thieme.de/fz/klinneuro
Freq: Quarterly; **Annual Sub.:** EUR 280,80; **Circ:** 3,700
Editor: R. Dengler
Profile: The Journal of nervous system function testing. The whole range: EEG, EMG, ENG, EVP, functional imaging, ultrasonography, interventional neurophysiology; Established expertise: CME-certified education and training; Systematic Reviews; original research with clinical studies, case reports of interest; Informative image findings.
Language(s): German
ADVERTISING RATES:
Full Page Mono .... EUR 2000
Full Page Colour .... EUR 3110
Mechanical Data: Type Area: 248 x 175 mm, No. of Columns (Display): 4, Col Widths (Display): 40 mm
Official Journal of: Organ d. Dt. u. d. Österr. Ges. f. klin. Neurophysiologie
BUSINESS: HEALTH & MEDICAL: Mental Health

KLINISCHE PÄDIATRIE 732882G56A-6020
Editorial: Moorenstr. 5, 40225 DÜSSELDORF
Email: goebel@med.uni-duesseldorf.de **Web site:** http://www.thieme.de/fz/klin_padiatr.html
Freq: 7 issues yearly; **Annual Sub.:** EUR 386,80; **Circ:** 470
Editor: Ulrich Göbel
Profile: The forum for scientific information in pediatrics. Selected original works from all areas of pediatrics. Visite: Your forum for interesting patient stories and unusual case studies. Recent advances in diagnosis and therapy. Results of pediatric oncology plus medicine and the market. Date information from the industry.
Language(s): English; German
ADVERTISING RATES:
Full Page Mono .... EUR 750
Full Page Colour .... EUR 1890
Mechanical Data: Type Area: 248 x 175 mm, No. of Columns (Display): 4, Col Widths (Display): 40 mm
BUSINESS: HEALTH & MEDICAL

KMA DAS GESUNDHEITSWIRTSCHAFTS-MAGAZIN 732877G56C-4
Editorial: Neue Grünstr. 17, 10179 BERLIN
Tel: 30 3309190 **Fax:** 30 33091929
Email: redaktion@kma-medien.de **Web site:** http://www.kma-online.de
Freq: Monthly; Free to qualifying individuals
Annual Sub.: EUR 98,00; **Circ:** 10,729
Editor: Claudia Dirks; **Advertising Manager:** Gerhard Hirz

rofile: Journal about hospital, clinic management nd administration. Twitter: http://twitter.com/ namedien.
anguage(s): German
DVERTISING RATES:
ull Page Mono .... EUR 3350
ull Page Colour .... EUR 4660
echanical Data: Type Area: 241 x 177 mm, No. of olumns (Display): 3, Col Widths (Display): 55 mm
opy instructions: *Copy Date:* 20 days prior to ublication
fficial Journal of: Organ d. Fachvereinigung rankenhaustechnik e.V., d. Österr. Verb. d. rankenhaus-Techniker u. d. BundesArGe Leitender rankenpflegepersonen e.V. f. Deutschland
upplement(s): Hauptstadtkongress Supplement; ma report bauen & planen; kma report beratung; rankenhaus-Technik
USINESS: HEALTH & MEDICAL: Hospitals

KNEE SURGERY SPORTS TRAUMATOLOGY ARTHROSCOPY 732909G56A-6040

ditorial: Tiergartenstr. 17, 69121 HEIDELBERG
el: 6221 4870 **Fax:** 6221 4878366
mail: subscriptions@springer.com **Web site:** http:// ww.springerlink.com
req: Monthly; **Annual Sub.:** EUR 1672,00; **Circ:** ,700
ditor: J. Karlsson; **Advertising Manager:** Noëla rischer
rofile: European journal covering all aspects of knee urgery, sports traumatology and arthroscopy.
anguage(s): English
DVERTISING RATES:
ull Page Mono .... EUR 1270
ull Page Colour .... EUR 2310
echanical Data: Type Area: 240 x 175 mm
fficial Journal of: Organ d. European Society of ports Traumatology, Knee Surgery and Arthroscopy
USINESS: HEALTH & MEDICAL

KNEIPP JOURNAL 732912G74G-800

ditorial: Adolf-Scholz-Allee 6, 86825 BAD VÖRISHOFEN **Tel:** 8247 3002162
ax: 8247 3002199
mail: kneippjournal@kneippbund.de **Web site:** ttp://www.kneippverlag.de
req: Monthly; Free to qualifying individuals
nnual Sub.: EUR 30,00; **Circ:** 102,816
ditor: Beate Seeßlen-Hurler
rofile: Magazine containing information on healthy festyles and eating.
anguage(s): German
DVERTISING RATES:
ull Page Mono .... EUR 3264
ull Page Colour .... EUR 5064
echanical Data: Type Area: 250 x 176 mm, No. of olumns (Display): 2, Col Widths (Display): 86 mm
ONSUMER: WOMEN'S INTEREST CONSUMER MAGAZINES: Slimming & Health

KOCHEN LEICHT GEMACHT 1601201G74P-991

ditorial: Römerstr. 90, 79618 RHEINFELDEN
el: 7623 964166 **Fax:** 7623 964459
mail: info@oz-verlag.de **Web site:** http://www. z-verlag.de
req: 6 issues yearly; **Annual Sub.:** EUR 13,00; **Circ:** 5,000
ditor: Anne Bühring
rofile: Cooking Guide with easy-to-follow recipes om ingredients of the season or for special ccasions.
anguage(s): German
DVERTISING RATES:
ull Page Mono .... EUR 1360
ull Page Colour .... EUR 1680
echanical Data: Type Area: 226 x 159 mm, No. of olumns (Display): 4, Col Widths (Display): 35 mm

OCHEN MIT LIEBE 1882191G74P-1273

ditorial: Römerstr. 90, 79618 RHEINFELDEN
el: 7623 964166 **Fax:** 7623 964459
mail: info@oz-verlag.de **Web site:** http://www. z-verlag.de
req: Quarterly; **Cover Price:** EUR 2,50; **Circ:** 80,000
rofile: Magazine about cooking.
anguage(s): German
DVERTISING RATES:
ull Page Mono .... EUR 1360
ull Page Colour .... EUR 1680
echanical Data: Type Area: 251 x 183 mm

KOCHEN & GENIESSEN 732936G74P-500

ditorial: Burchardstr. 11, 20095 HAMBURG
el: 40 30195170 **Fax:** 40 30195175
mail: info@kochen-und-geniessen.de **Web site:** ttp://www.kochen-und-geniessen.de
req: Monthly; **Annual Sub.:** EUR 34,80; **Circ:** 206,271
ditor: Götz Poggensee
rofile: kochen & genießen is guide, source of nformation and ideas at the expert level. The magazine is long used and collected as a reference. he intense exchange of letters and phone calls to he editors give evidence to a very close reader oyalty. The readers are true experts in the areas of ooking and baking. They constantly grapple with these issues. The readers are interested in recipes, in hospitality and daily life and are looking for ideas for clever variations of classicals. Facebook: http:// www.facebook.com/lecker.de/ Twitter: http:// twitter.com/LECKER_de.
Language(s): German
Readership: Aimed at people with an interest in cookery.
ADVERTISING RATES:
Full Page Mono .... EUR 13836
Full Page Colour .... EUR 13836
Mechanical Data: Type Area: 261 x 196 mm
Copy instructions: *Copy Date:* 42 days prior to publication
CONSUMER: WOMEN'S INTEREST CONSUMER MAGAZINES: Food & Cookery

KOCH-METSCHNIKOW JOURNAL 1799535G56A-11463

Editorial: Brandenburgische Str. 18, 10707 BERLIN
Tel: 30 8867490 **Fax:** 30 88674999
Email: info@grosse-verlag.de **Web site:** http://www. grosse-verlag.de
Freq: Quarterly; Free to qualifying individuals
Annual Sub.: EUR 60,50; **Circ:** 2,900
Editor: Hartmut Hübner; **Advertising Manager:** Douglas Grosse
Profile: Medicine magazine.
Language(s): German; Russian
Mechanical Data: Type Area: 280 x 210 mm
Official Journal of: Organ d. Koch-Metschnikow Forum e.V.

KOEHLER RUNDSCHAU 732950G36-6

Editorial: Hauptstr. 2, 77704 OBERKIRCH
Tel: 7802 814340 **Fax:** 7802 815340
Email: ruth.karcher@koehlerpaper.com **Web site:** http://www.koehlerpaper.com
Freq: 3 issues yearly; **Cover Price:** Free; **Circ:** 4,000
Editor: Ruth Karcher
Profile: Magazine for employees of August Koehler AG.
Language(s): German

KOELN.DE 1662078G80-14366

Editorial: Am Coloneum 9, 50829 KÖLN
Tel: 221 2222880 **Fax:** 221 2222988
Email: efranzmann@netcologne.de **Web site:** http:// www.koeln.de
Freq: Daily; **Cover Price:** Paid; **Circ:** 2,024,299 Unique Users
Editor: Edgar Franzmann; **Advertising Manager:** Jörg Severin
Profile: Ezine: Magazine for city and region, concentrating on events, gastronomy, music, arts and events.
Language(s): German
CONSUMER: RURAL & REGIONAL INTEREST

KOLLOQUIUM 732999G56A-6060

Editorial: Unter den Eichen 5, 65195 WIESBADEN
Tel: 611 97460 **Fax:** 611 9746304
Email: kontakt@medical-tribune.de **Web site:** http:// www.medical-tribune.de
Freq: 11 issues yearly; **Circ:** 67,200
Editor: Ulrike Hennemann; **Advertising Manager:** Katja Fuchs
Profile: The training supplement in the Medical Tribune looks at each issue with a central focus for the primary care medical practice, such as pain, cardiology and diabetes. The supplement reports with attractive categories in all journalistic representations on current research, advances in treatment, and highlights of national and international conferences. Each issue gives the doctor a clear and effective overview of the State of Art target group: all general practitioners, practitioners and internists.
Language(s): German
ADVERTISING RATES:
Full Page Mono .... EUR 5590
Full Page Colour .... EUR 7150
Mechanical Data: Type Area: 280 x 190 mm
Copy instructions: *Copy Date:* 21 days prior to publication
Supplement to: Medical Tribune

KÖLN 8 AKTUELL 732954G72-6232

Editorial: Stolberger Str. 114a, 50933 KÖLN
Tel: 221 9544140 **Fax:** 221 954414499
Email: redaktion@koelner-wochenspiegel.de **Web site:** http://www.rheinische-anzeigenblaetter.de
Freq: Weekly; **Cover Price:** Free; **Circ:** 22,896
Editor: Angelika Koenig; **Advertising Manager:** Astrid Rehm
Profile: Advertising journal (house-to-house) concentrating on local stories.
Language(s): German
ADVERTISING RATES:
Full Page Mono .... EUR 1961
Full Page Colour .... EUR 2843
Mechanical Data: Type Area: 430 x 282 mm, No. of Columns (Display): 6, Col Widths (Display): 45 mm
Copy instructions: *Copy Date:* 5 days prior to publication
LOCAL NEWSPAPERS

KÖLN. DIE STADT 1826201G89A-12384

Editorial: Kardinal-Höffner-Platz 1, 50667 KÖLN
Tel: 221 22123328 **Fax:** 221 22123320
Email: ralf.rudolf@koelntourismus.de **Web site:** http://www.koelntourismus.de
Freq: Annual; **Cover Price:** EUR 2,00; **Circ:** 25,000
Editor: Georg Wohlrab; **Advertising Manager:** Georg Wohlrab
Profile: Guides for Cologne.
Language(s): German
Mechanical Data: Type Area: 210 x 105 mm

KÖLN MAGAZIN 1794858G14A-9981

Editorial: Von-der-Wettern-Str. 25, 51149 KÖLN
Tel: 2203 35840 **Fax:** 2203 3584185
Email: info@maenken.com **Web site:** http://www. maenken.com
Freq: Quarterly; **Cover Price:** Free; **Circ:** 8,500
Editor: Volker Bittner; **Advertising Manager:** Thomas Müllenborn
Profile: Magazine is aimed at managers of large and medium-sized businesses and independent and informed in an appropriate context of developments in the economic area of Cologne. The expert report is complemented by thematic focus of company profiles and interviews with personalities from the economy and public life.
Language(s): German
ADVERTISING RATES:
Full Page Mono .... EUR 3330
Full Page Colour .... EUR 3330
Mechanical Data: Type Area: 240 x 190 mm, No. of Columns (Display): 3, Col Widths (Display): 60 mm
Copy instructions: *Copy Date:* 30 days prior to publication

KÖLN-BONN MANAGER 1931000G14A-10383

Editorial: Braschoßer Str. 55, 53721 SIEGBURG
Tel: 2241 234260 **Fax:** 2241 2342626
Email: lmc_mediaconsult@t-online.de **Web site:** http://www.koeln-bonn-manager.de
Freq: 6 issues yearly; **Annual Sub.:** EUR 28,00; **Circ:** 18,736
Profile: In addition to regionally relevant economic issues and well-researched background information and interviews, company profiles and contributions will be presented on interesting personalities. Similarly, topics that address the purchasing power manager as a person and individual.
Language(s): German
ADVERTISING RATES:
Full Page Mono .... EUR 2490
Full Page Colour .... EUR 2490
Mechanical Data: Type Area: 260 x 188 mm, No. of Columns (Display): 4, Col Widths (Display): 44 mm

KÖLNER GASTRO-SPECIAL 732963G89A-2820

Editorial: Vorgebirgstr. 59, 50677 KÖLN
Tel: 221 93472736 **Fax:** 221 93472742
Email: talk@koelner.de **Web site:** http://www. koelner.de
Freq: Half-yearly; **Cover Price:** Free; **Circ:** 25,000
Editor: Achim Göbel; **Advertising Manager:** Achim Göbel
Profile: The Cologne City Guide is published twice a year (summer / winter) as inserts in the Kölner Illustrierte. He always informed about the catering and leisure facilities in Cologne. Provide more than a thousand well-researched entries Cologne cafes, bistros, bars, restaurants, cinemas, theaters, live clubs and Pubs. Reports on new openings, area-portraits, stories and tests are also available.
Language(s): German
ADVERTISING RATES:
Full Page Mono .... EUR 2200
Full Page Colour .... EUR 3250
Mechanical Data: Type Area: 260 x 190 mm
Copy instructions: *Copy Date:* 14 days prior to publication
Supplement to: Kölner Illustrierte

KÖLNER ILLUSTRIERTE 732956G80-6260

Editorial: Vorgebirgstr. 59, 50677 KÖLN
Tel: 221 35558715 **Fax:** 221 355587411
Email: talk@koelner.de **Web site:** http://www. koelner.de
Freq: Monthly; **Annual Sub.:** EUR 10,00; **Circ:** 18,070
Editor: Irma Wagner; **Advertising Manager:** Achim Göbel
Profile: Since 1985, monthly city magazines. In appealing features and interviews regionally interesting topics. An extensive daily calendar informed of all significant events in Cologne. In addition to culture and politics are also lifestyle issues, such as going out, shopping, travel and parties not to short.
Language(s): German
ADVERTISING RATES:
Full Page Mono .... EUR 2200
Full Page Colour .... EUR 3250
Mechanical Data: Type Area: 260 x 190 mm, No. of Columns (Display): 4, Col Widths (Display): 44 mm
Copy instructions: *Copy Date:* 13 days prior to publication
Supplement(s): Kölner Gastro-Special; Kölner Uni-Special
CONSUMER: RURAL & REGIONAL INTEREST

KÖLNER STADT-ANZEIGER 732962G67B-8120

Editorial: Amsterdamer Str. 192, 50735 KÖLN
Tel: 221 2240 **Fax:** 221 2242524
Email: redaktion-ksta@mds.de **Web site:** http:// www.ksta.de
Freq: 312 issues yearly; **Circ:** 333,956
Editor: Peter Pauls; **Advertising Manager:** Karsten Hundhausen
Profile: Regional daily newspaper covering politics, economics, sports, travel and technology. Facebook: http://www.facebook.com/pages/KSTA/ 141063022950 Twitter: http://twitter.com/ksta_news This Outlet offers RSS (Really Simple Syndication).
Language(s): German
ADVERTISING RATES:
SCC .... EUR 551,00
Mechanical Data: Type Area: 430 x 285 mm, No. of Columns (Display): 6, Col Widths (Display): 45 mm
Copy instructions: *Copy Date:* 2 days prior to publication
Supplement(s): doppio; Magazin am Wochenende; prisma
REGIONAL DAILY & SUNDAY NEWSPAPERS: Regional Daily Newspapers

KÖLNER WOCHENSPIEGEL - AUSG. STADTBEZIRK EHRENFELD 725957G72-3376

Editorial: Stolberger Str. 114a, 50933 KÖLN
Tel: 221 9544140 **Fax:** 221 954414499
Email: redaktion@koelner-wochenspiegel.de **Web site:** http://www.rheinische-anzeigenblaetter.de
Freq: Weekly; **Cover Price:** Free; **Circ:** 52,793
Editor: Angelika Koenig; **Advertising Manager:** Astrid Rehm
Profile: Advertising journal (house-to-house) concentrating on local stories.
Language(s): German
ADVERTISING RATES:
Full Page Mono .... EUR 2528
Full Page Colour .... EUR 3666
Mechanical Data: Type Area: 430 x 282 mm, No. of Columns (Display): 6, Col Widths (Display): 45 mm
Copy instructions: *Copy Date:* 5 days prior to publication
LOCAL NEWSPAPERS

KÖLNERLEBEN 732959G74N-400

Editorial: Ottmar-Pohl-Platz 1, 51103 KÖLN
Tel: 221 22127508 **Fax:** 221 22127019
Email: koelnerleben@stadt-koeln.de **Web site:** http:// www.stadt-koeln.de
Freq: 6 issues yearly; **Annual Sub.:** EUR 12,00; **Circ:** 30,500
Editor: Lydia Schneider-Benjamin; **Advertising Manager:** Klaus Posthum
Profile: The magazine informs older cologne citizens about interesting topics. It provides information, advice, entertainment and a full event summary for the active, enterprising, and mobile health-conscious older generation beyond working life. The magazine has a circulation of over 32,000 pharmacies and public institutions for free distribution to citizens.
Language(s): German
ADVERTISING RATES:
Full Page Mono .... EUR 1550
Full Page Colour .... EUR 1820
Mechanical Data: Type Area: 252 x 185 mm, No. of Columns (Display): 3, Col Widths (Display): 61 mm
Copy instructions: *Copy Date:* 30 days prior to publication

KÖLNISCHE RUNDSCHAU 732973G67B-8140

Editorial: Stolkgasse 25, 50667 KÖLN
Tel: 221 1632558 **Fax:** 221 1632557
Email: print@kr-redaktion.de **Web site:** http://www. rundschau-online.de
Freq: 312 issues yearly; **Circ:** 333,956
Editor: Engelbert Greis; **Advertising Manager:** Karsten Hundhausen
Profile: Regional daily newspaper covering politics, economics, sports, travel and technology. Facebook: http://www.facebook.com/pages/Kolnische-Rundschau/147616463739 This Outlet offers RSS (Really Simple Syndication).
Language(s): German
ADVERTISING RATES:
SCC .... EUR 551,00
Mechanical Data: Type Area: 430 x 285 mm, No. of Columns (Display): 6, Col Widths (Display): 45 mm
Copy instructions: *Copy Date:* 2 days prior to publication
Supplement(s): doppio; prisma
REGIONAL DAILY & SUNDAY NEWSPAPERS: Regional Daily Newspapers

KOLPING MAGAZIN 733000G87-7720

Editorial: Kolpingplatz 5, 50667 KÖLN
Tel: 221 20701195 **Fax:** 221 20701186
Email: joachim.flieher@kolping.de **Web site:** http:// www.kolping.de
Freq: 11 issues yearly; Free to qualifying individuals
Annual Sub.: EUR 14,40; **Circ:** 171,796
Editor: Martin Grünewald
Profile: Magazine and official paper of Kolpingwerk Germany.
Language(s): German
ADVERTISING RATES:
Full Page Mono .... EUR 4745
Full Page Colour .... EUR 6880
Mechanical Data: Type Area: 300 x 215 mm, No. of Columns (Display): 3, Col Widths (Display): 57 mm
Copy instructions: *Copy Date:* 30 days prior to publication
CONSUMER: RELIGIOUS

DER KOMET 733008G64A-4
Editorial: Molkenbrunner Str. 10, 66954 PIRMASENS
Tel: 6331 513220 **Fax:** 6331 31480
Email: redaktion@komet-pirmasens.de **Web site:** http://www.komet-pirmasens.de
Freq: 36 issues yearly; **Annual Sub.:** EUR 142,00; **Circ:** 7,000
Editor: Detlef Weide; **Advertising Manager:** Birgit Jennewein
Profile: Magazine covering the fairs and travelling shows trade.
Language(s): German
ADVERTISING RATES:
Full Page Mono .... EUR 2430
Full Page Colour .... EUR 2916
Mechanical Data: Type Area: 300 x 221 mm, No. of Columns (Display): 9, Col Widths (Display): 22 mm
Copy instructions: *Copy Date:* 6 days prior to publication
Official Journal of: Organ d. Dt. Schaustellerbund e.V. u. d. Bundesverb. Dt. Schausteller u. Marktleute e.V.
BUSINESS: OTHER CLASSIFICATIONS: Amusement Trade

KOMM TK IT 1836983G18B-2182
Editorial: Paula-Thiede-Ufer 10, 10179 BERLIN
Tel: 30 69562461 **Fax:** 30 69563716
Email: redaktion.komm@verdi.de **Web site:** http://tk-it.verdi.de
Freq: 9 issues yearly; **Circ:** 126,032
Editor: Christoph Heil
Profile: Union magazine for the telecommunications and information technology sectors.
Language(s): German
ADVERTISING RATES:
Full Page Mono .... EUR 4962
Full Page Colour .... EUR 6450
Mechanical Data: Type Area: 266 x 183 mm, No. of Columns (Display): 4, Col Widths (Display): 42 mm

KOMMJUR 1657580G1A-3569
Editorial: August-Bebel-Allee 6, 53175 BONN
Tel: 228 9596229 **Fax:** 228 9596234
Email: uwe.zimmermann@dstgb.de **Web site:** http://www.kommunaljurist.de
Freq: Monthly; **Annual Sub.:** EUR 177,11; **Circ:** 1,100
Editor: Uwe Zimmermann
Profile: Magazine about legal counselling for communes, local districts, communal associations and communal companies.
Language(s): German
ADVERTISING RATES:
Full Page Mono .... EUR 590
Full Page Colour .... EUR 1715
Mechanical Data: Type Area: 251 x 185 mm

KOMMUNAL DIREKT 733029G32A-1740
Editorial: Stotznocken 5, 45239 ESSEN
Tel: 201 8496074 **Fax:** 201 8496075
Email: essen@kommunaldirekt.de **Web site:** http://www.kommunaldirekt.de
Freq: 6 issues yearly; Free to qualifying individuals **Annual Sub.:** EUR 33,00; **Circ:** 22,921
Editor: Franz Huckewitz; **Advertising Manager:** Dieter Ulischberger
Profile: Journal provides current topics on products, services, etc. around the local procurement market.
Language(s): German
Readership: Aimed at managers within the field.
ADVERTISING RATES:
Full Page Mono .... EUR 3140
Full Page Colour .... EUR 4230
Mechanical Data: Type Area: 280 x 190 mm, No. of Columns (Display): 3, Col Widths (Display): 60 mm
Copy instructions: *Copy Date:* 21 days prior to publication
BUSINESS: LOCAL GOVERNMENT, LEISURE & RECREATION: Local Government

KOMMUNALE FAHRZEUGE 733033G49E-982
Editorial: Bert-Brecht-Str. 15, 78054 VILLINGEN-SCHWENNINGEN **Tel:** 7720 394163
Fax: 7720 394175
Email: bethge@kuhnverlag.de **Web site:** http://www.kuhn-kataloge.de
Freq: Annual; **Cover Price:** EUR 17,00; **Circ:** 5,751
Editor: Axel Bethge; **Advertising Manager:** Konrad Baumann
Profile: Journal providing information on German railways.
Language(s): German
ADVERTISING RATES:
Full Page Mono .... EUR 2440
Full Page Colour .... EUR 3055
Mechanical Data: Type Area: 254 x 180 mm
BUSINESS: TRANSPORT: Railways

KOMMUNALE STEUER-ZEITSCHRIFT 733038G32C-100
Editorial: Luisenstr. 100, 53721 SIEGBURG
Tel: 2241 938340 **Fax:** 2241 9383433
Email: redaktion@kstz-online.de **Web site:** http://www.kstz-online.de
Freq: Monthly; **Annual Sub.:** EUR 136,28; **Circ:** 2,100
Editor: Peter Heine; **Advertising Manager:** Gerald Böke
Profile: The KStZ has its place in the municipal finance literature. Articles on current issues, particularly on taxes, fees and contributions and the reproduction of the relevant case law make it an indispensable tool for finance departments, local tax offices and law offices and the county, city and municipal administrations in general. The KStZ is read primarily by the mayors, government agencies and department heads and administrators of the municipalities and the counties and local businesses.
Language(s): German
Readership: Read by local government officials.
ADVERTISING RATES:
Full Page Mono .... EUR 700
Full Page Colour .... EUR 700
Mechanical Data: Type Area: 258 x 184 mm
Copy instructions: *Copy Date:* 7 days prior to publication
BUSINESS: LOCAL GOVERNMENT, LEISURE & RECREATION: Local Government Finance

KOMMUNALES ECHO 733037G14L-6827
Editorial: Josef-Görres-Platz 17, 56068 KOBLENZ
Tel: 261 35766 **Fax:** 261 38257
Email: rp@komba.de **Web site:** http://www.komba.de
Freq: 10 issues yearly; Free to qualifying individuals ; **Circ:** 5,200
Editor: Bardo Kraus
Profile: Municipal trades union magazine.
Language(s): German
ADVERTISING RATES:
Full Page Mono .... EUR 480
Mechanical Data: Type Area: 270 x 185 mm, No. of Columns (Display): 3, Col Widths (Display): 58 mm
BUSINESS: COMMERCE, INDUSTRY & MANAGEMENT: Trade Unions

KOMMUNAL-KASSEN-ZEITSCHRIFT 733040G32C-20
Editorial: Luisenstr. 100, 53721 SIEGBURG
Tel: 2241 938340 **Fax:** 2241 9383433
Email: info@reckinger.de **Web site:** http://www.reckinger.de
Freq: Monthly; **Annual Sub.:** EUR 138,28; **Circ:** 2,800
Editor: Karola Singer; **Advertising Manager:** Gerald Böke
Profile: The local cash journal is the organs of the Association of the Municipal Treasurer Association Practical essays and publishing topic-relevant case law make it the guide for the municipal funds and enforcement practice. The KKZ is read primarily by the authorities and department heads and administrators of the finance departments, funds and enforcement authorities of the municipalities and the counties and local businesses.
Language(s): German
ADVERTISING RATES:
Full Page Mono .... EUR 870
Full Page Colour .... EUR 870
Mechanical Data: Type Area: 258 x 184 mm
Copy instructions: *Copy Date:* 10 days prior to publication
BUSINESS: LOCAL GOVERNMENT, LEISURE & RECREATION: Local Government Finance

KOMMUNALTECHNIK 733045G4D-12
Editorial: Heidecker Weg 112, 31275 LEHRTE
Tel: 5132 859140 **Fax:** 5132 8599940
Email: redaktion@beckmann-verlag.de **Web site:** http://www.kommunaltechnik.net
Freq: 7 issues yearly; **Annual Sub.:** EUR 41,00; **Circ:** 14,531
Editor: Hans-Günter Dörpmund; **Advertising Manager:** Edward Kurdzielewicz
Profile: Magazine about technology and control.
Language(s): German
ADVERTISING RATES:
Full Page Mono .... EUR 3104
Full Page Colour .... EUR 4035
Mechanical Data: Type Area: 270 x 190 mm, No. of Columns (Display): 4, Col Widths (Display): 45 mm
BUSINESS: ARCHITECTURE & BUILDING: Planning & Housing

KOMMUNALWISSENSCHAFT-LICHE DISSERTATIONEN 733052G4D-7
Editorial: Zimmerstr. 13, 10969 BERLIN
Tel: 30 39001279 **Fax:** 30 39001160
Email: graeber@difu.de **Web site:** http://www.difu.de
Freq: Annual; **Annual Sub.:** EUR 20,00; **Circ:** 325
Editor: Rita Gräber
Profile: Magazine for local politicians.
Language(s): German

KOMMUNIKATION & RECHT 733055G18B-1974
Editorial: Mainzer Landstr. 251, 60326 FRANKFURT
Tel: 69 75951151 **Fax:** 69 75952780
Email: kutschke@betriebs-berater.de **Web site:** http://www.kommunikationundrecht.de
Freq: 11 issues yearly; **Annual Sub.:** EUR 348,00; **Circ:** 2,000
Editor: Torsten Kutschke; **Advertising Manager:** Marion Gertzen
Profile: Magazine providing information on legal matters related to the telecommunications industry.
Language(s): German
ADVERTISING RATES:
Full Page Mono .... EUR 1495
Full Page Colour .... EUR 2375
Mechanical Data: Type Area: 257 x 180 mm, No. of Columns (Display): 4, Col Widths (Display): 43 mm
Copy instructions: *Copy Date:* 20 days prior to publication
BUSINESS: ELECTRONICS: Telecommunications

KOMPAKT GASTROENTEROLOGIE 1998526G56A-11676
Editorial: Otto-Hahn-Str. 7, 50997 KÖLN
Tel: 2236 376408 **Fax:** 2236 376999
Email: dk@biermann.net **Web site:** http://www.ge-kompakt.de
Freq: 6 issues yearly; **Annual Sub.:** EUR 39,00; **Circ:** 3,200
Editor: Dieter Kaulard; **Advertising Manager:** Larissa Apisa
Profile: Kompakt Gastroenterologie is aimed at gastroenterologists and gastroenterology specialists working in hospitals or established practice in Germany. It reports on all areas of clinical gastroenterology. The focus will be annotated abstracts from major scientific publications, tables of contents of leading international journals and conference dates and announcements from the industry.
Language(s): German
ADVERTISING RATES:
Full Page Mono .... EUR 1866
Full Page Colour .... EUR 3021
Mechanical Data: Type Area: 312 x 220 mm
Copy instructions: *Copy Date:* 21 days prior to publication

KOMPAKT PNEUMOLOGIE 1998527G56A-11677
Editorial: Otto-Hahn-Str. 7, 50997 KÖLN
Tel: 2236 376408 **Fax:** 2236 376999
Email: dk@biermann.net **Web site:** http://www.pneumo-online.de
Freq: 6 issues yearly; **Annual Sub.:** EUR 39,00; **Circ:** 3,700
Editor: Dieter Kaulard; **Advertising Manager:** Larissa Apisa
Profile: Kompakt Pneumologie aimed at all pulmonologists in clinic or established practice in Germany. The newsletter reports on all areas of clinical pulmonary medicine and the diagnosis and treatment of respiratory diseases. Topics are current reports from the international medical, abstracts from scientific publications, tables of contents of leading international journals, conference dates and reports from the industry.
Language(s): German
ADVERTISING RATES:
Full Page Mono .... EUR 1866
Full Page Colour .... EUR 3021
Mechanical Data: Type Area: 312 x 220 mm
Copy instructions: *Copy Date:* 21 days prior to publication

KOMPASS VOR ORT 1824184G58-1786
Editorial: Hunscheidtstr. 18, 44789 BOCHUM
Tel: 234 316295 **Fax:** 234 316378
Email: pr@bergbau-bg.de **Web site:** http://www.bergbau-bg.de
Freq: Quarterly; **Cover Price:** Free; **Circ:** 35,000
Editor: Norbert Ulitzka
Profile: Magazine for employees of mining companies in Germany in the fields of lignite, coal, salt and Erze.Themen: the Occupational Safety and Health mining.
Language(s): German
Mechanical Data: Type Area: 295 x 189 mm, No. of Columns (Display): 3, Col Widths (Display): 50 mm
Copy instructions: *Copy Date:* 20 days prior to publication

KOMPASS VOR ORT 1824184G58-1823
Editorial: Hunscheidtstr. 18, 44789 BOCHUM
Tel: 234 316295 **Fax:** 234 316378
Email: pr@bergbau-bg.de **Web site:** http://www.bergbau-bg.de
Freq: Quarterly; **Cover Price:** Free; **Circ:** 35,000
Editor: Norbert Ulitzka
Profile: Magazine for employees of mining companies in Germany in the fields of lignite, coal, salt and Erze.Themen: the Occupational Safety and Health mining.
Language(s): German
Mechanical Data: Type Area: 295 x 189 mm, No. of Columns (Display): 3, Col Widths (Display): 50 mm
Copy instructions: *Copy Date:* 20 days prior to publication

KOMPETENT FÜR KOMMUNIKATION - AUSG. KARLSRUHE/ NORDSCHWARZWALD/RHEIN-NECKAR/PFALZ/SAAR 733067G2A-2260
Editorial: Schubartstr. 24, 73529 SCHWÄBISCH GMÜND **Tel:** 7171 4959473 **Fax:** 7171 4959474
Email: info@kompetent.de **Web site:** http://www.kompetent.de
Freq: Annual; **Cover Price:** EUR 10,00; **Circ:** 4,500
Editor: Andreas Grötsch
Profile: Publication with information, addresses and contacts for advertising, public relations, sales promotion and marketing in the city of Karlsruhe and the regions of Nordschwarzwald, Rhein-Neckar, Pfa and Saar.
Language(s): German
ADVERTISING RATES:
Full Page Mono .... EUR 49
Full Page Colour .... EUR 69
Mechanical Data: Type Area: 190 x 120 mm
Copy instructions: *Copy Date:* 45 days prior to publication

KOMPETENT FÜR KOMMUNIKATION - AUSG. SÜDBADEN/BODENSEE 733065G2A-222
Editorial: Schubartstr. 24, 73529 SCHWÄBISCH GMÜND **Tel:** 7171 4959473 **Fax:** 7171 4959474
Email: info@kompetent.de **Web site:** http://www.kompetent.de
Freq: Annual; **Cover Price:** EUR 10,00; **Circ:** 4,500
Editor: Andreas Grötsch
Profile: Publication with information, addresses and contacts for marketing, advertising, public relations and sales promotion.
Language(s): German
ADVERTISING RATES:
Full Page Mono .... EUR 49
Full Page Colour .... EUR 69
Mechanical Data: Type Area: 190 x 120 mm

KOMPETENT FÜR KOMMUNIKATION - AUSG. WÜRTTEMBERG 733066G2A-224
Editorial: Schubartstr. 24, 73529 SCHWÄBISCH GMÜND **Tel:** 7171 4959473 **Fax:** 7171 4959474
Email: info@kompetent.de **Web site:** http://www.kompetent.de
Freq: Annual; **Cover Price:** EUR 10,00; **Circ:** 4,500
Editor: Andreas Grötsch
Profile: Publication with information, addresses and contacts for advertising, public relations, sales promotion and marketing for the region of Württemberg.
Language(s): German
ADVERTISING RATES:
Full Page Mono .... EUR 49
Full Page Colour .... EUR 69
Mechanical Data: Type Area: 190 x 120 mm
Copy instructions: *Copy Date:* 45 days prior to publication

KOMPETENZ WASSER 1601538G57-264
Editorial: Ostmerheimer Str. 555, 51109 KÖLN
Tel: 221 22122407 **Fax:** 221 22124533
Email: elke.schlepuetz@steb-koeln.de **Web site:** http://www.steb-koeln.de
Freq: Annual; **Cover Price:** Free; **Circ:** 1,000
Editor: Elke Schlepütz
Profile: Cologne trade journal for waste water, flood protection and water.
Language(s): German
ADVERTISING RATES:
Full Page Mono .... EUR 87
Full Page Colour .... EUR 112
Mechanical Data: Type Area: 256 x 170 mm, No. of Columns (Display): 3, Col Widths (Display): 53 mm

KONDITOREI & CAFÉ 733073G8B-2
Editorial: Silberburgstr. 122, 70176 STUTTGART
Tel: 711 2133332 **Fax:** 711 2133280
Email: a.richter@matthaes.de **Web site:** http://www.koca-online.de
Freq: Monthly; **Annual Sub.:** EUR 234,00; **Circ:** 5,00
Editor: Wolf-Andreas Richter; **Advertising Manager:** Nicole M. Felger
Profile: Magazine about cafes and cakeshops.
Language(s): German
Readership: Aimed at the cafes and cakeshops in Germany.
ADVERTISING RATES:
Full Page Mono .... EUR 323
Full Page Colour .... EUR 323
Mechanical Data: Type Area: 261 x 187 mm, No. of Columns (Display): 4, Col Widths (Display): 43 mm
Official Journal of: Organ d. Dt. Konditorenbundes
BUSINESS: BAKING & CONFECTIONERY: Confectionery Manufacturing

KONGRESS KALENDER MEDIZIN INTERNATIONAL CONGRESS CALENDAR MEDICINE 733075G56A-608
Editorial: Ammonitenstr. 1, 72336 BALINGEN
Tel: 7433 952431 **Fax:** 7433 952381
Email: kongresse@spitta.de **Web site:** http://www.kongresskalender.spitta.de
Freq: Annual; **Cover Price:** EUR 26,80; **Circ:** 20,000
Editor: Ilona Tahir; **Advertising Manager:** Josefa Seydler
Profile: Manual for medical specialists and nurses with a list of all medical training conferences around the world.
Language(s): English; German
ADVERTISING RATES:
Full Page Mono .... EUR 420
Full Page Colour .... EUR 485
Mechanical Data: Type Area: 180 x 125 mm
Copy instructions: *Copy Date:* 49 days prior to publication

KÖNIGSTEINER WOCHE
732985G72-6268
Editorial: Theresenstr. 2, 61462 KÖNIGSTEIN
Tel: 6174 938555 **Fax:** 6174 938560
Email: redaktion-kw@hochtaunus.de **Web site:** http://www.hochtaunus.de/kw
Freq: Weekly; **Cover Price:** Free; **Circ:** 12,000
Editor: Elena Schemuth; **Advertising Manager:** Alexander Bommersheim
Profile: Advertising journal (house-to-house) concentrating on local stories.
Language(s): German
ADVERTISING RATES:
Full Page Mono .... EUR 1858
Full Page Colour .... EUR 1978
Mechanical Data: Type Area: 430 x 282 mm, No. of Columns (Display): 6, Col Widths (Display): 45 mm
Copy instructions: *Copy Date:* 2 days prior to publication
LOCAL NEWSPAPERS

KONKRET
733086G82-4900
Editorial: Ehrenbergstr. 59, 22767 HAMBURG
Tel: 40 8512530 **Fax:** 40 8512514
Email: redaktion@konkret-magazin.de **Web site:** http://www.konkret-verlage.de
Freq: Monthly; **Annual Sub.:** EUR 53,00; **Circ:** 41,508
Editor: Wolfgang Schneider; **Advertising Manager:** Thomas Schulz
Profile: Left popular magazine. From the fifties until today, the magazine stands for the rejection of war, military, defense, on superstition (also Christian), and ideology of exploitation, capitalism, Nazism, fascism, racism, anti-Semitism. Time and again, making the magazine the voice of opposition movements (anti-nuclear death and peace movement, student unrest and Apo, Young Socialists, Communists and political militancy, anti-nuclear movement, census boycott and solidarity with political prisoners). The harshest critics can be found in the magazine itself hardly a rebel movement, it has completely closed, and no one has joined the magazine. Since 1990, the magazine deals specially with the consequences of German reunification: the rise of nationalism, anti-Semitism and racism and the rise of neo-Nazi violence and the militarization of foreign policy.
Language(s): German
ADVERTISING RATES:
Full Page Mono .... EUR 2000
Full Page Colour .... EUR 2700
Mechanical Data: Type Area: 260 x 190 mm, No. of Columns (Display): 3, Col Widths (Display): 60 mm
Copy instructions: *Copy Date:* 28 days prior to publication
Supplement(s): literatur konkret
CONSUMER: CURRENT AFFAIRS & POLITICS

KONRADSBLATT
733089G87-7760
Editorial: Rudolf-Freytag-Str. 6, 76189 KARLSRUHE
Tel: 721 9545201 **Fax:** 721 9545210
Email: redaktion@konradsblatt.de **Web site:** http://www.konradsblatt-online.de
Freq: Weekly; **Annual Sub.:** EUR 97,20; **Circ:** 61,175
Editor: Klaus Nientiedt; **Advertising Manager:** Siegfried Fernschild
Profile: Catholic newspaper for the archdiocese of Freiburg.
Language(s): German
ADVERTISING RATES:
Full Page Mono .... EUR 3080
Full Page Colour .... EUR 6048
Mechanical Data: Type Area: 280 x 204 mm, No. of Columns (Display): 4, Col Widths (Display): 45 mm
Copy instructions: *Copy Date:* 11 days prior to publication
Supplement(s): Kirche aktiv; Kirche auf dem Weg
CONSUMER: RELIGIOUS

KONSTRUIEREN + GIESSEN
1655177G19E-1877
Editorial: Sohnstr. 70, 40237 DÜSSELDORF
Tel: 211 6871282 **Fax:** 211 6871265
Email: info@bdguss.de **Web site:** http://www.bdguss.de
Freq: Quarterly; **Cover Price:** Free; **Circ:** 3,000
Editor: Karl-Heinz Schütt
Profile: Magazine covering all aspects of technology.
Language(s): German

DER KONSTRUKTEUR
733098G19B-103
Editorial: Lise-Meitner-Str. 2, 55129 MAINZ
Tel: 6131 992238 **Fax:** 6131 992100
Email: m.doeppert@vfmz.de **Web site:** http://www.industrie-service.de
Freq: 11 issues yearly; **Annual Sub.:** EUR 92,00; **Circ:** 24,537
Editor: Michael Döppert; **Advertising Manager:** Bernd Kostbade
Profile: Der Konstrukteur reports competently and informatively on drive technology, fluid power technology, CAD/CAM/PLM, construction elements, automation technology, materials and joining technology. The reporting is focused on technical information as practical reports, research news, and reports on applications. The expertise knowledge of the editorial team ensures the right choice of topics and themes highly focused on the target group. Target group: pecialists in construction and development in OEM enterprises: namely known specialists and executives in technical design and construction functions.
Language(s): German
Readership: Aimed at engineers.
ADVERTISING RATES:
Full Page Mono .... EUR 5230
Full Page Colour .... EUR 6460
Mechanical Data: Type Area: 265 x 185 mm, No. of Columns (Display): 4, Col Widths (Display): 43 mm
Copy instructions: *Copy Date:* 14 days prior to publication
BUSINESS: ENGINEERING & MACHINERY: Engineering - Design

KONSTRUKTION
733099G19B-104
Editorial: VDI-Platz 1, 40468 DÜSSELDORF
Tel: 211 6103173 **Fax:** 211 6103148
Email: konstruktion@technikwissen.de **Web site:** http://www.konstruktion-online.de
Freq: 11 issues yearly; **Annual Sub.:** EUR 390,00; **Circ:** 20,172
Editor: Hans Hövelmann
Profile: The objective of the magazine is to provide mechanical engineering and design. Reputable authors from industry and research report on tasks and solutions. The editorial spectrum extends from the product idea up to the application in machine construction. The magazine section pro vides trade news and prod uct orientated reporting. Target group: Managers for design and development, test and development engineers in machine, apparatus and equip ment construction including 15,200 engineers of the VDI Society for Design Engineering.
Language(s): German
Readership: Read by engineers within the field.
ADVERTISING RATES:
Full Page Mono .... EUR 5016
Full Page Colour .... EUR 6291
Mechanical Data: Type Area: 270 x 185 mm, No. of Columns (Display): 4, Col Widths (Display): 45 mm
Copy instructions: *Copy Date:* 21 days prior to publication
Official Journal of: Organ d. VDI-Ges. Entwicklung Konstruktion Vertrieb u. d. VDI-Ges. Werkstofftechnik
BUSINESS: ENGINEERING & MACHINERY: Engineering - Design

KONSTRUKTION & ENTWICKLUNG
733101G42A-102
Editorial: Göggingerstr. 105a, 86199 AUGSBURG
Tel: 821 31988031 **Fax:** 821 31988080
Email: klieber@schluetersche.de **Web site:** http://www.konstruktion-entwicklung.de
Freq: 10 issues yearly; **Annual Sub.:** EUR 47,00; **Circ:** 24,828
Editor: Harald Klieber; **Advertising Manager:** Sebastian Lichtenberg
Profile: The reinforced editorial team of Konstruktion & Entwicklung informs design engineers and development engineers succinctly on trends, markets, doers and products of the fields of mechanical and plant engineering, electrical engineering as well as vehicle construction. The trend magazine for designers and developers stands for precise information based on sound background information and facts. Interviews as well as reports researched mainly by ourselves show in words and pictures what creative solutions look like and therefore provide a real additional value. Trend topics as well as news from research and development are also a fixed part of each issue. The carefully edited and professionally sound topics are tailored to the information needs of all groups of people involved in the decision process. News ranging from the fields of management to services complete the information and provide the readers with an insight into future developments relevant for them. Our photo-reportages or the "Kreative Zone" show that specialized information can be presented in a lively way. Here we introduce constructions and inventions that cannot be found in textbooks. Hence Konstruktion & Entwicklung is the indispensable information platform for many decision makers in the industry in order to plan the application of technology, to decide and to further develop for the future.
Language(s): German
ADVERTISING RATES:
Full Page Mono .... EUR 4420
Full Page Colour .... EUR 5650
Mechanical Data: Type Area: 272 x 188 mm, No. of Columns (Display): 4, Col Widths (Display): 44 mm
Copy instructions: *Copy Date:* 14 days prior to publication
BUSINESS: CONSTRUCTION

KONSTRUKTIONS PRAXIS
733100G19E-980
Editorial: Max-Planck-Str. 7, 97082 WÜRZBURG
Tel: 931 4180 **Fax:** 931 4182766
Email: redaktion@konstruktionspraxis.de **Web site:** http://www.konstruktionspraxis.de
Freq: 18 issues yearly; **Annual Sub.:** EUR 165,00; **Circ:** 23,141
Editor: Karl-Ullrich Höltkemeier; **Advertising Manager:** Bernd Weinig
Profile: konstruktions praxis is the special title for developers and design engineers coming from the mechanical engineering, apparatus engineering, electrical engineering, automotive engineering as well as metal working and plastics industries. From digital engineering (construction software for development, calculation and drawing, simulation and animation, hardware, design engineer workplace) to the choice of materials and constructional parts as well as the application of components for connection, fluid and drive technology, automation (sensors, controls, fieldbus, IPC, human-machine interface) and electrical engineering. konstruktionspraxis presents tendencies and trends, provides basic knowledge and background reports and enhances market transparency with user reports and product information. Facebook: http://www.facebook.com/pages/konstruktionspraxis/386224064781 Twitter: http://twitter.com/konstruktionspr This Outlet offers RSS (Really Simple Syndication).
Language(s): German
ADVERTISING RATES:
Full Page Mono .... EUR 4934
Full Page Colour .... EUR 6563
Mechanical Data: Type Area: 270 x 190 mm, No. of Columns (Display): 4, Col Widths (Display): 46 mm
Copy instructions: *Copy Date:* 25 days prior to publication
Supplement(s): kataloge orange
BUSINESS: ENGINEERING & MACHINERY: Machinery, Machine Tools & Metalworking

KONSTRUKTIONSPRAXIS.DE
1622279G42A-8
Editorial: Max-Planck-Str. 7, 97082 WÜRZBURG
Tel: 931 4182866 **Fax:** 931 4182766
Email: redaktion@konstruktionspraxis.de **Web site:** http://www.konstruktionspraxis.de
Freq: Daily; **Cover Price:** Paid; **Circ:** 79,448 Unique Users
Editor: Karl-Ullrich Höltkemeier; **Advertising Manager:** Bernd Weinig
Profile: Ezine: Portal for constructors, developers in the engineering, equipment engineering, electrical engineering and vehicle construction search engine. Facebook: http://www.facebook.com/pages/konstruktionspraxis/386224064781 Twitter: http://twitter.com/konstruktionspr This Outlet offers RSS (Really Simple Syndication).
Language(s): German
BUSINESS: CONSTRUCTION

KONTAKT
733117G58-980
Editorial: Heinrich-Böcking-Str. 10, 66121 SAARBRÜCKEN **Tel:** 681 6071150 **Fax:** 681 6071155
Email: neidhardt-armin@vse.de **Web site:** http://www.vse.de
Freq: 6 issues yearly; **Circ:** 7,000
Editor: Armin Neidhardt
Profile: Magazine for employees of VSE AG.
Language(s): German

KONTAKT CHANCE
1615562G90-7
Editorial: Im Mediapark 4d, 50670 KÖLN
Tel: 221 420400 **Fax:** 221 42040444
Email: info@kontaktchance.de **Web site:** http://www.kontaktchance.de
Freq: Weekly; **Annual Sub.:** EUR 69,80; **Circ:** 59,651
Editor: Alicia Berland; **Advertising Manager:** Alexander Pali
Language(s): Russian
ADVERTISING RATES:
SCC .... EUR 82,50
Mechanical Data: Type Area: 320 x 229 mm, No. of Columns (Display): 5, Col Widths (Display): 44 mm
Copy instructions: *Copy Date:* 7 days prior to publication
CONSUMER: ETHNIC

KONTAKTE
733124G14A-4040
Editorial: Joseph-Scherer-Str. 3, 44139 DORTMUND
Tel: 231 1354245 **Fax:** 231 135134245
Email: claus.rehse@signal-iduna.de **Web site:** http://www.signal-iduna.de
Freq: 3 issues yearly; **Cover Price:** Free; **Circ:** 21,000
Editor: Claus Rehse
Profile: Company publication published by Signal Iduna Gruppe.
Language(s): German

KONTAKTE
733124G14A-10439
Editorial: Joseph-Scherer-Str. 3, 44139 DORTMUND
Tel: 231 1354245 **Fax:** 231 135134245
Email: claus.rehse@signal-iduna.de **Web site:** http://www.signal-iduna.de
Freq: 3 issues yearly; **Cover Price:** Free; **Circ:** 21,000
Editor: Claus Rehse
Profile: Company publication published by Signal Iduna Gruppe.
Language(s): German

KONTAKTER
733130G2A-2280
Editorial: Hultschiner Str. 8, 81677 MÜNCHEN
Tel: 89 21837657 **Fax:** 89 21837850
Email: kontakt@kontakter.de **Web site:** http://kontakter.de
Freq: Weekly; **Annual Sub.:** EUR 775,00; **Circ:** 1,995
Editor: Jochen Kalka; **News Editor:** Klaus Wieking
Profile: Magazine providing a communications service for publicity professionals.
Language(s): German
ADVERTISING RATES:
Full Page Mono .... EUR 3000
Full Page Colour .... EUR 3950
Mechanical Data: Type Area: 250 x 179 mm
Copy instructions: *Copy Date:* 5 days prior to publication
BUSINESS: COMMUNICATIONS, ADVERTISING & MARKETING

KONTAKTER.DE
1622866G2A-5487
Editorial: Hultschiner Str. 8, 81677 MÜNCHEN
Tel: 89 21837026 **Fax:** 89 21837849
Email: jochen.kalka@kontakter.de **Web site:** http://www.kontakter.de
Freq: Daily; **Cover Price:** Paid; **Circ:** 58,765 Unique Users
Editor: Jochen Kalka; **Advertising Manager:** Andreas Schneider
Profile: Ezine: Magazine providing a communications service for publicity professionals.
Language(s): German
BUSINESS: COMMUNICATIONS, ADVERTISING & MARKETING

DIE KONTAKTLINSE
733132G56E-240
Editorial: Ernst-Mey-Str. 8, 70771 LEINFELDEN-ECHTERDINGEN **Tel:** 711 7594295
Fax: 711 7594397
Email: kl.redaktion@konradin.de **Web site:** http://www.kon-online.de
Freq: 10 issues yearly; **Annual Sub.:** EUR 111,00; **Circ:** 2,656
Editor: Wolfgang Cagnolati; **Advertising Manager:** Ines Scholz
Profile: International journal about contact lenses.
Language(s): German
ADVERTISING RATES:
Full Page Mono .... EUR 1790
Full Page Colour .... EUR 2960
Mechanical Data: Type Area: 270 x 188 mm, No. of Columns (Display): 4, Col Widths (Display): 44 mm
Official Journal of: Organ d. Vereinigung Dt. Contactlinsenspezialisten e.V.
BUSINESS: HEALTH & MEDICAL: Optics

KONTUREN
733145G56A-11184
Editorial: Frankfurter Allee 40, 10247 BERLIN
Tel: 30 20687034 **Fax:** 30 20687036
Email: konturen@do-suchthilfe.de **Web site:** http://www.konturen.de
Freq: 6 issues yearly; **Annual Sub.:** EUR 25,50; **Circ:** 4,000
Editor: Beate Bollig
Profile: Drug report, particularly concerned with products related to HIV and AIDS.
Language(s): German
Readership: Aimed at doctors, psychologists and pharmacists.
ADVERTISING RATES:
Full Page Mono .... EUR 770
Full Page Colour .... EUR 1345
Mechanical Data: Type Area: 240 x 176 mm, No. of Columns (Display): 4, Col Widths (Display): 45 mm
Copy instructions: *Copy Date:* 30 days prior to publication
BUSINESS: HEALTH & MEDICAL

DER KONZERN
1665717G14A-9740
Editorial: Luxemburger Str. 449, 50939 KÖLN
Tel: 221 943737080 **Fax:** 221 943737203
Email: der-konzern@heymanns.com **Web site:** http://www.wolterskluwer.de
Freq: Monthly; **Circ:** 650
Editor: Philipp Caspar Kind
Profile: Magazine for entrepreneurs with focus on taxes and economy.
Language(s): German
ADVERTISING RATES:
Full Page Mono .... EUR 850
Full Page Colour .... EUR 1744
Mechanical Data: Type Area: 270 x 186 mm, No. of Columns (Display): 4, Col Widths (Display): 45 mm

KONZERTNEWS
1606262G76D-5961
Editorial: Agnes-Bernauer-Str. 129, 80687 MÜNCHEN **Tel:** 89 6936560 **Fax:** 89 69365656
Email: info@inpunkto-media.de **Web site:** http://www.inpunkto-media.de
Freq: Quarterly; **Cover Price:** Free; **Circ:** 129,765
Editor: Andreas Schessl
Profile: Program preview of Munich concert promoter MünchenMusik.
Language(s): German
ADVERTISING RATES:
Full Page Colour .... EUR 5900
Mechanical Data: Type Area: 262 x 174 mm
CONSUMER: MUSIC & PERFORMING ARTS: Music

KOPF FIT
733171G94H-7220
Editorial: Otto-Hahn-Str. 16, 47608 GELDERN
Tel: 2831 13000 **Fax:** 2831 130020
Email: mail@sud-verlag.de **Web site:** http://www.kopf-fit.com
Freq: Monthly; **Circ:** 155,450
Editor: Ursula Bissinger; **Advertising Manager:** Marcus H. Thielen
Profile: Mind and memory training successfully, that is the final action of the pharmacy customer magazine head-fit. In addition to physical fitness is also the mental agility that is memory-jogging exercises the brain, an effective cure for aging. Maintain the level or new integration of daily life, after severe physical, mental or psychological disorder, by Brain Training, is the alternative way to train alongside their concentration but also the memory and to challenge the mind.
Language(s): German
Readership: Aimed at members of the general public.

ADVERTISING RATES:
Full Page Mono .... EUR 1368
Full Page Colour .... EUR 1932
Mechanical Data: Type Area: 175 x 175 mm
Copy instructions: *Copy Date:* 60 days prior to publication
CONSUMER: OTHER CLASSIFICATIONS: Customer Magazines

KOPO KOMMUNALPOLITISCHE BLÄTTER 733042G82-4860
Editorial: Klingelhöferstr. 8, 10785 BERLIN
Tel: 30 22070471 **Fax:** 30 22070478
Email: g.grabowski@kopo.de **Web site:** http://www.kopo.de
Freq: 11 issues yearly; **Annual Sub.:** EUR 70,80; **Circ:** 7,343
Editor: Gaby Grabowski
Profile: Journal covering national, regional and European political news.
Language(s): German
ADVERTISING RATES:
Full Page Colour .... EUR 3780
Mechanical Data: Type Area: 243 x 180 mm, No. of Columns (Display): 3, Col Widths (Display): 50 mm
Copy instructions: *Copy Date:* 28 days prior to publication
Official Journal of: Organ d. Kommunalpolit. Vereinigung d. CDU/CSU
Supplement(s): Unternehmerin Kommune + Forum Neue Länder
CONSUMER: CURRENT AFFAIRS & POLITICS

KOR 760077G14A-9253
Editorial: Grafenberger Allee 293, 40237 DÜSSELDORF **Tel:** 211 8871448 **Fax:** 211 8872803
Email: kor.redaktion@fachverlag.de **Web site:** http://www.kor-ifrs.de
Freq: 11 issues yearly; **Annual Sub.:** EUR 246,00; **Circ:** 2,657
Editor: Annette Jünger-Fuhr; **Advertising Manager:** Ralf Pötzsch
Profile: Journal with issues of accounting and auditing from the perspective of capital market oriented companies.
Language(s): German
ADVERTISING RATES:
Full Page Mono .... EUR 1710
Full Page Colour .... EUR 1820
Mechanical Data: Type Area: 252 x 178 mm
Copy instructions: *Copy Date:* 15 days prior to publication
BUSINESS: COMMERCE, INDUSTRY & MANAGEMENT

KOREA CONTACT 1881558G14C-4786
Editorial: Ritterstr. 2b, 10969 BERLIN
Tel: 30 61508926 **Fax:** 30 61508927
Email: pt@owc.de **Web site:** http://www.owc.de
Freq: Annual; **Cover Price:** Free; **Circ:** 12,000
Editor: Peter Tichauer; **Advertising Manager:** Norbert Mayer
Profile: Magazine focusing on future business negotiations with Korea. Also contains market analyses and trends.
Language(s): German
ADVERTISING RATES:
Full Page Mono .... EUR 2500
Full Page Colour .... EUR 3200
Mechanical Data: Type Area: 265 x 175 mm

KORNWESTHEIM & KREIS LUDWIGSBURG 1740312G67B-8160_500
Editorial: Rechbergstr. 10, 70806 KORNWESTHEIM
Tel: 7154 13120 **Fax:** 7154 131270
Email: redaktion@kornwestheimer-zeitung.zgs.de
Web site: http://www.kornwestheimer-zeitung.de
Freq: 312 issues yearly; **Circ:** 4,504
Advertising Manager: Daniel Schwarz
Profile: Regional daily newspaper covering politics, economics, sport, travel and technology. Facebook: http://www.facebook.com/stuttgarternachrichten.
Language(s): German
ADVERTISING RATES:
SCC .... EUR 38,00
Mechanical Data: Type Area: 492 x 321 mm, No. of Columns (Display): 7, Col Widths (Display): 44 mm
Copy instructions: *Copy Date:* 1 day prior to publication
Supplement to: Kornwestheimer Zeitung, Stuttgarter Nachrichten, Stuttgarter Zeitung
REGIONAL DAILY & SUNDAY NEWSPAPERS: Regional Daily Newspapers

KORNWESTHEIMER STADT ANZEIGER 733180G72-6288
Editorial: Rechbergstr. 10, 70806 KORNWESTHEIM
Tel: 7154 13120 **Fax:** 7154 131270
Email: redaktion@kornwestheimer-zeitung.zgs.de
Web site: http://www.kornwestheimer-zeitung.de
Freq: Weekly; **Cover Price:** Free; **Circ:** 14,000
Editor: Werner Waldner; **Advertising Manager:** Daniel Schwarz
Profile: Advertising journal (house-to-house) concentrating on local stories.
Language(s): German
ADVERTISING RATES:
Full Page Mono .... EUR 5890
Full Page Colour .... EUR 8714
Mechanical Data: Type Area: 492 x 321 mm, No. of Columns (Display): 7, Col Widths (Display): 45 mm
Copy instructions: *Copy Date:* 2 days prior to publication
LOCAL NEWSPAPERS

KORNWESTHEIMER ZEITUNG 733181G67B-8160
Editorial: Rechbergstr. 10, 70806 KORNWESTHEIM
Tel: 7154 13120 **Fax:** 7154 131270
Email: redaktion@kornwestheimer-zeitung.zgs.de
Web site: http://www.kornwestheimer-zeitung.de
Freq: 312 issues yearly; **Circ:** 43,578
Advertising Manager: Daniel Schwarz
Profile: Daily newspaper with regional news and a local sports section. Facebook: http://www.facebook.com/stuttgarternachrichten.
Language(s): German
ADVERTISING RATES:
SCC .... EUR 397,20
Mechanical Data: Type Area: 492 x 321 mm, No. of Columns (Display): 7, Col Widths (Display): 45 mm
Copy instructions: *Copy Date:* 2 days prior to publication
Supplement(s): Kornwestheim & Kreis Ludwigsburg
REGIONAL DAILY & SUNDAY NEWSPAPERS: Regional Daily Newspapers

KOSMETIK INTERNATIONAL 733191G15A-100
Editorial: Medienplatz 1, 76571 GAGGENAU
Tel: 7225 9160 **Fax:** 7225 916249
Email: redaktion@ki-verlag.de **Web site:** http://www.ki-online.de
Freq: Monthly; **Annual Sub.:** EUR 78,00; **Circ:** 24,947
Editor: Waltraud Ellerich-Minareci; **Advertising Manager:** Christian Schikora
Profile: Journal for cosmetics professionals. The editorial coverage includes the entire range of applied cosmetics (including basic and advanced training), hand and nail care and nail design, pedicure, permanent makeup, spa, Visagismus and color and style analysis. The magazine regularly reports on news and trends in cosmetic research and development and in the fields of medicine and psychology, nutrition and fitness, marketing and trade shows. In addition, the reader current information about companies and associations as well as product innovations. The journal presents a market overview of each issue are presented in the products at a specific focal point: a brief description of products and details of the distribution and source.
Language(s): German
Readership: Aimed at beauticians.
ADVERTISING RATES:
Full Page Mono .... EUR 4370
Full Page Colour .... EUR 4370
Mechanical Data: Type Area: 232 x 165 mm, No. of Columns (Display): 4, Col Widths (Display): 47 mm
Copy instructions: *Copy Date:* 28 days prior to publication
Official Journal of: Organ d. Cosmetica-Fachmessen & akzente
Supplement(s): Ki Kontakt
BUSINESS: COSMETICS & HAIRDRESSING: Cosmetics

KOSMETISCHE MEDIZIN 733194G56A-6120
Editorial: Friedrichstr. 41, 01067 DRESDEN
Tel: 351 4801210 **Fax:** 30 88674999
Email: info@grosse-verlag.de **Web site:** http://www.grosse-verlag.de
Freq: 6 issues yearly; Free to qualifying individuals
Annual Sub.: EUR 95,00; **Circ:** 3,451
Editor: Uwe Wollina; **Advertising Manager:** Antje Himmel
Profile: International magazine focusing on medical cosmetology and dermatology.
Language(s): English; German
Readership: Aimed at dermatologists and surgeons.
ADVERTISING RATES:
Full Page Colour .... EUR 2427
Mechanical Data: Type Area: 235 x 184 mm, No. of Columns (Display): 3, Col Widths (Display): 56 mm
Copy instructions: *Copy Date:* 21 days prior to publication
Official Journal of: Organ d. Österr. Ges. f. dermatolog. Kosmetologie u. Altersforschung, d. Dt. Ges. f. Ästhet. Dermatologie, Vereinigung f. ästhet. Dermatologie u. Laseranwendung, d. Dt. Ges. f. ästhet. Botulinumtoxin-Therapie, ArGe Assoziierter Dermatolog. Inst.'e e.V. u. d. Austrian Academy of Aesthetic Surgery
BUSINESS: HEALTH & MEDICAL

KÖTZTINGER UMSCHAU 732991G67B-8180
Editorial: Margaretenstr. 4, 93047 REGENSBURG
Tel: 941 20765 **Fax:** 941 207142
Email: mz-redaktion@mittelbayerische.de **Web site:** http://www.mittelbayerische.de
Freq: 312 issues yearly; **Circ:** 15,538
Profile: Daily newspaper with regional news and a local sports section.
Language(s): German
ADVERTISING RATES:
SCC .... EUR 40,00
Mechanical Data: Type Area: 430 x 281 mm, No. of Columns (Display): 6, Col Widths (Display): 45 mm
Copy instructions: *Copy Date:* 1 day prior to publication
Supplement(s): Mittelbayerische jun.
REGIONAL DAILY & SUNDAY NEWSPAPERS: Regional Daily Newspapers

KÖTZTINGER ZEITUNG 732992G67B-8200
Editorial: Ludwigsplatz 30, 94315 STRAUBING
Tel: 9421 9404601 **Fax:** 9421 9404609
Email: landkreis@straubinger-tagblatt.de **Web site:** http://www.idowa.de
Freq: 312 issues yearly; **Circ:** 9,205
Advertising Manager: Klaus Huber
Profile: Regional daily newspaper with news on politics, economy, culture, sports, travel, technology, etc. She is a local issue by Straubinger Tagblatt for the old County Kötzting. Twitter: http://twitter.com/idowa This Outlet offers RSS (Really Simple Syndication).
Language(s): German
ADVERTISING RATES:
SCC .... EUR 15,30
Mechanical Data: Type Area: 430 x 282 mm, No. of Columns (Display): 6, Col Widths (Display): 45 mm
Copy instructions: *Copy Date:* 1 day prior to publication
Supplement(s): Zuhause
REGIONAL DAILY & SUNDAY NEWSPAPERS: Regional Daily Newspapers

KQ KUNSTQUARTAL 722326G84A-500
Editorial: Zeppelinstr. 32, 73760 OSTFILDERN
Tel: 711 4405226 **Fax:** 711 4405228
Email: r.palmer@kqkunstquartal.de **Web site:** http://www.kqkunstquartal.de
Freq: Quarterly; **Annual Sub.:** EUR 32,00; **Circ:** 20,000
Editor: Renate Palmer; **Advertising Manager:** Renate Palmer
Profile: International preview of exhibitions and auctions.
Language(s): German
Readership: Aimed at people interested in art and exhibitions.
ADVERTISING RATES:
Full Page Mono .... EUR 700
Full Page Colour .... EUR 1000
Mechanical Data: Type Area: 205 x 115 mm
Copy instructions: *Copy Date:* 40 days prior to publication
CONSUMER: THE ARTS & LITERARY: Arts

KR KREFELD LIFE 765101G50-1185
Editorial: Dießemer Bruch 167, 47805 KREFELD
Tel: 2151 5100126 **Fax:** 2151 5100215
Email: natalie.klein-kutz@stuenings.de **Web site:** http://www.kr-life.de
Freq: Annual; **Cover Price:** EUR 1,50; **Circ:** 20,000
Editor: Nina Multhoff; **Advertising Manager:** Natalie Klein-Kutz
Profile: City and restaurant guides in three languages, 124 pages. Information about city, sightseeing, dining, shopping, culture, sports, business and events for locals and tourists.
Language(s): Dutch; English; German
ADVERTISING RATES:
Full Page Colour .... EUR 818
Mechanical Data: Type Area: 194 x 90 mm, No. of Columns (Display): 2
Copy instructions: *Copy Date:* 30 days prior to publication

KRADBLATT 1643474G77B-27
Editorial: Auf dem Berge 26, 28844 WEYHE
Tel: 421 841330 **Fax:** 421 8092348
Email: redaktion@kradblatt.de **Web site:** http://www.kradblatt.de
Freq: Monthly; **Cover Price:** Free; **Circ:** 20,000
Editor: Berthold Reinken; **Advertising Manager:** Berthold Reinken
Profile: Regional, free motorcycle magazine with event tips and travel reports, which is published monthly in northern Germany. The magazine is free of charge for as plenty of motorcycle and accessory retailers, and at many stations, but can be purchased on a subscription.
Language(s): German
ADVERTISING RATES:
Full Page Mono .... EUR 750
Full Page Colour .... EUR 1275
Mechanical Data: Type Area: 230 x 155 mm, No. of Columns (Display): 3, Col Widths (Display): 48 mm

KRAFTHAND 733226G31A-160
Editorial: Walter-Schulz-Str. 1, 86825 BAD WÖRISHOFEN **Tel:** 8247 300750 **Fax:** 8247 300773
Email: gottfried.karpstein@krafthand.de **Web site:** http://www.krafthand.de
Freq: 20 issues yearly; **Annual Sub.:** EUR 100,00; **Circ:** 22,529
Editor: Gottfried Karpstein; **Advertising Manager:** Klaus Peter Lang
Profile: Technology magazine for free and branded garages. The power goes hand as a guide for automotive entrepreneur and workshop professionals. Editorial Focus: workshop practice, automotive, parts & systems, workshop law, corporate practice.
Language(s): German
Readership: Aimed at personnel interested in the motor trade.
ADVERTISING RATES:
Full Page Mono .... EUR 5220
Full Page Colour .... EUR 6945
Mechanical Data: Type Area: 270 x 187 mm, No. of Columns (Display): 4, Col Widths (Display): 43 mm
BUSINESS: MOTOR TRADE: Motor Trade Accessories

KRAFTSTOFF 1826030G27-3059
Editorial: Allersberger Str. 185/F, 90461 NÜRNBERG
Tel: 911 4804990 **Fax:** 911 48049929
Email: redaktion@kraftstoff-online.com **Web site:** http://www.kraftstoff-online.com
Freq: Half-yearly; **Cover Price:** EUR 6,00; **Circ:** 9,000
Editor: Max Groll; **Advertising Manager:** Max Groll
Profile: Business magazine for car rental companies.
Language(s): German
ADVERTISING RATES:
Full Page Mono .... EUR 2510
Full Page Colour .... EUR 2900
Mechanical Data: Type Area: 277 x 190 mm, No. of Columns (Display): 2, Col Widths (Display): 87 mm
Copy instructions: *Copy Date:* 30 days prior to publication

KRAFTVERKEHRSHANDBUCH 733232G49A-860
Editorial: Aschauer Str. 30, 81549 MÜNCHEN
Tel: 89 2030430 **Fax:** 89 2030432280
Email: mathias.schmidt@springer.com **Web site:** http://www.springer-transport-media.de
Freq: Annual; **Cover Price:** EUR 22,36; **Circ:** 2,000
Editor: Mathias Schmidt
Profile: Magazine on recent laws concerning road transports.
Language(s): German

KRAICHGAU STIMME 733234G67B-8220
Editorial: Allee 2, 74072 HEILBRONN **Tel:** 7131 6150
Fax: 7131 615373
Email: redaktion@stimme.de **Web site:** http://www.stimme.de
Freq: 312 issues yearly; **Circ:** 6,674
Advertising Manager: Martin Kufner
Profile: Daily newspaper with regional news and a local sports section. Once again, the Kraichgau Stimme included in the International Color Quality Club, which puts them among the 50 daily newspapers with the world's best image and print quality. Facebook: http://www.facebook.com/pages/Heilbronner-Stimme/141931462525928 Twitter: http://twitter.com/stimmeonline This Outlet offers RSS (Really Simple Syndication).
Language(s): German
Mechanical Data: Type Area: 490 x 327 mm, No. of Columns (Display): 7, Col Widths (Display): 45 mm
Copy instructions: *Copy Date:* 1 day prior to publication
Supplement(s): autoStimme; sole; WirtschaftsStimme
REGIONAL DAILY & SUNDAY NEWSPAPERS: Regional Daily Newspapers

KRAN & BÜHNE 733255G10-260
Editorial: Sundgauallee 15, 79114 FREIBURG
Tel: 761 8978660 **Fax:** 761 8866814
Email: rk@vertikal.net **Web site:** http://www.vertikal.net
Freq: 8 issues yearly; **Annual Sub.:** EUR 26,00; **Circ:** 8,623
Editor: Rüdiger Kopf; **Advertising Manager:** Karlheinz Kopp
Profile: Magazine for crane operators and working platforms users.
Language(s): German
ADVERTISING RATES:
Full Page Mono .... EUR 2301
Full Page Colour .... EUR 3132
Mechanical Data: Type Area: 268 x 184 mm
Copy instructions: *Copy Date:* 21 days prior to publication
BUSINESS: MATERIALS HANDLING

KRAN & HEBETECHNIK 737421G49A-2356
Editorial: Wilhelm-Giese-Str. 26, 27616 BEVERSTEDT **Tel:** 4747 8741301 **Fax:** 4747 8741222
Email: hpeimann@kran-und-hebetechnik.de **Web site:** http://www.kran-und-hebetechnik.de
Freq: 7 issues yearly; **Annual Sub.:** EUR 30,00; **Circ:** 12,194
Editor: Herbert Peimann; **Advertising Manager:** Frank Stüven
Profile: Magazine on the optimal usage of crane and elevation technology.
Language(s): German
Mechanical Data: Type Area: 250 x 184 mm, No. of Columns (Display): 4, Col Widths (Display): 43 mm
Copy instructions: *Copy Date:* 21 days prior to publication
BUSINESS: TRANSPORT

DAS KRANKENHAUS 733243G56C-6
Editorial: Hansaallee 201, 40549 DÜSSELDORF
Tel: 211 88290910 **Fax:** 211 88290929
Email: peter.ossen@kohlhammer.de **Web site:** http://www.daskrankenhaus.de
Freq: Monthly; **Annual Sub.:** EUR 211,80; **Circ:** 3,319
Editor: Peter Ossen
Profile: Official publication of the Society of German Hospitals.
Language(s): German
ADVERTISING RATES:
Full Page Mono .... EUR 1860
Full Page Colour .... EUR 3210
Mechanical Data: Type Area: 260 x 185 mm, No. of Columns (Display): 2, Col Widths (Display): 90 mm

Copy instructions: *Copy Date:* 20 days prior to publication
BUSINESS: HEALTH & MEDICAL: Hospitals

KRANKENHAUS-HYGIENE + INFEKTIONSVERHÜTUNG
733245G56C-7
Editorial: Siemensstr. 18, 35394 GIESSEN
Tel: 641 9790520 **Fax:** 641 9790534
Email: momberger@iki-giessen.de
Freq: 6 issues yearly; **Annual Sub.:** EUR 103,00; **Circ:** 2,250
Editor: Burkhard Wille
Profile: Magazine about hygiene, sanitation and preventing the spread of infection in hospitals.
Language(s): German
ADVERTISING RATES:
Full Page Mono .... EUR 1600
Full Page Colour .... EUR 2920
Mechanical Data: Type Area: 240 x 175 mm
Official Journal of: Organ d. Vereinigung d. Hygiene-Fachkräfte in d. BRD
BUSINESS: HEALTH & MEDICAL: Hospitals

KRANKENHAUSHYGIENE UP2DATE
1794358G56A-11447
Editorial: Cuno-Niggl-Str. 3, 83278 TRAUNSTEIN
Email: ines.kappstein@klinikum-traunstein.de **Web site:** http://www.thieme.de/fz/krankenhaushygiene-u2d
Freq: Quarterly; **Annual Sub.:** EUR 155,40; **Circ:** 1,250
Editor: Ines Kappstein
Profile: Krankenhaushygiene up2date at a glance: Best Practice of Hospital Hygiene, CME-certified training; Well-researched review articles in an attractive layout.
Language(s): German
ADVERTISING RATES:
Full Page Mono .... EUR 1630
Full Page Colour .... EUR 2800
Mechanical Data: Type Area: 248 x 175 mm

KRANKENHAUSPHARMAZIE
733246G37-1100
Editorial: Birkenwaldstr. 44, 70191 STUTTGART
Tel: 711 2582234 **Fax:** 711 2582283
Email: kph@deutscher-apotheker-verlag.de **Web site:** http://www.krankenhauspharmazie.de
Freq: Monthly; Free to qualifying individuals
Annual Sub.: EUR 295,80; **Circ:** 3,000
Editor: Tanja Liebing; **Advertising Manager:** Kornelia Wind
Profile: Journal of ADKA - the Association of German Hospital Pharmacists.
Language(s): German
Readership: Aimed at pharmacists.
ADVERTISING RATES:
Full Page Mono .... EUR 2292
Full Page Colour .... EUR 3700
Mechanical Data: Type Area: 262 x 182 mm, No. of Columns (Display): 3, Col Widths (Display): 55 mm
Copy instructions: *Copy Date:* 21 days prior to publication
BUSINESS: PHARMACEUTICAL & CHEMISTS

KRANKENPFLEGE JOURNAL
733251G56B-1648
Editorial: Birkenstr. 13, 89257 ILLERTISSEN
Tel: 7303 910030 **Fax:** 7303 5299
Email: redaktion@krankenpflege-journal.de **Web site:** http://www.krankenpflege-journal.com
Freq: 10 issues yearly; **Annual Sub.:** EUR 32,00; **Circ:** 23,760
Editor: Thomas Backe
Profile: Information on health and aged care, healthcare, pharmaceutical, utilities, medical devices.
Language(s): German
ADVERTISING RATES:
Full Page Mono .... EUR 2500
Full Page Colour .... EUR 4300
Mechanical Data: Type Area: 270 x 185 mm, No. of Columns (Display): 2, Col Widths (Display): 90 mm
Copy instructions: *Copy Date:* 14 days prior to publication
BUSINESS: HEALTH & MEDICAL: Nursing

KRAUT&RÜBEN
733257G93-680
Editorial: Lothstr. 29, 80797 MÜNCHEN
Tel: 89 127051 **Fax:** 89 12705354
Email: redkraut-u-rueben@dlv.de **Web site:** http://www.krautundrueben.de
Freq: Monthly; **Annual Sub.:** EUR 55,50; **Circ:** 87,839
Editor: Ulrike Schäfner; **Advertising Manager:** Thomas Herrmann
Profile: "kraut&rüben" is the magazine for the environmentally conscious gardening and planting reader. "Natural " is the philosophy of life (lifestyle) for garden, work, home and leisure. "kraut&rüben" represents this lifestyle in the course of time, for over 25 years, contemporary and in a unique style. "kraut&rüben" provides ideas for the active" green leisure activity ", the nature-based design of ornamental and vegetable gardens, healthy, natural, organic food and environmentally conscious lifestyle. Adventure, fun, learning and dealing with a natural (organic)-oriented environment are at the forefront. "kraut&rüben" corresponds with the change in environmental awareness, the high interest in organic gardening and natural living.
Language(s): German
ADVERTISING RATES:
Full Page Mono .... EUR 5211
Full Page Colour .... EUR 8528
Mechanical Data: Type Area: 252 x 184 mm, No. of Columns (Display): 4, Col Widths (Display): 43 mm
Copy instructions: *Copy Date:* 42 days prior to publication
CONSUMER: GARDENING

KREATIV MAGAZIN
741245G74A-3319
Editorial: Im Buhles 4, 61479 SCHLOSSBORN
Tel: 6174 9994000 **Fax:** 6174 9994099
Email: mailbox@logikpark.de **Web site:** http://www.logikpark.de
Freq: 9 issues yearly; **Cover Price:** Free; **Circ:** 70,802
Editor: Peter Pfeiffer; **Advertising Manager:** Frank Krauthäuser
Profile: Magazine providing advice and information to promote a healthier lifestyle, including tips on diet and exercise.
Language(s): German
Readership: Aimed at slimmers and the health conscious.
ADVERTISING RATES:
Full Page Mono .... EUR 2900
Full Page Colour .... EUR 2900
Mechanical Data: Type Area: 250 x 185 mm, No. of Columns (Display): 4, Col Widths (Display): 44 mm
Copy instructions: *Copy Date:* 36 days prior to publication
CONSUMER: WOMEN'S INTEREST CONSUMER MAGAZINES: Women's Interest

KREDIT UND KAPITAL
733264G1G-19
Editorial: Simrockstr. 4, 53113 BONN
Tel: 228 2045758 **Fax:** 228 2045735
Email: redaktion.kredit-und-kapital@dsgv.de **Web site:** http://www.kredit-und-kapital.de
Freq: Quarterly; **Annual Sub.:** EUR 88,00; **Circ:** 600
Advertising Manager: Arlett Günther
Profile: Publication focusing on monetary economics and finance.
Language(s): English; German
Readership: Read by financial advisors and bankers.
ADVERTISING RATES:
Full Page Mono .... EUR 550
Mechanical Data: Type Area: 185 x 115 mm
BUSINESS: FINANCE & ECONOMICS: Credit Trading

KREIS-ANZEIGER
733272G67B-8260
Editorial: Zeppelinstr. 11, 63667 NIDDA
Tel: 6043 5020 **Fax:** 6043 50220
Email: redaktion@kreis-anzeiger.de **Web site:** http://www.kreis-anzeiger.de
Freq: 312 issues yearly; **Circ:** 13,136
Advertising Manager: Aline Cloos
Profile: Daily newspaper with regional news and a local sports section. This Outlet offers RSS (Really Simple Syndication).
Language(s): German
ADVERTISING RATES:
SCC .... EUR 30,60
Mechanical Data: Type Area: 430 x 278 mm, No. of Columns (Display): 6, Col Widths (Display): 45 mm
Copy instructions: *Copy Date:* 1 day prior to publication
REGIONAL DAILY & SUNDAY NEWSPAPERS: Regional Daily Newspapers

KREIS-ANZEIGER
733269G72-6320
Editorial: Gabelsbergerstr. 1, 89407 DILLINGEN
Tel: 9071 79360 **Fax:** 9071 793650
Email: verlag@kreisanzeiger.de **Web site:** http://www.kreisanzeiger.de
Freq: Weekly; **Cover Price:** Free; **Circ:** 40,397
Editor: Udo Skwara; **Advertising Manager:** Brigitte Musselmann
Profile: Advertising journal (house-to-house) concentrating on local stories.
Language(s): German
ADVERTISING RATES:
Full Page Mono .... EUR 1659
Full Page Colour .... EUR 2157
Mechanical Data: Type Area: 326 x 233 mm, No. of Columns (Display): 5, Col Widths (Display): 45 mm
Copy instructions: *Copy Date:* 4 days prior to publication
LOCAL NEWSPAPERS

KREISBOTE WEILHEIM-SCHONGAU
733281G72-6348
Editorial: Am Weidenbach 8, 82362 WEILHEIM
Tel: 881 68616 **Fax:** 881 68653
Email: redaktion-wm@kreisbote.de **Web site:** http://www.kreisbote.de
Freq: Weekly; **Cover Price:** Free; **Circ:** 45,222
Editor: Maria Hofstetter; **Advertising Manager:** Helmut Ernst
Profile: Advertising journal (house-to-house) concentrating on local stories.
Language(s): German
ADVERTISING RATES:
Full Page Mono .... EUR 4247
Full Page Colour .... EUR 5521
Mechanical Data: Type Area: 474 x 324 mm, No. of Columns (Display): 7, Col Widths (Display): 45 mm
Copy instructions: *Copy Date:* 2 days prior to publication
LOCAL NEWSPAPERS

KREISSTADT ECHO
733300G72-6396
Editorial: Hauptstr. 68, 65719 HOFHEIM
Tel: 6192 902607 **Fax:** 6192 23120
Email: hz-redaktion@vrm.de **Web site:** http://www.hofheimer-zeitung.de
Freq: Weekly; **Cover Price:** Free; **Circ:** 23,580
Editor: Kirsten Weber
Profile: Advertising journal (house-to-house) concentrating on local stories.
Language(s): German
ADVERTISING RATES:
Full Page Mono .... EUR 3663
Full Page Colour .... EUR 5880
Mechanical Data: Type Area: 480 x 325 mm, No. of Columns (Display): 7, Col Widths (Display): 45 mm
Copy instructions: *Copy Date:* 1 day prior to publication
LOCAL NEWSPAPERS

KREISZEITUNG
733304G67B-8360
Editorial: Bahnhofstr. 27, 71034 BÖBLINGEN
Tel: 7031 620030 **Fax:** 7031 227443
Email: krz@bb-live.de **Web site:** http://www.bb-live.de
Freq: 312 issues yearly; **Circ:** 16,769
Editor: Otto Kühnle; **Advertising Manager:** Georg Schwenk
Profile: Daily newspaper with regional news and a local sports section. Facebook: http://www.facebook.com/pages/bb-live-KREISZEITUNG-Boblinger-Bote/357599107961.
Language(s): German
ADVERTISING RATES:
SCC .... EUR 40,20
Mechanical Data: Type Area: 485 x 324 mm, No. of Columns (Display): 7, Col Widths (Display): 45 mm
Copy instructions: *Copy Date:* 1 day prior to publication
REGIONAL DAILY & SUNDAY NEWSPAPERS: Regional Daily Newspapers

KREISZEITUNG
733305G67B-8380
Editorial: Am Ristedter Weg 17, 28857 SYKE
Tel: 4242 58300 **Fax:** 4242 58332
Email: redaktion@kreiszeitung.de **Web site:** http://www.kreiszeitung.de
Freq: 312 issues yearly; **Circ:** 27,799
Editor: Hans Willms; **News Editor:** Gregor Diekmann; **Advertising Manager:** Axel Berghoff
Profile: The Kreiszeitung publishing group is the fifth largest newspaper in Niedersachsen, with a daily circulation of over 82,000 copies. Regional daily newspaper covering politics, economics, sport, travel and technology. Facebook: http://www.facebook.com/pages/Kreiszeitung This Outlet offers RSS (Really Simple Syndication).
Language(s): German
ADVERTISING RATES:
SCC .... EUR 69,60
Mechanical Data: Type Area: 472 x 325 mm, No. of Columns (Display): 7, Col Widths (Display): 45 mm
Copy instructions: *Copy Date:* 1 day prior to publication
REGIONAL DAILY & SUNDAY NEWSPAPERS: Regional Daily Newspapers

KREISZEITUNG ELBE GEEST WOCHENBLATT
733306G72-6400
Editorial: Von-Somnitz-Ring 4a, 21423 WINSEN
Tel: 4171 88110 **Fax:** 4171 881133
Email: red-buch@kreiszeitung-wochenblatt.de **Web site:** http://www.kreiszeitung-wochenblatt.de
Freq: Weekly; **Cover Price:** Free; **Circ:** 49,400
Editor: Reinhard Schrader; **Advertising Manager:** Ingo Schnackenbeck
Profile: Advertising journal (house-to-house) concentrating on local stories.
Language(s): German
ADVERTISING RATES:
Full Page Mono .... EUR 4092
Full Page Colour .... EUR 4387
Mechanical Data: Type Area: 440 x 285 mm, No. of Columns (Display): 6, Col Widths (Display): 45 mm
Copy instructions: *Copy Date:* 2 days prior to publication
LOCAL NEWSPAPERS

KREISZEITUNG NEUE BUXTEHUDER WOCHENBLATT
733308G72-6404
Editorial: Bahnhofstr. 46, 21614 BUXTEHUDE
Tel: 4161 506326 **Fax:** 4161 506333
Email: red-bux@kreiszeitung.net **Web site:** http://www.kreiszeitung.net
Freq: Weekly; **Cover Price:** Free; **Circ:** 51,400
Editor: Reinhard Schrader; **Advertising Manager:** Christoph Kunst
Profile: Advertising journal (house-to-house) concentrating on local stories.
Language(s): German
ADVERTISING RATES:
Full Page Mono .... EUR 4092
Full Page Colour .... EUR 4387
Mechanical Data: Type Area: 440 x 280 mm, No. of Columns (Display): 6, Col Widths (Display): 45 mm
Copy instructions: *Copy Date:* 2 days prior to publication
LOCAL NEWSPAPERS

KREISZEITUNG NEUE STADER WOCHENBLATT
733309G72-6408
Editorial: Hinterm Hagedorn 4, 21682 STADE
Tel: 4141 40950 **Fax:** 4141 409533
Email: red-bux@kreiszeitung.net **Web site:** http://www.kreiszeitung.net
Freq: Weekly; **Cover Price:** Free; **Circ:** 47,650
Editor: Reinhard Schrader; **Advertising Manager:** Christoph Kunst
Profile: Advertising journal (house-to-house) concentrating on local stories.
Language(s): German
ADVERTISING RATES:
Full Page Mono .... EUR 4092
Full Page Colour .... EUR 4387
Mechanical Data: Type Area: 440 x 280 mm, No. of Columns (Display): 6, Col Widths (Display): 45 mm
Copy instructions: *Copy Date:* 2 days prior to publication
LOCAL NEWSPAPERS

KREISZEITUNG NORDHEIDE/ ELBE&GEEST WOCHENBLATT ZUM WOCHENENDE
733310G72-6416
Editorial: Bendestorfer Str. 3, 21244 BUCHHOLZ
Tel: 4181 200350 **Fax:** 4181 200355
Email: red-buch@kreiszeitung-wochenblatt.de **Web site:** http://www.kreiszeitung-wochenblatt.de
Freq: Weekly; **Cover Price:** Free; **Circ:** 102,000
Editor: Reinhard Schrader; **Advertising Manager:** Martin R. Roesnick
Profile: Advertising journal (house-to-house) concentrating on local stories.
Language(s): German
ADVERTISING RATES:
Full Page Mono .... EUR 6336
Full Page Colour .... EUR 6926
Mechanical Data: Type Area: 440 x 285 mm, No. of Columns (Display): 6, Col Widths (Display): 45 mm
Copy instructions: *Copy Date:* 2 days prior to publication
LOCAL NEWSPAPERS

KREISZEITUNG WESERMARSCH
733312G67B-8400
Editorial: Bahnhofstr. 36, 26954 NORDENHAM
Tel: 4731 943110 **Fax:** 4731 943101
Email: nordenham.redaktion@kreiszeitung-wesermarsch.de **Web site:** http://www.kreiszeitung-wesermarsch.de
Freq: 312 issues yearly; **Circ:** 6,723
Advertising Manager: Matthias Ditzen-Blanke
Profile: Daily newspaper with regional news and a local sports section.
Language(s): German
ADVERTISING RATES:
SCC .... EUR 27,90
Mechanical Data: Type Area: 487 x 324 mm, No. of Columns (Display): 7, Col Widths (Display): 45 mm
Copy instructions: *Copy Date:* 1 day prior to publication
Supplement(s): Bäderzeitung; Ferienjournal; Wesermarsch magazin
REGIONAL DAILY & SUNDAY NEWSPAPERS: Regional Daily Newspapers

KRESS KÖPFE
1859113G2A-5783
Editorial: Wieblinger Weg 17, 69123 HEIDELBERG
Tel: 6221 33100 **Fax:** 6221 3310222
Email: office@kress.de **Web site:** http://www.kress.de
Freq: Annual; **Annual Sub.:** EUR 61,50; **Circ:** 3,000
Advertising Manager: Anke Graewer
Profile: Journal covering communications and marketing. Facebook: http://www.facebook.com/pages/kress/224519924203.
Language(s): German
ADVERTISING RATES:
Full Page Mono .... EUR 2600
Full Page Colour .... EUR 2600
Mechanical Data: Type Area: 240 x 170 mm

KRESS REPORT
733316G2A-2300
Editorial: Wieblinger Weg 17, 69123 HEIDELBERG
Tel: 6221 3310231 **Fax:** 6221 3310299
Email: eckhard.mueller@kress.de **Web site:** http://www.kress.de
Freq: 25 issues yearly; **Annual Sub.:** EUR 414,00; **Circ:** 2,475
Editor: Eckhard Müller; **Advertising Manager:** Milosz Lipski
Profile: The kressreport reported as a professional companion for professionals on current events, people and key figures from the media and communications industry. The main topics of the magazine are printed media, TV, radio, internet, mobile, advertising and PR. Readers of the reports are kress top decision-makers and media strategists in media, marketing departments and agencies.
Language(s): German
Readership: Read by people in the marketing industry.
ADVERTISING RATES:
Full Page Mono .... EUR 2950
Full Page Colour .... EUR 2950
Mechanical Data: Type Area: 240 x 180 mm, No. of Columns (Display): 3, Col Widths (Display): 60 mm
Copy instructions: *Copy Date:* 7 days prior to publication
BUSINESS: COMMUNICATIONS, ADVERTISING & MARKETING

KRESS.DE 1621609G2A-5458

Editorial: Wieblinger Weg 17, 69123 HEIDELBERG
Tel: 6221 3310201 **Fax:** 6221 3310299
Email: post@kress.de **Web site:** http://www.kress.de
Freq: Daily; **Cover Price:** Paid; **Circ:** 974,864 Unique Users
Editor: Eckhard Müller; **Advertising Manager:** Lutz Nahold
Profile: Ezine: Information Service of the communications industry - with news from print media, TV & Radio Industry, Internet & digital world, advertising and public relations scene Facebook: http://www.facebook.com/pages/kress/224519924203 Twitter: http://twitter.com/#!/kressZwitscher This Outlet offers RSS (Really Simple Syndication).
Language(s): German
BUSINESS: COMMUNICATIONS, ADVERTISING & MARKETING

KRESSTHEMA LUXUS 1659615G2A-5569

Editorial: Wieblinger Weg 17, 69123 HEIDELBERG
Tel: 6221 3310231 **Fax:** 6221 3310299
Email: eckhard.mueller@kress.de **Web site:** http://www.kress.de
Freq: Annual; **Cover Price:** EUR 8,50; **Circ:** 2,580
Editor: Eckhard Müller; **Advertising Manager:** Anke Graewer
Profile: Magazine about people, companies and concepts dealing with luxury goods. Facebook: http://www.facebook.com/pages/kress/224519924203.
Language(s): German
Mechanical Data: Type Area: 240 x 180 mm

KREUZER 733318G80-6460

Editorial: Brühl 54, 04109 LEIPZIG **Tel:** 341 2698020
Fax: 341 2698088
Email: chefredaktion@kreuzer-leipzig.de **Web site:** http://www.kreuzer-leipzig.de
Freq: Monthly; **Annual Sub.:** EUR 27,00; **Circ:** 10,589
Editor: Robert Schimke; **Advertising Manager:** Egbert Pietsch
Profile: Illustrated magazine for the city of Leipzig.
Language(s): German
ADVERTISING RATES:
Full Page Mono .... EUR 1990
Full Page Colour .... EUR 1990
Mechanical Data: Type Area: 260 x 190 mm, No. of Columns (Display): 6, Col Widths (Display): 30 mm
Copy instructions: *Copy Date:* 18 days prior to publication
Supplement(s): dok.ma; Jolle; :logbuch; u:boot
CONSUMER: RURAL & REGIONAL INTEREST

KREUZFAHRT-ZEITUNG 1895933G89A-12455

Editorial: Dielingerstr. 1, 49074 OSNABRÜCK
Tel: 2571 957784
Email: redaktion@kreuzfahrt-zeitung.de **Web site:** http://www.kreuzfahrt-zeitung.de
Freq: Quarterly; **Annual Sub.:** EUR 10,00; **Circ:** 350,000
Editor: Silvia Rütter; **Advertising Manager:** Thomas Rolf
Profile: Information lovers and newcomers to Exclusive Cruises Facebook: http://www.facebook.com/kreuzfahrtzeitung This Outlet offers RSS (Really Simple Syndication).
Language(s): German
ADVERTISING RATES:
Full Page Mono .... EUR 13900
Full Page Colour .... EUR 13900
Mechanical Data: Type Area: 294 x 226 mm
Copy instructions: *Copy Date:* 21 days prior to publication

DER KRIMINALIST 733335G44-3121

Editorial: Zur Stumpfen Eiche 5, 51580 REICHSHOF
Tel: 2261 56470 **Fax:** 2261 56473
Email: der.kriminalist@bdk.de **Web site:** http://www.bdk.de
Freq: 11 issues yearly; Free to qualifying individuals
Annual Sub.: EUR 45,00; **Circ:** 16,778
Editor: Rolf Rainer Jäger
Profile: Magazine for members of the West German Criminologists Organisation. Facebook: http://www.facebook.com/pages/BDK-Bund-Deutscher-Kriminalbeamter/113719188109.
Language(s): German
ADVERTISING RATES:
Full Page Mono .... EUR 2230
Full Page Colour .... EUR 3640
Mechanical Data: Type Area: 270 x 185 mm, No. of Columns (Display): 3, Col Widths (Display): 59 mm
Copy instructions: *Copy Date:* 28 days prior to publication
BUSINESS: LEGAL

KRIMINALISTIK 733336G44-3122

Editorial: Römerstr. 2, 69115 HEIDELBERG
Tel: 6221 991000 **Fax:** 3212 8947908
Email: kriminalistik@gmx.de **Web site:** http://www.kriminalistik.de
Freq: 11 issues yearly; **Annual Sub.:** EUR 172,95; **Circ:** 1,800
Editor: Bernd Fuchs; **Advertising Manager:** Isabell Henze
Profile: Magazine focusing on the science, theory and practice of criminology and criminalistics.
Language(s): German
Readership: Aimed at managers in the police force, criminology students, lecturers, lawyers, judges and public prosecutors.
ADVERTISING RATES:
Full Page Mono .... EUR 1300
Full Page Colour .... EUR 1800
Mechanical Data: Type Area: 257 x 178 mm, No. of Columns (Display): 2, Col Widths (Display): 86 mm
BUSINESS: LEGAL

KRITISCHE JUSTIZ 733346G44-1400

Editorial: Große Scharrnstr. 59, 15230 FRANKFURT/ODER **Tel:** 335 55342777 **Fax:** 335 55342779
Email: kj-redaktion@europa-uni.de **Web site:** http://www.kj-online.de
Freq: Quarterly; **Annual Sub.:** EUR 78,31; **Circ:** 1,800
Editor: Eva Kocher
Profile: Journal containing essays, reports and comment on all contemporary legal matters.
Language(s): German
ADVERTISING RATES:
Full Page Mono .... EUR 900
Full Page Colour .... EUR 2025
Mechanical Data: Type Area: 215 x 137 mm
BUSINESS: LEGAL

KRV DIE KRANKENVERSICHERUNG 733253G1D-445

Editorial: Holsteinische Str. 16, 10717 BERLIN
Email: joachim.odenbach@googlemail.com **Web site:** http://www.krvdigital.de
Freq: Monthly; **Annual Sub.:** EUR 106,40; **Circ:** 1,200
Editor: Joachim Odenbach; **Advertising Manager:** Peter Taprogge
Profile: Journal covering all matters relating to health insurance.
Language(s): German
ADVERTISING RATES:
Full Page Mono .... EUR 1300
Full Page Colour .... EUR 2200
Mechanical Data: Type Area: 262 x 172 mm
BUSINESS: FINANCE & ECONOMICS: Insurance

KSA KINDERSCHUTZ AKTUELL 733357G32G-1500

Editorial: Hainhölzer Str. 13, 30159 HANNOVER
Tel: 511 6461633
Email: ksa-redaktion@duesenberg-kontext.de **Web site:** http://www.kinderschutzbund.de
Freq: Quarterly; **Circ:** 50,000
Editor: Swaantje Düsenberg
Profile: Magazine containing information about lobbying for children's rights, care and protection.
Language(s): German
BUSINESS: LOCAL GOVERNMENT, LEISURE & RECREATION: Community Care & Social Services

KSTA.DE KÖLNER STADT-ANZEIGER 1621596G67B-16585

Editorial: Amsterdamer Str. 192, 50735 KÖLN
Tel: 221 2240 **Fax:** 221 2242524
Email: online@ksta.de **Web site:** http://www.ksta.de
Freq: Daily; **Cover Price:** Paid; **Circ:** 4,381,480 Unique Users
Editor: Peter Pauls; **News Editor:** Wolfgang Brüser; **Advertising Manager:** Susanne Diessner
Profile: The Internet portal of the regional newspaper Kölner Stadt-Anzeiger offers news from Cologne and the region as well as information from the political, economic, panorama, culture, debate, cars, travel, technology, campus, health, magazine and youth. Facebook: http://www.facebook.com/pages/KSTA/141063022950 Twitter: http://twitter.com/ksta_news This Outlet offers RSS (Really Simple Syndication).
Language(s): German
REGIONAL DAILY & SUNDAY NEWSPAPERS: Regional Daily Newspapers

KTM KRANKENHAUS TECHNIK + MANAGEMENT 733248G56C-9

Editorial: Keltenstr. 3, 86343 KÖNIGSBRUNN
Tel: 8231 9574666 **Fax:** 8231 9574668
Email: ktm-redaktion@pn-verlag.de **Web site:** http://www.ktm-journal.de
Freq: 10 issues yearly; Free to qualifying individuals
Annual Sub.: EUR 80,00; **Circ:** 10,045
Editor: Eugen Mühlberger; **Advertising Manager:** Claudia Langlinderer
Profile: Publication focusing on hospital and medical technology.
Language(s): German
ADVERTISING RATES:
Full Page Mono .... EUR 3080
Full Page Colour .... EUR 4370
Mechanical Data: Type Area: 265 x 175 mm, No. of Columns (Display): 3, Col Widths (Display): 55 mm
Copy instructions: *Copy Date:* 22 days prior to publication
Official Journal of: Organ d. Fachverb. Biomedizin. Technik e.V.
BUSINESS: HEALTH & MEDICAL: Hospitals

KU GESUNDHEITSMANAGEMENT 733249G56C-10

Editorial: E.-C.-Baumann-Str. 5, 95326 KULMBACH
Tel: 9221 949310 **Fax:** 9221 949377
Email: d.schuette@mg-oberfranken.de **Web site:** http://www.ku-gesundheitsmanagement.de
Freq: Monthly; **Annual Sub.:** EUR 205,00; **Circ:** 4,995
Editor: Daniela Schütte; **Advertising Manager:** Alexander Schiffauer
Profile: Magazine about all aspects of hospital management.
Language(s): German
Readership: Read by clinicians.
ADVERTISING RATES:
Full Page Mono .... EUR 2360
Full Page Colour .... EUR 3580
Mechanical Data: Type Area: 264 x 186 mm, No. of Columns (Display): 4, Col Widths (Display): 45 mm
Copy instructions: *Copy Date:* 18 days prior to publication
Official Journal of: Organ d. Verb. d. Krankenhausdirektoren Deutschlands u. d. Dt. Ges. d. Ärzte im Krankenhausmanagement e.V.
BUSINESS: HEALTH & MEDICAL: Hospitals

KU GESUNDHEITSMANAGEMENT 1704538G56R-11326

Editorial: E.-C.-Baumann-Str. 5, 95326 KULMBACH
Tel: 9221 949393 **Fax:** 9221 949377
Email: bfv@mg-oberfranken.de **Web site:** http://www.ku-gesundheitsmanagement.de
Cover Price: Paid; **Circ:** 14,328 Unique Users
Editor: Angelika Volk; **Advertising Manager:** Alexander Schiffauer
Profile: Ezine: Magazine about all aspects of hospital management.
Language(s): German
BUSINESS: HEALTH & MEDICAL: Health Medical Related

KÜCHE 733369G11A-960

Editorial: Brembach 5a, 36129 GERSFELD
Tel: 6654 919230 **Fax:** 6654 919231
Email: s.romeis@t-online.de **Web site:** http://www.kueche-magazin.de
Freq: Monthly; Free to qualifying individuals
Annual Sub.: EUR 74,90; **Circ:** 17,609
Editor: Sabine Romeis; **Advertising Manager:** Rachid Attaoua
Profile: Magazine containing information relating to the catering industry.
Language(s): German
ADVERTISING RATES:
Full Page Mono .... EUR 5071
Full Page Colour .... EUR 7125
Mechanical Data: Type Area: 256 x 186 mm, No. of Columns (Display): 4, Col Widths (Display): 43 mm
Copy instructions: *Copy Date:* 28 days prior to publication
BUSINESS: CATERING: Catering, Hotels & Restaurants

KÜCHE & BAD FORUM 733376G23C-180

Editorial: Andernacher Str. 5a, 90411 NÜRNBERG
Tel: 911 9557860 **Fax:** 911 9557811
Email: redaktion@ritthammer-verlag.de **Web site:** http://www.kuecheundbadforum.de
Freq: Monthly; **Annual Sub.:** EUR 60,00; **Circ:** 12,282
Editor: Helmut Merkel; **Advertising Manager:** Andreas Müller-Buck
Profile: Magazine on kitchen and bathroom furniture with information about events and innovations.
Language(s): German
ADVERTISING RATES:
Full Page Mono .... EUR 4330
Full Page Colour .... EUR 5950
Mechanical Data: Type Area: 275 x 196 mm, No. of Columns (Display): 4, Col Widths (Display): 46 mm
Official Journal of: Organ d. Verb. d. dt. Küchenmöbelindustrie, d. dt. Möbelindustrie e.V., d. Hauptverb. d. dt. Holzindustrie u. d. Kunststoffe verarbeitenden Industrie u. verwandter Industriezweige e.V.
Supplement to: Möbelmarkt
BUSINESS: FURNISHINGS & FURNITURE: Furnishings & Furniture - Kitchens & Bathrooms

KÜCHEN HANDEL 733370G23C-200

Editorial: Rotländerweg 13, 59846 SUNDERN
Tel: 2933 5071 **Fax:** 2933 7400
Email: willach@interieur-verlag.de **Web site:** http://www.kuechenhandel-online.de
Freq: 6 issues yearly; **Annual Sub.:** EUR 53,00; **Circ:** 4,500
Editor: Stefanie Willach; **Advertising Manager:** Matthias Brünnich
Profile: Magazine with information on kitchen furniture and household appliances.
Language(s): German
Readership: Read by kitchen retailers.
ADVERTISING RATES:
Full Page Mono .... EUR 2600
Full Page Colour .... EUR 4040
Mechanical Data: Type Area: 258 x 176 mm, No. of Columns (Display): 3, Col Widths (Display): 56 mm
Copy instructions: *Copy Date:* 20 days prior to publication
BUSINESS: FURNISHINGS & FURNITURE: Furnishings & Furniture - Kitchens & Bathrooms

KÜCHEN NEWS 733371G23C-220

Editorial: Rotländerweg 13, 59846 SUNDERN
Tel: 2933 5071 **Fax:** 2933 7400
Email: willach@interieur-verlag.de **Web site:** http://www.kuechennews.de
Freq: 22 issues yearly; **Annual Sub.:** EUR 155,23; **Circ:** 1,300
Editor: Stefanie Willach; **Advertising Manager:** Matthias Brünnich
Profile: Magazine focusing on the kitchen equipment trade. Twitter: https://twitter.com/#!/kuechennews This Outlet offers RSS (Really Simple Syndication).
Language(s): German
ADVERTISING RATES:
Full Page Mono .... EUR 660
Full Page Colour .... EUR 1000
Mechanical Data: No. of Columns (Display): 3, Col Widths (Display): 58 mm, Type Area: 230 x 190 mm
Copy instructions: *Copy Date:* 3 days prior to publication
BUSINESS: FURNISHINGS & FURNITURE: Furnishings & Furniture - Kitchens & Bathrooms

DER KÜCHENPLANER 733372G23C-240

Editorial: Hegede 17, 33617 BIELEFELD
Tel: 521 139413 **Fax:** 521 139430
Email: d.biermann@strobel-verlag.de **Web site:** http://www.kuechenplaner-magazin.de
Freq: 8 issues yearly; **Annual Sub.:** EUR 53,70; **Circ:** 6,047
Editor: Dirk Biermann; **Advertising Manager:** Stefan Schütte
Profile: Magazine about kitchen design and installation.
Language(s): German
Readership: Aimed at kitchen designers, fitters and manufacturers.
ADVERTISING RATES:
Full Page Mono .... EUR 3364
Full Page Colour .... EUR 4661
Mechanical Data: Type Area: 265 x 184 mm, No. of Columns (Display): 4, Col Widths (Display): 43 mm
BUSINESS: FURNISHINGS & FURNITURE: Furnishings & Furniture - Kitchens & Bathrooms

DER KÜCHENPROFI 733373G23C-485

Editorial: Weidestr. 120a, 22083 HAMBURG
Tel: 40 63201847 **Fax:** 40 6307510
Email: heike.lorenz@holzmann.de **Web site:** http://www.derkuechenprofi.de
Freq: 3 issues yearly; **Annual Sub.:** EUR 13,80; **Circ:** 10,617
Editor: Heike Lorenz; **Advertising Manager:** Anke Zimmer
Profile: Magazine about kitchen installations and equipment. Facebook: http://www.facebook.com/pages/mobel-kultur/124172594286549.
Language(s): German
ADVERTISING RATES:
Full Page Mono .... EUR 4560
Full Page Colour .... EUR 6180
Mechanical Data: Type Area: 263 x 180 mm, No. of Columns (Display): 4, Col Widths (Display): 42 mm
Copy instructions: *Copy Date:* 28 days prior to publication
BUSINESS: FURNISHINGS & FURNITURE: Furnishings & Furniture - Kitchens & Bathrooms

KULT AM PULT 733403G41B-10

Editorial: Fasanenweg 18, 70771 LEINFELDEN-ECHTERDINGEN **Tel:** 711 7591305
Fax: 711 75913775
Email: rtimter@bitverlag.de **Web site:** http://www.kultampult.de
Freq: Quarterly; **Annual Sub.:** EUR 18,00; **Circ:** 6,084
Editor: Reiner Timter; **Advertising Manager:** Joachim Ahnfeldt
Profile: Journal of the nicest aspects of writing. It informed about news from the world of high-quality writing instruments and office accessories. But KULT AM PULT is more than just a pen or paper journal: Cities reports tell you interesting things about cities from the perspective of art and (write) culture lover. Interesting interviews with contemporaries of Trade and Industry provide personal perspectives on office culture. Reports of collections and exhibitions around the issues paper, writing and editorial offices are also part of the spectrum, such as time signature of the focal points of industry events: fairs, collectors meetings and discussion forums. Last but not least, are examples of successful store design, the manufacturer reports, sales and customer goods an essential part of reporting.
Language(s): German
ADVERTISING RATES:
Full Page Mono .... EUR 2860
Full Page Colour .... EUR 4180
Mechanical Data: Type Area: 242 x 172 mm, No. of Columns (Display): 3, Col Widths (Display): 57 mm
Copy instructions: *Copy Date:* 27 days prior to publication
BUSINESS: PRINTING & STATIONERY: Stationery

KULTUR POLITIK 733463G84A-1560

Editorial: Weberstr. 61, 53113 BONN
Tel: 228 216107 **Fax:** 228 96699690
Email: info@bbk-bundesverband.de **Web site:** http://www.bbk-bundesverband.de
Freq: Quarterly; Free to qualifying individuals
Annual Sub.: EUR 13,00; **Circ:** 13,200
Editor: Werner Schaub; **Advertising Manager:** Ursula Cramer
Profile: Art and culture magazine.
Language(s): German
Readership: Aimed at people interested in the arts and culture.

ADVERTISING RATES:
Full Page Mono .... EUR 696
Mechanical Data: Type Area: 260 x 185 mm, No. of Columns (Display): 3, Col Widths (Display): 58 mm
Copy instructions: *Copy Date:* 40 days prior to publication
CONSUMER: THE ARTS & LITERARY: Arts

KULTUR & TECHNIK 733503G64P-11
Editorial: Gistlstr. 63, 82049 PULLACH
Tel: 89 12116712 **Fax:** 89 12116727
Email: landes@folio-muc.de
Freq: Quarterly; Free to qualifying individuals
Annual Sub.: EUR 29,30; **Circ:** 18,600
Editor: Sabrina Landes; **Advertising Manager:** Fritz Lebherz
Profile: Journal of the German Museum in Munich.
Language(s): German
ADVERTISING RATES:
Full Page Mono .... EUR 1900
Full Page Colour .... EUR 1900
Mechanical Data: Type Area: 242 x 187 mm, No. of Columns (Display): 3, Col Widths (Display): 59 mm
BUSINESS: OTHER CLASSIFICATIONS: Museums

KULTURNEWS 733456G80-6620
Editorial: Friedensallee 7, 22765 HAMBURG
Tel: 40 3808976 **Fax:** 40 38089773
Email: redaktion@bunkverlag.de **Web site:** http://www.kulturnews.de
Freq: Monthly; **Annual Sub.:** EUR 21,00; **Circ:** 200,100
Editor: Jutta Rossellit; **Advertising Manager:** Helge Löbel
Profile: culture is the lead news magazine in the entertainment field. As a basic medium for music, film, literature, culture and entertainment offers kulturnews monthly a credible and competent selection of the best new releases and events. The successful concept of range, journalistic Competence, efficiency and credibility in the target group of young urbans makes the track one of the leading advertising medium in the entertainment segment.
Language(s): German
Readership: Aimed at tourists, visitors and local residents.
ADVERTISING RATES:
Full Page Colour .... EUR 13600
Mechanical Data: Type Area: 250 x 180 mm
Copy instructions: *Copy Date:* 13 days prior to publication
Supplement(s): citymag; citymag; citymag; citymag; citymag; citymag; citymag; citymag; citymag; citymag
CONSUMER: RURAL & REGIONAL INTEREST

KULTURSPIEGEL 733489G84A-1600
Editorial: Brandstwiete 19, 20457 HAMBURG
Tel: 40 30072306 **Fax:** 40 30072793
Email: spiegel@spiegel.de **Web site:** http://www.spiegel.de/kulturspiegel
Freq: 6 issues yearly; **Cover Price:** Free; **Circ:** 900,298
Editor: Marianne Wellershoff; **Advertising Manager:** Norbert Facklam
Profile: Every last Monday of the month the KulturSPIEGEL is a supplement of DER SPIEGEL. The program magazine reportes in detail on current cultural issues and trends. With stories, portraits and interviews, young and controversial issues in addition to the mainstream as well as an extensive service section with CD and DVD reviews and numerous book and audio book specific recommendation are given from the KulturSpiegel to its readers. KulturSPIEGEL with a circulation of over 900 000 copies and a reach of 1.35 million readers is Germany's largest cultural magazine. Facebook: http://www.facebook.com/kulturspiegel This Outlet offers RSS (Really Simple Syndication).
Language(s): German
ADVERTISING RATES:
Full Page Mono .... EUR 23806
Full Page Colour .... EUR 23806
Mechanical Data: Type Area: 233 x 168 mm, No. of Columns (Display): 3, Col Widths (Display): 53 mm
Copy instructions: *Copy Date:* 21 days prior to publication
Supplement to: Der Spiegel
CONSUMER: THE ARTS & LITERARY: Arts

KULTUS UND UNTERRICHT
733513G80-14111
Editorial: Neues Schloss, 70173 STUTTGART
Tel: 711 2792831
Email: martha.sauser@km.kv.bwl.de
Freq: 22 issues yearly; **Annual Sub.:** EUR 68,85
Editor: Günther Hörz; **Advertising Manager:** Uwe Stockburger
Profile: Publication of the Ministry of Education and Arts for all places of learning in Baden-Württemberg.
Language(s): German
Readership: Aimed at teachers in schools and colleges within the area.
CONSUMER: RURAL & REGIONAL INTEREST

KUNST+KULTUR 1663679G2A-5614
Editorial: Neckarhalde 27a, 72070 TÜBINGEN
Tel: 7071 940180 **Fax:** 7071 940887
Email: burkhard.baltzer@verdi.de **Web site:** http://www.kunstundkultur-online.de
Freq: Quarterly; Free to qualifying individuals
Annual Sub.: EUR 26,00; **Circ:** 28,000
Editor: Burkhard Baltzer
Profile: Cultural political magazine of the ver.di Trade Union.
Language(s): German
ADVERTISING RATES:
Full Page Mono .... EUR 3550
Full Page Colour .... EUR 6200
Mechanical Data: Type Area: 420 x 255 mm, No. of Columns (Display): 3, Col Widths (Display): 75 mm
Copy instructions: *Copy Date:* 28 days prior to publication
Supplement to: ver.di Publik

KUNST + UNTERRICHT
733558G62B-1320
Editorial: Im Brande 17, 30926 SEELZE
Tel: 511 40004228 **Fax:** 511 40004219
Email: redaktion.ku@friedrich-verlag.de **Web site:** http://www.friedrich-verlag.de
Freq: 10 issues yearly; **Annual Sub.:** EUR 108,00; **Circ:** 7,000
Editor: Ute Zander-Hering; **Advertising Manager:** Bernd Schrader
Profile: Just in the exhibition - now at Kunst + Unterricht! Kunst + Unterricht is the place to become the subject of art. The magazine is based on the art, thinking out of the classroom and offers valuable incentives to new artistic methods. Examples of contemporary art and art history will show you practical approaches for all school levels. In each issue of the knowledge flows from 40 years of Kunst + Unterricht activities. You benefit from: high-quality images: up to date and directly usable, good ideas and materials fund that offers everything for the comprehensive treatment of a subject and with the extra booklet digression to trace the complex didactic discussion and discourse of art at the height time.
Language(s): German
ADVERTISING RATES:
Full Page Mono .... EUR 1290
Full Page Colour .... EUR 1940
Mechanical Data: Type Area: 243 x 175 mm, No. of Columns (Display): 3, Col Widths (Display): 55 mm
Copy instructions: *Copy Date:* 49 days prior to publication
Supplement(s): bildung+medien; bildung+reisen; bildung+science
BUSINESS: CHURCH & SCHOOL EQUIPMENT & EDUCATION: Education Teachers

KUNSTCHRONIK 733530G7-162
Editorial: Katharina-von-Bora-Str. 10, 80333 MÜNCHEN **Tel:** 89 28927559 **Fax:** 89 28927607
Email: kunstchronik@zikg.lrz-muenchen.de
Freq: 11 issues yearly; **Annual Sub.:** EUR 69,90; **Circ:** 1,800
Editor: Christine Tauber; **Advertising Manager:** Wolf-Dieter Schoyerer
Profile: Magazine covering all aspects of the antiques trade.
Language(s): German
ADVERTISING RATES:
Full Page Mono .... EUR 414
Mechanical Data: Type Area: 210 x 145 mm, No. of Columns (Display): 2, Col Widths (Display): 66 mm
Copy instructions: *Copy Date:* 30 days prior to publication
BUSINESS: ANTIQUES

KUNSTHANDWERK & DESIGN
733534G84A-220
Editorial: Eifelstr. 19, 50674 KÖLN **Tel:** 221 9231621
Fax: 221 9231622
Email: uta.klotz@t-online.de **Web site:** http://www.kunsthandwerk-design.de
Freq: 6 issues yearly; **Annual Sub.:** EUR 46,00; **Circ:** 4,500
Editor: Uta Klotz; **Advertising Manager:** Uta Klotz
Profile: Publication covering different aspects of contemporary art, craft and design.
Language(s): German
Readership: Aimed at artists, craftsmen, owners of galleries and museums, exhibitions, collectors and those who have an interest in art and design.
ADVERTISING RATES:
Full Page Mono .... EUR 880
Full Page Colour .... EUR 1250
Mechanical Data: Type Area: 246 x 169 mm, No. of Columns (Display): 3, Col Widths (Display): 53 mm
Copy instructions: *Copy Date:* 40 days prior to publication
CONSUMER: THE ARTS & LITERARY: Arts

KUNSTSTOFF MAGAZIN
733546G39-65
Editorial: Havelstr. 9, 64295 DARMSTADT
Tel: 6151 380419 **Fax:** 6151 38099419
Email: droege@hoppenstedt.de **Web site:** http://www.kunststoff-magazin.de
Freq: 6 issues yearly; **Annual Sub.:** EUR 92,00; **Circ:** 17,833
Editor: Meinolf Droege; **Advertising Manager:** Heike Heckmann
Profile: Magazine about rubber, plastic and recycling. Facebook: http://www.facebook.com/pages/Kunststoff-Magazin/103413906367239.
Language(s): German
ADVERTISING RATES:
Full Page Mono .... EUR 3820
Full Page Colour .... EUR 5440
Mechanical Data: Type Area: 252 x 180 mm, No. of Columns (Display): 3, Col Widths (Display): 56 mm
Copy instructions: *Copy Date:* 14 days prior to publication
Supplement(s): kataloge orange
BUSINESS: PLASTICS & RUBBER

KUNSTSTOFFE 733391G39-80
Editorial: Kolbergerstr. 22, 81679 MÜNCHEN
Tel: 89 99830621 **Fax:** 89 99830625
Email: kunststoffe@hanser.de **Web site:** http://www.kunststoffe.de
Freq: Monthly; **Annual Sub.:** EUR 208,00; **Circ:** 16,275
Editor: Gerhard Gotzmann; **Advertising Manager:** Heike Herchenröther-Rosenstein
Profile: Kunststoffe up to date and reliable information on technical developments and trends in the plastics industry: from practice to practice! Exclusive insider reports are the trademarks of Kunststoffe. They shape the profile of this journal as a guiding carrier for information the plastics industry. Added within the German plastics trade press Kunststoffe by far the highest paid circulation.
Language(s): German
Readership: Read by members of both the Association and Society.
ADVERTISING RATES:
Full Page Mono .... EUR 4000
Full Page Colour .... EUR 6160
Mechanical Data: Type Area: 250 x 175 mm, No. of Columns (Display): 4, Col Widths (Display): 41 mm
Official Journal of: Organ d. PlasticsEurope Deutschland e.V., d. Gesamtverb. kunststoffverarbeitende Industrie e.V., d. VDI Ges. Kunststofftechnik, d. Normenausschuss Kunststoffe im DIN, d. AVK Industrievereinigung Verstärkte Kunststoffe e.V.
BUSINESS: PLASTICS & RUBBER

KUNSTSTOFFVERARBEITUNG DEUTSCHLAND 733550G13-1520
Editorial: Bert-Brecht-Str. 15, 78054 VILLINGEN-SCHWENNINGEN **Tel:** 7720 394118
Fax: 7720 394175
Email: findeisen@kuhnverlag.de **Web site:** http://www.kuhn-kataloge.de
Freq: Annual; **Cover Price:** EUR 17,00; **Circ:** 6,151
Editor: Steffi Findeisen; **Advertising Manager:** Konrad Baumann
Profile: Magazine for the synthetic materials industry including a special on surface technology.
Language(s): German
ADVERTISING RATES:
Full Page Mono .... EUR 2440
Full Page Colour .... EUR 3055
Mechanical Data: Type Area: 254 x 180 mm
BUSINESS: CHEMICALS

DER KURIER 733593G72-6504
Editorial: Marktplatz 14, 63500 SELIGENSTADT
Tel: 6182 22821 **Fax:** 6182 28283
Email: redaktion@der-kurier.de **Web site:** http://www.der-kurier.de
Freq: Weekly; **Cover Price:** Free; **Circ:** 21,800
Editor: Patrick Schad; **Advertising Manager:** Marco Schwarzkopf
Profile: Advertising journal (house-to-house) concentrating on local stories.
Language(s): German
ADVERTISING RATES:
Full Page Mono .... EUR 4066
Full Page Colour .... EUR 4616
Mechanical Data: Type Area: 480 x 326 mm, No. of Columns (Display): 7, Col Widths (Display): 44 mm
LOCAL NEWSPAPERS

KURIER AM SONNTAG
733596G72-6512
Editorial: Martinistr. 43, 28195 BREMEN
Tel: 421 36710 **Fax:** 421 36711000
Email: redaktion@weser-kurier.de **Web site:** http://www.weser-kurier.de
Freq: Weekly; **Cover Price:** EUR 1,00; **Circ:** 164,204
Editor: Helge Matthiesen
Profile: Regional daily newspaper with news on politics, economy, culture, sports, travel, technology, etc.
Language(s): German
ADVERTISING RATES:
SCC .... EUR 293,50
Mechanical Data: Type Area: 490 x 333 mm, No. of Columns (Display): 7, Col Widths (Display): 45 mm
Copy instructions: *Copy Date:* 2 days prior to publication
LOCAL NEWSPAPERS

KURIER OCHRONY ROSLIN
733600G21A-2400
Editorial: Alfred-Nobel-Str. 50, 40789 MONHEIM
Tel: 2173 383540 **Fax:** 2173 383454
Email: bernhard.grupp@bayercropscience.com **Web site:** http://www.agrocourier.com
Freq: 3 issues yearly; **Cover Price:** Free; **Circ:** 10,000
Editor: Bernhard Grupp
Profile: Company publication published by Bayer CropScience.
Language(s): Polish

KURS 733609G1C-980
Editorial: Rommersdorfer Str. 9, 53604 BAD HONNEF **Tel:** 2224 978756 **Fax:** 2224 978757
Email: george.clegg@t-online.de **Web site:** http://www.kurs-magazin.de
Freq: Monthly; **Annual Sub.:** EUR 120,00; **Circ:** 18,942
Editor: George Clegg; **Advertising Manager:** Anne Forst
Profile: Kurs is the monthly magazine for the full range of financial services from insurance companies, investment companies, banks and building societies. With high business value and berulichen Kurs informed in the sales, consulting and brokerage services and financial decision makers active in sales and marketing via the market and competition, providers and the new offerings, acquisitions and sales and displays product reviews and performance analysis.
Language(s): German
ADVERTISING RATES:
Full Page Mono .... EUR 4450
Full Page Colour .... EUR 4450
Mechanical Data: Type Area: 248 x 180 mm, No. of Columns (Display): 3, Col Widths (Display): 56 mm
Copy instructions: *Copy Date:* 22 days prior to publication
BUSINESS: FINANCE & ECONOMICS: Banking

KURS KIEL 1615117G89A-11570
Editorial: Andreas-Gayk-Str. 31, 24103 KIEL
Tel: 431 6791028 **Fax:** 431 6791099
Email: n.grimm@kiel-marketing.de **Web site:** http://www.kurskiel.de
Freq: Quarterly; Free to qualifying individuals
Annual Sub.: EUR 12,00; **Circ:** 38,000
Editor: Nicolas Grimm; **Advertising Manager:** Nicolas Grimm
Profile: City guide and calendar with events for visitors and citizens of the city of Kiel.
Language(s): German
ADVERTISING RATES:
Full Page Mono .... EUR 980
Full Page Colour .... EUR 980
Mechanical Data: Type Area: 196 x 84 mm
Copy instructions: *Copy Date:* 40 days prior to publication

KURSANA MAGAZIN
1641792G74N-840
Editorial: Friedrichstr. 90, 10117 BERLIN
Tel: 30 20252525 **Fax:** 30 20252540
Email: mehls@dussmann.de **Web site:** http://www.kursana.de
Freq: Half-yearly; **Circ:** 35,000
Editor: Michaela Mehls
Profile: Magazine for the elderly.
Language(s): German

KURVE 733651G77B-80
Editorial: Hertinger Str. 60, 59423 UNNA
Tel: 2303 985521 **Fax:** 2303 985309
Email: efoe@syburger.de **Web site:** http://www.syburger.de
Freq: Monthly; **Annual Sub.:** EUR 19,20; **Circ:** 28,000
Editor: Erik Förster; **Advertising Manager:** Jessica Kwasny
Profile: Motorcycle magazine for the northern region of Niedersachsen, Hamburg, Bremen, Schleswig-Holstein, Osnabrück, Mecklenburg-Vorpommern. The editorial focus is on regional news, plus get driving reports, tests, and travel. The magazine for active bikers, because they only exist in the motorcycle trade and meeting places.
Language(s): German
Readership: Read by enthusiasts.
ADVERTISING RATES:
Full Page Mono .... EUR 821
Full Page Colour .... EUR 1149
Mechanical Data: Type Area: 232 x 155 mm, No. of Columns (Display): 3, Col Widths (Display): 48 mm
CONSUMER: MOTORING & CYCLING: Motorcycling

KURZ-INFOS AUS STEUER UND WIRTSCHAFT FÜR DEN BERATER 1664573G1A-3599
Editorial: Portastr. 2, 32423 MINDEN **Tel:** 571 23729
Fax: 571 28768
Email: info@wiadok.de **Web site:** http://www.wiadok.de
Freq: Monthly; **Annual Sub.:** EUR 117,60; **Circ:** 120
Editor: von Knobelsdorf
Profile: Magazine containing information about tax law for tax advisors.
Language(s): German

KV BLATT BERLIN 733667G56A-6180
Editorial: Masurenallee 6a, 14057 BERLIN
Tel: 30 31003223 **Fax:** 30 31003210
Email: kvblatt-berlin@kvberlin.de **Web site:** http://www.kvberlin.de
Freq: Monthly; **Circ:** 14,000
Editor: Reinhold Schlitt
Profile: Journal containing features on regional and national medical policy, news items and health information.
Language(s): German
Readership: Read by doctors.
ADVERTISING RATES:
Full Page Mono .... EUR 1470
Full Page Colour .... EUR 2215
Mechanical Data: Type Area: 257 x 169 mm, No. of Columns (Display): 3, Col Widths (Display): 53 mm

Copy instructions: *Copy Date:* 18 days prior to publication
BUSINESS: HEALTH & MEDICAL

KV RHEINLAND-PFALZ PRAXIS
1818592G56A-11514
Editorial: Isaac-Fulda-Allee 14, 55124 MAINZ
Tel: 6131 326326 **Fax:** 6131 326327
Email: kvpraxis@kv-rlp.de **Web site:** http://www.kv-rlp.de
Freq: Quarterly; **Circ:** 6,500
Editor: Ricada Busch
Profile: In the newsletter, "KV Rheinland-Pfalz Praxis" informed the Doctors Association of Rhineland-Palatinate its members regularly informed of current issues in the contract medical and contract psychotherapeutical care.
Language(s): German

KVN-PRO
1820099G56A-11520
Editorial: Berliner Allee 22, 30175 HANNOVER
Tel: 511 3803133 **Fax:** 511 3803491
Email: detlef.haffke@kvn.de **Web site:** http://www.kvn.de
Freq: Quarterly; **Cover Price:** Free; **Circ:** 1,500
Editor: Detlef Haffke
Profile: Statistical data from the Chamber of Resident Doctors in Lower Saxony.
Language(s): German

KW KORRESPONDENZ WASSERWIRTSCHAFT
1832739G4E-7217
Editorial: Theodor-Heuss-Allee 17, 53773 HENNEF
Tel: 2242 872190 **Fax:** 2242 872151
Email: bringewski@dwa.de **Web site:** http://www.gfa-kw.de
Freq: Monthly; **Circ:** 2,094
Editor: Frank Bringewski; **Advertising Manager:** Andrea Vogel
Profile: The KW Korrespondenz Wasserwirtschaft is the organ of the DWA for general water management issues: hydrology, water management, water and soil, hydraulic engineering, hydropower, water ecology, groundwater, hydraulic mechanics, flood protection. There are also cross-cutting issues such as law, business, education, international cooperation. In addition to detailed technical papers, it offers comprehensive information "from the industry, " News from the work of the DWA and their bodies, the latest news from science and practice as well as text messages - everything that is important for water managers - names and heads, case law, dissertations, books and other media, events.
Language(s): German
ADVERTISING RATES:
Full Page Mono .... EUR 1260
Full Page Colour .... EUR 2190
Mechanical Data: Type Area: 256 x 176 mm, No. of Columns (Display): 3, Col Widths (Display): 56 mm
Copy instructions: *Copy Date:* 35 days prior to publication
Supplement(s): gewässer-info

L.A. MULTIMEDIA
733759G62B-1380
Editorial: Kirchhörder Str. 28, 44229 DORTMUND
Tel: 2392 5345906 **Fax:** 2392 5345939
Email: luga@redaktionsbuero-education.de **Web site:** http://www.lamultimedia.de
Freq: Quarterly; **Circ:** 18,500
Editor: Jürgen Luga; **Advertising Manager:** Jürgen Luga
Profile: Magazine containing information on multimedia, IT, the Internet and software, in order to enable school teachers to choose appropriate programs.
Language(s): German
ADVERTISING RATES:
Full Page Mono .... EUR 2600
Full Page Colour .... EUR 4160
Mechanical Data: Type Area: 264 x 185 mm, No. of Columns (Display): 3, Col Widths (Display): 60 mm
Copy instructions: *Copy Date:* 49 days prior to publication
BUSINESS: CHURCH & SCHOOL EQUIPMENT & EDUCATION: Education Teachers

LABO
733687G55-3898
Editorial: Havelstr. 9, 64295 DARMSTADT
Tel: 6151 380268 **Fax:** 6151 38099268
Email: hundrieser@hoppenstedt.de **Web site:** http://www.labo.de
Freq: Monthly; **Annual Sub.:** EUR 102,00; **Circ:** 24,879
Editor: Hans-Jürgen Hundrieser; **Advertising Manager:** Robert Horn
Profile: The magazine of quality laboratory reports on application-based products for industry and research laboratories. In addition to the detailed product view, the editorial content through market surveys, experts and opinion articles and reports is completed. Facebook: http://www.facebook.com/pages/LABO/353567256411.
Language(s): German
Readership: Aimed at laboratory technicians.
ADVERTISING RATES:
Full Page Mono .... EUR 5600
Full Page Colour .... EUR 6800
Mechanical Data: Type Area: 252 x 180 mm, No. of Columns (Display): 4, Col Widths (Display): 42 mm
Copy instructions: *Copy Date:* 14 days prior to publication
BUSINESS: APPLIED SCIENCE & LABORATORIES

LABORATORIUMSMEDIZIN / JOURNAL OF LABORATORY MEDICINE
733691G55-65
Editorial: Genthiner Str. 13, 10785 BERLIN
Tel: 30 26005220 **Fax:** 30 26005325
Email: jlm.editorial@degruyter.com **Web site:** http://www.degruyter.de/journals/labmed
Freq: 6 issues yearly; **Annual Sub.:** EUR 385,00; **Circ:** 4,100
Editor: Matthias Nauck
Profile: Official magazine of German Society for Laboratory Medicine, reporting about current developments from the different areas of this medical discipline.
Language(s): English; German
Readership: Read by laboratory technicians.
ADVERTISING RATES:
Full Page Mono .... EUR 1900
Full Page Colour .... EUR 3370
Mechanical Data: Type Area: 250 x 170 mm, No. of Columns (Display): 2, Col Widths (Display): 83 mm
Copy instructions: *Copy Date:* 28 days prior to publication
Official Journal of: Organ d. Dt. Vereinten Ges. f. Klin. Chemie u. Laboratoriumsmedizin e.V.
BUSINESS: APPLIED SCIENCE & LABORATORIES

LABORPRAXIS
733694G13-1640
Editorial: Max-Planck-Str. 7, 97082 WÜRZBURG
Tel: 931 4182352 **Fax:** 931 4182750
Email: marc.platthaus@vogel.de **Web site:** http://www.laborpraxis.de
Freq: Monthly; **Annual Sub.:** EUR 125,00; **Circ:** 20,877
Editor: Marc Platthaus; **Advertising Manager:** Ludwig Springauf
Profile: Journal for laboratory analysis and life sciences in industry, research and science. informed decision-makers in chemical, physical, analytical and biotechnology laboratories of the latest developments and products. Experts report with technical articles on innovations in instrumental analysis. Specials such as combinatorial chemistry, laboratory automation, LIMS, bio-and genetic engineering, pharmaceutical analysis, chromatography and spectroscopy, and national and international trade reports and product information about the latest trends in the industry worldwide. Facebook: http://www.facebook.com/laborpraxis.
Language(s): German
ADVERTISING RATES:
Full Page Mono .... EUR 5690
Full Page Colour .... EUR 7230
Mechanical Data: Type Area: 270 x 190 mm, No. of Columns (Display): 4, Col Widths (Display): 46 mm
Copy instructions: *Copy Date:* 30 days prior to publication
BUSINESS: CHEMICALS

LACKIERERBLATT
733699G16A-2
Editorial: Ernst-Mey-Str. 8, 70771 LEINFELDEN-ECHTERDINGEN **Tel:** 711 7594532
Fax: 711 7594397
Email: michael.rehm@konradin.de **Web site:** http://www.lackiererblatt.de
Freq: 7 issues yearly; **Annual Sub.:** EUR 70,70; **Circ:** 5,278
Editor: Michael Rehm; **Advertising Manager:** Carola Gayda
Profile: Magazine containing information about the painting and decorating trade.
Language(s): German
ADVERTISING RATES:
Full Page Mono .... EUR 2550
Full Page Colour .... EUR 3990
Mechanical Data: Type Area: 270 x 188 mm, No. of Columns (Display): 4, Col Widths (Display): 44 mm
Official Journal of: Organ d. Bundesfachgruppe Fahrzeuglackierer im Hauptverb. Farbe, Gestaltung, Bautenschutz
BUSINESS: DECORATING & PAINT

LADYSLOUNGE
1732852G74A-3494
Editorial: Körnerstr. 28, 53175 BONN
Tel: 228 9354800 **Fax:** 228 93548020
Email: info@kernkern.de **Web site:** http://www.golfwelt.net
Freq: Quarterly; **Cover Price:** EUR 3,50; **Circ:** 77,400
Editor: Karin Aigner; **Advertising Manager:** Rusha Kern
Profile: Women's magazine around the golf ball with issues such as: emotions, luxury, lifestyle and golf.
Language(s): German
ADVERTISING RATES:
Full Page Mono .... EUR 9870
Full Page Colour .... EUR 9870
Mechanical Data: Type Area: 265 x 181 mm

LAHNDILL WIRTSCHAFT
747578G63-1060
Editorial: Friedenstr. 2, 35578 WETZLAR
Tel: 6441 94481140 **Fax:** 6441 94481190
Email: boikat@lahndill.ihk.de **Web site:** http://www.ihk-lahndill.de
Freq: 11 issues yearly; Free to qualifying individuals
Annual Sub.: EUR 28,12; **Circ:** 18,000
Editor: Ingrid Lemp
Profile: Journal of the Lahn-Dill Chamber of Trade and Industry.
Language(s): German
ADVERTISING RATES:
Full Page Mono .... EUR 1541
Full Page Colour .... EUR 2466
Mechanical Data: Type Area: 247 x 185 mm, No. of Columns (Display): 3, Col Widths (Display): 58 mm
BUSINESS: REGIONAL BUSINESS

LAHRER ZEITUNG
733743G67B-8460
Editorial: Kreuzstr. 9, 77933 LAHR
Tel: 7821 2783162 **Fax:** 7821 2783150
Email: redaktion@lahrer-zeitung.de
Freq: 312 issues yearly; **Circ:** 10,351
Advertising Manager: Ulrike Lambart
Profile: Regional daily newspaper with news on politics, economy, culture, sports, travel, technology, etc. The Mittelbadische Presse are Offenburger Tageblatt, Kehler Zeitung, Lahrer Zeitung and Acher-Rench-Zeitung. With a total circulation of about 60,000 specimens come from the media company Reiff, "the" home of the newspapers Ortenau. Partly for nearly 200 years we have * Absolute proximity to the readers, because the reader is himself in the newspaper * Regional expertise * Information Platform of the events and life in the region * instrument of human communication, commerce, economics and politics in the Ortenau and therefore ideal promotional tool. Newspapers are, six days a week: * News * Independent * unique - they are always subject.
Language(s): German
ADVERTISING RATES:
SCC .... EUR 33,90
Mechanical Data: Type Area: 435 x 280 mm, No. of Columns (Display): 6, Col Widths (Display): 45 mm
Copy instructions: *Copy Date:* 1 day prior to publication
REGIONAL DAILY & SUNDAY NEWSPAPERS: Regional Daily Newspapers

LAK KONKRET
733749G37-1120
Editorial: Im Lohe 13, 29331 LACHENDORF
Tel: 5145 98700 **Fax:** 5145 987070
Email: draxler@t-online.de
Freq: 6 issues yearly; **Cover Price:** EUR 5,62
Free to qualifying individuals ; **Circ:** 5,900
Editor: Jürgen R. Draxler
Profile: Magazine on health and social politics, pharmacy management and official magazine of the Pharmaceutical Board.
Language(s): German

LAMINAT MAGAZIN
733756G46-11
Editorial: Fasanenweg 18, 70771 LEINFELDEN-ECHTERDINGEN **Tel:** 711 7591306
Fax: 711 7591440
Email: info@drw-verlag.de **Web site:** http://www.drw-verlag.de
Freq: Annual; **Cover Price:** EUR 5,00; **Circ:** 13,000
Editor: Karsten Koch; **Advertising Manager:** Oliver Heinz
Profile: Magazine focusing on the ecological perspective of the timber industry.
Language(s): English; German
Readership: Read by managers in the timber trade.
ADVERTISING RATES:
Full Page Mono .... EUR 5000
Full Page Colour .... EUR 6680
Mechanical Data: Type Area: 270 x 175 mm, No. of Columns (Display): 4, Col Widths (Display): 40 mm
Copy instructions: *Copy Date:* 34 days prior to publication
Supplement to: HK Holz- und Kunststoffverarbeitung, Holz-Zentralblatt
BUSINESS: TIMBER, WOOD & FORESTRY

LAMPERTHEIMER ZEITUNG
733758G67B-8480
Editorial: Alte Viernheimer Str. 9, 68623 LAMPERTHEIM **Tel:** 6206 952060 **Fax:** 6206 952066
Email: lokal@lampertheimer-zeitung.de **Web site:** http://www.lampertheimer-zeitung.de
Freq: 312 issues yearly; **Circ:** 5,377
Profile: Daily newspaper with regional news and a local sports section. Facebook: http://www.facebook.com/pages/Allgemeine-Zeitung/255951758912.
Language(s): German
ADVERTISING RATES:
SCC .... EUR 38,50
Mechanical Data: Type Area: 480 x 325 mm, No. of Columns (Display): 7, Col Widths (Display): 45 mm
Copy instructions: *Copy Date:* 1 day prior to publication
Supplement(s): pepper; rtv
REGIONAL DAILY & SUNDAY NEWSPAPERS: Regional Daily Newspapers

LAND FRAUEN JOURNAL
1925381G21A-4436
Editorial: Dorfstr. 1, 14513 TELTOW
Tel: 3328 319300 **Fax:** 3328 319305
Email: blv_ev@t-online.de **Web site:** http://www.brandenburger-landfrauen.de
Freq: Annual; **Circ:** 2,500
Editor: Anja-Christin Faber
Profile: Information for countrywomen.
Language(s): German

LAND & FORST
733838G21A-2460
Editorial: Kabelkamp 6, 30179 HANNOVER
Tel: 511 67806112 **Fax:** 511 67806110
Email: landundforst@dlv.de **Web site:** http://www.landundforst.de
Freq: Weekly; **Annual Sub.:** EUR 96,90; **Circ:** 63,676
Editor: Ralf Stephan; **Advertising Manager:** Jens Riegamer
Profile: Weekly for farmers, their families and country life.
Language(s): German
ADVERTISING RATES:
Full Page Mono .... EUR 7236
Full Page Colour .... EUR 11124
Mechanical Data: Type Area: 270 x 190 mm, No. of Columns (Display): 4, Col Widths (Display): 45 mm
Copy instructions: *Copy Date:* 10 days prior to publication
BUSINESS: AGRICULTURE & FARMING

LAND & MEER
733860G89A-12105
Editorial: Neumühlen 46, 22763 HAMBURG
Tel: 40 3907681 **Fax:** 40 3907682
Email: mail@landundmeer.de **Web site:** http://www.landundmeer.de
Freq: Annual; **Cover Price:** EUR 6,40; **Circ:** 100,000
Editor: Undine Schaper; **Advertising Manager:** Undine Schaper
Profile: Land & Meer is the leading magazine for the north of Germany - and the holiday makers from all over Germany and neighboring countries, especially Switzerland. With journalistic quality, it offers its readers a broad cross-section of tourism highlights between the North and Baltic Sea coast. Facebook: http://www.facebook.com/pages/Land-Meer-Verlag/125059514190416 This Outlet offers RSS (Really Simple Syndication).
Language(s): German
ADVERTISING RATES:
Full Page Mono .... EUR 6580
Full Page Colour .... EUR 6580
Mechanical Data: No. of Columns (Display): 4, Type Area: 230 x 170 mm, Col Widths (Display): 40 mm
Copy instructions: *Copy Date:* 66 days prior to publication

LAND & MEER FAHRRAD WANDERN-WALKING
1864382G89A-12425
Editorial: Neumühlen 46, 22763 HAMBURG
Tel: 40 3907681 **Fax:** 40 3907682
Email: mail@landundmeer.de **Web site:** http://www.landundmeer.de
Freq: Annual; **Cover Price:** EUR 5,90; **Circ:** 100,000
Editor: Undine Schaper; **Advertising Manager:** Undine Schaper
Profile: About regional cycling magazine with tours in Schleswig-Holstein, Lower Saxony, Mecklenburg Vorpommern, Hamburg and Bremen. More than 50 routes between the North and Baltic Seas. Facebook: http://www.facebook.com/pages/Land-Meer-Verlag/125059514190416 This Outlet offers RSS (Really Simple Syndication).
Language(s): German
ADVERTISING RATES:
Full Page Mono .... EUR 4500
Full Page Colour .... EUR 4500
Mechanical Data: Type Area: 170 x 127 mm

LANDAUER NEUE PRESSE
733764G67B-8500
Editorial: Medienstr. 5, 94036 PASSAU
Tel: 851 8020 **Fax:** 851 802256
Email: pnp@vgp.de **Web site:** http://www.pnp.de
Freq: 312 issues yearly; **Circ:** 1,424
Advertising Manager: Gerhard Koller
Profile: Daily newspaper with regional news and a local sports section. Twitter: http://twitter.com/pnp_online This Outlet offers RSS (Really Simple Syndication).
Language(s): German
ADVERTISING RATES:
SCC .... EUR 15,30
Mechanical Data: Type Area: 482 x 325 mm, No. of Columns (Display): 7, Col Widths (Display): 45 mm
Copy instructions: *Copy Date:* 2 days prior to publication
REGIONAL DAILY & SUNDAY NEWSPAPERS: Regional Daily Newspapers

LANDAUER ZEITUNG
733765G67B-8520
Editorial: Ludwigsplatz 30, 94315 STRAUBING
Tel: 9421 9404601 **Fax:** 9421 9404609
Email: landkreis@straubinger-tagblatt.de **Web site:** http://www.idowa.de
Freq: 312 issues yearly; **Circ:** 8,105
Advertising Manager: Klaus Huber
Profile: Regional daily newspaper with news on politics, economy, culture, sports, travel, technology, etc. She is a local issue by Straubinger Tagblatt for the old County Landau. Twitter: http://twitter.com/idowa This Outlet offers RSS (Really Simple Syndication).
Language(s): German
ADVERTISING RATES:
SCC .... EUR 14,70
Mechanical Data: Type Area: 430 x 282 mm, No. of Columns (Display): 6, Col Widths (Display): 45 mm
Copy instructions: *Copy Date:* 1 day prior to publication
Supplement(s): Zuhause
REGIONAL DAILY & SUNDAY NEWSPAPERS: Regional Daily Newspapers

LANDESZEITUNG FÜR DIE LÜNEBURGER HEIDE

733793G67B-8540

Editorial: Am Sande 18, 21335 LÜNEBURG
Tel: 4131 740250 **Fax:** 4131 740213
Email: redaktion@landeszeitung.de **Web site:** http://www.landeszeitung.de
Freq: 312 issues yearly; **Circ:** 31,474
Editor: Christoph Steiner; **News Editor:** Werner Kolbe; **Advertising Manager:** Dieter Borchardt
Profile: Regional daily newspaper with news on politics, economy, culture, sports, travel technology and Others Those who want to reach people in our distribution area is in Local newspaper to the right place. The results of our latest reader survey, underline the outstanding position the Landeszeitung as the leading Daily newspaper in our region. Facebook: http://www.facebook.com/pages/Landeszeitung-Luneburg/106727649360868.
Language(s): German
ADVERTISING RATES:
SCC .... EUR 74,00
Mechanical Data: Type Area: 435 x 282 mm, No. of Columns (Display): 6, Col Widths (Display): 45 mm
Copy instructions: *Copy Date:* 1 day prior to publication
Supplement(s): Auto Journal; Bauen & Wohnen; Baugebiete in Lüneburg und Umgebung; Clever Magazin; Garten Journal; Gesundheits-Kompass; Green ...golfen im Norden; Konfirmationen in Stadt und Land; LZ Leserreisen; Sattelfest; Schlemmen & Genießen Spezial; Senioren; Trau Dich!
REGIONAL DAILY & SUNDAY NEWSPAPERS: Regional Daily Newspapers

LANDESZEITUNG FÜR DIE LÜNEBURGER HEIDE ONLINE

1621648G67B-16592

Editorial: Am Sande 16, 21335 LÜNEBURG
Tel: 4131 740290 **Fax:** 4131 740213
Email: jj@landeszeitung.de **Web site:** http://www.landeszeitung.de
Freq: Daily; **Cover Price:** Paid; **Circ:** 251,211 Unique Users
Editor: Hans Herbert Jenckel; **Advertising Manager:** Dieter Borchardt
Profile: Ezine: Regional daily newspaper covering politics, economics, sport, travel and technology. Facebook: http://www.facebook.com/pages/Landeszeitung-Luneburg/106727649360868.
Language(s): German
REGIONAL DAILY & SUNDAY NEWSPAPERS: Regional Daily Newspapers

LANDFRAUEN AKTUELL

725420G21A-1280

Editorial: Claire-Waldoff-Str. 7, 10117 BERLIN
Tel: 30 284492910 **Fax:** 30 284492919
Email: zimmermann@landfrauen.info **Web site:** http://www.landfrauen.info
Freq: Quarterly; **Annual Sub.:** EUR 7,50; **Circ:** 11,000
Editor: Ursula Zimmermann; **Advertising Manager:** Gabriele Wittkowski
Profile: LandFrauen Aktuell keep on all important issues and developments affecting rural women and rural areas, offers wide range of information, practical ideas and methodological support for the life of the country, reported on the priorities in the organization work of the individual state associations, informed regularly about activities, actions, events and developments in the rural women work at the federal level, contains assistance for the preparation of topics for the association's work, eg References and contacts. For all those looking out beyond the edge of their own village, they for women and developments in rural areas are active or who simply like to live in the countryside, LandFrauen Aktuell is the right magazine.
Language(s): German

LANDGENUSS

2086410G74P-1390

Editorial: An der Halle 400 1, 24143 KIEL
Tel: 431 20076665 **Fax:** 431 20076650
Email: redaktion@landgenuss-magazin.de **Web site:** http://www.landgenuss-magazin.de
Freq: 6 issues yearly; **Annual Sub.:** EUR 27,90; **Circ:** 80,000
Editor: Hanna Kirstein
Profile: LandGenuss brings pleasure to the reader the cuisine of different regions in more detail with lots of great recipes from the country, enriched with authentic features all about the best theme of country life. We serve them many indigenous recipes that inspire you to cook at home and wallow memories. Our editors visit the people from the country, browse the best, also thought to be lost on recipes, meet for a coffee chat with the cake bakers of the courtyard cafés and tell them why grandma's red cabbage always tastes particularly well. In addition they provide facts to garden & decoration, events and restaurant tips and to stay in their favorite gourmet region. Join us on a culinary journey through the bakeries, farms, domestic kitchens and the producers from different regions. Every two months, we offer the reader a comprehensive, expert insight into the seasonal, national and sometimes international isolated country's cuisine - down to earth and sometimes romantic, but always authentic. Facebook: http://www.facebook.com/Land.Genuss.
Language(s): German
ADVERTISING RATES:
Full Page Colour .... EUR 10120
Mechanical Data: Type Area: 297 x 232 mm

DER LANDKREIS

733804G32A-2000

Editorial: Lennéstr. 11, 10785 BERLIN
Tel: 30 590097319 **Fax:** 30 590097412
Email: presse@landkreistag.de **Web site:** http://www.landkreistag.de
Freq: 10 issues yearly; **Annual Sub.:** EUR 98,90; **Circ:** 1,765
Editor: Hans-Günter Henneke
Profile: Publication about municipal self-administration.
Language(s): German
ADVERTISING RATES:
Full Page Mono .... EUR 1320
Full Page Colour .... EUR 2550
Mechanical Data: Type Area: 260 x 185 mm, No. of Columns (Display): 2, Col Widths (Display): 90 mm
Copy instructions: *Copy Date:* 30 days prior to publication
BUSINESS: LOCAL GOVERNMENT, LEISURE & RECREATION: Local Government

LANDKÜCHE WOCHE DER FRAU

2086901G74P-1399

Editorial: Rotweg 8, 76532 BADEN-BADEN
Tel: 7221 3501131 **Fax:** 7221 3501304
Email: wochederfrau@klambt.de
Freq: Half-yearly; **Circ:** 80,000
Advertising Manager: Martin Fischer
Profile: The trend toward natural and original pleasure is undiminished. No wonder that one remembers more and more on the old kitchen treasures - and that the proposals can be found in our recipe again. Autumn and winter pleasures, such as cabbage or root vegetables come when the right place, mushroom dishes, delicious quiches and pies - just good! The charm is in the original and simple, but by no means is boring. Rural recipes with traditional ingredients awaken childhood memories: sweet pastries, hearty stews, colorful vegetable dishes, sweets like to grandma's day, homemade bread and rolls, pancakes, hearty meat kitchen - with these recipe ideas for everyone!.
Language(s): German
ADVERTISING RATES:
Full Page Mono .... EUR 5370
Full Page Colour .... EUR 5370
Mechanical Data: Type Area: 250 x 195 mm, No. of Columns (Display): 4, Col Widths (Display): 45 mm
Copy instructions: *Copy Date:* 28 days prior to publication

LANDLUST

1732492G74P-1195

Editorial: Hülsebrockstr. 2, 48165 MÜNSTER
Tel: 2501 8016112 **Fax:** 2501 8016119
Email: redaktion@landlust.de **Web site:** http://www.landlust.de
Freq: 6 issues yearly; **Annual Sub.:** EUR 22,80; **Circ:** 843,953
Editor: Ute Frieling-Huchzermeyer; **Advertising Manager:** Ulrich Toholt
Profile: Landlust shows the best aspects of rural life with a unique natural and high authenticity. The magazine is distinguished by its high-quality performance, offers quiet layout and a natural, loving imagery. Landlust convinces with a unique concept. The magazine launched in the autumn of 2005 excited since the first edition ever more people. With over 1.4 million readers and a circulation of over 700,000 copies is Landlust like the top 20 consumer magazine in Germany. Part of the success is the particular view of the original rural life, the surprise and the reader's own natural habitat near brings. Therefore, country pleasure is perceived as beneficial by the readers differently. In every single page - even in the print ads - will pay attention to harmony and consistency. For the readers of Landlust expect a successful whole and again with each new edition. The garden is one of the favorite places in the land of pleasure readers. Here live the nature-loving readers in creative and design their personal environment to your heart's content. 84 percent of the Landlust readers have a garden that requires regular care and enjoy the view of flower beds. Ornamental gardens to dream or vegetable and herb beds for fresh produce from the garden at home are the focus of the garden section. A lot of importance on the editorial guidance and practical tips from garden design to proper care. Landlust lovers and readers are excellent hosts. In their home environment they want to feel at home, cook and bake with love and download like a guest. A beautiful environment is especially important to them. The reader interested in healthy eating and about 60 percent of the Landlust readers pay attention to good quality food. Easy to cook delicious recipes draw from the culinary side of Landlust. The selection of recipes based on seasonal offerings. Landlust readers love to stay beautiful. They have a keen interest in living and interior issues. Three quarters of the Landlust readers high output signal readiness for their house or apartment. Quality, rural feel, craft soundness and practicality are the benchmark for the establishment of home. The special feature to discover in things, to convey appreciation, it is oriented the Landlust editors. Landlust readers live in harmony with nature and yourself. They love of nature, love of animals and creativity are especially strong. You want to understand the nature and experience in their original form. Landlust speaks of this life with reference to credibility. In addition, interested readers of the Landlust for traditional craftsmanship, care for their fondness for nostalgia and historical traditions care or enjoy the rustic charm of a rural lifestyle. The editors of Landlust draws sensitive portraits of people living with and in nature, and true traditions combine with modern natural life.
Language(s): German
ADVERTISING RATES:
Full Page Mono .... EUR 32600
Full Page Colour .... EUR 32600
Mechanical Data: Type Area: 258 x 192 mm, No. of Columns (Display): 4, Col Widths (Display): 45 mm
Copy instructions: *Copy Date:* 35 days prior to publication

LANDPOST

733819G21A-2520

Editorial: Wollgrasweg 31, 70599 STUTTGART
Tel: 711 4512764 **Fax:** 711 456603
Email: dewald@neinhaus-verlag.de **Web site:** http://www.neinhaus-verlag.de
Freq: Weekly; **Annual Sub.:** EUR 51,00; **Circ:** 15,182
Editor: Kornelia Dewald; **Advertising Manager:** Carmen Balier
Profile: Newspaper containing news about all aspects of agriculture.
Language(s): German
ADVERTISING RATES:
Full Page Mono .... EUR 4264
Full Page Colour .... EUR 4889
Mechanical Data: Type Area: 260 x 195 mm, No. of Columns (Display): 4, Col Widths (Display): 45 mm
Copy instructions: *Copy Date:* 4 days prior to publication
BUSINESS: AGRICULTURE & FARMING

LANDSBERGER TAGBLATT

733822G67B-8700

Editorial: Curt-Frenzel-Str. 2, 86167 AUGSBURG
Tel: 821 7770 **Fax:** 821 7772067
Web site: http://www.augsburger-allgemeine.de
Freq: 312 issues yearly; **Circ:** 15,913
Advertising Manager: Herbert Dachs
Profile: Daily newspaper with regional news and a local sports section. Facebook: http://www.facebook.com/AugsburgerAllgemeine Twitter: http://twitter.com/AZ_Augsburg This Outlet offers RSS (Really Simple Syndication).
Language(s): German
ADVERTISING RATES:
SCC .... EUR 45,50
Mechanical Data: Type Area: 480 x 327 mm, No. of Columns (Display): 7, Col Widths (Display): 45 mm
Copy instructions: *Copy Date:* 1 day prior to publication
REGIONAL DAILY & SUNDAY NEWSPAPERS: Regional Daily Newspapers

LANDSCHAFT BAUEN & GESTALTEN

1691878G4E-7072

Editorial: Alexander-von-Humboldt-Str. 4, 53604 BAD HONNEF **Tel:** 2224 770717 **Fax:** 2224 770777
Email: bgl@galabau.de **Web site:** http://www.landschaft-bauen-und-gestalten.de
Freq: Monthly; Free to qualifying individuals
Annual Sub.: EUR 36,00; **Circ:** 5,950
Editor: Bettina Holleczek; **Advertising Manager:** Jörg Hengster
Profile: Journal of the Association of Gardening, landscaping and sports fields. It provides information on current relevant professional landscaping issues and developments in Economy, business, environment, politics, labor politics, law, taxation, research and development, training and teaching. It reports on association-specific news and provides a forum for professional and political interests discussions. The comprehensive service section provides tips for events, seminars, exhibition and conference dates and tips for the green industry.
Language(s): German
ADVERTISING RATES:
Full Page Mono .... EUR 1449
Full Page Colour .... EUR 2399
Mechanical Data: Type Area: 275 x 192 mm
Copy instructions: *Copy Date:* 28 days prior to publication

LANDSCHAFTSPFLEGE UND NATURSCHUTZ IN THÜRINGEN

1654959G57-2724

Editorial: Göschwitzer Str. 41, 07745 JENA
Tel: 3641 684352 **Fax:** 3641 684222
Email: andreas.noellert@tlug.thueringen.de **Web site:** http://www.tlug-jena.de
Freq: Quarterly; **Annual Sub.:** EUR 14,00; **Circ:** 1,800
Editor: Andreas Nöllert; **Advertising Manager:** Lutz Baseler
Profile: Magazine of the Thüringer Landesanstalt for Environment and Geology.
Language(s): German
ADVERTISING RATES:
Full Page Mono .... EUR 409
Full Page Colour .... EUR 600
Mechanical Data: Type Area: 255 x 180 mm, No. of Columns (Display): 3, Col Widths (Display): 58 mm
Copy instructions: *Copy Date:* 14 days prior to publication

LANDSCHAFTSPFLEGE UND NATURSCHUTZ IN THÜRINGEN

1654959G57-2962

Editorial: Göschwitzer Str. 41, 07745 JENA
Tel: 3641 684352 **Fax:** 3641 684222
Email: andreas.noellert@tlug.thueringen.de **Web site:** http://www.tlug-jena.de
Freq: Quarterly; **Annual Sub.:** EUR 14,00; **Circ:** 1,800
Editor: Andreas Nöllert; **Advertising Manager:** Lutz Baseler
Profile: Magazine of the Thüringer Landesanstalt for Environment and Geology.
Language(s): German
ADVERTISING RATES:
Full Page Mono .... EUR 409
Full Page Colour .... EUR 600
Mechanical Data: Type Area: 255 x 180 mm, No. of Columns (Display): 3, Col Widths (Display): 58 mm
Copy instructions: *Copy Date:* 14 days prior to publication

LANDSHUT AKTUELL

733826G72-6608

Editorial: Ländgasse 116, 84028 LANDSHUT
Tel: 871 850230 **Fax:** 871 850232
Email: redaktion@landshut-aktuell.de
Freq: Weekly; **Cover Price:** Free; **Circ:** 112,106
Editor: Christoph Reich; **Advertising Manager:** Josef Arndt
Profile: Advertising journal (house-to-house) concentrating on local stories.
Language(s): German
ADVERTISING RATES:
Full Page Mono .... EUR 3200
Full Page Colour .... EUR 4464
Mechanical Data: Type Area: 430 x 280 mm, No. of Columns (Display): 6, Col Widths (Display): 45 mm
Copy instructions: *Copy Date:* 2 days prior to publication
LOCAL NEWSPAPERS

LANDSHUTER WOCHENBLATT

733827G72-6612

Editorial: Maybachstr. 8, 84030 LANDSHUT
Tel: 871 1419151 **Fax:** 871 1419160
Email: michael.stolzenberg@wochenblatt.de **Web site:** http://www.wochenblatt.de
Freq: Weekly; **Cover Price:** Free; **Circ:** 82,600
Editor: Michael Stolzenberg; **Advertising Manager:** Thomas Ecker
Profile: Advertising journal (house-to-house) concentrating on local stories.
Language(s): German
ADVERTISING RATES:
Full Page Mono .... EUR 4444
Full Page Colour .... EUR 6680
Mechanical Data: Type Area: 460 x 280 mm, No. of Columns (Display): 6, Col Widths (Display): 43 mm
Copy instructions: *Copy Date:* 1 day prior to publication
LOCAL NEWSPAPERS

LANDSHUTER ZEITUNG

733828G67B-8720

Editorial: Altstadt 89, 84028 LANDSHUT
Tel: 871 8500 **Fax:** 871 850202
Email: stadtred@landshuter-zeitung.de **Web site:** http://www.idowa.de
Freq: 312 issues yearly; **Circ:** 36,796
Editor: Falk Bottke; **Advertising Manager:** Irmgard Haberger
Profile: Regional daily newspaper with news on politics, economy, culture, sports, travel, technology, etc. The newspaper group Straubinger Tagblatt / Landshuter Zeitungin addition to the Verlagsgruppe Passau's second largest publishing group in Lower Bavaria. Your head office is in Straubing, along with another publishing house exists in Landshut. For the newspaper group owns newspapers Straubinger Tagblatt, Landshuter Allgemeine Laber-Zeitung, Bogener Zeitung, Chamer Regional daily newspaper with news on politics, economy, culture, sports, travel, technology, etc. The newspaper group Straubinger Tagblatt / Landshut newspaper in addition to the Verlagsgruppe Passau's second largest publishing group in Lower Bavaria. Your head office is in Straubing, along with another publishing house exists in Landshut. For the newspaper group owns newspapers Straubinger Tagblatt, Landshuter Zeitung, Allgemeine Laber-Zeitung, Bogener Zeitungr, Chamer Zeitung, Dingolfinger Anzeiger, Donau-Anzeiger, Donau-Post, Hallertauer Zeitung, Kötztinger Zeitung, Landauer Zeitung, Moosburger Zeitung, Plattlinger Anzeiger, Vilsbiburger Zeitung. In the majority of their appearance area is only local newspaper. In the northern area of distribution, it has competition from the Mittelbayerischen Zeitung, on the east by the Passauer Neue Presse and the southern and western part of regional editions of the Münchner Merkur. Twitter: http://twitter.com/idowa RSS (Really Simple Syndication) is offered.Dingolfinger Gazette, Donau-Gazette, Donau-mail, Hallertau newspaper Kötztinger newspaper, Landauer newspaper, Moss Burger newspaper, Plattlinger Gazette, Vilsbiburg Newspapers . In the majority of their appearance area is only local newspaper. In the northern area of distribution, it has competition from the Middle Bavarian newspaper, on the east by the Passauer Neue Presse and the southern and western part of regional editions of the Munich Mercury. Twitter: http://twitter.com/idowa RSS (Really Simple Syndication) is offered.
Language(s): German
ADVERTISING RATES:
SCC .... EUR 67,60
Mechanical Data: Type Area: 430 x 282 mm, No. of Columns (Display): 6, Col Widths (Display): 45 mm
Copy instructions: *Copy Date:* 1 day prior to publication
Supplement(s): Zuhause
REGIONAL DAILY & SUNDAY NEWSPAPERS: Regional Daily Newspapers

LANDTECHNIK

733837G21E-3

Editorial: Bartningstr. 49, 64289 DARMSTADT
Tel: 6151 7001127 **Fax:** 6151 7001123
Email: landtechnik@ktbl.de **Web site:** http://www.landtechnik-online.eu

Freq: 6 issues yearly; **Annual Sub.:** EUR 162,60; **Circ:** 1,000
Editor: Isabel Benda; **Advertising Manager:** Andrea Trinoga
Profile: Agricultural Engineering magazine at a scientific level for the German speaking countries. In the center of their current coverage, the technical progress, as it is driven forward in the research and development departments, research institutes and agricultural engineering manufacturers. Renowned authors and aspiring young professionals available in the Landtechnik a sound platform for their professional contributions. Here, topics and trends identified and for discussion, their practical relevance is often before directly. All relevant sectors are represented: the technology of tractors as well as modern machinery and equipment for the outdoor industry. Innovations in the areas of planning, economy and interior Stallbau see the Landtechnik their rightful place. Reports on information technologies and the latest findings from the fields of environmental technology and renewable energy sources round out the picture.
Language(s): English; German
Readership: Aimed at scientists and economists.
ADVERTISING RATES:
Full Page Mono .... EUR 1750
Full Page Colour .... EUR 2000
Mechanical Data: Type Area: 268 x 186 mm, No. of Columns (Display): 4, Col Widths (Display): 46 mm
Copy instructions: *Copy Date:* 26 days prior to publication
BUSINESS: AGRICULTURE & FARMING: Agriculture - Machinery & Plant

LANDWIRTSCHAFTLICHES WOCHENBLATT WESTFALEN-LIPPE
733867G21J-43
Editorial: Hülsebrockstr. 2, 48165 MÜNSTER
Tel: 2501 801841 **Fax:** 2501 801836
Email: redaktion@wochenblatt.com **Web site:** http://www.wochenblatt.com
Freq: Weekly; **Circ:** 64,330
Editor: Karl-Heinz Tölle; **Advertising Manager:** Gabriele Wittkowski
Profile: Professional and family magazine for agriculture in Westfalen-Lippe.
Language(s): German
ADVERTISING RATES:
Full Page Mono .... EUR 7241
Full Page Colour .... EUR 11864
Mechanical Data: Type Area: 310 x 211 mm, No. of Columns (Display): 4, Col Widths (Display): 46 mm
Copy instructions: *Copy Date:* 6 days prior to publication
Official Journal of: Organ d. Westfäl.-Lipp. Landwirtschaftsverb. e.V., d. Landwirtschaftskammer NRW f. d. Landesteil Westfalen-Lippe u. d. Rhein. Westfäl. Genossenschaftsverb. e.V.
BUSINESS: AGRICULTURE & FARMING: Agriculture & Farming - Regional

LANGENBECK'S ARCHIVES OF SURGERY
733874G56A-6220
Editorial: Tiergartenstr. 17, 69121 HEIDELBERG
Tel: 6221 4870 **Fax:** 6221 4878366
Email: gabriele.schroeder@springer.com **Web site:** http://www.springerlink.com
Freq: 8 issues yearly; **Annual Sub.:** EUR 1161,00; **Circ:** 288
Editor: Hans G. Beger
Profile: Langenbeck's Archives of Surgery.
Language(s): English
ADVERTISING RATES:
Full Page Mono .... EUR 740
Full Page Colour .... EUR 1780
Mechanical Data: Type Area: 240 x 175 mm
Official Journal of: Organ d. Congress of the German Society of Surgery, d. German Association of Endocrine Surgeons, d. German Society of General and Visceral Surgery, d. German, Austrian and Swiss Surgical Associations for Minimal Invasive Surgery, d. Section for Surgical Research of the German Society of Surgery u. d. European Society of Endocrine Surgeons

LANGENSELBOLDER ZEITUNG
733880G67B-8740
Editorial: Donaustr. 5, 63452 HANAU
Tel: 6181 29030 **Fax:** 6181 2903300
Email: redaktion@hanauer.de **Web site:** http://www.hanauer.de
Freq: 312 issues yearly; **Circ:** 1,329
Advertising Manager: Klaus-Peter Reinert
Profile: Daily newspaper with regional news and a local sports section.
Language(s): German
ADVERTISING RATES:
SCC .... EUR 20,80
Mechanical Data: Type Area: 480 x 323 mm, No. of Columns (Display): 7, Col Widths (Display): 44 mm
Copy instructions: *Copy Date:* 1 day prior to publication
REGIONAL DAILY & SUNDAY NEWSPAPERS: Regional Daily Newspapers

LANLINE
733886G5E-180
Editorial: Landsberger Str. 396, 81241 MÜNCHEN
Tel: 89 452057212 **Fax:** 89 452057220
Email: joerg.schroeper@lanline.de **Web site:** http://www.lanline.de
Freq: Monthly; **Annual Sub.:** EUR 99,60; **Circ:** 41,600
Editor: Jörg Schröper
Profile: The magazine delivers competently researched information for network specialists, Managers and telecommunications specialists. Technically detailed application examples, professional tests and comprehensive market overviews help IT professionals in their daily work.
Language(s): German
ADVERTISING RATES:
Full Page Mono .... EUR 5260
Full Page Colour .... EUR 7950
Mechanical Data: Type Area: 270 x 188 mm, No. of Columns (Display): 4, Col Widths (Display): 44 mm
Copy instructions: *Copy Date:* 28 days prior to publication
BUSINESS: COMPUTERS & AUTOMATION: Data Transmission

LARGE FORMAT
733888G41A-1460
Editorial: Dietlindenstr. 18, 80802 MÜNCHEN
Tel: 89 36888189 **Fax:** 89 36888181
Email: mail@largeformat.de **Web site:** http://www.largeformat.de
Freq: 8 issues yearly; **Annual Sub.:** EUR 68,00; **Circ:** 5,000
Editor: Sonja Angerer; **Advertising Manager:** Hermann Will
Profile: Magazine focusing on large format printing, including new hardware and software, new supplies and applications.
Language(s): German
Readership: Read by printers and those in related industries.
ADVERTISING RATES:
Full Page Mono .... EUR 4039
Full Page Colour .... EUR 4039
Mechanical Data: Type Area: 265 x 193 mm, No. of Columns (Display): 4, Col Widths (Display): 45 mm
BUSINESS: PRINTING & STATIONERY: Printing

LÄRMBEKÄMPFUNG
748697G57-2600
Editorial: VDI-Platz 1, 40468 DÜSSELDORF
Tel: 211 6103343 **Fax:** 211 6103148
Email: zimmermann@technikwissen.de **Web site:** http://www.laermbekaempfung.de
Freq: 6 issues yearly; Free to qualifying individuals
Annual Sub.: EUR 195,50; **Circ:** 1,722
Editor: Elisabeth Zimmermann
Profile: The Journal Lärmbekämpfung is the only German-language magazine for the entire field of noise abatement. It reports on an interdisciplinary physical, medical, social and economic effects of noise. Fundamental and technical issues of noise measurement and assessment, but also technical, legal and organizational possibilities of Noise control are discussed in depth and detailed contributions. Furthermore, the magazine focuses on the effect of vibration and multiple loads.
Language(s): German
ADVERTISING RATES:
Full Page Mono .... EUR 1752
Full Page Colour .... EUR 2832
Mechanical Data: Type Area: 270 x 185 mm, No. of Columns (Display): 4, Col Widths (Display): 45 mm
Copy instructions: *Copy Date:* 21 days prior to publication
BUSINESS: ENVIRONMENT & POLLUTION

LARYNGO- RHINO- OTOLOGIE
733889G56A-6240
Editorial: Rüdigerstr. 14, 70469 STUTTGART
Tel: 711 8931532 **Fax:** 711 8931408
Email: silke.karl@thieme.de **Web site:** http://www.thieme.de/lro
Freq: Monthly; **Annual Sub.:** EUR 315,90; **Circ:** 1,960
Editor: Silke Karl
Profile: Scientifically based knowledge about recent discoveries in the field of otolaryngology. Under the heading, How I do it' and, Tips & Tricks' to be given valuable diagnostic and therapeutic indications. In the series, operative techniques' show Step-by-step illustrations, the steps of the operations in colorful drawings. The German Society for ENT Medicine publishes an annual summary of presentations and round table discussions of their annual meeting. All members of society have this issue.
Language(s): German
ADVERTISING RATES:
Full Page Mono .... EUR 1580
Full Page Colour .... EUR 2660
Mechanical Data: Type Area: 248 x 175 mm, No. of Columns (Display): 4, Col Widths (Display): 40 mm
Official Journal of: Organ d. Dt. u. d. Österr. Ges. f. Hals-Nasen-Ohren-Heilkunde, Kopf- u. Hals-Chirurgie
BUSINESS: HEALTH & MEDICAL

LASER
733890G18A-128_70
Editorial: Kolpingstr. 46, 86916 KAUFERING
Tel: 8191 964111 **Fax:** 8191 964141
Email: klinker@b-quadrat.de **Web site:** http://www.b-quadrat.de
Freq: Quarterly; **Annual Sub.:** EUR 65,00; **Circ:** 11,562
Editor: Wolfgang Klinker; **Advertising Manager:** Werner Duda
Profile: The journal laser technology, informed by principles and practice reports, interviews and reports and gives the readers a comprehensive overview of the possibilities and applications of laser technology. The range of topics extends from the material processing on the measurement technology and medical technology to sensor technology and optoelectronics.
Language(s): German
Readership: Read by scientists and engineers.
ADVERTISING RATES:
Full Page Mono .... EUR 3400
Full Page Colour .... EUR 4450
Mechanical Data: Type Area: 250 x 175 mm, No. of Columns (Display): 4, Col Widths (Display): 40 mm
BUSINESS: ELECTRONICS

LASER+PHOTONICS
1835495G19E-1943
Editorial: Kolbergerstr. 22, 81679 MÜNCHEN
Email: flinn@hanser.de **Web site:** http://www.laser-photonik.de
Freq: 5 issues yearly; **Annual Sub.:** EUR 64,00; **Circ:** 4,422
Profile: The journal Laser+Photonics predominantly targets developers of optical, optoelectronic and laser systems as well as decision-makers equipment purchases in the target markets of photonics, telecommunications, laser-based production technology, medical technology, machine and device engineering and in the automotive industry. Laser+Photonics keeps you informed on laser and light sources, on optical and opto electronic materials, components and assemblies, as well as on measuring technology and CAD/CAM tools.
Language(s): English
ADVERTISING RATES:
Full Page Mono .... EUR 4300
Full Page Colour .... EUR 4300
Mechanical Data: Type Area: 250 x 175 mm, No. of Columns (Display): 4, Col Widths (Display): 41 mm

LASER+PHOTONIK
733892G19E-1040
Editorial: Kolbergerstr. 22, 81679 MÜNCHEN
Tel: 89 99830650 **Fax:** 89 99830157
Email: flinn@hanser.de **Web site:** http://www.laser-photonik.de
Freq: 5 issues yearly; **Annual Sub.:** EUR 64,00; **Circ:** 12,718
Editor: Greorgy Flinn; **Advertising Manager:** Martin Ricchiuti
Profile: The journal Laser+Photonik predominantly targets developers of optical, optoelectronic and laser systems as well as decision-makers equipment purchases in the target markets of photonics, telecommunications, laser-based production technology, medical technology, machine and device engineering and in the automotive industry. Laser+Photonik keeps you informed on laser and light sources, on optical and opto electronic materials, components and assemblies, as well as on measuring technology and CAD/CAM tools.
Language(s): German
Readership: Aimed at the engineering industry.
ADVERTISING RATES:
Full Page Mono .... EUR 4370
Full Page Colour .... EUR 4370
Mechanical Data: Type Area: 250 x 175 mm, No. of Columns (Display): 4, Col Widths (Display): 41 mm
Official Journal of: Organ d. Dt. Industrieverb. f. opt., medizin. u. mechatron. Technologien e.V.
BUSINESS: ENGINEERING & MACHINERY: Machinery, Machine Tools & Metalworking

LASER+PRODUKTION
2077902G19E-1976
Editorial: Kolbergerstr. 22, 81679 MÜNCHEN
Tel: 89 99830650 **Fax:** 89 99830157
Email: flinn@hanser.de **Web site:** http://www.laser-photonik.de
Freq: Annual; **Circ:** 15,000
Editor: Greorgy Flinn; **Advertising Manager:** Martin Ricchiuti
Profile: Laser+Produktion shows the most important trade show, the Laser World of Photonics, the innovations in laser materials processing: the laser as a tool, the most powerful machines, the latest radiation sources and beamlines, systems engineering, robotics, laser measurement technology, innovative processing methods. Laser+Produktion brings together the industry know-how of leading journals in the fields of laser technology, sheet metal, plastic and micro-machining and tool and mold.
Language(s): German
ADVERTISING RATES:
Full Page Mono .... EUR 3925
Full Page Colour .... EUR 3925
Mechanical Data: Type Area: 250 x 175 mm, No. of Columns (Display): 4, Col Widths (Display): 41 mm
Copy instructions: *Copy Date:* 29 days prior to publication

LAST&KRAFT
733896G77A-1320
Editorial: Lise-Meitner-Str. 2, 55129 MAINZ
Tel: 6131 992143 **Fax:** 6131 992100
Email: redaktion@lastundkraft.de **Web site:** http://www.lastundkraft.de
Freq: 6 issues yearly; **Annual Sub.:** EUR 54,00; **Circ:** 8,655
Editor: Fritz Knebel; **Advertising Manager:** Michael Kaiser
Profile: Publication containing company portraits, technical developments and reports on utility vehicles.
Language(s): German
ADVERTISING RATES:
Full Page Mono .... EUR 1150
Full Page Colour .... EUR 1150
Mechanical Data: Type Area: 260 x 185 mm, No. of Columns (Display): 3, Col Widths (Display): 59 mm
Copy instructions: *Copy Date:* 30 days prior to publication

LASTAUTO OMNIBUS
733893G49D-1
Editorial: Handwerkstr. 15, 70565 STUTTGART
Tel: 711 7849819 **Fax:** 711 7849889
Email: thomas.rosenberger@etm-verlag.de **Web site:** http://www.lastauto.de
Freq: 11 issues yearly; **Annual Sub.:** EUR 46,20; **Circ:** 13,368
Editor: Thomas Rosenberger; **Advertising Manager:** Roland Schäfer
Profile: lastauto omnibus, the technically-oriented commercial vehicle magazine reported monthly barometer of tests, technology and trends in the commercial vehicle. In addition to detailed reports on trucks and vans also come Busthemen not too short. Tips for used car advice, repair and replacement costs as well as accessories and model cars are also part of lastauto omnibus.
Language(s): German
Readership: Read by manufacturers and operators of fleets of commercial vehicles.
ADVERTISING RATES:
Full Page Mono .... EUR 7820
Full Page Colour .... EUR 7820
Mechanical Data: Type Area: 263 x 196 mm, No. of Columns (Display): 3, Col Widths (Display): 62 mm
Supplement(s): Truck Sport Magazin; Who Is Who im Nutzfahrzeug-Flottenmarkt
BUSINESS: TRANSPORT: Commercial Vehicles

LASTAUTO OMNIBUS KATALOG
733894G49A-900
Editorial: Handwerkstr. 15, 70565 STUTTGART
Tel: 6374 91360
Email: frank.zeitzen@zeitzen-mathieu.de **Web site:** http://www.etm-verlag.de
Freq: Annual; **Cover Price:** EUR 14,90; **Circ:** 25,000
Editor: Frank Zeitzen; **Advertising Manager:** Roland Schäfer
Profile: Digest of Manufacturers and utility vehicles, trucks, buses, trailers, trailers and special vehicles. The catalog has been established for 40 years as an indispensable guide to the commercial vehicle industry. To give the reader a quick access to the catalog is divided into three parts: the first part, about 330 international manufacturers of trucks, vans, buses, trailers and bodies, as well as special vehicles made before. The second part lists the actual prices and technical data from 2200 truck, 1000 truck-bus models and 400. Are also found here costs around 500 calculations of the main trucks, vans and buses. The third part comprises the service section with approval and production numbers, addresses, buying advice, market overviews and important information and data from the commercial vehicle world. All three are written in German and English.
Language(s): German
ADVERTISING RATES:
Full Page Mono .... EUR 8740
Full Page Colour .... EUR 8740
Mechanical Data: Type Area: 263 x 196 mm, No. of Columns (Display): 2, Col Widths (Display): 95 mm
Copy instructions: *Copy Date:* 36 days prior to publication

LAUENBURGER RUFER
733907G72-6636
Editorial: Schefestr. 11, 21493 SCHWARZENBEK
Tel: 4151 88900 **Fax:** 4151 889044
Email: redaktion@lauenburger-rufer.de **Web site:** http://www.viebranz.de
Freq: Weekly; **Cover Price:** Free; **Circ:** 11,580
Editor: Christina Kriegs-Schmidt; **Advertising Manager:** Nicole Mettner
Profile: Advertising journal (house-to-house) concentrating on local stories.
Language(s): German
ADVERTISING RATES:
Full Page Mono .... EUR 2451
Full Page Colour .... EUR 2511
Mechanical Data: Type Area: 430 x 282 mm, No. of Columns (Display): 6, Col Widths (Display): 45 mm
Copy instructions: *Copy Date:* 1 day prior to publication
LOCAL NEWSPAPERS

LAUENBURGISCHE LANDESZEITUNG
733909G67B-8760
Editorial: Curslacker Neuer Deich 50, 21029 HAMBURG **Tel:** 40 72566211 **Fax:** 40 72566219
Email: redaktion@bergedorfer-zeitung.de **Web site:** http://www.bergedorfer-zeitung.de
Freq: 312 issues yearly; **Circ:** 17,776
Advertising Manager: Ulf Kowitz
Profile: Daily newspaper with regional news and a local sports section. Facebook: http://www.facebook.com/bergedorferzeitung.
Language(s): German
ADVERTISING RATES:
SCC .... EUR 57,10
Mechanical Data: Type Area: 430 x 282 mm, No. of Columns (Display): 6, Col Widths (Display): 45 mm
Copy instructions: *Copy Date:* 1 day prior to publication
REGIONAL DAILY & SUNDAY NEWSPAPERS: Regional Daily Newspapers

LAURA
733917G74A-1780
Editorial: Meßberg 1, 20095 HAMBURG
Tel: 40 30195462 **Fax:** 40 30195490
Email: laura@bauerredaktionen.de **Web site:** http://www.laura.de
Freq: Weekly; **Annual Sub.:** EUR 52,00; **Circ:** 223,650
Editor: Viola Wallmüller

Profile: Magazine containing articles about fashion, cosmetics, family life and recruitment. Facebook: http://www.facebook.com/pages/WUNDERWEIB/15113523707.
Language(s): German
Readership: Aimed at women aged between 20 and 50 years.
ADVERTISING RATES:
Full Page Mono .... EUR 13772
Full Page Colour .... EUR 13772
Mechanical Data: Type Area: 258 x 206 mm
Copy instructions: *Copy Date:* 28 days prior to publication
CONSUMER: WOMEN'S INTEREST CONSUMER MAGAZINES: Women's Interest

LAURA WOHNEN KREATIV
733918G74C-2160
Editorial: Charles-de-Gaulle-Str. 8, 81737 MÜNCHEN **Tel:** 89 67867610 **Fax:** 89 67867613
Email: elke.wagner@bauerredaktionen.de **Web site:** http://www.bauerverlag.de
Freq: Monthly; **Annual Sub.:** EUR 30,00; **Circ:** 100,489
Editor: Elke Wagner
Profile: The magazine provides regular residential housing advice, a furniture market survey and sales tips. Each issue will be taken into account all the rooms of the home - from living room to kitchen, bedroom, bathroom and hall to the nursery. Contents belongs to a regular housing advice from experienced interior designers who take on selected device problems. Examples of home and lifestyle reports encourage readers to making the design of your own four walls of their imagination. They are supported by current pages with new products and trends. For each issue, a 16-page special is the creative or presenting traditional crafts. Mega colorful format that seasonal topic pages with decorative accessories round out the concept of the magazine.
Language(s): German
ADVERTISING RATES:
Full Page Mono .... EUR 7875
Full Page Colour .... EUR 7875
Mechanical Data: Type Area: 268 x 200 mm, No. of Columns (Display): 3, Col Widths (Display): 64 mm
Copy instructions: *Copy Date:* 49 days prior to publication
CONSUMER: WOMEN'S INTEREST CONSUMER MAGAZINES: Home & Family

LAUSITZER RUNDSCHAU
733922G67B-8780
Editorial: Str. der Jugend 54, 03050 COTTBUS
Tel: 355 4810 **Fax:** 355 481246
Email: redaktion@lr-online.de **Web site:** http://www.lr-online.de
Freq: 312 issues yearly; **Circ:** 93,065
Editor: Johannes M. Fischer; **News Editor:** Jan Siegel; **Advertising Manager:** Detlef Hockun
Profile: Regional daily newspaper with news on politics, economy, culture, sports, travel, technology, etc. Facebook: http://www.facebook.com/lausitzerrundschau?ref=nf Twitter: http://twitter.com/lr_online This Outlet offers RSS (Really Simple Syndication).
Language(s): German
ADVERTISING RATES:
SCC .... EUR 197,10
Mechanical Data: Type Area: 481 x 326 mm, No. of Columns (Display): 7, Col Widths (Display): 44 mm
Copy instructions: *Copy Date:* 2 days prior to publication
Supplement(s): rtv
REGIONAL DAILY & SUNDAY NEWSPAPERS: Regional Daily Newspapers

LAUSITZER SEENLAND FERIENJOURNAL
1795360G89A-12295
Editorial: Parzellenstr. 21, 03050 COTTBUS
Tel: 355 4838730 **Fax:** 355 4838739
Email: info@verlag-semmler.de **Web site:** http://www.verlag-semmler.de
Freq: Annual; **Cover Price:** Free; **Circ:** 60,000
Profile: Regional Holiday Magazine for the Lusatian Lakeland.
Language(s): German

LAUT.DE
1662123G76D-6213
Editorial: Seilerstr. 7, 78467 KONSTANZ
Tel: 7531 6923800 **Fax:** 7531 6923811
Email: redaktion@laut.de **Web site:** http://www.laut.de
Freq: Daily; **Cover Price:** Paid; **Circ:** 1,890,566 Unique Users
Editor: Joachim Gauger
Language(s): German
CONSUMER: MUSIC & PERFORMING ARTS: Music

LAUTERBACHER ANZEIGER
733923G67B-8800
Editorial: Am Kreuz 10, 36304 ALSFELD
Tel: 6331 966960 **Fax:** 6331 966968
Email: redaktion@lauterbacher-anzeiger.de **Web site:** http://www.lauterbacher-anzeiger.de
Freq: 312 issues yearly; **Circ:** 6,404
Advertising Manager: Martin Hank
Profile: Daily newspaper with regional news and a local sports section.
Language(s): German
ADVERTISING RATES:
SCC .... EUR 22,80
Mechanical Data: Type Area: 430 x 278 mm, No. of Columns (Display): 6, Col Widths (Display): 45 mm
Copy instructions: *Copy Date:* 1 day prior to publication
Supplement(s): auf dem Vulkan; vital im leben
REGIONAL DAILY & SUNDAY NEWSPAPERS: Regional Daily Newspapers

LAVIVA
1859338G74A-3637
Editorial: Stubbenhuk 10, 20459 HAMBURG
Tel: 40 37030 **Fax:** 40 37035010
Email: redaktion@laviva.com **Web site:** http://www.laviva.com
Freq: Monthly; **Cover Price:** EUR 1,00; **Circ:** 325,878
Editor: Stefanie Hellge
Profile: LAVIVA offers its readers a colorful bouquet of topics such as fashion, beauty, enjoy, Body & Soul, travel and lifestyle. Easy, fun, diverse and full of useful tips. Over 96% of the readers of Laviva are women. The monthly women's magazine reaches 790,000 readers per issue.
Language(s): German
ADVERTISING RATES:
Full Page Mono .... EUR 18200
Full Page Colour .... EUR 18200
Mechanical Data: Type Area: 240 x 175 mm, No. of Columns (Display): 3, Col Widths (Display): 55 mm
Copy instructions: *Copy Date:* 45 days prior to publication

LDA - AUSG. WETZLAR
733739G72-6572
Editorial: Elsa-Brandström-Str. 18, 35578 WETZLAR
Tel: 6441 959281 **Fax:** 6441 75166
Email: redaktion.lda@mittelhessen.de **Web site:** http://www.lahn-dill-anzeiger.de
Freq: Weekly; **Cover Price:** Free; **Circ:** 83,100
Editor: Winfried Brandhoff; **Advertising Manager:** Peter Rother
Profile: Advertising journal (house-to-house) concentrating on local stories.
Language(s): German
ADVERTISING RATES:
Full Page Mono .... EUR 6243
Full Page Colour .... EUR 9364
Mechanical Data: Type Area: 490 x 330 mm, No. of Columns (Display): 7, Col Widths (Display): 44 mm
Copy instructions: *Copy Date:* 2 days prior to publication
LOCAL NEWSPAPERS

LEA
733938G74A-1800
Editorial: Rotweg 8, 76532 BADEN-BADEN
Tel: 7221 3501446 **Fax:** 7221 3501467
Email: lea@klambt.de **Web site:** http://www.klambt.de
Freq: Weekly; **Annual Sub.:** EUR 65,00; **Circ:** 168,242
Editor: Sabine Bartels
Profile: Lea is the magazine for modern women between 20 and 49 who have both feet in life that are healthy inquisitivenessand a positive attitude on the lookout for new ideas - a very communicative and active readership. High utility value characterizes the different subject areas, Send portable and affordable fashion ideas and styles for each type, tips from the fields of wellness, diet and nutrition, advice for health, business and everyday life, new recipes the family kitchen, leisure and vacation recommendations. Entertainment in the form of puzzles, horoscopes and reports on People of today. Authoritative information and advice coupled with an exciting and relaxing entertainment - that's the editorial basic concept of Lea.
Language(s): German
ADVERTISING RATES:
Full Page Mono .... EUR 7560
Full Page Colour .... EUR 7560
Mechanical Data: Type Area: 260 x 195 mm, No. of Columns (Display): 4, Col Widths (Display): 45 mm
Copy instructions: *Copy Date:* 28 days prior to publication
CONSUMER: WOMEN'S INTEREST CONSUMER MAGAZINES: Women's Interest

LEA EXTRA AUFLÄUFE & GRATINS
2086902G74P-1400
Editorial: Rotweg 8, 76532 BADEN-BADEN
Tel: 7221 3501446 **Fax:** 7221 3501467
Email: lea@klambt.de **Web site:** http://www.klambt.de
Freq: Annual; **Circ:** 80,000
Profile: Wonderfully crispy gratin with soft melting cheese in the cold season are particularly popular. We layers delicious casseroles with vegetables, spice residues on refined and airy soufflés get out of the tube! Delicious to melt away.
Language(s): German
ADVERTISING RATES:
Full Page Mono .... EUR 5370
Full Page Colour .... EUR 5370
Mechanical Data: Type Area: 250 x 195 mm, No. of Columns (Display): 4, Col Widths (Display): 45 mm
Copy instructions: *Copy Date:* 28 days prior to publication

LEA FÜR GÄSTE KÜCHEN KLASSIKER
2086903G74P-1401
Editorial: Rotweg 8, 76532 BADEN-BADEN
Tel: 7221 3501446 **Fax:** 7221 3501467
Email: lea@klambt.de **Web site:** http://www.klambt.de
Freq: Annual; **Circ:** 80,000
Profile: There are many ways to pamper guests. How about another go with a nice roast venison with homemade noodles? Or roast with smart stuffing? Sliced for the family? Not to despise: the pastry-ABC. And something sweet for the coffee table: From Frankfurter Kranz to Black Forest cherry cake!.
Language(s): German
ADVERTISING RATES:
Full Page Mono .... EUR 5370
Full Page Colour .... EUR 5370
Mechanical Data: Type Area: 250 x 195 mm, No. of Columns (Display): 4, Col Widths (Display): 45 mm
Copy instructions: *Copy Date:* 28 days prior to publication

LEA SPECIAL BASTELN
1614262G74A-3340
Editorial: Römerstr. 90, 79618 RHEINFELDEN
Tel: 7623 9640 **Fax:** 7623 964200
Email: info@oz-verlag.de **Web site:** http://www.oz-verlag.de
Freq: 3 issues yearly; **Cover Price:** EUR 2,95; **Circ:** 80,000
Profile: Craft magazine with ideas about a selected topic such as crafts for Easter or Christmas, crafts with children, make decorative cards, window color.. With pattern templates and simple instructions step by step.
Language(s): German

LEA SPECIAL FRISUREN
1606881G74A-3311
Editorial: Rotweg 8, 76532 BADEN-BADEN
Tel: 7221 3501446 **Fax:** 7221 3501467
Email: lea@klambt.de **Web site:** http://www.media.klambt.de
Freq: Quarterly; **Cover Price:** EUR 1,95; **Circ:** 101,000
Editor: Sabine Bartels
Profile: Magazine for women focusing on hair dressing.
Language(s): German
ADVERTISING RATES:
Full Page Mono .... EUR 3985
Full Page Colour .... EUR 4390
Mechanical Data: Type Area: 280 x 195 mm, No. of Columns (Display): 4, Col Widths (Display): 45 mm
Copy instructions: *Copy Date:* 28 days prior to publication

LEBEN? LEBEN!
1684021G94F-1864
Editorial: Gezelinallee 37, 51375 LEVERKUSEN
Tel: 214 310570 **Fax:** 214 3105719
Email: info@gfmk.com **Web site:** http://www.gfmk.com
Freq: Quarterly; **Cover Price:** Free; **Circ:** 29,708
Editor: Anke Tennemann; **Advertising Manager:** Kirsten Caspari
Profile: Journal of women self-help after cancer. Contains medical articles and reviews patient's questions, tips, recipes and useful addresses.
Language(s): German
ADVERTISING RATES:
Full Page Mono .... EUR 2540
Full Page Colour .... EUR 3810
Mechanical Data: Type Area: 240 x 178 mm, No. of Columns (Display): 3, Col Widths (Display): 48 mm
CONSUMER: OTHER CLASSIFICATIONS: Disability

LEBEN & ERZIEHEN
733994G74C-2180
Editorial: Böheimstr. 8, 86153 AUGSBURG
Tel: 821 45548151 **Fax:** 821 45548110
Email: redaktion@bayard-media.de **Web site:** http://www.leben-und-erziehen.de
Freq: Monthly; **Annual Sub.:** EUR 23,88; **Circ:** 125,521
Editor: Martina Kaiser; **Advertising Manager:** Armin Baier
Profile: Leben & erziehen is a competent guide through the pregnancy and the first exciting years with a child. The Guide magazine know what questions have young families. And gives reliable answers. Compact and clearly presented. The magazine moved that moves young parents. The magazine is an ideal advertising medium - because it is consistently focused on targeting young family and they anbegleitet from the beginning. The big issues in Leben & erziehen: to promote children from the start, health, baby care, nutrition, sleep, education and development. Topics that the magazine takes up virtually - so that parents share the tips in everyday family life in practice to be able to. Responsible and is currently the Advisor magazine on the issues, thereby offering an ideal and credible advertising environment. The journal is published since 1952.
Language(s): German
ADVERTISING RATES:
Full Page Mono .... EUR 8200
Full Page Colour .... EUR 8200
Mechanical Data: No. of Columns (Display): 4, Col Widths (Display): 40 mm, Type Area: 242 x 175 mm
CONSUMER: WOMEN'S INTEREST CONSUMER MAGAZINES: Home & Family

LEBEN&WEG
734003G94F-48
Editorial: Altkrautheimer Str. 20, 74238 KRAUTHEIM
Tel: 6294 428121 **Fax:** 6294 428129
Email: info@bsk-ev.org **Web site:** http://www.bsk-ev.org
Freq: 6 issues yearly; Free to qualifying individuals
Annual Sub.: EUR 28,00; **Circ:** 8,900
Editor: Ulrich Mannsbart; **Advertising Manager:** Peter Reichert
Profile: Magazine containing information for people with disabilities to lead an independent life.
Language(s): German
Readership: Aimed at those with disabilities who live independently.
ADVERTISING RATES:
Full Page Mono .... EUR 1623
Full Page Colour .... EUR 2109
Mechanical Data: No. of Columns (Display): 3, Col Widths (Display): 58 mm, Type Area: 260 x 180 mm
Copy instructions: *Copy Date:* 28 days prior to publication
CONSUMER: OTHER CLASSIFICATIONS: Disability

LEBENDE SPRACHEN
733948G84B-1460
Editorial: Genthiner Str. 13, 10785 BERLIN
Tel: 30 260050 **Fax:** 30 26005251
Email: info@degruyter.com **Web site:** http://www.degruyter.com
Annual Sub.: EUR 79,00
Profile: Magazine for translators and interpreters.
Language(s): German
Mechanical Data: Type Area: 190 x 115 mm
CONSUMER: THE ARTS & LITERARY: Literary

LEBENDIGE ERDE
1663502G21A-4319
Editorial: Brandschneise 1, 64295 DARMSTADT
Tel: 6155 84690 **Fax:** 6155 846911
Email: redaktion@lebendigeerde.de **Web site:** http://www.lebendigeerde.de
Freq: 6 issues yearly; **Annual Sub.:** EUR 40,00; **Circ:** 5,000
Editor: Michael Olbrich-Majer
Profile: Magazine about biological dynamic farming, nutrition and culture.
Language(s): German
ADVERTISING RATES:
Full Page Mono .... EUR 660
Mechanical Data: Type Area: 232 x 180 mm, No. of Columns (Display): 4, Col Widths (Display): 42 mm
Copy instructions: *Copy Date:* 35 days prior to publication

LEBENSBOGEN
768360G74N-809
Editorial: Bayernstr. 18, 63739 ASCHAFFENBURG
Tel: 6021 5822609 **Fax:** 6021 394998
Email: ellenheeg@gmx.de **Web site:** http://www.landkreis-aschaffenburg.de
Freq: Half-yearly; **Cover Price:** Free; **Circ:** 5,000
Editor: Ellen Heeg
Profile: Magazine for the elderly.
Language(s): German

LEBENSBOGEN
768360G74N-934
Editorial: Bayernstr. 18, 63739 ASCHAFFENBURG
Tel: 6021 5822609 **Fax:** 6021 394998
Email: ellenheeg@gmx.de **Web site:** http://www.landkreis-aschaffenburg.de
Freq: Half-yearly; **Cover Price:** Free; **Circ:** 5,000
Editor: Ellen Heeg
Profile: Magazine for the elderly.
Language(s): German

LEBENSHILFE ZEITUNG
733971G94F-50
Editorial: Leipziger Platz 15, 10117 BERLIN
Tel: 30 206411140 **Fax:** 30 206411240
Email: lhz-redaktion@lebenshilfe.de **Web site:** http://www.lebenshilfe.de
Freq: Quarterly; Free to qualifying individuals
Annual Sub.: EUR 12,00; **Circ:** 119,770
Editor: Jeanne Niklas-Faust
Profile: Magazine containing articles about counselling, service, shopping, legal and practical help, associations and links.
Language(s): German
Readership: Aimed at people with mental disabilities, their families, friends and carers.
ADVERTISING RATES:
Full Page Mono .... EUR 5988
Full Page Colour .... EUR 8683
Mechanical Data: Type Area: 413 x 281 mm, No. of Columns (Display): 5, Col Widths (Display): 53 mm
Copy instructions: *Copy Date:* 35 days prior to publication
Supplement(s): Magazin
CONSUMER: OTHER CLASSIFICATIONS: Disability

LEBENSLAUF >>
1825398G74N-928
Editorial: Bodenborn 43, 58452 WITTEN
Tel: 2302 93093810 **Fax:** 2302 93093899
Email: info@lebenslauf-magazin.net **Web site:** http://www.lebenslauf-magazin.net
Freq: 6 issues yearly; **Annual Sub.:** EUR 28,80; **Circ:** 13,000
Editor: Agnes Wedell; **Advertising Manager:** Thilo Cunz
Profile: Christian magazine for the elderly.
Language(s): German
ADVERTISING RATES:
Full Page Mono .... EUR 1530
Full Page Colour .... EUR 1882

Mechanical Data: Type Area: 258 x 188 mm, No. of Columns (Display): 4, Col Widths (Display): 44 mm
Copy instructions: *Copy Date:* 24 days prior to publication

LEBENSMITTEL PRAXIS
733978G22A-1340
Editorial: Am Hammergraben 14, 56567 NEUWIED
Tel: 2631 879127 **Fax:** 2631 879204
Email: redaktion@lebensmittelpraxis.de **Web site:** http://www.lebensmittelpraxis.de
Freq: 23 issues yearly; **Annual Sub.:** EUR 39,70; **Circ:** 60,188
Editor: Reiner Mihr
Profile: Magazine for the food industry and food trade. With practical, service-oriented and market-related information, the magazine almost all relevant decision makers and managers reached into the trade centers, self-employed in the retail sale and distribution and district leaders up to the market management. In the magazine, readers will find complete information about companies, business strategies, trends and current product range developments but also the most interesting innovations, the hottest selling tips and best promotions.
Language(s): German
Readership: Read by people in the food production industry.
ADVERTISING RATES:
Full Page Mono .... EUR 10630
Full Page Colour .... EUR 18600
Mechanical Data: Type Area: 256 x 185 mm, No. of Columns (Display): 4, Col Widths (Display): 43 mm
Copy instructions: *Copy Date:* 10 days prior to publication
BUSINESS: FOOD

LEBENSMITTEL TECHNIK
733980G22C-70
Editorial: Bugdahnstr. 5, 22767 HAMBURG
Tel: 40 38609380 **Fax:** 40 38609385
Email: v.herrmann@lebensmitteltechnik-online.de
Web site: http://www.lebensmitteltechnik-online.de
Freq: 10 issues yearly; Free to qualifying individuals
Annual Sub.: EUR 80,60; **Circ:** 9,003
Editor: Volker Herrmann; **Advertising Manager:** Uwe Miculcy
Profile: Official journal of the German Association of Food Technology. Includes trade news, reports and interviews regarding the production and packaging of food and drink.
Language(s): German
ADVERTISING RATES:
Full Page Mono .... EUR 3270
Full Page Colour .... EUR 4680
Mechanical Data: Type Area: 267 x 186 mm, No. of Columns (Display): 4, Col Widths (Display): 43 mm
Official Journal of: Organ d. Ges. Dt. Lebensmitteltechnologen e.V. u. d. Vereins Österr. Lebensmittel- u. Biotechnologen
BUSINESS: FOOD: Food Processing & Packaging

LEBENSMITTEL ZEITUNG
733984G22A-1400
Editorial: Mainzer Landstr. 251, 60326 FRANKFURT
Tel: 69 75951401 **Fax:** 69 75951400
Email: red-lz@dfv.de **Web site:** http://www.lebensmittelzeitung.net
Freq: Weekly; **Annual Sub.:** EUR 257,00; **Circ:** 40,676
Editor: Angela Wisken; **Advertising Manager:** Sven Lang
Profile: The newspaper is the leading trade and business magazine in the consumer goods industry in Germany. Who the latest news, analysis and background reports on marketing strategies, product range and sales concepts of German and international trade and industrial companies studied, they found in the LZ - often exclusively. The spectrum of coverage of food to nonfood to IT and logistics. Our core readers are decision makers: directors, managers, purchasing, selling, CM and Marketing Manager, IT and logistics managers, sales managers and independent retailers close. Facebook: http://www.facebook.com/Lebensmittel.Zeitung Twitter: http://twitter.com/LZNETnews.
Language(s): German
ADVERTISING RATES:
Full Page Mono .... EUR 20340
Full Page Colour .... EUR 20340
Mechanical Data: Type Area: 440 x 280 mm, No. of Columns (Display): 5, Col Widths (Display): 53 mm
Copy instructions: *Copy Date:* 10 days prior to publication
Supplement(s): Der Handel.; Lebensmittel Zeitung Nonfood trends; Lebensmittel Zeitung Spezial
BUSINESS: FOOD

LEBENSMITTEL ZEITUNG
1623012G22R-1
Editorial: Mainzer Landstr. 251, 60326 FRANKFURT
Tel: 69 75951454 **Fax:** 69 75951480
Email: wisken@lebensmittelzeitung.net **Web site:** http://www.lebensmittelzeitung.net
Freq: Daily; **Cover Price:** Paid
Annual Sub.: EUR 214,00; **Circ:** 409,091 Unique Users
Editor: Angela Wisken; **Advertising Manager:** Sven Lang
Profile: Ezine: Economic news for the food industry, database companies from trade and industry, online specials. Facebook: http://www.facebook.com/Lebensmittel.Zeitung Twitter: http://twitter.com/LZNETnews.
Language(s): German
BUSINESS: FOOD: Food Related

LEBENSMITTEL ZEITUNG DIREKT
733985G22A-1420
Editorial: Mainzer Landstr. 251, 60326 FRANKFURT
Tel: 69 75951691 **Fax:** 69 75951690
Email: marcelo.crescenti@dfv.de **Web site:** http://www.lebensmittelzeitung.net
Freq: Monthly; **Cover Price:** EUR 2,00; **Circ:** 69,763
Editor: Marcelo Crescenti; **Advertising Manager:** Sven Lang
Profile: Lebensmittel Zeitung direkt is the trade journal for the entire POS. It is aimed at decision makers and doers on the surface. From the store manager of the qualified technical staff to the seller. An understandable approach category - sales, sales promotion, POS marketing - a clear layout and handy magazine format support a tailored approach. The content is based on the information needs of the POS professionals: descriptions of highly successful and successful sales promotions, product information and category knowledge, tips on shelf management, promotions and product range. The Lebensmittel Zeitung direkt is delivered free to the outlets and from the market leaders laid out in the rest rooms. Facebook: http://www.facebook.com/Lebensmittel.Zeitung Twitter: http://twitter.com/LZNETnews.
Language(s): German
ADVERTISING RATES:
Full Page Mono .... EUR 16280
Full Page Colour .... EUR 16280
Mechanical Data: Type Area: 300 x 220 mm
BUSINESS: FOOD

LEBENSMITTEL ZEITUNG SPEZIAL
733986G22A-1440
Editorial: Mainzer Landstr. 251, 60326 FRANKFURT
Tel: 69 75951491 **Fax:** 69 75951490
Email: christiane.duethmann@lebensmittelzeitung.net
Web site: http://www.lebensmittelzeitung.net
Freq: Half-yearly; **Annual Sub.:** EUR 18,00; **Circ:** 40,714
Editor: Christiane Düthmann; **Advertising Manager:** Sven Lang
Profile: Lebensmittel Zeitung Spezial is the theme of the food magazine and newspaper published as a supplement to the Lebensmittel Zeitung. Facebook: http://www.facebook.com/Lebensmittel.Zeitung Twitter: http://twitter.com/LZNETnews.
Language(s): German
ADVERTISING RATES:
Full Page Colour .... EUR 19940
Mechanical Data: Type Area: 250 x 175 mm, No. of Columns (Display): 3, Col Widths (Display): 55 mm
Copy instructions: *Copy Date:* 28 days prior to publication
Supplement to: Lebensmittel Zeitung
BUSINESS: FOOD

LEBENSMITTELCHEMIE
733974G55-3900
Editorial: Ste.-Marie-aux-Mines-Str. 4, 76646 BRUCHSAL **Tel:** 7257 931230 **Fax:** 7257 931230
Email: lebensmittelchemie@t-online.de
Freq: 6 issues yearly; **Annual Sub.:** EUR 635,00; **Circ:** 3,230
Editor: Rüdiger Schneider; **Advertising Manager:** Marion Schulz
Profile: Magazine about chemicals used in food.
Language(s): German
Readership: Read by food chemists in research and administration, analytical chemists, toxicologists, ecologists and environmental chemists.
ADVERTISING RATES:
Full Page Mono .... EUR 2090
Full Page Colour .... EUR 3050
Mechanical Data: Type Area: 260 x 180 mm
Copy instructions: *Copy Date:* 30 days prior to publication
BUSINESS: APPLIED SCIENCE & LABORATORIES

LEBENSRAUM
733988G57-1040
Editorial: Taunusstr. 151, 61381 FRIEDRICHSDORF
Tel: 6172 71060 **Fax:** 6172 710610
Email: lebensraum-hessen@t-online.de **Web site:** http://www.agrinet.de/naturlandstiftung
Freq: Quarterly; Free to qualifying individuals
Annual Sub.: EUR 8,40; **Circ:** 4,000
Profile: Magazine about nature conservation in cultural landscapes.
Language(s): German
ADVERTISING RATES:
Full Page Mono .... EUR 480
Full Page Colour .... EUR 810
Mechanical Data: Type Area: 270 x 185 mm
Copy instructions: *Copy Date:* 30 days prior to publication

LEBENSRÄUME
722099G94H-1020
Editorial: Stresemannstr. 20, 47051 DUISBURG
Tel: 203 3052725 **Fax:** 203 30527820
Email: w.metzmacher@wohlfarth.de **Web site:** http://www.baustoffmarkt-online.de
Freq: Quarterly; **Circ:** 75,000
Editor: Wolfgang Metzmacher; **Advertising Manager:** Mechthild Kaiser
Profile: Customer magazine about DIY and building.
Language(s): German
ADVERTISING RATES:
Full Page Mono .... EUR 2600
Full Page Colour .... EUR 3530
Mechanical Data: Type Area: 259 x 178 mm
Copy instructions: *Copy Date:* 21 days prior to publication
CONSUMER: OTHER CLASSIFICATIONS: Customer Magazines

LEBENSRÄUME-SPEZIAL
722014G94H-1100
Editorial: Stresemannstr. 20, 47051 DUISBURG
Tel: 2054 8708044 **Fax:** 203 30527820
Email: r.schanze@wohlfarth.de **Web site:** http://www.baustoffmarkt-online.de
Freq: Quarterly; **Circ:** 21,000
Editor: Ralf Schanze; **Advertising Manager:** Mechthild Kaiser
Profile: Magazine about building materials and the ceramic tile trade.
Language(s): German
ADVERTISING RATES:
Full Page Mono .... EUR 2070
Full Page Colour .... EUR 3000
Mechanical Data: Type Area: 259 x 178 mm
Copy instructions: *Copy Date:* 21 days prior to publication
CONSUMER: OTHER CLASSIFICATIONS: Customer Magazines

LECKER
1695134G74P-1174
Editorial: Burchardstr. 11, 20095 HAMBURG
Tel: 40 30195170 **Fax:** 40 30195175
Email: lecker@hbv.de **Web site:** http://www.lecker.de
Freq: 10 issues yearly; **Annual Sub.:** EUR 30,00; **Circ:** 147,148
Editor: Jessika Brendel
Profile: LECKER is an innovative food magazine that presents both the classic cuisine and the trends of the young kitchen - always straightforward and in a challenging visual language. LECKER lives the joy of cooking and continues the trend of uncomplicated food with pleasure and passion on each side. The innovative landscape format and the simple recipe graphics are practical and clever. LECKER stands for cooking and drinks, always presents the "right tool" and "the set table". LECKER readers are leisure active men and women between 29 and 49 who are experimenting in the kitchen with joy and mood, even if they have not learned classical cooking. When cooking quality and freshness characterize the basic ingredients. Quality convenience products are no contradiction here, but simply given time. LECKER readers are young, creative, love life and like to invite friends over for dinner. Facebook: http://www.facebook.com/lecker.de.
Language(s): German
ADVERTISING RATES:
Full Page Mono .... EUR 11349
Full Page Colour .... EUR 11349
Mechanical Data: Type Area: 176 x 214 mm

LECKER KOCHEN & BACKEN
1638269G74P-1057
Editorial: Ruhrtalstr. 67, 45239 ESSEN
Tel: 201 24688222 **Fax:** 201 24688140
Email: k.franz@stegenwaller.de **Web site:** http://www.stegenwaller.de
Freq: 6 issues yearly; **Cover Price:** EUR 0,99; **Circ:** 47,675
Editor: Kerstin Franz; **Advertising Manager:** Oliver Schulte
Profile: Seasonal cooking and baking for beginners and professionals with a winning puzzle with great prices on the topic of cooking.
Language(s): German
ADVERTISING RATES:
Full Page Mono .... EUR 3800
Full Page Colour .... EUR 3800
Mechanical Data: Type Area: 237 x 196 mm

LECKERES AUS OMAS KÜCHE
1882169G74P-1272
Editorial: Römerstr. 90, 79618 RHEINFELDEN
Tel: 7623 9640 **Fax:** 7623 964200
Email: info@oz-verlag.de **Web site:** http://www.oz-verlag.de
Freq: 6 issues yearly; **Annual Sub.:** EUR 21,00; **Circ:** 80,000
Profile: Cooking Guide with easy-to-follow recipes from ingredients of the season or for special occasions.
Language(s): German
ADVERTISING RATES:
Full Page Mono .... EUR 1360
Full Page Colour .... EUR 1680
Mechanical Data: Type Area: 251 x 183 mm

LEDERWAREN REPORT
734008G52D-80
Editorial: Oberkasseler Str. 100, 40545 DÜSSELDORF **Tel:** 211 5770822 **Fax:** 211 5770812
Email: lr.redaktion@sternefeld.de **Web site:** http://www.sternefeld.de
Freq: Monthly; **Annual Sub.:** EUR 139,00; **Circ:** 6,450
Editor: Tobias Kurtz; **Advertising Manager:** Sabine Peters
Profile: Magazine concerning the manufacture and retail of leather goods.
Language(s): German
Readership: Aimed at manufacturers, buyers and sellers of leather goods.
ADVERTISING RATES:
Full Page Mono .... EUR 1866
Full Page Colour .... EUR 3186
Mechanical Data: Type Area: 264 x 174 mm, No. of Columns (Display): 4, Col Widths (Display): 40 mm
Official Journal of: Organ d. Bundesverb. d. Dt. Lederwaren-Einzelhandels e.V.
BUSINESS: GIFT TRADE: Leather

LEGACY
734009G76D-3040
Editorial: Lessingstr. 28, 66121 SAARBRÜCKEN
Tel: 681 3907660 **Fax:** 681 3907661
Email: redaktion@legacy.de **Web site:** http://www.legacy.de
Freq: 6 issues yearly; **Annual Sub.:** EUR 35,00; **Circ:** 1,562
Editor: Patric Knittel; **Advertising Manager:** Patric Knittel
Profile: LEGACY MAGAZINE - THE VOICE FROM THE DARK SIDE is the largest circulation Hard Stuff magazine in Europe. A professional scene-editing bimonthly on the latest bands and publications in the field of dark and hard music: Death, Thrash, Black Metal, metalcore, New Metal, Rock, Gothic, Dark, Industrial, Ritual, Neofolk, etc. On 240 pages is looked next to a 2-CD insert (including multimedia features) and four color posters and their horizons. There are numerous background reports on literature, art, philosophy, and an extensive multimedia section Performances of the latest DVDs, movies, games, radio plays, books and magazines. Think different - Be independent!.
Language(s): German
ADVERTISING RATES:
Full Page Mono .... EUR 2000
Full Page Colour .... EUR 2400
Mechanical Data: Type Area: 297 x 210 mm, No. of Columns (Display): 4, Col Widths (Display): 53 mm
Copy instructions: *Copy Date:* 14 days prior to publication
CONSUMER: MUSIC & PERFORMING ARTS: Music

LEHRER UND SCHULE HEUTE
734023G62B-3190
Editorial: Von-Bolanden-Str. 12, 66453 GERSHEIM
Tel: 6843 91190 **Fax:** 6843 91192
Freq: 10 issues yearly; **Circ:** 3,100
Editor: Herbert Buhr; **Advertising Manager:** Herbert Buhr
Profile: Journal of the Saarland Teachers' Association.
Language(s): German
ADVERTISING RATES:
Full Page Mono .... EUR 300
Mechanical Data: Type Area: 250 x 176 mm, No. of Columns (Display): 3, Col Widths (Display): 56 mm
Copy instructions: *Copy Date:* 15 days prior to publication
BUSINESS: CHURCH & SCHOOL EQUIPMENT & EDUCATION: Education Teachers

LEICHTATHLETIK SPECIAL
734033G75J-200
Editorial: Machabäerstr. 3, 50668 KÖLN
Tel: 221 922790 **Fax:** 221 9227979
Email: ermert@cng-media.de
Freq: 3 issues yearly; **Circ:** 4,931
Editor: Christian Ermert; **Advertising Manager:** Frank Krauthäuser
Profile: Official journal of the German Association of Track and Field Athletics.
Language(s): German
ADVERTISING RATES:
Full Page Mono .... EUR 2200
Full Page Colour .... EUR 2200
Mechanical Data: Type Area: 248 x 185 mm, No. of Columns (Display): 4, Col Widths (Display): 43 mm
Copy instructions: *Copy Date:* 3 days prior to publication
CONSUMER: SPORT: Athletics

LEICHTATHLETIK TRAINING
734036G62B-375
Editorial: Rektoratsweg 36, 48159 MÜNSTER
Tel: 251 2300566 **Fax:** 251 2300599
Email: lt@philippka.de **Web site:** http://www.philippka.de
Freq: 10 issues yearly; **Annual Sub.:** EUR 46,80; **Circ:** 6,532
Editor: Frank Müller; **Advertising Manager:** Peter Möllers
Profile: "leichtathletiktraining" provides coaches of all skill areas, especially youth coaches, on at least 40 pages per issue, with new, attractive training, exercises and forms of play for a motivating, diverse and performance-enhancing training. For the performance and high power range training plans and training sessions according to the annual plan (periodization) are offered, while the popular sports and physical education for specific programs are introduced. Additional contributions from the fields of sports medicine, biomechanics, sports physiotherapy, sports nutrition and sports psychology teach basic practical skills in a clear and didactically prepared manner.
Language(s): German
Readership: Aimed at teachers of physical education.
ADVERTISING RATES:
Full Page Mono .... EUR 1095
Full Page Colour .... EUR 1660

Mechanical Data: Type Area: 267 x 180 mm, No. of Columns (Display): 3, Col Widths (Display): 55 mm
Copy instructions: *Copy Date:* 28 days prior to publication
BUSINESS: CHURCH & SCHOOL EQUIPMENT & EDUCATION: Education Teachers

LEINE DEISTER ZEITUNG
734040G67B-8820
Editorial: Junkernstr. 13, 31028 GRONAU
Tel: 5182 92190 **Fax:** 5182 921939
Email: ldz-redaktion@leinetal-online.de **Web site:** http://www.leinetal-online.de
Freq: 312 issues yearly; **Circ:** 5,453
Advertising Manager: Manfred Mäckeler
Profile: Daily newspaper with regional news and a local sports section.
Language(s): German
ADVERTISING RATES:
SCC .... EUR 17,60
Mechanical Data: Type Area: 430 x 285 mm, No. of Columns (Display): 6, Col Widths (Display): 44 mm
Copy instructions: *Copy Date:* 1 day prior to publication
REGIONAL DAILY & SUNDAY NEWSPAPERS: Regional Daily Newspapers

LEINEN LOS!
1860324G40-989
Editorial: Gebrüder-Wright-Str. 5, 53125 BONN
Tel: 228 298743 **Fax:** 228 9251242
Email: leinenlos@gmx.net **Web site:** http://www.deutscher-marinebund.de
Freq: 6 issues yearly; Free to qualifying individuals
Annual Sub.: EUR 22,50; **Circ:** 18,000
Editor: Werner Schiebert
Profile: Magazine for members of the German Navy Association.
Language(s): German
ADVERTISING RATES:
Full Page Mono .... EUR 1128
Full Page Colour .... EUR 2128
Mechanical Data: Type Area: 270 x 182 mm
Copy instructions: *Copy Date:* 20 days prior to publication

LEINE-ZEITUNG GARBSEN SEELZE
1606071G67B-6520_506
Editorial: Rathausplatz 11, 30823 GARBSEN
Tel: 5131 467240 **Fax:** 5131 467221
Email: chefredaktion@heimatzeitungen.de
Freq: 312 issues yearly; **Circ:** 13,818
Editor: Peter Taubald; **Advertising Manager:** Olaf Kuhlwein
Profile: Regional daily newspaper covering politics, economics, sport, travel and technology.
Language(s): German
ADVERTISING RATES:
SCC .... EUR 28,10
Mechanical Data: Type Area: 370 x 257 mm, No. of Columns (Display): 5, Col Widths (Display): 45 mm
Copy instructions: *Copy Date:* 2 days prior to publication
Supplement to: Hannoversche Allgemeine Zeitung, Neue Presse
REGIONAL DAILY & SUNDAY NEWSPAPERS: Regional Daily Newspapers

LEINE-ZEITUNG NEUSTADT WUNSTORF
1606072G67B-6520_507
Editorial: Rathausplatz 11, 30823 GARBSEN
Tel: 5131 467210 **Fax:** 5131 467221
Email: chefredaktion@heimatzeitungen.de
Freq: 312 issues yearly; **Circ:** 15,757
Editor: Peter Taubald; **Advertising Manager:** Olaf Kuhlwein
Profile: Regional daily newspaper covering politics, economics, sport, travel and technology.
Language(s): German
ADVERTISING RATES:
SCC .... EUR 28,10
Mechanical Data: Type Area: 370 x 257 mm, No. of Columns (Display): 5, Col Widths (Display): 45 mm
Copy instructions: *Copy Date:* 2 days prior to publication
Supplement to: Hannoversche Allgemeine Zeitung, Neue Presse
REGIONAL DAILY & SUNDAY NEWSPAPERS: Regional Daily Newspapers

LEIPZIG IM FOKUS
2007300G89A-12570
Editorial: Gerberstr. 15, 04105 LEIPZIG
Tel: 341 9881440 **Fax:** 341 9881547
Email: magazin@leipzigimfokus.de **Web site:** http://www.wochenkurier.info
Freq: Quarterly; **Cover Price:** Free; **Circ:** 100,000
Profile: Leipziger tourism and events magazine. Information on city history and heritage, culture, current events makes Leipzig and tourists alike delight in a visit to the metropolis of Saxony.
Language(s): German
ADVERTISING RATES:
Full Page Mono .... EUR 2500
Full Page Colour .... EUR 2500
Mechanical Data: Type Area: 327 x 233 mm

LEIPZIG TAG & NACHT
1663262G89A-11945
Editorial: Brühl 54, 04109 LEIPZIG **Tel:** 341 2698020
Fax: 341 2698088
Email: chefredaktion@kreuzer-leipzig.de **Web site:** http://www.leipzigtagundnacht.de
Freq: Annual; **Cover Price:** EUR 6,00; **Circ:** 7,000
Editor: Robert Schimke; **Advertising Manager:** Egbert Pietsch
Profile: Restaurant Guide for Leipzig and surrounding area. Service pages with addresses of the major food stores, hotels and beer gardens. The reader can learn where he go out in the best brunch or sleep where there is the best coffees, teas, chocolates or home accessories in town. The magazine section covers topics such as healthy food, wine, coffee nightlife and fine food.
Language(s): German
ADVERTISING RATES:
Full Page Mono .... EUR 2400
Full Page Colour .... EUR 2400
Mechanical Data: Type Area: 244 x 177 mm, No. of Columns (Display): 3, Col Widths (Display): 60 mm
Copy instructions: *Copy Date:* 30 days prior to publication

LEIPZIG TAG & NACHT
2073856G89A-12588
Editorial: Brühl 54, 04109 LEIPZIG **Tel:** 341 2698020
Fax: 341 2698088
Email: chefredaktion@kreuzer-leipzig.de **Web site:** http://www.leipzigtagundnacht.de
Freq: Annual; **Cover Price:** EUR 5,20; **Circ:** 13,000
Editor: Robert Schimke; **Advertising Manager:** Egbert Pietsch
Profile: Restaurant Guide for Leipzig and surrounding area. Service pages with addresses of the major food stores, hotels and beer gardens. The reader can learn where he go out in the best brunch or sleep where there is the best coffees, teas, chocolates or home accessories in town. The magazine section covers topics such as healthy food, wine, coffee nightlife and fine food.
Language(s): German
ADVERTISING RATES:
Full Page Mono .... EUR 2400
Full Page Colour .... EUR 2400
Mechanical Data: Type Area: 191 x 140 mm, No. of Columns (Display): 3, Col Widths (Display): 60 mm
Copy instructions: *Copy Date:* 30 days prior to publication

LEIPZIGER LAND WOCHENKURIER - AUSG. BORNA
723412G72-2564
Editorial: Gerberstr. 15, 04105 LEIPZIG
Tel: 341 9881433 **Fax:** 341 9800541
Email: marliesdaeberitz@lwk-verlag.de **Web site:** http://www.wochenkurier.info
Freq: Weekly; **Cover Price:** Free; **Circ:** 30,326
Editor: Marlies Däberitz; **Advertising Manager:** Sina Häse
Profile: Advertising journal (house-to-house) concentrating on local stories.
Language(s): German
ADVERTISING RATES:
Full Page Mono .... EUR 2740
Full Page Colour .... EUR 3835
Mechanical Data: Type Area: 430 x 290 mm, No. of Columns (Display): 7, Col Widths (Display): 38 mm
Copy instructions: *Copy Date:* 3 days prior to publication
LOCAL NEWSPAPERS

LEIPZIGER LAND WOCHENKURIER - AUSG. GEITHAIN
728448G72-4164
Editorial: Gerberstr. 15, 04105 LEIPZIG
Tel: 341 9881433 **Fax:** 341 9800541
Email: marliesdaeberitz@lwk-verlag.de **Web site:** http://www.wochenkurier.info
Freq: Weekly; **Cover Price:** Free; **Circ:** 9,504
Editor: Marlies Däberitz; **Advertising Manager:** Sina Häse
Profile: Advertising journal (house-to-house) concentrating on local stories.
Language(s): German
ADVERTISING RATES:
Full Page Mono .... EUR 1746
Full Page Colour .... EUR 2445
Mechanical Data: Type Area: 430 x 290 mm, No. of Columns (Display): 7, Col Widths (Display): 38 mm
Copy instructions: *Copy Date:* 3 days prior to publication
LOCAL NEWSPAPERS

LEIPZIGER LAND WOCHENKURIER - AUSG. WURZEN
748406G72-16628
Editorial: Gerberstr. 15, 04105 LEIPZIG
Tel: 341 9881433 **Fax:** 341 9800541
Email: marliesdaeberitz@lwk-verlag.de **Web site:** http://www.wochenkurier.info
Freq: Weekly; **Cover Price:** Free; **Circ:** 25,088
Editor: Marlies Däberitz; **Advertising Manager:** Sina Häse
Profile: Advertising journal (house-to-house) concentrating on local stories.
Language(s): German
ADVERTISING RATES:
Full Page Mono .... EUR 2469
Full Page Colour .... EUR 3456
Mechanical Data: Type Area: 430 x 290 mm, No. of Columns (Display): 7, Col Widths (Display): 38 mm
Copy instructions: *Copy Date:* 3 days prior to publication
LOCAL NEWSPAPERS

LEIPZIGER RUNDSCHAU
734049G72-6696
Editorial: Floßplatz 6, 04107 LEIPZIG
Tel: 341 21812801 **Fax:** 341 21812746
Email: h.betat@leipziger-anzeigenblatt-verlag.de
Web site: http://www.leipziger-rundschau.de
Freq: Weekly; **Cover Price:** Free; **Circ:** 260,000
Editor: Heiko Betat; **Advertising Manager:** Helko Leischner
Profile: Advertising journal (house-to-house) concentrating on local stories.
Language(s): German
ADVERTISING RATES:
Full Page Mono .... EUR 6095
Full Page Colour .... EUR 9751
Mechanical Data: Type Area: 368 x 256 mm, No. of Columns (Display): 6, Col Widths (Display): 41 mm
Copy instructions: *Copy Date:* 2 days prior to publication
LOCAL NEWSPAPERS

LEIPZIGER VOLKSZEITUNG
734051G67B-8840
Editorial: Peterssteinweg 19, 04107 LEIPZIG
Tel: 341 21811205 **Fax:** 341 21811543
Email: chefredaktion@lvz.de **Web site:** http://www.lvz.de
Freq: 312 issues yearly; **Circ:** 218,476
Editor: Bernd Hilder; **News Editor:** André Böhmer; **Advertising Manager:** Harald Weiß
Profile: Regional daily newspaper with news on politics, economy, culture, sports, travel, technology, etc. Facebook: http://facebook.com/lvzonline Twitter: http://twitter.com/#!/lvzonline RSS (Really Simple Syndication) wird angeboten.
Language(s): German
ADVERTISING RATES:
SCC .... EUR 474,00
Mechanical Data: Col Widths (Display): 45 mm
Copy instructions: *Copy Date:* 2 days prior to publication
Supplement(s): Borna-Geithainer Zeitung; Delitzsch-Eilenburger Kreiszeitung; Gesund; Muldentaler Kreiszeitung; Nova Eventis; P.C. Paunsdorf Center Journal; prisma; Promenaden Express; Theke
REGIONAL DAILY & SUNDAY NEWSPAPERS: Regional Daily Newspapers

LEISTUNGSSPORT
734056G75A-2040
Editorial: Otto-Fleck-Schneise 12, 60528 FRANKFURT **Tel:** 69 6700243 **Fax:** 69 6772392
Email: nickel@dosb.de **Web site:** http://www.leistungssport.net
Freq: 6 issues yearly; **Annual Sub.:** EUR 39,60; **Circ:** 2,853
Editor: Peter Tschiene; **Advertising Manager:** Peter Möllers
Profile: "Leistungssport" offers coaches who look beyond the boundaries of their sport, practical information on new findings of sports science and transferable findings from other sports disciplines. Special emphasis is placed on the usefulness of the contributions to the practice. In its "Trainer Forum" practitioners get the opportunity to share their experiences. Under the heading of "Focus on" current issues are addressed, which are highly controversial among experts. "Leistungssport" thus addresses the "upper ten thousand " coachs in this country - a sophisticated, high-profile audience with a high multiplier effect.
Language(s): German
ADVERTISING RATES:
Full Page Mono .... EUR 750
Full Page Colour .... EUR 1355
Mechanical Data: Type Area: 267 x 180 mm, No. of Columns (Display): 3, Col Widths (Display): 55 mm
Copy instructions: *Copy Date:* 28 days prior to publication
CONSUMER: SPORT

LENA
734063G74A-1820
Editorial: Römerstr. 90, 79618 RHEINFELDEN
Tel: 7623 964408 **Fax:** 7623 964459
Email: info@oz-verlag.de **Web site:** http://www.oz-verlag.de
Freq: Monthly; **Annual Sub.:** EUR 49,20; **Circ:** 26,408
Editor: Regina Bühler
Profile: The monthly magazine presents diverse, individual and creative craft and craft ideas to decorate the house and garden with imaginative table and window decorations and lovely little things. Content focus are various embroidery techniques such as cross stitch, Hardanger, white and colored embroidery in all its facets. The creative reader finds but also various crochet and knit designs and attractive living ideas for sewing. Hot topics, such as for example Felting be taken individually. Beginners and professionals alike use. The course explains both traditional and trendy topics course in detail and with appropriate images. A simple but precise instructions makes it easier to rework part of the models.
Language(s): German
ADVERTISING RATES:
Full Page Colour .... EUR 2960
Mechanical Data: Type Area: 251 x 183 mm, No. of Columns (Display): 4, Col Widths (Display): 41 mm
Copy instructions: *Copy Date:* 70 days prior to publication
CONSUMER: WOMEN'S INTEREST CONSUMER MAGAZINES: Women's Interest

LEO
1613847G86B-644
Editorial: Rothmundstr. 6, 80337 MÜNCHEN
Tel: 89 552971619 **Fax:** 89 552971625
Email: redaktion@leo-magazin.de **Web site:** http://www.leo-live.de
Freq: Monthly; **Cover Price:** Free; **Circ:** 22,750
Editor: Bernd Müller; **Advertising Manager:** Kerstin Rode
Profile: Leo, the queer magazine in Munich and Bavaria, is with recent reports on politics, culture and party scene in Munich and Nuremberg as well as the extensive agenda and city guide since 2007, the guide to gay life in Bavaria.
Language(s): German
ADVERTISING RATES:
Full Page Mono .... EUR 2180
Full Page Colour .... EUR 2180
Mechanical Data: Type Area: 260 x 190 mm, No. of Columns (Display): 4, Col Widths (Display): 45 mm
Copy instructions: *Copy Date:* 15 days prior to publication
CONSUMER: ADULT & GAY MAGAZINES: Gay & Lesbian Magazines

LEONBERGER KREISZEITUNG
734077G67B-8860
Editorial: Stuttgarter Str. 7, 71229 LEONBERG
Tel: 7152 9372811 **Fax:** 7152 9372819
Email: redaktion@leonberger-kreiszeitung.zgs.de
Web site: http://www.leonberger-kreiszeitung.de
Freq: 312 issues yearly; **Circ:** 15,625
Editor: Michael Schmidt; **Advertising Manager:** Oliver Scheffler
Profile: Daily newspaper with regional news and a local sports section. Twitter: http://twitter.com/StZonline This Outlet offers RSS (Really Simple Syndication).
Language(s): German
ADVERTISING RATES:
SCC .... EUR 45,60
Mechanical Data: Type Area: 485 x 321 mm, No. of Columns (Display): 7, Col Widths (Display): 44 mm
Copy instructions: *Copy Date:* 2 days prior to publication
Supplement(s): Leonberg & Umgebung
REGIONAL DAILY & SUNDAY NEWSPAPERS: Regional Daily Newspapers

LEPORELLO
766902G50-1194
Editorial: Pleicher Kirchplatz 11, 97070 WÜRZBURG
Tel: 931 329160 **Fax:** 931 3291666
Email: kvv@kunstvoll-verlag.de **Web site:** http://www.kunstvoll-verlag.de
Freq: 10 issues yearly; **Cover Price:** Free; **Circ:** 12,500
Editor: Petra Jendryssek; **Advertising Manager:** Thomas Andres
Profile: Reports about culture, cultural support, children's culture, intercultural issues.
Language(s): German
ADVERTISING RATES:
Full Page Mono .... EUR 1500
Full Page Colour .... EUR 1650
Mechanical Data: Type Area: 273 x 192 mm, No. of Columns (Display): 4, Col Widths (Display): 45 mm
Copy instructions: *Copy Date:* 14 days prior to publication

LERN CHANCEN
734080G62A-2440
Editorial: Im Brande 17, 30926 SEELZE
Tel: 511 40004113 **Fax:** 511 40004975
Email: redaktion.lc@friedrich-verlag.de **Web site:** http://www.lernchancen.de
Freq: 6 issues yearly; **Annual Sub.:** EUR 75,40; **Circ:** 3,000
Editor: Kerstin Bembom; **Advertising Manager:** Bernd Schrader
Profile: No student may be left behind! Who now stands in front of the class, to be quite different performance needs students, accompany them on their individual learning path and support. As a teacher at a primary, secondary or comprehensive school, you also know that professional education is important, but you are just as important as a educator. Lern chancen, the magazine, the two together brings to you: In the theme of school do you find the answers: How to plan together with colleagues to improve teaching and disinterested parents for the concerns of their children gain or involves unusual projects breathe new life into school. The topic of teaching brings vivid examples of teaching that are feasible, even under difficult conditions. Reduced to the essentials, prepared with worksheets and materials that have proven themselves in practice. With Lern chancen are available: sample lessons that have been proven in heterogeneous groups of learners, effective support materials for weaker students, valuable tips and tools for your professional approach, sophisticated templates and worksheets.
Language(s): German
Readership: Read by teachers and students.
ADVERTISING RATES:
Full Page Mono .... EUR 970
Full Page Colour .... EUR 1460
Mechanical Data: Type Area: 254 x 183 mm
Copy instructions: *Copy Date:* 49 days prior to publication
Supplement(s): bildung+medien; bildung+reisen; bildung+science
BUSINESS: CHURCH & SCHOOL EQUIPMENT & EDUCATION: Education

LERNENDE SCHULE
734081G62A-2460
Editorial: Im Brande 17, 30926 SEELZE
Tel: 511 40004187 **Fax:** 511 40004219

Email: druschky@friedrich-verlag.de **Web site:** http://www.lernende-schule.de
Freq: Quarterly; **Annual Sub.:** EUR 64,00; **Circ:** 3,000
Editor: Petra Druschky; **Advertising Manager:** Bernd Schrader
Profile: The magazine for those who want to actively participate in shaping their school. Graphically: Take advantage of concrete action plans, methods and instruments, and selected practical examples of the pedagogical education development. Encouraging: receive numerous suggestions on how to destinations such as implement structured and partnership working, positive school climate and school as a habitat. Practical: Take advantage of the practical, immediately usable materials for the daily school and teaching development. Exemplary: Read in each issue opinions, to introduce the philosophical projects, processes, problems and experiences of "learner schools".
Language(s): German
ADVERTISING RATES:
Full Page Mono .... EUR 910
Full Page Colour .... EUR 1370
Mechanical Data: Type Area: 258 x 183 mm
Copy instructions: *Copy Date:* 49 days prior to publication
Supplement(s): bildung+medien; bildung+reisen; bildung+science
BUSINESS: CHURCH & SCHOOL EQUIPMENT & EDUCATION: Education

LESBENRING-INFO 734089G74A-1860
Editorial: Postfach 101642, 04016 LEIPZIG
Email: redaktion@lesbenring.de **Web site:** http://www.lesbenring.de
Freq: 6 issues yearly; **Circ:** 1,000
Editor: Karis Schneider
Profile: Magazine for lesbians.
Language(s): German
Copy instructions: *Copy Date:* 21 days prior to publication

LEVERKUSENER ANZEIGER 734111G67B-8880
Editorial: Amsterdamer Str. 192, 50735 KÖLN
Tel: 221 2240 **Fax:** 221 2242602
Email: redaktion-ksta@mds.de **Web site:** http://www.ksta.de
Freq: 312 issues yearly; **Circ:** 22,021
Advertising Manager: Karsten Hundhausen
Profile: Daily newspaper with regional news and a local sports section. Facebook: http://www.facebook.com/pages/KSTA/141063022950 Twitter: http://twitter.com/ksta_news This Outlet offers RSS (Really Simple Syndication).
Language(s): German
ADVERTISING RATES:
SCC .... EUR 69,00
Mechanical Data: Type Area: 430 x 285 mm, No. of Columns (Display): 6, Col Widths (Display): 45 mm
Copy instructions: *Copy Date:* 2 days prior to publication
Supplement(s): prisma
REGIONAL DAILY & SUNDAY NEWSPAPERS: Regional Daily Newspapers

LEVIATHAN 734114G32G-2967
Editorial: Reichpietschufer 50, 10785 BERLIN
Tel: 30 25491597
Email: blomert@wzb.eu **Web site:** http://www.leviathan-digital.de
Freq: Quarterly; **Annual Sub.:** EUR 121,00; **Circ:** 850
Editor: Reinhard Blomert; **Advertising Manager:** Yvonne Guderjahn
Profile: Publication for those working in the field of social sciences.
Language(s): German
ADVERTISING RATES:
Full Page Mono .... EUR 735
Full Page Colour .... EUR 1635
Mechanical Data: Type Area: 190 x 125 mm, No. of Columns (Display): 2, Col Widths (Display): 61 mm
BUSINESS: LOCAL GOVERNMENT, LEISURE & RECREATION: Community Care & Social Services

LFI LEICA FOTOGRAFIE INTERNATIONAL 1665848G85A-832
Editorial: Hammerbrookstr. 93, 20097 HAMBURG
Tel: 40 226211280 **Fax:** 40 226211270
Email: info@lfi-online.de **Web site:** http://www.lfi-online.de
Freq: 8 issues yearly; **Annual Sub.:** EUR 50,00; **Circ:** 9,344
Editor: Frank P. Lohstöter; **Advertising Manager:** Kirstin Ahrndt-Buchholz
Profile: Leica company photo magazine, German edition.
Language(s): German
ADVERTISING RATES:
Full Page Mono .... EUR 2730
Full Page Colour .... EUR 4200
Mechanical Data: Type Area: 245 x 183 mm, No. of Columns (Display): 4, Col Widths (Display): 42 mm
Copy instructions: *Copy Date:* 35 days prior to publication
CONSUMER: PHOTOGRAPHY & FILM MAKING: Photography

LFI LEICA FOTOGRAFIE INTERNATIONAL 1665849G85A-833
Editorial: Hammerbrookstr. 93, 20097 HAMBURG
Tel: 40 226211280 **Fax:** 40 226211270
Email: info@lfi-online.de **Web site:** http://www.lfi-online.de
Freq: 8 issues yearly; **Annual Sub.:** EUR 54,00; **Circ:** 6,442
Editor: Frank P. Lohstöter; **Advertising Manager:** Kirstin Ahrndt-Buchholz
Profile: Leica company photo magazine, English edition.
Language(s): English
ADVERTISING RATES:
Full Page Mono .... EUR 1101
Full Page Colour .... EUR 1695
Mechanical Data: Type Area: 245 x 183 mm, No. of Columns (Display): 4, Col Widths (Display): 42 mm
Copy instructions: *Copy Date:* 35 days prior to publication
CONSUMER: PHOTOGRAPHY & FILM MAKING: Photography

LGAD-NACHRICHTEN 1860265G14A-10215
Editorial: Max-Joseph-Str. 5, 80333 MÜNCHEN
Tel: 89 5459370 **Fax:** 89 54593730
Email: info@lgad.de **Web site:** http://www.lgad.de
Freq: 6 issues yearly; **Circ:** 1,000
Editor: Joachim Schwichtenberg
Profile: Magazine containing information on the wholesale trade.
Language(s): German
Official Journal of: Organ d. LV Groß- u. Außenhandel, Vertrieb u. Dienstleistungen Bayern (Unternehmer- u. Arbeitgeberverb. d. intermediären Wirtschaft e.V.)

LIBERAL 734127G82-5300
Editorial: Reinhardtstr. 16, 10117 BERLIN
Tel: 30 27572875 **Fax:** 30 27572880
Email: renate.metzenthin@liberalverlag.de **Web site:** http://www.liberalverlag.de
Freq: Quarterly; **Annual Sub.:** EUR 43,00; **Circ:** 2,600
Editor: Jürgen Frölich; **Advertising Manager:** Renate Metzenthin
Profile: Books for Politics and Culture, the magazine informs extensively and critically about what is going on in Germany, Europe and the world - political, economic and intellectual life.
Language(s): German
ADVERTISING RATES:
Full Page Mono .... EUR 1534
Mechanical Data: Type Area: 214 x 140 mm, No. of Columns (Display): 2, Col Widths (Display): 67 mm
Copy instructions: *Copy Date:* 30 days prior to publication
CONSUMER: CURRENT AFFAIRS & POLITICS

LIBORIUSBLATT 734132G87-8260
Editorial: Lange Str. 335, 59067 HAMM
Tel: 2381 940400 **Fax:** 2381 9404070
Email: redaktion.liboriusblatt@liborius.de **Web site:** http://www.liboriusblatt.de
Freq: Weekly; **Cover Price:** EUR 1,80; **Circ:** 38,927
Editor: Andrea Groß-Schulte; **Advertising Manager:** Manfred Schmitz
Profile: Catholic magazine.
Language(s): German
ADVERTISING RATES:
Full Page Mono .... EUR 3596
Full Page Colour .... EUR 5753
Mechanical Data: Type Area: 315 x 216 mm, No. of Columns (Display): 5, Col Widths (Display): 40 mm
Copy instructions: *Copy Date:* 10 days prior to publication
CONSUMER: RELIGIOUS

LICHT 734139G17-200_50
Editorial: Lazarettstr. 4, 80636 MÜNCHEN
Tel: 89 12607294 **Fax:** 89 12607304
Email: welk@pflaum.de **Web site:** http://www.lichtnet.de
Freq: 9 issues yearly; **Annual Sub.:** EUR 109,80; **Circ:** 10,718
Editor: Regina Welk; **Advertising Manager:** Michael Dietl
Profile: Publication of the Technical Lighting Association, the Trade Association for Lighting Advertisers and the Association of Lamp, Light and Accessories Industries. Covers technical and trade news, planning and design.
Language(s): English; German
ADVERTISING RATES:
Full Page Mono .... EUR 3480
Full Page Colour .... EUR 4410
Mechanical Data: Type Area: 272 x 184 mm, No. of Columns (Display): 3, Col Widths (Display): 58 mm
Copy instructions: *Copy Date:* 30 days prior to publication
Official Journal of: Organ d. Dt. Lichttechn. Ges. e.V., d. Normenausschusses Lichttechnik im DIN Dt. Inst. f. Normung e.V., d. Verb. Wohnraumleuchten-, Lampenschirm- u. Zubehör-Industrie e.V. u. d. Fachverb. Lichtwerbung e.V.
BUSINESS: ELECTRICAL

LICHT + RAUM 2084585G4E-7351
Editorial: Avenwedder Str. 55, 33335 GÜTERSLOH
Tel: 5241 8090884 **Fax:** 5241 80690880
Email: burkhard.froehlich@bauverlag.de **Web site:** http://www.dbz-lichtundraum.de
Freq: Quarterly; **Annual Sub.:** EUR 69,00; **Circ:** 18,000
Editor: Burkhard Fröhlich; **Advertising Manager:** Andreas Kirchgessner
Profile: With the two focal points of light + interior design, the relaunched title used since 2010 to the larger target group of lighting designers, interior designers, architects, facility managers as well as the exclusive lighting retailers and lighting, furniture and design studios. The editors of Licht + Raum reference to specific examples and projects are the way to define space. Light, material and design, space-shaping the interior and qualified interior design are the design factors which treated particularly are. Aspects which stand out in a particular example to be dealt with in depth and on projects. A holistic specification and product subject areas as well as interviews with designers and lighting designers, facility reports and show highlights will include a permanent part of Licht + Raum. The subject areas in which we are moving with Licht + Raum are stores, hotels, restaurants, bars, office, Events, Wellness, showrooms, education, museums and galleries.
Language(s): German
ADVERTISING RATES:
Full Page Mono .... EUR 5230
Full Page Colour .... EUR 8310
Mechanical Data: Type Area: 259 x 200 mm, No. of Columns (Display): 4, Col Widths (Display): 47 mm
Copy instructions: *Copy Date:* 14 days prior to publication
Supplement to: Bauwelt, DBZ Deutsche BauZeitschrift, Facility Management

LICHTENBERGER RATHAUSNACHRICHTEN 730446G46-7
Editorial: Rathausstr. 8, 10360 BERLIN
Tel: 30 902963312 **Fax:** 30 902963319
Email: redaktion@rathausnachrichten.de **Web site:** http://www.rathausnachrichten.de
Freq: Monthly; **Cover Price:** Free; **Circ:** 124,950
Editor: Christian Schwenkenbecher; **Advertising Manager:** Kai Bröske
Profile: Local official paper.
Language(s): German
ADVERTISING RATES:
Full Page Mono .... EUR 3254
Full Page Colour .... EUR 4556
Mechanical Data: Type Area: 327 x 233 mm, No. of Columns (Display): 5, Col Widths (Display): 45 mm
Copy instructions: *Copy Date:* 5 days prior to publication
Supplement(s): Bären Schaufenster Center am Tierpark

LICHT.FORUM 734152G17-1538
Editorial: Poststr. 9, 64293 DARMSTADT
Tel: 6151 399014 **Fax:** 6151 399022
Email: info@rfw-kom.de **Web site:** http://www.licht.de
Freq: Annual; **Cover Price:** Free; **Circ:** 350,000
Editor: Monika Schäfer-Feil
Profile: Information about illumination. From new trends in bathroom lighting to energy-efficient lighting for municipalities: The compact reader receives information on current issues - with many examples from practice.
Language(s): German

LIEGENSCHAFT AKTUELL 734171G1E-540
Editorial: Reinsburgstr. 82, 70178 STUTTGART
Tel: 711 238860 **Fax:** 711 2388625
Email: joerg.bleyhl@pressecompany.de **Web site:** http://www.immoclick24.de
Freq: 6 issues yearly; **Annual Sub.:** EUR 36,00; **Circ:** 12,695
Editor: Jörg Bleyhl; **Advertising Manager:** Karin Navaei
Profile: Magazine about the property business with relevant information about building, renovation and modernisation.
Language(s): German
Readership: Read by property developers and builders.
ADVERTISING RATES:
Full Page Mono .... EUR 4120
Full Page Colour .... EUR 5560
Mechanical Data: Type Area: 270 x 189 mm, No. of Columns (Display): 4, Col Widths (Display): 45 mm
Copy instructions: *Copy Date:* 15 days prior to publication
BUSINESS: FINANCE & ECONOMICS: Property

LIFE + SCIENCE 1659666G91D-10089
Editorial: Rotebühlstr. 77, 70178 STUTTGART
Tel: 711 66725738 **Fax:** 711 66722004
Email: a.mathes@klett.de **Web site:** http://www.lifeandscience.de
Freq: Quarterly; **Cover Price:** Free; **Circ:** 202,254
Editor: Dierk Suhr; **Advertising Manager:** Petra Sonnenfroh-Kost
Profile: Science and career magazine for students (Grades 10-13.) with topics from mathematics, computer science, science and technology combined with exciting content from industry and trade. In each issue features life + science training and study courses and shows the students' careers and prospects in industry, business and research. The didactic, scientific content can be also used as a teaching material in class.
Language(s): German
ADVERTISING RATES:
Full Page Mono .... EUR 9800
Full Page Colour .... EUR 9800
Mechanical Data: Type Area: 256 x 188 mm, No. of Columns (Display): 3, Col Widths (Display): 66 mm
Copy instructions: *Copy Date:* 30 days prior to publication
CONSUMER: RECREATION & LEISURE: Children & Youth

LIFE&STYLE 1842872G74A-3614
Editorial: Burchardstr. 19, 20095 HAMBURG
Tel: 40 30191202 **Fax:** 40 30191235
Email: katharina.gliese@bauerredaktionen.de **Web site:** http://www.bauerverlag.de
Freq: 26 issues yearly; **Cover Price:** EUR 1,90; **Circ:** 128,413
Editor: Tim Affeld
Profile: Life & Style is Germany's first weekly Fashion & People magazine. The unique blend of glam-gossip and highstreet fashion brings it right into the heart of ist readers and inspires their world by the look and the lives of stars. Beauty and Fashion environments are dominated in Life & Style by the hottest celebrities. Here Life & Style conveys, in addition to the weekly trend update, always specific styling tips to mimic the star looks. The readers are urban fashionistas between 20-39 years of age who orientate on the style of the stars. They are eager consumers, open to new things and love to discover trends and implement them for themselves.
Language(s): German
ADVERTISING RATES:
Full Page Mono .... EUR 8679
Full Page Colour .... EUR 8679
Mechanical Data: Type Area: 258 x 206 mm

LIFELINE 1662146G74G-1843
Editorial: Schwedter Str. 263, 10119 BERLIN
Tel: 30 884293920 **Fax:** 30 884293940
Email: info@bsmo.de **Web site:** http://www.lifeline.de
Freq: Daily; **Cover Price:** Paid; **Circ:** 847,426 Unique Users
Editor: Martin Trinkaus
Language(s): German
CONSUMER: WOMEN'S INTEREST CONSUMER MAGAZINES: Slimming & Health

LIFE@MAGAZIN 734176G2A-2380
Editorial: Steeler Bergstr. 96, 45276 ESSEN
Tel: 201 8508513 **Fax:** 201 8508514
Email: chrkolb@pressesprecher.de **Web site:** http://www.life-at.de
Freq: 6 issues yearly; **Cover Price:** Free; **Circ:** 49,000
Editor: Christian Kolb; **Advertising Manager:** Christian Kolb
Profile: Youth Media Magazine.
Language(s): German
ADVERTISING RATES:
Full Page Mono .... EUR 3500
Full Page Colour .... EUR 5000
Mechanical Data: Type Area: 297 x 210 mm

LIFT STUTTGART 734181G80-7180
Editorial: Falbenhennenstr. 17, 70180 STUTTGART
Tel: 711 60171717 **Fax:** 711 60171749
Email: info@lift-online.de **Web site:** http://www.lift-online.de
Freq: Monthly; **Annual Sub.:** EUR 22,00; **Circ:** 15,002
Editor: Ingmar Volkmann
Profile: City magazine for Stuttgart and the region. At about 180 pages to find the active, interested in culture and outgoing joyful lift Stuttgart readers everything that makes your life exciting in and around Stuttgart: people, city life, food, music, film, art, theater, clubs, shopping. The magazine publishes selected special topics. The special topics provide an ideal editorial environment to directly with your audience and your ad without reaching wastage. Facebook: http://www.facebook.com/LIFTStadtmagazin.
Language(s): German
ADVERTISING RATES:
Full Page Mono .... EUR 2020
Full Page Colour .... EUR 2960
Mechanical Data: Type Area: 260 x 190 mm
Copy instructions: *Copy Date:* 16 days prior to publication
CONSUMER: RURAL & REGIONAL INTEREST

LIGHT-EVENT + ARCHITECTURE 1639607G17-1557
Editorial: Braugasse 2, 59602 RÜTHEN
Tel: 2952 9759200 **Fax:** 2952 9759201
Email: info@highlight-verlag.de **Web site:** http://www.highlight-web.de
Freq: Half-yearly; **Cover Price:** EUR 7,00; **Circ:** 10,000
Editor: Markus Helle; **Advertising Manager:** Jutta Füser
Profile: Magazine about light in urban regions.
Language(s): German
ADVERTISING RATES:
Full Page Mono .... EUR 2375
Full Page Colour .... EUR 4025
Mechanical Data: Type Area: 275 x 196 mm, No. of Columns (Display): 4, Col Widths (Display): 46 mm

LIMNOLOGICA 734191G42C-38
Editorial: Universitätsstr. 5, 45141 ESSEN
Tel: 201 1833084 **Fax:** 201 1834442
Email: daniel.hering@uni-due.de
Freq: Quarterly; **Annual Sub.:** EUR 135,00

Editor: Daniel Hering
Profile: Journal covering ecology and management of inland waters.
Language(s): English; German
Official Journal of: Organ d. Dt. Ges. f. Limnologie
BUSINESS: CONSTRUCTION: Water Engineering

LINDAUER ZEITUNG
734192G67B-8900
Editorial: Rudolf-Roth-Str. 18, 88299 LEUTKIRCH
Tel: 7561 800 **Fax:** 7561 80134
Web site: http://www.szon.de
Freq: 312 issues yearly; **Circ:** 7,238
Profile: In its edition provides the "Lindauer Zeitung" its readers daily with the latest information from government, business, sports, culture and food from the local environment. Twitter: http://twitter.com/Schwaebische This Outlet offers RSS (Really Simple Syndication).
Language(s): German
ADVERTISING RATES:
SCC .... EUR 43,80
Mechanical Data: Type Area: 480 x 320 mm, No. of Columns (Display): 7, Col Widths (Display): 44 mm
Copy instructions: *Copy Date:* 1 day prior to publication
REGIONAL DAILY & SUNDAY NEWSPAPERS: Regional Daily Newspapers

LINGENER TAGESPOST
734198G67B-8920
Editorial: Breiter Gang 10, 49074 OSNABRÜCK
Tel: 541 3100 **Fax:** 541 310485
Email: redaktion@noz.de **Web site:** http://www.noz.de
Freq: 312 issues yearly; **Circ:** 21,709
Profile: Daily newspaper with regional news and a local sports section. Twitter: http://twitter.com/noz_de This Outlet offers RSS (Really Simple Syndication).
Language(s): German
ADVERTISING RATES:
SCC .... EUR 50,90
Mechanical Data: Type Area: 487 x 318 mm, No. of Columns (Display): 7, Col Widths (Display): 43 mm
Copy instructions: *Copy Date:* 2 days prior to publication
Supplement(s): Immo-Welt; Kfz-Welt
REGIONAL DAILY & SUNDAY NEWSPAPERS: Regional Daily Newspapers

LINIE INTERNATIONAL
734202G47B-1
Editorial: Neuer Zollhof 2, 40221 DÜSSELDORF
Tel: 211 22950500 **Fax:** 211 229505013
Email: j.neuhaus@linie-international.com **Web site:** http://www.linie-international.com
Freq: 5 issues yearly; **Annual Sub.:** EUR 71,00; **Circ:** 15,000
Advertising Manager: Julia Neuhaus
Profile: Specialist publication about underwear and lingerie, homewear and hosiery.
Language(s): German
ADVERTISING RATES:
Full Page Mono .... EUR 5500
Full Page Colour .... EUR 5500
Mechanical Data: Type Area: 260 x 190 mm
Copy instructions: *Copy Date:* 20 days prior to publication
BUSINESS: CLOTHING & TEXTILES: Lingerie, Hosiery/Swimwear

LINKS + RECHTS DER AUTOBAHN
734207G89A-3360
Editorial: Dießemer Bruch 167, 47805 KREFELD
Tel: 2151 5100129 **Fax:** 2151 510025129
Email: autobahn-guide@stuenings.de **Web site:** http://www.autobahn-guide.de
Freq: Annual; **Cover Price:** EUR 9,95; **Circ:** 128,000
Editor: Nina Otz; **Advertising Manager:** Verena Falk
Profile: Guide to top-to-date information on hotels, restaurants, gas stations and destinations in 22 European countries shows the guide once more how useful it is as a tour guide in the glove compartment. The trick: With Links+Rechts der Autobahn will reach the navigation device for supporting actor, because you, the easiest directions even without local knowledge of exactly what you wish your target.
Language(s): German
ADVERTISING RATES:
Full Page Colour .... EUR 2485
Mechanical Data: Type Area: 198 x 130 mm
Copy instructions: *Copy Date:* 75 days prior to publication

LINUX MAGAZIN
734214G5C-34_50
Editorial: Putzbrunner Str. 71, 81739 MÜNCHEN
Tel: 89 9934110 **Fax:** 89 99341199
Email: jkleinert@linux-magazin.de **Web site:** http://www.linux-magazin.de
Freq: Monthly; **Annual Sub.:** EUR 61,60; **Circ:** 47,000
Editor: Jan Kleinert; **Advertising Manager:** Hubert Wiest
Profile: Magazine for users of the Linux operating system with information about: system administration, virtualization, migrations, hardware and software for network and server, storage, security and anti-spam, high availability, clusters, databases, software and tools for commercial applications, programming and tools Cloud computing, Web development, product and industry news, events, trends such as smartphone operating systems and app development. Twitter: http://twitter.com/linuxmagazin Facebook: http://www.facebook.com/LinuxMagazin.
Language(s): German
Readership: Aimed at professionals in the IT industry.
ADVERTISING RATES:
Full Page Mono .... EUR 2780
Full Page Colour .... EUR 3680
Mechanical Data: Type Area: 266 x 184 mm
Copy instructions: *Copy Date:* 24 days prior to publication
BUSINESS: COMPUTERS & AUTOMATION: Professional Personal Computers

LION
1694961G32G-3101
Editorial: Deutz-Mülheimer Str. 227, 51063 KÖLN
Tel: 221 26007646 **Fax:** 611 9915420
Email: chefredakteur@lions.de
Freq: 11 issues yearly; **Circ:** 46,840
Editor: Ulrich Stoltenberg; **Advertising Manager:** Monika Droege
Profile: Journal of the German Lions Clubs.
Language(s): German
ADVERTISING RATES:
Full Page Mono .... EUR 2231
Full Page Colour .... EUR 3905
Mechanical Data: Type Area: 256 x 188 mm, No. of Columns (Display): 3, Col Widths (Display): 60 mm
Copy instructions: *Copy Date:* 31 days prior to publication
BUSINESS: LOCAL GOVERNMENT, LEISURE & RECREATION: Community Care & Social Services

LIPPISCHE LANDES-ZEITUNG
734234G67B-8940
Editorial: Ohmstr. 7, 32758 DETMOLD
Tel: 5231 911131 **Fax:** 5231 911145
Email: detmold@lz-online.de **Web site:** http://www.lz.de
Freq: 312 issues yearly; **Circ:** 41,620
Editor: Michael Dahl; **Advertising Manager:** Ralf Büschemann
Profile: The Lippische Landes-Zeitung has enjoyed a long history, is also always on the cutting edge. The success story of the LZ dates back to the year 1767, when the birth of the LZ in the form of the initial publication of the "Lippischen Intelligenzblätter" beat. Today, it not only the oldest newspaper has become in NRW, but also a local paper that feels Lippe and its people committed in a particular way. With a circulation of over 43,500 copies, the LZ now reaches about 148,000 readers - and over the Internet far more. Facebook: http://www.facebook.com/pages/Lippische-Landes-Zeitung/319567342628 Twitter: http://twitter.com/lzonline This Outlet offers RSS (Really Simple Syndication).
Language(s): German
ADVERTISING RATES:
SCC .... EUR 92,80
Mechanical Data: Type Area: 490 x 324 mm, No. of Columns (Display): 7, Col Widths (Display): 45 mm
Copy instructions: *Copy Date:* 1 day prior to publication
Supplement(s): prisma
REGIONAL DAILY & SUNDAY NEWSPAPERS: Regional Daily Newspapers

LISA
734239G74A-1900
Editorial: Hubert-Burda-Platz 1, 77652 OFFENBURG
Tel: 781 845147 **Fax:** 781 845122
Email: lisa@burda.com **Web site:** http://www.lisa.de
Freq: Weekly; **Annual Sub.:** EUR 59,80; **Circ:** 331,848
Editor: Maria Sandoval
Profile: Lisa sees the contemporary life of women particularly well and is in a superior manner to the diversity of life in all facets: family, job, partnership, and of course the own interests of modern women. That is why Lisa is chock full of tips and ideas on fashion, beauty, home and society and so excited every week millions of readers. The fact stand with both feet on, have fun, be informed, and seek advice, they are creative, relax and enjoy. And - they have their own little foibles endearing as cool perfectionism.
Language(s): German
Readership: Aimed at women between 25 and 35 years.
ADVERTISING RATES:
Full Page Mono .... EUR 16200
Full Page Colour .... EUR 16200
Mechanical Data: Type Area: 258 x 196 mm, No. of Columns (Display): 4, Col Widths (Display): 46 mm
Copy instructions: *Copy Date:* 21 days prior to publication
CONSUMER: WOMEN'S INTEREST CONSUMER MAGAZINES: Women's Interest

LISA BLUMEN & PFLANZEN
734241G93-240_50
Editorial: Hubert-Burda-Platz 1, 77652 OFFENBURG
Tel: 781 845238 **Fax:** 781 845244
Email: ursula.braun-bernhart@burda.com **Web site:** http://www.lisa.de
Freq: Monthly; **Annual Sub.:** EUR 20,40; **Circ:** 107,691
Editor: Ursula Braun-Bernhart; **Advertising Manager:** Caroline Müller
Profile: The monthly "Lisa Blumen & Pflanzen" aims at balcony, terrace and garden owners who love flowers and plants, who like digging, raking, weeding, watering, - but also want to be creative and still want to relax. "Lisa Blumen & Pflanzen" provides in an attractive form happy and colorful and thoroughly informative topics on the areas of balcony and terrace, garden, creative and DIY, food and wellness, housing and well-being, practical tips are scattered loosely into the colorful theme mix. Facebook: http://www.facebook.com/lisafreundeskreis.
Language(s): German
Readership: Aimed at people who do not own a garden.
ADVERTISING RATES:
Full Page Mono .... EUR 7650
Full Page Colour .... EUR 7650
Mechanical Data: Type Area: 280 x 220 mm, No. of Columns (Display): 4, Col Widths (Display): 52 mm
CONSUMER: GARDENING

LISA KOCHEN & BACKEN
734242G74P-983
Editorial: Hubert-Burda-Platz 1, 77652 OFFENBURG
Tel: 781 845235 **Fax:** 781 845240
Email: margit.schwend@burda.com **Web site:** http://www.daskochrezept.de/lisa-kochen-und-backen
Freq: Monthly; **Annual Sub.:** EUR 18,60; **Circ:** 112,220
Editor: Jutta Kässinger; **Advertising Manager:** Konstanze Hacke
Profile: All those who cook with fun, love to bake and eat with pleasure found in the variety of suggestions and ideas a source of inspiration. With a wealth of best recipes, the everyday of cooking in a daily experience of pleasure turns - ideal for households of young families with limited time budget and high expectations. An editorial and conceptually coordinated layout provides a quick overview of topics. Directly and easily the reader will find the meals to which they want to. In each issue culinary desires are fulfilled: the everyday kitchen with quick and economical meals as well as traditional and international cuisine. Easy to follow tips, current and interesting new products, knowledge about health and nutrition, and suggestions for kitchen appliances and household tips round out the issue concept.
Language(s): German
ADVERTISING RATES:
Full Page Mono .... EUR 12400
Full Page Colour .... EUR 12400
Mechanical Data: Type Area: 250 x 188 mm, No. of Columns (Display): 4, Col Widths (Display): 44 mm
Copy instructions: *Copy Date:* 42 days prior to publication
CONSUMER: WOMEN'S INTEREST CONSUMER MAGAZINES: Food & Cookery

LISA WOHNEN & DEKORIEREN
734245G74C-2300
Editorial: Hubert-Burda-Platz 1, 77652 OFFENBURG
Tel: 781 843368 **Fax:** 781 843382
Email: gertrud.hansmann@burda.com **Web site:** http://www.lisa-mehr-erleben.de
Freq: Monthly; **Annual Sub.:** EUR 26,40; **Circ:** 180,226
Editor: Manfred Heidt; **Advertising Manager:** Sabine Burda
Profile: Lisa Wohnen & Dekorieren each month shows the whole world of the home with new furniture trends, vibrant lifestyle reports, ideas for partys and useful information on topics such as building or insurance. Kitchen, bathroom, living room or children's room: The Lisa-living world is young, modern, creative, colorful - and full of emotional warmth. Each issue of Lisa Wohnen & Dekorieren reaches an average of 600,000 readers and inspires a new generation of lifestyle magazine readers: young, often still in the nestbuilding or family phase, with above-average income and a particularly highly motivated interest in living, design and furnishing. Facebook: http://www.facebook.com/lisafreundeskreis.
Language(s): German
Readership: Aimed at women interested in improving their home surroundings.
ADVERTISING RATES:
Full Page Mono .... EUR 11300
Full Page Colour .... EUR 11300
Mechanical Data: Type Area: 280 x 220 mm, No. of Columns (Display): 4, Col Widths (Display): 52 mm
Copy instructions: *Copy Date:* 60 days prior to publication
CONSUMER: WOMEN'S INTEREST CONSUMER MAGAZINES: Home & Family

LISSY.DE
1626166G91D-9893
Editorial: Karlsruher Str. 31, 76437 RASTATT
Tel: 7222 13506 **Fax:** 7222 13415
Email: susanne.stegbauer@vpm.de **Web site:** http://www.lissy.de
Freq: Monthly; **Cover Price:** Paid; **Circ:** 38,169 Unique Users
Editor: Susanne Stegbauer
Profile: Internet Media: Lissy.de is the site for young horse enthusiasts on the Internet. It addresses especially the target group of horse enthusiasts young girls aged 6 to 14 years and provides regular updates to your four-legged darlings. Complements the editorial content with information on comic book series, the main character, Lissy and your friends from the riding school. Other important components of Lissy.de are moving image contributions, sweepstakes, surveys, free online games and a horse's lexicon, which contains lots of facts about the handling of horses and their care and maintenance. An excellent platform for exchange among like-minded members of Lissy, the closed community, with its numerous forums. In addition, the members exclusive online games and news available and once a month, the newsletter Lissy fans about current topics.
Language(s): German
CONSUMER: RECREATION & LEISURE: Children & Youth

LITERATUREN
734259G76B-8165
Editorial: Knesebeckstr. 59, 10719 BERLIN
Tel: 30 25449580 **Fax:** 30 25449581
Email: redaktion@literaturen.de **Web site:** http://www.literaturen.de
Freq: 7 issues yearly; **Annual Sub.:** EUR 99,00; **Circ:** 17,000
Editor: Ronald Düker; **Advertising Manager:** Thomas Brovot
Profile: Illustrated journal of books and subjects: reviews, columns, features, profiles, essays, interviews and commentary. The journal provides entertaining, critical and professionally researched articles, a high-quality layout, attractive photos and illustrations. It extends beyond the traditional view of books on criticism and combines them with contemporary issues.
Language(s): German
ADVERTISING RATES:
Full Page Mono .... EUR 3450
Full Page Colour .... EUR 3450
Mechanical Data: No. of Columns (Display): 4, Col Widths (Display): 45 mm, Type Area: 250 x 180 mm
CONSUMER: MUSIC & PERFORMING ARTS: Theatre

LIVE!
734289G80-7220
Editorial: Vorgebirgstr. 59, 50677 KÖLN
Tel: 221 35558715 **Fax:** 221 93472730
Email: talk@koelner.de **Web site:** http://www.koelner.de
Freq: Monthly; **Cover Price:** Free; **Circ:** 41,592
Editor: Irma Wagner; **Advertising Manager:** Achim Göbel
Profile: Magazine for city and region, concentrating on gastronomy, music, arts and events.
Language(s): German
ADVERTISING RATES:
Full Page Mono .... EUR 3440
Full Page Colour .... EUR 5070
Mechanical Data: Type Area: 260 x 190 mm, No. of Columns (Display): 4, Col Widths (Display): 44 mm
Copy instructions: *Copy Date:* 15 days prior to publication
CONSUMER: RURAL & REGIONAL INTEREST

LIVE MAGAZIN
734294G80-7240
Editorial: Aschmattstr. 8, 76532 BADEN-BADEN
Tel: 7221 502340 **Fax:** 7221 502344
Email: livemagazin@baden-medien.de **Web site:** http://www.baden-medien.de
Freq: 6 issues yearly; **Annual Sub.:** EUR 18,00; **Circ:** 20,500
Editor: Marita Schneider; **Advertising Manager:** Manfred Schneider
Profile: Information from the region, large events calendar and regular sections on fashion and beauty, wellness and leisure, information, Cars & technology, decoration and living, art, culture, events, food & beverage, building renovation, and the horoscope.
Language(s): German
ADVERTISING RATES:
Full Page Colour .... EUR 2198
Mechanical Data: Type Area: 270 x 190 mm, No. of Columns (Display): 4, Col Widths (Display): 44 mm
Copy instructions: *Copy Date:* 15 days prior to publication
CONSUMER: RURAL & REGIONAL INTEREST

LIVING AT HOME
734298G74A-174
Editorial: Am Baumwall 11, 20459 HAMBURG
Tel: 40 37034246 **Fax:** 40 3703174246
Email: info@livingathome.de **Web site:** http://www.livingathome.de
Freq: Monthly; **Annual Sub.:** EUR 44,40; **Circ:** 150,569
Editor: Bettina Billerbeck
Profile: Living at Home shows the latest trends and lots of ideas for the mainplace of life: the personal housing and living room. The editorial foci on housing and kitchen and guests transform the own four walls into a comfort zone. Readers of Living At Home know that living is fun and how to be a charming hostess! Living At Home serves a very high quality standard and maintains a welcoming visual language - shiny, fresh, surprising. The lifestyle magazine reaches extremely attractive target groups: mobile cosmopolitan, luxury-oriented consumers and readers, who also have a high affinity for fashion, wellness and cosmetic care. And the far above average net household income sets the stage to be able to meet the existing needs.
Language(s): German
Readership: Read mainly by women.
ADVERTISING RATES:
Full Page Mono .... EUR 17600
Full Page Colour .... EUR 17600
Mechanical Data: Type Area: 235 x 181 mm, No. of Columns (Display): 3, Col Widths (Display): 57 mm
Copy instructions: *Copy Date:* 50 days prior to publication
CONSUMER: WOMEN'S INTEREST CONSUMER MAGAZINES: Women's Interest

LIVING AT HOME.DE
1626189G74P-1050
Editorial: Am Baumwall 11, 20459 HAMBURG
Tel: 40 37034214 **Fax:** 40 37034212

Email: info@livingathome.de **Web site:** http://www.livingathome.de
Freq: Daily; **Cover Price:** Paid; **Circ:** 907,741 Unique Users
Editor: Nadja Stavenhagen
Profile: Internet-portal of the publishing group Living - competent advice around the home, is the market leader in Germany in the segment of Living / lifestyle, provides users with information, services and trends in four areas and presents attractive products in shops and galleries.
Language(s): German
CONSUMER: WOMEN'S INTEREST CONSUMER MAGAZINES: Food & Cookery

LIVING BRIGITTE VON BOCH
763472G74C-3453
Editorial: Hildebrandtstr. 4, 40215 DÜSSELDORF
Tel: 211 501107 **Fax:** 211 501106
Email: utelaatz@brigittevonboch.de **Web site:** http://www.brigittevonbochliving.de
Freq: 6 issues yearly; **Annual Sub.:** EUR 30,00; **Circ:** 22,529
Editor: Brigitte von Boch; **Advertising Manager:** Ute Laatz
Profile: Lifestyle magazine, focused decoration and interiors. The magazine shows women between 29 and 49 not only set up, how they decorate, design the garden, cook. It provides, above all, a guide and shows the background and context of a lifestyle for the more and more people are interested.
Language(s): German
ADVERTISING RATES:
Full Page Mono .... EUR 8750
Full Page Colour .... EUR 8750
Mechanical Data: Type Area: 235 x 170 mm
CONSUMER: WOMEN'S INTEREST CONSUMER MAGAZINES: Home & Family

LÖBAUER WOCHENKURIER
734327G72-6812
Editorial: Wettiner Platz 10, 01067 DRESDEN
Tel: 351 491760 **Fax:** 351 4917674
Email: wochenkurier-dresden@dwk-verlag.de **Web site:** http://www.wochenkurier.info
Freq: Weekly; **Cover Price:** Free; **Circ:** 33,450
Editor: Regine Eberlein; **Advertising Manager:** Andreas Schönherr
Profile: Advertising journal (house-to-house) concentrating on local stories.
Language(s): German
ADVERTISING RATES:
Full Page Mono .... EUR 3010
Full Page Colour .... EUR 4214
Mechanical Data: Type Area: 430 x 290 mm, No. of Columns (Display): 7, Col Widths (Display): 38 mm
Copy instructions: *Copy Date:* 5 days prior to publication
LOCAL NEWSPAPERS

LOG. KOMPASS
1684024G10-533
Editorial: Nordkanalstr. 36, 20097 HAMBURG
Tel: 40 23714175 **Fax:** 40 23714226
Email: redaktion@logkompass.de **Web site:** http://www.logkompass.de
Freq: 10 issues yearly; Free to qualifying individuals
Annual Sub.: EUR 134,82; **Circ:** 20,043
Editor: Björn Helmke; **Advertising Manager:** Oliver Detje
Profile: Logistics.
Language(s): German
ADVERTISING RATES:
Full Page Colour .... EUR 5000
Mechanical Data: Type Area: 253 x 185 mm, No. of Columns (Display): 3, Col Widths (Display): 59 mm
Copy instructions: *Copy Date:* 14 days prior to publication
Official Journal of: Organ d. BVL Bundesvereinigung Logistik e.V.
BUSINESS: MATERIALS HANDLING

LOGISTIK FÜR UNTERNEHMEN
734357G49R-9
Editorial: VDI-Platz 1, 40468 DÜSSELDORF
Tel: 211 6103187 **Fax:** 211 6103148
Email: logistik@technikwissen.de **Web site:** http://www.logistik-fuer-unternehmen.de
Freq: 9 issues yearly; Free to qualifying individuals
Annual Sub.: EUR 154,50; **Circ:** 19,817
Editor: Anja Seeman
Profile: The trade magazine of the internal and external logistics aimed at the technical and commercial management and all logistics in the cross-section function decision makers active in industrial and commercial companies as well as logistics service providers. The future-oriented topics is aimed at the information needs of these high-profile target group. The magazine supports the ongoing processes of change of the sector and reports with editorial depth of all major logistics trends.
Language(s): German
Readership: Aimed at decision makers working in logistics within the industry and trade enterprises.
ADVERTISING RATES:
Full Page Mono .... EUR 4992
Full Page Colour .... EUR 6072
Mechanical Data: Type Area: 270 x 185 mm, No. of Columns (Display): 4, Col Widths (Display): 45 mm
Official Journal of: Organ d. VDI-Ges. Fördertechnik Materialfluß Logistik
BUSINESS: TRANSPORT: Transport Related

LOGISTIK HEUTE
734358G49R-10
Editorial: Joseph-Dollinger-Bogen 5, 80807 MÜNCHEN **Tel:** 89 32391212 **Fax:** 89 32391420
Email: redaktion@logistik-heute.de **Web site:** http://www.logistik-heute.de
Freq: 10 issues yearly; Free to qualifying individuals
Annual Sub.: EUR 187,80; **Circ:** 35,513
Editor: Petra Seebauer; **Advertising Manager:** Gabriele König
Profile: Procurement, production, distribution and disposal - all mixed with logistics. And therefore Logistik Heute, the magazine for managers in industry, commerce and service, has tailored its approach consistently to the entire supply chain. An independent editorial and technical contributors from research and practice to date on innovative logistics concepts, new products, ideas and trends along the entire supply chain. Detailed market surveys and business reportage, month after month, the logistical issues will include. Twitter:http://twitter.com/#!/LOGISTIK_HEUTE This Outlet offers RSS (Really Simple Syndication).
Language(s): German
Readership: Aimed at decision makers in the industrial, business and service sectors.
ADVERTISING RATES:
Full Page Mono .... EUR 5980
Full Page Colour .... EUR 8680
Mechanical Data: Type Area: 270 x 185 mm, No. of Columns (Display): 4, Col Widths (Display): 43 mm
Copy instructions: *Copy Date:* 23 days prior to publication
Supplement(s): update
BUSINESS: TRANSPORT: Transport Related

LOGISTIK JOURNAL
727578G49R-4
Editorial: Talhofstr. 24b, 82205 GILCHING
Tel: 8105 385378 **Fax:** 8105 385311
Email: m.weilacher@verlag-henrich.de **Web site:** http://www.logistik-journal.de
Freq: 6 issues yearly; **Annual Sub.:** EUR 80,00; **Circ:** 14,595
Editor: Michael Weilacher; **Advertising Manager:** Siegfried Kunert
Profile: Journal covering logistics and automation. Twitter: http://twitter.com/#!/logistikjournal.
Language(s): German
Readership: Aimed at managers and decision makers.
ADVERTISING RATES:
Full Page Mono .... EUR 5068
Full Page Colour .... EUR 6448
Mechanical Data: Type Area: 282 x 200 mm, No. of Columns (Display): 4, Col Widths (Display): 47 mm
Copy instructions: *Copy Date:* 14 days prior to publication
Supplement(s): i Quadrat
BUSINESS: TRANSPORT: Transport Related

LOGISTRA FUHRPARK
1931418G49A-2476
Editorial: Joseph-Dollinger-Bogen 5, 80807 MÜNCHEN **Tel:** 89 32391220 **Fax:** 89 32391417
Email: redaktion@logistra.de **Web site:** http://www.logistra.de
Freq: Quarterly; **Annual Sub.:** EUR 107,60; **Circ:** 14,503
Editor: Torsten Buchholz; **Advertising Manager:** Michaela Pech
Profile: The journal reports on new and proven solutions and products from all sectors of the commercial vehicle fleet and is aimed at fleet managers and fleet managers in industry and trade company with its own truck fleet (truck und/0der transporter) that perform quality transportation, part of the traffic. For distribution and procurement Commercial vehicles and trailers, means for securing loads, alternative engines and other technical and operational details shown and tested for their benefits for fleet management.
Language(s): German
ADVERTISING RATES:
Full Page Mono .... EUR 4980
Full Page Colour .... EUR 4980
Mechanical Data: Type Area: 270 x 185 mm, No. of Columns (Display): 4, Col Widths (Display): 43 mm
Supplement(s): Die Profi Werkstatt

LOGISTRA LAGERLOGISTIK
726617G49C-70
Editorial: Joseph-Dollinger-Bogen 5, 80807 MÜNCHEN **Tel:** 89 32391493 **Fax:** 89 32391417
Email: redaktion@logistra.de **Web site:** http://www.logistra.de
Freq: Quarterly; **Annual Sub.:** EUR 107,60; **Circ:** 14,503
Editor: Petra Seebauer; **Advertising Manager:** Gabriele König
Profile: The journal reports on new and proven solutions and products from all areas of warehousing and shipping and is aimed at storage and shipping managers in industrial and commercial enterprises. The presentation of tools and technical systems that can optimize the reader his intra-company processes, is in focus. Trucks, cranes, storage systems, etc. are just some examples.
Language(s): German
Readership: Read by HGV drivers, transport managers and anyone interested or connected with the logistics industry.
ADVERTISING RATES:
Full Page Mono .... EUR 4980
Full Page Colour .... EUR 4980
Mechanical Data: Type Area: 270 x 185 mm, No. of Columns (Display): 4, Col Widths (Display): 43 mm
BUSINESS: TRANSPORT: Freight

L.O.G.O.S. INTERDISZIPLINÄR
734371G56R-1240
Editorial: Alwinenstr. 10, 65189 WIESBADEN
Tel: 611 303680 **Fax:** 611 303688
Email: karen.ellger@t-online.de
Freq: Quarterly; **Annual Sub.:** EUR 69,00
Editor: Karen Ellger
Profile: Publication about speech and communication therapy.
Language(s): German
BUSINESS: HEALTH & MEDICAL: Health Medical Related

LOHN+GEHALT
734397G14A-4220
Editorial: Augustinusstr. 9d, 50226 FRECHEN
Tel: 2234 9661011 **Fax:** 2234 966109
Email: matt-keller@datakontext.com **Web site:** http://www.lohn-und-gehalt-zeitschrift.de
Freq: 8 issues yearly; **Annual Sub.:** EUR 129,00; **Circ:** 6,500
Editor: Markus Matt-Kellner; **Advertising Manager:** Kerstin Giffei
Profile: Journal about wages and salaries.
Language(s): German
ADVERTISING RATES:
Full Page Mono .... EUR 1785
Full Page Colour .... EUR 3124
Mechanical Data: Type Area: 230 x 175 mm, No. of Columns (Display): 3, Col Widths (Display): 55 mm
Copy instructions: *Copy Date:* 30 days prior to publication
BUSINESS: COMMERCE, INDUSTRY & MANAGEMENT

LÖHNER ZEITUNG
734330G67B-8980
Editorial: Brüderstr. 30, 32052 HERFORD
Tel: 5221 59080 **Fax:** 5221 590816
Freq: 312 issues yearly; **Circ:** 3,605
Profile: Daily newspaper with regional news and a local sports section.
Language(s): German
Mechanical Data: Type Area: 490 x 320 mm, No. of Columns (Display): 7, Col Widths (Display): 44 mm
Copy instructions: *Copy Date:* 1 day prior to publication
REGIONAL DAILY & SUNDAY NEWSPAPERS: Regional Daily Newspapers

LOHNSTEUER-MITTEILUNGEN
1627049G1A-3533
Editorial: Augustinusstr. 9d, 50226 FRECHEN
Tel: 2234 966100 **Fax:** 2234 966109
Email: fachverlag@datakontext.com **Web site:** http://www.datakontext.com
Freq: Monthly; **Annual Sub.:** EUR 54,00; **Circ:** 4,000
Editor: Michael Popp
Profile: Lohnsteuer-Mitteilungen is the advice letter for corporate income tax practice and provides in each issue: practice cases, practical tips, legally compliant solution of doubts, decisions of the tax jurisdiction, the financial management guidelines.
Language(s): German

LOHNUNTERNEHMEN
734398G21A-2680
Editorial: Heidecker Weg 112, 31275 LEHRTE
Tel: 5132 859140 **Fax:** 5132 8599940
Email: redaktion@beckmann-verlag.de **Web site:** http://www.lu-web.de
Freq: Monthly; Free to qualifying individuals
Annual Sub.: EUR 91,00; **Circ:** 4,924
Editor: Hans-Günter Dörpmund; **Advertising Manager:** Edward Kurdzielwicz
Profile: Official journal of the Society of Employers of Agricultural and Forestry Workers.
Language(s): German
ADVERTISING RATES:
Full Page Mono .... EUR 2432
Full Page Colour .... EUR 3818
Mechanical Data: Type Area: 270 x 190 mm, No. of Columns (Display): 4, Col Widths (Display): 45 mm
Official Journal of: Organ d. Lohnunternehmer-Berufsorganisation
BUSINESS: AGRICULTURE & FARMING

LOHRER ECHO
734399G67B-9000
Editorial: Weichertstr. 20, 63741 ASCHAFFENBURG
Tel: 6021 396229 **Fax:** 6021 396499
Email: redaktion@main-echo.de **Web site:** http://www.main-netz.de
Freq: 312 issues yearly; **Circ:** 6,137
Advertising Manager: Reinhard Fresow
Profile: Daily newspaper with regional news and a local sports section. Twitter: http://twitter.com/mainnetz This Outlet offers RSS (Really Simple Syndication).
Language(s): German
ADVERTISING RATES:
SCC .... EUR 18,10
Mechanical Data: Type Area: 480 x 366 mm, No. of Columns (Display): 8, Col Widths (Display): 44 mm
Copy instructions: *Copy Date:* 1 day prior to publication
Supplement(s): Gesundheit!
REGIONAL DAILY & SUNDAY NEWSPAPERS: Regional Daily Newspapers

LOKAL BOTE
734446G72-6920
Editorial: Maikäferweg 10, 29640 SCHNEVERDINGEN **Tel:** 40 7546118
Fax: 40 7546861
Email: info@lokalbote-hamburg.de **Web site:** http://www.lokalbote-hamburg.de
Freq: Monthly; **Cover Price:** Free; **Circ:** 40,000
Editor: Gisbert Müller; **Advertising Manager:** Gerd Hardenberg
Profile: Advertising journal (house-to-house) concentrating on local stories.
Language(s): German
ADVERTISING RATES:
Full Page Mono .... EUR 3000
Full Page Colour .... EUR 3130
Mechanical Data: Type Area: 438 x 286 mm, No. of Columns (Display): 6, Col Widths (Display): 46 mm
Copy instructions: *Copy Date:* 3 days prior to publication
LOCAL NEWSPAPERS

LOKALANZEIGER ANDERNACHER KURIER
734429G72-6956
Editorial: Hinter der Jungenstr. 22, 56218 MÜLHEIM-KÄRLICH **Tel:** 261 928193 **Fax:** 261 928199
Email: andernacher-kurier@vfa-online.de **Web site:** http://www.vfa-online.de
Freq: Weekly; **Cover Price:** Free; **Circ:** 31,200
Editor: Ralf Helfenstein; **Advertising Manager:** René Kuhmann
Profile: Advertising journal (house-to-house) concentrating on local stories.
Language(s): German
ADVERTISING RATES:
Full Page Mono .... EUR 4416
Mechanical Data: Type Area: 480 x 325 mm, No. of Columns (Display): 8, Col Widths (Display): 38 mm
Copy instructions: *Copy Date:* 3 days prior to publication
LOCAL NEWSPAPERS

LOKAL-ANZEIGER - AUSG. BARMBEK/WINTERHUDE
734415G72-6888
Editorial: Kattunbleiche 37, 22041 HAMBURG
Tel: 40 681988 **Fax:** 4552 9933081
Email: redaktion@lokalanzeiger.info **Web site:** http://www.lokal-anzeiger-hamburg.de
Freq: 26 issues yearly; **Cover Price:** Free; **Circ:** 34,800
Editor: Holger Bischoff; **Advertising Manager:** Matthias Bischoff
Profile: Advertising journal (house-to-house) concentrating on local stories.
Language(s): German
ADVERTISING RATES:
Full Page Mono .... EUR 2016
Full Page Colour .... EUR 2268
Mechanical Data: Type Area: 420 x 280 mm, No. of Columns (Display): 6, Col Widths (Display): 45 mm
Copy instructions: *Copy Date:* 6 days prior to publication
LOCAL NEWSPAPERS

LOKALANZEIGER LAHN-POST
734428G72-6952
Editorial: Ste.-Foy-Str. 27, 65549 LIMBURG
Tel: 6431 913338 **Fax:** 6431 23458
Email: lahn-post@vfa-online.de **Web site:** http://www.vfa-online.de
Freq: Weekly; **Cover Price:** Free; **Circ:** 83,300
Editor: Mirko Bader; **Advertising Manager:** René Kuhmann
Profile: Advertising journal (house-to-house) concentrating on local stories.
Language(s): German
ADVERTISING RATES:
Full Page Mono .... EUR 7680
Mechanical Data: Type Area: 480 x 325 mm, No. of Columns (Display): 8, Col Widths (Display): 38 mm
Copy instructions: *Copy Date:* 5 days prior to publication
LOCAL NEWSPAPERS

LOP LANDWIRTSCHAFT OHNE PFLUG
733868G21A-2560
Editorial: Oraniendamm 68, 13469 BERLIN
Tel: 30 40304336 **Fax:** 30 40304340
Email: lop@pfluglos.de **Web site:** http://www.pfluglos.de
Freq: 9 issues yearly; Free to qualifying individuals
Annual Sub.: EUR 43,20; **Circ:** 3,800
Editor: Konrad Steinert; **Advertising Manager:** Theresia Wirth
Profile: Magazine for farmers, consultants, research institutions and government agencies that deal with conservation tillage.
Language(s): German
Readership: Aimed at all those involved in agriculture including farmers.
ADVERTISING RATES:
Full Page Mono .... EUR 2722
Full Page Colour .... EUR 3780
Mechanical Data: Type Area: 252 x 186 mm, No. of Columns (Display): 3, Col Widths (Display): 45 mm
Copy instructions: *Copy Date:* 21 days prior to publication
BUSINESS: AGRICULTURE & FARMING

LOUIS
1865408G77A-2858

Editorial: Rungedamm 35, 21035 HAMBURG
Email: info@louis.de **Web site:** http://www.louis.de
Freq: Annual; **Cover Price:** Free; **Circ:** 1,200,000
Editor: Sven Kindel
Profile: Customer magazine from Louis bikers' equipment.
Language(s): German
ADVERTISING RATES:
Full Page Mono .... EUR 14990
Full Page Colour .... EUR 14990
Copy instructions: *Copy Date:* 77 days prior to publication

LÖWENKURIER
728664G14A-2660

Editorial: Adenauerring 7, 81737 MÜNCHEN
Tel: 89 51216300 **Fax:** 89 51211045
Email: presse@generali.de **Web site:** http://www.generali.de
Freq: 6 issues yearly; **Circ:** 18,000
Editor: Wolfgang Leix
Profile: Magazine for employees of Thuringia Generali Versicherungen.
Language(s): German

LÖWENZAHN
734350G91D-5040

Editorial: Wallstr. 59, 10179 BERLIN **Tel:** 30 240080
Fax: 30 24008599
Email: s.saydo@ehapa.de **Web site:** http://www.ehapa.de
Freq: Monthly; **Annual Sub.:** EUR 32,45; **Circ:** 24,299
Editor: Sanya Saydo
Profile: Magazine of the same name ZDF broadcast with stories of nature, environment and technology. Content: Photo stories for reading, reports, experiments, activities and puzzles. Currently, unusual and exciting for young and old knowledge is explained. In addition, there are plenty of instructions for self experimentation and research for the little ones 4-10 years. The magazine is based on the ZDF-success show. Presented and commented on the contents of the popular leader Fritz Fuchs.
Language(s): German
ADVERTISING RATES:
Full Page Mono .... EUR 4400
Full Page Colour .... EUR 4400
Mechanical Data: Type Area: 280 x 210 mm, No. of Columns (Display): 4, Col Widths (Display): 52 mm
CONSUMER: RECREATION & LEISURE: Children & Youth

LOYAL
734473G40-946

Editorial: Frankenallee 71, 60327 FRANKFURT
Tel: 69 75014219 **Fax:** 69 75014361
Email: fsd@fsd.de **Web site:** http://www.fsd.de
Freq: 11 issues yearly; **Annual Sub.:** EUR 35,00; **Circ:** 145,000
Editor: Rüdiger Moniac
Profile: German defence magazine.
Language(s): German
ADVERTISING RATES:
Full Page Mono .... EUR 3850
Full Page Colour .... EUR 7000
Mechanical Data: Type Area: 253 x 185 mm, No. of Columns (Display): 4, Col Widths (Display): 45 mm
Copy instructions: *Copy Date:* 26 days prior to publication
BUSINESS: DEFENCE

LPI LIGHTING PRESS INTERNATIONAL
1629388G43A-1510

Editorial: Bodelschwinghstr. 14, 58675 HEMER
Tel: 8131 565572 **Fax:** 8131 565510
Email: matthias.martin@l-p-i.de **Web site:** http://www.l-p-i.de
Freq: 8 issues yearly; **Annual Sub.:** EUR 44,00; **Circ:** 9,923
Editor: Matthias Martin; **Advertising Manager:** Gabriele Brunner
Profile: Magazine on illumination, light and building services engineering.
Language(s): English; German
ADVERTISING RATES:
Full Page Mono .... EUR 4480
Full Page Colour .... EUR 4480
Mechanical Data: Type Area: 306 x 211 mm
BUSINESS: ELECTRICAL RETAIL TRADE

LSV KOMPAKT
1914895G21A-4433

Editorial: Weißensteinstr. 72, 34131 KASSEL
Tel: 561 9359241 **Fax:** 561 9359244
Email: presse1@spv.lsv.de **Web site:** http://www.lsv.de
Freq: 5 issues yearly; **Circ:** 1,000,000
Editor: Albert Münz
Profile: Membership magazine of the agricultural social security reports on the topics of health and health care, accident prevention, contributions and design review, pensions .
Language(s): German

LSWB INFO
1860130G1A-3716

Editorial: Implerstr. 11, 81371 MÜNCHEN
Tel: 89 2732140 **Fax:** 89 2730656
Email: info@lswb.de **Web site:** http://www.lswb.de
Freq: 6 issues yearly; **Circ:** 6,500
Editor: Steffen Jahn; **Advertising Manager:** Stefan Kolleth
Profile: Information for accountants and auditors.
Language(s): German
Mechanical Data: Type Area: 290 x 210 mm
Copy instructions: *Copy Date:* 30 days prior to publication

LÜBBECKER KREISZEITUNG
734490G67B-9020

Editorial: Sudbrackstr. 14, 33611 BIELEFELD
Tel: 521 5850 **Fax:** 521 585489
Email: wb@westfalen-blatt.de **Web site:** http://www.westfalen-blatt.de
Freq: 312 issues yearly; **Circ:** 9,122
Advertising Manager: Gabriele Förster
Profile: Daily newspaper with regional news and a local sports section.
Language(s): German
Mechanical Data: Type Area: 490 x 320 mm, No. of Columns (Display): 7, Col Widths (Display): 44 mm
Copy instructions: *Copy Date:* 1 day prior to publication
Supplement(s): Mein Garten; www.wb-immo.net
REGIONAL DAILY & SUNDAY NEWSPAPERS: Regional Daily Newspapers

LÜBECKER NACHRICHTEN
734496G67B-9040

Editorial: Herrenholz 10, 23556 LÜBECK
Tel: 451 1440 **Fax:** 451 1441022
Email: ln-chefredaktion@ln-luebeck.de **Web site:** http://www.luebecker-nachrichten.de
Freq: 312 issues yearly; **Annual Sub.:** EUR 22,10; **Circ:** 99,395
Editor: Manfred von Thien; **News Editor:** Wilfried Schwanholz; **Advertising Manager:** Rüdiger Kruppa
Profile: Regional daily newspaper with news on politics, economy, culture, sports, travel, technology, etc. Facebook: http://www.facebook.com/pages/Lubecker-Nachrichten-Online/373673517230?ref=search&sid=1469388759.1445959996..1 Twitter: http://twitter.com/LN_online This Outlet offers RSS (Really Simple Syndication).
Language(s): German
ADVERTISING RATES:
SCC .... EUR 181,60
Mechanical Data: Type Area: 487 x 327 mm, No. of Columns (Display): 7, Col Widths (Display): 45 mm
Copy instructions: *Copy Date:* 1 day prior to publication
Supplement(s): TheaterZeit
REGIONAL DAILY & SUNDAY NEWSPAPERS: Regional Daily Newspapers

LÜBECKER NACHRICHTEN
1626167G67B-16714

Editorial: Herrenholz 10, 23556 LÜBECK
Tel: 451 1442263
Email: info@ln-online.de **Web site:** http://www.ln-online.de
Freq: Daily; **Cover Price:** Paid; **Circ:** 743,216 Unique Users
Editor: Holger Haase; **Advertising Manager:** Rüdiger Kruppa
Profile: Ezine: Regional daily newspaper covering politics, economics, sport, travel and technology. Twitter: http://twitter.com/LN_Online.
Language(s): German
REGIONAL DAILY & SUNDAY NEWSPAPERS: Regional Daily Newspapers

LÜDENSCHEIDER NACHRICHTEN
734500G67B-9060

Editorial: Schillerstr. 20, 58511 LÜDENSCHEID
Tel: 2351 1580 **Fax:** 2351 158223
Email: ln@come-on.de **Web site:** http://www.come-on.de
Freq: 312 issues yearly; **Circ:** 15,043
Advertising Manager: Guido Schröder
Profile: Daily newspaper with regional news and a local sports section. This Outlet offers RSS (Really Simple Syndication).
Language(s): German
ADVERTISING RATES:
SCC .... EUR 56,00
Mechanical Data: Type Area: 466 x 317 mm, No. of Columns (Display): 7, Col Widths (Display): 43 mm
Copy instructions: *Copy Date:* 1 day prior to publication
Supplement(s): prisma
REGIONAL DAILY & SUNDAY NEWSPAPERS: Regional Daily Newspapers

LUDWIG - SÜDOSTBAYERNS TRENDMAGAZIN, AUSG. RO-TS-BGL-AÖ-MÜ-PAN
734483G80-7320

Editorial: Rupertistr. 32, 83278 TRAUNSTEIN
Tel: 861 166290 **Fax:** 861 1662929
Email: info@ludwig-magazin.de **Web site:** http://www.ludwig-magazin.de
Freq: Monthly; **Cover Price:** Free; **Circ:** 25,750
Editor: Sebastian Ochs; **Advertising Manager:** Elli Boeddeker
Profile: Magazine for city and region, concentrating on gastronomy, music, arts and events.
Language(s): German
ADVERTISING RATES:
Full Page Mono .... EUR 2575
Full Page Colour .... EUR 2575
Mechanical Data: Type Area: 237 x 164 mm
CONSUMER: RURAL & REGIONAL INTEREST

LUDWIGSBURGER KREISZEITUNG
734486G67B-9080

Editorial: Körnerstr. 14, 71634 LUDWIGSBURG
Tel: 7141 130240 **Fax:** 7141 130340
Email: redaktion@lkz.de **Web site:** http://www.lkz.de
Freq: 260 issues yearly; **Circ:** 40,428
Editor: Ulrike Trampus; **News Editor:** Hubert Dreher; **Advertising Manager:** Jürgen Merkle
Profile: Regional daily newspaper covering politics, economics, sport, travel and technology. Twitter: http://twitter.com/lkz_online This Outlet offers RSS (Really Simple Syndication).
Language(s): German
ADVERTISING RATES:
SCC .... EUR 72,10
Mechanical Data: Type Area: 485 x 324 mm, No. of Columns (Display): 7, Col Widths (Display): 45 mm
Copy instructions: *Copy Date:* 2 days prior to publication
REGIONAL DAILY & SUNDAY NEWSPAPERS: Regional Daily Newspapers

LUDWIGSBURGER WOCHENBLATT
734487G72-7076

Editorial: Lindenstr. 15, 71634 LUDWIGSBURG
Tel: 7141 9620511 **Fax:** 7141 9620533
Email: redaktion@luwo.de **Web site:** http://www.ludwigsburger-wochenblatt.de
Freq: Weekly; **Cover Price:** Free; **Circ:** 151,500
Editor: Gerald Probst; **Advertising Manager:** Gerald Probst
Profile: Advertising journal (house-to-house) concentrating on local stories.
Language(s): German
ADVERTISING RATES:
Full Page Mono .... EUR 8760
Full Page Colour .... EUR 12256
Mechanical Data: Type Area: 485 x 325 mm, No. of Columns (Display): 7, Col Widths (Display): 45 mm
Copy instructions: *Copy Date:* 2 days prior to publication
LOCAL NEWSPAPERS

LUDWIGSLUSTER BLITZ AM SONNTAG
734489G72-7084

Editorial: Pampower Str. 3, 19061 SCHWERIN
Tel: 385 64584841 **Fax:** 385 64584820
Email: rita.brueckner@blitzverlag.de **Web site:** http://www.blitzverlag.de
Freq: Weekly; **Cover Price:** Free; **Circ:** 57,220
Editor: Rita Brückner
Profile: Advertising journal (house-to-house) concentrating on local stories.
Language(s): German
ADVERTISING RATES:
Full Page Mono .... EUR 2924
Full Page Colour .... EUR 3314
Mechanical Data: Type Area: 420 x 285 mm, No. of Columns (Display): 6, Col Widths (Display): 45 mm
Copy instructions: *Copy Date:* 2 days prior to publication
LOCAL NEWSPAPERS

LUFT- UND RAUMFAHRT
734515G6A-960

Editorial: Kolpingring 16, 82041 OBERHACHING
Tel: 89 6138900 **Fax:** 89 61389010
Email: aviatic@aviatic.de **Web site:** http://www.aviatic.de
Freq: 6 issues yearly
Editor: Peter Pletschacher; **Advertising Manager:** Judith Fischl
Profile: Magazine covering air and space travel and relevant technology.
Language(s): German
ADVERTISING RATES:
Full Page Mono .... EUR 2030
Full Page Colour .... EUR 3670
Mechanical Data: Type Area: 264 x 184 mm
BUSINESS: AVIATION & AERONAUTICS

LUFTHANSA EXCLUSIVE
1644037G94H-14398

Editorial: Stubbenhuk 10, 20459 HAMBURG
Tel: 40 37035065 **Fax:** 40 37035010
Email: lhmagazin@guj.de **Web site:** http://www.corporate-editors.com
Freq: 6 issues yearly; **Cover Price:** Free; **Circ:** 289,085
Editor: Christian Krug; **Advertising Manager:** Heiko Hager
Profile: On board magazine of the German Lufthansa airline.
Language(s): German
ADVERTISING RATES:
Full Page Mono .... EUR 19600
Full Page Colour .... EUR 19600
Mechanical Data: Type Area: 240 x 180 mm
Copy instructions: *Copy Date:* 59 days prior to publication
CONSUMER: OTHER CLASSIFICATIONS: Customer Magazines

LUFTRETTUNG
1609393G56R-2411

Editorial: Borsigstr. 30, 73249 WERNAU
Tel: 7153 923248
Email: info@wortweber.de **Web site:** http://www.wortweber.de
Freq: Quarterly; **Circ:** 325,000
Editor: Irina Wonneberg
Profile: Annual on Christianity related to sport.
Language(s): German
BUSINESS: HEALTH & MEDICAL: Health Medical Related

LUKULLUS
734522G94H-7640

Editorial: Am Flugplatz 4, Haus 49, 23560 LÜBECK
Tel: 451 50405681 **Fax:** 451 50405688
Email: redaktion@hanse-medienkontor.de
Freq: Weekly; **Cover Price:** Free; **Circ:** 263,271
Editor: Björn Hansen
Profile: Magazine containing information on cookery, as well as fitness and health.
Language(s): German
ADVERTISING RATES:
Full Page Mono .... EUR 17000
Full Page Colour .... EUR 17000
Mechanical Data: Type Area: 260 x 189 mm, No. of Columns (Display): 4, Col Widths (Display): 45 mm
CONSUMER: OTHER CLASSIFICATIONS: Customer Magazines

LURUPER WOCHENBLATT
734533G72-7100

Editorial: Harburger Rathausstr. 40, 21073 HAMBURG **Tel:** 40 85322933 **Fax:** 40 85322939
Email: post@wochenblatt-redaktion.de **Web site:** http://www.luruper-wochenblatt.de
Cover Price: Free
Editor: Olaf Zimmermann; **Advertising Manager:** Jürgen Müller
Profile: Advertising journal (house-to-house) concentrating on local stories.
Language(s): German
Supplement(s): Elbe-Einkaufszentrum Aktuell
LOCAL NEWSPAPERS

LUST AUF GENUSS
1832684G74P-1256

Editorial: Arabellastr. 23, 81925 MÜNCHEN
Tel: 89 92500 **Fax:** 89 92503030
Web site: http://www.lustaufgenuss.de
Freq: Monthly; **Annual Sub.:** EUR 49,40; **Circ:** 152,667
Editor: Birgitt Micha
Profile: "Experience is special, " With the success of the show the concept enthusiastic readers! Lust auf Genuss is the food and beverage magazine for sophisticated and open-minded readers who love the creative and the allure of the new: a passionate cook, try out and enjoy - best equal with friends. Culinary trends, seasonal highlights, the best in the world - optical quality and always innovative staging. A brand to revel and dream, but always focused on practical experience. The brand name clearly communicates the underlying life and the life-world. Lust auf Genuss is offset by the joy of life, openness to new things, for style and the beautiful side of life.
Language(s): German
ADVERTISING RATES:
Full Page Mono .... EUR 14900
Full Page Colour .... EUR 14900
Mechanical Data: Type Area: 246 x 192 mm, No. of Columns (Display): 4, Col Widths (Display): 45 mm

LUST AUFS LAND
733794G89A-3320

Editorial: Maarstr. 96, 53227 BONN **Tel:** 228 963020
Fax: 228 9630233
Email: bois@landselection.de **Web site:** http://www.landselection.de
Freq: Annual; **Cover Price:** EUR 10,00; **Circ:** 10,000
Editor: Silvia Bois; **Advertising Manager:** Bettina Zanella
Profile: Farm holiday magazine.
Language(s): German
ADVERTISING RATES:
Full Page Mono .... EUR 1200
Full Page Colour .... EUR 1500
Mechanical Data: Type Area: 190 x 120 mm
Copy instructions: *Copy Date:* 80 days prior to publication

LÜTTRINGHAUSER ANZEIGER
734505G72-7108

Editorial: Gertenbachstr. 20, 42899 REMSCHEID
Tel: 2191 50663 **Fax:** 2191 54598
Email: luettringhauser-anzeiger@t-online.de **Web site:** http://www.luettringhauser-anzeiger.de
Freq: Weekly; **Annual Sub.:** EUR 52,00; **Circ:** 9,150
Editor: Stefan Göllner; **Advertising Manager:** Stefan Göllner
Profile: Regional weekly covering politics, economics, sport, travel, technology and the arts.
Language(s): German
ADVERTISING RATES:
SCC .... EUR 18,50
Mechanical Data: Type Area: 430 x 285 mm, No. of Columns (Display): 6, Col Widths (Display): 45 mm
Copy instructions: *Copy Date:* 1 day prior to publication
LOCAL NEWSPAPERS

LUTZ'SCHES KURZ-INFO
1928134G57-2936

Editorial: Postfach 1420, 65764 KELKHEIM
Tel: 172 6712118 **Fax:** 6195 65118
Email: presse-lutz@gmx.net
Freq: Monthly; **Circ:** 20,000
Profile: The latest information on environmental protection.

Language(s): German
Mechanical Data: Type Area: 204 x 145 mm, No. of Columns (Display): 2, Col Widths (Display): 70 mm
Copy instructions: *Copy Date:* 8 days prior to publication

LUX 1929851G65A-180_106
Editorial: Hultschiner Str. 8, 81677 MÜNCHEN
Tel: 89 21837281 **Fax:** 89 21837213
Email: info@sv-onpact.de **Web site:** http://www.es-werde-lux.de
Freq: 6 issues yearly; **Circ:** 494,000
Editor: Herbert Lechner; **Advertising Manager:** Susanne Kögler
Profile: LUX - The magazine for intelligent energy appears every 2 months as a supplement to the Süddeutsche Zeitung has a circulation of about 490,000 copies. LUX transports the future topics "Renewable Energies" and "optimization of conventional energy technologies" in an unparalleled range by its carrier medium Süddeutsche Zeitung (ø 1.27 million readers *) to a premium target group. Like no other medium combines LUX information and value around the Energy. Innovative energy concepts, new techniques and devices achieve efficient with LUX regularly demanding SZ readership and thus decision- the multipliers and technical interest.
Language(s): German
ADVERTISING RATES:
Full Page Mono .... EUR 15100
Full Page Colour .... EUR 15100
Mechanical Data: Type Area: 245 x 196 mm, No. of Columns (Display): 3, Col Widths (Display): 63 mm
Copy instructions: *Copy Date:* 47 days prior to publication
Supplement to: Süddeutsche Zeitung
NATIONAL DAILY & SUNDAY NEWSPAPERS: Unabhängiges konservatives MdEP

LUXEMBURGER OBST- UND GARTENBAUFREUND
734547G21A-2700
Editorial: Hüttersdorfer Str. 29, 66839 SCHMELZ
Tel: 6887 9032999 **Fax:** 6887 9032998
Email: info@unsergarten-verlag.de **Web site:** http://www.unsergarten-verlag.de
Freq: 6 issues yearly; Free to qualifying individuals
Annual Sub.: EUR 10,80; **Circ:** 360
Editor: Monika Lambert-Debong; **Advertising Manager:** Monika Lambert-Debong
Profile: Magazine for members of the Luxembourger Association for Landscape Architecture, Fruit Growing and Gardening.
Language(s): German
Mechanical Data: Type Area: 264 x 189 mm, No. of Columns (Display): 4, Col Widths (Display): 45 mm
Copy instructions: *Copy Date:* 20 days prior to publication
Official Journal of: Organ d. Luxemburger Landes-Obst- u. Gartenbauvereins

L!VE 734292G89C-4811
Editorial: Mainzer Str. 23, 66111 SAARBRÜCKEN
Tel: 681 9601034 **Fax:** 681 9601035
Email: info@live-magazin.de **Web site:** http://www.live-magazin.de
Freq: Monthly; **Cover Price:** Free; **Circ:** 35,240
Editor: Marija Herceg
Profile: City magazine in the Saarland with information on music-, sports- and cultural events. Facebook: http://www.facebook.com/LiveMagazin.
Language(s): German
ADVERTISING RATES:
Full Page Mono .... EUR 1390
Full Page Colour .... EUR 2790
Mechanical Data: Type Area: 268 x 200 mm, No. of Columns (Display): 4, Col Widths (Display): 47 mm
Copy instructions: *Copy Date:* 14 days prior to publication
CONSUMER: HOLIDAYS & TRAVEL: Entertainment Guides

LVZ ONLINE 1621628G67B-16588
Editorial: Peterssteinweg 19, 04107 LEIPZIG
Tel: 341 21811595 **Fax:** 341 21811794
Email: holger.herzberg@lvz-online.de **Web site:** http://www.lvz-online.de
Freq: Daily; **Cover Price:** Paid; **Circ:** 1,486,449 Unique Users
Editor: Holger Herzberg
Profile: Leipziger Volkszeitung online: latest news from politics, business, sports, culture and society from Leipzig Facebook: http://facebook.com/lvzonline Twitter: http://twitter.com/#!/lvzonline This Outlet offers RSS (Really Simple Syndication).
Language(s): German
REGIONAL DAILY & SUNDAY NEWSPAPERS: Regional Daily Newspapers

LW HESSEN.RHEINLAND-PFALZ LANDWIRTSCHAFTLICHES WOCHENBLATT 734559G21A-2720
Editorial: Taunusstr. 151, 61381 FRIEDRICHSDORF
Tel: 6172 7106144 **Fax:** 6172 7106199
Email: c.mohr@lv-hessen.de **Web site:** http://www.lw-heute.de
Freq: Weekly; **Annual Sub.:** EUR 91,00; **Circ:** 21,870
Editor: Cornelius Mohr; **Advertising Manager:** Christa Schweitzer
Profile: Official weekly from the Association of Farmers in Hessen, the Hessische Landjugend and bulletin of agricultural and rural organizations. The audience is made up of farmers and representatives of rural cooperatives, the agricultural trade and agricultural machinery trade. Spread is the weekly addition of agricultural schools and departments, in dairies and for rural women and rural youth.
Language(s): German
ADVERTISING RATES:
Full Page Mono .... EUR 4543
Full Page Colour .... EUR 7678
Mechanical Data: Type Area: 275 x 192 mm, No. of Columns (Display): 4, Col Widths (Display): 45 mm
Copy instructions: *Copy Date:* 5 days prior to publication
Supplement(s): wochenblatt Magazin
BUSINESS: AGRICULTURE & FARMING

LW HESSEN.RHEINLAND-PFALZ LANDWIRTSCHAFTLICHES WOCHENBLATT 734560G21A-2740
Editorial: Weberstr. 9, 55130 MAINZ **Tel:** 6131 62050
Fax: 6131 620544
Email: c.mohr@lv-hessen.de **Web site:** http://www.fraund.de
Freq: Weekly; **Annual Sub.:** EUR 82,20; **Circ:** 7,325
Editor: Cornelius Mohr
Profile: Current news, agricultural politics and crops, are in addition to business management, animal husbandry and agricultural technology, the most commonly read sections. Market and price reports and classified advertisements are in the majority of respondents read regularly, even if no current intention to buy or sell.
Language(s): German
ADVERTISING RATES:
Full Page Mono .... EUR 2772
Full Page Colour .... EUR 4565
Mechanical Data: Type Area: 275 x 192 mm, No. of Columns (Display): 4, Col Widths (Display): 45 mm
Copy instructions: *Copy Date:* 5 days prior to publication
Official Journal of: Organ d. Bauern- u. Winzerverb. Rheinland-Pfalz Süd e.V. u. d. angeschlossenen Verbände, Amtsblatt d. Landwirtschaftskammer Rheinland-Pfalz u. d. landwirtschaftl. Fachverbände
Supplement(s): wochenblatt Magazin
BUSINESS: AGRICULTURE & FARMING

LWF AKTUELL 1792808G21A-4351
Editorial: Hans-Carl-von-Carlowitz-Platz 1, 85354 FREISING **Tel:** 8161 714881 **Fax:** 8161 714971
Email: redaktion@lwf.bayern.de **Web site:** http://www.lwf.bayern.de
Freq: 6 issues yearly; **Cover Price:** EUR 5,00
Free to qualifying individuals ; **Circ:** 1,600
Editor: Michael Mößnang
Profile: Magazine from the Bavarian Federal Organization for Forestry.
Language(s): German

LWF AKTUELL 1792808G21A-4453
Editorial: Hans-Carl-von-Carlowitz-Platz 1, 85354 FREISING **Tel:** 8161 714881 **Fax:** 8161 714971
Email: redaktion@lwf.bayern.de **Web site:** http://www.lwf.bayern.de
Freq: 6 issues yearly; **Cover Price:** EUR 5,00
Free to qualifying individuals ; **Circ:** 1,600
Editor: Michael Mößnang
Profile: Magazine from the Bavarian Federal Organization for Forestry.
Language(s): German

LYDIA 734567G74A-3276
Editorial: Dillerberg 1, 35614 ASSLAR **Tel:** 6443 6839
Fax: 6443 686839
Email: redaktion@lydia.net **Web site:** http://www.lydia.net
Freq: Quarterly; **Annual Sub.:** EUR 12,10; **Circ:** 115,938
Editor: Elisabeth Mittelstädt
Profile: Women's magazine. In each issue you will find practical, proven tips for everyday and refreshing wind for the challenges of life in marriage, in parenting, in Singlesein, work, in times of sickness and sorrow, in financial and relationship issues. LYDIA moving experience reports, interesting interviews with Christian women, practical tips, Impulse for religious life and much more. People openly talk about how they overcome difficulties and fears, how to meet God and amazing experience.
Language(s): German
ADVERTISING RATES:
Full Page Colour .... EUR 3675
Mechanical Data: Type Area: 244 x 181 mm, No. of Columns (Display): 3, Col Widths (Display): 58 mm
Copy instructions: *Copy Date:* 126 days prior to publication

LYMPHOLOGIE IN FORSCHUNG UND PRAXIS 734569G56A-6280
Editorial: Otto-Hahn-Str. 7, 50997 KÖLN
Tel: 2236 3760 **Fax:** 2236 376999
Email: aa@biermann.net **Web site:** http://www.viavital.net
Freq: Half-yearly; Free to qualifying individuals
Annual Sub.: EUR 60,00; **Circ:** 1,441
Editor: Hellmuth Zöltzer; **Advertising Manager:** Bettina Thiemeyer
Profile: The complexity of the functional processes associated with the concept of Lymphology, is supported in Lymphologie in Forschung und Praxis statement. It is clear that the Lymphology not exclusively with the diagnosis and treatment of lymphedema treated as equal, but rather as a multidisciplinary discipline. The journal provides comprehensive analysis and ongoing discussions, suggesting to the doctors and physical therapists interested in new insights and perspectives from research and clinical practice. Among the authors in addition to doctors and physiotherapists are also bandagists.
Language(s): German
Readership: Read by members of the Society, including dermatologists, surgeons and interns.
ADVERTISING RATES:
Full Page Mono .... EUR 1170
Full Page Colour .... EUR 2070
Mechanical Data: Type Area: 243 x 178 mm
Copy instructions: *Copy Date:* 21 days prior to publication
Official Journal of: Organ d. Dt. Ges. f. Lymphologie, d. Ges. Deutschsprachiger Lymphologen e.V. u. d. Ges. f. manuelle Lymphdrainage nach Dr. Vodder u. sonstige lympholog. Therapien e.V.
BUSINESS: HEALTH & MEDICAL

LZ RHEINLAND 734573G21J-32
Editorial: Rochusstr. 18, 53123 BONN
Tel: 228 52006534 **Fax:** 228 52006560
Email: stefan.sallen@lz-rheinland.de **Web site:** http://www.lz-rheinland.de
Freq: Weekly; **Annual Sub.:** EUR 95,50; **Circ:** 19,700
Editor: Stefan Sallen; **Advertising Manager:** Markus Schulz
Profile: Influenced by the strong agricultural region of Aachen, Cologne bay, the pig herds in the Lower Rhine and the dairy farms in the Eifel, the Bergischer and Oberbergischer Kreis, manage the readers of the LZ Rheinland over 520,000 hectares of agricultural land in the Rhineland. In addition to cereals are still sugar beet, potatoes and corn (maize silage and grain) to the most important crops of the Rhine farmer.
Language(s): German
ADVERTISING RATES:
Full Page Mono .... EUR 3356
Full Page Colour .... EUR 5687
Mechanical Data: Type Area: 275 x 198 mm, No. of Columns (Display): 4, Col Widths (Display): 46 mm
Copy instructions: *Copy Date:* 6 days prior to publication
Official Journal of: Organ d. Rhein. LandwirtschaftsVerb., d. LV Landwirtschaftl. Fachschulabsolventen u. d. Rhein. Landfrauenverb., Amtsblatt d. Landwirtschaftskammer Nordrhein-Westfalen, Verkündungsblatt d. Landesbeauftragten f. d. Landesteil Nordrhein
BUSINESS: AGRICULTURE & FARMING: Agriculture & Farming - Regional

M MENSCHEN MACHEN MEDIEN 736307G2D-15
Editorial: Paula-Thiede-Ufer 10, 10179 BERLIN
Tel: 30 69562326 **Fax:** 30 69563676
Email: karin.wenk@verdi.de **Web site:** http://mmm.verdi.de
Freq: 9 issues yearly; Free to qualifying individuals
Annual Sub.: EUR 36,00; **Circ:** 50,000
Editor: Karin Wenk
Profile: Media Political Magazine of ver.di for journalists, members and employees interested in the public service broadcasters, private radio, in cinemas, film production, publishing houses and agencies, and media policy in principle for all.
Language(s): German
Readership: Aimed at producers, broadcasters and journalists.
ADVERTISING RATES:
Full Page Mono .... EUR 2800
Full Page Colour .... EUR 4500
Mechanical Data: Type Area: 272 x 185 mm, No. of Columns (Display): 3, Col Widths (Display): 59 mm
Supplement to: ver.di Publik
BUSINESS: COMMUNICATIONS, ADVERTISING & MARKETING: Broadcasting

M+A MESSEPLANER
736702G14A-4260
Editorial: Mainzer Landstr. 251, 60326 FRANKFURT
Tel: 69 75951641 **Fax:** 69 75951640
Email: muamesseplaner-redaktion@dfv.de **Web site:** http://www.expodatabase.de
Freq: Half-yearly; **Annual Sub.:** EUR 214,00; **Circ:** 3,698
Editor: Dorit Vogel-Seib; **Advertising Manager:** Volker Schledt
Profile: Guide for fairs and exhibitions worldwide.
Language(s): German
ADVERTISING RATES:
Full Page Mono .... EUR 3170
Full Page Colour .... EUR 3890
Mechanical Data: Type Area: 266 x 184 mm, No. of Columns (Display): 3, Col Widths (Display): 58 mm
Copy instructions: *Copy Date:* 40 days prior to publication
Supplement(s): m+a service

M+A REPORT 736703G2C-40_50
Editorial: Mainzer Landstr. 251, 60326 FRANKFURT
Tel: 69 75951631 **Fax:** 69 75951630
Email: muareport-redaktion@dfv.de **Web site:** http://www.expodatabase.de
Freq: 8 issues yearly; **Annual Sub.:** EUR 98,44; **Circ:** 11,969
Editor: Christiane Appel; **Advertising Manager:** Volker Schledt
Profile: m+a report – The Global Exhibition Magazine is the market and opinion leader for the exhibition community and trade show industry. As a bilingual exhibition marketing magazine for exhibition makers with decision-making authority in industry, trade, the services sector and the association world, in eight issues a year m+a report delivers cross-sectoral practical tips on how successfully to design trade fairs and other marketing events. First-hand reports, market analyses, news and background coverage from the international exhibition industry round off the editorial spectrum. m+a report is a business and service magazine in one.
Language(s): English; German
Readership: Aimed at marketing professionals and managers involved with trade fairs and marketing events.
ADVERTISING RATES:
Full Page Mono .... EUR 3325
Full Page Colour .... EUR 4045
Mechanical Data: Type Area: 266 x 184 mm, No. of Columns (Display): 3, Col Widths (Display): 58 mm
Copy instructions: *Copy Date:* 28 days prior to publication
Supplement(s): m+a service
BUSINESS: COMMUNICATIONS, ADVERTISING & MARKETING: Conferences & Exhibitions

M&K MEDIEN & KOMMUNIKATIONSWISSEN-SCHAFT 735146G2A-3180
Editorial: Heimhuder Str. 21, 20148 HAMBURG
Tel: 40 45021741 **Fax:** 40 45021777
Email: c.matzen@hans-bredow-institut.de **Web site:** http://www.m-und-k.info
Freq: Quarterly; **Annual Sub.:** EUR 118,31; **Circ:** 1,800
Editor: Christiane Matzen
Profile: Forum for theoretical and empirical contributions about media and communications sciences.
Language(s): German
ADVERTISING RATES:
Full Page Mono .... EUR 800
Full Page Colour .... EUR 1550
Mechanical Data: No. of Columns (Display): 2, Col Widths (Display): 56 mm, Type Area: 185 x 117 mm

M & T METALLHANDWERK
736710G19E-1060
Editorial: Stolberger Str. 84, 50933 KÖLN
Tel: 221 5497248 **Fax:** 221 5497326
Email: red.metallhandwerk@coleman-verlag.de **Web site:** http://www.mt-metallhandwerk.de
Freq: Monthly; Free to qualifying individuals
Annual Sub.: EUR 122,00; **Circ:** 19,938
Editor: John-Thomas Siehoff; **Advertising Manager:** Thomas Füngerlings
Profile: M & T Metallhandwerk is the organ of the Association of metal. The comprehensive, specialized and targeted editorial content first-hand to make the magazine an indispensable basic medium for the entrepreneurs of the metal trades. It depends mainly on aluminum and steel fabricators, locksmith and precision engineering. Every month, informs them of new updates from the industry and taught in varying emphases specialized details.
Language(s): German
Readership: Aimed at metalworkers.
ADVERTISING RATES:
Full Page Mono .... EUR 3830
Full Page Colour .... EUR 5075
Mechanical Data: Type Area: 267 x 188 mm, No. of Columns (Display): 4, Col Widths (Display): 44 mm
Copy instructions: *Copy Date:* 30 days prior to publication
Official Journal of: Organ d. Bundesverb. Metall
BUSINESS: ENGINEERING & MACHINERY: Machinery, Machine Tools & Metalworking

M & T ONLINE 1622794G19E-1870
Editorial: Stolberger Str. 84, 50933 KÖLN
Tel: 221 5497271 **Fax:** 221 54976271
Email: red.metallhandwerk@coleman-verlag.de **Web site:** http://www.mt-metallhandwerk.de
Freq: Weekly; **Circ:** 73,000
Editor: John-Thomas Siehoff; **Advertising Manager:** Thomas Füngerlings
Profile: Ezine: Journal covering all aspects of metalworking.
Language(s): German

MA PRESSEMEDIEN 735013G2A-2460
Editorial: Am Weingarten 25, 60487 FRANKFURT
Tel: 69 1568050 **Fax:** 69 15680540
Email: agma@agma-mmc.de **Web site:** http://www.agma-mmc.de
Freq: Half-yearly; **Circ:** 1,200
Profile: National accounts of magazines, supplements, daily newspapers, confessional press, reader circles and cinemas.
Language(s): German

MA RADIO 735014G2A-2480
Editorial: Am Weingarten 25, 60487 FRANKFURT
Tel: 69 1568050 **Fax:** 69 15680540
Email: agma@agma-mmc.de **Web site:** http://www.agma-mmc.de

Freq: Half-yearly; **Circ:** 650
Profile: National accounts of radio.
Language(s): German

MACH MAL PAUSE 734579G74A-175
Editorial: Karlsruher Str. 31, 76437 RASTATT
Tel: 7222 13247 **Fax:** 7222 13434
Email: machmalpause@vpm.de **Web site:** http://www.vpm.de
Freq: Weekly; **Cover Price:** EUR 1,10; **Circ:** 116,073
Editor: Silvia Lass von Maydell
Profile: mach mal Pause offers its readers interesting puzzles, great odds, exciting entertainment and useful tips for everyday life. True to its motto: Puzzle, Win, fun. Stories about people, news reports, everyday, and almost incredible Distractions will be presented in entertaining written texts. There are many service issues such as wellness, health, delicious and healthy food and travel. Popular puzzle for short breaks in between or a quiet evening at home make a colorful mix of the magazine perfectly. This is your chance to win valuable prizes - with better opportunities than in many a television show.
Language(s): German
ADVERTISING RATES:
Full Page Mono .... EUR 4853
Full Page Colour .... EUR 4853
Mechanical Data: Type Area: 261 x 196 mm, No. of Columns (Display): 4, Col Widths (Display): 46 mm
Copy instructions: *Copy Date:* 34 days prior to publication
CONSUMER: WOMEN'S INTEREST CONSUMER MAGAZINES: Women's Interest

MACHER 1665994G14A-9742
Editorial: Hanns-Martin-Schleyer-Str. 8, 54294 TRIER **Tel:** 651 7199931 **Fax:** 651 7199978
Email: macher@volksfreund.de **Web site:** http://www.macher.volksfreund.de
Freq: 10 issues yearly; **Annual Sub.:** EUR 15,00; **Circ:** 20,000
Editor: Alexander Houben; **Advertising Manager:** Wolfgang Sturges
Profile: Regional business magazine for entrepreneurs and decision makers in the Saar-Mosele-Eifel-Hunsrück and Luxembourg.
Language(s): German
ADVERTISING RATES:
Full Page Mono .... EUR 2316
Full Page Colour .... EUR 2316
Mechanical Data: Type Area: 273 x 185 mm, No. of Columns (Display): 4, Col Widths (Display): 44 mm
Copy instructions: *Copy Date:* 10 days prior to publication

DAS MACHT SPASS! 1825402G74A-3571
Editorial: Sieker Landstr. 126, 22143 HAMBURG
Tel: 40 6739780 **Fax:** 40 67397821
Email: wmb@cpvkg.de **Web site:** http://www.conpart-verlag.de
Freq: Monthly; **Cover Price:** EUR 0,59; **Circ:** 96,738
Editor: Wolfgang M. Biehler
Profile: The magazine contains the following categories: Love & Life | House & Home | Healthy & Fit | Fashion & Chic | Rates & Win | Travel & Services | Tips, Tricks & more.
Language(s): German
ADVERTISING RATES:
Full Page Mono .... EUR 5000
Full Page Colour .... EUR 5000
Mechanical Data: Type Area: 262 x 194 mm, No. of Columns (Display): 4

MACWELT 1623160G5B-10
Editorial: Lyonel-Feininger-Str. 26, 80807 MÜNCHEN
Tel: 89 36086234 **Fax:** 89 36086304
Email: shirsch@macwelt.de **Web site:** http://www.macwelt.de
Freq: Daily; **Cover Price:** Paid; **Circ:** 2,167,982 Unique Users
Editor: Sebastian Hirsch; **Advertising Manager:** Andrea Weinholz
Profile: Ezine: Magazine focusing on Macintosh computers.
Language(s): German
BUSINESS: COMPUTERS & AUTOMATION: Data Processing

MACWELT 734588G5C-39_50
Editorial: Lyonel-Feininger-Str. 26, 80807 MÜNCHEN
Tel: 89 36086234 **Fax:** 89 36086124
Email: redaktion@macwelt.de **Web site:** http://www.macwelt.de
Freq: Monthly; **Annual Sub.:** EUR 70,80; **Circ:** 28,435
Editor: Sebastian Hirsch; **Advertising Manager:** Sascha Neubacher
Profile: Macwelt offers know how and special information for all Mac users. Relevant issues about the Mac and its surroundings published in comprehensive and funded articles. Actual: news, Information and trends about all mac relevant issues, fair reports and updates, background information from the macintosh scene; Test: individual test of hardware, software, special technique section offers background articles; Know How: more than 20 pages of know how articles; Tipps & Tricks: Basic information and Tipps about the mac operating sysems and many other issues for quick assistance for daily use.
Language(s): German
Readership: Aimed at users of Macintosh computers.
ADVERTISING RATES:
Full Page Mono .... EUR 4900
Full Page Colour .... EUR 6500
Mechanical Data: Type Area: 241 x 177 mm, No. of Columns (Display): 4, Col Widths (Display): 42 mm
Copy instructions: *Copy Date:* 28 days prior to publication
BUSINESS: COMPUTERS & AUTOMATION: Professional Personal Computers

MAD 734589G91D-5120
Editorial: Rotebühlstr. 87, 70178 STUTTGART
Tel: 711 947680 **Fax:** 711 9476830
Email: info@panini.de **Web site:** http://www.panini.de
Freq: 6 issues yearly; **Cover Price:** EUR 3,00; **Circ:** 19,513
Editor: Jo Löffler
Profile: Satirical magazine, in no doubt "the smartest magazine in the world " spared no expense or color to top events from movies, TV and the rest of the world belonging to pull his leg. Frech and absolutely iconic!.
Language(s): German
ADVERTISING RATES:
Full Page Mono .... EUR 2500
Full Page Colour .... EUR 2500
Mechanical Data: Type Area: 247 x 187 mm
CONSUMER: RECREATION & LEISURE: Children & Youth

MADAME 734590G74A-1980
Editorial: Leonrodstr. 52, 80636 MÜNCHEN
Tel: 89 551350 **Fax:** 89 55135299
Email: mailbox@madame.de **Web site:** http://www.madame.de
Freq: Monthly; **Annual Sub.:** EUR 63,00; **Circ:** 103,858
Editor: Katrin Riebartsch; **Advertising Manager:** Michaela Hammel
Profile: Madame sees itself as the lead magazine for strong, confident women who smartly and elegantly stage their life and thus are models and style icons. This image of women is the base of the journalistic claim: Madame is wide and deep, involves and inspires the reader. Top themes of fashion, beauty and wellness, lifestyle, culture and travel determine the content diversity of Madame. Every editorial review is staged modern and has substance. For Madame gets to the bottom. Intelligent and creative people share their insights and experiences with the readers and make them insiders, who are inspired by Madame to think ahead, be up-to-date and to indicate their high quality standards. Madame convinces by a clear structure and a strong, informative and exclusive visual language.
Language(s): German
ADVERTISING RATES:
Full Page Mono .... EUR 16790
Full Page Colour .... EUR 18180
Mechanical Data: Type Area: 253 x 190 mm, No. of Columns (Display): 3, Col Widths (Display): 60 mm
CONSUMER: WOMEN'S INTEREST CONSUMER MAGAZINES: Women's Interest

MÄDCHEN 734593G74F-122
Editorial: Leonrodstr. 52, 80636 MÜNCHEN
Tel: 89 69749302 **Fax:** 89 69749312
Email: redaktion@maedchen.de **Web site:** http://www.maedchen.de
Freq: 26 issues yearly; **Annual Sub.:** EUR 44,20; **Circ:** 134,622
Editor: Verena Volkhausen; **Advertising Manager:** Margit Böhmer
Profile: They are fascinated by the world, live in the Katy Perry and Robert Pattinson. You hear jealous the thrilling adventures of the big sister. Admire the girl from high school in secret for their cool style. And they are above all: love for the first time to our ears. The target group are girls between 12 and 17 years. Just in this world appears a girl: We have the latest gossip from Hollywood, give cool and smart styling tips and have the professional tricks for the first make-up. And very important: We advise the readers in all walks of life issues. Whether it's about boys and love, insecurities with their own bodies or to relieve stress in the family - we provide assistance for small and large everyday problems.
Language(s): German
Readership: Read by girls aged 14 to 19 years.
ADVERTISING RATES:
Full Page Mono .... EUR 13820
Full Page Colour .... EUR 13820
Mechanical Data: Type Area: 258 x 185 mm, No. of Columns (Display): 4, Col Widths (Display): 43 mm
CONSUMER: WOMEN'S INTEREST CONSUMER MAGAZINES: Teenage

MAERKISCHEALLGEMEINE.DE 1662175G67B-16740
Editorial: Friedrich-Engels-Str. 24, 14473 POTSDAM
Tel: 331 28400 **Fax:** 331 2840310
Email: chefredaktion@mazonline.de **Web site:** http://www.maerkischeallgemeine.de
Freq: Daily; **Cover Price:** Paid; **Circ:** 794,158 Unique Users
Editor: Klaus Rost
Profile: Ezine: Daily updated information on local politics, economy, culture, sports, travel and technology for Brandenburg, supplemented with interactive maps, photo galleries, videos, and the weather for all counties. Facebook: http://www.facebook.com/MAZonline Twitter: http://twitter.com/maz_aktuell This Outlet offers RSS (Really Simple Syndication).
Language(s): German
REGIONAL DAILY & SUNDAY NEWSPAPERS: Regional Daily Newspapers

MAFO 1683959G56E-398
Editorial: Papiermühlenweg 74, 40882 RATINGEN
Tel: 2102 16780 **Fax:** 2102 167828
Email: info@mafo-optics.com **Web site:** http://www.mafo-optics.com
Freq: 6 issues yearly; **Annual Sub.:** EUR 140,00; **Circ:** 2,500
Editor: Isabel Spangemacher; **Advertising Manager:** Constanze Claßen
Profile: Mafo is the independent journal for producers, managers and distributors in ophthalmic optics worldwide. It is designed to reflect the interests of all sectors, at every link in the global eyewear delivery chain, including the industry's importers and exporters. It also focuses on supplier's relationship with retail optics, especially chains, marketing and buying groups.
Language(s): English
ADVERTISING RATES:
Full Page Mono .... EUR 1750
Full Page Colour .... EUR 3310
Mechanical Data: Type Area: 257 x 184 mm
Copy instructions: *Copy Date:* 20 days prior to publication
BUSINESS: HEALTH & MEDICAL: Optics

MAGASCENE 734627G80-7400
Editorial: Lange Laube 22, 30159 HANNOVER
Tel: 511 15551 **Fax:** 511 1316169
Email: redaktion@stroetmann-verlag.de **Web site:** http://www.magascene.de
Freq: Monthly; **Cover Price:** Free; **Circ:** 39,422
Editor: Reinhard Stroetmann; **Advertising Manager:** Reinhard Stroetmann
Profile: City and event magazine, here we show you what is happening in the city and surrounding countryside. In the booklet you will find: The Interview of the month, event tips, top tips and the latest news from the scene.
Language(s): German
ADVERTISING RATES:
Full Page Mono .... EUR 1450
Full Page Colour .... EUR 2645
Mechanical Data: Type Area: 195 x 130 mm, No. of Columns (Display): 3, Col Widths (Display): 41 mm
Copy instructions: *Copy Date:* 10 days prior to publication
CONSUMER: RURAL & REGIONAL INTEREST

DAS MAGAZIN 734629G73-280
Editorial: Tieckstr. 8, 10115 BERLIN
Tel: 30 48496230 **Fax:** 30 48496236
Email: redaktion@dasmagazin.de **Web site:** http://www.dasmagazin.de
Freq: 11 issues yearly; **Annual Sub.:** EUR 28,00; **Circ:** 51,000
Editor: Manuela Thieme; **Advertising Manager:** Christian Hentschel
Profile: Das Magazin is a fun, visually unusual monthly magazine. It is dedicated to cultural themes, love and life plans as well as satire and achieved with the diverse of topics, especially the younger generation of orientation seeking academics. The practical format, the ironic tone and working with young writers, illustrators and photographers captures the spirit of the mobile, urban audience. Visual hallmark and symbol of the playful lightness is the illustrated cover. This maintains the sheet has a long tradition. It was founded in 1924, 1941 adjusted due to the war and opened in 1954 in East Berlin again. In recent years, Das Magazin has established itself in the German media market as a journalistic premium product. Meanwhile, a new generation of readers excited for the sheet. Das Magazin provides a friendly environment for advertisements. Thanks to the extensive and interesting reading material each issue contains several references in his hand, share ideas, and collected.
Language(s): German
ADVERTISING RATES:
Full Page Mono .... EUR 1900
Full Page Colour .... EUR 2900
Mechanical Data: Type Area: 208 x 140 mm, No. of Columns (Display): 2, Col Widths (Display): 68 mm
Copy instructions: *Copy Date:* 20 days prior to publication
CONSUMER: NATIONAL & INTERNATIONAL PERIODICALS

MAGAZIN 721489G80-900
Editorial: Homburger Landstr. 851, 60437 FRANKFURT **Tel:** 69 5074214 **Fax:** 69 5073444
Email: redaktion@rhein-main-magazin.de **Web site:** http://www.rhein-main-magazin.de
Freq: Monthly; **Annual Sub.:** EUR 40,00; **Circ:** 9,297
Editor: Sebastian Laux; **Advertising Manager:** Carmen De Martino
Profile: The magazin is a great family magazine for the region, is available at newsagents, supermarkets, kiosks, petrol stations, railway station bookshops and in all other stores, what newspapers and magazines conduct. It offers the most beautiful destinations in the region Frankfurt am Main, Hochtaunuskreis, the Wetteraukreis, the Main-Kinzig-Kreis, the Rheingau-Taunus-Kreis, the Lahn-Dill-Kreis, the district of Limburg-Weilburg, the Main-Taunus-Kreis, the district of Offenbach, the Vogelsbergkreis, and almost all major cities and towns in Hesse and Rhineland-Palatinate and parts of Bavaria.
Language(s): German
ADVERTISING RATES:
Full Page Mono .... EUR 2500
Full Page Colour .... EUR 3500
Mechanical Data: Type Area: 263 x 188 mm, No. of Columns (Display): 4, Col Widths (Display): 45 mm
Copy instructions: *Copy Date:* 15 days prior to publication
CONSUMER: RURAL & REGIONAL INTEREST

MAGAZIN 734509G89D-6
Editorial: Stubbenhuk 10, 20459 HAMBURG
Tel: 40 37035011 **Fax:** 40 37035099
Email: lhmagazin@guj.de **Web site:** http://www.corporate-editors.com
Freq: Monthly; **Annual Sub.:** EUR 54,00; **Circ:** 575,770
Editor: Christian Krug; **Advertising Manager:** Heiko Hager
Profile: Lufthansa inflight magazine with editorial emphasis in Travel, People, and Aviation.
Language(s): English; German
ADVERTISING RATES:
Full Page Mono .... EUR 29400
Full Page Colour .... EUR 29400
Mechanical Data: Type Area: 240 x 180 mm
Copy instructions: *Copy Date:* 56 days prior to publication
CONSUMER: HOLIDAYS & TRAVEL: In-Flight Magazines

MAGAZIN FREIE WERKSTATT 721638G77A-2826
Editorial: Philipp-Nicolai-Weg 3, 58313 HERDECKE
Tel: 2330 91830 **Fax:** 2330 13570
Email: info@verlag-kaufhold.de **Web site:** http://www.verlag-kaufhold.de
Freq: 3 issues yearly; **Cover Price:** Free; **Circ:** 250,000
Editor: Ralf Galow; **Advertising Manager:** Selina Wannke
Profile: Customer magazine on automobiles covering cars and garages as well as lifestyle.
Language(s): German
ADVERTISING RATES:
Full Page Mono .... EUR 5000
Full Page Colour .... EUR 5000
Mechanical Data: Type Area: 267 x 188 mm, No. of Columns (Display): 3, Col Widths (Display): 59 mm
Copy instructions: *Copy Date:* 28 days prior to publication

MAGDEBURGER KURIER 1657430G74N-853
Editorial: Alt Fermersleben 77, 39122 MAGDEBURG
Tel: 391 4011000 **Fax:** 391 5419805
Email: mdkurier@aol.com
Freq: Monthly; **Cover Price:** Free; **Circ:** 10,000
Editor: Gerda Bednarz
Profile: Magazine for the elderly in Magdeburg.
Language(s): German
ADVERTISING RATES:
Full Page Colour .... EUR 1522
Copy instructions: *Copy Date:* 20 days prior to publication

MAGDEBURGER VOLKSSTIMME 734677G67B-9100
Editorial: Bahnhofstr. 17, 39104 MAGDEBURG
Tel: 391 59990 **Fax:** 391 5999210
Email: chefredaktion@volksstimme.de **Web site:** http://www.volksstimme.de
Freq: 312 issues yearly; **Circ:** 45,362
Editor: Günther Tyllack; **News Editor:** Michael Bock; **Advertising Manager:** Rainer Pfeil
Profile: As the largest daily newspaper in northern Saxony-Anhalt, the Volksstimme reaches 536,000 readers a day* (MA 2010). From Monday to Saturday a team of highly qualified editors put together the latest information and news from the region and around the world. Thanks the 18 local editions is the Volksstimme always close to the action. Twitter: http://twitter.com/volksstimme This Outlet offers RSS (Really Simple Syndication).
Language(s): German
ADVERTISING RATES:
SCC .... EUR 416,80
Mechanical Data: Type Area: 480 x 327 mm, No. of Columns (Display): 7, Col Widths (Display): 45 mm
Copy instructions: *Copy Date:* 2 days prior to publication
Supplement(s): Allee-Center Aktuell; Anstoss in der Landeshauptstadt Magdeburg; bauRatgeber; Biber; Immobilien Spezial; Leser-Reisen; prisma; Standort Magdeburg
REGIONAL DAILY & SUNDAY NEWSPAPERS: Regional Daily Newspapers

MAGNUS.DE CONNECT 1704283G18B-2124
Editorial: Leuschnerstr. 1, 70174 STUTTGART
Tel: 711 1821696 **Fax:** 711 1821832
Email: dwaasen@wekanet.de **Web site:** http://www.connect.de
Freq: Daily; **Cover Price:** Paid; **Circ:** 1,134,579 Unique Users
Editor: Dirk Waasen; **Advertising Manager:** Klaus Ahlering
Profile: Ezine: Magazine for telecommunications. From his special point of view investigated and analyzed connect the adjacent border areas such as notebooks, PDAs, (mobile) internet and in particular the possibilities of networking devices, whether indoors (home connect) or outdoor. Specially

designed for use in mobile vehicle specific media such as navigation systems, infotainment and mobile office complete the range of topics in the Navigation category.
Language(s): German
BUSINESS: ELECTRONICS: Telecommunications

MAHLZEIT 734692G94H-8300
Editorial: Rosental 51, 41334 NETTETAL
Tel: 2153 916823 **Fax:** 2153 916827
Email: redaktion@mahlzeit-magazin.de **Web site:** http://www.grenzlandnachrichten.de
Freq: Monthly; **Cover Price:** Free; **Circ:** 50,000
Editor: Marita Offermanns; **Advertising Manager:** Klaus Gerits
Profile: Magazine about healthy eating, natural living and well-being.
Language(s): German
ADVERTISING RATES:
Full Page Mono .... EUR 1250
Full Page Colour .... EUR 1730
Mechanical Data: Type Area: 255 x 185 mm
Copy instructions: *Copy Date:* 16 days prior to publication
CONSUMER: OTHER CLASSIFICATIONS: Customer Magazines

MAILINGTAGE [NEWS] 1666282G2A-5626
Editorial: Englerstr. 26, 76275 ETTLINGEN
Tel: 7243 54000 **Fax:** 7243 540054
Email: braendli@im-marketing-forum.de **Web site:** http://www.mailingtage.de
Freq: Quarterly; **Cover Price:** Free; **Circ:** 35,000
Editor: Andrea Brändli; **Advertising Manager:** Christine Werner
Profile: Event of the newspaper Mailingtage, trade fair for modern direct and dialog marketing with the accompanying conference "meeting dialogue. " It reports on content and program of the event as well as news and facts from the direct and dialog marketing world. Facebook: http://www.facebook.com/dialogmarketing Twitter: http://twitter.com/#!/mailingtage_Nbg/.
Language(s): German

MAIN FEELING 1842243G65B-3_101
Editorial: Frankenallee 71, 60327 FRANKFURT
Tel: 69 75014352 **Fax:** 69 75014361
Email: redaktion@magazin-mainfeeling.de **Web site:** http://www.magazin-mainfeeling.de
Freq: Quarterly; **Cover Price:** EUR 3,50; **Circ:** 30,000
Editor: Ulrich Müller-Braun
Profile: Regional lifestyle magazine for the Rhine-Main region. To live is to feel good. To live well means to feel at ease. The magazine reflects this positive attitude to life in the Rhine-Main region with dramatic visual effects and main content contrary: With high-quality portraits of dedicated individuals who enjoy the discovery of worlds for all the senses and inspiring stories of society and regions. Open-minded, stylish and future-oriented: The people in Frankfurt and the Rhein-Main region know that can work and leisure facilities here to join a truly superb. Accordingly so, the standard by which the individual quality of life is measured. Whether innovative products, culinary discoveries and modern lifestyle - the lifestyle magazine offers its readers the highest level.
Language(s): German
ADVERTISING RATES:
Full Page Mono .... EUR 2300
Full Page Colour .... EUR 2300
Mechanical Data: Type Area: 258 x 180 mm
Copy instructions: *Copy Date:* 15 days prior to publication
Supplement to: Frankfurter Allgemeine Sonntagszeitung
NATIONAL DAILY & SUNDAY NEWSPAPERS: GB-Unabhängigkeits-MdEP

MAIN-ECHO 734701G67B-9120
Editorial: Weichertstr. 20, 63741 ASCHAFFENBURG
Tel: 6021 396229 **Fax:** 6021 396499
Email: redaktion@main-echo.de **Web site:** http://www.main-netz.de
Freq: 312 issues yearly; **Circ:** 78,072
Editor: Claus Morhart; **News Editor:** Renate Englert; **Advertising Manager:** Reinhard Fresow
Profile: Regional daily newspaper with news on politics, economy, culture, sport, travel, technology. Twitter: http://twitter.com/mainnetz This Outlet offers RSS (Really Simple Syndication).
Language(s): German
ADVERTISING RATES:
SCC .... EUR 123,00
Mechanical Data: Type Area: 480 x 366 mm, No. of Columns (Display): 8, Col Widths (Display): 44 mm
Copy instructions: *Copy Date:* 1 day prior to publication
Supplement(s): Gesundheit!; tv Sieben
REGIONAL DAILY & SUNDAY NEWSPAPERS: Regional Daily Newspapers

MAINPOST.DE 1621656G67B-16594
Editorial: Berner Str. 2, 97084 WÜRZBURG
Tel: 931 6001191 **Fax:** 931 6001285
Email: red.online@mainpost.de **Web site:** http://www.mainpost.de
Freq: Daily; **Cover Price:** Paid; **Circ:** 1,866,672 Unique Users
Editor: Roland Schmitt-Raiser; **Advertising Manager:** Christian Franz
Profile: Ezine: mainpost.de is the platform for people interested in news and advertising markets in Franken. Both as a supplement to the daily newspaper and also for the rapid and deep information. About 100 editors from the media group Main-Post are working around the clock on the current regional and national coverage in print, pictures and video. In the advertising markets related jobs, jobs, homes, cars, friendships, classifieds and more. Facebook: http://de-de.facebook.com/mainpost Twitter: http://twitter.com/#!/mainpost/ This Outlet offers RSS (Really Simple Syndication).
Language(s): German
REGIONAL DAILY & SUNDAY NEWSPAPERS: Regional Daily Newspapers

MAIN-SPITZE 734709G67B-9160
Editorial: Erich-Dombrowski-Str. 2, 55127 MAINZ
Tel: 6131 485805 **Fax:** 6131 485833
Web site: http://www.vrm.de
Freq: 312 issues yearly; **Circ:** 9,549
Advertising Manager: Gerhard Müller
Profile: Daily newspaper with regional news and a local sports section. This Outlet offers RSS (Really Simple Syndication).
Language(s): German
ADVERTISING RATES:
SCC .... EUR 47,40
Mechanical Data: Type Area: 480 x 325 mm, No. of Columns (Display): 7, Col Widths (Display): 45 mm
Copy instructions: *Copy Date:* 1 day prior to publication
Supplement(s): extra Familie; extra Gesundheit; extra Sport; extra Wissen; pepper; Start frei
REGIONAL DAILY & SUNDAY NEWSPAPERS: Regional Daily Newspapers

DER MAINZER 734711G80-7420
Editorial: 117er Ehrenhof 5, 55118 MAINZ
Tel: 6131 965330 **Fax:** 6131 9653399
Email: briefkasten@dermainzer.net **Web site:** http://www.dermainzer.net
Freq: Monthly; **Cover Price:** Free; **Circ:** 31,967
Editor: Marion Diehl; **Advertising Manager:** Werner Horn
Profile: Magazine for Mainz and Rheinhessen.
Language(s): German
Readership: Read by residents.
ADVERTISING RATES:
Full Page Mono .... EUR 1810
Full Page Colour .... EUR 2890
Mechanical Data: Type Area: 275 x 195 mm, No. of Columns (Display): 4, Col Widths (Display): 45 mm
Copy instructions: *Copy Date:* 14 days prior to publication
CONSUMER: RURAL & REGIONAL INTEREST

MAINZER RHEIN ZEITUNG 734714G67B-9200
Editorial: August-Horch-Str. 28, 56070 KOBLENZ
Tel: 261 892240 **Fax:** 261 892770
Email: redaktion@rhein-zeitung.de **Web site:** http://www.rhein-zeitung.de
Freq: 312 issues yearly; **Annual Sub.:** EUR 16,80; **Circ:** 7,259
Advertising Manager: Roswitha Kapp
Profile: Regional daily newspaper with news on politics, economy, culture, sports, travel, technology, etc. The Mainzer Rhein Zeitung is a local issue the in koblenz appearing Rhein-Zeitung. Facebook: http://www.facebook.com/rheinzeitung Twitter: http://www.rhein-zeitung.de/twitter.html This Outlet offers RSS (Really Simple Syndication). This Outlet offers RSS (Really Simple Syndication).
Language(s): German
ADVERTISING RATES:
SCC .... EUR 58,00
Mechanical Data: Type Area: 480 x 325 mm, No. of Columns (Display): 7, Col Widths (Display): 45 mm
Copy instructions: *Copy Date:* 1 day prior to publication
Supplement(s): MRZplus; SpielZeit
REGIONAL DAILY & SUNDAY NEWSPAPERS: Regional Daily Newspapers

MAINZER WOCHENBLATT 734716G72-7148
Editorial: Markt 17, 55116 MAINZ **Tel:** 6131 485570
Fax: 6131 485566
Email: redaktion@mainzer-wochenblatt.de **Web site:** http://www.mainzer-wochenblatt.de
Freq: Weekly; **Cover Price:** Free; **Circ:** 147,541
Editor: Rüdiger Benda; **Advertising Manager:** Rainer Baumann
Profile: Advertising journal (house-to-house) concentrating on local stories.
Language(s): German
ADVERTISING RATES:
Full Page Mono .... EUR 9005
Full Page Colour .... EUR 12264
Mechanical Data: Type Area: 480 x 325 mm, No. of Columns (Display): 7, Col Widths (Display): 45 mm
Copy instructions: *Copy Date:* 2 days prior to publication
LOCAL NEWSPAPERS

MAIS 734718G21A-2780
Editorial: Clemens-August-Str. 54, 53115 BONN
Tel: 228 926580 **Fax:** 228 9265820
Email: dmk@maiskomitee.de **Web site:** http://www.dlg-agrofoodmedien.de
Freq: Quarterly; **Annual Sub.:** EUR 30,50; **Circ:** 4,750
Editor: Helmut Meßner; **Advertising Manager:** Rainer Schluck
Profile: Journal covering maize cultivation.
Language(s): German
ADVERTISING RATES:
Full Page Mono .... EUR 1542
Full Page Colour .... EUR 2802
Mechanical Data: Type Area: 270 x 186 mm, No. of Columns (Display): 3, Col Widths (Display): 58 mm
Copy instructions: *Copy Date:* 21 days prior to publication
BUSINESS: AGRICULTURE & FARMING

MAIS INFORMATION 1655256G21A-4302
Editorial: Lockhauser Str. 68, 32052 HERFORD
Tel: 5221 76520 **Fax:** 5221 71853
Email: info@ragt.de **Web site:** http://www.ragt.de
Freq: Half-yearly; **Cover Price:** Free; **Circ:** 60,000
Editor: Thomas Mellinger
Profile: Company publication from the R.A.G.T Saaten Deutschland GmbH.
Language(s): German

MAISREPORT 2042363G21A-4472
Editorial: Pascalstr. 11, 47506 NEUKIRCHEN-VLUYN
Tel: 2845 9369724 **Fax:** 2845 936979
Email: info@agasaat-mais.de **Web site:** http://www.agasaat-mais.de
Freq: Quarterly; **Circ:** 70,000
Editor: Alexander Gnann
Profile: Company publication from the agaSaat Maishandelsges. mbH.
Language(s): German

MALER TASCHENBUCH 734729G4B-360
Editorial: Streitfeldstr. 35, 81673 MÜNCHEN
Tel: 89 436005175 **Fax:** 89 436005166
Email: redaktion@mappe.de **Web site:** http://www.mappe.de
Freq: Annual; **Circ:** 15,000
Editor: Matthias Heilig; **Advertising Manager:** Elmar Große
Profile: Magazine with practical advice for painters and varnishers.
Language(s): German
ADVERTISING RATES:
Full Page Mono .... EUR 1400
Full Page Colour .... EUR 2375
Mechanical Data: Type Area: 126 x 85 mm

DER MALER UND LACKIERERMEISTER 734730G16A-3
Editorial: Schloss Mindelburg, 87719 MINDELHEIM
Tel: 8261 999315 **Fax:** 8261 999395
Email: p.schmid@sachon.de **Web site:** http://www.dermaler.de
Freq: Monthly; Free to qualifying individuals
Annual Sub.: EUR 36,38; **Circ:** 21,162
Editor: Peter Schmid; **Advertising Manager:** Anita Elsäßer
Profile: Journal for master craftsmen in painting and varnishing.
Language(s): German
ADVERTISING RATES:
Full Page Mono .... EUR 4929
Full Page Colour .... EUR 7224
Mechanical Data: Type Area: 270 x 185 mm, No. of Columns (Display): 4, Col Widths (Display): 45 mm
Official Journal of: Organ d. Hauptverb. Farbe, Gestaltung, Bautenschutz, d. Landesinnungsverbände d. Maler- u. Lackiererhandwerks Bayern, Nordrhein, Sachsen, Sachsen-Anhalt, Niedersachsen, Thüringen, Westfalen sowie d. Bundesverb. Korrosionsschutz, d. Arbeitskreises Sachverständigenwesen f. Nordrhein u. Rheinland u. d. fachtechn. Betriebsberatungsstelle f. Nordrhein
BUSINESS: DECORATING & PAINT

MALERBLATT 734726G16A-65
Editorial: Ernst-Mey-Str. 8, 70771 LEINFELDEN-ECHTERDINGEN **Tel:** 711 7594496
Fax: 711 7594399
Email: malerblatt@konradin.de **Web site:** http://www.malerblatt.de
Freq: Monthly; **Annual Sub.:** EUR 116,40; **Circ:** 21,914
Editor: Ulrich Schweizer; **Advertising Manager:** Carola Gayda
Profile: What's happening in the market that can help companies in the painting and plastering of the craft to the front and a secure future? The Malerblatt provides answers to these existential questions of the companies on the removal trade. With a view to thinking outside the Malerblatt reported on the events of the industry strong opinions and unconventional. Design, engineering and business administration: by date information on these fundamental pillars of the craft entrepreneurs continue to be qualified and able to provide an advantage over their competition.
Language(s): German
Readership: Aimed at painters and professionals in the paint industry.
ADVERTISING RATES:
Full Page Mono .... EUR 5140
Full Page Colour .... EUR 7600
Mechanical Data: Type Area: 270 x 188 mm, No. of Columns (Display): 4, Col Widths (Display): 44 mm
Official Journal of: Organ d. Landesinnungsverbände Rheinland-Pfalz, Hessen u. Südbaden
BUSINESS: DECORATING & PAINT

MALLORCA GEHT AUS! 1616470G89A-12090
Editorial: Höherweg 287, 40231 DÜSSELDORF
Tel: 211 7357681 **Fax:** 211 7357680
Email: info@ueberblick.de **Web site:** http://www.ueberblick.de
Freq: Annual; **Cover Price:** EUR 9,80; **Circ:** 60,000
Editor: Martina Vogt; **Advertising Manager:** Andreas Huber
Profile: Gastronomy guide for Mallorca.
Language(s): German
ADVERTISING RATES:
Full Page Mono .... EUR 3580
Full Page Colour .... EUR 5280
Mechanical Data: Type Area: 260 x 190 mm, No. of Columns (Display): 4, Col Widths (Display): 44 mm
Copy instructions: *Copy Date:* 30 days prior to publication

MAMMA MIA! 1804973G56A-11480
Editorial: Altkönigstr. 31, 61476 KRONBERG
Tel: 6173 966403 **Fax:** 6173 966402
Email: eva.schumacher@mammamia-online.de **Web site:** http://www.mammamia-online.de
Freq: Quarterly; **Annual Sub.:** EUR 18,00; **Circ:** 20,000
Editor: Eva Schumacher-Wulf; **Advertising Manager:** Anne-Claire Brühl
Profile: Magazine provides information on the full range of conventional medicine to complementary treatments for breast cancer. Facebook: http://www.facebook.com/brustkrebsmagazin.mammamia Twitter: http://twitter.com/#!/MammaMiaMagazin.
Language(s): German
ADVERTISING RATES:
Full Page Mono .... EUR 2950
Full Page Colour .... EUR 2950
Mechanical Data: Type Area: 247 x 174 mm

MAN IST WAS MAN ISST 1988363G74P-1332
Editorial: Soesttor 12, 59555 LIPPSTADT
Tel: 2941 9589130
Email: redaktion@man-ist.de **Web site:** http://www.man-ist.de
Freq: Monthly; **Cover Price:** EUR 1,90; **Circ:** 130,000
Editor: Uwe Schmalenbach
Profile: The magazine focuses on journalistic manner with all aspects of the food and the food. The blade does all the bandwith on "food" in the look of the production of food on the selection and preparation of products, questions of table to consumption, including implications for health, welfare, environment. The joy of the ingredients, cooking and eating is in the foreground.
Language(s): German
ADVERTISING RATES:
Full Page Mono .... EUR 7500
Full Page Colour .... EUR 7500
Mechanical Data: Type Area: 324 x 223 mm
Copy instructions: *Copy Date:* 28 days prior to publication

MANAGE IT 1659331G5E-24
Editorial: Flossmannstr. 4, 85560 EBERSBERG
Tel: 8092 2470210 **Fax:** 8092 2470229
Email: redaktion@ap-verlag.de **Web site:** http://www.ap-verlag.de
Freq: 6 issues yearly; **Annual Sub.:** EUR 45,00; **Circ:** 10,316
Editor: Albert Absmeier
Profile: Magazine for the IT and telecommunications business.
Language(s): German
ADVERTISING RATES:
Full Page Mono .... EUR 4200
Full Page Colour .... EUR 5300
Mechanical Data: Type Area: 250 x 180 mm
Copy instructions: *Copy Date:* 14 days prior to publication
Supplement(s): Vertikal
BUSINESS: COMPUTERS & AUTOMATION: Data Transmission

MANAGE_HR 1852350G14A-10200
Editorial: Endenicher Str. 41, 53115 BONN
Tel: 228 9779135 **Fax:** 228 9779177
Email: redaktion@managerseminare.de **Web site:** http://www.managerseminare.de
Freq: Quarterly; **Circ:** 20,029
Editor: Nicole Bußmann; **Advertising Manager:** Gerhard May
Profile: Magazine supplement with information on practical knowledge in personnel work. Target groups are people in business and public administration with a need for know-how in human resources management.
Language(s): German
ADVERTISING RATES:
Full Page Mono .... EUR 2980
Full Page Colour .... EUR 3400
Mechanical Data: Type Area: 258 x 170 mm, No. of Columns (Display): 4, Col Widths (Display): 40 mm
Copy instructions: *Copy Date:* 31 days prior to publication
Supplement to: managerSeminare

MANAGEMENT REVUE
734746G14A-4320
Editorial: Marktplatz 5, 86415 MERING
Tel: 8233 4783 **Fax:** 8233 30755
Email: hampp@rhverlag.de **Web site:** http://www.hampp-verlag.de
Freq: Quarterly; **Annual Sub.:** EUR 150,00; **Circ:** 400
Editor: Rainer Hampp
Profile: Technical papers on management, personnel management and organization.
Language(s): English

MANAGEMENT & KRANKENHAUS
734747G56C-11
Editorial: Rößlerstr. 90, 64293 DARMSTADT
Tel: 6151 8090185 **Fax:** 6151 8090179
Email: ulrike.hoffrichter@wiley.com **Web site:** http://www.management-krankenhaus.de
Freq: Monthly; **Annual Sub.:** EUR 122,00; **Circ:** 28,638
Editor: Ulrike Hoffrichter; **Advertising Manager:** Manfred Böhler
Profile: As a trade newspaper for the inpatient health care, Management & Krankenhaus aimed specifically at all decision makers in hospitals, rehabilitation facilities and medical care centers. Its readers are the decision makers in administration and infrastructure management (controlling, purchasing, IT, human resources, technology etc.) and the decision makers in medical and nursing areas. Of course, also include the relevant associations and professional societies as well as key representatives from government, industry and science to the audience. In the heart of its approach, Management & Krankenhaus's many different functions of a decision that will be resolved, so that its area of responsibility can be successful. Here it reliable partner support from the industry. They have a future-oriented know-how, innovative products and useful services. In Management & Krankenhaus describe experts and opinion leaders from hospitals, academia, industry and policy successful concepts, explain their views to landmark developments and their backgrounds. Departments: Facility & management, health economics, health policy, hygiene, IT and communications, laboratory & diagnostics, medicine & technology, pharmaceuticals.
Language(s): German
Readership: Read by decision makers, management, the medical profession and nursing staff in German hospitals.
ADVERTISING RATES:
Full Page Mono .... EUR 11000
Full Page Colour .... EUR 11000
Mechanical Data: Type Area: 455 x 325 mm, No. of Columns (Display): 6, Col Widths (Display): 50 mm
BUSINESS: HEALTH & MEDICAL: Hospitals

MANAGER MAGAZIN
734750G14A-9258
Editorial: Dovenfleet 5, 20457 HAMBURG
Tel: 40 3080050 **Fax:** 40 30800549
Email: mm_redaktion@manager-magazin.de **Web site:** http://www.manager-magazin.de
Freq: Monthly; **Annual Sub.:** EUR 93,60; **Circ:** 114,075
Editor: Arno Balzer; **Advertising Manager:** Norbert Facklam
Profile: Business magazine for professional decision-makers and managers, with exclusive information, extensive case studies, sound analysis and critical background reports on all corporate and business sectors.
Language(s): German
Readership: Read by managers.
ADVERTISING RATES:
Full Page Mono .... EUR 22190
Full Page Colour .... EUR 22190
Mechanical Data: Type Area: 252 x 178 mm, No. of Columns (Display): 3, Col Widths (Display): 56 mm
Copy instructions: *Copy Date:* 22 days prior to publication
BUSINESS: COMMERCE, INDUSTRY & MANAGEMENT

MANAGERSEMINARE
734752G14A-4400
Editorial: Endenicher Str. 41, 53115 BONN
Tel: 228 9779135 **Fax:** 228 9779177
Email: redaktion@managerseminare.de **Web site:** http://www.managerseminare.de
Freq: Monthly; **Annual Sub.:** EUR 99,60; **Circ:** 21,054
Editor: Nicole Bußmann; **Advertising Manager:** Gerhard May
Profile: managerSeminare, the trade magazine for executives, self-employed and entrepreneurs, delivers in the categories management, knowledge, training and development monthly new impetus to the further education sector. Competent expert authors provide insight into key management issues and reveal future trends, such as: change in organizations (organizational development), change management, business, leadership & team development, leadership and management style, examples from the PE practice, trends in coaching, Expert opinions and interviews, reviews of current literature, tips and tricks for personal development, best practice reports and case studies from the corporate life. Each issue also contains a supplement, which is dedicated to a specific topic or a particular region and that in more detail. Finally, a comprehensive seminar market informs the readers about current seminars and providing their suppliers in detail.
Language(s): German
Readership: Aimed at human resources developers, trainers and managers.
ADVERTISING RATES:
Full Page Mono .... EUR 3740
Full Page Colour .... EUR 4580
Mechanical Data: Type Area: 262 x 185 mm, No. of Columns (Display): 4, Col Widths (Display): 45 mm
Copy instructions: *Copy Date:* 20 days prior to publication
Supplement(s): manage_HR
BUSINESS: COMMERCE, INDUSTRY & MANAGEMENT

MANDANTEN-KURIER
1663880G1F-1624
Editorial: Eyssenecksstr. 31, 60322 FRANKFURT
Tel: 69 15300611 **Fax:** 69 15300610
Email: info@isf-schweiz.ch **Web site:** http://www.isf-schweiz.ch
Freq: Annual; **Cover Price:** Free; **Circ:** 10,000
Editor: Klaus Hennig
Profile: Magazine containing background information about business and stock exchange.
Language(s): German

MANGFALL BOTE
734757G67B-9220
Editorial: Hafnerstr. 5, 83022 ROSENHEIM
Tel: 8031 213201 **Fax:** 8031 213216
Email: redaktion@ovb.net **Web site:** http://www.ovb-online.de
Freq: 312 issues yearly; **Circ:** 11,875
Advertising Manager: Max Breu
Profile: Regional daily newspaper with news on politics, economy, culture, sports, travel, technology, etc. The Mangfall Bote is a regional edition of the newspaper "Oberbayerisches Volksblatt".
Language(s): German
ADVERTISING RATES:
SCC .... EUR 58,70
Mechanical Data: Type Area: 474 x 324 mm, No. of Columns (Display): 7, Col Widths (Display): 45 mm
Copy instructions: *Copy Date:* 1 day prior to publication
Supplement(s): rtv
REGIONAL DAILY & SUNDAY NEWSPAPERS: Regional Daily Newspapers

MANNHEIMER MORGEN
734760G67B-9240
Editorial: Dudenstr. 12, 68167 MANNHEIM
Tel: 621 3921313 **Fax:** 621 3921376
Email: redaktion@mamo.de **Web site:** http://www.morgenweb.de
Freq: 312 issues yearly; **Circ:** 78,704
Editor: Horst Roth; **News Editor:** Michael Schröder; **Advertising Manager:** Gerhard Haeberle
Profile: Regional daily newspaper with news on politics, economy, culture, sports, travel, technology, etc. With nine local editions and a circulation of over 75,000 copies the Mannheimer Morgen the newspaper of the Rhine-Neckar region. Critical, emotional, credible and deeply rooted in the region that draws from the Mannheimer Morgen. Because some 70 journalists working at five locations in the region and correspondents around the world. Facebook: http://www.facebook.com/pages/morgenweb/105113719526519 Twitter: http://twitter.com/morgenweb This Outlet offers RSS (Really Simple Syndication).
Language(s): German
ADVERTISING RATES:
SCC .... EUR 169,50
Mechanical Data: Type Area: 490 x 320 mm, No. of Columns (Display): 7, Col Widths (Display): 44 mm
Copy instructions: *Copy Date:* 1 day prior to publication
Supplement(s): Das will ich; essen & genießen in der Metropolregion; Lust auf Genuss; Mannheim im Weihnachtszauber; Mode & Stil; Morgen Magazin; Natürlich; TV Morgen; 4 wände; Wirtschaftsmorgen; Wohlfühljournal
REGIONAL DAILY & SUNDAY NEWSPAPERS: Regional Daily Newspapers

MANUELLE MEDIZIN
734766G56A-6320
Editorial: Tiergartenstr. 17, 69121 HEIDELBERG
Tel: 6221 48780 **Fax:** 6221 4878366
Email: subscriptions@springer.com **Web site:** http://www.springerlink.com
Freq: 6 issues yearly; **Annual Sub.:** EUR 247,00; **Circ:** 10,606
Editor: L. Beyer; **Advertising Manager:** Elke Tismer
Profile: Manuelle Medizin deals with all aspects of manual medicine and its neighboring areas. It provides information on current developments in the field and addresses orthopedists, rheumatologists, internists, traumatologists as well as general practitioners and physiotherapists. Through its interdisciplinary approach the journal offers a wide scientific basis for current developments of manual medicine. Freely submitted original papers allow the presentation of important clinical studies and serve scientific exchange. Case reports feature interesting cases and aim at optimizing diagnostic and therapeutic strategies. Comprehensive reviews on a specific topical issue focus on providing evidenced based information on current findings.
Language(s): German
ADVERTISING RATES:
Full Page Mono .... EUR 1890
Full Page Colour .... EUR 3190
Mechanical Data: No. of Columns (Display): 3, Col Widths (Display): 54 mm, Type Area: 240 x 174 mm
Official Journal of: Organ d. Dt. Ges. f. Manuelle Medizin, d. Ärzteseminar Bln. e.V., d. Dr. Karl-Sell-Ärzteseminar Neutrauchburg e.V., d. Dt. Ges. f. Muskuloskeletale Medizin e.V., d. Österr. Ärzteges. f. Manuelle Medizin e.V., d. Österr. ArGe. f. Manuelle Medizin e.V. u. d. Schweizer. Ärzteges. f. Manuelle Medizin e.V.

MAPPE
734769G16A-4
Editorial: Streitfeldstr. 35, 81673 MÜNCHEN
Tel: 89 436005175 **Fax:** 89 436005166
Email: redaktion@mappe.de **Web site:** http://www.mappe.de
Freq: Monthly; **Annual Sub.:** EUR 117,00; **Circ:** 18,095
Editor: Matthias Heilig; **Advertising Manager:** Andreas Schneider
Profile: Magazine about colour mixing, indoor and outdoor painting, decorating and varnishing techniques and trade materials.
Language(s): German
Readership: Aimed at painters.
ADVERTISING RATES:
Full Page Mono .... EUR 5025
Full Page Colour .... EUR 7950
Mechanical Data: Type Area: 269 x 182 mm, No. of Columns (Display): 4, Col Widths (Display): 43 mm
Copy instructions: *Copy Date:* 31 days prior to publication
BUSINESS: DECORATING & PAINT

MARBACH & BOTTWARTAL
1740315G67B-9260_500
Editorial: König-Wilhelm-Platz 2, 71672 MARBACH
Tel: 7144 85000 **Fax:** 7144 5000
Email: redaktion@marbacher-zeitung.zgs.de **Web site:** http://www.marbacher-zeitung.de
Freq: 312 issues yearly; **Circ:** 7,897
Advertising Manager: Ulrich Eitel
Profile: Regional daily newspaper covering politics, economics, sport, travel and technology.
Language(s): German
ADVERTISING RATES:
SCC .... EUR 36,30
Mechanical Data: Type Area: 492 x 321 mm, No. of Columns (Display): 7, Col Widths (Display): 44 mm
Copy instructions: *Copy Date:* 1 day prior to publication
Supplement to: Marbacher Zeitung, Stuttgarter Nachrichten, Stuttgarter Zeitung
REGIONAL DAILY & SUNDAY NEWSPAPERS: Regional Daily Newspapers

MARBACHER ZEITUNG
734771G67B-9260
Editorial: König-Wilhelm-Platz 2, 71672 MARBACH
Tel: 7144 85000 **Fax:** 7144 5000
Email: redaktion@marbacher-zeitung.zgs.de **Web site:** http://www.marbacher-zeitung.de
Freq: 312 issues yearly; **Circ:** 43,578
Advertising Manager: Ulrich Eitel
Profile: Daily newspaper with regional news and a local sports section.
Language(s): German
ADVERTISING RATES:
SCC .... EUR 397,20
Mechanical Data: Type Area: 492 x 321 mm, No. of Columns (Display): 7, Col Widths (Display): 45 mm
Copy instructions: *Copy Date:* 2 days prior to publication
Supplement(s): Marbach & Bottwartal
REGIONAL DAILY & SUNDAY NEWSPAPERS: Regional Daily Newspapers

MARBURGER BUND ZEITUNG
734772G56A-6340
Editorial: Reinhardtstr. 36, 10117 BERLIN
Tel: 30 7468460 **Fax:** 30 240830329
Email: redaktion@marburger-bund.de **Web site:** http://www.marburger-bund-zeitung.de
Freq: 18 issues yearly; Free to qualifying individuals **Annual Sub.:** EUR 35,00; **Circ:** 109,107
Editor: Angelika Steimer-Schmid
Profile: The newspaper of the Marburger Bund doctors' union, trade union, health and professional-political interests of all salaried and permanent doctors in Germany.
Language(s): German
ADVERTISING RATES:
Full Page Mono .... EUR 9300
Full Page Colour .... EUR 11000
Mechanical Data: Type Area: 390 x 282 mm, No. of Columns (Display): 6, Col Widths (Display): 43 mm
Copy instructions: *Copy Date:* 21 days prior to publication
BUSINESS: HEALTH & MEDICAL

MARBURGER MAGAZIN EXPRESS
734773G80-7440
Editorial: Ernst-Giller-Str. 20a, 35039 MARBURG
Tel: 6421 68440 **Fax:** 6421 684444
Email: redaktion@marbuch-verlag.de **Web site:** http://www.marbuch-verlag.de
Freq: Weekly; **Cover Price:** Free; **Circ:** 14,087
Editor: Georg Kronenberg; **Advertising Manager:** Hans-Werner Hußmann
Profile: Magazine for the Marburg area.
Language(s): German
ADVERTISING RATES:
Full Page Mono .... EUR 1352
Full Page Colour .... EUR 1790
Mechanical Data: Type Area: 260 x 190 mm, No. of Columns (Display): 4, Col Widths (Display): 45 mm
Copy instructions: *Copy Date:* 3 days prior to publication
CONSUMER: RURAL & REGIONAL INTEREST

MARCELLINO'S DEUTSCHLAND HOTEL REPORT
1925304G89A-12509
Editorial: Kaistr. 12, 40221 DÜSSELDORF
Tel: 211 3006690 **Fax:** 211 30066930
Email: mail@marcellinos.de **Web site:** http://www.marcellinos.de
Freq: Annual; **Cover Price:** EUR 18,00; **Circ:** 13,000
Editor: Elisabeth M. Rohata; **Advertising Manager:** Marcellino M. Hudalla
Profile: Hotel guide for Germany.
Language(s): German
ADVERTISING RATES:
Full Page Mono .... EUR 2880
Full Page Colour .... EUR 2880
Mechanical Data: Type Area: 210 x 99 mm
Copy instructions: *Copy Date:* 55 days prior to publication

MARCELLINO'S DEUTSCHLAND RESTAURANT REPORT
1925306G89A-12511
Editorial: Kaistr. 12, 40221 DÜSSELDORF
Tel: 211 3006690 **Fax:** 211 30066930
Email: mail@marcellinos.de **Web site:** http://www.marcellinos.de
Freq: Annual; **Cover Price:** EUR 18,00; **Circ:** 8,000
Editor: Elisabeth M. Rohata; **Advertising Manager:** Marcellino M. Hudalla
Profile: Restaurant guide.
Language(s): German
ADVERTISING RATES:
Full Page Mono .... EUR 2348
Full Page Colour .... EUR 2348
Mechanical Data: Type Area: 210 x 99 mm
Copy instructions: *Copy Date:* 70 days prior to publication

MARCELLINO'S RESTAURANT REPORT - AUSG. BERLIN U. UMGEBUNG
1925307G89A-12512
Editorial: Kaistr. 12, 40221 DÜSSELDORF
Tel: 211 3006690 **Fax:** 211 30066930
Email: mail@marcellinos.de **Web site:** http://www.marcellinos.de
Freq: Annual; **Cover Price:** EUR 12,00; **Circ:** 12,610
Editor: Elisabeth M. Rohata; **Advertising Manager:** Marcellino M. Hudalla
Profile: Restaurant guide for the Berlin region.
Language(s): German
ADVERTISING RATES:
Full Page Mono .... EUR 2880
Full Page Colour .... EUR 2880
Mechanical Data: Type Area: 210 x 99 mm
Copy instructions: *Copy Date:* 60 days prior to publication

MARCELLINO'S RESTAURANT REPORT - AUSG. DÜSSELDORF KREFELD WUPPERTAL NEUSS MÖNCHENGLADBACH
1925308G89A-12513
Editorial: Kaistr. 12, 40221 DÜSSELDORF
Tel: 211 3006690 **Fax:** 211 30066930
Email: mail@marcellinos.de **Web site:** http://www.marcellinos.de
Freq: Annual; **Cover Price:** EUR 12,00; **Circ:** 12,610
Editor: Elisabeth M. Rohata; **Advertising Manager:** Marcellino M. Hudalla
Profile: Restaurant guide for Düsseldorf, Krefeld, Wuppertal, Neuss and Mönchengladbach.
Language(s): German
ADVERTISING RATES:
Full Page Mono .... EUR 2880
Full Page Colour .... EUR 2880
Mechanical Data: Type Area: 210 x 99 mm
Copy instructions: *Copy Date:* 65 days prior to publication

MARCELLINO'S RESTAURANT REPORT - AUSG. FRANKFURT U. UMGEBUNG
1925384G89A-12522
Editorial: Kaistr. 12, 40221 DÜSSELDORF
Tel: 211 3006690 **Fax:** 211 30066930
Email: mail@marcellinos.de **Web site:** http://www.marcellinos.de
Freq: Annual; **Cover Price:** EUR 12,00; **Circ:** 8,000
Editor: Elisabeth M. Rohata; **Advertising Manager:** Marcellino M. Hudalla
Profile: Restaurant guide for Frankfurt, Offenbach, Mainz, Wiesbaden and Eltville.
Language(s): German
ADVERTISING RATES:
Full Page Mono .... EUR 2348
Full Page Colour .... EUR 2348
Copy instructions: *Copy Date:* 70 days prior to publication

MARCELLINO'S RESTAURANT REPORT - AUSG. HAMBURG U. UMGEBUNG
1925385G89A-12523
Editorial: Kaistr. 12, 40221 DÜSSELDORF
Tel: 211 3006690 **Fax:** 211 30066930
Email: mail@marcellinos.de **Web site:** http://www.marcellinos.de
Freq: Annual; **Cover Price:** EUR 12,00; **Circ:** 12,610
Editor: Elisabeth M. Rohata; **Advertising Manager:** Marcellino M. Hudalla
Profile: Restaurant guide for the Hamburg region.
Language(s): German
ADVERTISING RATES:
Full Page Mono .... EUR 2880
Full Page Colour .... EUR 2880
Mechanical Data: Type Area: 210 x 99 mm
Copy instructions: *Copy Date:* 70 days prior to publication

MARCELLINO'S RESTAURANT REPORT - AUSG. KÖLN BONN BAD NEUENAHR BERGISCH GLADBACH
1925309G89A-12514
Editorial: Kaistr. 12, 40221 DÜSSELDORF
Tel: 211 3006690 **Fax:** 211 30066930
Email: mail@marcellinos.de **Web site:** http://www.marcellinos.de
Freq: Annual; **Cover Price:** EUR 12,00; **Circ:** 8,000
Editor: Elisabeth M. Rohata; **Advertising Manager:** Marcellino M. Hudalla
Profile: Restaurant and club reviews by guests for guests for Bonn, Bad Neuenahr and Bergisch Gladbach.
Language(s): German
ADVERTISING RATES:
Full Page Mono .... EUR 2348
Full Page Colour .... EUR 2348
Mechanical Data: Type Area: 210 x 99 mm
Copy instructions: *Copy Date:* 70 days prior to publication

MARCELLINO'S RESTAURANT REPORT - AUSG. MALLORCA
1925310G89A-12515
Editorial: Kaistr. 12, 40221 DÜSSELDORF
Tel: 211 3006690 **Fax:** 211 30066930
Email: mail@marcellinos.de **Web site:** http://www.marcellinos.de
Freq: Annual; **Cover Price:** EUR 12,00; **Circ:** 8,000
Editor: Elisabeth M. Rohata; **Advertising Manager:** Marcellino M. Hudalla
Profile: Restaurant guide for Mallorca.
Language(s): German
ADVERTISING RATES:
Full Page Mono .... EUR 2348
Full Page Colour .... EUR 2348
Mechanical Data: Type Area: 210 x 99 mm
Copy instructions: *Copy Date:* 55 days prior to publication

MARCELLINO'S RESTAURANT REPORT - AUSG. MÜNCHEN U. UMGEBUNG
1925311G89A-12516
Editorial: Kaistr. 12, 40221 DÜSSELDORF
Tel: 211 3006690 **Fax:** 211 30066930
Email: mail@marcellinos.de **Web site:** http://www.marcellinos.de
Freq: Annual; **Cover Price:** EUR 12,00; **Circ:** 12,610
Editor: Elisabeth M. Rohata; **Advertising Manager:** Marcellino M. Hudalla
Profile: Restaurant guide for Munich and surrounding regions.
Language(s): German
ADVERTISING RATES:
Full Page Mono .... EUR 2880
Full Page Colour .... EUR 2880
Copy instructions: *Copy Date:* 60 days prior to publication

MARCELLINO'S RESTAURANT REPORT - AUSG. RUHRGEBIET
1925312G89A-12517
Editorial: Kaistr. 12, 40221 DÜSSELDORF
Tel: 211 3006690 **Fax:** 211 30066930
Email: mail@marcellinos.de **Web site:** http://www.marcellinos.de
Freq: Annual; **Cover Price:** EUR 12,00; **Circ:** 8,000
Editor: Elisabeth M. Rohata; **Advertising Manager:** Marcellino M. Hudalla
Profile: Restaurant guide for the Ruhr Basin region.
Language(s): German
ADVERTISING RATES:
Full Page Mono .... EUR 2348
Full Page Colour .... EUR 2348
Mechanical Data: Type Area: 210 x 99 mm
Copy instructions: *Copy Date:* 70 days prior to publication

MARCELLINO'S RESTAURANT REPORT - AUSG. STUTTGART HEILBRONN TÜBINGEN ESSLINGEN BÖBLINGEN
1925313G89A-12518
Editorial: Kaistr. 12, 40221 DÜSSELDORF
Tel: 211 3006690 **Fax:** 211 30066930
Email: mail@marcellinos.de **Web site:** http://www.marcellinos.de
Freq: Annual; **Cover Price:** EUR 12,00; **Circ:** 8,000
Editor: Elisabeth M. Rohata; **Advertising Manager:** Marcellino M. Hudalla
Profile: Restaurant guide for Stuttgart, Heilbronn, Tübingen, Esslingen and Böblingen.
Language(s): German
ADVERTISING RATES:
Full Page Mono .... EUR 2348
Full Page Colour .... EUR 2348
Mechanical Data: Type Area: 210 x 99 mm
Copy instructions: *Copy Date:* 70 days prior to publication

MARCELLINO'S RESTAURANT REPORT - AUSG. SYLT, AMRUM U. FÖHR
1925316G89A-12521
Editorial: Kaistr. 12, 40221 DÜSSELDORF
Tel: 211 3006690 **Fax:** 211 30066930
Email: mail@marcellinos.de **Web site:** http://www.marcellinos.de
Freq: Annual; **Cover Price:** EUR 9,95; **Circ:** 5,820
Editor: Elisabeth M. Rohata; **Advertising Manager:** Marcellino M. Hudalla
Profile: Restaurant and club reviews from guests for guests for Sylt, Amrum and Föhr.
Language(s): German
ADVERTISING RATES:
Full Page Mono .... EUR 1900
Full Page Colour .... EUR 1900
Mechanical Data: Type Area: 210 x 99 mm
Copy instructions: *Copy Date:* 55 days prior to publication

MARE
734792G94J-320
Editorial: Pickhuben 2, 20457 HAMBURG
Tel: 40 3698590 **Fax:** 40 36985990
Email: mare@mare.de **Web site:** http://www.mare.de
Freq: 6 issues yearly; **Annual Sub.:** EUR 46,80; **Circ:** 26,200
Editor: Nikolaus K. Gelpke
Profile: mare is the award-winning magazine of the seas, whose reports and photo galleries among others the Lead Award, the World Press Award and the CNN Journalist Award has been awarded. mare puts the emphasis placed by the sea has a life, economic and cultural space for the people in the public consciousness. Every two months mare is so new thinking on economic, political, cultural, environmental and scientific themes that have their starting point from the perspective of the seas. Facebook: http://www.facebook.com/mareverlag.
Language(s): German
Readership: Focused on ecology - perceived from the unique viewpoint of the sea.
ADVERTISING RATES:
Full Page Colour .... EUR 7500
Mechanical Data: Type Area: 250 x 180 mm
Copy instructions: *Copy Date:* 47 days prior to publication
CONSUMER: OTHER CLASSIFICATIONS: Popular Science

MARINE FORUM
734814G45A-921
Editorial: Ulrich-von-Hassel-Str. 2, 53123 BONN
Tel: 228 9191521 **Fax:** 228 9191522
Email: marineforum@mov-moh.de **Web site:** http://www.marineforum.info
Freq: 10 issues yearly; Free to qualifying individuals
Annual Sub.: EUR 59,90; **Circ:** 10,093
Editor: Jürgen E. Kratzmann
Profile: Magazine focusing on the maritime industry.
Language(s): German
ADVERTISING RATES:
Full Page Mono .... EUR 2300
Full Page Colour .... EUR 3260
Mechanical Data: Type Area: 270 x 185 mm
Copy instructions: *Copy Date:* 30 days prior to publication
Official Journal of: Organ d. Marine-Offizier-Vereinigung
BUSINESS: MARINE & SHIPPING

MARITIM JOURNAL
734816G89B-80
Editorial: Külpstr. 2, 64293 DARMSTADT
Tel: 6151 905778 **Fax:** 6151 905707
Email: info.vkd@maritim.de **Web site:** http://www.maritim.de
Freq: Half-yearly; **Cover Price:** Free; **Circ:** 60,000
Advertising Manager: Carola Ehrhardt
Profile: Magazine of the Maritim hotel group.
Language(s): English; German
ADVERTISING RATES:
Full Page Mono .... EUR 3900
Full Page Colour .... EUR 4900
Mechanical Data: Type Area: 263 x 176 mm
Copy instructions: *Copy Date:* 42 days prior to publication
CONSUMER: HOLIDAYS & TRAVEL: Hotel Magazines

MARKANT HANDELSMAGAZIN
734817G53-115
Editorial: Medienplatz 1, 76571 GAGGENAU
Tel: 7225 916250 **Fax:** 7225 916291
Email: mehler@medialog.de **Web site:** http://www.medialog.de
Freq: 11 issues yearly; **Circ:** 11,684
Editor: Klaus Mehler; **Advertising Manager:** Matthias Stichling
Profile: Journal for executives in trade and economy.
Language(s): German
Readership: Aimed at retailers.
ADVERTISING RATES:
Full Page Mono .... EUR 5985
Full Page Colour .... EUR 7890
Mechanical Data: Type Area: 244 x 173 mm, No. of Columns (Display): 3, Col Widths (Display): 55 mm
Copy instructions: *Copy Date:* 28 days prior to publication
BUSINESS: RETAILING & WHOLESALING

MARKE41
1996733G2A-5907
Editorial: Ridlerstr. 35a, 80339 MÜNCHEN
Tel: 89 72959915 **Fax:** 89 72959918
Email: redaktion@marke41.de **Web site:** http://www.marke41.de
Freq: 6 issues yearly; **Annual Sub.:** EUR 90,00; **Circ:** 5,600
Editor: Friedrich M. Kirn
Profile: Ezine: Journal for hands-on marketing in print and online, includes skilled posts with informative charts on innovative brand management and efficient budget use, provides proven marketing approaches, effective tools and checklists for practice, summarizes the main aspects and making for a quick overview, presented competent partners marketing strategy and performance measurement.
Language(s): German
ADVERTISING RATES:
Full Page Mono .... EUR 5200
Full Page Colour .... EUR 5200
Mechanical Data: Type Area: 238 x 187 mm, No. of Columns (Display): 3, Col Widths (Display): 67 mm
Copy instructions: *Copy Date:* 15 days prior to publication

MARKENARTIKEL
734819G2A-170
Editorial: Nebendahlstr. 16, 22041 HAMBURG
Tel: 40 6090090 **Fax:** 40 60900977
Email: markenartikel@new-business.de **Web site:** http://www.new-business.de
Freq: 11 issues yearly; **Annual Sub.:** EUR 98,00; **Circ:** 3,398
Editor: Peter Strahlendorf; **Advertising Manager:** Jens Jansen
Profile: International journal containing articles about brand management. Facebook: http://www.facebook.com/SEATde.
Language(s): German
ADVERTISING RATES:
Full Page Mono .... EUR 4200
Full Page Colour .... EUR 4200
Mechanical Data: Type Area: 275 x 175 mm
Copy instructions: *Copy Date:* 25 days prior to publication
BUSINESS: COMMUNICATIONS, ADVERTISING & MARKETING

MARKENR
1882043G1A-3765
Editorial: Luxemburger Str. 449, 50939 KÖLN
Tel: 221 943730 **Fax:** 221 94373901
Web site: http://www.wolterskluwer.de
Freq: 10 issues yearly; **Annual Sub.:** EUR 165,00; **Circ:** 850
Profile: Magazine about German, European and international copyright law.
Language(s): German
ADVERTISING RATES:
Full Page Mono .... EUR 1039
Full Page Colour .... EUR 2146
Mechanical Data: Type Area: 255 x 184 mm
Copy instructions: *Copy Date:* 21 days prior to publication

MARKETING
1637462G2A-5523
Editorial: Von-Melle-Park 5, 20146 HAMBURG
Tel: 40 428386401
Email: editor@marketing-zfp.de **Web site:** http://www.marketing.beck.de
Freq: Quarterly; **Annual Sub.:** EUR 175,10; **Circ:** 700
Editor: Henrik Sattler
Profile: Magazine provides a forum for the dialogue between research and practice, analysis and problem solving in marketing, demonstration of modern quantitative and qualitative methods, exchange of findings and results.
Language(s): German

MARKETING INTERN
1647228G1C-1443
Editorial: Wilhelm-Haas-Platz 2, 63263 NEU-ISENBURG **Tel:** 69 6978139 **Fax:** 69 6978124
Email: ralf.galka@genossenschaftsverband.de **Web site:** http://www.genossenschaftsverband.de
Freq: Quarterly; **Circ:** 3,000
Editor: Ralf Galka; **Advertising Manager:** Brigitte Ott
Profile: Company publication published by Volksbanken und Raiffeisenbanken.
Language(s): German
ADVERTISING RATES:
Full Page Mono .... EUR 2730
Full Page Colour .... EUR 5187
Mechanical Data: Type Area: 266 x 179 mm, No. of Columns (Display): 3, Col Widths (Display): 56 mm
Copy instructions: *Copy Date:* 30 days prior to publication

MARKETINGAKTIONEN
1894858G50-1263
Editorial: Kaiserstr. 56, 60329 FRANKFURT
Tel: 69 21238800 **Fax:** 69 21237880
Email: info@infofrankfurt.de **Web site:** http://www.frankfurt-tourismus.de
Freq: Quarterly; **Circ:** 310
Profile: Information about tourism, hotels and the Frankfurt airport.
Language(s): German

MARKETING-CLUB DÜSSELDORF
2025908G2A-5915
Editorial: Kesselsbergweg 9, 40489 DÜSSELDORF
Tel: 211 6415065 **Fax:** 211 6415066
Email: info@marketing-club.net **Web site:** http://www.marketing-club.net
Circ: 1,000
Editor: Dirk Krüssenberg; **Advertising Manager:** Silvia Gertler
Profile: Mitgliederzeitschrift des Marketing-Club Düsseldorf.
Language(s): German

MARKGRÄFLER TAGBLATT
734829G67B-9300
Editorial: Am Alten Markt 2, 79539 LÖRRACH
Tel: 7621 40330 **Fax:** 7621 403381
Email: mt.redaktion@verlagshaus-jaumann.de **Web site:** http://www.die-oberbadische.de
Freq: 312 issues yearly; **Circ:** 3,848
Advertising Manager: Thomas Dunke
Profile: Daily newspaper with regional news and a local sports section.
Language(s): German
Mechanical Data: Type Area: 435 x 280 mm, No. of Columns (Display): 6, Col Widths (Display): 45 mm
Copy instructions: *Copy Date:* 1 day prior to publication
REGIONAL DAILY & SUNDAY NEWSPAPERS: Regional Daily Newspapers

MÄRKISCHE ALLGEMEINE
734606G67B-9320
Editorial: Friedrich-Engels-Str. 24, 14473 POTSDAM
Tel: 331 28400 **Fax:** 331 2840310
Email: chefredaktion@mazonline.de **Web site:** http://www.maerkischeallgemeine.de
Freq: 312 issues yearly; **Circ:** 140,080
Editor: Klaus Rost; **News Editor:** Henry Lohmar; **Advertising Manager:** Detlef Schiller
Profile: Regional daily newspaper with news on politics, economy, culture, sports, travel, technology, etc. Facebook: http://www.facebook.com/MAZonline Twitter: http://twitter.com/maz_aktuell This Outlet offers RSS (Really Simple Syndication).
Language(s): German
ADVERTISING RATES:
SCC .... EUR 236,20
Mechanical Data: Type Area: 479 x 324 mm, No. of Columns (Display): 7, Col Widths (Display): 45 mm
Copy instructions: *Copy Date:* 2 days prior to publication
Supplement(s): prisma
REGIONAL DAILY & SUNDAY NEWSPAPERS: Regional Daily Newspapers

DER MÄRKISCHE BOTE
734608G72-7192
Editorial: Wernerstr. 21, 03046 COTTBUS
Tel: 355 3813811 **Fax:** 355 3813120
Email: post@cga-verlag.de **Web site:** http://www.maerkischerbote.de
Freq: Weekly; **Cover Price:** Free; **Circ:** 108,000
Editor: Jürgen Heinrich; **Advertising Manager:** Petra Heinrich
Profile: Advertising journal (house-to-house) concentrating on local stories.
Language(s): German
ADVERTISING RATES:
Full Page Mono .... EUR 4560
Mechanical Data: Type Area: 435 x 277 mm, No. of Columns (Display): 6, Col Widths (Display): 43 mm
LOCAL NEWSPAPERS

MÄRKISCHE ODERZEITUNG
734609G67B-9340
Editorial: Kellenspring 6, 15230 FRANKFURT
Tel: 335 5530511 **Fax:** 335 5530538
Email: redaktion@moz.de **Web site:** http://www.moz.de
Freq: 312 issues yearly; Free to qualifying individuals ; **Circ:** 87,961
Editor: Frank Mangelsdorf; **News Editor:** Günter Marx; **Advertising Manager:** André Tackenberg
Profile: Regional daily newspaper with news on politics, economy, culture, sports, travel, technology, etc. She appears in the east of Brandenburg near Berlin to the Oder. Editorial office is Frankfurt (Oder). The distribution of MOZ is substantially identical to the former East German district of Frankfurt (Oder), a region with about 680,000 inhabitants. It extends from Schwedt and Angermünde in the north to Eisenhüttenstadt in the south, ranging from the city of Berlin in the west to the Oder in the east. The distribution area covers the counties Märkisch Oderland, Oder-Spree, Barnim, parts Uckermark and the independent city of Frankfurt (Oder). The Angermünde, Bad Freienwalde, Beeskow, Bernau, Eberswalde, Eisenhüttenstadt, Frankfurt (Oder), Fürstenwalde, Schwedt, Seelow and Strausberg appearing eleven o'clock local editions have a total of about 270,000 readers. Of the more than 88,000 copies sold well refer 82 809 readers of MOZ in the subscription. The MOZ sees itself as a "voice in East

Brandenburg" in the city of Potsdam and the Federal capital Berlin and maintains there own correspondent offices. The Märkische or newspaper in these days the Central Government currently available in order to make local attention on the region to represent their interests. A major focuses the Märkische Oderzeitung reporting from neighboring Poland. Every two months is the daily newspaper supplement "Brandenburgische Blätter" at. They see themselves as guides through the Brandenburg nature and culture, past and present. To this end, they gather as portraits of Prussia, architectural descriptions and historical reports. Facebook: http://www.facebook.com/maerkischeoderzeitung This Outlet offers RSS (Really Simple Syndication).
Language(s): German
ADVERTISING RATES:
SCC .... EUR 214,40
Mechanical Data: Type Area: 476 x 323 mm, No. of Columns (Display): 7, Col Widths (Display): 45 mm
Copy instructions: *Copy Date:* 2 days prior to publication
Supplement(s): prisma
REGIONAL DAILY & SUNDAY NEWSPAPERS: Regional Daily Newspapers

MÄRKISCHER MARKT - AUSG. BAD FREIENWALDE 734611G72-7200
Editorial: Kellenspring 6, 15230 FRANKFURT
Tel: 335 5530343 **Fax:** 335 5530353
Email: mm-badfreienwalde@moz.de **Web site:** http://www.maerkischer-markt.de
Freq: Weekly; **Cover Price:** Free; **Circ:** 14,875
Editor: Michael Petsch; **Advertising Manager:** André Tackenberg
Profile: Advertising journal (house-to-house) concentrating on local stories.
Language(s): German
ADVERTISING RATES:
Full Page Mono .... EUR 1733
Full Page Colour .... EUR 2513
Mechanical Data: Type Area: 476 x 323 mm, No. of Columns (Display): 7, Col Widths (Display): 45 mm
Copy instructions: *Copy Date:* 2 days prior to publication
LOCAL NEWSPAPERS

MÄRKISCHES ZENTRUM NEWS 1855855G74M-877
Editorial: Flutstr. 1, 12439 BERLIN **Tel:** 30 5426170
Web site: http://www.maerkisches-zentrum.de
Freq: 8 issues yearly; **Cover Price:** Free; **Circ:** 159,556
Editor: Frank Bürger; **Advertising Manager:** Johann Brunken
Profile: Shopping centre publication of the Märkisches Zentrum with reports and recommendations to the Shoppincenter.
Language(s): German

MÄRKLIN MAGAZIN 734622G79B-880
Editorial: Löwenstr. 46a, 70597 STUTTGART
Tel: 711 44080064 **Fax:** 711 44080066
Email: maerklin-magazin@3g-media.de **Web site:** http://www.maerklin.de/mm
Freq: 6 issues yearly; Free to qualifying individuals
Annual Sub.: EUR 30,00; **Circ:** 73,595
Editor: Peter Waldleitner
Profile: Publication for model railway enthusiasts.
Language(s): German
ADVERTISING RATES:
Full Page Mono .... EUR 2720
Full Page Colour .... EUR 3090
Mechanical Data: Type Area: 279 x 180 mm
CONSUMER: HOBBIES & DIY: Models & Modelling

MARKSCHEIDEWESEN 734831G30-3
Editorial: Wüllnerstr. 2, 52062 AACHEN
Tel: 241 8095687 **Fax:** 241 8092150
Email: preusse@ifm.rwth-aachen.de **Web site:** http://www.dmv-ev.de
Freq: 3 issues yearly; Free to qualifying individuals
Annual Sub.: EUR 82,00; **Circ:** 1,000
Editor: Axel Preuße
Profile: Research results covering all aspects of the mining industry.
Language(s): German

MARKT AM MITTWOCH - AUSG. BAD KISSINGEN 721737G72-1644
Editorial: Berner Str. 2, 97084 WÜRZBURG
Tel: 931 6001355 **Fax:** 931 6001478
Email: red.sonderpublikation@mainpost.de **Web site:** http://www.markt.mainpost.de
Freq: Weekly; **Cover Price:** Free; **Circ:** 40,300
Editor: Werner Barthel; **Advertising Manager:** Michael Schmitt
Profile: Advertising journal (house-to-house) concentrating on local stories.
Language(s): German
ADVERTISING RATES:
Full Page Mono .... EUR 3425
Full Page Colour .... EUR 4436
Mechanical Data: Type Area: 466 x 310 mm, No. of Columns (Display): 7, Col Widths (Display): 43 mm
Copy instructions: *Copy Date:* 2 days prior to publication
Supplement(s): main zuhause
LOCAL NEWSPAPERS

MARKT AM MITTWOCH - AUSG. KITZINGEN/GEROLZHOFEN/ MAINSCHLEIFE 732746G72-6176
Editorial: Berner Str. 2, 97084 WÜRZBURG
Tel: 931 6001355 **Fax:** 931 6001478
Email: red.sonderpublikation@mainpost.de **Web site:** http://www.markt.mainpost.de
Freq: Weekly; **Cover Price:** Free; **Circ:** 50,500
Editor: Werner Barthel; **Advertising Manager:** Karina Rösch
Profile: Advertising journal (house-to-house) concentrating on local stories.
Language(s): German
ADVERTISING RATES:
Full Page Mono .... EUR 3522
Full Page Colour .... EUR 4599
Mechanical Data: Type Area: 466 x 310 mm, No. of Columns (Display): 7, Col Widths (Display): 43 mm
Copy instructions: *Copy Date:* 5 days prior to publication
Supplement(s): Kitzingen-Gerolzhofen-Mainschleife Veranstaltungskalender; Kitzingen kompakt; markt visionen; Wiesentheid kompakt
LOCAL NEWSPAPERS

MARKT AM MITTWOCH - AUSG. RHÖN-GRABFELD 740454G72-10928
Editorial: Berner Str. 2, 97084 WÜRZBURG
Tel: 931 6001355 **Fax:** 931 6001478
Email: red.sonderpublikation@mainpost.de **Web site:** http://www.markt.mainpost.de
Freq: Weekly; **Cover Price:** Free; **Circ:** 38,000
Editor: Werner Barthel; **Advertising Manager:** Bernd Pieper
Profile: Advertising journal (house-to-house) concentrating on local stories.
Language(s): German
ADVERTISING RATES:
Full Page Mono .... EUR 3196
Full Page Colour .... EUR 4142
Mechanical Data: Type Area: 466 x 310 mm, No. of Columns (Display): 7, Col Widths (Display): 43 mm
Copy instructions: *Copy Date:* 2 days prior to publication
Supplement(s): main zuhause
LOCAL NEWSPAPERS

MARKT AM MITTWOCH - AUSG. SCHWEINFURT 741572G72-11840
Editorial: Berner Str. 2, 97084 WÜRZBURG
Tel: 931 6001355 **Fax:** 931 6001478
Email: red.sonderpublikation@mainpost.de **Web site:** http://www.markt.mainpost.de
Freq: Weekly; **Cover Price:** Free; **Circ:** 64,600
Editor: Werner Barthel; **Advertising Manager:** Norbert Schmitt
Profile: Advertising journal (house-to-house) concentrating on local stories.
Language(s): German
ADVERTISING RATES:
Full Page Mono .... EUR 5220
Full Page Colour .... EUR 6785
Mechanical Data: Type Area: 466 x 310 mm, No. of Columns (Display): 7, Col Widths (Display): 43 mm
Copy instructions: *Copy Date:* 2 days prior to publication
Supplement(s): Dittelbrunn kompakt; Mainbogen kompakt; main zuhause; markt visionen
LOCAL NEWSPAPERS

MARKT ANZEIGER OST 734845G14A-4440
Editorial: Am Teichfeld 24, 06567 BAD FRANKENHAUSEN **Tel:** 34671 63087
Fax: 34671 77539
Email: marktanzeigerost@t-online.de **Web site:** http://www.marktanzeiger-ost.de
Freq: 6 issues yearly; **Annual Sub.:** EUR 21,00; **Circ:** 4,000
Editor: Joachim Mühler; **Advertising Manager:** Joachim Mühler
Profile: Magazine with city and market events for the German New Federal States.
Language(s): German
ADVERTISING RATES:
Full Page Mono .... EUR 300
Full Page Colour .... EUR 390
Mechanical Data: Type Area: 190 x 125 mm, No. of Columns (Display): 2, Col Widths (Display): 59 mm
Copy instructions: *Copy Date:* 15 days prior to publication

MARKT IN GRÜN 734864G26C-220
Editorial: Stolberger Str. 84, 50933 KÖLN
Tel: 221 5497363 **Fax:** 221 54976357
Email: red.marktingruen@rohn.de **Web site:** http://www.markt-in-gruen.de
Freq: 10 issues yearly; **Annual Sub.:** EUR 114,00; **Circ:** 6,926
Editor: Ute Roggendorf; **Advertising Manager:** Verena Thiele
Profile: Magazine covering all sectors of the gardening trade. Contains reports, market analyses, surveys, details of new products, technology, equipment and supplies.
Language(s): German
Readership: Aimed at garden centres, DIY stores, gardening equipment retailers, florists, nurseries, seed specialists and hypermarkets.
ADVERTISING RATES:
Full Page Mono .... EUR 3330
Full Page Colour .... EUR 5640
Mechanical Data: Type Area: 267 x 188 mm, No. of Columns (Display): 3, Col Widths (Display): 60 mm
Copy instructions: *Copy Date:* 21 days prior to publication
BUSINESS: GARDEN TRADE

DER MARKT IN MITTELDEUTSCHLAND 734865G63-540
Editorial: Alter Markt 8, 39104 MAGDEBURG
Tel: 391 5693170 **Fax:** 391 5693193
Email: laudan@magdeburg.ihk.de **Web site:** http://www.magdeburg.ihk.de
Freq: Monthly; Free to qualifying individuals
Annual Sub.: EUR 28,00; **Circ:** 35,996
Editor: Frank Laudan; **Advertising Manager:** Marianne Schack
Profile: Publication of the Magdeburg Chamber of Trade and Industry.
Language(s): German
Readership: Aimed at commerce and industry.
ADVERTISING RATES:
Full Page Mono .... EUR 2650
Full Page Colour .... EUR 3950
Mechanical Data: Type Area: 260 x 185 mm, No. of Columns (Display): 3, Col Widths (Display): 58 mm
Copy instructions: *Copy Date:* 18 days prior to publication
BUSINESS: REGIONAL BUSINESS

MARKT INTERN APOTHEKE PHARMAZIE 734866G37-1220
Editorial: Grafenberger Allee 30, 40237 DÜSSELDORF **Tel:** 211 6698153 **Fax:** 211 6698188
Email: apotheke@markt-intern.de **Web site:** http://www.markt-intern.de
Freq: Weekly; **Annual Sub.:** EUR 343,92
Editor: Christoph Bach
Profile: Magazine about medicine, health and healthcare and new products.
Language(s): German
Readership: Read by pharmacists.
Supplement(s): markt intern Mittelstand
BUSINESS: PHARMACEUTICAL & CHEMISTS

MARKT INTERN INSTALLATION SANITÄR/HEIZUNG 734878G3D-833
Editorial: Grafenberger Allee 30, 40237 DÜSSELDORF **Tel:** 211 6698119 **Fax:** 211 6698175
Email: ish@markt-intern.de **Web site:** http://www.markt-intern.de
Freq: Weekly; **Annual Sub.:** EUR 343,92
Editor: Hans Georg Pauli
Profile: Magazine about installation, sanitation and heating.
Language(s): German
Readership: Read by skilled manual workers in the installation and sanitation trade.
Supplement(s): markt intern Mittelstand
BUSINESS: HEATING & VENTILATION: Heating & Plumbing

MARKT INTERN MITTELSTAND 734880G14A-4460
Editorial: Grafenberger Allee 30, 40237 DÜSSELDORF **Tel:** 211 6698129 **Fax:** 211 6698333
Email: mittelstand@markt-intern.de **Web site:** http://www.markt-intern.de
Freq: 25 issues yearly; **Annual Sub.:** EUR 163,36
Editor: Carsten Schmitt
Profile: Magazine about politics, the economy and law.
Language(s): German
Supplement to: markt intern Apotheke Pharmazie, markt intern Augenoptik Optometrie, markt intern Auto Tankstelle, markt intern Büro-Fachhandel, markt intern DOB-Fachhandel, markt intern Eisenwaren, Werkzeuge, Garten, markt intern Elektro-Fachhandel, markt intern Elektro-Installation, markt intern Foto-Fachhandel, markt intern HAKA-Fachhandel, markt intern Installation Sanitär/Heizung, markt intern Möbel-Fachhandel, markt intern Parfümerie Kosmetik, markt intern Schuh-Fachhandel, markt intern Spielwaren Modellbau, Basteln, markt intern Sport-Fachhandel, markt intern Telekommunikation, markt intern Uhren Schmuck, markt intern Unterhaltungs-Elektronik, markt intern Wolle, Stoffe Handarbeiten, markt intern Young Fashion Jeans/ Sportswear
BUSINESS: COMMERCE, INDUSTRY & MANAGEMENT

MARKT UND MITTELSTAND 734921G14A-4500
Editorial: Bismarckstr. 24, 61169 FRIEDBERG
Tel: 6031 7386192 **Fax:** 6031 738620
Email: boris.karkowski@marktundmittelstand.de
Web site: http://www.marktundmittelstand.de
Freq: 10 issues yearly; **Annual Sub.:** EUR 55,00; **Circ:** 101,625
Editor: Boris Karkowski; **Advertising Manager:** Sylvia Daun
Profile: In Markt und Mittelstand corporate decision makers from Mittelstand companies find all the information they need to boost their companies: practical, tried and tested and topical. Information that adds value. Our authors take on an entrepreneur's and manager's view on topics. They only cover business-relevant issues. Readers find practical advice from the typical fields of actions of medium-sized companies, gripping stories about enterprises and entrepreneurs. We have a 360°view on the corporate world. Markt und Mittelstand covers strategy, financing, manufacturing and sales, i.e. the entire value chain. It is designed not only for managing directors but also for financial executives or heads of sales. At the core of our magazine are growth companies, i.e. companies that develop quickly and therefore have an extraordinary demand for information and investments. Markt und Mittelstand focuses on companies with an annual sales volume of 3 to 250 million Euro or 25 to 250 employees. Rubrics: Strategy and Human Resources: Readers find all the information on how to develop a company. It is about the development of business models, the development of market access strategies, M&A, line extensions, the development of the value added chain and human resources topics. Financing: The financing rubric supports companies in financing their growth plans and offers important advice on accounting, invoicing or tax issues. Other typical topics in this rubric are: alternative financing, current developments in the credit sector or topical tax decisions. Technology and Production: No matter whether you work in a manufacturing - business or the service industry – production is the heart of your company. Therefore readers find important advice on production technology, process management, purchasing of semi-finished goods and manufacturing. In addition, we cover IT and telecommunication. Customers and Markets: No sales, no business. This rubric covers new distribution channels, organisation management of sales teams, sales financing, logistics and marketing.
Language(s): German
Readership: Aimed at managers.
ADVERTISING RATES:
Full Page Mono .... EUR 12260
Full Page Colour .... EUR 12260
Mechanical Data: Type Area: 236 x 169 mm, No. of Columns (Display): 3, Col Widths (Display): 53 mm
Copy instructions: *Copy Date:* 17 days prior to publication
Supplement(s): €uro spezial
BUSINESS: COMMERCE, INDUSTRY & MANAGEMENT

MARKT&TECHNIK 734922G18A-130
Editorial: Gruber Str. 46a, 85586 POING
Tel: 8121 951312 **Fax:** 8121 951399
Email: redaktion@markt-technik.de **Web site:** http://www.elektroniknet.de
Freq: Weekly; **Annual Sub.:** EUR 229,00; **Circ:** 31,528
Editor: Heinz Arnold; **Advertising Manager:** Christian Stadler
Profile: Markt&Technik, the independent weekly newspaper for electronics, includes upto-date information on the latest technology and its impact, business issues and trends, product development strategies, buying strategies, new product information and management techniques in the electronics industry. The editorial content meets the specific information requirements of decision makers in development, product planning, purchase, technical and administrative management. Clearly headed, extensive market surveys, focussed reports and product reports give a quick and reliable overview of all the important fields in electronics. Facebook: http://www.facebook.com/pages/elektroniknetde/121306857884722.
Language(s): German
ADVERTISING RATES:
Full Page Mono .... EUR 6140
Full Page Colour .... EUR 8580
Mechanical Data: Type Area: 260 x 195 mm, No. of Columns (Display): 4, Col Widths (Display): 45 mm
Copy instructions: *Copy Date:* 14 days prior to publication
BUSINESS: ELECTRONICS

MARKT & WIRTSCHAFT WESTFALEN 1837030G14A-10158
Editorial: Meisenstr. 96, 33607 BIELEFELD
Tel: 521 2997390 **Fax:** 5257 932175
Email: peters@mawi-westfalen.de **Web site:** http://www.mawi-westfalen.de
Freq: 8 issues yearly; **Annual Sub.:** EUR 18,00; **Circ:** 24,000
Editor: Christiane Peters; **Advertising Manager:** Stephanie Blume
Profile: Business magazine for entrepreneurs in Westfalen. In addition to reporting on regional business and economic issues, we place our emphasis on a comprehensive range of services that the readers can have an added value. We carry our media not only information and opinions, but we also understand as a service to the economy in the region of Westphalia. In addition to changing titles and special topics can be found in each issue researched reports and news in the categories: company & markets, law & finance, cover story, e-business, education & training. Twitter: http://twitter.com/#!/mawiwestfalen/.
Language(s): German
ADVERTISING RATES:
Full Page Mono .... EUR 1817
Full Page Colour .... EUR 2317
Mechanical Data: Type Area: 241 x 185 mm, No. of Columns (Display): 3, Col Widths (Display): 58 mm
Copy instructions: *Copy Date:* 21 days prior to publication

MARKT WOCHENMITTE - AUSG. LOHR/ MARKTHEIDENFELD 734402G72-6840
Editorial: Berner Str. 2, 97084 WÜRZBURG
Tel: 931 6001355 **Fax:** 931 6001478

Email: red.sonderpublikation@mainpost.de **Web site:** http://www.markt.mainpost.de
Freq: Weekly; **Cover Price:** Free; **Circ:** 36,200
Editor: Werner Barthel; **Advertising Manager:** Julius Schmitt
Profile: Advertising journal (house-to-house) concentrating on local stories.
Language(s): German
Mechanical Data: Type Area: 466 x 310 mm, No. of Columns (Display): 7, Col Widths (Display): 43 mm
Copy instructions: *Copy Date:* 3 days prior to publication
Supplement(s): Framersbach/Partenstein und Umgebung kompakt; Lohr kompakt; main zuhause; Marktheidenfeld kompakt; markt visionen
LOCAL NEWSPAPERS

MÄRKTE IM SAARLAND MIT WOCHENKALENDER
734623G14A-4540
Editorial: Virchowstr. 7, 66119 SAARBRÜCKEN
Tel: 681 5015925 **Fax:** 681 5015915
Email: statistik@lzd.saarland.de **Web site:** http://www.statistik.saarland.de
Freq: Annual; **Cover Price:** EUR 10,00; **Circ:** 400
Profile: Calendar lists unique and regularly scheduled events, from the flea market to the consumer show. Events by type, beginning and duration both in alphabetical order of the market place and in chronological order. Information on the Population of market places, a calendar and an administrative map of the Saarland supplement the information provided.
Language(s): German

MÄRKTE & TRENDS 1643560G1F-1551
Editorial: Theodor-Heuss-Allee 72, 60486 FRANKFURT
Email: maerkte.trends@db.com **Web site:** http://www.deutsche-bank.de/start
Freq: Quarterly; **Cover Price:** EUR 3,50; **Circ:** 500,000
Editor: Hans-Christian Schnack
Profile: Company publication from the Deutsche Bank.
Language(s): German
ADVERTISING RATES:
Full Page Mono .... EUR 15000
Full Page Colour .... EUR 15000
Mechanical Data: Type Area: 240 x 170 mm

MARKTFORSCHUNG ...
724014G2A-5421
Editorial: Friedrichstr. 187, 10117 BERLIN
Tel: 700 49907420 **Fax:** 700 49907421
Email: handbuch@bvm.org **Web site:** http://www.bvm.org
Freq: Annual; **Cover Price:** EUR 80,25
Free to qualifying individuals ; **Circ:** 2,000
Profile: Publication of the BVM Professional Association of German Market and Social Researchers with around 500 entries, the most comprehensive compendium of market research in German speaking countries.
Language(s): German
ADVERTISING RATES:
Full Page Mono .... EUR 1300
Full Page Colour .... EUR 1750

MARKTHEIDENFELDER ANZEIGENBLATT 734862G72-7356
Editorial: Baumhofstr. 37, 97828 MARKTHEIDENFELD **Tel:** 9391 98450
Fax: 9391 9845155
Email: broestler@anzeigenblatt-online.de **Web site:** http://www.anzeigenblatt-online.de
Freq: Weekly; **Cover Price:** Free; **Circ:** 18,475
Advertising Manager: Manfred Körber
Profile: Advertising journal (house-to-house) concentrating on local stories.
Language(s): German
ADVERTISING RATES:
Full Page Mono .... EUR 1402
Full Page Colour .... EUR 1892
Mechanical Data: Type Area: 310 x 201 mm, No. of Columns (Display): 4, Col Widths (Display): 45 mm
Copy instructions: *Copy Date:* 1 day prior to publication
LOCAL NEWSPAPERS

MARKTKORB 734890G72-7360
Editorial: Frankfurter Str. 8, 36043 FULDA
Tel: 661 280253 **Fax:** 661 280283
Email: redaktion@marktkorb.de **Web site:** http://www.marktkorb.de
Freq: Weekly; **Cover Price:** Free; **Circ:** 116,147
Editor: Wolfgang Weber; **Advertising Manager:** Kai Hengmith
Profile: Advertising journal (house-to-house) concentrating on local stories.
Language(s): German
ADVERTISING RATES:
Full Page Mono .... EUR 4154
Full Page Colour .... EUR 5625
Mechanical Data: Type Area: 432 x 280 mm, No. of Columns (Display): 6, Col Widths (Display): 45 mm
Copy instructions: *Copy Date:* 1 day prior to publication
LOCAL NEWSPAPERS

MARKTREDWITZER TAGBLATT FRANKENPOST 734901G67B-9360
Editorial: Poststr. 9, 95028 HOF **Tel:** 9281 8160
Fax: 9281 816283
Email: redaktion@frankenpost.de **Web site:** http://www.frankenpost.de
Freq: 312 issues yearly; **Circ:** 5,419
Advertising Manager: Stefan Sailer
Profile: Regional daily newspaper with news on politics, economy, culture, sports, travel, technology, etc. Marktredwitzer Tagblatt Frankenpost is a local edition of the newspaper Frankenpost. Facebook: http://www.facebook.com/pages/Frankenpost/330862476314 Twitter: http://twitter.com/frankenpost This Outlet offers RSS (Really Simple Syndication).
Language(s): German
ADVERTISING RATES:
SCC .... EUR 37,80
Mechanical Data: Type Area: 485 x 325 mm, No. of Columns (Display): 7, Col Widths (Display): 44 mm
Copy instructions: *Copy Date:* 1 day prior to publication
Supplement(s): rtv
REGIONAL DAILY & SUNDAY NEWSPAPERS: Regional Daily Newspapers

MARKTSPIEGEL 734915G72-7392
Editorial: Marktstr. 16, 31303 BURGDORF
Tel: 5136 89940 **Fax:** 5136 899430
Email: redaktion.burgdorf@marktspiegel-verlag.de
Web site: http://www.marktspiegel-verlag.de
Freq: Weekly; **Cover Price:** Free; **Circ:** 24,300
Editor: Jens Kamm; **Advertising Manager:** Klaus Hoffmann
Profile: Advertising journal (house-to-house) concentrating on local stories.
Language(s): German
ADVERTISING RATES:
Full Page Mono .... EUR 2890
Full Page Colour .... EUR 3329
Mechanical Data: Type Area: 430 x 277 mm, No. of Columns (Display): 6, Col Widths (Display): 45 mm
Copy instructions: *Copy Date:* 2 days prior to publication
LOCAL NEWSPAPERS

DER MARKTSPIEGEL
734910G72-17467
Editorial: Burgschmietstr. 2, 90419 NÜRNBERG
Tel: 911 3990846 **Fax:** 911 3990812
Email: media@marktspiegel.de **Web site:** http://www.marktspiegel.de
Freq: Weekly; **Cover Price:** Free; **Circ:** 43,000
Editor: John R. Braun; **Advertising Manager:** Claudia Gläß
Profile: Advertising journal (house-to-house) concentrating on local stories.
Language(s): German
ADVERTISING RATES:
Full Page Mono .... EUR 2376
Full Page Colour .... EUR 3564
Mechanical Data: Type Area: 440 x 282 mm, No. of Columns (Display): 6, Col Widths (Display): 45 mm
Copy instructions: *Copy Date:* 2 days prior to publication
LOCAL NEWSPAPERS

DER MARKTSPIEGEL
734911G72-18124
Editorial: Burgschmietstr. 2, 90419 NÜRNBERG
Tel: 911 3990846 **Fax:** 911 3990812
Email: media@marktspiegel.de **Web site:** http://www.marktspiegel.de
Freq: Weekly; **Cover Price:** Free; **Circ:** 51,000
Editor: John R. Braun; **Advertising Manager:** Claudia Gläß
Profile: Advertising journal (house-to-house) concentrating on local stories.
Language(s): German
ADVERTISING RATES:
Full Page Mono .... EUR 3564
Full Page Colour .... EUR 5346
Mechanical Data: Type Area: 440 x 282 mm, No. of Columns (Display): 6, Col Widths (Display): 45 mm
Copy instructions: *Copy Date:* 2 days prior to publication
LOCAL NEWSPAPERS

MARL AKTUELL SONNTAGSBLATT 734926G72-7400
Editorial: Sickingmühler Str. 99, 45772 MARL
Tel: 2365 65055 **Fax:** 2365 65400
Email: redaktion@vest-aktuell.de **Web site:** http://www.vest-aktuell.de
Freq: Weekly; **Cover Price:** Free; **Circ:** 42,300
Editor: Dietmar U. Grone; **Advertising Manager:** Dietmar Büttel
Profile: Advertising journal (house-to-house) concentrating on local stories.
Language(s): German
ADVERTISING RATES:
Full Page Mono .... EUR 3297
Full Page Colour .... EUR 3417
Mechanical Data: Type Area: 435 x 287 mm, No. of Columns (Display): 7, Col Widths (Display): 39 mm
Copy instructions: *Copy Date:* 2 days prior to publication
LOCAL NEWSPAPERS

MARLER ZEITUNG 734927G67B-9380
Editorial: Kampstr. 84b, 45772 MARL **Tel:** 2365 1070
Fax: 2365 1071490
Email: info@medienhaus-bauer.de **Web site:** http://www.medienhaus-bauer.de
Freq: 312 issues yearly; **Circ:** 14,044
Advertising Manager: Carsten Dingerkuss
Profile: Regional daily newspaper with news on politics, economy, culture, sports, travel, technology, etc. The newspaper offers a mix of local, regional and international News from all areas. Fun and interactive content such as forums, polls or betting games are also part of the program. Local out of the city and the neighborhood is the focus of attention. Facebook: http://www.facebook.com/medienhbauer This Outlet offers RSS (Really Simple Syndication).
Language(s): German
ADVERTISING RATES:
SCC .... EUR 33,30
Mechanical Data: Type Area: 487 x 325 mm, No. of Columns (Display): 7, Col Widths (Display): 43 mm
Copy instructions: *Copy Date:* 1 day prior to publication
Supplement(s): prisma
REGIONAL DAILY & SUNDAY NEWSPAPERS: Regional Daily Newspapers

MARNER ZEITUNG 734929G67B-9400
Editorial: Wulf-Isebrand-Platz 1, 25746 HEIDE
Tel: 481 6886200 **Fax:** 481 688690200
Email: redaktion@boyens-medien.de **Web site:** http://www.boyens-medien.de
Freq: 312 issues yearly; **Circ:** 9,151
Advertising Manager: Klaus Böhlke
Profile: Daily newspaper with reports on politics, economy, stock market, entertainment, events, culture and sport, are available from the Dithmarscher Landeszeitung with a large regional news and sports pages. Twitter: http://twitter.com/shz_de This Outlet offers RSS (Really Simple Syndication).
Language(s): German
ADVERTISING RATES:
SCC .... EUR 24,10
Mechanical Data: Type Area: 430 x 285 mm, No. of Columns (Display): 6, Col Widths (Display): 45 mm
Copy instructions: *Copy Date:* 1 day prior to publication
REGIONAL DAILY & SUNDAY NEWSPAPERS: Regional Daily Newspapers

MASCHINE + WERKZEUG
734944G19E-1080
Editorial: Talhofstr. 24b, 82205 GILCHING
Tel: 8105 385359 **Fax:** 8105 385311
Email: m.flohr@verlag-henrich.de **Web site:** http://www.maschinewerkzeug.de
Freq: 10 issues yearly; **Annual Sub.:** EUR 88,00; **Circ:** 22,683
Editor: Manfred Flohr; **Advertising Manager:** Christian M. Rosner
Profile: maschine+werkzeug especially addresses the executive technical management and production managers in the metal machining and metal processing industry. Manufacturing in Germany makes efficient production with the highest quality absolutely necessary. This is why the focus on the editorial reporting is on practise-oriented problem solving, including in the organisational and business environment. maschine+werkzeug also presents the latest subjects, special information focuses and in-depth themes in focuses, Extras or supplements/special editions and that with a target group-orientation. The information is supplemented cross-medial in the form of the online portal www.maschinewerkzeug.de and the weekly special newsletter. Our coverage, reports, market analyses and interviews provide the reader with a fundamental information basis and decision-making support when it comes to forthcoming investments.
Language(s): German
Readership: Aimed at people in the engineering industry.
ADVERTISING RATES:
Full Page Mono .... EUR 4610
Full Page Colour .... EUR 5990
Mechanical Data: Type Area: 282 x 200 mm, No. of Columns (Display): 4, Col Widths (Display): 47 mm
Copy instructions: *Copy Date:* 20 days prior to publication
Supplement(s): i Quadrat
BUSINESS: ENGINEERING & MACHINERY: Machinery, Machine Tools & Metalworking

MASCHINENBAU UND METALLBEARBEITUNG DEUTSCHLAND 735381G27-1800
Editorial: Bert-Brecht-Str. 15, 78054 VILLINGEN-SCHWENNINGEN **Tel:** 7720 394118
Fax: 7720 394175
Email: findeisen@kuhnverlag.de **Web site:** http://www.kuhn-kataloge.de
Freq: Annual; **Cover Price:** EUR 17,00; **Circ:** 11,487
Editor: Steffi Findeisen; **Advertising Manager:** Konrad Baumann
Profile: Magazine about the metal industry and engine construction.
Language(s): German
ADVERTISING RATES:
Full Page Mono .... EUR 3354
Full Page Colour .... EUR 4104
Mechanical Data: Type Area: 254 x 180 mm
BUSINESS: METAL, IRON & STEEL

MASCHINENDIAGNOSE-NEWS
2035542G19E-1968
Editorial: Köpenicker Str. 325/40, 12555 BERLIN
Tel: 30 65762565 **Fax:** 30 65762564
Email: mailbox@maschinendiagnose.de **Web site:** http://www.maschinendiagnose.de
Freq: Annual; **Cover Price:** Free; **Circ:** 4,200
Profile: Magazine for customers about machine diagnosis methods and their application.
Language(s): German

MASCHINENRING AKTUELL
765173G21A-4211
Editorial: Eschborner Landstr. 122, 60489 FRANKFURT **Tel:** 69 24788454 **Fax:** 69 24788480
Email: r.rupalla@dlg.org **Web site:** http://www.dlg-verlag.de
Freq: Quarterly; Free to qualifying individuals
Annual Sub.: EUR 16,00; **Circ:** 114,691
Editor: Rainer Rupalla; **Advertising Manager:** Viola Hilz
Profile: Magazine with news from agriculture and agricultural technologies.
Language(s): German
ADVERTISING RATES:
Full Page Mono .... EUR 6921
Full Page Colour .... EUR 8742
Mechanical Data: Type Area: 344 x 240 mm
BUSINESS: AGRICULTURE & FARMING

MASTERRIND 740496G21D-5
Editorial: Osterkrug 20, 27283 VERDEN
Tel: 4231 6795 **Fax:** 4231 679780
Email: info@masterrind.de **Web site:** http://www.masterrind.de
Freq: Quarterly; Free to qualifying individuals
Annual Sub.: EUR 9,20; **Circ:** 20,675
Editor: Hermann Bischoff
Profile: Magazine for cattle breeding, artificial insemination and marketing.
Language(s): German
ADVERTISING RATES:
Full Page Mono .... EUR 1377
Full Page Colour .... EUR 1973
Mechanical Data: Type Area: 271 x 190 mm, No. of Columns (Display): 4, Col Widths (Display): 43 mm
Copy instructions: *Copy Date:* 14 days prior to publication
BUSINESS: AGRICULTURE & FARMING: Livestock

MATE 1606046G86B-633
Editorial: Sophienstr. 8, 10178 BERLIN
Tel: 30 44319835 **Fax:** 30 44319877
Email: info@mate-magazin.com **Web site:** http://www.mate-magazine.com
Freq: 3 issues yearly; **Annual Sub.:** EUR 15,00; **Circ:** 37,884
Editor: Felix Just
Profile: Magazine for gays.
Language(s): German
ADVERTISING RATES:
Full Page Mono .... EUR 5600
Full Page Colour .... EUR 5600
Mechanical Data: Type Area: 235 x 190 mm, No. of Columns (Display): 6, Col Widths (Display): 27 mm
Copy instructions: *Copy Date:* 20 days prior to publication
CONSUMER: ADULT & GAY MAGAZINES: Gay & Lesbian Magazines

MATECO NEWS 1840017G4E-7225
Editorial: Bottroper Str. 16, 70376 STUTTGART
Tel: 711 9555659 **Fax:** 711 955561059
Email: mail@mateco.de **Web site:** http://www.mateco.de
Freq: Half-yearly; **Circ:** 4,000
Profile: Employee and customer magazine from the Mateco AG for man-carrying platforms.
Language(s): German

MATERIAL+TECHNIK MÖBEL
736709G23C-260
Editorial: Andernacher Str. 5a, 90411 NÜRNBERG
Tel: 911 9557887 **Fax:** 911 9557878
Email: barth@material-technik.de **Web site:** http://www.material-technik.de
Freq: 7 issues yearly; **Annual Sub.:** EUR 39,00; **Circ:** 10,517
Editor: Richard Barth; **Advertising Manager:** Olga Maier
Profile: International magazine on furniture for executives, suppliers and interior designers.
Language(s): English; German
ADVERTISING RATES:
Full Page Mono .... EUR 4330
Full Page Colour .... EUR 5950
Mechanical Data: Type Area: 275 x 196 mm, No. of Columns (Display): 4, Col Widths (Display): 46 mm
Copy instructions: *Copy Date:* 28 days prior to publication
Official Journal of: Organ d. Hauptverb. d. Dt. Holz u. Kunststoffe verarbeitenden Industrie u. verwandter Industriezweige e.V.
BUSINESS: FURNISHINGS & FURNITURE: Furnishings & Furniture - Kitchens & Bathrooms

MATERIALFLUSS 734962G49R-12
Editorial: Justus-von-Liebig-Str. 1, 86899 LANDSBERG **Tel:** 8191 125290 **Fax:** 8191 125483

Email: leo.breu@mi-verlag.de **Web site:** http://www.materialfluss.de
Freq: 11 issues yearly; **Annual Sub.:** EUR 108,00; **Circ:** 19,741
Editor: Leo Breu; **Advertising Manager:** Helmut Schempp
Profile: Materialfluss, the trade magazine for the intralogistics sector, is targeted at logistics managers and decision-makers in in-house logistics. Materialfluss provides cross-industry reports on technologies, trends, applications and products and consolidates opinions on all aspects of intralogistics in the form of knowledgeable and, at times, exclusive journalism. The end result delivers practical solutions on a monthly basis, helping you take the decisions necessary to make your logistics faster, cheaper and more reliable.
Language(s): German
Readership: Read by managers and executives.
ADVERTISING RATES:
Full Page Mono .... EUR 4700
Full Page Colour .... EUR 5980
Mechanical Data: Type Area: 257 x 178 mm, No. of Columns (Display): 4, Col Widths (Display): 41 mm
Copy instructions: *Copy Date:* 28 days prior to publication
BUSINESS: TRANSPORT: Transport Related

MATERIALS AND CORROSION WERKSTOFFE UND KORROSION
734965G19C-150
Editorial: Unter den Eichen 87, 12205 BERLIN
Tel: 30 81041732 **Fax:** 30 81041737
Email: juergen.mietz@bam.de
Freq: Monthly; **Annual Sub.:** EUR 2751,00; **Circ:** 1,000
Editor: Jürgen Mietz; **Advertising Manager:** Marion Schulz
Profile: Journal concerning the effects of corrosive environments, corrosion testing and protection of industrial materials.
Language(s): English
Readership: Aimed at scientists, mechanical engineers, chemists, equipment manufacturers, metallurgists and environmental scientists.
ADVERTISING RATES:
Full Page Mono .... EUR 2300
Full Page Colour .... EUR 3230
Mechanical Data: Type Area: 260 x 180 mm
Official Journal of: Organ d. Ges. f. Korrosionsschutz e.V., d. Dt. Ges. f. Chem. Apparatewesen, Chem. Technik u. Biotechnologie e.V. u. d. Europ. Föderation Korrosion
BUSINESS: ENGINEERING & MACHINERY: Finishing

MATERIALWISSENSCHAFT UND WERKSTOFFTECHNIK
734967G19R-80
Editorial: Boschstr. 12, 69469 WEINHEIM
Tel: 6201 606249 **Fax:** 6201 606509
Email: matsci@wiley.com **Web site:** http://www.wiley-vch.de
Freq: Monthly; **Annual Sub.:** EUR 2717,00; **Circ:** 1,000
Editor: Jörn Ritterbusch; **Advertising Manager:** Marion Schulz
Profile: Magazine focusing on material science and technology.
Language(s): English; German
ADVERTISING RATES:
Full Page Mono .... EUR 2300
Full Page Colour .... EUR 3230
Mechanical Data: Type Area: 260 x 180 mm
Official Journal of: Organ d. Dt. Ges. f. Materialkunde, d. Dt. Ges. f. Chem. Apparatewesen, Chem. Technik u. Biotechnologie e.V. u. d. Stahlinstitut VDEh
BUSINESS: ENGINEERING & MACHINERY: Engineering Related

MATHEMATICAL METHODS OF OPERATIONS RESEARCH
734969G14A-4580
Editorial: Am Weichselgarten 9, 91058 ERLANGEN
Email: alexander.martin@math.uni-erlangen.de **Web site:** http://www.springerlink.com
Freq: 6 issues yearly; **Annual Sub.:** EUR 1037,00; **Circ:** 453
Editor: Alexander Martin
Profile: Mathematical methods of operations research.
Language(s): English
ADVERTISING RATES:
Full Page Mono .... EUR 740
Full Page Colour .... EUR 1780
Mechanical Data: Type Area: 200 x 130 mm

MATHEMATICAL METHODS OF OPERATIONS RESEARCH
734969G14A-10100
Editorial: Am Weichselgarten 9, 91058 ERLANGEN
Email: alexander.martin@math.uni-erlangen.de **Web site:** http://www.springerlink.com
Freq: 6 issues yearly; **Annual Sub.:** EUR 1037,00; **Circ:** 453
Editor: Alexander Martin
Profile: Mathematical methods of operations research.
Language(s): English
ADVERTISING RATES:
Full Page Mono .... EUR 740
Full Page Colour .... EUR 1780
Mechanical Data: Type Area: 200 x 130 mm

MATHILDE
734976G74A-2020
Editorial: Postfach 130269, 64242 DARMSTADT
Tel: 6151 537937
Email: redaktion@mathilde-frauenzeitung.de **Web site:** http://www.mathilde-frauenzeitung.de
Freq: 6 issues yearly; **Annual Sub.:** EUR 18,00; **Circ:** 1,000
Editor: Gabriele Merziger
Profile: Regional magazine for women in Darmstadt featuring book reviews and political subjects.
Language(s): German
ADVERTISING RATES:
Full Page Mono .... EUR 300
Mechanical Data: Type Area: 240 x 180 mm

MAUERWERK
734982G4E-5280
Editorial: 01062 DRESDEN **Tel:** 351 46335010
Fax: 351 46337713
Email: w.jaeger@jaeger-ingenieure.de
Freq: 6 issues yearly; **Annual Sub.:** EUR 153,00; **Circ:** 4,500
Editor: Wolfram Jäger; **Advertising Manager:** Sylvie Krüger
Profile: Magazine about stonework and masonry.
Language(s): German
Readership: Aimed at people working within the building industry.
ADVERTISING RATES:
Full Page Mono .... EUR 2320
Full Page Colour .... EUR 3760
Mechanical Data: Type Area: 260 x 181 mm, No. of Columns (Display): 4, Col Widths (Display): 42 mm
BUSINESS: ARCHITECTURE & BUILDING: Building

MAUERWERK-KALENDER
734983G4E-5300
Editorial: Rotherstr. 21, 10245 BERLIN
Tel: 30 47031200 **Fax:** 30 47031270
Email: info@ernst-und-sohn.de **Web site:** http://www.ernst-und-sohn.de
Freq: Annual; **Cover Price:** EUR 135,00; **Circ:** 4,000
Editor: Wolfram Jäger; **Advertising Manager:** Sylvie Krüger
Profile: Annual for brick work builders with information on developments, reviews, standardised performance, creativity and product innovations.
Language(s): German
ADVERTISING RATES:
Full Page Mono .... EUR 1470
Full Page Colour .... EUR 2800
Mechanical Data: Type Area: 206 x 140 mm

MAURITIUS
1832632G74N-937
Editorial: Hambacher Weg 12, 96450 COBURG
Tel: 9561 354270 **Fax:** 9561 354269
Web site: http://www.mohr-stadtillu.de
Freq: Quarterly; **Cover Price:** Free; **Circ:** 8,000
Editor: Manfred Mehls; **Advertising Manager:** Manfred Mehls
Profile: Magazine for the elderly from the region of Coburg.
Language(s): German

MAV KOMPETENZ IN DER SPANENDEN FERTIGUNG
734940G19E-1856
Editorial: Ernst-Mey-Str. 8, 70771 LEINFELDEN-ECHTERDINGEN **Tel:** 711 7594389
Fax: 711 7594398
Email: mav.redaktion@konradin.de **Web site:** http://www.mav-online.de
Freq: 10 issues yearly; **Annual Sub.:** EUR 62,50; **Circ:** 20,031
Editor: Holger Röhr; **Advertising Manager:** Peter Hamberger
Profile: In the meantime more than 50 years the mav Kompetenz in der spanenden Fertigung has become a global information and media partner for the manufacturing industry in Germany. It offers tightly integrates the knowledge from professionals for professionals around the metal cutting. Competently, they report on theoretical solutions, practical applications, economic success concepts and interesting product innovations. As a mediator between information providers and information seekers, mav Kompetenz in der spanenden Fertigung has developed expertise in metal-cutting manufacturing a variety of innovative services. These include the industry-specific Internet portal www.mav-online.de, the e-paper with a link to the ads, online market surveys and databases, online business guide and career guide, which mav Techno-Tour, the retro-mav Guide.
Language(s): German
ADVERTISING RATES:
Full Page Mono .... EUR 4800
Full Page Colour .... EUR 5890
Mechanical Data: Type Area: 270 x 188 mm, No. of Columns (Display): 4, Col Widths (Display): 44 mm
BUSINESS: ENGINEERING & MACHINERY: Machinery, Machine Tools & Metalworking

MAVIDA
1791885G74N-905
Editorial: Weltenburger Str. 4, 81677 MÜNCHEN
Tel: 89 41969448 **Fax:** 89 4705364
Email: ssperle@avr-verlag.de **Web site:** http://www.avr-werbeagentur.de
Freq: Quarterly; **Cover Price:** EUR 2,40; **Circ:** 75,000
Editor: Simone Sperle; **Advertising Manager:** Katja Herrmann
Profile: The Magazine for dedicated power women on the topics of health, wellness, nutrition and fitness.
Language(s): German
ADVERTISING RATES:
Full Page Mono .... EUR 4900
Full Page Colour .... EUR 4900
Mechanical Data: Type Area: 240 x 170 mm, No. of Columns (Display): 3, Col Widths (Display): 55 mm

MAX
1686692G73-590
Editorial: Steinhauser Str. 1, 81677 MÜNCHEN
Tel: 89 92502404
Email: max@tomorrow-focus.de **Web site:** http://www.max.de
Cover Price: Paid; **Circ:** 630,166 Unique Users
Editor: Thomas Mende
Profile: Ezine: Men's lifestyle magazine, includes CD Roms, books, fashion, politics, economics and stockmarket.
Language(s): German
CONSUMER: NATIONAL & INTERNATIONAL PERIODICALS

MAXI
734994G74A-2040
Editorial: Burchardstr. 11, 20095 HAMBURG
Tel: 40 30195454 **Fax:** 40 30195449
Email: mail@maxi.de **Web site:** http://www.maxi.de
Freq: Monthly; **Annual Sub.:** EUR 30,00; **Circ:** 205,923
Editor: Ann Thorer
Profile: Magazine containing information about fashion, beauty, food, drink and travel. Also contains interviews. Facebook: http://www.facebook.com/pages/Maxi/496766860223.
Language(s): German
Readership: Aimed at young women.
ADVERTISING RATES:
Full Page Mono .... EUR 19980
Full Page Colour .... EUR 19980
Mechanical Data: Type Area: 248 x 191 mm, No. of Columns (Display): 4, Col Widths (Display): 46 mm
CONSUMER: WOMEN'S INTEREST CONSUMER MAGAZINES: Women's Interest

MAXIMUM TUNER
1739557G77A-2765
Editorial: Paffrather Str. 80, 51465 BERGISCH GLADBACH **Tel:** 2202 41857 **Fax:** 2202 41877
Email: info@eurotuner.de **Web site:** http://www.tuning2go.de
Freq: 6 issues yearly; **Annual Sub.:** EUR 18,00; **Circ:** 24,100
Editor: Olivier Fourcade; **Advertising Manager:** Olivier Fourcade
Profile: Tuning magazine for Japanese cars with news, show dates and information provider.
Language(s): German
ADVERTISING RATES:
Full Page Mono .... EUR 4100
Full Page Colour .... EUR 4990
Mechanical Data: Type Area: 267 x 181 mm, No. of Columns (Display): 4, Col Widths (Display): 42 mm
Copy instructions: *Copy Date:* 28 days prior to publication
CONSUMER: MOTORING & CYCLING: Motoring

MAXITY DRESDNER ELBLAND
1830256G89A-12408
Editorial: Prager Str. 2b, 01069 DRESDEN
Tel: 351 8007030 **Fax:** 351 8007070
Email: redaktion@maxity.de **Web site:** http://www.maxity.de
Freq: Annual; **Cover Price:** Free; **Circ:** 30,000
Editor: Christine Herzog; **Advertising Manager:** Cathleen Moosche
Profile: District guide for tourists and business travellers to the Saxony Elbland.
Language(s): German
Mechanical Data: Type Area: 126 x 85 mm

MAYENER WOCHENSPIEGEL
735005G72-7420
Editorial: Rosengasse, 56727 MAYEN
Tel: 2651 981816 **Fax:** 2651 981818
Email: red-mayen@wvm-verlag.de **Web site:** http://www.wochenspiegellive.de
Freq: Weekly; **Cover Price:** Free; **Circ:** 40,972
Editor: Mario Zender; **Advertising Manager:** Frank Günther
Profile: Advertising journal (house-to-house) concentrating on local stories.
Language(s): German
ADVERTISING RATES:
Full Page Mono .... EUR 3612
Full Page Colour .... EUR 5057
Mechanical Data: Type Area: 430 x 290 mm, No. of Columns (Display): 7, Col Widths (Display): 38 mm
Copy instructions: *Copy Date:* 2 days prior to publication
LOCAL NEWSPAPERS

MAZ MITTELHESSISCHE ANZEIGEN ZEITUNG - AUSG. ALSFELD
736256G72-8976
Editorial: Landgraf-Philipp-Str. 25, 34613 SCHWALMSTADT **Tel:** 6691 919168
Fax: 6691 21047
Email: redaktion-hr@maz-verlag.de **Web site:** http://www.maz-verlag.de
Freq: Weekly; **Cover Price:** Free; **Circ:** 17,620
Editor: Klaus Kächler; **Advertising Manager:** Arthur Reith
Profile: Advertising journal (house-to-house) concentrating on local stories.
Language(s): German
ADVERTISING RATES:
Full Page Mono .... EUR 1887
Full Page Colour .... EUR 2601
Mechanical Data: Type Area: 425 x 280 mm, No. of Columns (Display): 6, Col Widths (Display): 45 mm
Copy instructions: *Copy Date:* 1 day prior to publication
LOCAL NEWSPAPERS

MAZ MITTELHESSISCHE ANZEIGEN ZEITUNG - AUSG. HINTERLAND
736257G72-8968
Editorial: Katharinengasse 12, 35390 GIESSEN
Tel: 641 794657 **Fax:** 641 794656
Email: redaktion-mr@maz-verlag.de **Web site:** http://www.maz-verlag.de
Freq: Weekly; **Cover Price:** Free; **Circ:** 30,052
Editor: Klaus Kächler; **Advertising Manager:** Rainer Alt
Profile: Advertising journal (house-to-house) concentrating on local stories.
Language(s): German
ADVERTISING RATES:
Full Page Mono .... EUR 2270
Full Page Colour .... EUR 3162
Mechanical Data: Type Area: 425 x 280 mm, No. of Columns (Display): 6, Col Widths (Display): 45 mm
Copy instructions: *Copy Date:* 1 day prior to publication
LOCAL NEWSPAPERS

MAZ MOTOR AUTO ZEITUNG - AUSG. CHEMNITZ
1695623G77A-2737
Editorial: Ostra-Allee 20, 01067 DRESDEN
Tel: 351 48642408 **Fax:** 351 48642679
Email: korczynsky.joerg@dd-v.de **Web site:** http://www.maz-online.de
Freq: 16 issues yearly; **Cover Price:** Free; **Circ:** 20,000
Editor: Jörg Korczynsky; **Advertising Manager:** Jörg Korczynsky
Profile: Offer magazine used cars, motorcycles, construction equipment, commercial vehicles. Free Distribution of dispensaries with a focus on gas stations, beverage stores, car dealers and car accessories and driving schools. Part of the reading circle, reading sessions. Display in the branch network of the Saxon newspaper.
Language(s): German
ADVERTISING RATES:
Full Page Colour .... EUR 901
Mechanical Data: Type Area: 320 x 226 mm, No. of Columns (Display): 4, Col Widths (Display): 52 mm
Copy instructions: *Copy Date:* 8 days prior to publication

MAZ MOTOR AUTO ZEITUNG - AUSG. LEIPZIG/HALLE
1824004G77A-2819
Editorial: Ostra-Allee 20, 01067 DRESDEN
Email: korczynsky.joerg@dd-v.de **Web site:** http://www.maz-online.de
Freq: 16 issues yearly; **Cover Price:** Free; **Circ:** 30,000
Profile: Offer magazine used cars, motorcycles, construction equipment, commercial vehicles. Free Distribution of dispensaries with a focus on gas stations, beverage stores, car dealers and car accessories and driving schools. Part of the reading circle, reading sessions. Display in the branch network of the Saxon newspaper.
Language(s): German
ADVERTISING RATES:
Full Page Colour .... EUR 901
Mechanical Data: Type Area: 320 x 226 mm, No. of Columns (Display): 4, Col Widths (Display): 52 mm
Copy instructions: *Copy Date:* 8 days prior to publication

MB MARKETING BERATER
723723G47A-80
Editorial: An Lyskirchen 14, 50676 KÖLN
Tel: 221 92150940 **Fax:** 221 92150910
Email: jacobs@bte.de **Web site:** http://www.bte.de
Freq: Monthly; Free to qualifying individuals
Annual Sub.: EUR 35,10; **Circ:** 10,481
Editor: Siegfried Jacobs; **Advertising Manager:** Manuela Carlier
Profile: The mb marketing berater is a magazine for the owner and manager in the textile retail trade. Editorial focus is the commercial marketing of clothing and textiles.
Language(s): German
ADVERTISING RATES:
Full Page Mono .... EUR 2330
Full Page Colour .... EUR 3728
Mechanical Data: Type Area: 260 x 190 mm, No. of Columns (Display): 3, Col Widths (Display): 60 mm

Copy instructions: *Copy Date:* 15 days prior to publication
BUSINESS: CLOTHING & TEXTILES

MBZ METALLBAUZEITUNG
1827048G27-3063
Editorial: Am Gentenberg 117, 40489 DÜSSELDORF **Tel:** 211 4371350 **Fax:** 211 4371351
Email: ruhnke@adamas-media.de **Web site:** http://www.adamas-media.de
Freq: Monthly; **Annual Sub.:** EUR 30,00; **Circ:** 16,981
Editor: Karl Ruhnke
Profile: Journal containing information about the metalworking industry.
Language(s): German
ADVERTISING RATES:
Full Page Mono .... EUR 3289
Full Page Colour .... EUR 4389
Mechanical Data: Type Area: 267 x 185 mm, No. of Columns (Display): 4, Col Widths (Display): 43 mm
BUSINESS: METAL, IRON & STEEL

MD INTERNATIONAL DESIGNSCOUT FOR FURNITURE, INTERIOR AND DESIGN
736363G23C-380
Editorial: Ernst-Mey-Str. 8, 70771 LEINFELDEN-ECHTERDINGEN **Tel:** 711 7594262
Fax: 711 7594397
Email: md.redaktion@konradin.de **Web site:** http://www.md-magazine.com
Freq: Monthly; **Annual Sub.:** EUR 147,00; **Circ:** 10,703
Editor: Ulrich Büttner; **Advertising Manager:** Ines Scholz
Profile: md is the international Designscout for professional planers of interior – selective, inspiring, independent. md selects editorially the international range of furniture for contract and dwelling as well as products around interior design by formal and qualitative criteria. By concentrating on essentials, md provides architects, interior designers, interior outfitters, designers and premium sales outlets with invaluable product data and facts when confronted with a flood of crossmedia information, and a guide to correct product decision-taking for professionally handled projects. Therefore md is an important source of inspiration for the target group, shows novelties and trends and it is the ideal platform of communication for product and image advertising in this sector.
Language(s): English; French; German
ADVERTISING RATES:
Full Page Mono .... EUR 4250
Full Page Colour .... EUR 6110
Mechanical Data: Type Area: 283 x 205 mm, No. of Columns (Display): 4, Col Widths (Display): 49 mm
BUSINESS: FURNISHINGS & FURNITURE: Furnishings & Furniture - Kitchens & Bathrooms

MD MARKETING DIGEST
1825639G2A-5749
Editorial: Tiefenbronner Str. 65, 75175 PFORZHEIM
Tel: 7231 286277 **Fax:** 7231 286666
Email: marketingdigest@werbeliebe.de **Web site:** http://www.werbeliebe.de
Freq: Half-yearly; **Cover Price:** Free; **Circ:** 2,500
Profile: Students' magazine.
Language(s): German

MDF MAGAZIN
735043G46-12
Editorial: Fasanenweg 18, 70771 LEINFELDEN-ECHTERDINGEN **Tel:** 711 7591306
Fax: 711 7591440
Email: info@drw-verlag.de **Web site:** http://www.drw-verlag.de
Freq: Annual; **Cover Price:** EUR 5,00; **Circ:** 13,000
Editor: Karsten Koch; **Advertising Manager:** Oliver Heinz
Profile: Magazine focusing on the timber trade and machinery and tools used for timber processing.
Language(s): English; German
Readership: Read by people working in the timber trade.
ADVERTISING RATES:
Full Page Mono .... EUR 5000
Full Page Colour .... EUR 6680
Mechanical Data: Type Area: 270 x 175 mm, No. of Columns (Display): 4, Col Widths (Display): 40 mm
Copy instructions: *Copy Date:* 30 days prior to publication
Supplement to: HK Holz- und Kunststoffverarbeitung, Holz-Zentralblatt
BUSINESS: TIMBER, WOOD & FORESTRY

[ME] MECHATRONIK & ENGINEERING
719717G19D-10
Editorial: Schragenhoferstr. 35/A, 80992 MÜNCHEN
Tel: 89 15704612 **Fax:** 89 15704622
Email: schaefer@agt-verlag.de **Web site:** http://www.me-magazin.com
Freq: 6 issues yearly; **Annual Sub.:** EUR 66,00; **Circ:** 15,903
Editor: Peter Schäfer; **Advertising Manager:** Simone Hildenbrand
Profile: me is the industry magazine for developers, designers and automation engineers overcome the traditional approaches and think laterally. me is the communication platform (print and online) for those who develop the mechatronic approach consistently. The magazine reported on technological and economic consequences of mechatronics in mechanical engineering and electrical engineering. me describes the chances of mechatronic systems in promising sectors such as medical technology or the use of energy from sun and wind. me covers saving potential in the development of machinery and equipment, shows the way on energy efficiency and picks up ideas from research and science to the mechatronic approach to further develop Here are both components of mechatronic systems, mechatronic design and engineering in the foreground. me is critical and competent journalism and is aimed at managers in the design and automation responsibility. It serves as a decision support for mechanical and plant engineering, design, automation of industrial plants, plant designers, OEM's, electrical engineers, as well as for buyers echatronic components.
Language(s): German
ADVERTISING RATES:
Full Page Mono .... EUR 3690
Full Page Colour .... EUR 4920
Mechanical Data: Type Area: 270 x 185 mm, No. of Columns (Display): 4, Col Widths (Display): 43 mm
Copy instructions: *Copy Date:* 14 days prior to publication
BUSINESS: ENGINEERING & MACHINERY: Hydraulic Power

MECHATRONIK
728164G18A-233
Editorial: Oskar-Maria-Graf-Ring 23, 81737 MÜNCHEN **Tel:** 89 67369745 **Fax:** 89 67369761
Email: mechatronik@igt-verlag.de **Web site:** http://www.mechatronik.info
Freq: 8 issues yearly; **Annual Sub.:** EUR 163,60; **Circ:** 15,202
Editor: Wolfgang Patelay; **Advertising Manager:** Andrea Horn
Profile: Journal covering measuring techniques and precision engineering in the electronics and optics industries, includes electronics, telecommunications, domestic appliances and systems for the automotive industry.
Language(s): German
Readership: Aimed at designers.
ADVERTISING RATES:
Full Page Mono .... EUR 3760
Full Page Colour .... EUR 5360
Mechanical Data: Type Area: 256 x 175 mm, No. of Columns (Display): 4, Col Widths (Display): 41 mm
Official Journal of: Organ d. VDE/VDI-Ges. Mikroelektronik, Mikro- u. Feinwerktechnik
BUSINESS: ELECTRONICS

MECKLENBURGER BLITZ AM SONNTAG
735058G72-7480
Editorial: Eisenbahnstr. 3, 18273 GÜSTROW
Tel: 3843 7270341 **Fax:** 3843 7270370
Email: sabine.moll@blitzverlag.de **Web site:** http://www.blitzverlag.de
Freq: Weekly; **Cover Price:** Free; **Circ:** 45,016
Editor: Sabine Moll; **Advertising Manager:** André Wollbrecht
Profile: Advertising journal (house-to-house) concentrating on local stories.
Language(s): German
ADVERTISING RATES:
Full Page Mono .... EUR 3352
Full Page Colour .... EUR 372
Mechanical Data: Type Area: 420 x 280 mm, No. of Columns (Display): 6, Col Widths (Display): 45 mm
Copy instructions: *Copy Date:* 2 days prior to publication
LOCAL NEWSPAPERS

MEDIA41
2067505G2A-5925
Editorial: Ridlerstr. 35a, 80339 MÜNCHEN
Tel: 89 72959915 **Fax:** 89 72959918
Email: redaktion@media41.de **Web site:** http://www.media41.de
Freq: 6 issues yearly; **Annual Sub.:** EUR 90,00; **Circ:** 3,600
Editor: Friedrich M. Kirn
Profile: The journal is practical for media planners, provides know-how at first hand and provides media planners reliable and competent guidance. High-profile releases are background stories of renowned trade journalists, exclusive author contributions, current studies, case studies of successful media planning and realistic forecasts of future trends in media planning.
Language(s): German
ADVERTISING RATES:
Full Page Mono .... EUR 4850
Full Page Colour .... EUR 4850
Mechanical Data: Type Area: 238 x 187 mm, No. of Columns (Display): 3, Col Widths (Display): 67 mm

MEDIA DATEN FACHZEITSCHRIFTEN
1832661G2A-5769
Editorial: Abraham-Lincoln-Str. 46, 65189 WIESBADEN **Tel:** 611 7878317 **Fax:** 611 787878317
Email: cornelia.gerstenberg@mediadaten.com **Web site:** http://www.media-daten.com
Freq: Quarterly; **Annual Sub.:** EUR 654,00; **Circ:** 864
Editor: Cornelia Gerstenberg; **Advertising Manager:** Thomas Heusler
Profile: Magazine for media planners and buying agents.
Language(s): German
ADVERTISING RATES:
Full Page Mono .... EUR 2900
Full Page Colour .... EUR 4130
Mechanical Data: Type Area: 275 x 185 mm, No. of Columns (Display): 3, Col Widths (Display): 58 mm
Copy instructions: *Copy Date:* 54 days prior to publication

MEDIA DATEN RADIO/TV
1832681G2A-5770
Editorial: Abraham-Lincoln-Str. 46, 65189 WIESBADEN **Tel:** 611 7878317 **Fax:** 611 787878317
Email: cornelia.gerstenberg@mediadaten.com **Web site:** http://www.mediadaten.com
Freq: Quarterly; **Annual Sub.:** EUR 158,00; **Circ:** 801
Editor: Cornelia Gerstenberg; **Advertising Manager:** Thomas Heusler
Profile: Overview of national and regional public and private radio and TV stations.
Language(s): German
ADVERTISING RATES:
Full Page Mono .... EUR 2900
Full Page Colour .... EUR 4130
Mechanical Data: Type Area: 275 x 185 mm, No. of Columns (Display): 3, Col Widths (Display): 58 mm
Copy instructions: *Copy Date:* 54 days prior to publication

MEDIA DATEN ZEITSCHRIFTEN
1832682G2A-5771
Editorial: Abraham-Lincoln-Str. 46, 65189 WIESBADEN **Tel:** 611 7878317 **Fax:** 611 787878317
Email: cornelia.gerstenberg@mediadaten.com **Web site:** http://www.mediadaten.com
Freq: Quarterly; **Annual Sub.:** EUR 654,00; **Circ:** 813
Editor: Cornelia Gerstenberg; **Advertising Manager:** Thomas Heusler
Profile: Tariffs of periodicals.
Language(s): German
ADVERTISING RATES:
Full Page Mono .... EUR 2900
Full Page Colour .... EUR 4130
Mechanical Data: Type Area: 275 x 185 mm, No. of Columns (Display): 3, Col Widths (Display): 58 mm
Copy instructions: *Copy Date:* 54 days prior to publication

MEDIA DATEN ZEITUNGEN ANZEIGENBLÄTTER
1832683G2A-5772
Editorial: Abraham-Lincoln-Str. 46, 65189 WIESBADEN **Tel:** 611 7878317 **Fax:** 611 787878317
Email: cornelia.gerstenberg@mediadaten.com **Web site:** http://www.mediadaten.com
Freq: Quarterly; **Annual Sub.:** EUR 654,00; **Circ:** 938
Editor: Cornelia Gerstenberg; **Advertising Manager:** Thomas Heusler
Profile: Tariffs of regional and national subscription magazines.
Language(s): German
ADVERTISING RATES:
Full Page Mono .... EUR 2900
Full Page Colour .... EUR 4130
Mechanical Data: Type Area: 275 x 185 mm, No. of Columns (Display): 3, Col Widths (Display): 58 mm
Copy instructions: *Copy Date:* 54 days prior to publication

MEDIA GUIDE
735082G2A-2720
Editorial: Weyerstraßerweg 159, 50969 KÖLN
Tel: 221 376030 **Fax:** 221 374020
Email: redaktion@messetreff.com **Web site:** http://www.mediaguidebayern.de
Freq: Annual; **Cover Price:** EUR 12,00; **Circ:** 12,500
Editor: Manfred Kanzler
Profile: Magazine about electronic media.
Language(s): English; German
ADVERTISING RATES:
Full Page Mono .... EUR 3680
Full Page Colour .... EUR 3680
Mechanical Data: Type Area: 252 x 180 mm, No. of Columns (Display): 3, Col Widths (Display): 50 mm
Copy instructions: *Copy Date:* 30 days prior to publication

MEDIA GUIDE
735084G2A-2760
Editorial: Weyerstraßerweg 159, 50969 KÖLN
Tel: 221 376030 **Fax:** 221 374020
Email: media-guide@messetreff.com **Web site:** http://www.mediaguidenrw.de
Freq: Annual; **Cover Price:** EUR 12,00; **Circ:** 12,500
Editor: Manfred Kanzler
Profile: Magazine for electronic media in Nordrhein-Westfalen.
Language(s): English; German
ADVERTISING RATES:
Full Page Mono .... EUR 3680
Full Page Colour .... EUR 3680
Mechanical Data: Type Area: 252 x 180 mm, No. of Columns (Display): 3, Col Widths (Display): 50 mm
Copy instructions: *Copy Date:* 30 days prior to publication

MEDIA PERSPEKTIVEN
735091G2A-2820
Editorial: Bertramstr. 8/D-Bau, 60320 FRANKFURT
Tel: 69 15424310 **Fax:** 69 15424305
Email: redaktion@media-perspektiven.de **Web site:** http://www.media-perspektiven.de
Freq: Monthly; **Cover Price:** Free; **Circ:** 7,000
Editor: Christa-Maria Ridder
Profile: Magazine on current media issues (media markets - policy, research, role of mass media as advertising media).
Language(s): German

MEDIA PERSPEKTIVEN BASISDATEN
735092G2A-2840
Editorial: Bertramstr. 8/D-Bau, 60320 FRANKFURT
Tel: 69 15424310 **Fax:** 69 15424305
Email: redaktion@media-perspektiven.de **Web site:** http://www.media-perspektiven.de
Freq: Annual; **Cover Price:** EUR 15,00; **Circ:** 7,000
Editor: Christa-Maria Ridder
Profile: Publication with data describing the media situation in Germany.
Language(s): German

MEDIA PERSPEKTIVEN DOKUMENTATION
735093G2A-2860
Editorial: Bertramstr. 8/D-Bau, 60320 FRANKFURT
Tel: 69 15424310 **Fax:** 69 15424305
Email: redaktion@media-perspektiven.de **Web site:** http://www.media-perspektiven.de
Freq: Annual; **Cover Price:** EUR 10,00; **Circ:** 7,000
Editor: Christa-Maria Ridder
Profile: Documentation of relevant laws, judgements, decisions about media in Germany.
Language(s): German

MEDIA SPECTRUM
735097G2A-2900
Editorial: Abraham-Lincoln-Str. 46, 65189 WIESBADEN **Tel:** 611 7878638 **Fax:** 611 787878638
Email: imke.sander@media-daten.de **Web site:** http://www.media-spectrum.de
Freq: 8 issues yearly; **Annual Sub.:** EUR 159,00; **Circ:** 6,700
Editor: Anja Schüür-Langkau; **Advertising Manager:** Sabine Schüler
Profile: "media spectrum" is for over 30 years the trade magazine for communications and media planning. The magazine addresses the top decision makers at media agencies, advertisers and the media. In addition, "media spectrum" facilitates Media and Communication experts with the basis for their daily work and promotes the transfer between science and practice. In-depth background reports, interviews and portraits of trends and developments in the communications and media planning are analyzed. Moreover, each issue has a media relevant planning issue in focus, supplemented by studies, research methods, tables, graphics and reviews. Additional market surveys, rankings, posters and specials round out the editorial approach. Thus "media spectrum, " is the established magazine for successful communication and media planning.
Language(s): German
Readership: Read by media planners.
ADVERTISING RATES:
Full Page Mono .... EUR 3050
Full Page Colour .... EUR 4280
Mechanical Data: Type Area: 250 x 175 mm
BUSINESS: COMMUNICATIONS, ADVERTISING & MARKETING

MEDIASELLER
735096G43A-980
Editorial: Franz-Ludwig-Str. 7a, 96047 BAMBERG
Tel: 951 861115 **Fax:** 951 861158
Email: mediaseller@meisenbach.de **Web site:** http://www.mediaseller-online.de
Freq: 10 issues yearly; **Annual Sub.:** EUR 50,00; **Circ:** 14,686
Editor: Andreas Wischerhoff; **Advertising Manager:** Dominik Lippold
Profile: Magazine about the retail of home electronics such as computers and telecommunications equipment.
Language(s): German
ADVERTISING RATES:
Full Page Mono .... EUR 5358
Full Page Colour .... EUR 5358
Mechanical Data: Type Area: 260 x 194 mm
BUSINESS: ELECTRICAL RETAIL TRADE

MEDICA AKTUELL
735105G56A-6420
Editorial: Am Forsthaus Gravenbruch 5, 63263 NEU-ISENBURG **Tel:** 6102 506040 **Fax:** 6102 58740
Email: info@aerztezeitung.de **Web site:** http://www.aerztezeitung.de
Freq: Quarterly; **Cover Price:** Free; **Circ:** 14,500
Editor: Wolfgang van den Bergh; **Advertising Manager:** Ute Krille
Profile: Magazine for visitors and exhibitors at medical fairs.
Language(s): German
ADVERTISING RATES:
Full Page Mono .... EUR 3410
Full Page Colour .... EUR 4030
Mechanical Data: Type Area: 390 x 286 mm, No. of Columns (Display): 5, Col Widths (Display): 54 mm
Copy instructions: *Copy Date:* 10 days prior to publication

MEDICAL CORPS INTERNATIONAL FORUM
1861459G56A-11572
Editorial: Celsiusstr. 43, 53125 BONN
Tel: 228 919370 **Fax:** 228 9193723
Email: gianpiero.lupi@mci-forum.com **Web site:** http://www.mci-forum.com

Freq: Quarterly; **Annual Sub.:** EUR 58,20; **Circ:** 15,000
Editor: Gianpiero A. Lupi
Profile: At a time when the importance of the medical services in armed forces throughout the world is increasing with a view to resolving global crises and to providing professional assistance in natural or man-made disasters, the magazine Medical Corps International Forum (MCiF) makes an important contribution to global understanding. MCiF tackles a wide range of relevant topics from military medicine and emergency/disaster medicine.The magazine provides a topical and highly relevant platform for the crossborder dialogue between international medical services of the armed forces, cooperating institutions and aid organisations. MCiF therefore provides professionals from all over the world with a unique forum for an exchange of views and opinions about this specific range of subjects. MCiF offers you the outstanding opportunity of adequately approaching professionals in decision-making positions and of acquainting them with your company and its range of high-quality products and services.
Language(s): English
ADVERTISING RATES:
Full Page Colour .... EUR 4500
Mechanical Data: Type Area: 267 x 185 mm

MEDICAL MICROBIOLOGY AND IMMUNOLOGY 735111G56A-6520
Editorial: Paul-Ehrlich-Str. 40, 60596 FRANKFURT
Email: h.w.doerr@em.uni-frankfurt.de **Web site:** http://www.springerlink.com
Freq: Quarterly; **Annual Sub.:** EUR 1737,00; **Circ:** 78
Editor: H. W. Doerr
Profile: Medical microbiology and immunology.
Language(s): English
ADVERTISING RATES:
Full Page Mono .... EUR 740
Full Page Colour .... EUR 1780
Mechanical Data: Type Area: 240 x 175 mm

MEDICAL SPECIAL 735114G56A-6540
Editorial: Badestr. 7, 31020 SALZHEMMENDORF
Tel: 5153 1898 **Fax:** 5153 964814
Email: klueckmann@medical-special.de **Web site:** http://www.medical-special.de
Freq: 6 issues yearly; **Annual Sub.:** EUR 27,50; **Circ:** 27,200
Editor: Michael Klückmann; **Advertising Manager:** Brigitte Hoffmann
Profile: Publication focusing on current articles and trends into natural healing procedures and medical practices.
Language(s): German
Readership: Aimed at physicians, pharmacists, medical technicians practicing in clinics.
ADVERTISING RATES:
Full Page Mono .... EUR 2768
Full Page Colour .... EUR 3967
Mechanical Data: Type Area: 259 x 186 mm, No. of Columns (Display): 2, Col Widths (Display): 91 mm
Copy instructions: *Copy Date:* 21 days prior to publication
BUSINESS: HEALTH & MEDICAL

MEDICAL TRIBUNE 730545G56A-4980
Editorial: Unter den Eichen 5, 65195 WIESBADEN
Tel: 611 9746303 **Fax:** 611 9746304
Email: redaktion@medical-tribune.de **Web site:** http://www.medical-tribune.de
Freq: Quarterly; **Annual Sub.:** EUR 20,00; **Circ:** 6,623
Editor: Ulrike Hennemann; **Advertising Manager:** Katja Fuchs
Profile: Recent advances in diagnosis and therapy for Paediatricians and youth physicians. In the medical part is reported in attractive sections on recent advances in diagnosis and therapy as well as highlights of national and international conferences and also interdisciplinary, relevant topics. The range is supplemented by subject-specific information for health and ethics policies and economic issues. The editorial team is assisted in the drafting of the issues by a scientific advisory board.
Language(s): German
ADVERTISING RATES:
Full Page Mono .... EUR 2590
Full Page Colour .... EUR 3370
Mechanical Data: Type Area: 390 x 286 mm, No. of Columns (Display): 5
Copy instructions: *Copy Date:* 16 days prior to publication
Supplement(s): Gesunde Medizin

MEDICAL TRIBUNE 735116G56A-6560
Editorial: Unter den Eichen 5, 65195 WIESBADEN
Tel: 611 97460 **Fax:** 611 9746304
Email: redaktion@medical-tribune.de **Web site:** http://www.medical-tribune.de
Freq: Weekly; **Annual Sub.:** EUR 99,00; **Circ:** 65,492
Editor: Ulrike Hennemann; **Advertising Manager:** Katja Fuchs
Profile: Medicine, health policy and practice guidance for GP's, practitioners and internists. The optimum range of topics for the practitioner based on sound sources, professional research and is brand presents typical. Impressive illustrations and exciting and instructive case histories enrich the proven concept. Witty and cryptic cartoons commenting on the events and remind the reader that not to lose the humor in everyday practice.
Language(s): German
Readership: Aimed at doctors.
ADVERTISING RATES:
Full Page Mono .... EUR 9160
Full Page Colour .... EUR 10720
Mechanical Data: Type Area: 390 x 286 mm, No. of Columns (Display): 5, Col Widths (Display): 54 mm
Copy instructions: *Copy Date:* 21 days prior to publication
Supplement(s): Kolloquium
BUSINESS: HEALTH & MEDICAL

MEDICAL TRIBUNE 1799509G56A-11459
Editorial: Unter den Eichen 5, 65195 WIESBADEN
Tel: 611 97460 **Fax:** 611 9746304
Email: redaktion@medical-tribune.de **Web site:** http://www.medical-tribune.de
Freq: 6 issues yearly; **Annual Sub.:** EUR 30,00; **Circ:** 10,123
Editor: Ulrike Hennemann; **Advertising Manager:** Katja Fuchs
Profile: Highlights of national and international congresses and from the current literature for neurologists, psychiatrists and psychotherapists. In the medical part is reported in attractive sections on recent advances in diagnosis and therapy as well as highlights of national and international conferences and also interdisciplinary, relevant topics. The range is supplemented by subject-specific information for health and ethics policies and economic issues. The editorial team is assisted in the drafting of the issues by a scientific advisory board.
Language(s): German
ADVERTISING RATES:
Full Page Mono .... EUR 2800
Full Page Colour .... EUR 3580
Mechanical Data: Type Area: 390 x 286 mm

MEDICAL TRIBUNE 1799510G56A-11460
Editorial: Unter den Eichen 5, 65195 WIESBADEN
Tel: 611 97460 **Fax:** 611 9746304
Email: redaktion@medical-tribune.de **Web site:** http://www.medical-tribune.de
Freq: 6 issues yearly; **Annual Sub.:** EUR 30,00; **Circ:** 12,376
Editor: Ulrike Hennemann; **Advertising Manager:** Katja Fuchs
Profile: Highlights of national and international congresses and from the current literature for oncologists, hematologists, pulmonologists and oncologistic urologists. In the medical part is reported in attractive sections on recent advances in diagnosis and therapy as well as highlights of national and international conferences and also interdisciplinary, relevant topics. The range is supplemented by subject-specific information for health and ethics policies and economic issues. The editorial team is assisted in the drafting of the issues by a scientific advisory board.
Language(s): German
ADVERTISING RATES:
Full Page Mono .... EUR 3800
Full Page Colour .... EUR 4580
Mechanical Data: Type Area: 390 x 286 mm

MEDICAL TRIBUNE 730545G56A-11596
Editorial: Unter den Eichen 5, 65195 WIESBADEN
Tel: 611 9746303 **Fax:** 611 9746304
Email: redaktion@medical-tribune.de **Web site:** http://www.medical-tribune.de
Freq: Quarterly; **Annual Sub.:** EUR 20,00; **Circ:** 6,623
Editor: Ulrike Hennemann; **Advertising Manager:** Katja Fuchs
Profile: Recent advances in diagnosis and therapy for Paediatricians and youth physicians. In the medical part is reported in attractive sections on recent advances in diagnosis and therapy as well as highlights of national and international conferences and also interdisciplinary, relevant topics. The range is supplemented by subject-specific information for health and ethics policies and economic issues. The editorial team is assisted in the drafting of the issues by a scientific advisory board.
Language(s): German
ADVERTISING RATES:
Full Page Mono .... EUR 2590
Full Page Colour .... EUR 3370
Mechanical Data: Type Area: 390 x 286 mm, No. of Columns (Display): 5
Copy instructions: *Copy Date:* 16 days prior to publication
Supplement(s): Gesunde Medizin

MEDIEN BULLETIN 735126G2D-50
Editorial: Am Kurfürstenweg 2a, 85232 BERGKIRCHEN **Tel:** 8131 354759 **Fax:** 8131 354760
Email: redaktion@medienbulletin.de **Web site:** http://www.mebucom.de
Freq: 10 issues yearly; **Annual Sub.:** EUR 91,50; **Circ:** 5,000
Editor: Eckhard Eckstein; **Advertising Manager:** Christl Kaiser
Profile: MEDIEN BULLETIN is the only German-speaking media and broadcast magazine with a comprehensive integrated crossmedia approach. MEDIEN BULLETIN - now 30 years on the market - covers complete value chains from the production to the processing, the management, the archiving, the playout and the distribution of multimedia content on different distribution channels. MEDIEN BULLETIN has a strong focus on convergence subjects like the growing influence of telecommunications, information technology and Internet on the broadcasting business. MEDIEN BULLETIN reports about experts, decision-makers and companies in the media and broadcast industry, about the newest technologies, products and solutions, about all related economic and content-based aspects as well as about the media policy and regulatory framework conditions - always with with a close view to international developements. With this MEDIEN BULLETIN offers the wides spectrum of subjects in the area of media and broadcast magazines. Target group: decision makers, experts, service providers (technique, content, creation and planning). addressing: broadcasters, tv- and film-producers, studios and production houses, rental companies, system integrators, service providers, content owners and distributors, editorial departments, media regulators, media organizations and institutions, universities and educational facilities.
Language(s): German
ADVERTISING RATES:
Full Page Mono .... EUR 1990
Full Page Colour .... EUR 3530
Mechanical Data: Type Area: 254 x 185 mm
BUSINESS: COMMUNICATIONS, ADVERTISING & MARKETING: Broadcasting

MEDIENBRIEF 735125G2A-3220
Editorial: Bertha-von-Suttner-Platz 1, 40227 DÜSSELDORF **Tel:** 211 8998189 **Fax:** 211 8929264
Email: manfred.kremers@lvr.de **Web site:** http://www.medien-und-bildung.lvr.de
Freq: Half-yearly; **Cover Price:** Free; **Circ:** 6,000
Editor: Manfred Kremers
Profile: Media paedagogical magazine.
Language(s): German

MEDIENHANDBUCH.DE 1704544G2A-5679
Editorial: Bahrenfelder Str. 93, 22765 HAMBURG
Tel: 40 392225
Email: chefredaktion@medienhandbuch.de **Web site:** http://www.medienhandbuch.de
Freq: Daily; **Cover Price:** Paid; **Circ:** 34,326 Unique Users
Editor: Oliver Hein-Behrens
Language(s): German
BUSINESS: COMMUNICATIONS, ADVERTISING & MARKETING

MEDIENWIRTSCHAFT 1772567G2A-5691
Editorial: Finkenau 35, 22081 HAMBURG
Tel: 40 41346830 **Fax:** 40 41346810
Email: i.sjurts@hamburgmediaschool.com **Web site:** http://www.medienwirtschaft-online.de
Freq: Quarterly; **Annual Sub.:** EUR 78,00; **Circ:** 1,250
Editor: Insa Sjurts; **Advertising Manager:** Jens Jansen
Profile: Journal of current business and economic issues in the context of media companies, media markets, media management and media economics. The range of sectors covered range from the traditional media industries as part of book, newspaper, magazines, radio and television about the new online and mobile media markets part to telecommunications. The increasing dissolution of industry boundaries and the emergence of new markets with new products and competitors are given special attention. Using scientific methods, basic issues are processed, analyzed and discussed and classified the results into the context of the current scientific debate. The media industry is aimed at researchers and practitioners in the media as well as students of the respective disciplines.
Language(s): German
ADVERTISING RATES:
Full Page Mono .... EUR 1850
Full Page Colour .... EUR 1850
Mechanical Data: Type Area: 297 x 210 mm
Copy instructions: *Copy Date:* 28 days prior to publication

MEDIENWISSENSCHAFT 735149G2A-3200
Editorial: Wilhelm-Röpke-Str. 6a, 35039 MARBURG
Tel: 6421 2825587 **Fax:** 6421 2826989
Email: medrez@staff.uni-marburg.de **Web site:** http://www.medienwissenschaft-rezensionen.de
Freq: Quarterly; **Annual Sub.:** EUR 49,80; **Circ:** 600
Editor: Sven Stollfuß; **Advertising Manager:** Katrin Ahnemann
Profile: Magazine about media with reviews about books, press and audio visual media from movies, TV and video.
Language(s): German
ADVERTISING RATES:
Full Page Mono .... EUR 180
Mechanical Data: Type Area: 185 x 115 mm

MEDINTERN 1862821G56A-11577
Editorial: Frühlingstr. 9, 83125 EGGSTÄTT
Tel: 8056 1086
Email: claudia.sarkady@t-online.de **Web site:** http://www.med-intern.com
Freq: Quarterly; **Annual Sub.:** EUR 28,00; **Circ:** 40,000
Editor: Claudia Sarkady; **Advertising Manager:** Kornelia Huditz
Profile: Information service by doctors for doctors and independent practice.
Language(s): German
ADVERTISING RATES:
Full Page Mono .... EUR 1950
Full Page Colour .... EUR 1950
Mechanical Data: Type Area: 268 x 188 mm, No. of Columns (Display): 3
Copy instructions: *Copy Date:* 21 days prior to publication

MEDIUM 735154G2B-700
Editorial: Im Uhrig 31, 60433 FRANKFURT
Tel: 69 95297944 **Fax:** 69 95297945
Email: redaktion@mediummagazin.de **Web site:** http://www.mediummagazin.de
Freq: 8 issues yearly; **Annual Sub.:** EUR 49,00; **Circ:** 20,050
Editor: Annette Milz
Profile: "medium" offers useful aspects, the latest tips, well-researched background information, sensitive personal portraits. Contributions from the "medium" are cited in the "Spiegel", in "Zeit", in "focus", "FAZ", "Süddeutsche", in the "Welt". A lot of attention we devote to training issues, as well as "medium" takes care of the offspring.
Language(s): German
Readership: Aimed at journalists and PR managers.
ADVERTISING RATES:
Full Page Mono .... EUR 4470
Full Page Colour .... EUR 6705
Mechanical Data: Type Area: 252 x 188 mm
BUSINESS: COMMUNICATIONS, ADVERTISING & MARKETING: Press

MEDIZIN FÜR MANAGER 1739835G14A-9855
Editorial: Bergheimer Str. 104, 69115 HEIDELBERG
Tel: 6221 6530620 **Fax:** 6221 6530630
Email: info@medizin-fuer-manager.de **Web site:** http://www.medizin-fuer-manager.de
Freq: Annual; **Annual Sub.:** EUR 32,50; **Circ:** 15,000
Advertising Manager: Irene Naujoks
Profile: Regional magazine with medical information for manager.
Language(s): German
ADVERTISING RATES:
Full Page Mono .... EUR 4210
Full Page Colour .... EUR 4210
Mechanical Data: Type Area: 290 x 230 mm
BUSINESS: COMMERCE, INDUSTRY & MANAGEMENT

MEDIZIN FÜR MANAGER 1827052G14A-10084
Editorial: Bergheimer Str. 104, 69115 HEIDELBERG
Tel: 6221 6530620 **Fax:** 6221 6530630
Email: info@medizin-fuer-manager.de **Web site:** http://www.medizin-fuer-manager.de
Freq: Annual; **Annual Sub.:** EUR 32,50; **Circ:** 13,500
Advertising Manager: Irene Naujoks
Profile: Regional magazine with medical information for manager.
Language(s): German
ADVERTISING RATES:
Full Page Mono .... EUR 4210
Full Page Colour .... EUR 4210
Mechanical Data: Type Area: 290 x 230 mm

MEDIZIN FÜR MANAGER 1827055G14A-10087
Editorial: Bergheimer Str. 104, 69115 HEIDELBERG
Tel: 6221 6530620 **Fax:** 6221 6530630
Email: info@medizin-fuer-manager.de **Web site:** http://www.medizin-fuer-manager.de
Freq: Annual; **Annual Sub.:** EUR 32,50; **Circ:** 12,000
Advertising Manager: Irene Naujoks
Profile: Regional magazine with medical information for manager.
Language(s): German
ADVERTISING RATES:
Full Page Mono .... EUR 4210
Full Page Colour .... EUR 4210
Mechanical Data: Type Area: 290 x 230 mm

MEDIZIN FÜR MANAGER 1827057G14A-10089
Editorial: Bergheimer Str. 104, 69115 HEIDELBERG
Tel: 6221 6530620 **Fax:** 6221 6530630
Email: info@medizin-fuer-manager.de **Web site:** http://www.medizin-fuer-manager.de
Freq: Annual; **Annual Sub.:** EUR 32,50; **Circ:** 15,000
Advertising Manager: Irene Naujoks
Profile: Regional magazine with medical information for manager.
Language(s): German
ADVERTISING RATES:
Full Page Mono .... EUR 4210
Full Page Colour .... EUR 4210
Mechanical Data: Type Area: 290 x 230 mm

MEDIZIN, GESELLSCHAFT UND GESCHICHTE 735160G56R-2433
Editorial: Straußweg 17, 70184 STUTTGART
Tel: 711 46084171 **Fax:** 711 46084181
Web site: http://www.steiner-verlag.de/MedGG
Freq: Annual; **Annual Sub.:** EUR 40,80; **Circ:** 500
Editor: Sylvelyn Hähner-Rombach
Profile: Original contributions, social history of medicine, history of homeopathy and alternative healing methods, medicine and pharmacy history.
Language(s): English; German
Readership: Focused on health medical care.
ADVERTISING RATES:
Full Page Mono .... EUR 750

Mechanical Data: Type Area: 190 x 120 mm
BUSINESS: HEALTH & MEDICAL: Health Medical Related

MEDIZIN HISTORISCHES JOURNAL 1824622G56A-11522
Editorial: Oberer Neubergweg 10a, 97074 WÜRZBURG
Email: michael.stolberg@mail.uni-wuerzburg.de **Web site:** http://www.steiner-verlag.de/MedHist
Freq: Quarterly; **Annual Sub.:** EUR 148,20; **Circ:** 300
Editor: Michael Stolberg; **Advertising Manager:** Susanne Szoradi
Profile: Journal on medicine and the life sciences in history.
Language(s): English; French; German; Italian
ADVERTISING RATES:
Full Page Mono .... EUR 750
Mechanical Data: Type Area: 190 x 120 mm

MEDIZIN & PRAXIS SPEZIAL 1657630G56A-11308
Editorial: Vogelsang 28, 21682 STADE
Tel: 4141 801199 **Fax:** 4141 801197
Email: verlagbvhallern@t-online.de **Web site:** http://www.medizinundpraxis.de
Freq: 3 issues yearly; **Cover Price:** EUR 8,00; **Circ:** 23,500
Editor: Bernd von Hallern
Profile: Magazine about surgery, traumatology, orthopaedy, dermatology, phlebology and general medicine, hospital nurses and other care services, teachers at nurses' and elderly care schools.
Language(s): German
ADVERTISING RATES:
Full Page Mono .... EUR 1200
Full Page Colour .... EUR 1990
Mechanical Data: Type Area: 265 x 185 mm, No. of Columns (Display): 2, Col Widths (Display): 85 mm
Copy instructions: *Copy Date:* 30 days prior to publication

MEDIZINI MIT SUPER-POSTER 735164G91D-5320
Editorial: Konradshöhe, 82065 BAIERBRUNN
Tel: 89 744330 **Fax:** 89 74433330
Email: medizini@wortundbildverlag.de **Web site:** http://www.gesundheitpro.de
Freq: Monthly; **Cover Price:** Free; **Circ:** 1,714,909
Editor: Harald Lorenz; **Advertising Manager:** Brigitta Hackmann
Profile: Children Magazine distributed via pharmacists with entertainment, puzzles and poster.
Language(s): German
ADVERTISING RATES:
Full Page Mono .... EUR 34400
Full Page Colour .... EUR 34400
Mechanical Data: Type Area: 297 x 210 mm
Copy instructions: *Copy Date:* 56 days prior to publication
CONSUMER: RECREATION & LEISURE: Children & Youth

DIE MEDIZINISCHE FACHANGESTELLTE 721264G56R-140
Editorial: Eschstr. 22, 44629 HERNE
Tel: 2323 141700 **Fax:** 2323 141123
Email: b.switon@kiehl.de **Web site:** http://www.kiehl.de
Freq: Monthly; **Annual Sub.:** EUR 61,80; **Circ:** 5,761
Editor: Barbara Switon; **Advertising Manager:** Andreas Reimann
Profile: More success in education, certainly in all the tests go, to convince the job every day: „Die Medizinische Fachangestellte" (formerly: Die Arzthelferin) is the ideal resource for anyone who wants to take their career into their own hands. The magazine offers the latest information on all subjects that are important for the medical staff. For the regular (audit) training it also includes training exercises, review questions and sample cases with solutions. Even complicated issues can be described easily understandable. You benefit from the content without investing much time must be. "Real" examination questions with solutions enable optimal exam preparation. The lots of practical tips you can apply directly. The authors come from the training practice and knows what is important to you. On „Die Medizinische Fachangestellte" you can rely on, because the contributions of the journal based on the current training regulations and requirements of the professional world. The regular columns: medical expertise, accounting system, practice management, patient care, communication, information technology, law, economics and management, education and employment, the case in practice, the current keyword, From A to Z, check training schedule with training schedules, book and software tips news flashes.
Language(s): German
ADVERTISING RATES:
Full Page Mono .... EUR 1190
Full Page Colour .... EUR 1650
Mechanical Data: Type Area: 260 x 186 mm
Copy instructions: *Copy Date:* 30 days prior to publication
BUSINESS: HEALTH & MEDICAL: Health Medical Related

MEDIZINISCHE GENETIK 735165G56A-11261
Editorial: Inselkammerstr. 4, 82008 UNTERHACHING
Tel: 89 55027855 **Fax:** 89 55027856
Email: redaktion@medgenetik.de **Web site:** http://www.medgenetik.de
Freq: Quarterly; Free to qualifying individuals
Annual Sub.: EUR 110,00; **Circ:** 1,450
Editor: Christine Scholz; **Advertising Manager:** Sabine Weidner
Profile: The medizinische genetik is the largest trade journal for clinical and general human genetics in Germany. It is published by the German Society of Human Genetics (gfh). Its focus is on continuing education and training: well-known authors provide both basic theoretical and application-oriented knowledge in the form of topics and for the certified training. Updated articles on law, ethics and psycho-social aspects of human genetic diagnostics and advice give readers a broad and thorough overview of current health policy discussions. Not least is the GfH by the publication of its opinions and guidelines in the Journal medizinische genetik specific instructions and guidance for the competent implementation human genetic knowledge in clinical practice. The geneticist in Germany, Austria and Switzerland are responsible for quality assurance in Europe, which comes in large contributions to the internal and external quality management expressed.
Language(s): English; German
ADVERTISING RATES:
Full Page Mono .... EUR 1260
Full Page Colour .... EUR 2300
Mechanical Data: Type Area: 240 x 174 mm

MEDIZINISCHE KLINIK 735166G56C-110
Editorial: Aschauer Str. 30, 81549 MÜNCHEN
Tel: 89 2030431300 **Fax:** 89 2030431399
Email: daniela.oesterle@springer.com **Web site:** http://www.springermedizin.de
Freq: Monthly; Free to qualifying individuals
Annual Sub.: EUR 266,00; **Circ:** 20,118
Editor: Johannes Köbberling
Profile: The internal medicine journal „Medizinische Klinik" provides current, practical knowledge of internal medicine and its neighboring areas for clinicians and practicing internists with its own training module "practice", which is based CME. In the institution German Society of Internal Medicine will also original papers, review articles, published case reports, contributions from the health services research and specialized communications of the society published. Critical Journal Club reviews of international internal medicine trade press in the spring of first-class experts round off the paper.
Language(s): German
ADVERTISING RATES:
Full Page Mono .... EUR 2525
Full Page Colour .... EUR 3825
Mechanical Data: Type Area: 247 x 174 mm, No. of Columns (Display): 2, Col Widths (Display): 83 mm
Official Journal of: Organ d. Dt. Ges. f. Innere Medizin
BUSINESS: HEALTH & MEDICAL: Hospitals

MEDIZINISCHE KONGRESSE 1902505G56A-11601
Editorial: Mitteldicker Weg 1, 63263 NEU-ISENBURG **Tel:** 69 69500852 **Fax:** 69 69500827
Email: info@medizinische-kongresse.de **Web site:** http://www.medizinische-kongresse.de
Freq: Annual; **Cover Price:** EUR 34,50; **Circ:** 19,000
Editor: Ingrid Haack; **Advertising Manager:** André Oltersdorff
Profile: Magazine on medical congresses.
Language(s): German
ADVERTISING RATES:
Full Page Colour .... EUR 3988
Mechanical Data: Type Area: 187 x 131 mm
Copy instructions: *Copy Date:* 30 days prior to publication

DER MEDIZINISCHE SACHVERSTÄNDIGE 735169G56A-6880
Editorial: Forststr. 131, 70193 STUTTGART
Tel: 711 63672848 **Fax:** 711 63672711
Email: huett@gentnerverlag.de **Web site:** http://www.medsach.de
Freq: 6 issues yearly; **Annual Sub.:** EUR 158,80; **Circ:** 1,648
Editor: Norbert Rösner; **Advertising Manager:** Angela Grüssner
Profile: Medical newspaper containing the latest reports and developments within the field.
Language(s): German
ADVERTISING RATES:
Full Page Mono .... EUR 860
Full Page Colour .... EUR 1600
Mechanical Data: Type Area: 260 x 185 mm, No. of Columns (Display): 4, Col Widths (Display): 45 mm
Copy instructions: *Copy Date:* 30 days prior to publication
BUSINESS: HEALTH & MEDICAL

MEDIZINISCH-ORTHOPÄDISCHE TECHNIK 1928135G56A-11643
Editorial: Kaunstr. 34, 14163 BERLIN
Tel: 30 8011018 **Fax:** 30 8016661
Email: s.tischler@firmengruppe-tischler.de **Web site:** http://www.mot-magazin.de
Freq: 6 issues yearly; **Annual Sub.:** EUR 68,00; **Circ:** 6,650
Editor: B. Greitemann
Profile: Magazine focusing on technical orthopaedics.
Language(s): German
ADVERTISING RATES:
Full Page Mono .... EUR 1400
Full Page Colour .... EUR 2300
Mechanical Data: Type Area: 252 x 185 mm, No. of Columns (Display): 3, Col Widths (Display): 55 mm
Copy instructions: *Copy Date:* 28 days prior to publication
Official Journal of: Organ d. Internat. Society for Prothetics and Orthotics (ISPO) Deutschland, d. ISPO Österr., d. Amputierten Iniative e.V.

MEDR MEDIZINRECHT 735181G44-3064
Editorial: Albertus-Magnus-Platz, 50923 KÖLN
Tel: 221 4701400 **Fax:** 221 4701401
Email: medizinrecht@uni-koeln.de **Web site:** http://www.springerlink.com
Freq: Monthly; **Annual Sub.:** EUR 579,00; **Circ:** 1,300
Editor: Christian Katzenmeier; **Advertising Manager:** Fritz Lebherz
Profile: Journal focusing on the law relating to medicine.
Language(s): German
Readership: Aimed at lawyers.
ADVERTISING RATES:
Full Page Mono .... EUR 1660
Full Page Colour .... EUR 3310
Mechanical Data: Type Area: 260 x 186 mm, No. of Columns (Display): 2, Col Widths (Display): 90 mm
BUSINESS: LEGAL

MEDREPORT 735180G56R-91
Editorial: Rotherstr. 21, 10245 BERLIN
Tel: 30 47031432 **Fax:** 30 47031444
Email: medreports@wiley.com **Web site:** http://www.blackwell.de
Freq: 45 issues yearly; **Annual Sub.:** EUR 254,66
Editor: Beata Dümde; **Advertising Manager:** Rita Mattutat
Profile: Magazine about medical congresses.
Language(s): German
ADVERTISING RATES:
Full Page Mono .... EUR 2680
Full Page Colour .... EUR 3880
Mechanical Data: Type Area: 355 x 256 mm, No. of Columns (Display): 5, Col Widths (Display): 48 mm
Copy instructions: *Copy Date:* 35 days prior to publication
Official Journal of: Organ f. ärztl. Fortbildungskongresse
BUSINESS: HEALTH & MEDICAL: Health Medical Related

MEDREVIEW 1606836G56A-11161
Editorial: Rotherstr. 21, 10245 BERLIN
Tel: 30 47031432 **Fax:** 30 47031444
Email: medreview@wiley.com **Web site:** http://www.medreviews.de
Freq: Monthly; **Annual Sub.:** EUR 149,80; **Circ:** 3,617
Editor: Alexandra Pearl; **Advertising Manager:** Rita Mattutat
Profile: Magazine on congresses for medical further education. It appears as a follow-up assessment 6 weeks after an event.
Language(s): German
ADVERTISING RATES:
Full Page Mono .... EUR 2450
Full Page Colour .... EUR 3200
Mechanical Data: Type Area: 254 x 165 mm, No. of Columns (Display): 3, Col Widths (Display): 52 mm
Copy instructions: *Copy Date:* 21 days prior to publication

MEDWELT DIE MEDIZINISCHE WELT 735170G56A-6900
Editorial: Hölderlinstr. 3, 70174 STUTTGART
Tel: 711 2298737 **Fax:** 711 2298765
Email: peter.henning@schattauer.de **Web site:** http://www.die-medizinische-welt.de
Freq: 6 issues yearly; **Annual Sub.:** EUR 180,00; **Circ:** 14,578
Editor: Peter Henning; **Advertising Manager:** Christoph Brocker
Profile: In medical education and training provides the MedWelt Die Medizinische Welt an essential foundation for the practicing physician, the specialist for general medicine and specialist in internal medicine. The journal is devoted to each issue one or two key themes. Since 2004, the MedWelt cooperates with the competence networks in medicine. In the form of priority issues they present their scientific work in practice and contribute to the knowledge of the clinic at the practice. Original and review articles, clinical trials, conference proceedings, abstracts and news from research and industry, provide a comprehensive overview of current developments in medical research and diagnosis and treatment of diseases of the issues involved.
Language(s): German
ADVERTISING RATES:
Full Page Mono .... EUR 2540
Full Page Colour .... EUR 3790
Mechanical Data: Type Area: 243 x 179 mm, No. of Columns (Display): 3, Col Widths (Display): 57 mm
Copy instructions: *Copy Date:* 40 days prior to publication
BUSINESS: HEALTH & MEDICAL

MEER & FLAIR 735186G89A-12108
Editorial: Unter den Eichen 18, 26160 BAD ZWISCHENAHN **Tel:** 4403 61567 **Fax:** 4403 61499
Email: m.koesters@tg.bad-zwischenahn.de **Web site:** http://www.touristik-bad-zwischenahn.de
Freq: Monthly; **Cover Price:** Free; **Circ:** 14,000
Editor: Miriam Kösters
Profile: Tourist magazine about Bad Zwischenahn.
Language(s): German
ADVERTISING RATES:
Full Page Mono .... EUR 856
Full Page Colour .... EUR 1120
Mechanical Data: Type Area: 270 x 185 mm, No. of Columns (Display): 4, Col Widths (Display): 43 mm
Copy instructions: *Copy Date:* 14 days prior to publication

MEETING GUIDE 1799875G50-1247
Editorial: Am Karlsbad 11, 10785 BERLIN
Tel: 30 2647480 **Fax:** 30 264748968
Email: catrin.linde@btm.de **Web site:** http://www.visitberlin.de
Freq: Annual; **Cover Price:** Free; **Circ:** 5,000
Profile: Magazine for planning congresses and seminars in Berlin.
Language(s): English; German
ADVERTISING RATES:
Full Page Mono .... EUR 2340
Full Page Colour .... EUR 2340
Mechanical Data: Type Area: 254 x 175 mm
Copy instructions: *Copy Date:* 87 days prior to publication

MEGA HIRO 766897G91D-9862
Editorial: Rotebühlstr. 87, 70178 STUTTGART
Tel: 711 947680 **Fax:** 711 9476830
Email: info@panini.de **Web site:** http://www.panini.de
Freq: 13 issues yearly; **Cover Price:** EUR 2,99; **Circ:** 29,064
Editor: Jo Löffler
Profile: Mega Hiro is the Fun & anime magazine for boys between 9 and 14 years. There they find out all about the anime broadcast on RTL II (Pokemon, Naruto, Yu-Gi-Oh, 5D's, Blue Dragon, etc.), and also about DVDs, videos and games. There are puzzles, a TV Guide and exciting stuff!.
Language(s): German
ADVERTISING RATES:
Full Page Mono .... EUR 4900
Full Page Colour .... EUR 4900
Mechanical Data: Type Area: 250 x 180 mm
CONSUMER: RECREATION & LEISURE: Children & Youth

MEGAZIN 735194G80-7560
Editorial: Bergbräustr. 2, 85049 INGOLSTADT
Tel: 841 1560 **Fax:** 841 1406
Email: redaktion@megazin.de **Web site:** http://www.megazin.de
Freq: Monthly; **Cover Price:** Free; **Circ:** 14,796
Editor: Daniel Melegi; **Advertising Manager:** Daniel Melegi
Profile: Lifestyle magazine for the region of Ingolstadt.
Language(s): German
Readership: Aimed at 18 to 49 year olds.
ADVERTISING RATES:
Full Page Mono .... EUR 1320
Full Page Colour .... EUR 1860
Mechanical Data: Type Area: 275 x 189 mm, No. of Columns (Display): 4, Col Widths (Display): 45 mm
CONSUMER: RURAL & REGIONAL INTEREST

MEIER 735200G80-7580
Editorial: Melchiorstr. 1, 68167 MANNHEIM
Tel: 621 338800 **Fax:** 621 333367
Email: redaktion@meier-online.de **Web site:** http://www.meier-online.de
Freq: Monthly; **Annual Sub.:** EUR 25,00; **Circ:** 18,721
Editor: Ralf Laubscher
Profile: meier, the core product of Delta Media Publishing is for 25 years one of the most successful city magazines in Germany. meier reaches a broad, cross-generational audience that do not miss in every media planning. meier is the indispensable guide to life in the Rhein-Neckar-Delta and informs its readers a quick, reliable and entertaining on the main events and themes of the month. Facebook: http://www.facebook.com/pages/MEIER-Magazin/126690432908.
Language(s): German
ADVERTISING RATES:
Full Page Mono .... EUR 2017
Full Page Colour .... EUR 3367
Mechanical Data: Type Area: 260 x 190 mm, No. of Columns (Display): 4, Col Widths (Display): 43 mm
Copy instructions: *Copy Date:* 15 days prior to publication
Supplement(s): Festivalregion Rhein-Neckar; meier delta aktiv; meier Lange Nacht der Museen; meier schön + gut; meier summertime
CONSUMER: RURAL & REGIONAL INTEREST

MEIER SUMMERTIME 1865058G89A-12428
Editorial: Melchiorstr. 1, 68167 MANNHEIM
Tel: 621 338800 **Fax:** 621 333367
Email: info@meier-online.de **Web site:** http://www.meier-online.de
Freq: Annual; **Circ:** 30,000
Editor: Jana Klüber

Profile: meier summertime, the summer-Gastro-Guide. From the Meier espresso-editor summer freshly researched: beer gardens, street cafes, beach bars, ice cream shops, outdoor restaurants, tourist cafes - classics and newcomers. meier summertime reveals where there are fresh salads, cold beer and tasty cocktails and where you can dine outdoors - from rustic to elegant. meier summertime is an attractively designed and versatile guide on going out in the summer. Facebook: http://www.facebook.com/pages/MEIER-Magazin/126690432908.
Language(s): German
ADVERTISING RATES:
Full Page Mono .... EUR 1838
Full Page Colour .... EUR 2925
Mechanical Data: Type Area: 260 x 190 mm, No. of Columns (Display): 4, Col Widths (Display): 43 mm
Copy instructions: *Copy Date:* 30 days prior to publication
Supplement to: meier

MEIN BABY MEIN KIDSGO
1642013G74D-18
Editorial: Carl-Giesecke-Str. 4, 37079 GÖTTINGEN
Tel: 551 997250 **Fax:** 551 99725299
Email: redaktion@kidsgo.de **Web site:** http://www.kidsgo.de
Freq: Quarterly; **Cover Price:** Free; **Circ:** 34,816
Editor: Barbara Hirt; **Advertising Manager:** Barbara Hirt
Profile: Event magazine about pregnancy, birth, baby and family in Hamburg.
Language(s): German
ADVERTISING RATES:
Full Page Mono .... EUR 2800
Full Page Colour .... EUR 2800
Mechanical Data: Type Area: 272 x 185 mm, No. of Columns (Display): 3, Col Widths (Display): 57 mm
Copy instructions: *Copy Date:* 30 days prior to publication
CONSUMER: WOMEN'S INTEREST CONSUMER MAGAZINES: Child Care

MEIN BABY MEIN KIDSGO
1642014G74D-19
Editorial: Carl-Giesecke-Str. 4, 37079 GÖTTINGEN
Tel: 551 997250 **Fax:** 551 99725299
Email: redaktion@kidsgo.de **Web site:** http://www.kidsgo.de
Freq: Quarterly; **Cover Price:** Free; **Circ:** 21,432
Editor: Barbara Hirt; **Advertising Manager:** Barbara Hirt
Profile: Event magazine about pregnancy, birth, baby and family in Southern Lower Saxony / Northern Hessen.
Language(s): German
ADVERTISING RATES:
Full Page Mono .... EUR 1900
Full Page Colour .... EUR 1900
Mechanical Data: Type Area: 272 x 185 mm, No. of Columns (Display): 3, Col Widths (Display): 57 mm
Copy instructions: *Copy Date:* 30 days prior to publication
CONSUMER: WOMEN'S INTEREST CONSUMER MAGAZINES: Child Care

MEIN BABY MEIN KIDSGO - AUSG. BERLIN
1642010G74D-15
Editorial: Carl-Giesecke-Str. 4, 37079 GÖTTINGEN
Tel: 551 99725224 **Fax:** 551 99725299
Email: redaktion@kidsgo.de **Web site:** http://www.kidsgo.de
Freq: Quarterly; **Cover Price:** Free; **Circ:** 60,829
Editor: Barbara Hirt; **Advertising Manager:** Barbara Hirt
Profile: Event magazine about pregnancy, birth, baby and family in Berlin.
Language(s): German
ADVERTISING RATES:
Full Page Mono .... EUR 5520
Full Page Colour .... EUR 5520
Mechanical Data: Type Area: 272 x 185 mm, No. of Columns (Display): 3, Col Widths (Display): 57 mm
Copy instructions: *Copy Date:* 30 days prior to publication
CONSUMER: WOMEN'S INTEREST CONSUMER MAGAZINES: Child Care

MEIN BABY MEIN KIDSGO - AUSG. DÜSSELDORFER RAUM
1642012G74D-17
Editorial: Carl-Giesecke-Str. 4, 37079 GÖTTINGEN
Tel: 551 997250 **Fax:** 551 99725299
Email: redaktion@kidsgo.de **Web site:** http://www.kidsgo.de
Freq: Quarterly; **Cover Price:** Free; **Circ:** 30,369
Editor: Barbara Hirt; **Advertising Manager:** Barbara Hirt
Profile: Event magazine about pregnancy, birth, baby and family in Düsseldorf.
Language(s): German
ADVERTISING RATES:
Full Page Mono .... EUR 2460
Full Page Colour .... EUR 2460
Mechanical Data: Type Area: 272 x 185 mm, No. of Columns (Display): 3, Col Widths (Display): 57 mm
Copy instructions: *Copy Date:* 30 days prior to publication
CONSUMER: WOMEN'S INTEREST CONSUMER MAGAZINES: Child Care

MEIN BABY MEIN KIDSGO - AUSG. KÖLN
1642011G74D-16
Editorial: Carl-Giesecke-Str. 4, 37079 GÖTTINGEN
Tel: 551 997250 **Fax:** 551 99725299
Email: redaktion@kidsgo.de **Web site:** http://www.kidsgo.de
Freq: Quarterly; **Cover Price:** Free; **Circ:** 25,366
Editor: Barbara Hirt; **Advertising Manager:** Barbara Hirt
Profile: Event magazine about pregnancy, birth, baby and family in Cologne.
Language(s): German
ADVERTISING RATES:
Full Page Mono .... EUR 2330
Full Page Colour .... EUR 2330
Mechanical Data: Type Area: 272 x 185 mm, No. of Columns (Display): 3, Col Widths (Display): 57 mm
Copy instructions: *Copy Date:* 30 days prior to publication
CONSUMER: WOMEN'S INTEREST CONSUMER MAGAZINES: Child Care

MEIN BABY MEIN KIDSGO - AUSG. MÜNCHEN
1642009G74D-14
Editorial: Carl-Giesecke-Str. 4, 37079 GÖTTINGEN
Tel: 551 99725224 **Fax:** 551 99725299
Email: redaktion@kidsgo.de **Web site:** http://www.kidsgo.de
Freq: Quarterly; **Cover Price:** Free; **Circ:** 33,759
Editor: Barbara Hirt; **Advertising Manager:** Barbara Hirt
Profile: Event magazine about pregnancy, birth, baby and family in Munich.
Language(s): German
ADVERTISING RATES:
Full Page Mono .... EUR 2800
Full Page Colour .... EUR 2800
Mechanical Data: Type Area: 272 x 185 mm, No. of Columns (Display): 3, Col Widths (Display): 57 mm
Copy instructions: *Copy Date:* 30 days prior to publication
CONSUMER: WOMEN'S INTEREST CONSUMER MAGAZINES: Child Care

MEIN BEKENNTNIS
735204G74A-2060
Editorial: Sieker Landstr. 126/II, 22143 HAMBURG
Tel: 40 6739780 **Fax:** 40 67397821
Email: wmb@cpvkg.de **Web site:** http://www.conpart-verlag.de
Freq: 6 issues yearly; **Cover Price:** EUR 1,80; **Circ:** 100,000
Editor: Wolfgang M. Biehler
Profile: Women report in the journal of formative experiences that have influenced her life. Of courageous decisions, bitter truths, dramatic developments, unexpected twists and devastating consequences. It's about disturbing and distressing events, unsparing confessions, tormenting guilt, bitter disappointments and sad memories. And also to fateful encounters that ended in love, suffering or one's life worth living made. In addition, see "Mein Bekenntnis" different types of puzzles for a few relaxing minutes in between. The health tips and your own personal horoscope can help you through the day.
Language(s): German
ADVERTISING RATES:
Full Page Mono .... EUR 3000
Full Page Colour .... EUR 3000
Mechanical Data: Type Area: 300 x 220 mm, No. of Columns (Display): 4, Col Widths (Display): 55 mm

MEIN EIGENHEIM
735218G74C-2360
Editorial: Zeppelinstr. 10, 73760 OSTFILDERN
Tel: 711 28040600 **Fax:** 711 280406070
Email: redaktion@jfink-verlag.de **Web site:** http://www.mein-eigenheim.de
Freq: Quarterly; **Annual Sub.:** EUR 3,80; **Circ:** 1,923,491
Editor: Stefan Kriz
Profile: Magazine focusing on home decoration and renovation.
Language(s): German
Readership: Aimed at people buying and converting their homes.
ADVERTISING RATES:
Full Page Mono .... EUR 26950
Full Page Colour .... EUR 40720
Mechanical Data: Type Area: 261 x 195 mm, No. of Columns (Display): 4, Col Widths (Display): 45 mm
Copy instructions: *Copy Date:* 42 days prior to publication
CONSUMER: WOMEN'S INTEREST CONSUMER MAGAZINES: Home & Family

MEIN ERLEBNIS
735223G74A-2080
Editorial: Plauener Str. 160, 13053 BERLIN
Tel: 30 9830850 **Fax:** 30 98308510
Email: redaktion@publicaverlag.de **Web site:** http://www.publicaverlag.de
Freq: 6 issues yearly; **Annual Sub.:** EUR 13,20; **Circ:** 64,900
Editor: Brigitte Bauermeister
Profile: Women report in the journal of formative experiences that have influenced her life. Of courageous decisions, bitter truths, dramatic developments, unexpected twists and devastating consequences. It's about disturbing and distressing events, unsparing confessions, tormenting guilt, bitter disappointments and sad memories. And also to fateful encounters that ended in love, suffering or one's life worth living made. In addition, see "mein erlebnis" different types of puzzles for a few relaxing minutes in between. The health tips and your own personal horoscope can help you through the day.
Language(s): German
Readership: Aimed at women.
ADVERTISING RATES:
Full Page Mono .... EUR 1963
Full Page Colour .... EUR 3323
Mechanical Data: Type Area: 250 x 188 mm, No. of Columns (Display): 4, Col Widths (Display): 45 mm
CONSUMER: WOMEN'S INTEREST CONSUMER MAGAZINES: Women's Interest

MEIN GEHEIMNIS
735231G74A-2100
Editorial: Sieker Landstr. 126/II, 22143 HAMBURG
Tel: 40 6739780 **Fax:** 40 67397821
Email: wmb@cpvkg.de **Web site:** http://www.conpart-verlag.de
Freq: 6 issues yearly; **Cover Price:** EUR 1,90; **Circ:** 94,515
Editor: Wolfgang M. Biehler
Profile: Women report in the journal of formative experiences that have influenced her life. Of courageous decisions, bitter truths, dramatic developments, unexpected twists and devastating consequences. It's about disturbing and distressing events, unsparing confessions, tormenting guilt, bitter disappointments and sad memories. And also to fateful encounters that ended in love, suffering or one's life worth living made. In addition, see "Meine Geheimnis" different types of puzzles for a few relaxing minutes in between. The health tips and your own personal horoscope can help you through the day.
Language(s): German
ADVERTISING RATES:
Full Page Mono .... EUR 3000
Full Page Colour .... EUR 3000
Mechanical Data: Type Area: 280 x 210 mm, No. of Columns (Display): 4, Col Widths (Display): 52 mm

MEIN HOLZHAUS
722961G4E-6907
Editorial: Höhenstr. 17, 70736 FELLBACH
Tel: 711 5206244 **Fax:** 711 5206300
Email: bauen@fachschriften.de **Web site:** http://www.bautipps.de
Freq: Annual; **Circ:** 60,000
Editor: Harald Fritsche; **Advertising Manager:** Barbara Hoof
Profile: Publication about environmentally-friendly building and renovation.
Language(s): German
Readership: Architects, planners, environmentalists, homeowners, and the building industry.
ADVERTISING RATES:
Full Page Colour .... EUR 5180
Mechanical Data: Type Area: 247 x 187 mm, No. of Columns (Display): 4, Col Widths (Display): 43 mm
Copy instructions: *Copy Date:* 54 days prior to publication
Supplement to: pro fertig haus
BUSINESS: ARCHITECTURE & BUILDING: Building

MEIN LEBEN
735244G74A-2140
Editorial: Karlsruher Str. 31, 76437 RASTATT
Tel: 7222 13205 **Fax:** 7222 13351
Email: erlebnispresse@vpm.de **Web site:** http://www.vpm.de
Freq: 6 issues yearly; **Cover Price:** EUR 1,85; **Circ:** 56,800
Editor: Dietlinde Besch; **Advertising Manager:** Rainer Groß
Profile: Women report in the journal of formative experiences that have influenced her life. Of courageous decisions, bitter truths, dramatic developments, unexpected twists and devastating consequences. It's about disturbing and distressing events, unsparing confessions, tormenting guilt, bitter disappointments and sad memories. And also to fateful encounters that ended in love, suffering or one's life worth living made. In addition, see "Mein Leben" different types of puzzles for a few relaxing minutes in between. The health tips and your own personal horoscope can help you through the day.
Language(s): German
ADVERTISING RATES:
Full Page Mono .... EUR 1575
Full Page Colour .... EUR 2648
Mechanical Data: No. of Columns (Display): 4, Col Widths (Display): 47 mm, Type Area: 263 x 196 mm

MEIN SCHÖNER GARTEN
735255G93-740
Editorial: Hubert-Burda-Platz 1, 77652 OFFENBURG
Tel: 781 8401 **Fax:** 781 842254
Email: garten@burda.com **Web site:** http://www.mein-schoener-garten.de
Freq: Monthly; **Annual Sub.:** EUR 36,00; **Circ:** 404,676
Editor: Andrea Kögel; **Advertising Manager:** Malte Schwerdtfeger
Profile: The trend is clear: more and more people are spending more and more time in the garden. The garden is by far the favorite leisure time activity, increasing trend. Like any other and can in your own garden of relaxation, creativity and joy to be found and experienced. mein schöner Garten offers a monthly information and inspiration for an active, diverse interests and high-income target group. With high editorial competence and solid expertise of over 35 years, mein schöner Garten a demanding advisor.
Language(s): German
Readership: Aimed at people interested in gardening as a hobby.
ADVERTISING RATES:
Full Page Mono .... EUR 22500
Full Page Colour .... EUR 22500
Mechanical Data: Type Area: 253 x 194 mm, No. of Columns (Display): 4, Col Widths (Display): 45 mm
Copy instructions: *Copy Date:* 42 days prior to publication
CONSUMER: GARDENING

MEIN SCHÖNER GARTEN ONLINE
1621683G93-1013
Editorial: Am Kestendamm 1, 77652 OFFENBURG
Tel: 781 8401 **Fax:** 781 842254
Email: andrea.koegel@burda.com **Web site:** http://www.mein-schoener-garten.de
Freq: Weekly; **Cover Price:** Paid; **Circ:** 1,429,348 Unique Users
Editor: Andrea Kögel
Profile: Ezine: Magazine containing botanical and practical information about gardening, plus tips on garden layout and maintenance. Facebook: http://www.facebook.com/pages/Mein-schoner-Garten/371273748250.
Language(s): German
CONSUMER: GARDENING

MEIN SCHÖNES ZU HAUSE[3]
723013G74C-360
Editorial: Ehrig-Hahn-Str. 4, 16356 AHRENSFELDE
Tel: 30 43738124 **Fax:** 30 43738111
Email: info@biz-verlag.de **Web site:** http://www.zuhause3.de
Freq: 6 issues yearly; **Annual Sub.:** EUR 24,00; **Circ:** 112,960
Editor: Doris Neumann; **Advertising Manager:** Petra Beick
Profile: Magazine about the interior of one family houses. Facebook: http://www.facebook.com/pagesMein-Schönes-Zuhause-3/131254646943861.
Language(s): German
ADVERTISING RATES:
Full Page Mono .... EUR 7581
Full Page Colour .... EUR 7581
Mechanical Data: No. of Columns (Display): 4, Col Widths (Display): 45 mm, Type Area: 267 x 186 mm
Copy instructions: *Copy Date:* 50 days prior to publication
CONSUMER: WOMEN'S INTEREST CONSUMER MAGAZINES: Home & Family

MEINBERLIN.DE
1704085G80-14747
Editorial: Askanischer Platz 3, 10963 BERLIN
Tel: 30 290211860 **Fax:** 30 2902199918690
Email: redaktion@meinberlin.net **Web site:** http://www.urban-media-daten.de
Freq: Daily; **Cover Price:** Paid; **Circ:** 1,885,144 Unique Users
Advertising Manager: Gerd Stodiek
Profile: Ezine: Magazine for city and region, concentrating on events, gastronomy, music, arts and events.
Language(s): German
CONSUMER: RURAL & REGIONAL INTEREST

MEINE FAMILIE & ICH
735209G74P-220
Editorial: Arabellastr. 23, 81925 MÜNCHEN
Tel: 89 92503228 **Fax:** 89 92503030
Email: gabriele.angermeier@burda.com **Web site:** http://www.lustaufgenuss.de
Freq: 13 issues yearly; **Annual Sub.:** EUR 35,10; **Circ:** 328,936
Editor: Birgitt Micha
Profile: meine Familie & ich excited as Europe's largest food and beverage magazine four weekly its readers! The name must: meine Familie & ich offers its readers, the family managers, not only for everyday use recipes and suggestions, but under the slogan "live better" even a whole fireworks of practical tips on health, beauty, wellness, travel, cars, Budget, Finance and law - all that whar active, standed with both feet in life women interested. Twitter: http://twitter.com/daskochrezept.
Language(s): German
Readership: Aimed at women with a home and family.
ADVERTISING RATES:
Full Page Mono .... EUR 20900
Full Page Colour .... EUR 20900
Mechanical Data: Type Area: 246 x 192 mm, No. of Columns (Display): 4, Col Widths (Display): 45 mm
CONSUMER: WOMEN'S INTEREST CONSUMER MAGAZINES: Food & Cookery

MEINE GESCHICHTE
735212G74A-2260
Editorial: Plauener Str. 160, 13053 BERLIN
Tel: 30 9830850 **Fax:** 30 98308510
Email: redaktion@publicaverlag.de **Web site:** http://www.publicaverlag.de
Freq: 6 issues yearly; **Cover Price:** EUR 1,85; **Circ:** 27,128
Editor: Brigitte Bauermeister
Profile: Women report in the journal of formative experiences that have influenced her life. Of courageous decisions, bitter truths, dramatic developments, unexpected twists and devastating consequences. It's about disturbing and distressing events, unsparing confessions, tormenting guilt, bitter disappointments and sad memories. And also to fateful encounters that ended in love, suffering or

one's life worth living made. In addition, see "Meine Geschichte" different types of puzzles for a few relaxing minutes in between. The health tips and your own personal horoscope can help you through the day.
Language(s): German
Readership: Aimed at women.
ADVERTISING RATES:
Full Page Mono .... EUR 2066
Full Page Colour .... EUR 3477
Mechanical Data: Type Area: 250 x 188 mm, No. of Columns (Display): 4, Col Widths (Display): 45 mm
CONSUMER: WOMEN'S INTEREST CONSUMER MAGAZINES: Women's Interest

MEINE KREUZTALER SENIORENPOST
733326G74N-420
Editorial: Martin-Luther-Str. 2, 57223 KREUZTAL
Tel: 2732 582470 **Fax:** 2732 582472
Email: seniorenberatung@diakoniestation-kreuztal.de
Web site: http://www.diakoniestation-kreuztal.de
Freq: Half-yearly; **Cover Price:** Free; **Circ:** 2,500
Editor: Daniela Sadelkow-Geßner; **Advertising Manager:** Daniela Sadelkow-Geßner
Profile: Magazine for the elderly.
Language(s): German
ADVERTISING RATES:
Full Page Mono .... EUR 250
Full Page Colour .... EUR 300
Mechanical Data: Type Area: 253 x 180 mm

MEINE LAND KÜCHE
2070233G74P-1383
Editorial: Hubert-Burda-Platz 1, 77652 OFFENBURG
Tel: 781 843713
Email: eva.biegert@burda.com **Web site:** http://www.daskochrezept.de/meine-landkueche
Freq: 6 issues yearly; **Cover Price:** EUR 3,80; **Circ:** 30,276
Editor: Eva Biegert; **Advertising Manager:** Konstanze Hacke
Profile: meine Land Küche is a magazine about people and their passion for culinary experiences: The magazine invites you to discover the culinary diversity of the German gourmet regions and experience on the road itself. It is aimed at an audience who cooks with passion and from seasonal and regional traditions can inspire like new ideas. meine Land Küche is the genuine and unadulterated: authentic stories, local products, local cuisine and table manners, classic recipes and products. meine Land Küche is a magazine in which people find themselves featuring lively reports on original products or original crafts people will strive to revive old with a passion to lift thought to be forgotten treasures and discover lovely new.
Language(s): German
ADVERTISING RATES:
Full Page Mono .... EUR 9900
Full Page Colour .... EUR 9900
Mechanical Data: Type Area: 250 x 188 mm, No. of Columns (Display): 4, Col Widths (Display): 44 mm
Copy instructions: *Copy Date:* 34 days prior to publication

MEINE MELODIE
735222G76D-3220
Editorial: Karlsruher Str. 31, 76437 RASTATT
Tel: 7222 130 **Fax:** 7222 13351
Email: info@meinemelodie.de **Web site:** http://www.vpm.de
Freq: Monthly; **Annual Sub.:** EUR 25,20; **Circ:** 44,951
Editor: Volker Kithil; **Advertising Manager:** Rainer Gross
Profile: The competent magazine for folk music and popular songs. Let the music play: meine Melodie is the platform for stars and fans of the musicians' world between the North Sea beach and the Alps. Whether Heino or Patrick Lindner, Marianne & Michael, and Wolfgang Petry, with exclusive interviews and the famous look behind the scenes meine Melodie every month brings the latest news about the men and women who give us joy on stage, but also about the manager and presenters who are really in the million-dollar music industry calling the shots. meine Melodie is also a springboard for young talents and stage for passionate collectors, forum for fan clubs and bulletin board for interactive readership community. And meine Melodie spoiled: Every month the most interesting celebrity puzzles with attractive prices and valuable travel prizes to the home of the Stars. Also: concert tickets, Star-souvenirs and lots of brand-new CDs. meine Melodie, the magazine, that music makes transparent and open up lucrative markets.
Language(s): German
ADVERTISING RATES:
Full Page Mono .... EUR 3630
Full Page Colour .... EUR 5100
Mechanical Data: Type Area: 263 x 196 mm, No. of Columns (Display): 4, Col Widths (Display): 47 mm
Copy instructions: *Copy Date:* 55 days prior to publication
CONSUMER: MUSIC & PERFORMING ARTS: Music

MEINE PAUSE
1774827G74A-3509
Editorial: Ruhrtalstr. 67, 45239 ESSEN
Tel: 201 24688277 **Fax:** 201 24688100
Email: b.heyer@stegenwaller.de **Web site:** http://www.stegenwaller.de
Freq: Monthly; **Annual Sub.:** EUR 19,00; **Circ:** 139,441
Editor: Brigitta Heyer; **Advertising Manager:** Kerstin Franz
Profile: Meine Pause offers its readers pastime at its best: A common thread is the most popular puzzle types pass through the magazine and provide for diverse entertainment. But Meine Pause is much more than just a classic puzzle book: A large service section with topics related to financial, legal, medical and nursing information needs of the predominantly female readership. Delicious cooking and baking recipes make you want to try again, moving destiny reports offer exciting reading material, trend-fashion, travel reports and decorating ideas to show the beautiful side of life.
Language(s): German
ADVERTISING RATES:
Full Page Mono .... EUR 4500
Full Page Colour .... EUR 4500
Mechanical Data: Type Area: 260 x 196 mm, No. of Columns (Display): 4
Copy instructions: *Copy Date:* 20 days prior to publication

MEINE SCHICKSALS STORY
1833051G74A-3586
Editorial: Bäckerstr. 14, 25709 MARNE
Tel: 4851 964766 **Fax:** 4851 964767
Email: wmb@cpvkg.de **Web site:** http://www.conpart-verlag.de
Freq: 6 issues yearly; **Cover Price:** EUR 1,95; **Circ:** 100,000
Editor: Wolfgang M. Biehler
Profile: Women report in the journal of formative experiences that have influenced her life. Of courageous decisions, bitter truths, dramatic developments, unexpected twists and devastating consequences. It's about disturbing and distressing events, unsparing confessions, tormenting guilt, bitter disappointments and sad memories. And also to fateful encounters that ended in love, suffering or one's life worth living made. In addition, see "Meine Schicksals Story" different types of puzzles for a few relaxing minutes in between. The health tips and your own personal horoscope can help you through the day.
Language(s): German
ADVERTISING RATES:
Full Page Mono .... EUR 3000
Full Page Colour .... EUR 3000
Mechanical Data: Type Area: 300 x 220 mm, No. of Columns (Display): 4, Col Widths (Display): 55 mm

MEINE WAHRHEIT
735228G74A-2340
Editorial: Mühlenstieg 16, 22041 HAMBURG
Tel: 40 6828950 **Fax:** 40 68289550
Email: info@kelter.de **Web site:** http://www.kelter.de
Freq: Monthly; **Cover Price:** EUR 1,80; **Circ:** 645,000
Editor: Barbara Klawun
Profile: Women report in the journal of formative experiences that have influenced her life. Of courageous decisions, bitter truths, dramatic developments, unexpected twists and devastating consequences. It's about disturbing and distressing events, unsparing confessions, tormenting guilt, bitter disappointments and sad memories. And also to fateful encounters that ended in love, suffering or one's life worth living made. In addition, see "Meine Wahrheit" different types of puzzles for a few relaxing minutes in between. The health tips and your own personal horoscope can help you through the day.
Language(s): German
ADVERTISING RATES:
Full Page Mono .... EUR 3000
Mechanical Data: Type Area: 250 x 190 mm

MEINERZHAGENER ZEITUNG
735224G67B-9420
Editorial: Hauptstr. 42, 58540 MEINERZHAGEN
Tel: 2354 9270 **Fax:** 2354 927126
Email: mz@come-on.de **Web site:** http://www.come-on.de
Freq: 312 issues yearly; **Circ:** 7,117
Advertising Manager: Guido Schröder
Profile: Daily newspaper with regional news and a local sports section. This Outlet offers RSS (Really Simple Syndication).
Language(s): German
ADVERTISING RATES:
SCC .... EUR 35,60
Mechanical Data: Type Area: 466 x 317 mm, No. of Columns (Display): 7, Col Widths (Display): 43 mm
Copy instructions: *Copy Date:* 1 day prior to publication
Supplement(s): prisma
REGIONAL DAILY & SUNDAY NEWSPAPERS: Regional Daily Newspapers

MEISSNER TAGEBLATT
735264G72-7504
Editorial: Am Sand 1c, 01665 DIERA-ZEHREN
Tel: 3525 718642 **Fax:** 3525 718611
Email: tageblatt@satztechnik-meissen.de
Freq: 26 issues yearly; **Cover Price:** Free; **Circ:** 40,200
Editor: Toralf Grau; **Advertising Manager:** Lutz Barth
Profile: Advertising journal (house-to-house) concentrating on local stories.
Language(s): German
ADVERTISING RATES:
Full Page Mono .... EUR 4353
Full Page Colour .... EUR 5883
Mechanical Data: Type Area: 490 x 320 mm, No. of Columns (Display): 7, Col Widths (Display): 44 mm
Copy instructions: *Copy Date:* 6 days prior to publication
LOCAL NEWSPAPERS

MEISSNER WOCHENKURIER
735265G72-7508
Editorial: Wettiner Platz 10, 01067 DRESDEN
Tel: 351 491760 **Fax:** 351 4917674
Email: wochenkurier-dresden@dwk-verlag.de **Web site:** http://www.wochenkurier.info
Freq: Weekly; **Cover Price:** Free; **Circ:** 32,534
Editor: Regine Eberlein; **Advertising Manager:** Andreas Schönherr
Profile: Advertising journal (house-to-house) concentrating on local stories.
Language(s): German
ADVERTISING RATES:
Full Page Mono .... EUR 2860
Full Page Colour .... EUR 4004
Mechanical Data: Type Area: 430 x 290 mm, No. of Columns (Display): 7, Col Widths (Display): 38 mm
Copy instructions: *Copy Date:* 5 days prior to publication
LOCAL NEWSPAPERS

MELLER KREISBLATT
735274G67B-9460
Editorial: Breiter Gang 10, 49074 OSNABRÜCK
Tel: 541 3100 **Fax:** 541 310485
Email: redaktion@noz.de **Web site:** http://www.noz.de
Freq: 312 issues yearly; **Circ:** 9,139
Profile: Daily newspaper with regional news and a local sports section. Twitter: http://twitter.com/noz_de This Outlet offers RSS (Really Simple Syndication).
Language(s): German
ADVERTISING RATES:
SCC .... EUR 38,30
Mechanical Data: Type Area: 487 x 318 mm, No. of Columns (Display): 7, Col Widths (Display): 43 mm
Copy instructions: *Copy Date:* 2 days prior to publication
Supplement(s): Berufswahl; Immo-Welt; Kfz-Welt; melle-city.de; TheaterZeitung; Toaster
REGIONAL DAILY & SUNDAY NEWSPAPERS: Regional Daily Newspapers

MELLIAND TEXTILBERICHTE
735278G47A-820
Editorial: Mainzer Landstr. 251, 60326 FRANKFURT
Tel: 69 75951393 **Fax:** 69 75951390
Email: claudia.vanbonn@dfv.de **Web site:** http://www.melliand.de
Freq: Quarterly; **Annual Sub.:** EUR 172,80; **Circ:** 4,026
Editor: Claudia van Bonn; **Advertising Manager:** Dagmar Henning
Profile: European journal focusing on spinning, weaving, knitting, textile dyeing and finishing, ecology, textile testing, quality management and mill engineering. Also includes textile economic news and details of textile associations.
Language(s): English; German
Readership: Aimed at professionals in the textile industry.
ADVERTISING RATES:
Full Page Mono .... EUR 3415
Full Page Colour .... EUR 4740
Mechanical Data: Type Area: 256 x 185 mm, No. of Columns (Display): 3, Col Widths (Display): 57 mm
Copy instructions: *Copy Date:* 21 days prior to publication
Official Journal of: Organ d. Internat. Föderation v. Wirkerei- u. Strickereifachleuten Sektion Deutschland, d. Vereins dt. Textilveredelungsfachleute e.V. u. d. Vereins Österr. Textilchemiker u. Coloristen
Supplement(s): melliand Band- und Flechtindustrie
BUSINESS: CLOTHING & TEXTILES

MELSUNGER ALLGEMEINE
730354G67B-7160
Editorial: Frankfurter Str. 168, 34121 KASSEL
Tel: 561 20300 **Fax:** 561 2032406
Email: info@hna.de **Web site:** http://www.hna.de
Freq: 312 issues yearly; **Circ:** 8,832
Advertising Manager: Andrea Schaller-Öller
Profile: Regional daily newspaper with news on politics, economy, culture, sports, travel, technology, etc. The GMelsunger Allgemeine a local edition of theHNA Hessische/Niedersächsische Allgemeine. Twitter: http://twitter.com/hna_online This Outlet offers RSS (Really Simple Syndication).
Language(s): German
ADVERTISING RATES:
SCC .... EUR 36,80
Mechanical Data: Type Area: 430 x 285 mm, No. of Columns (Display): 6, Col Widths (Display): 45 mm
Copy instructions: *Copy Date:* 2 days prior to publication
REGIONAL DAILY & SUNDAY NEWSPAPERS: Regional Daily Newspapers

MEMMINGER KURIER
735287G72-7516
Editorial: Glendalestr. 8, 87700 MEMMINGEN
Tel: 8331 856118 **Fax:** 8331 856161
Email: redaktion@kurierverlag.de **Web site:** http://www.kurierverlag.de
Freq: Weekly; **Cover Price:** Free; **Circ:** 63,721
Editor: Eric Schneider
Profile: Advertising journal (house-to-house) concentrating on local stories.
Language(s): German
ADVERTISING RATES:
Full Page Mono .... EUR 6006
Full Page Colour .... EUR 7808
Mechanical Data: Type Area: 474 x 324 mm, No. of Columns (Display): 7, Col Widths (Display): 45 mm
Copy instructions: *Copy Date:* 2 days prior to publication
LOCAL NEWSPAPERS

MEMMINGER ZEITUNG
735288G67B-9480
Editorial: Heisinger Str. 14, 87437 KEMPTEN
Tel: 831 206439 **Fax:** 831 206123
Email: redaktion@azv.de **Web site:** http://www.all-in.de
Freq: 312 issues yearly; **Circ:** 20,867
Advertising Manager: Reinhard Melder
Profile: Regional daily newspaper with news on politics, economy, culture, sports, travel, technology, etc. Twitter: http://twitter.com/allgaeu This Outlet offers RSS (Really Simple Syndication).
Language(s): German
ADVERTISING RATES:
SCC .... EUR 62,00
Mechanical Data: Type Area: 480 x 327 mm, No. of Columns (Display): 7, Col Widths (Display): 45 mm
Copy instructions: *Copy Date:* 2 days prior to publication
Supplement(s): Allgäu-Dribbler; allgäu weit; allgäu weit Allgäuer Kultursommer; allgäu weit Gesundheit; allgäu weit Sommer; allgäu weit Winter; Golfregion Allgäu; rtv; Die Schwäbische Bäderstrasse Kraft-Quellen
REGIONAL DAILY & SUNDAY NEWSPAPERS: Regional Daily Newspapers

MEN'S HEALTH
735317G86C-140
Editorial: Leverkusenstr. 54, 22761 HAMBURG
Tel: 40 853303920 **Fax:** 40 853303933
Email: wmelcher@menshealth.de **Web site:** http://www.menshealth.de
Freq: Monthly; **Annual Sub.:** EUR 41,00; **Circ:** 250,221
Editor: Wolfgang Melcher; **Advertising Manager:** Sascha Gröschel
Profile: Men's Health - The comprehensive consultant for the modern man. Men think pragmatically - that's why Men's Health provides a monthly practical utility value on sport and fitness, partnership and sex, health and nutrition, fashion, style and occupation. Men's Health is written interesting and entertaining and helps its readers in their lives more pleasant, successful and confident. Men's Health met his readers as equals. It's good friend and an indispensable guide in one. Facebook: http://www.facebook.com/MensHealth.de Twitter: http://twitter.com/menshealth_de This Outlet offers RSS (Really Simple Syndication).
Language(s): German
Readership: Aimed at men.
ADVERTISING RATES:
Full Page Mono .... EUR 21500
Full Page Colour .... EUR 21500
Mechanical Data: Type Area: 255 x 189 mm
Copy instructions: *Copy Date:* 30 days prior to publication
CONSUMER: ADULT & GAY MAGAZINES: Men's Lifestyle Magazines

MEN'S HEALTH BEST FASHION
735318G86C-160
Editorial: Leverkusenstr. 54, 22761 HAMBURG
Tel: 40 853303920 **Fax:** 40 853303933
Email: wmelcher@menshealth.de **Web site:** http://www.bestfashion.de
Freq: Half-yearly; **Cover Price:** EUR 6,00; **Circ:** 60,000
Editor: Wolfgang Melcher; **Advertising Manager:** Sascha Gröschel
Profile: Men's Health Best Fashion - the Fashion Special. Men's Health Best Fashion is the special issue of Men's Health on fashion and appearance. With its vast photo galleries and comprehensive style and purchase deliberations, it was developed in view of the strong interest of the fashion Men's Health readers. Men's Health Best Fashion is for fashion greatly interested men who want to learn twice a year on the latest trends of designers from around the world. Topics: New Outfits: Get the latest trends from the fashion capitals of the world. Fashion Shopper: The Shopping Guide: Where to find really good fashion at a very low price? Body Fashion: Men's Health Best Fashion reports news and trends in body care. Fashion Report: Detailed background reports on all that interested about man fashion. Shoes: All about the matching shoes to the current outfit. Trends: Where is the fashion? New developments on the track. Fashion Know how: More knowledge about top designers, good style and the correct use of fashion. Watch: New contemporaries and old classics. Everything revolves around the Clock.
Language(s): German
ADVERTISING RATES:
Full Page Mono .... EUR 9500
Full Page Colour .... EUR 9500
Mechanical Data: Type Area: 268 x 195 mm

MENSCH & BÜRO
735308G54B-4
Editorial: Dischingerstr. 8, 69123 HEIDELBERG
Tel: 6221 644641 **Fax:** 6221 644640
Email: redaktion@menschundbuero.de **Web site:** http://www.office-work.net
Freq: 6 issues yearly; **Annual Sub.:** EUR 62,10; **Circ:** 16,432
Editor: David Wiechmann; **Advertising Manager:** Cornelia Huth-Neumann

Profile: Magazine containing information about providing a safe, comfortable and profitable office working environment.
Language(s): German
ADVERTISING RATES:
Full Page Mono .... EUR 4200
Full Page Colour .... EUR 6090
Mechanical Data: Type Area: 270 x 188 mm, No. of Columns (Display): 4, Col Widths (Display): 44 mm
BUSINESS: SAFETY & SECURITY: Safety

MENSCH & NATUR 1912300G74A-3681
Editorial: Wendenstr. 1a, 20097 HAMBURG
Tel: 40 5302405555 **Fax:** 40 5302402401
Email: info@mensch-natur-heute.de **Web site:** http://www.mensch-natur-heute.de
Freq: Quarterly; **Annual Sub.:** EUR 15,00; **Circ:** 35,000
Editor: Maria Köllner
Profile: The magazine reports on the health, nutrition, exercise, partnership, housing, environment and nature and is aimed at readers aged 40 and over.
Language(s): German
ADVERTISING RATES:
Full Page Mono .... EUR 3600
Full Page Colour .... EUR 3600
Mechanical Data: Type Area: 280 x 210 mm, No. of Columns (Display): 3, Col Widths (Display): 70 mm

MENSHEALTH.DE 1697666G86C-229
Editorial: Leverkusenstr. 54, 22761 HAMBURG
Tel: 40 853303922 **Fax:** 40 853303933
Email: dicheln@menshealth.de **Web site:** http://www.menshealth.de
Freq: Daily; **Cover Price:** Paid; **Circ:** 1,346,204 Unique Users
Editor: Detlef Icheln
Profile: The Internet portal supports men in the effort, your own well-being, enjoyment of life and personal sovereignty to increase. With information, suggestions, ideas and new perspectives as an integrated offering. Facebook: http://www.facebook.com/MensHealth.de Twitter: http://twitter.com/menshealth_de This Outlet offers RSS (Really Simple Syndication).
Language(s): German
CONSUMER: ADULT & GAY MAGAZINES: Men's Lifestyle Magazines

MEO 735320G63-580
Editorial: Am Waldthausenpark 2, 45127 ESSEN
Tel: 201 1892270 **Fax:** 201 1892173
Email: meo@essen.ihk.de **Web site:** http://www.essen.ihk24.de
Freq: 11 issues yearly; Free to qualifying individuals
Annual Sub.: EUR 25,00; **Circ:** 44,896
Editor: Gerald Püchel; **Advertising Manager:** Herbert Eick
Profile: meo the official journal of Commerce and Industry Chamber of Essen, Mulheim an der Ruhr, Oberhausen in Essen. The official notice of institution is designed as a regional business magazine and contains valuable information and tips, and news and reports, especially from medium-sized enterprises. meo addressed to all commercial enterprises of the District of the Chamber of Commerce (with the exception of the traditional crafts) and also by Subscription to establishments in neighboring regions.
Language(s): German
ADVERTISING RATES:
Full Page Mono .... EUR 2840
Full Page Colour .... EUR 3400
Mechanical Data: Type Area: 255 x 185 mm, No. of Columns (Display): 4, Col Widths (Display): 44 mm
Copy instructions: *Copy Date:* 27 days prior to publication
BUSINESS: REGIONAL BUSINESS

MEP MARKETING EVENT PRAXIS 735322G2A-3320
Editorial: Max-Planck-Str. 2, 64859 EPPERTSHAUSEN **Tel:** 6071 39410
Fax: 6071 344111
Email: mep@verlagshaus-gruber.de **Web site:** http://www.mep-online.de
Freq: 6 issues yearly; **Annual Sub.:** EUR 39,00; **Circ:** 11,500
Editor: Roland Gruber
Profile: Journal covering information on sales, merchandising and presentation techniques of event products.
Language(s): German
ADVERTISING RATES:
Full Page Mono .... EUR 1860
Full Page Colour .... EUR 2560
Mechanical Data: Type Area: 267 x 190 mm, No. of Columns (Display): 4, Col Widths (Display): 43 mm
BUSINESS: COMMUNICATIONS, ADVERTISING & MARKETING

MEPPENER TAGESPOST 735323G67B-9520
Editorial: Breiter Gang 10, 49074 OSNABRÜCK
Tel: 541 3100 **Fax:** 541 310485
Email: redaktion@noz.de **Web site:** http://www.n-oz.de
Freq: 312 issues yearly; **Circ:** 20,546
Profile: Daily newspaper with regional news and a local sports section.
Language(s): German
ADVERTISING RATES:
SCC .... EUR 49,50
Mechanical Data: Type Area: 487 x 318 mm, No. of Columns (Display): 7, Col Widths (Display): 43 mm
Copy instructions: *Copy Date:* 2 days prior to publication
Supplement(s): Immo-Welt; Kfz-Welt
REGIONAL DAILY & SUNDAY NEWSPAPERS: Regional Daily Newspapers

MERCEDES TUNER 1739558G77A-2766
Editorial: Paffrather Str. 80, 51465 BERGISCH GLADBACH **Tel:** 2202 41857 **Fax:** 2202 41877
Email: info@eurotuner.de **Web site:** http://www.tuning2go.de
Freq: 6 issues yearly; **Annual Sub.:** EUR 21,00; **Circ:** 21,900
Editor: Olivier Fourcade; **Advertising Manager:** Olivier Fourcade
Profile: Mercedes tuning magazine with news, show dates and information provider.
Language(s): German
ADVERTISING RATES:
Full Page Mono .... EUR 4100
Full Page Colour .... EUR 4990
Mechanical Data: Type Area: 267 x 181 mm, No. of Columns (Display): 4, Col Widths (Display): 42 mm
Copy instructions: *Copy Date:* 28 days prior to publication

MERCEDES-BENZ CLASSIC 1606202G77A-2552
Editorial: HPC E 402, 70546 STUTTGART
Tel: 711 1755285 **Fax:** 711 1754669
Email: ulrich.groening@daimler.com
Freq: 3 issues yearly; **Annual Sub.:** EUR 19,80; **Circ:** 75,000
Editor: Peter Michaely; **Advertising Manager:** Alexandra Velte
Profile: Mercedes-Benz Classic is the most extraordinary classic cars special magazine on the German market: Unlike all other established classic car magazines, Mercedes-Benz Classic deals only with the vehicles of one brand. Their illustrious history makes the mix of topics of this special-interest magazine as varied and exciting as the passion of many people who spend their precious leisure time with classic cars. Mercedes-Benz Classic presents milestones of the past and conveys the enthusiasm of the present. Presented are passionate collectors and their motorized treasures as well as pioneers of the automotive industry. Reports from the vintage and classic car scene and the special charisma of the classics are documented in impressive photo series. In addition, the Classic Car magazine reports on unusual travel tours and of course offers service stories about all issues of technology and restoration.
Language(s): German
ADVERTISING RATES:
Full Page Mono .... EUR 7800
Full Page Colour .... EUR 7800
Mechanical Data: Type Area: 244 x 181 mm
Copy instructions: *Copy Date:* 35 days prior to publication

MERCEDES-BENZ OMNIBUS 1633972G49A-2358
Editorial: Aschauer Str. 30, 81549 MÜNCHEN
Tel: 89 2030432570 **Fax:** 89 20304332570
Email: thomas.maier@springer.com **Web site:** http://www.springer-transport-media.de
Freq: Quarterly; **Cover Price:** Free; **Circ:** 48,500
Editor: Thomas Maier
Profile: Magazine on Mercedes-Benz coaches.
Language(s): German

MERCEDES-BENZ OMNIBUS 1633973G49A-2359
Editorial: Aschauer Str. 30, 81549 MÜNCHEN
Tel: 89 2030432570 **Fax:** 89 20304332570
Email: thomas.maier@springer.com **Web site:** http://www.springer-transport-media.de
Freq: Quarterly; **Cover Price:** Free; **Circ:** 4,500
Editor: Thomas Maier
Profile: Magazine about Mercedes-Benz coaches.
Language(s): English

MERCEDES-BENZ OMNIBUS 1633974G49A-2360
Editorial: Aschauer Str. 30, 81549 MÜNCHEN
Tel: 89 2030432570 **Fax:** 89 20304332570
Email: thomas.maier@springer.com **Web site:** http://www.springer-transport-media.de
Freq: Quarterly; **Cover Price:** Free; **Circ:** 3,500
Editor: Thomas Maier
Profile: Magazine about Mercedes-Benz coaches.
Language(s): French

MERCEDES-BENZ OMNIBUS 1633975G49A-2361
Editorial: Aschauer Str. 30, 81549 MÜNCHEN
Tel: 89 2030432570 **Fax:** 89 20304332570
Email: thomas.maier@springer.com **Web site:** http://www.springer-transport-media.de
Freq: Quarterly; **Cover Price:** Free; **Circ:** 6,000
Editor: Thomas Maier
Profile: Magazine about Mercedes-Benz coaches.
Language(s): Italian

MERCEDES-BENZ OMNIBUS 1633976G49A-2362
Editorial: Aschauer Str. 30, 81549 MÜNCHEN
Tel: 89 2030432570 **Fax:** 89 20304332570
Email: thomas.maier@springer.com **Web site:** http://www.springer-transport-media.de
Freq: Quarterly; **Cover Price:** Free; **Circ:** 1,500
Editor: Thomas Maier
Profile: Magazine about Mercedes-Benz coaches.
Language(s): Dutch

MERCEDES-BENZ OMNIBUS 1633977G49A-2363
Editorial: Aschauer Str. 30, 81549 MÜNCHEN
Tel: 89 2030432570 **Fax:** 89 20304332570
Email: thomas.maier@springer.com **Web site:** http://www.springer-transport-media.de
Freq: Quarterly; **Cover Price:** Free; **Circ:** 4,000
Editor: Thomas Maier
Profile: Magazine about Mercedes-Benz coaches.
Language(s): Spanish

MERCEDES-BENZ ROUTE 765206G49A-2310
Editorial: Völckersstr. 40, 22765 HAMBURG
Tel: 40 36967623 **Fax:** 40 36967639
Email: route@prhamburg.com **Web site:** http://www.prhamburg.com
Freq: 3 issues yearly; **Cover Price:** Free; **Circ:** 110,000
Editor: Lars Rauscher
Profile: Magazine for truckers.
Language(s): German
Mechanical Data: Type Area: 250 x 189 mm

MERCEDES-BENZ ROUTE 1860143G49A-2452
Editorial: Völckersstr. 40, 22765 HAMBURG
Tel: 40 3696760 **Fax:** 40 36967639
Email: route@prhamburg.com **Web site:** http://www.prhamburg.com
Freq: 3 issues yearly; **Cover Price:** Free; **Circ:** 18,000
Editor: Lars Rauscher
Profile: Magazine for truckers.
Language(s): Dutch
Mechanical Data: Type Area: 250 x 189 mm

MERCEDES-BENZ TRANSPORT 735327G49A-960
Editorial: Postcode Z602, 70546 STUTTGART
Tel: 711 1790468 **Fax:** 711 1790944
Email: monika.mezger@daimler.com **Web site:** http://www.mercedes-benz.com/emagazine
Freq: 3 issues yearly; **Annual Sub.:** EUR 18,00; **Circ:** 216,357
Editor: Lars Kruse
Profile: Company publication published by Daimler AG.
Language(s): German
ADVERTISING RATES:
Full Page Mono .... EUR 2539
Full Page Colour .... EUR 3893
Mechanical Data: Type Area: 255 x 193 mm
Copy instructions: *Copy Date:* 50 days prior to publication
BUSINESS: TRANSPORT

MERCEDESMAGAZIN 735326G94H-8580
Editorial: Tiefenklinger Weg 4, 69488 BIRKENAU
Tel: 6201 33841 **Fax:** 6201 393841
Email: jochen.kruse@presse-partner.com **Web site:** http://www.presse-partner.com
Freq: Quarterly; **Annual Sub.:** EUR 22,00; **Circ:** 633,111
Editor: Jochen Kruse
Profile: International magazine for owners of Mercedes cars.
Language(s): German
ADVERTISING RATES:
Full Page Mono .... EUR 20700
Full Page Colour .... EUR 20700
Mechanical Data: No. of Columns (Display): 3, Col Widths (Display): 56 mm, Type Area: 247 x 176 mm
Copy instructions: *Copy Date:* 45 days prior to publication
CONSUMER: OTHER CLASSIFICATIONS: Customer Magazines

MERIAN 735340G89A-11533
Editorial: Poßmoorweg 2, 22301 HAMBURG
Tel: 40 27172600 **Fax:** 40 27172628
Email: redaktion@merian.de **Web site:** http://www.merian.de
Freq: Monthly; **Annual Sub.:** EUR 81,50; **Circ:** 54,236
Editor: Andreas Hallaschka
Profile: Merian is synonymous for travel and culture at the highest level. Whether New York, Black Forest, Crete and Thailand every month MERIAN offers high performance in text and image and shows the diversity and uniqueness of a country, city or a region. Exclusively researched tips and detailed maps provide orientation and also lead to experiences off the beaten tourist paths. Text, photography, cartography and service section are tailored to a readership with the highest standards, not only in terms of travel. Facebook: http://www.facebook.com/merian.de/.
Language(s): German
Readership: Aimed at tourists.
ADVERTISING RATES:
Full Page Mono .... EUR 14200
Full Page Colour .... EUR 14200
Mechanical Data: Type Area: 247 x 170 mm, No. of Columns (Display): 3, Col Widths (Display): 56 mm
Copy instructions: *Copy Date:* 38 days prior to publication
CONSUMER: HOLIDAYS & TRAVEL: Travel

MERKUR-ONLINE.DE 1621686G67B-16597
Editorial: Paul-Heyse-Str. 2, 80336 MÜNCHEN
Tel: 89 5306188 **Fax:** 89 53068418
Email: markus.knall@merkur-online.de **Web site:** http://www.merkur-online.de
Freq: Daily; **Cover Price:** Paid; **Circ:** 3,249,369 Unique Users
Editor: Markus Knall; **Advertising Manager:** Mayumi Leitgeb
Profile: Ezine: Regional news and service portal for Munich and Upper Bavaria with news on politics, economy, culture, sports, travel, technology, etc. Facebook: http://www.facebook.com/merkuronline This Outlet offers RSS (Really Simple Syndication).
Language(s): German
REGIONAL DAILY & SUNDAY NEWSPAPERS: Regional Daily Newspapers

DER MERKURSTAB 735349G56A-6940
Editorial: Kladower Damm 221, 14089 BERLIN
Tel: 30 36501463 **Fax:** 30 36803891
Email: redaktion@merkurstab.de **Web site:** http://www.merkurstab.de
Freq: 6 issues yearly; **Annual Sub.:** EUR 80,00; **Circ:** 2,500
Profile: Magazine with illustrations of basic Anthroposophical medicine, medical-experimental work, Goethean nature and substance of observations, biographical studies, socio-hygienic articles, colloquia and therapeutic reports.
Language(s): German
ADVERTISING RATES:
Full Page Mono .... EUR 900
Full Page Colour .... EUR 1700
Mechanical Data: Type Area: 248 x 175 mm
Copy instructions: *Copy Date:* 28 days prior to publication

MESSAGE 735355G2B-28
Editorial: Menckestr. 27, 04155 LEIPZIG
Tel: 341 20040311 **Fax:** 341 20040321
Email: redaktion@message-online.com **Web site:** http://www.message-online.com
Freq: Quarterly; **Annual Sub.:** EUR 48,00; **Circ:** 3,000
Editor: Michael Haller
Profile: International magazine containing articles about journalism.
Language(s): German
Readership: Aimed at journalists and correspondents.
ADVERTISING RATES:
Full Page Colour .... EUR 1600
Mechanical Data: Type Area: 280 x 210 mm
Copy instructions: *Copy Date:* 15 days prior to publication
BUSINESS: COMMUNICATIONS, ADVERTISING & MARKETING: Press

DIE MESSEWIRTSCHAFTIBILANZ 735371G14A-4720
Editorial: Littenstr. 9, 10179 BERLIN
Tel: 30 24000140 **Fax:** 30 24000340
Email: h.koetter@auma.de **Web site:** http://www.auma.de
Freq: Annual; **Cover Price:** Free; **Circ:** 5,000
Editor: Harald Kötter
Profile: Account of German Trade Fair Committee.
Language(s): German

MESSTEC DRIVES AUTOMATION 735373G5A-6
Editorial: Rößlerstr. 90, 64293 DARMSTADT
Tel: 6151 8090162 **Fax:** 6151 8090183
Email: peter.ebert@wiley.com **Web site:** http://www.messtec.de
Freq: 7 issues yearly; **Annual Sub.:** EUR 113,00; **Circ:** 24,293
Editor: Peter Ebert; **Advertising Manager:** Oliver Scheel
Profile: The journal messtec drives Automation is 2010 from the merger of the two trade Mess Tec & Automation and drives & motion emerged. How to measure the subtitle "The magazine for measure I control I power I review" describes are in this title of the key aspects of automation technique combines in a single journal. The section provides an overview of automation products and solutions from the field of industrial communication including the corresponding peripherals (switchgear, power distribution, Wireless, power supply ...), connection equipment, industrial PCs, and Safety & Security. The category Drives & Motion has the issues of mechanical and electric drive technology and control technology and motion control to content and appropriate peripheral, which is for moving and driving of machinery and equipment necessary. The sensor Section deals with all types of sensors and components for process manufacturing,

and OEMs. Under the heading Inspection, the different facets of industrial image processing, cameras, materials testing and optables and dimensional measuring instruments together. In the section Test & Measurement, methods and equipment the signal detection and treatment analysis.
Language(s): German
Readership: Read by people in the manufacturing industry.
ADVERTISING RATES:
Full Page Mono .... EUR 4500
Full Page Colour .... EUR 5980
Mechanical Data: Type Area: 260 x 185 mm, No. of Columns (Display): 4, Col Widths (Display): 43 mm
BUSINESS: COMPUTERS & AUTOMATION: Automation & Instrumentation

METAL HAMMER 729752G76D-1840
Editorial: Mehringdamm 33, 10961 BERLIN
Tel: 30 3088188129 **Fax:** 30 3088188221
Email: redaktion@metal-hammer.de **Web site:** http://www.metal-hammer.de
Freq: Monthly; **Annual Sub.:** EUR 53,88; **Circ:** 42,077
Editor: Christof Leim; **Advertising Manager:** Oliver Horn
Profile: METAL HAMMER - the indispensable magazine for rock and metal fans. With a sense of new musical trends on the one hand and a sense of traditional values on the other hand, has developed the magazine since 1984, the most important institution for the fans of metal and rock music. The stylistic diversity, the dense network of information and the service transports the reader an unparalleled lifestyle. A life that never loses the editors in their intermediary role between the scene and artists from the eyes. This base near METAL HAMMER makes an indispensable member of a subculture. Facebook: http://www.facebook.com/MaximumMetalHammer Twitter: http://twitter.com/metalhammer_de.
Language(s): German
ADVERTISING RATES:
Full Page Mono .... EUR 6500
Full Page Colour .... EUR 6500
Mechanical Data: Type Area: 267 x 210 mm, No. of Columns (Display): 4, Col Widths (Display): 49 mm
Copy instructions: *Copy Date:* 30 days prior to publication
CONSUMER: MUSIC & PERFORMING ARTS: Music

METALL 735375G27-1740
Editorial: Hans-Böckler-Allee 9, 30173 HANNOVER
Tel: 511 73040 **Fax:** 511 7304157
Email: kammer@t-online.de **Web site:** http://www.metall-web.de
Freq: 10 issues yearly; **Annual Sub.:** EUR 215,00; **Circ:** 6,762
Editor: Catrin Kammer; **Advertising Manager:** Dennis Roß
Profile: International magazine covering all aspects of the non-ferrous metal industry.
Language(s): English; German
Readership: Aimed at people in the metal industry.
ADVERTISING RATES:
Full Page Mono .... EUR 2740
Full Page Colour .... EUR 3820
Mechanical Data: Type Area: 272 x 188 mm
Copy instructions: *Copy Date:* 14 days prior to publication
BUSINESS: METAL, IRON & STEEL

METALLBAU 735379G27-195
Editorial: Kirchplatz 8, 82538 GERETSRIED
Tel: 8171 911870 **Fax:** 8171 60974
Email: elgass@pse-redaktion.de **Web site:** http://www.metallbau-online.info
Freq: 11 issues yearly; **Annual Sub.:** EUR 103,20; **Circ:** 21,404
Editor: Stefan Elgaß; **Advertising Manager:** Axel Gase-Jochens
Profile: Metal construction-entrepreneurs and decision makers in metal craft have to get along in a broad range of tasks and make accurate, informed decisions. The trade journal metallbau is the groundbreaking communication tool for the structural metal construction. Current practices and actionable information provides the reader with the necessary competitive advantage. Editorial content constantly informed about technical developments in the areas of process and systems engineering, management and organization, safety and environmental protection, education and training. Technically oriented summaries explain new machines, processes and products intended for use in office or workshop. Essential part of the editorial planning, the practical issues treatment: experience and reviews from metal construction companies are a priority. Detailed market overviews provide an important aid in the capital equipment procurement or the selection of suppliers and service companies in the metal industry.
Language(s): German
Readership: Aimed at people working in the metal industry.
ADVERTISING RATES:
Full Page Mono .... EUR 4905
Full Page Colour .... EUR 5775
Mechanical Data: Type Area: 268 x 185 mm, No. of Columns (Display): 4, Col Widths (Display): 43 mm
Copy instructions: *Copy Date:* 15 days prior to publication
BUSINESS: METAL, IRON & STEEL

METALLOBERFLÄCHE MO 1898933G27-3108
Editorial: Oskar-Maria-Graf-Ring 23, 81737 MÜNCHEN **Tel:** 89 67369711 **Fax:** 89 67369761
Email: redaktion@metalloberfläche.de **Web site:** http://www.metalloberflaeche.de
Freq: Annual; **Circ:** 10,050
Editor: Lothar Zobel; **Advertising Manager:** Stefan Hrubesch
Profile: Journal focusing on metal and polymer surfacing techniques.
Language(s): German
ADVERTISING RATES:
Full Page Mono .... EUR 2906
Full Page Colour .... EUR 4650
Mechanical Data: Type Area: 250 x 181 mm, No. of Columns (Display): 3, Col Widths (Display): 55 mm
Copy instructions: *Copy Date:* 21 days prior to publication

METALLZEITUNG 730809G27-1060
Editorial: Wilhelm-Leuschner-Str. 79, 60329 FRANKFURT **Tel:** 800 4403825 **Fax:** 69 66932002
Email: metallzeitung@igmetall.de **Web site:** http://www.igmetall.de
Freq: Monthly; **Circ:** 2,209,752
Editor: Susanne Rohmund
Profile: Magazine for members of the German Industrial Union for Metal. Facebook: http://de-de.facebook.com/pages/IG-Metall/249296718436 Twitter: http://twitter.com/igmetall.
Language(s): German
ADVERTISING RATES:
Full Page Colour .... EUR 29270
Mechanical Data: No. of Columns (Display): 4, Col Widths (Display): 43 mm, Type Area: 268 x 197 mm
Copy instructions: *Copy Date:* 35 days prior to publication
BUSINESS: METAL, IRON & STEEL

METHODS 735389G56R-100
Editorial: Hölderlinstr. 3, 70174 STUTTGART
Tel: 711 2298737 **Fax:** 711 2298765
Email: peter.henning@schattauer.de **Web site:** http://www.methods-online.de
Freq: 6 issues yearly; **Annual Sub.:** EUR 228,00; **Circ:** 700
Editor: Peter Henning; **Advertising Manager:** Laura Lenz
Profile: Good medicine and good healthcare demand good information. Methods stresses the basic methodology and scientific fundamentals of processing data, information and knowledge in medicine and health care. It publishes original papers, reviews, reports, opinion papers, and editorials in medical informatics/health informatics and related disciplines such as medical biometry. It publishes papers in the whole range of processing data, information and knowledge in medicine and health care, including research in traditional as well as in new areas of this expanding field.
Language(s): English
ADVERTISING RATES:
Full Page Mono .... EUR 1090
Full Page Colour .... EUR 2230
Mechanical Data: Type Area: 243 x 179 mm, No. of Columns (Display): 3, Col Widths (Display): 57 mm
Copy instructions: *Copy Date:* 40 days prior to publication
Official Journal of: Organ d. European Federation of Medical Informatics u. Internat. Medical Informatics Association
BUSINESS: HEALTH & MEDICAL: Health Medical Related

DER METZGERMEISTER 735399G22D-200
Editorial: Lazarettstr. 4, 80636 MÜNCHEN
Tel: 89 12607228 **Fax:** 89 12607330
Email: fassmann@pflaum.de **Web site:** http://www.metzgermeister.de
Freq: Weekly; **Annual Sub.:** EUR 202,80; **Circ:** 6,226
Editor: Gerhard Fassmann; **Advertising Manager:** Michael Dietl
Profile: Official journal of the Society of Bavarian Butchers.
Language(s): German
ADVERTISING RATES:
Full Page Mono .... EUR 2190
Full Page Colour .... EUR 2970
Mechanical Data: Type Area: 270 x 187 mm, No. of Columns (Display): 4, Col Widths (Display): 43 mm
Copy instructions: *Copy Date:* 8 days prior to publication
Official Journal of: Organ d. Fleischerverb. Bayern u. d. Pfälz. Fleischerverb.
BUSINESS: FOOD: Meat Trade

METZINGER-URACHER GENERAL-ANZEIGER 735401G67B-9540
Editorial: Burgstr. 1, 72764 REUTLINGEN
Tel: 7121 3020 **Fax:** 7121 302677
Email: redaktion@gea.de **Web site:** http://www.gea.de
Freq: 312 issues yearly; **Circ:** 41,687
Advertising Manager: Stephan Körting
Profile: Daily newspaper with regional news and a local sports section. Twitter: http://twitter.com/geaonline This Outlet offers RSS (Really Simple Syndication).
Language(s): German
ADVERTISING RATES:
SCC .... EUR 91,90
Mechanical Data: Type Area: 480 x 320 mm, No. of Columns (Display): 7, Col Widths (Display): 44 mm
Copy instructions: *Copy Date:* 1 day prior to publication
Supplement(s): GEA Sport Magazin
REGIONAL DAILY & SUNDAY NEWSPAPERS: Regional Daily Newspapers

MFI MODELLFLUG INTERNATIONAL 735407G79B-940
Editorial: Schulstr. 12, 76532 BADEN-BADEN
Tel: 7221 952111 **Fax:** 7221 952145
Email: mfiredaktion@modellsport.de **Web site:** http://www.modellsport.de
Freq: Monthly; **Annual Sub.:** EUR 46,50; **Circ:** 29,000
Editor: Heinz Ongsieck; **Advertising Manager:** Steffen Weyrauch
Profile: Publication for model aeroplane enthusiasts.
Language(s): German
ADVERTISING RATES:
Full Page Mono .... EUR 1200
Full Page Colour .... EUR 2160
Mechanical Data: Type Area: 254 x 185 mm, No. of Columns (Display): 4, Col Widths (Display): 42 mm
CONSUMER: HOBBIES & DIY: Models & Modelling

MG KURIER 1664077G77A-2700
Editorial: Brehmstr. 73, 40239 DÜSSELDORF
Tel: 211 627621
Email: mg-kurier@mgcc.de **Web site:** http://www.mgcc.de
Freq: Quarterly; **Circ:** 1,000
Editor: Andreas Pichler; **Advertising Manager:** Karin von Buhrmeister
Profile: Magazine for MG drivers.
Language(s): German

M!GAMES 756225G78D-864
Editorial: Wallbergstr. 10, 86415 MERING
Tel: 8233 74010 **Fax:** 8233 740117
Email: redaktion@maniac.de **Web site:** http://www.maniac.de
Freq: Monthly; **Annual Sub.:** EUR 48,00; **Circ:** 50,000
Editor: Oliver Schultes; **Advertising Manager:** Andreas Knauf
Profile: Cross-system video game magazine for Playstation 3, Nintendo Wii, Xbox 360 and Handhelds.
Language(s): German
ADVERTISING RATES:
Full Page Colour .... EUR 6000
Mechanical Data: Type Area: 297 x 210 mm
Copy instructions: *Copy Date:* 30 days prior to publication
CONSUMER: CONSUMER ELECTRONICS: Games

MIBA 735413G79B-960
Editorial: Am Fohlenhof 9, 82256 FÜRSTENFELDBRUCK **Tel:** 8141 534810
Fax: 8141 53481200
Email: redaktion@miba.de **Web site:** http://www.miba.de
Freq: Monthly; **Annual Sub.:** EUR 79,80; **Circ:** 20,861
Editor: Martin Knaden; **Advertising Manager:** Elke Albrecht
Profile: Every month, more than 60 years, brings Miba, the oldest German model railway magazine, interesting model train systems proposal in all gauges, easy-assembly instructions and DIY tips for vehicles, buildings and landscape, and detailed picture reports of the easiest plants to perfectly designed super system. Practice tests and test reports give the reader some guidance in the vast range of industrial and small-scale manufacturers.
Language(s): German
Readership: Aimed at model railway enthusiasts.
ADVERTISING RATES:
Full Page Mono .... EUR 1860
Full Page Colour .... EUR 2680
Mechanical Data: Type Area: 268 x 180 mm, No. of Columns (Display): 3, Col Widths (Display): 57 mm
Copy instructions: *Copy Date:* 36 days prior to publication
CONSUMER: HOBBIES & DIY: Models & Modelling

MICROSYSTEM TECHNOLOGIES 735439G19A-600
Editorial: Tiergartenstr. 17, 69121 HEIDELBERG
Tel: 6221 4870 **Fax:** 6221 4878366
Email: dieter.merkle@springer.com **Web site:** http://www.springerlink.com
Freq: Monthly; **Annual Sub.:** EUR 1993,00; **Circ:** 111
Editor: B. Michel
Profile: Microsystem technologies: sensors, actuators, system integration.
Language(s): English
ADVERTISING RATES:
Full Page Mono .... EUR 740
Full Page Colour .... EUR 1780
Mechanical Data: Type Area: 240 x 175 mm

MIDRANGE MAGAZIN 735440G5B-90
Editorial: Kolpingstr. 26, 86916 KAUFERING
Tel: 8191 964926 **Fax:** 8191 964974
Email: redaktion@midrange.de **Web site:** http://www.midrange.de
Freq: Monthly; **Annual Sub.:** EUR 149,00; **Circ:** 10,956
Editor: Thomas Seibold; **Advertising Manager:** Brigitte Wildmann
Profile: Computer magazine about AS/400, Risc System/6000.
Language(s): German
ADVERTISING RATES:
Full Page Mono .... EUR 3850
Full Page Colour .... EUR 4750
Mechanical Data: Type Area: 231 x 172 mm, No. of Columns (Display): 3, Col Widths (Display): 54 mm
Copy instructions: *Copy Date:* 20 days prior to publication
BUSINESS: COMPUTERS & AUTOMATION: Data Processing

MIESBACHER MERKUR 735441G67B-9560
Editorial: Pfaffenrieder Str. 9, 82515 WOLFRATSHAUSEN **Tel:** 8171 2690
Fax: 8171 269240
Email: fsav@merkur-online.de **Web site:** http://www.merkur-online.de
Freq: 312 issues yearly; **Circ:** 16,666
Advertising Manager: Hans-Georg Bechthold
Profile: The Münchner Merkur with its own local newspapers, of which the Miesbacher Merkur is one that, the leading regional newspaper brand in the Munich area - the most affluent area of Germany. The combination of newspaper and region is the foundation on which to build the success of the title. This is the newspaper not only the factual news agency, but forms a community of solidarity with its readers and the local community. The clear focus on local reporting creates a high regard to human reader loyalty. She presses one hand in the very high number of close to 180,000 subscribers. Also for the high reader-commitment is the loyalty of the total current 827 000 daily readers, the Münchner Merkur or one of its local newspapers usually read over many years. The Münchner Merkur with its own local newspapers is a newspaper for the whole family, tradition and modern life for one of the most beautiful regions of Germany unites. Reliable, informative, critical: the Münchner Merkur is the indispensable daily newspaper for the region. Facebook: http://www.facebook.com/pages/merkur-online.de/190176143327 Twitter: http://twitter.com/mbmerkur This Outlet offers RSS (Really Simple Syndication).
Language(s): German
ADVERTISING RATES:
SCC .... EUR 43,60
Mechanical Data: Type Area: 474 x 324 mm, No. of Columns (Display): 7, Col Widths (Display): 45 mm
Copy instructions: *Copy Date:* 1 day prior to publication
REGIONAL DAILY & SUNDAY NEWSPAPERS: Regional Daily Newspapers

MIETERFORUM 735445G1K-2
Editorial: Märkische Str. 205, 44141 DORTMUND
Tel: 231 94790 **Fax:** 231 423963
Email: lely@report-age.de **Web site:** http://www.schulfundraising.de
Freq: Quarterly; **Circ:** 45,000
Editor: Uwe van der Lely
Profile: The magazine provides information on all things around the living, especially rent law, consumer protection, housing politics and local.
Language(s): German
Readership: Read by people renting accommodation.
Mechanical Data: Type Area: 270 x 181 mm, No. of Columns (Display): 3, Col Widths (Display): 57 mm
Copy instructions: *Copy Date:* 20 days prior to publication
BUSINESS: FINANCE & ECONOMICS: Rental Leasing

MIETERFORUM 735445G1K-11
Editorial: Märkische Str. 205, 44141 DORTMUND
Tel: 231 94790 **Fax:** 231 423963
Email: lely@report-age.de **Web site:** http://www.schulfundraising.de
Freq: Quarterly; **Circ:** 45,000
Editor: Uwe van der Lely
Profile: The magazine provides information on all things around the living, especially rent law, consumer protection, housing politics and local.
Language(s): German
Readership: Read by people renting accommodation.
Mechanical Data: Type Area: 270 x 181 mm, No. of Columns (Display): 3, Col Widths (Display): 57 mm
Copy instructions: *Copy Date:* 20 days prior to publication
BUSINESS: FINANCE & ECONOMICS: Rental Leasing

MIETERFORUM 735445G1K-11
Editorial: Märkische Str. 205, 44141 DORTMUND
Tel: 231 94790 **Fax:** 231 423963
Email: lely@report-age.de **Web site:** http://www.schulfundraising.de
Freq: Quarterly; **Circ:** 45,000
Editor: Uwe van der Lely
Profile: The magazine provides information on all things around the living, especially rent law, consumer protection, housing politics and local.
Language(s): German
Readership: Read by people renting accommodation.
Mechanical Data: Type Area: 270 x 181 mm, No. of Columns (Display): 3, Col Widths (Display): 57 mm
Copy instructions: *Copy Date:* 20 days prior to publication
BUSINESS: FINANCE & ECONOMICS: Rental Leasing

MIETERFORUM 735304G74K-75
Editorial: Brückstr. 58, 44787 BOCHUM
Tel: 234 9611444 **Fax:** 234 9611474
Email: mensch.mieter@mvbo.de **Web site:** http://www.mvbo.de
Freq: Quarterly; Free to qualifying individuals
Annual Sub.: EUR 2,00; **Circ:** 22,500
Editor: Aichard Hoffmann; **Advertising Manager:** Michael Wenzel
Profile: The magazine provides information on all things around the living, especially rent law, consumer protection, housing politics and local.
Language(s): German
Readership: Aimed at tenants.
CONSUMER: WOMEN'S INTEREST CONSUMER MAGAZINES: Home Purchase

MIETERZEITUNG 735449G1K-4
Editorial: Littenstr. 10, 10179 BERLIN **Tel:** 30 223230
Fax: 30 22323100
Email: info@mieterbund.de **Web site:** http://www.mieterbund.de
Freq: 6 issues yearly; Free to qualifying individuals
Annual Sub.: EUR 8,00; **Circ:** 615,641
Editor: Lukas Siebenkotten
Profile: Tenants newspaper with detailed information on laws, regulations, proposed legislation and court judgments that are used intensively by the readers. Guide articles, trends in the housing market and general consumer issues are addressed in the renter newspaper as competent as housing, tenancy and service topics.
Language(s): German
Readership: Aimed at tenants, lawyers and solicitors.
ADVERTISING RATES:
Full Page Mono .... EUR 4784
Full Page Colour .... EUR 7654
Mechanical Data: Type Area: 248 x 176 mm, No. of Columns (Display): 4, Col Widths (Display): 41 mm
Copy instructions: *Copy Date:* 42 days prior to publication
BUSINESS: FINANCE & ECONOMICS: Rental Leasing

MIKADO 735455G46-171_50
Editorial: Römerstr. 4, 86438 KISSING
Tel: 8233 237135 **Fax:** 8233 237111
Email: christoph.dauner@weka.de **Web site:** http://www.mikado-online.de
Freq: 11 issues yearly; **Annual Sub.:** EUR 98,00; **Circ:** 10,289
Editor: Christoph Maria Dauner; **Advertising Manager:** Christoph Maria Dauner
Profile: Business magazine for carpentry and timber construction companies in the German-speaking countries information on structural engineering and operations management. The reader receives the latest information, news or event announcements from the timber industry.
Language(s): German
Readership: Read by carpenters and architects.
ADVERTISING RATES:
Full Page Mono .... EUR 2960
Full Page Colour .... EUR 4730
Mechanical Data: Type Area: 260 x 185 mm, No. of Columns (Display): 4, Col Widths (Display): 45 mm
Copy instructions: *Copy Date:* 28 days prior to publication
Official Journal of: Organ d. Europ. Vereinigung d. Holzbaus u. d. Bundes Dt. Zimmermeister
Supplement(s): mikado plus
BUSINESS: TIMBER, WOOD & FORESTRY

MIKROKOSMOS 735458G55-85
Editorial: Königin-Luise-Str. 1, 14195 BERLIN
Tel: 30 83856475 **Fax:** 30 83856477
Email: hausmann@zedat.fu-berlin.de
Freq: 6 issues yearly; **Annual Sub.:** EUR 84,00
Editor: Klaus Hausmann
Profile: Journal about microscopy. Includes news about equipment, materials, forthcoming events and text books.
Language(s): German
Official Journal of: Organ d. Arbeitskreises Mikroskopie im Freundeskreis Botan. Garten Köln, d. Arbeitskreises Mikroskopie im Naturwissenschaftl. Verein zu Bremen, d. Berliner Mikroskop. Ges. e.V., d. Dt. Mikrobiolog. Ges. Stuttgart, d. Mikroskop. Vereinigung Hamburg, d. Mikrobiolog. Vereinigung München, d. Mikrograph. Ges. Wien, d. Mikroskop. ArGe d. Naturwissenschaftl. Vereinigung Hagen e.V., d. Mikroskop. ArGe'en Hannover Mainfranken u. Stuttgart, d. Mikroskop. Ges. Zürich u. d. Tübinger Mikroskop. Ges. e.V.
BUSINESS: APPLIED SCIENCE & LABORATORIES

MIKROPRODUKTION 1708260G17-1572
Editorial: Pittersdorf 5, 84104 RUDELZHAUSEN
Tel: 8752 869066
Email: deiter@mikroproduktion.com **Web site:** http://www.mikroproduktion.com
Freq: 6 issues yearly; **Annual Sub.:** EUR 68,00; **Circ:** 10,000
Editor: Frank Deiter
Profile: Mikroproduktion is a trade magazine specializing in applied micro technology, which contains reports on the complete processing chain for the manufacture of micro systems, miniaturized products and functional micro structures. Mikroproduktion presents new miniaturization technologies in the form of exclusive specialist articles from industry and R & D, and provides help in their implementation. In this connection, successfully completed applications by corporations leading the way in the market and the technology serve for reference purposes. Mikroproduktion is primarily aimed at production engineers, experts in research and development, chief executives and technical management staff in the fields of sensor technology, medical systems, machine manufacture, automotive engineering, semiconductors/microelectronics, the aerospace industry, tool and mold makers and precision engineering/optics.
Language(s): German
ADVERTISING RATES:
Full Page Mono .... EUR 2900
Full Page Colour .... EUR 3980
Mechanical Data: Type Area: 250 x 175 mm, No. of Columns (Display): 4, Col Widths (Display): 41 mm
Official Journal of: Organ d. Fachverb. Micro Technology

MILCH PUR 1848172G21A-4404
Editorial: Porschestr. 2, 87437 KEMPTEN
Tel: 831 571420 **Fax:** 831 79008
Email: baumgartner@milchpur.info **Web site:** http://www.milchpur.info
Freq: Quarterly; Free to qualifying individuals
Annual Sub.: EUR 10,00; **Circ:** 51,500
Editor: Christian Baumgartner; **Advertising Manager:** Karl König
Profile: The magazine of the Bavarian Society Milchprüfring is published 4 times a year and is the 45,000 milk producers in Bavaria sent free of charge through the milk collection truck driver. The magazine offers practical tips and practical information on a high level. Beginning with the birth of the calf, over the feeding of the cows up for enjoyable foods. It also provides entertainment and takes important technical discussions, research findings and developments to date. The authors are experts in their field.
Language(s): German
ADVERTISING RATES:
Full Page Colour .... EUR 4730
Mechanical Data: Type Area: 270 x 187 mm, No. of Columns (Display): 3, Col Widths (Display): 60 mm
Copy instructions: *Copy Date:* 30 days prior to publication

MILCH-MARKETING 735463G21G-4
Editorial: Rheintalstr. 6, 53498 BAD BREISIG
Tel: 2633 454015 **Fax:** 2633 97415
Email: wegerich@milch-marketing.de **Web site:** http://www.milch-marketing.de
Freq: Monthly; **Annual Sub.:** EUR 64,20; **Circ:** 6,291
Editor: Frank Wegerich; **Advertising Manager:** Carola Seiwert
Profile: Magazine about milk production and marketing.
Language(s): German
Readership: Aimed at dairy farmers, producers and suppliers of dairy products.
ADVERTISING RATES:
Full Page Mono .... EUR 4810
Full Page Colour .... EUR 4810
Mechanical Data: Type Area: 250 x 184 mm, No. of Columns (Display): 4, Col Widths (Display): 43 mm
Copy instructions: *Copy Date:* 28 days prior to publication
BUSINESS: AGRICULTURE & FARMING: Milk

MILCHPRAXIS 735464G21C-1
Editorial: Clemens-August-Str. 12, 53115 BONN
Tel: 228 9694230 **Fax:** 228 630311
Email: redaktion@dlg-agrofoodmedien.de **Web site:** http://www.dlg-agrofoodmedien.de
Freq: Quarterly; **Annual Sub.:** EUR 30,50; **Circ:** 9,231
Editor: Heinz-Peter Pütz; **Advertising Manager:** Rainer Schluck
Profile: Journal focusing on dairy farming and milk production.
Language(s): German
Readership: Read by dairy farmers.
ADVERTISING RATES:
Full Page Mono .... EUR 1770
Full Page Colour .... EUR 2390
Mechanical Data: Type Area: 270 x 186 mm, No. of Columns (Display): 3, Col Widths (Display): 58 mm
BUSINESS: AGRICULTURE & FARMING: Dairy Farming

MILCHRIND 735465G21C-2
Editorial: Hülsebrockstr. 2, 48165 MÜNSTER
Tel: 2501 801211 **Fax:** 2501 801215
Email: topf@lv.de **Web site:** http://www.milchrind.de
Freq: Quarterly; Free to qualifying individuals
Annual Sub.: EUR 32,00; **Circ:** 28,405
Editor: Christine Topf; **Advertising Manager:** Gabriele Wittkowski
Profile: milchrind is the leading specialist magazine for breeders and specialist dairy producers. milchrind, the powerful, specialized, and future-oriented breeding and milk production plants with high demand for equipment and capital goods reached. milchrind supplies sound and well-presented technical and background information from the fields of breeding and management. milchrind informed fully about the German and international Holstein breed. The magazine is not only a valuable guide in all breeding questions, but also reports on developments in dairy management. Here are a regular focus on health issues. In recent reports provide managers present their strategies in breeding and management.
Language(s): German
Readership: Aimed at farmers.
ADVERTISING RATES:
Full Page Mono .... EUR 3520
Full Page Colour .... EUR 5952
Mechanical Data: Type Area: 270 x 190 mm, No. of Columns (Display): 4, Col Widths (Display): 46 mm
Copy instructions: *Copy Date:* 29 days prior to publication
BUSINESS: AGRICULTURE & FARMING: Dairy Farming

MILCHWOCHE 735462G22A-1520
Editorial: Am Flugplatz 7, 31137 HILDESHEIM
Tel: 5121 9187040 **Fax:** 5121 9187059
Email: info@wemcard.de **Web site:** http://www.wemcard.de
Freq: Weekly; **Annual Sub.:** EUR 486,00; **Circ:** 1,958
Editor: Ralf Friederich; **Advertising Manager:** Sven Böttcher
Profile: Publication about milk and egg marketing.
Language(s): German
ADVERTISING RATES:
Full Page Mono .... EUR 2531
Full Page Colour .... EUR 3254
Mechanical Data: Type Area: 260 x 190 mm, No. of Columns (Display): 3, Col Widths (Display): 60 mm
Copy instructions: *Copy Date:* 7 days prior to publication
BUSINESS: FOOD

MILITARY TECHNOLOGY 735473G40-560
Editorial: Heilsbachstr. 26, 53123 BONN
Tel: 228 6483118 **Fax:** 228 6483109
Email: dpm@mpgbonn.de **Web site:** http://www.monch.com
Freq: Monthly; **Annual Sub.:** EUR 130,00; **Circ:** 23,397
Editor: Dennis-Peter Merklinghaus; **Advertising Manager:** Christa André
Profile: Military Technology was founded in 1977. It is the world's leading international tri-service defence monthly magazine in the English language. It covers all aspects of modern defence technology, requirements, procurements and programmes. Military Technology is the world's leading media platform for providing access to and influence within defence establishments worldwide, as well as the best platform for personal interaction with senior Politicians, Industrialists and Military officers across all services. By quarterly audit, it is the largest magazine of its type with recorded instances in writing of a pass-along rate of 30+ readers per copy, and audited circulation per issue of just under 25,000 copies. It is a unique strategic and tactical level resource to inform political, industrial and military decision-makers: Military Technology is "Required Reading for Defence Professionals".
Language(s): English
ADVERTISING RATES:
Full Page Mono .... EUR 4500
Full Page Colour .... EUR 7500
Mechanical Data: Type Area: 256 x 185 mm
Copy instructions: *Copy Date:* 30 days prior to publication
BUSINESS: DEFENCE

MINDELHEIMER ZEITUNG 735478G67B-9580
Editorial: Curt-Frenzel-Str. 2, 86167 AUGSBURG
Tel: 821 7770 **Fax:** 821 7772067
Web site: http://www.augsburger-allgemeine.de
Freq: 312 issues yearly; **Circ:** 13,906
Advertising Manager: Herbert Dachs
Profile: Regional daily newspaper with news on politics, economy, culture, sports, travel, technology, etc. Facebook: http://www.facebook.com/AugsburgerAllgemeine Twitter: http://twitter.com/AZ_Augsburg This Outlet offers RSS (Really Simple Syndication).
Language(s): German
ADVERTISING RATES:
SCC .... EUR 46,20
Mechanical Data: Type Area: 480 x 327 mm, No. of Columns (Display): 7, Col Widths (Display): 45 mm
Copy instructions: *Copy Date:* 1 day prior to publication
REGIONAL DAILY & SUNDAY NEWSPAPERS: Regional Daily Newspapers

---

MINDENER TAGEBLATT 735481G67B-9600
Editorial: Obermarktstr. 26, 32423 MINDEN
Tel: 571 8820 **Fax:** 571 882240
Email: mt@mt-online.de **Web site:** http://www.mt-online.de
Freq: 312 issues yearly; **Circ:** 33,319
Editor: Christoph Pepper; **News Editor:** Thomas Traue; **Advertising Manager:** Thomas Bouza Behm
Profile: Regional daily newspaper with news on politics, economy, culture, sports, travel, technology, etc. in the cities of Minden, Hille, Petershagen and Porta Westfalica. Facebook: http://www.facebook.com/pages/Mindener-Tageblatt/288611662122 Twitter: http://twitter.com/MT_ONLINE This Outlet offers RSS (Really Simple Syndication).
Language(s): German
ADVERTISING RATES:
SCC .... EUR 81,60
Mechanical Data: Type Area: 426 x 282 mm, No. of Columns (Display): 6, Col Widths (Display): 45 mm
Copy instructions: *Copy Date:* 1 day prior to publication
Supplement(s): prisma
REGIONAL DAILY & SUNDAY NEWSPAPERS: Regional Daily Newspapers

---

MINERALÖLTECHNIK 1829445G58-1791
Editorial: Jägerstr. 6, 10117 BERLIN
Tel: 30 755414400 **Fax:** 30 755414374
Email: info@uniti.de **Web site:** http://www.uniti.de
Freq: Monthly; **Annual Sub.:** EUR 72,90; **Circ:** 2,000
Editor: Edwin Leber; **Advertising Manager:** Carmen Fogel
Profile: International journal covering the latest in oil extraction techniques and the oil industry.
Language(s): English; German
ADVERTISING RATES:
Full Page Mono .... EUR 473
Mechanical Data: Type Area: 168 x 108 mm
Copy instructions: *Copy Date:* 45 days prior to publication
Official Journal of: Organ d. Uniti-Bundesverb. mittelständ. Mineralölunternehmen e. V.

MINI 735493G74A-2360
Editorial: Karlsruher Str. 31, 76437 RASTATT
Tel: 7222 13210 **Fax:** 7222 13505
Email: mini@vpm.de **Web site:** http://www.vpm.de
Freq: 17 issues yearly; **Cover Price:** EUR 0,89; **Circ:** 92,283
Editor: Silvia Lass von Maydell
Profile: Mini, this is the new price-performance category in the segment entertaining weekly women's magazines. Illustrated with large current reading fun, women's magazine with tips and tricks for everyday life, mysteries and travel journal. Recent reports, in-depth information, fast information about money & law make all the important home & garden, for body and soul to focus. Mini shows trends. Popular fashion, matching haircuts, the latest beauty trends. Cooking roast, fry, the editor knows the recipes. Ultimate Puzzle, great prizes.
Language(s): German
ADVERTISING RATES:
Full Page Mono .... EUR 3640
Full Page Colour .... EUR 3640
Mechanical Data: Type Area: 261 x 196 mm, No. of Columns (Display): 4, Col Widths (Display): 46 mm
Copy instructions: *Copy Date:* 35 days prior to publication
CONSUMER: WOMEN'S INTEREST CONSUMER MAGAZINES: Women's Interest

---

MINI EXTRA 735496G74P-660
Editorial: Karlsruher Str. 31, 76437 RASTATT
Tel: 7222 130 **Fax:** 7222 13218
Web site: http://www.vpm.de
Freq: Quarterly; **Cover Price:** EUR 1,95; **Circ:** 130,000
Editor: Silvia Lass von Maydell
Profile: Magazine containing baking recipes, advice on beverages and table decoration, calendar, shopping aid and advice on nutrition. All recipes have been tested by professionals and offer a "Guarantee to Success. " For each recipe there are practical assistance, such as "margins Angel ", but if in the preparation once something does not work, or an ingredient is not available. Drinks are an extra service proposals and original table decorations, seasonal calendars, smart shopping aids and of course valuable nutritional tips that make each Mini EXTRA an indispensable kitchen helper.
Language(s): German
ADVERTISING RATES:
Full Page Mono .... EUR 4500
Full Page Colour .... EUR 4500
Mechanical Data: Type Area: 261 x 196 mm
Copy instructions: *Copy Date:* 64 days prior to publication
CONSUMER: WOMEN'S INTEREST CONSUMER MAGAZINES: Food & Cookery

---

MINIMALLY INVASIVE NEUROSURGERY 735499G56A-7060
Editorial: Kriegsbergstr. 60, 70174 STUTTGART
Tel: 711 27833701 **Fax:** 711 27833709
Email: min@klinikum-stuttgart.de **Web site:** http://www.thieme.de/min
Freq: 6 issues yearly; **Annual Sub.:** EUR 271,80; **Circ:** 570
Editor: Nikolai Hopf
Profile: It is the content of the entire spectrum of modern neurosurgery shown: Keyhole Surgery, endoscopy, stereotactic-guided surgery, endovascular surgery, radiosurgery and surgical anatomy.
Language(s): English
ADVERTISING RATES:
Full Page Mono .... EUR 1060
Full Page Colour .... EUR 2170
Mechanical Data: Type Area: 248 x 175 mm, No. of Columns (Display): 4, Col Widths (Display): 40 mm
BUSINESS: HEALTH & MEDICAL

MIR MANAGEMENT INTERNATIONAL REVIEW 735514G14A-4780
Editorial: Abraham-Lincoln-Str. 46, 65189 WIESBADEN **Tel:** 611 7878272 **Fax:** 611 7878400
Email: ulrike.loercher@springer.com **Web site:** http://www.mir-online.de
Freq: 6 issues yearly; **Annual Sub.:** EUR 214,00; **Circ:** 1,200
Editor: Ulrike Lörcher; **Advertising Manager:** Yvonne Guderjahn
Profile: International review of management and business.
Language(s): English

Readership: Aimed at managers and decision makers.
ADVERTISING RATES:
Full Page Mono .... EUR 800
Full Page Colour .... EUR 1700
Mechanical Data: Type Area: 190 x 125 mm
BUSINESS: COMMERCE, INDUSTRY & MANAGEMENT

MISSY MAGAZINE 1860326G74A-3641
Editorial: Eschelsweg 4, 22767 HAMBURG
Tel: 40 20933967 **Fax:** 40 31792103
Email: redaktion@missy-mag.de **Web site:** http://www.missy-magazine.de
Freq: Quarterly; **Annual Sub.:** EUR 18,00; **Circ:** 20,000
Editor: Chris Köver; **Advertising Manager:** Margarita Tsomou
Profile: Missy Magazineis a magazine for a new generation of young women who are in the existing women's and lifestyle magazines Sleek as Vogue, Cosmopolitan Maxi or not find. With the following topics: Culture - From indie to mainstream, hip-hop to techno, contemporary and timeless - we report on innovative musicians, writers and filmmakers worldwide. Media blogs, social networks, online stores - we accompany the lives of our readers in the network and offer them there Orientierungshilfe. Fashion - Portraits, Interviews and lush photo spreads, trends on the street and on the catwalk - we talk to young designers, labels, and bloggers and staging the fashion trends of tomorrow. Sex - lust- and bedsteads layers, toys and positions - we test so that our readers have more fun during sex. DIY - DIY, knitting, cooking, screw on the bike or laminate cut - we show our readers how they can do things themselves. Technology and Gadgets - Smartphones, iPad, hardware and software - Missy is the technologically adept women's magazine, we will discuss news from the world of essential everyday electronics and are interested in crazy gadgets. Travel - Barcelona, Tel Aviv, New York - are cool women everywhere. Missy travels around the world and presents the secrets of local connoisseurs, in a special guide. Facebook: http://www.facebook.com/Goodtruebeautiful.
Language(s): German
ADVERTISING RATES:
Full Page Mono .... EUR 4350
Full Page Colour .... EUR 4350
Mechanical Data: Type Area: 266 x 194 mm

MITGLIEDERBRIEF BAYERISCHER ANWALTVERBAND 1833527G1A-3702
Editorial: Prinzregentenstr. 6, 83022 ROSENHEIM
Tel: 8031 9089433 **Fax:** 8031 9089477
Email: mitgliederbrief@bayerischer-anwaltverband.de
Web site: http://www.bayerischer-anwaltverband.de
Freq: 6 issues yearly; **Cover Price:** EUR 7,00
Free to qualifying individuals ; **Circ:** 11,000
Editor: Petra Rottmann
Profile: Information for members of the Bavarian Association for Advocates.
Language(s): German
ADVERTISING RATES:
Full Page Colour .... EUR 2490
Mechanical Data: Type Area: 257 x 190 mm, No. of Columns (Display): 4, Col Widths (Display): 45 mm

MITGLIEDERVERZEICHNIS 735581G2A-3360
Editorial: Grafenberger Allee 241, 40237 DÜSSELDORF **Tel:** 211 6907320 **Fax:** 211 674947
Email: lzverband@aol.com
Freq: Annual; **Circ:** 400
Profile: Magazine from the German Reader Circle Association.
Language(s): German
Mechanical Data: Type Area: 180 x 115 mm

MITTBAYNOT MITTEILUNGEN DES BAYERISCHEN NOTARVEREINS, DER NOTARKASSE UND DER LANDESNOTARKAMMER BAYERN 1638599G1A-3541
Editorial: Ottostr. 10, 80333 MÜNCHEN
Tel: 89 551660 **Fax:** 89 55166234
Email: mittbaynot@notarkasse.de **Web site:** http://www.notare.bayern.de
Freq: 6 issues yearly; Free to qualifying individuals
Annual Sub.: EUR 56,00; **Circ:** 3,500
Editor: Eliane Schuller
Profile: Official paper for notaries, lawyers and employees of notaries.
Language(s): German

MITTE JOURNAL 1855875G73-651
Editorial: Karl-Liebknecht-Str. 29, 10178 BERLIN
Tel: 30 293887456 **Fax:** 30 293887485
Email: schwenkenbecher@abendblatt-berlin.de **Web site:** http://www.abendblatt-berlin.de
Freq: Quarterly; **Cover Price:** Free; **Circ:** 22,000
Editor: Christian Schwenkenbecher
Profile: City magazine for Berlin with tips and trends.
Language(s): German

MITTE KOMPAKT 1898580G74M-889
Editorial: Bundesallee 23, 10717 BERLIN
Tel: 30 863030 **Fax:** 30 86303200
Email: info@bfb.de **Web site:** http://www.bfb.de
Freq: Annual; **Cover Price:** Free; **Circ:** 70,000
Profile: Industry district magazine. The core of this handy reference book is neatly sorted according to different themes of industry. Here you will find a plethora of vendors from the neighborhood. In preparation to the respective subject area raises a company, in an interview. To know your environment better, we present in the district windows, etc. beautiful places, monuments, museums, etc. For better orientation in the neighborhood also an integrated neighborhood with street plan is register. Furthermore, the county information you provide an overview of important phone numbers and agencies in your neighborhood.
Language(s): German
Mechanical Data: Type Area: 185 x 126 mm

MITTEILUNGEN AUS DER NNA 735635G57-1140
Editorial: Hof Möhr, 29640 SCHNEVERDINGEN
Tel: 5198 98938 **Fax:** 5198 989095
Email: nna@nna.niedersachsen.de **Web site:** http://www.nna.de
Freq: Half-yearly; **Cover Price:** EUR 2,60; **Circ:** 15,000
Editor: Renate Strohschneider
Profile: Information about activities of the Toepfer Akademie for Nature Conservation in the sectors E2158education, research and public relations.
Language(s): German
ADVERTISING RATES:
Full Page Mono .... EUR 500
Full Page Colour .... EUR 750

MITTEILUNGEN DES INSTITUTES FÜR TEXTILTECHNIK DER RHEINISCH-WESTFÄLISCHEN TECHNISCHEN HOCHSCHULE AACHEN 1862271G19A-1132
Editorial: Otto-Blumenthal-Str. 1, 52074 AACHEN
Tel: 241 8023490 **Fax:** 241 8022422
Email: ita@ita.rwth-aachen.de **Web site:** http://www.ita.rwth-aachen.de
Freq: Annual; **Cover Price:** EUR 50,00; **Circ:** 250
Editor: Thomas Gries
Profile: Publication from the Textile Technological Institute of the Technical University of Aachen.
Language(s): German

MITTEILUNGEN DES OBSTBAUVERSUCHSRINGES DES ALTEN LANDES E.V. AN DER ESTEBURG - OBSTBAUZENTRUM JORK 735711G26C-73
Editorial: Moorende 53, 21635 JORK
Tel: 4162 6016154 **Fax:** 4162 6016600
Email: redaktion@esteburg.de **Web site:** http://www.esteburg.de
Freq: Monthly; Free to qualifying individuals
Annual Sub.: EUR 62,00; **Circ:** 2,000
Editor: Karsten Klopp; **Advertising Manager:** Frank Fricke
Profile: International journal containing technical information about fruit cultivation.
Language(s): German
Readership: Aimed at fruit growers.
ADVERTISING RATES:
Full Page Mono .... EUR 1227
Full Page Colour .... EUR 2007
Mechanical Data: Type Area: 260 x 187 mm, No. of Columns (Display): 4, Col Widths (Display): 43 mm
Copy instructions: *Copy Date:* 21 days prior to publication
BUSINESS: GARDEN TRADE

MITTEILUNGSBLATT DEUTSCHER BRAUMEISTER- UND MALZMEISTER-BUND 736054G9B-6
Editorial: Arndtstr. 47, 44135 DORTMUND
Tel: 231 571121 **Fax:** 231 524261
Email: info@dbmb.de **Web site:** http://www.dbmb.de
Freq: 3 issues yearly; Free to qualifying individuals
Annual Sub.: EUR 77,90; **Circ:** 3,346
Editor: Gregor Schneider; **Advertising Manager:** Wolf-Dieter Schoyerer
Profile: Official journal of the Society of Brewers and Beer Distillers in Germany.
Language(s): German
ADVERTISING RATES:
Full Page Mono .... EUR 1723
Full Page Colour .... EUR 2821
Mechanical Data: Type Area: 275 x 185 mm, No. of Columns (Display): 3, Col Widths (Display): 58 mm
Copy instructions: *Copy Date:* 26 days prior to publication
BUSINESS: DRINKS & LICENSED TRADE: Brewing

MITTELBADISCHE PRESSE 1660626G67B-16737
Editorial: Marlener Str. 9, 77656 OFFENBURG
Tel: 781 5040 **Fax:** 781 5041319
Email: nachrichten@reiff.de **Web site:** http://www.baden-online.de
Freq: 312 issues yearly; **Circ:** 55,242
Editor: Jürgen Rohn; **News Editor:** Rüdiger Klausmann; **Advertising Manager:** Kurt Michelfelder
Profile: Regional daily newspaper covering politics, economics, sport, travel and technology.
Language(s): German
ADVERTISING RATES:
SCC .... EUR 125,50
Mechanical Data: Type Area: 420 x 284 mm, No. of Columns (Display): 6, Col Widths (Display): 44 mm
Copy instructions: *Copy Date:* 1 day prior to publication
REGIONAL DAILY & SUNDAY NEWSPAPERS: Regional Daily Newspapers

MITTELBAYERISCHE ZEITUNG FÜR DEN NÖRDLICHEN LANDKREIS REGENSBURG 736238G67B-9680
Editorial: Margaretenstr. 4, 93047 REGENSBURG
Tel: 941 20765 **Fax:** 941 207142
Email: mz-redaktion@mittelbayerische.de **Web site:** http://www.mittelbayerische.de
Freq: 312 issues yearly; **Circ:** 55,495
Profile: Regional daily newspaper with news on politics, economy, culture, sports, travel, technology, etc. What happened in his own front door is the most interesting news! Our Publisher product key is therefore to be the local newspaper. The desire for location-based information has led to our newspaper has become even more "local". The trend is increasingly ecoming the "editorial office" on site. Every city, every region has a permanent place in the newspaper. The Mittelbayerische Zeitung, with its 13 regional editions in the Upper Palatinate and large parts of Lower Bavaria, is the medium number one and reached with a circulation of 130,000 copies around 400,000 daily readers. As one of few newspapers in Germany, it entered against the prevailing trend circulation gains. Facebook: http://www.facebook.com/mittelbayerische Twitter: http://twitter.com/mz_de This Outlet offers RSS (Really Simple Syndication). This Outlet offers RSS (Really Simple Syndication).
Language(s): German
ADVERTISING RATES:
SCC .... EUR 134,40
Mechanical Data: Type Area: 430 x 281 mm, No. of Columns (Display): 6, Col Widths (Display): 45 mm
Copy instructions: *Copy Date:* 1 day prior to publication
Supplement(s): Mittelbayerische jun.; Regensburg Arcaden Aktuell
REGIONAL DAILY & SUNDAY NEWSPAPERS: Regional Daily Newspapers

MITTELBAYERISCHE ZEITUNG FÜR DEN SÜDLICHEN LANDKREIS REGENSBURG 736239G67B-9700
Editorial: Margaretenstr. 4, 93047 REGENSBURG
Tel: 941 20765 **Fax:** 941 207142
Email: mz-redaktion@mittelbayerische.de **Web site:** http://www.mittelbayerische.de
Freq: 312 issues yearly; **Circ:** 55,495
Profile: Regional daily newspaper with news on politics, economy, culture, sports, travel, technology, etc. What happened in his own front door is the most interesting news! Our Publisher product key is therefore to be the local newspaper. The desire for location-based information has led to our newspaper has become even more "local". The trend is increasingly ecoming the "editorial office" on site. Every city, every region has a permanent place in the newspaper. The Mittelbayerische Zeitung, with its 13 regional editions in the Upper Palatinate and large parts of Lower Bavaria, is the medium number one and reached with a circulation of 130,000 copies around 400,000 daily readers. As one of few newspapers in Germany, it entered against the prevailing trend circulation gains. Facebook: http://www.facebook.com/mittelbayerische Twitter: http://twitter.com/mz_de This Outlet offers RSS (Really Simple Syndication).
Language(s): German
ADVERTISING RATES:
SCC .... EUR 134,40
Mechanical Data: Type Area: 430 x 281 mm, No. of Columns (Display): 6, Col Widths (Display): 45 mm
Copy instructions: *Copy Date:* 1 day prior to publication
Supplement(s): Mittelbayerische jun.; Regensburg Arcaden Aktuell
REGIONAL DAILY & SUNDAY NEWSPAPERS: Regional Daily Newspapers

MITTELBAYERISCHE ZEITUNG FÜR HEMAU UND DEN WESTLICHEN LANDKREIS 736240G67B-9720
Editorial: Margaretenstr. 4, 93047 REGENSBURG
Tel: 941 20765 **Fax:** 941 207142
Email: mz-redaktion@mittelbayerische.de **Web site:** http://www.mittelbayerische.de
Freq: 312 issues yearly; **Circ:** 55,495
Profile: Regional daily newspaper with news on politics, economy, culture, sports, travel, technology, etc. What happened in his own front door is the most interesting news! Our Publisher product key is therefore to be the local newspaper. The desire for location-based information has led to our newspaper has become even more "local". The trend is increasingly ecoming the "editorial office" on site. Every city, every region has a permanent place in the newspaper. The Mittelbayerische Zeitung, with its 13 regional editions in the Upper Palatinate and large parts of Lower Bavaria, is the medium number one and reached with a circulation of 130,000 copies around 400,000 daily readers. As one of few newspapers in Germany, it entered against the prevailing trend circulation gains. Facebook: http://www.facebook.com/mittelbayerische Twitter: http://twitter.com/mz_de This Outlet offers RSS (Really Simple Syndication).
Language(s): German
ADVERTISING RATES:
SCC .... EUR 134,40
Mechanical Data: Type Area: 430 x 281 mm, No. of Columns (Display): 6, Col Widths (Display): 45 mm
Copy instructions: *Copy Date:* 1 day prior to publication
Supplement(s): Mittelbayerische jun.
REGIONAL DAILY & SUNDAY NEWSPAPERS: Regional Daily Newspapers

MITTELBAYERISCHE ZEITUNG FÜR KELHEIM, ABENSBERG UND NEUSTADT 736241G67B-9740
Editorial: Margaretenstr. 4, 93047 REGENSBURG
Tel: 941 20765 **Fax:** 941 207142
Email: mz-redaktion@mittelbayerische.de **Web site:** http://www.mittelbayerische.de
Freq: 312 issues yearly; **Circ:** 14,148
Profile: Regional daily newspaper with news on politics, economy, culture, sports, travel, technology, etc. What happened in his own front door is the most interesting news! Our Publisher product key is therefore to be the local newspaper. The desire for location-based information has led to our newspaper has become even more "local". The trend is increasingly ecoming the "editorial office" on site. Every city, every region has a permanent place in the newspaper. The Mittelbayerische Zeitung, with its 13 regional editions in the Upper Palatinate and large parts of Lower Bavaria, is the medium number one and reached with a circulation of 130,000 copies around 400,000 daily readers. As one of few newspapers in Germany, it entered against the prevailing trend circulation gains. Facebook: http://www.facebook.com/mittelbayerische Twitter: http://twitter.com/mz_de This Outlet offers RSS (Really Simple Syndication).
Language(s): German
ADVERTISING RATES:
SCC .... EUR 44,40
Mechanical Data: Type Area: 430 x 281 mm, No. of Columns (Display): 6, Col Widths (Display): 45 mm
Copy instructions: *Copy Date:* 1 day prior to publication
Supplement(s): Mittelbayerische jun.
REGIONAL DAILY & SUNDAY NEWSPAPERS: Regional Daily Newspapers

MITTELBAYERISCHE ZEITUNG FÜR NITTENAU UND BRUCK 736242G67B-9760
Editorial: Margaretenstr. 4, 93047 REGENSBURG
Tel: 941 20765 **Fax:** 941 207142
Email: mz-redaktion@mittelbayerische.de **Web site:** http://www.mittelbayerische.de
Freq: 312 issues yearly; **Circ:** 19,500
Profile: Regional daily newspaper with news on politics, economy, culture, sports, travel, technology, etc. What happened in his own front door is the most interesting news! Our Publisher product key is therefore to be the local newspaper. The desire for location-based information has led to our newspaper has become even more "local". The trend is increasingly ecoming the "editorial office" on site. Every city, every region has a permanent place in the newspaper. The Mittelbayerische Zeitung, with its 13 regional editions in the Upper Palatinate and large parts of Lower Bavaria, is the medium number one and reached with a circulation of 130,000 copies around 400,000 daily readers. As one of few newspapers in Germany, it entered against the prevailing trend circulation gains. Facebook: http://www.facebook.com/mittelbayerische Twitter: http://twitter.com/mz_de This Outlet offers RSS (Really Simple Syndication).
Language(s): German
ADVERTISING RATES:
SCC .... EUR 51,60
Mechanical Data: Type Area: 430 x 281 mm, No. of Columns (Display): 6, Col Widths (Display): 45 mm
Copy instructions: *Copy Date:* 1 day prior to publication
Supplement(s): Mittelbayerische jun.
REGIONAL DAILY & SUNDAY NEWSPAPERS: Regional Daily Newspapers

MITTELBAYERISCHE ZEITUNG FÜR REGENSBURG 736243G67B-9780
Editorial: Margaretenstr. 4, 93047 REGENSBURG
Tel: 941 20765 **Fax:** 941 207142
Email: mz-redaktion@mittelbayerische.de **Web site:** http://www.mittelbayerische.de
Freq: 312 issues yearly; **Circ:** 55,495
Editor: Manfred Sauerer; **News Editor:** Christian Kucznierz
Profile: Regional daily newspaper with news on politics, economy, culture, sports, travel, technology, etc. What happened in his own front door is the most interesting news! Our Publisher product key is therefore to be the local newspaper. The desire for

location-based information has led to our newspaper has become even more "local". The trend is increasingly ecoming the "editorial office" on site. Every city, every region has a permanent place in the newspaper. The Mittelbayerische Zeitung, with its 13 regional editions in the Upper Palatinate and large parts of Lower Bavaria, is the medium number one and reached with a circulation of 130,000 copies around 400,000 daily readers. As one of few newspapers in Germany, it entered against the prevailing trend circulation gains. Facebook: http://www.facebook.com/mittelbayerische Twitter: http://twitter.com/mz_de This Outlet offers RSS (Really Simple Syndication).
Language(s): German
ADVERTISING RATES:
SCC .... EUR 134,40
Mechanical Data: Type Area: 430 x 281 mm, No. of Columns (Display): 6, Col Widths (Display): 45 mm
Copy instructions: *Copy Date:* 1 day prior to publication
Supplement(s): Mittelbayerische jun.; Regensburg Arcaden Aktuell; Theater-Zeitung
REGIONAL DAILY & SUNDAY NEWSPAPERS: Regional Daily Newspapers

MITTELBAYERISCHE ZEITUNG FÜR SCHWANDORF, DAS STÄDTEDREIECK UND NEUNBURG 1614959G67B-16492

Editorial: Margaretenstr. 4, 93047 REGENSBURG
Tel: 941 20765 **Fax:** 941 207142
Email: mz-redaktion@mittelbayerische.de **Web site:** http://www.mittelbayerische.de
Freq: 312 issues yearly; **Circ:** 19,500
Profile: Regional daily newspaper with news on politics, economy, culture, sports, travel, technology, etc. What happened in his own front door is the most interesting news! Our Publisher product key is therefore to be the local newspaper. The desire for location-based information has led to our newspaper has become even more "local". The trend is increasingly ecoming the "editorial office" on site. Every city, every region has a permanent place in the newspaper. The Mittelbayerische Zeitung, with its 13 regional editions in the Upper Palatinate and large parts of Lower Bavaria, is the medium number one and reached with a circulation of 130,000 copies around 400,000 daily readers. As one of few newspapers in Germany, it entered against the prevailing trend circulation gains. Facebook: http://www.facebook.com/mittelbayerische Twitter: http://twitter.com/mz_de This Outlet offers RSS (Really Simple Syndication).
Language(s): German
ADVERTISING RATES:
SCC .... EUR 51,60
Mechanical Data: Type Area: 430 x 281 mm, No. of Columns (Display): 6, Col Widths (Display): 45 mm
Copy instructions: *Copy Date:* 1 day prior to publication
Supplement(s): Mittelbayerische jun.
REGIONAL DAILY & SUNDAY NEWSPAPERS: Regional Daily Newspapers

MITTELDEUTSCHE MITTEILUNGEN 1830248G19A-1122

Editorial: Wolframstr. 25, 39116 MAGDEBURG
Tel: 391 6239286 **Fax:** 391 6239286
Email: redaktion@schmidt-tdp.de
Freq: Quarterly; **Circ:** 5,000
Editor: Barbara Schmidt
Profile: Magazine from the German Engineers Association for Middle Germany.
Language(s): German

MITTELDEUTSCHE ZEITUNG 736249G67B-9800

Editorial: Delitzscher Str. 65, 06112 HALLE
Tel: 345 5654240 **Fax:** 345 5654350
Email: service@mz-web.de **Web site:** http://www.mz-web.de
Freq: 312 issues yearly; **Circ:** 223,943
Editor: Hans-Jürgen Greye; **News Editor:** Rainer Wozny; **Advertising Manager:** Rainer Pfeil
Profile: Regional daily newspaper with news on politics, economy, culture, sports, travel, technology, etc. Facebook: http://www.facebook.com/mzwebde Twitter: http://twitter.com/mzwebde This Outlet offers RSS (Really Simple Syndication).
Language(s): German
ADVERTISING RATES:
SCC .... EUR 446,40
Mechanical Data: Type Area: 484 x 327 mm, No. of Columns (Display): 7, Col Widths (Display): 45 mm
Copy instructions: *Copy Date:* 2 days prior to publication
Supplement(s): Galaxo; Pluspunkt; prisma; Rathaus-Center Aktuell; Zeitznah
REGIONAL DAILY & SUNDAY NEWSPAPERS: Regional Daily Newspapers

MITTELSCHWÄBISCHE NACHRICHTEN 736264G67B-9860

Editorial: Curt-Frenzel-Str. 2, 86167 AUGSBURG
Tel: 821 7770 **Fax:** 821 7772067
Web site: http://www.augsburger-allgemeine.de
Freq: 312 issues yearly; **Circ:** 7,908
Advertising Manager: Herbert Dachs
Profile: Daily newspaper with regional news and a local sports section. Facebook: http://www.facebook.com/AugsburgerAllgemeine Twitter: http://twitter.com/AZ_Augsburg This Outlet offers RSS (Really Simple Syndication).
Language(s): German
ADVERTISING RATES:
SCC .... EUR 43,20
Mechanical Data: Type Area: 480 x 327 mm, No. of Columns (Display): 7, Col Widths (Display): 45 mm
Copy instructions: *Copy Date:* 1 day prior to publication
Supplement(s): Freizeit journal
REGIONAL DAILY & SUNDAY NEWSPAPERS: Regional Daily Newspapers

DER MITTELSTAND. 1639822G14A-9579

Editorial: Leipziger Platz 15, 10117 BERLIN
Tel: 30 53320620 **Fax:** 30 53320650
Email: mittelstand@bvmw.de **Web site:** http://www.bvmw.de
Freq: 6 issues yearly; **Circ:** 28,149
Editor: Eberhard Vogt
Profile: Magazine of the Association of medium-sized business, with the topics of economic policy (Germany / Europe / International), business-oriented service and national coverage, it informs practice the entrepreneurial middle class.
Language(s): German
ADVERTISING RATES:
Full Page Mono .... EUR 2900
Full Page Colour .... EUR 2900
Mechanical Data: Type Area: 254 x 185 mm, No. of Columns (Display): 3, Col Widths (Display): 57 mm
Copy instructions: *Copy Date:* 14 days prior to publication

MITTELSTANDSMAGAZIN 735537G14A-4800

Editorial: Gärtnerkoppel 3, 24259 WESTENSEE
Tel: 4305 992992 **Fax:** 4305 992993
Email: gk@mitmagazin.com **Web site:** http://www.mitmagazin.com
Freq: 10 issues yearly; Free to qualifying individuals **Annual Sub.:** EUR 31,00; **Circ:** 38,371
Editor: Günter F. Kohl; **Advertising Manager:** Brigitte Kohl
Profile: Information and information for SMEs, business and management. The middle class magazine is the membership magazine of the SME and business association. It has approximately 40,000 members and supporters of the strongest and most influential political organization in the area of the middle class in Germany. At all levels, represents the interests of SMEs, the MIT and its companies. Its members include hundreds of parliamentarians of all political levels. The MIT-members, including self-employed, entrepreneurs, CEOs, managers, executives, architects, doctors, lawyers, pharmacists, Senior Executives, in chambers, business organizations and in science and management are committed to the principles of social market economy Ludwig Erhard.
Language(s): German
ADVERTISING RATES:
Full Page Mono .... EUR 7800
Full Page Colour .... EUR 7800
Mechanical Data: Type Area: 252 x 180 mm, No. of Columns (Display): 4, Col Widths (Display): 42 mm
Copy instructions: *Copy Date:* 20 days prior to publication
BUSINESS: COMMERCE, INDUSTRY & MANAGEMENT

MITTWOCH AKTUELL 736283G72-8996

Editorial: Harburger Str. 63, 29614 SOLTAU
Tel: 5191 808137 **Fax:** 5191 808146
Email: redaktion@boehme-zeitung.de **Web site:** http://www.mittwochaktuell.de
Freq: Weekly; **Cover Price:** Free; **Circ:** 28,670
Editor: Jörg Jung
Profile: Advertising journal (house-to-house) concentrating on local stories.
Language(s): German
ADVERTISING RATES:
Full Page Mono .... EUR 2532
Full Page Colour .... EUR 3654
Mechanical Data: Type Area: 435 x 282 mm, No. of Columns (Display): 6, Col Widths (Display): 45 mm
Copy instructions: *Copy Date:* 2 days prior to publication
LOCAL NEWSPAPERS

MIX 1659989G80-14277

Editorial: Goebenstr. 14, 28209 BREMEN
Tel: 421 6964340 **Fax:** 421 69643499
Email: presse@mix-online.de **Web site:** http://www.mix-online.de
Freq: Monthly; **Cover Price:** Free; **Circ:** 41,675
Editor: Torsten Höner; **Advertising Manager:** Torsten Höner
Profile: Magazine for Bremen, Bremerhaven and surrounding areas: Calendar of Events, events, dates, cinema, theater, concerts, music, parties, exhibitions, museums, nightlife and culture.
Language(s): German
ADVERTISING RATES:
Full Page Mono .... EUR 1360
Full Page Colour .... EUR 2260
Mechanical Data: Type Area: 190 x 128 mm
Copy instructions: *Copy Date:* 14 days prior to publication
CONSUMER: RURAL & REGIONAL INTEREST

MM LOGISTIK 1739837G10-545

Editorial: Max-Planck-Str. 7, 97082 WÜRZBURG
Tel: 931 4182203 **Fax:** 931 4182770
Email: ken.fouhy@vogel.de **Web site:** http://www.mm-logistik.de
Freq: 8 issues yearly; **Annual Sub.:** EUR 46,00; **Circ:** 14,942
Editor: Ken Fouhy; **Advertising Manager:** Markus Dalke
Profile: Magazine for logistics in industry and commerce. Contents: Products and applications that meets the information needs of manufacturing industry, commerce and the provider of logistics services. The topics range from the areas, handling, warehousing, packaging, distribution and management and IT currently supports and the important events in the logistics industry. MM Logistik focuses on the decision maker of logistic processes in companies with more than 100 employees, as well as freight forwarders and other logistics service providers. Twitter: http://twitter.com/MMLogistik.
Language(s): German
ADVERTISING RATES:
Full Page Mono .... EUR 4350
Full Page Colour .... EUR 5790
Mechanical Data: Type Area: 270 x 190 mm, No. of Columns (Display): 4, Col Widths (Display): 46 mm
Copy instructions: *Copy Date:* 20 days prior to publication
BUSINESS: MATERIALS HANDLING

MM MASCHINENMARKT 736306G19B-106

Editorial: Max-Planck-Str. 7, 97082 WÜRZBURG
Tel: 931 4182203 **Fax:** 931 4182770
Email: ken.fouhy@vogel.de **Web site:** http://www.maschinenmarkt.vogel.de
Freq: Weekly; **Annual Sub.:** EUR 241,00; **Circ:** 44,143
Editor: Ken Fouhy; **Advertising Manager:** Winfried Burkard
Profile: MM MaschinenMarkt is a weekly industry magazine full of up-to-date information on the entire manufacturing sector. Sections on "Production", "Automation" and "Design" report on technical trends and highlight new and improved products and their applications in the manufacturing process. Business news and reports from the management and IT world supplement the coverage of technical topics. The "Update" section contains information on important events and major developments in industry and the economy. maschinenmarkt.de is an online source of concise information on the range of topics which are covered in MM MaschinenMarkt and which help stimulate demand. The maschinenmarkt.de business platform meets the concrete needs of users who are looking for fast, pinpoint access to the well-structured information they need for their daily work.
Language(s): German
Readership: Read by toolmakers and machinists.
ADVERTISING RATES:
Full Page Mono .... EUR 6840
Full Page Colour .... EUR 8098
Mechanical Data: Type Area: 270 x 190 mm, No. of Columns (Display): 4, Col Widths (Display): 46 mm
Copy instructions: *Copy Date:* 21 days prior to publication
Supplement(s): kataloge orange
BUSINESS: ENGINEERING & MACHINERY: Engineering - Design

MM ZULIEFERER 749036G19R-5

Editorial: Max-Planck-Str. 7, 97082 WÜRZBURG
Tel: 931 4180 **Fax:** 931 4182100
Email: info@vogel.de **Web site:** http://www.zulieferer.de
Freq: Annual; **Cover Price:** EUR 25,00; **Circ:** 30,000
Advertising Manager: Fred Poelmann
Profile: Reference work with online print link for design, manufacturing and purchasing managers in manufacturing.
Language(s): German
ADVERTISING RATES:
Full Page Mono .... EUR 2784
Full Page Colour .... EUR 3989
Mechanical Data: Type Area: 270 x 190 mm
Copy instructions: *Copy Date:* 25 days prior to publication

MMP MEDIZINISCHE MONATSSCHRIFT FÜR PHARMAZEUTEN 736314G37-82_20

Editorial: Birkenwaldstr. 44, 70191 STUTTGART
Tel: 711 2582234 **Fax:** 711 2582283
Email: mmp@wissenschaftliche-verlagsgesellschaft.de **Web site:** http://www.deutscher-apotheker-verlag.de
Freq: Monthly; **Annual Sub.:** EUR 150,80; **Circ:** 6,296
Editor: Heike Oberpichler-Schwenk; **Advertising Manager:** Kornelia Wind
Profile: Magazine covering medicine and therapy.
Language(s): German
Readership: Aimed at pharmacists.
ADVERTISING RATES:
Full Page Mono .... EUR 1790
Full Page Colour .... EUR 3240
Mechanical Data: Type Area: 255 x 177 mm, No. of Columns (Display): 4, Col Widths (Display): 41 mm
Copy instructions: *Copy Date:* 21 days prior to publication
BUSINESS: PHARMACEUTICAL & CHEMISTS

MMW FORTSCHRITTE DER MEDIZIN 736318G56A-7160

Editorial: Aschauer Str. 30, 81549 MÜNCHEN
Tel: 89 2030431300 **Fax:** 89 2030431399
Email: dirk.einecke@springer.com **Web site:** http://www.mmw.de
Freq: Weekly; **Annual Sub.:** EUR 204,20; **Circ:** 58,659
Editor: Dirk Einecke; **Advertising Manager:** Claudia Plank
Profile: Medical journal providing up to date developments in the medical profession for further education and information. Also includes information about the economy and Internet in relation to general medical practice. The journal is the following substantive areas: »Regular-certified training courses in cooperation with the Bavarian State Medical Association and overviews of important medical practice issues, and training seminars on various commissions. »magazine section with current reports and reports of important meetings, interviews, view diagnostics, case reports and reader stories" in practice ". »Overview of selected international literature, lecture, and critical comments by experts. »Company doctor's office with tips on practice management, billing and other business issues with service part "MMW hotline".
Language(s): German
Readership: Aimed at GPs, long qualified practitioners and junior doctors.
ADVERTISING RATES:
Full Page Mono .... EUR 3530
Full Page Colour .... EUR 5320
Mechanical Data: Type Area: 240 x 174 mm
Copy instructions: *Copy Date:* 21 days prior to publication
Official Journal of: Organ d. Dt. Hochdruckliga-Dt. Hypertonie Ges., d. Bundesverb. d. Pneumologen, d. Dt. Migräne- u. Kopfschmerzges., d. Dt. Ges. z. Studium d. Schmerzes, d. Fachkommission Diabetes in Bayern, d. Saarländ.-Pfälz. Internistenges., d. Dt. Liga z. Bekämpfung v. Gefäßerkrankungen, d. Dt. Ges. f. Endokrinologie, d. Bundesverb. niedergelassener Kardiologen Deutschland u. d. Ärztl. Weiterbildungskreis f. Psychotherapie
Supplement(s): prodialog
BUSINESS: HEALTH & MEDICAL

MO MAGAZIN FÜR OBERFLÄCHENTECHNIK 736397G19C-60

Editorial: Oskar-Maria-Graf-Ring 23, 81737 MÜNCHEN **Tel:** 89 67369751 **Fax:** 89 67369761
Email: carsten.blumenstengel@metalloberflaeche.de
Web site: http://www.metalloberflaeche.de
Freq: 10 issues yearly; **Annual Sub.:** EUR 129,00; **Circ:** 9,785
Editor: Carsten Blumenstengel; **Advertising Manager:** Dagmar Batschat
Profile: Journal focusing on metal and polymer surfacing techniques.
Language(s): German
ADVERTISING RATES:
Full Page Mono .... EUR 3297
Full Page Colour .... EUR 4780
Mechanical Data: Type Area: 250 x 181 mm, No. of Columns (Display): 4, Col Widths (Display): 40 mm
Official Journal of: Organ d. EGL, Ges. f. Lackiertechnik e.V.

MO MAGAZIN FÜR OBERFLÄCHENTECHNIK 736397G19C-151

Editorial: Oskar-Maria-Graf-Ring 23, 81737 MÜNCHEN **Tel:** 89 67369751 **Fax:** 89 67369761
Email: carsten.blumenstengel@metalloberflaeche.de
Web site: http://www.metalloberflaeche.de
Freq: 10 issues yearly; **Annual Sub.:** EUR 129,00; **Circ:** 9,785
Editor: Carsten Blumenstengel; **Advertising Manager:** Dagmar Batschat
Profile: Journal focusing on metal and polymer surfacing techniques.
Language(s): German
ADVERTISING RATES:
Full Page Mono .... EUR 3297
Full Page Colour .... EUR 4780
Mechanical Data: Type Area: 250 x 181 mm, No. of Columns (Display): 4, Col Widths (Display): 40 mm
Official Journal of: Organ d. EGL, Ges. f. Lackiertechnik e.V.

MÖBEL FERTIGUNG 736361G23A-420

Editorial: Weidestr. 120a, 22083 HAMBURG
Tel: 40 63201853 **Fax:** 40 6307510
Email: tino.eggert@holzmann.de **Web site:** http://www.moebelfertigung.com
Freq: 5 issues yearly; **Annual Sub.:** EUR 32,64; **Circ:** 9,186
Editor: Tino Eggert; **Advertising Manager:** Hans-Christian Hahn
Profile: Magazine about all aspects of the furniture trade.
Language(s): English; German
ADVERTISING RATES:
Full Page Mono .... EUR 4560
Full Page Colour .... EUR 6180
Mechanical Data: Type Area: 263 x 183 mm, No. of Columns (Display): 4, Col Widths (Display): 42 mm
Copy instructions: *Copy Date:* 30 days prior to publication
BUSINESS: FURNISHINGS & FURNITURE

MÖBEL KULTUR
736364G23A-90

Editorial: Weidestr. 120a, 22083 HAMBURG
Tel: 40 6320180 **Fax:** 40 6307510
Email: arnd.ziemer@holzmann.de **Web site:** http://www.moebelkultur.de
Freq: Monthly; Free to qualifying individuals
Annual Sub.: EUR 105,93; **Circ:** 7,626
Editor: Arnd Ziemer; **Advertising Manager:** Jochen Holzmann
Profile: Magazine with news and information from the furniture industry. Facebook: http://www.facebook.com/pages/mobel-kultur/124172594286549.
Language(s): German
ADVERTISING RATES:
Full Page Mono .... EUR 4560
Full Page Colour .... EUR 6180
Mechanical Data: Type Area: 286 x 212 mm, No. of Columns (Display): 4, Col Widths (Display): 50 mm
Copy instructions: *Copy Date:* 30 days prior to publication
Official Journal of: Organ d. Bundesverb. d. Dt. Möbel-, Küchen- u. Einrichtungsfachhandels e.V. u. ZVG Möbel
BUSINESS: FURNISHINGS & FURNITURE

MÖBELMARKT
736365G23A-112

Editorial: Andernacher Str. 5a, 90411 NÜRNBERG
Tel: 911 9557860 **Fax:** 911 9557811
Email: redaktion@ritthammer-verlag.de **Web site:** http://www.moebelmarkt.de
Freq: Monthly; **Annual Sub.:** EUR 90,00; **Circ:** 11,869
Editor: Helmut Merkel
Profile: International journal regards itself as a mirror image of the furniture and interior scene Twitter: http://twitter.com/moebelmarkt This Outlet offers RSS (Really Simple Syndication).
Language(s): German
ADVERTISING RATES:
Full Page Mono .... EUR 4330
Full Page Colour .... EUR 5950
Mechanical Data: Type Area: 285 x 212 mm, No. of Columns (Display): 4, Col Widths (Display): 46 mm
Official Journal of: Organ d. Verb. d. Dt. Möbelindustrie e.V., d. Hauptverb. d. Dt. Holzindustrie u. Kunststoffe verarbeitenden Industrie u. verwandter Industriezweige e.V., d. Fachverb. d. Polstermöbelindustrie, d. Dt. Gütegemeinschaft Möbel, d. Fachverb. Serienmöbelbetriebe d. Handwerks, Arbeitskreis Klein- u. Dielenmöbel, d. Inst. d. Dt. Möbelwirtschaft, d. VdDK-Verb. d. dt. Küchenmöbelindustrie e.V. u. d. möbelonline e.V.
Supplement(s): küche & bad forum
BUSINESS: FURNISHINGS & FURNITURE

DER MÖBELSPEDITEUR
736366G49A-1180

Editorial: Schulstr. 53, 65795 HATTERSHEIM
Tel: 6190 989810 **Fax:** 6190 989820
Email: hochgesang@amoe.de **Web site:** http://www.brandeisweb.de
Freq: 25 issues yearly; **Annual Sub.:** EUR 142,50; **Circ:** 902
Editor: Dierk Hochgesang; **Advertising Manager:** Bernd Wylicil
Profile: Publication about the transport of furniture.
Language(s): German
Readership: Aimed at people in transport companies.
ADVERTISING RATES:
Full Page Mono .... EUR 900
Full Page Colour .... EUR 1485
Mechanical Data: Type Area: 260 x 185 mm, No. of Columns (Display): 3, Col Widths (Display): 58 mm
Copy instructions: *Copy Date:* 12 days prior to publication
Official Journal of: Organ d. Bundesverb. Möbelspedition AMÖ e.V. u. d. Gruppe Internat. Möbelspediteure e.V.
BUSINESS: TRANSPORT

MOBIL
736321G94F-1847

Editorial: Maximilianstr. 14, 53111 BONN
Tel: 228 7660623
Email: mobil.novack@rheuma-liga.de **Web site:** http://www.rheuma-liga.de
Freq: 6 issues yearly; Free to qualifying individuals
Annual Sub.: EUR 16,00; **Circ:** 200,784
Editor: Ines Nowack; **Advertising Manager:** Walter Krey
Profile: The Deutsche Rheuma-Liga (German rheumatic society) magazine – mobil – is the central information and advice medium on rheumatism in Germany. mobil represents competent advice and practical help – informative, authentic and entertaining. Professional editorial expertise and practice-oriented reporting in the dedicated categories, Medicine & Knowledge, Living & Everyday Life, Exercise & Nutrition, Rheuma-Liga Aktiv, Politica l& Social and Tips & Trends, constantly optimize the reader's loyalty to mobil.
Language(s): German
ADVERTISING RATES:
Full Page Mono .... EUR 4250
Full Page Colour .... EUR 5950
Mechanical Data: Type Area: 252 x 180 mm, No. of Columns (Display): 4, Col Widths (Display): 42 mm
CONSUMER: OTHER CLASSIFICATIONS: Disability

MOBIL
736320G94H-9200

Editorial: Stubbenhuk 10, 20459 HAMBURG
Tel: 40 37035050 **Fax:** 40 37035010
Email: gjcm.mm@guj.de **Web site:** http://www.corporate-editors.com
Freq: Monthly; **Annual Sub.:** EUR 25,00; **Circ:** 505,240
Editor: Jan Spielhagen; **Advertising Manager:** Christian Böge
Profile: Magazine read by travellers on Deutsche Bahn.
Language(s): German
ADVERTISING RATES:
Full Page Mono .... EUR 17300
Full Page Colour .... EUR 17300
Mechanical Data: Type Area: 252 x 186 mm
CONSUMER: OTHER CLASSIFICATIONS: Customer Magazines

MOBIL UND SICHER
736336G77A-175

Editorial: Bernard-Eyberg-Str. 60, 51427 BERGISCH GLADBACH **Tel:** 2204 25801 **Fax:** 2204 584977
Email: mobilundsicher@t-online.de **Web site:** http://www.mobilundsicher.de
Freq: 6 issues yearly; **Annual Sub.:** EUR 8,25; **Circ:** 22,768
Editor: Rita Bourauel; **Advertising Manager:** Christiane Kermel
Profile: Magazine of the Deutschen Verkehrswacht The editorial concept of mobile and secure combines unique guide function for the areas of road safety, Traffic education, transport policy, traffic engineering, traffic law, accident research and road / environment. The sections travel, media, jokes and games provide entertainment. Audience: members, supporters of the German road, the national, regional, district and local traffic safety and youth traffic safety, traffic police educators, presenters and technical adviser for safety, security interest car users and all road users.
Language(s): German
Readership: Aimed at members of the Road Safety Promotion Organisation.
ADVERTISING RATES:
Full Page Mono .... EUR 3360
Full Page Colour .... EUR 5376
Mechanical Data: Type Area: 260 x 185 mm, No. of Columns (Display): 4, Col Widths (Display): 43 mm
Copy instructions: *Copy Date:* 30 days prior to publication
CONSUMER: MOTORING & CYCLING: Motoring

MOBILE
736322G74D-163

Editorial: Hermann-Herder-Str. 4, 79104 FREIBURG
Tel: 761 2717295 **Fax:** 761 2717262
Email: redaktion@mobile-familienmagazin.de **Web site:** http://www.mobile-elternmagazin.de
Freq: 6 issues yearly; **Annual Sub.:** EUR 12,00; **Circ:** 276,683
Editor: Julia Ubbelohde; **Advertising Manager:** Bettina Schillinger
Profile: mobile is a parents magazine of the kindergarten time, the mothers and fathers in their parenting skills and support that deals with the world of children in preschool and school age. It uses mobile problems and questions of parents and deals with current views of the kindergarten day. mobile will provide young parents practical and intelligible about topics in the areas education and psychology, health and nutrition, safety and nature. In the forefront of all issues is the active engagement of parents with their children.
Language(s): German
Readership: Aimed at parents with children in nursery education.
ADVERTISING RATES:
Full Page Mono .... EUR 18950
Full Page Colour .... EUR 18950
Mechanical Data: Type Area: 233 x 175 mm
Copy instructions: *Copy Date:* 52 days prior to publication
CONSUMER: WOMEN'S INTEREST CONSUMER MAGAZINES: Child Care

MOBILE BUSINESS
2038087G14A-10468

Editorial: Bertram-Blank-Str. 8, 51427 BERGISCH GLADBACH **Tel:** 2204 92140 **Fax:** 2204 921430
Email: redaktion@mobilebusiness.de **Web site:** http://www.mobilebusiness.de
Freq: 10 issues yearly; **Annual Sub.:** EUR 75,00; **Circ:** 28,515
Editor: Guido Piech; **Advertising Manager:** Thomas Büchel
Profile: Mobile Business is the new trend magazine for the mobile generation and for decision makers in companies who consider mobile communication as the basis for growth in business. Mobile Business is a strongly practical oriented print & online magazine that shows how company processes are prepared for the mobile business. Experts of all fields as well as the users themselves describe the usage of mobile applications, their integration in companies and the effective creation of value. Users will find a lof of suggestions in handling with these technologies. Market trends, new products and overviews of mobile applications give an overview of the market developments. All reports are intimately connected with facts and figures. Mobile Business: Lifestyle and business in a single magazine!.
Language(s): German
ADVERTISING RATES:
Full Page Mono .... EUR 7500
Full Page Colour .... EUR 9150
Mechanical Data: Type Area: 244 x 181 mm, No. of Columns (Display): 3, Col Widths (Display): 57 mm
Copy instructions: *Copy Date:* 23 days prior to publication

MOBILE MASCHINEN
1837304G19E-1944

Editorial: Lise-Meitner-Str. 2, 55129 MAINZ
Tel: 6131 992352 **Fax:** 6131 992100
Email: m.pfister@vfmz.de **Web site:** http://www.industrie-service.de
Freq: Quarterly; **Annual Sub.:** EUR 60,00; **Circ:** 7,433
Editor: Michael Pfister; **Advertising Manager:** Andreas Zepig
Profile: Mobile Maschinen serves as exchange experience by practice reports, surveys, reports, interviews and market surveys. Interdisciplinary insights are offered for actual situation and technical developments of related markets - especially in the markets construction, agriculture, forestry, materials handling and local and special vehicles. Hereby the disciplines of electrical, hydraulic and mechanical drive and control technology for mobile equipment are in focus. For the interior of a cab, nonfatiguing Components with functionality and ergonomics aspects are presented. Additional Mobile Maschinen offers quality information on all topics, which help the designer of mobile Machines in their daily work, such as technical, economic, legal and design aspects. Actual information from the market of components and systems and services complement the editorial environment.
Language(s): German
ADVERTISING RATES:
Full Page Mono .... EUR 3700
Full Page Colour .... EUR 4930
Mechanical Data: Type Area: 265 x 185 mm, No. of Columns (Display): 4, Col Widths (Display): 43 mm
Copy instructions: *Copy Date:* 14 days prior to publication
Official Journal of: Organ d. "Forum Mobile Maschinen" im VDMA

MOBILE NEWS
1793984G18B-2148

Editorial: Von-Ketteler-Str. 16, 84416 TAUFKIRCHEN
Tel: 8084 4133660 **Fax:** 8084 4133661
Email: mobile.news@fs-on.de
Freq: 6 issues yearly; **Annual Sub.:** EUR 25,00; **Circ:** 40,216
Editor: Thomas Sagkob; **Advertising Manager:** Volker Sagkob
Profile: Magazine for mobile communications (mobile phone-navigation-Mobile PC- Accessories-tariffs).
Language(s): German
ADVERTISING RATES:
Full Page Mono .... EUR 4071
Full Page Colour .... EUR 5800
Mechanical Data: Type Area: 250 x 185 mm, No. of Columns (Display): 4, Col Widths (Display): 40 mm
Copy instructions: *Copy Date:* 30 days prior to publication

MOBILE ZEIT
1615922G18B-1979

Editorial: Goethestr. 73a, 01589 RIESA
Tel: 3525 5290737 **Fax:** 3525 5290733
Email: schneider@mobilezeit.de **Web site:** http://www.mobilewelt.com
Freq: 6 issues yearly; **Cover Price:** EUR 3,30; **Circ:** 60,000
Editor: Ulf Schneider; **Advertising Manager:** Dirk Stachowski
Profile: Magazine of hardware tests (mobile phone, organizer, notebook) and buy recommendations.
Language(s): German
ADVERTISING RATES:
Full Page Mono .... EUR 4619
Full Page Colour .... EUR 7118
Mechanical Data: Type Area: 264 x 180 mm

MOBILE.DE
1698215G77A-2747

Editorial: Marktplatz 1, 14532 KLEINMACHNOW
Tel: 30 81097500 **Fax:** 30 81097132
Email: ratgeber@team.mobile.de **Web site:** http://www.mobile.de
Freq: Daily; **Cover Price:** Paid; **Circ:** 63,309,696 Unique Users
Language(s): German
CONSUMER: MOTORING & CYCLING: Motoring

MOBILITY 2.0
2088978G77A-2990

Editorial: Nymphenburger Str. 86, 80636 MÜNCHEN
Tel: 89 50038361 **Fax:** 89 50038310
Email: mobility2.0@publish-industry.net **Web site:** http://www.mobility20.net
Freq: 3 issues yearly; **Annual Sub.:** EUR 19,20; **Circ:** 14,450
Editor: Karlhorst Klotz; **Advertising Manager:** Katharina Merz
Profile: Mobility 2.0 provides answers to these central questions of our time, focuses on current technologies, describes the background and connections between vehicles, infrastructure and transport concepts. The focus is on sustainable mobility in the future, which sought by different techniques can be: use on one side with increasingly lower-emission engines and fuels, on the other side with pure electric vehicles, electricity from renewable energy or hybrid vehicles that combine the best of both worlds. Mobility 2.0 examines the use of traditional fuels and natural gas and LPG as well as the development of alternative fuels or the use of hydrogen as a mobile power source. It discusses Mobility 2.0 is not only how the vehicles look of tomorrow and what technology components are used, but points to, is what materials and processing methods to achieve this. With regard to electric mobility explains the magazine, how effectively current battery systems are and how to build energy suppliers and network operators a comprehensive energy supply for loading of modern electric vehicles. Audience: Readers of Mobility 2.0 are experts in the automotive and motorcycle industry and its suppliers, energy suppliers and network operators, public and municipal facilities. You must know the state of mobility, infrastructure and traffic engineering as well as current trends and look beyond the boundaries of their respective field - professionals who influence the development of strategies in their companies and decide on next steps.
Language(s): German
ADVERTISING RATES:
Full Page Mono .... EUR 5338
Full Page Colour .... EUR 6280
Mechanical Data: Type Area: 232 x 178 mm

MOBILOGISCH!
731298G49A-760

Editorial: Exerzierstr. 20, 13357 BERLIN
Tel: 30 4927473 **Fax:** 30 4927972
Email: redaktion@mobilogisch.de **Web site:** http://www.mobilogisch.de
Freq: Quarterly; Free to qualifying individuals
Annual Sub.: EUR 40,00; **Circ:** 1,000
Editor: Stefan Lieb; **Advertising Manager:** Karl-Heinz Ludewig
Profile: Magzine for dedicated lay people, experts in planning offices, universities, parties and the press on Transport and Environment.
Language(s): German
ADVERTISING RATES:
Full Page Mono .... EUR 200
Mechanical Data: Type Area: 250 x 189 mm, No. of Columns (Display): 2, Col Widths (Display): 90 mm
Copy instructions: *Copy Date:* 15 days prior to publication

MODELL
736339G79B-1040

Editorial: Klosterring 1, 78050 VILLINGEN-SCHWENNINGEN **Tel:** 7721 89870 **Fax:** 7721 898750
Email: mueller@neckar-verlag.de **Web site:** http://www.neckar-verlag.de
Freq: Monthly; **Annual Sub.:** EUR 62,00; **Circ:** 34,500
Editor: Ralph Müller; **Advertising Manager:** Uwe Stockburger
Profile: Magazine about radio-controlled model-building. The magazine reports monthly on all key issues of remote controlled flight. All posts are written by experts, backed by an editorial team consists of experienced and active model athletes. In addition to test reports of models, remote controls and motors model reports monthly about tips and tricks in the model aircraft in the flight season from the event's highlights and major exhibitions. The heading "News from the market " presented every month on multiple pages, the most innovative solutions. A unique feature is the DVD, the feature in the magazine and additional issues will be taken an interesting and entertaining.
Language(s): German
Readership: Aimed at people interested in model flying.
Mechanical Data: Type Area: 265 x 185 mm, No. of Columns (Display): 4, Col Widths (Display): 42 mm
CONSUMER: HOBBIES & DIY: Models & Modelling

MODELL FAHRZEUG
1660478G79B-1717

Editorial: Postfach 551129, 90218 NÜRNBERG
Tel: 911 9404640 **Fax:** 911 9404650
Email: a.berse@die-redakteure.com **Web site:** http://www.modellfahrzeug.de
Freq: 6 issues yearly; **Annual Sub.:** EUR 29,90; **Circ:** 13,500
Editor: Andreas Berse
Profile: Vehicle model is the leading magazine for car miniatures. It delivers 6 x in current insider information for model car enthusiasts comprehensive reports, clear opinions, collector profiles, useful tips plus information on meetings and exhibitions.
Language(s): German
ADVERTISING RATES:
Full Page Mono .... EUR 1980
Full Page Colour .... EUR 3170
Mechanical Data: Type Area: 248 x 182 mm, No. of Columns (Display): 4, Col Widths (Display): 43 mm
CONSUMER: HOBBIES & DIY: Models & Modelling

MODELL MAGAZIN
736348G79B-1160

Editorial: Willstätterstr. 9, 40549 DÜSSELDORF
Tel: 211 5201334 **Fax:** 211 5201328
Email: mm@alba-verlag.de **Web site:** http://www.alba-verlag.de
Freq: Monthly; **Annual Sub.:** EUR 49,80; **Circ:** 6,050
Advertising Manager: Robert A. Braun
Profile: Magazine aimed at people collecting and modelling scale cars, trucks and motorcycles.
Language(s): German
Readership: Aimed at model making enthusiasts.
ADVERTISING RATES:
Full Page Mono .... EUR 1250
Full Page Colour .... EUR 1795
Mechanical Data: Type Area: 255 x 191 mm, No. of Columns (Display): 4, Col Widths (Display): 45 mm
Copy instructions: *Copy Date:* 21 days prior to publication
CONSUMER: HOBBIES & DIY: Models & Modelling

MODELLFAN
736346G79B-1140

Editorial: Infanteriestr. 11a, 80797 MÜNCHEN
Tel: 89 130699720 **Fax:** 89 130699700
Email: redaktion@modellfan.de **Web site:** http://www.modellfan.de
Freq: Monthly; Free to qualifying individuals
Annual Sub.: EUR 70,20; **Circ:** 21,200

Editor: Helge Schling; **Advertising Manager:** Helmut Kramer
Profile: Magazine about plastic model-making. The magazine reported extensively and in detail about all facets of the hobby. Experienced model builders provide month by month market information and expertise for all areas of model building - cars, airplanes, ships, figures and dioramas. The magazine offers in every issue thanks to the many detailed and step-by-step illustrations excellent construction reports on current-model kits and order and own buildings. In addition to detailed engineering model building, materials, tools and colors will be handled and provides many tips and tricks. In the presentation of the model releases, in book reviews and in extensive surveys of manufacturers and retailers will find the reader's current market information. Target group: Magazine for all model builders. There is a distinction to the interests of its readers - from beginners and returners to rounders to. Most readers are between 35 us 55 years ago.
Language(s): German
ADVERTISING RATES:
Full Page Colour .... EUR 2135
Mechanical Data: Type Area: 235 x 181 mm, No. of Columns (Display): 4, Col Widths (Display): 45 mm
Copy instructions: *Copy Date:* 30 days prior to publication
Official Journal of: Organ d. Dt. Plastik-Modellbau-Verb. e.V.
CONSUMER: HOBBIES & DIY: Models & Modelling

MODEL.SZENE.DE
1662248G91D-10176
Editorial: Max-Planck-Str. 6, 50858 KÖLN
Tel: 221 91116 **Fax:** 221 911169
Email: info@webpool.de **Web site:** http://www.model.szene.de
Cover Price: Paid
Language(s): German
CONSUMER: RECREATION & LEISURE: Children & Youth

MODERNE GEBÄUDETECHNIK
736350G4E-7053
Editorial: Am Friedrichshain 22, 10407 BERLIN
Tel: 30 42151386 **Fax:** 30 42151207
Email: bernd.schroeder@hussberlin.de **Web site:** http://www.tga-praxis.de
Freq: 10 issues yearly; **Annual Sub.:** EUR 95,00; **Circ:** 11,858
Editor: Bernd Schröder; **Advertising Manager:** Marco Fiolka
Profile: Magazine covering building techniques for cities.
Language(s): German
Readership: Aimed at builders and architects.
ADVERTISING RATES:
Full Page Mono .... EUR 3680
Full Page Colour .... EUR 4880
Mechanical Data: Type Area: 266 x 185 mm, No. of Columns (Display): 4, Col Widths (Display): 43 mm
Copy instructions: *Copy Date:* 20 days prior to publication
BUSINESS: ARCHITECTURE & BUILDING: Building

MODERNE METALLTECHNIK M
736351G27-1840
Editorial: Danziger Str. 20, 74321 BIETIGHEIM-BISSINGEN **Tel:** 7142 63782 **Fax:** 7142 61298
Freq: Monthly; **Annual Sub.:** EUR 86,40; **Circ:** 13,100
Editor: H.-J. Buldt
Profile: Magazine about training and jobs in the metal industry.
Language(s): German
ADVERTISING RATES:
Full Page Mono .... EUR 1155
Full Page Colour .... EUR 1682
Mechanical Data: Type Area: 265 x 185 mm, No. of Columns (Display): 4, Col Widths (Display): 42 mm
Copy instructions: *Copy Date:* 30 days prior to publication

MODERNISIERUNGS MAGAZIN FÜR BAUGESELLSCHAFTEN - NEUBAU UND BESTAND -
736354G4E-392
Editorial: Reinsburgstr. 82, 70178 STUTTGART
Tel: 711 238860 **Fax:** 711 2388625
Email: joerg.bleyhl@pressecompany.de **Web site:** http://www.immoclick24.de
Freq: 10 issues yearly; **Annual Sub.:** EUR 26,00; **Circ:** 12,132
Editor: Jörg Bleyhl; **Advertising Manager:** Karin Navaei
Profile: Magazine about house modernisation and general building and living matters.
Language(s): German
ADVERTISING RATES:
Full Page Mono .... EUR 4120
Full Page Colour .... EUR 5560
Mechanical Data: Type Area: 270 x 185 mm, No. of Columns (Display): 3, Col Widths (Display): 59 mm
Copy instructions: *Copy Date:* 15 days prior to publication
BUSINESS: ARCHITECTURE & BUILDING: Building

MOHR STADTILLU
1616483G80-13824
Editorial: Hambacher Weg 12, 96450 COBURG
Tel: 9561 354270
Email: redaktion.coburg@mohr-stadtillu.de **Web site:** http://www.mohr-stadtillu.de
Freq: Monthly; **Cover Price:** Free; **Circ:** 13,707
Advertising Manager: Heiko Bayerlieb
Profile: Magazine for city and region, concentrating on gastronomy, music, arts and events.
Language(s): German
ADVERTISING RATES:
Full Page Mono .... EUR 2550
Full Page Colour .... EUR 2550
CONSUMER: RURAL & REGIONAL INTEREST

MOHR STADTILLU
1616489G80-13826
Editorial: Untere Sandstr. 1, 96049 BAMBERG
Tel: 951 5090341
Email: redaktion.bamberg@mohr-stadtillu.de **Web site:** http://www.mohr-stadtillu.de
Freq: Monthly; **Cover Price:** Free; **Circ:** 8,026
Editor: Andreas Mack
Profile: Magazine for city and region, concentrating on gastronomy, music, arts and events.
Language(s): German
ADVERTISING RATES:
Full Page Mono .... EUR 1700
Full Page Colour .... EUR 1700
CONSUMER: RURAL & REGIONAL INTEREST

MOIN MOIN FLENSBURG
736384G72-9040
Editorial: Am Friedenshügel 2, 24941 FLENSBURG
Tel: 461 588300 **Fax:** 461 588333
Email: krumrey@moinmoin.de **Web site:** http://www.moinmoin.de
Freq: Weekly; **Cover Price:** Free; **Circ:** 80,500
Editor: Alice Krumrey; **Advertising Manager:** Jens-Uwe Boenigk
Profile: Advertising journal (house-to-house) concentrating on local stories.
Language(s): German
ADVERTISING RATES:
Full Page Mono .... EUR 7739
Full Page Colour .... EUR 11216
Mechanical Data: Type Area: 487 x 325 mm, No. of Columns (Display): 7, Col Widths (Display): 44 mm
Copy instructions: *Copy Date:* 2 days prior to publication
LOCAL NEWSPAPERS

MOIN MOIN KAPPELN/ANGELN
736382G72-9032
Editorial: Callisenstr. 1b, 24837 SCHLESWIG
Tel: 4621 964118 **Fax:** 4621 964117
Email: sl-redaktion@moinmoin.de **Web site:** http://www.moinmoin.de
Cover Price: Free
Editor: Stephanie Redwanz; **Advertising Manager:** Jens-Uwe Boenigk
Profile: Advertising journal (house-to-house) concentrating on local stories.
Language(s): German
LOCAL NEWSPAPERS

MOIN MOIN SCHLESWIG
736388G72-9056
Editorial: Callisenstr. 1b, 24837 SCHLESWIG
Tel: 4621 964118 **Fax:** 4621 964117
Email: sl-redaktion@moinmoin.de **Web site:** http://www.moinmoin.de
Freq: Weekly; **Cover Price:** Free; **Circ:** 36,500
Editor: Alice Krumrey; **Advertising Manager:** Jens-Uwe Boenigk
Profile: Advertising journal (house-to-house) concentrating on local stories.
Language(s): German
ADVERTISING RATES:
Full Page Mono .... EUR 5216
Full Page Colour .... EUR 7568
Mechanical Data: Type Area: 487 x 325 mm, No. of Columns (Display): 7, Col Widths (Display): 44 mm
Copy instructions: *Copy Date:* 2 days prior to publication
LOCAL NEWSPAPERS

MOIN MOIN SÜDTONDERN
736391G72-9068
Editorial: Norderstr. 22, 25813 HUSUM
Tel: 4841 835666 **Fax:** 4841 835670
Email: redaktion-nf@nf-palette.de **Web site:** http://www.moinmoin.de
Freq: Weekly; **Cover Price:** Free; **Circ:** 15,000
Editor: Marion Laß; **Advertising Manager:** Jens-Uwe Boenigk
Profile: Advertising journal (house-to-house) concentrating on local stories.
Language(s): German
ADVERTISING RATES:
Full Page Mono .... EUR 4603
Full Page Colour .... EUR 6682
Mechanical Data: Type Area: 487 x 325 mm, No. of Columns (Display): 7, Col Widths (Display): 44 mm
Copy instructions: *Copy Date:* 2 days prior to publication
LOCAL NEWSPAPERS

MOLECULAR NUTRITION & FOOD RESEARCH
736910G22A-165
Editorial: Boschstr. 12, 69469 WEINHEIM
Tel: 6201 606311 **Fax:** 6201 606172
Email: hkraus@wiley-vch.de **Web site:** http://www.mnf-journal.de
Freq: Monthly; **Annual Sub.:** EUR 1567,00; **Circ:** 1,200
Editor: Hans-Joachim Kraus; **Advertising Manager:** Hans-Joachim Kraus
Profile: Official journal of the German Institute for Food Research.
Language(s): English
ADVERTISING RATES:
Full Page Mono .... EUR 950
Full Page Colour .... EUR 1930
Mechanical Data: Type Area: 230 x 170 mm
Copy instructions: *Copy Date:* 29 days prior to publication
BUSINESS: FOOD

DIE MOLKEREIZEITUNG WELT DER MILCH
747124G21G-5
Editorial: Am Flugplatz 7, 31137 HILDESHEIM
Tel: 5121 9187040 **Fax:** 5121 9187059
Email: info@wemcard.de **Web site:** http://www.wemcard.de
Freq: Weekly; **Annual Sub.:** EUR 444,00; **Circ:** 2,093
Editor: Ralf Friederich; **Advertising Manager:** Böttcher
Profile: Magazine covering all aspects of milk manufacture.
Language(s): German
ADVERTISING RATES:
Full Page Mono .... EUR 1500
Full Page Colour .... EUR 1500
Mechanical Data: Type Area: 245 x 190 mm, No. of Columns (Display): 3, Col Widths (Display): 60 mm
Copy instructions: *Copy Date:* 14 days prior to publication
BUSINESS: AGRICULTURE & FARMING: Milk

MONATSSCHRIFT
736409G21A-2860
Editorial: Rochusstr. 18, 53123 BONN
Tel: 228 52006577 **Fax:** 228 52006555
Email: thomas.kuehlwetter@monatsschrift.de **Web site:** http://www.monatsschrift.de
Freq: Monthly; **Annual Sub.:** EUR 90,00; **Circ:** 6,600
Editor: Thomas Kühlwetter; **Advertising Manager:** Markus Schulz
Profile: Magazine about all aspects of professional gardening.
Language(s): German
ADVERTISING RATES:
Full Page Mono .... EUR 2668
Full Page Colour .... EUR 4563
Mechanical Data: Type Area: 270 x 185 mm, No. of Columns (Display): 4, Col Widths (Display): 45 mm
Copy instructions: *Copy Date:* 21 days prior to publication
Official Journal of: Organ d. Provinzialverb. Rhein. Obst- u. Gemüsebauer e.V. u. d. Bauern- u. Winzerverb. Rheinland-Pfalz Süd e.V.
BUSINESS: AGRICULTURE & FARMING

MONATSSCHRIFT FÜR DEUTSCHES RECHT MDR
736411G44-1480
Editorial: Gustav-Heinemann-Ufer 58, 50968 KÖLN
Tel: 221 93738501 **Fax:** 221 93738951
Email: mdr@otto-schmidt.de **Web site:** http://www.mdr.ovs.de
Freq: 24 issues yearly; **Annual Sub.:** EUR 256,90; **Circ:** 3,221
Editor: Natalie Malcolm; **Advertising Manager:** Thorsten Deuse
Profile: Magazine about German private law containing news, information and articles.
Language(s): German
Readership: Aimed at people working within the legal profession, lawyers and judges.
ADVERTISING RATES:
Full Page Mono .... EUR 1195
Full Page Colour .... EUR 2092
Mechanical Data: Type Area: 260 x 180 mm, No. of Columns (Display): 2, Col Widths (Display): 88 mm
BUSINESS: LEGAL

MONATSSCHRIFT FÜR KRIMINOLOGIE UND STRAFRECHTSREFORM
736412G44-1500
Editorial: Günterstalstr. 73, 79100 FREIBURG
Tel: 761 7081210 **Fax:** 761 7081316
Email: u.auerbach@mpicc.de **Web site:** http://www.mschrkrim.de
Freq: 6 issues yearly; **Annual Sub.:** EUR 122,60; **Circ:** 750
Editor: Hans-Jörg Albrecht
Profile: Magazine containing news and information about criminology and penal reform.
Language(s): German
ADVERTISING RATES:
Full Page Mono .... EUR 728
Full Page Colour .... EUR 1622
Mechanical Data: Type Area: 195 x 130 mm
BUSINESS: LEGAL

MONATSSCHRIFT KINDERHEILKUNDE
736413G56A-7180
Editorial: Tiergartenstr. 17, 69121 HEIDELBERG
Tel: 6221 4878741 **Fax:** 6221 48768741
Email: kathrin.muth@springer.com **Web site:** http://www.springerlink.com
Freq: Monthly; **Annual Sub.:** EUR 366,00; **Circ:** 14,717
Profile: Monatsschrift Kinderheilkunde is an internationally respected journal covering all areas of pediatrics and juvenile medicine. The focus is on prevention, diagnostic approaches, management of complications, and current therapy strategies. The journal provides information for all pediatricians working in practical and clinical environments and scientists who are particularly interested in issues of pediatrics. Freely submitted original papers allow the presentation of important clinical studies and serve scientific exchange. Comprehensive reviews on a specific topical issue focus on providing evidenced based information on diagnostics and therapy. Review articles under the rubric "Continuing Medical Education" present verified results of scientific research and their integration into daily practice.
Language(s): German
ADVERTISING RATES:
Full Page Mono .... EUR 2900
Full Page Colour .... EUR 4250
Mechanical Data: Type Area: 240 x 174 mm
Official Journal of: Organ d. Dt. Ges. f. Kinderheilkunde u. Jugendmedizin u. d. Österr. Ges. f. Kinder- u. Jugendheilkunde
BUSINESS: HEALTH & MEDICAL

LE MONDE DIPLOMATIQUE
736414G65A-220_102
Editorial: Rudi-Dutschke-Str. 23, 10969 BERLIN
Tel: 30 25902276 **Fax:** 30 25902676
Email: diplo@monde-diplomatique.de **Web site:** http://www.monde-diplomatique.de
Freq: Monthly; **Annual Sub.:** EUR 46,80; **Circ:** 85,400
Editor: Barbara Bauer; **Advertising Manager:** Lena Meier
Profile: Monthly newspaper for international politics and society. It is published worldwide in 61 editions (31 online and 30 print editions). Of the 1.5 million readers, which have a newspaper in Arabic or Italian in mind, others read it in Japanese, Serbian or Hungarian. Added 2006, the Russian and Finnish edition. None of these papers is a pure one-to-one translation of the French original, every editorial makes a selection of articles, sets its own accents or add your own contributions. Thus, the German edition has up to three of the Berlin editorial pages disputed, regularly presents international artists in front of selected works and prints on the last page of the newspaper from a specially drawn comic. LE MONDE diplomatique is a unique medium: modern, open, international, and left, ie a radical understanding of equal opportunities required. Illuminated by the newspaper reports from the reality of the consequences and context of globalization, pointing to economic and social distribution conflicts, and make it - our special trademark - with maps illustrate what interests are at stake. Facebook: http://www.facebook.com/pages/Le-Monde-diplomatique-der-globale-Blick/136860635948 Twitter: http://twitter.com/#!/Monde_diplo.
Language(s): German
ADVERTISING RATES:
Full Page Mono .... EUR 10430
Full Page Colour .... EUR 11430
Mechanical Data: Type Area: 422 x 287 mm, No. of Columns (Display): 5, Col Widths (Display): 54 mm
Copy instructions: *Copy Date:* 21 days prior to publication
Supplement to: taz.die tageszeitung
NATIONAL DAILY & SUNDAY NEWSPAPERS: National Daily Newspapers

MONEYMAKER
2038855G2A-5920
Editorial: Boslerstr. 29, 71088 HOLZGERLINGEN
Tel: 7031 7440 **Fax:** 7031 744195
Email: seitz@elite-magazinverlag.de **Web site:** http://www.moneymaker-magazin.de
Freq: Half-yearly; **Cover Price:** EUR 1,00; **Circ:** 25,000
Editor: Bernd Seitz
Profile: Magazine for all solid-and part-time earning opportunities.
Language(s): German
ADVERTISING RATES:
Full Page Mono .... EUR 2500
Full Page Colour .... EUR 2500
Mechanical Data: Type Area: 254 x 185 mm, No. of Columns (Display): 3, Col Widths (Display): 59 mm
Copy instructions: *Copy Date:* 21 days prior to publication

MONOKEL
736431G74N-460
Editorial: Heinrich-Kraak-Str. 33, 33617 BIELEFELD
Tel: 521 150948 **Fax:** 521 150354
Web site: http://www.monokel.eu
Freq: 6 issues yearly; **Cover Price:** Free; **Circ:** 18,000
Editor: Marianne Zander; **Advertising Manager:** Markus Galla
Profile: Magazine for the elderly.
Language(s): German
ADVERTISING RATES:
Full Page Mono .... EUR 849
Full Page Colour .... EUR 1250
Mechanical Data: Type Area: 280 x 190 mm, No. of Columns (Display): 4
Copy instructions: *Copy Date:* 8 days prior to publication

MONTAGETECHNIK

2040246G19A-1149

Editorial: Kolbergerstr. 22, 81679 MÜNCHEN
Email: graef@hanser.de **Web site:** http://www.montagetechnik-online.de
Freq: 6 issues yearly; **Annual Sub.:** EUR 60,00; **Circ:** 9,814
Profile: The magazine targets design engineers, assembly and plant managers and production managers in automotive, machinery and plant construction, in electrical engineering and in the manufacturing industry or similar sectors. All the facets of assembly technology are presented in magazine format: Design - assembly plant design engineers will find technical data and new options for application of components and systems. Irrespective whether they are designing plant for own use or for the market. Automation - assembly, plant and production managers always have two goals in mind: More output-less waste! The assembly must be automated in order to achieve this. The magazine offers solutions and reports from the field. Organization - company management organizes the execution of many tasks - also in the assembly section. Contributions dealing with theoretical approaches are thus as relevant to efficiently organized processes as are experiential reports. It is editorial structure to always include the following aspects of assembly technology: Assembly, Mechanics, Robotics, Handling, Joining, Driving, Control and testing, Disassembly, Micro-assembly.
Language(s): German
ADVERTISING RATES:
Full Page Mono .... EUR 2020
Full Page Colour .... EUR 2020
Mechanical Data: Type Area: 202 x 152 mm
Copy instructions: *Copy Date:* 28 days prior to publication

MOOSBURGER ZEITUNG

736446G67B-9900

Editorial: Altstadt 89, 84028 LANDSHUT
Tel: 871 8500 **Fax:** 871 850202
Email: redaktion@landshuter-zeitung.de **Web site:** http://www.idowa.de
Freq: 312 issues yearly; **Circ:** 36,796
Advertising Manager: Irmgard Haberger
Profile: Regional daily newspaper with news on politics, economy, culture, sports, travel, technology, etc. She is a local issue of the Landshuter Zeitung for the eastern part of County Freising. Twitter: http://twitter.com/idowa This Outlet offers RSS (Really Simple Syndication).
Language(s): German
ADVERTISING RATES:
SCC .... EUR 67,60
Mechanical Data: Type Area: 430 x 282 mm, No. of Columns (Display): 6, Col Widths (Display): 45 mm
Copy instructions: *Copy Date:* 1 day prior to publication
Supplement(s): Zuhause
REGIONAL DAILY & SUNDAY NEWSPAPERS: Regional Daily Newspapers

MORGENPOST AM SONNTAG

736450G72-9088

Editorial: Ostra-Allee 20, 01067 DRESDEN
Tel: 351 48642626 **Fax:** 351 48642467
Email: mopodd.sopo@dd-v.de **Web site:** http://www.sz-online.de
Freq: Weekly; **Circ:** 69,833
Editor: Peter Rzepus; **Advertising Manager:** Tobias Spitzhorn
Profile: Regional weekly newspaper with news on politics, economy, culture, sport, travel, technology, etc. It is the joint Sunday edition of the Chemnitzer Morgenpost and Dresdner Morgenpost. Facebook: http://www.facebook.com/szonline.
Language(s): German
ADVERTISING RATES:
SCC .... EUR 68,70
Mechanical Data: Type Area: 327 x 233 mm, No. of Columns (Display): 5, Col Widths (Display): 45 mm
Copy instructions: *Copy Date:* 3 days prior to publication
LOCAL NEWSPAPERS

MORITZ

736452G80-7800

Editorial: Kreuzenstr. 94, 74076 HEILBRONN
Tel: 7131 1530210 **Fax:** 7131 1530111
Email: redaktion@moritz.de **Web site:** http://www.moritz.de
Freq: Monthly; **Cover Price:** Free; **Circ:** 14,850
Editor: Tamara Baranyay; **Advertising Manager:** Ingo Eckert
Profile: City magazine for Neckar-Odenwald/Kraichgau: The major events of an entire month of scene, cinema, theater, art, music, parties, sports and local color - all this is found in the extensive calendar of events Moritz. To a happy read and much-used city magazine, a comprehensive journal is part of recent reports, profiles and interviews. A monthly changing themes part with attractive special topics and special issues provides the reader with additional information. The monthly service section with the calendar of events and the many among the most respected Classifieds standard, well-made city magazine. Last-but-not-least part of the scene shows the scene whisper a cross section through the events of the city. The scene-pics are often the first pages viewed and are true to the motto "see and be seen".
Language(s): German
ADVERTISING RATES:
Full Page Mono .... EUR 2160
Full Page Colour .... EUR 2520
Mechanical Data: Type Area: 265 x 184 mm, No. of Columns (Display): 4, Col Widths (Display): 43 mm
Copy instructions: *Copy Date:* 11 days prior to publication
CONSUMER: RURAL & REGIONAL INTEREST

MORITZ

736453G80-7820

Editorial: Kreuzenstr. 94, 74076 HEILBRONN
Tel: 7131 1530210 **Fax:** 7131 1530111
Email: redaktion@moritz.de **Web site:** http://www.moritz.de
Freq: Monthly; **Cover Price:** Free; **Circ:** 22,859
Editor: Tamara Baranyay; **Advertising Manager:** Ingo Eckert
Profile: City magazine for Heilbronn: The major events of an entire month of scene, cinema, theater, art, music, parties, sports and local color - all this is found in the extensive calendar of events Moritz. To a happy read and much-used city magazine, a comprehensive journal is part of recent reports, profiles and interviews. A monthly changing themes part with attractive special topics and special issues provides the reader with additional information. The monthly service section with the calendar of events and the many among the most respected Classifieds standard, well-made city magazine. Last-but-not-least part of the scene shows the scene whisper a cross section through the events of the city. The scene-pics are often the first pages viewed and are true to the motto "see and be seen".
Language(s): German
ADVERTISING RATES:
Full Page Mono .... EUR 2640
Full Page Colour .... EUR 3070
Mechanical Data: Type Area: 265 x 184 mm, No. of Columns (Display): 4, Col Widths (Display): 43 mm
Copy instructions: *Copy Date:* 11 days prior to publication
CONSUMER: RURAL & REGIONAL INTEREST

MORITZ

736454G80-7840

Editorial: Kreuzenstr. 94, 74076 HEILBRONN
Tel: 7131 1530210 **Fax:** 7131 1530111
Email: redaktion@moritz.de **Web site:** http://www.moritz.de
Freq: Monthly; **Cover Price:** Free; **Circ:** 19,973
Advertising Manager: Ingo Eckert
Profile: City magazine for Hohenlohe/Tauber-Franken: The major events of an entire month of scene, cinema, theater, art, music, parties, sports and local color - all this is found in the extensive calendar of events Moritz. To a happy read and much-used city magazine, a comprehensive journal is part of recent reports, profiles and interviews. A monthly changing themes part with attractive special topics and special issues provides the reader with additional information. The monthly service section with the calendar of events and the many among the most respected Classifieds standard, well-made city magazine. Last-but-not-least part of the scene shows the scene whisper a cross section through the events of the city. The scene-pics are often the first pages viewed and are true to the motto "see and be seen".
Language(s): German
ADVERTISING RATES:
Full Page Mono .... EUR 2160
Full Page Colour .... EUR 2520
Mechanical Data: Type Area: 265 x 184 mm, No. of Columns (Display): 4, Col Widths (Display): 43 mm
Copy instructions: *Copy Date:* 11 days prior to publication
CONSUMER: RURAL & REGIONAL INTEREST

MORITZ

736455G80-7860

Editorial: Dieselstr. 32, 70839 GERLINGEN
Tel: 7156 3071640 **Fax:** 7156 3071650
Email: stuttgart@moritz.de **Web site:** http://www.moritz.de
Freq: Monthly; **Cover Price:** Free; **Circ:** 14,980
Editor: Alexander Steinle; **Advertising Manager:** Ingo Eckert
Profile: City magazine for Tübingen/Reutlingen: The major events of an entire month of scene, cinema, theater, art, music, parties, sports and local color - all this is found in the extensive calendar of events Moritz. To a happy read and much-used city magazine, a comprehensive journal is part of recent reports, profiles and interviews. A monthly changing themes part with attractive special topics and special issues provides the reader with additional information. The monthly service section with the calendar of events and the many among the most respected Classifieds standard, well-made city magazine. Last-but-not-least part of the scene shows the scene whisper a cross section through the events of the city. The scene-pics are often the first pages viewed and are true to the motto "see and be seen".
Language(s): German
ADVERTISING RATES:
Full Page Mono .... EUR 2160
Full Page Colour .... EUR 2520
Mechanical Data: Type Area: 265 x 184 mm, No. of Columns (Display): 4, Col Widths (Display): 43 mm
Copy instructions: *Copy Date:* 11 days prior to publication
CONSUMER: RURAL & REGIONAL INTEREST

MORITZ

736457G80-7900

Editorial: Dieselstr. 32, 70839 GERLINGEN
Tel: 7156 3071640 **Fax:** 7156 3071650
Email: stuttgart@moritz.de **Web site:** http://www.moritz.de
Freq: Monthly; **Cover Price:** Free; **Circ:** 24,650
Editor: Holger Ber; **Advertising Manager:** Ingo Eckert
Profile: City magazine for Stuttgart: The major events of an entire month of scene, cinema, theater, art, music, parties, sports and local color - all this is found in the extensive calendar of events Moritz. To a happy read and much-used city magazine, a comprehensive journal is part of recent reports, profiles and interviews. A monthly changing themes part with attractive special topics and special issues provides the reader with additional information. The monthly service section with the calendar of events and the many among the most respected Classifieds standard, well-made city magazine. Last-but-not-least part of the scene shows the scene whisper a cross section through the events of the city. The scene-pics are often the first pages viewed and are true to the motto "see and be seen".
Language(s): German
ADVERTISING RATES:
Full Page Mono .... EUR 3100
Full Page Colour .... EUR 3420
Mechanical Data: Type Area: 265 x 184 mm, No. of Columns (Display): 4, Col Widths (Display): 43 mm
Copy instructions: *Copy Date:* 11 days prior to publication
CONSUMER: RURAL & REGIONAL INTEREST

MOSAIK

756315G91D-9614

Editorial: Lindenallee 5, 14050 BERLIN
Tel: 30 3069270 **Fax:** 30 30692729
Email: mosaik@abrafaxe.de **Web site:** http://www.abrafaxe.com
Freq: Monthly; **Annual Sub.:** EUR 24,00; **Circ:** 69,256
Editor: Jörg Reuter; **Advertising Manager:** Reinhard Fischer
Profile: Comic magazine.
Language(s): German
ADVERTISING RATES:
Full Page Mono .... EUR 3380
Full Page Colour .... EUR 5930
Mechanical Data: Type Area: 216 x 144 mm
Copy instructions: *Copy Date:* 28 days prior to publication
CONSUMER: RECREATION & LEISURE: Children & Youth

MOSEL-RUWERTALER WOCHENSPIEGEL

736467G72-9100

Editorial: Max-Planck-Str. 10, 54296 TRIER
Tel: 651 716560 **Fax:** 651 716569
Email: red-trier@tw-verlag.de **Web site:** http://www.wochenspiegellive.de
Freq: Weekly; **Cover Price:** Free; **Circ:** 27,158
Editor: Arnt Finkenberg; **Advertising Manager:** Antonia Britten
Profile: Advertising journal (house-to-house) concentrating on local stories.
Language(s): German
ADVERTISING RATES:
Full Page Mono .... EUR 2408
Full Page Colour .... EUR 3371
Mechanical Data: Type Area: 430 x 290 mm, No. of Columns (Display): 7, Col Widths (Display): 38 mm
Copy instructions: *Copy Date:* 2 days prior to publication
Supplement(s): Frauen 'xtra
LOCAL NEWSPAPERS

MOTALIA

736474G77A-1440

Editorial: Raiffeisenstr. 16, 36275 KIRCHHEIM
Tel: 6628 8687 **Fax:** 6628 915397
Email: motalia@motalia.de **Web site:** http://www.motalia.de
Freq: 10 issues yearly; **Annual Sub.:** EUR 22,00; **Circ:** 6,000
Editor: Felix Hasselbrink; **Advertising Manager:** Felix Hasselbrink
Profile: Magazine about Italian motorbikes.
Language(s): German
ADVERTISING RATES:
Full Page Mono .... EUR 162
Full Page Colour .... EUR 260
Mechanical Data: Type Area: 190 x 130 mm
Copy instructions: *Copy Date:* 15 days prior to publication

MOT-BAU

736475G42B-2

Editorial: Dießemer Bruch 167, 47805 KREFELD
Tel: 2151 5100118 **Fax:** 2151 5100215
Email: mot-bau@stuenings.de **Web site:** http://www.mot-bau.de
Freq: Monthly; **Annual Sub.:** EUR 65,00; **Circ:** 7,948
Editor: Lutz Gerritzen; **Advertising Manager:** Cornelia Assem
Profile: Magazine with news from the areas of technology, business, government and associations, events, events and the used machine / baufahrzeugmarkt. Topics from civil, road and building construction as well as the construction industry.
Language(s): German
Readership: Aimed at contractors, construction engineers, equipment retailers and manufacturers.
ADVERTISING RATES:
Full Page Mono .... EUR 2760
Full Page Colour .... EUR 4290
Mechanical Data: Type Area: 255 x 185 mm, No. of Columns (Display): 4, Col Widths (Display): 45 mm
Copy instructions: *Copy Date:* 14 days prior to publication
BUSINESS: CONSTRUCTION: Roads

MOTION WORLD

1606565G19E-1852

Editorial: Nägelsbachstr. 33, 91052 ERLANGEN
Tel: 9131 9192501 **Fax:** 9131 9192594
Email: publishing-magazines@publicis-erlangen.de
Web site: http://www.siemens.de/motionworld-lesen
Freq: Quarterly; **Cover Price:** Free; **Circ:** 6,500
Editor: Gabriele Stadlbauer
Profile: Company publication published by Siemens AG.
Language(s): German

MOTOCROSS ENDURO

735036G77B-90

Editorial: Birkenweiherstr. 14, 63505 LANGENSELBOLD **Tel:** 6184 923330
Fax: 6184 923355
Email: redaktion@ziegler-verlag.de **Web site:** http://www.ziegler-verlag.de
Freq: Monthly; **Annual Sub.:** EUR 42,00; **Circ:** 150,000
Advertising Manager: Ralf Ziegler
Profile: Magazine about offroad and motocross.
Language(s): German
ADVERTISING RATES:
Full Page Mono .... EUR 2320
Full Page Colour .... EUR 4190
Mechanical Data: Type Area: 265 x 195 mm, No. of Columns (Display): 4, Col Widths (Display): 45 mm
Copy instructions: *Copy Date:* 21 days prior to publication
CONSUMER: MOTORING & CYCLING: Motorcycling

MOTOR BIKE

1913861G77A-2896

Editorial: Windmühlenstr. 47, 50129 BERGHEIM
Tel: 2238 845649 **Fax:** 2238 929890
Email: redaktion@motoretta.de **Web site:** http://www.motoretta.de
Freq: Quarterly; **Annual Sub.:** EUR 11,60; **Circ:** 70,000
Editor: Norbert Meiszies; **Advertising Manager:** Susanne Klages
Profile: Magazine for beginners and returners in Scooter scene. Main topics are scooters and motorcycles in small and mid-displacement segment used in the media coverage usually too short. For this purpose motor bike delivers crisp, short tests in brisk language that is understandable to inexperienced. News, sports and scene belong to its repertoire as the view over the nose wheel, for example, current trends in music, fashion and computers taken. motor bike must not only inform but also entertain and arouse the desire to bicycle.
Language(s): German
ADVERTISING RATES:
Full Page Mono .... EUR 3330
Full Page Colour .... EUR 5925
Mechanical Data: Type Area: 270 x 184 mm, No. of Columns (Display): 4, Col Widths (Display): 43 mm
Copy instructions: *Copy Date:* 21 days prior to publication

MOTOR CHIEMGAU

1850162G77A-2847

Editorial: Staudacher Str. 22, 83250 MARQUARTSTEIN **Tel:** 8641 97810
Fax: 8641 978122
Email: info@wittich-chiemgau.de **Web site:** http://www.wittich.de
Freq: Quarterly; **Cover Price:** Free; **Circ:** 37,000
Profile: Regional magazine Car and Motorcycle classifieds used car market.
Language(s): German
ADVERTISING RATES:
Full Page Mono .... EUR 1650
Full Page Colour .... EUR 1650
Mechanical Data: Type Area: 275 x 185 mm, No. of Columns (Display): 4, Col Widths (Display): 43 mm
Copy instructions: *Copy Date:* 7 days prior to publication

MOTOR KLASSIK

736493G77F-1

Editorial: Leuschnerstr. 1, 70174 STUTTGART
Tel: 711 1821365 **Fax:** 711 1821140
Email: mjuergens@motorpresse.de **Web site:** http://www.motor-klassik.de
Freq: Monthly; **Annual Sub.:** EUR 49,90; **Circ:** 81,343
Editor: Malte Jürgens; **Advertising Manager:** Gerhard Merkel
Profile: Motor Klassik is the magazine for the vibrant culture of automobile classics. Motor Klassik devotes itself to the classics of automobile history and their very individual qualities, making it possible for readers to immerse themselves in this fascinating world and directly experience the unique character of these vehicles. This high aspiration is underscored by the respectful approach taken to each individual classic and the high journalistic quality of text and image. Motor Klassik places great importance on readers really experiencing the fascination of automobile classics through genuine driving reports. Motor Klassik readers are predominantly male. Most are in the 30-to-59 age bracket and have an above-average education. Motor Klassik readers are established in their career and enjoy a high net household income. Their consumer behaviour is characterised by a willingness to spend a good deal of money on quality products and luxury goods. They are individualists with a passion, who enjoy their life to the full and for whom it is very important to express their personal style. In this regard a major role is played by special cars, watches or furniture that cannot be found on every street corner. True class is for them less a question of money than of quality, aesthetics and durability. Despite not necessarily being fanatical about technology, they nevertheless love simply immersing themselves in the world of automobile classics. As well as being interested in concrete suggestions, they are seeking a platform

that allows them to indulge, share and cultivate their fascination and passion for genuine classics.
Language(s): German
Readership: Aimed at enthusiasts.
ADVERTISING RATES:
Full Page Mono .... EUR 9000
Full Page Colour .... EUR 9000
Mechanical Data: Type Area: 240 x 185 mm, No. of Columns (Display): 4, Col Widths (Display): 41 mm
CONSUMER: MOTORING & CYCLING: Veteran Cars

MOTOR MANIACS 1983722G77A-2939
Editorial: Markircher Str. 9a, 68229 MANNHEIM
Tel: 621 4836129 **Fax:** 621 4836153
Email: b.glatthaar@motor-maniacs.de **Web site:** http://www.motor-maniacs.de
Freq: 6 issues yearly; **Cover Price:** EUR 5,00; **Circ:** 50,000
Editor: Boris Glatthaar; **Advertising Manager:** Oliver Langguth
Profile: The magazine pays tribute to American and European automotive icons of the 40s to the 80s and enthusiastic drivers with hobbyists, and enthusiasts for the particular vintage and classic cars, hot rods, custom or muscle car. True to style, character pimped cars of modern times are also an issue - if they have an authentic basis. Motor maniacs tells the stories of dream cars and everyday vehicles reveals in features, features, and the portraits Experiences of people whispering behind the wheel, the latest from screwdrivers and events halls, clubs and the scene is a voice of like-minded people. The magazine carries out the passion by some tips to buying a car, registration, maintenance, construction and restoration. For those who consider themselves new, there are plump dates, classifieds and a brokerage.
Language(s): German
ADVERTISING RATES:
Full Page Mono .... EUR 2950
Full Page Colour .... EUR 2950
Mechanical Data: Type Area: 256 x 184 mm, No. of Columns (Display): 4, Col Widths (Display): 43 mm
Copy instructions: *Copy Date:* 30 days prior to publication

MOTOR SPORT XL 736528G77D-700
Editorial: Hauptstr. 31, 53797 LOHMAR
Tel: 2246 9480000 **Fax:** 2246 9480004
Email: monschauer@motorsport-xl.de **Web site:** http://www.motorsport-xl.de
Freq: Monthly; **Annual Sub.:** EUR 43,00; **Circ:** 25,000
Editor: Ralph Monschauer
Profile: The motor sports magazine with news, schedules, results and much more for the motor racing and karting. Target audience: people interested in motor sports (teams, drivers, fans) http://www.facebook.com/motorsport.xl This Outlet offers RSS (Really Simple Syndication).
Language(s): German
Readership: Aimed at people interested in motorsports.
ADVERTISING RATES:
Full Page Mono .... EUR 1600
Full Page Colour .... EUR 2100
Mechanical Data: Type Area: 303 x 216 mm
CONSUMER: MOTORING & CYCLING: Motor Sports

MOTORAVER MAGAZINE 1862064G77A-2853
Editorial: Harkortstr. 162, 22765 HAMBURG
Tel: 40 226228710 **Fax:** 40 226228720
Email: info@motoraver.de **Web site:** http://www.motoraver.de
Freq: Quarterly; **Annual Sub.:** EUR 20,00; **Circ:** 30,000
Editor: Helge Thomsen; **Advertising Manager:** Christian Böhner
Profile: Magazine about cars from the 60s and 70s.
Language(s): German
ADVERTISING RATES:
Full Page Colour .... EUR 3450
Mechanical Data: Type Area: 275 x 215 mm

MOTORETTA 758311G77A-2528
Editorial: Wickingstr. 1, 45657 RECKLINGHAUSEN
Tel: 2361 93580 **Fax:** 2361 16495
Email: redaktion@motoretta.de **Web site:** http://www.motoretta.de
Freq: 8 issues yearly; **Annual Sub.:** EUR 24,00; **Circ:** 341,870
Editor: Norbert Meiszies; **Advertising Manager:** Christoph Wisberg
Profile: Magazine for scooter riders. Especially for the young and young at heart Scooter and Motorcycle interested the magazine offers an authentic editorial concept, which covers all major topics from the scooter and motorcycle range. The editorial base form the extensive testing and engineering reports, the latest scooter models, the largest scooter classifieds section and the current affairs programs - supported by exciting photo galleries and refreshing reports with a very high information content. Thus, the scooter is shown as an active recreational resources. Here the newcomers as well informed as the die-hard cyclists. Readership: The readership base is formed by three major groups: the young, trendy target group which is allowed to drive over 16 years, a scooter or a motorcycle with a limited capacity. The older, but young at heart and large target group of drivers who may also take their driver's license certain models. Both are standing before a purchase decision and begin to deal with the different brands and products. The advanced form the third largest, and the age-independent regular readers, which has won the magazine through the 21-year anniversary of the title.
Language(s): German
ADVERTISING RATES:
Full Page Mono .... EUR 2500
Full Page Colour .... EUR 4445
Mechanical Data: Type Area: 270 x 184 mm, No. of Columns (Display): 4, Col Widths (Display): 43 mm
Copy instructions: *Copy Date:* 21 days prior to publication

MOTORETTA SPEZIAL MOTORROLLER 1862380G77A-2855
Editorial: Wickingstr. 1, 45657 RECKLINGHAUSEN
Tel: 2361 93580 **Fax:** 2361 16495
Email: redaktion@motoretta.de **Web site:** http://www.motoretta.de
Freq: Annual; **Cover Price:** EUR 6,95; **Circ:** 32,300
Editor: Norbert Meiszies; **Advertising Manager:** Christoph Wisberg
Profile: Scooter-Catalog, Scooter Test-Catalog, of the Buyer's Guide.
Language(s): German
ADVERTISING RATES:
Full Page Mono .... EUR 2450
Full Page Colour .... EUR 4320
Mechanical Data: Type Area: 205 x 147 mm, No. of Columns (Display): 4, Col Widths (Display): 43 mm
Copy instructions: *Copy Date:* 20 days prior to publication

MOTORETTA SPEZIAL MOTORROLLER 1642043G77B-23
Editorial: Wickingstr. 1, 45657 RECKLINGHAUSEN
Tel: 2361 93580 **Fax:** 2361 16495
Email: redaktion@motoretta.de **Web site:** http://www.motoretta.de
Freq: Annual; **Cover Price:** EUR 4,95; **Circ:** 32,300
Editor: Norbert Meiszies; **Advertising Manager:** Christoph Wisberg
Profile: Scooters catalog, standard reference work with the entire range of the scooter market. In addition to all the major model data, the editorial approach of technical competence and facts and other important themes that serve as a guide to buying a motor scooter is completed.
Language(s): German
ADVERTISING RATES:
Full Page Mono .... EUR 2450
Full Page Colour .... EUR 4320
Mechanical Data: Type Area: 270 x 184 mm, No. of Columns (Display): 4, Col Widths (Display): 43 mm
Copy instructions: *Copy Date:* 12 days prior to publication

MOTORETTA SPEZIAL QUAD 1645750G77B-30
Editorial: Wickingstr. 1, 45657 RECKLINGHAUSEN
Tel: 2361 93580 **Fax:** 2361 16495
Email: redaktion@motoretta.de **Web site:** http://www.motoretta.de
Freq: Annual; **Cover Price:** EUR 4,95; **Circ:** 25,000
Editor: Norbert Meiszies; **Advertising Manager:** Susanne Klages
Profile: Test Catalog, standard work for those who want to get a complete overview of the Quad & ATV scene. The catalog presents an extraordinary appearance, all new models of the year. Both advanced and beginner the fun of the Quad & ATV is taught in an impressive manner. Thanks to All dates, technical specifications and vehicle descriptions, it is the purchase decision process. Of course, service information comes to accessories, clothing and tuning measures are not enough.
Language(s): German
ADVERTISING RATES:
Full Page Mono .... EUR 2015
Full Page Colour .... EUR 3580
Mechanical Data: Type Area: 270 x 184 mm, No. of Columns (Display): 4, Col Widths (Display): 43 mm
Copy instructions: *Copy Date:* 19 days prior to publication

MOTORIK 736487G56L-49
Editorial: Steinwasenstr. 6, 73614 SCHORNDORF
Tel: 7181 4020 **Fax:** 7181 402111
Email: motorik@hofmann-verlag.de **Web site:** http://www.hofmann-verlag.de
Freq: Quarterly; **Annual Sub.:** EUR 46,80; **Circ:** 3,758
Editor: Klaus Fischer; **Advertising Manager:** Isabel von Terzi
Profile: Magazine about motorised physiotherapy.
Language(s): German
ADVERTISING RATES:
Full Page Mono .... EUR 650
Mechanical Data: Type Area: 260 x 175 mm
Copy instructions: *Copy Date:* 30 days prior to publication
Official Journal of: Organ d. Aktionskreis Psychomotorik e.V.
BUSINESS: HEALTH & MEDICAL: Disability & Rehabilitation

MOTORIST 736488G26B-110
Editorial: Stolberger Str. 84, 50933 KÖLN
Tel: 221 5497311 **Fax:** 221 5497278
Email: red.motorist@rohn.de **Web site:** http://www.motorist-online.de
Freq: 6 issues yearly; **Annual Sub.:** EUR 102,00; **Circ:** 6,388
Editor: Jürgen Krieger; **Advertising Manager:** Verena Thiele
Profile: Journal concerning motorised machines for forestry and garden care.
Language(s): German
Readership: Aimed at professional gardeners, landscaping companies and suppliers of gardening equipment.
ADVERTISING RATES:
Full Page Mono .... EUR 3800
Full Page Colour .... EUR 6050
Mechanical Data: Type Area: 267 x 188 mm, No. of Columns (Display): 3, Col Widths (Display): 60 mm
Copy instructions: *Copy Date:* 21 days prior to publication
BUSINESS: GARDEN TRADE: Garden Trade Supplies

MOTOROUTE MAGAZIN 1641054G77A-2629
Editorial: Ernststr. 6, 96476 RODACH **Tel:** 9564 8380 **Fax:** 9564 83855
Email: info@motoroute.de **Web site:** http://www.motoroute.de
Freq: Annual; **Cover Price:** EUR 2,50; **Circ:** 40,000
Editor: Thomas Vinzelberg
Profile: Travel magazine for motorcycle tour with recommendations, hotel information and technical tips.
Language(s): German

MOTORRAD 1622873G77B-17
Editorial: Leuschnerstr. 1, 70174 STUTTGART
Tel: 711 1821533 **Fax:** 711 1821165
Email: nloens@motorpresse.de **Web site:** http://www.motorradonline.de
Freq: Weekly; **Cover Price:** Paid; **Circ:** 1,123,900 Unique Users
Editor: Michael Pfeiffer; **Advertising Manager:** Marcus Schardt
Profile: Ezine: Publication about motorcycling, providing news items, test results and technical information.
Language(s): German
CONSUMER: MOTORING & CYCLING: Motorcycling

MOTORRAD 736495G77B-170
Editorial: Leuschnerstr. 1, 70174 STUTTGART
Tel: 711 1821146 **Fax:** 711 1821781
Email: leserbriefe_mrd@motorpresse.de **Web site:** http://www.motorradonline.de
Freq: 26 issues yearly; **Annual Sub.:** EUR 93,80; **Circ:** 116,751
Editor: Michael Pfeiffer; **Advertising Manager:** Marcus Schardt
Profile: Motorrad – the gerneralist for the whole world of motorcycling. Motorrad is Europe's biggest motorcycle magazine and the only true generalist on the German market. The modern editorial concept comprises everything worth knowing and reporting from the world of the motorcycle and is unequalled in scope, depth, topicality and design. Motorrad is the number one in the German-speaking world for industry, trade, motorcyclists and enthusiasts alike. Comprehensive coverage, always as up-to-date as possible and backed by the highest editorial competence, helps form opinions, provides buyer guidance and offers abundant entertainment value. Motorrad readers know more than others. Motorrad is moreover the political heavyweight of the motorcycle world and a mouthpiece for all matters that concern the motorcyclist. Motorrad reaches, accompanies and advises active motorcyclists and a constantly growing number of people returning to the sport – roughly one million young and young-at-heart readers in the German-speaking regions with an above-average income. These readers are opinion leaders, communicative and active consumers. They cover many miles each year by motorcycle and car, so qualify as extremely mobile – the outdoor kind of people who are hard to reach with other media. Facebook: http://www.facebook.com/pages/MOTORRAD/273776715492 Twitter: http://twitter.com/#!/motorradonline This Outlet offers RSS (Really Simple Syndication).
Language(s): German
ADVERTISING RATES:
Full Page Mono .... EUR 16500
Full Page Colour .... EUR 16500
Mechanical Data: Type Area: 248 x 185 mm, No. of Columns (Display): 4, Col Widths (Display): 43 mm
Copy instructions: *Copy Date:* 35 days prior to publication
CONSUMER: MOTORING & CYCLING: Motorcycling

MOTORRAD ABENTEUER 736496G77D-740
Editorial: Eifelring 28, 53879 EUSKIRCHEN
Tel: 2251 650460 **Fax:** 2251 6504699
Email: motorradabenteuer@nitschke-verlag.de **Web site:** http://www.motorradabenteuer.de
Freq: 6 issues yearly; **Annual Sub.:** EUR 26,40; **Circ:** 15,601
Editor: Till Kohlmey; **Advertising Manager:** Martina Jonas
Profile: Motorrad Abenteuer awakens in us the desire to attempt something again. Whether sleeping bag, sleeping pad and tent or toothbrush, credit card and hotel guide - in common is the bike that catapulted us into the world beyond the everyday. Whether with the 125 over the Alps, with the Enduro trip through Africa or Super Single on the sandy slopes of Mecklenburg-Western Pomerania, the adventure lures everywhere, you just have to look only. Motorrad Abenteuer is for suggestions and tips. A demanding reportage magazine, written with passion and humor for young people and young at heart.
Language(s): German
ADVERTISING RATES:
Full Page Mono .... EUR 2887
Full Page Colour .... EUR 4100
Mechanical Data: No. of Columns (Display): 3, Col Widths (Display): 57 mm, Type Area: 248 x 185 mm
Copy instructions: *Copy Date:* 21 days prior to publication
CONSUMER: MOTORING & CYCLING: Motor Sports

MOTORRAD CLASSIC 736498G77B-4
Editorial: Leuschnerstr. 1, 70174 STUTTGART
Tel: 711 1821146 **Fax:** 711 1821781
Email: leserbriefe_mrd_classic@motorpresse.de
Freq: 8 issues yearly; **Annual Sub.:** EUR 39,90; **Circ:** 19,475
Editor: Michael Pfeiffer; **Advertising Manager:** Marcus Schardt
Profile: Motorrad Classic ist the major German-language magazine devoted exclusively to every aspect of classic motorcycles and the continuously expanding scene that comprises vintage bikes and younger classics. Historic and technical milestones, historical bike racing, restoration, people and their lovingly cared-for vintage bikes are all key components of the editorial concept. Generous amounts of photographic material is combined with in-depth textual information. The quality of the presentation and the technical expertise that backs it are unmatched by any comparable title. Motorrad Classic is an indispensable magazine for lovers of classic motorbikes built between the birth of the motorcycle and the 1980s. Readers benefit from inside knowledge and suggestions for activities that lift them out from among all average. The bikes presented stand for individuality, technical progress, style and character. In older readers, Motorrad Classic awakens memories of their own motorcycling past. Motorrad Classic readers are individualists. They love motorcycles and the associated engineering in its purest form. Age-wise they represent a broader range than other motorcycle. titles, and being financially independent they have an affinity for quality brands.
Language(s): German
ADVERTISING RATES:
Full Page Mono .... EUR 6100
Full Page Colour .... EUR 6100
Mechanical Data: Type Area: 248 x 185 mm, No. of Columns (Display): 4, Col Widths (Display): 43 mm
Copy instructions: *Copy Date:* 30 days prior to publication
CONSUMER: MOTORING & CYCLING: Motorcycling

MOTORRAD GESPANNE 736502G77A-1580
Editorial: Oberschwaigstr. 5a, 92237 SULZBACH-ROSENBERG **Tel:** 9661 812900 **Fax:** 9661 812901
Email: redaktion@motorrad-gespanne.de **Web site:** http://www.motorrad-gespanne.de
Freq: 6 issues yearly; **Annual Sub.:** EUR 37,00; **Circ:** 11,000
Editor: Martin Franitza; **Advertising Manager:** Bernhard Götz
Profile: Magazine about motorcycles with sidecars. Facebook: http://www.facebook.com/Gespannfahrer Twitter: http://twitter.com/#!/Gespannmagazin.
Language(s): German
ADVERTISING RATES:
Full Page Mono .... EUR 1389
Full Page Colour .... EUR 1957
Mechanical Data: Type Area: 250 x 185 mm, No. of Columns (Display): 4, Col Widths (Display): 43 mm
Copy instructions: *Copy Date:* 31 days prior to publication
Official Journal of: Organ d. Bundesverb. d. Hersteller u. Importeure v. Krafträder m. Beiwagen

MOTORRAD JAHRBUCH 741214G77A-2060
Editorial: Schrempfstr. 8, 70597 STUTTGART
Tel: 711 24897600 **Fax:** 711 24897628
Email: redaktion@mo-web.de **Web site:** http://www.mo-web.de
Freq: Annual; **Cover Price:** EUR 7,70; **Circ:** 150,000
Editor: Wolf-Martin Riedel; **Advertising Manager:** Sabine Schermer
Profile: The "MOTORRAD JAHRBUCH" is the interested readers throughout the season help. A comprehensive catalog section, detailed buying advice and valuable tips about motorcycle make this reference work indispensable.
Language(s): German
ADVERTISING RATES:
Full Page Mono .... EUR 4250
Full Page Colour .... EUR 7140
Mechanical Data: Type Area: 262 x 187 mm, No. of Columns (Display): 4, Col Widths (Display): 43 mm
Copy instructions: *Copy Date:* 41 days prior to publication

MOTORRAD KATALOG 736505G77A-1620
Editorial: Leuschnerstr. 1, 70174 STUTTGART
Tel: 711 1821374 **Fax:** 711 1821165
Email: leserbriefe_mrd@motorpresse.de **Web site:** http://www.motorradonline.de
Freq: Annual; **Cover Price:** EUR 8,50; **Circ:** 135,000
Editor: Michael Pfeiffer; **Advertising Manager:** Marcus Schardt

Profile: The gold standard reference work with the complete range of motorcycle and scooter market. All photos, data, test scores and prices, accessories, clothing, advice and all addresses used.
Language(s): German
ADVERTISING RATES:
Full Page Mono .... EUR 10800
Full Page Colour .... EUR 10800
Mechanical Data: Type Area: 248 x 185 mm, No. of Columns (Display): 4, Col Widths (Display): 43 mm
Copy instructions: *Copy Date:* 44 days prior to publication

MOTORRAD KONTAKTE
736506G77B-6
Editorial: Hertinger Str. 60, 59423 UNNA
Tel: 2303 985531 **Fax:** 2303 98559
Email: efoe@syburger.de **Web site:** http://www.syburger.de
Freq: Monthly; **Annual Sub.:** EUR 19,20; **Circ:** 20,000
Editor: Erik Förster; **Advertising Manager:** Jessica Kwasny
Profile: Motorcycle magazine for the region of Göttingen, Braunschweig, Kassel, Hanover, OWL, Harz. The editorial focus is on regional news, plus get driving reports, tests, and travel. The magazine for active bikers, because they only exist in the motorcycle trade and meeting places.
Language(s): German
Readership: Aimed at motorbike owners.
ADVERTISING RATES:
Full Page Mono .... EUR 821
Full Page Colour .... EUR 1149
Mechanical Data: Type Area: 232 x 155 mm, No. of Columns (Display): 3, Col Widths (Display): 48 mm
CONSUMER: MOTORING & CYCLING: Motorcycling

MOTORRAD KURIER
1850164G77A-2848
Editorial: Grundweg 8, 89250 SENDEN
Tel: 7307 961026 **Fax:** 7307 961027
Email: krad-verlag@t-online.de **Web site:** http://www.motorrad-kurier.de
Freq: 11 issues yearly; **Cover Price:** Free; **Circ:** 7,000
Editor: Jürgen Greif; **Advertising Manager:** Jürgen Greif
Profile: Regional motorbike magazine.
Language(s): German
ADVERTISING RATES:
Full Page Mono .... EUR 600
Full Page Colour .... EUR 600
Mechanical Data: Type Area: 277 x 190 mm
Copy instructions: *Copy Date:* 12 days prior to publication

MOTORRAD MAGAZIN MO
736508G77B-200
Editorial: Schrempfstr. 8, 70597 STUTTGART
Tel: 711 24897600 **Fax:** 711 24897628
Email: redaktion@mo-web.de **Web site:** http://www.mo-web.de
Freq: Monthly; **Annual Sub.:** EUR 49,90; **Circ:** 27,606
Editor: Jochen Soppa; **Advertising Manager:** Sabine Schermer
Profile: PFor more than 30 years MO is successful on his way. More consistently and uniquely since the year 2009th With themes, which in motorcycle magazines in this form was not far. In MO enthusiasm and expertise are important, not too often kept a know-Tester Latin. MO readers will appreciate the combination of sophisticated texts, resource information and fascinating photographs. The particularly high-quality equipment underlines this claim.
Language(s): German
Readership: Aimed at enthusiasts.
ADVERTISING RATES:
Full Page Mono .... EUR 4250
Full Page Colour .... EUR 7140
Mechanical Data: Type Area: 262 x 187 mm, No. of Columns (Display): 4, Col Widths (Display): 43 mm
Copy instructions: *Copy Date:* 28 days prior to publication
CONSUMER: MOTORING & CYCLING: Motorcycling

MOTORRAD NEWS
736510G77B-210
Editorial: Hertinger Str. 60, 59423 UNNA
Tel: 2303 985300 **Fax:** 2303 985309
Email: motorradnews@syburger.de **Web site:** http://www.syburger.de
Freq: Monthly; **Annual Sub.:** EUR 25,80; **Circ:** 70,634
Editor: Frank Roedel; **Advertising Manager:** Jessica Kwasny
Profile: Magazine for motorcyclists. Concise and precise information, the magazine about new machines, testing and technology, tours and accessories. Breaking news from the scene and regional information. Twitter: http://twitter.com/MotorradNews This Outlet offers RSS (Really Simple Syndication).
Language(s): German
Readership: Aimed at motorcycle enthusiasts.
ADVERTISING RATES:
Full Page Mono .... EUR 5760
Full Page Colour .... EUR 6760
Mechanical Data: Type Area: 248 x 186 mm, No. of Columns (Display): 4, Col Widths (Display): 43 mm
Copy instructions: *Copy Date:* 20 days prior to publication
CONSUMER: MOTORING & CYCLING: Motorcycling

MOTORRAD PROFILE
1642139G77B-24
Editorial: Ludwigstr. 11, 86669 STENGELHEIM
Tel: 8433 929476 **Fax:** 8433 1726
Email: unitec_medienvertrieb@web.de **Web site:** http://www.unitec-medienvertrieb.de
Freq: Annual; **Cover Price:** EUR 11,50; **Circ:** 4,500
Editor: Reiner Scharfenberg
Profile: Magazine about oldtimer motorcycles.
Language(s): German

MOTORRAD ROLLER SPEZIAL
740582G77A-2040
Editorial: Leuschnerstr. 1, 70174 STUTTGART
Tel: 711 1821374 **Fax:** 711 1821165
Email: roller@motorpresse.de **Web site:** http://www.motorpresse.de
Freq: Annual; **Cover Price:** EUR 3,90; **Circ:** 36,600
Editor: Michael Pfeiffer; **Advertising Manager:** Marcus Schardt
Profile: Motorrad roller spezia as the standard work for all is a must, want to have an accurate overview of the extensive scooter market.
Language(s): German
ADVERTISING RATES:
Full Page Mono .... EUR 6400
Full Page Colour .... EUR 6400
Mechanical Data: Type Area: 248 x 185 mm, No. of Columns (Display): 4, Col Widths (Display): 43 mm
Copy instructions: *Copy Date:* 47 days prior to publication

MOTORRAD TESTBUCH
736518G77A-1720
Editorial: Schrempfstr. 8, 70597 STUTTGART
Tel: 711 24897600 **Fax:** 711 24897628
Web site: http://www.mo-web.de
Freq: Annual; **Cover Price:** EUR 6,90; **Circ:** 125,000
Editor: Jochen Soppa; **Advertising Manager:** Sabine Schermer
Profile: About 100 current cycles in the test mirror. Engine, suspension, brakes, fuel consumption, performance and equipment are valued piece by piece by our test editors. With this guide, the reader is at the motorcycle purchase the best advice.
Language(s): German
ADVERTISING RATES:
Full Page Mono .... EUR 4250
Full Page Colour .... EUR 7140
Mechanical Data: Type Area: 262 x 187 mm, No. of Columns (Display): 4, Col Widths (Display): 43 mm
Copy instructions: *Copy Date:* 31 days prior to publication

MOTORRAD TREFF
736519G77B-360
Editorial: Hertinger Str. 60, 59423 UNNA
Tel: 2303 985531 **Fax:** 2303 985309
Email: efoe@syburger.de **Web site:** http://www.syburger.de
Freq: Monthly; **Annual Sub.:** EUR 19,20; **Circ:** 20,000
Editor: Erik Förster; **Advertising Manager:** Jessica Kwasny
Profile: Motorcycle magazine for the states of Sachsen, Sachsen-Anhalt und Thüringen. The editorial focus is on regional news, plus get driving reports, tests, and travel. The magazine for active bikers, because they only exist in the motorcycle trade and meeting places.
Language(s): German
Readership: Aimed at motorcyclists in Sachsen and Thüringen.
ADVERTISING RATES:
Full Page Mono .... EUR 821
Full Page Colour .... EUR 1149
Mechanical Data: Type Area: 232 x 155 mm, No. of Columns (Display): 3, Col Widths (Display): 48 mm
CONSUMER: MOTORING & CYCLING: Motorcycling

MOTORRADFAHRER
736499G77B-5
Editorial: Eifelring 28, 53879 EUSKIRCHEN
Tel: 2251 650460 **Fax:** 2251 6504699
Email: motorradfahrer@nitschke-verlag.de **Web site:** http://www.motorradfahrer-online.de
Freq: Monthly; **Annual Sub.:** EUR 21,60; **Circ:** 55,762
Editor: Guido Saliger; **Advertising Manager:** Martina Jonas
Profile: The Motorradfahrer is No. 1 among the bikers monthly titles. Together with the magazine Tourenfahrer a significant market share in the segment of the motorcycle magazines is covered. The Motorradfahrer is one of the few innovations in the industry. With his concept - information intensive, high credibility, regardless of the social and environmental impact of the motorcycle - it managed to reach new readers who do not feel addressed by the established magazines. In-depth tests, profound ideas, practical Buying Guide, a comprehensive second hand market and the close contact with the motorcycle scene, the Motorradfahrer to have one of the most important voices in the industry.
Language(s): German
ADVERTISING RATES:
Full Page Mono .... EUR 6331
Full Page Colour .... EUR 8990
Mechanical Data: No. of Columns (Display): 4, Col Widths (Display): 43 mm, Type Area: 244 x 187 mm
Copy instructions: *Copy Date:* 28 days prior to publication
CONSUMER: MOTORING & CYCLING: Motorcycling

MOTORRADSZENE BAYERN
736517G77B-400
Editorial: Hertinger Str. 60, 59423 UNNA
Tel: 2303 985531 **Fax:** 2303 985309
Email: efoe@syburger.de **Web site:** http://www.syburger.de
Freq: Monthly; **Annual Sub.:** EUR 19,20; **Circ:** 22,000
Editor: Erik Förster; **Advertising Manager:** Jessica Kwasny
Profile: Motorcycle magazine for the state of Bavaria. The editorial focus is on regional news, plus get driving reports, tests, and travel. The magazine for active bikers, because they only exist in the motorcycle trade and meeting places.
Language(s): German
ADVERTISING RATES:
Full Page Mono .... EUR 905
Full Page Colour .... EUR 1267
Mechanical Data: Type Area: 232 x 155 mm, No. of Columns (Display): 3, Col Widths (Display): 48 mm
CONSUMER: MOTORING & CYCLING: Motorcycling

MOTORRADTRAINING TERMINE
1800740G77A-2792
Editorial: Gladbecker Str. 425, 45329 ESSEN
Tel: 201 835390 **Fax:** 201 8353999
Email: info@ifz.de **Web site:** http://www.ifz.de
Freq: Annual; **Cover Price:** Free; **Circ:** 100,000
Profile: Catalog of dates throughout Germany offer motorcycle safety training. The training sessions are listed by month, types of training, venue and organizers. Are tender and information on costs and charges it to the respective organizers. Based in cooperation with the ADAC and the German Road Safety events listed on the information of the hosting organizations. There is no claim to completeness. Changes that may affect the precipitation of events or a shift, are not excluded.
Language(s): German

MOTORRADTREFF SPINNER
1656984G77B-25
Editorial: Hertinger Str. 60, 59423 UNNA
Tel: 2303 985531 **Fax:** 2303 985309
Email: efoe@syburger.de **Web site:** http://www.syburger.de
Freq: Monthly; **Annual Sub.:** EUR 19,20; **Circ:** 15,000
Editor: Erik Förster; **Advertising Manager:** Jessica Kwasny
Profile: Motorcycle magazine for the states of Berlin and Brandenburg. The editorial focus is on regional news, plus get driving reports, tests, and travel. The magazine for active bikers, because they only exist in the motorcycle trade and meeting places.
Language(s): German
ADVERTISING RATES:
Full Page Mono .... EUR 821
Full Page Colour .... EUR 1149
Mechanical Data: Type Area: 232 x 155 mm, No. of Columns (Display): 3, Col Widths (Display): 48 mm
Copy instructions: *Copy Date:* 14 days prior to publication

MOTORSPORT-TOTAL.COM
1661559G77D-1299
Editorial: Sendlinger-Tor-Platz 10, 80336 MÜNCHEN
Tel: 89 51555820 **Fax:** 89 51555821
Email: redaktion@motorsport-total.com **Web site:** http://www.motorsport-total.com
Freq: Monthly; **Cover Price:** Paid; **Circ:** 2,629,689 Unique Users
Editor: Christian Nimmervoll
Profile: Portal for motor sport fans Twitter: http://www.motorsport-total.com/twitter.html This Outlet offers RSS (Really Simple Syndication).
Language(s): German
CONSUMER: MOTORING & CYCLING: Motor Sports

MOUNTAIN BIKE
736534G77C-140
Editorial: Mollenbachstr. 6, 71229 LEONBERG
Tel: 7152 941560 **Fax:** 7152 941566
Email: leserservice@mountainbike-magazin.de **Web site:** http://www.mountainbike-magazin.de
Freq: Monthly; **Annual Sub.:** EUR 49,50; **Circ:** 77,047
Editor: Jens Vögele; **Advertising Manager:** Bernd Holzhauer
Profile: Mountain Bike is one of more than ten years, the world's largest mountain bike magazines. Always on the pulse of the time it informed active and enthusiastic bikers on the latest products and trends, acts as a fitness consultant, month after month ago is the most beautiful bike tours and fascinates with its fascinating features. Beginners also receive all the tips on the first bike and the right equipment. In short: Mountain Bike is the perfect market information for mountain bikers. acts by its competence and timeliness as purchase adviser and opinion for the whole bike scene. The magazine serves with its broad and attractive range of topics consistent the interests of active mountain biker. Meaningful bike, accessories and clothing tests support the ambitious mountain bikers as well as beginners in the purchasing decision. Service issues and tuning tips round out the equipment segment. Training and nutrition tips provide valuable know-how on how to improve personal fitness with a bike. Demonstrates competence and the extensive travel section. It shows the most beautiful bike tours and trails in Germany, Europe and worldwide, and presents all relevant area information at a glance. Twitter: http://twitter.com/MB_InTheTweet.
Language(s): German
ADVERTISING RATES:
Full Page Mono .... EUR 5015
Full Page Colour .... EUR 7990
Mechanical Data: Type Area: 248 x 185 mm, No. of Columns (Display): 4, Col Widths (Display): 43 mm
Copy instructions: *Copy Date:* 24 days prior to publication
CONSUMER: MOTORING & CYCLING: Cycling

MOUNTAIN BIKE ONLINE
1704547G77C-482
Editorial: Leuschnerstr. 1, 70174 STUTTGART
Tel: 7152 941560 **Fax:** 7152 941566
Email: leserservice@mountainbike-magazin.de **Web site:** http://www.mountainbike-magazin.de
Freq: Daily; **Cover Price:** Paid; **Circ:** 183,826 Unique Users
Editor: Jens Vögele
Profile: Ezine: The website includes information on active and enthusiastic bikers on the latest products and trends, acts as a fitness consultant, month after month ago is the most beautiful bike tours and fascinates with its fascinating features. Beginners also receive all the tips on the first bike and the right equipment. In short: Mountain Bike is the perfect market information for mountain bikers. acts by its competence and timeliness as purchase adviser and opinion for the whole bike scene. The site served by an attractive and diverse range of topics consistent the interests of active mountain biker. Meaningful bike, accessories and clothing tests support the ambitious mountain bikers as well as beginners in the purchasing decision. Service issues and tuning tips round out the equipment segment. Training and nutrition tips provide valuable know-how on how to improve personal fitness with a bike. Demonstrates competence and the extensive travel section. It shows the most beautiful bike tours and trails in Germany, Europe and worldwide, and presents all relevant information area at a glance. Twitter: http://twitter.com/MB_InTheTweet.
Language(s): German
CONSUMER: MOTORING & CYCLING: Cycling

MOVE
1641325G14A-9593
Editorial: Otto-Lilienthal-Str. 1, 28199 BREMEN
Tel: 421 3500861 **Fax:** 421 3500638
Email: imke.reichert@bcdtravel.de **Web site:** http://www.bcdtravel.de
Freq: Quarterly; **Cover Price:** Free; **Circ:** 30,000
Editor: Imke Reichert; **Advertising Manager:** Kai Braess
Profile: Magazine on business travels and travel management.
Language(s): German
ADVERTISING RATES:
Full Page Mono .... EUR 4100
Full Page Colour .... EUR 4100
Mechanical Data: Type Area: 263 x 220 mm
Copy instructions: *Copy Date:* 28 days prior to publication

MOVE UP
1606566G19E-1853
Editorial: Nägelsbachstr. 33, 91052 ERLANGEN
Tel: 9131 9192501 **Fax:** 9131 9192594
Email: publishing-magazines@publicis-erlangen.de
Web site: http://www.siemens.de/moveup-lesen
Freq: Annual; **Cover Price:** Free; **Circ:** 5,000
Editor: Kerstin Purucker
Profile: Company publication published by Siemens AG.
Language(s): German

MOVIEBETA
1665220G80-14481
Editorial: Nirmerstr. 7, 52080 AACHEN
Tel: 241 9519600 **Fax:** 241 9519601
Email: gb@kulturzone.net **Web site:** http://www.moviebeta.de
Freq: Monthly; **Cover Price:** Free; **Circ:** 14,000
Editor: Gabor Baksay
Profile: Magazine about cinema movies.
Language(s): German
ADVERTISING RATES:
Full Page Mono .... EUR 700
Full Page Colour .... EUR 1200
Mechanical Data: Type Area: 265 x 190 mm, No. of Columns (Display): 4, Col Widths (Display): 44 mm
Copy instructions: *Copy Date:* 10 days prior to publication
CONSUMER: RURAL & REGIONAL INTEREST

MP MATERIALPRÜFUNG MATERIALS TESTING
1657009G19A-1091
Editorial: Kolbergerstr. 22, 81679 MÜNCHEN
Tel: 89 99830658 **Fax:** 89 99830624
Email: mp@hanser.de **Web site:** http://www.materialstesting.de
Freq: 9 issues yearly; **Annual Sub.:** EUR 548,00; **Circ:** 1,205
Editor: Thomas Böllinghaus; **Advertising Manager:** Hermann J. Kleiner
Profile: MP Materialprüfung Materials Testing is the only German-English language journal dealing with aspects of material and component testing in industrial application, in test laboratories and research. The magazine provides information on non-destructive, destructive, optical, physical and chemical test procedures, about the transferability of test results when scaling up from samples to components and from laboratory conditions to full-scale operation. It contains formative, exclusive

articles by experts with international reputations. MP Materialprüfung Materials Testing publishes news from research agencies, technical associations and the materials testing sector and also reports on new and further developments in the industry.
Language(s): English; German
ADVERTISING RATES:
Full Page Mono .... EUR 2240
Full Page Colour .... EUR 3320
Mechanical Data: Type Area: 250 x 175 mm, No. of Columns (Display): 4, Col Widths (Display): 41 mm

MPA MESSEN PRÜFEN AUTOMATISIEREN 736552G17-1100
Editorial: Kolpingstr. 46, 86916 KAUFERING
Tel: 8191 964111 **Fax:** 8191 964141
Email: klinker@b-quadrat.de **Web site:** http://www.b-quadrat.de
Freq: 9 issues yearly; Free to qualifying individuals
Annual Sub.: EUR 92,00; **Circ:** 14,612
Editor: Wolfgang Klinker; **Advertising Manager:** Werner Duda
Profile: mpa, the journal for applied metrology, testing procedures and automation engineering, provides the practical and theoretical knowledge necessary for engineers and designers in industry, R&D, and consultancy to cope with their tasks. The editorial scope comprises all areas of automation engineering, involving components and networks as well as even entire process control systems. The concern of R&D, manufacture, and quality control are central issues within the editorial programme, with metrology and testing as integral components of automated processes being the focus of reporting.Through specialist essays, interviews and reports, mpa transfers directly usable, practice-oriented information.mpa reports on product novelties, and publishes in each issue an up-to-date market survey from mpa's range of topics. Features on theoretical principles and latest research results round off the editorial picture.mpa is an indispensable source of information for both users and suppliers of components, devices, systems, and installations used in metrology, testing and automation, as well as in electrical and power engineering.
Language(s): German
ADVERTISING RATES:
Full Page Mono .... EUR 3400
Full Page Colour .... EUR 4450
Mechanical Data: Type Area: 250 x 175 mm, No. of Columns (Display): 4, Col Widths (Display): 40 mm
Copy instructions: *Copy Date:* 21 days prior to publication
Official Journal of: Organ d. AMA Fachverb. e.V.

MPA MESSEN PRÜFEN AUTOMATISIEREN 736553G17-1120
Editorial: Kolpingstr. 46, 86916 KAUFERING
Tel: 8191 964111 **Fax:** 8191 964141
Email: klinker@b-quadrat.de **Web site:** http://www.b-quadrat.de
Freq: Annual; **Circ:** 14,612
Editor: Wolfgang Klinker; **Advertising Manager:** Werner Duda
Profile: Overview on products, components, equipment, systems and plants of measuring, control and automation, electro and drive technologies.
Language(s): German
ADVERTISING RATES:
Full Page Mono .... EUR 3400
Full Page Colour .... EUR 4450
Mechanical Data: Type Area: 250 x 175 mm, No. of Columns (Display): 4, Col Widths (Display): 40 mm
Official Journal of: Organ d. AMA Fachverb. e.V.

MPT INTERNATIONAL METALLURGICAL PLANT AND TECHNOLOGY 736556G19A-1062
Editorial: Sohnstr. 65, 40237 DÜSSELDORF
Tel: 211 6707568 **Fax:** 211 6707388
Email: arnt.hannewald@stahleisen.de **Web site:** http://www.mpt-international.com
Freq: 6 issues yearly; **Annual Sub.:** EUR 199,00; **Circ:** 10,992
Editor: Arnt Hannewald; **Advertising Manager:** Sigrid Klinge
Profile: Magazine for managers in the metal processing and metal forming industries.
Language(s): English
ADVERTISING RATES:
Full Page Mono .... EUR 3555
Full Page Colour .... EUR 4353
Mechanical Data: Type Area: 260 x 174 mm
BUSINESS: ENGINEERING & MACHINERY

MSR MAGAZIN 736564G5A-7
Editorial: Lise-Meitner-Str. 2, 55129 MAINZ
Tel: 6131 992345 **Fax:** 6131 992340
Email: redaktion@msr-magazin.de **Web site:** http://www.industrie-service.de
Freq: 10 issues yearly; **Annual Sub.:** EUR 86,00; **Circ:** 16,887
Editor: Dirk Schaar; **Advertising Manager:** Oliver Jennen
Profile: MSR Magazin deals with the complete range of topics associated with the entire field of measurement, control, instrumentation and automation technology. It provides a highly informed technical insight into the current state of the art, the latest news from research and development, and practical application of systems and processes. At the same time, it provides practical users with an overview of new products and their application possibilities. The editorial concept is based on technical articles written by competent authors, application reports, topical features, interviews, fairs and conference reports, and a plethora of short descriptions of new and further developed products. The editorial spectrum encompasses not only the classic automation topics such as metrology/sensory analysis, data acquisition/signal processing, open-loop and closed-loop control technology, actuators, networks and process control systems, but also the components necessary for designing automation systems such as control panels/switchgear cabinets, power supply systems, interfaces, electrical connection components etc.
Language(s): German
ADVERTISING RATES:
Full Page Mono .... EUR 3640
Full Page Colour .... EUR 4870
Mechanical Data: Type Area: 265 x 185 mm, No. of Columns (Display): 4, Col Widths (Display): 43 mm
Copy instructions: *Copy Date:* 14 days prior to publication
BUSINESS: COMPUTERS & AUTOMATION: Automation & Instrumentation

MSZ 1795233G74N-909
Editorial: Aegidiimarkt 3, 48143 MÜNSTER
Tel: 251 315861
Email: hildegard.schulte@t-online.de **Web site:** http://www.muenster.org/msz
Freq: Quarterly; **Cover Price:** Free; **Circ:** 8,100
Editor: Hildegard Schulte; **Advertising Manager:** Aiga Kraß
Profile: Newspaper for the elderly living in Muenster.
Language(s): German
Copy instructions: *Copy Date:* 28 days prior to publication

MT MEDIZINTECHNIK 736574G56A-2590
Editorial: Margarethenstr. 48, 61231 BAD NAUHEIM
Tel: 641 3092513 **Fax:** 641 3092914
Email: schriftleitungmt@aol.com **Web site:** http://www.mt-medizintechnik.de
Freq: 6 issues yearly; **Annual Sub.:** EUR 73,70; **Circ:** 3,100
Editor: Martin Fiebich; **Advertising Manager:** Gudrun Karafiol
Profile: Magazine about medical technology and practice.
Language(s): German
ADVERTISING RATES:
Full Page Mono .... EUR 1070
Full Page Colour .... EUR 1655
Mechanical Data: Type Area: 250 x 183 mm, No. of Columns (Display): 3, Col Widths (Display): 49 mm
Copy instructions: *Copy Date:* 56 days prior to publication
Official Journal of: Organ d. Fachverb. Biomedizin. Technik e.V.
BUSINESS: HEALTH & MEDICAL

MTA DIALOG 736567G56J-21
Editorial: Havelstr. 9, 64295 DARMSTADT
Tel: 6151 380258 **Fax:** 6151 38099258
Email: drews@hoppenstedt.de **Web site:** http://www.mta-dialog.de
Freq: Monthly; Free to qualifying individuals
Annual Sub.: EUR 86,90; **Circ:** 21,171
Editor: Birgit Drews
Profile: The journal for medical-technical assistants, laboratory physicians, radiologists, clinical chemists and teachers. Date with technical papers from the laboratory, radiology and diagnostic function. Informed about current practice survey methods, and new developments in medical technology and diagnostics. In every issue: The calendar of events with a wide offer for qualified training. The job market with training and further education completes the offer.
Language(s): German
Readership: Read by researchers and radiologists.
ADVERTISING RATES:
Full Page Mono .... EUR 2960
Full Page Colour .... EUR 5100
Mechanical Data: Type Area: 252 x 180 mm, No. of Columns (Display): 4, Col Widths (Display): 42 mm
Copy instructions: *Copy Date:* 15 days prior to publication
BUSINESS: HEALTH & MEDICAL: Radiography

MTD MEDIZIN-TECHNISCHER DIALOG 736569G56G-120
Editorial: Schomburger Str. 11, 88279 AMTZELL
Tel: 7520 95820 **Fax:** 7520 95899
Email: schmid@mtd.de **Web site:** http://www.mtd.de
Freq: Monthly; **Annual Sub.:** EUR 147,60; **Circ:** 2,802
Editor: Rolf Schmid; **Advertising Manager:** Horst Bayer
Profile: Magazine for the trade in medical products.
Language(s): German
ADVERTISING RATES:
Full Page Mono .... EUR 1779
Full Page Colour .... EUR 2859
Mechanical Data: Type Area: 270 x 175 mm, No. of Columns (Display): 3, Col Widths (Display): 55 mm
Copy instructions: *Copy Date:* 31 days prior to publication
Official Journal of: Organ d. Bundesverb. d. Sanitätsfachhandels u. d. Zentralvereinigung Medizin-Technik
BUSINESS: HEALTH & MEDICAL: Medical Equipment

MTV 1704650G76D-6362
Editorial: Stralauer Allee 7, 10245 BERLIN
Tel: 30 7001000 **Fax:** 30 700100599
Email: kontakt@mtv.de **Web site:** http://www.mtv.de
Freq: Daily; **Cover Price:** Paid; **Circ:** 3,407,656 Unique Users
Editor: Ralf Osteroth
Language(s): German
CONSUMER: MUSIC & PERFORMING ARTS: Music

MTZ MOTORTECHNISCHE ZEITSCHRIFT 736584G31A-165
Editorial: Abraham-Lincoln-Str. 46, 65189 WIESBADEN **Tel:** 611 7878342 **Fax:** 611 7878462
Email: redaktion@atzonline.de **Web site:** http://www.atzonline.de
Freq: 11 issues yearly; **Annual Sub.:** EUR 222,00; **Circ:** 5,349
Editor: Johannes Winterhagen; **Advertising Manager:** Sabine Röck
Profile: Technical publication about internal combustion engines and gas turbines.
Language(s): English; German
Readership: Aimed at professionals in the technical and engineering industry.
ADVERTISING RATES:
Full Page Mono .... EUR 3400
Full Page Colour .... EUR 5950
Mechanical Data: Type Area: 240 x 175 mm, No. of Columns (Display): 3, Col Widths (Display): 55 mm
Copy instructions: *Copy Date:* 28 days prior to publication
Official Journal of: Organ d. Fachverb. Motoren im Verb. Dt. Maschinen- u. Anlagenbau e.V., d. Forschungsvereinigung Verbrennungskraftmaschinen e.V., d. Wissenschaftl. Ges. f. Kraftfahrzeug- u. Motorentechnik e.V. u. d. Österr. Vereins f. Kraftfahrzeugtechnik
BUSINESS: MOTOR TRADE: Motor Trade Accessories

MÜHLACKER TAGBLATT 736588G67B-9940
Editorial: Kißlingweg 35, 75417 MÜHLACKER
Tel: 7041 8050 **Fax:** 7041 80570
Email: redaktion@muehlacker-tagblatt.de **Web site:** http://www.muehlacker-tagblatt.de
Freq: 312 issues yearly; **Circ:** 8,388
Advertising Manager: Jochen Elmer
Profile: Daily newspaper with regional news and a local sports section.
Language(s): German
ADVERTISING RATES:
SCC .... EUR 27,30
Mechanical Data: Type Area: 485 x 320 mm, No. of Columns (Display): 7, Col Widths (Display): 44 mm
Copy instructions: *Copy Date:* 2 days prior to publication
REGIONAL DAILY & SUNDAY NEWSPAPERS: Regional Daily Newspapers

MÜHLDORFER ANZEIGER 736589G67B-9960
Editorial: Hafnerstr. 5, 83022 ROSENHEIM
Tel: 8031 213201 **Fax:** 8031 213216
Email: redaktion@ovb.net **Web site:** http://www.ovb-online.de
Freq: 312 issues yearly; **Circ:** 13,997
Advertising Manager: Max Breu
Profile: Regional daily newspaper with news on politics, economy, culture, sports, travel, technology, etc. The Mühldorfer Anzeiger is a regional edition of the newspaper "Oberbayerisches Volksblatt". This Outlet offers RSS (Really Simple Syndication).
Language(s): German
ADVERTISING RATES:
SCC .... EUR 63,60
Mechanical Data: Type Area: 474 x 324 mm, No. of Columns (Display): 7, Col Widths (Display): 45 mm
Copy instructions: *Copy Date:* 1 day prior to publication
Supplement(s): rtv
REGIONAL DAILY & SUNDAY NEWSPAPERS: Regional Daily Newspapers

MÜHLE + MISCHFUTTER 736590G21A-290
Editorial: Paulinenstr. 43, 32756 DETMOLD
Tel: 5231 92430 **Fax:** 5231 924343
Email: redaktion@vms-detmold.de **Web site:** http://www.muehle-online.de
Freq: 24 issues yearly; **Annual Sub.:** EUR 232,30; **Circ:** 3,200
Editor: Reinald Pottebaum; **Advertising Manager:** Silke Käßner
Profile: Magazine about grain cultivation, concentrated agricultural feed and related topics.
Language(s): German
ADVERTISING RATES:
Full Page Mono .... EUR 940
Full Page Colour .... EUR 1760
Mechanical Data: Type Area: 270 x 190 mm, No. of Columns (Display): 4, Col Widths (Display): 45 mm
Copy instructions: *Copy Date:* 14 days prior to publication
Supplement(s): Der Mühlstein
BUSINESS: AGRICULTURE & FARMING

MÜHLENMAGAZIN 1828476G57-2852
Editorial: Heerser Mühle 1, 32107 BAD SALZUFLEN
Tel: 5222 797151 **Fax:** 5222 707990
Email: umweltzentrum@badsalzuflen.de **Web site:** http://www.heerser-muehle.de
Freq: Half-yearly; **Circ:** 2,000
Editor: Martin Doering
Profile: Magazine about environment protection.
Language(s): German
Copy instructions: *Copy Date:* 15 days prior to publication

MÜLL UND ABFALL 736607G32B-35
Editorial: Beethovenstr. 51a, 38106 BRAUNSCHWEIG **Tel:** 531 3913969
Fax: 531 3914584
Email: redaktion.muell+abfall@esvmedien.de **Web site:** http://www.muellundabfall.de
Freq: Monthly; **Annual Sub.:** EUR 152,59; **Circ:** 2,100
Editor: Klaus Fricke; **Advertising Manager:** Peter Taprogge
Profile: Magazine containing waste disposal and waste management information.
Language(s): German
ADVERTISING RATES:
Full Page Mono .... EUR 1310
Full Page Colour .... EUR 2210
Mechanical Data: Type Area: 254 x 185 mm, No. of Columns (Display): 2, Col Widths (Display): 84 mm
Copy instructions: *Copy Date:* 28 days prior to publication
BUSINESS: LOCAL GOVERNMENT, LEISURE & RECREATION: Public Health & Cleaning

MULTIMEDIA MAGAZIN 764051G5F-17
Editorial: Max-Planck-Str. 38, 50858 KÖLN
Tel: 2234 99080 **Fax:** 2234 9908130
Email: dubbert@chilicommunication.de **Web site:** http://www.kms.eu
Freq: Half-yearly; **Cover Price:** Free; **Circ:** 13,000
Editor: Stefan Dubbert
Profile: Customer magazine.
Language(s): German

MULTIMEDIA.DE 1662284G5-4607
Editorial: Heinestr. 72, 72762 REUTLINGEN
Tel: 7121 348100 **Fax:** 7121 348111
Email: kontakt@multimedia.de **Web site:** http://www.multimedia.de
Cover Price: Paid
Advertising Manager: Uwe Thomas
Language(s): German
BUSINESS: COMPUTERS & AUTOMATION

MÜNCHBERG-HELMBRECHTSER TAGESZEITUNG 736610G67B-9980
Editorial: Poststr. 9, 95028 HOF **Tel:** 9281 8160
Fax: 9281 816283
Email: verlag@frankenpost.de **Web site:** http://www.frankenpost.de
Freq: 312 issues yearly; **Circ:** 9,126
Advertising Manager: Stefan Sailer
Profile: Regional daily newspaper with news on politics, economy, culture, sports, travel, technology, etc. Münchberg-Helmbrechtser Tageszeitung is a local edition of the newspaper Frankenpost. Facebook: http://www.facebook.com/pages/Frankenpost/330862476314 Twitter: http://twitter.com/frankenpost This Outlet offers RSS (Really Simple Syndication).
Language(s): German
ADVERTISING RATES:
SCC .... EUR 39,00
Mechanical Data: Type Area: 485 x 325 mm, No. of Columns (Display): 7, Col Widths (Display): 44 mm
Copy instructions: *Copy Date:* 1 day prior to publication
Supplement(s): rtv
REGIONAL DAILY & SUNDAY NEWSPAPERS: Regional Daily Newspapers

MÜNCHEN GEHT AUS 1865622G89A-12432
Editorial: Arcisstr. 68, 80801 MÜNCHEN
Tel: 89 5505660 **Fax:** 89 55056612
Email: go@gomuenchen.com **Web site:** http://www.gomuenchen.de
Freq: Annual; **Cover Price:** EUR 5,00; **Circ:** 25,000
Editor: Daniel Wiechmann; **Advertising Manager:** Susanne Straßer
Profile: Restaurant Guide for Munich.
Language(s): German
ADVERTISING RATES:
Full Page Mono .... EUR 2160
Full Page Colour .... EUR 3500
Mechanical Data: Type Area: 183 x 132 mm, No. of Columns (Display): 3, Col Widths (Display): 44 mm
Copy instructions: *Copy Date:* 30 days prior to publication

MÜNCHEN KAUFT EIN! 1836487G89A-12411
Editorial: Höherweg 287, 40231 DÜSSELDORF
Tel: 211 7357681 **Fax:** 211 7357680
Email: info@ueberblick.de **Web site:** http://www.ueberblick.de

Freq: Annual; **Cover Price:** EUR 6,00; **Circ:** 40,000
Editor: Julitta Ammerschläger
Profile: Munich shopping guide to the best shopping addresses.
Language(s): German
ADVERTISING RATES:
Full Page Mono .... EUR 2390
Full Page Colour .... EUR 3490
Mechanical Data: Type Area: 260 x 190 mm, No. of Columns (Display): 4, Col Widths (Display): 44 mm
Copy instructions: *Copy Date:* 31 days prior to publication

MÜNCHNER ÄRZTLICHE ANZEIGEN 736617G56A-7200
Editorial: Elsenheimer Str. 63, 80687 MÜNCHEN
Tel: 89 5471160 **Fax:** 89 54711699
Email: schriftleitung@aekbv.de
Freq: 26 issues yearly; Free to qualifying individuals
Annual Sub.: EUR 75,00; **Circ:** 17,000
Editor: Caroline Mayer; **Advertising Manager:** Manfred Wester
Profile: Journal containing medical information for doctors in Munich.
Language(s): German
Mechanical Data: Type Area: 240 x 180 mm, No. of Columns (Display): 2, Col Widths (Display): 87 mm
Copy instructions: *Copy Date:* 11 days prior to publication

MÜNCHNER KIRCHENZEITUNG 736620G87-9440
Editorial: Herzog-Wilhelm-Str. 5, 80331 MÜNCHEN
Tel: 89 23225200 **Fax:** 89 23225240
Email: redaktion@muenchner-kirchenzeitung.de **Web site:** http://www.muenchner-kirchenzeitung.de
Freq: Weekly; **Circ:** 34,187
Editor: Johannes Schießl; **Advertising Manager:** Michael Brandl
Profile: Catholic weekly for the archbishopric of Munich and Freising.
Language(s): German
ADVERTISING RATES:
Full Page Mono .... EUR 2520
Full Page Colour .... EUR 3675
Mechanical Data: Type Area: 324 x 222 mm, No. of Columns (Display): 5, Col Widths (Display): 42 mm
Copy instructions: *Copy Date:* 13 days prior to publication
CONSUMER: RELIGIOUS

MÜNCHNER MERKUR 736621G67B-10000
Editorial: Paul-Heyse-Str. 2, 80336 MÜNCHEN
Tel: 89 53060 **Fax:** 89 53068651
Email: redaktion@merkur-online.de **Web site:** http://www.merkur-online.de
Freq: 312 issues yearly; **Circ:** 14,412
Editor: Karl Schermann; **News Editor:** Lorenz von Stackelberg; **Advertising Manager:** Hans-Georg Bechthold
Profile: The Münchner Merkur with its own local newspapers, the leading regional newspaper brand in the Munich area - the most affluent area of Germany. The combination of newspaper and region is the foundation on which to build the success of the title. This is the newspaper not only the factual news agency, but forms a community of solidarity with its readers and the local community. The clear focus on local reporting creates a high regard to human reader loyalty. She presses one hand in the very high number of close to 180,000 subscribers. Also for the high reader-commitment is the loyalty of the total current 827 000 daily readers, the Münchner Merkur or one of its local newspapers usually read over many years. The Münchner Merkur with its own local newspapers is a newspaper for the whole family, tradition and modern life for one of the most beautiful regions of Germany unites. Reliable, informative, critical: the Münchner Merkur is the indispensable daily newspaper for the region. Facebook: http://www.facebook.com/pages/merkur-online.de/190176143327 This Outlet offers RSS (Really Simple Syndication).
Language(s): German
ADVERTISING RATES:
SCC .... EUR 43,60
Mechanical Data: Type Area: 474 x 324 mm, No. of Columns (Display): 7, Col Widths (Display): 45 mm
Copy instructions: *Copy Date:* 1 day prior to publication
Supplement(s): doppio
REGIONAL DAILY & SUNDAY NEWSPAPERS: Regional Daily Newspapers

MÜNCHNER STADTGESPRÄCHE 1855466G57-2885
Editorial: Landwehrstr. 64a, 80336 MÜNCHEN
Tel: 89 3077490 **Fax:** 89 30774920
Email: a21@umweltinstitut.org **Web site:** http://www.muenchner-stadtgespraeche.de
Freq: 3 issues yearly; **Cover Price:** Free; **Circ:** 12,000
Editor: Christina Hacker
Profile: Magazine about research in environmental pollution in Munich.
Language(s): German

MÜNCHNER WOCHEN ANZEIGER MOOSACHER ANZEIGER 736640G72-9196
Editorial: Moosacher Str. 56, 80809 MÜNCHEN
Tel: 89 5529460 **Fax:** 89 55294639
Email: info@wochenanzeiger.de **Web site:** http://www.wochenanzeiger.de
Freq: Weekly; **Cover Price:** Free; **Circ:** 24,600
Editor: Ernst Kreisl; **Advertising Manager:** Ernst Kreisl
Profile: Advertising journal (house-to-house) concentrating on local stories.
Language(s): German
ADVERTISING RATES:
Full Page Mono .... EUR 3492
Full Page Colour .... EUR 3492
Mechanical Data: Type Area: 430 x 288 mm, No. of Columns (Display): 7, Col Widths (Display): 39 mm
Copy instructions: *Copy Date:* 1 day prior to publication
Supplement(s): Olympia-Einkaufszentrum Aktuell
LOCAL NEWSPAPERS

MÜNCHNER WOCHEN ANZEIGER SENDLINGER ANZEIGER 736648G72-9228
Editorial: Luise-Kiesselbach-Platz 31, 81377 MÜNCHEN **Tel:** 89 45243630 **Fax:** 89 45243650
Email: redaktion@sendlinger.info **Web site:** http://www.sendlingeranzeiger.de
Freq: Weekly; **Cover Price:** Free; **Circ:** 113,150
Editor: Klaus D. Kiefer; **Advertising Manager:** Peter Kaiser
Profile: Advertising journal (house-to-house) concentrating on local stories.
Language(s): German
ADVERTISING RATES:
Full Page Mono .... EUR 5566
Full Page Colour .... EUR 6974
Mechanical Data: Type Area: 370 x 255 mm, No. of Columns (Display): 6, Col Widths (Display): 40 mm
Copy instructions: *Copy Date:* 2 days prior to publication
LOCAL NEWSPAPERS

MÜNDENER ALLGEMEINE 730355G67B-7180
Editorial: Frankfurter Str. 168, 34121 KASSEL
Tel: 561 20300 **Fax:** 561 2032406
Email: info@hna.de **Web site:** http://www.hna.de
Freq: 312 issues yearly; **Circ:** 6,290
Advertising Manager: Andrea Schaller-Öller
Profile: Regional daily newspaper with news on politics, economy, culture, sports, travel, technology, etc. The Mündener Allgemeine a local edition of the HNA Hessische/Niedersächsische Allgemeine. Twitter: http://twitter.com/hna_online This Outlet offers RSS (Really Simple Syndication).
Language(s): German
ADVERTISING RATES:
SCC .... EUR 34,60
Mechanical Data: Type Area: 430 x 285 mm, No. of Columns (Display): 6, Col Widths (Display): 45 mm
Copy instructions: *Copy Date:* 2 days prior to publication
REGIONAL DAILY & SUNDAY NEWSPAPERS: Regional Daily Newspapers

DAS MÜNSTER 736677G84A-2400
Editorial: Leibnizstr. 13, 93055 REGENSBURG
Tel: 941 787850 **Fax:** 941 7878516
Email: das.muenster@schnell-und-steiner.de **Web site:** http://www.schnell-und-steiner.de
Freq: 5 issues yearly; **Annual Sub.:** EUR 58,10; **Circ:** 2,100
Editor: Simone Buckreus; **Advertising Manager:** Jürgen Volk
Profile: Periodical containing reviews of art and art history.
Language(s): German
Readership: Aimed at people interested in art, history, preservation of historical monuments, architecture, monasteries and holy orders.
ADVERTISING RATES:
Full Page Mono .... EUR 690
Full Page Colour .... EUR 1380
Mechanical Data: Type Area: 254 x 186 mm, No. of Columns (Display): 3, Col Widths (Display): 58 mm
Copy instructions: *Copy Date:* 20 days prior to publication
CONSUMER: THE ARTS & LITERARY: Arts

MÜNSTER GEHT AUS 765175G89A-11434
Editorial: Goldstr. 16, 33602 BIELEFELD
Tel: 521 932560 **Fax:** 521 9325699
Email: kontakt@tips-verlag.de **Web site:** http://www.muenster-geht-aus.de
Freq: Half-yearly; **Cover Price:** Free; **Circ:** 20,000
Editor: Friedrich Flöttmann; **Advertising Manager:** Frank Schmidt
Profile: Gastronomy, catering and leisure guide for Münster service section, tips and addresses for day and night owls. Facebook: http://de-de.facebook.com/people/Münster-Geht-Aus/100000914817923.
Language(s): German
ADVERTISING RATES:
Full Page Mono .... EUR 1358
Full Page Colour .... EUR 2167
Mechanical Data: Type Area: 190 x 130 mm, No. of Columns (Display): 3, Col Widths (Display): 40 mm
Copy instructions: *Copy Date:* 15 days prior to publication

MÜNSTER KAUFT EIN 765176G74A-3259
Editorial: Königsstr. 46, 48143 MÜNSTER
Tel: 251 899340 **Fax:** 251 8993420
Email: kontakt@tips-verlag.de **Web site:** http://www.tips-verlag.de
Freq: Half-yearly; **Cover Price:** Free; **Circ:** 20,000
Editor: Frank Schmidt; **Advertising Manager:** Frank Schmidt
Profile: Shopping guide for Munster. Since 1999, Münster kauft ein twice a year by the wide range of local shoppingworld. The shopping guide is divided into a magazine section with the latest reports on new stores, specialty products and favorite pieces and an extensive service section with over 800 addresses: freshly updated by industry and with useful information on the opening times to the range of brands.
Language(s): German
ADVERTISING RATES:
Full Page Mono .... EUR 1358
Full Page Colour .... EUR 2167
Mechanical Data: Type Area: 190 x 130 mm, No. of Columns (Display): 3, Col Widths (Display): 40 mm
Copy instructions: *Copy Date:* 20 days prior to publication

MÜNSTER SPEZIAL SCHENKEN FEIERN LEBEN 765177G74A-3260
Editorial: Königsstr. 46, 48143 MÜNSTER
Tel: 251 899340 **Fax:** 251 8993420
Email: kontakt@tips-verlag.de **Web site:** http://www.tips-verlag.de
Freq: Annual; **Cover Price:** Free; **Circ:** 20,000
Editor: Frank Schmidt; **Advertising Manager:** Frank Schmidt
Profile: Gift guide for Münster, the magazine since 1999 to make the pleasure giving and Christmas in Münster. With stories, reports and detailed gift tips Cathedral retail. Special service: The Gift Reviews are ordered by price groups and call the local sources of supply.
Language(s): German
ADVERTISING RATES:
Full Page Mono .... EUR 1490
Full Page Colour .... EUR 2357
Mechanical Data: Type Area: 260 x 190 mm, No. of Columns (Display): 4, Col Widths (Display): 43 mm
Copy instructions: *Copy Date:* 20 days prior to publication

MÜNSTERLAND 765104G50-1186
Editorial: Siemensstr. 4, 48565 STEINFURT
Tel: 2552 920153 **Fax:** 2552 920150
Email: muensterland@tecklenborg-verlag.de **Web site:** http://www.tecklenborg-verlag.de
Freq: Quarterly; **Annual Sub.:** EUR 20,00; **Circ:** 16,300
Editor: Ingrid Mende; **Advertising Manager:** Brigitte Tecklenborg
Profile: Magazine about culture and economy from the Munster area. Content: city portraits, catering tips, calendar of events and interviews with personalities from the region.
Language(s): German
ADVERTISING RATES:
Full Page Mono .... EUR 1810
Full Page Colour .... EUR 2735
Mechanical Data: Type Area: 259 x 178 mm, No. of Columns (Display): 4, Col Widths (Display): 48 mm
Copy instructions: *Copy Date:* 16 days prior to publication

MÜNSTERLAND ZEITUNG 736684G67B-10040
Editorial: Neubrückenstr. 8, 48143 MÜNSTER
Tel: 251 5924051 **Fax:** 251 5928457
Email: redaktion.newsdesk@mdhl.de **Web site:** http://www.muensterschezeitung.de
Freq: 312 issues yearly; **Circ:** 19,894
Profile: Daily newspaper with regional news and a local sports section. Twitter: http://twitter.com/mz_muenster.
Language(s): German
ADVERTISING RATES:
SCC .... EUR 55,60
Mechanical Data: Type Area: 478 x 315 mm, No. of Columns (Display): 7, Col Widths (Display): 42 mm
Copy instructions: *Copy Date:* 2 days prior to publication
Supplement(s): Freizeit
REGIONAL DAILY & SUNDAY NEWSPAPERS: Regional Daily Newspapers

MÜNSTERLÄNDISCHE TAGESZEITUNG 736682G67B-10060
Editorial: Lange Str. 9, 49661 CLOPPENBURG
Tel: 4471 17850 **Fax:** 4471 17830
Email: info@mt-news.de **Web site:** http://www.mt-news.de
Freq: 312 issues yearly; **Circ:** 18,060
Editor: Angelika Hauke; **Advertising Manager:** Karl-Heinz Berghoff
Profile: The close, traditional ties with the inhabitants of the district of Cloppenburg - 90 percent of all ads will appear in the MT family - the high density layer and spread in an area with a population with purchasing power, the Münsterländische Tageszeitung provides a daily average of success for advertising. It is estimated that each copy is read by over 60,000 people. So the Münsterländische Tageszeitung reaches by far the largest population in this area of ??distribution, form the district of Cloppenburg and the surrounding communities. MT is the official publication Journal of th region and its associated towns and villages.
Language(s): German
ADVERTISING RATES:
SCC .... EUR 40,40
Mechanical Data: Type Area: 420 x 282 mm, No. of Columns (Display): 6, Col Widths (Display): 45 mm
Copy instructions: *Copy Date:* 2 days prior to publication
Supplement(s): Treffpunkt ist Löningen
REGIONAL DAILY & SUNDAY NEWSPAPERS: Regional Daily Newspapers

MÜNSTERLÄNDISCHE VOLKSZEITUNG 736683G67B-10080
Editorial: Bahnhofstr. 8, 48431 RHEINE
Tel: 5971 4040 **Fax:** 5971 404399
Email: redaktion@mv-online.de **Web site:** http://www.mv-online.de
Freq: 312 issues yearly; **Circ:** 15,716
Profile: Daily newspaper with regional news and a local sports section. Facebook: http://www.facebook.com/pages/Munsterlandische-Volkszeitung/227279498838 This Outlet offers RSS (Really Simple Syndication).
Language(s): German
ADVERTISING RATES:
SCC .... EUR 39,50
Mechanical Data: Type Area: 488 x 324 mm, No. of Columns (Display): 7, Col Widths (Display): 44 mm
Copy instructions: *Copy Date:* 1 day prior to publication
Supplement(s): prisma
REGIONAL DAILY & SUNDAY NEWSPAPERS: Regional Daily Newspapers

MÜNSTERSCHE ZEITUNG 736685G67B-10100
Editorial: Neubrückenstr. 8, 48143 MÜNSTER
Tel: 251 5924051 **Fax:** 251 5928457
Email: redaktion.newsdesk@mdhl.de **Web site:** http://www.muensterschezeitung.de
Freq: 312 issues yearly
Editor: Stefan Bergmann
Profile: Daily news and reports on politics, sports, business and culture Twitter: http://twitter.com/mz_muenster This Outlet offers RSS (Really Simple Syndication).
Language(s): German
ADVERTISING RATES:
SCC .... EUR 95,60
Mechanical Data: Type Area: 478 x 315 mm, No. of Columns (Display): 7, Col Widths (Display): 42 mm
Copy instructions: *Copy Date:* 2 days prior to publication
Supplement(s): doppio; Freizeit; Heimspiel; moritz; prisma
REGIONAL DAILY & SUNDAY NEWSPAPERS: Regional Daily Newspapers

MÜRITZ AKTUELL 1606117G89A-12138
Editorial: Röbeler Str. 9, 17209 SIETOW
Tel: 39931 57914 **Fax:** 39931 57930
Email: info@wittich-sietow.de **Web site:** http://www.wittich.de
Freq: 7 issues yearly; **Cover Price:** Free; **Circ:** 6,000
Editor: Hans-Joachim Groß; **Advertising Manager:** Hans-Joachim Groß
Profile: Tourist magazine for the Mueritz region.
Language(s): German
ADVERTISING RATES:
Full Page Mono .... EUR 847
Full Page Colour .... EUR 897
Mechanical Data: Type Area: 275 x 185 mm, No. of Columns (Display): 4, Col Widths (Display): 43 mm
Copy instructions: *Copy Date:* 10 days prior to publication

MURNAUER TAGBLATT 736716G67B-10140
Editorial: Pfaffenrieder Str. 9, 82515 WOLFRATSHAUSEN **Tel:** 8171 2690
Fax: 8171 269240
Email: fsav@merkur-online.de **Web site:** http://www.merkur-online.de
Freq: 312 issues yearly; **Circ:** 15,089
Advertising Manager: Hans-Georg Bechthold
Profile: The Münchner Merkur with its own local newspapers, of which the Murnauer Tagblatt is one that, the leading regional newspaper brand in the Munich area - the most affluent area of Germany. The combination of newspaper and region is the foundation on which to build the success of the title. This is the newspaper not only the factual news agency, but forms a community of solidarity with its readers and the local community. The clear focus on local reporting creates a high regard to human reader loyalty. She presses one hand in the very high number of close to 180,000 subscribers. Also for the high reader-commitment is the loyalty of the total current 827 000 daily readers, the Münchner Merkur or one of its local newspapers usually read over many years. The Münchner Merkur with its own local newspapers is a newspaper for the whole family, tradition and modern life for one of the most beautiful regions of Germany unites. Reliable, informative, critical: the Münchner Merkur is the indispensable daily newspaper for the region. Facebook: http://www.facebook.com/pages/merkur-online.de/

90176143327 This Outlet offers RSS (Really Simple Syndication).
Language(s): German
ADVERTISING RATES:
SCC .... EUR 43,60
Mechanical Data: Type Area: 474 x 324 mm, No. of Columns (Display): 7, Col Widths (Display): 45 mm
Copy instructions: *Copy Date:* 1 day prior to publication
REGIONAL DAILY & SUNDAY NEWSPAPERS: Regional Daily Newspapers

MURRHARDTER ZEITUNG
736717G67B-10160
Editorial: Grabenstr. 23, 71540 MURRHARDT
Tel: 7192 929020 **Fax:** 7192 929019
Email: redaktion@murrhardter-zeitung.de **Web site:** http://www.murrhardter-zeitung.de
Freq: 312 issues yearly; **Circ:** 2,606
Editor: Reinhard Fiedler; **Advertising Manager:** Michael Mauser
Profile: Daily newspaper with regional news and a local sports section.
Language(s): German
ADVERTISING RATES:
SCC .... EUR 28,80
Mechanical Data: Type Area: 485 x 327 mm, No. of Columns (Display): 7, Col Widths (Display): 45 mm
Copy instructions: *Copy Date:* 1 day prior to publication
Supplement(s): Fußball lokal; Handball lokal
REGIONAL DAILY & SUNDAY NEWSPAPERS: Regional Daily Newspapers

MUSEUMS IN DRESDEN
1830175G89A-12404
Editorial: Prager Str. 2b, 01069 DRESDEN
Tel: 351 8007030 **Fax:** 351 8007070
Email: redaktion@maxity.de **Web site:** http://www.maxity.de
Freq: Annual; **Cover Price:** Free; **Circ:** 20,000
Editor: Christine Herzog
Profile: Museum guide for Dresden. Overview of the Dresden museums, their opening times and admission prices completely in English.
Language(s): English; German
ADVERTISING RATES:
Full Page Mono .... EUR 1080
Full Page Colour .... EUR 1080
Mechanical Data: Type Area: 190 x 85 mm

MUSIK IN DER GRUNDSCHULE
736756G62B-1700
Editorial: Goethestr. 61a, 16548 GLIENICKE
Tel: 33056 224330
Email: studioneumann@t-online.de **Web site:** http://www.musikpaedagogik-online.de
Freq: Quarterly; **Annual Sub.:** EUR 32,00; **Circ:** 8,000
Editor: Friedrich Neumann; **Advertising Manager:** Dieter P. Schwarz
Profile: Magazine about the teaching of music in elementary schools.
Language(s): German
Readership: Aimed at music teachers in Germany.
ADVERTISING RATES:
Full Page Mono .... EUR 655
Full Page Colour .... EUR 819
Mechanical Data: Type Area: 260 x 185 mm
Copy instructions: *Copy Date:* 38 days prior to publication
BUSINESS: CHURCH & SCHOOL EQUIPMENT & EDUCATION: Education Teachers

MUSIK & ÄSTHETIK
736773G76D-5980
Editorial: Langackern 1, 79289 HORBEN
Fax: 1805 06034560095
Email: riklein@t-online.de **Web site:** http://www.musikundaesthetik.de
Freq: Quarterly; **Annual Sub.:** EUR 68,00; **Circ:** 1,000
Editor: Richard Klein; **Advertising Manager:** Friederike Kamann
Profile: Magazine containing analyses of musical works, articles on music aesthetics, new music and music politics. Also includes book reviews and new recordings.
Language(s): English; German
Readership: Aimed at professional musicians, philosophers and people who enjoy listening to music.
ADVERTISING RATES:
Full Page Mono .... EUR 600
Mechanical Data: Type Area: 192 x 120 mm, No. of Columns (Display): 2, Col Widths (Display): 58 mm
Copy instructions: *Copy Date:* 20 days prior to publication
CONSUMER: MUSIC & PERFORMING ARTS: Music

MUSIK & BILDUNG
736774G61-43
Editorial: Weihergarten 5, 55116 MAINZ
Tel: 6131 246846 **Fax:** 6131 246212
Email: caren.benischek@schott-music.com **Web site:** http://www.musikpaedagogik-online.de
Freq: Quarterly; **Annual Sub.:** EUR 32,00; **Circ:** 8,000
Editor: Caren Benischek; **Advertising Manager:** Dieter P. Schwarz
Profile: Magazine covering theory and methodology of music teaching.
Language(s): German
Readership: Aimed at school musicians.
ADVERTISING RATES:
Full Page Mono .... EUR 945
Full Page Colour .... EUR 1182
Mechanical Data: Type Area: 260 x 185 mm
Copy instructions: *Copy Date:* 28 days prior to publication
BUSINESS: MUSIC TRADE

MUSIK & KIRCHE
736776G76D-160_50
Editorial: Heinrich-Schütz-Allee 35, 34131 KASSEL
Tel: 561 3105154 **Fax:** 561 3105310
Email: redaktion@musikundkirche.de **Web site:** http://www.musikundkirche.de
Freq: 6 issues yearly; **Annual Sub.:** EUR 43,00; **Circ:** 2,500
Editor: Klaus Röhring; **Advertising Manager:** Kerstin Lehmann
Profile: Journal about church music.
Language(s): German
ADVERTISING RATES:
Full Page Mono .... EUR 500
Mechanical Data: Type Area: 208 x 141 mm
Copy instructions: *Copy Date:* 45 days prior to publication
CONSUMER: MUSIC & PERFORMING ARTS: Music

MUSIKEXPRESS.
736747G76E-100
Editorial: Mehringdamm 33, 10961 BERLIN
Tel: 30 3088188218 **Fax:** 30 3088188221
Email: rainer.schmidt@axel-springer.de **Web site:** http://www.musikexpress.de
Freq: Monthly; **Annual Sub.:** EUR 52,80; **Circ:** 52,998
Editor: Rainer Schmidt; **Advertising Manager:** Oliver Horn
Profile: MUSIKEXPRESS presents itself as a self-conscious and trend-oriented music magazine. Not only with news, portraits, Interviews, CD reviews and concert reviews, but also with elaborate and surprisingly composed dossiers unusual on-site reports, irreverent Bits & Pieces right across the page and various forums for passionate debate. An important dimension of popular culture is MUSIKEXPRESS the theme "Fashion ". Unusual, musikaffin staged fashion lines provide visually attractive lifestyle trends. The perfectly developed, comprehensive service range "Sounds", which includes over 100 CD reviews, lots of tour dates and concert reviews of course, Consumer Electronics, Movies and DVDs, games and literature, is one more reason why MUSIKEXPRESS of many other media is used as an information and reference source.
Language(s): German
Readership: Read mainly by men between 20 and 30 years.
ADVERTISING RATES:
Full Page Mono .... EUR 9000
Full Page Colour .... EUR 9000
Mechanical Data: Type Area: 288 x 206 mm, No. of Columns (Display): 4, Col Widths (Display): 47 mm
Copy instructions: *Copy Date:* 28 days prior to publication
CONSUMER: MUSIC & PERFORMING ARTS: Pop Music

DIE MUSIKFORSCHUNG
736749G61-57
Editorial: Heinrich-Schütz-Allee 35, 34131 KASSEL
Tel: 561 3105255 **Fax:** 561 3105254
Email: g.f.musikforschung@t-online.de **Web site:** http://www.musikforschung.de
Freq: Quarterly; Free to qualifying individuals
Annual Sub.: EUR 69,00; **Circ:** 2,500
Editor: Jürgen Heidrich; **Advertising Manager:** Kerstin Lehmann
Profile: Magazine about all aspects of music. including research and teaching.
Language(s): German
ADVERTISING RATES:
Full Page Mono .... EUR 500
Mechanical Data: Type Area: 208 x 153 mm
Copy instructions: *Copy Date:* 45 days prior to publication
BUSINESS: MUSIC TRADE

MUSIKHANDEL
736752G61-5
Editorial: Keltingstr. 18, 23795 BAD SEGEBERG
Tel: 4551 889530 **Fax:** 4551 889599
Email: mahler@musikhandel-online.de **Web site:** http://www.musikhandel-online.de
Freq: 6 issues yearly; Free to qualifying individuals
Annual Sub.: EUR 37,00; **Circ:** 2,700
Editor: Wolfgang Spahr
Profile: Magazine about all aspects of the music trade.
Language(s): German
Mechanical Data: Type Area: 262 x 176 mm, No. of Columns (Display): 4, Col Widths (Display): 42 mm
BUSINESS: MUSIC TRADE

MUSIK-KONZEPTE
736759G76D-5979
Editorial: Levelingstr. 6a, 81673 MÜNCHEN
Tel: 89 43600012 **Fax:** 89 43600019
Email: info@etk-muenchen.de **Web site:** http://www.etk-muenchen.de
Freq: Quarterly; **Annual Sub.:** EUR 45,00
Advertising Manager: Clemens Heucke
Profile: Magazine for musical composers.
Language(s): German
ADVERTISING RATES:
Full Page Mono .... EUR 650
Mechanical Data: Type Area: 197 x 115 mm
CONSUMER: MUSIC & PERFORMING ARTS: Music

MUSIKMARKT
736760G61-6
Editorial: Fürstenrieder Str. 265, 81377 MÜNCHEN
Tel: 89 74126400 **Fax:** 89 74126401
Email: redaktion@musikmarkt.de **Web site:** http://www.musikmarkt.de
Freq: Weekly; **Annual Sub.:** EUR 214,00; **Circ:** 5,050
Editor: Stefan Zarges; **Advertising Manager:** Franz Grosse
Profile: Journal about the record market. Twitter: http://twitter.com/#!/musikmarkt This Outlet offers RSS (Really Simple Syndication).
Language(s): German
Readership: Read by music enthusiasts.
ADVERTISING RATES:
Full Page Mono .... EUR 1700
Full Page Colour .... EUR 2600
Mechanical Data: Type Area: 253 x 186 mm, No. of Columns (Display): 4, Col Widths (Display): 43 mm
Copy instructions: *Copy Date:* 14 days prior to publication
BUSINESS: MUSIC TRADE

MUSIX
765293G76D-5931
Editorial: Schlossgut Weyhern, 82281 EGENHOFEN
Tel: 8134 555016 **Fax:** 8134 555066
Email: martin.buchenberger@musix.de **Web site:** http://www.musix.de
Freq: Monthly; **Annual Sub.:** EUR 20,00; **Circ:** 296,245
Editor: Martin Buchenberger; **Advertising Manager:** Christian Marks
Profile: Magazine about musicians performing in Germany. CD, DVD, movies and game software novelties.
Language(s): German
ADVERTISING RATES:
Full Page Mono .... EUR 7770
Full Page Colour .... EUR 10780
Mechanical Data: Type Area: 271 x 184 mm, No. of Columns (Display): 4, Col Widths (Display): 45 mm
Copy instructions: *Copy Date:* 13 days prior to publication
Supplement(s): moviex
CONSUMER: MUSIC & PERFORMING ARTS: Music

MUSKELREPORT
736781G94F-1200
Editorial: Im Moos 4, 79112 FREIBURG
Tel: 7665 94470 **Fax:** 7665 944720
Email: info@dgm.org **Web site:** http://www.dgm.org
Freq: Quarterly; Free to qualifying individuals
Annual Sub.: EUR 20,00; **Circ:** 8,000
Editor: Horst Ganter
Profile: Magazine covering exercise and healthy living.
Language(s): German
ADVERTISING RATES:
Full Page Mono .... EUR 1400
Full Page Colour .... EUR 1400
Mechanical Data: Type Area: 297 x 210 mm, No. of Columns (Display): 3, Col Widths (Display): 58 mm
Copy instructions: *Copy Date:* 30 days prior to publication
CONSUMER: OTHER CLASSIFICATIONS: Disability

MYCOSES
736798G56A-7260
Editorial: Rotherstr. 21, 10245 BERLIN
Tel: 30 47031450 **Fax:** 30 47031410
Email: klaus.mickus@wiley.com **Web site:** http://www.wiley.com
Freq: 6 issues yearly; **Annual Sub.:** EUR 547,00; **Circ:** 1,200
Editor: H. C. Korting; **Advertising Manager:** Tobias Trinkl
Profile: International forum for pathogenesis, diagnosis, therapy, prophylaxis and epidemiology of fungal infectious diseases in humans and animals as well as on the biology of pathogenic fungi.
Language(s): English
Mechanical Data: Type Area: 263 x 167 mm
Copy instructions: *Copy Date:* 28 days prior to publication

MYSELF
1696628G74A-3477
Editorial: Karlstr. 23, 80333 MÜNCHEN
Tel: 89 381040 **Fax:** 89 38104739
Email: info@myself.de **Web site:** http://www.myself.de
Freq: Monthly; **Annual Sub.:** EUR 36,00; **Circ:** 279,892
Editor: Sabine Hofmann; **News Editor:** Natascha Zeljko; **Advertising Manager:** Susanne Förg-Randazzo
Profile: The life of modern, self-confident women has more aspects than ever before. Just like myself. With an intelligent, entertaining and relaxed attitude, myself offers topics that are interesting, fascinating and touching. myself has a unique concept and combines interesting features with useful information and modern lifestyle. Career, family, partners and friends - myself tells you all about it – in a great visual style. Great stories and journalistic competence on a high level, yet with a laid-back feel. This is very appealing to the most sophisticated target group, the educated and well-paid women between 25 and 49. myself tells us about the real life and about success stories, inspires us with new decorating ideas and party recipes, or takes us to antastic travel destinations. It seduces us with beautiful fashion and beauty photographs. The spectrum of topics includes career, fashion, beauty, relationships, health, food, design and travel. myself is not just one magazine. myself has as many sides as life itself. This Outlet offers RSS (Really Simple Syndication).
Language(s): German
ADVERTISING RATES:
Full Page Mono .... EUR 21500
Full Page Colour .... EUR 21500
Mechanical Data: Type Area: 247 x 190 mm, No. of Columns (Display): 4, Col Widths (Display): 44 mm
Copy instructions: *Copy Date:* 29 days prior to publication
CONSUMER: WOMEN'S INTEREST CONSUMER MAGAZINES: Women's Interest

MZ-WEB.DE
1621737G67B-16608
Editorial: Delitzscher Str. 65, 06112 HALLE
Tel: 345 5655007 **Fax:** 345 5655010
Email: gero.hirschelmann@mz-web.de **Web site:** http://www.mz-web.de
Freq: Daily; **Cover Price:** Paid; **Circ:** 1,496,011 Unique Users
Editor: Robby Braune
Profile: News portal of the Mitteldeutsche Zeitung. mz-web.de offers daily updated and edited news from all departments from politics to sports and business to culture. Special attention is given to the reporting of the distribution area of the Mitteldeutsche Zeitung. Local and regional texts, images and video from Sachsen-Anhalt therefore constitute the editorial focus. An online survey in 2009 showed that users appreciate this mix of news from the world, especially from Germany and the home. Another strength of mz-web.de is the balanced mix of editorial and service that offers users in addition to the daily news, extensive additional training. Facebook: http://www.facebook.com/mzwebde Twitter: http://twitter.com/mzwebde This Outlet offers RSS (Really Simple Syndication).
Language(s): German
REGIONAL DAILY & SUNDAY NEWSPAPERS: Regional Daily Newspapers

N BAHN MAGAZIN
737023G79B-1280
Editorial: Willstätterstr. 9, 40549 DÜSSELDORF
Tel: 211 5201334 **Fax:** 211 5201328
Email: nbm@alba-verlag.de **Web site:** http://www.alba-verlag.de
Freq: 6 issues yearly; **Annual Sub.:** EUR 33,00; **Circ:** 12,662
Advertising Manager: Robert A. Braun
Profile: Magazine for model railway enthusiasts and collectors.
Language(s): German
ADVERTISING RATES:
Full Page Mono .... EUR 1320
Full Page Colour .... EUR 1890
Mechanical Data: Type Area: 255 x 191 mm, No. of Columns (Display): 4, Col Widths (Display): 45 mm
Copy instructions: *Copy Date:* 20 days prior to publication
CONSUMER: HOBBIES & DIY: Models & Modelling

N UND L NATURSCHUTZ UND LANDSCHAFTSPFLEGE IN BRANDENBURG
1626636G57-2707
Editorial: Seeburger Chaussee 2, 14476 GROSS GLIENICKE **Tel:** 33201 442223 **Fax:** 33201 442299
Email: matthias.hille@lugv.brandenburg.de **Web site:** http://www.lugv.brandenburg.de
Freq: Quarterly; **Annual Sub.:** EUR 12,00; **Circ:** 2,100
Editor: Matthias Hille
Profile: Journal of the modern conservation professional or voluntary workers and cooperating areas. Information and guidance material, results of the practical and theoretical work.
Language(s): German

N & R NETZWIRTSCHAFTEN & RECHT
1794912G1A-3662
Editorial: Mainzer Landstr. 251, 60326 FRANKFURT
Tel: 69 75951151 **Fax:** 69 75952780
Email: kutschke@betriebs-berater.de **Web site:** http://www.nundr.net
Freq: Quarterly; **Annual Sub.:** EUR 169,90; **Circ:** 1,300
Editor: Torsten Kutschke; **Advertising Manager:** Marion Gertzen
Profile: Magazine for lawyers, companies and tax advisors.
Language(s): German
ADVERTISING RATES:
Full Page Mono .... EUR 1035
Full Page Colour .... EUR 1875
Mechanical Data: Type Area: 257 x 180 mm, No. of Columns (Display): 4, Col Widths (Display): 43 mm
Copy instructions: *Copy Date:* 16 days prior to publication

NA NEWSLETTER
1654888G2A-5555
Editorial: Mittelweg 144, 20148 HAMBURG
Tel: 40 41132843 **Fax:** 40 41132876
Email: petersen@newsaktuell.de **Web site:** http://www.newsaktuell.de
Freq: Quarterly; **Circ:** 2,500
Editor: Jens Petersen
Profile: Magazine for customers of the news aktuell company.
Language(s): German

NA NEWSLETTER
1654888G2A-5865
Editorial: Mittelweg 144, 20148 HAMBURG
Tel: 40 41132843 **Fax:** 40 41132876

Email: petersen@newsaktuell.de **Web site:** http://www.newsaktuell.de
Freq: Quarterly; **Circ:** 2,500
Editor: Jens Petersen
Profile: Magazine for customers of the news aktuell company.
Language(s): German

NACHRICHTEN 732754G14A-3820
Editorial: Karl-Wiechert-Allee 61, 30625 HANNOVER
Tel: 511 28020 **Fax:** 511 28029999
Email: service@kkh-allianz.de **Web site:** http://www.kkh-allianz.de
Freq: Quarterly; **Cover Price:** Free; **Circ:** 500,000
Editor: Oliver Kölling
Profile: Company publication published by KKH Kaufmännische Krankenkasse.
Language(s): German
ADVERTISING RATES:
Full Page Mono .... EUR 8900
Full Page Colour .... EUR 8900
Mechanical Data: Type Area: 256 x 175 mm

NACHRICHTEN AUS DER CHEMIE 736821G13-1780
Editorial: Varrentrappstr. 40, 60486 FRANKFURT
Tel: 69 7917462 **Fax:** 69 79171462
Email: nachrichten@gdch.de **Web site:** http://www.gdch.de
Freq: 11 issues yearly; **Annual Sub.:** EUR 344,00; **Circ:** 28,593
Editor: Ernst Guggolz
Profile: The Nachrichten aus der Chemie are already in the 59th Born in the most important source of information for chemists in all fields: decision makers, thought leaders, opinion makers, opinion leaders with budget and personnel responsibility from industry, universities, government agencies, associations. They form the unique audience. The high demands of the readers to products and brands which corresponds editorial expertise. The broad spectrum of communications, the unique range of personal information, event and training schedule ensures high reader loyalty. PhD students, career start-and-riser value not only to labor market information and extensive career job market. For advertisers, the Nachrichten aus der Chemiel is an indispensable medium. The Nachrichten aus der Chemie, the magazine with the largest paid circulation for Chemistry in Germany. Four times a year, no messages from the chemicals with increased circulation and reach the 2,000 members of the Austrian Chemical Society.
Language(s): German
ADVERTISING RATES:
Full Page Mono .... EUR 5380
Full Page Colour .... EUR 6480
Mechanical Data: No. of Columns (Display): 4, Col Widths (Display): 45 mm, Type Area: 260 x 180 mm
Copy instructions: *Copy Date:* 30 days prior to publication
BUSINESS: CHEMICALS

NACHRICHTEN FÜR AUSSENHANDEL 1626629G14C-4736
Editorial: Rudolfstr. 22, 60327 FRANKFURT
Tel: 69 66563225 **Fax:** 69 66563222
Email: redaktion@maerkte-weltweit.de **Web site:** http://www.maerkte-weltweit.de
Freq: 250 issues yearly; **Circ:** 3,000
Editor: Martin Brückner; **Advertising Manager:** Shezad Malik
Profile: Magazine with current news on international markets and the export trade.
Language(s): German
ADVERTISING RATES:
Full Page Mono .... EUR 1450
Full Page Colour .... EUR 1750
Mechanical Data: Type Area: 372 x 256 mm
Copy instructions: *Copy Date:* 8 days prior to publication

NACHRICHTEN FÜR DIE LANDWIRTSCHAFT 736891G21A-2900
Editorial: Am Kamp 19, 24768 RENDSBURG
Tel: 4331 127761 **Fax:** 4331 127718
Email: kbv.rd-eck@bauernverbandsh.de **Web site:** http://www.bauernverbandsh.de
Freq: Quarterly; **Circ:** 3,500
Editor: Reimer Thun; **Advertising Manager:** Reimer Thun
Profile: Official publication of the Farmers Association from the districts of Rendsburg and Eckernförde.
Language(s): German
ADVERTISING RATES:
Full Page Mono .... EUR 480
Mechanical Data: Type Area: 250 x 180 mm, No. of Columns (Display): 2, Col Widths (Display): 90 mm
Copy instructions: *Copy Date:* 20 days prior to publication

NACHTFLUG - (AUSG. MK-SÜD/OE-GM) 1739840G80-14929
Editorial: Mathildenstr. 20, 58507 LÜDENSCHEID
Tel: 2351 985990 **Fax:** 2351 9859922
Email: wigginghaus@nachtflug-magazin.de **Web site:** http://www.nachtflug-magazin.de
Freq: 6 issues yearly; **Cover Price:** Free; **Circ:** 13,500
Editor: Jürgen Wigginghaus
Language(s): German
ADVERTISING RATES:
Full Page Mono .... EUR 995
Full Page Colour .... EUR 1420
Mechanical Data: Type Area: 260 x 190 mm, No. of Columns (Display): 4, Col Widths (Display): 44 mm
CONSUMER: RURAL & REGIONAL INTEREST

NAHDRAN 721872G14A-600
Editorial: 42271 WUPPERTAL **Tel:** 18500 991836
Fax: 18500 991489
Email: nahdran@barmer-gek.de **Web site:** http://www.barmer-gek.de
Freq: Quarterly; **Circ:** 650,000
Editor: Athanasios Drougias; **Advertising Manager:** Andreas Hipp
Profile: Magazine for entrepreneurs.
Language(s): German
ADVERTISING RATES:
Full Page Mono .... EUR 8000
Full Page Colour .... EUR 10000
Mechanical Data: Type Area: 297 x 210 mm

NAHE-GLAN WOCHENSPIEGEL 736907G72-9508
Editorial: Hauptstr. 330, 55743 IDAR-OBERSTEIN
Tel: 6781 947719 **Fax:** 6781 947777
Email: red-idaroberstein@sw-verlag.de **Web site:** http://www.wochenspiegellive.de
Freq: Weekly; **Cover Price:** Free; **Circ:** 19,744
Editor: Kai Brückner
Profile: Advertising journal (house-to-house) concentrating on local stories.
Language(s): German
ADVERTISING RATES:
Full Page Mono .... EUR 2649
Full Page Colour .... EUR 3703
Mechanical Data: Type Area: 430 x 290 mm, No. of Columns (Display): 7, Col Widths (Display): 38 mm
Copy instructions: *Copy Date:* 2 days prior to publication
LOCAL NEWSPAPERS

NÄHER > DRAN 1668218G50-1224
Editorial: Augustusplatz 9, 04109 LEIPZIG
Tel: 341 7104310 **Fax:** 341 7104301
Email: presse@ltm-leipzig.de **Web site:** http://www.naeherdran-leipzig.de
Freq: Quarterly; **Cover Price:** Free; **Circ:** 20,000
Editor: Andreas Schmidt; **Advertising Manager:** Andreas Schmidt
Profile: Quarterly magazine with information from the fields of culture, tourism and economy of the city of Leipzig and central Germany. The medium is aimed at executives and opinion leaders in tourism. The content includes exclusive researched topics and portraits of important personalities and corporate portraits, and with the event highlights in the current quarter.
Language(s): German
ADVERTISING RATES:
Full Page Mono .... EUR 950
Full Page Colour .... EUR 950
Mechanical Data: Type Area: 265 x 188 mm
Copy instructions: *Copy Date:* 14 days prior to publication

NAHE-ZEITUNG 736909G67B-10180
Editorial: August-Horch-Str. 28, 56070 KOBLENZ
Tel: 261 892240 **Fax:** 261 892770
Email: redaktion@rhein-zeitung.net **Web site:** http://www.rhein-zeitung.de
Freq: 312 issues yearly; **Circ:** 14,219
Profile: Regional daily newspaper with news on politics, economy, culture, sports, travel, technology, etc. The Nahe-Zeitung is a local issue the in koblenz appearing Rhein-Zeitung. Facebook: http://www.facebook.com/rheinzeitung Twitter: http://www.rhein-zeitung.de/twitter.html This Outlet offers RSS (Really Simple Syndication).
Language(s): German
ADVERTISING RATES:
SCC .... EUR 69,20
Mechanical Data: Type Area: 480 x 325 mm, No. of Columns (Display): 7, Col Widths (Display): 45 mm
Copy instructions: *Copy Date:* 1 day prior to publication
REGIONAL DAILY & SUNDAY NEWSPAPERS: Regional Daily Newspapers

DER NAHVERKEHR 736914G49A-75
Editorial: Willstätterstr. 9, 40549 DÜSSELDORF
Tel: 211 5201372 **Fax:** 211 5201378
Email: dnv@alba-verlag.de **Web site:** http://www.alba-verlag.de
Freq: 10 issues yearly; **Annual Sub.:** EUR 110,00; **Circ:** 1,684
Editor: Lothar Kuttig; **Advertising Manager:** Beatrice van Dijk
Profile: Magazine with information on local public transport.
Language(s): German
ADVERTISING RATES:
Full Page Mono .... EUR 2170
Full Page Colour .... EUR 2995
Mechanical Data: Type Area: 272 x 198 mm, No. of Columns (Display): 4, Col Widths (Display): 46 mm
Copy instructions: *Copy Date:* 17 days prior to publication
BUSINESS: TRANSPORT

NAHVERKEHRS...PRAXIS 736915G49A-80_50
Editorial: Siegburgstr. 5, 44359 DORTMUND
Tel: 231 33690 **Fax:** 231 336920
Email: g.schoenen@nahverkehrspraxis.de **Web site:** http://www.nahverkehrspraxis.de
Freq: 10 issues yearly; **Annual Sub.:** EUR 60,00; **Circ:** 5,442
Editor: Gudrun Arnold-Schoenen; **Advertising Manager:** Martina Kaczmarek
Profile: Publication about all forms of local transport.
Language(s): German
Readership: Aimed at people in the transport industry.
ADVERTISING RATES:
Full Page Mono .... EUR 1720
Full Page Colour .... EUR 2500
Mechanical Data: Type Area: 262 x 184 mm, No. of Columns (Display): 4, Col Widths (Display): 43 mm
Copy instructions: *Copy Date:* 18 days prior to publication
Official Journal of: Organ d. Freien Vereinigung d. Meister öffentl. Verkehrsbetriebe
BUSINESS: TRANSPORT

NASSAUER TAGEBLATT 736931G67B-10200
Editorial: Elsa-Brandström-Str. 18, 35578 WETZLAR
Tel: 6441 9590 **Fax:** 6441 959292
Email: redaktion.wnz@mittelhessen.de **Web site:** http://www.mittelhessen.de
Freq: 312 issues yearly; **Circ:** 9,413
Advertising Manager: Peter Rother
Profile: Daily newspaper with regional news and a local sports section.
Language(s): German
ADVERTISING RATES:
SCC .... EUR 35,00
Mechanical Data: Type Area: 490 x 328 mm, No. of Columns (Display): 7, Col Widths (Display): 44 mm
Copy instructions: *Copy Date:* 1 day prior to publication
Supplement(s): [f]amilie& freizeit; Fußball-Kalender; [g]esund!; Gut fahren!; rtv
REGIONAL DAILY & SUNDAY NEWSPAPERS: Regional Daily Newspapers

NASSAUER TAGEBLATT AM SONNTAG 1606887G72-17863
Editorial: Elsa-Brandström-Str. 18, 35578 WETZLAR
Tel: 6441 9590 **Fax:** 6441 959292
Email: redaktion.wnz@mittelhessen.de **Web site:** http://www.mittelhessen.de
Freq: Weekly; **Cover Price:** EUR 1,00; **Circ:** 9,413
Advertising Manager: Peter Rother
Profile: Regional weekly covering politics, economics, sport, travel, technology and the arts.
Language(s): German
ADVERTISING RATES:
SCC .... EUR 35,00
Mechanical Data: Type Area: 490 x 328 mm, No. of Columns (Display): 7, Col Widths (Display): 44 mm
Copy instructions: *Copy Date:* 2 days prior to publication
LOCAL NEWSPAPERS

NASSAUISCHE NEUE PRESSE 736933G67B-10220
Editorial: Frankenallee 71, 60327 FRANKFURT
Tel: 69 75010 **Fax:** 69 75014232
Email: redaktion@fnp.de **Web site:** http://www.fnp.de
Freq: 312 issues yearly; **Circ:** 24,286
Profile: The Nassauische Neue Presse is the leading daily newspaper in the country Nassauer Land between Westerburg, Bad Camberg, Weilburg, Diez and Limburg with the county as the center of their range. The head office is situated in Limburg. The Nassau ische Neue Presses joins the nationwide coverage of a big city newspaper with the special charm of a country connected local newspaper. It is a regional edition of the Frankfurter Neue Presse. Facebook: http://www.facebook.com/pages/FNP/115994585097103 This Outlet offers RSS (Really Simple Syndication).
Language(s): German
ADVERTISING RATES:
SCC .... EUR 57,60
Mechanical Data: Type Area: 528 x 371 mm, No. of Columns (Display): 8, Col Widths (Display): 45 mm
Copy instructions: *Copy Date:* 1 day prior to publication
REGIONAL DAILY & SUNDAY NEWSPAPERS: Regional Daily Newspapers

NASSAUISCHER VEREIN FÜR NATURKUNDE MITTEILUNGEN 1609447G57-2652
Editorial: Seifer Weg 25, 65232 TAUNUSSTEIN
Tel: 6128 71737
Email: b_toussaint@web.de **Web site:** http://www.naturkunde-online.de
Freq: Annual; **Circ:** 350
Editor: Benedikt Toussaint
Profile: Club news from the Association for Nature Studies in Nassau.
Language(s): German
Mechanical Data: Type Area: 260 x 170 mm, No. of Columns (Display): 2, Col Widths (Display): 80 mm
Copy instructions: *Copy Date:* 30 days prior to publication

NATIONAL GEOGRAPHIC DEUTSCHLAND 736936G89A-12109
Editorial: Am Baumwall 11, 20459 HAMBURG
Tel: 40 37035511 **Fax:** 40 37035598
Email: leserbriefe@nationalgeographic.de **Web site:** http://www.nationalgeographic.de
Freq: 5 issues yearly; **Annual Sub.:** EUR 52,20; **Circ:** 179,817
Editor: Erwin Brunner; **Advertising Manager:** Heiko Hager
Profile: Climate change, sustainability, foreign countries and exciting expeditions are the subject foci of NATIONAL GEOGRAPHIC GERMANY. The authentic sound and equally entertaining reports inspire 1.2 million readers each month. Many National Geographic writers and photographers have won awards. NATIONAL GEOGRAPHIC has in mind the health of our planet and its inhabitants - for since the founding of the National Geographic Society in 1888 the study and conservation of the earth is always in the center of policy. The philosophy of the brand with the yellow border: to make people aware for their own living space. National Geographic shows the beauty of natural resources, but also the threat of cultural diversity and natural resources. The reports and research projects create awareness of the crucial issues of the 21st Century. Facebook: http://www.facebook.com/nationalgeographic.de.
Language(s): German
ADVERTISING RATES:
Full Page Mono .... EUR 20550
Full Page Colour .... EUR 20550
Mechanical Data: Type Area: 228 x 142 mm, No. of Columns (Display): 3, Col Widths (Display): 45 mm
Copy instructions: *Copy Date:* 30 days prior to publication
CONSUMER: HOLIDAYS & TRAVEL: Travel

NATIONALPARK 736937G57-1220
Editorial: Bahnhofstr. 22, 94481 GRAFENAU
Tel: 8552 625060 **Fax:** 8552 920529
Email: redaktion@nationalparkzeitung.de **Web site:** http://www.nationalparkzeitung.de
Freq: Quarterly; **Annual Sub.:** EUR 24,00; **Circ:** 5,000
Editor: Eva Pongratz; **Advertising Manager:** Stefanie Ott
Profile: Wilderness, national parks, nature and travel in German and European landscapes. Write to National Park since 1974, renowned authors - dedicated wildlife filmmaker, tried and tested national park manager or profiled conservationists. Take the latest developments with independent expertise under the microscope and reported in exciting travel reports of spectacular natural areas. Outstanding nature and wildlife photographs are a hallmark of the magazine writer who was co-founded by Horst Stern Environmental Journalists. National Park makes you wish for nature and wildlife - and is thus very popular. The magazine is aimed at a broad audience of interested people to nature: national park visitors (inside), tourists in Germany's natural landscapes, hikers, volunteer conservationist of the major environmental organizations, professionals in environmental agencies and environmental education institutions and students.
Language(s): German
ADVERTISING RATES:
Full Page Mono .... EUR 1120
Full Page Colour .... EUR 1995
Mechanical Data: Type Area: 224 x 175 mm, No. of Columns (Display): 2, Col Widths (Display): 86 mm
Copy instructions: *Copy Date:* 30 days prior to publication

NATUR IN NRW 734328G21A-2660
Editorial: Leibnizstr. 10, 45659 RECKLINGHAUSEN
Tel: 2361 3053246 **Fax:** 2361 3053340
Email: bernd.stracke@nua.nrw.de **Web site:** http://www.lanuv.nrw.de
Freq: Quarterly; **Annual Sub.:** EUR 7,50; **Circ:** 9,500
Editor: Bernd Stracke
Profile: Journal of the National Office for Nature, Environment and Consumer Protection of Nordrhein-Westfalen.
Language(s): German

NATUR & HEILEN 736992G74G-1300
Editorial: Nikolaistr. 5, 80802 MÜNCHEN
Tel: 89 38015912 **Fax:** 89 38015916
Email: adevillard@naturundheilen.de **Web site:** http://www.naturundheilen.de
Freq: Monthly; **Annual Sub.:** EUR 45,60; **Circ:** 63,943
Editor: Anne Devillard; **Advertising Manager:** Eva Ziervogel
Profile: NATUR & HEILEN added to the editorial "health and healing of life in harmony with nature," a unique position in modern magazine scene. This unique position is already evident at first glance in their appearance: Format and Layout project from the mass of the event titles out - unique and pioneering. A quality that finds itself in the quality of their readership. The editorial team consists of a team of experienced journalists and authors in close collaboration with naturopathic doctors and health-oriented practitioners. Expertise, journalistic integrity and an understandable style, the quality characteristics, the estimated readership and binds to NATUR & HEILEN. The editorial approach includes the following topics: • holistic health care • alternative medicine • Nature-cure and treatments • advice and self-help • Healthy food, clothing and housing • organic gardening, ecology and conservation • meaningful way of life and spirituality The magazine • has interested lay paths to healthy living and natural healing. • provides assistance in all areas of holistic health care and treatment of diseases. • describe clearly and competently new and tried and tested in the field of natural healing, enhanced by practical

recommendations for self-medication and a healthier lifestyle. • is recognized as a reliable guide to the practical everyday life, which underlines the close reader-binding. The practical useful application for the reader is paramount, it is by book reviews, and presentation of products and services in the category "Company News" and on the advertising pages "addresses for your health" and "Dates and venues" selectively increased and kept up to date. Facebook: http://www.facebook.com/naturundheilen.
Language(s): German
ADVERTISING RATES:
Full Page Mono .... EUR 2300
Full Page Colour .... EUR 3400
Mechanical Data: Type Area: 208 x 140 mm, No. of Columns (Display): 3, Col Widths (Display): 44 mm
Copy instructions: *Copy Date:* 30 days prior to publication
CONSUMER: WOMEN'S INTEREST CONSUMER MAGAZINES: Slimming & Health

NATUR+KOSMOS 736994G57-1260
Editorial: Bretonischer Ring 13, 85630 GRASBRUNN
Tel: 89 45616240 **Fax:** 89 456169300
Email: redaktion@natur.de **Web site:** http://www.natur.de
Freq: Monthly; **Annual Sub.:** EUR 63,00; **Circ:** 58,974
Editor: Jan Berndorff; **Advertising Manager:** Jacqueline Lindner
Profile: The holistic natur + kosmos science magazine aimed at people interested in nature and the environment and have chosen personally for a natural, healthy and resource-saving way of life. Accordingly devoted to natur + kosmos three areas: FASCINATION Exciting stories and knowledge building strong reports from around the world offer new and fascinating views of animals, plants, landscapes and cultures. Inspiring photos by renowned nature photographers are complemented by sophisticated expertise. SUSTAINABILITY The magazine provides in-depth background reports on the most important current environmental issues. It provides profound insights into the relationships between man, nature and technology, and thereby enables the reader, competent to stand. Topics in nature + kosmos as "social business" or "greentech" will be to talk about and promote a new awareness and action. ORIENTATION natur + kosmos green orientation provides for a responsible, health-oriented life in harmony with nature. Consumer information and health tips help the individual life as part of an ecological, biological and socio-ethical consumerism.
Language(s): German
ADVERTISING RATES:
Full Page Mono .... EUR 5000
Full Page Colour .... EUR 7500
Mechanical Data: Type Area: 250 x 188 mm
Copy instructions: *Copy Date:* 28 days prior to publication
BUSINESS: ENVIRONMENT & POLLUTION

NATUR UND LANDSCHAFT 736996G57-1280
Editorial: Konstantinstr. 110, 53179 BONN
Tel: 228 84913210 **Fax:** 228 84919999
Email: karl-heinz-erdmann@bfn.de **Web site:** http://www.natur-und-landschaft.de
Freq: 11 issues yearly; **Annual Sub.:** EUR 78,30; **Circ:** 3,521
Editor: Karl-Heinz Erdmann
Profile: Journal reflecting current thought on the scientific, applied planning and legal aspects of the conservation of nature and the countryside. Also provides a forum for exchange of information.
Language(s): German
ADVERTISING RATES:
Full Page Mono .... EUR 1115
Full Page Colour .... EUR 1940
Mechanical Data: Type Area: 260 x 185 mm, No. of Columns (Display): 2, Col Widths (Display): 90 mm
Copy instructions: *Copy Date:* 25 days prior to publication
BUSINESS: ENVIRONMENT & POLLUTION

NATUR + UMWELT 1706811G57-2782
Editorial: Dr.-Johann-Maier-Str. 4, 93049 REGENSBURG **Tel:** 941 2972022 **Fax:** 941 2972031
Email: nu@bund-naturschutz.de **Web site:** http://www.bund-naturschutz.de
Freq: Quarterly; **Circ:** 100,501
Editor: Manfred Gößwald
Profile: The magazine Natur+Umwelt informed members of the Bund Naturschutz in Bayern eV since 1918 on the work of the Association and all aspects of nature and environmental protection. According to reader surveys, it is for the BN members far the most important medium in this sector. The modern magazine offers its readers today-depth background on environmental issues, fascinating nature reports, portraits of committed individuals, travel reports on Europe's most beautiful destinations, advice for healthy, environmentally sound life, large-format images of the most beautiful animals and plants, age-based fees for children and young people, offers of broad range of educational work, reports on the BN in all regions of Bavaria.
Language(s): German
ADVERTISING RATES:
Full Page Mono .... EUR 2000
Full Page Colour .... EUR 3485
Mechanical Data: Type Area: 242 x 188 mm
Copy instructions: *Copy Date:* 29 days prior to publication

NATURAMED 736950G21R-785
Editorial: Marienplatz 3, 80331 MÜNCHEN
Tel: 89 294770 **Fax:** 89 294775
Email: redbuero_ull@web.de
Freq: 6 issues yearly; Free to qualifying individuals
Annual Sub.: EUR 44,40; **Circ:** 26,238
Editor: Marcela Ullmann
Profile: The title Naturamed is the journalistic forum of the Committee for Research into Natural Medicine (KFN). Task is to convey all aspects of rational phytotherapy. The journal presents the complex effects of herbal medicines comprehensive and practical in the foreground.
Language(s): German
ADVERTISING RATES:
Full Page Mono .... EUR 3980
Full Page Colour .... EUR 5180
Mechanical Data: Type Area: 233 x 180 mm, No. of Columns (Display): 3, Col Widths (Display): 53 mm
Official Journal of: Organ d. Dt. Ges. f. Akupunktur u. Neuraltherapie
BUSINESS: AGRICULTURE & FARMING: Agriculture & Farming Related

NATURFREUNDE HAMBURG 729616G57-2660
Editorial: Postfach 203157, 20221 HAMBURG
Email: naturfreunde-hh@gmx.de **Web site:** http://www.naturfreunde-hh.de
Freq: Quarterly; **Circ:** 1,200
Editor: Walter Bräker
Profile: Magazine from the Association for Environmental Protection about leisurely tourism, sport and culture.
Language(s): German

NATURFREUNDIN 736958G75L-840
Editorial: Warschauer Str. 58a, 10243 BERLIN
Tel: 30 29773265 **Fax:** 30 29773280
Email: redaktion@naturfreundin.de **Web site:** http://www.naturfreundin.naturfreunde.de
Freq: Quarterly; Free to qualifying individuals
Annual Sub.: EUR 20,00; **Circ:** 56,000
Editor: Samuel Lehmberg; **Advertising Manager:** Samuel Lehmberg
Profile: Magazine containing articles on environmental protection, tourism and culture.
Language(s): German
Readership: Aimed at nature enthusiasts.
ADVERTISING RATES:
Full Page Mono .... EUR 3850
Full Page Colour .... EUR 3850
Mechanical Data: Type Area: 249 x 196 mm, No. of Columns (Display): 3-4
Copy instructions: *Copy Date:* 45 days prior to publication
Supplement(s): Grüner Aufstieg; Hertlingshausener Eckbach-Post; Mitteilungen der Karlsruher Naturfreunde; Der Naturfreund; "Naturfreunde Aktuell"; Natur Freunde Hessen Info; Wir Naturfreunde in Rheinland und Westfalen
CONSUMER: SPORT: Outdoor

DIE NATURHEILKUNDE 728818G56R-660
Editorial: Peterstr. 11, 26382 WILHELMSHAVEN
Tel: 4421 7556616 **Fax:** 4421 7556610
Email: chefredaktion@forum-medizin.de **Web site:** http://www.forum-medizin.de
Freq: 6 issues yearly; Free to qualifying individuals
Annual Sub.: EUR 36,00; **Circ:** 14,452
Editor: Maik Lehmkuhl; **Advertising Manager:** Maik Lehmkuhl
Profile: Journal covering the practice of healing by natural methods.
Language(s): German
ADVERTISING RATES:
Full Page Mono .... EUR 2015
Full Page Colour .... EUR 3205
Mechanical Data: Type Area: 246 x 178 mm, No. of Columns (Display): 3, Col Widths (Display): 56 mm
Copy instructions: *Copy Date:* 21 days prior to publication
BUSINESS: HEALTH & MEDICAL: Health Medical Related

NATUR-HEILKUNDE JOURNAL 1615812G37-1778
Editorial: Max-Planck-Str. 47, 53340 MECKENHEIM
Tel: 2225 945536 **Fax:** 2225 945537
Email: k.schwarzbach@naturheilkundejournal.de
Web site: http://www.naturheilkundejournal.de
Freq: Monthly; **Annual Sub.:** EUR 48,00; **Circ:** 12,700
Editor: Klaus Schwarzbach; **Advertising Manager:** Alexander Schiffauer
Profile: Magazine for general practitioners, dentists, pharmacists, alternative practitioners and psychotherapists interested in naturopathy.
Language(s): German
ADVERTISING RATES:
Full Page Mono .... EUR 2195
Full Page Colour .... EUR 2195
Mechanical Data: Type Area: 264 x 184 mm, No. of Columns (Display): 3, Col Widths (Display): 58 mm
Copy instructions: *Copy Date:* 13 days prior to publication

NATURHEILKUNDE & GESUNDHEIT 736962G94H-9380
Editorial: Otto-Hahn-Str. 16, 47608 GELDERN
Tel: 2831 13000 **Fax:** 2831 130020
Email: s.guckenbiehl@sud-verlag.de **Web site:** http://www.naturheilkunde-und-gesundheit.com
Freq: Monthly; **Circ:** 95,971
Editor: Sabine Guckenbiehl; **Advertising Manager:** Marcus H. Thielen
Profile: Magazine about natural health care, herbal remedies and alternative medicines.
Language(s): German
ADVERTISING RATES:
Full Page Mono .... EUR 2156
Full Page Colour .... EUR 5590
Mechanical Data: No. of Columns (Display): 3, Col Widths (Display): 60 mm, Type Area: 240 x 188 mm
Copy instructions: *Copy Date:* 60 days prior to publication
CONSUMER: OTHER CLASSIFICATIONS: Customer Magazines

NATURHEILPRAXIS MIT NATURMEDIZIN 736963G56A-7300
Editorial: Kirchberghof, 97724 BURGLAUER
Tel: 9733 3787 **Fax:** 9733 9637
Email: liebau@naturheilpraxis.de **Web site:** http://www.naturheilpraxis.de
Freq: Monthly; **Annual Sub.:** EUR 98,40; **Circ:** 15,923
Editor: Karl-Friedrich Liebau; **Advertising Manager:** Michael Dietl
Profile: Magazine focusing on naturopathy, homeopathic medicine and new products.
Language(s): German
Readership: Read by pharmacists, doctors and practitioners of alternative medicine.
ADVERTISING RATES:
Full Page Mono .... EUR 2100
Full Page Colour .... EUR 3330
Mechanical Data: Type Area: 256 x 185 mm, No. of Columns (Display): 4, Col Widths (Display): 46 mm
Copy instructions: *Copy Date:* 25 days prior to publication
Official Journal of: Organ d. Arbeitskreises f. Augendiagnostik u. Phänomenologie Josef Angerer e.V., d. Dt. Ges. f. Klass. Homöopathie e.V., d. Nederlandse Werkgroep van Praktizijns in de natuurlijke geneeskunst u. d. Dansk Naturopraktor Forbund
BUSINESS: HEALTH & MEDICAL

NATURKOST.DE 1621743G74G-1749
Editorial: Magnolienweg 23, 63741 ASCHAFFENBURG **Tel:** 6021 4489270
Fax: 6021 4489470
Email: muetze@naturkost.de **Web site:** http://www.naturkost.de
Freq: 100 times a year; **Cover Price:** Paid; **Circ:** 185,410 Unique Users
Editor: Rolf Mütze; **Advertising Manager:** Dietlind Arndt
Profile: Ezine: Customer magazine available in health-food shops, about healthy eating, organic foods, natural health and ecological matters.
Language(s): German
CONSUMER: WOMEN'S INTEREST CONSUMER MAGAZINES: Slimming & Health

NATURKUNDLICHE BEITRÄGE DES DJN 736971G57-1340
Editorial: Geiststr. 2, 37073 GÖTTINGEN
Email: philipp.meinecke@naturbeobachtung.de **Web site:** http://www.naturbeobachtung.de
Freq: Annual; Free to qualifying individuals ; **Circ:** 500
Editor: Philipp Meinecke
Profile: Publication containing reports on nature studies from the DJN.
Language(s): German

NATURKUNDLICHE BEITRÄGE DES DJN 736971G57-2933
Editorial: Geiststr. 2, 37073 GÖTTINGEN
Email: philipp.meinecke@naturbeobachtung.de **Web site:** http://www.naturbeobachtung.de
Freq: Annual; Free to qualifying individuals ; **Circ:** 500
Editor: Philipp Meinecke
Profile: Publication containing reports on nature studies from the DJN.
Language(s): German

NATÜRLICH VEGETARISCH 736949G74P-680
Editorial: Kanonierstr. 9, 48149 MÜNSTER
Tel: 40 2193590
Email: redaktion@vebu.de **Web site:** http://www.vebu.de
Freq: Quarterly; Free to qualifying individuals
Annual Sub.: EUR 14,00; **Circ:** 7,500
Editor: Katja Angenent
Profile: Magazine of the Society of Vegetarians in Germany. Facebook: http://www.facebook.com/vebu.de.
Language(s): German
ADVERTISING RATES:
Full Page Mono .... EUR 580
Full Page Colour .... EUR 890
Mechanical Data: Type Area: 277 x 220 mm, No. of Columns (Display): 3, Col Widths (Display): 56 mm
Copy instructions: *Copy Date:* 60 days prior to publication

NATURMAGAZIN 722416G57-180
Editorial: Friedensallee 21, 15834 RANGSDORF
Tel: 33708 20431 **Fax:** 33708 20433
Email: verlag@nut-online.de **Web site:** http://www.naturmagazin.info
Freq: Quarterly; Free to qualifying individuals
Annual Sub.: EUR 16,50; **Circ:** 23,000
Profile: Magazine on environmental protection in the regions of Berlin and Brandenburg.
Language(s): German
ADVERTISING RATES:
Full Page Mono .... EUR 985
Full Page Colour .... EUR 1872
Mechanical Data: Type Area: 255 x 180 mm, No. of Columns (Display): 3, Col Widths (Display): 57 mm
Copy instructions: *Copy Date:* 45 days prior to publication

NATURPARKTELLER 1818171G89A-12359
Editorial: Marktplatz 8, 71540 MURRHARDT
Tel: 7192 213888 **Fax:** 7192 213880
Email: info@naturpark-sfw.de **Web site:** http://www.naturpark-sfw.de
Freq: Annual; **Cover Price:** Free; **Circ:** 35,000
Editor: Andrea Bofinger
Profile: Restaurant Guide to the "Naturparktellern": Alle Naturparkteller are offered at a special price of 12 € and include • wine or request another drink from the region. The main ingredients are from local production. Some restaurants also offer children and senior citizens and vegetarian dishes Nature Park. A total of 82 restaurateurs participate in the local park.
Language(s): German

NATURSCHUTZ HEUTE 736979G57-1360
Editorial: Charitéstr. 3, 10117 BERLIN
Tel: 30 2849841500 **Fax:** 30 2849842500
Email: naturschutz.heute@nabu.de **Web site:** http://www.naturschutz-heute.de
Freq: Quarterly; Free to qualifying individuals
Annual Sub.: EUR 24,00; **Circ:** 280,115
Editor: Helge May
Profile: Natzrschutz heute is the membership magazine of the Nature Conservation Germany. The NABU is the oldest and, with around 460,000 members and supporters as one of the largest environmental organizations of the Federal Republic of Germany. The magazine has been published since 1969 and has the highest total circulation of all IVW-certified nature magazines. It reaches more than 750,000 nationwide nature lovers, conversationists, scientists, biologists, ornithologists, people with conversation-conscous who are actively engaged in conservation. Naturschutz heute offers its readers in every issue an exciting mix intelligible contributions from natural history, conservation, environmental and ecological life. Constantly Recurring items are the big title track, the people portrait, "NABU-world "and the book reviews. With the detailed service route is to a very attractive advertising environment available in which each issue will jewqeils several consumer issues presented.
Language(s): German
ADVERTISING RATES:
Full Page Mono .... EUR 3990
Full Page Colour .... EUR 5810
Mechanical Data: Type Area: 276 x 194 mm, No. of Columns (Display): 4, Col Widths (Display): 45 mm
Copy instructions: *Copy Date:* 49 days prior to publication
Supplement(s): Naturschutz in Rheinland-Pfalz
BUSINESS: ENVIRONMENT & POLLUTION

NATURSCHUTZ IM SAARLAND 1655630G57-2726
Editorial: Antoniusstr. 18, 66822 LEBACH
Tel: 6881 936190 **Fax:** 6881 9361911
Email: redaktion@nabu-saar.de **Web site:** http://www.nabu-saar.de/nis
Freq: Quarterly; Free to qualifying individuals
Annual Sub.: EUR 15,00; **Circ:** 10,500
Editor: Ute-Maria Meiser; **Advertising Manager:** Gabi Jank
Profile: Publication focusing on nature protection in the Saarland.
Language(s): German
ADVERTISING RATES:
Full Page Mono .... EUR 1053
Full Page Colour .... EUR 1178
Mechanical Data: Type Area: 260 x 174 mm, No. of Columns (Display): 3, Col Widths (Display): 54 mm
Copy instructions: *Copy Date:* 30 days prior to publication

NATURSCHUTZ IN HAMBURG 736982G57-1400
Editorial: Osterstr. 58, 20259 HAMBURG
Tel: 40 69708912 **Fax:** 40 69708919
Email: quellmalz@nabu-hamburg.de **Web site:** http://www.nabu-hamburg.de
Freq: Quarterly; Free to qualifying individuals
Annual Sub.: EUR 13,00; **Circ:** 14,000
Editor: Bernd Quellmalz; **Advertising Manager:** Tobias Hinsch
Profile: Publication focusing on nature protection in Hamburg.
Language(s): German
ADVERTISING RATES:
Full Page Mono .... EUR 680
Full Page Colour .... EUR 1020
Mechanical Data: Type Area: 247 x 184 mm, No. of Columns (Display): 3, Col Widths (Display): 49 mm

Copy instructions: *Copy Date:* 45 days prior to publication

NATURSCHUTZ UND LANDSCHAFTSPLANUNG

736984G57-1420

Editorial: Jahnstr. 22, 34454 BAD AROLSEN
Tel: 5691 7197 **Fax:** 5691 50211
Email: nul@jedicke.de **Web site:** http://www.nul-online.de
Freq: Monthly; **Annual Sub.:** EUR 109,20; **Circ:** 3,350
Editor: Eckard Jedicke; **Advertising Manager:** Anna Greiner
Profile: Journal covering applied ecology, environmental planning and nature conservation.
Language(s): German
Readership: Read by ecologists, planners, architects, biologists and nature conservation workers.
ADVERTISING RATES:
Full Page Mono .... EUR 948
Mechanical Data: Type Area: 260 x 185 mm, No. of Columns (Display): 4, Col Widths (Display): 45 mm
Copy instructions: *Copy Date:* 26 days prior to publication
BUSINESS: ENVIRONMENT & POLLUTION

NATURSCHUTZ UND NATURPARKE

736985G57-1440

Editorial: Niederhaverbeck 7, 29646 BISPINGEN
Tel: 5198 987030 **Fax:** 5198 987039
Email: vnp-info@t-online.de **Web site:** http://www.verein-naturschutzpark.de
Freq: 3 issues yearly; **Circ:** 5,000
Profile: Magazine about nature and landscape protection.
Language(s): German

NATURSCHUTZ-INFORMATIONEN

1824558G57-2840

Editorial: Am Schölerberg 8, 49082 OSNABRÜCK
Tel: 541 589184 **Fax:** 541 57528
Email: nabu-os@osnanet.de **Web site:** http://www.umweltforum-osnabrueck.de
Freq: Half-yearly; **Cover Price:** Free; **Circ:** 2,500
Profile: Information about environment protection projects in the Osnabrueck region.
Language(s): German
Mechanical Data: Type Area: 192 x 136 mm, No. of Columns (Display): 2, Col Widths (Display): 60 mm

NATURSTEIN

736987G30-100

Editorial: Karlstr. 41, 89073 ULM **Tel:** 731 1520168
Fax: 731 1520159
Email: naturstein@ebnerverlag.de **Web site:** http://www.natursteinonline.de
Freq: Monthly; **Annual Sub.:** EUR 112,20; **Circ:** 4,886
Editor: Bärbel Holländer
Profile: Aimed at stonemasons, stone dealers and those involved in quarrying, stone transforming and stone mounting.
Language(s): German
Readership: Aimed at stonemasons, stonedealers and those involved in quarrying, stone transforming and stone mounting.
ADVERTISING RATES:
Full Page Mono .... EUR 2270
Full Page Colour .... EUR 3390
Mechanical Data: Type Area: 268 x 185 mm, No. of Columns (Display): 4, Col Widths (Display): 43 mm
Copy instructions: *Copy Date:* 15 days prior to publication
BUSINESS: MINING & QUARRYING

NATURWISSENSCHAFTLICHE RUNDSCHAU NR

737698G55-100_50

Editorial: Birkenwaldstr. 44, 70191 STUTTGART
Tel: 711 2582295 **Fax:** 711 2582291
Email: nr@wissenschaftliche-verlagsgesellschaft.de
Web site: http://www.naturwissenschaftliche-rundschau.de
Freq: Monthly; **Annual Sub.:** EUR 168,60; **Circ:** 1,700
Editor: Klaus Rehfeld; **Advertising Manager:** Kornelia Wind
Profile: Journal about natural sciences.
Language(s): German
ADVERTISING RATES:
Full Page Mono .... EUR 1907
Full Page Colour .... EUR 2676
Mechanical Data: Type Area: 252 x 178 mm, No. of Columns (Display): 3, Col Widths (Display): 56 mm
Copy instructions: *Copy Date:* 21 days prior to publication
Official Journal of: Organ d. Ges. Dt. Naturforscher u. Ärzte
BUSINESS: APPLIED SCIENCE & LABORATORIES

NAUMBURGER TAGEBLATT

737012G67B-10240

Editorial: Delitzscher Str. 65, 06112 HALLE
Tel: 345 5650 **Fax:** 345 5654350
Freq: 312 issues yearly; **Circ:** 13,588
Editor: Albrecht Günther; **Advertising Manager:** Olaf Döring
Profile: Daily newspaper with regional news and a local sports section.
Language(s): German
ADVERTISING RATES:
SCC .... EUR 56,00
Mechanical Data: Type Area: 484 x 327 mm, No. of Columns (Display): 7, Col Widths (Display): 45 mm
Copy instructions: *Copy Date:* 2 days prior to publication
REGIONAL DAILY & SUNDAY NEWSPAPERS: Regional Daily Newspapers

NAUMBURGER TAGEBLATT ONLINE

1622453G67B-16700

Editorial: Salzstr. 8, 06618 NAUMBURG
Tel: 3445 2307810 **Fax:** 3445 2307819
Email: naumburger.tageblatt@mz-web.de **Web site:** http://www.naumburger-tageblatt.de
Freq: Daily; **Cover Price:** Paid; **Circ:** 44,231 Unique Users
Editor: Albrecht Günther; **Advertising Manager:** Olaf Döring
Profile: Ezine: Regional daily newspaper covering politics, economics, sport, travel and technology.
Language(s): German
REGIONAL DAILY & SUNDAY NEWSPAPERS: Regional Daily Newspapers

NAUNYN-SCHMIEDEBERG'S ARCHIVES OF PHARMACOLOGY

737013G56A-7340

Editorial: Tiergartenstr. 17, 69121 HEIDELBERG
Tel: 6221 4870 **Fax:** 6221 4878366
Email: subscriptions@springer.com **Web site:** http://www.springerlink.com
Freq: Monthly; **Annual Sub.:** EUR 2737,00; **Circ:** 175
Editor: M. C. Michel
Profile: Naunyn Schmiedeberg's Archives of Pharmacology.
Language(s): English
ADVERTISING RATES:
Full Page Mono .... EUR 740
Full Page Colour .... EUR 1780
Mechanical Data: Type Area: 240 x 175 mm

NCFERTIGUNG

737025G19E-1859

Editorial: Göggingerstr. 105a, 86199 AUGSBURG
Tel: 821 31988010 **Fax:** 821 31988080
Email: angeli@schluetersche.de **Web site:** http://www.nc-fertigung.de
Freq: Monthly; **Annual Sub.:** EUR 82,00; **Circ:** 21,869
Editor: Helmut Angeli; **Advertising Manager:** Franz Krauß
Profile: NCFertigung is a trade magazine for the technical management of the machining metalworking industry. Because of the ambitious journalistic method the form of the editorial content focuses on illustrative reportages on innovations and their practical application, on critical interviews with exposed managers, on sector analysis and statements about technological trends. The topics of NC Fertigung are CNC machine tools, precision tools, CNC-control– and programming systems, measuring and clamping technology as well as chip removal, cooling lubricants and their processing. Further key points are the integration of computers, all questions around the specific drive and control technology as well as the various aspects from the energy/energy efficiency and machine periphery. NCFertigung goes to metalworking companies of all sizes and branches in the whole German speaking area: from 1-man-jobshop to allied companies – from manufacturer of precision turned parts to universal companies of job order production up to the highly specialized machine-tool industry.
Language(s): German
ADVERTISING RATES:
Full Page Mono .... EUR 3990
Full Page Colour .... EUR 5220
Mechanical Data: Type Area: 272 x 188 mm, No. of Columns (Display): 4, Col Widths (Display): 44 mm
Copy instructions: *Copy Date:* 14 days prior to publication
BUSINESS: ENGINEERING & MACHINERY: Machinery, Machine Tools & Metalworking

NDS

737105G62A-2620

Editorial: Nünningstr. 11, 45141 ESSEN
Tel: 201 2940355 **Fax:** 201 2940314
Email: redaktion@nds-verlag.de **Web site:** http://www.nds-verlag.de
Freq: 10 issues yearly; Free to qualifying individuals
Annual Sub.: EUR 35,00; **Circ:** 46,000
Editor: Fritz Junkers
Profile: The journal is the organ of the Association of Education and Science Union in North Rhine-Westphalia. Give advice to schools and education policy issues and employment problems of workers in education. In addition, nds published pedagogical articles and book reviews.
Language(s): German
ADVERTISING RATES:
Full Page Mono .... EUR 1875
Full Page Colour .... EUR 2915
Mechanical Data: Type Area: 252 x 185 mm, No. of Columns (Display): 4, Col Widths (Display): 43 mm
BUSINESS: CHURCH & SCHOOL EQUIPMENT & EDUCATION: Education

NDSVBL. NIEDERSÄCHSISCHE VERWALTUNGSBLÄTTER

737027G44-286

Editorial: Carl-Orff-Weg 19, 31157 SARSTEDT
Tel: 5066 7134 **Fax:** 5066 984463
Email: albers.koeme@web.de
Freq: Monthly; **Annual Sub.:** EUR 197,40; **Circ:** 470
Editor: Heinrich Albers; **Advertising Manager:** Roland Schulz
Profile: Magazine about legal administration in Lower Saxony.
Language(s): German
ADVERTISING RATES:
Full Page Mono .... EUR 840
Full Page Colour .... EUR 1770
Mechanical Data: Type Area: 260 x 180 mm
Copy instructions: *Copy Date:* 28 days prior to publication
BUSINESS: LEGAL

NEBENWERTE JOURNAL

737030G1F-1000

Editorial: Leibstr. 61, 85540 HAAR **Tel:** 89 43571171
Fax: 89 43571381
Email: info@nebenwerte-journal.de **Web site:** http://www.nebenwerte-journal.de
Freq: Monthly; **Annual Sub.:** EUR 93,00; **Circ:** 3,500
Editor: Carsten Stern; **Advertising Manager:** Christina Stern
Profile: Journal containing information about the Stock Market and trading companies.
Language(s): German
ADVERTISING RATES:
Full Page Colour .... EUR 2780
Mechanical Data: Type Area: 265 x 181 mm
Copy instructions: *Copy Date:* 14 days prior to publication

NEBENWERTE JOURNAL

737030G1F-1840

Editorial: Leibstr. 61, 85540 HAAR **Tel:** 89 43571171
Fax: 89 43571381
Email: info@nebenwerte-journal.de **Web site:** http://www.nebenwerte-journal.de
Freq: Monthly; **Annual Sub.:** EUR 93,00; **Circ:** 3,500
Editor: Carsten Stern; **Advertising Manager:** Christina Stern
Profile: Journal containing information about the Stock Market and trading companies.
Language(s): German
ADVERTISING RATES:
Full Page Colour .... EUR 2780
Mechanical Data: Type Area: 265 x 181 mm
Copy instructions: *Copy Date:* 14 days prior to publication

NECKAR JOURNAL

737036G67B-5000_502

Editorial: Zeppelinstr. 116, 73730 ESSLINGEN
Tel: 711 9310342 **Fax:** 711 9310413
Email: neckarjournal@ez-online.de **Web site:** http://www.ez-online.de
Freq: Monthly; **Cover Price:** Free; **Circ:** 45,000
Editor: Jakob Panitz; **Advertising Manager:** Natalie Bankston
Profile: Magazine containing information about events in Neckar, includes music and theatre.
Language(s): German
Readership: Read by local residents and visitors to the region.
Mechanical Data: Type Area: 315 x 237 mm, No. of Columns (Display): 5, Col Widths (Display): 45 mm
Copy instructions: *Copy Date:* 13 days prior to publication
Supplement to: Eßlinger Zeitung
REGIONAL DAILY & SUNDAY NEWSPAPERS: Regional Daily Newspapers

NECKAR- UND ENZBOTE

737040G67B-10260

Editorial: Körnerstr. 14, 71634 LUDWIGSBURG
Tel: 7141 130240 **Fax:** 7141 130340
Email: redaktion@lkz.de **Web site:** http://www.lkz.de
Freq: 312 issues yearly; **Circ:** 5,880
Advertising Manager: Jürgen Merkle
Profile: Daily newspaper with regional news and a local sports section.
Language(s): German
ADVERTISING RATES:
SCC .... EUR 29,40
Mechanical Data: Type Area: 485 x 324 mm, No. of Columns (Display): 7, Col Widths (Display): 45 mm
Copy instructions: *Copy Date:* 2 days prior to publication
REGIONAL DAILY & SUNDAY NEWSPAPERS: Regional Daily Newspapers

NEON

1622732G74Q-4

Editorial: Weihenstephaner Str. 7, 81673 MÜNCHEN
Tel: 89 4152774 **Fax:** 89 4152779
Email: redaktion@neon-magazin.de **Web site:** http://www.neon.de
Freq: Monthly; **Annual Sub.:** EUR 37,20; **Circ:** 234,094
Editor: Michael Ebert
Profile: Special from the stern magazine aimed at people in their twenties. Facebook: http://www.facebook.com/neonmagazin Twitter: http://twitter.com/neon_magazin This Outlet offers RSS (Really Simple Syndication).
Language(s): German
ADVERTISING RATES:
Full Page Mono .... EUR 19900
Full Page Colour .... EUR 19900
Mechanical Data: Type Area: 247 x 191 mm, No. of Columns (Display): 4, Col Widths (Display): 44 mm
Copy instructions: *Copy Date:* 30 days prior to publication
CONSUMER: WOMEN'S INTEREST CONSUMER MAGAZINES: Lifestyle

DER NEPHROLOGE

1752578G56A-11409

Editorial: Tiergartenstr. 17, 69121 HEIDELBERG
Tel: 6221 4878820 **Fax:** 6221 48768820
Email: annette.gasser@springer.com **Web site:** http://www.springermedizin.de
Freq: 6 issues yearly; **Annual Sub.:** EUR 180,00; **Circ:** 2,800
Advertising Manager: Sigrid Christ
Profile: Der Nephrologe offers up-to-date information for all nephrologists working in practical and clinical environments and scientists who are particularly interested in issues of nephrology. The content covers all areas of applied nephrology and hypertensiology. The topics range from prevention to diagnostic approaches and management of complications to current therapy strategies. Comprehensive reviews on a specific topical issue provide evidenced based information on diagnostics and therapy. Review articles under the rubric "Continuing Medical Education" present verified results of scientific research and their integration into daily practice.
Language(s): German
ADVERTISING RATES:
Full Page Mono .... EUR 3180
Full Page Colour .... EUR 3180
Mechanical Data: Type Area: 240 x 174 mm
Official Journal of: Organ d. Dt. Ges. f. Innere Medizin u. d. Berufsverb. Dt. Internisten

DER NERVENARZT

737052G56N-60

Editorial: Tiergartenstr. 17, 69121 HEIDELBERG
Tel: 6221 4878741 **Fax:** 6221 48768741
Email: kathrin.muth@springer.com **Web site:** http://www.springermedizin.de
Freq: Monthly; **Annual Sub.:** EUR 331,00; **Circ:** 12,669
Profile: Der Nervenarzt is an internationally recognized journal addressing neurologists and psychiatrists working in clinical or practical environments. Essential findings and current information from neurology, psychiatry as well as neuropathology, neurosurgery up to psychotherapy are presented. Review articles provide an overview on selected topics and offer the reader a summary of current findings from all fields of neurology and psychiatry. Freely submitted original papers allow the presentation of important clinical studies and serve the scientific exchange. Review articles under the rubric 'Continuing Medical Education' present verified results of scientific research and their integration into daily practice. All articles of Der Nervenarzt are peer reviewed.
Language(s): German
ADVERTISING RATES:
Full Page Mono .... EUR 2720
Full Page Colour .... EUR 4050
Mechanical Data: Type Area: 240 x 174 mm
Official Journal of: Organ d. Dt. Ges. f. Psychiatrie, Psychotherapie u. Nervenheilkunde, d. Dt. Ges. f. Neurologie u. d. Dt. Schlaganfall-Ges.
BUSINESS: HEALTH & MEDICAL: Mental Health

NERVENHEILKUNDE

737053G56A-7380

Editorial: Hölderlinstr. 3, 70174 STUTTGART
Tel: 711 2298771 **Fax:** 711 2298765
Email: anja.borchers@schattauer.de **Web site:** http://www.nervenheilkunde-online.de
Freq: 11 issues yearly; Free to qualifying individuals
Annual Sub.: EUR 160,00; **Circ:** 29,506
Editor: Anja Borchers; **Advertising Manager:** Nicole Dörr
Profile: The Nervenheilkunde is one of the most advanced and further education journals for neurologists, psychiatrists and Nerve specialists. As family physicians for mental disorders are the first contact, almost always, and the course for a competent specialist treatment in their hands, the customer is also insane to primary physicians. Goal is not only the transfer of scientific findings to provide practical information to help to improve treatment of patients with neurological and psychiatric disorders. Consequently, readers of Neurology collect up to three per issue CME credits. Regularly recommendations or guidelines of the German Migraine and Headache Society and the German Muscular Dystrophy Association and published.
Language(s): German
ADVERTISING RATES:
Full Page Mono .... EUR 4125
Full Page Colour .... EUR 5680
Mechanical Data: Type Area: 243 x 179 mm, No. of Columns (Display): 3, Col Widths (Display): 57 mm
Copy instructions: *Copy Date:* 40 days prior to publication
Official Journal of: Organ d. Dt. Migräne- u. Kopfschmerzges., d. Dt. Ges. f. Muskelkranke u. d. Österr. Kopfschmerzges.
BUSINESS: HEALTH & MEDICAL

NET

737057G18B-1976

Editorial: Baltzerstr. 30, 15569 WOLTERSDORF
Tel: 3301 2029154 **Fax:** 3301 2029155
Email: brigitte.kasper@net-im-web.de **Web site:** http://www.net-im-web.de
Freq: 10 issues yearly; **Annual Sub.:** EUR 122,00; **Circ:** 6,074

Editor: Brigitte Kasper; **Advertising Manager:** Frank Backasch
Profile: Journal concerning applied telecommunications and corporate network solutions.
Language(s): German
Readership: Aimed at engineers and corporate users of telecommunication services.
ADVERTISING RATES:
Full Page Mono .... EUR 2200
Full Page Colour .... EUR 3190
Mechanical Data: Type Area: 248 x 182 mm, No. of Columns (Display): 3, Col Widths (Display): 57 mm
Copy instructions: *Copy Date:* 18 days prior to publication
BUSINESS: ELECTRONICS: Telecommunications

NETWORK-KARRIERE
1882044G2A-5799
Editorial: Boslerstr. 29, 71088 HOLZGERLINGEN
Tel: 7031 744201 **Fax:** 7031 744199
Email: herausgeber@network-karriere.com **Web site:** http://www.network-karriere.com
Freq: Monthly; **Annual Sub.:** EUR 38,00; **Circ:** 40,000
Editor: Bernd Seitz; **Advertising Manager:** Andrea Hiddemann
Profile: International journal for network marketing and direct sales.
Language(s): German
ADVERTISING RATES:
Full Page Mono .... EUR 9954
Full Page Colour .... EUR 9954
Mechanical Data: Type Area: 420 x 279 mm, No. of Columns (Display): 6, Col Widths (Display): 44 mm
Copy instructions: *Copy Date:* 25 days prior to publication

NETZ
1834031G57-2863
Editorial: Luitpoldstr. 7a, 97082 WÜRZBURG
Tel: 931 43972 **Fax:** 931 42553
Email: info@bn-wuerzburg.de **Web site:** http://www.wuerzburg.bund-naturschutz.de
Freq: Half-yearly; **Circ:** 3,300
Editor: Klaus Isberner; **Advertising Manager:** Klaus Isberner
Profile: Member magazine from the Nature Protection Union in Bavaria.
Language(s): German
ADVERTISING RATES:
Full Page Mono .... EUR 169
Mechanical Data: Type Area: 186 x 125 mm
Copy instructions: *Copy Date:* 60 days prior to publication

NETZPRAXIS
726792G17-480
Editorial: Waldstr. 58, 63128 DIETZENBACH
Tel: 6074 33680 **Fax:** 6074 25896
Email: guenter.fenchel@t-online.de **Web site:** http://www.ew-online.de
Freq: 10 issues yearly; **Annual Sub.:** EUR 99,00; **Circ:** 7,169
Editor: Wolfgang Böhmer
Profile: Journal covering all aspects of the electrical industry.
Language(s): German
ADVERTISING RATES:
Full Page Mono .... EUR 2325
Full Page Colour .... EUR 3255
Mechanical Data: Type Area: 268 x 185 mm, No. of Columns (Display): 4, Col Widths (Display): 42 mm
BUSINESS: ELECTRICAL

NETZWELT
1704548G78D-1022
Editorial: Osdorfer Landstr. 20, 22607 HAMBURG
Tel: 40 81992737 **Fax:** 40 81992739
Email: redaktion@netzwelt.de **Web site:** http://www.netzwelt.de
Cover Price: Paid; **Circ:** 7,293,376 Unique Users
Editor: Sascha Hottes
Language(s): German
CONSUMER: CONSUMER ELECTRONICS: Games

NETZWERK
728680G14A-2680
Editorial: Wilhelm-Haas-Platz, 63263 NEU-ISENBURG **Tel:** 69 6978491 **Fax:** 69 6978427
Email: joachim.prahst@genossenschaftsverband.de
Web site: http://www.genossenschaftsverband.de
Freq: 10 issues yearly; **Circ:** 8,000
Editor: Joachim Prahst; **Advertising Manager:** Andreas Petersen
Profile: Management magazine.
Language(s): German
ADVERTISING RATES:
Full Page Mono .... EUR 3300
Full Page Colour .... EUR 6270
Mechanical Data: Type Area: 247 x 186 mm, No. of Columns (Display): 3, Col Widths (Display): 59 mm
Copy instructions: *Copy Date:* 40 days prior to publication
Supplement(s): PerspektivePraxis.de; Raiffeisen Magazin

NEUBURGER EXTRA
726851G72-3684
Editorial: Monheimer Str. 8, 86633 NEUBURG
Tel: 8431 605520 **Fax:** 8431 605521
Email: extrand@t-online.de
Freq: Weekly; **Cover Price:** Free; **Circ:** 28,175
Editor: Alexandra Fitzek; **Advertising Manager:** Ernst Zettel
Profile: Advertising journal (house-to-house) concentrating on local stories.
Language(s): German
ADVERTISING RATES:
Full Page Mono .... EUR 3831
Full Page Colour .... EUR 5813
Mechanical Data: Type Area: 480 x 327 mm, No. of Columns (Display): 7, Col Widths (Display): 45 mm
Copy instructions: *Copy Date:* 3 days prior to publication
LOCAL NEWSPAPERS

NEUBURGER RUNDSCHAU
737081G67B-10300
Editorial: Curt-Frenzel-Str. 2, 86167 AUGSBURG
Tel: 821 7770 **Fax:** 821 7772067
Web site: http://www.augsburger-allgemeine.de
Freq: 312 issues yearly; **Circ:** 10,011
Advertising Manager: Herbert Dachs
Profile: Regional daily newspaper with news on politics, economy, culture, sports, travel, technology. Facebook: http://www.facebook.com/AugsburgerAllgemeine Twitter: http://twitter.com/AZ_Augsburg This Outlet offers RSS (Really Simple Syndication).
Language(s): German
ADVERTISING RATES:
SCC .... EUR 45,20
Mechanical Data: Type Area: 480 x 327 mm, No. of Columns (Display): 7, Col Widths (Display): 45 mm
Copy instructions: *Copy Date:* 1 day prior to publication
REGIONAL DAILY & SUNDAY NEWSPAPERS: Regional Daily Newspapers

DAS NEUE
737084G74A-2380
Editorial: Burchardstr. 11, 20095 HAMBURG
Tel: 40 30194864 **Fax:** 40 30194901
Email: felicitas.heyden@das-neue.de **Web site:** http://www.bauermedia.com
Freq: Weekly; **Cover Price:** EUR 1,50; **Circ:** 185,289
Editor: Jörg Mandt
Profile: Entertainment weekly women's magazine, reports on the latest happenings from the world of celebrities, recommended fashion and beauty tips, multi-faceted ideas for holidays and travel, as well as plenty of tasty recipe ideas.
Language(s): German
Readership: Aimed at women.
ADVERTISING RATES:
Full Page Mono .... EUR 4800
Full Page Colour .... EUR 4800
Mechanical Data: Type Area: 261 x 196 mm, No. of Columns (Display): 4, Col Widths (Display): 46 mm
Copy instructions: *Copy Date:* 30 days prior to publication
CONSUMER: WOMEN'S INTEREST CONSUMER MAGAZINES: Women's Interest

NEUE APOTHEKEN ILLUSTRIERTE
737085G94H-9520
Editorial: Carl-Mannich-Str. 26, 65760 ESCHBORN
Tel: 6196 928310 **Fax:** 6196 928223
Email: redaktion@nai.de **Web site:** http://www.nai.de
Freq: 24 issues yearly; **Cover Price:** Free; **Circ:** 1,034,796
Editor: Jutta Petersen-Lehmann; **Advertising Manager:** Edgar Opper
Profile: Customer magazine distributed in pharmacies. Covers health, alternative medicine, fitness and nutrition.
Language(s): German
ADVERTISING RATES:
Full Page Mono .... EUR 19900
Full Page Colour .... EUR 19900
Mechanical Data: Type Area: 258 x 193 mm, No. of Columns (Display): 4, Col Widths (Display): 45 mm
Copy instructions: *Copy Date:* 60 days prior to publication
CONSUMER: OTHER CLASSIFICATIONS: Customer Magazines

NEUE APOTHEKEN ILLUSTRIERTE EXTRA
737086G94H-9540
Editorial: Carl-Mannich-Str. 26, 65760 ESCHBORN
Tel: 6196 928310 **Fax:** 6196 928223
Email: redaktion@nai.de **Web site:** http://www.nai.de
Freq: 6 issues yearly; **Cover Price:** Free; **Circ:** 98,669
Editor: Jutta Petersen-Lehmann; **Advertising Manager:** Edgar Opper
Profile: Magazine containing information about health issues.
Language(s): German
Readership: Aimed at customers of pharmacies in Germany.
ADVERTISING RATES:
Full Page Mono .... EUR 8020
Full Page Colour .... EUR 8020
Mechanical Data: Type Area: 258 x 193 mm, No. of Columns (Display): 4, Col Widths (Display): 46 mm
Copy instructions: *Copy Date:* 56 days prior to publication
CONSUMER: OTHER CLASSIFICATIONS: Customer Magazines

NEUE ARZNEIMITTEL
737088G37-1300
Editorial: Birkenwaldstr. 44, 70191 STUTTGART
Tel: 711 2582238 **Fax:** 711 2582291
Email: daz@deutscher-apotheker-verlag.de **Web site:** http://www.deutscher-apotheker-verlag.de
Freq: Monthly; **Annual Sub.:** EUR 64,00; **Circ:** 54,000
Editor: Bettina Hellwig
Profile: Magazine about drugs and pharmacological research.
Language(s): German
Readership: Aimed at physicians and pharmacists.
Supplement to: AMT Arzneimitteltherapie, DAZ Deutsche ApothekerZeitung
BUSINESS: PHARMACEUTICAL & CHEMISTS

NEUE BILDPOST
737094G87-9740
Editorial: Lange Str. 335, 59067 HAMM
Tel: 2381 9404090 **Fax:** 2381 9404094
Email: kontakt@bildpost.de **Web site:** http://www.bildpost.de
Freq: Weekly; **Annual Sub.:** EUR 89,25; **Circ:** 10,830
Editor: Johannes Müller; **Advertising Manager:** Edeltraud Hüttmann
Profile: Newspaper presenting news from a Christian viewpoint.
Language(s): German
Readership: Read by practicing Christians.
ADVERTISING RATES:
Full Page Mono .... EUR 8846
Full Page Colour .... EUR 14152
Mechanical Data: Type Area: 486 x 312 mm, No. of Columns (Display): 7, Col Widths (Display): 42 mm
Copy instructions: *Copy Date:* 12 days prior to publication
CONSUMER: RELIGIOUS

DAS NEUE BLATT
737096G74A-2400
Editorial: Meßberg 1, 20095 HAMBURG
Tel: 40 30194801 **Fax:** 40 30194903
Email: dasneueblatt@bauerredaktionen.de **Web site:** http://www.bauermedia.com
Freq: Weekly; **Cover Price:** EUR 1,50; **Circ:** 475,556
Editor: Petra Hansen-Blank
Profile: Weekly entertainment magazine for women with recent reports on the European aristocracy, international and national celebrities from the fields of show, music, film and television. In the great service and advice of the new leaf is always the latest tips and real life settings. Emphasis will Topics: recipes, health, fashion, money and legal and travel.
Language(s): German
ADVERTISING RATES:
Full Page Mono .... EUR 12100
Full Page Colour .... EUR 12100
Mechanical Data: Type Area: 258 x 206 mm, No. of Columns (Display): 4, Col Widths (Display): 49 mm
Copy instructions: *Copy Date:* 30 days prior to publication
CONSUMER: WOMEN'S INTEREST CONSUMER MAGAZINES: Women's Interest

NEUE BRAUNSCHWEIGER
737099G72-9592
Editorial: Hamburger Str. 277, 38114 BRAUNSCHWEIG **Tel:** 531 3900750
Fax: 531 3900753
Email: nb-redaktion@nb-online.de **Web site:** http://www.nb-online.de
Freq: 104 issues yearly; **Cover Price:** Free
Editor: Ingeborg Obi-Preuß; **Advertising Manager:** Jens Richwien
Profile: Advertising journal (house-to-house) concentrating on local stories.
Language(s): German
Mechanical Data: Type Area: 435 x 282 mm, No. of Columns (Display): 6, Col Widths (Display): 46 mm
Copy instructions: *Copy Date:* 2 days prior to publication
LOCAL NEWSPAPERS

NEUE CARITAS
737103G87-9760
Editorial: Karlstr. 40, 79104 FREIBURG
Tel: 761 200410 **Fax:** 761 200509
Email: christiane.stieff@caritas.de **Web site:** http://www.neue-caritas.de
Freq: 22 issues yearly; **Annual Sub.:** EUR 79,69; **Circ:** 7,100
Editor: Gertrud Rogg
Profile: Magazine about social work and topics relevant to the profession such as poverty, drug abuse and the law.
Language(s): German
ADVERTISING RATES:
Full Page Mono .... EUR 1520
Full Page Colour .... EUR 2200
Mechanical Data: Type Area: 222 x 176 mm, No. of Columns (Display): 3, Col Widths (Display): 56 mm
Copy instructions: *Copy Date:* 28 days prior to publication
CONSUMER: RELIGIOUS

NEUE DEISTER-ZEITUNG
737104G67B-10320
Editorial: Bahnhofstr. 18, 31832 SPRINGE
Tel: 5041 7890 **Fax:** 5041 78980
Email: m.fuegmann@ndz.de **Web site:** http://www.ndz.de
Freq: 312 issues yearly; **Circ:** 6,359
Editor: Marc Fügmann; **Advertising Manager:** Thomas Kritscher
Profile: Daily newspaper with regional news and a local sports section. Facebook: http://www.facebook.com/pages/Neue-Deister-Zeitung/409564431118 This Outlet offers RSS (Really Simple Syndication).
Language(s): German
ADVERTISING RATES:
SCC .... EUR 18,70
Mechanical Data: Type Area: 430 x 281 mm, No. of Columns (Display): 6, Col Widths (Display): 45 mm
Copy instructions: *Copy Date:* 2 days prior to publication
REGIONAL DAILY & SUNDAY NEWSPAPERS: Regional Daily Newspapers

NEUE ENERGIE
737108G58-1160
Editorial: Marienstr. 19, 10117 BERLIN
Tel: 30 28482130 **Fax:** 30 28482139
Email: info@neueenergie.net **Web site:** http://www.neueenergie.net
Freq: Monthly; Free to qualifying individuals
Annual Sub.: EUR 78,00; **Circ:** 25,883
Editor: Hanne May
Profile: neue energie is Germany's leading trade magazine for the renewable industry. neue energie is the membership journal of the Association of Wind Energy Association - one of the world's largest renewable associations. The magazine also subscribed to by many readers from all renewable sectors - small and large companies, financial institutions, service providers, representatives from science and research, students, interested private citizens, politicians and media representatives. Background reports and articles on current topics from politics and economy and to new technologies in renewable energies - full of energy and current.
Language(s): German
ADVERTISING RATES:
Full Page Mono .... EUR 1700
Full Page Colour .... EUR 3400
Mechanical Data: Type Area: 277 x 185 mm, No. of Columns (Display): 3, Col Widths (Display): 58 mm
Copy instructions: *Copy Date:* 30 days prior to publication
BUSINESS: ENERGY, FUEL & NUCLEAR

DIE NEUE FRAU
737115G74A-2420
Editorial: Rotweg 8, 76532 BADEN-BADEN
Tel: 7221 3501131 **Fax:** 7221 3501304
Email: dieneuefrau@klambt.de
Freq: Weekly; **Annual Sub.:** EUR 54,60; **Circ:** 169,099
Editor: Britta Behrens; **Advertising Manager:** Martin Fischer
Profile: Die neue Frau is a contemporary magazine for young women. The editorial links the reading interest in typical Yellow-themes with service-oriented issues and the fun of guessing in a folder. Die neue Frau has all topics of interest to women, in a compact and easily consumable presentation. The reports of celebrities from show business, from the movie and television stars, athletes and people in public life and a little of the nobility by background reports informative and lively. Incidents complete the offer. A historical portrait in the glory of the crown and scepter just gives young readers insight into the origin of the European nobility. Created as a great adviser, the service issues with information on fashion and beauty, health (a medical series to modern diseases), with recipe ideas for the new kitchen, suggestions for living and life, reports on holidays and travel, with tips on money and law as well as latest market information. For recreational fun and gimmicks Die neue Frau, the 6-sided puzzle-Journal brings different rate forms and lucrative profits). Die neue Frau is a successful mix of entertainment, reports on current events, expert advice and factual information.
Language(s): German
Readership: Aimed at women aged 18 to 60 years.
ADVERTISING RATES:
Full Page Mono .... EUR 4317
Full Page Colour .... EUR 4317
Mechanical Data: No. of Columns (Display): 4, Col Widths (Display): 45 mm, Type Area: 260 x 195 mm
Copy instructions: *Copy Date:* 28 days prior to publication
CONSUMER: WOMEN'S INTEREST CONSUMER MAGAZINES: Women's Interest

DIE NEUE FRAU DIE BESTEN FRÜHLINGSTORTEN UND KUCHEN
2086904G74P-1402
Editorial: Rotweg 8, 76532 BADEN-BADEN
Tel: 7221 3501131 **Fax:** 7221 3501304
Email: dieneuefrau@klambt.de
Freq: Annual; **Circ:** 80,000
Advertising Manager: Martin Fischer
Profile: A fresh cake or a delicious cake make everyday life a little sweeter. Fruity, creamy or rather moved quickly: In this issue, guaranteeing the right recipe is there. Baked with cheese, quick & delicious: pound cake, fine-filled pies and tarts.
Language(s): German
ADVERTISING RATES:
Full Page Mono .... EUR 5370
Full Page Colour .... EUR 5370
Mechanical Data: Type Area: 250 x 195 mm, No. of Columns (Display): 4, Col Widths (Display): 45 mm
Copy instructions: *Copy Date:* 28 days prior to publication

DIE NEUE FRAU DIE BESTEN LANDFRAUEN-KUCHEN
2086905G74P-1403
Editorial: Rotweg 8, 76532 BADEN-BADEN
Tel: 7221 3501131 **Fax:** 7221 3501304
Email: dieneuefrau@klambt.de
Freq: Annual; **Circ:** 80,000
Advertising Manager: Martin Fischer

Profile: There's nothing like strudel or a plate crumb cake - preferably still warm! The classic baking recipes of rural women are being rediscovered and rightly so. Some are easy, sometimes very opulent - but they all provide for this wonderful well-being: The best cakes for the dinner table, yeast dough: sometimes fine, sometimes strong, strudel, the best nut cake.
Language(s): German
ADVERTISING RATES:
Full Page Mono .... EUR 5370
Full Page Colour .... EUR 5370
Mechanical Data: Type Area: 250 x 195 mm, No. of Columns (Display): 4, Col Widths (Display): 45 mm
Copy instructions: *Copy Date:* 28 days prior to publication

DER NEUE GROSSE FREIZEITFÜHRER FÜR DEUTSCHLAND 1828569G89A-12398
Editorial: Dr.-Andler-Str. 28, 78224 SINGEN
Tel: 7731 63544 **Fax:** 7731 62401
Email: info@reisefuehrer.com **Web site:** http://www.reisefuehrer.com
Freq: Annual; **Cover Price:** EUR 9,95; **Circ:** 50,000
Editor: Manfred Klemann; **Advertising Manager:** Evelyn Seyler
Profile: Publication featuring trip destinations for the whole family, is a super companion for recreation seekers, adventurers and explorers. With many ideas for the Arts around the corner or for exciting holiday Tripps.
Language(s): German
ADVERTISING RATES:
Full Page Colour .... EUR 790
Copy instructions: *Copy Date:* 48 days prior to publication

NEUE KIRCHENZEITUNG 737132G87-9800
Editorial: Schmilinskystr. 80, 20099 HAMBURG
Tel: 40 24877111 **Fax:** 40 24877119
Email: redaktion@neue-kirchenzeitung.de **Web site:** http://www.neue-kirchenzeitung.de
Freq: Weekly; **Annual Sub.:** EUR 59,40; **Circ:** 5,567
Editor: Andreas Hüser; **Advertising Manager:** Brigitte Jaschke
Profile: Magazine for the archbishopric of Hamburg.
Language(s): German
ADVERTISING RATES:
Full Page Mono .... EUR 2352
Full Page Colour .... EUR 3360
Mechanical Data: Type Area: 480 x 325 mm, No. of Columns (Display): 7, Col Widths (Display): 43 mm
Copy instructions: *Copy Date:* 10 days prior to publication
CONSUMER: RELIGIOUS

NEUE LANDSCHAFT 737139G4E-5500
Editorial: Koenigsallee 65, 14193 BERLIN
Tel: 30 89590360 **Fax:** 30 89590317
Email: redaktion.neuelandschaft@patzerverlag.de
Web site: http://www.neuelandschaft.de
Freq: Monthly; **Annual Sub.:** EUR 95,40; **Circ:** 6,918
Editor: Christian Münter; **Advertising Manager:** Bodo Ulbricht
Profile: Magazine on garden, landscape, playground and sports field design.
Language(s): German
ADVERTISING RATES:
Full Page Mono .... EUR 2195
Full Page Colour .... EUR 4256
Mechanical Data: Type Area: 261 x 184 mm, No. of Columns (Display): 4, Col Widths (Display): 43 mm
Copy instructions: *Copy Date:* 14 days prior to publication
Supplement(s): Pro Baum
BUSINESS: ARCHITECTURE & BUILDING: Building

NEUE OZ OSNABRÜCKER ZEITUNG 737172G67B-10340
Editorial: Breiter Gang 10, 49074 OSNABRÜCK
Tel: 541 3100 **Fax:** 541 310485
Email: redaktion@noz.de **Web site:** http://www.noz.de
Freq: 312 issues yearly; **Circ:** 280,570
Editor: Berthold Hamelmann; **News Editor:** Christof Haverkamp
Profile: Regional daily newspaper with news on politics, economy, culture, sports, travel, technology, etc.
Language(s): German
ADVERTISING RATES:
SCC .... EUR 506,70
Copy instructions: *Copy Date:* 2 days prior to publication
Supplement(s): Beim hautnah; Berufswahl; Immo-Welt; Kfz-Welt; melle-city.de; TheaterZeitung; Toaster; Treffpunkt Bramsche; wir für wallenhorst
REGIONAL DAILY & SUNDAY NEWSPAPERS: Regional Daily Newspapers

NEUE PEINER WOCHE AM SONNTAG 737173G72-9620
Editorial: Woltorfer Str. 118, 31224 PEINE
Tel: 5171 5069820 **Fax:** 5171 5069812
Email: redaktion@peiner-woche.de **Web site:** http://www.peiner-woche.de
Freq: Weekly; **Cover Price:** Free; **Circ:** 61,310
Editor: Jürgen Grütter; **Advertising Manager:** Horst Schubert
Profile: Advertising journal (house-to-house) concentrating on local stories.
Language(s): German
ADVERTISING RATES:
Full Page Mono .... EUR 4206
Full Page Colour .... EUR 5238
Mechanical Data: Type Area: 430 x 277 mm, No. of Columns (Display): 6, Col Widths (Display): 45 mm
Copy instructions: *Copy Date:* 3 days prior to publication
LOCAL NEWSPAPERS

NEUE POST 737176G74A-2440
Editorial: Burchardstr. 11, 20095 HAMBURG
Tel: 40 30194123 **Fax:** 40 30194133
Email: neuepost@bauerredaktionen.de **Web site:** http://www.neuepost.de
Freq: Weekly; **Cover Price:** EUR 1,50; **Circ:** 703,357
Editor: Hansjörn Muder
Profile: Entertainment weekly women's magazine, reports on the latest happenings from the world of celebrities. Exclusive stories, background reports and interviews from the nobility and the lives of national and international stars from film, television show and features of the magazine.
Language(s): German
ADVERTISING RATES:
Full Page Mono .... EUR 14740
Full Page Colour .... EUR 14740
Mechanical Data: Type Area: 258 x 206 mm, No. of Columns (Display): 4, Col Widths (Display): 48 mm
Copy instructions: *Copy Date:* 28 days prior to publication
CONSUMER: WOMEN'S INTEREST CONSUMER MAGAZINES: Women's Interest

NEUE PRESSE 737179G67B-10360
Editorial: Steinweg 51, 96450 COBURG
Tel: 9561 8500 **Fax:** 9561 850288
Email: redaktion@np-coburg.de **Web site:** http://www.np-coburg.de
Freq: 312 issues yearly; **Circ:** 25,690
Editor: Wolfgang Braunschmidt; **News Editor:** Martin Fleischmann; **Advertising Manager:** Ursula Friedrich
Profile: Regional daily newspaper covering politics, economics, sports, travel and technology.
Language(s): German
ADVERTISING RATES:
SCC .... EUR 84,80
Mechanical Data: Type Area: 475 x 325 mm, No. of Columns (Display): 7, Col Widths (Display): 44 mm
Copy instructions: *Copy Date:* 2 days prior to publication
Supplement(s): Impulse aus der Region; Neue Presse Kinderzeitung
REGIONAL DAILY & SUNDAY NEWSPAPERS: Regional Daily Newspapers

NEUE PRESSE 737180G67B-10380
Editorial: Stiftstr. 2, 30159 HANNOVER
Tel: 511 51010 **Fax:** 511 51012275
Email: hannover@neuepresse.de **Web site:** http://www.neuepresse.de
Freq: 312 issues yearly; **Circ:** 193,886
Editor: Harald John; **News Editor:** Claus Lingenauber; **Advertising Manager:** Olaf Kuhlwein
Profile: The Hannover Allgemeine Zeitung is a leader in Niedersachsen. The success is based on a simple yet sophisticated approach: the Hannoversche Allgemeine Zeitung combines the proximity of a local newspaper with the foresight of a national news media. As a joint team of newspaper advertising Neue Presse and Hannoversche Allgemeine Zeitung offer a powerful and sophisticated basis. Whether economic, local, sports, or the weekly supplements car, real estate, travel, or special publications. Twitter: http://twitter.com/neuepresse This Outlet offers RSS (Really Simple Syndication).
Language(s): German
ADVERTISING RATES:
SCC .... EUR 320,20
Mechanical Data: Type Area: 528 x 370 mm, No. of Columns (Display): 8, Col Widths (Display): 45 mm
Copy instructions: *Copy Date:* 1 day prior to publication
Supplement(s): aktiv im leben; Anzeiger Burgdorf & Uetze; Anzeiger Lehrte & Sehnde; Calenberger Zeitung; Deister-Anzeiger Springe Bad Münder; Ernst-August-Galerie Aktuell; Gesund; Leine-Nachrichten; Leine-Zeitung Garbsen Seelze; Leine-Zeitung Neustadt Wunstorf; Nordhannoversche Zeitung; RegionsJournal; Spielzeit; Zuhause in Hannover und der Region
REGIONAL DAILY & SUNDAY NEWSPAPERS: Regional Daily Newspapers

NEUE REIFENZEITUNG 737187G31A-9
Editorial: Harsefelder Str. 5, 21680 STADE
Tel: 4141 53360 **Fax:** 4141 609900
Email: klaus.haddenbrock@reifenpresse.de **Web site:** http://www.neuereifenzeitung.de
Freq: Monthly; **Annual Sub.:** EUR 119,60; **Circ:** 6,250
Editor: Klaus Haddenbrock; **Advertising Manager:** Ute Monsees
Profile: Journal of the tire dealers, tire specialist and the tire industry Facebook: http://www.facebook.com/pages/Reifenpressede/154939211224844 Twitter: http://twitter.com/#!/Reifenpresse This Outlet offers RSS (Really Simple Syndication).
Language(s): German
ADVERTISING RATES:
Full Page Mono .... EUR 2340
Full Page Colour .... EUR 3705
Mechanical Data: Type Area: 265 x 185 mm, No. of Columns (Display): 4, Col Widths (Display): 41 mm
Copy instructions: *Copy Date:* 21 days prior to publication
BUSINESS: MOTOR TRADE: Motor Trade Accessories

NEUE SÄCHSISCHE LEHRERZEITUNG 737202G62J-290
Editorial: Meißner Str. 69, 01445 RADEBEUL
Tel: 351 839220 **Fax:** 351 8392213
Email: slv.ev@t-online.de **Web site:** http://www.slv-online.de
Freq: 6 issues yearly; Free to qualifying individuals
Annual Sub.: EUR 23,50; **Circ:** 8,664
Editor: Jens Weichelt; **Advertising Manager:** Sabine Sperling
Profile: Newspaper focusing on education in the region of Saxony.
Language(s): German
Readership: Aimed at all teachers in the Saxony region.
ADVERTISING RATES:
Full Page Mono .... EUR 1300
Full Page Colour .... EUR 2080
Mechanical Data: Type Area: 270 x 190 mm, No. of Columns (Display): 4, Col Widths (Display): 44 mm
Copy instructions: *Copy Date:* 21 days prior to publication
BUSINESS: CHURCH & SCHOOL EQUIPMENT & EDUCATION: Teachers & Education Management

DAS NEUE SPRACHROHR ELEKTROHANDWERK NORD 1615768G17-1541
Editorial: Baumschulenallee 12, 30625 HANNOVER
Tel: 511 9575744 **Fax:** 511 9575799
Email: liv@eh-nb.de **Web site:** http://www.eh-nb.de
Freq: 10 issues yearly; Free to qualifying individuals
Annual Sub.: EUR 65,00; **Circ:** 4,000
Editor: Thomas von Wrangel; **Advertising Manager:** Diana Beier
Profile: Magazine for members of the Guild of Electro Technicians and Information engineers.
Language(s): German
ADVERTISING RATES:
Full Page Mono .... EUR 1240
Full Page Colour .... EUR 1900
Mechanical Data: Type Area: 270 x 185 mm, No. of Columns (Display): 4, Col Widths (Display): 44 mm
Copy instructions: *Copy Date:* 12 days prior to publication

NEUE SZENE AUGSBURG 737254G80-8100
Editorial: Am Katzenstadel 28, 86152 AUGSBURG
Tel: 821 153009 **Fax:** 821 158043
Email: redaktion@neue-szene.de **Web site:** http://www.neue-szene.de
Freq: Monthly; **Cover Price:** Free; **Circ:** 25,010
Editor: Walter Sianos; **Advertising Manager:** Charlie Sono
Profile: City magazine for Augsburg and the region with comprehensive event calendar, classified ads, a large part of music and many special publications.
Language(s): German
Readership: Aimed at visitors and local residents.
ADVERTISING RATES:
Full Page Mono .... EUR 1080
Full Page Colour .... EUR 1400
Mechanical Data: Type Area: 270 x 190 mm, No. of Columns (Display): 4, Col Widths (Display): 44 mm
CONSUMER: RURAL & REGIONAL INTEREST

DER NEUE TAG 737255G67B-10400
Editorial: Weigelstr. 16, 92637 WEIDEN **Tel:** 961 850
Fax: 961 418336
Web site: http://www.oberpfalznetz.de
Freq: 312 issues yearly; **Circ:** 89,908
Editor: Hans Klemm; **News Editor:** Albert Franz; **Advertising Manager:** Andreas Holch
Profile: Regional daily newspaper with news on politics, economy, culture, sports, travel, technology, etc. The new day is a regional daily newspaper based in Weiden. The newspaper is published with eight editions in the urban and rural districts of Neustadt an der Waldnaab, Amberg, Amberg-Sulzbach, Tirschenreuth and Schwandorf together with their regional editions Amberger Zeitung and Sulzbach-Rosenberger Zeitung. Facebook: http://www.facebook.com/oberpfalznetz Twitter: http://twitter.com/oberpfalznetz This Outlet offers RSS (Really Simple Syndication).
Language(s): German
ADVERTISING RATES:
SCC .... EUR 108,80
Mechanical Data: Type Area: 430 x 284 mm, No. of Columns (Display): 6, Col Widths (Display): 45 mm
Copy instructions: *Copy Date:* 1 day prior to publication
REGIONAL DAILY & SUNDAY NEWSPAPERS: Regional Daily Newspapers

NEUE VERPACKUNG 737756G35-80
Editorial: Im Weiher 10, 69121 HEIDELBERG
Tel: 6221 489213 **Fax:** 6221 489481
Email: matthias.mahr@huethig.de **Web site:** http://www.neue-verpackung.de
Freq: Monthly; **Annual Sub.:** EUR 246,40; **Circ:** 14,168
Editor: Matthias Mahr; **Advertising Manager:** Anja Breuer
Profile: neue verpackung is one of the leading packaging trade magazines in Europe. The editorial reported on all aspects of industrial packaging of food, chemicals, pharmaceuticals, cosmetics and non-food products, machine equipment, packaging materials and packaging design.
Language(s): German
ADVERTISING RATES:
Full Page Mono .... EUR 322[illegible]
Full Page Colour .... EUR 453[illegible]
Mechanical Data: Type Area: 257 x 178 mm, No. of Columns (Display): 4, Col Widths (Display): 41 mm
Copy instructions: *Copy Date:* 30 days prior to publication
Official Journal of: Organ d. Dt. Forschungsverbundes Verpackungs-, Entsorgungs- u. Umwelttechnik e.V., d. Industrieverb. Verpackungen u. Folien aus Kunststoff e.V. u. d. Dt. Verpackungsmuseum
BUSINESS: PACKAGING & BOTTLING

NEUE WELT 737266G74A-246[illegible]
Editorial: Münchener Str. 101/09, 85737 ISMANING
Tel: 89 272700 **Fax:** 89 272703490
Email: neuewelt@waz-zeitschriften.de
Freq: Weekly; **Annual Sub.:** EUR 88,40; **Circ:** 244,316
Editor: Kai Winckler
Profile: Neue Welt convinced for over 75 years by reliable information, expert health advice and an extra large puzzle part. Exclusive interviews, great articles and pictures from the world of royalty and celebrities for great entertainment.
Language(s): German
Readership: Read by women.
ADVERTISING RATES:
Full Page Mono .... EUR 740[illegible]
Full Page Colour .... EUR 740[illegible]
Mechanical Data: Type Area: 260 x 195 mm, No. of Columns (Display): 4, Col Widths (Display): 45 mm
Copy instructions: *Copy Date:* 30 days prior to publication
CONSUMER: WOMEN'S INTEREST CONSUMER MAGAZINES: Women's Interest

NEUE WESTFÄLISCHE 737269G67B-1042[illegible]
Editorial: Niedernstr. 21, 33602 BIELEFELD
Tel: 521 5550 **Fax:** 521 555349
Email: redaktion@neue-westfaelische.de **Web site:** http://www.nw-news.de
Freq: 312 issues yearly; **Circ:** 255,769
Editor: Thomas Seim; **News Editor:** Jörg Rinne; **Advertising Manager:** Michael-Joachim Appelt
Profile: The newspaper group Neue Westfälische is the highest circulation daily newspaper in combination Ostwestfalen-Lippe and reaches 682 000 readers a day (MA 2010) with a circulation of 244,021 copies (IVW copies sold 4 / 2010). Facebook: http://www.facebook.com/nwnews Twitter: http://twitter.com/nwnews This Outlet offers RSS (Really Simple Syndication).
Language(s): German
ADVERTISING RATES:
SCC .... EUR 396,40
Mechanical Data: Type Area: 490 x 324 mm, No. of Columns (Display): 7, Col Widths (Display): 45 mm
Copy instructions: *Copy Date:* 1 day prior to publication
Supplement(s): Anpfiff; Erwin; Fußball im Altkreis Warburg; Fußball im Kreis Höxter; Neue Westfälische Schulstart; Neue Westfälische Schulstart; Neue Westfälische Schulstart; Neue Westfälische Schulstart; Neue Westfälische Schulstart; Neue Westfälische Schulstart; Neue Westfälische Schulstart; Neue Westfälische Schulstart; Neue Westfälische Schulstart; Neue Westfälische Schulstart; NWEnergie sparen; NWFamilie; NWFerien; NWGarten; NWgesund; NWHandwerk; NWHochzeit; NWimmo; NWMode; NWplus; NWvital
REGIONAL DAILY & SUNDAY NEWSPAPERS: Regional Daily Newspapers

NEUE WOCHE 737273G74A-2480
Editorial: Hubert-Burda-Platz 1, 77652 OFFENBURG
Tel: 781 845164 **Fax:** 781 845123
Email: redaktion@neuewoche.de **Web site:** http://www.freizeitfreunde.de
Freq: Weekly; **Cover Price:** EUR 1,00; **Circ:** 309,293
Editor: Tessy Pavelková
Profile: Fresh, trendy, founded the neue woche entertains and advises readers with an exciting, colorful and informative mix: the-minute celebrity stories, exclusive interviews, Trends & Styles in Fashion & Beauty, Food & Living. Additional founded information about health, money, justice and partnership. On Friday, the readers learn all about their favorite celebrities and VIPs. Celebrities trust neue woche.
Language(s): German
Readership: Aimed at women of all ages.
ADVERTISING RATES:
Full Page Mono .... EUR 7850
Full Page Colour .... EUR 7850
Mechanical Data: Type Area: 239 x 197 mm, No. of Columns (Display): 4, Col Widths (Display): 46 mm
Copy instructions: *Copy Date:* 14 days prior to publication
CONSUMER: WOMEN'S INTEREST CONSUMER MAGAZINES: Women's Interest

IEUE ZEITSCHRIFT FÜR MUSIK
737283G76D-3780
ditorial: Weihergarten 5, 55116 MAINZ
el: 6131 246854 **Fax:** 6131 246212
nail: nzfm.redaktion@schott-music.com **Web site:** tp://www.musikderzeit.de
eq: 6 issues yearly; **Annual Sub.:** EUR 48,00; **Circ:** 000
litor: Rolf W. Stoll; **Advertising Manager:** Dieter P. chwarz
rofile: Music magazine focusing on contemporary, assical, traditional, new, jazz, world and crossover yles. Also includes information on improvisation, ound art and dance.
anguage(s): German
eadership: Aimed at concert-goers, record and dio listeners, lovers of new music, musicologists nd students.
OVERTISING RATES:
ull Page Mono .... EUR 975
echanical Data: Type Area: 260 x 185 mm
opy instructions: *Copy Date:* 28 days prior to ublication
ONSUMER: MUSIC & PERFORMING ARTS: lusic

IEUE ZEITSCHRIFT FÜR VEHRRECHT
737285G44-1560
ditorial: Luxemburger Str. 449, 50939 KÖLN
el: 221 943737000 **Fax:** 221 943737201
mail: info@wolterskluwer.de **Web site:** http://www. olterskluwer.de
eq: 6 issues yearly; **Annual Sub.:** EUR 119,00; irc: 1,000
ditor: Klaus Dau
rofile: Magazine about military and defence law.
anguage(s): German
eadership: Aimed at army and national service ersonnel, also solicitors.
OVERTISING RATES:
ull Page Mono .... EUR 480
ull Page Colour .... EUR 1545
echanical Data: Type Area: 215 x 140 mm
opy instructions: *Copy Date:* 21 days prior to ublication
USINESS: LEGAL

DIE NEUEN BÄDER
737157G23C-85
ditorial: Höhenstr. 17, 70736 FELLBACH
el: 711 5206274 **Fax:** 711 5206300
mail: jeni@fachschriften.de **Web site:** http://www. enovieren.de
req: Annual; **Cover Price:** EUR 4,80; **Circ:** 65,000
ditor: Kurt Jeni; **Advertising Manager:** Wolfgang oges
rofile: "Die neuen Bäder" shows all builders in the lanning or renovation should be aware of sanitation rofessionals.
anguage(s): German
eadership: Architects, planners, builders, ecorators.
ADVERTISING RATES:
ull Page Colour .... EUR 7000
Mechanical Data: Type Area: 247 x 187 mm, No. of Columns (Display): 4, Col Widths (Display): 43 mm
Copy instructions: *Copy Date:* 40 days prior to ublication
BUSINESS: FURNISHINGS & FURNITURE: urnishings & Furniture - Kitchens & Bathrooms

IEUES AUS DEM LAND DER IDEEN
1826751G14C-4776
ditorial: Unter den Linden 74, 10117 BERLIN
el: 30 2064590 **Fax:** 30 20645937
mail: info@land-der-ideen.de **Web site:** http://www. and-der-ideen.de
req: Monthly; **Circ:** 5,000
ditor: Mike de Vries
rofile: Magazine with information about evelopments in German sciences, economy, arts nd culture.
anguage(s): German

NEUES DEUTSCHLAND
737215G65A-160
Editorial: Franz-Mehring-Platz 1, 10243 BERLIN
el: 30 29781711 **Fax:** 30 29781710
Email: redaktion@nd-online.de **Web site:** http:// www.neues-deutschland.de
Freq: 312 issues yearly; **Circ:** 35,872
Editor: Jürgen Reents; **News Editor:** Reinhard Fricke; **Advertising Manager:** Friedrun Hardt
Profile: National daily newspaper with news on politics, economy, culture, sports, travel, technology, etc. Facebook: http://www.facebook.com/pages/ Berlin-Germany/Neues-Deutschland-Online/ 272534920495 Twitter: http://twitter.com/ndaktuell This Outlet offers RSS (Really Simple Syndication).
Language(s): German
Readership: Read predominantly by pensioners, students and public sector employees living in the former DDR.
ADVERTISING RATES:
SCC .... EUR 59,00
Mechanical Data: Type Area: 475 x 330 mm, No. of Columns (Display): 7, Col Widths (Display): 45 mm
Copy instructions: *Copy Date:* 2 days prior to publication
NATIONAL DAILY & SUNDAY NEWSPAPERS: National Daily Newspapers

NEUES! FÜR DIE HOLZBAUBRANCHE IN DEUTSCHLAND-ÖSTERREICH-SCHWEIZ
1866596G4E-7249
Editorial: Hauptstr 37, 85579 NEUBIBERG
Tel: 89 6144210 **Fax:** 89 61442144
Email: neues@dietrichs.com **Web site:** http://www. dietrichs.com
Freq: Annual; **Cover Price:** Free; **Circ:** 20,000
Editor: Manfred Götz
Profile: Company publication.
Language(s): German

NEUES GLAS NEW GLASS
737218G12B-6
Editorial: Eifelstr. 19, 50677 KÖLN **Tel:** 221 9231621
Fax: 221 9231622
Email: uta.klotz@t-online.de **Web site:** http://www. kunstwelt-online.de
Freq: Quarterly; **Annual Sub.:** EUR 36,00; **Circ:** 5,500
Editor: Uta M. Klotz; **Advertising Manager:** Uta Klotz
Profile: International magazine about all aspects of modern glass art.
Language(s): English; German
Readership: Read by architects, designers of glassware and museum curators.
ADVERTISING RATES:
Full Page Mono .... EUR 990
Full Page Colour .... EUR 1450
Mechanical Data: Type Area: 226 x 171 mm, No. of Columns (Display): 2, Col Widths (Display): 83 mm
Copy instructions: *Copy Date:* 42 days prior to publication
BUSINESS: CERAMICS, POTTERY & GLASS: Glass

NEUHAUSER NYMPHENBURGER ANZEIGER
736644G72-9212
Editorial: Donnersbergerstr. 22, 80634 MÜNCHEN
Tel: 89 8090920 **Fax:** 89 80909212
Email: info@muenchenanzeiger.de **Web site:** http:// www.muenchenanzeiger.de
Freq: Weekly; **Cover Price:** Free; **Circ:** 52,850
Editor: Ursula Löschau; **Advertising Manager:** Thomas Schwalb
Profile: Advertising journal (house-to-house) concentrating on local stories.
Language(s): German
ADVERTISING RATES:
Full Page Mono .... EUR 2220
Full Page Colour .... EUR 2886
Mechanical Data: Type Area: 324 x 231 mm, No. of Columns (Display): 5, Col Widths (Display): 45 mm
Copy instructions: *Copy Date:* 2 days prior to publication
LOCAL NEWSPAPERS

NEUMARKTER ANZEIGER
737300G67B-10440
Editorial: Hafnerstr. 5, 83022 ROSENHEIM
Tel: 8031 213301 **Fax:** 8031 213216
Email: redaktion@ovb.net **Web site:** http://www. ovb-online.de
Freq: 312 issues yearly; **Circ:** 13,997
Advertising Manager: Max Breu
Profile: Regional daily newspaper with news on politics, economy, culture, sports, travel, technology, etc. The CNeumarkter Anzeiger is a regional edition of the newspaper "Oberbayerisches Volksblatt". This Outlet offers RSS (Really Simple Syndication).
Language(s): German
ADVERTISING RATES:
SCC .... EUR 63,60
Mechanical Data: Type Area: 474 x 324 mm, No. of Columns (Display): 7, Col Widths (Display): 45 mm
Copy instructions: *Copy Date:* 1 day prior to publication
Supplement(s): rtv
REGIONAL DAILY & SUNDAY NEWSPAPERS: Regional Daily Newspapers

NEUMARKTER NACHRICHTEN
737301G67B-10460
Editorial: Marienstr. 9, 90402 NÜRNBERG
Tel: 911 2160 **Fax:** 911 2162432
Web site: http://www.nuernberger-nachrichten.de
Freq: 312 issues yearly; **Circ:** 7,938
Profile: Daily newspaper with regional news and a local sports section.
Language(s): German
ADVERTISING RATES:
SCC .... EUR 32,80
Mechanical Data: Type Area: 430 x 280 mm, No. of Columns (Display): 6, Col Widths (Display): 45 mm
Copy instructions: *Copy Date:* 2 days prior to publication
Supplement(s): sechs+sechzig
REGIONAL DAILY & SUNDAY NEWSPAPERS: Regional Daily Newspapers

NEUMARKTER TAGBLATT
737302G67B-10480
Editorial: Margaretenstr. 4, 93047 REGENSBURG
Tel: 941 20765 **Fax:** 941 207142
Email: mz-redaktion@mittelbayerische.de **Web site:** http://www.mittelbayerische.de
Freq: 312 issues yearly; **Circ:** 18,827
Profile: Regional daily newspaper with news on politics, economy, culture, sports, travel, technology, etc. What happened in his own front door is the most interesting news! Our Publisher product key is therefore to be the local newspaper. The desire for location-based information has led to our newspaper has become even more "local". The trend is increasingly ecoming the "editorial office" on site. Every city, every region has a permanent place in the newspaper. The Mittelbayerische Zeitung, with its 13 regional editions in the Upper Palatinate and large parts of Lower Bavaria, is the medium number one and reached with a circulation of 130,000 copies around 400,000 daily readers. As one of few newspapers in Germany, it entered against the prevailing trend circulation gains. Facebook: http:// www.facebook.com/mittelbayerische Twitter: http:// twitter.com/mz_de This Outlet offers RSS (Really Simple Syndication).
Language(s): German
ADVERTISING RATES:
SCC .... EUR 51,60
Mechanical Data: Type Area: 430 x 281 mm, No. of Columns (Display): 6, Col Widths (Display): 45 mm
Copy instructions: *Copy Date:* 1 day prior to publication
Supplement(s): Mittelbayerische jun.
REGIONAL DAILY & SUNDAY NEWSPAPERS: Regional Daily Newspapers

NEURO AKTUELL
737311G56A-7400
Editorial: Osterstr. 21, 25587 MÜNSTERDORF
Tel: 4821 85222 **Fax:** 4821 893738
Email: huhn@westermayer-verlag.de
Freq: 9 issues yearly; **Annual Sub.:** EUR 40,00; **Circ:** 7,052
Editor: Benno Huhn; **Advertising Manager:** Reinhilde Bossema-Collien
Profile: Medical journal containing information and news for specialists helping patients with nervous and trauma-related conditions.
Language(s): German
ADVERTISING RATES:
Full Page Mono .... EUR 2810
Full Page Colour .... EUR 2810
Mechanical Data: Type Area: 267 x 184 mm, No. of Columns (Display): 2, Col Widths (Display): 90 mm
BUSINESS: HEALTH & MEDICAL

NEURO FORUM
737314G56A-7440
Editorial: Robert-Rössle-Str. 10, 13092 BERLIN
Tel: 30 94063133 **Fax:** 30 94063819
Email: gibson@mdc-berlin.de **Web site:** http://nwg. glia.mdc-berlin.de
Freq: Quarterly; Free to qualifying individuals
Annual Sub.: EUR 65,00; **Circ:** 2,250
Editor: Helmut Kettenmann
Profile: Magazine about neurosciences. Facebook: http://www.facebook.com/pages/ Neurowissenschaftliche-Gesellschaft-e-V/ 385130447222.
Language(s): German
ADVERTISING RATES:
Full Page Mono .... EUR 790
Full Page Colour .... EUR 1390
Mechanical Data: Type Area: 243 x 175 mm, No. of Columns (Display): 3, Col Widths (Display): 58 mm
Copy instructions: *Copy Date:* 25 days prior to publication

NEURO-DEPESCHE
737312G56N-70_25
Editorial: Paul-Wassermann-Str. 15, 81829 MÜNCHEN **Tel:** 89 4366300 **Fax:** 89 436630210
Email: info@gfi-online.de **Web site:** http://www. gfi-medien.de
Freq: 10 issues yearly; **Annual Sub.:** EUR 60,00; **Circ:** 7,821
Editor: Jörg Lellwitz
Profile: Journal providing information and research concerning neurology and psychiatry.
Language(s): German
Readership: Aimed at specialists within these fields.
ADVERTISING RATES:
Full Page Mono .... EUR 1860
Full Page Colour .... EUR 3100
Mechanical Data: Type Area: 258 x 187 mm, No. of Columns (Display): 3, Col Widths (Display): 59 mm
BUSINESS: HEALTH & MEDICAL: Mental Health

NEUROLOGIE & REHABILITATION
737316G56L-50
Editorial: Bismarckstr. 8, 53604 BAD HONNEF
Tel: 2224 919480 **Fax:** 2224 919482
Email: verlag@hippocampus.de **Web site:** http:// www.hippocampus.de
Freq: 6 issues yearly; Free to qualifying individuals
Annual Sub.: EUR 140,50; **Circ:** 3,800
Editor: Brigitte Bülau; **Advertising Manager:** Ute Weihrauch
Profile: Journal about neurology and rehabilitation. Official publication of the German Society for Neurological Rehabilitation.
Language(s): English; German
Readership: Read by neurologists and nerve doctors in clinics and practices.
ADVERTISING RATES:
Full Page Mono .... EUR 1250
Full Page Colour .... EUR 2270
Mechanical Data: Type Area: 240 x 175 mm, No. of Columns (Display): 3, Col Widths (Display): 55 mm
Copy instructions: *Copy Date:* 21 days prior to publication
Official Journal of: Organ d. Dt. Ges. f. Neurolog. Rehabilitation, d. Dt. Ges. f. Neurotraumatologie u. Klin. Neuropsychologie, d. Schweizer. Ges. f. Neurorehabilitation u. d. Österr. Ges. f. Neurorehabilitation
BUSINESS: HEALTH & MEDICAL: Disability & Rehabilitation

NEURORADIOLOGY
737322G56A-7520
Editorial: Tiergartenstr. 17, 69121 HEIDELBERG
Tel: 6221 4870 **Fax:** 6221 4878366
Email: ute.heilmann@springer.com **Web site:** http:// www.springerlink.com
Freq: Monthly; **Annual Sub.:** EUR 1651,00; **Circ:** 1,300
Editor: James V. Byrne; **Advertising Manager:** Noëla Krischer
Profile: Magazine about neuroradiology.
Language(s): English
ADVERTISING RATES:
Full Page Mono .... EUR 1440
Full Page Colour .... EUR 2480
Mechanical Data: Type Area: 240 x 175 mm
Official Journal of: Organ d. European Society of Neuroradiology

NEUROREHA
1934193G56A-11654
Editorial: Rüdigerstr. 14, 70469 STUTTGART
Tel: 711 89310 **Fax:** 711 8931298
Email: neuroreha@thieme.de **Web site:** http://www. thieme.de/physioonline/neuroreha.html
Freq: Quarterly; **Annual Sub.:** EUR 95,20; **Circ:** 1,450
Profile: neuroreha combines research and therapy. Rapid advances in theory and practice of the neurorehabilitation require looking beyond the confines of their own profession, to know the latest scientific findings and integrate them into treatment. neuro-rehabilitation support these efforts and encourages the continuing education of physicians and therapists in neurological rehabilitation.
Language(s): German
ADVERTISING RATES:
Full Page Mono .... EUR 820
Full Page Colour .... EUR 1240
Mechanical Data: Type Area: 178 x mm, No. of Columns (Display): 238

NEUROSURGICAL REVIEW
737323G56A-7540
Editorial: Tiergartenstr. 17, 69121 HEIDELBERG
Tel: 6221 4870 **Fax:** 6221 4878366
Email: hilde.haala@springer.com **Web site:** http:// www.springerlink.com
Freq: Quarterly; **Annual Sub.:** EUR 805,00; **Circ:** 153
Editor: H. Bertalanffy
Profile: Neurosurgical review.
Language(s): English
ADVERTISING RATES:
Full Page Mono .... EUR 740
Full Page Colour .... EUR 1780
Mechanical Data: Type Area: 240 x 175 mm

NEUROTRANSMITTER
737324G56N-71_25
Editorial: Aschauer Str. 30, 81549 MÜNCHEN
Tel: 89 2030431300 **Fax:** 89 2030431399
Email: beate.huber@springer.com **Web site:** http:// www.springermedizin.de
Freq: 11 issues yearly; Free to qualifying individuals
Annual Sub.: EUR 223,00; **Circ:** 10,374
Editor: Beate Huber; **Advertising Manager:** Peter Urban
Profile: NeuroTransmitter itself as a leading expert information and professional political medium for all psychiatrists and neurologists. The Journal provides a comprehensive combination of current professional policies, sound training and practice-oriented reader service. Selected articles from the journal of the Bavarian Medical Association recognized as a certified training. As a organ of three professional associations is the NeuroTransmitter required reading in the target group.
Language(s): German
Readership: Read by members of the German National Union of Neurologists and Psychiatrists.
ADVERTISING RATES:
Full Page Mono .... EUR 2500
Full Page Colour .... EUR 4030
Mechanical Data: Type Area: 240 x 174 mm
Official Journal of: Organ d. Berufsverb. Dt. Nervenärzte e.V., d. Berufsverb. Dt. Neurologen e.V. u. d. Berufsverb. Dt. Psychiater
Supplement(s): In Balance
BUSINESS: HEALTH & MEDICAL: Mental Health

NEUSS=GREVENBROICHER ZEITUNG
737326G67B-10500
Editorial: Zülpicher Str. 10, 40549 DÜSSELDORF
Tel: 211 5050 **Fax:** 211 5047562
Email: redaktionssekretariat@rheinische.post.de
Web site: http://www.rp-online.de
Freq: 312 issues yearly; **Circ:** 46,699
Advertising Manager: Marc Arne Schümann
Profile: Daily newspaper with regional news and a local sports section. Facebook: http:// www.facebook.com/rponline This Outlet offers RSS (Really Simple Syndication).
Language(s): German
ADVERTISING RATES:
SCC .... EUR 98,80
Mechanical Data: Type Area: 480 x 325 mm, No. of Columns (Display): 7, Col Widths (Display): 45 mm

Copy instructions: *Copy Date:* 2 days prior to publication
REGIONAL DAILY & SUNDAY NEWSPAPERS: Regional Daily Newspapers

NEUSTÄDTER BERLIN
1913908G89A-12499
Editorial: Friedensallee 26, 22765 HAMBURG
Tel: 40 39908181 **Fax:** 40 39903182
Email: redaktion@neustaedter.de **Web site:** http://www.neustaedter.de
Freq: Annual; **Cover Price:** EUR 5,80; **Circ:** 35,000
Editor: Ulf Dubbels
Profile: All dates for Berlin in a book. For newcomers and people seeking accommodation in Berlin! With all the info about the neighborhoods, the apartment search, to move to offices and a huge recreational and sports guide.
Language(s): German
ADVERTISING RATES:
Full Page Mono .... EUR 2300
Full Page Colour .... EUR 2300
Mechanical Data: Type Area: 158 x 102 mm

NEUSTÄDTER HAMBURG
1913909G89A-12500
Editorial: Friedensallee 26, 22765 HAMBURG
Tel: 40 39908181 **Fax:** 40 39903182
Email: redaktion@neustaedter.de **Web site:** http://www.neustaedter.de
Freq: Annual; **Cover Price:** EUR 5,80; **Circ:** 35,000
Editor: Ulf Dubbels
Profile: All information for Hamburg in a book. For newcomers and people seeking accommodation in Hamburg! With all the info about the neighborhoods, the apartment search, to move to offices and a huge recreational and sports guide.
Language(s): German
ADVERTISING RATES:
Full Page Mono .... EUR 2300
Full Page Colour .... EUR 2300
Mechanical Data: Type Area: 158 x 102 mm

NEUSTÄDTER KÖLN
1913910G89A-12501
Editorial: Friedensallee 26, 22765 HAMBURG
Tel: 40 39908181 **Fax:** 40 39903182
Email: redaktion@neustaedter.de **Web site:** http://www.neustaedter.de
Freq: Annual; **Cover Price:** EUR 5,80; **Circ:** 25,000
Editor: Ulf Dubbels
Profile: All information for Cologne in a book. For newcomers and people seeking accommodation in Cologne! With all the info about the neighborhoods, the apartment search, to move to offices and a huge recreational and sports guide.
Language(s): German
ADVERTISING RATES:
Full Page Mono .... EUR 1800
Full Page Colour .... EUR 1800
Mechanical Data: Type Area: 158 x 102 mm

NEUSTÄDTER MÜNCHEN
1913911G89A-12502
Editorial: Friedensallee 26, 22765 HAMBURG
Tel: 40 39908181 **Fax:** 40 39903182
Email: redaktion@neustaedter.de **Web site:** http://www.neustaedter.de
Freq: Annual; **Cover Price:** EUR 5,80; **Circ:** 25,000
Editor: Ulf Dubbels
Profile: All dates for Munich, in a book. For newcomers and people seeking accommodation in Munich! With all the info about the neighborhoods, the apartment search, to move to offices and a huge recreational and sports guide.
Language(s): German
ADVERTISING RATES:
Full Page Mono .... EUR 1800
Full Page Colour .... EUR 1800
Mechanical Data: Type Area: 158 x 102 mm

NEU-ULMER ZEITUNG
737336G67B-10280
Editorial: Curt-Frenzel-Str. 2, 86167 AUGSBURG
Tel: 821 7770 **Fax:** 821 7772067
Web site: http://www.augsburger-allgemeine.de
Freq: 312 issues yearly; **Circ:** 9,456
Advertising Manager: Herbert Dachs
Profile: Regional daily newspaper with news on politics, economy, culture, sports, travel, technology, etc. Facebook: http://www.facebook.com/AugsburgerAllgemeine Twitter: http://twitter.com/AZ_Augsburg This Outlet offers RSS (Really Simple Syndication).
Language(s): German
ADVERTISING RATES:
SCC .... EUR 45,40
Mechanical Data: Type Area: 480 x 327 mm, No. of Columns (Display): 7, Col Widths (Display): 45 mm
Copy instructions: *Copy Date:* 1 day prior to publication
Supplement(s): leben:wohnen
REGIONAL DAILY & SUNDAY NEWSPAPERS: Regional Daily Newspapers

NEW BUSINESS
737340G2A-3440
Editorial: Nebendahlstr. 16, 22041 HAMBURG
Tel: 40 60900970 **Fax:** 40 60900977
Email: nebel@new-business.de **Web site:** http://www.new-business.de
Freq: Weekly; **Circ:** 1,062
Editor: Harald Nebel; **Advertising Manager:** Jens Jansen
Profile: Magazine about advertising and the media. Facebook: http://www.facebook.com/SEATde.
Language(s): German
ADVERTISING RATES:
Full Page Mono .... EUR 3200
Full Page Colour .... EUR 3200
Mechanical Data: Type Area: 277 x 175 mm
Copy instructions: *Copy Date:* 10 days prior to publication
BUSINESS: COMMUNICATIONS, ADVERTISING & MARKETING

NEW ENERGY
737347G58-1180
Editorial: Marienstr. 19, 10117 BERLIN
Tel: 30 28482130 **Fax:** 30 28482139
Email: info@neueenergie.net **Web site:** http://www.neueenergie.net
Freq: 6 issues yearly; Free to qualifying individuals
Annual Sub.: EUR 70,00; **Circ:** 4,000
Editor: Hanne May
Profile: Magazine for current and future operators, planners, manufacturers of the equipment regenrativen energy technology as well as friends and supporters of renewable energy.
Language(s): English
ADVERTISING RATES:
Full Page Mono .... EUR 1300
Full Page Colour .... EUR 2600
Mechanical Data: Type Area: 277 x 185 mm
Copy instructions: *Copy Date:* 24 days prior to publication

NEW METROPOLIS
1999604G74A-3751
Editorial: Friedländer Weg 45, 37085 GÖTTINGEN
Tel: 551 41121 **Fax:** 551 42270
Email: redaktion@new-metropolis.info **Web site:** http://www.new-metropolis.info
Freq: 6 issues yearly; **Annual Sub.:** EUR 48,00; **Circ:** 19,800
Editor: Edda Stahn; **Advertising Manager:** Antje Arndt
Profile: Lifestyle magazine in XXL format for the consumer-like upper class enjoy traveling in Berlin and Germany, as well as foreign visitors to Berlin Premium and all the ambassadors in Germany.
Language(s): English; German
ADVERTISING RATES:
Full Page Mono .... EUR 3200
Full Page Colour .... EUR 3200
Mechanical Data: Type Area: 291 x 220 mm, No. of Columns (Display): 3, Col Widths (Display): 68 mm
Copy instructions: *Copy Date:* 14 days prior to publication

DIE NEWS
721328G14A-360
Editorial: Löffelstr. 1, 70597 STUTTGART
Tel: 711 76963714 **Fax:** 711 76963729
Email: redaktion@dienews.net **Web site:** http://www.dienews.net
Freq: 10 issues yearly; **Annual Sub.:** EUR 71,00; **Circ:** 19,900
Editor: Andrea Przyklenk
Profile: Magazine for independent companies and medium-sized family. Current issues in business and science, finance and policy, IT and Telecommunications, advertising and marketing, training and staff development, but also of culture and leisure. Entrepreneurs and enterprises, income concepts and strategies for medium-sized family businesses are the focus of reporting.
Language(s): German
Readership: Aimed at self-employed business people in southern Germany.
ADVERTISING RATES:
Full Page Mono .... EUR 3250
Full Page Colour .... EUR 3950
Mechanical Data: Type Area: 260 x 172 mm, No. of Columns (Display): 3, Col Widths (Display): 54 mm
Copy instructions: *Copy Date:* 16 days prior to publication
BUSINESS: COMMERCE, INDUSTRY & MANAGEMENT

NEWS
737355G80-8200
Editorial: Ritterstr. 16, 32423 MINDEN
Tel: 571 828550 **Fax:** 571 8285510
Email: redaktion@news-dasmagazin.de **Web site:** http://www.news-dasmagazin.de
Freq: Monthly; **Cover Price:** Free; **Circ:** 14,457
Editor: Carsten Korfesmeyer; **Advertising Manager:** Carsten Witte
Profile: Magazine for city and region, concentrating on gastronomy, music, arts and events.
Language(s): German
ADVERTISING RATES:
Full Page Mono .... EUR 1461
Full Page Colour .... EUR 2118
Mechanical Data: No. of Columns (Display): 4, Col Widths (Display): 44 mm, Type Area: 270 x 190 mm
Copy instructions: *Copy Date:* 6 days prior to publication
CONSUMER: RURAL & REGIONAL INTEREST

NEWSCLICK.DE
1621767G67B-16614
Editorial: Hamburger Str. 277, 38114 BRAUNSCHWEIG **Tel:** 531 39000 **Fax:** 531 3900780
Email: tobias.rieger@newsclick.de **Web site:** http://www.newsclick.de
Freq: Daily; **Cover Price:** Paid; **Circ:** 1,102,265 Unique Users
Editor: Paul-Josef Raue
Profile: Ezine: Information Portal of the Brunswick newspaper publisher with news from the areas of local, world, culture, sports, leisure. Similarly, photo galleries and videos, job, real estate, automotive and Ratings range. Twitter: http://twitter.com/bs_zeitung This Outlet offers RSS (Really Simple Syndication).
Language(s): German
REGIONAL DAILY & SUNDAY NEWSPAPERS: Regional Daily Newspapers

NEWSOLUTIONS
737403G5C-41_25
Editorial: Zugspitzstr. 7, 86932 PÜRGEN
Tel: 8196 7084 **Fax:** 8196 1239
Email: iabenthum@newsolutions.de **Web site:** http://www.newsolutions.de
Freq: Monthly; **Annual Sub.:** EUR 150,60; **Circ:** 8,000
Editor: Isabella Pridat-Zapp; **Advertising Manager:** Ingrid Abenthum
Profile: Magazine focusing on AS400 servers. Offers solutions for all platforms and includes information on Windows NT and Unix.
Language(s): German
Readership: Aimed at IT managers.
ADVERTISING RATES:
Full Page Mono .... EUR 2746
Full Page Colour .... EUR 3230
Mechanical Data: Type Area: 250 x 178 mm
Copy instructions: *Copy Date:* 32 days prior to publication
BUSINESS: COMPUTERS & AUTOMATION: Professional Personal Computers

NFM NUTZFAHRZEUGE-MANAGEMENT
737423G49D-50
Editorial: Wilhelm-Giese-Str. 26, 27616 BEVERSTEDT **Tel:** 4747 8741301 **Fax:** 4747 8741222
Email: hpeimann@nfm-verlag.de **Web site:** http://www.nfm-verlag.de
Freq: Monthly; **Annual Sub.:** EUR 35,00; **Circ:** 24,486
Editor: Herbert Peimann
Profile: Commercial vehicles, transportation, logistics, fleet management and more - NFM provides online and in the popular print magazine about the trends and developments in the transport and commercial vehicle industry.
Language(s): German
ADVERTISING RATES:
Full Page Mono .... EUR 6600
Full Page Colour .... EUR 6600
Mechanical Data: Type Area: 250 x 184 mm, No. of Columns (Display): 4, Col Widths (Display): 43 mm
BUSINESS: TRANSPORT: Commercial Vehicles

NFZ WERKSTATT
737428G49B-16
Editorial: Dießemer Bruch 167, 47805 KREFELD
Tel: 2151 5100118 **Fax:** 2151 5100215
Email: nfz-werkstatt@stuenings.de **Web site:** http://www.nfz-werkstatt.de
Freq: Quarterly; **Circ:** 37,605
Editor: Lutz Gerritzen; **Advertising Manager:** Cornelia Assem
Profile: Magazine for trucks, buses and construction vehicle repair shops. Independent editorial of the priorities we report in each issue on products, processes, tools, equipment, workshop equipment, facilities, environment, workshop profile, presentation of workshop business, workshop activities, new businesses, events and exhibitions, training in the automotive trade, updates and news from Associations and institutions of the motor vehicle registration etc.
Language(s): German
ADVERTISING RATES:
Full Page Mono .... EUR 4920
Full Page Colour .... EUR 6420
Mechanical Data: Type Area: 255 x 185 mm, No. of Columns (Display): 4, Col Widths (Display): 45 mm
Copy instructions: *Copy Date:* 15 days prior to publication
Official Journal of: Organ d. VMI Verb. d. Motorinstandsetzungsbetriebe e.V.
Supplement to: Bus fahrt, KFZ anzeiger
BUSINESS: TRANSPORT: Bus & Coach Transport

NIBELUNGEN KURIER
737431G72-9800
Editorial: Prinz-Carl-Anlage 20, 67547 WORMS
Tel: 6241 95780 **Fax:** 6241 957878
Email: redaktion@nibelungen-kurier.de **Web site:** http://www.nibelungen-kurier.de
Freq: 104 issues yearly; **Cover Price:** Free; **Circ:** 62,070
Editor: Steffen Adolf Heumann; **Advertising Manager:** Frank Meinel
Profile: Advertising journal (house-to-house) concentrating on local stories.
Language(s): German
ADVERTISING RATES:
Full Page Mono .... EUR 3696
Full Page Colour .... EUR 4004
Mechanical Data: Type Area: 440 x 290 mm, No. of Columns (Display): 6, Col Widths (Display): 45 mm
Copy instructions: *Copy Date:* 2 days prior to publication
LOCAL NEWSPAPERS

NIEDERBAYERISCHE WIRTSCHAFT
737447G63-64
Editorial: Nibelungenstr. 15, 94032 PASSAU
Tel: 851 507235 **Fax:** 851 507280
Email: brunner@passau.ihk.de **Web site:** http://www.passau-ihk.de
Freq: 11 issues yearly; Free to qualifying individuals
Annual Sub.: EUR 21,50; **Circ:** 32,808
Editor: Martin Brunner; **Advertising Manager:** Christine Schenkenbach
Profile: The "Niederbayerische Wirtschaft" or simply "NIWI" is the official publication organ of the Chamber of Commerce and Industry of Lower Bavaria. She is now with a circulation of more than 35,000 copies, the largest and most important regional business magazine. The NIWI appears eleven times a year and informs the member companies, but also the public about the work of the Chamber of Commerce, presents analysis of the economic region of Lower Bavaria and provides useful advice for corporate practice. New laws and regulations are also subject, like the development of the site or messages from the companies. Monthly covers the NIWI current issues in the sections focus and emphasis. Other priorities are always closely monitored economic region of Lower Bavaria - Upper Austria - Bohemia, as well as many international issues and information for businesses. According to the latest survey, the Chamber of Commerce magazines by far the leader in nationwide Range comparison (CCI magazine 45.1%, 21.5% der Spiegel, Focus 20.9%) are. No other printed medium reaches the decision makers in the German middle class as wide as the Chamber of Commerce's Magazine.
Language(s): German
ADVERTISING RATES:
Full Page Mono .... EUR 186
Full Page Colour .... EUR 272
Mechanical Data: Type Area: 255 x 185 mm, No. of Columns (Display): 3, Col Widths (Display): 59 mm
Copy instructions: *Copy Date:* 28 days prior to publication
BUSINESS: REGIONAL BUSINESS

NIEDERELBE-ZEITUNG
737450G67B-1052
Editorial: Kaemmererplatz 2, 27472 CUXHAVEN
Tel: 4721 5850 **Fax:** 4721 585336
Email: redaktion@nez.de **Web site:** http://www.nez.de
Freq: 312 issues yearly; **Circ:** 9,210
Advertising Manager: Ralf Drossner
Profile: Daily newspaper with regional news and a local sports section. Facebook: http://www.facebook.com/pages/Niederelbe-Zeitung/117402991618350 Twitter: http://twitter.com/#!/NEZ_Online.
Language(s): German
ADVERTISING RATES:
SCC .... EUR 36,9
Mechanical Data: Type Area: 487 x 324 mm, No. of Columns (Display): 7, Col Widths (Display): 45 mm
Copy instructions: *Copy Date:* 1 day prior to publication
Supplement(s): Cuxjournal; Ferienjournal; Hemmoor Magazin
REGIONAL DAILY & SUNDAY NEWSPAPERS: Regional Daily Newspapers

DER NIEDERGELASSENE ARZT
737451G56A-758
Editorial: Otto-Hahn-Str. 7, 50997 KÖLN
Tel: 2236 376438 **Fax:** 2236 376999
Email: schweihoff@wpv.de **Web site:** http://www.wpv.de
Freq: Monthly; Free to qualifying individuals
Annual Sub.: EUR 52,80; **Circ:** 64,850
Editor: Monika Schweihoff; **Advertising Manager:** Isabelle Becker
Profile: der niedergelassene arzt is the news magazine for general practitioners, practitioners and internists. In addition to current news coverage for medical emphases, and conferences focus on the fields of politics and the economy. For the doctor tailored, expert contributions to support its practice management. Billing Tips (IGeL-Tip, EBM-tip GOÄ-tip) provide relevant advice for everyday practice. Particularly interesting is the practice published twice a year compared to GPs. The heading "Practice Exchange" is a treasure trove for everything related to the practice routine. News, politics, economics, medicine, young physicians, women and medicine, diabetes, pharmaceutical news and Training: Additional sections are. the practicing physician's offices, around the body of the NAV-Virchow-Association and at more than 10,000 members as a subscription-time delivered in writing.
Language(s): German
Readership: Read by doctors, medical consultants and surgeons.
ADVERTISING RATES:
Full Page Mono .... EUR 4002
Full Page Colour .... EUR 5217
Mechanical Data: Type Area: 240 x 180 mm, No. of Columns (Display): 3, Col Widths (Display): 56 mm
Copy instructions: *Copy Date:* 21 days prior to publication
BUSINESS: HEALTH & MEDICAL

NIEDERKASSEL AKTUELL MIT AMTSBLATT DER STADT NIEDERKASSEL
737453G72-9820
Editorial: Friedensplatz 2, 53721 SIEGBURG
Tel: 2241 9665130 **Fax:** 2241 9665498

mail: redaktion@extra-blatt.de **Web site:** http://www.rheinische-anzeigenblaetter.de
req: Weekly; **Cover Price:** Free; **Circ:** 18,796
ditor-in-Chief: Irmgard Bracker-Klinkhammels;
dvertising Manager: Klaus Vogel
rofile: Advertising journal (house-to-house) oncentrating on local stories.
anguage(s): German
DVERTISING RATES:
ull Page Mono .... EUR 1703
ull Page Colour .... EUR 2469
Mechanical Data: Type Area: 430 x 282 mm, No. of olumns (Display): 6, Col Widths (Display): 45 mm
opy instructions: *Copy Date:* 5 days prior to ublication
OCAL NEWSPAPERS

DIE NIEDERLAUSITZ URLAUBS- UND FREIZEITMAGAZIN

1794316G89A-12285
Editorial: Schlossbezirk 3, 03130 SPREMBERG
Tel: 3563 602340 **Fax:** 3563 602342
Email: info@niederlausitz.de **Web site:** http://www.niederlausitz.de
Freq: Annual; **Cover Price:** Free; **Circ:** 50,000
Profile: Regional holiday and leisure magazine for the ower Lausitz.
anguage(s): German
Copy instructions: *Copy Date:* 30 days prior to ublication

NIEDERRHEIN

1829369G89A-12400
Editorial: Tiergartenstr. 64, 47533 KLEVE
Tel: 2821 7115615 **Fax:** 2821 7115639
Email: niederrhein.redaktion@mediamixx.net **Web site:** http://www.magazin-niederrhein.de
Freq: Monthly; **Annual Sub.:** EUR 33,60; **Circ:** 15,000
Editor: Frank Wöbbeking
Profile: Magazine for the Lower Rhine area for ourism, leisure, sports, gastronomy, culture and rade. We reported to date, provide service and ntertainment, and our readers want, whether long stablished or approved travels, curious, make the typical Lower Rhine "again and again to rediscover. The heart of the magazine is, therefore, the extensive alendar of events, in which all major events are learly presented. In addition, we present attractive destinations that serve the high-quality gastronomic offer in the region and bring the domestic economy in he right light.
Language(s): German
ADVERTISING RATES:
Full Page Mono .... EUR 1700
Full Page Colour .... EUR 1700
Mechanical Data: Type Area: 274 x 188 mm, No. of Columns (Display): 4, Col Widths (Display): 43 mm

NIEDERRHEIN TENNIS

737478G75H-180
Editorial: Pomona 137, 41464 NEUSS
Tel: 2131 7404710 **Fax:** 2131 7404760
Email: km@molt-medienservice.de **Web site:** http://www.tvn-tennis.de
Freq: 6 issues yearly; Free to qualifying individuals
Annual Sub.: EUR 21,00; **Circ:** 19,859
Editor: Klaus Molt
Profile: Official magazine of the Tennis Association for the Lower Rhine area.
Language(s): German
ADVERTISING RATES:
Full Page Colour .... EUR 2880
Mechanical Data: Type Area: 250 x 185 mm, No. of Columns (Display): 4, Col Widths (Display): 43 mm
Copy instructions: *Copy Date:* 30 days prior to publication
CONSUMER: SPORT: Racquet Sports

NIEDERSACHSEN GLOBAL

2070787G14C-4793
Editorial: Lotzestr. 26, 37081 GÖTTINGEN
Tel: 551 5075122
Email: gruenewald@polygo.de **Web site:** http://www.polygo.de
Freq: Half-yearly; **Cover Price:** Free; **Circ:** 8,000
Editor: Sven Gruenewald; **Advertising Manager:** John D. Swenson
Profile: Facebook: http://www.facebook.com/RegJoHannover.
Language(s): English
ADVERTISING RATES:
Full Page Mono .... EUR 1800
Full Page Colour .... EUR 1800
Mechanical Data: Type Area: 297 x 210 mm
Copy instructions: *Copy Date:* 24 days prior to publication

DIE NIEDERSÄCHSISCHE GEMEINDE

737481G32A-2240
Editorial: Arnswaldtstr. 28, 30159 HANNOVER
Tel: 511 302850 **Fax:** 511 3028530
Email: nsgb@nsgb.de **Web site:** http://www.nsgb.info
Freq: 6 issues yearly; Free to qualifying individuals
Annual Sub.: EUR 42,15; **Circ:** 12,184
Editor: Rainer Timmermann; **Advertising Manager:** Ute Stautmeister
Profile: Publication about municipal self-government.
Language(s): German
ADVERTISING RATES:
Full Page Mono .... EUR 1500
Full Page Colour .... EUR 3600
Mechanical Data: Type Area: 266 x 185 mm, No. of Columns (Display): 3, Col Widths (Display): 58 mm
Copy instructions: *Copy Date:* 28 days prior to publication
BUSINESS: LOCAL GOVERNMENT, LEISURE & RECREATION: Local Government

NIEDERSÄCHSISCHE RECHTSPFLEGE

737482G80-14126
Editorial: Am Waterlooplatz 1, 30169 HANNOVER
Freq: Monthly; **Annual Sub.:** EUR 59,52; **Circ:** 2,300
Editor: Schmidt; **Advertising Manager:** Wilhelm Ahrens
Profile: Journal about the legal system in Lower Saxony.
Language(s): German
ADVERTISING RATES:
Full Page Mono .... EUR 500
Mechanical Data: Type Area: 260 x 170 mm
Copy instructions: *Copy Date:* 45 days prior to publication
CONSUMER: RURAL & REGIONAL INTEREST

NIEDERSÄCHSISCHE WIRTSCHAFT

737761G63-660
Editorial: Schiffgraben 49, 30175 HANNOVER
Tel: 511 3107269 **Fax:** 511 3107450
Email: nw@hannover.ihk.de **Web site:** http://www.hannover.ihk.de
Freq: Monthly; Free to qualifying individuals
Annual Sub.: EUR 69,50; **Circ:** 42,536
Editor: Stefan Noort
Profile: The Niedersächsische Wirtschaft - the regional business magazine of the Chamber of Commerce and Industry Hanover - provides information on new trends and themes that make up a sustainable and successful business management. The reader will find facts, tips and background reports from the areas of taxation, finance, law, (inter) national markets, technology, training, e-commerce and much more. The cover story offers a monthly benefit-oriented information on a current topic. Lively articles on companies, people and current developments in the region to provide interest and identification with the regional business magazine. With a monthly circulation of over 40,000 copies reached the Lower Saxony area-wide economic managers of large and medium-sized enterprises in industry, trade and services in the CCI field. The readership is characterized by a high education and living standards, a high purchasing power and a primary interest economic topics. The Lower Saxony economy offers local and regional companies, traders, Suppliers and service providers an ideal platform to address their customers at the highest level decision makers. Since the Chamber of Commerce magazines are read in the context of entrepreneurial activity, creates a specific effect of the advertising messages of advertising. Take the opportunity to build on this through sustainable and strategic business relationships.
Language(s): German
ADVERTISING RATES:
Full Page Mono .... EUR 3017
Full Page Colour .... EUR 4602
Mechanical Data: Type Area: 277 x 190 mm, No. of Columns (Display): 3, Col Widths (Display): 58 mm
BUSINESS: REGIONAL BUSINESS

NIEDERSÄCHSISCHER JÄGER

737483G75F-520
Editorial: Kabelkamp 6, 30179 HANNOVER
Tel: 511 6780142 **Fax:** 511 67806140
Email: jaeger@dlv.de **Web site:** http://www.niedersaechsischer-jaeger.de
Freq: 24 issues yearly; **Annual Sub.:** EUR 88,90; **Circ:** 19,578
Editor: Dieter Bartsch; **Advertising Manager:** Jens Riegamer
Profile: Official publication will be published in the state hunters of Lower Saxony and Bremen. The hunting magazine for the hunter in the province with the second highest rate of hunting license holders in Germany. Subscribers title that is not under membership fees of the National Hunting Association is based. Lower Saxony is the underlying share for hunters by hunters in northern Germany and therefore the perfect combination for hunting magazine Pirsch.
Language(s): German
ADVERTISING RATES:
Full Page Mono .... EUR 2538
Full Page Colour .... EUR 3542
Mechanical Data: Type Area: 270 x 184 mm, No. of Columns (Display): 4, Col Widths (Display): 43 mm
Copy instructions: *Copy Date:* 18 days prior to publication
CONSUMER: SPORT: Shooting

NIEDERSÄCHSISCHES ÄRZTEBLATT

737486G56A-7620
Editorial: Berliner Allee 20, 30175 HANNOVER
Tel: 511 3802220 **Fax:** 511 3802260
Email: presse@aekn.de **Web site:** http://www.haeverlag.de
Freq: Monthly; Free to qualifying individuals
Annual Sub.: EUR 54,00; **Circ:** 38,000
Editor: Jörg Blume; **Advertising Manager:** Hiltrud Steffen
Profile: The niedersächsische ärzteblatt is the official journal of the Medical Association of Lower Saxony and the physicians' association Lower Saxony. By far the most widely read book of medical specialists and professional press in the state of Lower Saxony addressed to all 35,000 doctors, including more than 11,500 "established" as well as currently 2,000 psychological Psy- psychotherapists The journal publishes announcements of the Medical Association and the physicians' association Lower Saxony, occupational and academic articles and notes for meetings and conventions. Because of its wideth information spectrum, combined with the high acceptance by the reader recommends the niedersächsische ärzteblatt as powerful advertising when it comes to effectively address the Lower Saxony doctors.
Language(s): German
Readership: Aimed at doctors in the Lower Saxony region of Germany.
ADVERTISING RATES:
Full Page Mono .... EUR 2290
Full Page Colour .... EUR 4185
Mechanical Data: Type Area: 252 x 175 mm, No. of Columns (Display): 3, Col Widths (Display): 55 mm
Copy instructions: *Copy Date:* 20 days prior to publication
BUSINESS: HEALTH & MEDICAL

DER NIEREN PATIENT

725250G94F-500
Editorial: Kopenhagener Str. 74, 10437 BERLIN
Tel: 30 44038482 **Fax:** 30 44038482
Email: monecke@bnev.de **Web site:** http://www.nierenpatient-online.de
Freq: 8 issues yearly; Free to qualifying individuals
Annual Sub.: EUR 29,60; **Circ:** 15,971
Editor: Angela Monecke; **Advertising Manager:** Björn Lindenau
Profile: Largest nationwide subscription magazine for chronic kidney disease. „Der Nieren Patient" informed current and patient closely on the topics of kidney dialysis and transplantation. Provides extra sections for new patients and experienced "professionals" as well as extensive leisure and travel reports and nutrition tips.
Language(s): German
Readership: Read by dialysis patients.
ADVERTISING RATES:
Full Page Mono .... EUR 1860
Full Page Colour .... EUR 2650
Mechanical Data: Type Area: 248 x 178 mm, No. of Columns (Display): 4, Col Widths (Display): 41 mm
Copy instructions: *Copy Date:* 28 days prior to publication
CONSUMER: OTHER CLASSIFICATIONS: Disability

NIEREN- UND HOCHDRUCKKRANKHEITEN

737500G56A-7640
Editorial: Podbielskistr. 380, 30659 HANNOVER
Tel: 511 9063291 **Fax:** 511 9063098
Email: sekretariat.brunkhorst.oststadt@klinikum-hannover.de
Freq: Monthly; **Annual Sub.:** EUR 188,00; **Circ:** 3,700
Editor: R. Brunkhorst; **Advertising Manager:** Christian Graßl
Profile: Magazine about nephrology, internal medicine, urology, pediatrics, intensive care, guard and dialysis center,.
Language(s): German
ADVERTISING RATES:
Full Page Mono .... EUR 1900
Full Page Colour .... EUR 2890
Mechanical Data: Type Area: 242 x 167 mm, No. of Columns (Display): 3, Col Widths (Display): 56 mm
Copy instructions: *Copy Date:* 28 days prior to publication
Official Journal of: Organ d. Dt. Hochdruckliga e.V.

NIESKYER WOCHENKURIER

737502G72-9900
Editorial: Wettiner Platz 10, 01067 DRESDEN
Tel: 351 491760 **Fax:** 351 4917674
Email: wochenkurier-dresden@dwk-verlag.de **Web site:** http://www.wochenkurier.info
Freq: Weekly; **Cover Price:** Free; **Circ:** 14,531
Editor: Regine Eberlein; **Advertising Manager:** Andreas Schönherr
Profile: Advertising journal (house-to-house) concentrating on local stories.
Language(s): German
ADVERTISING RATES:
Full Page Mono .... EUR 2168
Full Page Colour .... EUR 3035
Mechanical Data: Type Area: 430 x 290 mm, No. of Columns (Display): 7, Col Widths (Display): 38 mm
Copy instructions: *Copy Date:* 5 days prior to publication
LOCAL NEWSPAPERS

NISSAN LIVE

767205G94H-13924
Editorial: Gurlittstr. 15, 20099 HAMBURG
Tel: 40 397565 **Fax:** 40 3908786
Email: andreas.rommelspacher@hamburg.de **Web site:** http://www.redaktionsbuero-rommelspacher.de
Freq: Quarterly; **Cover Price:** Free; **Circ:** 154,566
Editor: Andreas Rommelspacher
Profile: Company publication published by Renault Nissan Deutschland AG.
Language(s): German
ADVERTISING RATES:
Full Page Colour .... EUR 6700
Mechanical Data: Type Area: 250 x 188 mm
Copy instructions: *Copy Date:* 44 days prior to publication
CONSUMER: OTHER CLASSIFICATIONS: Customer Magazines

NJ NEUE JUSTIZ

737128G44-1540
Editorial: Lessingstr. 45, 09599 FREIBERG
Tel: 3731 392979 **Fax:** 3731 394043
Email: ring@rewi.tu-freiberg.de **Web site:** http://www.neue-justiz.de
Freq: Monthly; **Annual Sub.:** EUR 172,62; **Circ:** 1,900
Editor: Gerhard Ring
Profile: International publication about all aspects of the law.
Language(s): German
ADVERTISING RATES:
Full Page Mono .... EUR 1580
Full Page Colour .... EUR 2705
Mechanical Data: Type Area: 277 x 190 mm
Copy instructions: *Copy Date:* 30 days prior to publication
BUSINESS: LEGAL

NJW NEUE JURISTISCHE WOCHENSCHRIFT

737520G44-1580
Editorial: Beethovenstr. 7b, 60325 FRANKFURT
Tel: 69 7560910 **Fax:** 69 75609149
Email: redaktion@beck-frankfurt.de **Web site:** http://www.njw.de
Freq: Weekly; **Circ:** 38,278
Editor: Tobias Freudenberg; **Advertising Manager:** Fritz Lebherz
Profile: The NJW Neue Juristische Wochenschrift, is the leading legal magazine in Germany. With more than 100,000 readers, reaches more regularly NJW lawyers than any other title. It provides comprehensive, informed and week to date on all areas of law. The NJW has Germany's largest print jobs for lawyers, and online at www.beck-stellenmarkt.de. According to BGH NJW verdict is the must-read for all lawyers in Germany. No other legal journal reached its widest audience and more lawyers: Lawyers WLK 92%. Top figures for reader-to-bound: 90% of readers NJW confirm the high professional value. 92% regularly read NJW, i.e. at least 6 of 12 issues. 94% of the NJW readers collect all 50 issues per year. NJW 93% read for more than 5 years.
Language(s): German
ADVERTISING RATES:
Full Page Mono .... EUR 4210
Full Page Colour .... EUR 6040
Mechanical Data: Type Area: 260 x 186 mm, No. of Columns (Display): 4, Col Widths (Display): 43 mm
Supplement(s): NJW Spezial; ZRP Zeitschrift für Rechtspolitik
BUSINESS: LEGAL

NK NEUE KRIMINALPOLITIK

737136G32F-1147
Editorial: Olshausenstr. 75, 24098 KIEL
Tel: 431 8803575 **Fax:** 431 8807608
Email: mfrommel@email.uni-kiel.de **Web site:** http://www.neue-kriminalpolitik.de
Freq: Quarterly; **Annual Sub.:** EUR 95,67; **Circ:** 1,000
Editor: Monika Frommel
Profile: Police journal looking at new ways to solve crime with the involvement of social workers, criminologists, politicians, psychologists and the judicial system.
Language(s): German
ADVERTISING RATES:
Full Page Mono .... EUR 600
Full Page Colour .... EUR 1725
Mechanical Data: Type Area: 255 x 180 mm
BUSINESS: LOCAL GOVERNMENT, LEISURE & RECREATION: Police

NKW PARTNER FÜR ERSATZTEILE UND REPARATUR VON NUTZFAHRZEUGEN

737522G49D-3
Editorial: Hagmoos 6a, 87616 MARKTOBERDORF
Tel: 8342 9184190
Email: kuss@schluetersche.de **Web site:** http://www.nkw-partner.de
Freq: Quarterly; **Annual Sub.:** EUR 31,00; **Circ:** 21,456
Editor: Klaus Kuss; **Advertising Manager:** Christian Welc
Profile: The NKW partner is the only trade magazine that targets the editorial focus exclusively on the full range of commercial vehicle service market. The commercial vehicles produced in close cooperation partner with the General Association Automotive Trade Association (GVA) and the Working Group AK truck and trailer parts aftermarket. The trusting relationship with the group of commercial vehicles is also reflected in the address material used by the publisher. By the continuous synchronization with the address list of well-known commercial vehicle parts wholesalers of commercial vehicles have a partner address quality that is unique on the market. This will be supplemented to address root-bound workshops in the commercial vehicle service market. Topics The NKW partner provides information and background information on new products and technologies in the commercial vehicle manufacturers and workshop technology. - covers key issues by changing the entire range of commercial vehicle service market. - shows the hand of professional workshop reports practical installation tips. - reports on new trends, including repair of marketing tips. - points to new trends in the commercial vehicle parts market may lead to more sales. - reports about the supply partner of the commercial vehicle workshops.
Language(s): German
ADVERTISING RATES:
Full Page Mono .... EUR 3870
Full Page Colour .... EUR 4650

Mechanical Data: Type Area: 272 x 188 mm, No. of Columns (Display): 3, Col Widths (Display): 60 mm
Copy instructions: *Copy Date:* 21 days prior to publication
BUSINESS: TRANSPORT: Commercial Vehicles

NL NEUE LANDWIRTSCHAFT

737141G21A-2940
Editorial: Berliner Str. 112a, 13189 BERLIN
Tel: 30 2939740 **Fax:** 30 29397459
Email: dlv.berlin@dlv.de **Web site:** http://www.neuelandwirtschaft.de
Freq: Monthly; **Annual Sub.:** EUR 98,00; **Circ:** 13,100
Editor: Klaus Böhme; **Advertising Manager:** Thomas Herrmann
Profile: Magazine about agrarian management.
Language(s): German
ADVERTISING RATES:
Full Page Mono .... EUR 3402
Full Page Colour .... EUR 5346
Mechanical Data: Type Area: 270 x 184 mm, No. of Columns (Display): 4, Col Widths (Display): 43 mm
Copy instructions: *Copy Date:* 30 days prior to publication

NMZ NEUE MUSIKZEITUNG

737528G61-75
Editorial: Brunnstr. 23, 93053 REGENSBURG
Tel: 941 9459316 **Fax:** 941 9459350
Email: nmz@nmz.de **Web site:** http://www.nmz.de
Freq: 10 issues yearly; Free to qualifying individuals
Annual Sub.: EUR 41,80; **Circ:** 17,890
Editor: Andreas Kolb; **Advertising Manager:** Martina Wagner
Profile: The nmz neue musikzeitung for almost 60 years for independent quality music journalism in the print area. Since 1997, a presence with an online version on the Internet, the Germany's largest music trade magazine for a full relaunch in 2008 online-date significant to national opera premieres, concert events and premieres, CD, sheet music and new books and cultural policy and music education issues. By advertising on our sites, you only reach the target audience you desire: a qualified audience, which operates more than 90 percent of music professionals and regularly attends concerts and festivals, an exceptionally high proportion of opinion leaders and opinion leaders in media, cultural and political institutions, Music schools and music industry. The cultural information center of power supplied to the town every hour with the latest news from the world of music and cultural policy. We always attach importance to * Independent reporting * In-depth background information * Conflicting views * comments, analyze, question and polarize.
Language(s): German
Readership: Aimed at people working professionally with music.
ADVERTISING RATES:
Full Page Mono .... EUR 2922
Full Page Colour .... EUR 4294
Mechanical Data: Type Area: 415 x 285 mm, No. of Columns (Display): 5, Col Widths (Display): 53 mm
Copy instructions: *Copy Date:* 10 days prior to publication
BUSINESS: MUSIC TRADE

NNA BERICHTE

737529G57-1560
Editorial: Hof Möhr, 29640 SCHNEVERDINGEN
Tel: 5199 98938 **Fax:** 5199 98946
Email: nna@nna.niedersachsen.de **Web site:** http://www.nna.de
Freq: Annual; **Circ:** 500
Editor: Renate Strohschneider
Profile: Magazine of the Toepfer Akademie für Naturschutz.
Language(s): English; German

NORD ANZEIGER

737588G72-9920
Editorial: Bert-Brecht-Str. 29, 45128 ESSEN
Tel: 201 8042879 **Fax:** 201 8041576
Email: redaktion@nordanzeiger-essen.de **Web site:** http://www.lokalkompass.de/essen-nord
Freq: 104 issues yearly; **Cover Price:** Free; **Circ:** 71,600
Editor: Sabine Pfeffer; **Advertising Manager:** Lars Staehler
Profile: Advertising journal (house-to-house) concentrating on local stories.
Language(s): German
ADVERTISING RATES:
Full Page Mono .... EUR 4860
Full Page Colour .... EUR 6561
Mechanical Data: Type Area: 445 x 315 mm, No. of Columns (Display): 7, Col Widths (Display): 42 mm
Copy instructions: *Copy Date:* 2 days prior to publication
Supplement(s): Allee-Center Aktuell
LOCAL NEWSPAPERS

NORD VERKEHR

1895053G49A-2463
Editorial: Bullerdeich 36, 20537 HAMBURG
Tel: 40 25470170 **Fax:** 40 25470175
Email: info@vshhamburg.de **Web site:** http://www.vshhamburg.de
Freq: 10 issues yearly; **Circ:** 1,100
Editor: Frank Wylezol
Profile: Magazine for the transport business.
Language(s): German
ADVERTISING RATES:
Full Page Mono .... EUR 590
Full Page Colour .... EUR 590

Mechanical Data: Type Area: 262 x 183 mm, No. of Columns (Display): 3, Col Widths (Display): 58 mm
Copy instructions: *Copy Date:* 26 days prior to publication

NORDBAYERISCHE NACHRICHTEN

737591G67B-10600
Editorial: Marienstr. 9, 90402 NÜRNBERG
Tel: 911 2160 **Fax:** 911 2162432
Web site: http://www.nuernberger-nachrichten.de
Freq: 312 issues yearly; **Circ:** 273,680
Profile: Regional daily newspaper with news on politics, economy, culture, sports, travel, technology, etc.
Language(s): German
ADVERTISING RATES:
SCC .... EUR 291,60
Mechanical Data: No. of Columns (Display): 6, Col Widths (Display): 45 mm
Copy instructions: *Copy Date:* 2 days prior to publication
Supplement(s): sechs+sechzig
REGIONAL DAILY & SUNDAY NEWSPAPERS: Regional Daily Newspapers

---

NORDBAYERISCHER KURIER

737592G67B-10620
Editorial: Theodor-Schmidt-Str. 17, 95448 BAYREUTH **Tel:** 921 500170 **Fax:** 921 500180
Email: redaktion@kurier.tmt.de **Web site:** http://www.nordbayerischer-kurier.de
Freq: 312 issues yearly; **Annual Sub.:** EUR 26,20; **Circ:** 35,530
Advertising Manager: Andreas Weiss
Profile: Daily newspaper with regional news and a local sports section. Facebook: http://www.facebook.com/pages/Bayreuth-TV/139288517485 Twitter: http://twitter.com/kurier_online This Outlet offers RSS (Really Simple Syndication).
Language(s): German
ADVERTISING RATES:
SCC .... EUR 50,10
Mechanical Data: Type Area: 430 x 282 mm, No. of Columns (Display): 6, Col Widths (Display): 45 mm
Copy instructions: *Copy Date:* 1 day prior to publication
Supplement(s): Kinder-Kurier; modernisieren
REGIONAL DAILY & SUNDAY NEWSPAPERS: Regional Daily Newspapers

---

NORDBAYERN.DE

1704549G67B-16759
Editorial: Marienstr. 9, 90402 NÜRNBERG
Tel: 911 2160 **Fax:** 911 2162989
Email: kontakt@nordbayern.de **Web site:** http://www.nordbayern.de
Freq: Daily; **Cover Price:** Paid; **Circ:** 2,308,585 Unique Users
Editor: Thomas Gerlach; **Advertising Manager:** Ute Rupprecht
Profile: Online news service of Nuremberg with its associated local newspapers and the Nürnberger Zeitung Facebook: http://www.facebook.com/nordbayern.de This Outlet offers RSS (Really Simple Syndication).
Language(s): German
REGIONAL DAILY & SUNDAY NEWSPAPERS: Regional Daily Newspapers

---

DER NORD-BERLINER

737593G72-9932
Editorial: Hermsdorfer Damm 149, 13467 BERLIN
Tel: 30 41909140 **Fax:** 30 41909135
Email: redaktion@nord-berliner.de **Web site:** http://www.nord-berliner.de
Freq: Weekly; **Annual Sub.:** EUR 25,00; **Circ:** 32,000
Editor: Michael Fischer; **Advertising Manager:** Gerhard Jarosch
Profile: Regional weekly newspaper with news on politics, economy, culture, sports, travel, technology, etc. to the north of Berlin and the northern hinterland (District Oberhavel).
Language(s): German
ADVERTISING RATES:
SCC .... EUR 21,50
Mechanical Data: Type Area: 410 x 278 mm, No. of Columns (Display): 6, Col Widths (Display): 43 mm
Copy instructions: *Copy Date:* 2 days prior to publication
LOCAL NEWSPAPERS

NORDDEUTSCHE GARTENBAU-MITTEILUNGEN

737595G26D-6
Editorial: Brennerhof 121, 22113 HAMBURG
Tel: 40 73601590 **Fax:** 40 787687
Email: info@gartenbauverband-nord.de **Web site:** http://www.wifoeg.de
Freq: 6 issues yearly; Free to qualifying individuals
Annual Sub.: EUR 15,00; **Circ:** 1,500
Editor: Paul Helle; **Advertising Manager:** Ingeborg Polomski
Profile: Magazine about horticulture and gardening in North Germany.
Language(s): German
Readership: Aimed at gardeners and professionals within the sector.
ADVERTISING RATES:
Full Page Mono .... EUR 970
Full Page Colour .... EUR 1450

Mechanical Data: Type Area: 257 x 185 mm, No. of Columns (Display): 4, Col Widths (Display): 45 mm
Copy instructions: *Copy Date:* 10 days prior to publication
BUSINESS: GARDEN TRADE: Garden Trade Horticulture

DIE NORDDEUTSCHE HAUSBESITZER ZEITUNG

737596G74K-1180
Editorial: Sophienblatt 3, 24103 KIEL
Tel: 431 6636116 **Fax:** 431 6636199
Email: info@nhz-online.de **Web site:** http://www.nhz-online.de
Freq: Monthly; Free to qualifying individuals
Annual Sub.: EUR 20,00; **Circ:** 63,058
Editor: Jürgen Kuhrt
Profile: In the 105th Year published Norddeutsche Hausbesitzer Zeitung is an organ of the Association of Schleswig-Holstein-House, housing and land-owners Association. In the newspaper are all matters of home, housing and real property treated, they will be sent to members for free.
Language(s): German
ADVERTISING RATES:
Full Page Mono .... EUR 6063
Full Page Colour .... EUR 9398
Mechanical Data: Type Area: 430 x 282 mm, No. of Columns (Display): 6, Col Widths (Display): 45 mm
Official Journal of: Organ d. LV Schleswig-Holstein d. Haus-, Wohnungs- u. Grundeigentümer e.V.
CONSUMER: WOMEN'S INTEREST CONSUMER MAGAZINES: Home Purchase

NORDDEUTSCHE HOTEL- UND GASTSTÄTTEN NACHRICHTEN

737597G11A-1240
Editorial: Fichtestr. 18, 30625 HANNOVER
Tel: 511 554048 **Fax:** 511 554040
Email: info@kwie.de **Web site:** http://www.nhgn.de
Freq: Monthly; **Circ:** 8,000
Editor: Stephan Kwiecinski
Profile: Magazine covering news about hotels and restaurants in Northern Germany.
Language(s): German
Readership: Aimed at decision makers in the hotel and gastronomy trade.
ADVERTISING RATES:
Full Page Mono .... EUR 3450
Full Page Colour .... EUR 6200
Mechanical Data: Type Area: 425 x 282 mm, No. of Columns (Display): 6, Col Widths (Display): 43 mm
Official Journal of: Organ d. Dt. Hotel- u. Gaststättenverb., LV Niedersachsen
BUSINESS: CATERING: Catering, Hotels & Restaurants

NORDDEUTSCHE NEUESTE NACHRICHTEN

737599G67B-10640
Editorial: Bergstr. 10, 18057 ROSTOCK
Tel: 381 491168706 **Fax:** 381 491168705
Email: nnn@nnn.de **Web site:** http://www.nnn.de
Freq: 312 issues yearly; **Circ:** 8,940
Editor: Dietmar Tahn; **Advertising Manager:** Bernd Bleitzhofer
Profile: Daily newspaper with regional news and a local sports section. Facebook: http://www.facebook.com/nnnonline This Outlet offers RSS (Really Simple Syndication).
Language(s): German
ADVERTISING RATES:
SCC .... EUR 75,50
Mechanical Data: Type Area: 480 x 325 mm, No. of Columns (Display): 7, Col Widths (Display): 45 mm
Copy instructions: *Copy Date:* 1 day prior to publication
Supplement(s): prisma
REGIONAL DAILY & SUNDAY NEWSPAPERS: Regional Daily Newspapers

---

NORDDEUTSCHE RUNDSCHAU

737604G67B-10660
Editorial: Nikolaistr. 7, 24937 FLENSBURG
Tel: 461 8080 **Fax:** 461 8081058
Email: redaktion@shz.de **Web site:** http://www.shz.de
Freq: 312 issues yearly; **Circ:** 22,618
Advertising Manager: Ingeborg Schwarz
Profile: Under the title "Königlich privilegiertes gemeinnütziges unterhaltendes Wochenblatt für Itzehoe und Umgebung" was published in 1817 for the first time the precursor of today's "Norddeutsche Rundschau". After turbulent times during the world wars, the newspaper was the first on 20 August 1949 spread among its current title. Facebook: http://www.facebook.com/shzonline Twitter: http://twitter.com/shz_de This Outlet offers RSS (Really Simple Syndication).
Language(s): German
ADVERTISING RATES:
SCC .... EUR 75,60
Mechanical Data: Type Area: 480 x 325 mm, No. of Columns (Display): 7, Col Widths (Display): 45 mm
Copy instructions: *Copy Date:* 1 day prior to publication
Supplement(s): nordisch gesund; Schleswig-Holstein Journal; tv magazin
REGIONAL DAILY & SUNDAY NEWSPAPERS: Regional Daily Newspapers

DER NORDDEUTSCHE SCHÜTZE

737605G75F-54
Editorial: Schulze-Delitzsch-Str. 35, 30938 BURGWEDEL **Tel:** 5139 899936 **Fax:** 5139 899950
Email: redaktion.nds@winkler-stenzel.de **Web site:** http://www.winkler-stenzel.de
Freq: Monthly; **Annual Sub.:** EUR 32,00; **Circ:** 5,650
Editor: Andreas Winkler; **Advertising Manager:** Kerstin Schökel
Profile: Official publication of North-German Shooters Association.
Language(s): German
ADVERTISING RATES:
Full Page Mono .... EUR 121
Full Page Colour .... EUR 175
Mechanical Data: Type Area: 270 x 185 mm, No. of Columns (Display): 4, Col Widths (Display): 44 mm
Copy instructions: *Copy Date:* 20 days prior to publication
Official Journal of: Organ d. norddt. Landesverbände im Dt. Schützenbund
CONSUMER: SPORT: Shooting

NORDDEUTSCHES HANDWERK

737606G63-11
Editorial: Hans-Böckler-Allee 7, 30173 HANNOVER
Tel: 511 85502455 **Fax:** 511 85502403
Email: nh.redaktion@schluetersche.de **Web site:** http://www.handwerk.com
Freq: 21 issues yearly; Free to qualifying individuals
Annual Sub.: EUR 45,50; **Circ:** 94,481
Editor: Irmke Frömling; **Advertising Manager:** Andreas Dirschauer
Profile: The Norddeutsches Handwerk, is the business newspaper of the chambers in Lower Saxony and Magdeburg. Whether background reports, technical information and specific tips for the craftsmen. The Norddeutsches Handwerk brings benefit-oriented texts to the point. Readers are Owner of the establishment, cooperating partners, managing directors and employed master. 86% of our readers make their own or with colleagues investment decisions. The Norddeutsches Handwerk offers you one of the highest circulations of craft papers in Germany: more than 95 000 copies. 100 percent presence in Lower Saxony and in Board District Madgeburg. 21 issues a year guarantee timeliness and targeting the decision makers. Facebook: http://www.facebook.com/home.php.
Language(s): German
ADVERTISING RATES:
Full Page Mono .... EUR 11217
Full Page Colour .... EUR 22158
Mechanical Data: Type Area: 475 x 325 mm, No. of Columns (Display): 6, Col Widths (Display): 50 mm
Copy instructions: *Copy Date:* 14 days prior to publication
BUSINESS: REGIONAL BUSINESS

NORDERNEYER BADEZEITUNG

737610G67B-10680
Editorial: Maiburger Str. 8, 26789 LEER
Tel: 491 97900 **Fax:** 491 9790201
Email: redaktion@ostfriesen-zeitung.de **Web site:** http://www.ostfriesen-zeitung.de
Freq: 312 issues yearly; **Circ:** 1,585
Advertising Manager: Uwe Boden
Profile: Daily newspaper with regional news and a local sports section.
Language(s): German
ADVERTISING RATES:
SCC .... EUR 26,00
Mechanical Data: Type Area: 420 x 282 mm, No. of Columns (Display): 6, Col Widths (Display): 43 mm
Copy instructions: *Copy Date:* 2 days prior to publication
REGIONAL DAILY & SUNDAY NEWSPAPERS: Regional Daily Newspapers

---

NORDFRIESLAND PALETTE

737616G72-9952
Editorial: Norderstr. 22, 25813 HUSUM
Tel: 4841 835666 **Fax:** 4841 835670
Email: redaktion-nf@nf-palette.de **Web site:** http://www.nf-palette.de
Freq: Weekly; **Cover Price:** Free; **Circ:** 40,200
Editor: Marion Laß
Profile: Advertising journal (house-to-house) concentrating on local stories.
Language(s): German
ADVERTISING RATES:
Full Page Mono .... EUR 5591
Full Page Colour .... EUR 8114
Mechanical Data: Type Area: 487 x 325 mm, No. of Columns (Display): 7, Col Widths (Display): 44 mm
Copy instructions: *Copy Date:* 2 days prior to publication
LOCAL NEWSPAPERS

NORDFRIESLAND TAGEBLATT

737617G67B-10700
Editorial: Nikolaistr. 7, 24937 FLENSBURG
Tel: 461 8080 **Fax:** 461 8081058
Email: redaktion@shz.de **Web site:** http://www.shz.de
Freq: 312 issues yearly; **Circ:** 8,896
Advertising Manager: Ingeborg Schwarz
Profile: The history of the various predecessors of the "Nordfriesland Tageblatt" can be traced back to 1879. In its present form it is the newspaper since 1970. The "Nordfriesland Tageblatt" is mainly distributed in the continental part of the old district Südtondern. Facebook: http://www.facebook.com/

shzonline Twitter: http://twitter.com/shz_de This
Outlet offers RSS (Really Simple Syndication).
Language(s): German
ADVERTISING RATES:
SCC .... EUR 55,60
Mechanical Data: Type Area: 480 x 325 mm, No. of
Columns (Display): 7, Col Widths (Display): 45 mm
Copy instructions: *Copy Date:* 1 day prior to
publication
Supplement(s): nordisch gesund; Schleswig-Holstein
Journal; tv magazin
**REGIONAL DAILY & SUNDAY NEWSPAPERS:
Regional Daily Newspapers**

NORDIC SPORTS MAGAZIN
742038G75J-150
Editorial: Heerstr. 5, 58540 MEINERZHAGEN
Tel: 2354 77990 **Fax:** 2354 779977
Email: a.hemmersbach@sportcombi.de **Web site:**
http://www.nordicsports.de
Freq: 6 issues yearly; **Annual Sub.:** EUR 24,30; **Circ:**
42,339
Editor: Arnd Hemmersbach; **Advertising Manager:**
Erik Hornung
Profile: Journal of Cross-country skiing, biathlon, trail
running and adventure racing.
Language(s): German
Readership: Aimed at skiers of all levels and
enthusiasts.
ADVERTISING RATES:
Full Page Mono .... EUR 3292
Full Page Colour .... EUR 5488
Mechanical Data: Type Area: 250 x 180 mm, No. of
Columns (Display): 4, Col Widths (Display): 41 mm
Copy instructions: *Copy Date:* 30 days prior to
publication
CONSUMER: SPORT: Athletics

NORDIS
737624G89A-11534
Editorial: Maxstr. 64, 45127 ESSEN **Tel:** 201 872290
Fax: 201 8942511
Email: verlag@nordis.com **Web site:** http://www.
skandinavien.de
Freq: 6 issues yearly; Free to qualifying individuals
Annual Sub.: EUR 28,00; **Circ:** 30,947
Editor: Lutz Stickeln
Profile: Northern Europe is increasingly becoming
the center of attention. There are good reasons:
increased political and economic integration,
pacemaker function in many areas, powerful trading
partner, a gateway to neighboring regions of
northwestern Russia and the Baltic states. Last but
not least, more and more central European feel of its
many natural beauties and attracted a wealth of
attractive destinations. The result: The need to be
knowledgeable and informed response to North
Europe, is increasing! Nordis - The Northern
European magazine that satisfies by far the largest
and most prestigious special-interest magazine for
North European issues on the German market, this
need! With current affairs, interviews and travel
accounts, carefully researched background stories,
with solid information and a clear layout inspired
Nordis - The Northern European magazine a wide
readership of Scandinavia fans and Northern Europe-
enthusiast: Individual and group travelers, families,
nature lovers, outdoor fans and lovers of culture.
Their feature is that they are traveling and
communicative, high income and have an above-
average buying interest in Scandinavian products.
Language(s): German
Readership: Aimed at tourists.
ADVERTISING RATES:
Full Page Mono .... EUR 2190
Full Page Colour .... EUR 3790
Mechanical Data: Type Area: 262 x 178 mm, No. of
Columns (Display): 4, Col Widths (Display): 41 mm
Copy instructions: *Copy Date:* 35 days prior to
publication
Supplement(s): DNF-Magazin
CONSUMER: HOLIDAYS & TRAVEL: Travel

NORD-KURIER
737626G1M-4
Editorial: Lornsenstr. 48, 24105 KIEL
Tel: 431 563065 **Fax:** 431 567637
Email: mail@nord-kurier.de **Web site:** http://www.
nord-kurier.de
Freq: 9 issues yearly; **Circ:** 23,500
Editor: Roger H. Müller
Profile: Magazine of the Federal taxpayers in
Hamburg, Schleswig-Holstein and Mecklenburg-
Vorpommern.
Language(s): German
BUSINESS: FINANCE & ECONOMICS: Taxation

NORDKURIER
737625G67B-10720
Editorial: Friedrich-Engels-Ring 29, 17033
NEUBRANDENBURG **Tel:** 395 45750
Fax: 395 4575550
Email: redaktion@nordkurier.de **Web site:** http://
www.nordkurier.de
Freq: 312 issues yearly; **Circ:** 88,203
Editor: Michael Seidel; **Advertising Manager:**
Carsten Kottwitz
Profile: Regional daily newspaper covering politics,
economics, sport, travel and technology. Facebook:
http://www.facebook.com/Nordkurier Twitter: http://
twitter.com/nordkurier This Outlet offers RSS (Really
Simple Syndication).
Language(s): German
ADVERTISING RATES:
SCC .... EUR 155,40
Mechanical Data: Type Area: 480 x 324 mm, No. of
Columns (Display): 7, Col Widths (Display): 45 mm
Copy instructions: *Copy Date:* 2 days prior to
publication
Supplement(s): prisma
**REGIONAL DAILY & SUNDAY NEWSPAPERS:
Regional Daily Newspapers**

NORDÖR ZEITSCHRIFT FÜR ÖFFENTLICHES RECHT IN NORDDEUTSCHLAND
737633G44-3125
Editorial: Schlüterstr. 28, 20149 HAMBURG
Tel: 40 428384965 **Fax:** 40 428385670
Email: redaktion@nordoer.de **Web site:** http://www.
nordoer.de
Freq: Monthly; **Annual Sub.:** EUR 198,04; **Circ:** 800
Editor: Ulrich Ramsauer
Profile: Magazine containing reports of recent legal
judgements in the area of provincial legislation.
Includes information about administration and law
courts.
Language(s): German
Readership: Read by judges, legal administrators
and law students.
ADVERTISING RATES:
Full Page Mono .... EUR 540
Full Page Colour .... EUR 1665
Mechanical Data: Col Widths (Display): 86 mm, Type
Area: 257 x 176 mm, No. of Columns (Display): 2
Copy instructions: *Copy Date:* 45 days prior to
publication
BUSINESS: LEGAL

NORDSÄCHSISCHER WOCHENKURIER - AUSG. EILENBURG
725989G72-3420
Editorial: Gerberstr. 15, 04105 LEIPZIG
Tel: 341 9881433 **Fax:** 341 9800541
Email: marliesdaeberitz@lwk-verlag.de **Web site:**
http://www.wochenkurier.info
Freq: Weekly; **Cover Price:** Free; **Circ:** 17,620
Editor: Marlies Däberitz; **Advertising Manager:** Sina
Häse
Profile: Advertising journal (house-to-house)
concentrating on local stories.
Language(s): German
ADVERTISING RATES:
Full Page Mono .... EUR 2378
Full Page Colour .... EUR 3330
Mechanical Data: Type Area: 430 x 290 mm, No. of
Columns (Display): 7, Col Widths (Display): 38 mm
Copy instructions: *Copy Date:* 3 days prior to
publication
LOCAL NEWSPAPERS

NORDSÄCHSISCHER WOCHENKURIER - AUSG. OSCHATZ
738358G72-10288
Editorial: Gerberstr. 15, 04105 LEIPZIG
Tel: 341 9881433 **Fax:** 341 9800541
Email: marliesdaeberitz@lwk-verlag.de **Web site:**
http://www.wochenkurier.info
Freq: Weekly; **Cover Price:** Free; **Circ:** 20,251
Editor: Marlies Däberitz; **Advertising Manager:** Sina
Häse
Profile: Advertising journal (house-to-house)
concentrating on local stories.
Language(s): German
ADVERTISING RATES:
Full Page Mono .... EUR 2408
Full Page Colour .... EUR 3372
Mechanical Data: Type Area: 430 x 290 mm, No. of
Columns (Display): 7, Col Widths (Display): 38 mm
Copy instructions: *Copy Date:* 3 days prior to
publication
LOCAL NEWSPAPERS

NORDSÄCHSISCHER WOCHENKURIER - AUSG. TORGAU
745205G72-14380
Editorial: Gerberstr. 15, 04105 LEIPZIG
Tel: 341 9881433 **Fax:** 341 9800541
Email: marliesdaeberitz@lwk-verlag.de **Web site:**
http://www.wochenkurier.info
Freq: Weekly; **Cover Price:** Free; **Circ:** 23,658
Editor: Marlies Däberitz; **Advertising Manager:** Sina
Häse
Profile: Advertising journal (house-to-house)
concentrating on local stories.
Language(s): German
ADVERTISING RATES:
Full Page Mono .... EUR 2559
Full Page Colour .... EUR 3582
Mechanical Data: Type Area: 430 x 290 mm, No. of
Columns (Display): 7, Col Widths (Display): 38 mm
Copy instructions: *Copy Date:* 3 days prior to
publication
LOCAL NEWSPAPERS

NORDSEE* URLAUBSMAGAZIN
1819888G89A-12365
Editorial: Zingel 5, 25813 HUSUM **Tel:** 4841 897575
Fax: 4841 4843
Email: info@nordseetourismus.de **Web site:** http://
www.nordseetourismus.de
Freq: Annual; **Cover Price:** Free; **Circ:** 200,000
Editor: Andrea Simons; **Advertising Manager:**
Sandra Milke
Profile: Mut flads safaris, endless beaches, white,
green or colorful, coastal delights and treasures from
the sea - the nordsee* urlaubsmagazin makes with
fascinating features in the mood for holiday.
Language(s): German

NORDSEE-HEILBAD BÜSUM URLAUBSMAGAZIN
1648495G89A-11863
Editorial: Südstrand 11, 25761 BÜSUM
Tel: 4834 9090 **Fax:** 4834 909166
Email: info@buesum.de **Web site:** http://www.
buesum.de
Freq: Annual; **Cover Price:** Free; **Circ:** 70,000
Editor: Malte Keller
Profile: Magazine for visitors and citizens of the
community of Büsum.
Language(s): German
ADVERTISING RATES:
Full Page Mono .... EUR 2390
Full Page Colour .... EUR 2812
Mechanical Data: Type Area: 265 x 197 mm
Copy instructions: *Copy Date:* 40 days prior to
publication

NORDSEE-ZEITUNG
737639G67B-10740
Editorial: Hafenstr. 140, 27576 BREMERHAVEN
Tel: 471 5970 **Fax:** 471 597314
Email: nzbremerhaven@nordsee-zeitung.de **Web
site:** http://www.nordsee-zeitung.de
Freq: 312 issues yearly; **Circ:** 61,876
Advertising Manager: Thomas Grupe
Profile: Daily newspaper with regional news and a
local sports section. Twitter: http://twitter.com/
nordseezeitung This Outlet offers RSS (Really Simple
Syndication).
Language(s): German
ADVERTISING RATES:
SCC .... EUR 149,00
Mechanical Data: Type Area: 487 x 324 mm, No. of
Columns (Display): 7, Col Widths (Display): 45 mm
Copy instructions: *Copy Date:* 1 day prior to
publication
Supplement(s): Cuxjournal; Ferienjournal;
Niederdeutsches Heimatblatt
**REGIONAL DAILY & SUNDAY NEWSPAPERS:
Regional Daily Newspapers**

NORDWEST EXPRESS
737646G72-9988
Editorial: Johann-Stelling-Str. 6, 19205
GADEBUSCH **Tel:** 3886 38388227
Fax: 3886 38388225
Email: nordwest-express@svz.de
Freq: Weekly; **Cover Price:** Free; **Circ:** 11,238
Editor: Mario Kuska; **Advertising Manager:** Dagmar
Albertsen
Profile: Advertising journal (house-to-house)
concentrating on local stories.
Language(s): German
ADVERTISING RATES:
Full Page Mono .... EUR 2420
Full Page Colour .... EUR 3159
Mechanical Data: Type Area: 480 x 325 mm, No. of
Columns (Display): 7, Col Widths (Display): 45 mm
Copy instructions: *Copy Date:* 3 days prior to
publication
LOCAL NEWSPAPERS

NORDWEST ZEITUNG
737648G67B-10760
Editorial: Peterstr. 28, 26121 OLDENBURG
Tel: 441 998801 **Fax:** 441 99882029
Email: red.oldenburg@nordwest-zeitung.de **Web
site:** http://www.nwzonline.de
Freq: 312 issues yearly; **Circ:** 123,447
Editor: Rolf Seelheim; **News Editor:** Herrmann
Gröblinghoff; **Advertising Manager:** Bodo M. Bauer
Profile: Regional daily newspaper covering politics,
economics, culture, sports, travel and technology.
Language(s): German
ADVERTISING RATES:
SCC .... EUR 148,40
Mechanical Data: Type Area: 420 x 282 mm, No. of
Columns (Display): 6, Col Widths (Display): 45 mm
Copy instructions: *Copy Date:* 2 days prior to
publication
Supplement(s): Abenteuer familie; Einfach tierisch...;
Faszination Reitsport; Kinder-NWZ; Love is in the air;
NWZ Inside; rtv; Spielzeit
**REGIONAL DAILY & SUNDAY NEWSPAPERS:
Regional Daily Newspapers**

NORTHEIMER NEUESTE NACHRICHTEN
730356G67B-7200
Editorial: Frankfurter Str. 168, 34121 KASSEL
Tel: 561 20300 **Fax:** 561 2032406
Email: info@hna.de **Web site:** http://www.hna.de
Freq: 312 issues yearly; **Circ:** 15,881
Advertising Manager: Andrea Schaller-Öller
Profile: Regional daily newspaper with news on
politics, economy, culture, sports, travel, technology,
etc. The Northeimer Neueste Nachrichten is a local
issue of HNA Hessische/Niedersächsische
Allgemeine. Twitter: http://twitter.com/hna_online
This Outlet offers RSS (Really Simple Syndication).
Language(s): German
ADVERTISING RATES:
SCC .... EUR 40,00
Mechanical Data: Type Area: 430 x 285 mm, No. of
Columns (Display): 6, Col Widths (Display): 45 mm
Copy instructions: *Copy Date:* 2 days prior to
publication
**REGIONAL DAILY & SUNDAY NEWSPAPERS:
Regional Daily Newspapers**

DER NOTARZT
737659G56P-2
Editorial: Sandweg 11, 97078 WÜRZBURG
Tel: 931 284770 **Fax:** 931 284746
Email: sefrin@agbn.de **Web site:** http://www.thieme.
de/notarzt
Freq: 6 issues yearly; Free to qualifying individuals
Annual Sub.: EUR 138,90; **Circ:** 11,100
Editor: Peter Sefrin
Profile: Provide you with "Der Notarzt" for your
regular emergency medical training: Knowledge up to
date: Case reports, original research and CME will
teach you the latest developments in emergency
medicine Practical tips on the best care and transport
of emergency patients Presentation of
interdisciplinary emergency situations and border
areas of emergency medicine ideal for your training:
vivid graphics EKG Examples Emergency
Pharmacology practical: Interesting case studies
from the everyday designated experts Regular
training: Earn 3 CME points with every issue. Also:
information about emergency medicine:
Comprehensive professional political news current
Releases Book reviews and conferences.
Language(s): German
Readership: Aimed at doctors on emergency call.
ADVERTISING RATES:
Full Page Mono .... EUR 2480
Full Page Colour .... EUR 3980
Mechanical Data: Type Area: 248 x 175 mm, No. of
Columns (Display): 3, Col Widths (Display): 55 mm
Official Journal of: Organ d. Bundesvereinigung d.
ArGe Notärzte Deutschlands u. d. Dt.
Interdisziplinären Vereinigung f. Intensiv- u.
Notfallmedizin
**BUSINESS: HEALTH & MEDICAL: Casualty &
Emergency**

NOTBZ
737660G44-3126
Editorial: Gustav-Heinemann-Ufer 58, 50968 KÖLN
Tel: 221 9373801 **Fax:** 221 93738900
Email: notbz@laendernotarkasse.de **Web site:** http://
www.notbz.de
Freq: Monthly; **Annual Sub.:** EUR 176,90; **Circ:** 1,110
Editor: Dirk-Ulrich Otto; **Advertising Manager:**
Thorsten Deuse
Profile: Magazine for the notaries' associations of
Brandenburg, Sachsen, Sachsen-Anhalt,
Mecklenburg and Thüringen.
Language(s): German
Readership: Read by lawyers and notaries.
ADVERTISING RATES:
Full Page Mono .... EUR 750
Full Page Colour .... EUR 1313
Mechanical Data: Type Area: 260 x 180 mm, No. of
Columns (Display): 2, Col Widths (Display): 88 mm
BUSINESS: LEGAL

NOTFALL + RETTUNGSMEDIZIN
737666G56P-3
Editorial: Tiergartenstr. 17, 69121 HEIDELBERG
Tel: 6221 4878218 **Fax:** 6221 48768218
Email: michal.baenfer@springer.com **Web site:**
http://www.springermedizin.de
Freq: 8 issues yearly; **Annual Sub.:** EUR 161,00;
Circ: 4,000
Advertising Manager: Odette Thomßen
Profile: "Notfall + Rettungsmedizin" presents its
interdisciplinary focus on preclinical and in-hospital
emergency care, the quality of management and
emergency medical services research. Contents:
Main topic with state-of-the-art overviews, guidelines,
quality management, case reports, Journal Club,
CME / Continuing Education - certified training, notes
of the GRC and ARC.
Language(s): German
ADVERTISING RATES:
Full Page Mono .... EUR 1850
Full Page Colour .... EUR 2890
Mechanical Data: Type Area: 240 x 174 mm
Official Journal of: Organ d. Dt. Interdisziplinäre
Vereinigung f. Intensiv- u. Notfallmedizin, d. ArGe
Südwestdt. Notärzte, d. Dt. Rat f. Wiederbelebung -
German Resuscitation Council u. d. Österr. Rat f.
Wiederbelebung - Austrian Resuscitation Council
**BUSINESS: HEALTH & MEDICAL: Casualty &
Emergency**

NOTFALLMEDIZIN UP2DATE
1794363G56A-11448
Editorial: Arnold-Heller-Str. 3, 24105 KIEL
Tel: 431 5977000 **Fax:** 431 59742018
Email: vv@uk-sh.de **Web site:** http://www.thieme.de/
fz/notfall-u2d
Freq: Quarterly; **Annual Sub.:** EUR 155,40; **Circ:**
2,980
Editor: Jens Scholz
Profile: Successful action in emergency medicine is
not an accident. It is the product faster decisions,
and resolute action. The Basics: First-class expertise.
Notfallmedizin up2date provides you with
professional training and expert information - up to
date, practical, reliable. Four times a year to-date and
reliable training in emergency medicine and rescue
service. Practice relevant topics reader-friendly
brought to the point. Date as a professional journal,
clearly structured like a textbook.
Language(s): German
ADVERTISING RATES:
Full Page Mono .... EUR 2220
Full Page Colour .... EUR 3420

Mechanical Data: Type Area: 248 x 175 mm

NOVUM
737693G2A-3580
Editorial: Dietlindenstr. 18, 80802 MÜNCHEN
Tel: 89 36888180 **Fax:** 89 36888181
Email: schulz@novumnet.de **Web site:** http://www.novumnet.de
Freq: Monthly; **Annual Sub.:** EUR 120,00; **Circ:** 9,520
Editor: Bettina Schulz
Profile: Journal focusing on design and communication. Includes a section called Novum Plus, providing information on technology within the field.
Language(s): English; German
ADVERTISING RATES:
Full Page Colour .... EUR 3720
Mechanical Data: Type Area: 271 x 205 mm, No. of Columns (Display): 4, Col Widths (Display): 47 mm
BUSINESS: COMMUNICATIONS, ADVERTISING & MARKETING

DIE NRW NACHRICHTEN
1799461G14A-9989
Editorial: Postfach 140155, 40071 DÜSSELDORF
Tel: 211 9917526 **Fax:** 211 9917550
Email: presse@steuerzahler-nrw.de **Web site:** http://www.steuerzahler-nrw.de
Freq: 11 issues yearly; **Circ:** 80,300
Editor: Bärbel Hildebrand
Profile: News from the fiscal policy, tax tips, reports on detected or prevented waste cases, the financial position of municipalities in Nordrhein-Westfalen. Details of the League of Taxpayers Nordrhein-Westfalen e V. It is a supplement of the journal "Der Steuerzahler".
Language(s): German
Supplement to: Der Steuerzahler

NRW-INFO
1788734G57-2806
Editorial: Merowingerstr. 88, 40225 DÜSSELDORF
Tel: 211 3020050 **Fax:** 211 30200526
Email: dirk.jansen@bund.net **Web site:** http://www.bund-nrw.de
Freq: Quarterly; **Circ:** 17,000
Editor: Dirk Jansen
Profile: Membermagazine from the German Association for Environment and Nature Protection.
Language(s): German

NRW.JETZT
1936775G14A-10405
Editorial: Max-Planck-Str. 6, 50858 KÖLN
Tel: 2234 91177662 **Fax:** 2234 91177667
Email: klaus.kelle@nrwjetzt.de **Web site:** http://www.nrwjetzt.de
Freq: 10 issues yearly; **Annual Sub.:** EUR 36,00; **Circ:** 21,000
Editor: Klaus Kelle
Profile: Magazine for decision makers in Nordrhein-Westfalen. It appears monthly and reports on interesting topics from business, politics, culture and way of life in Nordrhein-Westfalen. We let people have their say, have something to say. We come to issues on which it is worth thinking about. And we will show areas in which this state is very front or on the way to the top. Recipient: Members, managers, entrepreneurs, mayors, union, federation officials and chairman of large organizations from all sectors of public life. Facebook: http://www.facebook.com/pages/NRWjetzt/158445247805.
Language(s): German
ADVERTISING RATES:
Full Page Mono .... EUR 4800
Full Page Colour .... EUR 4800
Mechanical Data: Type Area: 245 x 180 mm, No. of Columns (Display): 3, Col Widths (Display): 57 mm
Copy instructions: *Copy Date:* 8 days prior to publication

NRZ NEUE RHEIN ZEITUNG
737703G67B-10800
Editorial: Friedrichstr. 34, 45128 ESSEN
Tel: 201 8040 **Fax:** 201 8042621
Email: redaktion@nrz.de **Web site:** http://www.derwesten.de
Freq: 312 issues yearly; **Annual Sub.:** EUR 20,90; **Circ:** 321,135
Editor: Rüdiger Oppers; **News Editor:** Michael Minholz; **Advertising Manager:** Christian Klaucke
Profile: Three years before the founding of the Federal Republic of Germany, on 13 July 1946, the NRZ was published. As a critical, helpful and contentious companion through the day it has always remained true to its self-image: open to citizens' concerns, discussion friendly, tolerant, courageous, tenacious, uncompromising. The NRZ is one of the largest regional newspapers in Germany. Its habitat is as complex and diverse, as the NRZ itself: on one hand a big city media for the Rhine Ruhr area and the City of Dusseldorf, on the other hand, a local paper for the Lower Rhine between Kleve and Moers. Enriched with reports from NRZ correspondents from Germany, Europe and around the world, the major newspaper in the Rhine and Ruhr Area offers an exciting, eclectic mix of news, reports with background and entertainment: refreshingly topical, refreshingly entertaining, refreshingly different! Facebook: http://www.facebook.com/derwesten Twitter: http://twitter.com/Am_Niederrhein This Outlet offers RSS (Really Simple Syndication).
Language(s): German
ADVERTISING RATES:
SCC .... EUR 780,00
Mechanical Data: Type Area: 445 x 320 mm, No. of Columns (Display): 7, Col Widths (Display): 44 mm
Copy instructions: *Copy Date:* 2 days prior to publication
Supplement(s): heimat am niederrhein; Mein Auto; Mein Beruf; Meine besten Jahre; Meine Familie; Meine Freizeit; Meine Weihnacht; Mein neues Jahr!; Mein Shopping; Mein Stil; Mein Team; Mein Urlaub; Mein Zuhause
REGIONAL DAILY & SUNDAY NEWSPAPERS: Regional Daily Newspapers

NRZ NEUE RUHR ZEITUNG
737704G67B-10820
Editorial: Friedrichstr. 34, 45128 ESSEN
Tel: 201 8040 **Fax:** 201 8042621
Email: redaktion@nrz.de **Web site:** http://www.derwesten.de
Freq: 312 issues yearly; **Annual Sub.:** EUR 20,90; **Circ:** 321,135
Editor: Rüdiger Oppers; **News Editor:** Manfred Pichl; **Advertising Manager:** Christian Klaucke
Profile: The NRZ is one of the largest regional newspapers in Germany. Its habitat is so complex and diverse as the NRZ itself: on one hand a big city media for the Rhine Ruhr area and the City of Dusseldorf, on the other hand a local paper for the Lower Rhine between Kleve and Moers. Enriched with reports from NRZ correspondents from Germany, Europe and around the world, the major newspaper in the Rhine and Ruhrarea offers an exciting, eclectic mix of news, reports with background and entertainment. Facebook: http://www.facebook.com/derwesten.
Language(s): German
ADVERTISING RATES:
SCC .... EUR 780,00
Mechanical Data: Type Area: 445 x 320 mm, No. of Columns (Display): 7, Col Widths (Display): 44 mm
Copy instructions: *Copy Date:* 2 days prior to publication
Supplement(s): Aktuell; Essen.Erleben.; Limbecker Platz Aktuell; Mein Auto; Mein Beruf; Meine besten Jahre; Meine Familie; Meine Freizeit; Mein Essen kompakt; Meine Weihnacht; Mein neues Jahr!; Mein Shopping; Mein Stil; Mein Team; Mein Urlaub; Mein Zuhause; NRZ Wirtschaft; Rhein-Ruhr Zentrum Aktuell
REGIONAL DAILY & SUNDAY NEWSPAPERS: Regional Daily Newspapers

NSTN NACHRICHTEN
737705G32A-2300
Editorial: Prinzenstr. 23, 30159 HANNOVER
Tel: 511 368940 **Fax:** 511 3689430
Email: redaktion@nst.de **Web site:** http://www.nst.de
Freq: 11 issues yearly; Free to qualifying individuals
Annual Sub.: EUR 48,00; **Circ:** 6,800
Editor: Heiger Scholz; **Advertising Manager:** Kerstin Schökel
Profile: Journal about local government in Lower Saxony.
Language(s): German
Readership: Aimed at councillors and civil servants.
ADVERTISING RATES:
Full Page Mono .... EUR 1705
Full Page Colour .... EUR 2245
Mechanical Data: Type Area: 262 x 180 mm, No. of Columns (Display): 3, Col Widths (Display): 53 mm
Copy instructions: *Copy Date:* 25 days prior to publication
BUSINESS: LOCAL GOVERNMENT, LEISURE & RECREATION: Local Government

NTI NEUE THÜRINGER ILLUSTRIERTE
764826G14A-9282
Editorial: Legefelder Hauptstr. 14a, 99438 WEIMAR
Tel: 3643 903224 **Fax:** 3643 511933
Email: wstgmbh.weimar@t-online.de **Web site:** http://www.nti-online.net
Freq: Monthly; **Annual Sub.:** EUR 18,00; **Circ:** 10,800
Editor: Jörg Schuster; **Advertising Manager:** Elisabeth Demmler
Profile: Magazine on economy, politics, tourism, sport and culture for executives and opinion- eaders in the Thüringen region.
Language(s): German
ADVERTISING RATES:
Full Page Mono .... EUR 1290
Full Page Colour .... EUR 1935
Mechanical Data: Type Area: 267 x 185 mm, No. of Columns (Display): 2, Col Widths (Display): 90 mm
Copy instructions: *Copy Date:* 15 days prior to publication

NTZ
737711G18B-1400
Editorial: Merianstr. 29, 63069 OFFENBACH
Tel: 69 8400061331 **Fax:** 69 8400061399
Email: ntz-redaktion@vde-verlag.de **Web site:** http://www.ntz-online.de
Freq: 6 issues yearly; **Annual Sub.:** EUR 107,00; **Circ:** 9,868
Editor: Walter A. Ströver; **Advertising Manager:** Markus Lehnert
Profile: Magazine containing information about electronic techniques and telecommunications matters.
Language(s): German
ADVERTISING RATES:
Full Page Mono .... EUR 2990
Full Page Colour .... EUR 4350
Mechanical Data: Type Area: 270 x 189 mm, No. of Columns (Display): 4, Col Widths (Display): 44 mm
Copy instructions: *Copy Date:* 22 days prior to publication
Official Journal of: Organ d. Informationstechn. Ges. im VDE e.V.
BUSINESS: ELECTRONICS: Telecommunications

NUN REDEN WIR
1616268G74N-815
Editorial: Friesenring 32, 48147 MÜNSTER
Tel: 251 212050 **Fax:** 251 2006613
Email: info@lsv-nrw.de **Web site:** http://www.lsv-nrw.de
Freq: Quarterly; **Cover Price:** Free; **Circ:** 3,000
Editor: Gaby Schnell
Profile: Magazine for the elderly from the German federal state of Nordrhein-Westfalen.
Language(s): German

NUN REDEN WIR
1616268G74N-1002
Editorial: Friesenring 32, 48147 MÜNSTER
Tel: 251 212050 **Fax:** 251 2006613
Email: info@lsv-nrw.de **Web site:** http://www.lsv-nrw.de
Freq: Quarterly; **Cover Price:** Free; **Circ:** 3,000
Editor: Gaby Schnell
Profile: Magazine for the elderly from the German federal state of Nordrhein-Westfalen.
Language(s): German

DER NÜRBURGER
737717G77B-450
Editorial: Hertinger Str. 60, 59423 UNNA
Tel: 2303 985531 **Fax:** 2303 985309
Email: efoe@syburger.de **Web site:** http://www.syburger.de
Freq: Monthly; **Annual Sub.:** EUR 19,20; **Circ:** 20,000
Editor: Erik Förster; **Advertising Manager:** Jessica Kwasny
Profile: Motorcycle magazine for the region of Köln, Aachen, Mittelrhein, Eifel. The editorial focus is on regional news, plus get driving reports, tests, and travel. The magazine for active bikers, because they only exist in the motorcycle trade and meeting places.
Language(s): German
Readership: Aimed at motorcyclists in the Rheinland-Pfalz region.
ADVERTISING RATES:
Full Page Mono .... EUR 905
Full Page Colour .... EUR 1267
Mechanical Data: Type Area: 232 x 155 mm, No. of Columns (Display): 3, Col Widths (Display): 48 mm
CONSUMER: MOTORING & CYCLING: Motorcycling

NÜRNBERGER NACHRICHTEN
737728G67B-10840
Editorial: Marienstr. 9, 90402 NÜRNBERG
Tel: 911 2160 **Fax:** 911 2162432
Web site: http://www.nuernberger-nachrichten.de
Freq: 312 issues yearly; **Circ:** 308,468
Editor: Heinz-Joachim Hauck
Profile: Regional daily newspaper with news on politics, economy, culture, sports, travel, technology, etc. Twitter: http://twitter.com/NN_Online This Outlet offers RSS (Really Simple Syndication).
Language(s): German
ADVERTISING RATES:
SCC .... EUR 291,60
Mechanical Data: No. of Columns (Display): 6, Col Widths (Display): 45 mm
Copy instructions: *Copy Date:* 2 days prior to publication
Supplement(s): sechs+sechzig
REGIONAL DAILY & SUNDAY NEWSPAPERS: Regional Daily Newspapers

NÜRNBERGER STADTANZEIGER
1621789G72-18245
Editorial: Marienstr. 9, 90402 NÜRNBERG
Tel: 911 2160 **Fax:** 911 2162432
Email: info@pressenetz.de **Web site:** http://www.stadtanzeiger.nordbayern.de
Freq: Weekly; **Cover Price:** Paid; **Circ:** 705,200 Unique Users
Editor: Hans-Joachim Hauck; **Advertising Manager:** Ute Rupprecht
Profile: Ezine: Advertising journal (house-to-house) concentrating on local stories.
Language(s): German
LOCAL NEWSPAPERS

NÜRTINGER ECHO
737733G72-10024
Editorial: Zeppelinstr. 116, 73730 ESSLINGEN
Tel: 711 758700160 **Fax:** 711 758700148
Email: redaktion@ihr-wochenblatt-echo.de **Web site:** http://www.ihr-wochenblatt-echo.de
Freq: Weekly; **Cover Price:** Free; **Circ:** 51,900
Editor: Barbara Scherer
Profile: Advertising journal (house-to-house) concentrating on local stories.
Language(s): German
ADVERTISING RATES:
Full Page Mono .... EUR 1980
Full Page Colour .... EUR 2609
Mechanical Data: Type Area: 370 x 255 mm, No. of Columns (Display): 5, Col Widths (Display): 45 mm
Copy instructions: *Copy Date:* 2 days prior to publication
LOCAL NEWSPAPERS

NÜRTINGER ZEITUNG
737734G67B-1086
Editorial: Carl-Benz-Str. 1, 72622 NÜRTINGEN
Tel: 7022 9464129 **Fax:** 7022 9464111
Email: forum@ntz.de **Web site:** http://www.ntz.de
Freq: 312 issues yearly; **Circ:** 22,088
Editor: Anneliese Lieb; **Advertising Manager:** Victor Stroner
Profile: Daily newspaper with regional news and a local sports section.
Language(s): German
ADVERTISING RATES:
SCC .... EUR 45,8
Mechanical Data: Type Area: 485 x 321 mm, No. of Columns (Display): 7, Col Widths (Display): 43 mm
Copy instructions: *Copy Date:* 2 days prior to publication
REGIONAL DAILY & SUNDAY NEWSPAPERS: Regional Daily Newspapers

NURTV
737749G76C-300
Editorial: Münchener Str. 101, 85737 ISMANING
Tel: 89 272707621 **Fax:** 89 272707690
Email: kontakt@nurtv.de **Web site:** http://www.gong-verlag.de
Freq: Monthly; **Annual Sub.:** EUR 15,60; **Circ:** 615,850
Editor: Katharina Lukas
Profile: Magazine containing TV listings.
Language(s): German
ADVERTISING RATES:
Full Page Mono .... EUR 9350
Full Page Colour .... EUR 9350
Mechanical Data: Type Area: 245 x 190 mm
Copy instructions: *Copy Date:* 22 days prior to publication
CONSUMER: MUSIC & PERFORMING ARTS: TV & Radio

NWB INTERNATIONALES STEUER- UND WIRTSCHAFTSRECHT IWB
731660G14C-58
Editorial: Eschstr. 22, 44629 HERNE
Tel: 2323 141237 **Fax:** 2323 141249
Web site: http://www.nwb.de/go/modul5
Freq: 24 issues yearly; **Annual Sub.:** EUR 423,60; **Circ:** 2,270
Editor: Thorsten Kunde; **Advertising Manager:** Andreas Reimann
Profile: Magazine covering international business.
Language(s): German
ADVERTISING RATES:
Full Page Mono .... EUR 1107
Full Page Colour .... EUR 1993
Mechanical Data: Type Area: 205 x 148 mm, No. of Columns (Display): 2, Col Widths (Display): 70 mm
Copy instructions: *Copy Date:* 14 days prior to publication
BUSINESS: COMMERCE, INDUSTRY & MANAGEMENT: International Commerce

NWB RECHNUNGSWESEN BBK
722200G14A-660
Editorial: Eschstr. 22, 44629 HERNE
Tel: 2323 141244 **Fax:** 2323 141248
Web site: http://www.nwb.de/go/modul2
Freq: 24 issues yearly; **Annual Sub.:** EUR 214,80; **Circ:** 8,670
Editor: Kordula Ziegelmann; **Advertising Manager:** Andreas Reimann
Profile: Magazine on book-keeping.
Language(s): German
ADVERTISING RATES:
Full Page Mono .... EUR 1456
Full Page Colour .... EUR 2620
Mechanical Data: Type Area: 205 x 148 mm, No. of Columns (Display): 2, Col Widths (Display): 58 mm
Copy instructions: *Copy Date:* 14 days prior to publication
BUSINESS: COMMERCE, INDUSTRY & MANAGEMENT

NWB STEUER- UND WIRTSCHAFTSRECHT
737759G1M-5
Editorial: Eschstr. 22, 44629 HERNE
Tel: 2323 141900 **Fax:** 2323 141205
Web site: http://www.nwb.de/go/modul1
Freq: Weekly; **Annual Sub.:** EUR 326,40; **Circ:** 33,025
Editor: Reinhild Foltzik; **Advertising Manager:** Andreas Reimann
Profile: The NWB provides its readers with a quick, reliable and comprehensive coverage to date information of all tax laws and information on all the tax law immediately contiguous areas of commercial law. Understandable commentaries and design recommendations and guidelines can complete the information on offer. The issues are legal, tax, commercial and illustrated in the economic impact.
Language(s): German
ADVERTISING RATES:
Full Page Mono .... EUR 3690
Full Page Colour .... EUR 5904
Mechanical Data: Type Area: 205 x 148 mm, No. of Columns (Display): 2, Col Widths (Display): 70 mm
Copy instructions: *Copy Date:* 12 days prior to publication
BUSINESS: FINANCE & ECONOMICS: Taxation

NWB UNTERNEHMENSTEUERN UND BILANZEN STUB
743763G1A-2980
Editorial: Eschstr. 22, 44629 HERNE
Tel: 2323 141242 **Fax:** 2323 141248
Web site: http://www.nwb.de/go/modul3
Freq: 24 issues yearly; **Annual Sub.:** EUR 259,20; **Circ:** 3,508
Editor: Patrick Zugehör; **Advertising Manager:** Andreas Reimann
Profile: Magazine for tax and economic advisors and accountancy experts.
Language(s): German
ADVERTISING RATES:
Full Page Mono .... EUR 1190
Full Page Colour .... EUR 1995
Mechanical Data: Type Area: 260 x 186 mm
Copy instructions: *Copy Date:* 14 days prior to publication
BUSINESS: FINANCE & ECONOMICS

NWZ GÖPPINGER KREISNACHRICHTEN
737763G67B-10880
Editorial: Rosenstr. 24, 73033 GÖPPINGEN
Tel: 7161 204143 **Fax:** 7161 204154
Email: nwz.redaktion@swp.de **Web site:** http://www.suedwest-aktiv.de
Freq: 312 issues yearly; **Circ:** 33,692
Profile: NWZ is a local edition of the Südwest Presse, Ulm.
Language(s): German
ADVERTISING RATES:
SCC .... EUR 93,60
Mechanical Data: Type Area: 480 x 320 mm, No. of Columns (Display): 7, Col Widths (Display): 44 mm
Copy instructions: *Copy Date:* 1 day prior to publication
Supplement(s): Das Magazin
REGIONAL DAILY & SUNDAY NEWSPAPERS: Regional Daily Newspapers

NWZ ONLINE
1621796G67B-16627
Editorial: Peterstr. 28, 26121 OLDENBURG
Tel: 441 99882000 **Fax:** 441 99882029
Email: online@nordwest-zeitung.de **Web site:** http://www.nwzonline.de
Freq: Daily; **Cover Price:** Paid
Annual Sub.: EUR 18,90; **Circ:** 1,905,822 Unique Users
Editor: Gaby Schneider-Schelling
Profile: NWZ online is the online service of the Nordwest-Zeitung. The website provides users with cutting-edge information, images routes to regional events and digital television. On the website daily updated news, reports and interviews from the region, the daily changing weatherman and TV reports to be seen. NWZ online users are local in the NWZ-circulation area resident. NWZ online.de is also used extensively: 59% of users visit NWZ online daily.
Language(s): German
REGIONAL DAILY & SUNDAY NEWSPAPERS: Regional Daily Newspapers

NZ NORDBAYERISCHE ZEITUNG
737766G67B-10900
Editorial: Marienstr. 9, 90402 NÜRNBERG
Tel: 911 23510 **Fax:** 911 23512000
Email: nz-redaktion@pressenetz.de **Web site:** http://www.nz-online.de
Freq: 312 issues yearly; **Circ:** 273,680
Profile: Daily newspaper with regional news and a local sports section. Facebook: http://www.facebook.com/nuernberger.zeitung.
Language(s): German
ADVERTISING RATES:
SCC .... EUR 291,60
Mechanical Data: No. of Columns (Display): 6, Col Widths (Display): 45 mm
Copy instructions: *Copy Date:* 2 days prior to publication
Supplement(s): sechs+sechzig
REGIONAL DAILY & SUNDAY NEWSPAPERS: Regional Daily Newspapers

NZ NÜRNBERGER ZEITUNG
737767G67B-10920
Editorial: Marienstr. 9, 90402 NÜRNBERG
Tel: 911 23510 **Fax:** 911 23512000
Email: nz-redaktion@pressenetz.de **Web site:** http://www.nz-online.de
Freq: 312 issues yearly; **Circ:** 122,313
Editor: Raimund Kirch
Profile: Regional daily newspaper covering politics, economics, sport, travel and technology. Facebook: http://www.facebook.com/nuernberger.zeitung Twitter: http://twitter.com/NZ_Online This Outlet offers RSS (Really Simple Syndication).
Language(s): German
ADVERTISING RATES:
SCC .... EUR 198,80
Mechanical Data: Type Area: 420 x 284 mm, No. of Columns (Display): 6, Col Widths (Display): 45 mm
Copy instructions: *Copy Date:* 2 days prior to publication
Supplement(s): sechs+sechzig
REGIONAL DAILY & SUNDAY NEWSPAPERS: Regional Daily Newspapers

N-ZONE
737768G78D-360
Editorial: Dr.-Mack-Str. 77, 90762 FÜRTH
Tel: 911 2872100 **Fax:** 911 2872200
Email: redaktion@n-zone.de **Web site:** http://www.n-zone.de
Freq: Monthly; **Annual Sub.:** EUR 42,00; **Circ:** 20,000
Editor: Petra Fröhlich; **Advertising Manager:** Gunnar Obermeier
Profile: Magazine focusing on computer games.
Language(s): German
ADVERTISING RATES:
Full Page Mono .... EUR 6400
Full Page Colour .... EUR 6400
Mechanical Data: Type Area: 280 x 210 mm, No. of Columns (Display): 4, Col Widths (Display): 52 mm
Copy instructions: *Copy Date:* 30 days prior to publication
CONSUMER: CONSUMER ELECTRONICS: Games

O+P
738432G19E-1300
Editorial: Lise-Meitner-Str. 2, 55129 MAINZ
Tel: 6131 992352 **Fax:** 6131 992340
Email: m.pfister@vfmz.de **Web site:** http://www.industrie-service.de
Freq: 11 issues yearly; **Annual Sub.:** EUR 157,00; **Circ:** 9,667
Editor: Michael Pfister; **Advertising Manager:** Andreas Zepig
Profile: O+P informs currently and permanently about the whole field of development and practice, of components and systems in fluid technology. It offers professional technological information for all topics in oil-hydraulic and pneumatic load transmission, control systems and closed loop control. The journal is a permanent forum for the dialog between producer and user, especially in the fields of planning, construction and economical application, tools, machines, plants and systems. With the focus on the practical side the main task of the journal is to help fitting the modern fluid technology to the specific needs in the companies and to offer optimal solutions. O+P is the main journal for the industrial sector that depends on the use of modern fluid technology.
Language(s): German
ADVERTISING RATES:
Full Page Mono .... EUR 3900
Full Page Colour .... EUR 5130
Mechanical Data: Type Area: 265 x 185 mm, No. of Columns (Display): 4, Col Widths (Display): 43 mm
Copy instructions: *Copy Date:* 14 days prior to publication
Official Journal of: Organ d. Forschungsfonds d. Fachverb. Fluidtechnik im VDMA
BUSINESS: ENGINEERING & MACHINERY: Machinery, Machine Tools & Metalworking

O+P KONSTRUKTIONS JAHRBUCH
738433G19E-1320
Editorial: Lise-Meitner-Str. 2, 55129 MAINZ
Tel: 6131 992352 **Fax:** 6131 992340
Email: m.pfister@vfmz.de **Web site:** http://www.industrie-service.de
Freq: Annual; **Cover Price:** EUR 38,00; **Circ:** 8,000
Editor: Michael Pfister; **Advertising Manager:** Andreas Zepig
Profile: The editorial capacity of the „O+P Konstruktions Jahrbuch" is exactly cut for the information needs of all application areas of fluid power engineering. At first glance the interested users finds formulas, momograms, standard conversions, guidelines, recommendations and thesises. With more than thousand single entries in clearly structured product-charts the user receives information about specially assembly types, ranges of application and the most interesting technical data of the available products - a real capacity-comparison.
Language(s): German
ADVERTISING RATES:
Full Page Mono .... EUR 3930
Full Page Colour .... EUR 5160
Mechanical Data: Type Area: 265 x 185 mm, No. of Columns (Display): 4, Col Widths (Display): 43 mm
Copy instructions: *Copy Date:* 20 days prior to publication
Official Journal of: Organ d. Forschungsfonds d. Fachverb. Fluidtechnik im VDMA

O+P REPORT
738434G19E-1340
Editorial: Lise-Meitner-Str. 2, 55129 MAINZ
Tel: 6131 992352 **Fax:** 6131 992340
Email: m.pfister@vfmz.de **Web site:** http://www.industrie-service.de
Freq: Annual; **Annual Sub.:** EUR 157,00; **Circ:** 10,000
Editor: Michael Pfister; **Advertising Manager:** Andreas Zepig
Profile: The o+p Report is important for 12.000 constructors, engineers, experts in hydraulic and pneumatic technology in the whole producing industry. In this special edition of O+P the expert in fluid technology finds the current offer for hydraulic and pneu- matic components, load transmission and drive and control systems. In clearly arranged short reports the reader finds information for example about pumps and drives, cylinders, valves and aggregates, lines and attachments.
Language(s): German
ADVERTISING RATES:
Full Page Mono .... EUR 3900
Full Page Colour .... EUR 5130
Mechanical Data: Type Area: 265 x 185 mm, No. of Columns (Display): 4, Col Widths (Display): 43 mm
Copy instructions: *Copy Date:* 18 days prior to publication
Official Journal of: Organ d. Forschungsfonds d. Fachverb. Fluidtechnik im VDMA

DIE OBERBADISCHE
737773G67B-10940
Editorial: Am Alten Markt 2, 79539 LÖRRACH
Tel: 7621 403350 **Fax:** 7621 403381
Email: ov.loerrach@verlagshaus-jaumann.de **Web site:** http://www.die-oberbadische.de
Freq: 312 issues yearly; **Circ:** 13,633
Editor: Guido Neidinger; **Advertising Manager:** Thomas Dunke
Profile: Daily newspaper with regional news and a local sports section.
Language(s): German
Mechanical Data: Type Area: 435 x 280 mm, No. of Columns (Display): 6, Col Widths (Display): 45 mm
Copy instructions: *Copy Date:* 1 day prior to publication
REGIONAL DAILY & SUNDAY NEWSPAPERS: Regional Daily Newspapers

OBERBAYERISCHES VOLKSBLATT
737776G67B-10980
Editorial: Hafnerstr. 5, 83022 ROSENHEIM
Tel: 8031 213201 **Fax:** 8031 213216
Email: redaktion@ovb.net **Web site:** http://www.ovb-online.de
Freq: 312 issues yearly; **Circ:** 31,440
Editor: Willi Börsch; **News Editor:** Willi Börsch; **Advertising Manager:** Max Breu
Profile: Regional daily newspaper with news on politics, economy, culture, sports, travel, technology, etc. The Oberbayerische Volksblatl (OVB) is a regional newspaper in the city and district of Rosenheim, Mühldorf am Inn, and in the Chiemsee area and western part of the district of Traunstein. They reached with their regional editions Chiemgau-Zeitung, Mangfall Bote, Mühldorfer Anzeiger, Neumarkter Anzteiger, Waldkraiburger Nachrichten and Wasserburger Zeitung a paid circulation of 69,645 copies. The jacket, which is the political, sports and business pages, comes from the Münchner Merkur, This Outlet offers RSS (Really Simple Syndication).
Language(s): German
ADVERTISING RATES:
SCC .... EUR 97,30
Mechanical Data: Type Area: 474 x 324 mm, No. of Columns (Display): 7, Col Widths (Display): 45 mm
Copy instructions: *Copy Date:* 1 day prior to publication
Supplement(s): rtv
REGIONAL DAILY & SUNDAY NEWSPAPERS: Regional Daily Newspapers

OBERBERGISCHE VOLKSZEITUNG
737778G67B-11000
Editorial: Stolkgasse 25, 50667 KÖLN
Tel: 221 1632558 **Fax:** 221 1632557
Email: print@kr-redaktion.de **Web site:** http://www.rundschau-online.de
Freq: 312 issues yearly; **Circ:** 33,431
Advertising Manager: Karsten Hundhausen
Profile: Daily newspaper with regional news and a local sports section. Facebook: http://www.facebook.com/pages/Kolnische-Rundschau/147616463739.
Language(s): German
ADVERTISING RATES:
SCC .... EUR 85,50
Mechanical Data: Type Area: 430 x 285 mm, No. of Columns (Display): 6, Col Widths (Display): 45 mm
Copy instructions: *Copy Date:* 2 days prior to publication
Supplement(s): prisma
REGIONAL DAILY & SUNDAY NEWSPAPERS: Regional Daily Newspapers

OBERBERGISCHER ANZEIGER
737777G67B-11020
Editorial: Amsterdamer Str. 192, 50735 KÖLN
Tel: 221 2240 **Fax:** 221 2242602
Email: redaktion-ksta@mds.de **Web site:** http://www.ksta.de
Freq: 312 issues yearly; **Circ:** 33,431
Advertising Manager: Karsten Hundhausen
Profile: Daily newspaper with regional news and a local sports section. Facebook: http://www.facebook.com/pages/KSTA/141063022950 Twitter: http://twitter.com/ksta_news This Outlet offers RSS (Really Simple Syndication).
Language(s): German
ADVERTISING RATES:
SCC .... EUR 85,50
Mechanical Data: Type Area: 430 x 285 mm, No. of Columns (Display): 6, Col Widths (Display): 45 mm
Copy instructions: *Copy Date:* 2 days prior to publication
Supplement(s): prisma
REGIONAL DAILY & SUNDAY NEWSPAPERS: Regional Daily Newspapers

OBERE EXTREMITÄT
1795088G56A-11452
Editorial: Tiergartenstr. 17, 69121 HEIDELBERG
Tel: 6221 4878814 **Fax:** 6221 48768814
Email: elster.steinkopff@springer.com **Web site:** http://www.springermedizin.de
Freq: Quarterly; **Annual Sub.:** EUR 180,00; **Circ:** 650
Advertising Manager: Noëla Krischer-Janka
Profile: The journal is dedicated to the treatment of injuries, consequences of injuries, and diseases of the upper extremity, i.e., of the shoulder joint, elbow joint, and hand. As a common communication and continuing education forum for all surgeons and orthopedists with the corresponding specialization, the journal is future oriented and fills an important gap in the information offered to orthopedic and trauma surgeons. In addition to original papers and review articles, special sections report on innovative treatment measures, difficulties concerning expert opinions, professional organization developments, and congress activities.
Language(s): German
ADVERTISING RATES:
Full Page Mono .... EUR 1680
Full Page Colour .... EUR 2700
Mechanical Data: Type Area: 240 x 174 mm
Official Journal of: Organ d. Dt. Vereinigung f. Schultern- u. Ellenbogenchirurgie (DVSE) e.V.

DER OBERHAUSENER
762834G89C-4705
Editorial: Uhlenbroicher Weg 30a, 47269 DUISBURG
Tel: 203 729207 **Fax:** 203 719378
Email: curran@design-werk.net
Freq: Monthly; **Cover Price:** Free; **Circ:** 4,900
Editor: Ralph Curran
Profile: Programme of events in Oberhausen.
Language(s): German
ADVERTISING RATES:
Full Page Mono .... EUR 586
Full Page Colour .... EUR 586
Mechanical Data: No. of Columns (Display): 3, Col Widths (Display): 31 mm, Type Area: 136 x 98 mm
Copy instructions: *Copy Date:* 20 days prior to publication
CONSUMER: HOLIDAYS & TRAVEL: Entertainment Guides

OBERHESSISCHE PRESSE
737793G67B-11080
Editorial: Franz-Tuczek-Weg 1, 35039 MARBURG
Tel: 6421 409301 **Fax:** 6421 409302
Email: info@op-marburg.de **Web site:** http://www.op-marburg.de
Freq: 312 issues yearly; **Circ:** 29,166
Editor: Wolfram Hitzeroth; **News Editor:** Till Conrad; **Advertising Manager:** Roger Schneider
Profile: Regional daily newspaper covering politics, economics, sport, travel and technology. Regional daily newspaper with news on politics, economy, culture, sports, travel, technology, etc. Is the flagship of the publishing Oberhessische PRESSE, a traditional daily newspaper that is founded local priorities. It is the largest daily newspaper in the county, around the university town of Marburg. Facebook: http://www.facebook.com/OberhessischePresse?ref=search&sid=1469388759.4095210341..1 Twitter: http://twitter.com/OPmarburg This Outlet offers RSS (Really Simple Syndication).
Language(s): German
ADVERTISING RATES:
SCC .... EUR 52,20
Mechanical Data: Type Area: 430 x 277 mm, No. of Columns (Display): 6, Col Widths (Display): 45 mm
Copy instructions: *Copy Date:* 1 day prior to publication
REGIONAL DAILY & SUNDAY NEWSPAPERS: Regional Daily Newspapers

OBERHESSISCHE ZEITUNG
737794G67B-11100
Editorial: Am Kreuz 10, 36304 ALSFELD
Tel: 6331 966911 **Fax:** 6331 966913
Email: redaktion@oberhessische-zeitung.de **Web site:** http://www.oberhessische-zeitung.de
Freq: 312 issues yearly; **Circ:** 6,721
Advertising Manager: Martin Hank
Profile: Daily newspaper with regional news and a local sports section.
Language(s): German
ADVERTISING RATES:
SCC .... EUR 22,80
Mechanical Data: Type Area: 430 x 282 mm, No. of Columns (Display): 6, Col Widths (Display): 45 mm
Copy instructions: *Copy Date:* 1 day prior to publication
Supplement(s): auf dem Vulkan; vital im leben
REGIONAL DAILY & SUNDAY NEWSPAPERS: Regional Daily Newspapers

OBERMAIN-TAGBLATT
737812G67B-11120
Editorial: Reundorfer Str. 2, 96215 LICHTENFELS
Tel: 9571 78820 **Fax:** 9571 78824
Email: redaktion@obermain.de **Web site:** http://www.obermain.de
Freq: 312 issues yearly; **Annual Sub.:** EUR 20,80; **Circ:** 12,309
Advertising Manager: Christa Robisch
Profile: Daily newspaper with regional news and a local sports section.
Language(s): German
ADVERTISING RATES:
SCC .... EUR 26,00
Mechanical Data: Type Area: 430 x 282 mm, No. of Columns (Display): 6, Col Widths (Display): 45 mm
Copy instructions: *Copy Date:* 1 day prior to publication
REGIONAL DAILY & SUNDAY NEWSPAPERS: Regional Daily Newspapers

OBERPFÄLZER WOCHENZEITUNG OWZ WOCHENBLATT - AUSG. WEIDEN/NEUSTADT

737832G72-10108
Editorial: Weigelstr. 16, 92637 WEIDEN
Tel: 961 85323 **Fax:** 961 85320
Email: redowz@zeitung.org **Web site:** http://www.oberpfalznetz.de
Freq: Weekly; **Cover Price:** Free; **Circ:** 86,800
Editor: Hans Luger; **Advertising Manager:** Andreas Holch
Profile: Advertising journal (house-to-house) concentrating on local stories.
Language(s): German
ADVERTISING RATES:
Full Page Mono .... EUR 3845
Full Page Colour .... EUR 5676
Mechanical Data: Type Area: 430 x 280 mm, No. of Columns (Display): 6, Col Widths (Display): 45 mm
Copy instructions: *Copy Date:* 2 days prior to publication
LOCAL NEWSPAPERS

OBERSCHWABEN MAGAZIN

737838G89A-3520
Editorial: Max-Stromeyer-Str. 116, 78467 KONSTANZ **Tel:** 7531 90710 **Fax:** 7531 907131
Email: jhummel@labhard.de **Web site:** http://www.labhard.de
Freq: Annual; **Cover Price:** EUR 3,90; **Circ:** 39,500
Editor: Jasmin Hummel; **Advertising Manager:** Claudia Manz
Profile: Current travel and leisure guide in magazine format for the holiday landscape Upper Swabia. Attractions, Upper Swabian Baroque Route, cycle Danube-Lake Constance, portraits of cities and towns, art, culture and history, health and wellness. Large Events and Museums guide, removable maps and addresses provide high utility and a lot of contacts. High quality, lavishly produced collection object. For 15 years on the market.
Language(s): German
ADVERTISING RATES:
Full Page Mono .... EUR 2010
Full Page Colour .... EUR 2010
Mechanical Data: Type Area: 263 x 188 mm
Copy instructions: *Copy Date:* 47 days prior to publication
CONSUMER: HOLIDAYS & TRAVEL: Travel

OBERSCHWABEN NATURNAH

755760G57-2621
Editorial: Briachhalde 15, 88255 BAINDT
Tel: 7501 43344
Email: d.o.weber@t-online.de **Web site:** http://www.bno-ev.de
Freq: Annual; **Cover Price:** EUR 8,00
Free to qualifying individuals ; **Circ:** 1,000
Editor: Dietrich Weber
Profile: Magazine for member of the association of nature conservation for the region of Oberschwaben.
Language(s): German

OBJEKT SPEKTRUM

737859G5R-657
Editorial: Toni-Schmid-Str. 10b, 81825 MÜNCHEN
Tel: 89 74995702 **Fax:** 89 74995703
Email: jens.coldewey@objektspektrum.de **Web site:** http://www.objektspektrum.de
Freq: 6 issues yearly; **Annual Sub.:** EUR 48,00; **Circ:** 14,000
Editor: Jens Coldewey
Profile: Magazine containing practical up to date information about developments in computer technology.
Language(s): German
ADVERTISING RATES:
Full Page Mono .... EUR 3005
Full Page Colour .... EUR 4365
Mechanical Data: Type Area: 250 x 181 mm
Copy instructions: *Copy Date:* 32 days prior to publication
BUSINESS: COMPUTERS & AUTOMATION: Computers Related

OBST & GARTEN

737865G26D-220
Editorial: Eulenbachweg 4, 79674 TODTNAU
Tel: 7671 999315 **Fax:** 7671 999316
Email: dspychalski@ulmer.de **Web site:** http://www.obst-und-garten.de
Freq: Monthly; **Annual Sub.:** EUR 40,00; **Circ:** 17,979
Editor: Rolf Heinzelmann; **Advertising Manager:** Anna Greiner
Profile: With a circulation of around 19,600 copies, offering Obst & Garten in Baden-Württemberg, particularly in the important fruit growing region near Lake Constance and in Baden a high range, but is appreciated all over Germany and neighboring countries as a garden guide and trade magazine. With special reference to fruit growing Obst & Garten informed about cultivation methods, crop protection, storage and utilization as well as new insights from science and research. Easily understandable advice for all gardening work, articles about the health value of fruits and vegetables and the news supplement content. Articles on nature and landscape protection and the association and club news from LOGL and LVEO make Obst & Garten a valuable views and information forum. The constant themes are fruit growing, crop protection, variety selection, harvesting and storage, orchards, fruit- and vegetable-exploitation, juice preparation, distillery, fruit-growing technology, marketing, wood & forestry, vegetables and ornamental plants, health, child & garden, landscape and nature conservation, events.
Language(s): German
Readership: Aimed at professional gardeners and fruit growers.
ADVERTISING RATES:
Full Page Mono .... EUR 3369
Full Page Colour .... EUR 4479
Mechanical Data: Type Area: 270 x 195 mm, No. of Columns (Display): 4, Col Widths (Display): 45 mm
Copy instructions: *Copy Date:* 18 days prior to publication
Official Journal of: Organ d. LV Erwerbsobstbau Baden-Württemberg e.V.
BUSINESS: GARDEN TRADE: Garden Trade Horticulture

OBSTBAU

737863G26C-75
Editorial: Claire-Waldoff-Str. 7, 10117 BERLIN
Tel: 30 20006523 **Fax:** 30 20006529
Email: disselborg-obstbau@g-net.de **Web site:** http://www.obstbau.org
Freq: Monthly; **Annual Sub.:** EUR 78,00; **Circ:** 7,000
Editor: Jörg Disselborg
Profile: Magazine covering all aspects of fruit growing.
Language(s): German
Readership: Aimed at fruit growers.
ADVERTISING RATES:
Full Page Mono .... EUR 1740
Full Page Colour .... EUR 2685
Mechanical Data: Type Area: 270 x 185 mm, No. of Columns (Display): 3, Col Widths (Display): 58 mm
Copy instructions: *Copy Date:* 10 days prior to publication
Official Journal of: Organ d. Landesfachgruppen Brandenburg, Hamburg, Mecklenburg Vorpommern, Niedersachsen, Rheinhessen, Sachsen-Anhalt, Schleswig-Holstein u. Thüringen, d. Obstbauverbände Baden-Württemberg, Bayern, Hessen, Sachsen u. Westfalen-Lippe, d. Obstbauberatungsringe: Schleswig-Holstein, Südoldenburg, Tettnang u. Überlingen u. d. ArGe Obstbau Pfalz u. Rheinland-Nassau
BUSINESS: GARDEN TRADE

ODENWÄLDER ECHO

737873G67B-11180
Editorial: Holzhofallee 25, 64295 DARMSTADT
Tel: 6151 3871 **Fax:** 6151 387307
Email: redaktion@darmstaedter-echo.de **Web site:** http://www.echo-online.de
Freq: 312 issues yearly; **Circ:** 13,133
Advertising Manager: Andreas Wohlfart
Profile: Daily newspaper with regional news and a local sports section.
Language(s): German
ADVERTISING RATES:
SCC .... EUR 22,00
Mechanical Data: Type Area: 491 x 339 mm, No. of Columns (Display): 7, Col Widths (Display): 45 mm
Copy instructions: *Copy Date:* 1 day prior to publication
Supplement(s): Generation; Gesund leben heute; handwerk aktuell; Die Hupe; i2 immobilien; Kinder Echo; Odenwälder Kartoffelsupp; Sonntags Echo; Start frei
REGIONAL DAILY & SUNDAY NEWSPAPERS: Regional Daily Newspapers

ODENWÄLDER ZEITUNG

737878G67B-11200
Editorial: Friedrichstr. 24, 69469 WEINHEIM
Tel: 6201 81160 **Fax:** 6201 81167
Email: oz@diesbachmedien.de **Web site:** http://www.wnoz.de
Freq: 312 issues yearly; **Circ:** 22,999
Advertising Manager: Wolfgang Schlösser
Profile: Daily newspaper with regional news and a local sports section. Facebook: http://www.facebook.com/pages/wnoz/295395650806.
Language(s): German
ADVERTISING RATES:
SCC .... EUR 40,00
Mechanical Data: Type Area: 490 x 320 mm, No. of Columns (Display): 7, Col Widths (Display): 44 mm
Copy instructions: *Copy Date:* 2 days prior to publication
REGIONAL DAILY & SUNDAY NEWSPAPERS: Regional Daily Newspapers

DER ODERLANDSPIEGEL - REG.-AUSG. FRANKFURT (ODER)/LANDKREIS MÄRK.-ODERLAND

737881G72-10160
Editorial: Rosa-Luxemburg-Str. 42, 15230 FRANKFURT **Tel:** 335 558990 **Fax:** 335 55899107
Email: redaktion@der-oderland-spiegel.de **Web site:** http://www.der-oderland-spiegel.de
Freq: Weekly; **Cover Price:** Free; **Circ:** 54,860
Editor: Irmtraut Ossowski; **Advertising Manager:** Bernd Helberg
Profile: Advertising journal (house-to-house) concentrating on local stories.
Language(s): German
ADVERTISING RATES:
Full Page Mono .... EUR 2942
Full Page Colour .... EUR 4118
Mechanical Data: Type Area: 430 x 279 mm, No. of Columns (Display): 6, Col Widths (Display): 44 mm
Copy instructions: *Copy Date:* 3 days prior to publication
Supplement(s): Der Ärzte Spiegel
LOCAL NEWSPAPERS

OFF ROAD

738146G77A-260_50
Editorial: Alte Landstr. 21, 85521 OTTOBRUNN
Tel: 89 608210 **Fax:** 89 60821200
Email: redaktion@off-road.de **Web site:** http://www.off-road.de
Freq: Monthly; **Annual Sub.:** EUR 40,80; **Circ:** 52,262
Editor: Cornelia Czerny; **Advertising Manager:** Walter Schneider
Profile: OFF ROAD is the leading magazine on the topics wheel-drive, off-road vehicles and SUVs. Each month, readers can expect a balance of topics in vehicle tests, service issues, accessory ideas, trip reports and the latest in Sports & scene. About Print and Web also offers off-road brand and experience world travel co-operation, driver training and events with partners from the auto and tire industry awards such as the OFF ROAD AWARD and high-quality competitions interesting additional advertising channels for product communication. With these exciting content reaches over 140,000 monthly OFF ROAD readers. The average reader of the OFF ROAD is male, extremely high income, young and eager consumers. He cultivated his outdoor lifestyle with many activities. The OFF ROAD readers will not only fully informed, but lives on the road vehicles and SUVs. OFF ROAD stands for credibility and competence: 89% of readers who rely on the authenticity of buying a new car OFF ROAD. With its clear positioning in the market and the free-spending, brand-oriented readership interested in innovative products OFF ROAD offers the ideal platform for your advertising activities with minimum wastage. Facebook: http://www.facebook.com/offroadmagazin.
Language(s): German
ADVERTISING RATES:
Full Page Mono .... EUR 5980
Full Page Colour .... EUR 9980
Mechanical Data: Type Area: 247 x 184 mm, No. of Columns (Display): 4, Col Widths (Display): 43 mm
Copy instructions: *Copy Date:* 21 days prior to publication
CONSUMER: MOTORING & CYCLING: Motoring

OFF ROAD SPECIAL ALLRADKATALOG

1702983G77A-2752
Editorial: Alte Landstr. 21, 85521 OTTOBRUNN
Tel: 89 608210 **Fax:** 89 60821200
Email: redaktion@off-road.de **Web site:** http://www.off-road.de
Freq: Annual; **Cover Price:** EUR 4,90; **Circ:** 60,000
Advertising Manager: Walter Schneider
Profile: Reference book for all-wheel-and off-road enthusiasts. All available in Germany, SUV and sport utility vehicles at a glance - with information, prices and addresses. An exclusive special section is also introducing 4x4 vehicles from the global production. The catalog is a valuable aid for decision. Facebook: http://www.facebook.com/offroadmagazin.
Language(s): German
ADVERTISING RATES:
Full Page Mono .... EUR 6950
Full Page Colour .... EUR 6950
Mechanical Data: Type Area: 247 x 184 mm
Copy instructions: *Copy Date:* 28 days prior to publication

OFF ROAD SPECIAL TESTJAHRBUCH

1702985G77A-2754
Editorial: Alte Landstr. 21, 85521 OTTOBRUNN
Tel: 89 608210 **Fax:** 89 60821200
Email: redaktion@off-road.de **Web site:** http://www.off-road.de
Freq: Annual; **Cover Price:** EUR 9,80; **Circ:** 50,000
Advertising Manager: Walter Schneider
Profile: At 244 pages, the Testjahrbuch a perfect overview of the major off-road vehicle of the current model year. All major vessels were checked by the editor through its paces - in tests, driving reports, presentations and in direct comparison. Facebook: http://www.facebook.com/offroadmagazin.
Language(s): German
ADVERTISING RATES:
Full Page Mono .... EUR 6950
Full Page Colour .... EUR 6950
Mechanical Data: Type Area: 247 x 184 mm
Copy instructions: *Copy Date:* 28 days prior to publication

OFFENBACHER WIRTSCHAFT

738099G63-700
Editorial: Frankfurter Str. 90, 63067 OFFENBACH
Tel: 69 8207245 **Fax:** 69 8207199
Email: redaktion@offenbach.ihk.de **Web site:** http://www.offenbach.ihk.de
Freq: 10 issues yearly; Free to qualifying individuals
Annual Sub.: EUR 23,00; **Circ:** 24,701
Editor: Klaus Linke
Profile: The Offenbacher Wirtschaft is the membership magazine of the Offenbacher Chamber of Commerce and Industry and the most important source of information for companies in the region. It reaches a monthly 24 407 entrepreneurs, businessmen, traders, managing medium-sized companies and chief executives of large companies and their employees.
Language(s): German
ADVERTISING RATES:
Full Page Mono .... EUR 3350
Full Page Colour .... EUR 3350
Mechanical Data: Type Area: 260 x 185 mm, No. of Columns (Display): 3, Col Widths (Display): 58 mm
Copy instructions: *Copy Date:* 15 days prior to publication
BUSINESS: REGIONAL BUSINESS

OFFENBACH-POST

738100G67B-11220
Editorial: Waldstr. 226, 63071 OFFENBACH
Tel: 69 850080 **Fax:** 69 85008298
Email: red.offenbach@op-online.de **Web site:** http://www.op-online.de
Freq: 312 issues yearly; **Circ:** 48,219
Editor: Frank Pröse; **News Editor:** Ulrich Kaiser;
Advertising Manager: Helmut Moser
Profile: Regional daily newspaper covering politics, economics, sport, travel and technology.
Language(s): German
ADVERTISING RATES:
SCC .... EUR 96,30
Mechanical Data: Type Area: 470 x 322 mm, No. of Columns (Display): 7, Col Widths (Display): 43 mm
Copy instructions: *Copy Date:* 1 day prior to publication
Supplement(s): Bieberer Heimatblatt; doppio; Heimatblatt für Bürgel und Rumpenheim; Start frei
REGIONAL DAILY & SUNDAY NEWSPAPERS: Regional Daily Newspapers

OFFENBACH-POST ONLINE

1621807G67B-16630
Editorial: Waldstr. 226, 63071 OFFENBACH
Tel: 69 85008311 **Fax:** 69 85008391
Email: service@op-online.de **Web site:** http://www.op-online.de
Freq: Daily; **Cover Price:** Paid; **Circ:** 639,329 Unique Users
Editor: Stefan Hautschek; **Advertising Manager:** Armin Schlarb
Profile: Ezine: The information and service platform for city and district of Offenbach provides the latest news and information about politics, economy, culture, sports, travel, technology, etc. Facebook: http://www.facebook.com/oponline.de Twitter: https://twitter.com/#!/OP_online This Outlet offers RSS (Really Simple Syndication).
Language(s): German
REGIONAL DAILY & SUNDAY NEWSPAPERS: Regional Daily Newspapers

OFFENBURGER TAGEBLATT

738102G67B-11240
Editorial: Marlener Str. 9, 77656 OFFENBURG
Tel: 781 5041331 **Fax:** 781 5041319
Email: lokales.offenburg@reiff.de **Web site:** http://www.baden-online.de
Freq: 312 issues yearly; **Circ:** 55,242
Advertising Manager: Kurt Michelfelder
Profile: Regional daily newspaper with news on politics, economy, culture, sports, travel, technology, etc. The Mittelbadische Presse are Offenburger Tageblatt, Kehler Zeitung, Lahrer Zeitung and Acher-Rench-Zeitung. With a total circulation of about 60,000 specimens come from the media company Reiff, "the" home of the newspapers Ortenau. Partly for nearly 200 years we have * Absolute readers around because the reader is with us in the self-Journal * Regional expertise * Information Platform of the events and life in the region * instrument of human communication, commerce, economics and politics in the Ortenau and therefore ideal promotional tool. Newspapers are, six days a week: * News * Independent * unique - they are always subject.
Language(s): German
ADVERTISING RATES:
SCC .... EUR 125,50
Mechanical Data: Type Area: 420 x 284 mm, No. of Columns (Display): 6, Col Widths (Display): 44 mm
Copy instructions: *Copy Date:* 1 day prior to publication
REGIONAL DAILY & SUNDAY NEWSPAPERS: Regional Daily Newspapers

DER ÖFFENTLICHE DIENST

737897G32K-2
Editorial: Luxemburger Str. 449, 50939 KÖLN
Tel: 221 943730 **Fax:** 221 94373901
Web site: http://www.wolterskluwer.de
Freq: 11 issues yearly; **Annual Sub.:** EUR 105,90; **Circ:** 1,200
Profile: Magazine for members of the civil service.
Language(s): German
ADVERTISING RATES:
Full Page Mono .... EUR 1134
Full Page Colour .... EUR 2028
Mechanical Data: Type Area: 270 x 186 mm, No. of Columns (Display): 4, Col Widths (Display): 45 mm
BUSINESS: LOCAL GOVERNMENT, LEISURE & RECREATION: Civil Service

ÖFFENTLICHER ANZEIGER

737900G67B-11260
Editorial: August-Horch-Str. 28, 56070 KOBLENZ
Tel: 261 892240 **Fax:** 261 892770
Email: redaktion@rhein-zeitung.net **Web site:** http://www.rhein-zeitung.de
Freq: 312 issues yearly; **Circ:** 18,650
Profile: Regional daily newspaper with news on politics, economy, culture, sports, travel, technology, etc. The Öffentlicher Anzeiger is a local issue the in koblenz appearing Rhein-Zeitung. Facebook: http://www.facebook.com/rheinzeitung Twitter: http://www.rhein-zeitung.de/twitter.html This Outlet offers RSS (Really Simple Syndication).
Language(s): German
ADVERTISING RATES:
SCC .... EUR 69,80
Mechanical Data: Type Area: 480 x 325 mm, No. of Columns (Display): 7, Col Widths (Display): 45 mm

Copy instructions: *Copy Date:* 1 day prior to
publication
**REGIONAL DAILY & SUNDAY NEWSPAPERS:
Regional Daily Newspapers**

OFFICE BRANDS
1799877G34-552
Editorial: Zimmerstr. 56, 10117 BERLIN
Tel: 30 47907118 **Fax:** 30 47907120
Email: rn@officeabc.de **Web site:** http://www.office-brands.de
Freq: Half-yearly; **Cover Price:** EUR 8,00; **Circ:** 29,570
Editor: Robert Nehring; **Advertising Manager:** Bärbel Skrzypczak
Profile: Magazine on office supplies, office technology and office space.
Language(s): German
ADVERTISING RATES:
Full Page Mono .... EUR 5795
Full Page Colour .... EUR 5795
Mechanical Data: Type Area: 240 x 178 mm, No. of Columns (Display): 3, Col Widths (Display): 56 mm
Copy instructions: *Copy Date:* 30 days prior to publication

OFFICE & PAPER
738134G34-531
Editorial: Aschmattstr. 8, 76532 BADEN-BADEN
Tel: 7221 502220 **Fax:** 7221 502222
Email: info@officeandpaper.de **Web site:** http://www.officeandpaper.de
Freq: 10 issues yearly; **Annual Sub.:** EUR 103,20; **Circ:** 6,846
Editor: Claudia Wasser; **Advertising Manager:** Yvonne Hilbert
Profile: Trade magazine for office supplies and stationery designed for the entire industry. Office & paper uses trends and innovations at an early stage and informed of future-oriented projects. The editorial staff attended trade fairs at home and abroad. Office paper is divided into a magazine (trade, industry, trade fairs) and a partial product. Regularly in the magazine: the heading Officetec with key information from the field of office technology. Facebook: http://www.facebook.com/pages/Officepaper/14002175290841 Twitter: http://twitter.com/#!/officeandpaper This Outlet offers RSS (Really Simple Syndication).
Language(s): German
Readership: Read by office managers.
ADVERTISING RATES:
Full Page Mono .... EUR 2400
Full Page Colour .... EUR 3840
Mechanical Data: Type Area: 240 x 179 mm, No. of Columns (Display): 3, Col Widths (Display): 57 mm
Copy instructions: *Copy Date:* 14 days prior to publication
BUSINESS: OFFICE EQUIPMENT

L'OFFICIEL HOMMES
1983075G86C-249
Editorial: Leonrodstr. 52, 80636 MÜNCHEN
Tel: 89 697490 **Fax:** 89 69749430
Email: lale.aktay@madame.de **Web site:** http://www.madame.de
Freq: Quarterly; **Circ:** 60,000
Editor: Lâle Aktay; **Advertising Manager:** Stefanie Beck
Profile: L'Officiel Hommes - one of the world's best fashion magazines for men. L'Officiel Hommes does not react to the fashion zeitgeist - it sets the fashion zeitgeist. On more than 250 pages, L'Officiel Hommes informs the sophisticated man four times a year about the most important trends in fashion, beauty and culture.
Language(s): German
ADVERTISING RATES:
Full Page Mono .... EUR 12000
Full Page Colour .... EUR 12000
Mechanical Data: Type Area: 295 x 225 mm

L'OFFICIEL HOMMES
1983075G86C-256
Editorial: Leonrodstr. 52, 80636 MÜNCHEN
Tel: 89 697490 **Fax:** 89 69749430
Email: lale.aktay@madame.de **Web site:** http://www.madame.de
Freq: Quarterly; **Circ:** 60,000
Editor: Lâle Aktay; **Advertising Manager:** Stefanie Beck
Profile: L'Officiel Hommes - one of the world's best fashion magazines for men. L'Officiel Hommes does not react to the fashion zeitgeist - it sets the fashion zeitgeist. On more than 250 pages, L'Officiel Hommes informs the sophisticated man four times a year about the most important trends in fashion, beauty and culture.
Language(s): German
ADVERTISING RATES:
Full Page Mono .... EUR 12000
Full Page Colour .... EUR 12000
Mechanical Data: Type Area: 295 x 225 mm

OFFIZIELLES SPEDITEUR-ADRESSBUCH
738141G49A-1500
Editorial: Nordkanalstr. 36, 20097 HAMBURG
Tel: 40 2371401 **Fax:** 40 23714333
Email: spa@dvz.de **Web site:** http://www.spediteur-adressbuch.de
Freq: Annual; **Cover Price:** EUR 116,00; **Circ:** 5,000
Advertising Manager: Ruth Christa Torz
Profile: Directory listing addresses relevant for forwarding agencies.
Language(s): German
ADVERTISING RATES:
Full Page Mono .... EUR 1329
Full Page Colour .... EUR 2229
Mechanical Data: Type Area: 200 x 140 mm
Copy instructions: *Copy Date:* 40 days prior to publication

OH LÀ LÀ FREIZEITMAGAZIN
1794260G89A-12284
Editorial: Ahornweg, 79804 DOGERN **Tel:** 7751 6186
Fax: 7751 700214
Email: erdenbrink@t-online.de **Web site:** http://www.ohlala-freizeitmagazin.com
Freq: Annual; **Cover Price:** EUR 3,50; **Circ:** 15,000
Editor: Monika Erdenbrink
Profile: Journal of leisure and travel tips, trip ideas, hiking, mountaineering, cycling, culture and events for Black Forest, Lake Constance and Switzerland. Walk like you love the mountains, water or musicals, cycling your hobby, you from looking and a luxury hotel and are you not good deals indifferent, that's Oh Lá Lá Leisure magazine just right for you.
Language(s): German
ADVERTISING RATES:
Full Page Mono .... EUR 1399
Full Page Colour .... EUR 1399
Mechanical Data: Type Area: 220 x 155 mm, No. of Columns (Display): 2, Col Widths (Display): 60 mm

OIL GAS EUROPEAN MAGAZINE
738163G33-60
Editorial: Neumann-Reichardt-Str. 34, 22041 HAMBURG **Tel:** 40 65694540 **Fax:** 40 65694553
Email: h.j.mager@oilgaspublisher.de **Web site:** http://www.oilgaspublisher.de
Freq: Quarterly; **Annual Sub.:** EUR 99,30; **Circ:** 5,860
Editor: Hans Jörg Mager; **Advertising Manager:** Harald Jordan
Profile: Magazine about the oil and gas industry in Europe.
Language(s): English
Readership: Aimed at professionals in the oil and gas industry.
ADVERTISING RATES:
Full Page Mono .... EUR 3050
Full Page Colour .... EUR 4100
Mechanical Data: Type Area: 260 x 185 mm, No. of Columns (Display): 3, Col Widths (Display): 60 mm
Copy instructions: *Copy Date:* 10 days prior to publication
BUSINESS: OIL & PETROLEUM

OK!
1833902G74A-3590
Editorial: Gänsemarkt 24, 20354 HAMBURG
Tel: 40 4118825101 **Fax:** 40 4118825102
Email: ulrike.behrens@ok-magazin.de **Web site:** http://www.ok-magazin.de
Freq: Weekly; **Annual Sub.:** EUR 27,95; **Circ:** 147,298
Editor: Alex Siemen
Profile: OK! is the largest People magazine in the world (to be published in 21 editions, reaching 37 million readers a month). The latest from the world of the beautiful & famous: Exclusive interviews and pictures, background stories and the highlights from movies, music and TV. Whether New York, Hollywood, London or Berlin - our reporters report from the red carpet and talk to the people who make the headlines. OK! is the exclusive magazine of the Stars. Each week kidnapped OK! in the glamorous world of Fashion & Beauty. Under the heading OK! Style, we present the latest looks from the international catwalks, speak with models and fashion designers, look in the closets of celebrities. OK! Style tells its readers what's hot today - with glamorous photo shoots, in-depth service stories and current trend reports. Facebook: http://www.facebook.com/OKMagazin.de Twitter: http://twitter.com/OKMagazin This Outlet offers RSS (Really Simple Syndication).
Language(s): German
ADVERTISING RATES:
Full Page Mono .... EUR 14000
Full Page Colour .... EUR 14000
Mechanical Data: Type Area: 252 x 200 mm, No. of Columns (Display): 3, Col Widths (Display): 68 mm

ÖKO TEST
737938G57-1640
Editorial: Kasseler Str. 1a, 60486 FRANKFURT
Tel: 69 97777136 **Fax:** 69 97777139
Email: redaktion@oekotest.de **Web site:** http://www.oekotest.de
Freq: Monthly; **Annual Sub.:** EUR 39,00; **Circ:** 150,519
Editor: Jürgen Stellpflug; **Advertising Manager:** Peter Stäsche
Profile: The focus of ÖKO TEST lies in extensive product and service tests. In every issue there are up to ten comparative tests from all walks of life, each with detailed information on area of interest. In addition, ÖKO TEST appear in-depth background information, news updates, expert interviews, articles and more customers. Each issue contains individual copy issue codes that the reader more information for free from the ÖKO- TEST Web site can download. ÖKO TEST is the highest reach of consumer magazine in Germany, in the monthly advertising can be switched. Facebook: ttp://www.facebook.com/oekotest This Outlet offers RSS (Really Simple Syndication).
Language(s): German
ADVERTISING RATES:
Full Page Mono .... EUR 6700
Full Page Colour .... EUR 10500
Mechanical Data: Type Area: 253 x 183 mm, No. of Columns (Display): 4, Col Widths (Display): 43 mm
Copy instructions: *Copy Date:* 38 days prior to publication
BUSINESS: ENVIRONMENT & POLLUTION

ÖKO TEST
1621806G57-2683
Editorial: Kasseler Str. 1a, 60486 FRANKFURT
Tel: 69 97777136 **Fax:** 69 97777139
Email: webteam@oekotest.de **Web site:** http://www.oekotest.de
Freq: Weekly; **Cover Price:** Paid; **Circ:** 515,035 Unique Users
Editor: Patrick Junker; **Advertising Manager:** Jelena Petric
Profile: Ezine: The focus of ÖKO TEST lies in extensive product and service tests. Facebook: ttp://www.facebook.com/oekotest This Outlet offers RSS (Really Simple Syndication).
Language(s): German
BUSINESS: ENVIRONMENT & POLLUTION

ÖKOLOGISCHES WIRTSCHAFTEN
737931G57-2662
Editorial: Potsdamer Str. 105, 10785 BERLIN
Tel: 30 88459429 **Fax:** 30 8825439
Email: redaktion@ioew.de **Web site:** http://www.ioew.de
Freq: Quarterly; **Annual Sub.:** EUR 64,65; **Circ:** 1,500
Editor: Christopher Garthe; **Advertising Manager:** Stefanie Ott
Profile: Magazine covering ecology and environmental management.
Language(s): German
ADVERTISING RATES:
Full Page Colour .... EUR 2550
Mechanical Data: Type Area: 225 x 175 mm, No. of Columns (Display): 3, Col Widths (Display): 55 mm
BUSINESS: ENVIRONMENT & POLLUTION

OLDENBURGISCHE VOLKSZEITUNG
738182G67B-11300
Editorial: Neuer Markt 2, 49377 VECHTA
Tel: 4441 9560300 **Fax:** 4441 9560310
Email: info@ov-online.de **Web site:** http://www.ov-online.de
Freq: 312 issues yearly; **Annual Sub.:** EUR 25,70; **Circ:** 21,853
Editor: Uwe Haring; **News Editor:** Giorgio Tzimurtas; **Advertising Manager:** Reinhard Brannekämper
Profile: Regional daily newspaper for the district of Vechta and the Oldenburgische Münsterland with news on politics, economy, culture, sports, travel, technology, etc. Facebook: http://www.facebook.com/OVonline This Outlet offers RSS (Really Simple Syndication). This Outlet offers RSS (Really Simple Syndication).
Language(s): German
ADVERTISING RATES:
SCC .... EUR 56,00
Mechanical Data: Type Area: 425 x 282 mm, No. of Columns (Display): 6, Col Widths (Display): 45 mm
Copy instructions: *Copy Date:* 2 days prior to publication
REGIONAL DAILY & SUNDAY NEWSPAPERS: Regional Daily Newspapers

OLDENBURGISCHE WIRTSCHAFT
1659935G63-1755
Editorial: Moslestr. 6, 26122 OLDENBURG
Tel: 441 2220210 **Fax:** 441 2220111
Email: michael.bruns@oldenburg.ihk.de **Web site:** http://www.ihk-oldenburg.de
Freq: Monthly; Free to qualifying individuals
Annual Sub.: EUR 22,00; **Circ:** 16,606
Editor: Michael Bruns; **Advertising Manager:** Ralf Niemeyer
Profile: Magazine from the Oldenburg Chamber of Trade and Industry.
Language(s): German
ADVERTISING RATES:
Full Page Mono .... EUR 2820
Full Page Colour .... EUR 2820
Mechanical Data: Type Area: 272 x 188 mm, No. of Columns (Display): 4, Col Widths (Display): 44 mm
BUSINESS: REGIONAL BUSINESS

OLDTIMER ANZEIGER
1828711G77A-2834
Editorial: Drostestr. 14, 30161 HANNOVER
Tel: 511 390910 **Fax:** 511 39091252
Email: zentrale@dhd.de **Web site:** http://www.dhd24.com
Freq: 6 issues yearly; **Cover Price:** EUR 2,80; **Circ:** 80,000
Advertising Manager: Curd Kitzelmann
Profile: Treasure trove for lovers of old cars. Nationwide Classifieds Photo and secure a wide range of exceptional vehicles. Upgrading and hobbyists offers vintage scoreboard beyond the right spare parts and related accessories.
Language(s): German
ADVERTISING RATES:
Full Page Mono .... EUR 999
Full Page Colour .... EUR 1500
Mechanical Data: Type Area: 280 x 191 mm, No. of Columns (Display): 4, Col Widths (Display): 45 mm
Copy instructions: *Copy Date:* 14 days prior to publication

OLDTIMER INSERAT
1861974G77A-2852
Editorial: Drostestr. 14, 30161 HANNOVER
Tel: 511 390910 **Fax:** 511 39091252
Email: zentrale@dhd.de **Web site:** http://www.dhd24.com
Freq: 6 issues yearly; **Annual Sub.:** EUR 16,00; **Circ:** 60,000
Advertising Manager: Lars Schnatmann
Profile: Whether Beetle Cabrio, Karmann Ghia or Triumph Spitfire, Oldtimer Inserat is the ideal treasure trove for lovers of old cars. Here you will find more than just used cars. Nationwide Classifieds Photo and ensure a broad offering of exceptional cars in your area. Upgrading and hobbyists offers classic car listing also related accessories as well as suitable replacement parts.
Language(s): German
ADVERTISING RATES:
Full Page Mono .... EUR 999
Full Page Colour .... EUR 999
Mechanical Data: Type Area: 280 x 191 mm, No. of Columns (Display): 4, Col Widths (Display): 45 mm
Copy instructions: *Copy Date:* 16 days prior to publication

OLDTIMER KATALOG
738189G77A-1840
Editorial: Gut Pottscheidt, 53639 KÖNIGSWINTER
Tel: 2223 923023 **Fax:** 2223 923013
Email: info@heel-verlag.de **Web site:** http://www.heel-verlag.de
Freq: Annual; **Cover Price:** EUR 17,90; **Circ:** 38,000
Editor: Günther Zink; **Advertising Manager:** Steffen Wagner
Profile: The latest edition of Europe's largest market leader in classic cars presented at the 25th now Output of some 1,100 vehicles over 150 manufacturers in detail in words and pictures. Facebook: http://www.facebook.com/HEELVerlag.
Language(s): German
ADVERTISING RATES:
Full Page Mono .... EUR 1150
Full Page Colour .... EUR 1725
Mechanical Data: Type Area: 269 x 187 mm
Copy instructions: *Copy Date:* 45 days prior to publication

OLDTIMER MARKT
738190G77F-165
Editorial: Lise-Meitner-Str. 2, 55129 MAINZ
Tel: 6131 9920 **Fax:** 6131 992100
Email: redaktion@oldtimer-markt.de **Web site:** http://www.oldtimer-markt.de
Freq: Monthly; **Annual Sub.:** EUR 35,40; **Circ:** 132,465
Editor: Peter Steinfurth; **Advertising Manager:** Michael Kaiser
Profile: Magazine about classic cars and motorcycles.
Language(s): German
Readership: Read by car enthusiasts.
ADVERTISING RATES:
Full Page Mono .... EUR 9760
Full Page Colour .... EUR 11400
Mechanical Data: Type Area: 260 x 185 mm, No. of Columns (Display): 4, Col Widths (Display): 43 mm
CONSUMER: MOTORING & CYCLING: Veteran Cars

OLDTIMER PRAXIS
738191G77F-2
Editorial: Lise-Meitner-Str. 2, 55129 MAINZ
Tel: 6131 9920 **Fax:** 6131 992100
Email: redaktion@oldtimer-praxis.de **Web site:** http://www.oldtimer-markt.de
Freq: Monthly; **Annual Sub.:** EUR 21,00; **Circ:** 98,261
Editor: Lars Rosenbrock; **Advertising Manager:** Michael Kaiser
Profile: OLDTIMER PRAXIS is the most technically-oriented counterpart to the OLDTIMER MARKT. The editorial focus is on detailed reports restoration of classic cars and motorcycles. They deal not only on the technical details of the restorations, including personal experiences of the owners come up with their classics do not go far enough. Visualized in technical articles, technical issues comprehensible on the subject of classic cars explained. Categories like "tips, tricks, gimmicks" provide easily understandable solutions to the toughest problems. In-depth workshops on specific subjects such as engine, chassis and body as well as market surveys and testing of tools, operating supplies and maintenance products round out the editorial approach of OLDTIMER PRAXIS and OLDTIMER MARKT offers its tech-savvy readers of entertainment and value equally and also provides inspiration and know-how "to do it. A continuous increase in circulation since its launch 20 years ago shows the high and growing acceptance of the readership. In the target group are similar and OldTIMER PRAXIS and PLDTIMER MARKT wherein by the practice, readers even more, "inventors and handymen" can be found. This makes it Europe's second most-selling classic car magazine just for suppliers of spare parts and auto accessories for essential advertising medium.
Language(s): German
Readership: Read by car enthusiasts.
ADVERTISING RATES:
Full Page Mono .... EUR 6100
Full Page Colour .... EUR 7400
Mechanical Data: Type Area: 260 x 185 mm, No. of Columns (Display): 4, Col Widths (Display): 43 mm
CONSUMER: MOTORING & CYCLING: Veteran Cars

OLDTIMER TRAKTOR

1732445G21A-4337

Editorial: Lise-Meitner-Str. 2, 55129 MAINZ
Tel: 6131 992143 **Fax:** 6131 992100
Email: redaktion@oldtimer-traktor.com **Web site:** http://www.oldtimer-traktor.com
Freq: 6 issues yearly; **Annual Sub.:** EUR 29,70; **Circ:** 50,392
Editor: Fritz Knebel; **Advertising Manager:** Michael Kaiser
Profile: The magazine is aimed at the classic car scene around classic tractors, stationary engines and Unimogs in all its facets. Content: Type histories, restoration reports and technical contributions with respect to maintenance and care.
Language(s): German
ADVERTISING RATES:
Full Page Mono .... EUR 1150
Full Page Colour .... EUR 1150
Mechanical Data: Type Area: 260 x 185 mm, No. of Columns (Display): 4, Col Widths (Display): 43 mm
Copy instructions: *Copy Date:* 28 days prior to publication
BUSINESS: AGRICULTURE & FARMING

OM ZEITSCHRIFT FÜR ORTHOMOLEKULARE MEDIZIN

1622405G56A-11236

Editorial: Oswald-Hesse-Str. 50, 70469 STUTTGART
Tel: 711 8931959 **Fax:** 711 8931748
Email: anke.niklas@medizinverlage.de **Web site:** http://www.medizinverlage.de
Freq: Quarterly; **Annual Sub.:** EUR 53,50; **Circ:** 11,300
Editor: Anke Niklas; **Advertising Manager:** Kathrin Thomas
Profile: Magazine about orthomolecular medicine.
Language(s): German
ADVERTISING RATES:
Full Page Mono .... EUR 1840
Full Page Colour .... EUR 2770
Mechanical Data: Type Area: 224 x 166 mm
Copy instructions: *Copy Date:* 35 days prior to publication

OMNIBUS NACHRICHTEN

738216G49A-1520

Editorial: Am Weitgarten 37, 53227 BONN
Tel: 228 9442853 **Fax:** 228 445280
Email: info@omnibusspiegel.de **Web site:** http://www.omnibusspiegel.de
Freq: 3 issues yearly; **Annual Sub.:** EUR 33,00; **Circ:** 1,100
Editor: Dieter Hanke; **Advertising Manager:** Dieter Hanke
Profile: Magazine with information on coach travel companies and transport.
Language(s): German
Mechanical Data: Type Area: 255 x 181 mm, No. of Columns (Display): 2
Copy instructions: *Copy Date:* 30 days prior to publication

OMNIBUS SPIEGEL

738218G49A-1560

Editorial: Am Weitgarten 37, 53227 BONN
Tel: 228 9442853 **Fax:** 228 445280
Email: info@omnibusspiegel.de **Web site:** http://www.omnibusspiegel.de
Freq: 9 issues yearly; **Annual Sub.:** EUR 59,00; **Circ:** 3,200
Editor: Dieter Hanke; **Advertising Manager:** Dieter Hanke
Profile: Magazine on coach production and transport in past and present.
Language(s): German
Mechanical Data: Type Area: 255 x 182 mm, No. of Columns (Display): 3, Col Widths (Display): 56 mm
Copy instructions: *Copy Date:* 30 days prior to publication

OMNIBUSREVUE

738217G49B-2

Editorial: Aschauer Str. 30, 81549 MÜNCHEN
Tel: 89 2030432173 **Fax:** 89 2030432167
Email: annekatrin@springer.com **Web site:** http://www.omnibusrevue.de
Freq: Monthly; **Annual Sub.:** EUR 98,90; **Circ:** 6,647
Editor: Anne Katrin Wieser; **Advertising Manager:** Marisa d'Arbonneau
Profile: Magazine containing information about bus and coach transport.
Language(s): German
ADVERTISING RATES:
Full Page Colour .... EUR 4860
Mechanical Data: Type Area: 268 x 199 mm, No. of Columns (Display): 4, Col Widths (Display): 43 mm
BUSINESS: TRANSPORT: Bus & Coach Transport

ONE TO ONE

738227G2A-3620

Editorial: Bei den Mühren 91, 20457 HAMBURG
Tel: 40 36983226 **Fax:** 40 36983236
Email: redaktion@onetoone.de **Web site:** http://www.onetoone.de
Freq: Monthly; **Annual Sub.:** EUR 69,00; **Circ:** 12,245
Profile: Magazine containing articles about marketing communication agencies, budgets and campaigns, enterprises, e-commerce, customer relationship management, database, logistics and services.
Language(s): German
Readership: Aimed at retailers.
ADVERTISING RATES:
Full Page Mono .... EUR 2950
Full Page Colour .... EUR 2950
Mechanical Data: Type Area: 272 x 212 mm, No. of Columns (Display): 4, Col Widths (Display): 50 mm
Copy instructions: *Copy Date:* 21 days prior to publication
BUSINESS: COMMUNICATIONS, ADVERTISING & MARKETING

ONE TO ONE BOOK

763050G2A-5399

Editorial: Bei den Mühren 91, 20457 HAMBURG
Tel: 40 3698320 **Fax:** 40 36983236
Email: redaktion@onetoone.de **Web site:** http://www.onetoone.de
Freq: Annual; **Cover Price:** EUR 29,00; **Circ:** 9,700
Advertising Manager: Birgit Haß
Profile: Publication providing knowledge about the direct marketing branch. Facebook: http://www.facebook.com/ONEtoONE.de Twitter: http://twitter.com/#!/ONEtoONE_de This Outlet offers RSS (Really Simple Syndication).
Language(s): German
ADVERTISING RATES:
Full Page Mono .... EUR 1680
Full Page Colour .... EUR 1680
Mechanical Data: Type Area: 272 x 212 mm

DER ONKOLOGE

738229G56A-7780

Editorial: Tiergartenstr. 17, 69121 HEIDELBERG
Tel: 6221 4878533 **Fax:** 6221 48768533
Email: charlotte.leisse@springer.com **Web site:** http://www.springerlink.com
Freq: Monthly; **Annual Sub.:** EUR 241,00; **Circ:** 2,800
Profile: Der Onkologe deals with relevant issues concerning the diagnosis and therapy of oncological diseases. Special emphasis is placed on oncology's interfaces with the fields of internal medicine, radiology and surgery. This interdisciplinary journal addresses the needs of researchers and doctors working in the field of oncology. The core of each issue consists of comprehensive reviews on a specific topical issue. Here the focus is on providing evidenced based information on diagnostics and therapy relevant for daily practice. After the topics are selected by an independent editorial board, established experts prepare the articles for each issue. Contributions under the rubric "Continuing Medical Education" present the verified results of scientific research and their integration into daily practice.
Language(s): German
Readership: Aimed at physicians.
ADVERTISING RATES:
Full Page Mono .... EUR 2250
Full Page Colour .... EUR 3550
Mechanical Data: Type Area: 240 x 174 mm
Official Journal of: Organ d. Dt. Krebsges. e.V.
BUSINESS: HEALTH & MEDICAL

ONKOLOGIE

738230G56A-7800

Editorial: Wilhelmstr. 20a, 79098 FREIBURG
Tel: 761 452070 **Fax:** 761 4520714
Email: information@karger.de **Web site:** http://www.karger.com
Freq: Monthly; Free to qualifying individuals
Annual Sub.: EUR 253,00; **Circ:** 4,520
Editor: H.-J. Schmoll; **Advertising Manager:** Ellen Zimmermann
Profile: Journal focusing on cancer research and treatment.
Language(s): English; German
ADVERTISING RATES:
Full Page Mono .... EUR 3200
Full Page Colour .... EUR 5240
Mechanical Data: Type Area: 242 x 180 mm, No. of Columns (Display): 2, Col Widths (Display): 90 mm
Copy instructions: *Copy Date:* 42 days prior to publication
Official Journal of: Organ d. Dt. u. d. Österr. Ges. f. Hämatologie u. Onkologie u. d. Österr. Krebsges.-Krebsliga
BUSINESS: HEALTH & MEDICAL

ONKOLOGIE HEUTE

1703354G56A-11389

Editorial: Südl. Auffahrtsallee 73, 80639 MÜNCHEN
Tel: 89 10119151 **Fax:** 89 174230
Email: ulliravens@aol.com **Web site:** http://www.onkologie-heute.org
Freq: 6 issues yearly; **Annual Sub.:** EUR 43,00; **Circ:** 13,651
Editor: Ulrich Ravens
Language(s): German
ADVERTISING RATES:
Full Page Mono .... EUR 2900
Full Page Colour .... EUR 4500
Mechanical Data: Type Area: 245 x 174 mm
BUSINESS: HEALTH & MEDICAL

ONKOLOGISCHE WELT

731544G56A-5500

Editorial: Hölderlinstr. 3, 70174 STUTTGART
Tel: 711 2298737 **Fax:** 711 2298765
Email: peter.henning@schattauer.de **Web site:** http://www.onkologische-welt.de
Freq: 6 issues yearly; **Annual Sub.:** EUR 72,00; **Circ:** 9,800
Editor: Peter Henning; **Advertising Manager:** Christoph Brocker
Profile: The main national and international cancer conferences are in the focus of the journal Onkologische Welt. With this offer, a short, serious convention coverage by renowned medical journalist is directed the Onkologische Welt - as a guide for practice - to all doctors who work in oncology standard care and on current developments and trends in their area quickly and still want to provide comprehensive. Beside the convention coverage, the magazine offers original scientific articles, interviews with opinion leaders and expert commentary and presents current studies. Changing topics, such as psycho-oncology, nutrition and sports or targeted side-effect management round off the program.
Language(s): German
ADVERTISING RATES:
Full Page Mono .... EUR 1940
Full Page Colour .... EUR 3075
Mechanical Data: Type Area: 243 x 179 mm, No. of Columns (Display): 3, Col Widths (Display): 57 mm
Copy instructions: *Copy Date:* 40 days prior to publication
BUSINESS: HEALTH & MEDICAL

OPEN AUTOMATION

738250G5A-8

Editorial: Merianstr. 29, 63069 OFFENBACH
Tel: 69 8400061331 **Fax:** 69 8400061399
Email: openautomation@vde-verlag.de **Web site:** http://www.openautomation.de
Freq: 6 issues yearly; **Annual Sub.:** EUR 59,50; **Circ:** 18,086
Editor: Ronald Heinze; **Advertising Manager:** Markus Lehnert
Profile: Magazine on open automation, providing critical analyses on developments, trends and innovations.
Language(s): German
Readership: Aimed at software developers, managers, engineers in electrical, mechanical engineering and plant construction.
ADVERTISING RATES:
Full Page Mono .... EUR 4100
Full Page Colour .... EUR 5450
Mechanical Data: Type Area: 246 x 175 mm, No. of Columns (Display): 3, Col Widths (Display): 56 mm
Copy instructions: *Copy Date:* 25 days prior to publication
BUSINESS: COMPUTERS & AUTOMATION: Automation & Instrumentation

OPERATIVE ORTHOPÄDIE UND TRAUMATOLOGIE

738253G56A-7840

Editorial: Aschauer Str. 30, 81549 MÜNCHEN
Tel: 89 2030431300 **Fax:** 89 2030431399
Email: gisa.falkowski@springer.com **Web site:** http://www.springermedizin.de
Freq: 5 issues yearly; **Annual Sub.:** EUR 334,00; **Circ:** 3,300
Editor: Gisa Falkowski
Profile: Operative Orthopädie und Traumatologie presents established and new surgical procedures in a coherent structured and elaborately illustrated contributions, and provides a constantly updated surgical teaching. Since 2005, organ-related issues appear, especially to established orthopedic and trauma surgeons.
Language(s): English; German
ADVERTISING RATES:
Full Page Mono .... EUR 1990
Full Page Colour .... EUR 3240
Mechanical Data: Type Area: 240 x 174 mm
Official Journal of: Organ d. Dt. Ges. f. Orthopädie u. Orthopäd. Chirurgie, d. Dt. Ges. f. Unfallchirurgie, d. Österr. Ges. f. Unfallchirurgie u. d. Schweizer. Ges. f. Traumatologie u. Versicherungsmedizin
BUSINESS: HEALTH & MEDICAL

DAS OPERNGLAS

738257G76F-200

Editorial: Grelckstr. 36, 22529 HAMBURG
Tel: 40 585501 **Fax:** 40 585505
Email: info@opernglas.de **Web site:** http://www.opernglas.de
Freq: 11 issues yearly; **Annual Sub.:** EUR 65,00; **Circ:** 19,000
Editor: Ralf Tiedemann
Profile: Magazine providing articles, reviews and performance listings for the opera, concerts and ballet.
Language(s): German
Readership: Aimed at lovers of music and dance.
ADVERTISING RATES:
Full Page Mono .... EUR 3400
Full Page Colour .... EUR 4200
Mechanical Data: Type Area: 242 x 177 mm, No. of Columns (Display): 4, Col Widths (Display): 40 mm
CONSUMER: MUSIC & PERFORMING ARTS: Opera

OPERNWELT

738259G76F-1

Editorial: Knesebeckstr. 59, 10719 BERLIN
Tel: 30 2544950 **Fax:** 30 25449512
Email: redaktion@opernwelt.de **Web site:** http://www.kultiversum.de/opernwelt
Freq: 11 issues yearly; **Annual Sub.:** EUR 137,60; **Circ:** 10,000
Editor: Stephan Mösch; **Advertising Manager:** Annika Kusche
Profile: Content of the magazine Opera: international premiere reports, fixtures of the leading opera houses, singer profiles, interviews, documentaries, cultural and political commentary, CD, DVD and book reviews.
Language(s): German
Readership: Read by opera lovers.
ADVERTISING RATES:
Full Page Mono .... EUR 3000
Full Page Colour .... EUR 3800
Mechanical Data: Type Area: 276 x 215 mm, No. of Columns (Display): 4, Col Widths (Display): 50 mm
Copy instructions: *Copy Date:* 36 days prior to publication
CONSUMER: MUSIC & PERFORMING ARTS: Opera

OPHTHALMOCHIRURGIE

738261G56E-387

Editorial: Maaßstr. 32/1, 69123 HEIDELBERG
Tel: 6221 1377630 **Fax:** 6221 29910
Email: heusel@kaden-verlag.de **Web site:** http://www.kaden-verlag.de
Freq: 6 issues yearly; **Annual Sub.:** EUR 91,50; **Circ:** 1,200
Editor: Jens Funk; **Advertising Manager:** Petra Hübler
Profile: Journal about ophthalmic surgery. Overview contributions, journal papers, health and professional politics, Congress Reports.
Language(s): German
ADVERTISING RATES:
Full Page Mono .... EUR 1455
Full Page Colour .... EUR 2580
Mechanical Data: Type Area: 230 x 178 mm, No. of Columns (Display): 3, Col Widths (Display): 56 mm
Copy instructions: *Copy Date:* 37 days prior to publication
BUSINESS: HEALTH & MEDICAL: Optics

OPHTHALMO-INDEX

1609451G56A-11166

Editorial: Papiermühlenweg 74, 40882 RATINGEN
Tel: 2102 167817 **Fax:** 2102 167828
Email: redaktion@augenspiegel.com **Web site:** http://www.augenspiegel.com
Freq: Annual; **Cover Price:** EUR 15,00; **Circ:** 5,800
Advertising Manager: Karin Lilge
Profile: Directory for ophthalmologists listing companies and medical products.
Language(s): German
ADVERTISING RATES:
Full Page Mono .... EUR 2387
Full Page Colour .... EUR 3950
Mechanical Data: Type Area: 228 x 188 mm
Copy instructions: *Copy Date:* 30 days prior to publication

DER OPHTHALMOLOGE

738262G56E-388

Editorial: Tiergartenstr. 17, 69121 HEIDELBERG
Tel: 6221 4878210 **Fax:** 6221 48768210
Email: christiane.jurek@springer.com **Web site:** http://www.springermedizin.de
Freq: Monthly; **Annual Sub.:** EUR 353,00; **Circ:** 5,800
Advertising Manager: Doris Brandl
Profile: Der Ophthalmologe is an internationally recognized journal dealing with all aspects of ophthalmology. The journal serves both the scientific exchange and the continuing education of ophthalmologists. Freely submitted original papers allow the presentation of important clinical studies and serve scientific exchange. Case reports feature interesting cases and aim at optimizing diagnostic and therapeutic strategies. Comprehensive reviews on a specific topical issue focus on providing evidenced based information on diagnostics and therapy. Review articles under the rubric 'Continuing Medical Education' present verified results of scientific research and their integration into daily practice.
Language(s): German
ADVERTISING RATES:
Full Page Mono .... EUR 2010
Full Page Colour .... EUR 3200
Mechanical Data: Type Area: 240 x 174 mm
Official Journal of: Organ d. Dt. Ophthalmolog. Ges. e.V.
BUSINESS: HEALTH & MEDICAL: Optics

OPHTHALMOLOGISCHE NACHRICHTEN

738264G56E-389

Editorial: Otto-Hahn-Str. 7, 50997 KÖLN
Tel: 2236 376408 **Fax:** 2236 376999
Email: dk@biermann.net **Web site:** http://www.ool.de
Freq: Monthly; **Annual Sub.:** EUR 98,00; **Circ:** 5,159
Editor: Dieter Kaulard; **Advertising Manager:** Michael Kesten
Profile: The „Ophthalmologischen Nachrichten" apply as an opinion-leading German Journal of Ophthalmology. Its report to date on all the relevant health professional and political events and important developments in conservative ophthalmology and ophthalmic surgery. Personal details and current schedule complete the offer. In case of eye doctors are especially popular among the major conferences of the subject as the AAD, DOC, and DOG appears ON Congress editions with real time reporting.
Language(s): German
ADVERTISING RATES:
Full Page Mono .... EUR 2956
Full Page Colour .... EUR 4111
Mechanical Data: Type Area: 430 x 315 mm, No. of Columns (Display): 5, Col Widths (Display): 53 mm
Supplement(s): IOL-Info
BUSINESS: HEALTH & MEDICAL: Optics

OP-JOURNAL

738265G56A-7820

Editorial: Im Kirchenhürstle 4, 79224 UMKIRCH
Tel: 7665 503241 **Fax:** 7665 503240
Email: atzorn.gabriela@synthes.com **Web site:** http://www.thieme.de/op-journal

Freq: 3 issues yearly; **Annual Sub.:** EUR 77,80; **Circ:** 3,000
Editor: Hans-Jörg Oestern
Profile: Magazine for physical doctors with scientific, clinical and technical information concerning surgery.
Language(s): German

OPTIK
738270G55-105
Editorial: Hochschulstr. 6, 64289 DARMSTADT
Tel: 6151 162022 **Fax:** 6151 164123
Email: theo.tschudi@physik.tu-darmstadt.de
Freq: 24 issues yearly; **Annual Sub.:** EUR 736,00
Editor: Theo Tschudi
Profile: International journal focusing on light and electron optics.
Language(s): English
Official Journal of: Organ d. Dt. Ges. f. Elektronenmikroskopie u. d. Dt. Ges. f. angewandte Optik
BUSINESS: APPLIED SCIENCE & LABORATORIES

OPTOINDEX
738279G56A-7940
Editorial: Papiermühlenweg 74, 40882 RATINGEN
Tel: 2102 167827 **Fax:** 2102 167828
Email: manuela.oltersdorf@mediawelt-services.de
Web site: http://www.opto-index.de
Freq: Annual; **Cover Price:** EUR 15,00; **Circ:** 13,600
Advertising Manager: Heike Bergfeld
Profile: Directory on ophthalmologist specialised trade in Germany, Austria and Switzerland.
Language(s): German
ADVERTISING RATES:
Full Page Mono .... EUR 2604
Full Page Colour .... EUR 4164
Mechanical Data: Type Area: 257 x 185 mm
Copy instructions: *Copy Date:* 30 days prior to publication

ORAL AND MAXILLOFACIAL SURGERY
736705G56A-7240
Editorial: Tiergartenstr. 17, 69121 HEIDELBERG
Tel: 6221 4870 **Fax:** 6221 4878366
Email: subscriptions@springer.com **Web site:** http://www.springerlink.com
Freq: Quarterly; **Annual Sub.:** EUR 306,00; **Circ:** 138
Editor: Friedrich-Wilhelm Neukam
Profile: Magazine about recent developments in mouth, jaw and face surgery.
Language(s): English; German
ADVERTISING RATES:
Full Page Mono .... EUR 740
Full Page Colour .... EUR 1780
Mechanical Data: Type Area: 240 x 175 mm

ORALPROPHYLAXE & KINDERZAHNHEILKUNDE
738282G56D-760
Editorial: Dieselstr. 2, 50859 KÖLN
Tel: 2234 7011241 **Fax:** 2234 7011515
Email: schubert@aerzteverlag.de **Web site:** http://www.zahnheilkunde.de
Freq: Quarterly; **Annual Sub.:** EUR 64,00; **Circ:** 5,749
Editor: Hans Gülzow; **Advertising Manager:** Marga Pinsdorf
Profile: Oralprophylaxe und Kinderzahnheilkunde (Oral Prophylaxis and Paediatric Dentistry) is the official publication of the German Society for Paediatric Dentistry (Deutsche Gesellschaft für Kinderzahnheilkunde, DGK) and its 1,408 members (as per July 2010) and the publication of the German Society for Conservative Dentistry (Deutsche Gesellschaft für Zahnerhaltung, DGZ). Oralprophylaxe & Kinderzahnheilkunde is a journal for dentists who are practically or scientifically active in oral prophylaxis or paedodontics, for dentists involved in group therapy for juvenile patients, general dental practitioners and their staff and students eager to learn more about these fields. Oralprophylaxe & Kinderzahnheilkunde provides very practical and well-founded scientific information on all regions of dental prophylaxis and paedodontics. It is distributed specifically to dentists who are actively committed to these topics.
Language(s): German
Readership: Read by dentists involved practically or scientifically in oral prophylaxis.
ADVERTISING RATES:
Full Page Mono .... EUR 1700
Full Page Colour .... EUR 2600
Mechanical Data: Type Area: 265 x 175 mm, No. of Columns (Display): 3, Col Widths (Display): 55 mm
Copy instructions: *Copy Date:* 30 days prior to publication
Official Journal of: Organ d. Dt. Ges. f. Zahnerhaltung e.V. u. d. Ges. f. Kinderzahnheilkunde
BUSINESS: HEALTH & MEDICAL: Dental

ORANIENBURGER GENERALANZEIGER
738284G67B-11320
Editorial: Lehnitzstr. 13, 16515 ORANIENBURG
Tel: 3301 59630 **Fax:** 3301 596350
Email: lokales@oranienburger-generalanzeiger.de
Web site: http://www.die-mark-online.de
Freq: 312 issues yearly; **Circ:** 11,736
Editor: Frank Mangelsdorf; **News Editor:** Claudia Duda; **Advertising Manager:** Tibor Szabo
Profile: Regional daily newspaper covering politics, economics, sport, travel and technology.
Language(s): German
ADVERTISING RATES:
SCC .... EUR 25,70
Mechanical Data: Type Area: 485 x 327 mm, No. of Columns (Display): 7, Col Widths (Display): 43 mm
Copy instructions: *Copy Date:* 3 days prior to publication
Supplement(s): rtv
REGIONAL DAILY & SUNDAY NEWSPAPERS: Regional Daily Newspapers

DAS ORCHESTER
738287G61-80
Editorial: Littenstr. 10, 10179 BERLIN
Tel: 30 8279080 **Fax:** 30 82790817
Email: chefredaktion@dasorchester.de **Web site:** http://www.dasorchester.de
Freq: 11 issues yearly; Free to qualifying individuals
Annual Sub.: EUR 75,00; **Circ:** 20,000
Editor: Gerald Mertens; **Advertising Manager:** Dieter P. Schwarz
Profile: magazine with the largest number of job offers for orchestral musicians throughout the world – also online with search function. It contains information on all topics concerning the orchestra – including training of musicians and performance practice, music and musicians' medicine, education in music and educational programmes, attraction of audiences and cultural funding, orchestra marketing and orchestra management. It takes a look at the international orchestra scene, reports on the work of radio choirs andpublishes studies on audience research. Reports on concert series, premieres, music festivals, competitions and conferences reflect the current musical life.In addition, it provides information on News for Musicians and on instrument making, newsflashes and detailed reviews of new books, scores, CDs and DVDs. Appears in 45 countries around the world.
Language(s): German
Readership: Aimed at amateur and professional musicians, opera and concert lovers, instrumental teachers, musicologists, music students and instrument manufacturers.
ADVERTISING RATES:
Full Page Mono .... EUR 1735
Full Page Colour .... EUR 2169
Mechanical Data: Type Area: 260 x 185 mm
Copy instructions: *Copy Date:* 34 days prior to publication
BUSINESS: MUSIC TRADE

ORGANISATIONSBERATUNG, SUPERVISION, COACHING (OSC)
738294G14A-5160
Editorial: Taunusstr. 126, 61440 OBERURSEL
Tel: 6171 708994
Email: kontakt@schmidt-lellek.de **Web site:** http://www.osc-digital.de
Freq: Quarterly; **Annual Sub.:** EUR 108,00; **Circ:** 1,150
Editor: Christoph J. Schmidt-Lellek; **Advertising Manager:** Yvonne Guderjahn
Profile: International forum for performance and counselling.
Language(s): German
ADVERTISING RATES:
Full Page Mono .... EUR 735
Full Page Colour .... EUR 1635
Mechanical Data: Type Area: 190 x 125 mm, No. of Columns (Display): 2, Col Widths (Display): 61 mm

ORGANISATIONSENT-WICKLUNG
738295S14A-740
Editorial: Postfach 150506, 80044 MÜNCHEN
Tel: 89 71998852 **Fax:** 89 71998851
Email: zoe.redaktion@fachverlag.de **Web site:** http://www.zoe.ch
Freq: Quarterly; **Annual Sub.:** EUR 98,00; **Circ:** 6,250
Editor: Katharina Rockinger; **Advertising Manager:** Ralf Pötzsch
Profile: The organizational development is the leading specialist on questions of organization and management development and change management journal. Concepts, approaches and practical guidelines for designing and implementing change processes. Critically reflected experience reports and case studies from many fields of application.
Language(s): German
ADVERTISING RATES:
Full Page Mono .... EUR 1135
Full Page Colour .... EUR 1850
Mechanical Data: Type Area: 265 x 175 mm, No. of Columns (Display): 2, Col Widths (Display): 85 mm
Copy instructions: *Copy Date:* 28 days prior to publication
BUSINESS: COMMERCE, INDUSTRY & MANAGEMENT

ORNITHOLOGISCHE MITTEILUNGEN
738324G81F-100
Editorial: An der Ronne 184, 50859 KÖLN
Tel: 2234 70584 **Fax:** 2234 79154
Freq: 11 issues yearly; **Annual Sub.:** EUR 56,40; **Circ:** 1,000
Editor: Walther Thiede
Profile: Magazine providing scientific information and research into the field of ornithology.
Language(s): German
Readership: Aimed at ornithologists.
ADVERTISING RATES:
Full Page Mono .... EUR 358
Mechanical Data: Type Area: 200 x 130 mm
Copy instructions: *Copy Date:* 30 days prior to publication
CONSUMER: ANIMALS & PETS: Birds

ORTHO PRESS
738339G94H-14429
Editorial: Hansaring 115, 50670 KÖLN
Tel: 221 9408250 **Fax:** 221 9408211
Email: info@orthopress.de **Web site:** http://www.orthopress.de
Freq: Quarterly; **Annual Sub.:** EUR 17,50; **Circ:** 898,735
Editor: Curt Findeisen
Profile: Orthopaedic journal for customers.
Language(s): German
ADVERTISING RATES:
Full Page Mono .... EUR 13500
Full Page Colour .... EUR 19575
Mechanical Data: Type Area: 238 x 176 mm, No. of Columns (Display): 3, Col Widths (Display): 56 mm
Copy instructions: *Copy Date:* 26 days prior to publication
CONSUMER: OTHER CLASSIFICATIONS: Customer Magazines

DER ORTHOPÄDE
738332G56A-7960
Editorial: Tiergartenstr. 17, 69121 HEIDELBERG
Tel: 6221 4878218 **Fax:** 6221 48768218
Email: michael.baenfer@springer.com **Web site:** http://www.springerlink.com
Freq: Monthly; **Annual Sub.:** EUR 335,00; **Circ:** 3,302
Editor: Volker Ewerbeck; **Advertising Manager:** Noëla Krischer-Janka
Profile: Der Orthopäde is an internationally recognized journal dealing with all aspects of orthopaedics and its neighboring areas. The journal serves both the scientific exchange and the continuing education of orthopaedists. Freely submitted original papers allow the presentation of important clinical studies and serve scientific exchange. Comprehensive reviews on a specific topical issue focus on providing evidenced based information on diagnostics and therapy. Review articles under the rubric 'Continuing Medical Education' present verified results of scientific research and their integration into daily practice.
Language(s): German
Readership: Aimed at orthopaedic surgeons.
ADVERTISING RATES:
Full Page Mono .... EUR 2040
Full Page Colour .... EUR 3230
Mechanical Data: Type Area: 240 x 174 mm
Official Journal of: Organ d. Dt. Ges. f. Orthopädie u. Orthopäd. Chirurgie u. d. Dt. Ges. f. Orthopädie u. Unfallchirurgie
BUSINESS: HEALTH & MEDICAL

ORTHOPÄDIE IM PROFIL
1924167G56A-11620
Editorial: Rößlerstr. 90, 64293 DARMSTADT
Tel: 6151 8090200 **Fax:** 6151 8090179
Email: ralf.mateblowski@wiley.com **Web site:** http://www.gitverlag.com
Freq: Half-yearly; **Cover Price:** EUR 12,60
Free to qualifying individuals ; **Circ:** 12,000
Editor: Ralf Mateblowski; **Advertising Manager:** Ralf Mateblowski
Profile: In the seventh year since its inception from the proven editorship of Prof. Dr. Georg Köster, chief physician at the Orthopaedic Surgery Clinic in Lorsch, the GIT is the successful special issue in 2011 again half a year out: Issue 1 / 2011 appears before the annual meeting of the Association of South German orthopedic association in Baden-Baden, Issue 2 / 2011 at the German Congress of Orthopaedics and Trauma Surgery in Berlin. Expert authors take a stand on current issues in orthopedic and trauma surgery. Focus on their application-oriented contributions - often in tandem with the developers and providers in this absolutely exciting and innovative profession - is of exceptionally high practical relevance.
Language(s): German
ADVERTISING RATES:
Full Page Colour .... EUR 3500
Mechanical Data: Type Area: 260 x 185 mm, No. of Columns (Display): 3, Col Widths (Display): 60 mm

ORTHOPÄDIE MITTEILUNGEN
738333G56A-7980
Editorial: Rüdigerstr. 14, 70469 STUTTGART
Tel: 711 8931617 **Fax:** 711 8931408
Email: kathrin.juergens@thieme.de **Web site:** http://www.thieme.de/ortho
Freq: 6 issues yearly; Free to qualifying individuals
Annual Sub.: EUR 202,40; **Circ:** 10,767
Editor: Fritz Uwe Niethard
Profile: Orthopädie Mitteilungen reports on current results and delivers news from orthopedic specialist organizations. It also offers interesting contributions to the clinic and practice environments and a detailed course and convention calendar. The journal reflects the current scientific and political situation and development of the subject and thus enjoys the highest awareness and acceptance among readers.
Language(s): German
ADVERTISING RATES:
Full Page Mono .... EUR 2900
Full Page Colour .... EUR 4490
Mechanical Data: Type Area: 250 x 175 mm, No. of Columns (Display): 4, Col Widths (Display): 40 mm

ORTHOPÄDIE SCHUHTECHNIK
738334G29-40
Editorial: Schubartstr. 21, 73312 GEISLINGEN
Tel: 7331 930154 **Fax:** 7331 930191
Email: wolfgang.best@ostechnik.de **Web site:** http://www.ostechnik.de
Freq: Monthly; **Annual Sub.:** EUR 118,45; **Circ:** 3,621
Editor: Wolfgang Best; **Advertising Manager:** Sibylle Lutz
Profile: Journal about orthopaedic shoe technology.
Language(s): German
Readership: Aimed at those involved in the shoe industry.
ADVERTISING RATES:
Full Page Mono .... EUR 1850
Full Page Colour .... EUR 3200
Mechanical Data: Type Area: 262 x 185 mm, No. of Columns (Display): 4, Col Widths (Display): 43 mm
Copy instructions: *Copy Date:* 20 days prior to publication
Official Journal of: Organ d. Zentralverb. Gesundheitshandwerk Orthopädieschuhtechnik u. d. Internat. Verb. d. Orthopädieschuhtechniker
BUSINESS: FOOTWEAR

ORTHOPÄDIE TECHNIK
1655633G14R-6054
Editorial: Reinoldistr. 7, 44135 DORTMUND
Tel: 231 55705052 **Fax:** 231 55705070
Email: boecker@ot-forum.de **Web site:** http://www.ot-forum.de
Freq: Monthly; **Annual Sub.:** EUR 112,00; **Circ:** 2,920
Editor: Dirk Böcker; **Advertising Manager:** Gudrun Bramsiepe
Profile: Magazine for orthopaedy and rehabilitation supply stores.
Language(s): English; German
ADVERTISING RATES:
Full Page Mono .... EUR 1590
Full Page Colour .... EUR 2820
Mechanical Data: Type Area: 265 x 185 mm, No. of Columns (Display): 4, Col Widths (Display): 43 mm
Copy instructions: *Copy Date:* 21 days prior to publication
Official Journal of: Organ d. Bundesinnungsverb. f. Orthopädie-Technik u. d. Interbor
Supplement(s): Orthopädie Technik; Orthopädie Technik Sport
BUSINESS: COMMERCE, INDUSTRY & MANAGEMENT: Commerce Related

ORTHOPÄDIE & RHEUMA
738336G56A-8000
Editorial: Aschauer Str. 30, 81549 MÜNCHEN
Tel: 89 2030431406 **Fax:** 89 2030431399
Email: brigitta.schneider@springer.com **Web site:** http://www.orthopaedieundrheuma.de
Freq: 11 issues yearly; Free to qualifying individuals
Annual Sub.: EUR 106,00; **Circ:** 6,138
Editor: Brigitta Schneider
Profile: Orthopädie & Rheuma reports from the field for the field to date on issues that are directly tailored to the area of interest of the target group. Experienced doctors from hospitals and practice and a scientific advisory board responsible for editorial and the contributions as authors of this journal. In addition to accounting technical, economic and legal issues affecting the profession and for medical training is in a practice orthopedics, rheumatology and applied modern pain therapy at the center. Selected contributions of the Bavarian Medical Association as certified education (CME) approved.
Language(s): German
Readership: Aimed at specialists in the fields of orthopaedics and rheumatology.
ADVERTISING RATES:
Full Page Mono .... EUR 2200
Full Page Colour .... EUR 3450
Mechanical Data: Type Area: 240 x 174 mm, No. of Columns (Display): 3, Col Widths (Display): 54 mm
Official Journal of: Organ d. Interdisziplinären Ges. f. orthopäd., unfallchirurg. u. allg. Schmerztherapie
BUSINESS: HEALTH & MEDICAL

ORTHOPÄDIE UND UNFALLCHIRUGIE UP2DATE
1697524G56A-11383
Editorial: Rüdigerstr. 14, 70469 STUTTGART
Tel: 711 8931617 **Fax:** 711 8931623
Email: kathrin.juergens@thieme.de **Web site:** http://www.thieme.de/fz/ou-u2d.html
Freq: 6 issues yearly; **Annual Sub.:** EUR 194,40; **Circ:** 6,000
Profile: Orthopädie und Unfallchirurgie up2date is the successful practice-oriented comprehensive textbook for the further CME education in the joint training times. Four high-quality colored designed individual contributions per issue, which are bound separately and can be stored individually by the subscribers in a ring binder.
Language(s): German
ADVERTISING RATES:
Full Page Mono .... EUR 1820
Full Page Colour .... EUR 3020
Mechanical Data: Type Area: 256 x 180 mm

ORTHOPÄDISCHE NACHRICHTEN
738337G56A-8020
Editorial: Otto-Hahn-Str. 7, 50997 KÖLN
Tel: 2236 3760 **Fax:** 2236 376999
Email: info@biermann.net **Web site:** http://www.biermann.net
Freq: Monthly; **Annual Sub.:** EUR 98,00; **Circ:** 7,784
Editor: Christian Heinemeyer; **Advertising Manager:** Katrin Gross
Profile: The ,,Orthopädische Nachrichten" are among the opinion-leading magazines of German orthopedics and trauma surgery. They report to date on all events, developments, personalities and conventions in the subject. The conference expenses for the annual meeting of the South German

orthopedists in May and the German Congress of Orthopaedics and Trauma Surgery in Berlin in October, noted for its daily news reporting exceptionally strong.
Language(s): German
ADVERTISING RATES:
Full Page Mono .... EUR 2956
Full Page Colour .... EUR 4111
Mechanical Data: Type Area: 378 x 285 mm, No. of Columns (Display): 5, Col Widths (Display): 53 mm
Copy instructions: *Copy Date:* 21 days prior to publication
BUSINESS: HEALTH & MEDICAL

ORTHOPÄDISCHE PRAXIS
738338G56A-8040
Editorial: Wilhelmshöher Allee 345, 34131 KASSEL
Tel: 561 3084231 **Fax:** 561 3084204
Email: werner.siebert@vitos-ok.de
Freq: Monthly; Free to qualifying individuals
Annual Sub.: EUR 122,25; **Circ:** 5,090
Editor: Werner Siebert; **Advertising Manager:** Brigitte Burandt
Profile: Official journal of the Orthopaedics Association of Southern Germany.
Language(s): German
ADVERTISING RATES:
Full Page Mono .... EUR 1581
Full Page Colour .... EUR 2731
Mechanical Data: Type Area: 235 x 175 mm, No. of Columns (Display): 3, Col Widths (Display): 45 mm
Copy instructions: *Copy Date:* 40 days prior to publication
Official Journal of: Organ d. Vereinigung Süddt. Orthopäden e.V.
BUSINESS: HEALTH & MEDICAL

OSCHATZER ALLGEMEINE
738355G67B-11340
Editorial: Peterssteinweg 19, 04107 LEIPZIG
Tel: 341 21810 **Fax:** 341 21811543
Email: chefredaktion@lvz.de **Web site:** http://www.lvz.de
Freq: 312 issues yearly; **Circ:** 8,455
Advertising Manager: Harald Weiß
Profile: Daily newspaper with regional news and a local sports section. Twitter: http://twitter.com/lvzonline This Outlet offers RSS (Really Simple Syndication).
Language(s): German
ADVERTISING RATES:
SCC .... EUR 42,40
Mechanical Data: Type Area: 528 x 371 mm, No. of Columns (Display): 8, Col Widths (Display): 45 mm
Copy instructions: *Copy Date:* 2 days prior to publication
Supplement(s): prisma
REGIONAL DAILY & SUNDAY NEWSPAPERS: Regional Daily Newspapers

OST|AUSSCHUSS INFORMATIONEN
1601570G14C-4714
Editorial: Breite Str. 29, 10178 BERLIN
Tel: 30 20281441 **Fax:** 30 20282441
Email: ost-ausschuss@bdi-online.de **Web site:** http://www.ost-ausschuss.de
Freq: 10 issues yearly; **Circ:** 5,000
Profile: Magazine containing information for companies and institutions about economic developments in Middle and Eastern Europe.
Language(s): German
ADVERTISING RATES:
Full Page Mono .... EUR 2200
Full Page Colour .... EUR 2800
Mechanical Data: Type Area: 265 x 175 mm
Copy instructions: *Copy Date:* 14 days prior to publication
Supplement to: Ost-West Contact

OSTBAU
1622406G4E-6958
Editorial: Legefelder Hauptstr. 14a, 99438 WEIMAR
Tel: 3643 903224 **Fax:** 3643 511933
Email: wstgmbh.weimar@t-online.de **Web site:** http://www.wst-verlag.de
Freq: 5 issues yearly; **Annual Sub.:** EUR 25,00; **Circ:** 8,100
Editor: Jörg Schuster; **Advertising Manager:** Ramona Fleck
Profile: Magazine on building conservation and accommodation economy of the German New Laender.
Language(s): German
ADVERTISING RATES:
Full Page Mono .... EUR 1465
Full Page Colour .... EUR 2235
Mechanical Data: Type Area: 267 x 185 mm

OSTBAYERN WINTERJOURNAL
1862620G89A-12421
Editorial: Luitpoldstr. 20, 93047 REGENSBURG
Tel: 941 585390 **Fax:** 941 5853939
Email: wullinger@ostbayern-tourismus.de **Web site:** http://www.ostbayern-tourismus.de
Freq: Annual; **Cover Price:** Free; **Circ:** 30,000
Editor: Regina Wullinger
Profile: Journal of the winter sports regions of eastern Bavaria with holiday offers.
Language(s): German

OSTEOLOGIE OSTEOLOGY
1853235S56A-2186
Editorial: Hölderlinstr. 3, 70174 STUTTGART
Tel: 711 2298735 **Fax:** 711 2298765
Email: claudia.stein@schattauer.de **Web site:** http://www.schattauer.de
Freq: Quarterly; Free to qualifying individuals
Annual Sub.: EUR 142,00; **Circ:** 2,050
Editor: Claudia Stein; **Advertising Manager:** Jasmin Thurner
Profile: The Osteologie Osteology is an interdisciplinary journal for continuing education and training in the field of osteology. It publishes in the form of focal point stapling review articles, original articles, case reports and short communications from all areas which have been experimentally or clinically deal with diseases of the musculoskeletal system, specifically bone and joint diseases. Other sections provide carefully selected and annotated presentations of current literature as well as short messages from research and industry. Regular recommendations and guidelines of the associated professional society in the magazine are published.
Language(s): English; German
ADVERTISING RATES:
Full Page Mono .... EUR 1505
Full Page Colour .... EUR 2665
Mechanical Data: Type Area: 243 x 179 mm, No. of Columns (Display): 3, Col Widths (Display): 57 mm
Copy instructions: *Copy Date:* 40 days prior to publication
Official Journal of: Organ d. Dt. Ges. f. Osteologie d. Orthopäd. Ges. f. Osteologie u. d. Dachverb. Osteologie e.V.

OSTEOPATHISCHE MEDIZIN
738384G56A-8060
Editorial: Annenhofer Weg 5, 24247 RODENBEK
Email: redaktion@osteopathische-medizin.de
Freq: Quarterly; **Annual Sub.:** EUR 161,00; **Circ:** 4,000
Profile: Magazine on holistic medicine.
Language(s): German
ADVERTISING RATES:
Full Page Mono .... EUR 1200
Full Page Colour .... EUR 2520
Mechanical Data: Type Area: 233 x 162 mm

OSTERBURGER VOLKSSTIMME
738386G67B-11360
Editorial: Bahnhofstr. 17, 39104 MAGDEBURG
Tel: 391 59990 **Fax:** 391 5999210
Email: chefredaktion@volksstimme.de **Web site:** http://www.volksstimme.de
Freq: 312 issues yearly; **Circ:** 31,795
Advertising Manager: Rainer Pfeil
Profile: As the largest daily newspaper in northern Saxony-Anhalt, the Volksstimme reaches 536,000 readers a day" (MA 2010). From Monday to Saturday a team of highly qualified editors put together the latest information and news from the region and around the world. Thanks the 18 local editions is the Volksstimme always close to the action. Twitter: http://twitter.com/volksstimme This Outlet offers RSS (Really Simple Syndication).
Language(s): German
ADVERTISING RATES:
SCC .... EUR 77,60
Mechanical Data: Type Area: 480 x 327 mm, No. of Columns (Display): 7, Col Widths (Display): 45 mm
Copy instructions: *Copy Date:* 2 days prior to publication
Supplement(s): Anstoss im Landkreis Stendal; bauRatgeber; Biber; Leser-Reisen; prisma; Standort Landkreis Stendal
REGIONAL DAILY & SUNDAY NEWSPAPERS: Regional Daily Newspapers

OSTERHOFENER ZEITUNG
738387G67B-11380
Editorial: Medienstr. 5, 94036 PASSAU
Tel: 851 8020 **Fax:** 851 802256
Email: pnp@vgp.de **Web site:** http://www.pnp.de
Freq: 312 issues yearly; **Circ:** 22,743
Advertising Manager: Gerhard Koller
Profile: Daily newspaper with regional news and a local sports section. Twitter: http://twitter.com/pnp_online This Outlet offers RSS (Really Simple Syndication).
Language(s): German
ADVERTISING RATES:
SCC .... EUR 62,50
Mechanical Data: Type Area: 482 x 325 mm, No. of Columns (Display): 7, Col Widths (Display): 45 mm
Copy instructions: *Copy Date:* 2 days prior to publication
REGIONAL DAILY & SUNDAY NEWSPAPERS: Regional Daily Newspapers

OSTERHOLZER ANZEIGER
738388G72-10308
Editorial: Bahnhofstr. 58, 27711 OSTERHOLZ-SCHARMBECK **Tel:** 4791 966566 **Fax:** 4791 966573
Email: redaktion@anzeiger-verlag.de **Web site:** http://www.marktplatz-osterholz.de
Freq: Weekly; **Cover Price:** Free; **Circ:** 52,700
Editor: Ulla Ingenhoven; **Advertising Manager:** Albert Michel
Profile: Advertising journal (house-to-house) concentrating on local stories.
Language(s): German
ADVERTISING RATES:
Full Page Mono .... EUR 5248
Full Page Colour .... EUR 5578
Mechanical Data: Type Area: 490 x 330 mm, No. of Columns (Display): 7, Col Widths (Display): 45 mm
Copy instructions: *Copy Date:* 2 days prior to publication
LOCAL NEWSPAPERS

OSTERIE D'ITALIA
1657226G89A-11883
Editorial: Grillparzerstr. 12, 81675 MÜNCHEN
Tel: 89 41981453 **Fax:** 89 41981123
Web site: http://www.graefe-und-unzer.de
Freq: Annual; **Cover Price:** EUR 29,90; **Circ:** 20,000
Profile: Completely revised and researched leads, "Osteria d'Italia" the travelers to Italy again in the finest taverns in the country. In all parts there are taverns, cafes and Enotec, bars and cake shops who have the original regional cuisine, initially prescribed hospitality and sensual pleasure, which is recommended by SLOW FOOD here the best 1732. Entertaining portraits of the inns and essays provide vivid insights on regional particularities. In addition, the reader tips for outstanding services such as wine or cheese and extensive culinary vocabulary helps with shopping and restaurant. This is "Osteria d'Italia" is the ideal companion for exploring the authentic Italian regional cuisine and lifestyle.
Language(s): German
Mechanical Data: Type Area: 195 x 100 mm

OSTERLÄNDER VOLKSZEITUNG
738391G67B-11400
Editorial: Peterssteinweg 19, 04107 LEIPZIG
Tel: 341 21810 **Fax:** 341 21811543
Email: chefredaktion@lvz.de **Web site:** http://www.lvz.de
Freq: 312 issues yearly; **Circ:** 13,898
Advertising Manager: Harald Weiß
Profile: Daily newspaper with regional news and a local sports section. Twitter: http://twitter.com/lvzonline This Outlet offers RSS (Really Simple Syndication).
Language(s): German
ADVERTISING RATES:
SCC .... EUR 54,80
Mechanical Data: Type Area: 528 x 371 mm, No. of Columns (Display): 8, Col Widths (Display): 45 mm
Copy instructions: *Copy Date:* 2 days prior to publication
Supplement(s): prisma
REGIONAL DAILY & SUNDAY NEWSPAPERS: Regional Daily Newspapers

OSTEUROPA
738392G82-6620
Editorial: Schaperstr. 30, 10719 BERLIN
Tel: 30 21478412 **Fax:** 30 21478414
Email: info@dgo-online.org **Web site:** http://www.dgo-online.org
Freq: Monthly; Free to qualifying individuals
Annual Sub.: EUR 96,00; **Circ:** 1,800
Editor: Manfred Sapper; **Advertising Manager:** Brigitta Weiss
Profile: Magazine about politics and current affairs in Eastern Europe.
Language(s): German
ADVERTISING RATES:
Full Page Mono .... EUR 500
Mechanical Data: Type Area: 205 x 122 mm
CONSUMER: CURRENT AFFAIRS & POLITICS

OSTEUROPA WIRTSCHAFT
738393G14C-70
Editorial: Beltweg 20, 80805 MÜNCHEN
Tel: 89 36105686
Email: franz_lothar_a@hotmail.com
Freq: Quarterly; **Annual Sub.:** EUR 56,00; **Circ:** 450
Editor: Franz-Lothar Altmann; **Advertising Manager:** Brigitta Weiss
Profile: International journal covering industry and commerce in Eastern Europe.
Language(s): German
ADVERTISING RATES:
Full Page Mono .... EUR 400
Mechanical Data: Type Area: 205 x 122 mm
BUSINESS: COMMERCE, INDUSTRY & MANAGEMENT: International Commerce

OSTFRIESEN ZEITUNG
738395G67B-11420
Editorial: Maiburger Str. 8, 26789 LEER
Tel: 491 9790100 **Fax:** 491 9790201
Email: redaktion@oz-online.de **Web site:** http://www.oz-online.de
Freq: 312 issues yearly; **Circ:** 38,829
Editor: Uwe Heitmann; **Advertising Manager:** Uwe Boden
Profile: The Ostfriesen-Zeitung is a regional daily newspaper for East Friesland (counties Aurich, Leer and Wittmund, Emden) with news on politics, economy, culture, sports, travel, technology, etc. The Ostfriesen-Zeitung is published as a morning newspaper six times a week (Monday to Saturday) in the Berliner format in four successive issues Leer, Emden/Norden, Aurich/Wittmund and Rheiderland. This Outlet offers RSS (Really Simple Syndication).
Language(s): German
ADVERTISING RATES:
SCC .... EUR 84,00
Mechanical Data: Type Area: 420 x 282 mm, No. of Columns (Display): 6, Col Widths (Display): 43 mm
Copy instructions: *Copy Date:* 2 days prior to publication
REGIONAL DAILY & SUNDAY NEWSPAPERS: Regional Daily Newspapers

OSTFRIESISCHE NACHRICHTEN
738397G67B-11440
Editorial: Kirchstr. 8, 26603 AURICH
Tel: 4941 170893 **Fax:** 4941 170848
Email: redaktion@on-online.de **Web site:** http://www.on-online.de
Freq: 312 issues yearly; **Circ:** 14,113
Editor: Ralf Klöker; **Advertising Manager:** Uwe Boden
Profile: Daily newspaper with regional news and a local sports section.
Language(s): German
ADVERTISING RATES:
SCC .... EUR 50,40
Mechanical Data: Type Area: 487 x 329 mm, No. of Columns (Display): 7, Col Widths (Display): 43 mm
Copy instructions: *Copy Date:* 2 days prior to publication
Supplement(s): Ostfriesische Kinder Nachrichten
REGIONAL DAILY & SUNDAY NEWSPAPERS: Regional Daily Newspapers

OSTFRIESISCHER KURIER
738398G67B-11460
Editorial: Stellmacherstr. 14, 26506 NORDEN
Tel: 4931 925230 **Fax:** 4931 925307
Email: ok-redaktion@skn.info **Web site:** http://www.skn.info
Freq: 312 issues yearly; **Circ:** 14,126
Editor: Thomas Aldick; **Advertising Manager:** Ludwig Freesemann
Profile: Since 07/02/1867, the Ostfriesische Kurier is the home newspaper for the city Norden and its surrounding communities and the North Sea islands Norderney, Juist and Baltrum. Today, the daily newspaper Ostfriesischer Kurier holds with 14,000 copies sold in its territory in the area of Norden a market share of about 90 percent.
Language(s): German
ADVERTISING RATES:
SCC .... EUR 42,80
Mechanical Data: Type Area: 420 x 282 mm, No. of Columns (Display): 6, Col Widths (Display): 45 mm
Copy instructions: *Copy Date:* 2 days prior to publication
REGIONAL DAILY & SUNDAY NEWSPAPERS: Regional Daily Newspapers

OSTFRIESLAND MAGAZIN
738399G80-8720
Editorial: Stellmacherstr. 14, 26506 NORDEN
Tel: 4931 925227 **Fax:** 4931 925360
Email: oma-redaktion@skn.info **Web site:** http://www.ostfriesland-magazin.de
Freq: Monthly; **Annual Sub.:** EUR 54,80; **Circ:** 11,055
Editor: Reinhard Former; **Advertising Manager:** Dorothea Christians
Profile: Magazine focusing on the Ostfriesland region of Northern Germany.
Language(s): German
ADVERTISING RATES:
Full Page Mono .... EUR 1595
Full Page Colour .... EUR 1870
Mechanical Data: Type Area: 275 x 187 mm, No. of Columns (Display): 4, Col Widths (Display): 45 mm
CONSUMER: RURAL & REGIONAL INTEREST

OSTHEIMER ZEITUNG
738400G67B-11480
Editorial: Paulinenstr. 32, 97645 OSTHEIM
Tel: 9777 518 **Fax:** 9777 1563
Freq: 156 issues yearly; **Circ:** 821
Advertising Manager: Jörg Gunzenheimer
Profile: Daily newspaper with regional news and a local sports section.
Language(s): German
ADVERTISING RATES:
SCC .... EUR 5,90
Mechanical Data: Type Area: 420 x 280 mm, No. of Columns (Display): 6, Col Widths (Display): 45 mm
Copy instructions: *Copy Date:* 3 days prior to publication
REGIONAL DAILY & SUNDAY NEWSPAPERS: Regional Daily Newspapers

OSTHOLSTEINER ANZEIGER
738401G67B-11500
Editorial: Nikolaistr. 7, 24937 FLENSBURG
Tel: 461 8080 **Fax:** 461 8081058
Email: redaktion@shz.de **Web site:** http://www.shz.de
Freq: 312 issues yearly; **Circ:** 7,407
Advertising Manager: Mathias Kordts
Profile: Daily newspaper with regional news and a local sports section. Facebook: http://www.facebook.com/shzonline Twitter: http://twitter.com/shz_de This Outlet offers RSS (Really Simple Syndication).
Language(s): German
ADVERTISING RATES:
SCC .... EUR 40,80
Mechanical Data: Type Area: 480 x 325 mm, No. of Columns (Display): 7, Col Widths (Display): 45 mm
Copy instructions: *Copy Date:* 1 day prior to publication

Supplement(s): nordisch gesund
REGIONAL DAILY & SUNDAY NEWSPAPERS: Regional Daily Newspapers

OSTSEE ZEITUNG 738410G67B-11520
Editorial: Richard-Wagner-Str. 1a, 18055 ROSTOCK
Tel: 381 3650 **Fax:** 381 365373
Email: redaktion@ostsee-zeitung.de **Web site:** http://www.ostsee-zeitung.de
Freq: 312 issues yearly; **Annual Sub.:** EUR 21,95; **Circ:** 146,189
Editor: Jan Emendörfer; **News Editor:** Jan-Peter Schröder; **Advertising Manager:** Michael Schottmann
Profile: Regional daily newspaper with news on politics, economy, culture, sports, travel, technology, etc. Facebook: http://www.facebook.com/pages/Ostsee-Zeitung/374927701107 Twitter: http://twitter.com/OZlive.
Language(s): German
ADVERTISING RATES:
SCC .... EUR 293,40
Mechanical Data: Type Area: 480 x 327 mm, No. of Columns (Display): 7, Col Widths (Display): 45 mm
Copy instructions: *Copy Date:* 2 days prior to publication
Supplement(s): Souffleurkasten
REGIONAL DAILY & SUNDAY NEWSPAPERS: Regional Daily Newspapers

OSTTHÜRINGER ZEITUNG OTZ 738413G67B-11540
Editorial: Alte Str. 3, 04626 LÖBICHAU
Tel: 3447 525911 **Fax:** 3447 525914
Email: redaktion@otz.de **Web site:** http://www.otz.de
Freq: 312 issues yearly; **Circ:** 113,196
Editor: Ullrich Erzigkeit; **News Editor:** Sebastian Helbing
Profile: Regional daily newspaper with news on politics, economy, culture, sports, travel, technology, etc. In the abbreviation Ostthüringen OTZ knows: Hardly anyone speaks of the Ostthüringer Zeitung if he thinks the biggest newspaper in the region. Is the name of the newspaper based in Gera not that old. He emerged in July 1991, when the Ostthüringer Nachrichten (OTN) as part of a major confrontation with the Trust Agency in Berlin stopped coming, and published thanks to the partnership of the WAZ media group, the Ostthüringer Zeitung. But the actual birth proposed in reversing January 1990. Exactly 19 January, 0.47 clock was the OTN in printing a new free newspaper for Eastern Thuringia, after the editor has broken the stranglehold of the Socialist Unity Party (SED). The clear separation between news and opinion, the revival of distance-critical reporting and give the reader a voice was from the start, the editor in chief credo of Ullrich Erzigkeit. This is the OTZ to the task of giving a more comprehensive service to readers in times of serious social change orientation and counseling. Above all, the OTZ is a regional newspaper in the local jurisdiction between Saale and white magpie. Twelve local editors provide the vital proximity to the audience. Down to earth and rooted in the region with a feel for the concerns and needs of the people. This ruling of a market research institute on the OTZ is an incentive for the future. Twitter: http://twitter.com/OTZonline This Outlet offers RSS (Really Simple Syndication).
Language(s): German
ADVERTISING RATES:
SCC .... EUR 298,80
Mechanical Data: Type Area: 480 x 326 mm, No. of Columns (Display): 7, Col Widths (Display): 44 mm
Copy instructions: *Copy Date:* 2 days prior to publication
Supplement(s): Extra TA OTZ TLZ
REGIONAL DAILY & SUNDAY NEWSPAPERS: Regional Daily Newspapers

OST-WEST CONTACT 738416G14C-1100
Editorial: Ritterstr. 2b, 10969 BERLIN
Tel: 30 6150890 **Fax:** 30 6150929
Email: jf@owc.de **Web site:** http://www.owc.de
Freq: Monthly; **Annual Sub.:** EUR 127,33; **Circ:** 8,792
Editor: Jutta Falkner; **Advertising Manager:** Norbert Mayer
Profile: Magazine containing information on business opportunities between Germany, Middle and Eastern Europe.
Language(s): German
ADVERTISING RATES:
Full Page Mono .... EUR 3100
Full Page Colour .... EUR 4100
Mechanical Data: Type Area: 265 x 175 mm
Official Journal of: Organ d. Ost- u. Mitteleuropa Verein Hbg.
Supplement(s): ostlausschuss informationen
BUSINESS: COMMERCE, INDUSTRY & MANAGEMENT: International Commerce

OSTWESTFÄLISCHE WIRTSCHAFT 738418G63-760
Editorial: Elsa-Brandström-Str. 1, 33602 BIELEFELD
Tel: 521 554203 **Fax:** 521 554114
Email: redaktion@bielefeld.ihk.de **Web site:** http://www.bielefeld.ihk.de
Freq: Monthly; Free to qualifying individuals
Annual Sub.: EUR 18,36; **Circ:** 48,120
Editor: Christoph von der Heiden; **Advertising Manager:** Anke Schwarzer
Profile: Magazine from the Chamber of Trade and Industry of Ostwestfalen, Bielefeld.
Language(s): German
ADVERTISING RATES:
Full Page Mono .... EUR 2582
Full Page Colour .... EUR 5402
Mechanical Data: Type Area: 260 x 185 mm, No. of Columns (Display): 4, Col Widths (Display): 43 mm
Copy instructions: *Copy Date:* 25 days prior to publication
BUSINESS: REGIONAL BUSINESS

OTC TOOLS 738422G2A-3640
Editorial: Ehrengutstr. 1, 80469 MÜNCHEN
Tel: 89 7210960 **Fax:** 89 7210979
Freq: 6 issues yearly; **Cover Price:** Free; **Circ:** 2,000
Profile: Magazine about market trends and strategies.
Language(s): German

OTZ.DE OSTTHÜRINGER ZEITUNG 1621821G67B-16635
Editorial: Alte Str. 3, 04626 LÖBICHAU **Tel:** 3447 524
Fax: 3447 525914
Email: redaktion@otz.de **Web site:** http://www.otz.de
Freq: Daily; **Cover Price:** Paid; **Circ:** 306,452 Unique Users
Editor: Ullrich Erzigkeit
Profile: Internet Portal der Ostthüringer Zeitung: local news, regional news, headlines and news on sports, politics, economy, culture, events. Twitter: http://twitter.com/OTZonline This Outlet offers RSS (Really Simple Syndication).
Language(s): German
REGIONAL DAILY & SUNDAY NEWSPAPERS: Regional Daily Newspapers

OUR CATS 738435G81C-2
Editorial: Monschauer Str. 2, 41068 MÖNCHENGLADBACH **Tel:** 2161 9463820
Fax: 2161 9463840
Email: redaktion@minervaverlag.de **Web site:** http://www.our-cats.de
Freq: Monthly; **Annual Sub.:** EUR 28,80; **Circ:** 51,000
Editor: Frank de la Motte
Profile: Magazine for cat owners and cat breeders. Monthly information on the absolute top topics related to the cat. Well-known authors and recognized experts are a permanent base and provide the author with readers brand new inside information, a broad base of knowledge and discuss the latest pet medical and behavioral approaches. Breed profiles that are on all the latest give an overview of the fascinating diversity of the cat world. Large, impressive features appeal to all cat lovers, including the issue of animal protection is in the hotel or its expression. Topics of general interest such as education, behavior and updates complete the whole thing.
Language(s): German
Readership: Read by cat owners and breeders.
ADVERTISING RATES:
Full Page Mono .... EUR 2028
Full Page Colour .... EUR 3448
Mechanical Data: Type Area: 260 x 192 mm, No. of Columns (Display): 4, Col Widths (Display): 45 mm
CONSUMER: ANIMALS & PETS: Cats

OUTDOOR 738440G75L-180
Editorial: Leuschnerstr. 1, 70174 STUTTGART
Tel: 7152 941586 **Fax:** 7152 941548
Email: info@outdoor-magazin.com **Web site:** http://www.outdoor-magazin.com
Freq: Monthly; **Annual Sub.:** EUR 55,00; **Circ:** 50,445
Editor: Olaf Beck; **Advertising Manager:** Bernd Holzhauer
Profile: outdoor is the magazine for all who like to be active outdoors in nature. From small suites or great adventure, whether a short walk or an extended trekking vacation, a tour on foot or by bike - outdoor is substantial tour tips and presents the most attractive destinations in the world for hiking, trekking fans, kayakers and tour cyclists. outdoor fueling the desire to travel, there are also plenty of tips for the same active recreation right outside the front door. Desire to travel, natural enthusiasm and sportsmanship are emphasized. In addition, outdoor supplies all of the right outdoor equipment - from hiking shoes to sleeping bag. This know-how and the in-depth equipment tests to make outdoor unique in its segment. outdoor is opinion leader and the market leader in the outdoor magazines. outdoor accompanies and dominates the booming outdoor sports. Regardless informed and committed outdoor hikers, bikers, canoeists and all other natural athletes on destinations and tours in Germany, Europe and worldwide. Meaningful accessories and clothing tests support the ambitious outdoor fans as well as the starter at the right purchasing decision. Service issues and a comprehensive buying advice round out the equipment segment. Facebook: http://www.facebook.com/outdoormagazin.
Language(s): German
ADVERTISING RATES:
Full Page Mono .... EUR 3585
Full Page Colour .... EUR 5350
Mechanical Data: No. of Columns (Display): 3, Col Widths (Display): 58 mm, Type Area: 248 x 185 mm
Copy instructions: *Copy Date:* 20 days prior to publication
CONSUMER: SPORT: Outdoor

OUTDOOR.MARKT 1818265G14A-10050
Editorial: Schanzenstr. 36/31, 51063 KÖLN
Tel: 221 9608400 **Fax:** 221 9680550
Email: info@outdoormarkt.com **Web site:** http://www.outdoormarkt.com
Freq: 10 issues yearly; **Annual Sub.:** EUR 40,00; **Circ:** 10,000
Editor: Andreas Mayer; **Advertising Manager:** Holger Henopp
Profile: outdoor.markt - the last 5 years, the b2b magazine for industry and commerce especially for outdoor activities. First-hand information, new products, Background knowledge, analysis and personal information will be provided.
Language(s): German
ADVERTISING RATES:
Full Page Mono .... EUR 3650
Full Page Colour .... EUR 3650
Mechanical Data: Type Area: 248 x 185 mm

OVERTIME 753749G89A-11720
Editorial: Alfons-Peter-Str. 4, 86971 PEITING
Tel: 8861 68232 **Fax:** 8861 68231
Email: info@ecpeiting.de **Web site:** http://www.ecpeiting.de
Cover Price: EUR 1,00; **Circ:** 2,500
Editor: Stefan Stets; **Advertising Manager:** Stefan Stets
Profile: Stadium magazine of ice hockey team Peiting.
Language(s): German
Copy instructions: *Copy Date:* 2 days prior to publication

OXMOX 738461G80-8740
Editorial: Böckmannstr. 15, 20099 HAMBURG
Tel: 40 248777 **Fax:** 40 249448
Email: klaus.schulz@oxmoxhh.de **Web site:** http://www.oxmoxhh.de
Freq: Monthly; **Annual Sub.:** EUR 18,00; **Circ:** 40,000
Editor: Klaus M. Schulz; **Advertising Manager:** Roxanne M. Schulz
Profile: Magazine providing news and cultural information for Hamburg and the surrounding area.
Language(s): German
Readership: Read by people between the ages of 20 and 30.
ADVERTISING RATES:
Full Page Mono .... EUR 2400
Full Page Colour .... EUR 3500
Mechanical Data: Type Area: 247 x 181 mm
Copy instructions: *Copy Date:* 10 days prior to publication
CONSUMER: RURAL & REGIONAL INTEREST

OZON INFORMATIONEN 738466G57-2638
Editorial: Porscheplatz, 45127 ESSEN
Tel: 201 8859219 **Fax:** 201 8859009
Email: thomas.ganeff@umweltamt.essen.de **Web site:** http://www.essen.de
Freq: 5 issues yearly; **Cover Price:** Free; **Circ:** 500
Editor: Thomas Ganeff
Profile: Publication containing information about the atmospheric ozone pollution in Essen.
Language(s): German

P9MAG 1826413G2A-5751
Editorial: Untermainkai 29, 60329 FRANKFURT
Tel: 69 83831214 **Fax:** 69 83831212
Email: fashion@pont9.de **Web site:** http://www.p9mag.de
Freq: Annual; **Cover Price:** Free; **Circ:** 4,900
Editor: Guido Braun
Profile: Advertising company publication.
Language(s): English; German
ADVERTISING RATES:
Full Page Colour .... EUR 1200

P&A 1739843G19E-1904
Editorial: Nymphenburger Str. 86, 80636 MÜNCHEN
Tel: 89 50038337 **Fax:** 89 50038310
Email: pua.redaktion@publish-industry.net **Web site:** http://www.pua24.net
Freq: 10 issues yearly; **Circ:** 16,197
Editor: Ulla Reutner; **Advertising Manager:** Susanne Meier
Language(s): German
ADVERTISING RATES:
Full Page Colour .... EUR 6210
Mechanical Data: Type Area: 232 x 178 mm, No. of Columns (Display): 4, Col Widths (Display): 42 mm
BUSINESS: ENGINEERING & MACHINERY: Machinery, Machine Tools & Metalworking

P & S PFLUG UND SPATEN 739757G21A-3120
Editorial: Bertha-von-Suttner-Str. 7, 34131 KASSEL
Tel: 561 93012400 **Fax:** 561 938545378
Email: info@verlag-ackerbau.de
Freq: Quarterly; **Cover Price:** EUR 0,60; **Circ:** 35,000
Editor: A. Münz
Profile: Magazine about agriculture.
Language(s): German

PACKAGING JOURNAL 1644073G35-167
Editorial: Emil-Hoffmann-Str. 55, 50996 KÖLN
Tel: 2236 84880 **Fax:** 2236 848824
Email: el@ella-verlag.de **Web site:** http://www.packaging-journal.de
Freq: 9 issues yearly; **Annual Sub.:** EUR 70,00; **Circ:** 12,900
Editor: Elke Latuperisa; **Advertising Manager:** Elke Latuperisa
Profile: Magazine for the packaging industry covering technology, logistics and marketing.
Language(s): English; German
ADVERTISING RATES:
Full Page Mono .... EUR 2575
Full Page Colour .... EUR 3990
Mechanical Data: Type Area: 262 x 186 mm, No. of Columns (Display): 3, Col Widths (Display): 50 mm
Copy instructions: *Copy Date:* 21 days prior to publication
BUSINESS: PACKAGING & BOTTLING

PACKMITTEL 738548G41A-1580
Editorial: Mainzer Landstr. 251, 60326 FRANKFURT
Tel: 69 75951545 **Fax:** 69 75951540
Email: redaktion@packreport.de **Web site:** http://www.packmittel-dfv.de
Freq: 6 issues yearly; **Annual Sub.:** EUR 132,70; **Circ:** 4,203
Editor: Thomas Röhl; **Advertising Manager:** Heidrun Dangl
Profile: Magazine about printing, refinement and processing of paper and plastic films.
Language(s): German
ADVERTISING RATES:
Full Page Mono .... EUR 2870
Full Page Colour .... EUR 3495
Mechanical Data: Type Area: 268 x 185 mm, No. of Columns (Display): 4, Col Widths (Display): 43 mm
BUSINESS: PRINTING & STATIONERY: Printing

PACKREPORT 738468G35-100
Editorial: Mainzer Landstr. 251, 60326 FRANKFURT
Tel: 69 75951545 **Fax:** 69 75951540
Email: thomas.roehl@packreport.de **Web site:** http://www.packreport.de
Freq: 10 issues yearly; **Annual Sub.:** EUR 123,10; **Circ:** 12,154
Editor: Thomas Röhl; **Advertising Manager:** Heidrun Dangl
Profile: Journal containing technical and marketing information about the packaging industry.
Language(s): German
Readership: Aimed at managers within the packaging industry.
ADVERTISING RATES:
Full Page Mono .... EUR 3345
Full Page Colour .... EUR 4180
Mechanical Data: Type Area: 268 x 185 mm, No. of Columns (Display): 4, Col Widths (Display): 43 mm
Copy instructions: *Copy Date:* 18 days prior to publication
Official Journal of: Organ d. VVL e.V.
BUSINESS: PACKAGING & BOTTLING

PÄD 738471G56A-8100
Editorial: Borsteler Chaussee 85, Haus 16, 22453 HAMBURG **Tel:** 40 232334 **Fax:** 40 230292
Email: info@omnimedonline.de **Web site:** http://www.omnimedonline.de
Freq: 6 issues yearly; **Annual Sub.:** EUR 53,50; **Circ:** 11,777
Editor: Michael Zinke; **Advertising Manager:** Vanessa Baack
Profile: Journal about medicine relating to the care of children.
Language(s): German
ADVERTISING RATES:
Full Page Mono .... EUR 1800
Full Page Colour .... EUR 3360
Mechanical Data: Type Area: 250 x 180 mm, No. of Columns (Display): 3, Col Widths (Display): 56 mm
Copy instructions: *Copy Date:* 28 days prior to publication
BUSINESS: HEALTH & MEDICAL

PÄDAGOGIK 738472G62B-3193
Editorial: Rothenbaumchaussee 11, 20148 HAMBURG **Tel:** 40 454595 **Fax:** 40 4108564
Email: info@paedagogische-beitraege-verlag.de
Web site: http://www.beltz.de
Freq: 11 issues yearly; **Annual Sub.:** EUR 67,00; **Circ:** 10,000
Editor: Johannes Bastian; **Advertising Manager:** Claudia Klinger
Profile: "Pädagogik" is the leading school educational journal in Germany. "Pädagogik" provides a detailed thematic focus and practical information for the design of instructional materials and school.
Language(s): German
ADVERTISING RATES:
Full Page Mono .... EUR 1500
Full Page Colour .... EUR 2250
Mechanical Data: Type Area: 267 x 175 mm, No. of Columns (Display): 4, Col Widths (Display): 42 mm
Copy instructions: *Copy Date:* 65 days prior to publication
BUSINESS: CHURCH & SCHOOL EQUIPMENT & EDUCATION: Education Teachers

PADDY AND WATER ENVIRONMENT 1638681G57-2718
Editorial: Tiergartenstr. 17, 69121 HEIDELBERG
Tel: 6221 4870 **Fax:** 6221 4878177

Email: subscriptions@springer.com **Web site:** http://www.springerlink.com
Freq: Quarterly; **Annual Sub.:** EUR 265,00; **Circ:** 637
Editor: Yoshisuke Nakano
Profile: Publication about the science and technology of water and environment related disciplines in paddyfarming.
Language(s): English
ADVERTISING RATES:
Full Page Mono .... EUR 830
Full Page Colour .... EUR 1870
Mechanical Data: Type Area: 240 x 175 mm

PÄDIATRIE
738486G56A-8120
Editorial: Aschauer Str. 30, 81549 MÜNCHEN
Tel: 89 2030431401 **Fax:** 89 2030431399
Email: markus.seidl@springer.com **Web site:** http://www.paediatrie-hautnah.de
Freq: 6 issues yearly; **Annual Sub.:** EUR 104,50; **Circ:** 8,115
Editor: Markus Seidl; **Advertising Manager:** Kornelia Echsel
Profile: pädiatrie is the training magazine of pediatricians for pediatricians. Hands-on review articles and case reports informs about the current state of diagnosis and therapy. In "Journal Club" of the magazine will speak and comment experts on the international specialized literature. "Congress compact" edited together the highlights of the major conferences. Finally, the reader is in the "clinic and practice" valuable practical tips and information on recent court rulings. And approved by the Bavarian Medical Association training module enables the acquisition of three CME credits per issue.
Language(s): German
ADVERTISING RATES:
Full Page Mono .... EUR 2140
Full Page Colour .... EUR 3740
Mechanical Data: Type Area: 240 x 174 mm
Official Journal of: Organ d. Netzwerk f. interdisziplinäre pädiatr. Dermatologie
BUSINESS: HEALTH & MEDICAL

PÄDIATRIE UP2DATE
1792948G56A-11439
Editorial: Langenbeckstr. 1, 55131 MAINZ
Tel: 6131 177326 **Fax:** 6131 173918
Email: zepp@kinder.klinik.uni-mainz.de **Web site:** http://www.thieme.de/fz/paediatrie-u2d.html
Freq: Quarterly; **Annual Sub.:** EUR 154,40; **Circ:** 3,200
Editor: Fred Zepp
Profile: Pädiatrie up2date is a CME-certified education and training journal in pediatrics. State-of-the-art contributions, educational contributions, current guidelines and study results from the main areas of pediatrics. The innovative concept of a self-updating and dynamic textbook, combining Pädiatrie up2date the perfect didactic and the modern layout of a textbook with the timeliness and continuity of a professional journal.
Language(s): German
ADVERTISING RATES:
Full Page Mono .... EUR 1490
Full Page Colour .... EUR 2660
Mechanical Data: Type Area: 250 x 175 mm

PÄDIATRISCHE PRAXIS
738489G56A-8160
Editorial: Bürkleinstr. 12, 80538 MÜNCHEN
Tel: 89 227988 **Fax:** 89 2904643
Email: office@marseille-verlag.com **Web site:** http://www.marseille-verlag.com
Freq: 7 issues yearly; **Annual Sub.:** EUR 325,75
Editor: S. Wirth
Profile: Magazine focusing on all aspects of paediatrics.
Language(s): German
Readership: Aimed at paediatricians in hospitals and practices.
BUSINESS: HEALTH & MEDICAL

PÄDIATRIX
1644145G56A-11294
Editorial: Sofienstr. 5, 69115 HEIDELBERG
Tel: 6221 137470 **Fax:** 6221 1374777
Email: volz-zang@biomedpark.de **Web site:** http://www.paediatrix.de
Freq: 8 issues yearly; **Cover Price:** Free; **Circ:** 9,331
Editor: Corinna Volz-Zang
Profile: Magazine on paediatrics.
Language(s): German
ADVERTISING RATES:
Full Page Mono .... EUR 980
Full Page Colour .... EUR 980
Mechanical Data: Type Area: 254 x 151 mm, No. of Columns (Display): 2, Col Widths (Display): 73 mm
Copy instructions: *Copy Date:* 30 days prior to publication
BUSINESS: HEALTH & MEDICAL

PAGE
738492G60A-80
Editorial: Borselstr. 28/I, 22765 HAMBURG
Tel: 40 85183400 **Fax:** 40 85183449
Email: info@page-online.de **Web site:** http://www.page-online.de
Freq: Monthly; **Annual Sub.:** EUR 103,30; **Circ:** 18,580
Editor: Gabriele Günder; **Advertising Manager:** Alexander Herz
Profile: Magazine about digital publishing and media production. Offers advice and suggestions in all areas of digital design and electronic publishing, irrespective of platform or manufacturer. Facebook: http://www.facebook.com/pagemag Twitter: http://twitter.com/#!/pagemag This Outlet offers RSS (Really Simple Syndication).
Language(s): German
ADVERTISING RATES:
Full Page Mono .... EUR 5170
Full Page Colour .... EUR 5170
Mechanical Data: Type Area: 265 x 185 mm
Copy instructions: *Copy Date:* 27 days prior to publication
Supplement(s): Page Extra
BUSINESS: PUBLISHING: Publishing & Book Trade

PALSTEK
738509G91A-80
Editorial: Eppendorfer Weg 57a, 20259 HAMBURG
Tel: 40 40196350 **Fax:** 40 40196341
Email: u.kronberg@palstek.de **Web site:** http://www.palstek.de
Freq: 6 issues yearly; **Annual Sub.:** EUR 31,80; **Circ:** 24,665
Editor: Ulrich Kronberg; **Advertising Manager:** Imke Feddersen
Profile: Publication about sailing, yachts, sportsboats and boating equipment. Facebook: http://www.facebook.com/pages/palstek/112002002158815 This Outlet offers RSS (Really Simple Syndication).
Language(s): German
Readership: Aimed at boat-owners.
ADVERTISING RATES:
Full Page Mono .... EUR 2350
Full Page Colour .... EUR 3785
Mechanical Data: Type Area: 265 x 165 mm, No. of Columns (Display): 4, Col Widths (Display): 42 mm
Copy instructions: *Copy Date:* 30 days prior to publication
CONSUMER: RECREATION & LEISURE: Boating & Yachting

PAPER MANAGER
738539G36-8
Editorial: Döllgaststr. 7, 86199 AUGSBURG
Tel: 821 344570 **Fax:** 821 3445719
Email: info@mkpublishing.de **Web site:** http://www.paper-manager.de
Freq: Half-yearly; **Cover Price:** Free; **Circ:** 7,500
Profile: Company publication published by Böwe Systec AG.
Language(s): German

PAPIER + TECHNIK
738545G36-9
Editorial: Dischingerstr. 8, 69123 HEIDELBERG
Tel: 6221 644625 **Fax:** 6221 644640
Email: verena.manek@haefner-verlag.de **Web site:** http://www.papierundtechnik.de
Freq: 10 issues yearly; **Cover Price:** EUR 1,00; **Circ:** 40,000
Advertising Manager: Sandra Rink
Profile: Journal containing information about paper production.
Language(s): German
ADVERTISING RATES:
Full Page Mono .... EUR 1300
Full Page Colour .... EUR 1885
Mechanical Data: Type Area: 260 x 178 mm
BUSINESS: PAPER

PARCHIMER BLITZ AM SONNTAG
738570G72-10404
Editorial: Pampower Str. 3, 19061 SCHWERIN
Tel: 385 64584841 **Fax:** 385 64584820
Email: rita.brueckner@blitzverlag.de **Web site:** http://www.blitzverlag.de
Freq: Weekly; **Cover Price:** Free; **Circ:** 34,785
Editor: Rita Brückner
Profile: Advertising journal (house-to-house) concentrating on local stories.
Language(s): German
ADVERTISING RATES:
Full Page Mono .... EUR 2571
Full Page Colour .... EUR 2961
Mechanical Data: Type Area: 420 x 285 mm, No. of Columns (Display): 6, Col Widths (Display): 45 mm
Copy instructions: *Copy Date:* 2 days prior to publication
LOCAL NEWSPAPERS

PARKETT IM HOLZHANDEL
2035553G4B-727
Editorial: Dorfstr. 1, 24850 HÜSBY **Tel:** 4621 41470
Fax: 4621 41073
Email: parkett@magazinparkett.de **Web site:** http://www.magazinparkett.de
Freq: 6 issues yearly; **Circ:** 5,200
Editor: Peter Mau
Profile: Publication about the manufacture and installation of parquet flooring.
Language(s): German
Mechanical Data: Type Area: 252 x 184 mm, No. of Columns (Display): 4, Col Widths (Display): 43 mm
Supplement to: Parkett magazin

PARKETT MAGAZIN
738579G4B-480
Editorial: Dorfstr. 1, 24850 HÜSBY **Tel:** 4621 41470
Fax: 4621 41073
Email: parkett@magazinparkett.de **Web site:** http://www.magazinparkett.de
Freq: 6 issues yearly; **Annual Sub.:** EUR 92,00; **Circ:** 5,053
Editor: Peter Mau
Profile: Publication about the manufacture and installation of parquet flooring.
Language(s): German
ADVERTISING RATES:
Full Page Mono .... EUR 2490
Full Page Colour .... EUR 4100
Mechanical Data: Type Area: 252 x 184 mm, No. of Columns (Display): 4, Col Widths (Display): 43 mm
Supplement(s): Parkett im Holzhandel
BUSINESS: ARCHITECTURE & BUILDING: Interior Design & Flooring

DAS PARLAMENT
738583G72-10408
Editorial: Platz der Republik 1, 11011 BERLIN
Tel: 30 22730515 **Fax:** 30 22736524
Email: redaktion.das-parlament@bundestag.de **Web site:** http://www.das-parlament.de
Freq: 38 issues yearly; **Annual Sub.:** EUR 34,90; **Circ:** 57,831
Editor: Jörg Biallas
Profile: Das Parlament is a political newspaper, published by the German Bundestag. It appears one to two a week and deals mainly with policy. The focus of the paper is on the German domestic politics. About a quarter of the issues deal only with a theme (Dossier), the remaining part deals with several current socio-political and historical issues that have a connection to the work of the Bundestag and the history of the Federal Republic of Germany. Regularly there are also book reviews published. In Parlament the parliamentary debates are well documented by the imprint of the mostly slightly abridged speeches of the Member of Parliament.
Language(s): German
ADVERTISING RATES:
Full Page Mono .... EUR 2990
Full Page Colour .... EUR 5430
Mechanical Data: Type Area: 527 x 360 mm, No. of Columns (Display): 5, Col Widths (Display): 68 mm
Copy instructions: *Copy Date:* 14 days prior to publication
Supplement(s): APuZ Aus Politik und Zeitgeschichte
LOCAL NEWSPAPERS

PARQUET INTERNATIONAL
1791038G4B-711
Editorial: Dorfstr. 1, 24850 HÜSBY **Tel:** 4621 41470
Fax: 4621 41073
Email: parkett@magazinparkett.de **Web site:** http://www.magazinparkett.de
Freq: 3 issues yearly; **Annual Sub.:** EUR 53,00; **Circ:** 4,200
Editor: Peter Mau
Profile: Publication about the manufacture and installation of parquet flooring.
Language(s): English
ADVERTISING RATES:
Full Page Mono .... EUR 2490
Full Page Colour .... EUR 4100
Mechanical Data: Type Area: 252 x 184 mm, No. of Columns (Display): 4, Col Widths (Display): 43 mm

PARTNER HUND
738592G81B-11
Editorial: Münchener Str. 101, 85737 ISMANING
Tel: 89 272707511 **Fax:** 89 272707590
Email: redaktion@herz-fuer-tiere.de **Web site:** http://www.partner-hund.de
Freq: Monthly; **Annual Sub.:** EUR 25,80; **Circ:** 38,487
Editor: Ursula Birr
Profile: Partner HUND is Europe's largest dog magazine. A team of veterinarians, animal psychologists, dog experts and breeders ensure the necessary competence. Editorial expertise and high utility pays: For over 15 years in the market reaches 0.56 million readers Partner HUND (AWA 2010). • Partner HUND accompanied than any other magazine to dog owners through all phases of his life four-legged friend. From choosing the right breed of the puppy time, the education phase and the choice of problem-leave it finds in the partner DOG complete and informative advice. • focus of the book is the extensive service and practical component. All questions and requests that occur when keeping a dog to be answered. Experts provide readers with advice and tips on nutrition, health, education, behavior and character of the dog. Every month, a rare and presented a popular breed and another breed with her celebrity and "ordinary" farmers. • For beats the entertainment section. Perplexing puzzles and games to talk at a high level and invite you to join in and relax. Facebook: http://www.facebook.com/PartnerHund.
Language(s): German
Readership: Read by dog lovers and breeders.
ADVERTISING RATES:
Full Page Mono .... EUR 3000
Full Page Colour .... EUR 4300
Mechanical Data: Type Area: 267 x 180 mm, No. of Columns (Display): 4, Col Widths (Display): 42 mm
Copy instructions: *Copy Date:* 35 days prior to publication
CONSUMER: ANIMALS & PETS: Dogs

PARTOUT
738597G80-8760
Editorial: Svendborger Str. 23, 24109 KIEL
Tel: 431 687875 **Fax:** 431 687897
Email: partout-fl@t-online.de **Web site:** http://www.partout-online.de
Freq: Monthly; **Annual Sub.:** EUR 20,00; **Circ:** 11,000
Editor: Dirk Schneekloth; **Advertising Manager:** Dirk Schneekloth
Profile: News magazine for the Flensburg area.
Language(s): German
ADVERTISING RATES:
Full Page Mono .... EUR 510
Full Page Colour .... EUR 1080
Mechanical Data: Type Area: 180 x 130 mm
Copy instructions: *Copy Date:* 12 days prior to publication
CONSUMER: RURAL & REGIONAL INTEREST

PASSAUER BISTUMSBLATT
738615G87-10260
Editorial: Domplatz 3, 94032 PASSAU
Tel: 851 3931320 **Fax:** 851 31893
Email: krinninger@passauer-bistumsblatt.de **Web site:** http://www.passauer-bistumsblatt.de
Freq: Weekly; **Circ:** 17,908
Editor: Wolfgang Krinninger; **Advertising Manager:** Irmgard Höltl
Profile: Church magazine for the Diocese of Passau.
Language(s): German
ADVERTISING RATES:
Full Page Mono .... EUR 980
Full Page Colour .... EUR 980
Mechanical Data: Type Area: 320 x 224 mm, No. of Columns (Display): 4, Col Widths (Display): 55 mm
Copy instructions: *Copy Date:* 8 days prior to publication
CONSUMER: RELIGIOUS

PASSAUER NEUE PRESSE
738616G67B-11560
Editorial: Medienstr. 5, 94036 PASSAU
Tel: 851 8020 **Fax:** 851 802256
Email: pnp@vgp.de **Web site:** http://www.pnp.de
Freq: 312 issues yearly; **Circ:** 179,621
Editor: Ernst Fuchs; **News Editor:** Martin Wanninger; **Advertising Manager:** Gerhard Koller
Profile: Regional daily newspaper covering politics, economics, sport, travel and technology. Facebook: http://www.facebook.com/passauerneuepresse?ref=search&sid=1469388759.688614946..1 Twitter: http://twitter.com/pnp_online This Outlet offers RSS (Really Simple Syndication).
Language(s): German
ADVERTISING RATES:
SCC .... EUR 330,70
Mechanical Data: Col Widths (Display): 45 mm
Copy instructions: *Copy Date:* 2 days prior to publication
Supplement(s): Unser wilder Wald
REGIONAL DAILY & SUNDAY NEWSPAPERS: Regional Daily Newspapers

PASSIVHAUS KOMPENDIUM
1818710G4E-7147
Editorial: Prof.-Schmieder-Str. 8c, 78476 ALLENSBACH **Tel:** 7533 98300 **Fax:** 7533 98301
Email: laible@phk-verlag.de **Web site:** http://www.phk-verlag.de
Freq: Annual; **Cover Price:** EUR 7,40; **Circ:** 24,500
Editor: Johannes Laible; **Advertising Manager:** Johannes Laible
Profile: The core target group consists of all key decision-makers around the passive house construction: information active builders, their architects deliberately choose and (with) decide on technical components, architects and planners with passive house experience, or those who approach new to the subject; Passive House skeptics, such as among property developers, in the local politics, building authorities.
Language(s): German
ADVERTISING RATES:
Full Page Mono .... EUR 2240
Full Page Colour .... EUR 2240
Mechanical Data: Type Area: 270 x 188 mm
Copy instructions: *Copy Date:* 45 days prior to publication

PASTA!
1641702G80-14186
Editorial: Römerstr. 3, 94032 PASSAU
Tel: 851 9290865 **Fax:** 851 9290866
Email: redaktion@pastaonline.de **Web site:** http://www.pastaonline.de
Freq: 10 issues yearly; **Cover Price:** Free; **Circ:** 9,840
Editor: Till Gabriel; **Advertising Manager:** Cornelius Lloyd Martens
Profile: Regional magazine for city and region, concentrating on gastronomy, music, arts and events.
Language(s): German
ADVERTISING RATES:
Full Page Mono .... EUR 1379
Full Page Colour .... EUR 1379
Mechanical Data: Type Area: 302 x 212 mm
Copy instructions: *Copy Date:* 10 days prior to publication
CONSUMER: RURAL & REGIONAL INTEREST

PATCHWORK MAGAZIN
1660540G74A-3429
Editorial: Im Buhles 4, 61479 SCHLOSSBORN
Tel: 6174 9994000 **Fax:** 6174 9994099
Email: j.eisenbeiser@patchworkmagazin.de **Web site:** http://www.patchworkmagazin.de
Freq: 6 issues yearly; **Annual Sub.:** EUR 34,20; **Circ:** 55,000
Editor: Jasmin Eisenbeiser
Profile: In each issue of the magazine 20-30 for rework, using current materials and seasonal patterns. For the corresponding levels from beginners

with basic knowledge to advanced. The current product information, company profiles, feedback, data, events and a pattern sheet in original size.
Language(s): German
ADVERTISING RATES:
Full Page Mono .... EUR 1440
Full Page Colour .... EUR 1800
Mechanical Data: Type Area: 250 x 185 mm, No. of Columns (Display): 4, Col Widths (Display): 44 mm
Copy instructions: *Copy Date:* 44 days prior to publication

DER PATHOLOGE 738637G56A-8200
Editorial: Tiergartenstr. 17, 69121 HEIDELBERG
Tel: 6221 4870 **Fax:** 6221 4878366
Email: elisabeth.althaus@springer.com **Web site:** http://www.springermedizin.de
Freq: 6 issues yearly; **Annual Sub.:** EUR 354,00; **Circ:** 1,100
Advertising Manager: Silvia Ziemann
Profile: Der Pathologe is an internationally recognized journal and combines practical relevance with scientific competence. The journal informs all pathologists working on departments and institutes as well as morphologically interested scientists about developments in the field of pathology. The journal serves both the scientific exchange and the continuing education of pathologists. Comprehensive reviews on a specific topical issue focus on providing evidenced based information under consideration of practical experience. Freely submitted original papers allow the presentation of important clinical studies and serve the scientific exchange.
Language(s): German
ADVERTISING RATES:
Full Page Mono .... EUR 1495
Full Page Colour .... EUR 2535
Mechanical Data: Type Area: 240 x 174 mm
Official Journal of: Organ d. Dt., d. Österr. u. d. Schweizer. Ges. f. Pathologie, d. Dt. Abt. d. Internat. Akademie f. Pathologie u. d. Berufsverb. Dt. Pathologen

DER PATRIOT 738640G67B-11580
Editorial: Hansastr. 2, 59557 LIPPSTADT
Tel: 2941 20100 **Fax:** 2941 201297
Email: redaktion@derpatriot.de **Web site:** http://www.derpatriot.de
Freq: 312 issues yearly; **Circ:** 25,377
Editor: Georg Böer; **Advertising Manager:** Andreas Grunig
Profile: The proximity to the reader is the guideline. And the events in the region, our big issue. Day after day. Informative to be, entertaining, critical and helpful - as understood by the Patriot's role that he perceives already since 1848. From the small beginnings of the newspaper's founder has become a modern media house, which looks back with pride on the past and at the same time introduces the new challenges of present and future. Through the diverse coverage - about local politics, community life, sport, culture and the local economy - the Patriot will raise awareness of home and origin, and simultaneously direct our attention to the country and the wide world.
Language(s): German
ADVERTISING RATES:
SCC .... EUR 64,80
Mechanical Data: Type Area: 466 x 316 mm, No. of Columns (Display): 7, Col Widths (Display): 43 mm
Copy instructions: *Copy Date:* 1 day prior to publication
Supplement(s): Heimatblätter; prisma
REGIONAL DAILY & SUNDAY NEWSPAPERS: Regional Daily Newspapers

PAULINUS 738645G87-10320
Editorial: Hinter dem Dom 6, 54290 TRIER
Tel: 651 7105610 **Fax:** 651 7105613
Email: redaktion@paulinus.de **Web site:** http://www.wochenzeitung.paulinus.de
Freq: Weekly; **Annual Sub.:** EUR 62,90; **Circ:** 31,155
Editor: Bruno Sonnen
Profile: Weekly newspaper from the diocese of Trier.
Language(s): German
ADVERTISING RATES:
Full Page Mono .... EUR 6048
Full Page Colour .... EUR 7560
Mechanical Data: Type Area: 480 x 323 mm, No. of Columns (Display): 7, Col Widths (Display): 44 mm
Copy instructions: *Copy Date:* 10 days prior to publication
CONSUMER: RELIGIOUS

PBI PRÉFA BÉTON INTERNATIONAL 1790310G4E-7118
Editorial: Industriestr. 180, 50999 KÖLN
Tel: 2236 962390 **Fax:** 2236 962396
Email: h.karutz@cpi-worldwide.com **Web site:** http://www.cpi-worldwide.com
Freq: 6 issues yearly; **Annual Sub.:** EUR 120,00; **Circ:** 2,500
Editor: Holger Karutz; **Advertising Manager:** Gerhard Klöckner
Profile: Magazine for concrete producers.
Language(s): French
Mechanical Data: Type Area: 260 x 180 mm, No. of Columns (Display): 3, Col Widths (Display): 56 mm
Copy instructions: *Copy Date:* 30 days prior to publication

PBS AKTUELL 738662G41B-25
Editorial: Fasanenweg 18, 70771 LEINFELDEN-ECHTERDINGEN **Tel:** 711 75913387
Fax: 711 75913775
Email: kweik@bitverlag.de **Web site:** http://www.pbsaktuell.de
Freq: 10 issues yearly; Free to qualifying individuals
Annual Sub.: EUR 30,00; **Circ:** 14,574
Editor: Kathrin Weik; **Advertising Manager:** Joachim Ahnfeldt
Profile: Journal of the wholesalers association writing, stationery and office supplies. The recipients are the customers organized in this association wholesalers, therefore, primarily the small and medium-PBS-shops and stationery shops with an assortment mix to books, toys, creative assortments and magazines. In this target group is pbs currently the only journal that is read regularly and continuously reaches all dealers. Material used as address current customer files of the wholesaler. With a circulation of 16,000 copies pbs currently by far the medium with the largest circulation in the PBS sector. The emphasis is on new product range, offers from manufacturers and large dealer groups, seasonal promotions as well as suggestions and tips for daily selling and dealing with customers. Assistance in business management and legal issues complements the range of topics. But do also take reports on the industry, from manufacturers and trade as well as current trends and developments, the reader is in range pbs date.
Language(s): German
Readership: Aimed at managers of small and medium-sized specialist stores and shops selling writing products.
ADVERTISING RATES:
Full Page Mono .... EUR 5030
Full Page Colour .... EUR 6950
Mechanical Data: Type Area: 297 x 210 mm
Copy instructions: *Copy Date:* 28 days prior to publication
BUSINESS: PRINTING & STATIONERY: Stationery

PBS REPORT 738663G34-533
Editorial: Sontraer Str. 6, 60386 FRANKFURT
Tel: 69 42090379 **Fax:** 69 42090370
Email: pietro.giarrizzo@zarbock.de **Web site:** http://www.pbs-report.de
Freq: 11 issues yearly; **Annual Sub.:** EUR 93,00; **Circ:** 7,877
Editor: Pietro Giarrizzo; **Advertising Manager:** Armin Schaum
Profile: Magazine about office supplies, stationery, office machines and furniture and gifts.
Language(s): German
ADVERTISING RATES:
Full Page Colour .... EUR 4200
Mechanical Data: Type Area: 270 x 170 mm, No. of Columns (Display): 3, Col Widths (Display): 55 mm
Copy instructions: *Copy Date:* 7 days prior to publication
BUSINESS: OFFICE EQUIPMENT

PC ACTION 738666G78D-400
Editorial: Dr.-Mack-Str. 83, 90762 FÜRTH
Tel: 911 2872100 **Fax:** 911 2872200
Email: leserbriefe@pcaction.de **Web site:** http://www.pcaction.de
Freq: Monthly; **Annual Sub.:** EUR 63,00; **Circ:** 29,666
Editor: Petra Fröhlich; **Advertising Manager:** Gunnar Obermeier
Profile: Magazine covering all aspects of personal computing.
Language(s): German
ADVERTISING RATES:
Full Page Mono .... EUR 7690
Full Page Colour .... EUR 7690
Mechanical Data: Col Widths (Display): 52 mm, Type Area: 280 x 210 mm, No. of Columns (Display): 4
Copy instructions: *Copy Date:* 30 days prior to publication
CONSUMER: CONSUMER ELECTRONICS: Games

PC GAMES 738673G78D-460
Editorial: Dr.-Mack-Str. 83, 90762 FÜRTH
Tel: 911 2872100 **Fax:** 911 2872200
Email: redaktion@pcgames.de **Web site:** http://www.pcgames.de
Freq: Monthly; **Annual Sub.:** EUR 63,00; **Circ:** 105,191
Editor: Thorsten Küchler; **Advertising Manager:** Gunnar Obermeier
Profile: Gaming magazine provides information to understand and competently about the latest PC games, created background stories and issues expert buying advice.
Language(s): German
ADVERTISING RATES:
Full Page Mono .... EUR 12500
Full Page Colour .... EUR 12500
Mechanical Data: Col Widths (Display): 52 mm, Type Area: 280 x 210 mm, No. of Columns (Display): 4
Copy instructions: *Copy Date:* 30 days prior to publication
CONSUMER: CONSUMER ELECTRONICS: Games

PC GAMES 1687275G78D-1003
Editorial: Dr.-Mack-Str. 83, 90762 FÜRTH
Tel: 911 2872100 **Fax:** 911 2872200
Email: redaktion.online@pcgames.de **Web site:** http://www.pcgames.de
Freq: Daily; **Cover Price:** Paid; **Circ:** 6,664,863 Unique Users
Editor: Florian Stangl
Profile: Ezine: Magazine focussing on computer games. Twitter: http://twitter.com/pcgamesde.
Language(s): German
CONSUMER: CONSUMER ELECTRONICS: Games

PC GAMES HARDWARE 738675G78D-500
Editorial: Dr.-Mack-Str. 83, 90762 FÜRTH
Tel: 911 2872100 **Fax:** 911 2872200
Email: redaktion@pcgameshardware.de **Web site:** http://www.pcgh.de
Freq: Monthly; **Annual Sub.:** EUR 63,00; **Circ:** 47,338
Editor: Thilo Bayer; **Advertising Manager:** Gunnar Obermeier
Profile: PC Games Hardware is the forum for IT and technology enthusiasts. The magazineilluminates the complex hardware world from the perspective of an experienced PC user. If the power supply buyers' guide, video cards, testing or tuning tips - everything revolves around the question: How can I get from my PC even more power? The answer is the competent editorial every month. Facebook: http://www.facebook.com/pcgameshardware Twitter: http://twitter.com/#!/pcgh.
Language(s): German
ADVERTISING RATES:
Full Page Mono .... EUR 7700
Full Page Colour .... EUR 7700
Mechanical Data: No. of Columns (Display): 4, Col Widths (Display): 52 mm, Type Area: 297 x 210 mm
Copy instructions: *Copy Date:* 30 days prior to publication
CONSUMER: CONSUMER ELECTRONICS: Games

PC GO 738677G5C-57
Editorial: Richard-Reitzner-Allee 2, 85540 HAAR
Tel: 89 255561173 **Fax:** 89 255561625
Email: redaktion@pcgo.de **Web site:** http://www.pcgo.de
Freq: Monthly; **Cover Price:** EUR 4,99; **Circ:** 134,508
Editor: Jörg Hermann; **Advertising Manager:** Gisela Nerke
Profile: Magazine analysing new IT products, services and systems, providing advice and recommendations.
Language(s): German
Readership: Aimed at IT professionals, teachers and students.
ADVERTISING RATES:
Full Page Mono .... EUR 8925
Full Page Colour .... EUR 11900
Mechanical Data: Type Area: 250 x 185 mm, No. of Columns (Display): 4, Col Widths (Display): 43 mm
Copy instructions: *Copy Date:* 28 days prior to publication
BUSINESS: COMPUTERS & AUTOMATION: Professional Personal Computers

PC MAGAZIN 738684G78E-1
Editorial: Richard-Reitzner-Allee 2, 85540 HAAR
Tel: 89 255561118 **Fax:** 89 255561621
Email: redaktion@pc-magazin.de **Web site:** http://www.pc-magazin.de
Freq: Monthly; **Cover Price:** EUR 4,99; **Circ:** 136,277
Editor: Wolfgang Koser; **Advertising Manager:** Gisela Nerke
Profile: Technology magazine for experienced IT professionals with a strong interest in PCs and background information on modern PC technology. Magazine is aimed at IT professionals who need firm and reliable information for their professional and personal decisions. To power users who want to work with the latest and most powerful hardware and software. Planning to professional users in many fields of work from creative design to design. Looking to administrators and service technicians, the tips and tools for everyday use.
Language(s): German
ADVERTISING RATES:
Full Page Mono .... EUR 9675
Full Page Colour .... EUR 12900
Mechanical Data: Type Area: 250 x 185 mm, No. of Columns (Display): 4, Col Widths (Display): 43 mm
Copy instructions: *Copy Date:* 28 days prior to publication
CONSUMER: CONSUMER ELECTRONICS: Home Computing

PC PR@XIS 738693G5C-6
Editorial: Merowingerstr. 30, 40223 DÜSSELDORF
Tel: 211 933470 **Fax:** 211 9334710
Email: redaktion@pcpraxis.de **Web site:** http://www.pcpraxis.de
Freq: Monthly; **Annual Sub.:** EUR 51,60; **Circ:** 81,384
Editor: Michael Dollny; **Advertising Manager:** Jörg Hausch
Profile: Magazine for advanced PC users, IT professionals and IT purchasing decision makers. PC World offers the latest tests and issues to the full range of IT Market. Specific purchase recommendations, product and solution-oriented workshops and practical know-how are the priorities.
Language(s): German
ADVERTISING RATES:
Full Page Mono .... EUR 6380
Full Page Colour .... EUR 7980
Mechanical Data: Type Area: 274 x 180 mm, No. of Columns (Display): 4, Col Widths (Display): 42 mm
Copy instructions: *Copy Date:* 20 days prior to publication
BUSINESS: COMPUTERS & AUTOMATION: Professional Personal Computers

PC WELT 738701G5C-11
Editorial: Lyonel-Feininger-Str. 26, 80807 MÜNCHEN
Tel: 89 36086222 **Fax:** 89 36086459
Email: pressemitteilung@pcwelt.de **Web site:** http://www.pcwelt.de
Freq: Monthly; **Annual Sub.:** EUR 59,88; **Circ:** 277,587
Editor: Harald Kuppek; **Advertising Manager:** Christoph Burkhart
Profile: Magazine for business users in professional and semi- professional applications operating on Windows, DOS and OS/2. Facebook: http://www.facebook.com/pcwelt Twitter: http://twitter.com/pcwelt This Outlet offers RSS (Really Simple Syndication).
Language(s): German
ADVERTISING RATES:
Full Page Mono .... EUR 15170
Full Page Colour .... EUR 16990
Mechanical Data: Type Area: 242 x 180 mm, No. of Columns (Display): 3, Col Widths (Display): 57 mm
BUSINESS: COMPUTERS & AUTOMATION: Professional Personal Computers

PC WELT 1623196G5C-29
Editorial: Lyonel-Feininger-Str. 26, 80807 MÜNCHEN
Tel: 89 36086222 **Fax:** 89 36086459
Email: pressemitteilung@pcwelt.de **Web site:** http://www.pcwelt.de
Freq: Daily; **Cover Price:** Paid; **Circ:** 9,699,409 Unique Users
Editor: Harald Kuppek; **Advertising Manager:** Petra Seeser
Profile: Ezine: Magazine for business users in professional and semi- professional applications operating on Windows, DOS and OS/2. Facebook: http://www.facebook.com/pcwelt.
Language(s): German
BUSINESS: COMPUTERS & AUTOMATION: Professional Personal Computers

PDP PSYCHODYNAMISCHE PSYCHOTHERAPIE 1638054G56A-11269
Editorial: Hölderlinstr. 3, 70174 STUTTGART
Tel: 711 2298754 **Fax:** 711 2298765
Email: jan.hueber@schattauer.de **Web site:** http://www.pdp-online.info
Freq: Quarterly; Free to qualifying individuals
Annual Sub.: EUR 92,00; **Circ:** 1,650
Editor: Jan Hueber; **Advertising Manager:** Nicole Dörr
Profile: In the spectrum of the psychoanalytic processes is the psychodynamically oriented psychotherapy is of particular importance. It has proved itself not only in the treatment of many mental illnesses, but is a widespread practice in patient care. Its large range of indications, its flexibility toward treatment innovations and its cost are just a few reasons for the wide acceptance of psychodynamically oriented psychotherapy for patients and therapists. The PDP informs medical and psychological psychotherapists about the evolution of psychoanalytically oriented psychotherapy in scientific articles, reports, treatment, communications and discussions that are relevant for daily practice.
Language(s): German
ADVERTISING RATES:
Full Page Mono .... EUR 1395
Full Page Colour .... EUR 2505
Mechanical Data: Type Area: 212 x 135 mm
Copy instructions: *Copy Date:* 40 days prior to publication
Official Journal of: Organ d. Dt. Fachges. f. Tiefenpsycholog. fundierte Psychotherapie e.V.

PEDIATRIC NEPHROLOGY 738708G56A-8240
Editorial: Tiergartenstr. 17, 69121 HEIDELBERG
Tel: 6221 4870 **Fax:** 6221 4878366
Email: subscriptions@springer.com **Web site:** http://www.springerlink.com
Freq: Monthly; **Annual Sub.:** EUR 3581,00; **Circ:** 1,512
Editor: O. Mehls
Profile: Paediatric nephrology.
Language(s): English
ADVERTISING RATES:
Full Page Mono .... EUR 1390
Full Page Colour .... EUR 2430
Mechanical Data: Type Area: 240 x 175 mm
Official Journal of: Organ d. Internat. Pediatric Nephrology Association

PEDIATRIC RADIOLOGY 1638483G56A-11276
Editorial: Tiergartenstr. 17, 69121 HEIDELBERG
Tel: 6221 4870 **Fax:** 6221 4878366
Email: subscriptions@springer.com **Web site:** http://www.springerlink.com
Freq: Monthly; **Annual Sub.:** EUR 1949,00; **Circ:** 1,650
Editor: Guy Sebag; **Advertising Manager:** Noëla Krischer
Profile: Paediatric radiology.
Language(s): English
ADVERTISING RATES:
Full Page Mono .... EUR 1440
Full Page Colour .... EUR 2480
Mechanical Data: Type Area: 240 x 175 mm
Official Journal of: Organ d. European Society of Pediatric Radiology, d. Society for Pediatric Radiology, d. Asian and Oceanic Society for Pediatric

Radiology u. d. Sociedad Latinoamericana de Radiologia Pediatrica

PEDIATRIC SURGERY INTERNATIONAL
738709G56A-8260

Editorial: Tiergartenstr. 17, 69121 HEIDELBERG
Tel: 6221 4870 **Fax:** 6221 4878366
Email: gabriele.schroeder@springer.com **Web site:** http://www.springerlink.com
Freq: Monthly; **Annual Sub.:** EUR 2019,00; **Circ:** 870
Editor: P. Puri
Profile: Magazine about international paediatric surgery.
Language(s): English
ADVERTISING RATES:
Full Page Mono .... EUR 920
Full Page Colour .... EUR 1960
Mechanical Data: Type Area: 240 x 175 mm
Official Journal of: Organ d. Society of Pediatric Surgical Research, d. Japanese Society of Pediatric Surgeons, d. Pediatric Colorectal Society u. d. Asian Association of Paediatric Surgeons

PEDOBIOLOGIA
738710G64F-1880

Editorial: Berliner Str. 28, 37073 GÖTTINGEN
Tel: 551 395557 **Fax:** 551 395448
Email: sscheu@gwdg.de
Freq: 6 issues yearly; **Annual Sub.:** EUR 261,00
Editor: Stefan Scheu
Profile: Magazine focusing on soil biology.
Language(s): English
BUSINESS: OTHER CLASSIFICATIONS: Biology

PEENE BLITZ AM SONNTAG
738712G72-10432

Editorial: Markt 3, 17489 GREIFSWALD
Tel: 3834 7737741 **Fax:** 3834 7737730
Email: mathias.kerber@blitzverlag.de **Web site:** http://www.blitzverlag.de
Freq: Weekly; **Cover Price:** Free; **Circ:** 46,512
Editor: Mathias Kerber; **Advertising Manager:** Frank Rohde
Profile: Advertising journal (house-to-house) concentrating on local stories.
Language(s): German
ADVERTISING RATES:
Full Page Mono .... EUR 2924
Full Page Colour .... EUR 3314
Mechanical Data: Type Area: 420 x 285 mm, No. of Columns (Display): 6, Col Widths (Display): 45 mm
Copy instructions: *Copy Date:* 2 days prior to publication
LOCAL NEWSPAPERS

PEGNITZ-ZEITUNG
738718G67B-11620

Editorial: Nürnberger Str. 19, 91207 LAUF
Tel: 9123 175155 **Fax:** 9123 175198
Email: redaktion@pegnitz-zeitung.de **Web site:** http://www.pegnitz-zeitung.de
Freq: 312 issues yearly; **Circ:** 12,476
Profile: Daily newspaper with regional news and a local sports section.
Language(s): German
ADVERTISING RATES:
SCC .... EUR 35,50
Mechanical Data: Type Area: 420 x 281 mm, No. of Columns (Display): 6, Col Widths (Display): 45 mm
Copy instructions: *Copy Date:* 2 days prior to publication
Supplement(s): Amtsblatt für den Landkreis Nürnberger Land; sechs+sechzig
REGIONAL DAILY & SUNDAY NEWSPAPERS: Regional Daily Newspapers

PEINER ALLGEMEINE ZEITUNG
738720G67B-11640

Editorial: Werderstr. 49, 31224 PEINE
Tel: 5171 406131 **Fax:** 5171 406133
Email: redaktion@paz-online.de **Web site:** http://www.paz-online.de
Freq: 312 issues yearly; **Circ:** 20,961
Editor: Dirk Borth; **Advertising Manager:** Carsten Winkler
Profile: Daily newspaper with regional news and a local sports section. This Outlet offers RSS (Really Simple Syndication).
Language(s): German
Mechanical Data: Type Area: 430 x 277 mm, No. of Columns (Display): 6, Col Widths (Display): 45 mm
Copy instructions: *Copy Date:* 2 days prior to publication
Supplement(s): City Magazin Peine; rtv
REGIONAL DAILY & SUNDAY NEWSPAPERS: Regional Daily Newspapers

PELIKANS BETEILIGUNGS-KOMPASS
1828554G1F-1734

Editorial: Altstadt 296, 84028 LANDSHUT
Tel: 871 4306330 **Fax:** 871 43063311
Email: info@beteiligungsreport.de **Web site:** http://www.beteiligungsreport.de
Freq: Annual; **Cover Price:** EUR 59,80; **Circ:** 8,000
Editor: Edmund Pelikan
Profile: Manual for the market of closed-end funds.
Language(s): German
ADVERTISING RATES:
Full Page Mono .... EUR 690

PENZBERGER MERKUR
738744G67B-11660

Editorial: Pfaffenrieder Str. 9, 82515 WOLFRATSHAUSEN **Tel:** 8171 2690
Fax: 8171 269240
Email: fsav@merkur-online.de **Web site:** http://www.merkur-online.de
Freq: 312 issues yearly; **Circ:** 12,145
Advertising Manager: Hans-Georg Bechthold
Profile: The Münchner Merkur with its own local newspapers, of which the Penzberger Merkur is one that, the leading regional newspaper brand in the Munich area - the most affluent area of Germany. The combination of newspaper and region is the foundation on which to build the success of the title. This is the newspaper not only the factual news agency, but forms a community of solidarity with its readers and the local community. The clear focus on local reporting creates a high regard to human reader loyalty. She presses one hand in the very high number of close to 180,000 subscribers. Also for the high reader-commitment is the loyalty of the total current 827 000 daily readers, the Münchner Merkur or one of its local newspapers usually read over many years. The Münchner Merkur with its own local newspapers is a newspaper for the whole family, tradition and modern life for one of the most beautiful regions of Germany unites. Reliable, informative, critical: the Münchner Merkur is the indispensable daily newspaper for the region. Facebook: http://www.facebook.com/pages/merkur-online.de/190176143327 This Outlet offers RSS (Really Simple Syndication).
Language(s): German
ADVERTISING RATES:
SCC .... EUR 43,60
Mechanical Data: Type Area: 474 x 324 mm, No. of Columns (Display): 7, Col Widths (Display): 45 mm
Copy instructions: *Copy Date:* 1 day prior to publication
REGIONAL DAILY & SUNDAY NEWSPAPERS: Regional Daily Newspapers

PERFORMANCE
767155G1C-1412

Editorial: Am Wuhlegrund 20, 16356 AHRENSFELDE
Tel: 30 93495562 **Fax:** 30 93495563
Email: redaktion@performance-online.de **Web site:** http://www.performance-online.de
Freq: 10 issues yearly; **Annual Sub.:** EUR 60,00; **Circ:** 8,975
Editor: Hans Pfeifer; **Advertising Manager:** Ivona Okanik
Profile: Magazine with information on finances focusing on sale, support, marketing and product design.
Language(s): German
ADVERTISING RATES:
Full Page Mono .... EUR 2831
Full Page Colour .... EUR 3775
Mechanical Data: No. of Columns (Display): 2, Col Widths (Display): 87 mm, Type Area: 252 x 176 mm
Copy instructions: *Copy Date:* 20 days prior to publication

PERFUSION
738756G56A-8280

Editorial: Storchenweg 20, 90617 PUSCHENDORF
Tel: 9101 9901110 **Fax:** 9101 9901119
Email: info@verlag-perfusion.de **Web site:** http://www.verlag-perfusion.de
Freq: 6 issues yearly; Free to qualifying individuals
Annual Sub.: EUR 35,70; **Circ:** 21,000
Editor: Brigitte Söllner; **Advertising Manager:** Sibylle Michna
Profile: Perfusion intensified dialogue between the clinic and practice, between clinical and industrial research. In Perfusion related diagnostic and therapeutic problems, a common forum. Be published editorials, guest editorials, review articles, original papers, short reports, forums, literature reviews, book reviews, conference reports, reports from industry and research. Target group: General practitioners and clinicians from all specialized (especially cardiology, angiology, phlebology, hemorheology, cardiac surgery / vascular surgery / neurosurgery, emergency medicine, general medicine) Topics: epidemiology, prevention, diagnosis, treatment and rehabilitation cerebro-and cardiovascular diseases, recent research from the fields hemorheology, microcirculation, atherogenesis, thrombogenesis, metabolic diseases, pharmacology.
Language(s): English; German
ADVERTISING RATES:
Full Page Mono .... EUR 2310
Full Page Colour .... EUR 3410
Mechanical Data: Type Area: 245 x 175 mm
Copy instructions: *Copy Date:* 8 days prior to publication
Official Journal of: Organ d. Dt. Ges. f. Arterioskleroseforschung

PERLENTAUCHER.DE
1662413G84A-3737

Editorial: Eichendorffstr. 21, 10115 BERLIN
Tel: 30 40055830 **Fax:** 30 40055839
Email: redaktion@perlentaucher.de **Web site:** http://www.perlentaucher.de
Freq: Daily; **Cover Price:** Paid; **Circ:** 635,553 Unique Users
Editor: Anja Seeliger; **Advertising Manager:** Thierry Chervel
Language(s): German
CONSUMER: THE ARTS & LITERARY: Arts

PERRY RHODAN HOMEPAGE
1692594G76B-8473

Editorial: Karlsruher Str. 31, 76437 RASTATT
Tel: 7222 130 **Fax:** 7222 13385
Email: kontakt@perry-rhodan.net **Web site:** http://www.perry-rhodan.net
Freq: 250 times a year; **Cover Price:** Paid; **Circ:** 41,169 Unique Users
Editor: Björn Berenz; **Advertising Manager:** Björn Berenz
Language(s): German
CONSUMER: MUSIC & PERFORMING ARTS: Theatre

PERSONAL
738773G14F-42

Editorial: Munzinger Str. 9, 79111 FREIBURG
Tel: 761 8983840 **Fax:** 761 898993840
Email: randolf.jessl@haufe-lexware.com **Web site:** http://www.personal-im-web.de
Freq: Monthly; **Annual Sub.:** EUR 198,00; **Circ:** 4,069
Editor: Randolf Jessl
Profile: Human resources management magazine with in-depth information for the daily operations and strategic new directions. This Outlet offers RSS (Really Simple Syndication).
Language(s): German
ADVERTISING RATES:
Full Page Mono .... EUR 1982
Full Page Colour .... EUR 3390
Mechanical Data: Type Area: 265 x 175 mm, No. of Columns (Display): 3, Col Widths (Display): 55 mm
Copy instructions: *Copy Date:* 25 days prior to publication
BUSINESS: COMMERCE, INDUSTRY & MANAGEMENT: Training & Recruitment

PERSONALBERATER
738778G14A-5460

Editorial: Brandenburgstr. 3, 40629 DÜSSELDORF
Tel: 211 6914535 **Fax:** 211 6914537
Email: info@management-karriere.de **Web site:** http://www.management-karriere.de
Freq: Annual; **Cover Price:** EUR 70,00; **Circ:** 3,000
Editor: Roma Sadler; **Advertising Manager:** Heinrich Sadler
Profile: Publication featuring information about staff management.
Language(s): German
ADVERTISING RATES:
Full Page Mono .... EUR 1012
Full Page Colour .... EUR 1866
Mechanical Data: Type Area: 210 x 140 mm
Copy instructions: *Copy Date:* 60 days prior to publication

PERSONALFÜHRUNG
738781G14F-45

Editorial: Niederkasseler Lohweg 16, 40547 DÜSSELDORF **Tel:** 211 5978161 **Fax:** 211 5978169
Email: personalfuehrung@dgfp.de **Web site:** http://www.dgfp.de
Freq: Monthly; Free to qualifying individuals
Annual Sub.: EUR 116,00; **Circ:** 7,301
Editor: Thomas Hartge; **Advertising Manager:** Hilde Regnier
Profile: Magazine containing information on personnel management.
Language(s): German
ADVERTISING RATES:
Full Page Mono .... EUR 2100
Full Page Colour .... EUR 3680
Mechanical Data: Type Area: 240 x 176 mm, No. of Columns (Display): 4, Col Widths (Display): 41 mm
BUSINESS: COMMERCE, INDUSTRY & MANAGEMENT: Training & Recruitment

PERSONALMAGAZIN
738786G14F-11

Editorial: Munzinger Str. 9, 79111 FREIBURG
Tel: 761 8983921 **Fax:** 761 8983112
Email: redaktion@personalmagazin.de **Web site:** http://www.personalmagazin.de
Freq: Monthly; **Annual Sub.:** EUR 122,00; **Circ:** 38,725
Editor: Randolf Jessl
Profile: Magazine focusing on trends and practice within personnel management. Includes articles covering wages and social rights. Twitter: http://twitter.com/personalmagazin.
Language(s): German
Readership: Read by personnel managers.
ADVERTISING RATES:
Full Page Mono .... EUR 7000
Full Page Colour .... EUR 7900
Mechanical Data: Type Area: 249 x 176 mm, No. of Columns (Display): 3, Col Widths (Display): 56 mm
Copy instructions: *Copy Date:* 30 days prior to publication
Supplement to: baV spezial
BUSINESS: COMMERCE, INDUSTRY & MANAGEMENT: Training & Recruitment

DER PERSONALRAT
738790G32K-155

Editorial: Staufenstr. 4, 60323 FRANKFURT
Tel: 69 71915843 **Fax:** 69 71915844
Email: derpersonalrat@bund-verlag.de **Web site:** http://www.bund-verlag.de
Freq: 11 issues yearly; **Annual Sub.:** EUR 129,60; **Circ:** 7,015
Editor: Michael Kröll; **Advertising Manager:** Peter Beuther
Profile: Journal covering legislation and individual rights within the civil service and public administration.
Language(s): German
Readership: Aimed at civil servants.
ADVERTISING RATES:
Full Page Mono .... EUR 1990
Full Page Colour .... EUR 2488
Mechanical Data: Type Area: 271 x 180 mm
Copy instructions: *Copy Date:* 20 days prior to publication
BUSINESS: LOCAL GOVERNMENT, LEISURE & RECREATION: Civil Service

PERSONALWIRTSCHAFT
738805G14F-48

Editorial: Luxemburger Str. 449, 50939 KÖLN
Tel: 221 943737653 **Fax:** 221 943737757
Email: personalwirtschaft@wolterskluwer.de **Web site:** http://www.personalwirtschaft.de
Freq: Monthly; **Annual Sub.:** EUR 169,80; **Circ:** 8,110
Editor: Erwin Stickling; **Advertising Manager:** Karin Kamphausen
Profile: The magazine reports on current trends in well-known German and international companies on new developments in the legal situation, Software innovations, developments in the education industry and much more. Information for HR managers in modern medium-sized enterprises and large corporations that focus on strategic and value adding human resources issues and is looking to participate in the company's success crucial.
Language(s): German
ADVERTISING RATES:
Full Page Mono .... EUR 2900
Full Page Colour .... EUR 3650
Mechanical Data: Type Area: 244 x 175 mm, No. of Columns (Display): 4, Col Widths (Display): 40 mm
Copy instructions: *Copy Date:* 28 days prior to publication
BUSINESS: COMMERCE, INDUSTRY & MANAGEMENT: Training & Recruitment

PERSPEKTIVEN
730339G46-115

Editorial: Kreuzstr. 108, 44137 DORTMUND
Tel: 231 91201025 **Fax:** 231 91201052
Email: pernse.nrw@tischler.de **Web site:** http://www.tischler-nrw.de
Freq: 17 issues yearly; Free to qualifying individuals ; **Circ:** 5,500
Editor: Ralf Bickert; **Advertising Manager:** Wolfgang Locker
Profile: Magazine concerning the manufacture of wood products.
Language(s): German
Readership: Aimed at owners and employees of wood product manufacturing outlets.
ADVERTISING RATES:
Full Page Mono .... EUR 3500
Full Page Colour .... EUR 3500
Mechanical Data: Type Area: 242 x 175 mm, No. of Columns (Display): 3, Col Widths (Display): 55 mm
Copy instructions: *Copy Date:* 21 days prior to publication
BUSINESS: TIMBER, WOOD & FORESTRY

PERSPEKTIVEN
1833381G58-1799

Editorial: Mohrenstr. 11, 50670 KÖLN
Tel: 221 9218290 **Fax:** 221 9218296
Email: akkus@die-fuehrungskraefte.de **Web site:** http://www.die-fuehrungskraefte.de
Freq: 6 issues yearly; **Circ:** 15,434
Editor: Ilhan Akkus
Profile: Magazine for managers.
Language(s): German
ADVERTISING RATES:
Full Page Colour .... EUR 2250
Mechanical Data: Type Area: 256 x 186 mm
Supplement(s): ULA Nachrichten

PERSPEKTIVEPRAXIS.DE
1824663G14A-10069

Editorial: Pariser Platz 3, 10117 BERLIN
Tel: 30 202416900 **Fax:** 30 202416985
Email: presse@dgrv.de **Web site:** http://www.perspektivepraxis.de
Freq: Quarterly; **Cover Price:** Free; **Circ:** 27,100
Editor: Andreas Wieg
Profile: Magazine with information for cooperative companies.
Language(s): German
Supplement to: netzwerk

PERSPEKTIVEPRAXIS.DE
1824663G14A-10400

Editorial: Pariser Platz 3, 10117 BERLIN
Tel: 30 202416900 **Fax:** 30 202416985
Email: presse@dgrv.de **Web site:** http://www.perspektivepraxis.de
Freq: Quarterly; **Cover Price:** Free; **Circ:** 27,100
Editor: Andreas Wieg
Profile: Magazine with information for cooperative companies.
Language(s): German
Supplement to: netzwerk

PERSV DIE PERSONALVERTRETUNG
738804G32A-2520

Editorial: Hamackstr. 7, 38116 BRAUNSCHWEIG
Tel: 531 512802 **Fax:** 531 512802

Email: redaktionpv@esvmedien.de **Web site:** http://www.persvdigital.de
Freq: Monthly; **Annual Sub.:** EUR 114,19; **Circ:** 3,600
Editor: Frank Bieler; **Advertising Manager:** Peter Taprogge
Profile: Magazine for personnel in local government and administration.
Language(s): German
ADVERTISING RATES:
Full Page Mono .... EUR 2770
Full Page Colour .... EUR 3670
Mechanical Data: Type Area: 254 x 172 mm, No. of Columns (Display): 2, Col Widths (Display): 84 mm
BUSINESS: LOCAL GOVERNMENT, LEISURE & RECREATION: Local Government

PET
738823G64E-1
Editorial: Am Erlengraben 8, 76275 ETTLINGEN
Tel: 7243 575230 **Fax:** 7243 575200
Email: r.majer-abele@daehne.de **Web site:** http://www.petonline.de
Freq: 11 issues yearly; **Annual Sub.:** EUR 92,00; **Circ:** 5,934
Editor: Ralf Majer-Abele; **Advertising Manager:** Thomas Heinen
Profile: pet is the specialist magazine for the German-speaking pet sector. Contributions from Austria and Switzerland are included to complement the reports on the German market. Every issue brings up-to-date and practical information on all the different aspects of the pet market. The magazine focuses on news and personnel announcements from the sector, trade fair reports, coverage of the specialty pet trade and the pet departments in garden centres and DIY stores, as well as reports on suppliers and service concepts. Regular market and product surveys, in addition to detailed keynote topics, deal with developments in a variety of different product areas. Expertly analysed statistics provide readers with information on the current state of the pet market.
Language(s): German
Readership: Read by animal keepers.
ADVERTISING RATES:
Full Page Mono .... EUR 1895
Full Page Colour .... EUR 3824
Mechanical Data: Type Area: 270 x 187 mm, No. of Columns (Display): 4, Col Widths (Display): 43 mm
BUSINESS: OTHER CLASSIFICATIONS: Pet Trade

PETRA
738829G74A-2540
Editorial: Poßmoorweg 2, 22301 HAMBURG
Tel: 40 27173009 **Fax:** 40 27173020
Email: redaktion@petra.de **Web site:** http://www.petra.de
Freq: Monthly; **Annual Sub.:** EUR 30,00; **Circ:** 234,743
Editor: Nina Maurischat; **Advertising Manager:** Tobias van Duynen
Profile: PETRA is Germany's most widely read monthly women's magazine for fashion, beauty and lifestyle. PETRA, means international fashion, lively entertainment, luxury and beauty topics around the own reality of life such as partnership, psychology, career and culture. PETRA is adult large optics and a completely positive attitude to life. Facebook: http://www.facebook.com/petra.
Language(s): German
Readership: Aimed at modern women.
ADVERTISING RATES:
Full Page Mono .... EUR 23000
Full Page Colour .... EUR 23000
Mechanical Data: Type Area: 252 x 178 mm, No. of Columns (Display): 4, Col Widths (Display): 40 mm
Copy instructions: *Copy Date:* 63 days prior to publication
CONSUMER: WOMEN'S INTEREST CONSUMER MAGAZINES: Women's Interest

PETTERSSON UND FINDUS
761296G91D-9657
Editorial: Rotebühlstr. 87, 70178 STUTTGART
Tel: 711 94768780 **Fax:** 711 94768830
Email: info@panini.de **Web site:** http://www.panini.de
Freq: 6 issues yearly; **Cover Price:** EUR 2,70; **Circ:** 35,412
Editor: Gabriele El Hag
Profile: Pettersson and Findus is the Activity Magazine for Kids! The colorful interactive booklet is based on the popular television characters Pettersson and Findus Sven Nordqvist. Faithful whose drawings will be staged, in riddles, stories and great extras.
Language(s): German
ADVERTISING RATES:
Full Page Mono .... EUR 3900
Full Page Colour .... EUR 3900
Mechanical Data: Type Area: 256 x 186 mm
CONSUMER: RECREATION & LEISURE: Children & Youth

PFAD
732657G32G-102
Editorial: Geisbergstr. 16, 10777 BERLIN
Tel: 30 94879423 **Fax:** 30 47985031
Email: margit.huber@pfad-bv.de **Web site:** http://www.pfad-bv.de
Freq: Quarterly; Free to qualifying individuals
Annual Sub.: EUR 19,95; **Circ:** 3,200
Editor: Margit Huber; **Advertising Manager:** Tanja Kern
Profile: Magazine focusing on child fostering and adoption.
Language(s): German
ADVERTISING RATES:
Full Page Mono .... EUR 805
Mechanical Data: Type Area: 260 x 180 mm, No. of Columns (Display): 2, Col Widths (Display): 87 mm
Copy instructions: *Copy Date:* 36 days prior to publication
BUSINESS: LOCAL GOVERNMENT, LEISURE & RECREATION: Community Care & Social Services

PFAFFENHOFENER KURIER
738845G67B-11680
Editorial: Stauffenbergstr. 2a, 85051 INGOLSTADT
Tel: 841 96660 **Fax:** 841 9666255
Email: redaktion@donaukurier.de **Web site:** http://www.donaukurier.de
Freq: 312 issues yearly; **Circ:** 15,255
Advertising Manager: Hermann Fetsch
Profile: Daily newspaper with regional news and a local sports section. Facebook: http://www.facebook.com/donaukurier.online.
Language(s): German
ADVERTISING RATES:
SCC .... EUR 31,80
Mechanical Data: Type Area: 435 x 282 mm, No. of Columns (Display): 6, Col Widths (Display): 45 mm
Copy instructions: *Copy Date:* 1 day prior to publication
REGIONAL DAILY & SUNDAY NEWSPAPERS: Regional Daily Newspapers

PFALZCLUB MAGAZIN
1740176G89A-12235
Editorial: Martin-Luther-Str. 69, 67433 NEUSTADT
Tel: 6321 912322 **Fax:** 6321 12881
Email: info@pfalz-marketing.de **Web site:** http://www.pfalz-marketing.de
Freq: Quarterly; **Circ:** 15,000
Editor: Detlev Janik
Profile: Club magazine with internal information.
Language(s): German
ADVERTISING RATES:
Full Page Mono .... EUR 3000
Full Page Colour .... EUR 3000

PFÄLZISCHER MERKUR
738841G67B-11700
Editorial: Hauptstr. 66, 66482 ZWEIBRÜCKEN
Tel: 6332 800050 **Fax:** 6332 800059
Email: merkur@pm-zw.de **Web site:** http://www.pfaelzischer-merkur.de
Freq: 312 issues yearly; **Circ:** 8,027
Editor: Peter Stefan Herbst; **Advertising Manager:** Michael Schmierer
Profile: Daily newspaper with regional news and a local sports section. This Outlet offers RSS (Really Simple Syndication).
Language(s): German
ADVERTISING RATES:
SCC .... EUR 43,20
Mechanical Data: Type Area: 480 x 326 mm, No. of Columns (Display): 7, Col Widths (Display): 44 mm
Copy instructions: *Copy Date:* 2 days prior to publication
Supplement(s): rtv; Theaterzeit; treff.region
REGIONAL DAILY & SUNDAY NEWSPAPERS: Regional Daily Newspapers

PFERD + SPORT IN SCHLESWIG-HOLSTEIN UND HAMBURG
738874G75E-150
Editorial: Im Dreieck 8, 21376 SALZHAUSEN
Tel: 4172 6699 **Fax:** 4172 6696
Email: dvpreussen@aol.com **Web site:** http://www.pferd-und-sport.de
Freq: Monthly; Free to qualifying individuals
Annual Sub.: EUR 61,20; **Circ:** 13,809
Editor: Donata von Preußen; **Advertising Manager:** Philip Rathmann
Profile: Magazine about equestrian sports in Hamburg and Schleswig-Holstein.
Language(s): German
ADVERTISING RATES:
Full Page Mono .... EUR 2155
Full Page Colour .... EUR 2755
Mechanical Data: Type Area: 245 x 188 mm, No. of Columns (Display): 4, Col Widths (Display): 44 mm
Copy instructions: *Copy Date:* 20 days prior to publication
CONSUMER: SPORT: Horse Racing

PFERDE ANZEIGER
738858G81D-6
Editorial: Drostestr. 14, 30161 HANNOVER
Tel: 511 390910 **Fax:** 511 39091252
Email: zentrale@dhd.de **Web site:** http://www.deine-tierwelt.de
Freq: Monthly; **Cover Price:** EUR 3,50; **Circ:** 60,000
Advertising Manager: Lars Schnatmann
Profile: Publication about horses and the sale of horses.
Language(s): German
Readership: Aimed at breeders and owners of horses.
ADVERTISING RATES:
Full Page Mono .... EUR 2408
Full Page Colour .... EUR 2766
Mechanical Data: Type Area: 280 x 191 mm, No. of Columns (Display): 4, Col Widths (Display): 45 mm
Copy instructions: *Copy Date:* 16 days prior to publication
CONSUMER: ANIMALS & PETS: Horses & Ponies

PFERDE FREUNDE FÜRS LEBEN
1615563G91D-9816
Editorial: Rotebühlstr. 87, 70178 STUTTGART
Tel: 711 947680 **Fax:** 711 9476830
Email: info@panini.de **Web site:** http://www.panini.de
Freq: Monthly; **Cover Price:** EUR 2,50; **Circ:** 38,331
Editor: Martin Klingseisen
Profile: Horse magazine for young girls. In an entertaining, emotional nature and in combination with beautiful photos get the girls all about their favorite subject: horses and riding. In each issue, readers also find two beautiful posters, an exciting photo story, a great comic, and many puzzles and raffles. Each issue features with high-quality trend Extra! Anhören Umschrift.
Language(s): German
ADVERTISING RATES:
Full Page Mono .... EUR 3900
Full Page Colour .... EUR 3900
Mechanical Data: Type Area: 250 x 180 mm
CONSUMER: RECREATION & LEISURE: Children & Youth

PFERDEFORUM
1613840G81X-3202
Editorial: Mars-la-Tour-Str. 4, 26121 OLDENBURG
Tel: 441 801221 **Fax:** 441 801249
Email: info@pferdeforum-online.de **Web site:** http://www.pferdeforum-online.de
Freq: Monthly; **Annual Sub.:** EUR 64,80; **Circ:** 12,095
Editor: Heiko Meinardus
Profile: Official publication of the Weser-Ems Riding Association.
Language(s): German
ADVERTISING RATES:
Full Page Mono .... EUR 2000
Full Page Colour .... EUR 2830
Mechanical Data: Type Area: 270 x 184 mm, No. of Columns (Display): 4, Col Widths (Display): 43 mm
Copy instructions: *Copy Date:* 31 days prior to publication
Official Journal of: Organ d. Springpferdezuchtverb. Oldenburg-Internat. e.V., d. Verb. d. Züchter d. Oldenburger Pferdes e.V. u. d. Pferdestammbuch Weser-Ems e.V.
CONSUMER: ANIMALS & PETS

PFERDEMARKT
738865G75E-400
Editorial: Hülsebrockstr. 2, 48165 MÜNSTER
Tel: 2501 801154 **Fax:** 2501 801334
Email: redaktion@pferdemarkt.de **Web site:** http://www.pferdemarkt.de
Freq: 6 issues yearly; **Annual Sub.:** EUR 35,50; **Circ:** 23,180
Editor: Markus Wörmann
Profile: Magazine all about riding and horse breeding for buyers, sellers and horse owners.
Language(s): German
Readership: Aimed at trainers and owners of riding stables, also read by participants in equestrian events.
ADVERTISING RATES:
Full Page Mono .... EUR 2666
Full Page Colour .... EUR 3994
Mechanical Data: Type Area: 280 x 193 mm, No. of Columns (Display): 4, Col Widths (Display): 46 mm
CONSUMER: SPORT: Horse Racing

PFERDESPORT JOURNAL
745930G81D-19
Editorial: Weberstr. 9, 55130 MAINZ
Tel: 6131 620538 **Fax:** 6131 620544
Email: s.schreiber@fraund.de **Web site:** http://www.fraund.de
Freq: Monthly; **Annual Sub.:** EUR 57,80; **Circ:** 11,014
Editor: Simone Schreiber; **Advertising Manager:** Manfred Schulz
Profile: Sport Horse Journal is the magazine about horses for competition and recreational athletes, horse lovers and horse breeder. with exciting reports, interesting editorials on legal, health or education, current results and an abundance of dates.
Language(s): German
ADVERTISING RATES:
Full Page Mono .... EUR 1610
Full Page Colour .... EUR 2815
Mechanical Data: Type Area: 270 x 185 mm, No. of Columns (Display): 4, Col Widths (Display): 43 mm
Copy instructions: *Copy Date:* 20 days prior to publication
Official Journal of: Organ d. Hess. Reit- u. Fahrverb. e.V., d. Verb. Hess. Pferdezüchter e.V., d. Verb. d. Ponyzüchter Hessen e.V., d. Kommission f. Pferdeleistungsprüfungen in Hessen, d. Pferdesportverb. Hessen, d. Pferdesportverb. Rheinland-Pfalz, d. Pferdezuchtverb. Rheinland-Pfalz-Saar und d. FLSE Luxemburg
CONSUMER: ANIMALS & PETS: Horses & Ponies

PFLEGE PARTNER
738895G56L-5
Editorial: Plathnerstr. 4c, 30175 HANNOVER
Tel: 511 9910313 **Fax:** 511 9910309
Email: angela.havers@vincentz.de **Web site:** http://www.vincentz-kundenmedien.de
Freq: 6 issues yearly; **Cover Price:** Free; **Circ:** 81,449
Editor: Angelika Havers; **Advertising Manager:** Henning-Lothar Litka
Profile: Magazine for carers of the disabled.
Language(s): German
ADVERTISING RATES:
Full Page Mono .... EUR 3680
Full Page Colour .... EUR 4000
Mechanical Data: Type Area: 258 x 185 mm, No. of Columns (Display): 4, Col Widths (Display): 42 mm
Copy instructions: *Copy Date:* 28 days prior to publication
BUSINESS: HEALTH & MEDICAL: Disability & Rehabilitation

PFLEGE- & KRANKENHAUSRECHT-PKR
738891G56C-12
Editorial: Stadtwaldpark 10, 34212 MELSUNGEN
Tel: 5661 734429 **Fax:** 5661 8360
Email: markus.boucsein@bibliomed.de **Web site:** http://www.bibliomed.de
Freq: Quarterly; **Annual Sub.:** EUR 52,00; **Circ:** 2,000
Editor: Markus Boucsein; **Advertising Manager:** Michael Menzer
Profile: Juridical magazine focusing on legal rights in hospital management regarding in- and out-patient care.
Language(s): German
ADVERTISING RATES:
Full Page Mono .... EUR 550
Full Page Colour .... EUR 1135
Mechanical Data: Type Area: 250 x 180 mm, No. of Columns (Display): 2, Col Widths (Display): 88 mm
BUSINESS: HEALTH & MEDICAL: Hospitals

PFLEGEZEITSCHRIFT
738896G56B-1650
Editorial: Heßbrühlstr. 69, 70565 STUTTGART
Tel: 711 78637253 **Fax:** 711 78638436
Email: pflegezeitschrift@kohlhammer.de **Web site:** http://www.pflegezeitschrift.de
Freq: Monthly; **Annual Sub.:** EUR 60,60; **Circ:** 6,038
Editor: Christian Heinemeyer
Profile: Journal about all aspects of nursing.
Language(s): German
ADVERTISING RATES:
Full Page Mono .... EUR 1575
Full Page Colour .... EUR 2970
Mechanical Data: Type Area: 260 x 185 mm, No. of Columns (Display): 3, Col Widths (Display): 53 mm
BUSINESS: HEALTH & MEDICAL: Nursing

PFORZHEIMER KURIER
738902G67B-11720
Editorial: Linkenheimer Landstr. 133, 76149 KARLSRUHE **Tel:** 721 7890 **Fax:** 721 789155
Email: redaktion@bnn.de
Freq: 312 issues yearly; **Circ:** 4,698
Advertising Manager: Jörg Stark
Profile: The Badische Neueste Nachrichten with a paid circulation of about 150,000 copies and 400,000 readers every day one of the major daily newspapers in the state of Baden-Wuerttemberg. This newspaper is understood in the concert of the leaves the country as a not to be hearing voices of Baden and the Palatinate region between and Ortenau, between the Black Forest and Rhine valley. Nine local editions in the distribution area in the Karlsruhe, Pforzheim and Bruchsal, Baden resources emphasize the character of this newspaper as Baden regional newspaper. On this image editing with a full working day with about 90 editors. Most of the editorial staff but provided in the local editors at ten locations in the distribution area the readers with local news. In addition to the BNN output Karlsruhe, Rastatt, Baden-Baden, Ettlingen arise then the Pforzheimer Kurier, the Bruchsaler Rundschau, the Brettener Nachrichten and not least the Acher- und Bühler Bote. Although the focus of reporting is very strong locally and regionally, the Badische Neueste Nachrichten offer their readers a broad and comprehensive news coverage.
Language(s): German
ADVERTISING RATES:
SCC .... EUR 25,50
Mechanical Data: Type Area: 480 x 360 mm, No. of Columns (Display): 8, Col Widths (Display): 43 mm
Copy instructions: *Copy Date:* 1 day prior to publication
REGIONAL DAILY & SUNDAY NEWSPAPERS: Regional Daily Newspapers

PFORZHEIMER ZEITUNG
738903G67B-11740
Editorial: Poststr. 5, 75172 PFORZHEIM
Tel: 7231 933185 **Fax:** 7231 933260
Email: redaktion@pz-news.de **Web site:** http://www.pz-news.de
Freq: 312 issues yearly; **Circ:** 38,253
Editor: Holger Knöferl; **News Editor:** Magnus Schlecht; **Advertising Manager:** Hartmut Döhl
Profile: Regional daily newspaper with news on politics, economy, culture, sports, travel, technology, etc. Facebook: http://www.facebook.com/pages/PZ-news-Pforzheimer-Zeitung-Online-wwwpz-newsde/254564920485?ref=nf Twitter: http://twitter.com/pznews This Outlet offers RSS (Really Simple Syndication).
Language(s): German
ADVERTISING RATES:
SCC .... EUR 59,30
Mechanical Data: Type Area: 486 x 320 mm, No. of Columns (Display): 7, Col Widths (Display): 44 mm
Copy instructions: *Copy Date:* 1 day prior to publication
REGIONAL DAILY & SUNDAY NEWSPAPERS: Regional Daily Newspapers

PHÄNOMEN FARBE 738907G16B-120

Editorial: Nördlinger Str. 15, 40597 DÜSSELDORF
Tel: 211 7182314 **Fax:** 211 7182366
Email: pf-verlag@t-online.de **Web site:** http://www.phaenomen-farbe.de
Freq: 6 issues yearly; **Annual Sub.:** EUR 108,00; **Circ:** 2,000
Editor: Friedrich M. Albert
Profile: Magazine containing information about paints, varnish, glues and printing colours.
Language(s): English; German
Readership: Read by suppliers and manufacturers.
ADVERTISING RATES:
Full Page Mono .... EUR 985
Full Page Colour .... EUR 985
Mechanical Data: Type Area: 255 x 190 mm, No. of Columns (Display): 3, Col Widths (Display): 59 mm
Copy instructions: *Copy Date:* 30 days prior to publication
BUSINESS: DECORATING & PAINT: Paint - Technical Manufacture

PHARMA KOMMUNIKATION 1824560G37-1851

Editorial: Am Forsthaus Gravenbruch 5, 63263 NEU-ISENBURG **Tel:** 6102 506135 **Fax:** 6102 506220
Email: info@aerztezeitung.de **Web site:** http://www.aerztezeitung.de
Freq: Quarterly; **Circ:** 3,600
Editor: Dieter Eschenbach; **Advertising Manager:** Ute Krille
Profile: Newspaper for the pharmaceutical industry containing information about products.
Language(s): German
ADVERTISING RATES:
Full Page Mono .... EUR 2500
Full Page Colour .... EUR 3400
Supplement to: Arzneimittel Zeitung

PHARMA MARKETING JOURNAL 738917G37-110

Editorial: Grafenberger Allee 293, 40237 DÜSSELDORF **Tel:** 211 8871427 **Fax:** 211 8871420
Email: p.hanser@fachverlag.de **Web site:** http://www.pharma-marketing.de
Freq: 6 issues yearly; **Annual Sub.:** EUR 80,00; **Circ:** 2,495
Editor: Peter Hanser; **Advertising Manager:** Regina Hamdorf
Profile: Informant for pharmaceutical marketing and supplier of operating instructions for the practice of marketing, sales and communications work in the pharmaceutical market.
Language(s): German
Readership: Aimed at those involved in the pharmaceutical and chemical industries and advertising agencies.
ADVERTISING RATES:
Full Page Mono .... EUR 2315
Full Page Colour .... EUR 2315
Mechanical Data: Type Area: 256 x 180 mm, No. of Columns (Display): 4, Col Widths (Display): 42 mm
Copy instructions: *Copy Date:* 15 days prior to publication
BUSINESS: PHARMACEUTICAL & CHEMISTS

PHARMA RUNDSCHAU 738920G37-1340

Editorial: Industriestr. 2, 63150 HEUSENSTAMM
Tel: 6104 606326 **Fax:** 6104 606117
Email: s.schmidtke@kepplermediengruppe.de **Web site:** http://www.pharmarundschau.de
Freq: 11 issues yearly; **Annual Sub.:** EUR 129,00; **Circ:** 22,978
Editor: Silvia Schmidtke; **Advertising Manager:** Reinald Korte
Profile: Official journal of the Association of German Pharmacists.
Language(s): German
ADVERTISING RATES:
Full Page Mono .... EUR 4620
Full Page Colour .... EUR 4620
Mechanical Data: Type Area: 263 x 185 mm, No. of Columns (Display): 3, Col Widths (Display): 58 mm
Copy instructions: *Copy Date:* 14 days prior to publication
BUSINESS: PHARMACEUTICAL & CHEMISTS

PHARMA+FOOD 738924G37-105

Editorial: Im Weiher 10, 69121 HEIDELBERG
Tel: 6221 489388 **Fax:** 6221 489490
Email: armin.scheuermann@huethig.de **Web site:** http://www.pharma-food.de
Freq: 7 issues yearly; **Annual Sub.:** EUR 82,80; **Circ:** 10,629
Editor: Armin Scheuermann; **Advertising Manager:** Sabine Wegmann
Profile: Pharma + Food is the leading trade magazine for decision makers in production, equipment and organization of the pharmaceutical, food and cosmetics industries. In the form of application reports, technical papers, interviews, product information and short report Pharma + Food knowledge and industry information to all who need to produce hygienic. As code-magazine reaches Pharma + Food professionals and managers, planners, decision makers and suppliers of components, systems and services of the health process technology and thus establishes direct contact with the investment decision-makers.
Language(s): German
Readership: Aimed at business executives and production managers within the industry.
ADVERTISING RATES:
Full Page Mono .... EUR 2940
Full Page Colour .... EUR 4040
Mechanical Data: Type Area: 257 x 178 mm, No. of Columns (Display): 4, Col Widths (Display): 41 mm
Copy instructions: *Copy Date:* 30 days prior to publication
BUSINESS: PHARMACEUTICAL & CHEMISTS

PHARMA WOCHE 739138G37-1769

Editorial: Am Forsthaus Gravenbruch 5, 63263 NEU-ISENBURG **Tel:** 6102 506145 **Fax:** 6102 506220
Email: info@aerztezeitung.de **Web site:** http://www.pmsline.de
Freq: 42 issues yearly; **Annual Sub.:** EUR 2140,00; **Circ:** 220
Editor: Bertold Schmitt-Feuerbach
Profile: Magazine for the pharmaceutical industry including information and investigation services.
Language(s): German
Mechanical Data: Type Area: 297 x 210 mm

PHARMA-AKTUELL 1646176G37-1799

Editorial: Lehmweg 11, 26316 VAREL
Tel: 4451 950395 **Fax:** 4451 950390
Email: gerigk@pharma-aktuell-online.de **Web site:** http://www.pharma-aktuell-online.de
Freq: Quarterly; **Annual Sub.:** EUR 65,00; **Circ:** 39,790
Editor: Maria Gerigk; **Advertising Manager:** Barbara Bepler
Profile: European Journal of Medicine, Pharmacy and finance. The magazine regularly informs all registered general practitioners and specialists about current diagnostic and therapeutic developments in medicine and pharmacy. The medical and scientific section of the Journal includes informative and practical articles by renowned writers of international renown, interviews with opinion leaders, practical training and professional reporting of conferences and symposia within the respective disciplines. The focus of the business section are business management issues. The latest information and tips from the financial, tax and insurance round out the spectrum.
Language(s): German
ADVERTISING RATES:
Full Page Mono .... EUR 4550
Full Page Colour .... EUR 5502
Mechanical Data: Type Area: 253 x 172 mm, No. of Columns (Display): 3, Col Widths (Display): 54 mm
Copy instructions: *Copy Date:* 14 days prior to publication

PHARMACOPSYCHIATRY 738914G56N-73

Editorial: Marie-Curie-Str. 9, 60439 FRANKFURT
Tel: 69 79829373
Email: pharmaco@thieme.de **Web site:** http://www.thieme.de/pharmaco
Freq: 6 issues yearly; **Circ:** 770
Editor: Walter E. Müller
Profile: Covering all new advances in psychotropic drugs, Pharmacopsychiatry provides psychiatrists and pharmacologists with key clinical insights and new avenues of research and treatment. The pharmacological, neurophysiological, and psychological basis of psychiatric disorders are explored using models and model theory as applied to clinical and experimental studies. Plus, reports of controlled clinical trials, case reports, and meeting proceedings serve as a state-of-the-art tool for advancing the field and setting European standards. Includes sections on: Psychiatry/Gerontopsychiatry, Pharmacology/Clinical Pharmacology, Neuro and Psychophysiology, Psychology and Neurobiology.
Language(s): English
ADVERTISING RATES:
Full Page Mono .... EUR 1050
Full Page Colour .... EUR 2190
Mechanical Data: Type Area: 248 x 175 mm, No. of Columns (Display): 3, Col Widths (Display): 55 mm
Official Journal of: Organ d. ArGe Neuropsychopharmakologie u. Pharmakopsychiatrie
BUSINESS: HEALTH & MEDICAL: Mental Health

PHARMAREPORT 738925G37-1766

Editorial: Dischingerstr. 8, 69123 HEIDELBERG
Tel: 6221 64460 **Fax:** 6221 644640
Email: redaktion@haefner-verlag.de **Web site:** http://www.haefner-verlag.de
Freq: 6 issues yearly; **Annual Sub.:** EUR 15,47; **Circ:** 2,400
Editor: Dieter Neumann
Profile: Magazine for employees of the pharmaceutical industry.
Language(s): German

PHARMATEC 756433G13-2326

Editorial: Max-Planck-Str. 7, 97082 WÜRZBURG
Tel: 931 4182594 **Fax:** 931 4182750
Email: anke.geipel-kern@vogel.de **Web site:** http://www.process.vogel.de/pharmaindustrie
Freq: 6 issues yearly; **Annual Sub.:** EUR 77,00; **Circ:** 10,771
Editor: Anke Geipel-Kern; **Advertising Manager:** Reiner Öttinger
Profile: Magazine about chemical and pharmaceutical technologies.
Language(s): German
ADVERTISING RATES:
Full Page Mono .... EUR 4820
Full Page Colour .... EUR 6005
Mechanical Data: Type Area: 270 x 190 mm, No. of Columns (Display): 4, Col Widths (Display): 46 mm
Copy instructions: *Copy Date:* 21 days prior to publication
BUSINESS: CHEMICALS

DIE PHARMAZIE 738927G37-1380

Editorial: Carl-Mannich-Str. 26, 65760 ESCHBORN
Tel: 6196 928262 **Fax:** 6196 928203
Email: pharmazie@govi.de **Web site:** http://www.govi.de/pharmazie.htm
Freq: Monthly; **Cover Price:** EUR 21,40; **Circ:** 400
Editor: Theodor Dingermann; **Advertising Manager:** Edgar Opper
Profile: The journal publishes original articles and summaries from all areas of pharmaceutical sciences. The recipients are institutions in research and teaching, mostly science-oriented pharmacists in officina, laboratory and hospital, nationally and internationally.
Language(s): English; German
Readership: Aimed at those within the pharmaceutical sector.
ADVERTISING RATES:
Full Page Mono .... EUR 286
Full Page Colour .... EUR 596
Mechanical Data: Type Area: 267 x 183 mm, No. of Columns (Display): 2
BUSINESS: PHARMACEUTICAL & CHEMISTS

PHARMAZIE IN UNSERER ZEIT 738928G37-1400

Editorial: Max-von-Laue-Str. 9, 60438 FRANKFURT
Tel: 69 79829650 **Fax:** 69 79829662
Email: dingermann@em.uni-frankfurt.de **Web site:** http://www.pharmuz.de
Freq: 6 issues yearly; **Annual Sub.:** EUR 255,00; **Circ:** 9,954
Editor: Theodor Dingermann; **Advertising Manager:** Imke Ridder
Profile: Official journal of the German Pharmacists' Association.
Language(s): German
ADVERTISING RATES:
Full Page Mono .... EUR 3040
Full Page Colour .... EUR 4390
Mechanical Data: Type Area: 260 x 185 mm, No. of Columns (Display): 4, Col Widths (Display): 45 mm
Copy instructions: *Copy Date:* 41 days prior to publication
BUSINESS: PHARMACEUTICAL & CHEMISTS

PHARMIND DIE PHARMAZEUTISCHE INDUSTRIE 738926G37-1767

Editorial: Baendelstockweg 20, 88326 AULENDORF
Tel: 7525 940159 **Fax:** 7525 940127
Email: redaktion@ecv.de **Web site:** http://www.pharmind.de
Freq: Monthly; **Annual Sub.:** EUR 248,00; **Circ:** 4,017
Editor: Claudius Arndt; **Advertising Manager:** Judith Scheller
Profile: Official journal of the association of the German pharmaceutical industry. Covers the production and distribution of pharmaceutical products and discusses health care and social politics.
Language(s): English; German
Readership: Aimed at pharmaceutical chemists within the industry.
ADVERTISING RATES:
Full Page Mono .... EUR 1590
Full Page Colour .... EUR 2580
Mechanical Data: Type Area: 270 x 187 mm, No. of Columns (Display): 4, Col Widths (Display): 46 mm
Copy instructions: *Copy Date:* 15 days prior to publication
Official Journal of: Organ d. Verbände d. Pharma-Industrie in Deutschland, Österr. u. d. Schweiz
BUSINESS: PHARMACEUTICAL & CHEMISTS

PHI PLANTA DE HORMIGÓN INTERNACIONAL 1668386G4E-7065

Editorial: Industriestr. 180, 50999 KÖLN
Tel: 2236 962390 **Fax:** 2236 962396
Email: h.karutz@cpi-worldwide.com **Web site:** http://www.cpi-worldwide.com
Freq: 6 issues yearly; **Annual Sub.:** EUR 120,00; **Circ:** 2,500
Editor: Holger Karutz; **Advertising Manager:** Gerhard Klöckner
Profile: The journals of "CPI-Worldwide" are the only source for cutting-edge technical data, news and information for the concrete industry - from around the world. This information processed editorially and professional - are aimed directly regardless of location to business owners, decision makers and managers. The articles are well-written by world-renowned and in their field well-known experts. Each topic is presented in a way that the audience important information available, it brings on the cutting edge of technology and so to increase productivity and operational performance contributes.
Language(s): Spanish
Mechanical Data: Type Area: 260 x 180 mm, No. of Columns (Display): 3, Col Widths (Display): 56 mm
Copy instructions: *Copy Date:* 30 days prior to publication

PHI PRODUKTIONSTECHNIK HANNOVER INFORMIERT 1828491G19A-1118

Editorial: Hollerithallee 6, 30419 HANNOVER
Tel: 511 27976500 **Fax:** 511 27976888
Email: redaktion@phi-hannover.de **Web site:** http://www.phi-hannover.de
Freq: Half-yearly; **Cover Price:** Free; **Circ:** 2,600
Editor: Meike Wiegand
Profile: Magazine from the Hanover Institute for Production Technologies.The journal of technological services in Hannover informed on issues of organization of production to the metal forming, from production to logistics, to laser technology, from high-performance processing to materials science.
Language(s): German

PHLEBOLOGIE 738951G56A-8320

Editorial: Hölderlinstr. 3, 70174 STUTTGART
Tel: 711 2298736 **Fax:** 711 2298765
Email: redaktion@phlebologieonline.de **Web site:** http://www.phlebologieonline.de
Freq: 6 issues yearly; Free to qualifying individuals
Annual Sub.: EUR 154,00; **Circ:** 2,350
Editor: Iris Weiche; **Advertising Manager:** Klaus Jansch
Profile: As a forum for European science phlebological is dedicated to certified CME journal phlebological all relevant topics in research and practice: New diagnostic procedures, preventive medical issues, and therapeutic measures are discussed in original and review articles. On the established practice of phlebotomists matched topics the state-of-the-art to provide a specific therapy or disease. The journal provides an opportunity to exchange experiences between the clinic and practice.
Language(s): English; French; German
ADVERTISING RATES:
Full Page Mono .... EUR 1505
Full Page Colour .... EUR 2645
Mechanical Data: Type Area: 243 x 179 mm, No. of Columns (Display): 3, Col Widths (Display): 57 mm
Copy instructions: *Copy Date:* 40 days prior to publication
Official Journal of: Organ d. ArGe Dermatolog. Angiologie d. Dt. Dermatolog. Ges. u. d. Berufsverb. d. Phlebologen, d. Dt. u. Schweizer. Ges. f. Phlebologie u. d. Bulletin de la Société Suisse de Phlébologie

PHOENIX SPEZIAL - MAGAZIN IHRES PHOENIX VERTRIEBSZENTRUMS, AUSG. AUGSBURG 767469G37-1736

Editorial: Pfingstweidstr. 10, 68199 MANNHEIM
Tel: 621 8505440 **Fax:** 621 8505599
Email: o.christiansen@phoenixgroup.eu **Web site:** http://www.phoenixgroup.eu
Freq: Quarterly; **Cover Price:** Free; **Circ:** 1,000
Editor: Olaf Christiansen
Profile: Magazine of a pharmaceutical wholesale trader.
Language(s): German

PHOENIX SPEZIAL - MAGAZIN IHRES PHOENIX VERTRIEBSZENTRUMS, AUSG. BAD KREUZNACH 767473G37-1740

Editorial: Pfingstweidstr. 10, 68199 MANNHEIM
Tel: 621 8505440 **Fax:** 621 8505599
Email: o.christiansen@phoenixgroup.eu **Web site:** http://www.phoenixgroup.eu
Freq: Quarterly; **Cover Price:** Free; **Circ:** 1,000
Editor: Olaf Christiansen
Profile: Magazine of a pharmaceutical wholesale trader, Bad Kreuznach edition.
Language(s): German

PHOENIX SPEZIAL - MAGAZIN IHRES PHOENIX VERTRIEBSZENTRUMS, AUSG. BERLIN 767472G37-1739

Editorial: Pfingstweidstr. 10, 68199 MANNHEIM
Tel: 621 8505440 **Fax:** 621 8505599
Email: o.christiansen@phoenixgroup.eu **Web site:** http://www.phoenixgroup.eu
Freq: Quarterly; **Cover Price:** Free; **Circ:** 1,000
Editor: Olaf Christiansen
Profile: Magazine of a pharmaceutical wholesale trader, Berlin edition.
Language(s): German

PHOENIX SPEZIAL - MAGAZIN IHRES PHOENIX VERTRIEBSZENTRUMS, AUSG. BIELEFELD 767470G37-1737

Editorial: Pfingstweidstr. 10, 68199 MANNHEIM
Tel: 621 8505440 **Fax:** 621 8505599
Email: o.christiansen@phoenixgroup.eu **Web site:** http://www.phoenixgroup.eu
Freq: Quarterly; **Cover Price:** Free; **Circ:** 1,000
Editor: Olaf Christiansen
Profile: Magazine of a pharmaceutical wholesale trader, Bielefeld edition.
Language(s): German

PHOENIX SPEZIAL - MAGAZIN IHRES PHOENIX VERTRIEBSZENTRUMS, AUSG. COTTBUS 767471G37-1738
Editorial: Pfingstweidstr. 10, 68199 MANNHEIM
Tel: 621 8505440 **Fax:** 621 8505599
Email: o.christiansen@phoenixgroup.eu **Web site:** http://www.phoenixgroup.eu
Freq: Quarterly; **Cover Price:** Free; **Circ:** 1,000
Editor: Olaf Christiansen
Profile: Magazine of a pharmaceutical wholesale trader, Cottbus edition.
Language(s): German

PHOENIX SPEZIAL - MAGAZIN IHRES PHOENIX VERTRIEBSZENTRUMS, AUSG. FREIBURG 1849216G37-1855
Editorial: Pfingstweidstr. 10, 68199 MANNHEIM
Tel: 621 8505440 **Fax:** 621 8505599
Email: o.christiansen@phoenixgroup.eu **Web site:** http://www.phoenixgroup.eu
Freq: Quarterly; **Cover Price:** Free; **Circ:** 800
Editor: Olaf Christiansen
Profile: Magazine of a pharmaceutical wholesale trader, Gotha edition.
Language(s): German

PHOENIX SPEZIAL - MAGAZIN IHRES PHOENIX VERTRIEBSZENTRUMS, AUSG. FÜRTH 767475G37-1742
Editorial: Pfingstweidstr. 10, 68199 MANNHEIM
Tel: 621 8505440 **Fax:** 621 8505599
Email: o.christiansen@phoenixgroup.eu **Web site:** http://www.phoenixgroup.eu
Freq: Quarterly; **Cover Price:** Free; **Circ:** 1,000
Editor: Olaf Christiansen
Profile: Magazine of a pharmaceutical wholesale trader, Fürth edition.
Language(s): German

PHOENIX SPEZIAL - MAGAZIN IHRES PHOENIX VERTRIEBSZENTRUMS, AUSG. GOTHA 767476G37-1743
Editorial: Pfingstweidstr. 10, 68199 MANNHEIM
Tel: 621 8505440 **Fax:** 621 8505599
Email: o.christiansen@phoenixgroup.eu **Web site:** http://www.phoenixgroup.eu
Freq: Quarterly; **Cover Price:** Free; **Circ:** 1,000
Editor: Olaf Christiansen
Profile: Magazine of a pharmaceutical wholesale trader, Gotha edition.
Language(s): German

PHOENIX SPEZIAL - MAGAZIN IHRES PHOENIX VERTRIEBSZENTRUMS, AUSG. GÖTTINGEN 767474G37-1741
Editorial: Pfingstweidstr. 10, 68199 MANNHEIM
Tel: 621 8505440 **Fax:** 621 8505599
Email: o.christiansen@phoenixgroup.eu **Web site:** http://www.phoenixgroup.eu
Freq: Quarterly; **Cover Price:** Free; **Circ:** 1,000
Editor: Olaf Christiansen
Profile: Magazine of a pharmaceutical wholesale trader, Göttingen edition.
Language(s): German

PHOENIX SPEZIAL - MAGAZIN IHRES PHOENIX VERTRIEBSZENTRUMS, AUSG. HAMBURG 767477G37-1744
Editorial: Pfingstweidstr. 10, 68199 MANNHEIM
Tel: 621 8505440 **Fax:** 621 8505599
Email: o.christiansen@phoenixgroup.eu **Web site:** http://www.phoenixgroup.eu
Freq: Quarterly; **Cover Price:** Free; **Circ:** 1,000
Editor: Olaf Christiansen
Profile: Magazine of a pharmaceutical wholesale trader, Hamburg edition.
Language(s): German

PHOENIX SPEZIAL - MAGAZIN IHRES PHOENIX VERTRIEBSZENTRUMS, AUSG. HANAU 767478G37-1745
Editorial: Pfingstweidstr. 10, 68199 MANNHEIM
Tel: 621 8505440 **Fax:** 621 8505599
Email: o.christiansen@phoenixgroup.eu **Web site:** http://www.phoenixgroup.eu
Freq: Quarterly; **Cover Price:** Free; **Circ:** 1,400
Editor: Olaf Christiansen
Profile: Magazine of a pharmaceutical wholesale trader, Hanau edition.
Language(s): German

PHOENIX SPEZIAL - MAGAZIN IHRES PHOENIX VERTRIEBSZENTRUMS, AUSG. HANNOVER 767479G37-1746
Editorial: Pfingstweidstr. 10, 68199 MANNHEIM
Tel: 621 8505440 **Fax:** 621 8505599
Email: o.christiansen@phoenixgroup.eu **Web site:** http://www.phoenixgroup.eu
Freq: Quarterly; **Cover Price:** Free; **Circ:** 1,000
Editor: Olaf Christiansen
Profile: Magazine of a pharmaceutical wholesale trader, Hanover edition.
Language(s): German

PHOENIX SPEZIAL - MAGAZIN IHRES PHOENIX VERTRIEBSZENTRUMS, AUSG. KÖLN 767480G37-1747
Editorial: Pfingstweidstr. 10, 68199 MANNHEIM
Tel: 621 8505440 **Fax:** 621 8505599
Email: o.christiansen@phoenixgroup.eu **Web site:** http://www.phoenixgroup.eu
Freq: Quarterly; **Cover Price:** Free; **Circ:** 1,000
Editor: Olaf Christiansen
Profile: Magazine of a pharmaceutical wholesale trader, Cologne edition.
Language(s): German

PHOENIX SPEZIAL - MAGAZIN IHRES PHOENIX VERTRIEBSZENTRUMS, AUSG. LEIPZIG 767481G37-1748
Editorial: Pfingstweidstr. 10, 68199 MANNHEIM
Tel: 621 8505440 **Fax:** 621 8505599
Email: o.christiansen@phoenixgroup.eu **Web site:** http://www.phoenixgroup.eu
Freq: Quarterly; **Cover Price:** Free; **Circ:** 1,000
Editor: Olaf Christiansen
Profile: Magazine of a pharmaceutical wholesale trader, Leipzig edition.
Language(s): German

PHOENIX SPEZIAL - MAGAZIN IHRES PHOENIX VERTRIEBSZENTRUMS, AUSG. MANNHEIM 767482G37-1749
Editorial: Pfingstweidstr. 10, 68199 MANNHEIM
Tel: 621 8505440 **Fax:** 621 8505599
Email: o.christiansen@phoenixgroup.eu **Web site:** http://www.phoenixgroup.eu
Freq: Quarterly; **Cover Price:** Free; **Circ:** 2,000
Editor: Olaf Christiansen
Profile: Magazine of a pharmaceutical wholesale trader, Mannheim edition.
Language(s): German

PHOENIX SPEZIAL - MAGAZIN IHRES PHOENIX VERTRIEBSZENTRUMS, AUSG. MÜNCHEN 767483G37-1750
Editorial: Pfingstweidstr. 10, 68199 MANNHEIM
Tel: 621 8505440 **Fax:** 621 8505599
Email: o.christiansen@phoenixgroup.eu **Web site:** http://www.phoenixgroup.eu
Freq: Quarterly; **Cover Price:** Free; **Circ:** 1,200
Editor: Olaf Christiansen
Profile: Magazine of a pharmaceutical wholesale trader, Munich edition.
Language(s): German

PHOENIX SPEZIAL - MAGAZIN IHRES PHOENIX VERTRIEBSZENTRUMS, AUSG. NEUHAUSEN 767484G37-1751
Editorial: Pfingstweidstr. 10, 68199 MANNHEIM
Tel: 621 8505440 **Fax:** 621 8505599
Email: o.christiansen@phoenixgroup.eu **Web site:** http://www.phoenixgroup.eu
Freq: Quarterly; **Cover Price:** Free; **Circ:** 1,000
Editor: Olaf Christiansen
Profile: Magazine of a pharmaceutical wholesale trader, Neuhausen edition.
Language(s): German

PHOENIX SPEZIAL - MAGAZIN IHRES PHOENIX VERTRIEBSZENTRUMS, AUSG. RUHR 767485G37-1752
Editorial: Pfingstweidstr. 10, 68199 MANNHEIM
Tel: 621 8505440 **Fax:** 621 8505599
Email: o.christiansen@phoenixgroup.eu **Web site:** http://www.phoenixgroup.eu
Freq: Quarterly; **Cover Price:** Free; **Circ:** 1,000
Editor: Olaf Christiansen
Profile: Magazine of a pharmaceutical wholesale trader, Ruhr edition.
Language(s): German

PHOENIX SPEZIAL - MAGAZIN IHRES PHOENIX VERTRIEBSZENTRUMS, AUSG. WESER-EMS 767486G37-1753
Editorial: Pfingstweidstr. 10, 68199 MANNHEIM
Tel: 621 8505440 **Fax:** 621 8505599
Email: o.christiansen@phoenixgroup.eu **Web site:** http://www.phoenixgroup.eu
Freq: Quarterly; **Cover Price:** Free; **Circ:** 1,000
Editor: Olaf Christiansen
Profile: Magazine of a pharmaceutical wholesale trader, Weser-Ems edition.
Language(s): German

PHOTO INTERNATIONAL 738971G85A-580
Editorial: Trappentreustr. 31, 80339 MÜNCHEN
Tel: 89 51997020
Email: hess@photo-international.de **Web site:** http://www.photo-international.de
Freq: 6 issues yearly; **Annual Sub.:** EUR 45,90; **Circ:** 10,200
Editor: Hans-Eberhard Hess
Profile: Magazine about photography.
Language(s): German
Readership: Aimed at amateurs.
ADVERTISING RATES:
Full Page Mono .... EUR 3200
Full Page Colour .... EUR 4950
Mechanical Data: Type Area: 258 x 190 mm, No. of Columns (Display): 4, Col Widths (Display): 45 mm
Copy instructions: *Copy Date:* 30 days prior to publication
CONSUMER: PHOTOGRAPHY & FILM MAKING: Photography

PHOTOGRAPHIE 738964G85A-600
Editorial: Innocentiastr. 33, 20144 HAMBURG
Tel: 40 189881130 **Fax:** 40 189881111
Email: f.spaeth@untitled-verlag.de **Web site:** http://www.photographie.de
Freq: 10 issues yearly; Free to qualifying individuals
Annual Sub.: EUR 45,00; **Circ:** 26,934
Editor: Frank Späth; **Advertising Manager:** Benjamin Heidke
Profile: Photo magazine for committed amateur photographers, semi-professionals and professionals.
Language(s): German
Readership: Read by photography enthusiasts.
ADVERTISING RATES:
Full Page Mono .... EUR 3400
Full Page Colour .... EUR 6500
Mechanical Data: Type Area: 275 x 202 mm, No. of Columns (Display): 4, Col Widths (Display): 47 mm
Copy instructions: *Copy Date:* 33 days prior to publication
Official Journal of: Organ d. DVF Dt. Verb. f. Fotografie e.V.
Supplement(s): DVF-journal
CONSUMER: PHOTOGRAPHY & FILM MAKING: Photography

PHOTON 738967G58-1220
Editorial: Jülicher Str. 376, 52070 AACHEN
Tel: 241 40030 **Fax:** 241 4003300
Email: redaktion@photon.de **Web site:** http://www.photon.de
Freq: Monthly; **Annual Sub.:** EUR 48,00; **Circ:** 44,313
Editor: Anne Kreutzmann
Profile: Solar Power magazine for art, science and management in the photovoltaic sector.
Language(s): German
ADVERTISING RATES:
Full Page Mono .... EUR 4914
Full Page Colour .... EUR 4914
Mechanical Data: Type Area: 265 x 174 mm, No. of Columns (Display): 3, Col Widths (Display): 55 mm
Copy instructions: *Copy Date:* 28 days prior to publication
BUSINESS: ENERGY, FUEL & NUCLEAR

PHOTON 1860097G58-1804
Editorial: Jülicher Str. 376, 52070 AACHEN
Tel: 241 40030 **Fax:** 241 4003300
Email: blanca.diaz@photon.com.es **Web site:** http://www.photon.com.es
Freq: Monthly; **Annual Sub.:** EUR 48,00; **Circ:** 20,000
Advertising Manager: Julio Magdalena
Profile: Solar Power magazine for art, science and management in the photovoltaic sector.
Language(s): Spanish
ADVERTISING RATES:
Full Page Mono .... EUR 3780
Full Page Colour .... EUR 3780
Mechanical Data: Type Area: 265 x 174 mm, No. of Columns (Display): 3, Col Widths (Display): 55 mm
Copy instructions: *Copy Date:* 28 days prior to publication

PHOTON INTERNATIONAL 1626194G58-1720
Editorial: Jülicher Str. 376, 52070 AACHEN
Tel: 241 40030 **Fax:** 241 4003300
Email: editorial-office@photon-international.com
Web site: http://www.photon-international.com
Freq: Monthly; **Annual Sub.:** EUR 230,00; **Circ:** 28,000
Editor: Michael Schmela; **Advertising Manager:** Martin Lehmann
Profile: Solar Power magazine for art, science and management in the photovoltaic sector.
Language(s): English
ADVERTISING RATES:
Full Page Mono .... EUR 6330
Full Page Colour .... EUR 6330
Mechanical Data: Type Area: 265 x 174 mm, No. of Columns (Display): 3, Col Widths (Display): 55 mm
Copy instructions: *Copy Date:* 28 days prior to publication

PHOTONIK 738968G18A-236
Editorial: Saarlandstr. 28, 70734 FELLBACH
Tel: 711 95295116 **Fax:** 711 95295199
Email: kuppe@at-fachverlag.de **Web site:** http://www.photonik.de
Freq: 6 issues yearly; **Annual Sub.:** EUR 72,00; **Circ:** 17,860
Editor: Johannes Kuppe; **Advertising Manager:** Norbert Schöne
Profile: Journal for the current optical technologies with applications and application-specific product reports for developers and users.
Language(s): English; German
ADVERTISING RATES:
Full Page Mono .... EUR 5280
Full Page Colour .... EUR 6330
Mechanical Data: Type Area: 264 x 185 mm, No. of Columns (Display): 4, Col Widths (Display): 43 mm
Copy instructions: *Copy Date:* 20 days prior to publication
Official Journal of: Organ d. DGaO
BUSINESS: ELECTRONICS

PHOTOVOLTAIC PRODUCTION 2073858G57-2964
Editorial: Im Weiher 10, 69121 HEIDELBERG
Tel: 6221 489388 **Fax:** 6221 489490
Email: armin.scheuermann@huethig.de **Web site:** http://www.pv-production.de
Freq: Quarterly; **Annual Sub.:** EUR 59,00; **Circ:** 10,000
Editor: Armin Scheuermann; **Advertising Manager:** Sabine Wegmann
Profile: photovoltaic production describes the production technology along the entire value chain in the production of photovoltaic solutions: Starting with the wet chemical process, such as silicon preparation or the manufacture of chemicals for thin film or organic photovoltaics and the relevant materials, to cell manufacturing and on to finished modules, including power electronics. This also includes, for example, the presentation of the currently available equipment technology for PV processes: chemical plants and plant components, assembly lines for PV modules and automation and handling systems for manufacturing thin-film solar cells, but also inverters and electronic systems for PV production, to name just a few highlights of the contents. photovoltaic production concentrates the know-how of three competent trade journals from the Hüthig Publishers, each the leader in its market segment. The photovoltaic production publishing dates are synchronized with the key branch trade fairs. The English language magazine will be distributed both at German and international events.
Language(s): English
ADVERTISING RATES:
Full Page Mono .... EUR 3858
Full Page Colour .... EUR 4933
Mechanical Data: Type Area: 257 x 178 mm, No. of Columns (Display): 4, Col Widths (Display): 41 mm

PHOTOVOLTAIK 1818174G57-2831
Editorial: Zinnowitzer Str. 1, 10115 BERLIN
Tel: 30 726296333 **Fax:** 30 726296309
Email: fuhs@photovoltaik.eu **Web site:** http://www.photovoltaik.eu
Freq: Monthly; **Annual Sub.:** EUR 117,00; **Circ:** 25,014
Editor: Michael Fuhs
Profile: The B2B magazine photovoltaik there since June 2007 on the market. The booklet brings together themes of politics and society as a critical analysis of the EEG amendment, feel for trends in the photovoltaic business and offers tips on planning, installation, financing and insurance of solar power systems. It is aimed at professionals from trade, commerce, planning, engineering, industry, banking and insurance, and all decision makers in the photovoltaic industry. Compact market overviews and previews of dates round out the portfolio of B2B Magazine. Twitter: http://twitter.com/photovoltaik.
Language(s): German
ADVERTISING RATES:
Full Page Mono .... EUR 3450
Full Page Colour .... EUR 3450
Mechanical Data: Type Area: 254 x 183 mm, No. of Columns (Display): 3, Col Widths (Display): 54 mm
Copy instructions: *Copy Date:* 15 days prior to publication

PHYSIK JOURNAL 738975G55-108
Editorial: Boschstr. 12, 69469 WEINHEIM
Tel: 6201 606243 **Fax:** 6201 606328
Email: redaktion@physik-journal.de **Web site:** http://www.physik-journal.de
Freq: 11 issues yearly; Free to qualifying individuals
Annual Sub.: EUR 360,00; **Circ:** 57,284
Editor: Stefan Jorda; **Advertising Manager:** Änne Anders
Profile: Official journal of the German Society of Physics.
Language(s): German
ADVERTISING RATES:
Full Page Mono .... EUR 5800

Full Page Colour .... EUR 7450
Mechanical Data: Type Area: 260 x 185 mm, No. of Columns (Display): 4, Col Widths (Display): 45 mm
Copy instructions: *Copy Date:* 30 days prior to publication
Official Journal of: Organ d. Dt. Physikal. Ges.
BUSINESS: APPLIED SCIENCE & LABORATORIES

PHYSIKALISCHE MEDIZIN REHABILITATIONSMEDIZIN KURORTMEDIZIN 739476G56L-6

Editorial: Erlanger Allee 101, 07740 JENA
Email: physmed@thieme.de **Web site:** http://www.thieme.de/physmed
Freq: 6 issues yearly; Free to qualifying individuals
Annual Sub.: EUR 178,90; **Circ:** 1,350
Editor: U. C. Smolenski
Profile: The latest issue of physical medicine in hospitals and practices in selected original works. Learn more interdisciplinary - on all topics related to physical medicine, rehabilitation medicine, spa medicine: such as early rehabilitation, physical therapy and immune systems, climatology, physical medicine in dentistry, Thalasso therapy for atopic dermatitis, coordination exercises and back pain etc. Great part for training and continuing education. In addition, short posts around the subject, your society news, event calendar with courses and conferences.
Language(s): German
ADVERTISING RATES:
Full Page Mono .... EUR 1550
Full Page Colour .... EUR 2660
Mechanical Data: Type Area: 248 x 175 mm, No. of Columns (Display): 3, Col Widths (Display): 55 mm
Official Journal of: Organ d. Dt. Ges. f. Physikal. Medizin u. Rehabilitation, d. Berufsverb. d. Rehabilitationsärzte e.V., d. Österr. Ges. f. Balneologie u. Medizin. Klimatologie, d. Österr. Ges. f. Physik. Medizin u. Rehabilitation, d. Verb. österr. Kurärzte u. d. Berufsverb. Österr. Fachärzte f. Physikal. Medizin u. Rehabilitation
BUSINESS: HEALTH & MEDICAL: Disability & Rehabilitation

PICTORIAL 1934605G2A-5871

Editorial: Im Abtsgrüdel 5, 76744 WÖRTH
Tel: 7271 952076
Email: s.hartmann@pictorial-online.com **Web site:** http://www.pictorial-online.com
Freq: 6 issues yearly; **Annual Sub.:** EUR 36,00; **Circ:** 4,300
Editor: Stefan Hartmann
Profile: Photography and electronic imaging magazine. Facebook: http://www.facebook.com/UnitedArchives.
Language(s): German
ADVERTISING RATES:
Full Page Mono .... EUR 1200
Full Page Colour .... EUR 1680
Mechanical Data: Type Area: 273 x 186 mm
Copy instructions: *Copy Date:* 19 days prior to publication

PICTURE 738986G2A-3720

Editorial: Erscheckweg 1, 72664 KOHLBERG
Tel: 7025 102152 **Fax:** 7025 7111
Email: i.neher@ict.de **Web site:** http://www.ict.de
Freq: Annual; **Cover Price:** Free; **Circ:** 12,000
Editor: Isabel Neher
Profile: Company publication published by ict Innovative Communication Technologies AG.
Language(s): English; German

PICTURE 1703427G80-14736

Editorial: Wiedbachstr. 50, 56567 NEUWIED
Tel: 2631 964647 **Fax:** 2631 964640
Email: a.gras@hwg-media.de **Web site:** http://www.kulturspiegel.vg
Freq: Monthly; **Cover Price:** Free; **Circ:** 21,769
Editor: Anna-Lena Gras; **Advertising Manager:** Rolf Mohrs
Profile: Cultural magazine for the Middle Rhine region with information on events.
Language(s): German
CONSUMER: RURAL & REGIONAL INTEREST

PICTURES OF THE FUTURE 1819892G14A-10057

Editorial: Wittelsbacherplatz 2, 80333 MÜNCHEN
Tel: 89 63633246 **Fax:** 89 63635292
Email: ulrich.eberl@siemens.com **Web site:** http://www.siemens.com/pof
Freq: Half-yearly; **Circ:** 100,000
Editor: Ulrich Eberl
Profile: Magazine of Siemens AG.
Language(s): English

PID PSYCHOTHERAPIE IM DIALOG 738991G56N-83

Editorial: Pirmasenser Str. 23a, 66994 DAHN
Tel: 6391 409362 **Fax:** 6391 4090069
Email: pid-redaktion@gmx.de **Web site:** http://www.thieme.de/pid
Freq: Quarterly; **Annual Sub.:** EUR 119,90; **Circ:** 3,630
Editor: Andrea Dinger-Broda
Profile: Our concept: an issue, many perspectives. Each issue with a current focal point - image disturbance or setting. The theme from the perspective of different types of therapeutic approaches and occupational groups: The view outside the box extend your treatment skills. The topic of using detailed individual case studies, "Self-Experienced" can be transferred very well and understand. Originality is happening: PiD provides space for new ideas and experiences, even without rigorous scientific review. Our goal: integration, development, communication. Use knowledge and experience from other therapeutic approaches to enhance your game room and for a possible differential treatment of your patients. Integrate individual, unused, and a variety of suggestions in your therapy practice. Take an active part in the development of the discipline. Take the opportunity to talk with other therapists. Our contents: messages, suggestions, contradictions. State of the Art: Overview on the subject as an objective body of knowledge processing and "common ground". In practice: the case reports from very different directions. The résumé: a final word of the editors, which combines the individual contributions together and trying to make a comprehensive evaluation. The interview with people who really have something unique to say on the subject. Research in practice: the possibility for PT in private practice to initiate empirical studies and smaller to transport. The dialogue-left: service to our readers, to view more information and training opportunities on the topic, reports and comments to professional politics. In dialogue: a forum for discussion of the contents and to build local networks.
Language(s): German
Readership: Read by doctors and psychiatrists.
ADVERTISING RATES:
Full Page Mono .... EUR 1760
Full Page Colour .... EUR 2900
Mechanical Data: Type Area: 248 x 175 mm, No. of Columns (Display): 4, Col Widths (Display): 40 mm
BUSINESS: HEALTH & MEDICAL: Mental Health

DER PILGER 739000G87-10720

Editorial: Brunckstr. 17, 67346 SPEYER
Tel: 6232 318360 **Fax:** 6232 318379
Email: redaktion@pilger-speyer.de **Web site:** http://www.pilger-speyer.de
Freq: Weekly; **Circ:** 23,074
Editor: Norbert Rönn; **Advertising Manager:** Susanne Rottmann
Profile: Church magazine for the Diocese of Speyer.
Language(s): German
ADVERTISING RATES:
Full Page Mono .... EUR 1425
Full Page Colour .... EUR 2550
Mechanical Data: Type Area: 300 x 228 mm, No. of Columns (Display): 5, Col Widths (Display): 44 mm
Copy instructions: *Copy Date:* 9 days prior to publication
CONSUMER: RELIGIOUS

PINNEBERGER TAGEBLATT 739008G67B-11760

Editorial: Damm 9, 25421 PINNEBERG
Tel: 4101 5356101 **Fax:** 4101 5356106
Email: redaktion@a-beig.de **Web site:** http://www.pinneberger-tageblatt.de
Freq: 312 issues yearly; **Circ:** 12,796
Editor: Michael Kluth; **Advertising Manager:** Karsten Raasch
Profile: Regional daily newspaper covering politics, economics, sport, travel and technology. This Outlet offers RSS (Really Simple Syndication).
Language(s): German
ADVERTISING RATES:
SCC .... EUR 42,90
Mechanical Data: Type Area: 430 x 278 mm, No. of Columns (Display): 6, Col Widths (Display): 45 mm
Copy instructions: *Copy Date:* 1 day prior to publication
Supplement(s): nordisch gesund; Statt gespräch
REGIONAL DAILY & SUNDAY NEWSPAPERS: Regional Daily Newspapers

PIRANHA 739022G74F-135

Editorial: Sandstr. 3, 80335 MÜNCHEN
Tel: 89 30774212 **Fax:** 89 30774233
Email: christian.fischer@piranha-media.de **Web site:** http://www.piranha-media.de
Freq: 11 issues yearly; **Cover Price:** Free; **Circ:** 114,417
Editor: Christian Fischer; **Advertising Manager:** Jörg Sauer
Profile: Magazine focusing on music, sport, fashion and lifestyle.
Language(s): German
Readership: Aimed at teenagers.
ADVERTISING RATES:
Full Page Mono .... EUR 6000
Full Page Colour .... EUR 6000
Mechanical Data: Type Area: 297 x 210 mm
CONSUMER: WOMEN'S INTEREST CONSUMER MAGAZINES: Teenage

PIRNAER WOCHENKURIER 739027G72-10500

Editorial: Wettiner Platz 10, 01067 DRESDEN
Tel: 351 491760 **Fax:** 351 4917674
Email: wochenkurier-dresden@dwk-verlag.de **Web site:** http://www.wochenkurier.info
Freq: Weekly; **Cover Price:** Free; **Circ:** 45,426
Editor: Regine Eberlein; **Advertising Manager:** Andreas Schönherr
Profile: Advertising journal (house-to-house) concentrating on local stories.
Language(s): German
ADVERTISING RATES:
Full Page Mono .... EUR 3251
Full Page Colour .... EUR 4552
Mechanical Data: Type Area: 430 x 290 mm, No. of Columns (Display): 7, Col Widths (Display): 38 mm
Copy instructions: *Copy Date:* 5 days prior to publication
LOCAL NEWSPAPERS

PIRSCH 739028G75F-580

Editorial: Lothstr. 19, 80797 MÜNCHEN
Tel: 89 12705362 **Fax:** 89 12705542
Email: pirschredaktion@dlv.de **Web site:** http://www.jagderleben.de
Freq: 24 issues yearly; **Annual Sub.:** EUR 103,00; **Circ:** 34,279
Editor: Sascha Numßen; **Advertising Manager:** Thomas Herrmann
Profile: Game is hunting magazine that combines the experience of the hunting with hands-on factual information. For competent reporting include the types and Habitat protection, management and maintenance area, hunting equipment, weapon and shooting, game client, hunting dogs, politics and education.
Language(s): German
ADVERTISING RATES:
Full Page Mono .... EUR 2873
Full Page Colour .... EUR 5573
Mechanical Data: Type Area: 270 x 184 mm, No. of Columns (Display): 4, Col Widths (Display): 43 mm
Copy instructions: *Copy Date:* 24 days prior to publication
CONSUMER: SPORT: Shooting

PISTE 739029G80-8940

Editorial: Georgswerder Bogen 4, 21109 HAMBURG
Tel: 40 32093192 **Fax:** 40 32093198
Email: hamburg@piste.de **Web site:** http://www.piste.de
Freq: Monthly; **Cover Price:** Free; **Circ:** 24,615
Editor: Gideon Schier; **Advertising Manager:** Gideon Schier
Profile: City and scene magazine for Hamburg and the surrounding area: Party Shots, tips from the scene of life and city-specific topics. He reports and information about everything that interests the fashion-conscious readers between 18 and 40.
Language(s): German
ADVERTISING RATES:
Full Page Mono .... EUR 1420
Full Page Colour .... EUR 2480
Mechanical Data: Type Area: 266 x 188 mm, No. of Columns (Display): 4, Col Widths (Display): 44 mm
Copy instructions: *Copy Date:* 18 days prior to publication
CONSUMER: RURAL & REGIONAL INTEREST

PISTE 739031G80-8980

Editorial: Eutiner Str. 1, 23611 BAD SCHWARTAU
Tel: 451 7021167 **Fax:** 451 7021189
Email: luebeck@piste.de **Web site:** http://www.piste.de/luebeck
Freq: Monthly; **Cover Price:** Free; **Circ:** 15,940
Editor: André Vatankhah; **Advertising Manager:** André Vatankhah
Profile: Magazine for city and region, concentrating on gastronomy, music, arts and events.
Language(s): German
ADVERTISING RATES:
Full Page Mono .... EUR 1250
Full Page Colour .... EUR 2180
Mechanical Data: Type Area: 297 x 220 mm
CONSUMER: RURAL & REGIONAL INTEREST

PISTE 739032G80-9000

Editorial: Johannesstr. 15b, 17034 NEUBRANDENBURG **Tel:** 395 5824020
Fax: 395 5825635
Email: redaktion@piste-neubrandenburg.de **Web site:** http://www.piste.de
Freq: Monthly; **Cover Price:** Free; **Circ:** 15,160
Editor: Falk Emmaus; **Advertising Manager:** Falk Emmaus
Profile: Magazine for city and region, concentrating on gastronomy, music, arts and events.
Language(s): German
ADVERTISING RATES:
Full Page Mono .... EUR 970
Full Page Colour .... EUR 2055
Mechanical Data: Type Area: 266 x 188 mm, No. of Columns (Display): 4, Col Widths (Display): 44 mm
Copy instructions: *Copy Date:* 15 days prior to publication
CONSUMER: RURAL & REGIONAL INTEREST

PISTE 739033G80-9020

Editorial: Am Brink 4, 18057 ROSTOCK
Tel: 381 7698633 **Fax:** 381 7698645
Email: rostock@piste.de **Web site:** http://www.piste-rostock.de
Freq: Monthly; **Cover Price:** Free; **Circ:** 17,865
Editor: Thomas Zerbe; **Advertising Manager:** Dirk Wehmeyer
Profile: City and scene magazine for Rostock and Güstrow: Party Shots, tips from the scene of life and city-specific topics. He reports and information about everything that interests the fashion-conscious readers between 18 and 40.
Language(s): German
ADVERTISING RATES:
Full Page Mono .... EUR 1420
Full Page Colour .... EUR 2480
Mechanical Data: Type Area: 266 x 188 mm, No. of Columns (Display): 4, Col Widths (Display): 44 mm
Copy instructions: *Copy Date:* 10 days prior to publication
CONSUMER: RURAL & REGIONAL INTEREST

PISTE 739034G80-9040

Editorial: Mecklenburgstr. 67, 19053 SCHWERIN
Tel: 385 7788628 **Fax:** 385 7788629
Email: genschmer@piste.de **Web site:** http://www.piste-schwerin.de
Freq: Monthly; **Cover Price:** Free; **Circ:** 16,530
Editor: Heike Genschmer; **Advertising Manager:** Olaf Meißner
Profile: Magazine for city and region, concentrating on gastronomy, music, arts and events.
Language(s): German
ADVERTISING RATES:
Full Page Mono .... EUR 1250
Full Page Colour .... EUR 2180
Mechanical Data: Type Area: 297 x 220 mm
CONSUMER: RURAL & REGIONAL INTEREST

PKA AKTIV 739038G37-1768

Editorial: Birkenwaldstr. 44, 70191 STUTTGART
Tel: 711 2582238 **Fax:** 711 2582291
Email: daz@deutscher-apotheker-verlag.de **Web site:** http://www.deutscher-apotheker-verlag.de
Freq: 3 issues yearly; **Annual Sub.:** EUR 21,00; **Circ:** 30,262
Editor: Sabine Stute; **Advertising Manager:** Kornelia Wind
Profile: Magazine supplement for pharmaceutical-business employees.
Language(s): German
Mechanical Data: Type Area: 233 x 153 mm
Copy instructions: *Copy Date:* 30 days prior to publication
Supplement to: DAZ Deutsche ApothekerZeitung
BUSINESS: PHARMACEUTICAL & CHEMISTS

PKV PUBLIK 739040G1D-180

Editorial: Bayenthalgürtel 26, 50968 KÖLN
Tel: 221 376620 **Fax:** 221 3766210
Email: presse@pkv.de **Web site:** http://www.pkv.de
Freq: 10 issues yearly; **Annual Sub.:** EUR 11,00
Editor: Stephan Caspary
Profile: Journal of the Association of Private Health Insurers.
Language(s): German
Supplement to: Versicherungswirtschaft
BUSINESS: FINANCE & ECONOMICS: Insurance

PLAKATIV 739044G2A-3760

Editorial: Geheimrat-Hummel-Platz 4, 65239 HOCHHEIM **Tel:** 6146 605143 **Fax:** 6146 605204
Email: m.lehmann@eubuco.de **Web site:** http://www.plakativ-magazin.de
Freq: 5 issues yearly; **Annual Sub.:** EUR 36,50; **Circ:** 10,500
Editor: Jochen Gutzeit; **Advertising Manager:** Magda Lehmann
Profile: Magazine about large format printing advertising.
Language(s): German
ADVERTISING RATES:
Full Page Mono .... EUR 2250
Full Page Colour .... EUR 3600
Mechanical Data: Type Area: 290 x 220 mm, No. of Columns (Display): 5, Col Widths (Display): 40 mm
Copy instructions: *Copy Date:* 14 days prior to publication
Official Journal of: Organ d. Fachverb. Aussenwerbung e. V.

PLANERRECHTS-REPORT 1660430G4E-7031

Editorial: Nelkenstr. 24, 85521 RIEMERLING
Tel: 89 48002993
Freq: Monthly; **Annual Sub.:** EUR 40,64; **Circ:** 2,400
Editor: Michael Frikell
Profile: The VOB-Verlag Ernst Vögel OHG has focused entirely on practical publications on private construction law. Contractors, construction managers, architects, engineers, public and private clients and their advisors will find here lots of valuable information to building law. And in ways that it can be used immediately for daily practice. By the VOB-Verlag Ernst Vögel OHG monthly published fact sheets "BR Baurechts-Report", "Vergaberechts-Report" and "Planerrechts-Report" informed of all significant new choices for construction, procurement and planning law and enjoy a wide acceptance among readers. Thanks to the high circulations can ensure the VOB-Verlag Ernst Vögel OHG for his works a very favorable price-performance ratio.
Language(s): German

PLANETSNOW 1692599G75G-563

Editorial: Leuschnerstr. 1, 70174 STUTTGART
Tel: 7152 941575 **Fax:** 7152 941597
Email: msteinheil@motorpresse.de **Web site:** http://www.planetsnow.de
Cover Price: Paid; **Circ:** 9,308 Unique Users
Editor: Mario Steinheil
Language(s): German
CONSUMER: SPORT: Winter Sports

PLANUNG & ANALYSE
739072G2A-3800

Editorial: Mainzer Landstr. 251, 60326 FRANKFURT
Tel: 69 75952014 **Fax:** 69 75952017
Email: redaktion@planung-analyse.de **Web site:** http://www.planung-analyse.de
Freq: 7 issues yearly; **Annual Sub.:** EUR 179,00; **Circ:** 2,200
Editor: Gwen Kaufmann; **Advertising Manager:** Gwen Kaufmann
Profile: Journal focusing on market research and marketing.
Language(s): English; German
ADVERTISING RATES:
Full Page Mono .... EUR 3540
Full Page Colour .... EUR 3540
Mechanical Data: Type Area: 272 x 175 mm, No. of Columns (Display): 3, Col Widths (Display): 55 mm
Copy instructions: *Copy Date:* 28 days prior to publication
BUSINESS: COMMUNICATIONS, ADVERTISING & MARKETING

PLÄRRER
739041G83-15014

Editorial: Singerstr. 26, 90443 NÜRNBERG
Tel: 911 4247852 **Fax:** 911 4247899
Email: j.schmoldt@plaerrer.de **Web site:** http://www.plaerrer.de
Freq: Monthly; **Annual Sub.:** EUR 22,00; **Circ:** 7,095
Editor: Jochen Schmoldt; **Advertising Manager:** Silvia Höllerer
Profile: Magazine for students in Nürnberg.
Language(s): German
ADVERTISING RATES:
Full Page Mono .... EUR 1231
Full Page Colour .... EUR 2040
Mechanical Data: Type Area: 260 x 190 mm, No. of Columns (Display): 6, Col Widths (Display): 28 mm
Copy instructions: *Copy Date:* 15 days prior to publication
CONSUMER: STUDENT PUBLICATIONS

PLASTCOURIER-RUSSIA
1664128G13-2418

Editorial: Gleueler Str. 373, 50935 KÖLN
Tel: 221 439256 **Fax:** 221 438121
Email: f.vollmer@vm-verlag.com **Web site:** http://www.extrusion-info.com
Freq: 6 issues yearly; **Annual Sub.:** EUR 60,00; **Circ:** 2,970
Editor: Fritz Vollmer; **Advertising Manager:** Inge Böhle
Profile: Magazine about synthetic materials processing.
Language(s): Russian
ADVERTISING RATES:
Full Page Mono .... EUR 2450
Full Page Colour .... EUR 2450
Mechanical Data: Type Area: 250 x 185 mm, No. of Columns (Display): 2, Col Widths (Display): 90 mm
Copy instructions: *Copy Date:* 30 days prior to publication
BUSINESS: CHEMICALS

PLASTISCHE CHIRURGIE
764682G56A-11105

Editorial: Maaßstr. 32/1, 69123 HEIDELBERG
Tel: 6221 1377610 **Fax:** 6221 6599590
Email: kraemer@kaden-verlag.de **Web site:** http://www.kaden-verlag.de
Freq: Quarterly; Free to qualifying individuals
Annual Sub.: EUR 86,00; **Circ:** 2,000
Editor: Norbert Krämer; **Advertising Manager:** Ingo Rosenstock
Profile: Magazine on plastic surgery.
Language(s): German
ADVERTISING RATES:
Full Page Mono .... EUR 970
Full Page Colour .... EUR 2095
Mechanical Data: Type Area: 230 x 178 mm, No. of Columns (Display): 3, Col Widths (Display): 56 mm
Copy instructions: *Copy Date:* 17 days prior to publication

PLASTVERARBEITER
739076G39-110

Editorial: Im Weiher 10, 69121 HEIDELBERG
Tel: 6221 489347 **Fax:** 6221 489481
Email: annedore.munde@huethig.de **Web site:** http://www.plastverarbeiter.de
Freq: Monthly; **Annual Sub.:** EUR 204,80; **Circ:** 12,349
Editor: Annedore Munde; **Advertising Manager:** Rüdger Aulich
Profile: Plastverarbeiter: The magazine for decision-makers have increased market opportunities and efficient produce in the plastics processing industry - information from the field: solidly researched, easy to read, quick to implement. The Plastverarbeiter supports plastics processors in times of increasing cost pressures and increasing globalization and to produce resource-efficient to identify new market opportunities and to use it for their own commercial success. Its present innovative products and solutions as well as production and manufacturing strategies. The focus is on specific problems are in practice. In the editorial exclusively researched reports and trend reports combine facts and opinions and give the decision-making process involved experts and leaders in plastics processing, the relevant arguments to the hand - based on sound research, easy to read and implemented quickly.
Language(s): German
Readership: Aimed at decision makers within the industry.

ADVERTISING RATES:
Full Page Mono .... EUR 3430
Full Page Colour .... EUR 4860
Mechanical Data: Type Area: 257 x 178 mm, No. of Columns (Display): 4, Col Widths (Display): 41 mm
Copy instructions: *Copy Date:* 26 days prior to publication
BUSINESS: PLASTICS & RUBBER

DER PLATOW BRIEF
739079G1F-1180

Editorial: Stuttgarter Str. 25, 60329 FRANKFURT
Tel: 69 24263914 **Fax:** 69 236909
Email: frank.mahlmeister@platow.de **Web site:** http://www.platow.de
Freq: 156 issues yearly; **Annual Sub.:** EUR 520,00
Editor: Frank Mahlmeister; **Advertising Manager:** Sandra Paasche
Profile: Aimed at investment managers in banks, companies and the stock market.
Language(s): German
Readership: Aimed at investment managers in banks, companies and the stockmarket.
ADVERTISING RATES:
Full Page Colour .... EUR 7800
Mechanical Data: Type Area: 250 x 180 mm
Copy instructions: *Copy Date:* 7 days prior to publication
Supplement(s): Platow Immobilien
BUSINESS: FINANCE & ECONOMICS: Investment

PLATTLINGER ANZEIGER
739087G67B-11780

Editorial: Ludwigsplatz 30, 94315 STRAUBING
Tel: 9421 9404601 **Fax:** 9421 9404609
Email: landkreis@straubinger-tagblatt.de **Web site:** http://www.idowa.de
Freq: 312 issues yearly; **Circ:** 2,021
Advertising Manager: Klaus Huber
Profile: Regional daily newspaper with news on politics, economy, culture, sports, travel, technology, etc. She is a local issue by Straubinger Tagblatt for the southern part of County Deggendorf. Twitter: http://twitter.com/idowa This Outlet offers RSS (Really Simple Syndication).
Language(s): German
ADVERTISING RATES:
SCC .... EUR 12,70
Mechanical Data: Type Area: 430 x 282 mm, No. of Columns (Display): 6, Col Widths (Display): 45 mm
Copy instructions: *Copy Date:* 1 day prior to publication
Supplement(s): Zuhause
REGIONAL DAILY & SUNDAY NEWSPAPERS: Regional Daily Newspapers

PLATTLINGER ZEITUNG
739088G67B-11800

Editorial: Medienstr. 5, 94036 PASSAU
Tel: 851 8020 **Fax:** 851 802256
Email: pnp@vgp.de **Web site:** http://www.pnp.de
Freq: 312 issues yearly; **Circ:** 22,743
Advertising Manager: Gerhard Koller
Profile: Daily newspaper with regional news and a local sports section. Twitter: http://twitter.com/pnp_online This Outlet offers RSS (Really Simple Syndication).
Language(s): German
ADVERTISING RATES:
SCC .... EUR 62,50
Mechanical Data: Type Area: 482 x 325 mm, No. of Columns (Display): 7, Col Widths (Display): 45 mm
Copy instructions: *Copy Date:* 2 days prior to publication
REGIONAL DAILY & SUNDAY NEWSPAPERS: Regional Daily Newspapers

PLAYBOY
739093G86A-90

Editorial: Arabellastr. 21, 81925 MÜNCHEN
Tel: 89 92502786 **Fax:** 89 92501210
Email: team@playboy.de **Web site:** http://www.playboy.de
Freq: Monthly; **Annual Sub.:** EUR 58,80; **Circ:** 212,468
Editor: Florian Boitin; **Advertising Manager:** Katherine Kreiner
Profile: Playboy is THE premium lifestyle magazine for men. "All men fun" is the central message that issues of diversity and reporting are varied, sophisticated and setting standards. The Playboy tells of the exciting side of life. Of women who are beautiful and desirable. Of people to realize their dreams. He takes a stand on the important issues of the time, without losing sight of the conversation. With erotic photography, honest reports and interviews, combined with all issues of everyday lifestyle editors staged a monthly world, the men interested. With a reach of 1.77 million readers (AWA 2010) of Playboy's most successful titles in the market - and with a balanced age structure. Playboy is not a question of age but a way of life. Facebook: http://www.facebook.com/PlayboyGermany Twitter: http://twitter.com/#!/playboy_d This Outlet offers RSS (Really Simple Syndication).
Language(s): German
ADVERTISING RATES:
Full Page Mono .... EUR 24300
Full Page Colour .... EUR 24300
Mechanical Data: Type Area: 260 x 175 mm
CONSUMER: ADULT & GAY MAGAZINES: Adult Magazines

PLAYBOY
1621864G86C-211

Editorial: Arabellastr. 21, 81925 MÜNCHEN
Tel: 89 92501332 **Fax:** 89 92501220
Email: cyberclub@playboy.de **Web site:** http://www.playboy.de
Freq: Daily; **Cover Price:** Paid; **Circ:** 1,339,812 Unique Users
Editor: Florian Boitin
Profile: Playboy is THE premium lifestyle magazine for men. The mixture of erotic photography and sophisticated journalism leads to the success of the magazine. Facebook: http://www.facebook.com/PlayboyGermany Twitter: http://twitter.com/#!/playboy_d This Outlet offers RSS (Really Simple Syndication).
Language(s): German
CONSUMER: ADULT & GAY MAGAZINES: Men's Lifestyle Magazines

PLAZA MAGAZINE
1866732G74A-3653

Editorial: Kastanienallee 71, 10435 BERLIN
Tel: 30 61628115 **Fax:** 30 61628111
Email: berlin@plazamagazine.com **Web site:** http://www.plazamagazine.com
Freq: Quarterly; **Annual Sub.:** EUR 35,00; **Circ:** 22,000
Editor: Stephan Burkoff
Profile: Magazine with focus on design, modern living, fashion and cars.
Language(s): German
ADVERTISING RATES:
Full Page Mono .... EUR 5500
Full Page Colour .... EUR 5500

PLIETSCH*
1919864G14A-10337

Editorial: Kurt-Schumacher-Str. 24, 30159 HANNOVER **Tel:** 511 76072626 **Fax:** 511 76072619
Email: mussack@nds.de **Web site:** http://www.innovatives.niedersachsen.de
Freq: Quarterly; **Cover Price:** Free; **Circ:** 484,000
Editor: Barbara Mussack
Profile: Magazine offers information on the innovation potential of firms in Lower Saxony and one research directions.
Language(s): German

PLUS MAGAZIN
1644191G74N-845

Editorial: Lindenstr. 20, 50674 KÖLN
Tel: 221 277570 **Fax:** 221 2775710
Email: plusmagazin@bayard-media.de **Web site:** http://www.plus-mag.de
Freq: Monthly; **Annual Sub.:** EUR 39,60; **Circ:** 138,298
Editor: Jürgen Sinn; **Advertising Manager:** Armin Baier
Profile: High Quality Advisor magazine provides practical answers to all questions that interest people in the second phase of life really. This helps plus Magazin readers to enjoy this phase of life as rich and valuable. This high level of consulting expertise, the magazine has led to an unusually high proportion of subscribers. The high level of quality is also expressed in a long time spent reading from the plus Magazin readers. With five major subject areas, the magazine covers all important aspects of life of people off in the second half of life: health and fitness, beauty and fashion, food, drink, enjoyment, Food & Wine and Travel & Culture.
Language(s): German
ADVERTISING RATES:
Full Page Mono .... EUR 9500
Full Page Colour .... EUR 9500
Mechanical Data: Type Area: 217 x 175 mm, No. of Columns (Display): 4, Col Widths (Display): 39 mm
CONSUMER: WOMEN'S INTEREST CONSUMER MAGAZINES: Retirement

PLUS PRODUKTION VON LEITERPLATTEN UND SYSTEMEN
739113G18A-237

Editorial: Karlstr. 4, 88348 BAD SAULGAU
Tel: 7581 480122 **Fax:** 7581 480110
Email: charlotte.schade@leuze-verlag.de **Web site:** http://www.leiterplatten.com
Freq: Monthly; Free to qualifying individuals
Annual Sub.: EUR 72,55; **Circ:** 3,108
Editor: Charlotte Schade; **Advertising Manager:** Petra Istvan
Profile: Magazine providing news and information about the electronics industry. Includes articles on outsourcing, quality and environmental protection.
Language(s): English; German
Readership: Aimed at professionals directly involved in the industry.
ADVERTISING RATES:
Full Page Mono .... EUR 1020
Full Page Colour .... EUR 1500
Mechanical Data: Type Area: 200 x 135 mm, No. of Columns (Display): 2, Col Widths (Display): 65 mm
Copy instructions: *Copy Date:* 31 days prior to publication
Official Journal of: Organ d. Fachverbände FBDI e.V., FED e.V., Imaps Deutschland e.V., EITI e.V., ZVEI Electronic Components and systems, ZVEI PCB and Electronic Systems, 3-D MID e.V., DVS e.V.
BUSINESS: ELECTRONICS

PLUSPUNKTE
739122G74M-480

Editorial: Cheruskerring 19, 48147 MÜNSTER
Tel: 251 4838127
Freq: Quarterly; **Circ:** 35,000
Editor: Ralf Thier-Hinse
Profile: Magazine of the Familien-Wirtschaftsrjng Association about family policy and social law.
Language(s): German

P.M. HISTORY
739130G94J-400

Editorial: Weihenstephaner Str. 7, 81673 MÜNCHEN
Tel: 89 415200 **Fax:** 89 4152565
Email: rink.jana@muc.guj.de **Web site:** http://www.pm-history.de
Freq: Monthly; **Annual Sub.:** EUR 51,60; **Circ:** 59,979
Editor: Sascha Priester; **Advertising Manager:** Andrea Wörsdörfer
Profile: Popular scientific magazine.
Language(s): German
ADVERTISING RATES:
Full Page Mono .... EUR 9500
Full Page Colour .... EUR 9500
Mechanical Data: Type Area: 240 x 184 mm
Copy instructions: *Copy Date:* 35 days prior to publication
CONSUMER: OTHER CLASSIFICATIONS: Popular Science

P.M. LOGIK-TRAINER
739132G94J-440

Editorial: Weihenstephaner Str. 7, 81673 MÜNCHEN
Tel: 89 415200 **Fax:** 89 4152652
Email: pm.redaktion@muc.guj.de **Web site:** http://www.pm-magazin.de
Freq: Monthly; **Cover Price:** EUR 1,90; **Circ:** 70,000
Editor: Martin Tzschaschel; **Advertising Manager:** Nicole Schostak
Profile: Logic coaching magazine.
Language(s): German
ADVERTISING RATES:
Full Page Mono .... EUR 5300
Full Page Colour .... EUR 5300
Mechanical Data: Type Area: 280 x 195 mm
CONSUMER: OTHER CLASSIFICATIONS: Popular Science

P.M. MAGAZIN
739125G94J-360

Editorial: Weihenstephaner Str. 7, 81673 MÜNCHEN
Tel: 89 415200 **Fax:** 89 4152565
Email: pm.redaktion@muc.guj.de **Web site:** http://www.pm-magazin.de
Freq: 5 issues yearly; **Annual Sub.:** EUR 40,80; **Circ:** 282,708
Editor: Hans-Hermann Sprado; **Advertising Manager:** Andrea Wörsdörfer
Profile: Popular science magazine, contains articles about pharmacology, anthropology, biology, medicine and archaeology. Facebook: http://www.facebook.com/PMOnline This Outlet offers RSS (Really Simple Syndication).
Language(s): German
Readership: Read mainly by men aged 20 to 39 years.
ADVERTISING RATES:
Full Page Mono .... EUR 22900
Full Page Colour .... EUR 22900
Mechanical Data: Type Area: 240 x 184 mm, No. of Columns (Display): 3, Col Widths (Display): 59 mm
CONSUMER: OTHER CLASSIFICATIONS: Popular Science

PMA PRODUCTION MANAGEMENT
1865337G17-1616

Editorial: Dachauer Str. 37b, 85232 BERGKIRCHEN
Tel: 8131 5655167 **Fax:** 8131 56559167
Email: markus.wilmsmann@p-m-a.de **Web site:** http://www.p-m-a.de
Freq: 8 issues yearly; **Annual Sub.:** EUR 55,20; **Circ:** 7,100
Editor: Markus Wilmsmann; **Advertising Manager:** Elisabeth Wagenpfeil
Profile: Facebook: http://www.facebook.com/pages/pma-Production-Management/122487094447042.
Language(s): German
ADVERTISING RATES:
Full Page Mono .... EUR 2120
Full Page Colour .... EUR 3380
Mechanical Data: Type Area: 254 x 185 mm
Copy instructions: *Copy Date:* 28 days prior to publication

PM-REPORT
739135G2A-3840

Editorial: Suarezstr. 55, 14057 BERLIN
Tel: 30 54592770 **Fax:** 30 54592772
Email: redaktion@pm-report.de **Web site:** http://www.pm-report.de
Freq: Monthly; **Annual Sub.:** EUR 150,00; **Circ:** 1,950
Editor: Christian Sachse; **Advertising Manager:** Elke Magnus
Profile: Magazine about medical publications, pharma marketing, product management.
Language(s): German
ADVERTISING RATES:
Full Page Mono .... EUR 1400
Full Page Colour .... EUR 1915
Mechanical Data: Type Area: 271 x 185 mm, No. of Columns (Display): 3, Col Widths (Display): 58 mm
Copy instructions: *Copy Date:* 14 days prior to publication

PM-REPORT SPECIAL: SELBSTMEDIKATION
739137G2A-3860
Editorial: Suarezstr. 55, 14057 BERLIN
Tel: 30 54592770 **Fax:** 30 54592772
Email: redaktion@pm-report.de **Web site:** http://www.pm-report.de
Freq: Half-yearly; **Annual Sub.:** EUR 49,00; **Circ:** 1,900
Editor: Christian Sachse; **Advertising Manager:** Elke Magnus
Profile: Publication about pharma marketing.
Language(s): German
ADVERTISING RATES:
Full Page Mono .... EUR 1400
Full Page Colour .... EUR 1915
Mechanical Data: Type Area: 271 x 185 mm, No. of Columns (Display): 3, Col Widths (Display): 58 mm
Copy instructions: *Copy Date:* 14 days prior to publication

DER PNEUMOLOGE
1658213G56A-11311
Editorial: Tiergartenstr. 17, 69121 HEIDELBERG
Tel: 6221 4878891 **Fax:** 6221 48768891
Email: katharina.bernsmeier@springer.com **Web site:** http://www.springermedizin.de
Freq: 6 issues yearly; **Annual Sub.:** EUR 174,00; **Circ:** 2,400
Profile: Der Pneumologe offers up-to-date information for all pneumologists working in practical and clinical environments and scientists who are particularly interested in issues of pneumology. The focus is on current developments regarding prevention, diagnostic approaches, management of complications and current therapy strategies. Comprehensive reviews on a specific topical issue provide evidenced based information on diagnostics and therapy. Review articles under the rubric "Continuing Medical Education" present verified results of scientific research and their integration into daily practice.
Language(s): German
ADVERTISING RATES:
Full Page Mono .... EUR 1776
Full Page Colour .... EUR 2816
Mechanical Data: Type Area: 240 x 174 mm
Official Journal of: Organ d. Dt. Ges. f. Innere Medizin

PNEUMOLOGIE
739145G56A-8400
Editorial: Rüdigerstr. 14, 70469 STUTTGART
Tel: 711 8931434 **Fax:** 711 8931408
Email: andrea.stute@thieme.de **Web site:** http://www.thieme.de
Freq: Monthly; **Annual Sub.:** EUR 291,40; **Circ:** 3,700
Editor: Andrea Stute
Profile: Information on the progress of research results and the diagnosis and treatment in the field of pulmonary and respiratory diseases. In headings and recommendations reflects the work of 13 specialized sections of the German Society for Pneumology. The spectrum ranges from Allergology via endoscopy and Paediatric Pneumology through to cell biology. Society members receive the journal as part of their membership.
Language(s): German
ADVERTISING RATES:
Full Page Mono .... EUR 1980
Full Page Colour .... EUR 3210
Mechanical Data: Type Area: 248 x 175 mm, No. of Columns (Display): 4, Col Widths (Display): 40 mm
Official Journal of: Organ d. Dt. Ges. f. Pneumologie, d. Dt. Zentralkomitees z. Bekämpfung d. Tuberkulose u. d. Bundesverb. d. Pneumologen
BUSINESS: HEALTH & MEDICAL

PNEUMONEWS
1934262G56A-11656
Editorial: Aschauer Str. 30, 81549 MÜNCHEN
Tel: 89 2030431300 **Fax:** 89 2030431399
Email: beate.schumacher@springer.com **Web site:** http://www.pneumo-news.de
Freq: 6 issues yearly; **Annual Sub.:** EUR 94,50; **Circ:** 3,300
Editor: Beate Schumacher; **Advertising Manager:** Ines Spankau
Profile: PneumoNews offers practical training to all areas of respiratory medicine. The focus is of experts wrote and commented papers of the current international literature. In addition, in each issue to be offered two short and practical CME modules. The highlights of national and international pneumology congresses are presented in reports and interviews. For the theme "professional politics" and "Practice Management" is a collaboration with the Federation of pulmonologists.
Language(s): German
ADVERTISING RATES:
Full Page Mono .... EUR 1650
Full Page Colour .... EUR 2700
Mechanical Data: Type Area: 240 x 174 mm

PODOLOGIE
739152G56K-1
Editorial: Paul-Gerhardt-Allee 46, 81245 MÜNCHEN
Tel: 89 31890557 **Fax:** 89 31890553
Email: podologie.redaktion@vnmonline.de **Web site:** http://www.podologie.de
Freq: Monthly; **Annual Sub.:** EUR 95,00; **Circ:** 4,648
Editor: Angelika Schaller
Profile: Magazine about foot care and chiropody.
Language(s): German
ADVERTISING RATES:
Full Page Mono .... EUR 1541
Full Page Colour .... EUR 2697
Mechanical Data: Type Area: 260 x 185 mm, No. of Columns (Display): 4, Col Widths (Display): 43 mm
Copy instructions: *Copy Date:* 28 days prior to publication
BUSINESS: HEALTH & MEDICAL: Chiropody

POLITISCHE BILDUNG
739179G82-298
Editorial: Adolf-Damaschke-Str. 10, 65824 SCHWALBACH **Tel:** 6196 86065 **Fax:** 6196 86060
Email: info@wochenschau-verlag.de **Web site:** http://www.wochenschau-verlag.de
Freq: Quarterly; **Annual Sub.:** EUR 64,80; **Circ:** 1,000
Advertising Manager: Edith Beralli
Profile: Magazine about politics and current affairs. Also covers political education in schools and further education.
Language(s): German
ADVERTISING RATES:
Full Page Mono .... EUR 650
Mechanical Data: Type Area: 187 x 117 mm
Copy instructions: *Copy Date:* 40 days prior to publication
CONSUMER: CURRENT AFFAIRS & POLITICS

POLITISCHE ÖKOLOGIE
739181G57-18_70
Editorial: Waltherstr. 29, 80337 MÜNCHEN
Tel: 89 54418443 **Fax:** 89 54418449
Email: radloff@oekom.de **Web site:** http://www.oekom.de
Freq: Quarterly; **Annual Sub.:** EUR 67,95; **Circ:** 4,000
Editor: Jacob Radloff
Profile: Journal covering political issues surrounding ecology and the environment.
Language(s): German
ADVERTISING RATES:
Full Page Colour .... EUR 3300
Mechanical Data: Type Area: 225 x 175 mm, No. of Columns (Display): 3, Col Widths (Display): 51 mm
BUSINESS: ENVIRONMENT & POLLUTION

DIE POLIZEI
739185G32F-620
Editorial: Ruppiner Chaussee 263, 13503 BERLIN
Tel: 30 4311613 **Fax:** 30 4311613
Email: prof_m_knape@gmx.de
Freq: Monthly; **Annual Sub.:** EUR 109,90; **Circ:** 900
Editor: M. Knape
Profile: Journal containing news from the German police academies.
Language(s): German
ADVERTISING RATES:
Full Page Mono .... EUR 991
Full Page Colour .... EUR 1843
Mechanical Data: Type Area: 270 x 186 mm, No. of Columns (Display): 4, Col Widths (Display): 45 mm
Copy instructions: *Copy Date:* 33 days prior to publication
BUSINESS: LOCAL GOVERNMENT, LEISURE & RECREATION: Police

POLIZEI-HEUTE
739187G32F-640
Editorial: Barbarossastr. 21, 63517 RODENBACH
Tel: 6184 95080 **Fax:** 6184 54524
Email: redaktion@security-service.com **Web site:** http://www.security-service.com
Freq: 6 issues yearly; **Annual Sub.:** EUR 35,00; **Circ:** 3,400
Editor: Helmut Brückmann
Profile: Journal containing information on training and education within the police force.
Language(s): German
ADVERTISING RATES:
Full Page Mono .... EUR 1390
Full Page Colour .... EUR 2290
Mechanical Data: Type Area: 262 x 171 mm, No. of Columns (Display): 3, Col Widths (Display): 54 mm
Copy instructions: *Copy Date:* 28 days prior to publication
BUSINESS: LOCAL GOVERNMENT, LEISURE & RECREATION: Police

POLIZEISPIEGEL
739196G32F-1166
Editorial: Friedrichstr. 169, 10117 BERLIN
Tel: 30 47378123 **Fax:** 30 47378125
Email: dpolg@dbb.de **Web site:** http://www.dpolg.de
Freq: 10 issues yearly; Free to qualifying individuals
Annual Sub.: EUR 48,00; **Circ:** 57,588
Editor: Elisabeth Schnell; **Advertising Manager:** Katy Netz
Profile: Official news journal of the German police trade union.
Language(s): German
ADVERTISING RATES:
Full Page Mono .... EUR 3600
Full Page Colour .... EUR 4950
Mechanical Data: Type Area: 270 x 185 mm, No. of Columns (Display): 4, Col Widths (Display): 43 mm
Copy instructions: *Copy Date:* 42 days prior to publication
BUSINESS: LOCAL GOVERNMENT, LEISURE & RECREATION: Police

POLSTER FASHION
739204G23A-125
Editorial: Andernacher Str. 5a, 90411 NÜRNBERG
Tel: 911 9557860 **Fax:** 911 9557811
Email: redaktion@ritthammer-verlag.de **Web site:** http://www.moebelmarkt.de
Freq: 6 issues yearly; **Annual Sub.:** EUR 48,00; **Circ:** 15,120
Editor: Helmut Merkel; **Advertising Manager:** Andreas Müller-Buck
Profile: International magazine about upholstered furniture.
Language(s): English; German
ADVERTISING RATES:
Full Page Mono .... EUR 4410
Full Page Colour .... EUR 5730
Mechanical Data: Type Area: 310 x 235 mm, No. of Columns (Display): 4, Col Widths (Display): 50 mm
BUSINESS: FURNISHINGS & FURNITURE

POLYMER BULLETIN
739206G39-1
Editorial: Ackermannweg 10, 55128 MAINZ
Tel: 6131 379150 **Fax:** 6131 379350
Email: klaus.muellen@mpip-mainz.mpg.de **Web site:** http://www.springerlink.com
Freq: 18 issues yearly; **Annual Sub.:** EUR 2473,00; **Circ:** 370
Editor: Klaus Müllen
Profile: Polymer bulletin.
Language(s): English
ADVERTISING RATES:
Full Page Mono .... EUR 740
Full Page Colour .... EUR 1780
Mechanical Data: Type Area: 200 x 130 mm

POPCORN
739220G74G-1817
Editorial: Leonrodstr. 52, 80636 MÜNCHEN
Tel: 89 69749202 **Fax:** 89 69749201
Email: redaktion@popcorn-mag.de **Web site:** http://www.popcorn-mag.de
Freq: Monthly; **Annual Sub.:** EUR 24,60; **Circ:** 208,546
Editor: Norbert Lalla; **Advertising Manager:** Marit Böhmer
Profile: Popcorn has distinguished itself in the market as a visually and content valuable youth magazine. By consistently focusing on the positive youthful charm issues Popcorn could be "premium product" in the youth market be established. Popcorn is a celebrity magazine that captures the spirit of young people and reflects their lifestyle. Popcorn informs, entertains and provides a multitude of services for readers aged between 12 and 20 years. Popcorn is divided into four content areas: pop music, cinema and TV, youth counseling and service topics. Pop music: All current stars are described in detail in portraits, interviews, home stories, concert reviews, etc. are presented and illustrated a new, hip music trends to target groups. Cinema and TV: The most important films of the month are presented on six pages visually outstanding. In addition, there are great stories of the hottest stars of film and TV scene. Monthly statements about movies and series give the reader guidance. Youth counseling: Here popcorn distinguished by seriousness and credibility. The sensitive area of youth consulting (sex education, help with problems with school, parents, environment, etc.) is not treated voyeuristic, but the young people and their problems are taken seriously. Service topics: A high value in use take on the service issues. In addition to puzzles are psychological tests, games and trend reports, especially the posters (up to 20 in a booklet, of which at least two mega-size) an attractive offer. Even the look of Popcorn is a consistent way. Only high-quality, current photo material, a spacious and modern layout with high-quality tracks provide a compact, colorful and modern magazine for young people.
Language(s): German
Readership: Aimed at young people.
ADVERTISING RATES:
Full Page Mono .... EUR 13110
Full Page Colour .... EUR 13110
Mechanical Data: Type Area: 258 x 185 mm, No. of Columns (Display): 4, Col Widths (Display): 43 mm
CONSUMER: WOMEN'S INTEREST CONSUMER MAGAZINES: Slimming & Health

PORSCHE CLUB LIFE
739226G77E-340
Editorial: Adams-Lehmann-Str. 61, 80797 MÜNCHEN **Tel:** 89 327299911 **Fax:** 89 327299928
Email: frank@gindler.de **Web site:** http://www.porsche-club-deutschland.de
Freq: Quarterly; Free to qualifying individuals
Annual Sub.: EUR 49,00; **Circ:** 25,814
Editor: Frank J. Gindler; **Advertising Manager:** Anna Maria Artinger
Profile: Magazine containing information about Porsches.
Language(s): German
ADVERTISING RATES:
Full Page Mono .... EUR 3800
Full Page Colour .... EUR 4900
Mechanical Data: Type Area: 265 x 182 mm, No. of Columns (Display): 4, Col Widths (Display): 44 mm
Copy instructions: *Copy Date:* 14 days prior to publication
Official Journal of: Organ d. Porsche Club Deutschland e.V.
CONSUMER: MOTORING & CYCLING: Club Cars

PORSCHE FAHRER
1799763G77A-2785
Editorial: Rhönstr. 131, 60385 FRANKFURT
Tel: 69 40592361 **Fax:** 69 40592361
Email: jh.muche@heel-verlag.de **Web site:** http://www.pf-magazin.de
Freq: Quarterly; **Annual Sub.:** EUR 21,00; **Circ:** 20,800
Editor: Jan-Henrik Muche; **Advertising Manager:** Sabine Blüm
Profile: Magazine for at lovers of classic Porsche in particular as well as to Porsche enthusiasts in general. Model concepts, detailed technical features, fascinating stories from the motor sports history and tips on restoration.
Language(s): German
ADVERTISING RATES:
Full Page Mono .... EUR 4200
Full Page Colour .... EUR 5600
Mechanical Data: Type Area: 256 x 175 mm

PORT01.CITY-FLASH BREMEN
1777892G80-15082
Editorial: Parallelweg 31, 28219 BREMEN
Tel: 421 3800388 **Fax:** 421 3800343
Email: bremen@port01.com **Web site:** http://www.port01.com
Freq: Monthly; **Cover Price:** Free; **Circ:** 9,640
Editor: Stefan Ketzler
Profile: Facebook: http://www.facebook.com/port01Dresden.
Language(s): German
ADVERTISING RATES:
Full Page Mono .... EUR 680
Full Page Colour .... EUR 680
CONSUMER: RURAL & REGIONAL INTEREST

PORT01.CITY-FLASH CHEMNITZ
1777893G80-15083
Editorial: Lindenhöhe 16, 09434 KRUMHERMERSDORF **Tel:** 162 4230386
Email: chemnitz@port01.com **Web site:** http://www.port01.com
Freq: Monthly; **Cover Price:** Free; **Circ:** 9,262
Editor: Henri Grebler; **Advertising Manager:** Martin Löser
Profile: Facebook: http://www.facebook.com/port01Dresden.
Language(s): German
ADVERTISING RATES:
Full Page Mono .... EUR 650
Full Page Colour .... EUR 650
CONSUMER: RURAL & REGIONAL INTEREST

PORT01.CITY-FLASH DRESDEN
1777895G80-15085
Editorial: Brucknerstr. 4, 01309 DRESDEN
Tel: 351 21330077 **Fax:** 351 21330022
Email: dresden@port01.com **Web site:** http://www.port01.com
Freq: Monthly; **Cover Price:** Free; **Circ:** 8,783
Editor: Florian Kaminski; **Advertising Manager:** Florian Kaminski
Profile: Facebook: http://www.facebook.com/port01Dresden.
Language(s): German
ADVERTISING RATES:
Full Page Mono .... EUR 680
Full Page Colour .... EUR 680
CONSUMER: RURAL & REGIONAL INTEREST

PORT01.CITY-FLASH JENA WEIMAR
1777897G80-15087
Editorial: Bitterfelder Str. 7, 04129 LEIPZIG
Tel: 341 90986464 **Fax:** 341 90986469
Email: jena@port01.com **Web site:** http://www.port01.com
Freq: Monthly; **Cover Price:** Free; **Circ:** 8,920
Editor: Tim Wache
Profile: Facebook: http://www.facebook.com/port01Dresden.
Language(s): German
ADVERTISING RATES:
Full Page Mono .... EUR 650
Full Page Colour .... EUR 650
CONSUMER: RURAL & REGIONAL INTEREST

PORT01.CITY-FLASH LEIPZIG
1777898G80-15088
Editorial: Bitterfelder Str. 7, 04129 LEIPZIG
Tel: 341 90986464 **Fax:** 341 90986469
Email: leipzig@port01.com **Web site:** http://www.port01.com
Freq: Monthly; **Cover Price:** Free; **Circ:** 9,563
Editor: Stefan Bach
Profile: Facebook: http://www.facebook.com/port01Dresden.
Language(s): German
ADVERTISING RATES:
Full Page Mono .... EUR 680
Full Page Colour .... EUR 680
CONSUMER: RURAL & REGIONAL INTEREST

PORT01.CITY-FLASH PLAUEN ZWICKAU
1777901G80-15091
Editorial: Bahnhofstr. 12, 08523 PLAUEN
Tel: 3741 276055
Email: markus@port01.com **Web site:** http://www.port01.com
Freq: Monthly; **Cover Price:** Free; **Circ:** 9,209
Editor: Markus Schneider
Profile: Facebook: http://www.facebook.com/port01Dresden.
Language(s): German
ADVERTISING RATES:
Full Page Mono .... EUR 650
Full Page Colour .... EUR 650

Copy instructions: *Copy Date:* 15 days prior to publication
CONSUMER: RURAL & REGIONAL INTEREST

PORT01.CITY-FLASH STUTTGART LUDWIGSBURG
1777903G80-15092
Editorial: Heilbronner Str. 7, 70174 STUTTGART
Tel: 711 50629620 **Fax:** 351 21330022
Email: stuttgart@port01.com **Web site:** http://www.port01.com
Freq: Monthly; **Cover Price:** Free; **Circ:** 9,733
Editor: Yvonne C. Utz; **Advertising Manager:** Yvonne C. Utz
Profile: Facebook: http://www.facebook.com/port01Dresden.
Language(s): German
ADVERTISING RATES:
Full Page Mono .... EUR 680
Full Page Colour .... EUR 680
CONSUMER: RURAL & REGIONAL INTEREST

PORT01.CITY-FLASH WÜRZBURG
1777905G80-15093
Editorial: Jägerstr. 14, 97082 WÜRZBURG
Tel: 931 2876210 **Fax:** 931 4526959
Email: bhesi@port01.com **Web site:** http://www.port01.com
Freq: Monthly; **Cover Price:** Free; **Circ:** 9,570
Editor: Bettina Pfeuffer; **Advertising Manager:** Bettina Pfeuffer
Profile: Facebook: http://www.facebook.com/port01Dresden.
Language(s): German
ADVERTISING RATES:
Full Page Mono .... EUR 650
Full Page Colour .... EUR 650
CONSUMER: RURAL & REGIONAL INTEREST

PORTFOLIO INSTITUTIONELL
1832440G1C-1474
Editorial: Kleine Hochstr. 9, 60313 FRANKFURT
Tel: 69 85708112 **Fax:** 69 85708149
Email: kontakt@portfolio-verlag.com **Web site:** http://www.portfolio-institutionell.de
Freq: Monthly; **Annual Sub.:** EUR 225,00; **Circ:** 10,400
Editor: Patrick Eisele; **Advertising Manager:** Carsten Schieck
Profile: Magazine reporting on current and future trends in asset management, company pension shemes and investment law.
Language(s): German
ADVERTISING RATES:
Full Page Mono .... EUR 7800
Full Page Colour .... EUR 7800
Mechanical Data: Type Area: 255 x 192 mm

PORTFOLIO INTERNATIONAL
1832441G1C-1475
Editorial: Kleine Hochstr. 9, 60313 FRANKFURT
Tel: 69 85708112 **Fax:** 69 85708149
Email: redaktion@portfolio-verlag.com **Web site:** http://www.portfolio-international.de
Freq: 10 issues yearly; **Annual Sub.:** EUR 140,00; **Circ:** 19,643
Advertising Manager: Carsten Schieck
Profile: portfolio international is the leading B2B magazine for independent financial advisors, bank consultants and fund of funds managers in Germany. It supplies independent and reliable information and analyses on investment and insurance products, trends within the capital markets, product provider strategies, changes in legal or tax structure and distribution methods.
Language(s): German
ADVERTISING RATES:
Full Page Mono .... EUR 7800
Full Page Colour .... EUR 7800
Mechanical Data: Type Area: 324 x 245 mm

PORTUGUESE ECONOMIC JOURNAL
765626G1A-3497
Editorial: Tiergartenstr. 17, 69121 HEIDELBERG
Tel: 6221 4870 **Fax:** 6221 4878366
Email: subscriptions@springer.com **Web site:** http://www.springerlink.com
Freq: 3 issues yearly; **Annual Sub.:** EUR 227,50; **Circ:** 211
Editor: Paulo Brito
Profile: Journal aims to publish theoretical, empirical, applied or policy-oriented research papers on any field in economics.
Language(s): English
ADVERTISING RATES:
Full Page Mono .... EUR 740
Full Page Colour .... EUR 1780
Mechanical Data: Type Area: 200 x 130 mm
Official Journal of: Organ d. Instituto Superior de Economia e Gestão

PORZ AKTUELL
739233G72-10532
Editorial: Stolberger Str. 114a, 50933 KÖLN
Tel: 221 9544140 **Fax:** 221 954414499
Email: redaktion@koelner-wochenspiegel.de **Web site:** http://www.rheinische-anzeigenblaetter.de
Freq: Weekly; **Cover Price:** Free; **Circ:** 52,198
Editor: Angela Koenig; **Advertising Manager:** Astrid Rehm
Profile: Advertising journal (house-to-house) concentrating on local stories.
Language(s): German
ADVERTISING RATES:
Full Page Mono .... EUR 2993
Full Page Colour .... EUR 4340
Mechanical Data: Type Area: 430 x 282 mm, No. of Columns (Display): 6, Col Widths (Display): 45 mm
Copy instructions: *Copy Date:* 5 days prior to publication
LOCAL NEWSPAPERS

POSITION
739241G14F-50
Editorial: Breite Str. 29, 10178 BERLIN
Tel: 30 203081604 **Fax:** 30 2030851604
Email: huels.klaudia@berlin.dihk.de
Freq: Quarterly; **Annual Sub.:** EUR 9,20; **Circ:** 66,954
Editor: Klaudia Hüls
Profile: Magazine providing practical information about career advancement in banking, insurance, industry, transport and the local hotel and catering trade.
Language(s): German
ADVERTISING RATES:
Full Page Mono .... EUR 2040
Full Page Colour .... EUR 3260
Mechanical Data: Type Area: 247 x 180 mm, No. of Columns (Display): 3, Col Widths (Display): 56 mm
Copy instructions: *Copy Date:* 45 days prior to publication
BUSINESS: COMMERCE, INDUSTRY & MANAGEMENT: Training & Recruitment

POSITIONEN ZU POLITIK, WIRTSCHAFT UND GESELLSCHAFT
1642147G1D-465
Editorial: Wilhelmstr. 43/43G, 10117 BERLIN
Tel: 30 20205115 **Fax:** 30 20206115
Email: positionen@gdv.de **Web site:** http://www.gdv.de
Freq: 6 issues yearly; **Circ:** 30,000
Editor: Holger Schmitt
Profile: Magazine with issues from the insurance business.
Language(s): German

P.O.S.KOMPAKT
2090770G14A-10513
Editorial: Bargkoppelweg 72, 22145 HAMBURG
Tel: 40 79699771 **Fax:** 40 79699773
Email: redaktion@pos-kompakt.net **Web site:** http://www.pos-kompakt.net
Freq: 8 issues yearly; **Annual Sub.:** EUR 58,00; **Circ:** 12,850
Editor: Thomas Weppler; **Advertising Manager:** Thorsten Brandmann
Profile: P.O.S. kompakt, the trade magazine for all topics, products and services is around the point of sale. P.O.S. kompakt about brands, retailers, packaging, POS materials, point of sales reports, multimedia, POS design, advertising, communications, strategies & analysis for point of sale and provides a comprehensive overview of all relevant aspects of the sell-in, sell-through and sell-out.
Language(s): German
ADVERTISING RATES:
Full Page Mono .... EUR 3975
Full Page Colour .... EUR 3975
Mechanical Data: Type Area: 261 x 185 mm, No. of Columns (Display): 4, Col Widths (Display): 46 mm

POS-MAIL
753942G2A-5440
Editorial: Freiligrathring 18, 40878 RATINGEN
Tel: 2102 20270 **Fax:** 2102 202790
Email: t.bloemer@cat-verlag.de **Web site:** http://www.pos-mail.de
Freq: Monthly; **Annual Sub.:** EUR 60,00; **Circ:** 15,396
Editor: Thomas Blömer; **Advertising Manager:** Ralf Gruna
Profile: Information for high-tech marketing retail consumer electronics, telecom, PC + peripherals, photo, video, infotainment.
Language(s): German
ADVERTISING RATES:
Full Page Mono .... EUR 4920
Full Page Colour .... EUR 6396
Mechanical Data: Type Area: 400 x 277 mm, No. of Columns (Display): 4, Col Widths (Display): 65 mm
Copy instructions: *Copy Date:* 20 days prior to publication
BUSINESS: COMMUNICATIONS, ADVERTISING & MARKETING

POS-MANAGER TECHNOLOGY
763104G14A-9264
Editorial: Businesspark A96, 86842 TÜRKHEIM
Tel: 8245 96760160 **Fax:** 8245 96760100
Email: ck@th-medien.com **Web site:** http://www.th-medien.com
Freq: 6 issues yearly; Free to qualifying individuals
Annual Sub.: EUR 44,00; **Circ:** 12,330
Editor: Carolin Kober; **Advertising Manager:** Angelika Eigner
Profile: Magazine on trade marketing.
Language(s): English; German
ADVERTISING RATES:
Full Page Mono .... EUR 3500
Full Page Colour .... EUR 3950
Mechanical Data: Type Area: 260 x 185 mm, No. of Columns (Display): 3, Col Widths (Display): 57 mm

POS.NEWS
1873512G14A-10259
Editorial: Auf dem Dattel 17, 56332 HATZENPORT
Tel: 2605 8499722 **Fax:** 2605 8499727
Email: redaktion@posnews.de **Web site:** http://www.posnews.de
Freq: 8 issues yearly; **Annual Sub.:** EUR 32,00; **Circ:** 13,687
Editor: Peter Schlotmann; **Advertising Manager:** Peter Schlotmann
Profile: Magazine for executives in trade.
Language(s): German
ADVERTISING RATES:
Full Page Mono .... EUR 3950
Full Page Colour .... EUR 3950
Mechanical Data: Type Area: 241 x 180 mm
Copy instructions: *Copy Date:* 10 days prior to publication

DER POSTILLION
739247G72-10544
Editorial: Kasinostr. 28, 53840 TROISDORF
Tel: 2241 2600 **Fax:** 2241 260259
Email: redaktion@rmp.de **Web site:** http://www.ortszeitungen.de
Freq: 26 issues yearly; **Cover Price:** Free; **Circ:** 11,900
Editor: Wolfgang Mannek; **Advertising Manager:** Engelbert Krips
Profile: Advertising journal (house-to-house) concentrating on local stories.
Language(s): German
ADVERTISING RATES:
Full Page Mono .... EUR 818
Full Page Colour .... EUR 901
Mechanical Data: Type Area: 280 x 185 mm, No. of Columns (Display): 4, Col Widths (Display): 43 mm
Copy instructions: *Copy Date:* 3 days prior to publication
LOCAL NEWSPAPERS

POSTMICHEL-BRIEF
1616362G74N-819
Editorial: Ritterstr. 16, 73728 ESSLINGEN
Tel: 711 35123108 **Fax:** 711 3512552614
Email: renate.schaumburg@esslingen.de **Web site:** http://www.senioren.esslingen.de
Freq: Quarterly; **Cover Price:** Free; **Circ:** 2,000
Editor: Renate Schaumburg; **Advertising Manager:** Franz Auer
Profile: Magazine for elderly citizens of the city of Esslingen.
Language(s): German
ADVERTISING RATES:
Full Page Mono .... EUR 133
Full Page Colour .... EUR 133
Mechanical Data: Type Area: 245 x 165 mm
Copy instructions: *Copy Date:* 45 days prior to publication

POTSDAM AM SONNTAG
739276G72-10552
Editorial: Platz der Einheit 14, 14467 POTSDAM
Tel: 331 2376155 **Fax:** 331 2376400
Email: pams.pnn@pnn.de **Web site:** http://www.pams.de
Freq: Weekly; **Cover Price:** Free; **Circ:** 110,000
Editor: Michael Erbach; **Advertising Manager:** Marcel Pelletier
Profile: Advertising journal (house-to-house) concentrating on local stories.
Language(s): German
ADVERTISING RATES:
Full Page Mono .... EUR 5676
Full Page Colour .... EUR 7260
Mechanical Data: Type Area: 440 x 277 mm, No. of Columns (Display): 6, Col Widths (Display): 45 mm
Copy instructions: *Copy Date:* 4 days prior to publication
LOCAL NEWSPAPERS

DER POTSDAMER
739277G72-10556
Editorial: Behlertstr. 35, 14467 POTSDAM
Tel: 331 298220 **Fax:** 331 2982231
Email: info@der-potsdamer.biz **Web site:** http://www.derpotsdamer-online.de
Freq: Weekly; **Cover Price:** Free; **Circ:** 135,500
Editor: André Großmann
Profile: Advertising journal (house-to-house) concentrating on local stories.
Language(s): German
ADVERTISING RATES:
Full Page Mono .... EUR 5725
Full Page Colour .... EUR 8587
Mechanical Data: Type Area: 435 x 281 mm, No. of Columns (Display): 7, Col Widths (Display): 38 mm
Copy instructions: *Copy Date:* 5 days prior to publication
LOCAL NEWSPAPERS

POTSDAMER NEUESTE NACHRICHTEN
739279G67B-11840
Editorial: Platz der Einheit 14, 14467 POTSDAM
Tel: 331 2376132 **Fax:** 331 2376300
Email: redaktion.pnn@pnn.de **Web site:** http://www.pnn.de
Freq: 312 issues yearly; **Circ:** 10,803
Editor: Michael Erbach; **News Editor:** Peter Tiede; **Advertising Manager:** Marcel Pelletier
Profile: Every day from Monday to Saturday seems the core product "Potsdamer Neueste Nachrichten (PNN) with a paid circulation of 11,000 copies. The first issue appeared on 1 May 1951. The newspaper was also the GDR period as a civil alternative to the faithful line SED newspaper, and was happy to read about self-employed and "free spirits". The PNN is the only daily newspaper in the new states with growing support - thanks to the dynamic development of the region of Potsdam, but also thanks to a focus on news from Potsdam and Berlin in a newspaper. The PNN readership is characterized today by far above average educational and income patterns, coupled with an often work-related, high interest in events in the city of Potsdam, but also at Berlin's issues. This is fortunate, because the sister newspaper Potsdamer Neueste Nachrichten is "Der Tagesspiegel", Berlin. This provides a day for the coat approved quality part of the PNN. Resulting in Potsdam with a young and well educated editors, the Potsdam local directory, local content to national policy in Brandenburg, as well as cultural, sports and business in the region. This Outlet offers RSS (Really Simple Syndication).
Language(s): German
ADVERTISING RATES:
SCC .... EUR 28,50
Mechanical Data: Type Area: 528 x 370 mm, No. of Columns (Display): 8, Col Widths (Display): 45 mm
Copy instructions: *Copy Date:* 2 days prior to publication
Supplement(s): doppio; Potsdam Tipps; rtv; Ticket
REGIONAL DAILY & SUNDAY NEWSPAPERS: Regional Daily Newspapers

PPI FORUM
1833434G1C-1476
Editorial: Moorfuhrtweg 13, 22301 HAMBURG
Tel: 40 2274330 **Fax:** 40 227433333
Web site: http://www.ppi.de
Freq: 3 issues yearly; **Cover Price:** Free; **Circ:** 4,500
Editor: Michael Ballauff
Profile: Customer magazine from the 'PPI Finacial Systems' company containing information on IT for banks and creditt institutions.
Language(s): German

PPMP PSYCHOTHERAPIE PSYCHOSOMATIK MEDIZINISCHE PSYCHOLOGIE
739289G56N-72
Editorial: Stoystr. 3, 07740 JENA
Email: bernhard.strauss@med.uni-jena.de **Web site:** http://www.thieme.de/ppmp
Freq: 10 issues yearly; **Annual Sub.:** EUR 212,80; **Circ:** 1,380
Editor: Bernhard Strauß
Profile: Reflection of the research. Pure knowledge. Original work with current research on diagnosis and therapy. CME-certified education and training. Systematic reviews. Instructive case reports. Introduction of new treatment approaches. Questions of the readers to research practice answered accurately. Summaries of international studies.
Language(s): German
ADVERTISING RATES:
Full Page Mono .... EUR 1180
Full Page Colour .... EUR 2290
Mechanical Data: Type Area: 248 x 175 mm, No. of Columns (Display): 4, Col Widths (Display): 40 mm
BUSINESS: HEALTH & MEDICAL: Mental Health

PPT PSYCHOPHARMAKOTHERAPIE
739290G56N-71_50
Editorial: Birkenwaldstr. 44, 70191 STUTTGART
Tel: 711 2582234 **Fax:** 711 2582283
Email: ppt@wissenschaftliche-verlagsgesellschaft.de **Web site:** http://www.ppt-online.de
Freq: 6 issues yearly; **Annual Sub.:** EUR 112,80; **Circ:** 10,347
Editor: Heike Oberpichler-Schwenk; **Advertising Manager:** Kornelia Wind
Profile: Aimed at psychiatrists, neurologists, GPs and clinics.
Language(s): German
Readership: Aimed at phyciatrists, neurologists, GPs and clinics.
ADVERTISING RATES:
Full Page Mono .... EUR 1813
Full Page Colour .... EUR 3016
Mechanical Data: Type Area: 262 x 182 mm, No. of Columns (Display): 3, Col Widths (Display): 56 mm
Copy instructions: *Copy Date:* 21 days prior to publication
Official Journal of: Organ d. Inst. f. Arzneimittelsicherheit in d. Psychiatrie
BUSINESS: HEALTH & MEDICAL: Mental Health

PR MAGAZIN
739477G2E-130
Editorial: Mainzer Str. 16, 53424 REMAGEN
Tel: 2228 931123 **Fax:** 2228 931137
Email: prmagazin@rommerskirchen.com **Web site:** http://www.prmagazin.de
Freq: Monthly; **Annual Sub.:** EUR 198,50; **Circ:** 4,189
Editor: Thomas Rommerskirchen
Profile: Magazine presents information and importance to the theory and practice of the communications industry.
Language(s): German
ADVERTISING RATES:
Full Page Mono .... EUR 2650
Full Page Colour .... EUR 4120
Mechanical Data: Col Widths (Display): 43 mm, Type Area: 260 x 185 mm, No. of Columns (Display): 4
Copy instructions: *Copy Date:* 15 days prior to publication

Supplement(s): Fakten; Themen; ViaVision
BUSINESS: COMMUNICATIONS, ADVERTISING & MARKETING: Public Relations

PR REPORT 739672G2E-135
Editorial: Weidestr. 122a, 22083 HAMBURG
Tel: 40 69206200 **Fax:** 40 69206333
Email: red.prreport@haymarket.de **Web site:** http://www.prreport.de
Freq: 11 issues yearly; **Annual Sub.:** EUR 198,50; **Circ:** 4,832
Editor: Uwe Förster; **Advertising Manager:** Jan Philipp Rost
Profile: Magazine for all who communicate more professionally. It is aimed at decision makers in companies, organizations and associations as well as agencies and service providers in the PR industry. The PR Report accompanies this dynamic and diverse market as a strong opinion magazine, analyzes current developments and provides guidance. This Outlet offers RSS (Really Simple Syndication).
Language(s): German
Readership: Aimed at those working in the field of public relations.
ADVERTISING RATES:
Full Page Colour .... EUR 4500
Mechanical Data: Type Area: 242 x 188 mm
Copy instructions: *Copy Date:* 20 days prior to publication
BUSINESS: COMMUNICATIONS, ADVERTISING & MARKETING: Public Relations

PR REPORT COMPENDIUM 1639611G2A-5535
Editorial: Weidestr. 122a, 22083 HAMBURG
Tel: 40 69206200 **Fax:** 40 69206333
Email: compendium@haymarket.de **Web site:** http://www.prreport.de
Freq: Annual; **Cover Price:** EUR 40,00; **Circ:** 2,000
Editor: Uwe Förster; **Advertising Manager:** Jan Philipp Rost
Profile: Publication listing German public relations agencies.
Language(s): German
ADVERTISING RATES:
Full Page Colour .... EUR 3800
Mechanical Data: Type Area: 242 x 188 mm
Copy instructions: *Copy Date:* 30 days prior to publication

DER PRAKTIKER 739299G27-1960
Editorial: Aachener Str. 172, 40223 DÜSSELDORF
Tel: 211 1591276 **Fax:** 211 1591350
Email: dietmar.rippegather@dvs-hg.de **Web site:** http://www.dvs-media.info
Freq: Monthly; **Annual Sub.:** EUR 99,00; **Circ:** 8,724
Editor: Dietmar Rippegather; **Advertising Manager:** Iris Jansen
Profile: Magazine about welding and soldering techniques.
Language(s): German
Readership: Aimed at welders.
ADVERTISING RATES:
Full Page Mono .... EUR 2950
Full Page Colour .... EUR 3950
Mechanical Data: Type Area: 253 x 176 mm, No. of Columns (Display): 3, Col Widths (Display): 58 mm
Copy instructions: *Copy Date:* 44 days prior to publication
BUSINESS: METAL, IRON & STEEL

PRAKTISCHE METALLOGRAPHIE PRACTICAL METALLOGRAPHY 739303G19C-100
Editorial: Postfach 151150, 66041 SAARBRÜCKEN
Tel: 681 3022048 **Fax:** 681 3024876
Email: pm-editor@matsci.uni-sb.de **Web site:** http://www.practical-metallography.com
Freq: Monthly; **Annual Sub.:** EUR 157,20; **Circ:** 1,300
Editor: Frank Mücklich; **Advertising Manager:** Hermann J. Kleiner
Profile: Praktische Metallographie Practical Metallography is the practical journal for microscopic characterization of materials. It is considered a standard and reference for all questions on the metallography and Materialography. The PM also reported on the work of the Committee of Experts Metallography of DGM. Of special interest for the readers of this PM to the products and processes from the fields of image analysis, image archiving, documentation, microscopy, hardness testing, preparation, vacuum technology, and metallographic services.
Language(s): English; German
Readership: Aimed at metallurgists.
ADVERTISING RATES:
Full Page Mono .... EUR 840
Full Page Colour .... EUR 1335
Mechanical Data: Type Area: 180 x 130 mm
Copy instructions: *Copy Date:* 30 days prior to publication
Official Journal of: Organ d. Practical Metallography
BUSINESS: ENGINEERING & MACHINERY: Finishing

DER PRAKTISCHE TIERARZT 739304G64H-260
Editorial: Gneisenaustr. 10, 30175 HANNOVER
Tel: 511 858060 **Fax:** 511 858045
Email: info@tierpraxis.de **Web site:** http://www.tierpraxis.de
Freq: Monthly; **Annual Sub.:** EUR 120,00; **Circ:** 7,973
Editor: Birgit Leopold-Temmler; **Advertising Manager:** Bettina Kruse
Profile: Veterinary practice journal.
Language(s): German
ADVERTISING RATES:
Full Page Mono .... EUR 2170
Full Page Colour .... EUR 3309
Mechanical Data: Type Area: 272 x 188 mm, No. of Columns (Display): 4, Col Widths (Display): 44 mm
Copy instructions: *Copy Date:* 25 days prior to publication
Official Journal of: Organ d. Bundesverb. Praktizierender Tierärzte e.V.
BUSINESS: OTHER CLASSIFICATIONS: Veterinary

PRÄVENTION 739296G56R-2440
Editorial: Am Sonnenberg 17, 55270 SCHWABENHEIM **Tel:** 6130 7760 **Fax:** 6130 7971
Email: peter.sabo@t-online.de **Web site:** http://www.zeitschrift-praevention.de
Freq: Quarterly; **Annual Sub.:** EUR 24,50; **Circ:** 1,900
Editor: Peter Sabo; **Advertising Manager:** Peter Sabo
Profile: Magazine about developments in medicine.
Language(s): German
ADVERTISING RATES:
Full Page Mono .... EUR 614
Mechanical Data: Type Area: 247 x 183 mm, No. of Columns (Display): 3, Col Widths (Display): 57 mm
Copy instructions: *Copy Date:* 45 days prior to publication
BUSINESS: HEALTH & MEDICAL: Health Medical Related

PRÄVENTION UND GESUNDHEITSFÖRDERUNG 1706875G56A-11392
Editorial: Tiergartenstr. 17, 69121 HEIDELBERG
Tel: 6221 4878434 **Fax:** 6221 4878576
Email: christine.lodge@springer.com **Web site:** http://praevention.springer.de
Freq: Quarterly; **Annual Sub.:** EUR 159,00; **Circ:** 323
Editor: Christine Lodge
Profile: Germany is an economic high-performance society that spends a lot of repair and compensation for health problems and little for their prevention. Prävention + Gesundheitsförderung is the organ for the publication of scientific papers on preventive measures in the following areas of society: • in kindergartens and schools, • in enterprises, service institutions and administrative • in organizations of employers and trade unions, • in the state with its various authorities, • in the institutions of social protection, • throughout the healthcare industry with all its facilities, • in education and science. Here, the work will be divided into four subject areas with the following key messages: Creating knowledge for prevention and health promotion Investment in health rather than cure and compensation More self-responsibility and support for employees Innovative health management rather than early retirement or premature curation Prävention + Gesundheitsförderung aims to contribute high-quality work will also mean that institutions that promote the health of detectable them belonging to people who are rewarded, those who produce the avoidable social costs charged accordingly.
Language(s): German
ADVERTISING RATES:
Full Page Mono .... EUR 740
Full Page Colour .... EUR 1780
Mechanical Data: Type Area: 240 x 175 mm

PRÄVENTION UND REHABILITATION 739297G56L-57
Editorial: Buchenhöhe 46, 83471 BERCHTESGADEN
Freq: Quarterly; **Annual Sub.:** EUR 82,50; **Circ:** 1,500
Editor: J. Lecheler; **Advertising Manager:** Christian Graßl
Profile: Publication containing information and articles about rehabilitation and how to prevent disease and illness.
Language(s): German
ADVERTISING RATES:
Full Page Mono .... EUR 1065
Full Page Colour .... EUR 2055
Mechanical Data: Type Area: 242 x 167 mm, No. of Columns (Display): 3, Col Widths (Display): 56 mm
Copy instructions: *Copy Date:* 28 days prior to publication
BUSINESS: HEALTH & MEDICAL: Disability & Rehabilitation

PRAXIS 739315G56G-180
Editorial: Ottostr. 12, 50859 KÖLN
Tel: 2234 7011148 **Fax:** 2234 7011149
Email: praxiscomputer@aerzteblatt.de **Web site:** http://www.aerzteblatt.de
Freq: 5 issues yearly; **Annual Sub.:** EUR 18,00; **Circ:** 100,000
Editor: Heinz Stüwe; **Advertising Manager:** Petra Pahlke-Schäfers
Profile: Magazine for modern technologies and management in the doctor's office (Supplement Deutsches Ärzteblatt) Facebook: http://www.facebook.com/aerzteblatt.
Language(s): German
Readership: Aimed at established physicians.
ADVERTISING RATES:
Full Page Mono .... EUR 5100
Full Page Colour .... EUR 6890
Mechanical Data: Type Area: 260 x 185 mm
Supplement to: Deutsches Ärzteblatt
BUSINESS: HEALTH & MEDICAL: Medical Equipment

PRAXIS DER KINDERPSYCHOLOGIE UND KINDERPSYCHIATRIE 739318G56A-11148
Editorial: Hartwigstr. 2c, 28209 BREMEN
Tel: 421 21868607
Email: kniebank@uni-bremen.de **Web site:** http://www.v-r.de
Freq: 10 issues yearly; **Annual Sub.:** EUR 74,00; **Circ:** 2,000
Editor: Kay Niebank; **Advertising Manager:** Anja Kütemeyer
Profile: Magazine with results from psychoanalysis, psychology and family therapy.
Language(s): German
ADVERTISING RATES:
Full Page Mono .... EUR 700
Mechanical Data: Type Area: 190 x 120 mm

PRAXIS DER PSYCHOMOTORIK 739323G56R-1820
Editorial: Schleefstr. 14, 44287 DORTMUND
Tel: 231 128008 **Fax:** 231 128009
Email: redaktion@verlag-modernes-lernen.de **Web site:** http://www.verlag-modernes-lernen.de
Freq: Quarterly; **Annual Sub.:** EUR 32,00; **Circ:** 3,921
Editor: Kerstin Weingarten; **Advertising Manager:** Gudrun Luck
Profile: Magazine on psychomotorics.
Language(s): German
ADVERTISING RATES:
Full Page Mono .... EUR 570
Full Page Colour .... EUR 656
Mechanical Data: Type Area: 252 x 171 mm, No. of Columns (Display): 4, Col Widths (Display): 38 mm
Copy instructions: *Copy Date:* 28 days prior to publication
BUSINESS: HEALTH & MEDICAL: Health Medical Related

PRAXIS DEUTSCH 739328G62B-2240
Editorial: Im Brande 17, 30926 SEELZE
Tel: 511 400040 **Fax:** 511 40004219
Email: redaktion.pd@friedrich-verlag.de **Web site:** http://www.praxis-deutsch.de
Freq: 6 issues yearly; **Annual Sub.:** EUR 57,94; **Circ:** 11,400
Editor: Katharina Reich; **Advertising Manager:** Bernd Schrader
Profile: Competent German lessons at the cutting edge. The leading magazine for the German language lessons offers a wealth of good texts and innovative materials for your classes. With the image and text documents, spreadsheets, slides and material cards you can put the students nearby flexible teaching ideas. With Praxis Deutsch, you always know what issues are important and how good German lessons is made. Experienced teachers and specialists from the training and education show how to do it. The team of renowned editors consists all the emphasis and checked on teaching ideas carefully to its practicability. This gives you the security you need in the school day.
Language(s): German
ADVERTISING RATES:
Full Page Mono .... EUR 2320
Full Page Colour .... EUR 2320
Mechanical Data: Type Area: 256 x 187 mm
Copy instructions: *Copy Date:* 35 days prior to publication
Supplement(s): bildung+medien; bildung+reisen; bildung+science
BUSINESS: CHURCH & SCHOOL EQUIPMENT & EDUCATION: Education Teachers

PRAXIS ERGOTHERAPIE 739330G56R-1840
Editorial: Schleefstr. 14, 44287 DORTMUND
Tel: 231 128008 **Fax:** 231 128009
Email: redaktion@verlag-modernes-lernen.de **Web site:** http://www.verlag-modernes-lernen.de
Freq: 6 issues yearly; **Annual Sub.:** EUR 34,00; **Circ:** 5,347
Editor: Dorothea Becker; **Advertising Manager:** Gudrun Luck
Profile: Magazine on ergotherapy.
Language(s): German
ADVERTISING RATES:
Full Page Mono .... EUR 640
Full Page Colour .... EUR 736
Mechanical Data: Type Area: 252 x 171 mm, No. of Columns (Display): 4, Col Widths (Display): 38 mm
Copy instructions: *Copy Date:* 28 days prior to publication
BUSINESS: HEALTH & MEDICAL: Health Medical Related

PRAXIS FREMDSPRACHENUNTERRICHT 727973G62B-820
Editorial: Rosenheimer Str. 145, 81671 MÜNCHEN
Tel: 89 450510 **Fax:** 89 45051310
Email: holler@oldenbourg.de **Web site:** http://www.praxis-fremdsprachenunterricht.de
Freq: 6 issues yearly; **Annual Sub.:** EUR 64,90; **Circ:** 3,980
Editor: Stefan Holler; **Advertising Manager:** Christian Schwarzbauer
Profile: Publication about the teaching of foreign languages.
Language(s): English; French; German; Russian
ADVERTISING RATES:
Full Page Mono .... EUR 815
Full Page Colour .... EUR 1305
Mechanical Data: Type Area: 260 x 184 mm
Copy instructions: *Copy Date:* 35 days prior to publication
BUSINESS: CHURCH & SCHOOL EQUIPMENT & EDUCATION: Education Teachers

PRAXIS GEOGRAPHIE 739331G62B-2260
Editorial: Georg-Westermann-Allee 66, 38104 BRAUNSCHWEIG **Tel:** 531 708388 **Fax:** 531 708374
Email: pg@westermann.de **Web site:** http://www.praxisgeographie.de
Freq: 11 issues yearly; **Annual Sub.:** EUR 100,10; **Circ:** 10,000
Editor: Peter Just; **Advertising Manager:** Peter Kniep
Profile: Magazine providing practical advice concerning the teaching of geography, including suggested sample worksheets.
Language(s): German
Readership: Aimed at Geography teachers.
ADVERTISING RATES:
Full Page Mono .... EUR 1200
Full Page Colour .... EUR 1920
Mechanical Data: No. of Columns (Display): 4, Col Widths (Display): 43 mm, Type Area: 264 x 185 mm
Copy instructions: *Copy Date:* 49 days prior to publication
BUSINESS: CHURCH & SCHOOL EQUIPMENT & EDUCATION: Education Teachers

PRAXIS GESCHICHTE 739332G62B-2280
Editorial: Georg-Westermann-Allee 66, 38104 BRAUNSCHWEIG **Tel:** 531 708383 **Fax:** 531 708374
Email: pgs@westermann.de **Web site:** http://www.praxisgeschichte.de
Freq: 6 issues yearly; **Annual Sub.:** EUR 54,60; **Circ:** 10,000
Editor: Florian Cebulla
Profile: Magazine providing information about the teaching of history, including photocopiable teaching material.
Language(s): German
Readership: Aimed at history teachers.
ADVERTISING RATES:
Full Page Mono .... EUR 1200
Full Page Colour .... EUR 1920
Mechanical Data: No. of Columns (Display): 4, Col Widths (Display): 43 mm, Type Area: 264 x 185 mm
Copy instructions: *Copy Date:* 49 days prior to publication
BUSINESS: CHURCH & SCHOOL EQUIPMENT & EDUCATION: Education Teachers

PRAXIS GRUNDSCHULE 739333G62C-22
Editorial: Georg-Westermann-Allee 66, 38104 BRAUNSCHWEIG **Tel:** 531 708382 **Fax:** 531 708374
Email: pgru@westermann.de **Web site:** http://www.praxisgrundschule.de
Freq: 6 issues yearly; **Annual Sub.:** EUR 62,40; **Circ:** 22,000
Editor: Katrin Bokemeyer; **Advertising Manager:** Peter Kniep
Profile: Magazine for primary school teachers, students and junior faculty.
Language(s): German
ADVERTISING RATES:
Full Page Mono .... EUR 3100
Full Page Colour .... EUR 4960
Mechanical Data: No. of Columns (Display): 4, Col Widths (Display): 43 mm, Type Area: 264 x 185 mm
Copy instructions: *Copy Date:* 49 days prior to publication
BUSINESS: CHURCH & SCHOOL EQUIPMENT & EDUCATION: Junior Education

PRAXIS KLINISCHE VERHALTENSMEDIZIN UND REHABILITATION 739348G56A-8540
Editorial: Lange Koppel 10, 24248 MÖNKEBERG
Email: mzielke@ahg.de **Web site:** http://www.psychologie-aktuell.com/pkv
Freq: Quarterly; **Annual Sub.:** EUR 49,00; **Circ:** 980
Editor: Manfred Zielke; **Advertising Manager:** Wolfgang Pabst
Profile: Magazine about clinical behaviour medicine and rehabilitation.
Language(s): German
ADVERTISING RATES:
Full Page Mono .... EUR 500
Mechanical Data: Type Area: 265 x 180 mm, No. of Columns (Display): 3, Col Widths (Display): 55 mm
Copy instructions: *Copy Date:* 42 days prior to publication

PRAXIS MAGAZIN 729965G56A-4720
Editorial: Gewerbestr. 9, 79219 STAUFEN
Tel: 7633 933200 **Fax:** 7633 9332020
Email: praxismagazin@pacs-online.com **Web site:** http://www.pacs-online.com
Freq: 10 issues yearly; **Annual Sub.:** EUR 31,00; **Circ:** 9,900

Editor: Rolf-Günther Sommer; **Advertising Manager:** Christoph Knüttel
Profile: Magazine about homeopathy and natural healing.
Language(s): German
ADVERTISING RATES:
Full Page Mono .... EUR 1844
Full Page Colour .... EUR 2870
Mechanical Data: Type Area: 268 x 187 mm, No. of Columns (Display): 3, Col Widths (Display): 53 mm
Copy instructions: *Copy Date:* 36 days prior to publication

PRAXIS SCHULE 5-10

739362G62C-23
Editorial: Kolbstr. 28, 44269 DORTMUND
Tel: 231 5345906 **Fax:** 231 5345939
Email: luga@redaktionsbuero-education.de **Web site:** http://www.praxisschule.de
Freq: 6 issues yearly; **Annual Sub.:** EUR 54,60; **Circ:** 3,500
Editor: Jürgen Luga
Profile: Magazine providing practical information about teaching children aged 10 to 16 years. Focuses particularly on Maths, German and English, including teaching material.
Language(s): German
Readership: Aimed at teachers of the secondary schools.
ADVERTISING RATES:
Full Page Mono .... EUR 950
Full Page Colour .... EUR 1520
Mechanical Data: No. of Columns (Display): 4, Col Widths (Display): 43 mm, Type Area: 264 x 185 mm
Copy instructions: *Copy Date:* 49 days prior to publication
BUSINESS: CHURCH & SCHOOL EQUIPMENT & EDUCATION: Junior Education

PRAXISCHECK

1606207G4E-6900
Editorial: Römerstr. 4, 86438 KISSING
Tel: 8233 2304001 **Fax:** 8233 237400
Email: emre.onur@weka.de **Web site:** http://www.weka-praxis-check.de
Freq: Quarterly; **Annual Sub.:** EUR 60,00; **Circ:** 3,765
Editor: Emre Onur
Profile: Magazine for architects and engineers on planning and managing building projects.
Language(s): German
ADVERTISING RATES:
Full Page Mono .... EUR 1700
Full Page Colour .... EUR 1700
Mechanical Data: No. of Columns (Display): 3, Col Widths (Display): 54 mm, Type Area: 267 x 178 mm

PRAXIS-DEPESCHE

739317G56A-8500
Editorial: Paul-Wassermann-Str. 15, 81829 MÜNCHEN **Tel:** 89 436630230 **Fax:** 89 436630211
Email: ehnert@gfi-online.de **Web site:** http://www.gfi-medien.de
Freq: Monthly; **Annual Sub.:** EUR 36,00; **Circ:** 53,937
Editor: Wilfried Ehnert
Profile: Publication containing information on diagnosis and therapy.
Language(s): German
Readership: Aimed at general practitioners.
ADVERTISING RATES:
Full Page Mono .... EUR 3510
Full Page Colour .... EUR 4940
Mechanical Data: Type Area: 258 x 187 mm, No. of Columns (Display): 3, Col Widths (Display): 59 mm
Copy instructions: *Copy Date:* 21 days prior to publication
BUSINESS: HEALTH & MEDICAL

PREDPRINIMATEL

1978900G14A-10413
Editorial: Koblenzer Str. 97, 32584 LÖHNE
Tel: 5731 981040 **Fax:** 5731 6641009
Email: post@bem-media.de **Web site:** http://www.predprinimatel.de
Freq: Monthly; **Circ:** 2,000
Profile: Russian language newspaper for Germany.
Language(s): Russian
ADVERTISING RATES:
Full Page Mono .... EUR 1039
Full Page Colour .... EUR 1039
Mechanical Data: Type Area: 297 x 210 mm

PREMEDIA NEWSLETTER

1829451G2A-5759
Editorial: Adalbert-Seifriz-Str. 53, 69151 NECKARGEMÜND **Tel:** 6223 74757 **Fax:** 6223 74139
Email: karl.malik@premedianewsletter.de **Web site:** http://www.premedianewsletter.de
Freq: Monthly; **Annual Sub.:** EUR 186,00; **Circ:** 6,390
Editor: Karl Malik
Profile: Newsletter about marketing, management, international media markets.
Language(s): German
ADVERTISING RATES:
Full Page Mono .... EUR 1447
Full Page Colour .... EUR 2980
Mechanical Data: Type Area: 275 x 185 mm, No. of Columns (Display): 3, Col Widths (Display): 57 mm
Copy instructions: *Copy Date:* 4 days prior to publication

PREMIUS

1994805G74M-958
Editorial: Ölmühle 9, 20357 HAMBURG
Tel: 40 18086753
Email: redaktion@premius-online.de **Web site:** http://www.premius-online.de
Freq: Quarterly; **Cover Price:** EUR 2,00; **Circ:** 100,000
Editor: Andreas Busch
Profile: Magazine for sophisticated, rational consumers with buying interest in tests and investigations for the price and quality of products and services.
Language(s): German
ADVERTISING RATES:
Full Page Mono .... EUR 9900
Full Page Colour .... EUR 9900
Mechanical Data: Type Area: 260 x 190 mm

PRENZLAUER BERG KOMPAKT

1898583G74M-890
Editorial: Bundesallee 23, 10717 BERLIN
Tel: 30 863030 **Fax:** 30 86303200
Email: info@bfb.de **Web site:** http://www.bfb.de
Freq: Annual; **Cover Price:** Free; **Circ:** 96,000
Profile: Industry district magazine. The core of this handy reference book is neatly sorted according to different themes of industry. Here you will find a plethora of vendors from the neighborhood. In preparation to the respective subject area raises a company, in an interview. To know your environment better, we present in the district windows, etc. beautiful places, monuments, museums, etc. For better orientation in the neighborhood also an integrated neighborhood with street plan is register. Furthermore, the county information you provide an overview of important phone numbers and agencies in your neighborhood.
Language(s): German
Mechanical Data: Type Area: 185 x 126 mm

PREPRESS WORLD OF PRINT

739400G41A-74
Editorial: Freiligrathring 18, 40878 RATINGEN
Tel: 2102 20270 **Fax:** 2102 202790
Email: info@worldofprint.de **Web site:** http://www.worldofprint.de
Freq: 10 issues yearly; **Annual Sub.:** EUR 50,00; **Circ:** 11,374
Editor: Daniela Blömer; **Advertising Manager:** Oliver Göpfert
Profile: Magazine containing information about graphic arts and publishing.
Language(s): German
Readership: Read by graphic designers and publishers.
ADVERTISING RATES:
Full Page Colour .... EUR 4992
Mechanical Data: Type Area: 253 x 180 mm, No. of Columns (Display): 3, Col Widths (Display): 56 mm
Copy instructions: *Copy Date:* 14 days prior to publication
BUSINESS: PRINTING & STATIONERY: Printing

PRESSE REPORT

739407G60C-20
Editorial: Nebendahlstr. 16, 22041 HAMBURG
Tel: 40 6090080 **Fax:** 40 60900988
Email: ralf.deppe@presse-fachverlag.de **Web site:** http://www.presse-fachverlag.de
Freq: Monthly; **Annual Sub.:** EUR 33,60; **Circ:** 47,096
Editor: Ralf Deppe; **Advertising Manager:** Lars Lücke
Profile: Magazine for the press wholesale trade.
Language(s): German
ADVERTISING RATES:
Full Page Mono .... EUR 5225
Full Page Colour .... EUR 5225
Mechanical Data: No. of Columns (Display): 3, Col Widths (Display): 55 mm, Type Area: 262 x 175 mm
BUSINESS: PUBLISHING: Newsagents

PRESSESPRECHER

1639754G2A-5537
Editorial: Werderscher Markt 13, 10117 BERLIN
Tel: 30 848590 **Fax:** 30 84859200
Email: sg@pressesprecher.com **Web site:** http://www.pressesprecher.com
Freq: 10 issues yearly; **Annual Sub.:** EUR 120,00; **Circ:** 8,000
Editor: Sebastian Gülde; **Advertising Manager:** Norman Wittig
Profile: Magazine for public relations and communications for press officers and communication departments in companies, associations and institutions Twitter: http://twitter.com/#!/pressesprecher.
Language(s): German
ADVERTISING RATES:
Full Page Mono .... EUR 4600
Full Page Colour .... EUR 4600
Mechanical Data: Type Area: 257 x 180 mm, No. of Columns (Display): 4, Col Widths (Display): 40 mm
Copy instructions: *Copy Date:* 16 days prior to publication

PRIGNITZ EXPRESS

739428G72-10572
Editorial: Berliner Str. 1, 19348 PERLEBERG
Tel: 3876 79958280 **Fax:** 3876 79958285
Email: prignitz-express@prignitzer.de
Freq: Weekly; **Cover Price:** Free; **Circ:** 33,849
Editor: Marina Lenth; **Advertising Manager:** Dagmar Albertsen
Profile: Advertising journal (house-to-house) concentrating on local stories.
Language(s): German
ADVERTISING RATES:
Full Page Mono .... EUR 2420
Full Page Colour .... EUR 3159
Mechanical Data: Type Area: 480 x 325 mm, No. of Columns (Display): 7, Col Widths (Display): 45 mm
Copy instructions: *Copy Date:* 3 days prior to publication
LOCAL NEWSPAPERS

DER PRIGNITZER

739427G67B-11860
Editorial: Gutenbergstr. 1, 19061 SCHWERIN
Tel: 385 63780 **Fax:** 385 3975140
Email: redaktion@svz.de **Web site:** http://www.svz.de
Freq: 312 issues yearly; **Circ:** 10,555
Advertising Manager: Dagmar Albertsen
Profile: Daily newspaper with regional news and a local sports section. This Outlet offers RSS (Really Simple Syndication).
Language(s): German
ADVERTISING RATES:
SCC .... EUR 64,50
Mechanical Data: Type Area: 480 x 325 mm, No. of Columns (Display): 7, Col Widths (Display): 45 mm
Copy instructions: *Copy Date:* 1 day prior to publication
Supplement(s): prisma
REGIONAL DAILY & SUNDAY NEWSPAPERS: Regional Daily Newspapers

PRIMUS RIND

1793293G21A-4352
Editorial: Lothstr. 29, 80797 MÜNCHEN
Tel: 89 12705294 **Fax:** 89 12705546
Email: reddlz@dlv.de **Web site:** http://www.dlz-agrarmagazin.de
Freq: Monthly; **Annual Sub.:** EUR 81,50; **Circ:** 32,369
Editor: Maren Diersing-Espenhorst; **Advertising Manager:** Thomas Herrmann
Profile: primus rind is the supplementary Expert Information Supplement in dlz agrarmagazin for specialized - and growth companies in the dairy and meat production. Performance-oriented production, animal health management with qualified national and international competition orientation is the concept of professional editorial primus rind. Distribution areas are the core regions of the German milk and meat production. dlz primus bark is almost exclusively to subscribers to the paid dlz agrarmagazin.
Language(s): German
ADVERTISING RATES:
Full Page Mono .... EUR 2750
Full Page Colour .... EUR 4370
Mechanical Data: Type Area: 267 x 175 mm, No. of Columns (Display): 4, Col Widths (Display): 40 mm
Copy instructions: *Copy Date:* 24 days prior to publication
Supplement to: dlz agrarmagazin

PRIMUS SCHWEIN

1793294G21A-4353
Editorial: Lothstr. 29, 80797 MÜNCHEN
Tel: 89 12705294 **Fax:** 89 12705546
Email: reddlz@dlv.de **Web site:** http://www.dlz-agrarmagazin.de
Freq: Monthly; **Annual Sub.:** EUR 81,50; **Circ:** 21,500
Editor: Uwe Bräunig; **Advertising Manager:** Thomas Herrmann
Profile: Agricultural journal covering management production and technology.
Language(s): German
ADVERTISING RATES:
Full Page Mono .... EUR 2560
Full Page Colour .... EUR 4140
Mechanical Data: Type Area: 267 x 175 mm, No. of Columns (Display): 4, Col Widths (Display): 40 mm
Copy instructions: *Copy Date:* 24 days prior to publication
Supplement to: dlz agrarmagazin

PRINT & PRODUKTION

739444G41A-1800
Editorial: Geheimrat-Hummel-Platz 4, 65239 HOCHHEIM **Tel:** 6146 605102 **Fax:** 6146 605204
Email: redaktion@print-und-produktion.de **Web site:** http://www.print-und-produktion.de
Freq: 10 issues yearly; **Annual Sub.:** EUR 53,50; **Circ:** 10,484
Editor: Alexander Bötel; **Advertising Manager:** Magda Lehmann
Profile: Magazine containing articles about all aspects of the printing and production business.
Language(s): German
Readership: Aimed at typesetters, reproduction company employees and producers in advertising agencies and publishing companies.
ADVERTISING RATES:
Full Page Mono .... EUR 3700
Full Page Colour .... EUR 4900
Mechanical Data: Type Area: 290 x 220 mm, No. of Columns (Display): 5, Col Widths (Display): 40 mm
Copy instructions: *Copy Date:* 11 days prior to publication
Official Journal of: Organ d. EWPA, d. Digicom e.V. u. d. Arbeitskreis Prägefolien e.V.
BUSINESS: PRINTING & STATIONERY: Printing

PRINT.DE

1621897G41A-2144
Editorial: Riedstr. 25, 73760 OSTFILDERN
Tel: 711 4481720 **Fax:** 711 442099
Email: b.niemela@print.de **Web site:** http://www.print.de
Freq: Daily; **Cover Price:** Paid; **Circ:** 111,167 Unique Users
Editor: Bernhard Niemela
Profile: Ezine: www.print.de (formerly www.publish.de) is convincing thanks to a selection of information that's chosen especially for executives in the entire printing industry, in advertising and marketing departments, and in production and advertising agencies. print.de not only offers all business-relevant specialized information about pre-printing, printing and post-processing, we also offer exclusive and comprehensive research options. Whether it's gigantic full-text research in our online archive, the huge job market of the printing industry, extensive overviews of the market, a detailed index of suppliers or special dossiers: in each case, users will find high-quality content in every form, prepared and evaluated, and accompanied by commentaries written by a team of renowned journalists and authors. Facebook: http://www.facebook.com/print.de Twitter: http://twitter.com/#!/print_de.
Language(s): German
BUSINESS: PRINTING & STATIONERY: Printing

PRINZ

739448G80-9180
Editorial: Poßmoorweg 2, 22301 HAMBURG
Tel: 40 27171450 **Fax:** 40 27171490
Email: redaktion@prinz.de **Web site:** http://www.prinz.de
Freq: Monthly; **Circ:** 38,254
Editor: Jörg Schumacher; **Advertising Manager:** Sönke Grahl
Profile: Prinz (issue Hamburg) is the magazine for city living. Prinz is based around a unique concept: it combines an urban attitude to life with region-specific tips and information. Prinz is a monthly magazine, read by people across Germany, which celebrates the heroes, ideas and personalities of 13 German cities. Prinz combines a high-class journalistic concept with a unique service brief, and hits the right notes with 20–40-something urbanites both in its content and on an emotional level. Prinz expresses opinions, gives ratings and creates classifications. It offers its readers context and guidance through the multitude of possibilities in Germany's cities. Prinz presents its readers with a fresh perspective on contemporary issues and paints them a portrait of urban lifestyle in sections entitled Report, Music, Party, Film, Fashion, Beauty, Design, Technology, Motoring and Travel.
Language(s): German
ADVERTISING RATES:
Full Page Mono .... EUR 2350
Full Page Colour .... EUR 3690
Mechanical Data: Type Area: 201 x 146 mm
CONSUMER: RURAL & REGIONAL INTEREST

PRISMA

739457G67B-20_500
Editorial: Stolkgasse 25, 50667 KÖLN
Tel: 221 1632631 **Fax:** 221 1632636
Email: info@prisma-redaktion.de **Web site:** http://www.prisma.de
Freq: Weekly; **Cover Price:** Free; **Circ:** 4,047,018
Editor: Detlef Hartlap
Profile: TV supplement to more than 50 Trägerzeitungen.Woche week prism provides for his readers a special target group topic at the center of the editors. And a clear recycled TV program gives many good tips prism million households in the coveted regular place on the TV.
Language(s): German
ADVERTISING RATES:
Full Page Mono .... EUR 45756
Full Page Colour .... EUR 59159
Mechanical Data: Type Area: 242 x 193 mm, No. of Columns (Display): 4, Col Widths (Display): 46 mm
Copy instructions: *Copy Date:* 21 days prior to publication
Supplement to: Aachener Nachrichten, Aachener Zeitung, Ahlener Tageblatt, Ahlener Zeitung, Allgemeiner Anzeiger, Allgemeine Zeitung, Altenaer Kreisblatt, Bergische Landeszeitung, Berliner Morgenpost, Billerbecker Anzeiger, Bocholter Borkener Volksblatt, Börde Volksstimme, Bonner Rundschau, Borkener Zeitung, Braunschweiger Zeitung, Burger Volksstimme, B.Z., Dattelner Morgenpost, Döbelner Allgemeine Zeitung, Dorstener Zeitung, Dresdner Neueste Nachrichten, Dülmener Zeitung, Dürener Nachrichten, Dürener Zeitung, Eifeler Nachrichten, Eifeler Zeitung, Emsdettener Volkszeitung, Eschweiler Nachrichten, Eschweiler Zeitung, Gardelegener Volksstimme, Geilenkirchener Zeitung, General-Anzeiger, Genthiner Volksstimme, Gescherer Zeitung, Geseker Zeitung, Die Glocke, Goslarsche Zeitung, Halberstädter Volksstimme, Haldensleber Volksstimme, Halterner Zeitung, Harzer Volksstimme, Havelberger Volksstimme, Heinsberger Nachrichten, Heinsberger Zeitung, Hellweger Anzeiger, Hertener Allgemeine, Ibbenbürener Volkszeitung, Jülicher Nachrichten, Jülicher Zeitung, Klötzer Volksstimme, Kölner Stadt-Anzeiger, Kölnische Rundschau, Leipziger Volkszeitung, Leverkusener Anzeiger, Lüdenscheider Nachrichten, Märkische Allgemeine, Märkische Oderzeitung, Magdeburger Volksstimme, Marler Zeitung, Meinerzhagener Zeitung, Mindener Tageblatt, Mitteldeutsche Zeitung, Münsterländische Volkszeitung, Münstersche Zeitung, Norddeutsche Neueste Nachrichten, Nordkurier, Oberbergischer Anzeiger, Oberbergische Volkszeitung, Oschatzer Allgemeine, Osterburger Volksstimme, Osterländer Volkszeitung, Der Patriot, Der Prignitzer, Recklinghäuser Zeitung, Rheinische Post, Rhein-Sieg-Anzeiger, Rhein-Sieg Rundschau, Rhön- und Streubote, Ruhr Nachrichten, Salzgitter-Zeitung, Salzwedeler Volksstimme, Schönebecker Volksstimme, Schweriner Volkszeitung, Siegener Zeitung, Soester Anzeiger, Staßfurter Volksstimme, Steinfurter Kreisblatt, Stendaler Volksstimme, Stimberg Zeitung, Stolberger Nachrichten, Stolberger Zeitung, Süderländer Tageblatt, Süderländer Volksfreund, Tageblatt für den Kreis Steinfurt, Trierischer Volksfreund, Uckermark Kurier, Usedom Kurier, Vlothoer Anzeiger, Waltroper Zeitung,

Germany

Wermelskirchener General-Anzeiger, Westdeutsche Zeitung, Westfälische Nachrichten, Westfälischer Anzeiger, Westfalen-Blatt, Wolfsburger Nachrichten, WZ Bergischer Volksbote, Zerbster Volksstimme
REGIONAL DAILY & SUNDAY NEWSPAPERS: Regional Daily Newspapers

PRIVATE WEALTH 1832714G73-641
Editorial: Südliche Auffahrtsallee 29, 80639 MÜNCHEN **Tel:** 89 25543916 **Fax:** 89 25542971
Email: km@private-wealth.de **Web site:** http://www.private-wealth.de
Freq: Quarterly; **Cover Price:** EUR 15,00; **Circ:** 20,000
Editor: Klaus Meitinger
Profile: The magazine is the only premium magazine combines business expertise with all facets of the sophisticated lifestyle in one concept. The editorial reports on major companies and their success stories. She introduces advanced management ideas and objectively analyzed the smartest investment strategies. It provides suggestions for an enjoyable life in prosperity - exclusive destinations and hotels, the most beautiful cars, boats and shares. And it is dedicated to the topics of charity, education and health.
Language(s): German
ADVERTISING RATES:
Full Page Mono .... EUR 11100
Full Page Colour .... EUR 11100
Mechanical Data: Type Area: 285 x 217 mm
Copy instructions: *Copy Date:* 42 days prior to publication

PRO 739484G2A-3980
Editorial: Steinbühlstr. 3, 35578 WETZLAR
Tel: 6441 915156 **Fax:** 6441 915157
Email: dippel@pro-medienmagazin.de **Web site:** http://www.pro-medienmagazin.de
Freq: 6 issues yearly; **Cover Price:** Free; **Circ:** 74,000
Editor: Andreas Dippel; **Advertising Manager:** Christoph Görlach
Profile: Christian magazine about media with reports, portraits and interviews on current issues from society, culture, politics and church.
Language(s): German
ADVERTISING RATES:
Full Page Mono .... EUR 1890
Full Page Colour .... EUR 2100
Mechanical Data: Type Area: 250 x 177 mm, No. of Columns (Display): 3, Col Widths (Display): 55 mm
Supplement(s): Israelreport

PRO-4-PRO 1864623G14A-10233
Editorial: Rößlerstr. 90, 64293 DARMSTADT
Tel: 6151 8090162 **Fax:** 6151 8090183
Email: peter.ebert@wiley.com **Web site:** http://www.pro-4-pro.com
Freq: Annual; **Circ:** 30,000
Editor: Peter Ebert; **Advertising Manager:** Peter Ebert
Profile: Every year the same question: to be invested now in print advertising budget (= display) or on the Internet? The special edition PRO-4-PRO (messtec drives automation 7-8/10) makes you the answer: do both simultaneously! The annual summer special edition is published with a circulation of 30,000 copies a "best of" of the GIT Online industry portal PRO-4-PRO ("Products for Professionals"). In cooperation with the magazines and INSPECT GIT SECURITY + MANAGEMENT We provide the readers the latest products from the fields of automation, sensors, inspection methods and measurement technology in the form of PR / text ads before. The layout and the text of your ad takes care of the GIT. All products that are published in PRO-4-PRO appear simultaneously for a year on www.pro-4-pro.com/msr.
Language(s): German
ADVERTISING RATES:
Full Page Mono .... EUR 3560
Full Page Colour .... EUR 3560
Mechanical Data: Type Area: 260 x 185 mm, No. of Columns (Display): 4, Col Widths (Display): 43 mm
Copy instructions: *Copy Date:* 14 days prior to publication

PRO ALTER 739485G56B-1300
Editorial: An der Pauluskirche 3, 50677 KÖLN
Tel: 221 9318410 **Fax:** 221 9318476
Email: proalter@kda.de **Web site:** http://www.proalter.de
Freq: 6 issues yearly; **Annual Sub.:** EUR 29,90; **Circ:** 6,000
Editor: Peter Michell-Auli; **Advertising Manager:** Simone Helck
Profile: Magazine for the professional, voluntary and private work with seniors, elderly care, elderly care with all relevant information. With reports, features, interviews and commentary on important and topical questions about age and aging.
Language(s): German
Readership: Read by nursing staff.
ADVERTISING RATES:
Full Page Colour .... EUR 3500
Mechanical Data: Type Area: 264 x 177 mm
BUSINESS: HEALTH & MEDICAL: Nursing

PRO FAMILIA MAGAZIN 739543G74C-2840
Editorial: Stresemannallee 3, 60596 FRANKFURT
Tel: 69 639002 **Fax:** 69 639852
Email: magazin@profamilia.de **Web site:** http://www.profamilia.de
Freq: Quarterly; Free to qualifying individuals
Annual Sub.: EUR 19,50; **Circ:** 7,500
Profile: Magazine about sexual pedagogy and family planning.
Language(s): German
ADVERTISING RATES:
Full Page Mono .... EUR 1015
Full Page Colour .... EUR 1735
Mechanical Data: Type Area: 245 x 180 mm, No. of Columns (Display): 3, Col Widths (Display): 55 mm
Copy instructions: *Copy Date:* 30 days prior to publication
CONSUMER: WOMEN'S INTEREST CONSUMER MAGAZINES: Home & Family

PRO FERTIG HAUS 739544G79A-150
Editorial: Höhenstr. 17, 70736 FELLBACH
Tel: 711 5206228 **Fax:** 711 5206300
Email: pro-fertighaus@fachschriften.de **Web site:** http://www.bautipps.de
Freq: 6 issues yearly; **Cover Price:** EUR 1,50; **Circ:** 37,658
Editor: Harald Fritsche; **Advertising Manager:** Barbara Hoof
Profile: Magazine about practical DIY and building and maintaining a home.
Language(s): German
Readership: Aimed at homeowners and housebuilders, architects and planners.
ADVERTISING RATES:
Full Page Colour .... EUR 9550
Mechanical Data: Type Area: 247 x 187 mm, No. of Columns (Display): 4, Col Widths (Display): 43 mm
Copy instructions: *Copy Date:* 40 days prior to publication
Supplement(s): baugui.de; mein Holzhaus
CONSUMER: HOBBIES & DIY

PRO MEDIA 739636G2A-4000
Editorial: Greifswalder Str. 38, 12623 BERLIN
Tel: 30 56301618 **Fax:** 30 56301619
Email: promediabb@t-online.de **Web site:** http://www.promedia-berlin.de
Freq: Monthly; **Annual Sub.:** EUR 222,00; **Circ:** 2,200
Editor: Helmut Hartung
Profile: Media service for the regions of Berlin and Brandenburg.
Language(s): German
ADVERTISING RATES:
Full Page Mono .... EUR 900
Full Page Colour .... EUR 1300
Mechanical Data: Type Area: 258 x 180 mm

PRO MOBIL 739642G91B-50
Editorial: Leuschnerstr. 1, 70174 STUTTGART
Tel: 711 1822471 **Fax:** 711 1822479
Email: redaktion@promobil.de **Web site:** http://www.promobil.de
Freq: Monthly; **Annual Sub.:** EUR 41,00; **Circ:** 76,786
Editor: Kai Feyerabend; **Advertising Manager:** Peter Steinbach
Profile: Magazine about mobile homes. The magazine focuses on vehicles and accessory tests as well as the latest additions to all parts of RV sector - from leisure-mobile to luxury liners. Authentic travel reports and extremely useful pratical tips are just as much a part of the pro mobil repertoire as reader-focused service topics, news from the RV-site scene and a very popular, in-depth collectable reference section. pro mobil tests are respected for their sound expertise and high credibility, for the pro mobil editors are acknowledged and accredited experts. The new product presentations alsways represent the latest developments and are often covered exclusively. The specific mix and variety of topics mke the magazine both an essential buyer's guide and an opinion leader that shapes the market. pro mobil readers like to travel flexibly and independently. They are particularly active motor home users and the motor home is an integral part of their life. They also take on the role of opinion leaders and are important sources of information for others. They enjoy traveling and do so frequently. In their travels they also often actively participate in sports. Their well over average income allows them to be generous consumers. Twitter: http://twitter.com/promobil This Outlet offers RSS (Really Simple Syndication).
Language(s): German
ADVERTISING RATES:
Full Page Mono .... EUR 5220
Full Page Colour .... EUR 8330
Mechanical Data: Type Area: 248 x 185 mm, No. of Columns (Display): 4, Col Widths (Display): 43 mm
Copy instructions: *Copy Date:* 28 days prior to publication
CONSUMER: RECREATION & LEISURE: Camping & Caravanning

PRO RUHRGEBIET 1659903G14A-9648
Editorial: Semperstr. 51, 45138 ESSEN
Tel: 201 8941523 **Fax:** 201 8941510
Email: info@proruhrgebiet.de **Web site:** http://www.proruhrgebiet.de
Freq: Quarterly; **Circ:** 2,000
Profile: Magazine of the Pro Ruhrgebiet Association.
Language(s): German

PROCESS 739496G13-1960
Editorial: Max-Planck-Str. 7, 97082 WÜRZBURG
Tel: 931 4182536 **Fax:** 931 4182750
Email: gerd.kielburger@vogel.de **Web site:** http://www.process.de
Freq: Monthly; **Annual Sub.:** EUR 87,00; **Circ:** 24,098
Editor: Gerd Kielburger; **Advertising Manager:** Reiner Öttinger
Profile: Process is the trade magazine for the community of specialist and management personnel in the chemicals, pharmaceuticals and process engineering sectors in all areas of the process industry – and opens up the path to further information channels. It thereby highlights technical aspects and the life cycle of components, systems, procedures and systems, including complete services - from use in the pilot plant to production. This includes the latest industry information as well as product innovations, technological developments and especially their specific usefulness for business practice. The magazine supports the discussion on technical trends and developments in the industry, to provide necessary background information, and so promote dialogue between producers and users in the process industry. Audience: engineers and technicians, professionals and executives in the chemical and pharmaceutical, oil and gas industry, biotechnology and water and wastewater sector. Twitter: http://twitter.com/Process_de This Outlet offers RSS (Really Simple Syndication).
Language(s): German
Readership: Read by process engineers and managers.
ADVERTISING RATES:
Full Page Mono .... EUR 5845
Full Page Colour .... EUR 7230
Mechanical Data: Type Area: 270 x 190 mm, No. of Columns (Display): 4, Col Widths (Display): 46 mm
Copy instructions: *Copy Date:* 21 days prior to publication
BUSINESS: CHEMICALS

PROCONTRA 1808709G1F-1711
Editorial: Schumannstr. 17, 10117 BERLIN
Tel: 30 21960830 **Fax:** 30 21960832
Email: redaktion@alsterspree-verlag.de **Web site:** http://www.procontra-online.de
Freq: 6 issues yearly; **Annual Sub.:** EUR 20,00; **Circ:** 40,600
Editor: Philipp B. Siebert; **Advertising Manager:** Daniel Ravensberger
Profile: Trade journal for financial professionals. The aim of the procontra is founded trends, developments, products and markets the industry's controversial, analytical and journalistic prepare. The readers use Is procontra information source and guide for their daily consulting work. The independent report provides readers with a trusted view of moods, Opinions and products of the financial services market. Facebook: http://www.facebook.com/procontra Twitter: http://twitter.com/#!/procontra_mag.
Language(s): German
ADVERTISING RATES:
Full Page Mono .... EUR 7100
Full Page Colour .... EUR 7100
Mechanical Data: Type Area: 228 x 187 mm
Copy instructions: *Copy Date:* 28 days prior to publication

PROCONTRA 1808709G1F-1818
Editorial: Schumannstr. 17, 10117 BERLIN
Tel: 30 21960830 **Fax:** 30 21960832
Email: redaktion@alsterspree-verlag.de **Web site:** http://www.procontra-online.de
Freq: 6 issues yearly; **Annual Sub.:** EUR 20,00; **Circ:** 40,600
Editor: Philipp B. Siebert; **Advertising Manager:** Daniel Ravensberger
Profile: Trade journal for financial professionals. The aim of the procontra is founded trends, developments, products and markets the industry's controversial, analytical and journalistic prepare. The readers use Is procontra information source and guide for their daily consulting work. The independent report provides readers with a trusted view of moods, Opinions and products of the financial services market. Facebook: http://www.facebook.com/procontra Twitter: http://twitter.com/#!/procontra_mag.
Language(s): German
ADVERTISING RATES:
Full Page Mono .... EUR 7100
Full Page Colour .... EUR 7100
Mechanical Data: Type Area: 228 x 187 mm
Copy instructions: *Copy Date:* 28 days prior to publication

PRODIALOG 1622930G56A-11254
Editorial: Aschauer Str. 30, 81549 MÜNCHEN
Tel: 89 2030431300 **Fax:** 89 2030431399
Email: carin.szostecki@springer.com **Web site:** http://www.springermedizin.de
Freq: Monthly; **Circ:** 61,000
Editor: Carin Szostecki
Profile: Joint initiative of the AOK Federal Association and the Münchener Medizinischen Wochenschrift. The newsletter for practitioners is once a month "MMW Fortschritte der Medizin ". He reported hands-on health policy and medical issues, highlights the background and presents joint projects between doctors and AOK..
Language(s): German
Supplement to: MMW Fortschritte der Medizin

PRODUCTION ENGINEERING 1832490G19A-1131
Editorial: An der Universität 2, 30823 GARBSEN
Tel: 511 7622533 **Fax:** 511 7625115
Email: info@ifw.uni-hannover.de
Freq: 6 issues yearly; **Annual Sub.:** EUR 713,00; **Circ:** 378
Editor: Berend Denkena
Profile: This journal will help researchers to learn more about some of the top-rated developments in production engineering and production organization for modern industry.
Language(s): English
ADVERTISING RATES:
Full Page Mono .... EUR 740
Full Page Colour .... EUR 1780
Mechanical Data: Type Area: 240 x 175 mm
Official Journal of: Organ d. German Academic Society for Production Engineering - Wissenschaftl. Ges. f. Produktionstechnik

PRODUCTION PARTNER 739504G2D-620
Editorial: Emil-Hoffmann-Str. 13, 50996 KÖLN
Tel: 2236 962170 **Fax:** 2236 962175
Email: redaktion@production-partner.de **Web site:** http://www.production-partner.de
Freq: 10 issues yearly; **Annual Sub.:** EUR 61,00; **Circ:** 4,894
Editor: Walter Wehrhan; **Advertising Manager:** Angelika Müller
Profile: PRODUCTION PARTNER is now almost 20 years, the market-leading and largest circulation publication in the field of professional studio and stage equipment in Germany. The immense variety of topics in this market segment has led to the PRODUCTION PARTNER now on the topics of focus, which are primarily in live productions (including theatrical and industrial productions) used: sound, light, event technology, Stage technique and projection.
Language(s): German
ADVERTISING RATES:
Full Page Mono .... EUR 2211
Full Page Colour .... EUR 4053
Mechanical Data: Type Area: 254 x 185 mm, No. of Columns (Display): 4, Col Widths (Display): 43 mm
BUSINESS: COMMUNICATIONS, ADVERTISING & MARKETING: Broadcasting

PRODUCTIVITY MANAGEMENT 764902G19E-1845
Editorial: Detmolder Str. 62, 10715 BERLIN
Tel: 331 9773355 **Fax:** 331 9773406
Email: hanna.theuer@gito.de **Web site:** http://www.productivity-management.de
Freq: 5 issues yearly; **Annual Sub.:** EUR 109,00; **Circ:** 11,287
Editor: Hanna Theuer; **Advertising Manager:** Martina Braun
Profile: Magazine about enterprise resource planning in production and logistics.
Language(s): German
ADVERTISING RATES:
Full Page Colour .... EUR 3360
Mechanical Data: Type Area: 234 x 175 mm, No. of Columns (Display): 3, Col Widths (Display): 55 mm
Copy instructions: *Copy Date:* 30 days prior to publication

PRODUCTRONIC 739505G18A-238
Editorial: Im Weiher 10, 69121 HEIDELBERG
Tel: 6221 489360 **Fax:** 6221 489482
Email: productronic@huethig.de **Web site:** http://www.productronic.de
Freq: 9 issues yearly; **Annual Sub.:** EUR 123,00; **Circ:** 9,928
Editor: Hilmar Beine; **Advertising Manager:** Andreas Bausch
Profile: productronic is aimed at decision makers and professionals in the electronics manufacturing and to those concerned with the development of technology or services in the area of electronics manufacturing. As an opinion leader and the productronic itself fully informed and researched all aspects of an effective and economic electronic manufacturing. productronic is the electronics manufacturing industry in German-speaking comprehensively.
Language(s): German
ADVERTISING RATES:
Full Page Mono .... EUR 3974
Full Page Colour .... EUR 5049
Mechanical Data: Type Area: 257 x 178 mm, No. of Columns (Display): 4, Col Widths (Display): 41 mm
BUSINESS: ELECTRONICS

PRODUKTION 739512G14B-40
Editorial: Justus-von-Liebig-Str. 1, 86899 LANDSBERG **Tel:** 8191 125681 **Fax:** 8191 125312
Email: redaktion@produktion.de **Web site:** http://www.produktion.de
Freq: Weekly; **Annual Sub.:** EUR 97,80; **Circ:** 39,730
Editor: Eduard Altmann; **Advertising Manager:** Michael Klotz
Profile: The trade newspaper Produktion achieved with their mix of topics from technology and business, the whole decision chain of manufacturing industry of professionals and specialists (brand decision-makers) to heads of manufacturing and production-related departments such as engineering and logistics (quantities and technology decision-makers) to managers and technology executives (financial decisions). Production supports them with technical know-how and product information on the shop floor, with practical examples and management tips for process optimization and competitive and market analysis for business decisions. The strengths of the specialist title production lies in its large

industrial range, the target group-specific issues spectrum, the high quality of its factual reporting and the big news in connection with newspaper typically quick overview.
Language(s): German
ADVERTISING RATES:
Full Page Mono .... EUR 11200
Full Page Colour .... EUR 11200
Mechanical Data: No. of Columns (Display): 5, Col Widths (Display): 47 mm, Type Area: 371 x 249 mm
Copy instructions: *Copy Date:* 15 days prior to publication
Supplement(s): kataloge orange
BUSINESS: COMMERCE, INDUSTRY & MANAGEMENT: Industry & Factories

PROFESSIONAL LIGHTING DESIGN
1741708G17-1575
Editorial: Marienfelder Str. 18, 33330 GÜTERSLOH
Tel: 5241 307260 **Fax:** 5241 3072640
Email: jritter@via-internet.com **Web site:** http://via-verlag.com
Freq: 6 issues yearly; **Annual Sub.:** EUR 71,90; **Circ:** 2,500
Editor: Joachim Ritter; **Advertising Manager:** Frank Paskarbeit
Profile: Magazine with information on product novelties and recent trends in lighting design.
Language(s): English
ADVERTISING RATES:
Full Page Mono .... EUR 5350
Full Page Colour .... EUR 2930
Mechanical Data: Type Area: 275 x 210 mm, No. of Columns (Display): 4, Col Widths (Display): 48 mm
Copy instructions: *Copy Date:* 21 days prior to publication
Official Journal of: Organ d. Professional Lighting Designers' Association e.V.

PROFESSIONAL LIGHTING DESIGN
1829642G17-1597
Editorial: Marienfelder Str. 18, 33330 GÜTERSLOH
Tel: 5241 307260 **Fax:** 5241 3072640
Email: jritter@via-internet.com **Web site:** http://via-verlag.com
Freq: 6 issues yearly; **Annual Sub.:** EUR 57,00; **Circ:** 7,000
Editor: Joachim Ritter; **Advertising Manager:** Frank Paskarbeit
Profile: Magazine with information on product novelties and recent trends in lighting design.
Language(s): German
ADVERTISING RATES:
Full Page Mono .... EUR 3300
Full Page Colour .... EUR 3300
Mechanical Data: Type Area: 275 x 210 mm, No. of Columns (Display): 4, Col Widths (Display): 48 mm
Copy instructions: *Copy Date:* 21 days prior to publication
Official Journal of: Organ d. Professional Lighting Designers' Association e.V.

PROFESSIONAL LIGHTING DESIGN
1741708G17-1598
Editorial: Marienfelder Str. 18, 33330 GÜTERSLOH
Tel: 5241 307260 **Fax:** 5241 3072640
Email: jritter@via-internet.com **Web site:** http://via-verlag.com
Freq: 6 issues yearly; **Annual Sub.:** EUR 71,90; **Circ:** 2,500
Editor: Joachim Ritter; **Advertising Manager:** Frank Paskarbeit
Profile: Magazine with information on product novelties and recent trends in lighting design.
Language(s): English
ADVERTISING RATES:
Full Page Mono .... EUR 5350
Full Page Colour .... EUR 2930
Mechanical Data: Type Area: 275 x 210 mm, No. of Columns (Display): 4, Col Widths (Display): 48 mm
Copy instructions: *Copy Date:* 21 days prior to publication
Official Journal of: Organ d. Professional Lighting Designers' Association e.V.

PROFESSIONAL PRODUCTION
739546G2D-60
Editorial: Postfach 101215, 86882 LANDSBERG
Tel: 8191 922606 **Fax:** 8191 922607
Email: redaktion@professional-production.de **Web site:** http://www.professional-production.de
Freq: 8 issues yearly; **Annual Sub.:** EUR 54,57; **Circ:** 5,951
Editor: Ruodlieb Neubauer; **Advertising Manager:** Joyce Hoch
Profile: Magazine about broadcasting, media and film production.
Language(s): German
Readership: Read by television and film producers and technicians.
ADVERTISING RATES:
Full Page Mono .... EUR 1400
Full Page Colour .... EUR 2500
Mechanical Data: Type Area: 272 x 188 mm, No. of Columns (Display): 3, Col Widths (Display): 60 mm
BUSINESS: COMMUNICATIONS, ADVERTISING & MARKETING: Broadcasting

PROFI
739548G4B-620
Editorial: Hünefeldstr. 42a, 46236 BOTTROP
Tel: 2041 766648 **Fax:** 2041 769402
Email: frank.spiess@dieschnittstelle.com **Web site:** http://www.tomsit.de
Freq: Quarterly; **Cover Price:** Free; **Circ:** 40,000
Editor: Frank Spieß
Profile: Company publication published by Henkel Bautechnik.
Language(s): German

PROFI
739549G21E-110
Editorial: Hülsebrockstr. 2, 48165 MÜNSTER
Tel: 2501 801900 **Fax:** 2501 801901
Email: redaktion@profi.de **Web site:** http://www.profi.de
Freq: Monthly; **Annual Sub.:** EUR 91,80; **Circ:** 70,593
Editor: Manfred Neunaber; **Advertising Manager:** Gabriele Wittkowski
Profile: Magazine for professional agricultural technology. Agricultural technology-interested reader month by month thorough and practical information. Extensive reviews of new and used equipment, DIY solutions, repair manuals, workshop tricks, feature articles, the electronics and valuable tips on care and maintenance of the machines are editorial priorities. The magazine always has an eye for the practice. It tests examined and evaluated all the machines in practical use and gives you valuable tips for practitioners. Thus, it is preparing investment decisions are arguments and contributes to the formation of opinions. Target groups: • technically savvy, investment-strong farmers • Farmers use machines with überbetrieblichem • powerful contractors • farm equipment dealers and mechanics • farm equipment manufacturers and development departments.
Language(s): German
ADVERTISING RATES:
Full Page Mono .... EUR 5728
Full Page Colour .... EUR 9165
Mechanical Data: Type Area: 270 x 190 mm, No. of Columns (Display): 4, Col Widths (Display): 46 mm
Copy instructions: *Copy Date:* 10 days prior to publication
Supplement(s): traktorpool das Magazin
BUSINESS: AGRICULTURE & FARMING: Agriculture - Machinery & Plant

PROFI CLUBSHOP
1864921G4E-7244
Editorial: Hohe Kanzelstr. 4, 65527 NIEDERNHAUSEN **Tel:** 6127 991818
Fax: 6127 991819
Email: fahrerclub@zeppelin.com **Web site:** http://www.fahrerclub.de
Freq: Quarterly; **Circ:** 23,000
Editor: Birgit Friedmann
Profile: Magazine for Zeppelin building machinery operators.
Language(s): German
Mechanical Data: No. of Columns (Display): 4
Copy instructions: *Copy Date:* 14 days prior to publication

PROFI KOSMETIK
739552G15A-100_50
Editorial: Neuhauser Str. 21, 78464 KONSTANZ
Tel: 7531 812250 **Fax:** 7531 812299
Email: eberhardt.arntzen@t-online.de **Web site:** http://www.profikosmetik.de
Freq: 11 issues yearly; **Annual Sub.:** EUR 48,00; **Circ:** 15,013
Editor: Hannelore Eberhardt-Arntzen; **Advertising Manager:** Hans-Jörg Schmidt
Profile: Journal focusing on applied cosmetics in institutes for manicure and pedicure.
Language(s): German
Readership: Read by beauticians.
ADVERTISING RATES:
Full Page Mono .... EUR 2800
Full Page Colour .... EUR 2800
Mechanical Data: Type Area: 252 x 176 mm, No. of Columns (Display): 4, Col Widths (Display): 40 mm
Copy instructions: *Copy Date:* 30 days prior to publication
BUSINESS: COSMETICS & HAIRDRESSING: Cosmetics

DIE PROFI WERKSTATT
2002772G49A-2486
Editorial: Joseph-Dollinger-Bogen 5, 80807 MÜNCHEN **Tel:** 89 32391492 **Fax:** 89 32391417
Email: redaktion@profi-werkstatt.net **Web site:** http://www.profi-werkstatt.net
Circ: 45,000
Editor: Thomas Pietsch; **Advertising Manager:** Frank Hochhäusler
Profile: The special edition The PROFI-Werkstatt can be directed to readers who perform in a special shop service and maintenance work on commercial vehicles or carried out by independent garages. The print run is attributed to the magazines Transport, Logistra and busplaner. In order to ensure the professional workshop an extensive market penetration in van, truck and bus workshops in Germany. The wide range of topics from A to Z for exhaust emission testing cylinder head gasket sell offers an ideal advertising environment for all the accessories, wear parts and attachments for commercial vehicles and equipment repairers or service providers are in the industry. With hands-on technical reports and reports on trends and developments in the commercial vehicle technology and workshop equipment, the PROFI-Werkstatt provides the reader with important information for upcoming purchase decisions and processes in his work area.
Language(s): German
ADVERTISING RATES:
Full Page Mono .... EUR 6880
Full Page Colour .... EUR 6880
Mechanical Data: Type Area: 270 x 185 mm, No. of Columns (Display): 4, Col Widths (Display): 43 mm
Supplement to: busplaner International, Logistra Fuhrpark, Transport

PROFIBÖRSE
739550G4R-780
Editorial: Crüwellstr. 11, 33615 BIELEFELD
Tel: 521 124044 **Fax:** 521 124088
Email: bernd.lochmueller@musb.de **Web site:** http://www.fz-profiboerse.de
Freq: 6 issues yearly; **Annual Sub.:** EUR 35,00; **Circ:** 3,530
Editor: Bernd Lochmüller; **Advertising Manager:** Bernd Lochmüller
Profile: Magazine for the construction industry covering tools, machines, industrial news, security systems, building requirements and equipment.
Language(s): German
ADVERTISING RATES:
Full Page Mono .... EUR 1596
Full Page Colour .... EUR 2600
Mechanical Data: Type Area: 270 x 184 mm, No. of Columns (Display): 4, Col Widths (Display): 43 mm
Copy instructions: *Copy Date:* 21 days prior to publication
BUSINESS: ARCHITECTURE & BUILDING: Building Related

PROFIFOTO
739551G38-85
Editorial: Mürmeln 83b, 41363 JÜCHEN
Tel: 2165 872173 **Fax:** 2167 872174
Email: profifoto@buero-grg.de **Web site:** http://www.profifoto.de
Freq: 10 issues yearly; **Annual Sub.:** EUR 70,00; **Circ:** 16,954
Editor: Thomas Gerwers; **Advertising Manager:** Walter Hauck
Profile: ProfiFoto is Germany's leading media brand for professional Photographers and everyone who aspires to become a pro. Month after Month, the print version of ProfiFoto delivers more than 100 pages of reports on the latest photo technology and professional photography news.
Language(s): German
Readership: Read by professional photographers.
ADVERTISING RATES:
Full Page Mono .... EUR 3000
Full Page Colour .... EUR 5200
Mechanical Data: Type Area: 276 x 205 mm, No. of Columns (Display): 4, Col Widths (Display): 47 mm
Copy instructions: *Copy Date:* 41 days prior to publication
BUSINESS: PHOTOGRAPHIC TRADE

PROFIL
728677G21A-2040
Editorial: Türkenstr. 22, 80333 MÜNCHEN
Tel: 89 28683402 **Fax:** 89 28683405
Email: profil@gv-bayern.de **Web site:** http://www.gv-bayern.de
Freq: Monthly; **Annual Sub.:** EUR 45,00; **Circ:** 6,000
Editor: Jürgen Gros; **Advertising Manager:** Margit Edhofer
Profile: Magazine for Bavarian cooperatives.
Language(s): German
ADVERTISING RATES:
Full Page Mono .... EUR 1540
Full Page Colour .... EUR 3180
Mechanical Data: Type Area: 260 x 185 mm, No. of Columns (Display): 3, Col Widths (Display): 59 mm
Copy instructions: *Copy Date:* 15 days prior to publication
Supplement(s): Raiffeisen Magazin

DAS PROFIL
1865339G27-3089
Editorial: Rheinmetall-Platz 1, 40476 DÜSSELDORF
Tel: 211 47304 **Fax:** 211 4734157
Email: rolf-dieter.schneider@rheinmetall.com **Web site:** http://www.rheinmetall.com
Freq: 5 issues yearly; **Circ:** 20,000
Editor: Rolf Dieter Schneider
Profile: Magazine for employees of Rheinmetall AG.
Language(s): German

PROFIL
739554G62D-2296
Editorial: Friedrichstr. 169, 10117 BERLIN
Tel: 30 40816789 **Fax:** 30 40816788
Email: info@dphv.de **Web site:** http://www.dphv.de
Freq: 10 issues yearly; Free to qualifying individuals
Annual Sub.: EUR 18,41; **Circ:** 49,518
Editor: Eva Hertzfeld; **Advertising Manager:** Caroline Dassow
Profile: Membership magazine of the German teachers' association. It provides information and views on education and training policies and issues on science and research, business and politics. Audience: teachers in secondary school, universities, and total and managers in education authorities and entities of federal, state and local authorities.
Language(s): German
ADVERTISING RATES:
Full Page Mono .... EUR 2444
Full Page Colour .... EUR 4067
Mechanical Data: Type Area: 270 x 185 mm, No. of Columns (Display): 4, Col Widths (Display): 43 mm
BUSINESS: CHURCH & SCHOOL EQUIPMENT & EDUCATION: Secondary Education

PROFILE
746189G1A-3140
Editorial: Gasselstiege 33, 48159 MÜNSTER
Tel: 251 535860 **Fax:** 251 5358660
Email: info@stbv.de **Web site:** http://www.stbv.de
Freq: 6 issues yearly; **Circ:** 3,000
Editor: Hans W. Haubruck
Profile: Magazine about tax law.
Language(s): German
ADVERTISING RATES:
Full Page Mono .... EUR 800
Full Page Colour .... EUR 1040
Mechanical Data: Type Area: 257 x 170 mm
Copy instructions: *Copy Date:* 42 days prior to publication

PROFILE
746189G1A-3790
Editorial: Gasselstiege 33, 48159 MÜNSTER
Tel: 251 535860 **Fax:** 251 5358660
Email: info@stbv.de **Web site:** http://www.stbv.de
Freq: 6 issues yearly; **Circ:** 3,000
Editor: Hans W. Haubruck
Profile: Magazine about tax law.
Language(s): German
ADVERTISING RATES:
Full Page Mono .... EUR 800
Full Page Colour .... EUR 1040
Mechanical Data: Type Area: 257 x 170 mm
Copy instructions: *Copy Date:* 42 days prior to publication

PROFILE
725666G15A-60
Editorial: Scheidtweilerstr. 17, 50933 KÖLN
Tel: 221 5892088 **Fax:** 221 9526124
Email: ctheis@markenverlag.de **Web site:** http://www.markenverlag.de
Freq: 7 issues yearly; Free to qualifying individuals
Annual Sub.: EUR 42,00; **Circ:** 7,500
Editor: Christof Theis; **Advertising Manager:** Christof Theis
Profile: Profile has the premium range of perfumery trade magazines profiled as a modern classic and is aimed at the privately run perfume stores and perfumery companies and perfumery department stores. The readers of Profile, owner of perfumes and their employees expect, the latest trends from the major sectors of perfumery - Skincare, Cosmetics, perfumes and accessories, POS marketing, employee and customer orientation, service spectrum - balanced selected and intelligently analyzed. Profile is aesthetic in the visual language, reliable information at superior level.
Language(s): German
ADVERTISING RATES:
Full Page Mono .... EUR 4800
Full Page Colour .... EUR 4800
Mechanical Data: Type Area: 264 x 188 mm, No. of Columns (Display): 4, Col Widths (Display): 44 mm
Copy instructions: *Copy Date:* 23 days prior to publication
BUSINESS: COSMETICS & HAIRDRESSING: Cosmetics

PROFIRMA
739567G14A-5920
Editorial: Munzinger Str. 9, 79111 FREIBURG
Tel: 761 8983031 **Fax:** 761 8983112
Email: online@haufe-lexware.com **Web site:** http://www.profirma.de
Freq: 11 issues yearly; **Annual Sub.:** EUR 64,00; **Circ:** 79,441
Editor: Dieter Römer; **Advertising Manager:** Bernd Junker
Profile: ProFirma is the magazine for the innovative entrepreneur. Owners and managers from the large field of SMEs ProFirma provides valuable information for strategic management, to financial, legal, tax and marketing and the latest trends in IT and investment issues. Competent, easy and quite safe. The focus of the utility is following the motto "Learn from the best". The resort "We entrepreneurs" can innovative business leaders to speak, showcases excellent business ideas with readers contributions and addresses current debates. ProFirma are medium-sized lobby. Target audience: owners, managers and self-employed in medium-sized companies across all industries.
Language(s): German
Readership: Aimed at managers and business executives.
ADVERTISING RATES:
Full Page Mono .... EUR 8400
Full Page Colour .... EUR 10500
Mechanical Data: Type Area: 249 x 176 mm, No. of Columns (Display): 3, Col Widths (Display): 56 mm
Copy instructions: *Copy Date:* 20 days prior to publication
Supplement to: baV spezial, ProFirma Professional
BUSINESS: COMMERCE, INDUSTRY & MANAGEMENT

PROFITS
728768G1C-50
Editorial: Am Wallgraben 115, 70565 STUTTGART
Tel: 711 7821236 **Fax:** 711 7821288
Email: frank.bantle@dsv-gruppe.de **Web site:** http://www.dsv-gruppe.de
Freq: 6 issues yearly; **Annual Sub.:** EUR 23,70; **Circ:** 47,389
Editor: Thomas Stoll; **Advertising Manager:** Anneli Baumann
Profile: Magazine of the German Savings Bank Group covering business and finance.
Language(s): German
Readership: Aimed at executives, financiers and business managers.
ADVERTISING RATES:
Full Page Mono .... EUR 4050

Full Page Colour .... EUR 5200
Mechanical Data: Type Area: 236 x 174 mm, No. of Columns (Display): 3, Col Widths (Display): 56 mm
Copy instructions: *Copy Date:* 32 days prior to publication
BUSINESS: FINANCE & ECONOMICS: Banking

PROJEKT PSYCHOTHERAPIE
1813733G56A-11508
Editorial: Schwimmbadstr. 22, 79100 FREIBURG
Tel: 761 7910245 **Fax:** 761 7910243
Email: bvvp@bvvp.de **Web site:** http://www.bvvp.de
Freq: Quarterly; **Cover Price:** EUR 6,00
Free to qualifying individuals ; **Circ:** 5,000
Editor: Martin Klett
Profile: Publication from the Federal Association of Psychotherapists.
Language(s): German
ADVERTISING RATES:
Full Page Mono .... EUR 1500
Full Page Colour .... EUR 1900
Mechanical Data: Type Area: 236 x 190 mm

PROJEKTMANAGEMENT AKTUELL
765178G14A-9286
Editorial: Am Grauen Stein, 51105 KÖLN
Tel: 221 8063514 **Fax:** 221 8063510
Email: anke.piwetzki@de.tuv.com **Web site:** http://www.tuev-media.de
Freq: 5 issues yearly; Free to qualifying individuals
Annual Sub.: EUR 75,25; **Circ:** 6,500
Advertising Manager: Gudrun Karafiol
Profile: Magazine with information for project managers in industry, building business, advising and engineering offices.
Language(s): German
ADVERTISING RATES:
Full Page Mono .... EUR 854
Full Page Colour .... EUR 1439
Mechanical Data: Type Area: 250 x 183 mm, No. of Columns (Display): 3, Col Widths (Display): 49 mm
Copy instructions: *Copy Date:* 56 days prior to publication

PROMOBIL.DE
1691887G77A-2735
Editorial: Leuschnerstr. 1, 70174 STUTTGART
Tel: 7152 941575 **Fax:** 7152 941597
Email: msteinheil@motorpresse.de **Web site:** http://www.promobil.de
Freq: Daily; **Cover Price:** Paid; **Circ:** 192,531 Unique Users
Editor: Mario Steinheil; **Advertising Manager:** Peter Steinbach
Profile: Ezine: Magazine about mobile homes.
Language(s): German
CONSUMER: MOTORING & CYCLING: Motoring

PROMOTION PRODUCTS
2035555G2A-5917
Editorial: Waltherstr. 49, 51069 KÖLN
Tel: 221 6891130 **Fax:** 221 6891110
Email: pohl@waorg.com **Web site:** http://www.promotionproducts.biz
Freq: 6 issues yearly; **Annual Sub.:** EUR 36,00; **Circ:** 29,750
Editor: Heike Pohl; **Advertising Manager:** Sarah Vieten
Profile: Magazine about new promotional products. With ideas and suggestions for the successful use of promotional products. Each issue presents a wide range of effective and trendy promotional items, clearly divided into product categories and finished with guidance on the optimum use - from the giveaway for the next event on bonuses for loyal customers or employees to promotional onpacks. Best practice examples, current market news, trade show reports and interviews from the world of haptic advertising round out the coverage.
Language(s): German
ADVERTISING RATES:
Full Page Mono .... EUR 2150
Full Page Colour .... EUR 2150
Mechanical Data: Type Area: 234 x 190 mm, No. of Columns (Display): 3, Col Widths (Display): 64 mm

PROPELLANTS, EXPLOSIVES, PYROTECHNICS
739648G13-158
Editorial: Postfach 1240, 76318 PFINZTAL
Tel: 721 4640139 **Fax:** 721 4640111
Email: pep@ict.fhg.de
Freq: 6 issues yearly; **Annual Sub.:** EUR 1572,00
Editor: Peter Elsner
Profile: Official journal of the International Pyrotechnics Society. The journal deals with scientific and technological aspects of energetic materials.
Language(s): English
Official Journal of: Organ d. Internat. Pyrotechnics Society
BUSINESS: CHEMICALS

PROPHYLAXE IMPULS
739650G56D-800
Editorial: Danckelmannstr. 9, 14059 BERLIN
Tel: 30 30127881 **Fax:** 30 30127882
Email: hpcm-hp@t-online.de
Freq: Quarterly; **Annual Sub.:** EUR 19,00; **Circ:** 6,865
Editor: Hedi von Bergh; **Advertising Manager:** Heike Müller-Wüstenfeld
Profile: Publication about developments in dentistry, particularly in the field of oral hygiene.
Language(s): German
ADVERTISING RATES:
Full Page Mono .... EUR 2040
Full Page Colour .... EUR 3045
Mechanical Data: Type Area: 245 x 176 mm, No. of Columns (Display): 3, Col Widths (Display): 46 mm
Copy instructions: *Copy Date:* 42 days prior to publication
BUSINESS: HEALTH & MEDICAL: Dental

PROSIEBEN
1662469G76A-1551
Editorial: Medienallee 6, 85774 UNTERFÖHRING
Tel: 89 950710 **Fax:** 89 95078901
Email: info@sevenoneintermedia.de **Web site:** http://www.prosieben.de
Freq: Daily; **Cover Price:** Paid; **Circ:** 112,094,564 Unique Users
Editor: Daniel Grey
Profile: Website for the Nationwide private TV channel Pro Sieben with information for the films, series, documentaries and news. Twitter: http://twitter.com/ProSiebenTV.
Language(s): German
CONSUMER: MUSIC & PERFORMING ARTS: Cinema

PROTECTOR
739659G54C-3
Editorial: Oskar-Maria-Graf-Ring 23, 81737 MÜNCHEN **Tel:** 89 67369752 **Fax:** 89 67369761
Email: hagen.zumpe@igt-verlag.de **Web site:** http://www.sicherheit.info
Freq: 10 issues yearly; **Annual Sub.:** EUR 115,50; **Circ:** 10,162
Editor: Hagen Zumpe; **Advertising Manager:** Gabriele Strixner
Profile: Journal covering security and fire protection.
Language(s): German
ADVERTISING RATES:
Full Page Mono .... EUR 2284
Full Page Colour .... EUR 3654
Mechanical Data: Type Area: 265 x 175 mm, No. of Columns (Display): 3, Col Widths (Display): 55 mm
Copy instructions: *Copy Date:* 30 days prior to publication
BUSINESS: SAFETY & SECURITY: Security

PROVOCATEUR
2084586G86C-260
Editorial: Bruderstr. 10, 80538 MÜNCHEN
Tel: 89 54877700
Email: michael.brunnbauer@provocateur-magazin.de **Web site:** http://www.provocateur-magazin.de
Freq: 6 issues yearly; **Annual Sub.:** EUR 25,80; **Circ:** 50,000
Editor: Michael Brunnbauer
Profile: Provocateur is the magazine for the whole world of men. As the only magazine in Germany, which holds for all men will find a suitable living environment, there Provocateur for a clear line: men of sport, men of art, men of business, men with format or men's lifestyles, men with a sense of fashion and cosmetics. For each type, there is a personal column, with his personal issues and must-haves. With its current themes and his sense for trends, Provocateur aimed at a sophisticated and cosmopolitan audience with a sense of the finer things in life (watches, cars, technology, fashion ...). In addition to information Provocateur offers entertainment with men - from exclusive interviews and exciting reports on provocative photo spreads to new perspectives. Target group: male 30 +, decision makers and self-employed, high income and ready for sale luxury and quality-oriented, urban, and early adopter.
Language(s): German
ADVERTISING RATES:
Full Page Colour .... EUR 6460
Mechanical Data: Type Area: 230 x 170 mm

PRÜMER WOCHENSPIEGEL
739675G72-10604
Editorial: Max-Planck-Str. 10, 54296 TRIER
Tel: 6561 958015 **Fax:** 6561 958081
Email: red-bitburg@tw-verlag.de **Web site:** http://www.eifellive.de
Freq: Weekly; **Cover Price:** Free; **Circ:** 13,848
Editor: Helmut Müller; **Advertising Manager:** Andreas Noll
Profile: Advertising journal (house-to-house) concentrating on local stories.
Language(s): German
ADVERTISING RATES:
Full Page Mono .... EUR 2348
Full Page Colour .... EUR 3281
Mechanical Data: Type Area: 430 x 290 mm, No. of Columns (Display): 7, Col Widths (Display): 38 mm
Copy instructions: *Copy Date:* 2 days prior to publication
LOCAL NEWSPAPERS

PS
739678G77D-1080
Editorial: Leuschnerstr. 1, 70174 STUTTGART
Tel: 711 1821606 **Fax:** 711 1821781
Email: ps@motorpresse.de **Web site:** http://www.ps-online.de
Freq: Monthly; **Annual Sub.:** EUR 39,90; **Circ:** 41,922
Editor: Michael Pfeiffer; **Advertising Manager:** Marcus Schardt
Profile: Every month the modern editorial concept offers readers a fresh package of elaborate, down-to-earth tests and comprehensive service. Naturally PS reports extensively on the national and international motorcycle racing scene and offers action-packed tests and coverage from the tuning and off-road scenes. PS reaches a clearly defined readership of sport-keen and technically oriented readers through the consistently sport-based emphasis of the magazine. Sport motorcycles represent the largest markt sector, with the biggest turnover and the clientele most willing to spend. PS is compulsory reading for all motorcycle sports fans, as the magazine is partner to the Superbike World Championships and other national race series.
Language(s): German
ADVERTISING RATES:
Full Page Mono .... EUR 8900
Full Page Colour .... EUR 8900
Mechanical Data: Type Area: 248 x 185 mm, No. of Columns (Display): 4, Col Widths (Display): 43 mm
Copy instructions: *Copy Date:* 24 days prior to publication
CONSUMER: MOTORING & CYCLING: Motor Sports

PS DAS AUTOMAGAZIN
1615179G77A-2562
Editorial: Gögginger Str. 2, 72505 KRAUCHENWIES
Tel: 7576 961850 **Fax:** 7576 9618599
Freq: 10 issues yearly; **Cover Price:** Free; **Circ:** 11,500
Editor: Mathias R. Albert
Profile: Motorbike magazine.
Language(s): German
ADVERTISING RATES:
Full Page Mono .... EUR 784
Full Page Colour .... EUR 1800
Mechanical Data: Type Area: 280 x 180 mm, No. of Columns (Display): 4
Copy instructions: *Copy Date:* 4 days prior to publication

PS PÄDAGOGEN SERVICE
741411G62A-3100
Editorial: Helmlinger Str. 1, 77839 LICHTENAU
Tel: 7227 505010 **Fax:** 7227 505050
Email: martina.wollmer@b-b-v.de **Web site:** http://www.b-b-v.de
Freq: Annual; **Cover Price:** EUR 5,00; **Circ:** 35,000
Profile: Reference work in education for teachers with hands-on reports and about 500 useful addresses for the school day with e-mail and Internet.
Language(s): German
ADVERTISING RATES:
Full Page Mono .... EUR 2575
Full Page Colour .... EUR 2575
Mechanical Data: Type Area: 180 x 125 mm
Copy instructions: *Copy Date:* 62 days prior to publication
BUSINESS: CHURCH & SCHOOL EQUIPMENT & EDUCATION: Education

PSI JOURNAL
739685G2A-4040
Editorial: Dekan-Laist-Str. 17, 55129 MAINZ
Tel: 6131 9583601 **Fax:** 6131 958366
Email: geppert@edit-line.de
Freq: 11 issues yearly; **Circ:** 7,568
Editor: Manfred Schlösser; **Advertising Manager:** Tanja Damrath
Profile: Official journal of the German Promotional Articles Association.
Language(s): English; French; German
ADVERTISING RATES:
Full Page Mono .... EUR 2012
Full Page Colour .... EUR 2854
Mechanical Data: Type Area: 260 x 185 mm, No. of Columns (Display): 3, Col Widths (Display): 58 mm
Copy instructions: *Copy Date:* 20 days prior to publication
BUSINESS: COMMUNICATIONS, ADVERTISING & MARKETING

PSO MAGAZIN
739687G56A-11187
Editorial: Seewartenstr. 10, 20459 HAMBURG
Tel: 40 2233990 **Fax:** 40 22339922
Email: info@psoriasis-bund.de **Web site:** http://www.psoriasis-bund.de
Freq: 6 issues yearly; **Circ:** 6,852
Editor: Hans-Detlev Kunz; **Advertising Manager:** Hans-Detlev Kunz
Profile: Magazine for members of German Psoriasis Association.
Language(s): German
ADVERTISING RATES:
Full Page Mono .... EUR 1400
Full Page Colour .... EUR 2060
Mechanical Data: Type Area: 263 x 180 mm, No. of Columns (Display): 3, Col Widths (Display): 56 mm
Copy instructions: *Copy Date:* 45 days prior to publication
BUSINESS: HEALTH & MEDICAL

PSYCH. PFLEGE HEUTE
739692G56N-6
Editorial: Remter Weg 69, 33617 BIELEFELD
Email: michael.schulz@evkb.de **Web site:** http://www.thieme.de/fz/psychpflege.html
Freq: 6 issues yearly; **Annual Sub.:** EUR 99,50; **Circ:** 1,750
Editor: Michael Schulz
Profile: The journal Psych. Pflege Heute provides information about the work field of psychiatric nurses and promotes the critical examination with relevant issues. It caters to psychiatric care in all its forms and provide impetus for further nursing activities. Psychiatric hospitals are only one possible location for psychiatric care: even in forensics or in psychiatric settings is done gerontopsychiatric care, outpatient or inpatient basis, equipped with special interventions - the field is more colorful. In nursing education, psychiatric care is more important today, and also the education and training of psychiatric nurses is becoming increasingly important. Maintenance is by far the largest professional group in mental health care. The psychiatric nursing services are provided 7 days a week, 24 hours. In this power - and also on the creativity and responsibility, which belong to this profession - the nurses are proud of.
Language(s): German
ADVERTISING RATES:
Full Page Mono .... EUR 1340
Full Page Colour .... EUR 2090
Mechanical Data: Type Area: 248 x 175 mm
BUSINESS: HEALTH & MEDICAL: Mental Health

DIE PSYCHIATRIE
1697345G56A-11382
Editorial: Hölderlinstr. 3, 70174 STUTTGART
Tel: 711 2298754 **Fax:** 711 2298765
Email: jan.hueber@schattauer.de **Web site:** http://www.die-psychiatrie-online.de
Freq: Quarterly; **Annual Sub.:** EUR 128,00; **Circ:** 2,400
Editor: Jan Hueber; **Advertising Manager:** Nicole Dörr
Profile: Die Psychiatrie is probably the most versatile of all medical disciplines, which reflects as no other the relationship of body, soul and society. The journal Die Psychiatrie represents the fascinating complexity of the subject and its many facets. The heading "Pharmacotherapeutic Satellite Forum", the expert authors introduce in modern psycho-pharmacological treatment strategies, rounds off the comprehensive concept of the magazine. Die Psychiatrie is a magazine that documented the psychiatrist, the foundations of his professional medical practice, prompting a confrontation with one's own subject and allows him to find the personal site in the complex, multidimensional space of his science and his work life. In the best sense so it becomes an identity cause forum.
Language(s): English; German
ADVERTISING RATES:
Full Page Mono .... EUR 1420
Full Page Colour .... EUR 2560
Mechanical Data: Type Area: 242 x 174 mm
Copy instructions: *Copy Date:* 40 days prior to publication
Official Journal of: Organ d. Dt. Ges. f. Psychiatrie, Psychotherapie u. Nervenheilkunde

PSYCHIATRIE & NEUROLOGIE
1643874S56A-2043
Editorial: Sac.-Baumgärtl-Str. 1, 94350 FALKENFELS **Tel:** 9961 701565 **Fax:** 9961 701566
Email: n.mittermaier@rosenfluh.ch **Web site:** http://www.rosenfluh.ch
Freq: Quarterly; **Annual Sub.:** CHF 40,00; **Circ:** 5,200
Editor: Norbert Mittermaier
Profile: Magazine about further education for psychiatrists.
Language(s): German
ADVERTISING RATES:
Full Page Mono .... CHF 3280
Full Page Colour .... CHF 4880
Mechanical Data: Type Area: 238 x 175 mm
Copy instructions: *Copy Date:* 31 days prior to publication

PSYCHIATRIE & NEUROLOGIE
1643874S56A-2174
Editorial: Sac.-Baumgärtl-Str. 1, 94350 FALKENFELS **Tel:** 9961 701565 **Fax:** 9961 701566
Email: n.mittermaier@rosenfluh.ch **Web site:** http://www.rosenfluh.ch
Freq: Quarterly; **Annual Sub.:** CHF 40,00; **Circ:** 5,200
Editor: Norbert Mittermaier
Profile: Magazine about further education for psychiatrists.
Language(s): German
ADVERTISING RATES:
Full Page Mono .... CHF 3280
Full Page Colour .... CHF 4880
Mechanical Data: Type Area: 238 x 175 mm
Copy instructions: *Copy Date:* 31 days prior to publication

PSYCHIATRIE UND PSYCHOTHERAPIE UP2DATE
1826715G56A-11528
Editorial: Ratzeburger Allee 160, 23538 LÜBECK
Tel: 451 5002440 **Fax:** 451 5002603
Email: fritz.hohagen@psychiatrie.uk-sh.de **Web site:** http://www.thieme.de/fz/psychiatrie-u2d.html
Freq: 6 issues yearly; **Annual Sub.:** EUR 176,40; **Circ:** 1,970
Editor: Fritz Hohagen
Profile: Training with system. Pure training - in all relevant areas of psychiatry and psychotherapy. Up to 72 CME credits per year - every magazine with 4 training articles as well as Pro and Contra, short presentations and case studies. State-of-the-art articles from the following categories: organic mental disorders, disorders due to psychoactive substances, schizophrenia, schizophreniform and delusional

disorders, affective disorders, neurotic, somatoform and stress disorders, mental disorders with physical factors, personality disorders, Special Topics. Reader and looking up friendly like a textbook - with info boxes, practice notes, case reports and key messages. Design your guide - all bound contributions separately archived for easy pickup folder.
Language(s): German
ADVERTISING RATES:
Full Page Mono .... EUR 1840
Full Page Colour .... EUR 3010
Mechanical Data: Type Area: 248 x 175 mm, No. of Columns (Display): 3, Col Widths (Display): 55 mm

PSYCHIATRISCHE PRAXIS
739693G56N-79
Editorial: Philipp-Rosenthal-Str. 55, 04103 LEIPZIG
Email: sonja.kolb@medizin.uni-leipzig.de **Web site:** http://www.thieme.de/psychiat-praxis
Freq: 8 issues yearly; **Annual Sub.:** EUR 216,80; **Circ:** 1,700
Editor: Steffi G. Riedel-Heller
Profile: Psychiatry in the spotlight. Social psychiatric-oriented. Recent papers and solid overviews. Pro-counterpoint debates on burning issues. Informative case studies. Conception of international studies, new books and interesting developments in the subject.
Language(s): German
ADVERTISING RATES:
Full Page Mono .... EUR 1270
Full Page Colour .... EUR 2410
Mechanical Data: Type Area: 248 x 175 mm, No. of Columns (Display): 4, Col Widths (Display): 40 mm
Official Journal of: Organ d. Dt. Ges. f. Gerontopsychiatrie u. -psychotherapie, d. Arbeitskreis d. Chefärzte u. Chefärztinnen v. Kliniken f. Psychiatrie u. Psychotherapie an Allgemeinkrankenhäusern in Deutschland u. d. Bundeskonferenz Dt. Kliniken f. Psychiatrie u. Psychotherapie
BUSINESS: HEALTH & MEDICAL: Mental Health

PSYCHOANALYTISCHE FAMILIENTHERAPIE
1638451G56A-11271
Editorial: Walltorstr. 10, 35390 GIESSEN
Tel: 641 9699780 **Fax:** 641 96997819
Email: hjw@psychosozial-verlag.de **Web site:** http://www.psychosozial-verlag.de
Freq: Half-yearly; Free to qualifying individuals
Annual Sub.: EUR 28,00; **Circ:** 400
Editor: Trin Haland-Wirth
Profile: Magazine about couple, family and social therapy.
Language(s): German
ADVERTISING RATES:
Full Page Mono .... EUR 300
Full Page Colour .... EUR 450
Mechanical Data: Type Area: 168 x 106 mm
Copy instructions: *Copy Date:* 60 days prior to publication

PSYCHOLOGICAL RESEARCH
739697G56A-8700
Editorial: Heidelberger Platz 3, 14197 BERLIN
Tel: 30 827870 **Fax:** 30 8214091
Email: hommel@fsw.leidenuniv.nl **Web site:** http://www.springer.com
Freq: 6 issues yearly; **Annual Sub.:** EUR 1497,00; **Circ:** 160
Editor: Bernhard Hommel
Profile: International journal about psychological research.
Language(s): English
ADVERTISING RATES:
Full Page Mono .... EUR 740
Full Page Colour .... EUR 1780
Mechanical Data: Type Area: 240 x 175 mm

PSYCHOLOGIE HEUTE
739698G56N-80
Editorial: Werderstr. 10, 69469 WEINHEIM
Tel: 6201 6007379 **Fax:** 6201 6007382
Email: redaktion@psychologie-heute.de **Web site:** http://www.psychologie-heute.de
Freq: Monthly; **Annual Sub.:** EUR 64,00; **Circ:** 88,123
Editor: Heiko Ernst; **Advertising Manager:** Claudia Klinger
Profile: Psycholgie Heute is the leading german-language magazine for psychology and related sciences such as sociology, philosophy, biology, brain research and anthropology. Understandable and entertaining written and lavishly illustrated spreads the Journal each month the topics of life: happiness and self-development, love and partnership, body and well-being, childhood and personality, upbringing and education. Each issue also brings news from the psychological research and from the health and social sciences. A large part non-fiction at the end of the book provides a detailed overview of the new publications on the subject spectrum. Psycholgie Heute is targeted at professionals (psychologists, physicians, teachers) and more generally to people who want to understand themselves and others better and not be content with surfaces. They all find in this magazine of current research findings, which they can use for their particular situation.
Language(s): German
Readership: Aimed at people studying psychology and others interested in psychology.

ADVERTISING RATES:
Full Page Mono .... EUR 4470
Full Page Colour .... EUR 6260
Mechanical Data: Type Area: 256 x 180 mm, No. of Columns (Display): 4, Col Widths (Display): 42 mm
Copy instructions: *Copy Date:* 49 days prior to publication
BUSINESS: HEALTH & MEDICAL: Mental Health

PSYCHOLOGIE IN ERZIEHUNG UND UNTERRICHT
739699G62A-2960
Editorial: Leopoldstr. 13, 80802 MÜNCHEN
Tel: 89 21805191 **Fax:** 89 21805137
Email: peu@psy.lmu.de
Freq: Quarterly; **Annual Sub.:** EUR 84,00; **Circ:** 900
Editor: Sabine Walper
Profile: Magazine focusing on the role of psychology in development and teaching.
Language(s): English; German
ADVERTISING RATES:
Full Page Mono .... EUR 625
Full Page Colour .... EUR 1555
Mechanical Data: Type Area: 200 x 130 mm, No. of Columns (Display): 2, Col Widths (Display): 63 mm
Copy instructions: *Copy Date:* 31 days prior to publication
Official Journal of: Organ d. Dt. Ges. f. Psychologie
BUSINESS: CHURCH & SCHOOL EQUIPMENT & EDUCATION: Education

PSYCHOPHARMACOLOGY
739707G56A-8740
Editorial: Tiergartenstr. 17, 69121 HEIDELBERG
Tel: 6221 4870 **Fax:** 6221 4878366
Email: subscriptions@springer.com **Web site:** http://www.springerlink.com
Freq: 24 issues yearly; **Annual Sub.:** EUR 6736,00; **Circ:** 495
Profile: Publication about psychopharmacology.
Language(s): English
ADVERTISING RATES:
Full Page Mono .... EUR 830
Full Page Colour .... EUR 1870
Mechanical Data: Type Area: 240 x 175 mm

PSYCHOTHERAPEUT
739712G56A-8760
Editorial: Klugstr. 39, 80638 MÜNCHEN
Tel: 89 51603658 **Fax:** 89 51604742
Email: regine.karcher-reiners@springer.com **Web site:** http://www.springermedizin.de
Freq: 6 issues yearly; **Annual Sub.:** EUR 189,00; **Circ:** 1,900
Profile: The journal Psychotherapeut aims at specialists and psychologists who have acquired psychotherapeutic competence or are about to complete their education in this field. The contents of Psychotherapeut are based on a conception that is independent from individual schools and disciplines, and the journal aims to foster the convergence of and professional exchange between the different schools of psychotherapy. Comprehensive reviews provide an overview on selected topics and offer the reader evidenced based information on diagnostics and therapy. Freely submitted original papers allow the presentation of important clinical studies and serve the scientific exchange. Review articles under the rubric "Continuing Medical Education" present verified results of scientific research and their integration into daily practice.
Language(s): German
ADVERTISING RATES:
Full Page Mono .... EUR 1850
Full Page Colour .... EUR 3040
Mechanical Data: Type Area: 240 x 174 mm
Official Journal of: Organ d. Berufsverb. Dt. Psychologinnen u. Psychologen e.V., Bundesverb. d. Vertragspsychotherapeuten e.V., Dt. Ges. f. Psychologie, Dt. Ges. f. Psychoanalyse, Psychotherapie, Psychosomatik u. Tiefenpsychologie e.V.

PSYCHOTHERAPEUTEN-JOURNAL
1632933G56N-25
Editorial: St.-Paul-Str. 9, 80336 MÜNCHEN
Tel: 89 51555519 **Fax:** 89 51555525
Email: welsch@ptk-bayern.de **Web site:** http://www.psychotherapeutenjournal.de
Freq: Quarterly; **Annual Sub.:** EUR 72,00; **Circ:** 38,868
Editor: Karin Welsch
Profile: The journal publishes articles that are directly or indirectly to the prevention treatment and rehabilitation of mental disorders and psychological aspects of somatic diseases, scientific, gesundheitspolitische, professional and socio-legal aspects of education, training and continuing education and professional practice of psychologists Relating psychotherapists and child and adolescent psychotherapist.
Language(s): German
ADVERTISING RATES:
Full Page Mono .... EUR 2225
Full Page Colour .... EUR 2725
Mechanical Data: Type Area: 257 x 178 mm, No. of Columns (Display): 3, Col Widths (Display): 56 mm
Copy instructions: *Copy Date:* 40 days prior to publication
BUSINESS: HEALTH & MEDICAL: Mental Health

PSYCHOTHERAPIE IM ALTER
1641974G56A-11291
Editorial: Felsengarten 9, 34225 BAUNATAL
Tel: 561 48040 **Fax:** 564 4804402
Email: j.kipp@psychotherapie-im-alter.de **Web site:** http://www.psychotherapie-im-alter.de
Freq: Quarterly; **Annual Sub.:** EUR 55,90; **Circ:** 500
Editor: Johannes Kipp
Profile: The magazine is aimed at all professionals who work with older people in psychotherapy, advice and support through these psychosocial interventions. It wants to address the above-mentioned professional groups in private practice in counseling centers, specialty clinics, departments and institutions for the elderly and the nursing work. Another major goal of the journal is to provide a forum for the socio-therapy and psychotherapy of aging to create and promote professional exchanges about therapy schools and professional groups.
Language(s): German
ADVERTISING RATES:
Full Page Mono .... EUR 350
Full Page Colour .... EUR 500
Mechanical Data: Type Area: 168 x 114 mm
Copy instructions: *Copy Date:* 60 days prior to publication

P.T. MAGAZIN FÜR WIRTSCHAFT UND POLITIK
1613842G14A-9402
Editorial: Melscher Str. 1, 04299 LEIPZIG
Tel: 341 2406100 **Fax:** 341 2406166
Email: info@op-pt.de **Web site:** http://www.pt-magazin.de
Freq: 6 issues yearly; **Annual Sub.:** EUR 16,00; **Circ:** 39,855
Editor: Helfried Schmidt; **Advertising Manager:** Petra Tröger
Profile: The magazine offers midsize businesses a new communications platform in comparison to other business magazines. The entrepreneur is addressed as personally liable and most active artist and innovator, as a decision of outsourcing tasks to staff and technical investment.
Language(s): German
ADVERTISING RATES:
Full Page Colour .... EUR 5400
Mechanical Data: Type Area: 297 x 210 mm
Copy instructions: *Copy Date:* 20 days prior to publication
Official Journal of: Organ d. Oskar-Patzelt-Stiftung
BUSINESS: COMMERCE, INDUSTRY & MANAGEMENT

PT ZEITSCHRIFT FÜR PHYSIOTHERAPEUTEN
733242G56R-1120
Editorial: Lazarettstr. 4, 80636 MÜNCHEN
Tel: 89 126070 **Fax:** 89 12607333
Email: pt.redaktion@pflaum.de **Web site:** http://www.physiotherapeuten.de
Freq: Monthly; **Annual Sub.:** EUR 100,80; **Circ:** 26,408
Editor: Michael Dietl; **Advertising Manager:** Michael Dietl
Profile: The magazine is aimed at physical therapists of all disciplines and fields and adjacent to interested professionals. The headings of science, theory, magazine and practice comprise research, commentaries, interviews, reviews, reports, meetings, Short Articles and events.. The journal bridges the gap between practice and science - and between science and practice. All categories are closely linked in the magazine. pt sees itself as a professionally competent companion on the road to academisation and professionalism in physiotherapy. Target groups: Physiotherapists, massage therapists and medical bath attendants, occupational therapists and doctors.
Language(s): German
ADVERTISING RATES:
Full Page Mono .... EUR 2460
Full Page Colour .... EUR 3870
Mechanical Data: Type Area: 256 x 185 mm, No. of Columns (Display): 3, Col Widths (Display): 59 mm
Copy instructions: *Copy Date:* 31 days prior to publication
Official Journal of: Organ d. Dt. Verb. f. Physiotherapie - Zentralverb. d. Physiotherapeuten/ Krankengymnasten e.V.
Supplement(s): ZVK Journal
BUSINESS: HEALTH & MEDICAL: Health Medical Related

PTA DIE PTA IN DER APOTHEKE
739718G37-90
Editorial: Otto-Volger-Str. 15, 65843 SULZBACH
Tel: 6196 7667245 **Fax:** 6196 7676269
Email: p.kreuter@uzv.de **Web site:** http://www.pta-aktuell.de
Freq: Monthly; **Annual Sub.:** EUR 72,00; **Circ:** 26,791
Editor: Petra Kreuter; **Advertising Manager:** Norbert Stahl
Profile: Magazine for professionals in the pharmacy. Core target group are pharmaceutical technicians and pharmaceutical engineers. Contains current foundation contributions to pharmacy practice. Focus: Self-medication and counseling. Information about new products and applications, PTA and PKA training.
Language(s): German
Readership: Aimed at those involved in the pharmaceutical trade.
ADVERTISING RATES:
Full Page Mono .... EUR 2750
Full Page Colour .... EUR 4260
Mechanical Data: Type Area: 237 x 186 mm, No. of Columns (Display): 4, Col Widths (Display): 44 mm
Copy instructions: *Copy Date:* 21 days prior to publication
Supplement(s): DGE info
BUSINESS: PHARMACEUTICAL & CHEMISTS

PTA FORUM
1606208G37-1755
Editorial: Carl-Mannich-Str. 26, 65760 ESCHBORN
Tel: 6196 928280 **Fax:** 6196 928275
Email: pta-forum@govi.de **Web site:** http://www.pta-forum.de
Freq: Monthly; Free to qualifying individuals
Annual Sub.: EUR 35,76; **Circ:** 38,028
Editor: Daniel Rücker; **Advertising Manager:** Edgar Opper
Profile: Supplement the "PZ Pharmaceutical newspaper, " Regular Categories: Herbs Portraits: The self-medication-related plants, self-medication / advice in hand sale: On the basis of important groups of drugs or diseases, support for counseling, politics: the latest information and developments in health care, tips for Practice: Integrated into the articles, the interaction of medicines: examples from practice, Alternative Healing: Holistic therapies, Market Compass: Reviews and News from industry, communication: professional dealing with difficult customers, reports from the PTA schools, PTA-service training and congresses. The contributions offer subject-specific designed base and background knowledge on selected topics relevant to the activities of the PTA useful and important. The publication of phone numbers and addresses of advice or information points is the readers-makers use rate. This illustrates the positive response.
Language(s): German
ADVERTISING RATES:
Full Page Mono .... EUR 4110
Full Page Colour .... EUR 4110
Mechanical Data: Type Area: 260 x 178 mm, No. of Columns (Display): 3, Col Widths (Display): 56 mm
Copy instructions: *Copy Date:* 15 days prior to publication
Supplement to: PZ Pharmazeutische Zeitung

PTA HEUTE
739717G37-88
Editorial: Birkenwaldstr. 44, 70191 STUTTGART
Tel: 711 2582238 **Fax:** 711 2582291
Email: rberger@deutscher-apotheker-verlag.de **Web site:** http://www.ptaheute.de
Freq: 24 issues yearly; Free to qualifying individuals
Annual Sub.: EUR 69,80; **Circ:** 47,302
Editor: Reinhild Berger; **Advertising Manager:** Kornelia Wind
Profile: Magazine for the pharmaceutical-technical assistant. PTA Heute takes on all topics around the pharmacy: the focus is drug and support. Furthermore, it is about Dermocosmetics, nutrition and dietary supplements and medical-pharmaceutical products.
Language(s): German
Readership: Aimed at pharmacists and retailers of pharmaceutical products.
ADVERTISING RATES:
Full Page Mono .... EUR 3720
Full Page Colour .... EUR 5630
Mechanical Data: Type Area: 238 x 182 mm, No. of Columns (Display): 3, Col Widths (Display): 56 mm
Copy instructions: *Copy Date:* 20 days prior to publication
BUSINESS: PHARMACEUTICAL & CHEMISTS

PTT PERSÖNLICHKEITS-STÖRUNGEN THEORIE UND THERAPIE
739721G56A-8780
Editorial: Hölderlinstr. 3, 70174 STUTTGART
Tel: 711 2298734 **Fax:** 711 2298765
Email: birgit.lang@schattauer.de **Web site:** http://www.ptt-online.info
Freq: Quarterly; **Annual Sub.:** EUR 98,00; **Circ:** 2,150
Advertising Manager: Nicole Dörr
Profile: The number of patients with personality disorders in the practices of neurologists, psychiatrists and psychotherapists is constantly increasing. The therapy makes considerable demands on their competence and professionalism. Comorbidity with depression requiring treatment with medication to some extent, forced and anxiety disorders is common. First editor of the periodical, Prof. Kernberg, is considered the world's leading scientist in the field of personality disorders. Requested overview and original works by renowned authors in memorable graphic design form the basis for the work of practicing neurologists and psychotherapists.
Language(s): German
ADVERTISING RATES:
Full Page Mono .... EUR 1395
Full Page Colour .... EUR 2505
Mechanical Data: Type Area: 212 x 137 mm, No. of Columns (Display): 2
Copy instructions: *Copy Date:* 40 days prior to publication
Official Journal of: Organ d. Ges. z. Erforschung u. Therapie v. Persönlichkeitsstörungen

PTV COMPASS
1663527G18B-2087
Editorial: Stumpfstr. 1, 76131 KARLSRUHE
Tel: 721 96510 **Fax:** 721 9651699
Email: public.relations@ptv.de **Web site:** http://www.ptv.de
Freq: 3 issues yearly; **Cover Price:** Free; **Circ:** 10,000
Editor: Kristina Stifter

Profile: Customer magazine on travel-, traffic- and transport planning in the B2B sector.
Language(s): German

PUBLIC 739723G80-9360

Editorial: Schwemannstr. 8, 31134 HILDESHEIM
Tel: 5121 37073 **Fax:** 5121 132458
Email: public@esprit-media.de **Web site:** http://www.stadtmagazin-public.de
Freq: Monthly; **Cover Price:** Free; **Circ:** 8,888
Editor: Jan Fuhrhop; **Advertising Manager:** Daniel Rothert
Profile: Magazine for city and region, concentrating on gastronomy, music, arts and events.
Language(s): German
ADVERTISING RATES:
Full Page Mono .... EUR 1100
Full Page Colour .... EUR 1580
Mechanical Data: Type Area: 285 x 187 mm, No. of Columns (Display): 4, Col Widths (Display): 44 mm
Copy instructions: *Copy Date:* 15 days prior to publication
CONSUMER: RURAL & REGIONAL INTEREST

PUBLIC MARKETING 1895943G2A-5803

Editorial: Nebendahlstr. 16, 22041 HAMBURG
Tel: 40 60900974 **Fax:** 40 60900977
Email: wodzak@new-business.de **Web site:** http://www.publicmarketing.eu
Freq: 10 issues yearly; **Annual Sub.:** EUR 120,00; **Circ:** 2,500
Editor: Yvonne Wodzak; **Advertising Manager:** Milosz Lipski
Profile: Magazine about public marketing.
Language(s): German
ADVERTISING RATES:
Full Page Mono .... EUR 2490
Full Page Colour .... EUR 2490
Mechanical Data: Type Area: 262 x 175 mm
Copy instructions: *Copy Date:* 18 days prior to publication

PUBLIC RELATIONS FORUM FÜR WISSENSCHAFT UND PRAXIS 739727G2E-140

Editorial: Wächterstr. 2, 90489 NÜRNBERG
Tel: 911 22814 **Fax:** 911 22815
Email: antim-verlag@t-online.de
Freq: Quarterly; **Annual Sub.:** EUR 40,00; **Circ:** 4,150
Editor: Werner Wunder; **Advertising Manager:** Lydia Kastenhuber
Profile: Magazine about all aspects of public relations.
Language(s): German
ADVERTISING RATES:
Full Page Mono .... EUR 1800
Full Page Colour .... EUR 2700
Mechanical Data: Type Area: 260 x 176 mm, No. of Columns (Display): 2, Col Widths (Display): 72 mm
Copy instructions: *Copy Date:* 15 days prior to publication
BUSINESS: COMMUNICATIONS, ADVERTISING & MARKETING: Public Relations

PUBLIK-FORUM 739730G87-11000

Editorial: Krebsmühle, 61440 OBERURSEL
Tel: 6171 70030 **Fax:** 6171 700340
Email: redaktion@publik-forum.de **Web site:** http://www.publik-forum.de
Freq: 24 issues yearly; **Circ:** 36,742
Editor: Wolfgang Kessler; **Advertising Manager:** Barbara Wetzel
Profile: Magazine covering the economy, business, politics, theology of the church.
Language(s): German
ADVERTISING RATES:
Full Page Mono .... EUR 2681
Full Page Colour .... EUR 3888
Mechanical Data: Type Area: 261 x 190 mm, No. of Columns (Display): 3, Col Widths (Display): 62 mm
Copy instructions: *Copy Date:* 17 days prior to publication
CONSUMER: RELIGIOUS

PUBLIZISTIK 739734G2A-4080

Editorial: Expo-Plaza 12, 30539 HANNOVER
Tel: 511 3100484 **Fax:** 511 3100400
Email: gunter.reus@ijk.hmt-hannover.de **Web site:** http://www.publizistik-digital.de
Freq: Quarterly; **Annual Sub.:** EUR 129,00; **Circ:** 680
Editor: Gunter Reus; **Advertising Manager:** Yvonne Guderjahn
Profile: Magazine about press and publicity.
Language(s): German
ADVERTISING RATES:
Full Page Mono .... EUR 735
Full Page Colour .... EUR 1635
Mechanical Data: Type Area: 190 x 125 mm
BUSINESS: COMMUNICATIONS, ADVERTISING & MARKETING

PUK PROZESSTECHNIK UND KOMPONENTEN 739748G19E-1520

Editorial: Blumenstr. 15, 90402 NÜRNBERG
Tel: 911 20180 **Fax:** 911 2018100
Email: puk@harnisch.com **Web site:** http://www.harnisch.com
Freq: Annual; **Annual Sub.:** EUR 12,00; **Circ:** 21,701
Editor: Silke Watkins; **Advertising Manager:** Ursula Hahn
Profile: PuK Prozesstechnik und Komponenten is the immediate replacement for "Pumpen und Kompressoren mit Druckluft- und Vakuumtechnik" which existed for over 50 years. Of course this new format will contain all previous features. To explain the vast range of applications of pumps and compressors, four special topics have been determined according to economic and research needs: • Water/Wastewater/Environmental engineering • Chemistry/Pharma/Bioengineering • Energy/Oil/Gas • Food and beverage industry. In the future, not only do we view singular elements but increasingly integrated system solutions as well. In addition, the components will take up more room. To top off the content, company news and innovations as well as a shopping guide with dot index and trade mark registry have been included.
Language(s): German
ADVERTISING RATES:
Full Page Mono .... EUR 5625
Full Page Colour .... EUR 8156
Mechanical Data: Type Area: 250 x 189 mm

PUMUCKL MAGAZIN 739752G91D-6620

Editorial: Rotebühlstr. 87, 70178 STUTTGART
Tel: 711 94768780 **Fax:** 711 94768830
Email: info@panini.de **Web site:** http://www.panini.de
Freq: 6 issues yearly; **Cover Price:** EUR 2,70; **Circ:** 25,728
Editor: Gabriele El Hag
Profile: The magazine offers panini puck strengths Pumuckl two comics and a lot of fun and action. There are competitions with klabauterstarken prices and great extras.
Language(s): German
ADVERTISING RATES:
Full Page Mono .... EUR 3900
Full Page Colour .... EUR 3900
Mechanical Data: Type Area: 260 x 190 mm
CONSUMER: RECREATION & LEISURE: Children & Youth

THE PUNCHLINER 1657435G73-512

Editorial: Hauptstr. 16b, 38527 MEINE
Tel: 5304 501783 **Fax:** 5304 501796
Email: reiffer@verlag-reiffer.de **Web site:** http://www.verlag-reiffer.de
Freq: Annual; **Annual Sub.:** EUR 15,00; **Circ:** 500
Editor: Andreas Reiffer; **Advertising Manager:** Andreas Reiffer
Profile: Magazine about literature, sub culture and satire.
Language(s): German
Copy instructions: *Copy Date:* 30 days prior to publication

PUNKT 1657720G1C-1449

Editorial: Brienner Str. 18, 80333 MÜNCHEN
Tel: 89 217126724 **Fax:** 89 217121250
Email: punkt@bayernlb.de
Freq: Quarterly; **Circ:** 9,000
Editor: Sabine Ratschiller
Profile: Magazine of the Bayerische Landesbank.
Language(s): German

PUNKT 756443G14A-9238

Editorial: Frankfurter Str. 720, 51145 KÖLN
Tel: 2203 937507 **Fax:** 2203 937191
Email: pressestelle@gruener-punkt.de **Web site:** http://www.gruener-punkt.de
Freq: 3 issues yearly; **Cover Price:** Free; **Circ:** 6,000
Editor: Klaus Hillebrand
Profile: Magazine from the Duales System Deutschland company about waste disposal management and the environment, saving of resources and recycling.
Language(s): German
BUSINESS: COMMERCE, INDUSTRY & MANAGEMENT

PUNKT.RBW 1826972G14A-10080

Editorial: Friedrich-Ebert-Str., 51429 BERGISCH GLADBACH **Tel:** 2204 97630 **Fax:** 2204 976399
Email: info@rbw.de **Web site:** http://www.rbw.de
Freq: Quarterly; **Circ:** 5,500
Editor: Erik Werdel; **Advertising Manager:** Natascha Ern
Profile: Regional economy magazine.
Language(s): German
ADVERTISING RATES:
Full Page Mono .... EUR 725
Full Page Colour .... EUR 1125
Mechanical Data: Type Area: 278 x 185 mm

PUPPEN & SPIELZEUG 739766G79K-1620

Editorial: Stresemannstr. 20, 47051 DUISBURG
Tel: 203 3052748 **Fax:** 203 30527820
Email: r.ndouop.kalajian@wohlfarth.de **Web site:** http://www.puppen-und-spielzeug.de
Freq: 6 issues yearly; **Annual Sub.:** EUR 37,20; **Circ:** 7,900
Editor: Frank Wohlfarth; **Advertising Manager:** Jutta Nagels
Profile: Magazine focusing on the history of dolls. Includes collection advice, details on prices and auctions and profiles of antique and modern dolls.
Language(s): German
Readership: Aimed at collectors of dolls.
ADVERTISING RATES:
Full Page Mono .... EUR 880
Full Page Colour .... EUR 1650
Mechanical Data: Type Area: 259 x 178 mm
Copy instructions: *Copy Date:* 46 days prior to publication
CONSUMER: HOBBIES & DIY: Collectors Magazines

PUR 1640382G80-14165

Editorial: Ludwigstr. 37, 60327 FRANKFURT
Tel: 69 974600 **Fax:** 69 97460163
Email: redaktion@welovepur.de **Web site:** http://www.frankfurt-pur.de
Freq: Monthly; **Cover Price:** Free; **Circ:** 30,285
Advertising Manager: Melanie Hennemann
Profile: Magazine for city and region, concentrating on gastronomy, music, arts and events. Facebook: http://www.facebook.com/welovepur This Outlet offers RSS (Really Simple Syndication).
Language(s): German
ADVERTISING RATES:
Full Page Mono .... EUR 2340
Full Page Colour .... EUR 3560
Mechanical Data: Type Area: 270 x 195 mm
Copy instructions: *Copy Date:* 9 days prior to publication
CONSUMER: RURAL & REGIONAL INTEREST

PURE BY PREMIUMPARK 1977633G19B-124

Editorial: Herzogparkstr. 1, 81679 MÜNCHEN
Tel: 89 80032070
Email: guenther@premiumpark.de **Web site:** http://www.premiumpark.de
Freq: 6 issues yearly; **Annual Sub.:** EUR 55,00; **Circ:** 22,000
Editor: Andreas Günther; **Advertising Manager:** Johannes Ruf
Profile: Magazine for business, design and sustainability. It is a competent guide through the most important product ranges - from housing to travel from work enjoy. pure discovered the best products from these worlds - a model of design and sustainability. At the same time, the magazine raises his index finger and warns of products or companies that are no longer accurate and timely act or. There is thus a unique orientation medium for the conscious consumers and at the same time to the welcome stage for companies, are defined by values such as design and sustainability. Even if the magazine focuses on the core values, it is not ecologically or alternatively konsumverneinend. Rather, it promotes the responsible consumption and therefore represents a contemporary understanding of luxury. Finally, it lays claim to this authority does not, it is rather based on a panel of scientific competence and the media. Internationally renowned experts will support pure act and in the selection of topics and products. And for pure write-known authors.
Language(s): German
ADVERTISING RATES:
Full Page Mono .... EUR 8000
Full Page Colour .... EUR 8000
Mechanical Data: Type Area: 340 x 240 mm

PV MAGAZINE 2001873G58-1836

Editorial: Zinnowitzer Str. 1, 10115 BERLIN
Tel: 30 726296458 **Fax:** 30 726296309
Email: neidlein@pv-magazine.com **Web site:** http://www.pv-magazine.com
Freq: Monthly; **Annual Sub.:** EUR 179,00; **Circ:** 20,200
Editor: Hans-Christoph Neidlein; **Advertising Manager:** Andrea Jeremias
Profile: The magazine provides information on the photovoltaic market and the latest technological developments. With its independent, technology-focused reporting, pv magazine concentrates on covering the latest PV news, topical technological trends and worldwide market developments. Categories covered include: markets & trends, research & development, applications & installations, industry & suppliers, careers & recruitment, and products. Facebook: http://www.facebook.com/pvmagazine Twitter: http://twitter.com/#!/pvmagazine This Outlet offers RSS (Really Simple Syndication).
Language(s): English
ADVERTISING RATES:
Full Page Mono .... EUR 3450
Full Page Colour .... EUR 3450
Mechanical Data: Type Area: 254 x 183 mm

PVH MAGAZIN 739775G14A-6020

Editorial: EDE-Platz 1, 42389 WUPPERTAL
Tel: 202 6096865 **Fax:** 202 609670739
Email: wolfgang.pott@ede.de **Web site:** http://www.ede.de
Freq: 5 issues yearly; **Circ:** 7,000
Editor: Wolfgang Pott; **Advertising Manager:** Claudia Berlinghof
Profile: Magazine for the production-associated trade in the range of focus tools / machine tools, equipment, fastening systems, hardware / Security / components, construction equipment / safety / technical trade, steel and plumbing / heating.
Language(s): German
ADVERTISING RATES:
Full Page Colour .... EUR 2050
Mechanical Data: Type Area: 247 x 169 mm, No. of Columns (Display): 3, Col Widths (Display): 53 mm
Copy instructions: *Copy Date:* 30 days prior to publication

PVS POLITISCHE VIERTELJAHRESSCHRIFT 739184G82-9487

Editorial: Schneiderberg 50, 30167 HANNOVER
Tel: 511 7625703
Email: pvs-redaktion@ipw.uni-hannover.de **Web site:** http://www.pvs-digital.de
Freq: Quarterly; **Annual Sub.:** EUR 177,00; **Circ:** 1,080
Editor: Rainer Schmalz-Bruns
Profile: Magazine containing articles about the current political situation in Germany.
Language(s): German
Mechanical Data: Type Area: 190 x 125 mm, No. of Columns (Display): 2, Col Widths (Display): 61 mm
CONSUMER: CURRENT AFFAIRS & POLITICS

PVT POLIZEI VERKEHR + TECHNIK 739202G32F-760

Editorial: Nietzschestr. 46, 53117 BONN
Tel: 228 3240995 **Fax:** 228 3240995
Email: redaktion@polizei-verkehr-technik.de **Web site:** http://www.polizei-verkehr-technik.de
Freq: 6 issues yearly; **Annual Sub.:** EUR 37,30; **Circ:** 3,683
Editor: Helmut Kimmerle; **Advertising Manager:** Dorina Schulze
Profile: Magazine for all members of the BOS and for police and other security companies and services with content areas for police, traffic and safety engineering and management.
Language(s): German
ADVERTISING RATES:
Full Page Mono .... EUR 1950
Full Page Colour .... EUR 2950
Mechanical Data: Type Area: 260 x 180 mm, No. of Columns (Display): 3, Col Widths (Display): 57 mm
Copy instructions: *Copy Date:* 28 days prior to publication
BUSINESS: LOCAL GOVERNMENT, LEISURE & RECREATION: Police

PYRMONTER NACHRICHTEN 739782G67B-11920

Editorial: Baustr. 44, 31785 HAMELN **Tel:** 5151 2000
Fax: 5151 200435
Email: redaktion@dewezet.de **Web site:** http://www.dewezet.de
Freq: 312 issues yearly; **Circ:** 5,150
Advertising Manager: Rolf Grummel
Profile: Daily newspaper with regional news and a local sports section. This Outlet offers RSS (Really Simple Syndication).
Language(s): German
ADVERTISING RATES:
SCC .... EUR 25,40
Mechanical Data: Type Area: 430 x 281 mm, No. of Columns (Display): 6, Col Widths (Display): 44 mm
Copy instructions: *Copy Date:* 1 day prior to publication
REGIONAL DAILY & SUNDAY NEWSPAPERS: Regional Daily Newspapers

PYRMONTER RUNDBLICK 739783G72-10628

Editorial: Baustr. 44, 31785 HAMELN
Tel: 5151 578814 **Fax:** 5151 578816
Email: e.hesse@wrw-hameln.de **Web site:** http://www.wrw-hameln.de
Freq: Weekly; **Cover Price:** Free; **Circ:** 17,000
Editor: Guido-Erol Hesse-Öztanil; **Advertising Manager:** Claudia Reisch
Profile: Advertising journal (house-to-house) concentrating on local stories.
Language(s): German
ADVERTISING RATES:
Full Page Mono .... EUR 1599
Full Page Colour .... EUR 2499
Mechanical Data: Type Area: 430 x 281 mm, No. of Columns (Display): 6, Col Widths (Display): 44 mm
Copy instructions: *Copy Date:* 3 days prior to publication
LOCAL NEWSPAPERS

PZ PHARMAZEUTISCHE ZEITUNG 739786G37-1460

Editorial: Carl-Mannich-Str. 26, 65760 ESCHBORN
Tel: 6196 928280 **Fax:** 6196 928275
Email: redaktion@govi.de **Web site:** http://www.pharmazeutische-zeitung.de
Freq: Weekly; Free to qualifying individuals
Annual Sub.: EUR 156,00; **Circ:** 37,096
Editor: Daniel Rücker; **Advertising Manager:** Edgar Opper
Profile: Due to the wide range of views and current reports, the PZ PHARMAZEUTISCHE ZEITUNG is ranked in the first place of the weekly journals among the readers. The PZ is characterized as close to practice and to reader-needs edited information. Through the current reporting and focus on the needs of the target group PZ-readers are generally better informed than many doctors. As confirmed by reader surveys. The PT informs neutrally about the benefits and risks of new medicines: factually, professionally, objectively. With this section, the PT is recommended as an independent medium for commerce and

industry. The diversity of themes and opinions in the PZ find a great deal of attention within the entire pharmacy team. The reader-friendly, diverse structured editorial content permanently provides new impulses and and reading incentives: - contributions convey the latest scientific findings in a compact manner. - The heading Drug Commission is an official service for pharmacists. Informs, among other things, about recalls, . - Contributions from pharmacy and medicine, health and social work, profession and politics, science, economy and trade cover a wide field of interests. - Summaries of original contributions underline the range of expertise. - Of great interest are the contributions from the chambers and associations, local and specialist-oriented groups as well as from universities.
Language(s): German
ADVERTISING RATES:
Full Page Mono .... EUR 5720
Full Page Colour .... EUR 5720
Mechanical Data: Type Area: 251 x 177 mm, No. of Columns (Display): 3, Col Widths (Display): 55 mm
Copy instructions: *Copy Date:* 10 days prior to publication
Supplement(s): pta Forum
BUSINESS: PHARMACEUTICAL & CHEMISTS

PZ PHARMAZEUTISCHE ZEITUNG ONLINE 1685596G37-1822
Editorial: Carl-Mannich-Str. 26, 65760 ESCHBORN
Tel: 6196 928280 **Fax:** 6196 928275
Email: redaktion@govi.de **Web site:** http://www.pharmazeutische-zeitung.de
Freq: Daily; **Cover Price:** Paid; **Circ:** 292,629 Unique Users
Editor: Sven Siebenand; **Advertising Manager:** Achim Heinemann
Profile: Internet Media: PZ Pharmazeutische Zeitung is the largest online portal, when it comes to pharmacists as well as to achieve PTA online. The portal brings together the online archives information on approximately 350 new drugs, more than 500 NRF recipe instructions and almost 16,000 articles and PT has the largest German pharmaceutical link collection with more than 2000 links together. On this page you will supply the pharmaceutical newspaper succinctly presented in alphabetical order.
Language(s): German
BUSINESS: PHARMACEUTICAL & CHEMISTS

PZ PIRMASENSER ZEITUNG 739787G67B-11940
Editorial: Schachenstr. 1, 66954 PIRMASENS
Tel: 6331 80050 **Fax:** 6331 800581
Email: redaktion@pirmasenser-zeitung.de **Web site:** http://www.pirmasenser-zeitung.de
Freq: 312 issues yearly; **Circ:** 13,015
Editor: Franz-Josef Majer; **Advertising Manager:** Alexander Hoffmann
Profile: Regional daily newspaper covering politics, economics, sport, travel and technology.
Language(s): German
ADVERTISING RATES:
SCC .... EUR 45,80
Mechanical Data: Type Area: 485 x 320 mm, No. of Columns (Display): 7, Col Widths (Display): 44 mm
Copy instructions: *Copy Date:* 1 day prior to publication
REGIONAL DAILY & SUNDAY NEWSPAPERS: Regional Daily Newspapers

PZ PRISMA 765152G37-1725
Editorial: Carl-Mannich-Str. 26, 65760 ESCHBORN
Tel: 6196 928262 **Fax:** 6196 928203
Email: redaktion@govi.de **Web site:** http://www.govi.de
Freq: Quarterly; **Annual Sub.:** EUR 50,00; **Circ:** 1,500
Editor: Axel Helmstädter; **Advertising Manager:** Edgar Opper
Profile: Magazine on further education for pharmacists. The magazine is primarily aimed at pharmacists in training as a specialist pharmacist, a qualification that for several years after graduation as in the areas Offizinpharmazie, clinical pharmacy, pharmaceutical technology or medical information can be acquired.
Language(s): German
ADVERTISING RATES:
Full Page Mono .... EUR 806
Full Page Colour .... EUR 1336
Mechanical Data: Type Area: 250 x 176 mm
Copy instructions: *Copy Date:* 28 days prior to publication

QM-INFOCENTER.DE 1704565G14R-6144
Editorial: Kolbergerstr. 22, 81679 MÜNCHEN
Tel: 89 99830258 **Fax:** 89 99830156
Email: redaktion@qm-infocenter.de **Web site:** http://www.qm-infocenter.de
Freq: Daily; **Cover Price:** Paid; **Circ:** 28,158 Unique Users
Editor: Petra Weber; **Advertising Manager:** Bianca Diekmann
Profile: Online portal on quality management and quality assurance.
Language(s): German
BUSINESS: COMMERCE, INDUSTRY & MANAGEMENT: Commerce Related

QUALIMEDIC 1703654G74G-1856
Editorial: Brückenstr. 1, 50667 KÖLN **Tel:** 221 27050
Fax: 221 2705555
Email: funk@qualimedic.de **Web site:** http://www.qualimedic.de
Cover Price: Paid; **Circ:** 1,239,350 Unique Users
Editor: Miriam Funk
Language(s): German
CONSUMER: WOMEN'S INTEREST CONSUMER MAGAZINES: Slimming & Health

QUALITY ENGINEERING 733144G14K-100
Editorial: Ernst-Mey-Str. 8, 70771 LEINFELDEN-ECHTERDINGEN **Tel:** 711 7594451
Fax: 711 75941451
Email: qe.redaktion@konradin.de **Web site:** http://www.qe-online.de
Freq: 6 issues yearly; **Annual Sub.:** EUR 68,40; **Circ:** 20,490
Editor: Werner Götz; **Advertising Manager:** Andreas Hugel
Profile: Journal competently addresses the market- and application-oriented to the quality management and quality assurance and production measurement. Editorial focus on quality / environmental management, Dimensional measurement, image processing / machine vision, optical metrology, materials testing and metrology. The readers are experts in quality assurance, management and production measurement technology in innovative companies in all industries. A major part is involved in investment decisions.
Language(s): German
Readership: Aimed at those who work in quality assurance.
ADVERTISING RATES:
Full Page Mono .... EUR 4620
Full Page Colour .... EUR 5685
Mechanical Data: Type Area: 270 x 188 mm, No. of Columns (Display): 4, Col Widths (Display): 44 mm
BUSINESS: COMMERCE, INDUSTRY & MANAGEMENT: Quality Assurance

QUARTER HORSE JOURNAL 739810G75E-160
Editorial: Sonnenstr. 2, 65529 WALDEMS
Tel: 6126 989220
Email: redaktion@quarter-horse-journal.de **Web site:** http://www.quarter-horse-journal.de
Freq: Monthly; Free to qualifying individuals
Annual Sub.: EUR 48,00; **Circ:** 23,600
Editor: Friederike Fritz; **Advertising Manager:** Maren Arndt
Profile: The current monthly magazine for Western Horse breeding, sport, lifestyle and leisure. As an official member of several organizations in Western Riding QHJ whose members receive as part of their membership. The American Quarter Horse is the American dream of riding and is numerically the largest breed of horse in the world, with more than 4 million registered horses in 85 countries.
Language(s): German
ADVERTISING RATES:
Full Page Mono .... EUR 952
Full Page Colour .... EUR 1464
Mechanical Data: Type Area: 250 x 190 mm, No. of Columns (Display): 4, Col Widths (Display): 43 mm
Copy instructions: *Copy Date:* 25 days prior to publication
Official Journal of: Organ d. Dt., Austrian/Swiss Quarter Horse Association e.V., d. NSBA u. NCHA o.G. e.V.
CONSUMER: SPORT: Horse Racing

QUARTERLY JOURNAL OF INTERNATIONAL AGRICULTURE 739811G21A-3220
Editorial: Eschborner Landstr. 122, 60489 FRANKFURT **Tel:** 69 247880 **Fax:** 69 24788480
Email: dlg-verlag@dlg.org **Web site:** http://www.dlg-verlag.de
Freq: Quarterly; **Annual Sub.:** EUR 117,00; **Circ:** 350
Advertising Manager: Viola Hilz
Profile: Contributions to agrarian sciences and rural developments in the international context.
Language(s): English

QUEENS 1703426G80-14735
Editorial: Wiedbachstr. 50, 56567 NEUWIED
Tel: 2631 964647 **Fax:** 2631 964611
Email: a.gras@hwg-media.de **Web site:** http://www.queens.vg
Freq: Monthly; **Cover Price:** Free; **Circ:** 14,694
Editor: Anna Lena Gras; **Advertising Manager:** Rolf Mohrs
Language(s): German
CONSUMER: RURAL & REGIONAL INTEREST

QUER DURCH HAMBURG/ SCHLESWIG-HOLSTEIN SCHIFFFAHRT UND TRANSPORT 739793G49A-1580
Editorial: Nordkanalstr. 36, 20097 HAMBURG
Tel: 40 23714136 **Fax:** 40 23714333
Email: marijana.mikulic@dvvmedia.com **Web site:** http://www.dvvmedia.com
Freq: Annual; **Cover Price:** EUR 29,90; **Circ:** 4,000
Editor: Marijana Mikulic; **Advertising Manager:** Oliver Detje
Profile: Directory for the transport business.
Language(s): German
ADVERTISING RATES:
Full Page Mono .... EUR 1280
Full Page Colour .... EUR 2180
Mechanical Data: Type Area: 122 x 82 mm
Copy instructions: *Copy Date:* 42 days prior to publication

QUICKBORNER TAGEBLATT 739840G67B-11960
Editorial: Damm 9, 25421 PINNEBERG
Tel: 4101 5356101 **Fax:** 4101 5356106
Email: redaktion@a-beig.de **Web site:** http://www.quickborner-tageblatt.de
Freq: 312 issues yearly; **Circ:** 12,796
Advertising Manager: Karsten Raasch
Profile: Daily newspaper with regional news and a local sports section. This Outlet offers RSS (Really Simple Syndication).
Language(s): German
ADVERTISING RATES:
SCC .... EUR 42,90
Mechanical Data: Type Area: 430 x 278 mm, No. of Columns (Display): 6, Col Widths (Display): 45 mm
Copy instructions: *Copy Date:* 1 day prior to publication
Supplement(s): nordisch gesund
REGIONAL DAILY & SUNDAY NEWSPAPERS: Regional Daily Newspapers

QUIP 739843G14A-9537
Editorial: Breite Str. 29, 10178 BERLIN
Tel: 30 203081520 **Fax:** 30 203081522
Email: quip@wjd.de **Web site:** http://www.wjd.de
Freq: 6 issues yearly; Free to qualifying individuals
Annual Sub.: EUR 24,60; **Circ:** 12,210
Editor: Karsten Taruttis; **Advertising Manager:** Daniel Mayershofer
Profile: The magazine of the Junior Chamber Germany "quip"deals with current issues in the fields of economy, society and politics, and offers its readers find the association reporting date background information on economic issues, industry trends and issues of strategic business development.
Language(s): German
ADVERTISING RATES:
Full Page Mono .... EUR 1980
Full Page Colour .... EUR 3300
Mechanical Data: Type Area: 259 x 189 mm, No. of Columns (Display): 3, Col Widths (Display): 59 mm
Supplement(s): B4B Mittelstand
BUSINESS: COMMERCE, INDUSTRY & MANAGEMENT

QZ QUALITÄT UND ZUVERLÄSSIGKEIT 739849G14K-200
Editorial: Kolbergerstr. 22, 81679 MÜNCHEN
Tel: 89 99830618 **Fax:** 89 99830624
Email: qz@hanser.de **Web site:** http://www.qm-infocenter.de
Freq: Monthly; Free to qualifying individuals
Annual Sub.: EUR 179,00; **Circ:** 18,213
Editor: Fritz Taucher; **Advertising Manager:** Hermann J. Kleiner
Profile: QZ Qualität und Zuverlässigkeit is the premier specialist journal on the subject of Quality Management in the industry and service sector. It provides practice-based information across all branches of industry for quality experts on subjects such as quality systems and methods, applicable standards, product liability, CAQ software, measurement and testing technology and the latest trends and career opportunities. As the mouthpiece of the German Association of Quality Management, QZ reaches an exclusive readership positioned within the middle to top management sector. Providing practically-oriented technical articles and product reports, QZ helps keep readers abreast of the latest trends and developments. With varied and interesting reports, interviews and comment, QZ provides valuable orientation in the professional environment.
Language(s): German
ADVERTISING RATES:
Full Page Mono .... EUR 3980
Full Page Colour .... EUR 5810
Mechanical Data: Type Area: 250 x 175 mm, No. of Columns (Display): 4, Col Widths (Display): 41 mm
Official Journal of: Organ d. Dt. Ges. f. Qualität u. d. Quality Austria
BUSINESS: COMMERCE, INDUSTRY & MANAGEMENT: Quality Assurance

R RATGEBER FRAU UND FAMILIE 740668G74A-2620
Editorial: Wehratalstr. 3, 79664 WEHR
Tel: 7761 9350 **Fax:** 7761 57691
Email: redaktion.hess@weck.de **Web site:** http://www.weck.de
Freq: Monthly; **Annual Sub.:** EUR 25,80; **Circ:** 161,399
Editor: Eberhard Hackelsberger; **News Editor:** Eberhard Hackelsberger; **Advertising Manager:** Eberhard Hackelsberger
Profile: Magazine for women with practical tips with an emphasis on food and drink, health, medicine and fashion.
Language(s): German
ADVERTISING RATES:
Full Page Mono .... EUR 8000
Full Page Colour .... EUR 8000
Mechanical Data: No. of Columns (Display): 3, Col Widths (Display): 47 mm, Type Area: 192 x 152 mm
Copy instructions: *Copy Date:* 53 days prior to publication
CONSUMER: WOMEN'S INTEREST CONSUMER MAGAZINES: Women's Interest

R RATGEBER FRAU UND FAMILIE SPEZIAL WEIHNACHTEN 1644955G74A-3416
Editorial: Wehratalstr. 3, 79664 WEHR
Tel: 7761 9350 **Fax:** 7761 57691
Email: ratgeber@weck.de **Web site:** http://www.weck.de
Freq: Annual; **Cover Price:** EUR 1,99; **Circ:** 200,000
Editor: Eberhard Hackelsberger; **Advertising Manager:** Eberhard Hackelsberger
Profile: Guide magazine, Christmas Special from J. Weck GmbH u. Co. KG.
Language(s): German
ADVERTISING RATES:
Full Page Mono .... EUR 3000
Full Page Colour .... EUR 3000
Mechanical Data: Type Area: 218 x 168 mm, No. of Columns (Display): 3, Col Widths (Display): 53 mm
Copy instructions: *Copy Date:* 60 days prior to publication

R+S RECHT UND SCHADEN 740066G1D-48
Editorial: Tagetesweg 15, 51143 KÖLN
Tel: 2203 84819
Email: johannes.waelder@netcologne.de
Freq: Monthly; **Annual Sub.:** EUR 214,70; **Circ:** 1,700
Editor: Johannes Wälder; **Advertising Manager:** Fritz Lebherz
Profile: Journal about insurance and compensation.
Language(s): German
ADVERTISING RATES:
Full Page Mono .... EUR 1460
Full Page Colour .... EUR 2960
Mechanical Data: Type Area: 260 x 186 mm, No. of Columns (Display): 4, Col Widths (Display): 43 mm
BUSINESS: FINANCE & ECONOMICS: Insurance

R + S ROLLLADEN + SONNENSCHUTZ 740831G4B-692
Editorial: Hopmannstr. 2, 53177 BONN
Tel: 228 952100 **Fax:** 228 9521010
Email: redaktion@rs-fachzeitschrift.de **Web site:** http://www.rs-fachzeitschrift.de
Freq: 10 issues yearly; Free to qualifying individuals
Annual Sub.: EUR 60,00; **Circ:** 2,450
Editor: Christoph Silber-Bonz
Profile: Magazine about roller shutters, venetian blinds, marquees, windows and similar equipment. Facebook: http://www.facebook.com/pages/Bundesverband-Rollladen-Sonnenschutz-eV/146674152049952.
Language(s): German
ADVERTISING RATES:
Full Page Mono .... EUR 560
Full Page Colour .... EUR 956
Mechanical Data: Type Area: 260 x 189 mm, No. of Columns (Display): 3, Col Widths (Display): 59 mm
Copy instructions: *Copy Date:* 28 days prior to publication

DER RABE RALF 1664254G57-2747
Editorial: Prenzlauer Allee 8, 10405 BERLIN
Tel: 30 44339147 **Fax:** 30 44339133
Email: raberalf@grueneliga.de **Web site:** http://www.raberalf.grueneliga-berlin.de
Freq: 6 issues yearly; Free to qualifying individuals ; **Circ:** 10,000
Editor: Leif Miller
Profile: Magazine about the environment of the Berlin region.
Language(s): German
ADVERTISING RATES:
Full Page Mono .... EUR 684
Full Page Colour .... EUR 1197
Mechanical Data: Type Area: 285 x 207 mm, No. of Columns (Display): 4, Col Widths (Display): 48 mm
Copy instructions: *Copy Date:* 10 days prior to publication

DER RADIOLOGE 739871G56J-180
Editorial: Tiergartenstr. 17, 69121 HEIDELBERG
Tel: 6221 4878519 **Fax:** 6221 48768519
Email: claudia.zappe@springer.com **Web site:** http://www.springermedizin.de
Freq: Monthly; **Annual Sub.:** EUR 417,00; **Circ:** 3,100
Editor: Maximilian Reiser; **Advertising Manager:** Odette Thomßen
Profile: Der Radiologe is an internationally recognized journal dealing with all aspects of radiology and serving the continuing medical education of radiologists in clinical and practical environments. The focus is on x-ray diagnostics, angiography computer tomography, interventional radiology, magnet resonance tomography, digital picture processing, radio oncology and nuclear medicine. Comprehensive reviews on a specific topical issue focus on providing evidenced based information on diagnostics and therapy. Freely submitted original papers allow the presentation of important clinical studies and serve the scientific exchange. Review articles under the rubric 'Continuing Medical Education' present verified results of scientific research and their integration into daily practice.
Language(s): German

ADVERTISING RATES:
Full Page Mono .... EUR 2020
Full Page Colour .... EUR 3210
Mechanical Data: Type Area: 240 x 174 mm
Official Journal of: Organ d. Berufsverb. d. Dt. Radiologen e.V.
BUSINESS: HEALTH & MEDICAL: Radiography

RADIOLOGIE TECHNOLGIE
739872G56R-1940
Editorial: Unterm Berg 91, 26123 OLDENBURG
Tel: 441 36258
Email: radiassi@nwn.de
Freq: Quarterly; **Annual Sub.:** EUR 15,10; **Circ:** 2,739
Editor: Anke Ohmstede; **Advertising Manager:** Christiane Kermel
Profile: Magazine for assistants in medical radiology.
Language(s): German
ADVERTISING RATES:
Full Page Mono .... EUR 1020
Full Page Colour .... EUR 1938
Mechanical Data: Type Area: 266 x 184 mm, No. of Columns (Display): 4, Col Widths (Display): 43 mm
Copy instructions: *Copy Date:* 42 days prior to publication
BUSINESS: HEALTH & MEDICAL: Health Medical Related

RADIOLOGIE UP2DATE
1606838A56A-2007
Editorial: Carl-Neuberg-Str. 1, 30625 HANNOVER
Email: galanski.m@mh-hannover.de **Web site:** http://www.thieme.de/fz/rad-u2d-impressum.html
Freq: Quarterly; **Annual Sub.:** EUR 173,40; **Circ:** 3,410
Editor: Michael Galanski
Profile: Compressed and concise information with high relevance, immediately actionable knowledge for practice. Each issue contains four CME Individual contributions, which are bound separately and are archived by the subscribers in a handy ring binder.
Language(s): German
ADVERTISING RATES:
Full Page Mono .... EUR 1560
Full Page Colour .... EUR 2730
Mechanical Data: Type Area: 250 x 175 mm

RADIOPRAXIS
1892740G56A-11591
Editorial: Rüdigerstr. 14, 70469 STUTTGART
Tel: 711 8931405 **Fax:** 711 8931564
Email: susanne.huiss@thieme.de **Web site:** http://www.thieme.de/fz/radiopraxis.html
Freq: Quarterly; **Annual Sub.:** EUR 69,90; **Circ:** 3,100
Editor: Susanne Huiss
Profile: Radiopraxis, the training journal provides the radiology team knowledge for daily practice. The publication also awards points for the certified training of medical-technical radiology assistants and radiology technologists. Radiopraxis provides information about Radiological Diagnostic, Nuclear Medicine and Radiotherapy. Reports on education, association news, science news and book reviews round out the content set.
Language(s): German
ADVERTISING RATES:
Full Page Mono .... EUR 1420
Full Page Colour .... EUR 2470
Mechanical Data: Type Area: 248 x 175 mm
Official Journal of: Organ d. RTaustria-Verb. d. RadiologietechnologInnen Österr. u. der VMTB-Vereinigung d. Med.-Techn. Berufe in d. DRG

RADMARKT
739881G31B-2
Editorial: Niederwall 53, 33602 BIELEFELD
Tel: 521 595522 **Fax:** 521 595518
Email: radmarkt@bva-bielefeld.de **Web site:** http://www.radmarkt.de
Freq: Monthly; **Annual Sub.:** EUR 102,00; **Circ:** 4,994
Editor: Michael Bollschweiler
Profile: Journal about the cycle and motorcycle trade, providing technical research, development and business news.
Language(s): German
Readership: Aimed at cycle and motorcycle manufacturers, retailers and repairers.
ADVERTISING RATES:
Full Page Colour .... EUR 3030
Mechanical Data: Type Area: 271 x 185 mm, No. of Columns (Display): 4, Col Widths (Display): 43 mm
Copy instructions: *Copy Date:* 28 days prior to publication
BUSINESS: MOTOR TRADE: Motorcycle Trade

RADWELT
739893G77C-300
Editorial: Grünenstr. 8, 28199 BREMEN
Tel: 421 346290 **Fax:** 421 3462950
Email: radwelt@adfc.de **Web site:** http://www.adfc.de
Freq: 6 issues yearly; Free to qualifying individuals
Annual Sub.: EUR 25,00; **Circ:** 76,034
Editor: Alexandra Kirsch; **Advertising Manager:** Petra Wedel
Profile: The magazine of the ADFC reports on the transport policy work of ADFC. It communicates the cycling fun. The main topics of trekking and bike magazine: * Move: with policy and traffic issues, content from the ADFC life and activities, with background information on laws and legal help * Technology: Driving with reports, background information and product comparisons * Travel with travel stories, tips and tour destinations.
Language(s): German
ADVERTISING RATES:
Full Page Mono .... EUR 3730
Full Page Colour .... EUR 5400
Mechanical Data: Type Area: 260 x 185 mm, No. of Columns (Display): 4, Col Widths (Display): 45 mm
CONSUMER: MOTORING & CYCLING: Cycling

RADZEIT
739894G77C-320
Editorial: Brunnenstr. 28, 10119 BERLIN
Tel: 30 4484724 **Fax:** 30 44340520
Email: kontakt@radzeit.de **Web site:** http://www.adfc-berlin.de
Freq: 6 issues yearly; Free to qualifying individuals
Annual Sub.: EUR 10,00; **Circ:** 41,595
Editor: Michaela Müller; **Advertising Manager:** David Greve
Profile: Magazine for leisure time bicyclists.
Language(s): German
ADVERTISING RATES:
Full Page Mono .... EUR 1025
Full Page Colour .... EUR 1400
Mechanical Data: No. of Columns (Display): 2, Col Widths (Display): 60 mm, Type Area: 180 x 125 mm
Copy instructions: *Copy Date:* 12 days prior to publication
CONSUMER: MOTORING & CYCLING: Cycling

RAIFFEISEN MAGAZIN
739925G21A-3240
Editorial: Pariser Platz 3, 10117 BERLIN
Tel: 30 856214430 **Fax:** 30 856214432
Email: windbergs@drv.raiffeisen.de **Web site:** http://www.raiffeisen.de
Freq: 6 issues yearly; **Circ:** 28,000
Editor: Monika Windbergs; **Advertising Manager:** Monika Windbergs
Profile: Magazine from the German Raiffeisen Association about agrarian economy, marketing, cooperatives and agrarian politics.
Language(s): German
ADVERTISING RATES:
Full Page Mono .... EUR 1500
Full Page Colour .... EUR 3450
Mechanical Data: Type Area: 258 x 163 mm, No. of Columns (Display): 3, Col Widths (Display): 60 mm
Copy instructions: *Copy Date:* 14 days prior to publication
Supplement to: netzwerk, Profil

RAMP
1852382G77A-2850
Editorial: Obere Wässere 5, 72764 REUTLINGEN
Tel: 7121 4330470 **Fax:** 7121 73304710
Email: info@ramp-magazin.de **Web site:** http://www.ramp-magazin.de
Freq: Quarterly; **Annual Sub.:** EUR 60,00; **Circ:** 40,000
Editor: Michael Köckritz; **Advertising Manager:** Patrick Morda
Profile: ramp is coffee-table book and car magazine with multithematischem access and strong standards. Immediately, authentic, intense. Fresh Change of perspective, to a fine sense of nuance and dramatic mix. Always new, always exciting. The layout is a useful means the experience-intensive production. Cars fascinate and delight like few things in this world. Their presence, their stories, their shapes, their opportunities, the sound of their engines raise passions. ramp will affect cars enter, start, go to experience - and share this experience with his readers. As intensively as possible, subjective rather than objective untouchable. ramp offers stories from driving and photo galleries as road movies in Cinemascope. The enthusiasm for the car connected with the love of life. The car in the context of music and fashion, culture and lifestyle, design and art. Pure car culture: the myths, the stories and anecdotes about models and brands.
Language(s): German
ADVERTISING RATES:
Full Page Mono .... EUR 9000
Full Page Colour .... EUR 9000
Mechanical Data: Type Area: 259 x 206 mm
Copy instructions: *Copy Date:* 38 days prior to publication

RAPIDX
2077903G19E-1977
Editorial: Kolbergerstr. 22, 81679 MÜNCHEN
Tel: 89 99830611 **Fax:** 89 99830623
Email: fachtan@hanser.de **Web site:** http://www.form-werkzeug.de
Freq: 3 issues yearly; **Circ:** 7,000
Editor: Richard Fachtan; **Advertising Manager:** Dietmar von der Au
Profile: rapidX deals with Rapid Prototyping RP. These include rapid tooling RT and Rapid Manufacturing RM. In view of their wide application fields is called generative manufacturing processes. RP, RT, RM enable it to develop work pieces, parts and products very quickly according to individual customer requirements to design and produce cost-effective. In conjunction with other technologies such as reverse engineering (reverse development, so that reconstruction and replica), the whole process chain from RP, RT, RM of product development as a Rapid Product Development RPD is called. The magazine reports on each area of this main topics: RP model provides components and unique pieces based on her design data (CAD) with tool-free production and puts it directly and quickly through the layer manufacturing (using a laser printer or laser machines) in order to work or end products. RT made by layer manufacturing CAD data from complicated parts of molds. So you can check its functionality using near-series / series of the same components implement (design and function) and a short-term as more economical production of small series. RM made by layer manufacturing from CAD data quickly and flexible components, finished products and series. It uses the materials such as glass, metal, ceramics, plastics and new materials. RM simulated prior to manufacture your product in the virtual stage and can analyze and optimize it. The wide choice of material allows less waste and effective use of materials and is ecologically and economically. RapidX served as a high-tech magazine with large, modern layout with all these aspects and contribution of research, development and manufacturing and has a competent and interested audience.
Language(s): German
ADVERTISING RATES:
Full Page Mono .... EUR 2000
Full Page Colour .... EUR 3200
Mechanical Data: Type Area: 250 x 175 mm, No. of Columns (Display): 4, Col Widths (Display): 41 mm
Copy instructions: *Copy Date:* 29 days prior to publication

RAPS
739945G21A-3260
Editorial: Clemens-August-Str. 12, 53115 BONN
Tel: 228 9694230 **Fax:** 228 630311
Email: redaktion@dlg-agrofoodmedien.de **Web site:** http://www.dlg-agrofoodmedien.de
Freq: Quarterly; **Annual Sub.:** EUR 30,50; **Circ:** 14,875
Editor: Heinz-Peter Pütz; **Advertising Manager:** Rainer Schluck
Profile: Journal about oil and plant protein.
Language(s): German
Readership: Read by arable farmers.
ADVERTISING RATES:
Full Page Mono .... EUR 2340
Full Page Colour .... EUR 3870
Mechanical Data: Type Area: 270 x 186 mm, No. of Columns (Display): 3, Col Widths (Display): 58 mm
Official Journal of: Organ d. Union z. Förderung v. Oel- u. Proteinpflanzen e.V.
BUSINESS: AGRICULTURE & FARMING

RAS INTERNATIONAL
739951G3B-80
Editorial: Goethestr. 75, 40237 DÜSSELDORF
Tel: 211 9149408 **Fax:** 211 9149490
Email: n.klein@krs-redaktion.de **Web site:** http://www.ras-online.com
Freq: Monthly; **Annual Sub.:** EUR 60,00; **Circ:** 9,704
Editor: Nikolaus Klein; **Advertising Manager:** Alke Schmeis
Profile: Magazine focusing on plumbing, sanitation and heating.
Language(s): German
Readership: Read by plumbers and installation engineers.
ADVERTISING RATES:
Full Page Mono .... EUR 2750
Full Page Colour .... EUR 4675
Mechanical Data: Type Area: 257 x 185 mm, No. of Columns (Display): 2, Col Widths (Display): 88 mm
Official Journal of: Organ d. DG Haustechnik
BUSINESS: HEATING & VENTILATION: Industrial Heating & Ventilation

RASCHE NACHRICHTEN
739948G14A-6100
Editorial: Rheinlandstr. 5, 42579 HEILIGENHAUS
Tel: 2056 98290 **Fax:** 2056 982920
Email: info@system-management.com **Web site:** http://www.system-management.com
Freq: Quarterly; **Cover Price:** Free; **Circ:** 1,200
Editor: Walter Braun; **Advertising Manager:** Walter Braun
Profile: Magazine for managers about business and personnel development.
Language(s): German
ADVERTISING RATES:
Full Page Mono .... EUR 511

RATGEBER AUS IHRER APOTHEKE
739956G94H-10260
Editorial: Duisburger Str. 375/C-Geb., 46049 OBERHAUSEN **Tel:** 208 8480224 **Fax:** 208 8480242
Email: birgit.voelkel@storckverlag.de **Web site:** http://www.storckverlag.de
Freq: 24 issues yearly; **Cover Price:** Free; **Circ:** 2,269,223
Editor: Wilhelm Gössling; **Advertising Manager:** Michael Herrmann
Profile: Magazine containing information about healthy living, natural remedies and medicines available from pharmacies.
Language(s): German
ADVERTISING RATES:
Full Page Mono .... EUR 32800
Full Page Colour .... EUR 32800
Mechanical Data: No. of Columns (Display): 4, Col Widths (Display): 43 mm, Type Area: 258 x 184 mm
Copy instructions: *Copy Date:* 58 days prior to publication
CONSUMER: OTHER CLASSIFICATIONS: Customer Magazines

RATGEBER BAUEN
739957G74C-207
Editorial: Von-der-Wettern-Str. 25, 51149 KÖLN
Tel: 2203 3584131 **Fax:** 2203 3584185
Email: info@maenken.com **Web site:** http://www.maenken.com
Freq: Quarterly; **Cover Price:** EUR 2,50; **Circ:** 40,000
Editor: Wieland Mänken; **Advertising Manager:** Andreas Borchert
Profile: Main issue with the areas new construction, renovation, reconstruction, rehabilitation. Preservation and house ideas.
Language(s): German
ADVERTISING RATES:
Full Page Mono .... EUR 4870
Full Page Colour .... EUR 4870
Mechanical Data: Type Area: 270 x 191 mm, No. of Columns (Display): 3, Col Widths (Display): 57 mm
Copy instructions: *Copy Date:* 35 days prior to publication
CONSUMER: WOMEN'S INTEREST CONSUMER MAGAZINES: Home & Family

RATGEBER FÜR DEN GARTENLIEBHABER
739958G21A-3300
Editorial: Berliner Str. 10, 59505 BAD SASSENDORF
Tel: 2921 55045 **Fax:** 2921 944518
Email: manfred-terbrueggen@t-online.de
Freq: Monthly; **Annual Sub.:** EUR 16,80; **Circ:** 2,457
Editor: Manfred Terbrüggen; **Advertising Manager:** Monika Lambert-Debong
Profile: Magazine from the Association of Fruit Growers and Gardeners, Small Scale and Hobby Gardeners in the region of Nordrhein-Westfalen.
Language(s): German
ADVERTISING RATES:
Full Page Mono .... EUR 615
Full Page Colour .... EUR 1490
Mechanical Data: Type Area: 264 x 189 mm, No. of Columns (Display): 4, Col Widths (Display): 45 mm
Copy instructions: *Copy Date:* 20 days prior to publication
BUSINESS: AGRICULTURE & FARMING

RATGEBER-AKTUELL
1863791G74M-879
Editorial: Gustav-Adolf-Str. 7, 04105 LEIPZIG
Tel: 341 7113136 **Fax:** 341 7113125
Email: verlag@dzb.de **Web site:** http://www.dzb.de
Freq: Monthly; **Annual Sub.:** EUR 15,36; **Circ:** 250
Editor: Gabi Schulze; **Advertising Manager:** Sylvia Thormann
Profile: Magazine for the blind (braille).
Language(s): German

RATHAUSCONSULT
1638900G32A-7195
Editorial: Egermannstr. 2, 53359 RHEINBACH
Tel: 2226 8020 **Fax:** 2226 802222
Email: verlag@ubgnet.de **Web site:** http://www.rathausconsult.de
Freq: Quarterly; **Circ:** 5,717
Editor: Andreas Oberholz; **Advertising Manager:** Hans Peter Steins
Profile: Magazine with information for elected municipal officers and managers, communal politics.
Language(s): German
ADVERTISING RATES:
Full Page Colour .... EUR 4500
Mechanical Data: Type Area: 247 x 185 mm
BUSINESS: LOCAL GOVERNMENT, LEISURE & RECREATION: Local Government

RATIONELL REINIGEN
739979G4F-6
Editorial: Gewerbestr. 2, 86825 BAD WÖRISHOFEN
Tel: 8247 354164 **Fax:** 8247 354270
Email: peter.hartmann@holzmann-medien.de **Web site:** http://www.rationell-reinigen.de
Freq: Monthly; **Annual Sub.:** EUR 99,00; **Circ:** 25,252
Editor: Peter Hartmann; **Advertising Manager:** Gerti Strobel
Profile: Journal of cleaning technology informed about all important activities of the service building. In addition, efficiently clean the accompanying changes in the industry in new business areas. Articles on subjects such as cleaning equipment, hygiene, facilities management, special clothing, equipment operation are priorities of the reporting. Recognized technical authors write about business and leadership, and provide tips for sales professionals. Twitter: twitter.com/#!/rr_News.
Language(s): German
ADVERTISING RATES:
Full Page Mono .... EUR 3550
Full Page Colour .... EUR 5250
Mechanical Data: Type Area: 266 x 185 mm, No. of Columns (Display): 4, Col Widths (Display): 43 mm
Copy instructions: *Copy Date:* 15 days prior to publication
Official Journal of: Organ d. Bundesinnungsverb. d. Gebäudereiniger-Handwerks u. d. Landesinnung Niederösterreich d. Denkmal-, Fassaden- u. Gebäudereiniger
BUSINESS: ARCHITECTURE & BUILDING: Cleaning & Maintenance

RÄTSEL-AKTUELL
739897G94H-10280
Editorial: Otto-Hahn-Str. 16, 47608 GELDERN
Tel: 2831 13000 **Fax:** 2831 130020
Email: info@sud-verlag.de **Web site:** http://www.raetsel-aktuell.com
Freq: Monthly; **Circ:** 256,000
Editor: Hannelore von Berg; **Advertising Manager:** Marcus H. Thielen
Profile: The pharmacy customer magazine is 50% of medical topics and displays as well as 50% of puzzles, which are characterized by difficulty with asterisks. To give all the puzzles friends the opportunity to heranzutrauen difficult tasks, the

solutions in each issue is published. Puzzle currently published monthly, in the unique square format nationwide and is a paid subscription sold through pharmacies.
Language(s): German
Readership: Aimed at the general public.
ADVERTISING RATES:
Full Page Mono .... EUR 2232
Full Page Colour .... EUR 3025
Mechanical Data: Type Area: 175 x 175 mm, No. of Columns (Display): 2, Col Widths (Display): 65 mm
Copy instructions: *Copy Date:* 60 days prior to publication
CONSUMER: OTHER CLASSIFICATIONS: Customer Magazines

DER RAUBFISCH
739984G64F-2728
Editorial: Erich-Kästner-Str. 2, 56379 SINGHOFEN
Tel: 2604 978350 **Fax:** 2604 978360
Email: rf@paulparey.de **Web site:** http://www.raubfisch.de
Freq: 6 issues yearly; **Annual Sub.:** EUR 21,50; **Circ:** 24,654
Editor: Thomas Wendt; **Advertising Manager:** Sylvia Lühert
Profile: Magazine about fishing for predatory fish.
Language(s): German
Readership: Aimed at people interested in fishing.
ADVERTISING RATES:
Full Page Mono .... EUR 1545
Full Page Colour .... EUR 2621
Mechanical Data: Type Area: 253 x 186 mm, No. of Columns (Display): 4, Col Widths (Display): 43 mm
BUSINESS: OTHER CLASSIFICATIONS: Biology

RAUF AUF DIE BERGE
727193G89A-1440
Editorial: Maarstr. 96, 53227 BONN
Tel: 228 9630210 **Fax:** 228 9630233
Email: hoitz@bauernhofurlaub.com **Web site:** http://www.bauernhofurlaub.com
Freq: Annual; **Cover Price:** EUR 8,90; **Circ:** 10,000
Editor: Sabine Hoitz; **Advertising Manager:** Sabine Hoitz
Profile: Travel guide for farm holidays in Bavaria, Austria, the South Tyrol and Switzerland.
Language(s): German
Mechanical Data: Type Area: 190 x 120 mm
Copy instructions: *Copy Date:* 60 days prior to publication

RAUMBRAND
1641797G2A-5544
Editorial: Hultschiner Str. 8, 81677 MÜNCHEN
Tel: 89 21837254 **Fax:** 89 21837213
Email: jan.esche@raumbrand.de **Web site:** http://www.raumbrand.de
Freq: Quarterly; **Annual Sub.:** EUR 24,00; **Circ:** 8,000
Editor: Jan Esche; **Advertising Manager:** Susanne Kögler
Profile: Magazine about all aspects of design and branding.
Language(s): German
ADVERTISING RATES:
Full Page Mono .... EUR 2550
Full Page Colour .... EUR 2550
Mechanical Data: Type Area: 235 x 180 mm
Copy instructions: *Copy Date:* 20 days prior to publication

RAUMFORSCHUNG UND RAUMORDNUNG
739990G6C-4
Editorial: Hohenzollernstr. 11, 30161 HANNOVER
Tel: 511 3484236 **Fax:** 511 3484241
Email: klee@arl-net.de **Web site:** http://www.arl-net.de
Freq: 6 issues yearly; **Annual Sub.:** EUR 302,00; **Circ:** 1,200
Editor: Andreas Klee
Profile: Journal about space research.
Language(s): English; German
Mechanical Data: Type Area: 270 x 186 mm, No. of Columns (Display): 4, Col Widths (Display): 45 mm
BUSINESS: AVIATION & AERONAUTICS: Space Research

RAUMPLANUNG
739992G4D-8
Editorial: Hansastr. 26, 44137 DORTMUND
Tel: 231 759570 **Fax:** 231 759597
Email: redaktion@ifr-ev.de **Web site:** http://www.ifr-ev.de
Freq: 5 issues yearly; Free to qualifying individuals
Annual Sub.: EUR 91,00; **Circ:** 1,900
Editor: Lutz Meltzer; **Advertising Manager:** Uschi Moering
Profile: Magazine for spacial and city planning.
Language(s): German
ADVERTISING RATES:
Full Page Mono .... EUR 1250
Mechanical Data: Type Area: 255 x 165 mm, No. of Columns (Display): 2, Col Widths (Display): 80 mm
Copy instructions: *Copy Date:* 35 days prior to publication

RAUS AUFS LAND
1640262G89A-11821
Editorial: Maarstr. 96, 53227 BONN **Tel:** 228 963020
Fax: 228 9630233
Email: hoitz@bauernhofurlaub.com **Web site:** http://www.bauernhofurlaub.com
Freq: Annual; **Cover Price:** EUR 9,90; **Circ:** 40,000
Editor: Sabine Hoitz; **Advertising Manager:** Sabine Hoitz
Profile: Travel guide to holidays on the farm with information on more than 1,000 holiday houses from all over Germany.
Language(s): German
Mechanical Data: Type Area: 190 x 120 mm

RAVELINE
740000G91D-6800
Editorial: Hospeltstr. 32, 50825 KÖLN
Tel: 221 5708120 **Fax:** 221 570812121
Email: svenman@raveline.de **Web site:** http://www.raveline.de
Freq: Monthly; **Annual Sub.:** EUR 48,00; **Circ:** 73,172
Editor: Sven Schäfer; **Advertising Manager:** Johannes Mertmann
Profile: Raveline has long been the largest circulation journal in the field of electronic music. As a bonus feature on every issue there is an exclusive DJ mix for Raveline readers as a free download. Every month supply Raveline his readers with exclusive interviews, breaking news, hundreds of record reviews and art news and reviews to product launches in lifestyle, nightlife, fashion, games and Kino-/DVD-Themen. Always up to date, focused Raveline constantly new trends and developments in the DJ, producer and club scene and is primarily aimed at the urban, affluent consumers between 18 and 35.
Language(s): German
ADVERTISING RATES:
Full Page Mono .... EUR 7900
Full Page Colour .... EUR 7900
Mechanical Data: Type Area: 297 x 210 mm
Copy instructions: *Copy Date:* 15 days prior to publication
CONSUMER: RECREATION & LEISURE: Children & Youth

RBN RUNDBRIEF DES BERGISCHEN NATURSCHUTZVEREIN
1606267G57-2648
Editorial: Schmitzbüchel 2, 51491 OVERATH
Tel: 2204 7977 **Fax:** 2204 74258
Email: rbnoverath@t-online.de **Web site:** http://www.bergischer-naturschutzverein.de
Freq: 3 issues yearly; **Circ:** 1,300
Editor: Mark vom Hofe
Profile: Publication containing information from the Bergischer Naturschutzverein.
Language(s): German

RBN RUNDBRIEF DES BERGISCHEN NATURSCHUTZVEREIN
1606267G57-2934
Editorial: Schmitzbüchel 2, 51491 OVERATH
Tel: 2204 7977 **Fax:** 2204 74258
Email: rbnoverath@t-online.de **Web site:** http://www.bergischer-naturschutzverein.de
Freq: 3 issues yearly; **Circ:** 1,300
Editor: Mark vom Hofe
Profile: Publication containing information from the Bergischer Naturschutzverein.
Language(s): German

RDE - RECHT DER ENERGIEWIRTSCHAFT
740012G44-1640
Editorial: Luxemburger Str. 449, 50939 KÖLN
Tel: 221 943730 **Fax:** 221 94373901
Web site: http://www.wolterskluwer.de
Freq: 10 issues yearly; **Annual Sub.:** EUR 189,00; **Circ:** 1,350
Editor: Markus Moraing
Profile: Journal focusing on the law concerning energy economics.
Language(s): German
ADVERTISING RATES:
Full Page Mono .... EUR 991
Full Page Colour .... EUR 1840
Mechanical Data: Type Area: 260 x 186 mm, No. of Columns (Display): 4, Col Widths (Display): 45 mm
Copy instructions: *Copy Date:* 32 days prior to publication
BUSINESS: LEGAL

RDV RECHT DER DATENVERARBEITUNG
740016G5B-131
Editorial: Pariser Str. 37, 53117 BONN
Tel: 228 694313 **Fax:** 228 695638
Email: klug@gdd.de **Web site:** http://www.rdv-fachzeitschrift.de
Freq: 6 issues yearly; Free to qualifying individuals
Annual Sub.: EUR 139,00; **Circ:** 4,070
Editor: Peter Gola; **Advertising Manager:** Thomas Reinhard
Profile: Magazine about data protection and developments in IT.
Language(s): German
ADVERTISING RATES:
Full Page Mono .... EUR 1182
Full Page Colour .... EUR 2068
Mechanical Data: Type Area: 255 x 186 mm, No. of Columns (Display): 2, Col Widths (Display): 92 mm
Copy instructions: *Copy Date:* 31 days prior to publication
BUSINESS: COMPUTERS & AUTOMATION: Data Processing

RDW KURZREPORT AUS STEUERN UND RECHT
740017G44-1680
Editorial: Scharrstr. 2, 70563 STUTTGART
Tel: 711 73850 **Fax:** 711 7385100
Email: k.krohn@boorberg.de **Web site:** http://www.boorberg.de
Freq: 24 issues yearly; **Annual Sub.:** EUR 181,20; **Circ:** 4,460
Editor: Klaus Krohn; **Advertising Manager:** Roland Schulz
Profile: Magazine about business law.
Language(s): German
ADVERTISING RATES:
Full Page Mono .... EUR 945
Full Page Colour .... EUR 1875
Mechanical Data: Type Area: 172 x 120 mm
Copy instructions: *Copy Date:* 21 days prior to publication
BUSINESS: LEGAL

READER'S DIGEST DEUTSCHLAND
740019G73-360
Editorial: Vordernbergstr. 6, 70191 STUTTGART
Tel: 711 6602428 **Fax:** 711 6602858
Email: redaktion@readersdigest.de **Web site:** http://www.readersdigest.de
Freq: Monthly; **Annual Sub.:** EUR 39,90; **Circ:** 707,564
Editor: Michael Kallinger; **Advertising Manager:** Anett Groch
Profile: Reader's Digest magazine in Germany, the current affairs For over 60 years, Reader's Digest in Germany follows this claim, which is a source of motivation: genuine pleasure to read through constructive journalism for a living and positive self-esteem. Not loud sensation, but reliable information and challenging issues that always the people at the center, which makes the value and the editorial authority of Reader's Digest - and the magazine non-changeable. Reader's Digest Germany is the medium for legitimate 45plus - The key generation.
Language(s): German
ADVERTISING RATES:
Full Page Mono .... EUR 16600
Full Page Colour .... EUR 16600
Mechanical Data: Type Area: 165 x 110 mm, No. of Columns (Display): 2, Col Widths (Display): 54 mm
Copy instructions: *Copy Date:* 45 days prior to publication
CONSUMER: NATIONAL & INTERNATIONAL PERIODICALS

READER'S DIGEST ÖSTERREICH
1749672G73-611
Editorial: Vordernbergstr. 6, 70191 STUTTGART
Tel: 711 66020 **Fax:** 711 6602858
Email: redaktion@readersdigest.de **Web site:** http://www.readersdigest.at
Freq: Monthly; **Annual Sub.:** EUR 39,90; **Circ:** 48,450
Editor: Michael Kallinger; **Advertising Manager:** Anett Groch
Profile: Magazine containing articles of universal interest reprinted from international publications.
Language(s): German
ADVERTISING RATES:
Full Page Colour .... EUR 5400
Mechanical Data: Type Area: 165 x 110 mm
Copy instructions: *Copy Date:* 45 days prior to publication

REBE & WEIN
740028G21H-5
Editorial: Bopserstr. 17, 70180 STUTTGART
Tel: 711 2140145 **Fax:** 711 2360232
Email: eberenz@bwagrar.de **Web site:** http://www.rebeundwein.de
Freq: Monthly; **Annual Sub.:** EUR 34,80; **Circ:** 5,695
Editor: Walter Eberenz; **Advertising Manager:** Sonja Fischer
Profile: Rebe & Wein is the magazine for viticulture and wine industry in Wurttemberg and Franconia. Rebe & Wein is the organ of the wine associations in Wurttemberg and Franconia and combined with the technical information for winemakers and wine industry. Practical technical articles provide comprehensive information on key topics. Viticulture, enology, business management and marketing are the focus. Complement the current industry information specialist part. The constant themes are wine-growing practices (including technology, process, plant protection, varieties), wine making (with technology, methods), business management, marketing, industry information (with dates, news, association news, events), wine-growing in other regions. With a circulation of over 5,800 Rebe & Wein offers copies in two growing regions a wide range.
Language(s): German
ADVERTISING RATES:
Full Page Mono .... EUR 2350
Full Page Colour .... EUR 3340
Mechanical Data: Type Area: 260 x 186 mm, No. of Columns (Display): 4, Col Widths (Display): 45 mm
Copy instructions: *Copy Date:* 12 days prior to publication
Official Journal of: Organ d. Weinbauverb. Württ. e.V. u. d. Weingärtnergenossenschaften
BUSINESS: AGRICULTURE & FARMING: Vine Growing

RECCE
1866840G40-998
Editorial: Bennebeker Chaussee 100, 24848 KROPP
Tel: 4624 301440 **Fax:** 4624 301199
Email: info@recce.de **Web site:** http://www.recce.de
Freq: Quarterly; Free to qualifying individuals
Annual Sub.: EUR 11,00; **Circ:** 2,500
Editor: Martin Huber; **Advertising Manager:** Matthias Nehls
Profile: Magazine with information about the air force.
Language(s): German
ADVERTISING RATES:
Full Page Mono .... EUR 120
Full Page Colour .... EUR 205
Copy instructions: *Copy Date:* 31 days prior to publication

RECHT DER FINANZINSTRUMENTE
2055973G1A-3838
Editorial: Mainzer Landstr. 251, 60326 FRANKFURT
Tel: 69 75952741 **Fax:** 69 75952730
Email: koster@betriebs-berater.de **Web site:** http://www.rdf-online.de
Freq: 6 issues yearly; **Annual Sub.:** EUR 389,00; **Circ:** 1,000
Editor: Martina Koster; **Advertising Manager:** Marion Gertzen
Profile: Journal for company advisers.
Language(s): German
ADVERTISING RATES:
Full Page Mono .... EUR 1800
Full Page Colour .... EUR 2300
Mechanical Data: Type Area: 272 x 198 mm, No. of Columns (Display): 2, Col Widths (Display): 96 mm

RECHT DER INTERNATIONALEN WIRTSCHAFT
740035G44-3138
Editorial: Mainzer Landstr. 251, 60326 FRANKFURT
Tel: 69 75952751 **Fax:** 69 75952780
Email: abele@betriebs-berater.de **Web site:** http://www.betriebs-berater.de
Freq: 11 issues yearly; **Annual Sub.:** EUR 549,00; **Circ:** 2,450
Editor: Roland Abele; **Advertising Manager:** Marion Gertzen
Profile: Journal providing legal information concerning international commerce and industry.
Language(s): German
ADVERTISING RATES:
Full Page Mono .... EUR 1995
Full Page Colour .... EUR 2485
Mechanical Data: Type Area: 257 x 180 mm, No. of Columns (Display): 4, Col Widths (Display): 43 mm
Copy instructions: *Copy Date:* 17 days prior to publication
BUSINESS: LEGAL

RECHT DEUTLICH
2090096G74M-974
Editorial: Heinrich-Lorenz-Str. 2, 09120 CHEMNITZ
Tel: 371 5289178 **Fax:** 371 5289179
Email: b.schilder@wvd-mediengruppe.de **Web site:** http://www.wochenspiegel-sachsen.de
Freq: Annual; **Circ:** 30,000
Editor: Bernadette Schilder; **Advertising Manager:** Bernadette Schilder
Profile: All aspects of a healthy lifestyle - from "A for Active 50 + to Z for dental health" are the focus of the Magazine Gesundleben. Published by the Wochenspiegel Sachsen Verlag is published quarterly since May 2006 and is aimed at people who want to be active for their physical and mental well-being and are interested for health issues. Because each issue to a cover story is devoted to the graphic provides all information about a focused, healthy life for many readers is a coveted collector's item. The magazine is free in doctors' offices and other delivery points available in southwest Saxony.
Language(s): German
ADVERTISING RATES:
Full Page Mono .... EUR 1560
Full Page Colour .... EUR 2028
Mechanical Data: Type Area: 250 x 185 mm

DIE RECHTSANWALTS- UND NOTARFACHANGESTELLTEN
765585G1A-3463
Editorial: Eschstr. 22, 44629 HERNE
Tel: 2323 141900 **Fax:** 2323 141123
Email: c.ziegler@kiehl.de **Web site:** http://www.kiehl.de
Freq: Monthly; **Annual Sub.:** EUR 61,80; **Circ:** 3,863
Editor: Corinna Ziegler; **Advertising Manager:** Andreas Reimann
Profile: The magazine „Die Rechtsanwalts- und Notarfachangestellten", accompanies the readers from the start of vocational training and also provides the knowledge needed in their daily work in the office. The simple and clear presentation of technical subjects, many practical examples, numerous review questions with solutions, diagrams, patterns formulations, etc. facilitate understanding. In each edition supports a post-training test the systematic learning.
Language(s): German
ADVERTISING RATES:
Full Page Mono .... EUR 990
Full Page Colour .... EUR 1390
Mechanical Data: Type Area: 260 x 186 mm
Copy instructions: *Copy Date:* 30 days prior to publication
BUSINESS: FINANCE & ECONOMICS

Germany

RECHTSMEDIZIN 740051G56A-8820
Editorial: Tiergartenstr. 17, 69121 HEIDELBERG
Tel: 6221 4870 **Fax:** 6221 4878366
Email: subscriptions@springer.com **Web site:** http://www.springerlink.com
Freq: 6 issues yearly; Free to qualifying individuals
Annual Sub.: EUR 447,00; **Circ:** 750
Editor: Klaus Püschel
Profile: Rechtsmedizin is an internationally recognized journal dealing with all aspects of forensic medicine. It provides information on current developments in forensic pathology, traumatology, traffic medicine, toxicology, serology, insurance medicine, psychopathology and legal medical issues. Freely submitted original papers allow the presentation of important clinical studies and serve scientific exchange. Case reports feature interesting and unique cases thus providing a platform for scientific information and critical discussion. Comprehensive reviews on a specific topical issue focus on providing evidenced based information on all aspects of the field. Review articles under the rubric "Continuing Medical Education" present verified results of scientific research and their integration into daily practice.
Language(s): German
ADVERTISING RATES:
Full Page Mono .... EUR 830
Full Page Colour .... EUR 1870
Mechanical Data: No. of Columns (Display): 3, Col Widths (Display): 54 mm, Type Area: 240 x 175 mm
Official Journal of: Organ d. Dt. Ges. f. Rechtsmedizin e.V.

RECKLINGHÄUSER ZEITUNG 740070G67B-12020
Editorial: Kampstr. 84b, 45772 MARL **Tel:** 2365 1070
Fax: 2365 1071490
Email: info@medienhaus-bauer.de **Web site:** http://www.medienhaus-bauer.de
Freq: 312 issues yearly; **Circ:** 61,911
Editor: Kurt Bauer; **News Editor:** Thomas Bartel;
Advertising Manager: Carsten Dingerkuss
Profile: Regional daily newspaper with news on politics, economy, culture, sports, travel, technology, etc. The newspaper offers a mix of local, regional and international News from all areas. Fun and interactive content such as forums, polls or betting games are also part of the program. Local out of the city and the neighborhood is the focus of attention. Facebook: http://www.facebook.com/medienhbauer This Outlet offers RSS (Really Simple Syndication).
Language(s): German
ADVERTISING RATES:
SCC .... EUR 85,20
Mechanical Data: Type Area: 487 x 325 mm, No. of Columns (Display): 7, Col Widths (Display): 43 mm
Copy instructions: *Copy Date:* 1 day prior to publication
Supplement(s): prisma
REGIONAL DAILY & SUNDAY NEWSPAPERS: Regional Daily Newspapers

RECYCLING MAGAZIN 740076G32B-42
Editorial: Hackerbrücke 6, 80335 MÜNCHEN
Tel: 89 89817371 **Fax:** 89 89817350
Email: info@recyclingmagazin.de **Web site:** http://www.recyclingmagazin.de
Freq: 24 issues yearly; **Annual Sub.:** EUR 194,90;
Circ: 2,797
Editor: Stephan Peter Krafzik; **Advertising Manager:** Christa Manghard
Profile: Magazine about the handling and recycling of waste material and primary and secondary raw material trading.
Language(s): German
Readership: Read by people in the recycling industry.
ADVERTISING RATES:
Full Page Mono .... EUR 2099
Full Page Colour .... EUR 2990
Mechanical Data: Type Area: 248 x 180 mm, No. of Columns (Display): 4, Col Widths (Display): 42 mm
Copy instructions: *Copy Date:* 14 days prior to publication
BUSINESS: LOCAL GOVERNMENT, LEISURE & RECREATION: Public Health & Cleaning

RECYCLING TECHNOLOGY 1830895G49A-2443
Editorial: Joseph-Dollinger-Bogen 5, 80807 MÜNCHEN **Tel:** 89 32391270 **Fax:** 89 32391416
Email: andreas.schleinkofer@huss-verlag.de **Web site:** http://www.recyclingtechnology.de
Freq: 8 issues yearly; **Annual Sub.:** EUR 107,60;
Circ: 4,601
Editor: Andreas Schleinkofer
Profile: Detailed information on technological developments, new equipment, maintenance and safety. It is aimed at recycling and disposal business, department heads, in d. municipalities, technical buyers in recycling companies and technical manager for recycling and disposal.
Language(s): German
ADVERTISING RATES:
Full Page Colour .... EUR 3080
Mechanical Data: Type Area: 270 x 185 mm

RED BOX 1639938G2A-5538
Editorial: Nebendahlstr. 16, 22041 HAMBURG
Tel: 40 4501500 **Fax:** 40 45015098
Email: info@redbox.de **Web site:** http://www.redbox.de
Freq: Annual; **Cover Price:** EUR 49,00; **Circ:** 3,000
Editor: Magdalena Kluge; **Advertising Manager:** Ingrid Blank
Profile: Manual of the advertising and communications sectors.
Language(s): German
Mechanical Data: Type Area: 188 x 190 mm, No. of Columns (Display): 3, Col Widths (Display): 60 mm

REDAKTIONS ADRESS 1832685G2A-5773
Editorial: Abraham-Lincoln-Str. 46, 65189 WIESBADEN **Tel:** 611 7878317 **Fax:** 611 787878317
Email: cornelia.gerstenberg@mediadaten.com **Web site:** http://www.mediadaten.com
Freq: Half-yearly; **Annual Sub.:** EUR 435,00; **Circ:** 350
Editor: Cornelia Gerstenberg; **Advertising Manager:** Thomas Heusler
Profile: Directory listing addresses of journalists and editorial departments.
Language(s): German
ADVERTISING RATES:
Full Page Mono .... EUR 880
Full Page Colour .... EUR 1480
Mechanical Data: Type Area: 275 x 185 mm, No. of Columns (Display): 3, Col Widths (Display): 58 mm

DIE REGENSBURGER STADTZEITUNG 740117G80-9440
Editorial: Margaretenstr. 8, 93047 REGENSBURG
Tel: 941 53836 **Fax:** 941 560242
Email: rsz@regensburger-stadtzeitung.de **Web site:** http://www.regensburger-stadtzeitung.de
Freq: 10 issues yearly; **Cover Price:** Free; **Circ:** 32,010
Editor: Peter Kittel; **Advertising Manager:** Margot Pillhatsch
Profile: The Regensburg city newspaper is the most established and has long been the largest city magazines of Eastern Bavaria. Target group is the active and public-spending readers aged 25 to 65 and more.
Language(s): German
ADVERTISING RATES:
Full Page Mono .... EUR 1475
Full Page Colour .... EUR 2028
Mechanical Data: Type Area: 270 x 190 mm, No. of Columns (Display): 4, Col Widths (Display): 44 mm
Copy instructions: *Copy Date:* 10 days prior to publication
CONSUMER: RURAL & REGIONAL INTEREST

REGENSBURGER WOCHENBLATT - AUSG. LANDKREIS 740118G72-10724
Editorial: Im Gewerbepark B10, 93059 REGENSBURG **Tel:** 941 4604150 **Fax:** 941 4604155
Email: christian.eckl@wochenblatt.de **Web site:** http://www.wochenblatt.de
Freq: Weekly; **Cover Price:** Free; **Circ:** 74,300
Editor: Christian Eckl; **Advertising Manager:** Günter Schmidmeister
Profile: Advertising journal (house-to-house) concentrating on local stories.
Language(s): German
ADVERTISING RATES:
Full Page Mono .... EUR 4416
Full Page Colour .... EUR 5189
Mechanical Data: Type Area: 460 x 280 mm, No. of Columns (Display): 6, Col Widths (Display): 43 mm
Copy instructions: *Copy Date:* 1 day prior to publication
Supplement(s): erlebnis magazin
LOCAL NEWSPAPERS

REGENWALD REPORT 740120G57-1800
Editorial: Jupiterweg 15, 22391 HAMBURG
Tel: 40 4103804 **Fax:** 40 4500144
Email: info@regenwald.org **Web site:** http://www.regenwald.org
Freq: Quarterly; **Cover Price:** Free; **Circ:** 150,000
Editor: Klaus Schenck
Profile: Journal of the Association "Rettet den Regenwald" to protect tropical forests and Indians, the exploitation of tropical forests by logging and commercial plantations to monocultures.
Language(s): German

REGIONAL ENVIRONMENTAL CHANGE 740137G57-1820
Editorial: Postfach 601203, 14412 POTSDAM
Tel: 331 2882637 **Fax:** 331 2882600
Email: rec@pik-potsdam.de **Web site:** http://www.springerlink.com
Freq: Quarterly; **Annual Sub.:** EUR 282,00; **Circ:** 54
Editor: Wolfgang Cramer
Profile: Magazine about environmental change.
Language(s): German
ADVERTISING RATES:
Full Page Mono .... EUR 740
Full Page Colour .... EUR 1780
Mechanical Data: Type Area: 240 x 175 mm

REGIONALE RUNDSCHAU 740138G67B-12100
Editorial: Martinistr. 43, 28195 BREMEN
Tel: 421 36710 **Fax:** 421 36711000
Email: redaktion@weser-kurier.de **Web site:** http://www.weser-kurier.de
Freq: 312 issues yearly; **Circ:** 13,414
Profile: Daily newspaper with regional news and a local sports section.
Language(s): German
ADVERTISING RATES:
SCC .... EUR 26,50
Mechanical Data: Type Area: 490 x 333 mm, No. of Columns (Display): 7, Col Widths (Display): 45 mm
Copy instructions: *Copy Date:* 2 days prior to publication
Supplement(s): wochen Journal
REGIONAL DAILY & SUNDAY NEWSPAPERS: Regional Daily Newspapers

REGIONALEUROPÄISCHER WIRTSCHAFTS-SPIEGEL 740146G14A-6220
Editorial: Timmerhellstr. 39, 45478 MÜLHEIM
Tel: 208 377080 **Fax:** 208 380077
Email: info@iwn-verlag.de **Web site:** http://www.iwn-verlag.de
Freq: 6 issues yearly; **Annual Sub.:** EUR 28,00; **Circ:** 10,141
Editor: Kay Kolodziej
Profile: Magazine with information on companies, markets, technologies and innovations from industry, trade and service in German-speaking Europe.
Language(s): German
Mechanical Data: Type Area: 266 x 184 mm, No. of Columns (Display): 4, Col Widths (Display): 41 mm
BUSINESS: COMMERCE, INDUSTRY & MANAGEMENT

REGIOTRANS 740160G49E-720
Editorial: Bert-Brecht-Str. 15, 78054 VILLINGEN-SCHWENNINGEN **Tel:** 7720 394163
Fax: 7720 394167
Email: bethge@kuhnverlag.de **Web site:** http://www.kuhn-kataloge.de
Freq: Annual; **Cover Price:** EUR 17,00; **Circ:** 5,133
Editor: Axel Bethge; **Advertising Manager:** Konrad Baumann
Profile: Magazine for bus companies and Deutsche Bahn.
Language(s): German
ADVERTISING RATES:
Full Page Mono .... EUR 2440
Full Page Colour .... EUR 3055
Mechanical Data: Type Area: 254 x 180 mm
BUSINESS: TRANSPORT: Railways

DIE REHABILITATION 740166G56L-7
Editorial: Rüdigerstr. 14, 70469 STUTTGART
Tel: 711 89310 **Fax:** 711 8931258
Email: rehabilitation@thieme.de **Web site:** http://www.thieme.de/rehabilitation
Freq: 6 issues yearly; **Annual Sub.:** EUR 217,90;
Circ: 1,200
Editor: W. H. Jäckel
Profile: Rehabilitation, quality management, new concepts and models of care for use of the ICF, movement therapy. Rehabilitation Research: Ptactice relevant results, methods and assessments, guidelines development, socio-medical questions. About legal, political and social conditions. News of trade associations.
Language(s): German
ADVERTISING RATES:
Full Page Mono .... EUR 1180
Full Page Colour .... EUR 2320
Mechanical Data: Type Area: 248 x 175 mm, No. of Columns (Display): 4, Col Widths (Display): 40 mm
Official Journal of: Organ d. Dt. Vereinigung f. Rehabilitation Behinderter, d. Bundes-ArGe f. Rehabilitation u. d. Dt. Ges. f. Rehabilitationswissenschaften
BUSINESS: HEALTH & MEDICAL: Disability & Rehabilitation

REHAUER TAGBLATT FRANKENPOST 740168G67B-12120
Editorial: Poststr. 9, 95028 HOF **Tel:** 9281 8160
Fax: 9281 816283
Email: redaktion@frankenpost.de **Web site:** http://www.frankenpost.de
Freq: 312 issues yearly; **Circ:** 2,635
Advertising Manager: Stefan Sailer
Profile: Regional daily newspaper with news on politics, economy, culture, sports, travel, technology, etc. Rehauer Tagblatt Frankenpost is a local edition of the newspaper Frankenpost. Facebook: http://www.facebook.com/pages/Frankenpost/330862476314 Twitter: http://twitter.com/frankenpost This Outlet offers RSS (Really Simple Syndication).
Language(s): German
ADVERTISING RATES:
SCC .... EUR 109,60
Mechanical Data: Type Area: 485 x 325 mm, No. of Columns (Display): 7, Col Widths (Display): 44 mm
Copy instructions: *Copy Date:* 1 day prior to publication
Supplement(s): rtv
REGIONAL DAILY & SUNDAY NEWSPAPERS: Regional Daily Newspapers

REICHENHALLER TAGBLATT 740176G67B-12140
Editorial: Schachtstr. 4, 83435 BAD REICHENHALL
Tel: 8651 9810 **Fax:** 8651 981160
Email: info@bgl-medien.de **Web site:** http://www.bgl-medien.de
Freq: 312 issues yearly; **Circ:** 10,058
Editor: Sabine Zehringer; **Advertising Manager:** Hans Straniak
Profile: The Reichenhaller Tagblatt (founded 1840) is the daily newspaper for the town of Bad Reichenhall, that after the incorporation of Charles Stein and Marzoll counts 17,000 inhabitants. The audience extends beyond the area of Berchtesgaden in the northern district of country: Anger, Aufham, Teisendorf, Bayerisch Gmain, Högl, Piding, Schneizlreuth and Weißbach a. d. Alpenstraße. The world bath Bad Reichenhall, as well as the recreational and health resorts of the range have a year-round season and a strong addition to the spas leisure tourism. Based on these factors, the vast purchasing power of the population and particularly the level of well-kept shops, all the buyer needs to meet all budgets.
Language(s): German
ADVERTISING RATES:
SCC .... EUR 24,00
Mechanical Data: Type Area: 420 x 280 mm, No. of Columns (Display): 6, Col Widths (Display): 44 mm
Copy instructions: *Copy Date:* 1 day prior to publication
REGIONAL DAILY & SUNDAY NEWSPAPERS: Regional Daily Newspapers

REIFENWELT 1948996G27-3121
Editorial: Stiftswaldstr. 60, 67657 KAISERSLAUTERN
Tel: 631 53487169 **Fax:** 631 534872007
Email: redaktion@reifenwelt.de **Web site:** http://www.reifenwelt.de
Freq: 10 issues yearly; **Annual Sub.:** EUR 45,00;
Circ: 14,500
Editor: Peter Schmidt; **Advertising Manager:** Marc Fuchs
Profile: The trade publication for all types of companies that deal in tires. It reports on the entire spectrum of the tire industry and highlights of Trade and Industry, significant developments in technology and economy car segment.
Language(s): German
ADVERTISING RATES:
Full Page Mono .... EUR 4400
Full Page Colour .... EUR 4400
Mechanical Data: Type Area: 355 x 255 mm

REIFEZEIT 1789688G74N-903
Editorial: Heimstr. 70, 27749 DELMENHORST
Tel: 4221 155350 **Fax:** 4221 155352
Email: info@reifezeit.net **Web site:** http://www.reifezeit.net
Freq: 6 issues yearly; **Circ:** 32,000
Editor: Gerlinde Kläner
Profile: Seniors newspaper with news information services for the elderly.
Language(s): German
Mechanical Data: Type Area: 420 x 280 mm

REINICKENDORF KOMPAKT 1898585G74M-891
Editorial: Bundesallee 23, 10717 BERLIN
Tel: 30 863030 **Fax:** 30 86303200
Email: info@bfb.de **Web site:** http://www.bfb.de
Freq: Annual; **Cover Price:** Free; **Circ:** 128,000
Profile: Industry district magazine. The core of this handy reference book is neatly sorted according to different themes of industry. Here you will find a plethora of vendors from the neighborhood. In preparation to the respective subject area raises a company, in an interview. To know your environment better, we present in the district windows, etc. beautiful places, monuments, museums, etc. For better orientation in the neighborhood also an integrated neighborhood with street plan is register. Furthermore, the county information you provide an overview of important phone numbers and agencies in your neighborhood.
Language(s): German
ADVERTISING RATES:
Full Page Mono .... EUR 990
Full Page Colour .... EUR 990
Mechanical Data: Type Area: 185 x 126 mm

REINIGUNGS MARKT 740191G4F-8
Editorial: Mittlerer Hubweg 5, 72227 EGENHAUSEN
Tel: 7453 9385787 **Fax:** 7453 9385797
Email: info@knittler.de **Web site:** http://www.knittler.de
Freq: 10 issues yearly; Free to qualifying individuals
Annual Sub.: EUR 52,80; **Circ:** 11,986
Editor: Reinhard Knittler
Profile: Magazine containing articles about the technical and chemical cleaning of buildings, hygiene, safety at work and management.
Language(s): German
Readership: Read by managers of cleaning companies, hotels, restaurants, hospitals, local authorities and facility managers.
ADVERTISING RATES:
Full Page Mono .... EUR 3072
Full Page Colour .... EUR 4773
Mechanical Data: Type Area: 262 x 179 mm, No. of Columns (Display): 4, Col Widths (Display): 42 mm
Copy instructions: *Copy Date:* 21 days prior to publication

Official Journal of: Organ d. ISSA f. Deutschland, Österr. u. d. Schweiz
BUSINESS: ARCHITECTURE & BUILDING: Cleaning & Maintenance

REISE MOTORRAD RIDE ON!
740205G77B-8
Editorial: Markircher Str. 9a, 68229 MANNHEIM
Tel: 621 483614401 **Fax:** 621 483614411
Email: a.sacher@huber-verlag.de **Web site:** http://www.reisemotorrad.de
Freq: 6 issues yearly; **Annual Sub.:** EUR 27,00; **Circ:** 22,222
Editor: Anton Sacher; **Advertising Manager:** Katrin Schumann
Profile: For 20 years heard REISE MOTORRAD in all German-speaking countries of the leading magazines for avid travelers motorcyclists. The high quality and modern styling, and professional journalism are the trademarks of REISE MOTORRAD. Fascination: Top-researched travel reports with great photos and lots of information from near and far. Technology: Practice Tests motorcycle touring capabilities, filled with targeted information. Services: clothing, accessories, navigation, hotel tips, tour operators and major addresses from all over the world.
Language(s): German
ADVERTISING RATES:
Full Page Colour .... EUR 5990
Mechanical Data: Type Area: 256 x 184 mm, No. of Columns (Display): 4, Col Widths (Display): 43 mm
Copy instructions: *Copy Date:* 30 days prior to publication
CONSUMER: MOTORING & CYCLING: Motorcycling

REISE & PREISE
740216G89A-11537
Editorial: Hauptstr. 14, 21614 BUXTEHUDE
Tel: 4161 71690 **Fax:** 4161 716915
Email: redaktion@reise-preise.de **Web site:** http://www.reise-preise.de
Freq: Quarterly; **Annual Sub.:** EUR 18,60; **Circ:** 77,214
Editor: Oliver Kühn; **Advertising Manager:** Torsten Kühn
Profile: Magazine about air travel and planning a holiday. Attractively illustrated, special features on particular countries, exciting reports on trips, competent industry contributions and any amount of inside information - all this not only creates travel dreams but also provides an ideal environment for your advertising. The magazine Reise & Preise is intended for demanding individual, package holiday and business travellers who spend a fair amount of money on their holiday. Facebook: http://www.facebook.com/pages/REISEPREISE/376441376729 Twitter: http://twitter.com/#!/reise_preise.
Language(s): German
ADVERTISING RATES:
Full Page Mono .... EUR 6990
Full Page Colour .... EUR 6990
Mechanical Data: Type Area: 270 x 187 mm, No. of Columns (Display): 4, Col Widths (Display): 43 mm
Copy instructions: *Copy Date:* 45 days prior to publication
CONSUMER: HOLIDAYS & TRAVEL: Travel

REISEDIENST
740196G89A-12110
Editorial: Dießemer Bruch 167, 47805 KREFELD
Tel: 2151 51000 **Fax:** 2151 5100105
Email: medien@stuenings.de **Web site:** http://www.reise-dienst.com
Freq: Annual; **Cover Price:** EUR 2,50; **Circ:** 67,000
Editor: Jörg Montag; **Advertising Manager:** Dennis Feegers
Profile: Leisure recreation planner for trips to destinations on the Lower Rhine, the Ruhr area, in the Münsterland and in the Netherlands. With lots of information about hotels, restaurants, leisure, culture, events. At 124 pages the reader will find useful tips and suggestions for leisure time on the Lower Rhine, the Ruhr area, in the Münsterland and in the Netherlands border. Whether sports, cities, monuments, culture, nature, fun and relaxation - with the Reise-Dienst, there are exciting things in his own front door to discover. Those who want to experience the Lower Rhine and Münsterland in all its aspects related with the "Reise-Dienst" is the ideal companion. Whether by bicycle between Bocholt and Vreden or on the trail of the Romans in the LVR-Archeological Park Xanten, the reader numerous recreational and cultural tips obtained for every taste.
Language(s): German
ADVERTISING RATES:
Full Page Colour .... EUR 1980
Mechanical Data: Type Area: 250 x 184 mm, No. of Columns (Display): 4, Col Widths (Display): 43 mm
Copy instructions: *Copy Date:* 60 days prior to publication

REISEFIEBER
740197G89A-11536
Editorial: Auf den Höhen 13, 93138 LAPPERSDORF
Tel: 941 2802402 **Fax:** 941 2802404
Email: magazin.reisefieber@gmx.de **Web site:** http://www.reisefieber-magazin.de
Freq: Quarterly; **Annual Sub.:** EUR 12,00; **Circ:** 70,000
Editor: Andreas Langer; **Advertising Manager:** Sabina Langer
Profile: Travel magazine for tourists with features including global lifestyle and fitness topics.
Language(s): German
ADVERTISING RATES:
Full Page Mono .... EUR 3100
Full Page Colour .... EUR 4900
Mechanical Data: Type Area: 252 x 200 mm
Copy instructions: *Copy Date:* 40 days prior to publication
CONSUMER: HOLIDAYS & TRAVEL: Travel

REISEHANDBUCH SKANDINAVIEN
760149G89A-11417
Editorial: Maxstr. 64, 45127 ESSEN **Tel:** 201 872290
Fax: 201 8942511
Email: verlag@nordis.com **Web site:** http://www.skandinavien.de
Freq: Annual; **Cover Price:** EUR 9,80; **Circ:** 80,000
Editor: Lutz Stickeln
Profile: Travel guide for Scandinavia and North Europe.
Language(s): German
ADVERTISING RATES:
Full Page Mono .... EUR 3150
Full Page Colour .... EUR 4250
Mechanical Data: Type Area: 239 x 148 mm, No. of Columns (Display): 3, Col Widths (Display): 45 mm
Copy instructions: *Copy Date:* 105 days prior to publication

REISEMAGAZIN
740201G89A-12111
Editorial: Ottostr. 12, 50859 KÖLN
Tel: 2234 7011120 **Fax:** 2234 7011142
Email: verlag@aerzteblatt.de **Web site:** http://www.aerzteblatt.de
Freq: 3 issues yearly; **Circ:** 149,000
Editor: Heinz Stüwe; **Advertising Manager:** Petra Pahlke-Schäfers
Profile: Travel magazine for doctors, dentists and clinicians (Supplement: Deutsches Ärzteblatt and zm Zahnärztliche Mitteilungen) Facebook: http://www.facebook.com/aerzteblatt.
Language(s): German
ADVERTISING RATES:
Full Page Mono .... EUR 5100
Full Page Colour .... EUR 6890
Mechanical Data: Type Area: 260 x 185 mm, No. of Columns (Display): 4
Supplement to: Deutsches Ärzteblatt, zm Zahnärztliche Mitteilungen

REISEMOBIL INTERNATIONAL
740203G77A-1960
Editorial: Postwiesenstr. 5a, 70327 STUTTGART
Tel: 711 1346610 **Fax:** 711 1346668
Email: wagner@doldemedien.de **Web site:** http://www.reisemobil-international.de
Freq: Monthly; **Annual Sub.:** EUR 37,80; **Circ:** 48,711
Editor: Ingo Wagner; **Advertising Manager:** Sylke Wohlschiess
Profile: Motorhome Magazine: Test, technology and service around the theme motorhome, travel destinations, parking and camping Facebook: http://facebook.com/reisemobil.international.
Language(s): German
ADVERTISING RATES:
Full Page Mono .... EUR 3410
Full Page Colour .... EUR 5560
Mechanical Data: Type Area: 252 x 184 mm, No. of Columns (Display): 4, Col Widths (Display): 43 mm
Copy instructions: *Copy Date:* 20 days prior to publication
CONSUMER: MOTORING & CYCLING: Motoring

REISEMOBIL INTERNATIONAL BORDATLAS
740204G77A-1980
Editorial: Postwiesenstr. 5a, 70327 STUTTGART
Tel: 711 1346610 **Fax:** 711 1346668
Email: bordatlas@reisemobil-international.de **Web site:** http://www.bordatlas.de
Freq: Annual; **Cover Price:** EUR 21,90; **Circ:** 65,000
Advertising Manager: Sylke Wohlschiess
Profile: International camping guide for motorhome and caravan drivers. Facebook: http://www.facebook.com/reisemobil.international.
Language(s): German
ADVERTISING RATES:
Full Page Mono .... EUR 2170
Full Page Colour .... EUR 3500
Mechanical Data: Type Area: 252 x 184 mm, No. of Columns (Display): 4, Col Widths (Display): 43 mm
Copy instructions: *Copy Date:* 40 days prior to publication

REISEN EXCLUSIV
763247G89A-11424
Editorial: Emil-Hoffmann-Str. 55, 50999 KÖLN
Tel: 2236 848813 **Fax:** 2236 848824
Email: jl@ella-verlag.de **Web site:** http://www.reisenexclusiv.com
Freq: Quarterly; **Cover Price:** EUR 6,50; **Circ:** 56,000
Editor: Jennifer Latuperisa; **Advertising Manager:** Susanne Julia Gorny
Profile: reisen EXCLUSIV is the premium-magazine for travellers who associate luxury and the quality of life with the exploration of foreign cultures. reisen EXCLUSIV offers a wide variety of topics and possible destinations. The magazine entertains with authentic and comprehensive articles which are investigated directly at the location by our editorial journalists. The reading pleasure in regard to travel and luxury not only provides new incentives to the demanding target group of widely travelled educated and prosperous men and women to discover new worthwhile destinations but also sheds a new light on familiar locations. How? With reports in respect to fascinating destinations, unusual hotels, cultural highlights and culinary discoveries to be made. Reading pleasure combined with visual and mind-broadening experience – this is what reisen EXCLUSIV is all about. The spectrum of topics is enlivened with own lifestyle productions which present fashion, beauty and accessories on an aesthetically high standard. The reader will be able to find topics regarding worthwhile luxury hotels, Germany's highlights and recommendable getaways for all seasons in each and every issue of the premium magazine. But that's not all: The fourth and last issue of the year does combine the favorite topics of our readers (Hotels and Gourmet) with the standard topics! To put it short, you can rely on reisen EXCLUSIV! Twitter: http://twitter.com/#!/reisenEXCLUSIV.
Language(s): German
ADVERTISING RATES:
Full Page Mono .... EUR 6200
Full Page Colour .... EUR 6200
Mechanical Data: Type Area: 240 x 175 mm

REISEN.DE
1662553G89A-11926
Editorial: Planegger Str. 16, 82110 GERMERING
Tel: 1805 618000 **Fax:** 1805 618099
Email: redaktion@reisen.de **Web site:** http://www.reisen.de
Cover Price: Paid; **Circ:** 5,582,011 Unique Users
Editor: Ellen Teßmann
Language(s): German
CONSUMER: HOLIDAYS & TRAVEL: Travel

REISE-PREISE.DE
1692998G91B-2511
Editorial: Hauptstr. 14, 21614 BUXTEHUDE
Tel: 4161 71690 **Fax:** 4161 716915
Email: redaktion@reise-preise.de **Web site:** http://www.reise-preise.de
Freq: Daily; **Cover Price:** Paid; **Circ:** 80,331 Unique Users
Editor: Oliver Kühn; **Advertising Manager:** Thorsten Kühn
Profile: Ezine: Magazine about air travel and planning a holiday. Facebook: http://www.facebook.com/pages/REISEPREISE/376441376729 Twitter: http://twitter.com/#!/reise_preise.
Language(s): German
CONSUMER: RECREATION & LEISURE: Camping & Caravanning

REISEWELT
1997383G65B-2_100
Editorial: Markt 1, 45127 ESSEN **Tel:** 201 1095195
Fax: 201 1095141
Email: info@markt1-verlag.de **Web site:** http://www.cp-verlagsgesellschaft.de
Freq: Monthly; **Circ:** 413,887
Editor: Alfred Harke
Profile: Current topics related to culture and arts, recreation and sports, cities and shopping, and more.
Language(s): German
ADVERTISING RATES:
Full Page Mono .... EUR 18550
Full Page Colour .... EUR 18550
Mechanical Data: Type Area: 175 x mm, No. of Columns (Display): 267
Supplement to: Welt am Sonntag
NATIONAL DAILY & SUNDAY NEWSPAPERS: GB-Unabhängigkeits-MdEP

REITEN UND ZUCHT IN BERLIN UND BRANDENBURG-ANHALT
740224G81D-10
Editorial: Ehrig-Hahn-Str. 4, 16356 AHRENSFELDE
Tel: 30 41909551 **Fax:** 30 41909553
Email: redaktion@reiten-zucht.de **Web site:** http://www.reiten-zucht.de
Freq: Monthly; **Annual Sub.:** EUR 58,80; **Circ:** 5,685
Editor: Björn Schroeder; **Advertising Manager:** Martina Palenker
Profile: Magazine about equestrian sports and horse-breeding in Berlin-Brandenburg. Facebook: http://www.facebook.com/pages/Reiten-und-Zucht-in-Berlin-und-Brandenburg-Anhalt/321409567346?ref=nf Twitter: http://twitter.com/#!/reitenundzucht.
Language(s): German
ADVERTISING RATES:
Full Page Mono .... EUR 710
Full Page Colour .... EUR 1349
Mechanical Data: Type Area: 261 x 191 mm, No. of Columns (Display): 4, Col Widths (Display): 44 mm
Copy instructions: *Copy Date:* 14 days prior to publication
Official Journal of: Organ d. LV Pferdesport Berlin-Brandenburg e.V., d. Reg.-Verb. d. Reit- u. Fahrvereine Berlin e.V., d. Landeskommission f. Pferdeleistungsprüfungen Berlin-Brandenburg u. d. Pferdezuchtverb. Brandenburg-Anhalt e.V.
CONSUMER: ANIMALS & PETS: Horses & Ponies

REITER REVUE INTERNATIONAL
740228G75E-200
Editorial: Erich-Kästner-Str. 2, 56379 SINGHOFEN
Tel: 2604 978201 **Fax:** 2604 9786201
Email: brief@reiterrevue.de **Web site:** http://www.reiterrevue.de
Freq: Monthly; Free to qualifying individuals
Annual Sub.: EUR 57,00; **Circ:** 29,888
Editor: Susanne Hennig; **Advertising Manager:** Bärbel Labonte
Profile: The trade magazine for equestrian sport, Pfedezucht and maintenance is one of the leading special-interest magazines in Germany. Riding on the classical European warmbloods prescribed Reiter Revue International covers the diverse range of topics from around the sports and leisure partners horse. Critical background reports, current reports from Germany and abroad, and teaching contributions from renowned instructors and experts round out the professional range. Several times a year Film Reviews DVD deepen the contents of the magazine. The DVD can also be targeted for advertising of the manufacturers and service providers used in the equine sector.
Language(s): German
ADVERTISING RATES:
Full Page Mono .... EUR 3414
Full Page Colour .... EUR 5873
Mechanical Data: Type Area: 253 x 186 mm, No. of Columns (Display): 4, Col Widths (Display): 43 mm
Official Journal of: Organ d. Förderkreises f. Amateur- u. Berufsreitsport e.V.
CONSUMER: SPORT: Horse Racing

REITER & PFERDE IN WESTFALEN
740231G81D-14
Editorial: Sudmühlenstr. 31, 48157 MÜNSTER
Tel: 251 6861683 **Fax:** 251 6861689
Email: reiterredaktion@lv.de **Web site:** http://www.reiter-und-pferde.de
Freq: Monthly; Free to qualifying individuals
Annual Sub.: EUR 52,80; **Circ:** 26,953
Editor: Jasmin Wiedemann; **Advertising Manager:** Gabriele Wittkowski
Profile: Journal of equestrian sports in Westfalen. It provides essential technical information on all topics relating to horse breeding, housing, feeding, horse health, training of horse and rider, gear and much more. The journal gives detailed information on breeding and sporting events in Westphalia and the activities in the clubs. It publishes the complete tournament calls and appointments.
Language(s): German
ADVERTISING RATES:
Full Page Mono .... EUR 2649
Full Page Colour .... EUR 4317
Mechanical Data: Type Area: 270 x 190 mm, No. of Columns (Display): 4, Col Widths (Display): 46 mm
Copy instructions: *Copy Date:* 21 days prior to publication
Official Journal of: Organ d. Pferdesportverb. Westfalen e.V. u. d. Westfäl. Pferdestammbuches e.V.
CONSUMER: ANIMALS & PETS: Horses & Ponies

DIE REITERIN
1983621G74A-3742
Editorial: Mandichostr. 18, 86504 MERCHING
Tel: 8233 381135 **Fax:** 8233 381212
Email: rosina.jennissen@die-reiterin.net **Web site:** http://www.die-reiterin.net
Freq: 6 issues yearly; **Annual Sub.:** EUR 27,00; **Circ:** 60,000
Editor: Rosina Jennissen
Profile: The most beautiful aspects of the equestrian life, riding features, stylish furnishing and living, fashion and beauty, celebrities, health, wellness, holiday and news from the scene - the magazine reflects the environment of their readers.
Language(s): German
ADVERTISING RATES:
Full Page Mono .... EUR 3900
Full Page Colour .... EUR 3900
Mechanical Data: Type Area: 265 x 190 mm, No. of Columns (Display): 4, Col Widths (Display): 45 mm

REITERJOURNAL
740226G75E-223
Editorial: Motorstr. 38, 70499 STUTTGART
Tel: 711 80608225 **Fax:** 711 80608250
Email: reiterjournal@matthaesmedien.de **Web site:** http://www.reiterjournal.com
Freq: Monthly; Free to qualifying individuals
Annual Sub.: EUR 62,00; **Circ:** 17,448
Editor: Hugo Matthaes; **Advertising Manager:** Hugo Matthaes
Profile: Magazine for equestrian sport and breeding in Baden-Wuerttemberg. The Journal tab is the voice for riders and breeders in the Southwest. as the official organ of various professional associations and organizations with the reader about all important issues are informed about the horse. With the regular sections finds a large audience bond instead of the equestrian Journal: RJ-date - tournaments - training of rider and horse - markets and auctions - Breeding Journal - from the clubs - Youth in the saddle - about horses - RJ-special - horses, and most important: in the green part of any special regulations of tournaments including the schedule. The Journal tab is the required reading of the riders, horse breeders, veterinarians, show organizers and judges. All are interested in comprehensive information about equestrian sports, horses, horse breeding and use the schedule of tournament contracts.
Language(s): German
ADVERTISING RATES:
Full Page Mono .... EUR 1985
Full Page Colour .... EUR 3210
Mechanical Data: Type Area: 273 x 190 mm, No. of Columns (Display): 4, Col Widths (Display): 43 mm
Copy instructions: *Copy Date:* 20 days prior to publication
Official Journal of: Organ d. Pferdezuchtverb. Baden-Württemberg e.V., Amt f. Landwirtschaft, Landschafts- u. Bodenkultur Ludwigsburg, Pferdesportverb. Baden-Württemberg e.V., Landeskommission f. Pferdeleistungsprüfungen, Württ. Pferdesportverb., Pferdesportverb. Südbaden, Verb. d. Pferdesportvereine Nordbaden
CONSUMER: SPORT: Horse Racing

REITSPORT MAGAZIN
740233G75E-520
Editorial: Misburger Str. 119, 30625 HANNOVER
Tel: 511 56059930 **Fax:** 511 56059939
Email: redaktion@paragon.de **Web site:** http://www.reitsport-magazin.de
Freq: Monthly; **Annual Sub.:** EUR 63,00; **Circ:** 9,841
Editor: Birgit Springmann; **Advertising Manager:** Alexandra Duesmann
Profile: "Reitsport Magazin" reports monthly on the Sport in Niedersachsen and Bremen. It is the association's journal the equestrian federations Hanover and Bremen. Here you will find the tournament alerts and reporting on the tournament.
Language(s): German
ADVERTISING RATES:
Full Page Mono .... EUR 1808
Full Page Colour .... EUR 3072
Mechanical Data: Type Area: 255 x 190 mm, No. of Columns (Display): 4, Col Widths (Display): 45 mm
Copy instructions: *Copy Date:* 30 days prior to publication
Official Journal of: Organ d. Pferdesportverbände Hannover e.V. u. Bremen e.V.
CONSUMER: SPORT: Horse Racing

REMSCHEIDER GENERAL-ANZEIGER
740246G67B-12180
Editorial: Konrad-Adenauer-Str. 2, 42853 REMSCHEID **Tel:** 2191 909211 **Fax:** 2191 909185
Email: redaktion@rga-online.de **Web site:** http://www.rga-online.de
Freq: 312 issues yearly; **Circ:** 19,034
News Editor: Axel Richter
Profile: Daily newspaper with regional news and a local sports section. Twitter: http://twitter.com/rgaonline This Outlet offers RSS (Really Simple Syndication).
Language(s): German
ADVERTISING RATES:
SCC .... EUR 65,40
Mechanical Data: Type Area: 430 x 282 mm, No. of Columns (Display): 6, Col Widths (Display): 45 mm
Copy instructions: *Copy Date:* 1 day prior to publication
Supplement(s): prisma; Radio RSG News
REGIONAL DAILY & SUNDAY NEWSPAPERS: Regional Daily Newspapers

REMS-ZEITUNG
740247G67B-12160
Editorial: Paradiesstr. 12, 73525 SCHWÄBISCH GMÜND **Tel:** 7171 600640 **Fax:** 7171 600659
Email: redaktion@rems-zeitung.de **Web site:** http://www.rems-zeitung.de
Freq: 312 issues yearly; **Circ:** 15,147
Editor: Meinrad Sigg; **Advertising Manager:** Andreas Lonardoni
Profile: Daily newspaper with regional news and a local sports section.
Language(s): German
ADVERTISING RATES:
SCC .... EUR 66,20
Mechanical Data: Type Area: 480 x 320 mm, No. of Columns (Display): 7, Col Widths (Display): 43 mm
Copy instructions: *Copy Date:* 1 day prior to publication
REGIONAL DAILY & SUNDAY NEWSPAPERS: Regional Daily Newspapers

RENDITE
2073308G1F-1867
Editorial: Düsseldorfer Str. 16, 60329 FRANKFURT
Tel: 69 2732342 **Fax:** 69 2732264
Email: rendite@boersenzeitung.de **Web site:** http://www.boersen-zeitung.com/index.php?li=338
Freq: Quarterly; **Circ:** 40,000
Editor: Claus Döring; **Advertising Manager:** Jens Zinke
Profile: And investment magazine supplement of Börsen-Zeitung, is aimed at decision makers in the financial sector and provides them with solid information on new investment trends, strategies, and products. The magazine, which is at more than 40,000 assets, and investment advisors nationwide and sent out in German speaking countries and also included the stock market newspaper, published in the three-month intervals. Focus of the report are issues relating to funds, certificates, exchange traded funds, alternative investments and equities. This investment strategies and new products are analyzed and evaluated. Yield - The investment magazine of the stock market newspaper, focused on the specific interest of the experts and decision makers. The benefit of this target group is clearly in the foreground. In addition, yield but also the sophisticated private investor has in mind.
Language(s): German
ADVERTISING RATES:
Full Page Mono .... EUR 11856
Full Page Colour .... EUR 11856
Mechanical Data: Type Area: 244 x 170 mm
Copy instructions: *Copy Date:* 28 days prior to publication
Supplement to: Börsen-Zeitung

RENOPRAXIS
1687397G1A-3608
Editorial: Feldstiege 100, 48161 MÜNSTER
Tel: 2533 9300671 **Fax:** 2533 930050
Email: hilke.arnau@lexisnexis.de **Web site:** http://www.lexisnexis.de
Freq: Monthly; **Annual Sub.:** EUR 98,00; **Circ:** 5,500
Editor: Hilke Arnau; **Advertising Manager:** Anja Christiansen
Profile: Magazine for lawyers specialised in law of obligations.
Language(s): German
ADVERTISING RATES:
Full Page Mono .... EUR 800
Full Page Colour .... EUR 1550
Mechanical Data: Type Area: 243 x 176 mm

RENTE & CO
1792953G74N-906
Editorial: Lindenstr. 20, 50674 KÖLN
Tel: 221 277570 **Fax:** 221 2775710
Email: plusmagazin@bayard-media.de **Web site:** http://www.plus-mag.de
Freq: Quarterly; **Cover Price:** EUR 3,95; **Circ:** 65,000
Editor: Jürgen Sinn; **Advertising Manager:** Armin Baier
Profile: Rente & Co is the German pensions magazine. Four times a year helps "Rente & Co " the workers, pensioners, as well as officials to gain financial security for old age. Whether statutory retirement or pension, whether occupational or personal pensions - "Rente & Co " the Guide magazine is about your pension. Complementing the topics related to health insurance, care insurance, investing and taxes. Want to "Rente & Co" is therefore the perfect guide magazine for all the concrete value and expert advice have.
Language(s): German
ADVERTISING RATES:
Full Page Mono .... EUR 6500
Full Page Colour .... EUR 6500

DIE RENTENVERSICHERUNG RV
740265G1H-200
Editorial: Einsteinstr. 10, 53757 ST. AUGUSTIN
Tel: 2241 31640 **Fax:** 2241 316436
Email: info@asgard.de **Web site:** http://www.asgard.de
Freq: Monthly; Free to qualifying individuals
Annual Sub.: EUR 78,90; **Circ:** 580
Editor: Stefan Maus; **Advertising Manager:** Stefan Maus
Profile: Magazine for pension, retirement, social policy.
Language(s): German
ADVERTISING RATES:
Full Page Mono .... EUR 820
Full Page Colour .... EUR 1070
Mechanical Data: Type Area: 262 x 175 mm, No. of Columns (Display): 2, Col Widths (Display): 85 mm
Copy instructions: *Copy Date:* 10 days prior to publication
Official Journal of: Organ f. d. Bundesverb. d. Sozialrechts- u. Rentenberater e.V.
BUSINESS: FINANCE & ECONOMICS: Pensions

REPORT NATURHEILKUNDE
1928145G56A-11644
Editorial: Kaunstr. 34, 14163 BERLIN
Tel: 30 8011018 **Fax:** 30 8016661
Email: verlagsgesellschaft@firmengruppe-tischler.de
Web site: http://www.report-naturheilkunde.de
Freq: 6 issues yearly; **Annual Sub.:** EUR 20,00; **Circ:** 15,420
Editor: H. P. Becker
Profile: Magazine for alternative practitioners and naturopathy.
Language(s): German
ADVERTISING RATES:
Full Page Mono .... EUR 1400
Full Page Colour .... EUR 2600
Mechanical Data: Type Area: 260 x 180 mm, No. of Columns (Display): 3, Col Widths (Display): 59 mm
Copy instructions: *Copy Date:* 30 days prior to publication

REPRODUCTION IN DOMESTIC ANIMALS
740297G64H-280
Editorial: Rotherstr. 21, 10245 BERLIN
Tel: 30 47031465 **Fax:** 30 47031477
Email: suzanne.albrecht@wiley.com **Web site:** http://www.wiley.com
Freq: 6 issues yearly; **Annual Sub.:** EUR 818,00; **Circ:** 400
Editor: H. Rodriguez-Martinez; **Advertising Manager:** Tobias Trinkl
Profile: Publication about animal reproduction and biotechnology with special regard to investigations in applied and clinical research.
Language(s): English
Mechanical Data: Type Area: 250 x 175 mm, No. of Columns (Display): 2, Col Widths (Display): 85 mm
Official Journal of: Organ d. European Society for Domestic Animal Reproduction, d. European Veterinary Society for Small Animal Reproduction u. d. Spanish Society of Animal Reproduction
BUSINESS: OTHER CLASSIFICATIONS: Veterinary

RESEARCH & RESULTS
1752681G2A-5687
Editorial: Haldenbergerstr. 28, 80997 MÜNCHEN
Tel: 89 149027910 **Fax:** 89 149027929
Email: reitmeier@research-results.de **Web site:** http://www.research-results.de
Freq: 7 issues yearly; **Annual Sub.:** EUR 149,80; **Circ:** 3,685
Editor: Hans Reitmeier
Profile: Research & Results is a leading magazine in the field of market research. Seven issues per year and an average circulation of over 3,500 enable it to reach its target group perfectly. The readership primarily consists of decision-makers in market research, marketing, media planning and media research. The main sections are trade articles, news, appointments, events and the Omnibus overview. Modern Content - keeping our finger on the pulse of the industry in Germany, Europe and worldwide with the latest news and in-depth reports - profiles of companies, studies and methodology ensure high value to readers-career section including personal success stories, current appointments, and education and training possibilities - practical service section with market reports on seminars, available studies, service providers and omnibus surveys.
Language(s): German
ADVERTISING RATES:
Full Page Mono .... EUR 2330
Full Page Colour .... EUR 3340
Mechanical Data: Type Area: 254 x 180 mm, No. of Columns (Display): 3, Col Widths (Display): 57 mm
Copy instructions: *Copy Date:* 28 days prior to publication
Supplement(s): Nutzenforschung Report

RE-SOLUT
1616652G74N-823
Editorial: Dürerstr. 5, 45659 RECKLINGHAUSEN
Email: maria.tamm@gmx.de **Web site:** http://www.seniorenbeirat-recklinghausen.de
Freq: Quarterly; **Cover Price:** Free; **Circ:** 3,500
Editor: Hans-Friedrich Tamm
Profile: Magazine for the elderly from the region of Recklinghausen.
Language(s): German

RESOURCE
736605G57-1180
Editorial: Dorfstr. 51, 16816 NEURUPPIN
Tel: 3391 45450 **Fax:** 3391 454510
Email: tkverlag@vivis.de **Web site:** http://www.muellmagazin.de
Freq: Quarterly; **Annual Sub.:** EUR 52,00; **Circ:** 2,700
Editor: Karl Thomé-Kozmiensky; **Advertising Manager:** Steffi Nerlinger
Profile: Magazine reports on current research results, methods and approaches to waste minimization and pollution prevention at home and abroad, analysis of environmental trends and discussion of new waste treatment processes, etc.
Language(s): German
ADVERTISING RATES:
Full Page Mono .... EUR 1100
Full Page Colour .... EUR 1790
Mechanical Data: Type Area: 254 x 182 mm, No. of Columns (Display): 3, Col Widths (Display): 56 mm
Copy instructions: *Copy Date:* 28 days prior to publication
BUSINESS: ENVIRONMENT & POLLUTION

RESTAURO
740318G94B-460
Editorial: Streitfeldstr. 35, 81673 MÜNCHEN
Tel: 89 436005175 **Fax:** 89 436005113
Email: m.heilig@restauro.de **Web site:** http://www.restauro.de
Freq: 8 issues yearly; **Annual Sub.:** EUR 122,00; **Circ:** 4,054
Editor: Matthias Heilig; **Advertising Manager:** Andreas Schneider
Profile: Journal about conservation techniques and museums.
Language(s): German
ADVERTISING RATES:
Full Page Mono .... EUR 1360
Full Page Colour .... EUR 2650
Mechanical Data: No. of Columns (Display): 4, Col Widths (Display): 42 mm, Type Area: 269 x 183 mm
Copy instructions: *Copy Date:* 32 days prior to publication
CONSUMER: OTHER CLASSIFICATIONS: Historic Buildings

RESTORATION OF BUILDINGS AND MONUMENTS
1614693G19A-1073
Editorial: Schlierbergstr. 80, 79100 FREIBURG
Tel: 761 8818652 **Fax:** 761 8818651
Email: wittmann@aedificat.de **Web site:** http://www.aedificat.de
Freq: 6 issues yearly; Free to qualifying individuals
Annual Sub.: EUR 137,50; **Circ:** 250
Editor: Folker H. Wittmann
Profile: International journal for restoration of buildings and monuments.
Language(s): English; German
ADVERTISING RATES:
Full Page Mono .... EUR 605
Full Page Colour .... EUR 1445
Mechanical Data: Type Area: 246 x 168 mm

RESULTS
1892627G14A-10273
Editorial: Harvestehuder Weg 42, 20149 HAMBURG
Tel: 40 44188456 **Fax:** 40 44188309
Email: cp@hoca.de **Web site:** http://cp.hoca.de
Freq: 3 issues yearly; **Cover Price:** Free; **Circ:** 30,000
Editor: Boris Burauel
Profile: Company publication.
Language(s): German

RETTUNGS MAGAZIN
740326G56P-6
Editorial: Kurt-Schumacher-Allee 2, 28329 BREMEN
Tel: 421 468860 **Fax:** 421 4688630
Email: redaktion@rettungsmagazin.de **Web site:** http://www.rettungsdienst.de
Freq: 6 issues yearly; **Annual Sub.:** EUR 25,00; **Circ:** 13,668
Editor: Lars Schmitz-Eggen
Profile: Independent trade magazine for all employees of the emergency services. Positioning: Presentation of the work in the organizations. This includes field reports, in which specialists write about your experiences. This ranges from the mountain rescue service on the rescue on the streets and disasters to the rescue at sea. Development of vehicles and equipment are presented. Description of medical techniques. Glossary section. The rescue magazine is for the whole team in the emergency service is a valuable source of information. Target group: All in the emergency service workers such as paramedics, assistants, doctors, members of the aid agencies, firefighters, armed forces members Facebook: http://www.facebook.com/rettungsdienst This Outlet offers RSS (Really Simple Syndication).
Language(s): German
Readership: Read by people employed in the emergency care services.
ADVERTISING RATES:
Full Page Mono .... EUR 2342
Full Page Colour .... EUR 3680
Mechanical Data: Type Area: 243 x 188 mm, No. of Columns (Display): 4, Col Widths (Display): 45 mm
BUSINESS: HEALTH & MEDICAL: Casualty & Emergency

RETTUNGSDIENST
740325G56P-5
Editorial: Rathausstr. 1, 26188 EDEWECHT
Tel: 4405 918115 **Fax:** 4405 918130
Email: dahlstrom@skverlag.de **Web site:** http://www.skverlag.de
Freq: Monthly; **Annual Sub.:** EUR 44,50; **Circ:** 22,500
Editor: Detlef Dahlstrom
Profile: Magazine for all the emergency medical service workers and clinicians who are involved in the emergency medical service, for aid agencies and fire departments and the Occupational Health Service. Contents: - with real case examples and current information from the field of prehospital emergency medicine, and many more emergency services, training, emergency surgery, legal, professional policy - the diversity of the rescue scene at home and abroad, comprehensive- - Job Market.
Language(s): German
ADVERTISING RATES:
Full Page Mono .... EUR 1600
Full Page Colour .... EUR 2800
Mechanical Data: Type Area: 252 x 184 mm, No. of Columns (Display): 4, Col Widths (Display): 49 mm
Copy instructions: *Copy Date:* 21 days prior to publication
BUSINESS: HEALTH & MEDICAL: Casualty & Emergency

REUTLINGER GENERAL-ANZEIGER
740336G67B-12200
Editorial: Burgstr. 1, 72764 REUTLINGEN
Tel: 7121 3020 **Fax:** 7121 302677
Email: redaktion@gea.de **Web site:** http://www.gea.de
Freq: 312 issues yearly; **Circ:** 41,687
Editor: Hartmut Troebs; **News Editor:** Christoph Irion; **Advertising Manager:** Stephan Körting
Profile: The GEA - or the "Generaler" - as it is called in the population, was founded in 1887. Tradition: The GEA is now the largest circulation national daily newspaper and the only full production in the region of Reutlingen and Neckar-Alb. Independent and owner led by the Reutlinger publishing family Lehari. Our editors work on, comprehensive reports from the city and region of Reutlingen, Baden-Württemberg, Germany and the world every day, they illuminate the background, analyze and comment on current events. The General-Anzeiger, with the subtitles Echaz-Bote and Metzinger-Uracher General-Anzeiger reaches a daily circulation of 43,000 copies, about 118,000 people in its overall distribution area and is therefore not only the leading source of information in the Neckar-Alb Region, but also a powerful advertising medium. Twitter: http://twitter.com/geaonline This Outlet offers RSS (Really Simple Syndication).
Language(s): German
ADVERTISING RATES:
SCC .... EUR 91,90
Mechanical Data: Type Area: 480 x 320 mm, No. of Columns (Display): 7, Col Widths (Display): 44 mm
Copy instructions: *Copy Date:* 1 day prior to publication
Supplement(s): GEA Sport Magazin
REGIONAL DAILY & SUNDAY NEWSPAPERS: Regional Daily Newspapers

REUTLINGER NACHRICHTEN
740339G67B-12220
Editorial: Albstr. 4, 72764 REUTLINGEN
Tel: 7121 93020 **Fax:** 7121 930246
Email: rn.redaktion@swp.de **Web site:** http://www.suedwest-aktiv.de
Freq: 312 issues yearly; **Circ:** 12,513
Advertising Manager: Otto Hirt
Profile: Daily newspaper with regional news and a local sports section. Twitter: http://twitter.com/SWPde This Outlet offers RSS (Really Simple Syndication).
Language(s): German
ADVERTISING RATES:
SCC .... EUR 14,50
Mechanical Data: Type Area: 480 x 320 mm, No. of Columns (Display): 7, Col Widths (Display): 44 mm
Copy instructions: *Copy Date:* 1 day prior to publication
REGIONAL DAILY & SUNDAY NEWSPAPERS: Regional Daily Newspapers

REUTLINGER WOCHENBLATT

740342G72-10832

Editorial: Marktplatz 16, 72764 REUTLINGEN
Tel: 7121 938134 **Fax:** 7121 938111
Email: chmielewski@wobla-rt.de **Web site:** http://www.reutlinger-wochenblatt.de
Freq: Weekly; **Cover Price:** Free; **Circ:** 121,350
Editor: Anja Chmielewski; **Advertising Manager:** Claudia Münzing
Profile: Advertising journal (house-to-house) concentrating on local stories.
Language(s): German
ADVERTISING RATES:
Full Page Mono .... EUR 6149
Full Page Colour .... EUR 8333
Mechanical Data: Type Area: 480 x 320 mm, No. of Columns (Display): 7, Col Widths (Display): 44 mm
Copy instructions: *Copy Date:* 1 day prior to publication
LOCAL NEWSPAPERS

REVIER MANAGER 1832761G14A-10134

Editorial: Alfredstr. 279, 45133 ESSEN
Tel: 201 294260 **Fax:** 201 2942610
Email: to@rm-redaktion.de **Web site:** http://www.revier-manager.de
Freq: 10 issues yearly; **Annual Sub.:** EUR 28,00; **Circ:** 27,950
Editor: Tamara Olschewski; **Advertising Manager:** Sophia Butt
Profile: In addition to regionally relevant economic issues and well-researched background information and interviews, company profiles and contributions will be presented on interesting personalities. Similarly, topics that address the purchasing power manager as a person and individual.
Language(s): German
ADVERTISING RATES:
Full Page Mono .... EUR 4624
Full Page Colour .... EUR 4624
Mechanical Data: Type Area: 260 x 188 mm, No. of Columns (Display): 4, Col Widths (Display): 44 mm

REVIEW GERMAN TRADE FAIR INDUSTRY

728741G14A-2700

Editorial: Littenstr. 9, 10179 BERLIN
Tel: 30 24000140 **Fax:** 30 24000330
Email: info@auma.de **Web site:** http://www.auma.de
Freq: Annual; **Cover Price:** Free; **Circ:** 1,000
Editor: Harald Kötter
Profile: Magazine by German Trade Fair Committee.
Language(s): English

REZEPTE MIT PFIFF 740368G74P-740

Editorial: Rotweg 8, 76532 BADEN-BADEN
Tel: 7221 3501446 **Fax:** 7221 3501467
Email: rezeptemitpfiff@klambt.de
Freq: Monthly; **Annual Sub.:** EUR 26,40; **Circ:** 31,589
Editor: Sabine Bartels
Profile: Consumption has a name: Rezepte mit Pfiff. "One should offer the body any good, so that the soul wants to live in it", the great Winston Churchill (1874-1965). How right he was still with it! And how little it as a surprise that another proverb says: Heart is through his stomach ... And who cook women mostly? Right, for their loved! It should be tasty, easy, fast and affordable for every day. But even for those special occasions in life are found in Rezepte mit Pfiff every month a lot of ideas and suggestions. Seasoned with the delicious variety of valuable tips and tricks that make cooking easier - and bring a touch of sophistication in the preparation. And of course, we also place great emphasis on the sweet side of life: seductive fruit cake, creamy cakes, muffins and more - with Rezepte mit Pfiff every day is a pleasure!.
Language(s): German
Readership: Aimed at people with an interest in food and cookery.
ADVERTISING RATES:
Full Page Mono .... EUR 5370
Full Page Colour .... EUR 5370
Mechanical Data: Type Area: 280 x 195 mm, No. of Columns (Display): 4, Col Widths (Display): 45 mm
Copy instructions: *Copy Date:* 28 days prior to publication
CONSUMER: WOMEN'S INTEREST CONSUMER MAGAZINES: Food & Cookery

REZEPTE PUR 1622887G74P-1045

Editorial: Burchardstr. 11, 20095 HAMBURG
Tel: 40 30194945 **Fax:** 40 30195220
Email: rezeptepur@bauerredaktionen.de **Web site:** http://www.rezepte-pur.de
Freq: Monthly; **Annual Sub.:** EUR 16,68; **Circ:** 107,775
Editor: Gudrun Hoffmüller
Profile: "REZEPTE pur" is the ideal title for those who like to concentrate on the essentials, are cooking beginners or have little time to cook. The recipe collection provides low-cost alternatives for every day. In a creative and easy way "REZEPTE pur" makes every day situations in the kitchen more easy in a creative and easy way - competent, pure and cheap! The readers value a tasteful and healthy diet and enjoy this from time to time in budget-low recipes and ingredients. Facebook: http://www.facebook.com/lecker.de.
Language(s): German
ADVERTISING RATES:
Full Page Mono .... EUR 8156
Full Page Colour .... EUR 8156
Mechanical Data: Type Area: 237 x 195 mm, No. of Columns (Display): 4, Col Widths (Display): 45 mm
Copy instructions: *Copy Date:* 28 days prior to publication
CONSUMER: WOMEN'S INTEREST CONSUMER MAGAZINES: Food & Cookery

RFE ELEKTRO HÄNDLER EH

725953G43A-360

Editorial: Am Friedrichshain 22, 10407 BERLIN
Tel: 30 42151315 **Fax:** 30 42151208
Email: waltraud.schwass@hussberlin.de **Web site:** http://www.rfe-eh.de
Freq: 10 issues yearly; **Annual Sub.:** EUR 78,00; **Circ:** 15,249
Editor: Horst Winkler; **Advertising Manager:** Bringfriede Trester
Profile: Journal for the retailer in the electrical wholesale and retail, in the kitchen retail and household goods trade, and in the electrical trade with attached shop and magazine for solutions of the Consumer Electronic (CE), the multi-media technology (PC) and the Communications Electronics (TK) in stores. Topics: Consumer electronics, consumer electronics, computer technology and multimedia, telecommunications, electronic measuring equipment, antennas and satellite technology, security systems, Internet and computer, show reports, articles and practice issues from trade and industry.
Language(s): German
ADVERTISING RATES:
Full Page Mono .... EUR 4150
Full Page Colour .... EUR 5290
Mechanical Data: Type Area: 266 x 185 mm, No. of Columns (Display): 4, Col Widths (Display): 43 mm
Copy instructions: *Copy Date:* 20 days prior to publication
BUSINESS: ELECTRICAL RETAIL TRADE

RFL RUNDSCHAU FÜR FLEISCHHYGIENE UND LEBENSMITTELÜBERWACHUNG

740372G22D-221

Editorial: Prinz-Eugen-Str. 19, 04277 LEIPZIG
Tel: 341 3013128
Email: g.schiefer@web.de
Freq: Monthly; **Annual Sub.:** EUR 74,70; **Circ:** 3,660
Editor: Georg Schiefer; **Advertising Manager:** Bettina Kruse
Profile: Magazine containing information on the technology and equipment used in the meat trade and related industries.
Language(s): German
ADVERTISING RATES:
Full Page Mono .... EUR 990
Full Page Colour .... EUR 1590
Mechanical Data: Type Area: 272 x 188 mm, No. of Columns (Display): 4, Col Widths (Display): 44 mm
Copy instructions: *Copy Date:* 21 days prior to publication
BUSINESS: FOOD: Meat Trade

RGA-ONLINE 1621933G72-18249

Editorial: Konrad-Adenauer-Str. 2, 42853 REMSCHEID **Tel:** 2191 909301 **Fax:** 2191 909174
Email: kratz@rga-online.de **Web site:** http://www.rga-online.de
Freq: Daily; **Cover Price:** Paid; **Circ:** 231,615 Unique Users
Editor: Andreas Kratz; **Advertising Manager:** Andreas Kratz
Profile: Ezine: Advertising journal (house-to-house) concentrating on local stories.
Language(s): German
LOCAL NEWSPAPERS

RHEIDERLAND 740374G67B-12240

Editorial: Risiusstr. 6, 26826 WEENER
Tel: 4951 9300 **Fax:** 4951 930120
Email: redaktion@rheiderland.de **Web site:** http://www.rheiderland.de
Freq: 312 issues yearly; **Circ:** 5,676
Editor: Gunther Faupel; **Advertising Manager:** Lothar Schoormann
Profile: Daily newspaper with regional news and a local sports section.
Language(s): German
ADVERTISING RATES:
SCC .... EUR 37,80
Mechanical Data: Type Area: 487 x 318 mm, No. of Columns (Display): 7, Col Widths (Display): 43 mm
Copy instructions: *Copy Date:* 2 days prior to publication
Supplement(s): Immo-Welt; Kfz-Welt
REGIONAL DAILY & SUNDAY NEWSPAPERS: Regional Daily Newspapers

RHEINER ANZEIGER

740390G72-10896

Editorial: Poststr. 1, 48431 RHEINE
Tel: 5971 404664 **Fax:** 5971 404699
Email: redaktion@rheiner-anzeiger.de **Web site:** http://www.rheiner-anzeiger.de
Freq: Weekly; **Cover Price:** Free; **Circ:** 47,000
Editor: Reiner Wellmann; **Advertising Manager:** Adolf Hartmann
Profile: Advertising journal (house-to-house) concentrating on local stories.
Language(s): German
ADVERTISING RATES:
Full Page Mono .... EUR 3416
Full Page Colour .... EUR 4407
Mechanical Data: Type Area: 488 x 323 mm, No. of Columns (Display): 7, Col Widths (Display): 45 mm
Copy instructions: *Copy Date:* 2 days prior to publication
LOCAL NEWSPAPERS

RHEINGAUER WOCHENBLATT

740393G72-10904

Editorial: Langgasse 21, 65183 WIESBADEN
Tel: 611 3552360 **Fax:** 611 3552343
Email: redaktion@rheingauer-wochenblatt.de **Web site:** http://www.rheingauer-wochenblatt.de
Freq: Weekly; **Cover Price:** Free; **Circ:** 29,547
Editor: Rüdiger Benda; **Advertising Manager:** Rainer Baumann
Profile: Advertising journal (house-to-house) concentrating on local stories.
Language(s): German
ADVERTISING RATES:
Full Page Mono .... EUR 2991
Full Page Colour .... EUR 4066
Mechanical Data: Type Area: 480 x 325 mm, No. of Columns (Display): 7, Col Widths (Display): 45 mm
Copy instructions: *Copy Date:* 2 days prior to publication
LOCAL NEWSPAPERS

RHEINGOLD MOVE 740394G2A-4220

Editorial: Kaiser-Wilhelm-Ring 46, 50672 KÖLN
Tel: 221 91277738 **Fax:** 221 91277755
Email: pfuhler@rheingold-online.de **Web site:** http://www.rheingold-online.de
Freq: Half-yearly; **Cover Price:** Free; **Circ:** 7,000
Editor: Rainer Pfuhler
Profile: Company publication published by rheingold.
Language(s): German

RHEINHESSISCHES WOCHENBLATT 740396G72-10908

Editorial: Wormser Str. 4, 55276 OPPENHEIM
Tel: 6133 2708 **Fax:** 6133 70432
Email: redaktion@rheinhessisches-wochenblatt.de
Web site: http://www.rheinhessisches-wochenblatt.de
Freq: Weekly; **Cover Price:** Free; **Circ:** 26,162
Editor: Rüdiger Benda; **Advertising Manager:** Rainer Baumann
Profile: Advertising journal (house-to-house) concentrating on local stories.
Language(s): German
ADVERTISING RATES:
Full Page Mono .... EUR 2991
Full Page Colour .... EUR 4066
Mechanical Data: Type Area: 480 x 325 mm, No. of Columns (Display): 7, Col Widths (Display): 45 mm
Copy instructions: *Copy Date:* 2 days prior to publication
LOCAL NEWSPAPERS

RHEIN-HUNSRÜCK-ZEITUNG

740398G67B-12280

Editorial: August-Horch-Str. 28, 56070 KOBLENZ
Tel: 261 892240 **Fax:** 261 892770
Email: redaktion@rhein-zeitung.net **Web site:** http://www.rhein-zeitung.de
Freq: 312 issues yearly; **Circ:** 13,705
Profile: Regional daily newspaper with news on politics, economy, culture, sports, travel, technology, etc. The Rhein-Hunsrück-Zeitung is a local issue the in koblenz appearing Rhein-Zeitung. Facebook: http://www.facebook.com/rheinzeitung Twitter: http://www.rhein-zeitung.de/twitter.html This Outlet offers RSS (Really Simple Syndication).
Language(s): German
ADVERTISING RATES:
SCC .... EUR 65,10
Mechanical Data: Type Area: 480 x 325 mm, No. of Columns (Display): 7, Col Widths (Display): 45 mm
Copy instructions: *Copy Date:* 1 day prior to publication
REGIONAL DAILY & SUNDAY NEWSPAPERS: Regional Daily Newspapers

RHEINISCHE BAUERNZEITUNG

740400G21A-3340

Editorial: Karl-Tesche-Str. 3, 56073 KOBLENZ
Tel: 261 3042201006 **Fax:** 261 304221000
Email: redaktion@rheinische-bauernzeitung.de **Web site:** http://www.lv-net.de
Freq: Weekly; **Annual Sub.:** EUR 73,20; **Circ:** 11,800
Editor: Josef Derstappen; **Advertising Manager:** Michael Nau
Profile: Farming journal.
Language(s): German
Readership: Read by farmers in the Rhein region.
ADVERTISING RATES:
Full Page Mono .... EUR 3534
Full Page Colour .... EUR 5704
Mechanical Data: Type Area: 310 x 212 mm, No. of Columns (Display): 4, Col Widths (Display): 50 mm
Copy instructions: *Copy Date:* 4 days prior to publication
Official Journal of: Organ d. Bauern- u. Winzerverb. Rheinland-Nassau, Amtsblatt d. Landwirtschaftskammer Rheinland-Pfalz, Mttbl. d. Bauernverb. Saar, d. Landwirtschaftskammer f. d. Saarland u. d. LV Gartenbau
BUSINESS: AGRICULTURE & FARMING

RHEINISCHE POST 740404G67B-12400

Editorial: Zülpicher Str. 10, 40549 DÜSSELDORF
Tel: 211 5050 **Fax:** 211 5047562
Email: redaktionssekretariat@rheinische-post.de
Web site: http://www.rp-online.de
Freq: 312 issues yearly; **Circ:** 363,799
Editor: Sven Gösmann; **News Editor:** Martin Kessler; **Advertising Manager:** Marc Arne Schümann
Profile: The Rheinische Post is the largest circulation daily newspaper in the Rhineland and one of the largest subscription newspapers in Germany. As a modern quality paper, it reflects the cultural, social and sporting life of the region and also provides precise researched contributions to world affairs, analytical views and pointed opinions. Largely responsible for this high-quality and comprehensive reporting are 236 editors and volunteers, a large number of freelancers and a network of correspondents in many cities in the world. Not least, the Rheinische Post achieve over 1 million discerning readers with above-average income and education level. The Rheinische Post is available to people in the region, time, place, and emotionally closer than any other medium and gives all ages an optimal contribution to the active lifestyle. Facebook: http://www.facebook.com/rponline Twitter: http://twitter.com/rpo_topnews This Outlet offers RSS (Really Simple Syndication).
Language(s): German
ADVERTISING RATES:
SCC .... EUR 504,00
Mechanical Data: Type Area: 480 x 325 mm, No. of Columns (Display): 7, Col Widths (Display): 45 mm
Copy instructions: *Copy Date:* 2 days prior to publication
Supplement(s): doppio; in Düsseldorf; prisma
REGIONAL DAILY & SUNDAY NEWSPAPERS: Regional Daily Newspapers

RHEINISCHES ÄRZTEBLATT

740407G56A-8960

Editorial: Tersteegenstr. 9, 40474 DÜSSELDORF
Tel: 211 43021245 **Fax:** 211 43021244
Email: rheinisches-aerzteblatt@aekno.de **Web site:** http://www.aekno.de
Freq: Monthly; Free to qualifying individuals
Annual Sub.: EUR 80,00; **Circ:** 51,500
Editor: Horst Schumacher
Profile: The RHEINISCHE ÄRZTEBLATT is the official organ of the Medical Association of North Rhine and the physicians' association and all the doctors in the country part of the state of North Rhine-Westphalia (administrative districts of Cologne and Dusseldorf) sent. The journal publishes notices of the Medical Association and the KV Nordrhein, occupational and written contributions to science as well as information on conferences and congresses. The Rheinisches Ärzteblatt also informed his readers about issues of health policy, ethics in medicine and the regional medical and scientific training. These are topics that give everyone / m North Rhine doctor or physician for his / her daily work necessary information and / causing him / her to be RHEINISCHE ÄRZTEBLATT carefully.
Language(s): German
Readership: Aimed at doctors in the Rhein region.
ADVERTISING RATES:
Full Page Mono .... EUR 2830
Full Page Colour .... EUR 5230
Mechanical Data: Type Area: 255 x 179 mm, No. of Columns (Display): 4, Col Widths (Display): 43 mm
Copy instructions: *Copy Date:* 27 days prior to publication
BUSINESS: HEALTH & MEDICAL

RHEINISCHES ZAHNÄRZTEBLATT 740410G56D-820

Editorial: Lindemannstr. 34, 40237 DÜSSELDORF
Tel: 211 9684217 **Fax:** 211 9684332
Email: rzb@kzvnr.de **Web site:** http://www.kzvnr.de
Freq: 11 issues yearly; Free to qualifying individuals
Annual Sub.: EUR 38,50; **Circ:** 10,900
Editor: Uwe Neddermeyer
Profile: Dentistry magazine for the Rhein area.
Language(s): German
Readership: Read by dentists in Nordheim.
ADVERTISING RATES:
Full Page Mono .... EUR 1290
Full Page Colour .... EUR 2010
Mechanical Data: Type Area: 260 x 185 mm, No. of Columns (Display): 3, Col Widths (Display): 58 mm
BUSINESS: HEALTH & MEDICAL: Dental

RHEINISCH-WESTFÄLISCHER JÄGER 740412G75F-600

Editorial: Hülsebrockstr. 2, 48165 MÜNSTER
Tel: 2501 801332 **Fax:** 2501 801333
Email: kruse@lv.de **Web site:** http://www.rwj-online.de
Freq: Monthly; Free to qualifying individuals
Annual Sub.: EUR 54,60; **Circ:** 63,775
Editor: Matthias Kruse; **Advertising Manager:** Gabriele Wittkowski
Profile: The Rheinisch-Westfälische Jäger is the monthly magazine of the members of the National Hunting Association of North Rhine-Westphalia. Here's the basic professional interested in hunting will find information on all topics related to hunting. He is much-used forum for discussion and exchange of opinions, trends and background information. In a special section to find dates and information on events and meetings in the area.
Language(s): German
ADVERTISING RATES:
Full Page Mono .... EUR 3709
Full Page Colour .... EUR 6046

Mechanical Data: Type Area: 270 x 190 mm, No. of Columns (Display): 4, Col Widths (Display): 46 mm
CONSUMER: SPORT: Shooting

RHEIN-LAHN-ZEITUNG
740417G67B-12300
Editorial: August-Horch-Str. 28, 56070 KOBLENZ
Tel: 261 892240 **Fax:** 261 892770
Email: redaktion@rhein-zeitung.de **Web site:** http://www.rhein-zeitung.de
Freq: 312 issues yearly; **Circ:** 16,937
Profile: Regional daily newspaper with news on politics, economy, culture, sports, travel, technology, etc. The Rhein-Lahn-Zeitung is a local issue the in koblenz appearing Rhein-Zeitung. Facebook: http://www.facebook.com/rheinzeitung Twitter: http://www.rhein-zeitung.de/twitter.html This Outlet offers RSS (Really Simple Syndication).
Language(s): German
ADVERTISING RATES:
SCC .... EUR 182,20
Mechanical Data: Type Area: 480 x 325 mm, No. of Columns (Display): 7, Col Widths (Display): 45 mm
Copy instructions: *Copy Date:* 1 day prior to publication
REGIONAL DAILY & SUNDAY NEWSPAPERS: Regional Daily Newspapers

RHEINLANDS REITER+PFERDE
740424G81D-15
Editorial: Weißenstein 52, 40764 LANGENFELD
Tel: 2173 3945959 **Fax:** 2173 3945958
Email: redaktion@reiter-pferde.de **Web site:** http://www.reiter-pferde.de
Freq: Monthly; **Free to qualifying individuals**
Annual Sub.: EUR 48,00; **Circ:** 16,628
Editor: Ilja Waßenhoven; **Advertising Manager:** Sandra Reitenbach
Profile: Official publication of the Rheinland Riding Association.
Language(s): German
ADVERTISING RATES:
Full Page Mono .... EUR 1600
Full Page Colour .... EUR 2360
Mechanical Data: Type Area: 264 x 185 mm, No. of Columns (Display): 4, Col Widths (Display): 44 mm
Copy instructions: *Copy Date:* 20 days prior to publication
Official Journal of: Organ d. Pferdesportverb. Rheinland e.V., d. Kommission f. Pferdeleistungsprüfungen Rheinland u. d. Rhein. Pferdestammbuch e.V.
CONSUMER: ANIMALS & PETS: Horses & Ponies

RHEIN-MAIN.NET
1622231G89A-11689
Editorial: Frankenallee 71, 60327 FRANKFURT
Tel: 69 75014063 **Fax:** 69 75014069
Email: info@rhein-main.net **Web site:** http://www.rhein-main.net
Freq: Daily; **Cover Price:** Paid; **Circ:** 132,386 Unique Users
Editor: Thomas Krohn; **Advertising Manager:** Julia Faller
Profile: Ezine: Magazine for city and region, concentrating on events, gastronomy, music, arts and events.
Language(s): German
CONSUMER: HOLIDAYS & TRAVEL: Travel

RHEIN-MOSEL WOCHENSPIEGEL
740427G72-10884
Editorial: Johann-Trarbach-Str. 16, 55469 SIMMERN
Tel: 6761 950116 **Fax:** 6761 950120
Email: red-hunsrueck@sw-verlag.de **Web site:** http://www.wochenspiegellive.de
Freq: Weekly; **Cover Price:** Free; **Circ:** 18,469
Editor: Kai Brückner
Profile: Advertising journal (house-to-house) concentrating on local stories.
Language(s): German
ADVERTISING RATES:
Full Page Mono .... EUR 2649
Full Page Colour .... EUR 3703
Mechanical Data: Type Area: 430 x 290 mm, No. of Columns (Display): 7, Col Widths (Display): 38 mm
Copy instructions: *Copy Date:* 2 days prior to publication
LOCAL NEWSPAPERS

RHEIN-NECKAR-ZEITUNG
740431G67B-12320
Editorial: Neugasse 2, 69117 HEIDELBERG
Tel: 6221 5191 **Fax:** 6221 22369
Email: marlies.pritschke@rnz.de **Web site:** http://www.rnz.de
Freq: 312 issues yearly; **Circ:** 90,586
Editor: Klaus Welzel; **News Editor:** Klaus Welzel; **Advertising Manager:** Inge Hölzcke
Profile: Regional daily newspaper with news on politics, economy, culture, sports, travel, technology, etc. The Rhein-Neckar-Zeitung (RNZ) will appear in Heidelberg with a paid circulation of 91 523 copies and is the regionally dominant newspaper. The distribution area stretches alongside Heidelberg of Weinheim, Sinsheim, Schwetzingen, Mosbach and Buchen. Twitter: http://twitter.com/RNZonline This Outlet offers RSS (Really Simple Syndication).
Language(s): German
ADVERTISING RATES:
SCC .... EUR 174,40
Mechanical Data: Col Widths (Display): 45 mm

Copy instructions: *Copy Date:* 1 day prior to publication
REGIONAL DAILY & SUNDAY NEWSPAPERS: Regional Daily Newspapers

DIE RHEINPFALZ
740432G67B-12420
Editorial: Amtsstr. 5, 67059 LUDWIGSHAFEN
Tel: 621 590201 **Fax:** 621 5902272
Email: redaktion@rheinpfalz.de **Web site:** http://www.rheinpfalz.de
Freq: 312 issues yearly; **Circ:** 243,917
Editor: Michael Garthe; **Advertising Manager:** Jan Puhlmann
Profile: Regional daily newspaper with news on politics, economy, culture, sports, travel, technology, etc. Twitter: http://twitter.com/rheinpfalz This Outlet offers RSS (Really Simple Syndication).
Language(s): German
ADVERTISING RATES:
SCC .... EUR 271,50
Mechanical Data: Type Area: 485 x 320 mm, No. of Columns (Display): 7, Col Widths (Display): 44 mm
Copy instructions: *Copy Date:* 1 day prior to publication
Supplement(s): Der Frankenthaler; Landauer Leben; Leo; neue Lu; Rotunde
REGIONAL DAILY & SUNDAY NEWSPAPERS: Regional Daily Newspapers

RHEIN-SIEG RUNDSCHAU
740439G67B-12360
Editorial: Stolkgasse 25, 50667 KÖLN
Tel: 221 1632558 **Fax:** 221 1632557
Email: print@kr-redaktion.de **Web site:** http://www.rundschau-online.de
Freq: 312 issues yearly; **Circ:** 38,003
Advertising Manager: Karsten Hundhausen
Profile: Daily newspaper with regional news and a local sports section. Facebook: http://www.facebook.com/pages/Kolnische-Rundschau/147616463739 This Outlet offers RSS (Really Simple Syndication).
Language(s): German
ADVERTISING RATES:
SCC .... EUR 87,00
Mechanical Data: Type Area: 430 x 285 mm, No. of Columns (Display): 6, Col Widths (Display): 45 mm
Copy instructions: *Copy Date:* 2 days prior to publication
Supplement(s): prisma
REGIONAL DAILY & SUNDAY NEWSPAPERS: Regional Daily Newspapers

RHEIN-SIEG-ANZEIGER
740438G67B-12340
Editorial: Amsterdamer Str. 192, 50735 KÖLN
Tel: 221 2240 **Fax:** 221 2242524
Email: redaktion-ksta@mds.de **Web site:** http://www.ksta.de
Freq: 312 issues yearly; **Circ:** 38,003
Advertising Manager: Karsten Hundhausen
Profile: Daily newspaper with regional news and a local sports section. Facebook: http://www.facebook.com/pages/KSTA/141063022950 Twitter: http://twitter.com/ksta_news This Outlet offers RSS (Really Simple Syndication).
Language(s): German
ADVERTISING RATES:
SCC .... EUR 87,00
Mechanical Data: Type Area: 430 x 285 mm, No. of Columns (Display): 6, Col Widths (Display): 45 mm
Copy instructions: *Copy Date:* 2 days prior to publication
Supplement(s): prisma
REGIONAL DAILY & SUNDAY NEWSPAPERS: Regional Daily Newspapers

RHEINZEIGER
1828500G14A-10097
Editorial: Gottfried-Hagen-Str. 60, 51105 KÖLN
Tel: 221 839110 **Fax:** 221 8391111
Email: heinz.bettmann@rheinzeiger.de **Web site:** http://www.rheinzeiger.de
Freq: Half-yearly; **Circ:** 2,300
Editor: Heinz Bettmann
Profile: Regional start up magazine.
Language(s): German
ADVERTISING RATES:
Full Page Mono .... EUR 1000
Full Page Colour .... EUR 1450
Mechanical Data: Type Area: 297 x 210 mm

RHEIN-ZEITUNG
740446G67B-12380
Editorial: August-Horch-Str. 28, 56070 KOBLENZ
Tel: 261 892240 **Fax:** 261 892770
Email: redaktion@rhein-zeitung.net **Web site:** http://www.rhein-zeitung.de
Freq: 312 issues yearly; **Circ:** 199,806
Editor: Christian Lindner; **News Editor:** Manfred Ruch
Profile: Regional daily newspaper with news on politics, economy, culture, sports, travel, technology, etc. The Rhein-Zeitung published in 16 local editions with eight different titles: Rhein-Zeitung (under the name appearing in the city of Koblenz and the districts Ahrweiler, Altenkirchen, Cochem-Zell, Mayen-Koblenz, Neuwied), Kirner Zeitung (municipality and city Kirn), Mainzer Rhein-Zeitung (city and around Mainz), Nahe-Zeitung (Kreis Birkenfeld), Öffentlicher Anzeiger (Kreis Bad Kreuznach), Rhein-Hunsrück-Zeitung (Rhein-Hunsrück-Kreis), Rhein-Lahn-Zeitung (Rhein-Lahn-Kreis) and Westerwälder Zeitung (Westerwaldkreis)

Facebook: http://www.facebook.com/rheinzeitung Twitter: http://www.rhein-zeitung.de/twitter.html This Outlet offers RSS (Really Simple Syndication).
Language(s): German
ADVERTISING RATES:
SCC .... EUR 466,60
Mechanical Data: Type Area: 480 x 325 mm, No. of Columns (Display): 7, Col Widths (Display): 45 mm
Copy instructions: *Copy Date:* 1 day prior to publication
Supplement(s): Handwerk Special; kulturInfo
REGIONAL DAILY & SUNDAY NEWSPAPERS: Regional Daily Newspapers

RHEIN-ZEITUNG.DE
1621939G67B-16651
Editorial: August-Horch-Str. 28, 56070 KOBLENZ
Tel: 261 892330 **Fax:** 261 892358
Email: onlinered@rhein-zeitung.net **Web site:** http://www.rhein-zeitung.de
Freq: Daily; **Cover Price:** Paid; **Circ:** 1,605,514 Unique Users
Editor: Marcus Schwarze
Profile: Ezine: Regional daily newspaper covering politics, economics, culture, sports, travel, technology and entertainment. Facebook: http://www.facebook.com/rheinzeitung Twitter: http://www.rhein-zeitung.de/twitter.html This Outlet offers RSS (Really Simple Syndication).
Language(s): German
REGIONAL DAILY & SUNDAY NEWSPAPERS: Regional Daily Newspapers

RHEUMATOLOGY INTERNATIONAL
740448G56A-8980
Editorial: Tiergartenstr. 17, 69121 HEIDELBERG
Tel: 6221 4870 **Fax:** 6221 4878366
Email: subscriptions@springer.com **Web site:** http://www.springerlink.com
Freq: Monthly; **Annual Sub.:** EUR 2090,00; **Circ:** 258
Editor: E. M. Lemmel
Profile: International magazine about rheumatology.
Language(s): English
ADVERTISING RATES:
Full Page Mono .... EUR 740
Full Page Colour .... EUR 1780
Mechanical Data: Type Area: 240 x 175 mm

RHÖN- U. SAALEPOST
740457G67B-12440
Editorial: Industriestr. 8, 97616 BAD NEUSTADT
Tel: 9771 919334 **Fax:** 9771 919355
Email: redaktion@rhoen-undsaalepost.de
Freq: 312 issues yearly; **Circ:** 5,104
Advertising Manager: Wolfgang Markert
Profile: Daily newspaper with regional news and a local sports section.
Language(s): German
ADVERTISING RATES:
SCC .... EUR 14,90
Mechanical Data: Type Area: 466 x 310 mm, No. of Columns (Display): 7, Col Widths (Display): 43 mm
Copy instructions: *Copy Date:* 3 days prior to publication
REGIONAL DAILY & SUNDAY NEWSPAPERS: Regional Daily Newspapers

RHÖN- UND STREUBOTE
740458G67B-12460
Editorial: Friedenstr. 9, 97638 MELLRICHSTADT
Tel: 9776 812112 **Fax:** 9776 812144
Email: redaktion.rsb@rhoenundstreubote.de **Web site:** http://www.mack-druck.de
Freq: 312 issues yearly; **Circ:** 2,946
Editor: B. Städtler
Profile: Daily newspaper with regional news and a local sports section.
Language(s): German
ADVERTISING RATES:
SCC .... EUR 20,50
Mechanical Data: Type Area: 466 x 310 mm, No. of Columns (Display): 7, Col Widths (Display): 43 mm
Copy instructions: *Copy Date:* 1 day prior to publication
Supplement(s): prisma
REGIONAL DAILY & SUNDAY NEWSPAPERS: Regional Daily Newspapers

RHW MANAGEMENT
739978G4F-17
Editorial: Paul-Gerhardt-Allee 46, 81245 MÜNCHEN
Tel: 89 31890520 **Fax:** 89 31890553
Email: robert.schwabe@vnmonline.de **Web site:** http://www.rationelle-hauswirtschaft.de
Freq: Monthly; **Annual Sub.:** EUR 92,00; **Circ:** 6,092
Editor: Robert Schwabe
Profile: Journal concerned with efficient housekeeping, and in particular institutional households.
Language(s): German
ADVERTISING RATES:
Full Page Mono .... EUR 2024
Full Page Colour .... EUR 3543
Mechanical Data: Type Area: 260 x 185 mm, No. of Columns (Display): 4, Col Widths (Display): 43 mm
Copy instructions: *Copy Date:* 30 days prior to publication
BUSINESS: ARCHITECTURE & BUILDING: Cleaning & Maintenance

RHW PRAXIS
1615565G74C-3596
Editorial: Paul-Gerhardt-Allee 46, 81245 MÜNCHEN
Tel: 89 3189050 **Fax:** 89 31890553
Email: rhw.redaktion@vnmonline.de **Web site:** http://www.rhw-praxis.de
Freq: Quarterly; **Annual Sub.:** EUR 60,50; **Circ:** 2,910
Editor: Robert Schwabe
Profile: Magazine for managers in home economics.
Language(s): German
ADVERTISING RATES:
Full Page Mono .... EUR 1012
Full Page Colour .... EUR 1771
Mechanical Data: Type Area: 175 x 119 mm, No. of Columns (Display): 2, Col Widths (Display): 57 mm
Copy instructions: *Copy Date:* 31 days prior to publication
CONSUMER: WOMEN'S INTEREST CONSUMER MAGAZINES: Home & Family

RIA RECHT IM AMT
740464G44-1840
Editorial: Luxemburger Str. 449, 50939 KÖLN
Tel: 221 943737000 **Fax:** 221 943737201
Email: info@wolterskluwer.de **Web site:** http://www.personalamt-online.de
Freq: 6 issues yearly; **Annual Sub.:** EUR 115,00; **Circ:** 1,350
Editor: Norbert Fattler; **Advertising Manager:** Stefanie Szillat
Profile: Magazine covering the latest news and developments in the civil service.
Language(s): German
Readership: Aimed at civil servants.
ADVERTISING RATES:
Full Page Mono .... EUR 675
Full Page Colour .... EUR 1740
Mechanical Data: Type Area: 255 x 184 mm
Copy instructions: *Copy Date:* 28 days prior to publication
BUSINESS: LEGAL

RICHTER UND STAATSANWALT IN NRW
740467G44-3151
Editorial: Martin-Luther-Str. 11, 59065 HAMM
Tel: 2381 29814 **Fax:** 2381 22568
Email: rista@drb-nrw.de **Web site:** http://www.drb-nrw.de
Freq: 6 issues yearly; **Annual Sub.:** EUR 11,76; **Circ:** 7,500
Editor: Wolfgang Fey
Profile: Journal containing news and information for judges and attorneys in Nordrhein-Westfalen.
Language(s): German
ADVERTISING RATES:
Full Page Mono .... EUR 670
Full Page Colour .... EUR 1300
Mechanical Data: Type Area: 267 x 185 mm, No. of Columns (Display): 3, Col Widths (Display): 58 mm
BUSINESS: LEGAL

RIESAER WOCHENKURIER
740481G72-10960
Editorial: Wettiner Platz 10, 01067 DRESDEN
Tel: 351 491760 **Fax:** 351 4917674
Email: wochenkurier-dresden@dwk-verlag.de **Web site:** http://www.wochenkurier.info
Freq: Weekly; **Cover Price:** Free; **Circ:** 36,356
Editor: Regine Eberlein; **Advertising Manager:** Andreas Schönherr
Profile: Advertising journal (house-to-house) concentrating on local stories.
Language(s): German
ADVERTISING RATES:
Full Page Mono .... EUR 3131
Full Page Colour .... EUR 4383
Mechanical Data: Type Area: 430 x 290 mm, No. of Columns (Display): 7, Col Widths (Display): 38 mm
Copy instructions: *Copy Date:* 5 days prior to publication
LOCAL NEWSPAPERS

RIESER NACHRICHTEN
740488G67B-12480
Editorial: Curt-Frenzel-Str. 2, 86167 AUGSBURG
Tel: 821 7770 **Fax:** 821 7772067
Web site: http://www.augsburger-allgemeine.de
Freq: 312 issues yearly; **Circ:** 11,180
Advertising Manager: Herbert Dachs
Profile: Regional daily newspaper with news on politics, economy, culture, sports, travel, technology, etc. Facebook: http://www.facebook.com/AugsburgerAllgemeine Twitter: http://twitter.com/AZ_Augsburg This Outlet offers RSS (Really Simple Syndication).
Language(s): German
ADVERTISING RATES:
SCC .... EUR 45,30
Mechanical Data: Type Area: 480 x 327 mm, No. of Columns (Display): 7, Col Widths (Display): 45 mm
Copy instructions: *Copy Date:* 1 day prior to publication
REGIONAL DAILY & SUNDAY NEWSPAPERS: Regional Daily Newspapers

RIK
740495G86B-540
Editorial: Norbertstr. 2, 50670 KÖLN
Tel: 221 3906620 **Fax:** 221 3906622
Email: redaktion@rik-magazin.de **Web site:** http://rik.inqueery.de
Freq: Monthly; **Annual Sub.:** EUR 48,00; **Circ:** 25,915
Editor: Torsten Bless; **Advertising Manager:** Christian Beese

Profile: Rik is a gay metropolis magazine in the West. Since its launch in April 1985 and restarted in October 1998 it has grown steadily in size and circulation. Meanwhile, it provides a print run of 32,000 copies for the cover of Cologne, Dusseldorf, the Ruhr area and all major cities in North Rhine-Westphalia. The rik offers news on culture, politics, lifestyle and natural scene. Completed they will be part of a comprehensive service that provides information about dates and venues of the gay community. With its high editorial standards and its comprehensive service section, it is an indispensable source of information Rik is the delivery of more than 300 offices in Cologne, Dusseldorf and other locations in North Rhine-Westphalia.
Language(s): German
ADVERTISING RATES:
Full Page Mono .... EUR 2680
Full Page Colour .... EUR 2680
Mechanical Data: Type Area: 260 x 190 mm, No. of Columns (Display): 6, Col Widths (Display): 29 mm
Copy instructions: *Copy Date:* 11 days prior to publication
CONSUMER: ADULT & GAY MAGAZINES: Gay & Lesbian Magazines

RIND IM BILD
1836431G21A-4390
Editorial: Rendsburger Str. 178, 24537 NEUMÜNSTER **Tel:** 4321 905300 **Fax:** 4321 905396
Email: redaktion@rsheg.de **Web site:** http://www.rsheg.de
Freq: Quarterly; **Circ:** 9,000
Editor: Susanne Derner
Profile: Magazine for dairy cattle farmers.
Language(s): German
Copy instructions: *Copy Date:* 31 days prior to publication
Official Journal of: Organ d. Rinderzucht Schleswig-Holstein eG u. d. Landeskontrollverb. Schleswig-Holstein e.V.

RINDERZUCHT BRAUNVIEH
740497G21D-6
Editorial: Bayerstr. 57, 80335 MÜNCHEN
Tel: 89 53098944 **Fax:** 89 53098930
Email: redbraun@dlv.de **Web site:** http://www.rinderzucht-braunvieh.de
Freq: Quarterly; **Annual Sub.:** EUR 28,00
Editor: Johannes Urban; **Advertising Manager:** Thomas Herrmann
Profile: Rinderzucht Braunvieh is a special magazine for the Milch-/Rindviehhaltenden operating in the southern German and Alpine regions of Austria, Switzerland and South Tyrol. Rinderzucht Braunvieh is read by the breeders / farmers and farming advisors in the German and foreign breeding areas of this race. The editor of the magazines cattle Simmental and Brown Swiss cattle, the ASR (Association of South German cattle breeders). They are the official organs of the Association of South German cattle breeders. Editorial focuses on issues of domestic and European perspective to the modern, competitive breeding and farm management as well as the date of production. With the latest releases of the genetic value of great performance-based sires are presented. With the simultaneous presentation of the best international sire readers gain a comprehensive overview of the state of the Simmental and Brown Swiss. In addition, part of the contents of the current information of the ASR on markets, prices, dates and messages from organizations and associations.
Language(s): German
Mechanical Data: Type Area: 270 x 184 mm, No. of Columns (Display): 4, Col Widths (Display): 43 mm
Copy instructions: *Copy Date:* 30 days prior to publication
Official Journal of: Organ d. Interessengemeinschaft Brown Swiss, d. ArGe Dt. Braunvieh u. d. ArGe Süddt. Rinderzüchter
BUSINESS: AGRICULTURE & FARMING: Livestock

RINDERZUCHT FLECKVIEH
740498G21D-7
Editorial: Bayerstr. 57, 80335 MÜNCHEN
Tel: 89 53098944 **Fax:** 89 53098930
Email: redfleck@dlv.de **Web site:** http://www.dlv.de/fleckvieh
Freq: Quarterly; **Annual Sub.:** EUR 28,00; **Circ:** 15,152
Editor: Johannes Urban; **Advertising Manager:** Thomas Herrmann
Profile: Rinderzucht Fleckvieh is a special magazine for the Milch-/Rindviehhaltenden operating in the southern German and Alpine regions of Austria, Switzerland and South Tyrol. Rinderzucht Fleckvieh is read by the breeders / farmers and farming advisors in the German and foreign breeding areas of this race. The editor of the magazines cattle Simmental and Brown Swiss cattle, the ASR (Association of South German cattle breeders). They are the official organs of the Association of South German cattle breeders. Editorial focuses on issues of domestic and European perspective to the modern, competitive breeding and farm management as well as the date of production. With the latest releases of the genetic value of great performance-based sires are presented. With the simultaneous presentation of the best international sire readers gain a comprehensive overview of the state of the Simmental and Brown Swiss. In addition, part of the contents of the current information of the ASR on markets, prices, dates and messages from organizations and associations.
Language(s): German
ADVERTISING RATES:
Full Page Mono .... EUR 3510
Full Page Colour .... EUR 5141
Mechanical Data: Type Area: 270 x 184 mm, No. of Columns (Display): 4, Col Widths (Display): 45 mm
Copy instructions: *Copy Date:* 32 days prior to publication
Official Journal of: Organ d. ArGe Süddt. Rinderzüchter
BUSINESS: AGRICULTURE & FARMING: Livestock

RINDERZUCHT & MILCHPRODUKTION
1865887G21A-4425
Editorial: Nessestr. 1, 26789 LEER **Tel:** 491 800459
Fax: 491 800422
Email: f.beenenga@vost.de **Web site:** http://www.vostov.de
Freq: 5 issues yearly; **Annual Sub.:** EUR 15,00; **Circ:** 6,000
Editor: Fenna Beenenga; **Advertising Manager:** Fenna Beenenga
Profile: Magazine for dairy cattle farmers.
Language(s): German
ADVERTISING RATES:
Full Page Mono .... EUR 200
Full Page Colour .... EUR 495
Mechanical Data: Type Area: 270 x 184 mm, No. of Columns (Display): 3, Col Widths (Display): 58 mm
Copy instructions: *Copy Date:* 31 days prior to publication

RISIKO MANAGER
1657388G1C-1448
Editorial: Wendelinstr. 1, 50933 KÖLN
Tel: 221 5490532 **Fax:** 221 5490315
Email: frank.romeike@bank-verlag-medien.de **Web site:** http://www.risiko-manager.com
Freq: 25 issues yearly; **Annual Sub.:** EUR 386,27; **Circ:** 819
Editor: Roland Franz Erben; **Advertising Manager:** Stefan Hirschmann
Profile: RISIKO MANAGER is the leading magazine for all Financial Risk Management professionals in banks, savings banks and insurance companies. RISIKO MANAGER appeals to a growing community of banking professionals whose influence on decision-making is continuously increasing. These people are Chief Risk Officers, Operational Risk Managers, Credit Risk Managers, Market Risk Officers, Rating Analysts, Credit Analysts, Controllers, Risk Controllers, as well as Management Consultants, Auditors and Officers of DAX 100 companies. RISIKO MANAGER provides its readers with the information that is vitally important to their jobs. RISIKO MANAGER is written by risk managers, for risk managers. Facebook: http://www.facebook.com/pages/Risiko-Manager-Fachzeitschrift/170968359584670 Twitter: http://twitter.com/#!/Risiko_Manager This Outlet offers RSS (Really Simple Syndication).
Language(s): German
ADVERTISING RATES:
Full Page Mono .... EUR 2100
Full Page Colour .... EUR 2100
Mechanical Data: Type Area: 251 x 180 mm, No. of Columns (Display): 3, Col Widths (Display): 51 mm
Copy instructions: *Copy Date:* 14 days prior to publication
Supplement(s): RC&A Risk, Compliance & Audit

RKW MAGAZIN
748389G14A-8000
Editorial: Düsseldorfer Str. 40, 65760 ESCHBORN
Tel: 6196 4952813 **Fax:** 6196 4954801
Email: k.grossheim@rkw.de **Web site:** http://www.rkw.de
Freq: Quarterly; **Circ:** 3,000
Editor: Kathrin Grossheim
Profile: Journal containing articles and information concerning business and productivity.
Language(s): German
BUSINESS: COMMERCE, INDUSTRY & MANAGEMENT

RNOTZ RHEINISCHE NOTAR-ZEITSCHRIFT
740540G1A-2480
Editorial: Burgmauer 53, 50667 KÖLN
Tel: 221 2575292 **Fax:** 221 2575293
Email: rnotz@rhnotk.de **Web site:** http://www.rnotz.de
Freq: 10 issues yearly; Free to qualifying individuals
Annual Sub.: EUR 64,20; **Circ:** 1,800
Editor: Jan Link
Profile: Magazine from the Chamber of Notaries in Cologne.
Language(s): German
ADVERTISING RATES:
Full Page Mono .... EUR 1000
Mechanical Data: Type Area: 258 x 165 mm

ROBIN WOOD MAGAZIN
740543G57-1860
Editorial: Rosa-Luxemburg-Str. 24, 16303 SCHWEDT **Tel:** 3332 252010 **Fax:** 3332 252011
Email: magazin@robinwood.de **Web site:** http://www.robinwood.de
Freq: Quarterly; Free to qualifying individuals
Annual Sub.: EUR 12,00; **Circ:** 10,000
Editor: Christiane Weitzel; **Advertising Manager:** Christiane Weitzel
Profile: Magazine about environmental protection and ecology. Facebook: http://www.facebook.com/robinwood.ev.
Language(s): German
BUSINESS: ENVIRONMENT & POLLUTION

ROCK HARD
740550G76D-4600
Editorial: Paderborner Str. 17, 44143 DORTMUND
Tel: 231 5620140 **Fax:** 231 56201433
Email: megazine@rockhard.de **Web site:** http://www.rockhard.de
Freq: Monthly; **Annual Sub.:** EUR 63,00; **Circ:** 28,622
Editor: Götz Kühnemund; **Advertising Manager:** Daniela Lipka
Profile: ROCK HARD is not just any heavy metal magazine that "chance" to succeed, but an important institution in the musical forest of leaves of the Federal Republic. Founded in 1983 by Holger Stratmann and Uwe Lerch, ROCK HARD 1987 was the first German "fanzine" in a national distribution (an example that many others followed), and has now set its own power at the head of the European rock magazines. In addition, there were currently offshoots in France, Italy, Greece, Slovenia, Slovakia and the Czech Republic. The newspaper sees itself as a critical intermediary between fans, artists and industry and make a contribution every month for a music division, the crisis-ridden in the music industry is not wrong to still be relatively "healthy" is considered. There is really nothing that has not tackled ROCK HARD in the past 27 years. What started in September 1983 as a small metal and hard rock fanzine, has long since become an established size in the hard rock industry. ROCK HARD reached each month about 350,000 fans in German-speaking - and without commercial concessions to the record industry and trend surfing. For ROCK HARD sets trends rather own success and speaks to several generations of rock fans. Whether "old" idols or "young" heroes, only quality, reader interest and entertainment value are crucial when it comes to determining the topics of this issue. Our writers hold for many years excellent relations with many musical personalities who always like to talk out of school. Despite all the professionalism ROCK HARD feels since the founding days of the Underground committed and now covers almost all shades of hard rock music. But also as a communication interface meets ROCK HARD an important task. Letters to the six pages in each issue are in the music scene was just as unique as the legendary arguments with musicians (Slayer, Manowar, Anthrax ...). As a critical intermediary between fans, musicians and record companies has HARD ROCK attention to grievances or initiated discussions that are vital for a healthy, self-renewing scene. twitter.com/#!/rock_hard_de www.facebook.com/rockhardmegazine.
Language(s): German
Readership: Aimed at people who enjoy rock music and amateur musicians.
ADVERTISING RATES:
Full Page Mono .... EUR 3500
Full Page Colour .... EUR 5000
Mechanical Data: Type Area: 270 x 210 mm
CONSUMER: MUSIC & PERFORMING ARTS: Music

ROCK HARD ONLINE
1622296G76D-6042
Editorial: Paderborner Str. 17, 44143 DORTMUND
Tel: 231 5620140 **Fax:** 231 56201413
Email: sascha@rockhard.de **Web site:** http://www.rockhard.de
Cover Price: Paid; **Circ:** 200,582 Unique Users
Editor: Sascha Nieroba
Profile: Ezine: Magazine focusing on all aspects of rock music.
Language(s): German
CONSUMER: MUSIC & PERFORMING ARTS: Music

RODGAUPOST
740561G72-11016
Editorial: Waldstr. 226, 63071 OFFENBACH
Tel: 69 85008274 **Fax:** 69 85008296
Email: rodgaupost@stadtpost.de **Web site:** http://www.stadtpost.de
Freq: Weekly; **Cover Price:** Free; **Circ:** 27,800
Editor: Wolfgang Janz; **Advertising Manager:** Helmut Moser
Profile: Advertising journal (house-to-house) concentrating on local stories.
Language(s): German
ADVERTISING RATES:
Full Page Mono .... EUR 3619
Full Page Colour .... EUR 5067
Mechanical Data: Type Area: 470 x 322 mm, No. of Columns (Display): 7, Col Widths (Display): 43 mm
Copy instructions: *Copy Date:* 2 days prior to publication
LOCAL NEWSPAPERS

RÖFO FORTSCHRITTE AUF DEM GEBIET DER RÖNTGENSTRAHLEN UND DER BILDGEBENDEN VERFAHREN
1614982G56A-11201
Editorial: Rüdigerstr. 14, 70469 STUTTGART
Tel: 711 8931532 **Fax:** 711 8931408
Email: silke.karl@thieme.de **Web site:** http://www.thieme.de/roefo
Freq: Monthly; Free to qualifying individuals
Annual Sub.: EUR 581,80; **Circ:** 7,650
Editor: Silke Karl
Profile: Education and training highly scientifically in the field of radiological research and imaging procedure. New procedures are excellent illustrated in original work discussed. Also, the interventional radiology is becoming word, just as quality security.
Language(s): English; German
ADVERTISING RATES:
Full Page Mono .... EUR 2580
Full Page Colour .... EUR 3810
Mechanical Data: Type Area: 248 x 175 mm, No. of Columns (Display): 4, Col Widths (Display): 40 mm
Official Journal of: Organ d. Dt. u. d. Österr. Röntgenges.
Supplement(s): Current congress

ROHRBAU JOURNAL
1800082G4E-7124
Editorial: Legefelder Hauptstr. 14a, 99438 WEIMAR
Tel: 3643 903224 **Fax:** 3643 511933
Email: wstgmbh.weimar@t-online.de **Web site:** http://www.wst-verlag.de
Freq: Quarterly; **Annual Sub.:** EUR 20,00; **Circ:** 6,000
Editor: Jörg Schuster
Profile: Magazine about all aspects of plumbing and water engineering.
Language(s): German
ADVERTISING RATES:
Full Page Mono .... EUR 1465
Full Page Colour .... EUR 2235
Mechanical Data: Type Area: 267 x 185 mm
Copy instructions: *Copy Date:* 15 days prior to publication

ROI DIALOG
1655636G14A-9620
Editorial: Nymphenburger Str. 86, 80636 MÜNCHEN
Tel: 89 1215900 **Fax:** 89 12159010
Email: dialog@roi.de **Web site:** http://www.roi.de
Freq: 3 issues yearly; **Cover Price:** Free; **Circ:** 2,500
Editor: Hans-Georg Scheibe
Profile: Customer magazine.
Language(s): German

ROLF KAUKAS BUSSI BÄR
740579G91D-6840
Editorial: Karlsruher Str. 31, 76437 RASTATT
Tel: 7222 13293 **Fax:** 7222 13415
Email: ulrike.wagner@vpm.de **Web site:** http://www.bussibaer.de
Freq: Monthly; **Annual Sub.:** EUR 35,40; **Circ:** 71,205
Editor: Ulrike Wagner; **Advertising Manager:** Rainer Gross
Profile: Rolf Kaukas Bussi Bär is the most popular employment magazine for all children in preschool and first years of primary school. Since 1967 Rolf Kauka, founder and former editor of the children's magazine, Rolf Kaukas Bussi Bär can be with his golden heart, a friend of the children. Each issue is filled with large read-aloud stories, large extra-paper model, game pages, mathematical and writing games, songs, rhymes, cooking ideas for healthy eating, and selected topics of knowledge of nature and animals. Rolf Kaukas Bussi Bär - the magazine provides great entertainment for the young reader. Each issue also contains a carefully designed Toy Extra.
Language(s): German
ADVERTISING RATES:
Full Page Mono .... EUR 6187
Full Page Colour .... EUR 6187
Mechanical Data: Type Area: 260 x 192 mm
CONSUMER: RECREATION & LEISURE: Children & Youth

ROLLING STONE
740584G76E-3
Editorial: Mehringdamm 33, 10961 BERLIN
Tel: 30 3088188218 **Fax:** 30 3088188221
Email: rainer.schmidt@axelspringer.de **Web site:** http://www.rollingstone.de
Freq: Monthly; **Annual Sub.:** EUR 54,00; **Circ:** 61,797
Editor: Rainer Schmidt; **Advertising Manager:** Oliver Horn
Profile: Not without reason is ROLLING STONE worldwide as the "bible of rock music. " The German edition, for eleven years firmly established in the market, the unorthodox of topics has adapted and expanded edition of the U.S. for Germany: Pop as a focal point of youth culture, music in the context of social movements. Topics such as literature, film, internet and politics are a permanent range of ROLLING STONE. Music is understood as a reflection of societal trends and snacks instead of journalism there are ROLLING STONE detailed reading stories to see the bigger picture of Pop & Rock. "Who wants to hear, need to read" - the motto of the ROLLING STONE is more important than ever.
Language(s): German
Readership: Aimed at rock and pop music enthusiasts.
ADVERTISING RATES:
Full Page Mono .... EUR 8500
Full Page Colour .... EUR 8500
Mechanical Data: Type Area: 277 x 214 mm, No. of Columns (Display): 4, Col Widths (Display): 46 mm
Copy instructions: *Copy Date:* 30 days prior to publication
CONSUMER: MUSIC & PERFORMING ARTS: Pop Music

ROMANTISCH WOHNEN
1694600G74C-3683
Editorial: Wilhelm-Sinsteden-Str. 6, 47533 KLEVE
Tel: 2821 7139616 **Fax:** 2821 7139620
Email: s.hackel@wohnverlag.de **Web site:** http://www.wohnverlag.de
Freq: 6 issues yearly; **Annual Sub.:** EUR 26,90; **Circ:** 120,000
Editor: Stephanie Hackel; **Advertising Manager:** Dennis van Offern
Profile: Living magazine with exclusive interior design ideas. The contents provide an exclusive lifestyle with high enjoyment factor, the desire for romantic country

atmosphere and the right to family life. In addition, each issue provides suggestions for special decorations, lifestyle and enjoyment. In addition, ideas will be informed regularly about interesting housing issues, and it will open new insights in the field of furniture and accessories. Target group: Romantic Living is aimed at readers who own the home, living, adjusting and fine living attach great value and shows a special interest in the country house style. The vast number of readers have your own home or in the near future intends to own your own property. The age of the predominantly female readership is between 25 to 70 years.
Language(s): German
ADVERTISING RATES:
Full Page Colour .... EUR 8790
Mechanical Data: Type Area: 260 x 200 mm
CONSUMER: WOMEN'S INTEREST CONSUMER MAGAZINES: Home & Family

ROMANWOCHE
740595G74A-2680
Editorial: Karlsruher Str. 31, 76437 RASTATT
Tel: 7222 13205 **Fax:** 7222 13351
Email: erlebnispresse@vpm.de **Web site:** http://www.vpm.de
Freq: Quarterly; **Cover Price:** EUR 1,80; **Circ:** 34,800
Editor: Dietlinde Besch; **Advertising Manager:** Rainer Groß
Profile: The selected stories of the Romanwoche expect an explosion of sensual and heartbreaking episodes, seasoned with a dash of adventure and family romance. It is about love, happiness and passion, jealousy and reconciliation. You will find both romance and tender crackling erotic experiences, as well as amusing everyday stories and interesting love dramas. This sparkling mix makes the Romanwoche for a special reading experience. You also find into the Romanwoche many puzzles, a health adviser and your personal horoscope.
Language(s): German
ADVERTISING RATES:
Full Page Mono .... EUR 1626
Full Page Colour .... EUR 2701
Mechanical Data: Type Area: 263 x 196 mm, No. of Columns (Display): 4, Col Widths (Display): 47 mm

RONDO
740597G76D-4760
Editorial: Lucile-Grahn-Str. 37, 81675 MÜNCHEN
Tel: 89 45726140 **Fax:** 89 45726150
Email: kettner@inmedia.de **Web site:** http://www.rondomagazin.de
Freq: 6 issues yearly; **Annual Sub.:** EUR 22,00; **Circ:** 80,216
Editor: Markus Kettner; **Advertising Manager:** Eva Kluge
Profile: Aimed at music enthusiasts.
Language(s): German
Readership: Aimed at music enthusiastics.
ADVERTISING RATES:
Full Page Mono .... EUR 5260
Full Page Colour .... EUR 6230
Mechanical Data: Type Area: 256 x 182 mm
CONSUMER: MUSIC & PERFORMING ARTS: Music

ROSENBOGEN
740605G21A-3440
Editorial: Maria-Viktoria-Str. 12, 76530 BADEN-BADEN **Tel:** 7221 53975 **Fax:** 7221 181483
Email: an.koegel@t-online.de
Freq: Quarterly; **Circ:** 7,500
Editor: Andrea Kögel
Profile: Magazine from the Association of German Rose Friends.
Language(s): German
ADVERTISING RATES:
Full Page Mono .... EUR 332
Mechanical Data: Type Area: 170 x 144 mm
Copy instructions: *Copy Date:* 28 days prior to publication

ROSEN-JAHRBUCH
740607G21A-3420
Editorial: Waldseestr. 14, 76530 BADEN-BADEN
Tel: 7221 31302 **Fax:** 7221 38337
Email: info@rosenfreunde.de **Web site:** http://www.rosenfreunde.de
Freq: Annual; **Cover Price:** EUR 9,00
Free to qualifying individuals ; **Circ:** 7,500
Profile: Annual from the Association of German Rose Friends.
Language(s): German

ROSTOCKER BLITZ AM SONNTAG
740618G72-11060
Editorial: Am Kabutzenhof 21, 18057 ROSTOCK
Tel: 381 45959541 **Fax:** 381 45959590
Email: ilona.vent@blitzverlag.de **Web site:** http://www.blitzverlag.de
Freq: Weekly; **Cover Price:** Free; **Circ:** 105,651
Editor: Ilona Vent; **Advertising Manager:** Heike Kleinitz
Profile: Advertising journal (house-to-house) concentrating on local stories.
Language(s): German
ADVERTISING RATES:
Full Page Mono .... EUR 5418
Full Page Colour .... EUR 5808
Mechanical Data: Type Area: 420 x 285 mm, No. of Columns (Display): 6, Col Widths (Display): 45 mm
Copy instructions: *Copy Date:* 2 days prior to publication
LOCAL NEWSPAPERS

ROTARY MAGAZIN
740619G32G-2080
Editorial: Raboisen 30, 20095 HAMBURG
Tel: 40 3499970 **Fax:** 40 34999717
Email: redaktion@rotary.de **Web site:** http://www.rotary.de/magazin
Freq: Monthly; **Annual Sub.:** EUR 25,20; **Circ:** 57,770
Editor: René Nehring
Profile: The Rotary Magazin is the sophisticated readers' forum in our society. Each month the editorial staff is made in key topics dealing with current issues in politics, society, economy and culture. Whether federal minister or celebrity designer, whether a Nobel laureate or business leaders: In the Rotary Magazine renowned authors comment on the events and analyze important social developments. In recent years, the Rotary magazin has continuously increased the circulation and also content and design developed into a quality title with style. Accordingly, the positive approval among the audience. As entrepreneurs and social leaders of our readers are curious, highly competent and strong opinions. Precisely why they love the confrontation with the Rotary Magazine.
Language(s): German
ADVERTISING RATES:
Full Page Mono .... EUR 4400
Full Page Colour .... EUR 4400
Mechanical Data: Type Area: 215 x 139 mm, No. of Columns (Display): 3, Col Widths (Display): 43 mm
Copy instructions: *Copy Date:* 30 days prior to publication
BUSINESS: LOCAL GOVERNMENT, LEISURE & RECREATION: Community Care & Social Services

ROTENBURG-BEBRAER ALLGEMEINE
730357G67B-7220
Editorial: Frankfurter Str. 168, 34121 KASSEL
Tel: 561 20300 **Fax:** 561 2032406
Email: info@hna.de **Web site:** http://www.hna.de
Freq: 312 issues yearly; **Circ:** 7,935
Advertising Manager: Andrea Schaller-Öller
Profile: Regional daily newspaper with news on politics, economy, culture, sports, travel, technology, etc. The Rotenburg-Bebraer Allgemeine a local edition of the HNA Hessische/Niedersächsische Allgemeine. Twitter: http://twitter.com/hna_online This Outlet offers RSS (Really Simple Syndication).
Language(s): German
ADVERTISING RATES:
SCC .... EUR 36,80
Mechanical Data: Type Area: 430 x 285 mm, No. of Columns (Display): 6, Col Widths (Display): 45 mm
Copy instructions: *Copy Date:* 2 days prior to publication
REGIONAL DAILY & SUNDAY NEWSPAPERS: Regional Daily Newspapers

ROTENBURGER KREISZEITUNG
740625G67B-12520
Editorial: Große Str. 37, 27356 ROTENBURG
Tel: 4261 72330 **Fax:** 4261 72300
Email: redaktion.rotenburg@kreiszeitung.de **Web site:** http://www.kreiszeitung.de
Freq: 312 issues yearly; **Circ:** 10,403
Advertising Manager: Ingo Raeder
Profile: Daily newspaper with regional news and a local sports section. Facebook: http://www.facebook.com/pages/Kreiszeitung Twitter: http://twitter.com/kreiszeitung This Outlet offers RSS (Really Simple Syndication).
Language(s): German
ADVERTISING RATES:
SCC .... EUR 29,50
Mechanical Data: Type Area: 431 x 276 mm, No. of Columns (Display): 6, Col Widths (Display): 44 mm
Copy instructions: *Copy Date:* 1 day prior to publication
REGIONAL DAILY & SUNDAY NEWSPAPERS: Regional Daily Newspapers

ROTENBURGER RUNDSCHAU
740626G72-11064
Editorial: Große Str. 79, 27356 ROTENBURG
Tel: 4261 929030 **Fax:** 4261 929039
Email: redaktion@rotenburger-rundschau.de **Web site:** http://www.rotenburger-rundschau.de
Freq: Weekly; **Cover Price:** Free; **Circ:** 43,193
Editor: Gabriele Marienhagen; **Advertising Manager:** Jens Reiter
Profile: Advertising journal (house-to-house) concentrating on local stories.
Language(s): German
ADVERTISING RATES:
Full Page Mono .... EUR 4080
Full Page Colour .... EUR 4398
Mechanical Data: Type Area: 425 x 282 mm, No. of Columns (Display): 6, Col Widths (Display): 45 mm
Copy instructions: *Copy Date:* 2 days prior to publication
LOCAL NEWSPAPERS

ROTH-HILPOLTSTEINER VOLKSZEITUNG
740639G67B-12540
Editorial: Allee 2, 91154 ROTH **Tel:** 9171 970311
Fax: 9171 970326
Email: verlag@roth-hilpoltsteiner-volkszeitung.de **Web site:** http://www.roth-hilpoltsteiner-volkszeitung.de
Freq: 312 issues yearly; **Circ:** 11,116
Profile: Daily newspaper with regional news and a local sports section.
Language(s): German
ADVERTISING RATES:
SCC .... EUR 31,00
Mechanical Data: Type Area: 430 x 280 mm, No. of Columns (Display): 6, Col Widths (Display): 45 mm
Copy instructions: *Copy Date:* 2 days prior to publication
REGIONAL DAILY & SUNDAY NEWSPAPERS: Regional Daily Newspapers

ROTHKEHLCHEN
1790092G57-2809
Editorial: Weinbergweg 1, 91154 ROTH
Tel: 9171 81251 **Fax:** 9171 817251
Email: rothkehlchen@landratsamt-roth.de **Web site:** http://www.landratsamt-roth.de/rothkehlchen
Freq: Quarterly; **Cover Price:** Free; **Circ:** 52,000
Editor: Anne-Karina Landmann
Profile: Regional environment newspaper.
Language(s): German

ROTOR
740646G79B-1400
Editorial: Schulstr. 12, 76532 BADEN-BADEN
Tel: 7221 952113 **Fax:** 7221 952145
Email: rotorredaktion@modellsport.de **Web site:** http://www.modellsport.de
Freq: Monthly; **Annual Sub.:** EUR 73,00; **Circ:** 15,000
Editor: Markus Fiehn; **Advertising Manager:** Steffen Weyrauch
Profile: Magazine about model helicopters.
Language(s): German
Readership: Aimed at people who enjoy model-making.
ADVERTISING RATES:
Full Page Mono .... EUR 1000
Full Page Colour .... EUR 1800
Mechanical Data: Type Area: 254 x 185 mm, No. of Columns (Display): 4, Col Widths (Display): 42 mm
Copy instructions: *Copy Date:* 15 days prior to publication
CONSUMER: HOBBIES & DIY: Models & Modelling

ROTORBLATT
1865536G40-997
Editorial: Anne-Frank-Str. 2, 65197 WIESBADEN
Tel: 611 465316 **Fax:** 611 5659735
Email: rainer.herzberg@rotorblatt.de **Web site:** http://www.rotorblatt.de
Freq: Quarterly; **Annual Sub.:** EUR 22,00; **Circ:** 6,224
Editor: Rainer Herzberg; **Advertising Manager:** Klaus Macholz
Profile: Rotorblatt is the leading German helicopter magazine. Except for professionals, the magazine turns to the young pilots and people with high affinity on helicopters. News and portraits from the defense, police and border guards, air rescue, business aviation, technology and training, market & products. Facebook: http://www.facebook.com/pages/ROTORBLATT/262659394409.
Language(s): German
ADVERTISING RATES:
Full Page Mono .... EUR 2750
Full Page Colour .... EUR 2750
Mechanical Data: Type Area: 248 x 185 mm, No. of Columns (Display): 4, Col Widths (Display): 45 mm
Official Journal of: Organ d. Gemeinschaft d. Heeresflieger, d. Gemeinschaft Hubschrauber d. Luftwaffe, d. Bundesvereinigung fliegendes Personal d. Polizei u. d. Dt. Hubschrauber Verb.

ROTTALER ANZEIGER
740650G67B-12560
Editorial: Medienstr. 5, 94036 PASSAU
Tel: 851 8020 **Fax:** 851 802256
Email: pnp@vgp.de **Web site:** http://www.pnp.de
Freq: 312 issues yearly; **Circ:** 11,024
Advertising Manager: Gerhard Koller
Profile: Daily newspaper with regional news and a local sports section. Twitter: http://twitter.com/pnp_online This Outlet offers RSS (Really Simple Syndication).
Language(s): German
ADVERTISING RATES:
SCC .... EUR 43,00
Mechanical Data: Type Area: 482 x 325 mm, No. of Columns (Display): 7, Col Widths (Display): 45 mm
Copy instructions: *Copy Date:* 2 days prior to publication
REGIONAL DAILY & SUNDAY NEWSPAPERS: Regional Daily Newspapers

ROTTAL-INN WOCHENBLATT
723214G72-2424
Editorial: Stadtplatz 32, 84347 PFARRKIRCHEN
Tel: 8561 234615 **Fax:** 8561 5059
Email: holger.becker@wochenblatt.de **Web site:** http://www.wochenblatt.de
Freq: Weekly; **Cover Price:** Free; **Circ:** 40,200
Editor: Holger Becker; **Advertising Manager:** Therese Wimmer
Profile: Advertising journal (house-to-house) concentrating on local stories.
Language(s): German
ADVERTISING RATES:
Full Page Mono .... EUR 3699
Full Page Colour .... EUR 5548
Mechanical Data: Type Area: 460 x 280 mm, No. of Columns (Display): 6, Col Widths (Display): 43 mm
Copy instructions: *Copy Date:* 2 days prior to publication
LOCAL NEWSPAPERS

ROVER-BLATT
1800711G77A-2787
Editorial: Damaschkestr. 11, 52066 AACHEN
Tel: 241 9214900 **Fax:** 241 9214901
Email: info@dlrc.org **Web site:** http://www.dlrc.org
Freq: 6 issues yearly; **Circ:** 1,300
Editor: Jochen v. Arnim; **Advertising Manager:** Andreas Berger
Profile: Rover car club magazine with internal information.
Language(s): German
Mechanical Data: Type Area: 187 x 131 mm, No. of Columns (Display): 2, Col Widths (Display): 63 mm
Copy instructions: *Copy Date:* 30 days prior to publication

RP REPORT PSYCHOLOGIE
740664G56N-90
Editorial: Am Köllnischen Park 2, 10179 BERLIN
Tel: 30 209166620 **Fax:** 30 209166413
Email: verlag@psychologenverlag.de **Web site:** http://www.report-psychologie.de
Freq: 10 issues yearly; Free to qualifying individuals
Annual Sub.: EUR 54,00; **Circ:** 12,500
Editor: Christa Schaffmann; **Advertising Manager:** Ina Jungbluth
Profile: Journal containing news and developments in psychology. Also includes book reviews.
Language(s): German
Readership: Aimed at psychologists, students of psychology and people interested in psychology. .
ADVERTISING RATES:
Full Page Mono .... EUR 1300
Full Page Colour .... EUR 2140
Mechanical Data: Type Area: 259 x 177 mm
Copy instructions: *Copy Date:* 20 days prior to publication
BUSINESS: HEALTH & MEDICAL: Mental Health

RPAKTUELL
1789753G1D-481
Editorial: Theodor-Heuss-Ring 11, 50668 KÖLN
Tel: 221 9738678 **Fax:** 221 9738824
Email: marianne.kutzner@genre.com **Web site:** http://www.genre.com/business-school
Freq: Half-yearly; **Circ:** 1,500
Editor: Marianne Kutzner
Profile: Information from the insurance company General Reinsurance Corporation.
Language(s): German

RT RETAIL TECHNOLOGY
740321G53-200
Editorial: Spichernstr. 55, 50672 KÖLN
Tel: 221 5799340 **Fax:** 221 5799345
Email: lambertz@ehi.org **Web site:** http://www.ehi.org
Freq: Quarterly; Free to qualifying individuals
Annual Sub.: EUR 53,50; **Circ:** 11,400
Editor: Winfried Lambertz; **Advertising Manager:** Claudia Husseck
Profile: Magazine containing articles about new products, events, e-commerce, communications and technology, includes investments.
Language(s): German
Readership: Aimed at executives and managers in retail and marketing.
ADVERTISING RATES:
Full Page Mono .... EUR 3000
Full Page Colour .... EUR 4100
Mechanical Data: Type Area: 235 x 182 mm, No. of Columns (Display): 3, Col Widths (Display): 58 mm
Copy instructions: *Copy Date:* 14 days prior to publication
BUSINESS: RETAILING & WHOLESALING

RTR EUROPEAN RAIL TECHNOLOGY REVIEW
739929G49E-700
Editorial: Nordkanalstr. 36, 20097 HAMBURG
Tel: 40 23714230 **Fax:** 40 23714236
Email: ursula.hahn@dvvmedia.com **Web site:** http://www.eurailpress.de
Freq: Quarterly; **Annual Sub.:** EUR 60,00; **Circ:** 3,158
Editor: Eberhard Jänsch; **Advertising Manager:** Silke Härtel
Profile: International railway magazine.
Language(s): English
Readership: Read by railway engineers.
ADVERTISING RATES:
Full Page Mono .... EUR 2660
Full Page Colour .... EUR 3650
Mechanical Data: Type Area: 262 x 184 mm, No. of Columns (Display): 4, Col Widths (Display): 43 mm
Copy instructions: *Copy Date:* 21 days prior to publication
BUSINESS: TRANSPORT: Railways

RTS MAGAZIN
1831395G4E-7213
Editorial: Herner Str. 299, 44809 BOCHUM
Tel: 234 9539136 **Fax:** 234 9539130
Email: maren.meyerling@kleffmann-verlag.de **Web site:** http://www.rts-magazin.de
Freq: Monthly; **Annual Sub.:** EUR 107,00; **Circ:** 11,758
Editor: Maren Meyerling
Profile: Journal about the design and construction of shutters and blinds.
Language(s): English; German
ADVERTISING RATES:
Full Page Mono .... EUR 2370
Full Page Colour .... EUR 4120
Mechanical Data: Type Area: 258 x 178 mm, No. of Columns (Display): 4, Col Widths (Display): 42 mm
Supplement(s): Fassade

RTV 740689G67B-260_500
Editorial: Breslauer Str. 300, 90471 NÜRNBERG
Tel: 911 8920123 **Fax:** 911 8920189
Email: matthias.roth@rtv.de **Web site:** http://www.rtv.de
Freq: Weekly; **Circ:** 9,150,000
Editor: Matthias Roth; **Advertising Manager:** Martin Schumacher
Profile: TV programme supplement to regional dailies. Facebook: http://www.facebook.com/rtvde Twitter: http://twitter.com/rtvde This Outlet offers RSS (Really Simple Syndication).
Language(s): German
ADVERTISING RATES:
Full Page Mono .... EUR 81380
Full Page Colour .... EUR 99770
Mechanical Data: Type Area: 242 x 190 mm, No. of Columns (Display): 4, Col Widths (Display): 44 mm
Copy instructions: *Copy Date:* 15 days prior to publication
Supplement to: Aichacher Zeitung, Allgäuer Anzeigeblatt, Allgäuer Zeitung, Altmark Zeitung, Bayerische Rundschau, Berchtesgadener Anzeiger, Berliner Kurier, Berliner Zeitung, Bietigheimer Zeitung, Bönnigheimer Zeitung, Buchloer Zeitung, Cellesche Zeitung, Chiemgau-Zeitung, Coburger Tageblatt, Dill-Post, Dresdner Morgenpost, Elbmarsch-Post, Fehmarnsches Tageblatt, Fränkischer Tag, Frankenpost, Freie Presse, Freies Wort, Freitags-Anzeiger für Mörfelden-Walldorf, Kelsterbach und Zeppelinheim, Friedrichsfelder Wochenblatt für den Stadtteil Mannheim-Friedrichsfeld und das Gebiet Neu-Edingen, FW Meininger Tageblatt, Gelnhäuser Neue Zeitung, Gransee-Zeitung, Haigerer Zeitung, Hamburger Morgenpost, Herborner Tageblatt, Hinterländer Anzeiger, Hohenloher Tagblatt, Iserlohner Kreisanzeiger und Zeitung, Ladenburger Zeitung, Lampertheimer Zeitung, Lausitzer Rundschau, Lippische Wochenschau insider, Mangfall Bote, Memminger Zeitung, Mühldorfer Anzeiger, Nassauer Tageblatt, Neumarkter Anzeiger, Nordwest Zeitung, Oberbayerisches Volksblatt, Oranienburger Generalanzeiger, Peiner Allgemeine Zeitung, Potsdamer Neueste Nachrichten, Probsteier Herold, Ruppiner Anzeiger, Sachsenheimer Zeitung, Sächsische Zeitung, Sächsische Zeitung, Sächsische Zeitung, Schaafheimer Zeitung, Schaumburger Zeitung, Schaumburg-Lippische Landes-Zeitung, Selber Tagblatt Frankenpost, Solms-Braunfelser, Südthüringer Zeitung, Der Tagesspiegel, Thüringer Allgemeine, TLZ Eichsfeld Eichsfelder Tageblatt, TLZ Eisenach Eisenacher Presse, TLZ Erfurt Thüringische Landeszeitung, TLZ Gera Thüringische Landeszeitung, TLZ Gotha Gothaer Tagespost, TLZ Jena Thüringische Landeszeitung, TLZ Unstrut-Hainich Thüringische Landeszeitung, TLZ Weimar Thüringische Landeszeitung, Torgauer Zeitung, Vogtland-Anzeiger, Waldkraiburger Nachrichten, Wasserburger Zeitung, Weilburger Tageblatt, Werntal=Zeitung, Der Westallgäuer, Westdeutsche Allgemeine WAZ, Wetzlarer Neue Zeitung, Wiesbadener Kurier
REGIONAL DAILY & SUNDAY NEWSPAPERS: Regional Daily Newspapers

RUBS 740700G72-11096
Editorial: Junkernstr. 13, 31028 GRONAU
Tel: 5182 92190 **Fax:** 5182 921939
Email: rubs-redaktion@leinetal-online.de **Web site:** http://www.leinetal-online.de
Freq: Weekly; **Cover Price:** Free; **Circ:** 24,900
Editor: Hartmut Müller; **Advertising Manager:** Manfred Mäckeler
Profile: Advertising journal (house-to-house) concentrating on local stories.
Language(s): German
ADVERTISING RATES:
Full Page Mono .... EUR 2555
Full Page Colour .... EUR 3612
Mechanical Data: Type Area: 430 x 282 mm, No. of Columns (Display): 6, Col Widths (Display): 45 mm
Copy instructions: *Copy Date:* 2 days prior to publication
LOCAL NEWSPAPERS

RUDERSPORT 740704G75M-600
Editorial: Böblinger Str. 68/1, 71065 SINDELFINGEN
Tel: 7031 862822 **Fax:** 7031 862801
Email: rudersport@szbz.de
Freq: Monthly; **Annual Sub.:** EUR 79,80; **Circ:** 4,761
Editor: Brigitte Schurr; **Advertising Manager:** Yvonne Damast
Profile: Journal of the German Rowing Association.
Language(s): German
ADVERTISING RATES:
Full Page Mono .... EUR 760
Full Page Colour .... EUR 970
Mechanical Data: Type Area: 262 x 182 mm, No. of Columns (Display): 4, Col Widths (Display): 43 mm
Copy instructions: *Copy Date:* 28 days prior to publication
Official Journal of: Organ d. Dt. Ruderverb.
CONSUMER: SPORT: Water Sports

RÜGEN BLITZ AM SONNTAG 740714G72-11108
Editorial: Tribseer Damm 2, 18437 STRALSUND
Tel: 3831 2677451 **Fax:** 3838 2677402
Email: wilfried.stabenow@blitzverlag.de **Web site:** http://www.blitzverlag.de
Freq: Weekly; **Cover Price:** Free; **Circ:** 33,810
Editor: Wilfried Stabenow; **Advertising Manager:** André Holfert
Profile: Advertising journal (house-to-house) concentrating on local stories.
Language(s): German
ADVERTISING RATES:
Full Page Mono .... EUR 2546
Full Page Colour .... EUR 2936
Mechanical Data: Type Area: 420 x 285 mm, No. of Columns (Display): 6, Col Widths (Display): 45 mm
Copy instructions: *Copy Date:* 2 days prior to publication
LOCAL NEWSPAPERS

RUHR KURIER 740733G72-11124
Editorial: Westfalenstr. 288, 45276 ESSEN
Tel: 201 851330 **Fax:** 201 8513333
Email: redaktion@ruhrkurier-essen.de **Web site:** http://www.lokalkompass.de/essen-ruhr
Freq: 104 issues yearly; **Cover Price:** Free; **Circ:** 27,100
Editor: Beatrix von Lauff; **Advertising Manager:** Lars Staehler
Profile: Advertising journal (house-to-house) concentrating on local stories.
Language(s): German
ADVERTISING RATES:
Full Page Mono .... EUR 2773
Full Page Colour .... EUR 3743
Mechanical Data: Type Area: 445 x 315 mm, No. of Columns (Display): 7, Col Widths (Display): 42 mm
Copy instructions: *Copy Date:* 2 days prior to publication
LOCAL NEWSPAPERS

RUHR NACHRICHTEN 740734G67B-12600
Editorial: Westenhellweg 86, 44137 DORTMUND
Tel: 231 90590 **Fax:** 231 90598402
Email: redaktion.rn@mdhl.de **Web site:** http://www.ruhrnachrichten.de
Freq: 312 issues yearly; **Annual Sub.:** EUR 22,30; **Circ:** 309,009
Editor: Wolfram Kiwit; **News Editor:** Holger Niehaus; **Advertising Manager:** Ulf Spannagel
Profile: Regional daily newspaper with news on politics, economy, culture, sports, travel, technology, etc. Twitter: http://twitter.com/ruhrnachrichten This Outlet offers RSS (Really Simple Syndication).
Language(s): German
ADVERTISING RATES:
SCC .... EUR 426,80
Mechanical Data: No. of Columns (Display): 7, Col Widths (Display): 42 mm
Copy instructions: *Copy Date:* 2 days prior to publication
Supplement(s): doppio; Freizeit; prisma
REGIONAL DAILY & SUNDAY NEWSPAPERS: Regional Daily Newspapers

RUHR WIRTSCHAFT 740735G63-780
Editorial: Märkische Str. 120, 44141 DORTMUND
Tel: 231 5417257 **Fax:** 231 5417195
Email: g.schulte@dortmund.ihk.de **Web site:** http://www.dortmund.ihk24.de
Freq: 11 issues yearly; Free to qualifying individuals
Annual Sub.: EUR 48,75; **Circ:** 33,000
Editor: Georg Schulte
Profile: The Ruhr Wirtschaft is the magazine of Commerce and Industry Chamber of Dortmund, is a regional business magazine for all industries. It publishes the only economic and corporate reports from the region informed about environmental protection, Transport, foreign trade, law, taxation and finance, vocational education and training. The Ruhr Wirtschaft is widespread, with a circulation of 33,000 copies in the CCI region and to function as a date and reliable information and communication medium for more than 48,000 decision makers in the economy.
Language(s): German
ADVERTISING RATES:
Full Page Mono .... EUR 2179
Full Page Colour .... EUR 2942
Mechanical Data: Type Area: 260 x 185 mm, No. of Columns (Display): 3, Col Widths (Display): 58 mm
Copy instructions: *Copy Date:* 20 days prior to publication
BUSINESS: REGIONAL BUSINESS

RUHR-ANZEIGER WAZ 740728G67B-12580
Editorial: Friedrichstr. 34, 45128 ESSEN
Tel: 201 8040 **Fax:** 201 8046539
Email: zentralredaktion@waz.de **Web site:** http://www.derwesten.de
Freq: 312 issues yearly; **Circ:** 13,108
Advertising Manager: Christian Klaucke
Profile: Germany's largest regional newspaper. Inextricably linked with the development of the Ruhr area is the success story of the Westdeutsche Allgemeine WAZ. Since its first publication on 3.4.1948, it helped shaping the region Ruhr, Emscher and Lippe like no other medium. Licensee and publisher Erich Brost created a newspaper of Anglo-Saxon model. The focus was and is independent and nonpartisan. Together with the co-editor James Funke, he conducted the most successful newspaper start-up after the war. Today, the WAZ is Germany's largest regional newspaper, its range extends from the southern Münsterland to the Niederbergische Region, from the Lower Rhine up to the Region of Unna. The total area is approximately 4450 sq km. In the Ruhr area cities Essen, Bochum, Gelsenkirchen, Duisburg, Oberhausen and Mülheim an der Ruhr, WAZ is the leading daily newspaper. The newspaper of the Ruhr area has always listened to the citizens. In it people of the territory find themselves. In it the city happens. The WAZ reports and commentes close to its readers and unaffected. The Ruhr-Anzeiger WAZ is a regional edition of the Westdeutsche Allgemeine WAZ. Facebook: http://www.facebook.com/derwesten.
Language(s): German
ADVERTISING RATES:
SCC .... EUR 57,60
Mechanical Data: Type Area: 445 x 320 mm, No. of Columns (Display): 7, Col Widths (Display): 44 mm
Copy instructions: *Copy Date:* 2 days prior to publication
Supplement(s): Mein Auto; Mein Beruf; Meine besten Jahre; Meine Familie; Mein Freizeit; Meine Weihnacht; Mein neues Jahr!; Mein Shopping; Mein Stil; Mein Team; Mein Urlaub; Mein Zuhause
REGIONAL DAILY & SUNDAY NEWSPAPERS: Regional Daily Newspapers

RUHRWORT 740736G87-11340
Editorial: Alfredistr. 31, 45127 ESSEN
Tel: 201 810870 **Fax:** 201 8108740
Email: engelberg@ruhrwort.de **Web site:** http://www.ruhrwort.de
Freq: Weekly; **Annual Sub.:** EUR 68,40; **Circ:** 19,840
Editor: Ulrich Engelberg
Profile: Magazine for the Diocese of Essen.
Language(s): German
ADVERTISING RATES:
Full Page Mono .... EUR 3461
Full Page Colour .... EUR 5568
Mechanical Data: Type Area: 430 x 312 mm, No. of Columns (Display): 7, Col Widths (Display): 42 mm
Copy instructions: *Copy Date:* 5 days prior to publication
CONSUMER: RELIGIOUS

RUND UMS BABY 1662592G74C-3644
Editorial: Hauptstr. 33, 83684 TEGERNSEE
Tel: 8022 706390 **Fax:** 8022 7063940
Email: redaktion@rund-ums-baby.de **Web site:** http://www.rund-ums-baby.de
Freq: Weekly; **Cover Price:** Paid; **Circ:** 3,288,676 Unique Users
Editor: Heike Schneider
Profile: Online magazine for young parents.
Language(s): German
CONSUMER: WOMEN'S INTEREST CONSUMER MAGAZINES: Home & Family

RUNDBRIEF 1834621G21A-4388
Editorial: Taunusstr. 151, 61381 FRIEDRICHSDORF
Tel: 6172 77073 **Fax:** 6172 77075
Email: mail@lfv-hessen.de **Web site:** http://www.lfv-hessen.de
Freq: Half-yearly; **Circ:** 1,500
Advertising Manager: Doris Wirkner
Profile: Information from the Country Women's Association in Hesse.
Language(s): German

RUNDBRIEF DER NAJU HESSEN UND THÜRINGEN 1831325G57-2858
Editorial: Friedenstr. 26, 35578 WETZLAR
Tel: 6441 946903
Email: info@naju-hessen.de **Web site:** http://www.naju-hessen.de
Circ: 950
Profile: Paper about nature conservation in Hesse and Thuringia.
Language(s): German

RUNDBRIEF FILM & MEDIENBÜRO NIEDERSACHSEN 727319G2A-1380
Editorial: Lohstr. 45a, 49074 OSNABRÜCK
Tel: 541 28426 **Fax:** 541 29507
Email: info@filmbuero-nds.de **Web site:** http://www.filmbuero-nds.de
Freq: Quarterly; Free to qualifying individuals
Annual Sub.: EUR 14,00; **Circ:** 1,300
Editor: Karl Maier; **Advertising Manager:** Karl Maier
Profile: Magazine with information for managers and employees in media culture and media economy.
Language(s): German
ADVERTISING RATES:
Full Page Colour .... EUR 290
Mechanical Data: Type Area: 264 x 182 mm, No. of Columns (Display): 3, Col Widths (Display): 58 mm
Copy instructions: *Copy Date:* 14 days prior to publication

RUNDGESPRÄCHE DER KOMMISSION FÜR ÖKOLOGIE 1609324G57-2651
Editorial: Wolfratshauser Str. 27, 81379 MÜNCHEN
Tel: 89 7428270 **Fax:** 89 7242772
Email: info@pfeil-verlag.de **Web site:** http://www.pfeil-verlag.de
Freq: Quarterly; **Cover Price:** EUR 25,00; **Circ:** 800
Editor: Claudia Deigele
Profile: Publication containing correspondence from the Committee for Ecology.
Language(s): German

RUNDSCHAU 740819G47A-940
Editorial: Ohmstr. 15, 80802 MÜNCHEN
Tel: 89 38160542 **Fax:** 89 38160514
Email: meyer@rundschauverlag.de **Web site:** http://www.rundschauverlag.de
Freq: 11 issues yearly; **Annual Sub.:** EUR 112,00; **Circ:** 5,198
Editor: Friederike Meyer; **Advertising Manager:** Carola Frommer
Profile: Magazine on international fashion for women.
Language(s): German
ADVERTISING RATES:
Full Page Mono .... EUR 1810
Full Page Colour .... EUR 3220
Mechanical Data: Type Area: 265 x 185 mm, No. of Columns (Display): 4, Col Widths (Display): 42 mm
Official Journal of: Organ d. Bundesverb. d. Bekleidungshandwerks e.V.
BUSINESS: CLOTHING & TEXTILES

RUNDSCHAU 740820G47A-960
Editorial: Ohmstr. 15, 80802 MÜNCHEN
Tel: 89 38160542 **Fax:** 89 38160514
Email: meyer@rundschauverlag.de **Web site:** http://www.rundschauverlag.de
Freq: 10 issues yearly; **Annual Sub.:** EUR 112,00; **Circ:** 1,254
Editor: Friederike Meyer; **Advertising Manager:** Carola Frommer
Profile: Magazine on international fashion for men.
Language(s): German
ADVERTISING RATES:
Full Page Mono .... EUR 1810
Full Page Colour .... EUR 3220
Mechanical Data: Type Area: 265 x 185 mm, No. of Columns (Display): 4, Col Widths (Display): 42 mm
Official Journal of: Organ d. Bundesverb. d. Bekleidungshandwerks e.V.
BUSINESS: CLOTHING & TEXTILES

RUNDSCHAU 722180G72-1760
Editorial: Steinmarkt 12, 93413 CHAM
Tel: 9971 852233 **Fax:** 9971 852236
Email: josef.fischer@rundschau-mail.de **Web site:** http://www.mittelbayerische.de
Freq: Weekly; **Cover Price:** Free; **Circ:** 41,081
Editor: Martin Angerer; **Advertising Manager:** Michael Kusch
Profile: Advertising journal (house-to-house) concentrating on local stories.
Language(s): German
ADVERTISING RATES:
Full Page Mono .... EUR 2580
Full Page Colour .... EUR 3612
Mechanical Data: Type Area: 430 x 281 mm, No. of Columns (Display): 6, Col Widths (Display): 45 mm
Copy instructions: *Copy Date:* 2 days prior to publication
LOCAL NEWSPAPERS

RUNDSCHAU FÜR DEN LEBENSMITTELHANDEL 740825G53-210
Editorial: Medienplatz 1, 76571 GAGGENAU
Tel: 7225 916250 **Fax:** 7225 916291
Email: mehler@medialog.de **Web site:** http://www.rundschau.de
Freq: Monthly; **Annual Sub.:** EUR 18,60; **Circ:** 64,908
Editor: Klaus Mehler; **Advertising Manager:** Matthias Stichling
Profile: Magazine covering all aspects of the retail industry.
Language(s): German
ADVERTISING RATES:
Full Page Mono .... EUR 9330
Full Page Colour .... EUR 16275
Mechanical Data: Type Area: 242 x 194 mm, No. of Columns (Display): 3, Col Widths (Display): 60 mm
Copy instructions: *Copy Date:* 21 days prior to publication
BUSINESS: RETAILING & WHOLESALING

RUNDSCHAU FÜR DEN SCHWÄBISCHEN WALD 740826G67B-12620
Editorial: Grabenstr. 14, 74405 GAILDORF
Tel: 7971 958815 **Fax:** 7971 958823
Email: rundschau.redaktion@swp.de **Web site:** http://www.suedwest-aktiv.de
Freq: 312 issues yearly; **Annual Sub.:** EUR 25,90; **Circ:** 4,642
Advertising Manager: Michael Geissler
Profile: Daily newspaper with regional news and a local sports section.
Language(s): German
ADVERTISING RATES:
SCC .... EUR 26,40
Mechanical Data: Type Area: 420 x 274 mm, No. of Columns (Display): 6, Col Widths (Display): 44 mm
Copy instructions: *Copy Date:* 1 day prior to publication
Supplement(s): Das Magazin; Regio Business
REGIONAL DAILY & SUNDAY NEWSPAPERS: Regional Daily Newspapers

RUNDSCHREIBEN FÜR IHRE KUNDENZEITUNG 1864924G37-1859
Editorial: Boschstr. 16, 28857 SYKE **Tel:** 4242 9610 **Fax:** 4242 961110

Email: mariongoebber@ipagruppe.de **Web site:** http://www.ipaverlag.de
Freq: Monthly; **Annual Sub.:** EUR 100,00; **Circ:** 500
Editor: Marion Göbber
Profile: Magazine with information on magazines for pharmacists.
Language(s): German

RUNDY
1830153G2A-5765
Editorial: Am Glockenturm 6, 63814 MAINASCHAFF
Tel: 6021 583880 **Fax:** 6021 5838822
Email: tillmannrudorf@rundy.de **Web site:** http://www.rundy.de
Freq: 26 issues yearly; **Circ:** 1,705
Editor: Tillmann Rudorf; **Advertising Manager:** Markus Blümel
Profile: Magazine with information about media and politics.
Language(s): German
ADVERTISING RATES:
Full Page Mono .... EUR 2350
Full Page Colour .... EUR 2350
Mechanical Data: Type Area: 272 x 175 mm, No. of Columns (Display): 4, Col Widths (Display): 40 mm
Copy instructions: *Copy Date:* 7 days prior to publication

RUNDY TITELSCHUTZ JOURNAL
1830156G2A-5767
Editorial: Am Glockenturm 6, 63814 MAINASCHAFF
Tel: 6021 583880 **Fax:** 6021 5838822
Email: titelschutz@rundy.de **Web site:** http://www.titelschutzjournal.de
Freq: Weekly; **Cover Price:** Free; **Circ:** 3,640
Editor: Tillmann Rudorf; **Advertising Manager:** Svenja Reichert
Profile: Information service about copyrights of newspapers, magazines, radio, TV, movies, sound storage media, software.
Language(s): German
Mechanical Data: Type Area: 262 x 175 mm, No. of Columns (Display): 2, Col Widths (Display): 85 mm
Copy instructions: *Copy Date:* 3 days prior to publication

RUNNER'S WORLD
1637764G75J-474
Editorial: Leverkusenstr. 54, 22761 HAMBURG
Tel: 40 853303922 **Fax:** 40 853303722
Email: leserservice@runners-world.de **Web site:** http://www.runnersworld.de
Freq: Monthly; **Annual Sub.:** EUR 46,00; **Circ:** 64,713
Editor: Frank Hofmann; **Advertising Manager:** Sascha Gröschel
Profile: Runner's World is the largest running magazine in the world and the largest by far in Germany. For over ten years will be as the undisputed expertise in the market and provides an active, enthusiastic runners with all the essential guidance: of the latest facts and research findings about running and fitness, to sound advice about proper nutrition, the best equipment and the hip latest outfits. Reports from all the major events of the marathon and running scene complete the program. Readers of Runner's World are strong personalities. They are often a step ahead other and like to take the lead. A decent level of perseverance and determination are indispensable. In terms of consumption, they are too demanding, as they would thereby compromising. For them, pleasure and satisfaction of their personal desires to the fore. Money plays a minor role.
Language(s): German
ADVERTISING RATES:
Full Page Mono .... EUR 7600
Full Page Colour .... EUR 7600
Mechanical Data: Type Area: 248 x 185 mm, No. of Columns (Display): 3
Copy instructions: *Copy Date:* 35 days prior to publication
CONSUMER: SPORT: Athletics

RUPPINER ANZEIGER
740866G67B-12640
Editorial: Lehnitzstr. 13, 16515 ORANIENBURG
Tel: 3301 59630 **Fax:** 3301 596350
Email: lokales@oranienburger-generalanzeiger.de
Web site: http://www.die-mark-online.de
Freq: 312 issues yearly; **Circ:** 6,769
Advertising Manager: Tibor Szabo
Profile: Daily newspaper with regional news and a local sports section.
Language(s): German
ADVERTISING RATES:
SCC .... EUR 23,60
Mechanical Data: Type Area: 485 x 327 mm, No. of Columns (Display): 7, Col Widths (Display): 43 mm
Copy instructions: *Copy Date:* 3 days prior to publication
Supplement(s): rtv
REGIONAL DAILY & SUNDAY NEWSPAPERS: Regional Daily Newspapers

RURAL 21
726349G21A-1440
Editorial: Eschborner Landstr. 122, 60489 FRANKFURT **Tel:** 69 247880 **Fax:** 69 24788481
Email: s.richter@dlg.org **Web site:** http://www.rural21.com
Freq: 6 issues yearly; **Annual Sub.:** EUR 49,00; **Circ:** 10,000
Editor: Silvia Richter; **Advertising Manager:** Viola Hilz
Profile: Magazine about international trading, export and import.
Language(s): English; German
ADVERTISING RATES:
Full Page Mono .... EUR 669
Mechanical Data: Type Area: 240 x 178 mm, No. of Columns (Display): 3, Col Widths (Display): 59 mm
BUSINESS: AGRICULTURE & FARMING

RÜSSELSHEIMER ECHO
740717G67B-12680
Editorial: Holzhofallee 25, 64295 DARMSTADT
Tel: 6151 3871 **Fax:** 6151 387307
Email: redaktion@darmstaedter-echo.de **Web site:** http://www.echo-online.de
Freq: 312 issues yearly; **Circ:** 17,165
Advertising Manager: Andreas Wohlfart
Profile: Daily newspaper with regional news and a local sports section. This Outlet offers RSS (Really Simple Syndication).
Language(s): German
ADVERTISING RATES:
SCC .... EUR 26,70
Mechanical Data: Type Area: 491 x 339 mm, No. of Columns (Display): 7, Col Widths (Display): 45 mm
Copy instructions: *Copy Date:* 1 day prior to publication
Supplement(s): Generation; Gesund leben heute; Die Hupe; i2 immobilien; Kinder Echo; M55; Odenwälder Kartoffelsupp; Sonntags Echo; Start frei; theaterlzeitung
REGIONAL DAILY & SUNDAY NEWSPAPERS: Regional Daily Newspapers

RÜSSELSHEIMER WOCHENBLATT
740718G72-11336
Editorial: Friedensplatz 12, 65428 RÜSSELSHEIM
Tel: 6142 85561 **Fax:** 6142 85521
Email: redaktion@ruesselsheimer-wochenblatt.de
Web site: http://www.ruesselsheimer-wochenblatt.de
Freq: Weekly; **Cover Price:** Free; **Circ:** 39,839
Editor: Rüdiger Benda; **Advertising Manager:** Rainer Baumann
Profile: Advertising journal (house-to-house) concentrating on local stories.
Language(s): German
ADVERTISING RATES:
Full Page Mono .... EUR 3797
Full Page Colour .... EUR 5276
Mechanical Data: Type Area: 480 x 325 mm, No. of Columns (Display): 7, Col Widths (Display): 45 mm
Copy instructions: *Copy Date:* 2 days prior to publication
LOCAL NEWSPAPERS

RUTE & ROLLE
740871G92-220
Editorial: Hellgrundweg 109, 22525 HAMBURG
Tel: 40 2361300 **Fax:** 40 23613022
Email: kloeer@ruteundrolle.de **Web site:** http://www.ruteundrolle.de
Freq: Monthly; **Annual Sub.:** EUR 39,00; **Circ:** 62,371
Editor: Matthias Six; **Advertising Manager:** Matthias Six
Profile: A nature orientated and increasingly popular hobby end has changed: The fishing has become more diverse, modern and has emerged from the shadows of a media and markets previously often underrated pastime. Anglers have become a target group that is increasingly coming into focus in many companies and is being courted. This goes along with the increasingly positive representation of the observed fishing in the media: Fishing is clearly a trend. The ways to achieve, fishing as potential customers are changing and continue to change: editorial magazine articles and traditional print advertising are increasingly being supplemented by moving pictures as an information medium. Cross-media advertising and future-oriented marketing tools provide completely new ways to reach customers, not just to excite.
Language(s): German
Readership: Aimed at anglers.
ADVERTISING RATES:
Full Page Mono .... EUR 3200
Full Page Colour .... EUR 5360
Mechanical Data: Type Area: 248 x 185 mm, No. of Columns (Display): 4, Col Widths (Display): 43 mm
Copy instructions: *Copy Date:* 21 days prior to publication
CONSUMER: ANGLING & FISHING

RW TEXTILSERVICE
740857G47A-1620
Editorial: Gewerbestr. 2, 86825 BAD WÖRISHOFEN
Tel: 8247 354261 **Fax:** 8247 354270
Email: vanessa.ebert@holzmann-medien.de **Web site:** http://www.rw-textilservice.de
Freq: Monthly; **Annual Sub.:** EUR 89,00; **Circ:** 5,085
Editor: Vanessa Ebert; **Advertising Manager:** Angela Holzwarth
Profile: Magazine for managers in the textile service branch as well as cleaners of textiles, laundries and textile leasing companies.
Language(s): German
ADVERTISING RATES:
Full Page Mono .... EUR 2445
Full Page Colour .... EUR 4110
Mechanical Data: Type Area: 260 x 185 mm, No. of Columns (Display): 4, Col Widths (Display): 43 mm
Copy instructions: *Copy Date:* 20 days prior to publication
BUSINESS: CLOTHING & TEXTILES

RWE KOMPAKT
1882172G14A-10272
Editorial: Harvestehuder Weg 42, 20149 HAMBURG
Tel: 40 44188242 **Fax:** 40 44188309
Email: cp@hoca.de **Web site:** http://cp.hoca.de
Freq: Quarterly; **Circ:** 29,500
Editor: Jan H. Kolbaum
Profile: Company publication published by RWE Westfalen-Weser-Ems AG.
Language(s): German

RZ RAUM & AUSSTATTUNG
740887G16A-5
Editorial: Nymphenburger Str. 1, 80335 MÜNCHEN
Tel: 89 29001144 **Fax:** 89 29001199
Email: gaby.reckstat@winkler-online.de **Web site:** http://www.winkler-online.de
Freq: 11 issues yearly; Free to qualifying individuals
Annual Sub.: EUR 104,00; **Circ:** 5,729
Editor: Gabriela Reckstat; **Advertising Manager:** Gunnar Reckstat
Profile: Official journal of the Association of Interior Decorators.
Language(s): German
ADVERTISING RATES:
Full Page Mono .... EUR 3395
Full Page Colour .... EUR 5432
Mechanical Data: Type Area: 267 x 178 mm, No. of Columns (Display): 4, Col Widths (Display): 41 mm
Copy instructions: *Copy Date:* 15 days prior to publication
Official Journal of: Organ d. Zentralverb. Raum u. Ausstattung u. d. Bundesverb. d. vereidigten Sachverständigen f. Raum u. Ausstattung
BUSINESS: DECORATING & PAINT

SAALE-ZEITUNG
1703657G67B-16754
Editorial: Gutenbergstr. 1, 96050 BAMBERG
Tel: 951 1880 **Fax:** 951 188323
Email: redaktion@infranken.de **Web site:** http://www.infranken.de
Freq: 312 issues yearly; **Circ:** 14,068
Advertising Manager: Thomas Schlick
Profile: The Saale-Zeitung, headquartered in Bad Kissingen, is a regional newspaper with news on politics, economy, culture, sports, travel, technology, etc., which is read mainly in the territory of the Frankish Rhön. The main distribution area is the district of Bad Kissingen and the surrounding areas. Facebook: http://www.facebook.com/pages/inFrankende/209363937665 Twitter: http://twitter.com/infranken This Outlet offers RSS (Really Simple Syndication).
Language(s): German
ADVERTISING RATES:
SCC .... EUR 30,60
Mechanical Data: Type Area: 430 x 285 mm, No. of Columns (Display): 6, Col Widths (Display): 45 mm
Copy instructions: *Copy Date:* 1 day prior to publication
Supplement(s): doppio; rtv
REGIONAL DAILY & SUNDAY NEWSPAPERS: Regional Daily Newspapers

SAAR.AMATEUR
740893G75A-2420
Editorial: Gutenbergstr. 11, 66117 SAARBRÜCKEN
Tel: 681 5023710 **Fax:** 681 5023709
Email: g.mueller@saar-amateur.de **Web site:** http://www.saaramateur.de
Freq: 40 issues yearly; **Circ:** 5,391
Editor: Georg Müller; **Advertising Manager:** Michael Schmierer
Profile: Magazine for athletes in the Saarland.
Language(s): German
ADVERTISING RATES:
Full Page Mono .... EUR 1390
Full Page Colour .... EUR 1390
Mechanical Data: Type Area: 326 x 232 mm, No. of Columns (Display): 5, Col Widths (Display): 45 mm
Copy instructions: *Copy Date:* 4 days prior to publication
CONSUMER: SPORT

SAARBRÜCKER ZEITUNG
740895G67B-12740
Editorial: Gutenbergstr. 11, 66117 SAARBRÜCKEN
Tel: 681 5020 **Fax:** 681 502501
Email: sz-service@sz-sb.de **Web site:** http://www.saarbruecker-zeitung.de
Freq: 312 issues yearly; **Circ:** 155,444
Editor: Peter Stefan Herbst; **News Editor:** Ulrich Brenner; **Advertising Manager:** Michael Schmierer
Profile: Regional daily newspaper with news on politics, economy, culture, sports, travel, technology, etc. The Saarbrückener Zeitung with circulation over 150,000 copies and 510,000 readers of the leading media brand in the Saarland. Even nationally, it is one of the major regional newspapers. Facebook: http://www.facebook.com/group.php?gid=128213578634&ref=mf Twitter: http://twitter.com/szaktuell This Outlet offers RSS (Really Simple Syndication).
Language(s): German
ADVERTISING RATES:
SCC .... EUR 275,20
Mechanical Data: Type Area: 480 x 326 mm, No. of Columns (Display): 7, Col Widths (Display): 44 mm
Copy instructions: *Copy Date:* 2 days prior to publication
Supplement(s): tele.tipp; Theaterzeit; treff.region
REGIONAL DAILY & SUNDAY NEWSPAPERS: Regional Daily Newspapers

DER SAAR-HANDWERKER
740897G63-1725
Editorial: Grülingsstr. 115, 66113 SAARBRÜCKEN
Tel: 681 948610 **Fax:** 681 9486199
Email: sh@agvh.de **Web site:** http://www.saarhandwerker.de
Freq: Monthly; Free to qualifying individuals
Annual Sub.: EUR 213,00; **Circ:** 2,417
Editor: Martin Weisgerber; **Advertising Manager:** Christiane Aubertin
Profile: Official journal of the Saarbrücken Chamber of Commerce.
Language(s): German
ADVERTISING RATES:
Full Page Mono .... EUR 993
Full Page Colour .... EUR 1728
Mechanical Data: Type Area: 267 x 185 mm, No. of Columns (Display): 3, Col Widths (Display): 58 mm
Copy instructions: *Copy Date:* 12 days prior to publication
Official Journal of: Organ d. Arbeitgeberverb. d. Saarländ. Handwerks e.V. u. d. Innungen u. d. Handwerkskammer d. Saarlandes
BUSINESS: REGIONAL BUSINESS

SAARLÄNDISCHES ÄRZTEBLATT
740902G56A-9080
Editorial: Faktoreistr. 4, 66111 SAARBRÜCKEN
Tel: 681 4003272 **Fax:** 681 4003339
Email: aerzteblatt@aeksaar.de **Web site:** http://www.aerztekammer-saarland.de
Freq: Monthly; Free to qualifying individuals
Annual Sub.: EUR 109,00; **Circ:** 6,900
Editor: Andreas Kondziela; **Advertising Manager:** Melanie Bölsdorff
Profile: Journal for physicians and dentists in the Saarland.
Language(s): German
Readership: Aimed at doctors.
ADVERTISING RATES:
Full Page Mono .... EUR 1225
Full Page Colour .... EUR 2140
Mechanical Data: Type Area: 252 x 185 mm, No. of Columns (Display): 3, Col Widths (Display): 58 mm
Copy instructions: *Copy Date:* 20 days prior to publication
BUSINESS: HEALTH & MEDICAL

SABRINA
740917G74E-300
Editorial: Römerstr. 90, 79618 RHEINFELDEN
Tel: 7623 964164 **Fax:** 7623 964459
Email: info@oz-verlag.de **Web site:** http://www.oz-verlag.de
Freq: Monthly; **Annual Sub.:** EUR 33,60; **Circ:** 31,476
Editor: Petra Bäck
Profile: Each month the magazine brings the latest and trendy knits for replication. Super Easy to challenging proposals from a variety of wool fabrics offer a variety of styles for beginners knitting professionals. Target group: young creative women who prefer the individual fashion off the rack and appreciate the hobby of knitting as a hobby. In addition, they have a self-made garment niggling joy.
Language(s): German
ADVERTISING RATES:
Full Page Mono .... EUR 2080
Full Page Colour .... EUR 2560
Mechanical Data: Type Area: 251 x 183 mm, No. of Columns (Display): 4, Col Widths (Display): 41 mm
CONSUMER: WOMEN'S INTEREST CONSUMER MAGAZINES: Crafts

SABRINA WOMAN
1626652G74A-3390
Editorial: Römerstr. 90, 79618 RHEINFELDEN
Tel: 7623 964540 **Fax:** 7623 964451
Email: info@oz-verlag.de **Web site:** http://www.oz-verlag.de
Freq: Quarterly; **Annual Sub.:** EUR 15,00; **Circ:** 65,000
Editor: Dagmar Scholz
Profile: Magazine with sewing instructions for Ladies Large Sizes - sporty, lively and witty fashion for the home sewing nähbegeisterte "seamstresses".
Language(s): German
Mechanical Data: Type Area: 251 x 183 mm

SACHSEN MAGAZIN
1814430G89A-12350
Editorial: Saalhausener Str. 51b, 01159 DRESDEN
Tel: 351 79588313 **Fax:** 351 79588315
Email: ckaesler@labhard.de **Web site:** http://www.labhard.de
Freq: Annual; **Cover Price:** EUR 5,00; **Circ:** 80,000
Editor: Claudia Kaesler; **Advertising Manager:** Iris Kupferschmied
Profile: Year-round current travel and leisure guide in magazine format for Saxony. Under the motto "Discover - Experience - Enjoy" touristy relevant pieces of information: attractions, culture and leisure facilities, cities and regions, hotels and restaurants. A Saxon calendar of events, maps, timetables and service addresses, provide great benefits. The Sachsen Magazin is a high quality lavishly produced purchase object with collective character.
Language(s): German
ADVERTISING RATES:
Full Page Mono .... EUR 2793
Full Page Colour .... EUR 2793
Mechanical Data: Type Area: 260 x 180 mm
Copy instructions: *Copy Date:* 31 days prior to publication

SACHSENBUMMEL 740925G89A-12112
Editorial: Karsdorfer Str. 1, 01768 GLASHÜTTE
Tel: 3504 694950 **Fax:** 3504 6949529
Email: sachsenbummel@saxacon.de **Web site:** http://www.sachsenbummel.de
Freq: Quarterly; **Annual Sub.:** EUR 15,00; **Circ:** 10,000
Editor: Gernod Loose; **Advertising Manager:** Gernod Loose
Profile: Magazine about culture, history and tourism in Saxony including a programme of events.
Language(s): German
ADVERTISING RATES:
Full Page Colour .... EUR 1650
Mechanical Data: Type Area: 230 x 174 mm

SACHSENHEIMER ZEITUNG
740927G67B-12760
Editorial: Kronenbergstr. 10, 74321 BIETIGHEIM-BISSINGEN **Tel:** 7142 403410 **Fax:** 7142 403128
Email: redaktion@bietigheimerzeitung.de **Web site:** http://www.bietigheimerzeitung.de
Freq: 312 issues yearly; **Circ:** 12,204
Advertising Manager: Johannes Schwiderowski
Profile: Daily newspaper with regional news and a local sports section.
Language(s): German
ADVERTISING RATES:
SCC .... EUR 42,60
Mechanical Data: Type Area: 485 x 320 mm, No. of Columns (Display): 7, Col Widths (Display): 44 mm
Copy instructions: *Copy Date:* 2 days prior to publication
Supplement(s): rtv
REGIONAL DAILY & SUNDAY NEWSPAPERS: Regional Daily Newspapers

SÄCHSISCHE ZEITUNG
740942G67B-12780
Editorial: Ostra-Allee 20, 01067 DRESDEN
Tel: 351 48640 **Fax:** 351 48642282
Email: sz.chefredaktion@dd-v.de **Web site:** http://www.sz-online.de
Freq: 312 issues yearly
Advertising Manager: Tobias Spitzhorn
Profile: Daily newspaper with regional news and a local sports section. Facebook: http://www.facebook.com/szonline.
Language(s): German
ADVERTISING RATES:
SCC .... EUR 144,00
Mechanical Data: Type Area: 485 x 327 mm, No. of Columns (Display): 7, Col Widths (Display): 45 mm
Copy instructions: *Copy Date:* 2 days prior to publication
Supplement(s): chrismon; PluSZ; rtv
REGIONAL DAILY & SUNDAY NEWSPAPERS: Regional Daily Newspapers

SÄCHSISCHER BOTE - WOCHENZTG. F. DRESDEN, AUSG. NORD 740939G72-11448
Editorial: Devrientstr. 5, 01067 DRESDEN
Tel: 351 8657127 **Fax:** 351 8657110
Email: redaktion@saechsischer-bote.de **Web site:** http://www.saechsischer-bote.de
Freq: Weekly; **Cover Price:** Free; **Circ:** 57,100
Editor: Hans-Georg Prause; **Advertising Manager:** Petra Aehlig
Profile: Advertising journal (house-to-house) concentrating on local stories.
Language(s): German
ADVERTISING RATES:
Full Page Mono .... EUR 2813
Full Page Colour .... EUR 3819
Mechanical Data: Type Area: 430 x 282 mm, No. of Columns (Display): 6, Col Widths (Display): 45 mm
Copy instructions: *Copy Date:* 2 days prior to publication
LOCAL NEWSPAPERS

SÄCHSVBL. SÄCHSISCHE VERWALTUNGSBLÄTTER
740941G32A-2680
Editorial: Scharrstr. 2, 70563 STUTTGART
Tel: 711 73850 **Fax:** 711 7385330
Email: s.sonntag@boorberg.de **Web site:** http://www.boorberg.de
Freq: Monthly; **Annual Sub.:** EUR 197,40; **Circ:** 470
Editor: Jürgen Meng; **Advertising Manager:** Roland Schulz
Profile: Journal of public administration and law in the German region of Saxony.
Language(s): German
Readership: Read by legal and public administrators.
ADVERTISING RATES:
Full Page Mono .... EUR 840
Full Page Colour .... EUR 1770
Mechanical Data: Type Area: 260 x 180 mm, No. of Columns (Display): 2, Col Widths (Display): 88 mm
Copy instructions: *Copy Date:* 28 days prior to publication
BUSINESS: LOCAL GOVERNMENT, LEISURE & RECREATION: Local Government

DER SACHVERSTÄNDIGE
740936G14A-6320
Editorial: Beethovenstr. 7b, 60325 FRANKFURT
Tel: 69 7560910 **Fax:** 69 75609149
Email: ds@beck-frankfurt.de **Web site:** http://www.ds.beck.de
Freq: Monthly; **Annual Sub.:** EUR 121,80; **Circ:** 4,200
Editor: Elisabeth Jackisch; **Advertising Manager:** Fritz Lebherz
Profile: Magazine for experts, chambers, courts of law and authorities.
Language(s): German
ADVERTISING RATES:
Full Page Mono .... EUR 1840
Full Page Colour .... EUR 3640
Mechanical Data: Type Area: 260 x 186 mm, No. of Columns (Display): 4, Col Widths (Display): 43 mm

SALDO 740967G74M-520
Editorial: Neckargartacher Str. 90, 74080 HEILBRONN **Tel:** 7131 9133211 **Fax:** 7131 920970
Email: info@geldundverbraucher.de **Web site:** http://www.geldundverbraucher.de
Freq: Half-yearly; **Circ:** 4,000
Editor: Jürgen Buck; **Advertising Manager:** Bernd Martin
Profile: Customer magazine about investments, insurance, internet, the Euro, holidays, telecommunications and automobiles.
Language(s): German
ADVERTISING RATES:
Full Page Mono .... EUR 600
Full Page Colour .... EUR 600
Mechanical Data: Type Area: 220 x 174 mm, No. of Columns (Display): 3, Col Widths (Display): 55 mm
Copy instructions: *Copy Date:* 14 days prior to publication

SALES BUSINESS 740970G14A-6340
Editorial: Abraham-Lincoln-Str. 46, 65189 WIESBADEN **Tel:** 611 7878205 **Fax:** 611 7878435
Email: peter.rensch@springer.com **Web site:** http://www.salesbusiness.de
Freq: 10 issues yearly; **Annual Sub.:** EUR 99,00; **Circ:** 15,382
Editor: Peter Rensch; **Advertising Manager:** Eva Hanenberg
Profile: Magazine on sales management and marketing.
Language(s): German
ADVERTISING RATES:
Full Page Mono .... EUR 4690
Full Page Colour .... EUR 6160
Mechanical Data: Type Area: 240 x 175 mm, No. of Columns (Display): 4, Col Widths (Display): 44 mm
Copy instructions: *Copy Date:* 30 days prior to publication
BUSINESS: COMMERCE, INDUSTRY & MANAGEMENT

SALES GUIDE KÖLN COLOGNE
740971G50-840
Editorial: Weyerstraßerweg 159, 50969 KÖLN
Tel: 221 376030 **Fax:** 221 374020
Email: info@messetreff.com **Web site:** http://www.willkommeninkoeln.de
Freq: Annual; **Cover Price:** EUR 12,00; **Circ:** 12,500
Editor: Manfred Kanzler; **Advertising Manager:** Gabriele Fischer
Profile: Sales guide Cologne.
Language(s): English; German
ADVERTISING RATES:
Full Page Mono .... EUR 4350
Full Page Colour .... EUR 4350
Mechanical Data: Type Area: 257 x 184 mm, No. of Columns (Display): 4, Col Widths (Display): 46 mm
Copy instructions: *Copy Date:* 30 days prior to publication

SALES MANUAL 746271G50-1160
Editorial: Am Karlsbad 11, 10785 BERLIN
Tel: 30 2647480 **Fax:** 30 264748968
Email: catrin.linde@btm.de **Web site:** http://www.visitberlin.de
Freq: Annual; **Cover Price:** Free; **Circ:** 13,000
Profile: Sales manual with tourism related data and information for planning and organising trips to Berlin.
Language(s): English; German
ADVERTISING RATES:
Full Page Mono .... EUR 5300
Full Page Colour .... EUR 5300
Mechanical Data: Type Area: 260 x 188 mm
Copy instructions: *Copy Date:* 97 days prior to publication

SALZGITTER WOCHE AM SONNTAG 741002G72-11456
Editorial: Berliner Str. 11, 38226 SALZGITTER
Tel: 5341 17057 **Fax:** 5341 17132
Email: redaktion@salzgitter-woche.de **Web site:** http://www.salzgitter-woche.de
Freq: Weekly; **Cover Price:** Free; **Circ:** 64,225
Editor: Klaus-Jürgen Grütter; **Advertising Manager:** Hubert Schubert
Profile: Advertising journal (house-to-house) concentrating on local stories.
Language(s): German
ADVERTISING RATES:
Full Page Mono .... EUR 4206
Full Page Colour .... EUR 5186
Mechanical Data: Type Area: 430 x 277 mm, No. of Columns (Display): 6, Col Widths (Display): 45 mm
Copy instructions: *Copy Date:* 3 days prior to publication
LOCAL NEWSPAPERS

SALZGITTER-ZEITUNG
741004G67B-12860
Editorial: Hamburger Str. 277, 38114 BRAUNSCHWEIG **Tel:** 531 39000 **Fax:** 531 3900610
Email: redaktion@bzv.de **Web site:** http://www.newsclick.de
Freq: 312 issues yearly; **Circ:** 18,524
Advertising Manager: Raphael Feldmann
Profile: Regional daily newspaper with news on politics, economy, culture, sports, travel, technology, etc. Almost half a million readers between resin and the Lüneburg Heath and regularly access to the Braunschweiger Zeitung (BZ), the second largest newspaper in Lower Saxony. Salzgitter-Zeitung is a regional edition of the Braunschweiger Zeitung. The BZ appears weekdays and has an average paid circulation of 150,000 copies. With the main titles Braunschweiger Zeitung, Salzgitter-Zeitung and Wolfsburger Nachrichten and the seven local editions of the Braunschweiger Zeitung profiled as a strong regional newspaper in a historically significant landscape, the Brunswick Country. The Braunschweiger Zeitung considers itself not only as an information medium but also as a forum. Twitter: http://twitter.com/bs_zeitung This Outlet offers RSS (Really Simple Syndication).
Language(s): German
ADVERTISING RATES:
SCC .... EUR 62,40
Mechanical Data: Type Area: 435 x 282 mm, No. of Columns (Display): 6, Col Widths (Display): 45 mm
Copy instructions: *Copy Date:* 1 day prior to publication
Supplement(s): prisma
REGIONAL DAILY & SUNDAY NEWSPAPERS: Regional Daily Newspapers

SALZWEDELER VOLKSSTIMME
741014G67B-12880
Editorial: Bahnhofstr. 17, 39104 MAGDEBURG
Tel: 391 59990 **Fax:** 391 5999210
Email: chefredaktion@volksstimme.de **Web site:** http://www.volksstimme.de
Freq: 312 issues yearly; **Circ:** 20,759
Advertising Manager: Rainer Pfeil
Profile: As the largest daily newspaper in northern Saxony-Anhalt, the Volksstimme reaches 536,000 readers a day* (MA 2010). From Monday to Saturday a team of highly qualified editors put together the latest information and news from the region and around the world. Thanks the 18 local editions is the Volksstimme always close to the action. Twitter: http://twitter.com/volksstimme This Outlet offers RSS (Really Simple Syndication).
Language(s): German
ADVERTISING RATES:
SCC .... EUR 63,20
Mechanical Data: Type Area: 480 x 327 mm, No. of Columns (Display): 7, Col Widths (Display): 45 mm
Copy instructions: *Copy Date:* 2 days prior to publication
Supplement(s): Anstoss im Altmarkkreis Salzwedel; bauRatgeber; Biber; Immobilien Spezial; Leser-Reisen; prisma; Standort Altmarkkreis Salzwedel
REGIONAL DAILY & SUNDAY NEWSPAPERS: Regional Daily Newspapers

SANDRA 1882173G74A-3657
Editorial: Römerstr. 90, 79618 RHEINFELDEN
Tel: 7623 964408 **Fax:** 7623 964459
Email: info@oz-verlag.de **Web site:** http://www.oz-verlag.de
Freq: Quarterly; **Annual Sub.:** EUR 19,20; **Circ:** 60,000
Editor: Janne Graf
Profile: Knitwear for ladies, spring, summer, autumn and winter sweaters, large sizes, ponchos, scarves, bags.
Language(s): German
ADVERTISING RATES:
Full Page Mono .... EUR 2080
Full Page Colour .... EUR 2560
Mechanical Data: Type Area: 251 x 183 mm

SÄNGER & MUSIKANTEN
740951G76D-4840
Editorial: Lothstr. 29, 80797 MÜNCHEN
Tel: 89 127051 **Fax:** 89 12705335
Email: smz-redaktion@dlv.de **Web site:** http://www.dlv.de
Freq: 6 issues yearly; **Annual Sub.:** EUR 35,50; **Circ:** 5,093
Editor: Josef Focht; **Advertising Manager:** Thomas Herrmann
Profile: Publication about folk music.
Language(s): German
ADVERTISING RATES:
Full Page Mono .... EUR 767
Full Page Colour .... EUR 2071
Mechanical Data: Type Area: 203 x 135 mm, No. of Columns (Display): 2, Col Widths (Display): 65 mm
CONSUMER: MUSIC & PERFORMING ARTS: Music

SANITÄR + HEIZUNGSTECHNIK
741044G3D-700
Editorial: Bitterfelder Str. 7, 04129 LEIPZIG
Tel: 341 9029300 **Fax:** 341 9029307
Email: krammer-leipzig@t-online.de **Web site:** http://www.sht-online.de
Freq: Monthly; **Annual Sub.:** EUR 90,00; **Circ:** 23,712
Editor: Sigrid Wieschke; **Advertising Manager:** Alke Schmeis
Profile: The Sanitär + Heizungstechnik read heating, oil and gas installation, ventilation, air conditioning and plumbing specialists in trade, industry, planning and administration. It contains reports on the latest installation methods of problem solving, on time-saving planning and calculation methods, the legal requirements and standards. In addition, the most important innovations of the industry presented and published legal decisions of the household technology. An appendix refers to additional information on the Internet.
Language(s): German
Readership: Read by builders, plumbers and heating engineers.
ADVERTISING RATES:
Full Page Mono .... EUR 3600
Full Page Colour .... EUR 6120
Mechanical Data: Type Area: 257 x 185 mm, No. of Columns (Display): 2, Col Widths (Display): 88 mm
Copy instructions: *Copy Date:* 21 days prior to publication
Official Journal of: Organ d. Fachverbände Sanitär-, Heizungs- u. Klimatechnik Bayern, Rheinland/Rheinhessen, Sachsen u. Thüringen
BUSINESS: HEATING & VENTILATION: Heating & Plumbing

SANITÄRJOURNAL 747199G3B-160
Editorial: Eibenweg 20, 71364 WINNENDEN
Tel: 6223 74009 **Fax:** 6223 74148
Email: redaktion@heizungsjournal.de **Web site:** http://www.heizungsjournal.de
Freq: 6 issues yearly; **Annual Sub.:** EUR 49,90; **Circ:** 37,067
Editor: Dieter-Martin Funk; **Advertising Manager:** Elke Oechsner-Jung
Profile: Magazine containing news and information on air-conditioning, heating and ventilation.
Language(s): German
ADVERTISING RATES:
Full Page Mono .... EUR 6080
Full Page Colour .... EUR 6080
Mechanical Data: Type Area: 260 x 185 mm, No. of Columns (Display): 4, Col Widths (Display): 43 mm
Copy instructions: *Copy Date:* 21 days prior to publication
BUSINESS: HEATING & VENTILATION: Industrial Heating & Ventilation

SAT + KABEL 1609325G2A-5432
Editorial: Wallbergstr. 10, 86415 MERING
Tel: 8233 74010 **Fax:** 8233 740117
Email: jochen.wieloch@satundkabel.de **Web site:** http://www.satundkabel.de
Freq: 6 issues yearly; **Annual Sub.:** EUR 21,00; **Circ:** 22,362
Editor: Jochen Wieloch; **Advertising Manager:** Andreas Knauf
Profile: The magazine sat + kabel informed since November 2002 practically about all the facts in the digital TV, satellite, broadband and media industry in particular Focus on HDTV. In the magazine there are extensive tests of new consumer electronics, workshops for cable and satellite fans as well as current background reports.
Language(s): German
ADVERTISING RATES:
Full Page Colour .... EUR 6000
Mechanical Data: Type Area: 297 x 210 mm
BUSINESS: COMMUNICATIONS, ADVERTISING & MARKETING

SAUERLANDKURIER FÜR OLPE, DROLSHAGEN, WENDEN UND UMGEBUNG 741119G72-11524
Editorial: Löherweg 13, 57462 OLPE **Tel:** 2761 93990
Fax: 2761 939999
Email: olpe@sauerlandkurier.de **Web site:** http://www.sauerlandkurier.de
Freq: Weekly; **Cover Price:** Free; **Circ:** 25,510
Editor: Torsten-Eric Sendler; **Advertising Manager:** Thomas Hommerich
Profile: Advertising journal (house-to-house) concentrating on local stories.
Language(s): German
ADVERTISING RATES:
Full Page Mono .... EUR 1359
Full Page Colour .... EUR 1631
Mechanical Data: Type Area: 316 x 225 mm, No. of Columns (Display): 5, Col Widths (Display): 43 mm
Copy instructions: *Copy Date:* 2 days prior to publication
LOCAL NEWSPAPERS

SAUERLANDKURIER FÜR SCHMALLENBERG, AUE-W., ESLOHE UND UMGEBUNG
741120G72-11528
Editorial: Oberer Hagen 8, 57392 SCHMALLENBERG **Tel:** 2972 97870
Fax: 2972 978725
Email: meschede@sauerlandkurier.de **Web site:** http://www.sauerlandkurier.de
Freq: Weekly; **Cover Price:** Free; **Circ:** 17,290
Editor: Torsten-Eric Sendler; **Advertising Manager:** Dieter Richard
Profile: Advertising journal (house-to-house) concentrating on local stories.
Language(s): German
ADVERTISING RATES:
Full Page Mono .... EUR 1359
Full Page Colour .... EUR 1631
Mechanical Data: Type Area: 316 x 211 mm, No. of Columns (Display): 5, Col Widths (Display): 43 mm

Germany

Copy instructions: *Copy Date:* 2 days prior to publication
LOCAL NEWSPAPERS

SAVOIR VIVRE 1790147G89A-12268
Editorial: Cäcilienstr. 46, 50667 KÖLN
Tel: 221 277590 **Fax:** 221 27759100
Email: info@belgien-tourismus.de **Web site:** http://www.belgien-tourismus.de
Freq: Annual; **Cover Price:** Free; **Circ:** 40,000
Editor: Vanessa Gromer
Profile: Travel Information for Belgium on the tourist offer in Wallonia and Brussels Facebook: http://www.facebook.com/BelgienTourismus.
Language(s): German

SAVOIR-VIVRE 741127G74P-780
Editorial: Rothenbaumchaussee 27, 20148 HAMBURG **Tel:** 40 3708182030
Email: redaktion@go-presse.de **Web site:** http://www.savoirvivre.de
Freq: 6 issues yearly; **Cover Price:** EUR 5,00; **Circ:** 27,500
Editor: Karl-F. Lietz
Profile: News magazine for connoisseurs. The thematic focus is travel and enjoyment, test programs (restaurants, hotels, products), wine and the world of fine wine, diet tips for connoisseurs, table and dining culture as well exclusive coverage from all parts of Germany and from the neighboring countries. Also: wellness trends, spa treatments, special events and cultural highlights.
Language(s): German
ADVERTISING RATES:
Full Page Mono .... EUR 4200
Full Page Colour .... EUR 4200
Mechanical Data: Type Area: 240 x 172 mm
CONSUMER: WOMEN'S INTEREST CONSUMER MAGAZINES: Food & Cookery

---

SAX 741128G80-10000
Editorial: Bautzner Str. 22, 01099 DRESDEN
Tel: 351 8293918 **Fax:** 351 8293949
Email: redaktion@cybersax.de **Web site:** http://www.cybersax.de
Freq: Monthly; **Annual Sub.:** EUR 19,00; **Circ:** 5,151
Editor: Uwe Stuhrberg; **Advertising Manager:** Andreas Eichler
Profile: Magazine for city and region, concentrating on gastronomy, music, arts and events.
Language(s): German
ADVERTISING RATES:
Full Page Mono .... EUR 1450
Full Page Colour .... EUR 2040
Mechanical Data: Type Area: 260 x 190 mm, Col Widths (Display): 44 mm, No. of Columns (Display): 4
Copy instructions: *Copy Date:* 10 days prior to publication
CONSUMER: RURAL & REGIONAL INTEREST

SAZ BIKE 741129G31C-1
Editorial: Rumfordstr. 42, 80469 MÜNCHEN
Tel: 89 2121100 **Fax:** 89 21211019
Email: redbike@saz.de **Web site:** http://www.saz.de/sazbike/index.html
Freq: 24 issues yearly; **Annual Sub.:** EUR 112,00; **Circ:** 5,930
Editor: Horst O. Frankl; **Advertising Manager:** Eric Wollenberg
Profile: Journal of the bike trade for traders, sellers, buyers, owners and industry.
Language(s): German
Readership: Read by manufacturers, suppliers and retailers.
ADVERTISING RATES:
Full Page Mono .... EUR 2090
Full Page Colour .... EUR 2990
Mechanical Data: Type Area: 315 x 230 mm
Copy instructions: *Copy Date:* 11 days prior to publication
Supplement(s): saz college
BUSINESS: MOTOR TRADE: Bicycle Trade

SAZ SPORTSFASHION MAGAZIN 741131G48B-4
Editorial: Rumfordstr. 42, 80469 MÜNCHEN
Tel: 89 2121100 **Fax:** 89 21211019
Email: sazsport@saz.de **Web site:** http://www.saz.de
Freq: 8 issues yearly; **Annual Sub.:** EUR 70,00; **Circ:** 20,000
Editor: Horst O. Frankl; **Advertising Manager:** Kirsten Meuer
Profile: Magazine for sports fashion buyers in Germany, Austria and Switzerland. saz sportfashion magazin is a special issue of the magazine saz sport.
Language(s): German
Readership: Aimed at management of sportswear specialist retailers and manufacturers.
ADVERTISING RATES:
Full Page Mono .... EUR 5270
Full Page Colour .... EUR 5270
Mechanical Data: Type Area: 295 x 223 mm, No. of Columns (Display): 4, Col Widths (Display): 52 mm
Copy instructions: *Copy Date:* 14 days prior to publication
BUSINESS: TOY TRADE & SPORTS GOODS: Sports Goods

SB 1934607G4E-7320
Editorial: Am Sportpark Müngersdorf 3, 50933 KÖLN
Tel: 221 16802317 **Fax:** 221 16802323
Email: buehlbecker@iaks.info **Web site:** http://www.sb.iaks.info
Freq: 6 issues yearly; **Annual Sub.:** EUR 42,00; **Circ:** 5,500
Editor: Johannes Bühlbecker; **Advertising Manager:** Claudia Barz
Profile: Magazine on sport and swimming facility building.
Language(s): English; French; German; Spanish
ADVERTISING RATES:
Full Page Colour .... EUR 1900
Mechanical Data: Type Area: 297 x 210 mm
Official Journal of: Organ d. Internat. Vereinigung Sport- u. Freizeiteinrichtungen e.V.

SBR 741136G14A-6360
Editorial: Grafenberger Allee 293, 40237 DÜSSELDORF **Tel:** 211 8871427 **Fax:** 211 8871420
Email: p.hanser@fachverlag.de **Web site:** http://www.sbr-online.de
Freq: Quarterly; **Annual Sub.:** EUR 180,00; **Circ:** 2,700
Editor: Wolfgang Ballwieser; **Advertising Manager:** Ralf Pötzsch
Profile: Journal of Marketing Research, Rechnungslegung, Finance, Marketing, Decision Theory and New Institutional Economics.
Language(s): English
ADVERTISING RATES:
Full Page Mono .... EUR 1280
Full Page Colour .... EUR 2330
Mechanical Data: Type Area: 203 x 140 mm
Copy instructions: *Copy Date:* 30 days prior to publication
Official Journal of: Organ d. Schmalenbach-Ges. f. Betriebswirtschaft e.V.

SBZ MONTEUR 741137G3D-720
Editorial: Forststr. 131, 70193 STUTTGART
Tel: 2302 30771 **Fax:** 2302 30119
Email: scheele@sbz-online.de **Web site:** http://www.sbz-monteur.de
Freq: Monthly; Free to qualifying individuals
Annual Sub.: EUR 95,80; **Circ:** 6,048
Editor: Jörg Scheele; **Advertising Manager:** Bettina Landwehr
Profile: Magazine covering sanitation, heating and air-conditioning.
Language(s): German
ADVERTISING RATES:
Full Page Mono .... EUR 810
Full Page Colour .... EUR 1260
Mechanical Data: Type Area: 251 x 177 mm, No. of Columns (Display): 4, Col Widths (Display): 41 mm
Copy instructions: *Copy Date:* 28 days prior to publication
BUSINESS: HEATING & VENTILATION: Heating & Plumbing

SBZ SANITÄR.HEIZUNG.KLIMA 741138G3D-740
Editorial: Forststr. 131, 70193 STUTTGART
Tel: 711 63672844 **Fax:** 711 63672755
Email: schlattmann@sbz-online.de **Web site:** http://www.sbz-online.de
Freq: 21 issues yearly; **Annual Sub.:** EUR 159,60; **Circ:** 33,541
Editor: Dirk Schlattmann; **Advertising Manager:** Bettina Landwehr
Profile: The SBZ Sanitär.Heizung.Klima is a magazine being published in the 14-day rhythm which reports about the event in the HVAC and plumbing industry as well as about the technical and marketing developments currently. An official media partner of the central association is sanitarily heating climate the SBZ of HVAC trade associations. The magazine is mainly read of discriminators in skilled crafts and great trading concerns but also with associations in the industry and of sales representatives.
Language(s): German
Readership: Read by plumbing and heating engineers.
ADVERTISING RATES:
Full Page Mono .... EUR 5290
Full Page Colour .... EUR 6310
Mechanical Data: Type Area: 265 x 187 mm, No. of Columns (Display): 4, Col Widths (Display): 43 mm
Copy instructions: *Copy Date:* 20 days prior to publication
Official Journal of: Organ v. Landesfachverbänden u. d. Zentralverb. Sanitär, Heizung, Klima
BUSINESS: HEATING & VENTILATION: Heating & Plumbing

SCANIA BEWEGT 1852483A49A-600
Editorial: Handwerkstr. 15, 70565 STUTTGART
Tel: 89 7849880 **Fax:** 89 784980
Email: paul.goettl@etmservices.de **Web site:** http://www.scania.at
Freq: Quarterly; **Cover Price:** Free; **Circ:** 14,000
Editor: Paul Göttl
Profile: Company publication published by Scania Österreich.
Language(s): German

SCANIA BEWEGT 763999G49C-64
Editorial: Handwerkstr. 15, 70565 STUTTGART
Tel: 711 7849880 **Fax:** 711 784980
Email: paul.goettl@etmservices.de **Web site:** http://www.etm-verlag.de
Freq: Quarterly; **Cover Price:** Free; **Circ:** 19,600
Editor: Paul Göttl
Profile: Company publication published by Vogel MultiComServices.
Language(s): German
ADVERTISING RATES:
Full Page Colour .... EUR 3900
Mechanical Data: Type Area: 265 x 198 mm

SCHACH MAGAZIN 64 741145G79F-2280
Editorial: Nienstedt 16, 27211 BASSUM
Email: redaktion@schach-magazin.de **Web site:** http://www.schach-magazin.de
Freq: Monthly; Free to qualifying individuals
Annual Sub.: EUR 52,80; **Circ:** 4,895
Editor: Otto Borik; **Advertising Manager:** Karin Wachendorf
Profile: Magazine about chess. Contains articles, interviews and advice.
Language(s): German
Readership: Aimed at chess players of all levels.
ADVERTISING RATES:
Full Page Mono .... EUR 800
Full Page Colour .... EUR 800
Mechanical Data: Type Area: 260 x 185 mm, No. of Columns (Display): 4, Col Widths (Display): 45 mm
CONSUMER: HOBBIES & DIY: Games & Puzzles

SCHÄDELSPALTER 741149G80-10060
Editorial: Hallerstr. 27, 30161 HANNOVER
Tel: 511 3402445 **Fax:** 511 3402464
Email: redaktion@schaedelspalter.de **Web site:** http://www.schaedelspalter.de
Freq: Monthly; **Annual Sub.:** EUR 20,00; **Circ:** 7,052
Editor: André Buron; **Advertising Manager:** Reinhard Mahl
Profile: Magazine providing information on tourism and events in Hanover.
Language(s): German
ADVERTISING RATES:
Full Page Mono .... EUR 1535
Full Page Colour .... EUR 2630
Mechanical Data: Type Area: 260 x 190 mm, No. of Columns (Display): 4, Col Widths (Display): 44 mm
Copy instructions: *Copy Date:* 15 days prior to publication
Supplement(s): Hannover kauft ein
CONSUMER: RURAL & REGIONAL INTEREST

SCHAFZUCHT 725073G21D-1
Editorial: Mühlenweg 1, 53567 BUCHHOLZ
Tel: 2683 945463 **Fax:** 2683 945464
Email: gdierichs@ulmer.de **Web site:** http://www.schafzucht-online.de
Freq: 24 issues yearly; **Annual Sub.:** EUR 94,80; **Circ:** 7,031
Editor: Günther Dierichs; **Advertising Manager:** Irmtraud Kirchenbaur
Profile: The Schafzucht delivers tips and information about "life with sheep and goats" which is essential for the experienced sheep keepers as well as hobby shepherds and herd shepherds. In addition, all issues relating to goat breeding and keeping are dealt with in detail six times a year in the goat focus issues. With a circulation of over 8,100 copies, the Schafzucht offers a large cross-regional range. The Schafzucht is the organ of the Vereinigung Deutscher Landesschafzuchtverbände and the Bundesverband Deutscher Ziegenzüchter as well as of the affiliated state associations. It provides extensive knowledge in all areas of sheep and goat keeping. Schafzucht is published twice a month: once as an extensive, colour magazine and once as Schafzucht kompakt with up-to-date information, dates and market information. The focus is on: Practical, problem-solving information about life with sheep and goats. Alongside this, Schafzucht reports about current agricultural procedures and about exhibitions, events and association activities. Regular themes are Breeding, Keeping, Feeding and animal health, Information about sheepdogs, Preparing, processing and marketing meat, milk, wool and skin, Market information, Agricultural policies, Landscape conservation.
Language(s): German
ADVERTISING RATES:
Full Page Mono .... EUR 2754
Full Page Colour .... EUR 3894
Mechanical Data: Type Area: 270 x 186 mm, No. of Columns (Display): 4, Col Widths (Display): 45 mm
Copy instructions: *Copy Date:* 14 days prior to publication
Official Journal of: Organ d. Vereinigung Dt. Landesschafzuchtverbände u. d. Bundesverb. Dt. Ziegenzüchter
BUSINESS: AGRICULTURE & FARMING: Livestock

SCHAUFENSTER 741176G72-11580
Editorial: Zeppelinstr. 10, 37603 HOLZMINDEN
Tel: 5531 93040 **Fax:** 5531 930442
Email: redaktion@tah.de **Web site:** http://www.tah.de
Freq: Weekly; **Cover Price:** Free; **Circ:** 52,000
Editor: Gudrun Reinking; **Advertising Manager:** Thomas Kriegel
Profile: Advertising journal (house-to-house) concentrating on local stories.
Language(s): German
ADVERTISING RATES:
Full Page Mono .... EUR 2271
Full Page Colour .... EUR 3225
Mechanical Data: Type Area: 430 x 277 mm, No. of Columns (Display): 6, Col Widths (Display): 45 mm
Copy instructions: *Copy Date:* 5 days prior to publication
LOCAL NEWSPAPERS

SCHAUMBURGER NACHRICHTEN 742086G67B-1354
Editorial: Am Markt 12, 31655 STADTHAGEN
Tel: 5721 809230 **Fax:** 5721 2007
Email: sn@madsack.de **Web site:** http://www.sn-online.de
Freq: 312 issues yearly; **Circ:** 17,060
Editor: Uwe Graells; **Advertising Manager:** Arne Frank
Profile: Daily newspaper with regional news and a local sports section. Twitter: http://twitter.com/sn_online This Outlet offers RSS (Really Simple Syndication).
Language(s): German
ADVERTISING RATES:
SCC .... EUR 45,1
Mechanical Data: Type Area: 528 x 370 mm, No. of Columns (Display): 8, Col Widths (Display): 45 mm
Copy instructions: *Copy Date:* 2 days prior to publication
REGIONAL DAILY & SUNDAY NEWSPAPERS: Regional Daily Newspapers

---

SCHAUMBURGER ZEITUNG 741197G67B-1292
Editorial: Klosterstr. 32, 31737 RINTELN
Tel: 5751 40000 **Fax:** 5751 4000522
Email: sz-redaktion@schaumburger-zeitung.de **Web site:** http://www.schaumburger-zeitung.de
Freq: 312 issues yearly; **Circ:** 7,925
Editor: Stefan Reineking; **Advertising Manager:** Dirk Dreier
Profile: Daily newspaper with regional news and a local sports section. This Outlet offers RSS (Really Simple Syndication).
Language(s): German
ADVERTISING RATES:
SCC .... EUR 21,9
Mechanical Data: Type Area: 430 x 281 mm, No. of Columns (Display): 6, Col Widths (Display): 45 mm
Copy instructions: *Copy Date:* 1 day prior to publication
Supplement(s): rtv
REGIONAL DAILY & SUNDAY NEWSPAPERS: Regional Daily Newspapers

---

SCHAUMBURG-LIPPISCHE LANDES-ZEITUNG 741198G67B-1290
Editorial: Klosterstr. 32, 31737 RINTELN
Tel: 5751 40000 **Fax:** 5751 4000522
Email: lz-redaktion@landes-zeitung.de **Web site:** http://www.landes-zeitung.de
Freq: 312 issues yearly; **Circ:** 3,541
Advertising Manager: Dirk Dreier
Profile: Daily newspaper with regional news and a local sports section.
Language(s): German
ADVERTISING RATES:
SCC .... EUR 15,1
Mechanical Data: Type Area: 430 x 281 mm, No. of Columns (Display): 6, Col Widths (Display): 45 mm
Copy instructions: *Copy Date:* 1 day prior to publication
Supplement(s): rtv
REGIONAL DAILY & SUNDAY NEWSPAPERS: Regional Daily Newspapers

---

SCHENEFELDER TAGEBLATT 741212G67B-1296
Editorial: Damm 9, 25421 PINNEBERG
Tel: 4101 5356101 **Fax:** 4101 5356106
Email: redaktion@a-beig.de **Web site:** http://www.schenefelder-tageblatt.de
Freq: 312 issues yearly; **Circ:** 12,796
Advertising Manager: Karsten Raasch
Profile: Daily newspaper with regional news and a local sports section. This Outlet offers RSS (Really Simple Syndication).
Language(s): German
ADVERTISING RATES:
SCC .... EUR 42,90
Mechanical Data: Type Area: 430 x 278 mm, No. of Columns (Display): 6, Col Widths (Display): 45 mm
Copy instructions: *Copy Date:* 1 day prior to publication
Supplement(s): nordisch gesund
REGIONAL DAILY & SUNDAY NEWSPAPERS: Regional Daily Newspapers

---

SCHICKSALS-ERLEBNISSE 735252G74A-2160
Editorial: Sieker Landstr. 126/II, 22143 HAMBURG
Tel: 40 6739780 **Fax:** 40 67397821
Email: wmb@cpvkg.de **Web site:** http://www.conpart-verlag.de
Freq: 6 issues yearly; **Cover Price:** EUR 1,90; **Circ:** 110,000
Editor: Wolfgang M. Biehler
Profile: Magazine for women.
Language(s): German
ADVERTISING RATES:
Full Page Mono .... EUR 3000
Full Page Colour .... EUR 3000
Mechanical Data: Type Area: 280 x 210 mm, No. of Columns (Display): 4, Col Widths (Display): 52 mm

SCHIEDSVZ ZEITSCHRIFT FÜR SCHIEDSVERFAHREN

768820G1A-3478
Editorial: Bethmannstr. 50, 60311 FRANKFURT
Tel: 69 29908658 **Fax:** 69 29908108
Email: info@schiedsvz.de **Web site:** http://www.schiedsvz.de
Freq: 6 issues yearly; **Annual Sub.:** EUR 325,90; **Circ:** 1,600
Editor: Jörg Risse; **Advertising Manager:** Fritz Lebherz
Profile: Magazine containing essays, recent decisions and judgements.
Language(s): German
ADVERTISING RATES:
Full Page Mono .... EUR 1460
Full Page Colour .... EUR 2960
Mechanical Data: Type Area: 260 x 186 mm, No. of Columns (Display): 4, Col Widths (Display): 43 mm
BUSINESS: FINANCE & ECONOMICS

SCHIFF & HAFEN

741230G45A-680
Editorial: Nordkanalstr. 36, 20097 HAMBURG
Tel: 40 23714143 **Fax:** 40 23714154
Email: silke.sadowski@dvvmedia.com **Web site:** http://www.schiffundhafen.de
Freq: Monthly; Free to qualifying individuals
Annual Sub.: EUR 188,00; **Circ:** 6,779
Editor: Silke Sadowski; **Advertising Manager:** Florian Visser
Profile: Journal for marine, construction, marine engineering, implementation, financing, theory, ship suppliers, port construction, offshore, container traffic, Maritime Engineering.
Language(s): English; German
ADVERTISING RATES:
Full Page Mono .... EUR 2717
Full Page Colour .... EUR 4180
Mechanical Data: Type Area: 251 x 183 mm, No. of Columns (Display): 3, Col Widths (Display): 58 mm
Copy instructions: *Copy Date:* 29 days prior to publication
Official Journal of: Organ d. Verb. Dt. Kapitäne u. Schiffsoffiziere e.V., d. Ges. f. Maritime Technik e.V., d. Schiffbautechn. Ges. e.V. u. d. Center of Maritime Technologies e.V.
BUSINESS: MARINE & SHIPPING

SCHIFFAHRT HAFEN BAHN UND TECHNIK

741222G45A-720
Editorial: Siebengebirgsstr. 14, 53757 ST. AUGUSTIN **Tel:** 2241 1482517 **Fax:** 2241 1482518
Email: redaktion@schiffahrtundtechnik.de **Web site:** http://www.schifffahrtundtechnik.de
Freq: 8 issues yearly; **Annual Sub.:** EUR 53,50; **Circ:** 6,825
Editor: Hans-Wilhelm Dünner; **Advertising Manager:** Sylvia Guddat
Profile: Magazine about sailing and maritime matters.
Language(s): German
ADVERTISING RATES:
Full Page Mono .... EUR 2150
Full Page Colour .... EUR 2950
Mechanical Data: Type Area: 270 x 186 mm, No. of Columns (Display): 3, Col Widths (Display): 58 mm
Copy instructions: *Copy Date:* 14 days prior to publication
Official Journal of: Organ d. German Lloyd f. d. Binnenschiffahrt in Europa
BUSINESS: MARINE & SHIPPING

SCHIFFERSTADTER TAGBLATT

741224G67B-12980
Editorial: Bahnhofstr. 70, 67105 SCHIFFERSTADT
Tel: 6235 926916 **Fax:** 6235 926933
Email: redaktion@schifferstadter-tagblatt.de **Web site:** http://www.schifferstadter-tagblatt.de
Freq: 312 issues yearly; **Circ:** 2,082
Editor: Susanne Geier; **Advertising Manager:** Susanne Geier
Profile: Daily newspaper with regional news and a local sports section.
Language(s): German
ADVERTISING RATES:
SCC .... EUR 14,70
Mechanical Data: Type Area: 430 x 280 mm, No. of Columns (Display): 6, Col Widths (Display): 45 mm
Copy instructions: *Copy Date:* 1 day prior to publication
REGIONAL DAILY & SUNDAY NEWSPAPERS: Regional Daily Newspapers

SCHIFFS-INGENIEUR JOURNAL

741226G49A-1600
Editorial: Gurlittstr. 32, 20099 HAMBURG
Tel: 40 2803883 **Fax:** 40 2803565
Email: vsih-vdsi@t-online.de **Web site:** http://www.schiffsingenieure.de
Freq: 6 issues yearly; **Cover Price:** EUR 4,50
Free to qualifying individuals ; **Circ:** 1,500
Editor: Joachim Ortlepp
Profile: Magazine of the Association of Ship Engineers in Hamburg.
Language(s): German
ADVERTISING RATES:
Full Page Mono .... EUR 453
Full Page Colour .... EUR 761
Mechanical Data: Type Area: 250 x 170 mm, No. of Columns (Display): 3, Col Widths (Display): 54 mm
Copy instructions: *Copy Date:* 30 days prior to publication

SCHIFFSMODELL

741227G79B-1460
Editorial: Klosterring 1, 78050 VILLINGEN-SCHWENNINGEN **Tel:** 7721 89870 **Fax:** 7721 898750
Email: welz@neckar-verlag.de **Web site:** http://www.neckar-verlag.de
Freq: Monthly; **Annual Sub.:** EUR 53,80; **Circ:** 16,500
Editor: Hans-Jörg Welz; **Advertising Manager:** Klaus Pechmann
Profile: Magazine containing information about how to make and sail model boats.
Language(s): German
Readership: Aimed at people interested in building model ships.
ADVERTISING RATES:
Full Page Mono .... EUR 877
Full Page Colour .... EUR 1228
Mechanical Data: Type Area: 265 x 185 mm, No. of Columns (Display): 4, Col Widths (Display): 42 mm
CONSUMER: HOBBIES & DIY: Models & Modelling

SCHIFFSREISEN INTERN.

741228G50-880
Editorial: Dorotheenstr. 64, 22301 HAMBURG
Tel: 40 46856587 **Fax:** 40 46863297
Email: gerd.achilles@schiffsreisenportal.de **Web site:** http://www.schiffsreisenportal.de
Freq: 24 issues yearly; **Annual Sub.:** EUR 160,50; **Circ:** 3,620
Editor: Gerd Achilles; **Advertising Manager:** Irina Oldendorf
Profile: Magazine with news about shipping, cruises and ferries. Facebook: http://www.facebook.com/schiffsreisenintern Twitter: http://twitter.com/#!/kreuzfahrt2011 This Outlet offers RSS (Really Simple Syndication).
Language(s): German
ADVERTISING RATES:
Full Page Mono .... EUR 780
Full Page Colour .... EUR 780
Mechanical Data: Type Area: 265 x 182 mm
Copy instructions: *Copy Date:* 7 days prior to publication

SCHLANGENBRUT

741244G74A-2740
Editorial: Postfach 200922, 53139 BONN
Tel: 228 1802094 **Fax:** 228 1802092
Email: redaktion@schlangenbrut.de **Web site:** http://www.schlangenbrut.de
Freq: Quarterly; **Annual Sub.:** EUR 20,00; **Circ:** 3,000
Editor: Britta Hoffmann
Profile: Magazine aimed at feminists and women interested in religion.
Language(s): German
ADVERTISING RATES:
Full Page Mono .... EUR 735
Mechanical Data: Type Area: 251 x 180 mm, No. of Columns (Display): 3, Col Widths (Display): 57 mm
Copy instructions: *Copy Date:* 42 days prior to publication

SCHLÄNGER ZEITUNG

1638362G67B-16720
Editorial: Sudbrackstr. 14, 33611 BIELEFELD
Tel: 521 5850 **Fax:** 521 585489
Email: wb@westfalen-blatt.de **Web site:** http://www.westfalen-blatt.de
Freq: 260 issues yearly; **Annual Sub.:** EUR 23,10; **Circ:** 45,244
Advertising Manager: Gabriele Förster
Profile: Regional daily newspaper covering politics, economics, sport, travel and technology.
Language(s): German
Mechanical Data: Type Area: 490 x 320 mm, No. of Columns (Display): 7, Col Widths (Display): 44 mm
Copy instructions: *Copy Date:* 1 day prior to publication
Supplement(s): Mein Garten; www.wb-immo.net
REGIONAL DAILY & SUNDAY NEWSPAPERS: Regional Daily Newspapers

SCHLAUER STROMER

1703739G74M-783
Editorial: Heinrich-Böcking-Str. 10, 66121 SAARBRÜCKEN **Tel:** 681 90690 **Fax:** 681 90691575
Email: service@energis.de **Web site:** http://www.energis.de
Freq: Quarterly; **Cover Price:** Free; **Circ:** 420,000
Editor: Uwe Bongers
Profile: Customer magazine from the municipal utility company energis GmbH.
Language(s): German

SCHLECKER

741249G94H-10740
Editorial: Talstr. 21, 89584 EHINGEN
Tel: 7391 70770 **Fax:** 7391 707720
Email: info@sachs-marketing.de **Web site:** http://www.sachs-marketing.de
Freq: Monthly; **Cover Price:** Free; **Circ:** 1,485,667
Editor: Nadine Sachs
Profile: Company publication by the Schlecker drugstore company.
Language(s): German
ADVERTISING RATES:
Full Page Mono .... EUR 21500
Full Page Colour .... EUR 35000
Mechanical Data: Type Area: 236 x 180 mm, No. of Columns (Display): 4, Col Widths (Display): 42 mm
Copy instructions: *Copy Date:* 30 days prior to publication
CONSUMER: OTHER CLASSIFICATIONS: Customer Magazines

SCHLEI BOTE

741251G67B-13000
Editorial: Nikolaistr. 7, 24937 FLENSBURG
Tel: 461 8080 **Fax:** 461 8081058
Email: redaktion@shz.de **Web site:** http://www.shz.de
Freq: 312 issues yearly; **Circ:** 4,362
Advertising Manager: Ingeborg Schwarz
Profile: Founded in 1864, "Schlei Bote" in Kappeln is mainly in the district Schleswig-Flensburg along the loop to Süderbrarup and spread as far as Gelting. Facebook: http://www.facebook.com/shzonline Twitter: http://twitter.com/shz_de This Outlet offers RSS (Really Simple Syndication).
Language(s): German
ADVERTISING RATES:
SCC .... EUR 33,20
Mechanical Data: Type Area: 480 x 325 mm, No. of Columns (Display): 7, Col Widths (Display): 45 mm
Copy instructions: *Copy Date:* 1 day prior to publication
Supplement(s): nordisch gesund; tv magazin
REGIONAL DAILY & SUNDAY NEWSPAPERS: Regional Daily Newspapers

SCHLEIDENER WOCHENSPIEGEL

741252G72-11656
Editorial: Hermann-Kattwinkel-Str. 2, 53937 SCHLEIDEN **Tel:** 2444 959620 **Fax:** 2444 959629
Email: red-schleiden@weiss-verlag.de **Web site:** http://www.wochenspiegellive.de
Freq: Weekly; **Cover Price:** Free; **Circ:** 35,942
Editor: Alexander Lenders
Profile: Advertising journal (house-to-house) concentrating on local stories.
Language(s): German
ADVERTISING RATES:
Full Page Mono .... EUR 3071
Full Page Colour .... EUR 4305
Mechanical Data: Type Area: 430 x 290 mm, No. of Columns (Display): 7, Col Widths (Display): 38 mm
Copy instructions: *Copy Date:* 2 days prior to publication
LOCAL NEWSPAPERS

SCHLEIFEN + POLIEREN

741253G19E-1560
Editorial: Neustr. 163, 42553 VELBERT
Tel: 2053 981251 **Fax:** 2053 981256
Email: redaktion@fachverlag-moeller.de **Web site:** http://www.fachverlag-moeller.de
Freq: 6 issues yearly; **Annual Sub.:** EUR 30,00; **Circ:** 2,851
Editor: Erik Möller; **Advertising Manager:** Erik Möller
Profile: Magazine about grinding and burnishing techniques.
Language(s): German
ADVERTISING RATES:
Full Page Mono .... EUR 640
Full Page Colour .... EUR 1120
Mechanical Data: Type Area: 260 x 180 mm, No. of Columns (Display): 4, Col Widths (Display): 44 mm
Copy instructions: *Copy Date:* 14 days prior to publication

SCHLESWIGER NACHRICHTEN

741265G67B-13080
Editorial: Nikolaistr. 7, 24937 FLENSBURG
Tel: 461 8080 **Fax:** 461 8081058
Email: redaktion@shz.de **Web site:** http://www.shz.de
Freq: 312 issues yearly; **Circ:** 15,918
Advertising Manager: Ingeborg Schwarz
Profile: The "Schleswiger Nachrichten" was first published in 1812 under the title "Königlich privilegiertes Intelligenzblatt" - that is the newspaper of the oldest of the sh:z publications. The newspaper is read mainly in the town of Schleswig, and in parts of the district of Schleswig-Flensburg to Süderbrarup and Kropp. Facebook: http://www.facebook.com/shzonline Twitter: http://twitter.com/shz_de This Outlet offers RSS (Really Simple Syndication).
Language(s): German
ADVERTISING RATES:
SCC .... EUR 64,00
Mechanical Data: Type Area: 480 x 325 mm, No. of Columns (Display): 7, Col Widths (Display): 45 mm
Copy instructions: *Copy Date:* 1 day prior to publication
Supplement(s): nordisch gesund; Schleswig-Holstein Journal; tv magazin
REGIONAL DAILY & SUNDAY NEWSPAPERS: Regional Daily Newspapers

SCHLESWIG-HOLSTEINISCHE LANDESZEITUNG

741270G67B-13060
Editorial: Nikolaistr. 7, 24937 FLENSBURG
Tel: 461 8080 **Fax:** 461 8081058
Email: redaktion@shz.de **Web site:** http://www.shz.de
Freq: 312 issues yearly; **Circ:** 25,227
Advertising Manager: Ingeborg Schwarz
Profile: The "Schleswig-Holsteinische Landeszeitung" there since 1807. The second-oldest daily newspaper it is of the sh:z and belongs to the publisher since 1986. The local newspaper is the second largest after the title "Flensburger Tageblatt". Facebook: http://www.facebook.com/shzonline Twitter: http://twitter.com/shz_de This Outlet offers RSS (Really Simple Syndication).
Language(s): German
ADVERTISING RATES:
SCC .... EUR 73,60
Mechanical Data: Type Area: 480 x 325 mm, No. of Columns (Display): 7, Col Widths (Display): 45 mm
Copy instructions: *Copy Date:* 1 day prior to publication
Supplement(s): nordisch gesund; Schleswig-Holstein Journal; tv magazin
REGIONAL DAILY & SUNDAY NEWSPAPERS: Regional Daily Newspapers

SCHLESWIG-HOLSTEINISCHES ÄRZTEBLATT

758426G56A-11101
Editorial: Bismarckallee 8, 23795 BAD SEGEBERG
Tel: 4551 803119 **Fax:** 4551 803181
Email: aerzteblatt@aeksh.org **Web site:** http://www.aeksh.de
Freq: Monthly; **Annual Sub.:** EUR 46,00; **Circ:** 16,000
Editor: Karl-Werner Ratschko; **Advertising Manager:** Samira Rummler
Profile: Magazine for doctors in the Schleswig-Holstein region.
Language(s): German
ADVERTISING RATES:
Full Page Mono .... EUR 1880
Full Page Colour .... EUR 3572
Mechanical Data: Type Area: 200 x 140 mm, No. of Columns (Display): 3, Col Widths (Display): 45 mm
Copy instructions: *Copy Date:* 25 days prior to publication

SCHLITZER BOTE

741280G67B-13100
Editorial: Frankfurter Str. 8, 36043 FULDA
Tel: 661 2800 **Fax:** 661 280125
Email: verlag@parzeller.de **Web site:** http://www.parzeller.de
Freq: 312 issues yearly; **Circ:** 2,015
Profile: Daily newspaper with regional news and a local sports section.
Language(s): German
ADVERTISING RATES:
SCC .... EUR 24,40
Mechanical Data: Type Area: 420 x 280 mm, No. of Columns (Display): 6, Col Widths (Display): 45 mm
Copy instructions: *Copy Date:* 1 day prior to publication
REGIONAL DAILY & SUNDAY NEWSPAPERS: Regional Daily Newspapers

SCHLOSS + BESCHLAG MARKT

741288G54C-4
Editorial: Stresemannstr. 20, 47051 DUISBURG
Tel: 203 3052722 **Fax:** 203 30527820
Email: t.schmidt@wohlfarth.de **Web site:** http://www.schloss-und-beschlagmarkt.de
Freq: Monthly; **Annual Sub.:** EUR 56,50; **Circ:** 2,281
Editor: Thorsten Schmidt; **Advertising Manager:** Stefan Hillebrand
Profile: „schloss + beschlag markt" is the current industry trade magazine for the construction fittings and security industry. Monthly informed „schloss + beschlag markt" the decision makers first hand with the latest industry information - including the Finish hardware retailers, safe operations and key services, VdS-installer, the construction components retail trade and the industry. Similarly, using CID-counseling centers and service providers such as property and casualty insurers" „schloss + beschlag markt" as an important source of information for their work. This gives the editors reliably conveys the users the most important news from all sectors of business and industry, up to date with background information and reports quickly and directly from the major industry trade shows.
Language(s): German
Readership: Aimed at decision makers in the fittings and security market.
ADVERTISING RATES:
Full Page Mono .... EUR 1890
Full Page Colour .... EUR 3150
Mechanical Data: Type Area: 264 x 178 mm, No. of Columns (Display): 3, Col Widths (Display): 56 mm
Copy instructions: *Copy Date:* 21 days prior to publication
BUSINESS: SAFETY & SECURITY: Security

SCHLÖSSER BADEN-WÜRTTEMBERG

741281G80-10160
Editorial: Breitscheidstr. 69, 70176 STUTTGART
Tel: 711 6660115 **Fax:** 711 6660119
Email: b.erbsen-haim@staatsanzeiger.de **Web site:** http://www.schloesser-magazin.de
Freq: Quarterly; **Annual Sub.:** EUR 20,00; **Circ:** 14,924
Editor: Barbara Erbsen-Haim; **Advertising Manager:** Thomas Krieger
Profile: Magazine describing castles, abbeys and gardens in Baden-Württemberg.
Language(s): German
ADVERTISING RATES:
Full Page Mono .... EUR 1650
Full Page Colour .... EUR 2170
Mechanical Data: Type Area: 260 x 200 mm, No. of Columns (Display): 4, Col Widths (Display): 46 mm
Copy instructions: *Copy Date:* 40 days prior to publication
Supplement to: Staatsanzeiger
Supplement(s): Denkmalstiftung Baden-Württemberg
CONSUMER: RURAL & REGIONAL INTEREST

SCHLUMMER ATLAS

741297G89A-3920
Editorial: Schleefstr. 1, 44287 DORTMUND
Tel: 231 444770 **Fax:** 231 4447777
Email: hauptredaktion@busche.de **Web site:** http://www.schlummer-atlas.de

Freq: Annual; **Cover Price:** EUR 29,95; **Circ:** 42,318
Advertising Manager: Jörg Leu
Profile: Quality and high standard of the hotel are considered immutable requirement for entry into the Schlummer Atlas. The work offers the best accommodation address for city breaks, holidays and business trips. Current data and photos of selected hotels make travel planning easy. The guest receives reliable information on hospitality, service and ambience of the destination hotels. Valuation basis is the recognized sleep-star system, which uses an experienced, independent editorial team consistently. The Schlummer Atlas presents some 5,500 hotels in Germany, Belgium, Alsace, Luxembourg, Netherlands, Austria, South Tyrol and Switzerland. It contains detailed and extensive illustrated information on all hotels recherchirt. The data are objective and user-friendly form.
Language(s): German
ADVERTISING RATES:
Full Page Mono .... EUR 6100
Full Page Colour .... EUR 6100
Mechanical Data: Type Area: 205 x 142 mm

DER SCHMERZ
741304G56A-9100
Editorial: Tiergartenstr. 17, 69121 HEIDELBERG
Tel: 6221 4878618 **Fax:** 6221 48768618
Email: werner.roessling@springer.com **Web site:** http://www.springerlink.com
Freq: 6 issues yearly; **Annual Sub.:** EUR 267,00; **Circ:** 4,800
Advertising Manager: Odette Thomßen
Profile: „Der Schmerz" is intended for physicians of all specialties as well as psychologists who are engaged in the treatment of patients in pain or in pain research. The aim of the journal is to improve the treatment of pain patients in the long term. In original research reports on new findings in pain research, survey methods and contributions provide the physician with practical guidance on pain and its treatment. Posts under the rubric "education - certified education" present significant results of scientific research and medical experience make for daily practice.
Language(s): German
Readership: Aimed at physicians of all medical fields.
ADVERTISING RATES:
Full Page Mono .... EUR 2180
Full Page Colour .... EUR 3370
Mechanical Data: Type Area: 240 x 174 mm
Copy instructions: *Copy Date:* 21 days prior to publication
Official Journal of: Organ d. Dt. Ges. z. Studium d. Schmerzes, d. Schweizer. Ges. z. Studium d. Schmerzes, d. Österr. Schmerzges. u. d. Dt. Interdisziplinären Vereinigung f. Schmerztherapie
BUSINESS: HEALTH & MEDICAL

SCHMERZ & AKUPUNKTUR
1633980G56A-11266
Editorial: Osserstr. 40, 81679 MÜNCHEN
Tel: 89 8145252 **Fax:** 89 82000929
Email: kontakt@akupunktur.de **Web site:** http://www.akupunktur-arzt.de
Freq: Quarterly; **Annual Sub.:** EUR 96,00; **Circ:** 12,000
Editor: Gerhard Opitz; **Advertising Manager:** Barbara Kanters
Profile: The Journal Schmerz & Akupunktur is for anyone interested in school medicine in order to show you in treatment-resistant cases as an alternative the possibility of a scientifically based acupuncture and auriculomedicine. A major focus is the treatment of pain. Organ of Deutsche Akademie für Akupunktur und Aurikulomedizin e.V., Europäische Gesellschaft für biologische Lasertherapie und Akupunktur e.V., Österreichische Gesellschaft für kontrollierte Akupunktur, Schweizerische Ärztegesellschaft für Aurikulomedizin und Akupunktur, Nederlands-Belgische Stichting voor Aurikulomedicinae, Europäische Akademie für Akupunktur, affiliated members in England, USA, Canada, France, Spain, Italy and other 14 countries.
Language(s): English; German
ADVERTISING RATES:
Full Page Mono .... EUR 1220
Full Page Colour .... EUR 2300
Mechanical Data: Type Area: 240 x 170 mm, No. of Columns (Display): 2, Col Widths (Display): 80 mm
Copy instructions: *Copy Date:* 21 days prior to publication
Official Journal of: Organ d. Österr. Ges. f. Kontrollierte Akupunktur, d. Schweizer Ärzteges. f. Aurikulomedizin u. Akupunktur, d. Nederlands-Belg. Stichting voor Auriculomedicinae u. d. Europ. Akademie f. Akupunktur u. deren affilierten Mitgliedern

SCHMIEDE JOURNAL
741308G19E-1861
Editorial: Goldene Pforte 1, 58093 HAGEN
Tel: 2331 958828 **Fax:** 2331 958728
Email: bjansen@metalform.de **Web site:** http://www.metalform.de
Freq: Half-yearly; Free to qualifying individuals
Annual Sub.: EUR 26,00; **Circ:** 3,825
Editor: Barbara Jansen
Profile: European journal focusing on metalworking. Provides information about the use of aluminium in industry, the vehicle production and aeronautics sectors, along with articles concerning machinery, new technology and tools.
Language(s): German
Readership: Aimed at technical designers, planning and manufacturing engineers, analysts and specialists in the machine building industry.
ADVERTISING RATES:
Full Page Mono .... EUR 1950
Full Page Colour .... EUR 2925
Mechanical Data: Type Area: 270 x 186 mm, No. of Columns (Display): 3, Col Widths (Display): 59 mm
Copy instructions: *Copy Date:* 30 days prior to publication
BUSINESS: ENGINEERING & MACHINERY: Machinery, Machine Tools & Metalworking

SCHMÖLLNER NACHRICHTEN
741313G67B-13120
Editorial: Alte Str. 3, 04626 LÖBICHAU
Tel: 3447 525911 **Fax:** 3447 525914
Email: redaktion@otz.de **Web site:** http://www.otz.de
Freq: 312 issues yearly; **Circ:** 5,184
Profile: Daily newspaper with regional news and a local sports section.
Language(s): German
ADVERTISING RATES:
SCC .... EUR 86,00
Mechanical Data: Type Area: 480 x 326 mm, No. of Columns (Display): 7, Col Widths (Display): 44 mm
Copy instructions: *Copy Date:* 2 days prior to publication
REGIONAL DAILY & SUNDAY NEWSPAPERS: Regional Daily Newspapers

SCHNÄPPCHENFÜHRER DEUTSCHLAND
1643790G74M-680
Editorial: Metzinger Str. 40, 70794 FILDERSTADT
Tel: 711 7799738 **Fax:** 711 777206
Email: info@schnaeppchenfuehrer.com **Web site:** http://www.schnaeppchenfuehrer.com
Freq: Annual; **Cover Price:** EUR 12,90; **Circ:** 35,000
Editor: Florian Waldmüller; **Advertising Manager:** Florian Waldmüller
Profile: Shopping guide about direct sales in Germany.
Language(s): German
ADVERTISING RATES:
Full Page Mono .... EUR 995
Full Page Colour .... EUR 2400
Mechanical Data: Type Area: 200 x 120 mm

SCHNEVERDINGER ZEITUNG
741324G67B-13140
Editorial: Harburger Str. 63, 29614 SOLTAU
Tel: 5191 808135 **Fax:** 5191 808146
Email: redaktion@boehme-zeitung.de **Web site:** http://www.boehme-zeitung.de
Freq: 312 issues yearly; **Circ:** 11,434
Profile: Daily newspaper with regional news and a local sports section.
Language(s): German
ADVERTISING RATES:
SCC .... EUR 43,60
Mechanical Data: Type Area: 435 x 282 mm, No. of Columns (Display): 6, Col Widths (Display): 45 mm
Copy instructions: *Copy Date:* 1 day prior to publication
Supplement(s): Arena
REGIONAL DAILY & SUNDAY NEWSPAPERS: Regional Daily Newspapers

DER SCHNITT- & STANZWERKZEUGBAU
741326G27-2120
Editorial: Neustr. 163, 42553 VELBERT
Tel: 2053 981252 **Fax:** 2053 981256
Email: redaktion@fachverlag-moeller.de **Web site:** http://www.fachverlag-moeller.de
Freq: 6 issues yearly; **Annual Sub.:** EUR 30,00; **Circ:** 3,000
Editor: Harald Möller; **Advertising Manager:** Harald Möller
Profile: Magazine about tool design and construction for steel sheet forming companies.
Language(s): German
ADVERTISING RATES:
Full Page Mono .... EUR 640
Full Page Colour .... EUR 1120
Mechanical Data: Type Area: 260 x 180 mm, No. of Columns (Display): 4, Col Widths (Display): 44 mm
Copy instructions: *Copy Date:* 14 days prior to publication

SCHNITT-STELLE
2042255G18B-2246
Editorial: Vennhofallee 79, 33689 BIELEFELD
Tel: 5205 20888 **Fax:** 5205 20888
Email: ewald.bittner@t-online.de **Web site:** http://www.akribie.de
Freq: 3 issues yearly; Free to qualifying individuals
Annual Sub.: EUR 20,00; **Circ:** 300
Editor: Ewald Bittner
Profile: Journal of actual aspects of information science.
Language(s): English; German

SCHNÜSS
741328G80-10220
Editorial: Roonstr. 3a, 53175 BONN
Tel: 228 6047615 **Fax:** 228 6047620
Email: redaktion@schnuess.de **Web site:** http://www.schnuess.de
Freq: Monthly; **Cover Price:** Free; **Circ:** 15,000
Editor: Gitta List; **Advertising Manager:** Marcus Thye
Profile: Magazine containing information, news and articles about Bonn.
Language(s): German
ADVERTISING RATES:
Full Page Mono .... EUR 1200
Full Page Colour .... EUR 1700
Mechanical Data: Type Area: 260 x 190 mm, No. of Columns (Display): 4, Col Widths (Display): 44 mm
CONSUMER: RURAL & REGIONAL INTEREST

SCHOLZ FILM FERNSEH ABC
741368G76A-1280
Editorial: Dassauweg 4a, 22145 HAMBURG
Tel: 40 6781704 **Fax:** 40 6782833
Email: info@filmabc.de **Web site:** http://www.filmabc.de
Freq: Annual; **Cover Price:** EUR 45,00
Profile: Directory listing addresses from the film, radio and TV sectors in Germany.
Language(s): German
CONSUMER: MUSIC & PERFORMING ARTS: Cinema

DAS SCHÖNE ALLGÄU
741337G80-10240
Editorial: Porschestr. 2, 87437 KEMPTEN
Tel: 831 5714229 **Fax:** 831 71524
Email: a.kiechle@ava-verlag.de **Web site:** http://www.das-schoene-allgaeu-online.de
Freq: Monthly; **Annual Sub.:** EUR 76,00; **Circ:** 15,000
Editor: Andrea Kiechle; **Advertising Manager:** Marianne Kilger
Profile: Magazine providing articles and news concerning the Allgäu area of Germany. Includes details of tourist attractions, restaurants and hotels.
Language(s): German
Readership: Aimed at tourists, visitors to the area and local residents.
ADVERTISING RATES:
Full Page Mono .... EUR 1569
Full Page Colour .... EUR 1887
Mechanical Data: Type Area: 265 x 185 mm, No. of Columns (Display): 4, Col Widths (Display): 45 mm
Copy instructions: *Copy Date:* 14 days prior to publication
CONSUMER: RURAL & REGIONAL INTEREST

SCHÖNE FREIZEIT!
1825417G74A-3573
Editorial: Sieker Landstr. 126, 22143 HAMBURG
Tel: 40 6739780 **Fax:** 40 67397821
Email: wmb@cpvkg.de **Web site:** http://www.conpart-verlag.de
Freq: Monthly; **Cover Price:** EUR 0,59; **Circ:** 109,009
Editor: Wolfgang M. Biehler
Profile: The journal contains the following headings: Royals & Society | VIPs & Celebrities | Love & Life | House & Home | Healthy & Fit | Fashion & Chic | Rates & Win | Travel & Services | Tips, Tricks & more.
Language(s): German
ADVERTISING RATES:
Full Page Mono .... EUR 5000
Full Page Colour .... EUR 5000
Mechanical Data: Type Area: 278 x 209 mm, No. of Columns (Display): 4

SCHÖNE FREIZEIT! EINFACH BACKEN
1833052G74A-3587
Editorial: Sieker Landstr. 126/II, 22143 HAMBURG
Tel: 40 6739780 **Fax:** 40 67397821
Email: wmb@cpvkg.de **Web site:** http://www.conpart-verlag.de
Freq: 3 issues yearly; **Cover Price:** EUR 1,80; **Circ:** 130,000
Editor: Wolfgang M. Biehler
Profile: Magazine for women.
Language(s): German
ADVERTISING RATES:
Full Page Mono .... EUR 5000
Full Page Colour .... EUR 5000
Mechanical Data: Type Area: 280 x 210 mm, No. of Columns (Display): 4, Col Widths (Display): 52 mm

SCHÖNE WELT
1895141G74A-3662
Editorial: Ruhrtalstr. 67, 45239 ESSEN
Tel: 201 24688444 **Fax:** 201 24688100
Email: b.matten@stegenwaller.de **Web site:** http://www.stegenwaller.de
Freq: Monthly; **Cover Price:** EUR 0,49; **Circ:** 138,839
Editor: Britta Matten; **Advertising Manager:** Oliver Schulte
Profile: SCHÖNE WELT is good entertainment from the world of celebrities, the rich and famous. Whether folk music or pop stars, German or Hollywood actor, Adel world or great, young talent. It offers the perfect blend Boulevard. In addition, the reader may also look forward to puzzles, advice and travel tips, trend information, reports and fate delicious recipes.
Language(s): German
ADVERTISING RATES:
Full Page Mono .... EUR 4500
Full Page Colour .... EUR 4500
Mechanical Data: Type Area: 265 x 189 mm
Copy instructions: *Copy Date:* 29 days prior to publication

SCHÖNE WOCHE
741357G74A-2800
Editorial: Karlsruher Str. 31, 76437 RASTATT
Tel: 7222 13458 **Fax:** 7222 13431
Web site: http://www.vpm.de
Freq: Weekly; **Cover Price:** EUR 0,69; **Circ:** 184,617
Editor: Gitta Kabelitz
Profile: Schöne Woche comes in a fresh, cheerful layout. It combines joy of life with a puzzle pleasure. The young reader is to relax and have fun while reading. The editorial content includes a modern range of issues for young women between 20 and 49 years. Schöne Woche offers exciting travel stories, features, fashion and cosmetics as well as delicious recipes. The celebrity coverage is concerned mainly with young stars from show business. Schöne Woche is characterized by a high service orientation and orientation guide. In addition to classic topics such as domestic service, beauty and health, there are tips for all areas of life. An online rubric and many puzzles with attractive prizes complete the reading pleasure.
Language(s): German
ADVERTISING RATES:
Full Page Mono .... EUR 3321
Full Page Colour .... EUR 3321
Mechanical Data: Type Area: 261 x 196 mm, No. of Columns (Display): 5, Col Widths (Display): 36 mm
CONSUMER: WOMEN'S INTEREST CONSUMER MAGAZINES: Women's Interest

SCHÖNE ZEITEN
1660544G89A-11893
Editorial: Braunser Weg 12, 34454 BAD AROLSEN
Tel: 5691 878207 **Fax:** 5691 878407
Web site: http://www.ramada.de
Freq: 3 issues yearly; **Cover Price:** Free; **Circ:** 50,000
Editor: Geraldine Lübeck
Profile: The Ramada-travel magazine for regular customers, trade shows, travel agencies.
Language(s): German

SCHÖNE ZEITEN
1660544G89A-12263
Editorial: Braunser Weg 12, 34454 BAD AROLSEN
Tel: 5691 878207 **Fax:** 5691 878407
Web site: http://www.ramada.de
Freq: 3 issues yearly; **Cover Price:** Free; **Circ:** 50,000
Editor: Geraldine Lübeck
Profile: The Ramada-travel magazine for regular customers, trade shows, travel agencies.
Language(s): German

SCHÖNEBECKER VOLKSSTIMME
741340G67B-13160
Editorial: Bahnhofstr. 17, 39104 MAGDEBURG
Tel: 391 59990 **Fax:** 391 5999210
Email: chefredaktion@volksstimme.de **Web site:** http://www.volksstimme.de
Freq: 312 issues yearly; **Circ:** 12,091
Advertising Manager: Rainer Pfeil
Profile: As the largest daily newspaper in northern Saxony-Anhalt, the Volksstimme reaches 536,000 readers a day" (MA 2010). From Monday to Saturday a team of highly qualified editors put together the latest information and news from the region and around the world. Thanks the 18 local editions is the Volksstimme always close to the action. Twitter: http://twitter.com/volksstimme This Outlet offers RSS (Really Simple Syndication).
Language(s): German
ADVERTISING RATES:
SCC .... EUR 50,80
Mechanical Data: Type Area: 480 x 327 mm, No. of Columns (Display): 7, Col Widths (Display): 45 mm
Copy instructions: *Copy Date:* 2 days prior to publication
Supplement(s): Anstoss in Schönebeck; bauRatgeber; Biber; Leser-Reisen; prisma; Standort Landkreis Schönebeck
REGIONAL DAILY & SUNDAY NEWSPAPERS: Regional Daily Newspapers

SCHÖNER BAYERISCHER WALD
741347G89A-12114
Editorial: Bahnhofstr. 22, 94481 GRAFENAU
Tel: 8552 625060 **Fax:** 8552 920529
Email: redaktion@nationalparkzeitung.de **Web site:** http://www.schöner-bayerischer-wald.de
Freq: 6 issues yearly; **Annual Sub.:** EUR 26,00; **Circ:** 10,000
Editor: Eva Pongratz
Profile: Magazine about culture, leisure and entertainment in the Bayerischer Wald region.
Language(s): German
ADVERTISING RATES:
Full Page Mono .... EUR 1170
Full Page Colour .... EUR 1170
Mechanical Data: Type Area: 260 x 185 mm, No. of Columns (Display): 4, Col Widths (Display): 45 mm
Copy instructions: *Copy Date:* 21 days prior to publication

SCHÖNER FÜHLEN
1657739G74A-3427
Editorial: Taimerhofstr. 22, 81927 MÜNCHEN
Tel: 89 52302634 **Fax:** 89 52302635
Email: herschko@aol.com **Web site:** http://www.schoener-fuehlen.de
Freq: Quarterly; **Cover Price:** Free; **Circ:** 269,550
Editor: Philipp Herschkowitz
Profile: Company publication.
Language(s): German
ADVERTISING RATES:
Full Page Mono .... EUR 8800
Full Page Colour .... EUR 8800

Mechanical Data: Type Area: 232 x 180 mm, No. of Columns (Display): 4, Col Widths (Display): 45 mm
CONSUMER: WOMEN'S INTEREST CONSUMER MAGAZINES: Women's Interest

SCHÖNER WOHNEN 741351G74C-2980
Editorial: Am Baumwall 11, 20459 HAMBURG
Tel: 40 37032226 **Fax:** 40 37035676
Email: hoellein.dagmar@guj.de **Web site:** http://www.schoener-wohnen.de
Freq: Monthly; **Annual Sub.:** EUR 49,20; **Circ:** 41,184
Editor: Stephan Schäfer; **Advertising Manager:** Nicole Schostak
Profile: SCHÖNER WOHNEN is a synonym for living and class: style icon, realistic, relevant - the dominant medium for an entire industry. Every month SCHÖNER WOHNEN stages in a distinctive journalistic and aesthetic quality the best from the world of living. The Magazine inspires its readers to the themes, design, architecture, lifestyle, garden, travel, and inspires people to realize their personal dreams. In addition, the editors open with their great expertise and credibility the doors to good taste. SCHÖNER WOHNEN offers a unique of topic mix, shows celebrities with style, and gives practical advice, how to individually get and implement trends in the home. Facebook: http://www.facebook.com/schoenerwohnen Twitter: http://twitter.com/StephanSchaefer.
Language(s): German
Readership: Aimed at women interested in home decoration.
ADVERTISING RATES:
Full Page Mono .... EUR 29700
Full Page Colour .... EUR 29700
Mechanical Data: Type Area: 256 x 194 mm, No. of Columns (Display): 3, Col Widths (Display): 62 mm
Supplement(s): blue kompakt.
CONSUMER: WOMEN'S INTEREST CONSUMER MAGAZINES: Home & Family

SCHONGAUER NACHRICHTEN
741370G67B-13180
Editorial: Münzstr. 14, 86956 SCHONGAU
Tel: 8861 920 **Fax:** 8861 92136
Email: sog-nachrichten@merkur-online.de **Web site:** http://www.merkur-online.de
Freq: 312 issues yearly; **Circ:** 8,930
Advertising Manager: Hans-Georg Bechthold
Profile: Daily newspaper with regional news and a local sports section. Facebook: http://www.facebook.com/pages/merkur-online.de/190176143327 This Outlet offers RSS (Really Simple Syndication).
Language(s): German
ADVERTISING RATES:
SCC .... EUR 43,60
Mechanical Data: Type Area: 474 x 324 mm, No. of Columns (Display): 7, Col Widths (Display): 45 mm
Copy instructions: *Copy Date:* 1 day prior to publication
REGIONAL DAILY & SUNDAY NEWSPAPERS: Regional Daily Newspapers

DIE SCHÖNSTEN BACKREZEPTE 741361G74P-820
Editorial: Rotweg 8, 76532 BADEN-BADEN
Tel: 7221 3501841 **Fax:** 7221 3501288
Email: liliane.elomari@klambt.de **Web site:** http://www.media.klambt.de
Freq: Annual; **Cover Price:** EUR 1,95; **Circ:** 78,000
Editor: Liliane El Omari; **Advertising Manager:** Martin Fischer
Profile: It says the family throughout the year, when before Christmas cookies beautiful fragrance wafts through the house! Therefore, great biscuits parade is the culmination of this title. However, Christmas cakes and tarts are introduced. Here is a small selection of recipes: I Cookies I cake I Cakes I Punch I macaroons I Stollen I Chocolates I sweet decorations I Gingerbread House I Grandma's Bakery I Gifts from the kitchen I a baked Advent Calendar I fine tea and punch. All in all: a good meal!.
Language(s): German
ADVERTISING RATES:
Full Page Mono .... EUR 5370
Full Page Colour .... EUR 5370
Mechanical Data: Type Area: 250 x 195 mm
Copy instructions: *Copy Date:* 42 days prior to publication

SCHORNDORFER NACHRICHTEN 741378G67B-13200
Editorial: Albrecht-Villinger-Str. 10, 71332 WAIBLINGEN **Tel:** 7151 5660 **Fax:** 7151 566402
Email: info@redaktion.zvw.de **Web site:** http://www.zvw.de
Freq: 312 issues yearly; **Circ:** 16,000
Advertising Manager: Michael Feßler
Profile: Daily newspaper with regional news and a local sports section.
Language(s): German
ADVERTISING RATES:
SCC .... EUR 50,50
Mechanical Data: Type Area: 485 x 324 mm, No. of Columns (Display): 7, Col Widths (Display): 44 mm
Copy instructions: *Copy Date:* 2 days prior to publication
REGIONAL DAILY & SUNDAY NEWSPAPERS: Regional Daily Newspapers

SCHORNSTEINFEGERHANDWERK 741380G4F-10
Editorial: Westerwaldstr. 6, 53757 ST. AUGUSTIN
Tel: 2241 34070 **Fax:** 2241 340710
Email: ziv@schornsteinfeger.de **Web site:** http://www.schornsteinfeger.de
Freq: Monthly; Free to qualifying individuals
Annual Sub.: EUR 52,43; **Circ:** 11,250
Editor: Achim Heckel; **Advertising Manager:** Kathrin Seigner
Profile: Magazine for the chimney-sweeping trade.
Language(s): German
Readership: Aimed at chimney-sweepers.
ADVERTISING RATES:
Full Page Mono .... EUR 1137
Full Page Colour .... EUR 1537
Mechanical Data: Type Area: 232 x 180 mm, No. of Columns (Display): 3, Col Widths (Display): 56 mm
Copy instructions: *Copy Date:* 30 days prior to publication
BUSINESS: ARCHITECTURE & BUILDING: Cleaning & Maintenance

SCHREIBHEFT 741389G84B-2767
Editorial: Nieberdingstr. 18, 45147 ESSEN
Tel: 201 778111 **Fax:** 201 775174
Email: schreibheft@netcologne.de **Web site:** http://www.schreibheft.de
Freq: Half-yearly; **Annual Sub.:** EUR 40,00; **Circ:** 2,000
Editor: Norbert Wehr; **Advertising Manager:** Norbert Wehr
Profile: Magazine focusing on international literature.
Language(s): German
Readership: Aimed at people interested in the arts and culture.
ADVERTISING RATES:
Full Page Mono .... EUR 515
Mechanical Data: Type Area: 300 x 192 mm
Copy instructions: *Copy Date:* 30 days prior to publication
CONSUMER: THE ARTS & LITERARY: Literary

SCHROBENHAUSENER ZEITUNG 741406G67B-13220
Editorial: Stauffenbergstr. 2a, 85051 INGOLSTADT
Tel: 841 96660 **Fax:** 841 9666255
Email: redaktion@donaukurier.de **Web site:** http://www.donaukurier.de
Freq: 312 issues yearly; **Circ:** 7,426
Advertising Manager Hermann Fetsch
Profile: Daily newspaper with regional news and a local sports section. Facebook: http://www.facebook.com/donaukurier.online Twitter: http://twitter.com/donaukurier This Outlet offers RSS (Really Simple Syndication).
Language(s): German
ADVERTISING RATES:
SCC .... EUR 26,70
Mechanical Data: Type Area: 435 x 282 mm, No. of Columns (Display): 6, Col Widths (Display): 45 mm
Copy instructions: *Copy Date:* 1 day prior to publication
REGIONAL DAILY & SUNDAY NEWSPAPERS: Regional Daily Newspapers

SCHROT & KORN 741408G94H-10840
Editorial: Magnolienweg 23, 63741 ASCHAFFENBURG **Tel:** 6021 4489120
Fax: 6021 4489320
Email: redaktion@bioverlag.de **Web site:** http://www.schrotundkorn.de
Freq: Monthly; **Annual Sub.:** EUR 20,00; **Circ:** 725,225
Editor: Barbara Gruber; **Advertising Manager:** Ellen Heil
Profile: Customer magazine available in health-food shops, about healthy eating, organic foods, natural health and ecological matters.
Language(s): German
Readership: Aimed at the general public.
ADVERTISING RATES:
Full Page Mono .... EUR 8900
Full Page Colour .... EUR 12750
Mechanical Data: No. of Columns (Display): 3, Col Widths (Display): 58 mm, Type Area: 251 x 189 mm
Copy instructions: *Copy Date:* 37 days prior to publication
CONSUMER: OTHER CLASSIFICATIONS: Customer Magazines

SCHUHKURIER 741432G29-2
Editorial: Oberkasseler Str. 100, 40545 DÜSSELDORF **Tel:** 211 5770821 **Fax:** 211 5770812
Email: sk.redaktion@sternefeld.de **Web site:** http://www.schuhkurier.de
Freq: Weekly; **Annual Sub.:** EUR 196,00; **Circ:** 8,830
Editor: Petra Salewski; **Advertising Manager:** Sabine Peters
Profile: Magazine about all aspects of the German shoe trade.
Language(s): German
ADVERTISING RATES:
Full Page Mono .... EUR 2498
Full Page Colour .... EUR 4328
Mechanical Data: Type Area: 270 x 179 mm, No. of Columns (Display): 4, Col Widths (Display): 40 mm
Copy instructions: *Copy Date:* 10 days prior to publication
Supplement(s): I love shoes
BUSINESS: FOOTWEAR

SCHUHMARKT 741433G29-3
Editorial: Marktplatz 13, 65183 WIESBADEN
Tel: 611 3609874 **Fax:** 611 3609876
Email: peter.skop@chmielorz.de **Web site:** http://www.schuhmarkt-news.de
Freq: 26 issues yearly; **Annual Sub.:** EUR 197,00; **Circ:** 7,700
Editor: Peter Skop; **Advertising Manager:** Ilona Kirmes
Profile: The SchuhMarkt reports comprehensively, competently and date on all trade-related, economic and fashion themes. In the SchuhMarkt to reach the key decision-makers and an effective advertising platform to communicate with your target group. Take advantage of the high expertise of our editors.
Language(s): German
Readership: Read by members of association.
ADVERTISING RATES:
Full Page Colour .... EUR 4990
Mechanical Data: Type Area: 275 x 200 mm
BUSINESS: FOOTWEAR

SCHULE NRW 720259G80-14020
Editorial: Rudolf-Diesel-Str. 5, 50226 FRECHEN
Tel: 2234 18660 **Fax:** 2234 186690
Email: zeitschriften@ritterbach.de **Web site:** http://www.schul-welt.de
Freq: Monthly; **Annual Sub.:** EUR 56,00; **Circ:** 13,000
Profile: Official gazette for schools from the government of the German federal state of Nordrhein-Westfalen.
Language(s): German
ADVERTISING RATES:
Full Page Mono .... EUR 1315
Full Page Colour .... EUR 1980
Mechanical Data: Type Area: 257 x 176 mm, No. of Columns (Display): 2, Col Widths (Display): 86 mm
Copy instructions: *Copy Date:* 15 days prior to publication
CONSUMER: RURAL & REGIONAL INTEREST

SCHULMAGAZIN 5 BIS 10
741457G62D-2332
Editorial: Rosenheimer Str. 145, 81671 MÜNCHEN
Tel: 89 45051371 **Fax:** 89 45051310
Email: holler@oldenbourg.de **Web site:** http://www.schulmagazin5-10.de
Freq: 11 issues yearly; **Annual Sub.:** EUR 100,40; **Circ:** 4,385
Editor: Stefan Holler; **Advertising Manager:** Christian Schwarzbauer
Profile: Journal about the methodology, didactics and education in secondary education.
Language(s): German
ADVERTISING RATES:
Full Page Mono .... EUR 955
Full Page Colour .... EUR 1530
Mechanical Data: Type Area: 257 x 177 mm, No. of Columns (Display): 3, Col Widths (Display): 56 mm
Copy instructions: *Copy Date:* 35 days prior to publication
Supplement(s): Eine Welt in der Schule
BUSINESS: CHURCH & SCHOOL EQUIPMENT & EDUCATION: Secondary Education

SCHUL-MANAGEMENT
741458G62J-360
Editorial: Rosenheimer Str. 145, 81671 MÜNCHEN
Tel: 89 45051371 **Fax:** 89 45051310
Email: holler@oldenbourg.de **Web site:** http://www.schulmanagement-online.de
Freq: 6 issues yearly; **Annual Sub.:** EUR 58,90; **Circ:** 2,505
Editor: Stefan Holler; **Advertising Manager:** Christian Schwarzbauer
Profile: Journal about the management of schools.
Language(s): German
ADVERTISING RATES:
Full Page Mono .... EUR 795
Full Page Colour .... EUR 1270
Mechanical Data: Type Area: 248 x 177 mm, No. of Columns (Display): 3, Col Widths (Display): 56 mm
Copy instructions: *Copy Date:* 35 days prior to publication
BUSINESS: CHURCH & SCHOOL EQUIPMENT & EDUCATION: Teachers & Education Management

SCHULVERWALTUNG BW
741462G62J-380
Editorial: Adolf-Kolping-Str. 10, 96317 KRONACH
Tel: 9261 9694283 **Fax:** 9261 9694299
Email: bguentsch@wolterskluwer.de **Web site:** http://www.wolterskluwer.de
Freq: 11 issues yearly; **Annual Sub.:** EUR 129,10; **Circ:** 2,900
Editor: Bertram Güntsch; **Advertising Manager:** Marcel Müller
Profile: Magazine about school management in Baden-Württemberg.
Language(s): German
ADVERTISING RATES:
Full Page Mono .... EUR 1425
Mechanical Data: Type Area: 265 x 174 mm, No. of Columns (Display): 3, Col Widths (Display): 55 mm
BUSINESS: CHURCH & SCHOOL EQUIPMENT & EDUCATION: Teachers & Education Management

SCHULVERWALTUNG BY
741463G62J-400
Editorial: Adolf-Kolping-Str. 10, 96317 KRONACH
Tel: 9261 9694288 **Fax:** 9261 9694299
Email: abrehm@wolterskluwer.de **Web site:** http://www.schulleitung.de
Freq: 11 issues yearly; **Annual Sub.:** EUR 176,00; **Circ:** 1,950
Editor: Anne Brehm; **Advertising Manager:** Marcel Müller
Profile: Journal about school management and teaching in Bavaria.
Language(s): German
ADVERTISING RATES:
Full Page Mono .... EUR 1425
Mechanical Data: Type Area: 265 x 174 mm, No. of Columns (Display): 3, Col Widths (Display): 55 mm
BUSINESS: CHURCH & SCHOOL EQUIPMENT & EDUCATION: Teachers & Education Management

SCHULVERWALTUNG NRW
741468G62J-460
Editorial: Luxemburger Str. 449, 50939 KÖLN
Tel: 221 943737359 **Fax:** 221 9437317359
Email: bstock@wolterskluwer.de
Freq: 11 issues yearly; **Annual Sub.:** EUR 156,90; **Circ:** 3,250
Editor: Barbara Stock; **Advertising Manager:** Petra Schardt
Profile: Magazine about school management in Nordrhein-Westfalen.
Language(s): German
ADVERTISING RATES:
Full Page Mono .... EUR 1535
Full Page Colour .... EUR 2290
Mechanical Data: Type Area: 265 x 174 mm
BUSINESS: CHURCH & SCHOOL EQUIPMENT & EDUCATION: Teachers & Education Management

SCHULVERWALTUNGSBLATT FÜR NIEDERSACHSEN
741470G80-14142
Editorial: Schiffgraben 12, 30159 HANNOVER
Tel: 511 1207281 **Fax:** 511 1207449
Email: peter.wachtel@mk.niedersachsen.de
Freq: Monthly; **Annual Sub.:** EUR 33,75; **Circ:** 6,000
Editor: Peter Wachtel
Profile: Magazine about school management in Niedersachsen.
Language(s): German
ADVERTISING RATES:
Full Page Mono .... EUR 790
Full Page Colour .... EUR 1185
Mechanical Data: Type Area: 250 x 170 mm, No. of Columns (Display): 2, Col Widths (Display): 82 mm
Copy instructions: *Copy Date:* 15 days prior to publication
CONSUMER: RURAL & REGIONAL INTEREST

SCHÜTTGUT 741425G10-120
Editorial: Max-Planck-Str. 7, 97082 WÜRZBURG
Tel: 931 4182345 **Fax:** 931 4182290
Email: wolfgang.geisler@vogel.de **Web site:** http://www.schuettgut-transtech.com
Freq: 8 issues yearly; **Annual Sub.:** EUR 204,00; **Circ:** 4,985
Editor: Wolfgang Geisler; **Advertising Manager:** Klaus Göhler
Profile: The magazine Schüttgut informs professionals of the bulk industry on conveying, dosing, storage, characterization, processing, extraction, conditioning, transportation and handling of mineral and organic solids. The technical and scientific contributions include mechanical and procedural problems and their solutions, which are associated with the use, processing and transportation of bulk materials of interest. In addition reports on trade fairs, trade events and personalities.
Language(s): German
ADVERTISING RATES:
Full Page Mono .... EUR 2307
Full Page Colour .... EUR 3207
Mechanical Data: Type Area: 270 x 180 mm, No. of Columns (Display): 3, Col Widths (Display): 56 mm
Copy instructions: *Copy Date:* 21 days prior to publication
BUSINESS: MATERIALS HANDLING

SCHÜTZEN & ERHALTEN
1664617G4E-7056
Editorial: Hans-Willy-Mertens-Str. 2, 50858 KÖLN
Tel: 2234 48455 **Fax:** 2234 49314
Email: info@dhbv.de **Web site:** http://www.dhbv.de
Freq: Quarterly; Free to qualifying individuals
Annual Sub.: EUR 37,45; **Circ:** 1,000
Editor: Friedrich Remes; **Advertising Manager:** Michaela Meitz
Profile: Magazine about trends and solutions for all issues concerning wood and building conservation.
Language(s): German
ADVERTISING RATES:
Full Page Mono .... EUR 750
Full Page Colour .... EUR 1000
Mechanical Data: Type Area: 270 x 190 mm, No. of Columns (Display): 4, Col Widths (Display): 43 mm

SCHWABACHER TAGBLATT
741481G67B-13260
Editorial: Spitalberg 3, 91126 SCHWABACH
Tel: 9122 93800 **Fax:** 9122 836794
Email: redaktion@sc-tagblatt.de **Web site:** http://www.schwabacher-tagblatt.de
Freq: 312 issues yearly; **Circ:** 15,073
Profile: Daily newspaper with regional news and a local sports section.

Language(s): German
ADVERTISING RATES:
SCC .... EUR 29,50
Mechanical Data: Type Area: 430 x 280 mm, No. of Columns (Display): 6, Col Widths (Display): 45 mm
Copy instructions: *Copy Date:* 2 days prior to publication
Supplement(s): sechs+sechzig
REGIONAL DAILY & SUNDAY NEWSPAPERS: Regional Daily Newspapers

SCHWÄBISCHE POST
741495G67B-13280
Editorial: Bahnhofstr. 65, 73430 AALEN
Tel: 7361 594171 **Fax:** 7361 594161
Email: redaktion@schwaebische-post.de **Web site:** http://www.schwaebische-post.de
Freq: 312 issues yearly; **Circ:** 25,492
Editor: Rainer Wiese; **Advertising Manager:** Falko Pütz
Profile: Daily newspaper with regional news and a local sports section. Facebook: http://de-de.facebook.com/schwaepo Twitter: http://twitter.com/SchwaePo This Outlet offers RSS (Really Simple Syndication).
Language(s): German
ADVERTISING RATES:
SCC .... EUR 80,00
Mechanical Data: Type Area: 430 x 283 mm, No. of Columns (Display): 6, Col Widths (Display): 45 mm
Copy instructions: *Copy Date:* 1 day prior to publication
Supplement(s): Das Magazin
REGIONAL DAILY & SUNDAY NEWSPAPERS: Regional Daily Newspapers

SCHWÄBISCHE ZEITUNG
741501G67B-13300
Editorial: Rudolf-Roth-Str. 18, 88299 LEUTKIRCH
Tel: 7561 800 **Fax:** 7561 80134
Email: redaktion@schwaebische.de **Web site:** http://www.schwaebische.de
Freq: 312 issues yearly; **Circ:** 176,684
Editor: Hendrik Groth; **News Editor:** Peter Weißenberg; **Advertising Manager:** Reinhard Hofer
Profile: The Schwäbische Zeitung is the largest subscription newspaper in Baden-Wuerttemberg. In 22 local editions, some of which appear with different titles, provides the "Schwäbische Zeitung" its readers daily with the latest information from government, business, sports, culture, and of course from the local environment. Twitter: http://twitter.com/Schwaebische This Outlet offers RSS (Really Simple Syndication).
Language(s): German
ADVERTISING RATES:
SCC .... EUR 354,40
Mechanical Data: Type Area: 480 x 320 mm, No. of Columns (Display): 7, Col Widths (Display): 44 mm
Copy instructions: *Copy Date:* 1 day prior to publication
Supplement(s): Mein Stil
REGIONAL DAILY & SUNDAY NEWSPAPERS: Regional Daily Newspapers

SCHWÄBISCHE.DE
1662625G67B-16744
Editorial: Rudolf-Roth-Str. 18, 88299 LEUTKIRCH
Tel: 7561 80102 **Fax:** 7561 80378
Email: redaktion@schwaebische-zeitung.de **Web site:** http://www.schwaebische.de
Cover Price: Paid; **Circ:** 1,768,276 Unique Users
Editor: Ralf Geisenhanslüke; **Advertising Manager:** Andreas Huber
Profile: Ezine: Regional daily newspaper covering politics, culture, economics, sports, travel and technology. Twitter: http://twitter.com/Schwaebische This Outlet offers RSS (Really Simple Syndication).
Language(s): German
REGIONAL DAILY & SUNDAY NEWSPAPERS: Regional Daily Newspapers

SCHWÄBISCHES TAGBLATT
741500G67B-13320
Editorial: Uhlandstr. 2, 72072 TÜBINGEN
Tel: 7071 9340 **Fax:** 7071 35033
Email: redaktion@tagblatt.de **Web site:** http://www.tagblatt.de
Freq: 312 issues yearly; **Circ:** 42,096
Editor: Eckhard Ströbel; **Advertising Manager:** Wolfgang Dieter
Profile: Daily newspaper with regional news and a local sports section. Facebook: http://www.facebook.com/schwaebischestagblatt Twitter: http://twitter.com/TAGBLATT This Outlet offers RSS (Really Simple Syndication).
Language(s): German
ADVERTISING RATES:
SCC .... EUR 79,00
Mechanical Data: Type Area: 480 x 321 mm, No. of Columns (Display): 7, Col Widths (Display): 44 mm
Copy instructions: *Copy Date:* 1 day prior to publication
Supplement(s): Blatt
REGIONAL DAILY & SUNDAY NEWSPAPERS: Regional Daily Newspapers

SCHWABMÜNCHNER ALLGEMEINE
741483G67B-13340
Editorial: Curt-Frenzel-Str. 2, 86167 AUGSBURG
Tel: 821 7770 **Fax:** 821 7772067
Email: redaktion@augsburger-allgemeine.de **Web site:** http://www.augsburger-allgemeine.de
Freq: 312 issues yearly; **Circ:** 15,627
Advertising Manager: Herbert Dachs
Profile: Regional daily newspaper with news on politics, economy, culture, sports, travel, technology, etc. Facebook: http://www.facebook.com/AugsburgerAllgemeine Twitter: http://twitter.com/AZ_Augsburg This Outlet offers RSS (Really Simple Syndication).
Language(s): German
ADVERTISING RATES:
SCC .... EUR 42,60
Mechanical Data: Type Area: 480 x 327 mm, No. of Columns (Display): 7, Col Widths (Display): 45 mm
Copy instructions: *Copy Date:* 1 day prior to publication
Supplement(s): CiA City News
REGIONAL DAILY & SUNDAY NEWSPAPERS: Regional Daily Newspapers

SCHWACKELISTE LANDMASCHINEN
741488G27-2160
Editorial: Wilhelm-Röntgen-Str. 7, 63477 MAINTAL
Tel: 6181 4050 **Fax:** 6181 405111
Email: info@eurotaxschwacke.de **Web site:** http://www.schwacke.de
Freq: Half-yearly; **Annual Sub.:** EUR 263,00; **Circ:** 1,110
Editor: Ernst Fuchs
Profile: Directory listing agricultural machinery.
Language(s): German
ADVERTISING RATES:
Full Page Mono .... EUR 700
Full Page Colour .... EUR 1600
Mechanical Data: Type Area: 200 x 138 mm

SCHWACKELISTE NUTZFAHRZEUGE
741489G31-10
Editorial: Wilhelm-Röntgen-Str. 7, 63477 MAINTAL
Tel: 6181 405153 **Fax:** 6181 405111
Email: wolfgang.schwabe@eurotaxschwacke.de **Web site:** http://www.schwacke.de
Freq: Quarterly; **Annual Sub.:** EUR 251,00; **Circ:** 2,655
Editor: Wolfgang Schwabe
Profile: Directory listing commercial vehicles.
Language(s): German
ADVERTISING RATES:
Full Page Mono .... EUR 1000
Full Page Colour .... EUR 1900
Mechanical Data: Type Area: 200 x 138 mm

SCHWACKELISTE PKW
741490G31-11
Editorial: Wilhelm-Röntgen-Str. 7, 63477 MAINTAL
Tel: 6181 405144 **Fax:** 6181 405111
Email: roland.stach@eurotaxschwacke.de **Web site:** http://www.schwacke.de
Freq: Monthly; **Annual Sub.:** EUR 282,00; **Circ:** 4,520
Editor: Roland Stach
Profile: Directory listing prices for cars.
Language(s): German
ADVERTISING RATES:
Full Page Mono .... EUR 900
Full Page Colour .... EUR 1800
Mechanical Data: Type Area: 138 x 93 mm

SCHWACKELISTE SUPERSCHWACKE
741491G31-12
Editorial: Wilhelm-Röntgen-Str. 7, 63477 MAINTAL
Tel: 6181 405144 **Fax:** 6181 405111
Email: roland.stach@eurotaxschwacke.de **Web site:** http://www.schwacke.de
Freq: Monthly; **Annual Sub.:** EUR 640,00; **Circ:** 3,940
Editor: Roland Stach
Profile: Directory listing special models and vans.
Language(s): German
ADVERTISING RATES:
Full Page Mono .... EUR 1000
Full Page Colour .... EUR 1900
Mechanical Data: Type Area: 190 x 123 mm

SCHWACKELISTE ZWEIRAD
741493G31-13
Editorial: Wilhelm-Röntgen-Str. 7, 63477 MAINTAL
Tel: 6181 405147 **Fax:** 6181 405156
Email: tle@eurotaxschwacke.de **Web site:** http://www.schwacke.de
Freq: Quarterly; **Annual Sub.:** EUR 176,00; **Circ:** 3,205
Editor: Thomas Lemp
Profile: Directory listing two-wheelers.
Language(s): German
ADVERTISING RATES:
Full Page Mono .... EUR 700
Full Page Colour .... EUR 1600
Mechanical Data: Type Area: 138 x 93 mm
Copy instructions: *Copy Date:* 38 days prior to publication

SCHWÄLMER ALLGEMEINE
730358G67B-7240
Editorial: Frankfurter Str. 168, 34121 KASSEL
Tel: 561 20300 **Fax:** 561 2032406
Email: info@hna.de **Web site:** http://www.hna.de
Freq: 312 issues yearly; **Circ:** 8,065
Advertising Manager: Andrea Schaller-Öller
Profile: Regional daily newspaper with news on politics, economy, culture, sports, travel, technology, etc. The Schwälmer Allgemeine a local edition of the HNA Hessische/Niedersächsische Allgemeine. Twitter: http://twitter.com/hna_online This Outlet offers RSS (Really Simple Syndication).
Language(s): German
ADVERTISING RATES:
SCC .... EUR 36,80
Mechanical Data: Type Area: 430 x 285 mm, No. of Columns (Display): 6, Col Widths (Display): 45 mm
Copy instructions: *Copy Date:* 2 days prior to publication
REGIONAL DAILY & SUNDAY NEWSPAPERS: Regional Daily Newspapers

SCHWARMSTEDTER RUNDSCHAU
741514G72-11808
Editorial: Hauptstr. 10, 29690 SCHWARMSTEDT
Tel: 5071 961880 **Fax:** 5071 9618819
Email: anke.ullrich@aller-weser-verlag.de **Web site:** http://www.aller-weser-verlag.de
Freq: Weekly; **Cover Price:** Free; **Circ:** 15,250
Editor: Anke Ullrich; **Advertising Manager:** Sabine Düßmann
Profile: Advertising journal (house-to-house) concentrating on local stories.
Language(s): German
ADVERTISING RATES:
Full Page Mono .... EUR 1054
Full Page Colour .... EUR 1529
Mechanical Data: Type Area: 310 x 230 mm, No. of Columns (Display): 5, Col Widths (Display): 44 mm
Copy instructions: *Copy Date:* 3 days prior to publication
LOCAL NEWSPAPERS

SCHWARZENBACHER AMTS-BLATT
741521G67B-13360
Editorial: August-Bebel-Str. 22, 95126 SCHWARZENBACH **Tel:** 9284 349 **Fax:** 9284 800460
Email: hauptmann-verlag@t-online.de
Freq: Weekly; **Cover Price:** EUR 1,40; **Circ:** 1,851
Editor: Siegfried Hauptmann; **Advertising Manager:** Siegfried Hauptmann
Profile: Regional daily newspaper covering politics, economics, sport, travel and technology.
Language(s): German
ADVERTISING RATES:
SCC .... EUR 14,80
Mechanical Data: Type Area: 420 x 280 mm, No. of Columns (Display): 6, Col Widths (Display): 45 mm
Copy instructions: *Copy Date:* 1 day prior to publication
REGIONAL DAILY & SUNDAY NEWSPAPERS: Regional Daily Newspapers

SCHWARZENBEKER ANZEIGER
741522G72-11812
Editorial: Schefestr. 11, 21493 SCHWARZENBEK
Tel: 4151 88900 **Fax:** 4151 889044
Email: redaktion@schwarzenbeker-anzeiger.de **Web site:** http://www.viebranz.de
Freq: Weekly; **Cover Price:** Free; **Circ:** 12,130
Editor: Christa Möller; **Advertising Manager:** Astrid von Haugwitz-Schütt
Profile: Advertising journal (house-to-house) concentrating on local stories.
Language(s): German
ADVERTISING RATES:
Full Page Mono .... EUR 2451
Full Page Colour .... EUR 2511
Mechanical Data: Type Area: 430 x 282 mm, No. of Columns (Display): 6, Col Widths (Display): 45 mm
Copy instructions: *Copy Date:* 1 day prior to publication
LOCAL NEWSPAPERS

SCHWARZWALD GÄSTE-JOURNAL
762911G89A-12132
Editorial: Kirchtorstr. 14, 78727 OBERNDORF
Tel: 7423 78396 **Fax:** 7423 78367
Email: service@schwarzwaelder-bote.de **Web site:** http://www.schwarzwaelder-bote.de
Freq: 3 issues yearly; **Cover Price:** Free; **Circ:** 120,000
Editor: Frank Börnard; **Advertising Manager:** Hans-Carsten Steensen
Profile: Magazine for tourists of the Schwarzwald region. Distribution: health resorts, tourist information, hotels and offices of the "Schwarzwälder Boten".
Language(s): German
Mechanical Data: Type Area: 276 x 212 mm

SCHWARZWÄLDER BOTE
741558G67B-13380
Editorial: Kirchtorstr. 14, 78727 OBERNDORF
Tel: 7423 780 **Fax:** 7423 7873
Email: redaktion@schwarzwaelder-bote.de **Web site:** http://www.schwarzwaelder-bote.de
Freq: 312 issues yearly; **Circ:** 130,526
Editor: Klaus Siegmeier; **News Editor:** Christoph Bielecki
Profile: Regional daily newspaper covering politics, economics, sport, travel and technology. Facebook: http://www.facebook.com/SchwarzwaelderBote Twitter: http://twitter.com/schwarzwaelder This Outlet offers RSS (Really Simple Syndication).
Language(s): German
ADVERTISING RATES:
SCC .... EUR 240,6
Mechanical Data: No. of Columns (Display): 6, Col Widths (Display): 45 mm, Type Area: 435 x 280 mm
Copy instructions: *Copy Date:* 1 day prior to publication
Supplement(s): Alter aktiv; woodz magazin
REGIONAL DAILY & SUNDAY NEWSPAPERS: Regional Daily Newspapers

SCHWARZWEISS
741563G85A-68
Editorial: Siemensstr. 4, 48565 STEINFURT
Tel: 2552 920204 **Fax:** 2552 920150
Email: schwarzweiss@tecklenborg-verlag.de **Web site:** http://www.tecklenborg-verlag.de
Freq: 6 issues yearly; **Annual Sub.:** EUR 78,00; **Circ:** 6,530
Editor: Martin Lehmann; **Advertising Manager:** Marion Dües
Profile: Magazine containing information about black and white photography.
Language(s): German
Readership: Aimed at amateur photographers.
ADVERTISING RATES:
Full Page Mono .... EUR 265
Full Page Colour .... EUR 457
Mechanical Data: Type Area: 241 x 185 mm, No. of Columns (Display): 2, Col Widths (Display): 90 mm
Copy instructions: *Copy Date:* 22 days prior to publication
CONSUMER: PHOTOGRAPHY & FILM MAKING: Photography

SCHWEINFURTER TAGBLATT
741573G67B-1342
Editorial: Berner Str. 2, 97084 WÜRZBURG
Tel: 931 60010 **Fax:** 931 6001242
Web site: http://www.mainpost.de
Freq: 312 issues yearly; **Circ:** 25,264
Advertising Manager: Matthias Faller
Profile: Daily newspaper with regional news and a local sports section. Facebook: http://www.facebook.com/mainpost?ref=search&sid=1469388759.1899628925..1 Twitter: http://twitter.com/mainpost This Outlet offers RSS (Really Simple Syndication).
Language(s): German
ADVERTISING RATES:
SCC .... EUR 65,00
Mechanical Data: Type Area: 466 x 310 mm, No. of Columns (Display): 7, Col Widths (Display): 43 mm
Copy instructions: *Copy Date:* 1 day prior to publication
Supplement(s): Anstoß Schweinfurt; 4 Wände
REGIONAL DAILY & SUNDAY NEWSPAPERS: Regional Daily Newspapers

SCHWEISSEN UND SCHNEIDEN
741575G27-2260
Editorial: Aachener Str. 172, 40223 DÜSSELDORF
Tel: 211 1591276 **Fax:** 211 1591350
Email: dietmar.rippegather@dvs-hg.de **Web site:** http://www.dvs-media.info
Freq: Monthly; **Annual Sub.:** EUR 177,00; **Circ:** 4,996
Editor: Dietmar Rippegather; **Advertising Manager:** Iris Jansen
Profile: Official journal of the German Welding Society.
Language(s): German
Readership: Aimed at welders within the Society.
ADVERTISING RATES:
Full Page Mono .... EUR 2900
Full Page Colour .... EUR 3900
Mechanical Data: Type Area: 253 x 176 mm, No. of Columns (Display): 2, Col Widths (Display): 86 mm
Copy instructions: *Copy Date:* 45 days prior to publication
BUSINESS: METAL, IRON & STEEL

DIE SCHWEIZER BAUSTOFF-INDUSTRIE DSB
741585G30-171
Editorial: Hans-Böckler-Allee 9, 30173 HANNOVER
Tel: 511 7304134 **Fax:** 511 7304157
Email: v.mueller@giesel.de **Web site:** http://www.giesel-verlag.de
Freq: 6 issues yearly; Free to qualifying individuals
Annual Sub.: EUR 106,00; **Circ:** 2,579
Editor: Volker Müller; **Advertising Manager:** Berko Härtel
Profile: Journal of the Swiss Society of Sand and Gravel Merchants.
Language(s): French; German
Readership: Aimed at quarrymen and suppliers.
ADVERTISING RATES:
Full Page Mono .... EUR 1721
Full Page Colour .... EUR 2582
Mechanical Data: Type Area: 263 x 176 mm, No. of Columns (Display): 4, Col Widths (Display): 40 mm
Copy instructions: *Copy Date:* 20 days prior to publication
Official Journal of: Organ d. Fachverb. d. Schweizer. Kies- u. Betonindustrie, d. Schweizer. Mischgut-Industrie u. d. Verb. Schweizer. Hartsteinbrüche
BUSINESS: MINING & QUARRYING

SCHWEIZER PRÄZISIONS-FERTIGUNGSTECHNIK
741646G19E-1850
Editorial: Kolbergerstr. 22, 81679 MÜNCHEN
Tel: 89 99830682 **Fax:** 89 99830623

mail: hobohm@hanser.de **Web site:** http://www. anser.de
req: Annual; **Cover Price:** EUR 20,00; **Circ:** 25,500
ditor: Michael Hobohm; **Advertising Manager:** ietmar von der Au
rofile: For over 20 years, accompanied the ublication of Schweizer Präzisions- ertigungstechnik export activities of the Swiss achine tool industry. In cooperation with the WISSMEM the Schweizer Präzisions- ertigungstechnik reports in detail and hands-on nnovative metal-cutting methods and trends in anufacturing technology for the industrial metal. ust ahead of the leading exhibition EMO expect the eaders of our trade - WB Werkstatt+Betrieb and likroproduktion (focus points are ultra-precision achining, precision engineering, micro-machining, edical technics), both recipients of Schweizer räzisions-Fertigungstechnik, information about new roducts and developments in the Fields of machine ools, precision tools, automation, Test and easurement, information technology etc.
anguage(s): German
DVERTISING RATES:
ull Page Mono .... EUR 4300
ull Page Colour .... EUR 7000
echanical Data: Type Area: 250 x 175 mm, No. of olumns (Display): 4, Col Widths (Display): 41 mm
opy instructions: *Copy Date:* 36 days prior to ublication
upplement(s): Swiss Quality Production

SCHWEIZERISCHE ZEITSCHRIFT FÜR GANZHEITSMEDIZIN

1748923S56A-2089

ditorial: Wilhelmstr. 20a, 79098 FREIBURG
el: 761 4520730 **Fax:** 761 4520714
mail: a.eitner@karger.de **Web site:** http://www. arger.com
req: 6 issues yearly; Free to qualifying individuals
nnual Sub.: EUR 52,00; **Circ:** 4,000
ditor: Alexander Eitner; **Advertising Manager:** Ellen immermann
rofile: Journal of Applied Naturopathy, including the cientific models of thought.
anguage(s): English; German
DVERTISING RATES:
ull Page Mono .... EUR 2080
ull Page Colour .... EUR 2980
echanical Data: Type Area: 242 x 180 mm
fficial Journal of: Union schweizer. omplementärmed. Ärzteorganisationen

SCHWERINER BLITZ AM SONNTAG

741668G72-11852

ditorial: Pampower Str. 3, 19061 SCHWERIN
el: 385 64584841 **Fax:** 385 64584820
mail: rita.brueckner@blitzverlag.de **Web site:** http:// www.blitzverlag.de
req: Weekly; **Cover Price:** Free; **Circ:** 77,315
ditor: Rita Brückner
rofile: Advertising journal (house-to-house) concentrating on local stories.
anguage(s): German
DVERTISING RATES:
ull Page Mono .... EUR 3982
ull Page Colour .... EUR 4372
echanical Data: Type Area: 420 x 285 mm, No. of Columns (Display): 6, Col Widths (Display): 45 mm
opy instructions: *Copy Date:* 2 days prior to ublication
LOCAL NEWSPAPERS

SCHWERINER EXPRESS

741669G72-11856

Editorial: Gutenbergstr. 1, 19061 SCHWERIN
Tel: 385 63788671 **Fax:** 385 63788670
Email: biha@svz.de **Web site:** http://www.svz.de
Freq: Weekly; **Cover Price:** Free; **Circ:** 74,230
Editor: Birgitt Hamm; **Advertising Manager:** Jürgen Pröhl
Profile: Advertising journal (house-to-house) concentrating on local stories.
Language(s): German
ADVERTISING RATES:
Full Page Mono .... EUR 4839
Full Page Colour .... EUR 6284
Mechanical Data: Type Area: 480 x 325 mm, No. of Columns (Display): 7, Col Widths (Display): 45 mm
Copy instructions: *Copy Date:* 3 days prior to publication
LOCAL NEWSPAPERS

SCHWERINER KURIER

741670G72-11860

Editorial: Wismarsche Str. 146, 19053 SCHWERIN
Tel: 385 5905815 **Fax:** 385 5905854
Email: redaktion@schwerinonline.de **Web site:** http:// www.schwerinonline.de
Freq: Weekly; **Cover Price:** Free; **Circ:** 92,400
Editor: Irene Schwaß
Profile: Advertising journal (house-to-house) concentrating on local stories.
Language(s): German
ADVERTISING RATES:
Full Page Mono .... EUR 4976
Full Page Colour .... EUR 7203
Mechanical Data: Type Area: 435 x 281 mm, No. of Columns (Display): 7, Col Widths (Display): 38 mm
Copy instructions: *Copy Date:* 3 days prior to publication
LOCAL NEWSPAPERS

SCHWERINER VOLKSZEITUNG

741671G67B-13440

Editorial: Gutenbergstr. 1, 19061 SCHWERIN
Tel: 385 63780 **Fax:** 385 3975140
Email: redaktion@svz.de **Web site:** http://www.svz.de
Freq: 312 issues yearly; **Circ:** 95,587
Editor: Dieter Schulz; **Advertising Manager:** Andreas Gruczek
Profile: Regional daily newspaper with news on politics, economy, culture, sports, travel, technology, etc. This Outlet offers RSS (Really Simple Syndication).
Language(s): German
ADVERTISING RATES:
SCC .... EUR 295,50
Mechanical Data: Type Area: 480 x 325 mm, No. of Columns (Display): 7, Col Widths (Display): 45 mm
Copy instructions: *Copy Date:* 1 day prior to publication
Supplement(s): prisma
REGIONAL DAILY & SUNDAY NEWSPAPERS: Regional Daily Newspapers

SCHWERTRANSPORT MAGAZIN

1666027G49A-2444

Editorial: Hauptstr. 27, 67823 UNKENBACH
Tel: 6362 994016 **Fax:** 6362 994017
Email: redaktion@kmverlag.de **Web site:** http://www. schwertransportmagazin.de
Freq: 6 issues yearly; **Annual Sub.:** EUR 38,00; **Circ:** 35,000
Editor: Jens Buschmeyer
Profile: International trade magazine for heavy transport, heavy vehicles, engineering and logistics. The magazine regularly offers the following headings: News, Events, Marketing + Trade, Technology + Management, in action, financing, insurance, accessories, sport truck, StM-law, StM-Extra, StM-Mini.
Language(s): German
ADVERTISING RATES:
Full Page Mono .... EUR 2800
Full Page Colour .... EUR 3500
Mechanical Data: Type Area: 274 x 188 mm, No. of Columns (Display): 3, Col Widths (Display): 45 mm

DIE SCHWESTER DER PFLEGER

741674G56B-1651

Editorial: Stadtwaldpark 10, 34212 MELSUNGEN
Tel: 5661 734483 **Fax:** 5661 8360
Email: markus.boucsein@bibliomed.de **Web site:** http://www.bibliomed.de
Freq: Monthly; Free to qualifying individuals
Annual Sub.: EUR 45,00; **Circ:** 53,313
Editor: Markus Boucsein
Profile: The contents of the magazine Die Schwester Der Pfleger is addressed to all employees of nursing in hospitals and institutions of nursing homes. Success of Germany's largest nursing journal, the mixture of education, nursing practice, management and science. Latest news, conference reports, expert tips, book reviews and new product releases round out the program content. Since July 2006, is the sister of nurses, the official organ of the German Professional Association of Nursing.
Language(s): German
ADVERTISING RATES:
Full Page Mono .... EUR 4565
Full Page Colour .... EUR 4565
Mechanical Data: Type Area: 273 x 186 mm, No. of Columns (Display): 3, Col Widths (Display): 65 mm
Copy instructions: *Copy Date:* 14 days prior to publication
Official Journal of: Organ d. Dt. Bundesverb. f. Pflegeberufe e.V.
Supplement(s): Die Schwester Der Pfleger plus+
BUSINESS: HEALTH & MEDICAL: Nursing

SCHWETZINGER ZEITUNG

741677G67B-13460

Editorial: Carl-Theodor-Str. 1, 68723 SCHWETZINGEN **Tel:** 6202 2050 **Fax:** 6202 205392
Email: sz-redaktion@schwetzinger-zeitung.de **Web site:** http://www.schwetzinger-zeitung.de
Freq: 312 issues yearly; **Circ:** 16,218
Editor: Jürgen Gruler; **Advertising Manager:** Heiner Hugo
Profile: Daily newspaper with regional news and a local sports section. Facebook: http://www.facebook .com/pages/morgenweb/105113719526519 ?ref=search&sid=1469388759.1280026596..1 This Outlet offers RSS (Really Simple Syndication).
Language(s): German
ADVERTISING RATES:
SCC .... EUR 52,50
Mechanical Data: Type Area: 490 x 320 mm, No. of Columns (Display): 7, Col Widths (Display): 44 mm
Copy instructions: *Copy Date:* 2 days prior to publication
Supplement(s): Das will ich; essen & genießen in der Metropolregion; Lust auf Genuss; Mode & Stil; Morgen Magazin; Natürlich; TV Morgen; Wirtschaftsmorgen; Wohlfühljournal
REGIONAL DAILY & SUNDAY NEWSPAPERS: Regional Daily Newspapers

SCHWIMMBAD & SAUNA

741678G32E-7

Editorial: Höhenstr. 17, 70736 FELLBACH
Tel: 711 5206207 **Fax:** 711 5206276
Email: schwimmbad@fachschriften.de **Web site:** http://www.schwimmbad.de
Freq: 6 issues yearly; **Annual Sub.:** EUR 21,00; **Circ:** 18,627
Editor: Mark Böttger; **Advertising Manager:** Daniela Buchheim
Profile: Schwimmbad & Sauna reached an exclusive audience of homeowners and builders who are concerned with the installation of swimming pools, whirlpools, saunas, infrared cabins, steam rooms and solariums, or is in possession of a Plant and are planning to expand. Schwimmbad & Sauna for over 40 years the accepted medium for industry professionals.
Language(s): German
Readership: For architects, planners, homeowners, and the building trade.
ADVERTISING RATES:
Full Page Colour .... EUR 6400
Mechanical Data: Type Area: 276 x 184 mm, No. of Columns (Display): 3, Col Widths (Display): 58 mm
Copy instructions: *Copy Date:* 40 days prior to publication
BUSINESS: LOCAL GOVERNMENT, LEISURE & RECREATION: Swimming Pools

SCOOTER & SPORT

734673G77A-2600

Editorial: Ziegelstr. 24, 91126 REDNITZHEMBACH
Tel: 9122 630290 **Fax:** 9122 6302999
Email: info@scooterundsport.de **Web site:** http:// www.scooterundsport.de
Freq: 6 issues yearly; **Annual Sub.:** EUR 21,00; **Circ:** 15,373
Editor: Reinhold Wagner
Profile: Magazine about scooters with a focus on tests, comparison tests and buying advice on current vehicles.
Language(s): German
ADVERTISING RATES:
Full Page Mono .... EUR 2990
Full Page Colour .... EUR 5190
Mechanical Data: Type Area: 277 x 185 mm, No. of Columns (Display): 4, Col Widths (Display): 43 mm
Copy instructions: *Copy Date:* 28 days prior to publication
CONSUMER: MOTORING & CYCLING: Motoring

SCOOTER & SPORT KATALOG

741689G77A-2100

Editorial: Ziegelstr. 24, 91126 REDNITZHEMBACH
Tel: 9122 630290 **Fax:** 9122 6302999
Email: info@scooterundsport.de **Web site:** http:// www.scooterundsport.de
Freq: Annual; **Cover Price:** EUR 5,00; **Circ:** 36,800
Editor: Reinhold Wagner
Profile: The catalog presents a complete comprehensive range of scooters with a short test of brand scooters, buying advice, technical data and insurance cost comparison.
Language(s): German
ADVERTISING RATES:
Full Page Mono .... EUR 2990
Full Page Colour .... EUR 5190
Mechanical Data: Type Area: 277 x 185 mm

SCOPE

741690G19A-1065

Editorial: Havelstr. 9, 64295 DARMSTADT
Tel: 6151 380311 **Fax:** 6151 38099327
Email: scope-redaktion@hoppenstedt.de **Web site:** http://www.scope-online.de
Freq: Monthly; **Annual Sub.:** EUR 122,00; **Circ:** 79,753
Editor: Hajo Stotz; **Advertising Manager:** Heike Heckmann
Profile: Scope, the magazine industry for production and technology, is characterized by its strong presence in the German industry: Germany's highest circulation industry magazine with 80,000 copies monthly Scope reaches all important Industries. The range of issues of Scope professional includes engineering reports, best practice examples, management issues for decision makers in the industry, interviews, reports, background and review articles. This Outlet offers RSS (Really Simple Syndication).
Language(s): German
Readership: Aimed at sales and key account managers.
ADVERTISING RATES:
Full Page Mono .... EUR 6780
Full Page Colour .... EUR 8400
Mechanical Data: Type Area: 252 x 180 mm, No. of Columns (Display): 3, Col Widths (Display): 56 mm
Copy instructions: *Copy Date:* 21 days prior to publication
Supplement(s): kataloge orange
BUSINESS: ENGINEERING & MACHINERY

SCREEN DVD MAGAZIN

753748G76A-350

Editorial: Schanzenstr. 70, 20357 HAMBURG
Tel: 40 18888589 **Fax:** 40 18888588
Email: heldt@dvd-magazin.de **Web site:** http://www. dvd-magazin.de
Freq: 9 issues yearly; **Annual Sub.:** EUR 29,80; **Circ:** 39,911
Editor: Ulrich Heldt; **Advertising Manager:** Florian Kundt
Profile: TheScreen DVD Magazin is the film magazine program guide for DVDs and Blu-rays. It is sorted by genre with new releases practical assessment of the main points of the film, the picture and sound quality and the amenities included features. The Blu-ray reviews the editorial detailed with a special focus on the technical aspects. All available Blu-ray and DVD versions of a product are presented and compared. Several special topics complement the wide range and allow a deeper presence of individual topics (eg kids' DVDs, Asian films, documentaries, horror films). How important is obtaining the 3D technology in 2011? The magazine observed and reported extensively on the development of innovations in the hardware sector and the growing film program. The readers are not only Blu-ray and DVD fans, but also go regularly to the cinema to enjoy the latest film starts on the big screen. The magazine presents each issue in the current cinema hits and presents figures on production and composition as well as interesting background information. Anyone who wants to experience great adventures, not only as a spectator, who is in the games section to the right place. Periodically, the magazine hip games for all platforms before and specifically directed its focus on successful movie-in play area. What would be the most beautiful films without the corresponding high-quality equipment in the home theater? For this reason, the magazine regularly presents the latest home theater equipment on (TV, Blu-ray, DVD, receiver, sound, video projector). In addition, the reader through extensive specials on the latest technology is always up to date in terms of home entertainment and held film distributor and film-download services. Facebook: http:// www.facebook.com/screendvdmagazin This Outlet offers RSS (Really Simple Syndication).
Language(s): German
ADVERTISING RATES:
Full Page Mono .... EUR 5900
Full Page Colour .... EUR 5900
Mechanical Data: Type Area: 260 x 190 mm
CONSUMER: MUSIC & PERFORMING ARTS: Cinema

SEBNITZER WOCHENKURIER

741702G72-11872

Editorial: Wettiner Platz 10, 01067 DRESDEN
Tel: 351 491760 **Fax:** 351 4917674
Email: wochenkurier-dresden@dwk-verlag.de **Web site:** http://www.wochenkurier.info
Freq: Weekly; **Cover Price:** Free; **Circ:** 19,964
Editor: Regine Eberlein; **Advertising Manager:** Andreas Schönherr
Profile: Advertising journal (house-to-house) concentrating on local stories.
Language(s): German
ADVERTISING RATES:
Full Page Mono .... EUR 2469
Full Page Colour .... EUR 3456
Mechanical Data: Type Area: 430 x 290 mm, No. of Columns (Display): 7, Col Widths (Display): 38 mm
Copy instructions: *Copy Date:* 5 days prior to publication
LOCAL NEWSPAPERS

SECHZIG NA UND?

741704G74N-500

Editorial: Rheinhöhenweg 76, 53424 REMAGEN
Tel: 2228 912846 **Fax:** 2228 912271
Email: steinschulte.bonn@freenet.de **Web site:** http://www.sechzig-na-und.de
Freq: 6 issues yearly; **Annual Sub.:** EUR 20,00; **Circ:** 123,200
Editor: Sisu Steinschulte; **Advertising Manager:** Sabine Hübner
Profile: Seniors magazine for active people 50 plus, the fun and enjoy the finer things of life and also have the wherewithal to do so. Currently, the background information on the current situation in politics and business as well as the latest facts and figures from Berlin, Bonn and Brussels, etc., are interviews with celebrities of our day - but also with "people like you and me" belong to this division, as well Yesterday and today, when we face events of earlier years to current conditions. Art comes from ability, the saying goes. And skills of the other can give us pleasure or peace - to give in any case, valuable hours. No wonder that art is one of the most important issues in the ostrich "Current" is. In the section we wanted commitment organizations, associations and initiatives with their most important ideas and are employees - as an inspiration for those looking for a meaningful activity in old age. And our articles on fashion, beauty and wellness show us again and again: Not only women will enjoy the latest trends. Guides: Health wanted more than 80 percent of the Germans. We collect the latest news and reviews, as today also one of the other issues guide your right to pension, retirement and round about money. Tips for home and garden and cooking recipes from around the world ensure that our readers run out of ideas not at home. In the travel journal with us are descriptions of New Zealand and America are right next to the Bavarian Forest, Lake Constance and the Black Forest. The latest travel tips and trends entice with specific offers that are not necessarily found in the usual travel brochures. And our two monthly hotel performance will not only be read by our readers but also collected enthusiastically. The entertainment part should be fun: short stories, book reviews, the chart (once a year, the Chinese), the price puzzle, lots of humor and poetry in each issue are waiting for their readers.
Language(s): German
ADVERTISING RATES:
Full Page Mono .... EUR 3400
Full Page Colour .... EUR 4500
Mechanical Data: Type Area: 260 x 190 mm, No. of Columns (Display): 4, Col Widths (Display): 45 mm
Copy instructions: *Copy Date:* 21 days prior to publication
CONSUMER: WOMEN'S INTEREST CONSUMER MAGAZINES: Retirement

SECURITY INSIGHT
1851032G14A-10189
Editorial: Salisweg 30d, 63454 HANAU
Tel: 6181 966570 **Fax:** 6181 966571
Email: mh@security-insight.com **Web site:** http://www.security-insight.com
Freq: 6 issues yearly; **Annual Sub.:** EUR 68,00; **Circ:** 7,900
Editor: Marcus Heide; **Advertising Manager:** Ilse Klaus
Profile: Magazine for security decision makers in industry, business, commerce, administration and other organizations.
Language(s): German
ADVERTISING RATES:
Full Page Mono .... EUR 2450
Full Page Colour .... EUR 2800
Mechanical Data: Type Area: 280 x 186 mm, No. of Columns (Display): 3, Col Widths (Display): 57 mm
Copy instructions: *Copy Date:* 20 days prior to publication

SECURITY POINT
741712G54C-5
Editorial: Barbarossastr. 21, 63517 RODENBACH
Tel: 6184 95080 **Fax:** 6184 54524
Email: redaktion@security-service.com **Web site:** http://www.security-service.com
Freq: 6 issues yearly; **Annual Sub.:** EUR 30,00; **Circ:** 6,925
Editor: Helmut Brückmann; **Advertising Manager:** Inge Schuch
Profile: Magazine covering information about security products and the security industry.
Language(s): German
ADVERTISING RATES:
Full Page Mono .... EUR 3230
Full Page Colour .... EUR 3230
Mechanical Data: Type Area: 223 x 157 mm
BUSINESS: SAFETY & SECURITY: Security

SEEKARTEN UND BÜCHER KATALOG
1622813G49A-2345
Editorial: Bernhard-Nocht-Str. 78, 20359 HAMBURG
Tel: 40 31900 **Fax:** 40 31905000
Email: posteingang@bsh.de **Web site:** http://www.bsh.de
Cover Price: EUR 7,00; **Circ:** 1,500
Profile: Catalogue about nautical chards and books.
Language(s): English; German
Supplement to: Nachrichten für Seefahrer

SEENLAND SEENPLATTE
741718G89A-12116
Editorial: Reuchlinstr. 10, 10553 BERLIN
Tel: 30 36286431 **Fax:** 30 36286437
Email: presse@magazin-seenland.de **Web site:** http://www.magazin-seenland.de
Freq: Annual; **Cover Price:** EUR 5,90; **Circ:** 32,917
Advertising Manager: Florian Diesing
Profile: Guide and planning tool for visitors to the Mecklenburgischen Seenplatte with reports on people and places, trip suggestions and trip reports, including maps, business directory and events calendar Facebook: http://www.facebook.com/MagazinSeenland.
Language(s): German
ADVERTISING RATES:
Full Page Mono .... EUR 3550
Full Page Colour .... EUR 3550
Mechanical Data: Type Area: 270 x 180 mm
Copy instructions: *Copy Date:* 30 days prior to publication
CONSUMER: HOLIDAYS & TRAVEL: Travel

SEEREISENMAGAZIN
1704668G91B-2543
Editorial: Hofäckerweg 22, 63743 ASCHAFFENBURG **Tel:** 6021 6253030
Fax: 6021 6253031
Email: redaktion@seereisenmagazin.de **Web site:** http://www.seereisenmagazin.de
Freq: 6 times a year; **Cover Price:** Paid; **Circ:** 10,675 Unique Users
Editor: Egon Giebe
Profile: Internet portal for Cruises.
Language(s): German
CONSUMER: RECREATION & LEISURE: Camping & Caravanning

SEESPIEGEL
1687116G57-2759
Editorial: Kernerplatz 9, 70182 STUTTGART
Tel: 711 1261533 **Fax:** 711 1261509
Email: bruno.blattner@um.bwl.de **Web site:** http://www.seespiegel.de
Freq: Half-yearly; **Cover Price:** Free; **Circ:** 13,000
Editor: Bruno Blattner
Profile: Information on water quality of Lake Constance, and to the riparian zone and catchment area of the lake (natural environment, living and working space, residential and utility room, recovery room).
Language(s): German

SEGELN
741733G91A-110
Editorial: Troplowitzstr. 5, 22529 HAMBURG
Tel: 40 38906124 **Fax:** 40 38906125
Email: thorsten.hoege@segeln-magazin.de **Web site:** http://www.segeln-magazin.de
Freq: Monthly; Free to qualifying individuals
Annual Sub.: EUR 57,00; **Circ:** 32,466
Editor: Thorsten Höge; **Advertising Manager:** Nadine Querfurth
Profile: Since then almost 40 years, accompanied the magazine segeln with reports, outstanding utility as well as competent yacht and equipment testing this so varied leisure activities. The magazine has a clear reader focus: the cruising sailor. Over the decades, it is segeln to become an important instance. Strong partners ensure the highest editorial quality. segeln is a member institution of the Deutscher Hochseesportverband Hansa -DHH-, Germany's largest training facility for sailors and Kreuzer Yachtclub Deutschland. Also provides the World Cruising Club, world's largest blue-water organization, regular information.
Language(s): German
Readership: Aimed at boating and maritime enthusiasts.
ADVERTISING RATES:
Full Page Mono .... EUR 3164
Full Page Colour .... EUR 5488
Mechanical Data: Type Area: 248 x 185 mm, No. of Columns (Display): 4, Col Widths (Display): 45 mm
Copy instructions: *Copy Date:* 30 days prior to publication
Official Journal of: Organ d. KYCD Kreuzer Yachtclub Dt. u. d. DHH Deutscher Hochseesportverb. e.V.
CONSUMER: RECREATION & LEISURE: Boating & Yachting

SEGLER-ZEITUNG
741734G91A-120
Editorial: Schwertfegerstr. 1, 23556 LÜBECK
Tel: 451 898974 **Fax:** 451 898557
Email: redaktion@segler-zeitung.de **Web site:** http://www.segler-zeitung.de
Freq: Monthly; **Annual Sub.:** EUR 36,00; **Circ:** 28,000
Editor: Hermann Hell; **Advertising Manager:** Britta Stein
Profile: Official journal of the Schleswig-Holstein Sailing Association. Magazine for water sports, and information for cruising and racing sailors from the dinghy to the yacht. Tests, racing events, news, product information, news from the world of water sports.
Language(s): German
Readership: Aimed mainly at sailors.
ADVERTISING RATES:
Full Page Mono .... EUR 1600
Full Page Colour .... EUR 2480
Mechanical Data: Type Area: 250 x 180 mm, No. of Columns (Display): 4, Col Widths (Display): 43 mm
Copy instructions: *Copy Date:* 30 days prior to publication
CONSUMER: RECREATION & LEISURE: Boating & Yachting

SELBER MACHEN
741754G79A-140
Editorial: Poßmoorweg 2, 22301 HAMBURG
Tel: 40 27173182 **Fax:** 40 27172075
Email: redaktion@selbermachen.de **Web site:** http://www.selbermachen.de
Freq: Monthly; **Annual Sub.:** EUR 38,40; **Circ:** 85,762
Editor: Thomas Mauz; **Advertising Manager:** Roberto Sprengel
Profile: The practical monthly magazine is aimed at those who enjoy their own creativity in setting up the apartment, the modernization of the house, while beautifying the garden - there are so many options! selber machen supplies the ideas. By oneself is not mere theory: Any proposal, any suggestion the issue was previously developed in the studios of the editing, built and tested. Here, the pleasure is self-produced at the results in the foreground.
Language(s): German
ADVERTISING RATES:
Full Page Mono .... EUR 16900
Full Page Colour .... EUR 16900
Mechanical Data: Type Area: 253 x 187 mm, No. of Columns (Display): 4, Col Widths (Display): 43 mm
Copy instructions: *Copy Date:* 40 days prior to publication
CONSUMER: HOBBIES & DIY

SELBER TAGBLATT FRANKENPOST
741755G67B-13480
Editorial: Poststr. 9, 95028 HOF **Tel:** 9281 8160
Fax: 9281 816283
Email: redaktion@frankenpost.de **Web site:** http://www.frankenpost.de
Freq: 312 issues yearly; **Circ:** 5,309
Advertising Manager: Sebastian Anger
Profile: Regional daily newspaper with news on politics, economy, culture, sports, travel, technology, etc. Selber Tagblatt Frankenpost is a local edition of the newspaper Frankenpost. Facebook: http://www.facebook.com/pages/Frankenpost/330862476314 Twitter: http://twitter.com/frankenpost This Outlet offers RSS (Really Simple Syndication).
Language(s): German
ADVERTISING RATES:
SCC .... EUR 47,60
Mechanical Data: Type Area: 485 x 325 mm, No. of Columns (Display): 7, Col Widths (Display): 44 mm
Copy instructions: *Copy Date:* 1 day prior to publication
Supplement(s): rtv
REGIONAL DAILY & SUNDAY NEWSPAPERS: Regional Daily Newspapers

SELBST IST DER MANN
741763G79A-160
Editorial: Industriestr. 16, 50735 KÖLN
Tel: 221 7709502 **Fax:** 221 7709195
Email: selbst@selbst.de **Web site:** http://www.selbst.de
Freq: Monthly; **Annual Sub.:** EUR 42,00; **Circ:** 76,359
Editor: Nils Staehler
Profile: The home improvement magazine covers the entire spectrum of home improvement activities as a competent and entertaining guide. No other do-it-yourself magazine shows so consistently and in detail can be realized projects as "step-by-step" in their own work. The magazine provides detailed information on the latest developments in tools, materials and techniques.
Language(s): German
ADVERTISING RATES:
Full Page Mono .... EUR 17238
Full Page Colour .... EUR 17238
Mechanical Data: Type Area: 248 x 188 mm, No. of Columns (Display): 4, Col Widths (Display): 44 mm
Copy instructions: *Copy Date:* 35 days prior to publication
CONSUMER: HOBBIES & DIY

DER SELBSTÄNDIGE DSMAGAZIN
741758G14A-6540
Editorial: Westfalendamm 48, 44141 DORTMUND
Tel: 231 2250910 **Fax:** 231 22509129
Email: info@bds-nrw.de **Web site:** http://www.bds-nrw.de
Freq: 6 issues yearly; **Circ:** 10,000
Editor: Joachim Schäfer
Profile: Magazine for managers of medium sized companies, freelancers and service providers.
Language(s): German
ADVERTISING RATES:
Full Page Mono .... EUR 1990
Full Page Colour .... EUR 2900
Mechanical Data: Type Area: 265 x 192 mm, No. of Columns (Display): 4, Col Widths (Display): 45 mm

SELBST.DE
1621993G79A-298
Editorial: Burchardstr. 11, 20095 HAMBURG
Tel: 40 30190 **Fax:** 40 30191991
Email: detlev.garn@bauermedia.com **Web site:** http://www.selbst.de
Freq: Daily; **Cover Price:** Paid; **Circ:** 1,136,794 Unique Users
Editor: Detlev Garn
Profile: The DIY portal will handle the entire spectrum of home improvement activities as a competent and entertaining guide. No other do-it-yourself portal is so consistently and in detail can be realized projects as "step-by-step" in their own work. The website provides detailed information on the latest developments in tools, materials and techniques.
Language(s): German
CONSUMER: HOBBIES & DIY

SELECTION
741768G74P-880
Editorial: Erich-Dombrowski-Str. 2, 55127 MAINZ
Tel: 6131 5841136 **Fax:** 6131 5841102
Email: petra.muenster@konradin.de **Web site:** http://www.selection-online.com
Freq: Quarterly; **Annual Sub.:** EUR 16,80; **Circ:** 37,886
Editor: Petra Münster; **Advertising Manager:** Petra Binz-Lockenvitz
Profile: Wine and Gourmet magazine for the enjoyment affine end users can obtain information quickly, easily and without much knowledge of good luxury products and these may also want to order directly from the producer, with articles on the topics of wine, gourmet food, culture, travel and information on current consumption Events. The health magazine regularly carries out its own independent expert panel objective tasting pleasure goods and introduces his readers to new recommended products.
Language(s): German
Readership: Aimed at people with an interest in gastronomy.
ADVERTISING RATES:
Full Page Mono .... EUR 4390
Full Page Colour .... EUR 4390
Mechanical Data: Type Area: 260 x 204 mm, No. of Columns (Display): 3, Col Widths (Display): 64 mm
Copy instructions: *Copy Date:* 52 days prior to publication
CONSUMER: WOMEN'S INTEREST CONSUMER MAGAZINES: Food & Cookery

SEMINARS IN IMMUNOPATHOLOGY
742619G56A-9360
Editorial: Tiergartenstr. 17, 69121 HEIDELBERG
Tel: 6221 4870 **Fax:** 6221 4878366
Email: subscriptions@springer.com **Web site:** http://www.springerlink.com
Freq: 6 issues yearly; **Annual Sub.:** EUR 1284,00; **Circ:** 220
Editor: Shozo Izui
Profile: Journal for clinicians and pathologists in the field of immunopathology. Topics: recent developments, review articles, literature.
Language(s): English
ADVERTISING RATES:
Full Page Mono .... EUR 740
Full Page Colour .... EUR 1780
Mechanical Data: Type Area: 200 x 130 mm

SEMINARS IN IMMUNOPATHOLOGY
742619G56A-1166
Editorial: Tiergartenstr. 17, 69121 HEIDELBERG
Tel: 6221 4870 **Fax:** 6221 4878366
Email: subscriptions@springer.com **Web site:** http:/
www.springerlink.com
Freq: 6 issues yearly; **Annual Sub.:** EUR 1284,00; **Circ:** 220
Editor: Shozo Izui
Profile: Journal for clinicians and pathologists in the field of immunopathology. Topics: recent developments, review articles, literature.
Language(s): English
ADVERTISING RATES:
Full Page Mono .... EUR 74
Full Page Colour .... EUR 178
Mechanical Data: Type Area: 200 x 130 mm

SENFTENBERGER WOCHENKURIER
741798G72-1192
Editorial: Kreuzstr. 12, 01968 SENFTENBERG
Tel: 3573 363662 **Fax:** 3573 363668
Email: kerstintwarok@cwk-verlag.de **Web site:** http://www.wochenkurier.info
Freq: Weekly; **Cover Price:** Free; **Circ:** 42,616
Editor: Kerstin Twarok; **Advertising Manager:** Uwe Peschel
Profile: Advertising journal (house-to-house) concentrating on local stories.
Language(s): German
ADVERTISING RATES:
Full Page Mono .... EUR 337
Full Page Colour .... EUR 472
Mechanical Data: Type Area: 430 x 290 mm, No. of Columns (Display): 7, Col Widths (Display): 38 mm
Copy instructions: *Copy Date:* 3 days prior to publication
LOCAL NEWSPAPERS

SENIOREN AKTIV TERMINE
1861949G74N-96
Editorial: Junkerstr. 21, 53177 BONN
Tel: 228 559020 **Fax:** 228 5590222
Email: aktiv@idealbonn.de **Web site:** http://www.sen-aktiv.de
Freq: 6 issues yearly; **Annual Sub.:** EUR 18,00; **Circ:** 13,950
Editor: Detlef Hipp; **Advertising Manager:** Detlef Hipp
Profile: Magazine for the elderly.
Language(s): German
ADVERTISING RATES:
Full Page Mono .... EUR 185
Full Page Colour .... EUR 215
Mechanical Data: Type Area: 300 x 212 mm, No. of Columns (Display): 4, Col Widths (Display): 49 mm
Copy instructions: *Copy Date:* 21 days prior to publication

SENIOREN HEUTE
741803G74N-54
Editorial: Häuserstr. 15a, 37154 NORTHEIM
Tel: 5551 1589
Freq: 3 issues yearly; **Cover Price:** Free; **Circ:** 6,700
Editor: Rolf Hasenkrüger
Profile: Club magazine for the elderly.
Language(s): German

SENIOREN JOURNAL GOLDENER HERBST
1793702G74N-907
Editorial: Rathausplatz, 67240 BOBENHEIM-ROXHEIM **Tel:** 6239 99143
Web site: http://www.bobenheim-roxheim.de/gemeinde/senioren/index.htm
Freq: Annual; **Cover Price:** Free; **Circ:** 2,000
Editor: Harald Krauß
Profile: Magazine for the elderly from the elderly.
Language(s): German

SENIOREN RATGEBER
741807G94H-10880
Editorial: Konradshöhe, 82065 BAIERBRUNN
Tel: 89 744330 **Fax:** 89 74433460
Email: sr@wortundbildverlag.de **Web site:** http://www.senioren-ratgeber.de
Freq: Monthly; **Cover Price:** Free; **Circ:** 1,836,245
Editor: Claudia Röttger; **Advertising Manager:** Brigitta Hackmann
Profile: Magazine for the elderly with advice and information on how to keep fit.
Language(s): German
Readership: Aimed at people over 50 years.
ADVERTISING RATES:
Full Page Mono .... EUR 21900
Full Page Colour .... EUR 21900
Mechanical Data: Type Area: 186 x 148 mm, No. of Columns (Display): 2, Col Widths (Display): 69 mm
Copy instructions: *Copy Date:* 54 days prior to publication
CONSUMER: OTHER CLASSIFICATIONS: Customer Magazines

SENIOREN- UND PFLEGEMAGAZIN
2081153G74N-1033
Editorial: Saarlouiser Str. 18, 80997 MÜNCHEN
Tel: 89 381697750 **Fax:** 89 381697759

Email: presse@senioren-und-pflegemagazin.de **Web site:** http://www.senioren-und-pflegemagazin.de
Freq: Annual; **Cover Price:** Free; **Circ:** 6,900
Editor: Timon Royer; **Advertising Manager:** Roger Siers
Profile: The "Senioren- und Pflegemagazin" is a competent information service procurement for retirement and nursing facilities. Anyone care to be informed in the market about the latest products and best innovations will come at the "Senioren- und Pflegemagazin" a must. With a total circulation of print today, 7500 + 135 000 online requests each year (2009) - is the "Senioren- und Pflegemagazin" is now the highest reach of the industry leader for product innovations in the care market. There is nowhere else in such detail by top authors reported exclusively on the latest technologies and developments in the care market.
Language(s): German
ADVERTISING RATES:
Full Page Mono .... EUR 2995
Full Page Colour .... EUR 2995
Mechanical Data: Type Area: 245 x 185 mm, No. of Columns (Display): 4, Col Widths (Display): 43 mm
Copy instructions: *Copy Date:* 15 days prior to publication

SENIOREN ZEITSCHRIFT
741809G74N-560
Editorial: Hansaallee 150, 60320 FRANKFURT
Tel: 69 21233405 **Fax:** 69 21230741
Email: info.senioren-zeitschrift@stadt-frankfurt.de
Web site: http://www.senioren-zeitschrift-frankfurt.de
Freq: Quarterly; **Cover Price:** Free; **Circ:** 60,000
Editor: Jutta Perino
Profile: Magazine for the elderly. The Senioren Zeitschrift offers a mix of recent reports, important information and entertaining articles.
Language(s): German
ADVERTISING RATES:
Full Page Mono .... EUR 1915
Full Page Colour .... EUR 3177
Mechanical Data: Type Area: 275 x 185 mm, No. of Columns (Display): 3, Col Widths (Display): 59 mm
Copy instructions: *Copy Date:* 30 days prior to publication

SENIORENBLICKPUNKT
1623070G74N-830
Editorial: Huttenstr. 49, 76646 BRUCHSAL
Tel: 7251 385687 **Fax:** 7251 385685
Email: ksr.ka@web.de **Web site:** http://www.ksr-ka.de
Freq: 6 issues yearly; Free to qualifying individuals
Annual Sub.: EUR 9,60; **Circ:** 10,000
Editor: Brigitte Hübner
Profile: Magazine for the elderly from the regions of Karlsruhe, Bretten, Bruchsal and Ettlingen.
Language(s): German
ADVERTISING RATES:
Full Page Mono .... EUR 1213
Full Page Colour .... EUR 1577
Mechanical Data: Type Area: 245 x 170 mm, No. of Columns (Display): 3, Col Widths (Display): 54 mm
Copy instructions: *Copy Date:* 21 days prior to publication

SENIORENPROGRAMM
741806G74N-620
Editorial: Obere Königsstr. 8, 34117 KASSEL
Tel: 561 7875071 **Fax:** 561 7875299
Email: uwe.wolk@stadt-kassel.de **Web site:** http://www.stadt-kassel.de
Freq: Annual; **Cover Price:** Free; **Circ:** 12,000
Editor: Uwe Wolk
Profile: Magazine with events for the elderly.
Language(s): German

SENOLOGIE
1698006G56A-11384
Editorial: Rüdigerstr. 14, 70469 STUTTGART
Tel: 711 8931429 **Fax:** 711 8931408
Email: christiane.weseloh@thieme.de **Web site:** http://www.thieme.de/senologie
Freq: Quarterly; Free to qualifying individuals
Annual Sub.: EUR 94,80; **Circ:** 5,800
Editor: Christiane Weseloh
Profile: Forum of the German Society for Senology and cooperating international societies. Content focusing on the oncological diseases of the chest. Currently, an interdisciplinary approach (information from oncology, gynecology, radiology, plastic surgery, pathology). High quality training.
Language(s): German
ADVERTISING RATES:
Full Page Mono .... EUR 2600
Full Page Colour .... EUR 4550
Mechanical Data: Type Area: 256 x 180 mm
Copy instructions: *Copy Date:* 16 days prior to publication
Official Journal of: Organ d. Dt. Ges. f. Senologie, d. Österr. Ges. f. Senologie u. d. Schweizer. Ges. f. Senologie

SENSOR REPORT
1749683G17-1578
Editorial: Robert-Koch-Str. 20, 35410 HUNGEN
Tel: 6402 7727 **Fax:** 6402 9693
Email: gerhard.weissler@sensorreport.de **Web site:** http://www.sensorreport.de
Freq: 6 issues yearly; Free to qualifying individuals
Annual Sub.: CHF 125,00; **Circ:** 10,500
Editor: Gerhard A. Weissler
Profile: Magazine about sensor technology and picture processing for measurement technology and plant automation.
Language(s): German
ADVERTISING RATES:
Full Page Mono .... CHF 2000
Full Page Colour .... CHF 3200
Mechanical Data: Type Area: 255 x 183 mm, No. of Columns (Display): 3, Col Widths (Display): 58 mm
Copy instructions: *Copy Date:* 15 days prior to publication
Official Journal of: Organ d. AMA Fachverb. f. Sensorik e.V.

SEPARATOR'S DIGEST
1659940G19E-1885
Editorial: Werner-Habig-Str. 1, 59302 OELDE
Tel: 2522 772692 **Fax:** 2522 772678
Email: ws.publicrelations@geagroup.com **Web site:** http://www.westfalia-separator.com
Freq: 3 issues yearly; **Cover Price:** Free; **Circ:** 1,500
Editor: Peter Arens
Profile: Company publication published by the GEA Westfalia Separator GmbH.
Language(s): German

SERBSKE NOWINY
741825G67B-13500
Editorial: Tuchmacherstr. 27, 02625 BAUTZEN
Tel: 3591 577232 **Fax:** 3591 577202
Email: redaktion@serbske-nowiny.de **Web site:** http://www.serbske-nowiny.de
Freq: 260 issues yearly; **Circ:** 1,650
Editor: Benedikt Dyrlich; **Advertising Manager:** Manja Bujnowska
Profile: Regional daily newspaper for the Sorbian minority covering politics, economics, sport, travel and technology.
Language(s): Sorbian languages
Mechanical Data: Type Area: 390 x 280 mm, No. of Columns (Display): 5, Col Widths (Display): 52 mm
Copy instructions: *Copy Date:* 2 days prior to publication
REGIONAL DAILY & SUNDAY NEWSPAPERS: Regional Daily Newspapers

SERC 04
1703663G75G-566
Editorial: Zum Mooswäldle 9, 78054 VILLINGEN-SCHWENNINGEN **Tel:** 7720 97790 **Fax:** 7720 977915
Email: info@serc-wildwings.de **Web site:** http://www.serc-wildwings.de
Cover Price: Paid; **Circ:** 65,333 Unique Users
Editor: Christian Arnold
Profile: Facebook: http://www.facebook.com/sercwildwings.
Language(s): German
CONSUMER: SPORT: Winter Sports

SERVICE KURIER
1698582G74M-776
Editorial: Goßlerstr. 30, 12161 BERLIN
Tel: 30 8594010 **Fax:** 30 8594023
Email: deutscher_service_ring@web.de **Web site:** http://www.deutscher-service-ring.de
Freq: Quarterly; **Annual Sub.:** EUR 6,00; **Circ:** 50,000
Editor: Jörg-Bernd Jungmann
Profile: Target groups of the newspaper published for over 16 years in Berlin and the Brandenburg countryside, are senior citizens and people with disabilities. In the future, imagine the "Service Kurier" for more specific will go to the "days of action for quality of life and extensive exhibition of his readers. In addition, the "courier service" to the multi generational Thanks be considered stronger than the editors of the view that the demographic changes in our society is a challenge for all generations.
Language(s): German
ADVERTISING RATES:
Full Page Mono .... EUR 2943
Full Page Colour .... EUR 4415
Mechanical Data: Type Area: 327 x 233 mm, No. of Columns (Display): 5, Col Widths (Display): 45 mm

SESAMSTRASSE
756521G91D-9631
Editorial: Rotebühlstr. 87, 70178 STUTTGART
Tel: 711 94768780 **Fax:** 711 94768830
Email: info@panini.de **Web site:** http://www.panini.de
Freq: Quarterly; **Annual Sub.:** EUR 11,90; **Circ:** 49,392
Editor: Gabriele El Hag
Profile: The booklet of the beloved characters from the TV appears at Panini: The "Sesamstreet" magazine is the classic children's magazines. There are funny stories, craft and game tips, contests and strong extras.
Language(s): German
ADVERTISING RATES:
Full Page Mono .... EUR 3500
Full Page Colour .... EUR 3500
Mechanical Data: Type Area: 265 x 197 mm
CONSUMER: RECREATION & LEISURE: Children & Youth

SETRA FAMILIE
741846G49A-1620
Editorial: Neumann-Reichardt-Str. 27, 22041 HAMBURG **Tel:** 40 6710900 **Fax:** 40 67109029
Email: peter.pfaff@newport3.de **Web site:** http://www.newport3.de
Freq: Half-yearly; **Cover Price:** Free; **Circ:** 9,000
Editor: Peter Pfaff
Profile: Company publication published by Setra Omnibusse.
Language(s): German

SETRA FAMILIE
1626365G49A-2355
Editorial: Neumann-Reichardt-Str. 27, 22041 HAMBURG **Tel:** 40 6710900 **Fax:** 40 67109029
Email: peter.pfaff@newport3.de **Web site:** http://www.newport3.de
Freq: Half-yearly; **Cover Price:** Free; **Circ:** 3,000
Editor: Peter Pfaff
Profile: Company publication published by EvoBus, Setra Omnibusse.
Language(s): English

SEXUOLOGIE
741858G56A-9120
Editorial: Luisenstr. 57, 10117 BERLIN
Tel: 30 450529301 **Fax:** 30 450529992
Email: sexuologie@sexualmedizin-akademie.de
Freq: Half-yearly; **Annual Sub.:** EUR 156,00; **Circ:** 1,250
Profile: Magazine about sexual medical further education and research.
Language(s): German
ADVERTISING RATES:
Full Page Mono .... EUR 850
Full Page Colour .... EUR 1900
Mechanical Data: Type Area: 240 x 175 mm

SFT
1657907G76A-1513
Editorial: Dr.-Mack-Str. 83, 90762 FÜRTH
Tel: 911 2872100 **Fax:** 911 2872200
Email: redaktion@sft-magazin.de **Web site:** http://www.spielefilmetechnik.de
Freq: Monthly; **Annual Sub.:** EUR 49,00; **Circ:** 103,434
Editor: Christian Müller; **Advertising Manager:** Gunnar Obermeier
Profile: SFT is the test magazine for technology, movies, music and gaming. For everything that really gets a modern man's attention. For more fun in electronic entertainment and the digital lifestyle. SFT stands for high quality + journalistic competence + loads of content - 132 pages of magazine + DVD with a complete film and PC game.
Language(s): German
ADVERTISING RATES:
Full Page Mono .... EUR 11200
Full Page Colour .... EUR 11200
Mechanical Data: Type Area: 267 x 215 mm, No. of Columns (Display): 4, Col Widths (Display): 54 mm
Copy instructions: *Copy Date:* 28 days prior to publication
CONSUMER: MUSIC & PERFORMING ARTS: Cinema

SHAPE
761802G74A-3250
Editorial: Arabellastr. 33, 81925 MÜNCHEN
Tel: 89 9234233 **Fax:** 89 9234409
Email: gerald.buechelmaier@mvg.de **Web site:** http://www.shape.de
Freq: Monthly; **Annual Sub.:** EUR 29,00; **Circ:** 265,005
Editor: Gerald Büchelmaier; **Advertising Manager:** Andrea Seidl
Profile: Shape is the unique fitness and lifestyle magazine for women, with the aim to help them get in Shape while having fun. Shape is a personal trainer for body, mind and soul and motivates, spreads a love for life and combines fitness & food with the lifestyle topics beauty, fashion, travel & psychology. The inspirational concept addresses all areas of an active woman's life. Shape is a way of life and a must-have for all women who want to be stylish, sexy and fit. Shape is published in 30 countries and is the biggest fitness magazine for women. Facebook: http://www.facebook.com/pages/SHAPE-Magazin/113702771973890 This Outlet offers RSS (Really Simple Syndication).
Language(s): German
ADVERTISING RATES:
Full Page Mono .... EUR 17500
Full Page Colour .... EUR 17500
Mechanical Data: Type Area: 217 x 160 mm, No. of Columns (Display): 3, Col Widths (Display): 51 mm
Copy instructions: *Copy Date:* 40 days prior to publication
CONSUMER: WOMEN'S INTEREST CONSUMER MAGAZINES: Women's Interest

SHAPE
1749684G74A-3501
Editorial: Arabellastr. 33, 81925 MÜNCHEN
Tel: 89 9234233 **Fax:** 89 9234409
Email: gerald.buechelmaier@mvg.de **Web site:** http://www.shape.de
Freq: Monthly; **Annual Sub.:** CHF 58,00; **Circ:** 265,005
Editor: Gerald Büchelmaier; **Advertising Manager:** Marit Böhmer
Profile: Facebook: http://www.facebook.com/pages/SHAPE-Magazin/113702771973890.
Language(s): German
ADVERTISING RATES:
Full Page Mono .... CHF 16800
Full Page Colour .... CHF 16800
Mechanical Data: Type Area: 217 x 160 mm, No. of Columns (Display): 3, Col Widths (Display): 51 mm
Copy instructions: *Copy Date:* 40 days prior to publication
CONSUMER: WOMEN'S INTEREST CONSUMER MAGAZINES: Women's Interest

SHK PROFI
1749229G3D-860
Editorial: Avenwedder Str. 55, 33335 GÜTERSLOH
Tel: 5241 8090884 **Fax:** 5241 80690880
Email: christoph.brauneis@bauverlag.de **Web site:** http://www.shk-profi.com
Freq: 8 issues yearly; **Annual Sub.:** EUR 69,60; **Circ:** 29,818
Editor: Christoph Brauneis; **Advertising Manager:** Herbert Walhorn
Profile: The "SHK Profi" than the journal not only a current reflection of the industry, but has already points to the future tasks for the craft. Besides the "traditional" segments of plumbing, heating and HVAC fitters issues such as the targeted end customers address and consulting, air tightness of buildings and mold growth, risks and opportunities of trade cooperation are included. The trend towards multi-trade works is another important aspect of the "SHK Profi" picks. "Added value" is the keyword that this magazine for the reader speaks the language of artisans, describes most accurately.
Language(s): German
ADVERTISING RATES:
Full Page Mono .... EUR 3670
Full Page Colour .... EUR 4765
Mechanical Data: Type Area: 270 x 186 mm, No. of Columns (Display): 4, Col Widths (Display): 45 mm
Copy instructions: *Copy Date:* 14 days prior to publication
Supplement(s): RE Regenerative Energien
BUSINESS: HEATING & VENTILATION: Heating & Plumbing

SHK REPORT
741043G3D-680
Editorial: Goethestr. 75, 40237 DÜSSELDORF
Tel: 211 9149402 **Fax:** 211 9149490
Email: t.burska@krs-redaktion.de **Web site:** http://www.krammerag.de
Freq: 9 issues yearly; **Annual Sub.:** EUR 21,00; **Circ:** 24,878
Editor: Thomas Burska-Erler; **Advertising Manager:** Alke Schmeis
Profile: The SHK-REPORT is an indicator magazine for readers in the craft of plumbing, heating, oil and gas installation, ventilation and air conditioning industry as well as planners and architects. Rich illustrations and fluently written texts give a concentrated overview of operations and new developments in the subject.
Language(s): German
ADVERTISING RATES:
Full Page Mono .... EUR 4200
Full Page Colour .... EUR 6300
Mechanical Data: Type Area: 305 x 220 mm, No. of Columns (Display): 4, Col Widths (Display): 50 mm
BUSINESS: HEATING & VENTILATION: Heating & Plumbing

SHOP'N JOY
1615118G89A-11571
Editorial: Andreas-Gayk-Str. 31, 24103 KIEL
Tel: 431 6791050 **Fax:** 431 6791099
Email: j.schmidt@kiel-marketing.de **Web site:** http://www.stadtmarketing-kiel.de
Freq: Annual; **Annual Sub.:** EUR 2,50; **Circ:** 30,000
Editor: Janine-Christine Schmidt; **Advertising Manager:** Janine-Christine Schmidt
Profile: Adventure Guide with shopping focus for Kiel.
Language(s): English; German
ADVERTISING RATES:
Full Page Mono .... EUR 1200
Full Page Colour .... EUR 1200
Copy instructions: *Copy Date:* 123 days prior to publication

SHOWCASES
1814251G2A-5731
Editorial: Rölefeld 31, 51545 WALDBRÖL
Tel: 2296 900946 **Fax:** 2296 900947
Email: info@showcases.de **Web site:** http://www.showcases.de
Freq: Quarterly; **Annual Sub.:** EUR 26,00; **Circ:** 8,000
Editor: Kerstin Meisner; **Advertising Manager:** Jens Kahnert
Profile: Magazine for event and corporate communications.
Language(s): German
Copy instructions: *Copy Date:* 20 days prior to publication

SI INFORMATIONEN
742015G3D-760
Editorial: Saarlandstr. 28, 70734 FELLBACH
Tel: 711 95295133 **Fax:** 711 95295199
Email: si@at-fachverlag.de **Web site:** http://www.si-informationen.de
Freq: Monthly; **Annual Sub.:** EUR 72,60; **Circ:** 33,629
Editor: Mathias Müller; **Advertising Manager:** Monika Raiser
Profile: Magazine for entrepreneurs and executives in the HVAC industry - combined independent, free reference guide with the target group plumbing, heating engineers, air conditioning technicians, architects and planners. Fast, cascading tiered communication of information to the depth with lots of pictures and informative drawings. Practical illustration and description of the products. The recipient of the Si-find information on the magazine industry requirement with proof sent. Each individual reader is known by name, by job title, industry affiliation, size of company and phone number. Facebook: http://www.facebook.com/pages/Si-Informationen/325190941241 Twitter: http://twitter.com/#!/siinformationen This Outlet offers RSS (Really Simple Syndication).
Language(s): German

Readership: Aimed at plumbers and heating engineers.
ADVERTISING RATES:
Full Page Mono .... EUR 5220
Full Page Colour .... EUR 6360
Mechanical Data: Type Area: 264 x 185 mm, No. of Columns (Display): 4, Col Widths (Display): 43 mm
Supplement(s): Si Spezial
BUSINESS: HEATING & VENTILATION: Heating & Plumbing

SICHER IST SICHER ARBEITSSCHUTZ AKTUELL
721079G54B-12
Editorial: Genthiner Str. 30g, 10785 BERLIN
Tel: 30 2500850 **Fax:** 30 250085305
Email: sis-schriftleitung@t-online.de **Web site:** http://www.sisdigital.de
Freq: Monthly; **Annual Sub.:** EUR 85,39; **Circ:** 2,150
Editor: Ralf Pieper; **Advertising Manager:** Peter Taprogge
Profile: Magazine about work safety and related insurance. Practice-oriented technical journal on technical, environmental, economic and legal aspects of safety. Provides news from the legal practice and new regulations, contributions of the Country Committee for Occupational Safety and Safety Technology (LASI), and from the Federal Institute for Occupational Safety and Health BAuA) and information of the Federal Working Group for Safety and Health at Work.
Language(s): German
Readership: The magazine is read by safety officers and employees of manufacturing enterprises and services.
ADVERTISING RATES:
Full Page Mono .... EUR 1230
Full Page Colour .... EUR 2130
Mechanical Data: Type Area: 255 x 175 mm, No. of Columns (Display): 3, Col Widths (Display): 55 mm
Supplement(s): baua: Aktuell; BFSI aktuell
BUSINESS: SAFETY & SECURITY: Safety

SICHERHEITS MAGAZIN
741913G94H-10900
Editorial: Stresemannstr. 20, 47051 DUISBURG
Tel: 203 3052722 **Fax:** 203 30527820
Email: t.schmidt@wohlfarth.de **Web site:** http://www.schloss-und-beschlagmarkt.de
Freq: Half-yearly; **Circ:** 29,820
Editor: Thorsten Schmidt; **Advertising Manager:** Stefan Hillebrand
Profile: Magazine containing information about safety and security systems.
Language(s): German
ADVERTISING RATES:
Full Page Mono .... EUR 2810
Full Page Colour .... EUR 4700
Mechanical Data: Type Area: 258 x 178 mm, No. of Columns (Display): 3, Col Widths (Display): 56 mm
Copy instructions: *Copy Date:* 21 days prior to publication
CONSUMER: OTHER CLASSIFICATIONS: Customer Magazines

SICHERHEITS PROFI 1684605G49C-88
Editorial: Ottenser Hauptstr. 54, 22765 HAMBURG
Tel: 40 39801154
Email: ute.krohne@bg-verkehr.de **Web site:** http://www.bg-verkehr.de
Freq: 8 issues yearly; **Circ:** 230,000
Editor: Ute Krohne
Profile: Communications and information of the trade association for car ownership. Attachment to traffic Observations, Edition B. and get them to member companies of the road-based transport sector, aviation and inland waterways.
Language(s): German
Supplement to: verkehrs Rundschau

SICHERHEITSBEAUFTRAGTER
741910G54C-7
Editorial: Dischingerstr. 8, 69123 HEIDELBERG
Tel: 6221 644617 **Fax:** 6221 644640
Email: sicherheitsbeauftragter@konradin.de **Web site:** http://www.sicherheitsbeauftragter.de
Freq: 10 issues yearly; **Annual Sub.:** EUR 36,30; **Circ:** 13,605
Editor: Weigand Naumann; **Advertising Manager:** Sandra Rink
Profile: Magazine focusing on all aspects of security.
Language(s): German
Readership: Read by security officers.
ADVERTISING RATES:
Full Page Mono .... EUR 2100
Full Page Colour .... EUR 3045
Mechanical Data: Type Area: 270 x 188 mm
Copy instructions: *Copy Date:* 30 days prior to publication
Supplement(s): baua: Aktuell
BUSINESS: SAFETY & SECURITY: Security

SICHERHEITS-BERATER
1628212G14A-9551
Editorial: Alte Heerstr. 1, 53121 BONN
Tel: 228 9629388 **Fax:** 228 9629390
Email: redaktion@sicherheits-berater.de **Web site:** http://www.sicherheits-berater.de
Freq: 22 issues yearly; **Annual Sub.:** EUR 264,00; **Circ:** 2,100
Editor: Rainer v. zur Mühlen; **Advertising Manager:** Alice M. W. Hoffmann
Profile: Benefit-oriented information, checklist-like built-in problem representation and structured as a practical aid measures for the prevention of claims. Topics: Plant protection and property protection, telecommunications and IT security, IT security and auditing, fire safety, occupational safety, database backup, current warnings, background information, intelligence, legal issues. Target audience: senior management, property security, work safety, fire protection, auditing and controlling.
Language(s): German
ADVERTISING RATES:
Full Page Mono .... EUR 1000
Full Page Colour .... EUR 1750
Mechanical Data: Type Area: 270 x 162 mm, No. of Columns (Display): 4, Col Widths (Display): 41 mm
Copy instructions: *Copy Date:* 10 days prior to publication

SICHERHEITSINGENIEUR
741912G54B-6
Editorial: Dischingerstr. 8, 69123 HEIDELBERG
Tel: 6221 644617 **Fax:** 6221 644640
Email: sicherheitsingenieur@konradin.de **Web site:** http://www.si-magazin.de
Freq: Monthly; **Annual Sub.:** EUR 96,60; **Circ:** 4,061
Editor: Weigand Naumann; **Advertising Manager:** Sandra Rink
Profile: Journal containing information about safety contracting and engineering.
Language(s): German
Readership: Aimed at contractors and engineers.
ADVERTISING RATES:
Full Page Mono .... EUR 1260
Full Page Colour .... EUR 1827
Mechanical Data: Type Area: 270 x 188 mm
Copy instructions: *Copy Date:* 30 days prior to publication
Supplement(s): baua: Aktuell
BUSINESS: SAFETY & SECURITY: Safety

SICHERHEITSREPORT
741918G32A-2760
Editorial: Deelbögenkamp 4, 22297 HAMBURG
Tel: 40 51460 **Fax:** 40 51462146
Email: hv.hamburg@vbg.de **Web site:** http://www.vbg.de
Freq: Quarterly; **Circ:** 798,869
Editor: Manfred Fischer; **Advertising Manager:** Walter Piezonka
Profile: Official paper with information for companies, insurers, security experts and agents.
Language(s): German
ADVERTISING RATES:
Full Page Mono .... EUR 13970
Full Page Colour .... EUR 14450
Mechanical Data: Type Area: 221 x 170 mm, No. of Columns (Display): 3, Col Widths (Display): 53 mm
Copy instructions: *Copy Date:* 42 days prior to publication
BUSINESS: LOCAL GOVERNMENT, LEISURE & RECREATION: Local Government

SICHT 1834009G74N-940
Editorial: Lange Wende 16a, 59755 ARNSBERG
Tel: 2932 2012207 **Fax:** 2932 529056
Email: m.gerwin@arnsberg.de **Web site:** http://www.arnsberg.de/senioren
Freq: Quarterly; **Cover Price:** Free; **Circ:** 6,500
Profile: Magazine for the elderly.
Language(s): German

SICHT 1834009G74N-1003
Editorial: Lange Wende 16a, 59755 ARNSBERG
Tel: 2932 2012207 **Fax:** 2932 529056
Email: m.gerwin@arnsberg.de **Web site:** http://www.arnsberg.de/senioren
Freq: Quarterly; **Cover Price:** Free; **Circ:** 6,500
Profile: Magazine for the elderly.
Language(s): German

SICHT + SONNENSCHUTZ
1626532G4E-6966
Editorial: Gewerbestr. 2, 86825 BAD WÖRISHOFEN
Tel: 8247 354231 **Fax:** 8247 3544231
Email: reinhold.kober@holzmann-medien.de **Web site:** http://www.sicht-sonnenschutz.com
Freq: 11 issues yearly; **Annual Sub.:** EUR 70,40; **Circ:** 9,650
Editor: Reinhold Kober; **Advertising Manager:** Michaela Sammer
Profile: We constantly talk about: news, sun protection technology, textile sun protection, day lighting technics, exterior and interior sun protection, awning mechanism, shutter technics, control engineering, folding and sliding shutters, insect screens, door technology, functional glass, products and books.
Language(s): German
ADVERTISING RATES:
Full Page Mono .... EUR 2080
Full Page Colour .... EUR 3580
Mechanical Data: Type Area: 245 x 172 mm, No. of Columns (Display): 4, Col Widths (Display): 40 mm
Copy instructions: *Copy Date:* 21 days prior to publication
BUSINESS: ARCHITECTURE & BUILDING: Building

DER SIEBDRUCK & DIGITALDRUCK 741937G41A-1880
Editorial: Grapengießerstr. 30, 23556 LÜBECK
Tel: 451 8798861 **Fax:** 451 8798893
Email: verlag@draeger.de **Web site:** http://www.der-siebdruck.de
Freq: 10 issues yearly; **Annual Sub.:** EUR 42,00; **Circ:** 4,500
Editor: Peter Arndt; **Advertising Manager:** Monika Saß
Profile: Magazine about silkscreen printing, technology & advertising & m. digital print, plotter, sign-making, film technique, pad printing, etc.
Language(s): German
ADVERTISING RATES:
Full Page Mono .... EUR 1430
Full Page Colour .... EUR 2165
Mechanical Data: Type Area: 258 x 175 mm, No. of Columns (Display): 3, Col Widths (Display): 55 mm
Copy instructions: *Copy Date:* 20 days prior to publication
BUSINESS: PRINTING & STATIONERY: Printing

SIEDLUNG UND EIGENHEIM
741944G74K-1260
Editorial: Schleißheimer Str. 205a, 80809 MÜNCHEN
Tel: 89 3073660 **Fax:** 89 305970
Email: info@eigenheimerverband.de **Web site:** http://www.eigenheimerverband.de
Freq: Monthly; Free to qualifying individuals
Annual Sub.: EUR 15,00; **Circ:** 82,935
Editor: Friedrich Richler; **Advertising Manager:** James Hübner
Profile: Siedlung und Eigenheim is the monthly magazine for members of Eigenheimerverband Bayern e.V. and is available from over 82,000 members. The monthly magazine offers its readers detailed topics contributions from the fields of Home and comprehensive housing policy, legal and tax specialist information. Tips are added to the modernization and renovation. Reviews of vegetables, fruit and ornamental garden and garden design and garden equipment must not be missing, becausea rule have the reader about one-and two-familyhouses with large gardens . The size of the gardens is an average of 490 m^2. The magazine is read by high-spending, high-income people "in the best age (average age: 56 years) who invest regularly in the care and maintenance of house and garden. In the section garden and nature can be found next to the garden calendar for fruit, vegetable and ornamental garden regularly about issues such as new varieties, greenhouses and cold frames, garden tools, lawn and turf care, water garden and garden pond or irrigation systems. Posts around terrace, Canning and A- cook, and shredding and composting round out the variety of topics. In the category Home & Apartment are also contributions related to heating, and solar energy technology, winter garden, roof and roof construction, facade, modernization and renovation as well as to and extensions.
Language(s): German
Readership: Aimed at members.
ADVERTISING RATES:
Full Page Mono .... EUR 2093
Full Page Colour .... EUR 3347
Mechanical Data: Type Area: 260 x 181 mm, No. of Columns (Display): 4, Col Widths (Display): 43 mm
Copy instructions: *Copy Date:* 28 days prior to publication
CONSUMER: WOMEN'S INTEREST CONSUMER MAGAZINES: Home Purchase

SIEGENER ZEITUNG
741949G67B-13520
Editorial: Obergraben 39, 57072 SIEGEN
Tel: 271 59400 **Fax:** 271 5940239
Email: redaktion@siegener-zeitung.de **Web site:** http://www.siegener-zeitung.de
Freq: 312 issues yearly; **Circ:** 56,869
Editor: Dieter Sobotka; **News Editor:** Klaus-Jürgen Menn; **Advertising Manager:** Rolf-Eckard Dilling
Profile: Regional daily newspaper with news on politics, economy, culture, sports, travel, technology, etc. The Siegener Zeitung is the highest circulation daily newspaper in the county of Siegen-Wittgenstein. Facebook: http://www.facebook.com/siegenerzeitung Twitter: http://twitter.com/siegenerzeitung This Outlet offers RSS (Really Simple Syndication).
Language(s): German
ADVERTISING RATES:
SCC .... EUR 74,00
Mechanical Data: Type Area: 485 x 321 mm, No. of Columns (Display): 7, Col Widths (Display): 44 mm
Copy instructions: *Copy Date:* 1 day prior to publication
Supplement(s): prisma
REGIONAL DAILY & SUNDAY NEWSPAPERS: Regional Daily Newspapers

SIEGENER ZEITUNG ONLINE
1622003G67B-16661
Editorial: Obergraben 39, 57072 SIEGEN
Tel: 271 5940219 **Fax:** 271 5940239
Email: redaktion@siegener-zeitung.de **Web site:** http://www.siegener-zeitung.de
Freq: Daily; **Cover Price:** Paid; **Circ:** 173,378 Unique Users
Editor: Dieter Sobotka; **News Editor:** Werner Latsch; **Advertising Manager:** Rolf-Eckard Dilling
Profile: Ezine: Regional daily newspaper covering politics, economics, culture, sports, travel and technology.
Language(s): German
REGIONAL DAILY & SUNDAY NEWSPAPERS: Regional Daily Newspapers

SIEGESSÄULE 741962G86B-600
Editorial: Tempelhofer Ufer 11, 10963 BERLIN
Tel: 30 23553931 **Fax:** 30 23553919
Email: redaktion@siegessaeule.de **Web site:** http://www.siegessaeule.de
Freq: Monthly; **Cover Price:** Free; **Circ:** 50,074
Editor: Sirko Salka; **Advertising Manager:** Bernd Offermann
Profile: Berlin's city magazine for gays and lesbians - one big cover story and solid sections (stage, music, party, film, gossip, restaurant pages) and the program calendar for the current month. Facebook: http://www.facebook.com/pages/Siegessaule/108822659145336 Twitter: http://twitter.com/#!/GaySiegessaeule.
Language(s): German
Readership: Read by members of the gay and lesbian community, also German speaking tourists.
ADVERTISING RATES:
Full Page Mono .... EUR 3600
Full Page Colour .... EUR 3600
Mechanical Data: Type Area: 260 x 190 mm, No. of Columns (Display): 4, Col Widths (Display): 45 mm
Copy instructions: *Copy Date:* 15 days prior to publication
Supplement(s): Queer Wedding
CONSUMER: ADULT & GAY MAGAZINES: Gay & Lesbian Magazines

SIGNAL + DRAHT 741976G49E-780
Editorial: Nordkanalstr. 36, 20097 HAMBURG
Tel: 40 23714281 **Fax:** 40 23714205
Email: jennifer.schykowski@dvvmedia.com **Web site:** http://www.eurailpress.de
Freq: 10 issues yearly; **Annual Sub.:** EUR 134,00; **Circ:** 2,745
Editor: Karl-Heinz Suwe; **Advertising Manager:** Silke Härtel
Profile: Publication focusing on information and communication in the railway industry.
Language(s): German
Readership: Aimed at professionals in the railway industry.
ADVERTISING RATES:
Full Page Mono .... EUR 2340
Full Page Colour .... EUR 3330
Mechanical Data: Type Area: 265 x 182 mm, No. of Columns (Display): 4, Col Widths (Display): 42 mm
BUSINESS: TRANSPORT: Railways

LE SILLON 741986G21A-2620
Editorial: John-Deere-Str. 70, 68163 MANNHEIM
Tel: 621 8298418 **Fax:** 621 8298300
Email: rollersteven@johndeere.com **Web site:** http://www.johndeere.de
Freq: Quarterly; **Cover Price:** Free; **Circ:** 167,000
Editor: Steven Roller
Profile: Company publication published by Deere & Company.
Language(s): French

SIMPSONS COMICS 741995G91D-7260
Editorial: Rotebühlstr. 87, 70178 STUTTGART
Tel: 711 947680 **Fax:** 711 9476830
Email: info@panini.de **Web site:** http://www.panini.de
Freq: Monthly; **Cover Price:** EUR 2,50; **Circ:** 27,475
Editor: Jo Löffler
Profile: Simpsons Comics - the official comic into a cult cartoon series on ProSieben. Have begun to conquer the animated characters on television and seamlessly continued in the comic strip by Panini. A field day for all Simpsons fans!.
Language(s): German
ADVERTISING RATES:
Full Page Mono .... EUR 3900
Full Page Colour .... EUR 3900
Mechanical Data: Type Area: 237 x 149 mm
CONSUMER: RECREATION & LEISURE: Children & Youth

SINGLE.DE 1687118G86A-1422
Editorial: Max-Planck-Str. 6, 50858 KÖLN
Tel: 221 91116 **Fax:** 221 911169
Email: info@webpool.de **Web site:** http://www.single.de
Cover Price: Paid; **Circ:** 50,000,000 Unique Users
Language(s): German
CONSUMER: ADULT & GAY MAGAZINES: Adult Magazines

SINNIOR 1837042G74N-950
Editorial: Moltkestr. 2, 78467 KONSTANZ
Tel: 7531 71294
Email: info@akzent-magazin.com **Web site:** http://www.sinnior.com
Freq: Annual; **Cover Price:** EUR 4,50; **Circ:** 20,000
Editor: Anja Böhme; **Advertising Manager:** Alexander Schraut
Profile: Magazine for seniors on topics such as travel, technology, vital, legal and consumer advice.
Language(s): German
ADVERTISING RATES:
Full Page Mono .... EUR 4200
Full Page Colour .... EUR 4200

Mechanical Data: Type Area: 276 x 188 mm, No. of Columns (Display): 4, Col Widths (Display): 42 mm
Copy instructions: *Copy Date:* 30 days prior to publication

SIXTH SENSE
1655029G40-967
Editorial: Industriestr. 20, 33689 BIELEFELD
Tel: 5205 998660 **Fax:** 5205 9986629
Email: news@sixth-sense-newspaper.de **Web site:** http://www.sixthsense.bfgnet.de
Freq: Weekly; **Annual Sub.:** EUR 80,00; **Circ:** 12,000
Advertising Manager: Ilka Silvera
Profile: Regional weekly newspaper for the British forces in Germany covering politics, economics, sport, travel, technology and the arts.
Language(s): English
Mechanical Data: Type Area: 317 x 231 mm, No. of Columns (Display): 5
Copy instructions: *Copy Date:* 8 days prior to publication

SKÅL INTERNATIONAL JOURNAL DEUTSCHLAND
742028G50-1201
Editorial: Robert-Bosch-Str. 10, 63477 MAINTAL
Tel: 6181 94340 **Fax:** 6181 45719
Email: kramer@seitensatz.de **Web site:** http://www.skal-journal.de
Freq: Quarterly; Free to qualifying individuals
Annual Sub.: EUR 12,80; **Circ:** 5,000
Editor: Stefanie Kramer; **Advertising Manager:** Ulrike Minnich
Profile: Club magazine of the German Skål-Club.
Language(s): German
ADVERTISING RATES:
Full Page Mono .... EUR 1260
Full Page Colour .... EUR 2200
Mechanical Data: Type Area: 265 x 184 mm, No. of Columns (Display): 3, Col Widths (Display): 58 mm
Copy instructions: *Copy Date:* 21 days prior to publication

SKATEBOARD
742030G75X-4540
Editorial: An der Linde 11, 50668 KÖLN
Tel: 221 9140020 **Fax:** 221 9140099
Email: redaktion@skateboardmsm.de **Web site:** http://www.skateboardmsm.de
Freq: Monthly; **Annual Sub.:** EUR 38,40; **Circ:** 40,950
Editor: Oliver Tielsch; **Advertising Manager:** Carsten Bauer
Profile: The skateboard magazine is published monthly and interviews, the latest product news, photos and unique sequences, the biggest, most credible and most prestigious magazine of the European skate scene. Facebook: http://www.facebook.com/skateboardmsm Twitter: http://twitter.com/#!/skateboardmsmde This Outlet offers RSS (Really Simple Syndication).
Language(s): German
Readership: Aimed at skateboarders aged between 10 and 24 years old.
ADVERTISING RATES:
Full Page Mono .... EUR 3729
Full Page Colour .... EUR 4939
Mechanical Data: Type Area: 300 x 230 mm
CONSUMER: SPORT: Other Sport

SKELETAL RADIOLOGY
742034G56A-9160
Editorial: Tiergartenstr. 17, 69121 HEIDELBERG
Tel: 6221 4870 **Fax:** 6221 4878366
Email: subscriptions@springer.com **Web site:** http://www.springerlink.com
Freq: Monthly; **Annual Sub.:** EUR 1397,00; **Circ:** 1,500
Editor: Daniel I. Rosenthal
Profile: Skeletal radiology.
Language(s): English
ADVERTISING RATES:
Full Page Mono .... EUR 1440
Full Page Colour .... EUR 2480
Mechanical Data: Type Area: 240 x 175 mm
Official Journal of: Organ d. Internat. Skeletal Society

SKIMAGAZIN
742039G75G-420
Editorial: Landsberger Str. 482, 81241 MÜNCHEN
Tel: 89 242926530 **Fax:** 89 242926569
Email: f.tausch@sportcombi.de **Web site:** http://www.skimagazin.de
Freq: 5 issues yearly; Free to qualifying individuals
Annual Sub.: EUR 26,40; **Circ:** 123,215
Editor: Florian Tausch; **Advertising Manager:** Erik Hornung
Profile: Magazine for serious skiers, presents the full diversity of alpine skiing, the SkiMagazin test is one of the largest and most recognized ski tests and is published in eight other European countries.
Language(s): German
Readership: Read by all levels of skiing enthusiasts.
ADVERTISING RATES:
Full Page Mono .... EUR 6871
Full Page Colour .... EUR 11454
Mechanical Data: Type Area: 250 x 180 mm, No. of Columns (Display): 4, Col Widths (Display): 41 mm
Copy instructions: *Copy Date:* 30 days prior to publication
CONSUMER: SPORT: Winter Sports

SKIPPER
742041G91A-140
Editorial: Am Windfeld 15, 83714 MIESBACH
Tel: 8025 294101 **Fax:** 8025 294271
Email: keschneiders@skipperonline.de **Web site:** http://www.skippermagazin.de
Freq: Monthly; **Annual Sub.:** EUR 44,00; **Circ:** 17,567
Editor: Klaus E. Schneiders; **Advertising Manager:** Rainer Matthe
Profile: Skipper is one of the leading water sports magazines in the European market. Since 1978, Skipper covers every month from all relevant areas of motorized water sports. In addition to expert reviews of new boats, trailers vehicles and maritime equipment we offer useful information about technology and electronics that provide practical tips for professionals and beginners, exciting reports and the latest from the scene. In addition, we offer attractive boat territories from Germany - before and abroad and provide information on attractive regional features. Skipper reached water sports enthusiasts and readers of all ages and income levels is an important link between trade and consumers.
Language(s): German
ADVERTISING RATES:
Full Page Mono .... EUR 4960
Full Page Colour .... EUR 4960
Mechanical Data: Type Area: 250 x 186 mm, No. of Columns (Display): 4, Col Widths (Display): 43 mm
Copy instructions: *Copy Date:* 28 days prior to publication
CONSUMER: RECREATION & LEISURE: Boating & Yachting

SLEAZE
1840781G73-647
Editorial: Gürtelstr. 25, 10247 BERLIN
Tel: 30 32534730 **Fax:** 30 32534731
Email: yanah@sleazemag.de **Web site:** http://www.sleazemag.de
Freq: 6 issues yearly; **Cover Price:** Free; **Circ:** 54,000
Editor: Yanah Hölig; **Advertising Manager:** Danilo Opitz
Profile: Sleaze is a print magazine, which updates and timeless theme in some rough graphics. Focuses on politics and business, street art and tattoo, music and literature, youth and movement. Born of the frustration about the humorless and superficial equality of the magazines, there is a magazine of free minds of free spirits. Facebook: http://www.facebook.com/sleazemag.de?v=wall Twitter: http://twitter.com/#!/SLEAZEmagazin This Outlet offers RSS (Really Simple Syndication).
Language(s): German
ADVERTISING RATES:
Full Page Mono .... EUR 6000
Full Page Colour .... EUR 6000
Mechanical Data: Type Area: 297 x 210 mm
Copy instructions: *Copy Date:* 14 days prior to publication

SLEEP AND BREATHING
1832448G56A-11543
Editorial: Heidelberger Platz 3, 14197 BERLIN
Tel: 30 827870 **Fax:** 30 8214091
Email: subscriptions@springer.com **Web site:** http://www.springer.com
Freq: Quarterly; **Annual Sub.:** EUR 372,00; **Circ:** 1,789
Editor: N. C. Netzer
Profile: Sleep and Breathing reflects the international state of the science and practice of sleep medicine.
Language(s): English
ADVERTISING RATES:
Full Page Mono .... EUR 1130
Full Page Colour .... EUR 2170
Mechanical Data: Type Area: 240 x 175 mm
Official Journal of: Organ d. American, European u. Japanese Academy of Dental Sleep Medicine u. d. British Society of Dental Sleep Medicine

---

SLOGANS
1655598G2A-5558
Editorial: Mühlwiesenstr. 32, 70794 FILDERSTADT
Tel: 7158 9390241 **Fax:** 7158 9390277
Email: wolf.hirschmann@slogan.de **Web site:** http://www.slogan.de
Freq: Half-yearly; **Circ:** 1,200
Editor: Wolf Hirschmann
Profile: Magazine from the Slogan, Werbung, Marketing, consulting company.
Language(s): German

SLOW FOOD MAGAZIN
1812271G74P-1237
Editorial: Ziekowstr. 164, 13509 BERLIN
Tel: 30 49997449
Email: redaktion@slowfoodmagazin.de **Web site:** http://www.slowfood.de
Freq: 6 issues yearly; Free to qualifying individuals
Annual Sub.: EUR 20,00; **Circ:** 26,000
Editor: Martina Tschirner
Profile: Slow Food is a forum for lovers of responsibility. Well-known authors writing on current issues in the areas of sustainable food production, organic farming and biodiversity, Culinary & Catering, wine and wine culture, local cuisine, healthy baby food.
Language(s): German
ADVERTISING RATES:
Full Page Colour .... EUR 1420
Mechanical Data: Type Area: 252 x 175 mm

SMAG
742065G89C-4828
Editorial: Ruhrtalstr. 67, 45239 ESSEN
Tel: 201 246880 **Fax:** 201 24688100
Email: redaktion@stegenwaller.de **Web site:** http://www.mysmag.de
Freq: Monthly; **Annual Sub.:** EUR 20,00; **Circ:** 54,818
Editor: Dirk Stegenwaller; **Advertising Manager:** Alexander P. Jäger
Profile: Events magazine for the Rhine/Ruhr region with news and events calendar for parties, fashion, lifestyle and music. Facebook: http://www.facebook.com/smagmagazin This Outlet offers RSS (Really Simple Syndication).
Language(s): German
Readership: Read by local residents and visitors.
ADVERTISING RATES:
Full Page Colour .... EUR 4050
Mechanical Data: No. of Columns (Display): 4, Col Widths (Display): 45 mm, Type Area: 261 x 190 mm
Copy instructions: *Copy Date:* 6 days prior to publication
CONSUMER: HOLIDAYS & TRAVEL: Entertainment Guides

SMOKERS CLUB
742076G94H-10980
Editorial: Erich-Dombrowski-Str. 2, 55127 MAINZ
Tel: 6131 58410 **Fax:** 6131 5841101
Email: folker.kling@konradin.de **Web site:** http://www.smokersclub.de
Freq: Quarterly; **Annual Sub.:** EUR 18,80; **Circ:** 30,789
Editor: Folker Kling; **Advertising Manager:** Michael Günther
Profile: Publication for pipe smokers.
Language(s): German
ADVERTISING RATES:
Full Page Mono .... EUR 3630
Full Page Colour .... EUR 5450
Mechanical Data: Type Area: 244 x 178 mm, No. of Columns (Display): 4, Col Widths (Display): 41 mm
Copy instructions: *Copy Date:* 21 days prior to publication
CONSUMER: OTHER CLASSIFICATIONS: Customer Magazines

SNOWBOARDER
742083G75G-480
Editorial: Gabelsbergerstr. 36, 80333 MÜNCHEN
Tel: 89 5427200 **Fax:** 89 54272080
Email: info@snowboardermbm.de **Web site:** http://www.snowboardermbm.de
Freq: 7 issues yearly; **Annual Sub.:** EUR 25,90; **Circ:** 52,500
Editor: Sebastian Gogl; **Advertising Manager:** Martin Olesch
Profile: Magazine about snowboarding. For 20 years, accompanied the snowboarder Monster Backside Snowboard Magazine as the leading magazine in the German speaking the scene and its developments. Since its inception, the magazine's credo "by snowboarders for snowboarders," has remained faithful. Our philosophy includes the setting that both the needs of the core snowboarders and the weekenders want to become satisfied. This balancing act between scene Mainstream and mastering the MBM in the history of the magazine. Fascinating images from around the world, exceptional features, solid service issues, as well as gossip and shape the MBM. Rooted in the scene, the magazine brings new trends and developments in the target group authentic detail. Facebook: http://de-de.facebook.com/snowboardermbm Twitter: http://twitter.com/#!/snowboardermbm This Outlet offers RSS (Really Simple Syndication).
Language(s): German
Readership: Aimed at young people.
ADVERTISING RATES:
Full Page Colour .... EUR 5500
Mechanical Data: Type Area: 300 x 230 mm
CONSUMER: SPORT: Winter Sports

SO ISST ITALIEN
1895574G74P-1276
Editorial: An der Halle 400 1, 24143 KIEL
Tel: 431 20076600 **Fax:** 431 20076650
Email: redaktion@so-isst-italien.de **Web site:** http://www.soisstitalien.de
Freq: 6 issues yearly; **Annual Sub.:** EUR 24,90; **Circ:** 37,121
Editor: Kathrin Hoberg; **Advertising Manager:** Julia Buchholz
Profile: Cooking and lifestyle magazine all about the Italian lifestyle. Recipes, product tips, travel, excursions and restaurant information on Italy.
Language(s): German
ADVERTISING RATES:
Full Page Mono .... EUR 3500
Full Page Colour .... EUR 4700
Mechanical Data: Type Area: 297 x 232 mm

SO SCHMECKT MÜNCHEN!
1836496G89A-12412
Editorial: Höherweg 287, 40231 DÜSSELDORF
Tel: 211 7357681 **Fax:** 211 7357680
Email: info@ueberblick.de **Web site:** http://www.ueberblick.de
Freq: Annual; **Cover Price:** EUR 7,80; **Circ:** 50,000
Editor: Philipp Fischer
Profile: Munich restaurant guide with information on about 300 restaurants.
Language(s): German
ADVERTISING RATES:
Full Page Mono .... EUR 2670
Full Page Colour .... EUR 3975
Mechanical Data: Type Area: 260 x 190 mm, No. of Columns (Display): 4, Col Widths (Display): 44 mm

Copy instructions: *Copy Date:* 31 days prior to publication

SOESTER ANZEIGER
742102G67B-13560
Editorial: Schloitweg 19, 59494 SOEST
Tel: 2921 6880 **Fax:** 2921 688148
Email: stadtredaktion@soester-anzeiger.de **Web site:** http://www.soester-anzeiger.de
Freq: 312 issues yearly; **Circ:** 36,900
Advertising Manager: Steffen Schulle
Profile: Daily newspaper with regional news and a local sports section. Twitter: http://twitter.com/wa_online This Outlet offers RSS (Really Simple Syndication).
Language(s): German
ADVERTISING RATES:
SCC .... EUR 77,60
Mechanical Data: Type Area: 466 x 317 mm, No. of Columns (Display): 7, Col Widths (Display): 43 mm
Copy instructions: *Copy Date:* 1 day prior to publication
Supplement(s): prisma
REGIONAL DAILY & SUNDAY NEWSPAPERS: Regional Daily Newspapers

---

SOESTMAGAZIN
742103G80-10580
Editorial: Nelmannwall 4, 59494 SOEST
Tel: 2921 36090 **Fax:** 2921 360929
Email: info@fkwverlag.com **Web site:** http://www.fkwverlag.com
Freq: Monthly; **Cover Price:** Free; **Circ:** 23,500
Editor: Burkhard Salzmann; **Advertising Manager:** Rüdiger Deparade
Profile: City Magazine for Soest with Events to music, culture and sports.
Language(s): German
ADVERTISING RATES:
Full Page Mono .... EUR 1680
Mechanical Data: No. of Columns (Display): 4, Col Widths (Display): 43 mm
CONSUMER: RURAL & REGIONAL INTEREST

SÖFW JOURNAL
742099G13-2060
Editorial: Beethovenstr. 16, 86150 AUGSBURG
Tel: 821 325830 **Fax:** 821 3258323
Email: s.fischer@sofw.com **Web site:** http://www.sofw.com
Freq: Monthly; **Annual Sub.:** EUR 268,90; **Circ:** 907
Editor: Siegfried Fischer; **Advertising Manager:** Siegfried Fischer
Profile: Magazine for soap, perfume and detergent experts with information on new raw materials and testing methods.
Language(s): German
ADVERTISING RATES:
Full Page Mono .... EUR 1740
Full Page Colour .... EUR 2760
Mechanical Data: Type Area: 264 x 178 mm, No. of Columns (Display): 4, Col Widths (Display): 40 mm
Copy instructions: *Copy Date:* 14 days prior to publication
Official Journal of: Organ d. Vereinigung d. Seifen-, Parfüm- u. Waschmittelfachleute e.V.
BUSINESS: CHEMICALS

SOLARBRIEF
1829646G57-2854
Editorial: Frère-Roger-Str. 8, 52062 AACHEN
Tel: 241 511616 **Fax:** 241 535786
Email: zentrale@sfv.de **Web site:** http://www.sfv.de
Freq: Quarterly; **Cover Price:** EUR 6,00
Free to qualifying individuals ; **Circ:** 5,500
Editor: Wolf von Fabeck
Profile: Magazine about renewal energies. Facebook: http://www.facebook.com/pages/Solarenergie-Forderverein-Deutschland-eV-SFV/415318040608.
Language(s): German

SOLARTHEMEN
742110G58-1705
Editorial: Bültestr. 70b, 32584 LÖHNE
Tel: 5731 83460 **Fax:** 5731 83469
Email: redaktion@solarthemen.de **Web site:** http://www.solarthemen.de
Freq: 24 issues yearly; **Annual Sub.:** EUR 132,00; **Circ:** 2,562
Editor: Guido Bröer
Profile: Concise, up-to-date, research-competent. These are the key features of Solarthemen. Our information service for experts reaches decision-makers within the renewable energy sector, 24 times a year. This Outlet offers RSS (Really Simple Syndication).
Language(s): German
ADVERTISING RATES:
Full Page Mono .... EUR 1450
Full Page Colour .... EUR 1450
Mechanical Data: Type Area: 297 x 210 mm
Copy instructions: *Copy Date:* 14 days prior to publication
BUSINESS: ENERGY, FUEL & NUCLEAR

SOLARTHEMEN:KOM
2036260G57-2961
Editorial: Bültestr. 70b, 32584 LÖHNE
Tel: 5731 83460 **Fax:** 5731 83469
Email: redaktion@solarthemen.de **Web site:** http://www.solarthemen.de
Freq: Quarterly; **Annual Sub.:** EUR 22,00; **Circ:** 15,000

Editor: Guido Bröer
Profile: Renewable energy for cities and communities. Solar Topics: com is the only trade magazine for the local audience that is dedicated exclusively to renewable energies. This Outlet offers RSS (Really Simple Syndication).
Language(s): German
ADVERTISING RATES:
Full Page Mono .... EUR 3490
Full Page Colour .... EUR 3490
Mechanical Data: Type Area: 297 x 210 mm

SOLARZEITALTER 1615131G58-1709
Editorial: Kaiser-Friedrich-Str. 11, 53113 BONN
Tel: 228 362373 **Fax:** 228 361279
Email: solarzeitalter@eurosolar.de **Web site:** http://www.eurosolar.org
Freq: Quarterly; Free to qualifying individuals
Annual Sub.: EUR 20,00; **Circ:** 4,000
Editor: Irm Pontenagel; **Advertising Manager:** Antje Spindler
Profile: Magazine about politics and the economy of renewable energy.
Language(s): German
ADVERTISING RATES:
Full Page Mono .... EUR 650
Full Page Colour .... EUR 1500
Mechanical Data: Type Area: 202 x 142 mm
Copy instructions: *Copy Date:* 20 days prior to publication

IL SOLCO 742111G21A-2200
Editorial: John-Deere-Str. 8, 68163 MANNHEIM
Tel: 621 8298418 **Fax:** 621 8298300
Email: rollersteven@johndeere.com **Web site:** http://www.johndeere.com
Freq: Quarterly; **Cover Price:** Free; **Circ:** 42,000
Editor: Steven Roller
Profile: Company publication published by Deere & Company.
Language(s): Italian

SOLDAT IM VOLK 742113G40-720
Editorial: Rheinallee 55, 53173 BONN
Tel: 228 361007 **Fax:** 228 361008
Email: vds.bund.bonn@t-online.de
Freq: 6 issues yearly; **Annual Sub.:** EUR 22,00; **Circ:** 1,200
Profile: Publication of the Association of German Soldiers.
Language(s): German
ADVERTISING RATES:
Full Page Mono .... EUR 1030
Mechanical Data: Type Area: 270 x 185 mm, No. of Columns (Display): 3, Col Widths (Display): 58 mm
Copy instructions: *Copy Date:* 15 days prior to publication
BUSINESS: DEFENCE

DAS SOLINGER AM MITTWOCH 742122G72-12008
Editorial: Mummstr. 9, 42651 SOLINGEN
Tel: 212 299100 **Fax:** 212 299123
Email: b.boll@solinger-tageblatt.de **Web site:** http://www.solinger-tageblatt.de
Freq: Weekly; **Cover Price:** Free; **Circ:** 74,684
Editor: Stefan M. Kob; **Advertising Manager:** Matthias Köstner
Profile: Advertising journal (house-to-house) concentrating on local stories.
Language(s): German
ADVERTISING RATES:
Full Page Mono .... EUR 3741
Full Page Colour .... EUR 5522
Mechanical Data: Type Area: 430 x 282 mm, No. of Columns (Display): 6, Col Widths (Display): 45 mm
Copy instructions: *Copy Date:* 1 day prior to publication
LOCAL NEWSPAPERS

SOLINGER MORGENPOST 742121G67B-13580
Editorial: Zülpicher Str. 10, 40549 DÜSSELDORF
Tel: 211 5050 **Fax:** 211 5047562
Email: redaktionssekretariat@rheinische-post.de
Web site: http://www.rp-online.de
Freq: 312 issues yearly; **Circ:** 3,339
Advertising Manager: Marc Arne Schümann
Profile: Daily newspaper with regional news and a local sports section. Facebook: http://www.facebook.com/rponline Twitter: http://www.rp-online.de/app/feed/twitter This Outlet offers RSS (Really Simple Syndication).
Language(s): German
ADVERTISING RATES:
SCC .... EUR 29,10
Mechanical Data: Type Area: 480 x 325 mm, No. of Columns (Display): 7, Col Widths (Display): 45 mm
Copy instructions: *Copy Date:* 2 days prior to publication
REGIONAL DAILY & SUNDAY NEWSPAPERS: Regional Daily Newspapers

SOLINGER-TAGEBLATT.DE 1622060G67B-16663
Editorial: Mummstr. 9, 42651 SOLINGEN
Tel: 212 299106 **Fax:** 212 299123
Email: stefan.kob@solinger-tageblatt.de **Web site:** http://www.solinger-tageblatt.de
Freq: Daily; **Cover Price:** Paid; **Circ:** 267,108 Unique Users
Editor: Stefan M. Kob
Profile: Ezine: Regional daily newspaper covering politics, economics, sports, travel and technology. Facebook: http://www.facebook.com/sgtageblatt Twitter: http://twitter.com/#!/SGTageblatt.
Language(s): German
REGIONAL DAILY & SUNDAY NEWSPAPERS: Regional Daily Newspapers

SOLLINGER ALLGEMEINE 730359G67B-7260
Editorial: Frankfurter Str. 168, 34121 KASSEL
Tel: 561 20300 **Fax:** 561 2032406
Email: info@hna.de **Web site:** http://www.hna.de
Freq: 312 issues yearly; **Circ:** 15,881
Advertising Manager: Andrea Schaller-Öller
Profile: Regional daily newspaper with news on politics, economy, culture, sports, travel, technology, etc. The Sollinger Allgemeine is a local issue of HNA Hessische/Niedersächsische Allgemeine. Twitter: http://twitter.com/hna_online This Outlet offers RSS (Really Simple Syndication).
Language(s): German
ADVERTISING RATES:
SCC .... EUR 40,00
Mechanical Data: Type Area: 430 x 285 mm, No. of Columns (Display): 6, Col Widths (Display): 45 mm
Copy instructions: *Copy Date:* 2 days prior to publication
REGIONAL DAILY & SUNDAY NEWSPAPERS: Regional Daily Newspapers

SOLMS-BRAUNFELSER 742127G67B-13600
Editorial: Elsa-Brandström-Str. 18, 35578 WETZLAR
Tel: 6441 9590 **Fax:** 6441 959292
Email: redaktion.wnz@mittelhessen.de **Web site:** http://www.mittelhessen.de
Freq: 312 issues yearly; **Circ:** 25,825
Advertising Manager: Peter Rother
Profile: Daily newspaper with regional news and a local sports section.
Language(s): German
ADVERTISING RATES:
SCC .... EUR 66,50
Mechanical Data: Type Area: 490 x 328 mm, No. of Columns (Display): 7, Col Widths (Display): 44 mm
Copy instructions: *Copy Date:* 1 day prior to publication
Supplement(s): [f]amilie& freizeit; Fußball-Kalender; [g]esund!; Handball-Kalender; lahndillregio; rtv
REGIONAL DAILY & SUNDAY NEWSPAPERS: Regional Daily Newspapers

SOLMS-BRAUNFELSER AM SONNTAG 1606890G72-18521
Editorial: Elsa-Brandström-Str. 18, 35578 WETZLAR
Tel: 6441 9590 **Fax:** 6441 959292
Email: redaktion.wnz@mittelhessen.de **Web site:** http://www.mittelhessen.de
Freq: Weekly; **Cover Price:** EUR 1,00; **Circ:** 25,825
Advertising Manager: Peter Rother
Profile: Regional weekly covering politics, economics, sport, travel, technology and the arts.
Language(s): German
ADVERTISING RATES:
SCC .... EUR 66,50
Mechanical Data: Type Area: 490 x 328 mm, No. of Columns (Display): 7, Col Widths (Display): 44 mm
Copy instructions: *Copy Date:* 2 days prior to publication
LOCAL NEWSPAPERS

SOMMELIER MAGAZIN 756539G74P-981
Editorial: Maximilianstr. 7, 67433 NEUSTADT
Tel: 6321 890845 **Fax:** 6321 890873
Email: baeder@meininger.de **Web site:** http://www.sommelier-magazin.de
Freq: 6 issues yearly; Free to qualifying individuals
Annual Sub.: EUR 39,60; **Circ:** 4,216
Editor: Kristine Bäder; **Advertising Manager:** Ralf Clemens
Profile: The „Sommelier Magazin" is the service magazine for sommeliers and restaurateurs that covers all aspects of wine and spirits as well as other subjects associated with the pleasures of life. As the official publication of the Sommelier Union of Germany, it constitutes the connecting link between Union members, high-class gastronomy and hotel businesses and the producers and importers of high-quality wines and other beverages. The „Sommelier Magazin" places particular emphasis on practical value. The main area of editorial focus is concentrated information on cultivation areas, recommended producers and wines, specialized knowledge and further training, practical suggestions for combining wines and foods, beverage and cigar expertise and cellar management.
Language(s): German
ADVERTISING RATES:
Full Page Mono .... EUR 2855
Full Page Colour .... EUR 3075
Mechanical Data: Type Area: 260 x 195 mm, No. of Columns (Display): 4, Col Widths (Display): 45 mm
Copy instructions: *Copy Date:* 35 days prior to publication
Official Journal of: Organ d. Dt. Sommelier-Union e.V.
CONSUMER: WOMEN'S INTEREST CONSUMER MAGAZINES: Food & Cookery

SOMMERGASTRO 1666082G74P-1171
Editorial: Falbenhennenstr. 17, 70180 STUTTGART
Tel: 711 60171749 **Fax:** 711 60171729
Email: info@lift-online.de **Web site:** http://www.lift-online.de
Freq: Annual; **Cover Price:** Free; **Circ:** 30,000
Editor: Sabrina Schuler
Profile: The largest open-air guide Gastro guide for Stuttgart and the region with 400 top names from beer gardens, street cafes, beer gardens, city beaches and street fairs. The special issue is a constant companion throughout the open-air season, and is used throughout the summer. Facebook: http://www.facebook.com/pages/LIFT-Stadtmagazin/161318138841.
Language(s): German
ADVERTISING RATES:
Full Page Mono .... EUR 1815
Full Page Colour .... EUR 2405
Mechanical Data: Type Area: 260 x 190 mm, No. of Columns (Display): 4, Col Widths (Display): 44 mm
Copy instructions: *Copy Date:* 14 days prior to publication

SOMMEROASEN CHEMNITZ 1882127G89A-12446
Editorial: Prager Str. 2b, 01069 DRESDEN
Tel: 351 8007030 **Fax:** 351 8007070
Email: redaktion@maxity.de **Web site:** http://www.sommeroasen.de
Freq: Annual; **Cover Price:** Free; **Circ:** 15,000
Profile: Directory listing outdoor gastronomy facilities in Chemnitz.
Language(s): English; German
Mechanical Data: Type Area: 126 x 85 mm

SOMMEROASEN DRESDEN 1830257G89A-12409
Editorial: Prager Str. 2b, 01069 DRESDEN
Tel: 351 8007030 **Fax:** 351 8007070
Email: redaktion@maxity.de **Web site:** http://www.sommeroasen.de
Freq: Annual; **Cover Price:** Free; **Circ:** 15,000
Editor: Christine Herzog; **Advertising Manager:** Cathleen Moosche
Profile: Directory listing outdoor gastronomy facilities in Dresden.
Language(s): German
Mechanical Data: Type Area: 126 x 85 mm

SOMNOLOGIE 742137G56A-9220
Editorial: Tiergartenstr. 17, 69121 HEIDELBERG
Tel: 6221 4878819 **Fax:** 6221 48768819
Email: denskus.steinkopff@springer.com **Web site:** http://www.springer.com
Freq: Quarterly; **Annual Sub.:** EUR 189,00; **Circ:** 2,300
Advertising Manager: Sabine Weidner
Profile: Somnologie ist the official Journal of the German Sleep Society and the Austrian Sleep Research Association. On the basis of current, clinically relevant research results, the journal Somnologie is concerned with the etiology, pathophysiology, differential diagnostics and treatment of various sleep disorders. A scientific, comprehensive analysis of the various causes of sleep disorders requires the cooperation of several branches of medicine. Due to the cooperation of specialists in the areas of epidemiology, human genetics, ENT, OMF, internal medicine, pneumology, cardiology, gastroenterology, neurology, neurophysiology, physiology, psychology, pediatrics, and pharmacology, Somnologie fulfills the multidisciplinary requirements of sleep research and sleep medicine. In addition to experimental and clinical original articles, reviews, case reports, recommendations and guidelines are published. With the peer-review process and Online First publication of articles, the journal ensures international scientific standards.
Language(s): English; German
ADVERTISING RATES:
Full Page Mono .... EUR 1460
Full Page Colour .... EUR 2500
Mechanical Data: Type Area: 240 x 174 mm
Official Journal of: Organ d. Dt. Ges. f. Schlafforschung u. Schlafmedizin u. d. Österr. Ges. f. Schlafmedizin u. Schlafforschung

SONNE WIND & WÄRME 742154G58-1300
Editorial: Niederwall 53, 33602 BIELEFELD
Tel: 521 595515 **Fax:** 521 595556
Email: sonnewindwaerme@bva-bielefeld.de **Web site:** http://www.sonnewindwaerme.de
Freq: 18 issues yearly; **Annual Sub.:** EUR 99,00; **Circ:** 29,399
Editor: Volker Buddensiek
Profile: Magazine about the use of renewable energy and using energy-saving technology. Main topics: solar thermal, solar power, solar architecture, biomass, wind energy, cogeneration, fuel cells and heat pumps.
Language(s): German
ADVERTISING RATES:
Full Page Colour .... EUR 3300
Mechanical Data: Type Area: 260 x 190 mm, No. of Columns (Display): 3, Col Widths (Display): 60 mm
Copy instructions: *Copy Date:* 21 days prior to publication
BUSINESS: ENERGY, FUEL & NUCLEAR

SONNENENERGIE 765240G19A-1045
Editorial: Landgrabenstr. 94, 90443 NÜRNBERG
Tel: 911 37651630 **Fax:** 911 37651631
Email: sonnenenergie@dgs.de **Web site:** http://www.sonnenenergie.de
Freq: 6 issues yearly; Free to qualifying individuals
Annual Sub.: EUR 30,00; **Circ:** 8,500
Editor: Matthias Hüttmann
Profile: Magazine covering all aspects of solar technology.
Language(s): German
ADVERTISING RATES:
Full Page Mono .... EUR 2400
Full Page Colour .... EUR 2400
Mechanical Data: Type Area: 265 x 174 mm

SONNENENERGIE 765240G19A-1142
Editorial: Landgrabenstr. 94, 90443 NÜRNBERG
Tel: 911 37651630 **Fax:** 911 37651631
Email: sonnenenergie@dgs.de **Web site:** http://www.sonnenenergie.de
Freq: 6 issues yearly; Free to qualifying individuals
Annual Sub.: EUR 30,00; **Circ:** 8,500
Editor: Matthias Hüttmann
Profile: Magazine covering all aspects of solar technology.
Language(s): German
ADVERTISING RATES:
Full Page Mono .... EUR 2400
Full Page Colour .... EUR 2400
Mechanical Data: Type Area: 265 x 174 mm

DER SONNTAG 742158G87-11600
Editorial: Blumenstr. 76, 04155 LEIPZIG
Tel: 341 7114170 **Fax:** 341 7114160
Email: info@sonntag-sachsen.de **Web site:** http://www.sonntag-sachsen.de
Freq: Weekly; **Annual Sub.:** EUR 42,00; **Circ:** 10,308
Editor: Christine Reuther
Profile: Weekly from the Evangelical Lutheran national church in Saxony.
Language(s): German
ADVERTISING RATES:
Full Page Mono .... EUR 2436
Full Page Colour .... EUR 4263
Mechanical Data: Type Area: 406 x 282 mm, No. of Columns (Display): 6, Col Widths (Display): 45 mm
Copy instructions: *Copy Date:* 13 days prior to publication
CONSUMER: RELIGIOUS

DER SONNTAG 742162G87-11620
Editorial: Frankfurter Str. 9, 65549 LIMBURG
Tel: 6431 91130 **Fax:** 6431 911337
Email: h-kaiser@kirchenzeitung.de **Web site:** http://www.kirchenzeitung.de
Freq: Weekly; **Annual Sub.:** EUR 73,20; **Circ:** 10,016
Editor: Johannes Becher; **Advertising Manager:** Sylvia Ehrengard
Profile: Church magazine from the diocese of Limburg.
Language(s): German
ADVERTISING RATES:
Full Page Mono .... EUR 3206
Mechanical Data: Type Area: 458 x 325 mm, No. of Columns (Display): 7, Col Widths (Display): 45 mm
Copy instructions: *Copy Date:* 14 days prior to publication
CONSUMER: RELIGIOUS

SONNTAG AKTUELL 742163G72-12060
Editorial: Plieninger Str. 150, 70567 STUTTGART
Tel: 711 72050 **Fax:** 711 72051509
Email: redaktion@soak.zgs.de **Web site:** http://www.sonntag-aktuell.de
Freq: Weekly; **Cover Price:** EUR 1,30; **Circ:** 645,499
Editor: Christoph Reisinger
Profile: Regional weekly covering politics, economics, sports, travel, technology and the arts.
Language(s): German
ADVERTISING RATES:
SCC .... EUR 714,60
Mechanical Data: Type Area: 492 x 321 mm, No. of Columns (Display): 7, Col Widths (Display): 44 mm
Copy instructions: *Copy Date:* 4 days prior to publication
LOCAL NEWSPAPERS

SONNTAG EXPRESS 742165G72-12068
Editorial: Amsterdamer Str. 192, 50735 KÖLN
Tel: 221 2240 **Fax:** 221 2242700
Email: redaktion@express.de **Web site:** http://www.express.de
Freq: Weekly; **Circ:** 153,993
Advertising Manager: Karsten Hundhausen
Profile: 7th issue of the week for Express, Bonn and Dusseldorf Express. The local-based tabloid newspaper from the publisher M. DuMont Schauberg is the currently-cheeky voice of the region and the lawyer of his readers. Six times a week, the editors demonstrate their competence, for the Express, there are more than just sensational headline. Exciting coverage is combined with in-depth background information and critical comments. The Express is the leading newspaper purchase of the Rhineland with the highest competence in the region. He appears in the circulation area with three issues: in Cologne, Dusseldorf and Bonn, from the Eifel to the Oberbergische Land. The Express is characterized by recent, strong acceptance themes, series and service elements. His style is like the people on the Rhine: tolerant, cosmopolitan, humorous with a touch of

emotion. One of the very strong points of the Express: sport. Facebook: http://www.facebook.com/express.de.
Language(s): German
ADVERTISING RATES:
SCC .... EUR 136,70
Mechanical Data: Type Area: 430 x 285 mm, No. of Columns (Display): 6, Col Widths (Display): 45 mm
Copy instructions: *Copy Date:* 3 days prior to publication
LOCAL NEWSPAPERS

SONNTAGS POST FRECHEN
727881G72-3996
Editorial: Europaallee 33b, 50226 FRECHEN
Tel: 2234 95744130 **Fax:** 2234 95744499
Email: redaktion@sonntags-post.de **Web site:** http://www.rheinische-anzeigenblaetter.de
Freq: Weekly; **Cover Price:** Free; **Circ:** 24,933
Editor: Ulf Stefan Dahmen; **Advertising Manager:** Daniela Bauer
Profile: Advertising journal (house-to-house) concentrating on local stories.
Language(s): German
ADVERTISING RATES:
Full Page Mono .... EUR 1858
Full Page Colour .... EUR 2694
Mechanical Data: Type Area: 430 x 282 mm, No. of Columns (Display): 6, Col Widths (Display): 45 mm
Copy instructions: *Copy Date:* 2 days prior to publication
LOCAL NEWSPAPERS

SONNTAGS POST HÜRTH
730615G72-5716
Editorial: Europaallee 33b, 50226 FRECHEN
Tel: 2238 95744130 **Fax:** 2234 95744499
Email: redaktion@sonntags-post.de **Web site:** http://www.rheinische-anzeigenblaetter.de
Freq: Weekly; **Cover Price:** Free; **Circ:** 29,235
Editor: Ulf Stefan Dahmen; **Advertising Manager:** Daniela Bauer
Profile: Advertising journal (house-to-house) concentrating on local stories.
Language(s): German
ADVERTISING RATES:
Full Page Mono .... EUR 1858
Full Page Colour .... EUR 2694
Mechanical Data: Type Area: 430 x 282 mm, No. of Columns (Display): 6, Col Widths (Display): 45 mm
Copy instructions: *Copy Date:* 2 days prior to publication
LOCAL NEWSPAPERS

SONNTAGS POST PULHEIM
739740G72-10620
Editorial: Europaallee 33b, 50226 FRECHEN
Tel: 2234 95744130 **Fax:** 2234 95744499
Email: redaktion@sonntags-post.de **Web site:** http://www.rheinische-anzeigenblaetter.de
Freq: Weekly; **Cover Price:** Free; **Circ:** 33,336
Editor: Ulf Stefan Dahmen; **Advertising Manager:** Daniela Bauer
Profile: Advertising journal (house-to-house) concentrating on local stories.
Language(s): German
ADVERTISING RATES:
Full Page Mono .... EUR 2038
Full Page Colour .... EUR 2955
Mechanical Data: Type Area: 430 x 282 mm, No. of Columns (Display): 6, Col Widths (Display): 45 mm
Copy instructions: *Copy Date:* 2 days prior to publication
LOCAL NEWSPAPERS

SONNTAGSBLATT
742182G87-11640
Editorial: Birkerstr. 22, 80636 MÜNCHEN
Tel: 89 12172126 **Fax:** 89 12172304
Email: sonntagsblatt@epv.de **Web site:** http://www.sonntagsblatt-bayern.de
Freq: Weekly; **Annual Sub.:** EUR 69,00; **Circ:** 29,324
Editor: Helmut Frank
Profile: Newspaper about the Protestant church in Bavaria.
Language(s): German
ADVERTISING RATES:
Full Page Mono .... EUR 2052
Full Page Colour .... EUR 2850
Mechanical Data: Type Area: 285 x 212 mm, No. of Columns (Display): 4, Col Widths (Display): 45 mm
Copy instructions: *Copy Date:* 12 days prior to publication
CONSUMER: RELIGIOUS

SONNTAGSBLITZ
742191G72-12140
Editorial: Marienstr. 11, 90402 NÜRNBERG
Tel: 911 2162759 **Fax:** 911 2161560
Email: nn-redaktion-blitz@pressenetz.de **Web site:** http://www.sonntagsblitz.de
Freq: Weekly; **Cover Price:** Free; **Circ:** 405,115
Editor: Georg Klietz
Profile: Advertising journal (house-to-house) concentrating on local stories.
Language(s): German
ADVERTISING RATES:
Full Page Mono .... EUR 14784
Full Page Colour .... EUR 19944
Mechanical Data: Type Area: 430 x 280 mm, No. of Columns (Display): 6, Col Widths (Display): 45 mm
Copy instructions: *Copy Date:* 3 days prior to publication
LOCAL NEWSPAPERS

SONNTAGSNACHRICHTEN HALLESCHER KURIER
742208G72-12240
Editorial: Franckestr. 2, 06110 HALLE
Tel: 345 2040923 **Fax:** 345 2040990
Email: fschumann@saaleverlag.de **Web site:** http://www.sonntagsnachrichten.de
Freq: Weekly; **Cover Price:** Free; **Circ:** 158,586
Editor: Frank Schumann; **Advertising Manager:** Uwe Eggert
Profile: Advertising journal (house-to-house) concentrating on local stories.
Language(s): German
ADVERTISING RATES:
Full Page Mono .... EUR 7018
Full Page Colour .... EUR 7118
Mechanical Data: Type Area: 430 x 285 mm, No. of Columns (Display): 6, Col Widths (Display): 45 mm
Copy instructions: *Copy Date:* 2 days prior to publication
Supplement(s): hallescher feierabend
LOCAL NEWSPAPERS

SONNTAGSWOCHENBLATT - AUSG. TORGAU
742219G72-12244
Editorial: Elbstr. 3, 04860 TORGAU **Tel:** 3421 721047 **Fax:** 3421 721050
Email: torgau@sonntagswochenblatt.de **Web site:** http://www.sonntagswochenblatt.de
Freq: Weekly; **Cover Price:** Free; **Circ:** 31,020
Editor: Eckhard Baumbach; **Advertising Manager:** Carsten Brauer
Profile: Advertising journal (house-to-house) concentrating on local stories.
Language(s): German
ADVERTISING RATES:
Full Page Mono .... EUR 2428
Full Page Colour .... EUR 3763
Mechanical Data: Type Area: 435 x 277 mm, No. of Columns (Display): 6, Col Widths (Display): 45 mm
Copy instructions: *Copy Date:* 3 days prior to publication
LOCAL NEWSPAPERS

SONNTAGS-ZEITUNG AKTUELL - AUSG. NÖRDLINGEN
742223G72-12192
Editorial: Bei den Kornschrannen 18, 86720 NÖRDLINGEN **Tel:** 9092 968330 **Fax:** 9092 9683990
Email: redaktion.donauries@wochenzeitung.de
Freq: Weekly; **Cover Price:** Free; **Circ:** 34,356
Editor: Manfred Fink; **Advertising Manager:** Manfred Schindler
Profile: Advertising journal (house-to-house) concentrating on local stories.
Language(s): German
ADVERTISING RATES:
Full Page Mono .... EUR 3806
Full Page Colour .... EUR 4940
Mechanical Data: Type Area: 420 x 280 mm, No. of Columns (Display): 6, Col Widths (Display): 45 mm
Copy instructions: *Copy Date:* 2 days prior to publication
LOCAL NEWSPAPERS

SOUND & RECORDING
1743598G76D-6393
Editorial: Emil-Hoffmann-Str. 13, 50996 KÖLN
Tel: 2236 9621733 **Fax:** 2236 96217933
Email: redaktion@soundandrecording.de **Web site:** http://www.soundandrecording.de
Freq: Monthly; **Annual Sub.:** EUR 50,65; **Circ:** 11,016
Editor: Gerald Dellmann; **Advertising Manager:** Christiane Weyres
Profile: Sound&Recording is the fresh magazine for musicians, record their own songs and who value the best possible results. Usable shots start with proper equipment, authentic sounds and mastering the tricky perfectly rounded. Whether beginners or professionals, the new Sound & Recording on a monthly basis brings valuable practical insider tips and asis-depth information on equipment, sound and recording. Interesting background reports on the minds and stories in the trendy studios give the reader insights into the major musical productions. User-friendly song-writing tips, software and equipment tests and buy recommendations for every budget makes the new Sound & Recording the authentic information medium of the growing scene of young musicians and bands final record.
Language(s): German
Mechanical Data: Type Area: 262 x 176 mm, No. of Columns (Display): 4, Col Widths (Display): 40 mm
CONSUMER: MUSIC & PERFORMING ARTS: Music

SOUNDCHECK
726940G76E-210
Editorial: Dachauer Str. 37b, 85232 BERGKIRCHEN
Tel: 8131 565522 **Fax:** 8131 565510
Email: elmar.nuesslein@soundcheck.de **Web site:** http://www.soundcheck.de
Freq: Monthly; **Annual Sub.:** EUR 54,00; **Circ:** 6,092
Editor: Elmar Nüßlein; **Advertising Manager:** Karoline Lohner
Profile: Magazine covering new equipment and instruments, music, workshops, tuition and consumer product tests.
Language(s): German
Readership: Aimed at amateur rock and pop musicians.
ADVERTISING RATES:
Full Page Mono .... EUR 2590
Full Page Colour .... EUR 4090
Mechanical Data: Type Area: 254 x 185 mm, No. of Columns (Display): 4, Col Widths (Display): 43 mm
Copy instructions: *Copy Date:* 31 days prior to publication
CONSUMER: MUSIC & PERFORMING ARTS: Pop Music

SOURCING_ASIA
1704852G14C-4762
Editorial: Marienstr. 5, 70178 STUTTGART
Tel: 711 22558844 **Fax:** 711 22558811
Email: info@localglobal.de **Web site:** http://www.sourcing-asia.de
Freq: 6 issues yearly; **Annual Sub.:** EUR 149,40; **Circ:** 5,000
Editor: Hans Gäng
Profile: Provides information on current economic developments and changes in Asia being a leading trade publication for procurement, production and cooperation in Asia.
Language(s): English; German
ADVERTISING RATES:
Full Page Mono .... EUR 1800
Full Page Colour .... EUR 1800
Mechanical Data: Type Area: 270 x 192 mm
Copy instructions: *Copy Date:* 10 days prior to publication

SOUS
1662711G74A-3450
Editorial: Weltenburger Str. 4, 81677 MÜNCHEN
Tel: 89 41969424 **Fax:** 89 4705364
Email: info@avr-werbeagentur.de **Web site:** http://www.sous-magazin.de
Freq: Quarterly; **Cover Price:** EUR 12,50; **Circ:** 9,000
Editor: Bettina Klocke; **Advertising Manager:** Heike Schneider
Profile: Magazine about lingerie.
Language(s): German
ADVERTISING RATES:
Full Page Mono .... EUR 2660
Full Page Colour .... EUR 3680
Mechanical Data: Type Area: 241 x 160 mm
Copy instructions: *Copy Date:* 21 days prior to publication

SOVD ZEITUNG
742283G56B-1460
Editorial: Stralauer Str. 63, 10179 BERLIN
Tel: 30 726222140 **Fax:** 30 726222145
Email: redaktion@sovd.de **Web site:** http://www.sozialverband.de
Freq: Monthly; **Circ:** 400,003
Editor: Veronica Sina
Profile: Magazine from the German Social Association.
Language(s): German
Mechanical Data: Type Area: 420 x 286 mm, No. of Columns (Display): 5, Col Widths (Display): 54 mm
Copy instructions: *Copy Date:* 27 days prior to publication
BUSINESS: HEALTH & MEDICAL: Nursing

SOZIALE ARBEIT
742250G32G-2360
Editorial: Bernadottestr. 94, 14195 BERLIN
Tel: 30 83900137 **Fax:** 30 8314750
Email: gedschold@dzi.de **Web site:** http://www.dzi.de
Freq: 11 issues yearly; **Annual Sub.:** EUR 61,50; **Circ:** 800
Editor: Burkhard Wilke; **Advertising Manager:** Christian Gedschold
Profile: Magazine containing information only on published material relevant to social work. Covers general topics in social work also issues relating to health, education, youth and employment.
Language(s): German
Readership: Read by qualified and trainee social workers and scientists.
ADVERTISING RATES:
Full Page Mono .... EUR 310
Mechanical Data: Type Area: 218 x 136 mm, No. of Columns (Display): 2, Col Widths (Display): 65 mm
BUSINESS: LOCAL GOVERNMENT, LEISURE & RECREATION: Community Care & Social Services

SOZIALE SICHERHEIT
742257G32G-2400
Editorial: Poller Hauptstr. 25, 51105 KÖLN
Tel: 221 6308733 **Fax:** 221 8008298
Email: sozialtext@t-online.de **Web site:** http://www.bund-verlag.de
Freq: 11 issues yearly; **Annual Sub.:** EUR 110,40; **Circ:** 3,500
Editor: Hans Nakielski; **Advertising Manager:** Peter Beuther
Profile: Magazine about all aspects of social security and related legal issues.
Language(s): German
ADVERTISING RATES:
Full Page Mono .... EUR 1080
Full Page Colour .... EUR 1350
Mechanical Data: Type Area: 260 x 180 mm
Copy instructions: *Copy Date:* 20 days prior to publication
BUSINESS: LOCAL GOVERNMENT, LEISURE & RECREATION: Community Care & Social Services

SOZIALER FORTSCHRITT
742253G82-7820
Editorial: August-Croissant-Str. 5, 76829 LANDAU
Tel: 6341 28034170 **Fax:** 6341 28034171
Email: yollu@uni-landau.de **Web site:** http://www.sozialerfortschritt.de
Freq: Monthly; **Annual Sub.:** EUR 116,00; **Circ:** 580
Editor: Werner Sesselmeier; **Advertising Manager:** Arlett Günther
Profile: Magazine containing information about social policies.
Language(s): German
ADVERTISING RATES:
Full Page Mono .... EUR 600
Mechanical Data: Type Area: 255 x 170 mm
CONSUMER: CURRENT AFFAIRS & POLITICS

SOZIALMAGAZIN
742274G32G-2420
Editorial: Gaußstr. 18, 60316 FRANKFURT
Tel: 69 438999
Email: redaktion@sozmag.de **Web site:** http://www.juventa.de
Freq: 11 issues yearly; **Annual Sub.:** EUR 64,00; **Circ:** 4,000
Editor: Ria Puhl; **Advertising Manager:** Karola Weiss
Profile: Sozialmagazin offers inspiration for studies, profession and discipline. Sozialmagazin is the forum for all social policy issues, for the questions of social workers and the answers from science and practice. Sozialmagazin works with independent authors and is no association, no party, no institution and no church committed, only to its readers. Sozialmagazin is the magazine for social reality. Sozialmagazin documented for over thirty years, the events and changes in social work. It does not mince words, but not lose sight of what is feasible. Sozialmagazin also tackles uncomfortable subjects, but always remain factual. Scientific papers, practice reports and social reports complement the respective priority issue of the magazine.
Language(s): German
ADVERTISING RATES:
Full Page Mono .... EUR 800
Full Page Colour .... EUR 1330
Mechanical Data: Type Area: 204 x 143 mm, No. of Columns (Display): 3, Col Widths (Display): 44 mm
Copy instructions: *Copy Date:* 50 days prior to publication
BUSINESS: LOCAL GOVERNMENT, LEISURE & RECREATION: Community Care & Social Services

SOZIALPSYCHIATRISCHE INFORMATIONEN
742279G56A-9240
Editorial: Rohdehof 5, 30853 LANGENHAGEN
Tel: 511 7300590 **Fax:** 511 7300518
Email: gabriele.witte.langenhagen@klinikum-hannover.de **Web site:** http://www.verlag.psychiatrie.de/zeitschriften/info
Freq: Quarterly; **Annual Sub.:** EUR 30,00; **Circ:** 2,000
Editor: Gabriele Witte; **Advertising Manager:** Cornelia Brodmann
Profile: Interdisciplinary forum for socialpsychiatry.
Language(s): German
ADVERTISING RATES:
Full Page Mono .... EUR 650
Full Page Colour .... EUR 900
Mechanical Data: Type Area: 243 x 181 mm, No. of Columns (Display): 2, Col Widths (Display): 86 mm
Copy instructions: *Copy Date:* 30 days prior to publication

SOZIALWIRTSCHAFT
742088G32G-2240
Editorial: Eichwaldstr. 45, 60385 FRANKFURT
Tel: 69 447401
Email: gerhard.pfannendoerfer@t-online.de **Web site:** http://www.sozialwirtschaft.nomos.de
Freq: 6 issues yearly; **Annual Sub.:** EUR 120,56; **Circ:** 1,400
Editor: Gerhard Pfannendörfer
Profile: Magazine for German social workers, focusing on innovation and organisation.
Language(s): German
ADVERTISING RATES:
Full Page Mono .... EUR 990
Full Page Colour .... EUR 2115
Mechanical Data: No. of Columns (Display): 3, Col Widths (Display): 56 mm, Type Area: 255 x 178 mm
BUSINESS: LOCAL GOVERNMENT, LEISURE & RECREATION: Community Care & Social Services

SOZIALWIRTSCHAFT AKTUELL
1633108G14A-9556
Editorial: Eichwaldstr. 45, 60385 FRANKFURT
Tel: 69 447401
Email: gerhard.pfannendoerfer@t-online.de **Web site:** http://www.gerhard.pfannendoerfer.de
Freq: 22 issues yearly; **Annual Sub.:** EUR 163,59; **Circ:** 1,200
Editor: Gerhard Pfannendörfer
Profile: Magazine for managers in social companies.
Language(s): German
ADVERTISING RATES:
Full Page Mono .... EUR 770
Mechanical Data: Type Area: 259 x 190 mm

SOZW SOZIALE WELT
742261G1R-4640
Editorial: Konradstr. 6, 80801 MÜNCHEN
Tel: 89 21802458 **Fax:** 89 21805945

Email: soziale.welt@soziologie.uni-muenchen.de **Web site:** http://www.soziale-welt.de
Freq: Quarterly; **Annual Sub.:** EUR 108,31; **Circ:** 1,200
Editor: Irmhild Saake
Profile: Journal about politics, current affairs and sociology.
Language(s): German
ADVERTISING RATES:
Full Page Mono .... EUR 590
Full Page Colour .... EUR 1715
Mechanical Data: No. of Columns (Display): 2, Col Widths (Display): 56 mm, Type Area: 195 x 118 mm
Copy instructions: *Copy Date:* 30 days prior to publication
BUSINESS: FINANCE & ECONOMICS: Financial Related

SPACEVIEW 742292G79L-2
Editorial: Gut Pottscheidt, 53639 KÖNIGSWINTER
Tel: 2241 3013930 **Fax:** 2241 3013008
Email: m.rhode@heel-verlag.de **Web site:** http://www.space-view.de
Freq: Quarterly; **Annual Sub.:** EUR 19,60; **Circ:** 16,100
Editor: Markus Rohde; **Advertising Manager:** Sabine Blüm
Profile: Space view - TV & Cinema combines the topics of film, video and television magazines in the genre Science- Fiction/Mystery/Fantasy through sound reporting on film and television, celebrity portraits, trends and scene news. Regularly advertised price puzzles and games provide a strong reader loyalty. Calendar of Events, TV and cinema tips round out a comprehensive reader service. The magazine has positioned itself with a modern look and issue its genre-specific reporting of successful films and series in the segment of film and television magazines for a media-interested public.
Language(s): German
Readership: Aimed at science fiction fans.
ADVERTISING RATES:
Full Page Mono .... EUR 2620
Full Page Colour .... EUR 3500
Mechanical Data: Type Area: 256 x 175 mm, No. of Columns (Display): 4, Col Widths (Display): 43 mm
Copy instructions: *Copy Date:* 35 days prior to publication
CONSUMER: HOBBIES & DIY: Fantasy Games & Science Fiction

SPA-GUIDE 1697011G89A-12174
Editorial: Max-Eyth-Str. 22, 71686 REMSECK
Tel: 7146 286330 **Fax:** 7146 286332
Email: mail@gay-saunas.eu **Web site:** http://www.gay-saunas.eu
Freq: Annual; **Cover Price:** Free; **Circ:** 25,000
Editor: Claus Lemanczyk; **Advertising Manager:** Claus Lemanczyk
Profile: Gay Guide: Saunas in Europe, with maps for Germany, Austria and Switzerland.
Language(s): English
ADVERTISING RATES:
Full Page Mono .... EUR 790
Full Page Colour .... EUR 790
Mechanical Data: Type Area: 190 x 74 mm

SPANDAUER VOLKSBLATT - SPANDAUER ZTG.- HAVELLÄND. ZTG.- SPANDAUER ANZEIGER, LOKALZTG. F. D. HAVELSTADT AUSG. NORD F. D. ORTSTEILE SPANDAU, FALKENHAGENER FELD, HAKENFELDE, HASELHORST U. SIEMENSSTADT 742295G72-12276
Editorial: Wilhelmstr. 139, 10963 BERLIN
Tel: 30 259178400 **Fax:** 30 259138465
Email: redaktion@berliner-woche.de **Web site:** http://www.spandauer-volksblatt.de
Freq: Weekly; **Cover Price:** Free; **Circ:** 59,110
Editor: Helmut Herold; **Advertising Manager:** Norbert Rowohl
Profile: Advertising journal (house-to-house) concentrating on local stories.
Language(s): German
ADVERTISING RATES:
Full Page Mono .... EUR 3483
Full Page Colour .... EUR 4877
Mechanical Data: Type Area: 430 x 284 mm, No. of Columns (Display): 6, Col Widths (Display): 44 mm
Copy instructions: *Copy Date:* 6 days prior to publication
LOCAL NEWSPAPERS

SPARGEL & ERDBEER PROFI 742302G21A-3760
Editorial: Rochusstr. 18, 53123 BONN
Tel: 228 52006577 **Fax:** 228 52006555
Email: thomas.kuehlwetter@monatsschrift.de **Web site:** http://www.spargel-erdbeerprofi.de
Freq: 5 issues yearly; **Annual Sub.:** EUR 53,50; **Circ:** 5,500
Editor: Thomas Kühlwetter; **Advertising Manager:** Markus Schulz
Profile: Journal of asparagus and strawberry growers, supermarkets, crop consultants, direct marketers, teaching and research institutes.
Language(s): German
ADVERTISING RATES:
Full Page Mono .... EUR 2055
Full Page Colour .... EUR 2515
Mechanical Data: Type Area: 270 x 185 mm, No. of Columns (Display): 4, Col Widths (Display): 45 mm
Copy instructions: *Copy Date:* 14 days prior to publication
Official Journal of: Organ d. Spargel-Erzeugerrings Südbayern e.V.

SPARKASSE 742305G1C-1100
Editorial: Charlottenstr. 47, 10117 BERLIN
Tel: 30 202255154 **Fax:** 30 20225230
Email: sparkasse@dsgv.de **Web site:** http://www.sparkasse-magazin.de
Freq: Monthly; **Annual Sub.:** EUR 138,00; **Circ:** 3,102
Editor: Oliver Fischer
Profile: Magazine providing information on German savings banks.
Language(s): German
ADVERTISING RATES:
Full Page Mono .... EUR 2900
Full Page Colour .... EUR 4370
Mechanical Data: Type Area: 272 x 190 mm, No. of Columns (Display): 4, Col Widths (Display): 42 mm
BUSINESS: FINANCE & ECONOMICS: Banking

SPARKASSEN MARKT 1640263G1C-1441
Editorial: Am Wallgraben 115, 70565 STUTTGART
Tel: 711 7822927 **Fax:** 711 7822880
Email: smarkt-redaktion@dsv-gruppe.de **Web site:** http://www.smarkt-online.de
Freq: 6 issues yearly; **Annual Sub.:** EUR 63,90; **Circ:** 1,926
Editor: Thomas Stoll
Profile: Magazine on market communications of the savings bank group focusing on marketing, markets, media, management, new products and financial services.
Language(s): German
ADVERTISING RATES:
Full Page Mono .... EUR 1580
Full Page Colour .... EUR 2180
Mechanical Data: Type Area: 272 x 190 mm, No. of Columns (Display): 4, Col Widths (Display): 42 mm
BUSINESS: FINANCE & ECONOMICS: Banking

DIE SPARKASSEN ZEITUNG 742308G1C-1120
Editorial: Charlottenstr. 47, 10117 BERLIN
Tel: 30 202255149 **Fax:** 30 202255151
Email: sparkassenzeitung@dsgv.de **Web site:** http://www.sparkassenzeitung.de
Freq: Weekly; **Annual Sub.:** EUR 128,00; **Circ:** 8,821
Editor: Hans Ulrich Eßlinger
Profile: The Sparkassen Zeitung, the business and financial newspaper for managers and decision makers in the member institutions of the Sparkassen finance group. The Sparkassen Zeitung informs about current events in the financial markets, and provides interesting background information. The newspaper has savings in the important decision makers in the Savings Banks Financial Group and other banks at a very high priority. Nearly 100% of the rest are subscribed. The Sparkassen Zeitung offers a targeted approach.
Language(s): German
ADVERTISING RATES:
Full Page Mono .... EUR 12100
Full Page Colour .... EUR 13660
Mechanical Data: Type Area: 451 x 321 mm, No. of Columns (Display): 5, Col Widths (Display): 61 mm
Copy instructions: *Copy Date:* 7 days prior to publication

SPAZZ 1685445G80-14532
Editorial: Schaffnerstr. 5, 89073 ULM
Tel: 731 3783293 **Fax:** 731 3783299
Email: gehlert@ksm-verlag.de **Web site:** http://www.ksm-verlag.de
Freq: Monthly; **Annual Sub.:** EUR 34,00; **Circ:** 16,386
Editor: Jens Gehlert; **Advertising Manager:** Sarah Klingel
Profile: Magazine for the cities of Ulm and Neu-Ulm - with themes of culture, society, sports, city life, leisure, politics and business.
Language(s): German
ADVERTISING RATES:
Full Page Mono .... EUR 1160
Full Page Colour .... EUR 1160
Mechanical Data: Type Area: 222 x 152 mm
Copy instructions: *Copy Date:* 10 days prior to publication
CONSUMER: RURAL & REGIONAL INTEREST

SPECIAL ANTRIEBSTECHNIK 1898949G19A-1134
Editorial: VDI-Platz 1, 40468 DÜSSELDORF
Tel: 211 6103173 **Fax:** 211 6103148
Email: konstruktion@technikwissen.de **Web site:** http://www.konstruktion-online.de
Freq: Half-yearly; **Annual Sub.:** EUR 351,00; **Circ:** 21,628
Editor: Hans Hövelmann
Profile: Reports on the full range of mechanical and electric drive technology. Of gears, electric motors and frequency of controls and machine parts to hydraulic and pneumatic systems and components. An essential part of the special drive systems are current and high quality technical papers by competent authors from industry and science.
Language(s): German
ADVERTISING RATES:
Full Page Mono .... EUR 4896
Full Page Colour .... EUR 6171
Mechanical Data: Type Area: 270 x 185 mm, No. of Columns (Display): 4, Col Widths (Display): 45 mm

---

SPECTATOR-DENTISTRY 1749236G56D-1317
Editorial: Dieselstr. 2, 50859 KÖLN
Tel: 2234 7011280 **Fax:** 2234 70116280
Email: schunk@aerzteverlag.de **Web site:** http://www.spectator.de
Freq: 10 issues yearly; **Annual Sub.:** EUR 36,00; **Circ:** 39,029
Editor: Bernd Schunk; **Advertising Manager:** Marga Pinsdorf
Profile: Deutscher Ärzte-Verlag offers SPECTATOR DENTISTRY to an interested dental audience, focusing on the world of dental events. Spectator Dentistry reports on everything that takes place at conferences, symposia and continuing-education events. It presents knowledge and disseminates opinions and reports on all that happens at dental events, making sure to reflect even the more controversial professional discussions. A detailed calendar, organized by dental disciplines, guides dentists through a "jungle" of events that has become ever denser since the summer of 2004, when dentists first became obliged to attend continuing education. Facebook: http://www.facebook.com/people/Redaktion-Spectator/100000729796701 In addition, SPECTATOR DENTISTRY is a keen observer of state-of-the-art research in universities and enterprises and keeps an eye on business developments relevant to the dental industry. Facebook: http://www.facebook.com/people/Redaktion-Spectator/100000729796701.
Language(s): German
ADVERTISING RATES:
Full Page Mono .... EUR 4950
Full Page Colour .... EUR 4950
Mechanical Data: Type Area: 391 x 281 mm, No. of Columns (Display): 5, Col Widths (Display): 52 mm
Supplement(s): Spectator team
BUSINESS: HEALTH & MEDICAL: Dental

SPECTRUM 1925933G4E-7301
Editorial: Kochstr. 6, 10969 BERLIN
Tel: 30 259229210 **Fax:** 30 259229219
Email: gf@betoninfo.de **Web site:** http://www.betoninfo.de
Freq: 6 issues yearly; **Circ:** 875
Profile: Magazine from the Building Association.
Language(s): German

SPEKTRUM DER MEDIATION 1836237G1A-3705
Editorial: Schulzengasse 5, 37290 WEIDENHAUSEN
Tel: 5657 8391 **Fax:** 5657 913460
Email: redaktion@bmev.de **Web site:** http://www.bmev.de
Freq: Quarterly; Free to qualifying individuals
Annual Sub.: EUR 46,00; **Circ:** 2,000
Editor: Erwin Ruhnau; **Advertising Manager:** Erwin Ruhnau
Profile: Member magazine form the German Society for Mediation.
Language(s): German
ADVERTISING RATES:
Full Page Mono .... EUR 500
Full Page Colour .... EUR 550
Mechanical Data: Type Area: 297 x 210 mm

SPEKTRUM DER WISSENSCHAFT 742347G94J-540
Editorial: Slevogtstr. 3, 69126 HEIDELBERG
Tel: 6221 9126711 **Fax:** 6221 9126729
Email: koenneker@spektrum.com **Web site:** http://www.spektrum.de
Freq: Monthly; **Annual Sub.:** EUR 84,00; **Circ:** 83,339
Editor: Carsten Könneker
Profile: The magazine analyzed the most current research trends long before they come to the general public consciousness. Spectrum readers are much earlier in the picture about pioneering and upcoming developments, they are able to take criticism - and best prepared to make yourself. Editorial quality is the outstanding qualifications of our hand-picked authors. Relevance and value characterize the contributions in the magazine: The editor selects what is important for research, technology, economy and society - and prepares it in a unique form carefully taught to a high level. Anyone who reads the magazine expanded on a continuous basis its knowledge horizon and his decision skills. Spectrum is the direct line to the designers of tomorrow's world. Our authors are German and international scientists from universities, research institutions and industrial research, the report on their own work areas.
Language(s): German
ADVERTISING RATES:
Full Page Mono .... EUR 9900
Full Page Colour .... EUR 9900
Mechanical Data: Type Area: 243 x 173 mm, No. of Columns (Display): 3, Col Widths (Display): 55 mm
Copy instructions: *Copy Date:* 30 days prior to publication
Supplement(s): SciTechs
CONSUMER: OTHER CLASSIFICATIONS: Popular Science

SPESSART 742363G57-2665
Editorial: Weichertstr. 20, 63741 ASCHAFFENBURG
Tel: 6021 396293 **Fax:** 6021 396396
Email: k.eymann@main-echo.de **Web site:** http://www.spessart-online.de
Freq: Monthly; **Annual Sub.:** EUR 26,00; **Circ:** 3,850
Editor: Klaus Eymann; **Advertising Manager:** Reinhard Fresow
Profile: Magazine about the history and nature at the Untermain and Spessart regions.
Language(s): German
ADVERTISING RATES:
Full Page Mono .... EUR 500
Full Page Colour .... EUR 600
Mechanical Data: Type Area: 260 x 184 mm, No. of Columns (Display): 4, Col Widths (Display): 44 mm
Copy instructions: *Copy Date:* 20 days prior to publication

SPEX 742364G76D-5972
Editorial: Köpenicker Str. 178, 10997 BERLIN
Email: redaktion@spex.de **Web site:** http://www.spex.de
Freq: 6 issues yearly; **Annual Sub.:** EUR 28,00; **Circ:** 14,798
Editor: Wibke Wetzker; **Advertising Manager:** Jörg Sauer
Profile: Magazine about music and culture. Facebook: http://www.facebook.com/spexmagazin Twitter: http://twitter.com/#!/spex This Outlet offers RSS (Really Simple Syndication).
Language(s): German
Readership: Aimed at young people.
ADVERTISING RATES:
Full Page Mono .... EUR 3500
Full Page Colour .... EUR 3500
Mechanical Data: Type Area: 295 x 230 mm
CONSUMER: MUSIC & PERFORMING ARTS: Music

SPEZIAL SCHENKEN FEIERN LEBEN 2008852G74A-3757
Editorial: Goldstr. 16, 33602 BIELEFELD
Tel: 521 932560 **Fax:** 521 9325699
Email: redaktion@tips-verlag.de **Web site:** http://www.tips-verlag.de
Freq: Annual; **Circ:** 20,000
Editor: Friedrich Flöttmann
Profile: Shopping guide for Gütersloh.
Language(s): German
ADVERTISING RATES:
Full Page Mono .... EUR 1747
Full Page Colour .... EUR 2784
Mechanical Data: Type Area: 260 x 190 mm, No. of Columns (Display): 4, Col Widths (Display): 43 mm
Copy instructions: *Copy Date:* 30 days prior to publication

DER SPIEGEL 742375G82-9938
Editorial: Brandstwiete 19, 20457 HAMBURG
Tel: 40 30070 **Fax:** 40 30072247
Email: spiegel@spiegel.de **Web site:** http://www.spiegel.de
Freq: Weekly; **Annual Sub.:** EUR 189,90; **Circ:** 961,958
Editor: Georg Mascolo; **Advertising Manager:** Norbert Facklam
Profile: DER SPIEGEL - the German Newsmagazine is a synonym for "investigative" journalism in Germany. The way it researches facts and informs its readers - sets him apart from other media in the country. DER SPIEGEL is characterized by good information, good research and reliable quality. The main focus of reporting is on political and social events. Key points of DER SPIEGEL concept are: - more background - a balanced mix of short and long stories - author texts with pointed opinions - Opening of talk and discussion forums - intensive engagement with the cover story - a reader-friendly layout The DER SPIEGEL reaches its core target groups not only by great accuracy, but also archieces highest ranges in many marketing-relevant target groups: for example, people with high education, in professions and with a high purchasing power, which makes a selective consumption possible. In the judgements of the DER SPIEGEL readers its unique concept and its high journalistic reputation become visible. Readers confirm DER SPIEGEL editors a distinctive style. Facebook: http://www.facebook.com/spiegelonline Twitter: http://twitter.com/SPIEGEL_alles This Outlet offers RSS (Really Simple Syndication).
Language(s): German
ADVERTISING RATES:
Full Page Mono .... EUR 56150
Full Page Colour .... EUR 56150
Mechanical Data: Type Area: 261 x 185 mm, No. of Columns (Display): 3, Col Widths (Display): 59 mm
Copy instructions: *Copy Date:* 21 days prior to publication
Editions:
Der Spiegel (UK Office)
Supplement(s): KulturSpiegel; Uni Spiegel
CONSUMER: CURRENT AFFAIRS & POLITICS

SPIEGEL DER FORSCHUNG 1638901G56A-11280
Editorial: Ludwigstr. 23, 35390 GIESSEN
Tel: 641 9912040 **Fax:** 641 9912049
Email: christel.lauterbach@admin.uni-giessen.de
Web site: http://www.uni-giessen.de/spiegel-der-forschung
Freq: Half-yearly; **Cover Price:** Free; **Circ:** 7,500
Editor: Christel Lauterbach
Profile: Current research projects and results by members of the University of Giessen.

Language(s): German

SPIEGEL ONLINE 1623199G82-9597

Editorial: Brandstwiete 19, 20457 HAMBURG
Tel: 40 38080222 **Fax:** 40 38080223
Email: spiegel_online@spiegel.de **Web site:** http://www.spiegel.de
Freq: Daily; **Cover Price:** Paid
Annual Sub.: EUR 192,40; **Circ:** 136,751,370 Unique Users
Editor: Rüdiger Ditz; **Advertising Manager:** Norbert Facklam
Profile: SPIEGEL ONLINE (www.spiegel.de) is the leading German online news magazine. It provides round the clock news and opinions, analysis and debates, news and background information, interviews and articles from the fields of politics, economics, network world, panorama, culture, science, travel, car and sport. Depending on the news situation leads the 60-member editorial team by more than a hundred updates per day. Rounding out the current range of service elements such as stock quotes, car and travel reports, an extensive database of reviews and critiques of books, CD-ROMs and music titles, rate calculator for telephone, Internet and electricity, access to SPIEGEL ONLINE Archive and to each of the last 52 editions of Der Spiegel as well as a discussion forum on various topics.
Language(s): German
CONSUMER: CURRENT AFFAIRS & POLITICS

SPIELBOX 742382G79F-2440

Editorial: Bahnhofstr. 22, 96117 MEMMELSDORF
Tel: 951 406660 **Fax:** 951 4066649
Email: redaktion@spielbox.de **Web site:** http://www.spielbox.de
Freq: 7 issues yearly; **Annual Sub.:** EUR 39,90; **Circ:** 15,600
Editor: Matthias Hardel; **Advertising Manager:** Barbara Nostheide
Profile: Magazine containing games and puzzles. Facebook: http://www.facebook.com/pages/spielbox/447680240472 Twitter: http://twitter.com/#!/spielbox.
Language(s): German
ADVERTISING RATES:
Full Page Mono .... EUR 1850
Full Page Colour .... EUR 2400
Mechanical Data: Type Area: 303 x 216 mm, No. of Columns (Display): 4, Col Widths (Display): 43 mm
Copy instructions: *Copy Date:* 21 days prior to publication
CONSUMER: HOBBIES & DIY: Games & Puzzles

SPIELEN UND LERNEN 742385G74D-210

Editorial: Schnewlinstr. 6, 79098 FREIBURG
Tel: 761 70578558 **Fax:** 761 70578657
Email: spielen-und-lernen@familymedia.de **Web site:** http://www.familie.de
Freq: Monthly; **Annual Sub.:** EUR 47,40; **Circ:** 111,815
Editor: Stephan Wessolek; **Advertising Manager:** Sabine Mecklenburg
Profile: Education and support for the family life, advice and entertainment role for the whole family with a special parents' section, which primarily takes up the education day, the "play with " / "do with "/ "meeting place"children's section and the common part of the family under the Motto "Join-it-yourself".
Language(s): German
Readership: Aimed at parents of young children.
ADVERTISING RATES:
Full Page Mono .... EUR 10200
Full Page Colour .... EUR 10200
Mechanical Data: Type Area: 243 x 170 mm, No. of Columns (Display): 4, Col Widths (Display): 60 mm
Copy instructions: *Copy Date:* 44 days prior to publication
CONSUMER: WOMEN'S INTEREST CONSUMER MAGAZINES: Child Care

SPIELETIPPS.DE 1662725G78D-964

Editorial: Bahnhofstr. 18b, 61250 USINGEN
Tel: 6081 5828733 **Fax:** 6081 5828734
Email: presse@spieletipps.de **Web site:** http://www.spieletipps.de
Freq: Daily; **Cover Price:** Paid; **Circ:** 8,032,484 Unique Users
Editor: Oliver Hartmann
Language(s): German
CONSUMER: CONSUMER ELECTRONICS: Games

SPIELMITTEL 742394G74C-3100

Editorial: Bahnhofstr. 22, 96117 MEMMELSDORF
Tel: 951 4066622 **Fax:** 951 4066649
Email: nostheide@nostheide.de **Web site:** http://www.nostheide.de
Freq: 5 issues yearly; **Circ:** 10,500
Editor: Thorsten Heinermann; **Advertising Manager:** Barbara Nostheide
Profile: Magazine with information about toys for educationists and consumer.
Language(s): German
Readership: Aimed at parents.
ADVERTISING RATES:
Full Page Mono .... EUR 1900
Full Page Colour .... EUR 2800
Mechanical Data: Type Area: 255 x 184 mm, No. of Columns (Display): 3, Col Widths (Display): 57 mm
Copy instructions: *Copy Date:* 21 days prior to publication
CONSUMER: WOMEN'S INTEREST CONSUMER MAGAZINES: Home & Family

DAS SPIELZEUG 758446G48A-323

Editorial: Franz-Ludwig-Str. 7a, 96047 BAMBERG
Tel: 951 861163 **Fax:** 951 861149
Email: p.lang@meisenbach.de **Web site:** http://www.dasspielzeug.de
Freq: Monthly; **Annual Sub.:** EUR 93,00; **Circ:** 7,517
Editor: Peter Lang; **Advertising Manager:** Doris Hanft
Profile: International magazine for the toy industry.
Language(s): English; German
ADVERTISING RATES:
Full Page Mono .... EUR 2634
Full Page Colour .... EUR 4114
Mechanical Data: Type Area: 264 x 185 mm, No. of Columns (Display): 3, Col Widths (Display): 59 mm
Copy instructions: *Copy Date:* 20 days prior to publication
Official Journal of: Organ d. Dt. Verb. d. Spielwaren-Industrie e.V.
BUSINESS: TOY TRADE & SPORTS GOODS: Toy Trade

SPIELZEUG INTERNATIONAL 742470G48A-240

Editorial: Debert 32, 91320 EBERMANNSTADT
Tel: 9194 73780 **Fax:** 9194 737820
Email: spielzeug@spielzeuginternational.de **Web site:** http://www.spielzeuginternational.de
Freq: 11 issues yearly; **Annual Sub.:** EUR 80,25; **Circ:** 7,374
Editor: Alfred G. Kropfeld; **Advertising Manager:** Ingrid Kropfeld
Profile: Ezine: International magazine concerning games, hobbies, gifts, video games, entertainment and related topics.
Language(s): English; German
Readership: Aimed at importers, exporters, wholesalers, retailers and manufacturers.
ADVERTISING RATES:
Full Page Mono .... EUR 2249
Full Page Colour .... EUR 3936
Mechanical Data: Type Area: 267 x 175 mm, No. of Columns (Display): 3, Col Widths (Display): 55 mm
Copy instructions: *Copy Date:* 15 days prior to publication
Official Journal of: Organ d. TTE Toy Traders of Europe, d. Europ. Vereinigung d. Spielwaren-Detailhandels u. d. Europ. Föderation d. Spielwaren-Groß- u. Außenhandels
BUSINESS: TOY TRADE & SPORTS GOODS: Toy Trade

SPIRIDON 742481G75J-360

Editorial: Dorfstr. 18a, 40699 ERKRATH
Tel: 211 726364 **Fax:** 211 786823
Email: spiridon@gmx.com **Web site:** http://www.laufmagazin-spiridon.de
Freq: Monthly; **Annual Sub.:** EUR 39,00; **Circ:** 11,000
Editor: Manfred Steffny; **Advertising Manager:** Dominik Steffny
Profile: Running and athletics journal.
Language(s): German
ADVERTISING RATES:
Full Page Mono .... EUR 1200
Full Page Colour .... EUR 2040
Mechanical Data: Type Area: 251 x 184 mm, No. of Columns (Display): 3, Col Widths (Display): 58 mm
Copy instructions: *Copy Date:* 16 days prior to publication
CONSUMER: SPORT: Athletics

SPIRIT 742482G94X-190

Editorial: Adam-Klein-Str. 156, 90431 NÜRNBERG
Tel: 911 47790730 **Fax:** 911 47790777
Email: redaktion@spiritmagazin.de **Web site:** http://www.spiritmagazin.de
Freq: 6 issues yearly; **Annual Sub.:** EUR 24,90; **Circ:** 1,000
Editor: Holger Schmidt
Profile: Magazine about cheerleading.
Language(s): German
ADVERTISING RATES:
Full Page Mono .... EUR 400
Full Page Colour .... EUR 400
Mechanical Data: Type Area: 260 x 178 mm, No. of Columns (Display): 3, Col Widths (Display): 56 mm
Copy instructions: *Copy Date:* 20 days prior to publication
CONSUMER: OTHER CLASSIFICATIONS: Miscellaneous

SPONGEBOB 1641064G91D-10012

Editorial: Wallstr. 59, 10179 BERLIN **Tel:** 30 240080
Fax: 30 24008455
Email: s.saydo@ehapa.de **Web site:** http://www.ehapa.de
Freq: 13 issues yearly; **Cover Price:** EUR 2,99; **Circ:** 74,576
Editor: Sanya Saydo
Profile: In the center of the magazine is the little yellow sponge, SpongeBob from the eponymous TV series. Together with his friends, he and his friends do in "Bikini Bottom" every month a new adventure. In each issue, readers ages 4 to 10 years are filled with unique addition to humorous stories and columns, with puzzles, tests and underwater features a SpongeBob-Extra.
Language(s): German
ADVERTISING RATES:
Full Page Mono .... EUR 6400
Full Page Colour .... EUR 6400
Mechanical Data: Type Area: 260 x 175 mm, No. of Columns (Display): 4, Col Widths (Display): 43 mm
CONSUMER: RECREATION & LEISURE: Children & Youth

SPORT1 1662744G75A-3699

Editorial: Münchener Str. 101g, 85737 ISMANING
Tel: 89 960662700 **Fax:** 89 960662709
Email: info@sport1.de **Web site:** http://www.sport1.de
Freq: Daily; **Cover Price:** Paid; **Circ:** 30,338,487 Unique Users
Editor: Roland Schekelinski
Profile: Twitter: http://twitter.com/sport1_news.
Language(s): German
CONSUMER: SPORT

SPORT AUTO 742504G77D-1120

Editorial: Leuschnerstr. 1, 70174 STUTTGART
Tel: 711 18201 **Fax:** 711 1821786
Email: hsaurma-jeltsch@motorpresse.de **Web site:** http://www.sportauto-online.de
Freq: Monthly; Free to qualifying individuals
Annual Sub.: EUR 46,80; **Circ:** 52,206
Editor: Horst von Saurma-Jeltsch; **Advertising Manager:** Stefan Granzer
Profile: Pleasure to the limit. In the toughest race tracks are brought all sporty cars from sport auto to the limits of their high-performance technology. Representing the compelling editorial concept is the sport auto super test. It takes place where belong sporty cars on the Nürburgring Nordschleife and the Hockenheim Ring. Includes lap and sector times, lateral acceleration data and aerodynamic Check the wind tunnel. The goal of sport auto is to answer the all-important question: Is it a sports car? Or will it be one? These detailed reports of new vehicle concepts and competently and thoroughly researched motor sports analysis and background reports. Every month in this journal will fascinating cars emotional experience. Twitter: http://twitter.com/sportauto.
Language(s): German
ADVERTISING RATES:
Full Page Mono .... EUR 10400
Full Page Colour .... EUR 10400
Mechanical Data: Type Area: 251 x 190 mm, No. of Columns (Display): 4, Col Widths (Display): 43 mm
Copy instructions: *Copy Date:* 30 days prior to publication
CONSUMER: MOTORING & CYCLING: Motor Sports

SPORT BÄDER FREIZEIT BAUTEN 742505G32E-10

Editorial: Beuttenmüllerstr. 30, 76530 BADEN-BADEN **Tel:** 7221 97990 **Fax:** 7221 979970
Email: sbf@kannewischer.com **Web site:** http://www.sbf-bauten.de
Freq: Quarterly; Free to qualifying individuals
Annual Sub.: EUR 40,00; **Circ:** 3,820
Editor: Jürgen Kannewischer; **Advertising Manager:** Renate Nagel
Profile: Magazine covering aquatic sports and leisure centre facilities.
Language(s): German
Readership: Read by building contractors, architects, engineers, swimming pool specialists and members of sports associations.
ADVERTISING RATES:
Full Page Mono .... EUR 1200
Full Page Colour .... EUR 2100
Mechanical Data: Type Area: 257 x 185 mm, No. of Columns (Display): 2, Col Widths (Display): 88 mm
Copy instructions: *Copy Date:* 28 days prior to publication
Official Journal of: Organ d. Internat. Akademie f. Bäder-, Sport- u. Freizeitbauten e.V., d. Dt. Inst. f. Bäder-, Sport- u. Freizeitbauten e.V. d. Schwimmstättenausschusses, d. Dt. Schwimmverb., d. Zentralen Beratungsstelle f. d. kommunalen Sportstättenbau
BUSINESS: LOCAL GOVERNMENT, LEISURE & RECREATION: Swimming Pools

SPORT IN BERLIN 742524G75A-2620

Editorial: Jesse-Owens-Allee 2, 14053 BERLIN
Tel: 30 30002109 **Fax:** 30 30002119
Email: sib@lsb-berlin.de **Web site:** http://www.lsb-berlin.de
Freq: 8 issues yearly; **Circ:** 6,500
Editor: Angela Baufeld
Profile: Publication about sport in Berlin.
Language(s): German
ADVERTISING RATES:
Full Page Mono .... EUR 450
Full Page Colour .... EUR 900
Mechanical Data: No. of Columns (Display): 3, Type Area: 254 x 175 mm, Col Widths (Display): 55 mm
CONSUMER: SPORT

SPORT ORTHOPÄDIE TRAUMATOLOGIE 742547G56A-9280

Editorial: Am Finkenhügel 1, 49076 OSNABRÜCK
Tel: 541 4056200 **Fax:** 541 4056299
Email: martin.engelhardt@klinikum-os.de
Freq: Quarterly; **Annual Sub.:** EUR 141,00; **Circ:** 1,400
Editor: Martin Engelhardt
Profile: Magazine covering sport orthopaedics and traumatology.
Language(s): English; German
ADVERTISING RATES:
Full Page Mono .... EUR 2210
Full Page Colour .... EUR 3530
Mechanical Data: Type Area: 240 x 175 mm
Official Journal of: Organ d. Ges. f. Orthopäd.-Traumatolog. Sportmedizin u. d. Verbandsärzte Deutschland e.V.

SPORT PRAXIS 742550G62B-2520

Editorial: Industriepark 3, 56291 WIEBELSHEIM
Tel: 6766 903212 **Fax:** 6766 903341
Email: ebert@limpert.de **Web site:** http://www.sportpraxis.com
Freq: Monthly; **Annual Sub.:** EUR 53,45; **Circ:** 7,500
Editor: Carsten Ebert
Profile: Journal for sports teachers.
Language(s): German
ADVERTISING RATES:
Full Page Colour .... EUR 980
Mechanical Data: Type Area: 249 x 181 mm, No. of Columns (Display): 3, Col Widths (Display): 57 mm
Copy instructions: *Copy Date:* 31 days prior to publication
Supplement(s): Der Übungsleiter
BUSINESS: CHURCH & SCHOOL EQUIPMENT & EDUCATION: Education Teachers

SPORT REVUE 1638608G75Q-251

Editorial: Rosenheimer Str. 22, 83043 BAD AIBLING
Tel: 8061 3899827 **Fax:** 8061 3899820
Email: redaktion@sportrevue.info **Web site:** http://www.sportrevue.info
Freq: Monthly; **Annual Sub.:** EUR 49,50; **Circ:** 35,000
Editor: Hans Joachim Wieland; **Advertising Manager:** Petra Robben
Profile: Bodybuilding & Fitness Lifestyle Magazine.
Language(s): German
CONSUMER: SPORT: Combat Sports

SPORTMEDIZIN IN NORDRHEIN 742543G56A-9300

Editorial: Am Sportpark Müngersdorf 6, 50933 KÖLN
Tel: 221 493785 **Fax:** 221 493207
Email: sportaerztebundnr@t-online.de **Web site:** http://www.sportaerztebund.de
Freq: Half-yearly; **Circ:** 700
Advertising Manager: Gabriele Wenzel-Wontka
Profile: Magazine on sports medicine in the Nordrhein-Westfalen region.
Language(s): German
ADVERTISING RATES:
Full Page Mono .... EUR 500
Full Page Colour .... EUR 1000
Copy instructions: *Copy Date:* 30 days prior to publication

SPORTSCHIPPER 742558G91A-160

Editorial: Schwertfegerstr. 1, 23556 LÜBECK
Tel: 451 898974 **Fax:** 451 898557
Email: redaktion@sport-schipper.de **Web site:** http://www.svg-verlag.de
Freq: Monthly; Free to qualifying individuals
Annual Sub.: EUR 16,00; **Circ:** 8,200
Editor: Hermann Hell
Profile: Magazine about boats and water sports in Lower Saxony and Bremen.
Language(s): German
ADVERTISING RATES:
Full Page Mono .... EUR 650
Full Page Colour .... EUR 1040
Mechanical Data: Type Area: 267 x 185 mm, No. of Columns (Display): 2, Col Widths (Display): 90 mm
Copy instructions: *Copy Date:* 15 days prior to publication
CONSUMER: RECREATION & LEISURE: Boating & Yachting

SPORTVERLETZUNG SPORTSCHADEN 742582G56A-9320

Editorial: Rüdigerstr. 14, 70469 STUTTGART
Tel: 711 8931630 **Fax:** 711 8931499
Email: anna.hecker@thieme.de **Web site:** http://www.thieme.de/sport
Freq: Quarterly; **Annual Sub.:** EUR 162,80; **Circ:** 1,200
Editor: Hanns-Peter Scharf
Profile: Your Forum - The magazine Sportverletzung Sportschaden. Information from A to Z: basics, prevention and rehabilitation. Hot topics: timely picture of the injury/prevention, resulting from Trend Sports (focal length). Diverse range: physiotherapy, applied research, new products and appliances, etc. Current issues with real value. Sports Traumatology: Prevention, treatment, rehabilitation. Sports Physiotherapy: Foundations, biomechanics, manual therapy, functional therapy, exercise therapy in sports, equipment, trends.
Language(s): German
ADVERTISING RATES:
Full Page Mono .... EUR 1230
Full Page Colour .... EUR 2340
Mechanical Data: Type Area: 248 x 175 mm, No. of Columns (Display): 4, Col Widths (Display): 40 mm
BUSINESS: HEALTH & MEDICAL

SPORT-WELT 742583G75E-540

Editorial: Im Mediapark 8, 50670 KÖLN
Tel: 221 2587260 **Fax:** 221 2587212
Email: sportwelt@sportverlag.de **Web site:** http://www.sportverlag.de
Freq: 156 issues yearly; **Annual Sub.:** EUR 410,00; **Circ:** 14,000
Editor: Hans Reski
Profile: Publication about thoroughbred horse-breeding and racing.
Language(s): German
ADVERTISING RATES:
Full Page Mono .... EUR 4000
Full Page Colour .... EUR 5200
Mechanical Data: Type Area: 525 x 285 mm, No. of Columns (Display): 6, Col Widths (Display): 45 mm
Copy instructions: *Copy Date:* 2 days prior to publication
CONSUMER: SPORT: Horse Racing

SPOT MARKT 742594G23A-135

Editorial: Weidestr. 120a, 22083 HAMBURG
Tel: 40 71370953 **Fax:** 40 71370952
Email: yvonne.brombach@holzmann.de **Web site:** http://www.holzmann.de
Freq: 20 issues yearly; **Annual Sub.:** EUR 276,06; **Circ:** 1,000
Editor: Yvonne Brombach; **Advertising Manager:** Sarah Albrecht
Profile: Magazine focusing on furniture. Facebook: http://www.facebook.com/pages/mobel-kultur/124172594286549.
Language(s): German
Readership: Read by managers in the furniture trade.
ADVERTISING RATES:
Full Page Mono .... EUR 2800
Mechanical Data: Type Area: 267 x 188 mm, No. of Columns (Display): 4, Col Widths (Display): 44 mm
Copy instructions: *Copy Date:* 14 days prior to publication
BUSINESS: FURNISHINGS & FURNITURE

SPOT ON 742595G91D-9747

Editorial: Fraunhoferstr. 22, 82152 PLANEGG
Tel: 89 85681311 **Fax:** 89 85681320
Email: spoton@spotlight-verlag.de **Web site:** http://www.spoton.de
Freq: Monthly; **Annual Sub.:** EUR 48,00; **Circ:** 27,330
Editor: Judith Gilbert; **Advertising Manager:** Axel Zettler
Profile: Spot on is the leading youth magazine "in easy English" for readers from ages 14 to 16. Every month, young people from English-speaking countries worldwide deliver insights on their lives, plans, dreams and activities. Regular features in Spot on include exclusive interviews with international celebrities as well as exciting reports on music, society, movies, literature, job opportunities abroad, and youth travel. The magazine also provides translations and/or explanations for difficult vocabulary and current colloquialisms. Complementing texts, easily comprehensible podcasts plus a choice of additional audio files are available on www.spoton.de. Spot on moere! – the supplementary exercise book – rounds off an editorial concept which for 12 years now has been a great success with our teenage audience. Facebook: http://www.facebook.com/pages/Spot-on/114293385262484.
Language(s): English; German
ADVERTISING RATES:
Full Page Mono .... EUR 2155
Full Page Colour .... EUR 3592
Mechanical Data: Type Area: 246 x 186 mm, No. of Columns (Display): 4, Col Widths (Display): 43 mm
Copy instructions: *Copy Date:* 35 days prior to publication
Supplement(s): Spot on In The Classroom
CONSUMER: RECREATION & LEISURE: Children & Youth

SPOTLIGHT 742590G88B-1000

Editorial: Fraunhoferstr. 22, 82152 PLANEGG
Tel: 89 85681211 **Fax:** 89 85681105
Email: i.sharp@spotlight-verlag.de **Web site:** http://www.spotlight-online.de
Freq: Monthly; **Annual Sub.:** EUR 69,90,; **Circ:** 73,836
Editor: Inez Sharp; **Advertising Manager:** Axel Zettler
Profile: For more than 30 years Spotlight has been reflecting the social and cultural life in the English-speaking parts of the world. Politics, society, the arts, cultural news, language skills and travel form a regular part of this unique magazine concept. With great journalistic expertise Spotlight elegantly blends efficient language training with thoroughly researched background information. Each month, nearly 55,000 discerning subscribers alone appreciate the well-founded reports and exciting views on the social and cultural developments in English-speaking countries worldwide, supplied by an international network of native correspondents, from North America to New Zealand. Facebook: http://www.facebook.com/pages/Spotlight/146418090870.
Language(s): English; German
ADVERTISING RATES:
Full Page Mono .... EUR 6268
Full Page Colour .... EUR 10446
Mechanical Data: Type Area: 246 x 186 mm, No. of Columns (Display): 4, Col Widths (Display): 43 mm
Copy instructions: *Copy Date:* 35 days prior to publication
Supplement(s): Spotlight In the Classroom
CONSUMER: EDUCATION: Adult Education

SPRACHE - STIMME - GEHÖR 742600G56L-150

Editorial: Rüdigerstr. 14, 70469 STUTTGART
Tel: 711 89310 **Fax:** 711 8931258
Email: ssg@thieme.de **Web site:** http://www.thieme.de/ssg
Freq: Quarterly; **Annual Sub.:** EUR 95,80; **Circ:** 2,550
Editor: M. Ptok
Profile: Each issue contains one main topic. Categories: Listen - Identify - Understand: voice, speech and language disorders to listen, the audio samples you find online. For you read, heard for you: National and international studies summarized for you and to the point. New momentum: The successful completion work of the tray. The little coach: Basic Terminology and brief. Patient information: The main themes as a template for your patients. SSG-quiz: Answer questions on the main topic and you win a forum-band speech therapy!.
Language(s): German
ADVERTISING RATES:
Full Page Mono .... EUR 1320
Full Page Colour .... EUR 2460
Mechanical Data: Type Area: 248 x 175 mm, No. of Columns (Display): 4, Col Widths (Display): 40 mm
Official Journal of: Organ d. Lehrervereinigung Schlaffhorst-Andersen e.V
BUSINESS: HEALTH & MEDICAL: Disability & Rehabilitation

DIE SPRACHHEILARBEIT 742602G56L-155

Editorial: Schieferberg 8, 31840 HESSISCH OLDENDORF **Tel:** 5152 2950 **Fax:** 5152 528774
Email: redaktion@sprachheilarbeit.eu
Freq: 6 issues yearly; Free to qualifying individuals
Annual Sub.: EUR 40,00; **Circ:** 7,800
Editor: Uwe Förster; **Advertising Manager:** Gudrun Luck
Profile: Publication covering new developments in speech therapy.
Language(s): German
ADVERTISING RATES:
Full Page Mono .... EUR 715
Full Page Colour .... EUR 858
Mechanical Data: Type Area: 252 x 171 mm, No. of Columns (Display): 4, Col Widths (Display): 38 mm
Copy instructions: *Copy Date:* 45 days prior to publication
BUSINESS: HEALTH & MEDICAL: Disability & Rehabilitation

SPRACHROHR 742605G2A-4500

Editorial: Köpenicker Str. 30, 10179 BERLIN
Tel: 30 88664106 **Fax:** 30 88664902
Freq: 6 issues yearly; Free to qualifying individuals
Annual Sub.: EUR 4,60; **Circ:** 18,000
Editor: Andreas Köhn
Profile: Magazine from the Trade Union ver.di for the media.
Language(s): German
ADVERTISING RATES:
Full Page Mono .... EUR 1483
Mechanical Data: Type Area: 270 x 194 mm, No. of Columns (Display): 4, Col Widths (Display): 45 mm
Copy instructions: *Copy Date:* 20 days prior to publication

SPREE 723973G83-1520

Editorial: Reuchlinstr. 10, 10553 BERLIN
Tel: 30 36286432 **Fax:** 30 36286437
Email: redaktion@stadtstudenten.de **Web site:** http://www.stadtstudenten.de
Freq: 6 issues yearly; **Cover Price:** Free; **Circ:** 29,920
Editor: Alexander Florin; **Advertising Manager:** Florian Diesing
Profile: Student magazine. Distributed in the university, high schools, cafés and bars.
Language(s): German
Readership: Read by students living in Berlin.
ADVERTISING RATES:
Full Page Mono .... EUR 2079
Full Page Colour .... EUR 2310
Mechanical Data: Type Area: 258 x 188 mm, No. of Columns (Display): 4, Col Widths (Display): 44 mm
Copy instructions: *Copy Date:* 19 days prior to publication
CONSUMER: STUDENT PUBLICATIONS

SPREE-NEISSE WOCHENKURIER - AUSG. FORST 727657G72-3920

Editorial: Hermannstr. 5, 03149 FORST
Tel: 3562 691801 **Fax:** 3562 698559
Email: kerstintwarok@cwk-verlag.de **Web site:** http://www.wochenkurier.info
Freq: Weekly; **Cover Price:** Free; **Circ:** 14,680
Editor: Kerstin Twarok; **Advertising Manager:** Uwe Peschel
Profile: Advertising journal (house-to-house) concentrating on local stories.
Language(s): German
ADVERTISING RATES:
Full Page Mono .... EUR 2258
Full Page Colour .... EUR 3161
Mechanical Data: Type Area: 430 x 290 mm, No. of Columns (Display): 7, Col Widths (Display): 38 mm
Copy instructions: *Copy Date:* 6 days prior to publication
LOCAL NEWSPAPERS

SPREE-NEISSE WOCHENKURIER - AUSG. GUBEN 729355G72-4864

Editorial: Karl-Marx-Str. 68, 03044 COTTBUS
Tel: 355 4312680 **Fax:** 355 472910
Email: kerstintwarok@cwk-verlag.de **Web site:** http://www.wochenkurier.info
Freq: Weekly; **Cover Price:** Free; **Circ:** 12,747
Editor: Kerstin Twarok; **Advertising Manager:** Uwe Peschel
Profile: Advertising journal (house-to-house) concentrating on local stories.
Language(s): German
ADVERTISING RATES:
Full Page Mono .... EUR 2258
Full Page Colour .... EUR 3161
Mechanical Data: Type Area: 430 x 290 mm, No. of Columns (Display): 7, Col Widths (Display): 38 mm
Copy instructions: *Copy Date:* 6 days prior to publication
LOCAL NEWSPAPERS

SPREE-NEISSE WOCHENKURIER - AUSG. SPREMBERG 742616G72-12296

Editorial: Lange Str. 22b, 03130 SPREMBERG
Tel: 3563 603248 **Fax:** 3563 94748
Email: kerstintwarok@cwk-verlag.de **Web site:** http://www.wochenkurier.info
Freq: Weekly; **Cover Price:** Free; **Circ:** 17,048
Editor: Kerstin Twarok; **Advertising Manager:** Uwe Peschel
Profile: Advertising journal (house-to-house) concentrating on local stories.
Language(s): German
ADVERTISING RATES:
Full Page Mono .... EUR 2378
Full Page Colour .... EUR 3330
Mechanical Data: Type Area: 430 x 290 mm, No. of Columns (Display): 7, Col Widths (Display): 38 mm
Copy instructions: *Copy Date:* 6 days prior to publication
LOCAL NEWSPAPERS

SPREEWÄLDER WOCHENKURIER - AUSG. CALAU 724049G72-2912

Editorial: Schloßstr. 11, 03205 CALAU
Tel: 3546 186649 **Fax:** 3546 8197
Email: kerstintwarok@cwk-verlag.de **Web site:** http://www.wochenkurier.info
Freq: Weekly; **Cover Price:** Free; **Circ:** 20,493
Editor: Kerstin Twarok; **Advertising Manager:** Uwe Peschel
Profile: Advertising journal (house-to-house) concentrating on local stories.
Language(s): German
ADVERTISING RATES:
Full Page Mono .... EUR 2348
Full Page Colour .... EUR 3287
Mechanical Data: Type Area: 430 x 290 mm, No. of Columns (Display): 7, Col Widths (Display): 38 mm
Copy instructions: *Copy Date:* 5 days prior to publication
LOCAL NEWSPAPERS

SPREEWÄLDER WOCHENKURIER - AUSG. LÜBBEN 734493G72-7044

Editorial: Hauptstr. 3, 15907 LÜBBEN
Tel: 3546 186649 **Fax:** 3546 8197
Email: kerstintwarok@cwk-verlag.de **Web site:** http://www.wochenkurier.info
Freq: Weekly; **Cover Price:** Free; **Circ:** 14,641
Editor: Kerstin Twarok; **Advertising Manager:** Uwe Peschel
Profile: Advertising journal (house-to-house) concentrating on local stories.
Language(s): German
ADVERTISING RATES:
Full Page Mono .... EUR 2047
Full Page Colour .... EUR 2866
Mechanical Data: Type Area: 430 x 290 mm, No. of Columns (Display): 7, Col Widths (Display): 38 mm
Copy instructions: *Copy Date:* 6 days prior to publication
LOCAL NEWSPAPERS

SPREEWÄLDER WOCHENKURIER - AUSG. LUCKAU 734480G72-7064

Editorial: Hauptstr. 3, 15907 LÜBBEN
Tel: 3546 186648 **Fax:** 3546 8197
Email: kerstintwarok@cwk-verlag.de **Web site:** http://www.wochenkurier.info
Freq: Weekly; **Cover Price:** Free; **Circ:** 8,718
Editor: Kerstin Twarok; **Advertising Manager:** Uwe Peschel
Profile: Advertising journal (house-to-house) concentrating on local stories.
Language(s): German
ADVERTISING RATES:
Full Page Mono .... EUR 1837
Full Page Colour .... EUR 2571
Mechanical Data: Type Area: 430 x 290 mm, No. of Columns (Display): 7, Col Widths (Display): 38 mm
Copy instructions: *Copy Date:* 4 days prior to publication
LOCAL NEWSPAPERS

SPRINGERMEDIZIN 1662287G56A-11380

Editorial: Schwedter Str. 263, 10119 BERLIN
Tel: 30 884293942 **Fax:** 30 884293940
Email: kundenservice@springermedizin.de **Web site:** http://www.springermedizin.de
Freq: Daily; **Cover Price:** Paid; **Circ:** 131,906 Unique Users
Profile: Internet Media: the Internet for medical doctors, pharmacists and other healthcare professionals.
Language(s): German
BUSINESS: HEALTH & MEDICAL

SPS MAGAZIN 742623G18A-239

Editorial: Zu den Sandbeeten 2, 35043 MARBURG
Tel: 6421 308639 **Fax:** 6421 308618
Email: info@sps-magazin.de **Web site:** http://www.sps-magazin.de
Freq: 13 issues yearly; **Annual Sub.:** EUR 99,00; **Circ:** 26,140
Editor: Kai Binder; **Advertising Manager:** Wiebke Tilhof
Profile: Magazine about industrial electronics, operating machinery, production and relevant legal matters.
Language(s): German
Readership: Aimed at electronic and industrial engineers.
ADVERTISING RATES:
Full Page Mono .... EUR 5190
Full Page Colour .... EUR 6580
Mechanical Data: Type Area: 270 x 185 mm, No. of Columns (Display): 4, Col Widths (Display): 45 mm
Copy instructions: *Copy Date:* 30 days prior to publication
BUSINESS: ELECTRONICS

SRTOUR STEUER- UND RECHTSBRIEF TOURISTIK 1833138G50-1254

Editorial: Postfach 1428, 48634 COESFELD
Tel: 2541 926330 **Fax:** 2541 970494
Email: hj.hillmer@web.de **Web site:** http://www.srtourdigital.de
Freq: Monthly; **Annual Sub.:** EUR 207,79; **Circ:** 1,000
Editor: Hans-Jürgen Hillmer; **Advertising Manager:** Peter Taprogge
Profile: Magazine with current infirmation on taxes for travel offices and agencies.
Language(s): German
ADVERTISING RATES:
Full Page Mono .... EUR 1000
Full Page Colour .... EUR 1900
Mechanical Data: Type Area: 228 x 155 mm

ST. GEORG 741057G75E-244

Editorial: Troplowitzstr. 5, 22529 HAMBURG
Tel: 40 38906101 **Fax:** 40 38906308
Email: gabriele.pochhammer@st-georg.de **Web site:** http://www.st-georg.de
Freq: Monthly; Free to qualifying individuals
Annual Sub.: EUR 60,00; **Circ:** 40,716
Editor: Gabriele Pochhammer; **Advertising Manager:** Jasmin Seitter
Profile: St. Georg is the oldest equestrian magazine and one of the opinion leaders in the equestrian scene! The current, competent and critical Reporting, accompanied by the St. Georg riding and breeding, and the attractive design of St. Georg make an indispensable equestrian magazine. St. Georg offers a wealth of information every month and pure entertainment.
Language(s): German
ADVERTISING RATES:
Full Page Mono .... EUR 3696
Full Page Colour .... EUR 6200
Mechanical Data: Type Area: 248 x 185 mm, No. of Columns (Display): 4, Col Widths (Display): 45 mm
Copy instructions: *Copy Date:* 27 days prior to publication
Official Journal of: Organ d. Dt. Reiter- u. Fahrer-Verb.
CONSUMER: SPORT: Horse Racing

ST SENIOREN TANZEN 741808G74N-85

Editorial: Hemmstr. 202, 28215 BREMEN
Tel: 421 441180 **Fax:** 421 4986217
Email: verband@seniorentanz.de **Web site:** http://www.seniorentanz.de
Freq: Quarterly; **Circ:** 7,200
Editor: Anita Brunberg
Profile: Club magazine for the elderly about dancing.
Language(s): German
Readership: Aimed at senior citizens.
Mechanical Data: Type Area: 250 x 185 mm, No. of Columns (Display): 3, Col Widths (Display): 57 mm
Copy instructions: *Copy Date:* 30 days prior to publication
CONSUMER: WOMEN'S INTEREST CONSUMER MAGAZINES: Retirement

ST SOLINGER TAGEBLATT 743758G67B-13660

Editorial: Mummstr. 9, 42651 SOLINGEN
Tel: 212 299100 **Fax:** 212 299123
Email: b.boll@solinger-tageblatt.de **Web site:** http://www.solinger-tageblatt.de
Freq: 312 issues yearly; **Circ:** 24,262

Editor: Stefan M. Kob; **News Editor:** Hans-Peter Meurer; **Advertising Manager:** Matthias Köstner
Profile: Daily newspaper with regional news and a local sports section. Facebook: http://www.facebook.com/sgtageblatt Twitter: http://twitter.com/#!/SGTageblatt.
Language(s): German
ADVERTISING RATES:
SCC .... EUR 86,60
Mechanical Data: Type Area: 430 x 282 mm, No. of Columns (Display): 6, Col Widths (Display): 45 mm
Copy instructions: *Copy Date:* 2 days prior to publication
Supplement(s): Berufswahl ...; prisma; ST Althaus; ST Sport extra; ST Wirtschaftsraum Solingen
REGIONAL DAILY & SUNDAY NEWSPAPERS: Regional Daily Newspapers

STAATSANZEIGER 742640G80-14143
Editorial: Breitscheidstr. 69, 70176 STUTTGART
Tel: 711 666010 **Fax:** 711 6660158
Email: redaktion@staatsanzeiger.de **Web site:** http://www.staatsanzeiger.de
Freq: Weekly; **Annual Sub.:** EUR 78,00; **Circ:** 14,882
Editor: Breda Nussbaum; **Advertising Manager:** Thomas Krieger
Profile: Journal covering local and central government in Baden-Württemberg includes local politics and culture.
Language(s): German
Readership: Aimed at individuals in public service and the private sector.
Mechanical Data: Type Area: 485 x 324 mm, No. of Columns (Display): 6, Col Widths (Display): 51 mm
Copy instructions: *Copy Date:* 4 days prior to publication
Supplement(s): Landesausschreibungsblatt Baden-Württemberg LBW; Momente; Schlösser Baden-Württemberg
CONSUMER: RURAL & REGIONAL INTEREST

STADER TAGEBLATT 742651G67B-13700
Editorial: Glückstädter Str. 10, 21682 STADE
Tel: 4141 936333 **Fax:** 4141 936294
Email: redaktion-std@tageblatt.de **Web site:** http://www.tageblatt.de
Freq: 312 issues yearly
Editor: Wolfgang Stephan; **Advertising Manager:** Georg Lempke
Profile: Daily newspaper with regional news and a local sports section. Twitter: http://twitter.com/tageblattonline This Outlet offers RSS (Really Simple Syndication).
Language(s): German
ADVERTISING RATES:
SCC .... EUR 121,50
Mechanical Data: Type Area: 487 x 324 mm, No. of Columns (Display): 7, Col Widths (Display): 45 mm
Copy instructions: *Copy Date:* 1 day prior to publication
Supplement(s): Ferienjournal; Stader Buxtehuder Altländer Tageblatt Freizeit Magazin; Stader Buxtehuder Altländer Tageblatt Steilpass
REGIONAL DAILY & SUNDAY NEWSPAPERS: Regional Daily Newspapers

STADT ANZEIGER CITY-ANZEIGER 724376G72-2964
Editorial: Ostwall 5, 44135 DORTMUND
Tel: 231 56229634 **Fax:** 231 5600159
Email: redaktion@cityanzeiger-dortmund.de **Web site:** http://www.cityanzeiger-dortmund.de
Freq: 104 issues yearly; **Cover Price:** Free; **Circ:** 54,000
Editor: Antje Geiß; **Advertising Manager:** Lars Staehler
Profile: Advertising journal (house-to-house) concentrating on local stories.
Language(s): German
Mechanical Data: Type Area: 445 x 315 mm, No. of Columns (Display): 7, Col Widths (Display): 42 mm
Copy instructions: *Copy Date:* 2 days prior to publication
LOCAL NEWSPAPERS

STADT ANZEIGER NORD-ANZEIGER 737590G72-9928
Editorial: Ostwall 5, 44135 DORTMUND
Tel: 231 56229632 **Fax:** 231 5600159
Email: redaktion@nordanzeiger-dortmund.de **Web site:** http://www.nordanzeiger-dortmund.de
Freq: 104 issues yearly; **Cover Price:** Free; **Circ:** 37,800
Editor: Ralf K. Braun; **Advertising Manager:** Lars Staehler
Profile: Advertising journal (house-to-house) concentrating on local stories.
Language(s): German
Mechanical Data: Type Area: 445 x 315 mm, No. of Columns (Display): 7, Col Widths (Display): 42 mm
Copy instructions: *Copy Date:* 2 days prior to publication
LOCAL NEWSPAPERS

STADT ANZEIGER OST-ANZEIGER 738375G72-10296
Editorial: Ostwall 5, 44135 DORTMUND
Tel: 231 56229632 **Fax:** 231 5600159
Email: redaktion@ostanzeiger-dortmund.de **Web site:** http://www.ostanzeiger-dortmund.de
Freq: 104 issues yearly; **Cover Price:** Free; **Circ:** 39,000
Editor: Ralf K. Braun; **Advertising Manager:** Lars Staehler
Profile: Advertising journal (house-to-house) concentrating on local stories.
Language(s): German
Mechanical Data: Type Area: 445 x 315 mm, No. of Columns (Display): 7, Col Widths (Display): 42 mm
Copy instructions: *Copy Date:* 2 days prior to publication
LOCAL NEWSPAPERS

STADT ANZEIGER SÜD-ANZEIGER 743896G72-13024
Editorial: Wiggerstr. 5, 44263 DORTMUND
Tel: 231 9411070 **Fax:** 231 422379
Email: redaktion@suedanzeiger-dortmund.de **Web site:** http://www.suedanzeiger-dortmund.de
Freq: 104 issues yearly; **Cover Price:** Free; **Circ:** 82,400
Editor: Peter Weigel; **Advertising Manager:** Lars Staehler
Profile: Advertising journal (house-to-house) concentrating on local stories.
Language(s): German
Mechanical Data: Type Area: 445 x 315 mm, No. of Columns (Display): 7, Col Widths (Display): 42 mm
Copy instructions: *Copy Date:* 2 days prior to publication
LOCAL NEWSPAPERS

STADT ANZEIGER WEST-ANZEIGER 747263G72-15212
Editorial: Ostwall 5, 44135 DORTMUND
Tel: 231 5622960 **Fax:** 231 5600159
Email: redaktion@westanzeiger-dortmund.de **Web site:** http://www.westanzeiger-dortmund.de
Freq: 104 issues yearly; **Cover Price:** Free; **Circ:** 70,800
Editor: Andreas Meier; **Advertising Manager:** Lars Staehler
Profile: Advertising journal (house-to-house) concentrating on local stories.
Language(s): German
Mechanical Data: Type Area: 445 x 315 mm, No. of Columns (Display): 7, Col Widths (Display): 42 mm
Copy instructions: *Copy Date:* 2 days prior to publication
LOCAL NEWSPAPERS

STADT BAUWELT 742694G4E-5820
Editorial: Schlüterstr. 42, 10707 BERLIN
Tel: 30 88410626 **Fax:** 30 8835167
Email: boris.schade-buensow@bauverlag.de **Web site:** http://www.bauwelt.de
Freq: Quarterly; **Annual Sub.:** EUR 85,20; **Circ:** 13,000
Editor: Boris Schade-Bünsow; **Advertising Manager:** Andreas Kirchgessner
Profile: Bauwelt - weekly forum for involved critical analysis and commentary on current issues in architecture. Formulated positions, provides material for discussion, forms opinions on a competent readers with decision-making authority over high volume of orders in large architectural firms and building authorities. Each issue focusing on the key issues, e.g. to business and administrative buildings, renovations, residential, industrial and public construction. Four times a year special edition Stadt Bauwelt on issues of urban design with increased support in addition to recipients of republic, states and municipalities.
Language(s): German
ADVERTISING RATES:
Full Page Mono .... EUR 4780
Full Page Colour .... EUR 7490
Mechanical Data: Type Area: 266 x 211 mm, No. of Columns (Display): 4, Col Widths (Display): 50 mm
Copy instructions: *Copy Date:* 14 days prior to publication

STADT UND GEMEINDE INTERAKTIV 742851G32A-2960
Editorial: Marienstr. 6, 12207 BERLIN
Tel: 30 77307225 **Fax:** 30 77307222
Email: kristin.schwarzbach@dstgb.de **Web site:** http://www.stadt-und-gemeinde.de
Freq: 10 issues yearly; **Annual Sub.:** EUR 78,00; **Circ:** 6,000
Editor: Gerd Landsberg; **Advertising Manager:** Kerstin Schökel
Profile: Journal about municipal administration within the different regions of Germany.
Language(s): German
Readership: Aimed at local government officials.
ADVERTISING RATES:
Full Page Mono .... EUR 1660
Full Page Colour .... EUR 2560
Mechanical Data: Type Area: 262 x 170 mm, No. of Columns (Display): 3, Col Widths (Display): 52 mm
Copy instructions: *Copy Date:* 25 days prior to publication
BUSINESS: LOCAL GOVERNMENT, LEISURE & RECREATION: Local Government

STADT + GRÜN 742852G32D-1
Editorial: Am Südtor 25, 30880 LAATZEN
Tel: 511 826541 **Fax:** 511 8669449
Email: ursula.kellner@patzerverlag.de **Web site:** http://www.stadtundgruen.de
Freq: Monthly; **Annual Sub.:** EUR 96,60; **Circ:** 2,445
Editor: Ursula Kellner; **Advertising Manager:** Bodo Ulbricht
Profile: Journal concerning the maintenance of parks and public gardens.
Language(s): German
ADVERTISING RATES:
Full Page Mono .... EUR 2065
Full Page Colour .... EUR 3958
Mechanical Data: Type Area: 261 x 184 mm, No. of Columns (Display): 4, Col Widths (Display): 43 mm
Copy instructions: *Copy Date:* 14 days prior to publication
Official Journal of: Organ d. Ständige Konferenz d. Gartenamtsleiter beim Dt. Städtetag
Supplement(s): Pro Baum
BUSINESS: LOCAL GOVERNMENT, LEISURE & RECREATION: Parks

STADT UND RAUM 742856G4E-5840
Editorial: Alte Schule Bannetze, 29308 WINSEN
Tel: 5146 98860 **Fax:** 5146 988629
Email: info@stadtundraum.de **Web site:** http://www.stadt-und-raum.de
Freq: 6 issues yearly; **Annual Sub.:** EUR 43,50; **Circ:** 7,000
Editor: Rolf von der Horst
Profile: The themes: urban and exterior design, landscape architecture, parks and public green areas, residential areas, playgrounds, playground design, Kita-outdoor spaces, recreation, safety and standards, game pieces, mobility and transport systems, leisure (sports) facilities and exercise rooms, computer for local authorities and planners ... The contents: Multi-generation concepts for higher residential, quality of leisure and life, game rooms and a "town full of life and environmental design" ... The issue categories: regular, recurring headings include In addition to the overarching themes "Stadt und Raum" and "game room planning," especially the "standards" book box, book information, FLL-date, magazine, market & media (with the manufacturer information), the market from A to Z, The Last, calendar ...
Language(s): German
Readership: Read by decision makers, landscape architects, council and municipal employees and those working in education.
ADVERTISING RATES:
Full Page Mono .... EUR 1892
Full Page Colour .... EUR 3376
Mechanical Data: Type Area: 270 x 186 mm

STADT UND RAUM 742856G4E-7321
Editorial: Alte Schule Bannetze, 29308 WINSEN
Tel: 5146 98860 **Fax:** 5146 988629
Email: info@stadtundraum.de **Web site:** http://www.stadt-und-raum.de
Freq: 6 issues yearly; **Annual Sub.:** EUR 43,50; **Circ:** 7,000
Editor: Rolf von der Horst
Profile: The themes: urban and exterior design, landscape architecture, parks and public green areas, residential areas, playgrounds, playground design, Kita-outdoor spaces, recreation, safety and standards, game pieces, mobility and transport systems, leisure (sports) facilities and exercise rooms, computer for local authorities and planners ... The contents: Multi-generation concepts for higher residential, quality of leisure and life, game rooms and a "town full of life and environmental design" ... The issue categories: regular, recurring headings include In addition to the overarching themes "Stadt und Raum" and "game room planning," especially the "standards" book box, book information, FLL-date, magazine, market & media (with the manufacturer information), the market from A to Z, The Last, calendar ...
Language(s): German
Readership: Read by decision makers, landscape architects, council and municipal employees and those working in education.
ADVERTISING RATES:
Full Page Mono .... EUR 1892
Full Page Colour .... EUR 3376
Mechanical Data: Type Area: 270 x 186 mm

STADTBLATT LIVE 742703G89A-4460
Editorial: Georgstr. 14, 49074 OSNABRÜCK
Tel: 541 3578723 **Fax:** 541 24602
Email: live@stadtblatt-osnabrueck.de **Web site:** http://www.stadtblatt-osnabrueck.de
Freq: Half-yearly; **Cover Price:** Free; **Circ:** 20,000
Editor: Andreas Bekemeier
Profile: City Journal is the imported live magazine for lovers of good cuisine. The restaurant guide is concerned with the diverse gastronomic scene in and around Osnabrück. Facebook: http://www.facebook.com/pages/STADTBLATT/116839888330562.
Language(s): German
ADVERTISING RATES:
Full Page Mono .... EUR 1120
Full Page Colour .... EUR 1120
Mechanical Data: Type Area: 191 x 146 mm

STADTBLATT OSNABRÜCK 742698G80-10740
Editorial: Georgstr. 14, 49074 OSNABRÜCK
Tel: 541 3578723 **Fax:** 541 24602
Email: redaktion@stadtblatt-osnabrueck.de **Web site:** http://www.stadtblatt-osnabrueck.de
Freq: Monthly; **Annual Sub.:** EUR 19,00; **Circ:** 3,049
Editor: Andreas Bekemeier
Profile: Magazine for city and region, concentrating on gastronomy, music, arts and events. Facebook: http://www.facebook.com/pages/STADTBLATT/116839888330562.
Language(s): German
ADVERTISING RATES:
Full Page Mono .... EUR 680
Full Page Colour .... EUR 1160
Mechanical Data: Type Area: 260 x 190 mm, No. of Columns (Display): 4, Col Widths (Display): 44 mm
Copy instructions: *Copy Date:* 12 days prior to publication
CONSUMER: RURAL & REGIONAL INTEREST

STÄDTE UND GEMEINDERAT 742892G32A-2980
Editorial: Kaiserswerther Str. 199, 40474 DÜSSELDORF **Tel:** 211 4587230 **Fax:** 211 4587211
Email: redaktion@kommunen-in-nrw.de **Web site:** http://www.nwstgb.de
Freq: 10 issues yearly; **Annual Sub.:** EUR 78,00; **Circ:** 14,708
Editor: Martin Lehrer; **Advertising Manager:** Alke Schmeis
Profile: Magazine from the German Association of Towns and Municipalities about communal and federal policies.
Language(s): German
ADVERTISING RATES:
Full Page Mono .... EUR 1620
Full Page Colour .... EUR 2835
Mechanical Data: Type Area: 270 x 180 mm, No. of Columns (Display): 4, Col Widths (Display): 45 mm
Copy instructions: *Copy Date:* 21 days prior to publication
BUSINESS: LOCAL GOVERNMENT, LEISURE & RECREATION: Local Government

STADTKURIER 742756G72-12720
Editorial: Bismarckallee 8, 79098 FREIBURG
Tel: 761 207190 **Fax:** 761 2071919
Email: redaktion@stadtkurier.de **Web site:** http://www.stadtkurier.de
Freq: Weekly; **Cover Price:** Free; **Circ:** 115,000
Editor: Stefan Ummenhöfer
Profile: Advertising journal (house-to-house) concentrating on local stories.
Language(s): German
ADVERTISING RATES:
Full Page Mono .... EUR 5796
Full Page Colour .... EUR 8442
Mechanical Data: Type Area: 420 x 280 mm, No. of Columns (Display): 6, Col Widths (Display): 45 mm
Copy instructions: *Copy Date:* 2 days prior to publication
LOCAL NEWSPAPERS

STADTLICHTER 1684118G80-14531
Editorial: Vor dem Bardowicker Tore 6, 21339 LÜNEBURG **Tel:** 4131 735715 **Fax:** 4131 760482
Email: redaktion@stadtlichter.com **Web site:** http://www.stadtlichter.com
Freq: 11 issues yearly; **Cover Price:** Free; **Circ:** 13,875
Editor: Katja Müller; **Advertising Manager:** Katja Müller
Profile: City magazine.
Language(s): German
ADVERTISING RATES:
Full Page Mono .... EUR 1017
Full Page Colour .... EUR 1320
Mechanical Data: Type Area: 264 x 192 mm
CONSUMER: RURAL & REGIONAL INTEREST

DER STADTPLAN 1826202G89A-12385
Editorial: Kardinal-Höffner-Platz 1, 50667 KÖLN
Tel: 221 22123328 **Fax:** 221 22123320
Email: ralf.rudolph@koelntourismus.de **Web site:** http://www.koelntourismus.de
Freq: Annual; **Cover Price:** EUR 0,20; **Circ:** 275,000
Editor: Georg Wohlrab
Profile: Cologne city map with information on attractions part.
Language(s): German

STADTPOST DREIEICH 742792G72-12756
Editorial: Waldstr. 226, 63071 OFFENBACH
Tel: 69 85008270 **Fax:** 69 85008296
Email: stadtpost.dreieich@stadtpost.de **Web site:** http://www.stadtpost.de
Freq: Weekly; **Cover Price:** Free; **Circ:** 37,550
Editor: Wolfgang Janz; **Advertising Manager:** Helmut Moser
Profile: Advertising journal (house-to-house) concentrating on local stories.
Language(s): German
ADVERTISING RATES:
Full Page Mono .... EUR 3521
Full Page Colour .... EUR 4929
Mechanical Data: Type Area: 470 x 322 mm, No. of Columns (Display): 7, Col Widths (Display): 43 mm
Copy instructions: *Copy Date:* 2 days prior to publication
Supplement(s): Isenburg-Zentrum Aktuell
LOCAL NEWSPAPERS

STADTPOST LANGEN-EGELSBACH 742794G72-12764
Editorial: Waldstr. 226, 63071 OFFENBACH
Tel: 69 85008270 **Fax:** 69 85008296

Email: stadtpost.langen@stadtpost.de **Web site:** http://www.op-online.de
Cover Price: Free
Editor: Wolfgang Janz; **Advertising Manager:** Helmut Moser
Profile: Advertising journal (house-to-house) concentrating on local stories.
Language(s): German
Supplement(s): Isenburg-Zentrum Aktuell
LOCAL NEWSPAPERS

STADTPOST OFFENBACH
742797G72-12776
Editorial: Waldstr. 226, 63071 OFFENBACH
Tel: 69 85008272 **Fax:** 69 85008296
Email: stadtpost.offenbach@stadtpost.de **Web site:** http://www.stadtpost.de
Freq: Weekly; **Cover Price:** Free; **Circ:** 41,850
Editor: Wolfgang Janz; **Advertising Manager:** Helmut Moser
Profile: Advertising journal (house-to-house) concentrating on local stories.
Language(s): German
ADVERTISING RATES:
Full Page Mono .... EUR 3784
Full Page Colour .... EUR 5297
Mechanical Data: Type Area: 470 x 322 mm, No. of Columns (Display): 7, Col Widths (Display): 43 mm
Copy instructions: *Copy Date:* 2 days prior to publication
Supplement(s): Isenburg-Zentrum Aktuell
LOCAL NEWSPAPERS

STADTPOST RÖDERMARK
742798G72-12780
Editorial: Waldstr. 226, 63071 OFFENBACH
Tel: 69 850080 **Fax:** 69 850080296
Email: stadtpost.roedermark@stadtpost.de **Web site:** http://www.op-online.de
Cover Price: Free
Editor: Wolfgang Janz; **Advertising Manager:** Helmut Moser
Profile: Advertising journal (house-to-house) concentrating on local stories.
Language(s): German
LOCAL NEWSPAPERS

STADTREPORT OBERHAUSEN
742801G89C-3740
Editorial: Schwartzstr. 62, 46045 OBERHAUSEN
Tel: 208 8245733 **Fax:** 208 8245721
Email: helmut.kawohl@tmo.oberhausen.de **Web site:** http://www.oberhausen-tourismus.de
Freq: Monthly; **Cover Price:** EUR 1,30; **Circ:** 8,000
Editor: Helmut Kawohl
Profile: Magazine about culture, business and life in Oberhausen.
Language(s): German
ADVERTISING RATES:
Full Page Mono .... EUR 320
Full Page Colour .... EUR 490
Mechanical Data: Type Area: 270 x 190 mm
CONSUMER: HOLIDAYS & TRAVEL: Entertainment Guides

STADTREVUE
742802G80-10700
Editorial: Maastrichter Str. 49, 50672 KÖLN
Tel: 221 95154126 **Fax:** 221 95154111
Email: bernd.willberg@stadtrevue.de **Web site:** http://www.stadtrevue.de
Freq: Monthly; **Annual Sub.:** EUR 22,00; **Circ:** 19,217
Editor: Bernd Wilberg; **Advertising Manager:** Michael Meiger
Profile: Magazine for the Cologne area. Facebook: http://www.facebook.com/stadtrevue Twitter: http://twitter.com/#!/stadtrevue.
Language(s): German
ADVERTISING RATES:
Full Page Mono .... EUR 2290
Full Page Colour .... EUR 3300
Mechanical Data: Type Area: 262 x 190 mm, No. of Columns (Display): 4, Col Widths (Display): 44 mm
Supplement(s): immergrün; Laufen und Skaten in Köln; Raum 5; StadtRevue spezial Weiterbildung
CONSUMER: RURAL & REGIONAL INTEREST

STADTREVUE SPEZIAL WEITERBILDUNG
1827777G57-2848
Editorial: Maastrichter Str. 49, 50672 KÖLN
Tel: 221 95154126 **Fax:** 221 95154111
Email: bren.wilberg@stadtrevue.de **Web site:** http://www.stadtrevue.de
Freq: Annual; **Cover Price:** Free; **Circ:** 30,000
Editor: Bernd Wilberg; **Advertising Manager:** Michael Meiger
Profile: Special issue on service and education training in Cologne. The provider commented directory of more than 200 addresses each year, new research. Distribution: Free distribution of targeted and insert in the September issue of the city revue.
Language(s): German
ADVERTISING RATES:
Full Page Mono .... EUR 1390
Full Page Colour .... EUR 1920
Mechanical Data: Type Area: 184 x 124 mm, No. of Columns (Display): 2, Col Widths (Display): 58 mm
Copy instructions: *Copy Date:* 56 days prior to publication
Supplement to: StadtRevue

STADTSTREICHER
742839G89C-4829
Editorial: Am Feldschlößchen 18, 09116 CHEMNITZ
Tel: 371 383800 **Fax:** 371 3838038
Email: info@stadtstreicher.de **Web site:** http://www.stadtstreicher.de
Freq: Monthly; **Cover Price:** Free; **Circ:** 17,237
Editor: Jenny Zichner; **Advertising Manager:** Markus Wolf
Profile: Events and leisure guide for Chemnitz and its surroundings.
Language(s): German
ADVERTISING RATES:
Full Page Mono .... EUR 2574
Full Page Colour .... EUR 2574
Mechanical Data: Type Area: 260 x 190 mm, No. of Columns (Display): 6, Col Widths (Display): 28 mm
Copy instructions: *Copy Date:* 10 days prior to publication
CONSUMER: HOLIDAYS & TRAVEL: Entertainment Guides

STADTVERKEHR
742858G49A-90
Editorial: Lörracher Str. 16, 79115 FREIBURG
Tel: 761 7031020 **Fax:** 761 7031053
Email: stefan.goebel@stadtverkehr.de **Web site:** http://www.stadtverkehr.de
Freq: 10 issues yearly; **Annual Sub.:** EUR 48,00; **Circ:** 5,465
Editor: Stefan Göbel; **Advertising Manager:** Waltraud Gänßmantel
Profile: Journal focusing on all aspects of public transport.
Language(s): German
ADVERTISING RATES:
Full Page Mono .... EUR 1350
Full Page Colour .... EUR 2150
Mechanical Data: Type Area: 260 x 186 mm, No. of Columns (Display): 2, Col Widths (Display): 90 mm
Copy instructions: *Copy Date:* 28 days prior to publication
BUSINESS: TRANSPORT

STAFETTE
743070G91D-7540
Editorial: Lina-Ammon-Str. 30, 90471 NÜRNBERG
Tel: 911 6600163 **Fax:** 911 6600110
Email: stafette@sailer-verlag.de **Web site:** http://www.sailer-verlag.de
Freq: Monthly; **Annual Sub.:** EUR 28,80; **Circ:** 78,968
Editor: Ronald Rothenburger; **Advertising Manager:** Armin Baier
Profile: Explore the world with Stafette. The strong student magazine reached as the core target group of children and adolescents between 8 and 13 years. Stafette is their recipe for success for decades remained true: With variety of topics Stafette promotes the pleasure of reading, inspires creativity, provides knowledge and above all offers lots of entertainment. At 60 pages there are interesting reports, computer news, competitions, tests, comics, jokes, sports stories, news from the music, movie and TV scene, and a giant poster in each issue.
Language(s): German
Readership: Aimed at children.
ADVERTISING RATES:
Full Page Mono .... EUR 6000
Full Page Colour .... EUR 6000
Mechanical Data: Type Area: 252 x 188 mm
CONSUMER: RECREATION & LEISURE: Children & Youth

STAGEREPORT
743071G2A-4520
Editorial: Hopfenfeld 5, 31311 UETZE
Tel: 5173 98270 **Fax:** 5173 982739
Email: info@stagereport.de **Web site:** http://www.stagereport.de
Freq: Monthly; **Annual Sub.:** EUR 59,50; **Circ:** 2,000
Editor: Peter Blach; **Advertising Manager:** Stefan Winterfeldt
Profile: Magazine with business information about event service providers and event organisers as well as representatives of the show and entertainment branches.
Language(s): German
ADVERTISING RATES:
Full Page Mono .... EUR 1320
Full Page Colour .... EUR 1980
Mechanical Data: No. of Columns (Display): 3, Col Widths (Display): 55 mm, Type Area: 253 x 175 mm
Copy instructions: *Copy Date:* 8 days prior to publication
Supplement(s): PocketEvent

STAHL UND EISEN
743079G27-2320
Editorial: Sohnstr. 65, 40237 DÜSSELDORF
Tel: 211 6707570 **Fax:** 211 6707436
Email: gerd.krause@stahleisen.de **Web site:** http://www.stahleisen.de
Freq: Monthly; **Annual Sub.:** EUR 222,00; **Circ:** 6,397
Editor: Gerd Krause; **Advertising Manager:** Sabine Dudek
Profile: International science and engineering-based trade journal. Includes a target-group-specific business section.
Language(s): English; German
Readership: Aimed at managers in the steel industry.
ADVERTISING RATES:
Full Page Mono .... EUR 2596
Full Page Colour .... EUR 3394
Mechanical Data: Type Area: 260 x 180 mm, No. of Columns (Display): 3, Col Widths (Display): 56 mm
Copy instructions: *Copy Date:* 14 days prior to publication
Official Journal of: Organ d. Stahlinst. VDEh, Wirtschaftsvereinigung Stahl unter Mitarbeit d. Centre de Recherches Métallurgiques, d. European Coil Coating Association u. d. Verb. d. Führungskräfte d. Eisen- u. Stahlerzeugung u. -verarbeitung e.V.
BUSINESS: METAL, IRON & STEEL

STAHLBAU
743074G27-270
Editorial: Rotherstr. 21, 10245 BERLIN
Tel: 30 47031248 **Fax:** 30 47031270
Email: stahlbau@ernst-und-sohn.de **Web site:** http://www.ernst-und-sohn.de
Freq: Monthly; **Annual Sub.:** EUR 446,00; **Circ:** 2,158
Editor: Karl-Eugen Kurrer; **Advertising Manager:** Norbert Schippel
Profile: Journal about steel, metal construction, building methods, planning, investigation, estimates and developments in the industry.
Language(s): German
Readership: Aimed at Civil Engineers and Consultants in the steel construction industry.
ADVERTISING RATES:
Full Page Mono .... EUR 2740
Full Page Colour .... EUR 4285
Mechanical Data: Type Area: 260 x 180 mm, No. of Columns (Display): 4, Col Widths (Display): 42 mm
BUSINESS: METAL, IRON & STEEL

STAHLBAU NACHRICHTEN
743075G27-270_50
Editorial: Biebricher Allee 11b, 65187 WIESBADEN
Tel: 611 846515 **Fax:** 611 801252
Email: mwiederspahn@verlagsgruppewiederspahn.de **Web site:** http://www.stahlbau-nachrichten.de
Freq: Quarterly; Free to qualifying individuals
Annual Sub.: EUR 40,00; **Circ:** 5,760
Editor: Michael Wiederspahn; **Advertising Manager:** Ulla Leitner
Profile: Magazine containing articles about steel constructions, building and civil engineering.
Language(s): German
ADVERTISING RATES:
Full Page Mono .... EUR 1700
Full Page Colour .... EUR 2400
Mechanical Data: Type Area: 268 x 185 mm, No. of Columns (Display): 3, Col Widths (Display): 58 mm
Copy instructions: *Copy Date:* 21 days prior to publication
BUSINESS: METAL, IRON & STEEL

DER STAHLFORMENBAUER
743076G27-271
Editorial: Neustr. 163, 42553 VELBERT
Tel: 2053 981250 **Fax:** 2053 981256
Email: redaktion@fachverlag-moeller.de **Web site:** http://www.fachverlag-moeller.de
Freq: 6 issues yearly; **Annual Sub.:** EUR 30,00; **Circ:** 2,797
Editor: Karl-Heinz Möller; **Advertising Manager:** Erik Möller
Profile: Journal about tools, moulding and casting.
Language(s): German
Readership: Read by people in the metal industry.
ADVERTISING RATES:
Full Page Mono .... EUR 640
Full Page Colour .... EUR 1120
Mechanical Data: Type Area: 260 x 180 mm, No. of Columns (Display): 4, Col Widths (Display): 44 mm
Copy instructions: *Copy Date:* 14 days prior to publication
BUSINESS: METAL, IRON & STEEL

STAHLMARKT
743077G27-2340
Editorial: Sohnstr. 65, 40237 DÜSSELDORF
Tel: 211 6707538 **Fax:** 211 6707540
Email: stahlmarkt@stahleisen.de **Web site:** http://www.stahleisen.de
Freq: Monthly; **Annual Sub.:** EUR 99,00; **Circ:** 7,854
Editor: Wiebke Sanders; **Advertising Manager:** Ruth Jentsch
Profile: Journal containing technical news about the steel industry, production, trade and processing.
Language(s): English; German
Readership: Aimed at the steel industry.
ADVERTISING RATES:
Full Page Mono .... EUR 2564
Full Page Colour .... EUR 3362
Mechanical Data: Type Area: 260 x 184 mm, No. of Columns (Display): 3, Col Widths (Display): 58 mm
Copy instructions: *Copy Date:* 21 days prior to publication
BUSINESS: METAL, IRON & STEEL

STAHLREPORT
743078G27-2360
Editorial: Max-Planck-Str. 1, 40237 DÜSSELDORF
Tel: 211 864970 **Fax:** 211 8649722
Email: wolfgart-bds@stahlhandel.com **Web site:** http://www.stahlhandel.com
Freq: Monthly; Free to qualifying individuals
Annual Sub.: EUR 86,40; **Circ:** 3,453
Editor: Ludger Wolfgart; **Advertising Manager:** Ksenija Sandek
Profile: Journal about steel manufacture, trading, processing and production.
Language(s): German
ADVERTISING RATES:
Full Page Mono .... EUR 2080
Full Page Colour .... EUR 3640
Mechanical Data: Type Area: 235 x 180 mm, No. of Columns (Display): 4, Col Widths (Display): 42 mm
Copy instructions: *Copy Date:* 12 days prior to publication
BUSINESS: METAL, IRON & STEEL

STAMM
743081G2A-5417
Editorial: Goldammerweg 16, 45134 ESSEN
Tel: 201 8430041 **Fax:** 201 8430015
Email: redaktion@stamm.de **Web site:** http://www.stamm.de
Freq: Annual; **Cover Price:** EUR 149,00; **Circ:** 3,000
Editor: Ulrich Tewes
Profile: Annual directory about press and media.
Language(s): German
ADVERTISING RATES:
Full Page Mono .... EUR 990
Mechanical Data: Type Area: 222 x 146 mm
Copy instructions: *Copy Date:* 120 days prior to publication

STANDARDS
724645G49R-2
Editorial: Maarweg 133, 50825 KÖLN
Tel: 221 947140 **Fax:** 221 94714990
Email: info@gs1-germany.de **Web site:** http://www.gs1-germany.de
Freq: Quarterly; Free to qualifying individuals
Annual Sub.: EUR 16,40; **Circ:** 42,000
Editor: Malte Hendriksen
Profile: Standards, processes, services jointly develop and deploy, that's the basic idea of GS1 Germany. The magazine provides with practical experience reports on application and process descriptions. It promotes the exchange of opinions and forecasts are development of technology and organization. In addition, it provides recommendations for practical implementation of commerce, industry and service for the common benefit of all The GS1 magazine offers an overview of the seminars and conferences, as well as professional publications. The reader is informed of service providers through a variety of hardware and software vendors for identification, communications and logistics solutions. With a circulation of over 40,000 copies away by GS1 magazine the decision makers in the consumer goods, automotive, pharmaceutical, DIY and textile industries and related sectors. Facebook: http://www.facebook.com/GS1.Germany Twitter: http://twitter.com/gs1germany.
Language(s): German
ADVERTISING RATES:
Full Page Mono .... EUR 3220
Full Page Colour .... EUR 4570
Mechanical Data: Type Area: 252 x 175 mm, No. of Columns (Display): 3, Col Widths (Display): 55 mm
BUSINESS: TRANSPORT: Transport Related

STANDPUNKTE
743093G17-1420
Editorial: Kapstadtring 10, 22297 HAMBURG
Tel: 40 63784231 **Fax:** 40 63784234
Email: haas@nordmetall.de **Web site:** http://www.nordmetall.de
Freq: 6 issues yearly; **Cover Price:** Free; **Circ:** 5,000
Editor: Peter Haas
Profile: Official publication of the Metal and Electro Industry Association for the region of Norddeutschland with information for employees, managers and external target groups.
Language(s): German

STAPLER WORLD
1641879G10-525
Editorial: Schäferstr. 2, 55257 BUDENHEIM
Tel: 6139 293443 **Fax:** 6139 960455
Email: oba@staplerworld.com **Web site:** http://www.staplerworld.com
Freq: 6 issues yearly; **Annual Sub.:** EUR 120,00; **Circ:** 9,922
Editor: Oliver Bachmann; **Advertising Manager:** Albert Mumm
Profile: Magazine on pallet carriers.
Language(s): German
ADVERTISING RATES:
Full Page Mono .... EUR 2765
Full Page Colour .... EUR 3890
Mechanical Data: Type Area: 245 x 184 mm, No. of Columns (Display): 3, Col Widths (Display): 58 mm
Copy instructions: *Copy Date:* 10 days prior to publication
BUSINESS: MATERIALS HANDLING

STARCH
743099G22A-1860
Editorial: Boschstr. 12, 69469 WEINHEIM
Tel: 6201 6060 **Fax:** 6201 606172
Email: starch@wiley-vch.de **Web site:** http://www.starch-journal.de
Freq: 6 issues yearly; **Annual Sub.:** EUR 1488,00; **Circ:** 965
Editor: Christine Mayer; **Advertising Manager:** Patricia Filler
Profile: Journal focusing on investigation, processing and use of carbohydrates and their derivatives.
Language(s): English
Readership: Read by specialists in the food, paper, adhesive, textile, chemical, synthetic materials and pharmaceutical industries.
ADVERTISING RATES:
Full Page Mono .... EUR 1600
Full Page Colour .... EUR 2950
Mechanical Data: Type Area: 260 x 180 mm, No. of Columns (Display): 3, Col Widths (Display): 60 mm
BUSINESS: FOOD

STARKENBURGER ECHO
743921G67B-14080
Editorial: Holzhofallee 25, 64295 DARMSTADT
Tel: 6151 3871 **Fax:** 6151 387218

Email: redaktion@darmstaedter-echo.de **Web site:** http://www.echo-online.de
Freq: 312 issues yearly; **Circ:** 5,947
Advertising Manager: Andreas Wohlfart
Profile: Daily newspaper with regional news and a local sports section. This Outlet offers RSS (Really Simple Syndication).
Language(s): German
ADVERTISING RATES:
SCC .... EUR 18,50
Mechanical Data: Type Area: 491 x 339 mm, No. of Columns (Display): 7, Col Widths (Display): 45 mm
Copy instructions: *Copy Date:* 1 day prior to publication
Supplement(s): Generation; Gesund leben heute; Die Hupe; i2 immobilien; Kinder Echo; Sonntags Echo
REGIONAL DAILY & SUNDAY NEWSPAPERS: Regional Daily Newspapers

STARNBERGER MERKUR
743106G67B-13720
Editorial: Pfaffenrieder Str. 9, 82515 WOLFRATSHAUSEN **Tel:** 8171 2690
Fax: 8171 269240
Email: fsav@merkur-online.de **Web site:** http://www.merkur-online.de
Freq: 312 issues yearly; **Circ:** 10,118
Advertising Manager: Hans-Georg Bechthold
Profile: The Münchner Merkur with its own local newspapers, of which the Starnberger Merkur is one that, the leading regional newspaper brand in the Munich area - the most affluent area of Germany. The combination of newspaper and region is the foundation on which to build the success of the title. This is the newspaper not only the factual news agency, but forms a community of solidarity with its readers and the local community. The clear focus on local reporting creates a high regard to human reader loyalty. She presses one hand in the very high number of close to 180,000 subscribers. Also for the high reader-commitment is the loyalty of the total current 827 000 daily readers, the Münchner Merkur or one of its local newspapers usually read over many years. The Münchner Merkur with its own local newspapers is a newspaper for the whole family, tradition and modern life for one of the most beautiful regions of Germany unites. Reliable, informative, critical: the Münchner Merkur is the indispensable daily newspaper for the region. Facebook: http://www.facebook.com/pages/merkur-online.de/190176143327 This Outlet offers RSS (Really Simple Syndication).
Language(s): German
ADVERTISING RATES:
SCC .... EUR 43,60
Mechanical Data: Type Area: 474 x 324 mm, No. of Columns (Display): 7, Col Widths (Display): 45 mm
Copy instructions: *Copy Date:* 1 day prior to publication
REGIONAL DAILY & SUNDAY NEWSPAPERS: Regional Daily Newspapers

STARTING UP
1641146G14A-9592
Editorial: Sämannstr. 14a, 82166 GRÄFELFING
Tel: 89 7415300 **Fax:** 89 74153019
Email: cbuechner@starting-up.de **Web site:** http://www.starting-up.de
Freq: Quarterly; **Annual Sub.:** EUR 21,90; **Circ:** 30,480
Editor: Cornelius Büchner; **Advertising Manager:** Ingrid Drechsler
Profile: StartingUp is the magazine for entrepreneurs and young entrepreneurs in Germany. The focal points are e.g. Questions about funding and financing, the latest marketing trends and current tax and legal advice. But the reader also learns how to effectively acquired customer or with the stress of everyday life especially in the grueling finish up phase. Facebook: http://www.facebook.com/StartingUp.
Language(s): German
ADVERTISING RATES:
Full Page Mono .... EUR 5600
Full Page Colour .... EUR 5600
Mechanical Data: Type Area: 240 x 178 mm
Copy instructions: *Copy Date:* 21 days prior to publication
BUSINESS: COMMERCE, INDUSTRY & MANAGEMENT

STASSFURTER VOLKSSTIMME
743118G67B-13740
Editorial: Bahnhofstr. 17, 39104 MAGDEBURG
Tel: 391 59990 **Fax:** 391 5999210
Email: chefredaktion@volksstimme.de **Web site:** http://www.volksstimme.de
Freq: 312 issues yearly; **Circ:** 9,748
Advertising Manager: Rainer Pfeil
Profile: As the largest daily newspaper in northern Saxony-Anhalt, the Volksstimme reaches 536,000 readers a day* (MA 2010). From Monday to Saturday a team of highly qualified editors put together the latest information and news from the region and around the world. Thanks the 18 local editions is the Volksstimme always close to the action. Twitter: http://twitter.com/volksstimme This Outlet offers RSS (Really Simple Syndication).
Language(s): German
ADVERTISING RATES:
SCC .... EUR 46,00
Mechanical Data: Type Area: 480 x 327 mm, No. of Columns (Display): 7, Col Widths (Display): 45 mm
Copy instructions: *Copy Date:* 2 days prior to publication
Supplement(s): Anstoss in Staßfurt; bauRatgeber; Biber; Leser-Reisen; prisma; Standort Landkreis Aschersleben-Stassfurt
REGIONAL DAILY & SUNDAY NEWSPAPERS: Regional Daily Newspapers

STATION TO STATION
743121G80-10880
Editorial: Exerzierplatz 14, 24103 KIEL
Tel: 431 702100 **Fax:** 431 7021010
Email: station@station.de **Web site:** http://www.station.de
Freq: Monthly; **Annual Sub.:** EUR 22,00; **Circ:** 11,000
Editor: Dörte Wohlenberg; **Advertising Manager:** Dörte Wohlenberg
Profile: Entertainment guide to Kiel. Includes music, theatre and cinema listings.
Language(s): German
CONSUMER: RURAL & REGIONAL INTEREST

STATISTIK DER ENERGIEWIRTSCHAFT
1656855G58-1735
Editorial: Richard-Wagner-Str. 41, 45128 ESSEN
Tel: 201 8108433 **Fax:** 201 81084733
Email: a.stemmer@vik.de **Web site:** http://www.vik.de
Freq: Annual; **Cover Price:** EUR 94,50; **Circ:** 1,000
Editor: Ansgar Stemmer
Profile: Statistical data of the energy economy.
Language(s): German
ADVERTISING RATES:
Full Page Mono .... EUR 1350
Full Page Colour .... EUR 2160
Mechanical Data: Type Area: 256 x 173 mm

STATISTISCHES HANDBUCH FÜR DEN MASCHINENBAU
743295G19E-1660
Editorial: Lyoner Str. 18, 60528 FRANKFURT
Tel: 69 66031374 **Fax:** 69 66032374
Email: gesine.schneider@vdma.org **Web site:** http://www.vdma.org
Freq: Annual; **Cover Price:** EUR 60,00; **Circ:** 800
Profile: Statistics about engine construction.
Language(s): German

STAUFENBIEL WIRTSCHAFT-SWISSENSCHAFTLER
722559G88C-20
Editorial: Maria-Hilf-Str. 15, 50677 KÖLN
Tel: 221 91266345 **Fax:** 221 9126639
Email: thomas.friedenberger@staufenbiel.de **Web site:** http://www.staufenbiel.de
Freq: Half-yearly; **Cover Price:** EUR 15,00; **Circ:** 35,000
Editor: Thomas Friedenberger; **Advertising Manager:** Holger Fäßler
Profile: Publication dealing with career planning, education and occupational issues.
Language(s): German
Readership: Aimed at people studying for leading positions.
ADVERTISING RATES:
Full Page Colour .... EUR 5260
Mechanical Data: Type Area: 210 x 146 mm
CONSUMER: EDUCATION: Careers

STAZ DAS STANDESAMT
743338G44-1980
Editorial: Hanauer Landstr. 197, 60314 FRANKFURT
Tel: 69 4058940 **Fax:** 69 405894900
Email: staz@vfst.de **Web site:** http://www.vfst.de
Freq: Monthly; **Annual Sub.:** EUR 152,50; **Circ:** 5,800
Editor: Tobias Helms; **Advertising Manager:** Dietmar Ingenbleek
Profile: Journal of the registry office system, family law, nationality law, personal law, private international law at home and abroad: - Essays from science and practice - Court decisions - Information and materials on international law - Population Statistics - Laws, regulations and orders of federal and state inform the reader up to date and thorough researchers and practitioners and provide a forum for debate on new legal developments and controversial state of opinion.
Language(s): German
ADVERTISING RATES:
Full Page Mono .... EUR 1370
Full Page Colour .... EUR 1370
Mechanical Data: Type Area: 258 x 177 mm, No. of Columns (Display): 2, Col Widths (Display): 86 mm
Copy instructions: *Copy Date:* 15 days prior to publication
Supplement(s): Verbandsnachrichten und Mitteilungen des Bundesverbandes und der Landesverbände der Deutschen Standesbeamtinnen und Standesbeamten (VBStA)
BUSINESS: LEGAL

STBG DIE STEUERBERATUNG
743343G1A-2600
Editorial: Bobert-Blum-Str. 11, 17489 GREIFSWALD
Email: bert.kaminski@t-online.de **Web site:** http://www.die-steuerberatung.de
Freq: Monthly; Free to qualifying individuals
Annual Sub.: EUR 172,05; **Circ:** 34,500
Editor: Bert Kaminski; **Advertising Manager:** Carsten Priesel
Profile: Magazine for tax advisors.
Language(s): German
ADVERTISING RATES:
Full Page Mono .... EUR 2990
Full Page Colour .... EUR 4590
Mechanical Data: Type Area: 260 x 180 mm, No. of Columns (Display): 4, Col Widths (Display): 43 mm
Copy instructions: *Copy Date:* 21 days prior to publication

STBP DIE STEUERLICHE BETRIEBSPRÜFUNG
743477G1B-35
Editorial: Henrichstr. 1, 33790 HALLE
Tel: 5201 735535 **Fax:** 5201 735244
Email: j.hille@esvmedien.de **Web site:** http://www.stbpdigital.de
Freq: Monthly; **Annual Sub.:** EUR 135,19; **Circ:** 1,600
Editor: Jürgen Hille; **Advertising Manager:** Peter Taprogge
Profile: Journal about company audits.
Language(s): German
ADVERTISING RATES:
Full Page Mono .... EUR 1575
Full Page Colour .... EUR 2475
Mechanical Data: Type Area: 248 x 171 mm, No. of Columns (Display): 2, Col Widths (Display): 84 mm
BUSINESS: FINANCE & ECONOMICS: Accountancy

STEEL CONSTRUCTION
1924068G4E-7299
Editorial: Rotherstr. 21, 10245 BERLIN
Tel: 30 47031248 **Fax:** 30 47031270
Email: karl-eugen.kurrer@wiley.com **Web site:** http://www.ernst-und-sohn.de
Freq: Quarterly; **Annual Sub.:** EUR 158,00; **Circ:** 4,800
Editor: Karl-Eugen Kurrer; **Advertising Manager:** Norbert Schippel
Profile: The journal publishes peer-reviewed papers on the whole research and engineering practice of structural steel, particularly in the areas of composites, bridges, engineering high, rope, membrane, facades, glass and metal light construction but also the crane, pole, tower, steel, water, container and chimney construction and fire protection.
Language(s): English
ADVERTISING RATES:
Full Page Mono .... EUR 2650
Full Page Colour .... EUR 4150
Mechanical Data: Type Area: 260 x 181 mm, No. of Columns (Display): 2, Col Widths (Display): 88 mm
Copy instructions: *Copy Date:* 35 days prior to publication

STEEL RESEARCH
743351G27-2959
Editorial: Boschstr. 12, 69469 WEINHEIM
Tel: 6201 606355 **Fax:** 6201 606510
Email: editor@steel-research.de **Web site:** http://www.wiley-vch.de
Freq: Monthly; **Annual Sub.:** EUR 309,00; **Circ:** 1,500
Editor: Sibylle Meyer; **Advertising Manager:** Patricia Filler
Profile: International magazine about all aspects of steel research.
Language(s): English
Readership: Read by scientists and engineers.
ADVERTISING RATES:
Full Page Mono .... EUR 1070
Full Page Colour .... EUR 1640
Mechanical Data: Type Area: 260 x 180 mm, No. of Columns (Display): 2, Col Widths (Display): 87 mm
Copy instructions: *Copy Date:* 20 days prior to publication

STEEL RESEARCH
743351G27-3114
Editorial: Boschstr. 12, 69469 WEINHEIM
Tel: 6201 606355 **Fax:** 6201 606510
Email: editor@steel-research.de **Web site:** http://www.wiley-vch.de
Freq: Monthly; **Annual Sub.:** EUR 309,00; **Circ:** 1,500
Editor: Sibylle Meyer; **Advertising Manager:** Patricia Filler
Profile: International magazine about all aspects of steel research.
Language(s): English
Readership: Read by scientists and engineers.
ADVERTISING RATES:
Full Page Mono .... EUR 1070
Full Page Colour .... EUR 1640
Mechanical Data: Type Area: 260 x 180 mm, No. of Columns (Display): 2, Col Widths (Display): 87 mm
Copy instructions: *Copy Date:* 20 days prior to publication

STEELER KURIER
743350G72-12844
Editorial: Westfalenstr. 288, 45276 ESSEN
Tel: 201 8513321 **Fax:** 201 8513333
Email: redaktion@steelerkurier-essen.de **Web site:** http://www.lokalkompass.de/essen-steele
Freq: 104 issues yearly; **Cover Price:** Free; **Circ:** 39,900
Editor: Detlef Leweux; **Advertising Manager:** Lars Staehler
Profile: Advertising journal (house-to-house) concentrating on local stories.
Language(s): German
ADVERTISING RATES:
Full Page Mono .... EUR 3614
Full Page Colour .... EUR 4879
Mechanical Data: Type Area: 445 x 315 mm, No. of Columns (Display): 7, Col Widths (Display): 42 mm
Copy instructions: *Copy Date:* 2 days prior to publication
LOCAL NEWSPAPERS

STEGLITZ KOMPAKT
1898588G74M-892
Editorial: Bundesallee 23, 10717 BERLIN
Tel: 30 863030 **Fax:** 30 86303200
Email: info@bfb.de **Web site:** http://www.bfb.de
Freq: Annual; **Cover Price:** Free; **Circ:** 105,000
Profile: Industry district magazine. The core of this handy reference book is neatly sorted according to different themes of industry. Here you will find a plethora of vendors from the neighborhood. In preparation to the respective subject area raises a company, in an interview. To know your environment better, we present in the district windows, etc. beautiful places, monuments, museums, etc. For better orientation in the neighborhood also an integrated neighborhood with street plan is register. Furthermore, the county information you provide an overview of important phone numbers and agencies in your neighborhood.
Language(s): German
ADVERTISING RATES:
Full Page Mono .... EUR 990
Full Page Colour .... EUR 990
Mechanical Data: Type Area: 185 x 126 mm

STEIN
743359G30-130
Editorial: Streitfeldstr. 35, 81673 MÜNCHEN
Tel: 89 436005194 **Fax:** 89 436005113
Email: w.hafner@s-stein.com **Web site:** http://www.s-stein.com
Freq: Monthly; **Annual Sub.:** EUR 129,00; **Circ:** 5,572
Editor: Willy Hafner; **Advertising Manager:** Andreas Schneider
Profile: Magazine containing information about stone and stone products.
Language(s): German
ADVERTISING RATES:
Full Page Mono .... EUR 2340
Full Page Colour .... EUR 3600
Mechanical Data: Type Area: 268 x 185 mm, No. of Columns (Display): 4, Col Widths (Display): 43 mm
Copy instructions: *Copy Date:* 20 days prior to publication
BUSINESS: MINING & QUARRYING

STEIN KERAMIK SANITÄR
743377G12A-75
Editorial: Meerkamp 120, 41238 MÖNCHENGLADBACH **Tel:** 2166 984183
Fax: 2166 984185
Email: redaktion.sks@stein-keramik-sanitaer.de **Web site:** http://www.stein-keramik-sanitaer.de
Freq: 6 issues yearly; **Annual Sub.:** EUR 18,00; **Circ:** 10,103
Editor: Gerhard Köhler
Profile: Journal of Planning and designing with ceramics, natural stones and sanitary facilities for planners, architects, retailers and processors.
Language(s): German
Readership: Read by architects, ceramic floor layers and distributors of ceramic tiles and bathroom fittings.
ADVERTISING RATES:
Full Page Mono .... EUR 2200
Full Page Colour .... EUR 3600
Mechanical Data: Type Area: 266 x 190 mm
Copy instructions: *Copy Date:* 15 days prior to publication
BUSINESS: CERAMICS, POTTERY & GLASS: Ceramics & Pottery

STEINBEISSER
1657926G57-2730
Editorial: Prof.-Virchow-Str. 8, 08280 AUE
Tel: 371 8321272
Email: gesteinsabbau@grueneliga.de **Web site:** http://www.grueneliga.de/gesteinsabbau
Freq: 6 issues yearly; Free to qualifying individuals
Annual Sub.: EUR 25,00; **Circ:** 250
Editor: Ulrich Wieland
Profile: Magazine from NGOs about nature and soil conservation.
Language(s): German

STEINBRUCH UND SANDGRUBE
743363G30-4
Editorial: Andechser Str. 10, 82205 GILCHING
Tel: 8105 772386 **Fax:** 8105 377076
Email: moehle@redaktion-susa.de **Web site:** http://www.steinbruch-und-sandgrube.de
Freq: Monthly; **Annual Sub.:** EUR 56,00; **Circ:** 10,319
Editor: Ute Möhle; **Advertising Manager:** Susann Buglass
Profile: Trade magazine about mining and quarrying, stone and earth, cement, construction materials and recycling.
Language(s): German
ADVERTISING RATES:
Full Page Mono .... EUR 1986
Full Page Colour .... EUR 3083
Mechanical Data: Type Area: 272 x 188 mm, No. of Columns (Display): 4, Col Widths (Display): 44 mm
Copy instructions: *Copy Date:* 21 days prior to publication
BUSINESS: MINING & QUARRYING

Germany

STEINE+ERDEN 731004G4E-4720
Editorial: Theodor-Heuss-Str. 160, 30853 LANGENHAGEN **Tel:** 511 72570 **Fax:** 511 7257100
Email: joerg.nierzwicki@bgrci.de **Web site:** http://www.steine-und-erden.net
Freq: 6 issues yearly; Free to qualifying individuals
Annual Sub.: EUR 73,50; **Circ:** 8,500
Editor: Jörg Nierzwicki; **Advertising Manager:** Rolf Gerdun
Profile: Magazine about stone, earth and concrete.
Language(s): German
Readership: Aimed at industrialists, qualified employees of the security sector and employees.
ADVERTISING RATES:
Full Page Mono .... EUR 2125
Full Page Colour .... EUR 2500
Mechanical Data: Type Area: 260 x 180 mm, No. of Columns (Display): 3, Col Widths (Display): 56 mm
Copy instructions: *Copy Date:* 12 days prior to publication
BUSINESS: ARCHITECTURE & BUILDING: Building

STEINFURTER KREISBLATT 743371G67B-13760
Editorial: An der Hansalinie 1, 48163 MÜNSTER
Tel: 251 6900 **Fax:** 251 690717
Email: redaktion@westfaelische-nachrichten.de **Web site:** http://www.westfaelische-nachrichten.de
Freq: 312 issues yearly; **Circ:** 12,558
Profile: Daily newspaper with regional news and a local sports section. Facebook: http://www.facebook.com/wnonline.
Language(s): German
ADVERTISING RATES:
SCC .... EUR 36,70
Mechanical Data: Type Area: 488 x 323 mm, No. of Columns (Display): 7, Col Widths (Display): 44 mm
Copy instructions: *Copy Date:* 1 day prior to publication
Supplement(s): lenz; prisma; yango family
REGIONAL DAILY & SUNDAY NEWSPAPERS: Regional Daily Newspapers

STEINKOHLE 1825985G58-1788
Editorial: Shamrockring 1, 44623 HERNE
Tel: 2323 153671 **Fax:** 2323 153759
Email: steinkohle@rag.de **Web site:** http://www.rag-deutsche-steinkohle.de
Freq: Annual; **Circ:** 30,000
Editor: Jost Beckebaum
Profile: Staff magazine for the coal mining.
Language(s): German

STEINZEUG-INFORMATION 743385G4E-5980
Editorial: Alfred-Nobel-Str. 17, 50226 FRECHEN
Tel: 2234 507271 **Fax:** 2234 507204
Email: fachverband@steinzeug.com **Web site:** http://www.fachverband-steinzeug.de
Freq: Annual; **Circ:** 10,000
Editor: Heiko Daun
Profile: Magazine from the Association of the Stoneware Industry.
Language(s): German

STELLENANZEIGEN.DE 1704569G94K-812
Editorial: Rablstr. 26, 81669 MÜNCHEN
Tel: 89 650761 00 **Fax:** 89 650761 99
Email: info@stellenanzeigen.de **Web site:** http://www.stellenanzeigen.de
Cover Price: Paid; **Circ:** 769,904 Unique Users
Editor: Michael Weideneder
Language(s): German
CONSUMER: OTHER CLASSIFICATIONS: Job Seekers

STELLEN-ONLINE.DE 1662775G94K-790
Editorial: Reinhold-Frank-Str. 63, 76133 KARLSRUHE **Tel:** 721 9205533 **Fax:** 721 9205544
Email: info@stellen-online.de **Web site:** http://www.stellen-online.de
Freq: Daily; **Cover Price:** Paid; **Circ:** 38,114 Unique Users
Advertising Manager: Susanne Beyer
Profile: Online job market. The range includes positions for specialists and executives in various industries. Facebook: http://www.facebook.com/stellenonline Twitter: http://twitter.com/#!/stellenonline This Outlet offers RSS (Really Simple Syndication).
Language(s): German
CONSUMER: OTHER CLASSIFICATIONS: Job Seekers

STEMWEDER ZEITUNG 1638383G67B-16721
Editorial: Sudbrackstr. 14, 33611 BIELEFELD
Tel: 521 5850 **Fax:** 521 585489
Email: wb@westfalen-blatt.de **Web site:** http://www.westfalen-blatt.de
Freq: 260 issues yearly; **Circ:** 9,122
Advertising Manager: Gabriele Förster
Profile: Regional daily newspaper covering politics, economics, sport, travel and technology.
Language(s): German
Mechanical Data: Type Area: 490 x 320 mm, No. of Columns (Display): 7, Col Widths (Display): 44 mm
Copy instructions: *Copy Date:* 1 day prior to publication
Supplement(s): Mein Garten; www.wb-immo.net
REGIONAL DAILY & SUNDAY NEWSPAPERS: Regional Daily Newspapers

STENDALER VOLKSSTIMME 743430G67B-13800
Editorial: Bahnhofstr. 17, 39104 MAGDEBURG
Tel: 391 59990 **Fax:** 391 5999210
Email: chefredaktion@volksstimme.de **Web site:** http://www.volksstimme.de
Freq: 312 issues yearly; **Circ:** 31,795
Advertising Manager: Rainer Pfeil
Profile: As the largest daily newspaper in northern Saxony-Anhalt, the Volksstimme reaches 536,000 readers a day" (MA 2010). From Monday to Saturday a team of highly qualified editors put together the latest information and news from the region and around the world. Thanks the 18 local editions is the Volksstimme always close to the action. Twitter: http://twitter.com/volksstimme This Outlet offers RSS (Really Simple Syndication).
Language(s): German
ADVERTISING RATES:
SCC .... EUR 77,60
Mechanical Data: Type Area: 480 x 327 mm, No. of Columns (Display): 7, Col Widths (Display): 45 mm
Copy instructions: *Copy Date:* 2 days prior to publication
Supplement(s): Anstoss im Landkreis Stendal; Biber; Leser-Reisen; prisma; Standort Landkreis Stendal
REGIONAL DAILY & SUNDAY NEWSPAPERS: Regional Daily Newspapers

STEP 743433G29-5
Editorial: Oberkasseler Str. 100, 40545 DÜSSELDORF **Tel:** 211 5770821 **Fax:** 211 5770812
Email: step.redaktion@sternefeld.de **Web site:** http://www.stepverlag.de
Freq: Quarterly; **Annual Sub.:** EUR 46,00; **Circ:** 15,000
Editor: Petra Salewski; **Advertising Manager:** Sabine Peters
Profile: Magazine about shoes, leather goods and accessories.
Language(s): German
Readership: Aimed at those involved in the shoe industry.
ADVERTISING RATES:
Full Page Mono .... EUR 4900
Full Page Colour .... EUR 4900
Mechanical Data: Type Area: 270 x 179 mm, No. of Columns (Display): 4, Col Widths (Display): 40 mm
BUSINESS: FOOTWEAR

STEREO 743437G78A-340
Editorial: Eifelring 28, 53879 EUSKIRCHEN
Tel: 2251 650460 **Fax:** 2251 6504699
Email: stereo@nitschke-verlag.de **Web site:** http://www.stereo.de
Freq: Monthly; **Annual Sub.:** EUR 54,00; **Circ:** 21,320
Editor: Reiner H. Nitschke; **Advertising Manager:** Ilhami Düzgün
Profile: Stereo information as a modern hi-fi magazine extensively about trends and innovations. Core are the tests of hi-qualified, high-end and multichannel components. The service is not neglected. In addition to the factual reporting has been devoted to stereo, in words, photos and layout, the fascination of HiFi convey. Reviews of new releases from the pop, jazz and classical music performances as well as expert DVD and audiophile tips from the CD and vinyl records offer build a bridge to the music.
Language(s): German
ADVERTISING RATES:
Full Page Mono .... EUR 4000
Full Page Colour .... EUR 6700
Mechanical Data: Type Area: 248 x 185 mm, No. of Columns (Display): 4, Col Widths (Display): 44 mm
Copy instructions: *Copy Date:* 35 days prior to publication
CONSUMER: CONSUMER ELECTRONICS: Hi-Fi & Recording

STEREOPLAY 743438G78A-360
Editorial: Leuschnerstr. 1, 70174 STUTTGART
Tel: 711 182373 **Fax:** 711 1821832
Email: redaktion@stereoplay.de **Web site:** http://www.stereoplay.de
Freq: Monthly; **Cover Price:** EUR 5,30; **Circ:** 21,764
Editor: Holger Biermann; **Advertising Manager:** Michael Hackenberg
Profile: Magazine for quality-conscious and eager HiFi and surround enthusiasts. For those who want to understand exactly how this works HiFi. The stereoplay tomorrow is a test-oriented HiFi magazine. By tight links with the factory test here new measurements are being developed that make it to the consumer and the industry easier to get transparency.
Language(s): German
ADVERTISING RATES:
Full Page Mono .... EUR 6713
Full Page Colour .... EUR 8950
Mechanical Data: Type Area: 250 x 185 mm, No. of Columns (Display): 4, Col Widths (Display): 43 mm
Copy instructions: *Copy Date:* 31 days prior to publication
CONSUMER: CONSUMER ELECTRONICS: Hi-Fi & Recording

STERN 743439G73-380
Editorial: Am Baumwall 11, 20459 HAMBURG
Tel: 40 37033541 **Fax:** 40 37035631
Email: stern@stern.de **Web site:** http://www.stern.de
Freq: Weekly; **Annual Sub.:** EUR 169,00; **Circ:** 857,231
Editor: Thomas Osterkorn; **News Editor:** Hans-Peter Junker; **Advertising Manager:** Lars Niemann
Profile: The particular mix of topics, clear position on current social issues, the spacious appearance and the strong social commitment make the stern unique in the German media landscape. The stern brings the most important things of current affairs: Today man is inundated with information. To cope with this, he does not need more facts and figures. He wants a magazine that selects classifies, orders and evaluates. The stern helps to focus, as it offers not only "content", but also the context. The stern shows the human side of the news: the story of a human or even a single facial expression says more about the significance of an event than dry numbers. Stories in the stern are concrete and emotional. The stern provides practical decision aids: in the past, the phone came from the post office, the occupational guidance from Papa and the power from the socket. Today everyone can and must choose from a plethora of options. The stern supports its readers in making complex decisions in everyday life. Great pictures are shown large: for its titles, reports and photographs, ir regularly receives national and international awards. Its opulence and visual power make the stern unique. The stern is a symbol of social commitment: Many magazines feel committed to critical reporting and disclosure. But none takes the initiative and takes position as often as the stern, with actions such as "Jugend forscht" or "StartUp". Facebook: http://www.facebook.com/stern Twitter: http://twitter.com/sternde This Outlet offers RSS (Really Simple Syndication).
Language(s): German
ADVERTISING RATES:
Full Page Mono .... EUR 55200
Full Page Colour .... EUR 55200
Mechanical Data: Type Area: 268 x 200 mm, No. of Columns (Display): 4, Col Widths (Display): 47 mm
Copy instructions: *Copy Date:* 21 days prior to publication
Supplement(s): stern tv magazin
CONSUMER: NATIONAL & INTERNATIONAL PERIODICALS

STERN GESUND LEBEN 1626671G74G-1756
Editorial: Am Baumwall 11, 20459 HAMBURG
Tel: 40 37037228 **Fax:** 40 37035861
Email: gesundleben@stern.de **Web site:** http://www.stern.de/gesund-leben
Freq: 6 issues yearly; **Annual Sub.:** EUR 37,20; **Circ:** 90,643
Editor: Sabine Kartte; **Advertising Manager:** Helma Spieker
Profile: The magazine provides information about prevention and treatment of diseases, healthy nutrition, fitness, wellness and relaxation.
Language(s): German
ADVERTISING RATES:
Full Page Mono .... EUR 13600
Full Page Colour .... EUR 13600
Mechanical Data: Type Area: 245 x 172 mm, No. of Columns (Display): 3, Col Widths (Display): 57 mm
Copy instructions: *Copy Date:* 28 days prior to publication
CONSUMER: WOMEN'S INTEREST CONSUMER MAGAZINES: Slimming & Health

STERN.DE 1622053G73-489
Editorial: Am Baumwall 11, 20459 HAMBURG
Tel: 40 37032652 **Fax:** 40 37035833
Web site: http://www.stern.de
Freq: Daily; **Cover Price:** Paid; **Circ:** 22,254,453 Unique Users
Editor: Frank Thomsen; **News Editor:** Dirk Benninghoff
Profile: Ezine: Magazine covering news, politics, economics, debate and interviews with prominent people. Facebook: http://www.facebook.com/stern Twitter: http://twitter.com/sternde This Outlet offers RSS (Really Simple Syndication).
Language(s): German
CONSUMER: NATIONAL & INTERNATIONAL PERIODICALS

STERNE UND WELTRAUM 743442G94J-640
Editorial: Königstuhl 17, 69117 HEIDELBERG
Tel: 6221 5281 **Fax:** 6221 528246
Email: suw@spektrum.com **Web site:** http://www.astronomie-heute.de
Freq: Monthly; **Annual Sub.:** EUR 85,20; **Circ:** 18,671
Editor: Uwe Reichert; **Advertising Manager:** Karin Schmidt
Profile: Journal of Astronomy reports, comprehensive, clear and informative about all areas of astronomy, space research and amateur astronomy. Experts present intelligible the current results of astronomical research and describe the development of new instruments, observatories and measurement techniques. Amateur astronomers provide tips for observing interesting celestial objects and phenomena, most telescopes and their many accessories and give the amateur astronomer sound instructions for independent exploration of the heavens, for astrophotography, and to evaluate their observations. Products for amateur astronomy are presented alongside the most beautiful pictures of galaxies, star clusters and colored mists.Reports from the history of astronomy and articles on issues of scientific world view, book reviews, interviews and reports on the activities of amateur astronomy groups complete the spectrum of topics.
Language(s): German
ADVERTISING RATES:
Full Page Mono .... EUR 2080
Full Page Colour .... EUR 2080
Mechanical Data: Type Area: 264 x 179 mm, No. of Columns (Display): 3, Col Widths (Display): 57 mm
Copy instructions: *Copy Date:* 21 days prior to publication
CONSUMER: OTHER CLASSIFICATIONS: Popular Science

DAS STEUER- UND GROLLBLATT BERLIN 1837501G1A-3706
Editorial: Motzstr. 32, 10777 BERLIN
Tel: 30 21473040 **Fax:** 30 21473041
Email: info@dstg-berlin.de **Web site:** http://www.dstg-berlin.de
Freq: 11 issues yearly; **Circ:** 7,500
Editor: Detlef Dames
Profile: Trade union member magazine.
Language(s): German
ADVERTISING RATES:
Full Page Mono .... EUR 575

STEUER + STUDIUM 743484G1A-2740
Editorial: Eschstr. 22, 44629 HERNE
Tel: 2323 141900 **Fax:** 2323 141249
Web site: http://www.nwb.de/go/modul6
Freq: Monthly; **Annual Sub.:** EUR 145,20; **Circ:** 10,605
Editor: Corinna Groß; **Advertising Manager:** Andreas Reimann
Profile: Magazine for further education in tax law.
Language(s): German
ADVERTISING RATES:
Full Page Mono .... EUR 1976
Full Page Colour .... EUR 3755
Mechanical Data: No. of Columns (Display): 4, Col Widths (Display): 43 mm, Type Area: 260 x 186 mm
Copy instructions: *Copy Date:* 14 days prior to publication
BUSINESS: FINANCE & ECONOMICS

STEUER UND WIRTSCHAFT 743485G1M-9
Editorial: Albertus-Magnus-Platz, 50931 KÖLN
Tel: 221 4702271 **Fax:** 221 4705027
Email: joachim.lang@uni-koeln.de **Web site:** http://www.uni-koeln.de
Freq: Quarterly; **Annual Sub.:** EUR 248,90; **Circ:** 714
Editor: Joachim Lang; **Advertising Manager:** Thorsten Deuse
Profile: Magazine covering all aspects of taxation. Facebook: http://www.facebook.com/universitaet.koeln.
Language(s): German
ADVERTISING RATES:
Full Page Mono .... EUR 1115
Full Page Colour .... EUR 1951
Mechanical Data: No. of Columns (Display): 2, Col Widths (Display): 88 mm, Type Area: 260 x 180 mm
BUSINESS: FINANCE & ECONOMICS: Taxation

STEUER- UND WIRTSCHAFTS-NACHRICHTEN DER LANDWIRTSCHAFTLICHEN BUCHSTELLEN IM HLBS 1928840G21A-4446
Editorial: Kölnstr. 202, 53757 ST. AUGUSTIN
Tel: 2241 8661718 **Fax:** 2241 8661729
Email: verband@hlbs.de **Web site:** http://www.hlbs.de
Freq: Monthly; **Annual Sub.:** EUR 13,80; **Circ:** 4,550
Editor: Hans-Josef Hartmann
Profile: Magazine for large scale farmers.
Language(s): German
ADVERTISING RATES:
Full Page Mono .... EUR 520
Mechanical Data: Type Area: 185 x 117 mm
Copy instructions: *Copy Date:* 12 days prior to publication

STEUERANWALTSMAGAZIN 743460G1A-3475
Editorial: Scharrstr. 2, 70563 STUTTGART
Tel: 711 73850 **Fax:** 711 7385100
Email: mail@boorberg.de **Web site:** http://www.boorberg.de
Freq: 6 issues yearly; **Annual Sub.:** EUR 105,00; **Circ:** 1,100
Editor: Kirsten Bäumel
Profile: Magazine from the tax law workgroup in the German Lawyers' Association.
Language(s): German
ADVERTISING RATES:
Full Page Mono .... EUR 810
Full Page Colour .... EUR 1740
Mechanical Data: Type Area: 260 x 180 mm
Copy instructions: *Copy Date:* 28 days prior to publication

DER STEUERBERATER
743463G1M-6
Editorial: Mainzer Landstr. 251, 60326 FRANKFURT
Tel: 69 75952703 **Fax:** 69 75952780
Email: weber@betriebs-berater.de **Web site:** http://www.betriebs-berater.de
Freq: 11 issues yearly; **Annual Sub.:** EUR 219,00; **Circ:** 4,500
Editor: Martin Weber; **Advertising Manager:** Marion Gertzen
Profile: Magazine for tax consultants.
Language(s): German
ADVERTISING RATES:
Full Page Mono .... EUR 1795
Full Page Colour .... EUR 2455
Mechanical Data: Type Area: 257 x 180 mm, No. of Columns (Display): 4, Col Widths (Display): 43 mm
Copy instructions: *Copy Date:* 19 days prior to publication
BUSINESS: FINANCE & ECONOMICS: Taxation

STEUERBERATER WOCHE
1647163G1A-3559
Editorial: Gustav-Heinemann-Ufer 58, 50968 KÖLN
Tel: 221 93738152 **Fax:** 221 93738902
Email: verlag@otto-schmidt.de **Web site:** http://www.stbwoche.de
Freq: 25 issues yearly; **Annual Sub.:** EUR 271,90; **Circ:** 1,630
Editor: Sixten Abeling; **Advertising Manager:** Thorsten Deuse
Profile: Magazine containing information about financial law jurisdiction and financial administration.
Language(s): German
ADVERTISING RATES:
Full Page Mono .... EUR 850
Full Page Colour .... EUR 1488
Mechanical Data: Type Area: 260 x 180 mm

STEUERCONSULTANT
724607G1A-460
Editorial: Munzinger Str. 9, 79111 FREIBURG
Tel: 761 8983213 **Fax:** 761 8983112
Email: redaktion@steuer-consultant.de **Web site:** http://www.steuer-consultant.de
Freq: Monthly; **Annual Sub.:** EUR 182,00; **Circ:** 20,308
Editor: Anke Kolb-Leistner; **Advertising Manager:** Bernd Junker
Profile: Magazine for accountants, auditors, financial managers in companies and financial services. Information is compact and easily understandable fashion journalism. The reader all the information necessary to carry out their activities in a journal: tax, consulting and law firm knowledge management. Tax consultant dedicated to tax in more detail than other journals on the consulting and management firm. Besides legal framework to analyze market trends, wealth creation, tax-efficient investment and corporate finance on a regular basis and displayed. Twitter: http://twitter.com/SteuerCons.
Language(s): German
Readership: Aimed at tax consultants, chartered accountants and economists.
ADVERTISING RATES:
Full Page Mono .... EUR 6300
Full Page Colour .... EUR 6900
Mechanical Data: Type Area: 249 x 176 mm, No. of Columns (Display): 3, Col Widths (Display): 56 mm
Copy instructions: *Copy Date:* 20 days prior to publication
Supplement to: baV spezial
BUSINESS: FINANCE & ECONOMICS

DIE STEUERFACHANGESTELLTEN
743472G1M-7
Editorial: Eschstr. 22, 44629 HERNE
Tel: 2323 141900 **Fax:** 2323 141123
Email: c.kehrein@kiehl.de **Web site:** http://www.kiehl.de
Freq: Monthly; **Annual Sub.:** EUR 61,80; **Circ:** 19,082
Editor: Claudia Kehrein; **Advertising Manager:** Andreas Reimann
Profile: The magazine „Die Steuerfachangestellten" not only helps to systematically prepare for the exam, it also conveys the knowledge that is needed in their daily work in practice. For the regular refreshing of knowledge, even after the exam, practice exercises and cases with solutions to help. Who „Die Steuerfachangestellten" reads is also informed of all current issues of tax law, accounting and profession law.
Language(s): German
ADVERTISING RATES:
Full Page Mono .... EUR 1950
Full Page Colour .... EUR 2750
Mechanical Data: Type Area: 260 x 186 mm
Copy instructions: *Copy Date:* 30 days prior to publication
BUSINESS: FINANCE & ECONOMICS: Taxation

STEUER-TELEX
1655777G1A-3564
Editorial: Oststr. 11, 50996 KÖLN **Tel:** 221 9370180
Fax: 221 93701890
Email: kundenservice@deubner-verlag.de **Web site:** http://www.steuer-telex.de
Freq: Weekly; **Annual Sub.:** EUR 399,00; **Circ:** 4,000
Editor: Pia Reuter
Profile: Magazine containing information for certified accountants and tax lawyers.
Language(s): German

DIE STEUER-WARTE
743487G1A-2780
Editorial: In den Gärtlesäckern 24, 70771 LEINFELDEN-ECHTERDINGEN **Tel:** 711 66735700
Fax: 711 66735710
Email: theigenthaler@aol.com
Freq: 10 issues yearly; Free to qualifying individuals
Annual Sub.: EUR 49,90; **Circ:** 72,000
Editor: Thomas Eigenthaler; **Advertising Manager:** Elke Schmidt
Profile: Magazine for employees in tax administrations and tax advisors.
Language(s): German
ADVERTISING RATES:
Full Page Mono .... EUR 2550
Full Page Colour .... EUR 4239
Mechanical Data: Type Area: 270 x 185 mm, No. of Columns (Display): 2, Col Widths (Display): 87 mm
Copy instructions: *Copy Date:* 30 days prior to publication
Supplement to: DSTG magazin

DER STEUERZAHLER
743488G1M-140
Editorial: Französische Str. 9, 10117 BERLIN
Tel: 30 2593960 **Fax:** 30 25939625
Email: presse@steuerzahler.de **Web site:** http://www.steuerzahler.de
Freq: 11 issues yearly; **Circ:** 313,017
Editor: Reiner Holznagel
Profile: Journal about the taxpayer.
Language(s): German
ADVERTISING RATES:
Full Page Mono .... EUR 9840
Full Page Colour .... EUR 12740
Mechanical Data: Type Area: 268 x 180 mm, No. of Columns (Display): 4, Col Widths (Display): 44 mm
Copy instructions: *Copy Date:* 20 days prior to publication
Supplement(s): Die NRW Nachrichten
BUSINESS: FINANCE & ECONOMICS: Taxation

STICKS
743501G76D-5220
Editorial: Emil-Hoffmann-Str. 13, 50996 KÖLN
Tel: 2236 9621734 **Fax:** 2236 96217934
Email: redaktion@sticks.de **Web site:** http://www.sticks.de
Freq: Monthly; **Annual Sub.:** EUR 50,00; **Circ:** 5,090
Editor: Axel Mikolajczak; **Advertising Manager:** Christiane Weyres
Profile: STICKS reached the only German-language monthly magazine for drums and percussion a readership in both professional musicians and amateurs, Drum teachers and students alike are represented. A recent study from April 2008 also shows that there has developed a uniform age structure of the STICKS reader, in the age group "13 - 20 Years", "20 - 30 years", "30 - 40 years" and "40-50 Year "represents strong. Main focus is on interviews with national and international musicians, historical and current features on drums and percussion vendors as well as drum events, reviews of tools and accessories, workshops and transcriptions as well as current information and scores on the JAM-Playalongs the STICKS CD . JAM STICKS Playalongs previous editions are available for paid download on the Web site at www.sticks.de STICKS / Playalongs available. Also offers access to comprehensive www.sticks.de STICKS archives as an article published in STICKS-download all interviews, reports, reviews and workshops. As recent polls showing reviews draw in STICKS by high competence and credibility and have proven to have a large share of the purchasing decisions of readers. The continuous evaluation of hundreds of monthly incoming correspondence enables STICKS editorial current reference to the wishes and suggestions of topics STICKS reader. This ensures that STICKS will continue to be the current and competent professional magazine by musicians for musicians.
Language(s): German
Readership: Read by professional and amateur drummers.
Mechanical Data: Type Area: 254 x 185 mm, No. of Columns (Display): 4, Col Widths (Display): 43 mm
Copy instructions: *Copy Date:* 26 days prior to publication
CONSUMER: MUSIC & PERFORMING ARTS: Music

DER STIFTSBOTE
743504G74N-680
Editorial: Bingstr. 30, 90480 NÜRNBERG
Tel: 911 40300 **Fax:** 911 4030241
Email: stiftsleitung@wohnstift-am-tiergarten.de **Web site:** http://www.wohnstift-am-tiergarten.de
Freq: 6 issues yearly; **Circ:** 800
Editor: Doris Dietrich-Heß
Profile: Magazine for the elderly.
Language(s): German

DIE STIFTUNG
1898963G14A-10294
Editorial: Hofmannstr. 7a, 81379 MÜNCHEN
Tel: 89 200033947 **Fax:** 89 200033939
Email: jungheim@die-stiftung.de **Web site:** http://www.die-stiftung.de
Freq: 6 issues yearly; **Annual Sub.:** EUR 48,00; **Circ:** 16,306
Editor: Gregor Jungheim; **Advertising Manager:** Alexandra Rößer
Profile: Magazine all about the foundation system on Germany, Austria and Switzerland.
Language(s): German
ADVERTISING RATES:
Full Page Mono .... EUR 4800
Full Page Colour .... EUR 4800
Mechanical Data: Type Area: 258 x 186 mm, No. of Columns (Display): 3, Col Widths (Display): 58 mm
Copy instructions: *Copy Date:* 14 days prior to publication

STIFTUNGSBRIEF
1623023G56A-11255
Editorial: Behringstr. 28a, 22765 HAMBURG
Tel: 40 28418730 **Fax:** 40 28418733
Email: info@mbmed.de **Web site:** http://www.mbmed.de
Freq: Quarterly; **Circ:** 75,000
Editor: Peter Müller
Profile: Details of the Health Foundation on current issues in the areas of health policy, practice management and marketing, legal and Internet.
Language(s): German

STIL & MARKT
743508G52C-60
Editorial: Franz-Ludwig-Str. 7a, 96047 BAMBERG
Tel: 951 861181 **Fax:** 951 861158
Email: s.stenzel@meisenbach.de **Web site:** http://www.stilundmarkt.de
Freq: Monthly; **Annual Sub.:** EUR 90,00; **Circ:** 8,583
Editor: Sabine Stenzel; **Advertising Manager:** Susanne Mirza
Profile: Magazine with information about dining rooms, kitchen equipment, gifts and lifestyle.
Language(s): German
Readership: Read by wholesalers, exporters and importers.
ADVERTISING RATES:
Full Page Mono .... EUR 2836
Full Page Colour .... EUR 4205
Mechanical Data: Type Area: 260 x 184 mm, No. of Columns (Display): 3
Copy instructions: *Copy Date:* 21 days prior to publication
BUSINESS: GIFT TRADE: Fancy Goods

STIMBERG ZEITUNG
743509G67B-13820
Editorial: Kampstr. 84b, 45772 MARL **Tel:** 2365 1070
Fax: 2365 1071490
Email: info@medienhaus-bauer.de **Web site:** http://www.medienhaus-bauer.de
Freq: 312 issues yearly; **Circ:** 5,049
Advertising Manager: Carsten Dingerkuss
Profile: Regional daily newspaper with news on politics, economy, culture, sports, travel, technology, etc. The newspaper offers a mix of local, regional and international News from all areas. Fun and interactive content such as forums, polls or betting games are also part of the program. Local out of the city and the neighborhood is the focus of attention. Facebook: http://www.facebook.com/medienhbauer This Outlet offers RSS (Really Simple Syndication).
Language(s): German
ADVERTISING RATES:
SCC .... EUR 25,60
Mechanical Data: Type Area: 487 x 325 mm, No. of Columns (Display): 7, Col Widths (Display): 43 mm
Copy instructions: *Copy Date:* 1 day prior to publication
Supplement(s): prisma
REGIONAL DAILY & SUNDAY NEWSPAPERS: Regional Daily Newspapers

STOLBERGER NACHRICHTEN
743539G67B-13840
Editorial: Dresdener Str. 3, 52068 AACHEN
Tel: 241 5101310 **Fax:** 241 5101360
Email: redaktion@zeitungsverlag-aachen.de **Web site:** http://www.an-online.de
Freq: 312 issues yearly; **Circ:** 29,821
Advertising Manager: Christian Kretschmer
Profile: Daily newspaper with regional news and a local sports section. Facebook: http://facebook.com/aachenernachrichten This Outlet offers RSS (Really Simple Syndication).
Language(s): German
ADVERTISING RATES:
SCC .... EUR 62,80
Mechanical Data: Type Area: 480 x 324 mm, No. of Columns (Display): 7, Col Widths (Display): 44 mm
Copy instructions: *Copy Date:* 1 day prior to publication
Supplement(s): prisma
REGIONAL DAILY & SUNDAY NEWSPAPERS: Regional Daily Newspapers

STOLBERGER ZEITUNG
743540G67B-13860
Editorial: Dresdener Str. 3, 52068 AACHEN
Tel: 241 5101310 **Fax:** 241 5101360
Email: redaktion@zeitungsverlag-aachen.de **Web site:** http://www.aachener-zeitung.de
Freq: 312 issues yearly; **Circ:** 29,821
Advertising Manager: Christian Kretschmer
Profile: Daily newspaper with regional news and a local sports section. Facebook: http://facebook.com/aachenerzeitung This Outlet offers RSS (Really Simple Syndication).
Language(s): German
ADVERTISING RATES:
SCC .... EUR 62,80
Mechanical Data: Type Area: 480 x 324 mm, No. of Columns (Display): 7, Col Widths (Display): 44 mm
Copy instructions: *Copy Date:* 1 day prior to publication
Supplement(s): prisma
REGIONAL DAILY & SUNDAY NEWSPAPERS: Regional Daily Newspapers

STONEPLUS
743543G4E-6000
Editorial: Ringstr. 58, 91080 UTTENREUTH
Tel: 9131 50532 **Fax:** 9131 50544
Email: redaktion@stoneplus.de **Web site:** http://www.stoneplus.de
Freq: 6 issues yearly; **Annual Sub.:** EUR 50,40; **Circ:** 7,943
Editor: Robert Mächtel; **Advertising Manager:** Karin Böhm
Profile: Journal about granite and natural stone used in building and tombstones.
Language(s): German
Readership: Aimed at architects, designers, builders, stonemasons and funeral directors.
ADVERTISING RATES:
Full Page Mono .... EUR 1670
Full Page Colour .... EUR 2860
Mechanical Data: Type Area: 265 x 180 mm, No. of Columns (Display): 3, Col Widths (Display): 59 mm
Copy instructions: *Copy Date:* 14 days prior to publication
BUSINESS: ARCHITECTURE & BUILDING: Building

STORES + SHOPS
743544G4E-402
Editorial: Spichernstr. 55, 50672 KÖLN
Tel: 221 5799340 **Fax:** 221 5799345
Email: lambertz@ehi.org **Web site:** http://www.ehi.org
Freq: 6 issues yearly; **Annual Sub.:** EUR 53,50; **Circ:** 16,500
Editor: Winfried Lambertz; **Advertising Manager:** Claudia Husseck
Profile: With topics related to equipment and furnishings for shops stores + shops provides precise information for the target group. The focus of reporting is on new store concepts and shop construction projects from all over the world and from all sectors as well as store design and visual merchandising. Investment trends in store expansions, strategies for successful POP marketing and management of retail properties are also part of the editorial concept, such as new products and important industry events. The research results of the EHI-Working Group "Store Planning & Design", readers of stores + shops learn of the first.
Language(s): English; German
Readership: Aimed at managers, decision makers in construction, capital goods buyers and marketing managers of major retail companies in Europe.
ADVERTISING RATES:
Full Page Mono .... EUR 3000
Full Page Colour .... EUR 4200
Mechanical Data: Type Area: 235 x 182 mm
Copy instructions: *Copy Date:* 14 days prior to publication
BUSINESS: ARCHITECTURE & BUILDING: Building

STORMARNER TAGEBLATT
743545G67B-13880
Editorial: Nikolaistr. 7, 24937 FLENSBURG
Tel: 461 8080 **Fax:** 461 8081058
Email: redaktion@shz.de **Web site:** http://www.shz.de
Freq: 312 issues yearly; **Circ:** 6,028
Advertising Manager: Ingeborg Schwarz
Profile: The "Stormarner Tageblatt" - the only daily newspaper for the Stormarn - one of the most traditional local newspapers in Schleswig-Holstein. Founded on 6 April 1839 as "Oldesloer Wochenblatt" was the newspaper for generations owned by the family of printing Schütte until 1993 sh:z was acquired. The "Stormarner Tageblatt" informed daily readers throughout Stormarn. Facebook: http://www.facebook.com/shzonline Twitter: http://twitter.com/shz_de This Outlet offers RSS (Really Simple Syndication).
Language(s): German
ADVERTISING RATES:
SCC .... EUR 39,60
Mechanical Data: Type Area: 430 x 282 mm, No. of Columns (Display): 6, Col Widths (Display): 45 mm
Copy instructions: *Copy Date:* 1 day prior to publication
Supplement(s): nordisch gesund; Schleswig-Holstein Journal; tv magazin
REGIONAL DAILY & SUNDAY NEWSPAPERS: Regional Daily Newspapers

STRAFVERTEIDIGER
743837G44-2040
Editorial: Luxemburger Str. 449, 50939 KÖLN
Tel: 221 943737000 **Fax:** 221 943737201
Email: stvredaktion@wolterskluwer.de **Web site:** http://www.strafverteidiger-stv.de
Freq: Monthly; **Annual Sub.:** EUR 189,90; **Circ:** 2,900
Editor: Klaus Lüderssen
Profile: Publication about defence counsel and related legal matters.
Language(s): German
ADVERTISING RATES:
Full Page Mono .... EUR 1050
Full Page Colour .... EUR 2115
Mechanical Data: Type Area: 255 x 184 mm
Copy instructions: *Copy Date:* 21 days prior to publication
BUSINESS: LEGAL

STRAHLENSCHUTZ PRAXIS
743552G56J-220
Editorial: Pappelweg 38, 75334 STRAUBENHARDT
Tel: 7082 40246 **Fax:** 7082 40206
Email: rupprecht@maushart.com
Freq: Quarterly; Free to qualifying individuals
Annual Sub.: EUR 58,70; **Circ:** 2,150

Editor: Rupprecht Maushart; **Advertising Manager:** Gudrun Karafiol
Profile: Publication containing information on how to maintain a safe environment when working with ionised and un-ionised radiation.
Language(s): German
ADVERTISING RATES:
Full Page Mono .... EUR 945
Full Page Colour .... EUR 1530
Mechanical Data: Type Area: 254 x 160 mm, No. of Columns (Display): 3, Col Widths (Display): 50 mm
Copy instructions: *Copy Date:* 56 days prior to publication
BUSINESS: HEALTH & MEDICAL: Radiography

STRAHLENTELEX MIT ELEKTROSMOG-REPORT
743553G57-2020
Editorial: Waldstr. 49, 15566 SCHÖNEICHE
Tel: 30 4352840 **Fax:** 30 64329167
Email: strahlentelex@t-online.de **Web site:** http://www.strahlentelex.de
Freq: Monthly; **Annual Sub.:** EUR 72,00; **Circ:** 800
Editor: Thomas Dersee
Profile: Publication containing information about radiation and effects on environment and health.
Language(s): German

STRAHLENTHERAPIE UND ONKOLOGIE
743554G56A-9380
Editorial: Aschauer Str. 30, 81549 MÜNCHEN
Tel: 89 2030431300 **Fax:** 89 2030431399
Email: elisabeth.renatus@springer.com **Web site:** http://www.springermedizin.de
Freq: Monthly; Free to qualifying individuals
Annual Sub.: EUR 525,00; **Circ:** 2,300
Editor: Elisabeth Renatus; **Advertising Manager:** Renate Senfft
Profile: Founded in 1912 and published monthly, Strahlentherapie und Onkologie is a scientific journal that covers all aspects of oncology with focus on radiooncology, radiation biology and radiation physics. The articles are of interest not only to radiooncologists but to all physicians interested in oncology, as well as to radiation biologists and radiation physicists. The peer-reviewed journal publishes original articles, review articles and case studies, scientific short communications and a literature review with annotated articles that inform the reader of new developments in the disciplines concerned. This allows for a sound overview of the latest results in radiooncology research. Contributions are published in English and German, with all articles having English summaries and legends. The journal is the official publication of several scientific radiooncological societies and publishes the relevant communications of these societies.
Language(s): English; German
ADVERTISING RATES:
Full Page Mono .... EUR 1650
Full Page Colour .... EUR 2900
Mechanical Data: Type Area: 240 x 174 mm
Copy instructions: *Copy Date:* 28 days prior to publication
Official Journal of: Organ d. Dt., Österr., Griech., Rumän. u. Ung. Ges. f. Radioonkologie, d. Schweizer. wissenschaftl. Ges. f. Radioonkologie, d. AG Radioonkologie d. Dt. Krebsges., d. Dt. Röntgenges., d. Dt. Ges. f. Medizin. Physik u. d. Dt. Krebsges.

STRALSUNDER BLITZ AM SONNTAG
743556G72-12936
Editorial: Tribseer Damm 2, 18437 STRALSUND
Tel: 3831 267714 **Fax:** 3831 267711
Email: antje.rudolph@blitzverlag.de **Web site:** http://www.blitzverlag.de
Freq: Weekly; **Cover Price:** Free; **Circ:** 44,070
Editor: Antje Rudolph; **Advertising Manager:** André Holfert
Profile: Advertising journal (house-to-house) concentrating on local stories.
Language(s): German
ADVERTISING RATES:
Full Page Mono .... EUR 2924
Full Page Colour .... EUR 3314
Mechanical Data: Type Area: 420 x 285 mm, No. of Columns (Display): 6, Col Widths (Display): 45 mm
Copy instructions: *Copy Date:* 2 days prior to publication
LOCAL NEWSPAPERS

STRANDGUT
743557G80-10940
Editorial: Ederstr. 10, 60486 FRANKFURT
Tel: 69 9791030 **Fax:** 69 7075125
Email: info@strandgut.de **Web site:** http://www.strandgut.de
Freq: Monthly; **Cover Price:** Free; **Circ:** 32,176
Editor: Kurt Otterbacher; **Advertising Manager:** Dietmar Lüning
Profile: Magazine for the Frankfurt area.
Language(s): German
ADVERTISING RATES:
Full Page Mono .... EUR 1760
Full Page Colour .... EUR 2550
Mechanical Data: Type Area: 270 x 190 mm, No. of Columns (Display): 4, Col Widths (Display): 45 mm
Copy instructions: *Copy Date:* 10 days prior to publication
CONSUMER: RURAL & REGIONAL INTEREST

STRASSE UND AUTOBAHN
743569G42B-20
Editorial: Im Mondsröttchen 45, 51429 BERGISCH GLADBACH **Tel:** 2204 916812 **Fax:** 2204 916813
Email: strasse-und-autobahn.redaktion@kirschbaum.de
Freq: Monthly; Free to qualifying individuals
Annual Sub.: EUR 109,00; **Circ:** 6,446
Editor: Hans Walter Horz; **Advertising Manager:** Volker Rutkowski
Profile: Publication of the Research Organisation for Road, Transport and Communications, and the National Association for Road and Transport Engineers. The journal concerns the building of roads, highways, bridges, and other sites, as well as noise prevention.
Language(s): German
Readership: Aimed at road and construction engineers.
ADVERTISING RATES:
Full Page Mono .... EUR 2850
Full Page Colour .... EUR 3860
Mechanical Data: Type Area: 260 x 185 mm, No. of Columns (Display): 4, Col Widths (Display): 44 mm
Official Journal of: Organ d. Bundesvereinigung d. Straßenbau- u. Verkehrsingenieure, d. Forschungsges. f. Straßen- u. Verkehrswesen u. d. FSV Wien
BUSINESS: CONSTRUCTION: Roads

STRASSEN- UND TIEFBAU ST
743565G42B-3
Editorial: Hans-Böckler-Allee 9, 30173 HANNOVER
Tel: 511 7304134 **Fax:** 511 7304157
Email: v.mueller@giesel.de **Web site:** http://www.giesel-verlag.de
Freq: 10 issues yearly; Free to qualifying individuals
Annual Sub.: EUR 119,00; **Circ:** 3,978
Editor: Volker Müller; **Advertising Manager:** Berko Härtel
Profile: Magazine concerning the development of modern roads, bridges, civil-engineering practices, traffic systems, equipment and fittings.
Language(s): German
ADVERTISING RATES:
Full Page Mono .... EUR 1793
Full Page Colour .... EUR 2690
Mechanical Data: Type Area: 268 x 188 mm, No. of Columns (Display): 4, Col Widths (Display): 44 mm
Copy instructions: *Copy Date:* 20 days prior to publication
Official Journal of: Organ d. Straßen- u. Tiefbaugewerbes im ZDB
BUSINESS: CONSTRUCTION: Roads

STRASSENVERKEHRS-TECHNIK
743566G49A-1680
Editorial: Im Mondsröttchen 45, 51429 BERGISCH GLADBACH **Tel:** 2204 916812 **Fax:** 2204 916813
Email: strassenverkehrstechnik.redaktion@kirschbaum.de
Freq: Monthly; Free to qualifying individuals
Annual Sub.: EUR 109,00; **Circ:** 3,463
Editor: Hans Walter Horz; **Advertising Manager:** Volker Rutkowski
Profile: Publication covering traffic and transport technology. Areas covered include transport planning, management, technology as well as town-planning and transport policies.
Language(s): German
ADVERTISING RATES:
Full Page Mono .... EUR 1990
Full Page Colour .... EUR 3050
Mechanical Data: Type Area: 260 x 185 mm, No. of Columns (Display): 4, Col Widths (Display): 44 mm
Copy instructions: *Copy Date:* 30 days prior to publication
Official Journal of: Organ d. Bundesvereinigung d. Straßenbau- u. Verkehrsingenieure u. d. Forschungsges. f. Straßen- u. Verkehrswesen u. d. FSV Wien
BUSINESS: TRANSPORT

STRASSENWÄRTER
753995G49A-1690
Editorial: Rösrather Str. 565, 51107 KÖLN
Tel: 2203 503110 **Fax:** 2203 5031120
Email: antoniusdommers@vdstra.de **Web site:** http://www.vdstra.de
Freq: 10 issues yearly; Free to qualifying individuals
Annual Sub.: EUR 19,80; **Circ:** 15,000
Editor: Antonius J. Dommers; **Advertising Manager:** Margret Lüke
Profile: Magazine for employees in road maintenance services and traffic security.
Language(s): German
ADVERTISING RATES:
Full Page Mono .... EUR 980
Full Page Colour .... EUR 1580
Mechanical Data: Type Area: 270 x 185 mm
Copy instructions: *Copy Date:* 15 days prior to publication

STRATEGIE & TECHNIK
742114G40-740
Editorial: Hochkreuzallee 1, 53175 BONN
Tel: 228 3680400 **Fax:** 228 3680402
Email: info@strategie-technik.de **Web site:** http://www.strategie-technik.de
Freq: Monthly; **Annual Sub.:** EUR 84,50; **Circ:** 6,847
Editor: Peter Boßdorf
Profile: Technical publication from the Ministry of Defence covering logistics, defence research, technology, technical news and the latest information from the armed forces.
Language(s): German
ADVERTISING RATES:
Full Page Mono .... EUR 3690
Full Page Colour .... EUR 5090
Mechanical Data: Type Area: 257 x 176 mm, No. of Columns (Display): 4, Col Widths (Display): 42 mm
Copy instructions: *Copy Date:* 20 days prior to publication
BUSINESS: DEFENCE

STRAUBINGER TAGBLATT
743573G67B-13900
Editorial: Ludwigsplatz 30, 94315 STRAUBING
Tel: 9421 9404601 **Fax:** 9421 9404609
Email: landkreis@straubinger-tagblatt.de **Web site:** http://www.idowa.de
Freq: 312 issues yearly; **Circ:** 26,804
Editor: Hans Götzl; **News Editor:** Hans Götzl; **Advertising Manager:** Klaus Huber
Profile: Regional daily newspaper with news on politics, economy, culture, sports, travel, technology, etc. The newspaper group Straubinger Tagblatt / Landshuter Zeitungin addition to the Verlagsgruppe Passau's second largest publishing group in Lower Bavaria. Your head office is in Straubing, along with another publishing house exists in Landshut. For the newspaper group owns newspapers Straubinger Tagblatt, Landshuter Allgemeine Laber-Zeitung, Bogener Zeitung, Chamer Regional daily newspaper with news on politics, economy, culture, sports, travel, technology, etc. The newspaper group Straubinger Tagblatt / Landshut newspaper in addition to the Verlagsgruppe Passau's second largest publishing group in Lower Bavaria. Your head office is in Straubing, along with another publishing house exists in Landshut. For the newspaper group owns newspapers Straubinger Tagblatt, Landshuter Zeitung, Allgemeine Laber-Zeitung, Bogener Zeitungr, Chamer Zeitung, Dingolfinger Anzeiger, Donau-Anzeiger, Donau-Post, Hallertauer Zeitung, Kötztinger Zeitung, Landauer Zeitung, Moosburger Zeitung, Plattlinger Anzeiger, Vilsbiburger Zeitung. In the majority of their appearance area is only local newspaper. In the northern area of distribution, it has competition from the Mittelbayerischen Zeitung, on the east by the Passauer Neue Presse and the southern and western part of regional editions of the Münchner Merkur. Twitter: http://twitter.com/idowa RSS (Really Simple Syndication) is offered.Dingolfinger Gazette, Donau-Gazette, Donau-mail, Hallertau newspaper Kötztinger newspaper, Landauer newspaper, Moss Burger newspaper, Plattlinger Gazette, Vilsbiburg Newspapers . In the majority of their appearance area is only local newspaper. In the northern area of distribution, it has competition from the Middle Bavarian newspaper, on the east by the Passauer Neue Presse and the southern and western part of regional editions of the Munich Mercury. Twitter: http://twitter.com/idowa RSS (Really Simple Syndication) is offered.
Language(s): German
ADVERTISING RATES:
SCC .... EUR 62,90
Mechanical Data: Type Area: 430 x 282 mm, No. of Columns (Display): 6, Col Widths (Display): 45 mm
Copy instructions: *Copy Date:* 1 day prior to publication
Supplement(s): Zuhause
REGIONAL DAILY & SUNDAY NEWSPAPERS: Regional Daily Newspapers

STRAUBINGER WOCHENBLATT
743574G72-12940
Editorial: Hirschberger Ring 29, 94315 STRAUBING
Tel: 9421 992121 **Fax:** 9421 992131
Email: dominic.casdorf@wochenblatt.de **Web site:** http://www.wochenblatt.de
Freq: Weekly; **Cover Price:** Free; **Circ:** 48,100
Editor: Dominic Casdorf; **Advertising Manager:** Stefan Sussbauer
Profile: Advertising journal (house-to-house) concentrating on local stories.
Language(s): German
ADVERTISING RATES:
Full Page Mono .... EUR 3892
Full Page Colour .... EUR 4665
Mechanical Data: Type Area: 460 x 280 mm, No. of Columns (Display): 6, Col Widths (Display): 43 mm
Copy instructions: *Copy Date:* 2 days prior to publication
LOCAL NEWSPAPERS

STREETWEAR TODAY
1641880G74A-3410
Editorial: Alte Hattinger Str. 29, 44789 BOCHUM
Tel: 234 6239789
Email: mm@stw2d.com **Web site:** http://www.streetwear-today.com
Freq: Quarterly; **Cover Price:** EUR 5,00; **Circ:** 22,800
Editor: Martin Magielka
Profile: Fashion magazine. Facebook: http://www.facebook.com/pages/streetwear-today/128170897202897?ref=ts.
Language(s): English; German
ADVERTISING RATES:
Full Page Mono .... EUR 6090
Full Page Colour .... EUR 6090
Mechanical Data: Type Area: 340 x 240 mm
Copy instructions: *Copy Date:* 20 days prior to publication

STRICKTRENDS
1882181G74A-3658
Editorial: Römerstr. 90, 79618 RHEINFELDEN
Tel: 7623 964408 **Fax:** 7623 964459
Email: info@oz-verlag.de **Web site:** http://www.oz-verlag.de
Freq: Quarterly; **Annual Sub.:** EUR 15,00; **Circ:** 100,000
Editor: Petra Bäck
Profile: Knitwear for ladies, spring, summer, autumn and winter sweaters, large sizes, ponchos, scarves, bags.
Language(s): German
ADVERTISING RATES:
Full Page Mono .... EUR 2480
Full Page Colour .... EUR 2960
Mechanical Data: Type Area: 274 x 183 mm

STROM PRAXIS
743752G43A-1280
Editorial: Reinhardtstr. 32, 10117 BERLIN
Tel: 30 284494190 **Fax:** 30 284494170
Email: strompraxis@ew-online.de **Web site:** http://www.ew-online.de
Freq: 6 issues yearly; **Annual Sub.:** EUR 59,00; **Circ:** 5,191
Editor: Wolfgang Rönspieß; **Advertising Manager:** Christa Fischer
Profile: Publication containing news and advice about the electrical trade.
Language(s): German
ADVERTISING RATES:
Full Page Mono .... EUR 3150
Full Page Colour .... EUR 4080
Mechanical Data: Type Area: 268 x 185 mm, No. of Columns (Display): 4, Col Widths (Display): 42 mm
Copy instructions: *Copy Date:* 14 days prior to publication
BUSINESS: ELECTRICAL RETAIL TRADE

STUDENT UND PRAKTIKANT
743767G37-1620
Editorial: Birkenwaldstr. 44, 70191 STUTTGART
Tel: 711 2582238 **Fax:** 711 2582291
Email: daz@deutscher-apotheker-verlag.de **Web site:** http://www.deutscher-apotheker-verlag.de
Freq: 6 issues yearly; **Circ:** 30,262
Editor: Wolfgang Caesar
Profile: Publication containing information about pharmaceutical products.
Language(s): German
Readership: Read by pharmaceutical students.
Supplement to: DAZ Deutsche ApothekerZeitung
BUSINESS: PHARMACEUTICAL & CHEMISTS

STUDIEREN IN MAGDEBURG
745766G83-12800
Editorial: Zum Handelshof 7, 39108 MAGDEBURG
Tel: 391 7325230 **Fax:** 391 7325231
Email: kontakt@dates-online.de **Web site:** http://www.bewegungsmelder.de/dates
Freq: Annual; **Cover Price:** Free; **Circ:** 10,325
Editor: Conrad Engelhardt; **Advertising Manager:** Jörg Segler
Profile: Magazine for students in Magdeburg.
Language(s): German
ADVERTISING RATES:
Full Page Mono .... EUR 690
Full Page Colour .... EUR 1190
Mechanical Data: No. of Columns (Display): 6, Col Widths (Display): 30 mm, Type Area: 261 x 185 mm
CONSUMER: STUDENT PUBLICATIONS

STUFF
1663381G86C-224
Editorial: Haußmannstr. 240, 70188 STUTTGART
Tel: 711 99797264 **Fax:** 711 99797393
Email: redaktion@stuff-mag.de **Web site:** http://www.stuff-mag.de
Freq: 6 issues yearly; **Annual Sub.:** EUR 21,00; **Circ:** 55,000
Editor: Udo Wöhrle; **Advertising Manager:** Beate Müller
Profile: Information for readers interested in gadgets, tech, lifestyle, multimedia.
Language(s): German
ADVERTISING RATES:
Full Page Mono .... EUR 5900
Full Page Colour .... EUR 5900
Mechanical Data: Type Area: 272 x 200 mm

STUTTGART GEHT AUS
1638879G89A-11806
Editorial: Falbenhennenstr. 17, 70180 STUTTGART
Tel: 711 60171717 **Fax:** 711 60171749
Email: info@lift-online.de **Web site:** http://www.lift-online.de
Freq: Annual; **Cover Price:** EUR 7,90; **Circ:** 30,000
Editor: Sabrina Schuler
Profile: The big gastronomic guide for Stuttgart and the region and shows the 1,500 best restaurants, bistros, wine bars, pubs, cafes, lounges and clubs in Stuttgart and region. Stuttgart geht aus told stories of going out and eat or drink, served a multitude of services and of course there are nightlife tips for the whole year. Facebook: http://www.facebook.com/pages/LIFT-Stadtmagazin/161318138841.
Language(s): German
ADVERTISING RATES:
Full Page Mono .... EUR 2340
Full Page Colour .... EUR 3380
Mechanical Data: Type Area: 260 x 190 mm, No. of Columns (Display): 4, Col Widths (Display): 44 mm
Copy instructions: *Copy Date:* 34 days prior to publication

STUTTGARTER AMTSBLATT
720380G72-856
Editorial: Rathauspassage 2, 70173 STUTTGART
Tel: 711 2162453 **Fax:** 711 2167705
Email: amtsblatt@stuttgart.de **Web site:** http://www.stuttgart.de
Freq: Weekly; **Annual Sub.:** EUR 28,20; **Circ:** 33,000
Editor: Markus Vogt
Profile: Magazine containing articles about events, functions and meetings in Stuttgart.
Language(s): German
Readership: Aimed at citizens of Stuttgart.
LOCAL NEWSPAPERS

STUTTGARTER NACHRICHTEN
743820G67B-13920
Editorial: Plieninger Str. 150, 70567 STUTTGART
Tel: 711 72050 **Fax:** 711 72057138
Email: cvd@stn.zgs.de **Web site:** http://www.stuttgarter-nachrichten.de
Freq: 312 issues yearly; **Circ:** 204,304
Editor: Christoph Reisinger; **News Editor:** Wolfgang Molitor
Profile: Regional daily newspaper with news on politics, economy, culture, sports, travel, technology, etc. Facebook: http://www.facebook.com/stuttgarternachrichten Twitter: http://twitter.com/StN_News This Outlet offers RSS (Really Simple Syndication).
Language(s): German
ADVERTISING RATES:
SCC .... EUR 358,00
Mechanical Data: Type Area: 492 x 321 mm, No. of Columns (Display): 7, Col Widths (Display): 44 mm
Copy instructions: *Copy Date:* 1 day prior to publication
Supplement(s): Kornwestheim & Kreis Ludwigsburg; Lesemomente; Marbach & Bottwartal; S-taff; Strohgäu Extra
REGIONAL DAILY & SUNDAY NEWSPAPERS: Regional Daily Newspapers

STUTTGARTER WOCHENBLATT
743832G72-13012
Editorial: Plieninger Str. 150, 70567 STUTTGART
Tel: 711 72083322 **Fax:** 711 72083340
Email: redaktion@stw.zgs.de **Web site:** http://www.stuttgarter-wochenblatt.de
Freq: Weekly; **Cover Price:** Free; **Circ:** 360,025
Editor: Bernd Ruof; **Advertising Manager:** Sven Gernhardt
Profile: Advertising journal (house-to-house) concentrating on local stories.
Language(s): German
ADVERTISING RATES:
Full Page Mono .... EUR 17737
Full Page Colour .... EUR 21284
Mechanical Data: Type Area: 492 x 321 mm, No. of Columns (Display): 7, Col Widths (Display): 44 mm
Copy instructions: *Copy Date:* 2 days prior to publication
LOCAL NEWSPAPERS

STUTTGARTER ZEITUNG
743833G67B-13940
Editorial: Plieninger Str. 150, 70567 STUTTGART
Tel: 711 72050 **Fax:** 711 72051234
Email: redaktion@stz.zgs.de **Web site:** http://www.stuttgarter-zeitung.de
Freq: 312 issues yearly; **Circ:** 204,304
Editor: Joachim Dorfs; **News Editor:** Rainer Pörtner
Profile: Regional daily newspaper covering politics, economics, sport, travel and technology. Twitter: http://twitter.com/StZonline This Outlet offers RSS (Really Simple Syndication).
Language(s): German
ADVERTISING RATES:
SCC .... EUR 358,00
Mechanical Data: Type Area: 492 x 321 mm, No. of Columns (Display): 7, Col Widths (Display): 44 mm
Copy instructions: *Copy Date:* 1 day prior to publication
Supplement(s): Kornwestheim & Kreis Ludwigsburg; Leonberg & Umgebung; Lesemomente; Marbach & Bottwartal; S-taff; Strohgäu Extra
REGIONAL DAILY & SUNDAY NEWSPAPERS: Regional Daily Newspapers

STYLE GUIDE
741189G2A-4320
Editorial: Theresienstr. 9, 94032 PASSAU
Tel: 851 9320012 **Fax:** 851 9320049
Email: info@style-guide.biz **Web site:** http://www.style-guide.biz
Freq: 10 issues yearly; **Annual Sub.:** EUR 104,00; **Circ:** 8,033
Editor: Helmut Lippl; **Advertising Manager:** Hans Isaak
Profile: Source of information for display advertising manager, salaried and freelance visual merchandising visual marketing, retailers, and the visual merchandising industry.
Language(s): German
ADVERTISING RATES:
Full Page Mono .... EUR 1825
Full Page Colour .... EUR 3193
Mechanical Data: Type Area: 239 x 190 mm, No. of Columns (Display): 3, Col Widths (Display): 60 mm
Copy instructions: *Copy Date:* 20 days prior to publication

STYLEPARK
1664861G4B-705
Editorial: Brönnerstr. 22, 60313 FRANKFURT
Tel: 69 29722222 **Fax:** 69 29722223
Email: magazin@stylepark.com **Web site:** http://www.stylepark.com
Freq: Quarterly; **Annual Sub.:** EUR 32,00; **Circ:** 22,000
Editor: Antonia Henschel
Profile: B2B magazine showcases the latest product and interior design by renowned international designers. It is aimed at architects, interior architects and designers in Germany.
Language(s): English; German
ADVERTISING RATES:
Full Page Mono .... EUR 3500
Full Page Colour .... EUR 3500
Mechanical Data: Type Area: 260 x 185 mm
Copy instructions: *Copy Date:* 45 days prior to publication

STYLEPARK
1704570G4E-7097
Editorial: Brönnerstr. 22, 60313 FRANKFURT
Tel: 69 29722222 **Fax:** 69 29722223
Email: redaktion@stylepark.com **Web site:** http://www.stylepark.com
Cover Price: Paid; **Circ:** 420,410 Unique Users
Editor: Dimitrios Tsatsas; **Advertising Manager:** Nicole Weßlin
Language(s): German
BUSINESS: ARCHITECTURE & BUILDING: Building

SUBKUTAN
765299G56A-11194
Editorial: Kopenhagener Str. 74, 10437 BERLIN
Tel: 30 44038482
Email: monecke@subkutan-online.de **Web site:** http://www.subkutan-online.de
Freq: 6 issues yearly; Free to qualifying individuals
Annual Sub.: EUR 16,00; **Circ:** 23,401
Editor: Angela Monecke; **Advertising Manager:** Björn Lindenau
Profile: Magazine of Diabetes Association in Brandenburg, Bremen, Hessen, Nordrhein-Westfalen, Rheinland-Pfalz, Schleswig-Holstein and Thüringen. Journal reports on the personal experiences of people with diabetes, innovations in diabetes care, current developments in the area of health policy, from the work of state associations and the Federation as well as innovations in the pharmaceutical industry.
Language(s): German
ADVERTISING RATES:
Full Page Mono .... EUR 2735
Full Page Colour .... EUR 2735
Mechanical Data: Type Area: 245 x 178 mm, No. of Columns (Display): 4, Col Widths (Display): 40 mm
Copy instructions: *Copy Date:* 28 days prior to publication
Official Journal of: Organ d. DDB-Landesverbände Berlin, Brandenburg, Bremen, Hessen, Nordrhein-Westfalen, Rheinland-Pfalz, Schleswig-Holstein u. Thüringen

SUBMISSIONS-ANZEIGER
1656856G4E-7014
Editorial: Schopenstehl 15, 20095 HAMBURG
Tel: 40 40194017 **Fax:** 40 40194031
Email: ausschreibungen@submission.de **Web site:** http://www.submission.de
Freq: 260 issues yearly; **Circ:** 10,000
Editor: Hans-Joachim Busch; **Advertising Manager:** Jürgen Klose
Profile: Magazine focusing on the building business, administration, industry, craftsmen, trade, architects and engineering offices.
Language(s): German
ADVERTISING RATES:
Full Page Mono .... EUR 980
Full Page Colour .... EUR 1100
Mechanical Data: Type Area: 278 x 210 mm, No. of Columns (Display): 4, Col Widths (Display): 45 mm
Copy instructions: *Copy Date:* 2 days prior to publication

SUBWAY
743880G80-11080
Editorial: Kohlmarkt 2, 38100 BRAUNSCHWEIG
Tel: 531 243200 **Fax:** 531 2432023
Email: chefredaktion@subway.de **Web site:** http://www.subway.de
Freq: Monthly; **Cover Price:** Free; **Circ:** 20,966
Editor: Christian Göttner; **Advertising Manager:** Michael Hoffmann
Profile: The traditional and widely read city magazine for free from Braunschweig is situated on over 400 delivery locations in the city. It covers 84 pages with detailed from regional and national reports and interviews from the fields of culture, society, lifestyle, sports, film, music, education and extensive event tips the full range of social life. Facebook: http://www.facebook.com/SUBWAYMagazin This Outlet offers RSS (Really Simple syndication).
Language(s): German
Readership: Read by tourists and residents of the area.
ADVERTISING RATES:
Full Page Mono .... EUR 1365
Full Page Colour .... EUR 2269
Mechanical Data: No. of Columns (Display): 4, Col Widths (Display): 45 mm, Type Area: 260 x 190 mm
Copy instructions: *Copy Date:* 15 days prior to publication
CONSUMER: RURAL & REGIONAL INTEREST

SUCH & FIND
743886G2A-5918
Editorial: Rosa-Luxemburg-Str. 27, 04301 LEIPZIG
Tel: 341 913750 **Fax:** 341 9137555
Email: dtp@sufi-ost.de **Web site:** http://www.sufi-ost.de
Freq: Weekly; **Cover Price:** EUR 1,70; **Circ:** 18,000
Editor: Stefan Ruffer
Profile: The SUCH & FIND appears every week Thursday at the kiosk in Saxony, Saxony-Anhalt, Thuringia, Brandenburg, Mecklenburg-Vorpommern about 20,000 private and commercial ads. The role of private Classifieds is free, commercial ads must be purchased.
Language(s): German
ADVERTISING RATES:
Full Page Mono .... EUR 1875
Full Page Colour .... EUR 2025
Mechanical Data: Type Area: 325 x 232 mm, No. of Columns (Display): 5, Col Widths (Display): 45 mm
Copy instructions: *Copy Date:* 1 day prior to publication

SUCH & FIND
743886G94X-7000
Editorial: Rosa-Luxemburg-Str. 27, 04301 LEIPZIG
Tel: 341 913750 **Fax:** 341 9137555
Email: dtp@sufi-ost.de **Web site:** http://www.sufi-ost.de
Freq: Weekly; **Cover Price:** EUR 1,70; **Circ:** 18,000
Editor: Stefan Ruffer
Profile: The SUCH & FIND appears every week Thursday at the kiosk in Saxony, Saxony-Anhalt, Thuringia, Brandenburg, Mecklenburg-Vorpommern about 20,000 private and commercial ads. The role of private Classifieds is free, commercial ads must be purchased.
Language(s): German
ADVERTISING RATES:
Full Page Mono .... EUR 1875
Full Page Colour .... EUR 2025
Mechanical Data: Type Area: 325 x 232 mm, No. of Columns (Display): 5, Col Widths (Display): 45 mm
Copy instructions: *Copy Date:* 1 day prior to publication

SUCHTMEDIZIN IN FORSCHUNG UND PRAXIS
743883G56A-9420
Editorial: Justus-von-Liebig-Str. 1, 86899 LANDSBERG **Tel:** 8191 125500 **Fax:** 8191 125492
Email: susanne.fischer@hjr-verlag.de **Web site:** http://www.ecomed-medizin.de/suchtmedizin
Freq: 6 issues yearly; **Annual Sub.:** EUR 178,00; **Circ:** 1,000
Editor: Susanne Fischer; **Advertising Manager:** Reingard Herbst
Profile: Interdisciplinary forum on addiction medicine.
Language(s): German
ADVERTISING RATES:
Full Page Mono .... EUR 1870
Full Page Colour .... EUR 2650
Mechanical Data: Type Area: 235 x 177 mm, No. of Columns (Display): 2, Col Widths (Display): 85 mm
Copy instructions: *Copy Date:* 42 days prior to publication

SUCHTTHERAPIE
743885G56A-9440
Editorial: Martinistr. 52, 20246 HAMBURG
Tel: 40 428035121 **Fax:** 40 428035121
Email: farnbacher@uke.uni-hamburg.de **Web site:** http://www.thieme.de/suchttherapie/index.html
Freq: Quarterly; **Annual Sub.:** EUR 123,80; **Circ:** 1,650
Editor: Jens Reimer
Profile: From practice for practice: Compact expertise. Original Articles and Overviews. Case reports and treatment reports. New trends in addiction medicine, addiction psychology, addictions social works. InternationalerStudien summaries, meeting reports, right, interviews. Studied internationally - look across the border.
Language(s): German
Readership: Aimed at doctors, psychiatrists and scientists in psychosomatic clinics.
ADVERTISING RATES:
Full Page Mono .... EUR 1430
Full Page Colour .... EUR 2600
Mechanical Data: Type Area: 248 x 175 mm, No. of Columns (Display): 4, Col Widths (Display): 40 mm
Official Journal of: Organ d. Dt. Ges. f. Suchtmedizin e.V. u. d. Dt. Ges. f. Suchtpsychologie e.V.
BUSINESS: HEALTH & MEDICAL

SÜD ANZEIGER
743894G72-13016
Editorial: Bert-Brecht-Str. 29, 45128 ESSEN
Tel: 201 8042510 **Fax:** 201 8041576
Email: redaktion@stadtspiegel-essen.de **Web site:** http://www.lokalkompass.de/essen-sud
Freq: 104 issues yearly; **Cover Price:** Free; **Circ:** 82,300
Editor: Dirk Bütefür; **Advertising Manager:** Lars Staehler
Profile: Advertising journal (house-to-house) concentrating on local stories.
Language(s): German
ADVERTISING RATES:
Full Page Mono .... EUR 5265
Full Page Colour .... EUR 7107
Mechanical Data: Type Area: 445 x 315 mm, No. of Columns (Display): 7, Col Widths (Display): 42 mm
Copy instructions: *Copy Date:* 2 days prior to publication
LOCAL NEWSPAPERS

SÜD-AFRIKA
767434G89A-12134
Editorial: Heilsbachstr. 17, 53123 BONN
Tel: 228 919320 **Fax:** 228 9193217
Email: info@latka.de **Web site:** http://www.sued-afrika.de
Freq: Quarterly; **Annual Sub.:** EUR 16,00; **Circ:** 24,500
Editor: Sigrid Latka-Jöhring; **Advertising Manager:** Benno M. Wildemann
Profile: Magazine about travel, lifestyle, culture and politics in Southern Africa.
Language(s): German
ADVERTISING RATES:
Full Page Colour .... EUR 4290
Mechanical Data: Type Area: 256 x 178 mm, No. of Columns (Display): 3, Col Widths (Display): 56 mm
Copy instructions: *Copy Date:* 40 days prior to publication

SÜDDEUTSCHE BAUWIRTSCHAFT UND ZEITSCHRIFT FÜR DENKMALSCHUTZ
743899G4E-6882
Editorial: Wilhelm-Hertz-Str. 14, 70192 STUTTGART
Tel: 711 2573333 **Fax:** 711 2573422
Email: horst.kimmich@googlemail.com
Freq: Monthly; **Annual Sub.:** EUR 22,00; **Circ:** 5,000
Editor: Horst Kimmich; **Advertising Manager:** Martina Vogel
Profile: Magazine about the building industry in Southern Germany.
Language(s): German
ADVERTISING RATES:
Full Page Mono .... EUR 1025
Full Page Colour .... EUR 1745
Mechanical Data: Type Area: 250 x 180 mm, No. of Columns (Display): 4, Col Widths (Display): 42 mm
Copy instructions: *Copy Date:* 20 days prior to publication

SÜDDEUTSCHE ZEITUNG
743904G65A-180
Editorial: Hultschiner Str. 8, 81677 MÜNCHEN
Tel: 89 21830 **Fax:** 89 2183787
Email: redaktion@sueddeutsche.de **Web site:** http://www.sueddeutsche.de
Freq: 312 issues yearly; **Circ:** 530,743
Editor: Kurt Kister; **News Editor:** Hendrik Munsberg; **Advertising Manager:** Jürgen Maukner
Profile: Broadsheet-sized quality newspaper providing in-depth coverage of national and international news, politics, finance, economics, culture and sport.
Language(s): German
Readership: Read by company directors, executives, managers and office personnel.
ADVERTISING RATES:
SCC .... EUR 746,00
Mechanical Data: Type Area: 528 x 371 mm, No. of Columns (Display): 8, Col Widths (Display): 45 mm
Copy instructions: *Copy Date:* 1 day prior to publication
Supplement(s): audiophil; BerufSZiel; buchjournal; chrismon; Hamburg: Das Magazin aus der Metropole; LeonArt; Lux; münchen erleben; The New York Times; Punkt. Bildung neu denken; Süddeutsche Zeitung Fernsehen; Süddeutsche Zeitung golf spielen; Süddeutsche Zeitung Magazin; Süddeutsche Zeitung Wohlfühlen; SZ Süddeutsche Zeitung Extra; Uni & Job; Urlaub in Tirol; Vielfalt erleben
NATIONAL DAILY & SUNDAY NEWSPAPERS: National Daily Newspapers

SÜDDEUTSCHE ZEITUNG DAS MAGAZIN ZUM JAHRESWECHSEL
1796236G73-617
Editorial: Hultschiner Str. 8, 81677 MÜNCHEN
Tel: 89 2183408 **Fax:** 89 21838482
Email: redaktion@sz-magazin.de **Web site:** http://www.sueddeutsche.de
Freq: Annual; **Cover Price:** EUR 6,00; **Circ:** 120,000
Editor: Kurt Kister; **Advertising Manager:** Anne Sasse
Profile: Special of the Sueddeutsche Zeitung, review of the year's events Facebook: http://www.facebook.com/sueddeutsche.
Language(s): German
ADVERTISING RATES:
Full Page Mono .... EUR 9900
Full Page Colour .... EUR 9900
Mechanical Data: Type Area: 241 x 184 mm
Copy instructions: *Copy Date:* 36 days prior to publication

SÜDDEUTSCHE ZEITUNG GOLF SPIELEN
744198G65A-180_102
Editorial: Fasanengartenstr. 138, 81549 MÜNCHEN
Tel: 89 2183391 **Fax:** 89 21838216
Email: ludwig.rembold@sueddeutsche.de **Web site:** http://www.sueddeutsche.de
Freq: Quarterly; **Circ:** 489,391
Editor: Ludwig Rembold; **Advertising Manager:** Anne Sasse
Profile: golf spielenf is the supplement of the Süddeutsche Zeitung for golfers and golf enthusiasts. With the SZ Supplement play golf you will meet the high readership of the Süddeutsche Zeitung. With 1.20 million readers (AWA 2010), it achieves the greatest reach among the nationwide subscription newspapers. This unique editorial approach and the high prevalence of type play golf of your advertising while the necessary drive. Besides the four issues per year offers to play golf at the golf tournaments SZ

(Business Golf Cup) the opportunity to reach your target audience. Facebook: http:// www.facebook.com/sueddeutsche Twitter: http:// twitter.com/sueddeutschede This Outlet offers RSS (Really Simple Syndication).
Language(s): German
ADVERTISING RATES:
Full Page Mono .... EUR 15100
Full Page Colour .... EUR 15100
Mechanical Data: Type Area: 246 x 191 mm, No. of Columns (Display): 4, Col Widths (Display): 44 mm
Supplement to: Süddeutsche Zeitung
NATIONAL DAILY & SUNDAY NEWSPAPERS: National Daily Newspapers

SÜDDEUTSCHE ZEITUNG MAGAZIN
743905G65A-180_103
Editorial: Hultschiner Str. 8, 81677 MÜNCHEN
Tel: 89 21839540 **Fax:** 89 21839570
Email: szmagazin@sz-magazin.de **Web site:** http:// www.sz-magazin.de
Freq: Weekly; **Circ:** 585,693
Editor: Timm Klotzek; **Advertising Manager:** Anne Sasse
Profile: As a magazine in Germany, great quality newspaper, we surprise our readers every Friday with creative journalism the highest level. We tie them up with a graphic design that is unparalleled. We tell stories that are remembered. And we bring together what is rarely together: Lifestyle and quality journalism. We feel well in both disciplines and combine them with elegance in the writing and thinking. This unique combination gives the Süddeutsche Zeitung Magazin something that other magazines can only dream of: Friends and fans.
Language(s): German
ADVERTISING RATES:
Full Page Mono .... EUR 15400
Full Page Colour .... EUR 15400
Mechanical Data: Type Area: 247 x 191 mm, No. of Columns (Display): 4, Col Widths (Display): 44 mm
Copy instructions: *Copy Date:* 24 days prior to publication
Supplement to: Süddeutsche Zeitung
NATIONAL DAILY & SUNDAY NEWSPAPERS: National Daily Newspapers

SÜDDEUTSCHE ZEITUNG WOHLFÜHLEN
1691945G65A-180_104
Editorial: Fasanengartenstr. 138, 81549 MÜNCHEN
Tel: 89 2183391 **Fax:** 89 21838315
Email: ludwig.rembold@sueddeutsche.de **Web site:** http://www.sueddeutsche.de/wohlfuehlen
Freq: Quarterly; **Cover Price:** Free; **Circ:** 493,364
Editor: Ludwig Rembold; **Advertising Manager:** Anne Sasse
Profile: Wohlfühlen is the supplement of the Süddeutsche Zeitung for wellness, fitness and health. Wohlfühlen achieved with four issues a year, a growing group of people who want to know how and where they draw new strength and energy quickly, and effectively promote their health improve.Wohlfühlen is for better quality of life and holistic well-being, combined with modern lifestyle. With its high service character Wohlfühlen guidance in the choice is all on the wellness market. Wohlfühlen informed of the high quality of journalism Süddeutsche Zeitung founded on wellness issues for body, mind and soul. This makes it the ideal environment for your advertising, because of Wohlfühlen g to reach the 1.20 million readers of the Süddeutsche Zeitung (AWA 2010).
Language(s): German
ADVERTISING RATES:
Full Page Mono .... EUR 15400
Full Page Colour .... EUR 15400
Mechanical Data: Type Area: 246 x 191 mm
Copy instructions: *Copy Date:* 33 days prior to publication
Supplement to: Süddeutsche Zeitung
NATIONAL DAILY & SUNDAY NEWSPAPERS: National Daily Newspapers

SÜDERELBE WOCHENBLATT
743907G72-13036
Editorial: Harburger Rathausstr. 40, 21073 HAMBURG **Tel:** 40 85322933 **Fax:** 40 85322939
Email: post@wochenblatt-redaktion.de **Web site:** http://www.suederelbe-wochenblatt.de
Freq: Weekly; **Cover Price:** Free; **Circ:** 36,361
Editor: Olaf Zimmermann; **Advertising Manager:** Jürgen Müller
Profile: Advertising journal (house-to-house) concentrating on local stories.
Language(s): German
ADVERTISING RATES:
Full Page Mono .... EUR 3793
Full Page Colour .... EUR 3913
Mechanical Data: Type Area: 430 x 282 mm, No. of Columns (Display): 6, Col Widths (Display): 45 mm
Copy instructions: *Copy Date:* 2 days prior to publication
LOCAL NEWSPAPERS

SÜDERLÄNDER TAGEBLATT
743909G67B-14020
Editorial: An der Lohmühle 7, 58840 PLETTENBERG
Tel: 2391 90930 **Fax:** 2391 909340
Email: st@mzv.net **Web site:** http://www.suederlaender-tageblatt.de
Freq: 312 issues yearly; **Circ:** 5,238
Profile: Daily newspaper with regional news and a local sports section.
Language(s): German
ADVERTISING RATES:
SCC .... EUR 35,60
Mechanical Data: Type Area: 466 x 317 mm, No. of Columns (Display): 7, Col Widths (Display): 43 mm
Copy instructions: *Copy Date:* 1 day prior to publication
Supplement(s): prisma
REGIONAL DAILY & SUNDAY NEWSPAPERS: Regional Daily Newspapers

SÜDERLÄNDER VOLKSFREUND
743910G67B-14040
Editorial: Freiheitstr. 24, 58791 WERDOHL
Tel: 2392 500570 **Fax:** 2392 500576
Email: sv@come-on.de **Web site:** http://www.come-on.de
Freq: 312 issues yearly; **Circ:** 3,256
Advertising Manager: Guido Schröder
Profile: Daily newspaper with regional news and a local sports section. This Outlet offers RSS (Really Simple Syndication).
Language(s): German
ADVERTISING RATES:
SCC .... EUR 29,60
Mechanical Data: Type Area: 466 x 317 mm, No. of Columns (Display): 7, Col Widths (Display): 43 mm
Copy instructions: *Copy Date:* 1 day prior to publication
Supplement(s): prisma
REGIONAL DAILY & SUNDAY NEWSPAPERS: Regional Daily Newspapers

SÜDHESSEN MORGEN
743912G67B-14060
Editorial: Dudenstr. 12, 68167 MANNHEIM
Tel: 621 3921313 **Fax:** 621 3921376
Email: redaktion@mamo.de **Web site:** http://www.morgenweb.de
Freq: 312 issues yearly
Advertising Manager: Gerhard Haeberle
Profile: Daily newspaper with regional news and a local sports section. Facebook: http:// www.facebook.com/pages/morgenweb/ 105113719526519.
Language(s): German
ADVERTISING RATES:
SCC .... EUR 31,50
Mechanical Data: Type Area: 490 x 320 mm, No. of Columns (Display): 7, Col Widths (Display): 44 mm
Copy instructions: *Copy Date:* 1 day prior to publication
Supplement(s): Das will ich; essen & genießen in der Metropolregion; Lust auf Genuss; Mannheim im Weihnachtszauber; Mode & Stil; Morgen Magazin; Natürlich; TV Morgen; 4 wände; Wirtschaftsmorgen; Wohlfühljournal
REGIONAL DAILY & SUNDAY NEWSPAPERS: Regional Daily Newspapers

SUDHOFFS ARCHIV
743893G56A-9460
Editorial: Luisenstr. 57, 10117 BERLIN
Tel: 30 450529351 **Fax:** 30 450529950
Web site: http://www.steiner-verlag.de/Sudhoff
Freq: Half-yearly; **Annual Sub.:** EUR 179,80; **Circ:** 500
Editor: Paul U. Unschuld; **Advertising Manager:** Susanne Szoradi
Profile: Magazine about the history of science.
Language(s): English; French; German
ADVERTISING RATES:
Full Page Mono .... EUR 750
Mechanical Data: Type Area: 190 x 120 mm

SÜDKURIER
743923G67B-14100
Editorial: Max-Stromeyer-Str. 178, 78467 KONSTANZ **Tel:** 7531 9990 **Fax:** 7531 9991576
Email: redaktion@suedkurier.de **Web site:** http:// www.suedkurier.de
Freq: 312 issues yearly; **Circ:** 142,723
Editor: Stefan Lutz; **Advertising Manager:** Michael Beyer
Profile: Regional daily newspaper covering politics, economics, culture, sports, travel and technology. Facebook: http://www.facebook.com/pages/ SUDKURIER/346232178065 Twitter: http:// twitter.com/SUEDKURIER This Outlet offers RSS (Really Simple Syndication).
Language(s): German
ADVERTISING RATES:
SCC .... EUR 278,90
Mechanical Data: Type Area: 440 x 290 mm, No. of Columns (Display): 6, Col Widths (Display): 45 mm
Copy instructions: *Copy Date:* 1 day prior to publication
REGIONAL DAILY & SUNDAY NEWSPAPERS: Regional Daily Newspapers

SÜDKURIER FRIEDRICHSHAFEN
743924G67B-14120
Editorial: Max-Stromeyer-Str. 178, 78467 KONSTANZ **Tel:** 7531 9990 **Fax:** 7531 9991576
Email: redaktion@suedkurier.de **Web site:** http:// www.suedkurier.de
Freq: 312 issues yearly; **Circ:** 20,499
Profile: Daily newspaper with regional news and a local sports section. Facebook: http:// www.facebook.com/pages/SUDKURIER/ 346232178065 Twitter: http://twitter.com/ SUEDKURIER This Outlet offers RSS (Really Simple Syndication).
Language(s): German
ADVERTISING RATES:
SCC .... EUR 49,70
Mechanical Data: Type Area: 440 x 290 mm, No. of Columns (Display): 6, Col Widths (Display): 45 mm
Copy instructions: *Copy Date:* 1 day prior to publication
REGIONAL DAILY & SUNDAY NEWSPAPERS: Regional Daily Newspapers

SÜDKURIER SNOW&FUN
1632936G89A-11728
Editorial: Max-Stromeyer-Str. 178, 78467 KONSTANZ **Tel:** 7531 9991262 **Fax:** 7531 9991566
Email: ferienzeitung@suedkurier.de **Web site:** http:// www.suedkurier-medienhaus.de
Freq: Annual; **Cover Price:** Free; **Circ:** 38,000
Editor: Katrin Dollinger
Profile: Magazine for skiers and boarders. In the new handy format and fresh layout, it will present the finest winter sports areas in the prospering area of the western Alps - reached in a day distance and for the winter holidays with short commutes. This magazine will always provide decision support in the increasingly short-term booking patterns of snow sports. The portraits are accompanied by field reports on winter sports equipment trends and tips, family offers, fun parks to events in the season. Target Group: Purchasing power skiers and winter sports day visitors from the region of Bodensee / Schwarzwald / Oberschwaben / Allgäu are the target group of this current season-magazine - valid from November to early April. Printed on newsprint, a greater play of the wire-stitched, color magazine in the distribution of its regional strengths: Attached in Südkurier (Bodensee region I and II), and additional free distribution to over 100 sport-affinity sites.
Language(s): German
Mechanical Data: Type Area: 450 x 325 mm, No. of Columns (Display): 6, Col Widths (Display): 51 mm

SÜDTHÜRINGER ZEITUNG STZ
1622068G67B-16665
Editorial: Andreasstr. 11, 36433 BAD SALZUNGEN
Tel: 3695 555050 **Fax:** 3695 555051
Email: online-redaktion@stz-online.de **Web site:** http://www.stz-online.de
Freq: Daily; **Cover Price:** Paid; **Circ:** 50,617 Unique Users
Editor: Berthold Dücker
Profile: Ezine: Regional daily newspaper covering politics, economics, sport, travel and technology.
Language(s): German
REGIONAL DAILY & SUNDAY NEWSPAPERS: Regional Daily Newspapers

SÜDWEST PRESSE
743951G67B-14160
Editorial: Hindenburgstr. 6, 72555 METZINGEN
Tel: 7123 945120 **Fax:** 7123 945201
Email: muv.redaktion@swp.de **Web site:** http://www.swp.de
Freq: 312 issues yearly; **Circ:** 12,513
Editor: Jürgen Kühnemund; **Advertising Manager:** Eberhard Euchner
Profile: Daily newspaper with regional news and a local sports section. Twitter: http://twitter.com/swpde This Outlet offers RSS (Really Simple Syndication).
Language(s): German
ADVERTISING RATES:
SCC .... EUR 14,50
Mechanical Data: Type Area: 480 x 320 mm, No. of Columns (Display): 7, Col Widths (Display): 44 mm
Copy instructions: *Copy Date:* 1 day prior to publication
REGIONAL DAILY & SUNDAY NEWSPAPERS: Regional Daily Newspapers

SÜDWEST PRESSE
743952G67B-14180
Editorial: Uhlandstr. 2, 72072 TÜBINGEN
Tel: 7071 9340 **Fax:** 7071 35033
Email: nc@tagblatt.de **Web site:** http://www.neckar-chronik.de
Freq: 312 issues yearly; **Circ:** 5,218
Editor: Eckhard Ströbel; **Advertising Manager:** Wolfgang Dieter
Profile: Daily newspaper with regional news and a local sports section.
Language(s): German
ADVERTISING RATES:
SCC .... EUR 28,90
Mechanical Data: Type Area: 480 x 321 mm, No. of Columns (Display): 7, Col Widths (Display): 44 mm
Copy instructions: *Copy Date:* 1 day prior to publication
REGIONAL DAILY & SUNDAY NEWSPAPERS: Regional Daily Newspapers

SÜDWEST PRESSE
743953G67B-14200
Editorial: Frauenstr. 77, 89073 ULM **Tel:** 731 1560
Fax: 731 156308
Email: redaktion@swp.de **Web site:** http://www.swp.de
Freq: 312 issues yearly; **Circ:** 308,082
Editor: Hans-Jörg Wiedenhaus; **News Editor:** Lothar Tolks; **Advertising Manager:** Dieter Müller
Profile: Regional daily newspaper covering politics, economics, cultur, sports, travel and technology. Twitter: http://twitter.com/swpde This Outlet offers RSS (Really Simple Syndication).
Language(s): German
ADVERTISING RATES:
SCC .... EUR 587,20
Mechanical Data: Col Widths (Display): 44 mm
Copy instructions: *Copy Date:* 1 day prior to publication
Supplement(s): Das Blaumännle; Langenau aktuell; leben:wohnen; Das Magazin
REGIONAL DAILY & SUNDAY NEWSPAPERS: Regional Daily Newspapers

SÜDWEST PRESSE DIE NECKARQUELLE
743954G67B-14220
Editorial: Bert-Brecht-Str. 15, 78054 VILLINGEN-SCHWENNINGEN **Tel:** 7720 394160
Fax: 7720 394222
Email: redaktion@kuhnverlag.de **Web site:** http:// www.nq-online.de
Freq: 312 issues yearly; **Circ:** 8,064
Editor: Günther Baumann; **Advertising Manager:** Axel Ziegler
Profile: Daily newspaper with regional news and a local sports section. Facebook: http:// www.facebook.com/neckarquelle.
Language(s): German
ADVERTISING RATES:
SCC .... EUR 38,10
Mechanical Data: Type Area: 420 x 280 mm, No. of Columns (Display): 6, Col Widths (Display): 45 mm
Copy instructions: *Copy Date:* 1 day prior to publication
REGIONAL DAILY & SUNDAY NEWSPAPERS: Regional Daily Newspapers

SÜDWESTDEUTSCHE PILZRUNDSCHAU
1837113G21A-4397
Editorial: Danziger Str. 27, 73262 REICHENBACH
Web site: http://www.pilzverein.de
Freq: Half-yearly; Free to qualifying individuals
Annual Sub.: EUR 20,00; **Circ:** 800
Editor: Ernst Dittrich
Profile: Magazinedealing with mushrooms.
Language(s): German
Mechanical Data: Type Area: 180 x 125 mm

SÜDWESTDEUTSCHE PILZRUNDSCHAU
1837113G21A-4463
Editorial: Danziger Str. 27, 73262 REICHENBACH
Web site: http://www.pilzverein.de
Freq: Half-yearly; Free to qualifying individuals
Annual Sub.: EUR 20,00; **Circ:** 800
Editor: Ernst Dittrich
Profile: Magazinedealing with mushrooms.
Language(s): German
Mechanical Data: Type Area: 180 x 125 mm

SÜDWESTFALEN MANAGER
1832763G14A-10135
Editorial: Möhnestr. 55, 59755 ARNSBERG
Tel: 2932 977511 **Fax:** 2932 977525
Email: to@suedwestfalen-manager.de **Web site:** http://www.suedwestfalen-manager.de
Freq: 10 issues yearly; **Annual Sub.:** EUR 28,00; **Circ:** 22,643
Editor: Tamara Olschewski; **Advertising Manager:** Torben Feil
Profile: In addition to regionally relevant economic issues and well-researched background information and interviews, company profiles and contributions will be presented on interesting personalities. Similarly, topics that address the purchasing power manager as a person and individual.
Language(s): German
ADVERTISING RATES:
Full Page Mono .... EUR 3450
Full Page Colour .... EUR 3450
Mechanical Data: Type Area: 260 x 188 mm, No. of Columns (Display): 4, Col Widths (Display): 44 mm

SUEDDEUTSCHE.DE
1622066G65A-269
Editorial: Hultschiner Str. 8, 81677 MÜNCHEN
Tel: 89 21830 **Fax:** 89 21838586
Email: wir@sueddeutsche.de **Web site:** http://www.sueddeutsche.de
Freq: Daily; **Cover Price:** Paid; **Circ:** 32,663,349 Unique Users
Editor: Stefan Plöchinger; **News Editor:** Lutz Knappmann
Profile: Online news platform: In addition to the "Süddeutsche Zeitung" be prepared international, national and regional hot topics varied and substantial. Current and comprehensive information in the sections politics, economics, finance, culture, sports, life & style, work & career, München, Bayern, panorama, cars, mobile, digital, knowledge, health, travel, real estate. Sueddeutsche.de to find popular columns such as Jürgen Schmieder's "Projekt 15" and "Flügelflitzer" or Bernd Graff's "Körperwelten". Furthermore sueddeutsche.de offers its users many more values, such as a bank compass, a pension calculator and a Glossary and application guide, a course search, an Internet dictionary and virus warnings and more than 200 large files and many special topics. Facebook: http://www.facebook.com/ sueddeutsche Twitter: http://twitter.com/ sueddeutschede This Outlet offers RSS (Really Simple Syndication).
Language(s): German
NATIONAL DAILY & SUNDAY NEWSPAPERS: National Daily Newspapers

SUGAR INDUSTRY ZUCKER INDUSTRIE
748980G22A-3160
Editorial: Lückhoffstr. 16, 14129 BERLIN
Tel: 30 8035678 **Fax:** 30 8032049
Email: sugarindustry@bartens.com **Web site:** http://www.bartens.com
Freq: Monthly; **Annual Sub.:** EUR 345,00; **Circ:** 2,170
Editor: Jürgen Bruhns; **Advertising Manager:** Ilsa Diller
Profile: International magazine concerning the sugar and sweetener industry.
Language(s): English; French; German; Spanish
Readership: Aimed at those involved in the food industry.
ADVERTISING RATES:
Full Page Mono .... EUR 1470
Full Page Colour .... EUR 2130
Mechanical Data: Type Area: 260 x 183 mm, No. of Columns (Display): 2, Col Widths (Display): 89 mm
Copy instructions: *Copy Date:* 10 days prior to publication
Official Journal of: Organ d. Vereins d. Zuckerindustrie, d. Vereins Dt. Zuckertechniker u. d. Vereins d. Kaufleute d. Dt. Zuckerindustrie
Supplement(s): ZSB
BUSINESS: FOOD

SUIZIDPROPHYLAXE
743970G56A-9480
Editorial: In der Obern Au 12, 93055 REGENSBURG
Tel: 941 7992270 **Fax:** 941 795198
Email: info@roderer-verlag.de **Web site:** http://www.roderer-verlag.de
Freq: Quarterly; Free to qualifying individuals
Annual Sub.: EUR 84,00; **Circ:** 700
Editor: Hans Wedler
Profile: Official publication from the German and Austrian Association for Suicide Prevention.
Language(s): German
Mechanical Data: Type Area: 250 x 170 mm

SULCO
743971G21A-3800
Editorial: John-Deere-Str. 70, 68163 MANNHEIM
Tel: 621 8298416 **Fax:** 621 8298300
Email: hironjeanclaude@johndeere.com **Web site:** http://www.johndeere.com
Freq: Quarterly; **Cover Price:** Free; **Circ:** 25,000
Editor: Jean-Claude Hiron
Profile: Company publication published by Deere & Company.
Language(s): Portuguese

SULINGER KREISZEITUNG
743973G67B-14240
Editorial: Am Ristedter Weg 17, 28857 SYKE
Tel: 4242 58300 **Fax:** 4242 58332
Email: redaktion@kreiszeitung.de **Web site:** http://www.kreiszeitung.de
Freq: 312 issues yearly; **Circ:** 16,282
Advertising Manager: Axel Berghoff
Profile: The Kreiszeitung publishing group is the fifth largest newspaper in Niedersachsen, with a daily circulation of over 82,000 copies. Regional daily newspaper covering politics, economics, sport, travel and technology. Facebook: http://www.facebook.com/pages/Kreiszeitung Twitter: http://twitter.com/kreiszeitung This Outlet offers RSS (Really Simple Syndication).
Language(s): German
ADVERTISING RATES:
SCC .... EUR 53,60
Mechanical Data: Type Area: 472 x 325 mm, No. of Columns (Display): 7, Col Widths (Display): 45 mm
Copy instructions: *Copy Date:* 1 day prior to publication
REGIONAL DAILY & SUNDAY NEWSPAPERS: Regional Daily Newspapers

SULZBACH-ROSENBERGER ZEITUNG
743976G67B-14260
Editorial: Luitpoldplatz 22, 92237 SULZBACH-ROSENBERG **Tel:** 9661 872910 **Fax:** 9661 872933
Email: redsul@zeitung.org
Freq: 312 issues yearly; **Circ:** 7,076
Profile: Regional daily newspaper with news on politics, economy, culture, sports, travel, technology, etc. It is a regional edition of the newspaper "Der neue Tag". Facebook: http://www.facebook.com/oberpfalznetz Twitter: http://twitter.com/oberpfalznetz This Outlet offers RSS (Really Simple Syndication).
Language(s): German
ADVERTISING RATES:
SCC .... EUR 22,00
Mechanical Data: Type Area: 430 x 284 mm, No. of Columns (Display): 6, Col Widths (Display): 45 mm
Copy instructions: *Copy Date:* 1 day prior to publication
REGIONAL DAILY & SUNDAY NEWSPAPERS: Regional Daily Newspapers

SUN & WIND ENERGY
1646081G57-2723
Editorial: Niederwall 53, 33602 BIELEFELD
Tel: 521 595548 **Fax:** 521 595556
Email: vb@sunwindenergy.com **Web site:** http://www.sunwindenergy.com
Freq: Monthly; **Annual Sub.:** EUR 134,00; **Circ:** 25,000
Editor: Volker Buddensiek
Profile: Magazine with articles about solar heating, solar electricity, solar architecture, wind energy, biomass, Concentrated Solar Power. This Outlet offers RSS (Really Simple Syndication).
Language(s): English
ADVERTISING RATES:
Full Page Colour .... EUR 3470
Mechanical Data: Type Area: 260 x 190 mm
Copy instructions: *Copy Date:* 21 days prior to publication

SUPER FREIZEIT
1836367G74A-3598
Editorial: Rotweg 8, 76532 BADEN-BADEN
Tel: 7221 3501722 **Fax:** 7221 3501799
Email: manuela.hirn@klambt.de
Freq: Monthly; **Cover Price:** EUR 0,55; **Circ:** 380,000
Editor: Herbert Martin
Profile: Puzzle magazine for women.
Language(s): German
ADVERTISING RATES:
Full Page Mono .... EUR 6200
Full Page Colour .... EUR 6200
Mechanical Data: Type Area: 265 x 207 mm

SUPER ILLU
743994G73-400
Editorial: Zimmerstr. 28, 10969 BERLIN
Tel: 30 23876400 **Fax:** 30 23876496
Email: post@super-illu.de **Web site:** http://www.super-illu.de
Freq: Weekly; **Annual Sub.:** EUR 83,20; **Circ:** 383,519
Editor: Robert Schneider
Profile: Super illu is the most widely read consumer magazine in Eastern Germany and absolutely dominant with a record coverage of 22.8% in Eastern Germany. Super illu reports for the East Germans, not about them. Super illu presents the current mix of current affairs, politics, advice and entertainment. Facebook: http://www.facebook.com/superillu This Outlet offers RSS (Really Simple Syndication).
Language(s): German
ADVERTISING RATES:
Full Page Mono .... EUR 22200
Full Page Colour .... EUR 22200
Mechanical Data: Type Area: 289 x 191 mm, No. of Columns (Display): 4, Col Widths (Display): 44 mm
Copy instructions: *Copy Date:* 22 days prior to publication
CONSUMER: NATIONAL & INTERNATIONAL PERIODICALS

SUPER ILLU.DE
1622069G73-490
Editorial: Zimmerstr. 28, 10969 BERLIN
Tel: 30 23876400 **Fax:** 30 23876496
Email: post@super-illu.de **Web site:** http://www.super-illu.de
Freq: Daily; **Cover Price:** Paid; **Circ:** 380,799 Unique Users
Editor: Rex Jakob
Profile: Ezine: General interest illustrated magazine.
Language(s): German
CONSUMER: NATIONAL & INTERNATIONAL PERIODICALS

SUPER MITTWOCH - AUSG. STOLBERG
743998G72-13124
Editorial: Dresdener Str. 3, 52068 AACHEN
Tel: 241 5101590 **Fax:** 241 5101550
Email: info@supermittwoch.de **Web site:** http://www.supersonntag.de
Freq: Weekly; **Cover Price:** Free; **Circ:** 26,730
Editor: Astrid van Megeren; **Advertising Manager:** Jürgen Carduck
Profile: Advertising journal (house-to-house) concentrating on local stories.
Language(s): German
ADVERTISING RATES:
Full Page Mono .... EUR 1901
Full Page Colour .... EUR 2662
Mechanical Data: Type Area: 322 x 241 mm, No. of Columns (Display): 6, Col Widths (Display): 38 mm
Copy instructions: *Copy Date:* 2 days prior to publication
LOCAL NEWSPAPERS

SUPER SONNTAG - AUSG. ALSDORF - HERZOGENRATH
744001G72-13128
Editorial: Dresdener Str. 3, 52068 AACHEN
Tel: 241 5101591 **Fax:** 241 5101550
Email: info@supersonntag.de **Web site:** http://www.supersonntag.de
Freq: Weekly; **Cover Price:** Free; **Circ:** 96,350
Editor: Astrid van Megeren; **Advertising Manager:** Jürgen Carduck
Profile: Advertising journal (house-to-house) concentrating on local stories.
Language(s): German
ADVERTISING RATES:
Full Page Mono .... EUR 8268
Full Page Colour .... EUR 11575
Mechanical Data: Type Area: 480 x 323 mm, No. of Columns (Display): 8, Col Widths (Display): 38 mm
Copy instructions: *Copy Date:* 3 days prior to publication
LOCAL NEWSPAPERS

SUPER SONNTAG - AUSG. BENDORF
744014G72-13180
Editorial: Hinter der Jungenstr. 22, 56218 MÜLHEIM-KÄRLICH **Tel:** 261 928122 **Fax:** 261 928199
Email: kai-thomas.willig@vfa-online.de **Web site:** http://www.super-sonntag.com
Freq: Weekly; **Cover Price:** Free; **Circ:** 15,500
Editor: Kai-Thomas Willig; **Advertising Manager:** Detlev Ohlemacher
Profile: Advertising journal (house-to-house) concentrating on local stories.
Language(s): German
ADVERTISING RATES:
Full Page Mono .... EUR 3456
Mechanical Data: Type Area: 480 x 325 mm, No. of Columns (Display): 8, Col Widths (Display): 38 mm
Copy instructions: *Copy Date:* 2 days prior to publication
LOCAL NEWSPAPERS

SUPER SONNTAG - AUSG. DÜREN-JÜLICH
744002G72-13132
Editorial: Dresdener Str. 3, 52068 AACHEN
Tel: 241 5101591 **Fax:** 241 5101550
Email: info@supersonntag.de **Web site:** http://www.supersonntag.de
Freq: Weekly; **Cover Price:** Free; **Circ:** 118,350
Editor: Astrid van Megeren; **Advertising Manager:** Jürgen Carduck
Profile: Advertising journal (house-to-house) concentrating on local stories.
Language(s): German
ADVERTISING RATES:
Full Page Mono .... EUR 8945
Full Page Colour .... EUR 12523
Mechanical Data: Type Area: 480 x 323 mm, No. of Columns (Display): 8, Col Widths (Display): 38 mm
Copy instructions: *Copy Date:* 3 days prior to publication
LOCAL NEWSPAPERS

SUPER TRABI
744027G77A-2220
Editorial: Markt 9, 09456 ANNABERG-BUCHHOLZ
Tel: 3733 5002935 **Fax:** 3733 5002934
Email: o.seifert@erz-art.de **Web site:** http://www.supertrabi.de
Freq: 5 issues yearly; Free to qualifying individuals
Annual Sub.: EUR 18,00; **Circ:** 10,000
Editor: Olaf Seifert; **Advertising Manager:** Gerd Mädler
Profile: Magazine for Trabant car fans.
Language(s): German
ADVERTISING RATES:
Full Page Mono .... EUR 1600
Full Page Colour .... EUR 2556
Mechanical Data: Type Area: 270 x 182 mm, No. of Columns (Display): 4, Col Widths (Display): 42 mm
Copy instructions: *Copy Date:* 14 days prior to publication

SUPER TROOPER
748442G40-840
Editorial: Marlener Str. 2, 77656 OFFENBURG
Tel: 781 955042 **Fax:** 781 955050
Email: redaktion@super-trooper.com **Web site:** http://www.super-trooper.com
Freq: Quarterly; **Cover Price:** Free; **Circ:** 35,000
Editor: Marco Wirth
Profile: Journal of soldiers from 18-48 years. Free delivery in the HBG-cafeterias of the army barracks.
Language(s): German
ADVERTISING RATES:
Full Page Mono .... EUR 3000
Full Page Colour .... EUR 3000
Mechanical Data: Type Area: 240 x 186 mm

SUPPLY
722566G10-40
Editorial: Ernst-Mey-Str. 8, 70771 LEINFELDEN-ECHTERDINGEN **Tel:** 711 7594431
Fax: 711 7594221
Email: ba.redaktion@konradin.de **Web site:** http://www.beschaffung-aktuell.de
Freq: Annual; **Circ:** 11,000
Editor: Daniel Zabota; **Advertising Manager:** Klaus-Dieter Mehnert
Profile: With the special publication "Supply" - The partners in the procurement Beschaffung aktuell serves the information needs of readers regarding vendors, service providers and products. Supply company information conveyed to the purchasing decision makers and is a source of inspiration for future procurement needs.
Language(s): German
ADVERTISING RATES:
Full Page Colour .... EUR 3460
Mechanical Data: Type Area: 270 x 188 mm
Copy instructions: *Copy Date:* 35 days prior to publication
Supplement to: Beschaffung aktuell

SUPPORTIVE CARE IN CANCER
744030G56A-9500
Editorial: Tiergartenstr. 17, 69121 HEIDELBERG
Tel: 6221 4870 **Fax:** 6221 4878366
Email: subscriptions@springer.com **Web site:** http://www.springerlink.com
Freq: Monthly; **Annual Sub.:** EUR 1089,00; **Circ:** 1,089
Editor: H. J. Senn
Profile: Official journal of the Multinational Association of Supportive Care in Cancer (MASCC). Aims at interested individuals, groups and institutions with scientific and social information on all aspects of supportive care in cancer patients. Covers medical, te.
Language(s): English
ADVERTISING RATES:
Full Page Mono .... EUR 1040
Full Page Colour .... EUR 2080
Mechanical Data: Type Area: 240 x 175 mm
Official Journal of: Organ d. Multinational Association of Supportive Care in Cancer

SURF
744032G75M-760
Editorial: Steinerstr. 15, 81369 MÜNCHEN
Tel: 89 7296010 **Fax:** 89 72960111
Email: teams@surf-magazin.de **Web site:** http://www.surf-magazin.de
Freq: 10 issues yearly; **Annual Sub.:** EUR 42,00; **Circ:** 22,411
Editor: Andreas Erbe; **Advertising Manager:** Ingo van Holt
Profile: Magazine about windsurfing. SURF embodies the true spirit and magic of this sport. Today the magazine is one of the best known brands in the industry. The editorial team's fearless unconventional style has influenced the surfing scene for decades. Incisive editorial combined with breathtaking photography of awesome destinations.
Language(s): German
Readership: Aimed at people interested in water sports .
ADVERTISING RATES:
Full Page Mono .... EUR 7100
Full Page Colour .... EUR 7100
Mechanical Data: Type Area: 254 x 192 mm, No. of Columns (Display): 4, Col Widths (Display): 45 mm
Copy instructions: *Copy Date:* 42 days prior to publication
CONSUMER: SPORT: Water Sports

SURFERS
744034G75M-780
Editorial: Gabelsbergerstr. 36, 80333 MÜNCHEN
Tel: 40 48000778 **Fax:** 89 54272080
Email: info@surfersmag.de **Web site:** http://www.surfersmag.de
Freq: 5 issues yearly; **Annual Sub.:** EUR 16,00; **Circ:** 38,887
Editor: Lars Jacobsen
Profile: Surfers with exciting interviews, the latest product news, photos and unique sequences, it is the biggest, most credible and most prestigious magazine of the German surf scene. Facebook: http://www.facebook.com/surfersmag Twitter: http://twitter.com/#!/surfersmag This Outlet offers RSS (Really Simple Syndication).
Language(s): German
CONSUMER: SPORT: Water Sports

SUS SCHWEINEZUCHT UND SCHWEINEMAST
744040G21D-9
Editorial: Hülsebrockstr. 2, 48165 MÜNSTER
Tel: 2501 801640 **Fax:** 2501 801654
Email: susredaktion@lv.de **Web site:** http://www.susonline.de
Freq: 6 issues yearly; **Annual Sub.:** EUR 43,80; **Circ:** 14,811
Editor: Heinrich Niggemeyer; **Advertising Manager:** Peter Wiggers
Profile: Publication about pig breeding, pig disease, management and feeding.
Language(s): German
Readership: Aimed at pig owners, advisors, veterinary surgeons and authorities.
ADVERTISING RATES:
Full Page Mono .... EUR 2985
Full Page Colour .... EUR 4953
Mechanical Data: Type Area: 270 x 190 mm, No. of Columns (Display): 4, Col Widths (Display): 46 mm
Copy instructions: *Copy Date:* 21 days prior to publication
Official Journal of: Organ d. Zentralverb. d. Dt. Schweineproduktion e.V.
BUSINESS: AGRICULTURE & FARMING: Livestock

SVK SÜDDEUTSCHER VERKEHRSKURIER
743901G49A-1700
Editorial: Leonrodstr. 48, 80636 MÜNCHEN
Tel: 89 12662934 **Fax:** 89 12662925
Email: svk@lbt.de **Web site:** http://www.lbt.de
Freq: Monthly; **Circ:** 3,895
Editor: Christian Durmann; **Advertising Manager:** Christian Durmann
Profile: Journal concerning transport in Southern Germany.
Language(s): German
ADVERTISING RATES:
Full Page Mono .... EUR 1278
Full Page Colour .... EUR 2337
Mechanical Data: Type Area: 240 x 175 mm, No. of Columns (Display): 3, Col Widths (Display): 57 mm
Copy instructions: *Copy Date:* 20 days prior to publication
BUSINESS: TRANSPORT

SVR STRASSENVERKEHRSRECHT
1657535G1A-3568
Editorial: Bunsenstr. 18, 69115 HEIDELBERG
Email: wferner@ferner.de **Web site:** http://www.strassenverkehrsrecht-online.de
Freq: Monthly; **Annual Sub.:** EUR 177,11; **Circ:** 1,000
Editor: Wolfgang Ferner

Profile: Magazine for traffic lawyers.
Language(s): German
ADVERTISING RATES:
Full Page Mono .... EUR 650
Full Page Colour .... EUR 1775
Mechanical Data: Type Area: 250 x 185 mm
Copy instructions: *Copy Date:* 30 days prior to publication

SWISS QUALITY PRODUCTION
1660365G19E-1879
Editorial: Kolbergerstr. 22, 81679 MÜNCHEN
Tel: 89 99830682 **Fax:** 89 99830623
Email: hobohm@hanser.de **Web site:** http://www.hanser.de
Freq: Annual; **Cover Price:** EUR 20,00; **Circ:** 20,000
Editor: Michael Hobohm; **Advertising Manager:** Dietmar von der Au
Profile: For over 20 years, accompanied the publication of Schweizer Präzisions-Fertigungstechnik export activities of the Swiss machine tool industry. In cooperation with the SWISSMEM the Schweizer Präzisions-Fertigungstechnik reports in detail and hands-on innovative metal-cutting methods and trends in manufacturing technology for the industrial metal.
Language(s): English
ADVERTISING RATES:
Full Page Mono .... EUR 4300
Full Page Colour .... EUR 7000
Mechanical Data: Type Area: 250 x 175 mm, No. of Columns (Display): 4, Col Widths (Display): 41 mm
Copy instructions: *Copy Date:* 34 days prior to publication
Supplement to: Schweizer Präzisions-Fertigungstechnik

DER SYBURGER
744154G77B-470
Editorial: Hertinger Str. 60, 59423 UNNA
Tel: 2303 985531 **Fax:** 2303 985309
Email: efoe@syburger.de **Web site:** http://www.syburger.de
Freq: Monthly; **Annual Sub.:** EUR 19,20; **Circ:** 33,000
Editor: Erik Förster; **Advertising Manager:** Jessica Kwasny
Profile: Motorcycle magazine for the Ruhrgebiet, Niederrhein, Münsterland, Siegen, Sauerland. The editorial focus is on regional news, plus get driving reports, tests, and travel. The magazine for active bikers, because they only exist in the motorcycle trade and meeting places.
Language(s): German
ADVERTISING RATES:
Full Page Mono .... EUR 1093
Full Page Colour .... EUR 1530
Mechanical Data: Type Area: 232 x 155 mm, No. of Columns (Display): 3, Col Widths (Display): 48 mm
CONSUMER: MOTORING & CYCLING: Motorcycling

SYLT GEHT AUS!
1819996G89A-12370
Editorial: Höherweg 287, 40231 DÜSSELDORF
Tel: 211 7357681 **Fax:** 211 7357680
Email: info@ueberblick.de **Web site:** http://www.ueberblick.de
Freq: Annual; **Cover Price:** EUR 7,80; **Circ:** 30,000
Editor: Britta Schmidt
Profile: Restaurant guide for Sylt.
Language(s): German
ADVERTISING RATES:
Full Page Mono .... EUR 2060
Full Page Colour .... EUR 3070
Mechanical Data: Type Area: 260 x 190 mm, No. of Columns (Display): 4, Col Widths (Display): 44 mm
Copy instructions: *Copy Date:* 30 days prior to publication

SYLT MAGAZIN
744157G89A-12117
Editorial: Gärtnerkoppel 3, 24259 WESTENSEE
Tel: 4305 992992 **Fax:** 4305 992993
Email: gkprkiel@t-online.de **Web site:** http://www.syltmagazin.de
Freq: Annual; **Cover Price:** EUR 7,00; **Circ:** 40,000
Editor: Günter Kohl
Profile: Magazine for tourists and islanders with tips, trends and events, reports, nature and environment, lifestyle, restaurants, addresses, news, celebrity talk.
Language(s): German
ADVERTISING RATES:
Full Page Colour .... EUR 3230
Mechanical Data: Type Area: 270 x 185 mm

SYLTER RUNDSCHAU
744158G67B-14280
Editorial: Nikolaistr. 7, 24937 FLENSBURG
Tel: 461 8080 **Fax:** 461 8081058
Email: redaktion@shz.de **Web site:** http://www.shz.de
Freq: 312 issues yearly; **Circ:** 5,786
Advertising Manager: Ingeborg Schwarz
Profile: The history of "Sylter Rundschau" dates back to 1865. Since 1971, the newspaper is part of the sh:z. The newspaper is now with the Islanders as in Sylt guests alike. Many of them can be the "Sylter Rundschau" even send home. Facebook: http://www.facebook.com/shzonline Twitter: http://twitter.com/shz_de This Outlet offers RSS (Really Simple Syndication).
Language(s): German
ADVERTISING RATES:
SCC .... EUR 44,40
Mechanical Data: Type Area: 480 x 325 mm, No. of Columns (Display): 7, Col Widths (Display): 45 mm
Copy instructions: *Copy Date:* 1 day prior to publication
Supplement(s): nordisch gesund; Schleswig-Holstein Journal; tv magazin
REGIONAL DAILY & SUNDAY NEWSPAPERS: Regional Daily Newspapers

SYLTER SPIEGEL
744159G72-13244
Editorial: Bomhoffstr. 2, 25980 WESTERLAND
Tel: 4651 26166 **Fax:** 4651 24400
Email: info@sylterspiegel.de **Web site:** http://www.sylterspiegel.de
Freq: Weekly; **Cover Price:** Free; **Circ:** 20,000
Editor: Christiane Retzlaff; **Advertising Manager:** Frank Rasmußen
Profile: Advertising journal (house-to-house) concentrating on local stories.
Language(s): German
ADVERTISING RATES:
Full Page Mono .... EUR 2672
Full Page Colour .... EUR 2810
Mechanical Data: Type Area: 420 x 280 mm, No. of Columns (Display): 6, Col Widths (Display): 45 mm
Copy instructions: *Copy Date:* 2 days prior to publication
LOCAL NEWSPAPERS

SYMPRAXIS
744164G2A-4620
Editorial: Stafflenbergstr. 32, 70184 STUTTGART
Tel: 711 947670 **Fax:** 711 9476787
Email: pr@sympra.de **Web site:** http://www.sympra.de
Freq: Annual; **Circ:** 1,000
Editor: Veit Mathauer
Profile: Company publication published by Sympra.
Language(s): German

SYNFACTS
1703055G37-1828
Editorial: Rüdigerstr. 14, 70469 STUTTGART
Tel: 711 8931786 **Fax:** 711 8931777
Email: susanne.haak@thieme.de **Web site:** http://www.thieme-chemistry.com/de/formate/zeitschriften/synfacts.html
Freq: Monthly; **Annual Sub.:** EUR 347,60; **Circ:** 600
Editor: Susanne Haak
Profile: In Synfacts current research results in synthetic organic chemistry, as they appear in the primary literature, are screened, selected, evaluated, summarized, and enriched with personal comments by experts in their fields.
Language(s): English
ADVERTISING RATES:
Full Page Mono .... EUR 770
Full Page Colour .... EUR 1460
Mechanical Data: Type Area: 250 x 175 mm, No. of Columns (Display): 4, Col Widths (Display): 40 mm

SYNLETT
756623G37-1722
Editorial: Rüdigerstr. 14, 70469 STUTTGART
Tel: 711 8931786 **Fax:** 711 8931777
Email: susanne.haak@thieme.de **Web site:** http://www.thieme-chemistry.com/de/formate/zeitschriften/synlett.html
Freq: 20 issues yearly; **Annual Sub.:** EUR 335,90; **Circ:** 1,310
Editor: Susanne Haak
Profile: Synlett is an international journal reporting research results and trends in synthetic organic chemistry in short personalized reviews and preliminary communications.
Language(s): English
ADVERTISING RATES:
Full Page Mono .... EUR 1410
Full Page Colour .... EUR 2550
Mechanical Data: Type Area: 250 x 175 mm, No. of Columns (Display): 4, Col Widths (Display): 40 mm

SYNTHESIS
756624G37-1723
Editorial: Rüdigerstr. 14, 70469 STUTTGART
Tel: 711 8931786 **Fax:** 711 8931777
Email: susanne.haak@thieme.de **Web site:** http://www.thieme-chemistry.com/en/products/journals/synthesis.html
Freq: 24 issues yearly; **Annual Sub.:** EUR 500,90; **Circ:** 1,600
Editor: Susanne Haak
Profile: Synthesis is a journal of international character devoted to the advancement of the science of synthetic chemistry, covering all fields of organic chemistry, including organometallic, medicinal, biological, and photochemistry, but also related disciplines.
Language(s): English
ADVERTISING RATES:
Full Page Mono .... EUR 1330
Full Page Colour .... EUR 2470
Mechanical Data: Type Area: 250 x 175 mm, No. of Columns (Display): 4, Col Widths (Display): 40 mm

SZ SEGEBERGER ZEITUNG
744194G67B-14300
Editorial: Hamburger Str. 26, 23795 BAD SEGEBERG **Tel:** 4551 9040 **Fax:** 4551 90483
Email: redaktion@segeberger-zeitung.de **Web site:** http://www.segeberger-zeitung.de
Freq: 312 issues yearly; **Circ:** 12,110
Editor: Stephan Ures; **Advertising Manager:** Thorsten Dücker
Profile: Daily newspaper with regional news and a local sports section. This Outlet offers RSS (Really Simple Syndication).
Language(s): German
ADVERTISING RATES:
SCC .... EUR 47,40
Mechanical Data: Type Area: 430 x 281 mm, No. of Columns (Display): 7, Col Widths (Display): 45 mm
Copy instructions: *Copy Date:* 1 day prior to publication
REGIONAL DAILY & SUNDAY NEWSPAPERS: Regional Daily Newspapers

SZ SINDELFINGER ZEITUNG
744195G67B-14320
Editorial: Böblinger Str. 76, 71065 SINDELFINGEN
Tel: 7031 862210 **Fax:** 7031 862202
Email: redaktion@szbz.de **Web site:** http://www.szbz.de
Freq: 312 issues yearly; **Circ:** 12,333
Editor: Jürgen Haar; **Advertising Manager:** Gabriele Karl
Profile: Daily newspaper with regional news and a local sports section. Facebook: http://www.facebook.com/szbz.de?ref=search&sid=1469388759.4198281248..1 Twitter: http://twitter.com/SZBZ This Outlet offers RSS (Really Simple Syndication).
Language(s): German
ADVERTISING RATES:
SCC .... EUR 43,20
Mechanical Data: Type Area: 485 x 320 mm, No. of Columns (Display): 7, Col Widths (Display): 44 mm
Copy instructions: *Copy Date:* 1 day prior to publication
REGIONAL DAILY & SUNDAY NEWSPAPERS: Regional Daily Newspapers

SZ SINDELFINGER ZEITUNG BZ BÖBLINGER ZEITUNG
744196G67B-14340
Editorial: Böblinger Str. 76, 71065 SINDELFINGEN
Tel: 7031 862210 **Fax:** 7031 862202
Email: redaktion@szbz.de **Web site:** http://www.szbz.de
Freq: 312 issues yearly; **Circ:** 12,333
Advertising Manager: Gabriele Karl
Profile: Daily newspaper with regional news and a local sports section. Facebook: http://www.facebook.com/szbz.de?ref=search&sid=1469388759.4198281248..1 Twitter: http://twitter.com/SZBZ This Outlet offers RSS (Really Simple Syndication).
Language(s): German
ADVERTISING RATES:
SCC .... EUR 43,20
Mechanical Data: Type Area: 485 x 320 mm, No. of Columns (Display): 7, Col Widths (Display): 44 mm
Copy instructions: *Copy Date:* 1 day prior to publication
REGIONAL DAILY & SUNDAY NEWSPAPERS: Regional Daily Newspapers

SZENE HAMBURG ESSEN + TRINKEN
1825375G89A-12377
Editorial: Behringstr. 14, 22765 HAMBURG
Tel: 40 4328420 **Fax:** 40 43284230
Email: sonderobjekte@szene-hamburg.de **Web site:** http://www.szene-hamburg.de
Freq: Annual; **Cover Price:** EUR 7,90; **Circ:** 30,000
Editor: Lisa Scheide; **Advertising Manager:** Christian Kröger
Profile: Gastronomy guide for Hamburg.
Language(s): German
ADVERTISING RATES:
Full Page Mono .... EUR 1840
Full Page Colour .... EUR 3200
Mechanical Data: Type Area: 260 x 190 mm, No. of Columns (Display): 4, Col Widths (Display): 44 mm
Copy instructions: *Copy Date:* 30 days prior to publication

SZENE HAMBURG KAUFT EIN!
1826353G89A-12388
Editorial: Behringstr. 14, 22765 HAMBURG
Tel: 40 4328420 **Fax:** 40 43284230
Email: sonderobjekte@szene-hamburg.de **Web site:** http://www.szene-hamburg.de
Freq: Annual; **Cover Price:** EUR 6,00; **Circ:** 20,000
Editor: Lisa Scheide; **Advertising Manager:** Christian Kröger
Profile: Shopping guide for Hamburg. It includes reports on the latest fashion trends, reports on interesting companies, interviews with regional personalities and those which will be soon. But it also navigates you safely through the city in the world of fashion, jewelry, beauty, sport, audio recordings, children, furniture and more. The best shopping areas in the annual bulletin, clearly organized by category, are presented and are of course provided with address, phone, opening times and web address. The guide is an excellent guide for bargain hunters, trend scouts, newcomers, shoppers and shopping experts. He always appears in the commercial end of November, but can also be purchased over the Internet.
Language(s): German
ADVERTISING RATES:
Full Page Mono .... EUR 1840
Full Page Colour .... EUR 2990
Mechanical Data: Type Area: 260 x 190 mm, No. of Columns (Display): 4, Col Widths (Display): 44 mm
Copy instructions: *Copy Date:* 30 days prior to publication

SZENE KÖLN / BONN
744182G80-11180
Editorial: Rheinallee 71, 53173 BONN
Tel: 228 363433 **Fax:** 228 363401
Email: e.breinlinger@szeneonline.de **Web site:** http://www.szeneonline.de
Freq: Monthly; **Cover Price:** Free; **Circ:** 10,000
Editor: Eberhard A. Breinlinger; **Advertising Manager:** Eberhard A. Breinlinger
Profile: City magazine presenting items on events, new books, comics, CDs, computer and cinema news.
Language(s): German
Readership: Read by people between 15 to 45 years of age with a high disposable income.
ADVERTISING RATES:
Full Page Mono .... EUR 595
Full Page Colour .... EUR 1239
Mechanical Data: Type Area: 190 x 135 mm, No. of Columns (Display): 3, Col Widths (Display): 43 mm
Copy instructions: *Copy Date:* 15 days prior to publication
CONSUMER: RURAL & REGIONAL INTEREST

SZENE KULTUR
744187G80-11220
Editorial: Poststr. 11, 88239 WANGEN
Tel: 7522 795030 **Fax:** 7522 795050
Email: redaktion@szene-kultur.de **Web site:** http://www.szene-kultur.de
Freq: 11 issues yearly; **Cover Price:** Free; **Circ:** 16,000
Editor: Michael Pertl; **Advertising Manager:** Michael Pertl
Profile: Magazine for the regions of Allgäu, Bodensee and Ravensburg.
Language(s): German
Readership: Read by local residents.
ADVERTISING RATES:
Full Page Mono .... EUR 890
Full Page Colour .... EUR 1150
Mechanical Data: Type Area: 270 x 190 mm
Copy instructions: *Copy Date:* 15 days prior to publication
CONSUMER: RURAL & REGIONAL INTEREST

SZENE LÜBECK
744188G89C-4830
Editorial: Langenfelde 11, 23611 BAD SCHWARTAU
Tel: 451 21047 **Fax:** 451 26039
Email: lokamedia@arcor.de **Web site:** http://www.szeneluebeck.de
Freq: Monthly; **Cover Price:** Free; **Circ:** 14,640
Editor: Lothar Kruse
Profile: Magazine containing information about entertainment and local events in Luebeck and the surrounding districts.
Language(s): German
Readership: Aimed at visitors and local residents.
ADVERTISING RATES:
Full Page Mono .... EUR 1000
Full Page Colour .... EUR 1400
Mechanical Data: Type Area: 265 x 184 mm
CONSUMER: HOLIDAYS & TRAVEL: Entertainment Guides

SZENE ROSTOCK
744190G89C-4831
Editorial: Wollenweberstr. 59, 18055 ROSTOCK
Tel: 381 37706965 **Fax:** 381 37706961
Email: katharina.leppin@szenerostock.de **Web site:** http://www.szenerostock.de
Freq: Monthly; **Cover Price:** Free; **Circ:** 15,000
Editor: Katharina Leppin; **Advertising Manager:** Helge Joswig
Profile: Magazine containing information about entertainment and local events in Rostock.
Language(s): German
Readership: Aimed at visitors and local residents.
ADVERTISING RATES:
Full Page Mono .... EUR 1100
Full Page Colour .... EUR 1600
Mechanical Data: Type Area: 297 x 210 mm
Copy instructions: *Copy Date:* 15 days prior to publication
CONSUMER: HOLIDAYS & TRAVEL: Entertainment Guides

SZ-ONLINE.DE
1622083G67B-16669
Editorial: Ostra-Allee 20, 01067 DRESDEN
Tel: 351 48642601 **Fax:** 351 48642606
Email: presse@sz-online.de **Web site:** http://www.sz-online.de
Freq: Daily; **Cover Price:** Paid; **Circ:** 1,907,269 Unique Users
Editor: Mirko Jakubowsky; **Advertising Manager:** Norbert Föckel
Profile: Online portal of Sächsische Zeitung. On more than 2000 individual sites let users find not only the latest news and photo galleries from Saxony and the world. With its numerous service and shopping offers from the ticket service to the travel booking and available on the website portals, satellite is the first stop portal on the web. Facebook: http://www.facebook.com/szonline Twitter: http://twitter.com/#!/szonline This Outlet offers RSS (Really Simple Syndication).
Language(s): German
REGIONAL DAILY & SUNDAY NEWSPAPERS: Regional Daily Newspapers

TAB
744203G4F-12
Editorial: Avenwedder Str. 55, 33335 GÜTERSLOH
Tel: 5241 807958 **Fax:** 5241 8067958

Email: christoph.brauneis@bauverlag.de **Web site:** http://www.tab.de
Freq: 11 issues yearly; **Annual Sub.:** EUR 148,80; **Circ:** 10,423
Editor: Christoph Brauneis; **Advertising Manager:** Herbert Walhorn
Profile: The TAB Technik am Bau is one of the leading journals of the technical building equipment. It is a forum of the substantive discussion. TAB engineers for heating, ventilation, air conditioning, refrigeration, plumbing and electrical are intermediaries between innovation and application, between industry, planning and practice. The editorial approach corresponds to the profile of the TAB readers: In each issue a comprehensive structural analysis appears under the aspect of the whole technology upgrades with pictures, tables, laying plans, circuit diagrams and scale, in their own characters studio-built drawings. This takes the TAB a special position, so that it is used by professionals as a permanent equipment in daily practice. Tailored to the varied activities of the TAB engineers, the technical papers will be processed accordingly and published exclusively in the TAB. Recent reports and the presentation of new products complement each issue the editorial environment. This Outlet offers RSS (Really Simple Syndication).
Language(s): German
Readership: Aimed at builders and property owners.
ADVERTISING RATES:
Full Page Mono .... EUR 4090
Full Page Colour .... EUR 5710
Mechanical Data: Type Area: 270 x 186 mm, No. of Columns (Display): 4, Col Widths (Display): 45 mm
Copy instructions: *Copy Date:* 14 days prior to publication
Official Journal of: Organ d. Bundesindustrieverb. Heizung-, Klima-, Sanitärtechnik/Techn. Gebäudesysteme e.V.
Supplement(s): Brandschutz in öffentlichen und privatwirtschaftlichen Gebäuden; computer spezial; RE Regenerative Energien
BUSINESS: ARCHITECTURE & BUILDING: Cleaning & Maintenance

TACHO METER 744206G31R-28

Editorial: Gerresheimer Landstr. 119, 40627 DÜSSELDORF **Tel:** 211 925950 **Fax:** 211 9259590
Email: info@kfz-nrw.de
Freq: 10 issues yearly; Free to qualifying individuals
Annual Sub.: EUR 35,00; **Circ:** 7,364
Profile: Magazine about the motor industry in Nordrhein- Westfalen.
Language(s): German
ADVERTISING RATES:
Full Page Mono .... EUR 2050
Full Page Colour .... EUR 2050
Mechanical Data: Type Area: 255 x 178 mm, No. of Columns (Display): 4, Col Widths (Display): 45 mm
Copy instructions: *Copy Date:* 21 days prior to publication
BUSINESS: MOTOR TRADE: Motor Trade Related

TAG DES HERRN 744215G87-12000

Editorial: Stammerstr. 11, 04159 LEIPZIG
Tel: 341 4677729 **Fax:** 341 467777809
Email: tdh@st-benno.de **Web site:** http://www.tag-des-herrn.de
Freq: Weekly; **Circ:** 24,419
Editor: Matthias Holluba; **Advertising Manager:** Maria Körner
Profile: Magazine for Catholic Christians in the dioceses of Dresden-Meissen.
Language(s): German
ADVERTISING RATES:
Full Page Mono .... EUR 3360
Full Page Colour .... EUR 5040
Mechanical Data: Type Area: 480 x 325 mm, No. of Columns (Display): 7, Col Widths (Display): 43 mm
Copy instructions: *Copy Date:* 10 days prior to publication
CONSUMER: RELIGIOUS

TAGEBLATT FÜR DEN KREIS STEINFURT 744218G67B-14360

Editorial: Bahnhofstr. 18, 48607 OCHTRUP
Tel: 2553 939434 **Fax:** 2553 939467
Email: redaktion@tageblatt-online.de **Web site:** http://www.tageblatt-online.de
Freq: 312 issues yearly; **Circ:** 4,205
Advertising Manager: Ulrich Mikat
Profile: Daily newspaper with regional news and a local sports section.
Language(s): German
ADVERTISING RATES:
SCC .... EUR 20,10
Mechanical Data: Type Area: 488 x 324 mm, No. of Columns (Display): 7, Col Widths (Display): 44 mm
Copy instructions: *Copy Date:* 1 day prior to publication
Supplement(s): prisma
REGIONAL DAILY & SUNDAY NEWSPAPERS: Regional Daily Newspapers

---

DIE TAGESPOST 744221G65A-200

Editorial: Dominikanerplatz 8, 97070 WÜRZBURG
Tel: 931 3086310 **Fax:** 931 3086333
Email: info@die-tagespost.de **Web site:** http://www.die-tagespost.de
Freq: 104 issues yearly; **Circ:** 11,658
Editor: Markus Reder; **News Editor:** Markus Reder; **Advertising Manager:** Anja Stichnoth
Profile: For more than 60 years"DIE TAGESPOST" informs on Tuesdays, Thursdays and Saturdays about facts from the church, politics, society and culture from a Catholicpoint of view. A special attention is paid to the exclusive Vatican Special. To provide guidance and to address questions of faith is a priority for the newspaper. "DIE TAGESPOST" is the only Catholic daily newspaper in the German language area, readers are Catholics who are deeply rooted in the faith of the Church.
Language(s): German
ADVERTISING RATES:
SCC .... EUR 10,90
Mechanical Data: Type Area: 465 x 320 mm, No. of Columns (Display): 7, Col Widths (Display): 44 mm
Copy instructions: *Copy Date:* 6 days prior to publication
NATIONAL DAILY & SUNDAY NEWSPAPERS: National Daily Newspapers

---

DER TAGESSPIEGEL 744222G67B-14380

Editorial: Askanischer Platz 3, 10963 BERLIN
Tel: 30 2902114005 **Fax:** 30 2902199914090
Email: redaktion@tagesspiegel.de **Web site:** http://www.tagesspiegel.de
Freq: 364 issues yearly; **Circ:** 132,683
Editor: Stephan-Andreas Casdorff; **News Editor:** Lutz Haverkamp; **Advertising Manager:** Jens Robotta
Profile: Regional daily newspaper with news on politics, economy, culture, sports, travel, technology, etc. Facebook: http://www.facebook.com/pages/Tagesspiegelde/59381221492 Twitter: http://twitter.com/tagesspiegel_de This Outlet offers RSS (Really Simple Syndication).
Language(s): German
ADVERTISING RATES:
SCC .... EUR 161,00
Mechanical Data: Type Area: 528 x 370 mm, No. of Columns (Display): 8, Col Widths (Display): 45 mm
Copy instructions: *Copy Date:* 1 day prior to publication
Supplement(s): Berliner Zugpferde; chrismon; doppio; Potsdam Tipps; Ticket
REGIONAL DAILY & SUNDAY NEWSPAPERS: Regional Daily Newspapers

---

DER TAGESSPIEGEL ONLINE 1622092G67B-16674

Editorial: Askanischer Platz 3, 10963 BERLIN
Tel: 30 2902114015
Email: online-redaktion@tagesspiegel.de **Web site:** http://www.tagesspiegel.de
Freq: Daily; **Cover Price:** Paid; **Circ:** 5,098,061 Unique Users
Editor: Markus Hesselmann
Profile: Ezine: Tagesspiegel.de is the ultimate platform for Berlin. Who or what is important in the capital is to be found. Fast, high-quality news in politics, economy and culture make tagesspiegel.de to opinion-forming media in Berlin and Germany. Facebook: http://www.facebook.com/pages/Tagesspiegelde/59381221492 Twitter: http://twitter.com/tagesspiegel_de This Outlet offers RSS (Really Simple Syndication).
Language(s): German
REGIONAL DAILY & SUNDAY NEWSPAPERS: Regional Daily Newspapers

---

TÄGLICHER ANZEIGER 744209G67B-14400

Editorial: Zeppelinstr. 10, 37603 HOLZMINDEN
Tel: 5531 93040 **Fax:** 5531 930442
Email: redaktion@tah.de **Web site:** http://www.tah.de
Freq: 312 issues yearly; **Circ:** 10,652
Editor: K. Mahnkopf; **Advertising Manager:** Karl Niebergall
Profile: The Täglicher Anzeiger is the leading advertising medium and the highest circulation daily newspaper in the district of Holzminden. The Täglicher Anzeiger is the Gazette of the city and the county of Holzminden, the district courts, the Tax Office and other agencies. This Outlet offers RSS (Really Simple Syndication).
Language(s): German
ADVERTISING RATES:
SCC .... EUR 18,80
Mechanical Data: Type Area: 430 x 277 mm, No. of Columns (Display): 6, Col Widths (Display): 45 mm
Copy instructions: *Copy Date:* 2 days prior to publication
REGIONAL DAILY & SUNDAY NEWSPAPERS: Regional Daily Newspapers

---

TAGNACHT 744225G89A-11020

Editorial: Maastrichter Str. 49, 50672 KÖLN
Tel: 221 95154126 **Fax:** 221 95154111
Email: tagnacht@stadtrevue.de **Web site:** http://www.stadtrevue.de
Freq: Annual; **Cover Price:** EUR 9,80; **Circ:** 25,000
Editor: Bernd Wilberg; **Advertising Manager:** Michael Meiger
Profile: Gastronomy and city guide for Cologne.
Language(s): German
ADVERTISING RATES:
Full Page Mono .... EUR 2930
Full Page Colour .... EUR 4210
Mechanical Data: Type Area: 300 x 224 mm
Copy instructions: *Copy Date:* 65 days prior to publication

TAGUNGSHOTELS 1740113G89A-12233

Editorial: Schleefstr. 1, 44287 DORTMUND
Tel: 231 444770 **Fax:** 231 4447777
Email: hauptredaktion@busche.de **Web site:** http://www.tagungshotels.de
Freq: Annual; **Cover Price:** Free; **Circ:** 40,674
Advertising Manager: Jörg Leu
Profile: International reference for selecting the right conference hotel. The catalog is based on meeting the needs of decision makers. Conference hotels in Germany and neighboring European countries are presented clearly with numerous illustrations. The advantages of the presented conference hotels and the facilities subject to the reader immediately into the eye. A map section with location-specific hotel and a hotel matrix entries with relevant information and meeting facilities complement the product. The catalog is an indispensable intermediary between industry and hotel industry.
Language(s): German
ADVERTISING RATES:
Full Page Mono .... EUR 4200
Full Page Colour .... EUR 4200
Mechanical Data: Type Area: 276 x 208 mm

TAGUNGSPLANER.DE 741423G14A-6480

Editorial: Friedrichstr. 76, 10117 BERLIN
Tel: 30 20625900 **Fax:** 30 206259400
Email: info@mice.ag **Web site:** http://www.tagungsplaner.de
Freq: Annual; **Cover Price:** Free; **Circ:** 37,900
Profile: The Practical Guide tagungsplaner.de is the indispensable planning tool for planners, organizers and purchasers of events. tagungsplaner.de is considered most used reference book of the event industry.
Language(s): German
BUSINESS: COMMERCE, INDUSTRY & MANAGEMENT

TAIWAN CONTACT 1799539G14C-4772

Editorial: Ritterstr. 2b, 10969 BERLIN
Tel: 30 61508926 **Fax:** 30 61508927
Email: pt@owc.de **Web site:** http://www.owc.de
Freq: Annual; **Cover Price:** Free; **Circ:** 9,000
Editor: Peter Tichauer; **Advertising Manager:** Norbert Mayer
Profile: Magazine focusing on future business negotiations with Taiwan. Also contains market analyses and trends.
Language(s): German
ADVERTISING RATES:
Full Page Mono .... EUR 2500
Full Page Colour .... EUR 3200
Mechanical Data: Type Area: 265 x 175 mm
Supplement to: China Contact

TAKE! 744232G74F-153

Editorial: Luisenstr. 88, 53721 SIEGBURG
Tel: 2241 66115 **Fax:** 2241 67862
Email: redaktion@take-online.de **Web site:** http://www.take-online.de
Freq: Quarterly; **Cover Price:** Free; **Circ:** 18,400
Editor: Patrick Schaab
Profile: Magazine for young people about lifestyle, fashion, multimedia, fitness, films and travel.
Language(s): German
CONSUMER: WOMEN'S INTEREST CONSUMER MAGAZINES: Teenage

T>AKT 756626G80-13567

Editorial: Zittauer Str. 30, 99091 ERFURT
Tel: 361 7308880 **Fax:** 361 7308885
Email: info@takt-magazin.de **Web site:** http://www.takt-magazin.de
Freq: Monthly; **Annual Sub.:** EUR 28,00; **Circ:** 32,292
Editor: Sylvia Obst; **Advertising Manager:** Endrik Schubert
Profile: Culture and Leisure magazine with event calendar for food, music, art and events in the major cities of Thuringia. Facebook: http://www.facebook.com/taktmagazin.
Language(s): German
ADVERTISING RATES:
Full Page Mono .... EUR 2254
Full Page Colour .... EUR 3266
Mechanical Data: No. of Columns (Display): 4, Col Widths (Display): 44 mm, Type Area: 260 x 190 mm
Copy instructions: *Copy Date:* 15 days prior to publication
CONSUMER: RURAL & REGIONAL INTEREST

TALBLICK TANNHEIMER TAL 1616158G89A-12146

Editorial: Kleine Grottenau 1, 86150 AUGSBURG
Tel: 821 4405427 **Fax:** 821 4405429
Email: talblick@vmm-wirtschaftsverlag.de **Web site:** http://www.tannheimertal.com
Freq: Quarterly; **Cover Price:** Free; **Circ:** 60,000
Editor: Melanie Wollscheid; **Advertising Manager:** Hans Peter Engel
Profile: The official guests of the Tourism Association magazine Tannheimer valley. Contains everything you need to know across the most beautiful valley in Europe and appetite for the next holiday. A colorful array of images and stories, people profiles and is supplemented with topics such as "guest and hospitality" and "mind and body. ".
Language(s): German
ADVERTISING RATES:
Full Page Mono .... EUR 2990
Full Page Colour .... EUR 2990
Mechanical Data: Type Area: 264 x 182 mm
Copy instructions: *Copy Date:* 8 days prior to publication

TALBLICK TANNHEIMER TAL 1616158G89A-12577

Editorial: Kleine Grottenau 1, 86150 AUGSBURG
Tel: 821 4405427 **Fax:** 821 4405429
Email: talblick@vmm-wirtschaftsverlag.de **Web site:** http://www.tannheimertal.com
Freq: Quarterly; **Cover Price:** Free; **Circ:** 60,000
Editor: Melanie Wollscheid; **Advertising Manager:** Hans Peter Engel
Profile: The official guests of the Tourism Association magazine Tannheimer valley. Contains everything you need to know across the most beautiful valley in Europe and appetite for the next holiday. A colorful array of images and stories, people profiles and is supplemented with topics such as "guest and hospitality" and "mind and body. ".
Language(s): German
ADVERTISING RATES:
Full Page Mono .... EUR 2990
Full Page Colour .... EUR 2990
Mechanical Data: Type Area: 264 x 182 mm
Copy instructions: *Copy Date:* 8 days prior to publication

TANDEM MAGAZIN 744240G14A-7420

Editorial: 117er Ehrenhof 3, 55118 MAINZ
Tel: 6131 218080 **Fax:** 6131 2180890
Email: info@tandem-media.de **Web site:** http://www.tandem-piazza.org
Freq: Quarterly; **Cover Price:** Free; **Circ:** 17,000
Advertising Manager: Elisabeth Schröder
Profile: Presentation of products and services in the fields of environmental protection and occupational safety in operation, products and suppliers directory.
Language(s): German

TANGO 744241G80-11300

Editorial: Poststr. 36, 20354 HAMBURG
Tel: 40 288096710 **Fax:** 431 288096720
Email: redaktion.hamburg@tango-online.de **Web site:** http://www.tango-online.de
Freq: Monthly; **Cover Price:** Free; **Circ:** 14,500
Editor: Jan Hempel
Profile: Lifestyle magazine and events guide to the cities of Hamburg.
Language(s): German
Readership: Aimed at people aged between 20 and 45 years old.
ADVERTISING RATES:
Full Page Mono .... EUR 2810
Full Page Colour .... EUR 2810
Mechanical Data: Type Area: 265 x 200 mm, No. of Columns (Display): 4, Col Widths (Display): 44 mm
CONSUMER: RURAL & REGIONAL INTEREST

TANKSTELLE 744245G31R-29

Editorial: Veilchenweg 22, 74369 LÖCHGAU
Tel: 7143 870797 **Fax:** 7143 870799
Email: rongisch@tankstelle-magazin.de **Web site:** http://www.tankstelle-magazin.de
Freq: Monthly; Free to qualifying individuals
Annual Sub.: EUR 49,20; **Circ:** 15,048
Editor: Hans Rongisch; **Advertising Manager:** Björn Lindenau
Profile: Journal containing information about service-stations.
Language(s): German
Readership: Read by service station operators.
ADVERTISING RATES:
Full Page Mono .... EUR 4750
Full Page Colour .... EUR 4750
Mechanical Data: Type Area: 260 x 180 mm, No. of Columns (Display): 4, Col Widths (Display): 42 mm
Copy instructions: *Copy Date:* 28 days prior to publication
Official Journal of: Organ d. Bundesverb. Tankstellen u. Gewerbl. Autowäsche Deutschland e.V., d. Fachverb. Tankstellengewerbe Bayern u. d. Tankstellenverb. Deutschland e.V.
BUSINESS: MOTOR TRADE: Motor Trade Related

TANKSTELLEN MARKT 744247G31R-31

Editorial: Aschauer Str. 30, 81549 MÜNCHEN
Tel: 89 2030431184 **Fax:** 89 2030431181
Email: tm.tankstellenmarkt@springer.com **Web site:** http://www.tankstellenmarkt.com
Freq: 10 issues yearly; Free to qualifying individuals
Annual Sub.: EUR 55,00; **Circ:** 15,687
Editor: Manfred Ruopp; **Advertising Manager:** Michael Harms
Profile: Magazine focusing on petrol stations, shopping and services.
Language(s): German
Readership: Read by owners and managers.
ADVERTISING RATES:
Full Page Mono .... EUR 4140
Full Page Colour .... EUR 6110
Mechanical Data: Type Area: 240 x 175 mm
Copy instructions: *Copy Date:* 25 days prior to publication
Official Journal of: Organ d. Dachverb. ZTG m. sämtl. Landesverbänden, d. IG Esso u. d. EPSI-Office
BUSINESS: MOTOR TRADE: Motor Trade Related

TANZSPIEGEL 744258G76G-240
Editorial: Otto-Fleck-Schneise 12, 60528 FRANKFURT **Tel:** 69 67736780 **Fax:** 69 67728530
Email: tanzspiegel@tanzsport.de **Web site:** http://www.tanzsport.de
Freq: Monthly; Free to qualifying individuals
Annual Sub.: EUR 33,00; **Circ:** 15,000
Editor: Ulrike Sander-Reis
Profile: Publication of the German Dance Association.
Language(s): German
ADVERTISING RATES:
Full Page Mono .... EUR 950
Full Page Colour .... EUR 1300
Mechanical Data: Type Area: 297 x 210 mm, No. of Columns (Display): 3, Col Widths (Display): 49 mm
Copy instructions: *Copy Date:* 30 days prior to publication
Supplement(s): nord tanzsport; swing&step; tanzjournal; tanz mit uns
CONSUMER: MUSIC & PERFORMING ARTS: Dance

TASCHENBUCH FÜR ARBEITSSICHERHEIT 756646G58-1681
Editorial: Taunusstr. 54, 65183 WIESBADEN
Fax: 611 9030379
Email: michael.fritton@universum.de
Freq: Annual; **Cover Price:** EUR 11,12; **Circ:** 16,850
Editor: Michael Fritton
Profile: Annual for safety at work for energy supplying companies.
Language(s): German

TASCHENBUCH FÜR SICHERHEITSBEAUFTRAGTE - AUSG. METALL 744279G27-2400
Editorial: Taunusstr. 54, 65183 WIESBADEN
Tel: 611 9030333 **Fax:** 611 9030379
Email: michael.fritton@universum.de
Freq: Annual; **Cover Price:** EUR 8,05; **Circ:** 89,000
Editor: Michael Fritton
Profile: Calendar with issues of safety and health at work, focus on metal industry.
Language(s): German

TASPO 744297G21A-3840
Editorial: Frankfurter Str. 3d, 38122 BRAUNSCHWEIG **Tel:** 531 3800411
Fax: 531 3800440
Email: red.taspo@haymarket.de **Web site:** http://www.taspo.de
Freq: Weekly; **Annual Sub.:** EUR 169,20; **Circ:** 13,614
Editor: Iris Anger; **Advertising Manager:** Christian Rueß
Profile: Magazine about production, trade and services in horticulture.
Language(s): German
ADVERTISING RATES:
Full Page Mono .... EUR 6360
Full Page Colour .... EUR 7578
Mechanical Data: Type Area: 400 x 282 mm, No. of Columns (Display): 6, Col Widths (Display): 45 mm
Copy instructions: *Copy Date:* 3 days prior to publication
Supplement(s): Taspo Das Magazin
BUSINESS: AGRICULTURE & FARMING

TASPO BAUMZEITUNG 722022G57-100
Editorial: Frankfurter Str. 3d, 38122 BRAUNSCHWEIG **Tel:** 531 3800411
Fax: 531 3800449
Email: red.baumzeitung@haymarket.de **Web site:** http://www.baumzeitung.de
Freq: 6 issues yearly; **Annual Sub.:** EUR 71,10; **Circ:** 3,139
Editor: Iris Anger; **Advertising Manager:** Christian Rueß
Profile: Magazine of tree care companies, landscape companies, parks departments and Aboristik. Rights issues around the tree, practical advice on tree care work or updates from the tree are among the research subjects. Audience: arborists, landscape companies with tree care, participants in forestry education and training, parks departments, Arborist, Tree Friends, dendrologists and tree experts.
Language(s): German
ADVERTISING RATES:
Full Page Colour .... EUR 2860
Mechanical Data: Type Area: 272 x 186 mm, No. of Columns (Display): 4, Col Widths (Display): 45 mm
BUSINESS: ENVIRONMENT & POLLUTION

TASPO DAS MAGAZIN 744298G26D-7
Editorial: Frankfurter Str. 3d, 38122 BRAUNSCHWEIG **Tel:** 531 3800410
Fax: 531 3800440
Email: red.taspo@haymarket.de **Web site:** http://www.taspo.de
Freq: 6 issues yearly; **Annual Sub.:** EUR 75,60; **Circ:** 13,067
Editor: Iris Anger; **Advertising Manager:** Christian Rueß
Profile: Journal containing information about horticultural production and management.
Language(s): German
Readership: Aimed at managers and professionals within the horticultural industry.
ADVERTISING RATES:
Full Page Mono .... EUR 3428
Full Page Colour .... EUR 4682
Mechanical Data: Type Area: 272 x 186 mm, No. of Columns (Display): 4, Col Widths (Display): 45 mm
Supplement to: Taspo
BUSINESS: GARDEN TRADE: Garden Trade Horticulture

TASPO GARTEN DESIGN 733753G4E-5060
Editorial: Hauptstr. 54, 79356 EICHSTETTEN
Tel: 7663 608666 **Fax:** 7663 9129669
Email: red.taspo-gartendesign@haymarket.de **Web site:** http://www.taspo-gartendesign.de
Freq: 6 issues yearly; **Annual Sub.:** EUR 94,80; **Circ:** 3,444
Editor: Matthias Hinkelammert; **Advertising Manager:** Christian Rueß
Profile: Magazine for landscape companies, planners, landscape architects and garden designers. It is planned and implemented traveled garden projects in practice.
Language(s): German
ADVERTISING RATES:
Full Page Mono .... EUR 2950
Full Page Colour .... EUR 2950
Mechanical Data: Type Area: 272 x 186 mm, No. of Columns (Display): 4, Col Widths (Display): 45 mm
BUSINESS: ARCHITECTURE & BUILDING: Building

TATENDRANG 1837047G14A-10159
Editorial: Zeuggasse 7, 86150 AUGSBURG
Email: erne@tatendrang.info **Web site:** http://www.tatendrang.info
Freq: 3 issues yearly; **Circ:** 1,800
Editor: Ingrid Erne
Profile: Regional business magazine.
Language(s): German
ADVERTISING RATES:
Full Page Mono .... EUR 300
Mechanical Data: Type Area: 260 x 200 mm

TÄTOWIER MAGAZIN 744211G84A-3200
Editorial: Markircher Str. 9a, 68229 MANNHEIM
Tel: 621 4836194 **Fax:** 621 4836173
Email: postmaster@taetowiermagazin.de **Web site:** http://www.taetowiermagazin.de
Freq: Monthly; **Annual Sub.:** EUR 52,00; **Circ:** 29,105
Editor: Dirk-Boris Rödel; **Advertising Manager:** Steffen Bickelhaupt
Profile: Every month, the world's best tattoo artists and newcomers are presented. Detailed reports on the major national and international tattoo conventions. An important part of the magazine are features on tattoo and piercing rites in primitive cultures, which are often in Tätowier Magazin first reported in Western literature. In addition, the magazine every month portraits of famous tattooed personalities from the arts and culture as well as by musicians of various styles. The case list in the booklet is a comprehensive overview of events in the scene. Facebook: http://www.facebook.com/TatowierMagazin.
Language(s): German
ADVERTISING RATES:
Full Page Colour .... EUR 2205
Mechanical Data: Type Area: 256 x 184 mm, No. of Columns (Display): 4, Col Widths (Display): 43 mm
Copy instructions: *Copy Date:* 39 days prior to publication
CONSUMER: THE ARTS & LITERARY: Arts

TATSACHEN 756647G14A-9232
Editorial: Stenglingser Weg 4, 58642 ISERLOHN
Tel: 2374 504350 **Fax:** 2374 504353
Email: joerg.mueller@lobbe.de **Web site:** http://www.lobbe.de
Freq: Half-yearly; **Cover Price:** Free; **Circ:** 5,500
Editor: Jörg Mueller
Profile: Magazine for employees of Lobbe.
Language(s): German

TAUBER-ZEITUNG 744309G67B-14420
Editorial: Ledermarkt 8, 97980 BAD MERGENTHEIM
Tel: 7931 59634 **Fax:** 7931 59644
Email: redaktion.tbz@swp.de **Web site:** http://www.suedwest-aktiv.de
Freq: 312 issues yearly; **Circ:** 5,576
Editor: Oliver Bauer; **News Editor:** Joachim Ilg; **Advertising Manager:** Ariane Kolb
Profile: Daily newspaper with regional news and a local sports section. Twitter: http://twitter.com/SWPde This Outlet offers RSS (Really Simple Syndication).
Language(s): German
ADVERTISING RATES:
SCC .... EUR 23,70
Mechanical Data: Type Area: 420 x 274 mm, No. of Columns (Display): 6, Col Widths (Display): 44 mm
Copy instructions: *Copy Date:* 1 day prior to publication
Supplement(s): Bad Mergentheimer Kur-Zeitung; Regio Business
REGIONAL DAILY & SUNDAY NEWSPAPERS: Regional Daily Newspapers

TAUCHEN 744311G75M-800
Editorial: Troplowitzstr. 5, 22529 HAMBURG
Tel: 40 38906191 **Fax:** 40 38906199
Email: redaktion@tauchen.de **Web site:** http://www.tauchen.de
Freq: Monthly; **Annual Sub.:** EUR 64,80; **Circ:** 29,369
Editor: Carolyn Martin; **Advertising Manager:** Evelyn Diekmann
Profile: Germany's most widely read magazine appear divers for over 30 years. tauchen is No. 1 in readership: A subscriber share of 49% of the paid circulation proves the high reader loyalty. tauchen is international: Divers in Austria and Switzerland will be addressed with its own focus. tauchen is the magazine for beginners and professionals. We offer exciting travel reports and reports of wreck exploration, test news from science and biology, the latest equipment and available to readers with advice and competence. tauchen brings the world below sea level on the surface.
Language(s): German
ADVERTISING RATES:
Full Page Mono .... EUR 3109
Full Page Colour .... EUR 4956
Mechanical Data: Type Area: 248 x 185 mm, No. of Columns (Display): 4, Col Widths (Display): 43 mm
Copy instructions: *Copy Date:* 27 days prior to publication
CONSUMER: SPORT: Water Sports

TAUNUS ZEITUNG 744317G67B-14440
Editorial: Frankenallee 71, 60327 FRANKFURT
Tel: 69 75010 **Fax:** 69 75014232
Email: redaktion@fnp.de **Web site:** http://www.fnp.de
Freq: 312 issues yearly; **Circ:** 33,075
Profile: The Taunus Zeitung is the most widely read daily newspaper in Hochtaunuskreis. She takes the dialogue with readers very seriously and has in Bad Homburg and Usingen two local editorial sites. No daily newspapers reported detailed on events in the cities and towns in the Hochtaunus district. It is particularly active in the event area. It organizes lectures, take part in trade fairs and is in major regional events like the Bad Homburg summer, the theater in the park or the town festival in Usingen site. Facebook: http://www.facebook.com/pages/FNP/115994585097103.
Language(s): German
ADVERTISING RATES:
SCC .... EUR 68,00
Mechanical Data: Type Area: 528 x 371 mm, No. of Columns (Display): 8, Col Widths (Display): 45 mm
Copy instructions: *Copy Date:* 1 day prior to publication
REGIONAL DAILY & SUNDAY NEWSPAPERS: Regional Daily Newspapers

TAUSENDFÜSSLER 1739952G74C-3723
Editorial: Gottlieb-Daimler-Str. 9, 24568 KALTENKIRCHEN **Tel:** 4191 722770
Fax: 4191 7227711
Email: redaktion@tausendfuessler.de **Web site:** http://www.tausendfuessler.de
Freq: Annual; **Cover Price:** Free; **Circ:** 157,590
Advertising Manager: Detlef Willner-van Laak
Profile: Yellow Pages for parents, educators and children in and around Hamburg.
Language(s): German
Mechanical Data: Type Area: 190 x 147 mm, No. of Columns (Display): 3, Col Widths (Display): 47 mm
CONSUMER: WOMEN'S INTEREST CONSUMER MAGAZINES: Home & Family

TAXI 744321G64G-3
Editorial: Aschauer Str. 30, 81549 MÜNCHEN
Tel: 89 2030432269 **Fax:** 89 2030432398
Email: dieter.fund@springer.com **Web site:** http://www.taxi-zeitschrift.de
Freq: 8 issues yearly; Free to qualifying individuals
Annual Sub.: EUR 38,90; **Circ:** 36,067
Editor: Dietmar Fund; **News Editor:** Silke Bub; **Advertising Manager:** Marisa D'Arbonneau
Profile: Journal of the taxi and rental car companies in Germany.
Language(s): German
ADVERTISING RATES:
Full Page Colour .... EUR 8580
Mechanical Data: Type Area: 250 x 185 mm, No. of Columns (Display): 4, Col Widths (Display): 43 mm
Copy instructions: *Copy Date:* 30 days prior to publication
BUSINESS: OTHER CLASSIFICATIONS: Taxi Trade

TAXI HEUTE 1830894G49A-2442
Editorial: Joseph-Dollinger-Bogen 5, 80807 MÜNCHEN **Tel:** 89 32391252 **Fax:** 89 32391163
Email: redaktion@taxi-heute.de **Web site:** http://www.taxi-heute.de
Freq: 8 issues yearly; **Annual Sub.:** EUR 55,60; **Circ:** 16,951
Editor: Jürgen Hartmann; **Advertising Manager:** Angelika König
Profile: taxi heute is the oldest, independent, IVW-audited, trade journal for the Taxi and rental car companies in Germany. taxi heute about news reports in each issue of cars and vans, as well as through mobile communication, transport, switching and billing systems for the taxi operators. Further information is critical to insurance and financing as a permanent editorial concept and practical tips on business management and personnel management of the taxi and car rental company.
Language(s): German
ADVERTISING RATES:
Full Page Mono .... EUR 4230
Full Page Colour .... EUR 6330
Mechanical Data: Type Area: 270 x 185 mm, No. of Columns (Display): 4, Col Widths (Display): 43 mm

TAXI RUNDSCHAU 1663993G49A-2385
Editorial: Alsterdorfer Str. 276, 22297 HAMBURG
Tel: 40 448643 **Fax:** 40 453551
Email: info@taxiverband-hamburg.de **Web site:** http://www.taxiverband-hamburg.de
Freq: 6 issues yearly; **Circ:** 2,000
Editor: Dirk Schütte; **Advertising Manager:** Alexander Lux
Profile: Magazine with information for the taxi and rented car business.
Language(s): German
ADVERTISING RATES:
Full Page Mono .... EUR 185
Full Page Colour .... EUR 185
Mechanical Data: Type Area: 185 x 122 mm
Copy instructions: *Copy Date:* 7 days prior to publication

TAXI RUNDSCHAU 1663993G49A-2472
Editorial: Alsterdorfer Str. 276, 22297 HAMBURG
Tel: 40 448643 **Fax:** 40 453551
Email: info@taxiverband-hamburg.de **Web site:** http://www.taxiverband-hamburg.de
Freq: 6 issues yearly; **Circ:** 2,000
Editor: Dirk Schütte; **Advertising Manager:** Alexander Lux
Profile: Magazine with information for the taxi and rented car business.
Language(s): German
ADVERTISING RATES:
Full Page Mono .... EUR 185
Full Page Colour .... EUR 185
Mechanical Data: Type Area: 185 x 122 mm
Copy instructions: *Copy Date:* 7 days prior to publication

TAZ.DE 1704201G65A-282
Editorial: Rudi-Dutschke-Str. 23, 10969 BERLIN
Tel: 30 259020 **Fax:** 30 2513003
Email: chefred@taz.de **Web site:** http://www.taz.de
Freq: Daily; **Cover Price:** Paid; **Circ:** 4,325,254 Unique Users
Editor: Ines Pohl
Profile: Ezine: The big left news portal of the "tageszeitung" from Berlin. Categories: breaking news, politics, future, power, debate, life, sports, truth, Berlin, North, newspaper archives, Service, Shop Facebook: http://www.facebook.com/group.php?gid=2209620560 Twitter: http://twitter.com/taz_online This Outlet offers RSS (Really Simple Syndication).
Language(s): German
NATIONAL DAILY & SUNDAY NEWSPAPERS: National Daily Newspapers

TAZ.DIE TAGESZEITUNG 744223G65A-220
Editorial: Rudi-Dutschke-Str. 23, 10969 BERLIN
Tel: 30 259020
Email: redaktion@taz.de **Web site:** http://www.taz.de
Freq: 312 issues yearly; **Circ:** 68,021
Editor: Ines Pohl; **Advertising Manager:** Margit Jöhnk
Profile: What began the left, loud Project on 17 April 1979, is now a recognized quality newspaper and a institution in the German press. The taz.die tageszeitung is a company that remains committed to the counter-public, and thus an indispensable source of information is for above-average educated, high income readers with a large proportion of opinion leaders and decision makers in media, business and administration. The taz.die tageszeitung has 87% exclusive readers, i.e. this important target group can be reached only in the taz.die tageszeitung! In 2008 by Prof. Dr. Wolfgang Donsbach of the Technical University of Dresden, led by taz readership survey among 4,000 subscribers to the high level of education and the willingness to take responsibility of the taz-readers has confirmed. Published since April 2009, the taz.die tageszeitung in a new layout and is in the weekend edition, which appears Saturdays, fully colored. In addition to news reporting, see the sonntaz to 20 pages of exciting topics such as everyday life, consumption, body and movements another section for your ads to the regular prices of federal edition. Facebook: http://www.facebook.com/group.php?gid=2209620560 Twitter: http://twitter.com/taz_online This Outlet offers RSS (Really Simple Syndication).
Language(s): German
Readership: Read mainly by public sector employees.
ADVERTISING RATES:
SCC .... EUR 102,00
Mechanical Data: Type Area: 430 x 285 mm, No. of Columns (Display): 6, Col Widths (Display): 44 mm
Copy instructions: *Copy Date:* 2 days prior to publication
Supplement(s): halbstark; Le Monde diplomatique; StadtZeit Kassel Magazin
NATIONAL DAILY & SUNDAY NEWSPAPERS: National Daily Newspapers

TEAM 740875G33-240
Editorial: 22284 HAMBURG **Tel:** 40 63246546
Fax: 40 63246814

Email: bianca.boedeker@shell.com Web site: http://www.shell.de
Freq: Quarterly; Circ: 14,000
Editor: Bianca Bödeker; Advertising Manager: Bianca Bödeker
Profile: Magazine for employees of Shell.
Language(s): German

TEAM WORK 1615547G56D-1271
Editorial: Hauptstr. 1, 86925 FUCHSTAL
Tel: 8243 96920 Fax: 8243 969222
Email: redaktion.tw@teamwork-media.de Web site: http://www.teamwork-media.de
Freq: 7 issues yearly; Annual Sub.: EUR 92,00; Circ: 9,591
Editor: Ralf Suckert
Profile: Interdisciplinary magazine on prothetical odontology.
Language(s): German
ADVERTISING RATES:
Full Page Colour .... EUR 3500
Mechanical Data: Type Area: 260 x 185 mm
Copy instructions: *Copy Date:* 28 days prior to publication
BUSINESS: HEALTH & MEDICAL: Dental

TECCHANNEL 1622099G5R-674
Editorial: Lyonel-Feininger-Str. 26, 80807 MÜNCHEN
Tel: 89 36086887 Fax: 89 3608699897
Email: redaktion@tecchannel.de Web site: http://www.tecchannel.de
Freq: Daily; Cover Price: Paid; Circ: 1,177,454 Unique Users
Editor: Michael Eckert; Advertising Manager: Sebastian Woerle
Profile: Twitter: http://twitter.com/TecChannel.
Language(s): German
BUSINESS: COMPUTERS & AUTOMATION: Computers Related

TECHNIK IN BAYERN
744371G14R-5340
Editorial: Westendstr. 199, 80686 MÜNCHEN
Tel: 89 57912456 Fax: 89 57912161
Email: tib@bv-muenchen.vdi.de Web site: http://www.technik-in-bayern.de
Freq: 6 issues yearly; Free to qualifying individuals
Annual Sub.: EUR 36,00; Circ: 24,778
Editor: Jochen Lösch
Profile: Member magazine for engineers in Upper Bavaria, Lower Bavaria and southern Bavaria with news from technology, science and business. In each issue we are addressing a key topic in the field of engineering, to comment on the skilled professionals and also look into the periphery. In addition, we bring industry reports, regional news from VDI and VDE, Preview of technical trade fairs and scientific meetings and information from research institutes and the TÜV Bayern.
Language(s): German
ADVERTISING RATES:
Full Page Mono .... EUR 2000
Full Page Colour .... EUR 2450
Mechanical Data: Type Area: 255 x 185 mm, No. of Columns (Display): 4, Col Widths (Display): 43 mm
Copy instructions: *Copy Date:* 30 days prior to publication
BUSINESS: COMMERCE, INDUSTRY & MANAGEMENT: Commerce Related

TECHNIK+EINKAUF
1667869G14A-9751
Editorial: Justus-von-Liebig-Str. 1, 86899 LANDSBERG Tel: 8191 125681 Fax: 8191 125312
Email: redaktion@technikundeinkauf.de Web site: http://www.technikundeinkauf.de
Freq: 9 issues yearly; Annual Sub.: EUR 78,00; Circ: 19,192
Editor: Eduard Altmann; Advertising Manager: Michael Klotz
Profile: The magazine focuses on a trade magazine for the manufacturing industry holistically with the procurement process and all its decision makers. This suggests the Journal as a cross-departmental team title at the bridge between the "procurement system" decision-makers involved in purchasing, design and production. With cost, time and quality pressures, the importance of these system-makers continues to grow. This also increases the demand on their skills: technik+Einkauf technology gives more purchasing authority for this purpose, purchasing more technology-and knowledge throughout the decision-team efficiency. Runs as a unifying element in the system concept Total Cost of Ownership (TCO) through the whole sheet: Current trend reports, market analysis and product information provide the hard facts. The Soft-Facts about expert advice, practical examples and background reports.
Language(s): German
ADVERTISING RATES:
Full Page Mono .... EUR 6600
Full Page Colour .... EUR 6600
Mechanical Data: Type Area: 257 x 178 mm, No. of Columns (Display): 4, Col Widths (Display): 41 mm
Copy instructions: *Copy Date:* 30 days prior to publication
Supplement(s): kataloge orange
BUSINESS: COMMERCE, INDUSTRY & MANAGEMENT

TECHNIKGESCHICHTE
744370G19A-880
Editorial: Str. des 17. Juni 135, 10623 BERLIN
Tel: 30 31424085 Fax: 30 31425962
Email: technikgeschichte@tu-berlin.de Web site: http://www.edition-sigma.de/tg
Freq: Quarterly; Free to qualifying individuals
Annual Sub.: EUR 78,00; Circ: 631
Editor: Katharina Zeitz; Advertising Manager: R. Bohn
Profile: Journal for history of technology research. TECHNIKGESCHICHTE publishes original contributions on the historical development of technology in their academic, social, economic and political contexts. TECHNIKGESCHICHTE turns with its interdisciplinary approach not only for engineering researchers and historians of technology, but also to social scientists of all disciplines, people involved in technical development etc. want to associations, corporations and politics as well as interested lay people, the technical and social change reflected in his involvement in the historical process. TECHNIKGESCHICHTE fully informed about the latest technology historical research: a comprehensive review section with reviews in German and foreign literature on the subject, through museums and exhibition reviews and a regular magazine show with information on topics related articles in other journals, and internationally.
Language(s): German
ADVERTISING RATES:
Full Page Mono .... EUR 350
Mechanical Data: Type Area: 193 x 120 mm
Copy instructions: *Copy Date:* 50 days prior to publication

TECHNISCHE KOMMUNIKATION 744375G18A-168
Editorial: Rotebühlstr. 64, 70178 STUTTGART
Tel: 711 6570454 Fax: 711 6570499
Email: redaktion@tekom.de Web site: http://www.tekom.de
Freq: 6 issues yearly; Free to qualifying individuals
Annual Sub.: EUR 48,20; Circ: 8,898
Editor: Gregor Schäfer; Advertising Manager: Bernd Dürrmeier
Profile: Magazine focusing on telecom and communications technology and documentation.
Language(s): German
ADVERTISING RATES:
Full Page Mono .... EUR 1355
Full Page Colour .... EUR 2575
Mechanical Data: Type Area: 252 x 182 mm, No. of Columns (Display): 3, Col Widths (Display): 58 mm
Copy instructions: *Copy Date:* 42 days prior to publication
BUSINESS: ELECTRONICS

TECHNISCHE SICHERHEIT
744382G19A-900
Editorial: VDI-Platz 1, 40468 DÜSSELDORF
Tel: 211 6103343 Fax: 211 6103148
Email: zimmermann@technikwissen.de Web site: http://www.technischesicherheit.de
Freq: 9 issues yearly; Annual Sub.: EUR 207,50; Circ: 4,349
Editor: Elisabeth Zimmermann
Profile: "Technische Sicherheit" covers recent developments in the fields of safety technology, health and safety at work and environmental monitoring. It features incidents in safety related installations, which have resulted in harm or injury, and highlights the measures that should be adopted to avoid personal injury or environmental damage. Experts and maintenance engineers, who have responsibility in their organisations for the safety of installations, health and safety at work and environmental protection. Engineers specialist insurance engineers, public service engineers as well as engineers in the fire service, hospitals and municipal services. Manufacturers, suppliers and service providers who deal with fire prevention, explosive safety, health and safety at work, boiler technology, plumbing, traffic safety, process measurement, lifts and transport of dangerous goods.
Language(s): German
ADVERTISING RATES:
Full Page Mono .... EUR 2688
Full Page Colour .... EUR 3678
Mechanical Data: Type Area: 270 x 185 mm, No. of Columns (Display): 4, Col Widths (Display): 45 mm
Copy instructions: *Copy Date:* 21 days prior to publication
Supplement(s): baua: Aktuell
BUSINESS: ENGINEERING & MACHINERY

TECHNOLOGISCH 1828518G4E-7207
Editorial: Theaterstr. 74, 52062 AACHEN
Tel: 241 889700 Fax: 241 8897042
Email: info@tema.de Web site: http://www.tema.de
Freq: Half-yearly; Circ: 25,000
Profile: Company publication from the Kieback&Peter GmbH & Co. KG.
Language(s): German

TECHNOLOGISCH 1828518G4E-7324
Editorial: Theaterstr. 74, 52062 AACHEN
Tel: 241 889700 Fax: 241 8897042
Email: info@tema.de Web site: http://www.tema.de
Freq: Half-yearly; Circ: 25,000
Profile: Company publication from the Kieback&Peter GmbH & Co. KG.
Language(s): German

TECHNOLOGY REVIEW
1626868G14A-9540
Editorial: Karl-Wiechert-Allee 10, 30625 HANNOVER
Tel: 511 5352764 Fax: 511 5352767
Email: manfred.pietschmann@heise.de Web site: http://www.technologyreview.de
Freq: Monthly; Annual Sub.: EUR 89,50; Circ: 32,801
Editor: Manfred Pietschmann; Advertising Manager: Michael Hanke
Profile: The journal bridges the gap between science and industry, between research and application and accompanies the entire innovation process from lab to market.
Language(s): German
ADVERTISING RATES:
Full Page Mono .... EUR 6000
Full Page Colour .... EUR 6000
Mechanical Data: Type Area: 238 x 178 mm
BUSINESS: COMMERCE, INDUSTRY & MANAGEMENT

DER TECKBOTE 744391G67B-14460
Editorial: Alleenstr. 158, 73230 KIRCHHEIM
Tel: 7021 975022 Fax: 7021 975044
Email: redaktion@teckbote.de Web site: http://www.teckbote.de
Freq: 312 issues yearly; Circ: 15,472
Editor: Frank Hoffmann; Advertising Manager: Bernd Köhle
Profile: Daily newspaper with regional news and a local sports section.
Language(s): German
ADVERTISING RATES:
SCC .... EUR 35,30
Mechanical Data: Type Area: 480 x 321 mm, No. of Columns (Display): 7, Col Widths (Display): 44 mm
Copy instructions: *Copy Date:* 1 day prior to publication
REGIONAL DAILY & SUNDAY NEWSPAPERS: Regional Daily Newspapers

TECNOLOGIA MILITAR
744392G40-800
Editorial: Heilsbachstr. 26, 53123 BONN
Tel: 228 64830 Fax: 228 6483109
Email: tecmil@mpgbonn.de Web site: http://www.monch.com
Freq: Quarterly; Annual Sub.: EUR 25,00; Circ: 9,517
Editor: Franz Thiele; Advertising Manager: Christa André
Profile: Publication about military technology.
Language(s): Portuguese; Spanish
ADVERTISING RATES:
Full Page Mono .... EUR 3950
Full Page Colour .... EUR 6500
Mechanical Data: Type Area: 256 x 185 mm
BUSINESS: DEFENCE

TEENSMAG 744398G74F-155
Editorial: Bodenborn 43, 58452 WITTEN
Tel: 2302 93093830 Fax: 2302 93093899
Email: info@teensmag.net Web site: http://www.teensmag.net
Freq: 6 issues yearly; Annual Sub.: EUR 25,20; Circ: 28,000
Editor: Annette Penno; Advertising Manager: Thilo Cunz
Profile: teensmag is the youth magazine with depth that the teens want to be in an increasingly confused world guidance. Issues such as occultism, drugs, sexuality, school, etc. access the experiences of young people to encourage and to find their own position. Similarly, talking photo stories, current reports, testimonials and creative tips from music, sports, film, fashion, religion, trends and everyday life of teenagers.
Language(s): German
Readership: Aimed at Christian teenagers.
ADVERTISING RATES:
Full Page Mono .... EUR 1122
Full Page Colour .... EUR 1420
Mechanical Data: Type Area: 258 x 188 mm, No. of Columns (Display): 4, Col Widths (Display): 44 mm
Copy instructions: *Copy Date:* 25 days prior to publication
CONSUMER: WOMEN'S INTEREST CONSUMER MAGAZINES: Teenage

TEGERNSEER ZEITUNG
744405G67B-14480
Editorial: Rosenstr. 2, 83684 TEGERNSEE
Tel: 8022 916821 Fax: 8022 916820
Email: teg-zeitung@merkur-online.de Web site: http://www.merkur-online.de
Freq: 312 issues yearly; Circ: 16,666
Advertising Manager: Hans-Georg Bechthold
Profile: The Münchner Merkur with its own local newspapers, of which the Tegernseer Zeitung is one that, the leading regional newspaper brand in the Munich area - the most affluent area of Germany. The combination of newspaper and region is the foundation on which to build the success of the title. This is the newspaper not only the factual news agency, but forms a community of solidarity with its readers and the local community. The clear focus on local reporting creates a high regard to human reader loyalty. She presses one hand in the very high number of close to 180,000 subscribers. Also for the high reader-commitment is the loyalty of the total current 827 000 daily readers, the Münchner Merkur or one of its local newspapers usually read over many years. The Münchner Merkur with its own local newspapers is a newspaper for the whole family, tradition and modern life for one of the most beautiful regions of Germany unites. Reliable, informative, critical: the Münchner Merkur is the indispensable daily newspaper for the region. Facebook: http://www.facebook.com/pages/merkur-online.de/190176143327 This Outlet offers RSS (Really Simple Syndication).
Language(s): German
ADVERTISING RATES:
SCC .... EUR 43,60
Mechanical Data: Type Area: 474 x 324 mm, No. of Columns (Display): 7, Col Widths (Display): 45 mm
Copy instructions: *Copy Date:* 1 day prior to publication
REGIONAL DAILY & SUNDAY NEWSPAPERS: Regional Daily Newspapers

TELECOM HANDEL 744416G18B-1977
Editorial: Bayerstr. 16a, 80335 MÜNCHEN
Tel: 89 74117151 Fax: 89 74117101
Email: redaktion@telecom-handel.de Web site: http://www.telecom-handel.de
Freq: 26 issues yearly; Annual Sub.: EUR 138,75; Circ: 17,986
Editor: Roland Bernhard; Advertising Manager: Angelika Hochmuth
Profile: Newspaper containing information about telecommunications, providing news on equipment, technology, suppliers and market trends. Facebook: http://www.facebook.com/telecomhandel.
Language(s): German
Readership: Aimed at the TK- industry.
ADVERTISING RATES:
Full Page Mono .... EUR 8350
Full Page Colour .... EUR 8350
Mechanical Data: Type Area: 335 x 260 mm, No. of Columns (Display): 5, Col Widths (Display): 48 mm
Copy instructions: *Copy Date:* 14 days prior to publication
Supplement(s): Telecom Handel
BUSINESS: ELECTRONICS: Telecommunications

TELEMONAT 744437G94H-12440
Editorial: Eimsbütteler Str. 64, 22769 HAMBURG
Tel: 40 4325890 Fax: 40 43258950
Email: kontakt@auc-hamburg.de Web site: http://www.auc-hamburg.de
Freq: Monthly; Circ: 206,721
Editor: Gerhard Balazs; Advertising Manager: Gerhard Balazs
Profile: TV listings magazine.
Language(s): German
ADVERTISING RATES:
Full Page Mono .... EUR 5400
Full Page Colour .... EUR 7200
Mechanical Data: Type Area: 190 x 133 mm
Copy instructions: *Copy Date:* 15 days prior to publication
CONSUMER: OTHER CLASSIFICATIONS: Customer Magazines

TELERAT-NACHRICHTEN
744438G18B-2006
Editorial: Josef-Nawrocki-Str. 30, 12587 BERLIN
Tel: 30 7550090 Fax: 30 75500911
Email: info@telerat.de Web site: http://www.telerat.de
Freq: Monthly; Cover Price: Free; Circ: 1,000
Editor: Rainer Hartlep
Profile: Company publication published by Telerat GmbH.
Language(s): German

TELETALK 744443G18B-1740
Editorial: Podbielskistr. 325, 30659 HANNOVER
Tel: 511 3348466 Fax: 511 3348499
Email: feldt@teletalk.de Web site: http://www.teletalk.de
Freq: Monthly; Annual Sub.: EUR 76,00; Circ: 8,482
Editor: Susanne Feldt
Profile: Magazine about the German telecommunications industry, call centres, telemarketing and voice telephony.
Language(s): German
ADVERTISING RATES:
Full Page Mono .... EUR 3945
Full Page Colour .... EUR 4780
Mechanical Data: Type Area: 251 x 175 mm
BUSINESS: ELECTRONICS: Telecommunications

TEMA 744459G19A-1066
Editorial: Baumschulweg 6, 53639 KÖNIGSWINTER
Tel: 2244 92427 Fax: 2244 924299
Email: bvt-online@online.de Web site: http://www.bvt-online.de
Freq: 6 issues yearly; Circ: 25,000
Editor: Harald Schulte; Advertising Manager: G. Wolny
Profile: Technician Job and Education Magazine. tema is the official organ of the Association of higher professions of engineering, business and design eV (BAT) and is intended for all who work in technical, economic and design professions. This is the journal editorial focusing on a report in the form of technical reports and product information, professional and socio-political information and reports from schools for technology, business and design and association news.
Language(s): German
ADVERTISING RATES:
Full Page Mono .... EUR 2300
Full Page Colour .... EUR 4090
Mechanical Data: Type Area: 241 x 171 mm

Copy instructions: *Copy Date:* 50 days prior to publication
BUSINESS: ENGINEERING & MACHINERY

TEMPELHOF KOMPAKT
1898594G74M-893
Editorial: Bundesallee 23, 10717 BERLIN
Tel: 30 863030 **Fax:** 30 86303200
Email: info@bfb.de **Web site:** http://www.bfb.de
Freq: Annual; **Cover Price:** Free; **Circ:** 96,000
Profile: Industry district magazine. The core of this handy reference book is neatly sorted according to different themes of industry. Here you will find a plethora of vendors from the neighborhood. In preparation to the respective subject area raises a company, in an interview. To know your environment better, we present in the district windows, etc. beautiful places, monuments, museums, etc. For better orientation in the neighborhood also an integrated neighborhood with street plan is register. Furthermore, the county information you provide an overview of important phone numbers and agencies in your neighborhood.
Language(s): German
ADVERTISING RATES:
Full Page Mono .... EUR 990
Full Page Colour .... EUR 990
Mechanical Data: Type Area: 185 x 126 mm

TEMPRA 365
1655396G34-544
Editorial: Zimmerstr. 56, 10117 BERLIN
Tel: 30 47907116 **Fax:** 30 47907120
Email: kw@officeabc.de **Web site:** http://www.tempra365.de
Freq: 6 issues yearly; Free to qualifying individuals
Annual Sub.: EUR 39,00; **Circ:** 6,750
Editor: Kirsten Waldheim; **Advertising Manager:** Bärbel Skrzypczak
Profile: Magazine on office and computing.
Language(s): German
ADVERTISING RATES:
Full Page Mono .... EUR 3600
Full Page Colour .... EUR 3600
Mechanical Data: Type Area: 240 x 178 mm, No. of Columns (Display): 3, Col Widths (Display): 56 mm
Copy instructions: *Copy Date:* 15 days prior to publication

TENNIS MAGAZIN
744473G75H-320
Editorial: Troplowitzstr. 5, 22529 HAMBURG
Tel: 40 38906511 **Fax:** 40 38906301
Email: redaktion@tennismagazin.de **Web site:** http://www.tennismagazin.de
Freq: 10 issues yearly; **Annual Sub.:** EUR 45,00; **Circ:** 20,457
Editor: Dieter Genske; **Advertising Manager:** Holger Henopp
Profile: The tennis magazin, since 1976 leader of the German Tennis magazine, has a subscriber share of over 70% of a loyal and affluent audience. The tennis magazin offers something for everyone: both for the serious amateur players and any fan of the pro game. The booklet is divided into the following areas: Tour & Tournament, Practice & Fitness, Test & Equipment, Travel, German scene, Fifteen All for Kids and Grand Slam for the elderly. Facebook: http://www.facebook.com/tennismagazin.
Language(s): German
ADVERTISING RATES:
Full Page Mono .... EUR 3930
Full Page Colour .... EUR 5496
Mechanical Data: No. of Columns (Display): 4, Col Widths (Display): 45 mm, Type Area: 248 x 185 mm
Copy instructions: *Copy Date:* 28 days prior to publication
CONSUMER: SPORT: Racquet Sports

TENNISSPORT
744475G75H-360
Editorial: Böblinger Str. 68/1, 71065 SINDELFINGEN
Tel: 7031 862811 **Fax:** 7031 862801
Email: sekretariat@deutsche-tennis-zeitung.de **Web site:** http://www.deutsche-tennis-zeitung.de
Freq: 6 issues yearly; **Annual Sub.:** EUR 34,80; **Circ:** 3,799
Editor: Brigitte Schurr; **Advertising Manager:** Timo Wagenblast
Profile: Magazine containing news and information about tennis.
Language(s): German
ADVERTISING RATES:
Full Page Mono .... EUR 1000
Full Page Colour .... EUR 1600
Mechanical Data: Type Area: 262 x 185 mm, No. of Columns (Display): 4, Col Widths (Display): 43 mm
Copy instructions: *Copy Date:* 35 days prior to publication
Official Journal of: Organ d. Dt. Tennis Bund, d. Internat. Tennis Federation, d. Tennislehrer-Verb. d. Schweiz, d. Verb. d. Tennisinstruktoren Österr. u. d. Professional Tennis Registry
CONSUMER: SPORT: Racquet Sports

TENSIDE SURFACTANTS DETERGENTS
744478G13-2100
Editorial: Am Kreuzberg 5, 41334 NETTETAL
Tel: 2153 952540 **Fax:** 2153 952541
Email: tenside@hanser.de **Web site:** http://www.tsd-journal.com
Freq: 6 issues yearly; **Annual Sub.:** EUR 384,60; **Circ:** 1,090
Editor: Beatrix Föllner; **Advertising Manager:** Hermann J. Kleiner
Profile: International special journal and official organ of the Gesellschaft Deutscher Chemiker GDCh Division of Detergency & Formulations with results of the latest research of universities and industry in the field of cleaning technology. Main focuses amongst others are fundamental research, technologies and application into surfactants.
Language(s): English; German
ADVERTISING RATES:
Full Page Mono .... EUR 2540
Full Page Colour .... EUR 3740
Mechanical Data: Type Area: 250 x 175 mm, No. of Columns (Display): 4, Col Widths (Display): 41 mm
Official Journal of: Organ d. Ges. Dt. Chemiker Division of Detergency & Formulation
BUSINESS: CHEMICALS

TERRATECH
744483G57-2040
Editorial: Lise-Meitner-Str. 2, 55129 MAINZ
Tel: 6131 992343 **Fax:** 6131 992100
Email: redaktion@terratech.de **Web site:** http://www.industrie-service.de
Freq: Quarterly; **Circ:** 2,142
Editor: Eva Linder; **Advertising Manager:** Gundula Unverzagt
Profile: Journal covering industrial site rehabilitation and soil conservation.
Language(s): German
ADVERTISING RATES:
Full Page Mono .... EUR 1770
Full Page Colour .... EUR 2535
Mechanical Data: Type Area: 265 x 185 mm, No. of Columns (Display): 4, Col Widths (Display): 43 mm
Copy instructions: *Copy Date:* 14 days prior to publication
BUSINESS: ENVIRONMENT & POLLUTION

TEST
760176G74M-624
Editorial: Lützowplatz 11, 10785 BERLIN
Tel: 30 26312283 **Fax:** 30 26312425
Email: test@stiftung-warentest.de **Web site:** http://www.test.de
Freq: Monthly; **Annual Sub.:** EUR 47,50; **Circ:** 540,000
Editor: Hubertus Primus
Profile: Magazine of the Stiftung Warentest featuring research results about goods and services from the consumer sector.
Language(s): German

TEXT INTERN
744522G2A-4720
Editorial: Beim Schlump 13 a, 20144 HAMBURG
Tel: 40 2292636 **Fax:** 40 2278676
Email: redaktion@textintern.de **Web site:** http://www.textintern.de
Freq: Weekly; **Annual Sub.:** EUR 537,36; **Circ:** 2,087
Editor: Christian Personn
Profile: Magazine providing an information service for media and marketing, containing articles and reports.
Language(s): German
Readership: Aimed at professionals in the fields of media, advertising, PR and marketing.
ADVERTISING RATES:
Full Page Colour .... EUR 2790
Mechanical Data: Type Area: 270 x 185 mm, No. of Columns (Display): 3, Col Widths (Display): 60 mm
Copy instructions: *Copy Date:* 3 days prior to publication
BUSINESS: COMMUNICATIONS, ADVERTISING & MARKETING

TEXTILE NETWORK
734939G47A-740
Editorial: Nordhäuser Str. 34, 37115 DUDERSTADT
Tel: 5527 979440 **Fax:** 5527 979441
Email: textile-network@meisenbach.de **Web site:** http://www.textile-network.de
Freq: 9 issues yearly; **Annual Sub.:** EUR 128,00; **Circ:** 7,021
Editor: Iris Schlomski; **Advertising Manager:** Roland de la Rosée
Profile: Technical journal for the knitting and knitwear finishing industries. Also includes details on fashion trends.
Language(s): German
ADVERTISING RATES:
Full Page Mono .... EUR 2759
Full Page Colour .... EUR 4669
Mechanical Data: Type Area: 270 x 180 mm, No. of Columns (Display): 3, Col Widths (Display): 48 mm
Copy instructions: *Copy Date:* 26 days prior to publication
BUSINESS: CLOTHING & TEXTILES

TEXTILEFORUM
744509G47A-1280
Editorial: Friedenstr. 5, 30175 HANNOVER
Tel: 511 817006 **Fax:** 511 813108
Email: tfs@etn-net.org **Web site:** http://www.tfs-etn.com
Freq: Quarterly; **Annual Sub.:** EUR 50,00; **Circ:** 4,000
Editor: Beatrijs Sterk; **Advertising Manager:** Beatrijs Sterk
Profile: Journal giving information on textiles, fashion design, art and craft. Facebook: http://www.facebook.com/pages/Hannover-Germany/Textile-Forum-magazine/69840154954.
Language(s): English
ADVERTISING RATES:
Full Page Mono .... EUR 920
Full Page Colour .... EUR 1420
Mechanical Data: Type Area: 272 x 184 mm, No. of Columns (Display): 4, Col Widths (Display): 43 mm
Copy instructions: *Copy Date:* 30 days prior to publication
BUSINESS: CLOTHING & TEXTILES

TEXTILWIRTSCHAFT
744518G47A-1320
Editorial: Mainzer Landstr. 251, 60326 FRANKFURT
Tel: 69 75951301 **Fax:** 69 75951300
Email: redaktiontw@dfv.de **Web site:** http://www.textilwirtschaft.de
Freq: Weekly; **Annual Sub.:** EUR 307,00; **Circ:** 23,043
Editor: Michael Werner; **Advertising Manager:** Timo Holste
Profile: Magazine covering all aspects of the textiles industry. Facebook: http://www.facebook.com/TextilWirtschaft Twitter: http://twitter.com/TW_online.
Language(s): German
ADVERTISING RATES:
Full Page Mono .... EUR 11210
Full Page Colour .... EUR 11210
Mechanical Data: Type Area: 300 x 230 mm, No. of Columns (Display): 4, Col Widths (Display): 49 mm
Copy instructions: *Copy Date:* 8 days prior to publication
Official Journal of: Organ d. Bundesverb. d. Dt. Textileinzelhandels e.V. u. d. Europ. Vereinigung d. Spitzenverbände d. Textileinzelhandels
BUSINESS: CLOTHING & TEXTILES

TEXTILWIRTSCHAFT ONLINE
1704318G47A-1662
Editorial: Mainzer Landstr. 251, 60326 FRANKFURT
Tel: 69 75951304 **Fax:** 69 75951309
Email: juergen.mueller@textilwirtschaft.de **Web site:** http://www.textilwirtschaft.de
Freq: Daily; **Cover Price:** Paid; **Circ:** 468,219 Unique Users
Editor: Jürgen Müller; **Advertising Manager:** Anna Kempf
Profile: Facebook: http://www.facebook.com/TextilWirtschaft Twitter: http://twitter.com/TW_online.
Language(s): German
BUSINESS: CLOTHING & TEXTILES

TGA FACHPLANER
1606418G3D-827
Editorial: Forststr. 131, 70193 STUTTGART
Tel: 700 36256620 **Fax:** 700 36256699
Email: vorlaender@tga-fachplaner.de **Web site:** http://www.tga-fachplaner.de
Freq: Monthly; Free to qualifying individuals
Annual Sub.: EUR 157,80; **Circ:** 8,186
Editor: Jochen Vorländer; **Advertising Manager:** Sandra Bayer
Profile: Magazine for executives and engineers in technical building services engineering.
Language(s): German
ADVERTISING RATES:
Full Page Mono .... EUR 3015
Full Page Colour .... EUR 4025
Mechanical Data: Type Area: 265 x 187 mm, No. of Columns (Display): 4, Col Widths (Display): 43 mm
Copy instructions: *Copy Date:* 35 days prior to publication
Official Journal of: Organ d. Bundesverb. d. Haus- u. Betriebstechniker e.V.
BUSINESS: HEATING & VENTILATION: Heating & Plumbing

TH ARBEITSSCHUTZ AKTUELL
1958009G27-3123
Editorial: Plathnerstr. 4c, 30175 HANNOVER
Tel: 511 9910331 **Fax:** 511 9910342
Email: bernhard.flacke@vincentz.net **Web site:** http://www.technischerhandel.com
Freq: Annual; **Circ:** 25,000
Editor: Bernhard Flacke; **Advertising Manager:** Henning-Lothar Litka
Profile: The A + A in Duesseldorf is the world's most important trade fair for all facets of occupational health and safety. At this trade fair technical trade information in the "Supplement Arbeitsschutz Aktuell" about the relevant issues in the health and safety.
Language(s): German
ADVERTISING RATES:
Full Page Mono .... EUR 4800
Full Page Colour .... EUR 6390
Mechanical Data: Type Area: 256 x 175 mm
Supplement to: TH Technischer Handel

TH TECHNISCHER HANDEL
744380G10-528
Editorial: Plathnerstr. 4c, 30175 HANNOVER
Tel: 511 9910331 **Fax:** 511 9910399
Email: bernhard.flacke@vincentz.net **Web site:** http://www.technischerhandel.com
Freq: Monthly; **Annual Sub.:** EUR 97,37; **Circ:** 1,009
Editor: Bernhard Flacke; **Advertising Manager:** Henning-Lothar Litka
Profile: Journal of the Association of Technical Traders.
Language(s): German
ADVERTISING RATES:
Full Page Mono .... EUR 1510
Full Page Colour .... EUR 2755
Mechanical Data: Type Area: 256 x 175 mm, No. of Columns (Display): 4, Col Widths (Display): 42 mm
Copy instructions: *Copy Date:* 20 days prior to publication
Official Journal of: Organ d. Verb. d. Techn. Handels e.V.
Supplement(s): TH Arbeitsschutz Aktuell
BUSINESS: MATERIALS HANDLING

THEATER HEUTE
744564G76B-6620
Editorial: Knesebeckstr. 59, 10719 BERLIN
Tel: 30 25449510 **Fax:** 30 25449512
Email: redaktion@theaterheute.de **Web site:** http://www.theaterheute.de
Freq: 11 issues yearly; **Annual Sub.:** EUR 135,00; **Circ:** 15,000
Editor: Franz Wille; **Advertising Manager:** Martin Kraemer
Profile: Theatre and drama magazine. Each issue includes a complete and unabridged script by a world-famous playwright. Also includes theatre dates, international productions and festivals, book reviews and TV drama.
Language(s): German
ADVERTISING RATES:
Full Page Mono .... EUR 3000
Full Page Colour .... EUR 3800
Mechanical Data: Type Area: 276 x 215 mm, No. of Columns (Display): 4, Col Widths (Display): 50 mm
Copy instructions: *Copy Date:* 36 days prior to publication
CONSUMER: MUSIC & PERFORMING ARTS: Theatre

THEDINGHÄUSER ZEITUNG
744626G67B-14500
Editorial: Am Ristedter Weg 17, 28857 SYKE
Tel: 4242 58300 **Fax:** 4242 58332
Email: redaktiojn@kreiszeitung.de **Web site:** http://www.kreiszeitung.de
Freq: 312 issues yearly; **Circ:** 22,726
Advertising Manager: Axel Berghoff
Profile: The Kreiszeitung publishing group is the fifth largest newspaper in Niedersachsen, with a daily circulation of over 82,000 copies. Regional daily newspaper covering politics, economics, sport, travel and technology. Facebook: http://www.facebook.com/pages/Kreiszeitung.
Language(s): German
ADVERTISING RATES:
SCC .... EUR 64,80
Mechanical Data: Type Area: 472 x 325 mm, No. of Columns (Display): 7, Col Widths (Display): 45 mm
Copy instructions: *Copy Date:* 1 day prior to publication
REGIONAL DAILY & SUNDAY NEWSPAPERS: Regional Daily Newspapers

THEMEN
744636G2A-4740
Editorial: Mainzer Str. 16, 53424 REMAGEN
Tel: 2228 931121 **Fax:** 2228 931135
Email: themen@rommerskirchen.com **Web site:** http://www.rommerskirchen.com
Freq: Monthly; **Cover Price:** Free; **Circ:** 46,546
Profile: Magazine featuring reports, portraits and announcements concerning topics of interest to journalists.
Language(s): German
Supplement to: journalist, pr magazin
BUSINESS: COMMUNICATIONS, ADVERTISING & MARKETING

THE THORACIC AND CARDIOVASCULAR SURGEON
744674G56A-9640
Editorial: Benekestr. 2, 61231 BAD NAUHEIM
Tel: 711 8931 **Fax:** 711 8931-
Email: thoracic@thieme.de **Web site:** http://www.thieme.de/thoracic
Freq: 8 issues yearly; **Circ:** 1,400
Editor: W. P. Klövekorn
Profile: The Thoracic and Cardiovascular Surgeon publishes articles of the highest standard from internationally recognized thoracic and cardiovascular surgeons, cardiologists, anesthesiologists, physiologists, and pathologists. Original articles, case reports, and important meeting announcements keep you abreast of key clinical advances, as well as providing the theoretical background of cardiovascular and thoracic surgery. This journal is an essential tool for anyone working in this field.
Language(s): English
ADVERTISING RATES:
Full Page Mono .... EUR 1310
Full Page Colour .... EUR 2450
Mechanical Data: Type Area: 248 x 175 mm, No. of Columns (Display): 3, Col Widths (Display): 55 mm
Official Journal of: Organ d. German Society for Thoracic and Cardiovascular Surgery
BUSINESS: HEALTH & MEDICAL

THROMBOSIS AND HAEMOSTASIS
744675G56A-9660
Editorial: Hölderlinstr. 3, 70174 STUTTGART
Tel: 711 2298763 **Fax:** 711 2298765
Email: elinor.switzer@schattauer.de **Web site:** http://www.thrombosis-online.com
Freq: Monthly; **Annual Sub.:** EUR 396,00; **Circ:** 3,180
Editor: Elinor Switzer; **Advertising Manager:** Laura Lenz
Profile: Thrombosis and Haemostasis publishes original articles with a broad scope in basic research and clinical studies in vascular biology and medicine, covering blood coagulation, fibrinolysis and cellular haemostasis; platelets and blood cells; wound

healing and inflammation/infection; endothelium and vascular development; cardiovascular biology and cell signalling; cellular proteolysis and oncology; new technologies, diagnostic tools and drugs; animal models.
Language(s): English
Readership: Read by haematologists, angiologists, cardiologists, surgeons and laboratory physicians.
ADVERTISING RATES:
Full Page Mono .... EUR 1775
Full Page Colour .... EUR 3160
Mechanical Data: Type Area: 246 x 183 mm, No. of Columns (Display): 2, Col Widths (Display): 85 mm
Copy instructions: *Copy Date:* 40 days prior to publication
Official Journal of: Organ d. Working Group on Thrombosis of the European Society of Cardiology u. d. Società Italiana per lo Studio dell'Emostasi e della Trombosi
BUSINESS: HEALTH & MEDICAL

THÜRINGER ALLGEMEINE

744680G67B-14520
Editorial: Gottstedter Landstr. 6, 99092 ERFURT
Tel: 361 2275101 **Fax:** 361 2275144
Email: redaktion@thueringer-allgemeine.de **Web site:** http://www.thueringer-allgemeine.de
Freq: 312 issues yearly; **Circ:** 200,789
Editor: Paul-Josef Raue; **News Editor:** Axel Fick; **Advertising Manager:** Matthias Gauß
Profile: Regional daily newspaper covering politics, economics, sport, travel and technology. The Thüringer Allgemeine, based in the state capital Erfurt is the largest of the Thuringian newspapers. It derives its name, however, only since 1990, when publishers and editors the old name "Das Volk" pointedly renamed. Progress and innovation are closely interconnected with the TA. It was after the turn of the first newspaper in the East, that subscribe to AP and Reuters, "Western" agencies. The content-orientation to a critical and objective fair journalism, combined with a high added value for readers in 1990 was crucial in the cooperation with the WAZ media group. Investment in advanced editing and printing technology provided a solid foothold in the market. With her coat and 14 local editions between Nordhausen and Ilmenau, between Eisenach and Apolda the TA staff make for a much-page newspaper demanding reader. Facebook: http://www.facebook.com/pages/thueringer-allgemeinede/97398174719?ref=ts Twitter: http://twitter.com/taonline This Outlet offers RSS (Really Simple Syndication).
Language(s): German
ADVERTISING RATES:
SCC .... EUR 488,40
Mechanical Data: Type Area: 480 x 326 mm, No. of Columns (Display): 7, Col Widths (Display): 44 mm
Copy instructions: *Copy Date:* 2 days prior to publication
Supplement(s): Extra TA OTZ TLZ; rtv
REGIONAL DAILY & SUNDAY NEWSPAPERS: Regional Daily Newspapers

THÜRINGER ALLGEMEINE ONLINE

1622112G67B-16677
Editorial: Gottstedter Landstr. 6, 99092 ERFURT
Tel: 361 2275025 **Fax:** 361 2275144
Email: online@thueringer-allgemeine.de **Web site:** http://www.thueringer-allgemeine.de
Freq: Daily; **Cover Price:** Paid; **Circ:** 558,857 Unique Users
Editor: Jan Hollitzer
Profile: Ezine: Online daily newspaper covering politics, economics, culture, sports, travel and technologyand more. Facebook: http://www.facebook.com/pages/thueringer-allgemeinede/97398174719?ref=ts Twitter: http://twitter.com/taonline.
Language(s): German
REGIONAL DAILY & SUNDAY NEWSPAPERS: Regional Daily Newspapers

THÜRVBL. THÜRINGER VERWALTUNGSBLÄTTER

744686G32A-6520
Editorial: Lindenallee 15, 98617 MEININGEN
Tel: 3693 509350 **Fax:** 3693 509399
Freq: Monthly; **Annual Sub.:** EUR 197,40; **Circ:** 420
Editor: Friedrich-Wilhelm Gülsdorff; **Advertising Manager:** Roland Schulz
Profile: Journal of public administration and law for the Thüringer region in Germany.
Language(s): German
Readership: Aimed at local government and legal officials.
ADVERTISING RATES:
Full Page Mono .... EUR 820
Full Page Colour .... EUR 1750
Mechanical Data: Type Area: 260 x 180 mm
Copy instructions: *Copy Date:* 28 days prior to publication
BUSINESS: LOCAL GOVERNMENT, LEISURE & RECREATION: Local Government

TIERÄRZTLICHE PRAXIS G

744729G64H-340
Editorial: Hölderlinstr. 3, 70174 STUTTGART
Tel: 711 2298749 **Fax:** 711 2298765
Email: tp-lektorat@arcor.de **Web site:** http://www.tieraerztliche-praxis.de
Freq: 6 issues yearly; **Annual Sub.:** EUR 140,00; **Circ:** 1,599
Editor: Gisela Jöhnssen; **Advertising Manager:** Klaus Jansch
Profile: The Tierärztliche Praxis with its two rows as the only veterinary medical journal is aimed at explicitly to the large animal or small animal practitioners, thereby ensuring a highly targeted approach. For the specialists, it offers original or review articles on new therapy and surgical techniques or the use of modern imaging techniques. The less specialized veterinarian or newcomer, at his daily work tailored practical contributions in the training section "From the study and practice." Highlighted with the "Conclusion for practice" at the end of each article is also the piece gives readers a quick overview of the main contents of this modern-designed magazine with many high-quality, mostly color illustrations. Each issue provides an ATF-approved training to acquire a product ATF-hour.
Language(s): German
Readership: Aimed at vets caring for large and working animals.
ADVERTISING RATES:
Full Page Mono .... EUR 1430
Full Page Colour .... EUR 2075
Mechanical Data: Type Area: 243 x 179 mm, No. of Columns (Display): 3, Col Widths (Display): 57 mm
Copy instructions: *Copy Date:* 40 days prior to publication
Official Journal of: Organ d. DVG-Fachgruppen Innere Medizin u. klin. Labordiagnostik, Geflügel, Krankheiten d. kleinen Wiederkäuer u. d. dt.-sprachigen Gruppe d. European Association of Avian Veterinarians
BUSINESS: OTHER CLASSIFICATIONS: Veterinary

TIERÄRZTLICHE PRAXIS K

744730G64H-360
Editorial: Hölderlinstr. 3, 70174 STUTTGART
Tel: 711 2298749 **Fax:** 711 2298765
Email: tp-lektorat@arcor.de **Web site:** http://www.tieraeztliche-praxis.de
Annual Sub.: EUR 184,00; **Circ:** 2,305
Editor: Gisela Jöhnssen; **Advertising Manager:** Klaus Jansch
Profile: The Tierärztliche Praxis with its two rows as the only veterinary medical journal is aimed at explicitly to the large animal or small animal practitioners, thereby ensuring a highly targeted approach. For the specialists, it offers original or review articles on new therapy and surgical techniques or the use of modern imaging techniques. The less specialized veterinarian or newcomer, at his daily work tailored practical contributions in the training section "From the study and practice." Highlighted with the "Conclusion for practice" at the end of each article is also the piece gives readers a quick overview of the main contents of this modern-designed magazine with many high-quality, mostly color illustrations. Each issue provides an ATF-approved training to acquire a product ATF-hour.
Language(s): German
Official Journal of: Organ d. DVG-Fachgruppen Innere Medizin u. klin. Labordiagnostik, Geflügel, Krankheiten d. kleinen Wiederkäuer u. d. dt.-sprachigen Gruppe d. European Association of Avian Veterinarians
BUSINESS: OTHER CLASSIFICATIONS: Veterinary

TIERE FREUNDE FÜRS LEBEN

744732G91D-8180
Editorial: Rotebühlstr. 87, 70178 STUTTGART
Tel: 711 947680 **Fax:** 711 9476830
Email: info@panini.de **Web site:** http://www.panini.de
Freq: 6 issues yearly; **Cover Price:** EUR 2,80; **Circ:** 34,425
Editor: Gabriele El Hag
Profile: The magazine for girls who love animals! The cute animal magazine for girls who love animals. 36 pages, readers will find interesting features from the realm of the fantastic animals and useful information about the proper handling of their favorites. Good mood make attractive competitions, the exciting photo novel, the funny comic, and many puzzles and jokes. In each issue of this 4 trading cards, posters and Tier 2 great great extras.
Language(s): German
ADVERTISING RATES:
Full Page Mono .... EUR 3900
Full Page Colour .... EUR 3900
Mechanical Data: Type Area: 250 x 180 mm
CONSUMER: RECREATION & LEISURE: Children & Youth

TIHO-ANZEIGER

744756G64H-400
Editorial: Bünteweg 2, 30559 HANNOVER
Tel: 511 9538002 **Fax:** 511 953828002
Email: presse@tiho-hannover.de **Web site:** http://www.tiho-hannover.de
Freq: Quarterly; Free to qualifying individuals
Annual Sub.: EUR 18,00; **Circ:** 2,805
Editor: Sonja von Brethorst; **Advertising Manager:** Bettina Kruse
Profile: Journal of the Hanover School of Veterinary Medicine.
Language(s): German
Mechanical Data: Type Area: 272 x 188 mm, No. of Columns (Display): 4, Col Widths (Display): 44 mm
BUSINESS: OTHER CLASSIFICATIONS: Veterinary

TINA

744762G74A-2940
Editorial: Burchardstr. 11, 20095 HAMBURG
Tel: 40 30192555 **Fax:** 40 30194131
Email: tina@bauermedia.com **Web site:** http://www.bauermedia.com
Freq: Weekly; **Annual Sub.:** EUR 65,00; **Circ:** 587,112
Editor: Sabine Ingwersen
Profile: European magazine for women covering fashion, beauty, home decoration, food and drink.
Language(s): German
ADVERTISING RATES:
Full Page Mono .... EUR 32989
Full Page Colour .... EUR 32989
Mechanical Data: Type Area: 258 x 206 mm, No. of Columns (Display): 4, Col Widths (Display): 49 mm
Copy instructions: *Copy Date:* 28 days prior to publication
CONSUMER: WOMEN'S INTEREST CONSUMER MAGAZINES: Women's Interest

TINA KOCH & BACK-IDEEN

744763G74P-920
Editorial: Burchardstr. 11, 20095 HAMBURG
Tel: 40 30194909 **Fax:** 40 30195220
Email: tik@bauerredaktionen.de **Web site:** http://www.tinakochen.de
Freq: Monthly; **Annual Sub.:** EUR 27,00; **Circ:** 108,716
Editor: Karina Bárány; **Advertising Manager:** Michael Linke
Profile: The journal is the ideal companion for the woman, for whom cooking and baking and are part of everyday life and relaxation. tina Koch&Back-Ideen provides recipes for everyday life that are fast and easy to implement. In addition, the reader finds recipes and decorating tips for special occasions as well as useful information on the subjects household customer goods. The readers master any life situation in the areas of cooking and baking with ease. They are living life and have in most cases founded a family. The women manage profession and family every day life. Facebook: http://www.facebook.com/lecker.de.
Language(s): German
ADVERTISING RATES:
Full Page Mono .... EUR 9884
Full Page Colour .... EUR 9884
Mechanical Data: Type Area: 258 x 206 mm, No. of Columns (Display): 4, Col Widths (Display): 48 mm
Copy instructions: *Copy Date:* 36 days prior to publication
CONSUMER: WOMEN'S INTEREST CONSUMER MAGAZINES: Food & Cookery

TINA WOMAN

1793706G74A-3525
Editorial: Burchardstr. 11, 20095 HAMBURG
Tel: 40 30194168 **Fax:** 40 30194131
Email: tina@bauerredaktionen.de **Web site:** http://www.bauermedia.com
Freq: Quarterly; **Cover Price:** EUR 2,70; **Circ:** 200,000
Editor: Sabine Ingwersen
Profile: Magazine for women. tina woman lays emphasis on the areas of fashion, beauty and reports.
Language(s): German
ADVERTISING RATES:
Full Page Mono .... EUR 8500
Full Page Colour .... EUR 8500
Mechanical Data: Type Area: 258 x 206 mm

TIP AM SONNTAG

739009G72-10488
Editorial: Damm 9, 25421 PINNEBERG
Tel: 4101 5356220 **Fax:** 4101 5356006
Email: tip@a-beig.de **Web site:** http://www.a-beig.de
Freq: Weekly; **Cover Price:** Free; **Circ:** 44,690
Editor: Felix Middendorf-Bräuner; **Advertising Manager:** Karsten Raasch
Profile: Advertising journal (house-to-house) concentrating on local stories.
Language(s): German
ADVERTISING RATES:
Full Page Mono .... EUR 3432
Full Page Colour .... EUR 5160
Mechanical Data: Type Area: 430 x 278 mm, No. of Columns (Display): 6, Col Widths (Display): 45 mm
Copy instructions: *Copy Date:* 2 days prior to publication
LOCAL NEWSPAPERS

TIP AM SONNTAG

746999G72-14988
Editorial: Damm 9, 25421 PINNEBERG
Tel: 4101 5356220 **Fax:** 4101 5356606
Email: tip@a-beig.de **Web site:** http://www.a-beig.de
Freq: Weekly; **Cover Price:** Free; **Circ:** 33,896
Editor: Felix Middendorf-Bräuner; **Advertising Manager:** Karsten Raasch
Profile: Advertising journal (house-to-house) concentrating on local stories.
Language(s): German
ADVERTISING RATES:
Full Page Mono .... EUR 2838
Full Page Colour .... EUR 4257
Mechanical Data: Type Area: 430 x 278 mm, No. of Columns (Display): 6, Col Widths (Display): 45 mm
Copy instructions: *Copy Date:* 2 days prior to publication
LOCAL NEWSPAPERS

TIP BERLIN

744959G80-11440
Editorial: Karl-Liebknecht-Str. 29, 10178 BERLIN
Tel: 30 250030 **Fax:** 30 25003399
Email: redaktion@tip-berlin.de **Web site:** http://www.tip-berlin.de
Freq: 26 issues yearly; **Annual Sub.:** EUR 70,70; **Circ:** 40,203
Editor: Heiko Zwirner; **Advertising Manager:** Martin Stedler
Profile: City magazine for Berlin with a cultural offer of the capital in all its diversity and in all its depth. Simultaneously, the complex variety of the Berlin event market is here ordered, sorted, evaluated and commented. The tip Berlin is Germany's largest city magazine for the reader and an indispensable companion for 14 days of culture and live scene. Trends, tips and recommendations with high competence in Berlin culture and urban life and policy, provide for the common use of each issue. Facebook: http://www.facebook.com/pages/tip-Berlin/59810144647 Twitter: http://twitter.com/#!/tip_berlin This Outlet offers RSS (Really Simple Syndication).
Language(s): German
ADVERTISING RATES:
Full Page Mono .... EUR 4290
Full Page Colour .... EUR 5790
Mechanical Data: Type Area: 254 x 180 mm, No. of Columns (Display): 4, Col Widths (Display): 42 mm
Copy instructions: *Copy Date:* 9 days prior to publication
Supplement(s): tip Fernsehen
CONSUMER: RURAL & REGIONAL INTEREST

TIP DER WOCHE - AUSG. AHLEN

1638989G72-18574
Editorial: Karl-Wüst-Str. 15, 74076 HEILBRONN
Tel: 7132 945612
Email: eva.gross@tip-werbeverlag.de **Web site:** http://www.tip-werbeverlag.de
Freq: Weekly; **Cover Price:** Free; **Circ:** 26,838
Editor: Eva Groß; **Advertising Manager:** Andreas Riekötter
Profile: Advertising journal (house-to-house) concentrating on local stories.
Language(s): German
ADVERTISING RATES:
Full Page Mono .... EUR 840
Mechanical Data: Type Area: 280 x 205 mm, No. of Columns (Display): 5, Col Widths (Display): 40 mm
Copy instructions: *Copy Date:* 7 days prior to publication
LOCAL NEWSPAPERS

TIP DER WOCHE - AUSG. DRESDEN-KOHLESTR.

744844G72-17544
Editorial: Karl-Wüst-Str. 15, 74076 HEILBRONN
Tel: 7132 945612
Email: eva.gross@tip-werbeverlag.de **Web site:** http://www.tip-werbeverlag.de
Freq: Weekly; **Cover Price:** Free; **Circ:** 15,419
Editor: Eva Groß; **Advertising Manager:** Andreas Riekötter
Profile: Advertising journal (house-to-house) concentrating on local stories.
Language(s): German
ADVERTISING RATES:
Full Page Mono .... EUR 1078
Mechanical Data: Type Area: 280 x 205 mm, No. of Columns (Display): 5, Col Widths (Display): 40 mm
Copy instructions: *Copy Date:* 7 days prior to publication
LOCAL NEWSPAPERS

TIPP

1649839G17-1560
Editorial: Dr.-Stiebel-Str., 37603 HOLZMINDEN
Tel: 5531 70295684 **Fax:** 5531 70295584
Email: michael.birke@stiebel-eltron.de **Web site:** http://www.stiebel-eltron.de
Freq: 3 issues yearly; **Cover Price:** Free; **Circ:** 105,000
Editor: Michael Birke
Profile: Magazine for experts and traders in the electro, sanitary and heating branches.
Language(s): German

DER TIPP DES TAGES

744957G14A-7480
Editorial: Fraunhoferstr. 5, 82152 PLANEGG
Tel: 89 89517224 **Fax:** 89 89517290
Email: online@haufe.de **Web site:** http://www.haufe.de
Freq: Annual; **Cover Price:** EUR 14,80; **Circ:** 5,000
Editor: Jasmin Jallad
Profile: Business calendar for lawyers, small and medium sized company managers and freelancers about law, economy and data processing.
Language(s): German

TIPPS

744975G4E-6220
Editorial: Hildesheimer Str. 309, 30519 HANNOVER
Tel: 511 9872530 **Fax:** 511 9872545
Email: rolf.schaper@bgbau.de **Web site:** http://www.bgbau.de
Freq: Half-yearly; **Circ:** 700,000
Editor: Rolf Schaper
Profile: Building industry magazine about safety at work and health protection.
Language(s): German

TIRAGE LIMITÉ

744983G73-476
Editorial: Postfach 4024, 40687 ERKRATH
Tel: 2104 1384968 **Fax:** 2104 1384969
Email: elite@tirage-limite.com **Web site:** http://www.tirage-limite.com

Freq: Quarterly; **Annual Sub.:** EUR 79,80; **Circ:** 104,000
Advertising Manager: Amadeo Tusa
Profile: Lifestyle magazine. The range of topics offers Culture & Art - Antiques & Beverage - Recreation & Tourism - Fashion and Architecture - Real Estate & Movable - Luxury & Lifestyle - Luxury Services & trends - etc. The magazine is partly in the 5-star hotels and VIP lounges their airports, as a board medium at some airlines.
Language(s): Dutch; English; French; German
ADVERTISING RATES:
Full Page Mono .... EUR 16000
Full Page Colour .... EUR 16000
Mechanical Data: Type Area: 288 x 200 mm, No. of Columns (Display): 3, Col Widths (Display): 63 mm
Copy instructions: *Copy Date:* 21 days prior to publication

TIS GALA BAU 1898595G21A-4428
Editorial: Avenwedder Str. 55, 33335 GÜTERSLOH
Tel: 5241 8090884 **Fax:** 5241 80690880
Email: roland.herr@bauverlag.de **Web site:** http://www.tis.de
Freq: Quarterly; **Circ:** 19,665
Editor: Roland Herr; **Advertising Manager:** Christian Reinke
Profile: All activities - up to 1 meter below the turf - both running and road construction companies as well as gardening and landscaping firms in this special edition tis GalaBau to be treated!.
Language(s): German
ADVERTISING RATES:
Full Page Mono .... EUR 3595
Full Page Colour .... EUR 5350
Mechanical Data: Type Area: 270 x 186 mm, No. of Columns (Display): 4, Col Widths (Display): 45 mm

TIS TIEFBAU INGENIEURBAU STRASSENBAU 745016G42B-4
Editorial: Avenwedder Str. 55, 33335 GÜTERSLOH
Tel: 5241 8090884 **Fax:** 5241 80690880
Email: roland.herr@bauverlag.de **Web site:** http://www.tis.de
Freq: 10 issues yearly; Free to qualifying individuals
Annual Sub.: EUR 129,60; **Circ:** 11,718
Editor: Roland Herr; **Advertising Manager:** Christian Reinke
Profile: tis Tiefbau Ingenieurbau Straßenbau is a trade journal concerned with modern process technology and construction. It gives qualified information about the areas road construction, civil engineering, bridge construction, tunnel construction, earthworks, foundations, sewer construction and hydraulic engineering. Four key issues to inform practice on transmission lines and the grave-free building. This is complemented by a detailed reporting of information about new products on the market for construction equipment, commercial vehicles, building materials, components, equipment and facilities as well as instructions for their rational use. Besides technical information, the target group of contractors, engineers and construction officer in the civil engineering road construction technical information on the successful management of a construction company as well as information about economic developments and trends in the market. Details of the training and continuing education, literature, meetings and legal matters as well as reports from companies and organizations complete the offering.
Language(s): German
ADVERTISING RATES:
Full Page Mono .... EUR 3140
Full Page Colour .... EUR 4940
Mechanical Data: Type Area: 270 x 186 mm, No. of Columns (Display): 4, Col Widths (Display): 45 mm
Copy instructions: *Copy Date:* 14 days prior to publication
BUSINESS: CONSTRUCTION: Roads

TISCHLERMEISTER NORD 729622G23A-240
Editorial: Albert-Schweitzer-Ring 10, 22045 HAMBURG **Tel:** 40 6686540 **Fax:** 40 66865470
Email: hkh-nord@tischler.de **Web site:** http://www.tischlerhandwerk.org
Freq: Quarterly; **Circ:** 2,000
Editor: Frank Schütt; **Advertising Manager:** Frank Fricke
Profile: Publication about carpentry.
Language(s): German
Readership: Aimed at carpenters and joiners in Hamburg.
ADVERTISING RATES:
Full Page Mono .... EUR 1664
Full Page Colour .... EUR 2736
Mechanical Data: Type Area: 265 x 185 mm, No. of Columns (Display): 4, Col Widths (Display): 45 mm
Official Journal of: Organ d. Fachverb. Holz u. Kunststoff Nord
BUSINESS: FURNISHINGS & FURNITURE

TISCHTENNIS 725061G75H-140
Editorial: Rektoratsweg 36, 48159 MÜNSTER
Tel: 251 2300550 **Fax:** 251 2300599
Email: tt@philippka.de **Web site:** http://www.philippka.de
Freq: Monthly; Free to qualifying individuals
Annual Sub.: EUR 43,20; **Circ:** 14,124
Editor: Rahul Nelson; **Advertising Manager:** Peter Möllers
Profile: The practical benefit for players, coaches and the makers in the clubs, intend the content of the only national color magazine for table tennis in Germany. Training tips and exercise programs, equipment tests, organizational and planning assistance as well as practical articles on subjects such as sports medicine, sports nutrition and club management complement the extensive background coverage of national and international top events. Reports and portraits of clubs, players and coaches complete the range of topics. Four regional sections (North, West, Southwest and South) also inform in detail about everything that goes on in the state associations, districts and clubs at the base.
Language(s): German
ADVERTISING RATES:
Full Page Mono .... EUR 1485
Full Page Colour .... EUR 2095
Mechanical Data: Type Area: 267 x 180 mm, No. of Columns (Display): 3, Col Widths (Display): 55 mm
Copy instructions: *Copy Date:* 28 days prior to publication
CONSUMER: SPORT: Racquet Sports

TITANIC 745018G82-8320
Editorial: Sophienstr. 8, 60487 FRANKFURT
Tel: 69 9705040 **Fax:** 69 97050497
Email: info@titanic-magazin.de **Web site:** http://www.titanic-magazin.de
Freq: Monthly; **Annual Sub.:** EUR 43,20; **Circ:** 99,760
Editor: Leo Fischer
Profile: Political satire magazine with event calendar, readings, exhibitions and other events.
Language(s): German
Readership: Aimed at people interested in humour and politics.
ADVERTISING RATES:
Full Page Mono .... EUR 2800
Full Page Colour .... EUR 5000
Mechanical Data: Type Area: 260 x 190 mm
CONSUMER: CURRENT AFFAIRS & POLITICS

DER TITELSCHUTZ ANZEIGER 745020G2A-4780
Editorial: Nebendahlstr. 16, 22041 HAMBURG
Tel: 40 60900961 **Fax:** 40 60900966
Email: titelschutz-anzeiger@presse-fachverlag.de
Web site: http://www.titelschutzanzeiger.de
Freq: Weekly; **Annual Sub.:** EUR 80,00; **Circ:** 3,100
Editor: Angela Lautenschläger; **Advertising Manager:** Angela Lautenschläger
Profile: Germany's special medium for title protection. Recipients: Media lawyers / legal experts, in-house counsels, CEOs and decision makers in publishing, radio and TV stations, producers of audio-visual, digital and electronic media (film, television, video, audio recordings, software).
Language(s): German
ADVERTISING RATES:
Full Page Mono .... EUR 925
Mechanical Data: Type Area: 262 x 175 mm, No. of Columns (Display): 2, Col Widths (Display): 85 mm

DER TITELSCHUTZ ANZEIGER MIT DER SOFTWARE TITEL 745021G2A-4800
Editorial: Nebendahlstr. 16, 22041 HAMBURG
Tel: 40 60900961 **Fax:** 40 60900966
Email: titelschutz-anzeiger@presse-fachverlag.de
Web site: http://www.titelschutzanzeiger.de
Freq: Monthly; **Annual Sub.:** EUR 80,00; **Circ:** 5,200
Editor: Angela Lautenschläger; **Advertising Manager:** Angela Lautenschläger
Profile: Index of copyrights for newspapers, magazines, books, sound storage media, radio, TV and movies.
Language(s): German
ADVERTISING RATES:
Full Page Mono .... EUR 1660
Mechanical Data: Type Area: 262 x 175 mm, No. of Columns (Display): 2, Col Widths (Display): 85 mm
Copy instructions: *Copy Date:* 14 days prior to publication

TJI TOBACCO JOURNAL INTERNATIONAL 745052G51-100
Editorial: Erich-Dombrowski-Str. 2, 55127 MAINZ
Tel: 6131 5841138 **Fax:** 6131 5841102
Email: stefanie.rossel@konradin.de **Web site:** http://www.tobaccojournal.com
Freq: 6 issues yearly; **Annual Sub.:** EUR 93,50; **Circ:** 6,100
Editor: Stefanie Rossel; **Advertising Manager:** Stefanie Scherrer
Profile: Magazine for the international tobacco industry.
Language(s): English
ADVERTISING RATES:
Full Page Mono .... EUR 4230
Full Page Colour .... EUR 4230
Mechanical Data: Type Area: 255 x 176 mm, No. of Columns (Display): 3, Col Widths (Display): 56 mm
Copy instructions: *Copy Date:* 28 days prior to publication
BUSINESS: TOBACCO

TK AKTUELL 745023G94H-12520
Editorial: Bramfelder Str. 140, 22305 HAMBURG
Tel: 40 69092187
Email: redaktion@tk-online.de **Web site:** http://www.tk-online.de
Freq: 3 issues yearly; **Circ:** 4,900,000
Editor: Roderich Vollmer-Rupprecht
Profile: Magazine containing articles about medicine, health and insurance.
Language(s): German
ADVERTISING RATES:
Full Page Mono .... EUR 43200
Full Page Colour .... EUR 43200
Mechanical Data: Type Area: 263 x 182 mm
Copy instructions: *Copy Date:* 60 days prior to publication
CONSUMER: OTHER CLASSIFICATIONS: Customer Magazines

TKREPORT 744728G22E-1
Editorial: Siegfriedstr. 5, 63785 OBERNBURG
Tel: 6022 61980 **Fax:** 6022 619823
Email: redaktion@tk-report.de **Web site:** http://www.tk-report.de
Freq: 10 issues yearly; **Annual Sub.:** EUR 78,00; **Circ:** 7,500
Editor: Albert Vollmer
Profile: Leading German-language journal in the field of frozen food, ice cream and TK-Technik/Logistik, the organ and driving force of the entire telecommunications industry.
Language(s): German
ADVERTISING RATES:
Full Page Mono .... EUR 2880
Full Page Colour .... EUR 3660
Mechanical Data: Type Area: 280 x 184 mm, No. of Columns (Display): 4, Col Widths (Display): 45 mm
BUSINESS: FOOD: Frozen Food

TLZ EISENACH EISENACHER PRESSE 745030G67B-14600
Editorial: Marienstr. 14, 99423 WEIMAR
Tel: 3643 2063 **Fax:** 3643 206422
Email: redaktion@tlz.de **Web site:** http://www.tlz.de
Freq: 312 issues yearly; **Circ:** 18,930
Profile: Regional daily newspaper with news on politics, economy, culture, sports, travel, technology, etc. The Thüringische Landeszeitung your publisher based in Weimar and Thuringia is the oldest newspaper. It appears not only along the "chain of pearls of culture", ie from about Gera Jena, Weimar and Erfurt, Gotha and Eisenach up, but also in Bad Langensalza, Mühlhausen and Eichsfeld. Particularly noteworthy is the cultural profile of the TLZ, highlighting among other things, a regular cultural supplement. From time immemorial, TLZ a critical spirit breathed between the lines. The particular closeness to the readers has always been her concern. Many actions in the immediate vicinity of the audience are proof of this.Significant investment in technical equipment in the early 90s allow the TLZ up to date. The cooperation with the newspaper group Thuringia ensure the editorial independence and a solid economic base. The journalistic self-understanding of TLZ is: We write plain text! Facebook: http://www.facebook.com/pages/TLZ/130099667004470 Twitter: http://twitter.com/tlznews This Outlet offers RSS (Really Simple Syndication).
Language(s): German
ADVERTISING RATES:
SCC .... EUR 61,20
Mechanical Data: Type Area: 480 x 326 mm, No. of Columns (Display): 7, Col Widths (Display): 44 mm
Copy instructions: *Copy Date:* 2 days prior to publication
Supplement(s): Extra TA OTZ TLZ; rtv
REGIONAL DAILY & SUNDAY NEWSPAPERS: Regional Daily Newspapers

TLZ ERFURT THÜRINGISCHE LANDESZEITUNG 745031G67B-14620
Editorial: Marienstr. 14, 99423 WEIMAR
Tel: 3643 2063 **Fax:** 3643 206422
Email: redaktion@tlz.de **Web site:** http://www.tlz.de
Freq: 312 issues yearly; **Circ:** 36,049
Profile: Regional daily newspaper with news on politics, economy, culture, sports, travel, technology, etc. The Thüringische Landeszeitung your publisher based in Weimar and Thuringia is the oldest newspaper. It appears not only along the "chain of pearls of culture", ie from about Gera Jena, Weimar and Erfurt, Gotha and Eisenach up, but also in Bad Langensalza, Mühlhausen and Eichsfeld. Particularly noteworthy is the cultural profile of the TLZ, highlighting among other things, a regular cultural supplement. From time immemorial, TLZ a critical spirit breathed between the lines. The particular closeness to the readers has always been her concern. Many actions in the immediate vicinity of the audience are proof of this. Significant investment in technical equipment in the early 90s allow the TLZ up to date. The cooperation with the newspaper group Thuringia ensure the editorial independence and a solid economic base. The journalistic self-understanding of TLZ is: We write plain text! Facebook: http://www.facebook.com/pages/TLZ/130099667004470 Twitter: http://twitter.com/tlznews This Outlet offers RSS (Really Simple Syndication).
Language(s): German
ADVERTISING RATES:
SCC .... EUR 93,60
Mechanical Data: Type Area: 480 x 326 mm, No. of Columns (Display): 7, Col Widths (Display): 44 mm
Copy instructions: *Copy Date:* 2 days prior to publication
Supplement(s): ESC aktuell; Extra TA OTZ TLZ; rtv
REGIONAL DAILY & SUNDAY NEWSPAPERS: Regional Daily Newspapers

TLZ GERA THÜRINGISCHE LANDESZEITUNG 745032G67B-14640
Editorial: Marienstr. 14, 99423 WEIMAR
Tel: 3643 2063 **Fax:** 3643 206422
Email: redaktion@tlz.de **Web site:** http://www.tlz.de
Freq: 312 issues yearly; **Circ:** 28,221
Profile: Regional daily newspaper with news on politics, economy, culture, sports, travel, technology, etc. The Thüringische Landeszeitung your publisher based in Weimar and Thuringia is the oldest newspaper. It appears not only along the "chain of pearls of culture", ie from about Gera Jena, Weimar and Erfurt, Gotha and Eisenach up, but also in Bad Langensalza, Mühlhausen and Eichsfeld. Particularly noteworthy is the cultural profile of the TLZ, highlighting among other things, a regular cultural supplement. From time immemorial, TLZ a critical spirit breathed between the lines. The particular closeness to the readers has always been her concern. Many actions in the immediate vicinity of the audience are proof of this. Significant investment in technical equipment in the early 90s allow the TLZ up to date. The cooperation with the newspaper group Thuringia ensure the editorial independence and a solid economic base. The journalistic self-understanding of TLZ is: We write plain text! Facebook: http://www.facebook.com/pages/TLZ/130099667004470 Twitter: http://twitter.com/tlznews This Outlet offers RSS (Really Simple Syndication).
Language(s): German
ADVERTISING RATES:
SCC .... EUR 86,00
Mechanical Data: Type Area: 480 x 326 mm, No. of Columns (Display): 7, Col Widths (Display): 44 mm
Copy instructions: *Copy Date:* 2 days prior to publication
Supplement(s): Extra TA OTZ TLZ; rtv
REGIONAL DAILY & SUNDAY NEWSPAPERS: Regional Daily Newspapers

TLZ GOTHA GOTHAER TAGESPOST 745033G67B-14660
Editorial: Marienstr. 14, 99423 WEIMAR
Tel: 3643 2063 **Fax:** 3643 206422
Email: redaktion@tlz.de **Web site:** http://www.tlz.de
Freq: 312 issues yearly; **Circ:** 21,751
Profile: Regional daily newspaper with news on politics, economy, culture, sports, travel, technology, etc. The Thüringische Landeszeitung your publisher based in Weimar and Thuringia is the oldest newspaper. It appears not only along the "chain of pearls of culture", ie from about Gera Jena, Weimar and Erfurt, Gotha and Eisenach up, but also in Bad Langensalza, Mulhouse and Eichsfeld. Particularly noteworthy is the cultural profile of the TLZ, highlighting among other things, a regular cultural supplement. From time immemorial, TLZ a critical spirit breathed between the lines. The particular closeness to the readers has always been her concern. Many actions in the immediate vicinity of the audience are proof of this. Significant investment in technical equipment in the early 90s allow the TLZ up to date. The cooperation with the newspaper group Thuringia ensure the editorial independence and a solid economic base. The journalistic self-understanding of TLZ is: We write plain text! Facebook: http://www.facebook.com/pages/TLZ/130099667004470 Twitter: http://twitter.com/tlznews This Outlet offers RSS (Really Simple Syndication).
Language(s): German
ADVERTISING RATES:
SCC .... EUR 61,60
Mechanical Data: Type Area: 480 x 326 mm, No. of Columns (Display): 7, Col Widths (Display): 44 mm
Copy instructions: *Copy Date:* 2 days prior to publication
Supplement(s): Extra TA OTZ TLZ; rtv
REGIONAL DAILY & SUNDAY NEWSPAPERS: Regional Daily Newspapers

TLZ JENA THÜRINGISCHE LANDESZEITUNG 745034G67B-14680
Editorial: Marienstr. 14, 99423 WEIMAR
Tel: 3643 2063 **Fax:** 3643 206402
Email: redaktion@tlz.de **Web site:** http://www.tlz.de
Freq: 312 issues yearly; **Circ:** 22,742
Profile: Regional daily newspaper with news on politics, economy, culture, sports, travel, technology, etc. The Thüringische Landeszeitung your publisher based in Weimar and Thuringia is the oldest newspaper. It appears not only along the "chain of pearls of culture", ie from about Gera Jena, Weimar and Erfurt, Gotha and Eisenach up, but also in Bad Langensalza, Mühlhausen and Eichsfeld. Particularly noteworthy is the cultural profile of the TLZ, highlighting among other things, a regular cultural supplement. From time immemorial, TLZ a critical spirit breathed between the lines. The particular closeness to the readers has always been her concern. Many actions in the immediate vicinity of the audience are proof of this. Significant investment in technical equipment in the early 90s allow the TLZ up to date. The cooperation with the newspaper group Thuringia ensure the editorial independence and a solid economic base. The journalistic self-understanding of TLZ is: We write plain text! Facebook: http://www.facebook.com/pages/TLZ/130099667004470 Twitter: http://twitter.com/tlznews This Outlet offers RSS (Really Simple Syndication).
Language(s): German
ADVERTISING RATES:
SCC .... EUR 68,80
Mechanical Data: Type Area: 480 x 326 mm, No. of Columns (Display): 7, Col Widths (Display): 44 mm
Copy instructions: *Copy Date:* 2 days prior to publication
Supplement(s): Extra TA OTZ TLZ; rtv
REGIONAL DAILY & SUNDAY NEWSPAPERS: Regional Daily Newspapers

TLZ.DE 1622118G67B-16678

Editorial: Marienstr. 14, 99423 WEIMAR
Tel: 3643 206420 **Fax:** 3643 206422
Email: online@tlz.de **Web site:** http://www.tlz.de
Freq: Daily; **Cover Price:** Paid
Editor: Hans Hoffmeister; **News Editor:** Norbert Block
Profile: Internet-Portal der Thüringer Landeszeitung : local news, regional news, headlines and news on sports, politics, economy, culture, events. Facebook: http://www.facebook.com/tlz.de Twitter: http://twitter.com/#!/TLZnews This Outlet offers RSS (Really Simple Syndication).
Language(s): German
REGIONAL DAILY & SUNDAY NEWSPAPERS: Regional Daily Newspapers

TM 745041G47A-1400

Editorial: Hildebrandtstr. 24, 40215 DÜSSELDORF
Tel: 211 83030 **Fax:** 211 324862
Email: bilder@bb-mediacompany.com **Web site:** http://www.bb-mediacompany.com
Freq: 10 issues yearly; **Annual Sub.:** EUR 229,00; **Circ:** 24,270
Editor: Rainer Schlatmann; **Advertising Manager:** Maike Prelle
Profile: TM delivers every issue with the relevant trends and ideas from the fashion business for the decision makers in commerce and industry. Exclusive reports, interviews with opinion leaders in the industry, pioneering store concepts and differentiated illuminated track topics arise in direct dialogue with decision makers from industry and trade. Magazine for trend analysis and decision making in fashion. As a high fashion magazine to design sophisticated layout and a clearly structured guide readers characterized TM. For this purpose are: analytical, market-trend information exclusive editorial photo shoots, visually high-class retail reports, interviews with depth, reports away from the mainstream, economically sound economic and sales data.
Language(s): German
ADVERTISING RATES:
Full Page Mono .... EUR 10930
Full Page Colour .... EUR 10930
Mechanical Data: Type Area: 299 x 232 mm
Copy instructions: *Copy Date:* 14 days prior to publication
BUSINESS: CLOTHING & TEXTILES

TM TECHNISCHES MESSEN

745049G19A-1067
Editorial: Rosenheimer Str. 145, 81671 MÜNCHEN
Tel: 89 45051288 **Fax:** 89 45051292
Email: julia.multerer@oldenbourg.de **Web site:** http://www.tm-technisches-messen.de
Freq: 11 issues yearly; Free to qualifying individuals
Annual Sub.: EUR 364,00; **Circ:** 781
Editor: Julia Multerer; **Advertising Manager:** Julia Multerer
Profile: Magazine providing information relating to all aspects of engineering.
Language(s): English; German
ADVERTISING RATES:
Full Page Mono .... EUR 2175
Full Page Colour .... EUR 3315
Mechanical Data: Type Area: 254 x 170 mm, No. of Columns (Display): 2, Col Widths (Display): 81 mm
Official Journal of: Organ d. AMA, Fachverb. f. Sensorik e.V. u. d. NAMUR, Interessengemeinschaft Prozessleittechnik d. chem. u. pharmazeut. Industrie
BUSINESS: ENGINEERING & MACHINERY

TÖLZER KURIER 745059G67B-14740

Editorial: Pfaffenrieder Str. 9, 82515 WOLFRATSHAUSEN **Tel:** 8171 2690
Fax: 8171 269240
Email: fsav@merkur-online.de
Freq: 312 issues yearly; **Circ:** 9,806
Advertising Manager: Hans-Georg Bechthold
Profile: The Münchner Merkur with its own local newspapers, of which the Tölzer Kurier is one that, the leading regional newspaper brand in the Munich area - the most affluent area of Germany. The combination of newspaper and region is the foundation on which to build the success of the title. This is the newspaper not only the factual news agency, but forms a community of solidarity with its readers and the local community. The clear focus on local reporting creates a high regard to human reader loyalty. She presses one hand in the very high number of close to 180,000 subscribers. Also for the high reader-commitment is the loyalty of the total current 827 000 daily readers, the Münchner Merkur or one of its local newspapers usually read over many years. The Münchner Merkur with its own local newspapers is a newspaper for the whole family, tradition and modern life for one of the most beautiful regions of Germany unites. Reliable, informative, critical: the Münchner Merkur is the indispensable daily newspaper for the region. This Outlet offers RSS (Really Simple Syndication).
Language(s): German
ADVERTISING RATES:
SCC .... EUR 43,60
Mechanical Data: Type Area: 474 x 324 mm, No. of Columns (Display): 7, Col Widths (Display): 45 mm
Copy instructions: *Copy Date:* 1 day prior to publication
REGIONAL DAILY & SUNDAY NEWSPAPERS: Regional Daily Newspapers

TOMONTOUR SUMMER

1827813G89A-12393
Editorial: Birkenleiten 11, 81543 MÜNCHEN
Tel: 89 62439772 **Fax:** 89 62439771
Email: fs@tomontour.de **Web site:** http://www.tomontour.de
Freq: Annual; **Cover Price:** Free; **Circ:** 172,000
Editor: Frank Störbrauck; **Advertising Manager:** Tom Dedek
Profile: Gay guide to worldwide destinations Facebook: http://www.facebook.com/pages/TOM-ON-TOUR/80220127132 Twitter: http://twitter.com/#!/tomontour.
Language(s): English; German

TOMONTOUR WINTER

1860215G89A-12417
Editorial: Birkenleiten 11, 81543 MÜNCHEN
Tel: 89 62439772 **Fax:** 89 62439771
Email: fs@tomontour.de **Web site:** http://www.tomontour.de
Freq: Annual; **Cover Price:** Free; **Circ:** 172,000
Editor: Frank Störbrauck; **Advertising Manager:** Tom Dedek
Profile: Gay guide to worldwide destinations Facebook: http://www.facebook.com/pages/TOM-ON-TOUR/80220127132 Twitter: http://twitter.com/#!/tomontour.
Language(s): English; German
Mechanical Data: Type Area: 280 x 216 mm

TOP5 1929676G14A-10380

Editorial: Ihmeplatz 2, 30449 HANNOVER
Tel: 511 4301673 **Fax:** 511 4301871
Email: andrea.zimmermann@enercity.de **Web site:** http://www.enercity.de
Freq: 3 issues yearly; **Cover Price:** Free; **Circ:** 17,000
Editor: Andrea Zimmermann
Profile: Newsletter focusing on the use of electricity in business.
Language(s): German

TOP AGRAR 745087G21A-3880

Editorial: Hülsebrockstr. 2, 48165 MÜNSTER
Tel: 2501 801640 **Fax:** 2501 801654
Email: redaktion@topagrar.com **Web site:** http://www.topagrar.com
Freq: Monthly; **Annual Sub.:** EUR 87,00; **Circ:** 115,645
Editor: Heinz-Günter Topüth; **Advertising Manager:** Peter Wiggers
Profile: Agricultural trade magazine for agricultural and livestock farms with high input use and investment. Facebook: http://www.facebook.com/pages/top-agrar/269807686281 Twitter: http://twitter.com/#!/topagrar This Outlet offers RSS (Really Simple Syndication).
Language(s): German
ADVERTISING RATES:
Full Page Mono .... EUR 9530
Full Page Colour .... EUR 14918
Mechanical Data: Type Area: 270 x 190 mm, No. of Columns (Display): 4, Col Widths (Display): 46 mm
Copy instructions: *Copy Date:* 30 days prior to publication
BUSINESS: AGRICULTURE & FARMING

TOP AGRAR ONLINE

1622122G21A-4261
Editorial: Hülsebrockstr. 2, 48165 MÜNSTER
Tel: 251 801654 **Fax:** 251 801204
Email: redaktion@topagrar.com **Web site:** http://www.topagrar.com
Freq: Daily; **Cover Price:** Paid; **Circ:** 581,709 Unique Users
Editor: Heinz-Günter Topüth; **Advertising Manager:** Peter Wiggers
Profile: Ezine: Magazine about European farming methods. Facebook: http://www.facebook.com/pages/top-agrar/269807686281 Twitter: http://twitter.com/#!/topagrar RSS (Really Simple Syndication) wird angeboten.
Language(s): German
BUSINESS: AGRICULTURE & FARMING

TOP HAIR INTERNATIONAL FASHION 745155G15B-320

Editorial: Medienplatz 1, 76571 GAGGENAU
Tel: 7225 916329 **Fax:** 7225 916320
Email: info@tophair.de **Web site:** http://www.tophair.de
Freq: 24 issues yearly; **Annual Sub.:** EUR 93,00; **Circ:** 30,156
Editor: Rebecca Kandler
Profile: European trade magazine for hairdressers with trends, news and interviews from the major fashion capitals of the world. The magazine is the undisputed market leader in Germany. For every first of the month the magazine delivers a four-language inside everything about hair fashion, styling and products.
Language(s): German
ADVERTISING RATES:
Full Page Mono .... EUR 4570
Full Page Colour .... EUR 6480
Mechanical Data: Type Area: 284 x 199 mm, No. of Columns (Display): 4, Col Widths (Display): 48 mm
Copy instructions: *Copy Date:* 31 days prior to publication
BUSINESS: COSMETICS & HAIRDRESSING: Hairdressing

TOP HOTEL 745156G11A-1440

Editorial: Celsiusstr. 7, 86899 LANDSBERG
Tel: 8191 9471620 **Fax:** 8191 9471666
Email: karsch@tophotel.de **Web site:** http://www.tophotel.de
Freq: 10 issues yearly; Free to qualifying individuals
Annual Sub.: EUR 50,00; **Circ:** 18,403
Editor: Thomas Karsch; **Advertising Manager:** Martin Frey
Profile: Magazine about hotel management. Official journal of the Hotel Sales and Marketing Association.
Language(s): German
ADVERTISING RATES:
Full Page Mono .... EUR 5530
Full Page Colour .... EUR 8080
Mechanical Data: Type Area: 270 x 184 mm, No. of Columns (Display): 3, Col Widths (Display): 59 mm
Copy instructions: *Copy Date:* 14 days prior to publication
Official Journal of: Organ d. FCSI Deutschland-Österr. e.V., d. FBMA e.V., d. VSR e.V., d. Flair Hotels e.V., d. Landidyll e.V. u. d. GAD e.V.
Supplement(s): HIZ Hotellerie in Zahlen
BUSINESS: CATERING: Catering, Hotels & Restaurants

TOP MAGAZIN DÜSSELDORF

745170G80-11620
Editorial: Corneliusstr. 85, 40215 DÜSSELDORF
Tel: 211 865120 **Fax:** 211 8651232
Email: duesseldorf@top-magazin.de **Web site:** http://www.top-magazin-duesseldorf.de
Freq: Quarterly; **Annual Sub.:** EUR 15,00; **Circ:** 14,000
Editor: Albert H. Bitter; **Advertising Manager:** Albert H. Bitter
Profile: Regionales Lifestylemagazin für Düsseldorf. Das Magazin ist konzipiert für all diejenigen, die das Außergewöhnliche, das Schöne und das Exklusive suchen. Zudem berichten wir über das Neueste aus Wirtschaft & Gesellschaft, Kultur & Freizeit, Gesundheit & Medizin, Mode, Luxus, Wellness und Sport. Das Magazin präsentiert besondere Persönlichkeiten, interessante Unternehmen und bieten anspruchsvolle Berichtsterstattung mit nationalem Flair.
Language(s): German
ADVERTISING RATES:
Full Page Mono .... EUR 2350
Full Page Colour .... EUR 2350
Mechanical Data: Type Area: 272 x 186 mm, No. of Columns (Display): 3, Col Widths (Display): 63 mm
CONSUMER: RURAL & REGIONAL INTEREST

TOP MAGAZIN HOCHZEITSTRÄUME

1792726G74A-3521
Editorial: Kantstr. 151, 10623 BERLIN
Tel: 30 2062673 **Fax:** 30 20626750
Email: redaktion@tmm.de **Web site:** http://www.tmm.de
Freq: Annual; **Cover Price:** Free; **Circ:** 25,000
Editor: Antje Naumann
Profile: The practical guide about weddings from A to Z for array schedule, service, styling, celebrations - tips, ideas and information and checklists for the big day and its preparation.
Language(s): German
ADVERTISING RATES:
Full Page Mono .... EUR 1490
Full Page Colour .... EUR 1490
Mechanical Data: Type Area: 272 x 186 mm

TOP MAGAZIN RUHRSTADT DORTMUND 745168G80-11580

Editorial: Lindemannstr. 81, 44137 DORTMUND
Tel: 231 22227700 **Fax:** 231 22227788
Email: dortmund@top-magazin.de **Web site:** http://www.top-magazin.de
Freq: Quarterly; **Annual Sub.:** EUR 16,00; **Circ:** 12,000
Editor: Steffi Tenhaven
Profile: Regional lifestyle magazine for Dortmund. The magazine is designed for those who seek the extraordinary, the beautiful and the exclusive. In addition, we report on the latest news from industry & Society, Culture & Sports, Health & Medicine, Fashion, luxury, wellness and sports. The magazine presents special personalities, interesting company and provide sophisticated reporting with a national flair. Anhören Umschrift.
Language(s): German
ADVERTISING RATES:
Full Page Mono .... EUR 2470
Full Page Colour .... EUR 2470
Mechanical Data: Type Area: 275 x 185 mm
CONSUMER: RURAL & REGIONAL INTEREST

TOP MAGAZIN STUTTGART

745179G80-11800
Editorial: Zettachring 2, 70567 STUTTGART
Tel: 711 9008001 **Fax:** 711 7227100
Email: stuttgart@top-magazin.de **Web site:** http://www.top-magazin-stuttgart.de
Freq: Quarterly; **Annual Sub.:** EUR 24,00; **Circ:** 20,000
Editor: Matthias Gaul; **Advertising Manager:** Karin Endress
Profile: Regional lifestyle magazine for Stuttgart. The magazine is designed for those who seek the extraordinary, the beautiful and the exclusive. In addition, we report on the latest news from industry & Society, Culture & Sports, Health & Medicine, Fashion, luxury, wellness and sports. The magazine presents special personalities, interesting company and provide sophisticated reporting with a national flair.
Language(s): German
ADVERTISING RATES:
Full Page Mono .... EUR 2880
Full Page Colour .... EUR 2880
Mechanical Data: Type Area: 275 x 185 mm
CONSUMER: RURAL & REGIONAL INTEREST

TOP MAGAZIN WUPPERTAL

745181G80-11840
Editorial: Otto-Hausmann-Ring 185, 42115 WUPPERTAL **Tel:** 202 271440 **Fax:** 202 7160093
Email: redaktion@top-wuppertal.de **Web site:** http://www.top-wuppertal.de
Freq: Quarterly; **Annual Sub.:** EUR 10,40; **Circ:** 10,000
Editor: Hendrik Walder; **Advertising Manager:** Stephan Sieper
Profile: Regional lifestyle magazine for the region Wuppertal. The magazine is designed for those who seek the extraordinary, the beautiful and the exclusive. In addition, we report on the latest news from industry & Society, Culture & Sports, Health & Medicine, Fashion, luxury, wellness and sports. The magazine presents special personalities, interesting company and provide sophisticated reporting with a national flair.
Language(s): German
ADVERTISING RATES:
Full Page Mono .... EUR 1390
Full Page Colour .... EUR 1390
Mechanical Data: Type Area: 272 x 186 mm
Copy instructions: *Copy Date:* 20 days prior to publication
CONSUMER: RURAL & REGIONAL INTEREST

TOP PRISMA 1863317G37-1857

Editorial: Pfingstweidstr. 10, 68199 MANNHEIM
Tel: 621 85058020 **Fax:** 621 85058023
Email: g.wuest@phoenixgroup.eu
Freq: 11 issues yearly; **Cover Price:** Free; **Circ:** 22,500
Advertising Manager: Wilmar Becker
Profile: Magazine for pharmacists.
Language(s): German
Mechanical Data: Type Area: 225 x 160 mm
Copy instructions: *Copy Date:* 30 days prior to publication

TOP SPIN 745194G75H-380

Editorial: Martin-Luther-Str. 56, 60389 FRANKFURT
Tel: 69 9459230
Email: michael.otto@htv-tennis.de **Web site:** http://www.htv-tennis.de
Freq: 8 issues yearly; **Annual Sub.:** EUR 28,00; **Circ:** 5,000
Editor: Michael Otto; **Advertising Manager:** Michael Otto
Profile: Magazine of the Hessen Tennis Association.
Language(s): German
ADVERTISING RATES:
Full Page Mono .... EUR 925
Full Page Colour .... EUR 1620
Mechanical Data: Type Area: 244 x 184 mm, No. of Columns (Display): 4, Col Widths (Display): 43 mm
CONSUMER: SPORT: Racquet Sports

TOPKONTAKT MARKETING & WERBUNG 1833538G2A-5775

Editorial: Landsberger Str. 77, 82205 GILCHING
Tel: 8105 376390 **Fax:** 8105 376392
Email: info@top-kontakt.de **Web site:** http://www.top-kontakt.de
Freq: 5 issues yearly; **Cover Price:** Free; **Circ:** 20,000
Profile: The output marketing and advertising to reach marketing and advertising manager of large and medium-sized enterprises. They come with this issue without much wastage directly to your competent partner. The high acceptance of this issue our customers achieve without great expense, using high resonance. Crucial is the good address address quality of our suppliers.
Language(s): German
ADVERTISING RATES:
Full Page Mono .... EUR 2300
Full Page Colour .... EUR 2300
Mechanical Data: Type Area: 297 x 210 mm

TOPNEWS 758482G1C-1403

Editorial: Siemensstr. 27, 61352 BAD HOMBURG
Tel: 6172 495510 **Fax:** 6172 495550
Email: marketing@bca.de **Web site:** http://www.bca.de
Freq: Quarterly; **Circ:** 18,091
Profile: Company publication published by BCA.
Language(s): German
ADVERTISING RATES:
Full Page Mono .... EUR 3750
Full Page Colour .... EUR 4950
Mechanical Data: Type Area: 253 x 180 mm

Copy instructions: *Copy Date:* 28 days prior to publication
BUSINESS: FINANCE & ECONOMICS: Banking

TOPOS
745186G26D-270
Editorial: Streitfeldstr. 35, 81673 MÜNCHEN
Tel: 89 436005150 **Fax:** 89 436005147
Email: r.schaefer@topos.de **Web site:** http://www.topos.de
Freq: Quarterly; **Annual Sub.:** EUR 120,00; **Circ:** 3,700
Editor: Robert Schäfer; **Advertising Manager:** Elmar Große
Profile: European landscape magazine focusing on the design aspects of landscape architecture.
Language(s): English; German
Readership: Aimed at professionals within the sector.
ADVERTISING RATES:
Full Page Mono .... EUR 2000
Full Page Colour .... EUR 3650
Mechanical Data: Type Area: 263 x 200 mm
BUSINESS: GARDEN TRADE: Garden Trade Horticulture

TORGAUER ZEITUNG
745206G67B-14780
Editorial: Peterssteinweg 19, 04107 LEIPZIG
Tel: 341 21810 **Fax:** 341 21811543
Email: chefredaktion@lvz.de **Web site:** http://www.lvz-online.de
Freq: 312 issues yearly; **Circ:** 10,255
Editor: Thomas Stöber; **Advertising Manager:** Harald Weiß
Profile: Daily newspaper with regional news and a local sports section. Facebook: http://facebook.com/lvzonline Twitter: http://twitter.com/torgauerzeitung This Outlet offers RSS (Really Simple Syndication).
Language(s): German
ADVERTISING RATES:
SCC .... EUR 53,20
Mechanical Data: Type Area: 528 x 371 mm, No. of Columns (Display): 8, Col Widths (Display): 45 mm
Copy instructions: *Copy Date:* 2 days prior to publication
Supplement(s): rtv
REGIONAL DAILY & SUNDAY NEWSPAPERS: Regional Daily Newspapers

TOUR SPEZIAL RENNRAD MARKT
745215G77C-380
Editorial: Steinerstr. 15d, 81369 MÜNCHEN
Tel: 89 7296030 **Fax:** 89 72960333
Email: redaktion@tour-magazin.de **Web site:** http://www.tour-magazin.de
Freq: Annual; **Cover Price:** EUR 6,50; **Circ:** 60,000
Editor: Thomas Musch; **Advertising Manager:** Ingeborg Bockstette
Profile: Catalog for racing enthusiasts with a current survey of racing bicycles with prices and all the technical details, as well as accessories, clothing and components.
Language(s): German
Readership: Aimed at cycling enthusiasts.
ADVERTISING RATES:
Full Page Mono .... EUR 2640
Full Page Colour .... EUR 4320
Mechanical Data: Type Area: 254 x 192 mm, No. of Columns (Display): 3, Col Widths (Display): 64 mm
Copy instructions: *Copy Date:* 42 days prior to publication
CONSUMER: MOTORING & CYCLING: Cycling

TOURENFAHRER
745216G77B-10
Editorial: Eifelring 28, 53879 EUSKIRCHEN
Tel: 2251 650460 **Fax:** 2251 6504639
Email: tourenfahrer@nitschke-verlag.de **Web site:** http://www.tourenfahrer.de
Freq: Monthly; **Annual Sub.:** EUR 54,00; **Circ:** 39,506
Editor: Reiner H. Nitschke; **Advertising Manager:** Martina Jonas
Profile: The Tourenfahrer is regarded as a visual style trendsetter Motorcycle Tour Magazine. Together with the Motorradfahrer, a significant market share in the segment of the motorcycle magazines is covered. The Tourenfahrer since 1981, the standards when it comes to communicating the fascination of motorcycle travel. The unmatched quality of its color lines earned him the reputation as "Geo in the motorcyclingfield". The competence of the motorcycle and accessory tests makes the tour driver to medium for all products relating to the active motorcycle spare time. Here, the palette ranges from the classic touring, via chopper, naked bikes, sport touring bike to the top Enduros.
Language(s): German
ADVERTISING RATES:
Full Page Mono .... EUR 5831
Full Page Colour .... EUR 8280
Mechanical Data: No. of Columns (Display): 4, Col Widths (Display): 43 mm, Type Area: 246 x 187 mm
Copy instructions: *Copy Date:* 30 days prior to publication
CONSUMER: MOTORING & CYCLING: Motorcycling

TOURISMUS REPORT HAMBURG
1794693G50-1246
Editorial: Beim Schlump 13a, 20144 HAMBURG
Tel: 40 480665510 **Fax:** 40 465130
Email: tourismus-report@bgup.de **Web site:** http://www.bgup.de
Freq: Quarterly; **Circ:** 2,500
Profile: Magazine from the Association of Tourism in Hamburg.
Language(s): German
ADVERTISING RATES:
Full Page Mono .... EUR 950
Full Page Colour .... EUR 950
Mechanical Data: Type Area: 254 x 188 mm

TOURISTIK AKTUELL
745228G50-1020
Editorial: Geheimrat-Hummel-Platz 4, 65239 HOCHHEIM **Tel:** 6146 605132 **Fax:** 6146 605203
Email: redaktion@touristik-aktuell.de **Web site:** http://www.touristik-aktuell.de
Freq: Weekly; **Annual Sub.:** EUR 41,00; **Circ:** 30,848
Editor: Matthias Gürtler; **Advertising Manager:** Bianca Peters
Profile: The magazine is one of the leading travel trade magazines and is characterized by the weekly frequency, timeliness and diversity of content as well as concise and clear treatment of topics. Hot and comprehensive information aimed primarily at vendors and decision makers in travel agencies. Even employees of tour operators, airlines, railways, tourist offices, hotel and rental car companies regularly read ta. Numerous Special Topics deepen sales and expertise. In a nutshell facts of related events, over- and perspective. Facebook: http://www.facebook.com/touristikaktuell This Outlet offers RSS (Really Simple Syndication).
Language(s): German
Readership: Aimed at personnel in travel agencies.
ADVERTISING RATES:
Full Page Mono .... EUR 5000
Full Page Colour .... EUR 6500
Mechanical Data: Type Area: 310 x 220 mm, No. of Columns (Display): 4, Col Widths (Display): 52 mm
Copy instructions: *Copy Date:* 14 days prior to publication
BUSINESS: TRAVEL & TOURISM

TOURISTIK MEDIEN
745230G50-1060
Editorial: Loisachufer 26, 82515 WOLFRATSHAUSEN **Tel:** 8171 41866
Fax: 8171 16967
Email: fvp@srt-redaktion.de **Web site:** http://www.touristikpr.de
Freq: Annual; **Cover Price:** EUR 75,00; **Circ:** 2,000
Editor: Fabian von Poser; **Advertising Manager:** Sybille Boolakee
Profile: Magazine with addresses of tourism-related editorial offices, magazines, special interest magazines, TV and new media, editors and employees as well as providing background information.
Language(s): German
ADVERTISING RATES:
Full Page Mono .... EUR 2145
Full Page Colour .... EUR 2145
Mechanical Data: Type Area: 184 x 116 mm
Copy instructions: *Copy Date:* 90 days prior to publication

TOYOTA MAGAZIN
1642052G94H-14384
Editorial: Nymphenburger Str. 81, 80636 MÜNCHEN
Tel: 89 35759310 **Fax:** 89 35759359
Email: gerhard.brauer@tpd.de **Web site:** http://www.tpd.de
Freq: Quarterly; **Cover Price:** EUR 3,50; **Circ:** 363,271
Editor: Gerhard Brauer
Profile: Company publication published by Toyota.
Language(s): German
ADVERTISING RATES:
Full Page Mono .... EUR 7950
Full Page Colour .... EUR 7950
Mechanical Data: Type Area: 230 x 184 mm
CONSUMER: OTHER CLASSIFICATIONS: Customer Magazines

TOYS
745241G48A-320
Editorial: Aschmattstr. 8, 76532 BADEN-BADEN
Tel: 7221 502231 **Fax:** 7221 502222
Email: dorndorf@goeller-verlag.de **Web site:** http://www.toys-online.net
Freq: 10 issues yearly; **Annual Sub.:** EUR 88,00; **Circ:** 5,565
Editor: Sibylle Dorndorf; **Advertising Manager:** Nicole Velten
Profile: Publication for the toy trade market.
Language(s): German
Readership: Read by manufacturers, suppliers and retailers.
ADVERTISING RATES:
Full Page Mono .... EUR 2350
Full Page Colour .... EUR 3850
Mechanical Data: Type Area: 273 x 191 mm, No. of Columns (Display): 4, Col Widths (Display): 44 mm
BUSINESS: TOY TRADE & SPORTS GOODS: Toy Trade

TR TECHNISCHE REVUE
744379G14A-255
Editorial: Ruhrallee 185, 45136 ESSEN
Tel: 201 8945210 **Fax:** 201 894558210
Email: j.wirtz@tim-europe.com **Web site:** http://www.technische-revue.eu
Freq: 10 issues yearly; **Cover Price:** Free; **Circ:** 19,205
Editor: Jürgen Wirtz; **Advertising Manager:** Oliver Schrader
Profile: Magazine for developers, designers and members of technical management in the areas of machine and plant construction and electrical / electronics. Facebook: http://www.facebook.com/pages/Technische-Revue/126655910681487?v=app_4949752878&ref=ts Twitter: Twitter:http://twitter.com/#!/technischerevue.
Language(s): German
ADVERTISING RATES:
Full Page Mono .... EUR 6565
Full Page Colour .... EUR 6565
Mechanical Data: Type Area: 271 x 184 mm
Copy instructions: *Copy Date:* 21 days prior to publication
BUSINESS: COMMERCE, INDUSTRY & MANAGEMENT

TRACE ELEMENTS AND ELECTROLYTES
745249G56A-9700
Editorial: Albert-Schweitzer-Str. 33, 48149 MÜNSTER
Freq: Quarterly; **Annual Sub.:** EUR 145,00; **Circ:** 2,000
Editor: K. H. Rahn; **Advertising Manager:** Jörg Feistle
Profile: Journal publishes reviews and editorials, original papers, short communications, and reports on recent advances in the entire field of trace elements.
Language(s): English
Mechanical Data: Type Area: 242 x 167 mm, No. of Columns (Display): 3, Col Widths (Display): 56 mm
Copy instructions: *Copy Date:* 28 days prior to publication
Official Journal of: Organ d. Society of Magnesium Research Germany u. d. German Working Group "Trace Elements and Electrolytes in Radiation Oncology" AKTE

TRADE FAIRS INTERNATIONAL
731529G14A-3540
Editorial: Oberfeld 32, 82319 STARNBERG
Tel: 8151 277907 **Fax:** 8151 277909
Email: info@tfi-publications.com **Web site:** http://www.tfi-publications.com
Freq: 5 issues yearly; **Annual Sub.:** EUR 40,00; **Circ:** 12,097
Editor: Peter Borstel; **Advertising Manager:** Axel Thunig
Profile: Magazine for the fair business, exhibitors, constructors and suppliers, fair locations and companies.
Language(s): English; German
ADVERTISING RATES:
Full Page Mono .... EUR 3590
Full Page Colour .... EUR 3990
Mechanical Data: Type Area: 252 x 184 mm, No. of Columns (Display): 4, Col Widths (Display): 43 mm
Copy instructions: *Copy Date:* 17 days prior to publication
BUSINESS: COMMERCE, INDUSTRY & MANAGEMENT

TRADERS'
764441G1F-1477
Editorial: Barbarastr. 31, 97074 WÜRZBURG
Tel: 931 452260 **Fax:** 931 4522613
Email: lothar@traders-mag.com **Web site:** http://www.traders-mag.com
Freq: Monthly; **Annual Sub.:** EUR 54,00; **Circ:** 15,000
Editor: Lothar Albert
Profile: The magazine has established itself as an information base for the Trader's elite. Current information on technical, mathematical tools and psychological aspects of the markets will be discussed in both professional articles and interviews. Here the professional investor base its dialogue to be to update and expand knowledge.
Language(s): German
ADVERTISING RATES:
Full Page Mono .... EUR 4500
Full Page Colour .... EUR 4500
Mechanical Data: Type Area: 297 x 210 mm
Copy instructions: *Copy Date:* 15 days prior to publication

TRADERS'
764441G1F-1732
Editorial: Barbarastr. 31, 97074 WÜRZBURG
Tel: 931 452260 **Fax:** 931 4522613
Email: lothar@traders-mag.com **Web site:** http://www.traders-mag.com
Freq: Monthly; **Annual Sub.:** EUR 54,00; **Circ:** 15,000
Editor: Lothar Albert
Profile: The magazine has established itself as an information base for the Trader's elite. Current information on technical, mathematical tools and psychological aspects of the markets will be discussed in both professional articles and interviews. Here the professional investor base its dialogue to be to update and expand knowledge.
Language(s): German
ADVERTISING RATES:
Full Page Mono .... EUR 4500
Full Page Colour .... EUR 4500
Mechanical Data: Type Area: 297 x 210 mm
Copy instructions: *Copy Date:* 15 days prior to publication

TRAILER
758484G76A-1443
Editorial: Dr.-C.-Otto-Str. 196, 44879 BOCHUM
Tel: 234 941910 **Fax:** 234 9419191
Email: info@trailer-kinokultur.de **Web site:** http://www.trailer-ruhr.de
Freq: Monthly; **Cover Price:** Free; **Circ:** 34,863
Editor: Joachim Berndt
Profile: Magazine about cinema, culture and movies. Facebook: http://www.facebook.com/pages/trailer-Ruhr/387614582993.
Language(s): German
ADVERTISING RATES:
Full Page Mono .... EUR 2800
Full Page Colour .... EUR 3600
Mechanical Data: Type Area: 265 x 190 mm, No. of Columns (Display): 4, Col Widths (Display): 44 mm
Copy instructions: *Copy Date:* 15 days prior to publication
CONSUMER: MUSIC & PERFORMING ARTS: Cinema

TRAINER
745261G62B-750
Editorial: Karl-Friedrich-Str. 14, 76133 KARLSRUHE
Tel: 721 165124 **Fax:** 721 165148
Email: constantin.wilser@health-and-beauty.com
Web site: http://www.trainer-magazine.com
Freq: 6 issues yearly; **Annual Sub.:** EUR 42,00; **Circ:** 7,100
Editor: Max Barth; **Advertising Manager:** Olaf Schneider
Profile: Magazine containing information about sports, courses and training methods. Official publication of SAFS/BETA and BSA Training Centres.
Language(s): German
Readership: Aimed at PE instructors and trainers.
ADVERTISING RATES:
Full Page Mono .... EUR 1400
Full Page Colour .... EUR 1930
Mechanical Data: Type Area: 252 x 171 mm, No. of Columns (Display): 3, Col Widths (Display): 53 mm
BUSINESS: CHURCH & SCHOOL EQUIPMENT & EDUCATION: Education Teachers

TRAINER + SEMINARANBIETER
745262G14A-7560
Editorial: Brandenburgstr. 3, 40629 DÜSSELDORF
Tel: 211 6914535 **Fax:** 211 6914537
Email: info@management-karriere.de **Web site:** http://www.management-karriere.de
Freq: Annual; **Cover Price:** EUR 65,45; **Circ:** 3,000
Editor: Roma Sadler; **Advertising Manager:** Heinrich Sadler
Profile: Publication featuring information about personnel development, management training and further education.
Language(s): German
ADVERTISING RATES:
Full Page Mono .... EUR 1012
Full Page Colour .... EUR 1866
Mechanical Data: Type Area: 210 x 140 mm
Copy instructions: *Copy Date:* 60 days prior to publication

TRAINING AKTUELL
745264G14F-80
Editorial: Endenicher Str. 41, 53115 BONN
Tel: 228 9779135 **Fax:** 228 9779177
Email: redaktion@managerseminare.de **Web site:** http://www.trainingaktuell.de
Freq: Monthly; **Annual Sub.:** EUR 85,00; **Circ:** 1,600
Editor: Nicole Bußmann; **Advertising Manager:** Gerhard May
Profile: Journal containing information concerning management development through training.
Language(s): German
ADVERTISING RATES:
Full Page Mono .... EUR 1290
Full Page Colour .... EUR 1590
Mechanical Data: Type Area: 243 x 180 mm, No. of Columns (Display): 3, Col Widths (Display): 60 mm
Copy instructions: *Copy Date:* 17 days prior to publication
BUSINESS: COMMERCE, INDUSTRY & MANAGEMENT: Training & Recruitment

DER TRAKEHNER
1744934G81X-3336
Editorial: Achtern Knick 9, 24306 BÖSDORF
Tel: 4523 880589 **Fax:** 4523 880588
Email: imke.eppers@t-online.de **Web site:** http://www.dertrakehner.de
Freq: Monthly; **Annual Sub.:** EUR 60,00; **Circ:** 4,775
Editor: Imke Eppers; **Advertising Manager:** Philip Rathmann
Language(s): German
ADVERTISING RATES:
Full Page Mono .... EUR 1024
Full Page Colour .... EUR 1864
Mechanical Data: Type Area: 245 x 188 mm, No. of Columns (Display): 4, Col Widths (Display): 44 mm
CONSUMER: ANIMALS & PETS

TRAKTOR CLASSIC
1840866G77A-2842
Editorial: Infanteriestr. 11a, 80797 MÜNCHEN
Tel: 89 130699765 **Fax:** 89 130699700
Email: traktorclassic@geramond.de **Web site:** http://www.traktorclassic.de
Freq: 6 issues yearly; **Annual Sub.:** EUR 26,46; **Circ:** 46,000
Editor: Bernhard Kramer; **Advertising Manager:** Helmut Kramer
Profile: Tractor Classic offers everything for the vintage tractor fan: Tractor Portraits of pre-war rarities to recent classics, magazine stories about scene, museums, clubs and collectors. To a large part of service, which offers a historic technology to the current location of spare parts and manuals for restoration of all the interested tractor.
Language(s): German

ADVERTISING RATES:
Full Page Colour .... EUR 950
Mechanical Data: Type Area: 235 x 181 mm, No. of Columns (Display): 4, Col Widths (Display): 45 mm
Copy instructions: *Copy Date:* 30 days prior to publication

TRAKTOR OLDTIMER KATALOG
1920422G77A-2903
Editorial: Gut Pottscheidt, 53639 KÖNIGSWINTER
Tel: 2223 923047 **Fax:** 2223 923026
Email: info@heel-verlag.de **Web site:** http://www.heel-verlag.de
Freq: Annual; **Cover Price:** EUR 14,95; **Circ:** 38,500
Editor: Udo Paulitz; **Advertising Manager:** Steffen Wagner
Profile: Catalogue providing an overview, technical data and prices of oldtimer tractors. Facebook: http://www.facebook.com/HEELVerlag.
Language(s): German
ADVERTISING RATES:
Full Page Mono .... EUR 1150
Full Page Colour .... EUR 1750
Mechanical Data: Type Area: 269 x 187 mm
Copy instructions: *Copy Date:* 40 days prior to publication

TRANS AKTUELL
745275G49A-1800
Editorial: Handwerkstr. 15, 70565 STUTTGART
Tel: 711 7849833 **Fax:** 711 7849859
Email: matthias.rathmann@etm-verlag.de **Web site:** http://www.transaktuell.de
Freq: 26 issues yearly; **Annual Sub.:** EUR 69,60; **Circ:** 58,660
Editor: Matthias Rathmann; **Advertising Manager:** Werner Faas
Profile: Magazine for the management of transport companies, freight forwarders and carriers for the fleet. trans aktuell is the 14-daily newspaper for Transport, transport and management. trans aktuell offers its readers quick information on traffic and transport policy in Germany and Europe. Other priorities include transport management and corporate governance. Whether it's current legislative changes or the latest market trends in transportation is: in trans aktuell managers currently find the information they need for their daily work. Currently, precise and practical.
Language(s): German
ADVERTISING RATES:
Full Page Mono .... EUR 15420
Full Page Colour .... EUR 15420
Mechanical Data: Type Area: 420 x 288 mm, No. of Columns (Display): 6, Col Widths (Display): 43 mm
Copy instructions: *Copy Date:* 14 days prior to publication
Supplement(s): KEP aktuell; Truck Sport Magazin; Who Is Who im Nutzfahrzeug-Flottenmarkt
BUSINESS: TRANSPORT

TRANS AKTUELL SPEZIAL
745276G49A-1820
Editorial: Handwerkstr. 15, 70565 STUTTGART
Tel: 711 7849880 **Fax:** 711 7849875
Email: thomas.goettl@etmservices.de **Web site:** http://www.etmservices.de
Freq: Annual; **Cover Price:** EUR 13,50
Free to qualifying individuals ; **Circ:** 40,000
Editor: Thomas Paul Göttl; **Advertising Manager:** Svetlana Maric
Profile: As trans aktuell spezial DEKRA fuel list appears in the 18 Year with a circulation of 40,000 copies. It has long since become required reading for professionals in car rental and fleet. Manufacturers and distributors of lubricants appreciate the DEKRA fuel-list as an indispensable guide, not least because of the large tables and comprehensive professional articles. Besides the comprehensive overview of fats, oils, lubricants, coolants, etc., are also the requirements and the addresses of the fuel supplier of the vehicle manufacturers contents of the magazine.
Language(s): English; German
ADVERTISING RATES:
Full Page Mono .... EUR 8090
Full Page Colour .... EUR 8090
Mechanical Data: Type Area: 260 x 185 mm, No. of Columns (Display): 4, Col Widths (Display): 43 mm
Copy instructions: *Copy Date:* 35 days prior to publication

TRANSFER
1644678G2A-5548
Editorial: Bonner Str. 271, 50968 KÖLN
Tel: 221 9347825 **Fax:** 221 9347788
Email: eisend@transfer-zeitschrift.net **Web site:** http://www.transfer-zeitschrift.net
Freq: Quarterly; Free to qualifying individuals
Annual Sub.: EUR 65,00; **Circ:** 4,800
Editor: Martin Eisend; **Advertising Manager:** Milosz Lipski
Profile: Magazine about the analysis and control of advertising effects of brands, products and campaigns.
Language(s): German
ADVERTISING RATES:
Full Page Mono .... EUR 2500
Full Page Colour .... EUR 2500
Mechanical Data: Type Area: 237 x 175 mm
Copy instructions: *Copy Date:* 33 days prior to publication

TRANSFER
1605536G49C-65
Editorial: Rellinger Str. 64a, 20257 HAMBURG
Tel: 40 8531330 **Fax:** 40 85313322
Email: mail@stroomer-pr.de **Web site:** http://www.stroomer-pr.de
Freq: 3 issues yearly; **Circ:** 10,000
Editor: Christian Stephan
Profile: Customer and employee magazine of Geis Gruppe.
Language(s): German

TRANSFUSION MEDICINE AND HEMOTHERAPY
1614907G56A-11199
Editorial: Wilhelmstr. 20a, 79098 FREIBURG
Tel: 761 452070 **Fax:** 761 4520714
Email: information@karger.de **Web site:** http://www.karger.com/tmh
Freq: 6 issues yearly; Free to qualifying individuals
Annual Sub.: EUR 173,00; **Circ:** 2,750
Editor: A. Sputtek; **Advertising Manager:** Verena Hering
Profile: Ezine: Magazine about transfusion medicine and haemotherapy.
Language(s): English; German
ADVERTISING RATES:
Full Page Mono .... EUR 2580
Full Page Colour .... EUR 4200
Mechanical Data: Type Area: 242 x 180 mm, No. of Columns (Display): 2, Col Widths (Display): 90 mm
Copy instructions: *Copy Date:* 42 days prior to publication
Official Journal of: Organ d. Dt. Ges. f. Transfusionsmedizin u. Immunhämatologie

TRANSPARENT
1914535G4E-7292
Editorial: Vaihinger Str. 151, 70567 STUTTGART
Tel: 711 7873369 **Fax:** 711 787388369
Email: verena.mikeleit@rib-software.com **Web site:** http://www.rib-software.com
Freq: Half-yearly; **Circ:** 2,500
Editor: Verena Mikeleit
Profile: Publication from the RIB company about software and services for the building industry.
Language(s): English; German

TRANSPLANTATIONSMEDIZIN
745295G56A-9720
Editorial: Eichengrund 28, 49525 LENGERICH
Tel: 5484 308 **Fax:** 5484 550
Email: wp@pabst-publishers.de **Web site:** http://www.transplantation.de
Freq: Quarterly; **Annual Sub.:** EUR 32,00; **Circ:** 1,650
Advertising Manager: Wolfgang Pabst
Profile: Publication about transplantation medicine.
Language(s): English; German
ADVERTISING RATES:
Full Page Mono .... EUR 540
Full Page Colour .... EUR 698
Mechanical Data: Type Area: 240 x 177 mm, No. of Columns (Display): 3, Col Widths (Display): 55 mm
Copy instructions: *Copy Date:* 30 days prior to publication
Official Journal of: Organ d. Dt. Transplantationsges.

TRANSPORT
1931038G49A-2473
Editorial: Joseph-Dollinger-Bogen 5, 80807 MÜNCHEN **Tel:** 89 32391220 **Fax:** 89 32391417
Email: redaktion@transport-online.de **Web site:** http://www.transport-online.de
Freq: 22 issues yearly; **Annual Sub.:** EUR 112,20; **Circ:** 21,446
Editor: Torsten Buchholz; **Advertising Manager:** Frank Hochhäuser
Profile: The trade journal Transport directed every two weeks consistently to carriers and freight forwarders that perform on behalf of trade, industry and logistics service providers with their own transport fleet. For Transport, the independent newspaper, which gives exclusively focused on this group and up to date, critical and founded an overview of the entire industry. A competent editorial observed trends and markets, and works-oriented themes to use bold, clear and reader-friendly to. Renowned experts will discuss opportunities and risks of transport and logistics industry.
Language(s): German
ADVERTISING RATES:
Full Page Mono .... EUR 4560
Full Page Colour .... EUR 6180
Mechanical Data: Type Area: 430 x 283 mm, No. of Columns (Display): 6, Col Widths (Display): 43 mm
Copy instructions: *Copy Date:* 14 days prior to publication
Supplement(s): Die Profi Werkstatt

TRAUMA UND BERUFSKRANKHEIT
745309G56A-9760
Editorial: Tiergartenstr. 17, 69121 HEIDELBERG
Tel: 6221 4870 **Fax:** 6221 4878366
Email: subscriptions@springer.com **Web site:** http://www.springerlink.com
Freq: Quarterly; **Annual Sub.:** EUR 145,00; **Circ:** 850
Editor: C. Jürgens; **Advertising Manager:** Christine Jürgens
Profile: Trauma und Berufskrankheit represents a holistic information to questions from the field of accident and reconstructive surgery, occupational diseases, and for handling all aspects of statutory accident insurance. In this framework, issues of accident prevention, diagnosis, operative and conservative therapy, the subsequent damage or intervention, rehabilitation and legal principles, criteria for compensation and aspects of retraining, treated.
Language(s): German
Readership: Read by medical professionals, social workers and employers.
ADVERTISING RATES:
Full Page Mono .... EUR 1200
Full Page Colour .... EUR 2240
Mechanical Data: No. of Columns (Display): 3, Col Widths (Display): 54 mm, Type Area: 240 x 175 mm
Official Journal of: Organ d. Berufsgenossenschaftl. Unfallkliniken u. Unfallkrankenhäuser, d. Haupt- u. Landesverb. d. gewerbl. Berufsgenossenschaften, d. Bundesverb. d. Unfallkassen u. d. Bundesverb. d. landwirtschaftl. Berufsgenossenschaften
BUSINESS: HEALTH & MEDICAL

TRAUMHAFTE HOCHZEIT REGIONAL
1789368G74A-3514
Editorial: Im Schlangengarten 56, 76877 OFFENBACH **Tel:** 6348 959391 **Fax:** 6348 959392
Email: mauer@hoema-verlag.de **Web site:** http://www.traumhochzeit-magazin.de
Freq: Half-yearly; **Cover Price:** Free; **Circ:** 20,000
Editor: Dieter Mauer
Profile: Magazine with information about wedding plannings.
Language(s): German
Mechanical Data: Type Area: 264 x 176 mm
Copy instructions: *Copy Date:* 14 days prior to publication

TRAUNREUTER ANZEIGER
745311G67B-14800
Editorial: Gabelsbergerstr. 4, 83308 TROSTBERG
Tel: 8621 80825 **Fax:** 8621 80868
Email: redaktion@trostberger-tagblatt.de **Web site:** http://www.chiemgau-online.de
Freq: 312 issues yearly; **Circ:** 19,154
Advertising Manager: Christian von Hobe
Profile: Daily newspaper with regional news and a local sports section.
Language(s): German
ADVERTISING RATES:
SCC .... EUR 47,20
Mechanical Data: Type Area: 430 x 280 mm, No. of Columns (Display): 6, Col Widths (Display): 45 mm
Copy instructions: *Copy Date:* 3 days prior to publication
REGIONAL DAILY & SUNDAY NEWSPAPERS: Regional Daily Newspapers

TRAUNSTEINER TAGBLATT
745312G67B-14820
Editorial: Marienstr. 12, 83278 TRAUNSTEIN
Tel: 861 98770 **Fax:** 861 9877119
Email: lokales@traunsteiner-tagblatt.de **Web site:** http://www.traunsteiner-tagblatt.de
Freq: 312 issues yearly; **Circ:** 15,208
Editor: Martin Miller; **News Editor:** Gunter Kasper
Profile: Regional daily newspaper covering politics, economics, sports, culture, travel and technology.
Language(s): German
ADVERTISING RATES:
SCC .... EUR 45,00
Mechanical Data: Type Area: 420 x 280 mm, No. of Columns (Display): 6, Col Widths (Display): 45 mm
Copy instructions: *Copy Date:* 2 days prior to publication
REGIONAL DAILY & SUNDAY NEWSPAPERS: Regional Daily Newspapers

TRAVEL TRIBUNE
745322G50-1140
Editorial: Unterster Zwerchweg 8, 60599 FRANKFURT **Tel:** 69 625025 **Fax:** 69 625026
Email: info@travel-tribune.de **Web site:** http://www.travel-tribune.de
Freq: Weekly; **Annual Sub.:** EUR 292,14; **Circ:** 5,000
Editor: Hans-Joachim Brings; **Advertising Manager:** Marco Tron
Profile: Pan-European magazine which provides a news service for the tourism business.
Language(s): German
ADVERTISING RATES:
Full Page Mono .... EUR 1600
Full Page Colour .... EUR 2495
Mechanical Data: Type Area: 265 x 185 mm, No. of Columns (Display): 4, Col Widths (Display): 46 mm
Copy instructions: *Copy Date:* 7 days prior to publication
BUSINESS: TRAVEL & TOURISM

TRAVEL.ONE
740195G50-680
Editorial: Hilpertstr. 3, 64295 DARMSTADT
Tel: 6151 3907930 **Fax:** 6151 3907939
Email: redaktion@travel-one.net **Web site:** http://www.travel-one.net
Freq: 25 issues yearly; **Annual Sub.:** EUR 25,00; **Circ:** 20,347
Editor: Christian Schmicke
Profile: News magazine for the tourism business. It supports motivated tourism experts in their day-to-day business with information on products and destinations as well as practical tips. Clearly structured categories give you a quick overview and keep you up to date with developments, trends and events in the tourism industry. In every issue, cover stories and features provide a look behind the scenes of the business. And regular surveys on current subjects give our readers the opportunity to voice their opinions. As a renowned specialist magazine, Travel One writes for all those who work in professional travel marketing.
Language(s): German
ADVERTISING RATES:
Full Page Mono .... EUR 6450
Full Page Colour .... EUR 6450
Mechanical Data: Type Area: 255 x 181 mm, No. of Columns (Display): 3, Col Widths (Display): 56 mm
Copy instructions: *Copy Date:* 14 days prior to publication
BUSINESS: TRAVEL & TOURISM

TRAVELTALK
745320G50-1120
Editorial: Wandsbeker Allee 1, 22041 HAMBURG
Tel: 40 41448288 **Fax:** 40 41448299
Email: redaktion@fvw-mediengruppe.de **Web site:** http://www.traveltalk.de
Freq: Weekly; **Annual Sub.:** EUR 18,00; **Circ:** 30,938
Editor: Matthias Ehbrecht; **Advertising Manager:** Matthias Schulz
Profile: The young weekly magazine for travel agents. TravelTalk is a travel trade magazine with a difference. TravelTalk informs, entertains, is competent and easyto read.TravelTalk gets to the heart of the most important tourism news – up to the minute, colorful and inspiring.
Language(s): German
ADVERTISING RATES:
Full Page Mono .... EUR 7750
Full Page Colour .... EUR 7750
Mechanical Data: Type Area: 241 x 195 mm
Copy instructions: *Copy Date:* 7 days prior to publication
BUSINESS: TRAVEL & TOURISM

TREFF
745350G91D-8420
Editorial: Schnewlinstr. 6, 79098 FREIBURG
Tel: 761 70578552 **Fax:** 761 70578654
Email: info@treffmagazin.de **Web site:** http://www.treffmagazin.de
Freq: Monthly; **Annual Sub.:** EUR 34,80; **Circ:** 50,000
Editor: Hauke Johannsen; **Advertising Manager:** Sabine Mecklenburg
Profile: Treff - The science magazine for pupil addressed with a broad range of topics in all nine-to fourteen-year-old girls and boys and said the wishes and needs of this target group age. Actual articles about school, stars, leisure, travel, nature, history, politics, media, environment, animals and sports are presented in vivid reporting, discussions, profiles, interviews and reports. In addition, every month for its own trading card, small encyclopedia of knowledge, letters and reviews, posters and great prizes and surprises. In addition, each month: an action with fun craft ideas, exciting experiments for Cooking and delicious recipes. These selected tips for books and audio books, movies, DVDs and games. Treff - an ideal addition to school and meaningful leisure time! Facebook: www.facebook.com/treffmagazin.
Language(s): German
ADVERTISING RATES:
Full Page Mono .... EUR 1790
Full Page Colour .... EUR 3220
Mechanical Data: Type Area: 243 x 168 mm, No. of Columns (Display): 3, Col Widths (Display): 59 mm
Copy instructions: *Copy Date:* 60 days prior to publication
CONSUMER: RECREATION & LEISURE: Children & Youth

TR€FFPUNKT
745346G94H-12620
Editorial: Am Wallgraben 115, 70565 STUTTGART
Tel: 711 7821724 **Fax:** 711 7821288
Email: treffpunkt@dsv-gruppe.de **Web site:** http://www.dsv-gruppe.de
Freq: Quarterly; **Annual Sub.:** EUR 21,00; **Circ:** 212,000
Editor: Thomas Stoll; **Advertising Manager:** Anneli Baumann
Profile: Magazine focusing on personal finance, including articles about investment and leisure.
Language(s): German
Readership: Aimed at customers of the German Savings Bank.
ADVERTISING RATES:
Full Page Mono .... EUR 4150
Full Page Colour .... EUR 5500
Mechanical Data: No. of Columns (Display): 3, Col Widths (Display): 54 mm, Type Area: 236 x 174 mm
CONSUMER: OTHER CLASSIFICATIONS: Customer Magazines

TREFFPUNKT 55 PLUS
1622750G74N-829
Editorial: Waldstr. 26, 82194 GRÖBENZELL
Tel: 8142 667884 **Fax:** 8142 667885
Email: info@vios-medien.de **Web site:** http://www.vios-medien.de
Freq: 3 issues yearly; **Annual Sub.:** EUR 9,00; **Circ:** 39,800
Editor: Armin Herb
Profile: Treffpunkt 55plus informed about the wide range of cultural, educational and leisure activities in and around Munich. The magazine suggests to get active and stay. It reports on initiatives and opportunities to engage with like-minded people or to do something. It deals with sound and expert topics and issues relevant to people over 55 years of interest: Health, Travel, Law & Finance, Internet.
Language(s): German
ADVERTISING RATES:
Full Page Mono .... EUR 3010
Full Page Colour .... EUR 3340

Mechanical Data: Type Area: 252 x 185 mm, No. of Columns (Display): 4, Col Widths (Display): 42 mm
Copy instructions: *Copy Date:* 49 days prior to publication

TREFFPUNKT DÜSSELDORF
1640571G89A-11827
Editorial: Weg zur Platte 15a, 45133 ESSEN
Tel: 201 413482 **Fax:** 201 411272
Email: hewesgmbh45133@aol.com **Web site:** http://www.treff-punkt.info
Freq: Monthly; **Cover Price:** Free; **Circ:** 20,000
Profile: City guide for Duesseldorf.
Language(s): German

TREFFPUNKT ESSEN
1616031G89A-11669
Editorial: Weg zur Platte 15a, 45133 ESSEN
Tel: 201 413482 **Fax:** 201 411272
Email: hewesgmbh45133@aol.com **Web site:** http://www.treff-punkt.info
Freq: Monthly; **Cover Price:** Free; **Circ:** 10,000
Profile: City guide for Essen.
Language(s): German
Mechanical Data: Type Area: 200 x 100 mm
Copy instructions: *Copy Date:* 10 days prior to publication

TREFFPUNKT KINO
745340G76A-1340
Editorial: Weihenstephaner Str. 7, 81673 MÜNCHEN
Tel: 89 45114110 **Fax:** 89 45114441
Email: u.hoecherl@e-media.de **Web site:** http://www.kino.de
Freq: Monthly; **Cover Price:** Free; **Circ:** 680,234
Editor: Ulrich Höcherl; **Advertising Manager:** Susanne Hübner
Profile: Film magazine about the latest cinema and video releases.
Language(s): German
ADVERTISING RATES:
Full Page Mono .... EUR 29380
Full Page Colour .... EUR 29380
Mechanical Data: Type Area: 231 x 180 mm, No. of Columns (Display): 4, Col Widths (Display): 42 mm
CONSUMER: MUSIC & PERFORMING ARTS: Cinema

TREND FRISUREN
745359G74H-100
Editorial: Hansaring 97, 50670 KÖLN
Tel: 221 9574270 **Fax:** 221 95742777
Email: marken-info@markenverlag.de **Web site:** http://www.markenverlag.de
Freq: Half-yearly; **Cover Price:** EUR 2,95; **Circ:** 80,000
Advertising Manager: Frank Krauthäuser
Profile: TREND FRISUREN targeted exactly to your head. Whether blonde or brown, or short, whether long, TREND Frisuren offers for each type a variety of proposals. Hairstyle trends that are tailored to the current fashion, just like to know around the hair and its care, image consulting and more! 2 times a year you can check the hairy trends, get ideas and tips.
Language(s): German
ADVERTISING RATES:
Full Page Mono .... EUR 2900
Full Page Colour .... EUR 2900
Mechanical Data: Type Area: 265 x 184 mm, No. of Columns (Display): 4, Col Widths (Display): 46 mm
Copy instructions: *Copy Date:* 42 days prior to publication
CONSUMER: WOMEN'S INTEREST CONSUMER MAGAZINES: Hair & Beauty

TRENDS&FUN
745367G80-11980
Editorial: Rudolf-Wissell-Str. 18, 37075 GÖTTINGEN
Tel: 551 3890042 **Fax:** 551 3890011
Email: drees@trends-fun.de **Web site:** http://www.trends-fun.de
Freq: 10 issues yearly; **Cover Price:** Free; **Circ:** 9,900
Editor: Ulrich Drees; **Advertising Manager:** Sylvia Stein
Profile: Magazine for city and region, concentrating on gastronomy, music, arts and events.
Language(s): German
ADVERTISING RATES:
Full Page Mono .... EUR 930
Full Page Colour .... EUR 930
Mechanical Data: Type Area: 270 x 190 mm
CONSUMER: RURAL & REGIONAL INTEREST

TREPTOW KOMPAKT
1898597G74M-894
Editorial: Bundesallee 23, 10717 BERLIN
Tel: 30 863030 **Fax:** 30 86303200
Email: info@bfb.de **Web site:** http://www.bfb.de
Freq: Annual; **Cover Price:** Free; **Circ:** 77,000
Profile: Industry district magazine. The core of this handy reference book is neatly sorted according to different themes of industry. Here you will find a plethora of vendors from the neighborhood. In preparation to the respective subject area raises a company, in an interview. To know your environment better, we present in the district windows, etc. beautiful places, monuments, museums, etc. For better orientation in the neighborhood also an integrated neighborhood with street plan is register. Furthermore, the county information you provide an overview of important phone numbers and agencies in your neighborhood.
Language(s): German
ADVERTISING RATES:
Full Page Mono .... EUR 990
Full Page Colour .... EUR 990
Mechanical Data: Type Area: 185 x 126 mm

TREUCHTLINGER KURIER
745374G67B-14840
Editorial: Hauptstr. 19, 91757 TREUCHTLINGEN
Tel: 9142 966110 **Fax:** 9142 966118
Email: verlag@treuchtlinger-kurier.de **Web site:** http://www.treuchtlinger-kurier.de
Freq: 312 issues yearly; **Circ:** 10,694
Profile: Daily newspaper with regional news and a local sports section.
Language(s): German
ADVERTISING RATES:
SCC .... EUR 21,80
Mechanical Data: Type Area: 430 x 280 mm, No. of Columns (Display): 6, Col Widths (Display): 45 mm
Copy instructions: *Copy Date:* 2 days prior to publication
REGIONAL DAILY & SUNDAY NEWSPAPERS: Regional Daily Newspapers

TRIBÜNE
745380G87-13482
Editorial: Habsburgerallee 72, 60385 FRANKFURT
Tel: 69 9433000 **Fax:** 69 94330023
Email: tribuene_verlag@t-online.de **Web site:** http://www.tribuene-verlag.de
Freq: Quarterly; **Annual Sub.:** EUR 34,00; **Circ:** 5,000
Editor: Otto R. Romberg; **Advertising Manager:** Elisabeth Reisch
Profile: Magazine about history and present, anti-Semitism, Democracy and Civic Education.
Language(s): German
ADVERTISING RATES:
Full Page Mono .... EUR 1300
Full Page Colour .... EUR 2290
Mechanical Data: Type Area: 194 x 122 mm
Copy instructions: *Copy Date:* 30 days prior to publication
CONSUMER: RELIGIOUS

TRIERER WOCHENSPIEGEL
745395G72-14400
Editorial: Max-Planck-Str. 10, 54296 TRIER
Tel: 651 716560 **Fax:** 651 716569
Email: red-trier@tw-verlag.de **Web site:** http://www.wochenspiegellive.de
Freq: Weekly; **Cover Price:** Free; **Circ:** 46,687
Editor: Arnt Finkenberg; **Advertising Manager:** Antonia Britten
Profile: Advertising journal (house-to-house) concentrating on local stories.
Language(s): German
ADVERTISING RATES:
Full Page Mono .... EUR 3281
Full Page Colour .... EUR 4605
Mechanical Data: Type Area: 430 x 290 mm, No. of Columns (Display): 7, Col Widths (Display): 38 mm
Copy instructions: *Copy Date:* 2 days prior to publication
Supplement(s): Frauen 'xtra
LOCAL NEWSPAPERS

TRIERISCHER VOLKSFREUND
745398G67B-14860
Editorial: Hanns-Martin-Schleyer-Str. 8, 54294 TRIER **Tel:** 651 71990 **Fax:** 651 7199990
Email: redaktion@volksfreund.de **Web site:** http://www.volksfreund.de
Freq: 312 issues yearly; **Circ:** 99,679
Editor: Isabell Funk; **Advertising Manager:** Wolfgang Sturges
Profile: Regional daily newspaper with news on politics, economy, culture, sports, travel, technology, etc. Facebook: http://de-de.facebook.com/Volksfreund Twitter: http://twitter.com/Volksfreund This Outlet offers RSS (Really Simple Syndication).
Language(s): German
ADVERTISING RATES:
SCC .... EUR 153,60
Mechanical Data: Type Area: 490 x 326 mm, No. of Columns (Display): 7, Col Widths (Display): 44 mm
Copy instructions: *Copy Date:* 2 days prior to publication
Supplement(s): Anstoss; Lucky; prisma; rendezvous
REGIONAL DAILY & SUNDAY NEWSPAPERS: Regional Daily Newspapers

TRIFELS KURIER
745401G72-14412
Editorial: Hauptstr. 24, 76855 ANNWEILER
Tel: 6346 965967 **Fax:** 6346 965968
Email: suewe@wobla.de
Freq: Weekly; **Cover Price:** Free; **Circ:** 12,200
Editor: Jürgen Bender
Profile: Advertising journal (house-to-house) concentrating on local stories.
Language(s): German
ADVERTISING RATES:
Full Page Mono .... EUR 1072
Full Page Colour .... EUR 41392
Mechanical Data: Type Area: 320 x 228 mm, No. of Columns (Display): 5, Col Widths (Display): 44 mm
Copy instructions: *Copy Date:* 3 days prior to publication
LOCAL NEWSPAPERS

TROCKENBAU AKUSTIK
745404G4B-70
Editorial: Stolberger Str. 84, 50933 KÖLN
Tel: 221 5497279 **Fax:** 221 54976294
Email: red.trockenbau@rudolf-mueller.de **Web site:** http://www.trockenbau-akustik.de
Freq: Monthly; **Annual Sub.:** EUR 135,00; **Circ:** 14,874
Editor: Thomas Grüning; **Advertising Manager:** Thomas Füngerlings
Profile: Magazine focusing on interior design, drylining, partitions, ceilings and finishing.
Language(s): German
Readership: Aimed at building contractors and architects.
ADVERTISING RATES:
Full Page Mono .... EUR 4295
Full Page Colour .... EUR 7070
Mechanical Data: Type Area: 267 x 188 mm, No. of Columns (Display): 4, Col Widths (Display): 44 mm
Official Journal of: Organ d. Gütegemeinschaft Trockenbau e.V.
BUSINESS: ARCHITECTURE & BUILDING: Interior Design & Flooring

TROSSINGER ZEITUNG
745416G67B-14880
Editorial: Jägerhofstr. 4, 78532 TUTTLINGEN
Tel: 7461 70150 **Fax:** 7461 701547
Web site: http://www.schwaebische.de
Freq: 312 issues yearly; **Circ:** 22,517
Advertising Manager: Tarkan Tekin
Profile: In its edition provides the "Trossinger Zeitung" its readers daily with the latest information from government, business, sports, culture and food from the local environment. Twitter: http://twitter.com/Schwaebische This Outlet offers RSS (Really Simple Syndication).
Language(s): German
ADVERTISING RATES:
SCC .... EUR 77,20
Mechanical Data: Type Area: 480 x 320 mm, No. of Columns (Display): 7, Col Widths (Display): 44 mm
Copy instructions: *Copy Date:* 1 day prior to publication
Supplement(s): rtv
REGIONAL DAILY & SUNDAY NEWSPAPERS: Regional Daily Newspapers

TROSTBERGER TAGBLATT
745417G67B-14900
Editorial: Gabelsbergerstr. 4, 83308 TROSTBERG
Tel: 8621 80825 **Fax:** 8621 80868
Email: redaktion@trostberger-tagblatt.de **Web site:** http://www.chiemgau-online.de
Freq: 312 issues yearly; **Circ:** 19,154
Editor: Karlheinz Kas; **News Editor:** Karlheinz Kas; **Advertising Manager:** Christian von Hobe
Profile: Regional daily newspaper covering politics, economics, culture, sports, travel and technology.
Language(s): German
ADVERTISING RATES:
SCC .... EUR 47,20
Mechanical Data: Type Area: 430 x 280 mm, No. of Columns (Display): 6, Col Widths (Display): 45 mm
Copy instructions: *Copy Date:* 3 days prior to publication
REGIONAL DAILY & SUNDAY NEWSPAPERS: Regional Daily Newspapers

DER TROTTER
745418G89A-12118
Editorial: Rußhütter Str. 26, 66287 QUIERSCHIED
Tel: 700 45623876
Email: redaktion@dertrotter.de **Web site:** http://www.globetrotter.org
Freq: 5 issues yearly; Free to qualifying individuals
Annual Sub.: EUR 40,00; **Circ:** 1,000
Editor: Norbert Lüdtke; **Advertising Manager:** Norbert Lüdtke
Profile: Magazine about worldwide travels.
Language(s): German
Mechanical Data: Type Area: 180 x 120 mm, No. of Columns (Display): 2, Col Widths (Display): 58 mm
Copy instructions: *Copy Date:* 42 days prior to publication

TRUCK, BUS + CO
1616367G49A-2332
Editorial: Aschauer Str. 30, 81549 MÜNCHEN
Tel: 89 2030432945 **Fax:** 89 2030432477
Web site: http://www.springer-transport-media.de
Freq: Half-yearly; **Cover Price:** Free; **Circ:** 26,000
Advertising Manager: Ute Unkel
Profile: Company publication published by DKV.
Language(s): German

TRUCK MOBILES INTERNATIONAL
1864103G49A-2456
Editorial: An der Strusbek 23, 22926 AHRENSBURG
Tel: 4102 47870 **Fax:** 4102 478794
Email: vertrieb@daz-verlag.de **Web site:** http://www.daz-verlag.de
Freq: 26 issues yearly; **Annual Sub.:** EUR 79,25; **Circ:** 13,968
Advertising Manager: Dirk Spars
Profile: The TRUCK MOBILES INTERNATIONAL is the largest and best selling truck magazine ads in Europe It impresses with its eye-catching format and is available with two week 20 250 * IVW sales coies Europe's market leader in commercial vehicle tested and construction equipment quotes. Nationwide coverage and beyond Europe's borders has been one of the INTERNATIONAL TRUCK MOBILE 18 years now required reading for all decision makers in the fields of commercial vehicle Trade and fleet management. In addition, the TRUCK MOBILES INTERNATIONALL is more than a customer-oriented subscription service a large number of potential customers. To meet international customer requirements, provides TRUCK MOBILES INTERNATIONAL their readers a range of IT tools in local languages for better understanding of display. To preserve the clarity and the abundance of supply and demand needs to be, appears TRUCK MOBILES INTERNATIONAL sorted by categories every 14 days in the new semi-Nordic format.
Language(s): English; German
ADVERTISING RATES:
Full Page Mono .... EUR 1882
Full Page Colour .... EUR 1882
Mechanical Data: Type Area: 355 x 250 mm, No. of Columns (Display): 5, Col Widths (Display): 46 mm
Copy instructions: *Copy Date:* 10 days prior to publication

TRUCKER
745425G49D-130
Editorial: Aschauer Str. 30, 81549 MÜNCHEN
Tel: 89 2030432982 **Fax:** 89 2030432983
Email: trucker@springer.com **Web site:** http://www.trucker.de
Freq: Monthly; **Annual Sub.:** EUR 38,90; **Circ:** 48,342
Editor: Johannes Reichel; **Advertising Manager:** Matthias Pioro
Profile: TRUCKER – the magazine for long-distance truck drivers. For more than 30 years. TRUCKER has been the specialized magazine for truck drivers. Month after month, new trucks and technologies are introduced and compared. Driving reports, service topics and exciting everyday reports complete the picture. The readers are primarily professional truck drivers covering long distances, as well as self-driving hauliers.
Language(s): German
ADVERTISING RATES:
Full Page Colour .... EUR 9260
Mechanical Data: Type Area: 268 x 199 mm, No. of Columns (Display): 4, Col Widths (Display): 43 mm
BUSINESS: TRANSPORT: Commercial Vehicles

TRUCKMARKET
731531G49A-780
Editorial: Aschauer Str. 30, 81549 MÜNCHEN
Tel: 89 2030432294 **Fax:** 89 2030432100
Email: anzeigen.truckmarket@springer.com **Web site:** http://www.truckmarket.de
Freq: 26 issues yearly; **Circ:** 30,000
Profile: Since 1997, the advertisement magazine TruckMarket has been published in Germany and abroad, giving you an overview of current offers of used commercial vehicles (trailers, lorries, construction vehicles, etc.) every 14 days.
Language(s): German
ADVERTISING RATES:
Full Page Mono .... EUR 880
Full Page Colour .... EUR 1315
Mechanical Data: Type Area: 251 x 190 mm, No. of Columns (Display): 3, Col Widths (Display): 60 mm

TRUCKMARKET
1704675G49A-2404
Editorial: Aschauer Str. 30, 81549 MÜNCHEN
Tel: 89 2030432294 **Fax:** 89 2030432100
Email: anzeigen.truckmarket@springer.com **Web site:** http://www.truckmarket.de
Freq: Daily; **Cover Price:** Paid; **Circ:** 851,390 Unique Users
Profile: Ezine: Ad magazine on used commercial vehicles for businessmen and executives in the transport business, vehicle fleets and garages.
Language(s): German
BUSINESS: TRANSPORT

TU
745465G62B-2760
Editorial: Lichtenbergstr. 18, 79114 FREIBURG
Tel: 761 83759 **Fax:** 761 8975283
Email: sachs@ph-freiburg.de
Freq: Quarterly; **Annual Sub.:** EUR 24,00; **Circ:** 3,000
Editor: Burkhard Sachs; **Advertising Manager:** Uwe Stockburger
Profile: Journal covering teaching methods.
Language(s): German
Readership: Read by teachers at primary and secondary levels.
BUSINESS: CHURCH & SCHOOL EQUIPMENT & EDUCATION: Education Teachers

TU TIERÄRZTLICHE UMSCHAU
745540G64H-420
Editorial: Neuhauser Str. 21, 78464 KONSTANZ
Tel: 7531 812226 **Fax:** 7531 812299
Email: redaktion-tu@terra-verlag.de **Web site:** http://www.tu-online.de
Freq: Monthly; **Annual Sub.:** EUR 89,00; **Circ:** 5,845
Editor: Margund Mrozek
Profile: Journal covering veterinary medicine.
Language(s): German
Readership: Aimed at vets, students and people in pharmaceutical companies, colleges and universities.
ADVERTISING RATES:
Full Page Mono .... EUR 1750
Full Page Colour .... EUR 3060
Mechanical Data: Type Area: 260 x 175 mm, No. of Columns (Display): 4, Col Widths (Display): 41 mm
Copy instructions: *Copy Date:* 28 days prior to publication
BUSINESS: OTHER CLASSIFICATIONS: Veterinary

TÜBINGER WOCHENBLATT
745475G72-14416

Editorial: Marktplatz 16, 72764 REUTLINGEN
Tel: 7121 938139 **Fax:** 7121 938111
Email: hupp@wobla-rt.de **Web site:** http://www.tuebinger-wochenblatt.de
Freq: Weekly; **Cover Price:** Free; **Circ:** 54,850
Editor: Petra Hupp; **Advertising Manager:** Claudia Münzing
Profile: Advertising journal (house-to-house) concentrating on local stories.
Language(s): German
ADVERTISING RATES:
Full Page Mono .... EUR 4167
Full Page Colour .... EUR 5746
Mechanical Data: Type Area: 480 x 320 mm, No. of Columns (Display): 7, Col Widths (Display): 44 mm
Copy instructions: *Copy Date:* 1 day prior to publication
LOCAL NEWSPAPERS

TUKAN
1834287G57-2866

Editorial: Siesmayerstr. 61, 60323 FRANKFURT
Tel: 69 751550 **Fax:** 69 752182
Email: mail@tropica-verde.de **Web site:** http://www.tropica-verde.de
Freq: Annual; **Circ:** 2,500
Editor: Annekathrin Eppenstein
Profile: Publication focusing on the protection of tropical forests, information about club activities in Germany and projects in Costa Rica as well as international environmental issues, botanical and zoological information.
Language(s): German

TUMORDIAGNOSTIK & THERAPIE
745485G56A-9800

Editorial: Rüdigerstr. 14, 70469 STUTTGART
Tel: 711 8931502 **Fax:** 711 8931408
Email: marion.rukavina@thieme.de **Web site:** http://www.thieme.de/tumor
Freq: 6 issues yearly; **Annual Sub.:** EUR 260,90; **Circ:** 5,700
Editor: Jochen Schütte
Profile: The magazine has set the promotion of interdisciplinary cooperation in the field of cancer to the goal. Clinicians and experts inform you about the current progress in the broad field between oncology screening and follow-up. Training works and overviews lead the reader into the subject. Editorial shell portion with a priority issue. After each of the headings diagnosis, treatment, aftercare and preventive treats is an indication of proven professionals. Original research on topics outline, review articles, industrial forum "Medicine and the market" for the news of pharmaceutical and medical technics.
Language(s): German
ADVERTISING RATES:
Full Page Mono .... EUR 1870
Full Page Colour .... EUR 3310
Mechanical Data: Type Area: 248 x 175 mm, No. of Columns (Display): 3, Col Widths (Display): 55 mm
BUSINESS: HEALTH & MEDICAL

TUNING
745488G77A-2300

Editorial: Steinerstr. 15/D, 81369 MÜNCHEN
Tel: 89 72960250 **Fax:** 89 72960333
Email: info@tuning-magazin.de **Web site:** http://www.tuning-magazin.de
Freq: 6 issues yearly; **Annual Sub.:** EUR 19,20; **Circ:** 57,500
Editor: Andreas Becker; **Advertising Manager:** Sigrid Pinke
Profile: TUNING - is driving more than one car. For over 20 years of tuning is the voice of a different car addicts. All that has boring, downtuning, styling, finishing, making hot to do tuning and cruising reflected TUNING. The Journal of gasoline, rubber, speed and drive thinks, feels, and polarized the community - it's the scene. Clear layout, uncompromising language, and stepped into the limelight vehicles we celebrate as heroes, because TUNING cars are the stars. In tuning the fans feel of mobile "mood guns", "PS"monsters, "cruise ships", "Drift-Queens" well - everything else is for our readers but only "factory" TUNING discovers trends, hyped trends! generates new trends -. everything else is "copy-paste" TUNING came as the first German-language magazine in 1986 in the world of car dressing before TUNING is the number one of our readers and bring every two months, the exciting world of a different love of freedom to four. Wheels to the point headings such as TUNING News -. everything about the latest products of diverse aftermarket, tuning hi-fi news - mobile entertainment, TUNING Fun unlimited - Tests of the hottest auto games, TUNING SCENE-News, TUNING How to do - Built-in specials to interesting accessories and TUNING Toolbox - the sound guide, complete the "auto Phil " special interest Bible. Facebook: http://www.facebook.com/TuningMagazin.
Language(s): German
ADVERTISING RATES:
Full Page Mono .... EUR 5050
Full Page Colour .... EUR 5660
Mechanical Data: Type Area: 262 x 185 mm, No. of Columns (Display): 4, Col Widths (Display): 43 mm
Copy instructions: *Copy Date:* 28 days prior to publication
CONSUMER: MOTORING & CYCLING: Motoring

TUNNEL
745490G42A-101

Editorial: Avenwedder Str. 55, 33335 GÜTERSLOH
Tel: 5241 8088730 **Fax:** 5241 80690880
Email: roland.herr@bauverlag.de **Web site:** http://www.tunnel-online.info
Freq: 8 issues yearly; **Annual Sub.:** EUR 147,00; **Circ:** 4,000
Editor: Roland Herr; **Advertising Manager:** Christian Reinke
Profile: As a technical, practical magazine, tunnel devoted to the construction and planning as well as research, technical equipment, maintenance and refurbishment of all underground structures. Tunneling can not be viewed solely in national terms. Almost all related themes are of comprehensive international interest. Therefore appears tunnel in both English and German, all contributions are full length translated professionally and played. The magazine is adapted to the current building, distributed internationally. A large part of future construction projects will take new buildings and repairs of existing tunnel to complete and form a corresponding emphasis in the reporting.
Language(s): English; German
ADVERTISING RATES:
Full Page Mono .... EUR 2350
Full Page Colour .... EUR 3895
Mechanical Data: Type Area: 270 x 186 mm, No. of Columns (Display): 4, Col Widths (Display): 45 mm
Copy instructions: *Copy Date:* 14 days prior to publication
Official Journal of: Organ d. Studienges. f. unterird. Verkehrsanlagen e.V.
BUSINESS: CONSTRUCTION

TUNNELBAU
745491G4E-6320

Editorial: Montebruchstr. 2, 45219 ESSEN
Tel: 2054 924114 **Fax:** 2054 924119
Email: kb@vge.de **Web site:** http://www.vge.de
Freq: Annual; **Cover Price:** EUR 32,00; **Circ:** 4,000
Editor: Katrin Brummermann; **Advertising Manager:** Monika Motzfeld
Profile: Magazine on tunnel building and tunnel building technology.
Language(s): German
ADVERTISING RATES:
Full Page Mono .... EUR 1720
Full Page Colour .... EUR 2770
Mechanical Data: Type Area: 125 x 81 mm

L' TUR NIX WIE WEG.
1704541G91B-2542

Editorial: Augustaplatz 8, 76530 BADEN-BADEN
Tel: 1805 212121 **Fax:** 1805 212196
Email: impressum@ltur.de **Web site:** http://www.ltur.de
Freq: Daily; **Cover Price:** Paid; **Circ:** 3,416,871 Unique Users
Advertising Manager: Andrea Scharner
Language(s): German
CONSUMER: RECREATION & LEISURE: Camping & Caravanning

TÜRKIYE
1638957G73-635

Editorial: Starkenburgstr. 7, 64546 MÖRFELDEN-WALLDORF **Tel:** 6105 9813131 **Fax:** 6105 9813170
Email: redaktion@ihlas.de **Web site:** http://www.turkiyegazetesi.de
Freq: 364 issues yearly; **Cover Price:** EUR 1,00; **Circ:** 45,000
Editor: Nihat Furat; **Advertising Manager:** Ahmet Dörtkasli
Profile: National Turkish daily covering politics, economics, culture, sports, travel and the arts.
Language(s): Turkish
Mechanical Data: Type Area: 525 x 356 mm, No. of Columns (Display): 9
Copy instructions: *Copy Date:* 3 days prior to publication

TÜR-TOR-FENSTER REPORT
745478G4A-238

Editorial: Hengsener Str. 14, 44309 DORTMUND
Tel: 231 92505553 **Fax:** 231 92505559
Email: goetz@vfz-verlag.de **Web site:** http://www.vfz-verlag.de
Freq: 6 issues yearly; **Annual Sub.:** EUR 63,00; **Circ:** 4,900
Editor: Ulrike Götz; **Advertising Manager:** Andrea Goodall
Profile: Magazine for gate, door and window manufacturers, safety equipment and fire protection.
Language(s): English; German
Readership: Aimed at producers, users, architects and engineers.
ADVERTISING RATES:
Full Page Mono .... EUR 1630
Full Page Colour .... EUR 2390
Mechanical Data: Type Area: 265 x 187 mm, No. of Columns (Display): 3, Col Widths (Display): 59 mm
Copy instructions: *Copy Date:* 30 days prior to publication
BUSINESS: ARCHITECTURE & BUILDING: Architecture

TUSH
1789516G74A-3515

Editorial: Barmbeker Str. 33, 22303 HAMBURG
Tel: 40 28004466 **Fax:** 40 28004488
Email: info@tushmagazine.com **Web site:** http://www.tushmagazine.com
Freq: Quarterly; **Annual Sub.:** EUR 24,00; **Circ:** 19,000
Editor: Armin Morbach
Profile: Comments on Aesthetics & Society - with this motto TUSH presents four times a year about 250 glossy pages withf the topicsbeauty, fashion, lifestyle, design and art in a new, larger context. TUSH is the arena of the world's best photographers, hair and make-up artists, top models and art directors. Source of inspiration for beauty, fashion and lifestyle industry. TUSH offers readers the feeling to be in the middle and at the same time a piece ahead.
Language(s): English; German
ADVERTISING RATES:
Full Page Mono .... EUR 9000
Full Page Colour .... EUR 9000
Mechanical Data: Type Area: 285 x 220 mm
Copy instructions: *Copy Date:* 30 days prior to publication

TÜV SÜD JOURNAL
745481G19A-940

Editorial: Westendstr. 199, 80686 MÜNCHEN
Tel: 89 57912648 **Fax:** 89 57912224
Email: joerg.riedle@tuev-sued.de **Web site:** http://www.tuev-sued.de/journal
Freq: Quarterly; **Cover Price:** Free; **Circ:** 45,000
Editor: Jörg Riedle
Profile: Magazine for employees of TÜV Süddeutschland.
Language(s): English; German

TV14
745595G76C-600

Editorial: Burchardstr. 11, 20095 HAMBURG
Tel: 40 30190 **Fax:** 40 30194032
Web site: http://www.tv14.de
Freq: 26 issues yearly; **Cover Price:** EUR 1,00; **Circ:** 2,432,587
Editor: Uwe Bokelmann
Profile: tv14 combines the wide range of topics weekly TV titles with the modern layout and the compactness of bi-daily titles. In addition to a clear-TV program to eight pages per broadcasting day tv14 offers a varied mix of topics in 14 categories: TV background, cinema, stars and multimedia are included as well as travel, food, nature and sports.
Language(s): German
Readership: Aimed at young people aged 20 to 40 years.
ADVERTISING RATES:
Full Page Mono .... EUR 38856
Full Page Colour .... EUR 38856
Mechanical Data: Type Area: 258 x 206 mm
Copy instructions: *Copy Date:* 31 days prior to publication
CONSUMER: MUSIC & PERFORMING ARTS: TV & Radio

TV 4X7
1640849G76C-930

Editorial: Rindermarkt 6, 80331 MÜNCHEN
Tel: 89 18912874 **Fax:** 89 55058670
Email: sibille.mierscheid@blattgold.tv **Web site:** http://www.tvundmehr.de
Freq: Monthly; **Annual Sub.:** EUR 16,25; **Circ:** 181,628
Editor: Sandra Schönbein
Profile: TV program guide with four weeks of full program, many of the program guide and TV highlights of the trendy pocket format. In addition, there 's Star-News of music, cinema and film, multimedia special with travel stories, tips cinema, CD and DVD hits as well as tips and trends querbeet ...
Language(s): German
ADVERTISING RATES:
Full Page Mono .... EUR 6100
Full Page Colour .... EUR 6100
Mechanical Data: Type Area: 216 x 152 mm, No. of Columns (Display): 3, Col Widths (Display): 48 mm
Copy instructions: *Copy Date:* 28 days prior to publication
CONSUMER: MUSIC & PERFORMING ARTS: TV & Radio

TV DIGITAL
1643522G76C-933

Editorial: Axel-Springer-Platz 1, 20355 HAMBURG
Tel: 40 34729720 **Fax:** 40 34729629
Email: leserservice@tvdigital.de **Web site:** http://www.tvdigital.de
Freq: 26 issues yearly; **Annual Sub.:** EUR 48,10; **Circ:** 1,779,640
Editor: Christian Hellmann; **Advertising Manager:** Arne Bergmann
Profile: TV listings guide focused on Pay-TV and digital channels, also includes lifestyle articles. Twitter: http://www.twitter.com/TVDIGITALnews This Outlet offers RSS (Really Simple Syndication).
Language(s): German
ADVERTISING RATES:
Full Page Mono .... EUR 47300
Full Page Colour .... EUR 47300
Mechanical Data: Type Area: 265 x 202 mm, No. of Columns (Display): 3, Col Widths (Display): 63 mm
CONSUMER: MUSIC & PERFORMING ARTS: TV & Radio

TV DIREKT
745554G76C-620

Editorial: Münchener Str. 101, 85737 ISMANING
Tel: 89 272707620 **Fax:** 89 272707690
Email: kontakt@tvdirekt.de **Web site:** http://www.tvdirekt.de
Freq: 26 issues yearly; **Annual Sub.:** EUR 32,50; **Circ:** 1,181,857
Editor: Katharina Lukas
Profile: TV listings magazine.
Language(s): German
ADVERTISING RATES:
Full Page Mono .... EUR 15900
Full Page Colour .... EUR 15900
Mechanical Data: No. of Columns (Display): 4, Col Widths (Display): 46 mm, Type Area: 260 x 196 mm
Copy instructions: *Copy Date:* 20 days prior to publication
CONSUMER: MUSIC & PERFORMING ARTS: TV & Radio

TV DISKURS
745555G2A-4920

Editorial: Heidestr. 3, 10557 BERLIN **Tel:** 30 2308360
Fax: 30 23083670
Email: tvdiskurs@fsf.de **Web site:** http://www.fsf.de
Freq: Quarterly; **Circ:** 2,400
Editor: Joachim von Gottberg
Profile: Magazine with information about protecting youth from the media, media research and media paedagogics.
Language(s): German

TV GESUND & LEBEN
758487G76C-901

Editorial: Rathausstr. 28, 22941 BARGTEHEIDE
Tel: 4532 28670 **Fax:** 4532 286750
Email: info@tvgesund.de **Web site:** http://www.tvgesund.de
Freq: 26 issues yearly; **Cover Price:** Free; **Circ:** 443,486
Editor: Roman Köster; **Advertising Manager:** Michael Holzknecht
Profile: Health customer magazine TV program for pharmacy customers with reports, comments and advice on medical, beauty, wellness and prevention. In addition to a 14-day TV program, we present a specific selection of the most important health programs on TV. Competitions, puzzles, children's page and many tips in the service section round the magazine TV Health & Life from.
Language(s): German
ADVERTISING RATES:
Full Page Mono .... EUR 9850
Full Page Colour .... EUR 9850
Mechanical Data: Type Area: 260 x 182 mm
CONSUMER: MUSIC & PERFORMING ARTS: TV & Radio

TV HÖREN UND SEHEN
745564G76C-700

Editorial: Burchardstr. 11, 20095 HAMBURG
Tel: 40 30190 **Fax:** 40 30194032
Email: susanne.gritzbach@bauermedia.com **Web site:** http://www.tvhus.de
Freq: Weekly; **Annual Sub.:** EUR 72,80; **Circ:** 796,721
Editor: Uwe Bokelmann
Profile: Program guide in which all programs and all programs are comprehensively presented and informative program to twelve pages. Hearing and seeing the TV program particularly valuable diamond-TV movies highlights.
Language(s): German
ADVERTISING RATES:
Full Page Mono .... EUR 33869
Full Page Colour .... EUR 33869
Mechanical Data: Type Area: 258 x 206 mm, No. of Columns (Display): 4, Col Widths (Display): 48 mm
Copy instructions: *Copy Date:* 28 days prior to publication
CONSUMER: MUSIC & PERFORMING ARTS: TV & Radio

TV KLAR
745568G76C-740

Editorial: Burchardstr. 11, 20067 HAMBURG
Tel: 40 30194153 **Fax:** 40 30192148
Email: tvklar@bauerredaktionen.de **Web site:** http://www.bauermedia.com
Freq: Weekly; **Cover Price:** EUR 0,79; **Circ:** 251,080
Editor: Michael Heun
Profile: TV klar provides its readers with a clearly articulated program and offer a wide and varied mix of reportage, stories, advice columns and puzzles profit entertainment and relaxation.
Language(s): German
ADVERTISING RATES:
Full Page Mono .... EUR 16450
Full Page Colour .... EUR 16450
Mechanical Data: Type Area: 258 x 206 mm
Copy instructions: *Copy Date:* 28 days prior to publication
CONSUMER: MUSIC & PERFORMING ARTS: TV & Radio

TV KOCHEN
1639660G74P-1386

Editorial: Münchener Str. 101, 85737 ISMANING
Tel: 89 272707621 **Fax:** 89 272707690
Email: kontakt@gongverlag.de **Web site:** http://www.gong-verlag.de
Freq: 13 issues yearly; **Cover Price:** EUR 0,99; **Circ:** 200,000
Editor: Katharina Lukas; **Advertising Manager:** Benita Ahsendorf
Profile: Magazine for children about animals.
Language(s): German
ADVERTISING RATES:
Full Page Mono .... EUR 4900
Full Page Colour .... EUR 4900
Mechanical Data: Type Area: 245 x 190 mm

TV KOCHEN
1639660G91D-9954

Editorial: Münchener Str. 101, 85737 ISMANING
Tel: 89 272707621 **Fax:** 89 272707690

Germany

Email: kontakt@gongverlag.de **Web site:** http://www.gong-verlag.de
Freq: 13 issues yearly; **Cover Price:** EUR 0,99; **Circ:** 200,000
Editor: Katharina Lukas; **Advertising Manager:** Benita Ahsendorf
Profile: Magazine for children about animals.
Language(s): German
ADVERTISING RATES:
Full Page Mono .... EUR 4900
Full Page Colour .... EUR 4900
Mechanical Data: Type Area: 245 x 190 mm

TV MOVIE 745571G76C-760
Editorial: Meßberg 1, 20095 HAMBURG
Tel: 40 30193603 **Fax:** 40 30193605
Email: agnes.diaz@tvmovie.de **Web site:** http://www.tvmovie.de
Freq: 26 issues yearly; **Annual Sub.:** EUR 49,40; **Circ:** 1,382,512
Editor: Stefan Westendorp
Profile: TV program guide with emphasis on film. In addition to exciting reports and background to film and cinema delivers TV Movie Highlights interviews and columns from the source - stars up close. Moreover, in every TV Movie: Top-Sport, the latest trends in multimedia and telecommunications and of course the most important new releases on DVD and BLU-RAY.
Language(s): German
ADVERTISING RATES:
Full Page Mono .... EUR 52983
Full Page Colour .... EUR 52983
Mechanical Data: Type Area: 258 x 206 mm
Copy instructions: *Copy Date:* 32 days prior to publication
Supplement(s): Wetten Dass..?
CONSUMER: MUSIC & PERFORMING ARTS: TV & Radio

TV MOVIE.DE 1622138G76C-917
Editorial: Meßberg 1, 20095 HAMBURG
Tel: 40 30190 **Fax:** 40 30191991
Email: amely.brouwers@bauermedia.com **Web site:** http://www.tvmovie.de
Freq: Daily; **Cover Price:** Paid; **Circ:** 10,131,124 Unique Users
Editor: Amely Brouwers
Profile: Ezine: TVMovie.de with the famous MovieStar complements the expertise of the printed mark is the interactivity of the online medium. The core competencies are the current clear-TV program and the latest news from the film and DVD industry. The portal also offers an editorial guide for the new WebTV program in Germany. The offer is completed in detail the categories sports and multimedia. There are innovative features like an iPhone application or a mobile version of the proposal offered to the user. The users are young, high income, predominantly male with a large Interest in new technological developments in telecommunications and consumer electronics. Facebook: http://www.facebook.com/TVMovie Twitter: http://twitter.com/tvmoviede This Outlet offers RSS (Really Simple Syndication).
Language(s): German
CONSUMER: MUSIC & PERFORMING ARTS: TV & Radio

TV NEU 745573G76C-780
Editorial: Axel-Springer-Platz 1, 20355 HAMBURG
Tel: 40 34700 **Fax:** 40 34722601
Email: tvneu.leser@axelspringer.de **Web site:** http://www.axelspringer.de
Freq: 20 issues yearly; **Annual Sub.:** EUR 51,48; **Circ:** 100,199
Editor: Jan von Frenckell; **Advertising Manager:** Arne Bergmann
Profile: TVneu is the young program guide for all those who attach importance to concise information at a reasonable price, want to be entertained and expert advice. All about television, about everyday life. TVneu readers spend their leisure time actively. They therefore place great value on current information, which focus on the essentials and offer great benefits. TVneu consistently goes to these needs and puts emphasis in the major areas of life, the reader. TVneu - concise information for leisure active people.
Language(s): German
ADVERTISING RATES:
Full Page Mono .... EUR 9000
Full Page Colour .... EUR 9000
Mechanical Data: Type Area: 270 x 206 mm, No. of Columns (Display): 4, Col Widths (Display): 50 mm
Copy instructions: *Copy Date:* 21 days prior to publication
CONSUMER: MUSIC & PERFORMING ARTS: TV & Radio

TV PICCOLINO 1638958G76C-928
Editorial: Rindermarkt 6, 80331 MÜNCHEN
Tel: 89 18912874 **Fax:** 89 55058670
Email: info@blattgold.tv **Web site:** http://www.tvpiccolino.de
Freq: 26 issues yearly; **Annual Sub.:** EUR 19,50; **Circ:** 180,741
Editor: Sandra Schönbein
Profile: TV program guide, 14 days full program with many of the program guide and TV highlights of the trendy pocket format. This 's Star-News of music, cinema and film, travel tips, recipes for collecting, puzzle-fun and much more.
Language(s): German
ADVERTISING RATES:
Full Page Mono .... EUR 5100
Full Page Colour .... EUR 5100
Mechanical Data: Type Area: 220 x 160 mm
Copy instructions: *Copy Date:* 20 days prior to publication
CONSUMER: MUSIC & PERFORMING ARTS: TV & Radio

TV PUR 745584G76C-800
Editorial: Meßberg 1, 20095 HAMBURG
Tel: 40 30193603 **Fax:** 40 30193605
Email: agnes.diaz@tvmovie.de **Web site:** http://www.bauermediagroup.de
Freq: Monthly; **Cover Price:** EUR 0,99; **Circ:** 618,381
Editor: Stefan Westendorp
Profile: Magazine providing a comprehensive guide to TV listings. Program guide with about 124 pages - including 112 pages of pure program- information.
Language(s): German
ADVERTISING RATES:
Full Page Mono .... EUR 17581
Full Page Colour .... EUR 17581
Mechanical Data: Type Area: 252 x 184 mm
Copy instructions: *Copy Date:* 33 days prior to publication
CONSUMER: MUSIC & PERFORMING ARTS: TV & Radio

TV SPIELFILM 745586G76C-820
Editorial: Christoph-Probst-Weg 1, 20251 HAMBURG **Tel:** 40 41312203 **Fax:** 40 41312299
Email: echo@tvspielfilm.de **Web site:** http://www.tvspielfilm.de
Freq: Monthly; **Annual Sub.:** EUR 49,40; **Circ:** 406,361
Editor: Lutz Carstens; **Advertising Manager:** Daniela Henning
Profile: TV Spielfilm appeals especially to young opinion-forming groups, which are high income and consumption-oriented. TV Spielfilm is tailored to the demanding TV generation, constantly adapting to the innovations in the TV market. The high editorial quality is as much a core competence, such as the timeliness and breadth of coverage in modern media and lifestyle. The TV and cinema experts from the editorial staff assess competently, independently and critically, by selected criteria such as movies, series, documentaries and reports. Facebook: http://www.facebook.com/TVspielfilm Twitter: http://twitter.com/TV_Spielfilm1.
Language(s): German
ADVERTISING RATES:
Full Page Mono .... EUR 58636
Full Page Colour .... EUR 58636
Mechanical Data: Type Area: 265 x 198 mm
Copy instructions: *Copy Date:* 28 days prior to publication
CONSUMER: MUSIC & PERFORMING ARTS: TV & Radio

TV SPIELFILM ONLINE 1622139G76C-937
Editorial: Steinhauser Str. 1, 81677 MÜNCHEN
Tel: 89 92502404
Email: tvspielfilm@tomorrow-focus.de **Web site:** http://www.tvspielfilm.de
Freq: Daily; **Cover Price:** Paid; **Circ:** 14,663,808 Unique Users
Editor: Thomas Mende
Profile: TV Spielfilm Online is the personal program guide on the web. It offers information about television, news, reviews and background on the current program offering. There are the TV highlights, sorted by categories like movies, sports, reportage, editorial, and presented updated hourly. The more than 150 channels (including all-digital and pay TV channels) are divided by the favorite channel function, and the editorial pre-selected channel packages. In addition, the theater program and DVD news will be retrieved. The star database contains information on all stars and celebrities as well as when each actor can be seen on TV. The site speaks mostly sophisticated, educated and high-income users to mid-30 at. The typical TV Spielfilm Online user is 20 years and older has at least attended secondary school, is employed or in training and has a household income of about 3.000 €. Facebook: http://www.facebook.com/TVspielfilm Twitter: http://twitter.com/TV_Spielfilm1.
Language(s): German
CONSUMER: MUSIC & PERFORMING ARTS: TV & Radio

TV TODAY 745590G76C-880
Editorial: Christoph-Probst-Weg 1, 20251 HAMBURG **Tel:** 40 41312203 **Fax:** 40 41312299
Email: service@tvtoday.de **Web site:** http://www.tvtoday.de
Freq: Monthly; **Annual Sub.:** EUR 45,50; **Circ:** 406,361
Editor: Lutz Carstens; **Advertising Manager:** Lutz Nierhoff
Profile: TV Today appeals especially to young opinion-forming groups, which are high income and consumption-oriented. TV Today is tailored to the demanding TV generation, constantly adapting to the innovations in the TV market. The high editorial quality is as much a core competence, such as the timeliness and breadth of coverage in modern media and lifestyle. The TV and cinema experts from the editorial staff assess competently, independently and critically, by selected criteria such as movies, series, documentaries and reports. Facebook: http://www.facebook.com/TVtoday Twitter: http://twitter.com/TV_Today.
Language(s): German
ADVERTISING RATES:
Full Page Mono .... EUR 58636
Full Page Colour .... EUR 58636
Mechanical Data: Type Area: 265 x 198 mm
Copy instructions: *Copy Date:* 28 days prior to publication
CONSUMER: MUSIC & PERFORMING ARTS: TV & Radio

TV TODAY ONLINE 1622140G76C-919
Editorial: Christoph-Probst-Weg 1, 20251 HAMBURG **Tel:** 40 41312203 **Fax:** 40 41312299
Email: service@tvtoday.de **Web site:** http://www.tvtoday.de
Freq: Daily; **Cover Price:** Paid; **Circ:** 5,009,587 Unique Users
Editor: Lutz Carstens
Profile: Ezine: The TV portal provides information to users at a glance quickly and directly about the current TV program. Every day, over 2,000 listed programs, TV-day tips and search functions are the core services of TV Today Online. The users are predominantly male (68%) with above-average interest in the subject computer, insurance, digital TV and telecommunications. The extra entertainment department informed of new films at the cinema, games and music. For users with high affinity to Homentertainment it is a week before the latest movies on DVD and shows the latest technology trends. An additional service consisting Quiz coach, horoscopes, competitions, user forums on TV and entertainment topics, as well as stars in the Web service completes the offerings of entertainment. Facebook: http://www.facebook.com/HubertBurdaMedia Twitter: http://twitter.com/burda_news.
Language(s): German
CONSUMER: MUSIC & PERFORMING ARTS: TV & Radio

TW TAGUNGSREGIONEN 745604G14A-7680
Editorial: Mainzer Landstr. 251, 60326 FRANKFURT
Tel: 69 75951906 **Fax:** 69 75951900
Email: mewis@tw-media.com **Web site:** http://www.tagungsregionen.com
Freq: 5 issues yearly; **Circ:** 16,000
Editor: Dirk Mewis
Profile: Supplement the TW Meetings Industry in Germany, Austria and Switzerland. Directory of event cities / locations, convention and exhibition centers, conference hotels, conference and event venues ships.
Language(s): German
ADVERTISING RATES:
Full Page Colour .... EUR 1450
Mechanical Data: Type Area: 255 x 180 mm
Supplement to: TW The Global Magazine for Meeting, Incentive and Event Professionals

TW THE GLOBAL MAGAZINE FOR MEETING, INCENTIVE AND EVENT PROFESSIONALS 745605G2C-90
Editorial: Mainzer Landstr. 251, 60326 FRANKFURT
Tel: 69 75951906 **Fax:** 69 75951900
Email: mewis@tw-media.com **Web site:** http://www.tw-media.com
Freq: 5 issues yearly; **Annual Sub.:** EUR 68,00; **Circ:** 19,928
Editor: Dirk Mewis; **Advertising Manager:** Christine Fuchs
Profile: Magazine covering facts, figures, facilities, services and management practice in the meetings and incentive travel industry.
Language(s): English; German
ADVERTISING RATES:
Full Page Colour .... EUR 6200
Mechanical Data: Type Area: 255 x 186 mm, No. of Columns (Display): 4, Col Widths (Display): 44 mm
Copy instructions: *Copy Date:* 14 days prior to publication
Supplement(s): TW TagungsRegionen
BUSINESS: COMMUNICATIONS, ADVERTISING & MARKETING: Conferences & Exhibitions

TW THEMA WIRTSCHAFT 744633G63-860
Editorial: Mercatorstr. 22, 47051 DUISBURG
Tel: 203 2821200 **Fax:** 203 2821248
Email: tw-redaktion@niederrhein.ihk.de **Web site:** http://www.ihk-niederrhein.de
Freq: 10 issues yearly; Free to qualifying individuals
Annual Sub.: EUR 28,60; **Circ:** 52,088
Editor: Alfred Kilian
Profile: Journal of the Chamber of Trade and Industry in Duisburg for decision makers in medium-sized enterprises.
Language(s): German
ADVERTISING RATES:
Full Page Mono .... EUR 2791
Mechanical Data: Type Area: 262 x 184 mm, No. of Columns (Display): 3, Col Widths (Display): 59 mm
Copy instructions: *Copy Date:* 21 days prior to publication
BUSINESS: REGIONAL BUSINESS

TW.DIREKT 745601G49A-20
Editorial: Friedenstr. 41, 44139 DORTMUND
Tel: 231 9145463500 **Fax:** 231 9145463590
Email: info@vsp-business-media.de **Web site:** http://www.tw-direkt.de
Freq: Quarterly; **Annual Sub.:** EUR 28,00; **Circ:** 20,000
Editor: Peter H. Voß
Profile: tw.direkt addresses decision makers in industry, trade and logistics. Achieved with a circulation of 20,000 copies each issue an average of 48 000 readers. At selected events additional copies will be printed and laid on the ground. Readers of the tw.direkt are averaging 40 to 50 years old and have an income of 50,000 € per year. This and the wide range of topics make TWdirekt interesting as a display medium for the various industries. Ranging from hotels and meeting high quality writing instruments through to business books and magazines, fashion, jewelry, insurance, cars and many TWdirekt offers the perfect advertising environment.
Language(s): German
Readership: Aimed at senior management in the logistics and transport industries.
ADVERTISING RATES:
Full Page Mono .... EUR 4800
Full Page Colour .... EUR 4800
Mechanical Data: Type Area: 271 x 161 mm

TZ 745612G67B-14920
Editorial: Paul-Heyse-Str. 2, 80336 MÜNCHEN
Tel: 89 53060 **Fax:** 89 5306552
Web site: http://www.tz-online.de
Freq: 260 issues yearly; **Circ:** 134,046
Editor: Rudolf Bögel; **News Editor:** Klaus Rimpel;
Advertising Manager: Hans-Georg Bechthold
Profile: Regional daily newspaper covering politics, economics, sport, travel and technology. Facebook: http://www.facebook.com/pages/TZ-Online/95100047797 This Outlet offers RSS (Really Simple Syndication).
Language(s): German
ADVERTISING RATES:
SCC .... EUR 103,40
Mechanical Data: Type Area: 474 x 324 mm, No. of Columns (Display): 7, Col Widths (Display): 45 mm
Copy instructions: *Copy Date:* 1 day prior to publication
Supplement(s): doppio
REGIONAL DAILY & SUNDAY NEWSPAPERS: Regional Daily Newspapers

TZ 1704676G67B-16764
Editorial: Paul-Heyse-Str. 2, 80336 MÜNCHEN
Tel: 89 53068434 **Fax:** 89 5306607
Email: sekretariat@tz-online.de **Web site:** http://www.tz-online.de
Freq: Daily; **Cover Price:** Paid; **Circ:** 4,264,201 Unique Users
Editor: Markus Knall
Profile: Ezine: Regional daily newspaper covering politics, economics, sport, travel and technology. Facebook: http://www.facebook.com/pages/TZ-Online/95100047797.
Language(s): German
REGIONAL DAILY & SUNDAY NEWSPAPERS: Regional Daily Newspapers

TZB THÜRINGER ZAHNÄRZTE BLATT 745613G56D-860
Editorial: Barbarossahof 16, 99092 ERFURT
Tel: 361 7432136 **Fax:** 361 7432150
Email: ptz@lzkth.de **Web site:** http://www.lzkth.de
Freq: 11 issues yearly; Free to qualifying individuals
Annual Sub.: EUR 53,91; **Circ:** 2,700
Editor: Karl-Heinz Müller; **Advertising Manager:** Wolfgang Klaus
Profile: Official magazine of the Landeszahnärztekammer Thüringen and of the Kassenzahnärztliche Vereinigung Thüringen.
Language(s): German
Readership: Read by dentists.
ADVERTISING RATES:
Full Page Colour .... EUR 1380
Mechanical Data: Type Area: 297 x 210 mm
Copy instructions: *Copy Date:* 25 days prior to publication
Official Journal of: Organ d. Landeszahnärztekammer Thüringen u. d. Kassenzahnärztl. Vereinigung Thüringen
BUSINESS: HEALTH & MEDICAL: Dental

Ü 745623G62B-770
Editorial: Von-Coels-Str. 390, 52080 AACHEN
Tel: 241 9581019 **Fax:** 241 9581010
Email: redaktion@m-m-sports.com **Web site:** http://www.dersportverlag.de
Freq: 6 issues yearly; **Annual Sub.:** EUR 21,00; **Circ:** 30,000
Editor: Pia Pauly; **Advertising Manager:** Kirsten Schiffer
Profile: The instructor magazine "Ü" is a treasure trove for trainers, coaches, teachers, educators, parents, etc. For groups of all ages offers Ü newer and sports cross Suggestions for the creative design of lessons.
Language(s): German
Readership: Read by trainers involved with the German Gymnastics Association.
ADVERTISING RATES:
Full Page Mono .... EUR 1280
Full Page Colour .... EUR 2480
Mechanical Data: Type Area: 248 x 165 mm
Copy instructions: *Copy Date:* 40 days prior to publication

Supplement to: NTB-Magazin
BUSINESS: CHURCH & SCHOOL EQUIPMENT & EDUCATION: Education Teachers

ÜBEN & MUSIZIEREN
745624G62B-2840
Editorial: Weihergarten 5, 55116 MAINZ
Tel: 6131 246855 **Fax:** 6131 246212
Email: ruediger.behschnitt@schott-music.com **Web site:** http://www.musikpaedagogik-online.de
Freq: 6 issues yearly; **Annual Sub.:** EUR 46,00; **Circ:** 6,000
Editor: Rüdiger Behschnitt; **Advertising Manager:** Dieter P. Schwarz
Profile: Magazine concerning the teaching of music in schools, colleges and at home.
Language(s): German
ADVERTISING RATES:
Full Page Mono .... EUR 875
Mechanical Data: Type Area: 260 x 185 mm
Copy instructions: *Copy Date:* 34 days prior to publication
BUSINESS: CHURCH & SCHOOL EQUIPMENT & EDUCATION: Education Teachers

ÜBER LAND
1861170G21A-4412
Editorial: Dieperzbergweg 13, 57610 ALTENKIRCHEN **Tel:** 2681 95160 **Fax:** 2681 70206
Email: info@lja.de **Web site:** http://www.lja.de
Freq: Half-yearly; **Cover Price:** EUR 6,00
Free to qualifying individuals ; **Circ:** 800
Editor: Hans-Heiner Heuser
Profile: Perspectives on land and ecology.
Language(s): German

UCKERMARK KURIER
745621G67B-14940
Editorial: Friedrich-Engels-Ring 29, 17033 NEUBRANDENBURG **Tel:** 395 45750
Fax: 395 4575694
Email: redaktion@nordkurier.de **Web site:** http://www.nordkurier.de
Freq: 312 issues yearly; **Circ:** 107,725
Advertising Manager: Carsten Kottwitz
Profile: Daily newspaper with regional news and a local sports section. Facebook: http://www.facebook.com/pages/Nordkurier/102742776465803.
Language(s): German
ADVERTISING RATES:
SCC .... EUR 41,10
Mechanical Data: Type Area: 480 x 324 mm, No. of Columns (Display): 7, Col Widths (Display): 45 mm
Copy instructions: *Copy Date:* 2 days prior to publication
Supplement(s): prisma
REGIONAL DAILY & SUNDAY NEWSPAPERS: Regional Daily Newspapers

UDZ UNTERNEHMEN DER ZUKUNFT
745976G14A-7720
Editorial: Pontdriesch 14, 52062 AACHEN
Tel: 241 477050 **Fax:** 241 47705199
Email: redaktion-udz@fir.rwth-aachen.de **Web site:** http://www.fir.rwth-aachen.de
Freq: 3 issues yearly; **Circ:** 3,500
Editor: Astrid Giernalczyk
Profile: Magazine for organisation and occupation in production and service.
Language(s): English; German
ADVERTISING RATES:
Full Page Mono .... EUR 650
Mechanical Data: Type Area: 247 x 144 mm, No. of Columns (Display): 3, Col Widths (Display): 45 mm
Copy instructions: *Copy Date:* 30 days prior to publication

UECKER-RANDOW BLITZ AM SONNTAG
745643G72-14448
Editorial: Friedrich-Engels-Ring 7a, 17033 NEUBRANDENBURG **Tel:** 395 5632113
Fax: 395 5632100
Email: ute.koepke@blitzverlag.de **Web site:** http://www.blitzverlag.de
Freq: Weekly; **Cover Price:** Free; **Circ:** 37,346
Editor: Ute Köpke; **Advertising Manager:** Petra Göring
Profile: Advertising journal (house-to-house) concentrating on local stories.
Language(s): German
ADVERTISING RATES:
Full Page Mono .... EUR 2772
Full Page Colour .... EUR 3162
Mechanical Data: Type Area: 420 x 285 mm, No. of Columns (Display): 6, Col Widths (Display): 45 mm
Copy instructions: *Copy Date:* 2 days prior to publication
LOCAL NEWSPAPERS

UETERSENER NACHRICHTEN
745651G67B-14960
Editorial: Großer Sand 3, 25436 UETERSEN
Tel: 4122 92500 **Fax:** 4122 1858
Email: redaktion@uena.de **Web site:** http://www.uena.de
Freq: 312 issues yearly; **Circ:** 5,002
Editor: Roland von Ziehlberg; **Advertising Manager:** Gisa Köhler
Profile: Daily newspaper with regional news and a local sports section.
Language(s): German
ADVERTISING RATES:
SCC .... EUR 31,20
Mechanical Data: Type Area: 430 x 282 mm, No. of Columns (Display): 6, Col Widths (Display): 45 mm
Copy instructions: *Copy Date:* 1 day prior to publication
REGIONAL DAILY & SUNDAY NEWSPAPERS: Regional Daily Newspapers

UFZ-NEWSLETTER
1793994G57-2816
Editorial: Permoserstr. 15, 04318 LEIPZIG
Tel: 341 2351269 **Fax:** 341 2352649
Email: info@ufz.de **Web site:** http://www.ufz.de
Freq: Quarterly; **Cover Price:** Free; **Circ:** 5,000
Editor: Doris Böhme
Profile: Information from the Helmholtz Centre for Environmental Research.
Language(s): German

UGB-FORUM
745656G56A-11188
Editorial: Sandusweg 3, 35435 WETTENBERG
Tel: 641 8089613 **Fax:** 641 8089650
Email: ulrike.becker@ugb.de **Web site:** http://www.ugb.de
Freq: 6 issues yearly; Free to qualifying individuals
Annual Sub.: EUR 45,00; **Circ:** 5,200
Editor: Ulrike Becker; **Advertising Manager:** Stefan Weigt
Profile: Magazine about health support, nutrition and wellbeing.
Language(s): German

UHREN MAGAZIN
745662G79K-340_50
Editorial: Riedstr. 25, 73760 OSTFILDERN
Tel: 711 44007610 **Fax:** 711 44007611
Email: redaktion@uhrenmagazin.de **Web site:** http://www.watchtime.net
Freq: 10 issues yearly; **Annual Sub.:** EUR 67,30; **Circ:** 5,726
Editor: Thomas Wanka; **Advertising Manager:** Andrea Scheungrab
Profile: Purchasing advice round the clock at the Clock is at the center magazine. As a high-class special-interest magazine that Uhren-Magazin is both content and optical for endless fascination watches. In addition to the rational and technical information on the mechanics and design gives the Uhren-Magazin to its readers the emotional component, and the joy of holding a high-quality mechanical clock. The designated competent test subjects magazine divers and pilots watches under harsh field conditions most accurate tests. Extensive market surveys, helpful service information and fascinating knowledge contributions, and the ten-time appearance a year provide the proverbial high relevance and acceptance of the oldest German watch magazine. The motto around the Clock is made in the Uhren-Magazin literally. We carry the watch enthusiasts of the most exciting destinations that exist for watch enthusiasts: In the workshops of the great watchmakers in the Swiss Jura and Geneva, in the studios of German watchmaking to Glashütte or to Munich. The only watch magazine organized the Uhren-Magazin readers exclusive trips that left a feverish gleam in the eyes of the enthusiastic participants. Facebook: http://www.facebook.com/watchtime.net.
Language(s): German
ADVERTISING RATES:
Full Page Mono .... EUR 5280
Full Page Colour .... EUR 5280
Mechanical Data: Type Area: 254 x 191 mm, No. of Columns (Display): 3, Col Widths (Display): 61 mm
Copy instructions: *Copy Date:* 31 days prior to publication
CONSUMER: HOBBIES & DIY: Collectors Magazines

U.J.S. UHREN JUWELEN SCHMUCK
745660G52A-43
Editorial: Klasingstr. 1, 33602 BIELEFELD
Tel: 521 987853820 **Fax:** 521 987853838
Email: dietmar.krebs@chmielorz.de **Web site:** http://www.ujs.info
Freq: Monthly; **Annual Sub.:** EUR 111,00; **Circ:** 8,026
Editor: Dietmar Krebs; **Advertising Manager:** Franz Stypa
Profile: U.J.S. Uhren Juwelen Schmuck is the opinion-leading journal for qualified retailers. The latest industry news and the latest insights from the fields of watchmaking technology, jewelry design and manufacturing and gemology are a focus of reporting. The jeweler found in U.J.S. sound advice in the areas of: business administration, computer and inventory management, purchasing, sales, assortment, store design and window dressing. A comprehensive overview of the current offerings from industry and the wholesale offer special exhibition issues and the monthly in the magazine apprehended priorities. Portraits, critical interviews to appeal-issues of retail and the global report on developments abroad complete the profile of U.J.S. and strengthen the high-loyalty from readers. The supplement U.J.S. FashionGuide establishes the links between fashion, cosmetics, accessories, watches and jewelry. It prepares the dealer well before the talks with his customers, makes suggestions for the design range and provides him with clear information about the brand worlds. For this reason, the U.J.S. FashionGuide is an important guide for staff in the shop. Facebook: http://www.facebook.com/pages/edit/pages/UJS-Uhren-Juwelen-Schmuck/122763151083889.
Language(s): German
ADVERTISING RATES:
Full Page Mono .... EUR 2750
Full Page Colour .... EUR 4020
Mechanical Data: Type Area: 274 x 203 mm, No. of Columns (Display): 4, Col Widths (Display): 47 mm
Official Journal of: Organ d. Zentralverb. f. Uhren, Schmuck u. Zeitmesstechnik u. d. Bundesgroßhandelsverb. f. Uhren
BUSINESS: GIFT TRADE: Jewellery

UK PT KONTAKT
1896647G18B-2196
Editorial: Frankenallee 71, 60327 FRANKFURT
Tel: 69 75014576 **Fax:** 69 75014877
Email: verlag@fsd.de **Web site:** http://www.fsd.de
Freq: Quarterly; **Circ:** 80,000
Editor: Stefan Sochatzy
Profile: Magazine of the Accident Insurance Post and Telecom is the official journal of the accident fund and Telefon. It is aimed at the over 140 member companies of the accident fund. For this, the German Post AG and the German Telekom AG and its subsidiaries as well as a number of other companies and organizations with more than 409 000 employees. It will reach the decision makers, opinion leaders and employees for actions of prevention and rehabilitation in the member companies.
Language(s): German
ADVERTISING RATES:
Full Page Mono .... EUR 1720
Full Page Colour .... EUR 3100
Mechanical Data: Type Area: 260 x 180 mm
Copy instructions: *Copy Date:* 46 days prior to publication

UK UNSERE KIRCHE
745894G87-12380
Editorial: Cansteinstr. 1, 33647 BIELEFELD
Tel: 521 94400 **Fax:** 521 9440181
Email: redaktion@unserekirche.de **Web site:** http://www.unserekirche.de
Freq: Weekly; **Annual Sub.:** EUR 62,40; **Circ:** 50,626
Editor: Wolfgang Riewe; **Advertising Manager:** Michael Pijahn
Profile: Magazine for the Protestant Church.
Language(s): German
ADVERTISING RATES:
Full Page Mono .... EUR 5400
Full Page Colour .... EUR 7680
Mechanical Data: Type Area: 395 x 285 mm, No. of Columns (Display): 6, Col Widths (Display): 45 mm
Copy instructions: *Copy Date:* 15 days prior to publication
CONSUMER: RELIGIOUS

ULMER WOCHENBLATT
745675G72-14472
Editorial: Frauenstr. 77, 89073 ULM **Tel:** 731 156271
Fax: 731 156860
Email: uwo@swp.de **Web site:** http://www.wochenblatt-aktiv.de
Freq: Weekly; **Cover Price:** Free; **Circ:** 139,570
Editor: Karin Zeger; **Advertising Manager:** Thomas Baumann
Profile: Advertising journal (house-to-house) concentrating on local stories.
Language(s): German
ADVERTISING RATES:
Full Page Mono .... EUR 6351
Full Page Colour .... EUR 9543
Mechanical Data: Type Area: 480 x 320 mm, No. of Columns (Display): 7, Col Widths (Display): 44 mm
Copy instructions: *Copy Date:* 1 day prior to publication
LOCAL NEWSPAPERS

ULTIMO
745680G80-12100
Editorial: Eichenweg 2, 24214 NOER **Tel:** 431 86757
Fax: 431 82330
Email: info@ultimo-kiel.de **Web site:** http://www.ultimo-kiel.de
Freq: Monthly; **Cover Price:** Free; **Circ:** 12,365
Editor: Wolfgang Buhmann
Profile: Magazine about the Kiel region.
Language(s): German
ADVERTISING RATES:
Full Page Mono .... EUR 500
Full Page Colour .... EUR 500
Mechanical Data: Type Area: 180 x 124 mm, No. of Columns (Display): 3, Col Widths (Display): 37 mm
Copy instructions: *Copy Date:* 10 days prior to publication
CONSUMER: RURAL & REGIONAL INTEREST

ULTIMO
745681G80-12120
Editorial: Wahmstr. 39, 23552 LÜBECK
Tel: 451 72031 **Fax:** 451 74850
Email: info@ultimo-luebeck.de **Web site:** http://www.ultimo-luebeck.de
Freq: Monthly; **Cover Price:** Free; **Circ:** 14,630
Editor: Thomas Lender; **Advertising Manager:** Avni Mahnoli
Profile: Magazine for city and region, concentrating on gastronomy, music, arts and events. Facebook: http://www.facebook.com/pages/Lubeck/Ultimo-Stadtmagazin-Lubeck/462788195113.
Language(s): German
ADVERTISING RATES:
Full Page Mono .... EUR 920
Full Page Colour .... EUR 1480
Mechanical Data: Type Area: 180 x 124 mm, No. of Columns (Display): 2, Col Widths (Display): 60 mm
Copy instructions: *Copy Date:* 14 days prior to publication
CONSUMER: RURAL & REGIONAL INTEREST

ULTIMO
745682G89C-4833
Editorial: Herforder Str. 237, 33609 BIELEFELD
Tel: 521 441812
Email: info@ultimo-bielefeld.de **Web site:** http://www.ultimo-bielefeld.de
Freq: 22 issues yearly; **Cover Price:** Free; **Circ:** 13,900
Editor: Thomas Friedrich
Profile: Entertainment guide for Bielefeld.
Language(s): German
Readership: Read by people aged between 15 and 35 years.
ADVERTISING RATES:
Full Page Mono .... EUR 780
Full Page Colour .... EUR 1200
Mechanical Data: Type Area: 260 x 190 mm, No. of Columns (Display): 4, Col Widths (Display): 44 mm
CONSUMER: HOLIDAYS & TRAVEL: Entertainment Guides

ULTRASCHALL IN DER MEDIZIN EUROPEAN JOURNAL OF ULTRASOUND
745687G56A-9820
Editorial: Rüdigerstr. 14, 70469 STUTTGART
Tel: 711 89310 **Fax:** 711 8931298
Email: ultraschall@thieme.de **Web site:** http://www.thieme.de/ultraschall
Freq: 6 issues yearly; Free to qualifying individuals
Annual Sub.: EUR 328,90; **Circ:** 14,550
Editor: M. Bachmann Nielsen
Profile: Guiding themes magazine for all practical and clinical applications of ultrasound. Scientifically sound, with current categories of high practical value.
Language(s): English; German
ADVERTISING RATES:
Full Page Mono .... EUR 2930
Full Page Colour .... EUR 4400
Mechanical Data: Type Area: 248 x 175 mm, No. of Columns (Display): 4, Col Widths (Display): 40 mm
Official Journal of: Organ d. European Federation of Societies for Ultrasound in Medicine and Biology, d. Dt. Ges. f. Ultraschall in d. Medizin, d. Österr. Ges. f. Ultraschall in d. Medizin, d. Schweizer. Ges. f. Ultraschall in d. Medizin, d. Danish Society of Diagnostic Ultrasound, d. Norwegian Society for Diagnostic Ultrasound in Medicine, d. Latvian Society of Ultrasound in Medicine, d. Flemish Society of Ultrasound, d. Macedonian Ultrasound u. d. Croatian Society for Ultrasound in Medicine and Biology
BUSINESS: HEALTH & MEDICAL

UMBAUEN & MODERNISIEREN
745691G74C-3160
Editorial: Schwanthalerstr. 10, 80336 MÜNCHEN
Tel: 89 59908111 **Fax:** 89 59908133
Email: redaktion@cpz.de **Web site:** http://www.bau-welt.de
Freq: 6 issues yearly; **Annual Sub.:** EUR 12,00; **Circ:** 43,464
Editor: Claudia Mannschott; **Advertising Manager:** Sebastian Schmidt
Profile: The title of "Umbauen & Modernisieren" is a program. It is aimed at house and apartment owners, tenants and to buyers of used homes, and meets the increasing trend of renovation and do it yourself. In view of the heirs of this generation market will experience a further boom in the area of modernization. Thus, the reader an objective and credible documentation that supports the editors own sites. This alteration, extension and modernization projects are monitored on the site and photographed. Step by step shows is that used when the individual trades. Through extensive market surveys and material science, the reader an overview of the latest products and offers.
Language(s): German
ADVERTISING RATES:
Full Page Mono .... EUR 6130
Full Page Colour .... EUR 8500
Mechanical Data: Type Area: 270 x 180 mm, No. of Columns (Display): 4, Col Widths (Display): 42 mm
Copy instructions: *Copy Date:* 40 days prior to publication
Supplement(s): Bäder & Küchen; Dach, Wand & Boden; Erneuerbare Energien; Fenster, Türen & Garagentore; Heizung & Energiesparen; Smart Wohnen: Haustechnik & Sicherheit
CONSUMER: WOMEN'S INTEREST CONSUMER MAGAZINES: Home & Family

UMFELD UMWELT
1788740G57-2807
Editorial: Brennhausgasse 14, 09599 FREIBERG
Tel: 3731 392297 **Fax:** 3731 394060
Web site: http://www.ioez.tu-freiberg.de
Freq: Annual; **Circ:** 500
Profile: Ecology magazine.
Language(s): German

UMFORMTECHNIK
758489G27-2948
Editorial: Franz-Ludwig-Str. 7a, 96047 BAMBERG
Tel: 951 861119 **Fax:** 951 861170
Email: umformtechnik@meisenbach.de **Web site:** http://www.umformtechnik.net
Freq: Quarterly; **Annual Sub.:** EUR 83,00; **Circ:** 4,843
Editor: Wolfgang Fili; **Advertising Manager:** Georg Meisenbach

Profile: Magazine for the production of piece goods and semi manufactured products by massive forming.
Language(s): German
ADVERTISING RATES:
Full Page Mono .... EUR 2255
Full Page Colour .... EUR 3611
Mechanical Data: Type Area: 260 x 184 mm, No. of Columns (Display): 3, Col Widths (Display): 59 mm
Copy instructions: *Copy Date:* 20 days prior to publication
Official Journal of: Organ d. ICFG, CIRP
BUSINESS: METAL, IRON & STEEL

UMID UMWELT UND MENSCH - INFORMATIONSDIENST
1864874G56A-11579
Editorial: Corrensplatz 1, 14195 BERLIN
Tel: 30 89031443 **Fax:** 30 89031830
Email: kerstin.gebuhr@uba.de **Web site:** http://www.umweltbundesamt.de
Freq: 3 issues yearly; **Circ:** 1,100
Editor: Kerstin Gebuhr
Profile: Magazine with information about environment, health and consumer protection.
Language(s): German

[UMRISSE]
756770G4E-6810
Editorial: Biebricher Allee 11b, 65187 WIESBADEN
Tel: 611 846515 **Fax:** 611 801252
Email: mwiederspahn@verlagsgruppewiederspahn.de **Web site:** http://www.umrisse.de
Freq: 6 issues yearly; **Annual Sub.:** EUR 63,00; **Circ:** 8,785
Editor: Michael Wiederspahn; **Advertising Manager:** Stephanie Dechant
Profile: Magazine for architects, building engineers, town planners, building companies, constructors, banks, insurance companies and real estate experts.
Language(s): German
ADVERTISING RATES:
Full Page Mono .... EUR 2100
Full Page Colour .... EUR 3200
Mechanical Data: No. of Columns (Display): 3, Col Widths (Display): 58 mm, Type Area: 268 x 185 mm
Copy instructions: *Copy Date:* 28 days prior to publication

DER UMSATZ STEUER-BERATER
745698G1A-3000
Editorial: Gustav-Heinemann-Ufer 58, 50968 KÖLN
Tel: 221 93738152 **Fax:** 221 93738902
Email: verlag@otto-schmidt.de **Web site:** http://www.ustb.de
Freq: Monthly; **Annual Sub.:** EUR 176,90; **Circ:** 2,863
Editor: Monika Neu; **Advertising Manager:** Thorsten Deuse
Profile: Magazine about value added tax law.
Language(s): German
ADVERTISING RATES:
Full Page Mono .... EUR 875
Full Page Colour .... EUR 1532
Mechanical Data: No. of Columns (Display): 2, Col Widths (Display): 88 mm, Type Area: 260 x 180 mm
BUSINESS: FINANCE & ECONOMICS

UMWELT
1656858G57-2728
Editorial: 11055 BERLIN
Web site: http://www.bmu.de
Freq: 11 issues yearly; **Annual Sub.:** EUR 21,47; **Circ:** 8,500
Editor: Karl Tempel
Profile: National official paper.
Language(s): German

UMWELT AKTUELL
739763G57-1760
Editorial: Marienstr. 19, 10117 BERLIN
Tel: 30 678177582 **Fax:** 30 678177580
Email: redaktion@dnr.de **Web site:** http://www.umwelt-aktuell.eu
Freq: 10 issues yearly; **Annual Sub.:** EUR 66,45; **Circ:** 3,300
Editor: Matthias Bauer
Profile: Magazine focusing on the environment and ecology. Feature articles on environmental pollution and protection as well as ecological policy.
Language(s): German
ADVERTISING RATES:
Full Page Mono .... EUR 1530
Full Page Colour .... EUR 2780
Mechanical Data: Type Area: 225 x 175 mm
Copy instructions: *Copy Date:* 14 days prior to publication
BUSINESS: ENVIRONMENT & POLLUTION

DER UMWELT BEAUFTRAGTE
1660112G57-2733
Editorial: Usrainer Ring 81, 72076 TÜBINGEN
Tel: 7071 6878160
Email: schumacher@oekom.de **Web site:** http://www.oekom.de
Freq: 11 issues yearly; **Annual Sub.:** EUR 132,35; **Circ:** 1,700
Editor: Jochen Schumacher
Profile: Magazine containing environmental issues.
Language(s): German
ADVERTISING RATES:
Full Page Mono .... EUR 1200
Full Page Colour .... EUR 2150
Mechanical Data: Type Area: 260 x 185 mm

UMWELT DEPESCHE
1836918G57-2874
Editorial: Stephanusstr. 25, 30449 HANNOVER
Tel: 511 443303
Email: umweltdepesche@biu-hannover.de **Web site:** http://www.biu-hannover.de
Freq: Half-yearly; **Cover Price:** Free; **Circ:** 4,000
Editor: Ralf Strobach; **Advertising Manager:** Ralf Strobach
Profile: Magazine from the Bürgerinitiative Umweltschutz.
Language(s): German

UMWELT JOURNAL
1695144G57-2769
Editorial: von-Werthern-Str. 6, 96487 DÖRFLES-ESBACH **Tel:** 9561 858013
Email: r.mueller@zaw-coburg.de **Web site:** http://www.zaw-coburg.de
Freq: Half-yearly; **Cover Price:** Free; **Circ:** 139,500
Editor: Robert Müller
Profile: Company publication about environment protection.
Language(s): German

UMWELT JOURNAL RHEINLAND-PFALZ
745719G57-2140
Editorial: Kaiser-Friedrich-Str. 1, 55116 MAINZ
Tel: 6131 164433 **Fax:** 6131 164629
Email: ralph.plugge@mufv.rlp.de **Web site:** http://www.umdenken.de
Freq: Quarterly; **Cover Price:** Free; **Circ:** 15,000
Profile: Publication containing information about environmental policy in Rheinland-Pfalz.
Language(s): German

UMWELT MAGAZIN
745721G57-2180
Editorial: VDI-Platz 1, 40468 DÜSSELDORF
Tel: 211 6103326 **Fax:** 211 6103148
Email: umweltmagazin@technikwissen.de **Web site:** http://www.umweltmagazin.de
Freq: 8 issues yearly; Free to qualifying individuals
Annual Sub.: EUR 111,50; **Circ:** 14,802
Editor: Oliver Gehrmann
Profile: Environmental magazine - The magazine for decision makers and management technology - helps executives, the course in the company to set the record straight. With theme ideas, products and procedures presented to the subscription market leader market opportunities and solutions for the future of companies. The themes of water / sewage, waste management, recycling, pollution, air- pollution control, renewable energies, measurement, control and analytical techniques for decision makers in industry, consulting and engineering firms, municipalities, associations and policy competently prepared. The latest trends not only in technology but also in management, legal and IT to create short messages in a quick overview. Reports and statements from the Practice go into the depths. Magazine's prestigious environmental decision-makers know-how for the practice.
Language(s): German
ADVERTISING RATES:
Full Page Mono .... EUR 4272
Full Page Colour .... EUR 5427
Mechanical Data: Type Area: 270 x 185 mm, No. of Columns (Display): 4, Col Widths (Display): 45 mm
Copy instructions: *Copy Date:* 21 days prior to publication
Official Journal of: Organ d. VBU-Verb. d. Betriebsbeauftragten f. Umweltschutz e.V., d. VDI-Koordinierungsstelle Umwelttechnik, d. European Environmental Press u. d. VNU-Verb. f. nachhaltiges Umweltmanagement
BUSINESS: ENVIRONMENT & POLLUTION

UMWELT & VERKEHR KARLSRUHE
1605032G57-2645
Editorial: Kronenstr. 9, 76133 KARLSRUHE
Tel: 721 380575
Email: redaktion@umverka.de **Web site:** http://www.umverka.de
Freq: 3 issues yearly; Free to qualifying individuals
Annual Sub.: EUR 10,00; **Circ:** 2,000
Editor: Uwe Haack; **Advertising Manager:** Mari Däschner
Profile: Magazine about environment and traffic.
Language(s): German

UMWELTBRIEFE
1659912G57-2732
Editorial: Kaiser-Friedrich-Str. 90, 10585 BERLIN
Tel: 30 21298723 **Fax:** 30 21298730
Email: umweltbriefe@raabe.de **Web site:** http://www.umweltbriefe.de
Freq: 24 issues yearly; **Annual Sub.:** EUR 249,90; **Circ:** 1,000
Editor: Tim Bartels
Profile: Newsletter provides information on trends and perspectives from the environment. Content: news, research reports, expert opinions and information including a citizen to the issues of waste management, energy, transportation, climate protection and nature conservation, urban ecology, environmental management, environmental law and Local Agenda 21.
Language(s): German
ADVERTISING RATES:
Full Page Mono .... EUR 999
Mechanical Data: Type Area: 232 x 184 mm, No. of Columns (Display): 3, Col Widths (Display): 58 mm
Copy instructions: *Copy Date:* 7 days prior to publication

UMWELTDIREKT
745712G57-2100
Editorial: Hostackerweg 21, 69198 SCHRIESHEIM
Tel: 6220 6562 **Fax:** 6220 911023
Email: nischwitz@umweltdirekt.de **Web site:** http://www.umweltdirekt.de
Freq: Quarterly; **Annual Sub.:** EUR 15,00; **Circ:** 25,000
Editor: Anke Nischwitz; **Advertising Manager:** Christine Noe-Knust
Profile: Umwelt Direkt is the environmental magazine for the Rhine-Neckar region and offers interesting reports on all major issues of environmentally conscious life. Each issue contains a current focal point with a wealth of informative and entertaining articles, carefully researched and prepared journalistic professional. Umwelt Direkt is made by people who live here in the region, maintain contacts and business presence. People who make an informative and offensive environment magazine for their readers - for you.
Language(s): German
ADVERTISING RATES:
Full Page Mono .... EUR 1290
Full Page Colour .... EUR 1650
Mechanical Data: Type Area: 253 x 195 mm, No. of Columns (Display): 5
Copy instructions: *Copy Date:* 14 days prior to publication

UMWELTINSTITUT MÜNCHEN E.V. INFOBRIEF
1824855G57-2841
Editorial: Landwehrstr. 64 a, 80336 MÜNCHEN
Tel: 89 3077490 **Fax:** 89 30774920
Email: redaktion@umweltinstitut.org **Web site:** http://www.umweltinstitut.org
Freq: Half-yearly; **Cover Price:** Free; **Circ:** 40,000
Editor: Christina Hacker
Profile: Newsletter of the Environmental Institute Munich with work reports to investigate and reduce environmental impact.
Language(s): German

UMWELTMAGAZIN SAAR
1856068G57-2886
Editorial: Evangelisch-Kirch-Str. 8, 66111 SAARBRÜCKEN **Tel:** 681 813700 **Fax:** 681 813720
Email: info@bund-saar.de **Web site:** http://www.bund-saar.de
Freq: Quarterly; **Cover Price:** Free; **Circ:** 11,000
Editor: Christoph Hassel; **Advertising Manager:** Petra Petry
Profile: Magazine about environmental protection in the Saar region.
Language(s): German

UMWELT-MEDIZIN GESELLSCHAFT
745722G56A-9840
Editorial: Frielinger Str. 31, 28215 BREMEN
Tel: 421 4984251 **Fax:** 421 4984252
Email: info@umg-verlag.de **Web site:** http://www.umwelt-medizin-gesellschaft.de
Freq: Quarterly; Free to qualifying individuals
Annual Sub.: EUR 38,00; **Circ:** 3,000
Editor: Erik Petersen; **Advertising Manager:** Erik Petersen
Profile: Environmental medicine, human ecology, social responsibility, global survival.
Language(s): German
ADVERTISING RATES:
Full Page Mono .... EUR 470
Mechanical Data: Type Area: 277 x 184 mm, No. of Columns (Display): 2, Col Widths (Display): 70 mm
Copy instructions: *Copy Date:* 21 days prior to publication
Official Journal of: Organ d. Dt. Berufsverb. d. Umweltmediziner, d. Dt. Ges. f. Umwelt- u. Humantoxikologie, d. Interdisziplinären Ges. f. Umweltmedizin u. d. Ökolog. Ärztebundes

UMWELTMEDIZIN IN FORSCHUNG UND PRAXIS
745723G56A-9860
Editorial: Justus-von-Liebig-Str. 1, 86899 LANDSBERG **Tel:** 8191 125500 **Fax:** 8191 125492
Email: susanne.fischer@hjr-verlag.de **Web site:** http://www.ecomed-medizin.de/umweltmedizin
Freq: 6 issues yearly; **Annual Sub.:** EUR 214,00; **Circ:** 1,000
Editor: Susanne Fischer; **Advertising Manager:** Reingard Herbst
Profile: Official journal of the International Society of Environmental Medicine.
Language(s): German
ADVERTISING RATES:
Full Page Mono .... EUR 1780
Full Page Colour .... EUR 2515
Mechanical Data: Type Area: 235 x 177 mm, No. of Columns (Display): 2, Col Widths (Display): 85 mm
Copy instructions: *Copy Date:* 42 days prior to publication
Official Journal of: Organ d. Internat. Society of Environmental Medicine u. d. Ges. f. Hygiene u. Umweltmedizin
BUSINESS: HEALTH & MEDICAL

UMWELTWISSENSCHAFTEN UND SCHADSTOFF-FORSCHUNG
745736G57-2280
Editorial: Tiergartenstr. 17, 69121 HEIDELBERG
Tel: 6221 4870 **Fax:** 6221 4878177
Email: subscriptions@springer.com **Web site:** http://www.springer.com
Freq: 6 issues yearly; **Annual Sub.:** EUR 313,50; **Circ:** 700
Editor: Almut Heinrich
Profile: Journal focusing on environmental chemistry and ecology.
Language(s): English; German
ADVERTISING RATES:
Full Page Mono .... EUR 830
Full Page Colour .... EUR 1870
Mechanical Data: Type Area: 240 x 175 mm
Copy instructions: *Copy Date:* 42 days prior to publication
Official Journal of: Organ d. Verb. f. Geoökologie in Deutschland u. d. Eco-Informa
BUSINESS: ENVIRONMENT & POLLUTION

UNABHÄNGIGE BAUERNSTIMME
1860331G21A-4411
Editorial: Bahnhofstr. 31, 59065 HAMM
Tel: 2381 492289 **Fax:** 2381 492221
Email: redaktion@bauernstimme.de **Web site:** http://www.bauernstimme.de
Freq: 11 issues yearly; **Annual Sub.:** EUR 36,00; **Circ:** 7,000
Editor: Marcus Nürnberger; **Advertising Manager:** Vera Thiel
Profile: Magazine for farmers.
Language(s): German
ADVERTISING RATES:
Full Page Mono .... EUR 2220
Mechanical Data: Type Area: 296 x 229 mm, No. of Columns (Display): 5, Col Widths (Display): 42 mm

UNCLESALLY*S
745745G76D-5967
Editorial: Waldemarstr. 37, 10999 BERLIN
Tel: 30 69409663 **Fax:** 30 6913137
Email: caroline@sallys.net **Web site:** http://www.sallys.net
Freq: 10 issues yearly; **Annual Sub.:** EUR 15,00; **Circ:** 111,432
Editor: Caroline Frey
Profile: Music and entertainment magazine for the core target group 14 to 29 years on the subject: Music, movies, DVDs, sports, computer games, books, comics, radio plays, fashion, etc..
Language(s): German
ADVERTISING RATES:
Full Page Colour .... EUR 6540
Mechanical Data: Type Area: 250 x 200 mm
Supplement(s): sally*scout
CONSUMER: MUSIC & PERFORMING ARTS: Music

DER UNFALLCHIRURG
745751G56P-250
Editorial: Tiergartenstr. 17, 69121 HEIDELBERG
Tel: 6221 4878731 **Fax:** 6221 48768731
Email: isabelle.duerk@springer.com **Web site:** http://www.springerlink.com
Freq: Monthly; **Annual Sub.:** EUR 346,00; **Circ:** 4,100
Advertising Manager: Noëla Krischer
Profile: Der Unfallchirurg is an internationally respected publication organ. The journal is devoted to all aspects of the accident and reconstructive surgery and is used for training by established and working in the hospital trauma surgeons and surgeons. Practice-oriented review articles draw on selected topics and provide the reader with a compilation of current knowledge from all fields of trauma surgery. In addition to the provision of relevant background knowledge, the focus is on the evaluation of scientific results in the light of practical experience. The reader is given specific recommendations for action. Free submitted original papers allow the presentation of important clinical studies and serve the scientific exchange. Articles in the section "CME: Continuing Education - Certified Education" present assured results of scientific research and medical experience make for daily practice. After reading the articles the reader can verify the acquired knowledge and receive online CME points. The section is based on the training procedure of the field.
Language(s): German
Readership: Aimed at casualty and orthopaedic surgeons.
ADVERTISING RATES:
Full Page Mono .... EUR 1920
Full Page Colour .... EUR 3110
Mechanical Data: Type Area: 240 x 174 mm
Official Journal of: Organ d. Dt. Ges. f. Unfallchirurgie u. d. Dt. Ges. f. Orthopädie u. Unfallchirurgie
BUSINESS: HEALTH & MEDICAL: Casualty & Emergency

UNI FRIZZ
745770G83-12840
Editorial: Varrentrappstr. 53, 60486 FRANKFURT
Tel: 69 97951730 **Fax:** 69 97951729
Email: halder@frizz-frankfurt.de **Web site:** http://www.frizz-frankfurt.de
Freq: Half-yearly; **Cover Price:** Free; **Circ:** 20,225
Editor: Daniela Halder; **Advertising Manager:** Erk Walter
Profile: Magazine containing articles about entertainment and a listings-guide.
Language(s): German

Readership: Read by students in Frankfurt.
Mechanical Data: Type Area: 270 x 195 mm, No. of Columns (Display): 4, Col Widths (Display): 45 mm
CONSUMER: STUDENT PUBLICATIONS

UNI JOURNAL FRANKFURT
745779G83-12960
Editorial: Ludwigstr. 37, 60327 FRANKFURT
Tel: 69 97460285 **Fax:** 69 97460400
Email: chefredaktion@mmg.de **Web site:** http://www.journal-frankfurt.de
Freq: Half-yearly; **Cover Price:** Free; **Circ:** 24,985
Editor: Nils Bremer; **Advertising Manager:** Melanie Hennemann
Profile: Students' magazine.
Language(s): German
ADVERTISING RATES:
Full Page Mono .... EUR 1690
Full Page Colour .... EUR 2520
Mechanical Data: Type Area: 270 x 195 mm, No. of Columns (Display): 4, Col Widths (Display): 45 mm
CONSUMER: STUDENT PUBLICATIONS

UNI SPIEGEL
745808G83-15012
Editorial: Brandstwiete 19, 20457 HAMBURG
Tel: 40 30072303 **Fax:** 40 30072220
Email: unispiegel@spiegel.de **Web site:** http://www.spiegel.de/unispiegel
Freq: 6 issues yearly; **Cover Price:** Free; **Circ:** 213,848
Editor: Georg Mascolo; **Advertising Manager:** Norbert Facklam
Profile: UniSPIEGEL, the magazine for students, appears six times a year - three times per semester. Exclusive, with analysis and reports, interviews and reports SPIEGEL editors and staff inform about the university scene. Facebook: http://www.facebook.com/unispiegel.
Language(s): German
ADVERTISING RATES:
Full Page Mono .... EUR 14307
Full Page Colour .... EUR 14307
Mechanical Data: Type Area: 231 x 163 mm, No. of Columns (Display): 3, Col Widths (Display): 51 mm
Supplement to: Der Spiegel
CONSUMER: STUDENT PUBLICATIONS

UNICOMPACT
745760G83-13340
Editorial: Dillwächterstr. 4, 80686 MÜNCHEN
Tel: 89 76900310 **Fax:** 89 76900329
Email: david.lins@unicompact.de **Web site:** http://www.unicompact.de
Freq: 5 issues yearly; **Cover Price:** Free; **Circ:** 243,000
Editor: David Lins; **Advertising Manager:** Nicolai Haase
Profile: Lifestyle magazine for German students.
Language(s): German
ADVERTISING RATES:
Full Page Mono .... EUR 6798
Full Page Colour .... EUR 10980
Mechanical Data: Type Area: 244 x 172 mm, No. of Columns (Display): 4, Col Widths (Display): 42 mm
Copy instructions: *Copy Date:* 21 days prior to publication
CONSUMER: STUDENT PUBLICATIONS

UNICUM
745761G83-13360
Editorial: Ferdinandstr. 13, 44789 BOCHUM
Tel: 234 9615154 **Fax:** 234 9615111
Email: redaktion@unicum-verlag.de **Web site:** http://www.unicum.de
Freq: Monthly; **Cover Price:** Free; **Circ:** 400,819
Editor: Uwe Heinrich; **Advertising Manager:** Joachim Senk
Profile: Students' magazine.
Language(s): German
ADVERTISING RATES:
Full Page Mono .... EUR 12990
Full Page Colour .... EUR 17900
Mechanical Data: Type Area: 250 x 180 mm, No. of Columns (Display): 4, Col Widths (Display): 42 mm
Copy instructions: *Copy Date:* 25 days prior to publication
CONSUMER: STUDENT PUBLICATIONS

UNICUM ABI
745762G88A-300
Editorial: Ferdinandstr. 13, 44789 BOCHUM
Tel: 234 9615153 **Fax:** 234 9615111
Email: redaktion@unicum-verlag.de **Web site:** http://www.unicum.de
Freq: 9 issues yearly; **Cover Price:** Free; **Circ:** 251,056
Editor: Simone Ackfeld; **Advertising Manager:** Joachim Senk
Profile: UNICUM ABI offers what look young and adolescents in an important phase of life: guidance, advice and information, entertainment, fun and lifestyle. The topics have one thing in common: They burn the 15 - to 19-year-olds under the nails. Whether it is the question of whether it should continue after school study or vocational training, whether "Shooter" to make stupid, what you may disclose in a community, or why love can be a darn difficult subject. UNICUM ABI offers to these questions and many more tips, suggestions, analysis, advice and entertainment. The magazine provides insights into attractive career fields, urges to self-critical analysis of strengths and weaknesses, provides guidance and shows which requirements are imposed in such work and studies. All this with not a raised index finger, but entertaining, lively, honest, authentic and very close to the target group. UNICUM ABI provides a talking point and is sometimes even school subject: about the "English edition," which is completely in English and is used by teachers and students as a reading in the classroom. Or by interviews with celebrities from politics, sports, music and film world. To give a voice to students themselves, in their own school environment, the magazine organizes the competition "school of the year," says the editor of the detail. In short: UNICUM ABI offers benefits, fun and orientation for a moving stage of life!.
Language(s): German
Readership: Aimed at students, pupils and teachers.
ADVERTISING RATES:
Full Page Mono .... EUR 8980
Full Page Colour .... EUR 11900
Mechanical Data: No. of Columns (Display): 4, Col Widths (Display): 43 mm, Type Area: 215 x 165 mm
CONSUMER: EDUCATION

UNICUM BERUF
745763G62H-940
Editorial: Ferdinandstr. 13, 44789 BOCHUM
Tel: 234 9615151 **Fax:** 234 9615111
Email: redaktion@unicum-verlag.de **Web site:** http://www.unicum.de
Freq: Quarterly; **Cover Price:** Free; **Circ:** 151,591
Editor: Uwe Heinrich; **Advertising Manager:** Joachim Senk
Profile: Magazine containing information about jobs, business affairs, careers, money and lifestyle.
Language(s): German
Readership: Read by students and young professionals.
ADVERTISING RATES:
Full Page Mono .... EUR 7260
Full Page Colour .... EUR 9900
Mechanical Data: Type Area: 250 x 180 mm, No. of Columns (Display): 4, Col Widths (Display): 42 mm
BUSINESS: CHURCH & SCHOOL EQUIPMENT & EDUCATION: Careers

UNICUM.DE
1639831G62H-1184
Editorial: Ferdinandstr. 13, 44789 BOCHUM
Tel: 234 9615198 **Fax:** 234 9615111
Email: konter@unicum-verlag.de **Web site:** http://www.unicum.de
Freq: Daily; **Cover Price:** Paid; **Circ:** 442,298 Unique Users
Editor: Linda Konter
Profile: Ezine: Students' magazine.
Language(s): German
BUSINESS: CHURCH & SCHOOL EQUIPMENT & EDUCATION: Careers

UNI-GIG
745772G83-12880
Editorial: Sauerländer Weg 2a, 48145 MÜNSTER
Tel: 251 987230 **Fax:** 251 9872350
Email: office@gig-online.de **Web site:** http://www.gig-online.de
Freq: Half-yearly; **Cover Price:** Free; **Circ:** 25,400
Editor: Hubert Steinert; **Advertising Manager:** Martin Lückemeier
Profile: Students' magazine.
Language(s): German
ADVERTISING RATES:
Full Page Mono .... EUR 1200
Full Page Colour .... EUR 1750
Mechanical Data: Type Area: 250 x 180 mm, No. of Columns (Display): 4, Col Widths (Display): 42 mm
Copy instructions: *Copy Date:* 9 days prior to publication
CONSUMER: STUDENT PUBLICATIONS

UNILIFE
746522G74G-170
Editorial: Siemensstr. 6, 61352 BAD HOMBURG
Tel: 6172 670132 **Fax:** 6172 670519
Email: redaktion@unilife.de **Web site:** http://www.unilife.de
Freq: 6 issues yearly; **Circ:** 280,613
Editor: Wolfgang Frenken; **Advertising Manager:** Walter Krey
Profile: Magazine covering health, work, social life, relations and pastime activities from a health perspective.
Language(s): German
Readership: Aimed at young people.
ADVERTISING RATES:
Full Page Mono .... EUR 7000
Full Page Colour .... EUR 7000
Mechanical Data: Type Area: 250 x 189 mm
CONSUMER: WOMEN'S INTEREST CONSUMER MAGAZINES: Slimming & Health

UNISCENE
745799G83-13500
Editorial: Gertrudenkirchhof 10, 20095 HAMBURG
Tel: 40 37423600 **Fax:** 40 374236023
Email: redaktion@hey-hoffmann.de **Web site:** http://www.uniscene.de
Freq: 7 issues yearly; **Annual Sub.:** EUR 18,00; **Circ:** 30,000
Editor: Kai Hoffmann; **Advertising Manager:** Jan-Hinrich Hey
Profile: Students' magazine.
Language(s): German
ADVERTISING RATES:
Full Page Mono .... EUR 1900
Full Page Colour .... EUR 2470
Mechanical Data: Type Area: 280 x 210 mm
CONSUMER: STUDENT PUBLICATIONS

UNISCENE
745800G83-13520
Editorial: Lange Laube 22, 30159 HANNOVER
Tel: 511 15551 **Fax:** 511 1316169
Email: redaktion@stroetmann-verlag.de **Web site:** http://www.stroetmann-verlag.de
Freq: Half-yearly; **Cover Price:** Free; **Circ:** 14,390
Editor: Jens Bielke; **Advertising Manager:** Reinhard Stroetmann
Profile: Students' magazine.
Language(s): German
ADVERTISING RATES:
Full Page Mono .... EUR 1260
Full Page Colour .... EUR 2100
Mechanical Data: Type Area: 270 x 190 mm, No. of Columns (Display): 4, Col Widths (Display): 44 mm
Copy instructions: *Copy Date:* 10 days prior to publication
CONSUMER: STUDENT PUBLICATIONS

UNIVERSITAS
745842G84A-3320
Editorial: Happelstr. 12, 69120 HEIDELBERG
Tel: 6221 804827
Email: universitas@heidelberger-lese-zeiten-verlag.de **Web site:** http://www.heidelberger-lese-zeiten-verlag.de
Freq: Monthly; **Annual Sub.:** EUR 163,80; **Circ:** 3,000
Editor: Dirk Katzschmann
Profile: Magazine about interdisciplinary studies and culture.
Language(s): German
Readership: Read by academics and students of science, law and economics.
ADVERTISING RATES:
Full Page Mono .... EUR 990
Full Page Colour .... EUR 1755
Mechanical Data: Type Area: 190 x 114 mm, No. of Columns (Display): 2, Col Widths (Display): 55 mm
Copy instructions: *Copy Date:* 30 days prior to publication
Supplement(s): kinderUniversitas
CONSUMER: THE ARTS & LITERARY: Arts

UNIVERSITYJOURNAL
738251G14A-5120
Editorial: Dillwächterstr. 4, 80686 MÜNCHEN
Tel: 89 76900351 **Fax:** 89 76900329
Email: redaktion@university-journal.de **Web site:** http://www.university-journal.de
Freq: 5 issues yearly; **Cover Price:** EUR 6,00; **Circ:** 36,000
Editor: Nicolai Haase; **Advertising Manager:** Torsten Neubert
Profile: Journal for academic staff of the innovation-related subject areas of engineering and natural sciences. Editorial permanent focal points are: spin-off, career, innovations from universities and non-university research, equipment at the College and the Institute.
Language(s): German
ADVERTISING RATES:
Full Page Mono .... EUR 5980
Full Page Colour .... EUR 5980
Mechanical Data: Type Area: 297 x 210 mm

UNIZEIT
745835G83-13580
Editorial: Schloss, Neuer Graben, 49074 OSNABRÜCK **Tel:** 541 9694516 **Fax:** 541 9694570
Email: oliver.schmidt@uni-osnabrueck.de **Web site:** http://www.uni-osnabrueck.de
Freq: Quarterly; **Cover Price:** Free; **Circ:** 5,000
Editor: Oliver Schmidt; **Advertising Manager:** Oliver Schmidt
Profile: Newsletter about the University of Osnabrück.
Language(s): German
Readership: Read by university members.
ADVERTISING RATES:
Full Page Mono .... EUR 420
Full Page Colour .... EUR 420
Mechanical Data: Type Area: 277 x 190 mm, No. of Columns (Display): 4, Col Widths (Display): 44 mm
Copy instructions: *Copy Date:* 14 days prior to publication
CONSUMER: STUDENT PUBLICATIONS

UNSER GARTEN
745915G93-996
Editorial: Hüttersdorfer Str. 29, 66839 SCHMELZ
Tel: 6887 9032999 **Fax:** 6887 9032998
Email: info@unsergarten-verlag.de **Web site:** http://www.unsergarten-verlag.de
Freq: Monthly; **Annual Sub.:** EUR 16,80; **Circ:** 10,845
Editor: Monika Lambert-Debong; **Advertising Manager:** Monika Lambert-Debong
Profile: Magazine containing tips and information about gardening.
Language(s): German
Readership: Aimed at gardeners and nature enthusiasts.
ADVERTISING RATES:
Full Page Mono .... EUR 1160
Full Page Colour .... EUR 2300
Mechanical Data: Type Area: 264 x 189 mm, No. of Columns (Display): 4, Col Widths (Display): 45 mm
Copy instructions: *Copy Date:* 20 days prior to publication
Official Journal of: Verb. d. Gartenbauvereine Saarland/Rheinland-Pfalz e.V.-Verb. f. Garten- u. Landespflege
CONSUMER: GARDENING

UNSER HAUS FÜR DIE GANZE FAMILIE
764595G74C-3455
Editorial: Schwanthalerstr. 10, 80336 MÜNCHEN
Tel: 89 59908122 **Fax:** 89 59908133
Email: redaktion@cpz.de **Web site:** http://www.bau-welt.de
Freq: 6 issues yearly; **Annual Sub.:** EUR 6,00; **Circ:** 55,424
Editor: Claudia Mannschott; **Advertising Manager:** Sebastian Schmidt
Profile: Magazine for young families planning to build a house. It is focused on domestic examples for all budgets, in different architectural styles, designs, room layouts, facilities. The magazine is particularly the energy-efficiency, sustainability and environmental aspects of the houses in the foreground. Healthy living is also an important aspect as well as the energy-saving design. It presents examples next to house many tips and suggestions for planning and interior design, legal and financial support, guide to technology issues, and many new and interesting facts about the topic of new construction. Unser Haus für die ganze Familie presents a lot of tips and ideas for planning and interior design, legal and financial tools, advice for technical issues and many new and interesting facts about the topic of new construction. It accompanies and regularly interviewed clients in their works and details the construction experience of these families.
Language(s): German
ADVERTISING RATES:
Full Page Mono .... EUR 5740
Full Page Colour .... EUR 8200
Mechanical Data: Type Area: 270 x 180 mm, No. of Columns (Display): 4, Col Widths (Display): 42 mm
Copy instructions: *Copy Date:* 40 days prior to publication
Supplement(s): Bäder & Küchen; Dach, Wand & Boden; Erneuerbare Energien; Fenster, Türen & Garagentore; Heizung & Energiesparen; Smart Wohnen: Haustechnik & Sicherheit
CONSUMER: WOMEN'S INTEREST CONSUMER MAGAZINES: Home & Family

UNSER RASSEHUND
745935G81B-15
Editorial: Westfalendamm 174, 44141 DORTMUND
Tel: 231 565000 **Fax:** 231 592440
Email: info@vdh.de **Web site:** http://www.unserrassehund.de
Freq: Monthly; **Annual Sub.:** EUR 33,00; **Circ:** 30,000
Editor: Bernhard Meyer; **Advertising Manager:** Mariangela Böhme
Profile: Magazine containing information about pedigree dogs, general care and breeders.
Language(s): German
Readership: Aimed at dog lovers.
ADVERTISING RATES:
Full Page Mono .... EUR 1500
Full Page Colour .... EUR 3000
Mechanical Data: Type Area: 260 x 189 mm, No. of Columns (Display): 4, Col Widths (Display): 45 mm
Copy instructions: *Copy Date:* 30 days prior to publication
CONSUMER: ANIMALS & PETS: Dogs

UNSER WALD
745944G46-174
Editorial: Meckenheimer Allee 79, 53115 BONN
Tel: 228 9459835 **Fax:** 228 9459833
Email: unser-wald@sdw.de **Web site:** http://www.sdw.de
Freq: 6 issues yearly; **Annual Sub.:** EUR 17,50; **Circ:** 10,000
Editor: Sabine Krömer-Butz; **Advertising Manager:** Sabine Krömer-Butz
Profile: Journal about the protection of German forests, for Members of the SDW, foresters, hunters, timber industry and environmental public interest.
Language(s): German
ADVERTISING RATES:
Full Page Colour .... EUR 1950
Mechanical Data: Type Area: 257 x 185 mm, No. of Columns (Display): 3, Col Widths (Display): 58 mm
Copy instructions: *Copy Date:* 30 days prior to publication
BUSINESS: TIMBER, WOOD & FORESTRY

UNSERE BESTEN FREUNDE
745874G94H-12840
Editorial: Otto-Hahn-Str. 16, 47608 GELDERN
Tel: 2831 13000 **Fax:** 2831 130020
Email: s.guckenbiehl@sud-verlag.de **Web site:** http://www.sud-verlag.de
Freq: Monthly; **Cover Price:** Free; **Circ:** 160,414
Editor: Sabine Guckenbiehl; **Advertising Manager:** Marcus H. Thielen
Profile: Magazine about the care of domestic animals for customers of pharmacists.
Language(s): German
ADVERTISING RATES:
Full Page Mono .... EUR 4038
Full Page Colour .... EUR 4788
Mechanical Data: No. of Columns (Display): 2, Col Widths (Display): 92 mm, Type Area: 240 x 188 mm
Copy instructions: *Copy Date:* 60 days prior to publication
CONSUMER: OTHER CLASSIFICATIONS: Customer Magazines

UNSERE GEMEINDE
756779G94F-1703
Editorial: Ständeplatz 18, 34117 KASSEL
Tel: 561 7394051 **Fax:** 561 7394052
Email: ilenborg@dafeg.de **Web site:** http://www.dafeg.de
Freq: Monthly; **Annual Sub.:** EUR 18,00; **Circ:** 4,729

Editor: Ronald Ilenborg
Profile: Magazine by evangelical deaf people covering topics from spiritual welfare and basic knowledge of the Christian faith to recent reports about deaf people as well as providing information about technical, social and political events.
Language(s): German
ADVERTISING RATES:
Full Page Mono .... EUR 820
Mechanical Data: Type Area: 270 x 175 mm, No. of Columns (Display): 3, Col Widths (Display): 55 mm
Copy instructions: *Copy Date:* 15 days prior to publication
CONSUMER: OTHER CLASSIFICATIONS: Disability

UNSERE JAGD 745891G75L-1334

Editorial: Berliner Str. 112a, 13189 BERLIN
Tel: 30 2939740 **Fax:** 30 29397439
Email: unserejagd@dlv.de **Web site:** http://www.dlv.de
Freq: Monthly; Free to qualifying individuals
Annual Sub.: EUR 47,90; **Circ:** 39,103
Editor: Michael Cosack; **Advertising Manager:** Thomas Herrmann
Profile: unsere Jagd - The monthly magazine for hunters and nature lovers. Committed, critical, down to earth. The spokesman for the Weidmann, not only in East Germany. The lawyer for the forward-hunting.
Language(s): German
ADVERTISING RATES:
Full Page Mono .... EUR 2873
Full Page Colour .... EUR 5573
Mechanical Data: Type Area: 270 x 188 mm, No. of Columns (Display): 4, Col Widths (Display): 43 mm
Copy instructions: *Copy Date:* 31 days prior to publication
Supplement(s): Thüringer Jäger; Wir Jäger
CONSUMER: SPORT: Outdoor

UNSERE JUGEND 745893G32G-2981

Editorial: Franklinstr. 28, 10587 BERLIN
Email: schriftleitunguj@web.de
Freq: 10 issues yearly; **Annual Sub.:** EUR 56,00; **Circ:** 1,800
Editor: Sabine Behn
Profile: Magazine about issues facing young people and their care in the community.
Language(s): German
Readership: Aimed at social workers.
ADVERTISING RATES:
Full Page Mono .... EUR 625
Full Page Colour .... EUR 1555
Mechanical Data: Type Area: 200 x 130 mm, No. of Columns (Display): 2, Col Widths (Display): 63 mm
Copy instructions: *Copy Date:* 31 days prior to publication
BUSINESS: LOCAL GOVERNMENT, LEISURE & RECREATION: Community Care & Social Services

UNSERE REGION 725654G21A-1320

Editorial: Gustav-Siegle-Str. 16, 70193 STUTTGART
Tel: 711 2535900 **Fax:** 711 25359028
Email: post@energie-medien-verlag.de **Web site:** http://www.energie-medien-verlag.de
Freq: Quarterly; **Cover Price:** Free; **Circ:** 116,000
Profile: Company publication published by VWEW.
Language(s): German
ADVERTISING RATES:
Full Page Colour .... EUR 4400
Mechanical Data: Type Area: 270 x 190 mm
Copy instructions: *Copy Date:* 28 days prior to publication

UNTERALLGÄU RUNDSCHAU 745960G72-14588

Editorial: Maximilianstr. 14, 87719 MINDELHEIM
Tel: 8261 991342 **Fax:** 8261 991359
Email: harald.klofat@mindelheimer-zeitung.de **Web site:** http://www.mindelheimer-zeitung.de
Freq: Weekly; **Cover Price:** Free; **Circ:** 36,933
Editor: Harald Klofat; **Advertising Manager:** Johannes Högel
Profile: Advertising journal (house-to-house) concentrating on local stories.
Language(s): German
ADVERTISING RATES:
Full Page Mono .... EUR 3495
Full Page Colour .... EUR 5309
Mechanical Data: Type Area: 480 x 327 mm, No. of Columns (Display): 7, Col Widths (Display): 45 mm
Copy instructions: *Copy Date:* 2 days prior to publication
LOCAL NEWSPAPERS

UNTERNEHMEN STELLEN SICH VOR 745979G88C-110

Editorial: Moorbeker Str. 31, 26197 GROSSENKNETEN **Tel:** 4435 96120
Fax: 4435 961296
Email: info@berufsstart.de **Web site:** http://www.berufsstart.de
Freq: Annual; **Cover Price:** Free; **Circ:** 10,000
Profile: Publication providing information about careers with various companies.
Language(s): German
Readership: Read by students graduating from higher education.
ADVERTISING RATES:
Full Page Mono .... EUR 900
Full Page Colour .... EUR 1890
Mechanical Data: Type Area: 185 x 180 mm
Copy instructions: *Copy Date:* 15 days prior to publication
CONSUMER: EDUCATION: Careers

UNTERNEHMENSERGEBNISSE BUCHFÜHRENDER BETRIEBE IN NRW 745978G21A-3980

Editorial: Siebengebirgsstr. 200, 53229 BONN
Tel: 228 7031233 **Fax:** 228 703191223
Email: hans-peter.rehse@lwk.nrw.de **Web site:** http://www.landwirtschaftskammer.de
Freq: Annual; **Cover Price:** EUR 25,00; **Circ:** 750
Editor: Hans Peter Rehse
Profile: Magazine for accountants and tax advisors.
Language(s): German

UNTERNEHMER EDITION 1860332G14A-10218

Editorial: Hofmannstr. 7a, 81379 MÜNCHEN
Tel: 89 200033925 **Fax:** 89 200033939
Email: hofelich@goingpublic.de **Web site:** http://www.unternehmeredition.de
Freq: 6 issues yearly; **Annual Sub.:** EUR 48,00; **Circ:** 15,800
Editor: Markus Hofelich; **Advertising Manager:** Denise Hoser
Profile: Know-how for the middle class.
Language(s): German
ADVERTISING RATES:
Full Page Mono .... EUR 2900
Full Page Colour .... EUR 2900
Mechanical Data: Type Area: 246 x 164 mm, No. of Columns (Display): 2, Col Widths (Display): 80 mm

UNTERNEHMERBRIEF BAUWIRTSCHAFT 727371G1A-940

Editorial: Walter-Benjamin-Platz 6, 10629 BERLIN
Tel: 30 8851010 **Fax:** 30 8852030
Email: michael.sarry@gniosdorz.de
Freq: Monthly; **Annual Sub.:** EUR 192,00; **Circ:** 1,840
Editor: Michael Sarry; **Advertising Manager:** Fred Doischer
Profile: Magazine with advice on finances and taxes for the building industry.
Language(s): German
ADVERTISING RATES:
Full Page Mono .... EUR 1210
Full Page Colour .... EUR 1510
Mechanical Data: Type Area: 260 x 181 mm

UNTERNEHMERMAGAZIN 745984G14A-7760

Editorial: Schlossallee 10, 53179 BONN
Tel: 228 9545985 **Fax:** 228 9545980
Email: verlag@unternehmermagazin.de **Web site:** http://www.unternehmermagazin.de
Freq: 8 issues yearly; **Annual Sub.:** EUR 75,00; **Circ:** 69,557
Editor: Reinhard Nenzel; **Advertising Manager:** Reinhard Nenzel
Profile: Magazine about economics and finance.
Language(s): German
Readership: Read by decision makers, managing directors and entrepreneurs.
ADVERTISING RATES:
Full Page Mono .... EUR 9750
Full Page Colour .... EUR 10500
Mechanical Data: Type Area: 252 x 178 mm, No. of Columns (Display): 3, Col Widths (Display): 56 mm
Copy instructions: *Copy Date:* 14 days prior to publication
BUSINESS: COMMERCE, INDUSTRY & MANAGEMENT

UNTERRICHT BIOLOGIE 745986G62B-2960

Editorial: Im Brande 17, 30926 SEELZE
Tel: 511 40004228 **Fax:** 511 40004219
Email: redaktion.ub@friedrich-verlag.de **Web site:** http://www.unterricht-biologie.de
Freq: 10 issues yearly; **Annual Sub.:** EUR 109,00; **Circ:** 10,181
Editor: Barbara Dulitz; **Advertising Manager:** Bernd Schrader
Profile: With Unterricht Biologie clarify the questions of life. From climate change to Noro-virus with Unterricht Biologie, you get the current science in the classroom. Compact compiled and processed reliably contains Unterricht Biologie, all you need to know. So you can be sure that you do not miss anything. In the unique combination of proven teaching models with complete course materials you receive photocopiable illustrations, charts, tasks, knowledge, texts with scientific data and studies and experiments and games. So you can work out the lesson topics really extensively. The regular compact books Unterricht Biologie is now even more practical and offers generously illustrated student materials or suggestions you can use for your personal development and in the specialist group.
Language(s): German
ADVERTISING RATES:
Full Page Mono .... EUR 1450
Full Page Colour .... EUR 2180
Mechanical Data: Type Area: 258 x 180 mm, No. of Columns (Display): 3, Col Widths (Display): 57 mm
Copy instructions: *Copy Date:* 42 days prior to publication
Supplement(s): bildung+medien; bildung+reisen; bildung+science
BUSINESS: CHURCH & SCHOOL EQUIPMENT & EDUCATION: Education Teachers

UNTERRICHTSBLÄTTER 745988G40-948

Editorial: Postfach 140334, 53058 BONN
Freq: Monthly; **Annual Sub.:** EUR 157,95; **Circ:** 2,000
Editor: Michael Streffer; **Advertising Manager:** Isabell Henze
Profile: Publication covering training, further education and administration in the armed forces.
Language(s): German
ADVERTISING RATES:
Full Page Mono .... EUR 1300
Mechanical Data: Type Area: 257 x 178 mm
Copy instructions: *Copy Date:* 14 days prior to publication
BUSINESS: DEFENCE

UNTERTAUNUS WOCHENBLATT 745994G72-14620

Editorial: Langgasse 21, 65183 WIESBADEN
Tel: 611 3552370 **Fax:** 611 3552343
Email: redaktion@untertaunus-wochenblatt.de **Web site:** http://www.untertaunus-wochenblatt.de
Freq: Weekly; **Cover Price:** Free; **Circ:** 26,973
Editor: Marion Dehmer-Sehn; **Advertising Manager:** Rainer Baumann
Profile: Advertising journal (house-to-house) concentrating on local stories.
Language(s): German
ADVERTISING RATES:
Full Page Mono .... EUR 3260
Full Page Colour .... EUR 4503
Mechanical Data: Type Area: 480 x 325 mm, No. of Columns (Display): 7, Col Widths (Display): 45 mm
Copy instructions: *Copy Date:* 2 days prior to publication
Supplement(s): Stadt Postille
LOCAL NEWSPAPERS

UNTERTÜRKHEIMER ZEITUNG 745995G67B-14980

Editorial: Wilhelmstr. 18, 70372 STUTTGART
Tel: 711 955680 **Fax:** 711 9556883
Web site: http://www.untertuerkheimer-zeitung.de
Freq: 312 issues yearly; **Circ:** 8,719
Advertising Manager: Sigfried Baumann
Profile: Regional daily newspaper with news on politics, economy, culture, sports, travel, technology, etc. She is a local edition of the Cannstatter Zeitung. Facebook: http://www.facebook.com/pages/Esslinger-Zeitung/332067873971.
Language(s): German
ADVERTISING RATES:
SCC .... EUR 40,80
Mechanical Data: Type Area: 485 x 324 mm, No. of Columns (Display): 7, Col Widths (Display): 45 mm
Copy instructions: *Copy Date:* 1 day prior to publication
REGIONAL DAILY & SUNDAY NEWSPAPERS: Regional Daily Newspapers

UNTERWASSER 746002G75M-860

Editorial: Badstr. 4, 90402 NÜRNBERG
Tel: 911 2162241 **Fax:** 911 2162723
Email: redaktion@unterwasser.de **Web site:** http://www.unterwasser.de
Freq: Monthly; **Annual Sub.:** EUR 58,80; **Circ:** 24,445
Editor: Lars Brinkmann; **Advertising Manager:** Axel Nieber
Profile: Magazine about scuba diving, dive tourism, travel reports, portfolios, diving equipment, underwater photos, video, underwater photography, marine biology.
Language(s): German
ADVERTISING RATES:
Full Page Mono .... EUR 2810
Full Page Colour .... EUR 4600
Mechanical Data: Type Area: 250 x 195 mm, No. of Columns (Display): 4, Col Widths (Display): 45 mm
Copy instructions: *Copy Date:* 35 days prior to publication
CONSUMER: SPORT: Water Sports

UNTERWASSER.DE 1704678G75M-1080

Editorial: Badstr. 4, 90402 NÜRNBERG
Tel: 911 2162241 **Fax:** 911 2162723
Email: k.wunderlich@unterwasser.de **Web site:** http://www.unterwasser.de
Freq: Daily; **Cover Price:** Paid; **Circ:** 28,240 Unique Users
Editor: Kristin Wunderlich; **Advertising Manager:** Marco Lutz
Profile: Ezine: Diving magazine.
Language(s): German
CONSUMER: SPORT: Water Sports

UNTERWEGS 746006G87-12440

Editorial: Ludolfusstr. 2, 60487 FRANKFURT
Tel: 69 242521150 **Fax:** 69 242521159
Email: unterwegs@emk.de **Web site:** http://www.emk.de
Freq: 26 issues yearly; **Circ:** 7,500
Editor: Volker Kiemle
Profile: Religious magazine.
Language(s): German
Readership: Read by members of the Methodist Evangelist Church.
ADVERTISING RATES:
Full Page Mono .... EUR 869
Full Page Colour .... EUR 1169
Mechanical Data: Type Area: 255 x 187 mm, No. of Columns (Display): 4, Col Widths (Display): 43 mm
Copy instructions: *Copy Date:* 14 days prior to publication
CONSUMER: RELIGIOUS

UNUS 1826465G14A-10078

Editorial: Kirchenstr. 15, 81675 MÜNCHEN
Tel: 89 4195990 **Fax:** 89 41959912
Email: redaktion@unus-online.de **Web site:** http://www.unus-online.de
Freq: Quarterly; **Circ:** 25,000
Editor: Alexander Pschera
Profile: unus Unternehmer & Selbständige is a magazine for self-employed people and medium-sized companies as well as for decision makers in medium-sized and regional political field. With a circulation of 25,000 copies unus Unternehmer & Selbständige is both the official organ of association for approximately 20,000 members of the Federation of Self-employed (BDS) - Trade association Bayern e.V. and an economic-political and regional-political magazine. In addition, it will all mayors and district administrators in the state. The report focuses on economic and socio-political themes with high relevance for SMEs, regional development and advice. Strong expertise of the editors, systematic focus on the interests of medium-sized businesses, prominent and interesting interview partners, exclusive and timely topics and strong regional presence and a high acceptance in the target group make unus Unternehmer & Selbständige to a unique format in Bavaria.
Language(s): German
ADVERTISING RATES:
Full Page Mono .... EUR 3500
Full Page Colour .... EUR 3500
Mechanical Data: Type Area: 263 x 166 mm

UP TREND 1914751G74A-3691

Editorial: Bernhard-Nocht-Str. 99, 20359 HAMBURG
Tel: 40 30068216 **Fax:** 40 30068222
Email: volker.paulun@speedpool.com **Web site:** http://www.speedpool.com
Freq: Quarterly; **Cover Price:** EUR 8,00; **Circ:** 30,000
Editor: Mark Schneider
Profile: Lifestyle Magazine from ABT Sportsline, exciting reports provide interesting insights behind the scenes of the Allgäuer firm and its partners from tuning & motorsport.
Language(s): German
ADVERTISING RATES:
Full Page Mono .... EUR 5000
Full Page Colour .... EUR 5000
Mechanical Data: Type Area: 300 x 230 mm

UPDATE 738462G76A-1200

Editorial: Böckmannstr. 15, 20099 HAMBURG
Tel: 40 248777 **Fax:** 40 249448
Email: update@oxmoxhh.de **Web site:** http://www.oxmoxhh.de
Freq: Monthly; **Cover Price:** Free; **Circ:** 43,903
Editor: Klaus M. Schulz; **Advertising Manager:** Roxanne M. Schulz
Profile: Magazine for city and region, concentrating on gastronomy, music, arts and events.
Language(s): German
ADVERTISING RATES:
Full Page Mono .... EUR 2125
Full Page Colour .... EUR 3140
Mechanical Data: Type Area: 260 x 190 mm, No. of Columns (Display): 4, Col Widths (Display): 44 mm
Copy instructions: *Copy Date:* 14 days prior to publication
CONSUMER: MUSIC & PERFORMING ARTS: Cinema

UR UMSATZSTEUER-RUNDSCHAU 745699G1M-11

Editorial: Gustav-Heinemann-Ufer 58, 50968 KÖLN
Tel: 221 93738151 **Fax:** 221 93738902
Email: verlag@otto-schmidt.de **Web site:** http://www.umsatzsteuerrundschau.de
Freq: 24 issues yearly; **Annual Sub.:** EUR 291,90; **Circ:** 3,020
Editor: Rolf-Peter Humbert; **Advertising Manager:** Thorsten Deuse
Profile: Magazine focusing on VAT throughout Germany and the European Union.
Language(s): German
ADVERTISING RATES:
Full Page Mono .... EUR 1195
Full Page Colour .... EUR 2091
Mechanical Data: No. of Columns (Display): 2, Type Area: 260 x 180 mm, Col Widths (Display): 88 mm
BUSINESS: FINANCE & ECONOMICS: Taxation

URBANES 1925321G74N-989

Editorial: Unterberg 15b, 21033 HAMBURG
Tel: 40 41189880
Email: h.grossbongardt@großbongardt.com
Freq: Quarterly; **Cover Price:** Free; **Circ:** 25,000
Editor: Heinrich Großbongardt
Profile: Magazine for the over 50s in the metropolitan region of Hamburg. It presents topics from politics

and society, prevention & finance, health & beauty, travel & lifestyle, culture & science.
Language(s): German
ADVERTISING RATES:
Full Page Colour .... EUR 1900
Mechanical Data: Type Area: 270 x 186 mm, No. of Columns (Display): 3, Col Widths (Display): 50 mm
Copy instructions: *Copy Date:* 28 days prior to publication

URLAUB PERFEKT 1615190G89A-12142
Editorial: Wandsbeker Allee 1, 22041 HAMBURG
Tel: 40 41448230 **Fax:** 40 41448718
Email: redaktion@urlaubperfekt.de **Web site:** http://www.fvw-mediengruppe.de
Freq: 3 issues yearly; **Cover Price:** EUR 1,80; **Circ:** 110,000
Editor: Monika Spielberger; **Advertising Manager:** Michael Körner
Profile: TRAVEL IS OUR PROFESSION For your best customers - passengers in style The travel motives are based on the wishes of the reader. Whether a cultural event, activity holidays or Strandfan, countries that speak stories and themes cruise the needs of the target group directly. A look behind the scenes promoting the knowledge about relationships and gives customers a say. Perfect holiday readers are enlightened. Learn how a pilot trained in the simulator as an airport in the back office functions, such as the emergency center of an international health insurer is working. Food and Health take on vacation a special significance. Perfect holiday shows the best wellness hotels, relaxing bike rides along the popular wine routes, famous chefs and their recipes. The great documentary tells the story of dreams fulfilled life, from travel, remain long in memory. In each issue, the latest holiday trends. The close proximity to the holiday industry is perfect an information advantage that is reflected in the content and the unique position of expanding Perfect as a holiday, the travel magazine of the professionals even more. Holidays are the perfect travel magazine that is consistently focused on the needs of the best customers of tour operators and travel agents.
Language(s): German
ADVERTISING RATES:
Full Page Mono .... EUR 11900
Full Page Colour .... EUR 11900
Mechanical Data: Type Area: 241 x 195 mm, No. of Columns (Display): 4
CONSUMER: HOLIDAYS & TRAVEL: Travel

URLAUB UND FREIZEIT
746030G89A-12121
Editorial: Stadtplatz 11, 94209 REGEN
Tel: 9921 80334 **Fax:** 9921 6632
Email: verlag-groener@t-online.de **Web site:** http://www.verlag-groener.de
Freq: 7 issues yearly; **Cover Price:** Free; **Circ:** 40,000
Editor: Hans Gröner; **Advertising Manager:** Marion Gröner
Profile: Magazine for tourists and residents of the Bayerischer Wald region.
Language(s): German
ADVERTISING RATES:
Full Page Mono .... EUR 1197
Full Page Colour .... EUR 1225
Mechanical Data: Type Area: 277 x 194 mm, No. of Columns (Display): 4, Col Widths (Display): 45 mm
Copy instructions: *Copy Date:* 10 days prior to publication

URLAUBS LOTSE 2038524G89A-12584
Editorial: Markt 25, 18528 BERGEN
Tel: 3838 2014811 **Fax:** 3838 2014824
Email: ruegen@urlaubs-lotse.de
Freq: Weekly; **Cover Price:** Free; **Circ:** 25,000
Editor: Wolfgang Urban
Profile: Information for tourists on the island of Rügen.
Language(s): German

URLAUBS- UND GÄSTEZEITUNG ROMANTISCHER RHEIN
1657684G89A-11886
Editorial: Adolfstr. 17, 56112 LAHNSTEIN
Tel: 2621 187290 **Fax:** 2621 187292
Email: info@heimatlinks.de
Freq: Annual; **Cover Price:** Free; **Circ:** 100,000
Editor: Stefanie Friesenhahn
Profile: Magazine for tourists in the Mittelrhein region.
Language(s): German
ADVERTISING RATES:
Full Page Mono .... EUR 1200
Full Page Colour .... EUR 1500
Mechanical Data: Type Area: 319 x 227 mm

URLAUBSWELTEN 1657052G89A-11882
Editorial: Marktplatz 64, 72250 FREUDENSTADT
Tel: 7441 864711 **Fax:** 7441 864777
Email: petra.rau@freudenstadt.de **Web site:** http://www.freudenstadt-tourismus.de
Freq: Annual; **Cover Price:** Free; **Circ:** 50,000
Editor: Michael Krause; **Advertising Manager:** Petra Rau
Profile: Holiday magazine for Freudenstadt and Loßburg.
Language(s): German

DER UROLOGE 746035G56A-9940
Editorial: Tiergartenstr. 17, 69121 HEIDELBERG
Tel: 6221 4878618 **Fax:** 6221 48768618
Email: werner.roessling@springer.com **Web site:** http://www.springerlink.com
Freq: Monthly; Free to qualifying individuals
Annual Sub.: EUR 416,00; **Circ:** 7,244
Profile: Der Urologe is an internationally respected journal covering all areas of urology. The focus is on prevention, diagnostic approaches, management of complications, and current therapy strategies. The journal provides information for all urologists working in practical and clinical environments and scientists who are particularly interested in issues of urology. Comprehensive reviews on a specific topical issue focus on providing evidenced based information on diagnostics and therapy. Freely submitted original papers allow the presentation of important clinical studies and serve scientific exchange. Case reports feature interesting cases and aim at optimizing diagnostic and therapeutic strategies. Review articles under the rubric 'Continuing Medical Education' present verified results of scientific research and their integration into daily practice.
Language(s): German
ADVERTISING RATES:
Full Page Mono .... EUR 2850
Full Page Colour .... EUR 4150
Mechanical Data: Type Area: 240 x 174 mm
Official Journal of: Organ d. Dt. Ges. f. Urologie e.V., d. Berufsverb. d. Dt. Urologen u. d. Berufsverb. Österr. Urologen

UROLOGISCHE NACHRICHTEN
746039G56A-9980
Editorial: Otto-Hahn-Str. 7, 50997 KÖLN
Tel: 2236 376408 **Fax:** 2236 376999
Email: dk@biermann.net **Web site:** http://www.uro.de
Freq: Monthly; **Annual Sub.:** EUR 98,00; **Circ:** 3,604
Editor: Dieter Kaulard; **Advertising Manager:** Daniel Helmers
Profile: The „Urologische Nachrichten" are among the opinion-leading magazines of German urology. They report to date on all events, developments, personalities and conventions in the subject. Especially the issue to Congress annual meeting of the "German Society of Urology" is respected for its daily news reporting exceptionally strong.
Language(s): German
ADVERTISING RATES:
Full Page Mono .... EUR 2956
Full Page Colour .... EUR 4111
Mechanical Data: Type Area: 378 x 285 mm, No. of Columns (Display): 5, Col Widths (Display): 53 mm
Copy instructions: *Copy Date:* 21 days prior to publication
BUSINESS: HEALTH & MEDICAL

URO-NEWS 746040G56A-9920
Editorial: Aschauer Str. 30, 81549 MÜNCHEN
Tel: 89 2030431403 **Fax:** 89 2030431399
Email: claudia.maeck@springer.com **Web site:** http://www.uro-news-online.de
Freq: 11 issues yearly; **Annual Sub.:** EUR 143,00; **Circ:** 4,068
Editor: Claudia Mäck; **Advertising Manager:** Paul Berger
Profile: By urologists for urologists established - according to the headnote Uro-News as an independent monthly journal of professional political information, valuable tips on practice management and practical training by internationally recognized expert authors on all topics, from the urology. A CME-module with selected contributions that are recognized by the Bavarian State Medical Association to offer certified training, the readers in each issue of the ability to earn continuing education credits. The broad range of topics will be complemented by short presentations from the international literature. In addition, Uro-News is a forum for discussion of current issues around the urology.
Language(s): German
Readership: Aimed at doctors specialising in the field.
ADVERTISING RATES:
Full Page Mono .... EUR 2200
Full Page Colour .... EUR 3450
Mechanical Data: Type Area: 240 x 174 mm
Official Journal of: Organ d. ArGe kreativ kooperierender Urologen in d. DGU
BUSINESS: HEALTH & MEDICAL

USEDOM KURIER 746046G67B-15000
Editorial: Friedrich-Engels-Ring 29, 17033 NEUBRANDENBURG **Tel:** 395 45750
Fax: 395 4575694
Email: kurierverlag@nordkurier.de **Web site:** http://www.nordkurier.de
Freq: 312 issues yearly; **Circ:** 7,215
Advertising Manager: Carsten Kottwitz
Profile: Daily newspaper with regional news and a local sports section. Facebook: http://www.facebook.com/pages/Nordkurier/102747776465803 Twitter: http://twitter.com/nordkurier This Outlet offers RSS (Really Simple Syndication).
Language(s): German
ADVERTISING RATES:
SCC .... EUR 31,20
Mechanical Data: Type Area: 480 x 324 mm, No. of Columns (Display): 7, Col Widths (Display): 45 mm
Copy instructions: *Copy Date:* 2 days prior to publication
Supplement(s): prisma
REGIONAL DAILY & SUNDAY NEWSPAPERS: Regional Daily Newspapers

USHÜTT 746049G27-2720
Editorial: Werkstr. 1, 66763 DILLINGEN
Tel: 6831 473126 **Fax:** 6831 473078
Email: nicole.munninger@dillinger.biz **Web site:** http://www.dillinger.de
Freq: Quarterly; **Cover Price:** Free; **Circ:** 8,000
Editor: Nicole Munninger
Profile: Magazine for employees of Dillinger Hütte.
Language(s): German

USINGER ANZEIGENBLATT
746050G72-14632
Editorial: Am Riedborn 20, 61250 USINGEN
Tel: 6081 105451 **Fax:** 6081 105450
Email: redaktion@usinger-anzeiger.de **Web site:** http://www.usinger-anzeiger.de
Freq: Weekly; **Cover Price:** Free; **Circ:** 25,500
Editor: Frank Bugge; **Advertising Manager:** Heiko Selzer
Profile: Advertising journal (house-to-house) concentrating on local stories.
Language(s): German
ADVERTISING RATES:
Full Page Mono .... EUR 1806
Full Page Colour .... EUR 2529
Mechanical Data: Type Area: 430 x 280 mm, No. of Columns (Display): 6, Col Widths (Display): 45 mm
Copy instructions: *Copy Date:* 2 days prior to publication
LOCAL NEWSPAPERS

USINGER ANZEIGER
746051G67B-15020
Editorial: Am Riedborn 20, 61250 USINGEN
Tel: 6081 1050 **Fax:** 6081 105100
Email: redaktion@usinger-anzeiger.de **Web site:** http://www.usinger-anzeiger.de
Freq: 312 issues yearly; **Circ:** 5,665
Advertising Manager: Heiko Selzer
Profile: Daily newspaper with regional news and a local sports section.
Language(s): German
ADVERTISING RATES:
SCC .... EUR 23,10
Mechanical Data: Type Area: 430 x 278 mm, No. of Columns (Display): 6, Col Widths (Display): 45 mm
Copy instructions: *Copy Date:* 1 day prior to publication
REGIONAL DAILY & SUNDAY NEWSPAPERS: Regional Daily Newspapers

USP MENSCHEN IM MARKETING 1789852G2A-5693
Editorial: Saarbrücker Str. 36, 10405 BERLIN
Tel: 30 34806330 **Fax:** 30 348063333
Email: mattheis@marketingclubberlin.de **Web site:** http://www.mattheis-berlin.de
Freq: Quarterly; **Cover Price:** EUR 7,00
Free to qualifying individuals ; **Circ:** 4,000
Editor: Claudia Mattheis
Profile: Regional marketing magazine.
Language(s): German
ADVERTISING RATES:
Full Page Mono .... EUR 1600
Full Page Colour .... EUR 1950
Mechanical Data: Type Area: 249 x 185 mm
Copy instructions: *Copy Date:* 32 days prior to publication

UVP REPORT 746066G57-2340
Editorial: Sachsenweg 9, 59073 HAMM
Tel: 2381 52129 **Fax:** 2381 52195
Email: info@uvp.de **Web site:** http://www.uvp.de
Freq: 5 issues yearly; Free to qualifying individuals
Annual Sub.: EUR 95,00; **Circ:** 1,500
Editor: Frank Scholles
Profile: Journal containing information about environmental planning and policy for Germany and abroad. Also includes details on environmental issues concerning commerce and industry.
Language(s): German
ADVERTISING RATES:
Full Page Mono .... EUR 565
Mechanical Data: Type Area: 262 x 180 mm, No. of Columns (Display): 3, Col Widths (Display): 51 mm
Copy instructions: *Copy Date:* 31 days prior to publication
BUSINESS: ENVIRONMENT & POLLUTION

UVR UMSATZSTEUER- UND VERKEHRSSTEUER-RECHT
746067G1A-3060
Editorial: Dechenstr. 7, 53115 BONN **Tel:** 228 7240
Fax: 228 72493081
Email: info@stollfuss.de **Web site:** http://www.stollfuss.de
Freq: Monthly; **Circ:** 1,300
Editor: Jörg Kraeusel; **Advertising Manager:** Carsten Priesel
Profile: Publication about value added tax law.
Language(s): German
ADVERTISING RATES:
Full Page Mono .... EUR 1140
Full Page Colour .... EUR 1765
Mechanical Data: Type Area: 260 x 180 mm, No. of Columns (Display): 2, Col Widths (Display): 88 mm
Copy instructions: *Copy Date:* 21 days prior to publication

UWF UMWELT WIRTSCHAFTS FORUM 746070G57-2380
Editorial: Tiergartenstr. 17, 69121 HEIDELBERG
Tel: 6221 4870 **Fax:** 6221 4878366
Email: subscriptions@springer.com **Web site:** http://www.springerlink.com
Freq: Quarterly; **Annual Sub.:** EUR 227,00; **Circ:** 266
Profile: Magazine focusing on the environment and economy.
Language(s): German
Readership: Aimed at executives, scientists and people concerned with the environment.
ADVERTISING RATES:
Full Page Mono .... EUR 740
Full Page Colour .... EUR 1780
Mechanical Data: Type Area: 240 x 175 mm
BUSINESS: ENVIRONMENT & POLLUTION

V + T BETRIEBSPRAXIS UND RATIONALISIERUNG
746773G49A-2020
Editorial: Heinrichstr. 1, 33790 HALLE
Tel: 5201 735535 **Fax:** 5201 735244
Email: j.hille@esvmedien.de **Web site:** http://www.esv.info
Freq: Monthly; **Circ:** 1,902
Editor: Jürgen Hille; **Advertising Manager:** Peter Taprogge
Profile: Official magazine for local public transport, transport techniques, transport economy and transport politics.
Language(s): German
ADVERTISING RATES:
Full Page Mono .... EUR 1720
Full Page Colour .... EUR 2590
Mechanical Data: Type Area: 250 x 176 mm, No. of Columns (Display): 3, Col Widths (Display): 56 mm
Copy instructions: *Copy Date:* 30 days prior to publication
Official Journal of: Organ f. d. öffentl. Personennahverkehr
Supplement to: V + T Verkehr und Technik

V + T VERKEHR UND TECHNIK
746774G49A-2040
Editorial: Heinrichstr. 1, 33790 HALLE
Tel: 5201 735535 **Fax:** 5201 735244
Email: j.hille@esvmedien.de **Web site:** http://www.vtdigital.de
Freq: Monthly; **Annual Sub.:** EUR 131,59; **Circ:** 1,078
Editor: Jürgen Hille; **Advertising Manager:** Peter Taprogge
Profile: Journal about public transport, including business and technical information.
Language(s): German
ADVERTISING RATES:
Full Page Mono .... EUR 1750
Full Page Colour .... EUR 2650
Mechanical Data: Type Area: 250 x 176 mm, No. of Columns (Display): 3, Col Widths (Display): 56 mm
Copy instructions: *Copy Date:* 30 days prior to publication
Official Journal of: Organ f. d. öffentl. Personennahverkehr
Supplement(s): V + T Betriebspraxis und Rationalisierung
BUSINESS: TRANSPORT

VAA MAGAZIN 1667872G13-2421
Editorial: Mohrenstr. 11, 50670 KÖLN
Tel: 221 160010 **Fax:** 221 160016
Email: info@vaa.de **Web site:** http://www.vaa.de
Freq: 6 issues yearly; **Circ:** 26,970
Editor: Martin Kraushaar; **Advertising Manager:** Ursula Statz-Kriegel
Profile: The VAA Magazin is published six times a year. It includes reports on companies, products, inventors, and reports on the latest from the association's policies and the Voluntary Sector. A chemical diary belongs to this free service for members. The members of the association are a very interesting target group for government and industry. Through regular surveys, the association has over valuable empirical material. Members receive the salary survey overview of the salary levels in the industry. The income situation of pensioners is illustrated by the pensioner survey. The VAA provides the company with the well-being survey, where potential improvements are in working conditions.
Language(s): German
ADVERTISING RATES:
Full Page Mono .... EUR 3600
Mechanical Data: Type Area: 251 x 180 mm, No. of Columns (Display): 3, Col Widths (Display): 56 mm
Copy instructions: *Copy Date:* 16 days prior to publication
Supplement(s): ULA Nachrichten
BUSINESS: CHEMICALS

VAF REPORT 1832378G18B-2179
Editorial: Otto-Hahn-Str. 16, 40721 HILDEN
Tel: 2103 700250 **Fax:** 2103 700106
Email: info@vaf-ev.de **Web site:** http://www.vaf-ev.de
Freq: Quarterly; **Circ:** 2,500
Editor: Martin Bürstenbinder; **Advertising Manager:** Andrea Siebel
Profile: Information from the Federal Association for Telecommunications.
Language(s): German
ADVERTISING RATES:
Full Page Mono .... EUR 1450
Full Page Colour .... EUR 1450
Mechanical Data: Type Area: 240 x 180 mm

Germany

Copy instructions: *Copy Date:* 14 days prior to publication

VAIHINGER KREISZEITUNG
746077G67B-15040
Editorial: Marktplatz 15, 71665 VAIHINGEN
Tel: 7042 91950 **Fax:** 7042 91999
Email: info@vkz.de **Web site:** http://www.vkz.de
Freq: 312 issues yearly; **Circ:** 7,367
Advertising Manager: Detlef Großmann
Profile: Daily newspaper with regional news and a local sports section.
Language(s): German
ADVERTISING RATES:
SCC .... EUR 32,30
Mechanical Data: Type Area: 485 x 320 mm, No. of Columns (Display): 7, Col Widths (Display): 44 mm
Copy instructions: *Copy Date:* 2 days prior to publication
REGIONAL DAILY & SUNDAY NEWSPAPERS: Regional Daily Newspapers

VAKO
1613968G21A-4230
Editorial: John-Deere-Str. 70, 68163 MANNHEIM
Tel: 621 8298416 **Fax:** 621 8298300
Email: hironjeanclaude@johndeere.com **Web site:** http://www.johndeere.com
Freq: Quarterly; **Cover Price:** Free; **Circ:** 26,000
Editor: Jean-Claude Hiron
Profile: Company publication published by Deere & Company.
Language(s): Finnish

VAKUUM IN FORSCHUNG UND PRAXIS
746082G19A-130
Editorial: Aachener Str. 67, 52382 NIEDERZIER
Tel: 2428 902717 **Fax:** 2428 902718
Email: redaktion_vip@t-online.de
Freq: 6 issues yearly; Free to qualifying individuals
Annual Sub.: EUR 355,00; **Circ:** 2,773
Editor: Johann Scherle; **Advertising Manager:** Änne Anders
Profile: Journal containing news and developments in vacuum technology, surfaces and thin films, including problem solving and new products and equipment.
Language(s): German
ADVERTISING RATES:
Full Page Mono .... EUR 3800
Full Page Colour .... EUR 4970
Mechanical Data: Type Area: 250 x 187 mm, No. of Columns (Display): 4, Col Widths (Display): 45 mm
Copy instructions: *Copy Date:* 39 days prior to publication
Official Journal of: Organ d. DVG-Dt. Vakuum-Ges. e.V.
BUSINESS: ENGINEERING & MACHINERY

VAMOS ELTERN-KIND-REISEN
1626682G89A-12083
Editorial: Hindenburgstr. 27, 30175 HANNOVER
Tel: 511 4007990 **Fax:** 511 40079999
Email: kontakt@vamos-reisen.de **Web site:** http://www.vamos-reisen.de
Freq: Half-yearly; **Cover Price:** Free; **Circ:** 35,000
Editor: Silvia Augustin
Profile: Customer travel magazine for Vamos-Reisen.
Language(s): German

VAMOS ELTERN-KIND-REISEN
1626682G89A-12563
Editorial: Hindenburgstr. 27, 30175 HANNOVER
Tel: 511 4007990 **Fax:** 511 40079999
Email: kontakt@vamos-reisen.de **Web site:** http://www.vamos-reisen.de
Freq: Half-yearly; **Cover Price:** Free; **Circ:** 35,000
Editor: Silvia Augustin
Profile: Customer travel magazine for Vamos-Reisen.
Language(s): German

DER VARTA-FÜHRER
1865179G89A-12429
Editorial: Zeppelinstr. 39, 73760 OSTFILDERN
Tel: 711 4502182 **Fax:** 711 4502185
Email: varta-fuehrer@mairdumont.com **Web site:** http://www.varta-guide.de
Freq: Annual; **Cover Price:** EUR 29,95; **Circ:** 30,000
Editor: Holger Pirsch
Profile: Review about hotels and restaurants in Germany.
Language(s): German

VASOMED
746094G56A-10000
Editorial: Otto-Hahn-Str. 7, 50997 KÖLN
Tel: 2236 3760 **Fax:** 2236 37692530
Email: kb@biermann.net **Web site:** http://www.viavital.net
Freq: 6 issues yearly; **Annual Sub.:** EUR 49,00; **Circ:** 5,328
Editor: Eberhard Rabe; **Advertising Manager:** Bettina Thiemeyer
Profile: vasomed is the journal of vascular diseases. The current original works of Phlebology, Angiology, wound healing and Lymphology give the reader a comprehensive insight into the latest developments. Among the authors are renowned experts in vascular medicine regularly. vasomed look outside the box - international authors discuss their work here. In the congress editions of vasomed the speakers make their presentations before. Rounding out the range of information with news from the pharmaceutical industry and medical technology.
Language(s): German
Readership: Read by doctors and pharmacists.
ADVERTISING RATES:
Full Page Mono .... EUR 1835
Full Page Colour .... EUR 2885
Mechanical Data: Type Area: 253 x 184 mm, No. of Columns (Display): 3, Col Widths (Display): 58 mm
Copy instructions: *Copy Date:* 21 days prior to publication
BUSINESS: HEALTH & MEDICAL

VATER - MUTTER - KIND
1696506G94H-14925
Editorial: Sigmund-Freud-Str. 77a, 60435 FRANKFURT **Tel:** 69 7561900 **Fax:** 69 75619040
Email: sbuettner@buemed.de **Web site:** http://www.eltern-infothek.de
Freq: Half-yearly; **Cover Price:** Free; **Circ:** 287,550
Editor: Sven Büttner; **Advertising Manager:** Sven Büttner
Language(s): German
ADVERTISING RATES:
Full Page Mono .... EUR 12550
Full Page Colour .... EUR 19110
Mechanical Data: Type Area: 264 x 180 mm, No. of Columns (Display): 3, Col Widths (Display): 55 mm
Copy instructions: *Copy Date:* 28 days prior to publication
CONSUMER: OTHER CLASSIFICATIONS: Customer Magazines

VB VERKEHRSGESCHICHTLICHE BLÄTTER
746100G49E-983
Editorial: Ulmenstr. 2a, 13467 BERLIN
Tel: 30 4046146
Web site: http://www.verkehrsgeschichtliche-blaetter.de
Freq: 6 issues yearly; **Annual Sub.:** EUR 13,80; **Circ:** 1,950
Editor: Michael Günther; **Advertising Manager:** Hans-Joachim Pohl
Profile: Journal about the history of rail transport in Berlin and Brandenburg.
Language(s): German
ADVERTISING RATES:
Full Page Mono .... EUR 200
Mechanical Data: Type Area: 255 x 185 mm, No. of Columns (Display): 2, Col Widths (Display): 90 mm
Copy instructions: *Copy Date:* 35 days prior to publication
BUSINESS: TRANSPORT: Railways

VB VERSICHERUNGSBETRIEBE
746102G1D-240
Editorial: Gewerbestr. 2, 86825 BAD WÖRISHOFEN
Tel: 8247 354107 **Fax:** 8247 354108
Email: redgivb@holzmann-medien.de **Web site:** http://www.versicherungsbetriebe.de
Freq: Quarterly; **Annual Sub.:** EUR 68,00; **Circ:** 3,384
Editor: Erwin Ströbele; **Advertising Manager:** Thomas Pohl
Profile: The journal addresses the problems of the insurance industry for more than three decades and provides IT decision makers and managers to competently prepared information on the topics of information technology, management, communication and organization. Our own research of the editors are supplemented by the cooperation of renowned experts, managers and practitioners from the industry.
Language(s): German
ADVERTISING RATES:
Full Page Mono .... EUR 2725
Full Page Colour .... EUR 3895
Mechanical Data: Type Area: 255 x 185 mm, No. of Columns (Display): 4, Col Widths (Display): 43 mm
Copy instructions: *Copy Date:* 22 days prior to publication
BUSINESS: FINANCE & ECONOMICS: Insurance

VBLBW VERWALTUNGSBLÄTTER FÜR BADEN-WÜRTTEMBERG
746389G32A-6700
Editorial: Scharrstr. 2, 70563 STUTTGART
Tel: 711 73850 **Fax:** 711 7385100
Email: mail@boorberg.de **Web site:** http://www.boorberg.de
Freq: Monthly; **Annual Sub.:** EUR 245,40; **Circ:** 830
Editor: Karlheinz Schenk; **Advertising Manager:** Roland Schulz
Profile: Journal about legal administration in Baden-Württemberg.
Language(s): German
ADVERTISING RATES:
Full Page Mono .... EUR 892
Full Page Colour .... EUR 1822
Mechanical Data: Type Area: 260 x 180 mm, No. of Columns (Display): 2, Col Widths (Display): 88 mm
Copy instructions: *Copy Date:* 28 days prior to publication
BUSINESS: LOCAL GOVERNMENT, LEISURE & RECREATION: Local Government

VCOT VETERINARY AND COMPARATIVE ORTHOPAEDICS AND TRAUMATOLOGY
746109G64H-440
Editorial: Hölderlinstr. 3, 70174 STUTTGART
Tel: 711 2298758 **Fax:** 711 2298765
Email: laura.lenz@schattauer.de **Web site:** http://www.vcot-online.com
Freq: 6 issues yearly; **Annual Sub.:** EUR 198,00; **Circ:** 1,750
Editor: Laura Lenz; **Advertising Manager:** Christian Matthe
Profile: VCOT deals with orthopaedics and traumatology in veterinary medicine, whilst also covering common approaches in human and veterinary medicine. The Journal meets its readers demands by focusing on both traumatological and practical aspects. Articles of a high scientific standard are published by international authors. Review articles, original research papers, clinical communications, case reports, letters to the Editor, as well as the latest news in basic research inform the reader about new operating techniques and improvements.
Language(s): English
ADVERTISING RATES:
Full Page Mono .... EUR 1110
Full Page Colour .... EUR 1710
Mechanical Data: Type Area: 243 x 179 mm, No. of Columns (Display): 3, Col Widths (Display): 57 mm
Copy instructions: *Copy Date:* 40 days prior to publication
Official Journal of: Organ d. British Veterinary Orthopaedic Association, d. European Society of Veterinary Orthopaedics and Traumatology, d. Veterinary Orthopedic Society USA + Canada, d. Societa Española de Traumatología y Ortopedia Veterinaria u. d. Hellenic Association of Veterinary Orthopaedics & Traumatology, d. Italian Society of Veterinary Orthopaedics, d. AOVET, Grupo de Especialistas Veterinarios en Traumatología y Ortopedia, d. Associção Brasiliera de Orthopedia e Traumatologia Veterinária u. d. Grupo de Interesse Especial da APMVEAC em Traumatologia e Ortopedia
BUSINESS: OTHER CLASSIFICATIONS: Veterinary

VDB MAGAZIN
1698593G1C-1463
Editorial: Wilhelm-Epstein-Str. 14, 60431 FRANKFURT **Tel:** 69 95662237 **Fax:** 69 95663103
Email: post@vdb.dbb.de **Web site:** http://www.vdb.dbb.de
Freq: Quarterly; Free to qualifying individuals
Annual Sub.: EUR 10,00; **Circ:** 8,000
Editor: Harald Bauer
Profile: Appears quarterly "VdB Magazine", the journal of the Association VdB Federal Bank union. This is reported on the work of the dbb and treated on the work of the entire VdB and other useful / interesting topics.
Language(s): German
ADVERTISING RATES:
Full Page Mono .... EUR 1500
Mechanical Data: Type Area: 252 x 190 mm
Copy instructions: *Copy Date:* 42 days prior to publication

VDBUM INFORMATION
2042083G19E-1969
Editorial: Henleinstr. 8a, 28816 STUHR
Tel: 421 871680 **Fax:** 421 8716888
Email: zentrale@vdbum.de **Web site:** http://www.vdbum.de
Freq: 6 issues yearly; Free to qualifying individuals
Annual Sub.: EUR 42,00; **Circ:** 19,750
Editor: Udo Kiesewalter; **Advertising Manager:** Jens Engel
Profile: Journal concerning engineering machinery.
Language(s): German
ADVERTISING RATES:
Full Page Mono .... EUR 1630
Full Page Colour .... EUR 3575
Mechanical Data: Type Area: 252 x 184 mm, No. of Columns (Display): 3, Col Widths (Display): 58 mm
Copy instructions: *Copy Date:* 15 days prior to publication

VDI NACHRICHTEN
746116G19A-1068
Editorial: VDI-Platz 1, 40468 DÜSSELDORF
Tel: 211 6188316 **Fax:** 211 6188306
Email: redaktion@vdi-nachrichten.com **Web site:** http://www.vdi-nachrichten.com
Freq: Weekly; Free to qualifying individuals
Annual Sub.: EUR 118,00; **Circ:** 165,510
Editor: Rudolf Schulze
Profile: VDI news are the leading opinion-weekly newspaper for engineers and technical management. As the only of its kind, informed more than 298 000 readers (AWA 2010) expert on technological developments and innovations with particular reference to the stress field of technology, economy and socio-political issues. Twitter: http://twitter.com/vdinachrichten This Outlet offers RSS (Really Simple Syndication).
Language(s): German
Readership: Aimed at engineers, specialists in technology and science and heads of personnel departments.
ADVERTISING RATES:
SCC .... EUR 132,60
Mechanical Data: Type Area: 528 x 371 mm, No. of Columns (Display): 8, Col Widths (Display): 45 mm
Copy instructions: *Copy Date:* 6 days prior to publication
Supplement(s): Ingenieur Karriere; SciTechs
BUSINESS: ENGINEERING & MACHINERY

VDI-NACHRICHTEN.COM
1704203G14R-6140
Editorial: VDI-Platz 1, 40468 DÜSSELDORF
Tel: 211 61880 **Fax:** 211 6188112
Email: r.schulze@vdi-nachrichten.com **Web site:** http://www.vdi-nachrichten.com
Freq: Weekly; **Cover Price:** Paid; **Circ:** 292,682 Unique Users
Editor: Rudolf Schulze
Profile: Ezine: National weekly specialising in technology and economy.
Language(s): German
BUSINESS: COMMERCE, INDUSTRY & MANAGEMENT: Commerce Related

VDI-Z INTEGRIERTE PRODUKTION
746118G19A-110
Editorial: VDI-Platz 1, 40468 DÜSSELDORF
Tel: 211 6103335 **Fax:** 211 6103148
Email: heidecker@technikwissen.de **Web site:** http://www.vdi-z.de
Freq: Monthly; **Annual Sub.:** EUR 213,50; **Circ:** 12,477
Editor: Birgit Etmanski
Profile: Engineering journal covering development, construction and production.
Language(s): German
ADVERTISING RATES:
Full Page Mono .... EUR 4248
Full Page Colour .... EUR 5478
Mechanical Data: Type Area: 270 x 185 mm, No. of Columns (Display): 4, Col Widths (Display): 45 mm
Copy instructions: *Copy Date:* 30 days prior to publication
Official Journal of: Organ d. VDI-Ges. Produktionstechnik
BUSINESS: ENGINEERING & MACHINERY

VDK ZEITUNG
746119G74N-760
Editorial: In den Ministergärten 4, 10117 BERLIN
Tel: 30 726290405 **Fax:** 30 726290499
Email: presse@vdk.de **Web site:** http://www.vdk.de
Freq: 10 issues yearly; Free to qualifying individuals
Annual Sub.: EUR 9,95; **Circ:** 1,398,938
Profile: Association magazine d. social association VdK Germany with info's on issues of social security, political trends, health care and travel.
Language(s): German
ADVERTISING RATES:
Full Page Mono .... EUR 31520
Full Page Colour .... EUR 36189
Mechanical Data: Type Area: 426 x 281 mm, No. of Columns (Display): 5, Col Widths (Display): 53 mm
CONSUMER: WOMEN'S INTEREST CONSUMER MAGAZINES: Retirement

VDL-JOURNAL
1637626G21A-4287
Editorial: Anton-Aulke-Str. 11, 48167 MÜNSTER
Tel: 2506 811805 **Fax:** 2506 811805
Email: dr-barth@muenster.de **Web site:** http://www.vdl.de
Freq: 6 issues yearly; **Circ:** 5,700
Editor: Dieter Barth
Profile: Magazine for agricultural engineers, nutrition scientists as well as managers and counsellors in economy and administrations.
Language(s): German
ADVERTISING RATES:
Full Page Mono .... EUR 1592
Full Page Colour .... EUR 2628
Mechanical Data: Type Area: 248 x 180 mm, No. of Columns (Display): 4, Col Widths (Display): 42 mm

VDMA NACHRICHTEN
746122G19E-1720
Editorial: Lyoner Str. 18, 60528 FRANKFURT
Tel: 69 66031808 **Fax:** 69 66032808
Email: rebecca.pini@vdma.org **Web site:** http://www.vdma.org
Freq: Monthly; **Circ:** 6,900
Editor: Rebecca Pini; **Advertising Manager:** Manfred Otawa
Profile: Association journal with contributions for the entrepreneurs and executives of the capital goods industry and market topics Konjuktur, management, technology and environment.
Language(s): German
ADVERTISING RATES:
Full Page Colour .... EUR 4500
Mechanical Data: Type Area: 270 x 180 mm, No. of Columns (Display): 3, Col Widths (Display): 57 mm
Copy instructions: *Copy Date:* 21 days prior to publication
BUSINESS: ENGINEERING & MACHINERY: Machinery, Machine Tools & Metalworking

VDV MAGAZIN
746314G4C-4
Editorial: Postfach 2140, 53744 ST. AUGUSTIN
Tel: 171 2805778 **Fax:** 2241 201678
Email: bull@vdv-online.de **Web site:** http://www.vdv-online.de
Freq: 6 issues yearly; Free to qualifying individuals
Annual Sub.: EUR 84,00; **Circ:** 5,991
Editor: Rolf Bull; **Advertising Manager:** Franz Stypa
Profile: The association journal of the Association of German Surveying Engineers is one of the most widely read journals of surveying in German speaking countries. In the subject are practical topics from all fields of Surveying and Mapping. In addition, each issue will be presented on 10-15 pages new products, literature and developments from the

hardware and software. The Bildungswerk VDV presented here have wide range of seminar offers. An extensive calendar of events for surveying and geographic information system is another focus of the VDV messages.
Language(s): German
Readership: Aimed at members.
ADVERTISING RATES:
Full Page Mono .... EUR 2330
Full Page Colour .... EUR 3875
Mechanical Data: Type Area: 260 x 176 mm, No. of Columns (Display): 2, Col Widths (Display): 86 mm
Copy instructions: *Copy Date:* 21 days prior to publication
BUSINESS: ARCHITECTURE & BUILDING: Surveying

VEGETARISCH FIT! 1660554G74P-1146
Editorial: Hansaring 97, 50670 KÖLN
Tel: 221 5892088 **Fax:** 221 9526124
Email: ctheis@markenverlag.de **Web site:** http://www.markenverlag.de
Freq: 6 issues yearly; **Annual Sub.:** EUR 19,90; **Circ:** 70,000
Editor: Christof Theis
Profile: Vegetarian Fit is the first German periodical titles (since 1993), which deals exclusively with a vegetarian diet. The journal contains many recipes with nutritional information, detailed product information, nutrition tips and much more. Also environmental issues and animal welfare are not neglected.
Language(s): German
ADVERTISING RATES:
Full Page Mono .... EUR 2900
Full Page Colour .... EUR 2900
Mechanical Data: Type Area: 250 x 185 mm, No. of Columns (Display): 4, Col Widths (Display): 44 mm

VEGETARISCH-EINKAUFEN.DE
1691896G74P-1172
Editorial: Lossiusstr. 2, 21337 LÜNEBURG
Tel: 4131 268678 **Fax:** 721 151459750
Email: eva.wester@vegetarisch-einkaufen.de **Web site:** http://www.vegetarisch-einkaufen.de
Cover Price: Paid
Editor: Eva Wester; **Advertising Manager:** Armin Mück
Language(s): German
CONSUMER: WOMEN'S INTEREST CONSUMER MAGAZINES: Food & Cookery

VELBERTER ZEITUNG WAZ
746137G67B-15060
Editorial: Friedrichstr. 34, 45128 ESSEN
Tel: 201 8040 **Fax:** 201 8046539
Email: zentralredaktion@waz.de **Web site:** http://www.derwesten.de
Freq: 312 issues yearly; **Circ:** 12,987
Advertising Manager: Christian Klaucke
Profile: Germany's largest regional newspaper. Inextricably linked with the development of the Ruhr area is the success story of the Westdeutsche Allgemeine WAZ. Since its first publication on 3.4.1948, it helped shaping the region Ruhr, Emscher and Lippe like no other medium. Licensee and publisher Erich Brost created a newspaper of Anglo-Saxon model. The focus was and is independent and nonpartisan. Together with the co-editor James Funke, he conducted the most successful newspaper start-up after the war. Today, the WAZ is Germany's largest regional newspaper, its range extends from the southern Münsterland to the Niederbergische Region, from the Lower Rhine up to the Region of Unna. The total area is approximately 4450 sq km. In the Ruhr area cities Essen, Bochum, Gelsenkirchen, Duisburg, Oberhausen and Mülheim an der Ruhr, WAZ is the leading daily newspaper. The newspaper of the Ruhr area has always listened to the citizens. In it people of the territory find themselves. In it they happens. The WAZ reports and commentes close to its readers and unaffected. The Velberter Zeitung WAZ is a regional edition of the Westdeutsche Allgemeine WAZ. Facebook: http://www.facebook.com/derwesten.
Language(s): German
ADVERTISING RATES:
SCC .... EUR 63,20
Mechanical Data: Type Area: 445 x 320 mm, No. of Columns (Display): 7, Col Widths (Display): 44 mm
Copy instructions: *Copy Date:* 2 days prior to publication
Supplement(s): Mein Auto; Mein Beruf; Meine besten Jahre; Meine Familie; Meine Freizeit; Meine Weihnacht; Mein neues Jahr!; Mein Shopping; Mein Stil; Mein Team; Mein Urlaub; Mein Zuhause; Rhein-Ruhr Zentrum Aktuell
REGIONAL DAILY & SUNDAY NEWSPAPERS: Regional Daily Newspapers

VENTURECAPITAL 756795G1F-1468
Editorial: Hofmannstr. 7a, 81379 MÜNCHEN
Tel: 89 200033920 **Fax:** 89 200033939
Email: passmann@vc-magazin.de **Web site:** http://www.vc-magazin.de
Freq: 11 issues yearly; **Annual Sub.:** EUR 148,00; **Circ:** 6,144
Editor: Torsten Passmann; **Advertising Manager:** Denise Hoser
Profile: Magazine for financial investors and managers.
Language(s): German
ADVERTISING RATES:
Full Page Mono .... EUR 2900
Full Page Colour .... EUR 2900
Mechanical Data: Type Area: 246 x 164 mm, No. of Columns (Display): 2, Col Widths (Display): 80 mm
Copy instructions: *Copy Date:* 12 days prior to publication

DER VERA F. BIRKENBIHL-BRIEF 746149G73-440
Editorial: Welserstr. 1, 81373 MÜNCHEN
Tel: 89 71046664 **Fax:** 89 71046661
Email: barbara.voit@olzog.de **Web site:** http://www.birkenbihlbrief.de
Freq: Monthly; **Annual Sub.:** EUR 119,00; **Circ:** 800
Profile: Publication about training mental abilities.
Language(s): German

VERANSTALTUNGSKALENDER
1914991G2A-5851
Editorial: Hammacherstr. 33, 45127 ESSEN
Tel: 201 2480358 **Fax:** 201 2480348
Email: seminare@junge-presse.de **Web site:** http://www.junge-presse.de
Freq: Half-yearly; **Cover Price:** Free; **Circ:** 5,000
Editor: Felix Winnands; **Advertising Manager:** Felix Winnands
Profile: Programme of seminars and events.
Language(s): German
Copy instructions: *Copy Date:* 20 days prior to publication

VERANSTALTUNGS-PROGRAMM 746176G2A-4940
Editorial: Alte Steige 17, 73732 ESSLINGEN
Tel: 711 9378930 **Fax:** 711 9378939
Email: info@werbeagentur-beck.de **Web site:** http://www.werbeagentur-beck.de
Freq: Half-yearly; **Circ:** 4,000
Profile: Programme with events of the Communications Association Stuttgart.
Language(s): German
ADVERTISING RATES:
Full Page Mono .... EUR 384
Full Page Colour .... EUR 532
Mechanical Data: Type Area: 195 x 85 mm

VERBANDSNACHRICHTEN
746188G1A-3120
Editorial: Willy-Brandt-Ufer 10, 24143 KIEL
Tel: 431 997970 **Fax:** 431 9979717
Email: info@stbvsh.de **Web site:** http://www.stbvsh.de
Freq: Quarterly; **Circ:** 2,500
Editor: Maike Neelsen; **Advertising Manager:** Maike Neelsen
Profile: Magazine from the Association of Tax Advisors in Schleswig-Holstein.
Language(s): German
ADVERTISING RATES:
Full Page Mono .... EUR 400
Full Page Colour .... EUR 650
Copy instructions: *Copy Date:* 14 days prior to publication

VERBANDSNACHRICHTEN
746187G1M-12
Editorial: Littenstr. 10, 10179 BERLIN
Tel: 30 27595980 **Fax:** 30 27595988
Email: info@stbverband-berlin-bb.de **Web site:** http://www.stbverband-berlin-bb.de
Freq: 5 issues yearly; Free to qualifying individuals
Annual Sub.: EUR 50,00; **Circ:** 2,517
Editor: Wolfgang Wawro; **Advertising Manager:** Peter Gesellius
Profile: Journal containing articles and information about taxation in Berlin.
Language(s): German
ADVERTISING RATES:
Full Page Mono .... EUR 850
Full Page Colour .... EUR 1275
Mechanical Data: Type Area: 260 x 185 mm, No. of Columns (Display): 2, Col Widths (Display): 90 mm
BUSINESS: FINANCE & ECONOMICS: Taxation

VERBRAUCHER KONKRET
746194G74M-580
Editorial: Elsenstr. 106, 12435 BERLIN
Tel: 30 5360733 **Fax:** 30 53607345
Email: mail@verbraucher.org **Web site:** http://www.verbraucher.org
Freq: 6 issues yearly; Free to qualifying individuals
Annual Sub.: EUR 15,00; **Circ:** 10,000
Editor: Georg Abel; **Advertising Manager:** Georg Abel
Profile: Magazine for employees of Die Verbraucher Initiative e. V.
Language(s): German
ADVERTISING RATES:
Full Page Mono .... EUR 700
Full Page Colour .... EUR 1000
Mechanical Data: Type Area: 259 x 185 mm, No. of Columns (Display): 4
Copy instructions: *Copy Date:* 21 days prior to publication

VERDAUUNGSKRANKHEITEN
746200G56A-10020
Editorial: Ricarda-Huch-Weg 43, 07743 JENA
Tel: 3641 425688
Email: h.bosseck@web.de
Freq: 6 issues yearly; Free to qualifying individuals
Annual Sub.: EUR 110,00; **Circ:** 3,600
Editor: H. Bosseckert; **Advertising Manager:** Christian Graßl
Profile: Journal about gastroenterology and the treatment of digestive illnesses.
Language(s): German
Readership: Aimed at specialists in the fields of gastroenterology, radiology and surgeons.
ADVERTISING RATES:
Full Page Mono .... EUR 1900
Full Page Colour .... EUR 2890
Mechanical Data: Type Area: 242 x 167 mm, No. of Columns (Display): 3, Col Widths (Display): 56 mm
Copy instructions: *Copy Date:* 28 days prior to publication
BUSINESS: HEALTH & MEDICAL

VERDENER ALLER-ZEITUNG
746202G67B-15080
Editorial: Am Ristedter Weg 17, 28857 SYKE
Tel: 4242 58300 **Fax:** 4242 58332
Email: redaktion@kreiszeitung.de **Web site:** http://www.kreiszeitung.de
Freq: 312 issues yearly; **Circ:** 22,726
Advertising Manager: Axel Berghoff
Profile: The Kreiszeitung publishing group is the fifth largest newspaper in Niedersachsen, with a daily circulation of over 82,000 copies. Regional daily newspaper covering politics, economics, sport, travel and technology. Facebook: http://www.facebook.com/pages/Kreiszeitung.
Language(s): German
ADVERTISING RATES:
SCC .... EUR 64,80
Mechanical Data: Type Area: 472 x 325 mm, No. of Columns (Display): 7, Col Widths (Display): 45 mm
Copy instructions: *Copy Date:* 1 day prior to publication
REGIONAL DAILY & SUNDAY NEWSPAPERS: Regional Daily Newspapers

VERDENER NACHRICHTEN
746203G67B-15100
Editorial: Martinistr. 43, 28195 BREMEN
Tel: 421 36710 **Fax:** 421 36711000
Email: redaktion@bremer-nachrichten.de **Web site:** http://www.bremer-nachrichten.de
Freq: 312 issues yearly; **Circ:** 11,909
Profile: Daily newspaper with regional news and a local sports section.
Language(s): German
ADVERTISING RATES:
SCC .... EUR 24,00
Mechanical Data: Type Area: 490 x 333 mm, No. of Columns (Display): 7, Col Widths (Display): 45 mm
Copy instructions: *Copy Date:* 2 days prior to publication
Supplement(s): Ferienjournal; wochen Journal
REGIONAL DAILY & SUNDAY NEWSPAPERS: Regional Daily Newspapers

VER.DI HANDEL 1601715G14A-9352
Editorial: Prinzessinnenstr. 30, 10969 BERLIN
Tel: 30 6139360 **Fax:** 30 61393618
Email: info@bleifrei-berlin.de **Web site:** http://www.bleifrei-berlin.de
Freq: Quarterly; **Circ:** 303,748
Editor: Andreas Hamann
Profile: Member Magazine of the German trade union ver.di.
Language(s): German
Supplement to: ver.di Publik

VER.DI PUBLIK 760215G14L-6768
Editorial: Paula-Thiede-Ufer 10, 10179 BERLIN
Tel: 30 69561057 **Fax:** 30 69563012
Email: maria.kniesburges@verdi.de **Web site:** http://www.verdi-publik.de
Freq: 9 issues yearly; Free to qualifying individuals
Annual Sub.: EUR 18,00; **Circ:** 1,953,864
Editor: Maria Kniesburges
Profile: ver.di PUBLIK its readers informed professional journalistic quality of society, economy, politics and culture and of course about the activities of Verdi and general trade policy issues. In fixed sections is also reported on education, consumer and health issues. According to reader surveysver.di PUBLIK is read-intensive. For example, the reading time of culture or about 3 times as high as indicated by daily newspapers. ver.di PUBLIK appear nationwide, regional variations and subject-specific supplements. With ver.di PUBLIK away, according to each reader survey Issue about 3.5 million people whose consumption patterns of daily to demanding to be classified.
Language(s): German
ADVERTISING RATES:
Full Page Mono .... EUR 24500
Full Page Colour .... EUR 35000
Mechanical Data: Type Area: 430 x 285 mm, No. of Columns (Display): 5, Col Widths (Display): 52 mm
Copy instructions: *Copy Date:* 21 days prior to publication
Supplement(s): be.wegen ver.di; drei.; Druck + Papier; Kunst+Kultur; M Menschen Machen Medien; ver.di Handel
BUSINESS: COMMERCE, INDUSTRY & MANAGEMENT: Trade Unions

VERENA STRICKEN 746249G74A-3020
Editorial: Bahnhofstr. 50, 29556 SUDERBURG
Tel: 5826 958950 **Fax:** 5826 9589520
Email: redaktion@verena-stricken.com **Web site:** http://www.verena-stricken.com
Freq: Quarterly; **Annual Sub.:** EUR 25,00; **Circ:** 65,998
Editor: Anja Busse; **Advertising Manager:** Hartmut Sroka
Profile: Magazine for creative women who enjoy knitting.
Language(s): German
ADVERTISING RATES:
Full Page Mono .... EUR 3000
Full Page Colour .... EUR 5000
Mechanical Data: Type Area: 253 x 194 mm, No. of Columns (Display): 4, Col Widths (Display): 45 mm

VERFAHRENSTECHNIK
746251G19F-2
Editorial: Lise-Meitner-Str. 2, 55129 MAINZ
Tel: 6131 992325 **Fax:** 6131 992100
Email: e.linder@vfmz.de **Web site:** http://www.industrie-service.de
Freq: 10 issues yearly; Free to qualifying individuals
Annual Sub.: EUR 93,00; **Circ:** 19,526
Editor: Eva Linder; **Advertising Manager:** Gundula Unverzagt
Profile: Verfahrenstechnik informs competent, well informed, practical and actual about systems and components for the technical implementation of the chemical transformation. Verfahrenstechnik is more than just chemical engineering. Machines, apparatus and plants for the transformation are in the center of the editorial report, as well as special measurement and Automation technology. Conveying and storage equipment, and safety and environmental technology complete the range of information. Verfahrenstechnik is therefore the all-around title in mechanical engineering. More than 40 years the journal serves across all sectors as a communication turnover in the market and ensures a real dialogue between manufacturers and Users.
Language(s): German
ADVERTISING RATES:
Full Page Mono .... EUR 4600
Full Page Colour .... EUR 5830
Mechanical Data: Type Area: 265 x 185 mm, No. of Columns (Display): 4, Col Widths (Display): 43 mm
Copy instructions: *Copy Date:* 12 days prior to publication
BUSINESS: ENGINEERING & MACHINERY: Production & Mechanical Engineering

VERGABERECHTS-REPORT
746259G4E-6420
Editorial: Carl-Zeiss-Ring 14, 85737 ISMANING
Freq: Monthly; **Annual Sub.:** EUR 40,64; **Circ:** 5,000
Editor: H.-P. Burchardt
Profile: The VOB-Verlag Ernst Vögel OHG has focused entirely on practical publications on private construction law. Contractors, construction managers, architects, engineers, public and private clients and their advisors will find here lots of valuable information to building law. And in ways that it can be used immediately for daily practice. By the VOB-Verlag Ernst Vögel OHG monthly published fact sheets "BR Baurechts-Report", "Vergaberechts-Report" and "Planerrechts-Report" informed of all significant new choices for construction, procurement and planning law and enjoy a wide acceptance among readers. Thanks to the high circulations can ensure the VOB-Verlag Ernst Vögel OHG for his works a very favorable price-performance ratio.
Language(s): German

VERHALTENSTHERAPIE
746262G56A-10040
Editorial: Wilhelmstr. 20a, 79098 FREIBURG
Tel: 761 452070 **Fax:** 761 4520714
Email: information@karger.de **Web site:** http://www.karger.com
Freq: Quarterly; Free to qualifying individuals
Annual Sub.: EUR 146,00; **Circ:** 3,680
Editor: W. Rief; **Advertising Manager:** Ellen Zimmermann
Profile: Magazine on behaviour therapy.
Language(s): English; German
ADVERTISING RATES:
Full Page Mono .... EUR 2370
Full Page Colour .... EUR 3990
Mechanical Data: Type Area: 242 x 180 mm, No. of Columns (Display): 2, Col Widths (Display): 90 mm
Copy instructions: *Copy Date:* 42 days prior to publication
Official Journal of: Organ d. AFKV-Ausbildungsinst. f. Klin. Verhaltenstherapie in NW gem. e.V., d. APV-Ges. f. Angewandte Psychologie u. Verhaltensmedizin, d. AVM-ArGe f. Verhaltensmodifikation (Schweiz, Deutschland, Österr.), d. BAP-Bayer. Private Akademie f. Psychotherapie, d. CIP-Centrum f. Integrative Psychotherapie, d. DÄVT-Dt. Ärztl. Ges. f. Verhaltenstherapie e.V., d. DVT-Dt. Fachverb. f. Verhaltenstherapie e.V., d. GAP-Ges. f. Ausbildung in Psychotherapie, d. IFKV-Inst. f. Fort- u. Weiterbildung in Klin. Verhaltenstherapie, d. IVB-Inst. f. Verhaltenstherapie Berlin e.V., d. ÖGVT-Österr. Ges. f. Verhaltenstherapie, d. SGVT-Schweizer. Ges. f. Verhaltenstherapie, d. TAVT-Private Tübinger Akademie f. Verhaltenstherapie, d. Vereinigung d. Kassenpsychotherapeuten u. d. VFKV-Verein z. Förderung d. Klin. Verhaltenstherapie, d. Dt. Ges. f. Verhaltensmedizin u. Verhaltensmodifikation

VERKEHRS RUNDSCHAU - SICHERHEITSPROFI D. BG VERKEHR, AUSG. B 746299G49A-2160

Editorial: Aschauer Str. 30, 81549 MÜNCHEN
Tel: 89 2030432521 **Fax:** 89 2030432384
Email: birgit.bauer@springer.com **Web site:** http://www.verkehrsrundschau.de
Freq: 8 issues yearly; Free to qualifying individuals
Annual Sub.: EUR 169,90; **Circ:** 198,496
Editor: Birgit Bauer; **News Editor:** Sebastian Bollig; **Advertising Manager:** Matthias Pioro
Profile: VerkehrsRundschau B is published 8x per year as the official newsletter of the professional organization of registered keepers of vehicles.
Language(s): German
ADVERTISING RATES:
Full Page Colour .... EUR 13660
Mechanical Data: Type Area: 250 x 185 mm, No. of Columns (Display): 4, Col Widths (Display): 43 mm
Supplement(s): Sicherheits Profi
BUSINESS: TRANSPORT

VERKEHRS RUNDSCHAU - WOCHENMAGAZIN F. SPEDITION, TRANSPORT U. LOGISTIK, AUSG. A 746298G49A-2140

Editorial: Aschauer Str. 30, 81549 MÜNCHEN
Tel: 89 2030432521 **Fax:** 89 2030432384
Email: birgit.bauer@springer.com **Web site:** http://www.verkehrsrundschau.de
Freq: 29 issues yearly; **Annual Sub.:** EUR 169,90; **Circ:** 19,702
Editor: Birgit Bauer; **News Editor:** Sebastian Bollig; **Advertising Manager:** Matthias Pioro
Profile: VerkehrsRundschau A is the weekly independent magazine for transport and logistics. Regardless of transport type, it is aimed at all decision makers in all companies involved in organizing logistics supply chains: carriers, haulage contractors, and logistics service providers.
Language(s): German
ADVERTISING RATES:
Full Page Colour .... EUR 6160
Mechanical Data: Type Area: 250 x 185 mm, No. of Columns (Display): 4, Col Widths (Display): 43 mm
BUSINESS: TRANSPORT

VERKEHRS RUNDSCHAU - WOCHENMAGAZIN F. SPEDITION, TRANSPORT U. LOGISTIK, AUSG. C 1684646G49A-2394

Editorial: Aschauer Str. 30, 81549 MÜNCHEN
Tel: 89 2030432521 **Fax:** 89 2030432384
Email: birgit.bauer@springer.com **Web site:** http://www.verkehrsrundschau.de
Freq: Monthly; **Annual Sub.:** EUR 169,90; **Circ:** 30,350
Editor: Birgit Bauer; **News Editor:** Sebastian Bollig; **Advertising Manager:** Matthias Pioro
Profile: The issue C of TÜV Nord, TÜV Rheinland, TÜV Süd used as information carriers and shipped to customers in increased circulation of the companies. The editorial spectrum sets priorities in the areas of logistics, shippers, traffic, workshop, fleet management and internal logistics.
Language(s): German
ADVERTISING RATES:
Full Page Colour .... EUR 8010
Mechanical Data: Type Area: 250 x 185 mm, No. of Columns (Display): 4, Col Widths (Display): 43 mm
Supplement(s): KEP Spezial
BUSINESS: TRANSPORT

DER VERKEHRSANWALT

1639997G1A-3546
Editorial: Wachsbleiche 7, 53111 BONN
Tel: 228 919117 **Fax:** 228 9191123
Email: kontakt@anwaltverlag.de **Web site:** http://www.anwaltverlag.de
Freq: Quarterly; Free to qualifying individuals
Annual Sub.: EUR 47,60; **Circ:** 6,800
Profile: Magazine for lawyers specialising in traffic law.
Language(s): German
ADVERTISING RATES:
Full Page Mono .... EUR 1420
Full Page Colour .... EUR 2290
Mechanical Data: Type Area: 260 x 186 mm, No. of Columns (Display): 2, Col Widths (Display): 90 mm

VERKEHRSBLATT 746287G49R-29

Editorial: Schleefstr. 14, 44287 DORTMUND
Tel: 231 128047 **Fax:** 231 128009
Email: redaktion@verkehrsblatt.de **Web site:** http://www.verkehrsblatt.de
Freq: 24 issues yearly; **Annual Sub.:** EUR 76,80; **Circ:** 10,100
Editor-in-Chief: Dieter Borgmann; **Advertising Manager:** Gudrun Nucaro
Profile: Bulletin of the Federal Ministry of Traffic in Germany.
Language(s): German
ADVERTISING RATES:
Full Page Mono .... EUR 1280
Mechanical Data: Type Area: 245 x 167 mm, No. of Columns (Display): 3, Col Widths (Display): 52 mm
Copy instructions: *Copy Date:* 14 days prior to publication
BUSINESS: TRANSPORT: Transport Related

VERKEHRSDIENST 746288G49R-110

Editorial: Aschauer Str. 30, 81549 MÜNCHEN
Tel: 89 2030432262 **Fax:** 89 2030432207
Web site: http://www.springer-transport-media.de
Freq: Monthly; **Annual Sub.:** EUR 109,80; **Circ:** 1,500
Editor: Nicola Treitz; **Advertising Manager:** Elisabeth Huber
Profile: Journal about legal issues relating to traffic and transport.
Language(s): German
ADVERTISING RATES:
Full Page Mono .... EUR 560
Full Page Colour .... EUR 718
Mechanical Data: Type Area: 172 x 130 mm, No. of Columns (Display): 2, Col Widths (Display): 60 mm
Copy instructions: *Copy Date:* 23 days prior to publication
BUSINESS: TRANSPORT: Transport Related

VERKEHRSWIRTSCHAFT UND LOGISTIK NRW 1604973G49A-2319

Editorial: Erkrather Str. 141, 40233 DÜSSELDORF
Tel: 211 7347814 **Fax:** 211 7347831
Email: hover@vvwl.de **Web site:** http://www.vvwl-transport.de
Freq: 10 issues yearly; **Circ:** 3,700
Editor: Marcus Hover
Profile: Magazine for the transport and freight business, logistics and forwarding agencies.
Language(s): German
ADVERTISING RATES:
Full Page Mono .... EUR 900
Full Page Colour .... EUR 900
Mechanical Data: No. of Columns (Display): 3, Type Area: 240 x 180 mm
Copy instructions: *Copy Date:* 14 days prior to publication

VERKEHRSZEICHEN

746304G49A-2260
Editorial: Eduardstr. 4, 45468 MÜLHEIM
Tel: 208 33031 **Fax:** 208 3881588
Email: redaktion@verkehrszeichen-online.de **Web site:** http://www.verkehrszeichen-online.de
Freq: Quarterly; **Annual Sub.:** EUR 21,00; **Circ:** 1,200
Editor: Klaus-Peter Kalwitzki; **Advertising Manager:** Klaus-Peter Kalwitzki
Profile: Magazine for city and transport planners, traffic pedagogues and psychologists dealing with transport and mobility.
Language(s): German
ADVERTISING RATES:
Full Page Mono .... EUR 840
Mechanical Data: Type Area: 270 x 180 mm, No. of Columns (Display): 3, Col Widths (Display): 56 mm
Copy instructions: *Copy Date:* 21 days prior to publication

VERLER ZEITUNG 1638401G67B-16722

Editorial: Sudbrackstr. 14, 33611 BIELEFELD
Tel: 521 5850 **Fax:** 521 585489
Email: wb@westfalen-blatt.de **Web site:** http://www.westfalen-blatt.de
Freq: 260 issues yearly; **Circ:** 4,972
Advertising Manager: Gabriele Förster
Profile: Regional daily newspaper covering politics, economics, sport, travel and technology.
Language(s): German
Mechanical Data: Type Area: 490 x 320 mm, No. of Columns (Display): 7, Col Widths (Display): 44 mm
Copy instructions: *Copy Date:* 1 day prior to publication
Supplement(s): Mein Garten; www.wb-immo.net
REGIONAL DAILY & SUNDAY NEWSPAPERS: Regional Daily Newspapers

VERMESSUNG BRANDENBURG

1789519G19A-1110
Editorial: Heinrich-Mann-Allee 103, 14473 POTSDAM **Tel:** 331 8844210 **Fax:** 331 884416123
Email: schriftleitung@geobasis-bb.de **Web site:** http://www.geobasis-bb.de
Freq: Half-yearly; **Cover Price:** EUR 2,50; **Circ:** 1,500
Editor: Heinrich Tilly
Profile: Magazine with reports and news about surveying in the Federal State of Brandenburg.
Language(s): German

VERMÖGEN & STEUERN

746319G1A-3472
Editorial: Am Flutgraben 10, 52388 NÖRVENICH
Tel: 2426 5103 **Fax:** 2426 5727
Email: m.badura@badura.com **Web site:** http://www.vunds.de
Freq: Monthly; **Annual Sub.:** EUR 216,84; **Circ:** 877
Editor: Karl-Heinz Badura; **Advertising Manager:** Uwe Cappel
Profile: Magazine focusing on law and taxation.
Language(s): German
ADVERTISING RATES:
Full Page Mono .... EUR 2950
Full Page Colour .... EUR 4090
Mechanical Data: Type Area: 270 x 170 mm, No. of Columns (Display): 3, Col Widths (Display): 54 mm
Copy instructions: *Copy Date:* 15 days prior to publication
BUSINESS: FINANCE & ECONOMICS

VERMÖGENSBERATER

746317G1F-1360
Editorial: Schanzenstr. 70, 20357 HAMBURG
Tel: 40 46883227 **Fax:** 40 46883232
Email: guenther@jdb.de **Web site:** http://www.dvag-magazin.de
Freq: Quarterly; **Cover Price:** EUR 1,75; **Circ:** 742,283
Editor: Jens de Buhr
Profile: Magazine with reports on current and important financial topics Facebook: http://www.facebook.com/DVAG.DE Twitter: http://twitter.com/dvag This Outlet offers RSS (Really Simple Syndication).
Language(s): German
ADVERTISING RATES:
Full Page Mono .... EUR 18600
Full Page Colour .... EUR 22500
Mechanical Data: Type Area: 227 x 185 mm
Copy instructions: *Copy Date:* 30 days prior to publication
BUSINESS: FINANCE & ECONOMICS: Investment

VERORDNUNGSBLATT DES KATHOLISCHEN MILITÄRBISCHOFS FÜR DIE DEUTSCHE BUNDESWEHR

1637469G40-958
Editorial: Am Weidendamm 2, 10117 BERLIN
Tel: 30 206170 **Fax:** 30 20617199
Web site: http://www.katholische-militaerseelsorge.de
Freq: Quarterly; **Circ:** 300
Profile: Magazine containing information about Catholic pastoral care in the army.
Language(s): German

VERPFLEGUNGS-MANAGEMENT 1613852G11A-1568

Editorial: Lausitzer Str. 9, 63075 OFFENBACH
Tel: 69 86711404 **Fax:** 69 86711406
Email: info@jamverlag.de **Web site:** http://www.jamverlag.de
Freq: 10 issues yearly; **Annual Sub.:** EUR 54,00; **Circ:** 9,932
Editor: Ulrike Grohmann; **Advertising Manager:** Jutta Müller
Profile: Ezine: Journal concerning primary education.
Language(s): German
ADVERTISING RATES:
Full Page Mono .... EUR 2625
Full Page Colour .... EUR 3750
Mechanical Data: Type Area: 260 x 180 mm, No. of Columns (Display): 4, Col Widths (Display): 45 mm
Copy instructions: *Copy Date:* 16 days prior to publication
BUSINESS: CATERING: Catering, Hotels & Restaurants

DER VERSANDHAUSBERATER

746353G14A-9531
Editorial: Koblenzer Str. 99, 53177 BONN
Tel: 228 9550600 **Fax:** 228 354472
Email: gro@fid-verlag.de **Web site:** http://www.versandhausberater.de
Freq: Weekly; **Cover Price:** EUR 10,65; **Circ:** 1,200
Editor: Martin Groß-Albenhausen; **Advertising Manager:** Gabriele Drexler
Profile: Magazine with information for mail order companies.
Language(s): German
ADVERTISING RATES:
Full Page Mono .... EUR 1650
Full Page Colour .... EUR 2250
Mechanical Data: Type Area: 270 x 185 mm, No. of Columns (Display): 2, Col Widths (Display): 93 mm
Copy instructions: *Copy Date:* 7 days prior to publication
Supplement(s): Der Versandhausberater Spezial

DER VERSANDHAUSBERATER SPEZIAL 746354G14A-7840

Editorial: Koblenzer Str. 99, 53177 BONN
Tel: 228 9550600 **Fax:** 228 354472
Email: chefredaktion@versandhausberater.de **Web site:** http://www.versandhausberater.de
Freq: 6 issues yearly; **Circ:** 5,000
Editor: Martin Groß-Albenhausen; **Advertising Manager:** Gabriele Drexler
Profile: Magazine containing information for mail-order companies, online traders and direct-marketing companies.
Language(s): German
ADVERTISING RATES:
Full Page Mono .... EUR 2900
Full Page Colour .... EUR 3500
Mechanical Data: Type Area: 380 x 266 mm
Supplement to: Der Versandhausberater

VERSICHERUNGS MAGAZIN

746359G1D-300
Editorial: Abraham-Lincoln-Str. 46, 65189 WIESBADEN **Tel:** 611 7878203 **Fax:** 611 7878435
Email: bernhard.rudolf@springer.com **Web site:** http://www.versicherungsmagazin.de
Freq: Monthly; **Annual Sub.:** EUR 132,00; **Circ:** 12,991
Editor: Bernhard Rudolf; **Advertising Manager:** Annette Oberländer-Renner
Profile: Magazine for insurance intermediaries. Twitter: http://twitter.com/vm_news.
Language(s): German
ADVERTISING RATES:
Full Page Mono .... EUR 4000
Full Page Colour .... EUR 6100
Mechanical Data: Type Area: 240 x 175 mm, No. of Columns (Display): 4, Col Widths (Display): 40 mm
Copy instructions: *Copy Date:* 21 days prior to publication
BUSINESS: FINANCE & ECONOMICS: Insurance

VERSICHERUNGSJOURNAL EXTRABLATT 1793412G1D-483

Editorial: Rathausstr. 15, 22926 AHRENSBURG
Tel: 4102 7777880
Email: kontakt@versicherungsjournal.de **Web site:** http://www.versicherungsjournal.de
Freq: Quarterly; **Cover Price:** Free; **Circ:** 11,180
Profile: Information service for the insurance industry.
Language(s): German
ADVERTISING RATES:
Full Page Colour .... EUR 4990
Mechanical Data: Type Area: 280 x 210 mm
Copy instructions: *Copy Date:* 30 days prior to publication

VERSICHERUNGSMEDIZIN

746361G56A-10060
Editorial: Klosestr. 20, 76137 KARLSRUHE
Tel: 721 3509159 **Fax:** 721 3509201
Email: zoller@vvw.de **Web site:** http://www.vvw.de
Freq: Quarterly; **Annual Sub.:** EUR 24,00; **Circ:** 9,460
Editor: Gerd-Marko Ostendorf; **Advertising Manager:** Benjamin Bittmann
Profile: Magazine about medical prognosis, therapy and assessment.
Language(s): German
ADVERTISING RATES:
Full Page Mono .... EUR 1500
Mechanical Data: Type Area: 270 x 190 mm, No. of Columns (Display): 3, Col Widths (Display): 60 mm
Copy instructions: *Copy Date:* 14 days prior to publication
BUSINESS: HEALTH & MEDICAL

DIE VERSICHERUNGSPRAXIS

1865361G1D-492
Editorial: Breite Str. 98, 53111 BONN
Tel: 228 982230 **Fax:** 228 631651
Email: versicherungspraxis@dvs-schutzverband.de **Web site:** http://www.dvs-schutzverband.de
Freq: Monthly; Free to qualifying individuals
Annual Sub.: EUR 55,00; **Circ:** 2,600
Editor: Philipp Andreae; **Advertising Manager:** Philipp Andreae
Profile: Official magazine covering all aspects of the insurance business.
Language(s): German
ADVERTISING RATES:
Full Page Mono .... EUR 900
Full Page Colour .... EUR 1525
Mechanical Data: Type Area: 248 x 167 mm, No. of Columns (Display): 2, Col Widths (Display): 81 mm
Copy instructions: *Copy Date:* 15 days prior to publication

VERSICHERUNGS-VERMITTLUNG 1664097G1D-469

Editorial: Kekuléstr. 12, 53115 BONN
Tel: 228 2280516 **Fax:** 228 2280550
Email: h.d.schaefer@bvk.de **Web site:** http://www.bvk.de
Freq: 10 issues yearly; Free to qualifying individuals
Annual Sub.: EUR 65,00; **Circ:** 12,000
Editor: Hans-Dieter Schäfer; **Advertising Manager:** Katrin Weißenfels
Profile: Trade journal for independent insurance brokers and home loan merchants - is a treasure trove of information: compact and competent. association policy, professional issues, technical articles, taxation, business management, court rulings and more.
Language(s): German
ADVERTISING RATES:
Full Page Mono .... EUR 2100
Full Page Colour .... EUR 4050
Mechanical Data: No. of Columns (Display): 3, Col Widths (Display): 50 mm, Type Area: 237 x 162 mm
Copy instructions: *Copy Date:* 25 days prior to publication

VERSICHERUNGSWIRTSCHAFT

746367G1D-380
Editorial: Klosestr. 20, 76137 KARLSRUHE
Tel: 721 3509166 **Fax:** 721 3509202
Email: redaktion-vw@vvw.de **Web site:** http://www.vvw.de
Freq: 24 issues yearly; **Annual Sub.:** EUR 195,00; **Circ:** 5,519
Editor: Rita Lansch; **Advertising Manager:** Benjamin Bittmann
Profile: Magazine focusing on the personal insurance business.
Language(s): German
ADVERTISING RATES:
Full Page Mono .... EUR 2950
Full Page Colour .... EUR 5163
Mechanical Data: Type Area: 267 x 185 mm, No. of Columns (Display): 4, Col Widths (Display): 45 mm

Copy instructions: *Copy Date:* 9 days prior to publication
Supplement(s): PKV Publik
BUSINESS: FINANCE & ECONOMICS: Insurance

VERSORGUNGSWIRTSCHAFT
746368G58-1500
Editorial: Fraunhoferstr. 17, 80469 MÜNCHEN
Tel: 89 2023144 **Fax:** 89 2023055
Email: kundenservice@verlag-versorgungswirtschaft.de **Web site:** http://www.verlag-versorgungswirtschaft.de
Freq: Monthly; **Annual Sub.:** EUR 244,50; **Circ:** 1,300
Editor: Karl F. Markmiller; **Advertising Manager:** Maria Pauthner
Profile: Magazine containing news and developments about electricity, gas and water.
Language(s): German
ADVERTISING RATES:
Full Page Mono .... EUR 1250
Mechanical Data: Type Area: 252 x 175 mm, No. of Columns (Display): 3, Col Widths (Display): 55 mm
Copy instructions: *Copy Date:* 11 days prior to publication
BUSINESS: ENERGY, FUEL & NUCLEAR

VERTRÄGLICH REISEN
754026G89A-12122
Editorial: Niebuhrstr. 16b, 53113 BONN
Tel: 228 9858545 **Fax:** 228 9858550
Email: redaktion@fairkehr.de **Web site:** http://www.vertraeglich-reisen.de
Freq: Annual; **Cover Price:** EUR 3,90; **Circ:** 215,000
Editor: Regine Gwinner
Profile: Magazine listing environmentally-friendly apartments in Europe. Facebook: http://www.facebook.com/pages/Vertraglich-Reisen/159255957441197.
Language(s): German
ADVERTISING RATES:
Full Page Colour .... EUR 6900
Mechanical Data: Type Area: 256 x 185 mm, No. of Columns (Display): 4
Copy instructions: *Copy Date:* 80 days prior to publication

VERTRAULICHE MITTEILUNGEN AUS POLITIK, WIRTSCHAFT UND GELDANLAGE
746383G14A-7900
Editorial: Stemmerstr. 91, 78266 BÜSINGEN
Tel: 7734 6061 **Fax:** 7734 7112
Email: vertrauliche-mitteilungen@vertrauliche-mitteilungen.de **Web site:** http://www.vertrauliche-mitteilungen.de
Freq: Weekly; **Annual Sub.:** EUR 151,20; **Circ:** 20,000
Editor: Thomas Brügmann
Profile: Magazine containing selected information about politics, economics and investment.
Language(s): German

DIE VERWALTUNG
746386G44-2240
Editorial: Platz der Universität 3, 79085 FREIBURG
Freq: Quarterly; **Annual Sub.:** EUR 124,00; **Circ:** 500
Editor: Friedrich Schoch; **Advertising Manager:** Arlett Günther
Profile: European magazine featuring books on law, economics and social services, history, politics, philosophy, literary studies and natural sciences.
Language(s): German
ADVERTISING RATES:
Full Page Mono .... EUR 600
Mechanical Data: Type Area: 185 x 115 mm
BUSINESS: LEGAL

VERWALTUNGSRUNDSCHAU VR
746394G32A-6720
Editorial: Zweigertstr. 28, 45130 ESSEN
Tel: 201 827770 **Fax:** 201 8277799
Email: vr@schmittmann.de **Web site:** http://www.verwaltungsrundschau.de
Freq: Monthly; **Annual Sub.:** EUR 129,00; **Circ:** 1,000
Editor: Jens M. Schmittmann
Profile: Discussion forum for employees working in municipal administration at all levels.
Language(s): German
ADVERTISING RATES:
Full Page Mono .... EUR 850
Full Page Colour .... EUR 2185
Mechanical Data: Type Area: 260 x 185 mm
Copy instructions: *Copy Date:* 20 days prior to publication
BUSINESS: LOCAL GOVERNMENT, LEISURE & RECREATION: Local Government

---

VERWALTUNGSZEITUNG BADEN-WÜRTTEMBERG
746396G32A-6740
Editorial: Panoramastr. 27, 70174 STUTTGART
Tel: 711 2263262 **Fax:** 711 2263280
Email: info@vdv-bw.de **Web site:** http://www.vdv-bw.de
Freq: 5 issues yearly; Free to qualifying individuals
Annual Sub.: EUR 20,00; **Circ:** 7,500
Editor: Harald Gentsch
Profile: Magazine about administration in Baden-Württemberg.
Language(s): German
ADVERTISING RATES:
Full Page Mono .... EUR 1415
Mechanical Data: Type Area: 260 x 185 mm, No. of Columns (Display): 4, Col Widths (Display): 45 mm
BUSINESS: LOCAL GOVERNMENT, LEISURE & RECREATION: Local Government

---

VERZEICHNIS DER SCHRIFTEN ZUR WEINGESCHICHTE
1826674G74P-1250
Editorial: Schloßbergstr. 17, 55452 RÜMMELSHEIM
Tel: 6721 43489
Email: gerhard.stumm@gmx.de **Web site:** http://www.geschichte-des-weines.de
Freq: Quarterly; Free to qualifying individuals
Annual Sub.: EUR 40,00; **Circ:** 1,500
Editor: Gerhard Stumm
Profile: Magazine of the Society for the History of Wine.
Language(s): German

VERZEICHNIS DES VERSANDHANDELS
746355G14A-7860
Editorial: Koblenzer Str. 99, 53177 BONN
Tel: 228 9550600 **Fax:** 228 354472
Email: chefredaktion@versandhausberater.de **Web site:** http://www.versandhausberater.de
Freq: Annual; **Cover Price:** EUR 317,79; **Circ:** 1,500
Editor: Martin Groß-Albenhausen; **Advertising Manager:** Gabriele Drexler
Profile: Directory for mail-order companies in Germany, Austria and Switzerland.
Language(s): German
ADVERTISING RATES:
Full Page Mono .... EUR 2200
Full Page Colour .... EUR 2800
Mechanical Data: Type Area: 265 x 166 mm

VET IMPULSE
746435G64H-460
Editorial: Hindenburgstr. 71, 27442 GNARRENBURG
Tel: 4763 6280340 **Fax:** 4763 6280342
Email: vetimpulse@t-online.de **Web site:** http://www.vetimpulse.de
Freq: 24 issues yearly; **Annual Sub.:** EUR 28,00; **Circ:** 13,300
Editor: Manuela Tölle; **Advertising Manager:** Bärbel Lüers
Profile: Magazine for veterinarians.
Language(s): German
ADVERTISING RATES:
Full Page Mono .... EUR 4650
Full Page Colour .... EUR 5400
Mechanical Data: Type Area: 410 x 280 mm, No. of Columns (Display): 4, Col Widths (Display): 67 mm
Copy instructions: *Copy Date:* 28 days prior to publication
BUSINESS: OTHER CLASSIFICATIONS: Veterinary

VFDB ZEITSCHRIFT
746441G54A-120_50
Editorial: Pasteurstr. 17a, 50735 KÖLN
Tel: 221 7766472 **Fax:** 221 7766499
Email: mschnell@vds.de **Web site:** http://www.vfdb.de
Freq: Quarterly; **Annual Sub.:** EUR 83,20; **Circ:** 3,000
Editor: Michael Schnell
Profile: Journal focusing on research and technology in fire protection.
Language(s): German
ADVERTISING RATES:
Full Page Mono .... EUR 1133
Full Page Colour .... EUR 2050
Mechanical Data: Type Area: 243 x 188 mm, No. of Columns (Display): 3, Col Widths (Display): 68 mm
Copy instructions: *Copy Date:* 38 days prior to publication
BUSINESS: SAFETY & SECURITY: Fire Fighting

VGB POWERTECH
746451G58-1520
Editorial: Klinkestr. 27, 45136 ESSEN
Tel: 201 8128300 **Fax:** 201 8128302
Email: pr@vgb.org **Web site:** http://www.vgb.org
Freq: 11 issues yearly; Free to qualifying individuals
Annual Sub.: EUR 275,00; **Circ:** 4,100
Editor: Christopher Weßelmann; **Advertising Manager:** Ana Rios
Profile: Magazine about large power stations.
Language(s): English; German
ADVERTISING RATES:
Full Page Mono .... EUR 1900
Full Page Colour .... EUR 2750
Mechanical Data: Type Area: 262 x 182 mm, No. of Columns (Display): 3, Col Widths (Display): 58 mm
Copy instructions: *Copy Date:* 20 days prior to publication
BUSINESS: ENERGY, FUEL & NUCLEAR

VIADUKT
765243G14A-9289
Editorial: Komturhof 2, 08527 PLAUEN
Tel: 3741 1232111 **Fax:** 3741 1232112
Email: mail@viadukt-online.de **Web site:** http://www.viadukt-online.de
Freq: Quarterly; **Cover Price:** EUR 1,30; **Circ:** 20,000
Editor: Christina Michel; **Advertising Manager:** Katja Martin
Profile: Magazine for business and life in the region Vogtland and Saxony South-West with a variety of sections: Cover Story, Business, Portrait, Life, Data Library.
Language(s): German
ADVERTISING RATES:
Full Page Mono .... EUR 1750
Mechanical Data: Type Area: 247 x 187 mm

VIDEO HOMEVISION
1639513G78A-471
Editorial: Richard-Reitzner-Allee 2, 85540 HAAR
Tel: 89 255561111 **Fax:** 89 255561625
Email: redaktion@video-homevision.de **Web site:** http://www.video-homevision.de
Freq: Monthly; **Cover Price:** EUR 4,30; **Circ:** 46,088
Editor: Andreas Stumptner; **Advertising Manager:** Vedran Budimir
Profile: Video-HomeVision is the practically-oriented test & technology magazine covering all relevant topics and products of the fascinating world of home entertainment. Video-HomeVision advises interested newcomers in an comprehensive manner on the purchase of suitable equipment for their entry in the world of home entertainment. Both dedicated amateur users and professionals with technical know-how can find the necessary information on innovations in the increasingly merging markets of image, sound and PC technology. The flat screen TV in the living room serves increasingly as multimedia control desk within home networks. HDTV and 3D-TV gain rapidly in importance. Video-HomeVision tests not only the newest televisions, but also the key components: sat receivers, Blu-ray players and complete systems, network players, DVD and Blu-ray films as well as video-on-demand services. The focus of our tests on loudspeakers, AV receivers, music servers, compact systems and home theatre solutions is put on getting the right sound to go with the perfect picture – be it stereo, 2.1, 5.1 or 7.1 surround sound. Video-HomeVision provides a wealth of information both for beginners who appreciate high image quality and demanding home entertainment users with intention to instal a high-end home theatre with projector and high-class multi-channel sound system. Video-HomeVision covers the complete range of video: if HD camcorder or video editing workshops, up to video mobile phones and tablet PCs. Our magazine offers tests, reports, interviews, professional advice, workshops and background reports on any kind of application or demand. The Video-HomeVision film editors provide numerous reviews of new DVDs, Blu-rays and movies that serve as exquisite source of information for all technophiles and cineasts. he neutral test competence of both Video-HomeVision laboratories in Poing and Stuttgart is absolutely undisputed and highly acknowledged by technology developers of the international consumer electronics indstries. Test procedures and test equipment are constantly enhanced and developed to keep the state-of-the-art standards. This grants the highest possible test level for our readers. Due to its editorial focus on high-quality products and its targeted distribution, Video-HomeVision is a must-read for every committed home entertainment expert in the specialist retail trade. Twitter: http://twitter.com/videohomevision.
Language(s): German
ADVERTISING RATES:
Full Page Mono .... EUR 7875
Full Page Colour .... EUR 10500
Mechanical Data: Type Area: 250 x 185 mm, No. of Columns (Display): 4, Col Widths (Display): 43 mm
Copy instructions: *Copy Date:* 28 days prior to publication
CONSUMER: CONSUMER ELECTRONICS: Hi-Fi & Recording

VIDEO KAMERA OBJEKTIV
737857G85B-30
Editorial: Eggenfeldener Str. 14, 84326 FALKENBERG **Tel:** 8727 910094
Email: loehneysen@objektiv.org **Web site:** http://www.objektiv.org
Freq: 6 issues yearly; **Annual Sub.:** EUR 41,40; **Circ:** 12,800
Editor: Ulrich von Löhneysen; **Advertising Manager:** Stefanie Richer
Profile: Magazine containing articles on film and video.
Language(s): German
Readership: Aimed at people who enjoy filming.
ADVERTISING RATES:
Full Page Mono .... EUR 2630
Full Page Colour .... EUR 4000
Mechanical Data: Type Area: 263 x 185 mm, No. of Columns (Display): 4, Col Widths (Display): 43 mm
Copy instructions: *Copy Date:* 28 days prior to publication
CONSUMER: PHOTOGRAPHY & FILM MAKING: Film Making

VIDEOAKTIV DIGITAL
746485G85B-1
Editorial: Postfach 1101, 71567 OPPENWEILER
Tel: 7191 342043 **Fax:** 7191 342044
Email: redaktion@videoaktiv.de **Web site:** http://www.videoaktiv.de
Freq: 6 issues yearly; **Annual Sub.:** EUR 40,80; **Circ:** 8,044
Editor: Hans Ernst
Profile: Videoaktiv Digital is the test magazine for video and photo technique. The articles are geared towards easy understanding and comprehensible results, obtained in our own internationally renowned test laboratory. Target group: digital video professionals and interested laymen.
Language(s): German
Readership: Aimed at amateur and professional filmmakers.
ADVERTISING RATES:
Full Page Mono .... EUR 3100
Full Page Colour .... EUR 4545
Mechanical Data: Type Area: 280 x 215 mm, No. of Columns (Display): 3, Col Widths (Display): 58 mm
Copy instructions: *Copy Date:* 31 days prior to publication
CONSUMER: PHOTOGRAPHY & FILM MAKING: Film Making

VIDEOFILMEN
746486G78A-472
Editorial: Postfach 602462, 22239 HAMBURG
Tel: 40 28054041 **Fax:** 3212 5115115
Email: redaktion@videofilmen.de **Web site:** http://www.videofilmen.de
Freq: 6 issues yearly; **Annual Sub.:** EUR 39,60; **Circ:** 5,962
Editor: Egin Altenmüller; **Advertising Manager:** Stefan Nepita
Profile: videofilmen is Germany's oldest magazine for serious amateurs. For more than 20 years, is testing videofilmen video cameras, camcorders, editing equipment and accessories and reports about all aspects of access to technology and the post-processing, tips and tricks from the video practice. Focus of the editorial coverage are: Camera Reviews, product launches, trade show reports, equipment, solutions for post production, workshops on common software tools.
Language(s): German
ADVERTISING RATES:
Full Page Mono .... EUR 3196
Full Page Colour .... EUR 5593
Mechanical Data: Type Area: 277 x 190 mm, No. of Columns (Display): 4, Col Widths (Display): 45 mm
Copy instructions: *Copy Date:* 40 days prior to publication
CONSUMER: CONSUMER ELECTRONICS: Hi-Fi & Recording

VIDEOMEDIA
724059G78B-1
Editorial: Postfach 1151, 30927 BURGWEDEL
Tel: 5139 894507 **Fax:** 5139 894508
Email: info@videomedia-online.de **Web site:** http://www.videomedia-online.de
Freq: Quarterly; **Annual Sub.:** EUR 20,00; **Circ:** 13,500
Editor: Hans-Henning Mathe; **Advertising Manager:** Birgitta Mathe
Profile: Videomedia is a magazine for serious videographers with digital camcorder techniques and editing equipment.
Language(s): German
ADVERTISING RATES:
Full Page Colour .... EUR 4660
Mechanical Data: Type Area: 246 x 169 mm
Copy instructions: *Copy Date:* 30 days prior to publication
CONSUMER: CONSUMER ELECTRONICS: Video & DVD

VIDEOTIPP
746491G78B-12
Editorial: Weihenstephaner Str. 7, 81673 MÜNCHEN
Tel: 89 45114110 **Fax:** 89 45114441
Email: u.hoecherl@e-media.de **Web site:** http://www.mediabiz.de
Freq: Monthly; **Cover Price:** Free; **Circ:** 144,220
Editor: Ulrich Höcherl; **Advertising Manager:** Susanne Hübner
Profile: Home entertainment magazine.
Language(s): German
ADVERTISING RATES:
Full Page Mono .... EUR 7880
Full Page Colour .... EUR 7880
Mechanical Data: Type Area: 231 x 185 mm, No. of Columns (Display): 4, Col Widths (Display): 42 mm
CONSUMER: CONSUMER ELECTRONICS: Video & DVD

VIECHTACHER BAYERWALD-BOTE
746495G67B-15120
Editorial: Medienstr. 5, 94036 PASSAU
Tel: 851 8020 **Fax:** 851 802256
Email: pnp@vgp.de **Web site:** http://www.pnp.de
Freq: 312 issues yearly; **Circ:** 17,847
Advertising Manager: Gerhard Koller
Profile: Daily newspaper with regional news and a local sports section. Twitter: http://twitter.com/pnp_online This Outlet offers RSS (Really Simple Syndication).
Language(s): German
ADVERTISING RATES:
SCC .... EUR 43,50
Mechanical Data: Type Area: 482 x 325 mm, No. of Columns (Display): 7, Col Widths (Display): 45 mm
Copy instructions: *Copy Date:* 2 days prior to publication
REGIONAL DAILY & SUNDAY NEWSPAPERS: Regional Daily Newspapers

---

VIEL SPASS
746497G74A-3060
Editorial: Ruhrtalstr. 67, 45239 ESSEN
Tel: 201 246880 **Fax:** 201 24688100
Email: seg@stegenwaller.de **Web site:** http://www.vielspass.de
Freq: Weekly; **Annual Sub.:** EUR 44,20; **Circ:** 232,248
Editor: Andrea Richartz
Profile: Fresh, happy and cheeky - and always on the side of women „Viel Spaß" has everything that makes life more beautiful. Over 500,000 readers each week love this vibrant, young, entertaining mix:

Exclusive star interviews, latest celebrity news, expert advice on topics such as health, household, money and law. And the best puzzles in Germany. Viel Spaß offers a compact world of experience with many interactive elements. For entertainment and activity or just to enjoy.
Language(s): German
Readership: Aimed at women aged between 18 and 59 years old.
ADVERTISING RATES:
Full Page Mono .... EUR 6500
Full Page Colour .... EUR 6500
Mechanical Data: Type Area: 276 x 204 mm, No. of Columns (Display): 4, Col Widths (Display): 48 mm
CONSUMER: WOMEN'S INTEREST CONSUMER MAGAZINES: Women's Interest

VIER TORE BLITZ AM SONNTAG
746513G72-14712
Editorial: Friedrich-Engels-Ring 7a, 17033 NEUBRANDENBURG **Tel:** 395 5632111
Fax: 395 5632100
Email: gerhard.koehn@blitzverlag.de **Web site:** http://www.blitzverlag.de
Freq: Weekly; **Cover Price:** Free; **Circ:** 58,854
Editor: Gerhard Köhn; **Advertising Manager:** Petra Göring
Profile: Advertising journal (house-to-house) concentrating on local stories.
Language(s): German
ADVERTISING RATES:
Full Page Mono .... EUR 3503
Full Page Colour .... EUR 3893
Mechanical Data: Type Area: 420 x 285 mm, No. of Columns (Display): 6, Col Widths (Display): 45 mm
Copy instructions: *Copy Date:* 2 days prior to publication
LOCAL NEWSPAPERS

VIERNHEIMER TAGEBLATT
746503G67B-15140
Editorial: Rathausstr. 43, 68519 VIERNHEIM
Tel: 6204 96660 **Fax:** 6204 966666
Email: redaktion@viernheimertageblatt.de
Freq: 312 issues yearly; **Circ:** 5,827
Editor: Wolfgang Martin; **Advertising Manager:** Michaela Paliska
Profile: Daily newspaper with regional news and a local sports section.
Language(s): German
ADVERTISING RATES:
SCC .... EUR 12,90
Mechanical Data: Type Area: 460 x 280 mm, No. of Columns (Display): 6, Col Widths (Display): 45 mm
Copy instructions: *Copy Date:* 3 days prior to publication
REGIONAL DAILY & SUNDAY NEWSPAPERS: Regional Daily Newspapers

VIEW
1841557G14A-10175
Editorial: Willy-Brandt-Ring 13, 41747 VIERSEN
Tel: 2162 8179901 **Fax:** 2162 8179180
Email: info@wfg-kreis-viersen.de **Web site:** http://www.wfg-kreis-viersen.de
Cover Price: Free; **Circ:** 5,000
Editor: Axel Schaefers
Profile: Regional entrepreneur magazine.
Language(s): German

VIGO
768172G94H-13941
Editorial: Siemensstr. 6, 61352 BAD HOMBURG
Tel: 6172 670124 **Fax:** 6172 670181
Email: t.ceynowa@wdv.de **Web site:** http://www.vigo.de
Freq: 6 issues yearly; **Circ:** 1,125,602
Editor: Torsten Ceynowa; **Advertising Manager:** Walter Krey
Profile: Company publication published by AOK Rheinland.
Language(s): German
ADVERTISING RATES:
Full Page Mono .... EUR 11000
Full Page Colour .... EUR 11000
Mechanical Data: Type Area: 250 x 189 mm
Copy instructions: *Copy Date:* 30 days prior to publication
CONSUMER: OTHER CLASSIFICATIONS: Customer Magazines

VIK MITTEILUNGEN
1655819G58-1734
Editorial: Richard-Wagner-Str. 41, 45128 ESSEN
Tel: 201 8108415 **Fax:** 201 81084715
Email: r.schmied@vik.de **Web site:** http://www.vik.de
Freq: 6 issues yearly; **Annual Sub.:** EUR 115,00; **Circ:** 1,000
Editor: Roland Schmied; **Advertising Manager:** Roland Schmied
Profile: Association journal of the VIK Federation of Industrial Energy and Power Industry Association, with technical articles and information on politics and the economy: General and industrial energy and power industry, energy costs and energy prices, energy and environmental law, production and use of energy, technology, industrial ener.
Language(s): German
ADVERTISING RATES:
Full Page Mono .... EUR 950
Full Page Colour .... EUR 1550
Mechanical Data: Type Area: 260 x 185 mm

VILSBIBURGER ZEITUNG
746530G67B-15160
Editorial: Altstadt 89, 84028 LANDSHUT
Tel: 871 8500 **Fax:** 871 850202
Email: service@idowa.de **Web site:** http://www.idowa.de
Freq: 312 issues yearly; **Circ:** 8,636
Advertising Manager: Irmgard Haberger
Profile: Regional daily newspaper with news on politics, economy, culture, sports, travel, technology, etc. She is a Local issue of the Landshuter Zeitung for the old County Vilsbiburg. Twitter: http://twitter.com/idowa This Outlet offers RSS (Really Simple Syndication).
Language(s): German
ADVERTISING RATES:
SCC .... EUR 20,90
Mechanical Data: Type Area: 430 x 282 mm, No. of Columns (Display): 6, Col Widths (Display): 45 mm
Copy instructions: *Copy Date:* 1 day prior to publication
Supplement(s): Zuhause
REGIONAL DAILY & SUNDAY NEWSPAPERS: Regional Daily Newspapers

VILSHOFENER ANZEIGER
746531G67B-15180
Editorial: Medienstr. 5, 94036 PASSAU
Tel: 851 8020 **Fax:** 851 802256
Email: pnp@vgp.de **Web site:** http://www.pnp.de
Freq: 312 issues yearly; **Circ:** 8,059
Advertising Manager: Gerhard Koller
Profile: Daily newspaper with regional news and a local sports section. Twitter: http://twitter.com/pnp_online This Outlet offers RSS (Really Simple Syndication).
Language(s): German
ADVERTISING RATES:
SCC .... EUR 31,50
Mechanical Data: Type Area: 482 x 325 mm, No. of Columns (Display): 7, Col Widths (Display): 45 mm
Copy instructions: *Copy Date:* 2 days prior to publication
REGIONAL DAILY & SUNDAY NEWSPAPERS: Regional Daily Newspapers

VIP INTERNATIONAL HONEYMOONER
1626689G89A-12084
Editorial: Industriestr. 131c, 50996 KÖLN
Tel: 221 6501166 **Fax:** 221 65011688
Email: info@bm-medien-verlag.de **Web site:** http://www.bm-medien-verlag.de
Freq: Annual; **Cover Price:** EUR 7,00; **Circ:** 60,000
Editor: Michaela Scholl; **Advertising Manager:** Petra Schmidt
Profile: Magazine for wedding presents wonderful Inspiration for the precious time together. Idyllic luxury destinations such as created for newlyweds and still-lovers.
Language(s): English; German
ADVERTISING RATES:
Full Page Mono .... EUR 9000
Full Page Colour .... EUR 9000
Mechanical Data: Type Area: 325 x 280 mm

VIP INTERNATIONAL TRAVELLER
756827G89A-11675
Editorial: Industriestr. 131c, 50996 KÖLN
Tel: 221 6501166 **Fax:** 221 65011688
Email: info@bm-medien-verlag.de **Web site:** http://www.bm-medien-verlag.de
Freq: Half-yearly; **Cover Price:** EUR 7,00; **Circ:** 60,000
Editor: Michaela Scholl; **Advertising Manager:** Petra Schmidt
Profile: VIP International Traveller magazine reveals the wonderful world of luxury travel.
Language(s): English; German
ADVERTISING RATES:
Full Page Mono .... EUR 12000
Full Page Colour .... EUR 12000
Mechanical Data: Type Area: 330 x 235 mm

VIP INTERNATIONAL TRAVELLER GOLD EDITION
1666852G89A-11966
Editorial: Industriestr. 131c, 50996 KÖLN
Tel: 221 6501166 **Fax:** 221 65011688
Email: info@bm-medien-verlag.de **Web site:** http://www.bm-medien-verlag.de
Freq: Annual; **Cover Price:** EUR 9,00; **Circ:** 60,000
Editor: Michaela Scholl; **Advertising Manager:** Petra Schmidt
Profile: Special edition of the VIP International Traveler with selected travel addresses and hand-picked residences. Exquisite luxury hotels and resorts around the world, portraits of international style icons, interesting society news, hip venue, fashion, lifestyle and luxury and fine cuisine.
Language(s): English; German
ADVERTISING RATES:
Full Page Mono .... EUR 14000
Full Page Colour .... EUR 14000
Mechanical Data: Type Area: 330 x 235 mm

V.I.P. REISE MAGAZIN
746547G89A-12052
Editorial: Haeselerstr. 22c, 14050 BERLIN
Tel: 30 3028145
Email: dirk.jacobs@vip-reisemagazin.de **Web site:** http://www.vip-reisemagazin.de
Freq: 3 issues yearly; **Cover Price:** EUR 8,00; **Circ:** 78,000
Editor: Dirk Jacobs; **Advertising Manager:** Dirk Jacobs
Profile: Luxury travel magazine with reports on selected, exclusive destinations, first class hotels, airline and cruise programs portraits, exclusive rail travel, world travel, flights cross country specials, automotive, specials, etc.
Language(s): Arabic; German
ADVERTISING RATES:
Full Page Colour .... EUR 4100
Mechanical Data: Type Area: 264 x 178 mm, No. of Columns (Display): 2, Col Widths (Display): 89 mm
Copy instructions: *Copy Date:* 14 days prior to publication

VIRCHOWS ARCHIV
746548G56A-10080
Editorial: Tiergartenstr. 17, 69121 HEIDELBERG
Tel: 6221 4870 **Fax:** 6221 4878366
Email: subscriptions@springer.com **Web site:** http://www.springerlink.com
Freq: Monthly; **Annual Sub.:** EUR 2192,00; **Circ:** 733
Editor: Heinz Höfler
Profile: Archive about pathology.
Language(s): English
ADVERTISING RATES:
Full Page Mono .... EUR 830
Full Page Colour .... EUR 1870
Mechanical Data: Type Area: 240 x 175 mm
Official Journal of: Organ d. European Society of Pathology

VISAVIS WEB-BUSINESS
1882133G65A-27_107
Editorial: Auguststr. 19, 53229 BONN
Tel: 228 307940 **Fax:** 228 3079410
Email: w.haselbauer@visavis.de **Web site:** http://www.visavis.de
Freq: Annual; **Circ:** 120,000
Editor: Wolfgang Haselbauer; **Advertising Manager:** Bernhard Haselbauer
Profile: IT information for mid-sized.
Language(s): German
ADVERTISING RATES:
Full Page Mono .... EUR 12847
Full Page Colour .... EUR 14929
Mechanical Data: Type Area: 240 x 189 mm, No. of Columns (Display): 4, Col Widths (Display): 45 mm
Supplement to: Financial Times Deutschland
NATIONAL DAILY & SUNDAY NEWSPAPERS: Unabhängiges konservatives MdEP

VISIONS
746566G76E-230
Editorial: Heiliger Weg 1, 44135 DORTMUND
Tel: 231 5571310 **Fax:** 231 55713131
Email: plauk@visions.de **Web site:** http://www.visions.de
Freq: Monthly; **Annual Sub.:** EUR 60,00; **Circ:** 25,910
Editor: Dennis Plauk
Profile: VISIONS - music with a passion. For over 20 years, we rock in all its forms a labor of love: from metal, hardcore and punk, indie, noise, and an alternative to post-rock, Brit Pop and Singer / Songwriter - good music is our only criterion. VISIONS is a magazine for readers who live music as passionately as we do. Without blinkers and with dedication.
Language(s): German
Readership: Aimed at amateur rock and pop musicians.
ADVERTISING RATES:
Full Page Mono .... EUR 6790
Full Page Colour .... EUR 6790
Mechanical Data: Type Area: 300 x 225 mm, No. of Columns (Display): 4, Col Widths (Display): 46 mm
CONSUMER: MUSIC & PERFORMING ARTS: Pop Music

VISSELHÖVEDER NACHRICHTEN
746571G67B-15200
Editorial: Große Str. 37, 27356 ROTENBURG
Tel: 4261 72330 **Fax:** 4261 72300
Email: redaktion@rotenburger-kreiszeitung.de **Web site:** http://www.kreiszeitung.de
Freq: 312 issues yearly; **Circ:** 10,403
Advertising Manager: Axel Berghoff
Profile: Daily newspaper with regional news and a local sports section. Facebook: http://www.facebook.com/pages/Kreiszeitung.
Language(s): German
ADVERTISING RATES:
SCC .... EUR 29,50
Mechanical Data: Type Area: 431 x 276 mm, No. of Columns (Display): 6, Col Widths (Display): 44 mm
Copy instructions: *Copy Date:* 1 day prior to publication
REGIONAL DAILY & SUNDAY NEWSPAPERS: Regional Daily Newspapers

VISUELL
746575G2A-5000
Editorial: Lothar-von-Kübel-Str. 18, 76547 SINZHEIM
Tel: 7221 3017564 **Fax:** 7221 3017570
Email: redaktion@piag.de **Web site:** http://www.visuell-online.de
Freq: Quarterly; **Annual Sub.:** EUR 25,00; **Circ:** 4,200
Editor: Dieter Franzen
Profile: Journal covering all aspects of the photographic trade.
Language(s): English; German
Readership: Aimed at graphic and photographic users, photographers and photo agencies.
ADVERTISING RATES:
Full Page Mono .... EUR 1200
Full Page Colour .... EUR 1200
Mechanical Data: Type Area: 193 x 141 mm, No. of Columns (Display): 2, Col Widths (Display): 68 mm
Copy instructions: *Copy Date:* 30 days prior to publication
BUSINESS: COMMUNICATIONS, ADVERTISING & MARKETING

VISZERALMEDIZIN
724295G56A-2060
Editorial: Wilhelmstr. 20a, 79098 FREIBURG
Tel: 761 452070 **Fax:** 761 4520714
Email: information@karger.de **Web site:** http://www.karger.com/vim
Freq: Quarterly; **Annual Sub.:** EUR 197,00; **Circ:** 3,750
Advertising Manager: Ellen Zimmermann
Profile: Covering both clinical practice and research in gastroenterology and visceral surgery, this interdisciplinary journal is unique in its field. Invited reviews and supplemental issues provide an overview of topical subjects, while articles and case reports illuminate in more detail specific topics in major surgery, pre- and postsurgical therapy, and minimally invasive surgery. In the section 'interdisciplinary discussions' gastroenterologists, internists and radiologists, as well as general, vascular and abdominal surgeons will find practical answers to specific questions. The journal is thus a valuable source of information, imparting an essential and evolving knowledge of surgical gastroenterology.
Language(s): English; German
ADVERTISING RATES:
Full Page Mono .... EUR 2580
Full Page Colour .... EUR 4200
Mechanical Data: Type Area: 242 x 180 mm, No. of Columns (Display): 2, Col Widths (Display): 90 mm
Copy instructions: *Copy Date:* 42 days prior to publication

VITAL
746583G74G-180_50
Editorial: Poßmoorweg 2, 22301 HAMBURG
Tel: 40 27173100 **Fax:** 40 27173564
Email: redaktion@vital.de **Web site:** http://www.vital.de
Freq: Monthly; **Annual Sub.:** EUR 26,40; **Circ:** 246,738
Editor: Katja Burghardt; **Advertising Manager:** Tobias van Duynen
Profile: vital is the magazine for active, self-and body-conscious women who are are living life. vital presents its readers everything they need to keep body and mind in balance, to feel good all round. The high quality of reporting, carefully researched details, recent information and understandable presented relationships form the foundation of this unique women's magazine. In addition to high quality information vital offers to its readers at the same time stimulation, relaxation and certification with a focus on the three core competences beauty / fitness, health and nutrition. As part of the integration of "Healthy Living", there is now the "Healthy Living Dossier". Facebook: http://www.facebook.com/Kreativkommando.
Language(s): German
ADVERTISING RATES:
Full Page Mono .... EUR 16100
Full Page Colour .... EUR 16100
Mechanical Data: Type Area: 229 x 172 mm, No. of Columns (Display): 4, Col Widths (Display): 40 mm
Copy instructions: *Copy Date:* 34 days prior to publication
CONSUMER: WOMEN'S INTEREST CONSUMER MAGAZINES: Slimming & Health

VITANET.DE
1687710G74G-1831
Editorial: Ganghoferstr. 68, 80339 MÜNCHEN
Tel: 89 41856050 **Fax:** 89 418560519
Email: info@vitanet.de **Web site:** http://www.vitanet.de
Cover Price: Paid; **Circ:** 190,905 Unique Users
Editor: Karin Lindinger
Language(s): German
CONSUMER: WOMEN'S INTEREST CONSUMER MAGAZINES: Slimming & Health

VIVERITO
1810177G74N-917
Editorial: Am Luftschacht 20, 45307 ESSEN
Tel: 201 896260 **Fax:** 201 8962626
Email: k.freisle derer@mediabunt.de **Web site:** http://www.viverito.de
Freq: Quarterly; **Cover Price:** Free; **Circ:** 100,000
Editor: Karin Freislederer; **Advertising Manager:** Tanja Tengler
Profile: Magazine for Best-Ager with issues of culture, housing, travel and enjoy.
Language(s): German
ADVERTISING RATES:
Full Page Mono .... EUR 2800
Full Page Colour .... EUR 2800
Mechanical Data: Type Area: 274 x 184 mm
Copy instructions: *Copy Date:* 21 days prior to publication

VKU VERKEHRSUNFALL UND FAHRZEUGTECHNIK
746303G49A-2328
Editorial: Aschauer Str. 30, 81549 MÜNCHEN
Tel: 89 2030431136 **Fax:** 89 2030431205
Email: thomas.seidenstuecker@springer.com

Freq: 11 issues yearly; **Annual Sub.:** EUR 318,00; **Circ:** 1,891
Editor: Thomas Seidenstuecker; **Advertising Manager:** Michael Harms
Profile: Magazine for car and traffic experts, on car technology and the transport business.
Language(s): German
Mechanical Data: Type Area: 240 x 175 mm, No. of Columns (Display): 3, Col Widths (Display): 55 mm

VLOTHOER ANZEIGER
746599G67B-15220
Editorial: Obermarktstr. 26, 32423 MINDEN
Tel: 571 8820 **Fax:** 571 882240
Email: mt@mt-online.de **Web site:** http://www.mt-online.de
Freq: 312 issues yearly; **Circ:** 1,658
Advertising Manager: Thomas Bouza Behm
Profile: Daily newspaper with regional news and a local sports section. Facebook: http://www.facebook.com/pages/Mindener-Tageblatt/288611662122.
Language(s): German
ADVERTISING RATES:
SCC .... EUR 26,00
Mechanical Data: Type Area: 426 x 282 mm, No. of Columns (Display): 6, Col Widths (Display): 45 mm
Copy instructions: *Copy Date:* 1 day prior to publication
Supplement(s): prisma
REGIONAL DAILY & SUNDAY NEWSPAPERS: Regional Daily Newspapers

DIE VOGELWELT
746635G64F-2480
Editorial: Industriepark 3, 56291 WIEBELSHEIM
Tel: 6766 903141 **Fax:** 6766 903320
Email: vogelwelt@aula-verlag.de **Web site:** http://www.vogelwelt.com
Freq: Quarterly; **Annual Sub.:** EUR 62,95; **Circ:** 2,500
Editor: Volker Dierschke
Profile: Magazine about birds.
Language(s): English; German
ADVERTISING RATES:
Full Page Mono .... EUR 480
Full Page Colour .... EUR 960
Mechanical Data: No. of Columns (Display): 2, Col Widths (Display): 75 mm, Type Area: 220 x 155 mm
Copy instructions: *Copy Date:* 30 days prior to publication
Official Journal of: Organ d. Dachverb. Dt. Avifaunisten
BUSINESS: OTHER CLASSIFICATIONS: Biology

VOGTLAND-ANZEIGER
746636G67B-15260
Editorial: Martin-Luther-Str. 50, 08525 PLAUEN
Tel: 3741 597711 **Fax:** 3741 597747
Email: redaktion@vogtland-anzeiger.de **Web site:** http://www.vogtland-anzeiger.de
Freq: 312 issues yearly; **Circ:** 7,176
Editor: Marjon Thümmel; **Advertising Manager:** Winfried Forster
Profile: Daily newspaper with regional news and a local sports section. Facebook: http://www.facebook.com/pages/Vogtland-Anzeiger/152649588094102.
Language(s): German
ADVERTISING RATES:
SCC .... EUR 53,60
Mechanical Data: Type Area: 485 x 325 mm, No. of Columns (Display): 7, Col Widths (Display): 44 mm
Copy instructions: *Copy Date:* 1 day prior to publication
Supplement(s): rtv
REGIONAL DAILY & SUNDAY NEWSPAPERS: Regional Daily Newspapers

VOGUE
746640G74B-210
Editorial: Karlstr. 23, 80333 MÜNCHEN
Tel: 89 381040 **Fax:** 89 38104230
Email: bettina.gauss@vogue.de **Web site:** http://www.vogue.de
Freq: Monthly; **Annual Sub.:** EUR 62,40; **Circ:** 136,442
Editor: Christiane Arp; **Advertising Manager:** Susanne Förg-Randazzo
Profile: VOGUE is a synonym for fashion and style, opinion-forming and style-setting – the modern legend among women's magazines. Month after month, VOGUE presents the best from the international world of fashion in a unique journalistic and artistic way and Introduces young talents and tomorrow's trends. VOGUE gathers experts from the cosmetics industry and reveals their secrets for sophisticated, intelligent and high-spending readers. With interviews, features and portraits, VOGUE guides us through the world of art and culture, discovers new travel destinations and fantastic hideaways. The VOGUE reader is a self-confident young woman, who loves luxury and the beautiful things in life. She has an above-average education and a high net household income that allows her to fulfill her wishes. With an actual readership of 1.4 million readers*, VOGUE once again holds the leading position in the top segment of monthly women's magazines, ahead of ELLE and MADAME.
Language(s): German
Readership: Aimed at financially independent modern women.
ADVERTISING RATES:
Full Page Mono .... EUR 27900
Full Page Colour .... EUR 27900
Mechanical Data: Type Area: 247 x 190 mm
CONSUMER: WOMEN'S INTEREST CONSUMER MAGAZINES: Women's Interest - Fashion

VOLKSBLATT
746651G67B-15280
Editorial: Berner Str. 2, 97084 WÜRZBURG
Tel: 931 60010 **Fax:** 931 6001242
Web site: http://www.mainpost.de
Freq: 312 issues yearly; **Circ:** 41,923
Profile: Regional daily newspaper covering politics, economics, sport, travel and technology. Twitter: http://twitter.com/mainpost This Outlet offers RSS (Really Simple Syndication).
Language(s): German
ADVERTISING RATES:
SCC .... EUR 92,00
Mechanical Data: Type Area: 466 x 310 mm, No. of Columns (Display): 7, Col Widths (Display): 43 mm
Copy instructions: *Copy Date:* 1 day prior to publication
REGIONAL DAILY & SUNDAY NEWSPAPERS: Regional Daily Newspapers

VOLKSWAGEN MAGAZIN
746674G94H-13100
Editorial: Stubbenhuk 10, 20459 HAMBURG
Tel: 40 37035050 **Fax:** 40 37035010
Email: redaktion-volkswagen-magazin@guj.de **Web site:** http://www.corporate-editors.com
Freq: Quarterly; **Circ:** 615,469
Editor: Jan Spielhagen; **Advertising Manager:** Christian Böge
Profile: Magazine focusing on Volkswagen cars.
Language(s): German
Readership: Aimed at Volkswagen owners.
ADVERTISING RATES:
Full Page Mono .... EUR 19900
Full Page Colour .... EUR 19900
Mechanical Data: Type Area: 256 x 183 mm
Supplement(s): Volkswagen Club Magazin
CONSUMER: OTHER CLASSIFICATIONS: Customer Magazines

VOLKSZEITUNG
746676G67B-15300
Editorial: Berner Str. 2, 97084 WÜRZBURG
Tel: 931 30910 **Fax:** 931 13758
Email: red.volkszeitung@mainpost.de **Web site:** http://www.mainpost.de
Freq: 312 issues yearly; **Circ:** 46,618
Profile: Daily newspaper with regional news and a local sports section. Twitter: http://twitter.com/mainpost This Outlet offers RSS (Really Simple Syndication).
Language(s): German
ADVERTISING RATES:
SCC .... EUR 93,10
Mechanical Data: Type Area: 466 x 310 mm, No. of Columns (Display): 7, Col Widths (Display): 43 mm
Copy instructions: *Copy Date:* 1 day prior to publication
REGIONAL DAILY & SUNDAY NEWSPAPERS: Regional Daily Newspapers

VOLLBLUT
746677G75E-280
Editorial: Im Mediapark 8, 50670 KÖLN
Tel: 221 2587350 **Fax:** 221 2587212
Email: vollblut@sportverlag.de **Web site:** http://www.sportverlag.de
Freq: Quarterly; **Annual Sub.:** EUR 35,60; **Circ:** 2,800
Editor: Peter Scheid; **Advertising Manager:** Anja Diekmann
Profile: Publication for German stable-owners and thoroughbred horse-breeders focused on gallop.
Language(s): German
ADVERTISING RATES:
Full Page Mono .... EUR 1200
Full Page Colour .... EUR 1200
Mechanical Data: Type Area: 240 x 184 mm
Copy instructions: *Copy Date:* 14 days prior to publication
CONSUMER: SPORT: Horse Racing

VOLLEYBALL MAGAZIN
725113G75X-34
Editorial: Rektoratsweg 36, 48159 MÜNSTER
Tel: 251 2300552 **Fax:** 251 2300599
Email: vm@philippka.de **Web site:** http://www.volleyball.de
Freq: Monthly; **Annual Sub.:** EUR 47,40; **Circ:** 6,233
Editor: Klaus Wegener; **Advertising Manager:** Peter Möllers
Profile: The "volleyball Magazin" is the only national magazine for volleyball indoor and outdoor. The full color monthly magazine provides information in detailed reports and background reports - illustrated with large color photos - all the major national and international volleyball events portrays players and coaches, especially supplies a lot of information on sports medicine, sports nutrition, club management and organization, and other topics with practical utility.
Language(s): German
ADVERTISING RATES:
Full Page Mono .... EUR 1285
Full Page Colour .... EUR 1795
Mechanical Data: Type Area: 267 x 180 mm, No. of Columns (Display): 3, Col Widths (Display): 55 mm
Copy instructions: *Copy Date:* 28 days prior to publication
CONSUMER: SPORT: Other Sport

VON FRAU ZU FRAU
1828729G74A-3580
Editorial: Bärheide 1, 38442 WOLFSBURG
Tel: 5362 949733
Email: redaktion@allesguteverlag.de **Web site:** http://www.allesguteverlag.de
Freq: 11 issues yearly; **Cover Price:** EUR 0,70; **Circ:** 165,002
Editor: Bodo Scharffetter
Profile: Women's magazine: fashion & beauty, news & stories, health & nutrition, cooking & baking, guide, travel and wellness tips.
Language(s): German
ADVERTISING RATES:
Full Page Mono .... EUR 10500
Full Page Colour .... EUR 10500
Mechanical Data: Type Area: 277 x 207 mm

VON HAUS ZU HAUS
746695G72-14764
Editorial: Denzlinger Str. 42, 79312 EMMENDINGEN
Tel: 7641 938014 **Fax:** 7641 938010
Email: redaktion@von-haus-zu-haus.de **Web site:** http://www.wzo.de
Freq: Weekly; **Cover Price:** Free; **Circ:** 16,850
Editor: Christian von Löwensprung; **Advertising Manager:** Clemens Merkle
Profile: Advertising journal (house-to-house) concentrating on local stories.
Language(s): German
ADVERTISING RATES:
Full Page Mono .... EUR 2142
Full Page Colour .... EUR 2924
Mechanical Data: Type Area: 420 x 285 mm, No. of Columns (Display): 6, Col Widths (Display): 45 mm
Copy instructions: *Copy Date:* 2 days prior to publication
LOCAL NEWSPAPERS

VORPOMMERN BLITZ AM SONNTAG
746726G72-14780
Editorial: Tribseer Damm 2, 18437 STRALSUND
Tel: 3831 2677451 **Fax:** 3831 2677402
Email: wilfried.stabenow@blitzverlag.de **Web site:** http://www.blitzverlag.de
Freq: Weekly; **Cover Price:** Free; **Circ:** 15,395
Editor: Wilfried Stabenow; **Advertising Manager:** André Holfert
Profile: Advertising journal (house-to-house) concentrating on local stories.
Language(s): German
ADVERTISING RATES:
Full Page Mono .... EUR 1815
Full Page Colour .... EUR 2205
Mechanical Data: Type Area: 420 x 285 mm, No. of Columns (Display): 6, Col Widths (Display): 45 mm
Copy instructions: *Copy Date:* 2 days prior to publication
LOCAL NEWSPAPERS

VORSCHAU
746729G50-1180
Editorial: Augustusplatz 8, 04109 LEIPZIG
Tel: 341 12700 **Fax:** 341 1270200
Email: publicrelations@gewandhaus.de **Web site:** http://www.gewandhaus.de
Freq: Half-yearly; **Cover Price:** Free; **Circ:** 3,000
Advertising Manager: Katja Roloff
Profile: Programme of events.
Language(s): German
ADVERTISING RATES:
Full Page Colour .... EUR 350
Mechanical Data: Type Area: 190 x 85 mm
Copy instructions: *Copy Date:* 90 days prior to publication

VORSICHT
746736G80-12480
Editorial: Bleichstr. 25, 55543 BAD KREUZNACH
Tel: 671 839930 **Fax:** 671 8399339
Email: vorsicht@ess.de **Web site:** http://www.ess.de
Freq: Monthly; **Cover Price:** Free; **Circ:** 14,855
Editor: Torsten Strauß; **Advertising Manager:** Michael Wies
Profile: Magazine for the Rhine area.
Language(s): German
ADVERTISING RATES:
Full Page Mono .... EUR 1245
Full Page Colour .... EUR 1465
Mechanical Data: Type Area: 265 x 185 mm
Copy instructions: *Copy Date:* 10 days prior to publication
CONSUMER: RURAL & REGIONAL INTEREST

VORWÄRTS
746750G82-8840
Editorial: Stresemannstr. 30, 10963 BERLIN
Tel: 30 25594320 **Fax:** 30 25594390
Email: redaktion@vorwaerts.de **Web site:** http://www.vorwaerts.de
Freq: 10 issues yearly; Free to qualifying individuals
Annual Sub.: EUR 22,00; **Circ:** 420,638
Editor: Uwe Knüpfer; **Advertising Manager:** Michael Blum
Profile: Social democratic magazine. Facebook: http://www.facebook.com/pages/vorwarts/99923813221 Twitter: http://twitter.com/vorwaerts_de This Outlet offers RSS (Really Simple Syndication).
Language(s): German
ADVERTISING RATES:
Full Page Mono .... EUR 15300
Full Page Colour .... EUR 18000
Mechanical Data: Type Area: 323 x 225 mm, No. of Columns (Display): 4, Col Widths (Display): 52 mm
Supplement(s): Bayern vorwärts; NordOstPost; SPD Niedersachsen vorwärts; vorwärtsBerlin; vorwärtsExtra; vorwärtsExtra; vorwärtsHessen; vorwärts RLP; vorwärts: Saarland; Wir in Sachsen-Anhalt WISA vorwärts für Sachsen-Anhalt
CONSUMER: CURRENT AFFAIRS & POLITICS

VR FUTURE
731967G91D-3660
Editorial: Alter Wall 55, 20457 HAMBURG
Tel: 40 6568550 **Fax:** 40 65685517
Email: redaktion@vr-future.de **Web site:** http://www.vr-future.de
Freq: Quarterly; **Cover Price:** Free; **Circ:** 136,330
Editor: Marietta Miehlich
Profile: Company publication published by Bausparkasse Schwäbisch Hall.
Language(s): German
CONSUMER: RECREATION & LEISURE: Children & Youth

VR PRIMAX
1614042G91D-9797
Editorial: Leipziger Str. 35, 65191 WIESBADEN
Tel: 611 50660 **Fax:** 611 5066500
Email: direct@dgverlag.de **Web site:** http://www.vr-primax.de
Freq: Monthly; **Cover Price:** Free; **Circ:** 363,481
Editor: Gerhard Bayer
Profile: Company publication published by Volksbanken.
Language(s): German
CONSUMER: RECREATION & LEISURE: Children & Youth

VR. VERPACKUNGS-RUNDSCHAU
746352G35-160
Editorial: Industriestr. 2, 63150 HEUSENSTAMM
Tel: 6104 606379 **Fax:** 6104 606323
Email: vr@kepplermediengruppe.de **Web site:** http://www.verpackungsrundschau.de
Freq: Monthly; **Annual Sub.:** EUR 193,00; **Circ:** 13,780
Editor: Norbert Sauermann; **Advertising Manager:** Marion Neckermann
Profile: Magazine covering all aspects of packaging.
Language(s): English; German
Readership: Read by packaging engineers.
ADVERTISING RATES:
Full Page Mono .... EUR 2900
Full Page Colour .... EUR 4175
Mechanical Data: Type Area: 262 x 184 mm, No. of Columns (Display): 4, Col Widths (Display): 43 mm
Copy instructions: *Copy Date:* 21 days prior to publication
Official Journal of: Organ d. BDVI-Das Verpackungsnetzwerk
BUSINESS: PACKAGING & BOTTLING

VSYA EVROPA
1639851G90-35
Editorial: Großbeerenstr. 186, 12277 BERLIN
Tel: 30 26947260 **Fax:** 30 26947160
Email: europa@wernermedia.de **Web site:** http://www.vsya-evropa.com
Freq: 6 issues yearly; **Annual Sub.:** EUR 29,00; **Circ:** 72,768
Editor: Nicholas Werner; **Advertising Manager:** Natalja Huneke
Profile: Russian luxury magazine for wealthy Russian-speaking Europeans. The magazine specializes in exclusive themes for the elite of European fashion, design, architecture, culture, innovative technology and the economy with contributions to the legendary fashion houses, the trends of the season, billboard for two months, premieres, concerts, fairs and exhibitions; exclusive interviews with decision makers and creators behind the iconic brands, unique jewelry, accessories, haute couture and cosmetics, exotic hobbies and interests, travel from Europe and the world, in every issue: exclusive photo shoots; News from the world of yachts, cars and jets in design and technology, recipes from the chefs of Europe's most famous restaurants.
Language(s): Russian
ADVERTISING RATES:
Full Page Mono .... EUR 7330
Full Page Colour .... EUR 7330
Mechanical Data: Type Area: 247 x 188 mm
Copy instructions: *Copy Date:* 35 days prior to publication
CONSUMER: ETHNIC

VW CLASSIC
2041770G77A-2961
Editorial: Anton-Günther-Str. 4, 26180 RASTEDE
Tel: 4402 9822310 **Fax:** 4402 9822319
Email: t.fuths@vw-classic-magazin.de **Web site:** http://www.vw-classic-magazin.de
Freq: Half-yearly; **Cover Price:** EUR 5,50; **Circ:** 120,000
Editor: Thomas Fuths; **Advertising Manager:** Sigrid Pinke
Profile: Magazine for historic Volkswagen. The separation in lovely vintage car (Beetle, Karmann and Co. - air cooled) and affordable classic cars (Corrado, K70 and comrades - water-cooled) is passé. The result is a rather different spectrum of automobile fascination. For these vehicles - the classical pool of highest-volume car manufacturer in Europe - there has been no media platform. VW Classic is now on this platform. At the same time increasing the value of tradition. In an era when the new indicator, often soulless products from the retort, people are looking for the familiar, for things that have any substance and history. VW Classic delivers both. In addition: No brand is also closer to humans than Volkswagen. The label VW is therefore in the era of virtual trade marks, a real guarantee of honesty and soundness; of history and vitality, of romance and Selbsterlebtem. A more emotional than ever perceived brand that is loved with all my heart. And that's why the time is ripe for VW Classic - for the love of Volkswagen and love of an era that has created real value.
Language(s): German

ADVERTISING RATES:
Full Page Mono .... EUR 5500
Full Page Colour .... EUR 5500
Mechanical Data: Type Area: 254 x 192 mm, No. of Columns (Display): 4, Col Widths (Display): 45 mm
Copy instructions: *Copy Date:* 35 days prior to publication

VW GOLF & CO. 746802G77A-2380

Editorial: Hertener Markt 7, 45699 HERTEN
Tel: 2366 8080 **Fax:** 2366 808149
Email: red.vw@vest-netz.de
Freq: 6 issues yearly; **Annual Sub.:** EUR 38,00; **Circ:** 31,522
Editor: Arno Rudolf Welke
Profile: Magazine for Volkswagen-Golf fans.
Language(s): German
ADVERTISING RATES:
Full Page Mono .... EUR 4760
Full Page Colour .... EUR 6700
Mechanical Data: Type Area: 252 x 184 mm, No. of Columns (Display): 3, Col Widths (Display): 58 mm
Copy instructions: *Copy Date:* 37 days prior to publication

VW GOLF & CO. 746802G77A-2925

Editorial: Hertener Markt 7, 45699 HERTEN
Tel: 2366 8080 **Fax:** 2366 808149
Email: red.vw@vest-netz.de
Freq: 6 issues yearly; **Annual Sub.:** EUR 38,00; **Circ:** 31,522
Editor: Arno Rudolf Welke
Profile: Magazine for Volkswagen-Golf fans.
Language(s): German
ADVERTISING RATES:
Full Page Mono .... EUR 4760
Full Page Colour .... EUR 6700
Mechanical Data: Type Area: 252 x 184 mm, No. of Columns (Display): 3, Col Widths (Display): 58 mm
Copy instructions: *Copy Date:* 37 days prior to publication

VW SCENE INTERNATIONAL 746803G77E-455

Editorial: Hertener Mark 7, 45699 HERTEN
Tel: 2366 808104 **Fax:** 2366 808149
Email: red.vw@vest-netz.de **Web site:** http://www.vw-scene.de
Freq: Monthly; **Annual Sub.:** EUR 42,00; **Circ:** 31,370
Editor: Arno Rudolf Welke
Profile: VW SCENE International - from enthusiasm for VW. Beetle, Golf, Bulli - the list of Volkswagen, which have become over time could be a cult car, almost endless. Time and again young people's enthusiasm as well as long-term drivers for the VW brand. They spice up their beetle. For a VW is not a distant dream car, a VW is tangible excitement. For over twenty years accompanied SCENE VW enthusiasts of these vehicles. VW SCENE tells the story of the individually styled original or restored cars and their owners. The well-preserved 70-year- Passat is also shown the door-powered car in the flip-flop paint and painfully revived Karmann Ghia. They are all part of the scene. Whether air or water cooled - month after month, the editorial presents the latest trends, introduces new products prior and informed directly from the scene. For VW SCENE is local: at events and fairs, excursions. This includes a comprehensive calendar - in the magazine as well online.Die editorial team has an open ear for the concerns and needs of readers. For such close contact is the interactive section of the homepage www.vw scene.de all-user capabilities. With one click it lands directly in the editor, after a short registration are additional content available to him. VW SCENE - this is pure enthusiasm. At the kiosk, the Internet, on-site. At our core target group are mainly young male adults aged 16-39 years who make their everyday active in their free time to travel a lot and the car have made it their hobby. They are outgoing, very eager consumers and are full of adventure and zest for life. They are also very ready experimental, particularly as relates to new and modern products, from consumer electronics, fashion and technology.
Language(s): German
ADVERTISING RATES:
Full Page Mono .... EUR 3000
Full Page Colour .... EUR 4300
Mechanical Data: Type Area: 252 x 184 mm, No. of Columns (Display): 3, Col Widths (Display): 58 mm
Copy instructions: *Copy Date:* 28 days prior to publication
CONSUMER: MOTORING & CYCLING: Club Cars

VW SPEED 746804G77E-460

Editorial: Am Sandfeld 15a, 76149 KARLSRUHE
Tel: 721 627380 **Fax:** 721 6273811
Email: redaktion@vw-speed.de **Web site:** http://www.vw-speed.de
Freq: Monthly; **Annual Sub.:** EUR 39,50; **Circ:** 51,350
Editor: Stefan Matern; **Advertising Manager:** Sigrid Pinke
Profile: For over 15 years is one of the most successful VW SPEED th special interest magazines in the tuning segment. VW SPEED is the bible for fans old and new tuned Volkswagen. Formative for VW SPEED is the mixture of competent journalistic Texts, the high, spectacular photo-quality, unique layout, and ease in dealing with the topic VW tuning. VW SPEED tracks down the latest trends and places them in the limelight. VW SPEED is always up to date and reporting regularly on the most important meetings. VW SPEED writes not only about the scene - VW SPEED lives in the scene. It is the dream of every VW fans, his car to once present in VW SPEED. Readers - for readers is the recipe for success. A real, while most vibrant and lively scene sheet.
Language(s): German
Readership: Aimed at owners of VW cars and car enthusiasts.
ADVERTISING RATES:
Full Page Mono .... EUR 2850
Full Page Colour .... EUR 3800
Mechanical Data: Type Area: 232 x 185 mm, No. of Columns (Display): 4, Col Widths (Display): 43 mm
Copy instructions: *Copy Date:* 40 days prior to publication
CONSUMER: MOTORING & CYCLING: Club Cars

VW&AUDI TUNER MAGAZIN 1799983G77A-2786

Editorial: Paffrather Str. 80, 51465 BERGISCH GLADBACH **Tel:** 2202 41857 **Fax:** 2202 41877
Email: info@eurotuner.de **Web site:** http://www.tuning2go.de
Freq: 6 issues yearly; **Annual Sub.:** EUR 18,00; **Circ:** 26,200
Editor: Olivier Fourcade; **Advertising Manager:** Olivier Fourcade
Profile: European Magazine with a focus on automotive technology and tuned vehicles for VW and Audi Facebook: http://www.facebook.com/pages/VWAudi-Tuner-Magazin/344540676536.
Language(s): German
ADVERTISING RATES:
Full Page Mono .... EUR 4100
Full Page Colour .... EUR 4990
Mechanical Data: Type Area: 267 x 181 mm, No. of Columns (Display): 4, Col Widths (Display): 42 mm
Copy instructions: *Copy Date:* 28 days prior to publication

W&B WIRTSCHAFT UND BERUFSERZIEHUNG 748383G14F-100

Editorial: Am Buchenhang 14, 53115 BONN
Tel: 228 232501 **Fax:** 228 232501
Email: rainer.m.kieslinger@gmx.net **Web site:** http://www.w-und-b.com
Freq: Monthly; **Annual Sub.:** EUR 109,00; **Circ:** 1,400
Editor: Rainer M. Kieslinger; **Advertising Manager:** Sibylle Schönert
Profile: Magazine about occupational training.
Language(s): German
ADVERTISING RATES:
Full Page Mono .... EUR 499
Full Page Colour .... EUR 599
Mechanical Data: Type Area: 257 x 184 mm
Copy instructions: *Copy Date:* 28 days prior to publication
BUSINESS: COMMERCE, INDUSTRY & MANAGEMENT: Training & Recruitment

W&S 748390G54C-45

Editorial: Oskar-Maria-Graf-Ring 23, 81737 MÜNCHEN **Tel:** 89 67369742 **Fax:** 89 67369761
Email: britta.kalscheuer@igt-verlag.de **Web site:** http://www.sicherheit.info
Freq: 6 issues yearly; **Annual Sub.:** EUR 146,50; **Circ:** 9,782
Editor: Britta Kalscheuer; **Advertising Manager:** Ulrich Bornschein
Profile: Magazine covering security in the work place.
Language(s): German
Readership: Read by suppliers of security technology.
ADVERTISING RATES:
Full Page Mono .... EUR 2324
Full Page Colour .... EUR 3440
Mechanical Data: Type Area: 257 x 178 mm, No. of Columns (Display): 4, Col Widths (Display): 41 mm
Official Journal of: Organ d. BHE Bundesverb. d. Hersteller- u. Errichterfirmen v. Sicherheitssystemen e.V.
BUSINESS: SAFETY & SECURITY: Security

W&V 748391G2A-5060

Editorial: Hultschiner Str. 8, 81677 MÜNCHEN
Tel: 89 21837133 **Fax:** 89 21837850
Email: chefredakteur@wuv.de **Web site:** http://www.wuv.de
Freq: Weekly; **Annual Sub.:** EUR 249,00; **Circ:** 31,948
Editor: Jochen Kalka; **News Editor:** Lena Herrmann
Profile: Werben & Verkaufen provides information, utility and guidance for advertisers, agencies and media. The magazine of the communications and media industry is aimed primarily at decision makers and opinion leaders in marketing, advertising and sales. Facebook: http://www.facebook.com/pages/Werben-Verkaufen/371000506665 Twitter: http://twitter.com/#!/wuvonline This Outlet offers RSS (Really Simple Syndication).
Language(s): German
ADVERTISING RATES:
Full Page Colour .... EUR 9500
Mechanical Data: Type Area: 282 x 206 mm
Copy instructions: *Copy Date:* 10 days prior to publication
Supplement(s): einser; Page Extra; W&V Analyse; W&V Extra; W&V Guide; W&V Society
BUSINESS: COMMUNICATIONS, ADVERTISING & MARKETING

W&V ANALYSE 756886G2A-5391

Editorial: Hultschiner Str. 8, 81677 MÜNCHEN
Tel: 89 21837657 **Fax:** 89 21837849
Email: chefredakteur@wuv.de **Web site:** http://www.wuv.de
Circ: 32,211
Editor: Jochen Kalka
Profile: The supplement combines the areas of marketing, market research and consulting firm. It includes comprehensive contributions to research topics, information about important current market studies and brings news from the consulting and market research industry. Facebook: http://www.facebook.com/pages/Werben-Verkaufen/371000506665.
Language(s): German
ADVERTISING RATES:
Full Page Colour .... EUR 9500
Mechanical Data: Type Area: 281 x 184 mm
Copy instructions: *Copy Date:* 27 days prior to publication
Supplement to: W&V
BUSINESS: COMMUNICATIONS, ADVERTISING & MARKETING

W&V BOOKING 1637502G2A-5524

Editorial: Hultschiner Str. 8, 81677 MÜNCHEN
Tel: 89 21837131 **Fax:** 89 21837861
Web site: http://www.wuv.de
Freq: Annual; **Cover Price:** EUR 75,00; **Circ:** 2,000
Profile: Data and portraits of German speaking radio and TV stations. Facebook: http://www.facebook.com/pages/Werben-Verkaufen/371000506665.
Language(s): German
ADVERTISING RATES:
Full Page Colour .... EUR 2600
Mechanical Data: Type Area: 270 x 180 mm, No. of Columns (Display): 3, Col Widths (Display): 60 mm
Copy instructions: *Copy Date:* 26 days prior to publication

W&V DIGITAL 1622855G2A-5495

Editorial: Hultschiner Str. 8, 81677 MÜNCHEN
Tel: 89 21837999 **Fax:** 89 21837868
Email: chefredakteur@wuv.de **Web site:** http://www.emar.de
Freq: Daily; **Cover Price:** Paid; **Circ:** 55,750 Unique Users
Editor: Jochen Kalka
Profile: Ezine: Magazine focusing on developments in e-commerce.
Language(s): German
BUSINESS: COMMUNICATIONS, ADVERTISING & MARKETING

W&V EXTRA 1666529G2A-5627

Editorial: Hultschiner Str. 8, 81677 MÜNCHEN
Tel: 89 21837657 **Fax:** 89 21837849
Email: chefredakteur@wuv.de **Web site:** http://www.wuv.de
Circ: 32,211
Editor: Jochen Kalka
Profile: The journal is devoted to future developments related to the communications industry and beyond - from the pure theory of implementation in daily work to the use of single products. Facebook: http://www.facebook.com/pages/Werben-Verkaufen/371000506665.
Language(s): German
ADVERTISING RATES:
Full Page Colour .... EUR 9500
Mechanical Data: Type Area: 266 x 188 mm
Supplement to: W&V

W&V GUIDE 1976911G2A-5895

Editorial: Hultschiner Str. 8, 81677 MÜNCHEN
Tel: 89 21837657 **Fax:** 89 21837849
Email: chefredakteur@wuv.de **Web site:** http://www.wuv.de
Circ: 32,211
Editor: Jochen Kalka
Profile: The guide summarizes background information and user-oriented tips about a specific topic from the advertising industry together concise. In the pocket he is stuck on the cover of the W&V's total circulation. Facebook: http://www.facebook.com/pages/Werben-Verkaufen/371000506665 Twitter: http://twitter.com/#!/wuvonline RSS (Really Simple Syndication) wird angeboten.
Language(s): German
ADVERTISING RATES:
Full Page Colour .... EUR 7500
Mechanical Data: Type Area: 200 x 141 mm
Supplement to: W&V

W&V MEDIA 1621677G2A-5460

Editorial: Hultschiner Str. 8, 81677 MÜNCHEN
Tel: 89 21837999 **Fax:** 89 21837868
Email: wuvmedia@efv.de **Web site:** http://media.wuv.de
Freq: Daily; **Cover Price:** Paid; **Circ:** 48,897 Unique Users
Editor: Jochen Kalka
Profile: Ezine: Magazine about media and marketing.
Language(s): German
BUSINESS: COMMUNICATIONS, ADVERTISING & MARKETING

W&V ONLINE 1622897G2A-5489

Editorial: Hultschiner Str. 8, 81677 MÜNCHEN
Tel: 89 21837999 **Fax:** 89 21837868
Email: chefredaktion@wuv.de **Web site:** http://www.wuv.de
Freq: Daily; **Cover Price:** Paid; **Circ:** 1,273,092 Unique Users
Editor: Jochen Kalka
Profile: Ezine: Magazine about advertising, marketing, media and sales. Facebook: http://www.facebook.com/pages/Werben-Verkaufen/371000506665.
Language(s): German
BUSINESS: COMMUNICATIONS, ADVERTISING & MARKETING

W&V SOCIETY 1932189G2A-5866

Editorial: Hultschiner Str. 8, 81677 MÜNCHEN
Tel: 89 21837657 **Fax:** 89 21837849
Email: chefredakteur@wuv.de **Web site:** http://www.wuv.de
Circ: 32,211
Editor: Jochen Kalka
Profile: Supplement to the werben & verkaufen magazine Facebook: http://www.facebook.com/pages/Werben-Verkaufen/371000506665.
Language(s): German
ADVERTISING RATES:
Full Page Colour .... EUR 9500
Mechanical Data: Type Area: 266 x 188 mm
Supplement to: W&V

W&V SPOTS FERNSEHEN PLANUNGSDATEN 1637531G2A-5525

Editorial: Hultschiner Str. 8, 81677 MÜNCHEN
Tel: 89 21837131 **Fax:** 89 21837861
Web site: http://wuv.de
Freq: Quarterly; **Annual Sub.:** EUR 240,00; **Circ:** 1,500
Profile: Publication about all German-speaking TV stations.
Language(s): German
ADVERTISING RATES:
Full Page Colour .... EUR 2430
Mechanical Data: Type Area: 270 x 180 mm, No. of Columns (Display): 3, Col Widths (Display): 60 mm
Copy instructions: *Copy Date:* 27 days prior to publication

W&V SPOTS HÖRFUNK PLANUNGSDATEN 1637532G2A-5526

Editorial: Hultschiner Str. 8, 81677 MÜNCHEN
Tel: 89 21837131 **Fax:** 89 21837861
Web site: http://wuv.de
Freq: Quarterly; **Annual Sub.:** EUR 240,00; **Circ:** 1,500
Profile: Publication about all German-speaking radio stations.
Language(s): German
ADVERTISING RATES:
Full Page Colour .... EUR 2500
Mechanical Data: Type Area: 270 x 180 mm, No. of Columns (Display): 3, Col Widths (Display): 60 mm
Copy instructions: *Copy Date:* 27 days prior to publication

WA WERBEARTIKEL NACHRICHTEN 746967G2A-5080

Editorial: Waltherstr. 49, 51069 KÖLN
Tel: 221 6891130 **Fax:** 221 6891110
Email: delbrouck@waorg.com **Web site:** http://www.wanachrichten.de
Freq: Monthly; **Annual Sub.:** EUR 42,00; **Circ:** 9,753
Editor: Mischa Delbrouck; **Advertising Manager:** Sarah Vieten
Profile: Magazine for German-speaking promotional items resellers.
Language(s): German
ADVERTISING RATES:
Full Page Mono .... EUR 1480
Full Page Colour .... EUR 2350
Mechanical Data: Type Area: 260 x 182 mm, No. of Columns (Display): 3, Col Widths (Display): 58 mm
Copy instructions: *Copy Date:* 21 days prior to publication
BUSINESS: COMMUNICATIONS, ADVERTISING & MARKETING

WA WETTBEWERBE AKTUELL 747308G4A-11

Editorial: Maximilianstr. 5, 79100 FREIBURG
Tel: 761 774550 **Fax:** 761 7745511
Email: redaktion@wettbewerbe-aktuell.de **Web site:** http://www.wettbewerbe-aktuell.de
Freq: Monthly; **Annual Sub.:** EUR 139,80; **Circ:** 8,469
Editor: Thomas Hoffmann-Kuhnt; **Advertising Manager:** Jan Sievers
Profile: Journal detailing current architectural competitions open for competitive tender.
Language(s): German
Readership: Aimed at architects and engineers.
ADVERTISING RATES:
Full Page Mono .... EUR 4665
Full Page Colour .... EUR 6690
Mechanical Data: Type Area: 257 x 185 mm, No. of Columns (Display): 3, Col Widths (Display): 59 mm
Copy instructions: *Copy Date:* 20 days prior to publication
BUSINESS: ARCHITECTURE & BUILDING: Architecture

WA WOCHEN ANZEIGER
746971G72-14808
Editorial: Allee 2, 91154 ROTH **Tel:** 9171 970311
Fax: 9171 970326
Email: wochenanzeiger.roth-schwabach@pressenetz.de **Web site:** http://www.wa-wochenanzeiger.de
Freq: Weekly; **Cover Price:** Free; **Circ:** 80,474
Editor: Detlef Gsänger; **Advertising Manager:** Dieter Vitzthum
Profile: Advertising journal (house-to-house) concentrating on local stories.
Language(s): German
ADVERTISING RATES:
Full Page Mono .... EUR 3277
Full Page Colour .... EUR 4412
Mechanical Data: Type Area: 430 x 280 mm, No. of Columns (Display): 6, Col Widths (Display): 45 mm
Copy instructions: *Copy Date:* 2 days prior to publication
LOCAL NEWSPAPERS

WAGO DIRECT
1656861G17-1561
Editorial: Hansastr. 27, 32423 MINDEN
Tel: 571 887448 **Fax:** 571 887305
Email: martin.witzsch@wago.com **Web site:** http://www.wago.com
Freq: 3 issues yearly; **Cover Price:** Free; **Circ:** 150,000
Editor: Martin Witzsch
Profile: Customer magazine about electrotechnics, electronics, industry automation, energy economies and building services engineering.
Language(s): German

WAGO DIRECT INTERNATIONAL
1659552G17-1562
Editorial: Hansastr. 27, 32423 MINDEN
Tel: 571 887448 **Fax:** 571 887305
Email: martin.witzsch@wago.com **Web site:** http://www.wago.com
Cover Price: Free; **Circ:** 10,000
Editor: Martin Witzsch
Profile: Customer magazine about electrotechnics, electronics, industry automation, energy economies, building services engineering and similar issues.
Language(s): English

WAHRE GESCHICHTEN
746827G74A-3315
Editorial: Karlsruher Str. 31, 76437 RASTATT
Tel: 7222 13205 **Fax:** 7222 13351
Email: erlebnispresse@vpm.de **Web site:** http://www.vpm.de
Freq: 6 issues yearly; **Cover Price:** EUR 1,95; **Circ:** 107,000
Editor: Dietlinde Besch; **Advertising Manager:** Rainer Gross
Profile: Intimate confessions, dramatic stories: When reading wahre Geschichten you can watch the whole range of emotions that brought the storytellers to the brink of despair, which made them sad, proud or happy. You describe moments that made them look into the abyss or they have magic moments, bitter insights and joyful surprises, experiences of anger and sadness, joy and pain, hope and happiness. wahre Geschichten offers a variety of lived experience that to heart. You will also find in wahre Geschichten numerous puzzles, health news and your personal horoscope.
Language(s): German
ADVERTISING RATES:
Full Page Mono .... EUR 1575
Full Page Colour .... EUR 2648
Mechanical Data: Type Area: 263 x 196 mm, No. of Columns (Display): 4, Col Widths (Display): 47 mm

WAIBLINGER KREISZEITUNG
746831G67B-15320
Editorial: Albrecht-Villinger-Str. 10, 71332 WAIBLINGEN **Tel:** 7151 5660 **Fax:** 7151 566402
Email: info@redaktion.zvw.de **Web site:** http://www.waiblinger-kreiszeitung.de
Freq: 312 issues yearly; **Circ:** 16,211
Editor: Frank Nipkau; **News Editor:** Martin Winterling; **Advertising Manager:** Michael Feßler
Profile: Daily newspaper with regional news and a local sports section.
Language(s): German
ADVERTISING RATES:
SCC .... EUR 51,50
Mechanical Data: Type Area: 485 x 324 mm, No. of Columns (Display): 7, Col Widths (Display): 44 mm
Copy instructions: *Copy Date:* 2 days prior to publication
REGIONAL DAILY & SUNDAY NEWSPAPERS: Regional Daily Newspapers

DER WALDBAUER
746834G21A-4040
Editorial: Tegernseer Str. 8, 83607 HOLZKIRCHEN
Tel: 8024 48037 **Fax:** 8024 49429
Email: info@wbv-holzkirchen.de **Web site:** http://www.wbv-holzkirchen.de
Freq: Quarterly; **Circ:** 2,500
Editor: Gerhard Penninger; **Advertising Manager:** Gerhard Penninger
Profile: Official publication from the Association of Forest Owners of Holzkirchen.
Language(s): German
Mechanical Data: No. of Columns (Display): 3
Copy instructions: *Copy Date:* 30 days prior to publication

DIE WALDBAUERN IN NRW
765244G46-19
Editorial: Kappeler Str. 227, 40599 DÜSSELDORF
Tel: 211 1799835 **Fax:** 211 1799834
Email: info@waldbauernverband.de **Web site:** http://www.waldbauernverband.de
Freq: 6 issues yearly; Free to qualifying individuals
Annual Sub.: EUR 19,00; **Circ:** 2,300
Editor: Heidrun Buß-Schöne
Profile: Magazine with information for professional forestry workers.
Language(s): German
ADVERTISING RATES:
Full Page Mono .... EUR 640
Full Page Colour .... EUR 1056
Mechanical Data: Type Area: 270 x 190 mm, No. of Columns (Display): 4, Col Widths (Display): 46 mm
Copy instructions: *Copy Date:* 21 days prior to publication

DER WALDBESITZER
1663541G21A-4322
Editorial: Burgenlandstr. 7, 55543 BAD KREUZNACH
Tel: 671 7931114 **Fax:** 671 7931199
Email: dr.schuh@waldbesitzerverband-rlp.de
Freq: 3 issues yearly; **Annual Sub.:** EUR 10,00; **Circ:** 15,250
Editor: Wolfgang Schuh
Profile: Magazine for forestowners.
Language(s): German
ADVERTISING RATES:
Full Page Colour .... EUR 1090
Copy instructions: *Copy Date:* 28 days prior to publication

WALDECKISCHE ALLGEMEINE
730361G67B-7280
Editorial: Frankfurter Str. 168, 34121 KASSEL
Tel: 561 20300 **Fax:** 561 2032406
Email: info@hna.de **Web site:** http://www.hna.de
Freq: 312 issues yearly; **Circ:** 5,289
Advertising Manager: Andrea Schaller-Öller
Profile: Regional daily newspaper with news on politics, economy, culture, sports, travel, technology, etc. The Waldeckische Allgemeine a local edition of the HNA Hessische/Niedersächsische Allgemeine. Twitter: http://twitter.com/hna_online This Outlet offers RSS (Really Simple Syndication).
Language(s): German
ADVERTISING RATES:
SCC .... EUR 28,50
Mechanical Data: Type Area: 430 x 285 mm, No. of Columns (Display): 6, Col Widths (Display): 45 mm
Copy instructions: *Copy Date:* 2 days prior to publication
REGIONAL DAILY & SUNDAY NEWSPAPERS: Regional Daily Newspapers

WALDECKISCHE LANDESZEITUNG
746840G67B-15340
Editorial: Lengefelder Str. 6, 34497 KORBACH
Tel: 5631 560150 **Fax:** 5631 6994
Email: redaktion@wlz-fz.de **Web site:** http://www.wlz-fz.de
Freq: 312 issues yearly; **Circ:** 18,231
Editor: Jörg Kleine; **Advertising Manager:** Marina Kieweg
Profile: Regional daily newspaper covering politics, economics, culture, sports, travel and technology. Consistent four-color, clear, strong in the local section, funded research on the political background and daily special pages - these are the success factors, to appreciate the readers. This Outlet offers RSS (Really Simple Syndication).
Language(s): German
ADVERTISING RATES:
SCC .... EUR 43,10
Mechanical Data: Type Area: 430 x 277 mm, No. of Columns (Display): 6, Col Widths (Display): 45 mm
Copy instructions: *Copy Date:* 2 days prior to publication
REGIONAL DAILY & SUNDAY NEWSPAPERS: Regional Daily Newspapers

WALDKRAIBURGER NACHRICHTEN
746848G67B-15360
Editorial: Hafnerstr. 5, 83022 ROSENHEIM
Tel: 8031 213201 **Fax:** 8031 213216
Email: redaktion@ovb.net **Web site:** http://www.ovb-online.de
Freq: 312 issues yearly; **Circ:** 13,997
Advertising Manager: Max Breu
Profile: Regional daily newspaper with news on politics, economy, culture, sports, travel, technology, etc. The Waldkraiburger Nachrichten is a regional edition of the newspaper "Oberbayerisches Volksblatt". This Outlet offers RSS (Really Simple Syndication).
Language(s): German
ADVERTISING RATES:
SCC .... EUR 63,60
Mechanical Data: Type Area: 474 x 324 mm, No. of Columns (Display): 7, Col Widths (Display): 45 mm
Copy instructions: *Copy Date:* 1 day prior to publication
Supplement(s): rtv
REGIONAL DAILY & SUNDAY NEWSPAPERS: Regional Daily Newspapers

DER WALDWIRT
746858G46-13
Editorial: Danneckerstr. 37, 70182 STUTTGART
Tel: 711 2364737 **Fax:** 711 2361123
Email: hilt@foka.de **Web site:** http://www.foka.de
Freq: 6 issues yearly; **Annual Sub.:** EUR 30,00,; **Circ:** 3,990
Editor: Jörg Hilt; **Advertising Manager:** Ruth Reschke
Profile: Official journal of the Baden- Württemberg Forestry Commission.
Language(s): German
Readership: Aimed at forestry owners workers and those interested in the environment.
ADVERTISING RATES:
Full Page Mono .... EUR 1458
Mechanical Data: Type Area: 270 x 187 mm, No. of Columns (Display): 4, Col Widths (Display): 44 mm
BUSINESS: TIMBER, WOOD & FORESTRY

WALLSTREET:ONLINE
1662991G1F-1841
Editorial: Winsstr. 62, 10405 BERLIN
Tel: 30 20456420 **Fax:** 30 20456350
Email: redaktion@wallstreet-online.de **Web site:** http://www.wallstreet-online.de
Freq: Daily; **Cover Price:** Paid; **Circ:** 4,362,221 Unique Users
Editor: Sabrina Manthey
Language(s): German
BUSINESS: FINANCE & ECONOMICS: Investment

WALSRODER MARKT
746869G72-14872
Editorial: Lange Str. 26, 29964 WALSRODE
Tel: 5161 600941 **Fax:** 5161 600929
Email: redaktion.walsrode@aller-weser-verlag.de
Web site: http://www.aller-weser-verlag.de
Freq: Weekly; **Cover Price:** Free; **Circ:** 25,200
Editor: Michael Fischer; **Advertising Manager:** Sabine Düßmann
Profile: Advertising journal (house-to-house) concentrating on local stories.
Language(s): German
ADVERTISING RATES:
Full Page Mono .... EUR 2640
Full Page Colour .... EUR 3828
Mechanical Data: Type Area: 440 x 276 mm, No. of Columns (Display): 6, Col Widths (Display): 44 mm
Copy instructions: *Copy Date:* 5 days prior to publication
LOCAL NEWSPAPERS

WALSRODER ZEITUNG
746870G67B-15380
Editorial: Lange Str. 14, 29664 WALSRODE
Tel: 5161 60050 **Fax:** 5161 600528
Email: walsroderzeitung@wz-net.de **Web site:** http://www.wz-net.de
Freq: 312 issues yearly; **Circ:** 11,548
Advertising Manager: Ulrike Schomburg
Profile: Daily newspaper with regional news and a local sports section.
Language(s): German
ADVERTISING RATES:
SCC .... EUR 33,70
Mechanical Data: Type Area: 425 x 280 mm, No. of Columns (Display): 6, Col Widths (Display): 43 mm
Copy instructions: *Copy Date:* 1 day prior to publication
REGIONAL DAILY & SUNDAY NEWSPAPERS: Regional Daily Newspapers

WALT DISNEY MICKY MAUS MAGAZIN
746877G91D-8940
Editorial: Wallstr. 59, 10179 BERLIN **Tel:** 30 240080
Fax: 30 24008599
Email: p.hoepfner@ehapa.de **Web site:** http://www.disney.de/micky-maus-magazin
Freq: Weekly; **Annual Sub.:** EUR 102,00; **Circ:** 184,420
Editor: Peter Höpfner
Profile: Funny comics from Duckburg, current editorial content and every week new strong extras made the comic magazine is the undisputed leader among children's magazines.
Language(s): German
ADVERTISING RATES:
Full Page Mono .... EUR 14900
Full Page Colour .... EUR 14900
Mechanical Data: Type Area: 260 x 175 mm, No. of Columns (Display): 4, Col Widths (Display): 43 mm
Copy instructions: *Copy Date:* 54 days prior to publication
CONSUMER: RECREATION & LEISURE: Children & Youth

WALTROPER ZEITUNG
746881G67B-15400
Editorial: Kampstr. 84b, 45772 MARL **Tel:** 2365 1070
Fax: 2365 1071490
Email: info@medienhaus-bauer.de **Web site:** http://www.medienhaus-bauer.de
Freq: 312 issues yearly; **Circ:** 5,571
Advertising Manager: Carsten Dingerkuss
Profile: Regional daily newspaper with news on politics, economy, culture, sports, travel, technology, etc. The newspaper offers a mix of local, regional and international News from all areas. Fun and interactive content such as forums, polls or betting games are also part of the program. Local out of the city and the neighborhood is the focus of attention. Facebook: http://www.facebook.com/medienhbauer This Outlet offers RSS (Really Simple Syndication).
Language(s): German
ADVERTISING RATES:
SCC .... EUR 24,90
Mechanical Data: Type Area: 487 x 325 mm, No. of Columns (Display): 7, Col Widths (Display): 43 mm
Copy instructions: *Copy Date:* 1 day prior to publication
Supplement(s): prisma
REGIONAL DAILY & SUNDAY NEWSPAPERS: Regional Daily Newspapers

DAS WANDERWELTMAGAZIN
1646273G89A-11857
Editorial: Poststr. 7, 57392 SCHMALLENBERG
Tel: 2972 97400 **Fax:** 2792 974026
Email: info@schmallenberger-sauerland.de **Web site:** http://www.schmallenberger-sauerland.de
Freq: Annual; **Cover Price:** Free; **Circ:** 40,000
Advertising Manager: Hubertus Schmidt
Profile: Accommodation directory and information about a holiday in Schmallenberg Sauerland and the holiday region Eslohe.
Language(s): German

DAS WAR . . .
1881551G73-655
Editorial: Am Baumwall 11, 20459 HAMBURG
Tel: 40 37030
Web site: http://www.guj.de
Freq: Annual; **Cover Price:** EUR 35,00; **Circ:** 30,000
Profile: Annual of the general interest magazine Stern.
Language(s): German

WARNOW KURIER AM MITTWOCH
746913G72-14928
Editorial: Doberaner Str. 115, 18057 ROSTOCK
Tel: 381 4979750 **Fax:** 381 4979754
Email: redaktion@rostockonline.de **Web site:** http://www.warnowkurier.de
Freq: Weekly; **Cover Price:** Free; **Circ:** 125,617
Editor: Torben Godenrath; **Advertising Manager:** Torben Godenrath
Profile: Advertising journal (house-to-house) concentrating on local stories.
Language(s): German
ADVERTISING RATES:
Full Page Mono .... EUR 5695
Full Page Colour .... EUR 8070
Mechanical Data: Type Area: 435 x 281 mm, No. of Columns (Display): 7, Col Widths (Display): 38 mm
Copy instructions: *Copy Date:* 5 days prior to publication
LOCAL NEWSPAPERS

WARSTEINER
746915G80-12600
Editorial: Nelmannwall 4, 59494 SOEST
Tel: 2921 36090 **Fax:** 2921 360929
Email: info@fkwverlag.com **Web site:** http://www.fkwverlag.com
Freq: Monthly; **Cover Price:** Free; **Circ:** 13,500
Editor: Burkhard Salzmann
Profile: Illustrated magazine for the Warstein region.
Language(s): German
ADVERTISING RATES:
Full Page Mono .... EUR 1479
Full Page Colour .... EUR 1922
Copy instructions: *Copy Date:* 10 days prior to publication
CONSUMER: RURAL & REGIONAL INTEREST

WASSER UND ABFALL
746966G57-2460
Editorial: Dieselstr. 20, 65197 WIESBADEN
Tel: 611 9884915 **Fax:** 611 9884916
Email: wasser.abfall@t-online.de **Web site:** http://www.all4engineers.com
Freq: 10 issues yearly; Free to qualifying individuals
Annual Sub.: EUR 169,00; **Circ:** 5,278
Editor: Markus Porth; **Advertising Manager:** Peter Schmidtmann
Profile: Wasser und Abfall (Water and Waste) is the specialist magazine published by the German Association of Engineers for Water Management, Waste Management and Land Improvement (BWK). In addition to monthly cover stories, Wasser und Abfall reports on the following areas: waste management/soil protection/ground contamination, waste water/water protection, drinking water/ground water protection, water management/water engineering. The range of editorial topics is rounded off by reports on new legislation and local authority regulations as well as special subjects. Wasser und Abfall reaches experts and decision-makers in national, regional and local environmental authorities, in industry, water engineering, service providing companies and engineering offices.
Language(s): German
Readership: Read by managers of waste disposal companies and directors of industrial concerns.
ADVERTISING RATES:
Full Page Mono .... EUR 2122
Full Page Colour .... EUR 3022
Mechanical Data: Type Area: 240 x 175 mm, No. of Columns (Display): 3, Col Widths (Display): 55 mm
Copy instructions: *Copy Date:* 23 days prior to publication
BUSINESS: ENVIRONMENT & POLLUTION

WASSERBURGER ZEITUNG
746933G67B-15420
Editorial: Hafnerstr. 5, 83022 ROSENHEIM
Tel: 8031 213201 **Fax:** 8031 213216
Email: redaktion@ovb.net **Web site:** http://www.ovb-online.de
Freq: 312 issues yearly; **Circ:** 10,921
Advertising Manager: Max Breu
Profile: Regional daily newspaper with news on politics, economy, culture, sports, travel, technology, etc. The Wasserburger Zeitung is a regional edition of the newspaper "Oberbayerisches Volksblatt". This Outlet offers RSS (Really Simple Syndication).
Language(s): German
ADVERTISING RATES:
SCC .... EUR 58,70
Mechanical Data: Type Area: 474 x 324 mm, No. of Columns (Display): 7, Col Widths (Display): 45 mm
Copy instructions: *Copy Date:* 1 day prior to publication
Supplement(s): rtv
REGIONAL DAILY & SUNDAY NEWSPAPERS: Regional Daily Newspapers

WASSERKRAFT & ENERGIE
746936G58-1580
Editorial: Paulinenstr. 43, 32756 DETMOLD
Tel: 5231 92430 **Fax:** 5231 924343
Email: redaktion@vms-detmold.de **Web site:** http://www.wasserkraft-und-energie.de
Freq: Quarterly; **Annual Sub.:** EUR 62,50; **Circ:** 2,000
Editor: Anton Zeller; **Advertising Manager:** Silke Käßner
Profile: International quarterly about renewable energy.
Language(s): German
ADVERTISING RATES:
Full Page Mono .... EUR 889
Full Page Colour .... EUR 1239
Mechanical Data: Type Area: 212 x 135 mm
Copy instructions: *Copy Date:* 30 days prior to publication

WASSERSPORT
746941G75M-920
Editorial: Schwertfegerstr. 1, 23556 LÜBECK
Tel: 451 898974 **Fax:** 451 898557
Email: redaktion@svg-wassersport.de **Web site:** http://www.svg-wassersport.de
Freq: Monthly; **Annual Sub.:** EUR 36,00; **Circ:** 12,000
Editor: Hermann Hell; **Advertising Manager:** Gisela Deutschländer
Profile: Magazine about sailing and motorboats in Rheinland and Westphalia.
Language(s): German
ADVERTISING RATES:
Full Page Mono .... EUR 1430
Full Page Colour .... EUR 2270
Mechanical Data: Type Area: 250 x 180 mm, No. of Columns (Display): 4, Col Widths (Display): 43 mm
Copy instructions: *Copy Date:* 30 days prior to publication
Official Journal of: Organ d. Dt. Motoryachtverb.
CONSUMER: SPORT: Water Sports

WASSERSPORT-WIRTSCHAFT
746942G45E-100
Editorial: Schwertfegerstr. 1, 23556 LÜBECK
Tel: 451 898974 **Fax:** 451 898557
Email: redaktion@wassersport-wirtschaft.de **Web site:** http://www.wassersport-wirtschaft.de
Freq: Quarterly; **Annual Sub.:** EUR 20,00; **Circ:** 9,500
Editor: Hermann Hell
Profile: Magazine about water sports and leisure boats.
Language(s): German
Readership: Aimed at manufacturers of sport and leisure boats.
ADVERTISING RATES:
Full Page Mono .... EUR 805
Full Page Colour .... EUR 1260
Mechanical Data: Type Area: 250 x 180 mm, No. of Columns (Display): 4, Col Widths (Display): 43 mm
Copy instructions: *Copy Date:* 21 days prior to publication
Official Journal of: Organ d. Bundesverb. Wassersportwirtschaft e.V.
BUSINESS: MARINE & SHIPPING: Boat Trade

WASSERTRIEBWERK
746944G58-1600
Editorial: Steinbachweg 34, 83324 RUHPOLDING
Tel: 8663 9888 **Fax:** 8663 300
Email: antonzeller@t-online.de **Web site:** http://www.wassertriebwerk.de
Freq: Monthly; Free to qualifying individuals
Annual Sub.: EUR 60,15; **Circ:** 2,800
Editor: Anton Zeller; **Advertising Manager:** Silke Käßner
Profile: Journal about hydro-electric power.
Language(s): German
ADVERTISING RATES:
Full Page Mono .... EUR 889
Full Page Colour .... EUR 1239
Mechanical Data: Type Area: 208 x 135 mm
Copy instructions: *Copy Date:* 30 days prior to publication
Official Journal of: Organ d. Bundesverb. Dt. Wasserkraftwerke e.V. u. d. ArGe'en Wasserkraftwerke d. Länder
BUSINESS: ENERGY, FUEL & NUCLEAR

WASSERWIRTSCHAFT
746947G42C-6
Editorial: Abraham-Lincoln-Str. 46, 65189 WIESBADEN **Tel:** 611 7878284 **Fax:** 611 787878284
Email: stephan@heimerl.net **Web site:** http://www.umwelt.viewegteubner.de
Freq: 10 issues yearly; **Annual Sub.:** EUR 177,00; **Circ:** 2,608
Editor: Stephan Heimerl; **Advertising Manager:** Peter Schmidtmann
Profile: Specialist magazine for "Water and the Environment", is now in its 100th year of publication and is aimed at experts and decision makers in industry, construction companies for the entire water industry, authorities, planning offices for local, regional and national authorities, as well as service providers, engineering consultants, scientists and research institutes. The specialist magazine offers practice-oriented articles and well researched reports from research and science on the following subjects:hydroelectric power/turbines/small hydroelectric power plants, drinking water/ groundwater/inshore waterways, ecology, soil & land, pipes/pumps/fittings/containers, measuring technology/hydromechanics, hydraulics, water engineering/water management, hydrology, energy. The range of editoria ltopics is rounded off by the latest background reports on companies and products. As the organ of numerous associations and organisations, WasserWirtschaft reaches in particular those decision-makers who are responsible for awarding public contracts.
Language(s): German
Mechanical Data: Type Area: 240 x 175 mm, No. of Columns (Display): 4, Col Widths (Display): 40 mm
Official Journal of: Organ d. Wasserwirtschaftsverb. Baden-Württemberg, d. Ruhrverband., d. Dt. TalsperrenKomitees, d. ArGe Alpine Wasserkraft, d. Dt. Wasserhistor. Ges. u. d. Ges. f. Weiterbildung in d. Wasserwirtschaft
BUSINESS: CONSTRUCTION: Water Engineering

WASSERZEITUNG ZVK
1826292G74M-861
Editorial: Dorfstr. 4, 23936 GREVESMÜHLEN
Tel: 3881 75544 **Fax:** 3881 75545
Email: susann.galda@spree-pr.com **Web site:** http://www.spree-pr.com
Freq: Half-yearly; **Cover Price:** Free; **Circ:** 27,400
Editor: Susann Galda
Profile: Customer magazine from the water supplier and sewage company Zweckverband Kuehlung.
Language(s): German
Mechanical Data: Type Area: 327 x 233 mm, No. of Columns (Display): 5, Col Widths (Display): 42 mm

WB WERKSTATT+BETRIEB
746975G19E-1760
Editorial: Kolbergerstr. 22, 81679 MÜNCHEN
Tel: 89 99830661 **Fax:** 89 99830623
Email: damm@hanser.de **Web site:** http://www.werkstatt-betrieb.de
Freq: 10 issues yearly; **Annual Sub.:** EUR 128,00; **Circ:** 14,719
Editor: Helmut Damm; **Advertising Manager:** Dietmar von der Au
Profile: WB Werkstatt+Betrieb publishes practice-related articles on machining. Emphasis is laid on the production engineering prerequisites essential for cost-effective machining of metals. These include not only metalworking tools, machinery and plant but also related automation and information technology. The readers of WB Werkstatt+Betrieb are technical managers, production directors and engineers and metalworking professionals in mechanical and automotive engineering and other important areas of the metalworking industry.
Language(s): German
ADVERTISING RATES:
Full Page Mono .... EUR 3550
Full Page Colour .... EUR 5520
Mechanical Data: Type Area: 250 x 175 mm, No. of Columns (Display): 4, Col Widths (Display): 41 mm
Supplement(s): kataloge orange
BUSINESS: ENGINEERING & MACHINERY: Machinery, Machine Tools & Metalworking

WEBEN+
746991G74E-330
Editorial: Werkhof Kukate, 29496 WADDEWEITZ
Tel: 5849 468 **Fax:** 5849 1202
Email: info@werkhof-kukate.de **Web site:** http://www.webenplus.de
Freq: Half-yearly; Free to qualifying individuals
Annual Sub.: EUR 16,40; **Circ:** 1,200
Editor: Inge Seelig
Profile: Journal about weaving, spinning and dyeing.
Language(s): German
ADVERTISING RATES:
Full Page Mono .... EUR 520
Mechanical Data: Type Area: 258 x 181 mm, No. of Columns (Display): 2, Col Widths (Display): 89 mm
CONSUMER: WOMEN'S INTEREST CONSUMER MAGAZINES: Crafts

WEDEL-SCHULAUER TAGEBLATT
746998G67B-15440
Editorial: Damm 9, 25421 PINNEBERG
Tel: 4101 5356101 **Fax:** 4101 5356106
Email: redaktion@a-beig.de **Web site:** http://www.wedel-schulauer-tageblatt.de
Freq: 312 issues yearly; **Circ:** 4,049
Advertising Manager: Karsten Raasch
Profile: Daily newspaper with regional news and a local sports section. This Outlet offers RSS (Really Simple Syndication).
Language(s): German
ADVERTISING RATES:
SCC .... EUR 29,40
Mechanical Data: Type Area: 430 x 278 mm, No. of Columns (Display): 6, Col Widths (Display): 45 mm
Copy instructions: *Copy Date:* 1 day prior to publication
Supplement(s): nordisch gesund
REGIONAL DAILY & SUNDAY NEWSPAPERS: Regional Daily Newspapers

WEGWEISER OBERSTAUFEN MIT OFFIZIELLEM ORTSPLAN UND FREIZEITKARTE DER UMGEBUNG
747030G89A-11260
Editorial: Grüntenseestr. 26, 87466 OY-MITTELBERG **Tel:** 8361 3330 **Fax:** 8361 3338
Email: info@titze-verlag.de
Freq: Annual; **Cover Price:** Free; **Circ:** 20,000
Editor: Hermann Titze; **Advertising Manager:** Hermann Titze
Profile: Map for the spa resort Oberstaufen.
Language(s): German
ADVERTISING RATES:
Full Page Mono .... EUR 1050
Full Page Colour .... EUR 1150
Mechanical Data: Type Area: 210 x 90 mm
Copy instructions: *Copy Date:* 60 days prior to publication

WEHRMEDIZIN UND WEHRPHARMAZIE
1861225G40-990
Editorial: Celsiusstr. 43, 53125 BONN
Tel: 228 9193725 **Fax:** 228 9193723
Email: andreas.hoelscher@beta-publishing.com **Web site:** http://www.wehrmed.de
Freq: Quarterly; **Annual Sub.:** EUR 33,00; **Circ:** 8,100
Editor: Andreas Hölscher; **Advertising Manager:** Peter C. Franz
Profile: Publication about further education for the medical corps in the army.
Language(s): German
ADVERTISING RATES:
Full Page Mono .... EUR 2780
Full Page Colour .... EUR 3980
Mechanical Data: Type Area: 270 x 185 mm, No. of Columns (Display): 3, Col Widths (Display): 58 mm
Copy instructions: *Copy Date:* 36 days prior to publication

WEHRMEDIZINISCHE MONATSSCHRIFT
1863810G40-995
Editorial: Thorner Str. 9, 80993 MÜNCHEN
Tel: 89 768782
Email: ernst.juergen.finke@online.de **Web site:** http://www.wehrmed.de
Freq: 8 issues yearly; Free to qualifying individuals
Annual Sub.: EUR 35,00; **Circ:** 5,000
Editor: Ernst-Jürgen Finke; **Advertising Manager:** Peter C. Franz
Profile: Magazine for physicians and reserve ranks in the German army.
Language(s): German
ADVERTISING RATES:
Full Page Mono .... EUR 2340
Full Page Colour .... EUR 3240
Mechanical Data: Type Area: 260 x 180 mm, No. of Columns (Display): 3, Col Widths (Display): 60 mm
Official Journal of: Organ d. Sanitätsdienstes d. Bundeswehr

WEIDWERK IN MECKLENBURG VORPOMMERN
747040G75F-920
Editorial: Forsthof 1, 19374 DAMM **Tel:** 3871 63120
Fax: 3871 631212
Email: info@ljv-mecklenburg-vorpommern.de **Web site:** http://www.ljv-mecklenburg-vorpommern.de
Freq: Monthly; **Circ:** 11,000
Editor: Rüdiger Brandt; **Advertising Manager:** Sylvia Lühert
Profile: Magazine of the Hunting Association of Mecklenburg Vorpommern.
Language(s): German
ADVERTISING RATES:
Full Page Mono .... EUR 897
Full Page Colour .... EUR 1432
Mechanical Data: Type Area: 253 x 186 mm, No. of Columns (Display): 4, Col Widths (Display): 43 mm
Copy instructions: *Copy Date:* 29 days prior to publication
Supplement(s): Wald & Wild
CONSUMER: SPORT: Shooting

WEIGHT WATCHERS
756850G73-462
Editorial: Derendorfer Allee 295, 40476 DÜSSELDORF **Tel:** 211 9686216 **Fax:** 211 9686290
Email: cbachhausen@weight-watchers.de **Web site:** http://www.weightwatchers.de
Freq: 6 issues yearly; **Annual Sub.:** EUR 17,40; **Circ:** 104,893
Editor: Claudia Bachhausen-Dewart
Profile: Weight Watchers magazine.This attractive magazine for the well-being and more is packed with news, great recipes, success stories (before / after), many tips and information about a healthy diet. In addition, the magazine presents the latest beauty and styling ideas, fitness and wellness topics. Plus, there's lots of info on exclusive offers and products that assist in weight reduction.
Language(s): German
ADVERTISING RATES:
Full Page Mono .... EUR 7500
Full Page Colour .... EUR 7500
Mechanical Data: Type Area: 253 x 180 mm
Copy instructions: *Copy Date:* 42 days prior to publication
CONSUMER: NATIONAL & INTERNATIONAL PERIODICALS

DIE WEIHNACHTSMÄRKTE
1826214G89A-12386
Editorial: Kardinal-Höffner-Platz 1, 50667 KÖLN
Tel: 221 22130400 **Fax:** 221 22130410
Email: info@koelntourismus.de **Web site:** http://www.koelntourismus.de
Freq: Annual; **Cover Price:** Free; **Circ:** 100,000
Advertising Manager: Georg Wohlrab
Profile: Information to the Christmas markets in Cologne.
Language(s): Dutch; English; French; German
ADVERTISING RATES:
Full Page Mono .... EUR 2800
Full Page Colour .... EUR 2800
Mechanical Data: Type Area: 205 x 100 mm

WEILBURGER TAGEBLATT
747049G67B-15460
Editorial: Elsa-Brandström-Str. 18, 35578 WETZLAR
Tel: 6441 9590 **Fax:** 6441 959292
Email: redaktion.wnz@mittelhessen.de **Web site:** http://www.mittelhessen.de
Freq: 312 issues yearly; **Circ:** 9,413
Advertising Manager: Peter Rother
Profile: Daily newspaper with regional news and a local sports section.
Language(s): German
ADVERTISING RATES:
SCC .... EUR 35,00
Mechanical Data: Type Area: 490 x 328 mm, No. of Columns (Display): 7, Col Widths (Display): 44 mm
Copy instructions: *Copy Date:* 1 day prior to publication
Supplement(s): [f]amilie& freizeit; Fußball-Kalender; [g]esund!; Gut fahren!; rtv; Weilburg live
REGIONAL DAILY & SUNDAY NEWSPAPERS: Regional Daily Newspapers

WEILER ZEITUNG
747050G67B-15480
Editorial: Am Alten Markt 2, 79539 LÖRRACH
Tel: 7621 40330 **Fax:** 7621 403381
Email: wz.redaktion@verlagshaus-jaumann.de **Web site:** http://www.die-oberbadische.de
Freq: 312 issues yearly; **Circ:** 13,633
Advertising Manager: Thomas Dunke
Profile: Daily newspaper with regional news and a local sports section.
Language(s): German
Mechanical Data: Type Area: 435 x 280 mm, No. of Columns (Display): 6, Col Widths (Display): 45 mm
Copy instructions: *Copy Date:* 1 day prior to publication
REGIONAL DAILY & SUNDAY NEWSPAPERS: Regional Daily Newspapers

WEILHEIMER TAGBLATT
747052G67B-15500
Editorial: Pfaffenrieder Str. 9, 82515 WOLFRATSHAUSEN **Tel:** 8171 2690
Fax: 8171 269240
Email: fsav@merkur-online.de **Web site:** http://www.merkur-online.de
Freq: 312 issues yearly; **Circ:** 12,145
Advertising Manager: Hans-Georg Bechthold
Profile: The Münchner Merkur with its own local newspapers, of which the Weilheimer Tagblatt is one that, the leading regional newspaper brand in the Munich area - the most affluent area of Germany. The combination of newspaper and region is the foundation on which to build the success of the title. This is the newspaper not only the factual news agency, but forms a community of solidarity with its readers and the local community. The clear focus on local reporting creates a high regard to human reader loyalty. She presses one hand in the very high number of close to 180,000 subscribers. Also for the high reader-commitment is the loyalty of the total current 827 000 daily readers, the Münchner Merkur or one of its local newspapers usually read over many years. The Münchner Merkur with its own local newspapers is a newspaper for the whole family, tradition and modern life for one of the most beautiful regions of Germany unites. Reliable, informative, critical: the Münchner Merkur is the indispensable daily newspaper for the region. Facebook: http://www.facebook.com/pages/merkur-online.de/190176143327 This Outlet offers RSS (Really Simple Syndication).
Language(s): German
ADVERTISING RATES:
SCC .... EUR 43,60
Mechanical Data: Type Area: 474 x 324 mm, No. of Columns (Display): 7, Col Widths (Display): 45 mm
Copy instructions: *Copy Date:* 1 day prior to publication
REGIONAL DAILY & SUNDAY NEWSPAPERS: Regional Daily Newspapers

VEILIMDORFER ANZEIGER MIT IEBEL-NACHRICHTEN.
747053G72-15024
ditorial: Bessemerstr. 7, 70435 STUTTGART
el: 711 8200050 **Fax:** 711 8200059
mail: redaktion@eheinz.de **Web site:** http://www.heinz.de
req: Weekly; **Cover Price:** Free; **Circ:** 23,700
ditor: Peter Heinz; **Advertising Manager:** Peter leinz
rofile: Advertising journal (house-to-house) oncentrating on local stories.
anguage(s): German
DVERTISING RATES:
ull Page Mono .... EUR 2683
ull Page Colour .... EUR 2882
lechanical Data: Type Area: 485 x 320 mm, No. of olumns (Display): 7, Col Widths (Display): 43 mm
opy instructions: *Copy Date:* 2 days prior to ublication
OCAL NEWSPAPERS

WEIN+MARKT
747067G21A-4100
ditorial: Weberstr. 9, 55130 MAINZ
el: 6131 620512 **Fax:** 6131 914652
mail: w.engelhard@fraund.de **Web site:** http://www.wein-und-markt.de
req: Monthly; **Annual Sub.:** EUR 88,80; **Circ:** 7,020
ditor: Werner Engelhard; **Advertising Manager:** Dietlind Drees
rofile: Wein+Markt is the specialized magazine for rade, import, distribution and marketing of wine, sparkling wine and related products. An international eam of experienced wine-economy journalists provides the industry and distributors with the oundations for successful business. The trade eaders use the information gathered by Wein+Markt as a basis for decisions on purchasing, assortment ayout and sales. Wein+Markt is the important onnecting link and at the same time part of the wine-business in Germany.
anguage(s): German
ADVERTISING RATES:
Full Page Mono .... EUR 4100
Full Page Colour .... EUR 4100
Mechanical Data: Type Area: 260 x 185 mm, No. of Columns (Display): 4, Col Widths (Display): 43 mm
Copy instructions: *Copy Date:* 16 days prior to publication
BUSINESS: AGRICULTURE & FARMING

WEIN-BOULEVARD
1926422G74P-1303
Editorial: In der Halde 20, 72657 ALTENRIET
Tel: 7127 9315807 **Fax:** 7127 9315808
Email: info@wager.de **Web site:** http://www.wager.de
Freq: Annual; **Cover Price:** Free; **Circ:** 20,000
Editor: Wulf Wager; **Advertising Manager:** Sabine Kaupp
Profile: Wein-Boulevard offers a variety of information about wine in general and to the Stuttgart wines in particular. The best-known wine experts from the region give tips to quality, taste, storage and recreational activities around the theme of wine.
Language(s): German

WEINHEIMER NACHRICHTEN
747060G67B-15520
Editorial: Friedrichstr. 24, 69469 WEINHEIM
Tel: 6201 81160 **Fax:** 6201 81163
Email: wn@diesbachmedien.de **Web site:** http://www.wnoz.de
Freq: 312 issues yearly; **Circ:** 22,999
Advertising Manager: Wolfgang Schlösser
Profile: Daily newspaper with regional news and a local sports section. Facebook: http://www.facebook.com/pages/wnoz/295395650806.
Language(s): German
ADVERTISING RATES:
SCC .... EUR 40,00
Mechanical Data: Type Area: 490 x 320 mm, No. of Columns (Display): 7, Col Widths (Display): 44 mm
Copy instructions: *Copy Date:* 2 days prior to publication
Supplement(s): Wirtschaftsmorgen
REGIONAL DAILY & SUNDAY NEWSPAPERS: Regional Daily Newspapers

WEINWELT
747071G74P-980
Editorial: Maximilianstr. 7, 67433 NEUSTADT
Tel: 6321 890893 **Fax:** 6321 890884
Email: lindemann@meininger.de **Web site:** http://www.weinwelt.info
Freq: 6 issues yearly; **Annual Sub.:** EUR 29,40; **Circ:** 44,133
Editor: Ilka Lindemann; **Advertising Manager:** Ralf Clemens
Profile: weinwelt is the special interest publication for the wine drinker who wants to buy top-quality wines from good grapes at a fair price and enjoy them without complication. weinwelt focuses on the passion for enjoyment - the reader receives numerous practical orientation aids and lots of tips concerning all aspects of wine. Lifestyle-orientated topics, such as travel, gastronomy and spirits, as well as interviews with celebrities, round off the editorial concept. The reader concentrates on the good things in life and belongs to the high-consumption, quality-conscious and brand-orientated target group aged between 30 and 50.
Language(s): German
ADVERTISING RATES:
Full Page Mono .... EUR 5350
Full Page Colour .... EUR 5850
Mechanical Data: Type Area: 260 x 195 mm, No. of Columns (Display): 4, Col Widths (Display): 45 mm
Copy instructions: *Copy Date:* 34 days prior to publication
CONSUMER: WOMEN'S INTEREST CONSUMER MAGAZINES: Food & Cookery

WEINWIRTSCHAFT
747072G9C-6
Editorial: Maximilianstr. 7, 67433 NEUSTADT
Tel: 6321 890869 **Fax:** 6321 890873
Email: pilz@meininger.de **Web site:** http://www.weinwirtschaft.de
Freq: 26 issues yearly; **Annual Sub.:** EUR 156,00; **Circ:** 6,888
Editor: Hermann Pilz; **Advertising Manager:** Ralf Clemens
Profile: Weinwirtschaft is the German trade paper serving the entire professional trade in wines and spirits with the highest number of copies sold. Its circulation has been verified by the German Association for Verification of the Circulation of Advertising Media. Weinwirtschaft is written by professionals for professionals, providing informed comment, analysing trends, and anticipating future market developments. Weinwirtschaft is an essential element in any communications strategy designed to address industry professionals in charge of purchase decisions. Weinwirtschaft is of quite vital importance to producers and importers seeking to maintain and boost existing sales levels. Weinwirtschaft is Germany's No. 1 for wine.
Language(s): German
ADVERTISING RATES:
Full Page Mono .... EUR 3200
Full Page Colour .... EUR 4465
Mechanical Data: Type Area: 260 x 185 mm, No. of Columns (Display): 4, Col Widths (Display): 43 mm
Copy instructions: *Copy Date:* 14 days prior to publication
BUSINESS: DRINKS & LICENSED TRADE: Licensed Trade, Wines & Spirits

WEISSENBURGER TAGBLATT
747079G67B-15540
Editorial: Wildbadstr. 16, 91781 WEISSENBURG
Tel: 9141 859090 **Fax:** 9141 859030
Email: redaktion@weissenburger-tagblatt.com **Web site:** http://www.weissenburger-tagblatt.com
Freq: 312 issues yearly; **Circ:** 10,694
Profile: Daily newspaper with regional news and a local sports section.
Language(s): German
ADVERTISING RATES:
SCC .... EUR 21,80
Mechanical Data: Type Area: 430 x 280 mm, No. of Columns (Display): 6, Col Widths (Display): 45 mm
Copy instructions: *Copy Date:* 2 days prior to publication
REGIONAL DAILY & SUNDAY NEWSPAPERS: Regional Daily Newspapers

WEISSENSEE KOMPAKT
1898600G74M-895
Editorial: Bundesallee 23, 10717 BERLIN
Tel: 30 863030 **Fax:** 30 86303200
Email: info@bfb.de **Web site:** http://www.bfb.de
Freq: Annual; **Cover Price:** Free; **Circ:** 53,000
Profile: Industry district magazine. The core of this handy reference book is neatly sorted according to different themes of industry. Here you will find a plethora of vendors from the neighborhood. In preparation to the respective subject area raises a company, in an interview. To know your environment better, we present in the district windows, etc. beautiful places, monuments, museums, etc. For better orientation in the neighborhood also an integrated neighborhood with street plan is register. Furthermore, the county information you provide an overview of important phone numbers and agencies in your neighborhood.
Language(s): German
ADVERTISING RATES:
Full Page Mono .... EUR 990
Full Page Colour .... EUR 990
Mechanical Data: Type Area: 185 x 126 mm

WEISSWASSERANER WOCHENKURIER
747088G72-15052
Editorial: Wettiner Platz 10, 01067 DRESDEN
Tel: 351 491760 **Fax:** 351 4917674
Email: wochenkurier-dresden@dwk-verlag.de **Web site:** http://www.wochenkurier.info
Freq: Weekly; **Cover Price:** Free; **Circ:** 20,355
Editor: Regine Eberlein; **Advertising Manager:** Andreas Schönherr
Profile: Advertising journal (house-to-house) concentrating on local stories.
Language(s): German
ADVERTISING RATES:
Full Page Mono .... EUR 2439
Full Page Colour .... EUR 3414
Mechanical Data: Type Area: 430 x 290 mm, No. of Columns (Display): 7, Col Widths (Display): 38 mm
Copy instructions: *Copy Date:* 5 days prior to publication
LOCAL NEWSPAPERS

WEITERBILDUNG
728396G88B-460
Editorial: Luxemburger Str. 449, 50939 KÖLN
Tel: 221 943737646 **Fax:** 221 943737757
Email: weiterbildung@wolterskluwer.de **Web site:** http://www.weiterbildung-zeitschrift.de
Freq: 6 issues yearly; **Annual Sub.:** EUR 129,00; **Circ:** 2,000
Editor: Jörg E. Feuchthofen; **Advertising Manager:** Rolf Ganzer
Profile: International journal about further education.
Language(s): German
ADVERTISING RATES:
Full Page Mono .... EUR 700
Full Page Colour .... EUR 1640
Mechanical Data: Type Area: 260 x 184 mm, No. of Columns (Display): 2, Col Widths (Display): 90 mm
CONSUMER: EDUCATION: Adult Education

WELCOME ABOARD
747099G89A-12078
Editorial: von-Tschirsky-Weg 12, 32602 VLOTHO
Tel: 5733 960458 **Fax:** 5733 960459
Email: susanne.mueller@welcome-aboard.de **Web site:** http://www.welcome-aboard.de
Freq: Annual; **Cover Price:** EUR 8,50; **Circ:** 30,000
Editor: Susanne Müller
Profile: Magazine for boat trips with portraits of sea-going cruise ships, sailing, river cruisers, freighters and ferries, cruise reports and a service area for beginners and advanced.
Language(s): German
ADVERTISING RATES:
Full Page Colour .... EUR 3900
Mechanical Data: Type Area: 250 x 200 mm
Copy instructions: *Copy Date:* 60 days prior to publication

WELCOME! MAGAZIN
741345G89A-12113
Editorial: Inselkammerstr. 8, 82008 UNTERHACHING
Tel: 89 6201030 **Fax:** 89 62010325
Freq: Quarterly; **Annual Sub.:** EUR 9,60; **Circ:** 385,280
Editor: Anja Keul
Profile: Customer magazine for owners of the World of TUI Card about travelling, holidays, culture and lifestyle.
Language(s): German
ADVERTISING RATES:
Full Page Mono .... EUR 7600
Full Page Colour .... EUR 7600
Mechanical Data: Type Area: 244 x 190 mm
CONSUMER: HOLIDAYS & TRAVEL: Travel

WELDING AND CUTTING
1793349G27-3037
Editorial: Aachener Str. 172, 40223 DÜSSELDORF
Tel: 211 1591276 **Fax:** 211 1591350
Email: dietmar.rippegather@dvs-hg.de **Web site:** http://www.dvs-media.info
Freq: 6 issues yearly; **Annual Sub.:** EUR 136,00; **Circ:** 10,000
Editor: Dietmar Rippegather; **Advertising Manager:** Iris Jansen
Profile: Official journal of the German Welding Society.
Language(s): English
ADVERTISING RATES:
Full Page Mono .... EUR 2200
Full Page Colour .... EUR 3200
Mechanical Data: Type Area: 253 x 176 mm, No. of Columns (Display): 2, Col Widths (Display): 86 mm

WELLNESS BODY & SPIRIT
1660704G89A-11896
Editorial: Dr.-Andler-Str. 28, 78224 SINGEN
Tel: 7731 912310 **Fax:** 7731 9123130
Email: info@hohentwielverlag.de **Web site:** http://www.hohentwielverlag.de
Freq: Annual; **Cover Price:** EUR 2,00; **Circ:** 40,000
Editor: Pablo Klemann
Profile: Relaxation and recreation at Lake Constance. With Wellness Body & Spirit, we invite you to experience and enjoy the variety of health and wellness offerings. Example, you can discover the power of the sea of beauty and health with the Thalasso therapy. If you are looking for individual treatments and therapies, you will find plenty in Wellness Body & Spirit suggestions. Learn background information on different methods and find answers to the questions as the effect of treatment and indications for which it is suitable. The same applies to the area of alternative careers in the health and wellness area. The rapidly growing need for people to rest, regenerate and conscious life has created many new job around the body, mind and soul. Look forward to seeing some very interesting ways to change your career or further training.
Language(s): German
ADVERTISING RATES:
Full Page Colour .... EUR 1670
Mechanical Data: Type Area: 264 x 190 mm
Copy instructions: *Copy Date:* 10 days prior to publication

DIE WELT
747116G65A-260
Editorial: Axel-Springer-Str. 65, 10969 BERLIN
Tel: 30 25910 **Fax:** 30 259171606
Email: redaktion@welt.de **Web site:** http://www.welt.de
Freq: 312 issues yearly; **Circ:** 274,137
Editor: Jan-Eric Peters; **Advertising Manager:** Michael Haufe
Profile: "DIE WELT" is the national quality newspaper for traditional elites, facing challenges. WELT KOMPAKT, the modern tabloid, is the newspaper for the makers of the modern generation. In the categories politics, economics, finance, and feature DIE WELT offers clearly structured news, analysis and commentaries. Two daily regional editions in Berlin and Hamburg report on local affairs. Additional compact boxes in the different departments also allow the time-poor readers a short, quick information overview. In addition to the current website of WELT ONLINE "DIE WELT" offers many articles under various web addresses, which point directly to topic-related web sources with additional information. Facebook: http://www.facebook.com/weltonline Twitter: http://twitter.com/weltonline This Outlet offers RSS (Really Simple Syndication).
Language(s): German
Readership: Readership includes senior and middle managers, civil servants, decision-makers, the business community, university students and academics.
ADVERTISING RATES:
SCC .... EUR 846,00
Mechanical Data: Col Widths (Display): 45 mm
Copy instructions: *Copy Date:* 1 day prior to publication
Supplement(s): Bier Report; doppio; Feine Welt; KarriereWelt; MotorKompakt
NATIONAL DAILY & SUNDAY NEWSPAPERS: National Daily Newspapers

WELT AKTUELL
1936587G65A-289
Editorial: Axel-Springer-Str. 65, 10969 BERLIN
Tel: 30 25910 **Fax:** 30 259171606
Email: redaktion@welt.de **Web site:** http://www.welt.de
Freq: 260 issues yearly; **Cover Price:** Free; **Circ:** 41,000
Editor: Jan-Eric Peters; **Advertising Manager:** Michael Wittke
Profile: Since January 2010 WELT AKTUELL provides the business and economy class passengers on all Lufthansa flights within Germany on every trading day from 16.30 o'clock on with the most important news of the current day. And since April 2010 the newspaper accompanies the passengers in the first Class of Deutsche Bahn. On the train readers gain the business update of the day already at 15.30 o'clock. WELT AKTUELL reports fast, compact and easy on twelve informative pages in tabloid format. The newspaper presents news from business, government, enterprises, markets and international financial centers. Additionally there are analyses, commentaries and exclusive stories directly from the integrated print and online editorial team of the WELT- group. Facebook: http://www.facebook.com/weltonline.
Language(s): German
ADVERTISING RATES:
SCC .... EUR 172,50
Mechanical Data: No. of Columns (Display): 5, Col Widths (Display): 45 mm, Type Area: 370 x 248 mm
Copy instructions: *Copy Date:* 3 days prior to publication
NATIONAL DAILY & SUNDAY NEWSPAPERS: Unabhängiges konservatives MdEP

WELT AM SONNTAG
747117G65B-2
Editorial: Axel-Springer-Str. 65, 10969 BERLIN
Tel: 30 25910 **Fax:** 30 259177804
Web site: http://www.welt.de
Freq: Weekly; **Annual Sub.:** EUR 114,40; **Circ:** 422,277
Editor: Jan-Eric Peters; **Advertising Manager:** Michael Wittke
Profile: Welt am Sonntag - Germany's large Sunday newspaper. Welt am Sonntag is the market leader of quality Sunday newspapers. Welt am Sonntag publishes a large extent, with a modern look and opulent contents. Numerous photos, diagrams and information boxes help to understand complicated topics. At the same time the Welt am Sonntag is an author medium, where the focus is on the word and on sound arguments. In politics and economy, it is up to date and the news are strong. Editorial diversity is owned to analysis and forecasts from the financial world, exciting sports repots are just as exclusive as contributions from the fields of style and culture, real estate, travel and motor. Facebook: http://www.facebook.com/weltonline Twitter: http://twitter.com/weltonline This Outlet offers RSS (Really Simple Syndication).
Language(s): German
ADVERTISING RATES:
SCC .... EUR 456,50
Mechanical Data: Type Area: 528 x 374 mm, No. of Columns (Display): 8, Col Widths (Display): 45 mm
Copy instructions: *Copy Date:* 2 days prior to publication
Supplement(s): Feine Welt; Feine Welt; Feine Welt; Feine Welt; Feine Welt; Gesund; Icon; MotorKompakt; reiseWelt; Unternehmen an Rhein, Ruhr und Lippe
NATIONAL DAILY & SUNDAY NEWSPAPERS: National Sunday Newspapers

WELT DER FARBEN
747120G16B-150
Editorial: Ostlandstr. 1, 50858 KÖLN
Tel: 2234 73488 **Fax:** 2234 73598
Email: redaktion@welt-der-farben.de **Web site:** http://www.welt-der-farben.de
Freq: 11 issues yearly; **Annual Sub.:** EUR 70,00; **Circ:** 1,500
Editor: Renate Wittsack; **Advertising Manager:** Sabine Esener
Profile: Magazine containing information about the paint, varnish and related industries.
Language(s): German
ADVERTISING RATES:
Full Page Mono .... EUR 1550
Full Page Colour .... EUR 2600

Mechanical Data: Type Area: 250 x 175 mm
Copy instructions: *Copy Date:* 16 days prior to publication
BUSINESS: DECORATING & PAINT: Paint - Technical Manufacture

WELT DER FRAU 1843753G74A-3620
Editorial: Warnstedtstr. 57a, 22525 HAMBURG
Tel: 40 3553870 **Fax:** 40 35538712
Email: weltderfrau@fsmedienservice.de **Web site:** http://www.klambt.de
Freq: Monthly; **Annual Sub.:** EUR 12,00; **Circ:** 133,807
Editor: Andreas Fuchs
Profile: Welt der Frau consciously sets new accents in the world of entertaining women's magazines. It considers itself an engrossing supplement to the palette of informative women's publications and puts the spotlight on itself thanks to its generous size (230 x 295 mm) and elegant high gloss covers. Readers appreciate the well-organized and structured presentation of the topics – fashion, beauty, cooking, travel, health and dietary programme hits. On its 64 pages, this magazine covers the entire spectrum of a modern woman's life in detail. It provides lots of information and carefully researched editorial content. The generously designed visuals make the presentation of photos in the fashion, beauty care, recipe and travel segments particularly attractive. The news reports focus on stories depicting the destinies of "people just like you and I" hands-on. Expert advice complements the journalistic reports. Readers receive genuine assistance on topics such as excessive debt, emergencies, love, marriage, partnership, living with neighbours and educational issues. Emigration? Debt traps? Unemployment? Compelled to sell your house or farm? Neighbourhood topics that move all of us. Everything that affects the lives of women. The latest travel reports take readers through Germany; introduce metropolises such as Hamburg and Bremen. The segment also provides topical information on vacation destinations we all dream to visit – such as Mallorca, Tenerife or South Africa. The magazine introduces the most beautiful beaches, most romantic restaurants and the newest shopping malls. In the self-help section, experts offer readers advice on topics such as rent, money, pensions, vacations – even cats and dogs. The specialists are also available to take reader phone calls and have all of the right answers. Welt der Frau brings beauty and more value to women's lives – thanks to positive journalism!.
Language(s): German
ADVERTISING RATES:
Full Page Mono .... EUR 7450
Full Page Colour .... EUR 7450
Mechanical Data: Type Area: 258 x 209 mm, No. of Columns (Display): 4, Col Widths (Display): 46 mm

WELT DES KINDES 747126G62C-25
Editorial: Karlstr. 40, 79104 FREIBURG
Tel: 761 200270 **Fax:** 761 200671
Email: wdk@caritas.de **Web site:** http://www.welt-des-kindes.info
Freq: 6 issues yearly; Free to qualifying individuals
Annual Sub.: EUR 38,30; **Circ:** 10,000
Editor: Dagmar Wolf
Profile: Journal covering primary education, in and out of school.
Language(s): German
Readership: Aimed at academics, specialists and interested parents.
ADVERTISING RATES:
Full Page Mono .... EUR 850
Full Page Colour .... EUR 1100
Mechanical Data: Type Area: 225 x 172 mm, No. of Columns (Display): 3, Col Widths (Display): 54 mm
BUSINESS: CHURCH & SCHOOL EQUIPMENT & EDUCATION: Junior Education

WELT ONLINE 1663023G65A-276
Editorial: Axel-Springer-Str. 65, 10969 BERLIN
Tel: 30 25910 **Fax:** 30 259117606
Email: redaktion@welt.de **Web site:** http://www.welt.de
Freq: Daily; **Cover Price:** Paid; **Circ:** 34,215,304 Unique Users
Editor: Jan-Eric Peters
Profile: Ezine: Premium news portal in the world group. In addition to extensive coverage in the main categories of politics, economy, money, Panorama and Sport, the portal provides a variety of benefit issues, among others, from the travel, motor, culture and games. Photos and information graphics round - in addition to Facebook and Twitter channel - from the multimedia information. The archive search is one more service component - you can draw on almost 1 million items since 1995. Facebook: http://www.facebook.com/weltonline Twitter: http://twitter.com/weltonline This Outlet offers RSS (Really Simple Syndication).
Language(s): German
NATIONAL DAILY & SUNDAY NEWSPAPERS: National Daily Newspapers

WELTHANDEL 747131G14C-82
Editorial: Postfach 650909, 22369 HAMBURG
Tel: 40 6004670 **Fax:** 40 6013114
Freq: Quarterly; **Annual Sub.:** EUR 15,00; **Circ:** 20,000
Editor: Matthias Grosse; **Advertising Manager:** Peter Fuchs
Profile: The international business magazine informed about events on the world market. Economic analysis, forecasts, briefings and tips, supplemented by recent national reports, come in their streamlined shape, contrary to the information behavior of management.
Language(s): German
ADVERTISING RATES:
Full Page Mono .... EUR 3500
Full Page Colour .... EUR 6125
Mechanical Data: Type Area: 258 x 175 mm, No. of Columns (Display): 3, Col Widths (Display): 55 mm
Copy instructions: *Copy Date:* 20 days prior to publication
BUSINESS: COMMERCE, INDUSTRY & MANAGEMENT: International Commerce

WELTKUNST 747133G84A-3624
Editorial: Balanstr. 73/Geb.8, 81541 MÜNCHEN
Tel: 89 12699029 **Fax:** 89 12699015
Email: ute.stimmer@weltkunst.de **Web site:** http://www.zeitkunstverlag.de
Freq: 14 issues yearly; **Annual Sub.:** EUR 139,30; **Circ:** 20,000
Editor: Holger Christmann; **Advertising Manager:** Stephanie Förster
Profile: Weltkunst is the most respected magazine for art and antiques in German-speaking Europe. Sensual, opulent and professional based Weltkunst focuses on the offers of art trade, galleries and auctioneers, shows what is collected and traded and presented in museums - all in four- teen issues per year. Aside new sections and columns glitter in Weltkunst: art journeys accompanied by reportages and insider tips, visiting studios of interesting artists and museums with important persons, the style guide and the column of famous Florian Illies. As leading magazine for art Weltkunst appeals to private art collectors and art lovers as well as to professionals: art traders, gallery owners, auctioneers and art historian esteem the well-informed variety. The sophisticated claims of this well-educated and quality conscious readership are uniquely satisfied by the expertise of Weltkunst. Facebook: http://www.facebook.com/weltkunst.
Language(s): German
Readership: Aimed at antiques and art dealers.
ADVERTISING RATES:
Full Page Mono .... EUR 1770
Full Page Colour .... EUR 2540
Mechanical Data: Type Area: 271 x 188 mm, No. of Columns (Display): 4, Col Widths (Display): 43 mm
Copy instructions: *Copy Date:* 30 days prior to publication
Official Journal of: Organ d. Bundesverb. d. Dt. Kunst- u. Antiquitätenhandels e.V., d. Berufsgruppe d. österr. Antiquitätenhandels, d. Verb. schweizer. Antiquare u. Kunsthändler u. d. Vereinigung d. Händler in alter Kunst in d. Niederlanden
Supplement(s): Kunst in Salzburg
CONSUMER: THE ARTS & LITERARY: Arts

WELZHEIMER ZEITUNG 747151G67B-15560
Editorial: Albrecht-Villinger-Str. 10, 71332 WAIBLINGEN **Tel:** 7151 5660 **Fax:** 7151 566402
Email: welzheim@redaktion.zvw.de **Web site:** http://www.welzheimer-zeitung.de
Freq: 312 issues yearly; **Circ:** 3,465
Advertising Manager: Michael Feßler
Profile: Daily newspaper with regional news and a local sports section.
Language(s): German
ADVERTISING RATES:
SCC .... EUR 25,00
Mechanical Data: Type Area: 485 x 324 mm, No. of Columns (Display): 7, Col Widths (Display): 44 mm
Copy instructions: *Copy Date:* 2 days prior to publication
Supplement(s): Schaufenster
REGIONAL DAILY & SUNDAY NEWSPAPERS: Regional Daily Newspapers

WENDLINGER ZEITUNG 747159G67B-15580
Editorial: Carl-Benz-Str. 1, 72622 NÜRTINGEN
Tel: 7022 9464129 **Fax:** 7022 9464111
Email: forum@ntz.de **Web site:** http://www.ntz.de
Freq: 312 issues yearly; **Circ:** 22,088
Advertising Manager: Victor Stroner
Profile: Daily newspaper with regional news and a local sports section.
Language(s): German
ADVERTISING RATES:
SCC .... EUR 45,80
Mechanical Data: Type Area: 485 x 321 mm, No. of Columns (Display): 7, Col Widths (Display): 43 mm
Copy instructions: *Copy Date:* 2 days prior to publication
REGIONAL DAILY & SUNDAY NEWSPAPERS: Regional Daily Newspapers

WENDLINGER ZEITUNG NÜRTINGER ZEITUNG 1621791G67B-16625
Editorial: Carl-Benz-Str. 1, 72622 NÜRTINGEN
Tel: 7022 94640 **Fax:** 7022 9464111
Email: forum@ntz.de **Web site:** http://www.ntz.de
Freq: Daily; **Cover Price:** Paid; **Circ:** 68,702 Unique Users
Advertising Manager: Daniel Gebühr
Profile: Ezine: Daily newspaper with regional news and a local sports section.
Language(s): German
REGIONAL DAILY & SUNDAY NEWSPAPERS: Regional Daily Newspapers

WENDY 747160G91D-9100
Editorial: Wallstr. 59, 10179 BERLIN **Tel:** 30 240080
Fax: 30 24008455
Email: s.saydo@ehapa.de **Web site:** http://www.wendy.de
Freq: 26 issues yearly; **Annual Sub.:** EUR 65,00; **Circ:** 62,623
Editor: Sanya Saydo
Profile: Youth magazine for horse enthusiasts girls. And it's only in Wendy! Listen to pages 23 pages comic adventure. Dream up with the photo story to fantastic scenes of the most beautiful horses. Learn all about the great horses of the world. And get the tendigsten Extras! Wendy - horse up close! Every 2 weeks new!.
Language(s): German
Readership: Aimed at girls between the ages of 8 and 15 years.
ADVERTISING RATES:
Full Page Mono .... EUR 6900
Full Page Colour .... EUR 6900
Mechanical Data: Type Area: 297 x 210 mm, No. of Columns (Display): 4, Col Widths (Display): 52 mm
CONSUMER: RECREATION & LEISURE: Children & Youth

WERDEN KURIER 747182G72-15096
Editorial: Hauptstr. 48, 45219 ESSEN
Tel: 2054 923718 **Fax:** 2054 85545
Email: redaktion@werdenkurier-essen.de **Web site:** http://www.lokalkompass.de/essen-werden
Freq: 104 issues yearly; **Cover Price:** Free; **Circ:** 10,700
Editor: Melanie Hohmann; **Advertising Manager:** Lars Staehler
Profile: Advertising journal (house-to-house) concentrating on local stories.
Language(s): German
ADVERTISING RATES:
Full Page Mono .... EUR 2025
Full Page Colour .... EUR 2734
Mechanical Data: Type Area: 445 x 315 mm, No. of Columns (Display): 7, Col Widths (Display): 42 mm
Copy instructions: *Copy Date:* 2 days prior to publication
LOCAL NEWSPAPERS

WERDENER NACHRICHTEN 747180G72-15100
Editorial: Grafenstr. 41, 45239 ESSEN
Tel: 201 849419 **Fax:** 201 849422
Email: redaktion@werdener-nachrichten.de
Freq: Weekly; **Cover Price:** EUR 0,95; **Circ:** 3,373
Editor: Gereon Buchholz; **Advertising Manager:** Oliver Nothelfer
Profile: Regional weekly covering politics, economics, sport, travel, technology and the arts.
Language(s): German
ADVERTISING RATES:
SCC .... EUR 25,20
Mechanical Data: Type Area: 445 x 325 mm, No. of Columns (Display): 7, Col Widths (Display): 45 mm
Copy instructions: *Copy Date:* 2 days prior to publication
LOCAL NEWSPAPERS

WERKSTATT: PRAXIS 1752898G4E-7104
Editorial: Deichmanns Aue 31, 53179 BONN
Tel: 22899 4011594
Email: nina.wilke@bbr.bund.de
Cover Price: Free; **Circ:** 800
Profile: Publication of practical results on the topics of Spatial and Urban Planning, Housing and Construction.
Language(s): German

WERKSTOFFE IN DER FERTIGUNG 747200G19E-145
Editorial: Sonnenblumenring 35, 86415 MERING
Tel: 8233 780205 **Fax:** 8233 32762
Email: info@werkstoffzeitschrift.de **Web site:** http://www.werkstoffzeitschrift.de
Freq: 6 issues yearly; **Annual Sub.:** EUR 64,20; **Circ:** 10,900
Editor: Manfred Kittel; **Advertising Manager:** Tina Tauscher
Profile: Journal covering production materials.
Language(s): German
ADVERTISING RATES:
Full Page Mono .... EUR 2880
Full Page Colour .... EUR 3330
Mechanical Data: Type Area: 276 x 185 mm, No. of Columns (Display): 4, Col Widths (Display): 44 mm
Copy instructions: *Copy Date:* 14 days prior to publication
BUSINESS: ENGINEERING & MACHINERY: Machinery, Machine Tools & Metalworking

WERKZEUG & FORMENBAU 747203G19E-1800
Editorial: Justus-von-Liebig-Str. 1, 86899 LANDSBERG **Tel:** 8191 125697 **Fax:** 8191 125822
Email: richard.pergler@mi-verlag.de **Web site:** http://www.werkzeugundformenbau.de
Freq: 5 issues yearly; **Annual Sub.:** EUR 72,80; **Circ:** 10,131
Editor: Richard Pergler; **Advertising Manager:** Helmut Schempp
Profile: Premium Magazine for the tooling, molds, dies, jigs and fixtures industry. For content tool & mold building is aligned with the core products in the industry and thus a mirror image of the professional world of his receivers. The magazine offers its readers, therefore, a unique, fast and direct access to industry-related information. A holistic view of technological and organizational process chain in the form of feature articles, trend reports, user stories and product reviews, the magazine also provides the basis for the economic optimization of workflows.
Language(s): German
Readership: Aimed at those involved in the engineering sector.
ADVERTISING RATES:
Full Page Mono .... EUR 404
Full Page Colour .... EUR 538
Mechanical Data: Type Area: 257 x 178 mm, No. of Columns (Display): 4, Col Widths (Display): 41 mm
Copy instructions: *Copy Date:* 28 days prior to publication
BUSINESS: ENGINEERING & MACHINERY: Machinery, Machine Tools & Metalworking

WERRA-RUNDSCHAU 747219G67B-15640
Editorial: Vor dem Berge 2, 37269 ESCHWEGE
Tel: 5651 335933 **Fax:** 5651 335944
Email: redaktion@werra-rundschau.de **Web site:** http://www.werra-rundschau.de
Freq: 312 issues yearly; **Circ:** 11,065
Editor: Dieter Salzmann; **Advertising Manager:** Uwe Hammann
Profile: Daily newspaper with regional news and a local sports section.
Language(s): German
ADVERTISING RATES:
SCC .... EUR 24,70
Mechanical Data: Type Area: 430 x 285 mm, No. of Columns (Display): 6, Col Widths (Display): 45 mm
Copy instructions: *Copy Date:* 2 days prior to publication
REGIONAL DAILY & SUNDAY NEWSPAPERS: Regional Daily Newspapers

WERTHEIMER ZEITUNG 747227G67B-15660
Editorial: Weichertstr. 20, 63741 ASCHAFFENBURG
Tel: 6021 396299 **Fax:** 6021 396499
Email: redaktion@main-echo.de **Web site:** http://www.main-netz.de
Freq: 312 issues yearly; **Circ:** 4,512
Advertising Manager: Reinhard Fresow
Profile: Daily newspaper with regional news and a local sports section. Twitter: http://twitter.com/mainnetz This Outlet offers RSS (Really Simple Syndication).
Language(s): German
ADVERTISING RATES:
SCC .... EUR 18,10
Mechanical Data: Type Area: 480 x 366 mm, No. of Columns (Display): 8, Col Widths (Display): 44 mm
Copy instructions: *Copy Date:* 1 day prior to publication
Supplement(s): Gesundheit!
REGIONAL DAILY & SUNDAY NEWSPAPERS: Regional Daily Newspapers

WERTINGER ZEITUNG 747229G67B-15680
Editorial: Curt-Frenzel-Str. 2, 86167 AUGSBURG
Tel: 821 7770 **Fax:** 821 7772067
Web site: http://www.augsburger-allgemeine.de
Freq: 312 issues yearly; **Circ:** 5,366
Advertising Manager: Herbert Dachs
Profile: Daily newspaper with regional news and a local sports section. Facebook: http://www.facebook.com/AugsburgerAllgemeine Twitter: http://twitter.com/AZ_Augsburg This Outlet offers RSS (Really Simple Syndication).
Language(s): German
ADVERTISING RATES:
SCC .... EUR 40,10
Mechanical Data: Type Area: 480 x 327 mm, No. of Columns (Display): 7, Col Widths (Display): 45 mm
Copy instructions: *Copy Date:* 1 day prior to publication
REGIONAL DAILY & SUNDAY NEWSPAPERS: Regional Daily Newspapers

WESER LOTSE LOGISTICS PILOT 747246G45A-922
Editorial: Stader Str. 35, 28205 BREMEN
Tel: 421 7929996 **Fax:** 421 323891
Email: konrad@moskito.de **Web site:** http://www.moskito.de
Freq: 6 issues yearly; **Cover Price:** EUR 4,00
Free to qualifying individuals ; **Circ:** 4,000
Editor: Jürgen W. Konrad; **Advertising Manager:** Claudia Stuhrmann
Profile: Magazine for the transportation and logistics industry information, practical with exclusive background reports and analysis and carefully recherierten contributions. Per issue, the magazine has one main theme, a special and the following headings: News from ports + transport industry, company profile, e-Logistics, book reviews, Fairs and Congresses Spedition + fleet + insurance + law banks, training and careers, lines + agencies and personal.
Language(s): English; German
ADVERTISING RATES:
Full Page Mono .... EUR 1235
Full Page Colour .... EUR 1895
Mechanical Data: Type Area: 268 x 184 mm

opy instructions: *Copy Date:* 17 days prior to
blication
USINESS: MARINE & SHIPPING

/ESER-EMS MANAGER
1896369G14A-10284
litorial: Brückenort 15, 49565 BRAMSCHE
el: 5461 940222 **Fax:** 5461 940220
mail: n.salagaray@verlagkroeber.de **Web site:**
:p://weser-ems-manager.de
eq: 11 issues yearly; **Annual Sub.:** EUR 28,00;
rc: 19,685
litor: Nicholas Salagaray; **Advertising Manager:**
artin Bock
rofile: Business Magazine Weser-Ems. The journal
ll act as a voice for diverse operating companies,
ambers, guilds and associations and support the
esence of this dynamic economic region. The
agazine provides information and reports on
gional economic issues and provides relevant
ackground, industry-specific reports. Market
rveys and company rankings give you guidance in
lecting suppliers and customer acquisition. The
agazine features in particular the regional
tegration of issues of great value and especially as
valuable aid to management.
anguage(s): German
OVERTISING RATES:
ull Page Mono .... EUR 2490
ull Page Colour .... EUR 2490
echanical Data: Type Area: 260 x 188 mm

/ESER-KURIER
747245G67B-15700
ditorial: Martinistr. 43, 28195 BREMEN
el: 421 36710 **Fax:** 421 328327
mail: redaktion@weser-kurier.de **Web site:** http://
ww.weser-kurier.de
req: 312 issues yearly; **Circ:** 169,335
ditor: Helge Matthiesen
rofile: Regional daily newspaper with news on
olitics, economy, culture, sports, travel, technology,
c. Facebook: http://www.facebook.com/pages/
eser-kurierde/48412147711 Twitter: http://
vitter.com/WESER_KURIER This Outlet offers RSS
Really Simple Syndication).
anguage(s): German
OVERTISING RATES:
CC .... EUR 284,50
echanical Data: Type Area: 490 x 334 mm, No. of
olumns (Display): 7, Col Widths (Display): 46 mm
opy instructions: *Copy Date:* 1 day prior to
ublication
upplement(s): bremer kirchenzeitung; Ferienjournal;
ochen Journal
EGIONAL DAILY & SUNDAY NEWSPAPERS:
egional Daily Newspapers

/ESER-KURIER ONLINE
1622198G67B-16687
ditorial: Martinistr. 43, 28195 BREMEN
el: 421 36713575 **Fax:** 421 36711000
mail: online@weser-kurier.de **Web site:** http://www.
eser-kurier.de
req: Daily; **Cover Price:** Paid; **Circ:** 1,225,845
nique Users
ditor: Iris Hetscher
rofile: Ezine: Regional daily newspaper covering
olitics, economics, culture, sport, travel and
echnology.
anguage(s): German
EGIONAL DAILY & SUNDAY NEWSPAPERS:
egional Daily Newspapers

WEST ANZEIGER
747262G72-15208
ditorial: Bert-Brecht-Str. 29, 45128 ESSEN
el: 201 8042068 **Fax:** 201 8042995
mail: redaktion@westanzeiger-essen.de **Web site:**
ttp://www.lokalkompass.de/essen-west
req: 104 issues yearly; **Cover Price:** Free; **Circ:**
1,600
ditor: Frank Blum; **Advertising Manager:** Lars
Staehler
rofile: Advertising journal (house-to-house)
oncentrating on local stories.
anguage(s): German
ADVERTISING RATES:
Full Page Mono .... EUR 3334
Full Page Colour .... EUR 4500
Mechanical Data: Type Area: 445 x 315 mm, No. of
Columns (Display): 7, Col Widths (Display): 42 mm
Copy instructions: *Copy Date:* 2 days prior to
publication
LOCAL NEWSPAPERS

DER WESTALLGÄUER
747261G67B-15720
Editorial: Fridolin-Holzer-Str. 18, 88171 WEILER-SIMMERBERG **Tel:** 8387 3990 **Fax:** 8387 2729
Email: redaktion@westallgaeuer-zeitung.de **Web site:** http://www.westallgaeuer-zeitung.de
Freq: 312 issues yearly; **Circ:** 8,019
Advertising Manager: Claus Helmbrecht
Profile: Daily newspaper with regional news and a local sports section.
Language(s): German
ADVERTISING RATES:
SCC .... EUR 46,10
Mechanical Data: Type Area: 480 x 327 mm, No. of Columns (Display): 7, Col Widths (Display): 45 mm
Copy instructions: *Copy Date:* 2 days prior to publication
Supplement(s): allgäu weit; allgäu weit Allgäuer Kultursommer; allgäu weit Gesundheit; allgäu weit Sommer; allgäu weit Winter; Golfregion Allgäu; rtv; Die Schwäbische Bäderstrasse Kraft-Quellen; Westallgäu-Dribbler
REGIONAL DAILY & SUNDAY NEWSPAPERS:
Regional Daily Newspapers

WESTDEUTSCHE ALLGEMEINE WATTENSCHEIDER ZEITUNG WAZ
747266G67B-15740
Editorial: Friedrichstr. 34, 45128 ESSEN
Tel: 201 8040 **Fax:** 201 8046539
Email: zentralredaktion@waz.de **Web site:** http://www.derwesten.de
Freq: 312 issues yearly; **Circ:** 57,900
Advertising Manager: Christian Klaucke
Profile: Germany's largest regional newspaper. Inextricably linked with the development of the Ruhr area is the success story of the Westdeutsche Allgemeine WAZ. Since its first publication on 3.4.1948, it helped shaping the region Ruhr, Emscher and Lippe like no other medium. Licensee and publisher Erich Brost created a newspaper of Anglo-Saxon model. The focus was and is independent and nonpartisan. Together with the co-editor James Funke, he conducted the most successful newspaper start-up after the war. Today, the WAZ is Germany's largest regional newspaper, its range extends from the southern Münsterland to the Niederbergische Region, from the Lower Rhine up to the Region of Unna. The total area is approximately 4450 sq km. In the Ruhr area cities Essen, Bochum, Gelsenkirchen, Duisburg, Oberhausen and Mülheim an der Ruhr, WAZ is the leading daily newspaper. The newspaper of the Ruhr area has always listened to the citizens. In it people of the territory find themselves. In the city happens. The WAZ reports and commentes close to its readers and unaffected. The Westdeutsche Allgemeine Wattenscheider Zeitung WAZ is a regional edition of the Westdeutsche Allgemeine WAZ. Facebook: http://www.facebook.com/derwesten.
Language(s): German
ADVERTISING RATES:
SCC .... EUR 150,80
Mechanical Data: Type Area: 445 x 320 mm, No. of Columns (Display): 7, Col Widths (Display): 44 mm
Copy instructions: *Copy Date:* 2 days prior to publication
Supplement(s): Aufsteiger; Mein Auto; Mein Beruf; Meine besten Jahre; Meine Familie; Meine Freizeit; Meine Weihnacht; Mein neues Jahr!; Mein Shopping; Mein Stil; Mein Team; Mein Urlaub; Mein Zuhause; Theaterzeitung
REGIONAL DAILY & SUNDAY NEWSPAPERS:
Regional Daily Newspapers

WESTDEUTSCHE ALLGEMEINE WAZ
747267G67B-15760
Editorial: Friedrichstr. 34, 45128 ESSEN
Tel: 201 8040 **Fax:** 201 8046539
Email: zentralredaktion@waz.de **Web site:** http://www.derwesten.de
Freq: 312 issues yearly; **Circ:** 594,230
Editor: Ulrich Reitz; **News Editor:** Yvonne Szabo;
Advertising Manager: Christian Klaucke
Profile: Germany's largest regional newspaper. Inextricably linked with the development of the Ruhr area is the success story of the Westdeutsche Allgemeine WAZ. Since its first publication on 3.4.1948, it helped shaping the region Ruhr, Emscher and Lippe like no other medium. Licensee and publisher Erich Brost created a newspaper of Anglo-Saxon model. The focus was and is independent and nonpartisan. Together with the co-editor James Funke, he conducted the most successful newspaper start-up after the war. Today, the WAZ is Germany's largest regional newspaper, its range extends from the southern Münsterland to the Niederbergische Region, from the Lower Rhine up to the Region of Unna. The total area is approximately 4450 sq km. In the Ruhr area cities Essen, Bochum, Gelsenkirchen, Duisburg, Oberhausen and Mülheim an der Ruhr, WAZ is the leading daily newspaper. The newspaper of the Ruhr area has always listened to the citizens. In it people of the territory find themselves. In the city happens. The WAZ reports and commentes close to its readers and unaffected. Facebook: http://www.facebook.com/derwesten.
Language(s): German
ADVERTISING RATES:
SCC .... EUR 1435,60
Mechanical Data: Type Area: 445 x 320 mm, No. of Columns (Display): 7, Col Widths (Display): 44 mm
Copy instructions: *Copy Date:* 2 days prior to publication
Supplement(s): Aktuell; Aufsteiger; Durch Blick; Essen.Erleben.; Limbecker Platz Aktuell; Mein Auto; Mein Beruf; Meine besten Jahre; Meine Familie; Meine Freizeit; Mein Essen kompakt; Meine Weihnacht; Mein neues Jahr!; Mein Shopping; Mein Stil; Mein Team; Mein Urlaub; Mein Zuhause; Rathaus Galerie Essen Journal; Rhein-Ruhr Zentrum Aktuell; rtv; Theater Dortmund; Theaterzeitung; WAZ Wirtschaft
REGIONAL DAILY & SUNDAY NEWSPAPERS:
Regional Daily Newspapers

WESTDEUTSCHE ZEITUNG
748444G67B-16300
Editorial: Königsallee 27, 40212 DÜSSELDORF
Tel: 211 83820 **Fax:** 211 83822392
Email: westdeutsche.zeitung@wz-newsline.de **Web site:** http://www.wz-newsline.de
Freq: 312 issues yearly; **Circ:** 123,603
Editor: Martin Vogler; **News Editor:** Alexander Marinos; **Advertising Manager:** Thomas Müllenborn
Profile: Regional daily newspaper covering politics, economics, culture, sports, travel and technology. This Outlet offers RSS (Really Simple Syndication).
Language(s): German
ADVERTISING RATES:
SCC .... EUR 452,50
Mechanical Data: Type Area: 430 x 282 mm, No. of Columns (Display): 6, Col Widths (Display): 45 mm
Copy instructions: *Copy Date:* 2 days prior to publication
Supplement(s): prisma
REGIONAL DAILY & SUNDAY NEWSPAPERS:
Regional Daily Newspapers

DER WESTERWALD
747277G57-2520
Editorial: Koblenzer Str. 17, 56410 MONTABAUR
Tel: 2602 9496690 **Fax:** 2602 9496691
Email: info@westerwaldverein.de **Web site:** http://www.westerwaldverein.de
Freq: Quarterly; **Circ:** 5,700
Profile: Magazine about nature conservation, tourism and environmental protection in the Westerwald region.
Language(s): German
ADVERTISING RATES:
Full Page Mono .... EUR 383
Mechanical Data: Type Area: 214 x 146 mm, No. of Columns (Display): 2, Col Widths (Display): 70 mm
Copy instructions: *Copy Date:* 30 days prior to publication

WESTERWÄLDER ZEITUNG
747276G67B-15780
Editorial: August-Horch-Str. 28, 56070 KOBLENZ
Tel: 261 892240 **Fax:** 261 892770
Email: redaktion@rhein-zeitung.net **Web site:** http://www.rhein-zeitung.de
Freq: 312 issues yearly; **Circ:** 25,424
Profile: Regional daily newspaper with news on politics, economy, culture, sports, travel, technology, etc. The Westerwälder Zeitung is a local issue the in koblenz appearing Rhein-Zeitung. Facebook: http://www.facebook.com/rheinzeitung Twitter: http://www.rhein-zeitung.de/twitter.html This Outlet offers RSS (Really Simple Syndication).
Language(s): German
ADVERTISING RATES:
SCC .... EUR 81,60
Mechanical Data: Type Area: 480 x 325 mm, No. of Columns (Display): 7, Col Widths (Display): 45 mm
Copy instructions: *Copy Date:* 1 day prior to publication
Supplement(s): kulturInfo
REGIONAL DAILY & SUNDAY NEWSPAPERS:
Regional Daily Newspapers

WESTFALEN REPORTER
747292G33-340
Editorial: Industrieweg 43, 48155 MÜNSTER
Tel: 251 695309 **Fax:** 251 69573309
Email: redaktion@westfalen-ag.de **Web site:** http://www.westfalen-ag.de
Freq: 3 issues yearly; **Circ:** 6,700
Editor: Jürgen Erwert
Profile: Company publication published by Westfalen AG.
Language(s): German

WESTFALEN-BLATT
747290G67B-15800
Editorial: Sudbrackstr. 14, 33611 BIELEFELD
Tel: 521 5850 **Fax:** 521 585489
Email: wb@westfalen-blatt.de **Web site:** http://www.westfalen-blatt.de
Freq: 312 issues yearly; **Circ:** 131,283
Editor: André Best; **News Editor:** Andreas Kolesch;
Advertising Manager: Gabriele Förster
Profile: Regional daily newspaper covering politics, economics, culture, sports, travel and technology.
Language(s): German
Mechanical Data: Type Area: 490 x 320 mm, No. of Columns (Display): 7, Col Widths (Display): 44 mm
Copy instructions: *Copy Date:* 1 day prior to publication
Supplement(s): Bielefeld heute; Denkste; Fit Besser leben; Mein Garten; prisma; Scheinfrei; Wir Generation 60 plus; www.wb-immo.net
REGIONAL DAILY & SUNDAY NEWSPAPERS:
Regional Daily Newspapers

WESTFALENSPIEGEL
747294G80-12980
Editorial: An den Speichern 6, 48157 MÜNSTER
Tel: 251 4132215 **Fax:** 251 413220
Email: sluka@westfalenspiegel.de **Web site:** http://www.westfalenspiegel.de
Freq: 6 issues yearly; **Annual Sub.:** EUR 21,60; **Circ:** 14,000
Editor: Klaudia Sluka; **Advertising Manager:** Ulrike Schulze Schwienhorst
Profile: Magazine covering culture, events and tourism in the Westfalen area.
Language(s): German
ADVERTISING RATES:
Full Page Mono .... EUR 1360
Full Page Colour .... EUR 2160
Mechanical Data: No. of Columns (Display): 3, Col Widths (Display): 55 mm, Type Area: 260 x 175 mm
Copy instructions: *Copy Date:* 31 days prior to publication
CONSUMER: RURAL & REGIONAL INTEREST

WESTFÄLISCHE NACHRICHTEN
747281G67B-15820
Editorial: An der Hansalinie 1, 48163 MÜNSTER
Tel: 251 6900 **Fax:** 251 690717
Email: redaktion@westfaelische-nachrichten.de **Web site:** http://www.westfaelische-nachrichten.de
Freq: 312 issues yearly; **Circ:** 231,800
Profile: Daily newspaper with regional news and a local sports section. Facebook: http://www.facebook.com/wnonline Twitter: http://twitter.com/WN_Muenster This Outlet offers RSS (Really Simple Syndication).
Language(s): German
ADVERTISING RATES:
SCC .... EUR 368,90
Mechanical Data: Type Area: 488 x mm, No. of Columns (Display): 7
Copy instructions: *Copy Date:* 1 day prior to publication
Supplement(s): lenz; prisma; yango family
REGIONAL DAILY & SUNDAY NEWSPAPERS:
Regional Daily Newspapers

WESTFÄLISCHER ANZEIGER
747282G67B-15840
Editorial: Gutenbergstr. 1, 59065 HAMM
Tel: 2381 105242 **Fax:** 2381 105239
Email: redaktion@wa.de **Web site:** http://www.wa.de
Freq: 312 issues yearly; **Circ:** 141,826
Advertising Manager: Steffen Schulle
Profile: Regional daily newspaper covering politics, economics, sport, travel and technology. Twitter: http://twitter.com/wa_online This Outlet offers RSS (Really Simple Syndication).
Language(s): German
ADVERTISING RATES:
SCC .... EUR 334,00
Mechanical Data: Type Area: 466 x 317 mm, No. of Columns (Display): 7, Col Widths (Display): 43 mm
Copy instructions: *Copy Date:* 1 day prior to publication
Supplement(s): prisma
REGIONAL DAILY & SUNDAY NEWSPAPERS:
Regional Daily Newspapers

WESTFÄLISCHES ÄRZTEBLATT
747283G56A-10160
Editorial: Gartenstr. 210, 48147 MÜNSTER
Tel: 251 9292102 **Fax:** 251 9292149
Email: pressestelle@aekwl.de **Web site:** http://www.aekwl.de
Freq: Monthly; Free to qualifying individuals
Annual Sub.: EUR 79,20; **Circ:** 37,200
Editor: Klaus Dercks; **Advertising Manager:** Elke Adick
Profile: The "Westfälische Ärzteblatt" is the official journal of the Medical Association of Westfalen-Lippe. The newspaper is editorially and technically supervised by the press office and informed members of the editorial content of activities and positions of their body. Also includes the "Westfälische Ärzteblatt" all important official notices, decisions and relevant legal requirements. Most importantly, it provides comprehensive information on events organized by Academy for joint medical training of the Medical Association of Westfalen-Lippe doctors' association and the Westfalen-Lippe.
Language(s): German
ADVERTISING RATES:
Full Page Mono .... EUR 2270
Full Page Colour .... EUR 3460
Mechanical Data: Type Area: 250 x 185 mm, No. of Columns (Display): 4, Col Widths (Display): 44 mm
Copy instructions: *Copy Date:* 20 days prior to publication
BUSINESS: HEALTH & MEDICAL

WESTFÄLISCHES VOLKSBLATT
747285G67B-15860
Editorial: Imadstr. 40, 33102 PADERBORN
Tel: 5251 8960 **Fax:** 5251 896112
Email: redaktion@westfaelisches-volksblatt.de
Freq: 312 issues yearly; **Circ:** 45,244
Profile: Daily newspaper with regional news and a local sports section.
Language(s): German
Mechanical Data: Type Area: 490 x 320 mm, No. of Columns (Display): 7, Col Widths (Display): 44 mm
Copy instructions: *Copy Date:* 1 day prior to publication
REGIONAL DAILY & SUNDAY NEWSPAPERS:
Regional Daily Newspapers

WESTLINE
1622201G67B-16690
Editorial: Westenhellweg 86, 44137 DORTMUND
Tel: 231 90597905 **Fax:** 231 90598707
Email: redaktion@westline.de **Web site:** http://www.westline.de
Freq: Daily; **Cover Price:** Paid; **Circ:** 1,008,496 Unique Users
Profile: Ezine: Regional daily newspaper covering politics, economics, sport, travel and technology.
Language(s): German
REGIONAL DAILY & SUNDAY NEWSPAPERS:
Regional Daily Newspapers

WESTPFALZ-INFORMATIONEN
1856088G14A-10209
Editorial: Bahnhofstr. 1, 67655 KAISERSLAUTERN
Tel: 631 20577411 **Fax:** 631 20577420

Email: clev@westpfalz.de **Web site:** http://www.westpfalz.de
Freq: 3 issues yearly; **Cover Price:** Free; **Circ:** 850
Editor: Hans-Günther Clev
Profile: Regional magazine about environment, economy, transportation and tourism in Western Palatinate.
Language(s): German

WESTRICHER RUNDSCHAU
747303G72-15232
Editorial: Europaallee 2, 54343 FÖHREN
Tel: 6502 91470 **Fax:** 6502 7240
Email: redaktion@wittich-foehren.de **Web site:** http://www.wittich.de
Freq: Weekly; **Circ:** 5,200
Editor: Monika Rube; **Advertising Manager:** Klaus Wirth
Profile: Local official paper.
Language(s): German
ADVERTISING RATES:
Full Page Mono .... EUR 594
Full Page Colour .... EUR 664
Mechanical Data: Type Area: 275 x 185 mm, No. of Columns (Display): 2, Col Widths (Display): 90 mm
Copy instructions: *Copy Date:* 5 days prior to publication
LOCAL NEWSPAPERS

WETTERAUER ZEITUNG
747312G67B-15880
Editorial: Marburger Str. 18, 35390 GIESSEN
Tel: 641 30030 **Fax:** 641 3003305
Email: redaktion@wetterauer-zeitung.de **Web site:** http://www.wetterauer-zeitung.de
Freq: 312 issues yearly; **Circ:** 21,643
Advertising Manager: Wilfried Kämpf
Profile: Regional daily newspaper with news on politics, economy, culture, sports, travel, technology, etc. The Wetterauer Zeitung is the leading daily newspaper of the Wetterau district with a range of over 65,000 readers daily in the area of distribution. The percentage of subscribers to the paid circulation is 94%.
Language(s): German
ADVERTISING RATES:
SCC .... EUR 43,20
Mechanical Data: Type Area: 430 x 282 mm, No. of Columns (Display): 6, Col Widths (Display): 45 mm
Copy instructions: *Copy Date:* 1 day prior to publication
Supplement(s): streifzug
REGIONAL DAILY & SUNDAY NEWSPAPERS: Regional Daily Newspapers

WETTER.COM
1703755G91B-2535
Editorial: Werner-von-Siemens-Str. 22, 78224 SINGEN **Tel:** 7731 8380 **Fax:** 7731 83819
Email: contact@wetter.com **Web site:** http://www.wetter.com
Freq: Daily; **Cover Price:** Paid; **Circ:** 82,081,602 Unique Users
Editor: Hartmut Mühlbauer
Language(s): German
CONSUMER: RECREATION & LEISURE: Camping & Caravanning

WETZLARER NEUE ZEITUNG
747320G67B-15900
Editorial: Elsa-Brandström-Str. 18, 35578 WETZLAR
Tel: 6441 9590 **Fax:** 6441 959292
Email: redaktion.wnz@mittelhessen.de **Web site:** http://www.mittelhessen.de
Freq: 312 issues yearly; **Circ:** 25,825
Editor: Uwe Röndigs; **News Editor:** Michael Klein; **Advertising Manager:** Peter Rother
Profile: Regional daily newspaper covering politics, economics, culture, sports, travel and technology. This Outlet offers RSS (Really Simple Syndication).
Language(s): German
ADVERTISING RATES:
SCC .... EUR 66,50
Mechanical Data: Type Area: 490 x 328 mm, No. of Columns (Display): 7, Col Widths (Display): 44 mm
Copy instructions: *Copy Date:* 1 day prior to publication
Supplement(s): [f]amilie& freizeit; Fußball-Kalender; [g]esund!; Handball-Kalender; lahndillregio; rtv; Wetzlarer Hefte Das Stadtmagazin
REGIONAL DAILY & SUNDAY NEWSPAPERS: Regional Daily Newspapers

WETZLARER NEUE ZEITUNG AM SONNTAG
1606897G72-17865
Editorial: Elsa-Brandström-Str. 18, 35578 WETZLAR
Tel: 6441 9590 **Fax:** 6441 959292
Email: redaktion.wnz@mittelhessen.de **Web site:** http://www.mittelhessen.de
Freq: Weekly; **Cover Price:** EUR 1,00; **Circ:** 25,825
Editor: Alois Kösters; **News Editor:** Michael Klein; **Advertising Manager:** Peter Rother
Profile: Regional weekly covering politics, economics, culture, sports, travel, technology and the arts. This Outlet offers RSS (Really Simple Syndication).
Language(s): German
ADVERTISING RATES:
SCC .... EUR 66,50
Mechanical Data: Type Area: 490 x 328 mm, No. of Columns (Display): 7, Col Widths (Display): 44 mm

Copy instructions: *Copy Date:* 2 days prior to publication
LOCAL NEWSPAPERS

WHEELIES
1818431G77A-2815
Editorial: Am Kühnbach 27, 74523 SCHWÄBISCH HALL **Tel:** 791 53864 **Fax:** 791 959243
Email: info@wheelies.de **Web site:** http://www.wheelies.de
Freq: 8 issues yearly; **Cover Price:** Free; **Circ:** 35,000
Editor: Eberhard Hermann; **Advertising Manager:** Eberhard Hermann
Profile: Motorcycle Magazine.
Language(s): German
ADVERTISING RATES:
Full Page Mono .... EUR 900
Full Page Colour .... EUR 900
Mechanical Data: Type Area: 272 x 188 mm
Copy instructions: *Copy Date:* 12 days prior to publication

WHO IS WHO FACILITY MANAGEMENT
1637470G4E-6977
Editorial: Avenwedder Str. 55, 33335 GÜTERSLOH
Tel: 5241 8090884 **Fax:** 5241 80690880
Email: kerstin.galenza@bauverlag.de **Web site:** http://www.fm-whoiswho.de
Freq: Annual; **Cover Price:** EUR 41,90; **Circ:** 10,000
Editor: Kerstin Galenza; **Advertising Manager:** Herbert Walhorn
Profile: Directory about facility management.
Language(s): German
ADVERTISING RATES:
Full Page Mono .... EUR 2450
Full Page Colour .... EUR 2450
Mechanical Data: Type Area: 190 x 100 mm
Copy instructions: *Copy Date:* 50 days prior to publication

WHO IS WHO IM FLOTTENMARKT
1794812G49A-2424
Editorial: Handwerkstr. 15, 70565 STUTTGART
Tel: 711 784980 **Fax:** 711 7849824
Email: hanno.boblenz@etm-verlag.de **Web site:** http://www.who.firmenauto.de
Freq: Annual; **Circ:** 52,500
Editor: Hanno Boblenz; **Advertising Manager:** Thomas Beck
Profile: This unique reference work for the fleet market offers important information for the fleet manager. News, info, numbers, dates, names, addresses and contact with the principal players in the industry from the fields of manufacturing, leasing / management, tire / workshops, communication, service and trade, and tank management. Our editorial team makes all Provider in detail before, with address, contact national / regional, firm size, distribution channels, Brief descriptions and characteristics as body text.
Language(s): German
ADVERTISING RATES:
Full Page Mono .... EUR 5450
Full Page Colour .... EUR 5450
Mechanical Data: Type Area: 180 x 118 mm
Copy instructions: *Copy Date:* 48 days prior to publication
Supplement to: Firmenauto

WHO IS WHO IM TROCKENBAU
1861672G4E-7238
Editorial: Stolberger Str. 84, 50933 KÖLN
Tel: 221 5497279 **Fax:** 221 54976294
Email: red.trockenbau@rudolf-mueller.de **Web site:** http://www.trockenbau-akustik.de
Freq: Annual; **Cover Price:** EUR 32,00; **Circ:** 10,000
Editor: Thomas Grüning; **Advertising Manager:** Thomas Füngerlings
Profile: Directory listing addresses of the dry mortarless construction business.
Language(s): German
ADVERTISING RATES:
Full Page Mono .... EUR 1850
Full Page Colour .... EUR 3585
Mechanical Data: Type Area: 170 x 130 mm, No. of Columns (Display): 2, Col Widths (Display): 60 mm
Copy instructions: *Copy Date:* 65 days prior to publication

WHO'S WHO EUROPA MAGAZIN
747339G14A-8140
Editorial: Postfach 1427, 61404 OBERURSEL
Tel: 6171 51055 **Fax:** 6171 53542
Email: europamagazin@who-magazine.com **Web site:** http://www.who-magazine.com
Freq: Quarterly; **Annual Sub.:** EUR 40,00; **Circ:** 20,000
Editor: Wilma K. Bosse; **Advertising Manager:** Monika Würz
Profile: Magazine for decision makers in the European economy. Representation of companies with the specific range of services, corporate and business portraits.
Language(s): English; German
Readership: Aimed at enterprise managers.
ADVERTISING RATES:
Full Page Mono .... EUR 8250
Full Page Colour .... EUR 8250
Mechanical Data: Type Area: 245 x 180 mm

Copy instructions: *Copy Date:* 20 days prior to publication
BUSINESS: COMMERCE, INDUSTRY & MANAGEMENT

WI WIRTSCHAFTSINFORMATIK
747725G5B-170
Editorial: Universitätsstr. 24, 35032 MARBURG
Tel: 6421 2823894 **Fax:** 6421 2826554
Email: redaktion@wirtschaftsinformatik.de **Web site:** http://www.wirtschaftsinformatik.de
Freq: 6 issues yearly; **Annual Sub.:** EUR 243,00; **Circ:** 3,800
Editor: Ulrich Hasenkamp; **Advertising Manager:** Carmen Reths
Profile: Publication focusing on computer applications in business, administration, economics and related areas.
Language(s): English; German
ADVERTISING RATES:
Full Page Mono .... EUR 1980
Full Page Colour .... EUR 2880
Mechanical Data: Type Area: 240 x 175 mm, No. of Columns (Display): 3, Col Widths (Display): 55 mm
Official Journal of: Organ d. Ges. f. Informatik, FB Wirtschaftsinformatik u. d. Verb. d. Hochschullehrer f. Betriebswirtschaft e.V., Wissenschaftl. Kommission Wirtschaftsinformatik
BUSINESS: COMPUTERS & AUTOMATION: Data Processing

WI WOHNUNGSPOLITISCHE INFORMATIONEN
748278G74K-1420
Editorial: Tangstedter Landstr. 83, 22415 HAMBURG
Tel: 40 52010320 **Fax:** 40 52010312
Email: redaktion@hammonia.de **Web site:** http://www.hammonia.de
Freq: Weekly; **Annual Sub.:** EUR 104,00; **Circ:** 2,470
Editor: Manfred Neuhöfer; **Advertising Manager:** Heike Tiedemann
Profile: Magazine about property in Cologne.
Language(s): German
Copy instructions: *Copy Date:* 6 days prior to publication
CONSUMER: WOMEN'S INTEREST CONSUMER MAGAZINES: Home Purchase

WIDESCREEN
1613606G76A-1480
Editorial: Dr.-Mack-Str. 83, 90762 FÜRTH
Tel: 911 2872100 **Fax:** 911 2872200
Email: redaktion@widescreen-online.de **Web site:** http://www.widescreen-online.de
Freq: Monthly; **Annual Sub.:** EUR 73,00; **Circ:** 39,000
Editor: Christian Müller; **Advertising Manager:** Gunnar Obermeier
Profile: Widescreen - The test magazine for Blu-ray, DVD & Movies: DVD, Blu-ray movies - Widescreen illuminated all facets of the world of experience of film. With current movie reviews, detailed reviews of new DVD and Blu-ray, tests of home theater equipment, background reports and star interviews.
Language(s): German
ADVERTISING RATES:
Full Page Mono .... EUR 5990
Full Page Colour .... EUR 5990
Mechanical Data: Type Area: 297 x 210 mm, No. of Columns (Display): 4, Col Widths (Display): 52 mm
CONSUMER: MUSIC & PERFORMING ARTS: Cinema

WIESBADENER ERBENHEIMER ANZEIGER
726392G67B-16745
Editorial: Wandersmannstr. 15, 65205 WIESBADEN
Tel: 611 976160 **Fax:** 611 712429
Email: info@breuerpresse.de **Web site:** http://www.breuerpresse.de
Freq: Weekly; **Circ:** 6,000
Editor: Dieter Breuer; **Advertising Manager:** Ruth Göbel
Profile: We are the weekend and local newspaper for the families in 19 eastern suburbs of Wiesbaden, Hochheim and Hofheim. Comprehensive is our coverage of local events with sporting, cultural and local political events in the region. Unions have an important forum for their activities. Correspondents from the various suburbs regularly report on local conditions. Extensively are interested in the topics that the young and young at heart people. A handsome sports section provides information on small and big games, tournaments and sporting events in the region down to the most recent game classes.
Language(s): German
ADVERTISING RATES:
SCC .... EUR 18,00
Mechanical Data: Type Area: 430 x 285 mm, No. of Columns (Display): 6, Col Widths (Display): 45 mm
Copy instructions: *Copy Date:* 1 day prior to publication
Supplement(s): Wiesbadener Anzeiger
REGIONAL DAILY & SUNDAY NEWSPAPERS: Regional Daily Newspapers

WIESBADENER KURIER
747405G67B-15920
Editorial: Langgasse 21, 65183 WIESBADEN
Tel: 611 3550 **Fax:** 611 3553333
Email: kurier-redaktion@vrm.de **Web site:** http://www.wiesbadener-kurier.de
Freq: 312 issues yearly; **Circ:** 63,127

Editor: Stefan Schröder; **News Editor:** Christian Stang; **Advertising Manager:** Gerhard Müller
Profile: The Wiesbadener Kurier is a daily newspape published in the capital of Hessen. The newspaper includes News on politics, economy, culture, sports travel and technology. Facebook: http://www.facebook.com/pages/Wiesbadener-Kurier/262129856053 Twitter: http://twitter.com/wknachrichten This Outlet offers RSS (Really Simple Syndication).
Language(s): German
ADVERTISING RATES:
SCC .... EUR 143,2
Mechanical Data: Type Area: 480 x 325 mm, No. o Columns (Display): 7, Col Widths (Display): 45 mm
Copy instructions: *Copy Date:* 1 day prior to publication
Supplement(s): extra Familie; extra Gesundheit; extra Sport; extra Wissen; pepper; rtv; Start frei; Untertaunus anzeiger; vorOrt
REGIONAL DAILY & SUNDAY NEWSPAPERS: Regional Daily Newspapers

WIESBADENER TAGBLATT
747406G67B-1594
Editorial: Langgasse 21, 65183 WIESBADEN
Tel: 611 3492230 **Fax:** 611 3492233
Email: wt-stadtzeitung@vrm.de **Web site:** http://www.wiesbadener-tagblatt.de
Freq: 312 issues yearly; **Circ:** 63,127
Advertising Manager: Gerhard Müller
Profile: The Wiesbadener Tagblatt is a daily newspaper published in the capitol of Hessen. The newspaper includes News on politics, economy, culture, sports, travel and technology. Facebook: http://www.facebook.com/pages/Allgemeine-Zeitung/255951758912.
Language(s): German
ADVERTISING RATES:
SCC .... EUR 143,2
Mechanical Data: Type Area: 480 x 325 mm, No. of Columns (Display): 7, Col Widths (Display): 45 mm
Copy instructions: *Copy Date:* 1 day prior to publication
Supplement(s): extra Familie; extra Gesundheit; extra Sport; extra Wissen; pepper; Start frei; vorOrt
REGIONAL DAILY & SUNDAY NEWSPAPERS: Regional Daily Newspapers

WIESBADENER WOCHENBLATT
747407G72-1527
Editorial: Langgasse 21, 65183 WIESBADEN
Tel: 611 3552330 **Fax:** 611 3552343
Email: redaktion@wiesbadener-wochenblatt.de **Web site:** http://www.wiesbadener-wochenblatt.de
Freq: Weekly; **Cover Price:** Free; **Circ:** 132,916
Editor: Rüdiger Benda; **Advertising Manager:** Raine Baumann
Profile: Advertising journal (house-to-house) concentrating on local stories.
Language(s): German
ADVERTISING RATES:
Full Page Mono .... EUR 893
Full Page Colour .... EUR 1213
Mechanical Data: Type Area: 480 x 325 mm, No. of Columns (Display): 7, Col Widths (Display): 45 mm
Copy instructions: *Copy Date:* 2 days prior to publication
LOCAL NEWSPAPERS

WIF PORTAL
1819958G14A-1006
Editorial: Robert-Bosch-Str. 6, 73037 GÖPPINGEN
Tel: 7161 5023585 **Fax:** 7161 5023581
Email: wif@wif-gp.de **Web site:** http://www.wif-gp.d
Freq: Annual; **Cover Price:** Free; **Circ:** 2,000
Editor: Reiner Lohse
Profile: Regional business magazine.
Language(s): German

WIK ZEITSCHRIFT FÜR DIE SICHERHEIT DER WIRTSCHAFT
747414G54C-9
Editorial: Lise-Meitner-Str. 4, 55435 GAU-ALGESHEIM **Tel:** 6725 93040 **Fax:** 6725 5994
Email: redaktion.wik@secumedia.de **Web site:** http:/ www.wik.info
Freq: 6 issues yearly; Free to qualifying individuals **Annual Sub.:** EUR 105,00; **Circ:** 8,297
Editor: Horst Schärges
Profile: Publication containing information about security including marketing, products, technology, business development and related issues.
Language(s): German
Readership: Read by retailers and manufacturers.
ADVERTISING RATES:
Full Page Mono .... EUR 1940
Full Page Colour .... EUR 2900
Mechanical Data: Type Area: 246 x 170 mm
Official Journal of: Organ d. ArGe f. Sicherheit in d. Wirtschaft e.V.
BUSINESS: SAFETY & SECURITY: Security

WIKO WIRTSCHAFTSKOMPASS
747730G63-1480
Editorial: Graf-Schack-Allee 12, 19053 SCHWERIN
Tel: 385 5103114 **Fax:** 385 5103148
Email: kraus@schwerin.ihk.de **Web site:** http://www.ihkzuschwerin.de
Freq: 10 issues yearly; **Circ:** 19,409
Editor: Andreas Kraus

rofile: Business Magazine of Trade and Industry for chwerin and area. The annually published in ten ditions magazine is the most important medium of e Schwerin Chamber of Commerce for information, transport reviews, reports and numerous non-cash s. All Chamber member companies and in addition a broad audience in administration and policy, the agazine delivered free of charge. Readers are erefore primarily the decision makers in companies, ut also many interested representatives from overnment and politics.
anguage(s): German
DVERTISING RATES:
ull Page Colour .... EUR 1650
echanical Data: Type Area: 260 x 185 mm, No. of olumns (Display): 3, Col Widths (Display): 58 mm
opy instructions: *Copy Date:* 10
USINESS: REGIONAL BUSINESS

VILD UND HUND 747425G75F-960
ditorial: Erich-Kästner-Str. 2, 56379 SINGHOFEN
el: 2604 978401 Fax: 2604 978402
mail: wuh@paulparey.de Web site: http://www.ildundhund.de
req: 24 issues yearly; Annual Sub.: EUR 103,00;
irc: 63,326
ditor: Heiko Hornung; Advertising Manager: Sylvia Ehert
rofile: Magazine for hunters and nature lovers. The urnal reports on wildlife, water area, hunting, unters from the provinces, over hunting practices, unting equipment and policies.
anguage(s): German
DVERTISING RATES:
ull Page Mono .... EUR 4533
ull Page Colour .... EUR 8107
echanical Data: Type Area: 253 x 186 mm, No. of olumns (Display): 4, Col Widths (Display): 43 mm
opy instructions: *Copy Date:* 23 days prior to ublication
ONSUMER: SPORT: Shooting

WILDESHAUSER ZEITUNG 747423G67B-15980
ditorial: Bahnhofstr. 13, 27793 WILDESHAUSEN
el: 4431 9891143 Fax: 4431 9891149
mail: redaktion.wildeshausen@kreiszeitung.de
req: 312 issues yearly; Circ: 2,669
rofile: The Kreiszeitung publishing group is the fifth argest newspaper in Niedersachsen, with a daily irculation of over 82,000 copies. Regional daily ewspaper covering politics, economics, sport, travel nd technology. Facebook: http://www.facebook com/pages/Kreiszeitung-Syke/146798206489 ref=search&sid=1264453500.2068226289..1 Twitter: ttp://twitter.com/kreiszeitung This Outlet offers RSS Really Simple Syndication).
anguage(s): German
DVERTISING RATES:
CC .... EUR 21,60
Mechanical Data: Type Area: 472 x 325 mm, No. of Columns (Display): 7, Col Widths (Display): 45 mm
Copy instructions: *Copy Date:* 1 day prior to ublication
REGIONAL DAILY & SUNDAY NEWSPAPERS: Regional Daily Newspapers

WILDWECHSEL - AUSG. KASSEL/PADERBORN 747428G80-13020
Editorial: Sternstr. 40, 34414 WARBURG
Tel: 5641 60094 Fax: 5641 60813
Email: redaktion@wildwechsel.de Web site: http://www.wildwechsel.de
Freq: Monthly; Annual Sub.: EUR 19,00; Circ: 13,246
Editor: Fedor Waldschmidt; Advertising Manager: Fedor Waldschmidt
Profile: The Wildwechsel is a monthly regional magazine for Kassel and Paderborn. In the Wildwechsel can be found first of all important issues and trends in the region - from social development to cultural events, concerts and festivals. The centerpiece is the calendar of events, in which everything is related to what happened a month ago in the region - with data, facts and often short descriptions of events. In addition, there are also articles on national issues. Regularly new movies, comics and records are reviewed. In selected current CDs can come listen to the music hotline. Finally, there are current raffles and the classifieds section . Facebook: http://www.facebook.com/ wildwechsel.magazin.
Language(s): German
ADVERTISING RATES:
Full Page Mono .... EUR 971
Full Page Colour .... EUR 1457
Mechanical Data: Type Area: 190 x 130 mm, No. of Columns (Display): 3, Col Widths (Display): 40 mm
Copy instructions: *Copy Date:* 15 days prior to publication
CONSUMER: RURAL & REGIONAL INTEREST

WILDWECHSEL - AUSG. MARBURG/KASSEL/FULDA 747429G80-13040
Editorial: Sternstr. 40, 34414 WARBURG
Tel: 5641 60094 Fax: 5641 60813
Email: redaktion@wildwechsel.de Web site: http:// www.wildwechsel.de
Freq: Monthly; Annual Sub.: EUR 19,00; Circ: 10,999
Editor: Fedor Waldschmidt; Advertising Manager: Fedor Waldschmidt
Profile: The Wildwechsel is a monthly regional magazine for Marburg, Kassel and Fulda. In the Wildwechsel can be found first of all important issues and trends in the region - from social development to cultural events, concerts and festivals. The centerpiece is the calendar of events, in which everything is related to what happened a month ago in the region - with data, facts and often short descriptions of events. In addition, there are also articles on national issues. Regularly new movies, comics and records are reviewed. In selected current CDs can come listen to the music hotline. Finally, there are current raffles and the classifieds section . Facebook: http://www.facebook.com/ wildwechsel.magazin.
Language(s): German
ADVERTISING RATES:
Full Page Mono .... EUR 737
Full Page Colour .... EUR 1106
Mechanical Data: Type Area: 190 x 130 mm, No. of Columns (Display): 3, Col Widths (Display): 40 mm
Copy instructions: *Copy Date:* 15 days prior to publication
CONSUMER: RURAL & REGIONAL INTEREST

WILHELMSBURGER WOCHENBLATT 747435G72-15300
Editorial: Harburger Rathausstr. 40, 21073 HAMBURG Tel: 40 85322933 Fax: 40 85322939
Email: post@wochenblatt-redaktion.de Web site: http://www.wilhelmsburger-wochenblatt.de
Freq: Weekly; Cover Price: Free; Circ: 25,099
Editor: Olaf Zimmermann; Advertising Manager: Jürgen Müller
Profile: Advertising journal (house-to-house) concentrating on local stories.
Language(s): German
ADVERTISING RATES:
Full Page Mono .... EUR 3483
Full Page Colour .... EUR 3603
Mechanical Data: Type Area: 430 x 282 mm, No. of Columns (Display): 6, Col Widths (Display): 45 mm
Copy instructions: *Copy Date:* 2 days prior to publication
LOCAL NEWSPAPERS

WILHELMSHAVENER ZEITUNG 747438G67B-16000
Editorial: Parkstr. 8, 26382 WILHELMSHAVEN
Tel: 4421 4880 Fax: 4421 488430
Email: redaktion@wzonline.de Web site: http://www.wzonline.de
Freq: 312 issues yearly; Circ: 21,683
Editor: Gerd Abeldt; Advertising Manager: Thomas Schipper
Profile: Daily newspaper with regional news and a local sports section. Facebook: http:// www.facebook.com/wzonline.
Language(s): German
ADVERTISING RATES:
SCC .... EUR 43,80
Mechanical Data: Type Area: 420 x 282 mm, No. of Columns (Display): 6, Col Widths (Display): 45 mm
Copy instructions: *Copy Date:* 1 day prior to publication
Supplement(s): Kompass für Wilhelmshaven und Friesland; Theaterzeitung; WZ Teleblick
REGIONAL DAILY & SUNDAY NEWSPAPERS: Regional Daily Newspapers

WILLKOMMEN IM ERZGEBIRGE 747446G89A-12123
Editorial: Markt 20, 09111 CHEMNITZ
Tel: 371 3349114 Fax: 371 3349133
Email: redaktion@pagepro-media.de Web site: http://www.pagepro-media.de
Freq: Half-yearly; Cover Price: EUR 4,40; Circ: 45,000
Advertising Manager: Kerstin Adam
Profile: Tourism magazine for the Erzgebirge region with events and sightseeing tips, recommendations for walking tours, gastronomy and culture.
Language(s): German
ADVERTISING RATES:
Full Page Mono .... EUR 2310
Full Page Colour .... EUR 2310
Mechanical Data: Type Area: 268 x 195 mm, No. of Columns (Display): 3, Col Widths (Display): 63 mm
Copy instructions: *Copy Date:* 60 days prior to publication

WILLKOMMEN IM NATURTHEATER GREIFENSTEINE 747448G89A-12125
Editorial: Markt 8, 09456 ANNABERG-BUCHHOLZ
Tel: 3733 14123100 Fax: 371 65627310
Email: jutta.kolmorgen@blick.de Web site: http:// www.blick.de
Freq: Annual; Cover Price: EUR 1,50; Circ: 2,000
Editor: Jutta Kolmorgen; Advertising Manager: Jutta Kolmorgen
Profile: Magazine for tourists.
Language(s): German
ADVERTISING RATES:
Full Page Mono .... EUR 1836
Full Page Colour .... EUR 1836
Mechanical Data: Type Area: 268 x 195 mm, No. of Columns (Display): 3, Col Widths (Display): 63 mm

WILLKOMMEN IM VOGTLAND 747449G89A-12126
Editorial: Markt 20, 09111 CHEMNITZ
Tel: 371 3349114 Fax: 371 3349133
Email: redaktion@pagepro-media.de Web site: http://www.pagepro-media.de
Freq: Half-yearly; Cover Price: EUR 3,90; Circ: 30,000
Advertising Manager: Angela Hopfe
Profile: Magazine for tourists in the Vogtland region.
Language(s): German
ADVERTISING RATES:
Full Page Mono .... EUR 1977
Full Page Colour .... EUR 1977
Mechanical Data: Type Area: 268 x 195 mm, No. of Columns (Display): 3, Col Widths (Display): 63 mm

WILSTERSCHE ZEITUNG 747454G67B-16020
Editorial: Nikolaistr. 7, 24937 FLENSBURG
Tel: 461 8080 Fax: 461 8081058
Email: redaktion@shz.de Web site: http://www.shz.de
Freq: 312 issues yearly; Circ: 22,618
Advertising Manager: Ingeborg Schwarz
Profile: The "Wilstersche Zeitung" was founded in 1890 and was published until the end of 1998 the publisher Johann Schwarck Söhne. Since 1 January 1999 is the Wilstersche newspaper to sh:z. Facebook: http://www.facebook.com/shzonline Twitter: http://twitter.com/shz_de This Outlet offers RSS (Really Simple Syndication).
Language(s): German
ADVERTISING RATES:
SCC .... EUR 75,60
Mechanical Data: Type Area: 480 x 325 mm, No. of Columns (Display): 7, Col Widths (Display): 45 mm
Copy instructions: *Copy Date:* 1 day prior to publication
Supplement(s): nordisch gesund; Schleswig-Holstein Journal; tv magazin
REGIONAL DAILY & SUNDAY NEWSPAPERS: Regional Daily Newspapers

WIM WIRTSCHAFT IN MITTELFRANKEN 747590G63-1240
Editorial: Hauptmarkt 25, 90403 NÜRNBERG
Tel: 911 1335379 Fax: 911 1335300
Email: kurt.hesse@nuernberg.ihk.de Web site: http:// www.wim-magazin.de
Freq: Monthly; Free to qualifying individuals
Annual Sub.: EUR 24,00; Circ: 104,880
Editor: Kurt Hesse; Advertising Manager: Rüdiger Sander
Profile: "WiM - WIRTSCHAFT IN MITTELFRANKEN" is the official magazine of the Regional Economic Chamber of Commerce and Industry for Nuremberg and Central Franconia. Each month it addresses all companies from industry, commerce and services in Middle Franconia, the sixth largest economy in Germany. With a circulation of over 104,000 copies, the "WiM - WIRTSCHAFT IN MITTELFRANKEN" reaches all self-employed, large enterprises, medium-sized enterprises and individual entrepreneurs without any wastage. The readership is characterized by a high standard of living and education and corporate interest.
Language(s): German
ADVERTISING RATES:
Full Page Mono .... EUR 4950
Full Page Colour .... EUR 7920
Mechanical Data: Type Area: 253 x 188 mm, No. of Columns (Display): 4, Col Widths (Display): 44 mm
Copy instructions: *Copy Date:* 20 days prior to publication
BUSINESS: REGIONAL BUSINESS

WIN WOODWORKING INTERNATIONAL 747482G46-175
Editorial: Blumenstr. 15, 90402 NÜRNBERG
Tel: 911 2018210 Fax: 911 2018100
Email: robert.sax@harnisch.com Web site: http:// www.harnisch.com/win
Freq: Quarterly; Annual Sub.: EUR 62,00; Circ: 12,000
Editor: Robert Sax; Advertising Manager: Benno Keller
Profile: Publication for the woodworking and furniture industry.
Language(s): English
Readership: Aimed at professionals in the woodworking and furniture industry.
ADVERTISING RATES:
Full Page Mono .... EUR 3490
Full Page Colour .... EUR 4840
Mechanical Data: No. of Columns (Display): 4, Col Widths (Display): 44 mm, Type Area: 270 x 190 mm
BUSINESS: TIMBER, WOOD & FORESTRY

WIND ENERGY MARKET 1791432G58-1765
Editorial: Marienstr. 19, 10117 BERLIN
Tel: 30 28482106 Fax: 30 28482107
Email: service@wind-energie.de Web site: http:// www.wind-energie.de
Freq: Annual; Annual Sub.: EUR 35,00,; Circ: 3,800
Editor: Thorsten Paulsen
Profile: Annual with a market overview on renewable energy.
Language(s): English; German
ADVERTISING RATES:
Full Page Mono .... EUR 1400
Full Page Colour .... EUR 2800
Mechanical Data: Type Area: 262 x 177 mm, No. of Columns (Display): 3, Col Widths (Display): 58 mm
Official Journal of: Organ d. Bundesverb. Wind-Energie e.V.

WIND ENERGY MARKET 1935242G58-1827
Editorial: Marienstr. 19, 10117 BERLIN
Tel: 30 28482106 Fax: 30 28482107
Email: service@wind-energie.de Web site: http:// www.wind-energie.de
Freq: Annual; Annual Sub.: EUR 35,00,; Circ: 2,000
Editor: Thorsten Paulsen
Profile: Annual with a market overview on renewable energy.
Language(s): English
ADVERTISING RATES:
Full Page Mono .... EUR 1400
Full Page Colour .... EUR 2800
Mechanical Data: Type Area: 262 x 177 mm, No. of Columns (Display): 3, Col Widths (Display): 58 mm

WIND TURBINE MARKET 747462G58-1640
Editorial: Hans-Böckler-Allee 7, 30173 HANNOVER
Tel: 511 85502563 Fax: 511 85502500
Email: redaktion@sunmediaverlag.de Web site: http://www.erneuerbareenergien.de
Freq: Annual; Cover Price: EUR 25,00; Circ: 3,000
Editor: Karsten Schäfer; Advertising Manager: Patrick Krumbach
Profile: Overview on worldwide offered wind power plants.
Language(s): English; German; Spanish
ADVERTISING RATES:
Full Page Mono .... EUR 1300
Full Page Colour .... EUR 2260
Mechanical Data: Type Area: 261 x 190 mm, No. of Columns (Display): 4, Col Widths (Display): 44 mm
Supplement to: Erneuerbare Energien

WINDBRIEF SÜDWESTFALEN 1732602G74M-793
Editorial: Am Wördehoff 2, 59597 ERWITTE
Tel: 2945 963212 Fax: 2945 963213
Email: mk@windinvestor.de Web site: http://www.windinvestor.de
Freq: 3 issues yearly; Cover Price: Free; Circ: 4,300
Editor: Jürgen Spykers
Profile: The letter provides information on wind renewable energy with emphasis in Southern Westphalia.
Language(s): German

WINDSHEIMER ZEITUNG 747468G67B-16060
Editorial: Kegetstr. 11, 91438 BAD WINDSHEIM
Tel: 9841 9030 Fax: 9841 90315
Email: info@windsheimer-zeitung.de Web site: http://www.delp-druck.de
Freq: 312 issues yearly; Circ: 4,347
Profile: Daily newspaper with regional news and a local sports section.
Language(s): German
ADVERTISING RATES:
SCC .... EUR 15,90
Mechanical Data: Type Area: 430 x 280 mm, No. of Columns (Display): 6, Col Widths (Display): 45 mm
Copy instructions: *Copy Date:* 2 days prior to publication
REGIONAL DAILY & SUNDAY NEWSPAPERS: Regional Daily Newspapers

WINING & DINING 2071873G74P-1385
Editorial: Wilhelm-Sinsteden-Str. 6, 47533 KLEVE
Tel: 2821 7139616 Fax: 2821 7139620
Email: s.hackel@wohnverlag.de Web site: http:// www.wohnverlag.de
Freq: Half-yearly; Cover Price: EUR 5,00; Circ: 55,000
Editor: Stephanie Hackel; Advertising Manager: Dennis van Offern
Profile: Magazine reported internationally about renowned Star Cooks, regional food events and gourmet hotspots Feinschemcker.
Language(s): German
ADVERTISING RATES:
Full Page Mono .... EUR 7950
Full Page Colour .... EUR 7950
Mechanical Data: Type Area: 245 x 195 mm

WINKE FÜR DEN BIOGÄRTNER 756868G21A-4204
Editorial: Nonnengasse 16, 36037 FULDA
Tel: 661 9024531 Fax: 661 9024545
Email: garten@abtei-fulda.de Web site: http://www.abtei-fulda.de
Freq: 3 issues yearly; Annual Sub.: EUR 15,00; Circ: 3,500
Editor: Christa Weinrich
Profile: Biological magazine for gardeners.
Language(s): German

DER WINKELMESSER 1616492G77B-13
Editorial: Obergasse 20b, 61184 KARBEN
Tel: 6039 938643
Email: lutz.hollmann@winkelmesser-frankfurt.de Web site: http://www.winkelmesser-frankfurt.de
Freq: Annual; Cover Price: Free; Circ: 4,500
Editor: Lutz Hollmann
Profile: Regional motorcycling magazine.
Language(s): German

DER WINKELMESSER

1616492G77B-608

Editorial: Obergasse 20b, 61184 KARBEN
Tel: 6039 938643
Email: lutz.hollmann@winkelmesser-frankfurt.de **Web site:** http://www.winkelmesser-frankfurt.de
Freq: Annual; **Cover Price:** Free; **Circ:** 4,500
Editor: Lutz Hollmann
Profile: Regional motorcycling magazine.
Language(s): German

WINKLERS ILLUSTRIERTE

747474G88B-1360

Editorial: Georg-Westermann-Allee 66, 38104 BRAUNSCHWEIG **Tel:** 531 7080 **Fax:** 531 708343
Email: service@winklers.de **Web site:** http://www.winklers-illustrierte.de
Freq: 11 issues yearly; **Annual Sub.:** EUR 20,35; **Circ:** 15,000
Editor: Karl Wilhelm Henke
Profile: Journal containing information about shorthand, typewriting and office practice.
Language(s): German
ADVERTISING RATES:
Full Page Mono .... EUR 1000
Full Page Colour .... EUR 2000
Mechanical Data: Type Area: 260 x 176 mm
Copy instructions: *Copy Date:* 42 days prior to publication
CONSUMER: EDUCATION: Adult Education

WINLOAD.DE

1663056G78D-974

Editorial: Chausseestr. 8, 10115 BERLIN
Tel: 30 9210640 **Fax:** 30 92106431
Email: info@econa.com **Web site:** http://www.winload.de
Freq: Daily; **Cover Price:** Paid; **Circ:** 2,479,235 Unique Users
Editor: Tom Fuchs; **Advertising Manager:** Anika Böttcher
Profile: Internet Media: Download portal with more than 18,000 programs in 100 categories. Audience: IT and tech-savvy people This Outlet offers RSS (Really Simple Syndication).
Language(s): German
CONSUMER: CONSUMER ELECTRONICS: Games

WINNENDER ZEITUNG

747476G67B-16080

Editorial: Albrecht-Villinger-Str. 10, 71332 WAIBLINGEN **Tel:** 7151 5660 **Fax:** 7151 566402
Email: info@redaktion.zvw.de **Web site:** http://www.winnender-zeitung.de
Freq: 312 issues yearly; **Circ:** 8,275
Advertising Manager: Michael Feßler
Profile: Daily newspaper with regional news and a local sports section.
Language(s): German
ADVERTISING RATES:
SCC .... EUR 25,00
Mechanical Data: Type Area: 485 x 324 mm, No. of Columns (Display): 7, Col Widths (Display): 44 mm
Copy instructions: *Copy Date:* 2 days prior to publication
REGIONAL DAILY & SUNDAY NEWSPAPERS: Regional Daily Newspapers

WINSENER ANZEIGER

747478G67B-16100

Editorial: Schloßring 5, 21423 WINSEN
Tel: 4171 658110 **Fax:** 4171 658140
Email: redaktion@winsener-anzeiger.de **Web site:** http://www.winsener-anzeiger.de
Freq: 312 issues yearly; **Circ:** 9,565
Editor: Jürgen Peter Ravens; **Advertising Manager:** Lebrecht Maack
Profile: Daily newspaper with regional news and a local sports section.
Language(s): German
ADVERTISING RATES:
SCC .... EUR 49,30
Mechanical Data: Type Area: 430 x 282 mm, No. of Columns (Display): 6, Col Widths (Display): 45 mm
Copy instructions: *Copy Date:* 1 day prior to publication
REGIONAL DAILY & SUNDAY NEWSPAPERS: Regional Daily Newspapers

WINTERBETONNUNG DER DEUTSCHEN KÜSTENGEWÄSSER

756869G49A-2303

Editorial: Bernhard-Nocht-Str. 78, 20359 HAMBURG
Tel: 40 31900 **Fax:** 40 31905000
Email: posteingang@bsh.de **Web site:** http://www.bsh.de
Freq: Annual; **Cover Price:** EUR 8,00; **Circ:** 500
Profile: Nautical charts.
Language(s): German

WIR

747491G56A-11190

Editorial: Adenauerallee 134, 53113 BONN
Tel: 228 688460 **Fax:** 228 6884644
Email: dlfhbonn@kinderkrebsstiftung.de **Web site:** http://www.kinderkrebsstiftung.de
Freq: Quarterly; **Annual Sub.:** EUR 8,60; **Circ:** 14,000
Editor: Klaus Riddering
Profile: Magazine of the German Leukaemia Research Association - Project for Children suffering with Cancer.
Language(s): German
ADVERTISING RATES:
Full Page Mono .... EUR 2499
Full Page Colour .... EUR 2989
Mechanical Data: Type Area: 262 x 175 mm, No. of Columns (Display): 3, Col Widths (Display): 55 mm
Copy instructions: *Copy Date:* 20 days prior to publication

WIR

747583G63-1120

Editorial: Ernst-Barlach-Str. 1, 18055 ROSTOCK
Tel: 381 338701 **Fax:** 381 338709
Email: olsen@rostock.ihk.de **Web site:** http://www.rostock.ihk24.de
Freq: 10 issues yearly; Free to qualifying individuals
Annual Sub.: EUR 21,20; **Circ:** 33,068
Editor: Sven Olsen
Profile: The monthly magazine provides information on the work of the Rockstock Chamber of Commerce, on current topics and trends of regional economic activity, gives tips for business practice and brings detailed reports each month focusing on a theme. Official announcements of the CCI is to be published as well as current business news from the region.
Language(s): German
ADVERTISING RATES:
Full Page Mono .... EUR 1815
Full Page Colour .... EUR 2904
Mechanical Data: Type Area: 260 x 185 mm, No. of Columns (Display): 3, Col Widths (Display): 58 mm
Copy instructions: *Copy Date:* 35 days prior to publication
BUSINESS: REGIONAL BUSINESS

WIR

747498G74N-780

Editorial: Augustastr. 11, 45525 HATTINGEN
Tel: 2324 501882
Email: info@kick-unruhe.de **Web site:** http://www.hattingen.de
Freq: 5 issues yearly; **Cover Price:** Free; **Circ:** 5,000
Editor: Inge Berger
Profile: Magazine for the elderly.
Language(s): German
ADVERTISING RATES:
Full Page Mono .... EUR 340
Full Page Colour .... EUR 340
Mechanical Data: Type Area: 255 x 181 mm, No. of Columns (Display): 4, Col Widths (Display): 43 mm
Copy instructions: *Copy Date:* 30 days prior to publication

WIR AKTUELL

747506G1D-452

Editorial: Ruhrallee 92, 44139 DORTMUND
Tel: 231 9192255 **Fax:** 231 9193094
Email: presse@continentale.de **Web site:** http://www.continentale.de
Freq: Quarterly; **Circ:** 5,500
Editor: Gerhard W. Stry
Profile: Magazine for employees of Continentale Krankenversicherung.
Language(s): German

WIR AKTUELL

747506G1D-499

Editorial: Ruhrallee 92, 44139 DORTMUND
Tel: 231 9192255 **Fax:** 231 9193094
Email: presse@continentale.de **Web site:** http://www.continentale.de
Freq: Quarterly; **Circ:** 5,500
Editor: Gerhard W. Stry
Profile: Magazine for employees of Continentale Krankenversicherung.
Language(s): German

WIR FRAUEN

727847G74A-1180

Editorial: Luxemburger Str. 202, 50937 KÖLN
Tel: 221 448545 **Fax:** 221 444305
Email: mail@papyrossa.de **Web site:** http://www.papyrossa.de
Freq: Annual; **Cover Price:** EUR 9,50; **Circ:** 6,300
Editor: Florence Hervé
Profile: Calendar for women.
Language(s): German
ADVERTISING RATES:
Full Page Mono .... EUR 511
Mechanical Data: Type Area: 125 x 90 mm
Copy instructions: *Copy Date:* 90 days prior to publication

WIR FÜR EUCH

1866456G74N-973

Editorial: Langemarkstr. 19, 46042 OBERHAUSEN
Tel: 208 8252724 **Fax:** 208 2056264
Email: wfe@oberhausen.de **Web site:** http://bibliothek.oberhausen.de/seniorenzeitung
Freq: Quarterly; **Cover Price:** Free; **Circ:** 10,000
Editor: Rita Weller
Profile: Magazine for the elderly from the elderly.
Language(s): German

WIR IM SPORT

747528G75A-3440

Editorial: Friedrich-Alfred-Str. 25, 47055 DUISBURG
Tel: 203 7381830 **Fax:** 203 7381615
Email: joachim.lehmann@lsb-nrw.de **Web site:** http://www.wir-im-sport.de
Freq: 10 issues yearly; Free to qualifying individuals
Annual Sub.: EUR 15,00; **Circ:** 32,000
Editor: Joachim Lehmann
Profile: Magazine covering sports news for the Nordhein Westfalen area. Includes information about holiday activities and travel.
Language(s): German
ADVERTISING RATES:
Full Page Mono .... EUR 4645
Full Page Colour .... EUR 4645
Mechanical Data: Type Area: 253 x 188 mm, No. of Columns (Display): 4, Col Widths (Display): 44 mm
Copy instructions: *Copy Date:* 15 days prior to publication
CONSUMER: SPORT

WIR UND DIE WIRTSCHAFT

747860G63-1727

Editorial: Ferdinand-Sauerbruch-Str. 9, 56073 KOBLENZ **Tel:** 261 4040633 **Fax:** 261 4040626
Email: wiwi@vem.de **Web site:** http://www.vem.de
Freq: Monthly; **Circ:** 30,000
Editor: Siegbert Pinger
Profile: "Wir und die Wirtschaft" is the magazine of the companies and their employers' association vem.die arbeitgeber M+E, Industrie- und Dienstleistungsverband Rheinland-Rheinhessen for employees of establishments that gives insight into the fascinating world of the social market economy. Read factual information and reports on the functioning of the social market economy. Issues that burn the plants and their workers to give the nails, the magazine every month in easily understandable language. Reports from the working world, the bridge to our own experience. They are the trademark of "Wir und die Wirtschaft". Problems and their solutions are exemplified by companies from the region show. A wide service section supplements the core of the business-oriented magazine and adds value for the whole family. Facebook: http://www.facebook.com/vem.pinger.
Language(s): German
Supplement(s): M+E Zeitung
BUSINESS: REGIONAL BUSINESS

WIR ZIFKRAS

1928854G40-1003

Editorial: Ahrweg 140, 53347 ALFTER
Email: sonneck@zifkras.de
Circ: 150
Profile: Officers club magazine with internal information.
Language(s): German

WIRE

758518G27-2947

Editorial: Franz-Ludwig-Str. 7a, 96047 BAMBERG
Tel: 951 861118 **Fax:** 951 861170
Email: wire@meisenbach.de **Web site:** http://www.wireweb.de
Freq: Half-yearly; **Annual Sub.:** EUR 32,00; **Circ:** 3,900
Editor: Jörg Dambock; **Advertising Manager:** Georg Meisenbach
Profile: Magazine for manufacturers and processors of wire and cable.
Language(s): English
ADVERTISING RATES:
Full Page Mono .... EUR 2468
Full Page Colour .... EUR 3722
Mechanical Data: Type Area: 260 x 184 mm, No. of Columns (Display): 3, Col Widths (Display): 59 mm
Copy instructions: *Copy Date:* 20 days prior to publication
Official Journal of: Organ d. IWMA, ICFG
BUSINESS: METAL, IRON & STEEL

WIRTSCHAFT

747561G63-980

Editorial: Max-Joseph-Str. 2, 80333 MÜNCHEN
Tel: 89 5116222 **Fax:** 89 5116407
Email: adam@muenchen.ihk.de **Web site:** http://www.muenchen.ihk.de
Freq: 11 issues yearly; **Circ:** 98,900
Editor: Bernhard Adam
Profile: Journal of the Munich and Oberbayern Chamber of Trade and Industry. It offers readers compact expertise. The magazine takes the economy and economic policy from a regional perspective. It says regional policies from the perspective of entrepreneurs and provides tips for the daily management practice. The magazine provides information on taxes, finance, law, foreign trade, sales, trade, transport, vocational training or further education and helps to develop new markets. It reaches everywhere companies, medium-sized enterprises and individual entrepreneurs and professionals with high income levy without any wastage. The recipients of the magazine to decide on the investments in their businesses and as individuals are also affluent consumers.
Language(s): German
ADVERTISING RATES:
Full Page Mono .... EUR 5800
Full Page Colour .... EUR 7400
Mechanical Data: Type Area: 255 x 185 mm, No. of Columns (Display): 4, Col Widths (Display): 43 mm
Copy instructions: *Copy Date:* 32 days prior to publication
BUSINESS: REGIONAL BUSINESS

WIRTSCHAFT AKTUELL

747571G14A-8260

Editorial: Boschstr. 1, 48703 STADTLOHN
Tel: 2563 929210 **Fax:** 2563 929900
Email: redaktion@wirtschaft-aktuell.de **Web site:** http://www.wirtschaft-aktuell.de
Freq: Quarterly; **Annual Sub.:** EUR 16,00; **Circ:** 3,12
Editor: Christoph Almering; **Advertising Manager:** Rolf Koßmann
Profile: Business magazine for Coesfeld.
Language(s): German
ADVERTISING RATES:
Full Page Mono .... EUR 111
Full Page Colour .... EUR 159
Mechanical Data: Type Area: 270 x 189 mm, No. of Columns (Display): 4, Col Widths (Display): 45 mm
Copy instructions: *Copy Date:* 21 days prior to publication

WIRTSCHAFT AKTUELL

747572G14A-828

Editorial: Boschstr. 1, 48703 STADTLOHN
Tel: 2563 929210 **Fax:** 2563 929900
Email: redaktion@wirtschaft-aktuell.de **Web site:** http://www.wirtschaft-aktuell.de
Freq: Quarterly; **Annual Sub.:** EUR 16,00; **Circ:** 6,12
Editor: Christoph Almering; **Advertising Manager:** Rolf Koßmann
Profile: Business magazine for Borken.
Language(s): German
ADVERTISING RATES:
Full Page Mono .... EUR 126
Full Page Colour .... EUR 175
Mechanical Data: Type Area: 270 x 189 mm, No. of Columns (Display): 4, Col Widths (Display): 45 mm
Copy instructions: *Copy Date:* 21 days prior to publication

WIRTSCHAFT AKTUELL

747573G14A-830

Editorial: Boschstr. 1, 48703 STADTLOHN
Tel: 2563 929210 **Fax:** 2563 929900
Email: redaktion@wirtschaft-aktuell.de **Web site:** http://www.wirtschaft-aktuell.de
Freq: Quarterly; **Annual Sub.:** EUR 16,00; **Circ:** 2,05
Editor: Christoph Almering; **Advertising Manager:** Rolf Koßmann
Profile: Business magazine for the Grafschaft Bentheim region.
Language(s): German
ADVERTISING RATES:
Full Page Mono .... EUR 111
Full Page Colour .... EUR 159
Mechanical Data: Type Area: 270 x 189 mm, No. of Columns (Display): 4, Col Widths (Display): 45 mm
Copy instructions: *Copy Date:* 21 days prior to publication

WIRTSCHAFT AKTUELL - AUSG. EMSLAND

747570G14A-824

Editorial: Boschstr. 1, 48703 STADTLOHN
Tel: 2563 929210 **Fax:** 2563 929900
Email: redaktion@wirtschaft-aktuell.de **Web site:** http://www.wirtschaft-aktuell.de
Freq: Quarterly; **Annual Sub.:** EUR 16,00; **Circ:** 4,025
Editor: Christoph Almering; **Advertising Manager:** Rolf Koßmann
Profile: Business magazine for the Emsland region.
Language(s): German
ADVERTISING RATES:
Full Page Mono .... EUR 1265
Full Page Colour .... EUR 1750
Mechanical Data: Type Area: 270 x 189 mm, No. of Columns (Display): 4, Col Widths (Display): 45 mm
Copy instructions: *Copy Date:* 21 days prior to publication

WIRTSCHAFT AKTUELL - AUSG. OSNABRÜCK

747574G14A-8320

Editorial: Boschstr. 1, 48703 STADTLOHN
Tel: 2563 929210 **Fax:** 2563 929900
Email: redaktion@wirtschaft-aktuell.de **Web site:** http://www.wirtschaft-aktuell.de
Freq: Quarterly; **Annual Sub.:** EUR 16,00; **Circ:** 4,100
Editor: Christoph Almering; **Advertising Manager:** Rolf Koßmann
Profile: Business magazine for Osnabrück.
Language(s): German
ADVERTISING RATES:
Full Page Mono .... EUR 1265
Full Page Colour .... EUR 1750
Mechanical Data: Type Area: 270 x 189 mm, No. of Columns (Display): 4, Col Widths (Display): 45 mm
Copy instructions: *Copy Date:* 21 days prior to publication

WIRTSCHAFT AKTUELL - AUSG. STEINFURT

747569G14A-8220

Editorial: Boschstr. 1, 48703 STADTLOHN
Tel: 2563 929210 **Fax:** 2563 929900
Email: redaktion@wirtschaft-aktuell.de **Web site:** http://www.wirtschaft-aktuell.de
Freq: Quarterly; **Annual Sub.:** EUR 16,00; **Circ:** 4,550
Editor: Christoph Almering; **Advertising Manager:** Rolf Koßmann
Profile: Business magazine for Steinfurt.
Language(s): German
ADVERTISING RATES:
Full Page Mono .... EUR 1265
Full Page Colour .... EUR 1750
Mechanical Data: Type Area: 270 x 189 mm, No. of Columns (Display): 4, Col Widths (Display): 45 mm
Copy instructions: *Copy Date:* 21 days prior to publication

WIRTSCHAFT AKTUELL - AUSG. WARENDORF
747568G14A-8200

Editorial: Boschstr. 1, 48703 STADTLOHN
Tel: 2563 929210 **Fax:** 2563 929900
Email: redaktion@wirtschaft-aktuell.de **Web site:** http://www.wirtschaft-aktuell.de
Freq: Quarterly; **Annual Sub.:** EUR 16,00; **Circ:** 3,600
Editor: Christoph Almering; **Advertising Manager:** Rolf Koßmann
Profile: Business magazine for Warendorf.
Language(s): German
ADVERTISING RATES:
Full Page Mono .... EUR 1114
Full Page Colour .... EUR 1599
Mechanical Data: Type Area: 270 x 189 mm, No. of Columns (Display): 4, Col Widths (Display): 45 mm
Copy instructions: *Copy Date:* 21 days prior to publication

WIRTSCHAFT AM BAYERISCHEN UNTERMAIN
747576G63-1040

Editorial: Kerschensteinerstr. 9, 63741 ASCHAFFENBURG **Tel:** 6021 880111
Fax: 6021 88022127
Email: info@aschaffenburg.ihk.de **Web site:** http://www.aschaffenburg.ihk.de
Freq: 11 issues yearly; Free to qualifying individuals
Annual Sub.: EUR 18,41; **Circ:** 24,000
Editor: Horst Dommermuth; **Advertising Manager:** Sabine Weipert
Profile: Official journal of the Aschaffenburg Chamber of Trade and Industry. With a theme-related reporting, the journal informs about current, macro-economic developments and specific aspects of regional markets. Development themes are company announcements, information for business practice, thematic essays and reports from the Chamber of Commerce event.
Language(s): German
ADVERTISING RATES:
Full Page Mono .... EUR 1404
Full Page Colour .... EUR 2457
Mechanical Data: Type Area: 250 x 184 mm, No. of Columns (Display): 4, Col Widths (Display): 44 mm
Copy instructions: *Copy Date:* 20 days prior to publication
BUSINESS: REGIONAL BUSINESS

WIRTSCHAFT IM DIALOG
1828588G14A-10098

Editorial: Europaallee 33, 50226 FRECHEN
Tel: 2234 955680 **Fax:** 2234 9556868
Email: info@wfg-rhein-erft.de **Web site:** http://www.wfg-rhein-erft.de
Freq: Quarterly; **Cover Price:** Free; **Circ:** 8,500
Editor: Martin Schmitz; **Advertising Manager:** Goetz Römmelt
Profile: Regional business magazine.
Language(s): German
ADVERTISING RATES:
Full Page Mono .... EUR 2875
Full Page Colour .... EUR 2875
Mechanical Data: Type Area: 252 x 180 mm, No. of Columns (Display): 3, Col Widths (Display): 57 mm
Copy instructions: *Copy Date:* 14 days prior to publication

WIRTSCHAFT IM SÜDWESTEN
747586G63-1180

Editorial: Schnewlinstr. 11, 79098 FREIBURG
Tel: 761 151050 **Fax:** 761 3858398
Email: wis@freiburg.ihk.de **Web site:** http://www.wirtschaft-im-suedwesten.de
Freq: 11 issues yearly; Free to qualifying individuals
Annual Sub.: EUR 17,60; **Circ:** 62,332
Editor: Ulrich Plankenhorn; **Advertising Manager:** Achim Hartkopf
Profile: Magazine from the Freiburg Chamber of Trade and Industry. It is aimed at entrepreneurs and executives from industry, commerce, tourism, service and transport, with reports from the region for the region. Useful tips for everyday business. Standing about education and training.
Language(s): German
ADVERTISING RATES:
Full Page Mono .... EUR 4368
Full Page Colour .... EUR 5647
Mechanical Data: Type Area: 250 x 185 mm, No. of Columns (Display): 4, Col Widths (Display): 43 mm
Copy instructions: *Copy Date:* 27 days prior to publication
BUSINESS: REGIONAL BUSINESS

WIRTSCHAFT IN BREMEN
747587G63-1200

Editorial: Zweite Schlachtpforte 7, 28195 BREMEN
Tel: 421 3690372 **Fax:** 421 3690334
Email: backhaus@pressecontor.de **Web site:** http://www.schuenemann-verlag.de
Freq: Monthly; Free to qualifying individuals
Annual Sub.: EUR 22,80; **Circ:** 13,550
Editor: Christine Backhaus; **Advertising Manager:** Karin Wachendorf
Profile: Official magazine of the Bremen Chamber of Trade and Industry.
Language(s): German
ADVERTISING RATES:
Full Page Mono .... EUR 2365
Full Page Colour .... EUR 3775
Mechanical Data: Type Area: 261 x 190 mm, No. of Columns (Display): 4, Col Widths (Display): 45 mm
Copy instructions: *Copy Date:* 26 days prior to publication
BUSINESS: REGIONAL BUSINESS

WIRTSCHAFT IN MAINFRANKEN
747589G63-1220

Editorial: Mainaustr. 33, 97082 WÜRZBURG
Tel: 931 4194319 **Fax:** 931 4194100
Email: wim@wuerzburg.ihk.de **Web site:** http://www.wuerzburg.ihk.de
Freq: Monthly; **Cover Price:** Free; **Circ:** 13,899
Editor: Radu Ferendino; **Advertising Manager:** Daniela Dobresko
Profile: Journal of the Chamber of Trade and Industry for the Würzburg-Schweinfurt region.
Language(s): German
ADVERTISING RATES:
Full Page Mono .... EUR 2030
Full Page Colour .... EUR 2610
Mechanical Data: Type Area: 260 x 185 mm, No. of Columns (Display): 4, Col Widths (Display): 45 mm
Copy instructions: *Copy Date:* 8 days prior to publication
BUSINESS: REGIONAL BUSINESS

WIRTSCHAFT IN SÜDWESTSACHSEN
747593G63-1300

Editorial: Str. der Nationen 25, 09111 CHEMNITZ
Tel: 371 69001112 **Fax:** 371 69001114
Email: fiedler@chemnitz.ihk.de **Web site:** http://www.chemnitz.ihk24.de
Freq: 10 issues yearly; Free to qualifying individuals
Annual Sub.: EUR 25,56; **Circ:** 71,264
Editor: Marion Fiedler; **Advertising Manager:** Bernadette Schilder
Profile: Journal of the Chamber of Commerce and Industry for the Südwestsachsen region. It publishes important economic information from the region for the region. Companies in the industrial, commercial, service and transport by the Chamber of Commerce magazine supplied with technical information that can give any company.
Language(s): German
ADVERTISING RATES:
Full Page Mono .... EUR 3000
Full Page Colour .... EUR 4500
Mechanical Data: Type Area: 250 x 185 mm, No. of Columns (Display): 4, Col Widths (Display): 43 mm
Copy instructions: *Copy Date:* 23 days prior to publication
BUSINESS: REGIONAL BUSINESS

WIRTSCHAFT INFORM
1928853G14A-10379

Editorial: Münsterstr. 5, 59065 HAMM
Tel: 2381 9293406 **Fax:** 2381 9293222
Email: britta.wagner@wf-hamm.de **Web site:** http://www.wf-hamm.de
Freq: Quarterly; **Cover Price:** Free; **Circ:** 3,000
Editor: Britta Wagner
Profile: Newsletter of the Economic Development Hamm.
Language(s): German

WIRTSCHAFT MÜNSTERLAND FÜR DEN KREIS STEINFURT
1841561G14A-10176

Editorial: Siemensstr. 4, 48565 STEINFURT
Tel: 2552 920205 **Fax:** 2552 920210
Email: wirtschaft@tecklenborg-verlag.de **Web site:** http://www.tecklenborg-verlag.de
Freq: Quarterly; **Annual Sub.:** EUR 12,00; **Circ:** 8,450
Editor: Michael Hemschemeier; **Advertising Manager:** Hubert Tecklenborg
Profile: Magazine with events, information, tips and celebrity interviews from the Münsterland region.
Language(s): German
ADVERTISING RATES:
Full Page Mono .... EUR 1810
Full Page Colour .... EUR 2350
Mechanical Data: Type Area: 252 x 184 mm, No. of Columns (Display): 4, Col Widths (Display): 44 mm
Copy instructions: *Copy Date:* 19 days prior to publication

WIRTSCHAFT NECKAR-ALB
747597G63-1320

Editorial: Hindenburgstr. 54, 72762 REUTLINGEN
Tel: 7121 201174 **Fax:** 7121 2014174
Email: heise@reutlingen.ihk.de **Web site:** http://www.reutlingen.ihk.de
Freq: 10 issues yearly; Free to qualifying individuals
Annual Sub.: EUR 40,00; **Circ:** 18,509
Editor: Christoph Heise
Profile: Magazine of the Reutlingen Chamber of Trade and Industry.
Language(s): German
ADVERTISING RATES:
Full Page Mono .... EUR 1788
Full Page Colour .... EUR 2750
Mechanical Data: Type Area: 250 x 185 mm, No. of Columns (Display): 3, Col Widths (Display): 58 mm
Copy instructions: *Copy Date:* 30 days prior to publication
BUSINESS: REGIONAL BUSINESS

WIRTSCHAFT OSTFRIESLAND & PAPENBURG
747601G63-1380

Editorial: Ringstr. 4, 26721 EMDEN **Tel:** 4921 89010
Fax: 4921 890133
Email: ihk@emden.ihk.de **Web site:** http://www.ihk-emden.de
Freq: Monthly; Free to qualifying individuals
Annual Sub.: EUR 16,00; **Circ:** 12,764
Editor: Torsten Slink; **Advertising Manager:** Ralf Niemeyer
Profile: Magazine of the Chamber of Trade and Industry for the Papenburg and Ostfriesland regions.
Language(s): German
ADVERTISING RATES:
Full Page Mono .... EUR 2070
Full Page Colour .... EUR 2070
Mechanical Data: Type Area: 260 x 185 mm, No. of Columns (Display): 4, Col Widths (Display): 44 mm
Copy instructions: *Copy Date:* 25 days prior to publication
BUSINESS: REGIONAL BUSINESS

WIRTSCHAFT REGION FULDA
747603G63-1400

Editorial: Heinrichstr. 8, 36037 FULDA **Tel:** 661 2840
Fax: 661 28444
Email: info@fulda.ihk.de **Web site:** http://www.ihk-fulda.de
Freq: 11 issues yearly; Free to qualifying individuals
Annual Sub.: EUR 12,00; **Circ:** 11,213
Editor: Stefan Schunck
Profile: Publication of the Fulda Chamber of Trade and Industry.
Language(s): German
ADVERTISING RATES:
Full Page Mono .... EUR 920
Full Page Colour .... EUR 1070
Mechanical Data: Type Area: 250 x 185 mm, No. of Columns (Display): 3, Col Widths (Display): 59 mm
Copy instructions: *Copy Date:* 15 days prior to publication
BUSINESS: REGIONAL BUSINESS

WIRTSCHAFT REGIONAL
747602G14A-8380

Editorial: Bahnhofstr. 65, 73430 AALEN
Tel: 7361 594163 **Fax:** 7361 594231
Email: w.hofele@sdz-medien.de **Web site:** http://www.wirtschaft-regional.de
Freq: Monthly; **Annual Sub.:** EUR 46,00; **Circ:** 10,158
Editor: Winfried Hofele; **Advertising Manager:** Jürgen Stirner
Profile: Business magazine for the East Württemberg region.
Language(s): German
ADVERTISING RATES:
Full Page Mono .... EUR 6115
Full Page Colour .... EUR 8385
Mechanical Data: Type Area: 430 x 282 mm, No. of Columns (Display): 6, Col Widths (Display): 45 mm
Copy instructions: *Copy Date:* 14 days prior to publication
BUSINESS: COMMERCE, INDUSTRY & MANAGEMENT

WIRTSCHAFT REGIONAL
764952G14A-9283

Editorial: Richthofenstr. 96, 32756 DETMOLD
Tel: 5231 981000 **Fax:** 5231 9810033
Email: redaktion@wirtschaftregional.info **Web site:** http://www.wirtschaftregional.info
Freq: Monthly; **Annual Sub.:** EUR 20,00; **Circ:** 35,300
Editor: Peer-Michael Press; **Advertising Manager:** Günter Press
Profile: "Wirtschaft Regional" is an independent business magazine for executives in small and medium-sized companies, regardless of interests of individual organizations or companies. A strong media partner that provides competent, dedicated and themed with text, image, video presentations and one in the center: your business. The magazine helps promote the economic success of businesses in the region by bringing the issues of businesses in an interested public. We report on companies, people, politics, trends, markets and products.
Language(s): German
ADVERTISING RATES:
Full Page Mono .... EUR 4151
Full Page Colour .... EUR 5395
Mechanical Data: Type Area: 253 x 169 mm, No. of Columns (Display): 3, Col Widths (Display): 58 mm
Copy instructions: *Copy Date:* 18 days prior to publication

WIRTSCHAFT UND ERZIEHUNG
747842G62H-1120

Editorial: Alte Försterei 9, 33142 BÜREN
Tel: 2955 748558
Email: sandmann@vlw.de **Web site:** http://www.vlw.de
Freq: 10 issues yearly; Free to qualifying individuals
Annual Sub.: EUR 34,99; **Circ:** 16,620
Editor: Detlef Sandmann
Profile: Publication about training and careers in business.
Language(s): German
ADVERTISING RATES:
Full Page Mono .... EUR 970
Full Page Colour .... EUR 1625
Mechanical Data: Type Area: 257 x 187 mm
Copy instructions: *Copy Date:* 23 days prior to publication
BUSINESS: CHURCH & SCHOOL EQUIPMENT & EDUCATION: Careers

WIRTSCHAFT & MARKT
747844G14A-8400

Editorial: Zimmerstr. 55, 10117 BERLIN
Tel: 30 2789450 **Fax:** 30 27894523
Email: liebsch@wirtschaftundmarkt.de **Web site:** http://www.wirtschaftundmarkt.de
Freq: 10 issues yearly; Free to qualifying individuals
Annual Sub.: EUR 30,00; **Circ:** 30,350
Editor: Helfried Liebsch; **Advertising Manager:** Margit Eschment
Profile: The business magazine aimed at the middle class, especially the new federal states and reaches in every single member of the regional transit Business organizations in East Germany and Berlin. It has been 21 years the magazine for women and decision makers in business, politics and administration. Creative journalism, and a high profile account the special problems and needs in small and medium enterprises. "Wirtschaft & Markt" is the only national business magazine of the new countries skills and experience up close to the action provides on-site. With good contacts with players in the economy and policy guarantees, the magazine's readers reviews of high relevance and competence. The magazine cuts to his extensive service section to finance, business management, law, tax, investment, insurance, real estate to the specific needs of innovative SMEs, thereby ensuring accurate guide shaft. It is published monthly focusing on topics for entrepreneurs.
Language(s): German
ADVERTISING RATES:
Full Page Mono .... EUR 4200
Full Page Colour .... EUR 6300
Mechanical Data: Type Area: 250 x 182 mm, No. of Columns (Display): 3, Col Widths (Display): 59 mm
Copy instructions: *Copy Date:* 20 days prior to publication

WIRTSCHAFT UND RECHT IN OSTEUROPA WIRO
756873G14C-4703

Editorial: Postfach 340164, 80098 MÜNCHEN
Tel: 89 52314693 **Fax:** 89 52389921
Email: wiro@bohata.com **Web site:** http://www.bohata.com
Freq: Monthly; **Annual Sub.:** EUR 398,00; **Circ:** 1,000
Editor: Petr Bohata; **Advertising Manager:** Fritz Lebherz
Profile: Magazine on legal and economic developments in Middle and Eastern European States.
Language(s): German
ADVERTISING RATES:
Full Page Mono .... EUR 1460
Full Page Colour .... EUR 2960
Mechanical Data: Type Area: 260 x 186 mm, No. of Columns (Display): 4, Col Widths (Display): 43 mm

WIRTSCHAFT+WEITER-BILDUNG
747849G62H-1140

Editorial: Munzinger Str. 9, 79111 FREIBURG
Tel: 761 8983921 **Fax:** 761 8983112
Email: online@haufe-lexware.com **Web site:** http://www.wuw-magazin.de
Freq: 10 issues yearly; **Annual Sub.:** EUR 108,00; **Circ:** 15,647
Editor: Martin Pichler; **Advertising Manager:** Klaus A. Sturm
Profile: Journal about further education.
Language(s): German
ADVERTISING RATES:
Full Page Mono .... EUR 4000
Full Page Colour .... EUR 4800
Mechanical Data: Type Area: 249 x 176 mm, No. of Columns (Display): 3, Col Widths (Display): 56 mm
Copy instructions: *Copy Date:* 20 days prior to publication
BUSINESS: CHURCH & SCHOOL EQUIPMENT & EDUCATION: Careers

WIRTSCHAFT & WISSENSCHAFT
747850G14A-8440

Editorial: Barkhovenallee 1, 45239 ESSEN
Tel: 201 8401181 **Fax:** 201 8401459
Email: mail@stifterverband.de **Web site:** http://www.stifterverband.de
Freq: Quarterly; **Circ:** 7,500
Editor: Michael Sonnabend
Profile: Magazine for members of the Foundation Association, university and science politics.
Language(s): German

WIRTSCHAFT ZWISCHEN NORD- UND OSTSEE - AUSG. LÜBECK
747852G63-1440

Editorial: Fackenburger Allee 2, 23554 LÜBECK
Tel: 451 6006169 **Fax:** 451 60064169
Email: vogel@ihk-luebeck.de **Web site:** http://www.ihk-schleswig-holstein.de
Freq: 11 issues yearly; Free to qualifying individuals
Annual Sub.: EUR 22,00; **Circ:** 95,550
Editor: Klemens Vogel; **Advertising Manager:** Christiane Kermel
Profile: Journal of Commerce and Industry Chamber of Schleswig-Holstein with regional section Lübeck, Kiel or Flensburg. The magazine provides detailed

information about the companies in the northernmost province. It provides useful information inter alia to the areas of tax, legal, vocational training, trade, tourism, foreign trade and innovation and technology transfer. The leaders and managers in all major business districts in the IHK Flensburg, Kiel and Luebeck are among the readers of the Chamber of Commerce magazine. Thus it is the medium for the target group to reach the decision makers in the industry in Schleswig-Holstein.
Language(s): German
ADVERTISING RATES:
Full Page Mono .... EUR 5357
Full Page Colour .... EUR 8572
Mechanical Data: Type Area: 260 x 185 mm, No. of Columns (Display): 3, Col Widths (Display): 58 mm
BUSINESS: REGIONAL BUSINESS

WIRTSCHAFTS BILD
747605G14A-8580
Editorial: Egermannstr. 2, 53359 RHEINBACH
Tel: 2226 8020 **Fax:** 2226 802222
Email: verlag@ubgnet.de **Web site:** http://www.wirtschaftsbild.de
Freq: 25 issues yearly; **Annual Sub.:** EUR 674,10; **Circ:** 3,000
Editor: Andreas Oberholz; **Advertising Manager:** Hans Peter Steins
Profile: Journal providing economic and business news about Germany and the European Union.
Language(s): German
ADVERTISING RATES:
Full Page Mono .... EUR 1850
Full Page Colour .... EUR 1850
Mechanical Data: Col Widths (Display): 80 mm, Type Area: 243 x 170 mm, No. of Columns (Display): 2
Copy instructions: *Copy Date:* 20 days prior to publication
BUSINESS: COMMERCE, INDUSTRY & MANAGEMENT

WIRTSCHAFTS JOURNAL SÜD-WEST
1830024G14A-10114
Editorial: Koblenzer Str. 75, 57482 WENDEN
Tel: 2762 985228 **Fax:** 2762 985229
Email: info@wirtschaftsjournalsuedwest.de **Web site:** http://www.wirtschaftsjournalsuedwest.de
Freq: 8 issues yearly; **Annual Sub.:** EUR 48,00; **Circ:** 22,500
Editor: Andreas F. Lehmann; **Advertising Manager:** Marcus J. Lehmann
Profile: The magazine provides information about economics, economic policy and business in the south-west of North Rhine-Westphalia. It is distributed free to executives in medium-sized enterprises in south-west of North Rhine-Westphalia.
Language(s): German
ADVERTISING RATES:
Full Page Colour .... EUR 4295
Mechanical Data: Type Area: 260 x 190 mm
Copy instructions: *Copy Date:* 14 days prior to publication

WIRTSCHAFTS NACHRICHTEN
747749G14A-8740
Editorial: Dießemer Bruch 167, 47805 KREFELD
Tel: 2151 5100175 **Fax:** 2151 5100104
Email: wirtschafts-nachrichten@stuenings.de **Web site:** http://www.wirtschafts-nachrichten.de
Freq: Quarterly; **Annual Sub.:** EUR 20,00; **Circ:** 11,900
Editor: Jörg Montag; **Advertising Manager:** Julia Dahmen
Profile: Wirtschafts nachrichten is the independent, regional economic information in the region of North Rhine for entrepreneurs and decision makers. Reporting with a clear focus on regional economies focused on the economy in North Rhine (Niederrhein Dusseldorf and western Ruhr area). The Wirtschafts nachrichten used by entrepreneurs and executives from industry, commerce, crafts and services, whose interests are represented critical and independent association of the editors. Since 1956.
Language(s): German
ADVERTISING RATES:
Full Page Mono .... EUR 2100
Full Page Colour .... EUR 2700
Mechanical Data: Type Area: 255 x 185 mm, No. of Columns (Display): 4, Col Widths (Display): 43 mm
Copy instructions: *Copy Date:* 20 days prior to publication

WIRTSCHAFTS REPORT
747763G63-1560
Editorial: Koblenzer Str. 121, 57072 SIEGEN
Tel: 271 3302317 **Fax:** 271 330244317
Email: tanja.bauschert@siegen.ihk.de **Web site:** http://www.ihk-siegen.de
Freq: Monthly; **Annual Sub.:** EUR 36,60; **Circ:** 22,300
Editor: Tanja Bauschert
Profile: Journal of the Siegen Chamber of Trade and Industry. Each month the editorial team together an interesting mix of topics and would like to give a good overview of the economic life in the districts of Siegen-Wittgenstein and Olpe. At the same time it provides member companies a number of practical examples and will keep the company up to date - whether in developments in domestic companies, changes in legislation or on topics of general interest.
Language(s): German
ADVERTISING RATES:
Full Page Mono .... EUR 1600
Full Page Colour .... EUR 2560
Mechanical Data: Type Area: 260 x 185 mm, No. of Columns (Display): 4, Col Widths (Display): 46 mm

Copy instructions: *Copy Date:* 17 days prior to publication
BUSINESS: REGIONAL BUSINESS

WIRTSCHAFTS SPIEGEL
730820G63-420
Editorial: Sentmaringer Weg 61, 48151 MÜNSTER
Tel: 251 707319 **Fax:** 251 707358
Email: wirtschaftsspiegel@ihk-nordwestfalen.de **Web site:** http://www.ihk-nordwestfalen.de
Freq: 11 issues yearly; Free to qualifying individuals
Annual Sub.: EUR 19,80; **Circ:** 50,048
Editor: Guido Krüdewagen; **Advertising Manager:** Lars Lehmanski
Profile: Official Journal of Commerce and Industry Chamber Nord Westfalen (Münster). The official notice of institution is designed as a regional business magazine and contains valuable information and tips, and news and reports, especially from medium-sized enterprises. The magazine is aimed at all commercial enterprises of the district of Münster (Münsterland and Emscher-Lippe region), also via subscription to many companies in the adjacent regions. With a monthly circulation of approximately 52 200 copies are made in this area nationwide large enterprises, medium-sized enterprises and individual entrepreneurs and professionals with high income levy without any wastage. The number of such readers is made up of owners, managers and board members and executives. This readership is characterized by high living and standard of education and entrepreneurial interest.
Language(s): German
ADVERTISING RATES:
Full Page Mono .... EUR 3491
Full Page Colour .... EUR 5771
Mechanical Data: Type Area: 255 x 185 mm, No. of Columns (Display): 4, Col Widths (Display): 44 mm
Copy instructions: *Copy Date:* 21 days prior to publication
BUSINESS: REGIONAL BUSINESS

WIRTSCHAFTSBLATT
2090772G14A-10515
Editorial: Graf-Adolf-Platz 1, 40213 DÜSSELDORF
Tel: 211 31120600 **Fax:** 211 311206030
Email: redaktion@wirtschaftsblatt.de **Web site:** http://www.wirtschaftsblatt.de
Freq: 5 issues yearly; **Circ:** 10,000
Editor: Marc Daniel Schmelzer
Profile: The Wirtschaftsblatt is available for business reporting with local relevance. As an information organ of economic development agencies, institutions and associations as a forum for stakeholders and as a marketplace of businesses and service providers, it is the media platform of the economy. With the Wirtschaftsblatt are entrepreneurs at the site are well informed, interesting vendors who may be only a few kilometers from a resident to do something competitive and offer customers and what offers and services, the economic development agencies, associations and institutions.
Language(s): German
ADVERTISING RATES:
Full Page Mono .... EUR 2550
Full Page Colour .... EUR 2550
Mechanical Data: Type Area: 245 x 189 mm, No. of Columns (Display): 3, Col Widths (Display): 60 mm

---

WIRTSCHAFTSBLATT
2090773G14A-10516
Editorial: Graf-Adolf-Platz 1, 40213 DÜSSELDORF
Tel: 211 31120600 **Fax:** 211 311206030
Email: redaktion@wirtschaftsblatt.de **Web site:** http://www.wirtschaftsblatt.de
Freq: 5 issues yearly; **Circ:** 10,000
Editor: Marc Daniel Schmelzer
Profile: The Wirtschaftsblatt is available for business reporting with local relevance. As an information organ of economic development agencies, institutions and associations as a forum for stakeholders and as a marketplace of businesses and service providers, it is the media platform of the economy. With the Wirtschaftsblatt are entrepreneurs at the site are well informed, interesting vendors who may be only a few kilometers from a resident to do something competitive and offer customers and what offers and services, the economic development agencies, associations and institutions.
Language(s): German
ADVERTISING RATES:
Full Page Mono .... EUR 2550
Full Page Colour .... EUR 2550
Mechanical Data: Type Area: 245 x 189 mm, No. of Columns (Display): 3, Col Widths (Display): 60 mm

---

WIRTSCHAFTSBLATT
2090774G14A-10517
Editorial: Graf-Adolf-Platz 1, 40213 DÜSSELDORF
Tel: 211 31120600 **Fax:** 211 311206030
Email: redaktion@wirtschaftsblatt.de **Web site:** http://www.wirtschaftsblatt.de
Freq: 5 issues yearly; **Circ:** 13,000
Editor: Marc Daniel Schmelzer
Profile: The Wirtschaftsblatt is available for business reporting with local relevance. As an information organ of economic development agencies, institutions and associations as a forum for stakeholders and as a marketplace of businesses and service providers, it is the media platform of the economy. With the Wirtschaftsblatt are entrepreneurs at the site are well informed, interesting vendors who may be only a few kilometers from a resident to do something competitive and offer customers and what offers and services, the economic development agencies, associations and institutions.
Language(s): German
ADVERTISING RATES:
Full Page Mono .... EUR 2550
Full Page Colour .... EUR 2550
Mechanical Data: Type Area: 245 x 189 mm, No. of Columns (Display): 3, Col Widths (Display): 60 mm

---

WIRTSCHAFTSBLATT
2090775G14A-10518
Editorial: Graf-Adolf-Platz 1, 40213 DÜSSELDORF
Tel: 211 31120600 **Fax:** 211 311206030
Email: redaktion@wirtschaftsblatt.de **Web site:** http://www.wirtschaftsblatt.de
Freq: 5 issues yearly; **Circ:** 10,000
Editor: Marc Daniel Schmelzer
Profile: The Wirtschaftsblatt is available for business reporting with local relevance. As an information organ of economic development agencies, institutions and associations as a forum for stakeholders and as a marketplace of businesses and service providers, it is the media platform of the economy. With the Wirtschaftsblatt are entrepreneurs at the site are well informed, interesting vendors who may be only a few kilometers from a resident to do something competitive and offer customers and what offers and services, the economic development agencies, associations and institutions.
Language(s): German
ADVERTISING RATES:
Full Page Mono .... EUR 2550
Full Page Colour .... EUR 2550
Mechanical Data: Type Area: 245 x 189 mm, No. of Columns (Display): 3, Col Widths (Display): 60 mm

---

WIRTSCHAFTSBLATT
2090776G14A-10519
Editorial: Graf-Adolf-Platz 1, 40213 DÜSSELDORF
Tel: 211 31120600 **Fax:** 211 311206030
Email: redaktion@wirtschaftsblatt.de **Web site:** http://www.wirtschaftsblatt.de
Freq: 5 issues yearly; **Circ:** 12,000
Editor: Marc Daniel Schmelzer
Profile: The Wirtschaftsblatt is available for business reporting with local relevance. As an information organ of economic development agencies, institutions and associations as a forum for stakeholders and as a marketplace of businesses and service providers, it is the media platform of the economy. With the Wirtschaftsblatt are entrepreneurs at the site are well informed, interesting vendors who may be only a few kilometers from a resident to do something competitive and offer customers and what offers and services, the economic development agencies, associations and institutions.
Language(s): German
ADVERTISING RATES:
Full Page Mono .... EUR 2550
Full Page Colour .... EUR 2550
Mechanical Data: Type Area: 245 x 189 mm, No. of Columns (Display): 3, Col Widths (Display): 60 mm

---

WIRTSCHAFTSBLATT
2090777G14A-10520
Editorial: Graf-Adolf-Platz 1, 40213 DÜSSELDORF
Tel: 211 31120600 **Fax:** 211 311206030
Email: redaktion@wirtschaftsblatt.de **Web site:** http://www.wirtschaftsblatt.de
Freq: 5 issues yearly; **Circ:** 12,000
Editor: Marc Daniel Schmelzer
Profile: The Wirtschaftsblatt is available for business reporting with local relevance. As an information organ of economic development agencies, institutions and associations as a forum for stakeholders and as a marketplace of businesses and service providers, it is the media platform of the economy. With the Wirtschaftsblatt are entrepreneurs at the site are well informed, interesting vendors who may be only a few kilometers from a resident to do something competitive and offer customers and what offers and services, the economic development agencies, associations and institutions.
Language(s): German
ADVERTISING RATES:
Full Page Mono .... EUR 2550
Full Page Colour .... EUR 2550
Mechanical Data: Type Area: 245 x 189 mm, No. of Columns (Display): 3, Col Widths (Display): 60 mm

---

WIRTSCHAFTSBLATT
2090778G14A-10521
Editorial: Graf-Adolf-Platz 1, 40213 DÜSSELDORF
Tel: 211 31120600 **Fax:** 211 311206030
Email: redaktion@wirtschaftsblatt.de **Web site:** http://www.wirtschaftsblatt.de
Freq: 5 issues yearly; **Circ:** 10,000
Editor: Marc Daniel Schmelzer
Profile: The Wirtschaftsblatt is available for business reporting with local relevance. As an information organ of economic development agencies, institutions and associations as a forum for stakeholders and as a marketplace of businesses and service providers, it is the media platform of the economy. With the Wirtschaftsblatt are entrepreneurs at the site are well informed, interesting vendors who may be only a few kilometers from a resident to do something competitive and offer customers and what offers and services, the economic development agencies, associations and institutions.
Language(s): German
ADVERTISING RATES:
Full Page Mono .... EUR 2550
Full Page Colour .... EUR 2550

Mechanical Data: Type Area: 245 x 189 mm, No. of Columns (Display): 3, Col Widths (Display): 60 mm

---

WIRTSCHAFTSBLATT NIEDERRHEIN
1996206G14A-1043
Formerly: Wirtschaftsblatt
Editorial: Graf-Adolf-Platz 1, 40213 DÜSSELDORF
Tel: 211 31120600 **Fax:** 211 311206030
Email: redaktion@wirtschaftsblatt.de **Web site:** http://www.wirtschaftsblatt.de
Circ: 11,000
Editor: Marc Daniel Schmelzer
Profile: The Wirtschaftsblatt is available for business reporting with local relevance. As an information organ of economic development agencies, institutions and associations as a forum for stakeholders and as a marketplace of businesses and service providers, it is the media platform of the economy. With the Wirtschaftsblatt are entrepreneurs at the site are well informed, interesting vendors who may be only a few kilometers from a resident to do something competitive and offer customers and what offers and services, the economic development agencies, associations and institutions.
Language(s): German
ADVERTISING RATES:
Full Page Mono .... EUR 2550
Full Page Colour .... EUR 2550
Mechanical Data: Type Area: 245 x 189 mm, No. of Columns (Display): 3, Col Widths (Display): 60 mm

---

WIRTSCHAFTSDIENST VERSICHERUNGSMAKLER
747713G1D-420
Editorial: Max-Planck-Str. 7, 97082 WÜRZBURG
Tel: 931 4183070 **Fax:** 931 4183080
Email: wvm@iww.de **Web site:** http://www.iww.de
Freq: Monthly
Editor: Norbert Rettner
Profile: Magazine providing business news relating to insurance.
Language(s): German
BUSINESS: FINANCE & ECONOMICS: Insurance

WIRTSCHAFTSECHO
1852426G14A-10201
Editorial: Holzhofallee 25, 64295 DARMSTADT
Tel: 6151 3871 **Fax:** 6151 387307
Email: redaktion@wirtschaftsecho.de **Web site:** http://www.wirtschaftsecho.de
Freq: 6 issues yearly; **Annual Sub.:** EUR 18,00; **Circ:** 20,000
Editor: Hans Werner Mayer; **Advertising Manager:** Andreas Wohlfart
Profile: WirtschaftsEcho is an information platform for industry, trade and professionals. Committed useful, relevant, - As an ally of the companies in the region. Magazine for makers and markets in South Hesse. Each issue is devoted to a conthoughtful ideas on various topics such as: fleet, financing for SMEs or the modern office. Regular basic economic knowledge to students and trainees will be offered to encourage the identification of the young generation with the market, the market economy and the economic region of southern Hesse.
Language(s): German
ADVERTISING RATES:
Full Page Mono .... EUR 3857
Mechanical Data: Type Area: 322 x 231 mm, No. of Columns (Display): 5, Col Widths (Display): 43 mm
Copy instructions: *Copy Date:* 21 days prior to publication

WIRTSCHAFTSFORUM
747719G14A-8480
Editorial: Sassestr. 14, 48431 RHEINE
Tel: 5971 921640 **Fax:** 5971 92164838
Email: info@wirtschaftsforum-verlag.de **Web site:** http://www.wirtschaftsforum.de
Freq: Monthly; **Circ:** 10,203
Editor: Manfred Brinkmann; **Advertising Manager:** Karin Schmidt
Language(s): German
ADVERTISING RATES:
Full Page Mono .... EUR 3050
Full Page Colour .... EUR 4450
Mechanical Data: Type Area: 260 x 204 mm, No. of Columns (Display): 4, Col Widths (Display): 48 mm
Copy instructions: *Copy Date:* 14 days prior to publication
BUSINESS: COMMERCE, INDUSTRY & MANAGEMENT

WIRTSCHAFTSFORUM NAH- UND MITTELOST
756871G14A-9239
Editorial: Jägerstr. 63d, 10117 BERLIN
Tel: 30 2064100 **Fax:** 30 20641010
Email: numov@numov.de **Web site:** http://www.numov.de
Freq: 6 issues yearly; Free to qualifying individuals
Annual Sub.: EUR 240,00; **Circ:** 2,500
Editor: Helene Rang
Profile: Magazine on business developments and business opportunities for Members of Middle East Association.
Language(s): English; German

WIRTSCHAFTSKURIER
747731G14A-8640
Editorial: Parkring 4, 85748 GARCHING
Tel: 89 6389810 **Fax:** 89 63898120
Email: redaktion@wirtschaftskurier.de **Web site:** http://www.wirtschaftskurier.de
Freq: 11 issues yearly; **Annual Sub.:** EUR 27,50; **Circ:** 50,359
Editor: Elwine Happ-Frank; **News Editor:** Daniel Medhin; **Advertising Manager:** Alexandra Nohe
Profile: The WirtschaftsKurier is aimed at decision makers from politics and business. Newspaper resorts: - "The World in mind" Economic Policy (analysis, commentary, interviews), opinion (by prominent authors) - "Industry & Markets" portraits of large enterprises and medium-sized companies, industry developments, interviews with executives and managers - "Finance & Markets" "analyzes the financial markets, reports from banks and insurance companies, interviews with the heads of large financial institutions - "Energy efficiency" hot topics of the industry, portraits of utility companies, interviews with experts - "Innovation & IT " reports on the latest innovations in research and development, technological trends. The WirtschaftsKurier is read by directors and company owners. He is for all elected officials in the German Bundestag and in many countries parliaments. In addition, the economic courier at many fairs and congresses, at the airports and airlines as well as in many upscale hotels are represented. Especially in the important focus for the future target group of students as a separate distribution to universities and colleges. Because of its economic competence of the courier was included in the group of exchange duty sheets.
Language(s): German
ADVERTISING RATES:
Full Page Colour .... EUR 17800
Mechanical Data: Type Area: 445 x 314 mm, No. of Columns (Display): 6, Col Widths (Display): 49 mm
Copy instructions: *Copy Date:* 4 days prior to publication
BUSINESS: COMMERCE, INDUSTRY & MANAGEMENT

WIRTSCHAFTSMAGAZIN BODENSEE
747733G14A-8520
Editorial: Max-Stromeyer-Str. 116, 78467 KONSTANZ **Tel:** 7531 90710 **Fax:** 7531 907131
Email: twillauer@labhard.de **Web site:** http://www.labhard.de
Freq: Annual; **Cover Price:** EUR 5,00; **Circ:** 25,000
Editor: Thomas Willauer; **Advertising Manager:** Carola Buchwald
Profile: The Business Magazine is the business card of the international economic area of Bodensee. It communicates the hard and soft location factors in the region, combining business, culture and tourism. It provides detailed facts and figures and names of important institutions and contact persons. Politics and administration take a position on the opportunities and challenges of the international Bodensee region. Successful companies promote themselves and the location of Bodensee. Universities introduce themselves and show the quality of the educational landscape of Bodensee. Topics: Locations - Branches - Company - Institute - Research - Technology - Infrastructure - Investments - Property - Trade Shows - Conferences - Conventions - Counties - Cities - Municipalities - boards - Initiatives - Associations - Education - Universities - Labour Market - Job opportunities - Career Opportunities - Quality of Life - Culture - Nature.
Language(s): English; German
ADVERTISING RATES:
Full Page Colour .... EUR 1580
Mechanical Data: Type Area: 255 x 183 mm
Copy instructions: *Copy Date:* 44 days prior to publication

WIRTSCHAFTSMAGAZIN FÜR DEN FRAUENARZT
747739G56A-10200
Editorial: Otto-Hahn-Str. 7, 50997 KÖLN
Tel: 2236 376438 **Fax:** 2236 376999
Email: schweihoff@wpv.de **Web site:** http://www.wpv.de
Freq: 6 issues yearly; Free to qualifying individuals
Annual Sub.: EUR 22,50; **Circ:** 10,527
Editor: Monika Schweihoff; **Advertising Manager:** Isabelle Becker
Profile: The Wirtschaftsmagazin für den Frauenarzt is focused on issues that are important to physicians in everyday practice: billing tips, medical and tax law, summarizing medical topic and industry news, analysis of insurance and investment field, practice comparison.
Language(s): German
ADVERTISING RATES:
Full Page Mono .... EUR 2488
Full Page Colour .... EUR 3463
Mechanical Data: Type Area: 240 x 180 mm, No. of Columns (Display): 3, Col Widths (Display): 56 mm
Copy instructions: *Copy Date:* 21 days prior to publication
Official Journal of: Organ d. VWA Verb. Wirtschaft u. Arzt e.V.
BUSINESS: HEALTH & MEDICAL

WIRTSCHAFTSMAGAZIN FÜR DEN HAUTARZT
747740G56A-10220
Editorial: Otto-Hahn-Str. 7, 50997 KÖLN
Tel: 2236 376438 **Fax:** 2236 37692530
Email: schweihoff@wpv.de **Web site:** http://www.wpv.de
Freq: 6 issues yearly; Free to qualifying individuals
Annual Sub.: EUR 22,50; **Circ:** 4,539
Editor: Monika Schweihoff; **Advertising Manager:** Isabelle Becker
Profile: The Wirtschaftsmagazin für den Hautarzt is focused on issues that are important to physicians in everyday practice: billing tips, medical and tax law, summarizing medical topic and industry news, analysis of insurance and investment field, practice comparison.
Language(s): German
ADVERTISING RATES:
Full Page Mono .... EUR 1798
Full Page Colour .... EUR 2773
Mechanical Data: Type Area: 240 x 180 mm, No. of Columns (Display): 3, Col Widths (Display): 56 mm
Copy instructions: *Copy Date:* 21 days prior to publication
Official Journal of: Organ d. VWA Verb. Wirtschaft u. Arzt e.V.
BUSINESS: HEALTH & MEDICAL

WIRTSCHAFTSMAGAZIN FÜR DEN KINDERARZT
747741G56A-10240
Editorial: Otto-Hahn-Str. 7, 50997 KÖLN
Tel: 2236 376438 **Fax:** 2236 37692530
Email: schweihoff@wpv.de **Web site:** http://www.wpv.de
Freq: 6 issues yearly; Free to qualifying individuals
Annual Sub.: EUR 22,50; **Circ:** 6,779
Editor: Monika Schweihoff; **Advertising Manager:** Isabelle Becker
Profile: The Wirtschaftsmagazin für den Kinderarzt is focused on issues that are important to physicians in everyday practice: billing tips, medical and tax law, summarizing medical topic and industry news, analysis of insurance and investment field, practice comparison.
Language(s): German
ADVERTISING RATES:
Full Page Mono .... EUR 1798
Full Page Colour .... EUR 2773
Mechanical Data: Type Area: 240 x 180 mm, No. of Columns (Display): 3, Col Widths (Display): 56 mm
Copy instructions: *Copy Date:* 21 days prior to publication
Official Journal of: Organ d. VWA Verb. Wirtschaft u. Arzt e.V.
BUSINESS: HEALTH & MEDICAL

WIRTSCHAFTSMAGAZIN FÜR DEN NERVENARZT
747742G56A-10260
Editorial: Otto-Hahn-Str. 7, 50997 KÖLN
Tel: 2236 376438 **Fax:** 2236 37692530
Email: schweihoff@wpv.de **Web site:** http://www.wpv.de
Freq: 6 issues yearly; Free to qualifying individuals
Annual Sub.: EUR 22,50; **Circ:** 6,088
Editor: Monika Schweihoff; **Advertising Manager:** Isabelle Becker
Profile: The Wirtschaftsmagazin für den Nervenarzt is focused on issues that are important to physicians in everyday practice: billing tips, medical and tax law, summarizing medical topic and industry news, analysis of insurance and investment field, practice comparison.
Language(s): German
ADVERTISING RATES:
Full Page Mono .... EUR 1798
Full Page Colour .... EUR 2773
Mechanical Data: Type Area: 240 x 180 mm, No. of Columns (Display): 3, Col Widths (Display): 56 mm
Copy instructions: *Copy Date:* 21 days prior to publication
Official Journal of: Organ d. VWA Verb. Wirtschaft u. Arzt e.V.
BUSINESS: HEALTH & MEDICAL

WIRTSCHAFTSMAGAZIN FÜR DEN ORTHOPÄDEN
747743G56A-10280
Editorial: Otto-Hahn-Str. 7, 50997 KÖLN
Tel: 2236 376438 **Fax:** 2236 37692530
Email: schweihoff@wpv.de **Web site:** http://www.wpv.de
Freq: 6 issues yearly; Free to qualifying individuals
Annual Sub.: EUR 22,50; **Circ:** 6,208
Editor: Monika Schweihoff; **Advertising Manager:** Isabelle Becker
Profile: The Wirtschaftsmagazin für den Orthopäden is focused on issues that are important to physicians in everyday practice: billing tips, medical and tax law, summarizing medical topic and industry news, analysis of insurance and investment field, practice comparison.
Language(s): German
ADVERTISING RATES:
Full Page Mono .... EUR 1858
Full Page Colour .... EUR 2833
Mechanical Data: Type Area: 240 x 180 mm, No. of Columns (Display): 3, Col Widths (Display): 56 mm
Copy instructions: *Copy Date:* 21 days prior to publication
Official Journal of: Organ d. VWA - Verb. Wirtschaft u. Arzt e.V.
BUSINESS: HEALTH & MEDICAL

WIRTSCHAFTSMAGAZIN FÜR DEN UROLOGEN
747744G56A-10300
Editorial: Otto-Hahn-Str. 7, 50997 KÖLN
Tel: 2236 376438 **Fax:** 2236 37692530
Email: schweihoff@wpv.de **Web site:** http://www.wpv.de
Freq: 6 issues yearly; Free to qualifying individuals
Annual Sub.: EUR 30,00; **Circ:** 2,952
Editor: Monika Schweihoff; **Advertising Manager:** Isabelle Becker
Profile: The Wirtschaftsmagazin für den Urologen is focused on issues that are important to physicians in everyday practice: billing tips, medical and tax law, summarizing medical topic and industry news, analysis of insurance and investment field, practice comparison.
Language(s): German
ADVERTISING RATES:
Full Page Mono .... EUR 1733
Full Page Colour .... EUR 2708
Mechanical Data: Type Area: 240 x 180 mm, No. of Columns (Display): 3, Col Widths (Display): 56 mm
Copy instructions: *Copy Date:* 21 days prior to publication
Official Journal of: Organ d. VWA - Verb. Wirtschaft u. Arzt e.V.
BUSINESS: HEALTH & MEDICAL

DIE WIRTSCHAFTSPRÜFUNG WPG
747756G1B-5
Editorial: Tersteegenstr. 14, 40474 DÜSSELDORF
Tel: 211 4561280 **Fax:** 211 4561277
Email: armeloh@idw-verlag.de **Web site:** http://www.wpg.de
Freq: 24 issues yearly; **Circ:** 8,259
Editor: Karl-Heinz Armeloh
Profile: Journal about auditing.
Language(s): German
ADVERTISING RATES:
Full Page Mono .... EUR 2900
Full Page Colour .... EUR 3800
Mechanical Data: Type Area: 242 x 180 mm, No. of Columns (Display): 3, Col Widths (Display): 58 mm
Copy instructions: *Copy Date:* 14 days prior to publication
BUSINESS: FINANCE & ECONOMICS: Accountancy

WIRTSCHAFTSPSYCHOLOGIE AKTUELL
1609420G14A-9380
Editorial: Pettenkoferstr. 24, 80336 MÜNCHEN
Tel: 89 26026620 **Fax:** 89 26026631
Email: redaktion@wirtschaftspsychologie-aktuell.de
Web site: http://www.wirtschaftspsychologie-aktuell.de
Freq: Quarterly; Free to qualifying individuals
Annual Sub.: EUR 72,00; **Circ:** 2,800
Editor: Bärbel Schwertfeger; **Advertising Manager:** Tobias Frindte
Profile: Magazine about economy, seen from the psychological point of view. Subjects are personnel management, organisation, communications as well as marketing, environment, health, media and finance psychology. Twitter: http://twitter.com/#!/wipsychologie.
Language(s): German
ADVERTISING RATES:
Full Page Mono .... EUR 1100
Full Page Colour .... EUR 2000
Mechanical Data: No. of Columns (Display): 3, Col Widths (Display): 50 mm, Type Area: 257 x 178 mm
Copy instructions: *Copy Date:* 28 days prior to publication
BUSINESS: COMMERCE, INDUSTRY & MANAGEMENT

WIRTSCHAFTSSPIEGEL
1657103G14A-9628
Editorial: Hellersbergstr. 14, 41460 NEUSS
Tel: 162 8608416 **Fax:** 2131 220312
Freq: Monthly; Free to qualifying individuals
Annual Sub.: EUR 95,00; **Circ:** 4,400
Editor: Norbert Becker-Harzheim
Profile: Magazine for managers and entrepreneurs.
Language(s): German
ADVERTISING RATES:
Full Page Mono .... EUR 2100
Full Page Colour .... EUR 2520
Mechanical Data: Type Area: 270 x 185 mm, No. of Columns (Display): 3, Col Widths (Display): 59 mm
Copy instructions: *Copy Date:* 14 days prior to publication

WIRTSCHAFTSSPIEGEL
1660706G14A-9657
Editorial: Dr.-Andler-Str. 28, 78224 SINGEN
Tel: 7731 83816 **Fax:** 7731 9123130
Email: c.black@gmx.de **Web site:** http://www.wirtschaftsspiegel-bodensee.de
Freq: Annual; **Cover Price:** EUR 2,00; **Circ:** 20,000
Editor: Christiane Schwarz; **Advertising Manager:** Christiane Schwarz
Profile: Magazine of the businesses and services in Hegau.
Language(s): German
ADVERTISING RATES:
Full Page Colour .... EUR 825
Mechanical Data: Type Area: 275 x 230 mm

WIRTSCHAFTSTIPP DERMATOLOGEN/ ALLERGOLOGEN
747771G56A-10340
Editorial: Am Forsthaus Gravenbruch 5, 63263 NEU-ISENBURG **Tel:** 6102 5060 **Fax:** 6102 58870
Email: wi@aerztezeitung.de **Web site:** http://www.aerztezeitung.de
Freq: Monthly; **Annual Sub.:** EUR 21,40; **Circ:** 4,328
Editor: Wolfgang van den Bergh; **Advertising Manager:** Ute Krille
Profile: Journal with information, advice and problem-solving for dermatologists.
Language(s): German
ADVERTISING RATES:
Full Page Mono .... EUR 2250
Full Page Colour .... EUR 3500
Mechanical Data: Type Area: 280 x 210 mm
BUSINESS: HEALTH & MEDICAL

WIRTSCHAFTSTIPP GYNÄKOLOGEN
747772G56A-10360
Editorial: Am Forsthaus Gravenbruch 5, 63263 NEU-ISENBURG **Tel:** 6102 5060 **Fax:** 6102 58870
Email: wi@aerztezeitung.de **Web site:** http://www.aerztezeitung.de
Freq: Monthly; **Annual Sub.:** EUR 21,40; **Circ:** 8,372
Editor: Wolfgang van den Bergh; **Advertising Manager:** Ute Krille
Profile: Information for gynaecologists in Germany.
Language(s): German
ADVERTISING RATES:
Full Page Mono .... EUR 3230
Full Page Colour .... EUR 4480
Mechanical Data: Type Area: 280 x 210 mm
BUSINESS: HEALTH & MEDICAL

WIRTSCHAFTSTIPP ORTHOPÄDEN/ RHEUMATOLOGEN
1640186G56A-11285
Editorial: Am Forsthaus Gravenbruch 5, 63263 NEU-ISENBURG **Tel:** 6102 5060 **Fax:** 6102 58870
Email: wi@aerztezeitung.de **Web site:** http://www.aerztezeitung.de
Freq: Monthly; **Annual Sub.:** EUR 21,40; **Circ:** 4,175
Editor: Wolfgang van den Bergh; **Advertising Manager:** Ute Krille
Profile: Magazine on financial matters for orthopaedists.
Language(s): German
ADVERTISING RATES:
Full Page Mono .... EUR 2300
Full Page Colour .... EUR 3550
Mechanical Data: Type Area: 280 x 210 mm

WIRTSCHAFTSTIPP PÄDIATER
747774G56A-10400
Editorial: Am Forsthaus Gravenbruch 5, 63263 NEU-ISENBURG **Tel:** 6102 5060 **Fax:** 6102 58870
Email: wi@aerztezeitung.de **Web site:** http://www.aerztezeitung.de
Freq: Monthly; **Annual Sub.:** EUR 21,40; **Circ:** 5,472
Editor: Wolfgang van den Bergh; **Advertising Manager:** Ute Krille
Profile: Medical journal focusing on paediatrics.
Language(s): German
ADVERTISING RATES:
Full Page Mono .... EUR 2250
Full Page Colour .... EUR 3550
Mechanical Data: Type Area: 280 x 210 mm
BUSINESS: HEALTH & MEDICAL

WIRTSCHAFTSTIPP UROLOGEN
747775G56A-10420
Editorial: Am Forsthaus Gravenbruch 5, 63263 NEU-ISENBURG **Tel:** 6102 5060 **Fax:** 6102 58870
Email: wi@aerztezeitung.de **Web site:** http://www.aerztezeitung.de
Freq: Monthly; **Annual Sub.:** EUR 21,40; **Circ:** 2,375
Editor: Wolfgang van den Bergh; **Advertising Manager:** Ute Krille
Profile: Medical journal focusing on urology.
Language(s): German
ADVERTISING RATES:
Full Page Mono .... EUR 1950
Full Page Colour .... EUR 3200
Mechanical Data: Type Area: 280 x 210 mm
BUSINESS: HEALTH & MEDICAL

WIRTSCHAFTSWOCHE
747840G14A-8560
Editorial: Kasernenstr. 67, 40213 DÜSSELDORF
Tel: 211 8870 **Fax:** 211 887972114
Email: wiwo@wiwo.de **Web site:** http://www.wiwo.de
Freq: Weekly; **Annual Sub.:** EUR 198,00; **Circ:** 183,395
Editor: Roland Tichy
Profile: Business magazine. Monday for Monday are prepared to review current business related issues clear and informative for decision makers in the economy. More than 100 experts analyzed using a global correspondent and partner network, the most important developments and global trends in the departments: People of the economy, The Economist, Policy and the World Economy, business, markets, technology and knowledge, management and success, money and exchange and Perspectives and debate. Facebook: http://www.facebook.com/Wirtschaftswoche Twitter: http://twitter.com/#!/wiwo This Outlet offers RSS (Really Simple Syndication).
Language(s): German
Readership: Aimed at senior managers.
ADVERTISING RATES:
Full Page Mono .... EUR 25200
Full Page Colour .... EUR 25200
Mechanical Data: Type Area: 244 x 184 mm, No. of Columns (Display): 3, Col Widths (Display): 58 mm

Copy instructions: *Copy Date:* 14 days prior to publication
BUSINESS: COMMERCE, INDUSTRY & MANAGEMENT

WISMARER BLITZ AM SONNTAG
747873G72-15376
Editorial: Lübsche Str. 21, 23966 WISMAR
Tel: 3841 6280843 **Fax:** 3841 6280830
Email: kerstin.vogt@blitzverlag.de **Web site:** http://www.blitzverlag.de
Freq: Weekly; **Cover Price:** Free; **Circ:** 41,700
Editor: Kerstin Vogt; **Advertising Manager:** Georg Brandt
Profile: Advertising journal (house-to-house) concentrating on local stories.
Language(s): German
ADVERTISING RATES:
Full Page Mono .... EUR 2722
Full Page Colour .... EUR 3112
Mechanical Data: Type Area: 420 x 285 mm, No. of Columns (Display): 6, Col Widths (Display): 45 mm
Copy instructions: *Copy Date:* 2 days prior to publication
LOCAL NEWSPAPERS

WISSEN+KARRIERE
1882050G14A-10269
Editorial: Boslerstr. 29, 71088 HOLZGERLINGEN
Tel: 7031 7440 **Fax:** 7031 744195
Email: red@wissen-karriere.com **Web site:** http://www.wissen-karriere.com
Freq: 6 issues yearly; **Annual Sub.:** EUR 21,00; **Circ:** 30,000
Editor: Bernd Seitz; **Advertising Manager:** Andrea Hiddemann
Profile: Magazine for personal development, motivation, education and training.
Language(s): German
ADVERTISING RATES:
Full Page Mono .... EUR 4224
Full Page Colour .... EUR 4224
Mechanical Data: Type Area: 267 x 185 mm, No. of Columns (Display): 4, Col Widths (Display): 45 mm
Copy instructions: *Copy Date:* 20 days prior to publication

WISSENS MANAGEMENT
766488G14A-9320
Editorial: Westheimer Str. 18, 86356 NEUSÄSS
Tel: 821 48685290 **Fax:** 821 48685293
Email: lehnert@wissensmanagement.net **Web site:** http://www.wissensmanagement.net
Freq: 8 issues yearly; Free to qualifying individuals
Annual Sub.: EUR 84,90; **Circ:** 9,420
Editor: Oliver Lehnert
Language(s): German
ADVERTISING RATES:
Full Page Mono .... EUR 2980
Full Page Colour .... EUR 4030
Mechanical Data: Type Area: 250 x 180 mm, No. of Columns (Display): 4, Col Widths (Display): 42 mm
Copy instructions: *Copy Date:* 21 days prior to publication
BUSINESS: COMMERCE, INDUSTRY & MANAGEMENT

WISSENSCHAFT WIRTSCHAFT POLITIK
747885G14A-8820
Editorial: Rheinaustr. 37, 53225 BONN
Tel: 228 972003
Email: schmitz@wwponline.de **Web site:** http://www.wwponline.de
Freq: Weekly; **Annual Sub.:** EUR 295,00; **Circ:** 100
Editor: Ulrich Schmitz
Profile: Magazine about research and development for decision makers in sciences, economy and politics.
Language(s): German

WISSENSCHAFTS-MANAGEMENT
747882G55-190
Editorial: Matthias-Grünewald-Str. 1, 53175 BONN
Tel: 228 4213718 **Fax:** 228 4213729
Email: wissenschaftsmanagement@lemmens.de
Web site: http://www.lemmens.de
Freq: 6 issues yearly; **Annual Sub.:** EUR 125,73; **Circ:** 2,000
Editor: Klaudia Gerhardt
Profile: Journal of management issues and innovations in higher education, research and science management.
Language(s): German
ADVERTISING RATES:
Full Page Mono .... EUR 920
Full Page Colour .... EUR 1612
Mechanical Data: Type Area: 235 x 180 mm
Copy instructions: *Copy Date:* 14 days prior to publication
BUSINESS: APPLIED SCIENCE & LABORATORIES

WISSENSCHAFTS-MANAGEMENT SPECIAL
1665695G14A-9739
Editorial: Matthias-Grünewald-Str. 1, 53175 BONN
Tel: 228 421370 **Fax:** 228 4213729
Email: info@lemmens.de **Web site:** http://www.lemmens.de
Freq: Half-yearly; **Cover Price:** Free; **Circ:** 2,000
Editor: Markus Lemmers
Profile: Journal about science management nationally and internationally.
Language(s): German
ADVERTISING RATES:
Full Page Mono .... EUR 1228
Full Page Colour .... EUR 1612
Mechanical Data: Type Area: 240 x 170 mm

WISTRA
747887G44-2360
Editorial: Heger-Tor-Wall 14, 49078 OSNABRÜCK
Tel: 541 9694696
Email: wistra@uni-osnabrueck.de **Web site:** http://www.wistra-online.com
Freq: Monthly; **Annual Sub.:** EUR 377,95; **Circ:** 1,600
Editor: Erich Samson; **Advertising Manager:** Isabell Henze
Profile: Journal dealing with industrial, tax and criminal law.
Language(s): German
ADVERTISING RATES:
Full Page Mono .... EUR 1300
Mechanical Data: Type Area: 257 x 178 mm, No. of Columns (Display): 2, Col Widths (Display): 86 mm
BUSINESS: LEGAL

WITCH
747889G91D-9300
Editorial: Wallstr. 59, 10179 BERLIN **Tel:** 30 240080
Fax: 30 24008599
Email: p.hoepfner@ehapa.de **Web site:** http://www.witchmagazin.de
Freq: Monthly; **Cover Price:** EUR 2,95; **Circ:** 27,823
Editor: Peter Höpfner
Profile: Comic, Witch is the name of five girls: Will, Irma, Taranee, Cornelia and Hay Lin. The five friends are actually quite normal teenagers who fall in love with guys and sometimes have trouble in school ... with one difference: they possess magical powers that help them protect the world from dark forces. Witch - Magical, mystical, super-strong!.
Language(s): German
ADVERTISING RATES:
Full Page Mono .... EUR 3700
Full Page Colour .... EUR 3700
Mechanical Data: Type Area: 260 x 170 mm, No. of Columns (Display): 4, Col Widths (Display): 42 mm
CONSUMER: RECREATION & LEISURE: Children & Youth

WITTLAGER KREISBLATT
747900G67B-16120
Editorial: Breiter Gang 10, 49074 OSNABRÜCK
Tel: 541 3100 **Fax:** 541 310485
Email: redaktion@noz.de **Web site:** http://www.noz.de
Freq: 312 issues yearly; **Circ:** 6,037
Profile: Daily newspaper with regional news and a local sports section. Twitter: http://twitter.com/noz_de This Outlet offers RSS (Really Simple Syndication).
Language(s): German
ADVERTISING RATES:
SCC .... EUR 35,10
Mechanical Data: Type Area: 487 x 318 mm, No. of Columns (Display): 7, Col Widths (Display): 43 mm
Copy instructions: *Copy Date:* 2 days prior to publication
Supplement(s): Berufswahl; Immo-Welt; Kfz-Welt; melle-city.de; TheaterZeitung; Toaster; Treffpunkt Bramsche
REGIONAL DAILY & SUNDAY NEWSPAPERS: Regional Daily Newspapers

WITZENHÄUSER ALLGEMEINE
730362G67B-7300
Editorial: Frankfurter Str. 168, 34121 KASSEL
Tel: 561 20300 **Fax:** 561 2032406
Email: info@hna.de **Web site:** http://www.hna.de
Freq: 312 issues yearly; **Circ:** 8,098
Advertising Manager: Andrea Schaller-Öller
Profile: Regional daily newspaper with news on politics, economy, culture, sports, travel, technology, etc. The Witzenhäuser Allgemeine a local edition of the HNA Hessische/Niedersächsische Allgemeine. Twitter: http://twitter.com/hna_online This Outlet offers RSS (Really Simple Syndication).
Language(s): German
ADVERTISING RATES:
SCC .... EUR 34,60
Mechanical Data: Type Area: 430 x 285 mm, No. of Columns (Display): 6, Col Widths (Display): 45 mm
Copy instructions: *Copy Date:* 2 days prior to publication
REGIONAL DAILY & SUNDAY NEWSPAPERS: Regional Daily Newspapers

WIWO.DE
1687713G14A-9768
Editorial: Kasernenstr. 67, 40213 DÜSSELDORF
Tel: 211 8872192 **Fax:** 211 887972192
Email: online-pr@wiwo.de **Web site:** http://www.wiwo.de
Freq: Daily; **Cover Price:** Paid; **Circ:** 1,781,272 Unique Users
Editor: Roland Tichy
Profile: Ezine: Magazine containing information on business and economics. Facebook: http://www.facebook.com/Wirtschaftswoche Twitter: http://twitter.com/#!/wiwo This Outlet offers RSS (Really Simple Syndication).
Language(s): German
BUSINESS: COMMERCE, INDUSTRY & MANAGEMENT

WKSB
747907G4E-6680
Editorial: Postfach 210565, 67005 LUDWIGSHAFEN
Tel: 621 4701601 **Fax:** 621 4701606
Freq: Half-yearly; **Annual Sub.:** EUR 20,00; **Circ:** 3,500
Profile: Magazine for architects, building physicians and dry mortal constructors.
Language(s): German
ADVERTISING RATES:
Full Page Mono .... EUR 1770
Full Page Colour .... EUR 2925
Mechanical Data: Type Area: 275 x 185 mm, No. of Columns (Display): 2, Col Widths (Display): 90 mm

WLB WASSER, LUFT UND BODEN
747910G57-2540
Editorial: Lise-Meitner-Str. 2, 55129 MAINZ
Tel: 6131 992343 **Fax:** 6131 992100
Email: redaktion@wasser-luft-und-boden.de **Web site:** http://www.industrie-service.de
Freq: Quarterly; **Annual Sub.:** EUR 64,00; **Circ:** 14,360
Editor: Eva Linder; **Advertising Manager:** Gundula Unverzagt
Profile: wlb Wasser, Luft und Boden (Water, Air and Soil) accompanied developments in environmental protection and environmental engineering in Germany as a specialist journal for more than 50 years. WLB reports on the latest equipment, plants, processes and services in the environmental engineering industry, measurement and analysis techniques and equipment, as well as the latest technology, associated resources and materials. It also contains a plethora of practical information together with the statutory requirements and relevant regulations pertaining to water/wastewater treatment, air pollution control, waste disposal, soil conservation and the rehabilitation of industrial sites. Its topic-related classification of features and the high proportion of product-related short reports make sure full today's information requirements.
Language(s): German
Readership: Read by people concerned with the environment.
ADVERTISING RATES:
Full Page Mono .... EUR 3780
Full Page Colour .... EUR 5010
Mechanical Data: Type Area: 265 x 185 mm, No. of Columns (Display): 4, Col Widths (Display): 43 mm
Copy instructions: *Copy Date:* 14 days prior to publication
BUSINESS: ENVIRONMENT & POLLUTION

WM WAFFENMARKT-INTERN/ MESSERMARKT INTERN
747926G27-2960
Editorial: Theodor-Heuss-Ring 62, 50668 KÖLN
Tel: 221 2005412 **Fax:** 221 2005423
Email: spindler@waffenmarkt.de **Web site:** http://www.waffenmarkt.de
Freq: Monthly; **Annual Sub.:** EUR 50,00; **Circ:** 2,000
Editor: Maggy Spindler; **Advertising Manager:** Manuela Bache
Profile: Industry information for retailers, manufacturers and suppliers from the fields guns, outdoor, security, hunting, shooting and cutting edge goods.
Language(s): German
Readership: Read by licensed firearms dealers.
ADVERTISING RATES:
Full Page Mono .... EUR 2300
Full Page Colour .... EUR 3000
Mechanical Data: Type Area: 253 x 186 mm, No. of Columns (Display): 4, Col Widths (Display): 43 mm
Copy instructions: *Copy Date:* 14 days prior to publication
BUSINESS: METAL, IRON & STEEL

WO BEKOMME ICH MEIN BABY?
747936G94H-13560
Editorial: Sigmund-Freud-Str. 77a, 60435 FRANKFURT **Tel:** 69 7561900 **Fax:** 69 75619041
Email: sbuettner@buemed.de **Web site:** http://www.eltern-infothek.de
Freq: Annual; **Cover Price:** Free; **Circ:** 295,225
Advertising Manager: Jürgen Büttner
Profile: Guide for pregnant women.
Language(s): German
ADVERTISING RATES:
Full Page Mono .... EUR 23860
Full Page Colour .... EUR 38200
Mechanical Data: Type Area: 264 x 180 mm
CONSUMER: OTHER CLASSIFICATIONS: Customer Magazines

WOCHE DER FRAU
747942G74A-3220
Editorial: Rotweg 8, 76532 BADEN-BADEN
Tel: 7221 3501131 **Fax:** 7221 3501304
Email: wochederfrau@klambt.de
Freq: Weekly; **Annual Sub.:** EUR 54,60; **Circ:** 140,331
Editor: Britta Behrens; **Advertising Manager:** Martin Fischer
Profile: To already have an interest from young women about 35 years for the stories of the beautiful, successful people and celebrities from the world of film, television and the nobility, Woche der Frau present in a spacious look and with trenchant scene photos. Relevance determines the choice of celebrities: the photo of the week - a snapshot that moves. News of the Week - Highlights from the world of showbiz. Events of the week - which will meet the celebrities from film, television and sport. Cover story of the week - People-Stories, close to bring the celebrities to be touched. Feature of the Week - celebrities who are committed to others and role model. People of the Week - celebrities, about which one speaks. Two topics to give Woche der Frau a special USP: The film-novel - in each issue is presented with stills, even before the theatrical release, the latest film on four sides. The Astro-Guide - every week, readers gain a comprehensive chart of which shows the current constellation of stars and their chances for each zodiac sign both a look at a picture and after each decade divided in detail. A portrait of the astrologer underscores the seriousness of the horoscopes. The service and advice part in Woche der Frau is also tailored for younger women: I Fashion and Beauty - combines excitation in the current look of a concrete utility for its own type. I Cooking, eating and drinking - this is the trend towards "light cuisine" taken up and presented dishes that can be prepared quickly. Here, the appearance of the photos and recipes is fresh and seductive. I Health and Medicine - reports on new and valuable information from research and practice that deals with current topics on disease prevention and wellness tips. I Travel & Tourism - a photo report of a tourist area is awakened the desire to travel and supplemented with concrete information on people and places, sports and leisure facilities as well as information on tour operators. I Housing, household and Ratings - with decorating ideas, decorating tips, news and consumer information, test results and legal issues. I Arts - a TV preview with the TV-Tips of the Week and a Puzzle page with tricky puzzles.
Language(s): German
Readership: Aimed at women.
ADVERTISING RATES:
Full Page Mono .... EUR 4450
Full Page Colour .... EUR 4450
Mechanical Data: Type Area: 260 x 195 mm, No. of Columns (Display): 4, Col Widths (Display): 45 mm
Copy instructions: *Copy Date:* 28 days prior to publication
CONSUMER: WOMEN'S INTEREST CONSUMER MAGAZINES: Women's Interest

WOCHE DER FRAU DIE 90 BESTEN WEIHNACHTSPLÄTZCHEN
2086909G74P-1404
Editorial: Rotweg 8, 76532 BADEN-BADEN
Tel: 7221 3501131 **Fax:** 7221 3501304
Email: wochederfrau@klambt.de
Freq: Annual; **Circ:** 80,000
Advertising Manager: Martin Fischer
Profile: They simply belong to the little goodies for Advent. Traditional cookie recipes are well represented in this issue as new bakery trends that you can surprise your loved ones: airy and delicious: macaroons, cookies with fruit filling, chocolate hits, with Christmas baking spices.
Language(s): German
ADVERTISING RATES:
Full Page Mono .... EUR 5370
Full Page Colour .... EUR 5370
Mechanical Data: Type Area: 250 x 195 mm, No. of Columns (Display): 4, Col Widths (Display): 45 mm
Copy instructions: *Copy Date:* 28 days prior to publication

WOCHE DER FRAU EXTRA UNSERE 111 LIEBLINGSREZEPTE
2086910G74P-1405
Editorial: Rotweg 8, 76532 BADEN-BADEN
Tel: 7221 3501131 **Fax:** 7221 3501304
Email: wochederfrau@klambt.de
Freq: Quarterly; **Circ:** 80,000
Advertising Manager: Martin Fischer
Profile: The hit list of 111 favorite recipes for the whole family. In spring the mood for fresh is especially great: fresh herb cuisine, fish for everyone, new ideas with poultry, fruit tarts. You'll be surprised what can conjure up everything from seasonal ingredients ... 111 inspirations for delicious and healthy summer food. These recipes will change on the plate: Light summer roasts, salads as a full meal, fruits dreams, holiday cooking. Here, anyone who likes to enjoy, find it! Autumn is harvest time - rare is the table of Mother Nature covered so rich as now. 111 delicious recipes for seasonal and everyday use kitchen can be found in the autumn edition: of the classic kitchen - pumpkin! Delicious with apples, hearty goulash variations, fine eggs and pastries. With these recipes for the winter season can conjure up great meals every day for the whole family. And of course, be missing and festive recipes for the Christmas season not: Feast with Hack, classic with cabbage, roast hard, juicy buns and much more!.
Language(s): German
ADVERTISING RATES:
Full Page Mono .... EUR 5370
Full Page Colour .... EUR 5370
Mechanical Data: Type Area: 250 x 195 mm, No. of Columns (Display): 4, Col Widths (Display): 45 mm
Copy instructions: *Copy Date:* 28 days prior to publication

WOCHE HEUTE
1841563G74A-3606
Editorial: Karlsruher Str. 31, 76437 RASTATT
Tel: 7222 13518 **Fax:** 7222 13224

Email: regina.focht@vpm.de **Web site:** http://www.woche-heute.de
Freq: 17 issues yearly; **Cover Price:** EUR 0,70; **Circ:** 193,668
Editor: Volker Kithil
Profile: Entertainment and professional service to find the readers of Woche Heute for week by week. Everything from the world of celebrities, travel reports, delicious recipes and lush advice pages. To 22 pages to enter the blazing stars of TV, cinema, national and international pop music as a rendezvous like kings, princes and princesses from all over the world. Two large series themes ("women made history" and "time travel") to give the issue a high value. In addition to nearly 40 entertaining pages of puzzles, travel, advice and recipes is the great medical part of the Woche Heute the heart of it. Health Journal with the information and address boxes, detailed illustrations include 11 pages. Of these dedicated 4 pages in great detail the "theme of the week", "Escape from the stress," for example "stop the pain," or "menopause". The best remedies and the latest trends in alternative medicine are presented in the same category. Well known specialists are the editorial advice and assistance. Here, the medical part is easily written and understandable. For to provide clear, sensible and professional concerns of the first week is today.
Language(s): German
ADVERTISING RATES:
Full Page Mono .... EUR 4550
Full Page Colour .... EUR 4550
Mechanical Data: Type Area: 265 x 207 mm, No. of Columns (Display): 4, Col Widths (Display): 49 mm

DIE WOCHE IM BLICKPUNKT
723128G72-2224
Editorial: Schulstr. 13, 25335 ELMSHORN
Tel: 4121 2971800 **Fax:** 4121 2971818
Email: redaktion.elmshorn@shz.de **Web site:** http://www.shz.de
Freq: Weekly; **Cover Price:** Free; **Circ:** 70,080
Editor: Rainer Strandmann
Profile: Advertising journal (house-to-house) concentrating on local stories.
Language(s): German
ADVERTISING RATES:
Full Page Mono .... EUR 3354
Full Page Colour .... EUR 4128
Mechanical Data: Type Area: 430 x 282 mm, No. of Columns (Display): 6, Col Widths (Display): 45 mm
Copy instructions: *Copy Date:* 2 days prior to publication
LOCAL NEWSPAPERS

WOCHEN SPIEGEL AM SONNTAG
748143G72-15624
Editorial: Lange Str. 14, 29664 WALSRODE
Tel: 5161 60050 **Fax:** 5161 600528
Email: wochenspiegel@wz-net.de **Web site:** http://www.wz-net.de
Freq: Weekly; **Cover Price:** Free; **Circ:** 42,639
Editor: Kurt Sohnemann; **Advertising Manager:** Ulrike Schomburg
Profile: Advertising journal (house-to-house) concentrating on local stories.
Language(s): German
ADVERTISING RATES:
Full Page Mono .... EUR 3111
Full Page Colour .... EUR 5024
Mechanical Data: Type Area: 425 x 280 mm, No. of Columns (Display): 6, Col Widths (Display): 43 mm
Copy instructions: *Copy Date:* 3 days prior to publication
LOCAL NEWSPAPERS

WOCHEN ZEITUNG WZ AKTUELL - AUSG. ANSBACH
748223G72-15752
Editorial: Kanalstr. 16, 91522 ANSBACH
Tel: 981 970150 **Fax:** 981 97015990
Email: redaktion.ansbach@wochenzeitung.de
Freq: Weekly; **Cover Price:** Free; **Circ:** 55,830
Editor: Fabian Reisch; **Advertising Manager:** Martina Horand
Profile: Advertising journal (house-to-house) concentrating on local stories.
Language(s): German
ADVERTISING RATES:
Full Page Mono .... EUR 3579
Full Page Colour .... EUR 4662
Mechanical Data: Type Area: 420 x 280 mm, No. of Columns (Display): 6, Col Widths (Display): 45 mm
Copy instructions: *Copy Date:* 3 days prior to publication
LOCAL NEWSPAPERS

WOCHEN ZEITUNG WZ AKTUELL - AUSG. DINKELSBÜHL
748218G72-15732
Editorial: Altrathausplatz 9, 91550 DINKELSBÜHL
Tel: 9851 57300 **Fax:** 9851 5730990
Email: redaktion.dinkelsbuehl@wochenzeitung.de
Freq: Weekly; **Cover Price:** Free; **Circ:** 30,620
Editor: Elvira Steinseifer; **Advertising Manager:** Elvira Steinseifer
Profile: Advertising journal (house-to-house) concentrating on local stories.
Language(s): German
ADVERTISING RATES:
Full Page Mono .... EUR 3176
Full Page Colour .... EUR 4133
Mechanical Data: Type Area: 420 x 280 mm, No. of Columns (Display): 6, Col Widths (Display): 45 mm
Copy instructions: *Copy Date:* 3 days prior to publication
LOCAL NEWSPAPERS

WOCHEN ZEITUNG WZ AKTUELL - AUSG. HEIDENHEIM
748219G72-15736
Editorial: Wilhelmstr. 25, 89518 HEIDENHEIM
Tel: 7321 986414 **Fax:** 7321 9864990
Email: redaktion.heidenheim@wochenzeitung.de
Freq: Weekly; **Cover Price:** Free; **Circ:** 64,858
Editor: Robin Füchtner; **Advertising Manager:** Maike Wagner
Profile: Advertising journal (house-to-house) concentrating on local stories.
Language(s): German
ADVERTISING RATES:
Full Page Mono .... EUR 4511
Full Page Colour .... EUR 5872
Mechanical Data: Type Area: 420 x 280 mm, No. of Columns (Display): 6, Col Widths (Display): 45 mm
Copy instructions: *Copy Date:* 3 days prior to publication
LOCAL NEWSPAPERS

WOCHENANZEIGER FÜR DIE STÄDTE MÜNSINGEN, HAYINGEN UND TROCHTELFINGEN, DIE ORTE ENGSTINGEN, GOMADINGEN, HOHENSTEIN, HEROLDSTATT, MEHRSTETTEN, PFRONSTETTEN, RÖMERSTEIN, ZWIEFALTEN UND WEITERE 53 ORTSCHAFTEN AUF DER MITTLEREN ALB
747952G72-15756
Editorial: Gutenbergstr. 1, 72525 MÜNSINGEN
Tel: 7381 18730 **Fax:** 7381 18735
Email: alb-bote.redaktion@swp.de
Freq: Weekly; **Cover Price:** Free; **Circ:** 17,783
Editor: Jürgen Kühnemund; **Advertising Manager:** Helmut Schepper
Profile: Advertising journal (house-to-house) concentrating on local stories.
Language(s): German
ADVERTISING RATES:
Full Page Mono .... EUR 4637
Full Page Colour .... EUR 7090
Mechanical Data: Type Area: 480 x 320 mm, No. of Columns (Display): 7, Col Widths (Display): 44 mm
Copy instructions: *Copy Date:* 2 days prior to publication
LOCAL NEWSPAPERS

WOCHENBLATT
726426G72-3568
Editorial: Landshuter Str. 47a, 85435 ERDING
Tel: 8122 979215 **Fax:** 8122 979225
Email: christian.bluemel@wochenblatt.de **Web site:** http://www.wochenblatt.de
Freq: Weekly; **Cover Price:** Free; **Circ:** 44,000
Editor: Christian Blümel; **Advertising Manager:** Reinhard Michalski
Profile: Advertising journal (house-to-house) concentrating on local stories.
Language(s): German
ADVERTISING RATES:
Full Page Mono .... EUR 2124
Full Page Colour .... EUR 3168
Mechanical Data: Type Area: 360 x 232 mm, No. of Columns (Display): 5, Col Widths (Display): 43 mm
Copy instructions: *Copy Date:* 1 day prior to publication
LOCAL NEWSPAPERS

WOCHENBLATT
747966G72-15776
Editorial: Rosenstr. 24, 73033 GÖPPINGEN
Tel: 7161 204143 **Fax:** 7161 204154
Email: nwz.redaktion@swp.de **Web site:** http://www.wochenblatt-aktiv.de
Freq: Weekly; **Cover Price:** Free; **Circ:** 113,191
Editor: Rüdiger Gramsch; **Advertising Manager:** Mario Bayer
Profile: Advertising journal (house-to-house) concentrating on local stories.
Language(s): German
ADVERTISING RATES:
Full Page Mono .... EUR 6989
Full Page Colour .... EUR 10484
Mechanical Data: Type Area: 480 x 320 mm, No. of Columns (Display): 7, Col Widths (Display): 44 mm
Copy instructions: *Copy Date:* 2 days prior to publication
LOCAL NEWSPAPERS

WOCHENBLATT - AUSG. BIBERACH
747992G72-15880
Editorial: Radgasse 12, 88400 BIBERACH
Tel: 7351 189930 **Fax:** 7351 189915
Email: redaktion.bc@wbrv.de **Web site:** http://www.wochenblatt-online.de
Freq: Weekly; **Cover Price:** Free; **Circ:** 53,359
Editor: Wolfgang Gröner; **Advertising Manager:** Cornelis-Rik Wotke
Profile: Advertising journal (house-to-house) concentrating on local stories.
Language(s): German
ADVERTISING RATES:
Full Page Mono .... EUR 5772
Full Page Colour .... EUR 8669
Mechanical Data: Type Area: 480 x 320 mm, No. of Columns (Display): 7, Col Widths (Display): 44 mm
Copy instructions: *Copy Date:* 2 days prior to publication
LOCAL NEWSPAPERS

WOCHENBLATT - AUSG. FRIEDRICHSHAFEN/ ÜBERLINGEN
747988G72-15864
Editorial: Charlottenstr. 49, 88045 FRIEDRICHSHAFEN **Tel:** 7541 374140
Fax: 7541 374129
Email: redaktion.fn@wbrv.de **Web site:** http://www.wochenblatt-online.de
Freq: Weekly; **Cover Price:** Free; **Circ:** 84,190
Editor: Wolfgang Gröner; **Advertising Manager:** Cornelis-Rik Wotke
Profile: Advertising journal (house-to-house) concentrating on local stories.
Language(s): German
ADVERTISING RATES:
Full Page Mono .... EUR 5495
Full Page Colour .... EUR 8232
Mechanical Data: Type Area: 480 x 320 mm, No. of Columns (Display): 7, Col Widths (Display): 44 mm
Copy instructions: *Copy Date:* 2 days prior to publication
LOCAL NEWSPAPERS

WOCHENBLATT - AUSG. RAVENSBURG
747987G72-15860
Editorial: Olgastr. 8, 88214 RAVENSBURG
Tel: 751 370940 **Fax:** 751 370936
Email: redaktion.rv@wbrv.de **Web site:** http://www.wochenblatt-online.de
Freq: Weekly; **Cover Price:** Free; **Circ:** 70,591
Editor: Wolfgang Gröner; **Advertising Manager:** Cornelis-Rik Wotke
Profile: Advertising journal (house-to-house) concentrating on local stories.
Language(s): German
ADVERTISING RATES:
Full Page Mono .... EUR 6286
Full Page Colour .... EUR 9442
Mechanical Data: Type Area: 480 x 320 mm, No. of Columns (Display): 7, Col Widths (Display): 44 mm
Copy instructions: *Copy Date:* 2 days prior to publication
LOCAL NEWSPAPERS

WOCHENBLATT - AUSG. RIEDLINGEN
747986G72-15856
Editorial: Radgasse 12, 88400 BIBERACH
Tel: 7351 189948 **Fax:** 7351 189915
Email: redaktion.rie@wbrv.de **Web site:** http://www.wochenblatt-online.de
Freq: Weekly; **Cover Price:** Free; **Circ:** 15,627
Editor: Wolfgang Gröner; **Advertising Manager:** Cornelis-Rik Wotke
Profile: Advertising journal (house-to-house) concentrating on local stories.
Language(s): German
ADVERTISING RATES:
Full Page Mono .... EUR 3637
Full Page Colour .... EUR 5444
Mechanical Data: Type Area: 480 x 320 mm, No. of Columns (Display): 7, Col Widths (Display): 44 mm
Copy instructions: *Copy Date:* 2 days prior to publication
LOCAL NEWSPAPERS

WOCHENBLATT DER TAUBER-ZEITUNG
748007G72-15940
Editorial: Ledermarkt 8, 97980 BAD MERGENTHEIM
Tel: 7931 59625 **Fax:** 7931 59679
Email: wobla.tbz@swp.de **Web site:** http://www.tauber-zeitung.de
Freq: Weekly; **Cover Price:** Free; **Circ:** 35,050
Editor: Barbara Homolka; **Advertising Manager:** Ariane Kolb
Profile: Advertising journal (house-to-house) concentrating on local stories.
Language(s): German
ADVERTISING RATES:
Full Page Mono .... EUR 2394
Full Page Colour .... EUR 3579
Mechanical Data: Type Area: 420 x 274 mm, No. of Columns (Display): 6, Col Widths (Display): 44 mm
Copy instructions: *Copy Date:* 2 days prior to publication
LOCAL NEWSPAPERS

WOCHENBLATT FRANKENTHAL
748013G72-15964
Editorial: Schmiedgasse 47, 67227 FRANKENTHAL
Tel: 6233 607955 **Fax:** 6233 667428
Email: red-fra@wobla.de
Freq: Weekly; **Cover Price:** Free; **Circ:** 33,350
Editor: Ulrich Arndt; **Advertising Manager:** Stephan Feindel
Profile: Advertising journal (house-to-house) concentrating on local stories.
Language(s): German
ADVERTISING RATES:
Full Page Mono .... EUR 3395
Full Page Colour .... EUR 4414
Mechanical Data: Type Area: 485 x 320 mm, No. of Columns (Display): 7, Col Widths (Display): 44 mm
Copy instructions: *Copy Date:* 2 days prior to publication
LOCAL NEWSPAPERS

WOCHENBLATT FÜR PAPIERFABRIKATION
748015G36-11
Editorial: Mainzer Landstr. 251, 60326 FRANKFURT
Tel: 69 75951547 **Fax:** 69 75951239
Email: kerstin.graf@dfv.de **Web site:** http://www.wochenblatt-dfv.de
Freq: Monthly; **Annual Sub.:** EUR 134,20; **Circ:** 2,860
Editor: Kerstin Graf; **Advertising Manager:** Dagmar Henning
Profile: Journal for the pulp and paper industry, including features on cellulose production and mechanical pulp manufacture, stock preparation, grading, sheet manufacture, paper finishing, conversion and coating.
Language(s): German
ADVERTISING RATES:
Full Page Mono .... EUR 2160
Full Page Colour .... EUR 2950
Mechanical Data: Type Area: 268 x 185 mm, No. of Columns (Display): 4, Col Widths (Display): 43 mm
Copy instructions: *Copy Date:* 21 days prior to publication
Official Journal of: Organ d. Vereinigung Gernsbacher Papiermacher e.V., d. Papiermacher Berufsgenossenschaft Mainz, d. Akadem. Papier-Ingenieur-Vereine e.V. an d. Techn. Univ'en. Darmstadt u.. Dresden
BUSINESS: PAPER

WOCHENBLATT GERMERSHEIM MIT LINGENFELD
748021G72-15988
Editorial: Industriestr. 15, 76829 LANDAU
Tel: 6341 649512 **Fax:** 6341 649540
Email: red-ger@wobla.de **Web site:** http://www.wobla.de
Freq: Weekly; **Cover Price:** Free; **Circ:** 16,950
Editor: Ulrich Arndt; **Advertising Manager:** Stephan Feindel
Profile: Advertising journal (house-to-house) concentrating on local stories.
Language(s): German
ADVERTISING RATES:
Full Page Mono .... EUR 2581
Full Page Colour .... EUR 3395
Mechanical Data: Type Area: 485 x 320 mm, No. of Columns (Display): 7, Col Widths (Display): 44 mm
Copy instructions: *Copy Date:* 2 days prior to publication
LOCAL NEWSPAPERS

WOCHENBLATT HASSLOCH
748022G72-15992
Editorial: Parkstr. 13, 67454 HASSLOCH
Tel: 6324 59980 **Fax:** 6324 58854
Email: suewe@wobla.de **Web site:** http://www.wobla.de
Freq: Weekly; **Cover Price:** Free; **Circ:** 19,650
Editor: Ulrich Arndt; **Advertising Manager:** Stephan Feindel
Profile: Advertising journal (house-to-house) concentrating on local stories.
Language(s): German
ADVERTISING RATES:
Full Page Mono .... EUR 2886
Full Page Colour .... EUR 3769
Mechanical Data: Type Area: 485 x 320 mm, No. of Columns (Display): 7, Col Widths (Display): 44 mm
Copy instructions: *Copy Date:* 2 days prior to publication
LOCAL NEWSPAPERS

WOCHENBLATT KAISERSLAUTERN
748028G72-16008
Editorial: Pariser Str. 16, 67655 KAISERSLAUTERN
Tel: 631 3737269 **Fax:** 631 3737286
Email: red-kai@wobla.de **Web site:** http://www.wobla.de
Freq: Weekly; **Cover Price:** Free; **Circ:** 77,500
Editor: Ulrich Arndt; **Advertising Manager:** Stephan Feindel
Profile: Advertising journal (house-to-house) concentrating on local stories.
Language(s): German
ADVERTISING RATES:
Full Page Mono .... EUR 5772
Full Page Colour .... EUR 7537
Mechanical Data: Type Area: 485 x 320 mm, No. of Columns (Display): 7, Col Widths (Display): 44 mm
Copy instructions: *Copy Date:* 2 days prior to publication
LOCAL NEWSPAPERS

WOCHENBLATT KIRCHHEIMBOLANDEN MIT GÖLLHEIM UND EISENBERG
748017G72-15972
Editorial: Vorstadt 35, 67292 KIRCHHEIMBOLANDEN **Tel:** 6352 5533
Fax: 6352 5533

Email: red-kib@wobla.de **Web site:** http://www.wobla.de
Freq: Weekly; **Cover Price:** Free; **Circ:** 20,150
Editor: Klaus Mayer; **Advertising Manager:** Stephan Feindel
Profile: Advertising journal (house-to-house) concentrating on local stories.
Language(s): German
ADVERTISING RATES:
Full Page Mono .... EUR 1344
Full Page Colour .... EUR 1760
Mechanical Data: Type Area: 320 x 228 mm, No. of Columns (Display): 5, Col Widths (Display): 44 mm
Copy instructions: *Copy Date:* 2 days prior to publication
LOCAL NEWSPAPERS

WOCHENBLATT LANDAU

748031G72-16020
Editorial: Industriestr. 15, 76829 LANDAU
Tel: 6341 649510 **Fax:** 6341 649540
Email: red-lan@wobla.de **Web site:** http://www.wobla.de
Freq: Weekly; **Cover Price:** Free; **Circ:** 43,600
Editor: Ulrich Arndt; **Advertising Manager:** Stephan Feindel
Profile: Advertising journal (house-to-house) concentrating on local stories.
Language(s): German
ADVERTISING RATES:
Full Page Mono .... EUR 3294
Full Page Colour .... EUR 4312
Mechanical Data: Type Area: 485 x 320 mm, No. of Columns (Display): 7, Col Widths (Display): 44 mm
Copy instructions: *Copy Date:* 2 days prior to publication
LOCAL NEWSPAPERS

WOCHENBLATT LUDWIGSHAFEN

748033G72-16028
Editorial: Amtsstr. 5, 67059 LUDWIGSHAFEN
Tel: 621 5902373 **Fax:** 621 5902499
Email: red-lud@wobla.de **Web site:** http://www.wobla.de
Freq: Weekly; **Cover Price:** Free; **Circ:** 95,600
Editor: Ulrich Arndt; **Advertising Manager:** Stephan Feindel
Profile: Advertising journal (house-to-house) concentrating on local stories.
Language(s): German
ADVERTISING RATES:
Full Page Mono .... EUR 6111
Full Page Colour .... EUR 7945
Mechanical Data: Type Area: 485 x 320 mm, No. of Columns (Display): 7, Col Widths (Display): 44 mm
Copy instructions: *Copy Date:* 2 days prior to publication
LOCAL NEWSPAPERS

WOCHENBLATT MAGAZIN

1818432G21A-4374
Editorial: Bopserstr. 17, 70180 STUTTGART
Tel: 711 2140141 **Fax:** 711 2360232
Email: redaktion-lw@bwagrar.de **Web site:** http://www.bwagrar.de
Freq: 6 issues yearly; **Circ:** 182,900
Editor: Heiner Krehl; **Advertising Manager:** Gerhard Kretschmer
Profile: The wochenblatt Magazin informs and advises farmers and farm managers depth about a particular priority issue. The topics are thoroughly researched and presented in detail. So they are a perfect complement to the current coverage of the carrier track. The five participating professional editorial noards guarantee a high level of editorial quality and prepare the information independently and easily understood in the modern magazine layout.
Language(s): German
ADVERTISING RATES:
Full Page Mono .... EUR 11440
Full Page Colour .... EUR 15310
Mechanical Data: Type Area: 275 x 195 mm, No. of Columns (Display): 4, Col Widths (Display): 46 mm
Supplement to: BBZ Badische Bauern Zeitung, BW agrar Landwirtschaftliches Wochenblatt, BW agrar Schwäbischer Bauer, LW hessen.rheinland-pfalz Landwirtschaftliches Wochenblatt, LW hessen.rheinland-Pfalz Landwirtschaftliches Wochenblatt

WOCHENBLATT MARSCH & HEIDE

748035G72-16036
Editorial: Schloßring 5, 21423 WINSEN
Tel: 4171 658222 **Fax:** 4171 658140
Email: redaktion@winsener-anzeiger.de **Web site:** http://www.wochenblatt.biz
Freq: Weekly; **Cover Price:** Free; **Circ:** 53,500
Editor: Marcel Maack; **Advertising Manager:** Lebrecht Maack
Profile: Advertising journal (house-to-house) concentrating on local stories.
Language(s): German
ADVERTISING RATES:
Full Page Mono .... EUR 3303
Full Page Colour .... EUR 4619
Mechanical Data: Type Area: 430 x 280 mm, No. of Columns (Display): 6, Col Widths (Display): 45 mm
Copy instructions: *Copy Date:* 2 days prior to publication
LOCAL NEWSPAPERS

WOCHENBLATT MIT AMTSBLATT STADT MANNHEIM

748034G72-16032
Editorial: Melchiorstr. 1, 68167 MANNHEIM
Tel: 621 1279235 **Fax:** 621 1279220
Email: red-ma@wobla.de **Web site:** http://www.wobla.de
Freq: Weekly; **Cover Price:** Free; **Circ:** 190,450
Editor: Ulrich Arndt; **Advertising Manager:** Stephan Feindel
Profile: Advertising journal (house-to-house) concentrating on local stories.
Language(s): German
ADVERTISING RATES:
Full Page Mono .... EUR 10898
Full Page Colour .... EUR 14158
Mechanical Data: Type Area: 485 x 320 mm, No. of Columns (Display): 7, Col Widths (Display): 44 mm
Copy instructions: *Copy Date:* 2 days prior to publication
Supplement(s): Amtsblatt Stadt Mannheim
LOCAL NEWSPAPERS

WOCHENBLATT PASSAUER WOCHE

738618G72-10420
Editorial: Spitalhofstr. 94, 94032 PASSAU
Tel: 851 501426 **Fax:** 851 501432
Email: stefan.brandl@wochenblatt.de **Web site:** http://www.wochenblatt.de
Freq: Weekly; **Cover Price:** Free; **Circ:** 100,900
Editor: Stefan Brandl; **Advertising Manager:** Gerhard Haiböck
Profile: Advertising journal (house-to-house) concentrating on local stories.
Language(s): German
ADVERTISING RATES:
Full Page Mono .... EUR 4775
Full Page Colour .... EUR 7149
Mechanical Data: Type Area: 460 x 280 mm, No. of Columns (Display): 6, Col Widths (Display): 43 mm
Copy instructions: *Copy Date:* 2 days prior to publication
LOCAL NEWSPAPERS

WOCHENBLATT PIRMASENS

748037G72-16044
Editorial: Schachenstr. 3, 66953 PIRMASENS
Tel: 6331 800452 **Fax:** 6331 800453
Email: red-pir@wobla.de **Web site:** http://www.wobla.de
Freq: Weekly; **Cover Price:** Free; **Circ:** 31,000
Editor: Ulrich Arndt; **Advertising Manager:** Stephan Feindel
Profile: Advertising journal (house-to-house) concentrating on local stories.
Language(s): German
ADVERTISING RATES:
Full Page Mono .... EUR 3226
Full Page Colour .... EUR 4176
Mechanical Data: Type Area: 485 x 320 mm, No. of Columns (Display): 7, Col Widths (Display): 44 mm
Copy instructions: *Copy Date:* 2 days prior to publication
LOCAL NEWSPAPERS

WOCHENBLATT RÜLZHEIM, BELLHEIM, JOCKGRIM

748023G72-15996
Editorial: Industriestr. 15, 76829 LANDAU
Tel: 6341 649512 **Fax:** 6341 649540
Email: red-rue@wobla.de **Web site:** http://www.wobla.de
Freq: Weekly; **Cover Price:** Free; **Circ:** 18,150
Editor: Ulrich Arndt; **Advertising Manager:** Stephan Feindel
Profile: Advertising journal (house-to-house) concentrating on local stories.
Language(s): German
ADVERTISING RATES:
Full Page Mono .... EUR 2581
Full Page Colour .... EUR 3090
Mechanical Data: Type Area: 485 x 320 mm, No. of Columns (Display): 7, Col Widths (Display): 44 mm
Copy instructions: *Copy Date:* 2 days prior to publication
LOCAL NEWSPAPERS

WOCHENBLATT SPEYER

748040G72-16056
Editorial: Heydenreichstr. 5, 67346 SPEYER
Tel: 6232 676415 **Fax:** 6232 676411
Email: red-spe@wobla.de **Web site:** http://www.wobla.de
Freq: Weekly; **Cover Price:** Free; **Circ:** 40,950
Editor: Ulrich Arndt; **Advertising Manager:** Stephan Feindel
Profile: Advertising journal (house-to-house) concentrating on local stories.
Language(s): German
ADVERTISING RATES:
Full Page Mono .... EUR 3633
Full Page Colour .... EUR 4686
Mechanical Data: Type Area: 485 x 320 mm, No. of Columns (Display): 7, Col Widths (Display): 44 mm
Copy instructions: *Copy Date:* 2 days prior to publication
LOCAL NEWSPAPERS

WOCHENBLATT + SACHSENHEIM POST

748042G72-16064
Editorial: Marktplatz 15, 71665 VAIHINGEN
Tel: 7042 91950 **Fax:** 7042 91999
Email: info@vkz.de **Web site:** http://www.vkz.de
Freq: Weekly; **Cover Price:** Free; **Circ:** 41,500
Editor: Albert Arning; **Advertising Manager:** Detlef Großmann
Profile: Advertising journal (house-to-house) concentrating on local stories.
Language(s): German
ADVERTISING RATES:
Full Page Mono .... EUR 5487
Full Page Colour .... EUR 7931
Mechanical Data: Type Area: 485 x 320 mm, No. of Columns (Display): 7, Col Widths (Display): 44 mm
Copy instructions: *Copy Date:* 3 days prior to publication
Supplement(s): Amtsblatt für die Grosse Kreisstadt Vaihingen an der Enz
LOCAL NEWSPAPERS

WOCHENBLATT ZUM SONNTAG

748045G72-16072
Editorial: Kreuztor 8, 38126 BRAUNSCHWEIG
Tel: 531 3800025 **Fax:** 531 3800020
Email: redaktion@braunschweigreport.de
Freq: Weekly; **Cover Price:** Free; **Circ:** 63,000
Editor: Klaus Knodt; **Advertising Manager:** Ursula Manegold
Profile: Advertising journal (house-to-house) concentrating on local stories.
Language(s): German
ADVERTISING RATES:
Full Page Mono .... EUR 6915
Full Page Colour .... EUR 1037
Mechanical Data: Type Area: 430 x 280 mm, No. of Columns (Display): 6, Col Widths (Display): 45 mm
Copy instructions: *Copy Date:* 2 days prior to publication
LOCAL NEWSPAPERS

WOCHENEND ANZEIGER

748051G72-16088
Editorial: Schefestr. 11, 21493 SCHWARZENBEK
Tel: 4151 889088 **Fax:** 4151 889044
Email: redaktion@wochenend-anzeiger.de **Web site:** http://www.viebranz.de
Freq: Weekly; **Cover Price:** Free; **Circ:** 49,205
Editor: Olaf Kührmann; **Advertising Manager:** Sabine Riege
Profile: Advertising journal (house-to-house) concentrating on local stories.
Language(s): German
ADVERTISING RATES:
Full Page Mono .... EUR 4025
Full Page Colour .... EUR 4130
Mechanical Data: Type Area: 430 x 282 mm, No. of Columns (Display): 6, Col Widths (Display): 45 mm
Copy instructions: *Copy Date:* 1 day prior to publication
LOCAL NEWSPAPERS

WOCHENEND TZ

748052G67B-16140
Editorial: Paul-Heyse-Str. 2, 80336 MÜNCHEN
Tel: 89 53060 **Fax:** 89 5306552
Web site: http://www.tz-online.de
Freq: Weekly; **Circ:** 177,381
Editor: Rudolf Bögel; **News Editor:** Klaus Rimpel; **Advertising Manager:** Hans-Georg Bechthold
Profile: Regional weekly covering politics, economics, culture, sports, travel, technology and the arts. Facebook: http://www.facebook.com/pages/TZ-Online/95100047797 This Outlet offers RSS (Really Simple Syndication).
Language(s): German
ADVERTISING RATES:
SCC .... EUR 112,10
Mechanical Data: Type Area: 474 x 324 mm, No. of Columns (Display): 7, Col Widths (Display): 45 mm
Copy instructions: *Copy Date:* 1 day prior to publication
REGIONAL DAILY & SUNDAY NEWSPAPERS: Regional Daily Newspapers

WOCHENENDE KREISBOTE WEILHEIM UND MURNAU

733279G72-6340
Editorial: Am Weidenbach 8, 82362 WEILHEIM
Tel: 881 68616 **Fax:** 881 68653
Email: redaktion-wm@kreisbote.de **Web site:** http://www.kreisbote.de
Freq: Weekly; **Cover Price:** Free; **Circ:** 44,163
Editor: Maria Hofstetter; **Advertising Manager:** Helmut Ernst
Profile: Advertising journal (house-to-house) concentrating on local stories.
Language(s): German
ADVERTISING RATES:
Full Page Mono .... EUR 3749
Full Page Colour .... EUR 4874
Mechanical Data: Type Area: 474 x 324 mm, No. of Columns (Display): 7, Col Widths (Display): 45 mm
Copy instructions: *Copy Date:* 3 days prior to publication
LOCAL NEWSPAPERS

WOCHENJOURNAL WO

747933G72-15408
Editorial: Stephanienstr. 1, 76530 BADEN-BADEN
Tel: 7221 2151286 **Fax:** 7221 2151394
Email: wo.red@badisches-tagblatt.de **Web site:** http://www.badisches-tagblatt.de
Freq: Weekly; **Cover Price:** Free; **Circ:** 163,052
Editor: Thomas Riedinger; **Advertising Manager:** Stefan Hörig
Profile: Advertising journal (house-to-house) concentrating on local stories.
Language(s): German
ADVERTISING RATES:
Full Page Mono .... EUR 6813
Full Page Colour .... EUR 8874
Mechanical Data: Type Area: 435 x 282 mm, No. of Columns (Display): 6, Col Widths (Display): 44 mm
Copy instructions: *Copy Date:* 1 day prior to publication
LOCAL NEWSPAPERS

WOCHENSPIEGEL BAD BELZIG TREUENBRIETZEN

748147G72-16312
Editorial: Schillerstr. 1, 14913 JÜTERBOG
Tel: 3372 41920 **Fax:** 3372 419220
Email: redaktion.jbl@wochenspiegel-brb.de **Web site:** http://www.wochenspiegel-brb.de
Freq: Weekly; **Cover Price:** Free; **Circ:** 18,305
Editor: Iris Krüger
Profile: Advertising journal (house-to-house) concentrating on local stories.
Language(s): German
ADVERTISING RATES:
Full Page Mono .... EUR 2046
Full Page Colour .... EUR 2864
Mechanical Data: Type Area: 479 x 324 mm, No. of Columns (Display): 7, Col Widths (Display): 45 mm
Copy instructions: *Copy Date:* 5 days prior to publication
LOCAL NEWSPAPERS

WOCHENSPIEGEL BLIESTAL/ MANDELBACHTAL

748151G72-16328
Editorial: Von-der-Leyen-Str. 31, 66440 BLIESKASTEL **Tel:** 6842 924784 **Fax:** 6842 924729
Email: redaktion-bli@swvgmbh.de **Web site:** http://www.wochenspiegelonline.de
Freq: Weekly; **Cover Price:** Free; **Circ:** 18,560
Editor: Sandra Brettar; **Advertising Manager:** Günter Österreicher
Profile: Advertising journal (house-to-house) concentrating on local stories.
Language(s): German
ADVERTISING RATES:
Full Page Mono .... EUR 3394
Full Page Colour .... EUR 4604
Mechanical Data: Type Area: 480 x 326 mm, No. of Columns (Display): 7, Col Widths (Display): 44 mm
Copy instructions: *Copy Date:* 2 days prior to publication
LOCAL NEWSPAPERS

WOCHENSPIEGEL DILLINGEN MIT DILLINGER STADTRUNDSCHAU

725304G72-3136
Editorial: Hüttenwerkstr. 12, 66763 DILLINGEN
Tel: 6831 7616314 **Fax:** 6831 7616322
Email: redaktion-dil@swvgmbh.de **Web site:** http://www.wochenspiegelonline.de
Freq: Weekly; **Cover Price:** Free; **Circ:** 27,820
Editor: Alois Martin; **Advertising Manager:** Günter Österreicher
Profile: Advertising journal (house-to-house) concentrating on local stories.
Language(s): German
ADVERTISING RATES:
Full Page Mono .... EUR 3461
Full Page Colour .... EUR 4704
Mechanical Data: Type Area: 480 x 326 mm, No. of Columns (Display): 7, Col Widths (Display): 44 mm
Copy instructions: *Copy Date:* 2 days prior to publication
LOCAL NEWSPAPERS

WOCHENSPIEGEL HOCHWALD MIT HOCHWALD RUNDSCHAU

730394G72-5556
Editorial: Trierer Str. 10, 66663 MERZIG
Tel: 6861 9392214 **Fax:** 6861 9392222
Email: redaktion-mzg@swvgmbh.de **Web site:** http://www.wochenspiegel-saarland.de
Freq: Weekly; **Cover Price:** Free; **Circ:** 16,885
Editor: Klaus-Dieter Tiator; **Advertising Manager:** Günter Österreicher
Profile: Advertising journal (house-to-house) concentrating on local stories.
Language(s): German
ADVERTISING RATES:
Full Page Mono .... EUR 2352
Full Page Colour .... EUR 3159
Mechanical Data: Type Area: 480 x 326 mm, No. of Columns (Display): 7, Col Widths (Display): 44 mm
Copy instructions: *Copy Date:* 2 days prior to publication
LOCAL NEWSPAPERS

WOCHENSPIEGEL HOMBURG
748161G72-16344
Editorial: Talstr. 40, 66424 HOMBURG
Tel: 6841 924714 **Fax:** 6841 924729
Email: redaktion-hom@swvgmbh.de **Web site:** http://www.wochenspiegelonline.de
Freq: Weekly; **Cover Price:** Free; **Circ:** 39,495
Editor: Hartwig Fischer; **Advertising Manager:** Günter Österreicher
Profile: Advertising journal (house-to-house) concentrating on local stories.
Language(s): German
ADVERTISING RATES:
Full Page Mono .... EUR 4066
Full Page Colour .... EUR 5477
Mechanical Data: Type Area: 480 x 326 mm, No. of Columns (Display): 7, Col Widths (Display): 44 mm
Copy instructions: *Copy Date:* 2 days prior to publication
LOCAL NEWSPAPERS

WOCHENSPIEGEL ILLTAL MIT ILLTAL RUNDSCHAU
748162G72-16348
Editorial: Oberer Markt 19, 66538 NEUNKIRCHEN
Tel: 6821 9127314 **Fax:** 6821 9127322
Email: redaktion-nk@swvgmbh.de **Web site:** http://www.wochenspiegelonline.de
Freq: Weekly; **Cover Price:** Free; **Circ:** 21,405
Editor: Jürgen Ecker; **Advertising Manager:** Günter Österreicher
Profile: Advertising journal (house-to-house) concentrating on local stories.
Language(s): German
ADVERTISING RATES:
Full Page Mono .... EUR 3360
Full Page Colour .... EUR 4536
Mechanical Data: Type Area: 480 x 326 mm, No. of Columns (Display): 7, Col Widths (Display): 44 mm
Copy instructions: *Copy Date:* 2 days prior to publication
LOCAL NEWSPAPERS

WOCHENSPIEGEL MERZIG MIT MERZIGER STADTRUNDSCHAU
735353G72-7528
Editorial: Trierer Str. 10, 66663 MERZIG
Tel: 6861 9392214 **Fax:** 6861 9392222
Email: redaktion-mzg@swvgmbh.de **Web site:** http://www.wochenspiegelonline.de
Freq: Weekly; **Cover Price:** Free; **Circ:** 29,050
Editor: Klaus-Dieter Tiator; **Advertising Manager:** Günter Österreicher
Profile: Advertising journal (house-to-house) concentrating on local stories.
Language(s): German
ADVERTISING RATES:
Full Page Mono .... EUR 3461
Full Page Colour .... EUR 4704
Mechanical Data: Type Area: 480 x 326 mm, No. of Columns (Display): 7, Col Widths (Display): 44 mm
Copy instructions: *Copy Date:* 2 days prior to publication
LOCAL NEWSPAPERS

WOCHENSPIEGEL SAARBRÜCKEN
748180G72-16400
Editorial: Bleichstr. 21, 66111 SAARBRÜCKEN
Tel: 681 388020 **Fax:** 681 38802169
Email: redaktion-sbr@wochenspiegelonline.de **Web site:** http://www.wochenspiegelonline.de
Freq: Weekly; **Cover Price:** Free; **Circ:** 90,690
Editor: Thomas Trapp; **Advertising Manager:** Günter Österreicher
Profile: Advertising journal (house-to-house) concentrating on local stories.
Language(s): German
ADVERTISING RATES:
Full Page Mono .... EUR 7728
Full Page Colour .... EUR 10416
Mechanical Data: Type Area: 480 x 326 mm, No. of Columns (Display): 7, Col Widths (Display): 44 mm
Copy instructions: *Copy Date:* 2 days prior to publication
LOCAL NEWSPAPERS

WOCHENSPIEGEL SAARLOUIS MIT SAARLOUISER STADTRUNDSCHAU
740907G72-11416
Editorial: Kaiser-Friedrich-Ring 4, 66740 SAARLOUIS **Tel:** 6831 4888334 **Fax:** 6831 4888339
Email: redaktion-sls@swvgmbh.de **Web site:** http://www.wochenspiegelonline.de
Freq: Weekly; **Cover Price:** Free; **Circ:** 57,670
Editor: Rainer Selzer; **Advertising Manager:** Günter Österreicher
Profile: Advertising journal (house-to-house) concentrating on local stories.
Language(s): German
ADVERTISING RATES:
Full Page Mono .... EUR 5847
Full Page Colour .... EUR 7896
Mechanical Data: Type Area: 480 x 326 mm, No. of Columns (Display): 7, Col Widths (Display): 44 mm
Copy instructions: *Copy Date:* 2 days prior to publication
LOCAL NEWSPAPERS

WOCHENSPIEGEL ST. INGBERT
748182G72-16408
Editorial: Rickertstr. 38, 66386 ST. INGBERT
Tel: 6894 926472 **Fax:** 6894 926429
Email: redaktion-igb@swvgmbh.de **Web site:** http://www.wochenspiegelonline.de
Freq: Weekly; **Cover Price:** Free; **Circ:** 18,805
Editor: Jörg Jung; **Advertising Manager:** Günter Österreicher
Profile: Advertising journal (house-to-house) concentrating on local stories.
Language(s): German
ADVERTISING RATES:
Full Page Mono .... EUR 3394
Full Page Colour .... EUR 4602
Mechanical Data: Type Area: 480 x 326 mm, No. of Columns (Display): 7, Col Widths (Display): 44 mm
Copy instructions: *Copy Date:* 2 days prior to publication
LOCAL NEWSPAPERS

WOCHENSPIEGEL SULZBACHTAL/ FISCHBACHTAL
748187G72-16416
Editorial: Bleichstr. 21, 66111 SAARBRÜCKEN
Tel: 681 38802164 **Fax:** 681 38802169
Email: redaktion-igb@swvgmbh.de **Web site:** http://www.wochenspiegelonline.de
Freq: Weekly; **Cover Price:** Free; **Circ:** 33,480
Editor: Jürgen Becker; **Advertising Manager:** Günter Österreicher
Profile: Advertising journal (house-to-house) concentrating on local stories.
Language(s): German
ADVERTISING RATES:
Full Page Mono .... EUR 4066
Full Page Colour .... EUR 5477
Mechanical Data: Type Area: 440 x 326 mm, No. of Columns (Display): 7, Col Widths (Display): 44 mm
Copy instructions: *Copy Date:* 2 days prior to publication
LOCAL NEWSPAPERS

WOCHENSPIEGEL VÖLKLINGEN MIT VÖLKLINGER STADTRUNDSCHAU
746614G72-14756
Editorial: Poststr. 11, 66333 VÖLKLINGEN
Tel: 6898 501514 **Fax:** 6898 501529
Email: redaktion-vk@wochenspiegelonline.de **Web site:** http://www.wochenspiegelonline.de
Freq: Weekly; **Cover Price:** Free; **Circ:** 24,820
Editor: Doris Schmidt; **Advertising Manager:** Günter Österreicher
Profile: Advertising journal (house-to-house) concentrating on local stories.
Language(s): German
ADVERTISING RATES:
Full Page Mono .... EUR 3394
Full Page Colour .... EUR 4604
Mechanical Data: Type Area: 480 x 326 mm, No. of Columns (Display): 7, Col Widths (Display): 44 mm
Copy instructions: *Copy Date:* 2 days prior to publication
LOCAL NEWSPAPERS

WOCHEN-TIPP FÜR SYKE, STUHR, WEYHE UND BRUCHHAUSEN-VILSEN
748199G72-15720
Editorial: Werkstr. 2, 28857 SYKE **Tel:** 4242 58285 **Fax:** 4242 58288
Email: manuela.beer@aller-weser-verlag.de **Web site:** http://www.aller-weser-verlag.de
Freq: Weekly; **Cover Price:** Free; **Circ:** 37,500
Editor: Manuela Beer; **Advertising Manager:** Sabine Düßmann
Profile: Advertising journal (house-to-house) concentrating on local stories.
Language(s): German
ADVERTISING RATES:
Full Page Mono .... EUR 3271
Full Page Colour .... EUR 4743
Mechanical Data: Type Area: 472 x 325 mm, No. of Columns (Display): 7, Col Widths (Display): 45 mm
Copy instructions: *Copy Date:* 3 days prior to publication
LOCAL NEWSPAPERS

WOCHENZEITUNG EMMENDINGER TOR
726578G72-3660
Editorial: Denzlinger Str. 42, 79312 EMMENDINGEN
Tel: 7641 938012 **Fax:** 7641 938010
Email: redaktion@emmendinger-tor.de **Web site:** http://www.wzo.de
Freq: Weekly; **Cover Price:** Free; **Circ:** 25,700
Editor: Birte Pippon
Profile: Advertising journal (house-to-house) concentrating on local stories.
Language(s): German
ADVERTISING RATES:
Full Page Mono .... EUR 2621
Full Page Colour .... EUR 3579
Mechanical Data: Type Area: 420 x 285 mm, No. of Columns (Display): 6, Col Widths (Display): 45 mm
Copy instructions: *Copy Date:* 2 days prior to publication
Supplement(s): Emmendingen Aktuell; Teninger Nachrichten
LOCAL NEWSPAPERS

WOHLAU-STEINAUER HEIMATBLATT
748242G94D-2860
Editorial: Langes Gräthlein 45, 97078 WÜRZBURG
Tel: 931 24006 **Fax:** 931 29201
Email: info@goldammer.com **Web site:** http://www.goldammer.com
Freq: Monthly; **Annual Sub.:** EUR 36,00; **Circ:** 2,000
Editor: Clemens Hümpfner
Profile: Magazine featuring articles and history concerning the Wohlau-Steinauer area.
Language(s): German
Readership: Read by previous and current occupants of the area.
Mechanical Data: Type Area: 280 x 185 mm, No. of Columns (Display): 4, Col Widths (Display): 44 mm
Copy instructions: *Copy Date:* 30 days prior to publication
CONSUMER: OTHER CLASSIFICATIONS: Expatriates

WOHNBADEN
748245G23C-200_50
Editorial: Goethestr. 75, 40237 DÜSSELDORF
Tel: 211 9149414 **Fax:** 211 9149490
Email: m.heinrich@krs-redaktion.de **Web site:** http://www.krammerag.de
Freq: Half-yearly; **Cover Price:** EUR 5,00; **Circ:** 6,621
Editor: Marcus Heinrich; **Advertising Manager:** Alke Schmeis
Profile: Wohnbaden is aimed at residential consumers, builders and renovators who deal with the new installation, renovation and modernization of the bath. News reports on all topics related to the bathroom and sauna, spa, fitness: sanitary equipment, installation, maintenance and costs. Special Issue Part 1: wall and floor coverings. Special Issue Part 2: kitchen faucets and radiators.
Language(s): German
Readership: Aimed at manufacturers, suppliers, showroom managers and fitters.
ADVERTISING RATES:
Full Page Mono .... EUR 4200
Full Page Colour .... EUR 6300
Mechanical Data: Type Area: 257 x 185 mm, No. of Columns (Display): 4, Col Widths (Display): 42 mm
Copy instructions: *Copy Date:* 35 days prior to publication
BUSINESS: FURNISHINGS & FURNITURE: Furnishings & Furniture - Kitchens & Bathrooms

WOHN!DESIGN
748247G74C-3240
Editorial: Mörikestr. 67, 70199 STUTTGART
Tel: 711 96666412 **Fax:** 711 96666415
Email: stephan.demmrich@wohndesign.de **Web site:** http://www.wohndesign.de
Freq: 7 issues yearly; **Annual Sub.:** EUR 35,00; **Circ:** 44,322
Editor: Stephan Demmrich; **Advertising Manager:** Ulrike Ehlers
Profile: Journal of residential and architectural features from around the world, scene reports and presentation of cutting-edge products from the furniture and lifestyle sector. Looking for information on the topics of housing and architecture? If you are in terms of design with the times? Then offers living! design just the right reading material! Six times a year brings home! design is a wealth of current topics that revolve around the beautiful shape! Top-class residential and architectural features from around the world belong to its repertoire, such as scene reports from the world of design. The focus is the presentation of cutting-edge products from the furniture and lifestyle range: From kitchen accessories to the Bathroom to the sofa - home design sense trends, tips and trends for you and shows you every two months the latest hotspots! the design scene!.
Language(s): German
ADVERTISING RATES:
Full Page Mono .... EUR 6800
Full Page Colour .... EUR 8800
Mechanical Data: Type Area: 252 x 190 mm
Copy instructions: *Copy Date:* 32 days prior to publication
CONSUMER: WOMEN'S INTEREST CONSUMER MAGAZINES: Home & Family

WOHNEN
748254G94H-13600
Editorial: Beim Strohhause 27, 20097 HAMBURG
Tel: 40 413639122 **Fax:** 40 41363911
Email: briese@hmc.de **Web site:** http://www.wohnen-magazin.de
Freq: Quarterly; **Cover Price:** EUR 0,95; **Circ:** 1,051,835
Editor: Ekkehard Briese
Profile: Building society magazine about home purchase.
Language(s): German
ADVERTISING RATES:
Full Page Mono .... EUR 28460
Full Page Colour .... EUR 35900
Mechanical Data: Type Area: 260 x 190 mm, No. of Columns (Display): 4, Col Widths (Display): 44 mm
Copy instructions: *Copy Date:* 35 days prior to publication
Supplement(s): FinanzSpezial
CONSUMER: OTHER CLASSIFICATIONS: Customer Magazines

WOHNEN & GARTEN
723939G74C-420
Editorial: Hubert-Burda-Platz 1, 77652 OFFENBURG
Tel: 781 8401 **Fax:** 781 843522
Email: redaktion@wohnen-und-garten.com **Web site:** http://www.wohnen-und-garten.de
Freq: Monthly; **Annual Sub.:** EUR 45,60; **Circ:** 274,547
Editor: Andrea Kögel
Profile: At a time in the house and garden are more important than private wellness world, celebrated Wohnen & Garten the atmospheric home. With an emotional image and an opulent look is the fusion of inside and outside of home, garden and hospitality to a world of life, a lifestyle, staged. Posh decorating tips living reports and advice, garden design or unusual recipes for partys - Wohnen & Garten brings the best ideas for a sophisticated living environment in the "classic style". Facebook: http://www.facebook.com/pages/Wohnen-Garten/172955759406736.
Language(s): German
Readership: Read by women aged between 25 and 50, with above average incomes.
ADVERTISING RATES:
Full Page Mono .... EUR 16000
Full Page Colour .... EUR 16000
Mechanical Data: Type Area: 268 x 200 mm, No. of Columns (Display): 4, Col Widths (Display): 47 mm
Copy instructions: *Copy Date:* 42 days prior to publication
CONSUMER: WOMEN'S INTEREST CONSUMER MAGAZINES: Home & Family

WOHNIDEE
748262G74C-3380
Editorial: Charles-de-Gaulle-Str. 8, 81737 MÜNCHEN **Tel:** 89 67867603 **Fax:** 89 67867630
Email: andrea.wolf@wohnidee.de **Web site:** http://www.wohnidee.de
Freq: Monthly; **Annual Sub.:** EUR 38,40; **Circ:** 152,577
Editor: Simone Wendt
Profile: The magazine stands out due to very good sense of decor, furnishings, color and materials on housing and home furnishings. Thus, the journal presents stylish and shows the variety of design options. In addition, the reader at Wohnidee about all topics concerning decoration, decorating is competent and informed advice. The magazine takes great care in furnishing suggestions realistic, loving decorating ideas and solutions that not only conceivable, but are also feasible. With great features and attractive image galleries on recycled decoration, decorating Wohnidee offers helpful tips and information on lifestyle trends and design all types of housing and real estate. Behind all this is at Wohnidee thorough research, which is prepared as needed and utilitarian. Wohnidee delivers functionality and beauty that are permanent. It is bordered from the magazine well of excessive design experiments. For Wohnidee is the focus, not to earth and not to be lifted. Wohnidee considers it important to always shine with a high quality.
Language(s): German
ADVERTISING RATES:
Full Page Mono .... EUR 21644
Full Page Colour .... EUR 21664
Mechanical Data: Type Area: 256 x 186 mm, No. of Columns (Display): 4, Col Widths (Display): 43 mm
Copy instructions: *Copy Date:* 50 days prior to publication
CONSUMER: WOMEN'S INTEREST CONSUMER MAGAZINES: Home & Family

WOHNUNG + GESUNDHEIT
748279G4E-6700
Editorial: Holzham 25, 83115 NEUBEUERN
Tel: 8035 2039 **Fax:** 8035 8164
Email: institut@baubiologie.de **Web site:** http://www.baubiologie.de
Freq: Quarterly; **Annual Sub.:** EUR 36,00; **Circ:** 8,000
Editor: Anton Schneider; **Advertising Manager:** Elisabeth Krause
Profile: Magazine focusing on ecological building and living, also architecture.
Language(s): German
Readership: Read by people in the building industry.
ADVERTISING RATES:
Full Page Mono .... EUR 1280
Full Page Colour .... EUR 1490
Mechanical Data: Type Area: 238 x 174 mm
BUSINESS: ARCHITECTURE & BUILDING: Building

WOLFENBÜTTELER SCHAUFENSTER
748291G72-16492
Editorial: Großer Zimmerhof 25, 38300 WOLFENBÜTTEL **Tel:** 5331 98990 **Fax:** 5331 989956
Email: redaktion@schaufenster-wf.de **Web site:** http://www.schaufenster-wf.de
Freq: 104 issues yearly; **Cover Price:** Free; **Circ:** 55,500
Editor: Thorsten Raedlein; **Advertising Manager:** Nicole Volkstedt
Profile: Advertising journal (house-to-house) concentrating on local stories.
Language(s): German
ADVERTISING RATES:
Full Page Mono .... EUR 4748
Full Page Colour .... EUR 6760
Mechanical Data: Type Area: 430 x 280 mm, No. of Columns (Display): 6, Col Widths (Display): 45 mm
Copy instructions: *Copy Date:* 2 days prior to publication
LOCAL NEWSPAPERS

WOLFHAGER ALLGEMEINE
730363G67B-7320
Editorial: Frankfurter Str. 168, 34121 KASSEL
Tel: 561 20300 **Fax:** 561 2032406
Email: info@hna.de **Web site:** http://www.hna.de
Freq: 312 issues yearly; **Circ:** 15,903
Advertising Manager: Andrea Schaller-Öller

Profile: Regional daily newspaper with news on politics, economy, culture, sports, travel, technology, etc. The Wolfhager Allgemeine a local edition of the HNA Hessische/Niedersächsische Allgemeine. Facebook: http://www.facebook.com/HNA?ref=ts Twitter: http://twitter.com/hna_online This Outlet offers RSS (Really Simple Syndication).
Language(s): German
ADVERTISING RATES:
SCC .... EUR 37,10
Mechanical Data: Type Area: 430 x 285 mm, No. of Columns (Display): 6, Col Widths (Display): 45 mm
Copy instructions: *Copy Date:* 2 days prior to publication
REGIONAL DAILY & SUNDAY NEWSPAPERS: Regional Daily Newspapers

WOLFSBURGER ALLGEMEINE
748298G67B-16160
Editorial: Porschestr. 74, 38440 WOLFSBURG
Tel: 5361 200138 **Fax:** 5361 200124
Email: redaktion@waz-online.de **Web site:** http://www.waz-online.de
Freq: 312 issues yearly; **Circ:** 38,268
Editor: Carsten Baschin; **Advertising Manager:** Joachim Böhme
Profile: Daily newspaper with regional news and a local sports section. This Outlet offers RSS (Really Simple Syndication).
Language(s): German
ADVERTISING RATES:
SCC .... EUR 51,40
Mechanical Data: Type Area: 430 x 277 mm, No. of Columns (Display): 6, Col Widths (Display): 45 mm
Copy instructions: *Copy Date:* 1 day prior to publication
REGIONAL DAILY & SUNDAY NEWSPAPERS: Regional Daily Newspapers

WOLFSBURGER KURIER
748299G72-16508
Editorial: Poststr. 41, 38440 WOLFSBURG
Tel: 5361 20000 **Fax:** 5361 200022
Email: redaktion@wolfsburger-kurier.de **Web site:** http://www.wolfsburger-kurier.de
Freq: 104 issues yearly; **Cover Price:** Free
Editor: Oliver Fricke; **Advertising Manager:** Jutta Höll
Profile: Advertising journal (house-to-house) concentrating on local stories.
Language(s): German
ADVERTISING RATES:
Full Page Mono .... EUR 6837
Full Page Colour .... EUR 7227
Mechanical Data: Type Area: 430 x 282 mm, No. of Columns (Display): 6, Col Widths (Display): 45 mm
Copy instructions: *Copy Date:* 2 days prior to publication
LOCAL NEWSPAPERS

WOLFSBURGER NACHRICHTEN
748300G67B-16180
Editorial: Hamburger Str. 277, 38114 BRAUNSCHWEIG **Tel:** 531 39000 **Fax:** 531 3900610
Email: redaktion@bzv.de **Web site:** http://www.newsclick.de
Freq: 312 issues yearly; **Circ:** 27,701
Advertising Manager: Raphael Feldmann
Profile: Regional daily newspaper with news on politics, economy, culture, sports, travel, technology, etc. Almost half a million readers between resin and the Lüneburg Heath and regularly access to the Braunschweiger Zeitung (BZ), the second largest newspaper in Lower Saxony. Wolfsburger Nachrichten is a regional edition of the Braunschweiger Zeitung. The BZ appears weekdays and has an average paid circulation of 150,000 copies. With the main titles Braunschweiger Zeitung, Salzgitter-Zeitung and Wolfsburger Nachrichten and the seven local editions of the Braunschweiger Zeitung profiled as a strong regional newspaper in a historically significant landscape, the Brunswick Country. The Braunschweiger Zeitung considers itself not only as an information medium but also as a forum. Twitter: http://twitter.com/bs_zeitung This Outlet offers RSS (Really Simple Syndication).
Language(s): German
ADVERTISING RATES:
SCC .... EUR 66,00
Mechanical Data: Type Area: 435 x 282 mm, No. of Columns (Display): 6, Col Widths (Display): 45 mm
Copy instructions: *Copy Date:* 1 day prior to publication
Supplement(s): prisma
REGIONAL DAILY & SUNDAY NEWSPAPERS: Regional Daily Newspapers

WOLFSBURGER RUNDBLICK AM SONNTAG
748301G72-16512
Editorial: Porschestr. 58, 38440 WOLFSBURG
Tel: 5361 200144 **Fax:** 5361 200122
Email: redaktion@rundblick-wob.de **Web site:** http://www.rundblick-wob.de
Freq: Weekly; **Cover Price:** Free; **Circ:** 81,620
Editor: Frank Hitzschke; **Advertising Manager:** Horst Schubert
Profile: Advertising journal (house-to-house) concentrating on local stories.
Language(s): German
ADVERTISING RATES:
Full Page Mono .... EUR 5341
Full Page Colour .... EUR 6657
Mechanical Data: Type Area: 430 x 277 mm, No. of Columns (Display): 6, Col Widths (Display): 45 mm

Copy instructions: *Copy Date:* 3 days prior to publication
LOCAL NEWSPAPERS

WOMAN IN THE CITY
1895654G74A-3663
Editorial: Friedrich-Lueg-Str. 10, 44867 BOCHUM
Tel: 2327 991490 **Fax:** 2327 9914911
Email: kirsten.engelhardt@woman-itc.de **Web site:** http://www.woman-itc.de
Freq: Monthly; **Cover Price:** Free; **Circ:** 19,800
Editor: Kirsten Engelhardt; **Advertising Manager:** Jürgen Tkocz
Profile: Free women's magazine for Bochum, Witten and Dortmund. With the latest fashion, beauty and lifestyle trends, politics, art, culture, cuisine, city news, profiles, interviews and reports. Facebook: http://www.facebook.com/womaninthecity.hamburg Twitter: http://twitter.com/#!/WomanInHamburg.
Language(s): German
ADVERTISING RATES:
Full Page Mono .... EUR 1300
Full Page Colour .... EUR 1300
Mechanical Data: Type Area: 276 x 190 mm, No. of Columns (Display): 4, Col Widths (Display): 45 mm
Copy instructions: *Copy Date:* 10 days prior to publication

WOMAN IN THE CITY
1895655G74A-3664
Editorial: Friedrich-Lueg-Str. 10, 44867 BOCHUM
Tel: 2327 991490 **Fax:** 2327 9914911
Email: kirsten.engelhardt@woman-itc.de **Web site:** http://www.woman-itc.de
Freq: 11 issues yearly; **Cover Price:** Free; **Circ:** 19,800
Editor: Kirsten Engelhardt; **Advertising Manager:** Jürgen Tkocz
Profile: Free women's magazine for Wuppertal and Düsseldorf. With the latest fashion, beauty and lifestyle trends, politics, art, culture, cuisine, city news, profiles, interviews and reports. Facebook: http://www.facebook.com/womaninthecity.hamburg Twitter: http://twitter.com/#!/WomanInHamburg.
Language(s): German
ADVERTISING RATES:
Full Page Mono .... EUR 1300
Full Page Colour .... EUR 1300
Mechanical Data: Type Area: 276 x 190 mm, No. of Columns (Display): 4, Col Widths (Display): 45 mm
Copy instructions: *Copy Date:* 10 days prior to publication

WOMAN IN THE CITY
2080659G74A-3821
Editorial: Gertigstr. 44, 20251 HAMBURG
Tel: 40 278682760 **Fax:** 40 49219403
Email: info@witc-verlag.de **Web site:** http://www.witc-verlag.de
Freq: Monthly; **Cover Price:** Free; **Circ:** 15,000
Editor: Ilona Lütje
Profile: Free women's magazine for Hamburg Winterhude and Eppendorf. With the latest fashion, beauty and lifestyle trends, politics, art, culture, cuisine, city news, profiles, interviews and reports.
Language(s): German
ADVERTISING RATES:
Full Page Mono .... EUR 990
Full Page Colour .... EUR 990
Mechanical Data: Type Area: 271 x 185 mm, No. of Columns (Display): 3, Col Widths (Display): 57 mm
Copy instructions: *Copy Date:* 24 days prior to publication

WOMAN IN THE CITY
2080661G74A-3823
Editorial: Holzkoppelweg 15, 24118 KIEL
Fax: 4349 919544
Email: info@witc-verlag.de **Web site:** http://www.witc-verlag.de
Freq: Monthly; **Cover Price:** Free; **Circ:** 15,000
Editor: Dietmar Wagner
Profile: Free women's magazine for Schleswig-Holstein & Kiel. With the latest fashion, beauty and lifestyle trends, politics, art, culture, cuisine, city news, profiles, interviews and reports.
Language(s): German
ADVERTISING RATES:
Full Page Mono .... EUR 990
Full Page Colour .... EUR 990
Mechanical Data: Type Area: 271 x 185 mm, No. of Columns (Display): 3, Col Widths (Display): 57 mm
Copy instructions: *Copy Date:* 24 days prior to publication

WOMAN'S WORLD
1743747G74A-3496
Editorial: Stubbenhuk 10, 20459 HAMBURG
Tel: 40 37035065 **Fax:** 40 37035010
Email: lhmagazin@guj.de **Web site:** http://www.corporate-editors.com
Freq: Quarterly; **Circ:** 184,787
Editor: Christian Krug; **Advertising Manager:** Heiko Hager
Language(s): German
ADVERTISING RATES:
Full Page Mono .... EUR 15500
Full Page Colour .... EUR 15500
Mechanical Data: Type Area: 240 x 180 mm

Copy instructions: *Copy Date:* 56 days prior to publication
CONSUMER: WOMEN'S INTEREST CONSUMER MAGAZINES: Women's Interest

WORKING@OFFICE
748321G14F-6
Editorial: Abraham-Lincoln-Str. 46, 65189 WIESBADEN **Tel:** 611 7878159 **Fax:** 611 7878490
Email: workingoffice@gabler.de **Web site:** http://www.workingoffice.de
Freq: Monthly; **Annual Sub.:** EUR 94,00; **Circ:** 29,867
Editor: Annette Rompel; **Advertising Manager:** Eva Hanenberg
Profile: Magazine focusing on office working practice, new products and office management. Includes information about workshops, training courses and careers guidance.
Language(s): German
Readership: Read by secretaries, office managers and PAs.
ADVERTISING RATES:
Full Page Mono .... EUR 4345
Full Page Colour .... EUR 5995
Mechanical Data: Type Area: 240 x 175 mm, No. of Columns (Display): 4, Col Widths (Display): 40 mm
Copy instructions: *Copy Date:* 30 days prior to publication
Supplement(s): english@office; travel management
BUSINESS: COMMERCE, INDUSTRY & MANAGEMENT: Training & Recruitment

WÖRKSHOP
748229G2A-5240
Editorial: Uhlandring 18, 72829 ENGSTINGEN
Tel: 7129 930180 **Fax:** 7129 930184
Email: woerkshop@qontur.de **Web site:** http://www.qontur.de
Freq: 6 issues yearly; **Annual Sub.:** EUR 44,94; **Circ:** 8,949
Editor: Christoph R. Quattlender
Profile: Magazine containing information of relevance to advertising companies.
Language(s): German
Readership: Aimed at decision makers in PR departments, marketing and sales managers.
ADVERTISING RATES:
Full Page Mono .... EUR 3460
Full Page Colour .... EUR 3460
Mechanical Data: Type Area: 295 x 215 mm, No. of Columns (Display): 4, Col Widths (Display): 50 mm
BUSINESS: COMMUNICATIONS, ADVERTISING & MARKETING

WORLD JOURNAL OF UROLOGY
748325G56A-10460
Editorial: Fleischmannstr. 42, 17489 GREIFSWALD
Email: subscriptions@springer.com **Web site:** http://www.springerlink.com
Freq: 6 issues yearly; **Annual Sub.:** EUR 1125,00; **Circ:** 186
Editor: M. Burchardt
Profile: International publication about urology.
Language(s): English
ADVERTISING RATES:
Full Page Mono .... EUR 740
Full Page Colour .... EUR 1780
Mechanical Data: Type Area: 240 x 175 mm
Official Journal of: Organ d. Urological Research Society

WORLD OF BIKE
1616370G31B-3
Editorial: Ochsenfurter Str. 56, 97286 SOMMERHAUSEN **Tel:** 9333 904990
Fax: 9333 9049915
Email: wob-redaktion@world-of-bike.de **Web site:** http://www.world-of-bike.de
Freq: Monthly; **Cover Price:** Free; **Circ:** 7,221
Editor: Stefan Böhm; **Advertising Manager:** Daliah Wohlfeil
Profile: World of Bike is the industry magazine for motorcycle, scooter and quad trade in Germany. Since January 2006, appears the industry magazine also at stores in Austria and Switzerland. It sees itself as a guidebook for the motorcycle trade and professional workshop. The main topics include: garage, sales, consulting, corporate management, clothing and accessories.
Language(s): German
ADVERTISING RATES:
Full Page Mono .... EUR 2990
Full Page Colour .... EUR 3397
Mechanical Data: Type Area: 260 x 176 mm, No. of Columns (Display): 4, Col Widths (Display): 41 mm
Copy instructions: *Copy Date:* 17 days prior to publication
BUSINESS: MOTOR TRADE: Motorcycle Trade

WORLD OF METALLURGY - ERZMETALL
726523G27-2956
Editorial: Paul-Ernst-Str. 10, 38678 CLAUSTHAL-ZELLERFELD **Tel:** 5323 937920 **Fax:** 5323 937237
Email: redaktion@gdmb.de **Web site:** http://www.gdmb.de
Freq: 6 issues yearly; Free to qualifying individuals
Annual Sub.: EUR 230,00; **Circ:** 2,138
Editor: Jürgen Zuchowski; **Advertising Manager:** Ulrich Waschki
Profile: International magazine about finding, processing, smelting and analysing raw materials. Also focuses on environmental technology.
Language(s): English; German
Readership: Aimed at mining engineers and those involved in the metal industry.

ADVERTISING RATES:
Full Page Mono .... EUR 2240
Full Page Colour .... EUR 3029
Mechanical Data: Type Area: 270 x 180 mm, No. of Columns (Display): 3, Col Widths (Display): 56 mm
BUSINESS: METAL, IRON & STEEL

WORLD OF MINING - SURFACE UNDERGROUND
744033G30-5
Editorial: Paul-Ernst-Str. 10, 38678 CLAUSTHAL-ZELLERFELD **Tel:** 5323 93720 **Fax:** 5323 937237
Email: redaktion@gdmb.de **Web site:** http://www.gdmb.de
Freq: 6 issues yearly; Free to qualifying individuals
Annual Sub.: EUR 230,00; **Circ:** 2,161
Editor: Jürgen Zuchowski; **Advertising Manager:** Ulrich Waschki
Profile: Journal about surface mining.
Language(s): English; German
Readership: Read by geologists, mining engineers, manufacturers of machinery and those concerned with the environment.
ADVERTISING RATES:
Full Page Mono .... EUR 2240
Full Page Colour .... EUR 3029
Mechanical Data: Type Area: 270 x 180 mm, No. of Columns (Display): 3, Col Widths (Display): 56 mm
Copy instructions: *Copy Date:* 30 days prior to publication
BUSINESS: MINING & QUARRYING

WORLD OF PLASTICS
726913G19E-340
Editorial: Gleueler Str. 373, 50935 KÖLN
Tel: 221 439256 **Fax:** 221 438121
Email: f.vollmer@vm-verlag.com **Web site:** http://www.extrusion-info.com
Freq: Half-yearly; **Cover Price:** Free; **Circ:** 6,800
Editor: Fritz Vollmer; **Advertising Manager:** Inge Böhle
Profile: Magazine about synthetic materials processing.
Language(s): Chinese; English
ADVERTISING RATES:
Full Page Mono .... EUR 3300
Full Page Colour .... EUR 3300
Mechanical Data: Type Area: 250 x 185 mm, No. of Columns (Display): 3, Col Widths (Display): 59 mm
Copy instructions: *Copy Date:* 30 days prior to publication

WORMSER WOCHENBLATT
748333G72-16560
Editorial: Adenauerring 2, 67547 WORMS
Tel: 6241 84561 **Fax:** 6241 84548
Email: redaktion@wormser-wochenblatt.de **Web site:** http://www.rhein-main-wochenblatt.de
Freq: Weekly; **Cover Price:** Free; **Circ:** 58,370
Editor: Rüdiger Benda
Profile: Advertising journal (house-to-house) concentrating on local stories.
Language(s): German
ADVERTISING RATES:
Full Page Mono .... EUR 3932
Full Page Colour .... EUR 5276
Mechanical Data: Type Area: 480 x 325 mm, No. of Columns (Display): 7, Col Widths (Display): 45 mm
Copy instructions: *Copy Date:* 2 days prior to publication
LOCAL NEWSPAPERS

WORMSER ZEITUNG
748334G67B-16200
Editorial: Erich-Dombrowski-Str. 2, 55127 MAINZ
Tel: 6131 485805 **Fax:** 6131 485833
Web site: http://www.vrm.de
Freq: 312 issues yearly; **Circ:** 17,614
Advertising Manager: Gerhard Müller
Profile: Daily newspaper with regional news and a local sports section. Twitter: http://twitter.com/wznachrichten.
Language(s): German
ADVERTISING RATES:
SCC .... EUR 67,10
Mechanical Data: Type Area: 480 x 325 mm, No. of Columns (Display): 7, Col Widths (Display): 45 mm
Copy instructions: *Copy Date:* 1 day prior to publication
Supplement(s): extra Familie; extra Gesundheit; extra Sport; extra Wissen; pepper
REGIONAL DAILY & SUNDAY NEWSPAPERS: Regional Daily Newspapers

WÖRTHER ANZEIGER
748230G67B-16220
Editorial: Margaretenstr. 4, 93047 REGENSBURG
Tel: 941 207339 **Fax:** 941 207957
Email: mz-redaktion@mittelbayerische.de **Web site:** http://www.mittelbayerische.de
Freq: 312 issues yearly; **Circ:** 55,495
Profile: Daily newspaper with regional news and a local sports section.
Language(s): German
ADVERTISING RATES:
SCC .... EUR 134,40
Mechanical Data: Type Area: 430 x 281 mm, No. of Columns (Display): 6, Col Widths (Display): 45 mm
Copy instructions: *Copy Date:* 1 day prior to publication

Supplement(s): Mittelbayerische jun.
REGIONAL DAILY & SUNDAY NEWSPAPERS: Regional Daily Newspapers

WP WESTFALENPOST
748350G67B-16240
Editorial: Schürmannstr. 4, 58097 HAGEN
Tel: 2331 9170 **Fax:** 2331 9174206
Email: westfalenpost@westfalenpost.de **Web site:** http://www.westfalenpost.de
Freq: 312 issues yearly; **Circ:** 492,685
Editor: Stefan Kläsener; **News Editor:** Eberhard Einhoff
Profile: Regional daily newspaper for South Westphalia with news on politics, economy, culture, sports, travel, technology Facebook: http://www.facebook.com/derwesten Twitter: http://twitter.com/derwesten This Outlet offers RSS (Really Simple Syndication).
Language(s): German
ADVERTISING RATES:
SCC .... EUR 1056,00
Mechanical Data: Type Area: 445 x 320 mm, No. of Columns (Display): 7, Col Widths (Display): 44 mm
Copy instructions: *Copy Date:* 2 days prior to publication
Supplement(s): Mein Auto; Mein Beruf; Meine besten Jahre; Meine Freizeit; Mein Shopping; Mein Stil; Mein Urlaub; Mein Zuhause
REGIONAL DAILY & SUNDAY NEWSPAPERS: Regional Daily Newspapers

WPK MAGAZIN
1893506G1A-3769
Editorial: Rauchstr. 26, 10787 BERLIN
Tel: 30 7261610 **Fax:** 30 726161228
Email: magazin@wpk.de **Web site:** http://www.wpk.de
Freq: Quarterly; Free to qualifying individuals
Annual Sub.: EUR 68,00; **Circ:** 22,500
Editor: Peter Maxl
Profile: Information from the Chamber of Auditors for all certified accountants, auditors, audit firms and audit firms in Germany. The official organ of the Chamber of Auditors includes news, information and reports on legal developments that are important to the daily life of every professional accountant and auditor. Target group: you can reach all 2,600 operating in Germany economic and accounting firms as well as the approximately 17,200 individual accountants and certified accountants, of which a large part, accountants and lawyers. Because many accountants work in management consulting, you reach an audience that acts as a multiplier in all listed corporations and the most important medium-sized enterprises into it.
Language(s): German
ADVERTISING RATES:
Full Page Mono .... EUR 4660
Full Page Colour .... EUR 5220
Mechanical Data: Type Area: 243 x 175 mm, No. of Columns (Display): 3, Col Widths (Display): 55 mm

WR WESTFÄLISCHE RUNDSCHAU
748356G67B-16260
Editorial: Brüderweg 9, 44135 DORTMUND
Tel: 231 95730 **Fax:** 231 95731364
Email: mk.newsdesk@westfaelische-rundschau.de **Web site:** http://www.westfaelische-rundschau.de
Freq: 312 issues yearly; **Circ:** 492,685
Editor: Malte Hinz; **News Editor:** Torsten Droop
Profile: In Dortmund, the Eastern Ruhr area in Southern Westphalia the Westfälische Rundschau is at home. Today, more than 200 editors work for the current issues of the WR, to consolidate the reputation acquired in six decades: "Better the Rundschau". A dense network of 30 local newsrooms, editorial offices and district editors provide a dense local coverage of the cities of Dortmund and Hagen as well as the districts of Unna, Olpe, Siegen-Wittgenstein, Arnsberg, Ennepe-Ruhr-Kreis and the Mark Brandenburg district. In the central editorial office in Dortmund also the message streams of text, images and graphics from half a dozen international agencies working to be evaluated to provide a comprehensive and updated picture of the events in the region and around the world - clearly and competently. In the main countries, the WR is represented by its own correspondents. This means for your readers: background reports and news from the source. This compelling mix of regional and national reports, critical commentary, as well as its major social engagement made the WR a readers' forum, which is recognized by the readers and rewarded with loyalty.
Language(s): German
ADVERTISING RATES:
SCC .... EUR 1056,00
Mechanical Data: Type Area: 445 x 320 mm, No. of Columns (Display): 7, Col Widths (Display): 44 mm
Copy instructions: *Copy Date:* 2 days prior to publication
Supplement(s): Aufsteiger; Mein Auto; Mein Beruf; Meine besten Jahre; Meine Freizeit; Mein Shopping; Mein Stil; Mein Urlaub; Mein Zuhause; :Programm; Theater Dortmund
REGIONAL DAILY & SUNDAY NEWSPAPERS: Regional Daily Newspapers

WRP
748354G44-3159
Editorial: Kirchenstr. 2, 68782 BRÜHL
Tel: 6202 22282 **Fax:** 6202 5177241
Email: redaktion@wrp.de **Web site:** http://www.wrp.de
Freq: Monthly; **Annual Sub.:** EUR 725,00; **Circ:** 1,141
Editor: Günter Karl; **Advertising Manager:** Marion Gertzen
Profile: Journal focusing on the theory and practice of law.
Language(s): German
ADVERTISING RATES:
Full Page Mono .... EUR 1940
Full Page Colour .... EUR 3365
Mechanical Data: Type Area: 261 x 171 mm, No. of Columns (Display): 2, Col Widths (Display): 83 mm
Copy instructions: *Copy Date:* 13 days prior to publication
BUSINESS: LEGAL

WRP WÄSCHEREI + REINIGUNGS/PRAXIS
748355G28-1
Editorial: An der Alster 21, 20099 HAMBURG
Tel: 40 2484540 **Fax:** 40 2803788
Email: wrp@snfachpresse.de **Web site:** http://www.wrp-textilpflege.de
Freq: 11 issues yearly; **Annual Sub.:** EUR 80,00; **Circ:** 5,049
Editor: Michael Steinert
Profile: Publication about industrial laundries, marketing, cleaning and modern textiles.
Language(s): German
ADVERTISING RATES:
Full Page Mono .... EUR 2670
Full Page Colour .... EUR 4660
Mechanical Data: Type Area: 252 x 184 mm, No. of Columns (Display): 4, Col Widths (Display): 43 mm
Copy instructions: *Copy Date:* 28 days prior to publication
Official Journal of: Organ d. Gesamtverb. d. Fachverb. f. Wäscherei-, Textil- u. Versorgungsmanagement e.V., d. Industrieverb. Textil Service e.V., d. Dt. Textilreinigungsverb. e.V., d. Europ. Forschungsvereinigung Innovative Textilpflege e.V. u. d. Gütegemeinschaft sachgemäße Wäschepflege e.V.
BUSINESS: LAUNDRY & DRY CLEANING

WT WEHRTECHNIK
748364G40-900
Editorial: Heilsbachstr. 26, 53123 BONN
Tel: 228 64830 **Fax:** 228 6483109
Email: wehrtechnik@mpgbonn.de **Web site:** http://www.monch.com
Freq: Quarterly; **Annual Sub.:** EUR 45,00; **Circ:** 13,485
Editor: Rudolf K. Schiwon; **Advertising Manager:** Christa André
Profile: Defence magazine covering economics and politics, the forces, and international arms co-operation.
Language(s): German
ADVERTISING RATES:
Full Page Mono .... EUR 4500
Full Page Colour .... EUR 7500
Mechanical Data: Type Area: 256 x 185 mm
Copy instructions: *Copy Date:* 28 days prior to publication
BUSINESS: DEFENCE

WÜLFRATHER RUNDSCHAU
748369G72-16580
Editorial: Otto-Hausmann-Ring 185, 42115 WUPPERTAL **Tel:** 202 271440 **Fax:** 202 7160093
Email: redaktion@wuppertaler-rundschau.de **Web site:** http://www.wuppertaler-rundschau.de
Freq: Weekly; **Cover Price:** Free; **Circ:** 10,300
Editor: Hendrik Walder; **Advertising Manager:** Stephan Sieper
Profile: Advertising journal (house-to-house) concentrating on local stories.
Language(s): German
ADVERTISING RATES:
Full Page Mono .... EUR 1368
Mechanical Data: Type Area: 430 x 282 mm, No. of Columns (Display): 6, Col Widths (Display): 45 mm
Copy instructions: *Copy Date:* 2 days prior to publication
LOCAL NEWSPAPERS

WUND MANAGEMENT
1819832G56A-11517
Editorial: Marktplatz 13, 65183 WIESBADEN
Tel: 611 5059335 **Fax:** 611 5059311
Email: wm@mhp-verlag.de **Web site:** http://www.mhp-verlag.de
Freq: 6 issues yearly; Free to qualifying individuals
Annual Sub.: EUR 42,50; **Circ:** 4,588
Editor: Barbara Springer; **Advertising Manager:** Walter Bockemühl
Profile: The magazine "Wund Management" is a platform for all those concerned with the care, prevention and treatment of chronic wounds. The open information and experience for practical problems has its place here as well as scientific papers and reports related to wound care management and health economics. With current information from research and practice gives the reader a good overview of developments in the management of acute and chronic wounds. A particular concern is the strengthening of constructive cooperation in the treatment as well as identification of pragmatic approaches to standardized measures through dialogue between all parties involved.
Language(s): German
ADVERTISING RATES:
Full Page Mono .... EUR 1390
Full Page Colour .... EUR 2405
Mechanical Data: Type Area: 267 x 170 mm, No. of Columns (Display): 3, Col Widths (Display): 53 mm
Copy instructions: *Copy Date:* 14 days prior to publication
Official Journal of: Organ d. Initiative Chron. Wunden e.V., d. Wundzentrums Hamburg e.V., d. Wundverbundes Südwest e.V. u. d. d. Wundverbund Nord e.V.

WUPPERTALER RUNDSCHAU AM MITTWOCH
748397G72-16596
Editorial: Otto-Hausmann-Ring 185, 42115 WUPPERTAL **Tel:** 202 271440 **Fax:** 202 7160093
Email: redaktion@wuppertaler-rundschau.de **Web site:** http://www.wuppertaler-rundschau.de
Freq: Weekly; **Cover Price:** Free; **Circ:** 181,000
Editor: Hendrik Walder; **Advertising Manager:** Stephan Sieper
Profile: Advertising journal (house-to-house) concentrating on local stories.
Language(s): German
ADVERTISING RATES:
Full Page Mono .... EUR 9392
Full Page Colour .... EUR 13184
Mechanical Data: Type Area: 430 x 282 mm, No. of Columns (Display): 6, Col Widths (Display): 45 mm
Copy instructions: *Copy Date:* 2 days prior to publication
LOCAL NEWSPAPERS

WÜRZBURGER KATHOLISCHES SONNTAGSBLATT
748376G87-13180
Editorial: Kardinal-Döpfner-Platz 5, 97070 WÜRZBURG **Tel:** 931 38611250 **Fax:** 931 38611299
Email: info@sobla.de **Web site:** http://www.sobla.de
Freq: Weekly; **Annual Sub.:** EUR 58,80; **Circ:** 33,473
Editor: Wolfgang Bullin; **Advertising Manager:** Josef Berger
Profile: Catholic Sunday paper from the diocese of Würzburg.
Language(s): German
ADVERTISING RATES:
Full Page Mono .... EUR 1946
Full Page Colour .... EUR 2955
Mechanical Data: Type Area: 270 x 210 mm, No. of Columns (Display): 4, Col Widths (Display): 45 mm
Copy instructions: *Copy Date:* 14 days prior to publication
CONSUMER: RELIGIOUS

WUW WIRTSCHAFT UND WETTBEWERB
748409G44-2380
Editorial: Grafenberger Allee 293, 40237 DÜSSELDORF **Tel:** 211 8871435
Fax: 211 887971435
Email: wuw@fachverlag.de **Web site:** http://www.wuw-online.de
Freq: 11 issues yearly; **Annual Sub.:** EUR 384,00; **Circ:** 1,500
Editor: Lioba Jüttner-Kramny; **Advertising Manager:** Ralf Pötzsch
Profile: Legal journal concerning German and European competition law.
Language(s): German
ADVERTISING RATES:
Full Page Mono .... EUR 750
Full Page Colour .... EUR 1260
Mechanical Data: Type Area: 200 x 125 mm
Copy instructions: *Copy Date:* 21 days prior to publication
BUSINESS: LEGAL

WVV ENERGIE PLUS
1820333G58-1784
Editorial: Haugerring 5, 97070 WÜRZBURG
Tel: 931 361765
Email: florian.doktorczyk@wvv.de **Web site:** http://www.wvv.de
Freq: Quarterly; **Cover Price:** Free; **Circ:** 800
Editor: Susanne Pörtner
Profile: Company publication.
Language(s): German

WVV ENERGIE PLUS
1820333G58-1834
Editorial: Haugerring 5, 97070 WÜRZBURG
Tel: 931 361765
Email: florian.doktorczyk@wvv.de **Web site:** http://www.wvv.de
Freq: Quarterly; **Cover Price:** Free; **Circ:** 800
Editor: Susanne Pörtner
Profile: Company publication.
Language(s): German

WWF MAGAZIN
758539G57-2625
Editorial: Rebstöcker Str. 55, 60326 FRANKFURT
Tel: 69 79144156 **Fax:** 69 79144112
Email: e.redaktion@wwf.de **Web site:** http://www.wwf.de
Freq: Quarterly; Free to qualifying individuals
Annual Sub.: EUR 40,00; **Circ:** 170,000
Editor: Donné Norbert Beyer; **Advertising Manager:** Susanne Kögler
Profile: Magazine of the World Wide Fund For Nature, Germany. Facebook: http://www.facebook.com/pages/WWF-Deutschland/218786540044 This Outlet offers RSS (Really Simple Syndication).
Language(s): German
ADVERTISING RATES:
Full Page Mono .... EUR 7260
Full Page Colour .... EUR 9510
Mechanical Data: Type Area: 250 x 190 mm
Copy instructions: *Copy Date:* 63 days prior to publication

WWK-FORUM
748418G1D-453
Editorial: Marsstr. 37, 80335 MÜNCHEN
Tel: 89 51143531 **Fax:** 89 51142765
Email: thomas.emlinger@wwk.de **Web site:** http://www.wwk.de
Freq: Quarterly; **Circ:** 4,500
Editor: Ansgar Eckert
Profile: Magazine for employees of WWK Lebensversicherung.
Language(s): German

WWT WASSERWIRTSCHAFT WASSERTECHNIK
746948G32B-110
Editorial: Am Friedrichshain 22, 10407 BERLIN
Tel: 30 42151221 **Fax:** 30 42151234
Email: peter-michael.fritsch@hussberlin.de **Web site:** http://www.wwt-online.de
Freq: 9 issues yearly; **Annual Sub.:** EUR 136,80; **Circ:** 7,214
Editor: Peter-Michael Fritsch; **Advertising Manager:** Udo Magister
Profile: Magazine with information for sewage disposal and water supply, sewage disposal and water supply information, profound and practical way, quickly and comprehensively on the most important segments of their industry. Regularly provides an overview of new legislation and changes in the law says. About the EU water legislation will wwt-informed readers up to date. Management and personnel of the areas: Sewage treatment / disposal, water supply, pipe and sewer construction and remediation, use of rainwater / seepage and water conservation and flood control. The reader success stories and product information to assist investment decisions. The magazine supported with current professional contributions of recognized experts, the work of planners, engineers, technicians and service providers in the industry. wwt provides in-depth, hands-on expertise on sanitation, water supply, sewer and pipeline construction, law and justice, management and controlling, and market trends and reports news from the "water scene ". presented detailed ideas on the subject: pumps, measurement and analysis technology, decentralized wastewater treatment, membrane technology, industry + water, mud treatment / disposal, and sewer construction and remediation.
Language(s): German
Readership: Aimed at councillors and government officials.
ADVERTISING RATES:
Full Page Mono .... EUR 2280
Full Page Colour .... EUR 3330
Mechanical Data: Type Area: 265 x 185 mm, No. of Columns (Display): 4, Col Widths (Display): 42 mm
Copy instructions: *Copy Date:* 10 days prior to publication
BUSINESS: LOCAL GOVERNMENT, LEISURE & RECREATION: Public Health & Cleaning

WWW.DIEHALLOS.DE IN THÜRINGEN ZUM SONNTAG - AUSG. BAD SALZUNGEN
729521G19F-1
Editorial: Clemdastr. 2, 99817 EISENACH
Tel: 3691 204622 **Fax:** 3691 204620
Email: redaktionbadsalzungen@diehallos.de **Web site:** http://www.diehallos.de
Freq: Weekly; **Cover Price:** Free; **Circ:** 39,600
Editor: Susanne Jirschim; **Advertising Manager:** Michael Krämer
Profile: Advertising journal (house-to-house) concentrating on local stories.
Language(s): German
ADVERTISING RATES:
Full Page Mono .... EUR 2058
Full Page Colour .... EUR 2985
Mechanical Data: Type Area: 420 x 285 mm, No. of Columns (Display): 7, Col Widths (Display): 39 mm
Copy instructions: *Copy Date:* 3 days prior to publication

WWW.DIEHALLOS.DE IN THÜRINGEN ZUM SONNTAG - AUSG. WEIMAR U. APOLDA
729592G72-5160
Editorial: Jakobstr. 16, 99423 WEIMAR
Tel: 3643 853418 **Fax:** 3643 804083
Email: redaktionweimar@diehallos.de **Web site:** http://www.diehallos.de
Freq: Weekly; **Cover Price:** Free; **Circ:** 67,500
Editor: Klaus Schorcht; **Advertising Manager:** Michael Krämer
Profile: Advertising journal (house-to-house) concentrating on local stories.
Language(s): German
ADVERTISING RATES:
Full Page Mono .... EUR 2940
Full Page Colour .... EUR 4263
Mechanical Data: Type Area: 420 x 285 mm, No. of Columns (Display): 7, Col Widths (Display): 39 mm
Copy instructions: *Copy Date:* 3 days prior to publication
LOCAL NEWSPAPERS

WWW.ONLINESPIELE.DE

1663133G78D-976

Editorial: Römerturmstr. 25, 73547 LORCH
Tel: 7172 926060 **Fax:** 7172 9260699
Email: info@duesicomputersoftware.de **Web site:** http://www.onlinespiele.de
Freq: Quarterly; **Cover Price:** Paid; **Circ:** 231,260 Unique Users
Editor: Daniel Schwinn
Language(s): German
CONSUMER: CONSUMER ELECTRONICS: Games

WZ BERGISCHER VOLKSBOTE

748439G67B-16280

Editorial: Königsallee 27, 40212 DÜSSELDORF
Tel: 211 83820 **Fax:** 211 83822392
Email: zentralredaktion@westdeutsche-zeitung.de
Web site: http://www.wz-newsline.de
Freq: 312 issues yearly; **Cover Price:** EUR 0,90; **Circ:** 1,584
Advertising Manager: Thomas Müllenborn
Profile: Daily newspaper with regional news and a local sports section.
Language(s): German
ADVERTISING RATES:
SCC .... EUR 35,00
Mechanical Data: Type Area: 430 x 282 mm, No. of Columns (Display): 6, Col Widths (Display): 45 mm
Copy instructions: *Copy Date:* 2 days prior to publication
Supplement(s): prisma
REGIONAL DAILY & SUNDAY NEWSPAPERS: Regional Daily Newspapers

WZ NEWSLINE

1622235G67B-16696

Editorial: Königsallee 27, 40212 DÜSSELDORF
Tel: 211 83822373 **Fax:** 211 83822392
Email: martin.vogler@westdeutsche-zeitung.de **Web site:** http://www.wz-newsline.de
Freq: Daily; **Cover Price:** Paid; **Circ:** 1,343,741 Unique Users
Editor: Martin Vogler; **Advertising Manager:** Thomas Kösters
Profile: Ezine: Regional daily newspaper covering politics, economics, culture, sports, travel and technology. This Outlet offers RSS (Really Simple Syndication).
Language(s): German
REGIONAL DAILY & SUNDAY NEWSPAPERS: Regional Daily Newspapers

WZS WEGE ZUR SOZIALVERSICHERUNG

748443G32G-2880

Editorial: Genthiner Str. 30g, 10785 BERLIN
Tel: 30 2500850 **Fax:** 30 250085305
Email: esv@esvmedien.de **Web site:** http://www.wzsdigital.de
Freq: Monthly; **Annual Sub.:** EUR 69,56; **Circ:** 645
Profile: Journal about social security, health insurance and citizens' rights.
Language(s): German
ADVERTISING RATES:
Full Page Mono .... EUR 820
Full Page Colour .... EUR 1070
Mechanical Data: Type Area: 262 x 175 mm, No. of Columns (Display): 2, Col Widths (Display): 85 mm
Copy instructions: *Copy Date:* 10 days prior to publication
BUSINESS: LOCAL GOVERNMENT, LEISURE & RECREATION: Community Care & Social Services

XCENTRIC

748449G80-13400

Editorial: Unter dem Schöneberg 1, 34212 MELSUNGEN **Tel:** 5661 731402 **Fax:** 5661 731400
Email: bjoern.schoenewald@bernecker.de **Web site:** http://www.xcentric.de
Freq: Monthly; **Annual Sub.:** EUR 24,00; **Circ:** 20,000
Editor: Björn Schönewald; **Advertising Manager:** Ralf Spohr
Profile: Xcentric stands for over 14 years as a concept for the magazine scene in the region of Kassel and Göttingen. Intricately researched and attention to detail produces trendy, month after month, the magazine stories and pictures, seeing and knowing, and a calendar of events in the area of distribution. Special themes, games, hotline and an online presence with archives and galleries round out the offerings. Facebook: http://www.facebook.com/xcentric.de.
Language(s): German
ADVERTISING RATES:
Full Page Mono .... EUR 1200
Full Page Colour .... EUR 1690
Mechanical Data: Type Area: 260 x 186 mm, No. of Columns (Display): 3, Col Widths (Display): 59 mm
Copy instructions: *Copy Date:* 12 days prior to publication
CONSUMER: RURAL & REGIONAL INTEREST

XIA INTELLIGENTE ARCHITEKTUR

731420G4A-200

Editorial: Fasanenweg 18, 70771 LEINFELDEN-ECHTERDINGEN **Tel:** 711 7591286
Fax: 711 7591410
Email: ddanner@xia-online.de **Web site:** http://www.xia-online.de
Freq: Quarterly; **Annual Sub.:** EUR 48,80; **Circ:** 16,758
Editor: Dietmar Danner; **Advertising Manager:** Judith Hageloch
Profile: xia intelligente architektur is the magazine for innovative construction. Their particular form of architecture view includes design, building and operating aspects (facilities management). Integral planning, life cycle of a building, solar and energy efficient building and the intelligent use of materials, components and technical building equipment are the key themes. An outstanding projects and plans as well as in technical papers xia intelligente architektur shows the current state of theory and practice.
Language(s): German
Readership: Read by architects and designers.
ADVERTISING RATES:
Full Page Mono .... EUR 3640
Full Page Colour .... EUR 5785
Mechanical Data: Type Area: 280 x 212 mm, No. of Columns (Display): 4, Col Widths (Display): 50 mm
Copy instructions: *Copy Date:* 30 days prior to publication
BUSINESS: ARCHITECTURE & BUILDING: Architecture

Y

748459G40-920

Editorial: Kurt-Schumacher-Damm 41, 13405 BERLIN **Tel:** 30 49813526 **Fax:** 30 49813525
Email: chefredakteur@y-magazin.de **Web site:** http://www.y-magazin.de
Freq: 10 issues yearly; **Annual Sub.:** EUR 37,00; **Circ:** 50,000
Editor: Norbert Stäblein
Profile: Magazine is published on behalf of the armed forces of the Federal Minister of Defense and the Inspector General of the Bundeswehr troops in the information. Troops in the service information is information on topics related to the armed forces and the "citizens in uniform", including political education. As a magazine of the Bundeswehr Y reported about people, facts and background. We provide comprehensive information medium timeliness claim, however, with the aim of backgrounds and a larger context of his current themes. We therefore consider ourselves as a complementary medium to the daily and weekly periodicals from the current media mix of troop information.
Language(s): German
ADVERTISING RATES:
Full Page Mono .... EUR 2100
Full Page Colour .... EUR 3780
Mechanical Data: No. of Columns (Display): 4, Type Area: 241 x 169 mm, Col Widths (Display): 45 mm

YACHT

748460G91A-280

Editorial: Raboisen 8, 20095 HAMBURG
Tel: 40 3396660 **Fax:** 40 33966699
Email: mail@yacht.de **Web site:** http://www.yacht.de
Freq: 25 issues yearly; **Annual Sub.:** EUR 90,00; **Circ:** 48,438
Editor: Jochen Rieker; **Advertising Manager:** Ingo van Holt
Profile: Special-interest magazine with information on water sports in the German speaking region with information about yachts, power cruisers, dinghies, sports boats and equipment.
Language(s): German
ADVERTISING RATES:
Full Page Mono .... EUR 6980
Full Page Colour .... EUR 9950
Mechanical Data: Type Area: 254 x 192 mm, No. of Columns (Display): 4, Col Widths (Display): 45 mm
Copy instructions: *Copy Date:* 36 days prior to publication
CONSUMER: RECREATION & LEISURE: Boating & Yachting

YAEZ

1656043G91D-10049

Editorial: Kornbergstr. 44, 70176 STUTTGART
Tel: 711 9979830 **Fax:** 711 99798322
Email: pm@yaez.de **Web site:** http://www.yaez-verlag.de
Freq: 7 issues yearly; **Cover Price:** Free; **Circ:** 380,196
Editor: Janos Burghardt; **Advertising Manager:** Michael Hartung
Profile: Youth magazine for pupils, reports on social and political issues about friendship, first love, on the prospects in study and education about stars and students who have achieved something special.
Language(s): German
ADVERTISING RATES:
Full Page Mono .... EUR 13480
Full Page Colour .... EUR 13480
Mechanical Data: No. of Columns (Display): 3, Col Widths (Display): 75 mm, Type Area: 320 x 225 mm
Copy instructions: *Copy Date:* 7 days prior to publication
CONSUMER: RECREATION & LEISURE: Children & Youth

YAM.DE

1687186G91D-10299

Editorial: Leonrodstr. 52, 80636 MÜNCHEN
Tel: 89 69749361 **Fax:** 89 69749430
Email: hella.brunke@vision-media.de **Web site:** http://www.yam.de
Freq: Daily; **Cover Price:** Paid; **Circ:** 457,268 Unique Users
Editor: Fabian Knecht; **Advertising Manager:** Marit Böhmer
Profile: Youth and music portal with news, specials and many interactive features.
Language(s): German
CONSUMER: RECREATION & LEISURE: Children & Youth

YOU + ME

748474G80-13420

Editorial: Tannenbergstr. 35, 42103 WUPPERTAL
Tel: 202 3717045 **Fax:** 202 3717023
Email: marcuss.westphal@bewegungsmelder.de
Web site: http://www.youandme.de
Freq: Monthly; **Cover Price:** Free; **Circ:** 24,650
Editor: Marcuß Westphal; **Advertising Manager:** Uschi Schumacher
Profile: City magazine for Mettmann, Düsseldorf and Neuss with Events on music, culture, sports, exhibitions and shopping.
Language(s): German
ADVERTISING RATES:
Full Page Mono .... EUR 2450
Full Page Colour .... EUR 2450
CONSUMER: RURAL & REGIONAL INTEREST

YOUNG LOOK

748479G74H-150

Editorial: Hans-Henny-Jahnn-Weg 53, 22085 HAMBURG **Tel:** 40 226585 **Fax:** 40 22658333
Email: younglook@salaction.de **Web site:** http://www.bgw-online.de
Freq: Quarterly; **Circ:** 49,000
Editor: Daniela Bühe
Profile: Journal of the trade association for health care and welfare has many interesting topics for beginners. The magazine offers tips, trends and brings you news shows for work and play. Young Look would like to be partner, sponsor and platform for the period of training as a hairdresser to be - with information, ideas and discussions.
Language(s): German
Readership: Aimed at people interested in modern fashion and beauty.
CONSUMER: WOMEN'S INTEREST CONSUMER MAGAZINES: Hair & Beauty

YOUNGTIMER

1873104G77A-2865

Editorial: Leuschnerstr. 1, 70174 STUTTGART
Tel: 711 1821365 **Fax:** 711 1821140
Email: mjuergens@motorpresse.de **Web site:** http://www.motorpresse.de
Freq: Quarterly; **Cover Price:** EUR 4,50; **Circ:** 80,000
Editor: Malte Jürgens; **Advertising Manager:** Stephen Brand
Profile: Youngtimer is the magazine about cars of the last 20 to 30 years that have left an indelible mark on the hearts of car enthusiasts.Youngtimer captures the experience of how thesestill seemingly everyday cars turn into the classics of tomorrow. Alongside driving reports and purchasing recommendations, Youngtimer always focuses on the memorable experiences that people associate with these cars. After all, the classics of tomorrow are more than just a particular passion for Youngtimer readers – they were andare the automobile dreams of their youth. The great thing is – whereas back then these carswere mostly out of reach, today the readers are able to fulfil these dreams. The readers of Youngtimer are men in the prime of life who, as they approach 40, have retained a good deal of youthful vigour. In addition to their job and family, they still manage to keep enough space for the things they have always enjoyed most. Youngtimer readers are a target group that can get enthusiastic – and enthuse others too.
Language(s): German
ADVERTISING RATES:
Full Page Mono .... EUR 5400
Full Page Colour .... EUR 5400
Mechanical Data: Type Area: 240 x 185 mm, No. of Columns (Display): 3, Col Widths (Display): 57 mm

DIE ZAHNARZT WOCHE DZW

748510G56D-920

Editorial: Kurt-Schumacher-Str. 6, 53113 BONN
Tel: 228 2892160 **Fax:** 228 28921620
Email: redaktion@dzw.de **Web site:** http://www.dzw.de
Freq: Weekly; **Annual Sub.:** EUR 57,00; **Circ:** 45,955
Editor: Marion Marschall; **Advertising Manager:** Heike Müller-Wüstenfeld
Profile: The magazine as an independent medium provides its readers in articles, commentaries and interviews, current information on developments in public health, dentistry and all relevant areas to help them to work professionally successful and future-oriented to. The magazine offers readers to know on all topics related to dentistry, professional and economic policy, training, practice management, quality of life and general health. This Outlet offers RSS (Really Simple Syndication).
Language(s): German
Readership: Aimed at dentists in Germany.
ADVERTISING RATES:
Full Page Mono .... EUR 4900
Full Page Colour .... EUR 6280
Mechanical Data: Type Area: 380 x 265 mm, No. of Columns (Display): 6, Col Widths (Display): 40 mm
Copy instructions: *Copy Date:* 12 days prior to publication
Supplement(s): DZW Kompakt; DZW Orale Implantologie; DZW ZahnTechnik
BUSINESS: HEALTH & MEDICAL: Dental

ZAHNÄRZTEBLATT

748498G56D-980

Editorial: Schützenhöhe 11, 01099 DRESDEN
Tel: 351 8066276 **Fax:** 351 8066279
Email: izz.presse@lzk-sachsen.de **Web site:** http://www.zahnaerzte-in-sachsen.de
Freq: 11 issues yearly; Free to qualifying individuals
Annual Sub.: EUR 59,15; **Circ:** 5,037
Editor: Thomas Breyer; **Advertising Manager:** Sabine Sperling
Profile: Official journal of the Sachsen Dental Board.
Language(s): German
ADVERTISING RATES:
Full Page Mono .... EUR 1175
Full Page Colour .... EUR 1973
Mechanical Data: Type Area: 270 x 185 mm, No. of Columns (Display): 4, Col Widths (Display): 42 mm
Copy instructions: *Copy Date:* 30 days prior to publication
Official Journal of: Organ d. Landeszahnärztekammer Sachsen u. d. Kassenzahnärztl. Vereinigung
BUSINESS: HEALTH & MEDICAL: Dental

ZAHNÄRZTEBLATT WESTFALEN-LIPPE

748500G56D-1000

Editorial: Auf der Horst 25, 48147 MÜNSTER
Tel: 251 507176 **Fax:** 251 507288
Email: manfred.sietz@zahnaerzte-wl.de **Web site:** http://www.zahnaerzte-wl.de
Freq: 6 issues yearly; Free to qualifying individuals
Annual Sub.: EUR 19,20; **Circ:** 7,900
Editor: Manfred Sietz
Profile: Official magazine of the Chamber of Dentistry for the region Westfalen-Lippe.
Language(s): German
Readership: Aimed at dentists.
ADVERTISING RATES:
Full Page Mono .... EUR 1070
Full Page Colour .... EUR 1840
Mechanical Data: Type Area: 247 x 185 mm, No. of Columns (Display): 3, Col Widths (Display): 58 mm
BUSINESS: HEALTH & MEDICAL: Dental

DIE ZAHNMEDIZINISCHE FACHANGESTELLTE

766714G56R-2404

Editorial: Eschstr. 22, 44629 HERNE
Tel: 2323 141900 **Fax:** 2323 141123
Email: b.switon@kiehl.de **Web site:** http://www.kiehl.de
Freq: Monthly; **Annual Sub.:** EUR 61,80; **Circ:** 3,160
Editor: Barbara Switon; **Advertising Manager:** Andreas Reimann
Profile: The magazine reports in an easy and understandable way. It conveys specialized knowledge with picture documentaries and practical cases. Furthermore, the accounting system, practice management and key issues around education (such as labor law, labor protection, etc.) are contain. A regular training of knowledge on all subjects rounds out the magazine.
Language(s): German
ADVERTISING RATES:
Full Page Mono .... EUR 990
Full Page Colour .... EUR 1390
Mechanical Data: Type Area: 260 x 186 mm
Copy instructions: *Copy Date:* 30 days prior to publication
BUSINESS: HEALTH & MEDICAL: Health Medical Related

ZANDERA

748518G21A-4120

Editorial: Potsdamer Str. 187, 14469 POTSDAM
Web site: http://www.gartenbaubuecherei.de
Freq: Half-yearly; Free to qualifying individuals
Annual Sub.: EUR 30,00; **Circ:** 300
Editor: Clemens A. Wimmer
Profile: Magazine about historical gardening books, the history of horticulture, reviews and librarianship.
Language(s): English; German
Mechanical Data: Type Area: 180 x 115 mm

ZAP ZEITSCHRIFT FÜR DIE ANWALTSPRAXIS

748638G44-3161

Editorial: Feldstiege 100, 48161 MÜNSTER
Tel: 2533 93000 **Fax:** 2533 930050
Email: hilke.arnau@lexisnexis.de **Web site:** http://www.zap-verlag.de
Freq: 24 issues yearly; **Annual Sub.:** EUR 220,80; **Circ:** 7,300
Editor: Günter Lange; **Advertising Manager:** Anja Christensen
Profile: Legal journal.
Language(s): German
ADVERTISING RATES:
Full Page Mono .... EUR 1235
Full Page Colour .... EUR 1985
Mechanical Data: Type Area: 192 x 130 mm
Copy instructions: *Copy Date:* 14 days prior to publication
BUSINESS: LEGAL

ZAR ZEITSCHRIFT FÜR AUSLÄNDERRECHT UND AUSLÄNDERPOLITIK

748523G44-2400

Editorial: Universitätsplatz 10a, 06099 HALLE
Email: winfried.kluth@jura.uni-halle.de **Web site:** http://www.zar.nomos.de
Freq: 10 issues yearly; **Annual Sub.:** EUR 175,30; **Circ:** 1,400
Editor: Winfried Kluth
Profile: Magazine about foreign policy, laws and politics.
Language(s): German
ADVERTISING RATES:
Full Page Mono .... EUR 990
Full Page Colour .... EUR 2115
Mechanical Data: Type Area: 260 x 180 mm
BUSINESS: LEGAL

ZAU ZEITSCHRIFT FÜR ANGEWANDTE UMWELTFORSCHUNG
748526G57-2580

Editorial: Paffenbergstr. 95, 67663 KAISERSLAUTERN **Tel:** 631 2054513 **Fax:** 631 2055084
Email: junkernh@rhrk.uni-kl.de **Web site:** http://www.zau-net.de
Freq: Quarterly; **Annual Sub.:** EUR 101,25; **Circ:** 700
Editor: Martin Junkernheinrich
Profile: Magazine about applied environmental research for libraries, environmental institutions, public authorities, scientists and individuals from the domains of environment, law, economy and technology.
Language(s): German
ADVERTISING RATES:
Full Page Mono .... EUR 600
Mechanical Data: Type Area: 200 x 120 mm

ZBI ZAKLADY BETONOWE INTERNATIONAL
1863493G4E-7243

Editorial: Industriestr. 180, 50999 KÖLN
Tel: 2236 962390 **Fax:** 2236 962396
Email: h.karutz@cpi-worldwide.com **Web site:** http://www.cpi-worldwide.com
Freq: 6 issues yearly; Free to qualifying individuals
Annual Sub.: EUR 120,00; **Circ:** 2,000
Editor: Holger Karutz; **Advertising Manager:** Gerhard Klöckner
Profile: The journals of "CPI-Worldwide" are the only source for cutting-edge technical data, news and information for the concrete industry - from around the world. This information processed editorially and professional - are aimed directly regardless of location to business owners, decision makers and managers. The articles are well-written by world-renowned and in their field well-known experts. Each topic is presented in a way that the audience important information available, it brings on the cutting edge of technology and so to increase productivity and operational performance contributes.
Language(s): Polish
Mechanical Data: Type Area: 260 x 180 mm, No. of Columns (Display): 3, Col Widths (Display): 56 mm
Copy instructions: *Copy Date:* 30 days prior to publication

ZBW ZEITSCHRIFT FÜR BERUFS- UND WIRTSCHAFTSPÄDAGOGIK
748538G62B-800_50

Editorial: Friedrich-Ebert-Str. 91, 35039 MARBURG
Tel: 6421 42629
Web site: http://www.steiner-verlag.de/ZBW
Freq: Quarterly; **Annual Sub.:** EUR 159,00; **Circ:** 800
Editor: Gerhard Hauptmeier; **Advertising Manager:** Susanne Szoradi
Profile: Journal concerning the teaching of careers and business.
Language(s): German
ADVERTISING RATES:
Full Page Mono .... EUR 810
Mechanical Data: Type Area: 190 x 120 mm
BUSINESS: CHURCH & SCHOOL EQUIPMENT & EDUCATION: Education Teachers

ZDNET.DE
1622244G5B-190

Editorial: Willy-Brandt-Allee 2, 81829 MÜNCHEN
Tel: 89 25555700 **Fax:** 89 25555750
Email: kai.schmerer@cbs.com **Web site:** http://www.zdnet.de
Freq: Daily; **Cover Price:** Paid; **Circ:** 2,012,216 Unique Users
Editor: Kai Schmerer
Profile: Internet portal on the topic IT Facebook: http://www.facebook.com/ZDNet.de Twitter: http://twitter.com/#!/zdnet_de This Outlet offers RSS (Really Simple Syndication).
Language(s): German
BUSINESS: COMPUTERS & AUTOMATION: Data Processing

ZEHLENDORF KOMPAKT
1898603G74M-896

Editorial: Bundesallee 23, 10717 BERLIN
Tel: 30 863030 **Fax:** 30 86303200
Email: info@bfb.de **Web site:** http://www.bfb.de
Freq: Annual; **Cover Price:** Free; **Circ:** 67,000
Profile: Industry district magazine. The core of this handy reference book is neatly sorted according to different themes of industry. Here you will find a plethora of vendors from the neighborhood. In preparation to the respective subject area raises a company, in an interview. To know your environment better, we present in the district windows, etc. beautiful places, monuments, museums, etc. For better orientation in the neighborhood also an integrated neighborhood with street plan is register. Furthermore, the county information you provide an overview of important phone numbers and agencies in your neighborhood.
Language(s): German
ADVERTISING RATES:
Full Page Mono .... EUR 990
Full Page Colour .... EUR 990
Mechanical Data: Type Area: 185 x 126 mm

DIE ZEIT
748563G65J-1

Editorial: Speersort 1, 20095 HAMBURG
Tel: 40 32800 **Fax:** 40 327111
Email: diezeit@zeit.de **Web site:** http://www.zeit.de
Freq: Weekly; **Annual Sub.:** EUR 175,85; **Circ:** 534,624
Editor: Giovanni di Lorenzo; **Advertising Manager:** Matthias Weidling
Profile: DIE ZEIT is Germany's leading opinion-forming weekly. It reports on issues from politics and economy, culture and science, technology and medicine, society and education, travel, lifestyle and sports. In-depth background reports, thoroughly researched facts and rigorous analysis make DIE ZEIT to an important current source of information. DIE ZEIT issues items, takes position, discusses prospects and shapes opinions. ZEIT magazin offers entertainment at the highest level. Briefly characterized DIE ZEIT means - passionate journalism - challenging articles and contrasting views - incisive comments, subtle details and precise analysis The quality of journalism and an award-winning layout make the time a heavily used medium, with readers who belong mainly to the upper educational, occupational and income levels and thus bring the best conditions for a strong consumer behavior. Facebook: http://www.facebook.com/zeitonline Twitter: http://twitter.com/zeitonline This Outlet offers RSS (Really Simple Syndication).
Language(s): German
ADVERTISING RATES:
SCC .... EUR 550,00
Mechanical Data: Type Area: 528 x 371 mm, No. of Columns (Display): 8, Col Widths (Display): 45 mm
Copy instructions: *Copy Date:* 3 days prior to publication
Supplement(s): Bad Design; Berliner Zugpferde; chrismon; Zeit Chancen Abi; Zeit Literatur
NATIONAL DAILY & SUNDAY NEWSPAPERS: National Weekly Newspapers

ZEIT FÜR DIE FRAU
1827715G74A-3578

Editorial: Papyrusweg 17, 22117 HAMBURG
Tel: 40 76119930
Email: buhk@redaktionsbuero-ch-buhk.de
Freq: 6 issues yearly; **Cover Price:** EUR 0,59; **Circ:** 350,000
Editor: Christina Buhk
Profile: Women's magazine with a variety of topics such as fashion and beauty, diet and cooking, wellness and health, reportage and puzzles, travel and competition, wildlife and TV news, advice and financial counseling.
Language(s): German
ADVERTISING RATES:
Full Page Colour .... EUR 4950
Mechanical Data: Type Area: 286 x 207 mm

ZEIT FÜR DIE FRAU
1827715G74A-3690

Editorial: Papyrusweg 17, 22117 HAMBURG
Tel: 40 76119930
Email: buhk@redaktionsbuero-ch-buhk.de
Freq: 6 issues yearly; **Cover Price:** EUR 0,59; **Circ:** 350,000
Editor: Christina Buhk
Profile: Women's magazine with a variety of topics such as fashion and beauty, diet and cooking, wellness and health, reportage and puzzles, travel and competition, wildlife and TV news, advice and financial counseling.
Language(s): German
ADVERTISING RATES:
Full Page Colour .... EUR 4950
Mechanical Data: Type Area: 286 x 207 mm

ZEIT ONLINE
1622245G72-18264

Editorial: Speersort 1, 20095 HAMBURG
Tel: 40 32800 **Fax:** 40 32805003
Email: kontakt@zeit.de **Web site:** http://www.zeit.de
Freq: Daily; **Cover Price:** Paid; **Circ:** 20,985,182 Unique Users
Editor: Wolfgang Blau; **News Editor:** Karin Geil
Profile: Internet portal of the national weekly newspaper Die Zeit: latest news, commentary and news from politics, economy, society, culture, knowledge, digital, career, lifestyle, travel, cars and sports. The core competence of Zeit Online is the analytical classification of world affairs, in trenchant, opinion strong comments in excellent visual design and sophisticated readers in excellent debates. The dialogue between readers and editors are not only found on www.zeit.de, but also take on social platforms like Facebook, Twitter, YouTube, and the VZ networks. The keynote of Zeit Online is critical, but optimistic. The serious, serious Zeit Online reputation is in standard categories such as politics, economy and culture complemented by a very sensual imagery and emotional topics in the departments of life and travel. Minute news for Internet users for granted. In addition to the editorial content, the portal provides quality services such as the online job market, the course search engine and access to the offerings at the Zeit Verlag, such as Zeit Reisen and the Zeit store. The editorial content and services are for the readers and via mobile devices easily accessible. For smart phones, eReader, or tablets, such as the innovative iPad Buying formats are developed that meet the specific capabilities of each device optimally. Facebook: http://www.facebook.com/zeitonline Twitter: http://twitter.com/zeitonline This Outlet offers RSS (Really Simple Syndication).
Language(s): German
LOCAL NEWSPAPERS

ZEIT WISSEN
1692229G74A-3473

Editorial: Speersort 1, 20095 HAMBURG
Tel: 40 32800 **Fax:** 40 32800553
Email: kontakt@zeit-wissen.de **Web site:** http://www.zeit-wissen.de
Freq: 6 issues yearly; **Annual Sub.:** EUR 31,80; **Circ:** 86,660
Editor: Jan Schweitzer; **Advertising Manager:** Matthias Weidling
Profile: The magazine combines serious journalism, reliable information, profound research - with high-quality, entertaining photojournalism. In the four departments of science, health, technology and life magazine topics from the world of knowledge.
Language(s): German
ADVERTISING RATES:
Full Page Mono .... EUR 12500
Full Page Colour .... EUR 12500
Mechanical Data: Type Area: 237 x 188 mm
Copy instructions: *Copy Date:* 22 days prior to publication

ZEITLOS
1793709G74N-908

Editorial: Dollendorfer Str. 72, 53639 KÖNIGSWINTER **Tel:** 2244 925385 **Fax:** 2244 925388
Email: alexander.helbach@aeternitas.de **Web site:** http://www.aeternitas.de
Freq: Quarterly; **Cover Price:** EUR 2,00
Free to qualifying individuals ; **Circ:** 19,000
Editor: Alexander Helbach
Profile: The magazine of the Aeternitas eV, which gives the consumer initiative for burial culture knowledge of trends and ideas in the funeral industry. The magazine is a positive dealing with issues such as dying and death, burial and funeral culture, which are often repressed in our society. It is a "journal for conscious life" that promotes an active engagement with death and a new form of cultural mourning. In addition, it includes information on healthy nutrition, travel destinations for seniors, financial provision in old age, culture, literature, music, etc..
Language(s): German
ADVERTISING RATES:
Full Page Mono .... EUR 1400
Full Page Colour .... EUR 2000
Mechanical Data: Type Area: 275 x 185 mm
Copy instructions: *Copy Date:* 36 days prior to publication

ZEITPUNKT
748575G80-13460

Editorial: Mendelssohnstr. 3, 04109 LEIPZIG
Tel: 341 2122124 **Fax:** 341 2111118
Email: info@zeitpunkt-kulturmagazin.de **Web site:** http://www.zeitpunkt-kulturmagazin.de
Freq: Monthly; **Cover Price:** Free; **Circ:** 40,354
Editor: Christian Nóvé; **Advertising Manager:** Jan Thielbeer
Profile: Magazine for city and region, concentrating on gastronomy, music, arts and events.
Language(s): German
ADVERTISING RATES:
Full Page Mono .... EUR 2267
Full Page Colour .... EUR 3317
Mechanical Data: Type Area: 260 x 190 mm, No. of Columns (Display): 4, Col Widths (Display): 44 mm
CONSUMER: RURAL & REGIONAL INTEREST

ZEITPUNKT HOTEL- UND GASTRONOMIEFÜHRER
1809034G89A-12324

Editorial: Mendelssohnstr. 3, 04109 LEIPZIG
Tel: 341 2122124 **Fax:** 341 2111118
Email: info@zeitpunkt-kulturmagazin.de **Web site:** http://www.zeitpunkt-kulturmagazin.de
Freq: Annual; **Cover Price:** EUR 3,50; **Circ:** 12,000
Editor: Christian Nóvé; **Advertising Manager:** Jan Thielbeer
Profile: Gastronomy guide for Leipzig and Halle.
Language(s): German
ADVERTISING RATES:
Full Page Mono .... EUR 1266
Full Page Colour .... EUR 1808
Mechanical Data: Type Area: 260 x 190 mm, No. of Columns (Display): 4, Col Widths (Display): 44 mm
Copy instructions: *Copy Date:* 21 days prior to publication

ZEITSCHRIFT FÜR ARBEITSWISSENSCHAFT
748615G14R-150

Editorial: Germannstr. 31, 64409 MESSEL
Tel: 6159 253388 **Fax:** 6159 202185
Email: zfa-redaktion@zfa-online.de **Web site:** http://www.zfa-online.de
Freq: Quarterly; Free to qualifying individuals
Annual Sub.: EUR 80,00; **Circ:** 899
Editor: Kurt Landau
Profile: Journal of industrial engineering on issues related to ergonomics, organization, technology, sociology, psychology and physiology of work and profession.
Language(s): German
ADVERTISING RATES:
Full Page Mono .... EUR 1200
Mechanical Data: Type Area: 260 x 180 mm, No. of Columns (Display): 2, Col Widths (Display): 88 mm
Copy instructions: *Copy Date:* 30 days prior to publication
Supplement(s): ASUprotect
BUSINESS: COMMERCE, INDUSTRY & MANAGEMENT: Commerce Related

ZEITSCHRIFT FÜR ARZNEI- & GEWÜRZPFLANZEN
748617G37-1770

Editorial: Klein Sachau 4, 29459 CLENZE
Tel: 5844 9711880 **Fax:** 5844 9711889
Email: peter.erling@agrimedia.com **Web site:** http://www.zag-info.de
Freq: Quarterly; **Annual Sub.:** EUR 127,80; **Circ:** 1,000
Editor: Peter Erling; **Advertising Manager:** Karin Monneweg
Profile: The journal is a forum for all partners who are connected to the field of medicinal and aromatic plants. The main part of the application-oriented magazine form, wissenschaftliche original contributions related to primary production, processing, standardization, trade and economics.
Language(s): English; German
ADVERTISING RATES:
Full Page Mono .... EUR 790
Full Page Colour .... EUR 1560
Mechanical Data: Type Area: 252 x 180 mm
Copy instructions: *Copy Date:* 28 days prior to publication

ZEITSCHRIFT FÜR AUDIOLOGIE
748619G56A-10500

Editorial: Im Breitspiel 11a, 69126 HEIDELBERG
Tel: 6221 905090 **Fax:** 6221 9050920
Email: info@median-verlag.de **Web site:** http://www.median-verlag.de
Freq: Quarterly; Free to qualifying individuals
Annual Sub.: EUR 51,00; **Circ:** 1,800
Editor: Jürgen Kießling; **Advertising Manager:** Kyra Schiffke
Profile: Official publication from the German Society for Audiology.
Language(s): English; German
ADVERTISING RATES:
Full Page Mono .... EUR 865
Full Page Colour .... EUR 1690
Mechanical Data: Type Area: 250 x 188 mm, No. of Columns (Display): 3, Col Widths (Display): 60 mm
Copy instructions: *Copy Date:* 28 days prior to publication

ZEITSCHRIFT FÜR BEAMTENRECHT
748624G44-2440

Editorial: Am Wolfshof 5a, 53604 BAD HONNEF
Tel: 2224 978310 **Fax:** 2224 978310
Email: redaktion@zbr-online.de **Web site:** http://www.zbr-zeitschrift.de
Freq: 10 issues yearly; **Annual Sub.:** EUR 144,90; **Circ:** 1,795
Editor: Matthias Pechstein
Profile: Journal focusing on law and the civil service.
Language(s): German
ADVERTISING RATES:
Full Page Mono .... EUR 1400
Full Page Colour .... EUR 2210
Mechanical Data: Type Area: 260 x 185 mm, No. of Columns (Display): 2, Col Widths (Display): 90 mm
Copy instructions: *Copy Date:* 30 days prior to publication
BUSINESS: LEGAL

ZEITSCHRIFT FÜR BEWÄSSERUNGSWIRTSCHAFT
748627G21A-4140

Editorial: Eschborner Landstr. 122, 60489 FRANKFURT **Tel:** 69 247880 **Fax:** 69 24788480
Email: dlg-verlag@dlg.org **Web site:** http://www.dlg-verlag.de
Freq: Half-yearly; **Annual Sub.:** EUR 92,00; **Circ:** 200
Editor: Peter Wolff; **Advertising Manager:** Viola Hilz
Profile: Bilingual journal of Applied Irrigation Science containing English and German articles focuses on the solution of problems faced by irrigators in industrialised and Third World Countries. Topics: Applied geographical analysis and examination of technical,.
Language(s): English; German

ZEITSCHRIFT FÜR CHEMOTHERAPIE
748629G56A-10520

Editorial: Eichenallee 36a, 14050 BERLIN
Tel: 30 3125059 **Fax:** 30 3124742
Email: redaktion@zct-berlin.de **Web site:** http://www.zct-berlin.de
Freq: 6 issues yearly; **Annual Sub.:** EUR 36,00; **Circ:** 5,000
Editor: Hartmut Lode; **Advertising Manager:** Heidi Pretorius
Profile: Magazine with information for doctors and pharmacists for rational therapy of infection.
Language(s): German
Mechanical Data: No. of Columns (Display): 3, Col Widths (Display): 57 mm
Copy instructions: *Copy Date:* 10 days prior to publication

ZEITSCHRIFT FÜR DAS FÜRSORGEWESEN ZFF
748630G32G-2900

Editorial: Arndtstr. 1, 30167 HANNOVER
Web site: http://www.boorberg.de
Freq: Monthly; **Annual Sub.:** EUR 94,80; **Circ:** 1,760
Editor: Ulrich Harmening; **Advertising Manager:** Roland Schulz
Profile: Magazine focusing on welfare.
Language(s): German

ADVERTISING RATES:
Full Page Mono .... EUR 766
Full Page Colour .... EUR 1696
Mechanical Data: Type Area: 260 x 180 mm, No. of Columns (Display): 2, Col Widths (Display): 88 mm
Copy instructions: *Copy Date:* 31 days prior to publication
BUSINESS: LOCAL GOVERNMENT, LEISURE & RECREATION: Community Care & Social Services

ZEITSCHRIFT FÜR DAS GESAMTE FAMILIENRECHT MIT BETREUUNGSRECHT ERBRECHT VERFAHRENSRECHT ÖFFENTLICHEM RECHT FAMRZ

748631G44-2480
Editorial: Dr.-Gessler-Str. 20, 93051 REGENSBURG
Tel: 941 799031 **Fax:** 941 799033
Email: famrz@gieseking-verlag.de **Web site:** http://www.famrz.de
Freq: 24 issues yearly; **Annual Sub.:** EUR 235,00; **Circ:** 13,000
Editor: Dieter Schwab; **Advertising Manager:** Barbara Brante
Profile: Magazine about all aspects of family law.
Language(s): German
ADVERTISING RATES:
Full Page Mono .... EUR 1995
Full Page Colour .... EUR 3795
Mechanical Data: Type Area: 260 x 185 mm
Copy instructions: *Copy Date:* 18 days prior to publication
BUSINESS: LEGAL

ZEITSCHRIFT FÜR DAS GESAMTE KREDITWESEN

748634G1C-1380
Editorial: Aschaffenburger Str. 19, 60599 FRANKFURT **Tel:** 69 97083338 **Fax:** 69 7078400
Email: red.zfgk@kreditwesen.de **Web site:** http://www.kreditwesen.de
Freq: 24 issues yearly; **Annual Sub.:** EUR 477,36; **Circ:** 2,269
Editor: Berthold Morschhäuser; **Advertising Manager:** Ralf Werner
Profile: Journal covering all aspects of the credit business.
Language(s): German
ADVERTISING RATES:
Full Page Mono .... EUR 4220
Full Page Colour .... EUR 6320
Mechanical Data: Type Area: 265 x 185 mm, No. of Columns (Display): 3, Col Widths (Display): 58 mm
Copy instructions: *Copy Date:* 9 days prior to publication
Supplement(s): Ausgabe Technik
BUSINESS: FINANCE & ECONOMICS: Banking

ZEITSCHRIFT FÜR DIE GESAMTE VERSICHERUNGS-WISSENSCHAFT

748640G14A-8960
Editorial: Königsworther Platz 1, 30167 HANNOVER
Tel: 511 7625083 **Fax:** 511 7625081
Email: jms@ivbl.uni-hannover.de **Web site:** http://www.zverswiss.de
Freq: 5 issues yearly; **Annual Sub.:** EUR 156,00; **Circ:** 1,600
Editor: J.-M. Graf v. d. Schulenburg
Profile: Magazine about insurance.
Language(s): German
ADVERTISING RATES:
Full Page Mono .... EUR 1130
Full Page Colour .... EUR 2170
Mechanical Data: Type Area: 200 x 130 mm

ZEITSCHRIFT FÜR ENERGIEWIRTSCHAFT

748646G58-1725
Editorial: Sternwartstr. 17a, 81679 MÜNCHEN
Tel: 89 99884459 **Fax:** 89 99884698
Email: zfe@wiso.uni-koeln.de **Web site:** http://www.zeitschrift-fuer-energiewirtschaft.de
Freq: Quarterly; **Annual Sub.:** EUR 350,47; **Circ:** 1,050
Editor: Katrin Spitzer; **Advertising Manager:** Peter Schmidtmann
Profile: Magazine containing information about energy used in business and industry.
Language(s): German
Readership: Aimed at managers within the energy sector.
Mechanical Data: Type Area: 240 x 175 mm, No. of Columns (Display): 3, Col Widths (Display): 55 mm

ZEITSCHRIFT FÜR EPILEPTOLOGIE

726373G56A-3040
Editorial: Tiergartenstr. 17, 69121 HEIDELBERG
Tel: 6221 4878823 **Fax:** 6221 48768823
Email: ines.marberg@springer.com **Web site:** http://www.springermedizin.de
Freq: Quarterly; Free to qualifying individuals
Annual Sub.: EUR 218,00; **Circ:** 1,600
Profile: The aim of the Zeitschrift für Epileptologie is the presentation and discussion of current knowledge about epilepsy in German speaking area with a focus on clinically relevant topics. Basic knowledge about epilepsy as well as research results are also considered. The Zeitschrift für Epileptologie is primarily aimed at neurologists and paediatricians with a special interest about epilepsy diagnosis and therapy. As special categories, the magazine offers - Issues of the German Society for Epileptology - Communications from the Michael Foundation - Communications of the Association for presurgical epilepsy diagnosis and surgical treatment of epilepsy - The epilepsy surgery case - Epilepsy and law - Journal Club - book reviews.
Language(s): German
ADVERTISING RATES:
Full Page Mono .... EUR 1830
Full Page Colour .... EUR 2870
Mechanical Data: Type Area: 240 x 174 mm
Official Journal of: Organ d. Dt. Ges. f. Epileptologie

ZEITSCHRIFT FÜR EVIDENZ, FORTBILDUNG UND QUALITÄT IM GESUNDHEITSWESEN

748602G56A-10480
Editorial: Postfach 120264, 10592 BERLIN
Tel: 221 4848915 **Fax:** 221 4848916
Email: buerger@azq.de
Freq: 10 issues yearly; **Annual Sub.:** EUR 84,00; **Circ:** 2,050
Editor: Günter Ollenschläger
Profile: Magazine on medical further education.
Language(s): German
ADVERTISING RATES:
Full Page Mono .... EUR 1190
Full Page Colour .... EUR 2510
Mechanical Data: Type Area: 240 x 175 mm
Official Journal of: Organ d. Dt. Netzwerk Evidenzbasierte Medizin, Cochrane-Zentrum, ArGe d. wissenschaftl. medizin. Fachges. u. d. Ärztl. Zentrums f. Qualität in d. Medizin

ZEITSCHRIFT FÜR GANZHEITLICHE TIERMEDIZIN

748659G64H-500
Editorial: Oswald-Hesse-Str. 50, 70469 STUTTGART
Tel: 711 8931712 **Fax:** 711 8931706
Email: christina.lauer@medizinverlage.de **Web site:** http://www.sonntag-verlag.com
Freq: Quarterly; Free to qualifying individuals
Annual Sub.: EUR 73,50; **Circ:** 3,300
Editor: Christina Lauer; **Advertising Manager:** Ilona Reiser
Profile: Journal containing articles, case studies and information concerning alternative or complementary therapies for treating pets and farm animals.
Language(s): English; German
Readership: Read by veterinary surgeons and farm care personnel.
ADVERTISING RATES:
Full Page Mono .... EUR 1050
Full Page Colour .... EUR 1900
Mechanical Data: No. of Columns (Display): 3, Col Widths (Display): 55 mm, Type Area: 241 x 175 mm
Copy instructions: *Copy Date:* 35 days prior to publication
BUSINESS: OTHER CLASSIFICATIONS: Veterinary

ZEITSCHRIFT FÜR GASTROENTEROLOGIE

1615047G56A-11202
Editorial: Rüdigerstr. 14, 70469 STUTTGART
Tel: 711 8931429 **Fax:** 711 8931408
Email: christiane.weseloh@thieme.de **Web site:** http://www.thieme.de/fz/zfg.html
Freq: Monthly; Free to qualifying individuals
Annual Sub.: EUR 295,40; **Circ:** 6,160
Editor: Guido Adler
Profile: First-class works from all disciplines. Current information on morphological, endoscopic and radiological progress. Broad literature survey, part of extensive presentations, calendar of events, convention editions.
Language(s): English; German
ADVERTISING RATES:
Full Page Mono .... EUR 3580
Full Page Colour .... EUR 4840
Mechanical Data: Type Area: 248 x 175 mm, No. of Columns (Display): 3, Col Widths (Display): 55 mm
Official Journal of: Organ d. Gastroenterolog. ArGe Rheinland-Pfalz, Saarland, Ges. f. Gastroenterologie in Bayern, Nordrhein-Westfalen, d. Norddt. Ges. f. Gastroenterologie, d. Mitteldt. Ges. f. Gastroenterologie, d. Österr. u. d. Ungar. Ges. f. Gastroenterologie u. Hepatologie, d. Südwestdt. Ges. f. Gastroenterologie
Supplement(s): BVGD Info; Current congress

ZEITSCHRIFT FÜR GERONTOLOGIE + GERIATRIE

748666G56A-10600
Editorial: Tiergartenstr. 17, 69121 HEIDELBERG
Tel: 6221 4870 **Fax:** 6221 4878366
Email: subscriptions@springer.com **Web site:** http://www.springer.com
Freq: 6 issues yearly; **Annual Sub.:** EUR 186,00; **Circ:** 1,800
Profile: The fact that more and more people are getting older and decisive role in shaping our image of society, not least, we owe an intensive research on aging and medicine, past and present. Which the Zeitschrift für Gerontologie und Geriatrie with many years account by informing with its wide range of interested readers of all developments in aging research. Thematic issues addressed in the detailed manner all the issues of gerontology, biology and basic research of aging, geriatric research, psychology and sociology, as well as the practical nursing.
Language(s): German
ADVERTISING RATES:
Full Page Mono .... EUR 930
Full Page Colour .... EUR 1970
Mechanical Data: Type Area: 240 x 175 mm
Official Journal of: Organ d. Dt. Ges. f. Gerontologie u. Geriatrie, d. Bundesverb. Geriatrie e.V.
BUSINESS: HEALTH & MEDICAL

ZEITSCHRIFT FÜR GESUNDHEITSPSYCHOLOGIE

748669G56N-140
Editorial: Rohnsweg 25, 37085 GÖTTINGEN
Tel: 551 496090 **Fax:** 551 4960988
Email: verlag@hogrefe.de **Web site:** http://www.hogrefe.de/zeitschriften/zgp
Freq: Quarterly; **Annual Sub.:** EUR 86,95; **Circ:** 1,600
Editor: Arnold Lohaus; **Advertising Manager:** Nadine Teichert
Profile: Journal covering all aspects of psychology.
Language(s): German
Readership: Aimed at psychologists, doctors and people in health authorities.
ADVERTISING RATES:
Full Page Mono .... EUR 450
Mechanical Data: Type Area: 250 x 170 mm, No. of Columns (Display): 2, Col Widths (Display): 85 mm
Copy instructions: *Copy Date:* 42 days prior to publication
BUSINESS: HEALTH & MEDICAL: Mental Health

ZEITSCHRIFT FÜR HERZ-, THORAX- UND GEFÄSSCHIRURGIE

748674G56A-10640
Editorial: Tiergartenstr. 17, 69121 HEIDELBERG
Tel: 6221 4878820 **Fax:** 6221 48768820
Email: annette.gasser@springer.com **Web site:** http://www.springermedizin.de
Freq: 6 issues yearly; **Annual Sub.:** EUR 179,00; **Circ:** 600
Advertising Manager: Noëla Krischer-Janka
Profile: The „Zeitschrift für Herz-, Thorax- und Gefäßchirurgie" as the official training institution of the German Society for Thoracic and Cardiovascular Surgery, the information platform for the crucial developments in the field. Want to stay It is aimed at young doctors in training and to specialists, the most up to date. The journal state-of-the-art surgery provides the indication to treatment, current surgical and technological trends and information on new research directions. The core of each issue is a comprehensive review article, prepared and evaluated for daily practice. Case reports show unusual patterns of illness and treatment. They are dedicated to legal issues.
Language(s): German
ADVERTISING RATES:
Full Page Mono .... EUR 1190
Full Page Colour .... EUR 2230
Mechanical Data: Type Area: 240 x 174 mm
Official Journal of: Organ d. Dt. Ges. f. Thorax-, Herz- u. Gefäßchirurgie
BUSINESS: HEALTH & MEDICAL

ZEITSCHRIFT FÜR HISTORISCHE FORSCHUNG

748675G84B-2769
Editorial: Domplatz 20, 48143 MÜNSTER
Email: zhf.redaktion@uni-muenster.de
Freq: Quarterly; **Annual Sub.:** EUR 102,00; **Circ:** 600
Editor: Barbara Stollberg-Rilinger; **Advertising Manager:** Arlett Günther
Profile: European magazine featuring books on law, economics and social services, history, politics, philosophy, literary studies and natural sciences.
Language(s): German
ADVERTISING RATES:
Full Page Mono .... EUR 600
Mechanical Data: Type Area: 185 x 115 mm
CONSUMER: THE ARTS & LITERARY: Literary

ZEITSCHRIFT FÜR INDIVIDUALPSYCHOLOGIE

748678G56N-150
Editorial: Robert-Koch-Str. 10, 50931 KÖLN
Email: ulla.breuer@uk-koeln.de
Freq: Quarterly; Free to qualifying individuals
Annual Sub.: EUR 64,00; **Circ:** 2,400
Editor: Ulla Breuer; **Advertising Manager:** Anja Kütemeyer
Profile: Medical journal focusing on psychology.
Language(s): English; German
Readership: Journal read by psychologists, doctors, psychotherapists, teachers, child-behaviour specialists, neurologists and members of many public sector jobs and organisations.
ADVERTISING RATES:
Full Page Mono .... EUR 680
Mechanical Data: Type Area: 190 x 120 mm
BUSINESS: HEALTH & MEDICAL: Mental Health

ZEITSCHRIFT FÜR KLASSISCHE HOMÖOPATHIE

748687G56A-10700
Editorial: Oswald-Hesse-Str. 50, 70469 STUTTGART
Tel: 711 8931732 **Fax:** 711 8931748
Email: daniela.elsasser@medizinverlage.de **Web site:** http://www.medizinverlage.de
Freq: Quarterly; Free to qualifying individuals
Annual Sub.: EUR 89,40; **Circ:** 2,000
Editor: Daniela Elsasser; **Advertising Manager:** Nancy Ruhland
Profile: Magazine on basic and advanced homeopathy.
Language(s): German
ADVERTISING RATES:
Full Page Mono .... EUR 1160
Full Page Colour .... EUR 2080
Mechanical Data: Type Area: 210 x 140 mm
Copy instructions: *Copy Date:* 30 days prior to publication

ZEITSCHRIFT FÜR KLINISCHE PSYCHOLOGIE UND PSYCHOTHERAPIE

748689G56A-10720
Editorial: Rohnsweg 25, 37085 GÖTTINGEN
Tel: 551 496090 **Fax:** 551 4960988
Email: verlag@hogrefe.de **Web site:** http://www.hogrefe.de/zeitschriften/zkp
Freq: Quarterly; **Annual Sub.:** EUR 111,95; **Circ:** 3,600
Advertising Manager: Nadine Teichert
Profile: Magazine with Articles relating to psychological problems and disorders, psychological disorders and mental disorders co-determined physical.
Language(s): German
ADVERTISING RATES:
Full Page Mono .... EUR 1050
Mechanical Data: Type Area: 250 x 170 mm, No. of Columns (Display): 2, Col Widths (Display): 85 mm
Copy instructions: *Copy Date:* 42 days prior to publication
Official Journal of: Organ d. Dt. Ges. f. Psychologie zugleich Organ d. Fachgruppe Klin. Psychologie u. Psychiatrie in d. Dt. Ges. f. Psychologie u. d. ArGe f. Verhaltens Modifikation e.V., d. Berufsverb. Dt. Psychologen, Sektion Klin. Psychologie, d. Dt. Ges. f. Verhaltenstherapie e.V., d. Ges. f. wissenschaftl. Gesprächspsychotherapie e.V. u. d. Berufsverb. Österr. Psychologen, Sektion Klin. Psychologie

ZEITSCHRIFT FÜR KONFLIKT-MANAGEMENT

748690G1A-3380
Editorial: Gustav-Heinemann-Ufer 58, 50968 KÖLN
Tel: 221 93738821 **Fax:** 221 93738926
Email: redaktion-zkm@mediate.de **Web site:** http://www.centrale-fuer-mediation.de
Freq: 6 issues yearly; Free to qualifying individuals
Annual Sub.: EUR 133,90; **Circ:** 1,490
Editor: Karen Engler; **Advertising Manager:** Thorsten Deuse
Profile: Magazine about extrajudicial conflict solving.
Language(s): German
ADVERTISING RATES:
Full Page Mono .... EUR 780
Full Page Colour .... EUR 1365
Mechanical Data: Col Widths (Display): 88 mm, No. of Columns (Display): 2, Type Area: 260 x 180 mm
Copy instructions: *Copy Date:* 28 days prior to publication

ZEITSCHRIFT FÜR MEDIZINISCHE ETHIK

748701G56R-250
Editorial: Platz der Universität, 79085 FREIBURG
Tel: 761 2171708 **Fax:** 761 2032096
Email: verena.wetzstein@t-online.de
Freq: Quarterly; **Annual Sub.:** EUR 64,00; **Circ:** 1,200
Editor: Verena Wetzstein; **Advertising Manager:** Sabrina Reusch
Profile: Publication about medical ethics.
Language(s): German
ADVERTISING RATES:
Full Page Mono .... EUR 450
Full Page Colour .... EUR 561
Mechanical Data: Type Area: 188 x 121 mm, No. of Columns (Display): 2, Col Widths (Display): 58 mm
Copy instructions: *Copy Date:* 28 days prior to publication
BUSINESS: HEALTH & MEDICAL: Health Medical Related

ZEITSCHRIFT FÜR MEDIZINISCHE PHYSIK

748702G56J-90
Editorial: Theodor-Kutzer-Ufer 1, 68167 MANNHEIM
Tel: 6221 3835121 **Fax:** 6221 3835123
Email: lothar.schad@medma.uni-heidelberg.de
Freq: Quarterly; **Annual Sub.:** EUR 99,00; **Circ:** 1,900
Editor: Lothar Schad
Profile: Magazine containing articles about radiotherapy, X-ray diagnosis and nuclear medicine.
Language(s): English; French; German
Readership: Read by members of the medical profession.
ADVERTISING RATES:
Full Page Mono .... EUR 1170
Full Page Colour .... EUR 2490
Mechanical Data: Type Area: 240 x 175 mm
Official Journal of: Organ d. Dt., Österr. u. Schweizer. Ges. f. Medizin. Physik
BUSINESS: HEALTH & MEDICAL: Radiography

ZEITSCHRIFT FÜR NATURHEILKUNDE
748709G56R-2380
Editorial: Kasernenstr. 26, 42651 SOLINGEN
Tel: 212 47285 **Fax:** 212 42711
Email: redaktion@verlag-zfn.de **Web site:** http://www.verlag-zfn.de
Freq: Monthly; **Annual Sub.:** EUR 41,41; **Circ:** 5,800
Editor: Hartmut Lockenvitz; **Advertising Manager:** Hartmut Lockenvitz
Profile: Magazine about homeopathy and naturopathy.
Language(s): German
ADVERTISING RATES:
Full Page Mono .... EUR 1594
Full Page Colour .... EUR 2473
Mechanical Data: Type Area: 257 x 175 mm, No. of Columns (Display): 2, Col Widths (Display): 85 mm
Copy instructions: *Copy Date:* 40 days prior to publication
Official Journal of: Organ d. Union Dt. Heilpraktiker e.V.
BUSINESS: HEALTH & MEDICAL: Health Medical Related

ZEITSCHRIFT FÜR ORTHOPÄDIE UND UNFALLCHIRURGIE
748718G56A-10780
Editorial: Zeppelinstr. 58, 69121 HEIDELBERG
Tel: 6221 5886820 **Fax:** 6221 5886821
Email: zfou@thieme.de **Web site:** http://www.thieme.de/fz/zfou
Freq: 6 issues yearly; **Annual Sub.:** EUR 364,40; **Circ:** 1,830
Profile: Originated from the Zeitschrift für Orthopädie und ihre Grenzgebiete and the Aktuellen Traumatologie it carries the substantive development of the new common multiple orthopedic and trauma surgery bill and delivers a pure subscription title and contents of major scientific developments. It is the German-speaking orthopedic and trauma surgery journal with the highest scientific prestige.
Language(s): German
ADVERTISING RATES:
Full Page Mono .... EUR 1540
Full Page Colour .... EUR 2635
Mechanical Data: Type Area: 248 x 175 mm, No. of Columns (Display): 3, Col Widths (Display): 55 mm
Official Journal of: Organ d. Dt. Ges. f. Orthopädie u. Orthopäd. Chirurgie
BUSINESS: HEALTH & MEDICAL

ZEITSCHRIFT FÜR PALLIATIVMEDIZIN
748722G56A-10800
Editorial: Rüdigerstr. 14, 70469 STUTTGART
Tel: 711 8931593 **Fax:** 711 8931408
Email: silvia.geuenich@thieme.de **Web site:** http://www.thieme.de/palliativmedizin
Freq: 6 issues yearly; Free to qualifying individuals
Annual Sub.: EUR 126,90; **Circ:** 5,400
Editor: Silvia Geuenich
Profile: Make life worth living! The aim of palliative care is to care for critically ill patients and to improve their quality of life. The patient's life should be as active, happy, pain-and symptom-free as possible. The Palliative care is an area that represents an increasingly important area in medicine. With the Zeitschrift für Palliativmedizin, stay tuned, because you will find, in scientific and practical information, mapped the entire spectrum of palliative care. Heading "Science": State of the research; case reports from the everyday medical practice, CME-certified training: 3 points per item. Heading "Care": The practice with the help you cope with the daily challenges in caring for palliative patients. From practice for practice: four pages plus section extra-care nursing supplement with many practical tips. Section "Forum": Short refereed scientific information. Notices of the German Society for Palliative Medicine. Heading "Outlook": Interdisciplinary reflections on palliative care from the perspective of other disciplines, eg by pastors or physiotherapist.
Language(s): German
ADVERTISING RATES:
Full Page Mono .... EUR 1970
Full Page Colour .... EUR 3140
Mechanical Data: Type Area: 248 x 175 mm, No. of Columns (Display): 3, Col Widths (Display): 55 mm
Official Journal of: Organ d. Dt. Ges. f. Palliativmedizin zus. m. d. Österr. Palliativges.

ZEITSCHRIFT FÜR PERSONALFORSCHUNG
748726G14A-8980
Editorial: Marktplatz 5, 86415 MERING
Tel: 8233 4783 **Fax:** 8233 30755
Email: hampp@rhverlag.de **Web site:** http://www.hampp-verlag.de
Freq: Quarterly; **Annual Sub.:** EUR 80,00; **Circ:** 500
Editor: Rainer Hampp
Profile: Magazine containing scientific contributions about employees, leadership and management.
Language(s): English; German

ZEITSCHRIFT FÜR PHYTOTHERAPIE
748731G56A-10820
Editorial: Oswald-Hesse-Str. 50, 70469 STUTTGART
Tel: 711 8931738 **Fax:** 711 8931706
Email: hanno.kretschmer@medizinverlage.de **Web site:** http://www.medizinverlage.de
Freq: 6 issues yearly; Free to qualifying individuals
Annual Sub.: EUR 85,90; **Circ:** 4,200
Editor: Hanno Kretschmer; **Advertising Manager:** Markus Stehle
Profile: Magazine about phytotherapy.
Language(s): German
ADVERTISING RATES:
Full Page Mono .... EUR 1478
Full Page Colour .... EUR 2500
Mechanical Data: No. of Columns (Display): 3, Col Widths (Display): 55 mm, Type Area: 235 x 175 mm
Copy instructions: *Copy Date:* 30 days prior to publication
Official Journal of: Organ d. Ges. f. Phytotherapie e.V.

ZEITSCHRIFT FÜR PSYCHIATRIE, PSYCHOLOGIE UND PSYCHOTHERAPIE
1615049S56A-2132
Editorial: Grazer Str. 6, 28359 BREMEN
Tel: 421 2184618
Email: helmsen@uni-bremen.de
Freq: Quarterly; **Annual Sub.:** CHF 177,00; **Circ:** 500
Advertising Manager: H.R. Schindler
Profile: Magazine for psychologists and psychotherapists.
Language(s): German
ADVERTISING RATES:
Full Page Mono .... CHF 640
Full Page Colour .... CHF 1390
Mechanical Data: Type Area: 250 x 170 mm, No. of Columns (Display): 2, Col Widths (Display): 85 mm
Copy instructions: *Copy Date:* 47 days prior to publication

ZEITSCHRIFT FÜR PSYCHOSOMATISCHE MEDIZIN UND PSYCHOTHERAPIE
748738G56A-11150
Editorial: Bebelstr. 31, 37081 GÖTTINGEN
Email: gwitte@gwdg.de
Freq: Quarterly; **Annual Sub.:** EUR 99,00; **Circ:** 1,900
Editor: Gabriele Witte-Lakemann; **Advertising Manager:** Anja Kütemeyer
Profile: Publication about psychosomatic medicine and psychotherapy.
Language(s): German
ADVERTISING RATES:
Full Page Mono .... EUR 520
Mechanical Data: Type Area: 190 x 121 mm

ZEITSCHRIFT FÜR PSYCHOTRAUMATOLOGIE PSYCHOTHERAPIEWISSENSCHAFT PSYCHOLOGISCHE MEDIZIN ZPPM
1646277G56A-11299
Editorial: Bernhard-Feilchenfeld-Str. 11, 50969 KÖLN
Email: eichenberg@uni-koeln.de **Web site:** http://www.christianeeichenberg.de
Freq: Quarterly; **Annual Sub.:** EUR 64,40; **Circ:** 1,000
Profile: ZPPM has as its object, knowledge of psycho-trauma in disciplines and fields of practice to anchor, referred to collectively as the disciplines of psychological medicine. The aim is a broad interdisciplinary dialogue in order to meet the challenges of our time, since disasters, accidents, wars and violence - incidents which often lead to psychological trauma - are making the population more. Psychotraumatology can be analogous to the somatic traumatology (from ancient greek = Traumatic injury), rewritten as a theory of psychological injuries in prevention, treatment and rehabilitation Target groups: psychotherapists, psychoanalysts, physicians, psychiatrists, teachers and students at universities, counselors.
Language(s): English; German
ADVERTISING RATES:
Full Page Mono .... EUR 500
Mechanical Data: Type Area: 224 x 135 mm, No. of Columns (Display): 2, Col Widths (Display): 65 mm
Copy instructions: *Copy Date:* 42 days prior to publication

ZEITSCHRIFT FÜR REGENERATIVE MEDIZIN
1793089G56A-11442
Editorial: Johannisplatz 30, 04103 LEIPZIG
Email: frank-emmrich@medizin.uni-leipzig.de **Web site:** http://www.zuckschwerdtverlag.de
Freq: Quarterly; **Cover Price:** EUR 18,00; **Circ:** 1,300
Editor: Frank Emmrich
Profile: Magazine from the German Association for Regenerative Medicine.
Language(s): German
ADVERTISING RATES:
Full Page Mono .... EUR 1400
Full Page Colour .... EUR 2420
Mechanical Data: Type Area: 258 x 177 mm, No. of Columns (Display): 3, Col Widths (Display): 55 mm
Official Journal of: Organ d. Dt. Ges. f. Regenerative Medizin

ZEITSCHRIFT FÜR RHEUMATOLOGIE
748741G56A-10880
Editorial: Tiergartenstr. 17, 69121 HEIDELBERG
Tel: 6221 4878218 **Fax:** 6221 48768218
Email: michael.baenfer@springer.com **Web site:** http://www.springermedizin.de
Freq: 10 issues yearly; **Annual Sub.:** EUR 249,00; **Circ:** 2,100
Advertising Manager: Noëla Krischer-Janka
Profile: Zeitschrift für Rheumatologie is an internationally recognized journal dealing with all aspects of clinical rheumatology, the therapy of rheumatic diseases, and fundamental research in the field of rheumatology. The journal addresses both rheumatologists with own practices and those working in hospitals. Comprehensive reviews on a specific topical issue focus on providing evidenced based information on diagnostics and therapy. Case reports feature interesting cases and aim at optimizing diagnostic and therapeutic strategies. Review articles under the rubric "Continuing Medical Education" present verified results of scientific research and their integration into daily practice.
Language(s): German
ADVERTISING RATES:
Full Page Mono .... EUR 1280
Full Page Colour .... EUR 2320
Mechanical Data: Type Area: 240 x 174 mm
Official Journal of: Organ d. Dt. u. d. Schweizer. Ges. f. Rheumatologie, d. Österr. Ges. f. Rheumatologie & Rehabilitation, d. Berufsverb. Dt. Rheumatologen u. d. Dt. Ges. f. Innere Medizin
BUSINESS: HEALTH & MEDICAL

ZEITSCHRIFT FÜR SEXUALFORSCHUNG
748747G56A-10900
Editorial: Martinistr. 52, 20246 HAMBURG
Tel: 40 741053214 **Fax:** 40 741056406
Email: dekker@uke.uni-hamburg.de **Web site:** http://www.thieme.de/sexualforschung
Freq: Quarterly; Free to qualifying individuals
Annual Sub.: EUR 126,80; **Circ:** 810
Editor: Peer Briken
Profile: Represent sexuality - think sexuality. Wide range of topics: original works from empirical and clinical research, recent studies on sex and gender theory, informative case reports.
Language(s): German
ADVERTISING RATES:
Full Page Mono .... EUR 850
Full Page Colour .... EUR 1990
Mechanical Data: Type Area: 210 x 140 mm
Official Journal of: Organ d. Dt. Ges. f. Sexualforschung

ZEITSCHRIFT FÜR STOFFRECHT STOFFR
1828537G1A-3700
Editorial: Güntzelstr. 63, 10717 BERLIN
Tel: 30 81450615 **Fax:** 30 81450622
Email: kickum@lexxion.de **Web site:** http://www.lexxion.de
Freq: 6 issues yearly; **Annual Sub.:** EUR 197,46; **Circ:** 600
Editor: Christina Kickum
Profile: Magazine for jurists.
Language(s): German
ADVERTISING RATES:
Full Page Mono .... EUR 615
Mechanical Data: Type Area: 248 x 175 mm
Copy instructions: *Copy Date:* 21 days prior to publication

ZEITSCHRIFT FÜR SYSTEMISCHE THERAPIE UND BERATUNG
748756G56N-180
Editorial: Am Weinberg 12, 35037 MARBURG
Tel: 6421 590870 **Fax:** 6421 5908713
Email: zstb@mics.de **Web site:** http://www.mics.de
Freq: Quarterly; **Annual Sub.:** EUR 33,00; **Circ:** 1,345
Editor: Klaus G. Deissler; **Advertising Manager:** Gudrun Luck
Profile: Journal containing articles about the theory and practice of psychiatry, psychotherapy and other related fields.
Language(s): German
Readership: Read by psychotherapists, psychiatrists and social workers.
ADVERTISING RATES:
Full Page Mono .... EUR 405
Mechanical Data: Type Area: 206 x 135 mm, No. of Columns (Display): 2, Col Widths (Display): 63 mm
Copy instructions: *Copy Date:* 25 days prior to publication
BUSINESS: HEALTH & MEDICAL: Mental Health

ZEITSCHRIFT FÜR UMWELTPOLITIK & UMWELTRECHT
748763G57-120
Editorial: Holstenhofweg 85, 22043 HAMBURG
Tel: 40 65412886 **Fax:** 40 65413726
Email: kwzi@hsu-hh.de **Web site:** http://www.dfv.de
Freq: Quarterly; **Annual Sub.:** EUR 350,00; **Circ:** 600
Editor: Klaus W. Zimmermann; **Advertising Manager:** Marion Gertzen
Profile: Journal covering environmental politics.
Language(s): German
ADVERTISING RATES:
Full Page Mono .... EUR 980
Mechanical Data: Type Area: 200 x 135 mm, No. of Columns (Display): 2, Col Widths (Display): 67 mm
Copy instructions: *Copy Date:* 14 days prior to publication
BUSINESS: ENVIRONMENT & POLLUTION

ZEITSCHRIFT FÜR VERKEHRSSICHERHEIT ZVS
748767G49R-170
Editorial: Corneliusstr. 31, 42329 WUPPERTAL
Tel: 202 731000 **Fax:** 202 731184
Email: roensch-hasselhorn@zvs-online.de **Web site:** http://www.zvs-online.de
Freq: Quarterly; **Annual Sub.:** EUR 95,70; **Circ:** 550
Editor: Barbro Rönsch-Hasselhorn; **Advertising Manager:** Gudrun Karafiol
Profile: Magazine for those responsible for road safety in institutions and enterprises in the automotive industry and Verkehsingenieure, psychologists and lawyers. Topics: efficiency of security measures and security technology in stationary and moving traffic, analysis of accidents.
Language(s): German
ADVERTISING RATES:
Full Page Mono .... EUR 512
Full Page Colour .... EUR 1097
Mechanical Data: Type Area: 260 x 180 mm, No. of Columns (Display): 3, Col Widths (Display): 57 mm
Copy instructions: *Copy Date:* 56 days prior to publication
BUSINESS: TRANSPORT: Transport Related

ZEITSCHRIFT FÜR VERKEHRSWISSENSCHAFT
748768G49R-30
Editorial: Universitätsstr. 22, 50923 KÖLN
Tel: 221 4702312 **Fax:** 221 4705183
Email: h.baum@uni-koeln.de **Web site:** http://www.uni-koeln.de
Freq: 3 issues yearly; **Annual Sub.:** EUR 66,00; **Circ:** 750
Editor: Herbert Baum
Profile: Journal containing scientific articles relating to traffic. Facebook: http://www.facebook.com/universitaet.koeln.
Language(s): German
BUSINESS: TRANSPORT: Transport Related

ZEITSCHRIFT FÜR WIRTSCHAFTSPOLITIK
748772G14C-100
Editorial: Pohligstr. 1, 50969 KÖLN **Tel:** 221 4705347 **Fax:** 221 4705350
Email: rickmeyer@wiso.uni-koeln.de **Web site:** http://www.iwp.uni-koeln.de/de/publikationen/zfw/index.htm
Freq: 3 issues yearly; **Annual Sub.:** EUR 102,00; **Circ:** 650
Editor: Dagmar Rickmeyer; **Advertising Manager:** Sybille Egger
Profile: Magazine about German, European and international business and politics.
Language(s): English; German
ADVERTISING RATES:
Full Page Mono .... EUR 400
Mechanical Data: Type Area: 205 x 120 mm
Copy instructions: *Copy Date:* 30 days prior to publication
BUSINESS: COMMERCE, INDUSTRY & MANAGEMENT: International Commerce

ZEITSCHRIFT FÜR WIRTSCHAFTSRECHT ZIP
748773G44-2780
Editorial: Aachener Str. 222, 50931 KÖLN
Tel: 221 4008813 **Fax:** 221 4008828
Email: redaktion-zip@rws-verlag.de **Web site:** http://www.zip-online.de
Freq: Weekly; **Annual Sub.:** EUR 702,00; **Circ:** 4,500
Editor: Katherine Knauth; **Advertising Manager:** Karl-Heinz Schneider
Profile: Journal about commercial law.
Language(s): German
ADVERTISING RATES:
Full Page Mono .... EUR 1400
Full Page Colour .... EUR 2450
Mechanical Data: Type Area: 260 x 185 mm, No. of Columns (Display): 2, Col Widths (Display): 85 mm
Copy instructions: *Copy Date:* 7 days prior to publication
Supplement(s): Entscheidungen zum Wirtschaftsrecht EWiR
BUSINESS: LEGAL

ZEITSCHRIFT FÜR WUNDHEILUNG
765300G56A-11111
Editorial: Bleibtreustr. 12a, 10623 BERLIN
Tel: 30 32708233 **Fax:** 30 32708234
Email: info@congress-compact.de **Web site:** http://www.congress-compact.de
Freq: 6 issues yearly; Free to qualifying individuals
Annual Sub.: EUR 38,00; **Circ:** 9,724
Editor: Thomas Ruttkowski; **Advertising Manager:** Antje Müller
Profile: Magazine on wound healing.
Language(s): German
ADVERTISING RATES:
Full Page Mono .... EUR 1330
Full Page Colour .... EUR 2325
Mechanical Data: Type Area: 254 x 170 mm, No. of Columns (Display): 3, Col Widths (Display): 53 mm
Copy instructions: *Copy Date:* 14 days prior to publication
Official Journal of: Organ d. Dt. Ges. f. Wundheilung u. Wundbehandlung, d. Österr. Ges. f. Wundbehandlung u. d. Schweizer. Ges. f. Wundbehandlung
BUSINESS: HEALTH & MEDICAL

ZEITSCHRIFTEN 748599G2A-5360
Editorial: Guldenbachstr. 1, 50935 KÖLN
Tel: 221 460140 **Fax:** 221 4601425
Email: banger@banger.de **Web site:** http://www.banger.de
Freq: Annual; **Cover Price:** EUR 118,00; **Circ:** 2,500
Advertising Manager: Günter Jepsen
Profile: Directory with order-addresses for magazines for booksellers in Germany, Austria and Switzerland.
Language(s): German
ADVERTISING RATES:
Full Page Mono .... EUR 850
Mechanical Data: Type Area: 215 x 140 mm, No. of Columns (Display): 2, Col Widths (Display): 70 mm
Copy instructions: *Copy Date:* 40 days prior to publication

DIE ZEITUNG 1912897G74A-3683
Editorial: Nevinghoff 40, 48147 MÜNSTER
Tel: 251 2376409 **Fax:** 251 2376408
Email: info@wllv.de **Web site:** http://www.wllv.de
Freq: Annual; **Circ:** 46,000
Editor: Hildegard Kuhlmann
Profile: Magazine of the Westfalen-Lippe section of Landfrauen Deutschland.
Language(s): German

ZELLER WOCHENSPIEGEL
748806G72-16664
Editorial: Rosengasse, 56727 MAYEN
Tel: 2651 981806 **Fax:** 2651 981814
Email: red-cochem@wvm-verlag.de **Web site:** http://www.wochenspiegellive.de
Freq: Weekly; **Cover Price:** Free; **Circ:** 7,702
Editor: Mario Zender; **Advertising Manager:** Frank Günther
Profile: Advertising journal (house-to-house) concentrating on local stories.
Language(s): German
ADVERTISING RATES:
Full Page Mono .... EUR 2077
Full Page Colour .... EUR 2920
Mechanical Data: Type Area: 430 x 290 mm, No. of Columns (Display): 7, Col Widths (Display): 38 mm
Copy instructions: *Copy Date:* 2 days prior to publication
LOCAL NEWSPAPERS

ZENTRADA.MAGAZIN
748824G14A-9020
Editorial: Kantstr. 38, 97074 WÜRZBURG
Tel: 931 3598132 **Fax:** 931 3598133
Email: redaktion@zentrada.de **Web site:** http://www.zentrada.de
Freq: 26 issues yearly; **Annual Sub.:** EUR 89,88; **Circ:** 17,700
Editor: Martina Schimmel; **Advertising Manager:** Hubert Wanner
Profile: Magazine focusing on all aspects of business trade.
Language(s): German
ADVERTISING RATES:
Full Page Mono .... EUR 1950
Full Page Colour .... EUR 1950
Mechanical Data: Type Area: 289 x 209 mm, No. of Columns (Display): 4, Col Widths (Display): 50 mm
Copy instructions: *Copy Date:* 5 days prior to publication
BUSINESS: COMMERCE, INDUSTRY & MANAGEMENT

ZENTRALBLATT FÜR ARBEITSMEDIZIN, ARBEITSSCHUTZ UND ERGONOMIE 748812G56A-10940
Editorial: Dischingerstr. 8, 69123 HEIDELBERG
Tel: 6221 644860 **Fax:** 6221 644640
Email: zentralblatt@konradin.de **Web site:** http://www.zentralblatt-online.de
Freq: Monthly; **Annual Sub.:** EUR 160,20; **Circ:** 1,000
Editor: David Groneberg; **Advertising Manager:** Sandra Rink
Profile: Journal covering work-related medicine and safety provisions for workers.
Language(s): German
ADVERTISING RATES:
Full Page Mono .... EUR 720
Full Page Colour .... EUR 1044
Mechanical Data: Type Area: 250 x 172 mm, No. of Columns (Display): 4, Col Widths (Display): 44 mm
Copy instructions: *Copy Date:* 30 days prior to publication
Supplement(s): baua: Aktuell
BUSINESS: HEALTH & MEDICAL

ZENTRALBLATT FÜR CHIRURGIE 748813G56A-10960
Editorial: Rüdigerstr. 14, 70469 STUTTGART
Tel: 711 89310 **Fax:** 711 8931298
Email: zblchir@thieme.de **Web site:** http://www.thieme.de/fz/zblchir
Freq: 6 issues yearly; Free to qualifying individuals
Annual Sub.: EUR 274,90; **Circ:** 1,320
Editor: H. Lippert
Profile: Concentrated expertise from research and practice. Zentralblatt für Chirurgie - all the news from the General, Visceral and Vascular Surgery. Your forum for practice-related surgery. News from hospitals, academia and research. Modern layout: Clear layout, color illustrations, structured tables. Sections with real utility: Interesting, rare or unusual cases from clinic and practice: "casuistry"; important and interesting publications in international journals and summarized succinctly: "Short lecture"; structural and technological developments in medicine: "Current Surgery". The Latest from the jurisprudence. Lawyers evaluate current judgments to medical disputes: "legal".
Language(s): English; German
ADVERTISING RATES:
Full Page Mono .... EUR 1250
Full Page Colour .... EUR 2420
Mechanical Data: Type Area: 248 x 175 mm, No. of Columns (Display): 4, Col Widths (Display): 40 mm
Official Journal of: Organ d. Thüring. Ges. f. Chirurgie, d. Sächs. Chirurgenvereinigung, d. Berliner Chirurg. Ges., d. Chirurgenvereinigung Sachsen-Anhalt, d. Vereinigungen d. Mittelrhein., Niederrhein.-Westfäl., Nordwestdt. u. Bayer. Chirurgen u. d. Österr. Ges. f. Chirurgie, ArGe f. Minimal Invasive Chirurgie
BUSINESS: HEALTH & MEDICAL

ZENTRALSTERILISATION CENTRAL SERVICE 748826G56C-13
Editorial: Marktplatz 13, 65183 WIESBADEN
Tel: 611 5059335 **Fax:** 611 5059311
Email: zentrsteril@mhp-verlag.de **Web site:** http://www.mhp-verlag.de
Freq: 6 issues yearly; Free to qualifying individuals
Annual Sub.: EUR 57,60; **Circ:** 3,850
Editor: Gudrun Westermann; **Advertising Manager:** Walter Bockemühl
Profile: Communication organ of the German Society for Sterile with current issues in the preparation and sterile, especially the nomination of control and sterilization procedures, and automated cleaning and disinfection. The journal is a forum for all those everyday, scientific research and technological development in shaping the field. In a balanced, reader-friendly compilation of the magazine contains scientific articles, reports from practice, recommendations of professional societies, relevant press and news from the industry. Because not only interdisciplinary but also international cooperation to ensure a high quality standard in the sterile supply is necessary, will be published in the CSSD all contributions in German and English.
Language(s): English; German
Readership: Aimed at managers, technicions and employees connected with the sterilising of equipment in hospitals and clinicians.
ADVERTISING RATES:
Full Page Mono .... EUR 1850
Full Page Colour .... EUR 2865
Mechanical Data: Type Area: 273 x 179 mm, No. of Columns (Display): 3, Col Widths (Display): 57 mm
Copy instructions: *Copy Date:* 14 days prior to publication
Official Journal of: Organ d. Dt. Ges. f. Sterilgutversorgung e.V.
BUSINESS: HEALTH & MEDICAL: Hospitals

ZEO2 1853661G57-2883
Editorial: Paul-Lincke-Ufer 7a, 10999 BERLIN
Fax: 30 39105133
Email: franken@zeozwei.de **Web site:** http://www.zeozwei.de
Freq: Quarterly; **Annual Sub.:** EUR 12,00; **Circ:** 20,000
Editor: Marcus Franken; **Advertising Manager:** Michael Hadamczik
Profile: The focus of the magazine are the climate, energy and transport policies. The energy crisis and new world energy order, climate change and the response of the international community will, mass mobility, resource and supply problems - these are the big issues. Conservation and consumer issues to complete the editorial approach.
Language(s): German
ADVERTISING RATES:
Full Page Mono .... EUR 1950
Mechanical Data: Type Area: 297 x 210 mm

ZERBSTER VOLKSSTIMME
748830G67B-16320
Editorial: Bahnhofstr. 17, 39104 MAGDEBURG
Tel: 391 59990 **Fax:** 391 5999210
Email: chefredaktion@volksstimme.de **Web site:** http://www.volksstimme.de
Freq: 312 issues yearly; **Circ:** 6,559
Advertising Manager: Rainer Pfeil
Profile: As the largest daily newspaper in northern Saxony-Anhalt, the Volksstimme reaches 536,000 readers a day" (MA 2010). From Monday to Saturday a team of highly qualified editors put together the latest information and news from the region and around the world. Thanks the 18 local editions is the Volksstimme always close to the action. Twitter: http://twitter.com/volksstimme This Outlet offers RSS (Really Simple Syndication).
Language(s): German
ADVERTISING RATES:
SCC .... EUR 34,80
Mechanical Data: Type Area: 480 x 327 mm, No. of Columns (Display): 7, Col Widths (Display): 45 mm
Copy instructions: *Copy Date:* 2 days prior to publication
Supplement(s): Anstoss in Zerbst; bauRatgeber; Biber; Leser-Reisen; prisma; Rathaus-Center Aktuell; Standort Landkreis Anhalt-Zerbst
REGIONAL DAILY & SUNDAY NEWSPAPERS: Regional Daily Newspapers

ZEUS 1665841G1A-3600
Editorial: Postfach 15110, 66041 SAARBRÜCKEN
Tel: 681 3023237 **Fax:** 681 3024369
Email: zeus@europainstitut.de **Web site:** http://europainstitut.de
Freq: Quarterly; **Annual Sub.:** EUR 63,00; **Circ:** 800
Editor: Anja Trautmann; **Advertising Manager:** Brigitta Weiss
Profile: Dedicated to all current problems of European integration, Europe and international law and sets a focus on European media law, European human rights protection and European and International Economic Law.
Language(s): English; German
ADVERTISING RATES:
Full Page Mono .... EUR 400
Mechanical Data: Type Area: 210 x 130 mm
Copy instructions: *Copy Date:* 20 days prior to publication

DIE ZEUS 748834G27-2900
Editorial: Celler Str. 47, 29614 SOLTAU
Tel: 5191 802833 **Fax:** 5191 98664833
Email: liane.biermann@zeus-online.de **Web site:** http://www.zeus-online.de
Freq: 3 issues yearly; **Cover Price:** Free; **Circ:** 7,000
Editor: Liane Biermann; **Advertising Manager:** Liane Biermann
Profile: Magazine for DIY, hardware, gardening centers, motorists as well as wood wholesale and retail traders.
Language(s): German
ADVERTISING RATES:
Full Page Mono .... EUR 1480
Full Page Colour .... EUR 3070
Mechanical Data: Type Area: 257 x 175 mm, No. of Columns (Display): 3, Col Widths (Display): 55 mm
Copy instructions: *Copy Date:* 35 days prior to publication

ZEV ZEITSCHRIFT FÜR ERBRECHT UND VERMÖGENSNACHFOLGE
756914G1A-3453
Editorial: Wilhelmstr. 9, 80801 MÜNCHEN
Tel: 89 38189470 **Fax:** 89 38189123
Email: zev@beck.de **Web site:** http://www.zev.de
Freq: Monthly; **Annual Sub.:** EUR 297,20; **Circ:** 2,700
Editor: Karl-Heinz Sporer; **Advertising Manager:** Fritz Lebherz
Profile: Magazine about the law of succession, business law, tax law and donation law.
Language(s): German
ADVERTISING RATES:
Full Page Mono .... EUR 1660
Full Page Colour .... EUR 3310
Mechanical Data: Type Area: 260 x 186 mm, No. of Columns (Display): 4, Col Widths (Display): 43 mm
Copy instructions: *Copy Date:* 20 days prior to publication

ZEVENER ZEITUNG
748835G67B-16340
Editorial: Gartenstr. 4, 27404 ZEVEN
Tel: 4281 945201 **Fax:** 4281 945222
Email: redaktion@zevener-zeitung.de **Web site:** http://www.zevener-zeitung.de
Freq: 312 issues yearly; **Circ:** 8,833
Advertising Manager: Ursula Rudolph
Profile: Daily newspaper with regional news and a local sports section.
Language(s): German
ADVERTISING RATES:
SCC .... EUR 25,80
Mechanical Data: Type Area: 487 x 324 mm, No. of Columns (Display): 7, Col Widths (Display): 45 mm
Copy instructions: *Copy Date:* 1 day prior to publication
Supplement(s): Ferienjournal
REGIONAL DAILY & SUNDAY NEWSPAPERS: Regional Daily Newspapers

ZFA ZEITSCHRIFT FÜR ALLGEMEINMEDIZIN
748842G56A-11060
Editorial: Dieselstr. 2, 50859 KÖLN
Tel: 2234 7011374 **Fax:** 2234 70116374
Email: lampel@aerzteverlag.de **Web site:** http://www.aerzteverlag.de
Freq: 11 issues yearly; Free to qualifying individuals
Annual Sub.: EUR 114,00; **Circ:** 3,644
Editor: Heinz-Harald Abholz; **Advertising Manager:** Sylvia Thöne
Profile: The Zeitschrift für Allgemeinmedizin (ZFA) is the organ of the German Society of General Medicine and Family Medicine (DEGAM), the Association of University Professors of General Practice (GHA) and the Salzburger Society of General Medicine (SAGAM). The ZFA is a training track and offers science-based information relevant to the primary care practice. The high-quality contributions reflect the current state of general practice and provide a practical implementation of the knowledge gained in their professional life. The ZFA is thus aimed at continuing education interested general practitioners and (family doctor working) internists, doctors in training to become "specialist in general medicine" or "Internal and General Medicine, university teachers, lecturers and teaching general practitioners. The reader can gain CME points. Submitted full papers will be reviewed by the editors and also by at least two external experts (peer review "system). The manuscripts are also subject to a scientific and editorial work by the editor. Emphases on quality assurance are addressed, current controversies are discussed in general medicine, present studies from general practice and international studies. The ZFA is presented in the target group as a suitable forum for education and training.
Language(s): German
ADVERTISING RATES:
Full Page Mono .... EUR 1500
Mechanical Data: Type Area: 266 x 168 mm, No. of Columns (Display): 2, Col Widths (Display): 82 mm
Copy instructions: *Copy Date:* 28 days prior to publication
Official Journal of: Organ d. Dt. Ges. f. Allg.- u. Familienmedizin u. d. Ges. d. Hochschullehrer f. Allgemeinmedizin u. d. Salzburger Ges. f. Allgemeinmedizin
BUSINESS: HEALTH & MEDICAL

ZFA ZEITSCHRIFT FÜR ARBEITSRECHT 748843G44-2840
Editorial: Breite Str. 29, 10178 BERLIN
Tel: 30 20331210 **Fax:** 30 20332210
Email: redaktion.zfa@bda-online.de
Freq: Quarterly; **Annual Sub.:** EUR 125,00; **Circ:** 770
Editor: Barbara Braun
Profile: Journal about all aspects of employment rights.
Language(s): German
Readership: Aimed at members of the legal profession.
ADVERTISING RATES:
Full Page Mono .... EUR 789
Full Page Colour .... EUR 1683
Mechanical Data: Type Area: 195 x 130 mm
BUSINESS: LEGAL

ZFB ZEITSCHRIFT FÜR BETRIEBSWIRTSCHAFT
748847G14A-9140
Editorial: Abraham-Lincoln-Str. 46, 65189 WIESBADEN **Tel:** 611 7878232 **Fax:** 611 7878411
Email: annelie.meisenheimer@springer.com **Web site:** http://www.zfb-online.de
Freq: 11 issues yearly; **Annual Sub.:** EUR 218,00; **Circ:** 1,200
Editor: Annelie Meisenheimer; **Advertising Manager:** Yvonne Guderjahn
Profile: Magazine providing trendsetting knowledge in all fields of business economy.
Language(s): German
ADVERTISING RATES:
Full Page Mono .... EUR 800
Full Page Colour .... EUR 1700
Mechanical Data: Type Area: 190 x 125 mm
Copy instructions: *Copy Date:* 45 days prior to publication

ZFBF 748844G14A-9160
Editorial: Grafenberger Allee 293, 40237 DÜSSELDORF **Tel:** 211 8871427 **Fax:** 211 8871420
Email: p.hanser@fachverlag.de **Web site:** http://www.zfbf.de
Freq: 8 issues yearly; **Annual Sub.:** EUR 180,00; **Circ:** 2,700
Editor: Peter Hanser; **Advertising Manager:** Ralf Pötzsch
Profile: Business Research magazine. Information about the areas of accounting, finance, marketing, decision theory and new institutional economics.
Language(s): German
ADVERTISING RATES:
Full Page Mono .... EUR 1280
Full Page Colour .... EUR 2330
Mechanical Data: Type Area: 203 x 140 mm
Copy instructions: *Copy Date:* 25 days prior to publication
Official Journal of: Organ d. Schmalenbach-Ges. f. Betriebswirtschaft e.V.
BUSINESS: COMMERCE, INDUSTRY & MANAGEMENT

ZFBR ZEITSCHRIFT FÜR DEUTSCHES UND INTERNATIONALES BAU- UND VERGABERECHT 748845G44-385
Editorial: Meinekestr. 26, 10719 BERLIN
Email: zfbr-redaktionberlin@gmx.net
Freq: 8 issues yearly; **Annual Sub.:** EUR 205,80; **Circ:** 1,000
Editor: Hans-Georg Watzke
Profile: Official publication of the German Society for Building Laws and International Building Rights.
Language(s): German
ADVERTISING RATES:
Full Page Mono .... EUR 1660
Full Page Colour .... EUR 3310
Mechanical Data: Type Area: 260 x 186 mm, No. of Columns (Display): 4, Col Widths (Display): 43 mm
BUSINESS: LEGAL

ZFE ZEITSCHRIFT FÜR FAMILIEN- UND ERBRECHT
1605933G1A-3481
Editorial: Feldstiege 100, 48161 MÜNSTER
Tel: 2533 9300205 **Fax:** 2533 930055205
Email: karin.spriestersbach@lexisnexis.de **Web site:** http://www.zap-verlag.de
Freq: Monthly; **Annual Sub.:** EUR 151,20; **Circ:** 1,300

Editor: Karin Spriestersbach; **Advertising Manager:** Anja Christensen
Profile: Magazine for jurists.
Language(s): German
ADVERTISING RATES:
Full Page Mono .... EUR 600
Full Page Colour .... EUR 1350
Mechanical Data: Type Area: 263 x 170 mm
Copy instructions: *Copy Date:* 14 days prior to publication

ZFGG ZEITSCHRIFT FÜR DAS GESAMTE GENOSSENSCHAFTSWESEN
748632G14A-9348
Editorial: Findelgasse 7/9, 90402 NÜRNBERG
Tel: 911 20555922 **Fax:** 911 20555920
Email: redaktion@zfgg.de **Web site:** http://www.zfgg.de
Freq: Half-yearly; **Annual Sub.:** EUR 69,00; **Circ:** 450
Editor: Volker H. Peemöller
Profile: The magazine for the entire cooperative system (ZfgG) has set itself the task of questions and problems from the entire range of interdisciplinary cooperative system from an economic, managerial, legal and sociological perspective to deal with.
Language(s): German
ADVERTISING RATES:
Full Page Mono .... EUR 450
Mechanical Data: Type Area: 190 x 113 mm
Official Journal of: Organ f. Kooperationsforschung u. -praxis i. A. d. Genossenschaftsinst.'e an d. Univ.'en Erlangen-Nürnberg, Freiburg (Schweiz), Gießen, Hamburg, Hohenheim, Köln, Marburg, Münster, Wien

ZFK ZEITUNG FÜR KOMMUNALE WIRTSCHAFT
748849G58-164_50
Editorial: Neumarkter Str. 87, 81673 MÜNCHEN
Tel: 89 4319850 **Fax:** 89 4312258
Email: info@zfk.de **Web site:** http://www.zfk.de
Freq: Monthly; **Annual Sub.:** EUR 42,00; **Circ:** 14,555
Editor: Jürgen Pott; **News Editor:** Jadwiga Adamiak; **Advertising Manager:** Klaus Schachmayer
Profile: Journal covering news about energy, water and the environment.
Language(s): German
Readership: Read mainly by university graduates.
ADVERTISING RATES:
Full Page Mono .... EUR 10453
Full Page Colour .... EUR 15157
Mechanical Data: Type Area: 470 x 316 mm, No. of Columns (Display): 5, Col Widths (Display): 60 mm
Copy instructions: *Copy Date:* 30 days prior to publication
BUSINESS: ENERGY, FUEL & NUCLEAR

ZFO ZEITSCHRIFT FÜHRUNG + ORGANISATION
748850G14A-9180
Editorial: Universitätsstr. 14, 48143 MÜNSTER
Tel: 251 8322831 **Fax:** 251 8322836
Email: zfo@wiwi.uni-muenster.de **Web site:** http://www.zfo.de
Freq: 6 issues yearly; **Annual Sub.:** EUR 89,00; **Circ:** 4,700
Editor: Gerhard Schewe; **Advertising Manager:** Petra Bourscheid
Profile: Magazine about management and organisation in business.
Language(s): German
ADVERTISING RATES:
Full Page Mono .... EUR 2025
Full Page Colour .... EUR 3067
Mechanical Data: Type Area: 237 x 182 mm
Copy instructions: *Copy Date:* 30 days prior to publication

ZFPR ZEITSCHRIFT FÜR PERSONALVERTRETUNGS-RECHT
748727G44-2640
Editorial: Dreizehnmorgenweg 36, 53175 BONN
Tel: 228 3077890 **Fax:** 228 3077839
Email: zfpr-schriftleitung@dbb.de
Freq: Quarterly; Free to qualifying individuals
Annual Sub.: EUR 31,90; **Circ:** 19,536
Editor: Susanne Süllwold; **Advertising Manager:** Katy Netz
Profile: Journal for Staff Council members with information for the Staff Council practice.
Language(s): German
ADVERTISING RATES:
Full Page Mono .... EUR 2980
Full Page Colour .... EUR 2980
Mechanical Data: Type Area: 276 x 185 mm, No. of Columns (Display): 3, Col Widths (Display): 56 mm
BUSINESS: LEGAL

ZFP-ZEITUNG
748851G19A-1040
Editorial: Max-Planck-Str. 6, 12489 BERLIN
Tel: 30 67807103 **Fax:** 30 67807109
Email: zeitung@dgzfp.de **Web site:** http://www.dgzfp.de
Freq: 5 issues yearly; **Circ:** 3,300
Editor: Franziska Ahrens; **Advertising Manager:** Dörte Schnitger
Profile: Journal of holding the companies DGZfP, ÖGfZP and SGZP, specialist journal for Nondestructive Testing.
Language(s): German

ADVERTISING RATES:
Full Page Mono .... EUR 850
Full Page Colour .... EUR 1200
Mechanical Data: Type Area: 240 x 170 mm, No. of Columns (Display): 3, Col Widths (Display): 54 mm
Copy instructions: *Copy Date:* 24 days prior to publication

Z.F.R ZEITSCHRIFT FÜR REFERENDARE
748853G44-3163
Editorial: Böllerts Höfe 3, 45479 MÜLHEIM
Tel: 208 426502 **Fax:** 208 428271
Email: verlag@weimannpresse.de **Web site:** http://www.weimannpresse.de
Freq: Half-yearly; **Cover Price:** EUR 8,90; **Circ:** 8,000
Editor: Thomas Weimann
Profile: Legal journal focusing on referenda.
Language(s): German
Readership: Aimed at judges and legal professionals.
ADVERTISING RATES:
Full Page Mono .... EUR 2200
Full Page Colour .... EUR 3300
Mechanical Data: Type Area: 220 x 160 mm
BUSINESS: LEGAL

ZFSH/SGB
1882051G1A-3766
Editorial: Freisinger Str. 3, 85716 UNTERSCHLEISSHEIM **Tel:** 89 360070
Fax: 89 360073320
Web site: http://www.wolterskluwer.de
Freq: Monthly; **Annual Sub.:** EUR 194,00; **Circ:** 1,150
Profile: Social law in Germany and Europe.
Language(s): German
ADVERTISING RATES:
Full Page Mono .... EUR 1000
Full Page Colour .... EUR 2065
Mechanical Data: Type Area: 246 x 162 mm
Copy instructions: *Copy Date:* 28 days prior to publication

ZFSÖ ZEITSCHRIFT FÜR SOZIALÖKONOMIE
748751G1R-5700
Editorial: Salbeistr. 27, 26129 OLDENBURG
Tel: 441 36111797
Email: onken@sozialoekonomie.info **Web site:** http://www.sozialoekonomie-online.de
Freq: Quarterly; **Annual Sub.:** EUR 20,00; **Circ:** 1,200
Editor: Werner Onken; **Advertising Manager:** Christoph Gauke
Profile: Journal focusing on economic, social, financial and monetary policies.
Language(s): German
Readership: Aimed at financial specialists.
ADVERTISING RATES:
Full Page Mono .... EUR 155
Mechanical Data: Type Area: 203 x 140 mm, No. of Columns (Display): 2, Col Widths (Display): 68 mm
Copy instructions: *Copy Date:* 30 days prior to publication
BUSINESS: FINANCE & ECONOMICS: Financial Related

ZFV
748769G4C-5
Editorial: Im Tal 12, 86179 AUGSBURG
Tel: 821 2598911 **Fax:** 821 2598999
Email: juergen.mueller@dvw.de **Web site:** http://www.wissner.com/zfv
Freq: 6 issues yearly; Free to qualifying individuals
Annual Sub.: EUR 70,00; **Circ:** 8,100
Editor: Jürgen Müller; **Advertising Manager:** Sabine Schalwig
Profile: The technical-scientific journal for geodesy, geoinformation and land management reports on new developments in calculation methods, statistics and curve fitting, geodesy, land surveying, photogrammetry and remote sensing methods of positioning and navigation, engineering geodesy and special areas of surveying, GIS, cartography, land registry, land, land development, urban and regional planning, land management, valuation, management, organization and law, and basic science and neighboring.
Language(s): English; German
ADVERTISING RATES:
Full Page Mono .... EUR 1420
Full Page Colour .... EUR 1840
Mechanical Data: Type Area: 263 x 174 mm, No. of Columns (Display): 2, Col Widths (Display): 84 mm
Copy instructions: *Copy Date:* 30 days prior to publication
BUSINESS: ARCHITECTURE & BUILDING: Surveying

ZFW ZEITSCHRIFT FÜR WASSERRECHT
748859G44-2920
Editorial: Universitätsring 15, 54286 TRIER
Tel: 651 2012578 **Fax:** 651 2012580
Email: reinharm@uni-trier.de **Web site:** http://www.wasserrecht.uni-trier.de
Freq: Quarterly; **Annual Sub.:** EUR 128,30; **Circ:** 750
Editor: Michael Reinhardt
Profile: Legal journal relating to water.
Language(s): German
ADVERTISING RATES:
Full Page Mono .... EUR 583
Full Page Colour .... EUR 1435
Mechanical Data: Type Area: 195 x 130 mm
BUSINESS: LEGAL

ZFZ ZEITSCHRIFT FÜR ZÖLLE UND VERBRAUCHSTEUERN
748860G1M-14
Editorial: Dechenstr. 7, 53115 BONN **Tel:** 228 7240
Fax: 228 72493081
Email: info@stollfuss.de **Web site:** http://www.stollfuss.de
Freq: Monthly; **Circ:** 1,300
Editor: Reinhart Rüsken; **Advertising Manager:** Carsten Priesel
Profile: Journal about customs and excise duties.
Language(s): German
ADVERTISING RATES:
Full Page Mono .... EUR 1250
Full Page Colour .... EUR 1875
Mechanical Data: Type Area: 260 x 180 mm, No. of Columns (Display): 2, Col Widths (Display): 88 mm
Copy instructions: *Copy Date:* 21 days prior to publication
BUSINESS: FINANCE & ECONOMICS: Taxation

ZGM ZEITUNGSGRUPPE MÜNSTERLAND
1660638G67B-16738
Editorial: An der Hansalinie 1, 48163 MÜNSTER
Tel: 251 6900 **Fax:** 251 690717
Email: redaktion@zgm-muensterland.de **Web site:** http://www.zgm-muensterland.de
Freq: 260 issues yearly; **Circ:** 231,800
Editor: Norbert Tiemann; **News Editor:** Michael Giese; **Advertising Manager:** Sven Schubert
Profile: Regional daily newspaper covering politics, economics, culture, sports, travel and technology.
Language(s): German
ADVERTISING RATES:
SCC .... EUR 368,90
Mechanical Data: Type Area: 488 x mm, No. of Columns (Display): 7
Copy instructions: *Copy Date:* 1 day prior to publication
REGIONAL DAILY & SUNDAY NEWSPAPERS: Regional Daily Newspapers

ZGN ZEITSCHRIFT FÜR GEBURTSHILFE & NEONATOLOGIE
748662G56A-10580
Editorial: Rüdigerstr. 14, 70469 STUTTGART
Tel: 711 89310 **Fax:** 711 8931392
Email: zgn@thieme.de **Web site:** http://www.thieme.de/zgn
Freq: 6 issues yearly; Free to qualifying individuals
Annual Sub.: EUR 316,90; **Circ:** 1,450
Editor: Stephan Schmidt
Profile: Reliable supply from the beginning. The ZGN Zeitschrift für Geburtshilfe & Neonatologie accompanies you from the beginning: From the beginning of prenatal care to the confinement. Overview: Current research and development in obstetrics and neonatology. Unique: the only German-language journal in this specialty.
Language(s): German
ADVERTISING RATES:
Full Page Mono .... EUR 1350
Full Page Colour .... EUR 2460
Mechanical Data: Type Area: 248 x 175 mm, No. of Columns (Display): 3, Col Widths (Display): 55 mm
Official Journal of: Organ d. Dt. Ges. f. perinatale Medizin
BUSINESS: HEALTH & MEDICAL

ZGS ZEITSCHRIFT FÜR VERTRAGSGESTALTUNG, SCHULD- UND HAFTUNGSRECHT
1605932G1A-3480
Editorial: Feldstiege 100, 48161 MÜNSTER
Tel: 2533 9300687 **Fax:** 2533 930050
Email: matthias.uhlmann@lexisnexis.de **Web site:** http://www.zap-verlag.de
Freq: Monthly; **Annual Sub.:** EUR 201,20; **Circ:** 1,500
Editor: Hans Schulte-Nölke; **Advertising Manager:** Anja Christensen
Profile: Magazine for lawyers specialised in law of obligations.
Language(s): German
ADVERTISING RATES:
Full Page Mono .... EUR 1200
Full Page Colour .... EUR 1950
Mechanical Data: Type Area: 249 x 170 mm
Copy instructions: *Copy Date:* 14 days prior to publication

ZHH-INFORMATION
1826566G27-3060
Editorial: Eichendorffstr. 3, 40474 DÜSSELDORF
Tel: 211 470500 **Fax:** 211 4705029
Email: zhh@hartwaren.de **Web site:** http://www.zhh.de
Freq: 10 issues yearly; Free to qualifying individuals
Annual Sub.: EUR 51,49; **Circ:** 1,500
Editor: Stephanie Kawan; **Advertising Manager:** Claudia Koch
Profile: Magazine about the work of the Association for Trade in Goods.
Language(s): German
ADVERTISING RATES:
Full Page Mono .... EUR 750
Full Page Colour .... EUR 1290
Copy instructions: *Copy Date:* 14 days prior to publication

ZHR ZEITSCHRIFT FÜR DAS GESAMTE HANDELSRECHT UND WIRTSCHAFTSRECHT
748862G44-2940
Editorial: Adenauerallee 24, 53113 BONN
Email: karsten.schmidt@law-school.de
Freq: 6 issues yearly; **Annual Sub.:** EUR 319,00; **Circ:** 2,000
Editor: Karsten Schmidt; **Advertising Manager:** Marion Gertzen
Profile: Journal about the law relating to trade and commerce.
Language(s): German
ADVERTISING RATES:
Full Page Mono .... EUR 1065
Full Page Colour .... EUR 1625
Mechanical Data: Type Area: 190 x 118 mm
Copy instructions: *Copy Date:* 21 days prior to publication
BUSINESS: LEGAL

ZI ZIEGELINDUSTRIE INTERNATIONAL
748867G4E-6780
Editorial: Avenwedder Str. 55, 33335 GÜTERSLOH
Tel: 5241 8089264 **Fax:** 5241 80689264
Email: anett.fischer@bauverlag.de **Web site:** http://www.zi-international.com
Freq: 10 issues yearly; **Annual Sub.:** EUR 237,60; **Circ:** 4,857
Editor: Anett Fischer; **Advertising Manager:** Ingo Wanders
Profile: Zi Brick and Tile Industry International is considered by experts in the field to be the leading journal for the entire sector of the heavy clay industry, - clay bricks and tiles, vitrified clay pipes, the refractory and structural ceramics industries. Articles by noteworthy scientists and well-versed practitioners deal here with all questions and process innovations in regard to the production of heavy clay products - from the extraction of the raw material to the preparation and shaping up to the drying, firing and packaging methods. Considerable space is devoted to reporting on current problems. The journal informs the professionals on important structural problems and economic and social issues. The close links of the journal with the scientific research institutes provide a particularly broad basis for an exchange of experience with science and practice throughout the entire world. Since changing over to a complete German-English text the Zi Brick and Tile Industry International with the attainment meanwhile of worldwide circulation has developed in fact into the most highly regarded international journal in this sector. target group: brick plant. This Outlet offers RSS (Really Simple Syndication).
Language(s): English; German
ADVERTISING RATES:
Full Page Mono .... EUR 2380
Full Page Colour .... EUR 3525
Mechanical Data: Type Area: 270 x 190 mm, No. of Columns (Display): 4, Col Widths (Display): 45 mm
Copy instructions: *Copy Date:* 14 days prior to publication
BUSINESS: ARCHITECTURE & BUILDING: Building

ZIELPUNKTE REISEN
740214G89A-3820
Editorial: Eberle-Kögl-Str. 6, 87616 MARKTOBERDORF **Tel:** 8342 96420
Fax: 8342 964220
Email: service@zielpunkte.de **Web site:** http://www.zielpunkte.de
Freq: Annual; **Cover Price:** Free; **Circ:** 5,300
Editor: Herbert Kauer
Profile: Manual about group travel to Bavaria, Baden-Wuerttemberg, Austria and South Tyrol.
Language(s): German
ADVERTISING RATES:
Full Page Mono .... EUR 1190
Full Page Colour .... EUR 1190
Mechanical Data: No. of Columns (Display): 2, Col Widths (Display): 63 mm, Type Area: 190 x 130 mm
Copy instructions: *Copy Date:* 40 days prior to publication

ZI-JAHRBUCH
1635502G4E-6976
Editorial: Avenwedder Str. 55, 33335 GÜTERSLOH
Tel: 5241 8090884 **Fax:** 5241 80690880
Email: anett.fischer@bauverlag.de **Web site:** http://www.bauverlag.de
Freq: Annual; **Cover Price:** EUR 37,00; **Circ:** 3,000
Editor: Anett Fischer; **Advertising Manager:** Ingo Wanders
Profile: Magazine on production and application of architectural ceramics.
Language(s): English; German
ADVERTISING RATES:
Full Page Colour .... EUR 2995
Mechanical Data: Type Area: 270 x 190 mm

DER ZIMMERMANN
748879G46-176
Editorial: Stolberger Str. 84, 50933 KÖLN
Tel: 221 5497195 **Fax:** 221 5497326
Email: red.zimmermann@rudolf-mueller.de **Web site:** http://www.rudolf-mueller.de
Freq: Monthly; **Annual Sub.:** EUR 80,00; **Circ:** 10,259
Editor: Peter Kübler; **Advertising Manager:** Elke Herbst
Profile: Journal covering the carpentry trade.
Language(s): German
ADVERTISING RATES:
Full Page Mono .... EUR 2495

Full Page Colour .... EUR 4520
Mechanical Data: Type Area: 267 x 188 mm, No. of Columns (Display): 4, Col Widths (Display): 44 mm
Copy instructions: *Copy Date:* 20 days prior to publication
BUSINESS: TIMBER, WOOD & FORESTRY

ZINSO ZEITSCHRIFT FÜR DAS GESAMTE INSOLVENZRECHT
748633G44-3160
Editorial: Feldstiege 100, 48161 MÜNSTER
Tel: 2533 9300672 **Fax:** 2533 930050
Email: regina.dick@lexisnexis.de **Web site:** http://www.lexisnexis.de/zinso-zeitschrift
Freq: Weekly; **Annual Sub.:** EUR 615,00; **Circ:** 1,800
Editor: Hans Haarmeyer; **Advertising Manager:** Anja Christensen
Profile: Magazine providing information about the law concerning insolvency.
Language(s): German
Readership: Read by lawyers, liquidators and auditors.
ADVERTISING RATES:
Full Page Mono .... EUR 1345
Full Page Colour .... EUR 1945
Mechanical Data: Type Area: 249 x 174 mm
Copy instructions: *Copy Date:* 14 days prior to publication
BUSINESS: LEGAL

ZIR ZEITSCHRIFT INTERNE REVISION
748886G1M-170
Editorial: Ohmstr. 59, 60486 FRANKFURT
Tel: 69 7137690 **Fax:** 69 71376969
Email: info@diir.de **Web site:** http://www.zirdigital.de
Freq: 6 issues yearly; **Annual Sub.:** EUR 74,47; **Circ:** 3,500
Editor: Volker Hampel; **Advertising Manager:** Peter Taprogge
Profile: Professional contributions to date and to inform the future development of internal auditing while supporting the professional qualification and training. Against the background of legal and organizational initiatives ZIR the work of internal audit supports the concept of corporate governance and cooperation with other internal and external organs, institutions and professions.
Language(s): German
ADVERTISING RATES:
Full Page Mono .... EUR 1600
Full Page Colour .... EUR 2500
Mechanical Data: Type Area: 262 x 192 mm
Copy instructions: *Copy Date:* 18 days prior to publication
BUSINESS: FINANCE & ECONOMICS: Taxation

ZITTAUER WOCHENKURIER
748888G72-16684
Editorial: Wettiner Platz 10, 01067 DRESDEN
Tel: 351 491760 **Fax:** 351 4917674
Email: wochenkurier-dresden@dwk-verlag.de **Web site:** http://www.wochenkurier.info
Freq: Weekly; **Cover Price:** Free; **Circ:** 33,234
Editor: Regine Eberlein; **Advertising Manager:** Andreas Schönherr
Profile: Advertising journal (house-to-house) concentrating on local stories.
Language(s): German
ADVERTISING RATES:
Full Page Mono .... EUR 2980
Full Page Colour .... EUR 4172
Mechanical Data: Type Area: 430 x 290 mm, No. of Columns (Display): 7, Col Widths (Display): 38 mm
Copy instructions: *Copy Date:* 5 days prior to publication
LOCAL NEWSPAPERS

ZITTY BERLIN
1641068G80-14183
Editorial: Askanischer Platz 3, 10963 BERLIN
Tel: 30 290211860 **Fax:** 30 2902199918690
Email: redaktion@zitty.de **Web site:** http://www.urban-media-daten.de
Freq: Daily; **Cover Price:** Paid; **Circ:** 199,611 Unique Users
Editor: Kai Röger; **Advertising Manager:** Gerd Stodiek
Profile: Ezine: Magazine for city and region, concentrating on events, gastronomy, music, arts and events.
Language(s): German
CONSUMER: RURAL & REGIONAL INTEREST

ZITTY BERLIN
748889G89C-4835
Editorial: Askanischer Platz 3, 10963 BERLIN
Tel: 30 290210 **Fax:** 30 2902199941090
Email: redaktion@zitty.de **Web site:** http://www.zitty.de
Freq: 26 issues yearly; **Annual Sub.:** EUR 63,00; **Circ:** 34,676
Editor: Kai Röger; **Advertising Manager:** Bernd Maywald
Profile: Berlin entertainment guide covering music, cinema, theatre, literature, art and politics.
Language(s): German
ADVERTISING RATES:
Full Page Mono .... EUR 4800
Full Page Colour .... EUR 7100
Mechanical Data: Type Area: 260 x 190 mm, No. of Columns (Display): 4, Col Widths (Display): 44 mm
Copy instructions: *Copy Date:* 9 days prior to publication
CONSUMER: HOLIDAYS & TRAVEL: Entertainment Guides

ZKG INTERNATIONAL
748898G30-170
Editorial: Avenwedder Str. 55, 33335 GÜTERSLOH
Tel: 5241 8089366 **Fax:** 5241 80689366
Email: petra.strunk@bauverlag.de **Web site:** http://www.zkg-online.info
Freq: Monthly; **Annual Sub.:** EUR 387,60; **Circ:** 3,721
Editor: Petra Strunk; **Advertising Manager:** Christian Reinke
Profile: ZKG International has been more than eight decades as the leading international trade journal for the entire binder industry and its suppliers in the mechanical and plant engineering. The journal reports on the material basis of the binding cement building materials, lime and gypsum, the procedures of extraction and processing, the thermal and mechanical processes and the production control and quality control. The focus is on developments especially those which serve to improve production, reduce energy consumption, increase quality and improve environmental protection. With the technical and scientific treatment of new processes, their description and presentation of their performance and profitability, with reports and the publication of practical experience with new plant facilities in the world, with ZKG International is to inform professionals at home and abroad to date about their profession. In addition reports on innovations to companies, trade fairs, trade events, textbooks and personal. ZKG International is the magazine for the job market of cement, lime and plaster works and their related equipment industry.
Language(s): English; German
ADVERTISING RATES:
Full Page Mono .... EUR 2150
Full Page Colour .... EUR 3430
Mechanical Data: Type Area: 270 x 186 mm, No. of Columns (Display): 4, Col Widths (Display): 45 mm
Copy instructions: *Copy Date:* 12 days prior to publication
Official Journal of: Organ d. Bundesverb. d. Dt. Kalkindustrie u. d. Bundesverb. d. Gipsindustrie
BUSINESS: MINING & QUARRYING

ZLR
748899G44-2960
Editorial: Esplanade 41, 20354 HAMBURG
Tel: 40 356100 **Fax:** 40 35610180
Email: jagow@krohnlegal.de **Web site:** http://www.krohnlegal.de
Freq: 6 issues yearly; **Annual Sub.:** EUR 420,00; **Circ:** 800
Editor: Carl von Jagow; **Advertising Manager:** Marion Gertzen
Profile: Magazine about the law relating to food.
Language(s): German
ADVERTISING RATES:
Full Page Mono .... EUR 1390
Mechanical Data: Type Area: 200 x 135 mm
Copy instructions: *Copy Date:* 14 days prior to publication
BUSINESS: LEGAL

ZM ZAHNÄRZTLICHE MITTEILUNGEN
748942G56D-1160
Editorial: Behrenstr. 42, 10117 BERLIN
Tel: 30 28017949 **Fax:** 30 28017942
Email: e.maibach-nagel@zm-online.de **Web site:** http://www.zm-online.de
Freq: 24 issues yearly; **Annual Sub.:** EUR 168,00; **Circ:** 84,467
Editor: Egbert Maibach-Nagel; **Advertising Manager:** Marga Pinsdorf
Profile: zm – Zahnärztliche Mitteilungen (Dental News) is the official publication of the German Dental Association (Bundeszahnärztekammer, BZÄK) and the National Association of Statutory Health Insurance Dentists (Kassenzahnärztliche Bundesvereinigung, KZBV) and is sent out to all dentists in Germany. Content - Covers the full range of professional, health and social policies - Comprehensive scientific continuing-education section - Current topics in office management, including IT, business and law Special features - Interactive dental training based on the BZÄK and DGZMK training concepts - Comprehensive reader services with additional material and background information - Most copies are delivered to recipients' home addresses - Advertisements can be placed in Editions A and B separately - Classifieds appear in Edition A only - The target group includes all German dentists - zm is the only journal that reaches assistant dentists/interns.
Language(s): German
ADVERTISING RATES:
Full Page Mono .... EUR 5400
Full Page Colour .... EUR 7400
Mechanical Data: Type Area: 260 x 185 mm, No. of Columns (Display): 4, Col Widths (Display): 45 mm
Copy instructions: *Copy Date:* 12 days prior to publication
Supplement(s): ReiseMagazin
BUSINESS: HEALTH & MEDICAL: Dental

ZMK
748900G56D-1180
Editorial: Ammonitenstr. 1, 72336 BALINGEN
Tel: 7433 952319 **Fax:** 7433 952442
Email: redaktion@spitta.de **Web site:** http://www.zmk-aktuell.de
Freq: 10 issues yearly; **Annual Sub.:** EUR 62,00; **Circ:** 37,701
Editor: Ulrike Oßwald-Dame; **Advertising Manager:** Carolyn Piele
Profile: Journal covering dental care and practice management. Provides a forum for discussion, includes details of conferences and lifestyle articles.
Language(s): German
ADVERTISING RATES:
Full Page Mono .... EUR 4500
Full Page Colour .... EUR 5600
Mechanical Data: Type Area: 255 x 180 mm, No. of Columns (Display): 3, Col Widths (Display): 50 mm
Copy instructions: *Copy Date:* 34 days prior to publication
BUSINESS: HEALTH & MEDICAL: Dental

ZMR ZEITSCHRIFT FÜR MIET- UND RAUMRECHT
748940G44-2980
Editorial: Luxemburger Str. 449, 50939 KÖLN
Tel: 221 943737000 **Fax:** 221 943737201
Email: info@wolterskluwer.de **Web site:** http://www.wolterskluwer.de
Freq: Monthly; **Annual Sub.:** EUR 210,00; **Circ:** 2,800
Editor: Joachim Rau
Profile: Magazine about the law relating to tenancies and property.
Language(s): German
ADVERTISING RATES:
Full Page Mono .... EUR 1675
Full Page Colour .... EUR 2740
Mechanical Data: Type Area: 255 x 184 mm
Copy instructions: *Copy Date:* 21 days prior to publication
BUSINESS: LEGAL

ZNOTP ZEITSCHRIFT FÜR DIE NOTARPRAXIS
748944G44-3164
Editorial: Feldstiege 100, 48161 MÜNSTER
Tel: 2533 9300672 **Fax:** 2533 930050
Email: regina.dick@lexisnexis.de **Web site:** http://www.lexisnexis.de/znotp-zeitschrift
Freq: Monthly; **Annual Sub.:** EUR 172,00; **Circ:** 1,700
Editor: Norbert Frenz; **Advertising Manager:** Anja Christensen
Profile: Magazine providing information about all aspects of the legal profession.
Language(s): German
Readership: Aimed at solicitors.
ADVERTISING RATES:
Full Page Mono .... EUR 750
Full Page Colour .... EUR 1360
Mechanical Data: Type Area: 249 x 174 mm
Copy instructions: *Copy Date:* 20 days prior to publication
BUSINESS: LEGAL

ZÖGU ZEITSCHRIFT FÜR ÖFFENTLICHE UND GEMEINWIRTSCHAFTLICHE UNTERNEHMEN
748716G32A-7060
Editorial: Albertus-Magnus-Platz, 50923 KÖLN
Tel: 221 4706615 **Fax:** 221 4704999
Email: redaktion-zoegu@uni-koeln.de **Web site:** http://www.zoegu.de
Freq: Quarterly; **Annual Sub.:** EUR 133,31; **Circ:** 1,000
Editor: Frank Schulz-Nieswandt
Profile: Magazine about public service and municipal administration.
Language(s): German
Readership: Aimed at local government officials.
ADVERTISING RATES:
Full Page Mono .... EUR 650
Full Page Colour .... EUR 1775
Mechanical Data: Type Area: 186 x 118 mm
Copy instructions: *Copy Date:* 35 days prior to publication
Official Journal of: Organ d. Bundesverb. Öffentl. Dienstleistungen - Dt. Sektion d. CEEP e.V.
BUSINESS: LOCAL GOVERNMENT, LEISURE & RECREATION: Local Government

ZOLLERN-ALB KURIER
748950G67B-16360
Editorial: Grünewaldstr. 15, 72336 BALINGEN
Tel: 7433 266105 **Fax:** 7433 266118
Email: zak@zak.de **Web site:** http://www.zak.de
Freq: 312 issues yearly; **Circ:** 23,164
Advertising Manager: Kevin Jetter
Profile: Daily newspaper with regional news and a local sports section.
Language(s): German
ADVERTISING RATES:
SCC .... EUR 78,20
Mechanical Data: Type Area: 480 x 321 mm, No. of Columns (Display): 7, Col Widths (Display): 44 mm
Copy instructions: *Copy Date:* 1 day prior to publication
REGIONAL DAILY & SUNDAY NEWSPAPERS: Regional Daily Newspapers

DER ZOOLOGISCHE GARTEN
748960G64F-2640
Editorial: Am Tierpark 125, 10307 BERLIN
Tel: 30 51531104 **Fax:** 30 5124061
Freq: 6 issues yearly; **Annual Sub.:** EUR 129,00
Editor: Wolfgang Grummt
Profile: Journal about zoo biology. Covers breeding and keeping of zoo animals, behavioural science, veterinary medicine and book reviews.
Language(s): English; German
Official Journal of: Organ d. Verb. Dt. Zoodirektoren u. d. World Association of Zoos & Aquariums
BUSINESS: OTHER CLASSIFICATIONS: Biology

ZOOLOGISCHER ANZEIGER
748961G64F-2660
Editorial: Invalidenstr. 43, 10115 BERLIN
Email: carsten.lueter@mfn-berlin.de
Freq: Quarterly; **Annual Sub.:** EUR 178,00
Editor: Carsten Lüter
Profile: Magazine containing information on all aspects of zoology.
Language(s): English
BUSINESS: OTHER CLASSIFICATIONS: Biology

ZP ZAHNARZT & PRAXIS
1697467G56D-1309
Editorial: Ammonitenstr. 1, 72336 BALINGEN
Tel: 7433 952194 **Fax:** 7433 952442
Email: redaktion@spitta.de **Web site:** http://www.zp-aktuell.de
Freq: 6 issues yearly; **Annual Sub.:** EUR 40,00; **Circ:** 24,800
Editor: Felix Blankenstein
Profile: The magazine covers with practical articles and case studies, the comprehensive dental topics. The section "For you read - Science for practice " is preparing to current issues of scholarly journals as a resume. Place for the discussion of controversial topics ("pros and cons"). The category "Miscell" includes guest commentaries, reclamation instructive failures and interesting short messages around the dentistry. In its "practice management" expert authors provide information on funding, patient loyalty, practice organization, billing tips, law and taxes. The category "Industry Report" presents industry news in dialogue with users and industry.
Language(s): German
ADVERTISING RATES:
Full Page Colour .... EUR 4000
Mechanical Data: Type Area: 250 x 160 mm
BUSINESS: HEALTH & MEDICAL: Dental

ZPA
748969G56A-11080
Editorial: Maaßstr. 32/1, 69123 HEIDELBERG
Tel: 6221 1377610 **Fax:** 6221 29910
Email: blumroeder@kaden-verlag.de **Web site:** http://www.kaden-verlag.de
Freq: 11 issues yearly; **Annual Sub.:** EUR 108,00; **Circ:** 5,000
Editor: Annelie Burk; **Advertising Manager:** Petra Hübler
Profile: Magazine about ophthalmology.
Language(s): German
ADVERTISING RATES:
Full Page Mono .... EUR 2205
Full Page Colour .... EUR 3540
Mechanical Data: Type Area: 230 x 178 mm, No. of Columns (Display): 3, Col Widths (Display): 56 mm
Copy instructions: *Copy Date:* 28 days prior to publication

ZUCKERRÜBE
748981G21A-4160
Editorial: Clemens-August-Str. 12, 53115 BONN
Tel: 228 9694230 **Fax:** 228 630311
Email: redaktion@dlg-agrofoodmedien.de **Web site:** http://www.dlg-agrofoodmedien.de
Freq: 6 issues yearly; **Annual Sub.:** EUR 41,80; **Circ:** 16,247
Editor: Heinz-Peter Pütz; **Advertising Manager:** Rainer Schluck
Profile: Magazine about sugar beet growing.
Language(s): German
ADVERTISING RATES:
Full Page Mono .... EUR 2652
Full Page Colour .... EUR 4642
Mechanical Data: Type Area: 270 x 186 mm, No. of Columns (Display): 3, Col Widths (Display): 58 mm
Official Journal of: Organ d. Dachverb. Norddt. Zuckerrübenanbauer e.V., d. Vereins d. Zuckerindustrie, Bezirksgruppe Nord, d. ArGe d. Diamant-Verbände u. d. Verb. Rübenanbauer im Lippe-Weser-Raum e.V.
BUSINESS: AGRICULTURE & FARMING

ZUCKERRÜBEN-MAGAZIN
1837116G21A-4398
Editorial: Marktbreiter Str. 74, 97199 OCHSENFURT
Tel: 9331 91875 **Fax:** 9331 91874
Email: dzz@vsz.de **Web site:** http://www.vsz.de
Freq: Half-yearly; **Circ:** 22,389
Editor: Gudrun Walther
Profile: Supplement of Zeitung für Zuckerrübenbauern, the paper for sugar beet farmers.
Language(s): German
Supplement to: dzz Die Zucker Rübenzeitung

ZUFALL REPORT
1772724G49A-2419
Editorial: Robert-Bosch-Breite 11, 37079 GÖTTINGEN **Tel:** 551 607271 **Fax:** 551 607244
Email: carolin.heinrichs@zufall.de **Web site:** http://www.zufall.de
Freq: 3 issues yearly; **Circ:** 6,800
Editor: Carolin Heinrichs
Profile: Company publication from the Friedrich Zufall GmbH & Co. KG for international transports.
Language(s): German

ZUFFENHÄUSER WOCHE
749013G72-16700
Editorial: Bessemerstr. 7, 70435 STUTTGART
Tel: 711 8200050 **Fax:** 711 8200059
Email: redaktion@eheinz.de **Web site:** http://www.eheinz.de
Freq: Weekly; **Cover Price:** Free; **Circ:** 29,980
Editor: Peter Heinz; **Advertising Manager:** Peter Heinz
Profile: Advertising journal (house-to-house) concentrating on local stories.
Language(s): German
ADVERTISING RATES:
Full Page Mono .... EUR 3090
Full Page Colour .... EUR 3289
Mechanical Data: Type Area: 485 x 320 mm, No. of Columns (Display): 7, Col Widths (Display): 43 mm
Copy instructions: *Copy Date:* 2 days prior to publication
LOCAL NEWSPAPERS

ZÜGE
748985G79B-1640
Editorial: Klosterring 9, 87660 IRSEE
Tel: 8341 73410 **Fax:** 8341 73472
Freq: 6 issues yearly; **Annual Sub.:** EUR 27,00; **Circ:** 17,849
Editor: Klaus Eckert
Profile: Club members of the Eisenbahn-Romantik-Club get Züge six times a year for free. The magazine is aimed at model railroaders and hobby railroaders.
Language(s): German
ADVERTISING RATES:
Full Page Mono .... EUR 1240
Full Page Colour .... EUR 1840
Mechanical Data: Type Area: 250 x 172 mm
Copy instructions: *Copy Date:* 28 days prior to publication
CONSUMER: HOBBIES & DIY: Models & Modelling

ZUHAUSE WOHNEN
749027G74C-3440
Editorial: Poßmoorweg 2, 22301 HAMBURG
Tel: 40 27173131 **Fax:** 40 27173566
Email: redaktion@zuhause-wohnen.de **Web site:** http://www.zuhausewohnen.de
Freq: Monthly; **Annual Sub.:** EUR 38,40; **Circ:** 137,875
Editor: Regine Kuhlei; **Advertising Manager:** Roberto Sprengel
Profile: Stay at home, feel comfortable, relax, breathe, recharge your batteries ... ZUHAUSE WOHNEN is a magazine for people who do just that. People who achieve a lot and look for compensation in a very special life and living quality. ZUHAUSE WOHNEN is the magazine for individual readers who perceive and set up their environment with emotion and understanding relaxed. ZUHAUSE WOHNEN is a concept for discerning readers who value a stylish interior design and are willing to invest time and money in it. ZUHAUSE WOHNEN stands for vivid reports, that show people and their homes, makes proposals by Germany's most prominent interior designers and so links as the only classic lifestyle magazine sensibility and aesthetics with service, creativity and competence.
Language(s): German
Readership: Aimed at women aged between 30 and 50 years old.
ADVERTISING RATES:
Full Page Mono .... EUR 20900
Full Page Colour .... EUR 20900
Mechanical Data: Type Area: 257 x 193 mm, No. of Columns (Display): 4, Col Widths (Display): 45 mm
Supplement(s): zuhause wohnen Extra
CONSUMER: WOMEN'S INTEREST CONSUMER MAGAZINES: Home & Family

ZUHAUSE WOHNEN EXTRA
734301G93-700
Editorial: Poßmoorweg 2, 22301 HAMBURG
Tel: 40 27173131 **Fax:** 40 27173566
Email: redaktion@zuhause-wohnen.de **Web site:** http://www.zuhausewohnen.de
Freq: Monthly; **Circ:** 225,100
Editor: Regine Kuhlei; **Advertising Manager:** Roberto Sprengel
Profile: The supplement appears - connected by a band - together with a stock issue of ZUHAUSE WOHNEN.
Language(s): German
Readership: Read by people interested in gardens and gardening.
ADVERTISING RATES:
Full Page Mono .... EUR 12900
Full Page Colour .... EUR 12900
Mechanical Data: Type Area: 257 x 193 mm, No. of Columns (Display): 4, Col Widths (Display): 45 mm
Supplement to: zuhause wohnen
CONSUMER: GARDENING

ZUKUNFT JETZT
1739904G32G-3113
Editorial: Ruhrstr. 2, 10709 BERLIN
Tel: 30 86589120 **Fax:** 30 86589425
Email: redaktion@zj-online.de **Web site:** http://www.deutsche-rentenversicherung.de
Freq: Quarterly; **Cover Price:** Free; **Circ:** 2,275,000
Editor: Dirk von der Heide; **Advertising Manager:** Walter Piezonka
Profile: "zukunft jetzt" is the common customer magazine of the German pension insurance carrier. Consistently applied in dialogue, the magazine's readers met at eye level. It offers a wide range of topics surrounding the future pension and health - informative and entertaining. In this way, the magazine carried the core elements of the brand German Pension: competence, integrity and reliability. The sections pension, retirement and health reflect the core competencies of the German pension insurance. Conversations, interviews and portraits are available for their proximity to the environment of the customers. forward now is the modern, forward-looking customer magazine of the German pension insurance. It stands for safety, reliability and highly competent consulting the statutory scheme in all matters related to pensions. The editorial concept of the magazine is based on the cornerstones of information, utility and emotion. The presentation is reputable and high quality. The magazine can compete with popular titles in the financial and health care. Core target group of forward now are 30 - to 55-year-old insured. Communication goal is to convince this audience of the reliability of the PAYG pension and the need for additional capital-funded pensions. In addition, the comprehensive rehabilitation services and counseling skills of the statutory pension insurance in various areas of pensions are highlighted. Pension Security and return, contributions and benefits. Everything about the state pension, the first pillar of retirement provision in Germany. Pensions Riester, Rürup or company pension. Tips and figures on government-sponsored pension plans and the free offerings of the capital market. Health Prevention and rehabilitation. Benefits of the statutory pension insurance for the preservation of health and labor. Dialogue At eye level. The pension insurance policyholders in discussion with experts and celebrities on current topics of the time.
Language(s): German
ADVERTISING RATES:
Full Page Mono .... EUR 19836
Full Page Colour .... EUR 19836
Mechanical Data: Type Area: 236 x 182 mm, No. of Columns (Display): 4, Col Widths (Display): 42 mm
Copy instructions: *Copy Date:* 50 days prior to publication
BUSINESS: LOCAL GOVERNMENT, LEISURE & RECREATION: Community Care & Social Services

ZUKUNFTSMOTOR METROPOLREGION RHEIN-NECKAR
2010123G14A-10456
Editorial: Finkenstr. 10, 68623 LAMPERTHEIM
Tel: 6206 9390 **Fax:** 6206 939232
Email: simon@alphapublic.de **Web site:** http://www.alphapublic.de
Freq: Annual; **Cover Price:** Free; **Circ:** 20,500
Editor: Marcus Veith; **Advertising Manager:** Marcus Veith
Profile: Magazin für Journalisten, Ministerien, Verwaltungen, Kommunen, Kreise und Städte in der Metropolenregion Rhein-Neckar.
Language(s): German
ADVERTISING RATES:
Full Page Colour .... EUR 2650

ZULIEFERMARKT FÜR KONSTRUKTEURE UND TECHNISCHE EINKÄUFER
749037G17-1539
Editorial: Kolbergerstr. 22, 81679 MÜNCHEN
Tel: 89 99830648 **Fax:** 89 99830623
Email: pfeiffer@hanser.de **Web site:** http://www.zuliefermarkt.de
Freq: 7 issues yearly; **Annual Sub.:** EUR 58,00; **Circ:** 25,315
Editor: Frank Pfeiffer; **Advertising Manager:** Regine Schmidt
Profile: Today designers and technical buyers decide on the future of OEM products in teams consisting of members from several departments. As the first technical journal for this target group, ZulieferMarkt für Konstrukteure und technische Einkäufer (SupplyMarket) has provided competently prepared, practice-oriented specialized information on all aspects of the selection and procurement of individual components, entire assemblies and complex systems for over 25 years now. Topics range from drive technology to drawing parts. Articles focus both on economy over the entire service life of the products and their procurement management and on technical properties. ZulieferMarkt für Konstrukteure und technische Einkäufer is the technical journal for designers and purchasing decision-makers, e.g. in vehicle, mechanical and systems engineering, in the metal and plastics processing industry and in the electrical engineering sector. This Outlet offers RSS (Really Simple Syndication).
Language(s): German
Readership: Aimed at electricians.
ADVERTISING RATES:
Full Page Mono .... EUR 4560
Full Page Colour .... EUR 6990
Mechanical Data: Type Area: 250 x 175 mm, No. of Columns (Display): 4, Col Widths (Display): 41 mm
Supplement(s): kataloge orange
BUSINESS: ELECTRICAL

ZUM ZEITSCHRIFT FÜR URHEBER- UND MEDIENRECHT
749043G44-3000
Editorial: Salvatorplatz 1, 80333 MÜNCHEN
Tel: 89 29195470 **Fax:** 89 29195480
Email: redaktion@urheberrecht.org **Web site:** http://www.urheberrecht.org
Freq: Monthly; **Annual Sub.:** EUR 381,76; **Circ:** 1,500
Editor: Jürgen Becker
Profile: Journal about publicity and film rights.
Language(s): German
ADVERTISING RATES:
Full Page Mono .... EUR 890
Full Page Colour .... EUR 2015
Mechanical Data: Type Area: 246 x 180 mm, No. of Columns (Display): 2, Col Widths (Display): 85 mm
Copy instructions: *Copy Date:* 30 days prior to publication
BUSINESS: LEGAL

ZUR ZEITSCHRIFT FÜR UMWELTRECHT
749046G44-3020
Editorial: Universitätsallee GWI, 28359 BREMEN
Tel: 421 21866109 **Fax:** 421 21866108
Email: zur@uni-bremen.de **Web site:** http://www.zeitschrift-fuer-umweltrecht.de
Freq: Monthly; **Annual Sub.:** EUR 292,40; **Circ:** 1,100
Editor: Wolfgang Köck
Profile: Journal focusing on environmental law.
Language(s): German
ADVERTISING RATES:
Full Page Mono .... EUR 760
Full Page Colour .... EUR 1885
Mechanical Data: Type Area: 277 x 190 mm
Copy instructions: *Copy Date:* 35 days prior to publication
BUSINESS: LEGAL

ZVG GARTENBAU REPORT
749058G26D-8
Editorial: Godesberger Allee 142, 53175 BONN
Tel: 228 8100238 **Fax:** 228 8100233
Email: zvg-report@g-net.de **Web site:** http://www.g-net.de
Freq: 10 issues yearly; Free to qualifying individuals
Annual Sub.: EUR 35,00; **Circ:** 11,500
Editor: Franz-J. Jäger
Profile: Magazine concerning all aspects of horticulture.
Language(s): German
ADVERTISING RATES:
Full Page Mono .... EUR 1600
Full Page Colour .... EUR 2590
Mechanical Data: Type Area: 245 x 184 mm, No. of Columns (Display): 3, Col Widths (Display): 58 mm
Copy instructions: *Copy Date:* 15 days prior to publication
BUSINESS: GARDEN TRADE: Garden Trade Horticulture

ZVO REPORT
1894257G27-3098
Editorial: Max-Volmer-Str. 1, 40724 HILDEN
Tel: 2103 255610 **Fax:** 2103 255625
Email: mail@zvo.org **Web site:** http://www.zvo.org
Freq: 5 issues yearly; Free to qualifying individuals
Annual Sub.: EUR 10,00; **Circ:** 4,500
Editor: Christoph Matheis; **Advertising Manager:** Wolfgang Locker
Profile: Magazine of the Central Association for Surfacing Technology.
Language(s): German
ADVERTISING RATES:
Full Page Mono .... EUR 1980
Full Page Colour .... EUR 1980
Mechanical Data: Type Area: 262 x 184 mm, No. of Columns (Display): 3, Col Widths (Display): 59 mm
Copy instructions: *Copy Date:* 30 days prior to publication

ZWEIRAD
749073G77A-2460
Editorial: Boxdorfer Str. 13, 90765 FÜRTH
Tel: 911 3072970 **Fax:** 911 30709771
Email: redaktion@zweirad-online.de **Web site:** http://www.zweirad-online.de
Freq: 11 issues yearly; **Cover Price:** Free; **Circ:** 26,300
Editor: Mathias Thomaschek; **Advertising Manager:** Mathias Thomaschek
Profile: Northern Bavaria motorcycle magazine with regional issues, reader operations, striking features and over several hundred private offers, requests and personal ads in free classifieds section.
Language(s): German
ADVERTISING RATES:
Full Page Mono .... EUR 990
Full Page Colour .... EUR 990
Mechanical Data: Type Area: 285 x 195 mm, No. of Columns (Display): 4, Col Widths (Display): 45 mm
Copy instructions: *Copy Date:* 10 days prior to publication

ZWEIRAD
749073G77A-2918
Editorial: Boxdorfer Str. 13, 90765 FÜRTH
Tel: 911 3072970 **Fax:** 911 30709771
Email: redaktion@zweirad-online.de **Web site:** http://www.zweirad-online.de
Freq: 11 issues yearly; **Cover Price:** Free; **Circ:** 26,300
Editor: Mathias Thomaschek; **Advertising Manager:** Mathias Thomaschek
Profile: Northern Bavaria motorcycle magazine with regional issues, reader operations, striking features and over several hundred private offers, requests and personal ads in free classifieds section.
Language(s): German
ADVERTISING RATES:
Full Page Mono .... EUR 990
Full Page Colour .... EUR 990
Mechanical Data: Type Area: 285 x 195 mm, No. of Columns (Display): 4, Col Widths (Display): 45 mm
Copy instructions: *Copy Date:* 10 days prior to publication

ZWEIRAD ADRESSBUCH
749074G27-2940
Editorial: Tiroler Weg 1b, 79285 EBRINGEN
Tel: 7664 611511 **Fax:** 7664 611512
Email: info@kern-verlag.de **Web site:** http://www.zweirad-adressbuch.de
Freq: Annual; **Cover Price:** EUR 38,32; **Circ:** 4,500
Advertising Manager: Annette Dworak
Profile: Professional contacts for the bicycle industry, manufacturers and importers of products and brands in alphabetical order.
Language(s): English; German
ADVERTISING RATES:
Full Page Mono .... EUR 1520
Full Page Colour .... EUR 2120
Mechanical Data: Type Area: 260 x 185 mm, No. of Columns (Display): 3, Col Widths (Display): 58 mm
Copy instructions: *Copy Date:* 60 days prior to publication

ZWF ZEITSCHRIFT FÜR WIRTSCHAFTLICHEN FABRIKBETRIEB
749089G19F-3
Editorial: Pascalstr. 8, 10587 BERLIN
Tel: 30 22190553 **Fax:** 30 31425895
Email: zwf@mediatech-berlin.de
Freq: 10 issues yearly; **Annual Sub.:** EUR 428,00; **Circ:** 1,400
Editor: Yetvart Ficiciyan; **Advertising Manager:** Regine Schmidt
Profile: ZWF Zeitschrift für wirtschaftlichen Fabrikbetrieb provides technical papers in exclusive new findings of the current knowledge about production technology and industrial performance processes. The magazine is aimed at corporate executives and professionals in research and teaching. Key issue addressed by the ZWF is always the economics of production processes. The cost-cutting begins in product development and design, through to manufacturing and assembly, to sales and maintenance, and extends to the future in the return of decommissioned products. In addition, human performance has a significant importance. The modern and efficient plant operation thus requires an increasingly holistic approach, which makes the ZWF to guide their editorial work.
Language(s): German
ADVERTISING RATES:
Full Page Mono .... EUR 835
Full Page Colour .... EUR 1375
Mechanical Data: Type Area: 250 x 175 mm, No. of Columns (Display): 4, Col Widths (Display): 41 mm
Official Journal of: Organ d. Ges. f. Informatik e.V., CAP-Fachgruppe

ZWP ZAHNARZT WIRTSCHAFT PRAXIS
724490G56D-160
Editorial: Holbeinstr. 29, 04229 LEIPZIG
Tel: 341 48474321 **Fax:** 341 48474290
Email: isbaner@oemus-media.de **Web site:** http://www.oemus.com
Freq: Monthly; **Annual Sub.:** EUR 70,00; **Circ:** 40,289
Editor: Jürgen Isbaner; **Advertising Manager:** Stefan Thieme
Profile: For 17 years, the ZWP dental business practice leading business magazine for dentists. As a general-interest titles covering the ZWP the full range of dental practice management. With 12 issues per year, it is one of the frequency-and largest-circulation titles, and is undoubtedly one of the most respected sources of information in the German dental market.
Language(s): German
ADVERTISING RATES:
Full Page Mono .... EUR 4250
Full Page Colour .... EUR 4950
Mechanical Data: Type Area: 244 x 160 mm, No. of Columns (Display): 3, Col Widths (Display): 51 mm
Copy instructions: *Copy Date:* 14 days prior to publication
Supplement(s): ZWP spezial
BUSINESS: HEALTH & MEDICAL: Dental

ZZI ZEITSCHRIFT FÜR ZAHNÄRZTLICHE IMPLANTOLOGIE
748776G56D-1140
Editorial: Robert-Koch-Str. 40, 37075 GÖTTINGEN
Tel: 551 398343
Email: schliephake.henning@med.uni-goettingen.de
Web site: http://www.zahnheilkunde.de
Freq: Quarterly; **Annual Sub.:** EUR 152,00; **Circ:** 7,945
Editor: Henning Schliephake; **Advertising Manager:** Sylvia Thöne
Profile: ZZI – Zeitschrift für zahnärztliche Implantologie (Journal of Dental Implantology) is the most widely circulated journal for scientific implantology in Germany. It is the official publication of the German Society of Implantology (Deutsche Gesellschaft für Implantologie, DGI). With its 7,471 members (as per July 2010), the DGI is the largest German implantological association and also the largest in Europe. In 2005, ZZI also became the official publication of the Austrian Society of Implantology (Österreichische Gesellschaft für Implantologie in der Zahn-, Mund- und Kieferheilkunde, ÖGI). ZZI publishes peer-reviewed scientific articles as well as articles with a more practical orientation. Dental implantology is a field of dentistry that has developed and grown explosively over the past few years. Thanks to new materials and new implant shapes and procedures, dental implantology has spread widely. Successful and broadbased research performed in Switzerland, Austria and Germany has made the German-speaking countries global leaders in this specialist field.

Germany

Language(s): German
ADVERTISING RATES:
Full Page Mono .... EUR 1700
Full Page Colour .... EUR 2600
Mechanical Data: Type Area: 271 x 168 mm, No. of Columns (Display): 2, Col Widths (Display): 81 mm
Official Journal of: Organ d. Dt. Ges. f. Implantologie im Zahn-, Mund- u. Kieferbereich e.V. u. d. Österr. Ges. f. orale Chirurgie u. Implantation
BUSINESS: HEALTH & MEDICAL: Dental

ZZP ZEITSCHRIFT FÜR ZIVILPROZESS
748777G44-2800
Editorial: Luxemburger Str. 449, 50939 KÖLN
Tel: 221 943737095 **Fax:** 221 943737280
Email: mweber@wolterskluwer.de **Web site:** http://www.wolterskluwer.de
Freq: Quarterly; **Annual Sub.:** EUR 184,20; **Circ:** 750
Editor: Maike Weber; **Advertising Manager:** Stefanie Szillat
Profile: Journal about the German legal process.
Language(s): German
ADVERTISING RATES:
Full Page Mono .... EUR 750
Full Page Colour .... EUR 1602
Mechanical Data: Type Area: 195 x 130 mm
BUSINESS: LEGAL

Gibraltar

Time Difference: GMT + 1 hr (CET - Central European Time)
National Telephone Code: +350
Continent: Europe
Capital: Gibraltar
Principal Language: English, Spanish, Italian, Portuguese
Population: 27967
Monetary Unit: Gibraltar Pound (GIP)

EMBASSY HIGH

COMMISSION: Gibraltar Government London Office: Gibraltar House, 150 Strand, London WC2R 1JA,
Tel: 020 7836 0777
Fax: 020 7240 6612 Contact: Mr. Albert Poggio OBE (Government of Giblartar United Kingdom Representative)
Website: http://www.gibraltar.gov.uk
Email: info@gibraltar.gov.uk

GIBRALTAR CHRONICLE
1202429GI65A-5
Editorial: Watergate House, Casemates, PO Box 27
Tel: 200 71 627 **Fax:** 200 79 927
Email: letters@chronicle.gi **Web site:** http://www.chronicle.gi
Date Established: 1801; **Freq:** 313 issues yearly - Published Monday to Saturday; **Cover Price:** £0.50; **Circ:** 3,000
Usual Pagination: 24
Editor: Dominique Searle; **News Editor:** Paco Oliva; **Advertising Manager:** Lorraine Victory
Profile: Newspaper focusing on national and international news, business, politics and sport.
Language(s): English
Mechanical Data: Col Length: 400mm, Col Widths (Display): 50mm, No. of Columns (Display): 5, Film: Mono: Negative. Colour: Positive
NATIONAL DAILY & SUNDAY NEWSPAPERS: National Daily Newspapers

THE GIBRALTAR MAGAZINE
765008GI80-60
Editorial: PO Box 561, Imossi House, Irish Town, Suite 6377 **Tel:** 200 77 748 **Fax:** 200 77 748
Email: gibmag@gibraltar.gi **Web site:** http://www.thegibraltarmagazine.com
Date Established: 1995; **Freq:** 11 issues yearly - Not published in January; **Annual Sub.:** GIP 30.00; **Circ:** 8,000
Editor: Andrea Morton
Profile: Magazine containing articles on business and finance, community issues, history, leisure and sports, personality profiles and general interest features.
Language(s): English
Readership: Aimed at residents, frequent visitors and business visitors.
Supplement(s): At Home in Gibraltar - 1xY Business and Finance - 1xY.
CONSUMER: RURAL & REGIONAL INTEREST

INSIGHT MAGAZINE
765043GI80-85
Editorial: Suite D, 1st Floor, Ellesmere House, City Mill Lane **Tel:** 200 40 913 **Fax:** 200 48 665
Email: insight@gibtelecom.net **Web site:** http://www.insight-gibraltar.com
Date Established: 1992; **Freq:** Monthly; Free to qualifying individuals ; **Circ:** 6,000
Usual Pagination: 80
Editor: Charles Bosano; **Advertising Manager:** Jean King
Profile: Magazine focusing on local history, ecology, culture, business and finance, sport, health and well-being, social issues and current affairs.
Language(s): English
Readership: Aimed at residents, frequent visitors and business visitors.
CONSUMER: RURAL & REGIONAL INTEREST

PANORAMA
1202459GI65A-100
Editorial: 75 Irish Town, PO Box 225 **Tel:** 200 79 797
Fax: 200 74 664
Email: editorial@panorama.gi **Web site:** http://www.panorama.gi
Date Established: 1975; **Freq:** 260 issues yearly - Published Monday to Friday; **Cover Price:** GIP 0.50; **Circ:** 4,500
Editor: Joe Garcia; **Advertising Manager:** Douglas Cumming
Profile: Newspaper focusing on national and international news, business, politics and sport.
Language(s): English
NATIONAL DAILY & SUNDAY NEWSPAPERS: National Daily Newspapers

ROGTEC
1872959GI33-1
Editorial: Suite 4, 10th Floor, ICC, 2a Main Street, GIBRALTAR, PO BOX 516 **Tel:** 95 288 09 52
Fax: 95 290 42 30
Email: info@rogtecmagazine.com **Web site:** www.rogtecmagazine.com
Date Established: 2005; **Freq:** Monthly; **Circ:** 10,699
Editor: Nick Lucan
Profile: Magazine focusing on Russian & Caspian oil and gas issues.
Language(s): English; Russian
Readership: Targets oil professionals, region oil and gas engineers and oil experts.
ADVERTISING RATES:
Full Page Colour .... EUR 7500.00
Mechanical Data: Type Area: 205x275mm, Bleed Size: 211x281mm

VOX
1201192GI65J-80
Editorial: PO Box 306, Leon House, Suite 1
Tel: 200 77 414 **Fax:** 200 72 531
Email: info@vox.gi **Web site:** http://www.vox.gi
Date Established: 1955; **Freq:** Weekly - Published on Friday; **Cover Price:** GIP 0.50; **Circ:** 800
Editor: Derek McGrail
Profile: Newspaper focusing on national and international news, politics, business and sport.
Language(s): English
Mechanical Data: Type Area: 280 x 187mm, Col Length: 280mm, Page Width: 187mm
NATIONAL DAILY & SUNDAY NEWSPAPERS: Grünes MdEP

Greece

Time Difference: GMT + 2 hrs (EET - Eastern European Time)
National Telephone Code: +30
Continent: Europe
Capital: Athens
Principal Language: Greek
Population: 10706290
Monetary Unit: Euro (EUR)

EMBASSY HIGH

COMMISSION: Embassy of Greece: 1a Holland Park, London W11 3TP
Tel: 020 7221 6467
Fax: 020 7729 7221
Email: pressoffice@greekembassy.org.uk
Website:http://www.greekembassy.org.uk

2BOARD
1865030GR89D-1
Editorial: Ioannou Metaxa 80, Karelas, 194 00 KOROPI - ATTICA **Tel:** 210 6688201
Fax: 210 6688270
Email: siabou@liberis.gr **Web site:** http://mediakit.liberis.gr
Freq: Quarterly; **Cover Price:** Free; **Circ:** 10,000
Advertising Manager: Maria Theocharopouloy

Profile: Official magazine of 'Eleftherios Venizelos', represents and reflects validity of Athens International Airport (AIA), and at the same time presenting its activities.
Language(s): English; Greek
ADVERTISING RATES:
Full Page Colour .... EUR 9000
Mechanical Data: Type Area: 218x285mm
CONSUMER: HOLIDAYS & TRAVEL: In-Flight Magazines

AGGELIOFOROS
767745GR65A-41
Editorial: Tsimiski 45, 546 23 THESSALONIKI
Tel: 2310 77 91 11 **Fax:** 2310 24 38 52
Web site: http://www.agelioforos.gr
Freq: Daily; **Cover Price:** EUR 1.30; **Circ:** 8,000
Usual Pagination: 60
Editor: Evris Tsoumis; **Advertising Director:** Natasha Bouderakou; **Publisher:** Alexandros Mbakatselos
Profile: Newspaper covering national and international news, politics, economy, culture and social events.
Language(s): Greek
ADVERTISING RATES:
Full Page Colour .... EUR 4600.00
NATIONAL DAILY & SUNDAY NEWSPAPERS: National Daily Newspapers

ELEFTHEROTYPIA
1202547GR67B-15
Editorial: Minoos 10-16, 117 43 NEOS KOSMOS
Tel: 210 92 96 001 **Fax:** 210 90 28 311
Email: elef@enet.gr **Web site:** http://www.enet.gr
Date Established: 1980; **Freq:** Evenings; **Cover Price:** EUR 1.00; **Circ:** 75,000
Editor: Sifis Polimilis; **Advertising Director:** Ioanna Florou; **Publisher:** Thanasis Tegopoulos
Profile: Newspaper covering politics, economy, culture and social events.
Language(s): Greek
ADVERTISING RATES:
Full Page Mono .... EUR 9100.00
Full Page Colour .... EUR 13000.00
Mechanical Data: Trim Size: 355 x 265mm
REGIONAL DAILY & SUNDAY NEWSPAPERS: Regional Daily Newspapers

ESTIA
1202674GR65A-30
Editorial: Anthimou Gazi 9, 105 61 ATHINA
Tel: 210 32 20 481 **Fax:** 210 32 43 071
Email: estianews@otenet.gr
Date Established: 1876; **Freq:** Evenings; **Circ:** 13,000
Editor: Alexis Zaousis
Profile: Newspaper covering general news, politics, economy, culture, sport and entertainment.
Language(s): Greek
ADVERTISING RATES:
Full Page Mono .... EUR 3200.00
Full Page Colour .... EUR 4200.00
NATIONAL DAILY & SUNDAY NEWSPAPERS: National Daily Newspapers

ETHNOS
1691987GR65A-47
Editorial: Mpenaki & Aggiou Nektariou 5, 152 38 METAMORFOSI HALANDRIOU **Tel:** 210 60 61 000
Fax: 210 63 96 515
Email: ethnos@pegasus.gr **Web site:** http://www.ethnos.gr
Date Established: 1930; **Freq:** Daily; **Circ:** 100,000
Editor: Yiannis Floros; **Advertising Director:** Lida Thomakou; **Publisher:** Georgos Mpompolas
Profile: Newspaper covering national and international news with features on business and finance, lifestyle, entertainment and sport.
Language(s): Greek
ADVERTISING RATES:
Full Page Mono .... EUR 6900.00
Full Page Colour .... EUR 9600.00
NATIONAL DAILY & SUNDAY NEWSPAPERS: National Daily Newspapers

ETHNOS TIS KIRIAKIS
1691989GR65B-11
Editorial: Mpenaki & Aggiou Nektariou 5, 152 38 METAMORFOSI HALANDRIOU **Tel:** 210 60 61 000
Fax: 210 63 91 337
Email: ethnos@pegasus.gr **Web site:** http://www.ethnos.gr
Freq: Sunday; **Circ:** 200,000
Editor: Dimitris Douris; **Advertising Director:** Lida Thomakou; **Publisher:** Georgos Mpompolas
Profile: Newspaper covering national and international news with features on finance, entertainment and sport.
Language(s): Greek
ADVERTISING RATES:
Full Page Mono .... EUR 11600.00
Full Page Colour .... EUR 15300.00
NATIONAL DAILY & SUNDAY NEWSPAPERS: National Sunday Newspapers

KATHIMERINI
1202757GR65A-36
Editorial: Ethnarhou Makariou & 2 Falireos, 185 47 NEO FALIRO **Tel:** 210 4808000 **Fax:** 210 4808055
Email: info@kathimerini.gr **Web site:** http://www.kathimerini.gr
Date Established: 1998; **Freq:** Daily; **Cover Price:** EUR 1.00; **Circ:** 26,246

Editor: Nikos Ksidakis; **Managing Editor:** Nikos Konstandaros; **Advertising Director:** Regina Maselou; **Publisher:** Themistoklis Alafouzos
Profile: Newspaper covering politics, economy, culture and social events.
Language(s): English; Greek
ADVERTISING RATES:
Full Page Mono .... EUR 5200
Full Page Colour .... EUR 7400
Agency Commission: 10%
Mechanical Data: Type Area: 530 x 358mm, Col Length: 530mm, Page Width: 358mm
Copy instructions: *Copy Date:* 4 working days prior to publication date
NATIONAL DAILY & SUNDAY NEWSPAPERS: National Daily Newspapers

KERDOS
767735GR65A-39
Editorial: Vasileos Georgiou 44 kai Kalvou, 152 33 HALANDRI **Tel:** 210 67 47 881 **Fax:** 210 67 47 893
Email: mail@kerdos.gr **Web site:** http://www.kerdos.gr
Freq: Daily; **Cover Price:** EUR 1.00; **Circ:** 25,500
Editor: Dimitris Vasilandonakis; **Advertising Director:** Marilena Tseloni; **Publisher:** Vasilis Valamvanos
Profile: Newspaper covering national and international news, business and economics, politics and sport.
Language(s): Greek
ADVERTISING RATES:
Full Page Mono .... EUR 5800.00
Full Page Colour .... EUR 7128.00
NATIONAL DAILY & SUNDAY NEWSPAPERS: National Daily Newspapers

KIRIAKATIKI
1202669GR65B-26
Editorial: Minoos 10-16, 117 43 NEOS KOSMOS
Tel: 210 92 96 001 **Fax:** 210 90 28 311
Email: elef@enet.gr
Date Established: 1991; **Freq:** Weekly - Publish on Sunday; **Cover Price:** EUR 2.50; **Circ:** 280,000
Usual Pagination: 84
Editor: Vangelis Siafakas; **Advertising Director:** Panagiotis Georgopoulos; **Publisher:** Thanasis Tegopoulos
Profile: Newspaper covering politics, economy, culture and social events.
Language(s): Greek
ADVERTISING RATES:
Full Page Mono .... EUR 10700.00
Full Page Colour .... EUR 15000.00
Agency Commission: 20%
Mechanical Data: Type Area: 300 x 230mm, Film: Positive, right reading, emulsion side down, Screen: 60 lpc, Bleed Size: 310 x 235mm, Trim Size: 300 x 230mm, Col Length: 300mm, Page Width: 230mm
Copy instructions: *Copy Date:* 24 days prior to publication date
Average ad content per issue: 30%
Supplement(s): Epsilon - 52 x Y
NATIONAL DAILY & SUNDAY NEWSPAPERS: National Sunday Newspapers

MAKEDONIA
1202771GR67B-25
Editorial: Monastiriou 85, 546 27 THESSALONIKI
Tel: 2310 56 00 00 **Fax:** 2310 53 48 54
Email: pr@newspaper.gr
Freq: Mornings; **Cover Price:** EUR 1.00; **Circ:** 70,000
Editor: Georgos Trapezoidis; **Advertising Director:** Agamemnon Kumis; **Publisher:** Panagiotis Andonopoulos
Profile: Newspaper covering politics, economy, culture and social events.
Language(s): Greek
ADVERTISING RATES:
Full Page Mono .... EUR 550.00
Full Page Colour .... EUR 770.00
REGIONAL DAILY & SUNDAY NEWSPAPERS: Regional Daily Newspapers

NAFTEMPORIKI
1201207GR67B-30
Editorial: Lenorman 205, Kolonos, 104 42 ATHINA
Tel: 210 51 98 000 **Fax:** 2105139905
Email: editors@naftemporiki.gr **Web site:** http://www.naftemporiki.gr
Date Established: 1924; **Freq:** Daily - Greece; **Circ:** 22,000
Editor-in-Chief: Dimitrios Plakoutsis; **Advertising Manager:** Thanasis Kounias; **Publisher:** Marietta Athanassiadou
Profile: Financial newspaper covering all aspects of the economic and business environment.
Language(s): Greek
Readership: Aimed at business executives, investors, directors, managers, financial employees and others.
ADVERTISING RATES:
Full Page Mono .... EUR 5700
Full Page Colour .... EUR 7000
Agency Commission: 20%
Mechanical Data: Type Area: 350 x 266mm, Film: Positive, Col Length: 350mm, No. of Columns (Display): 6, Page Width: 266mm
REGIONAL DAILY & SUNDAY NEWSPAPERS: Regional Daily Newspapers

TA NEA
1202774GR65A-35
Editorial: Michalakopoulou 80, 115 28 ATHINA
Tel: 211 36 57 000 **Fax:** 211 36 58 301
Email: pressroom@tanea.gr **Web site:** http://www.tanea.gr

Date Established: 1946; **Freq:** Daily; **Cover Price:** EUR 1.00; **Circ:** 100,000
Editor: Panagiotis Kambilis; **Managing Editor:** Ilias Matsikas; **Publisher:** Christos Lambrakis
Profile: Newspaper covering politics, economy, current affairs and sport.
Language(s): Greek
ADVERTISING RATES:
Full Page Mono .... EUR 6900.00
Full Page Colour .... EUR 10350.00
NATIONAL DAILY & SUNDAY NEWSPAPERS: National Daily Newspapers

REAL NEWS
1902059GR65J-14
Editorial: 215 Kifisias Ave. 151, 24 ATHENS
Tel: 211 200 8 300 **Fax:** 211 200 8 399
Email: news@realnews.gr **Web site:** http://www.realnews.gr
Freq: Sunday; **Cover Price:** EUR 4.00; **Circ:** 110,000
Advertising Director: Stella Drosopoulou
Profile: Sunday newspaper with 4 supplements: reallife, realmoney, realplanet and realsports.
Language(s): Greek
ADVERTISING RATES:
Full Page Colour .... EUR 13000.00
NATIONAL DAILY & SUNDAY NEWSPAPERS: National Weekly Newspapers

RIZOSPASTIS
1626200GR65A-46
Editorial: Lefkis 134, 145 65 KRIONERI ATTIKIS
Tel: 210 62 97 000 **Fax:** 210 62 97 999
Email: mailbox@rizospastis.gr **Web site:** http://www.rizospastis.gr
Freq: Daily; **Circ:** 30,000
Editor: Takis Tsigkas; **Publisher:** Stefanos Loukas
Profile: National newspaper containing politics, economics, cultural and social issues.
Language(s): Greek
NATIONAL DAILY & SUNDAY NEWSPAPERS: National Daily Newspapers

TO VIMA
1500225GR65A-45
Editorial: Michalakopoulou 80, 115 28 ATHINA
Tel: 211 36 57 000 **Fax:** 211 36 58 004
Email: tovima@dolnet.gr **Web site:** http://www.tovima.gr
Freq: Daily; **Cover Price:** EUR 1.00; **Circ:** 15,100
Editor: Christos Nemis; **Advertising Director:** Thomas Granitsas
Profile: Newspaper focusing on national and international news, business, politics, culture and sport.
Language(s): Greek
ADVERTISING RATES:
Full Page Mono .... EUR 1900.00
Full Page Colour .... EUR 3100.00
NATIONAL DAILY & SUNDAY NEWSPAPERS: National Daily Newspapers

Hungary

Time Difference: GMT + 1 hr (CET - Central European Time)
National Telephone Code: +36
Continent: Europe
Capital: Budapest
Principal Language: Magyar (Hungarian)
Population: 10045407
Monetary Unit: Forint (HUF)
EMBASSY HIGH COMMISSION: Embassy of the Republic of Hungary: 35 Eaton Place, London SW1X 8BY
Tel: 0870 005 6721
Fax: 020 7823 1348 E-mail: office.lon@kum.hu Web: http://www.mfa.gov.hu/kulkepviselet/uk/hu

100XSZÉP
1689175HU74B-2
Editorial: Városmajor u. 11., 1122 BUDAPEST **Tel:** 1/488-5700 **Fax:** 1/488-5775
Circ: 53,058
Editor-in-Chief: Beatrix Vaskó
ADVERTISING RATES:
Full Page Colour .... HUF 1100000
CONSUMER: WOMEN'S INTEREST CONSUMER MAGAZINES: Women's Interest - Fashion

168 ÓRA
630077HU65A-1
Editorial: Bécsi út 3-5., 1023 BUDAPEST **Tel:** 1/438-5570 **Fax:** 1/438-5575
Email: hirdetes@168ora.hu **Web site:** http://www.168ora.hu
Cover Price: HUF 425; **Circ:** 42,294
Usual Pagination: 52
Profile: Newspaper covering national and international news, focusing on politics.
Readership: Aimed at well-educated people.
ADVERTISING RATES:
Full Page Mono .... HUF 693000
Full Page Colour .... HUF 1210000
NATIONAL DAILY & SUNDAY NEWSPAPERS: National Daily Newspapers

24 ÓRA
1688221HU67B-525
Editorial: Városmajor u. 11., 1122 BUDAPEST **Tel:** 1/488-5726 **Fax:** 1/488-5719
Circ: 21,409
Advertising Director: András Lengyel
ADVERTISING RATES:
Full Page Mono .... HUF 768000
Full Page Colour .... HUF 1032000
REGIONAL DAILY & SUNDAY NEWSPAPERS: Regional Daily Newspapers

3 DIMENZIÓ
1690666HU4A-69
Editorial: Kápolna u. 9., 6000 KECSKEMÉT **Tel:** 76/509-424 **Fax:** 76/509-426
Email: betapress@betapress.hu **Web site:** http://www.betapress.hu
Circ: 10,000
Editor-in-Chief: Csilla L. Horváth
Profile: Magazine focusing on construction, architecture and design.
BUSINESS: ARCHITECTURE & BUILDING: Architecture

4X4 - QUAD FUN MAGAZIN
630878HU77A-3
Editorial: Lehel út 61., 1135 BUDAPEST **Fax:** 1/577-2018
Email: 4x4@4x4.hu **Web site:** http://www.4x4.hu
Editor-in-Chief: László Góg
Profile: Magazine focusing on 4x4s and off-road rally cars, featuring news, introducing manufacturers and new vehicles. Also provides an in-depth coverage of all involved sports events.
Readership: Aimed at motorists, main dealers and motorsports enthusiasts.
CONSUMER: MOTORING & CYCLING: Motoring

ADÓ ÉS ELLENORZÉSI ÉRTESÍTO
1689109HU1M-31
Editorial: Mór u. 2-4., 1135 BUDAPEST **Tel:** 1/237-9843 **Fax:** 1/237-9841
Email: lap@saldo.hu **Web site:** http://www.adoertesito.hu
Circ: 15,000
Editor-in-Chief: János dr. Szikora
Profile: Magazine covering news and information on taxation matters.
BUSINESS: FINANCE & ECONOMICS: Taxation

ADÓ SZAKLAP
630539HU1M-20
Editorial: Prielle Kornélia u. 21-35., 1117 BUDAPEST
Tel: 40/464-565 **Fax:** 1/464-5637
Email: info@complex.hu **Web site:** http://www.ado.hu
Circ: 26,083
Profile: Magazine focusing on taxation and national insurance issues.
Readership: Aimed at financial staff, book-keepers and taxation advisers.
ADVERTISING RATES:
Full Page Mono .... HUF 435000
Full Page Colour .... HUF 560000
BUSINESS: FINANCE & ECONOMICS: Taxation

ADÓ TB-KALAUZ
1689108HU1M-30
Editorial: Prielle Kornélia u. 21-35., 1117 BUDAPEST
Tel: 40/464-565 **Fax:** 1/464-5637
Email: info@complex.hu **Web site:** http://www.ado.hu
Circ: 18,776
Profile: Magazine covering information on taxation and National Insurance matters.
ADVERTISING RATES:
Full Page Mono .... HUF 435000
Full Page Colour .... HUF 560000
BUSINESS: FINANCE & ECONOMICS: Taxation

ADÓ-KÓDEX
630562HU1M-25
Editorial: Prielle Kornélia u. 21-35., 1117 BUDAPEST
Tel: 40/464-565 **Fax:** 1/464-5637
Email: info@complex.hu **Web site:** http://www.ado.hu
Circ: 23,385
Profile: Magazine focusing specifically on changes in the Hungarian law regarding taxation and financial matters.
Readership: Aimed at all involved in taxation such as advisers, government bodies, book-keepers and self-employed individuals.
ADVERTISING RATES:
Full Page Mono .... HUF 435000
Full Page Colour .... HUF 560000
BUSINESS: FINANCE & ECONOMICS: Taxation

AGRÁRÁGAZAT
1689115HU21A-132
Editorial: Katona J. u. 6., 6400 KISKUNHALAS
Tel: 77/529-593 **Fax:** 77/529-593
Email: agraragazat@t-online.hu **Web site:** http://www.pointernet.pds.hu
Cover Price: HUF 2310; **Circ:** 20,000
Usual Pagination: 52
ADVERTISING RATES:
Full Page Mono .... HUF 249000
Full Page Colour .... HUF 279000
BUSINESS: AGRICULTURE & FARMING

ALAPRAJZ
633938HU4A-10
Editorial: Neumann János u. 1., 2040 BUDAÖRS
Tel: 23/422-455 **Fax:** 23/422-383
Email: mail@businessmedia.hu **Web site:** http://www.businessmedia.hu
Advertising Manager: Ágnes Berta
Profile: Magazine containing examples of architecture from all over the world, from a technical point of view.
Readership: Aimed at architects.
BUSINESS: ARCHITECTURE & BUILDING: Architecture

ALMALAP
630377HU5C-20
Editorial: Lehel út 61., 1135 BUDAPEST **Tel:** 1/452-7830 **Fax:** 1/452-7830
Email: 2009@almalap.hu **Web site:** http://www.almalap.hu
Cover Price: HUF 600
Profile: Magazine focusing on Macintosh computers and Mac applications.
Readership: Aimed at Macintosh users.
BUSINESS: COMPUTERS & AUTOMATION: Professional Personal Computers

AMELIE
1689341HU74B-6
Editorial: Lajos u. 48-66. B lph. II. em., 1036 BUDAPEST **Tel:** 1/489-8846 **Fax:** 1/430-1536
Email: hirdetes@amelie.hu
Cover Price: HUF 645
Annual Sub.: HUF 430; **Circ:** 23,437
Usual Pagination: 56
ADVERTISING RATES:
Full Page Colour .... HUF 500000
CONSUMER: WOMEN'S INTEREST CONSUMER MAGAZINES: Women's Interest - Fashion

AMS
1689162HU77A-33
Editorial: Angyali sziget 127., 2300 RÁCKEVE
Tel: 70/314-5544 **Fax:** 70/903-1611
Email: amsmagazin@amsmagazin.hu **Web site:** http://www.amsmagazin.hu
Cover Price: HUF 440; **Circ:** 15,000
Editor-in-Chief: Krisztina Bessenyey
CONSUMER: MOTORING & CYCLING: Motoring

ANYAGMOZGATÁS - CSOMAGOLÁS (A + CS)
633962HU10-10
Editorial: Újszolok u. 9. III/1., 2120 DUNAKESZI
Tel: 27/630-731 **Fax:** 333-8170
Email: acsirt@t-online.hu **Web site:** http://www.acsi.hu
Cover Price: HUF 600; **Circ:** 5,000
Usual Pagination: 56
Editor: Erzsébet Kovács
Profile: Publication providing technical and economic information regarding materials handling, packaging and logistics.
Readership: Aimed at those involved in logistics and packaging.
ADVERTISING RATES:
Full Page Mono .... HUF 96000
Full Page Colour .... HUF 220000
BUSINESS: MATERIALS HANDLING

ANYÁK LAPJA
1689150HU74C-87
Editorial: Váci út 168/B, 1138 BUDAPEST **Tel:** 1/238-0386 **Fax:** 1/450-1069
Email: anyaklapja@anyaklapja.hu **Web site:** http://www.anyaklapja.hu
Cover Price: HUF 550
Annual Sub.: HUF 430; **Circ:** 40,000
Usual Pagination: 116
Editor-in-Chief: Gyöngyi Cseszák
ADVERTISING RATES:
Full Page Colour .... HUF 960000
CONSUMER: WOMEN'S INTEREST CONSUMER MAGAZINES: Home & Family

ÁPOLÁSÜGY
1690380HU56B-1
Editorial: Pf. 190, 1431 BUDAPEST **Tel:** 1/266-5935
Fax: 1/266-5935
Email: mae@t-online.hu
Circ: 8,000
Editor-in-Chief: Márkné Mucha
BUSINESS: HEALTH & MEDICAL: Nursing

AQUA VÍZISPORT ÉS ÉLETMÓD MAGAZIN
706915HU91A-10
Editorial: Böszörményi út 3/A, 1126 BUDAPEST
Tel: 1/212-8182 **Fax:** 1/212-7951
Email: info@aquamagazin.hu **Web site:** http://www.aquamagazin.hu
Circ: 6,000
Editor-in-Chief: Gabriella Ország
Profile: Magazine focusing on water sports. Features national and international news, including articles on yachting, power boating, surfing, water skiing, diving and rafting.
Readership: Aimed at water sports enthusiasts.
CONSUMER: RECREATION & LEISURE: Boating & Yachting

ARANYSAS
1689153HU40-2
Editorial: Kerepesi út 29/B, 1087 BUDAPEST **Tel:** 1/323-1359 **Fax:** 1/323-1360
Web site: http://www.aranysas.hu
Circ: 25,000
Editor-in-Chief: István Törös
Profile: Magazine containing news about modern military aircrafts.
BUSINESS: DEFENCE

ÁSVÁNYVÍZ, ÜDÍTOITAL, GYÜMÖLCSLÉ
706917HU22C-10
Editorial: Fo u. 68., 1027 BUDAPEST **Tel:** 1/214-6691 **Fax:** 1/214-6692
Email: mail.mete@mtesz.hu
Managing Editor: Béla dr. Borszéki
Profile: Journal of the Association of Fruit Juice and Mineral Water Manufacturers, the Hungarian Association and Product Advice Bureau of Mineral Water Manufacturers and MÉTE. The publication includes scientific articles, trade union news, conferences, trade competitions, and the history of mineral water, fruit juice and soft drink manufacturing.
Readership: Aimed at technical professionals, marketing personnel, retailers and middle management involved in the manufacturing of mineral water, fruit juice and soft drinks.
BUSINESS: FOOD: Food Processing & Packaging

AZ AUTÓ
633751HU77A-4
Editorial: Rottenbiller u. 31., 1077 BUDAPEST **Tel:** 1/322-0421 **Fax:** 1/322-0421
Email: a2@hungary.net **Web site:** http://www.auto2.hu
Circ: 61,525
Usual Pagination: 72
Profile: Magazine providing in-depth coverage on all subjects connected to motoring. Features new models, tests, garages and main dealers, customer rights, car repairs, legal matters and technical news features.
Readership: Aimed at motorists, mechanics and enthusiasts.
ADVERTISING RATES:
Full Page Mono .... HUF 860000
Full Page Colour .... HUF 1080000
CONSUMER: MOTORING & CYCLING: Motoring

AUTO BILD MAGYARORSZÁG
1796668HU77A-86
Editorial: Városmajor u. 11., 1122 BUDAPEST **Tel:** 1/488-5700 **Fax:** 1/488-5579
Email: andras.furak@axelspringer.hu
Circ: 62,209
Editor-in-Chief: Róbert Szabó
ADVERTISING RATES:
Full Page Colour .... HUF 1130000
CONSUMER: MOTORING & CYCLING: Motoring

AUTÓ MOTOR
1600604HU77A-15
Editorial: Városmajor u. 11., 1122 BUDAPEST **Tel:** 1/488-5700 **Fax:** 1/488-5579
Email: andras.furak@axelspringer.hu
Circ: 61,090
Editor-in-Chief: Róbert Szabó
Profile: Publication focusing on motoring includes tests, car reviews, industry reports and articles on motorsports.
Readership: Aimed at motoring enthusiasts.
ADVERTISING RATES:
Full Page Colour .... HUF 1040000
CONSUMER: MOTORING & CYCLING: Motoring

AUTÓMAGAZIN
1200673HU77A-5
Editorial: Nagyszolos u. 11-15., 1113 BUDAPEST
Tel: 1/577-2600 **Fax:** 1/577-2690
Email: automagazin@motorpresse.hu **Web site:** http://www.automagazin.hu
Cover Price: HUF 695
Annual Sub.: HUF 5760; **Circ:** 28,583
Usual Pagination: 100
Profile: Magazine covering new products, tests and techniques, motor sports, equipment and features on popular cars.
Readership: Aimed at motorists, mechanics and enthusiasts.
ADVERTISING RATES:
Full Page Colour .... HUF 995000
CONSUMER: MOTORING & CYCLING: Motoring

AUTÓPIAC 1200668HU77A-10
Editorial: Nagyszolos u. 11-15., 1113 BUDAPEST
Tel: 1/577-2600 **Fax:** 1/577-2690
Email: autopiac@motorpresse.hu
Cover Price: HUF 195
Annual Sub.: HUF 6720; **Circ:** 26,260
Usual Pagination: 48
Editor-in-Chief: Roland Lamara
Profile: Magazine containing tests, technical articles and motor sport coverage as well as a detailed overview of the Hungarian market. Emphasis is on second-hand cars and how to reduce running costs. Provides up-to-date prices on second-hand and new cars, with tips and advice.
Readership: Aimed at car buyers, users and professionals.
ADVERTISING RATES:
Full Page Colour .... HUF 850000
CONSUMER: MOTORING & CYCLING: Motoring

AUTÓSÉLET 1689165HU77A-36
Editorial: Keveháza u. 1-3., 1119 BUDAPEST **Tel:** 1/357-6110 **Fax:** 1/357-6120
Email: autoselet@autoklub.hu
Circ: 75,000
Usual Pagination: 36
ADVERTISING RATES:
Full Page Mono .... HUF 520000
Full Page Colour .... HUF 800000
CONSUMER: MOTORING & CYCLING: Motoring

AUTÓTECHNIKA JAVÍTÁS ÉS KERESKEDELEM 633931HU31A-20
Editorial: Csaba u. 21., 9023 GYOR **Tel:** 96/618-074 **Fax:** 96/618-063
Email: auto@xmeditor.hu **Web site:** http://www.autotechnika.hu
Cover Price: HUF 9840; **Circ:** 4,000
Usual Pagination: 80
Editor-in-Chief: Iván dr. Nagyszokolyai
Profile: Publication focusing on car mechanics including car repair business news and professional developments.
Readership: Aimed at car mechanics and management in car repair centres.
ADVERTISING RATES:
Full Page Mono .... HUF 122400
Full Page Colour .... HUF 199700
BUSINESS: MOTOR TRADE: Motor Trade Accessories

AUTÓTESZT 1689166HU77A-37
Editorial: Budapesti út 87/A, 2040 BUDAÖRS
Tel: 30/302-0545
Email: info@autoteszt.com
Cover Price: HUF 245; **Circ:** 25,000
CONSUMER: MOTORING & CYCLING: Motoring

BABA MAGAZIN 1689180HU74D-1
Editorial: Váci út 168/B, 1138 BUDAPEST **Tel:** 1/238-0386 **Fax:** 1/450-1069
Email: babamagazin@anyaklapja.hu **Web site:** http://www.babamagazin.hu
Cover Price: HUF 550
Annual Sub.: HUF 430; **Circ:** 40,000
Usual Pagination: 116
Editor-in-Chief: Gyöngyi Cseszák
ADVERTISING RATES:
Full Page Colour .... HUF 960000
CONSUMER: WOMEN'S INTEREST CONSUMER MAGAZINES: Child Care

BABA PATIKA 1689184HU74D-2
Editorial: Váci út 168/B, 1138 BUDAPEST **Tel:** 1/238-0386 **Fax:** 1/450-1069
Email: babapatika@anyaklapja.hu **Web site:** http://www.babapatika.hu
Circ: 80,000
Usual Pagination: 56
Editor-in-Chief: Gyöngyi Cseszák
ADVERTISING RATES:
Full Page Colour .... HUF 960000
CONSUMER: WOMEN'S INTEREST CONSUMER MAGAZINES: Child Care

BABAINFO MAGAZIN 1796939HU74D-6
Editorial: Bolygó u. 1/B, 2000 SZENTENDRE **Tel:** 26/309-126 **Fax:** 26/500-291
Email: info@babainfomagazin.hu **Web site:** http://www.babainfomagazin.hu
Circ: 40,000
ADVERTISING RATES:
Full Page Colour .... HUF 795000
CONSUMER: WOMEN'S INTEREST CONSUMER MAGAZINES: Child Care

BABA-MAMA KALAUZ 1690748HU74D-5
Editorial: Tisza u. 6. V. em. 26., 1133 BUDAPEST
Tel: 1/359-3103 **Fax:** 1/359-3103
Email: k.pannonia@chello.hu **Web site:** http://www.viapannonia.hu
Circ: 30,000
CONSUMER: WOMEN'S INTEREST CONSUMER MAGAZINES: Child Care

BALATONI TIPP NYÁRI MAGAZIN 1690754HU89A-20
Editorial: Mikszáth u. 19/B, 8600 SIÓFOK **Tel:** 84/313-656 **Fax:** 84/313-656
Email: balatonpress@balatonpress.hu
Circ: 50,000
Editor-in-Chief: László Gyarmati
CONSUMER: HOLIDAYS & TRAVEL: Travel

BANK & TOZSDE 630474HU1A-2
Editorial: Október 6. u. 7., 1051 BUDAPEST **Tel:** 1/266-5372 **Fax:** 1/266-6391
Email: news@bankestozsde.hu **Web site:** http://www.bankestozsde.hu
Annual Sub.: EUR 21
Profile: Magazine focusing on business, economics and financial matters nationally and internationally.
Readership: Aimed at financial executives, decision-makers and investors.
BUSINESS: FINANCE & ECONOMICS

BASTEI ROMANTIK REGÉNYFÜZETEK 1690948HU74A-150
Editorial: Teréz krt. 38., 1066 BUDAPEST **Tel:** 1/428-2250 **Fax:** 1/428-2250
Email: kiado@ex-bb.hu **Web site:** http://www.ex-bb.hu
Cover Price: HUF 355; **Circ:** 25,000
Editor-in-Chief: Erzsébet Simonits
ADVERTISING RATES:
Full Page Mono .... HUF 70000
CONSUMER: WOMEN'S INTEREST CONSUMER MAGAZINES: Women's Interest

BEAUTY FORUM 634667HU15A-20
Editorial: Naphegy tér 8., 1016 BUDAPEST **Tel:** 1/457-0067 **Fax:** 1/201-3248
Email: szerkesztoseg@health-and-beauty.hu **Web site:** http://www.beauty-forum.hu
Annual Sub.: HUF 5990; **Circ:** 5,000
Profile: Official journal of the Hungarian Guild of Beauticians and the Hungarian Beauty Trade Fair. Introducing new products and methods, provides information on management, marketing, tax, insurance and legal issues.
Readership: Aimed at beauticians, owners and management of beauty salons, nail salons, sun-bed salons; also trainee beauticians and college trainers.
BUSINESS: COSMETICS & HAIRDRESSING: Cosmetics

BÉKÉS MEGYEI HÍRLAP 1688223HU67B-526
Editorial: Városmajor u. 11., 1122 BUDAPEST **Tel:** 1/488-5726 **Fax:** 1/488-5719
Circ: 30,817
Advertising Director: András Lengyel
ADVERTISING RATES:
Full Page Mono .... HUF 888000
Full Page Colour .... HUF 1272000
REGIONAL DAILY & SUNDAY NEWSPAPERS: Regional Daily Newspapers

BELVÁROSI TIMES DOWNTOWN 1689279HU89A-16
Editorial: Boróka u. 7., 2094 NAGYKOVÁCSI **Tel:** 26/355-106 **Fax:** 26/355-106
Email: maryon@externet.hu
Cover Price: HUF 680; **Circ:** 20,000
Editor-in-Chief: Piroska Kurali
CONSUMER: HOLIDAYS & TRAVEL: Travel

BESZÉLO 631080HU82-30
Editorial: Akadémia u. 1. fszt. 48-50., 1054 BUDAPEST **Tel:** 1/302-2912 **Fax:** 1/302-1271
Email: beszelo@enternet.hu **Web site:** http://www.beszelo.hu
Cover Price: HUF 689; **Circ:** 2,000
Editor-in-Chief: László Neményi
Profile: Magazine containing articles on political, historical and cultural issues.
Readership: Aimed at university students, teachers and historians.
CONSUMER: CURRENT AFFAIRS & POLITICS

BIKEMAG 634751HU77C-20
Editorial: Varrógépgyár 8-10., 1211 BUDAPEST
Tel: 70/336-9896 **Fax:** 22/596-069
Email: hirdetes@bikemag.hu **Web site:** http://www.bikemag.hu
Cover Price: HUF 745; **Circ:** 7,000
Profile: Magazine covering all aspects of leisure cycling. Featuring tests on various items, parts and products, medical issues, national and international news, race reviews (DH, DS, XC), cyclocross, BMX, reviews on bicycle lanes and tour guides.
Readership: Aimed at bicycle racers, their trainers and team; also at enthusiasts.
CONSUMER: MOTORING & CYCLING: Cycling

BIO INFO 1796940HU74Q-232
Editorial: Folyondár u. 15/A fszt. 5., 1037 BUDAPEST
Tel: 1/240-9549 **Fax:** 1/240-9549
Email: info@bio.info.hu **Web site:** http://www.bio.info.hu
Circ: 30,000
CONSUMER: WOMEN'S INTEREST CONSUMER MAGAZINES: Lifestyle

BLIKK 624256HU65A-121
Editorial: Szugló u. 81-85., 1141 BUDAPEST **Tel:** 1/460-2541 **Fax:** 1/460-2579
Email: gyartas@blikk.hu
Circ: 305,865
Usual Pagination: 20
Profile: Newspaper focusing on national and international news, politics, business, culture and sport.
ADVERTISING RATES:
Full Page Mono .... HUF 2745600
Full Page Colour .... HUF 3706560
NATIONAL DAILY & SUNDAY NEWSPAPERS: National Daily Newspapers

BLIKK NOK 1796934HU74A-161
Editorial: Szugló u. 81-85., 1141 BUDAPEST **Tel:** 1/460-4880 **Fax:** 1/460-4882
Cover Price: HUF 95; **Circ:** 184,046
Usual Pagination: 56
ADVERTISING RATES:
Full Page Colour .... HUF 1200000
CONSUMER: WOMEN'S INTEREST CONSUMER MAGAZINES: Women's Interest

BORÁSZATI FÜZETEK 634529HU9C-100
Tel: 30/231-6169
Email: barsi.nora@magyarmezogazdasag.hu **Web site:** http://www.magyarmezogazdasag.hu
Annual Sub.: HUF 5400
Profile: Publication providing in-depth coverage of all aspects of wine production. Features international standards, introduction of various wineries, trade news, meetings, national and international conferences, trade fairs and competitions, scientific articles on research subjects, legal and financial advice and trade history articles.
Readership: Aimed at owners and employees of wineries, retailers and importers.
BUSINESS: DRINKS & LICENSED TRADE: Licensed Trade, Wines & Spirits

BORBARÁT 630706HU74P-80
Editorial: Horvát u. 14-24. V.em, 1027 BUDAPEST
Tel: 24/460-833 **Fax:** 24/460-833
Email: marianna.dragon@borbarat.com **Web site:** http://www.borbarat.com
Cover Price: HUF 1495; **Circ:** 3,000
Editor-in-Chief: László Alkonyi
Profile: Magazine focusing on wine; introducing new vine yards, restaurants and breweries.
Readership: Aimed at wine producers and those who enjoy drinking wine.
CONSUMER: WOMEN'S INTEREST CONSUMER MAGAZINES: Food & Cookery

BORN TO BE WILD 1689209HU77A-38
Editorial: Gyarmat u. 53/B, 1145 BUDAPEST **Tel:** 1/250-5469 **Fax:** 1/250-5469
Email: info@wild.hu **Web site:** http://www.wild.hu
Cover Price: HUF 685; **Circ:** 20,000
Usual Pagination: 100
ADVERTISING RATES:
Full Page Colour .... HUF 260000
CONSUMER: MOTORING & CYCLING: Motoring

B.O.S.S. MAGAZIN 630583HU14A-40
Editorial: Diós árok 5., 1125 BUDAPEST **Tel:** 1/488-6060 **Fax:** 1/488-6061
Email: boss@bossmagazin.hu **Web site:** http://www.bossmagazin.hu
Cover Price: HUF 745
Annual Sub.: HUF 5960; **Circ:** 15,500
Usual Pagination: 104
Profile: Magazine covering economics, e-business, studies and information on management and business, with a hint of lifestyle and motoring news.
Readership: Aimed at executives and decision makers.
ADVERTISING RATES:
Full Page Colour .... HUF 920000
BUSINESS: COMMERCE, INDUSTRY & MANAGEMENT

BRAVO 1688626HU74F-1
Editorial: Szugló u. 81-85., 1141 BUDAPEST **Tel:** 1/460-4880 **Fax:** 1/460-4882
Cover Price: HUF 325; **Circ:** 58,415
Usual Pagination: 52
ADVERTISING RATES:
Full Page Colour .... HUF 1100000
CONSUMER: WOMEN'S INTEREST CONSUMER MAGAZINES: Teenage

BRAVO GIRL! 1689215HU74F-4
Editorial: Szugló u. 81-85., 1141 BUDAPEST **Tel:** 1/460-4880 **Fax:** 1/460-4882
Cover Price: HUF 350; **Circ:** 57,000
Usual Pagination: 60
ADVERTISING RATES:
Full Page Colour .... HUF 1100000
CONSUMER: WOMEN'S INTEREST CONSUMER MAGAZINES: Teenage

BUDAI POLGÁR 1688762HU72-60
Editorial: Bimbó út 1., 1022 BUDAPEST **Tel:** 1/316-3410 **Fax:** 1/316-3410
Email: budaipolgar@masodikkerulet.hu **Web site:** http://www.budaipolgar.hu
Circ: 50,000
Editor-in-Chief: Ildikó Tóth
LOCAL NEWSPAPERS

BUDAPEST GUIDE 1690760HU89C-88
Editorial: Március 15 tér. 7, 1056 BUDAPEST **Tel:** 1/266-5853 **Fax:** 1/338-4293
Email: info@budapestinfo.hu **Web site:** http://www.budapestinfo.hu
Circ: 1,000,000
CONSUMER: HOLIDAYS & TRAVEL: Entertainment Guides

BUDAPEST LIFE INGATLAN EXTRA 1796667HU1E-158
Editorial: Hajógyári sziget 132., 1033 BUDAPEST
Tel: 1/392-7964 **Fax:** 1/392-7963
Email: office@vtrend.hu **Web site:** http://www.ingatlan-extra.hu
Circ: 30,000
Profile: Magazine focusing on residential property investments, trends, developments, also includes analysis of property investments.
BUSINESS: FINANCE & ECONOMICS: Property

BUDAPEST LIFE MAGAZIN 1796666HU74Q-222
Editorial: Hajógyári sziget 132., 1033 BUDAPEST
Tel: 1/392-7964 **Fax:** 1/392-7963
Email: office@vtrend.hu **Web site:** http://www.budapestlife.hu
Circ: 25,000
CONSUMER: WOMEN'S INTEREST CONSUMER MAGAZINES: Lifestyle

BUDAPEST MENÜ 1690396HU74P-163
Editorial: Lechner Ödön fasor 1-2. A/818., 1095 BUDAPEST **Tel:** 1/555-2746
Email: budapestmenu@gmail.com
Circ: 40,000
CONSUMER: WOMEN'S INTEREST CONSUMER MAGAZINES: Food & Cookery

BUDAPEST PANORÁMA 1689220HU50-206
Editorial: Munkás u. 9., 1074 BUDAPEST **Tel:** 1/266-5853 **Fax:** 1/338-4293
Email: info@turizmus.com **Web site:** http://www.budapestpanorama.com
Circ: 25,000
BUSINESS: TRAVEL & TOURISM

BUDAPESTER ZEITUNG 630529HU82-40
Editorial: Kunigunda útja 18., 1037 BUDAPEST
Tel: 1/453-0752 **Fax:** 1/240-7583
Email: verlag@bzt.hu **Web site:** http://www.bzt.hu
Publisher: Jan Mainka
Profile: Magazine covering news on politics, economics and social events.
Readership: Aimed at business executives and German people living in Hungary.
ADVERTISING RATES:
Full Page Colour .... HUF 700000
CONSUMER: CURRENT AFFAIRS & POLITICS

BURDA 1797001HU74B-16
Editorial: Naphegy tér 8., 1016 BUDAPEST **Tel:** 1/267-0584 **Fax:** 1/267-0584
Email: info@burda.hu **Web site:** http://www.burda.hu
CONSUMER: WOMEN'S INTEREST CONSUMER MAGAZINES: Women's Interest - Fashion

BUSINESS HUNGARY 630656HU14A-70
Editorial: Király u. 16., 1061 BUDAPEST **Tel:** 1/887-4848 **Fax:** 1/887-4849
Email: sales@pxb.hu **Web site:** http://www.pxb.hu
Circ: 6,000
Usual Pagination: 44
Profile: Magazine focusing on economics and politics in Hungary.
Readership: Aimed at business executives and members of the American Chamber of Commerce.
ADVERTISING RATES:
Full Page Colour .... HUF 465000
BUSINESS: COMMERCE, INDUSTRY & MANAGEMENT

CADVILÁG
630091HU19J-40

Editorial: Koszeg u. 4., 1141 BUDAPEST **Tel:** 20/466-2014 **Fax:** 1/273-3411
Email: magazin@cadvilag.hu **Web site:** http://www.cadvilag.hu
Cover Price: HUF 882; **Circ:** 6,000
Editor-in-Chief: Éva N-Molnár
Profile: Magazine focusing on the field of computer aided design.
Readership: Aimed at architectural professionals, 3D information technologists and engineers.
BUSINESS: ENGINEERING & MACHINERY: CAD & CIM (Computer Integrated Manufacture)

CAFÉ & BAR
1827541HU11A-73

Editorial: József u. 26-28., 1084 BUDAPEST **Tel:** 1/327-0188 **Fax:** 1/266-8190
Email: cafebar@centralpress.hu **Web site:** http://www.centralpress.hu
Cover Price: HUF 800; **Circ:** 8,000
Editor-in-Chief: Noémi Szuna
BUSINESS: CATERING: Catering, Hotels & Restaurants

CAMION TRUCK & BUS MAGAZIN
631041HU49D-3

Editorial: Pf. 327, 1437 BUDAPEST **Tel:** 1/390-4474 **Fax:** 1/390-4474
Email: cambus@hu.inter.net
Profile: Publication providing in-depth coverage of a variety of issues connected to transportation. Featuring public transport, logistics, technical and mechanical news, legal advice, background industry news and business connections.
Readership: Aimed at everybody involved in transportation and logistics from drivers to executives.
ADVERTISING RATES:
Full Page Mono .... HUF 320000
Full Page Colour .... HUF 460000
BUSINESS: TRANSPORT: Commercial Vehicles

CÉGAUTÓ MAGAZIN
1796761HU77A-92

Editorial: Csantavér u. 9. I/4., 1146 BUDAPEST **Tel:** 23/444-070 **Fax:** 23/444-069
Email: info@moonandshark.hu
Cover Price: HUF 585; **Circ:** 25,000
Editor-in-Chief: Iván Hámor
CONSUMER: MOTORING & CYCLING: Motoring

CEO MAGAZIN
630670HU14A-100

Editorial: Haller u. 40., 1096 BUDAPEST **Tel:** 1/476-1080 **Fax:** 1/476-1085
Email: media@ceo.hu **Web site:** http://www.ceo.hu
Cover Price: HUF 2950; **Circ:** 10,000
Usual Pagination: 48
Editor-in-Chief: Piroska Szalai
Profile: Magazine containing articles from various Hungarian and international professors on subjects such as management, economics, finance, business theory and ethics.
Readership: Aimed at chief executives and decision makers in business.
ADVERTISING RATES:
Full Page Colour .... HUF 880000
BUSINESS: COMMERCE, INDUSTRY & MANAGEMENT

CHIP
1500105HU5D-10

Editorial: Nagyszolos u. 11-15., 1113 BUDAPEST **Tel:** 1/577-2600 **Fax:** 1/577-2690
Email: mbp@motorpresse.hu **Web site:** http://www.chipmagazin.hu
Cover Price: HUF 1495
Annual Sub.: HUF 17; **Circ:** 19,625
Usual Pagination: 132
Profile: Computer magazine about the developments in hardware and software applications. Focuses on PCs.
Readership: Aimed at managers and general PC users.
ADVERTISING RATES:
Full Page Colour .... HUF 775000
BUSINESS: COMPUTERS & AUTOMATION: Personal Computers

CINEMA MAGAZIN
1689236HU76A-2

Editorial: Falk Miksa u. 3., 1055 BUDAPEST **Tel:** 1/783-4486 **Fax:** 1/783-4486
Email: nagy.rita@geronia.hu
Cover Price: HUF 695; **Circ:** 20,000
CONSUMER: MUSIC & PERFORMING ARTS: Cinema

A CIPO
1689086HU29-1

Editorial: Donáti u. 69., 1015 BUDAPEST **Tel:** 30/294-0063 **Fax:** 1/325-7414
Email: gaborfanni@mail.datanet.hu **Web site:** http://www.acipo.hu
Circ: 3,000
Editor-in-Chief: Fanni Gábor
Profile: Magazine covering all aspects of the footwear industry. Includes trade news, machinery, materials and profiles.
BUSINESS: FOOTWEAR

CKM
631032HU86C-50

Editorial: Hajógyári sziget 213., 1033 BUDAPEST **Tel:** 1/505-0800 **Fax:** 1/505-0806
Cover Price: HUF 695; **Circ:** 38,063
Usual Pagination: 116
Profile: Men's magazine containing articles on cars, the Internet, relationships, travel, book reviews, music, films and theatre and careers.
Readership: Aimed at educated men aged between 20 and 50 years.
ADVERTISING RATES:
Full Page Colour .... HUF 1495000
CONSUMER: ADULT & GAY MAGAZINES: Men's Lifestyle Magazines

COMPUTERWORLD
630056HU5B-40

Editorial: Madách út 13-14. A/4, 1075 BUDAPEST **Tel:** 1/577-4300 **Fax:** 1/266-4343
Email: keriroda@idg.hu **Web site:** http://computerworld.hu
Circ: 10,000
Profile: Magazine focusing on information technology and business use of computers.
Readership: Aimed at computer and IT professionals.
BUSINESS: COMPUTERS & AUTOMATION: Data Processing

A CONTROLLER
1796854HU1A-156

Editorial: Homokos dulo 1., 1031 BUDAPEST **Tel:** 1/430-0571 **Fax:** 1/240-5670
Email: info@ecovit.hu **Web site:** http://www.ecovit.hu
Circ: 1,000
BUSINESS: FINANCE & ECONOMICS

CSAJOK MAGAZIN
1827483HU74C-132

Editorial: Dózsa Gy. út 32., 1071 BUDAPEST **Tel:** 1/343-1816 **Fax:** 1/413-7131
Email: csajokmagazin@csajokmagazin.hu **Web site:** http://www.csajokmagazin.hu
Circ: 50,000
Editor-in-Chief: Krisztina Széles
Profile: Magazine focused on family, health and lifestyle.
CONSUMER: WOMEN'S INTEREST CONSUMER MAGAZINES: Home & Family

CSALÁDI HÁZ MAGAZIN
630851HU4E-50

Editorial: Neumann János u. 1., 2040 BUDAÖRS **Tel:** 23/422-455 **Fax:** 23/422-456
Web site: http://csaladihaz.hu
Profile: Magazine providing in-depth coverage of house construction. Introduces homes from all over the country and internationally, building materials, building machinery, refurbishment and environmental issues.
Readership: Aimed at those who are in the process of building their own home, professional builders and managers of construction companies.
BUSINESS: ARCHITECTURE & BUILDING: Building

CUKORIPAR
634438HU22R-2

Editorial: Tolnai Lajos u. 25., 1084 BUDAPEST **Tel:** 1/323-2810 **Fax:** 1/214-6692
Email: mail.mete@mtesz.hu
Managing Editor: András dr. Zsigmond
Profile: Publication focusing on sugar manufacturing. Featuring technology, energetics and quality control of sugar manufacturing, also issues concerning natural ingredients, such as processing sugarbeet.
Readership: Aimed at sugar manufacturing engineers, manufacturers, research staff and product traders.
BUSINESS: FOOD: Food Related

DEBRECEN
1688895HU72-187

Editorial: Simonffy u. 2/A, 4025 DEBRECEN **Tel:** 52/581-818 **Fax:** 52/581-803
Email: kiado@deol.hu **Web site:** http://www.deol.hu
Circ: 90,000
Advertising Manager: Gabriella Bodnár
LOCAL NEWSPAPERS

DECANTER MAGAZIN
1796671HU21H-9

Editorial: Pálya u. 9., 1012 BUDAPEST **Tel:** 1/487-5200 **Fax:** 1/487-5203
Web site: http://www.decanter.com
Circ: 15,000
Usual Pagination: 80
ADVERTISING RATES:
Full Page Colour .... HUF 1100000
BUSINESS: AGRICULTURE & FARMING: Vine Growing

DÉLMAGYARORSZÁG
1688251HU67B-534

Editorial: Szabadkai út 20., 6729 SZEGED **Tel:** 62/567-888 **Fax:** 62/567-881
Email: szerkesztoseg@delmagyar.hu **Web site:** http://www.delmagyar.hu
Circ: 53,998
Editor-in-Chief: András Szetey
REGIONAL DAILY & SUNDAY NEWSPAPERS: Regional Daily Newspapers

DÉLPESTI KISHEKKI
1688694HU67B-507

Editorial: Kozma u. 9-11., 1108 BUDAPEST **Tel:** 1/210-0435 **Fax:** 1/210-0436
Email: szerkesztoseg@hekki.net **Web site:** http://www.amkiado.hu
Circ: 45,000
Editor-in-Chief: Gyula Kruppa
REGIONAL DAILY & SUNDAY NEWSPAPERS: Regional Daily Newspapers

DETEKTOR PLUSZ
631047HU54C-50

Editorial: Mogyoródi út 127/B, 1141 BUDAPEST **Tel:** 1/370-5018 **Fax:** 1/370-5018
Email: detektor@hu.inter.net
Profile: Publication providing in-depth coverage on personal and data security.
Readership: Aimed at security officers, managers and executives.
ADVERTISING RATES:
Full Page Colour .... HUF 255000
BUSINESS: SAFETY & SECURITY: Security

DIABETES
633059HU56A-145

Editorial: Hermina út 57-59., 1146 BUDAPEST **Tel:** 1/273-2840 **Fax:** 1/384-5399
Email: tudomany@tudomany-kiado.hu
Circ: 30,000
Profile: Publication providing in-depth coverage on diabetes. Featuring specialist doctors' articles, children with diabetes, dieticians' advice and news on the Diabetes Foundation.
Readership: Aimed at members of the medical profession and patients suffering from diabetes.
ADVERTISING RATES:
Full Page Colour .... HUF 358000
BUSINESS: HEALTH & MEDICAL

DIABETOLOGIA HUNGARICA
634685HU56A-53

Editorial: Hermina út 57-59., 1146 BUDAPEST **Tel:** 1/273-2840 **Fax:** 1/384-5399
Email: tudomany@tudomany-kiado.hu
Circ: 2,000
Profile: Journal focusing on diabetes and surgery.
Readership: Aimed at surgeons and doctors specialising in curing and researching diabetes.
BUSINESS: HEALTH & MEDICAL

DINING GUIDE
1690415HU74P-164

Editorial: Király u. 16., 1061 BUDAPEST **Tel:** 1/887-4848 **Fax:** 1/887-4849
Email: sales@pxb.hu **Web site:** http://www.pxb.hu
Circ: 30,000
Usual Pagination: 124
ADVERTISING RATES:
Full Page Colour .... HUF 270000
CONSUMER: WOMEN'S INTEREST CONSUMER MAGAZINES: Food & Cookery

DIPLOMACY & TRADE
1645392HU82-151

Editorial: Bécsi út 60., 1034 BUDAPEST **Tel:** 70/320-3051
Email: advertising@dteurope.com **Web site:** http://www.dteurope.com
Cover Price: HUF 490
Editor-in-Chief: András Badics
Profile: Magazine focusing on business, economy, trade, diplomacy, art, culture, politics and life style.
CONSUMER: CURRENT AFFAIRS & POLITICS

DRINFO EGÉSZSÉGMAGAZIN
1690066HU56A-144

Editorial: Czobor u. 82., 1147 BUDAPEST **Tel:** 1/363-1122
Email: info@diabetesonline.hu **Web site:** http://diabetesonline.hu
Circ: 30,000
Usual Pagination: 64
ADVERTISING RATES:
Full Page Colour .... HUF 360000
BUSINESS: HEALTH & MEDICAL

DUNAÚJVÁROSI HÍRLAP
1688299HU67B-546

Editorial: Vasmu u. 41. fszt. 6., 2400 DUNAÚJVÁROS **Tel:** 25/402-985 **Fax:** 25/402-986
Circ: 8,855
ADVERTISING RATES:
Full Page Mono .... HUF 485940
Full Page Colour .... HUF 680316
REGIONAL DAILY & SUNDAY NEWSPAPERS: Regional Daily Newspapers

DUNAÚJVÁROSI MARATON
1688475HU67J-16

Editorial: Házgyári út 12., 8200 VESZPRÉM **Tel:** 88/541-763 **Fax:** 88/541-688
Email: maraton@maraton.plt.hu **Web site:** http://www.maraton.hu
Circ: 23,970
ADVERTISING RATES:
Full Page Mono .... HUF 305270
REGIONAL DAILY & SUNDAY NEWSPAPERS: Regional Newspapers (excl. dailies)

DVD ÚJDONSÁGOK
1689285HU78B-1

Editorial: Perc u. 8., 1036 BUDAPEST **Tel:** 1/467-1400 **Fax:** 1/467-4242
Email: intercom@intercom.hu
Circ: 700
CONSUMER: CONSUMER ELECTRONICS: Video & DVD

ÉDESIPAR
706713HU8B-40

Editorial: Moszkva tér 5-7., 6725 SZEGED **Tel:** 62/546-030 **Fax:** 214-6692
Email: mail.mete@mtesz.hu
Managing Editor: Erno dr. Gyimes
Profile: Journal featuring the production of cocoa, chocolate, sugar and confectionery, biscuits and cakes, snacks and ice-cream. Providing information on new technology, economic analysis, quality control. Includes updates on trade and association news, conferences, new developments and the history of the industry. Contents and summaries are available in English, German and Russian as well as the main language.
Readership: Aimed at the members of the Association of Hungarian Confectionery Manufacturers and the Scientific Union of Nutrition Industries, also all those involved and interested in these industries.
BUSINESS: BAKING & CONFECTIONERY: Confectionery Manufacturing

ÉKSZER MAGAZIN
1689274HU52A-2

Editorial: Fehér út 10. (FMV) 8-as épület, 1106 BUDAPEST **Tel:** 1/260-1148 **Fax:** 1/260-4869
Email: direxmedia@direxmedia.hu **Web site:** http://www.ekszermagazin.hu
Cover Price: HUF 690; **Circ:** 10,000
BUSINESS: GIFT TRADE: Jewellery

ELEKTROINSTALLATEUR
706687HU17-75

Editorial: Balassi Bálint u. 7., 1055 BUDAPEST **Tel:** 1/301-3864 **Fax:** 1/301-3814
Email: elektro@mediprint.hu **Web site:** http://www.elektroinstallateur.hu
Annual Sub.: HUF 6000; **Circ:** 4,000
Profile: Journal of the Association of Industrial Electrical Businesses. Focuses on all electrical appliances, and systems involved in construction, wiring and alarm systems. Aims to give practical help to professionals in the technical, economic and retail fields. Provides information on new products and services.
Readership: Aimed at members of the Association of Industrial Electrical Businesses, also designers, builders and electrical retailers.
ADVERTISING RATES:
Full Page Colour .... HUF 550000
BUSINESS: ELECTRICAL

ELEKTRONET
630858HU18A-50

Editorial: Erzsébet királyné útja 125., 1142 BUDAPEST **Tel:** 1/231-4040
Email: info@elektro-net.hu **Web site:** http://www.elektro-net.hu
Cover Price: HUF 1350
Annual Sub.: HUF 8680; **Circ:** 9,200
Usual Pagination: 64
Profile: Magazine focusing on electronics. Content consists of theoretical and practical articles on professional issues, news and programs.
Readership: Aimed at qualified electronics specialists and executives showing an interest in the application of electronics in industry.
ADVERTISING RATES:
Full Page Colour .... HUF 472000
BUSINESS: ELECTRONICS

ELEKTROTECHNIKA
634002HU17-80

Editorial: Kossuth Lajos tér 6-8., 1055 BUDAPEST **Tel:** 1/353-1108 **Fax:** 1/353-4069
Email: elektrotechnika@mee.hu **Web site:** http://www.mee.hu
Cover Price: HUF 6300; **Circ:** 6,000
Profile: Publication of the Organisation of the Hungarian Electrotechnical Association, focuses on power generation, distribution, automation, heavy electrical machinery and apparatus.
Readership: Aimed at electrical and mechanical engineers, professors and students.
ADVERTISING RATES:
Full Page Colour .... HUF 290000
BUSINESS: ELECTRICAL

Hungary

ÉLELMEZÉS 1689294HU22A-140
Editorial: Eörsy Péter u. 25/A, 9024 GYOR **Tel:** 96/525-014 **Fax:** 96/525-015
Email: pentasys@t-online.hu **Web site:** http://www.elelmezes.hu
Annual Sub.: HUF 5100; **Circ:** 5,000
Usual Pagination: 52
Editor-in-Chief: János Benda
ADVERTISING RATES:
Full Page Mono .... HUF 108000
Full Page Colour .... HUF 180000
BUSINESS: FOOD

ÉLELMEZÉSI IPAR 634821HU22A-50
Editorial: Fo u. 68., 1027 BUDAPEST **Tel:** 1/225-0708 **Fax:** 1/214-6692
Email: mail.mete@mtesz.hu
Managing Editor: Zoltán dr. Hernádi
Profile: Journal focusing on food science, macro-economic trends, nutrition science, research, improvements and international news.
Readership: Aimed at food industrial engineers and executives of food retailing and wholesaling organisations.
BUSINESS: FOOD

ÉLELMISZER 766241HU22A-131
Editorial: Montevideo u. 3/B, 1037 BUDAPEST
Tel: 1/430-4544 **Fax:** 1/430-4549
Email: elelmiszer@elelmiszer.hu **Web site:** http://www.elelmiszer.hu
Cover Price: HUF 990; **Circ:** 18,000
Profile: Magazine for food and non-food products.
Readership: Read by decision-makers at purchasing departments, store managers, food and non-food producers, trading company managers and advertising agency executives.
BUSINESS: FOOD

ÉLET ÉS IRODALOM 631087HU82-50
Editorial: Rezso tér 15., 1089 BUDAPEST **Tel:** 1/210-5149 **Fax:** 1/303-9241
Email: es@es.hu **Web site:** http://www.es.hu
Cover Price: HUF 396; **Circ:** 21,000
Editor-in-Chief: Zoltán Kovács
Profile: Magazine containing articles on literature, politics, culture and news from the world of science.
Readership: Aimed at people with a general interest in current affairs.
ADVERTISING RATES:
Full Page Mono .... HUF 396000
Full Page Colour .... HUF 670000
CONSUMER: CURRENT AFFAIRS & POLITICS

ELITE MAGAZIN 1200814HU74A-5
Editorial: Lehel út 61., 1135 BUDAPEST **Tel:** 1/288-8560 **Fax:** 1/288-8570
Email: elite@elitemagazin.hu
Cover Price: HUF 627; **Circ:** 15,000
Usual Pagination: 128
Profile: Magazine covering lifestyle issues.
Readership: Aimed at those with a high disposable income, with an interest in culture and society.
ADVERTISING RATES:
Full Page Colour .... HUF 760000
CONSUMER: WOMEN'S INTEREST CONSUMER MAGAZINES: Women's Interest

ELIXÍR MAGAZIN 1689296HU74G-206
Editorial: Lehel u. 5. II/25., 1062 BUDAPEST **Tel:** 1/349-5933 **Fax:** 1/349-5933
Email: zita@elixir.hu
Cover Price: HUF 495
Annual Sub.: HUF 5520; **Circ:** 52,000
ADVERTISING RATES:
Full Page Colour .... HUF 650000
CONSUMER: WOMEN'S INTEREST CONSUMER MAGAZINES: Slimming & Health

ELLE 1689300HU74A-141
Editorial: Montevideo u. 9, 1037 BUDAPEST
Tel: 1 4373947 **Fax:** 1 4373181
Email: szilvia.csaki@sanomamedia.hu **Web site:** http://www.sanomamedia.hu
Freq: április 16./március 30., május 14./április 27.., június 11./május 25., július 16./június 29., augusztus 13./július 27., szeptember 17./augusztus 31., október 15./szeptember 28.., november 12./október 26., december 8./november 23; **Cover Price:** HUF 845; **Circ:** 37,500
Usual Pagination: 148
Editor-in-Chief: Virág Vass; **Advertising Manager:** Surányi Csáki Szilvia
Language(s): Hungarian
ADVERTISING RATES:
Full Page Colour .... HUF 1520000
Mechanical Data: Type Area: 170x239mm, Trim Size: 215x280 mm, Print Process: ofszet, 4+4 szin, Screen: 60 (150 lpi)
CONSUMER: WOMEN'S INTEREST CONSUMER MAGAZINES: Women's Interest

ENERGIAFOGYASZTÓK LAPJA 1690424HU58-31
Editorial: Köztársaság tér 7., 1081 BUDAPEST
Tel: 1/299-0267 **Fax:** 1/299-0268
Email: info@energetikaikiado.hu **Web site:** http://www.energetikaikiado.hu
Circ: 20,000
Usual Pagination: 36
Editor-in-Chief: László dr. Helm
ADVERTISING RATES:
Full Page Colour .... HUF 170000
BUSINESS: ENERGY, FUEL & NUCLEAR

ENERGIAGAZDÁLKODÁS 706719HU58-25
Editorial: Fo u. 68. V/525., 1027 BUDAPEST **Tel:** 1/353-2751 **Fax:** 1/353-3894
Circ: 1,500
Profile: Journal providing scientific articles on energy economics, energy efficiency and different issues involving the energy industry.
Readership: Aimed at the members of the Hungarian Scientific Society of Energy Economics and all those involved in the energy industry.
BUSINESS: ENERGY, FUEL & NUCLEAR

ENTREPRENEUR - AZ ÜZLETTÁRS 1797099HU14A-242
Editorial: Felsoerdosor u. 12-14., 1068 BUDAPEST
Tel: 1/769-1446 **Fax:** 1/785-6968
Email: info@azuzlettars.hu **Web site:** http://www.azuzlettars.hu
Cover Price: HUF 499; **Circ:** 10,000
Usual Pagination: 74
ADVERTISING RATES:
Full Page Colour .... HUF 1175000
BUSINESS: COMMERCE, INDUSTRY & MANAGEMENT

ÉPÍTO ÉLET 1827581HU4E-124
Editorial: Csengery út 22., 8800 NAGYKANIZSA
Tel: 20/423-0042 **Fax:** 93/516-984
Email: kalauz@t-online.hu **Web site:** http://www.epitoelet.hu
Circ: 3,800
Editor-in-Chief: Tamás Tóth
BUSINESS: ARCHITECTURE & BUILDING: Building

ÉPÍTOANYAG 1797039HU4E-118
Editorial: Fo u. 68., 1027 BUDAPEST **Tel:** 1/201-9360 **Fax:** 1/201-9360
Email: info@szte.org.hu **Web site:** http://www.szte.org.hu
Cover Price: HUF 1000; **Circ:** 800
Usual Pagination: 32
Editor-in-Chief: Réka Tóth-Asztalos
ADVERTISING RATES:
Full Page Mono .... HUF 58000
Full Page Colour .... HUF 105000
BUSINESS: ARCHITECTURE & BUILDING: Building

ÉPÍTOGÉPEK, ÉPÍTÉSGÉPESÍTÉS 1690694HU4E-102
Editorial: Ágoston u. 18., 1032 BUDAPEST **Tel:** 70/317-4380 **Fax:** 1/437-0166
Email: epitogepek@epitogepek.hu **Web site:** http://www.epitogepek.hu
Circ: 5,000
Usual Pagination: 100
ADVERTISING RATES:
Full Page Colour .... HUF 198000
BUSINESS: ARCHITECTURE & BUILDING: Building

ÉPÍTOIPARI SZAKILAP 1689309HU4E-94
Editorial: Péterfia u. 4., 4026 DEBRECEN **Tel:** 20/419-0016
Email: szakilap@szakilap.hu **Web site:** http://www.szakilap.hu
Circ: 70,000
Editor-in-Chief: Ibolya Marincsák
BUSINESS: ARCHITECTURE & BUILDING: Building

ÉPÍTOVILÁG 1843315HU4A-92
Editorial: Hársfa u. 21., 1074 BUDAPEST **Tel:** 1/342-7734 **Fax:** 1/342-7337
Email: kg.szakujsagiro@chello.hu **Web site:** http://www.etkkft.hu
Cover Price: HUF 420; **Circ:** 3,000
Editor-in-Chief: Gábor dr. Kiss
BUSINESS: ARCHITECTURE & BUILDING: Architecture

ERDOGAZDASÁG ÉS FAIPAR 1843362HU46-17
Editorial: Mirtusz u. 2., 1141 BUDAPEST **Tel:** 1/470-0411 **Fax:** 1/470-0410
Email: mmg@magyarmezogazdasag.hu
Cover Price: HUF 360
Usual Pagination: 32
BUSINESS: TIMBER, WOOD & FORESTRY

ESKÜVO ELOTT-ESKÜVO UTÁN 1796830HU74L-9
Editorial: Játék u. 8., 1221 BUDAPEST **Tel:** 1/229-0438 **Fax:** 1/229-0438
Email: delbszinfo@t-online.hu
Circ: 76,000
CONSUMER: WOMEN'S INTEREST CONSUMER MAGAZINES: Brides

ESKÜVOI DIVAT 1690697HU74L-18
Editorial: Kismartoni u. 55., 2040 BUDAÖRS-KAMARAERDO **Tel:** 23/444-438 **Fax:** 23/444-437
Email: eskuvo@eskuvoidivat.net **Web site:** http://www.eskuvoidivat.net
Cover Price: HUF 1180; **Circ:** 25,000
Usual Pagination: 400
Editor-in-Chief: Nóra Ömböly
ADVERTISING RATES:
Full Page Mono .... HUF 220000
Full Page Colour .... HUF 260000
CONSUMER: WOMEN'S INTEREST CONSUMER MAGAZINES: Brides

ÉSZAK-MAGYARORSZÁG 1688266HU67B-537
Editorial: Zsolcai kapu 3., 3526 MISKOLC **Tel:** 46/502-900 **Fax:** 46/501-260
Email: inform@inform.hu
Circ: 156,549
Usual Pagination: 16
ADVERTISING RATES:
Full Page Colour .... HUF 1416000
REGIONAL DAILY & SUNDAY NEWSPAPERS: Regional Daily Newspapers

ESZENCIA 1797133HU21H-12
Editorial: Kupeczky u. 9., 1025 BUDAPEST **Tel:** 1/346-0159 **Fax:** 1/346-0160
Email: rosenmayer@eszencia.co.hu **Web site:** http://www.eszencia.co.hu
Circ: 10,000
Editor-in-Chief: András Rosenmayer
BUSINESS: AGRICULTURE & FARMING: Vine Growing

EURÓPAI HÁZAK 1827432HU4A-84
Editorial: Szövo u. 31., 6726 SZEGED **Tel:** 62/425-787 **Fax:** 62/555-632
Email: szukits.kiado@vnet.hu **Web site:** http://www.europaihazak.hu
Cover Price: HUF 495
Editor-in-Chief: József Kószó
BUSINESS: ARCHITECTURE & BUILDING: Architecture

THE EXPLORER MAGAZIN 1796683HU89A-36
Editorial: Kelenhegyi út 29/A, 1118 BUDAPEST
Tel: 1/319-1539 **Fax:** 1/279-0253
Email: info@explorergroup.hu **Web site:** http://www.explorergroup.hu
Cover Price: HUF 595; **Circ:** 20,000
Profile: Magazine focused on outdoor sports activities.
CONSUMER: HOLIDAYS & TRAVEL: Travel

EXPRESSZ AUTÓ-MOTOR 1688360HU77A-26
Editorial: Babér u. 7., 1131 BUDAPEST **Tel:** 1/479-7919 **Fax:** 1/479-7916
Cover Price: HUF 348
ADVERTISING RATES:
Full Page Colour .... HUF 180000
CONSUMER: MOTORING & CYCLING: Motoring

EXTRA FRIZURA 1689582HU15A-21
Editorial: Lajos u. 48-66 B lhp II. em., 1036 BUDAPEST **Tel:** 1/489-8846 **Fax:** 1/430-1536
Email: extrafrizura@geomedia.hu
Cover Price: HUF 495
Usual Pagination: 64
ADVERTISING RATES:
Full Page Colour .... HUF 690000
BUSINESS: COSMETICS & HAIRDRESSING: Cosmetics

EZO TÉR MAGAZIN 1796684HU74Q-223
Editorial: Ritsmann Pál u. 25., 2051 BIATORBÁGY
Tel: 70/210-9833
Email: info@ezomedia.hu
Circ: 30,000
CONSUMER: WOMEN'S INTEREST CONSUMER MAGAZINES: Lifestyle

EZREDVÉG 634423HU84B-50
Editorial: Kupeczky u. 8., 1025 BUDAPEST **Tel:** 1/326-5759
Cover Price: HUF 350; **Circ:** 1,200
Usual Pagination: 80
Editor-in-Chief: András Simor
Profile: Magazine featuring literature, poems, novels, critics, arts and current affairs.
Readership: Aimed at the general public.
ADVERTISING RATES:
Full Page Mono .... HUF 40000
CONSUMER: THE ARTS & LITERARY: Literary

FANNY 1688324HU74A-133
Editorial: Városmajor u. 11., 1122 BUDAPEST **Tel:** 1/488-5700 **Fax:** 1/488-5775
Circ: 120,025
Editor-in-Chief: Aranka Stefanek
ADVERTISING RATES:
Full Page Colour .... HUF 880000
CONSUMER: WOMEN'S INTEREST CONSUMER MAGAZINES: Women's Interest

FEHÉRVÁRI 7 NAP 1688476HU67B-566
Editorial: Házgyári út 12., 8200 VESZPRÉM **Tel:** 88/541-763 **Fax:** 88/541-688
Email: maraton@maraton.plt.hu **Web site:** http://www.maraton.hu
Circ: 45,000
ADVERTISING RATES:
Full Page Mono .... HUF 576275
REGIONAL DAILY & SUNDAY NEWSPAPERS: Regional Daily Newspapers

FEHÉRVÁRI 7 NAP PLUSSZ 1688477HU67J-17
Editorial: Házgyári út 12., 8200 VESZPRÉM **Tel:** 88/541-763 **Fax:** 88/541-688
Email: maraton@maraton.plt.hu **Web site:** http://www.maraton.hu
Circ: 20,000
ADVERTISING RATES:
Full Page Mono .... HUF 336420
REGIONAL DAILY & SUNDAY NEWSPAPERS: Regional Newspapers (excl. dailies)

FEHÉRVÁRI START AUTÓS MAGAZIN 1689865HU77A-45
Editorial: Irányi D. u. 6., 8000 SZÉKESFEHÉRVÁR
Tel: 22/502-525 **Fax:** 22/502-526
Email: info@absurd.hu **Web site:** http://www.absurd.hu/start
Circ: 26,000
Editor-in-Chief: Anikó Baranyi
CONSUMER: MOTORING & CYCLING: Motoring

FEJÉR MEGYEI HÍRLAP 1688298HU67B-545
Editorial: Fo u. 17., 8000 SZÉKESFEHÉRVÁR
Tel: 22/316-590 **Fax:** 22/312-884
Circ: 46,395
ADVERTISING RATES:
Full Page Mono .... HUF 1420440
Full Page Colour .... HUF 1988616
REGIONAL DAILY & SUNDAY NEWSPAPERS: Regional Daily Newspapers

FÉSZEKRAKÓ MAGAZIN 1843452HU4A-93
Editorial: Teve u. 41., 1139 BUDAPEST **Tel:** 1/288-7070 **Fax:** 1/237-1209
Email: info@starfish.hu **Web site:** http://www.starfish.hu
Circ: 25,000
Profile: Magazine focusing on all aspects of interior design and architecture. Also includes advice and information on new products and trends.
ADVERTISING RATES:
Full Page Colour .... HUF 680000
BUSINESS: ARCHITECTURE & BUILDING: Architecture

FIDELIO EST 1689816HU89C-83
Editorial: Lajos u. 74-76., 1036 BUDAPEST **Tel:** 1/436-5000 **Fax:** 1/436-5001
Email: estmedia@estmedia.hu **Web site:** http://www.estmedia.hu
Circ: 50,000
CONSUMER: HOLIDAYS & TRAVEL: Entertainment Guides

FIT MUSCLE 1690446HU74G-219
Editorial: Telepes u. 51., 1147 BUDAPEST **Tel:** 1/222-6023 **Fax:** 1/363-3121
Email: art@scitecnutrition.hu **Web site:** http://www.fitmuscle.hu
Circ: 100,000
Editor-in-Chief: Zsolt Bengyel
CONSUMER: WOMEN'S INTEREST CONSUMER MAGAZINES: Slimming & Health

FITT MAMA 766359HU74C-82
Editorial: Hajógyári-sziget 213., 1033 BUDAPEST
Tel: 1/505-0800 **Fax:** 1/505-0806
Cover Price: HUF 495; **Circ:** 15,000
Usual Pagination: 108

Profile: Magazine focusing on health, fitness, nutrition, beauty and fashion topics for pregnant women and young mothers.
Readership: Aimed at expectant women and mothers of young children.
ADVERTISING RATES:
Full Page Colour .... HUF 890000
CONSUMER: WOMEN'S INTEREST CONSUMER MAGAZINES: Home & Family

FITTTIPP 2009
1690790HU75A-10
Editorial: Véghely D. u. 1., 8220 BALATONALMÁDI **Tel:** 70/383-6770
Email: iroda@marathon.hu **Web site:** http://www.marathon.hu
Circ: 30,000
Editor-in-Chief: Zsolt Németh
CONSUMER: SPORT

FORRÓ DRÓT
1689333HU58-27
Editorial: Fo u. 34-36., 1011 BUDAPEST **Tel:** 1/202-1092 **Fax:** 1/202-1534
Email: efabian@mvm.hu **Web site:** http://www.vd.hu
Circ: 25,000
BUSINESS: ENERGY, FUEL & NUCLEAR

FUTÁR
1688598HU67J-18
Tel: 42/501-510/4066 **Fax:** 42/501-970
Circ: 54,000
ADVERTISING RATES:
Full Page Colour .... HUF 440000
REGIONAL DAILY & SUNDAY NEWSPAPERS: Regional Newspapers (excl. dailies)

FUVARLEVÉL
1827478HU10-22
Editorial: Csengery út 22., 8800 NAGYKANIZSA **Tel:** 20/423-0042 **Fax:** 93/516-984
Email: kalauz@t-online.hu **Web site:** http://www.teher.hu
Circ: 7,000
Editor-in-Chief: Tamás Tóth
BUSINESS: MATERIALS HANDLING

GAMESTAR
630071HU78D-80
Editorial: Madách út 13-14. A ép. IV. em., 1075 BUDAPEST **Tel:** 1/577-4300 **Fax:** 1/266-4343
Email: keriroda@idg.hu **Web site:** http://gamestar.hu
Circ: 20,417
Profile: Magazine covering every aspect of computer technology use as entertainment.
Readership: Aimed at young computer game players.
CONSUMER: CONSUMER ELECTRONICS: Games

GARFIELD
1689346HU74F-5
Editorial: Fehér út 10., 1106 BUDAPEST **Tel:** 27/540-266 **Fax:** 27/540-266
Email: pildiko-semic@vnet.hu **Web site:** http://www.semic.hu
Circ: 37,500
Advertising Manager: Ildikó Pápai
ADVERTISING RATES:
Full Page Colour .... HUF 370000
CONSUMER: WOMEN'S INTEREST CONSUMER MAGAZINES: Teenage

GAZDASÁGI KALAUZ
1689351HU63-3
Editorial: Hosszúsétatér 4-6., 8000 SZÉKESFEHÉRVÁR **Tel:** 22/510-310 **Fax:** 22/510-312
Email: fmkik@fmkik.hu **Web site:** http://www.fmkik.hu
Circ: 50,000
BUSINESS: REGIONAL BUSINESS

GÉPGYÁRTÁS
1689358HU19E-2
Editorial: Fo u. 68., 1027 BUDAPEST **Tel:** 1/202-0656 **Fax:** 1/202-0252
Email: mail.gte@mtesz.hu
BUSINESS: ENGINEERING & MACHINERY: Machinery, Machine Tools & Metalworking

GÉPIPAR
1689359HU19A-86
Editorial: Fo u. 68., 1027 BUDAPEST **Tel:** 1/202-0656 **Fax:** 1/202-0252
Email: mail.gte@mtesz.hu
BUSINESS: ENGINEERING & MACHINERY

GLAMOUR
1690946HU74A-149
Editorial: Városmajor u. 11., 1122 BUDAPEST **Tel:** 1/488-5700 **Fax:** 1/488-5775
Circ: 72,350
Editor-in-Chief: Krisztina Maróy
ADVERTISING RATES:
Full Page Colour .... HUF 1640000
CONSUMER: WOMEN'S INTEREST CONSUMER MAGAZINES: Women's Interest

GUSTO
1689355HU21H-7
Editorial: Kapy u. 44., 1025 BUDAPEST **Tel:** 1/200-4545 **Fax:** 1/200-4971
Email: gusto@gusto.hu
Cover Price: HUF 980; **Circ:** 25,000
Editor-in-Chief: János Csillag
BUSINESS: AGRICULTURE & FARMING: Vine Growing

GYERMEKVILÁG KALAUZ
1690750HU81X-3
Editorial: Tisza u. 6. V. em. 26., 1133 BUDAPEST **Tel:** 1/359-3103 **Fax:** 1/359-3103
Email: k.pannonia@chello.hu **Web site:** http://www.viapannonia.hu
Circ: 30,000
CONSUMER: ANIMALS & PETS

GYÓGYHÍR MAGAZIN
1797251HU74G-242
Editorial: Üteg u. 49., 1139 BUDAPEST **Tel:** 1/349-6135 **Fax:** 1/452-0270
Email: info@pressgt.hu **Web site:** http://www.gyogyhirmagazin.hu
Cover Price: HUF 200
Annual Sub.: HUF 2400; **Circ:** 231,317
Usual Pagination: 24
Editor-in-Chief: Tibor Hollauer
ADVERTISING RATES:
Full Page Colour .... HUF 865000
CONSUMER: WOMEN'S INTEREST CONSUMER MAGAZINES: Slimming & Health

GYÓGYHÍREK
1689365HU56A-126
Editorial: Üllői út 86., 1089 BUDAPEST **Tel:** 1/459-9142 **Fax:** 1/459-9143
Email: buncsik@heimpalkorhaz.hu
Circ: 30,000
Usual Pagination: 16
ADVERTISING RATES:
Full Page Colour .... HUF 260000
BUSINESS: HEALTH & MEDICAL

GYÓGYSZERÉSZI HÍRLAP
1689360HU37-31
Editorial: Dózsa György út 19., 1146 BUDAPEST **Tel:** 1/467-8060 **Fax:** 1/363-9223
Email: galenus@galenus.hu **Web site:** http://www.patikamagazin.hu
Circ: 5,700
Usual Pagination: 32
ADVERTISING RATES:
Full Page Mono .... HUF 350000
Full Page Colour .... HUF 420000
BUSINESS: PHARMACEUTICAL & CHEMISTS

GYÓGYVÍZ KALAUZ
1690751HU89E-11
Editorial: Tisza u. 6. V. em. 26., 1133 BUDAPEST **Tel:** 1/359-3103 **Fax:** 1/359-3103
Email: k.pannonia@chello.hu **Web site:** http://www.viapannonia.hu
Circ: 30,000
CONSUMER: HOLIDAYS & TRAVEL: Holidays

GYÖNGY
1689172HU74A-138
Editorial: Városmajor u. 11., 1122 BUDAPEST **Tel:** 1/488-5700 **Fax:** 1/488-5775
Circ: 50,130
Editor-in-Chief: Klára Bokor
ADVERTISING RATES:
Full Page Colour .... HUF 1330000
CONSUMER: WOMEN'S INTEREST CONSUMER MAGAZINES: Women's Interest

HAJ ÉS STÍLUS
634674HU15B-50
Editorial: Naphegy tér 8., 1016 BUDAPEST **Tel:** 1/457-0067 **Fax:** 1/201-3248
Email: szerkesztoseg@health-and-beauty.hu **Web site:** http://www.haj-es-stilus.hu
Annual Sub.: HUF 4990; **Circ:** 6,000
Profile: Official journal of the Hungarian Guild of Hairdressers, providing information on news events, meetings and trade fairs. Introducing new products and materials and informing members of advanced courses and training.
Readership: Aimed at hairdressers, trainee hairdressers and their college teachers, owners and management of hairdressing salons, manufacturers and retailers of hairdressing goods.
BUSINESS: COSMETICS & HAIRDRESSING: Hairdressing

HAJDÚ-BIHARI NAPLÓ
1688268HU67B-539
Editorial: Dósa nádor tér 10., 4024 DEBRECEN **Tel:** 52/525-400 **Fax:** 52/525-405
Email: inform@inform.hu
Circ: 156,549
Usual Pagination: 16
ADVERTISING RATES:
Full Page Colour .... HUF 1296000
REGIONAL DAILY & SUNDAY NEWSPAPERS: Regional Daily Newspapers

HAJÓ MAGAZIN
1600730HU91A-30
Editorial: Bartók Béla út 152. H. III. em, 1115 BUDAPEST **Tel:** 1/275-4187 **Fax:** 1/275-4187
Email: hajo@hajomagazin.hu **Web site:** http://www.hajomagazin.hu
Cover Price: HUF 755
Editor-in-Chief: László Szekeres
Profile: Magazine providing information on sailing, power boating and water-skiing. Featuring articles on boating history, regattas, national and international news, and new products.
Readership: Aimed at all boating and water-sports enthusiasts.
CONSUMER: RECREATION & LEISURE: Boating & Yachting

HAMU ÉS GYÉMÁNT
1690479HU51-81
Editorial: Pálya u. 9., 1012 BUDAPEST **Tel:** 1/487-5200 **Fax:** 1/487-5203
Circ: 25,000
Usual Pagination: 140
ADVERTISING RATES:
Full Page Colour .... HUF 1350000
BUSINESS: TOBACCO

HASZON MAGAZIN
1689391HU14A-205
Editorial: Bécsi út 57-59., 1036 BUDAPEST **Tel:** 1/353-0575 **Fax:** 1/269-2051
Email: haszon@haszon.hu **Web site:** http://www.haszon.hu
Cover Price: HUF 490; **Circ:** 33,857
Usual Pagination: 84
ADVERTISING RATES:
Full Page Colour .... HUF 1260000
BUSINESS: COMMERCE, INDUSTRY & MANAGEMENT

HÁZIMOZI
1689398HU78B-3
Editorial: Budafoki út 60., 1117 BUDAPEST **Tel:** 1/464-3880 **Fax:** 1/382-0211
Email: janos.herceg@annex.hu
Cover Price: HUF 850; **Circ:** 15,000
CONSUMER: CONSUMER ELECTRONICS: Video & DVD

HEKUS BUNÜGYI MAGAZIN
1688666HU32F-3
Editorial: József nádor tér 9., 1051 BUDAPEST **Tel:** 1/266-7572 **Fax:** 1/266-7574
Email: titkarsag@hekusmagazin.hu
Circ: 25,000
BUSINESS: LOCAL GOVERNMENT, LEISURE & RECREATION: Police

HELYI TÉMA - AGGLOMERÁCIÓ
1797139HU72-440
Editorial: Fehérvári út 87., 1119 BUDAPEST **Tel:** 1/814-4755 **Fax:** 1/814-4756
Email: ertekesites@helyitema.hu
Circ: 51,800
ADVERTISING RATES:
Full Page Colour .... HUF 464311
LOCAL NEWSPAPERS

HEVES MEGYEI HÍRLAP
1688225HU67B-527
Editorial: Városmajor u. 11., 1122 BUDAPEST **Tel:** 1/488-5726 **Fax:** 1/488-5719
Circ: 22,176
Advertising Director: András Lengyel
ADVERTISING RATES:
Full Page Mono .... HUF 768000
Full Page Colour .... HUF 1032000
REGIONAL DAILY & SUNDAY NEWSPAPERS: Regional Daily Newspapers

HÍRADÁSTECHNIKA
633977HU18B-100
Editorial: Kossuth tér 6-8., 1055 BUDAPEST **Tel:** 1/353-1027
Profile: Publication providing professional and scientific coverage of telecommunications and technical issues about information technology.
Readership: Aimed at telecommunications and IT engineers.
BUSINESS: ELECTRONICS: Telecommunications

HITELEZÉS-KOCKÁZATKEZELÉS ÚJSÁG
1797105HU1A-160
Tel: 70/595-0123
Email: ugyfelszolgalat@nvo.hu **Web site:** http://www.nvo.hu
Circ: 100,000
Profile: Journal focusing on credit and risk management issues.
BUSINESS: FINANCE & ECONOMICS

HIVATÁSUNK
1797306HU56R-206
Editorial: Üllői út 82., 1082 BUDAPEST **Tel:** 1/323-2070 **Fax:** 1/323-2079
Email: meszk@meszk.hu **Web site:** http://www.meszk.hu
Circ: 50,000
Editor-in-Chief: Zoltán Balogh
BUSINESS: HEALTH & MEDICAL: Health Medical Related

HÖLGYVILÁG
631015HU74A-30
Editorial: Városmajor u. 11., 1122 BUDAPEST **Tel:** 1/488-5700 **Fax:** 1/488-5775
Circ: 63,208
Editor-in-Chief: Márta Palásti
Profile: Magazine focusing on lifestyle, beauty, fashion, family matters, health and travel.
Readership: Aimed at well educated women of all ages.
ADVERTISING RATES:
Full Page Colour .... HUF 1350000
CONSUMER: WOMEN'S INTEREST CONSUMER MAGAZINES: Women's Interest

HORIZON
1843406HU89D-1
Editorial: Lajos u. 48-66. B ép. II. em., 1036 BUDAPEST **Tel:** 1/489-8812 **Fax:** 1/430-1536
Email: hirdetes@geomedia.hu **Web site:** http://www.geomedia.hu
Circ: 20,000
Usual Pagination: 96
Editor-in-Chief: Gábor Szucs
ADVERTISING RATES:
Full Page Colour .... HUF 1320000
CONSUMER: HOLIDAYS & TRAVEL: In-Flight Magazines

HOT! MAGAZIN
1797263HU74A-164
Editorial: Szugló u. 81-85., 1141 BUDAPEST **Tel:** 1/460-4880 **Fax:** 1/460-4882
Cover Price: HUF 185; **Circ:** 135,773
Usual Pagination: 68
ADVERTISING RATES:
Full Page Colour .... HUF 1550000
CONSUMER: WOMEN'S INTEREST CONSUMER MAGAZINES: Women's Interest

HOTELEPROGRAM
1689426HU89B-1
Editorial: Pannónia u. 19., 1136 BUDAPEST **Tel:** 1/359-1826 **Fax:** 1/359-1826
Email: hoteleprogram@chello.hu
Circ: 25,000
Editor-in-Chief: Éva Erdos
CONSUMER: HOLIDAYS & TRAVEL: Hotel Magazines

HUNGARIAN AGRICULTURAL RESEARCH
1689767HU21A-141
Editorial: Páter K. u. 1., 2103 GÖDÖLLO **Tel:** 28/522-042 **Fax:** 28/522-042
Email: kiado@agroinform.com **Web site:** http://www.agroinform.com
Circ: 1,700
Editor-in-Chief: István Gyürk
BUSINESS: AGRICULTURE & FARMING

HUNGARY INFO
1690820HU89B-3
Editorial: Váci u. 78-80., 1056 BUDAPEST **Tel:** 1/266-3741 **Fax:** 1/267-0896
Email: marketing@hotelinfo.hu **Web site:** http://www.hotelinfo.hu
Circ: 50,000
CONSUMER: HOLIDAYS & TRAVEL: Hotel Magazines

A HÚS
633919HU22D-100
Editorial: Gubacsi út 6/B, 1097 BUDAPEST **Tel:** 1/215-7350 **Fax:** 1/214-6692
Email: mail.mete@mtesz.hu
Managing Editor: Kálmán dr. Incze
Profile: Magazine publishing research within the field of meat and nutrition under the following sections: Economical issues, meat science, meat and health, nature and technology, quality issues and livestock and meat production.
Readership: Aimed at dieticians, veterinary surgeons and those involved in the meat industry.
BUSINESS: FOOD: Meat Trade

HVG
1600490HU1A-4
Editorial: Montevideo u. 14., 1037 BUDAPEST **Tel:** 1/436-2020 **Fax:** 1/436-2089
Email: hirdet@hvg.hu **Web site:** http://www.hvg.hu
Cover Price: HUF 315; **Circ:** 105,430
Profile: Magazine focusing on the world economy with features covering financial, political, scientific and society matters. Contains interviews, opinion, weekly monitoring and portraits.
Readership: Aimed at business executives involved in finance and economics.
ADVERTISING RATES:
Full Page Mono .... HUF 1380000
Full Page Colour .... HUF 2800000
BUSINESS: FINANCE & ECONOMICS

Hungary

IDEÁL
631100HU74G-70
Editorial: Margit krt. 56. I/4., 1027 BUDAPEST **Tel:** 1/225-2012
Email: ideal@ideal.hu **Web site:** http://www.ideal.hu
Cover Price: HUF 485; **Circ:** 36,000
Usual Pagination: 96
Editor-in-Chief: József dr. Tamasi
Profile: Magazine focusing on lifestyle issues. Includes features on natural medicine, health, childcare and upbringing, organic recipes and mental health.
Readership: Aimed at women, aged between 18 and 50 years.
ADVERTISING RATES:
Full Page Mono .... HUF 440000
Full Page Colour .... HUF 760000
CONSUMER: WOMEN'S INTEREST CONSUMER MAGAZINES: Slimming & Health

INGATLAN ÉS BEFEKTETÉS
630571HU1E-150
Editorial: Károly krt. 9., 1075 BUDAPEST **Tel:** 1/342-8971 **Fax:** 1/352-7143
Email: info@immopress.hu **Web site:** http://www.ingatlanbefektetes.hu
Cover Price: HUF 560; **Circ:** 8,000
Editor-in-Chief: Zoltán Bogdán
Profile: Magazine containing articles on property investment, trend and development and analysis of investments.
Readership: Aimed at property agents, investment advisors and investors.
BUSINESS: FINANCE & ECONOMICS: Property

INGATLANRIPORT
1797107HU1E-168
Editorial: Bajcsy-Zsilinszky út 12., 1051 BUDAPEST **Tel:** 1/267-0161 **Fax:** 1/267-0253
Email: info@ingatlanriport.hu **Web site:** http://www.ingatlanriport.hu
Circ: 100,000
Profile: Magazine covering the Hungarian property market. Also includes articles and advise on property investment.
BUSINESS: FINANCE & ECONOMICS: Property

INTERCITY MAGAZIN
1690882HU89C-109
Editorial: Pálya u. 9., 1012 BUDAPEST **Tel:** 1/487-5200 **Fax:** 1/487-5203
Circ: 40,000
Usual Pagination: 64
ADVERTISING RATES:
Full Page Colour .... HUF 850000
CONSUMER: HOLIDAYS & TRAVEL: Entertainment Guides

ITBUSINESS
1688400HU5R-1
Editorial: Rákóczi út 28., 1072 BUDAPEST **Tel:** 1/577-7970 **Fax:** 1/577-7995
Email: info@itbusiness.hu **Web site:** http://www.itbusiness.hu
Cover Price: HUF 16; **Circ:** 8,252
Editor-in-Chief: Andrea Sziebig
BUSINESS: COMPUTERS & AUTOMATION: Computers Related

ITTHON
1827646HU50-217
Editorial: Miklós tér 1., 1033 BUDAPEST **Tel:** 20/661-1252 **Fax:** 1/242-4339
Email: vagi@itthonmagazin.net **Web site:** http://www.itthonmagazin.hu
Cover Price: HUF 390; **Circ:** 5,000
Usual Pagination: 64
Editor-in-Chief: József Vági
ADVERTISING RATES:
Full Page Colour .... HUF 200000
BUSINESS: TRAVEL & TOURISM

ITTHON OTTHON VAN
1691017HU89A-27
Editorial: Szobránc köz 6., 1143 BUDAPEST **Tel:** 1/210-8345 **Fax:** 1/210-8356
Email: gmentor@gmentor.hu **Web site:** http://www.itthonotthonvan.hu
Circ: 180,000
Editor-in-Chief: Sarolta Osváth
CONSUMER: HOLIDAYS & TRAVEL: Travel

JOY
631021HU74A-50
Editorial: Hajógyári sziget 213., 1033 BUDAPEST **Tel:** 1/505-0800 **Fax:** 1/505-0806
Circ: 89,086
Usual Pagination: 154
Profile: Women's trend and lifestyle magazine, featuring health, travel, fashion, legal and financial information.
Readership: Aimed at well-educated women aged between 16 and 30 years.
ADVERTISING RATES:
Full Page Colour .... HUF 1750000
CONSUMER: WOMEN'S INTEREST CONSUMER MAGAZINES: Women's Interest

JOY CELEBRITY
1827435HU74A-165
Editorial: Hajógyári sziget 213., 1033 BUDAPEST **Tel:** 1/505-0800 **Fax:** 1/505-0806
Cover Price: HUF 395; **Circ:** 40,000
Usual Pagination: 154
ADVERTISING RATES:
Full Page Colour .... HUF 1300000
CONSUMER: WOMEN'S INTEREST CONSUMER MAGAZINES: Women's Interest

KAMARAI ÁLLATORVOS
1797312HU64H-85
Editorial: István u. 2., 1078 BUDAPEST **Tel:** 1/478-4272 **Fax:** 1/478-4272
Email: maok@t-online.hu **Web site:** http://www.maok.hu
Circ: 3,100
Editor-in-Chief: János Perényi
BUSINESS: OTHER CLASSIFICATIONS: Veterinary

KANIZSA MAGAZIN
1689843HU74G-213
Editorial: Péterfai út 1/H Pf. 504, 8800 NAGYKANIZSA **Tel:** 30/969-3115 **Fax:** 93/326-905
Email: kanizsamagazin@chello.hu
Circ: 25,000
Editor-in-Chief: László Deregi
CONSUMER: WOMEN'S INTEREST CONSUMER MAGAZINES: Slimming & Health

KELET-MAGYARORSZÁG
1688267HU67B-538
Editorial: Dózsa Gy. u. 4-6., 4400 NYÍREGYHÁZA **Tel:** 42/501-510 **Fax:** 42/501-970
Email: inform@inform.hu
Circ: 156,549
Usual Pagination: 16
ADVERTISING RATES:
Full Page Colour .... HUF 1296000
REGIONAL DAILY & SUNDAY NEWSPAPERS: Regional Daily Newspapers

KÉPMÁS CSALÁDMAGAZIN
1689495HU74C-94
Editorial: Villányi út 5-7., 1114 BUDAPEST **Tel:** 1/365-1414 **Fax:** 1/365-1415
Email: kepmas@kepmas.hu **Web site:** http://www.kepmas.hu
Cover Price: HUF 450; **Circ:** 21,000
Usual Pagination: 100
Editor-in-Chief: Katalin Szám
ADVERTISING RATES:
Full Page Colour .... HUF 340000
CONSUMER: WOMEN'S INTEREST CONSUMER MAGAZINES: Home & Family

KERTBARÁT MAGAZIN
634560HU93-70
Editorial: Mirtusz u. 2., 1141 BUDAPEST **Tel:** 1/273-2290
Email: szerkesztoseg@kerteszetesszoleszet.hu
Annual Sub.: HUF 3060; **Circ:** 11,800
Profile: Magazine providing in-depth coverage of gardening, plants, vegetables and flowers. Features gardens, famous parks and castle grounds from around the world, flower shows, garden design, seasonal duties in the garden and seasonal decorating ideas.
Readership: Aimed at those who enjoy gardening, garden designers, weekend houseowners, allotment owners, garden centre staff and trainee garden designers.
CONSUMER: GARDENING

KERTÉSZET ÉS SZOLÉSZET
634557HU26C-70
Editorial: Mirtusz u. 2., 1141 BUDAPEST
Email: szerkesztoseg@kerteszetesszoleszet.hu
Annual Sub.: HUF 16; **Circ:** 8,500
Profile: Publication focusing on fruit, vegetable and flower gardening with special focus on wine-growing. Includes information on different processing centres, a detailed introduction of specific varieties, with tips and advice based on scientific research.
Readership: Aimed at medium to small gardening and wine-growing businesses and professional garden designers.
BUSINESS: GARDEN TRADE

KERTI KALENDÁRIUM
634585HU93-80
Editorial: Mirtusz u. 2., 1141 BUDAPEST **Tel:** 1/470-0411 **Fax:** 1/470-0410
Email: laczo@magyarmezogazdasag.hu **Web site:** http://www.magyarmezogazdasag.hu
Annual Sub.: HUF 2900; **Circ:** 9,600
Editor-in-Chief: Ferenc dr. Szent-Miklóssy
Profile: Magazine focusing on gardening. Includes articles on vegetable-, fruit-, plant- and grape-growing, wine processing and landscape gardening. Also provides information on major trade fairs, meetings and other gardening news.

Readership: Aimed at smallholders, medium and small vegetable, fruit, plant and flower businesses and home gardeners.
CONSUMER: GARDENING

KISALFÖLD
1688258HU67B-536
Editorial: Újlak u. 4/A, 9021 GYOR **Tel:** 96/504-444 **Fax:** 96/504-413
Circ: 79,998
ADVERTISING RATES:
Full Page Mono .... HUF 1713600
Full Page Colour .... HUF 2376000
REGIONAL DAILY & SUNDAY NEWSPAPERS: Regional Daily Newspapers

KISKEGYED
1688313HU74A-132
Editorial: Városmajor u. 11., 1122 BUDAPEST **Tel:** 1/488-5700 **Fax:** 1/488-5775
Circ: 252,027
Editor-in-Chief: Klára Bokor
ADVERTISING RATES:
Full Page Colour .... HUF 3250000
CONSUMER: WOMEN'S INTEREST CONSUMER MAGAZINES: Women's Interest

KISKEGYED KONYHÁJA
1689176HU74P-154
Editorial: Városmajor u. 11., 1122 BUDAPEST **Tel:** 1/488-5700 **Fax:** 1/488-5775
Circ: 82,680
Editor-in-Chief: Ágnes Dús
ADVERTISING RATES:
Full Page Colour .... HUF 700000
CONSUMER: WOMEN'S INTEREST CONSUMER MAGAZINES: Food & Cookery

KISPESTI MAGAZIN
1689505HU72H-1
Editorial: Kapisztrán u. 8., 1192 BUDAPEST **Tel:** 1/260-2449 **Fax:** 1/260-2449
Email: info@magazinlapok.hu **Web site:** http://www.magazinlapok.hu
Circ: 169,000
LOCAL NEWSPAPERS: Suburban Newspapers

KISTERMELOK LAPJA
633749HU21A-100
Editorial: Mirtusz u. 2., 1141 BUDAPEST **Tel:** 1/220-2226
Email: szerkesztoseg@kistermeloklapja.hu **Web site:** http://www.magyarmezogazdasag.hu
Annual Sub.: HUF 3600; **Circ:** 35,000
Profile: Magazine focusing on agriculture, livestock and poultry. Includes articles on veterinary medicine and all related subjects.
Readership: Aimed at farmers, self-employed smallholders and those involved in the agricultural industry.
BUSINESS: AGRICULTURE & FARMING

KIS-VÁROS-KÉP MAGAZIN
1797111HU74Q-236
Editorial: Fekete u. 3., 5100 JÁSZBERÉNY **Tel:** 20/913-4079
Email: kisvaroskep@kisvaroskep.hu
Circ: 13,000
Editor-in-Chief: Gábor Gedei
CONSUMER: WOMEN'S INTEREST CONSUMER MAGAZINES: Lifestyle

KÖNYVES EXTRA
1689513HU84A-97
Editorial: Rákóczi út 9., 1088 BUDAPEST **Tel:** 1/266-0025 **Fax:** 1/266-0025
Email: info@kepes-extra.hu
Circ: 15,000
Editor: Annamária Rojkó
ADVERTISING RATES:
Full Page Colour .... HUF 350000
CONSUMER: THE ARTS & LITERARY: Arts

KONZERVÚJSÁG
1689674HU22A-134
Editorial: Lakatos u. 3., 1164 BUDAPEST **Tel:** 20/962-1403 **Fax:** 1/214-6692
Email: mail.mete@mtesz.hu
Managing Editor: Mária Sósné dr. Gazdag
BUSINESS: FOOD

KÓRHÁZ
630958HU56C-100
Editorial: Balassi Bálint u. 7., 1055 BUDAPEST **Tel:** 1/461-7487 **Fax:** 1/461-0530
Email: korhaz@mediprint.hu **Web site:** http://www.magyarorvos.hu
Annual Sub.: HUF 9900; **Circ:** 5,250
Profile: Magazine focusing on issues involving healthcare personnel on all levels.

Readership: Aimed at hospital personnel, nurses and doctors, also government officials and national insurance personnel.
ADVERTISING RATES:
Full Page Colour .... HUF 540000
BUSINESS: HEALTH & MEDICAL: Hospitals

KÖRNYEZETVÉDELEM
633810HU57-90
Editorial: Balassi Bálint u. 7., 1055 BUDAPEST **Tel:** 1/301-3870 **Fax:** 1/301-3867
Email: kornyezetvedelem@mediprint.hu **Web site:** http://www.kornyezetvedelem.co.hu
Annual Sub.: HUF 4500; **Circ:** 3,802
Profile: Publication focusing on professional environmental engineering. Featuring ecology, environmental issues, technical news on waste-recycling from all around the world and industrial influences.
Readership: Aimed at local government officials, healthcare professionals and economical organisation managers.
ADVERTISING RATES:
Full Page Colour .... HUF 211000
BUSINESS: ENVIRONMENT & POLLUTION

KÖZÉLETI GAZDASÁGI KRÓNIKA
634591HU82-120
Editorial: Nagybányai út 74., 1025 BUDAPEST **Tel:** 30/992-6032 **Fax:** 1/394-2891
Email: kronika@t-online.hu **Web site:** http://www.kronika.info
Cover Price: HUF 179; **Circ:** 20,000
Usual Pagination: 40
Editor-in-Chief: Julianna Szabados
Profile: Magazine focusing on national and international politics and economics.
Readership: Aimed at all social classes, from manual workers to Government officials and chief executives.
ADVERTISING RATES:
Full Page Colour .... HUF 200000
CONSUMER: CURRENT AFFAIRS & POLITICS

A KUTYA
1689097HU81B-107
Editorial: Tétényi út 128/B-130., 1116 BUDAPEST **Tel:** 70/457-2761 **Fax:** 1/208-2305
Email: meoeszerk@t-online.hu
Circ: 25,000
Editor-in-Chief: Márta Harcsás
CONSUMER: ANIMALS & PETS: Dogs

LABINFÓ
630586HU56G-200
Editorial: Diós árok 5., 1125 BUDAPEST **Tel:** 1/488-6066 **Fax:** 1/488-6061
Email: labinfo@labinfo.hu
Profile: Magazine covering news on medical laboratory equipment.
Readership: Aimed at those who work in hospital, university and chemical laboratories.
BUSINESS: HEALTH & MEDICAL: Medical Equipment

LAKÁSFELÚJÍTÁS
1796792HU4E-133
Tel: 465-0248 **Fax:** 788-0379
Email: info@spektrumkiado.hu **Web site:** http://www.spektrumkiado.hu
Circ: 15,000
Usual Pagination: 48
Editor: Éva Szegedi
ADVERTISING RATES:
Full Page Colour .... HUF 325000
BUSINESS: ARCHITECTURE & BUILDING: Building

LAKÁSKULTÚRA
1689178HU74C-88
Editorial: Városmajor u. 11., 1122 BUDAPEST **Tel:** 1/488-5700 **Fax:** 1/488-5775
Circ: 67,421
Editor-in-Chief: Eszter Szucs
ADVERTISING RATES:
Full Page Colour .... HUF 2050000
CONSUMER: WOMEN'S INTEREST CONSUMER MAGAZINES: Home & Family

LG PHX
704833HU3C-40
Editorial: Balassi Bálint u. 7., 1055 BUDAPEST **Tel:** 1/301-3894 **Fax:** 1/301-3813
Email: phx@mediprint.hu **Web site:** http://www.muszakilapok.hu
Annual Sub.: HUF 3450; **Circ:** 5,000
Profile: Journal of the Association of Cooling and Climate Control Businesses. Featuring domestic and industrial refrigerator and cooling systems, individual and centralised air conditioning systems. Includes articles on new products, technologies and regulations. Provides news on latest developments and trade fairs.
Readership: Aimed at designers, manufacturers, installation, maintenance and repair companies, and construction engineers in the field of domestic and industrial refrigerating and cooling systems, also catering and hotel managers.
ADVERTISING RATES:
Full Page Colour .... HUF 420000
BUSINESS: HEATING & VENTILATION: Refrigeration & Ventilation

LÓERO 1688689HU77A-29
Editorial: Budafoki út 10/B fszt 3., 1111 BUDAPEST
Tel: 1/209-3834 **Fax:** 1/209-3835
Email: loero@loero.hu **Web site:** http://www.loero.hu
Circ: 50,000
Editor-in-Chief: Sándor Urai
CONSUMER: MOTORING & CYCLING: Motoring

MAGYAR ÁLLATORVOSOK LAPJA 634503HU64H-80
Tel: 341-3023
Email: szabo.judit@aotk.szie.hu **Web site:** http://www.magyarmezogazdasag.hu
Cover Price: HUF 1100
Profile: Journal featuring articles on animal health, scientific and practical issues.
Readership: Read by veterinarians, veterinarian assistants, teachers and students of veterinary medicine.
BUSINESS: OTHER CLASSIFICATIONS: Veterinary

MAGYAR ÁLLATTENYÉSZTOK LAPJA 634494HU21A-110
Editorial: Loportár u. 16., 1134 BUDAPEST **Tel:** 1/412-5000 **Fax:** 1/412-5001
Email: masz@t-online.hu **Web site:** http://www.magyarmezogazdasag.hu
Cover Price: HUF 230; **Circ:** 6,500
Profile: Publication of the Union of Hungarian Animal Breeders, featuring: Union news, including conferences and meetings; biology, including articles on recent research; dairy farming, sheep breeding, news of the European Animal Breeders Union, and international news.
Readership: Aimed at members of the Union of Hungarian Animal Breeders and the European Animal Breeders Union; also farm managers and self-employed farmers.
BUSINESS: AGRICULTURE & FARMING

MAGYAR ASZTALOS ÉS FAIPAR 1689570HU46-5
Editorial: Csaba u. 21., 9023 GYOR **Tel:** 96/618-060 **Fax:** 96/618-063
Email: faipar@xmeditor.hu
Circ: 4,800
Managing Editor: Tamás Hobör
BUSINESS: TIMBER, WOOD & FORESTRY

MAGYAR DEMOKRATA 1688435HU65J-6
Editorial: Andrássy út 124., 1062 BUDAPEST **Tel:** 1/354-2350 **Fax:** 1/354-2359
Email: demokrata@demokrata.hu
Circ: 36,588
Editor-in-Chief: András Bencsik
NATIONAL DAILY & SUNDAY NEWSPAPERS: National Weekly Newspapers

MAGYAR ELEKTRONIKA 633937HU18A-130
Editorial: Fogarasi út 5. 27. épület, 1148 BUDAPEST
Tel: 1/460-0289 **Fax:** 1/460-0289
Email: info@magyar-elektronika.hu
Cover Price: HUF 987; **Circ:** 3,000
Editor-in-Chief: Ferenc Tóth
Profile: Publication focusing on professional industrial electronics.
Readership: Aimed at engineers and development engineers.
BUSINESS: ELECTRONICS

MAGYAR ÉPÍTÉSTECHNIKA 634398HU4-80
Editorial: Balassi Bálint u. 7., 1055 BUDAPEST
Tel: 1/301-3894 **Fax:** 1/301-3813
Email: epitestechnika@mediprint.hu **Web site:** http://www.muszakilapok.hu
Annual Sub.: HUF 9240; **Circ:** 11,152
Profile: Publication covering all aspects of architecture, building and construction. Features news about IPOSZ, the Association of Hungarian Construction, national and international news, meetings and trade fairs.
Readership: Aimed at architects, designers, construction engineers, wholesalers and retailers of building materials, and those working in this field in scientific and educational institutions.
ADVERTISING RATES:
Full Page Colour .... HUF 580000
BUSINESS: ARCHITECTURE & BUILDING

MAGYAR ÉPÍTOIPAR 1689574HU4E-96
Editorial: Fo u. 68., 1027 BUDAPEST **Tel:** 1/201-8416 **Fax:** 1/201-8416
Email: info@eptud.hu
Cover Price: HUF 900; **Circ:** 2,500
Editor-in-Chief: László László
BUSINESS: ARCHITECTURE & BUILDING: Building

MAGYAR ÉPÜLETGÉPÉSZET 706758HU4E-85
Editorial: Fo u. 68. I/133., 1027 BUDAPEST **Tel:** 1/201-2562 **Fax:** 1/201-2562
Email: epgep.epte@mtesz.hu **Web site:** http://www.epgeponline.hu
Cover Price: HUF 4200
Editor-in-Chief: Lajos dr. Barna
Profile: Journal providing theoretical and practical information on construction engineering. Featuring news about recent projects and developments, as well as the history of the industry.
Readership: Aimed at construction engineers.
BUSINESS: ARCHITECTURE & BUILDING: Building

MAGYAR ESKÜVO 1690714HU74L-3
Editorial: Medve u. 24. V/1., 1027 BUDAPEST **Tel:** 1/355-0550 **Fax:** 1/225-0650
Email: terra@eskuvo.hu **Web site:** http://www.eskuvo.hu
Cover Price: HUF 890; **Circ:** 25,000
Managing Editor: Edina Dombovári
ADVERTISING RATES:
Full Page Mono .... HUF 230000
Full Page Colour .... HUF 300000
CONSUMER: WOMEN'S INTEREST CONSUMER MAGAZINES: Brides

MAGYAR FOGORVOS 1689592HU56D-1
Editorial: Balassi Bálint u. 7., 1055 BUDAPEST
Tel: 1/301-3879 **Fax:** 1/301-3893
Email: dental@mediprint.hu **Web site:** http://www.orvosilapok.hu
Circ: 5,802
ADVERTISING RATES:
Full Page Colour .... HUF 530000
BUSINESS: HEALTH & MEDICAL: Dental

MAGYAR GAZDASÁGI MAGAZIN 1691095HU14A-249
Editorial: Hársfa u. 21., 1074 BUDAPEST **Tel:** 1/413-6646 **Fax:** 1/413-6647
Email: szerkesztoseg@gazdasagimagazin.hu **Web site:** http://www.magygazd.hu
Circ: 2,000
Editor-in-Chief: Éva Szénási
BUSINESS: COMMERCE, INDUSTRY & MANAGEMENT

MAGYAR GRAFIKA 634747HU41A-1
Editorial: Fo u. 68. IV/416., 1027 BUDAPEST **Tel:** 1/457-0633 **Fax:** 1/202-0256
Email: faludi.pnyme@mtesz.hu **Web site:** http://www.mgonline.hu
Cover Price: HUF 1100
Annual Sub.: HUF 6900; **Circ:** 2,000
Usual Pagination: 40
Editor-in-Chief: Viktória Faludi
Profile: Journal of the Paper and Printing Industry's Mechanical Union, covering all aspects of printing. Features national and international news, research, statistics, human resources, and automation. Includes articles on European Union standards, and provides in-depth coverage of trade fairs and conferences.
Readership: Aimed at managers, engineers and all those working in the printing industry.
ADVERTISING RATES:
Full Page Colour .... HUF 240000
BUSINESS: PRINTING & STATIONERY: Printing

MAGYAR HÍRLAP 1500196HU65A-25
Editorial: Thököly út 105-107., 1145 BUDAPEST
Tel: 1/260-8404 **Fax:** 1/260-8404
Email: hirdetes@magyarhirlap.hu **Web site:** http://www.magyarhirlap.hu
Usual Pagination: 24
Profile: Newspaper concerning politics and economics.
ADVERTISING RATES:
Full Page Mono .... HUF 1050000
Full Page Colour .... HUF 1560000
NATIONAL DAILY & SUNDAY NEWSPAPERS: National Daily Newspapers

MAGYAR HORGÁSZ 1689586HU92-2
Editorial: Ó utca 3., 1066 BUDAPEST **Tel:** 1/311-3232 **Fax:** 1/311-3232
Email: mahor@t-online.hu **Web site:** http://www.mahor.hu
Circ: 92,000
Editor-in-Chief: Ferenc Szalay
CONSUMER: ANGLING & FISHING

MAGYAR INSTALLATEUR 704841HU4E-90
Editorial: Balassi Bálint u. 7., 1055 BUDAPEST
Tel: 1/301-3806 **Fax:** 1/301-3814
Email: pongracz.lajos@mediprint.hu **Web site:** http://www.magyarinstallateur.hu
Annual Sub.: HUF 6750; **Circ:** 5,252
Profile: Journal of the Association of Hungarian Construction Engineers. Focusing on building engineering, including water, gas, air-conditioning and heating systems. Provides examples of new products and technologies.
Readership: Aimed at system designers, construction engineers, retailers and consumers.
ADVERTISING RATES:
Full Page Colour .... HUF 550000
BUSINESS: ARCHITECTURE & BUILDING: Building

MAGYAR KÉMIKUSOK LAPJA 1689588HU13-81
Editorial: Fo u. 68. I/105., 1027 BUDAPEST **Tel:** 1/201-6883 **Fax:** 1/201-8056
Email: mail@mke.org.hu
Managing Editor: Tamás dr. Kiss
BUSINESS: CHEMICALS

MAGYAR KONYHA 634062HU74P-150
Editorial: Szentkirályi u. 1/B, 1088 BUDAPEST **Tel:** 1/267-0505 **Fax:** 1/267-0303
Email: szerkesztoseg@konyhamagazin.hu **Web site:** http://www.konyhamagazin.hu
Cover Price: HUF 375
Annual Sub.: HUF 3720; **Circ:** 35,000
Usual Pagination: 48
Profile: Magazine focusing on Hungarian cookery, introducing different regional and international dishes, finance, fitness and design for the home.
Readership: Aimed at housewives between the ages of 18 and 49 years.
ADVERTISING RATES:
Full Page Colour .... HUF 363000
CONSUMER: WOMEN'S INTEREST CONSUMER MAGAZINES: Food & Cookery

MAGYAR MEZOGAZDASÁG 633771HU21A-130
Editorial: Mirtusz u. 2., 1141 BUDAPEST **Tel:** 1/470-0411 **Fax:** 1/470-0410
Email: mmg@magyarmezogazdasag.hu
Cover Price: HUF 370
Annual Sub.: HUF 18; **Circ:** 8,200
Usual Pagination: 32
Profile: Publication providing in-depth coverage of agricultural issues. Focuses on livestock and medicine, food processing, machinery developments and news, gardening and viticulture.
Readership: Aimed at farmers, wine producers and those within the agricultural sector.
ADVERTISING RATES:
Full Page Mono .... HUF 385000
Full Page Colour .... HUF 490000
BUSINESS: AGRICULTURE & FARMING

MAGYAR NARANCS 631092HU82-150
Editorial: Naphegy tér 8., 1016 BUDAPEST **Tel:** 1/441-9000/2400 **Fax:** 1/356-9691
Email: magyar@narancs.hu **Web site:** http://www.narancs.hu
Editor-in-Chief: Endre Bojtár B.
Profile: Publication providing in-depth coverage of politics, literature, culture and current affairs.
Readership: Aimed at university students and those interested in current affairs.
CONSUMER: CURRENT AFFAIRS & POLITICS

MAGYAR NEMZET 1200640HU65A-30
Editorial: Wesselényi u. 8., 1075 BUDAPEST **Tel:** 1/342-6164 **Fax:** 1/342-6132
Email: titkarsag@mahirpress.hu
Circ: 75,696
Profile: Broadsheet-sized quality newspaper containing national and international news, current affairs, culture and in-depth stock market news. Provides Internet recommendations, information about Budapest and political issues worldwide.
Readership: Aimed at the general public.
ADVERTISING RATES:
Full Page Mono .... HUF 2200000
Full Page Colour .... HUF 2950000
NATIONAL DAILY & SUNDAY NEWSPAPERS: National Daily Newspapers

MAGYAR NOORVOSOK LAPJA 634627HU56A-261
Editorial: Podmaniczky u. 111., 1062 BUDAPEST
Tel: 1/475-2568 **Fax:** 1/475-2568
Circ: 1,400
Profile: Publication of the Semmelweis University of Health Sciences Department of Obstetrics and Gynaecology. Features articles on all aspects of gynaecology, including pregnancy, child birth and abortion.
Readership: Aimed at gynaecologists and medical students.
BUSINESS: HEALTH & MEDICAL

MAGYAR ORVOS 1689593HU56A-131
Editorial: Balassi Bálint u. 7., 1055 BUDAPEST
Tel: 1/461-7487 **Fax:** 1/461-0530
Email: magyarorvos@mediprint.hu **Web site:** http://www.magyarorvos.hu
Annual Sub.: HUF 9900; **Circ:** 29,000
ADVERTISING RATES:
Full Page Colour .... HUF 540000
BUSINESS: HEALTH & MEDICAL

MAGYAR TANTUSZ 1796739HU94D-11
Editorial: Borbátó u. 2., 4150 PÜSPÖKLADÁNY
Tel: 54/451-214 **Fax:** 54/451-214
Circ: 5,000
Editor-in-Chief: Attila Szilágyi
CONSUMER: OTHER CLASSIFICATIONS: Expatriates

MAGYARORSZÁGI BEDEKKER 1690844HU89A-25
Editorial: Buday László u. 5/B., 1024 BUDAPEST
Tel: 20/950-4601 **Fax:** 70/908-5075
Email: bedekker@mail.datanet.hu
Circ: 50,000
Editor-in-Chief: István Ferencz
CONSUMER: HOLIDAYS & TRAVEL: Travel

MAI PIAC 634811HU14A-254
Editorial: Montevideo u. 14., 1037 BUDAPEST **Tel:** 1/336-2472 **Fax:** 1/436-2087
Email: press@hvg.hu **Web site:** http://www.maipiac.hu
Circ: 16,500
Editor-in-Chief: Ágnes Orbán
Profile: Publication presenting macro-economic trends in Hungary, as well as general features and conditions of the FMCG (Fast Moving Consumer Goods) sector. Consists of five parts: Food retail and wholesale; shopping centres and hypermarkets; petrol station shops; the food industry and the media and advertising agencies specialising in this field.
Readership: Aimed at managers, industry executives, sales representatives in decision-making positions and service managers.
ADVERTISING RATES:
Full Page Colour .... HUF 790000
BUSINESS: COMMERCE, INDUSTRY & MANAGEMENT

MAMMUT MAGAZIN 1690551HU74Q-214
Editorial: Ribáry u. 1/B, 1022 BUDAPEST **Tel:** 1/275-5051 **Fax:** 1/275-5051
Email: mammutmag@t-online.hu **Web site:** http://www.mammut.hu
Circ: 70,000
Editor-in-Chief: Natasa Kalmár
CONSUMER: WOMEN'S INTEREST CONSUMER MAGAZINES: Lifestyle

MEDICUS UNIVERSALIS 634859HU56A-117
Editorial: Görgey u. 40., 1041 BUDAPEST **Tel:** 1/389-2595 **Fax:** 1/389-2595
Email: oali@oali.hu
Cover Price: HUF 600; **Circ:** 6,000
Profile: Medical journal providing general news, including new methods of treatment and medication, and updates on recent research and new developments.
Readership: Aimed at staff in the primary health care system, including general practitioners, health visitors and nurses.
BUSINESS: HEALTH & MEDICAL

MEGYEI NAPLÓ 1796997HU72-433
Editorial: Szabadság tér 9., 4400 NYÍREGYHÁZA
Tel: 42/411-826 **Fax:** 42/411-826
Email: info@nyhnaplo.hu
Circ: 85,000
Editor-in-Chief: Katalin dr. Daragóné Cservenyák
LOCAL NEWSPAPERS

MÉHÉSZET 634577HU21R-80
Editorial: Mirtusz u. 2., 1141 BUDAPEST **Tel:** 30/631-3512
Email: otto.nagy@t-online.hu **Web site:** http://www.magyarmezogazdasag.hu
Annual Sub.: HUF 4320; **Circ:** 14,900
Profile: Publication covering all aspects of honey processing.
Readership: Aimed at all those working in medium and small honey-processing businesses.
BUSINESS: AGRICULTURE & FARMING: Agriculture & Farming Related

METROPOL 630021HU67B-500
Editorial: Tüzér u. 39-41., 1134 BUDAPEST **Tel:** 1/431-6400 **Fax:** 1/431-6465
Email: hirdetes@metropol.hu **Web site:** http://www.metropol.hu
Circ: 320,386
Profile: Newspaper covering news and general interest subjects, featuring a job search, entertainment and interior design.
Readership: Aimed those living and working in Budapest.
ADVERTISING RATES:
Full Page Mono .... HUF 2984130
Full Page Colour .... HUF 3874470
REGIONAL DAILY & SUNDAY NEWSPAPERS: Regional Daily Newspapers

Hungary

MEZOHÍR
1689611HU21A-156
Editorial: Gyenes tér 1., 6000 KECSKEMÉT **Tel:** 30/943-9158
Email: info@mezohir.hu **Web site:** http://www.mezohir.hu
Circ: 18,917
BUSINESS: AGRICULTURE & FARMING

A MI OTTHONUNK
1689105HU74C-86
Editorial: Róna u. 120-122., 1149 BUDAPEST **Tel:** 1/469-6480 **Fax:** 1/469-6476
Email: info@amiotthonunk.hu **Web site:** http://www.amiotthonunk.hu
Cover Price: HUF 445; **Circ:** 35,000
Usual Pagination: 100
ADVERTISING RATES:
Full Page Colour .... HUF 680000
CONSUMER: WOMEN'S INTEREST CONSUMER MAGAZINES: Home & Family

MISKOLC INFO
1797177HU72-441
Editorial: Batthyány u. 1., 3525 MISKOLC **Tel:** 46/503-020 **Fax:** 46/344-657
Email: kultur@miskolcph.hu **Web site:** http://www.miskolc.hu
Circ: 60,000
Managing Editor: Vilmos Fedor
LOCAL NEWSPAPERS

MM MUSZAKI MAGAZIN
1689687HU19E-5
Editorial: Nagyszolos u. 11-15., 1113 BUDAPEST **Tel:** 1/577-2600 **Fax:** 1/577-2690
Email: mbp@motorpresse.hu **Web site:** http://www.mm-online.hu
Cover Price: HUF 900
Annual Sub.: HUF 8400; **Circ:** 8,540
Usual Pagination: 68
ADVERTISING RATES:
Full Page Colour .... HUF 450000
BUSINESS: ENGINEERING & MACHINERY: Machinery, Machine Tools & Metalworking

MODERN HÁZAK, LAKÁSOK
1690194HU4A-55
Editorial: Obsitos tér 1., 1155 BUDAPEST **Tel:** 1/415-0318 **Fax:** 1/415-0318
Email: azto@t-online.hu
BUSINESS: ARCHITECTURE & BUILDING: Architecture

MOTESZ MAGAZIN
1690557HU56R-211
Editorial: Nádor u. 36., 1051 BUDAPEST **Tel:** 1/312-3807 **Fax:** 1/383-7918
Email: szerkesztoseg@motesz.hu **Web site:** http://www.motesz.hu
Circ: 25,000
Editor-in-Chief: László Prof. Dr. Vécsei
BUSINESS: HEALTH & MEDICAL: Health Medical Related

MOTORREVÜ
1200658HU77B-5
Editorial: Nagyszolos u. 11-15., 1113 BUDAPEST **Tel:** 1/577-2600 **Fax:** 1/577-2691
Email: motorrevu@motorpresse.hu **Web site:** http://www.motorrevu.hu
Cover Price: HUF 790
Annual Sub.: HUF 6600; **Circ:** 26,483
Usual Pagination: 116
Profile: Magazine featuring tests and technical articles, topical reporting and motor sports.
Readership: Aimed at bike riders and enthusiasts, mechanics and trade professionals.
ADVERTISING RATES:
Full Page Mono .... HUF 510000
Full Page Colour .... HUF 590000
CONSUMER: MOTORING & CYCLING: Motorcycling

MOTORSPORT MAGYARORSZÁGON
1689691HU77A-42
Editorial: Pf. 23, 2473 VÁL **Tel:** 30/962-6310 **Fax:** 22/353-406
Email: motorsport@t-online.hu
Cover Price: HUF 498; **Circ:** 50,000
Editor-in-Chief: Anita Trejtnar
ADVERTISING RATES:
Full Page Mono .... HUF 260000
Full Page Colour .... HUF 360000
CONSUMER: MOTORING & CYCLING: Motoring

MUANYAG ÉS GUMI
1689357HU39-1
Editorial: Fo u. 68., 1027 BUDAPEST **Tel:** 1/202-0656 **Fax:** 1/202-0252
Email: mail.gte@mtesz.hu
BUSINESS: PLASTICS & RUBBER

MUANYAG- ÉS GUMIIPARI ÉVKÖNYV
634616HU39-4
Editorial: Nyugati tér. 8, 1056 BUDAPEST **Tel:** 1/349-3347 **Fax:** 1/339-8638
Email: infoprod@speednet.hu **Web site:** http://www.infoprod.hu
Profile: Publication of the Scientific Machinery Association, focusing on research and manufacturing news in the machinery industry. Features national and international trade news, including details of conferences and trade fairs.
Readership: Aimed at machinery engineers, trainee engineers, factory professionals and researchers in the field of scientific machinery.
BUSINESS: PLASTICS & RUBBER

NAPI ÁSZ
1690938HU67B-547
Editorial: Falk Miksa u. 3., 1055 BUDAPEST **Tel:** 1/783-4486 **Fax:** 1/783-4486
Email: szerk@napiasz.hu
Cover Price: HUF 88; **Circ:** 40,000
REGIONAL DAILY & SUNDAY NEWSPAPERS: Regional Daily Newspapers

NAPI GAZDASÁG
630009HU65A-33
Editorial: Csata u. 32., 1135 BUDAPEST **Tel:** 1/450-9600 **Fax:** 1/450-9601
Email: hirdetes@napi.hu **Web site:** http://www.napi.hu
Usual Pagination: 120
Profile: Newspaper focusing on national and international economics and finance.
Readership: Aimed at financial executives, investors and decision makers.
ADVERTISING RATES:
Full Page Mono .... HUF 629000
Full Page Colour .... HUF 865000
NATIONAL DAILY & SUNDAY NEWSPAPERS: National Daily Newspapers

NAPLÓ
1688297HU67B-544
Editorial: Almádi u. 3., 8200 VESZPRÉM **Tel:** 88/583-272 **Fax:** 88/583-270
Circ: 49,491
ADVERTISING RATES:
Full Page Mono .... HUF 1439130
Full Page Colour .... HUF 2014782
REGIONAL DAILY & SUNDAY NEWSPAPERS: Regional Daily Newspapers

NATURE KÖRNYEZETVÉDELMI MAGAZIN
1827466HU57-132
Editorial: Tamási Áron u. 18/B., 1124 BUDAPEST **Tel:** 20/663-4814
Email: info@naturemagazin.hu **Web site:** http://www.naturemagazin.hu
Circ: 10,000
Editor-in-Chief: Árpád Gyapay
BUSINESS: ENVIRONMENT & POLLUTION

NAVIGÁTOR
1689746HU10-14
Editorial: Klapka u. 6., 1134 BUDAPEST **Tel:** 1/349-2574 **Fax:** 1/210-5862
Email: postmaster@magyarkozlekedes.t-online.hu
Annual Sub.: HUF 5600; **Circ:** 2,500
Usual Pagination: 44
ADVERTISING RATES:
Full Page Mono .... HUF 330000
Full Page Colour .... HUF 520000
BUSINESS: MATERIALS HANDLING

NEMZETI SPORT
1500215HU65A-122
Editorial: Szugló u. 81-85., 1141 BUDAPEST **Tel:** 1/460-2541 **Fax:** 1/460-2579
Email: gyartas@nemzetisport.hu
Circ: 104,604
Usual Pagination: 20
Profile: Newspaper covering news from the world of sport. Featuring football, team and individual players nationally and worldwide.
Readership: Aimed at everybody interested in sport.
ADVERTISING RATES:
Full Page Mono .... HUF 1243620
Full Page Colour .... HUF 1678887
NATIONAL DAILY & SUNDAY NEWSPAPERS: National Daily Newspapers

NEMZETKÖZI KUTYA MAGAZIN
630882HU81B-100
Editorial: Budafoki út 93/C I/4., 1117 BUDAPEST **Tel:** 1/386-0223 **Fax:** 1/386-0223
Email: magazin@dingolapkiado.axelero.net
Cover Price: HUF 340; **Circ:** 25,000
Profile: Magazine containing articles on dog-keeping, caring for dogs, breeding and other issues.
Readership: Aimed at dog owners, dog-lovers and breeders.
CONSUMER: ANIMALS & PETS: Dogs

NÉPSZABADSÁG
1500231HU65A-40
Editorial: Bécsi út 122-124., 1034 BUDAPEST **Tel:** 1/436-4441 **Fax:** 1/250-1118
Email: hirdetes@nepszabadsag.hu **Web site:** http://www.nepszabadsag.hu
Circ: 131,816
Profile: National daily newspaper covering home and overseas news, economic and cultural news, sports news and features.
Readership: Aimed at the general public.
ADVERTISING RATES:
Full Page Mono .... HUF 2340000
Full Page Colour .... HUF 3150000
NATIONAL DAILY & SUNDAY NEWSPAPERS: National Daily Newspapers

NÉPSZAVA
629983HU65A-45
Editorial: Könyvek K. krt. 76., 1087 BUDAPEST **Tel:** 1/477-9030 **Fax:** 1/477-9033
Email: hirdetes@nepszava.hu **Web site:** http://www.nepszava.hu
Circ: 35,328
Usual Pagination: 16
Profile: Newspaper providing national and international news with specific focus on politics.
Readership: Aimed at the general public.
ADVERTISING RATES:
Full Page Mono .... HUF 1100000
Full Page Colour .... HUF 1700000
NATIONAL DAILY & SUNDAY NEWSPAPERS: National Daily Newspapers

NEXUS
1797180HU89A-30
Editorial: Munkás u. 9., 1074 BUDAPEST **Tel:** 1/266-5853 **Fax:** 1/338-4293
Email: info@turizmus.com
Circ: 15,000
CONSUMER: HOLIDAYS & TRAVEL: Travel

NIMRÓD VADÁSZÚJSÁG
1689759HU75F-3
Editorial: Medve u. 34-40., 1027 BUDAPEST **Tel:** 1/225-0748 **Fax:** 1/212-0340
Cover Price: HUF 545; **Circ:** 23,000
Usual Pagination: 52
Editor-in-Chief: Attila dr. Zoltán
ADVERTISING RATES:
Full Page Colour .... HUF 310000
CONSUMER: SPORT: Shooting

NYÍREGYHÁZI NAPLÓ
1689021HU72-304
Editorial: Szabadság tér 9., 4400 NYÍREGYHÁZA **Tel:** 70/933-9821 **Fax:** 42/411-826
Email: info@nyhnaplo.hu
Circ: 54,000
LOCAL NEWSPAPERS

ÓBUDA
1688763HU72-61
Editorial: Szentendrei út 32., 1035 BUDAPEST **Tel:** 1/235-0417 **Fax:** 1/430-1250
Email: obudaujsag@fecom.hu
Circ: 67,700
LOCAL NEWSPAPERS

OFFLINE MAGAZIN
1689774HU75L-4
Editorial: Kassai u. 84., 1142 BUDAPEST **Tel:** 1/363-8099 **Fax:** 1/363-8099
Email: info@offline.hu **Web site:** http://www.offline.hu
Cover Price: HUF 450; **Circ:** 23,000
CONSUMER: SPORT: Outdoor

OKTATÁSI MELLÉKLET
1796831HU67H-20
Editorial: Játék u. 8., 1221 BUDAPEST **Tel:** 1/229-0438 **Fax:** 1/229-0438
Email: delbszinfo@t-online.hu
Circ: 76,000
REGIONAL DAILY & SUNDAY NEWSPAPERS: Regional Colour Supplements

OLAJ, SZAPPAN, KOZMETIKA
634473HU13-80
Editorial: Kvassay J. u. 1., 1095 BUDAPEST **Tel:** 1/217-5240 **Fax:** 1/217-5241
Email: mail.mete@mtesz.hu
Managing Editor: Béla Kiss
Profile: Publication focusing on vegetable oil processing, household chemicals industry and cosmetics industry technology, including technical developments and research.
Readership: Aimed at chemical, industrial and retail professionals involved in the industry.
BUSINESS: CHEMICALS

ÓRA MAGAZIN
1689272HU52B-1
Editorial: Fehér út 10. (FMV) 8-as épület, 1106 BUDAPEST **Tel:** 1/260-1148 **Fax:** 1/260-4869
Email: direxmedia@direxmedia.hu **Web site:** http://www.oramagazin.hu
Cover Price: HUF 790
Annual Sub.: HUF 3950; **Circ:** 10,000
Usual Pagination: 60
ADVERTISING RATES:
Full Page Colour .... HUF 440000
BUSINESS: GIFT TRADE: Clocks & Watches

ORVOSOK LAPJA
1691056HU74G-234
Editorial: Istenhegyi út 29., 1125 BUDAPEST **Tel:** 1/224-5450 **Fax:** 1/224-5457
Email: recepcio@promenade.hu **Web site:** http://www.promenade.hu
Cover Price: HUF 13; **Circ:** 35,757
Usual Pagination: 40
ADVERTISING RATES:
Full Page Mono .... HUF 540000
Full Page Colour .... HUF 840000
CONSUMER: WOMEN'S INTEREST CONSUMER MAGAZINES: Slimming & Health

ÖTLETTÁR
630856HU4E-52
Editorial: Neumann János u. 1., 2040 BUDAÖRS **Tel:** 23/422-455 **Fax:** 23/422-456
Profile: Magazine providing ideas and advice for getting started with constructing a house. Featuring designers, constructors, new products and practical issues. Each issue contains 500 new designs.
Readership: Aimed at builders, trainee designers and those who are thinking of building a family home.
BUSINESS: ARCHITECTURE & BUILDING: Building

OTTHON TUDÓS MAGAZIN
1796616HU4B-3
Editorial: Dózsa Gy. út 32., 1071 BUDAPEST **Tel:** 1/343-1816 **Fax:** 1/413-7131
Email: otthontudos@otthontudos.hu **Web site:** http://www.otthontudos.hu
Cover Price: HUF 395
Editor-in-Chief: Krisztina Széles
BUSINESS: ARCHITECTURE & BUILDING: Interior Design & Flooring

PAPÍRIPAR
634738HU36-80
Editorial: Fo u. 68. IV/416., 1027 BUDAPEST **Tel:** 1/457-0633 **Fax:** 1/202-0256
Email: pnyme@mtesz.hu **Web site:** http://www.pnyme.hu/papiripar
Cover Price: HUF 600; **Circ:** 2,000
Usual Pagination: 40
Profile: Magazine featuring national and international news, research, statistics, human resources, finance and automation including trade fairs and conferences.
Readership: Aimed at chemical and mechanical engineers, technicians and retailers.
ADVERTISING RATES:
Full Page Colour .... HUF 240000
BUSINESS: PAPER

PATIKA MAGAZIN
1689799HU37-46
Editorial: Dózsa György út 19., 1146 BUDAPEST **Tel:** 1/467-8060 **Fax:** 1/363-9223
Email: galenus@galenus.hu **Web site:** http://www.patikamagazin.hu
Circ: 213,647
Usual Pagination: 24
ADVERTISING RATES:
Full Page Colour .... HUF 1100000
BUSINESS: PHARMACEUTICAL & CHEMISTS

PATIKA TÜKÖR
631051HU37-47
Editorial: Francia út 5. I/1., 1143 BUDAPEST **Tel:** 1/479-8020 **Fax:** 1/479-8029
Email: info@patikatukor.hu **Web site:** http://www.patikatukor.hu
Circ: 150,000
Profile: Publication containing health and medical issues. Featuring news and advice on maintaining a healthy lifestyle, including skin and eye care, beauty and homeopathy. Circulated in most pharmacies.
Readership: Aimed at the general public.
BUSINESS: PHARMACEUTICAL & CHEMISTS

PC GURU
630014HU5D-250
Editorial: Nagyszolos u. 11-15., 1113 BUDAPEST **Tel:** 1/577-2600 **Fax:** 1/577-2690
Email: mpb@motorpresse.hu **Web site:** http://www.pcguru.hu
Cover Price: HUF 1895
Annual Sub.: HUF 16; **Circ:** 24,250
Usual Pagination: 132
Profile: Magazine focusing on computing, covering useful tips and news on hardware, software and electronic entertainment.
Readership: Aimed at computer users.
ADVERTISING RATES:
Full Page Colour .... HUF 495000
BUSINESS: COMPUTERS & AUTOMATION: Personal Computers

PC WORLD 1600642HU5D-300
Editorial: Madách út 13-14. A/IV., 1075 BUDAPEST
Tel: 1/577-4300 **Fax:** 1/266-4343
Email: keriroda@idg.hu **Web site:** http://pcworld.hu
Circ: 26,733
Profile: Publication covering news, multimedia, networks, tests and product reviews.
Readership: Aimed at executives, users and developers and non-computer professionals interested in personal computers.
BUSINESS: COMPUTERS & AUTOMATION: Personal Computers

PÉNZÜGYI ÉVKÖNYV 1827561HU1A-168
Editorial: Maros u. 19-21., 1122 BUDAPEST **Tel:** 1/489-1165 **Fax:** 1/489-1159
Email: hirdetes@vg.hu
Profile: Magazine focusing on financial issues.
BUSINESS: FINANCE & ECONOMICS

PESTI EST 1688501HU89C-61
Editorial: Lajos u. 74-76., 1036 BUDAPEST **Tel:** 1/436-5000 **Fax:** 1/436-5001
Email: estmedi@estmedia.hu **Web site:** http://www.estmedia.hu
Circ: 121,346
CONSUMER: HOLIDAYS & TRAVEL: Entertainment Guides

PESTI MUSOR 630779HU84A-80
Editorial: Egyetem tér 5., 1053 BUDAPEST **Tel:** 1/318-5001 **Fax:** 1/318-5001
Email: info@geopress.hu **Web site:** http://www.pestimusor.hu
Cover Price: HUF 395; **Circ:** 30,000
Usual Pagination: 112
Editor-in-Chief: Attila Galambos
Profile: Magazine providing comprehensive listings of the capital's theatres, cinemas, museums and galleries. Also featuring new releases of films, videos, books and music.
Readership: Aimed at those aged between 25 and 45 who are interested in cultural events.
ADVERTISING RATES:
Full Page Colour .... HUF 585000
CONSUMER: THE ARTS & LITERARY: Arts

PETOFI NÉPE 1688229HU67B-529
Editorial: Városmajor u. 11., 1122 BUDAPEST **Tel:** 1/488-5726 **Fax:** 1/488-5719
Circ: 38,174
Advertising Director: András Lengyel
ADVERTISING RATES:
Full Page Mono .... HUF 1104000
Full Page Colour .... HUF 1464000
REGIONAL DAILY & SUNDAY NEWSPAPERS: Regional Daily Newspapers

PIAC ÉS PROFIT 631028HU1A-90
Editorial: Dózsa György út 144., 1134 BUDAPEST
Tel: 1/239-8400 **Fax:** 1/239-9595
Email: szerk@piacesprofit.hu **Web site:** http://www.piacesprofit.hu
Cover Price: HUF 680; **Circ:** 15,000
Profile: Magazine containing features on economics, information technology, also theatre, cinema, music and book reviews.
Readership: Aimed at decision-makers, executives and managers.
ADVERTISING RATES:
Full Page Colour £3024.00
BUSINESS: FINANCE & ECONOMICS

PIHENJ ITTHON 1797289HU89A-28
Editorial: Pf. 40, 2730 ALBERTIRSA **Tel:** 30/307-8439
Email: deis@deis.hu **Web site:** http://www.pihenjitthon.hu
Circ: 40,000
CONSUMER: HOLIDAYS & TRAVEL: Travel

PLAYBOY 766255HU86C-52
Editorial: Hajógyári sziget 213., 1033 BUDAPEST
Tel: 1/505-0872 **Fax:** 1/505-0806
Cover Price: HUF 795; **Circ:** 40,772
Usual Pagination: 120
Editor-in-Chief: Péter Radnai
Profile: Magazine focusing on male interest photographs. Includes articles on film, fashion, sport and cars.
Readership: Aimed at men aged between 25 and 45 years.
ADVERTISING RATES:
Full Page Colour .... HUF 1690000
CONSUMER: ADULT & GAY MAGAZINES: Men's Lifestyle Magazines

POLGÁRI OTTHON 1690224HU4A-56
Editorial: Nagybátonyi u. 4., 1037 BUDAPEST **Tel:** 1/439-1319 **Fax:** 1/240-4386
Email: polgariotthon@t-online.hu **Web site:** http://www.polgariotthon.hu
Cover Price: HUF 380
Editor-in-Chief: Gabriella Mátyás
BUSINESS: ARCHITECTURE & BUILDING: Architecture

POPCORN 1689174HU74F-3
Editorial: Városmajor u. 11., 1122 BUDAPEST **Tel:** 1/488-5700 **Fax:** 1/488-5775
Circ: 55,125
Editor-in-Chief: Beatrix Vaskó
ADVERTISING RATES:
Full Page Colour .... HUF 1100000
CONSUMER: WOMEN'S INTEREST CONSUMER MAGAZINES: Teenage

PRAXIS 1689829HU56A-136
Editorial: Krúdy Gyula u. 12. III/17., 1088 BUDAPEST
Tel: 1/266-1540 **Fax:** 1/266-1540
Email: praxiskiado@praxis.hu **Web site:** http://www.praxis.hu
Circ: 12,000
Editor-in-Chief: Balázs dr. Kollai
BUSINESS: HEALTH & MEDICAL

PRÍMA KONYHA MAGAZIN 1689831HU74P-160
Editorial: József krt. 31/B, 1085 BUDAPEST **Tel:** 1/230-3051 **Fax:** 1/220-3760
Email: info@primakonyha.hu
CONSUMER: WOMEN'S INTEREST CONSUMER MAGAZINES: Food & Cookery

PROGRAMME MAGAZINE 1690228HU14L-15
Editorial: Szegedi út 37-39., 1135 BUDAPEST **Tel:** 1/288-7702 **Fax:** 1/288-7703
Email: vivamedia1@t-online.hu
Circ: 50,000
BUSINESS: COMMERCE, INDUSTRY & MANAGEMENT: Trade Unions

PROGRESSZÍV MAGAZIN 1689840HU14A-226
Editorial: Rákospatak u. 70-72., 1142 BUDAPEST
Tel: 1/467-0618 **Fax:** 1/384-5307
Email: progressziv@crier.hu **Web site:** http://www.progressziv.hu
Circ: 18,000
BUSINESS: COMMERCE, INDUSTRY & MANAGEMENT

PROPERTY WATCH 1690390HU1E-157
Editorial: Lövoház u. 39., 1024 BUDAPEST **Tel:** 1/877-1000 **Fax:** 1/877-1001
Email: info@eston.hu
Circ: 20,000
Profile: Magazine focusing on news, trends and analysis of property investments.
BUSINESS: FINANCE & ECONOMICS: Property

RÁDIÓTECHNIKA 1689416HU43B-1
Editorial: Dagály u. 11/A I. emelet, 1138 BUDAPEST
Tel: 1/239-4933 **Fax:** 1/239-4933/34
Email: lapok@radiovilag.hu **Web site:** http://www.radiotechnika.hu
Editor-in-Chief: Ferenc Békei
BUSINESS: ELECTRICAL RETAIL TRADE: Radio & Hi-Fi

READER'S DIGEST 1200811HU73-100
Editorial: Népfürdo u. 22., 1138 BUDAPEST **Tel:** 1/66-61-730 **Fax:** 1/66-61-801
Email: marta.patai@readersdigest.hu **Web site:** http://www.rd.hu
Cover Price: HUF 680; **Circ:** 141,792
Usual Pagination: 144
Profile: General interest magazine.
Readership: Aimed at the general public.
ADVERTISING RATES:
Full Page Colour .... HUF 1100000
CONSUMER: NATIONAL & INTERNATIONAL PERIODICALS

ROLLING TONS 1689852HU49D-1
Editorial: Budapesti út 87/A, 2040 BUDAÖRS
Tel: 30/302-0545
Email: info@rollingtons.hu
Cover Price: HUF 245; **Circ:** 18,000
Editor-in-Chief: Szabolcs Chilkó
BUSINESS: TRANSPORT: Commercial Vehicles

RTV TIPP 1688514HU67B-503
Editorial: Almádi u. 3., 8200 VESZPRÉM **Tel:** 88/579-443 **Fax:** 88/583-267
Email: rtvtipp@plt.hu
Editor-in-Chief: István Györffy
REGIONAL DAILY & SUNDAY NEWSPAPERS: Regional Daily Newspapers

SAFETY & SECURITY 1827465HU54C-62
Editorial: Tamási Áron u. 18/B., 1124 BUDAPEST
Tel: 20/663-4814
Email: info@safsec.hu **Web site:** http://www.safsec.hu
Circ: 10,000
Editor-in-Chief: Árpád Gyapay
BUSINESS: SAFETY & SECURITY: Security

SHAPE 630760HU74G-200
Editorial: Hajógyári sziget 213., 1033 BUDAPEST
Tel: 1/505-0800 **Fax:** 1/505-0806
Cover Price: HUF 495; **Circ:** 28,469
Usual Pagination: 100
Profile: Magazine focusing on health, beauty and fitness issues.
Readership: Aimed at women aged 25 to 35 years.
ADVERTISING RATES:
Full Page Colour .... HUF 1250000
CONSUMER: WOMEN'S INTEREST CONSUMER MAGAZINES: Slimming & Health

SIKERES SPORTHORGÁSZ 1689862HU92-3
Editorial: Diósárok 26/B, 1125 BUDAPEST **Tel:** 20/915-7099 **Fax:** 1/209-2303
Email: sikeres@sport-horgasz.hu
Circ: 72,000
ADVERTISING RATES:
Full Page Colour .... HUF 350000
CONSUMER: ANGLING & FISHING

SOMOGYI HÍRLAP 1688231HU67B-530
Editorial: Városmajor u. 11., 1122 BUDAPEST **Tel:** 1/488-5726 **Fax:** 1/488-5719
Circ: 33,051
Advertising Director: András Lengyel
ADVERTISING RATES:
Full Page Mono .... HUF 984000
Full Page Colour .... HUF 1368000
REGIONAL DAILY & SUNDAY NEWSPAPERS: Regional Daily Newspapers

SÖRLEVÉL 1690606HU9B-1
Editorial: Vörösmarty tér 1., 1051 BUDAPEST **Tel:** 1/429-9094 **Fax:** 99/516-111
Email: eva.kiss@heineken.hu
Circ: 650
Editor-in-Chief: Éva Kiss
BUSINESS: DRINKS & LICENSED TRADE: Brewing

SPORT AUTO 1689863HU77A-44
Editorial: Bécsi út 57-61. I/11., 1136 BUDAPEST
Tel: 1/453-3310 **Fax:** 1/453-3313
Email: sportauto@sportauto.hu **Web site:** http://www.sportauto.hu
Cover Price: HUF 598; **Circ:** 35,000
Editor-in-Chief: László Fábián
ADVERTISING RATES:
Full Page Colour .... HUF 860000
CONSUMER: MOTORING & CYCLING: Motoring

SPORT PLUSSZ 1688517HU75A-3
Editorial: Angol u. 65-69., 1149 BUDAPEST **Tel:** 1/251-0000 **Fax:** 1/383-1773
Email: sport@naptv.hu
Circ: 80,000
CONSUMER: SPORT

STÍLUS & LENDÜLET MAGAZIN 1689683HU77A-41
Editorial: Pálya u. 9., 1012 BUDAPEST **Tel:** 1/487-5200 **Fax:** 1/487-5203
Circ: 365,000
Usual Pagination: 32
ADVERTISING RATES:
Full Page Colour .... HUF 920000
CONSUMER: MOTORING & CYCLING: Motoring

SUPPLY CHAIN MONITOR 1843424HU10-24
Editorial: Karinthy Frigyes u. 17., 1117 BUDAPEST
Tel: 1/789-4933 **Fax:** 1/788-0920
Email: scmonitor@scmonitor.hu **Web site:** http://www.scmonitor.hu
Annual Sub.: HUF 6300; **Circ:** 10,000
Editor-in-Chief: Szilvia Rapi-Jaubert
BUSINESS: MATERIALS HANDLING

SÜTOIPAROSOK, PÉKEK 634460HU8A-150
Editorial: Dombóvári út 5-7., 1117 BUDAPEST
Tel: 1/204-3809 **Fax:** 1/204-3809
Email: mail.mete@mtesz.hu
Managing Editor: András dr. Oláh
Profile: Publication of the Trade Union of Hungarian Bakers, featuring articles on trade news and general issues, scientific research, advice and help for self-employed bakers and news on trade union meetings and conferences.
Readership: Aimed at the members of the Trade Union of Hungarian Bakers and those working in bakeries.
BUSINESS: BAKING & CONFECTIONERY: Baking

SZABAD FÖLD 630028HU65A-80
Editorial: Lajos u. 48-66. B lph II. em., 1036 BUDAPEST **Tel:** 1/489-8846 **Fax:** 1/489-8849
Email: hirdetes@szabadfold.hu
Cover Price: HUF 195; **Circ:** 140,228
Usual Pagination: 40
Profile: Newspaper containing articles on national news, general interest subjects and advice sections covering various themes, with a focus on agriculture.
Readership: Aimed at families living in the country.
ADVERTISING RATES:
Full Page Mono .... HUF 2200000
Full Page Colour .... HUF 3080000
NATIONAL DAILY & SUNDAY NEWSPAPERS: National Daily Newspapers

SZEGEDI TÜKÖR 1688854HU72-146
Editorial: Szabadkai út 20., 6720 SZEGED **Tel:** 62/567-888 **Fax:** 62/567-881
Email: vecsey.agnes@szeged.eu
Circ: 72,000
Editor-in-Chief: Ágnes Vécsey
LOCAL NEWSPAPERS

SZÉP HÁZAK 1690255HU4A-62
Editorial: Disz tér 16., 1014 BUDAPEST **Tel:** 1/202-0185 **Fax:** 1/375-0462
Email: szephazak@szephazak.hu
Cover Price: HUF 395; **Circ:** 71,000
Usual Pagination: 100
ADVERTISING RATES:
Full Page Colour .... HUF 1100000
BUSINESS: ARCHITECTURE & BUILDING: Architecture

SZÉPLAK 1689880HU74C-98
Editorial: Ferenc tér 13. II/8., 1094 BUDAPEST
Tel: 1/456-8050 **Fax:** 1/218-0254
Email: szeplak@szeplak.hu **Web site:** http://www.szeplak.hu
Cover Price: HUF 485; **Circ:** 31,000
Usual Pagination: 96
Editor-in-Chief: János Berényi
ADVERTISING RATES:
Full Page Colour .... HUF 920000
CONSUMER: WOMEN'S INTEREST CONSUMER MAGAZINES: Home & Family

SZERENCSE MIX 1688523HU67J-1
Editorial: Csalogány u. 30-32., 1015 BUDAPEST
Tel: 1/224-3424 **Fax:** 1/224-3403
Email: szerencsemix@szrt.hu
Circ: 58,000
Editor-in-Chief: János Sz. Kiss
REGIONAL DAILY & SUNDAY NEWSPAPERS: Regional Newspapers (excl. dailies)

SZINERGIA 1690534HU1A-130
Editorial: Baross u. 91-95., 1047 BUDAPEST **Tel:** 1/399-5500 **Fax:** 1/399-5599
Email: info@synergon.hu **Web site:** http://www.synergon.hu
Circ: 3,000
Editor-in-Chief: lászló Lónyai
Profile: Magazine focusing on economics and information technology.
BUSINESS: FINANCE & ECONOMICS

SZÍNHÁZI KALAUZ 1690749HU76B-5
Editorial: Tisza u. 6. V. em. 26., 1133 BUDAPEST
Tel: 1/359-3103 **Fax:** 1/359-3103
Email: k.pannonia@chello.hu **Web site:** http://www.viapannonia.hu
Circ: 30,000
CONSUMER: MUSIC & PERFORMING ARTS: Theatre

SZOLOSI HÍREK 1843426HU1P-42
Editorial: Fo út 21., 5244 TISZASZOLOS **Tel:** 59/511-408 **Fax:** 59/511-408
Email: postmaster@phszolos.t-online.hu
BUSINESS: FINANCE & ECONOMICS: Fundraising

TEJGAZDASÁG 633912HU21G-180
Editorial: Guba S. u. 40., 7400 KAPOSVÁR **Tel:** 82/526-592 **Fax:** 82/526-593
Email: mail.mete@mtesz.hu
Managing Editor: Zoltán dr. Szakály
Profile: Publication featuring milk production, includes technology, quality control, marketing, nutritional science issues, legal issues and industry politics.
Readership: Aimed at executives and employees in the dairy industry.
BUSINESS: AGRICULTURE & FARMING: Milk

TEJIPARI HÍRLAP 633996HU21G-181
Editorial: Bartók Béla út 152/C I. em., 1115 BUDAPEST **Tel:** 1/204-5278 **Fax:** 1/204-5278
Email: tejiparihirlap@neteasy.hu
Circ: 10,000
Usual Pagination: 12
Profile: Publication focusing on the milk industry, includes economics and management.
Readership: Aimed at producers and retailers.
BUSINESS: AGRICULTURE & FARMING: Milk

TELECOM MAGAZIN 1689912HU18B-102
Editorial: Pacsirtamezo u. 32. II/29., 1036 BUDAPEST **Tel:** 1/237-0855 **Fax:** 1/237-0856
Email: telecom@telecommagazin.hu **Web site:** http://www.telecommagazin.hu
Editor-in-Chief: Attila Várnagy
BUSINESS: ELECTRONICS: Telecommunications

TERMÉKMIX 1689918HU14R-116
Editorial: Mogyoródi út 32., 1149 BUDAPEST **Tel:** 1/210-1830 **Fax:** 1/210-4150
Email: info@termekmix.hu **Web site:** http://www.termekmix.hu
Circ: 21,000
ADVERTISING RATES:
Full Page Colour .... HUF 600000
BUSINESS: COMMERCE, INDUSTRY & MANAGEMENT: Commerce Related

TERMÉSZETBÚVÁR 1690270HU57-115
Editorial: Október 6. u. 7., 1051 BUDAPEST **Tel:** 1/266-3036 **Fax:** 1/266-3343
Email: tbuvar@t-online.hu **Web site:** http://www.termeszetbuvar.hu
Cover Price: HUF 420; **Circ:** 16,000
Usual Pagination: 48
Editor-in-Chief: Imre Dosztányi
ADVERTISING RATES:
Full Page Colour .... HUF 300000
BUSINESS: ENVIRONMENT & POLLUTION

TERMÉSZETGYÓGYÁSZ MAGAZIN 630890HU56R-200
Editorial: Kapás u. 26-44. D. lph. IV/11., 1027 BUDAPEST **Tel:** 1/315-1725 **Fax:** 1/315-1725
Email: tgym@mail.datanet.hu **Web site:** http://www.tgy-magazin.hu
Circ: 60,000
Usual Pagination: 100
Editor-in-Chief: Katalin dr. Görgei
Profile: Magazine covering health and culture issues, also natural and complementary healing. Features aromatherapy, graphology, herbalism, holistics, introducing different parts of the human body, homeopathy, dream-reading, brain-control, meditation, yoga and bio-gardening.
Readership: Aimed at healthcare personnel, and all interested in natural health issues.
ADVERTISING RATES:
Full Page Mono .... HUF 460000
Full Page Colour .... HUF 580000
BUSINESS: HEALTH & MEDICAL: Health Medical Related

THEBUSINESSWOMAN 1690635HU74A-148
Editorial: Ady E. út 147/D fszt. 2., 1221 BUDAPEST **Tel:** 30/645-0390 **Fax:** 26/371-399
Email: marketing@thebusinesswoman.hu **Web site:** http://www.thebusinesswoman.hu
Circ: 15,000
Editor-in-Chief: Csilla dr. Marosi
CONSUMER: WOMEN'S INTEREST CONSUMER MAGAZINES: Women's Interest

TINA 1688591HU74A-137
Editorial: Szugló u. 81-85., 1145 BUDAPEST **Tel:** 1/460-4880 **Fax:** 1/460-4882
Cover Price: HUF 170; **Circ:** 69,109
Usual Pagination: 52
ADVERTISING RATES:
Full Page Colour .... HUF 1150000
CONSUMER: WOMEN'S INTEREST CONSUMER MAGAZINES: Women's Interest

T-MA 1690264HU14L-8
Editorial: Nádor u. 4., 1051 BUDAPEST **Tel:** 1/237-4347 **Fax:** 1/237-4349
Email: bardos@bm.gov.hu
Editor-in-Chief: László dr. Dura
BUSINESS: COMMERCE, INDUSTRY & MANAGEMENT: Trade Unions

TOLNA MEGYEI KRÓNIKA 1688744HU74C-85
Editorial: Csokonai u. 3. fszt. 1., 7100 SZEKSZÁRD **Tel:** 74/511-709 **Fax:** 74/414-853
Email: kafi50@t-online.hu
Circ: 50,000
CONSUMER: WOMEN'S INTEREST CONSUMER MAGAZINES: Home & Family

TOLNAI NÉPÚJSÁG 1688233HU67B-531
Editorial: Városmajor u. 11., 1122 BUDAPEST **Tel:** 1/488-5726 **Fax:** 1/488-5719
Circ: 20,948
Advertising Director: András Lengyel
ADVERTISING RATES:
Full Page Mono .... HUF 768000
Full Page Colour .... HUF 1032000
REGIONAL DAILY & SUNDAY NEWSPAPERS: Regional Daily Newspapers

TTG HUNGARY 706818HU50-190
Editorial: Zichy Jeno u. 4., 1066 BUDAPEST **Tel:** 1/321-1939 **Fax:** 1/301-7049
Email: info@ttghungary.hu **Web site:** http://www.ttghungary.hu
Circ: 5,000
Profile: Journal providing national and international news, information and trends in tourism.
Readership: Aimed at travel agents, tour guides, airlines and local governments.
ADVERTISING RATES:
Full Page Colour .... HUF 360000
BUSINESS: TRAVEL & TOURISM

TURIZMUS PANORÁMA 634402HU50-200
Editorial: Munkás u. 9., 1074 BUDAPEST **Tel:** 1/266-5853 **Fax:** 1/338-4293
Email: info@turizmus.com
Circ: 5,000
Profile: Publication focusing on professional tourism and hosting.
Readership: Aimed at travel agents, hotel owners and managers.
BUSINESS: TRAVEL & TOURISM

TURIZMUS TREND 766244HU50-201
Editorial: Montevideo u. 3/A, 1037 BUDAPEST **Tel:** 1/430-4562 **Fax:** 1/430-4569
Email: ttrend@ttrend.hu **Web site:** http://www.turizmusonline.hu
Cover Price: HUF 980; **Circ:** 3,009
Editor-in-Chief: Zoltán Szántó
Profile: Magazine focusing on Hungarian and international tourism.
Readership: Aimed at travel agents, hotel and transport company professionals.
BUSINESS: TRAVEL & TOURISM

TV PLUSZ MAGAZIN 1688599HU67B-504
Editorial: Dósa nádor tér 10., 4024 DEBRECEN **Tel:** 52/525-400 **Fax:** 52/525-405
Email: inform@inform.hu
Circ: 180,000
REGIONAL DAILY & SUNDAY NEWSPAPERS: Regional Daily Newspapers

TYPOGRAPHIA 1796768HU84A-169
Editorial: Benczúr u. 37. fszt. 1., 1068 BUDAPEST **Tel:** 1/266-0064 **Fax:** 1/266-0028
Email: typographia@nyomdaszok.t-online.net
Circ: 5,000
Editor-in-Chief: József Persovits
CONSUMER: THE ARTS & LITERARY: Arts

ÚJ DUNÁNTÚLI NAPLÓ 1688235HU67B-532
Editorial: Városmajor u. 11., 1122 BUDAPEST **Tel:** 1/488-5726 **Fax:** 1/488-5719
Circ: 48,389
Advertising Director: András Lengyel
ADVERTISING RATES:
Full Page Mono .... HUF 1104000
Full Page Colour .... HUF 1512000
REGIONAL DAILY & SUNDAY NEWSPAPERS: Regional Daily Newspapers

ÚJ MUVÉSZET 1689974HU84A-105
Editorial: Nagymezo u. 49., 1065 BUDAPEST **Tel:** 1/341-5598 **Fax:** 1/479-0232
Email: ujmuveszet@gmail.com **Web site:** http://www.uj-muveszet.hu
Cover Price: HUF 635; **Circ:** 3,800
Usual Pagination: 56
ADVERTISING RATES:
Full Page Colour .... HUF 250000
CONSUMER: THE ARTS & LITERARY: Arts

ÚJ NÉPLAP 1688237HU67B-533
Editorial: Városmajor u. 11., 1122 BUDAPEST **Tel:** 1/488-5726 **Fax:** 1/488-5719
Circ: 28,577
Advertising Director: András Lengyel
ADVERTISING RATES:
Full Page Mono .... HUF 912000
Full Page Colour .... HUF 1296000
REGIONAL DAILY & SUNDAY NEWSPAPERS: Regional Daily Newspapers

ÚJBUDA 1688771HU72-69
Editorial: Szent Gellért tér 1-3., 1111 BUDAPEST **Tel:** 1/372-0960 **Fax:** 1/372-0961
Email: media@ujbuda.hu
Circ: 82,000
Editor-in-Chief: Kinga Vincze
LOCAL NEWSPAPERS

AZ UTAZÓ 1689168HU89A-44
Editorial: Hajóállomás u. 1., 1095 BUDAPEST **Tel:** 1/323-3125 **Fax:** 1/323-3127
Email: emz@azutazo.hu **Web site:** http://www.azutazo.hu
Cover Price: HUF 495
Annual Sub.: HUF 2530; **Circ:** 22,000
Usual Pagination: 80
Editor-in-Chief: Zoltán dr. Érsek M.
ADVERTISING RATES:
Full Page Colour .... HUF 680000
CONSUMER: HOLIDAYS & TRAVEL: Travel

UTAZZ VELÜNK MAGAZIN 1796770HU50-215
Editorial: Nagy Lajos király útja 191., 1149 BUDAPEST **Tel:** 20/555-7998 **Fax:** 1/460-0795
Email: info@otthontar.com **Web site:** http://www.moutazzvelunkhungary.com
Cover Price: HUF 195; **Circ:** 10,000
BUSINESS: TRAVEL & TOURISM

ÜZLETI KALAUZ 1689749HU14A-225
Editorial: Nádor u. 29/B, 4400 NYÍREGYHÁZA **Tel:** 42/950-142 **Fax:** 42/406-913
Email: nemzetkozitukor@gmail.com **Web site:** http://www.nemzetkozitukor.hu
BUSINESS: COMMERCE, INDUSTRY & MANAGEMENT

VÁM-ZOLL 1689993HU1M-52
Editorial: Szegedi út 37-39., 1135 BUDAPEST **Tel:** 1/288-7702 **Fax:** 1/288-7703
Email: vivamedia1@t-online.hu
Cover Price: HUF 120
Annual Sub.: HUF 303; **Circ:** 50,000
Usual Pagination: 32
ADVERTISING RATES:
Full Page Mono .... HUF 100000
BUSINESS: FINANCE & ECONOMICS: Taxation

VÁROSHÁZI HÍRADÓ 1688782HU72-80
Editorial: Városház tér 11., 1221 BUDAPEST **Tel:** 1/482-0189 **Fax:** 1/482-0189
Email: ujsag@bp22.hu **Web site:** http://www.bp22.hu
Editor-in-Chief: György Bvalkó
LOCAL NEWSPAPERS

VAS NÉPE 1688296HU67B-543
Editorial: Fo tér 3-5., 9700 SZOMBATHELY **Tel:** 94/528-288 **Fax:** 94/528-290
Circ: 57,176
ADVERTISING RATES:
Full Page Mono .... HUF 1479625
Full Page Colour .... HUF 2071475
REGIONAL DAILY & SUNDAY NEWSPAPERS: Regional Daily Newspapers

VASÁRNAPI HÍREK 630888HU65B-1
Editorial: Avar u. 8., 1016 BUDAPEST **Tel:** 1/319-2333 **Fax:** 1/319-2333
Email: szerkesztoseg@vasarnapihirek.hu
Circ: 67,564
Editor-in-Chief: János Avar
Profile: Newspaper reviewing the news and events of the previous week.
Readership: Read mainly by men aged between 25 and 59 years.
NATIONAL DAILY & SUNDAY NEWSPAPERS: National Sunday Newspapers

VASUTAS MAGAZIN 1688751HU14L-12
Editorial: Andrássy út 73-75., 1062 BUDAPEST **Tel:** 1/511-3801 **Fax:** 1/511-4931
Email: ujsag@mav.hu
Circ: 25,000
BUSINESS: COMMERCE, INDUSTRY & MANAGEMENT: Trade Unions

VENDÉGLÁTÁS 633909HU11A-71
Editorial: József u. 26-28., 1084 BUDAPEST **Tel:** 1/327-0188 **Fax:** 1/266-8190
Email: vendeglatas@centralpress.hu **Web site:** http://www.vendeglatasonline.hu
Cover Price: HUF 1000
Annual Sub.: HUF 9500; **Circ:** 12,000
Editor-in-Chief: Miklós Niszkács
Profile: Publication containing general, financial, technical and legal news, programmes and events, interviews with chefs, village tourism, reviews of famous coffeehouses, international cuisine and gastronomic history.
Readership: Aimed at restaurateurs and hotel managers in private establishments and hotel-chains. Also aimed at managers of public catering facilities.
BUSINESS: CATERING: Catering, Hotels & Restaurants

VESZPRÉMI 7 NAP PLUSSZ 1688480HU67J-12
Editorial: Almádi u. 3., 8200 VESZPRÉM **Tel:** 88/400-400 **Fax:** 88/400-400
Email: veszpremmaraton@maraton.plt.hu **Web site:** http://www.maraton.hu
Circ: 27,198
ADVERTISING RATES:
Full Page Mono .... HUF 336420
REGIONAL DAILY & SUNDAY NEWSPAPERS: Regional Newspapers (excl. dailies)

VIDÉK ÍZE 1797137HU74P-175
Editorial: Lajos u. 48-66. B lph. II. em., 1036 BUDAPEST **Tel:** 1/489-8846 **Fax:** 1/489-8849
Email: hirdetes@videkize.hu
Cover Price: HUF 390; **Circ:** 22,963
Usual Pagination: 56
ADVERTISING RATES:
Full Page Colour .... HUF 539000
CONSUMER: WOMEN'S INTEREST CONSUMER MAGAZINES: Food & Cookery

VIDEO-PART MAGAZIN 1796804HU18A-134
Editorial: Ferenc krt. 26., 1092 BUDAPEST **Tel:** 1/456-3006 **Fax:** 1/217-1288
Email: pana@videopart.hu **Web site:** http://www.panashop.hu
Circ: 120,000
Editor-in-Chief: Zsuzsanna Kereskesné Pap
BUSINESS: ELECTRONICS

VIDEOPRAKTIKA 631083HU38-200
Editorial: Palotás u. 1., 1152 BUDAPEST **Tel:** 1/271-1118 **Fax:** 1/271-1119
Email: banach@videopraktika.hu **Web site:** http://www.videopraktika.hu
Cover Price: HUF 640; **Circ:** 6,000
Profile: Publication focusing on electronic picture production, digital pictures, also news and tips on video production and the Internet.
Readership: Aimed at professionals and enthusiasts.
BUSINESS: PHOTOGRAPHIC TRADE

VILÁGGAZDASÁG 629969HU65A-120
Editorial: Maros u. 19-21., 1122 BUDAPEST **Tel:** 1/489-1165 **Fax:** 1/489-1159
Email: hirdetes@vg.hu
Circ: 13,998
Profile: Newspaper covering all aspects of finance and business. Provides in-depth economic, stock market and international share analysis.
Readership: Aimed at highly qualified, senior management in business.
ADVERTISING RATES:
Full Page Mono .... HUF 960000
Full Page Colour .... HUF 1344000
NATIONAL DAILY & SUNDAY NEWSPAPERS: National Daily Newspapers

VILÁGJÁRÓ UTAZÁSI MAGAZIN 1690008HU89A-19
Editorial: Nagy Lajos király útja 210/A, 1149 BUDAPEST **Tel:** 1/300-1251 **Fax:** 1/300-1254
Email: info@vilagjaromagazin.hu **Web site:** http://www.vilagjaromagazin.hu
Circ: 30,000
CONSUMER: HOLIDAYS & TRAVEL: Travel

VILLANYSZERELOK LAPJA
1690012HU17-82
Editorial: Róbert Károly krt. 90., 1134 BUDAPEST
Tel: 1/450-0868 **Fax:** 1/236-0899
Email: hirdetes@villanylap.hu **Web site:** http://www.villanyszaklap.hu
Circ: 9,000
Usual Pagination: 48
ADVERTISING RATES:
Full Page Colour .... HUF 490000
BUSINESS: ELECTRICAL

VÍZMU PANORÁMA 1690294HU42C-1
Editorial: Sas u. 25., 1051 BUDAPEST **Tel:** 1/353-3241 **Fax:** 1/473-0055
Email: papp.maria@maviz.org **Web site:** http://www.maviz.org
Circ: 1,500
BUSINESS: CONSTRUCTION: Water Engineering

VOLKSWAGEN MAGAZIN
1690368HU77A-56
Editorial: Pálya u. 9., 1012 BUDAPEST **Tel:** 1/487-5200 **Fax:** 1/487-5203
Circ: 30,000
Usual Pagination: 48
ADVERTISING RATES:
Full Page Colour .... HUF 1050000
CONSUMER: MOTORING & CYCLING: Motoring

WAN2 MAGAZIN 1690015HU76D-7
Editorial: Pálya u. 9., 1012 BUDAPEST **Tel:** 1/487-5200 **Fax:** 1/487-5240
Circ: 27,000
Usual Pagination: 96
Editor-in-Chief: Tamás Ligeti Nagy
ADVERTISING RATES:
Full Page Colour .... HUF 900000
CONSUMER: MUSIC & PERFORMING ARTS: Music

WHERE MAGAZIN 1690017HU89B-2
Editorial: Király u. 16., 1061 BUDAPEST **Tel:** 1/887-4848 **Fax:** 1/887-4849
Email: sales@pxb.hu **Web site:** http://www.pxb.hu
Circ: 70,000
Usual Pagination: 40
ADVERTISING RATES:
Full Page Colour .... HUF 513000
CONSUMER: HOLIDAYS & TRAVEL: Hotel Magazines

XIII. KERÜLETI HÍRNÖK
1688773HU72-71
Editorial: Újpesti rkp. 7. Fszt. 2., 1137 BUDAPEST
Tel: 1/237-5060 **Fax:** 1/237-5069
Email: hirnok@sprintkiado.hu
Circ: 67,000
Editor-in-Chief: Ildikó Czeglédi
LOCAL NEWSPAPERS

ZALAI HÍRLAP 1688295HU67B-542
Editorial: Kossuth u. 45-49., 8900 ZALAEGERSZEG
Tel: 92/502-235 **Fax:** 92/312-580
Circ: 55,559
ADVERTISING RATES:
Full Page Mono .... HUF 1464050
Full Page Colour .... HUF 2049670
REGIONAL DAILY & SUNDAY NEWSPAPERS: Regional Daily Newspapers

ZÖLD DIMENZIÓ 1690899HU57-121
Editorial: Kápolna u. 9., 6000 KECSKEMÉT **Tel:** 76/509-424 **Fax:** 76/509-426
Email: betapress@betapress.hu **Web site:** http://www.betapress.hu
Circ: 8,000
Editor-in-Chief: Csilla L. Horváth
BUSINESS: ENVIRONMENT & POLLUTION

ZSIRÁF DIÁKMAGAZIN
1689079HU74F-2
Editorial: Lajos u. 42., 1036 BUDAPEST **Tel:** 1/318-4246 **Fax:** 1/318-4246
Email: ketzsiraf@zsiraf.hu **Web site:** http://www.zsiraf.hu
ADVERTISING RATES:
Full Page Colour .... HUF 350000
CONSUMER: WOMEN'S INTEREST CONSUMER MAGAZINES: Teenage

ZUGLÓI LAPOK 1688774HU72-72
Editorial: Pétervárad u. 7/B, 1145 BUDAPEST **Tel:** 1/467-2337 **Fax:** 1/467-2337
Email: deaka@t-online.hu **Web site:** http://www.zuglo.hu
Circ: 70,000
Editor-in-Chief: András dr. Deék
LOCAL NEWSPAPERS

Iceland

Time Difference: GMT
National Telephone Code: +354
Continent: Europe
Capital: Reykjavik
Principal Language: Icelandic, Danish, English, German
Population: 301931
Monetary Unit: Iceland Krona (ISK)

EMBASSY HIGH COMMISSION: Embassy of Iceland: 2a Hans Street, London SW1X 0JE
Tel: 020 7259 3999
Fax: 020 7245 9649
Email: icemb.london@utn.stjr.is
Website: http://www.iceland.org/uk

AEGIR 1550001IS45B-5
Editorial: Hafnarstraeti 82, 600 AKUREYRI
Tel: 461 51 35 **Fax:** 461 51 59
Email: oskar@athygli.is **Web site:** www.athygli.is
ISSN: 0001-9038
Date Established: 1905; **Freq:** Monthly; **Cover Price:** ISK 600.00
Annual Sub.: ISK 7600.00; **Circ:** 2,500
Editor: Oskar Halldorsson; **Advertising Manager:** Sigurlin Gudjonsdottir
Profile: Iceland fisheries magazine.
Language(s): Icelandic
Readership: Aimed at people, firms and others related to the fishing industry.
Mechanical Data: Col Length: 220mm, Page Width: 164mm
Copy instructions: *Copy Date:* Between the 10th and the 15th of each month
BUSINESS: MARINE & SHIPPING: Commercial Fishing

ATLANTICA 1600044IS89D-10
Editorial: Borgartún 23, 105 REYKJAVÍK
Tel: 512 75 75 **Fax:** 561 86 46
Email: atlantica@heimur.com **Web site:** http://www.icelandreview.com
Date Established: 1976; **Freq:** 6 issues yearly;
Cover Price: Free; **Circ:** 40,000
Usual Pagination: 100
Editor-in-Chief: Bjarni Brynjolfsson
Profile: Magazine focusing on travel, tourism and culture.
Language(s): English
Readership: Aimed at passengers on Icelandair airlines.
Agency Commission: 15%
Mechanical Data: Type Area: 248 x 171mm, Trim Size: 275 x 206mm, Screen: Mono: 54 lpc, Colour: 60 lpc, Print Process: Offset, Col Length: 248mm, Page Width: 171mm
Copy instructions: *Copy Date:* 2 months prior to publication date
CONSUMER: HOLIDAYS & TRAVEL: In-Flight Magazines

BLEIKT OG BLATT 1200855IS94X-5
Editorial: Linghalsi 5, 110 REYKJAVÍK **Tel:** 515 5500
Fax: 515 5588
Email: gudmundur@birtingur.is **Web site:** http://www.birtingur.is
ISSN: 1021-7130
Freq: 2 per day; **Circ:** 12,000
Editor: Gudmundur Arnarsson
Profile: Magazine focusing on issues and events related to sex and the relationship between the sexes.
Language(s): Icelandic
Readership: Aimed at all age groups of both sexes.
ADVERTISING RATES:
Full Page Mono .... ISK 49900.00
Full Page Colour .... ISK 87900.00
Agency Commission: 10%
Mechanical Data: Type Area: 253 x 173mm, Col Length: 253mm, Page Width: 173mm
CONSUMER: OTHER CLASSIFICATIONS: Miscellaneous

DAGBLADID VISIR 1500234IS65A-5
Editorial: Krokhalsi 6, 110 REYKJAVÍK **Tel:** 512 70 00
Fax: 515 55 99
Email: ritstjorn@dv.is **Web site:** www.dv.is
Date Established: 1910; **Freq:** Daily - Mondays to Fridays; **Cover Price:** ISK 295.00; **Circ:** 20,000
News Editor: Brynjolfur Thor Gudmundsson; **Editor-in-Chief:** Reynir Traustason
Profile: Newspaper covering news, sports and culture.
Language(s): Icelandic
NATIONAL DAILY & SUNDAY NEWSPAPERS: National Daily Newspapers

THE FARMERS MAGAZINE
1200832IS21A-5
Editorial: Farmers House, PO Box 7080, IS-127 REYKJAVIK **Tel:** 563 0300 **Fax:** 562 3068
Email: bbl@bondi.is **Web site:** http://www.bondi.is
Freq: 21 issues yearly; **Cover Price:** Free; **Circ:** 18,000
Usual Pagination: 40
Editor: Thorstur Haraldsson
Profile: Magazine featuring farming articles in general.
Language(s): Icelandic
Readership: Aimed at farm owners and managers.
BUSINESS: AGRICULTURE & FARMING

FREYR 1200828IS21A-10
Editorial: Farmers House, PO Box 7080, IS-127 REYKJAVIK **Tel:** 563 0300 **Fax:** 562 3068
Email: bbl@bondi.is **Web site:** http://www.bondi.is
ISSN: 0016-1209
Date Established: 1904; **Freq:** Quarterly; **Annual Sub.:** ISK 3600.00; **Circ:** 2,120
Usual Pagination: 40
Editor: Tjorvi Pjarnason
Profile: Magazine for agriculture and farming.
Language(s): Icelandic
Readership: Aimed at farm owners and managers.
Average ad content per issue: 5%
BUSINESS: AGRICULTURE & FARMING

GESTGJAFINN 1200853IS94G-5
Editorial: Linghalsi 5, 110 REYKJAVÍK **Tel:** 515 5500
Fax: 515 5599
Email: solveig@birtingur.is **Web site:** http://www.birtingur.is
ISSN: 1017-3552
Date Established: 1981; **Freq:** 17 issues yearly;
Cover Price: ISK 799.00
Annual Sub.: ISK 5432.00; **Circ:** 14,000
Usual Pagination: 100
Editor: Solveig Baldursdottir
Profile: Magazine featuring articles on gourmet food, drinks and restaurants.
Language(s): Icelandic
Readership: Aimed at visitors to Iceland.
ADVERTISING RATES:
Full Page Mono .... ISK 81500.00
Full Page Colour .... ISK 128700.00
Agency Commission: 10%
Mechanical Data: Type Area: 280 x 175mm, Col Length: 280mm, Page Width: 175mm
CONSUMER: OTHER CLASSIFICATIONS: Restaurant Guides

ICELAND REVIEW 1600540IS50-5
Editorial: Borgartún 23, 103 REYKJAVÍK
Tel: 512 75 75 **Fax:** 561 86 46
Email: icelandreview@icelandreview.com **Web site:** http://www.icelandreview.com
ISSN: 0019-1094
Date Established: 1963; **Freq:** Quarterly; **Cover Price:** ISK 899.00; **Circ:** 15,000
Usual Pagination: 100
Editor-in-Chief: Bjarni Brynjolfsson
Profile: Magazine featuring tourism, culture, news and travel.
Language(s): English
Readership: Read by travel agents, tour operators, tourists and Iceland enthusiasts.
ADVERTISING RATES:
Full Page Mono .... ISK 99.90
Full Page Colour .... ISK 121.90
Mechanical Data: Type Area: 245 x 172mm, Col Length: 245mm, Page Width: 172mm
BUSINESS: TRAVEL & TOURISM

MBL.IS 755521IS65A-9
Editorial: Hádegismóum 2, 110 REYKJAVIK
Tel: 569 11 00 **Fax:** 569 11 81
Email: netfrett@mbl.is **Web site:** http://www.mbl.is
Freq: Daily. Updated daily; **Cover Price:** Free
Editor: Gudmundur Hermannsson
Profile: E-zine version of Morgunbladid. Covers domestic and international news, economic and sport.
Language(s): Icelandic
NATIONAL DAILY & SUNDAY NEWSPAPERS: National Daily Newspapers

MORGUNBLADID 1201536IS65A-10
Editorial: Hádegismóum 2, 110 REYKJAVÍK
Tel: 569 11 00 **Fax:** 569 11 10
Email: morgunbladid@mbl.is **Web site:** http://www.mbl.is
Date Established: 1913; **Freq:** Daily; **Circ:** 55,000
News Editor: Gudmundur Hermannsson; **Editor-in-Chief:** Styrmir Gunnarsson; **Managing Director:** Einar Sigurdsson
Profile: Newspaper covering news, debate and entertainment.
Language(s): Icelandic
Readership: Aimed at readers aged between 12 and 80.
ADVERTISING RATES:
Full Page Mono .... ISK 187000.00
SCC .... ISK 339.20
Mechanical Data: Col Widths (Display): 47mm, Col Length: 390mm, No. of Columns (Display): 5
NATIONAL DAILY & SUNDAY NEWSPAPERS: National Daily Newspapers

NYTT LIF 1200841IS74B-5
Editorial: Lyngháls 5, IS-110 REYKJAVÍK
Tel: 515 5500 **Fax:** 515 5588
Email: nyttlif@birtingur.is **Web site:** http://www.birtingur.is/nyttlif
ISSN: 1017-3595
Date Established: 1978; **Freq:** 16 issues yearly - Every three weeks; **Cover Price:** ISK 1095.00; **Circ:** 16,000
Usual Pagination: 132
Editor: Asta Andresdottir
Profile: Magazine featuring articles on fashion, make-up, interior decoration, food and drink, also features lifestyle and culture and social issues articles.
Language(s): Icelandic
Readership: Aimed at middle to upper-class women and men between the ages of 20 and 40 years.
ADVERTISING RATES:
Full Page Mono .... ISK 83900.00
Full Page Colour .... ISK 131700.00
Agency Commission: 10%
Mechanical Data: Type Area: 260 x 180mm, Col Length: 260mm, Page Width: 180mm
CONSUMER: WOMEN'S INTEREST CONSUMER MAGAZINES: Women's Interest - Fashion

SED OG HEYRT 1200849IS76C-5
Editorial: Linghalsi 5, 110 REYKJAVÍK **Tel:** 515 5500
Fax: 515 5599
Email: loftur@birtingur.is **Web site:** http://www.birtingur.is
Date Established: 1996; **Freq:** Weekly; **Cover Price:** ISK 659.00; **Circ:** 23,000
Editor: Loftur Eiriksson
Profile: Magazine featuring people and celebrities, including a TV guide.
Language(s): Icelandic
Readership: Aimed at men and women between the ages of 15 and 45 years.
ADVERTISING RATES:
Full Page Mono .... ISK 81500.00
Full Page Colour .... ISK 128700.00
Agency Commission: 10%
Mechanical Data: Type Area: 275 x 203mm, Col Length: 275mm, Page Width: 203mm
CONSUMER: MUSIC & PERFORMING ARTS: TV & Radio

TÖLVUHEIMUR 755527IS5D-1000
Editorial: Borgartun 23, 105 REYKJAVÍK
Tel: 512 75 75 **Fax:** 861 86 46
Email: eyglo@heimur.is **Web site:** http://www.heimur.is
Date Established: 1995
Publisher: Benedikt Johannsesson
Profile: Magazine focusing on computers and information technology.
Language(s): Icelandic
Readership: Aimed at professionals and enthusiasts aged between 25 and 45 years.
BUSINESS: COMPUTERS & AUTOMATION: Personal Computers

VEIDIMADURINN 755531IS92-1000
Editorial: Bogartún 23, 101 REYKJAVÍK
Tel: 512 75 75
Email: bjarni@heimur.is **Web site:** http://www.heimur.is
Freq: 3 issues yearly; **Cover Price:** ISK 899; **Circ:** 6,000
Usual Pagination: 70
Editor: Bjarni Brynjolfsson
Profile: Magazine focusing on fishing and hunting.
Language(s): Icelandic
Readership: Aimed at fishing and hunting enthusiasts.
CONSUMER: ANGLING & FISHING

VIKAN 755534IS74C-1000
Editorial: Lynghåls 5, 110 REYKJAVÍK **Tel:** 515 5500
Fax: 515 5588
Email: vikan@birtingur.is **Web site:** http://www.birtingur.is
Freq: Weekly; **Cover Price:** ISK 659.00; **Circ:** 14,000
Usual Pagination: 64
Profile: Magazine featuring stories, interviews and crosswords for the whole family.
Language(s): Icelandic
Readership: Aimed at woman between 20 and 50 years old.
CONSUMER: WOMEN'S INTEREST CONSUMER MAGAZINES: Home & Family

WHAT'S ON IN REYKJAVÍK
1834364IS89C-1
Editorial: Borgartun 23, 105 REYKJAVIK
Tel: 512 75 47 **Fax:** 561 86 46
Email: ingvar@heimur.is **Web site:** www.whatson.is
Date Established: 1983; **Freq:** Monthly; **Cover Price:** Free; **Circ:** 110,000
Usual Pagination: 60
Editor: Ingvar Johann Kristjánsson

Iceland

Profile: Entertainment guide focusing on Reykjavik events.
Language(s): English
CONSUMER: HOLIDAYS & TRAVEL: Entertainment Guides

Irish Republic

Time Difference: Same as GMT
National Telephone Code: +353
Continent: Europe
Capital: Dublin
Principal Language: Irish, English
Population: 3917203
Monetary Unit: Euro (EUR)

EMBASSY HIGH COMMISSION: Embassy of Ireland: 17 Grosvenor Place, London SW1X 7HR
Tel: 020 7235 2171
Fax: 020 7245 6961 / londonembassymail@dfa.ie / http://www.embassyofireland.co.uk/home/index.aspx?id=33706

24/7
1666386E67H-5
Editorial: For all contact details see main record, Evening Echo
Freq: Weekly
Supplement to: Evening Echo
REGIONAL DAILY & SUNDAY NEWSPAPERS: Regional Colour Supplements

ACCOUNTANCY IRELAND
4136E1B-10
Editorial: Chartered Accountants House, 47-49 Pearse Street, DUBLIN 2 **Tel:** 1 637 7392
Fax: 1 523 3995
Email: editor@accountancyireland.ie **Web site:** http://www.accountancyireland.ie
ISSN: 0001-4699
Date Established: 1969; **Freq:** 6 issues yearly; Free to qualifying individuals
Annual Sub.: EUR 47; **Circ:** 25,879
Usual Pagination: 116
Editor: Daisy Downes; **Advertising Manager:** Joyce Kelly
Profile: Journal of the Institute of Chartered Accountants in Ireland covers accountancy, business and management, taxation, information technology, general news, leisure and lifestyle. Features include financial reporting, management accounting, company law and managing a business. The publication was first published in 1969 and has on average 116 pages per issue. Accountancy Ireland is published six times per year. Read by all members and students of The Institute of Chartered Accountants in Ireland and all members of the Institute of Accounting Technicians in Ireland. Twitter: http://twitter.com/accountancyire Facebook: http://www.facebook.com/pages/Accountancy-Ireland-Magazine/174330488205?ref=ts YouTube: http://www.youtube.com/accountancyireland.
Readership: Read by all members and students of The Institute of Chartered Accountants in Ireland and all members of the Institute of Accounting Technicians in Ireland.
ADVERTISING RATES:
Full Page Colour .... EUR 2800
Agency Commission: 15%
Mechanical Data: Film: Digital, Print Process: Sheet-fed litho, Type Area: 267 x 180mm, Col Length: 267mm, Page Width: 180mm, Trim Size: 297 x 210mm, Bleed Size: 307 x 220mm
Average ad content per issue: 25%
BUSINESS: FINANCE & ECONOMICS: Accountancy

ACCOUNTANCY PLUS
4138E1B-30
Formerly: CPA Journal of Accountancy
Editorial: 17 Harcourt Street, DUBLIN 2
Tel: 1 42 51 000 **Fax:** 14251001
Email: dfitzgerald@cpaireland.ie **Web site:** http://www.cpaireland.ie
Freq: Quarterly; Free to qualifying individuals
Annual Sub.: EUR 65; **Circ:** 6,000
Usual Pagination: 60
Editor: David Fitzgerald; **Advertising Manager:** Kelly-Marie Molloy
Profile: Magazine of the Institute of Certified Public Accountants in Ireland. Includes features on auditing, accounting, legislation, finance and banking, insurance, taxation, education, computing and business management.
Readership: Read by members of Accountancy Plus.
ADVERTISING RATES:
Full Page Colour .... EUR 1695
Mechanical Data: Trim Size: 280 x 216mm, Film: Digital, Bleed Size: 300 x 226mm, Type Area: 250 x 186mm, Col Length: 250mm, Page Width: 186mm
BUSINESS: FINANCE & ECONOMICS: Accountancy

ADMINISTRATION JOURNAL
4206E32A-20
Formerly: Administration
Editorial: Vergemount Hall, Clonskeagh, DUBLIN 6
Tel: 1 24 03 600 **Fax:** 12698644
Email: rboyle@ipa.ie **Web site:** http://www.ipa.ie
ISSN: 0001-8325
Date Established: 1953; **Freq:** Quarterly; Free to qualifying individuals
Annual Sub.: EUR 86; **Circ:** 2,500
Usual Pagination: 96
Editor: Richard Boyle
Profile: Journal covering all aspects of public administration.
Readership: Read by academics, students and senior public servants.
ADVERTISING RATES:
Full Page Mono .... EUR 2000
Mechanical Data: Trim Size: 216 x 138mm, Type Area: 180 x 103mm, Col Length: 180mm, Page Width: 103mm, Film: Digital
Copy instructions: *Copy Date:* 10 days prior to publication date
Average ad content per issue: 10%
BUSINESS: LOCAL GOVERNMENT, LEISURE & RECREATION: Local Government

AGEING MATTERS IN IRELAND
1639928E74N-1
Editorial: 30-31 Lower Camden Street, DUBLIN 2
Tel: 1 4756989 **Fax:** 14756011
Email: library@ageaction.ie **Web site:** http://www.ageaction.ie
ISSN: 1649-3484
Date Established: 1992; **Freq:** Monthly; **Cover Price:** Free; **Circ:** 2,500
Usual Pagination: 16
Editor: Eamon Timmins; **Advertising Manager:** Daragh Matthews
Profile: Magazine covering ageing issues in Ireland including lifestyle, security, sexuality, leisure, nostalgia, health, housing and finance.
Readership: Aimed at members of AgeAction Ireland; the elderly, politicians, students, academics, voluntary organisations interested in ageing issues and the general public.
CONSUMER: WOMEN'S INTEREST CONSUMER MAGAZINES: Retirement

ALIVE!
764509E87-5
Editorial: St. Mary's Priory, Tallaght, DUBLIN 24
Tel: 1 40 48 187 **Fax:** 14596784
Email: alivepaper@gmail.com **Web site:** http://www.alive.ie
Date Established: 1996; **Freq:** Monthly; **Cover Price:** Free; **Circ:** 380,000
Usual Pagination: 16
Advertising Manager: Breda Brennan; **Managing Editor:** Brian McKevitt
Profile: Family orientated newspaper containing religious and social, national and international information.
Readership: Aimed at the general public of all ages.
ADVERTISING RATES:
Full Page Mono .... EUR 6000
Full Page Colour .... EUR 6600
Mechanical Data: No. of Columns (Display): 6, Col Widths (Display): 45mm, Film: Digital
Average ad content per issue: 15%
CONSUMER: RELIGIOUS

A-MEN MAGAZINE
1881581E65B-44
Editorial: For all contact details see main record, The Irish Daily Star Sunday
Freq: Weekly
Supplement to: The Irish Daily Star Sunday
NATIONAL DAILY & SUNDAY NEWSPAPERS: National Sunday Newspapers

THE ANGLO-CELT
4302E72-3000
Editorial: Station House, CAVAN **Tel:** 49 43 31 100
Fax: 494332280
Email: linda@anglocelt.ie **Web site:** http://www.anglocelt.ie
Date Established: 1846; **Freq:** Weekly; **Cover Price:** EUR 1.95; **Circ:** 12,885
Usual Pagination: 48
Editor: Linda O'Reilly; **Advertising Manager:** Yvonne Jackson
ADVERTISING RATES:
Full Page Mono .... EUR 4458
Full Page Colour .... EUR 5638
Agency Commission: 15%
Mechanical Data: Type Area: 540 x 343mm, Col Length: 540mm, Page Width: 343mm
Average ad content per issue: 40%
LOCAL NEWSPAPERS

AQUACULTURE IRELAND
753058E45B-8
Formerly: Irish Aquaculture Directory and Guide
Editorial: Crofton Road, Dun Laoghaire, CO. DUBLIN
Tel: 1 66 80 043
Email: fiaccob@iol.ie **Web site:** http://www.aquaculture.ie
ISSN: 0790-0929
Date Established: 1982; **Freq:** Annual - Published in March; Free to qualifying individuals
Annual Sub.: EUR 50; **Circ:** 1,000
Usual Pagination: 40
Editor: Fiacc O Brolchain; **Advertising Manager:** Roger Cole
Profile: Journal of the Irish Aquaculture Industry Association. Contains information on all aspects of fish farming.
Readership: Aimed at fish farmers and aquaculture operations personnel, Government and Development body officials and researchers.
ADVERTISING RATES:
Full Page Mono .... EUR 1000
Full Page Colour .... EUR 1300
Agency Commission: 10%
Mechanical Data: Film: Digital, Type Area: 270 x 180mm, Bleed Size: 306 x 220mm, Col Length: 270mm, Page Width: 180mm, Trim Size: 297 x 210mm
Copy instructions: *Copy Date:* 21 days prior to publication date
Average ad content per issue: 25%
BUSINESS: MARINE & SHIPPING: Commercial Fishing

ARCHAEOLOGY IRELAND
629514E94X-4
Editorial: Media House, South County Business Park, Leopardstown, DUBLIN 18 **Tel:** 1 29 47 860
Fax: 1 29 47 861
Email: helen@wordwellbooks.com **Web site:** http://www.wordwellbooks.com
Date Established: 1987; **Freq:** Quarterly; **Cover Price:** EUR 6.50
Annual Sub.: EUR 24.00; **Circ:** 5,000
Usual Pagination: 48
Editor: Tom Condit; **Managing Director:** Nick Maxwell; **Advertising Manager:** Lorraine Lawlor
Profile: Magazine covering all aspects of Irish archaeology.
Readership: Aimed at archaeologists, students and others interested in archaeology.
Agency Commission: 15%
Copy instructions: *Copy Date:* 4 weeks prior to publication date
Average ad content per issue: 20%
CONSUMER: OTHER CLASSIFICATIONS: Miscellaneous

ARCHITECTURE IRELAND
4157E4A-40
Formerly: Architectural Ireland
Editorial: 19 Upper Fitz Willam Street, DUBLIN 2
Tel: 1 29 58 115 **Fax:** 1 29 59 350
Email: mail@architectureireland.ie **Web site:** http://www.architectureireland.ie
ISSN: 1649-5152
Date Established: 1980; **Freq:** 6 issues yearly Free to qualifying individuals
Annual Sub.: EUR 75; **Circ:** 3,500
Usual Pagination: 72
Advertising Manager: Cecil Maxwell
Profile: Official journal of the Royal Institute of the Architects of Ireland. First published in 1980, the publication has an average of 72 pages per issue. Aimed at architects, builders and government officials. Regular features: Arts Page Information on Arts exhibitions.; Book Review; Building Features 6 building features and reviews per issue.; Bulletin Features exhibition and conference news as well as competitions.; Dispatch Information update for RIAI members.; Editors Comment; President's Column Comment from the RIAI president.; Product Gallery; Product News; RIAI News, Exhibitions & Conferences The latest news regarding the Royal Institute of the Architects of Ireland.; Ten Questions for.... Questions and answers with an architect.
Readership: Aimed at architects, builders and government officials.
ADVERTISING RATES:
Full Page Mono .... EUR 1925
Full Page Colour .... EUR 2785
Agency Commission: 10%
Mechanical Data: Trim Size: 305 x 230mm, Film: Digital
BUSINESS: ARCHITECTURE & BUILDING: Architecture

ARENA
1659415E65H-19
Editorial: For all contact details see main record, The Irish Examiner
Freq: Weekly
Supplement to: The Irish Examiner
NATIONAL DAILY & SUNDAY NEWSPAPERS: National Colour Supplements

THE ARGUS
4324E72-3100
Editorial: Partnership Court, Park Street, Dundalk, CO. LOUTH **Tel:** 42 93 34 632 **Fax:** 429331643
Email: editorial@argus.ie **Web site:** http://www.argus.ie
Date Established: 1880; **Freq:** Weekly; **Circ:** 14,000
Editor: Jim Smyth; **Advertising Manager:** Deirdre McHugh
ADVERTISING RATES:
Full Page Mono .... EUR 280
Full Page Colour .... EUR 380
SCC .... EUR 11
Agency Commission: 15%
Mechanical Data: Col Length: 325mm, Col Widths (Display): 34.93mm, No. of Columns (Display): 7, Type Area: 325 x 262mm, Page Width: 262mm
Average ad content per issue: 50%
LOCAL NEWSPAPERS

ASHFORD & DROMOLAND CASTLE GUEST RELATIONS MAGAZINE
628782E89B-10
Formerly: Ashford & Dromoland Castle Souvenir Magazine
Editorial: Longboat Quay, 57-59 Sir John Rogerson Quay, DUBLIN 2 **Tel:** 1 43 22 200 **Fax:** 1 67 27 100
Email: info@ashville.com **Web site:** http://www.ashville.com
Date Established: 1995; **Freq:** Annual - Published in July/August; **Cover Price:** Free; **Circ:** 25,000
Usual Pagination: 88
Profile: Magazine guide to hotels and amenities in Eire as well as lifestyle features on art, literature, fashion and food.
Readership: Read by hotel guests.
ADVERTISING RATES:
Full Page Colour .... EUR 3600
Agency Commission: 15%
Mechanical Data: Bleed Size: +5mm, Trim Size: 297 x 210mm, Film: Digital
CONSUMER: HOLIDAYS & TRAVEL: Hotel Magazines

ASTIR
623473E62D-1
Editorial: Winetavern Street, DUBLIN 8
Tel: 1 60 40 160 **Fax:** 16719280
Email: gtuffy@asti.ie **Web site:** http://www.asti.ie
ISSN: 0790-6560
Freq: 6 issues yearly - Published between September and May; Free to qualifying individuals ; **Circ:** 18,000
Usual Pagination: 40
Editor: Gemma Tuffy
Profile: Magazine of the Association of Secondary Teachers of Ireland, containing news on events, campaigns, curriculum updates, advice on subjects from special needs to bullying and information for new teachers.
Readership: Read by the members of ASTI.
ADVERTISING RATES:
Full Page Colour .... EUR 2000
Agency Commission: 15%
Mechanical Data: Bleed Size: 303 x 216mm, Trim Size: 297 x 210mm, Film: Digital
Average ad content per issue: 20%
BUSINESS: CHURCH & SCHOOL EQUIPMENT & EDUCATION: Secondary Education

ASTRONOMY & SPACE
753084E94X-5
Editorial: PO Box 2888, DUBLIN 5 **Tel:** 1 84 70 777
Fax: 18470771
Email: editor@astronomy.ie **Web site:** http://www.astronomy.ie
ISSN: 0791-8062
Date Established: 1993; **Freq:** Monthly; **Annual Sub.:** EUR 40; **Circ:** 7,000
Usual Pagination: 48
Editor: David Moore
Profile: Magazine containing the latest information and articles on astronomy and space.
Readership: Aimed at the general public in the UK and Ireland.
CONSUMER: OTHER CLASSIFICATIONS: Miscellaneous

ATHLONE ADVERTISER
1817458E72-3150_100
Editorial: 21 Mardyke Street, Athlone, CO. WESTMEATH 0
Cover Price: Free
Part of Series, see entry for: Athlone Advertiser Series
LOCAL NEWSPAPERS

ATHLONE ADVERTISER SERIES
754396E72-3150
Formerly: Athlone Advertiser
Editorial: Unit 15-3rd Floor, Kilmartin N6 Centre, Athlone, CO. WESTMEATH **Tel:** 90 64 70 920
Fax: 90 64 79 646
Email: news@athloneadvertiser.ie **Web site:** http://www.athloneadvertiser.ie
Freq: Weekly; **Cover Price:** Free
Editor: Maria Daly
ADVERTISING RATES:
Full Page Colour .... EUR 2095
Agency Commission: 15%
Mechanical Data: Type Area: 355 x 263mm, Film: Digital, Col Length: 355mm, Page Width: 263mm, No. of Columns (Display): 7
Series owner and contact point for the following titles, see individual entries:
Athlone Advertiser athlone advertiser series
LOCAL NEWSPAPERS

ATHLONE ADVERTISER SERIES
1817459E72-3150_101
Editorial: 21 Mardyke Street, Athlone, CO. WESTMEATH 0
Freq: Weekly; **Cover Price:** Free; **Circ:** 5,921

Part of Series, see entry for: Athlone Advertiser Series
LOCAL NEWSPAPERS

ATHLONE TOPIC 754397E72-3155
Editorial: Arcade Buildings, Barrack Street, Athlone, CO. WESTMEATH **Tel:** 90 64 94 433 **Fax:** 906494964
Email: athlonetopic@eircom.net
Date Established: 1993; **Freq:** Weekly; **Cover Price:** EUR 1.80
Free to qualifying individuals ; **Circ:** 4,500
Editor: Tom Kiernan; **Advertising Manager:** Philomena Shanagher
ADVERTISING RATES:
Full Page Mono .... EUR 500
Full Page Colour .... EUR 500
SCC .... EUR 40
Agency Commission: 15%
Mechanical Data: No. of Columns (Display): 7, Film: Digital
Average ad content per issue: 40%
LOCAL NEWSPAPERS

AUTO IRELAND 628757E77D-10
Editorial: Rosemount House, Dundrum Road, Dundrum, DUBLIN 14 **Tel:** 1 240 5300
Fax: 1 661 9486
Email: automags@harmonia.ie **Web site:** http://www.harmonia.ie
ISSN: 0791-7635
Date Established: 1969; **Freq:** Annual - Published in December; **Cover Price:** EUR 3.99; **Circ:** 140,000
Usual Pagination: 108
Editor: Brian Soley
Profile: Magazine focusing on motoring and motor sports in Ireland and around the world. Includes a new car guide section, exclusive new car previews, motor industry news and motorsport fixtures. Read by car and motor sport enthusiasts.
Readership: Read by car and motor sport enthusiasts.
ADVERTISING RATES:
Full Page Colour .... EUR 4800
CONSUMER: MOTORING & CYCLING: Motor Sports

AUTO TRADE JOURNAL 714735E31A-69
Formerly: Irish Auto Trade Journal
Editorial: Glencree House, Lanesborough Road, ROSCOMMON TOWN **Tel:** 90 66 25 676
Fax: 906637410
Email: pdeane@autopub.ie **Web site:** http://www.autotrade.ie
Date Established: 1999; **Freq:** 6 issues yearly; Free to qualifying individuals
Annual Sub.: EUR 45; **Circ:** 7,800
Usual Pagination: 96
Editor: John Loughran; **Managing Editor:** Padraic Deane
Profile: Trade magazine covering all aspects of the motoring aftermarket industry for the Irish Republic and Northern Ireland.
Readership: Aimed at auto garages, auto dealerships, repair shops, bodyshops, motor factors, fleet managers, police and road safety authorities, recyclers and insurance managers.
ADVERTISING RATES:
Full Page Mono .... EUR 1700
Full Page Colour .... EUR 1900
Agency Commission: 15%
Mechanical Data: Col Length: 270mm, No. of Columns (Display): 4, Type Area: 270 x 185mm, Bleed Size: 303 x 216mm, Film: Digital, Page Width: 185mm
Average ad content per issue: 30%
BUSINESS: MOTOR TRADE: Motor Trade Accessories

AUTO TRADER REPUBLIC OF IRELAND 1665423E77A-203
Freq: Weekly; **Cover Price:** EUR 3.50; **Circ:** 17,401
Edition of: Auto Trader
CONSUMER: MOTORING & CYCLING: Motoring

AUTOBIZ 764510E31A-10
Editorial: Shangort, Knocknacarra, GALWAY XXX XXX **Tel:** 91 523 292 **Fax:** 91 584 411
Email: info@autobiz.ie **Web site:** http://www.autobiz.ie
Date Established: 1978; **Freq:** Monthly - Monthly except for July/Aug & Dec/Jan; Free to qualifying individuals ; **Circ:** 5,055
Usual Pagination: 76
Editor: Garry Falvey; **Advertising Manager:** Frank Falvey
Profile: Magazine containing information about used car parts, trade news and new products. First published in 1978, the publication has an average of 76 pages per issue. The magazine is packed full of interesting trade news and articles that relate to our motor trade customers. The listing of used parts and trade cars for sale is compiled from information pooled by subscribers, and published in the magazine each month. The car makes and models are listed alphabetically, in year order, with the final column showing the location by county. Aimed at people working in the motor trade, including car dealers, body shops, service garages, towing and breakdown firms, car dismantlers and motor factors.
Readership: Aimed at people working in the motor trade, including car dealers, body shops, service garages, towing and breakdown firms, car dismantlers and motor factors.
ADVERTISING RATES:
Full Page Mono .... EUR 800
Full Page Colour .... EUR 1400
Mechanical Data: Bleed Size: +3mm, Film: Digital, Type Area: 267 x 185mm, Trim Size: 297 x 210mm, Col Length: 267mm, Page Width: 185mm
BUSINESS: MOTOR TRADE: Motor Trade Accessories

THE AVONDHU 4304E72-3200
Editorial: 18 Lower Cork Street, Mitchelstown, CO. CORK **Tel:** 25 24 451 **Fax:** 2584463
Email: info@avondhupress.ie **Web site:** http://www.avondhupress.ie
Date Established: 1978; **Freq:** Weekly; **Cover Price:** EUR 1.80; **Circ:** 10,250
Usual Pagination: 56
Editor: John Barrett; **Advertising Manager:** James Barrett
ADVERTISING RATES:
Full Page Mono .... EUR 1080
Full Page Colour .... EUR 1350
Agency Commission: 17.5%
Mechanical Data: Col Length: 357mm, No. of Columns (Display): 8, Print Process: Web-fed offset litho, Type Area: 357 x 265mm, Page Width: 265mm, Col Widths (Display): 29.9mm, Film: Digital
Average ad content per issue: 30%
LOCAL NEWSPAPERS

BACKPACKER EUROPE 1639916E89A-201
Formerly: Backpacker
Editorial: Top Floor, 75-76 Camden Street, DUBLIN 2
Tel: 87 647 84 87 **Fax:** 14757301
Email: editor@backpacker-europe.com **Web site:** http://www.backpacker-europe.com
Date Established: 2001; **Freq:** Monthly; **Cover Price:** Free; **Circ:** 40,000
Usual Pagination: 68
Editor: Jillian Bolger
Profile: Magazine covering travel and lifestyle including tours, flights and hostels.
Readership: Aimed at in-coming and out-going travellers aged 18 to 32 years old as well as young professionals and students in Ireland.
ADVERTISING RATES:
Full Page Colour .... EUR 2550
Mechanical Data: Film: Digital, Trim Size: 297 x 210mm
CONSUMER: HOLIDAYS & TRAVEL: Travel

BACKSPIN GOLF MAGAZINE 628776E75D-10
Editorial: Birkdale, 4 Rathmichael Manor, Loughlinstown, CO. DUBLIN **Tel:** 1 28 27 269
Fax: 1 28 27 483
Email: golfbiz@eircom.net
Freq: 3 issues yearly - Published in April, July and November; **Cover Price:** EUR 3.75; **Circ:** 7,500
Usual Pagination: 108
Editor: Declan O'Donoghue; **Advertising Manager:** Declan O'Donoghue
Profile: Magazine focusing on golf in Ireland.
Readership: Aimed at golf enthusiasts.
ADVERTISING RATES:
Full Page Mono .... EUR 2000.00
Full Page Colour .... EUR 2000.00
Agency Commission: 10%
Mechanical Data: Type Area: 270 x 182mm, Col Length: 270mm, Page Width: 182mm, Bleed Size: 303 x 213mm, Trim Size: 297 x 210mm, Film: Digital
Copy instructions: *Copy Date:* 4 weeks prior to publication date
Average ad content per issue: 35%
CONSUMER: SPORT: Golf

THE BALLINCOLLIG NEWSLETTER 754415E72-3250
Editorial: Parknamore Lodge, West Village, Ballincollig, CO. CORK **Tel:** 21 48 77 665
Fax: 214871404
Email: dcgraph@indigo.ie
Freq: Weekly; **Cover Price:** Free; **Circ:** 4,000
Usual Pagination: 26
Advertising Manager: Derry Costello
ADVERTISING RATES:
Full Page Mono .... EUR 180
LOCAL NEWSPAPERS

BANKING IRELAND 4139E1C-4_50
Editorial: 1 North Wall Quay, DUBLIN 1
Tel: 1 61 16 500 **Fax:** 1 61 16 565
Email: info@bankers.ie **Web site:** http://www.bankers.ie
ISSN: 0791-1386
Date Established: 1898; **Freq:** Half-yearly - Published in January and June; **Circ:** 33,000
Usual Pagination: 32
Editor: Helen Naughton; **Advertising Manager:** Helen Naughton
Profile: Journal of the Institute of Bankers in Ireland.
Readership: Aimed at members.
BUSINESS: FINANCE & ECONOMICS: Banking

BIKE BUYERS GUIDE 1667827E77B-1
Editorial: 3rd Floor, Arena House, Arena Road, Sandyford Industrial Estate, DUBLIN 18
Tel: 1 240 5555 **Fax:** 1 240 5550
Email: justin@bikebuyersguide.ie **Web site:** http://www.bikebuyersguide.ie
Date Established: 2004; **Freq:** Monthly; **Cover Price:** EUR 4.99; **Circ:** 23,000
Usual Pagination: 100
Editor: Justin Delaney
Profile: Magazine covering all aspects of Irish motor bikes including new motor bike releases, Irish motor-cycling events, profiles of Irish riders as well as insurance and finance.
Readership: Aimed at those with an interest in motor cycles with specific reference to the Irish Market.
ADVERTISING RATES:
Full Page Colour .... EUR 995
Agency Commission: 15%
Mechanical Data: Type Area: 297 x 230mm, Col Length: 297mm, Page Width: 230mm, Film: Digital
CONSUMER: MOTORING & CYCLING: Motorcycling

BJUI 24449E56A-111
Formerly: BJU International
Editorial: 47 Eccles Street, DUBLIN 7
Tel: 1 80 32 098 **Fax:** 18034389
Email: editor.bjuint@mater.ie **Web site:** http://www.bjui.org
ISSN: 1464-4096
Freq: 26 issues yearly; **Annual Sub.:** £160; **Circ:** 10,000
Usual Pagination: 350
Editor: John Fitzpatrick; **Managing Editor:** Audrai O'Dwyer
Profile: Journal providing information on the latest technology, new instruments and treatments.
Readership: Aimed at clinicians working in the fields of urology, nephrology and other related areas.
ADVERTISING RATES:
Full Page Mono £582
Full Page Colour £1402
Agency Commission: 10%
Mechanical Data: Type Area: 245 x 180mm, Col Length: 245mm, Trim Size: 276 x 210mm, Bleed Size: 282 x 216mm, Print Process: Litho, Film: Digital, Page Width: 180mm
BUSINESS: HEALTH & MEDICAL

BLANCH GAZETTE 1644013E72-8205
Editorial: Block 3A, Mill Bank Industrial Estate, Lower Road, Lucan, CO. DUBLIN 0 **Tel:** 1 60 10 240
Fax: 16010251
Email: news@gazettegroup.com **Web site:** http://www.gazettegroup.com
Freq: Weekly; **Cover Price:** Free; **Circ:** 4,000
News Editor: Dawn Love
ADVERTISING RATES:
Full Page Colour .... EUR 1150
SCC .... EUR 60
Mechanical Data: Type Area: 340 x 260mm, Col Length: 340mm, No. of Columns (Display): 6, Film: Digital, Page Width: 260mm
LOCAL NEWSPAPERS

BOOKS IRELAND 4250E60A-10
Editorial: 11 Newgrove Avenue, DUBLIN 4
Tel: 1 26 92 185
Email: booksi@eircom.net **Web site:** http://www.islandireland.com/booksireland
ISSN: 0376-6039
Date Established: 1976; **Freq:** 6 issues yearly - Not published in January, July or August; **Cover Price:** EUR 3.50
Annual Sub.: EUR 35; **Circ:** 2,840
Usual Pagination: 36
Features Editor: Shirley Kelly; **Advertising Manager:** Lucy Tucker
Profile: Magazine listing and reviewing books of Irish authorship, publication or special interest. Contains interviews with authors and publishers and a seasonal list of forthcoming books. Aimed at librarians, booksellers, Irish studies academics and book collectors. Regular features: First Flush - First assessment of books of Irish interest Interviews - Interviews with authors of topical books of irish interest Reviews - Reviews of Irish-interest books by a panel of specialists.
Language(s): English; Gaelic
Readership: Aimed at librarians, booksellers, Irish studies academics and book collectors.
ADVERTISING RATES:
Full Page Colour .... EUR 620
Mechanical Data: Col Length: 275mm, Film: Digital, Type Area: 275 x 188mm, Print Process: Offset litho, Trim Size: 297 x 210mm, Page Width: 188mm
Average ad content per issue: 25%
BUSINESS: PUBLISHING: Publishing & Book Trade

BOOKVIEW IRELAND 629535E84B-40
Editorial: Unit 4, Campus Innovation Centre, Upper Newcastle Road, GALWAY **Tel:** 9 15 69 158
Email: info@emigrant.ie **Web site:** http://www.emigrant.ie
Freq: Monthly; **Cover Price:** Free; **Circ:** 16,000 Unique Users
Advertising Manager: Nualann O'Brien; **Publisher:** Liam Ferrie
Profile: Website featuring reviews of all the latest books of Irish interest.
Readership: Aimed at people interested in Ireland and Irish literature.
CONSUMER: THE ARTS & LITERARY: Literary

BRAY PEOPLE 4343E72-4700_106
Editorial: Channing House, Rowe Street, Wexford, CO. WEXFORD 0
Date Established: 1920; **Freq:** Weekly; **Cover Price:** EUR 1.50; **Circ:** 4,045
Usual Pagination: 65
ADVERTISING RATES:
Full Page Mono .... EUR 1640.07
Full Page Colour .... EUR 1823.36
SCC .... EUR 8.14
Part of Series, see entry for: Wexford People Series
LOCAL NEWSPAPERS

BS NEWS (BUILDING SERVICES NEWS) 4156E3B-10
Formerly: BSNews
Editorial: Carraig Court, Georges Avenue, Blackrock, CO. DUBLIN **Tel:** 1 28 85 001 **Fax:** 1 28 86 966
Email: pat@pressline.ie **Web site:** http://www.buildingservicesnews.com
ISSN: 0791-0878
Date Established: 1964; **Freq:** 11 issues yearly - Published in the last week of the cover month;
Annual Sub.: EUR 70.00; **Circ:** 2,500
Usual Pagination: 48
Editor: Pat Lehane; **Managing Director:** Pat Lehane;
Advertisement Director: Joe Warren
Profile: Magazine covering heating, air-conditioning, ventilation, refrigeration, sanitation, plumbing and maintenance.
Readership: Aimed at mechanical and electrical engineers in the construction industry.
ADVERTISING RATES:
Full Page Colour .... EUR 2400.00
Agency Commission: 10%
Mechanical Data: Bleed Size: +3mm, Trim Size: 297 x 210mm
Copy instructions: *Copy Date:* 2nd week of the month prior to publication date
Average ad content per issue: 40%
BUSINESS: HEATING & VENTILATION: Industrial Heating & Ventilation

BUDGET MAGAZINE 1659424E65H-24
Editorial: For all contact details see main record, The Sunday Business Post
Freq: Annual
Supplement to: The Sunday Business Post
NATIONAL DAILY & SUNDAY NEWSPAPERS: National Colour Supplements

BUSINESS 1666389E65H-16
Editorial: For all contact details see main record, Irish Independent
Freq: Weekly
Supplement to: Irish Independent
NATIONAL DAILY & SUNDAY NEWSPAPERS: National Colour Supplements

BUSINESS & FINANCE 4170E14A-15
Editorial: Unit 1a, Waters Edge, Charlotte Quay, DUBLIN 4 **Tel:** 1 41 67 800 **Fax:** 1 416 7898
Email: john.walsh@businessandfinance.ie **Web site:** http://www.businessandfinance.ie
Date Established: 1964; **Freq:** Monthly; **Annual Sub.:** EUR 50; **Circ:** 14,676
Usual Pagination: 108
Advertising Manager: Chris Simpson
Profile: Magazine covering all aspects of business, finance, economic policy and related political events in Ireland, Northern Ireland, the UK and Europe. Read by company managers, top company executives and general public. Twitter Handle: http://twitter.com/BandF Facebook: http://www.facebook.com/BusinessandFinance LinkedIn: http://www.linkedin.com/company/840693 Regular Features: Finance - News and analysis in finance Finance Review For the Record - News Roundup General Business News - News in business Life Sciences Review Marketing - Column examining current marketing strategies Markets Section - Comment and Analysis Motoring - Column looking at the latest news from the motoring industry, with road tests of new vehicles Politics - Political commentaries SMEs - Column looking at the small business sector Wealth Magazine Wine - Wine reviews Your Enterprise.
Readership: Read by company managers, top company executives and general public.
ADVERTISING RATES:
Full Page Colour .... EUR 3945
Agency Commission: 10%
Mechanical Data: Film: Digital, Col Length: 275mm, Page Width: 210mm, Type Area: 275 x 210mm, Bleed Size: +4mm
Average ad content per issue: 40%
Editions:
Business & Finance Who's Who in Irish Business
BUSINESS: COMMERCE, INDUSTRY & MANAGEMENT

BUSINESS LIMERICK MAGAZINE 1666167E63-2
Editorial: 48 O'Connell Street, Limerick, CO. LIMERICK **Tel:** 61 46 75 18 **Fax:** 61 40 49 40
Email: frank@businesslimerick.ie **Web site:** http://www.businesslimerick.ie
ISSN: 1649-4644
Date Established: 2003; **Freq:** Monthly - 12 (Monthly); **Cover Price:** EUR 3.50
Annual Sub.: EUR 60; **Circ:** 7,000
Usual Pagination: 84

Editor: Frank Collins; **Advertising Manager:** Marguerite Finnan
Profile: Business magazine containing news for the business community in the Limerick and Shannon area. Includes information about trade shows and trade fairs; the effect of budgets on local businesses, conference centres in the area, articles on the Chamber of Commerce and features on any issues affecting the local business community.
Readership: Aimed at decision makers in businesses in the Limerick and Shannon area, giving the business community an alternative platform to profile themselves and their services.
ADVERTISING RATES:
Full Page Colour .... EUR 1150
Agency Commission: 15%
Mechanical Data: Film: Digital, Bleed Size: 307 x 220mm, Trim Size: 297 x 210mm
Copy instructions: *Copy Date:* 7 days prior to publication date
Average ad content per issue: 40%
BUSINESS: REGIONAL BUSINESS

BUSINESS PLUS 4173E14A-21
Editorial: 30 Morehampton Road, DUBLIN 4
Tel: 1 660 8400 **Fax:** 1 660 4540
Email: info@businessplus.ie **Web site:** http://www.bizplus.ie
Date Established: 1998; **Freq:** Monthly - Combined May/June issue
Free to qualifying individuals ; **Circ:** 10,022
Usual Pagination: 120
Editor: Nick Mulcahy
Profile: Magazine providing information about Irish companies and developments of interest to them. Includes articles on entrepreneurs, quoted companies, fund-raising, IT, e-business, shares, investments, health, wine and cars. Aimed at SME owner managers and managers within large companies.
Readership: Aimed at SME owner managers and managers within large companies.
ADVERTISING RATES:
Full Page Colour .... EUR 3240
Agency Commission: 15%
Mechanical Data: Type Area: 270 x 180mm, Col Length: 270mm, Page Width: 180mm, Bleed Size: 307 x 220mm, Trim Size: 297 x 210mm
BUSINESS: COMMERCE, INDUSTRY & MANAGEMENT

BUSINESS THIS WEEK 1659439E65H-12
Formerly: Business Week
Editorial: For all contact details see main record, The Irish Times
Freq: Weekly
Supplement to: The Irish Times
NATIONAL DAILY & SUNDAY NEWSPAPERS: National Colour Supplements

BUSINESS TRAVEL 4231E50-2
Editorial: A12 Calmount Park, Ballymount, DUBLIN 12 **Tel:** 1 45 02 422 **Fax:** 14502954
Email: editor@biztravel.ie **Web site:** http://www.biztravel.ie
ISSN: 0021-1419
Date Established: 1994; **Freq:** Quarterly; **Annual Sub.:** EUR 25; **Circ:** 8,500
Editor: Michael Flood; **Features Editor:** Neil Steedman; **Advertising Manager:** Ian Bloomfield
Profile: Magazine covering all aspects of frequent business travel.
Readership: Read by senior executives of the top 1000 companies in Ireland.
ADVERTISING RATES:
Full Page Mono .... EUR 2010
Full Page Colour .... EUR 2910
Agency Commission: 10%
Mechanical Data: Type Area: 256 x 196mm, Col Length: 256mm, Page Width: 196mm, Bleed Size: 303 x 213mm, Trim Size: 297 x 210mm, Film: Digital
Average ad content per issue: 40%
BUSINESS: TRAVEL & TOURISM

CAR BUYER'S GUIDE 629538E77A-40
Editorial: 3rd Floor, Arena House, Arena Road, Sandyford Industrial Estate, DUBLIN 18
Tel: 1 24 05 555 **Fax:** 1 29 45 261
Email: karl@cbg.ie **Web site:** http://www.carbuyersguide.ie
ISSN: 1649-3214
Date Established: 1996; **Freq:** Weekly - Published on Thursday; **Cover Price:** EUR 1.99; **Circ:** 24,000
Usual Pagination: 200
Profile: Magazine covering all aspects of the used car industry.
Readership: Read by car buyers, enthusiasts and trade.
ADVERTISING RATES:
Full Page Colour .... EUR 2750
Agency Commission: 15%
Mechanical Data: Film: Digital, Trim Size: 297 x 230mm, Bleed Size: 307 x 240mm
Average ad content per issue: 40%
CONSUMER: MOTORING & CYCLING: Motoring

CAR BUYERS GUIDE - IRISH NEW CAR GUIDE 1775777E77A-204
Editorial: 3rd Floor, Arena House, Arena Road, Sandyford Industrial Estate, DUBLIN 18
Tel: 1 24 05 555 **Fax:** 12943303
Email: sandra@cbg.ie **Web site:** http://www.cbg.ie
ISSN: 1649-038X
Date Established: 2001; **Freq:** Monthly; **Cover Price:** EUR 4.95; **Circ:** 25,000
Usual Pagination: 146
Editor: Conor Twomey; **Advertising Manager:** Paul Rogers
Profile: Magazine covering Irish news, previews, reviews, interviews, twin tests, motor sport, gadgets and entertainment, which includes game consoles, TV DVD music and cameras. Also covers male lifestyle, fashion clothing, footwear and grooming products.
Readership: Aimed at new car buyers, motoring enthusiasts and Irish males with an interest in lifestyle products.
CONSUMER: MOTORING & CYCLING: Motoring

CARA MAGAZINE 4400E89D-50
Editorial: The Courtyard, 20E Castle Street, Dalkey, CO. DUBLIN 0 **Tel:** 1 66 38 949 **Fax:** 1 6638006
Email: info@maxmedia.ie **Web site:** http://www.maxmedia.ie/cara-magazine
Date Established: 1968; **Freq:** Quarterly - Combined issues for December/January, February/March, April/May and October/November; **Cover Price:** Free; **Circ:** 47,000
Usual Pagination: 112
Editor: Tony Clayton-Lea; **Managing Director:** Lisa Gaughran; **Advertising Director:** Mary Kershaw
Profile: Magazine covering travel, the arts and lifestyle.
Readership: Read by travellers on Aer Lingus flights.
ADVERTISING RATES:
Full Page Colour .... EUR 4995
Mechanical Data: Film: Digital, Col Length: 260mm, Page Width: 190mm, Type Area: 260 x 190mm, Trim Size: 290 x 220mm, Bleed Size: 296 x 226mm
CONSUMER: HOLIDAYS & TRAVEL: In-Flight Magazines

CARLOW PEOPLE 4344E72-4700_105
Editorial: Channing House, Rowe Street, Wexford, CO. WEXFORD 0
Date Established: 1996; **Freq:** Weekly; **Cover Price:** EUR 1.50; **Circ:** 3,728
Usual Pagination: 40
ADVERTISING RATES:
Full Page Mono .... EUR 900
Full Page Colour .... EUR 1050
SCC .... EUR 5.19
Part of Series, see entry for: Wexford People Series
LOCAL NEWSPAPERS

CARLOW TIMES 1668594E72-8210_103
Editorial: 5 Eglington Road, Bray, CO WICKLOW 0
Freq: 26 issues yearly; **Cover Price:** Free; **Circ:** 15,000
Part of Series, see entry for: Wicklow Times Series
LOCAL NEWSPAPERS

THE CARRICK DEMOCRAT 1813938E72-4300_102
Formerly: The Dundalk Life
Editorial: 11 Crowe Street, Dundalk, CO. LOUTH 0
Freq: Weekly
Free to qualifying individuals ; **Circ:** 10,000
Part of Series, see entry for: The Dundalk Democrat Series
LOCAL NEWSPAPERS

THE CARRIGDHOUN NEWSPAPER 754417E72-3410
Editorial: Wylie House, Main Street, Carrigaline, CO. CORK **Tel:** 21 43 73 557 **Fax:** 214373559
Email: carrigdhoun@eircom.net **Web site:** http://www.carrigdhoun.ie
Date Established: 1991; **Freq:** Weekly; **Cover Price:** EUR 1.20; **Circ:** 6,000
News Editor: Mary Scalley; **Publisher:** Vincent O'Donovan
ADVERTISING RATES:
Full Page Mono .... EUR 525
Full Page Colour .... EUR 525
Agency Commission: 15%
Mechanical Data: Col Length: 336mm, Page Width: 260mm, Type Area: 336 x 260mm, No. of Columns (Display): 6, No. of Columns (Display): 40mm
LOCAL NEWSPAPERS

CHECKOUT 4233E53-20
Formerly: Checkout Ireland
Editorial: Adelaide Hall, 3 Adelaide Street, Dun Laoghaire, CO. DUBLIN **Tel:** 1 23 00 322
Fax: 12365900
Email: editor@checkout.ie **Web site:** http://www.checkout.ie
Date Established: 1966; **Freq:** Monthly; Free to qualifying individuals
Annual Sub.: EUR 98; **Circ:** 5,302
Usual Pagination: 96
Editor: John Ruddy; **Publisher:** Kevin Kelly
Profile: Magazine covering all matters relating to the Irish grocery and drinks trade.
Readership: Aimed at independent retailers, food and drink manufacturers, off licences, wholesalers and distributors.
ADVERTISING RATES:
Full Page Colour .... EUR 2995
Agency Commission: 10%
Mechanical Data: Bleed Size: +4mm, Trim Size: 275 x 210mm, Film: Digital
Average ad content per issue: 35%
Supplement(s): What's in Store? - 1xY, Yearbook and Buyer's Guide - 1xY
BUSINESS: RETAILING & WHOLESALING

CHIC MAGAZINE 1659432E65H-32
Formerly: Star 7
Editorial: For all contact details see main record, The Irish Daily Star
Freq: Weekly
Supplement to: The Irish Daily Star
NATIONAL DAILY & SUNDAY NEWSPAPERS: National Colour Supplements

CHILDCARE.IE MAGAZINE 1754835E62C-31
Editorial: Burnaby Buildings, Church Road, Greystones, CO. WICKLOW **Tel:** 1 20 16 000
Fax: 1 20 16 002
Email: editor@childcare.ie **Web site:** http://www.childcare.ie
Date Established: 2001; **Freq:** 6 issues yearly; **Cover Price:** EUR 4.50
Free to qualifying individuals ; **Circ:** 8,940
Usual Pagination: 48
Editor: Jamie Lawlor; **Advertising Manager:** Jamie Lawlor
Profile: Magazine covering the early years of education.
Readership: Aimed at pre-school providers, teachers and carers.
BUSINESS: CHURCH & SCHOOL EQUIPMENT & EDUCATION: Junior Education

CIRCA ART MAGAZINE 629543E84A-175
Tel: 1 6401585
Email: editor@recirca.com **Web site:** http://www.recirca.com
ISSN: 0263-9475
Date Established: 1981; **Freq:** Quarterly; **Cover Price:** EUR 7.50
Annual Sub.: EUR 25; **Circ:** 2,500
Usual Pagination: 112
Editor: Peter FitzGerald; **Advertising Manager:** Barbara Knezevic
Profile: Magazine focusing on visual art and culture, particularly in Ireland.
Readership: Read by artists, designers, architects, arts administrators, art historian, students and all those interested in contemporary visual culture.
ADVERTISING RATES:
Full Page Colour .... EUR 895
Agency Commission: 15%
Mechanical Data: Bleed Size: 260 x 195mm, Trim Size: 255 x 210mm
Average ad content per issue: 6%
CONSUMER: THE ARTS & LITERARY: Arts

CITY WIDE NEWS 628740E72-3450
Editorial: 42 Northwood, Business Campus, DUBLIN 9 **Tel:** 1 86 23 939 **Fax:** 18306833
Email: lifetimesnewsdesk@me.com
Date Established: 1994; **Freq:** 26 issues yearly; **Cover Price:** Free; **Circ:** 31,574
Usual Pagination: 24
Editor: Edel Williams; **Advertising Manager:** Dermot Williams
ADVERTISING RATES:
Full Page Mono .... EUR 2350
Full Page Colour .... EUR 2937.50
SCC .... EUR 90
Agency Commission: 15%
Mechanical Data: Type Area: 332 x 258mm, Col Length: 332mm, Page Width: 258mm, Col Widths (Display): 29mm, No. of Columns (Display): 8, Film: Digital
Average ad content per issue: 35%
LOCAL NEWSPAPERS

THE CLARE CHAMPION 4303E72-3500
Editorial: Barrack Street, Ennis, CO. CLARE
Tel: 65 68 28 105 **Fax:** 656820374
Email: editor@clarechampion.ie **Web site:** http://www.clarechampion.ie
Date Established: 1903; **Freq:** Weekly; **Circ:** 16,691
Editor: Austin Hobbs; **Managing Director:** John Galvin; **Advertising Manager:** Ollie O'Regan
Language(s): English; Gaelic
ADVERTISING RATES:
Full Page Mono .... EUR 4752
Full Page Colour .... EUR 5832
SCC .... EUR 11
Agency Commission: 15%
Mechanical Data: Page Width: 380mm, Film: Digital, Type Area: 540 x 380mm, Col Length: 540mm, Col Widths (Display): 40mm, No. of Columns (Display): 9, Print Process: Web-fed litho
LOCAL NEWSPAPERS

CLARE COUNTY EXPRESS 754418E80-20
Editorial: Clonakilla, Ballynacally, Ennis, CO. CLARE 0 **Tel:** 65 68 26 464 **Fax:** 656826465
Email: patcosgrove@eircom.net
Date Established: 1979; **Freq:** Monthly; Free to qualifying individuals
Annual Sub.: EUR 50; **Circ:** 10,000
Usual Pagination: 16
Advertising Manager: Seamus O'Reilly
Profile: Newspaper containing local news and information for County Clare.
Readership: Aimed at residents and the surrounding areas.
CONSUMER: RURAL & REGIONAL INTEREST

CLARE COURIER 764340E72-3520
Editorial: Ballycasey Design Centre, Shannon, CO. CLARE **Tel:** 61 36 16 43 **Fax:** 61361178
Email: clareco@iol.ie **Web site:** http://www.clarecourier.ie
Date Established: 1990; **Freq:** 26 issues yearly; **Cover Price:** Free; **Circ:** 20,000
Editor: Eugene McCafferty
Profile: Newspaper containing news, sport and information for the Shannon, Ennis and South Clare area.
Language(s): English; Gaelic; Polish
ADVERTISING RATES:
Full Page Mono .... EUR 1250
Full Page Colour .... EUR 1800
Agency Commission: 10%
Mechanical Data: Film: Digital, Type Area: 335 x 275mm, Col Length: 335mm, Col Widths (Display): 35mm, No. of Columns (Display): 7, Page Width: 275mm
Average ad content per issue: 50%
LOCAL NEWSPAPERS

THE CLARE PEOPLE 1806118E72-8217_100
Editorial: Mill Road, ENNIS, CO.CLARE 0
Freq: Weekly; **Cover Price:** EUR 1.80; **Circ:** 11,129
Part of Series, see entry for: The Clare People Series
LOCAL NEWSPAPERS

THE CLARE PEOPLE SERIES 1741357E72-8217
Formerly: The Clare People
Editorial: Mill Road, ENNIS, CO.CLARE
Tel: 65 68 95 500 **Fax:** 656895501
Email: editor@clarepeople.ie **Web site:** http://www.clarepeople.com
Date Established: 2005; **Freq:** Weekly; **Circ:** 8,753
ADVERTISING RATES:
Full Page Mono .... EUR 2200
Full Page Colour .... EUR 2200
SCC .... EUR 13.30
Agency Commission: 15%
Mechanical Data: Type Area: 350 x 265mm, Col Length: 350mm, Page Width: 265mm, Col Widths (Display): 49.4mm, No. of Columns (Display): 5, Film: Digital
Series owner and contact point for the following titles, see individual entries:
The Clare People
LOCAL NEWSPAPERS

CLASSMATE 629549E62C-30
Editorial: Corporate Services, Communications Unit, 3 Palace Street, DUBLIN 2 **Tel:** 1 222 2266
Fax: 1 22223776
Email: comms@dublincity.ie **Web site:** http://www.dublincity.ie
Date Established: 1967; **Freq:** Quarterly; **Cover Price:** Free; **Circ:** 38,000
Usual Pagination: 16
Profile: Magazine focusing on issues concerning primary school education in Dublin.
Readership: Read by teachers, parents and children.
BUSINESS: CHURCH & SCHOOL EQUIPMENT & EDUCATION: Junior Education

CLONDALKIN GAZETTE 1698870E72-8204_100
Editorial: Block 3A, Mill Bank Business Park, Lower Road, Lucan, CO. DUBLIN 0
Freq: Weekly; **Cover Price:** Free
ADVERTISING RATES:
Full Page Colour .... EUR 1800
Part of Series, see entry for: Gazette Series
LOCAL NEWSPAPERS

COIN-OP NEWS EUROPE 4258E64A-30
Formerly: Coin-Op News
Editorial: 16 South Terrace, CORK **Tel:** 21 431 6776
Email: susan_mdassociates@eircom.net **Web site:** http://www.coin-opnews.eu
ISSN: 1649-3060
Date Established: 1984; **Freq:** Monthly; **Annual Sub.:** EUR 40; **Circ:** 5,000
Usual Pagination: 24
Publisher: Martin Dempsey
Profile: Journal covering the amusement and gaming trade in Europe and worldwide.
Language(s): Croatian; Czech; English; French; German; Hungarian; Italian; Polish; Russian; Serbian; Slovak; Spanish; Ukrainian
Readership: Aimed at people directly involved in the European or International amusement and gaming industry.

ADVERTISING RATES:
Full Page Colour £1600
Agency Commission: 10%
Mechanical Data: Type Area: 270 x 190mm, Col Length: 270mm, Page Width: 190mm, Bleed Size: 303 x 216mm, Trim Size: 297 x 210mm
BUSINESS: OTHER CLASSIFICATIONS: Amusement Trade

THE COLLEGE TIMES
754205E83-20
Editorial: 19 Clare Street, DUBLIN 2 **Tel:** 1 66 22 266 **Fax:** 16624981
Email: info@selectmedialtd.com
Date Established: 1999; **Freq:** 6 issues yearly; **Cover Price:** Free; **Circ:** 10,500
Usual Pagination: 36
Editor: Shane McGinley; **Publisher:** Robert Heuston
Profile: Magazine containing features, news and advice for students.
Readership: Aimed at students.
ADVERTISING RATES:
Full Page Colour .... EUR 1250
Agency Commission: 10%
Mechanical Data: Type Area: 270 x 182mm, Bleed Size: 303 x 216mm, Col Length: 270mm, Page Width: 182mm, Film: Digital, Trim Size: 297 x 210mm
CONSUMER: STUDENT PUBLICATIONS

COMHAR
4392E84B-50
Editorial: 5 Merrion Row, DUBLIN 2 **Tel:** 1 67 85 443 **Fax:** 16785443
Email: comhar@eircom.net
Date Established: 1942; **Freq:** Monthly
Annual Sub.: EUR 42
Usual Pagination: 32
Editor: Aindrias O Cathasaigh; **Advertising Manager:** Feargus O'Snodaigh
Profile: Magazine about literature, poetry and current affairs.
Language(s): Gaelic
Readership: Aimed at those interested in literature.
CONSUMER: THE ARTS & LITERARY: Literary

COMMERCIAL INTERIORS OF IRELAND
623601E4A-20
Editorial: Unit F5, Bymac Centre, North West Business Park, DUBLIN 15 **Tel:** 1 82 24 477 **Fax:** 18224485
Email: admin@pembrokepublishing.com
ISSN: 1649-1645
Freq: Annual - Published in June; **Cover Price:** Free; **Circ:** 6,000
Usual Pagination: 360
Advertising Manager: Michael Nash
Profile: Directory focusing on new building technology, architecture and interior design.
Readership: Aimed at architects, engineers and interior designers.
ADVERTISING RATES:
Full Page Colour .... EUR 2200
Agency Commission: 10%
Mechanical Data: Film: Digital, Trim Size: 297 x 210mm
BUSINESS: ARCHITECTURE & BUILDING: Architecture

COMMERCIAL LAW PRACTITIONER
4221E44-20
Editorial: 43 Fitzwilliam Place, DUBLIN 2 **Tel:** 1 66 25 301 **Fax:** 16625302
Email: martin.mccann@thomsonreuters.com **Web site:** http://www.roundhall.thomson.com
ISSN: 0791-895X
Freq: Monthly; **Annual Sub.:** EUR 625; **Circ:** 300
Usual Pagination: 28
Editor: Martin McCann
Profile: Journal about commercial and company law.
Readership: Read by solicitors, barristers, tax practitioners and accountants.
BUSINESS: LEGAL

COMMERCIAL PROPERTY & INTERIORS
1793559E1E-151
Editorial: 29 Charlemont Lane, Clontarf, DUBLIN 3 **Tel:** 1 83 30 560 **Fax:** 1 83 30 826
Email: trish.phelan@argyllcommunications.ie **Web site:** http://www.argyllcommunications.ie
Freq: Quarterly; **Annual Sub.:** EUR 29.95; **Circ:** 10,000
Usual Pagination: 88
Editor: Trish Phelan; **Managing Editor:** Trish Phelan
Profile: Magazine covering the commercial property and interiors market with the latest trends and developments in relation to hotels, offices and business parks.
Readership: Aimed at architects, specifiers, hoteliers and property developers.
ADVERTISING RATES:
Full Page Colour .... EUR 2500.00
Agency Commission: 10%
Mechanical Data: Bleed Size: 303 x 213mm, Trim Size: 297 x 210mm, Film: Digital
Copy instructions: *Copy Date:* 10 days prior to publication date
Average ad content per issue: 40%
BUSINESS: FINANCE & ECONOMICS: Property

COMMUNITY DENTAL HEALTH
40377E56D-11
Editorial: Oral Health Services Research Centre, University Dental School and Hospital, Wilton, CORK **Tel:** 21 49 01 210 **Fax:** 214545391
Email: cdh@ucc.ie **Web site:** http://www.fdi.org.uk
ISSN: 0256-539X
Freq: Quarterly; **Annual Sub.:** £93; **Circ:** 1,200
Usual Pagination: 64
Editor: Denis O'Mullane; **Advertising Manager:** Evan Carr
Profile: Journal of the British Association for the Study of Community Dentistry and the European Association of Dental Public Health.
Readership: Read by public dental health professionals.
ADVERTISING RATES:
Full Page Mono £260
Full Page Colour £380
Mechanical Data: Type Area: 270 x 179mm, Col Length: 270mm, Page Width: 179mm, Bleed Size: 303 x 216mm, Trim Size: 297 x 210mm, Film: Positive, right reading, emulsion side down. Digital
Average ad content per issue: 18%
BUSINESS: HEALTH & MEDICAL: Dental

COMPUSCHOOL MAGAZINE
1659462E62A-122
Editorial: For all contact details see main record, Teacher Magazine
Freq: 3 issues yearly
Supplement to: Teacher Magazine
BUSINESS: CHURCH & SCHOOL EQUIPMENT & EDUCATION: Education

COMPUTERS IN BUSINESS
1659427E65H-21
Editorial: For all contact details see main record, The Sunday Business Post
Freq: Monthly
Supplement to: The Sunday Business Post
NATIONAL DAILY & SUNDAY NEWSPAPERS: National Colour Supplements

COMPUTERSCOPE
4162E5B-5
Editorial: Media House, South County Business Park, Leopardstown, DUBLIN 18 **Tel:** 1 29 47 777 **Fax:** 12947799
Email: newsroom@mediateam.ie **Web site:** http://www.techcentral.ie
Date Established: 1985; **Freq:** Monthly - Published in the 1st week of the calendar month; Free to qualifying individuals
Annual Sub.: EUR 49; **Circ:** 8,000
Usual Pagination: 80
Advertising Manager: Brenda Smith; **Publisher:** John McDonald
Profile: Magazine with information about IT products, news, technology, networking and trends.
Readership: Aimed at the IT buyers of companies.
ADVERTISING RATES:
Full Page Colour .... EUR 4500
Agency Commission: 10%
Mechanical Data: Page Width: 227mm, Type Area: 337 x 227mm, Bleed Size: 363 x 253mm, Trim Size: 353 x 243mm, Film: Positive, right reading, emulsion side down, Col Length: 337mm
Copy instructions: *Copy Date:* 21 days prior to publication date
Average ad content per issue: 40%
BUSINESS: COMPUTERS & AUTOMATION: Data Processing

CONFERENCE & CONVENTION GUIDE
1659423E65H-22
Editorial: For all contact details see main record, The Sunday Business Post
Freq: Annual
Supplement to: The Sunday Business Post
NATIONAL DAILY & SUNDAY NEWSPAPERS: National Colour Supplements

CONFETTI
1639922E74L-151
Editorial: 1st Floor, Cunningham House, 130 Francis Street, DUBLIN 8 **Tel:** 1 41 67 900 **Fax:** 14167901
Email: ciara@dyflin.ie **Web site:** http://www.confetti.ie
Date Established: 2004; **Freq:** Quarterly
Annual Sub.: EUR 24; **Circ:** 5,805
Editor: Ciara Elliott
Profile: Magazine covering all aspects of wedding planning, including articles on venues, dresses, beauty, health and honeymoons.
Readership: Aimed at brides-to-be in Ireland.
ADVERTISING RATES:
Full Page Colour .... EUR 2200
Agency Commission: 10%
Mechanical Data: Trim Size: 297 x 230mm, Bleed Size: 307 x 240mm, Film: Digital
Average ad content per issue: 25%
CONSUMER: WOMEN'S INTEREST CONSUMER MAGAZINES: Brides

CONNACHT SENTINEL
4310E72-3600
Editorial: 15 Market Street, GALWAY **Tel:** 91 53 62 22 **Fax:** 91567242
Email: news@ctribune.ie **Web site:** http://www.galwaynews.co.uk
Date Established: 1925; **Freq:** Weekly; **Cover Price:** EUR 0.50; **Circ:** 5,241
Editor: Brendan Carroll
ADVERTISING RATES:
Full Page Mono .... EUR 1332
SCC .... EUR 16
Agency Commission: 10%
Mechanical Data: Print Process: Web-fed offset litho, Type Area: 340 x 265mm, Col Length: 340mm, Page Width: 265mm, No. of Columns (Display): 6, Film: Digital
LOCAL NEWSPAPERS

CONNACHT TRIBUNE
4311E72-3700
Editorial: 15 Market Street, GALWAY **Tel:** 91 53 62 22 **Fax:** 91567242
Email: news@ctribune.ie **Web site:** http://www.connacht-tribune.ie
Date Established: 1909; **Freq:** Weekly; **Annual Sub.:** EUR 80; **Circ:** 21,860
Editor: Brendan Carroll
ADVERTISING RATES:
Full Page Mono .... EUR 7776
Full Page Colour .... EUR 9720
SCC .... EUR 20
Mechanical Data: Col Length: 540mm, Film: Digital, No. of Columns (Display): 8, Type Area: 540 x 340mm, Print Process: Web-fed offset litho, Page Width: 340mm, Col Widths (Display): 40mm
LOCAL NEWSPAPERS

THE CONNAUGHT TELEGRAPH
4301E72-3800
Editorial: Cavendish Lane, Castlebar, CO. MAYO **Tel:** 94 90 21 711 **Fax:** 949024007
Email: tgillespie@con-telegraph.ie **Web site:** http://www.con-telegraph.ie
Date Established: 1828; **Freq:** Weekly; **Cover Price:** EUR 1.80; **Circ:** 19,261
Usual Pagination: 30
Editor: Tom Gillespie; **Advertising Manager:** Bernard Hughes
ADVERTISING RATES:
Full Page Mono .... EUR 5345
Full Page Colour .... EUR 6500
Agency Commission: 10%
Mechanical Data: Type Area: 538 x 386mm, Col Length: 538mm, Page Width: 386mm, No. of Columns (Display): 9, Col Widths (Display): 40mm, Film: Digital
LOCAL NEWSPAPERS

CONNECT
1667975E40-11
Editorial: For all contact details see main record, An Cosantóir Magazine
Freq: Monthly
Supplement to: An Cosantóir Magazine
BUSINESS: DEFENCE

CONNECTIONS
1775730E89D-52
Editorial: Level 5, Terminal Building, Dublin Airport, CO. DUBLIN **Tel:** 1 81 44 273
Email: neil.hayes@daa.ie
Freq: 6 issues yearly; **Cover Price:** Free; **Circ:** 65,000
Usual Pagination: 52
Editor: Neil Hayes
Profile: Magazine covering travel, lifestyle, food and drink and culture.
Readership: Aimed at passengers travelling through Dublin Airport.
ADVERTISING RATES:
Full Page Colour .... EUR 4600
Mechanical Data: Bleed Size: 276 x 221mm, Trim Size: 270 x 215mm, Print Process: Sheet-fed litho, Film: Digital
CONSUMER: HOLIDAYS & TRAVEL: In-Flight Magazines

CONSTRUCT IRELAND (FOR A SUSTAINABLE FUTURE)
1639917E4R-1
Formerly: Construct Ireland
Editorial: PO Box 9688, Blackrock, CO DUBLIN **Tel:** 1 21 07 513 **Fax:** 12107512
Email: info@constructireland.ie **Web site:** http://www.constructireland.ie
Freq: 6 issues yearly; **Cover Price:** EUR 4.75 Free to qualifying individuals
Annual Sub.: EUR 59; **Circ:** 7,703
Usual Pagination: 96
Advertising Manager: Jeff Colley
Profile: Magazine promoting the viability of sustainable construction and development in Ireland. Includes articles on energy efficiency, renewable energy, wastewater treatment, and eco building.
Readership: Aimed at local authorities, engineers, architects, builders, self-builders, developers, politicians and large energy users.
ADVERTISING RATES:
Full Page Colour .... EUR 1850
Mechanical Data: Type Area: 277 x 190mm, Bleed Size: 297 x 210mm, Col Length: 277mm, Page Width: 190mm
BUSINESS: ARCHITECTURE & BUILDING: Building Related

CONSTRUCTION
754207E42A-18
Editorial: Cunningham House, 130 Francis Street, DUBLIN 8 **Tel:** 1 41 67 900 **Fax:** 14167901
Email: brian@dyflin.ie **Web site:** http://www.dyflin.ie
Freq: Monthly; Free to qualifying individuals
Annual Sub.: EUR 60; **Circ:** 5,000
Usual Pagination: 64
Editor: Brian Foley; **Managing Director:** Philip McGaley; **Advertising Manager:** Joe Connolly;
Publisher: Karen Hesse
Profile: Official magazine of the Construction Industry Federation (CIF), focusing on construction, architecture, surveying and engineering.
Readership: Aimed at CIF Members, architects, surveyors, engineers and designers.
ADVERTISING RATES:
Full Page Colour .... EUR 2400
Agency Commission: 15%
Mechanical Data: Bleed Size: 307 x 220mm, Trim Size: 297 x 210mm, Col Length: 277mm, Page Width: 190mm, Type Area: 277 x 190mm, Film: Digital
Average ad content per issue: 30%
Supplement(s): The Essential Guide for Members - 1xY
BUSINESS: CONSTRUCTION

CONSTRUCTION AND PROPERTY NEWS
4218E42A-20
Editorial: Grattan House, Temple Road, Blackrock, CO. DUBLIN **Tel:** 1 76 42 700 **Fax:** 17642750
Email: m.martin@jemma.ie
Freq: Monthly; **Annual Sub.:** EUR 84; **Circ:** 3,846
Usual Pagination: 40
Editor: Maev Martin
Profile: Magazine concerning the construction and property trade.
Readership: Aimed at construction industry professionals.
ADVERTISING RATES:
Full Page Mono .... EUR 1800
Full Page Colour .... EUR 2400
Agency Commission: 10%
Mechanical Data: Type Area: 304 x 220mm, Col Length: 304mm, Page Width: 220mm, Trim Size: 345 x 243mm, Bleed Size: 351 x 249mm
Average ad content per issue: 33%
BUSINESS: CONSTRUCTION

CONSUMER CHOICE
623504E74C-10
Editorial: 43-44 Chelmsford Road, DUBLIN 6 **Tel:** 1 49 78 600 **Fax:** 1 4978601
Email: cai@consumerassociation.ie **Web site:** http://www.thecai.ie
ISSN: 0790-486X
Date Established: 1985; **Freq:** Monthly; **Annual Sub.:** EUR 130; **Circ:** 10,000
Usual Pagination: 40
Profile: Magazine published by the Consumers' Association of Ireland. Compares products in value, performance and reliability, reports on household goods, personal finance, cars, health, safety and the environment, also presents consumer law and case studies.
CONSUMER: WOMEN'S INTEREST CONSUMER MAGAZINES: Home & Family

CORK & COUNTY ADVERTISER INCORPORATING WEST CORK ADVERTISER
1682509E72-8211
Editorial: Shannon House, Connolly Street, Bandon, CO. CORK **Tel:** 23 88 29 048 **Fax:** 238829049
Email: westcorkad@eircom.net **Web site:** http://www.corkandcounty.com
Date Established: 2000; **Freq:** Weekly; **Cover Price:** Free; **Circ:** 20,000
Editor: Linda O'Leary
ADVERTISING RATES:
Full Page Mono .... EUR 400
Full Page Colour .... EUR 600
Agency Commission: 10%
Copy instructions: *Copy Date:* 4 days prior to publication date
Average ad content per issue: 70%
LOCAL NEWSPAPERS

CORK INDEPENDENT
4305E72-4800
Formerly: Inside Cork
Editorial: North Point House, North Point Business Park, New Mallow Road, CORK **Tel:** 21 42 88 566 **Fax:** 214288567
Email: editor@corkindependent.com **Web site:** http://www.corkindependent.com
Date Established: 1999; **Freq:** Weekly; **Cover Price:** Free; **Circ:** 27,754
Editor: Deirdre O'Shaughnessy
ADVERTISING RATES:
Full Page Colour .... EUR 2890
SCC .... EUR 20
Agency Commission: 15%
Mechanical Data: Film: Digital, Type Area: 332.5 x 260mm, Col Length: 332.5mm, Page Width: 260mm, Col Widths (Display): 34mm, No. of Columns (Display): 7
Average ad content per issue: 40%
LOCAL NEWSPAPERS

CORKLIFE
1666264E80-203
Editorial: 72 South Mall, CORK **Tel:** 21 42 22 404 **Fax:** 21 42 22 403
Email: info@corklife.ie **Web site:** http://www.corklife.ie

Date Established: 2002; **Freq:** 6 issues yearly; **Cover Price:** EUR 1.00
Free to qualifying individuals ; **Circ:** 10,000
Usual Pagination: 36
Editor: Keith Brown; **Advertising Manager:** Keith Brown
Profile: Magazine covering fashion, beauty, lifestyle, entertainment, shopping and health.
Readership: Aimed at residents and visitors to Cork.
ADVERTISING RATES:
Full Page Colour .... EUR 1200.00
Agency Commission: 15%
Mechanical Data: Type Area: 310 x 215mm, Col Length: 310mm, Page Width: 215mm
Average ad content per issue: 33%
CONSUMER: RURAL & REGIONAL INTEREST

THE CORKMAN (AVONDHU)
1667724E72-8202_106
Editorial: The Spa, Mallow, CO. CORK 0
Part of Series, see entry for: The Corkman Series
LOCAL NEWSPAPERS

THE CORKMAN (MUSKERRY EDITION)
768712E72-8202_104
Editorial: The Spa, Mallow, CO. CORK 0
Part of Series, see entry for: The Corkman Series
LOCAL NEWSPAPERS

THE CORKMAN (NORTH CORK)
768711E72-8202_105
Formerly: The Corkman (Main Edition)
Editorial: The Spa, Mallow, CO. CORK 0
Part of Series, see entry for: The Corkman Series
LOCAL NEWSPAPERS

THE CORKMAN SERIES
1638625E72-8202
Editorial: The Spa, Mallow, CO. CORK
Tel: 22 31 443 **Fax:** 2243183
Email: newsdesk@corkman.ie **Web site:** http://www.corkman.ie
Date Established: 1965; **Freq:** Weekly; **Cover Price:** EUR 1.80; **Circ:** 8,247
ADVERTISING RATES:
Full Page Mono .... EUR 5040
Full Page Colour .... EUR 5444
SCC .... EUR 11
Agency Commission: 15%
Mechanical Data: Film: Digital, Type Area: 563 x 340mm, Col Length: 563mm, Col Widths (Display): 8, Page Width: 340mm
Series owner and contact point for the following titles, see individual entries:
The Corkman (Avondhu)
The Corkman (Muskerry Edition)
The Corkman (North Cork)
LOCAL NEWSPAPERS

CORPORATE GOLF
1658142E75D-67
Editorial: For all contact details see main record, Golf Ireland-Irelands National Golf Magazine
Freq: Half-yearly
Supplement to: Golf Ireland-Irelands National Golf Magazine
CONSUMER: SPORT: Golf

AN COSANTÓIR MAGAZINE
4215E40-10
Editorial: Defence Forces Headquarters, Parkgate, Infirmary Road, DUBLIN 7 **Tel:** 1 80 42 691
Fax: 1 67 79 018
Email: ancosantoir@defenceforces.iol.ie **Web site:** http://www.military.ie
Date Established: 1940; **Freq:** 10 issues yearly; **Cover Price:** EUR 2.50
Annual Sub.: EUR 25.00; **Circ:** 5,000
Usual Pagination: 32
Editor: Willie Braine; **Advertising Manager:** Terry Mclaughlin
Profile: Official magazine of the Irish Defence Forces. Covers all aspects of Irish defence, including training, overseas service, charity work and new weapons and equipment.
Readership: Read by serving military personnel, military enthusiasts and reserve forces.
Supplement(s): Connect - 12xY
BUSINESS: DEFENCE

CREDIT FOCUS
623605E1G-70
Formerly: IICM Newsletter
Editorial: 17 Kildare Street, DUBLIN 2 **Tel:** 1 6099444
Fax: 1 6099445
Email: info@iicm.ie **Web site:** http://www.iicm.ie
Date Established: 1963; **Freq:** Quarterly; **Cover Price:** EUR 00
Free to qualifying individuals ; **Circ:** 2,000
Usual Pagination: 36
Profile: Newsletter of the Irish Institute of Credit Management giving advice and guidance on credit management issues.
Readership: Aimed at credit managers and controllers.
ADVERTISING RATES:
Full Page Colour .... EUR 750
Agency Commission: 10%
Mechanical Data: Trim Size: 297 x 210mm, Film: Digital
Average ad content per issue: 20%
BUSINESS: FINANCE & ECONOMICS: Credit Trading

CU FOCUS
754217E74M-35
Formerly: Credit Union News Magazine
Editorial: 33-41 Lower Mount Street, CO. DUBLIN
Tel: 1 61 46 914 **Fax:** 16146708
Email: kmcdonnell@creditunion.ie **Web site:** http://www.creditunion.ie
ISSN: 1649-377X
Freq: Quarterly; Free to qualifying individuals ; **Circ:** 11,000
Usual Pagination: 44
Advertising Manager: Kieran McDonnell
Profile: Publication of the Irish Credit Union movement. Includes advice on financial self-help.
Readership: Read by members.
ADVERTISING RATES:
Full Page Colour .... EUR 1600
Mechanical Data: Film: Digital, Type Area: 270 x 180mm, Col Length: 270mm, Trim Size: 297 x 210mm, Bleed Size: 306 x 220mm, Page Width: 180mm
Average ad content per issue: 10%
CONSUMER: WOMEN'S INTEREST CONSUMER MAGAZINES: Personal Finance

CUMHACHT
1666254E94F-1
Editorial: Foley Ryan Communications, Morrison Chambers, 32 Nassau Street, DUBLIN 2
Tel: 1 67 90 016 **Fax:** 1 67 90 056
Email: mairead@foleyryancommunications.com **Web site:** http://www.pwdi.ie
Date Established: 2001; **Freq:** Quarterly; **Cover Price:** Free; **Circ:** 9,000
Usual Pagination: 16
Editor: Mairéad Foley
Profile: Newsletter with news and articles relating to disability issues in Ireland. Covers physical, emotional, intellectual and mental disability.
Readership: Aimed at people with disabilities, their parents, partners and carers.
CONSUMER: OTHER CLASSIFICATIONS: Disability

DAIRY & FOOD INDUSTRIES MAGAZINE
4202E22C-51
Editorial: 7 Ballingarrane, Cahir Road, Clonmel, CO TIPPERRARY **Tel:** 52 70 767 **Fax:** 52 23 999
Email: mjmpublications@eircom.net
Freq: 6 issues yearly - Beginning of 2nd cover month; **Annual Sub.:** EUR 50.00; **Circ:** 2,700
Usual Pagination: 48
Editor: Jackie Joyce; **Managing Director:** Michael Kenna; **Advertising Manager:** Michael Kenna; **Publisher:** Michael Kenna
Profile: Magazine which specifically covers the food processing industry in Northern and Southern Ireland. Concentrates on dairies and co-operatives and the meat and bakery industries.
Readership: Aimed at decision makers within food processing industries.
ADVERTISING RATES:
Full Page Mono .... EUR 1295.00
Full Page Colour .... EUR 1795.00
Agency Commission: 15%
Mechanical Data: Type Area: 366 x 263mm, Bleed Size: 452 x 306mm, Trim Size: 420 x 297mm, Col Length: 263mm, Page Width: 366mm, No. of Columns (Display): 3
Copy instructions: *Copy Date:* 2 weeks prior to publication date
Average ad content per issue: 30%
BUSINESS: FOOD: Food Processing & Packaging

DAY & NIGHT MAGAZINE
1666391E65H-17
Editorial: For all contact details see main record, Irish Independent
Freq: Weekly
Supplement to: Irish Independent
NATIONAL DAILY & SUNDAY NEWSPAPERS: National Colour Supplements

DECISION
4174E14A-22
Editorial: PO Box 7130, DUBLIN 18 **Tel:** 1 27 80 841
Email: frank@decisionireland.com **Web site:** http://www.decisionireland.com
Date Established: 1996; **Freq:** 6 issues yearly; **Annual Sub.:** EUR 90; **Circ:** 5,000
Usual Pagination: 48
Advertising Manager: Frank Dillon
Profile: Management magazine with an emphasis on strategy and corporate leadership.
Readership: Aimed at senior decision-makers in the private sector.
ADVERTISING RATES:
Full Page Colour .... EUR 2500
Agency Commission: 15%
Mechanical Data: Film: Digital, Type Area: 234 x 190mm, Col Length: 234mm, Page Width: 190mm, Trim Size: 274 x 230mm, Bleed Size: 284 x 240mm
Supplement(s): Invesco Review of Pensions - 1xY
BUSINESS: COMMERCE, INDUSTRY & MANAGEMENT

DIABETES IRELAND
1639920E74G-176
Editorial: 25 Adelaide Street, Dun Loaghaire, CO DUBLIN **Tel:** 1 28 03 967
Email: mail@medmedia.ie **Web site:** http://www.diabetes.ie
ISSN: 1649-329X
Date Established: 2003; **Freq:** 6 issues yearly
Free to qualifying individuals ; **Circ:** 3,000
Usual Pagination: 48
Editor: Geraldine Meagan; **Advertising Manager:** Kieran O'Leary
Profile: Magazine of the Diabetes Federation of Ireland covering types of diabetes, weight control, nutrition, recipes, children with diabetes and new products as well as features on people who have the condition.
Readership: Aimed at those affected by diabetes, their families, carers and health professionals.
Agency Commission: 15%
Average ad content per issue: 30%
CONSUMER: WOMEN'S INTEREST CONSUMER MAGAZINES: Slimming & Health

DINING IN DUBLIN
628785E94G-1
Editorial: 35 Ferndale Court, Rathmichael, CO DUBLIN **Tel:** 1 2721188 **Fax:** 1 2721970
Email: sonya@dininginclublin.ie **Web site:** http://www.dininginclublin.ie
Date Established: 1998; **Freq:** Half-yearly - Published in May and November; **Cover Price:** EUR 3.99
Free to qualifying individuals ; **Circ:** 15,000
Usual Pagination: 80
Publisher: Sonya O'Donoghue
Profile: Magazine providing a menu guide to the best places to dine whilst staying in Dublin including full menus, write-ups and photos of restaurants.
Readership: Aimed at tourists visiting Dublin.
ADVERTISING RATES:
Full Page Colour .... EUR 1495
Agency Commission: 15%
Mechanical Data: Type Area: 270 x 190mm, Col Length: 270mm, Page Width: 190mm, Film: Digital, Bleed Size: 303 x 216mm, Trim Size: 297 x 210mm
CONSUMER: OTHER CLASSIFICATIONS: Restaurant Guides

DOCTRINE & LIFE
623534E87-20
Editorial: 42 Parnell Square, DUBLIN 1
Tel: 1 87 21 611 **Fax:** 1 87 31 760
Email: editor.doctrineandlife@dominicanpublications.com **Web site:** http://www.dominicanpublications.com
ISSN: 0012-466X
Date Established: 1951; **Freq:** 10 issues yearly; **Cover Price:** EUR 3.12
Annual Sub.: EUR 40.91; **Circ:** 1,500
Usual Pagination: 64
Editor: Bernard Treacy
Profile: European magazine focusing on religion.
Readership: Aimed at Christians.
CONSUMER: RELIGIOUS

DONEGAL DEMOCRAT
4309E72-4000
Editorial: Larkin House, Oldtown road, DONEGAL PE27DS **Tel:** 7491 28000
Email: editorial@donegaldemocrat.com **Web site:** http://www.donegaldemocrat.com
Date Established: 1919; **Freq:** 104 issues yearly; **Cover Price:** EUR 1.40; **Circ:** 23,792
Usual Pagination: 40
Editor: Michael Daly; **Advertising Manager:** Deidre McEnaney
ADVERTISING RATES:
Full Page Mono .... EUR 1921.70
Full Page Colour .... EUR 2690.40
SCC .... EUR 6.28
Agency Commission: 15%
Mechanical Data: No. of Columns (Display): 11, Col Widths (Display): 28mm, Trim Size: 560 x 328mm
Average ad content per issue: 40%
Supplement(s): Lifestyle - 52xY
LOCAL NEWSPAPERS

DONEGAL NEWS (DERRY PEOPLE)
4308E72-3900
Formerly: Derry People and Donegal News
Editorial: St. Annes Court, High Road, Letterkenny, CO. DONEGAL **Tel:** 74 91 21 491 **Fax:** 74 91 22 881
Email: editor@donegalnews.com **Web site:** http://www.donegalnews.com
Date Established: 1903; **Freq:** 104 issues yearly; **Cover Price:** EUR 1.50
Annual Sub.: EUR 186.15; **Circ:** 11,436
Editor: Columba Gill; **Advertising Manager:** Eunan McGlyn
ADVERTISING RATES:
Full Page Mono .... EUR 3900
Full Page Colour .... EUR 5460
Agency Commission: 12.5%
Mechanical Data: Bleed Size: 520 x 375mm, No. of Columns (Display): 10, Col Widths (Display): 34mm, Film: Digital
Average ad content per issue: 40%
Supplement(s): Gardens - 1xY, Wedding - 1xY
LOCAL NEWSPAPERS

DONEGAL ON SUNDAY
1663716E67C-1
Editorial: Larkin House, Oldtown Road, Letterkenny, DONEGAL **Tel:** 74 91 88 204 **Fax:** 749128001
Email: editorial@donegalonsunday.com **Web site:** http://www.donegalonsunday.com
Date Established: 2004; **Freq:** Sunday - Donegal; **Cover Price:** EUR 1.10; **Circ:** 3,702
Editor: Connie Duffy; **Advertising Manager:** Deidre McEnaney
Language(s): English; Gaelic
ADVERTISING RATES:
Full Page Mono .... EUR 1566.72
Full Page Colour .... EUR 2193.40
SCC .... EUR 5.12
Mechanical Data: Type Area: 340 x 268mm, Col Length: 340mm, Page Width: 268mm, Film: Digital, No. of Columns (Display): 9
Average ad content per issue: 25%
REGIONAL DAILY & SUNDAY NEWSPAPERS: Regional Sunday Newspapers

DONEGAL PEOPLE'S PRESS
623665E72-4050
Formerly: Donegal People's Press Series
Editorial: Larkin House, Oldtown Road, Letterkenny, CO. DONEGAL **Tel:** 74 91 28 000 **Fax:** 749128001
Email: editorial@donegaldemocrat.com **Web site:** http://www.donegaldemocrat.com
Freq: Weekly; **Cover Price:** EUR 1.35; **Circ:** 12,000
Editor: Paddy Walsh; **Advertising Manager:** Eamonn Davis
ADVERTISING RATES:
Full Page Mono .... EUR 1921.68
Full Page Colour .... EUR 2690.35
SCC .... EUR 6.28
Agency Commission: 15%
Average ad content per issue: 40%
LOCAL NEWSPAPERS

DOUGLAS NEWMAN GOOD CITY & TOWN MAGAZINE
1654817E74K-101
Formerly: Douglas Newman Good Homes Magazine
Editorial: 3rd Floor, Arena House, Arena Road, Sandyford Industrial Estate, DUBLIN 18
Tel: 1 24 05 540 **Fax:** 12405550
Email: laurahewson@page7media.ie **Web site:** http://www.dng.ie
ISSN: 2161-384X
Date Established: 2003; **Freq:** Quarterly; **Cover Price:** Free; **Circ:** 50,000
Usual Pagination: 96
Editor: Laura Hewson
Profile: Home and lifestyle magazine covering, home accessories, interiors, furniture, DIY, cooking, gardening and a where to buy guide as well as holidays and houses for sale.
Readership: Aimed at 25 to 55 year olds buying, selling or moving home and those interested in doing up their property.
ADVERTISING RATES:
Full Page Colour .... EUR 2900
Agency Commission: 15%
Mechanical Data: Trim Size: 297 x 210mm, Bleed Size: +5mm, Film: Digital
Average ad content per issue: 30%
CONSUMER: WOMEN'S INTEREST CONSUMER MAGAZINES: Home Purchase

DOWNTOWN
1666384E67B-52
Editorial: For all contact details see main record, Evening Echo
Freq: Weekly
Supplement to: Evening Echo
REGIONAL DAILY & SUNDAY NEWSPAPERS: Regional Daily Newspapers

DRINKS INDUSTRY IRELAND
754227E9A-8
Editorial: Louisville, Enniskerry, CO. WICKLOW NA
Tel: 1 20 46 230
Email: drinksinireland@gmail.com
Date Established: 2000; **Freq:** 6 issues yearly - Published in the middle of the cover month; Free to qualifying individuals
Annual Sub.: EUR 80; **Circ:** 3,900
Usual Pagination: 40
Editor: Pat Nolan
Profile: Magazine covering the drinks and the drink industry, with news of developments, interviews with decision makers and features on the latest trends.
Readership: Read by brewers, distillers, hotel, pub, night club and off-licence managers and retailers.
ADVERTISING RATES:
Full Page Colour .... EUR 2500
Agency Commission: 10%
Mechanical Data: Trim Size: 297 x 210mm, Film: Digital, Bleed Size: +6.36mm, Col Length: 272mm, Page Width: 192mm, Type Area: 272 x 192mm
Average ad content per issue: 30%
BUSINESS: DRINKS & LICENSED TRADE: Drinks, Licensed Trade, Wines & Spirits

DROGHEDA INDEPENDENT
1692641E72-4100_100
Editorial: 9 Shop Street, Drogheda, CO. LOUTH 0
Freq: Weekly; **Cover Price:** EUR 1.90
Part of Series, see entry for: Drogheda Independent Series
LOCAL NEWSPAPERS

DROGHEDA INDEPENDENT SERIES
4325E72-4100
Formerly: Drogheda Independent
Editorial: 9 Shop Street, Drogheda, CO. LOUTH
Tel: 41 98 38 658 **Fax:** 419834271
Email: editorial@drogheda-independent.ie **Web site:** http://www.drogheda-independent.ie
Date Established: 1885; **Freq:** Weekly; **Circ:** 10,328
Usual Pagination: 40
Editor: Hubert Murphy; **Advertising Manager:** Pat Gough; **Group Editor:** John Mulligan
ADVERTISING RATES:
Full Page Colour .... EUR 3000
SCC .... EUR 16
Series owner and contact point for the following titles, see individual entries:
Drogheda Independent
Mid Louth Independent
LOCAL NEWSPAPERS

DROGHEDA LEADER
628744E72-4130
Editorial: 35 Laurence Street, Drogheda, CO. LOUTH
Tel: 41 98 36 100 **Fax:** 419841517
Email: news@droghedaleader.ie **Web site:** http://www.droghedaleader.net
Date Established: 1995; **Freq:** Weekly; **Cover Price:** Free; **Circ:** 25,000
Usual Pagination: 28
News Editor: Gordon Hatch; **Managing Director:** Andrew Gates
ADVERTISING RATES:
Full Page Mono .... EUR 2340
Full Page Colour .... EUR 2925
SCC .... EUR 8.73
Mechanical Data: Page Width: 262mm, Film: Digital, Type Area: 345 x 262mm, Col Length: 345mm, Col Widths (Display): 32mm, No. of Columns (Display): 8
Average ad content per issue: 65%
LOCAL NEWSPAPERS

DRYSTOCK FARMER
4196E21D-50
Editorial: ICSA, 9 Lyster, Port Laose, CO LOIS
Tel: 57 86 62 120 **Fax:** 578662121
Email: info@icsaireland.com **Web site:** http://www.icsaireland.com
Freq: Quarterly; Free to qualifying individuals ; **Circ:** 10,000
Usual Pagination: 16
Editor: Ashling Deegan; **Advertising Manager:** Ciara Feehely
Profile: Magazine focusing on the production of lamb and beef.
Readership: Read by farmers and meat producers.
ADVERTISING RATES:
Full Page Colour .... EUR 1500
Mechanical Data: Trim Size: 297 x 210mm
Average ad content per issue: 30%
BUSINESS: AGRICULTURE & FARMING: Livestock

THE DUBLINER
712498E89C-30
Editorial: 3 Ely Place, DUBLIN 2 **Tel:** 1 48 04 700
Email: info@thedubliner.ie **Web site:** http://www.thedubliner.ie
Date Established: 2001; **Freq:** Monthly; **Cover Price:** EUR 2.95
Annual Sub.: EUR 44; **Circ:** 3,306
Usual Pagination: 140
Editor: Nicola Reddy; **Advertising Manager:** Paul Trainer
Profile: Magazine focusing on culture, style, entertainment, media and dining in Dublin.
Readership: Aimed at tourists and residents.
ADVERTISING RATES:
Full Page Colour .... EUR 3300
Agency Commission: 15%
Mechanical Data: Trim Size: 280 x 216mm, Bleed Size: 289 x 222mm, Film: Digital
Average ad content per issue: 35%
CONSUMER: HOLIDAYS & TRAVEL: Entertainment Guides

THE DUNDALK DEMOCRAT (COUNTY EDITION)
1813432E72-4300_101
Editorial: 11 Crowe Street, Dundalk, CO. LOUTH 0
Freq: Weekly; **Cover Price:** EUR 1.90
Part of Series, see entry for: The Dundalk Democrat Series
LOCAL NEWSPAPERS

THE DUNDALK DEMOCRAT SERIES
4326E72-4300
Formerly: The Dundalk Democrat
Editorial: 11 Crowe Street, Dundalk, CO. LOUTH 0
Tel: 42 93 34 058 **Fax:** 429331399
Email: editor@dundalkdemocrat.ie **Web site:** http://www.dundalktoday.com
Date Established: 1849; **Freq:** Weekly; **Circ:** 9,850
Usual Pagination: 42
Advertising Manager: Mark Matthews
ADVERTISING RATES:
Full Page Mono .... EUR 2618
Full Page Colour .... EUR 3367
SCC .... EUR 11
Agency Commission: 15%
Mechanical Data: Type Area: 340mm x266mm, Page Width: 266mm, Col Widths (Display): 35mm, Film: Digital, Col Length: 340mm, No. of Columns (Display): 9
Average ad content per issue: 45%
Series owner and contact point for the following titles, see individual entries:
The Carrick Democrat
The Dundalk Democrat (County Edition)
The Dundalk Democrat (Town Edition)
LOCAL NEWSPAPERS

THE DUNDALK DEMOCRAT (TOWN EDITION)
1813431E72-4300_100
Editorial: 11 Crowe Street, Dundalk, CO. LOUTH 0
Freq: Weekly; **Cover Price:** EUR 1.90
Part of Series, see entry for: The Dundalk Democrat Series
LOCAL NEWSPAPERS

DUNGARVAN LEADER
623669E72-4400
Editorial: 78 O'Connell Street, Dungarvan, CO. WATERFORD **Tel:** 58 41 203 **Fax:** 5845301
Email: dungarvanleader@cablesurf.com **Web site:** http://www.dungarvanleader.com
Date Established: 1938; **Freq:** Weekly; **Cover Price:** EUR 1.50; **Circ:** 10,000
Usual Pagination: 60
Editor: Colm Nagle; **Advertising Manager:** Anna Fahey
ADVERTISING RATES:
Full Page Mono .... EUR 1250
Full Page Colour .... EUR 1750
SCC .... EUR 12
Agency Commission: 15%
Mechanical Data: Type Area: 339.5 x 259mm, Col Length: 339.5mm, Col Widths (Display): 42mm, No. of Columns (Display): 6, Page Width: 259mm, Film: Digital
LOCAL NEWSPAPERS

DUNGARVAN OBSERVER
4335E72-4500
Editorial: Shandon, Dungarvan, CO. WATERFORD
Tel: 58 41 205 **Fax:** 5841559
Email: news@dungarvanobserver.com **Web site:** http://www.dungarvanobserver.ie
Freq: Weekly; **Cover Price:** EUR 1.70; **Circ:** 10,500
Advertising Manager: Marita Collins
ADVERTISING RATES:
SCC .... EUR 13
Agency Commission: 15%
Mechanical Data: Page Width: 335mm, Col Widths (Display): 39mm, Col Length: 516mm, Type Area: 516 x 335mm, No. of Columns (Display): 8, Print Process: Web-fed offset litho
Average ad content per issue: 25%
LOCAL NEWSPAPERS

EASY FOOD MAGAZINE
1640221E74P-202
Editorial: 1st Floor, 19 Railway Road, Dalkey, CO. DUBLIN **Tel:** 1 23 51 408 **Fax:** 12354434
Email: editoreasyfood@zahrapublishing.com **Web site:** http://www.easyfood.ie
ISSN: 1649-4253
Date Established: 2003; **Freq:** Monthly; **Circ:** 27,102
Usual Pagination: 84
Editor: Emma Parkin; **Advertising Manager:** Stephen Pearson; **Publisher:** Gina Miltiadou
Profile: Magazine covering quick and easy meals, wine reviews and nutritional issues.
Readership: Aimed at budget conscious, nutritionally aware home cooks.
ADVERTISING RATES:
Full Page Mono .... EUR 3250
Full Page Colour .... EUR 3250
Agency Commission: 15%
Mechanical Data: Type Area: 245 x 180mm, Bleed Size: 286 x 216mm, Trim Size: 276 x 206mm, Col Length: 245mm, Page Width: 180mm, Film: Digital
Average ad content per issue: 25%
CONSUMER: WOMEN'S INTEREST CONSUMER MAGAZINES: Food & Cookery

EASY HEALTH
1775846E74G-179
Editorial: 1st Floor, 19 Railway Road, Dalkey, CO. DUBLIN **Tel:** 1 23 51 408 **Fax:** 12354434
Email: editoreasyhealth@zahrapublishing.com **Web site:** http://www.easyhealth.ie
Date Established: 2006; **Freq:** 6 issues yearly; **Cover Price:** EUR 3.50; **Circ:** 11,007
Usual Pagination: 84
Editor: Emma Parkin; **Publisher:** Gina Miltiadou
Profile: Magazine covering family, kids', women's, men's and over 50s health, diet, nutrition, dental health and pets health.
Readership: Aimed at those looking for non-complicated and easy to understand health facts and information.
ADVERTISING RATES:
Full Page Mono .... EUR 2600
Full Page Colour .... EUR 3250
Agency Commission: 15%
Mechanical Data: Type Area: 245 x 180mm, Bleed Size: 286 x 216mm, Trim Size: 276 x 206mm, Col Length: 245mm, Page Width: 180mm
Average ad content per issue: 25%
CONSUMER: WOMEN'S INTEREST CONSUMER MAGAZINES: Slimming & Health

THE ECHO (BALLYFERMAT)
1824709E72-4550_103
Editorial: Village Green, Tallaght, DUBLIN 24
Cover Price: EUR 1.60
Part of Series, see entry for: The Echo Series
LOCAL NEWSPAPERS

THE ECHO (CLONDALKIN EDITION)
1659314E72-4550_101
Formerly: The Echo (West Edition)
Editorial: Village Green, Tallaght, DUBLIN 24
Freq: Weekly; **Cover Price:** EUR 1.60
Part of Series, see entry for: The Echo Series
LOCAL NEWSPAPERS

THE ECHO (LUCAN EDITION)
1813967E72-4550_102
Editorial: Village Green, Tallaght, DUBLIN 24
Freq: Weekly; **Cover Price:** EUR 1.60
Part of Series, see entry for: The Echo Series
LOCAL NEWSPAPERS

THE ECHO SERIES
764292E72-4550
Formerly: The Echo
Editorial: Village Green, Tallaght, DUBLIN 24
Tel: 1 46 64 500 **Fax:** 1 46 64 555
Email: editor@echo.ie **Web site:** http://www.echo.ie
ISSN: 1393-5496
Date Established: 1980; **Freq:** Weekly; **Circ:** 9,741
Editor: Emer Mulvaney; **Advertising Manager:** Dee Mackell
ADVERTISING RATES:
Full Page Mono .... EUR 2885
Full Page Colour .... EUR 3310
Mechanical Data: Col Widths (Display): 33mm, No. of Columns (Display): 7, Film: Digital, Col Length: 350mm, Page Width: 261mm, Type Area: 350 x 261mm
Series owner and contact point for the following titles, see individual entries:
The Echo (Ballyfermat)
The Echo (Clondalkin Edition)
The Echo (Lucan Edition)
The Echo (Tallaght Edition)
LOCAL NEWSPAPERS

THE ECHO SERIES (ENNISCORTHY)
623677E72-4650
Formerly: Gorey Echo
Editorial: Slaney Place, Enniscorthy, CO. WEXFORD
Tel: 53 92 33 231 **Fax:** 53 92 33 506
Email: editor@theecho.ie **Web site:** http://www.theecho.ie
Freq: Weekly; **Circ:** 20,000
Editor: Tom Mooney; **Advertising Manager:** Ray Mahon
ADVERTISING RATES:
Full Page Mono .... EUR 3094
Full Page Colour .... EUR 3808
SCC .... EUR 13
Agency Commission: 15%
Mechanical Data: Col Length: 340mm, Film: Digital, No. of Columns (Display): 7, Type Area: 340 x 262mm, Page Width: 262mm
Average ad content per issue: 35%
Series owner and contact point for the following titles, see individual entries:
The Enniscorthy Echo
The Gorey Echo
The New Ross Echo
The Wexford Echo
LOCAL NEWSPAPERS

THE ECHO (TALLAGHT EDITION)
1659313E72-4550_100
Formerly: Echo edition Tallaght/Templeogue
Editorial: Village Green, Tallaght, DUBLIN 24
Freq: Weekly; **Cover Price:** EUR 1.60
Part of Series, see entry for: The Echo Series
LOCAL NEWSPAPERS

THE ECONOMIC & SOCIAL REVIEW
623614E1A-25
Editorial: Department of Economics, University College Dublin, Belfield, DUBLIN 4 **Tel:** 1 71 68 239
Email: karl.whelan@ucd.ie **Web site:** http://www.esr.ie
Freq: Quarterly - Published in spring, summer/autumn and winter
Annual Sub.: EUR 30; **Circ:** 500
Usual Pagination: 100
Editor: Karl Whelan
Profile: Journal covering economics and applied social science. Based on selected papers from the Annual Conference of the Irish Economics Association.
Readership: Read by economists in university libraries.
BUSINESS: FINANCE & ECONOMICS

EDUCATION
1668294E32A-152
Editorial: For all contact details see main record, Local Authority News
Freq: Annual
Supplement to: Local Authority News
BUSINESS: LOCAL GOVERNMENT, LEISURE & RECREATION: Local Government

EDUCATION
4252E62A-50
Editorial: 9 Maypark, Malahide Road, DUBLIN 5
Tel: 1 83 29 243 **Fax:** 1 83 29 246
Email: education@keelaun.ie **Web site:** http://www.educationmagazine.ie
ISSN: 0791-6161
Freq: Quarterly; Free to qualifying individuals
Annual Sub.: EUR 50.00
Usual Pagination: 40
Editor: Niall Gormley
Profile: Magazine covering the Irish and UK education sector. Includes career opportunities, recruitment, higher education, new technology, IT in education, educational equipment and general news from universities, colleges and other educational establishments.
Readership: Read by teachers and education sector managers.
ADVERTISING RATES:
Full Page Mono .... EUR 2200.00
Full Page Colour .... EUR 2750.00
Agency Commission: 15%
Mechanical Data: Type Area: 273 x 183mm, Bleed Size: 304 x 214mm, Trim Size: 297 x 210mm, Col Length: 273mm, Page Width: 183mm, Print Process: Sheet-fed offset litho, Film: Negative, wrong reading, emulsion side up. Positive, right reading, emulsion side down
Copy instructions: *Copy Date:* 10 working days prior to publication date
BUSINESS: CHURCH & SCHOOL EQUIPMENT & EDUCATION: Education

ELECTRONICS COMPONENTS WORLD
1809291E18A-1
Editorial: 3 Inishkeen, Kilcoole, CO.WICKLOW
Tel: 86 24 85 842
Email: editorial@electronicscomponentsworld.com
Web site: http://www.electronicscomponentsworld.com
Freq: Daily; **Cover Price:** Free; **Circ:** 40,000 Unique Users
Editor: Donal McDonald
Profile: Electronics Industry Portal, featuring industry news, new products and technical articles.
Readership: Aimed at designers and engineers.
BUSINESS: ELECTRONICS

ELECTRONICS PRODUCTION WORLD
1809292E18A-2
Editorial: 3 Inishkeen, Kilcoole, CO. WICKLOW
Tel: 86 24 85 842
Email: donal@blackdotpublishing.com **Web site:** http://www.electronicsproductionworld.com
Freq: Daily; **Cover Price:** Free; **Circ:** 35,000 Unique Users
Editor: Donal McDonald
Profile: Electronics Industry portal featuring industry news, new products and technical articles.
Readership: Aimed at production engineers and plant managers.
BUSINESS: ELECTRONICS

EM
629579E58-100
Editorial: 27 Lower Fitzwilliam Street, DUBLIN 2
Tel: 1 70 27 402 **Fax:** 16760727
Email: bernie.healy@esb.ie **Web site:** http://www.esb.ie/em
ISSN: 0790-7508
Date Established: 1927; **Freq:** 6 issues yearly; **Cover Price:** Free; **Circ:** 6,000
Usual Pagination: 32
Editor: Bernie Healy
Profile: Publication of Ireland's main electricity supplier, containing information on supply, networks, generation events, safety, environment, international business and energy at home and in business. Also contains features of general interest for readers.
Readership: Read by customers, staff (current and retired), public representatives, external businesses, public bodies and newsdesks.
BUSINESS: ENERGY, FUEL & NUCLEAR

EMERGENCY SERVICES IRELAND
1639841E56P-1
Editorial: 14 Upper Fitzwilliam Street, DUBLIN 2
Tel: 1 67 85 165 **Fax:** 16785191
Email: emergencyservices@oceanpublishing.ie **Web site:** http://www.oceanpublishing.ie
Date Established: 2001; **Freq:** 6 issues yearly; **Cover Price:** Free; **Circ:** 2,000
Usual Pagination: 156
Advertising Manager: Grace Heneghan; **Publisher:** Patrick Aylward
Profile: Magazine covering the latest developments within the state and voluntary emergency services in Ireland, UK and overseas..
Readership: Aimed at the Garda Siochana, Fire and Ambulance Services, the Defence Forces, Irish Prison Service and the Irish Coast Guard, in addition to the voluntary services such as mountain rescue teams, RNLI and the Civil Defence.
ADVERTISING RATES:
Full Page Colour .... EUR 3995

Mechanical Data: Type Area: 264 x 185mm, Trim Size: 297 x 210mm, Bleed Size: 303 x 216mm, Col Length: 264mm, Film: Digital, Page Width: 185mm
BUSINESS: HEALTH & MEDICAL: Casualty & Emergency

EMPLOYMENT LAW REPORTS
4222E44-35
Editorial: 43 Fitzwilliam Place, DUBLIN 2
Tel: 1 66 25 301 **Fax:** 16625302
Email: terri.mcdonnell@thomsonreuters.com **Web site:** http://www.roundhall.ie
ISSN: 0791-2560
Date Established: 1989; **Freq:** 6 issues yearly;
Annual Sub.: EUR 465; **Circ:** 350
Usual Pagination: 72
Editor: Terri McDonnell
Profile: Publication reporting cases from the Labour Court, Equality Officers, Circuit Court and appeals to the Supreme Court in relation to employment law.
Readership: Aimed at solicitors and barristers concentrating on employment law.
BUSINESS: LEGAL

THE ENGINEERS JOURNAL
754651E19B-100
Formerly: IEI Journal
Editorial: 31 Deansgrange Road, Blackrock, CO. DUBLIN **Tel:** 1 28 93 305 **Fax:** 12896406
Email: bernard@ifpmedia.com **Web site:** http://www.engineersireland.ie
Freq: Monthly - Published in the 1st week of the month
Free to qualifying individuals ; **Circ:** 18,500
Usual Pagination: 64
Editor: Bernard Potter; **Advertising Manager:** John Sheehan
Profile: Magazine focusing on engineering projects in all fields including biomedical, chemical and process, electrical, electronics, ICT, infrastructure both civil and structural, mechanical and manufacturing.
Readership: Read by the engineering profession across all disciplines.
ADVERTISING RATES:
Full Page Colour .... EUR 2730
Agency Commission: 10%
Mechanical Data: Print Process: Offset litho, Col Length: 275mm, Page Width: 190mm, Type Area: 275 x 190mm, Trim Size: 297 x 210mm, Bleed Size: 302 x 215mm, Film: Digital
Average ad content per issue: 30%
BUSINESS: ENGINEERING & MACHINERY: Engineering - Design

ENNISCORTHY AND GOREY GUARDIAN
767640E72-4700_104
Formerly: Enniscorthy Guardian
Editorial: Channing House, Rowe Street, Wexford, CO. WEXFORD 0
Freq: Weekly; **Cover Price:** EUR 1.80; **Circ:** 7,372
ADVERTISING RATES:
Full Page Mono .... EUR 1640.70
Full Page Colour .... EUR 1850
SCC .... EUR 8.14
Part of Series, see entry for: Wexford People Series
LOCAL NEWSPAPERS

THE ENNISCORTHY ECHO
1659362E72-4650_100
Editorial: Slaney Place, Enniscorthy, CO. WEXFORD 0
Freq: Weekly; **Cover Price:** EUR 1.70
Part of Series, see entry for: The Echo Series (Enniscorthy)
LOCAL NEWSPAPERS

ENVIRONMENT & ENERGY MANAGEMENT
754233E57-35
Editorial: 51 Archville, Magheramappien, Convoy, CO. DONEGAL **Tel:** 74 91 34 242 **Fax:** 749134958
Email: donjsheridan@eircom.net **Web site:** http://www.enviroireland.com
Date Established: 2000; **Freq:** 6 issues yearly - Published in the last week of the 2nd cover month; Free to qualifying individuals
Annual Sub.: EUR 95; **Circ:** 14,000
Usual Pagination: 48
Editor: Don Sheridan
Profile: Magazine covering environmental and energy issues.
Readership: Aimed at local authority managers, process managers, executives and CEOs.
ADVERTISING RATES:
Full Page Colour .... EUR 2178
Agency Commission: 10%
Mechanical Data: Type Area: 274mm x 190mm, Col Length: 274mm, Bleed Size: 297 x 210mm, Col Widths (Display): 58mm, Screen: Litho, Film: Mono Negative, wrong reading, emulsion side up. Colour Positive, right reading, emulsion side down, Page Width: 190mm
BUSINESS: ENVIRONMENT & POLLUTION

ENVIRO-SOLUTIONS - NEWS UPDATE
1694455E57-41
Formerly: News Update
Editorial: 28 Venetian Hall, Howth Road, DUBLIN 5
Tel: 86 81 59 243
Email: neil@enviro-solutions.com **Web site:** http://www.enviro-solutions.com
Date Established: 2005; **Freq:** Weekly; **Annual Sub.:** EUR 65
Editor: Neil Flynn
Profile: Electronically delivered newsletter covering environmental management and energy efficiency developments at industrial, commercial and municipal levels.
Readership: Aimed at decision makers in both the private and public sectors, academics and central and local government.
BUSINESS: ENVIRONMENT & POLLUTION

EUROTIMES
1775860E56E-1
Editorial: Temple House, Temple Road, Blackrock, CO. DUBLIN **Tel:** 1 20 91 100 **Fax:** 12091112
Email: caroline.brick@escrs.org **Web site:** http://www.escrs.org
Date Established: 1997; **Freq:** Monthly; Free to qualifying individuals ; **Circ:** 32,019
Editor: Caroline Brick; **Executive Editor:** Colin Kerr; **Advertising Manager:** Caroline Anderson
Profile: Magazine focusing on the practice of ophthalmology in Europe. Featuring coverage of scientific congresses and events worldwide.
Readership: Aimed at ophthalmologists.
ADVERTISING RATES:
Full Page Colour .... EUR 7750
Agency Commission: 10%
Mechanical Data: Type Area: 320 x 270mm, Col Length: 320mm, Page Width: 270mm, Bleed Size: +3mm
BUSINESS: HEALTH & MEDICAL: Optics

EVENING ECHO
4272E67B-50
Editorial: City Quarter, Lapps Quay, CORK
Tel: 21 48 02 142 **Fax:** 21 48 02 135
Email: emma.connolly@eecho.ie **Web site:** http://www.eveningecho.ie
Freq: Daily - Not published on Sunday; **Cover Price:** EUR 1.20; **Circ:** 21,301
Usual Pagination: 86
Features Editor: John Dolan; **Advertising Manager:** Valerie Deane
Profile: The Evening Echo is a daily, evening tabloid paper published from Monday to Saturday and owned by Thomas Crosbie Holdings. The paper is based in Cork and Limerick, but is available throughout the province of Munster. The paper covers local news and sport around the cities and region of Munster as well as covering entertainment, lifestyle and leisure interests and motoring. Twitter handle: http://twitter.com/corkeveningecho.
ADVERTISING RATES:
Full Page Mono .... EUR 4600
Full Page Colour .... EUR 5520
SCC .... EUR 22.65
Mechanical Data: No. of Columns (Display): 7, Type Area: 320 x 265mm, Col Length: 320mm, Col Widths (Display): 35mm, Page Width: 265mm, Film: Digital
Supplement(s): 24/7 - 52xY, Downtown - 52xY, Friday Sport Special - 52xY, Grassroots - 52xY, Monday Sport Special - 52xY, The Pink Pages - 52xY, Women on Wednesday - 52xY
REGIONAL DAILY & SUNDAY NEWSPAPERS: Regional Daily Newspapers

EVENING HERALD
4274E65A-5
Editorial: Independent House, 27-32 Talbot Street, DUBLIN 1 **Tel:** 1 70 55 722 **Fax:** 1 70 55 784
Email: hnews@independent.ie **Web site:** http://www.herald.ie
Freq: Daily - Not published on Sunday; **Cover Price:** EUR 1.10; **Circ:** 65,435
Usual Pagination: 86
Editor: Fionnuala O'Leary; **Executive Editor:** Claire Grady; **Features Editor:** Dave Diebold
Profile: The Evening Herald is a tabloid evening newspaper published in Dublin by Independent News & Media. The newspaper covers local, national and international news, current affairs, business, entertainment, lifestyle and sport, providing news and classifieds from Dublin and Ireland. Twitter handle: http://twitter.com/eveningherald.
Readership: Read by executives, managers, office workers and students, the majority of whom live in urban areas.
ADVERTISING RATES:
Full Page Mono .... EUR 10430
Full Page Colour .... EUR 12365
SCC .... EUR 48.95
Mechanical Data: Page Width: 255mm, Film: Digital, Col Length: 330mm, Col Widths (Display): 40mm, No. of Columns (Display): 6, Type Area: 330 x 255mm
Average ad content per issue: 35%
Editions:
Evening Herald (City Final Edition)
NATIONAL DAILY & SUNDAY NEWSPAPERS: National Daily Newspapers

EVENING HERALD (CITY FINAL EDITION)
1693714E65A-5_500
Editorial: Independent House, 27-32 Talbot Street, DUBLIN 1
Freq: Daily
Edition of: Evening Herald
NATIONAL DAILY & SUNDAY NEWSPAPERS: National Daily Newspapers

THE EVENT GUIDE
629580E89C-35
Editorial: Regus House, Harcourt Road, DUBLIN 2
Tel: 1 47 73 933 **Fax:** 14029590
Email: info@eventguide.ie **Web site:** http://www.eventguide.ie
Date Established: 1984; **Freq:** 26 issues yearly;
Cover Price: Free; **Circ:** 24,000
Usual Pagination: 28
Profile: Magazine covering arts and entertainment listings, featuring preview articles and reviews of events in Ireland.
Readership: Read by people aged 15 to 50 years old living in or visiting Ireland.
ADVERTISING RATES:
Full Page Colour .... EUR 1700
Agency Commission: 10%
Mechanical Data: Film: Digital, Type Area: 375 x 262mm, Col Length: 375mm, Page Width: 262mm
Average ad content per issue: 40%
CONSUMER: HOLIDAYS & TRAVEL: Entertainment Guides

FACE UP
764156E74F-55
Editorial: 75 Orwell Road, Rathgar, DUBLIN 6
Tel: 1 49 22 488 **Fax:** 14927999
Email: info@faceup.ie **Web site:** http://www.faceup.ie
Date Established: 2001; **Freq:** Monthly; **Circ:** 10,000
Usual Pagination: 48
Editor: Gerard Moloney
Profile: Magazine containing features about pop stars, lifestyle and exam stress, includes a questions and answers column.
Readership: Aimed at teenagers between the ages of 14 and 17 years old.
ADVERTISING RATES:
Full Page Colour .... EUR 950
Mechanical Data: Col Length: 296mm, Page Width: 210mm, Type Area: 296 x 210mm, No. of Columns (Display): 4
Average ad content per issue: 10%
CONSUMER: WOMEN'S INTEREST CONSUMER MAGAZINES: Teenage

THE FAR EAST
623535E87-40
Editorial: St. Columbans, Navan, CO. MEATH
Tel: 46 90 21 525 **Fax:** 469071297
Web site: http://www.columban.com
Date Established: 1918; **Freq:** 6 issues yearly - Publishes two-monthly except for November and December, March and April; **Annual Sub.:** EUR 15; **Circ:** 100,000
Usual Pagination: 24
Editor: Cyril Lovett; **Circulation Manager:** Noel Daly
Profile: Publication containing reports of the work of Columban missionaries and articles about religious, social, peace and ecological issues.
Readership: Read by Christians in Britain and Ireland.
CONSUMER: RELIGIOUS

FARMER
1799350E72-8227
Editorial: Tone Street, Ballina, CO. MAYO
Freq: Weekly
ADVERTISING RATES:
Full Page Colour .... EUR 1200
Supplement to: Western People
LOCAL NEWSPAPERS

FARMING
1659412E65H-3
Formerly: The Farm Examiner
Editorial: For all contact details see main record, The Irish Examiner
Freq: Weekly
Supplement to: The Irish Examiner
NATIONAL DAILY & SUNDAY NEWSPAPERS: National Colour Supplements

FARMING
1775042E72-8228
Editorial: Unit 3, Hartley Business Park, Carrick-on-Shannon, CO. LEITRIM
Freq: Monthly
Supplement to: Leitrim Observer Series
LOCAL NEWSPAPERS

FARMING
1799362E72-8229
Editorial: 25 Michael Street, WATERFORD
Freq: Annual
Supplement to: Waterford News & Star
LOCAL NEWSPAPERS

FARMING
1744170E72-8230
Editorial: William Street, Tullamore, CO. OFFALY
Freq: Monthly
Supplement to: Tullamore Tribune
LOCAL NEWSPAPERS

FARMING
1744315E72-8231
Editorial: 34 High Street, KILKENNY
Freq: Quarterly
Supplement to: Kilkenny People
LOCAL NEWSPAPERS

FARMING INDEPENDENT
1666387E65H-4
Editorial: For all contact details see main record, Irish Independent
Freq: Weekly
Supplement to: Irish Independent
NATIONAL DAILY & SUNDAY NEWSPAPERS: National Colour Supplements

FEASTA
628753E84A-220
Editorial: 43 Na Cluainter, Trá Lí, CO CHIARRAÍ 2
Tel: 1 47 83 814
Email: feasta@eircom.net **Web site:** http://www.feasta.ie
ISSN: 0014-8946
Date Established: 1948; **Freq:** Monthly
Annual Sub.: EUR 75; **Circ:** 2,500
Usual Pagination: 32
Editor: Padraig MacFhearghusa
Profile: Magazine focusing on art and literature.
Language(s): Gaelic
Readership: Aimed at those interested in literature and art.
CONSUMER: THE ARTS & LITERARY: Arts

FEELGOOD
1659413E65H-27
Editorial: For all contact details see main record, The Irish Examiner
Freq: Weekly
Supplement to: The Irish Examiner
NATIONAL DAILY & SUNDAY NEWSPAPERS: National Colour Supplements

FESTIVAL - HEINEKEN GREEN ENERGY/OXEGEN
1659150E76E-101
Editorial: For all contact details see main record, Hot Press
Freq: Annual
Supplement to: Hot Press
CONSUMER: MUSIC & PERFORMING ARTS: Pop Music

FILM IRELAND
629583E85B-50
Editorial: Curved Street, DUBLIN 2 **Tel:** 1 67 96 716
Fax: 16796717
Email: editor@filmbase.ie **Web site:** http://www.filmireland.net
ISSN: 0791-7546
Date Established: 1987; **Freq:** 6 issues yearly
Annual Sub.: EUR 35; **Circ:** 3,250
Usual Pagination: 52
Editor: Niamh Creely; **Advertising Manager:** Grodon Gaffney
Profile: Magazine focusing on all aspects of filmmaking.
Readership: Aimed at cinephiles, film makers, emerging film makers and others interested in filmmaking.
ADVERTISING RATES:
Full Page Colour .... EUR 800
Agency Commission: 15%
CONSUMER: PHOTOGRAPHY & FILM MAKING: Film Making

FINANCE MAGAZINE
4134E1A-30
Editorial: 6 The Mall, Beacon Court, Sandyford, DUBLIN 18 **Tel:** 1 29 30 566 **Fax:** 12930560
Email: editorial@finance-magazine.com **Web site:** http://www.finance-magazine.com
ISSN: 0790-8628
Date Established: 1987; **Freq:** Monthly; **Annual Sub.:** EUR 225; **Circ:** 2,834
Usual Pagination: 16
Managing Director: Ken O'Brien; **Advertising Manager:** Martina Bermingham
Profile: European corporate financial and financial services magazine.
Readership: Aimed at senior financial executives in financial services and corporate Ireland.
ADVERTISING RATES:
Full Page Colour .... EUR 3500
BUSINESS: FINANCE & ECONOMICS

FINANCE MAGAZINE
1659426E65H-23
Editorial: For all contact details see main record, The Sunday Business Post
Freq: Annual
Supplement to: The Sunday Business Post
NATIONAL DAILY & SUNDAY NEWSPAPERS: National Colour Supplements

FINGAL INDEPENDENT (NORTH EDITION)
1692415E72-4570_100
Editorial: Shop Street, Drogheda, CO. LOUTH 0
Freq: Weekly; **Cover Price:** EUR 1.80
Part of Series, see entry for: Fingal Independent Series
LOCAL NEWSPAPERS

FINGAL INDEPENDENT SERIES
754384E72-4570
Formerly: Fingal Independent
Editorial: Shop Street, Drogheda, CO. LOUTH
Tel: 1 84 07 107 **Fax:** 1 84 07 022
Email: editorial@fingal-independent.ie **Web site:** http://www.fingal-independent.ie
Freq: Weekly; **Circ:** 3,677
Editor: Fergal Maddock; **Advertising Manager:** Patricia Caffrey
ADVERTISING RATES:
Full Page Colour .... EUR 3600
SCC .... EUR 11.50
Agency Commission: 10%
Average ad content per issue: 40%
Series owner and contact point for the following titles, see individual entries:
Fingal Independent (North Edition)
Fingal Independent (South Edition)
Supplement(s): Living in Fingal - 1xY
LOCAL NEWSPAPERS

FINGAL INDEPENDENT (SOUTH EDITION)
1692414E72-4570_101
Editorial: Shop Street, Drogheda, CO. LOUTH 0
Freq: Weekly; **Cover Price:** EUR 1.80
Part of Series, see entry for: Fingal Independent Series
LOCAL NEWSPAPERS

FIRST DAY AT SCHOOL
1866560E72-8258
Editorial: Unit 3, Hartley Business Park, Carrick-on-Shannon, CO. LEITRIM
Freq: Annual
Language(s): English; Gaelic
Supplement to: Leitrim Observer Series
LOCAL NEWSPAPERS

FITNESS
1799363E72-8232
Editorial: 25 Michael Street, WATERFORD
Freq: Annual
Supplement to: Waterford News & Star
LOCAL NEWSPAPERS

FLEET BUS AND COACH
1659454E49A-101
Formerly: Van/Truck/Bus & Coach Buyers Guide
Editorial: For all contact details see main record, Fleet Transport
Freq: 3 issues yearly
Supplement to: Fleet Transport
BUSINESS: TRANSPORT

FLEET CAR
1659451E49A-102
Formerly: Car Fleet
Editorial: D'Alton Street, Claremorris, CO. MAYO
Freq: 3 issues yearly
Supplement to: Fleet Transport
BUSINESS: TRANSPORT

FLEET MARITIME
1804089E49A-105
Editorial: For all contact details see main record, Fleet Transport
Freq: Quarterly
Supplement to: Fleet Transport
BUSINESS: TRANSPORT

FLEET TRAILER & BODY BUILDER
1804088E49A-104
Editorial: For all contact details see main record, Fleet Transport
Freq: Half-yearly
Supplement to: Fleet Transport
BUSINESS: TRANSPORT

FLEET TRANSPORT
4230E49A-30
Formerly: Fleet Management Magazine
Editorial: D'Alton Street, Claremorris, CO. MAYO
Tel: 94 93 72 819 **Fax:** 949373571
Email: jarlath@fleet.ie **Web site:** http://www.fleet.ie
ISSN: 1393-4856
Date Established: 1986; **Freq:** Monthly
Annual Sub.: EUR 65; **Circ:** 7,500
Usual Pagination: 60
Editor: Jarlath Sweeney; **Advertising Manager:** Orla Sweeney
Profile: Magazine covering all aspects of transport including news, views and road tests.
Readership: Aimed at road transport operators and decision makers.
ADVERTISING RATES:
Full Page Colour .... EUR 1950
Agency Commission: 15%
Mechanical Data: Type Area: 266 x 190mm, Col Length: 266mm, Page Width: 190mm, Bleed Size: 303 x 216mm, Trim Size: 297 x 210mm
Average ad content per issue: 40%
Supplement(s): Fleet Bus and Coach - 3xY, Fleet Car - 3xY, Fleet Maritime - 4xY, Fleet Trailer & Body Builder - 2xY, Fleet Van - 3xY
BUSINESS: TRANSPORT

FLEET VAN
1659458E49A-103
Editorial: For all contact details see main record, Fleet Transport
Freq: 3 issues yearly
Supplement to: Fleet Transport
BUSINESS: TRANSPORT

FOCUS
1685552E94F-3
Editorial: Whitworth Road, Drumcondra, DUBLIN 9
Tel: 1 83 07 033 **Fax:** 18307787
Email: joebollard2@eircom.net **Web site:** http://www.ncbi.ie/focus
Freq: Monthly; **Cover Price:** Free; **Circ:** 2,500
Editor: Joe Bollard
Profile: Audio magazine dealing with matters of vision impairment and other disabilities from Ireland and around the world.
Readership: Aimed at the visually impaired.
CONSUMER: OTHER CLASSIFICATIONS: Disability

FOINSE
623674E65J-1
Editorial: An Cheathru Rua, CO. NA GAILLIMHE
Tel: 9 15 95 520 **Fax:** 91595524
Email: nuacht@foinse.ie **Web site:** http://www.foinse.ie
Freq: Weekly; **Cover Price:** EUR 1.30; **Circ:** 4,152
Editor: Seân Tadhg Ó Gairbhí
Profile: Gaelic newspaper containing local and national news, current affairs and sport.
Language(s): Gaelic
ADVERTISING RATES:
Full Page Mono .... EUR 2400
Full Page Colour .... EUR 3190
SCC .... EUR 32
Agency Commission: 15%
Mechanical Data: Col Length: 387mm, Col Widths (Display): 40mm, Type Area: 387 x 257mm, No. of Columns (Display): 6, Page Width: 257mm
NATIONAL DAILY & SUNDAY NEWSPAPERS: National Weekly Newspapers

FOOD & DRINK BUSINESS EUROPE
37950E22A-41
Formerly: Food & Drink Business
Editorial: 51 Park West Enterprise Centre, Nangor Road, DUBLIN 12 **Tel:** 1 61 20 880 **Fax:** 16120881
Email: susan@prempub.com **Web site:** http://www.foodanddrinkbusiness.eu
ISSN: 1393-8436
Freq: Monthly - Published around the end of the cover month; Free to qualifying individuals
Annual Sub.: EUR 112.50; **Circ:** 24,900
Usual Pagination: 52
Editor: Susan Doyle; **Managing Director:** Ronan McGlade
Profile: Magazine covering all aspects of the food and drink industry. Includes bottling, packaging, logistics, distribution, materials, ingredients, IT, processing, manufacturing, control and automation.
Readership: Aimed at senior management and production engineers in food and drink manufacturing plants.
ADVERTISING RATES:
Full Page Mono £1595
Full Page Colour £2095
Mechanical Data: Bleed Size: 297 x 210mm, Trim Size: 303 x 216mm, Col Length: 274mm, Page Width: 190mm, Film: Digital, Type Area: 274 x 190mm, No. of Columns (Display): 3
BUSINESS: FOOD

FOOD & DRINK MAGAZINE
1659425E65H-39
Editorial: For all contact details see main record, The Sunday Business Post
Freq: Quarterly
Supplement to: The Sunday Business Post
NATIONAL DAILY & SUNDAY NEWSPAPERS: National Colour Supplements

FOOD & WINE
1799365E72-8233
Editorial: 25 Michael Street, WATERFORD
Freq: Half-yearly
Supplement to: Waterford News & Star
LOCAL NEWSPAPERS

FOOD & WINE MAGAZINE
629588E74P-60
Editorial: Rosemount House, Dundrum Road, Dundrum, DUBLIN 14 **Tel:** 1 24 05 300 **Fax:** 16619757
Email: foodandwine@harmonia.ie **Web site:** http://www.harmonia.ie
Date Established: 1997; **Freq:** Monthly - Double issues published in Dec/Jan and Jul/Aug; **Cover Price:** EUR 3.99
Annual Sub.: EUR 44; **Circ:** 7,815
Usual Pagination: 92
Profile: Magazine focusing on fine food and wine. Includes articles on recipes, dining out, restaurant reviews, wine profiles and spirit and beer guides. Also includes features on home entertaining, food-related travel, kitchen equipment, ingredient tests and kitchen interiors.
Readership: Aimed mainly at the 25 year old plus age group, consumers and catering professionals.
ADVERTISING RATES:
Full Page Colour .... EUR 2600
Agency Commission: 15%
Mechanical Data: Bleed Size: 310 x 235mm, Trim Size: 300 x 225mm, Type Area: 270 x 195mm, Col Length: 270mm, Page Width: 195mm, Print Process: Web-fed offset litho, Film: Digital
Average ad content per issue: 35%
CONSUMER: WOMEN'S INTEREST CONSUMER MAGAZINES: Food & Cookery

FOOD IRELAND
4203E22C-50
Editorial: Poolbeg House, 1-2 Poolbeg Street, DUBLIN 2 **Tel:** 1 24 13 095 **Fax:** 1 24 13 010
Email: foodireland@tarapublishingco.com **Web site:** http://www.tarapublishingco.com
Date Established: 1978; **Freq:** Annual - Published in June or July; Free to qualifying individuals
Annual Sub.: EUR 30.00; **Circ:** 3,125
Usual Pagination: 75
Editor: Kathleen Belton; **Advertising Manager:** Kathleen Belton
Profile: Journal covering the Irish food processing industry. Covers different aspects of food processing including plant, production, purchasing, finance, marketing, transport and research and development.
Readership: Aimed at food and beverage manufacturers in the Irish Republic.
ADVERTISING RATES:
Full Page Mono .... EUR 2795.00
Full Page Colour .... EUR 2795.00
Agency Commission: 10%
Mechanical Data: Film: Digital, Trim Size: 297 x 210mm, Bleed Size: 307 x 220mm, Type Area: 270 x 190mm, Col Length: 270mm, Page Width: 190mm
Average ad content per issue: 40%
BUSINESS: FOOD: Food Processing & Packaging

FORUM
4239E56A-1
Editorial: 25 Adelaide Street, Dun Laoghaire, CO. DUBLIN **Tel:** 1 28 03 967 **Fax:** 12807076
Email: geraldine@medmedia.ie **Web site:** http://www.medmedia.ie
Date Established: 1991; **Freq:** Monthly; Free to qualifying individuals
Annual Sub.: EUR 147; **Circ:** 3,500
Editor: Niall Hunter; **Publisher:** Geraldine Meagan
Profile: Journal covering all aspects of general practice in Ireland.
Readership: Read by general practitioners.
ADVERTISING RATES:
Full Page Mono .... EUR 1650
Full Page Colour .... EUR 1650
Agency Commission: 15%
Mechanical Data: No. of Columns (Display): 3, Film: Digital, Bleed Size: 303 x 216mm, Trim Size: 297 x 210mm, Type Area: 270 x 184mm, Col Length: 270mm, Page Width: 184mm, Col Widths (Display): 41mm
BUSINESS: HEALTH & MEDICAL

FREE ADS
1832619E72-8255
Editorial: 25 Michael Street, WATERFORD
Freq: Weekly
Supplement to: Waterford News & Star
LOCAL NEWSPAPERS

FRIDAY SPORT SPECIAL
1826364E67B-56
Editorial: For all contact details see main record, Evening Echo
Freq: Weekly - Published on Friday
Supplement to: Evening Echo
REGIONAL DAILY & SUNDAY NEWSPAPERS: Regional Daily Newspapers

THE FURROW
623538E87-43
Editorial: St. Patrick's College, Maynooth, CO. KILDARE **Tel:** 1 70 83 741 **Fax:** 17083908
Email: furrow.office@may.ie **Web site:** http://www.thefurrow.ie
ISSN: 0016-3120
Date Established: 1950; **Freq:** Monthly; **Cover Price:** EUR 2.75
Annual Sub.: EUR 50; **Circ:** 8,000
Usual Pagination: 64
Editor: Ronan Drury
Profile: Magazine covering all religious matters.
Readership: Aimed at clergy and lay people of all ages.
CONSUMER: RELIGIOUS

GALLERY
1852927E65H-40
Editorial: For all contact details see main record, The Irish Times
Freq: Weekly
Supplement to: The Irish Times
NATIONAL DAILY & SUNDAY NEWSPAPERS: National Colour Supplements

GALWAY ADVERTISER
4312E72-4600
Editorial: 41-42 Eyre Square, GALWAY 0
Tel: 91 53 09 00 **Fax:** 91565627
Email: dvarley@galwayadvertiser.ie **Web site:** http://www.advertiser.ie
Date Established: 1970; **Freq:** Weekly; **Cover Price:** Free; **Circ:** 29,093
Editor: Declan Varley
ADVERTISING RATES:
Full Page Mono .... EUR 2375
Full Page Colour .... EUR 2500
Mechanical Data: Trim Size: 355 x 263mm
Supplement(s): Property
LOCAL NEWSPAPERS

THE GALWAY CITY TRIBUNE
623663E72-3435
Formerly: City Tribune
Editorial: 15 Market Street, GALWAY
Tel: 91 53 62 22 **Fax:** 91567242
Email: news@ctribune.ie **Web site:** http://www.ctribune.ie
ISSN: 0791-1815
Freq: Weekly; **Circ:** 38,000
Usual Pagination: 40
Editor: Michael Glynn
ADVERTISING RATES:
Full Page Mono .... EUR 2916
Full Page Colour .... EUR 3645
SCC .... EUR 7.50
Agency Commission: 10%
Mechanical Data: Print Process: Web-fed offset litho, Page Width: 340mm, Type Area: 540 x 340mm, Col Length: 540mm, No. of Columns (Display): 8, Col Widths (Display): 40mm
LOCAL NEWSPAPERS

GALWAY INDEPENDENT
1659824E72-8207
Editorial: Unit 4, Galway Retail Park, Headford Road, GALWAY **Tel:** 91 56 90 00 **Fax:** 91569333
Email: editor@galwayindependent.com **Web site:** http://www.galwayindependent.com
Date Established: 2001; **Freq:** Weekly; **Cover Price:** Free; **Circ:** 25,009
Editor: Hilary Martyn
Language(s): English; Gaelic
ADVERTISING RATES:
Full Page Colour .... EUR 2895
SCC .... EUR 20
Mechanical Data: Type Area: 332.5 x 260mm, Col Length: 332.5mm, Page Width: 260mm, Col Widths (Display): 34.5mm, No. of Columns (Display): 7, Film: Digital
LOCAL NEWSPAPERS

GALWAYNOW
629598E80-50
Formerly: Galway Now
Editorial: Harris House, Tuam Road, CO. GALWAY
Tel: 91 38 43 50
Email: sinead@galwaynow.com **Web site:** http://www.galwaynow.com
Date Established: 1999; **Freq:** Monthly - Combined December/January issue; **Cover Price:** EUR 3.50
Annual Sub.: EUR 40; **Circ:** 50,000
Usual Pagination: 120
Editor: Sinead Ni Neachtain; **Managing Director:** Patricia McCrossan; **Advertising Manager:** Michelle Sweeney
Profile: Magazine focusing on positive living, lifestyle, health, fashion and interior design, based around traditions in the west of Ireland.
Language(s): English; Gaelic
Readership: Aimed at residents and those with an interest in the West of Ireland aged 25 years old and over.
ADVERTISING RATES:
Full Page Colour .... EUR 1450
Mechanical Data: Trim Size: 300 x 217mm, Film: Digital
CONSUMER: RURAL & REGIONAL INTEREST

GARDA REVIEW
4209E32F-30
Editorial: 5th Floor, Phibsboro Tower, DUBLIN 7
Tel: 1 83 03 533 **Fax:** 18303331
Email: editor@gardareview.ie **Web site:** http://www.gardareview.ie
Date Established: 1923; **Freq:** Monthly; **Annual Sub.:** EUR 52; **Circ:** 8,000
Usual Pagination: 44
Editor: Neil Ward
Profile: Journal of the Garda Representative Association, covering crime, security issues and industrial relation issues.
Language(s): English; Gaelic
Readership: Read by members of the Garda, journalists, politicians and government officials.
ADVERTISING RATES:
Full Page Mono .... EUR 1900
Full Page Colour .... EUR 2800
Agency Commission: 10%
Mechanical Data: Trim Size: 297 x 210mm
BUSINESS: LOCAL GOVERNMENT, LEISURE & RECREATION: Police

GARDENS
1750287E72-8234
Editorial: For all contact details see main record, Donegal News (Derry People)
Freq: Annual - Published in April
Supplement to: Donegal News (Derry People)
LOCAL NEWSPAPERS

GAY COMMUNITY NEWS
628747E86B-50
Editorial: Unit 2 Scarlet Row, West Essex Street, DUBLIN 8 **Tel:** 1 67 19 076 **Fax:** 16713549
Email: editor@gcn.ie **Web site:** http://www.gcn.ie
Date Established: 1988; **Freq:** Monthly; **Cover Price:** Free; **Circ:** 11,005
Usual Pagination: 60
Editor: Brian Finnegan; **Advertising Manager:** Conor Wilson
Profile: Magazine focusing on gay and lesbian culture, lifestyle, politics and entertainment.
Readership: Read by all ages of the gay and lesbian community.
ADVERTISING RATES:
Full Page Mono .... EUR 1119
Full Page Colour .... EUR 2315
Agency Commission: 10%
Mechanical Data: Film: Positive, right reading, emulsion side down, Print Process: Web-fed litho, Trim Size: 310 x 270mm, Bleed Size: 313 x 273mm
Average ad content per issue: 40%
CONSUMER: ADULT & GAY MAGAZINES: Gay & Lesbian Magazines

GAZETTE SERIES
1644012E72-8204
Formerly: Lucan Gazette
Editorial: Block 3A, Mill Bank Business Park, Lower Road, Lucan, CO. DUBLIN 0 **Tel:** 1 60 10 240
Fax: 16010251
Email: news@gazettegroup.com **Web site:** http://www.gazettegroup.com
Date Established: 2004; **Freq:** Weekly; **Cover Price:** Free; **Circ:** 4,500
News Editor: Dawn Love; **Advertising Manager:** Grainne O'Toole
Series owner and contact point for the following titles, see individual entries:
Clondalkin Gazette
Lucan Gazette
LOCAL NEWSPAPERS

GLOBAL COMPANY NEWS
1808730E1A-112
Editorial: Beech Park, Ennis, CO. CLARE
Tel: 65 68 24 751
Email: xltech@eircom.net
Date Established: 2006; **Freq:** Daily; **Circ:** 100 Unique Users
Editor: Patrick Corley
Profile: Email service containing financial and other listed company news, supplying real-time listed company news worldwide.
Readership: Aimed at financial database builders, editors of industry, investment and financial publications and the financial community.
BUSINESS: FINANCE & ECONOMICS

THE GLOSS
1775006E74A-148
Editorial: The Courtyard, 40 Main Street, Blackrock, CO. DUBLIN **Tel:** 1 27 55 130 **Fax:** 12755131
Web site: http://www.thegloss.ie
Date Established: 2006; **Freq:** Monthly - Double issue January and February; **Cover Price:** EUR 4.50
Free to qualifying individuals ; **Circ:** 20,000
Usual Pagination: 170
Editor: Sarah McDonnell; **Advertising Director:** Tracy Ormiston
Profile: Magazine covering fashion, lifestyle and culture including travel, arts, books, beauty, fashion and interiors.
Readership: Aimed at sophisticated women aged between 22 and 44 years old with a high disposable income.
ADVERTISING RATES:
Full Page Mono .... EUR 3000
Full Page Colour .... EUR 3000
Agency Commission: 10%
Mechanical Data: Bleed Size: 283 x 219mm, Trim Size: 277 x 213mm, Type Area: 267 x 203mm, Col Length: 267mm, Page Width: 203mm, Film: Digital
Average ad content per issue: 25%
CONSUMER: WOMEN'S INTEREST CONSUMER MAGAZINES: Women's Interest

GLOW*
1790527E74G-180
Formerly: Health, Living & Wellbeing
Editorial: 88 Lower Baggot Street, DUBLIN 2
Tel: 1 61 10 932
Email: marie@glowmagazine.ie **Web site:** http://www.glowmagazine.ie
Date Established: 2005; **Freq:** 6 issues yearly;
Cover Price: EUR 3.25
Annual Sub.: EUR 29.99; **Circ:** 30,000
Usual Pagination: 100
Editor: Marie Loftus; **Group Editor:** Marie Loftus
Profile: Magazine covering health, well-being and healthy lifestyle.
Readership: Aimed at ABC1 women.
ADVERTISING RATES:
Full Page Colour .... EUR 2500.00
Agency Commission: 15%
Mechanical Data: Type Area: 265 x 180mm, Bleed Size: 303 x 216mm, Trim Size: 297 x 210mm, Col Length: 265mm, Page Width: 180mm, Print Process: Litho, Film: Digital
Average ad content per issue: 40%
CONSUMER: WOMEN'S INTEREST CONSUMER MAGAZINES: Slimming & Health

GO
1852928E65H-41
Editorial: For all contact details see main record, The Irish Times
Freq: Weekly
Supplement to: The Irish Times
NATIONAL DAILY & SUNDAY NEWSPAPERS: National Colour Supplements

GOING PLACES MAGAZINE
1774779E89A-203
Editorial: 51 Allen Park Road, Stillorgan, CO DUBLIN
Tel: 1 20 56 895 **Fax:** 1 28 88 179
Email: goingplaces@ireland.com
Date Established: 2004; **Freq:** Quarterly; **Cover Price:** EUR 3.50; **Circ:** 10,000
Usual Pagination: 88
Editor: Suzanne Gunn; **Advertising Manager:** Brendan Dunn
Profile: Magazine covering travel, lifestyle, events, fashion and beauty.
Readership: Aimed at men and women aged 25 years old and over with a high disposable income.
ADVERTISING RATES:
Full Page Mono .... EUR 1800.00
Full Page Colour .... EUR 2400.00
Agency Commission: 15%
Mechanical Data: Type Area: 297 x 210mm, Bleed Size: 309 x 222mm, Trim Size: 297 x 210mm, Col Length: 297mm, Page Width: 210mm, Film: Digital
Copy instructions: *Copy Date:* 4 weeks prior to publication date
Average ad content per issue: 25%
CONSUMER: HOLIDAYS & TRAVEL: Travel

GOLF DIGEST IRELAND
1643545E75D-66
Editorial: E7 Calmount Office Park, Ballymount, DUBLIN 12 **Tel:** 1 41 99 604 **Fax:** 14293910
Email: john@golfdigest.ie **Web site:** http://www.golfdigest.ie
ISSN: 1649-3524
Date Established: 2003; **Freq:** Monthly; **Cover Price:** EUR 6.50; **Circ:** 18,000
Usual Pagination: 128
Editor: John Shortt
Profile: Magazine covering golf news, tips and techniques, instruction from top players and equipment reviews. With exclusive tuition in every issue from Tiger Woods, Phil Mickelson and Butch Harmon plus others.
Readership: Aimed at Irish Golfers.
ADVERTISING RATES:
Full Page Colour .... EUR 2700
Agency Commission: 15%
Mechanical Data: Trim Size: 297 x 230mm, Col Length: 257mm, Film: Digital
Average ad content per issue: 25%
CONSUMER: SPORT: Golf

GOLF IRELAND-IRELANDS NATIONAL GOLF MAGAZINE
764215E75D-65
Formerly: Golf Ireland
Editorial: PO Box 8111, Swords, CO. DUBLIN
Tel: 1 80 78 122 **Fax:** 18078203
Email: greg.irishgolfer@gmail.com **Web site:** http://www.irishgolf.tv
Date Established: 1996; **Freq:** 6 issues yearly;
Cover Price: EUR 5.99
Free to qualifying individuals ; **Circ:** 40,000
Usual Pagination: 124
Editor: Gregory Francis; **Advertising Manager:** Jonathan Kyle
Profile: Magazine focusing on golf containing features on competitions, equipment and contributions from famous golfers from around the world.
Language(s): English; French; German; Spanish
Readership: Aimed at ABC1 golf enthusiasts.
ADVERTISING RATES:
Full Page Colour .... EUR 2600
Agency Commission: 15%
Mechanical Data: Page Width: 185mm, Bleed Size: 303 x 216mm, Type Area: 274 x 185mm, Film: Digital, Col Length: 274mm, Trim Size: 297 x 210mm
Average ad content per issue: 33%
Supplement(s): Corporate Golf - 2xY, Golf Travel Ireland - 3xY, Irish Golfer - 2xY
CONSUMER: SPORT: Golf

GOLF TRAVEL IRELAND
1658117E75D-68
Editorial: For all contact details see main record, Golf Ireland-Irelands National Golf Magazine
Freq: 3 issues yearly
Supplement to: Golf Ireland-Irelands National Golf Magazine
CONSUMER: SPORT: Golf

THE GOREY ECHO
1692656E72-4650_103
Editorial: Slaney Place, Enniscorthy, CO. WEXFORD 0
Freq: Weekly; **Cover Price:** EUR 1.70
Part of Series, see entry for: The Echo Series (Enniscorthy)
LOCAL NEWSPAPERS

GRASSROOTS
1826363E67B-57
Editorial: For all contact details see main record, Evening Echo
Freq: Weekly - Published on Wednesday
Supplement to: Evening Echo
REGIONAL DAILY & SUNDAY NEWSPAPERS: Regional Daily Newspapers

GUIDELINE
623490E32G-100
Editorial: Heywood Community School, Ballinakill, CO. LAOIS **Tel:** 57 87 3333 **Fax:** 578733314
Email: guideline@eircom.net **Web site:** http://www.igc.ie
Freq: 3 issues yearly; **Cover Price:** Free; **Circ:** 1,300
Usual Pagination: 32
Advertising Manager: Fred Tuite
Profile: Magazine issued by the Institute of Guidance Counsellors, covering all aspects of a counsellor's work.
Readership: Read by guidance counsellors.
ADVERTISING RATES:
Full Page Mono .... EUR 600
Full Page Colour .... EUR 600
Mechanical Data: Bleed Size: 303 x 216mm
Average ad content per issue: 20%
BUSINESS: LOCAL GOVERNMENT, LEISURE & RECREATION: Community Care & Social Services

HANDLING NETWORK
760344E10-55
Editorial: 63 Granitefield, Dun Laoghaire, CO. DUBLIN **Tel:** 1 285 4004 **Fax:** 12854784
Email: anselm@eircom.net **Web site:** http://www.handling-network.com
Date Established: 1999; **Freq:** 6 issues yearly;
Cover Price: EUR 4.95
Free to qualifying individuals
Annual Sub.: EUR 40; **Circ:** 4,000
Usual Pagination: 52
Editor: Anselm Aherne; **Advertising Manager:** John Mannion
Profile: Magazine focusing on handling, logistics and distribution.
Readership: Read by handling and distribution industry professionals, project and maintenance engineers, warehouse managers, purchasing managers and safety officers.
ADVERTISING RATES:
Full Page Colour .... EUR 1500
Agency Commission: 15%
Mechanical Data: Film: Digital, Col Length: 277mm, Col Widths (Display): 63.3mm, No. of Columns (Display): 3, Page Width: 190mm, Bleed Size: 303 x 213mm, Type Area: 277 x190mm, Trim Size: 297 x 210mm
Average ad content per issue: 33%
BUSINESS: MATERIALS HANDLING

HEALING & DEVELOPMENT
623539E87-47
Editorial: Rosemount, Rosemount Terrace, Booterstown, CO.DUBLIN **Tel:** 1 28 87 180
Fax: 12834626
Email: info@mmmworldwide.org **Web site:** http://www.mmmworldwide.org
ISSN: 1393-8967
Date Established: 1940; **Freq:** Annual - Published in early December; **Annual Sub.:** EUR 70; **Circ:** 10,000
Usual Pagination: 48
Editor: Isabelle Smyth
Profile: Magazine covering the work of the Medical Missionaries of Mary.
Readership: Read by the general public, medical professionals, teachers and students interested in issues of developing world, especially in healthcare.
CONSUMER: RELIGIOUS

HEALTH & LIVING
1740587E65A-84
Editorial: For all contact details see main record, Irish Independent
Freq: Weekly - Published on Monday
Supplement to: Irish Independent
NATIONAL DAILY & SUNDAY NEWSPAPERS: National Daily Newspapers

HEALTH & SAFETY REVIEW
623619E54B-90
Editorial: 121-123 Ranelagh, DUBLIN 6
Tel: 1 66 71 152 **Fax:** 14972779
Email: hsr@eircom.net **Web site:** http://www.healthandsafetyreview.ie
Date Established: 1992; **Freq:** Monthly; **Annual Sub.:** EUR 260; **Circ:** 1,700
Usual Pagination: 32
Editor: Herbert Mulligan
Profile: Magazine covering all aspects of health and safety.
Readership: Aimed at health and safety officers, managers and company directors.
BUSINESS: SAFETY & SECURITY: Safety

HEALTHPLUS SUPPLEMENT
1659441E65H-9
Formerly: Health Supplement
Editorial: For all contact details see main record, The Irish Times
Freq: Weekly
Supplement to: The Irish Times
NATIONAL DAILY & SUNDAY NEWSPAPERS: National Colour Supplements

HERALD EXTRA
1775045E72-8235
Editorial: For all contact details see main record, The Tuam Herald
Freq: Weekly
Supplement to: The Tuam Herald
LOCAL NEWSPAPERS

HISTORY IRELAND
623480E94X-30
Editorial: 6 Palmerston Place, DUBLIN 7
Tel: 87 68 89 412
Email: editor@historyireland.com **Web site:** http://www.historyireland.com
Date Established: 1993; **Freq:** 6 issues yearly - Last week of January, March, May, July, September and November; **Circ:** 5,000
Usual Pagination: 68
Editor: Tommy Graham; **Advertising Manager:** Nick Maxwel
Profile: Magazine covering Irish history featuring maps, paintings, engravings and photographs for each period, book reviews, events, letters, local history, articles relating to the history syllabi, North and South, and interviews with historians.
Language(s): English; Gaelic
Readership: Aimed at those with an interest in Irish history.
ADVERTISING RATES:
Full Page Mono .... EUR 1100
Full Page Colour .... EUR 1100
Mechanical Data: Bleed Size: 303 x 216mm, Film: Digital, Trim Size: 265 x 180mm
CONSUMER: OTHER CLASSIFICATIONS: Miscellaneous

HOGAN STAND
629607E75A-100
Editorial: Kells Business Park, Kells, CO. MEATH
Tel: 46 92 41 923 **Fax:** 469241926
Email: lynnpublications@eircom.net **Web site:** http://www.hoganstand.com
ISSN: 0791-7244
Freq: Monthly; **Cover Price:** EUR 3.75
Annual Sub.: EUR 76.20; **Circ:** 30,000
Usual Pagination: 100
Editor: John Lynch; **Advertising Manager:** Peter Lynch
Profile: Magazine covering Gaelic football and hurling.
Readership: Read by Gaelic football fans.
CONSUMER: SPORT

HOLLY BOUGH
1791191E80F-1
Editorial: City Quarter, Lapps Key, CORK
Tel: 21 42 72 722 **Fax:** 214802135
Email: john.dolan@eecho.ie **Web site:** http://www.eveningecho.ie
Freq: Annual - Published in November; **Circ:** 60,900
Advertising Manager: John Dolan
Profile: Magazine covering Christmas nostalgia, Cork people and places, short stories, poems, children's section and sport.
Readership: Aimed at residents and former residents of Cork.
CONSUMER: RURAL & REGIONAL INTEREST: Regional Interest Northern Ireland

HOME & FRONT
1799364E72-8236
Editorial: 25 Michael Street, WATERFORD
Freq: Monthly
Supplement to: Waterford News & Star
LOCAL NEWSPAPERS

HOSPITALITY IRELAND
1663373E11A-15
Editorial: Adelaide Hall, 3 Adelaide Street, Dun Laoghaire, CO DUBLIN **Tel:** 1 23 65 880
Fax: 12300325
Email: mark.kelly@hospitality-ireland.com **Web site:** http://www.hospitality-ireland.com
Date Established: 2003; **Freq:** 6 issues yearly;
Cover Price: EUR 4.95
Free to qualifying individuals
Annual Sub.: EUR 75; **Circ:** 6,000
Usual Pagination: 68
Publisher: Mark Kelly
Profile: Magazine for the Irish food service and on-trade drinks industry.
Readership: Aimed at purchasing managers within the hospitality sectors, e.g. hotels, restaurants, pubs and bars. Also circulated to purchasing managers in schools, colleges, universities, sporting and social clubs, hospitals and nursing homes.
ADVERTISING RATES:
Full Page Colour .... EUR 2895
Agency Commission: 10%
Mechanical Data: Trim Size: 287 x 200mm, Bleed Size: 305 x 218mm, Film: Digital
Average ad content per issue: 30%
BUSINESS: CATERING: Catering, Hotels & Restaurants

HOT PRESS
4381E76E-100

Editorial: 13 Trinity Street, DUBLIN 2
Tel: 1 24 11 500 **Fax:** 12411538
Email: info@hotpress.ie **Web site:** http://www.hotpress.com
ISSN: 0332-0847
Date Established: 1977; **Freq:** 26 issues yearly; **Cover Price:** EUR 3.50; **Circ:** 17,725
Usual Pagination: 92
Editor: Niall Stokes
Profile: Magazine featuring popular music, movies, current affairs, fashion, comedy, sport, sex and popular culture. Includes news, reviews and interviews.
Readership: Aimed at young people in Ireland.
ADVERTISING RATES:
Full Page Mono .... EUR 3300
Full Page Colour .... EUR 4500
Mechanical Data: Film: Digital
Supplement(s): Festival - Heineken Green Energy/ Oxegen - 1xY, Hot Press Annual - 1xY, Hot Press Fashion - 3xY, Hot Press Students - 1xY
CONSUMER: MUSIC & PERFORMING ARTS: Pop Music

HOT PRESS ANNUAL
1659146E76E-103

Editorial: For all contact details see main record, Hot Press
Freq: Annual
Supplement to: Hot Press
CONSUMER: MUSIC & PERFORMING ARTS: Pop Music

HOT PRESS FASHION
1659149E76E-102

Editorial: For all contact details see main record, Hot Press
Freq: 3 issues yearly
Supplement to: Hot Press
CONSUMER: MUSIC & PERFORMING ARTS: Pop Music

HOT PRESS STUDENTS
1659147E83-251

Editorial: For all contact details see main record, Hot Press
Freq: Annual - For circulation figure see main record
Supplement to: Hot Press
CONSUMER: STUDENT PUBLICATIONS

HOTEL & RESTAURANT TIMES
629609E11A-12

Editorial: H and R House, Carton Court, Maynooth, CO. KILDARE **Tel:** 1 62 85 447 **Fax:** 16285447
Email: info@hotelandrestauranttimes.ie **Web site:** http://www.hotelandrestauranttimes.ie
Date Established: 1998; **Freq:** 6 issues yearly; **Cover Price:** EUR 3.65
Free to qualifying individuals ; **Circ:** 4,200
Usual Pagination: 52
Editor: Cyril McAree
Profile: Magazine containing information about the hotel, restaurant and hospitality industry in Ireland.
Readership: Read by hoteliers, restaurateurs, caterers, interior designers and architects.
BUSINESS: CATERING: Catering, Hotels & Restaurants

HOUSE
1692643E74C-208

Editorial: 9 Sandyford Office Park, Sandyford, DUBLIN 18 **Tel:** 1 29 58 115 **Fax:** 12959350
Email: mail@architectureireland.ie **Web site:** http://www.housearchitecture.ie
Date Established: 2005; **Freq:** Half-yearly - Published in March and October; **Circ:** 16,000
Editor: Emma Cullinan
Profile: Magazine containing practical advice on how to work with an architect when considering renovations, extensions or new build with floor plans, project and product information and garden design.
Readership: Aimed at those looking to renovate or extend their existing property or considering building a new one.
ADVERTISING RATES:
Full Page Colour .... EUR 2785
Agency Commission: 10%
Mechanical Data: Trim Size: 305 x 230mm, Bleed Size: 315 x 240mm, Film: Digital
Average ad content per issue: 40%
CONSUMER: WOMEN'S INTEREST CONSUMER MAGAZINES: Home & Family

HOUSE & HOME
1799351E72-8237

Editorial: Tone Street, Ballina, CO. MAYO
Freq: Weekly
ADVERTISING RATES:
Full Page Colour .... EUR 1200
Supplement to: Western People
LOCAL NEWSPAPERS

HOUSE AND HOME
1775043E72-8238

Editorial: Unit 3, Hartley Business Park, Carrick-on-Shannon, CO. LEITRIM
Freq: Monthly
Supplement to: Leitrim Observer Series
LOCAL NEWSPAPERS

HOUSE AND HOME
622964E74C-40

Editorial: 1st Floor, Cunningham House, 130 Francis Street, DUBLIN 8 **Tel:** 1 41 67 900 **Fax:** 1 41 67 901
Email: dara@houseandhome.ie **Web site:** http://www.houseandhome.ie
ISSN: 1393-3043
Date Established: 1996; **Freq:** 6 issues yearly; **Cover Price:** EUR 3.95; **Circ:** 15,385
Usual Pagination: 164
Editor: Dara Flynn; **Advertising Manager:** Imelda Crombie
Profile: Magazine containing ideas and advice for redecorating and renovating house interiors and exteriors. Read predominantly by women aged between 24 and 58 years old. Twitter Handle: http://twitter.com/houseandhomemag Facebook: http://www.facebook.com/houseandhomemag First Published: 1996 Average Pages per Issue: 164.
Readership: Read predominantly by women aged between 24 and 58 years old.
ADVERTISING RATES:
Full Page Colour .... EUR 3000
Agency Commission: 10%
Mechanical Data: Bleed Size: 307 x 220mm, Trim Size: 297 x 210mm, Film: Digital
Average ad content per issue: 33%
CONSUMER: WOMEN'S INTEREST CONSUMER MAGAZINES: Home & Family

HOUSING TIMES
629627E4E-30

Editorial: Construction House, Canal Road, DUBLIN 6 **Tel:** 1491 5000 **Fax:** 1496 6548
Email: housingtimes@gmail.com **Web site:** http://www.homebond.ie
Date Established: 1997; **Freq:** 3 issues yearly - Published in February, June and October; **Cover Price:** Free; **Circ:** 16,000
Usual Pagination: 52
Editor: Donal Buckley
Profile: Magazine about the housing industry, advising house-builders and others involved in the industry of market trends, opportunities, building standards, best practices and trends in planning, design, construction and products.
Readership: Read by home-builders, architects, specifiers, auctioneers, mortgage providers as well as planners, public servants and public representatives.
ADVERTISING RATES:
Full Page Colour .... EUR 1900
Agency Commission: 15%
Mechanical Data: Type Area: 287 x 200mm, Bleed Size: +4mm, Col Length: 287mm, Page Width: 200mm, Film: Digital
Average ad content per issue: 20%
BUSINESS: ARCHITECTURE & BUILDING: Building

HRD IRELAND
4181E14F-10

Formerly: Arena
Editorial: 38 Chestnut Meadows, Glanmire, CORK
Tel: 21 48 23 346
Email: rosecomm@indigo.ie **Web site:** http://www.iitd.com
ISSN: 1649-1599
Date Established: 1969; **Freq:** Quarterly; Free to qualifying individuals
Annual Sub.: EUR 53.33; **Circ:** 2,500
Usual Pagination: 32
Editor: Mary-Rose O'Sullivan; **Advertising Manager:** Sinead Heneghan; **Publisher:** Sinead Henaghan
Profile: Journal providing training and staff development news in Ireland and Europe. Includes personality profiles, features, case studies, book and training materials reviews, information on courses and regular employment law and advice columns for trainers and HR specialists.
Readership: Aimed at human resources, training and development personnel.
ADVERTISING RATES:
Full Page Mono .... EUR 1000
Full Page Colour .... EUR 1500
Agency Commission: 15%
Mechanical Data: Trim Size: 297 x 210mm, Film: Digital
BUSINESS: COMMERCE, INDUSTRY & MANAGEMENT: Training & Recruitment

IBEC AGENDA
4175E14A-25

Formerly: IBEC Newsletter
Editorial: Confederation House, 84-86 Lower Baggot Street, DUBLIN 2 **Tel:** 1 60 51 500 **Fax:** 16381508
Email: agenda@ibec.ie **Web site:** http://www.ibec.ie
Freq: Monthly; Free to qualifying individuals ; **Circ:** 7,500
Usual Pagination: 8
Editor: Reetta Suonpera
Profile: Official journal of the Irish Business and Employers' Confederation.
Readership: Aimed at IBEC members.
BUSINESS: COMMERCE, INDUSTRY & MANAGEMENT

ICARUS
764246E83-50

Editorial: House 6, Trinity College, DUBLIN 2
Tel: 1 89 62 335
Email: icaruseditor@gmail.com
Freq: 3 issues yearly - Published in February, April and November; **Cover Price:** Free; **Circ:** 1,500
Advertising Manager: Dan Sheehan
Profile: Informative publication for students.
Readership: Aimed at students of Trinity College Dublin, all Dublin Institute of Technology campuses, National College of Art & Design, Galway University and the Queen's University in Belfast.
Copy instructions: *Copy Date:* 7 days prior to publication date
Average ad content per issue: 4%
CONSUMER: STUDENT PUBLICATIONS

IMAGE
4354E74A-60

Editorial: Crofton Hall, 22 Crofton Road, Dun Laoghaire, CO. DUBLIN **Tel:** 1 28 08 415
Fax: 12808309
Email: melanie.morris@image.ie **Web site:** http://www.image.ie
ISSN: 0791-7570
Date Established: 1975; **Freq:** Monthly - Double issue published in December/January; **Cover Price:** EUR 4.25
Annual Sub.: EUR 65; **Circ:** 19,005
Usual Pagination: 252
Profile: Magazine covering fashion, beauty, travel and interiors. Includes articles on the theatre, book reviews, eating out and entertainment.
Readership: Aimed at affluent women aged 25 years and over.
Agency Commission: 10%
Average ad content per issue: 40%
Supplement(s): Business - 1xY, parenting - 1xY, Wedding - 1xY
CONSUMER: WOMEN'S INTEREST CONSUMER MAGAZINES: Women's Interest

IMAGE INTERIORS
4359E74C-60

Editorial: Crofton Hall, 22 Crofton Road, Dun Laoghaire, CO. DUBLIN **Tel:** 1 28 08 415
Fax: 12808309
Email: hazel@image.ie **Web site:** http://www.image-interiors.ie
Freq: 6 issues yearly; **Cover Price:** EUR 4.25; **Circ:** 9,070
Editor: Amanda Cochrane; **Advertising Manager:** Nicola Burns-Kirley
Profile: Magazine covering all aspects of homes and interiors.
Readership: Read by men and women between 25 and 50 years old living in urban areas.
ADVERTISING RATES:
Full Page Colour .... EUR 3400
Agency Commission: 10%
Mechanical Data: Type Area: 271 x 195mm, Print Process: Web-fed litho, Bleed Size: 306 x 224mm, Trim Size: 297 x 218mm, Col Length: 271mm, Page Width: 195mm, Film: Positive, right reading, emulsion side down. Digital
Average ad content per issue: 40%
CONSUMER: WOMEN'S INTEREST CONSUMER MAGAZINES: Home & Family

IN DUBLIN
1645721E80A-102

Editorial: 3rd Floor, Arena House, Arena Road, Sandyford Industrial Estate, DUBLIN 18
Tel: 1 24 05 500 **Fax:** 12943303
Email: brendan@indublin.ie **Web site:** http://www.indublin.ie
Date Established: 2004; **Freq:** Daily; **Cover Price:** Free; **Circ:** 129,000 Unique Users
Profile: Website covering what to do and where to go including, pubs, clubs, restaurants and entertainment as well as a TV listings section.
Readership: Aimed at residents and visitors to Dublin.
CONSUMER: RURAL & REGIONAL INTEREST: Rural Interest

IN TOUCH
4255E62J-70

Editorial: 35 Parnell Square, DUBLIN 1
Tel: 1 80 47 700 **Fax:** 18722462
Email: editor@into.ie **Web site:** http://www.into.ie
ISSN: 1393-4813
Date Established: 1997; **Freq:** 6 issues yearly; Free to qualifying individuals
Annual Sub.: EUR 25; **Circ:** 33,500
Usual Pagination: 64
Editor: Lori Kealy
Profile: Official magazine of the Irish National Teachers' Organisation, covering education, tips for teachers and trade union news.
Language(s): English; Gaelic
Readership: Aimed at primary educators.
ADVERTISING RATES:
Full Page Mono .... EUR 1560
Full Page Colour .... EUR 2142
SCC .... EUR 58
Agency Commission: 15%
Mechanical Data: Col Length: 275.5mm, Type Area: 275.5 x 191mm, Bleed Size: +5mm, Trim Size: 297 x 210mm, Page Width: 191mm
BUSINESS: CHURCH & SCHOOL EQUIPMENT & EDUCATION: Teachers & Education Management

INDUSTRIAL RELATIONS NEWS
629630E14B-50

Editorial: 121-123 Ranelagh, DUBLIN 6
Tel: 1 49 72 711 **Fax:** 14972779
Email: bsheehan@irn.ie **Web site:** http://www.irn.ie
Freq: Weekly; **Annual Sub.:** EUR 635; **Circ:** 1,100
Usual Pagination: 24
Editor: Brian Sheehan; **Advertising Manager:** Julie Colby
Profile: Magazine covering all industrial relations issues.
Readership: Aimed at HR managers and trade union executives.
ADVERTISING RATES:
Full Page Mono .... EUR 650
Agency Commission: 15%
Mechanical Data: Trim Size: 297 x 210mm, Type Area: 277 x 190mm, Col Length: 277mm, Page Width: 190mm, Film: Digital
Average ad content per issue: 10%
BUSINESS: COMMERCE, INDUSTRY & MANAGEMENT: Industry & Factories

INIS
1660269E84B-53

Editorial: 17 North Great George St., DUBLIN 1
Tel: 1 87 27 475 **Fax:** 18727476
Email: info@childrensbooksireland.ie **Web site:** http://www.childrensbooksireland.ie
Freq: Quarterly
Free to qualifying individuals ; **Circ:** 1,500
Usual Pagination: 62
Profile: Magazine covering all issues related to children's books including reviews of new titles.
Readership: Aimed at parents, teachers, librarians, authors and anyone with an interest in children's books.
CONSUMER: THE ARTS & LITERARY: Literary

THE INISH TIMES
754448E72-4780

Editorial: 33 Upper Main Street, Buncrana, Inishowen, CO. DONEGAL **Tel:** 74 93 41 055
Fax: 749341059
Email: info@inishtimes.com **Web site:** http://www.inishtimes.com
Date Established: 1999; **Freq:** Weekly; **Cover Price:** EUR 1.30; **Circ:** 5,269
Editor: John Gill
ADVERTISING RATES:
Full Page Mono .... EUR 1300
Full Page Colour .... EUR 1600
Agency Commission: 10%
Mechanical Data: Type Area: 335 x 260mm, Col Length: 335mm, Page Width: 260mm, No. of Columns (Display): 8, Col Widths (Display): 30mm, Film: Digital
LOCAL NEWSPAPERS

INITIATIVE (SME BUSINESS)
1666394E65H-26

Editorial: For all contact details see main record, Irish Independent
Freq: Monthly
Supplement to: Irish Independent
NATIONAL DAILY & SUNDAY NEWSPAPERS: National Colour Supplements

INNOVATION
1901982E65A-85

Editorial: The Irish Times Building, PO Box 74, 24-28 Tara Street, DUBLIN 2 **Tel:** 1 67 58 221
Email: mmcaleer@irishtimes.co.uk **Web site:** http://www.irishtimes.com/innovation
Freq: Monthly
Editor: Michael McAleer
Profile: Business magazine focusing on economics, green issues, profiles of leading members of the business community.
Supplement to: The Irish Times
NATIONAL DAILY & SUNDAY NEWSPAPERS: National Daily Newspapers

INSIDE GOVERNMENT
1780935E32R-81

Editorial: 19 Irishtown Road, DUBLIN 4
Tel: 1 23 13 593 **Fax:** 1 66 77 752
Email: ingov@eircom.net **Web site:** http://www.insidegovernment.ie
Date Established: 2003; **Freq:** 6 issues yearly; Free to qualifying individuals ; **Circ:** 5,200
Usual Pagination: 100
Editor: Joe Murphy; **Advertising Manager:** Joe Murphy
Profile: Publication about best practice and better management within the public sector.
Readership: Aimed at the public sector including government departments, healthcare and state agencies, local government, uniformed services and elected representatives.
ADVERTISING RATES:
Full Page Colour .... EUR 4290.00
Agency Commission: 10%
Mechanical Data: Type Area: 283 x 196mm, Bleed Size: 303 x 215mm, Col Length: 283mm, Page Width: 196mm, Print Process: Offset litho, Film: Digital
Copy instructions: *Copy Date:* 1 week prior to publication date
Average ad content per issue: 20%
BUSINESS: LOCAL GOVERNMENT, LEISURE & RECREATION: Local Government Related

INSIDE IRELAND INFORMATION SERVICE AND BI-MONTHLY E-NEWSLETTER
623575E73-60

Formerly: Inside Ireland Information Service and Quarterly Review
Editorial: PO Box 1886, DUBLIN 16 **Tel:** 1 49 31 359
Fax: 14934538
Email: insideireland@eircom.net **Web site:** http://www.insideireland.com
ISSN: 0332-2483

Date Established: 1978; **Freq:** 6 times a year; **Annual Sub.:** EUR 10; **Circ:** 2,000 Unique Users
Editor: Brenda Weir
Profile: Newsletter and information service containing information and articles about life and culture in Ireland past and present. Focuses on citizenship, retirement, folklore, real estate, genealogy, music, current affairs and culture, as well as covering financial and historical issues.
Readership: Aimed primarily at residents of the USA interested in Irish culture and those living abroad wishing to retire in Ireland.
CONSUMER: NATIONAL & INTERNATIONAL PERIODICALS

INSIDE MAGAZINE
1808572E4B-1
Editorial: 324 Clontarf Road, Clontarf, DUBLIN 3 **Tel:** 1 85 33 620
Email: interiorsassocmag@gmail.com
Date Established: 2006; **Freq:** 6 issues yearly; **Cover Price:** Free; **Circ:** 5,500
Usual Pagination: 100
Editor: Shane McGinley; **Advertising Manager:** Gary Mulhall; **Publisher:** Gary Mulhall
Profile: Official magazine of the Interiors Association containing features, news and advice from around the world about interior design.
Readership: Aimed at Irish interior designers.
ADVERTISING RATES:
Full Page Colour .... EUR 2895.00
Agency Commission: 15%
Mechanical Data: Bleed Size: 307 x 220mm, Trim Size: 297 x 210mm, Film: Digital
Copy instructions: *Copy Date:* 10 working days prior to publication date
Average ad content per issue: 40%
BUSINESS: ARCHITECTURE & BUILDING: Interior Design & Flooring

INSIDE SPORT
1659437E65H-29
Editorial: For all contact details see main record, The Irish Daily Star
Freq: Weekly
Supplement to: The Irish Daily Star
NATIONAL DAILY & SUNDAY NEWSPAPERS: National Colour Supplements

INSPIRE
1804086E74Q-154
Editorial: Meath Chronicle, Market Square, Navan, CO. MEATH **Tel:** 46 90 79 600 **Fax:** 46 90 23 565
Email: inspire@meathchronicle.ie
Date Established: 2007; **Freq:** Monthly - See main record for circulation figure
Editor: Meghan Smith
Profile: Lifestyle magazine with coverage of local events and personalities including features on restaurants, wine, fashion, beauty, health, motoring, travel, interiors and gardening.
ADVERTISING RATES:
Full Page Colour .... EUR 1500.00
Mechanical Data: Bleed Size: 342 x 266mm, Trim Size: 322 x 246mm, Film: Digital
Supplement to: The Meath Chronicle
CONSUMER: WOMEN'S INTEREST CONSUMER MAGAZINES: Lifestyle

INTERCOM
623540E87-49
Editorial: Catholic Communications Office, Columba Centre, Maynooth, CO KILDARE **Tel:** 1 50 53 000 **Fax:** 16016413
Email: fcousins@catholicbishops.ie **Web site:** http://www.veritas.ie
Date Established: 1970; **Freq:** Monthly; **Annual Sub.:** EUR 46; **Circ:** 6,000
Usual Pagination: 52
Editor: Francis Cousins
Profile: Magazine covering pastoral and liturgical resources.
Readership: Aimed at those in the Roman Catholic ministry.
ADVERTISING RATES:
Full Page Mono .... EUR 575
Full Page Colour .... EUR 875
Mechanical Data: Type Area: 271 x 181mm, Col Length: 271mm, Page Width: 181mm, Trim Size: 297 x 210mm, No. of Columns (Display): 2, Col Widths (Display): 57mm
Average ad content per issue: 15%
CONSUMER: RELIGIOUS

INTERMEZZO
1749827E89A-202
Editorial: 7 Cranford Centre, Montrose, DUBLIN 4 **Tel:** 1 26 01 114 **Fax:** 1 26 00 911
Email: intermezzoireland@gmail.com **Web site:** http://www.intermezzo.ie
Date Established: 2006; **Freq:** Quarterly; **Cover Price:** EUR 4.95; **Circ:** 12,000
Usual Pagination: 112
Editor: Kevin McParland; **Publisher:** Kevin McParland
Profile: Magazine covering food, wines, travel and life experiences.
Readership: Aimed at active, affluent food, wine and travel lovers aged 30 to 55 with a high disposable income.
ADVERTISING RATES:
Full Page Colour .... EUR 2895.00
SCC .... EUR 65.00
Agency Commission: 15%
Mechanical Data: Type Area: 244 x 175mm, Bleed Size: 278 x 203mm, Trim Size: 268 x 200mm, Col Length: 244mm, Page Width: 175mm, Film: Digital
Copy instructions: *Copy Date:* 2 weeks prior to publication date
Average ad content per issue: 20%
CONSUMER: HOLIDAYS & TRAVEL: Travel

INTERNATIONAL LIVING
1708236E74K-104
Editorial: Elysium House, Ballytruckle Road, WATERFORD **Tel:** 51 30 45 61
Email: editor@internationalliving.com **Web site:** http://www.internationalliving.com
Date Established: 1980; **Freq:** Monthly; **Annual Sub.:** $49.00; **Circ:** 55,000
Usual Pagination: 48
Editor: Laura Sheridan; **Advertising Manager:** Licinda Mytych; **Managing Editor:** Laura Sheridan
Profile: Magazine covering investment, lifestyle, real-estate and general information on buying property worldwide outside the USA and the cost of living and healthcare. Also includes practical information on living overseas.
Readership: Aimed at Americans looking to buy property or start a new life outside the United States of America.
CONSUMER: WOMEN'S INTEREST CONSUMER MAGAZINES: Home Purchase

INVESCO REVIEW OF PENSIONS
1667890E14A-27
Editorial: For all contact details see main record, Decision
Freq: Annual
Supplement to: Decision
BUSINESS: COMMERCE, INDUSTRY & MANAGEMENT

IPU REVIEW
4212E37-20
Editorial: Butterfield House, Butterfield Avenue, Rathfarnham, DUBLIN 14 **Tel:** 1 49 36 401 **Fax:** 14936626
Email: ipurev@ipu.ie **Web site:** http://www.ipu.ie
Date Established: 1976; **Freq:** Monthly; Free to qualifying individuals ; **Circ:** 2,650
Usual Pagination: 56
Editor: Marie Hogan; **Advertising Manager:** Janice Burke
Profile: Pharmacy magazine providing news and views for those working in the pharmaceutical profession. Highlights both professional and scientific matters relevant to pharmacy.
Readership: Read by pharmacists and those engaged in the pharmaceutical industry.
ADVERTISING RATES:
Full Page Mono .... EUR 900
Full Page Colour .... EUR 1200
Mechanical Data: Type Area: 273 x 185mm, Trim Size: 297 x 210mm, Bleed Size: 307 x 215mm, Film: Positive, right reading, emulsion side down. Digital, Col Length: 273mm, Page Width: 185mm
BUSINESS: PHARMACEUTICAL & CHEMISTS

IRELAND AFLOAT MAGAZINE
4401E91A-100
Formerly: Afloat
Editorial: 2 Lower Glenageary Road, Dun Laoghaire, CO. DUBLIN **Tel:** 1 28 46 161 **Fax:** 12846192
Email: info@afloat.ie **Web site:** http://www.afloat.ie
Date Established: 1952; **Freq:** 6 issues yearly
Annual Sub.: EUR 50; **Circ:** 8,000
Usual Pagination: 104
Editor: David O'Brien; **Advertising Manager:** Angela Bolton
Profile: Magazine about boating and yachting. Twitter: http://twitter.com/Afloatmagazine. Facebook: http://www.facebook.com/AfloatMagazine. Vimeo: http://vimeo.com/afloatmagazine. YouTube: :// www.youtube.com/afloatmagazine.
Readership: Aimed at water sports enthusiasts.
ADVERTISING RATES:
Full Page Colour .... EUR 2200
Agency Commission: 10%
Mechanical Data: Type Area: 250 x 180mm, Col Length: 250mm, Page Width: 180mm, Trim Size: 297 x 210mm, Bleed Size: 302 x 215mm, Film: Digital
Copy instructions: *Copy Date:* 14 days prior to publication date
Average ad content per issue: 30%
CONSUMER: RECREATION & LEISURE: Boating & Yachting

IRELAND OF THE WELCOMES
4398E89A-50
Editorial: Rosemount House, Dundrum Road, Dundrum, DUBLIN 14 **Tel:** 1 240 5300 **Fax:** 1 661 9486
Email: rhannaford@harmonia.ie
ISSN: 0021-0943
Date Established: 1952; **Freq:** 6 issues yearly; **Cover Price:** EUR 3.50; **Circ:** 38,138
Usual Pagination: 68
Editor: Richard Hannaford
Profile: Magazine celebrating the history, culture and lifestyle of Ireland.
Readership: Aimed at people with an interest in Ireland.
ADVERTISING RATES:
Full Page Colour .... EUR 3200
Mechanical Data: Bleed Size: 282 x 216mm, Film: Digital, Type Area: 256 x 190mm, Col Length: 256mm, Page Width: 190mm, Trim Size: 276 x 210mm
CONSUMER: HOLIDAYS & TRAVEL: Travel

IRELANDHOTELS.COM
628783E89B-20
Formerly: Be Our Guest
Editorial: 13 Northbrook Road, Ranelagh, DUBLIN 6 **Tel:** 1 49 76 459 **Fax:** 1 49 74 613
Email: info@ihf.ie **Web site:** http://www.ihf.ie
Circ: 350,000 Unique Users
Usual Pagination: 500
Editor: Miriam Young; **Advertising Manager:** Ronan Smyth
Profile: Magazine covering all aspects of the tourist trade in Eire, with special focus on hotels.
Readership: Aimed at tourists, travel agents and those seeking accommodation in Ireland.
CONSUMER: HOLIDAYS & TRAVEL: Hotel Magazines

IRELAND'S EYE
623507E73-70
Editorial: 6 Dominick Street, Mullingar, CO. WESTMEATH **Tel:** 44 93 48 868 **Fax:** 449343777
Email: topicadmin@eircom.net
ISSN: 0443-9056
Freq: Monthly; **Cover Price:** EUR 1.80
Annual Sub.: EUR 40; **Circ:** 25,000
Usual Pagination: 52
Editor: Tom Kiernan; **Advertising Manager:** Tom Kiernan
Profile: Magazine containing general interest articles and information, with particular emphasis on Irish culture. Includes letters, national news and features on local history.
Readership: Aimed at people of all age groups with an interest in Irish culture.
CONSUMER: NATIONAL & INTERNATIONAL PERIODICALS

IRELAND'S HORSE & PONY MAGAZINE
1752606E81D-101
Editorial: Agher, Summerhill, CO. MEATH **Tel:** 46 95 58 666 **Fax:** 469558667
Email: irelandshorseandpony@eircom.net
Freq: Monthly; **Circ:** 12,000
Usual Pagination: 68
Editor: Phil McGinley
Profile: Magazine covering all aspects of equestrian sport in Ireland.
Readership: Aimed at all those involved in equestrian sport from children and pony clubs to international riders.
ADVERTISING RATES:
Full Page Colour .... EUR 1600
Agency Commission: 15%
Mechanical Data: Trim Size: 297 x 210mm, Film: Digital
Average ad content per issue: 40%
CONSUMER: ANIMALS & PETS: Horses & Ponies

IRELAND'S HORSE REVIEW
623559E81D-100
Editorial: Garden Street, Ballina, CO. MAYO **Tel:** 96 73 500 **Fax:** 96 72 077
Email: horserev@iol.ie **Web site:** http://www.irelands-horsereview.com
Freq: Monthly; **Cover Price:** £1.95
Free to qualifying individuals ; **Circ:** 30,000
Editor: Liam Geddes; **Managing Director:** Liam Geddes; **Advertising Manager:** Deirdre Geddes
Profile: Magazine containing news from sports horses in Ireland and around the world, including dressage, showjumping, ponies, endurance and classifieds.
Readership: Aimed at those interested in equestrian sports.
ADVERTISING RATES:
Full Page Mono .... EUR 2400.00
Full Page Colour .... EUR 2460.00
Agency Commission: 15%
Mechanical Data: Type Area: 500 x 353mm
Copy instructions: *Copy Date:* 18th of the month prior to publication date
CONSUMER: ANIMALS & PETS: Horses & Ponies

IRELAND'S OWN
4349E73-80
Editorial: Channing House, Rowe Street, Wexford, CO. WEXFORD **Tel:** 53 91 40 100 **Fax:** 539140192
Email: irelands.own@peoplenews.ie **Web site:** http://www.finnvalley.ie/irelandsown
Date Established: 1902; **Freq:** Weekly; **Cover Price:** EUR 1.25
Annual Sub.: EUR 100; **Circ:** 39,574
Usual Pagination: 64
Editor: Sean Nolan
Profile: Magazine including short stories, historical articles, memory pieces, serials, a children's section, pen-pals and song lyrics.
Readership: Aimed at families.
ADVERTISING RATES:
Full Page Mono .... EUR 450
Full Page Colour .... EUR 600
Agency Commission: 15%
Mechanical Data: No. of Columns (Display): 4, Col Length: 235mm, Page Width: 175mm, Col Widths (Display): 40mm, Type Area: 235 x 175mm
CONSUMER: NATIONAL & INTERNATIONAL PERIODICALS

IRISH ANGLER
1660661E92-
Editorial: IPI Centre, Breaffy Road, Castlebar, CO. MAYO **Tel:** 94 90 27 656 **Fax:** 949027861
Email: irishanglereditor@eircom.net **Web site:** http://www.irishangler.ie
Date Established: 2004; **Freq:** Monthly; **Cover Price:** EUR 4.95; **Circ:** 6,000
Usual Pagination: 100
Editor: David Dinsmore; **Advertising Manager:** Michael Shanks
Profile: Magazine with instruction, stories and tackle reviews covering all forms of fishing. 50 per cent game fishing, 30 per cent sea fishing, 20 per cent coarse fishing to reflect angling trends in Ireland.
Readership: Aimed at fly, sea and coarse anglers in Ireland.
Average ad content per issue: 30%
CONSUMER: ANGLING & FISHING

IRISH ARTS REVIEW
628764E84A-300
Editorial: State Apartments, Dublin Castle, DUBLIN 2 **Tel:** 1 67 93 525 **Fax:** 1 63 34 417
Email: editorial@irishartsreview.com **Web site:** http://www.irishartsreview.com
ISSN: 1649-217X
Date Established: 1984; **Freq:** Quarterly; **Annual Sub.:** EUR 56.00; **Circ:** 11,039
Usual Pagination: 150
Editor: John Mulcahy; **Advertising Manager:** Yvonne Smalley; **Publisher:** Sonya Perkins
Profile: Journal on arts in Ireland, features painting, sculpture, architecture and decorative arts.
Readership: Aimed at people interested in art throughout Ireland.
ADVERTISING RATES:
Full Page Colour .... EUR 4000.00
Agency Commission: 15%
Mechanical Data: Type Area: 265 x 205mm, Bleed Size: 310 x 240mm, Trim Size: 300 x 230mm, Film: Digital, Page Width: 205mm, Col Length: 265mm
Copy instructions: *Copy Date:* 4 weeks prior to publication date
Average ad content per issue: 30%
Supplement(s): Price Guide to Irish Art - 1xY
CONSUMER: THE ARTS & LITERARY: Arts

THE IRISH BEEKEEPER (AN BEACHAIRE)
4197E21R-50
Editorial: Innisfail, Kickham Street, Thurles, CO. TIPPERARY **Tel:** 504 22 228
Email: jimbee@indigo.ie **Web site:** http://www.irishbeekeeping.ie
Date Established: 1947; **Freq:** Monthly; **Annual Sub.:** EUR 20; **Circ:** 1,500
Usual Pagination: 24
Editor: Jim Ryan
Profile: Official journal of the Federation of Irish Beekeepers.
Readership: Aimed at beekeepers in the Irish Republic.
BUSINESS: AGRICULTURE & FARMING: Agriculture & Farming Related

IRISH BODYSHOP JOURNAL
1667969E31R-1
Editorial: Glencree House, Lanesborough Road, ROSCOMMON TOWN **Tel:** 90 66 25 676 **Fax:** 906637410
Email: info@autopub.ie **Web site:** http://www.bodyshop.ie
Date Established: 2005; **Freq:** 6 issues yearly; Free to qualifying individuals
Annual Sub.: EUR 36; **Circ:** 7,600
Usual Pagination: 96
Editor: John Loughran; **Managing Editor:** Padraic Deane
Profile: Magazine covering news and features for the Irish auto bodyshop and refinishing industry.
Readership: Aimed at auto bodyshops, motor factors and all other related industries throughout Ireland.
ADVERTISING RATES:
Full Page Colour .... EUR 1600
Agency Commission: 15%
Mechanical Data: Type Area: 270 x 185mm, Bleed Size: 303 x 216mm, Trim Size: 297 x 210mm, Col Length: 270mm, Page Width: 185mm, No. of Columns (Display): 4, Film: Digital
Average ad content per issue: 30%
BUSINESS: MOTOR TRADE: Motor Trade Related

IRISH BRIDES MAGAZINE
4364E74L-50
Formerly: Irish Brides & Homes Magazine
Editorial: Crannagh House, 198 Rathfarnham Road, DUBLIN 14 **Tel:** 1 49 00 550 **Fax:** 14906763
Email: info@irishbrides.ie **Web site:** http://www.irishbrides.ie
ISSN: 0791-7694
Date Established: 1983; **Freq:** Quarterly; **Circ:** 5,809
Usual Pagination: 184
Editor: Emer McCarthy; **Publisher:** Mary McCarthy
Profile: Magazine for the modern Irish bride-to-be. Includes tips on fashion, beauty, practical advice on co-ordinating your wedding, reception and honeymoon ideas, the newest designer bridal gowns and accessories, as well as useful and up-to-date information on anything new in the bridal industry. Also features gift list and interiors ideas for your home.
Readership: Aimed at people planning a wedding.
ADVERTISING RATES:
Full Page Colour .... EUR 1500
Agency Commission: 15%

Mechanical Data: Col Length: 270mm, Page Width: 183mm, Type Area: 270 x 183mm, Bleed Size: 306 x 216mm, Trim Size: 297 x 210mm
CONSUMER: WOMEN'S INTEREST CONSUMER MAGAZINES: Brides

IRISH BROKER 1628223E1D-1
Editorial: 136 Baldoyle Industrial Estate, DUBLIN 13 **Tel:** 1 83 95 060 **Fax:** 18395062
Email: paul@irishbroker.ie
Date Established: 1984; **Freq:** Monthly; **Cover Price:** Free; **Circ:** 5,500
Editor: Paul Gibson
Profile: Magazine covering the insurance industry including life insurance, pensions and mortgages.
Readership: Aimed at brokers and investment companies.
BUSINESS: FINANCE & ECONOMICS: Insurance

IRISH BUILDING MAGAZINE 4160E4E-35
Editorial: 1 Windsor Mews, Summerhill Parade, Sandycove, CO. DUBLIN **Tel:** 1 44 29 264 **Fax:** 12846328
Email: info@irishbuildingmagazine.ie **Web site:** http://www.irishbuildingmagazine.ie
Date Established: 1982; **Freq:** 6 issues yearly; **Annual Sub.:** EUR 65; **Circ:** 4,500
Usual Pagination: 68
Editor: Noelette Walsh; **Managing Director:** Colin Walsh
Profile: Magazine covering business to business in the Irish construction industry.
Readership: Aimed at architects, consultants, consulting engineers, contractors, local authorities and corporations, quantity surveyors, property developers, clients, financial groups and government agencies.
ADVERTISING RATES:
Full Page Colour .... EUR 3595
Agency Commission: 10%
Mechanical Data: Film: Digital, Trim Size: 330 x 240mm, Bleed Size: 5mm
Average ad content per issue: 35%
BUSINESS: ARCHITECTURE & BUILDING: Building

IRISH CAR AND TRAVEL 623529E77A-85
Formerly: Irish Car Incorporating Irish 4 by 4 & Off Road
Editorial: 2 Sunbury, Kilcullen, CO. KILDARE **Tel:** 45 48 10 90
Email: irishcar@gmail.com **Web site:** http://www.irishcarnews.ie
ISSN: 0791-4792
Date Established: 1990; **Freq:** 6 issues yearly; **Cover Price:** EUR 3.20; **Circ:** 8,000
Usual Pagination: 54
Managing Editor: Brian Byrne
Profile: Magazine focusing on cars and travel, containing information about new models and comparisons as well as drives, destinations and travel tips.
Readership: Read by people considering purchasing a new car and by those with interests in travelling.
CONSUMER: MOTORING & CYCLING: Motoring

THE IRISH CATHOLIC 4395E87-50
Editorial: The Irish Farm Centre, Bluebell, DUBLIN 12 **Tel:** 1 42 76 400 **Fax:** 14276450
Email: news@irishcatholic.ie **Web site:** http://www.irishcatholic.ie
Date Established: 1888; **Freq:** Weekly - Published on Thursday; **Cover Price:** EUR 0.90; **Circ:** 27,000
Usual Pagination: 32
Editor: Garry O'Sullivan; **Features Editor:** Paul Keenan; **Advertising Manager:** Gerard Crowley
Profile: Weekly religious newspaper specialising in news, comment and analysis on events both inside and outside the Catholic Church.
Readership: Aimed at young Catholic families.
ADVERTISING RATES:
Full Page Mono .... EUR 2000
Full Page Colour .... EUR 2400
Agency Commission: 15%
Mechanical Data: Type Area: 350 x 265mm, Col Length: 350mm, Print Process: Web-fed offset litho, No. of Columns (Display): 6, Page Width: 265mm
CONSUMER: RELIGIOUS

IRISH COMPUTER 4163E5B-10
Editorial: Media House, South County Business Park, Leopardstown, DUBLIN 18 **Tel:** 1 29 47 772 **Fax:** 12947799
Email: cliff.hutton@mediateam.ie **Web site:** http://www.techcentral.ie
ISSN: 0342-0197
Date Established: 1977; **Freq:** Monthly - Published around the 2nd week of the month; **Cover Price:** £4.50; **Circ:** 4,000
Usual Pagination: 48
Editor: Cliff Hutton; **Publisher:** John McDonald
Profile: Journal containing news and information on the computer and communications industries.
Readership: Aimed at managers and IT professionals.
ADVERTISING RATES:
Full Page Colour .... EUR 3200
Agency Commission: 15%
Mechanical Data: Type Area: 272 x 184mm, Film: Positive, right reading, emulsion side down. Digital, Col Length: 272mm, Bleed Size: 303 x 216mm, Trim Size: 297 x 210mm, Page Width: 184mm
BUSINESS: COMPUTERS & AUTOMATION: Data Processing

IRISH CONSTRUCTION INDUSTRY MAGAZINE 4219E42A-60
Editorial: Quantum House, Temple Road, Blackrock, CO. DUBLIN **Tel:** 1 28 33 233 **Fax:** 12833254
Email: colin@irishconstruction.com **Web site:** http://www.irishconstruction.com
Date Established: 1990; **Freq:** Monthly - Published around the 1st week of the cover month; **Circ:** 3,374
Usual Pagination: 96
Group Editor: Denise Maguire; **Publisher:** Tony Cantwell
Profile: Magazine covering all aspects of the Irish construction industry.
Readership: Aimed at construction industry professionals.
ADVERTISING RATES:
Full Page Colour .... EUR 900
Agency Commission: 10%
Mechanical Data: Print Process: Sheet-fed offset litho, Type Area: 277 x 190mm, Film: Digital, Bleed Size: 304 x 218mm, Trim Size: 297 x 210mm, Col Length: 277mm, Page Width: 190mm
Copy instructions: *Copy Date:* 14 days prior to publication date
Average ad content per issue: 40%
BUSINESS: CONSTRUCTION

IRISH CURRENT LAW MONTHLY DIGEST 1667159E44-79
Editorial: 43 Fitzwilliam Place, DUBLIN 2 **Tel:** 1 60 24 808 **Fax:** 16625302
Email: pamela.morin@thomsonreuters.com **Web site:** http://www.roundhall.ie
ISSN: 1357-2679
Freq: Monthly; **Annual Sub.:** EUR 905.73
Usual Pagination: 90
Editor: Stephen Lucek
Profile: Journal covering all recent Irish legal developments.
Readership: Aimed at legal practitioners.
BUSINESS: LEGAL

IRISH CYCLING REVIEW 1660500E77C-1
Editorial: PO Box 7992, Dun Laoghaire, CO. DUBLIN **Tel:** 1 28 40 137 **Fax:** 1 28 40 137
Email: quinnfr@eircom.net
ISSN: 0790-0600
Freq: Quarterly; **Cover Price:** EUR 2.95; **Circ:** 10,000
Usual Pagination: 32
Editor: Frank Quinn; **Advertising Manager:** Frank Quinn; **Publisher:** Frank Quinn
Profile: Magazine covering Irish cycling and international events.
Readership: Aimed at cycling enthusiasts.
ADVERTISING RATES:
Full Page Mono £1400.00
Full Page Colour £1600.00
Agency Commission: 10%
Mechanical Data: Type Area: 268 x 184mm, Bleed Size: 303 x 218mm, Trim Size: 300 x 215mm, Col Length: 268mm, Page Width: 184mm, Film: Digital
Copy instructions: *Copy Date:* 2 weeks prior to publication date
Average ad content per issue: 25%
CONSUMER: MOTORING & CYCLING: Cycling

IRISH DAILY MAIL 1739542E65A-83
Editorial: 3rd Floor Embassy House, Herbert Park Lane, Ballsbridge, DUBLIN 4 **Tel:** 1 63 75 800 **Fax:** 16375920
Email: news@dailymail.ie
Freq: Daily - Irish Republic; **Circ:** 60,630
Editor: Ronan O'Reilly; **Features Editor:** Regina Lavelle
Profile: Irish edition of the Daily Mail tabloid newspaper, covering national and international news, features, travel, finance, sport, women's interest, entertainment and health. The Irish Daily Mail is published by Associated Newspapers. The paper was launched in February 2006.
ADVERTISING RATES:
Full Page Mono .... EUR 11550
Full Page Colour .... EUR 15960
Agency Commission: 15%
Copy instructions: *Copy Date:* 1 day prior to publication date
Average ad content per issue: 35%
NATIONAL DAILY & SUNDAY NEWSPAPERS: National Daily Newspapers

THE IRISH DAILY MIRROR 764348E65A-20
Formerly: The Irish Mirror
Editorial: Floor 4, Park House, 191-197 North Circular Road, DUBLIN 7 **Tel:** 1 86 88 600 **Fax:** 18688626
Email: news@irishmirror.ie
Freq: Daily - Irish Republic
Editor: Niall Moonan; **Features Editor:** Maeve Quigley; **Editor-in-Chief:** John Kierans
Profile: Irish edition of the Daily Mirror newspaper covering national and international news, sport, celebs and showbiz, culture and entertainment, with supplements featuring health, beauty, fashion and style and Irish football. Targets readers interested in politics, life features and sport.
ADVERTISING RATES:
Full Page Mono .... EUR 6664
Full Page Colour .... EUR 8925
SCC .... EUR 37.50
Agency Commission: 10%
Mechanical Data: Type Area: 341 x 265mm, Col Length: 265mm, No. of Columns (Display): 8, Col Widths (Display): 35mm, Page Width: 265mm, Film: Digital
NATIONAL DAILY & SUNDAY NEWSPAPERS: National Daily Newspapers

THE IRISH DAILY STAR 4261E65A-80
Formerly: Star
Editorial: Star House, 62A Terenure Road North, DUBLIN 6 **Tel:** 1 49 01 228 **Fax:** 14902193
Email: news@thestar.ie **Web site:** http://www.thestar.ie
Date Established: 1988; **Freq:** Daily - Irish Republic; **Cover Price:** EUR 1.40; **Circ:** 107,035
Editor: News Desk; **Features Editor:** Moira Hannon; **Managing Director:** Paul Cooke
Profile: The Irish Daily Star is a tabloid-sized newspaper with the crime and sensational coverage, focusing on celebrity matters, gossip and sports. Published in Ireland by the Independent Star Limited, being the Irish version of the UK tabloid Daily Star. It was first published on 29 February 1988.
ADVERTISING RATES:
Full Page Mono .... EUR 17690
SCC .... EUR 73.15
Mechanical Data: Type Area: 333 x 267mm, Col Length: 333mm, Col Widths (Display): 36mm, No. of Columns (Display): 7, Page Width: 267mm
Editions:
The Irish Daily Star (Northern Ireland Edition)
Supplement(s): Chic Magazine - 52xY, Inside Sport - 52xY, On Target - 52xY, Star Woman - 52xY, Weekend - 52xY
NATIONAL DAILY & SUNDAY NEWSPAPERS: National Daily Newspapers

THE IRISH DAILY STAR (NORTHERN IRELAND EDITION) 1693004E65A-80_500
Editorial: Star House, 62A Terenure Road North, DUBLIN 6
Freq: Daily
Edition of: The Irish Daily Star
NATIONAL DAILY & SUNDAY NEWSPAPERS: National Daily Newspapers

IRISH DIRECTOR 1976871E14A-29
Editorial: Top Floor, Block 43B, Yeats Way, Park West Business Park, Nangor Road, DUBLIN 12 **Tel:** 1 625 1480 **Fax:** 16251402
Email: id@businessandleadership.com **Web site:** http://www.irishdirector.ie
Freq: Quarterly; **Circ:** 5,132
Editor: Ann O'Dea
ADVERTISING RATES:
Full Page Colour .... EUR 3000
BUSINESS: COMMERCE, INDUSTRY & MANAGEMENT

IRISH EMIGRANT 629642E94D-100
Editorial: Unit 4, Campus Innovation Centre, Upper Newcastle Road, GALWAY **Tel:** 9 15 69 158
Email: info@emigrant.ie **Web site:** http://www.emigrant.ie
Date Established: 1987; **Freq:** Daily; **Cover Price:** Free; **Circ:** 150,000 Unique Users
Editor: Liam Ferrie
Profile: Website focusing on news and information of Irish interest.
Readership: Aimed at Irish people and people of Irish descent living overseas.
CONSUMER: OTHER CLASSIFICATIONS: Expatriates

THE IRISH EXAMINER 4273E65A-8
Formerly: The Examiner
Editorial: 4th Floor, City Quarter, Lapps Quay, CORK **Tel:** 21 42 72 722 **Fax:** 21 42 75 477
Email: news@examiner.ie **Web site:** http://www.irishexaminer.com
Date Established: 1841; **Freq:** Daily; **Cover Price:** EUR 1.80; **Circ:** 46,011
Editor: John O'Mahony; **Executive Editor:** Dolan O'Hagan; **Features Editor:** Vickie Maye
Profile: Broadsheet sized newspaper covering national and international news and current affairs, business, finance, politics, law, technology, property, sport, culture, health and topics of general interest. Sections on commercial property, money, careers and business culture. Supplements cover health and lifestyle issues, fashion, food, movies, television, books, as well as farming and agribusiness. The newspaper was first published in 1841. Twitter handle: http://twitter.com/irishexaminer.
ADVERTISING RATES:
Full Page Mono .... EUR 17400
Full Page Colour .... EUR 20100
SCC .... EUR 43.50
Mechanical Data: Film: Digital, No. of Columns (Display): 8
Editions:
The Irish Examiner (Cork & Kerry Edition)
Supplement(s): Arena - 52xY, Farming - 52xY, Feelgood - 52xY, Money & Jobs - 52xY, Weekend/ Property - 52xY
NATIONAL DAILY & SUNDAY NEWSPAPERS: National Daily Newspapers

THE IRISH EXAMINER (CORK & KERRY EDITION) 1666299E65A-8_110
Editorial: 4th Floor, City Quarter, Lapps Quay, CORK
Freq: Daily; **Cover Price:** EUR 1.80
Edition of: The Irish Examiner
NATIONAL DAILY & SUNDAY NEWSPAPERS: National Daily Newspapers

IRISH FARMERS JOURNAL 4193E21A-60
Editorial: Irish Farm Centre, Bluebell, DUBLIN 12 **Tel:** 1 41 99 500 **Fax:** 14520876
Email: edit@farmersjournal.ie **Web site:** http://www.farmersjournal.ie
Freq: Weekly - Published on Thursday; **Cover Price:** EUR 2.40
Annual Sub.: EUR 270; **Circ:** 70,405
Editor: Matt Dempsey; **News Editor:** Pat O'Keeffe; **Advertising Director:** John Grogan
Profile: Newspaper covering all aspects of Agriculture, food and rural living.
Readership: Aimed at Irish agricultural industry and farmers and rural dwellers.
ADVERTISING RATES:
Full Page Mono .... EUR 10584
Full Page Colour .... EUR 16200
SCC .... EUR 75
Agency Commission: 10%
Mechanical Data: Page Width: 262mm, Col Length: 360mm, Col Widths (Display): 40mm, No. of Columns (Display): 6, Type Area: 360 x 262mm, Trim Size: 360 x 290mm, Print Process: Web-fed offset litho
Supplement(s): Journal 2 - 52xY
BUSINESS: AGRICULTURE & FARMING

IRISH FARMERS MONTHLY 4194E21A-70
Editorial: 31 Deansgrange Road, Blackrock, CO. DUBLIN **Tel:** 1 28 93 305 **Fax:** 12896406
Email: margaret@ifpmedia.com **Web site:** http://www.ifpmedia.com
Date Established: 1975; **Freq:** Monthly; **Cover Price:** Free; **Circ:** 22,000
Usual Pagination: 68
Editor: Margaret Donnelly; **Advertising Manager:** John Sheehan
Profile: Magazine covering news, business advice and research within the agricultural industry.
Readership: Read by farmers and suppliers of agricultural supplies and equipment.
ADVERTISING RATES:
Full Page Colour .... EUR 3100
Agency Commission: 10%
Mechanical Data: Film: Digital, Type Area: 270 x 185mm, Col Length: 270mm, Page Width: 185mm, Bleed Size: 303 x 216mm, Trim Size: 297 x 210mm
Average ad content per issue: 25%
BUSINESS: AGRICULTURE & FARMING

THE IRISH FIELD 4388E75E-1000
Editorial: Irish Farm Centre, Bluebell, DUBLIN 12 **Tel:** 1 40 51 100 **Fax:** 14554008
Email: editorial@irishfield.ie **Web site:** http://www.irishfield.ie
Date Established: 1870; **Freq:** Weekly; **Cover Price:** EUR 3.10; **Circ:** 12,382
Usual Pagination: 112
Editor: Leo Powell
Profile: Newspaper focusing on Irish and international horse racing, breeding and sport horses.
Readership: Aimed at horse racing enthusiasts and equestrian.
ADVERTISING RATES:
Full Page Colour .... EUR 5650
Agency Commission: 10%
Mechanical Data: Bleed Size: 426 x 303mm, Trim Size: 420 x 297mm, Page Width: 262mm, Type Area: 360 x 262mm, Col Length: 360mm, Film: Digital
Average ad content per issue: 40%
CONSUMER: SPORT: Horse Racing

IRISH FOOD 4200E22A-40
Editorial: 31 Deansgrange Road, Blackrock, CO. DUBLIN **Tel:** 1 28 93 305 **Fax:** 12896406
Email: miriam@ifpmedia.com **Web site:** http://www.irishfoodmagazine.com
Freq: 6 issues yearly; **Cover Price:** Free; **Circ:** 3,500
Usual Pagination: 44
Editor: Miriam Atkins
Profile: International magazine promoting the Irish food industry at home and abroad.
Language(s): English; French; German; Italian; Japanese; Spanish
Readership: Read by buyers across Europe and internationally.
ADVERTISING RATES:
Full Page Colour .... EUR 2800
Mechanical Data: Film: Digital, Page Width: 185mm, Type Area: 270 x 185mm, Col Length: 270mm, Print Process: Offset litho, Trim Size: 297 x 210mm, Bleed Size: 303 x 216mm
Copy instructions: *Copy Date:* 14 days prior to publication date
Average ad content per issue: 30%
BUSINESS: FOOD

THE IRISH GARDEN 623519E93-90
Editorial: Media House, South Country Business Park, Leopardstown, DUBLIN 18 **Tel:** 1 2947777
Email: editor@theirishgarden.ie **Web site:** http://www.garden.ie
ISSN: 0791-6272
Date Established: 1992; **Freq:** Monthly; **Cover Price:** EUR 4.75
Annual Sub.: EUR 46; **Circ:** 11,459
Usual Pagination: 108
Editor: Gerry Daly; **Publisher:** John McDonald
Profile: Magazine focusing on gardening. Also contains articles on lifestyle and issues with particular relevance to Ireland.
Readership: Aimed at keen and beginner gardeners, mainly women aged 30 years old and over.
ADVERTISING RATES:
Full Page Colour .... EUR 2890
Agency Commission: 15%
Mechanical Data: Bleed Size: 310 x 240mm, Film: Digital, Trim Size: 300 x 230mm, Type Area: 280 x 210mm, Col Length: 280mm, Page Width: 210mm
Average ad content per issue: 20%
CONSUMER: GARDENING

IRISH GOLF REVIEW 1647142E75D-70
Editorial: 19 Clare Street, DUBLIN 2 **Tel:** 1 66 22 266
Fax: 16624981
Email: rheuston@selectmedialtd.com
Date Established: 1997; **Freq:** Quarterly; **Cover Price:** EUR 3.95; **Circ:** 10,500 Unique Users
Usual Pagination: 80
Publisher: Robert Heuston
Profile: Magazine covering golf clubs, courses, equipment reviews, destinations and resorts as well as tutorials.
Readership: Aimed at Irish golfers of all ages and all levels.
ADVERTISING RATES:
Full Page Colour .... EUR 1900
Mechanical Data: Trim Size: 297 x 210mm, Film: Digital
CONSUMER: SPORT: Golf

IRISH GOLF WORLD 623560E75D-71
Editorial: 19 Clare Street, DUBLIN 2 **Tel:** 1 66 22 266
Fax: 1 66 24 981
Email: info@selectmedialtd.com
Freq: Quarterly; **Cover Price:** Free; **Circ:** 22,500
Usual Pagination: 24
Editor: Robert Heuston; **Publisher:** Robert Heuston
Profile: Newspaper covering golf in Ireland.
Readership: Aimed at Irish golfers from both Northern and Southern Ireland.
ADVERTISING RATES:
Full Page Colour .... EUR 1800.00
Mechanical Data: Film: Digital
CONSUMER: SPORT: Golf

IRISH GOLFER 1658132E75D-69
Editorial: For all contact details see main record, Golf Ireland-Irelands National Golf Magazine
Freq: Half-yearly
Supplement to: Golf Ireland-Irelands National Golf Magazine
CONSUMER: SPORT: Golf

IRISH HAIRDRESSER INTERNATIONAL MAGAZINE 1691329E15B-1
Formerly: Irish Hairdressing Magazine
Editorial: PO Box 28, An Post Mail Centre, Dublin Road, ATHLONE **Tel:** 87 98 89 771 **Fax:** 906476300
Email: info@mohh.ie **Web site:** http://www.irishhairdressermagazine.ie
ISSN: 1393-4899
Date Established: 1996; **Freq:** 6 issues yearly; **Cover Price:** £3.35
Free to qualifying individuals ; **Circ:** 4,500
Usual Pagination: 68
Publisher: Maeve O'Healy-Harte
Profile: Magazine covering all aspects of the industry in Ireland and abroad including new products, industry news, interviews, salon profiles, people profiles, IHF news, OMC news, intercoiffure news, competition news and forthcoming events national and international.
Readership: Aimed at the hairdressing and beauty industry.
ADVERTISING RATES:
Full Page Colour .... EUR 1775
Mechanical Data: Trim Size: 297 x 210mm, Bleed Size: 303 x 216mm, Film: Digital
Copy instructions: *Copy Date:* 42 days prior to publication date
Average ad content per issue: 40%
BUSINESS: COSMETICS & HAIRDRESSING: Hairdressing

IRISH HARDWARE 4204E25-10
Editorial: Broom House, 65 Mulgrave Street, Dun Laoghaire, CO. DUBLIN **Tel:** 1 2147920
Fax: 1 2147950
Email: m.foran@jemma.ie **Web site:** http://www.irishhardware.com
Date Established: 1939; **Freq:** Monthly - Published around the middle of the cover month; **Annual Sub.:** EUR 74; **Circ:** 1,664
Editor: Martin Foran
Profile: Journal of the Irish Hardware Association, covering news and information on the hardware industry.
Readership: Aimed at those in hardware, building and gardening trades.
ADVERTISING RATES:
Full Page Colour .... EUR 2160
Agency Commission: 10%
Mechanical Data: Col Length: 270mm, Film: Digital, Trim Size: 297 x 210mm, Bleed Size: 304 x 216mm, Type Area: 270 x 190mm, Page Width: 190mm
Average ad content per issue: 40%
Supplement(s): Irish Hardware Paint Guide - 1xY, Irish Hardware Tools Guide - 1xY
BUSINESS: HARDWARE

IRISH HARDWARE PAINT GUIDE 1666674E25-11
Editorial: For all contact details see main record, Irish Hardware
Freq: Annual
Supplement to: Irish Hardware
BUSINESS: HARDWARE

IRISH HARDWARE TOOLS GUIDE 1666673E25-12
Editorial: For all contact details see main record, Irish Hardware
Freq: Annual
Supplement to: Irish Hardware
BUSINESS: HARDWARE

IRISH INDEPENDENT 4259E65A-10
Editorial: Independent House, 27-32 Talbot Street, DUBLIN 1 **Tel:** 1 70 55 333 **Fax:** 1 87 20 304
Email: info@independent.ie **Web site:** http://www.independent.ie
Freq: Daily - Not published on Sunday; **Cover Price:** EUR 1.80; **Circ:** 138,510
Editor: News Desk; **Features Editor:** Peter Carvosso
Profile: The Irish Independent is a national newspaper covering international and regional news, entertainment, recruitment, property and cars with sections providing sport coverage and business including analysis, key financial stories and market trends. Also features on cookery, wine and interiors. Published by Independent News and Media. Launched in 1905, replacing the Daily Irish Independent. Twitter handle: http://twitter.com/irishindo.
ADVERTISING RATES:
Full Page Mono .... EUR 29425
Full Page Colour .... EUR 36995
SCC .... EUR 75.15
Agency Commission: 10%
Mechanical Data: Film: Digital, Col Length: 530mm, Type Area: 530 x 340mm, Page Width: 340mm
Editions:
Irish Independent (Broadsheet Edition)
Irish Independent (Compact Edition)
Supplement(s): Business - 52xY, Day & Night Magazine - 52xY, Farming Independent - 52xY, Health & Living - 52xY, Initiative (SME Business) - 12xY, Mothers & Babies - 12xY, Property - 52xY, Sports Monthly - 12xY, Weekend Magazine - 52xY
NATIONAL DAILY & SUNDAY NEWSPAPERS: National Daily Newspapers

IRISH INDEPENDENT (BROADSHEET EDITION) 1692008E65A-10_500
Editorial: Independent House, 27-32 Talbot Street, DUBLIN 1
Freq: Daily; **Cover Price:** EUR 1.70; **Circ:** 82,771
Edition of: Irish Independent
NATIONAL DAILY & SUNDAY NEWSPAPERS: National Daily Newspapers

IRISH INDEPENDENT (COMPACT EDITION) 1692012E65A-10_501
Editorial: Independent House, 27-32 Talbot Street, DUBLIN 1
Freq: Daily; **Cover Price:** EUR 1.70; **Circ:** 81,431
Edition of: Irish Independent
NATIONAL DAILY & SUNDAY NEWSPAPERS: National Daily Newspapers

IRISH INTERIORS 623524E74C-90
Editorial: Unit F5, Bymac Centre, North West Business Park, DUBLIN 15 **Tel:** 1 82 24 477
Fax: 18224485
Email: admin@pembrokepublishing.com
Date Established: 1995; **Freq:** Half-yearly - Published in April and September; **Circ:** 30,000
Usual Pagination: 250
Editor: Alexander Fitzgerald; **Advertising Manager:** Declan Doran O'Reilly; **Publisher:** Michael Nash
Profile: Magazine featuring ideas on home furnishings, decoration and lifestyle.
Readership: Aimed at those with an interest in homes and interior design.
ADVERTISING RATES:
Full Page Colour .... EUR 2495
Agency Commission: 15%
Mechanical Data: Film: Digital, Trim Size: 297 x 210mm
CONSUMER: WOMEN'S INTEREST CONSUMER MAGAZINES: Home & Family

IRISH JOURNAL OF EDUCATION 4253E62A-121
Editorial: Educational Research Centre, St. Patrick's College, DUBLIN 9 **Tel:** 1 83 73 789 **Fax:** 18378997
Email: info@erc.ie **Web site:** http://www.erc.ie
ISSN: 0021-1257
Date Established: 1967; **Freq:** Annual; **Circ:** 550
Usual Pagination: 85
Editor: Thomas Kellaghan
Profile: Publication dealing with all aspects of education.
Readership: Aimed at teachers and academics.
BUSINESS: CHURCH & SCHOOL EQUIPMENT & EDUCATION: Education

IRISH JOURNAL OF FAMILY LAW 629650E44-55
Editorial: 43 Fitzwilliam Place, DUBLIN 2
Tel: 1 66 25 301 **Fax:** 16625302
Email: nicola.barrett@thomsonreuters.com **Web site:** http://www.roundhall.thomson.com
ISSN: 1393-7073
Freq: Quarterly; **Annual Sub.:** EUR 300; **Circ:** 500
Usual Pagination: 32
Editor: Nicola Barrett
Profile: Magazine containing articles on case law and legislation updates.
Readership: Aimed at law professionals, social workers and students.
BUSINESS: LEGAL

IRISH JOURNAL OF MEDICAL SCIENCE 4241E56A-5
Editorial: Frederick House, 19 South Frederick Street, DUBLIN 2 **Tel:** 1 63 34 820 **Fax:** 1 63 34 918
Email: journal@rami.ie **Web site:** http://www.ijms.ie
ISSN: 0021-1265
Date Established: 1832; **Freq:** Quarterly; **Cover Price:** EUR 42.00
Free to qualifying individuals
Annual Sub.: EUR 156.00; **Circ:** 8,000
Usual Pagination: 80
Editor: Helen Moore; **Advertising Manager:** Helen Moore
Profile: Official journal of the Royal Academy of Medicine in Ireland. Covers medical and allied topics.
Readership: Aimed at doctors, consultants and students world-wide.
ADVERTISING RATES:
Full Page Colour .... EUR 1270.00
Agency Commission: 10%
Mechanical Data: Type Area: 268 x 184mm, Col Length: 268mm, Bleed Size: +5mm, Trim Size: 288 x 204mm, Film: Digital, Page Width: 184mm
Copy instructions: *Copy Date:* 1st of the month prior to publication date
BUSINESS: HEALTH & MEDICAL

IRISH JURIST 629652E44-58
Editorial: 43 Fitzwilliam Place, DUBLIN 2
Tel: 1 66 25 301 **Fax:** 16625302
Web site: http://www.roundhall.thomson.com
Date Established: 1848; **Freq:** Annual; **Annual Sub.:** EUR 190; **Circ:** 500
Editor: Paul O'Connor; **Publisher:** Pamela Moran
Profile: Academic journal containing information on diverse aspects of the law.
Readership: Aimed at legal academics.
BUSINESS: LEGAL

IRISH LAW TIMES 4223E44-60
Formerly: Irish Law Times & Solicitors' Journal
Editorial: 43 Fitzwilliam Place, DUBLIN 2
Tel: 1 66 25 301 **Fax:** 16625302
Email: terri.mcdonnell@thomsonreuters.com **Web site:** http://www.roundhall.ie
ISSN: 0021-1281
Date Established: 1863; **Freq:** 26 issues yearly; **Annual Sub.:** EUR 605; **Circ:** 400
Usual Pagination: 16
Editor: Terri McDonnell
Profile: Magazine providing an information service and an ongoing report of developments in Irish law.
Readership: Read by legal practitioners.
ADVERTISING RATES:
Full Page Mono .... EUR 1200
Full Page Colour .... EUR 1500
Agency Commission: 15%
Mechanical Data: Bleed Size: 303 x 216mm, Trim Size: 297 x 210mm, Film: Digital
Average ad content per issue: 5%
Supplement(s): Irish Law Times Charities Directory - 1xY
BUSINESS: LEGAL

IRISH LAW TIMES CHARITIES DIRECTORY 1659450E44-80
Editorial: For all contact details see main record, Irish Law Times
Freq: Annual
ADVERTISING RATES:
Full Page Mono .... EUR 600.00
Supplement to: Irish Law Times
BUSINESS: LEGAL

IRISH MAIL ON SUNDAY 4262E65B-2
Formerly: Ireland On Sunday
Editorial: 3rd Floor Embassy House, Herbert Park Lane, Ballsbridge, DUBLIN 4 **Tel:** 1 63 75 800
Fax: 16375920
Email: news@mailonsunday.ie **Web site:** http://www.mailonsunday.ie
Freq: Sunday - Irish Republic; **Circ:** 123,919
Editor: Enda Leahy; **Editor-in-Chief:** Paul Field
Profile: Sunday edition of the Irish Daily Mail tabloid newspaper, covering national and international news with features on travel, finance, sport, women's interest, entertainment and health. Launched in 2006, replacing the British edition of the Mail on Sunday in the Irish market.
ADVERTISING RATES:
Full Page Mono .... EUR 9884.70
Full Page Colour .... EUR 13179.60
SCC .... EUR 40.95
Agency Commission: 10%
Mechanical Data: Type Area: 360 x 268mm, Print Process: Web-fed offset litho, Film: Digital, Col Length: 360mm, No. of Columns (Display): 7, Page Width: 268mm
Average ad content per issue: 20%
Sections:
The Title
Supplement(s): Style - 52xY, TV Week - 52xY
NATIONAL DAILY & SUNDAY NEWSPAPERS: National Sunday Newspapers

IRISH MARKETING JOURNAL 4153E2A-10
Editorial: 45 Upper Mount Street, DUBLIN 2
Tel: 1 66 11 660 **Fax:** 16611632
Email: editor@irishmarketingjournal.ie **Web site:** http://www.irishmarketingjournal.ie
ISSN: 0791-6809
Date Established: 1974; **Freq:** Monthly; **Annual Sub.:** EUR 160; **Circ:** 4,850
Usual Pagination: 64
Advertising Manager: Jennifer Komertzky; **Publisher:** John McGee
Profile: Magazine covering marketing, media and advertising affairs in Ireland.
Readership: Aimed at marketing and managing directors of Ireland's top companies, advertising agency personnel, media companies, state bodies and other marketing and advertising sector workers.
ADVERTISING RATES:
Full Page Colour .... EUR 3120
Agency Commission: 15%
Mechanical Data: Type Area: 295 x 195mm, Trim Size: 330 x 230mm, Film: Digital, Col Length: 295mm, Page Width: 195mm, Bleed Size: +5mm
Average ad content per issue: 40%
BUSINESS: COMMUNICATIONS, ADVERTISING & MARKETING

IRISH MEDICAL DIRECTORY 628810E56A-17
Editorial: PO Box 5049, DUBLIN 6 **Tel:** 1 49 26 040
Fax: 14926040
Email: mgueret@imd.ie **Web site:** http://www.imd.ie
Date Established: 1994; **Freq:** Annual - Published in May; Free to qualifying individuals
Annual Sub.: EUR 95; **Circ:** 6,500
Usual Pagination: 590
Editor: Maurice Guéret
Profile: Guide to health services in Ireland. Provides listings of family doctors, specialists, hospitals and staff, clinics, pharmaceutical and healthcare companies, patient support, medical schools and health organisations.
Readership: Aimed at healthcare, medical and industry personnel.
ADVERTISING RATES:
Full Page Colour .... EUR 2950
Agency Commission: 15%
Mechanical Data: Bleed Size: 303 x 215mm, Trim Size: 297 x 210mm
Average ad content per issue: 30%
BUSINESS: HEALTH & MEDICAL

IRISH MEDICAL JOURNAL 4242E56A-20
Editorial: IMO House, 10 Fitzwilliam Place, DUBLIN 2
Tel: 1 67 67 273 **Fax:** 16612758
Email: lduffy@imj.ie **Web site:** http://www.imj.ie
ISSN: 0332-3102
Date Established: 1867; **Freq:** Monthly; **Annual Sub.:** EUR 250; **Circ:** 9,000
Usual Pagination: 32
Editor: Lorna Duffy; **Advertising Manager:** Brighde Gallagher
Profile: Journal of the Irish Medical Association of Ireland that aims to educate medical students and postgraduates through scientific research, review articles and updates on contemporary clinical practices while providing an ongoing forum for medical debate.
Readership: Aimed at medical students and practitioners in Ireland.
BUSINESS: HEALTH & MEDICAL

IRISH MEDICAL NEWS 4243E56A-25
Editorial: Taney Hall, Eglinton Terrace, Dundrum, DUBLIN 14 **Tel:** 1 29 60 000 **Fax:** 12960383
Email: priscilla@imn.ie **Web site:** http://www.imn.ie

ate Established: 1984; **Freq:** Weekly; **Cover Price:** UR 4.25
ree to qualifying individuals ; **Circ:** 7,346
usual Pagination: 53
ditor: Priscilla Lynch; **Advertising Manager:** eather Angel
rofile: Journal covering all aspects of Irish medicine. ncludes news, features, opinion and clinical review rticles.
eadership: Read by doctors health policy makers, ther healthcare professionals, patient and health elated organisations/bodies and pharmaceutical ompanies.
DVERTISING RATES:
ull Page Colour .... EUR 1820
gency Commission: 10%
Mechanical Data: Type Area: 365 x 253mm, Col ength: 365mm, Bleed Size: 405 x 278mm, Trim Size: 95 x 273mm, No. of Columns (Display): 6, Col Vidths (Display): 38mm, Film: Digital, Page Width: 53mm
Copy instructions: *Copy Date:* 7 days prior to ublication date
verage ad content per issue: 50%
BUSINESS: HEALTH & MEDICAL

RISH MEDICAL TIMES 4244E56A-30

ditorial: 24-26 Upper Ormond Quay, DUBLIN 7 **el:** 1 81 76 300
mail: dara.gantly@imt.ie **Web site:** http://www.imt.e
SSN: 0047-1476
ate Established: 1967; **Freq:** Weekly; **Cover Price:** UR 6.30
ree to qualifying individuals ; **Circ:** 7,152
sual Pagination: 56
ditor: Dara Gantly
rofile: Journal containing news and information on developments in medicine.
eadership: Aimed at doctors.
ADVERTISING RATES:
ull Page Colour .... EUR 2250
gency Commission: 10%
Mechanical Data: Type Area: 365 x 251mm, Col ength: 365mm, Page Width: 251mm, Trim Size: 395 273mm, Bleed Size: 400 x 279mm, Film: Digital
Copy instructions: *Copy Date:* 14 days prior to ublication date
BUSINESS: HEALTH & MEDICAL

RISH MOTOR MANAGEMENT

4205E31A-70

Formerly: Irish Motor Industry
Editorial: 31 Deansgrange Road, Blackrock, CO. DUBLIN **Tel:** 1 28 93 305 **Fax:** 12896406
Email: bernard@ifpmedia.com **Web site:** http://www.ifpmedia.com/IMM.html
Date Established: 1969; **Freq:** 6 issues yearly; Free to qualifying individuals
Annual Sub.: EUR 100; **Circ:** 3,500
Usual Pagination: 48
Editor: Bernard Potter
Profile: Magazine covering all aspects of the Irish motor trade.
Readership: Read by manufacturers, suppliers, retailers and government officials.
ADVERTISING RATES:
Full Page Colour .... EUR 1650
Agency Commission: 10%
Mechanical Data: Bleed Size: 303 x 216mm, Film: Digital, Type Area: 270 x 185mm, Col Widths (Display): 270mm, Page Width: 185mm, Trim Size: 297 x 210mm
Average ad content per issue: 40%
BUSINESS: MOTOR TRADE: Motor Trade Accessories

IRISH MOUNTAIN LOG

629673E75L-150

Formerly: Mountain Log
Editorial: Sport HQ, 13 Joyce Way, Parkwest Business Park, DUBLIN 12 **Tel:** 1 62 51 115
Fax: 16251116
Email: info@mountaineering.ie **Web site:** http://www.mountaineering.ie
ISSN: 0790-8008
Date Established: 1987; **Freq:** Quarterly; **Cover Price:** EUR 3.20
Free to qualifying individuals ; **Circ:** 9,500
Usual Pagination: 52
Editor: Stuart Garland; **Advertising Manager:** Gay Needham
Profile: Magazine focusing on mountain climbing and walking.
Readership: Read by members of the Mountaineering Council of Ireland.
ADVERTISING RATES:
Full Page Colour .... EUR 1600
SCC .... EUR 21
Mechanical Data: Trim Size: 297 x 210mm, Bleed Size: 305 x 215mm, Type Area: 270 x 185mm, Col Length: 270mm, Page Width: 185mm, Film: Digital
Average ad content per issue: 25%
CONSUMER: SPORT: Outdoor

IRISH MUSIC MAGAZINE

623514E76D-60

Formerly: Irish Music
Editorial: 19 Clare Street, DUBLIN 2 **Tel:** 1 6622266
Fax: 1 6624981
Email: info@selectmedialtd.com **Web site:** http://www.irishmusicmagazine.com
Freq: Monthly; **Cover Price:** EUR 3.95; **Circ:** 10,500
Usual Pagination: 68
Editor: Robert Heuston
Profile: Magazine covering traditional and folk music in Ireland and Celtic countries.
Readership: Aimed at the music industry, musicians and fans.
ADVERTISING RATES:
Full Page Colour .... EUR 1180
Agency Commission: 10%
Mechanical Data: Page Width: 182mm, Type Area: 270 x 182mm, Print Process: Sheet-fed offset litho, Film: Digital, Bleed Size: 303 x 213mm, Trim Size: 297 x 210mm, Col Length: 270mm
CONSUMER: MUSIC & PERFORMING ARTS: Music

IRISH PHARMACHEM INDUSTRY BUYERS GUIDE

4213E37-40

Editorial: Poolbeg House, 1-2 Poolbeg Street, DUBLIN 2 **Tel:** 1 24 13 095 **Fax:** 12413010
Email: kathleenbelton@tarapublishingco.com **Web site:** http://www.irishpharmachem.com
Date Established: 1998; **Freq:** Annual - Published in August in 2010; Free to qualifying individuals
Annual Sub.: EUR 35; **Circ:** 2,500
Usual Pagination: 80
Editor: Kathleen Belton
Profile: Annual buyers guide and yearbook covering trends in the pharmaceutical and chemical industry, information on suppliers and scientific issues. In association with Pharmachemical Ireland.
Readership: Aimed at key management personnel within the pharmaceutical and chemical manufacturing industry.
ADVERTISING RATES:
Full Page Colour .... EUR 3295
Agency Commission: 15%
Mechanical Data: Film: Digital, Type Area: 267 x 180mm, Col Length: 267mm, Page Width: 180mm, Bleed Size: 307 x 220mm, Trim Size: 297 x 210mm
Average ad content per issue: 45%
BUSINESS: PHARMACEUTICAL & CHEMISTS

IRISH PHARMACIST 629656E37-51

Editorial: 7 Adelaide Court, Adelaide Road, DUBLIN 2 **Tel:** 1 4189799 **Fax:** 1 4789449
Email: maura@greencrosspublishing.ie **Web site:** http://www.greencrosspublishing.ie/publication.aspx?contentid=4
Date Established: 1998; **Freq:** Monthly; Free to qualifying individuals ; **Circ:** 2,300
Usual Pagination: 48
Profile: Magazine with news and comment plus clinical and business articles relating to both community and hospital pharmacy in Ireland and worldwide.
Readership: Aimed at community and hospital pharmacists.
BUSINESS: PHARMACEUTICAL & CHEMISTS

IRISH PHARMACY JOURNAL

4214E37-50

Editorial: 18 Shrewsbury Road, Ballsbridge, DUBLIN 4 **Tel:** 1 21 84 000 **Fax:** 1 28 37 678
Email: kate.oflaherty@pharmaceuticalsociety.ie **Web site:** http://www.pharmaceuticalsociety.ie
Date Established: 1923; **Freq:** 10 issues yearly;
Cover Price: EUR 56.75
Free to qualifying individuals ; **Circ:** 5,000
Usual Pagination: 48
Editor: Kate O'Flaherty; **Advertising Manager:** David O'Brien
Profile: Journal of the Pharmaceutical Society of Ireland.
Readership: Read by pharmacists and those engaged in the pharmaceutical industry.
ADVERTISING RATES:
Full Page Mono .... EUR 935.00
Full Page Colour .... EUR 1225.00
Mechanical Data: Col Length: 260mm, Page Width: 185mm, Type Area: 260 x 185mm, Bleed Size: 302 x 215mm, Trim Size: 297 x 210mm, Print Process: Sheet-fed litho, Film: Digital
Copy instructions: *Copy Date:* 20th of the month prior to publication date
BUSINESS: PHARMACEUTICAL & CHEMISTS

IRISH PLANNING & ENVIRONMENTAL LAW JOURNAL 4159E4D-50

Formerly: Irish Planning & Environmental Journal
Editorial: 43 Fitzwilliam Place, DUBLIN 2
Tel: 1 66 25 301 **Fax:** 16625302
Email: roundhall.reception@thomsonreuters.com
Web site: http://www.roundhall.ie
ISSN: 0791-9735
Date Established: 1994; **Freq:** Quarterly; **Annual Sub.:** EUR 292.83; **Circ:** 500
Usual Pagination: 40
Editor: Eamon Galligan
Profile: Magazine covering all aspects of planning and environmental development.
Readership: Read by lawyers specialising in environmental and planning law.
BUSINESS: ARCHITECTURE & BUILDING: Planning & Housing

IRISH PRINTER 4216E41A-10

Editorial: 1st Floor, Gratten House, Temple Road, Blackrock, CO. DUBLIN **Tel:** 1 76 42 700
Fax: 17642750
Email: g.burns@jemma.ie **Web site:** http://www.irishprinter.ie
ISSN: 0790-2026
Date Established: 1968; **Freq:** Monthly - Published on the 12th of the cover month; **Annual Sub.:** EUR 79.45; **Circ:** 1,472
Usual Pagination: 50
Editor: Grainne Burns; **Advertising Manager:** Frank Brennan
Profile: Magazine including features on technology, management, equipment, companies and events, market sector reports, trends in industry, business law and finance.
Readership: Aimed at the printing and graphic arts industry.
ADVERTISING RATES:
Full Page Colour .... EUR 2120
Agency Commission: 10%
Mechanical Data: Bleed Size: 307x 220mm, Trim Size: 297 x 210mm, Type Area: 270 x 190mm, Col Length: 270mm, Page Width: 190mm, Film: Digital
Average ad content per issue: 50%
BUSINESS: PRINTING & STATIONERY: Printing

THE IRISH PSYCHOLOGIST

623644E56N-80

Editorial: CX House, 2A Corn Exchange Place, Poolbeg Street, DUBLIN 2 **Tel:** 1 47 49 160
Fax: 11614749
Email: irishpsychologist@psihq.ie **Web site:** http://www.psihq.ie
ISSN: 0790-4789
Date Established: 1975; **Freq:** Monthly; Free to qualifying individuals
Annual Sub.: EUR 45; **Circ:** 2,500
Usual Pagination: 12
Editor: Suzanne Guerin; **Advertising Manager:** Yvonne Mikolajczyk
Profile: Newsletter containing news, articles and reports concerning the study of psychology.
Readership: Read by professional and student psychologists who are members of The Psychological Society of Ireland.
ADVERTISING RATES:
Full Page Mono .... EUR 1155
Full Page Colour .... EUR 1450
Mechanical Data: Page Width: 180mm, Type Area: 270 x 180mm, Col Length: 270mm, No. of Columns (Display): 2
Average ad content per issue: 25%
BUSINESS: HEALTH & MEDICAL: Mental Health

IRISH RED CROSS REVIEW

754297E56R-70

Formerly: Review - The Journal of the Irish Red Cross
Editorial: 16 Merrion Square, DUBLIN 2
Tel: 1 64 24 600 **Fax:** 16614461
Email: amaceoin@redcross.ie **Web site:** http://www.redcross.ie
Freq: Quarterly; **Cover Price:** Free; **Circ:** 8,000
Usual Pagination: 8
Editor: Aoife Mac Eoin
Profile: Magazine of the Irish Red Cross Society.
Readership: Read by members of the Irish Red Cross, donors, members of the Houses of the Oireachtas, libraries, aid agencies and government departments.
BUSINESS: HEALTH & MEDICAL: Health Medical Related

IRISH RUGBY REVIEW 4372E75C-186

Editorial: PO Box 7992, Dun Laoghaire, CO. DUBLIN
Tel: 1 28 40 137 **Fax:** 12840137
Email: quinnfr@eircom.net **Web site:** http://www.irishrugbyreview.com
ISSN: 0709-228X
Date Established: 1983; **Freq:** Monthly; **Cover Price:** EUR 2.95; **Circ:** 12,000
Usual Pagination: 32
Advertising Manager: Frank Quinn
Profile: Magazine covering rugby news, match schedules, competitions and information on Ireland (north and south) internationals, Six Nations, Heineken Cup, Magners League and AIB League.
Readership: Aimed at rugby enthusiasts.
ADVERTISING RATES:
Full Page Mono .... EUR 2300
Full Page Colour .... EUR 2650
Agency Commission: 15%
Mechanical Data: Trim Size: 300 x 215mm, Page Width: 184mm, Type Area: 268 x 184mm, Col Length: 268mm, Film: Digital
Average ad content per issue: 25%
CONSUMER: SPORT: Rugby

IRISH RUNNER 4376E75J-150

Editorial: Unit 19, Northwood Court, Northwood Business Campus, Santry, DUBLIN 9
Tel: 1 88 69 962 **Fax:** 18421334
Email: editor@irishrunner.ie **Web site:** http://www.irishrunner.ie
Date Established: 1981; **Freq:** 6 issues yearly;
Cover Price: EUR 4.95
Annual Sub.: EUR 30; **Circ:** 10,400
Usual Pagination: 80
Advertising Manager: Frank Greally
Profile: Magazine about recreational running and athletics.
Readership: Aimed at those interested in athletics.
ADVERTISING RATES:
Full Page Colour .... EUR 1500
CONSUMER: SPORT: Athletics

IRISH SHOOTER'S DIGEST

629660E75F-100

Editorial: Shannon Oughter, SLIGO **Tel:** 71 91 47 841
Fax: 71 91 47 841
Email: info@irishshootersdigest.ie **Web site:** http://www.irishshootersdigest.ie
ISSN: 1393-5151
Date Established: 1997; **Freq:** 11 issues yearly - Double issue for December/January; **Cover Price:** EUR 3.75
Annual Sub.: EUR 50.00; **Circ:** 8,000
Usual Pagination: 80
Editor: Eric Parkes; **Advertising Manager:** Eric Parkes
Profile: Magazine covering all forms of shooting - clay, game, rifle and shotgun. Also covering other field sports such as ferreting, falconry, gun dogs, game rearing and deer hunting.
Readership: Aimed at people interested in field sports.
ADVERTISING RATES:
Full Page Colour .... EUR 885.00
Agency Commission: 10%
Mechanical Data: Bleed Size: 303 x 216mm, Type Area: 270 x 190mm, Col Length: 270mm, Page Width: 190mm, Trim Size: 297 x 210mm, Film: Digital
Copy instructions: *Copy Date:* 10th of the month prior to publication date
Average ad content per issue: 40%
CONSUMER: SPORT: Shooting

THE IRISH SKIPPER 4226E45B-10

Editorial: Annagry, Letterkenny, CO DONEGAL
Tel: 74 95 62 843 **Fax:** 749548940
Email: skippereditor@iol.ie **Web site:** http://www.irishskipper.net
ISSN: 0791-2137
Date Established: 1964; **Freq:** Monthly; **Cover Price:** EUR 3.50
Annual Sub.: EUR 50; **Circ:** 5,500
Usual Pagination: 44
Editor: John Rafferty; **Advertising Manager:** Hugh Bonner
Profile: Newspaper representing the commercial fishing, fish processing and aquaculture industries throughout Ireland.
Readership: Aimed at commercial fishing and aquaculture industry personnel, marine academics and students.
ADVERTISING RATES:
Full Page Mono .... EUR 1200
Full Page Colour .... EUR 1450
Agency Commission: 10%
Mechanical Data: Trim Size: 330 x 230mm, No. of Columns (Display): 4, Film: Digital, Print Process: Offset litho, Col Length: 300mm, Col Widths (Display): 50mm, Type Area: 300 x 207mm, Page Width: 207mm
Average ad content per issue: 45%
BUSINESS: MARINE & SHIPPING: Commercial Fishing

THE IRISH SUN 767844E65A-82

Editorial: 4th Floor, Bishop's Square, Redmond's Hill, DUBLIN 2 **Tel:** 1 47 92 579 **Fax:** 14792590
Email: irishsun@the-sun.ie **Web site:** http://www.thesun.co.uk
Date Established: 1993; **Freq:** Daily - Irish Republic;
Cover Price: EUR 0.90; **Circ:** 108,783
News Editor: Damien Lane; **Features Editor:** Fiona Wynne
Profile: Irish edition of The Sun tabloid newspaper with latest news and features, celebrities, entertainment, television, show-biz, racing and sport. Launched in Ireland in 1993.
ADVERTISING RATES:
Full Page Mono .... EUR 9240
Full Page Colour .... EUR 11700
SCC .... EUR 41
Agency Commission: 15%
Mechanical Data: Type Area: 338 x 264mm, Col Length: 338mm, No. of Columns (Display): 7, Col Widths (Display): 34mm, Film: Digital, Page Width: 264mm
Average ad content per issue: 40%
NATIONAL DAILY & SUNDAY NEWSPAPERS: National Daily Newspapers

THE IRISH SUNDAY MIRROR

767843E65B-41

Editorial: Floor 4, Park House, 195-7 North Circular Road, DUBLIN 7 **Tel:** 1 86 88 629 **Fax:** 18688612
Freq: Sunday - Irish Republic; **Cover Price:** EUR 1.30; **Circ:** 84,104
Profile: Irish Sunday edition of the Sunday Mirror with latest news, sports, showbiz, and entertainment. Supplements cover celebrities and football. Published by Mirror Group Newspapers with a readership of 289,000 in total.
ADVERTISING RATES:
SCC .... EUR 24.28
Agency Commission: 15%
Mechanical Data: Type Area: 340 x 265mm, Col Length: 340mm, No. of Columns (Display): 7, Page Width: 265mm, Film: Digital
Average ad content per issue: 30%
NATIONAL DAILY & SUNDAY NEWSPAPERS: National Sunday Newspapers

Irish Republic

IRISH TATLER
601097E74A-65

Editorial: Rosemount House, Dundrum Road, Dundrum, DUBLIN 14 **Tel:** 1 24 05 300
Fax: 16619757
Email: jcollins@harmonia.ie **Web site:** http://www.ivenus.com
Date Established: 1890; **Freq:** Monthly; **Annual Sub.:** EUR 24; **Circ:** 23,536
Usual Pagination: 180
Editor: Jessie Collins
Profile: Glossy women's magazine focussing on style, beauty, social issues, relationships, interiors, food and travel.
Readership: Read by affluent women aged between 25 and 44 years old.
ADVERTISING RATES:
Full Page Colour .... EUR 3060
Agency Commission: 15%
Mechanical Data: Type Area: 270 x 195mm, Bleed Size: 310 x 235mm, Trim Size: 300 x 225mm, Col Length: 270mm, Page Width: 195mm, Film: Digital
CONSUMER: WOMEN'S INTEREST CONSUMER MAGAZINES: Women's Interest

IRISH TAX REVIEW
623590E1M-50

Editorial: South Block, Longboat Quay, Grand Canal Harbour, DUBLIN 2 **Tel:** 1 66 31 700 **Fax:** 16688387
Email: itr@taxireland.ie **Web site:** http://www.taxireland.ie
Date Established: 1980; **Freq:** 6 issues yearly; **Annual Sub.:** EUR 305; **Circ:** 6,200
Usual Pagination: 100
Editor: Maureen Travers
Profile: Magazine covering all issues relating to taxation in Ireland.
Readership: Read by members of the AITI.
ADVERTISING RATES:
Full Page Colour .... EUR 1550
Mechanical Data: Bleed Size: 307 x 220mm, Trim Size: 297 x 210mm, Film: Digital
Average ad content per issue: 10%
BUSINESS: FINANCE & ECONOMICS: Taxation

IRISH THEOLOGICAL QUARTERLY
623542E87-60

Editorial: St. Patrick's College, Maynooth, CO. KILDARE **Tel:** 1 70 83 496 **Fax:** 17083441
Email: itq.editor@may.ie **Web site:** http://itq.sagepub.com
ISSN: 0021-1400
Date Established: 1906; **Freq:** Quarterly; **Annual Sub.:** £34; **Circ:** 700
Usual Pagination: 96
Editor: Michael Conway
Profile: International journal concerning theology and related disciplines.
Readership: Aimed at academics and those trained in theology.
CONSUMER: RELIGIOUS

THE IRISH TIMES
4260E65A-30

Editorial: The Irish Times Building, PO Box 74, 24-28 Tara Street, DUBLIN 2 **Tel:** 1 67 58 000
Fax: 1 67 58 036
Email: newsdesk@irishtimes.com **Web site:** http://www.irishtimes.com
Date Established: 1859; **Freq:** Daily - Published Monday - Saturday; **Cover Price:** EUR 1.70; **Circ:** 102,543
Editor: News Desk; **Managing Director:** Liam Kavanagh; **Managing Editor:** Eoin McVey
Profile: The Irish Times was founded by Major Lawrence Knox and first published in 1859. Ireland's daily newspaper with news reporting from throughout Ireland, accompanied by reports from foreign correspondents, sports and business coverage, features and arts sections, lifestyle, jobs and property. Each issue contains analysis and assessment of the events of the day, and diversity of debate in the daily opinion columns. Supplements cover business and entertainment including movie, music and theatre reviews, interviews, articles, and media listings. Twitter handle: http://twitter.com/irishtimes.
ADVERTISING RATES:
Full Page Mono .... EUR 25900
Full Page Colour .... EUR 28350
SCC .... EUR 66.50
Agency Commission: 15%
Mechanical Data: Col Length: 540mm, Page Width: 372mm, Film: Digital, Type Area: 540 x 372mm, Col Widths (Display): 45mm, No. of Columns (Display): 8, Print Process: Web-fed offset litho
Copy instructions: *Copy Date:* 1 day prior to publication date
Average ad content per issue: 33%
Editions:
The Irish Times (International Edition UK)
The Irish Times (UK Office)
Supplement(s): Business This Week - 52xY, Gallery - 52xY, Go - 52xY, HealthPlus Supplement - 52xY, Innovation - 12xY, Irish Times Magazine - 52xY, Motors - 52xY, Property - 52xY, Sports Monday - 52xY, Sports Wednesday - 52xY, The Ticket - 52xY, Weekend Review - 52xY
NATIONAL DAILY & SUNDAY NEWSPAPERS: National Daily Newspapers

THE IRISH TIMES (INTERNATIONAL EDITION UK)
1691401E65A-30_500

Editorial: The Irish Times Building, PO Box 74, 24-28 Tara Street, DUBLIN 2
Freq: Daily
Edition of: The Irish Times
NATIONAL DAILY & SUNDAY NEWSPAPERS: National Daily Newspapers

IRISH TIMES MAGAZINE
1659440E65H-15

Editorial: The Irish Times Building, PO Box 74, 24-28 Tara Street, DUBLIN 2
Email: magazine@irishtimes.com
Freq: Weekly
Supplement to: The Irish Times
NATIONAL DAILY & SUNDAY NEWSPAPERS: National Colour Supplements

IRISH TRAVEL TRADE NEWS
4232E50-10

Editorial: A12 Calmount Park, Calmount Road, DUBLIN 12 **Tel:** 1 45 02 422 **Fax:** 14502954
Email: editor@irishtraveltradenews.com **Web site:** http://www.irishtraveltradenews.com
Date Established: 1971; **Freq:** Monthly; **Annual Sub.:** EUR 45; **Circ:** 2,200
Editor: Michael Flood; **News Editor:** Joe Jennings; **Features Editor:** Neil Steedman; **Advertising Manager:** Ian Bloomfield
Profile: Magazine focusing on travel and tourism.
Readership: Aimed at travel professionals throughout Ireland, Europe and the USA.
ADVERTISING RATES:
Full Page Mono £1640
Full Page Colour £2390
Agency Commission: 10%
Mechanical Data: Type Area: 256 x 196mm, Print Process: Litho, Bleed Size: 303 x 213mm, Trim Size: 297 x 210mm, Col Length: 256mm, Page Width: 196mm, Film: Digital
Average ad content per issue: 40%
BUSINESS: TRAVEL & TOURISM

IRISH TRUCKER
629663E49D-100

Editorial: Kells Business Park, Kells, CO. MEATH
Tel: 46 92 41 923 **Fax:** 46 92 41 926
Email: lynnpublications@eircom.net **Web site:** http://www.irishtrucker.com
Date Established: 1998; **Freq:** Monthly; **Cover Price:** EUR 38.00; **Circ:** 19,000
Usual Pagination: 100
Editor: John Lynch; **Advertising Manager:** Colm Lynch
Profile: Magazine focusing on commercial vehicles includes industry news and product reviews.
Readership: Aimed at fleet managers in national and multinational companies.
ADVERTISING RATES:
Full Page Colour .... EUR 1500.00
Agency Commission: 21%
Mechanical Data: Trim Size: 297 x 210mm, Film: Digital
Copy instructions: *Copy Date:* 2 weeks prior to publication date
Average ad content per issue: 40%
BUSINESS: TRANSPORT: Commercial Vehicles

IRISH VAN & TRUCK
623530E77A-88

Editorial: 2 Sunbury, Kilcullen, CO. KILDARE
Tel: 45 48 10 90
Email: irishcarnews@gmail.com **Web site:** http://www.irishcarnews.ie
ISSN: 1393-533X
Date Established: 1990; **Freq:** Quarterly; **Cover Price:** EUR 3.20; **Circ:** 8,000
Usual Pagination: 54
Editor: Brian Byrne; **Advertising Manager:** Patricia Whelan
Profile: Magazine containing information of vans and LCVs, including information about new models and comparisons.
Readership: Read by those considering purchasing a new van or truck.
CONSUMER: MOTORING & CYCLING: Motoring

IRISH VETERINARY JOURNAL
4417E64H-100

Editorial: 31 Deansgrange Road, Blackrock, CO. DUBLIN **Tel:** 1 28 93 305 **Fax:** 12896406
Email: vet@ifpmedia.com **Web site:** http://www.irishveterinaryjournal.com
ISSN: 0368-0762
Freq: Monthly; **Annual Sub.:** EUR 140; **Circ:** 2,600
Usual Pagination: 60
Editor: Robert Hogan
Profile: Journal focusing on veterinary issues.
Readership: Read by veterinary surgeons.
ADVERTISING RATES:
Full Page Colour .... EUR 2100
Agency Commission: 10%
Mechanical Data: Film: Digital, Type Area: 270 x 185mm, Bleed Size: 303 x 216mm, Trim Size: 279 x 210mm, Col Length: 270mm, Page Width: 185mm
Average ad content per issue: 30%
BUSINESS: OTHER CLASSIFICATIONS: Veterinary

IRISH WEDDING DIARY
1666372E74L-153

Editorial: 10 Rathgar Road, Rathmines, DUBLIN 6
T: 1 49 83 242 **Fax:** 14983217
Email: lisa@irishweddingdiary.ie **Web site:** http://www.irishweddingdiary.ie
Freq: Quarterly; **Circ:** 6,102
Usual Pagination: 200
Editor: Lisa Cannon
Profile: Magazine covering all aspects of weddings including, fashion, beauty, honeymoons, venues, car hire, photography and flowers.
Readership: Aimed at brides and grooms to be.
ADVERTISING RATES:
Full Page Colour .... EUR 1800
Agency Commission: 15%
Mechanical Data: Type Area: 270 x 183mm, Bleed Size: 306 x 216mm, Trim Size: 297 x 210mm, Col Length: 270mm, Page Width: 183mm, Print Process: Web-fed litho
Copy instructions: *Copy Date:* 14 days prior to publication date
Average ad content per issue: 40%
CONSUMER: WOMEN'S INTEREST CONSUMER MAGAZINES: Brides

IRISH YOUTH WORK SCENE
629667E91D-90

Editorial: Youth Work Ireland, 20 Lower Dominick Street, DUBLIN 1 **Tel:** 1 85 84 500 **Fax:** 1 87 242 183
Email: fbissett@youthworkireland.ie **Web site:** http://www.iywc.com
ISSN: 0791-6302
Date Established: 1992; **Freq:** Quarterly; **Annual Sub.:** EUR 20.00; **Circ:** 500
Usual Pagination: 24
Editor: Fran Bissett
Profile: Practice-based magazine focusing on youth work related issues.
Readership: Read by youth work practitioners and policy makers as well as senior volunteers.
CONSUMER: RECREATION & LEISURE: Children & Youth

IRISHTIMES.COM
713643E65A-81

Formerly: ireland.com
Editorial: The Irish Times Buildig, 24-28 Tara Street, DUBLIN 2 **Tel:** 1 67 58 000 **Fax:** 14727117
Email: news@irishtimes.com **Web site:** http://www.irishtimes.com
Date Established: 1994; **Freq:** Daily; **Circ:** 3,892,929 Unique Users
Profile: irishtimes.com is the online edition of The Irish Times including Irish and international news, business, sports and Irish and international weather. It aimed at Irish internet users and the Irish interest market. Launched in 1994. The Irish Times site moved from ireland.com to irishtimes.com following the integration of the print and online newsrooms in early 2008.
NATIONAL DAILY & SUNDAY NEWSPAPERS: National Daily Newspapers

JOURNAL 2
1659449E21A-201

Editorial: For all contact details see main record, Irish Farmers Journal
Freq: Weekly
Supplement to: Irish Farmers Journal
BUSINESS: AGRICULTURE & FARMING

JOURNAL OF CORPORATE REAL ESTATE
1750462U1E-393

Editorial: Jones Lang LaSalle, 10-11 Molesworth Street, DUBLIN 2
Email: clare.eriksson@eu.jll.com **Web site:** http://www.emeraldinsight.com/jcre.htm
ISSN: 1463-001X
Date Established: 1999; **Freq:** Quarterly; **Annual Sub.:** £399
Usual Pagination: 96
Editor: Aimee Wood
Profile: Publication dedicated to corporate real estate providing guidance on best practice, new developments, applied research and case studies on key strategic issues.
Readership: Aimed at corporate real estate executives.
BUSINESS: FINANCE & ECONOMICS: Property

JOURNAL OF THE IRISH DENTAL ASSOCIATION
4248E56D-10

Editorial: The Malthouse, 537 NCR, DUBLIN 1
Tel: 1 85 61 166 **Fax:** 18561169
Email: paul@thinkmedia.ie **Web site:** http://www.dentist.ie
ISSN: 0021-1133
Date Established: 1960; **Freq:** 6 issues yearly; Free to qualifying individuals
Annual Sub.: EUR 80; **Circ:** 3,246
Usual Pagination: 52
Editor: Paul O'Grady
Profile: Journal of the Irish Dental Association, covering scientific issues, business news and European news. Also features on dentistry related matters or personnel.
Readership: Read by dentists and practice managers.
ADVERTISING RATES:
Full Page Colour .... EUR 1800
Agency Commission: 15%
Mechanical Data: Type Area: 270 x 185mm, Bleed Size: 303 x 216mm, Trim Size: 297 x 210mm, Col Length: 270mm, Page Width: 185mm, Film: Digital
Average ad content per issue: 30%
BUSINESS: HEALTH & MEDICAL: Dental

KERRY LIFE
1743561E72-823

Editorial: Denny Street, Tralee, CO. KERRY
Freq: Weekly
Supplement to: The Kerryman Series
LOCAL NEWSPAPERS

THE KERRYMAN (NORTH EDITION)
768707E72-4900_10

Editorial: Denny Street, Tralee, CO. KERRY 0
Part of Series, see entry for: The Kerryman Series
LOCAL NEWSPAPERS

THE KERRYMAN SERIES
623727E72-4900

Formerly: Kerryman and Corkman Series
Editorial: Denny Street, Tralee, CO. KERRY
Tel: 66 71 45 500 **Fax:** 667145572
Email: news@kerryman.ie **Web site:** http://www.kerryman.ie
Freq: Weekly; **Cover Price:** EUR 1.80; **Circ:** 7,262
Editor: Declan Malone; **Advertising Manager:** Siobhan Murphy
ADVERTISING RATES:
SCC .... EUR 27.65
Agency Commission: 10%
Mechanical Data: Col Widths (Display): 34mm, Page Width: 340mm, Print Process: Web-fed offset litho, Film: Digital, Type Area: 560 x 340mm, Col Length: 560mm, No. of Columns (Display): 9
Average ad content per issue: 50%
Series owner and contact point for the following titles, see individual entries:
The Kerryman (North Edition)
The Kerryman (South Edition)
The Kerryman (Tralee Edition)
Supplement(s): Kerry Life - 52xY
LOCAL NEWSPAPERS

THE KERRYMAN (SOUTH EDITION)
768708E72-4900_101

Editorial: Denny Street, Tralee, CO. KERRY 0
Part of Series, see entry for: The Kerryman Series
LOCAL NEWSPAPERS

THE KERRYMAN (TRALEE EDITION)
768709E72-4900_102

Editorial: Denny Street, Tralee, CO. KERRY 0
Part of Series, see entry for: The Kerryman Series
LOCAL NEWSPAPERS

KERRY'S EYE
754420E72-4980

Editorial: 22 Ashe Street, Tralee, CO. KERRY
Tel: 66 71 49 200 **Fax:** 667123163
Email: news@kerryseye.com **Web site:** http://www.kerryseye.com
Date Established: 1974; **Freq:** Weekly; **Cover Price:** EUR 1.80; **Circ:** 26,000
Editor: Colin Lacey; **Advertising Manager:** Brendan Kennelly
ADVERTISING RATES:
Full Page Mono .... EUR 2650
Full Page Colour .... EUR 2900
Agency Commission: 15%
Mechanical Data: Type Area: 350 x 260mm, Col Length: 350mm, Col Widths (Display): 33.16mm, No. of Columns (Display): 7, Page Width: 260mm, Film: Digital
Average ad content per issue: 20%
LOCAL NEWSPAPERS

KILDARE NATIONALIST
754403E72-4990

Editorial: Liffey House, Edward Street, Newbridge, CO. KILDARE **Tel:** 45 43 21 47 **Fax:** 45433720
Email: news@kildare-nationalist.ie **Web site:** http://www.kildare-nationalist.ie
Date Established: 1992; **Freq:** Weekly; **Cover Price:** EUR 2.10; **Circ:** 6,000
Usual Pagination: 32
Editor: Barbara Sheridan; **Advertising Manager:** Mike Moore
ADVERTISING RATES:
SCC .... EUR 6.50
Mechanical Data: Col Widths (Display): 36mm, Type Area: 533 x 342mm, Col Length: 533mm, Page Width: 342mm, Film: Digital, No. of Columns (Display): 9
Average ad content per issue: 40%
Supplement(s): The Pulse - 52xY
LOCAL NEWSPAPERS

KILDARE POST
1799743E72-8224

Editorial: Unit W5D, Toughers Business Park, Newbridge, CO. KILDARE **Tel:** 45 40 93 50
Fax: 45409351
Email: editor@kildarepost.com
Date Established: 2006; **Freq:** Weekly; **Cover Price:** Free; **Circ:** 30,000
Managing Editor: Sian Busher
ADVERTISING RATES:
SCC .... EUR 10
Agency Commission: 15%
Mechanical Data: Type Area: 330 x 265mm, Col Length: 330mm, Page Width: 265mm, Col Widths (Display): 26.5mm, Film: Digital

verage ad content per issue: 70%
OCAL NEWSPAPERS

KILDARE TIMES 623794E80-60
ditorial: Unit 1, Eurospar, Fairgreen, Naas, CO. ILDARE **Tel:** 4 58 95 111 **Fax:** 45895099
mail: kildaretimes@eircom.net
req: Weekly; **Cover Price:** Free; **Circ:** 36,500
sual Pagination: 24
dvertising Manager: Terry O'Mahoney
rofile: Newspaper containing local news and formation.
eadership: Read by residents of Kildare.
DVERTISING RATES:
ull Page Mono .... EUR 1400
ull Page Colour .... EUR 1800
Mechanical Data: Page Width: 270mm, Film: Digital, ype Area: 315 x 270mm, Col Length: 315mm, No. of olumns (Display): 8
ditions:
orth Kildare Times
outh Kildare Times
ONSUMER: RURAL & REGIONAL INTEREST

KILKENNY ARTS FESTIVAL
1744314E72-8240
ditorial: 34 High Street, KILKENNY
req: Annual
upplement to: Kilkenny People
OCAL NEWSPAPERS

KILKENNY PEOPLE 4316E72-5000
ditorial: 34 High Street, KILKENNY
el: 56 77 21 015 **Fax:** 56 77 21 414
mail: editor@kilkennypeople.ie **Web site:** http:// www.kilkennypeople.ie
ate Established: 1892; **Freq:** Weekly; **Cover Price:** UR 1.85; **Circ:** 12,983
ditor: Brian Keyes; **Advertising Manager:** Bernie Moran
DVERTISING RATES:
ull Page Mono .... EUR 5248
ull Page Colour .... EUR 6560
CC .... EUR 10.80
gency Commission: 15%
echanical Data: Type Area: 538 x 343.5mm, Col ength: 538mm, Page Width: 343.5mm, No. of Columns (Display): 9, Col Widths (Display): 35mm, ilm: Digital
Supplement(s): Farming - 4xY, Kilkenny Arts Festival 1xY, Motors - 4xY, Property - 4xY, Weddings - 4xY
LOCAL NEWSPAPERS

KILLARNEY ADVERTISER
623791E72-5010
Editorial: Unit 1, Ballycasheen, Killarney, CO. KERRY **Tel:** 64 66 32 215 **Fax:** 64 66 327 22
Email: newsdesk@kilarneyadvertiser.ie **Web site:** http://www.killarneyadvertiser.ie
Date Established: 1973; **Freq:** Weekly; **Cover Price:** Free; **Circ:** 7,500
ADVERTISING RATES:
Full Page Colour .... EUR 440
Mechanical Data: Trim Size: 297 x 210mm
Average ad content per issue: 70%
LOCAL NEWSPAPERS

THE KINGDOM NEWSPAPER
623736E72-5040
Editorial: 65 New Street, Killarney, CO. KERRY
Tel: 64 66 31 392 **Fax:** 646634609
Email: news@thekingdom.ie **Web site:** http://www.the-kingdom.ie
ISSN: 0647-1140
Date Established: 1923; **Freq:** Weekly; **Cover Price:** EUR 1.70; **Circ:** 18,200
Editor: Mary Murphy; **Advertising Manager:** Catherine O'Sullivan
ADVERTISING RATES:
Full Page Mono .... EUR 1200
Full Page Colour .... EUR 1400
SCC .... EUR 60
Agency Commission: 15%
Mechanical Data: Page Width: 265mm, No. of Columns (Display): 7, Col Widths (Display): 37mm, Film: Digital, Type Area: 326 x 265mm, Col Length: 326mm
LOCAL NEWSPAPERS

KINSALE ADVERTISER
764506E72-5050
Editorial: Emmet Place, Kinsale, CO. CORK
Tel: 21 47 74 313 **Fax:** 214774339
Email: info@kinsaleadvertiser.iol.ie **Web site:** http:// www.kinsalenewsletter.com
Freq: Weekly; **Cover Price:** Free; **Circ:** 1,500
Advertising Manager: Niamh O'Connell
ADVERTISING RATES:
Full Page Mono .... EUR 88.33
Mechanical Data: No. of Columns (Display): 4, Film: Digital, Type Area: 173 x 131mm, Col Length: 173mm, Page Width: 131mm
Average ad content per issue: 100%
LOCAL NEWSPAPERS

KINSALE & DISTRICT NEWSLETTER 764505E80-70
Editorial: Emmet Place, Kinsale, CO. CORK
Tel: 21 47 74 313 **Fax:** 214774339
Email: info@kinsalenews.com **Web site:** http://www.kinsalenewsletter.com
Date Established: 1976; **Freq:** Monthly; **Cover Price:** EUR 2.75; **Circ:** 1,000
Usual Pagination: 32
Advertising Manager: Niamh O'Connell
Profile: Newsletter covering the latest in current affairs and a report of the monthly proceedings in Kinsale court. Each issue includes a different item of historical interest from the Kinsale & District Local History Society. Regular features include letters to the editor, photo's and details of local family milestones.
Readership: Aimed at local residents.
ADVERTISING RATES:
Full Page Mono .... EUR 73
Full Page Colour .... EUR 120
Mechanical Data: Trim Size: 238 x 199mm, Film: Digital
CONSUMER: RURAL & REGIONAL INTEREST

KISS 1640236E74F-56
Editorial: 2-4 Ely Place, DUBLIN 2 **Tel:** 1 48 04 700
Fax: 14807799
Email: info@kiss.ie **Web site:** http://www.kiss.ie
Date Established: 2003; **Freq:** Monthly; **Cover Price:** EUR 2.80; **Circ:** 22,469
Usual Pagination: 112
Advertising Manager: Jakki Brannigan
Profile: Magazine covering lifestyle, fashion, beauty, health, celebrity gossip and relationships.
Readership: Aimed at girls aged between 13 and 17 years old.
ADVERTISING RATES:
Full Page Colour .... EUR 3100
Agency Commission: 10%
Mechanical Data: Type Area: 250 x 174mm, Col Length: 250mm, Bleed Size: 280 x 210mm, Trim Size: 270 x 200mm, Page Width: 174mm
CONSUMER: WOMEN'S INTEREST CONSUMER MAGAZINES: Teenage

KITCHENS AND BATHROOMS
1666267E74C-206
Editorial: 1st Floor, Cunningham House, 130 Francis Street, DUBLIN 8 **Tel:** 1 41 67 900 **Fax:** 14167901
Email: karen@houseandhome.ie **Web site:** http:// www.houseandhome.ie
Date Established: 2002; **Freq:** Annual - Published in March; **Circ:** 20,000
Editor: Karen Hesse; **Advertising Manager:** Imelda Crombie
Profile: Magazine covering all aspects of planning or designing a new kitchen or bathroom or revamping and old one. Includes choosing fittings and finishes, appliances, colour schemes, flooring and lighting.
Readership: Aimed at those planning to update their kitchen or bathroom.
ADVERTISING RATES:
Full Page Colour .... EUR 2850
Agency Commission: 10%
Mechanical Data: Bleed Size: 307 x 220mm, Trim Size: 297 x 210mm, Film: Digital
CONSUMER: WOMEN'S INTEREST CONSUMER MAGAZINES: Home & Family

KNOWLEDGE IRELAND
1703196E5R-41
Editorial: Top Floor, 43B Yeats Way, Park West Business Park, Nangor Road, DUBLIN 12
Tel: 1 62 51 444 **Fax:** 16251402
Email: scorcoran@whitespace.ie **Web site:** http:// www.knowledgeireland.ie
Freq: 6 issues yearly; **Cover Price:** EUR 7.50 Free to qualifying individuals ; **Circ:** 5,753
Usual Pagination: 40
Editor: Sorcha Corcoran
Profile: Magazine covering strategy, change and technology management with news and analysis, product and website reviews, interviews and events.
Readership: Aimed at public and private sector management.
ADVERTISING RATES:
Full Page Colour .... EUR 3000
Agency Commission: 15%
Mechanical Data: Type Area: 267 x 180mm, Col Length: 267mm, Page Width: 180mm, Bleed Size: 307 x 216mm
Average ad content per issue: 25%
BUSINESS: COMPUTERS & AUTOMATION: Computers Related

LANDSCAPE AND GROUND MAINTENANCE 1668292E32A-151
Editorial: For all contact details see main record, Local Authority News
Freq: Annual
Supplement to: Local Authority News
BUSINESS: LOCAL GOVERNMENT, LEISURE & RECREATION: Local Government

LAOIS NATIONALIST 1659411E72-8212
Editorial: Coliseum Lane, PORTLAOISE
Tel: 57 86 70 216 **Fax:** 578661399
Email: news@laois-nationalist.ie **Web site:** http:// www.laois-nationalist.ie
Freq: Weekly; **Circ:** 4,500
Editor: Conal O'Boyle
ADVERTISING RATES:
Full Page Colour .... EUR 1965
SCC .... EUR 4.20
Mechanical Data: Col Widths (Display): 34mm, No. of Columns (Display): 9, Film: Digital, Type Area: 540 x 340mm, Col Length: 540mm, Page Width: 340mm
LOCAL NEWSPAPERS

LAW SOCIETY GAZETTE 4224E44-75
Editorial: Blackhall Place, DUBLIN 7 **Tel:** 1 67 24 828
Fax: 16724877
Email: gazette@lawsociety.ie **Web site:** http://www.lawsocietygazette.ie
Date Established: 1907; **Freq:** Monthly - Double issues Jan/Feb and Aug/Sept; **Cover Price:** EUR 3.75
Free to qualifying individuals
Annual Sub.: EUR 57; **Circ:** 11,200
Usual Pagination: 68
Editor: Mark McDermott; **Advertising Manager:** Seán Ó'hOisín
Profile: Official publication of the Law Society of Ireland.
Readership: Aimed at lawyers, members of the judiciary and students of law.
ADVERTISING RATES:
Full Page Mono .... EUR 2525
Full Page Colour .... EUR 3050
Agency Commission: 15%
Mechanical Data: Trim Size: 297 x 210mm, Bleed Size: 310 x 224mm, Type Area: 266 x 192mm, Col Length: 266mm, Film: Digital, Print Process: Litho, Page Width: 192mm
Average ad content per issue: 30%
BUSINESS: LEGAL

LEINSTER EXPRESS (LAOIS AND DISTRICTS) 4317E72-5100
Editorial: Dublin Road, Portlaoise, CO. LAOIS
Tel: 57 86 21 666 **Fax:** 578620491
Email: pat@leinsterexpress.ie **Web site:** http://www.leinsterexpress.ie
Date Established: 1837; **Freq:** Weekly
Annual Sub.: EUR 112.32; **Circ:** 12,493
Usual Pagination: 72
Editor: Pat Somers
ADVERTISING RATES:
Full Page Mono .... EUR 3452
Full Page Colour .... EUR 3935
SCC .... EUR 13.15
Agency Commission: 10%
Mechanical Data: Page Width: 260mm, Col Length: 340mm, Col Widths (Display): 34.5mm, No. of Columns (Display): 7, Type Area: 340 x 260mm, Print Process: Web-fed offset litho, Film: Digital
Average ad content per issue: 50%
LOCAL NEWSPAPERS

LEINSTER LEADER 4315E72-5200
Editorial: 19 South Main Street, Naas, CO. KILDARE
Tel: 45 89 73 02 **Fax:** 45871168
Email: editor@leinsterleader.ie **Web site:** http://www.leinsterleader.ie
Date Established: 1880; **Freq:** Weekly; **Circ:** 7,482
News Editor: Laura Coates; **Advertising Manager:** Emer Egan
ADVERTISING RATES:
Full Page Mono .... EUR 5145
Full Page Colour .... EUR 6208
SCC .... EUR 15.20
Agency Commission: 15%
Mechanical Data: Type Area: 520 x 348mm, Col Length: 520mm, Page Width: 348mm, No. of Columns (Display): 8, Col Widths (Display): 40mm, Film: Digital
LOCAL NEWSPAPERS

LEITRIM OBSERVER
1797205E72-5300_100
Editorial: Unit 3, Hartley Business Park, Carrick-on-Shannon, CO. LEITRIM 0
Freq: Weekly; **Cover Price:** EUR 1.90; **Circ:** 7,487
Usual Pagination: 40
Part of Series, see entry for: Leitrim Observer Series
LOCAL NEWSPAPERS

LEITRIM OBSERVER SERIES
4318E72-5300
Formerly: Leitrim Observer
Editorial: Unit 3, Hartley Business Park, Carrick-on-Shannon, CO. LEITRIM **Tel:** 71 96 20 025
Fax: 719620039
Email: editor@leitrimobserver.ie **Web site:** http:// www.leitrimobserver.ie
Date Established: 1890; **Freq:** Weekly; **Circ:** 8,286
Editor: Claire McGovern
Language(s): English; Gaelic
Agency Commission: 15%
Average ad content per issue: 40%
Series owner and contact point for the following titles, see individual entries:
Leitrim Observer
Supplement(s): Farming - 12xY, First Day at School - 1xY, House and Home - 12xY, Nostalgia, Style Magazine
LOCAL NEWSPAPERS

LETTERKENNY POST
1799742E72-8223
Editorial: River House, Diyarch Business Park, Letterkenny, CO. DONEGAL **Tel:** 74 91 94 800
Fax: 749194801
Email: chris@letterkennypost.com **Web site:** http:// www.letterkennypost.com
Freq: Weekly; **Cover Price:** Free; **Circ:** 15,000
Editor: Chris Ashmore
ADVERTISING RATES:
Full Page Colour .... EUR 1584
SCC .... EUR 60
Agency Commission: 15%
Mechanical Data: Type Area: 330 x 265mm, Col Length: 330mm, Page Width: 265mm, Col Widths (Display): 26.5mm, Film: Digital
Average ad content per issue: 70%
LOCAL NEWSPAPERS

LICENSING WORLD 4167E9A-20
Editorial: 1st Floor, Gratten House, Temple Road, Blackrock, CO. DUBLIN **Tel:** 1 76 42 700
Fax: 17642750
Email: n.tynan@jemma.ie **Web site:** http://www.licensingworld.ie
ISSN: 1393-0826
Date Established: 1942; **Freq:** Monthly - Published around the middle of the cover month; **Annual Sub.:** EUR 74; **Circ:** 3,120
Usual Pagination: 60
Editor: Nigel Tynan; **Advertising Manager:** Simon Grennan
Profile: Magazine for the licensed trade.
Readership: Aimed at managers of pubs, drinks companies, off licences, nightclubs and restaurants.
ADVERTISING RATES:
Full Page Colour .... EUR 2750
Agency Commission: 10%
Mechanical Data: Bleed Size: 307 x 220mm, Trim Size: 297 x 210mm, Type Area: 270 x 190mm, Col Length: 270mm, Page Width: 190mm, Film: Digital
Copy instructions: *Copy Date:* 7 days prior to publication date
Average ad content per issue: 25%
BUSINESS: DRINKS & LICENSED TRADE: Drinks, Licensed Trade, Wines & Spirits

LIFE AND TV 1750284E72-8242
Editorial: Channing House, Rowe Street, Wexford, CO. WEXFORD
Freq: Weekly
Supplement to: Wexford People Series
LOCAL NEWSPAPERS

LIFE MAGAZINE 1668500E65H-2
Editorial: Independent House, 27-32 Talbot Street, DUBLIN 1 **Tel:** 1 70 55 596 **Fax:** 17055779
Email: boconnor@unison.independent.ie **Web site:** http://www.unison.com
Date Established: 2004; **Freq:** Sunday - Irish Republic; **Circ:** 1,000,000
Usual Pagination: 56
Editor: Brendan O'Connor
Profile: Magazine covering beauty, fashion, lifestyle, health, food and eating out with TV previews and listings and life features including celebrity interviews.
ADVERTISING RATES:
Full Page Colour .... EUR 15627
Agency Commission: 10%
Mechanical Data: Type Area: 286 x 246mm, Bleed Size: 316 x 276mm, Trim Size: 310 x 270mm, Col Length: 286mm, Page Width: 246mm, No. of Columns (Display): 4, Film: Digital
Average ad content per issue: 30%
Supplement to: Sunday Independent
NATIONAL DAILY & SUNDAY NEWSPAPERS: National Colour Supplements

LIFESTYLE 1739819E72-8243
Editorial: Larkin House, Oldtown road, DONEGAL PE27DS
Freq: Weekly
Supplement to: Donegal Democrat
LOCAL NEWSPAPERS

LIFETIMES 623799E80-201
Editorial: 42 Northwood Business Park, Santry, DUBLIN 7 **Tel:** 1 86 23 939 **Fax:** 18306833
Email: lifetimesnewsdesk@me.com
Date Established: 1987; **Freq:** 26 issues yearly; **Cover Price:** Free; **Circ:** 80,000
Usual Pagination: 40
Editor: Edel Williams
Profile: Magazine containing information about events and lifestyle in Dublin. Also covers business, health and fitness, beauty and general medical matters.
Readership: Aimed at those living and working in Dublin.
ADVERTISING RATES:
Full Page Mono .... EUR 4200
Full Page Colour .... EUR 5250
SCC .... EUR 16
Agency Commission: 15%
Mechanical Data: Type Area: 332 x 258mm, Col Length: 332mm, Page Width: 258mm, No. of Columns (Display): 8, Col Widths (Display): 29mm, Film: Digital
Average ad content per issue: 45%
CONSUMER: RURAL & REGIONAL INTEREST

LIFFEY CHAMPION 623738E72-5350
Editorial: The Cornmill, Mill Lane, Leixlip, CO. KILDARE **Tel:** 1 62 45 533 **Fax:** 16243013
Email: editor@liffeychampion.net **Web site:** http://www.liffeychampion.net
Date Established: 1991; **Freq:** Weekly; **Cover Price:** EUR 1.90; **Circ:** 9,000
News Editor: Aideen Sutton; **Advertising Manager:** Marcella Faherty; **Managing Editor:** Vincent Sutton
ADVERTISING RATES:
Full Page Colour .... EUR 1680
Mechanical Data: Page Width: 265mm, Film: Digital, Type Area: 338 x 265mm, Col Length: 338mm, Col Widths (Display): 34mm, No. of Columns (Display): 7
Average ad content per issue: 20%
LOCAL NEWSPAPERS

LIMERICK CHRONICLE 768714E72-5500_101
Editorial: 54 O'Connell Street, LIMERICK 0
Freq: Weekly; **Cover Price:** EUR 0.85; **Circ:** 8,500
ADVERTISING RATES:
Full Page Mono .... EUR 1420
Full Page Colour .... EUR 1670
SCC .... EUR 6.55
Part of Series, see entry for: Limerick Leader & Chronicle Series
LOCAL NEWSPAPERS

LIMERICK LEADER & CHRONICLE SERIES 4320E72-5500
Formerly: Limerick Leader
Editorial: 54 O'Connell Street, LIMERICK
Tel: 61 21 45 00 **Fax:** 61401424
Email: editorial@limerickleader.ie **Web site:** http://www.limerickleader.ie
Date Established: 1889; **Freq:** Weekly; **Circ:** 70,619
Usual Pagination: 60
News Editor: Eugene Phelan; **Advertising Manager:** Robert Power
Profile: Twitter: http://twitter.com/limerick_leader .
ADVERTISING RATES:
Full Page Mono .... EUR 6800
Full Page Colour .... EUR 7330
SCC .... EUR 23.80
Agency Commission: 10%
Mechanical Data: Page Width: 263mm, Type Area: 393 x 263mm, Col Length: 393mm, No. of Columns (Display): 6, Col Widths (Display): 36mm
Series owner and contact point for the following titles, see individual entries:
Limerick Chronicle
Limerick Leader (City Edition)
Limerick Leader (County Edition)
Limerick Leader (Monday)
Limerick Leader (Wednesday)
Limerick Leader Weekender
LOCAL NEWSPAPERS

LIMERICK LEADER (CITY EDITION) 1693390E72-5500_102
Editorial: 54 O'Connell Street, LIMERICK 0
Freq: Weekly; **Cover Price:** EUR 1.85
ADVERTISING RATES:
SCC .... EUR 16.50
Part of Series, see entry for: Limerick Leader & Chronicle Series
LOCAL NEWSPAPERS

LIMERICK LEADER (COUNTY EDITION) 768713E72-5500_100
Formerly: Limerick Leader
Editorial: 54 O'Connell Street, LIMERICK 0
Freq: Weekly; **Cover Price:** EUR 1.85; **Circ:** 21,619
ADVERTISING RATES:
Full Page Mono .... EUR 6800
Full Page Colour .... EUR 7330
SCC .... EUR 23.80
Part of Series, see entry for: Limerick Leader & Chronicle Series
LOCAL NEWSPAPERS

LIMERICK LEADER (MONDAY) 1694861E72-5500_103
Editorial: 54 O'Connell Street, LIMERICK 0
Freq: Weekly; **Cover Price:** EUR 0.85; **Circ:** 7,500
ADVERTISING RATES:
Full Page Mono .... EUR 1535
Full Page Colour .... EUR 1805
SCC .... EUR 7.80
Part of Series, see entry for: Limerick Leader & Chronicle Series
LOCAL NEWSPAPERS

LIMERICK LEADER (WEDNESDAY) 1694862E72-5500_104
Editorial: 54 O'Connell Street, LIMERICK 0
Freq: Weekly; **Cover Price:** EUR 0.85; **Circ:** 8,000
ADVERTISING RATES:
Full Page Mono .... EUR 1535
Full Page Colour .... EUR 1805
SCC .... EUR 7.80
Part of Series, see entry for: Limerick Leader & Chronicle Series
LOCAL NEWSPAPERS

LIMERICK LEADER WEEKENDER 1794820E72-5500_105
Editorial: 54 O'Connell Street, LIMERICK 0
Date Established: 2006; **Freq:** Weekly; **Cover Price:** Free; **Circ:** 25,000
ADVERTISING RATES:
SCC .... EUR 6.50
Part of Series, see entry for: Limerick Leader & Chronicle Series
LOCAL NEWSPAPERS

LIMERICK NOW 1810694E80-207
Editorial: Harris House, Tuan Road, CO. GALWAY
Tel: 91 77 70 77 **Fax:** 91777080
Email: editor@limericknow.ie **Web site:** http://www.limericknow.ie
Date Established: 2007; **Freq:** Monthly; **Cover Price:** EUR 3.50; **Circ:** 50,000
Editor: Sinead Ni Neachtain; **Advertising Manager:** Kaitriona Dillon
Profile: Magazine focusing on positive living, lifestyle, health, fashion and interior design based in and around the traditions of South West Ireland.
Readership: Aimed at those with an interest in South West Ireland aged 25 years old plus.
ADVERTISING RATES:
Full Page Colour .... EUR 1450
Agency Commission: 15%
Mechanical Data: Type Area: 300 x 217mm, Col Length: 300mm, Page Width: 217mm, Film: Digital, Bleed Size: +3mm
Copy instructions: *Copy Date:* 21 days prior to publication date
CONSUMER: RURAL & REGIONAL INTEREST

LIMERICK POST 4321E72-5600
Editorial: 97 Henry Street, Rutland Street, LIMERICK
Tel: 61 41 33 22 **Fax:** 61417684
Email: news@limerickpost.ie **Web site:** http://www.limerickpost.ie
ISSN: 1393-8150
Date Established: 1986; **Freq:** Weekly; **Cover Price:** EUR 0.25
Free to qualifying individuals ; **Circ:** 17,369
Usual Pagination: 44
Editor: John O'Shaughnessy
ADVERTISING RATES:
Full Page Mono .... EUR 2336
Full Page Colour .... EUR 2536
SCC .... EUR 13.80
Agency Commission: 15%
Mechanical Data: Type Area: 339 x 260mm, Page Width: 260mm, Print Process: Web-fed offset litho, Film: Digital, No. of Columns (Display): 8, Col Widths (Display): 31mm, Col Length: 339mm
Average ad content per issue: 45%
LOCAL NEWSPAPERS

LIVING IN FINGAL 1800753E72-8244
Editorial: For all contact details see main record, Fingal Independent Series
Freq: Annual
Supplement to: Fingal Independent Series
LOCAL NEWSPAPERS

THE LOCAL NEWS (NORTH EDITION) 768717E72-5650_100
Editorial: Bank House Centre, 331 South Circular Road, DUBLIN 8
Freq: 26 issues yearly; **Cover Price:** Free
ADVERTISING RATES:
Full Page Mono .... EUR 1250
Full Page Colour .... EUR 1750
SCC .... EUR 8.90
Part of Series, see entry for: The Local News Series
LOCAL NEWSPAPERS

THE LOCAL NEWS SERIES 754388E72-5650
Formerly: Local News
Editorial: Bank House Centre, 331 South Circular Road, DUBLIN 8 **Tel:** 1 45 34 011 **Fax:** 14549024
Email: frank@localnews.ie **Web site:** http://www.localnews.ie
Date Established: 1988; **Freq:** 26 issues yearly; **Cover Price:** Free; **Circ:** 119,000
Agency Commission: 15%
Mechanical Data: Type Area: 375 x 255mm, Col Length: 375mm, Page Width: 255mm, No. of Columns (Display): 8, Col Widths (Display): 25mm
Average ad content per issue: 40%
Series owner and contact point for the following titles, see individual entries:
The Local News (North Edition)
The Local News (South Edition)
The Local News (West Edition)
LOCAL NEWSPAPERS

THE LOCAL NEWS (SOUTH EDITION) 768719E72-5650_102
Editorial: Bank House Centre, 331 South Circular Road, DUBLIN 8
Freq: 26 issues yearly; **Cover Price:** Free
ADVERTISING RATES:
Full Page Mono .... EUR 1250
Full Page Colour .... EUR 1750
SCC .... EUR 8.90
Part of Series, see entry for: The Local News Series
LOCAL NEWSPAPERS

THE LOCAL NEWS (WEST EDITION) 768718E72-5650_101
Editorial: Bank House Centre, 331 South Circular Road, DUBLIN 8
Freq: 26 issues yearly; **Cover Price:** Free
ADVERTISING RATES:
Full Page Mono .... EUR 1250
Full Page Colour .... EUR 1750
SCC .... EUR 8.90
Part of Series, see entry for: The Local News Series
LOCAL NEWSPAPERS

LONGFORD LEADER 4322E72-5700
Editorial: Leader House, Dublin Road, LONGFORD
Tel: 43 45 241 **Fax:** 4341489
Email: newsroom@longford-leader.ie **Web site:** http://www.longfordtoday.ie
Freq: Weekly; **Cover Price:** EUR 1.95; **Circ:** 8,079
Editor: Sheila Reilly; **News Editor:** Neil Halligan
ADVERTISING RATES:
Full Page Mono .... EUR 4897
Full Page Colour .... EUR 6130
SCC .... EUR 11.85
Agency Commission: 15%
Mechanical Data: Type Area: 540 x 340mm, Col Length: 540mm, No. of Columns (Display): 9, Page Width: 340mm, Film: Positive, right reading, emulsion side down
LOCAL NEWSPAPERS

THE LUCAN & CLONDALKIN NEWS 1835777E72-7340_101
Editorial: PO Box 3430, Tallaght, DUBLIN 24
Freq: Monthly; **Cover Price:** Free; **Circ:** 30,000
Part of Series, see entry for: The Tallaght News
LOCAL NEWSPAPERS

LUCAN GAZETTE 1698873E72-8204_101
Editorial: Block 3A, Mill Bank Business Park, Lower Road, Lucan, CO. DUBLIN 0
Freq: Weekly; **Cover Price:** Free; **Circ:** 41,653
ADVERTISING RATES:
Full Page Colour .... EUR 1800
Part of Series, see entry for: Gazette Series
LOCAL NEWSPAPERS

MANDATE NEWS 764496E14L-95
Editorial: 9 Cavendish Row, DUBLIN 1
Tel: 1 87 46 321 **Fax:** 18729581
Email: johndouglas@mandate.ie **Web site:** http://www.mandate.ie
Freq: Quarterly; **Cover Price:** Free; **Circ:** 10,000
Usual Pagination: 12
Editor: John Douglas
Profile: Newsletter of the trade union for retail, bar and administrative workers.
Readership: Read by members.
BUSINESS: COMMERCE, INDUSTRY & MANAGEMENT: Trade Unions

MARINE TIMES NEWSPAPER 4227E45B-100
Formerly: Marine Times Newspaper Ltd
Editorial: Ballymoon Industrial Estate, Kilcar, CO. DONEGAL **Tel:** 74 97 38 836 **Fax:** 749738841
Email: marinetimes@eircom.net **Web site:** http://www.marinetimes.ie
ISSN: 0791-1548
Date Established: 1989; **Freq:** Monthly; **Cover Price:** EUR 2.50
Annual Sub.: EUR 40; **Circ:** 6,500
Usual Pagination: 40
Editor: Mark McCarthy; **Advertising Manager:** Anne Murray
Profile: Newspaper providing information on the Irish commercial fishing and fish farming.
Readership: Aimed at anyone in the fishing and aquaculture industry.
ADVERTISING RATES:
Full Page Mono .... EUR 875
Full Page Colour .... EUR 1190
Agency Commission: 15%
Mechanical Data: Col Length: 340mm, Col Widths (Display): 40mm, Type Area: 340 x 265mm, Page Width: 265mm, Film: Digital
BUSINESS: MARINE & SHIPPING: Commercial Fishing

THE MARKET 1746106E14C-1
Editorial: The Plaza, Eastpoint Business Park, DUBLIN 3 **Tel:** 1 72 72 954
Email: mary.sweetman@enterprise-ireland.com **Web site:** http://www.the-market.ie
Freq: 6 issues yearly; Free to qualifying individuals
Annual Sub.: EUR 56.59; **Circ:** 5,500
Usual Pagination: 54
Editor: Mary Sweetman
Profile: Business publication, which aims to help companies to internationalise their businesses. It highlights export success stories and tries to identify the regions and market niches where the best opportunities lie. It also provides practical advice, with articles on marketing, selling, PR, trade shows and trade regulations.
Readership: Aimed at CEOs and people involved in export and business strategy.
BUSINESS: COMMERCE, INDUSTRY & MANAGEMENT: International Commerce

MARKETING 4154E2A-9
Editorial: 1 Albert Park, Sandycove, CO. DUBLIN
Tel: 1 28 44 456 **Fax:** 12807735
Email: cullen@marketing.ie **Web site:** http://www.marketing.ie
Date Established: 1990; **Freq:** Monthly; **Annual Sub.:** EUR 120; **Circ:** 3,000
Usual Pagination: 44
Editor: Michael Cullen; **Advertising Manager:** Jennifer Coen
Profile: Magazine focusing on all aspects of marketing.
Readership: Read by marketing and advertising executives, PR practitioners, researchers, designers, photographers, journalists and exhibition organisers.
ADVERTISING RATES:
Full Page Mono .... EUR 200
Full Page Colour .... EUR 200
Agency Commission: 15%
Mechanical Data: Screen: 60 lpc, Print Process: Offset, Film: Negative, right reading, emulsion side down, Bleed Size: 305 x 215mm, Trim Size: 270 x 180mm
BUSINESS: COMMUNICATIONS, ADVERTISING & MARKETING

MARKETING AGE 1812758E2A-9
Editorial: Top Floor, Block 43B, Yeats Way, Park West Business Park, Nangor Road, DUBLIN 12
Tel: 1 62 51 480 **Fax:** 16251402
Email: editorial@businessandleadership.com **Web site:** http://www.businessandleadership.com/magazines/marketing-age
Date Established: 2007; **Freq:** 6 issues yearly; Free to qualifying individuals
Annual Sub.: EUR 112; **Circ:** 4,882
Usual Pagination: 92
Editor: Grainne Rothery
Profile: Magazine focusing on marketing strategy. Features international marketing, salesforce leadership and digital marketing. Includes profiles and interviews with leading business figures.
Readership: Aimed at members of the Marketing Institute of Ireland, marketing directors and managers of top companies in Ireland.
ADVERTISING RATES:
Full Page Colour .... EUR 2500
Mechanical Data: Bleed Size: 307 x 220mm, Trim Size: 297 x 210mm, Film: Digital
BUSINESS: COMMUNICATIONS, ADVERTISING & MARKETING

MATERNITY 623586E74D-159
Formerly: Nationwide Maternity Hospital Magazine
Editorial: Longboat Quay, 57-59 Sir John Rogerson Quay, DUBLIN 2 **Tel:** 1 43 22 200 **Fax:** 16727100
Email: emily.manning@ashville.com **Web site:** http://www.ashville.com
Date Established: 1995; **Freq:** Annual - Published in June; **Cover Price:** Free; **Circ:** 50,000
Usual Pagination: 144
Editor: Emily Manning
Profile: Magazine covering all issues connected with ante and post-natal care.
Readership: Aimed at expectant mothers and maternity unit employees.
CONSUMER: WOMEN'S INTEREST CONSUMER MAGAZINES: Child Care

MATERNITY & INFANT 1792966E74D-160
Formerly: Infant
Editorial: Longboat Quay, 57-59 Sir John Rogerson Quay, DUBLIN 2 **Tel:** 1 43 22 200 **Fax:** 16727100
Email: editorial@maternityandinfant.ie **Web site:** http://www.maternityandinfant.ie
Freq: 6 issues yearly; **Cover Price:** EUR 3.95; **Circ:** 3,802
Usual Pagination: 112
Editor: Emily Manning; **Advertising Manager:** Regina Hinds
Profile: Magazine covering advice, expert opinion, parenting, questions and answers, fashion, competitions and tips.
Readership: Aimed at Irish mums-to-be and parents of pre-school and school age children.
ADVERTISING RATES:
Full Page Colour .... EUR 3400
Mechanical Data: Type Area: 275 x 188mm, Bleed Size: 305 x 220mm, Trim Size: 295 x 210mm, Col Length: 275mm, Page Width: 188mm, Film: Digital
Copy instructions: *Copy Date:* 28 days prior to publication date
Average ad content per issue: 25%
CONSUMER: WOMEN'S INTEREST CONSUMER MAGAZINES: Child Care

MAYO NEWS 4327E72-5900
Editorial: The Fairgreen, Westport, CO. MAYO
Tel: 98 25 311 **Fax:** 98 26 108
Email: editor@mayonews.ie **Web site:** http://www.mayonews.ie
Date Established: 1892; **Freq:** Weekly; **Cover Price:** EUR 1.95
Annual Sub.: EUR 185; **Circ:** 10,569

Editor: Michael Duffy; **News Editor:** Ciara Moynahan; **Managing Director:** Martin Reddington; **Advertising Manager:** Pat Cawley
ADVERTISING RATES:
Full Page Mono .... EUR 2376
Full Page Colour .... EUR 2970
SCC .... EUR 15
Mechanical Data: Page Width: 260mm, Type Area: 332.5 x 260mm, Col Length: 332.5mm, Col Widths (Display): 41mm, No. of Columns (Display): 6
LOCAL NEWSPAPERS

THE MEATH CHRONICLE
4329E72-6000
Editorial: Market Square, Navan, CO. MEATH
Tel: 46 90 79 600 **Fax:** 469023565
Email: info@meathchronicle.ie **Web site:** http://www.meathchronicle.ie
Date Established: 1897; **Freq:** Weekly; **Circ:** 12,171
Editor: Ken Davis
ADVERTISING RATES:
Full Page Mono .... EUR 5096
Full Page Colour .... EUR 5928
Mechanical Data: Type Area: 525 x 336mm, Col Length: 525mm, Page Width: 336mm, Film: Digital, No. of Columns (Display): 8
Supplement(s): Inspire - 12xY
LOCAL NEWSPAPERS

MEATH ECHO
1668589E72-8208
Editorial: Ratoath, CO. MEATH **Tel:** 1 82 54 434
Email: meathecho@gmail.com **Web site:** http://www.meathecho.ie
Date Established: 2002; **Freq:** 26 issues yearly; **Cover Price:** Free; **Circ:** 20,000
ADVERTISING RATES:
Full Page Colour .... EUR 899
SCC .... EUR 8.50
Agency Commission: 15%
Mechanical Data: Type Area: 330 x 255mm, Col Length: 330mm, Page Width: 255mm
LOCAL NEWSPAPERS

MEATH TOPIC
768720E72-6100_100
Editorial: 6 Dominick Street, Mullingar, CO. WESTMEATH 0
Freq: Weekly; **Cover Price:** EUR 1.75; **Circ:** 8,000
Part of Series, see entry for: Topic Series
LOCAL NEWSPAPERS

MEDICO - LEGAL JOURNAL OF IRELAND
1667147E44-78
Editorial: 43 Fitzwilliam Place, DUBLIN 2
Tel: 1 66 25 301 **Fax:** 16625302
Email: stephen.lucek@thomsonreuters.com **Web site:** http://www.roundhall.ie
ISSN: 1393-1792
Freq: Half-yearly - Published in April and November; **Annual Sub.:** EUR 245
Usual Pagination: 48
Editor: Stephen Lucek
Profile: Journal covering new developments as well as current legal and ethical issues related to patient care and the health services. Also provides an academic and scientific forum for debate on important medical legal issues.
Readership: Aimed at healthcare professionals and academics.
BUSINESS: LEGAL

METRO EIREANN
764293E90-150
Editorial: 46 Upper Dorset Street, DUBLIN 1
Tel: 1 87 83 223 **Fax:** 18783917
Email: editor@metroeireann.com **Web site:** http://www.metroeireann.com
Freq: Weekly
Annual Sub.: EUR 52; **Circ:** 10,000
Usual Pagination: 36
Editor: Chinedu Onyejelem
Profile: Publication concerning ethnic minorities in Ireland. Providing a source of news and information on Ireland's fast-growing immigrant community and ethnic minorities.
Language(s): English; French
Readership: Aimed at members of the Irish immigrant communities, ethnic minorities and those interested in multiculturalism.
ADVERTISING RATES:
Full Page Mono .... EUR 3072
Full Page Colour .... EUR 3456
SCC .... EUR 18
Agency Commission: 15%
Mechanical Data: Trim Size: 360 x 260mm, No. of Columns (Display): 6, Film: Digital, Col Widths (Display): 40mm
Average ad content per issue: 10%
CONSUMER: ETHNIC

METRO HERALD
1697235E67B-53
Formerly: Metro (Ireland)
Editorial: 3rd Floor Embassy House, Herbert Park Lane, Ballsbridge, DUBLIN 4 **Tel:** 1 63 75 900
Fax: 1 63 75 853
Email: news@metroherald.ie **Web site:** http://www.metroherald.ie
Date Established: 2005; **Freq:** Daily; **Cover Price:** Free; **Circ:** 59,041
News Editor: Joanne Ahern; **Managing Director:** Paul Crosbie

ADVERTISING RATES:
Full Page Mono .... EUR 6200
Full Page Colour .... EUR 7700
Agency Commission: 10%
Mechanical Data: Type Area: 360 x 268mm, Col Length: 360mm, Page Width: 268mm, Col Widths (Display): 35mm, No. of Columns (Display): 7, Film: Digital
Copy instructions: *Copy Date:* 2 days prior to publication date
Average ad content per issue: 32%
REGIONAL DAILY & SUNDAY NEWSPAPERS: Regional Daily Newspapers

MID LOUTH INDEPENDENT
1692419E72-4100_101
Editorial: 9 Shop Street, Drogheda, CO. LOUTH 0
Freq: Weekly; **Cover Price:** EUR 1.90
Part of Series, see entry for: Drogheda Independent Series
LOCAL NEWSPAPERS

MIDLAND TRIBUNE
4330E72-6200
Editorial: Main Street, Birr, CO. OFFALY
Tel: 57 91 20 003 **Fax:** 579120588
Email: editor@midlandtribune.ie
Date Established: 1881; **Freq:** Weekly; **Circ:** 10,460
Editor: John O'Callaghan; **Advertising Manager:** Phyllis Byrne
ADVERTISING RATES:
Full Page Mono .... EUR 5258
Full Page Colour .... EUR 6779
SCC .... EUR 16.07
Agency Commission: 15%
Mechanical Data: Type Area: 530 x 340mm, Col Length: 530mm, Page Width: 340mm, Col Widths (Display): 38mm, No. of Columns (Display): 8, Film: Digital
Average ad content per issue: 40%
LOCAL NEWSPAPERS

MIMS (IRELAND)
4245E56A-95
Editorial: 24-26 Upper Ormond Quay, DUBLIN 7
Tel: 1 81 76 300 **Fax:** 18176365
Email: info@mims.ie **Web site:** http://www.mims.ie
ISSN: 0300-8223
Freq: Monthly; Free to qualifying individuals
Annual Sub.: EUR 310; **Circ:** 7,500
Usual Pagination: 364
Profile: Directory containing listings and details of all prescription medicines available in Ireland.
Readership: Aimed at general practitioners, consultants and non-consultant hospital doctors, as well as pharmacists, nurses and other health workers.
ADVERTISING RATES:
Full Page Colour .... EUR 2285
Agency Commission: 10%
Mechanical Data: Bleed Size: 230 x 151mm, Trim Size: 210 x 148mm, Film: Digital
Copy instructions: *Copy Date:* 42 days prior to publication date
BUSINESS: HEALTH & MEDICAL

MODERN MEDICINE OF IRELAND
4246E56A-100
Editorial: 5-7 Clanwilliam Terrace, DUBLIN 2
Tel: 1 66 50 300 **Fax:** 16628041
Email: kfitzsimons@mandcgroup.ie
Date Established: 1971; **Freq:** 6 issues yearly; Free to qualifying individuals
Annual Sub.: EUR 70; **Circ:** 3,700
Usual Pagination: 68
Editor: Ken Fitzsimons; **Advertising Manager:** Amanda O'Keeffe
Profile: Journal covering all aspects of clinical medicine.
Readership: Aimed at Irish GPs and consultants.
ADVERTISING RATES:
Full Page Colour .... EUR 1520
Agency Commission: 10%
Mechanical Data: Type Area: 268 x 184mm, Col Length: 268mm, Bleed Size: +3mm, Film: Digital, Trim Size: 288 x 204mm, Page Width: 184mm, No. of Columns (Display): 3
Copy instructions: *Copy Date:* 14 days prior to publication date
Average ad content per issue: 40%
BUSINESS: HEALTH & MEDICAL

MODIFIED MOTORS
1640222E77A-201
Editorial: 3rd Floor, Arena House, Arena Road, Sandyford Industrial Estate, DUBLIN 18
Tel: 1 24 05 547 **Fax:** 12405550
Email: info@modifiedmotors.ie **Web site:** http://www.modifiedmotors.ie
Date Established: 2002; **Freq:** Monthly; **Cover Price:** EUR 4.95; **Circ:** 25,000
Usual Pagination: 100
Editor: Justin Delaney
Profile: Magazine covering modified cars with previews of shows and new product reviews. Also, men's lifestyle features include, games, DVDs, music and events.
Readership: Aimed predominantly at men aged between 16 and 30 years old.
ADVERTISING RATES:
Full Page Colour .... EUR 700
Mechanical Data: Bleed Size: 303 x 216mm
Average ad content per issue: 50%
CONSUMER: MOTORING & CYCLING: Motoring

MONDAY SPORT SPECIAL
1826365E67B-55
Editorial: For all contact details see main record, Evening Echo
Freq: Weekly - Publislhed on Monday
Supplement to: Evening Echo
REGIONAL DAILY & SUNDAY NEWSPAPERS: Regional Daily Newspapers

MONEY & JOBS
1659414E65H-18
Editorial: For all contact details see main record, The Irish Examiner
Freq: Weekly
Supplement to: The Irish Examiner
NATIONAL DAILY & SUNDAY NEWSPAPERS: National Colour Supplements

MOTHERS & BABIES
1638422E74D-151
Editorial: Whitespace Ltd, Top Floor, Block 43B, Yeats Way, Park West Business Park, Nangor Road, DUBLIN 12 **Tel:** 1 62 51 437 **Fax:** 16251402
Email: bmulligan@whitespace.ie **Web site:** http://www.whitespace.ie
Date Established: 2000; **Freq:** Monthly - See main record for circulation figure; **Cover Price:** Free
Usual Pagination: 48
Editor: Bernice Mulligan; **Advertising Manager:** Carol McMenamin
Profile: Magazine covering all issues relating to pregnancy, motherhood and parenting.
Readership: Aimed at parents of children from 0 to 4 years old and expectant mothers.
ADVERTISING RATES:
Full Page Colour .... EUR 8325
Agency Commission: 10%
Mechanical Data: Film: Digital, Type Area: 310 x 244mm, Bleed Size: 345 x 277mm, Trim Size: 337 x 269mm, Col Length: 310mm, No. of Columns (Display): 6, Page Width: 244mm
Copy instructions: *Copy Date:* 10 days prior to publication date
Average ad content per issue: 40%
Supplement to: Irish Independent
CONSUMER: WOMEN'S INTEREST CONSUMER MAGAZINES: Child Care

MOTORING
1799360E72-8245
Editorial: 25 Michael Street, WATERFORD
Freq: 3 issues yearly
Supplement to: Waterford News & Star
LOCAL NEWSPAPERS

MOTORING
1744169E72-8246
Editorial: William Street, Tullamore, CO. OFFALY
Freq: Monthly
Supplement to: Tullamore Tribune
LOCAL NEWSPAPERS

MOTORING LIFE
4383E77A-100
Editorial: 48 North Great Georges Street, DUBLIN 1
Tel: 1 87 80 444 **Fax:** 18787740
Email: info@motoringlife.ie **Web site:** http://www.motoringlife.ie
Date Established: 1947; **Freq:** 6 issues yearly; **Cover Price:** EUR 1.50; **Circ:** 10,000
Usual Pagination: 56
Editor: Geraldine Herbert; **Advertising Manager:** George Courtney
Profile: Magazine covering new car reviews, road tests, news, dealer information and a buyer's guide.
Readership: Aimed at car enthusiasts.
ADVERTISING RATES:
Full Page Colour .... EUR 2100
Agency Commission: 15%
Mechanical Data: Page Width: 179mm, Film: Digital, Type Area: 253 x 179mm, Bleed Size: +3mm, Trim Size: 289 x 215mm, Col Length: 253mm
CONSUMER: MOTORING & CYCLING: Motoring

MOTORS
1659442E65H-10
Formerly: Motoring
Editorial: For all contact details see main record, The Irish Times
Freq: Weekly
Supplement to: The Irish Times
NATIONAL DAILY & SUNDAY NEWSPAPERS: National Colour Supplements

MOTORS
1744313E72-8247
Editorial: 34 High Street, KILKENNY
Freq: Quarterly
Supplement to: Kilkenny People
LOCAL NEWSPAPERS

MOTORSHOW CAR BUYERS' GUIDE
628771E77A-150
Formerly: Motorshow
Editorial: Glencree House, Lanesborough Road, ROSCOMMON TOWN **Tel:** 90 66 25 676
Fax: 90 66 37 410
Email: pdeane@autopub.ie **Web site:** http://www.autopub.ie
ISSN: 1393-5313
Date Established: 1995; **Freq:** Annual - Published in November; **Cover Price:** EUR 4.95; **Circ:** 10,000
Usual Pagination: 136
Editor: Padraic Deane; **Advertising Manager:** John Loughran; **Managing Editor:** Padraic Deane;
Publisher: Padraic Deane
Profile: Annual car buyers' guide listings including details and verdicts on every new car model range available in Ireland. It also contains useful tips and statistics and had a detailed listing of all the new models to arrive in Ireland in the following 12-18 months.
Readership: Aimed predominantly at buyers of new and used cars. Also car owners, fleet managers and insurance managers.
CONSUMER: MOTORING & CYCLING: Motoring

MOVING IN MAGAZINE
628770E74K-100
Editorial: 29 Charlemont Lane, Clontarf, DUBLIN 3
Tel: 1 83 30 560 **Fax:** 18330826
Email: clodagh.edwards@argyllcommunications.ie
ISSN: 1393-7359
Date Established: 1998; **Freq:** 6 issues yearly; **Cover Price:** EUR 3.50
Annual Sub.: EUR 32; **Circ:** 25,000
Usual Pagination: 128
Managing Director: John Hogan; **Advertising Manager:** Clodagh Edwards; **Managing Editor:** Tommy Quinn
Profile: Magazine explaining issues concerning the purchase of new property and details necessary when moving home. Also includes articles on interiors.
Readership: Aimed at new home owners and those seeking to move home.
ADVERTISING RATES:
Full Page Colour .... EUR 2500
Agency Commission: 15%
Mechanical Data: Bleed Size: +3mm, Film: Digital, Type Area: 297 x 230mm, Col Length: 297mm, Page Width: 230mm
Average ad content per issue: 25%
CONSUMER: WOMEN'S INTEREST CONSUMER MAGAZINES: Home Purchase

MQ - MUSIC QUARTERLY - IMRO MAGAZINE
764227E61-100
Formerly: IMRO News
Editorial: Copyright House, Pembroke Row, Lower Baggot Street, DUBLIN 2 **Tel:** 1 66 14 844
Fax: 16763125
Email: keith.johnson@imro.ie **Web site:** http://www.imro.ie
Freq: Quarterly; Free to qualifying individuals ; **Circ:** 5,000
Usual Pagination: 24
Editor: Keith Johnson; **Advertising Manager:** Gillian Verrecchia
Profile: Publication containing information and news from the Irish Music Rights Organisation (IMRO).
Readership: Aimed at the members of the organisation, including songwriters, composers and music publishers.
ADVERTISING RATES:
Full Page Mono .... EUR 1800
Full Page Colour .... EUR 2750
Agency Commission: 15%
Mechanical Data: Trim Size: 297 x 210mm, Bleed Size: 303 x 216mm, Film: Digital
Average ad content per issue: 20%
BUSINESS: MUSIC TRADE

THE MUNSTER EXPRESS
4336E72-6300
Editorial: 37 The Quay, WATERFORD
Tel: 51 87 21 41 **Fax:** 51873452
Email: news@munster-express.ie **Web site:** http://www.munster-express.ie
Date Established: 1859; **Freq:** 104 issues yearly; **Cover Price:** EUR 1.80; **Circ:** 6,286
Editor: John O'Connor; **Advertising Manager:** Liz McGough
ADVERTISING RATES:
SCC .... EUR 9.97
Agency Commission: 15%
Mechanical Data: Col Widths (Display): 35mm, No. of Columns (Display): 9, Print Process: Offset litho, Type Area: 526 x 347mm, Film: Digital, Page Width: 347mm, Col Length: 526mm
Average ad content per issue: 43%
LOCAL NEWSPAPERS

MUNSTER INTERIORS
1664968E74C-204
Editorial: 76 Southbury Road, Wilton, CORK
Tel: 86 39 77 775 **Fax:** 18224485
Email: editor.munster.interiors@gmail.com
ISSN: 0188-2875
Date Established: 2005; **Freq:** Quarterly; **Cover Price:** EUR 3.95; **Circ:** 20,000
Usual Pagination: 160
Editor: Esther McCarthy; **Advertising Manager:** Darren Moran-Sheils
Profile: Magazine covering homes, style, decor, design, interior services and gardens.
Readership: Aimed at style lovers, home owners, interior designers and those purchasing a new home.
ADVERTISING RATES:
Full Page Colour .... EUR 1695
SCC .... EUR 20
Agency Commission: 15%
Mechanical Data: Trim Size: 297 x 210mm, Film: Digital

Average ad content per issue: 40%
CONSUMER: WOMEN'S INTEREST CONSUMER MAGAZINES: Home & Family

MUSGRAVE MAGAZINE
1640328E11A-14
Formerly: Musgrave Food Service Magazine
Editorial: 3rd Floor, Arena House, Arena Road, Sandyford Industrial Estate, DUBLIN 18
Tel: 1 24 05 556
Email: avril@page7media.ie
Date Established: 2003; **Freq:** Monthly - Published in the 1st week of the cover month; Free to qualifying individuals ; **Circ:** 23,500
Usual Pagination: 40
Editor: Avril Forde; **Advertising Manager:** Laura Hewson
Profile: Magazine with in-depth articles for both retailers and the hospitality sectors in Ireland.
Readership: Aimed at those working in all aspects of the grocery retail trade and hospitality sectors including symbol stores, independent retailers, forecourts, pubs, restaurants and hotels.
ADVERTISING RATES:
Full Page Colour .... EUR 3750
Mechanical Data: Trim Size: 297 x 210mm, Bleed Size: 307 x 220mm
Supplement(s): Musgrave Buyer's Guide - 1xY
BUSINESS: CATERING: Catering, Hotels & Restaurants

THE NATIONALIST & MUNSTER ADVERTISER
1808479E72-6600_100
Editorial: Queen Street, Clonmel, CO. TIPPERARY 0
Freq: Weekly; **Cover Price:** EUR 1.80; **Circ:** 14,162
Part of Series, see entry for: The Nationalist & Munster Advertiser Series
LOCAL NEWSPAPERS

THE NATIONALIST & MUNSTER ADVERTISER SERIES
4333E72-6600
Formerly: Nationalist & Munster Advertiser
Editorial: Queen Street, Clonmel, CO. TIPPERARY
Tel: 52 61 72500
Email: mheverin@nationalist.ie **Web site:** http://www.nationalist.ie
Date Established: 1890; **Freq:** Weekly; **Circ:** 11,087
Editor: Michael Heverin; **Advertising Manager:** Eimear McDonnell
Agency Commission: 10%
Mechanical Data: Col Length: 253mm, Col Widths (Display): 40mm, No. of Columns (Display): 9, Type Area: 253 x 330mm, Print Process: Web-fed offset litho, Film: Digital, Page Width: 330mm
Series owner and contact point for the following titles, see individual entries:
The Nationalist & Munster Advertiser
LOCAL NEWSPAPERS

THE NATIONALIST (CARLOW)
4300E72-6500
Formerly: The Nationalist & Leinster Times
Editorial: Hanover House, Hanover, CARLOW
Tel: 59 91 70 100 **Fax:** 599130301
Email: news@carlow-nationalist.ie **Web site:** http://www.carlow-nationalist.ie
Date Established: 1883; **Freq:** Weekly; **Cover Price:** EUR 2.10; **Circ:** 19,000
Editor: Conal O'Boyle; **News Editor:** Suzanne Pender
ADVERTISING RATES:
Full Page Mono .... EUR 4990
Full Page Colour .... EUR 6450
SCC .... EUR 14.85
Agency Commission: 15%
Mechanical Data: Film: Digital, No. of Columns (Display): 9, Col Widths (Display): 34mm
Average ad content per issue: 25%
LOCAL NEWSPAPERS

NCBI NEWS
1640010E56L-1
Editorial: NCBI (National Council for the Blind of Ireland), Head Office, Whitworth Road, Drumcondra, DUBLIN 9 **Tel:** 1 85 03 34 353 **Fax:** 18307787
Email: info@ncbi.ie **Web site:** http://www.ncbi.ie
Date Established: 1998; **Freq:** Quarterly; Free to qualifying individuals ; **Circ:** 4,500
Usual Pagination: 20
Editor: Frank Callery
Profile: Magazine covering issues relating to blindness and vision impairment.
Readership: Aimed at supporters, fundraisers and those with an interest in disability and rights in Ireland.
BUSINESS: HEALTH & MEDICAL: Disability & Rehabilitation

NENAGH GUARDIAN
4334E72-6700
Editorial: 13 Summerhill, Nenagh, CO. TIPPERARY
Tel: 67 31 214 **Fax:** 6733401
Email: editorial@nenaghguardian.ie **Web site:** http://www.nenaghguardian.ie
ISSN: 1649-0584
Date Established: 1838; **Freq:** Weekly; **Cover Price:** EUR 1.85; **Circ:** 7,364
Editor: Garry Cotter
ADVERTISING RATES:
Full Page Mono .... EUR 2510
Full Page Colour .... EUR 3110
Agency Commission: 15%
Mechanical Data: Page Width: 343mm, Col Length: 520mm, No. of Columns (Display): 9, Type Area: 520 x 343mm, Print Process: Offset litho
Average ad content per issue: 30%
LOCAL NEWSPAPERS

NEW GUIDE
1832618E72-8254
Editorial: 25 Michael Street, WATERFORD
Freq: Weekly
Supplement to: Waterford News & Star
LOCAL NEWSPAPERS

THE NEW ROSS ECHO
1659363E72-4650_101
Editorial: Slaney Place, Enniscorthy, CO. WEXFORD 0
Freq: Weekly; **Cover Price:** EUR 1.70
Part of Series, see entry for: The Echo Series (Enniscorthy)
LOCAL NEWSPAPERS

NEW ROSS STANDARD
4346E72-4700_101
Editorial: Channing House, Rowe Street, Wexford, CO. WEXFORD 0
Freq: Weekly; **Cover Price:** EUR 1.90; **Circ:** 5,905
ADVERTISING RATES:
Full Page Mono .... EUR 1640.70
Full Page Colour .... EUR 1850
SCC .... EUR 8.14
Part of Series, see entry for: Wexford People Series
LOCAL NEWSPAPERS

NORTH COUNTY LEADER
623827E72-8206
Editorial: Leader House, North Street, Swords, CO. DUBLIN **Tel:** 1 84 00 200 **Fax:** 18400550
Email: info@northcountyleader.ie **Web site:** http://www.northcountyleader.com
Date Established: 1994; **Freq:** Weekly; Free to qualifying individuals
Annual Sub.: EUR 116; **Circ:** 40,000
Usual Pagination: 28
Profile: Local news.
ADVERTISING RATES:
Full Page Mono .... EUR 2640
Full Page Colour .... EUR 3432
Agency Commission: 15%
Mechanical Data: Trim Size: 420 x 297mm, Page Width: 260mm, Film: Digital, Type Area: 320 x 260mm, Col Length: 320mm
Average ad content per issue: 40%
Supplement(s): North County Leader Motoring - 28xY, North County Leader Property - 28xY
LOCAL NEWSPAPERS

NORTH COUNTY LEADER MOTORING
1658257E77A-202
Editorial: For all contact details see main record, North County Leader
Freq: 28 issues yearly; **Cover Price:** Free
Supplement to: North County Leader
CONSUMER: MOTORING & CYCLING: Motoring

NORTH COUNTY LEADER PROPERTY
1658269E74K-102
Editorial: For all contact details see main record, North County Leader
Freq: 28 issues yearly
Supplement to: North County Leader
CONSUMER: WOMEN'S INTEREST CONSUMER MAGAZINES: Home Purchase

NORTH KILDARE TIMES
1659222E80-204
Editorial: For all contact details see main edition, Kildare Times
Freq: Weekly
Edition of: Kildare Times
CONSUMER: RURAL & REGIONAL INTEREST

NORTH WICKLOW TIMES
1659225E72-8210_100
Editorial: 5 Eglington Road, Bray, CO WICKLOW 0
Freq: Weekly; **Cover Price:** Free; **Circ:** 38,400
Part of Series, see entry for: Wicklow Times Series
LOCAL NEWSPAPERS

NORTHERN STANDARD
628737E72-6830
Editorial: The Diamond, MONAGHAN 0
Tel: 47 82 188 **Fax:** 4772257
Email: newsdesk@northern-standard.ie
Freq: Weekly; **Cover Price:** EUR 1.90; **Circ:** 14,500
Editor: Maurice Smyth; **Advertising Manager:** Ann Watterson
ADVERTISING RATES:
Full Page Mono .... EUR 5150
Full Page Colour .... EUR 6476
Mechanical Data: Film: Digital
LOCAL NEWSPAPERS

NORTHSIDE PEOPLE EAST EDITION
628748E72-6850
Editorial: 80-83 Omni Park, Santry, DUBLIN 9
Tel: 1 86 21 611 **Fax:** 18621626
Email: news@dublinpeople.com **Web site:** http://www.dublinpeople.com
Freq: Weekly; **Cover Price:** Free; **Circ:** 52,000
Editor: Pat O'Rourke
ADVERTISING RATES:
Full Page Mono .... EUR 4237
Full Page Colour .... EUR 5720
Agency Commission: 10%
Mechanical Data: Page Width: 260mm, Type Area: 343 x 260mm, Col Length: 343mm, No. of Columns (Display): 7, Col Widths (Display): 32mm, Film: Digital
Average ad content per issue: 55%
LOCAL NEWSPAPERS

NORTHSIDE PEOPLE WEST EDITION
623805E72-6860
Editorial: 80-83 Omni Park, Santry, DUBLIN 9
Tel: 1 86 21 611 **Fax:** 18621626
Email: news@dublinpeople.com **Web site:** http://www.dublinpeople.com
Date Established: 1995; **Freq:** Weekly; **Cover Price:** Free; **Circ:** 45,000
Editor: Jack Gleeson
ADVERTISING RATES:
Full Page Mono .... EUR 3916
Full Page Colour .... EUR 5286.60
SCC .... EUR 16.32
Mechanical Data: Page Width: 260mm, Type Area: 343 x 260mm, Col Length: 343mm, No. of Columns (Display): 7, Col Widths (Display): 32mm, Film: Digital
LOCAL NEWSPAPERS

NURSING IN THE COMMUNITY
629676E56B-15
Editorial: 25 Adelaide Street, Dun Laoghaire, CO. DUBLIN **Tel:** 1 28 03 967 **Fax:** 12807076
Email: alison@medmedia.ie **Web site:** http://www.medmedia.ie
ISSN: 1649-0657
Date Established: 1999; **Freq:** Quarterly; Free to qualifying individuals
Annual Sub.: EUR 75; **Circ:** 4,500
Usual Pagination: 36
Editor: Alison Moore; **Advertising Manager:** Leon Ellison
Profile: Clinical Guide for Irish nurses working in a community setting.
Readership: Read by practice nurses, public health nurses and clinical nurse specialists.
ADVERTISING RATES:
Full Page Colour .... EUR 1400
Mechanical Data: Type Area: 270 x 184mm, Col Length: 270mm, Page Width: 184mm, Bleed Size: 307 x 220mm, Trim Size: 297 x 210mm, Film: Digital
Average ad content per issue: 10%
BUSINESS: HEALTH & MEDICAL: Nursing

OBAIR
754317E4D-100
Editorial: 51 St. Stephen's Green, DUBLIN 2
Tel: 1 64 76 000 **Fax:** 16476491
Email: george.moir@opw.ie **Web site:** http://www.opw.ie
Freq: Half-yearly - Published in June and December; **Cover Price:** Free; **Circ:** 1,000
Usual Pagination: 32
Editor: Neil Ryan
Profile: Magazine covering current news and reports of The Office of Public Works in Ireland and abroad.
Readership: Aimed at OPW staff and customers.
BUSINESS: ARCHITECTURE & BUILDING: Planning & Housing

OBSERVER & STAR SERIES
754443E72-7660
Formerly: Weekly Observer
Editorial: 19 Bridge Street, Mallow, CO. CORK
Tel: 22 22 910 **Fax:** 2222959
Email: steve@valestar.ie
Freq: Weekly; **Cover Price:** EUR 1.80; **Circ:** 25,000
Editor: Steve Murphy; **Advertising Manager:** Sharon O'Brien
Series owner and contact point for the following titles, see individual entries:
Vale Star/Mallow Star
Weekly Observer
LOCAL NEWSPAPERS

OFFALY EXPRESS
4331E72-6900
Editorial: Bridge Street, Tullamore, CO. OFFALY
Tel: 57 93 21 744 **Fax:** 50651930
Email: grace@offalyexpress.ie
Freq: Weekly; **Circ:** 11,000
Editor: Grace O'Dea; **Advertising Manager:** Karen O'Connor
ADVERTISING RATES:
Full Page Mono .... EUR 3190
Full Page Colour .... EUR 3640
SCC .... EUR 16.75
Agency Commission: 15%
Mechanical Data: Type Area: 370 x 265mm, Col Length: 370mm, Page Width: 265mm, Film: Digital
LOCAL NEWSPAPERS

OFFALY INDEPENDENT
4341E72-7900
Editorial: The Mall, Tullamore, CO. OFFALY
Tel: 57 93 21 403 **Fax:** 579325184
Email: news@offalyindependent.ie **Web site:** http://www.offalyindependent.ie
Freq: Weekly; **Cover Price:** EUR 1.70; **Circ:** 10,000
ADVERTISING RATES:
Full Page Mono .... EUR 2112
Full Page Colour .... EUR 2669
SCC .... EUR 13.90
Agency Commission: 15%
Mechanical Data: Type Area: 320 x 254mm, Page Width: 254mm, Col Length: 320mm, Col Widths (Display): 39mm, No. of Columns (Display): 6, Film: Digital
Average ad content per issue: 30%
LOCAL NEWSPAPERS

OFFALY TOPIC
4339E72-6100_102
Editorial: 6 Dominick Street, Mullingar, CO. WESTMEATH 0
Freq: Weekly; **Cover Price:** EUR 1.75; **Circ:** 7,000
Part of Series, see entry for: Topic Series
LOCAL NEWSPAPERS

OLD MOORE'S ALMANAC
628800E94E-150
Editorial: Taney Hall, Eglinton Terrace, Dundrum, DUBLIN 14 **Tel:** 1 29 60 000 **Fax:** 1 29 60 383
Email: sarah@maccom.ie **Web site:** http://www.maccommunications.ie
ISSN: 0791-7716
Date Established: 1764; **Freq:** Annual - Published in November; **Cover Price:** EUR 3.50; **Circ:** 50,000
Usual Pagination: 100
Editor: Sarah McQuaid; **Advertising Manager:** Thomas O'Neill
Profile: Magazine covering agricultural fairs and marts, horse fixtures and information on sunrise, sunset and tidal times as well as gardening, recipes and horoscopes.
Readership: Aimed at those with an interest in agricultural affairs as well as the general reader.
ADVERTISING RATES:
Full Page Mono .... EUR 1000.00
Full Page Colour .... EUR 1500.00
Agency Commission: 15%
Mechanical Data: Type Area: 190 x 128mm, Bleed Size: 216 x 154mm, Trim Size: 210 x 148mm, Film: Digital, Col Length: 190mm, Page Width: 128mm
CONSUMER: OTHER CLASSIFICATIONS: Paranormal

ON TARGET
1659433E65H-31
Editorial: For all contact details see main record, The Irish Daily Star
Freq: Weekly
Supplement to: The Irish Daily Star
NATIONAL DAILY & SUNDAY NEWSPAPERS: National Colour Supplements

THE OPINION
764513E80-12
Formerly: Bandon Opinion
Editorial: 76 South Main Street, Bandon, CO. CORK
Tel: 23 42 288 **Fax:** 23 42 277
Email: editor@bandonopinion.com **Web site:** http://www.bandonopinion.com
Date Established: 1977; **Freq:** Monthly; **Cover Price:** EUR 3.95
Annual Sub.: EUR 78.00; **Circ:** 4,000
Usual Pagination: 76
Editor: Eddie Goggin; **Advertising Manager:** Eddie Goggin
Profile: News magazine featuring information about the social economic life of the West Cork area.
Readership: Aimed at the general public and businessmen.
ADVERTISING RATES:
Full Page Mono .... EUR 720.00
Full Page Colour .... EUR 970.00
Mechanical Data: Film: Digital, Trim Size: 261.5 x 190mm
CONSUMER: RURAL & REGIONAL INTEREST

ORGANIC MATTERS
1639926E57-48
Editorial: Main Street, Newtown Forbes, CO. LONGFORD **Tel:** 43 3342495 **Fax:** 433342496
Email: info@organicmattersmag.com **Web site:** http://www.organicmattersmag.com
Date Established: 1989; **Freq:** 6 issues yearly Free to qualifying individuals
Annual Sub.: EUR 35; **Circ:** 5,000
Usual Pagination: 36
Editor: Cáit Curran; **Advertising Director:** Frank McGouran
Profile: Magazine covering broad environmental issues, food, health and organic farming.
Readership: Aimed at environmentally minded people with interests such as farming and gardening.
ADVERTISING RATES:
Full Page Colour .... EUR 860
Agency Commission: 10%

Mechanical Data: Film: Digital, Trim Size: 297 x 210mm, Bleed Size: +7mm
Average ad content per issue: 30%
BUSINESS: ENVIRONMENT & POLLUTION

OUR GAMES - OFFICIAL GAA ANNUAL
1709124E75X-4
Editorial: 56 Carysfort Avenue, Blackrock, CO.DUBLIN **Tel:** 1 28 87 247 **Fax:** 1 28 83 583
Email: des@dbapublishing.ie **Web site:** http://www.dbapublishing.ie
ISSN: 1649-6256
Date Established: 2004; **Freq:** Annual - Published in November; **Cover Price:** EUR 9.95; **Circ:** 8,000
Usual Pagination: 100
Editor: Desmond Donegan
Profile: Magazine covering all aspects of Gaelic games including Gaelic football, hurling, carmogie, ladies' football and handball as well as a review of the year and player profiles.
Language(s): English; Gaelic
Readership: Aimed at GAA fans.
ADVERTISING RATES:
Full Page Colour .... EUR 1975.00
Mechanical Data: Bleed Size: 303 x 216mm, Trim Size: 297 x 210mm
CONSUMER: SPORT: Other Sport

OUTSIDER - IRELAND'S OUTDOOR MAGAZINE
1644389E75L-201
Formerly: Outsider
Editorial: 20 Fitzwilliam Street Upper, DUBLIN 2
Tel: 1 643-2308
Email: editor@outsider.ie **Web site:** http://www.outsider.ie
ISSN: 1649-3907
Date Established: 2003; **Freq:** 6 issues yearly; **Cover Price:** EUR 3.95; **Circ:** 15,000
Usual Pagination: 84
Editor: Roisin Finlay
Profile: Magazine covering outdoor and adventure sports including hill walking, skiing, snow-boarding, mountain biking, kayaking, canoeing, adventure racing, fell running, rock climbing and hiking as well as equipment reviews, travel destinations, health, fitness and nutrition.
Readership: Aimed at outdoor enthusiasts of all standards.
ADVERTISING RATES:
Full Page Mono .... EUR 2100
Full Page Colour .... EUR 2100
SCC .... EUR 22
Mechanical Data: Type Area: 277 x 190mm, Bleed Size: 303 x 216mm, Trim Size: 297 x 210mm, Film: Digital, Col Length: 277mm, Page Width: 190mm
CONSUMER: SPORT: Outdoor

PARENTING
1818822E74A-149
Editorial: For all contact details see main record, Image
Freq: Annual - Published in November. See main publication for circulation figure
Supplement to: Image
CONSUMER: WOMEN'S INTEREST CONSUMER MAGAZINES: Women's Interest

PC LIVE
4164E5D-100
Editorial: Media House, South County Business Park, Leopardstown, DUBLIN 18 **Tel:** 12 94 77 77
Fax: 12074299
Email: newsroom@mediateam.ie **Web site:** http://www.techcentral.ie
Freq: Monthly - Published at the beginning of the cover month; **Cover Price:** EUR 2.50; **Circ:** 4,316
Usual Pagination: 64
Profile: Magazine containing the latest PC news, with information about new products on the market, the Internet and computer games.
Readership: Aimed at managers of small to medium size companies using PCs as well as small-office, home-office computer and Internet users.
ADVERTISING RATES:
Full Page Mono .... EUR 2660
Full Page Colour .... EUR 3040
Agency Commission: 15%
Mechanical Data: Type Area: 280 x 210mm, Col Length: 280mm, Page Width: 210mm, Film: Positive, right reading, emulsion side down. Digital, Bleed Size: 310 x 240mm, Trim Size: 300 x 230mm, No. of Columns (Display): 4
Copy instructions: *Copy Date:* 21 days prior to publication date
Average ad content per issue: 35%
BUSINESS: COMPUTERS & AUTOMATION: Personal Computers

PEATLAND NEWS
629681E80A-100
Editorial: Irish Peatland Conservation Council, Lullymore, Rathangan, CO. KILDARE **Tel:** 45 86 01 33
Fax: 45 86 04 81
Email: bogs@ipcc.ie **Web site:** http://www.ipcc.ie
ISSN: 0791-2757
Date Established: 1985; **Freq:** Half-yearly - Published in April and October; **Cover Price:** EUR 5.00
Free to qualifying individuals ; **Circ:** 1,200
Usual Pagination: 24
Editor: Catherine O'Connell; **Advertising Manager:** Catherine O'Connell
Profile: Magazine of the Irish Peatland Conservation Council. Includes news, events and conservation and environmental issues relating to Irish peatlands.
Readership: Aimed at members.
ADVERTISING RATES:
Full Page Colour .... EUR 695.00
Mechanical Data: Page Width: 210mm, No. of Columns (Display): 3, Type Area: 295 x 210mm, Col Length: 295mm
Copy instructions: *Copy Date:* 1 month prior to publication date
CONSUMER: RURAL & REGIONAL INTEREST: Rural Interest

PENSIONS IRELAND
629655E1H-70
Formerly: Irish Pensions News
Editorial: 121-123 Ranelagh, DUBLIN 6
Tel: 1 49 72 711 **Fax:** 14972779
Email: jcolby@irn.ie **Web site:** http://www.pensionsirl.ie
Date Established: 1999; **Freq:** Monthly; Free to qualifying individuals
Annual Sub.: EUR 295; **Circ:** 500
Usual Pagination: 32
Editor: Julie Colby
Profile: Magazine covering all aspects of pension news.
Readership: Aimed at insurance brokers, bank managers and employees of pension companies.
ADVERTISING RATES:
Full Page Mono .... EUR 1600
Full Page Colour .... EUR 1600
Mechanical Data: Trim Size: 297 x 210mm
Copy instructions: *Copy Date:* 7 days prior to publication date
Average ad content per issue: 30%
BUSINESS: FINANCE & ECONOMICS: Pensions

PEOPLE FOCUS
754171E14F-30
Formerly: CIPD News
Editorial: 121-123 Ranelagh, DUBLIN 6
Tel: 1 49 72 711 **Fax:** 14972779
Email: jcolby@irn.ie **Web site:** http://www.cipd.ie
Freq: Quarterly; **Cover Price:** Free; **Circ:** 5,500
Usual Pagination: 40
Advertising Manager: Julie Colby
Profile: Publication containing information for those interested in the management and development of personnel.
Readership: Read by members of the Chartered Institute of Personnel and Development in Ireland.
ADVERTISING RATES:
Full Page Mono .... EUR 800
Full Page Colour .... EUR 1270
Agency Commission: 15%
Mechanical Data: Bleed Size: 303 x 216mm, Trim Size: 297 x 210mm, Col Length: 277mm, Page Width: 190mm, Film: Digital, Type Area: 277 x 190mm
Average ad content per issue: 20%
BUSINESS: COMMERCE, INDUSTRY & MANAGEMENT: Training & Recruitment

AN PHOBLACHT
1666220E82-181
Editorial: 58 Parnell Square, DUBLIN 1
Tel: 1 87 33 611 **Fax:** 1 87 33 074
Email: editor@anphoblacht.com **Web site:** http://www.anphoblacht.com
Freq: Weekly; **Cover Price:** EUR 1.10; **Circ:** 10,000
Usual Pagination: 20
Editor: Seán O Bradaigh
Profile: Political magazine offering news and views from a Republican point of view.
Readership: Aimed at those with an interest in politics and current affairs.
CONSUMER: CURRENT AFFAIRS & POLITICS

THE PHOENIX
4350E73-200
Editorial: 44 Lower Baggot Street, DUBLIN 2
Tel: 1 66 11 062 **Fax:** 16624532
Email: goldhawk@indigo.ie **Web site:** http://www.thephoenix.com
Date Established: 1983; **Freq:** 26 issues yearly; **Cover Price:** EUR 2.35; **Circ:** 16,601
Usual Pagination: 56
Editor: Paddy Prendiville; **Advertising Manager:** Biddy Mulcahy
Profile: Magazine covering current affairs and business news, with political satire and gossip.
Readership: Aimed at those interested in current affairs.
ADVERTISING RATES:
Full Page Colour .... EUR 4300
Agency Commission: 15%
Mechanical Data: Type Area: 270 x 186mm, Col Length: 270mm, Page Width: 186mm, Film: Digital, No. of Columns (Display): 4, Col Widths (Display): 44.5mm, Bleed Size: +5mm, Trim Size: 297 x 210mm
Average ad content per issue: 35%
CONSUMER: NATIONAL & INTERNATIONAL PERIODICALS

THE PINK PAGES
1666382E67H-2
Editorial: For all contact details see main record, Evening Echo
Freq: Weekly
Supplement to: Evening Echo
REGIONAL DAILY & SUNDAY NEWSPAPERS: Regional Colour Supplements

PIONEER
1646134E87-171
Editorial: 27 Upper Sherrard Street, DUBLIN 1
Tel: 1 87 49 464 **Fax:** 18748485
Email: pioneerceo@jesuit.ie **Web site:** http://www.pioneertotal.ie
Date Established: 1948; **Freq:** Monthly; **Cover Price:** EUR 1.55
Free to qualifying individuals ; **Circ:** 15,000
Usual Pagination: 32
Editor: Bernard McGuckian
Profile: Magazine with religious articles of general interest to the family and Pioneer work around the world as well as a young people's and children's section.
Readership: Aimed at all members of the family.
ADVERTISING RATES:
Full Page Colour .... EUR 990
CONSUMER: RELIGIOUS

PLAN
4158E4A-70
Editorial: Quantum House, Temple Road, Blackrock, CO DUBLIN **Tel:** 1 28 33 233 **Fax:** 12833045
Email: edit@planmagazine.ie **Web site:** http://www.planmagazine.ie
Date Established: 1969; **Freq:** Monthly; **Annual Sub.:** EUR 81; **Circ:** 3,800
Usual Pagination: 56
Editor: Denise Maguire; **Managing Director:** Tony Cantwell; **Advertising Manager:** Derek Moroney
Profile: Magazine covering architecture, interior design, construction, building design and project management in Ireland.
Readership: Read by architects, developers, consulting engineers and building contractors.
ADVERTISING RATES:
Full Page Colour .... EUR 2995
Agency Commission: 10%
Mechanical Data: Type Area: 277 x 210mm, Bleed Size: 308 x 240mm, Trim Size: 297 x 230mm, Print Process: Litho, Screen: 60 lpc, Col Length: 277mm, Page Width: 210mm
Average ad content per issue: 40%
BUSINESS: ARCHITECTURE & BUILDING: Architecture

POETRY IRELAND REVIEW
1639944E84B-51
Editorial: 2 Proud's Lane, Off St. Stephens Green, DUBLIN 2 **Tel:** 1 47 89 974 **Fax:** 1 47 80 205
Email: publications@poetryireland.ie **Web site:** http://www.poetryireland.ie
Freq: Quarterly; **Cover Price:** EUR 7.99
Annual Sub.: EUR 30.50; **Circ:** 1,000
Editor: Paul Lenehan; **Advertising Manager:** Ayoma Bowe
Profile: Magazine covering the best of Irish and International poetry and translation. Interviews with established and emerging poets. Essays and features. Reviews new collections and anthologies.
Readership: Aimed at anyone with an interest in poetry.
Average ad content per issue: 5%
CONSUMER: THE ARTS & LITERARY: Literary

PORTFOLIO
1666210E74Q-152
Editorial: Unit 8, Docklands Innovation Park, East Wall Road, DUBLIN 3 **Tel:** 1 67 25 831
Email: info@portfolio.ie **Web site:** http://www.portfolio.ie
Date Established: 2002; **Freq:** Monthly - Combined Dec/Jan issue; **Cover Price:** Free; **Circ:** 20,000
Usual Pagination: 32
Publisher: Gerry Proctor
Profile: Newspaper with news and features on future developments, human interest stories, sports, personal finance, business, property, travel, motoring, IT and lifestyle.
Readership: Aimed at local and business readers in Dublin both men and women aged between 24 and 34 years old.
ADVERTISING RATES:
Full Page Colour .... EUR 1750
Agency Commission: 15%
Mechanical Data: Type Area: 335 x 270mm, Col Length: 335mm, Page Width: 270mm, Col Widths (Display): 40mm, No. of Columns (Display): 6, Print Process: Heatset web offset, Film: Digital, Bleed Size: +5mm, Trim Size: 370 x 300mm
Average ad content per issue: 30%
CONSUMER: WOMEN'S INTEREST CONSUMER MAGAZINES: Lifestyle

PREGNANCY AND PARENTING
1640799E74D-152
Formerly: Kt parenting
Editorial: 51 Allen Park Road, Stillorgan, CO DUBLIN
Tel: 1 20 56 895 **Fax:** 1 28 88 179
Email: parenting@ireland.com
Date Established: 2000; **Freq:** Quarterly; **Cover Price:** EUR 3.95
Annual Sub.: EUR 17.50; **Circ:** 20,000
Usual Pagination: 54
Editor: Suzanne Gunn; **Advertising Manager:** Erika Gunn
Profile: Magazine covering all aspects of parenting including health, nutrition, early education and development as well as product news.
Readership: Aimed at parents, expectant mums, babies and toddlers aged 0 to 4 years old.
ADVERTISING RATES:
Full Page Colour .... EUR 2400.00
Agency Commission: 15%
Mechanical Data: Bleed Size: 297 x 197mm, Trim Size: 297 x 210mm, Type Area: 270 x 190mm, Col Length: 270mm, Page Width: 190mm, No. of Columns (Display): 3, Film: Digital
Copy instructions: *Copy Date:* 2 weeks prior to publication date
Average ad content per issue: 35%
CONSUMER: WOMEN'S INTEREST CONSUMER MAGAZINES: Child Care

PRICE GUIDE TO IRISH ART
1659468E84A-301
Editorial: For all contact details see main record, Irish Arts Review
Freq: Annual; **Circ:** 1,300
Supplement to: Irish Arts Review
CONSUMER: THE ARTS & LITERARY: Arts

PRIMARY TIMES IN DUBLIN
1645655E74D-155
Formerly: Primary Times in Dublin South
Editorial: 14 Eton Square, Tren, DUBLIN 6W
Tel: 1 49 25 923 **Fax:** 1 49 22 838
Email: primarytimesmoreilly@eircom.net **Web site:** http://www.primarytimesireland.com
Freq: Quarterly; **Cover Price:** Free; **Circ:** 45,000
Usual Pagination: 32
Editor: Marie O'Reilly; **Advertising Manager:** Marie O'Reilly
Profile: Magazine covering current educational issues and family matters as well as a what's on and where to go guide.
Readership: Aimed at teachers, parents and primary school children all over Dublin and North Wicklow.
Copy instructions: *Copy Date:* 2 weeks prior to publication date
CONSUMER: WOMEN'S INTEREST CONSUMER MAGAZINES: Child Care

PRIMARY TIMES IN LEINSTER
1645653E74D-154
Formerly: Primary Times in Kildare, Meath & Wicklow
Editorial: 18 Priory Walk, St. Raphaels Manor, Celbridge, CO KILDARE **Tel:** 1 62 75 785
Fax: 1 62 75 785
Email: primarytimes@iol.ie **Web site:** http://www.primarytimes.ie
Date Established: 2004; **Freq:** Quarterly; **Cover Price:** Free; **Circ:** 40,000
Usual Pagination: 32
Editor: Orla Kearney; **Advertising Manager:** Orla Kearney
Profile: Magazine covering educational issues and family matters as well as a what's on and where to go guide.
Readership: Aimed at teachers, parents and primary school children in Leinster.
Copy instructions: *Copy Date:* 2 weeks prior to publication date
CONSUMER: WOMEN'S INTEREST CONSUMER MAGAZINES: Child Care

PRIMARY TIMES IN THE WEST OF IRELAND
1692170E74D-157
Editorial: 28 Ardilaun Road, Newcastle, Galway
Tel: 91 52 72 32 **Fax:** 91 52 72 32
Email: primarytimeswest@eircom.net **Web site:** http://www.primarytimes.net
Date Established: 2005; **Freq:** Quarterly; **Cover Price:** Free; **Circ:** 35,000
Usual Pagination: 24
Editor: Chris Day; **Advertising Manager:** Chris Day
Profile: Magazine covering educational issues, news and family matters as well as a what's on guide, where to go guide and book reviews.
Language(s): English; Gaelic
Readership: Read by teachers, children and parents of children aged 4 to 12 years old in the West of Ireland.
CONSUMER: WOMEN'S INTEREST CONSUMER MAGAZINES: Child Care

PRIMARY TIMES SOUTH
1645642E74D-153
Formerly: Primary Times in Cork & Waterford
Editorial: Kilcalf, Tallow, CO WATERFORD
Tel: 58 56 838
Email: primarytimessouth@hotmail.com **Web site:** http://www.primarytimes.ie
Date Established: 2003; **Freq:** Quarterly - Published in March, May, September and November; Free to qualifying individuals
Annual Sub.: EUR 17.50; **Circ:** 44,310
Usual Pagination: 32
Editor: Tara McKeown; **Advertising Manager:** Tara McKeown
Profile: What's on guide featuring educational issues and forthcoming events.
Readership: For families, children, parents, carers and teachers of children under 12 in Cork, Waterford, Kerry and South Tipperary.
Copy instructions: *Copy Date:* 2 weeks prior to publication date
CONSUMER: WOMEN'S INTEREST CONSUMER MAGAZINES: Child Care

PRIVATE RESEARCH
4135E1A-110
Editorial: Coliemore House, Coliemore Road, Dalkey, CO. DUBLIN **Tel:** 1 28 48 911 **Fax:** 1 20 48 177

Email: info@privateresearch.ie **Web site:** http://www.privateresearch.ie
Date Established: 1994; **Freq:** Monthly; **Annual Sub.:** EUR 379.00; **Circ:** 20,000
Usual Pagination: 120
Editor: Mark O'Neill
Profile: Magazine providing financial and business information and analyses of corporate performance.
Readership: Read by senior management in all sectors.
BUSINESS: FINANCE & ECONOMICS

PROJECT MANAGEMENT
4217E42A-85
Formerly: Construction
Editorial: Acorn House, 38 St. Peter's Road, Phibsborough, DUBLIN 7 **Tel:** 1 86 86 640
Fax: 18686651
Email: production@aplgroup.net **Web site:** http://www.aplgroup.net
Date Established: 1999; **Freq:** 6 issues yearly; **Annual Sub.:** EUR 60; **Circ:** 5,108
Usual Pagination: 52
Editor: Tristan Burke; **Advertising Manager:** Helen Fairbrother
Profile: Project management publication for the construction and property sectors.
Readership: Read by investors, developers, architects, contractors, civil engineers, structural engineers, mechanical engineers, quantity surveyors, officers of local authorities, property and facilities managers, financial institutions and financial advisors.
ADVERTISING RATES:
Full Page Colour .... EUR 3250
Agency Commission: 10%
Mechanical Data: Film: Digital, Bleed Size: 307 x 220mm, Trim Size: 297 x 210mm
Average ad content per issue: 40%
BUSINESS: CONSTRUCTION

PROPERTY
1666390E65H-5
Editorial: For all contact details see main record, Irish Independent
Freq: Weekly
Supplement to: Irish Independent
NATIONAL DAILY & SUNDAY NEWSPAPERS: National Colour Supplements

PROPERTY
1659438E65H-11
Editorial: For all contact details see main record, The Irish Times
Freq: Weekly
Supplement to: The Irish Times
NATIONAL DAILY & SUNDAY NEWSPAPERS: National Colour Supplements

PROPERTY
1779367E72-8248
Editorial: 41-42 Eyre Square, GALWAY
ADVERTISING RATES:
Full Page Colour .... EUR 3950
Supplement to: Galway Advertiser
LOCAL NEWSPAPERS

PROPERTY
1744317E72-8249
Editorial: 34 High Street, KILKENNY
Freq: Quarterly
Supplement to: Kilkenny People
LOCAL NEWSPAPERS

THE PROPERTY PROFESSIONAL
629695E1E-100
Editorial: 129 Lower Baggot Street, DUBLIN 2
Tel: 1 67 90 380 **Fax:** 16761940
Email: tim@timryan.ie **Web site:** http://www.ipav.ie
Date Established: 1995; **Freq:** Quarterly; **Cover Price:** Free; **Circ:** 8,000
Usual Pagination: 32
Editor: Tim Ryan; **Advertising Manager:** Lee Ryan
Profile: Magazine covering issues of interest to members of the Institute of Auctioneers and Valuers.
Readership: Read by auctioneers, estate agents and those in related professions.
ADVERTISING RATES:
Full Page Mono .... EUR 1240
Full Page Colour .... EUR 1240
Agency Commission: 10%
Mechanical Data: Trim Size: 297 x 210mm, Bleed Size: 307 x 220mm, Type Area: 277 x 190mm, Col Length: 287mm, Film: Digital, Page Width: 190mm
Average ad content per issue: 20%
BUSINESS: FINANCE & ECONOMICS: Property

THE PROPERTY VALUER
4148E1E-150
Editorial: 38 Merrion Square, DUBLIN 2
Tel: 1 66 11 794 **Fax:** 1 66 11 797
Email: info@iavi.ie **Web site:** http://www.iavi.ie
Date Established: 1983; **Freq:** Quarterly; **Annual Sub.:** EUR 45.00; **Circ:** 3,300
Usual Pagination: 40
Editor: Valerie Bourke; **Advertising Manager:** Valerie Bourke
Profile: Journal of the Irish Auctioneers' and Valuers' Institute. Contains national and international property news.
Readership: Read by valuers and auctioneers.
ADVERTISING RATES:
Full Page Colour .... EUR 1300.00
Mechanical Data: Trim Size: 297 x 210mm, Print Process: Litho, Film: Positive, right reading, emulsion side down. Digital
Copy instructions: *Copy Date:* 16th of the month prior to publication date
BUSINESS: FINANCE & ECONOMICS: Property

PROPERTY WEST WEEKLY
1799200E72-8250
Editorial: Tone Street, Ballina, CO. MAYO
Freq: Weekly
ADVERTISING RATES:
Full Page Colour .... EUR 1200
Supplement to: Western People
LOCAL NEWSPAPERS

PRUDENCE
1659846E74A-142
Editorial: Cunningham House, 130 Francis Street, DUBLIN 8 **Tel:** 1 41 67 900 **Fax:** 14167901
Email: annette@prudence.ie **Web site:** http://www.prudence.ie
Date Established: 2004; **Freq:** 6 issues yearly; **Cover Price:** EUR 2.95; **Circ:** 11,290
Usual Pagination: 96
Editor: Annette O'Meara; **Advertising Manager:** Susan Bermingham
Profile: Magazine offering women in Ireland an A-list lifestyle at realistic prices. Guide to savvy living in Ireland, it offers an eclectic mix of designer, vintage and high street fashion as well as high-street alternatives to designer and celeb looks.
Readership: Aimed at women aged 22 to 44 years old.
ADVERTISING RATES:
Full Page Colour .... EUR 2800
Agency Commission: 15%
Mechanical Data: Film: Digital, Trim Size: 297 x 230mm, Bleed Size: 307 x 240mm
Average ad content per issue: 33%
CONSUMER: WOMEN'S INTEREST CONSUMER MAGAZINES: Women's Interest

PUBLIC SECTOR TIMES
4439E32G-200
Editorial: 5 Eglinton Road, Bray, CO. WICKLOW
Tel: 1 28 69 111 **Fax:** 12869074
Email: psted@localtimes.ie
Date Established: 1974; **Freq:** Monthly; Free to qualifying individuals
Annual Sub.: EUR 100; **Circ:** 10,200
Usual Pagination: 32
Editor: Shay Fitzmaurice; **News Editor:** Adrienne Kelly
Profile: Magazine covering all public service areas.
Readership: Aimed at decision makers in State offices, semi-state offices, government departments, Garda stations, hospitals and local authorities at middle to senior management level.
ADVERTISING RATES:
Full Page Colour .... EUR 2950
SCC .... EUR 18.50
Mechanical Data: Type Area: 345 x 270mm, No. of Columns (Display): 7, Col Length: 345mm, Page Width: 270mm, Print Process: Offset litho, Col Widths (Display): 35mm
BUSINESS: LOCAL GOVERNMENT, LEISURE & RECREATION: Community Care & Social Services

THE PULSE
1698608E72-8215
Editorial: Liffey House, Edward Street, Newbridge, CO. KILDARE
Freq: Weekly
ADVERTISING RATES:
SCC .... EUR 6.50
Supplement to: Kildare Nationalist
LOCAL NEWSPAPERS

RAIL BRIEF
629708E49E-500
Editorial: Iarnrd Ireann, Connolly Station, Amiens Street, DUBLIN 1 **Tel:** 1 70 32 627 **Fax:** 1 70 32 515
Email: railbrief@irishrail.ie **Web site:** http://www.irishrail.ie
Date Established: 1988; **Freq:** 6 issues yearly; **Cover Price:** Free; **Circ:** 5,500
Usual Pagination: 24
Editor: Joanne Bissett
Profile: Newsletter for staff members at Iarnród Éireann/Irish Rail.
Readership: Aimed at staff members.
BUSINESS: TRANSPORT: Railways

READ-OUT
4191E19A-130
Editorial: Caoran, Baile na Habhnan, CO GALWAY
Tel: 87 26 63 282 **Fax:** 91506872
Email: readout@iol.ie **Web site:** http://www.read-out.net
ISSN: 0791-4369
Date Established: 1989; **Freq:** 6 issues yearly; **Cover Price:** Free; **Circ:** 2,000
Usual Pagination: 20
Advertising Manager: Eoin O'Riain
Profile: Engineering publication specialising in instrumentation and control.
Language(s): English; Gaelic
Readership: Aimed at users and vendors in the instrumentation world.
ADVERTISING RATES:
Full Page Colour .... EUR 1500
Mechanical Data: Type Area: 275 x 180mm, Col Length: 275mm, Page Width: 180mm, Trim Size: 297 x 210mm
BUSINESS: ENGINEERING & MACHINERY

REALITY
4396E87-150
Editorial: 75 Orwell Road, Rathgar, DUBLIN 6
Tel: 1 49 22 488 **Fax:** 1 49 27 999
Email: info@redemptoristpublications.com **Web site:** http://www.redemptoristpublications.com
Freq: 11 issues yearly; **Cover Price:** EUR 1.70
Annual Sub.: EUR 22.00; **Circ:** 12,000
Usual Pagination: 48
Editor: Gerard Moloney; **Advertising Manager:** Paul Copeland
Profile: Journal about social and religious issues.
Readership: Aimed at Christian parents aged between 30 and 50 years old.
ADVERTISING RATES:
Full Page Colour .... EUR 850.00
Mechanical Data: Film: Digital
Copy instructions: *Copy Date:* 6 weeks prior to publication date
CONSUMER: RELIGIOUS

RELIGIOUS LIFE REVIEW
623548E87-152
Editorial: 42 Parnell Square, DUBLIN 1
Tel: 1 87 31 355 **Fax:** 1 87 31 760
Email: thomas.mccarthy@dominicanpublications.com **Web site:** http://www.dominicanpublications.com
Date Established: 1962; **Freq:** 6 issues yearly; **Cover Price:** EUR 4.09
Annual Sub.: EUR 23.05; **Circ:** 2,000
Editor: Thomas McCarthy; **Advertising Manager:** James Gray
Profile: Magazine covering various aspects of religious life.
Readership: Read by churchgoers.
ADVERTISING RATES:
Full Page Mono .... EUR 175.00
Mechanical Data: Film: Digital, Type Area: 175 x 100mm, Col Length: 175mm, Page Width: 100
Copy instructions: *Copy Date:* 4 weeks prior to publication date
Average ad content per issue: 10%
CONSUMER: RELIGIOUS

RENOVATE YOUR HOUSE AND HOME
1666265E74C-205
Editorial: 1st Floor, Cunningham House, 130 Francis Street, DUBLIN 8 **Tel:** 1 41 67 900 **Fax:** 14167901
Email: editor@houseandhome.ie **Web site:** http://www.houseandhome.ie
Date Established: 2004; **Freq:** Half-yearly - Published in June and October; **Cover Price:** EUR 3.95; **Circ:** 25,000
Editor: Karen Hesse; **Advertising Manager:** Imelda Crombie
Profile: Magazine covering all aspects of renovating your home and features on real home renovations.
Readership: Aimed at those looking to renovate their homes.
ADVERTISING RATES:
Full Page Colour .... EUR 2850
Agency Commission: 10%
Mechanical Data: Trim Size: 297 x 210mm, Bleed Size: 307 x 220mm, Film: Digital
Average ad content per issue: 15%
CONSUMER: WOMEN'S INTEREST CONSUMER MAGAZINES: Home & Family

RETAIL NEWS
4235E53-90
Editorial: Poolbeg House, 1-2 Poolbeg Street, DUBLIN 2 **Tel:** 1 24 13 095 **Fax:** 12413010
Email: kathleenbelton@tarapublishingco.com **Web site:** http://www.retailnews.ie
Date Established: 1957; **Freq:** Monthly - Combined issues in Jan/Feb and Jul/Aug; Free to qualifying individuals
Annual Sub.: EUR 110; **Circ:** 6,116
Usual Pagination: 76
Advertising Manager: Kathleen Belton
Profile: Magazine covering the grocery sector.
Readership: Read by multiples, independent grocers, symbol group members, forecourt retailers, off licences, buyers, relevant government departments, cash and carry outlets, wholesalers, suppliers and services companies in the FMCG market in the Republic of Ireland, including RGDTA, CSNA and NOFFLA members.
ADVERTISING RATES:
Full Page Colour .... EUR 3125
Agency Commission: 10%
Mechanical Data: Film: Digital, Type Area: 267 x 180mm, Bleed Size: 307 x 220mm, Trim Size: 290 x 210mm, Col Length: 267mm, Page Width: 180mm
Average ad content per issue: 40%
BUSINESS: RETAILING & WHOLESALING

RISK MANAGER
754693E54B-150
Editorial: 72 Tyrconnell Road, Inchicore, DUBLIN 8
Tel: 1 41 63 678 **Fax:** 14545119
Email: anndaly1@eircom.net
Date Established: 2002; **Freq:** Quarterly
Free to qualifying individuals ; **Circ:** 10,500
Usual Pagination: 62
Advertising Manager: Ann Daly
Profile: Magazine focusing on security, fire and risk management.
Readership: Aimed at security, facility managers, fire and risk managers and health and safety managers.
ADVERTISING RATES:
Full Page Colour .... EUR 175
Agency Commission: 15%
Mechanical Data: Trim Size: 297 x 210mm, Bleed Size: 307 x 220mm, Film: Digital
Average ad content per issue: 40%
BUSINESS: SAFETY & SECURITY: Safety

ROSCOMMON HERALD
1824094E72-7075_120
Editorial: St. Patrick Street, Boyle, CO. ROSCOMMON 00 353
Freq: Weekly
Part of Series, see entry for: Roscommon Herald Series
LOCAL NEWSPAPERS

ROSCOMMON HERALD MID/SOUTH
1824096E72-7075_140
Editorial: St. Patrick Street, Boyle, CO. ROSCOMMON 00 353
Freq: Weekly
Part of Series, see entry for: Roscommon Herald Series
LOCAL NEWSPAPERS

ROSCOMMON HERALD SERIES
754377E72-7075
Editorial: St. Patrick Street, Boyle, CO. ROSCOMMON **Tel:** 71 96 62 004 **Fax:** 719662926
Email: news@roscommonherald.com **Web site:** http://www.roscommonherald.com
Date Established: 1859; **Freq:** Weekly; **Cover Price:** EUR 1.80; **Circ:** 8,663
Editor: Christina McHugh; **Advertising Manager:** Claire Morgan
ADVERTISING RATES:
Full Page Mono .... EUR 2700
Full Page Colour .... EUR 3110
Mechanical Data: Film: Digital, Type Area: 524 x 340mm, Col Length: 524mm, Col Widths (Display): 39mm, No. of Columns (Display): 8, Page Width: 340mm
Copy instructions: *Copy Date:* 3 days prior to publication date
Series owner and contact point for the following titles, see individual entries:
Roscommon Herald
Roscommon Herald Mid/South
LOCAL NEWSPAPERS

ROSCOMMON PEOPLE
1804126E72-8226
Editorial: Abbey Street, Roscommon Town, ROSCOMMON **Tel:** 90 66 34 633 **Fax:** 906634303
Email: news@roscommonpeople.ie **Web site:** http://www.roscommonpeople.ie
Date Established: 2007; **Freq:** Weekly; **Cover Price:** Free; **Circ:** 15,000
ADVERTISING RATES:
Full Page Colour .... EUR 2000
SCC .... EUR 10
Agency Commission: 15%
Mechanical Data: Type Area: 330 x 260mm, Col Length: 330mm, Page Width: 260mm, Col Widths (Display): 34mm, No. of Columns (Display): 7, Film: Digital, Bleed Size: +4mm
Average ad content per issue: 35%
LOCAL NEWSPAPERS

RTE GUIDE
4380E76C-80
Editorial: TV Building, Donnybrook, DUBLIN 4
Tel: 1 20 82 920 **Fax:** 1 20 83 085
Email: rteguide@rte.ie **Web site:** http://www.rte.ie/rteguide
Date Established: 1961; **Freq:** Weekly - Published on Wednesday; **Cover Price:** EUR 1.70
Annual Sub.: EUR 95; **Circ:** 84,018
Usual Pagination: 96
Editor: Aoife Byrne
Profile: Official guide to Irish radio and television, delivering TV entertainment and lifestyle. Includes programme listings for RTÉ channels, TV3, TG4, 3e, BBC, UTV, and Channel 4, satellite channels. Launched on 1 December 1961 as the RTV Guide, changed its name in 1966. Facebook: http://www.facebook.com/rte123.
Readership: Aimed at Irish television and radio enthusiasts.
ADVERTISING RATES:
Full Page Colour .... EUR 6420
Agency Commission: 15%
Mechanical Data: No. of Columns (Display): 4, Type Area: 275 x 208mm, Col Length: 275mm, Bleed Size: 309 x 240mm, Trim Size: 297 x 228mm, Film: Digital, Page Width: 208mm
Copy instructions: *Copy Date:* 10 days prior to publication date
CONSUMER: MUSIC & PERFORMING ARTS: TV & Radio

RUNNING YOUR BUSINESS
623606E14H-150
Editorial: 24 Terenure Road East, Rathgar, DUBLIN 6
Tel: 1 49 02 244 **Fax:** 1 49 20 578

Email: info@ryb.ie **Web site:** http://www.runningyourbusiness.com
ISSN: 1393-1016
Date Established: 1995; **Freq:** 10 issues yearly - Joint issues in July/Aug and Dec/Jan; **Cover Price:** EUR 3.50
Annual Sub.: EUR 35.00; **Circ:** 30,000
Usual Pagination: 52
Editor: Donal McAuliffe; **Advertising Manager:** Donal McAuliffe; **Publisher:** Donal McAuliffe
Profile: Official magazine of the Small Firms' Association, providing information and advice on the management of small businesses.
Readership: Read by owners and managers of small businesses.
ADVERTISING RATES:
Full Page Mono .... EUR 3600.00
Full Page Colour .... EUR 4500.00
Agency Commission: 10%
Mechanical Data: Trim Size: 297 x 210mm, Film: Digital, No. of Columns (Display): 3, Type Area: 275 x 190mm, Bleed Size: 300 x 213mm, Col Length: 275mm, Page Width: 190mm
Copy instructions: *Copy Date:* 2 weeks prior to publication date
Average ad content per issue: 25%
BUSINESS: COMMERCE, INDUSTRY & MANAGEMENT: Small Business

THE SACRED HEART MESSENGER 623549E87-153
Editorial: 37 Lower Leeson Street, DUBLIN 2
Tel: 1 676 7491 **Fax:** 16767493
Email: sales@messenger.ie **Web site:** http://www.messenger.ie
Date Established: 1888; **Freq:** Monthly; **Cover Price:** EUR 1.10
Annual Sub.: EUR 20.40; **Circ:** 100,000
Usual Pagination: 56
Editor: John Looby
Profile: A Jesuit publication, magazine of the Apostleship of Prayer, covering various aspects of Christian living today, including the family and its problems, social issues, our Christian heritage, nature, the environment and the arts. It also contains material of an entertaining nature, and pages for the children.
Readership: Aimed at those who wish to live as Christians in the contemporary milieu.
CONSUMER: RELIGIOUS

SALESIAN BULLETIN 623550E87-155
Editorial: Salesian College, Celbridge, COUNTY KILDARE **Tel:** 1 62 75 060 **Fax:** 1 63 03 601
Email: sdbmedia@eircom.net **Web site:** http://homepage.eircom.net/~sdbmedia
ISSN: 0790-1216
Date Established: 1939; **Freq:** Quarterly; **Cover Price:** Free; **Circ:** 6,000
Usual Pagination: 24
Editor: Pat Egan
Profile: Bulletin published by the Salesians of Don Bosco as a means of communication and information about their work, especially for the young, at home and on the missions.
Readership: Read by supporters of Don Bosco's mission, Salesian families, parents and young people.
CONSUMER: RELIGIOUS

SALON IRELAND 1645553E15A-1
Editorial: Unit 17, Building 2, The Courtyard, Carmenhall Road, Sandyford, DUBLIN 18
Tel: 1 29 58 181
Email: chris.dunican@expo-events.com **Web site:** http://www.salonmagazine.ie
Freq: Monthly; **Circ:** 6,708
Usual Pagination: 64
Editor: Amy Fitzgibbon
Profile: Magazine covering beauty products, industry profiles and technical features.
Readership: Aimed at owners of hair beauty, tanning and nail salons.
ADVERTISING RATES:
Full Page Colour .... EUR 1507
SCC .... EUR 40
Agency Commission: 15%
Mechanical Data: Type Area: 277 x 190mm, Bleed Size: 286 x 219mm, Trim Size: 280 x 213mm, Col Length: 277mm, Page Width: 190mm, Film: Digital
Average ad content per issue: 50%
BUSINESS: COSMETICS & HAIRDRESSING: Cosmetics

SAOIRSE IRISH FREEDOM 629710E82-170
Editorial: 223 Parnell Street, DUBLIN 1
Tel: 1 87 29 747 **Fax:** 1 87 29 757
Email: saoirse@iol.ie **Web site:** http://www.saoirse.rr.nu
Date Established: 1914; **Freq:** Monthly; **Cover Price:** EUR 1.00
Usual Pagination: 16
Editor: Ruairí Óg Ó Brádaigh
Profile: Magazine focusing on the republican movement.
Readership: Aimed at Irish republicans.
CONSUMER: CURRENT AFFAIRS & POLITICS

SAOL 764361E62J-100
Editorial: 7 Cearnóg Mhuirfean, Baile Átha Cliath 2, DUBLIN 2 **Tel:** 1 83 13 333 **Fax:** 1 63 98 401
Email: saol@eircom.net **Web site:** http://www.forasnagaeilge.ie
Date Established: 1986; **Freq:** 11 issues yearly;
Cover Price: Free; **Circ:** 12,500
Usual Pagination: 20
Editor: Colm Ó Tórna; **Advertising Manager:** Colm Ó Tórna
Profile: Publication containing news, events and features about districts in Ireland as well as classes and communities around the world where the Gaelic language is still spoken or in the growing Irish language interest groups in Britain and America.
Language(s): Gaelic
Readership: Aimed at teachers, academics and individuals in schools and educational centres.
Mechanical Data: Trim Size: 420 x 297mm
BUSINESS: CHURCH & SCHOOL EQUIPMENT & EDUCATION: Teachers & Education Management

SCIENCE PLUS 1644183E88A-27
Editorial: Ground Floor, Block B, Liffey Valley Office Campus, DUBLIN 22 **Tel:** 1 61 66 490
Fax: 1 61 66 499
Email: editorial@cjfallon.ie **Web site:** http://www.cjfallon.ie
Date Established: 1987; **Freq:** 7 issues yearly;
Annual Sub.: EUR 25.00; **Circ:** 12,000
Usual Pagination: 48
Editor: Fintan Lane
Profile: Magazine covering biology, physics and chemistry as well as higher level mathematics including applied mathematics.
Readership: Aimed at higher level Leaving Certificate students.
CONSUMER: EDUCATION

SCIENCE SPIN 1667285E94J-1
Editorial: 5 Serpentine Road, DUBLIN 4
Tel: 1 66 83 066
Email: tom@sciencespin.com **Web site:** http://www.sciencespin.com
ISSN: 1649-3346
Date Established: 2003; **Freq:** 6 issues yearly; **Circ:** 6,000
Usual Pagination: 56
Editor: Tom Kennedy; **Advertising Manager:** Alan Doherty
Profile: Popular Science magazine with reports, in-depth features, interviews with scientists, research results, scholarships, appointments, diary section and what's on when and where.
Readership: Aimed at researchers, the scientists of tomorrow or simply those with an enquiring mind.
ADVERTISING RATES:
Full Page Colour .... EUR 2500
SCC .... EUR 30
Agency Commission: 10%
Mechanical Data: Trim Size: 275 x 210mm, Bleed Size: 281 x 216mm, Film: Digital, No. of Columns (Display): 3
Average ad content per issue: 40%
CONSUMER: OTHER CLASSIFICATIONS: Popular Science

SELECT INTERIORS 629715E74C-135
Editorial: 51 Southern Cross Business Park, Boghall Road, Bay, CO. WICKLOW **Tel:** 1 20 21 598
Email: brigid@selectmagazine.ie **Web site:** http://www.selectmagazine.ie
Date Established: 1991; **Freq:** Half-yearly; **Cover Price:** EUR 4.75; **Circ:** 20,000
Usual Pagination: 196
Editor: Brigid Whitehead
Profile: Magazine featuring furniture and interiors of Ireland.
Readership: Aimed at homemakers.
ADVERTISING RATES:
Full Page Colour .... EUR 2495
Agency Commission: 15%
Mechanical Data: Type Area: 270 x 210mm, Bleed Size: 306 x 236mm, Trim Size: 300 x 230mm, Col Length: 270mm, Page Width: 210mm, Film: Digital
Average ad content per issue: 30%
CONSUMER: WOMEN'S INTEREST CONSUMER MAGAZINES: Home & Family

SELECT KITCHENS AND BATHROOMS 1834429E23C-1
Editorial: 51 Southern Cross Business Park, Braye, CO. WICKLOW **Tel:** 1 20 21 598 **Fax:** 12021582
Email: editor@selectmagazine.ie **Web site:** http://www.selectmagazine.ie
Date Established: 2006; **Freq:** Annual - Published in May; **Cover Price:** EUR 4.75; **Circ:** 15,000
Usual Pagination: 130
Editor: Brigid Whitehead
Profile: Magazine covering the current trends for kitchens and bathrooms in Ireland.
Readership: Aimed at ABC1 readers.
ADVERTISING RATES:
Full Page Colour .... EUR 2495
BUSINESS: FURNISHINGS & FURNITURE: Furnishings & Furniture - Kitchens & Bathrooms

SENIOR TIMES 1639919E74Q-151
Editorial: Unit 1, 15 Oxford Lane, DUBLIN 6
Tel: 1 67 61 811 **Fax:** 16761944
Email: info@iol.ie **Web site:** http://www.seniortimes.ie
Date Established: 1999; **Freq:** 6 issues yearly;
Cover Price: EUR 3.95
Free to qualifying individuals
Annual Sub.: EUR 36; **Circ:** 15,000
Usual Pagination: 90
Editor: Brian McCabe; **Advertising Manager:** Brian McCabe
Profile: Magazine covering personal finance, health, travel, personality profiles, leisure activities, gardening, fishing, general news, computers and computer training.
Readership: Aimed at those aged over fifty.
ADVERTISING RATES:
Full Page Mono .... EUR 2100
Full Page Colour .... EUR 2500
Agency Commission: 10%
Mechanical Data: Bleed Size: 303 x 216mm, Trim Size: 297 x 210mm, Film: Digital
Average ad content per issue: 35%
CONSUMER: WOMEN'S INTEREST CONSUMER MAGAZINES: Lifestyle

SHELFLIFE 4236E53-100
Editorial: Media House, South County Business Park, Leopardstown, DUBLIN 18 **Tel:** 1 29 47 777
Fax: 12947799
Email: fionnuala.carolan@mediateam.ie **Web site:** http://www.shelflife.ie
ISSN: 1393-0753
Date Established: 1995; **Freq:** Monthly - Published in the 1st week of the cover month; Free to qualifying individuals
Annual Sub.: EUR 89; **Circ:** 7,631
Usual Pagination: 88
Editor: Fionnuala Carolan; **Managing Editor:** Colette O'Connor; **Publisher:** John McDonald
Profile: Magazine for the grocery FMCG market, especially the convenience, newsagent, off-trade and forecourt retail sectors.
Readership: Aimed at all those involved in the grocery and off-trade retail trade.
ADVERTISING RATES:
Full Page Mono .... EUR 2900
Full Page Colour .... EUR 2900
Agency Commission: 15%
Mechanical Data: Bleed Size: 350 x 250mm, Trim Size: 340 x 240mm, Type Area: 306 x 210mm, Col Length: 306mm, Page Width: 210mm, Film: Digital
Average ad content per issue: 40%
BUSINESS: RETAILING & WHOLESALING

SIGNAL 1786627E40-12
Editorial: 24 South Frederick Street, DUBLIN 2
Tel: 1 70 71 931 **Fax:** 17079941
Email: ruairi@eup.ie **Web site:** http://www.eup.ie
ISSN: 1649-7635
Date Established: 2002; **Freq:** Half-yearly; Free to qualifying individuals
Annual Sub.: EUR 38; **Circ:** 5,000
Usual Pagination: 80
Editor: Ruairi Kavanagh; **Advertising Manager:** Michael Kelly
Profile: The official magazine of RACO (Representative Association of Commissioned Officers), SIGNAL is distributed widely within both the military and civil structures of Irish defence. Provides strong analysis and in depth interviews with the key influences and participants in Irish defence and security.
Readership: Aimed at the officer corps and decision makers in the Irish Defence Forces and distributed to all officer personnel serving overseas. In addition it is circulated to all members of Parliament, MEPs and relevant government departments.
ADVERTISING RATES:
Full Page Mono .... EUR 3750
Full Page Colour .... EUR 4000
Agency Commission: 15%
Mechanical Data: Trim Size: 297 x 210mm
Copy instructions: *Copy Date:* 14 days prior to publication date
Average ad content per issue: 30%
BUSINESS: DEFENCE

SLAINTE MAGAZINE 623516E74G-175
Formerly: Slainte
Editorial: 167 Bluebell Woods, Oranmore, CO GALWAY **Tel:** 91 776472 **Fax:** 91 788526
Email: info@slaintemagazine.ie **Web site:** http://www.slaintemagazine.ie
Date Established: 1997; **Freq:** Quarterly; **Cover Price:** EUR 3.48
Free to qualifying individuals ; **Circ:** 24,000
Usual Pagination: 60
Editor: Maria McHale
Profile: Consumer health magazine covering all aspects of health, including food, dieting, nutrition, sport activities and lifestyle.
Readership: Aimed at those with an interest in a healthy lifestyle.
ADVERTISING RATES:
Full Page Colour .... EUR 2550
Agency Commission: 15%
Mechanical Data: Col Length: 270mm, Page Width: 190mm, Film: Digital, Trim Size: 297 x 210mm, Type Area: 270 x 190mm, Bleed Size: 303 x 213mm
Average ad content per issue: 42%
CONSUMER: WOMEN'S INTEREST CONSUMER MAGAZINES: Slimming & Health

SLIGO CHAMPION 4332E72-7100
Editorial: Connacht House, Markievicz Road, CO. SLIGO **Tel:** 71 91 69 222 **Fax:** 719169833
Email: editor@sligochampion.ie **Web site:** http://www.sligochampion.ie
ISSN: 1649-5721
Date Established: 1836; **Freq:** Weekly; **Cover Price:** EUR 1.90; **Circ:** 10,282
Editor: Jim Gray; **Advertising Manager:** Frances Higgins
ADVERTISING RATES:
Full Page Mono .... EUR 2835
Full Page Colour .... EUR 3500
SCC .... EUR 7.20
Agency Commission: 15%
Mechanical Data: Col Length: 530mm, Col Widths (Display): 34mm, Film: Digital, Type Area: 530 x 340mm, Print Process: Offset litho, Page Width: 340mm, No. of Columns (Display): 8
LOCAL NEWSPAPERS

SLIGO WEEKENDER 754380E72-7150
Editorial: Waterfront House, Bridge Street, SLIGO
Tel: 71 91 74 900 **Fax:** 719174911
Email: editor@sligoweekender.ie **Web site:** http://www.sligoweekender.ie
Freq: Weekly; **Cover Price:** EUR 1.80; **Circ:** 6,491
ADVERTISING RATES:
Full Page Mono .... EUR 1670
Full Page Colour .... EUR 2087
SCC .... EUR 90
Agency Commission: 15%
Mechanical Data: Film: Digital, No. of Columns (Display): 7, Page Width: 266.7mm
Average ad content per issue: 15%
Supplement(s): The Western Property - 52xY
LOCAL NEWSPAPERS

SMART COMPANY 1666298E5D-101
Editorial: Media House, South County Business Park, Leopardstown, DUBLIN 18 **Tel:** 1 29 47 777
Fax: 12074299
Email: paul.hearns@mediateam.ie **Web site:** http://www.smartcompany.ie
Date Established: 2002; **Freq:** 6 issues yearly
Free to qualifying individuals ; **Circ:** 22,000
Usual Pagination: 10
Editor: Paul Hearns
Profile: Magazine communicating the business benefits of IT to small and medium-sized businesses who do not employ a full-time IT manager.
Readership: Aimed at business owners and financial managers of small and medium-sized businesses.
ADVERTISING RATES:
Full Page Colour .... EUR 3200
Agency Commission: 10%
Mechanical Data: Bleed Size: +5mm, Trim Size: 297 x 210mm, Film: Digital, Type Area: 280 x 190mm, Col Length: 280mm, Page Width: 190mm
Average ad content per issue: 30%
BUSINESS: COMPUTERS & AUTOMATION: Personal Computers

SNAFFLE 1655080E75E-1001
Formerly: Dublin Horse
Editorial: 7 Cranford Centre, Montrose, DUBLIN 4
Tel: 1 26 00 899 **Fax:** 1 26 00 977
Email: jameswilliams30@gmail.com
Freq: Quarterly; **Cover Price:** EUR 5.00; **Circ:** 25,000
Usual Pagination: 120
Editor: James Williams; **Advertising Manager:** James Williams
Profile: Magazine covering the Dublin Horse Show and equestrian events worldwide including show-jumping, eventing and equestrian sport, as well as developments within the equestrian world.
Readership: Aimed at those interested in horses, particularly those attending horse shows.
ADVERTISING RATES:
Full Page Colour .... EUR 2200.00
Agency Commission: 15%
Mechanical Data: Bleed Size: 303 x 216mm, Trim Size: 297 x 210mm, Film: Digital
Copy instructions: *Copy Date:* 3 weeks prior to publication date
Average ad content per issue: 25%
CONSUMER: SPORT: Horse Racing

SOCIAL & PERSONAL 623588E74C-150
Editorial: 19 Nassau Street, DUBLIN 2
Tel: 1 63 33 993 **Fax:** 16334353
Email: editorial@socialandpersonal.ie **Web site:** http://www.socialandpersonal.ie
Date Established: 1934; **Freq:** Monthly; **Cover Price:** EUR 3.75
Annual Sub.: EUR 59; **Circ:** 19,056
Usual Pagination: 136
Editor: P. Gibbons; **Managing Director:** Richard Kavanagh; **Advertising Manager:** Sandra Bothwell
Profile: Magazine focusing on general lifestyle issues. Includes interviews with celebrities and features on home decoration, fashion, parties and people.
Readership: Aimed at women aged 24 years old and above.
ADVERTISING RATES:
Full Page Colour .... EUR 2500
Agency Commission: 15%
Mechanical Data: Trim Size: 300 x 215mm, Type Area: 282 x 195mm, Col Length: 282mm, Film: Digital, Bleed Size: 308 x 221mm, Page Width: 195mm
Average ad content per issue: 35%
CONSUMER: WOMEN'S INTEREST CONSUMER MAGAZINES: Home & Family

SOCIAL & PERSONAL LIVING
1793562E74C-210
Editorial: 19 Nassau Street, DUBLIN 2
Tel: 1 63 33 969 **Fax:** 16334353
Email: living@socialandpersonal.ie
Date Established: 2006; **Freq:** Quarterly; **Circ:** 25,000
Usual Pagination: 144
Editor: Declan Leavy
Profile: Magazine covering all aspects of interiors as well as product reviews and food.
Readership: Aimed at affluent households in Ireland.
ADVERTISING RATES:
Full Page Colour .... EUR 2100
Mechanical Data: Type Area: 277 x 210mm, Bleed Size: 303 x 236mm, Trim Size: 297 x 230mm, Col Length: 277mm, Page Width: 210mm, Film: Digital
CONSUMER: WOMEN'S INTEREST CONSUMER MAGAZINES: Home & Family

SOCIAL & PERSONAL WEDDINGS
1804095E74L-156
Editorial: 19 Nassau Street, DUBLIN 2
Tel: 1 63 99 993 **Fax:** 16334353
Email: weddings@socialandpersonal.ie **Web site:** http://www.socialandpersonal.ie
Date Established: 2007; **Freq:** Half-yearly - Published in February and September; **Cover Price:** EUR 4.95; **Circ:** 25,000
Usual Pagination: 114
Editor: Declan Leavy
Profile: Magazine covering all aspects of weddings including women's and men's fashion, venues and honeymoons.
Readership: Aimed at brides and grooms in Ireland.
ADVERTISING RATES:
Full Page Colour .... EUR 2100
Mechanical Data: Type Area: 277 x 210mm, Bleed Size: 303 x 236mm, Trim Size: 297 x 230mm, Col Length: 277mm, Page Width: 210mm, Film: Digital
CONSUMER: WOMEN'S INTEREST CONSUMER MAGAZINES: Brides

SOUTH KILDARE TIMES
1659221E80-205
Editorial: For all contact details see main edition, Kildare Times
Freq: Weekly
Edition of: Kildare Times
CONSUMER: RURAL & REGIONAL INTEREST

SOUTH TIPP TODAY
1775927E72-8219
Editorial: 21-22 Upper Irishtown, Clonmel, CO. TIPPERARY **Tel:** 52 61 27 342 **Fax:** 526129142
Email: editorial@southtipptoday.ie **Web site:** http://www.southtipptoday.ie
Date Established: 1995; **Freq:** Weekly; **Cover Price:** Free; **Circ:** 20,500
Editor: Tony Butler; **Advertising Manager:** Shioban Odwier
Readership: Aimed at the population of South Tipperary and West Waterford.
ADVERTISING RATES:
Full Page Mono .... EUR 1040
Full Page Colour .... EUR 1200
SCC .... EUR 6.20
Agency Commission: 15%
Mechanical Data: Type Area: 334 x 259mm, Col Length: 334mm, Page Width: 259mm, Col Widths (Display): 34mm, No. of Columns (Display): 7, Film: Digital
Average ad content per issue: 40%
LOCAL NEWSPAPERS

SOUTH WICKLOW TIMES
1659227E72-8210_101
Editorial: 5 Eglington Road, Bray, CO WICKLOW 0
Freq: Weekly; **Cover Price:** Free
Part of Series, see entry for: Wicklow Times Series
LOCAL NEWSPAPERS

SOUTHERN STAR
4306E72-7200
Editorial: Ilen Streeet, Skibbereen, CO. CORK
Tel: 28 21 200 **Fax:** 2821212
Email: editorial@southernstar.ie **Web site:** http://www.southernstar.ie
ISSN: 1649-900X
Date Established: 1889; **Freq:** Weekly; **Cover Price:** EUR 1.80; **Circ:** 15,000
Editor: Con Downing; **Advertising Manager:** John Hamilton
Profile: Local news and sport mainly for the West Cork area.
Readership: All ages within catchment area.
ADVERTISING RATES:
Full Page Mono .... EUR 3600
Full Page Colour .... EUR 5000
SCC .... EUR 11
Agency Commission: 15%
Mechanical Data: Film: Digital, Col Length: 540mm, No. of Columns (Display): 9, Type Area: 540 x 396mm, Print Process: Web-fed offset litho, Page Width: 396mm, Col Widths (Display): 40mm
LOCAL NEWSPAPERS

SOUTHSIDE PEOPLE
623812E72-7320
Formerly: Southside People West edition
Editorial: 80-83 Omni Park, Santry, DUBLIN 9
Tel: 1 86 21 611 **Fax:** 18621625
Email: news@dublinpeople.com **Web site:** http://www.dublinpeople.com
Freq: Weekly; **Cover Price:** Free; **Circ:** 45,000
Editor: Tony McCullagh; **Advertising Manager:** Sean Maguire
ADVERTISING RATES:
Full Page Mono .... EUR 4237
Full Page Colour .... EUR 5720
Agency Commission: 10%
Mechanical Data: Page Width: 260mm, Type Area: 343 x 260mm, Col Length: 343mm, No. of Columns (Display): 7, Col Widths (Display): 32mm, Film: Digital
Average ad content per issue: 55%
LOCAL NEWSPAPERS

SPECTRUM
4142E1C-18
Formerly: IBOA News
Editorial: IBOA House, Upper Stephen Street, DUBLIN 8 **Tel:** 1 47 55 908 **Fax:** 14780567
Email: info@iboa.ie **Web site:** http://www.iboa.ie
ISSN: 0790-066X
Date Established: 2008; **Freq:** Quarterly; Free to qualifying individuals ; **Circ:** 27,000
Usual Pagination: 40
Editor: Seamas Sheils; **Advertising Manager:** Tommy Kennedy
Profile: Publication containing financial news, covering economic and banking developments, trade union issues, lifestyle, sports, popular culture.
Readership: Aimed at IBOA members in the financial services sector in the Irish Republic, Northern Ireland and Great Britain.
Average ad content per issue: 5%
BUSINESS: FINANCE & ECONOMICS: Banking

SPIRITUALITY
623556E87-170
Editorial: 42 Parnell Square, DUBLIN 1
Tel: 1 87 21 611 **Fax:** 1 87 31 760
Email: editor.spirituality@dominicanpublications.com
Web site: http://www.dominicanpublications.com
ISSN: 1393-273X
Date Established: 1995; **Freq:** 6 issues yearly;
Cover Price: EUR 5.26
Annual Sub.: EUR 45.22; **Circ:** 3,000
Usual Pagination: 64
Editor: Tom Jordan Op
Profile: International magazine focusing on Christian spiritual traditions and contemporary experiences.
Readership: Aimed at Christians and those interested in and searching the topic of spirituality.
CONSUMER: RELIGIOUS

SPOKEOUT
1667274E94F-2
Editorial: Publication Dept, IWA, Blackheath Drive, Clontarf, DUBLIN 3 **Tel:** 1 81 86 456 **Fax:** 18333873
Email: joanna.marsden@iwa.ie **Web site:** http://www.iwa.ie
ISSN: 1393-8517
Freq: Quarterly
Free to qualifying individuals ; **Circ:** 20,000
Usual Pagination: 68
Editor: Joanna Marsden; **Advertising Manager:** Joseph Bourke
Profile: Health and lifestyle magazine covering subjects such as equality, disability, health, sport, access, home, adaptations and travel.
Readership: Aimed at those with limited mobility.
ADVERTISING RATES:
Full Page Colour .... EUR 2150
Agency Commission: 15%
Mechanical Data: Trim Size: 297 x 210mm, Bleed Size: 303 x 216mm, Film: Digital
Average ad content per issue: 30%
CONSUMER: OTHER CLASSIFICATIONS: Disability

SPORTS MONDAY
1666375E65H-6
Editorial: For all contact details see main record, The Irish Times
Freq: Weekly - Published on Monday
Supplement to: The Irish Times
NATIONAL DAILY & SUNDAY NEWSPAPERS: National Colour Supplements

SPORTS MONTHLY
1666393E65H-7
Editorial: For all contact details see main record, Irish Independent
Freq: Monthly
Supplement to: Irish Independent
NATIONAL DAILY & SUNDAY NEWSPAPERS: National Colour Supplements

SPORTS WEDNESDAY
1852929E65H-42
Editorial: For all contact details see main record, The Irish Times
Freq: Weekly - Published on Wednesday
Supplement to: The Irish Times
NATIONAL DAILY & SUNDAY NEWSPAPERS: National Colour Supplements

STAR WOMAN
1659435E65H-33
Editorial: For all contact details see main record, The Irish Daily Star
Freq: Weekly
Supplement to: The Irish Daily Star
NATIONAL DAILY & SUNDAY NEWSPAPERS: National Colour Supplements

STEERING WHEEL
623531E77A-200
Editorial: Ballindine, Claremorris, CO. MAYO
Tel: 94 93 64 054 **Fax:** 94 93 64 336
Email: ability@iol.ie
Date Established: 1980; **Freq:** Half-yearly - Published in June; **Cover Price:** EUR 2.00
Free to qualifying individuals ; **Circ:** 8,000
Usual Pagination: 40
Editor: Kenneth Fox; **Advertising Manager:** Kenneth Fox
Profile: Magazine providing articles across a diverse range of topics, including grants and bursaries, accessible holiday accommodation, air travel and airport parking, forthcoming events and exhibitions and disability legislation, with a focus on motoring and offers advice and information on all aspects of disabled driving.
Readership: Aimed at disabled drivers.
CONSUMER: MOTORING & CYCLING: Motoring

STUBBS GAZETTE
4176U14A-317_25
Editorial: 23 South Frederick Street, DUBLIN 2
Tel: 1 67 25 939 **Fax:** 1 67 62 984
Email: info@businesspro.ie **Web site:** http://www.businesspro.ie
Freq: Weekly; **Circ:** 2,500
Editor: Carmel Conroy; **Managing Director:** James Treacy
Profile: Publication providing financial information and reports on new technological developments, trends, business affairs and statistics.
Readership: Aimed at leaders in business and industry.
BUSINESS: COMMERCE, INDUSTRY & MANAGEMENT

STUDIES AND IRISH QUARTERLY REVIEW
629719E82-180
Formerly: Studies
Editorial: 36 Lower Leeson Street, DUBLIN 2
Tel: 1 67 66 785 **Fax:** 16725948
Email: studies@jesuit.ie **Web site:** http://www.studiesirishreview.com
ISSN: 0039-3459
Date Established: 1912; **Freq:** Quarterly
Annual Sub.: EUR 45.00; **Circ:** 1,300
Usual Pagination: 104
Editor: Fergus O'Donoghue; **Advertising Manager:** Margaret Dixon
Profile: Magazine covering review of humanities, science and religion, with emphasis on Irish interests.
Readership: Aimed at graduates who have an interdisciplinary interest.
Copy instructions: *Copy Date:* 1 month prior to publication date
CONSUMER: CURRENT AFFAIRS & POLITICS

THE SUNDAY BUSINESS POST
4263E65B-5
Editorial: 80 Harcourt Street, DUBLIN 2
Tel: 1 60 26 000 **Fax:** 1 67 96 496
Email: info@sbpost.ie **Web site:** http://www.thepost.ie
Freq: Sunday; **Cover Price:** EUR 2.40; **Circ:** 45,696
Editor: Gavin Daly
Profile: Sunday newspaper covering Irish business, financial, political and economic issues. The Sunday Business Post targets business people and key business decision makers with latest information and developments. It was launched in 1989 and has reached an adult readership of 162,000 in total. Twitter handle: http://twitter.com/sundaybusiness.
ADVERTISING RATES:
Full Page Mono .... EUR 13605
Full Page Colour .... EUR 18625
Agency Commission: 15%
Mechanical Data: Col Length: 540mm, Col Widths (Display): 39mm, No. of Columns (Display): 8, Type Area: 540 x 340mm, Print Process: Web-fed offset litho, Page Width: 340mm, Film: Digital
Average ad content per issue: 40%
Supplement(s): Budget Magazine - 1xY, Computers in Business - 12xY, Conference & Convention Guide - 1xY, Finance Magazine - 1xY, Food & Drink Magazine - 4xY
NATIONAL DAILY & SUNDAY NEWSPAPERS: National Sunday Newspapers

SUNDAY INDEPENDENT
4264E65B-10
Editorial: Independent House, 27-32 Talbot Street, DUBLIN 1 **Tel:** 1 70 55 333 **Fax:** 1 70 55 779
Email: mosullivan@independent.ie **Web site:** http://www.unison.ie
Freq: Sunday; **Circ:** 254,311
Usual Pagination: 72
Editor: Aengus Fanning; **News Editor:** Liam Collins; **Features Editor:** Mary O'Sullivan; **Advertising Manager:** Jo Collins
Profile: Ireland's Sunday newspaper with a comprehensive mix of comment, analysis, sport, business, current affairs and entertainment. Sports section contains 12 pages of Irish and international sport. The Living section includes a mix of interviews and lifestyle features, whilst the Business section investigates Irish and world business news, analyses the markets, interviews business personalities and explores personal finance options. It was first published in 1905.
ADVERTISING RATES:
Full Page Mono .... EUR 34115
Full Page Colour .... EUR 42170
Agency Commission: 10%
Mechanical Data: Type Area: 530 x 340mm, Col Length: 530mm, No. of Columns (Display): 8, Page Width: 340mm, Col Widths (Display): 40mm, Film: Digital
Average ad content per issue: 30%
Supplement(s): LIFE Magazine - 52xY
NATIONAL DAILY & SUNDAY NEWSPAPERS: National Sunday Newspapers

THE SUNDAY TIMES (IRELAND)
623659E65B-25
Formerly: The Sunday Times
Editorial: Bishop's Square, 4th Floor, Redmond's Hill, DUBLIN 2 **Tel:** 1 47 92 424 **Fax:** 14792421
Email: ireland@sunday-times.ie **Web site:** http://www.sunday-times.co.uk
Freq: Sunday - Irish Republic; **Cover Price:** EUR 2.50; **Circ:** 107,189
Profile: The Irish Edition of The Sunday Times newspaper. Broadsheet-sized quality Sunday newspaper containing Irish and international news, business, sport, culture and style, Irish cinema listings and schedules for RTE One and RTE Two. Launched in 1993. Twitter handle: http://twitter.com/SunTimesIreland.
Readership: Read by decision makers within business and industry, managers, academics and university students.
ADVERTISING RATES:
Full Page Mono .... EUR 19950
Full Page Colour .... EUR 26900
Agency Commission: 15%
Mechanical Data: No. of Columns (Display): 8, Page Width: 343mm, Type Area: 540 x 343mm, Col Length: 540mm, Col Widths (Display): 39mm, Film: Digital
NATIONAL DAILY & SUNDAY NEWSPAPERS: National Sunday Newspapers

SUNDAY WORLD
4266E65B-40
Editorial: Independent House, 27-32 Talbot Street, DUBLIN 1 **Tel:** 1 88 49 000 **Fax:** 1 88 49 001
Email: news@sundayworld.com **Web site:** http://www.sundayworld.com
ISSN: 0791-6760
Freq: Sunday; **Cover Price:** EUR 2.30; **Circ:** 251,334
Editor: Colm MacGinty; **News Editor:** John Donlon; **Managing Director:** Gerry Lennon; **Managing Editor:** Neil Leslie; **Advertising Director:** Mairead Kearns
Profile: The Sunday World is an Irish newspaper published by Sunday Newspapers Limited, a division of Independent News and Media. The newspaper covers Irish news, latest in showbiz and entertainment, celebrities and gossip, movies, Irish crime. Founded in 1973. In 2008, the newspaper won the prize for the Newspaper of the Year (Sunday) at the annual Chartered Institute of Public Relations Press and Broadcast Awards for Northern Ireland. Twitter handle: http://twitter.com/sundayworld.
ADVERTISING RATES:
Full Page Mono .... EUR 17500
Full Page Colour .... EUR 26700
SCC .... EUR 77
Mechanical Data: Type Area: 335 x 269mm, Col Length: 335mm, Col Widths (Display): 35mm, No. of Columns (Display): 7, Page Width: 269mm, Film: Digital
Supplement(s): Sunday World Magazine - 52xY
NATIONAL DAILY & SUNDAY NEWSPAPERS: National Sunday Newspapers

SUNDAY WORLD MAGAZINE
1626475E65H-1
Editorial: Independent House, 27-32 Talbot Street, DUBLIN 1 **Tel:** 1 88 49 000 **Fax:** 18849001
Email: swm@sundayworld.com **Web site:** http://www.sundayworld.com
Date Established: 2003; **Freq:** Weekly - Irish Republic; **Cover Price:** EUR 2.30; **Circ:** 273,000
Editor: Caoimhe Young
Profile: Magazine featuring celebrity and TV news, as well as lifestyle features including health, beauty, cookery, fashion, movies and music.
Readership: Aimed at a wide range of the general public.
ADVERTISING RATES:
Full Page Mono .... EUR 17500
Full Page Colour .... EUR 26700
SCC .... EUR 115
Agency Commission: 15%
Mechanical Data: Bleed Size: +3mm, Film: Digital, No. of Columns (Display): 4, Type Area: 287 x 269
Supplement to: Sunday World
NATIONAL DAILY & SUNDAY NEWSPAPERS: National Colour Supplements

THE TALLAGHT NEWS
754391E72-7340
Formerly: The News Series (Tallaght)
Editorial: PO Box 3430, Tallaght, DUBLIN 24
Tel: 1 45 19 000 **Fax:** 1 4519805
Email: info@tallaghtonline.ie **Web site:** http://www.tallaghtnews.com
Cover Price: Free; **Circ:** 63,000
Managing Editor: John Russell

ADVERTISING RATES:
Full Page Colour .... EUR 1195
Agency Commission: 15%
Mechanical Data: Film: Digital
Copy instructions: *Copy Date:* 4 days prior to publication date
Average ad content per issue: 40%
Series owner and contact point for the following titles, see individual entries:
The Lucan & Clondalkin News
The Tallaght News
LOCAL NEWSPAPERS

THE TALLAGHT NEWS
1835776E72-7340_100
Editorial: PO Box 3430, Tallaght, DUBLIN 24
Freq: 26 issues yearly; **Cover Price:** Free; **Circ:** 33,000
Part of Series, see entry for: The Tallaght News
LOCAL NEWSPAPERS

TECHNOLOGY IRELAND
4178E14B-150
Editorial: The Plaza, East Point Business Park, DUBLIN 3 **Tel:** 1 727 2954 **Fax:** 17272086
Email: technology.ireland@enterprise-ireland.com
Web site: http://www.technologyireland.ie
ISSN: 0040-1676
Date Established: 1968; **Freq:** 6 issues yearly - Published in the 1st week of the 1st cover month; Free to qualifying individuals
Annual Sub.: EUR 54; **Circ:** 7,000
Usual Pagination: 58
Editor: Teresa Meagh
Profile: Journal providing news and reviews of science and technology and its applications. Also contains information on industry throughout Ireland.
Readership: Aimed at government agency officials, industry leaders and third level colleges and researchers.
ADVERTISING RATES:
Full Page Colour .... EUR 1740
Agency Commission: 10%
Mechanical Data: Type Area: 277 x 192mm, Trim Size: 300 x 225mm, Bleed Size: 306 x 231mm, Col Length: 277mm, Page Width: 192mm
Average ad content per issue: 30%
BUSINESS: COMMERCE, INDUSTRY & MANAGEMENT: Industry & Factories

---

THE TICKET
1666380E65H-13
Editorial: For all contact details see main record, The Irish Times
Freq: Weekly
Supplement to: The Irish Times
NATIONAL DAILY & SUNDAY NEWSPAPERS: National Colour Supplements

---

TIPPERARY STAR
623756E72-7400
Editorial: Friar Street, Thurles, CO. TIPPERARY 0
Tel: 5 04 29 100 **Fax:** 50421110
Email: md@tipperarystar.ie **Web site:** http://www.tipperarystar.ie
Date Established: 1909; **Freq:** Weekly; **Cover Price:** EUR 1.90; **Circ:** 7,898
Usual Pagination: 36
Editor: Michael Dundon; **Advertising Manager:** Maria Woodlock
ADVERTISING RATES:
Full Page Mono .... EUR 4179
Full Page Colour .... EUR 5224
SCC .... EUR 8.75
Mechanical Data: Film: Positive, right reading, emulsion side down. Digital, Print Process: Offset litho, No. of Columns (Display): 9, Type Area: 538 x 343.5mm, Col Length: 538mm, Page Width: 343.5mm
LOCAL NEWSPAPERS

TIRCONAILL TRIBUNE
754450E72-7425
Editorial: Main Street, Milford, CO. DONEGAL
Tel: 74 91 53 600 **Fax:** 749153607
Email: tribune15@gmail.com **Web site:** http://www.tirconaill-tribune.com
Freq: Weekly; **Cover Price:** EUR 1.40; **Circ:** 6,500
Editor: John McAteer; **Advertising Manager:** Francis Daver
ADVERTISING RATES:
Full Page Mono .... EUR 550
Full Page Colour .... EUR 1000
Agency Commission: 10%
Mechanical Data: Type Area: 412 x 274mm, Film: Digital, Col Length: 412mm, Page Width: 274mm, Col Widths (Display): 31mm, No. of Columns (Display): 8
Average ad content per issue: 25%
LOCAL NEWSPAPERS

THE TITLE
767137E65B-2_700
Tel: 1 63 75 800 **Fax:** 1 63 75 830
Email: jack.white@irelandonsunday.com
Freq: Sunday - Published within Ireland on Sunday
Editor: Jack White
Profile: Section covering Gaelic and international sport.
ADVERTISING RATES:
Full Page Mono .... EUR 9884.00
Full Page Colour .... EUR 13179.00
Section of: Irish Mail on Sunday
NATIONAL DAILY & SUNDAY NEWSPAPERS: National Sunday Newspapers

---

TNT
1659466E83-252
Editorial: For all contact details see main record, Trinity News
Freq: 5 issues yearly; **Cover Price:** Free; **Circ:** 5,000
Supplement to: Trinity News
CONSUMER: STUDENT PUBLICATIONS

TODAY'S FARM
754343E21A-200
Editorial: Oak Park, CARLOW **Tel:** 59 91 70 200
Fax: 599183498
Email: mark.moore@teagasc.ie **Web site:** http://www.teagasc.ie
Freq: 6 issues yearly; Free to qualifying individuals
Annual Sub.: EUR 30.50; **Circ:** 46,000
Usual Pagination: 40
Advertising Manager: Frank McGouran
Profile: Magazine focusing on farming and agricultural issues.
Readership: Aimed at farmers in all areas of agricultural activity.
ADVERTISING RATES:
Full Page Colour .... EUR 2700
Agency Commission: 10%
Mechanical Data: Col Length: 272mm, Page Width: 182mm, Type Area: 272 x 182mm, Trim Size: 299 x 216mm, Bleed Size: 306 x 216mm
Average ad content per issue: 30%
BUSINESS: AGRICULTURE & FARMING

TODAY'S GROCERY MAGAZINE
4234E53-50
Formerly: Grocer Magazine
Editorial: The Mews, Eden Road Upper, Dun Laoghaire, CO. DUBLIN **Tel:** 1 28 09 466
Email: editorial@todaysgrocery.com **Web site:** http://www.todaysgrocery.com
Freq: Monthly; **Cover Price:** Free; **Circ:** 9,100
Usual Pagination: 52
Editor: Frank Madden; **Advertising Director:** Frank Madden
Profile: Magazine covering every aspect of the Irish food and grocery trade, including suppliers, multiples, independents, cash and carries, wholesalers and off-licence outlets.
Readership: Read by manufacturers, suppliers and retailers.
ADVERTISING RATES:
Full Page Colour .... EUR 2800.00
Agency Commission: 15%
Mechanical Data: Type Area: 271 x 184mm, Print Process: Sheet-fed litho, Bleed Size: 300 x 210mm, Trim Size: 297 x 210mm, Col Length: 271mm, Page Width: 184mm, Film: Digital
Copy instructions: *Copy Date:* 15th of the month prior to publication date
BUSINESS: RETAILING & WHOLESALING

TODAY'S PARENTS
764367E74D-130
Editorial: 19 Clare Street, DUBLIN 2 **Tel:** 1 66 22 266
Fax: 1 66 24 981
Email: info@selectmediaItd.com
Freq: Quarterly; **Cover Price:** EUR 1.90
Free to qualifying individuals
Annual Sub.: EUR 25.00; **Circ:** 10,500
Editor: Robert Heuston; **Advertising Manager:** Robert Heuston; **Publisher:** Robert Heuston
Profile: Magazine focusing on information for parents of babies and children. Containing features on education, activities, health and lifestyle.
Readership: Aimed at parents of babies and young children up to the age of 11.
ADVERTISING RATES:
Full Page Colour .... EUR 2095.00
Agency Commission: 10%
Mechanical Data: Film: Digital, Trim Size: 297 x 210mm, Bleed Size: 301 x 213mm
Average ad content per issue: 27%
CONSUMER: WOMEN'S INTEREST CONSUMER MAGAZINES: Child Care

TOPIC SERIES
4338E72-6100
Formerly: Meath Topic
Editorial: 6 Dominick Street, Mullingar, CO. WESTMEATH **Tel:** 44 93 48 868 **Fax:** 449343777
Email: news@westmeathtopic.com
Date Established: 1971; **Freq:** Weekly; **Circ:** 27,000
Usual Pagination: 56
Advertising Manager: Tom Kiernan
Series owner and contact point for the following titles, see individual entries:
Meath Topic
Offaly Topic
Westmeath Topic
LOCAL NEWSPAPERS

TOTALLY DUBLIN
1752608E80-206
Editorial: 7 Camden House, Camden Street, DUBLIN 2 **Tel:** 1 47 91 111 **Fax:** 14791116
Email: peter@hkm.ie
Freq: Monthly; **Cover Price:** Free; **Circ:** 49,868
Usual Pagination: 102
Publisher: Stefan Hallenius
Profile: Magazine covering Dublin culture and entertainment.
Readership: Aimed at residents in Dublin.
ADVERTISING RATES:
Full Page Colour .... EUR 2200
Agency Commission: 15%
Mechanical Data: Type Area: 335 x 227mm, Bleed Size: 370 x 270mm, Trim Size: 360 x 260mm, Col Length: 335mm, Page Width: 227mm, Film: Digital
Average ad content per issue: 40%
CONSUMER: RURAL & REGIONAL INTEREST

TRAVEL EXTRA
754344E89A-150
Editorial: Clownings, Straffan, KILDARE
Tel: 87 29 36 015 **Fax:** 16270126
Email: eoghan.corry@travelextra.ie **Web site:** http://www.travelextra.ie
Date Established: 1995; **Freq:** Monthly; Free to qualifying individuals
Annual Sub.: EUR 36.30; **Circ:** 22,000
Usual Pagination: 32
Editor: Eoghan Corry; **Features Editor:** Anne Cadwallader; **Managing Editor:** Gerry O'Hare
Profile: Magazine focusing on travel, holidays and entertainment in Ireland.
Readership: Aimed at those living in Ireland.
ADVERTISING RATES:
Full Page Colour .... EUR 2750
Agency Commission: 10%
Mechanical Data: No. of Columns (Display): 6, Col Widths (Display): 60mm, Type Area: 330 x 260mm, Bleed Size: +5mm, Trim Size: 370 x 285mm, Film: Digital, Col Length: 330mm, Page Width: 260mm
Average ad content per issue: 40%
CONSUMER: HOLIDAYS & TRAVEL: Travel

TRIBUNE MAGAZINE
1696055E65H-25
Formerly: i magazine
Editorial: For all contact details see main record, Sunday Tribune
Freq: Sunday
Supplement to: Sunday Tribune
NATIONAL DAILY & SUNDAY NEWSPAPERS: National Colour Supplements

---

TRINITY NEWS
4389E83-200
Editorial: 6 Trinity College, DUBLIN 2
Tel: 1 89 62 335
Email: editor@trinitynews.ie **Web site:** http://www.trinitynews.com
Freq: Monthly; **Cover Price:** Free; **Circ:** 5,000
Usual Pagination: 28
Editor: Martin McKenna; **Features Editor:** Emily Monk
Profile: Independent student newspaper of Trinity College, Dublin.
Readership: Aimed at students and staff in Dublin's city centre campus and inner-city Dublin.
Supplement(s): TNT - 5xY
CONSUMER: STUDENT PUBLICATIONS

THE TUAM HERALD
4313E72-7500
Editorial: Dublin Road, Tuam, CO. GALWAY
Tel: 93 24 183 **Fax:** 9324478
Email: editor@tuamherald.ie **Web site:** http://www.tuamherald.ie
Date Established: 1837; **Freq:** Weekly; **Cover Price:** EUR 1.50; **Circ:** 8,883
News Editor: Tony Galvin; **Advertising Manager:** Liz Gardiner
ADVERTISING RATES:
Full Page Mono .... EUR 2348
Full Page Colour .... EUR 3170
SCC .... EUR 5.35
Agency Commission: 15%
Mechanical Data: Type Area: 521 x 381mm, Col Length: 521mm, Col Widths (Display): 43mm, No. of Columns (Display): 8, Film: Digital, Page Width: 381mm
Average ad content per issue: 35%
Supplement(s): Herald eXtra - 52xY
LOCAL NEWSPAPERS

TULLAMORE TRIBUNE
754410E72-7525
Editorial: William Street, Tullamore, CO. OFFALY
Tel: 57 93 21 152 **Fax:** 579321927
Email: editor@tullamoretribune.ie **Web site:** http://www.tullamoretribune.ie
Date Established: 1978; **Freq:** Weekly; **Cover Price:** EUR 1.95; **Circ:** 16,000
News Editor: Gerard Scully; **Advertising Manager:** Phyllis Byrne
Profile: The Tullamore Tribune is a sister paper to the Midland Tribune. The Tullamore Tribune incorporates the Offaly Vindicator and the Leinster Reporter. It circulates in North and East Offaly and parts of Westmeath, Laois and Kildare. It has the highest circulation in the area and is innovative in maintaining its position.
Language(s): English; Gaelic
ADVERTISING RATES:
Full Page Mono .... EUR 5130.40
Full Page Colour .... EUR 6614.40
SCC .... EUR 12.10
Mechanical Data: No. of Columns (Display): 8, Col Widths (Display): 38mm, Film: Digital, Type Area: 530 x 340mm, Col Length: 530mm, Page Width: 340mm
Supplement(s): Farming - 12xY, Motoring - 12xY, Weddings - 12xY
LOCAL NEWSPAPERS

TV NOW!
623225E76C-100
Editorial: 2-4 Ely Place, DUBLIN 2 **Tel:** 1 48 07 700
Fax: 14804799
Email: deborah@tvnowmagazine.ie
Freq: Weekly; **Cover Price:** EUR 1,35; **Circ:** 29,204
Usual Pagination: 94
Editor: Deborah McGee
Profile: TV listings magazine containing features on soaps, celebrities, fashion, beauty and health.
Readership: Aimed at Irish television enthusiasts.
ADVERTISING RATES:
Full Page Colour .... EUR 3650
Agency Commission: 10%
Mechanical Data: Type Area: 277 x 200mm, Bleed Size: 307 x 230mm, Film: Digital, Trim Size: 297 x 220mm, Col Length: 277mm, Print Process: Web-fed offset litho, Page Width: 200mm
Average ad content per issue: 20%
CONSUMER: MUSIC & PERFORMING ARTS: TV & Radio

TV WEEK
1659429E65H-36
Editorial: For all contact details see main record, Irish Mail on Sunday
Freq: Weekly
ADVERTISING RATES:
Full Page Mono .... EUR 9884.00
Full Page Colour .... EUR 13179.00
Supplement to: Irish Mail on Sunday
NATIONAL DAILY & SUNDAY NEWSPAPERS: National Colour Supplements

---

TVB EUROPE
35697E2D-71
Editorial: 1st Floor, Suncourt House, 18-26 Essex Road, DUBLIN 18 **Tel:** 1 29 47 783
Fax: 20 7354 6049
Email: ienews@intentmedia.co.uk **Web site:** http://www.tvbeurope.com
ISSN: 1461-4197
Date Established: 1992; **Freq:** Monthly - Published on the 10th of the cover month; Free to qualifying individuals ; **Circ:** 7,402
Editor: Fergal Ringrose
Profile: Magazine containing features and information from within the television broadcasting industry, including new broadcasting innovations and technology. Aimed at TV operations chiefs, chief engineers, decision makers and management within the broadcasting industry. Regular features: H-D Update - Reports on high definition technologies within the industry.
Readership: Aimed at TV operations chiefs, chief engineers, decision makers and management within the broadcasting industry.
ADVERTISING RATES:
Full Page Colour £3550
Mechanical Data: Page Width: 228mm, Type Area: 314 x 228mm, Bleed Size: 340 x 250mm, Trim Size: 335 x 245mm, Film: Digital, Col Length: 314mm
BUSINESS: COMMUNICATIONS, ADVERTISING & MARKETING: Broadcasting

---

TYRE TRADE JOURNAL
628812E31A-80
Formerly: Irish Tyre Trade Journal & Aftermarket Times
Editorial: Glencree House, Lanesborough Road, ROSCOMMON TOWN **Tel:** 90 66 25 676
Fax: 906637410
Email: pdeane@autopub.ie **Web site:** http://www.tyretrade.ie
Date Established: 1996; **Freq:** 6 issues yearly; Free to qualifying individuals
Annual Sub.: EUR 45; **Circ:** 2,800
Usual Pagination: 84
Editor: Padraic Deane
Profile: Magazine containing information about tyres, tyre shop equipment, repair materials and a wide range of related automotive news and features of interest to the Irish republic and Northern Ireland retail and wholesale tyre trade plus many associate and interested businesses.
Readership: Aimed at wholesalers and retailers of tyre and fast-fit traders, fleet managers, agriculture equipment sellers, quarry managers, police and road safety authorities, insurance managers and management decision-makers throughout all of Ireland, north and south.
ADVERTISING RATES:
Full Page Colour .... EUR 1900
Agency Commission: 15%
Mechanical Data: Type Area: 270 x 185mm, Bleed Size: 303 x 216mm, Col Length: 270mm, No. of Columns (Display): 4, Film: Digital, Page Width: 185mm, Trim Size: 297 x 210mm
Average ad content per issue: 30%
BUSINESS: MOTOR TRADE: Motor Trade Accessories

U MAGAZINE
4356E74A-100
Editorial: Rosemount House, Dundrum Road, Dundrum, DUBLIN 14 **Tel:** 1 24 05 300
Fax: 16615797
Web site: http://www.ivenus.com
Date Established: 1980; **Freq:** 26 issues yearly; **Cover Price:** EUR 1.59; **Circ:** 27,564
Usual Pagination: 108
Editor: Jennifer Stevens
Profile: Magazine focusing on celebrities, beauty, fashion, sex, relationships and money.
Readership: Aimed at women between 18 and 35 years old.
ADVERTISING RATES:
Full Page Colour .... EUR 3520
Agency Commission: 15%

Mechanical Data: Type Area: 270 x 195mm, Bleed Size: 310 x 235mm, Trim Size: 300 x 225mm, Col Length: 270mm, Page Width: 195mm
Average ad content per issue: 25%
CONSUMER: WOMEN'S INTEREST CONSUMER MAGAZINES: Women's Interest

THE UCC EXPRESS
764368E83-15
Formerly: The University Express
Editorial: Forum, University College Cork, CORK **Tel:** 21 49 03 133 **Fax:** 214903219
Email: sucommunications@ucc.ie **Web site:** http://sin.ucc.ie
Freq: Monthly - Published fortnightly between September and June; **Cover Price:** Free; **Circ:** 4,000
Usual Pagination: 32
Editor: Caira Guiry; **News Editor:** Daniel Lynch; **Features Editor:** Stephen Collender
Profile: Student newspaper featuring information about the locality. Also includes articles on politics, music, reviews and entertainment.
Readership: Aimed at the students of University College Cork.
Average ad content per issue: 12%
CONSUMER: STUDENT PUBLICATIONS

UPSTAIRS DOWNSTAIRS
629775E74C-200
Editorial: U9 Killkerrin Business Park, Liosban, Tuam Road, CO. GALWAY **Tel:** 91 76 27 50 **Fax:** 91762753
Email: info@upstairsdownstairsltd.com **Web site:** http://www.upstairsdownstairsonline.com
Date Established: 1999; **Freq:** 6 issues yearly; **Circ:** 15,000
Usual Pagination: 96
Editor: Ann Leyden; **Advertising Manager:** Fionnuala Tarpey
Profile: Magazine containing articles on the home, gardening, products, services and ideas.
Readership: Aimed at householders living in Ireland.
ADVERTISING RATES:
Full Page Colour .... EUR 1350
Mechanical Data: Trim Size: 297 x 210mm, Film: Digital
Average ad content per issue: 33%
CONSUMER: WOMEN'S INTEREST CONSUMER MAGAZINES: Home & Family

UR DREAM HOME
1795194E74K-106
Editorial: Unit 12, Glenrock Business Park, Bothar na Minne, Ballybane, GALWAY **Tel:** 91 76 27 03
Fax: 91762843
Email: editor@urdreamhome.ie
Date Established: 2006; **Freq:** 6 issues yearly; **Circ:** 10,000
Usual Pagination: 100
Advertising Manager: Olga Magliocco
Profile: Magazine covering homes, interiors and gardens as well as finance, planning, an eco-friendly environment and art.
Readership: Aimed at home owners and potential home owners.
CONSUMER: WOMEN'S INTEREST CONSUMER MAGAZINES: Home Purchase

VALE STAR/MALLOW STAR
754439E72-7660_101
Editorial: 19 Bridge Street, Mallow, CO. CORK
Freq: Weekly; **Cover Price:** EUR 1.80; **Circ:** 12,500
Part of Series, see entry for: Observer & Star Series
LOCAL NEWSPAPERS

VIP MAGAZINE
4367E74Q-150
Editorial: 2-4 Ely Place, DUBLIN 2 **Tel:** 1 4804700
Fax: 1 4804799
Email: info@vipmagazine.ie
Date Established: 1999; **Freq:** Monthly; **Cover Price:** EUR 3.80; **Circ:** 24,113
Usual Pagination: 110
Advertising Manager: Jill Geoghegan
Profile: Magazine containing news, interviews and photo sessions with Irish celebrities. Includes coverage of weddings, births and celebrations.
Readership: Aimed at women aged between 19 and 47 years old.
ADVERTISING RATES:
Full Page Colour .... EUR 4300
Agency Commission: 10%
Mechanical Data: Type Area: 310 x 220mm, Col Length: 310mm, Page Width: 220mm, Film: Digital, Bleed Size: 340 x 250mm, Trim Size: 330 x 240mm
Average ad content per issue: 35%
CONSUMER: WOMEN'S INTEREST CONSUMER MAGAZINES: Lifestyle

VISITOR
623579E89A-200
Editorial: Taney Hall, Eglinton Terrace, Dundrum, DUBLIN 14
Email: info@maccom.ie **Web site:** http://www.maccommunications.ie
Date Established: 1988; **Freq:** Annual - Published in April; **Cover Price:** Free; **Circ:** 90,000
Usual Pagination: 52
Advertising Manager: Thomas O'Neill
Profile: Magazine covering travel, tourist attractions and historical articles.
Readership: Read by visitors to the Irish Republic.
ADVERTISING RATES:
Full Page Colour .... EUR 5000
Agency Commission: 10%
Mechanical Data: Trim Size: 297 x 210mm, Col Length: 277mm, Page Width: 190mm, Type Area: 277 x 190mm, Bleed Size: 303 x 216mm, Film: Digital
Average ad content per issue: 40%
CONSUMER: HOLIDAYS & TRAVEL: Travel

WALKING WORLD IRELAND
623518E75L-200
Editorial: Edelweiss, Cushina, Portlarlington, CO. LAOIS **Tel:** 57 86 45 343
Email: walkingworld@irl.ie **Web site:** http://www.walkingworldireland.com
ISSN: 0791-8801
Date Established: 1993; **Freq:** 6 issues yearly; **Annual Sub.:** EUR 32; **Circ:** 14,895
Usual Pagination: 56
Editor: Conor O'Hagan; **Advertising Manager:** Martin Joyce
Profile: Magazine containing information about walking routes in Ireland and abroad, equipment, related topics and the environment.
Readership: Read by walkers.
ADVERTISING RATES:
Full Page Colour .... EUR 1900
Agency Commission: 10%
Mechanical Data: Col Length: 267mm, Type Area: 267 x 185mm, Trim Size: 297 x 210mm, Bleed Size: 303 x 216mm, Film: Digital, Page Width: 185mm
Copy instructions: *Copy Date:* 27 days prior to publication date
Average ad content per issue: 30%
CONSUMER: SPORT: Outdoor

WATERFORD NEWS & STAR
4337E72-7600
Editorial: 25 Michael Street, WATERFORD
Tel: 51 874951 **Fax:** 51855281
Web site: http://www.waterford-news.com
Date Established: 1851; **Freq:** Weekly; **Circ:** 10,000
Editor: Mary Ryan; **Advertising Manager:** Ray Mahon
ADVERTISING RATES:
Full Page Mono .... EUR 2310
Full Page Colour .... EUR 2772
SCC .... EUR 10
Agency Commission: 15%
Mechanical Data: Col Widths (Display): 35mm, No. of Columns (Display): 7, Film: Digital
Copy instructions: *Copy Date:* 7 days prior to publication date
Supplement(s): Farming - 1xY, Fitness - 1xY, Food & Wine - 2xY, Free Ads - 52xY, Home & Front - 12xY, Motoring - 3xY, New Guide - 52xY, Weddings - 3xY
LOCAL NEWSPAPERS

WATERFORD TODAY
623814E80-150
Editorial: 36 Mayor's Walk, WATERFORD
Tel: 5 18 54 135 **Fax:** 51854140
Email: editor@waterford-today.ie **Web site:** http://www.waterford-today.ie
Date Established: 1989; **Freq:** Weekly; **Cover Price:** Free; **Circ:** 27,000
Usual Pagination: 44
Editor: Paddy Gallagher; **Advertising Manager:** Niall Morrissey
Profile: Newspaper containing information about Waterford and the surrounding area.
Language(s): English; Gaelic
Readership: Read by local residents and businesses.
ADVERTISING RATES:
Full Page Mono .... EUR 1900
Full Page Colour .... EUR 2375
Agency Commission: 15%
Mechanical Data: Col Widths (Display): 33mm, No. of Columns (Display): 7, Page Width: 259mm, Type Area: 344 x 259mm, Col Length: 344mm, Film: Digital
Average ad content per issue: 40%
CONSUMER: RURAL & REGIONAL INTEREST

WEDDING
1750285E72-8251
Editorial: For all contact details see main record, Donegal News (Derry People)
Freq: Annual - Published in March
Supplement to: Donegal News (Derry People)
LOCAL NEWSPAPERS

WEDDINGS
1744171E72-8252
Editorial: William Street, Tullamore, CO. OFFALY
Freq: Monthly
Supplement to: Tullamore Tribune
LOCAL NEWSPAPERS

WEDDINGS
1744316E72-8253
Editorial: 34 High Street, KILKENNY
Freq: Quarterly
Supplement to: Kilkenny People
LOCAL NEWSPAPERS

WEEKEND
1659436E65H-37
Editorial: For all contact details see main record, The Irish Daily Star
Freq: Weekly
Supplement to: The Irish Daily Star
NATIONAL DAILY & SUNDAY NEWSPAPERS: National Colour Supplements

WEEKEND MAGAZINE
1666392E65H-8
Editorial: Independent House, 27-32 Talbot Street, DUBLIN 1
Freq: Weekly
Editor: Edel Coffey; **Executive Editor:** Bairbre Power
Supplement to: Irish Independent
NATIONAL DAILY & SUNDAY NEWSPAPERS: National Colour Supplements

WEEKEND REVIEW
1666377E65H-14
Editorial: For all contact details see main record, The Irish Times
Freq: Weekly
Supplement to: The Irish Times
NATIONAL DAILY & SUNDAY NEWSPAPERS: National Colour Supplements

WEEKEND/PROPERTY
1659416E65H-38
Editorial: For all contact details see main record, The Irish Examiner
Freq: Weekly
Supplement to: The Irish Examiner
NATIONAL DAILY & SUNDAY NEWSPAPERS: National Colour Supplements

WEEKLY OBSERVER
768722E72-7660_100
Editorial: 19 Bridge Street, Mallow, CO. CORK
Freq: Weekly; **Cover Price:** EUR 1.80; **Circ:** 12,500
Part of Series, see entry for: Observer & Star Series
LOCAL NEWSPAPERS

WEST WICKLOW TIMES
1659229E72-8210_102
Editorial: 5 Eglington Road, Bray, CO WICKLOW 0
Freq: Weekly; **Cover Price:** Free
Part of Series, see entry for: Wicklow Times Series
LOCAL NEWSPAPERS

WESTERN PEOPLE
4328E72-7700
Editorial: Tone Street, Ballina, CO. MAYO
Tel: 96 60999 **Fax:** 96 73458
Email: info@westernpeople.com **Web site:** http://www.westernpeople.ie
Date Established: 1883; **Freq:** Weekly; **Cover Price:** EUR 1.50; **Circ:** 15,062
Editor: James Laffey
ADVERTISING RATES:
Full Page Mono .... EUR 7817.04
Full Page Colour .... EUR 8561.52
SCC .... EUR 16.80
Agency Commission: 15%
Mechanical Data: No. of Columns (Display): 9, Col Widths (Display): 34mm, Film: Digital, Type Area: 517 x 340mm, Col Length: 517mm, Page Width: 340mm
Supplement(s): Farmer - 52xY, House & Home - 52xY, Property West Weekly - 52xY, Western Extra - 52xY
LOCAL NEWSPAPERS

THE WESTERN PROPERTY
1697284E72-8213
Editorial: Waterfront House, Bridge Street, SLIGO
Freq: Weekly
Supplement to: Sligo Weekender
LOCAL NEWSPAPERS

WESTMEATH EXAMINER
4340E72-7800
Editorial: Blackhall Place, Mullingar, CO. WESTMEATH **Tel:** 44 93 46 700 **Fax:** 449330765
Email: news@westmeathexaminer.ie **Web site:** http://www.westmeathexaminer.ie
Date Established: 1882; **Freq:** Weekly
Annual Sub.: EUR 122.20; **Circ:** 6,183
Editor: Eilis Ryan
ADVERTISING RATES:
Full Page Mono .... EUR 4576
Full Page Colour .... EUR 5782
SCC .... EUR 11
Agency Commission: 15%
Mechanical Data: Col Length: 520mm, Col Widths (Display): 39mm, No. of Columns (Display): 8, Type Area: 520 x 340mm, Page Width: 340mm, Film: Digital
Average ad content per issue: 40%
LOCAL NEWSPAPERS

WESTMEATH INDEPENDENT
764221E72-7950
Editorial: 11 Sean Costello Street, Athlone, CO. WESTMEATH **Tel:** 90 64 34 300 **Fax:** 906474474
Email: editor@westmeathindependent.ie **Web site:** http://www.westmeathindependent.ie
Date Established: 1846; **Freq:** Weekly; **Cover Price:** EUR 1.95; **Circ:** 15,500
Editor: Tadhg Carey; **Advertising Manager:** Dale Greenwood
ADVERTISING RATES:
Full Page Mono .... EUR 4576
Full Page Colour .... EUR 5782
SCC .... EUR 11
Agency Commission: 15%
Mechanical Data: Col Widths (Display): 39mm, No. of Columns (Display): 8, Type Area: 530 x 340m, Col Length: 530mm, Page Width: 340mm, Film: Digital
Average ad content per issue: 40%
LOCAL NEWSPAPERS

WESTMEATH TOPIC
4342E72-6100_101
Editorial: 6 Dominick Street, Mullingar, CO. WESTMEATH 0
Email: topic@indigo.ie **Web site:** http://www.medialive.ie/press/provincial/provincial.html
Freq: Weekly; **Cover Price:** EUR 1.75; **Circ:** 12,000
Mechanical Data: Trim Size: 390 x 298mm
Part of Series, see entry for: Topic Series
LOCAL NEWSPAPERS

THE WEXFORD ECHO
1659361E72-4650_102
Editorial: Slaney Place, Enniscorthy, CO. WEXFORD 0
Freq: Weekly; **Cover Price:** EUR 1.70
Part of Series, see entry for: The Echo Series (Enniscorthy)
LOCAL NEWSPAPERS

WEXFORD PEOPLE
4347E72-4700_102
Formerly: The People (Wexford)
Editorial: Channing House, Rowe Street, Wexford, CO. WEXFORD 0
Email: editor@peoplenews.ie **Web site:** http://www.peoplenews.ie
Freq: Weekly; **Cover Price:** EUR 1.90; **Circ:** 11,439
ADVERTISING RATES:
Full Page Mono .... EUR 1890
Full Page Colour .... EUR 2080
SCC .... EUR 9.37
Part of Series, see entry for: Wexford People Series
LOCAL NEWSPAPERS

WEXFORD PEOPLE SERIES
4345E72-4700
Formerly: Gorey Guardian
Editorial: Channing House, Rowe Street, Wexford, CO. WEXFORD 0 **Tel:** 53 91 40 100
Fax: 53 91 40 195
Email: front.office@peoplenews.ie **Web site:** http://www.wexfordpeople.ie
Date Established: 1850; **Freq:** Weekly
Editor: Jim Hayes; **Advertising Manager:** Ann Jones
ADVERTISING RATES:
Full Page Mono £6882.45
Full Page Colour £8097.60
SCC £36.15
Agency Commission: 15%
Mechanical Data: Type Area: 320 x 261mm, Col Length: 320 mm, Col Widths (Display): 33, No. of Columns (Display): 7
Series owner and contact point for the following titles, see individual entries:
Bray People
Carlow People
Enniscorthy and Gorey Guardian
New Ross Standard
Wexford People
Wicklow People
Supplement(s): Life and TV - 52xY
LOCAL NEWSPAPERS

WHAT'S IN STORE?
1659460E53-103
Editorial: For all contact details see main record, Checkout
Freq: Annual
Supplement to: Checkout
BUSINESS: RETAILING & WHOLESALING

WICKLOW PEOPLE
4348E72-4700_103
Editorial: Channing House, Rowe Street, Wexford, CO. WEXFORD 0
Freq: Weekly; **Cover Price:** EUR 1.90; **Circ:** 10,521
ADVERTISING RATES:
Full Page Mono .... EUR 1890
Full Page Colour .... EUR 2080
SCC .... EUR 9.37
Part of Series, see entry for: Wexford People Series
LOCAL NEWSPAPERS

WICKLOW TIMES SERIES
754412E72-8210
Editorial: 5 Eglington Road, Bray, CO WICKLOW
Tel: 1 28 69 111 **Fax:** 12869074
Email: wicklowed@localtimes.ie
Date Established: 1986
Cover Price: Free; **Circ:** 53,400
News Editor: Adrienne Kelly; **Managing Editor:** Shay Fitzmaurice
ADVERTISING RATES:
Full Page Mono .... EUR 1700
Full Page Colour .... EUR 2300
Agency Commission: 15%

Mechanical Data: Col Length: 330mm, Film: Digital, ype Area: 330 x 270mm, Page Width: 270mm, No. f Columns (Display): 8, Col Widths (Display): 30mm
verage ad content per issue: 50%
eries owner and contact point for the following tles, see individual entries:
arlow Times
orth Wicklow Times
outh Wicklow Times
Vest Wicklow Times
OCAL NEWSPAPERS

WIN - WORLD OF IRISH IURSING & MIDWIFERY

4247E56B-20

Formerly: World of Irish Nursing
Editorial: 25 Adelaide Street, Dun Laoghaire, CO. DUBLIN **Tel:** 1 28 03 967 **Fax:** 12807076
Email: nursing@medmedia.ie **Web site:** http://www.medmedia.ie
SSN: 1393-8088
Date Established: 1994; **Freq:** Monthly - July/August joint issue; **Cover Price:** EUR 5.75
Free to qualifying individuals
Annual Sub.: EUR 145; **Circ:** 41,000
Usual Pagination: 72
Editor: Alison Moore; **Advertising Manager:** Leon Ellison
Profile: Magazine covering clinical nursing features, nursing management and research, professional development news including courses and industrial relations news.
Readership: Read by members of the Irish Nurses' Organisation and nurses in active practice in Ireland.
ADVERTISING RATES:
Full Page Mono .... EUR 2460
Full Page Colour .... EUR 2460
Agency Commission: 10%
Mechanical Data: Bleed Size: 303 x 216mm, Trim Size: 297 x 210mm, Film: Digital, Screen: 60 lpc, Page Width: 184mm, Type Area: 270 x 184mm, Col Length: 270mm
Average ad content per issue: 30%
BUSINESS: HEALTH & MEDICAL: Nursing

WMB WOMEN MEAN BUSINESS

1745614E74A-147

Editorial: 47 Harrington Street, DUBLIN 8
Tel: 1 41 55 056
Email: ed@womenmeanbusiness.com **Web site:** http://www.womenmeanbusiness.com
Date Established: 2006; **Freq:** 6 issues yearly; **Cover Price:** EUR 4.95; **Circ:** 3,808
Usual Pagination: 84
Managing Editor: Rosemary Delaney
Profile: Magazine covering women in the business world with profiles of business women and features on issues that affect women in business as well as lifestyle articles.
Readership: Aimed at women in the business world and in the workplace and entrepreneurs.
ADVERTISING RATES:
Full Page Colour .... EUR 3000
Agency Commission: 15%
Mechanical Data: Type Area: 275 x 210mm, Bleed Size: 281 x 216mm, Trim Size: 275 x 210mm, Col Length: 275mm, Page Width: 210mm, Film: Digital
Copy instructions: *Copy Date:* 28 days prior to publication date
Average ad content per issue: 8%
CONSUMER: WOMEN'S INTEREST CONSUMER MAGAZINES: Women's Interest

WOMAN'S WAY

4357E74A-120

Editorial: Rosemount House, Dundrum Road, Dundrum, DUBLIN 14 **Tel:** 1 24 05 300
Fax: 16622979
Email: atoner@harmonia.ie **Web site:** http://www.harmonia.ie
ISSN: 0043-7409
Date Established: 1963; **Freq:** Weekly; **Cover Price:** EUR 1.39; **Circ:** 22,197
Usual Pagination: 56
Editor: Áine Toner
Profile: Magazine featuring articles on fashion, cookery, beauty, real life, short stories, travel, celebrity interviews, soaps and TV, interiors, gardening, health, special features and interviews.
Readership: Aimed at Irish women with a home and family.
ADVERTISING RATES:
Full Page Colour .... EUR 3600
Agency Commission: 15%
Mechanical Data: Col Length: 270mm, Film: Digital, Col Widths (Display): 43mm, No. of Columns (Display): 4, Type Area: 270 x 180mm, Print Process: Web-fed offset litho, Bleed Size: 303 x 213mm, Trim Size: 297 x 210mm, Page Width: 180mm
Average ad content per issue: 30%
Supplement(s): Your New Baby - 4xY
CONSUMER: WOMEN'S INTEREST CONSUMER MAGAZINES: Women's Interest

WOMEN ON WEDNESDAY

1666383E67H-4

Editorial: For all contact details see main record, Evening Echo
Freq: Weekly
Supplement to: Evening Echo
REGIONAL DAILY & SUNDAY NEWSPAPERS: Regional Colour Supplements

WOMEN'S CLUB MAGAZINE

4358E74A-140

Editorial: 11 St. Peter's Road, Phibsboro, DUBLIN 7
Tel: 1 86 80 080
Email: womensclubs@mail.ie
ISSN: 0532-446X
Date Established: 1972; **Freq:** Half-yearly - Published in May and November; **Cover Price:** EUR 1.00; **Circ:** 5,000
Usual Pagination: 32
Editor: June Cooke; **Advertising Manager:** June Cooke
Profile: Official journal of the Irish Federation of Women's Clubs with club news, stories, poetry, topical articles, news from members, health and gardening.
Readership: Aimed at member of women's clubs in Southern Ireland.
CONSUMER: WOMEN'S INTEREST CONSUMER MAGAZINES: Women's Interest

WORK & LIFE

4182E14L-50

Formerly: Impact News
Editorial: Nerneys Court, Off Temple Street, DUBLIN 1 **Tel:** 1 81 71 538 **Fax:** 18171503
Email: bharbor@impact.ie **Web site:** http://www.impact.ie
Date Established: 2008; **Freq:** Quarterly; **Cover Price:** Free; **Circ:** 35,000
Usual Pagination: 50
Editor: Bernard Harbor; **Advertising Manager:** Frank Bambrick
Profile: Magazine for members of IMPACT trade union. Covers working life issues and other topical issues relating to public services and workers' rights. Also films, books, food, sport, gardening, health, music and other lifestyle issues.
Readership: Read by union members.
ADVERTISING RATES:
Full Page Colour .... EUR 2650
Agency Commission: 15%
Average ad content per issue: 40%
BUSINESS: COMMERCE, INDUSTRY & MANAGEMENT: Trade Unions

WORLD TRAVEL TRADE NEWS

1892609E50-11

Editorial: 3 Inishkeen, Kilcool, CO WICKLOW
Tel: 86 24 85 842
Email: donal@worldtraveltradenews.com **Web site:** http://www.worldtraveltradenews.com
Date Established: 2009; **Freq:** Daily; **Cover Price:** Free
Editor: Donal McDonald
Profile: Online magazine for the travel trade sector featuring global, cruise and technology news.
Readership: Aimed at professionals in the travel industry.
BUSINESS: TRAVEL & TOURISM

YEARBOOK AND BUYER'S GUIDE

1659461E53-104

Editorial: For all contact details see main record, Checkout
Freq: Annual
Supplement to: Checkout
BUSINESS: RETAILING & WHOLESALING

YOU & YOUR MONEY

1814273E74M-37

Editorial: Longboat Quay, 57-59 John Rogerson Quay, DUBLIN 2 **Tel:** 1 43 22 200 **Fax:** 16727100
Email: derek.owens@ashville.com **Web site:** http://www.youandyourmoney.ie
Date Established: 2007; **Freq:** Monthly; **Cover Price:** EUR 3.95
Annual Sub.: EUR 41; **Circ:** 6,909
Usual Pagination: 96
Advertising Manager: Colin Costello
Profile: Magazine covering choices about money whether you want to save it, make it or spend it.
Readership: Aimed at men and women aged 25 to 50 years old in the higher and middle income groups.
ADVERTISING RATES:
Full Page Colour .... EUR 4410
Agency Commission: 15%
Mechanical Data: Type Area: 271 x 203mm, Col Length: 271mm, Page Width: 203mm, Trim Size: 295 x 227mm
Average ad content per issue: 25%
CONSUMER: WOMEN'S INTEREST CONSUMER MAGAZINES: Personal Finance

YOUR NEW BABY

4361E74D-150

Editorial: Rosemount House, Dundrum Road, Dundrum, DUBLIN 14
Date Established: 1994; **Freq:** Quarterly - See Woman's Way for circulation figure; Free to qualifying individuals
Supplement to: Woman's Way
CONSUMER: WOMEN'S INTEREST CONSUMER MAGAZINES: Child Care

Italy

Time Difference: GMT + 1 hr (CET - Central European Time)
National Telephone Code: +39
Continent: Europe
Capital: Rome
Principal Language: Italian
Population: 58147733
Monetary Unit: Euro (EUR)

EMBASSY HIGH COMMISSION: Italian Embassy: 14 Three Kings Yard, Davies St, London W1K 4EH,
Tel: 020 7312 2200
Fax: 020 7312 2230 Head of Mission: HE Mr Alain Economides/ KCVO
Email: ambasciata.londra@esteri.it
Website: http://www.amblondra.esteri.it

18 KARATI - GOLD & FASHION

13764I52A-2

Editorial: Via Angelo della Pergola, 9, 20159 MILANO
Tel: 02 680189 **Fax:** 02 606298
Email: info@18karati.net **Web site:** http://www.18karati.net
Freq: 6 issues yearly; **Circ:** 20,000
Editor-in-Chief: Florinda Gaudio
Profile: International review on the art and culture of goldsmiths' work, design and gemstones.
Language(s): English; Italian; Spanish
Readership: Read by jewellers, gold- and silversmiths, importers, buyers and foreign representatives in Italy.
BUSINESS: GIFT TRADE: Jewellery

50 & PIU'

14231I74N-5

Editorial: L.go Arenula, 34, 00186 ROMA RM
Tel: 06 68134552 **Fax:** 0668139323
Email: redazione@50epiu.it **Web site:** http://www.50epiueditoriale.it
Freq: Monthly
Editor-in-Chief: Giovanna Vecchiotti
Profile: Magazine for people who are in their fifties and over.
Language(s): Italian
CONSUMER: WOMEN'S INTEREST CONSUMER MAGAZINES: Retirement

99 IDEE IL BAGNO

14164I74C-231

Editorial: Via Settembrini, 11, 20124 MILANO
Tel: 02 67495250 **Fax:** 02 67495333
Email: traffico@dibaio.com **Web site:** http://www.dibaio.com
Freq: Annual; **Circ:** 60,000
Editor-in-Chief: Giuseppe Maria Jonghi Lavarini
Profile: Publication about bathroom furnishing and fitments, technology, fashion, sportswear and cosmetics.
Language(s): Italian
CONSUMER: WOMEN'S INTEREST CONSUMER MAGAZINES: Home & Family

A4 AUTORUOTE 4X4

14351I77A-145

Editorial: Piazza Bonghi, 16, 10147 TORINO
Tel: 0112629577 **Fax:** 0112203441
Email: redazione@autoruote4x4.com **Web site:** http://www.autoruote4x4.com
Freq: Monthly; **Circ:** 20,000
Editor-in-Chief: Giorgio Rosato
Profile: Magazine covering all aspects of 4x4 motoring. Includes details of new products, reviews, test drives and articles on travel, tourism and adventure holidays.
Language(s): Italian
Readership: Aimed at motoring enthusiasts.
CONSUMER: MOTORING & CYCLING: Motoring

A ANNA

14093I74A-40

Editorial: Via A. Rizzoli 8, 20132 MILANO
Tel: 02 25841 **Fax:** 02 25843905
Web site: http://www.rcs.it
Freq: Weekly; **Circ:** 302,000
Editor: Paola Ventimiglia; **Editor-in-Chief:** Maria Latella
Profile: Women's magazine dealing with current affairs, health, beauty, cuisine and leisure.
Language(s): Italian
Readership: Aimed at women over 25 years.
CONSUMER: WOMEN'S INTEREST CONSUMER MAGAZINES: Women's Interest

A&V ELETTRONICA

13347I18A-5

Editorial: Via Console Flaminio, 19, 20134 MILANO
Tel: 02 210111250 **Fax:** 02 210111222
Email: redazione@tecnoimprese.it **Web site:** http://www.tecnoimprese.it
Freq: Monthly; **Circ:** 9,000
Editor: Laura Baronchelli; **Editor-in-Chief:** Silvio Baronchelli
Profile: Guide to electronic innovation, including features and new product information.
Language(s): Italian
Readership: Aimed at purchasers in the electronics industry.
BUSINESS: ELECTRONICS

A TAVOLA

14234I74P-20

Editorial: Via dei Gracchi 318, 00192 ROMA
Tel: 0632120148 **Fax:** 067232256
Email: redazione@atavolaweb.it **Web site:** http://www.atavolaweb.it
Freq: Monthly; **Circ:** 60,000
Editor-in-Chief: Guendalina Fortunati
Profile: Magazine covering general and Cordon Bleu cookery. Includes recipes and articles about tableware, cooking equipment, restaurants and wine.
Language(s): Italian
Readership: Aimed at women with a high disposable income.
CONSUMER: WOMEN'S INTEREST CONSUMER MAGAZINES: Food & Cookery

ABITARE

14137I74C-30

Editorial: Via Ventura, 5, 20134 MILANO
Tel: 02 210581 **Fax:** 02 21058316
Email: monica.guala@abitare.rcs.it **Web site:** http://www.abitare.it
Freq: Monthly
Editor-in-Chief: Mario Piazza
Profile: Journal containing articles on architecture and interior design. Reviews houses and objects from all over the world.
Language(s): English; Italian
Readership: Read by architects, designers, artists and students.
CONSUMER: WOMEN'S INTEREST CONSUMER MAGAZINES: Home & Family

AC - AUTOCARAVAN NOTIZIE

14541I91B-10

Editorial: Via Saliceto 22 E, 40013 CASTEL MAGGIORE (BO) **Tel:** 051 0933850 **Fax:** 051 0933869
Email: ac.autocaravan@acaciaedizioni.com **Web site:** http://www.acautocaravan.it
Freq: Monthly; **Circ:** 59,000
Editor-in-Chief: Bruno Andrea Ciattini
Profile: Magazine covering travel, holidays and adventure including modes of transport: car, caravan and camper. Also contains results of road tests.
Language(s): Italian
Readership: Aimed at campers.
CONSUMER: RECREATION & LEISURE: Camping & Caravanning

ACQUA & ARIA

13898I57-15

Editorial: Via Teocrito, 47, 20128 MILANO
Tel: 02 252071 **Fax:** 02 27000692
Email: acquaaria@bema.it **Web site:** http://www.bema.it
Freq: Monthly; **Circ:** 4,038
Editor-in-Chief: Gisella Bertini Malgarini
Profile: Magazine about environmental science and technology.
Language(s): Italian
Readership: Read by people in industries who have to deal with environmental issues.
BUSINESS: ENVIRONMENT & POLLUTION

ACS - AUDIOCARSTEREO

14393I78A-10

Editorial: Via Monte Nero, 101, 00012 GUIDONIA MONTECELIO (RM) **Tel:** 06 8720331
Fax: 06 87139141
Email: acs@newmediapro.eu **Web site:** http://www.audiocarstereo.it
Freq: Monthly; **Circ:** 30,000
Editor-in-Chief: Mauro Neri
Profile: Magazine about the latest in car stereos.
Language(s): Italian
CONSUMER: CONSUMER ELECTRONICS: Hi-Fi & Recording

ACTIVA FASHION DESIGN MANAGEMENT

622657I4B-20

Editorial: Via Lucano, 3, 20135 MILANO
Tel: 02 5516109 **Fax:** 02 5450120
Email: dde@designdiffusion.com **Web site:** http://www.designdiffusion.com
Editor-in-Chief: Carlo Russo
Profile: Magazine focusing on the applications of design in fashion, homes, cities and the workplace.
Language(s): English; Italian

Readership: Read by interior, fashion, car and concept designers and students.
BUSINESS: ARCHITECTURE & BUILDING: Interior Design & Flooring

AD ARCHITECTURAL DIGEST
14136I74C-25
Editorial: P.zza Castello 27, 20121 MILANO
Tel: 02 85612401 **Fax:** 02 8692363
Email: ad@condenast.it **Web site:** http://www.condenast.it
Freq: Monthly; **Circ:** 153,000
Editor: Mario Gerosa; **Editor-in-Chief:** Ettore Mocchetti
Profile: Italian edition of Architectural Digest, containing articles about beautiful houses throughout Italy.
Language(s): Italian
CONSUMER: WOMEN'S INTEREST CONSUMER MAGAZINES: Home & Family

ADV
76272212A-9
Editorial: Via Gian Battista Vico, 42, 20123 MILANO MI **Tel:** 02 81830313
Email: redazione@advertiser.it **Web site:** http://www.advertiser.it
Freq: Monthly; **Circ:** 4,500
Editor-in-Chief: Massimo Bolchi
Profile: Magazine focusing on advertising and marketing.
Language(s): Italian
BUSINESS: COMMUNICATIONS, ADVERTISING & MARKETING

AE - APPARECCHI ELETTRODOMESTICI
13623I43A-20
Editorial: Via Eritrea 21, 20157 MILANO
Tel: 02390901 **Fax:** 0239090331
Email: ae@tecnichenuove.com **Web site:** http://www.tecnichenuove.com
Freq: Monthly; **Circ:** 5,500
Editor-in-Chief: Paolo Thorausch
Profile: International magazine providing technical, economic and commercial information about electrical appliances, components and accessories, raw materials and services.
Language(s): English; Italian
Readership: Read by manufacturers of finished products, components, accessories and spare parts, also by suppliers of raw materials.
BUSINESS: ELECTRICAL RETAIL TRADE

AE-ATTUALITA' ELETTROTECNICA NEWS
13328I17-4
Editorial: Piazza Sant'Agostino, 22, 20123 MILANO
Tel: 0229412353 **Fax:** 02 29416826
Email: redazione@maestri.it **Web site:** http://www.maestri.it
Freq: Monthly; **Circ:** 16,000
Editor-in-Chief: Elena Martini
Profile: Magazine focusing on all aspects of the electrical industry. Covers domestic security, heating, ventilation and lighting and provides details of trade fairs and exhibitions. Also includes product reviews, information on services, software and developments in technology within the field.
Language(s): Italian
Readership: Aimed at electrical engineers, retailers and installers.
BUSINESS: ELECTRICAL

AEIT
13327I17-5
Editorial: Via Mauro Macchi, 32, 20124 MILANO MI
Tel: 0287389967 **Fax:** 0266989222
Email: redazione@federaeit.it **Web site:** http://www.federaeit.it
Freq: Monthly; **Circ:** 7,500
Editor-in-Chief: Maurizio Delfanti
Profile: Review of science and the electrical industry.
Language(s): Italian
BUSINESS: ELECTRICAL

AF DIGITALE
13631I43B-10
Editorial: Via Gadames, 123, 20151 MILANO MI
Tel: 02 365881 **Fax:** 02 36588222
Email: afdigitale@leditore.it **Web site:** http://www.afdigitale.it
Freq: Monthly
Editor-in-Chief: Massimo Bacchetti
Profile: Magazine concerning hi-fi, the music trade, records, musical instruments, video, audio and car stereo markets.
Language(s): Italian
BUSINESS: ELECTRICAL RETAIL TRADE: Radio & Hi-Fi

AFFARI & FINANZA (LA REPUBBLICA)
713656I74M-12
Editorial: Via Cristoforo Colombo, 90, 00147 ROMA
Tel: 0649821 **Fax:** 06 49822303
Email: segreteria_affari_finanza@repubblica.it **Web site:** http://www.repubblica.it
Freq: Weekly; **Circ:** 754,000
Editor: Luigi Gia
Profile: Newspaper containing articles about business and financial matters.
Language(s): Italian
CONSUMER: WOMEN'S INTEREST CONSUMER MAGAZINES: Personal Finance

L' AGENZIA DI VIAGGI
13744I50-10
Editorial: Via Tacito, 74, 00193 ROMA
Tel: 06 32600149 **Fax:** 06 32600168
Email: redazione@lagenziadiviaggi.it **Web site:** http://www.lagenziadiviaggi.it
Freq: Weekly; **Circ:** 14,500
Editor-in-Chief: Cristina Ambrosini
Profile: Newspaper for the travel trade.
Language(s): Italian
Readership: Read by travel agents and tour operators.
BUSINESS: TRAVEL & TOURISM

AGGIORNAMENTO MEDICO
13803I56A-20
Editorial: Via Luigi Zoja 30, 20153 MILANO
Tel: 02 48202740 **Fax:** 02 48201219
Email: agm@kurtis.it **Web site:** http://www.kurtis.it
Freq: Monthly; **Circ:** 40,500
Profile: Journal focusing on developments in medicine, including internal medicine, diseases, molecular and cellular biology, oncology, dermatology, neurology, gynaecology and specialised treatments and surgery. Also features medical legislation and social medicine.
Language(s): Italian
Readership: Read by general practitioners.
BUSINESS: HEALTH & MEDICAL

AGING
13895I56R-15
Editorial: Via Luigi Zoja, 30, 20153 MILANO
Tel: 02 48202740 **Fax:** 02 48201219
Email: aging@kurtis.it **Web site:** http://www.kurtis.it
Freq: 6 issues yearly; **Circ:** 2,500
Editor-in-Chief: Canzio Fuse'
Profile: Journal focusing on gerontology, geriatric assessment and epidemiology.
Language(s): English; Italian
Readership: Read by specialists in the treatment of the elderly.
BUSINESS: HEALTH & MEDICAL: Health Medical Related

AGRICOLTURA NUOVA
13399I21A-50
Editorial: Corso Vittorio Emanuele, 101, 00186 ROMA **Tel:** 06 6852397 **Fax:** 06 6861726
Email: agricoltura.nuova@confagricoltura.it **Web site:** http://www.confagricoltura.it
Freq: Monthly
Editor-in-Chief: Elisabetta Tufarelli Fangel
Profile: Journal of the National Association of Young Farmers.
Language(s): Italian
BUSINESS: AGRICULTURE & FARMING

AIR PRESS
13219I6A-30
Editorial: Via del Corso, 504, 00186 ROMA RM
Tel: 063217922 **Fax:** 06 3612368
Email: redazione@airpressonline.it **Web site:** http://www.airpressonline.it
Freq: Weekly; **Circ:** 10,000
Editor-in-Chief: Mauro Miccio
Profile: Magazine containing articles on general aviation, industry, cargo & air cargo, space, defence, political affairs, technology, research & telecommunications sectors.
Language(s): Italian
Readership: Industry executives and workers, civil and military aviation authorities, space and air transport managers, engineering and trading companies, airlines, airport management and related services, aviation clubs, ministries, political bodies and institutions.
BUSINESS: AVIATION & AERONAUTICS

AIRONE
14070I73-20
Editorial: Corso Magenta 55, 20123 MILANO
Tel: 02433131 **Fax:** 02 43313574
Email: airone@cairoeditore.it **Web site:** http://www.cairoeditore.it/Airone
Freq: Monthly; **Circ:** 100,000
Editor-in-Chief: Andrea Biavardi
Profile: General interest publication about nature and the world.
Language(s): Italian
CONSUMER: NATIONAL & INTERNATIONAL PERIODICALS

AL - ALLUMINIO E LEGHE
13493I27-15
Editorial: Via Brescia, 117, 25018 MONTICHIARI (BS)
Tel: 030 9981045 **Fax:** 030 9981055
Email: redazione@edimet.com **Web site:** http://www.edimet.com
Freq: 6 issues yearly; **Circ:** 6,000
Editor-in-Chief: Mario Conserva
Profile: International journal focusing on aluminium and its derivatives.
Language(s): English; French; German; Italian; Spanish
Readership: Aimed at those in the aluminium industry.
BUSINESS: METAL, IRON & STEEL

AL VOLANTE
624534I77A-391
Editorial: Corso di Porta Nuova, 3/a, 20121 MILANO
Tel: 02 63675455 **Fax:** 02 63675523
Email: segreteria@al-volante.com
Freq: Monthly; **Circ:** 600,000
Editor-in-Chief: Guido Costantini
Profile: Motoring magazine.
Language(s): Italian
Readership: Read by car enthusiasts.
CONSUMER: MOTORING & CYCLING: Motoring

ALAN FORD
1784323I91D-201
Editorial: Via Fatebenefratelli, 15, 20121 MILANO
Tel: 02 6592969 **Fax:** 02 6570226
Email: maxbunker@maxbunker.it **Web site:** http://www.maxbunker.it
Freq: Monthly; **Circ:** 105,000
Editor-in-Chief: Luciano Secchi
Language(s): Italian
CONSUMER: RECREATION & LEISURE: Children & Youth

ALLURE
14091I74A-25
Editorial: Via Cavour 50, 10123 TORINO
Tel: 01183921111 **Fax:** 0118125661
Email: redazione@allure.it **Web site:** http://www.allure.it
Freq: 6 issues yearly; **Circ:** 15,000
Editor-in-Chief: Roberto Pissimiglia
Profile: Magazine focusing on beauty. Includes articles on perfume, cosmetics and fashion accessories.
Language(s): Italian
CONSUMER: WOMEN'S INTEREST CONSUMER MAGAZINES: Women's Interest

ALTROCONSUMO
1784428I94H-1
Editorial: Via Valassina, 22, 20159 MILANO MI
Tel: 02 668901 **Fax:** 02 66890288
Email: silvia.franchina@euroconsumers.it **Web site:** http://www.altroconsumo.it
Freq: Monthly; **Circ:** 300,000
Editor: Alessandro Sessa; **Editor-in-Chief:** Rosanna Massarenti
Language(s): Italian
CONSUMER: OTHER CLASSIFICATIONS: Customer Magazines

AM AUTOMESE
14341I77A-15
Editorial: Via Del Lavoro, 7, 40068 SAN LAZZARO DI SAVENA BO **Tel:** 051 6227111 **Fax:** 051 6258310
Email: segreteria@am-automese.it **Web site:** http://www.am-automese.it
Freq: Monthly; **Circ:** 700,000
Editor: Marco Visani; **Editor-in-Chief:** Diego Eramo
Profile: International motoring journal. Tests out new cars on the market and contains a guide for buying new and second-hand vehicles.
Language(s): Italian
CONSUMER: MOTORING & CYCLING: Motoring

AMADEUS
14321I76D-25
Editorial: Via Alberto Mario 20 c/o Paragon Srl, 20149 MILANO **Tel:** 02 4816353 **Fax:** 02 4818968
Email: info@amadeusonline.net **Web site:** http://www.amadeusonline.net
Freq: Monthly; **Circ:** 65,000
Editor-in-Chief: Gaetano Santangelo
Profile: Classical music magazine covering early as well as contemporary music. Also includes articles about the ballet, instruments, history of music and contains critical analyses by world famous musicologists.
Language(s): Italian
Readership: Read by lovers of classical music.
CONSUMER: MUSIC & PERFORMING ARTS: Music

AMBIENTE CUCINA
13469I23C-5
Editorial: Via Pisacane 1, 20016 PERO MI
Tel: 02 30221 **Fax:** 0230226244
Email: anna.alberti@ilsole24ore.com **Web site:** http://www.shopping24.it
Freq: 6 issues yearly; **Circ:** 12,000
Editor-in-Chief: Antonio Greco
Profile: International journal of kitchen design. Includes trade news, new equipment, household products and kitchenware.
Language(s): English; Italian
Readership: Aimed at retailers of kitchen and kitchenware.
BUSINESS: FURNISHINGS & FURNITURE: Furnishings & Furniture - Kitchens & Bathrooms

AMBIENTE & SICUREZZA SUL LAVORO
13789I54B-10
Editorial: Via Dell'Acqua Traversa 187/189, 00135 ROMA **Tel:** 06 33245 1 **Fax:** 06 3313212
Email: amsl@epcperiodici.it **Web site:** http://www.epc.it
Freq: Monthly; **Circ:** 9,000
Editor-in-Chief: Michele Lepore
Profile: Journal focusing on health and safety at work.
Language(s): Italian
Readership: Read by facility managers and those responsible for safety and working conditions in medium- and large-sized companies and local government.
BUSINESS: SAFETY & SECURITY: Safety

AMBIENTE RISORSE SALUTE
13900I57-18_50
Editorial: Via Uguccio De Boso 11, 35124 PADOVA
Tel: 0498806109 **Fax:** 0498806109
Email: scienzaegoverno@scienzaegoverno.org **Web site:** http://www.scienzaegoverno.org
Freq: Quarterly; **Circ:** 10,000
Editor-in-Chief: Franco Spelzini
Profile: Environmental review covering scientific, technological and cultural developments.
Language(s): Italian
Readership: Read by public administrators and environmentalists.
BUSINESS: ENVIRONMENT & POLLUTION

AMICA
14092I74A-30
Editorial: Via A. Rizzoli 8, 20132 MILANO
Tel: 02 25841 **Fax:** 02 25843677
Email: amica@rcs.it **Web site:** http://www.rcs.it
Freq: Monthly; **Circ:** 215,000
Editor: Loredana Ranni; **Editor-in-Chief:** Cristina Lucchini
Profile: Magazine covering fashion, health, beauty, cuisine and leisure time.
Language(s): Italian
Readership: Aimed at women aged between 25 and 45 years.
CONSUMER: WOMEN'S INTEREST CONSUMER MAGAZINES: Women's Interest

AMICI DI CASA
706954I81X-10
Editorial: Via Torino, 51, 20063 CERNUSCO S.N.
Tel: 02 924321 **Fax:** 02 92432236
Email: editori@sprea.it **Web site:** http://www.sprea.it
Freq: 6 issues yearly
Editor-in-Chief: Luca Sprea
Profile: Magazine containing guidelines and information about pets and other animal welfare.
Language(s): Italian
Readership: Aimed at animal lovers.
CONSUMER: ANIMALS & PETS

AMMINISTRAZIONE & FINANZA
13021I1A-4
Editorial: Strada 1 Palazzo F. 6, 20090 MILANOFIORI ASSAGO MI **Tel:** 02 82476085 **Fax:** 02 82476800
Email: redazione.amministrazioneefinanza.ipsoa@wki.it **Web site:** http://www.ipsoa.it
Freq: Monthly; **Circ:** 20,000
Editor-in-Chief: Giulietta Lenni
Profile: Journal covering finance and business administration.
Language(s): Italian
Readership: Read by financial advisers, lawyers, magistrates, accountants and bankers.
BUSINESS: FINANCE & ECONOMICS

L' AMMONITORE
13384I19E-15
Editorial: Via Crispi, 19, 21100 VARESE
Tel: 0332 283039 **Fax:** 0332 234666
Email: redazione@ammonitore.it **Web site:** http://www.ammonitore.it
Freq: 24 issues yearly; **Circ:** 15,000
Editor-in-Chief: Giuseppe Tenaglia
Profile: Publication containing information about machinery, machine tools and metalworking.
Language(s): English; Italian
Readership: Read by managing directors, sales managers, managers, design draughtsmen and technicians in companies which use or produce machines.
BUSINESS: ENGINEERING & MACHINERY: Machinery, Machine Tools & Metalworking

ANNUARIO DEL SUONO
714453I78A-15
Editorial: Casella Postale 18340, 00164 ROMA - BRAVETTA **Tel:** 06 44702611 **Fax:** 06 44702612
Email: segreteria@suono.it **Web site:** http://www.suono.it
Freq: Annual; **Circ:** 35,000
Editor-in-Chief: Paolo Corciulo
Profile: Magazine featuring information and articles on hi-fi equipment. Includes market research and test results.
Language(s): Italian
CONSUMER: CONSUMER ELECTRONICS: Hi-Fi & Recording

ANTINCENDIO
13787I54A-10
Editorial: Via Dell'Acqua Traversa, 187/189, 00135 ROMA RM **Tel:** 06 33245208 **Fax:** 063313212
Email: antincendio@epcperiodici.it **Web site:** http://www.epcperiodici.it
Freq: Monthly; **Circ:** 10,000

Editor-in-Chief: Pier Roberto Pais
Profile: Journal focusing on fire prevention and civil protection.
Language(s): Italian
Readership: Read by managers in medium and large industrial operations, hospitals, banks and offices.
BUSINESS: SAFETY & SECURITY: Fire Fighting

ANTIQUARIATO 13223I7-10
Editorial: Corso Magenta, 55, 20123 MILANO MI
Tel: 02 43313425 **Fax:** 02 43313933
Email: antiquariato@cairoeditore.it **Web site:** http://www.cairoeditore.it
Freq: Monthly; **Circ:** 30,000
Editor: Maria Luisa Magagnoli; **Editor-in-Chief:** Michele Bonuomo
Profile: Magazine focusing on the antiques and art trade.
Language(s): Italian
BUSINESS: ANTIQUES

AO - AUTOMAZIONE OGGI 13164I5A-15
Editorial: SS Sempione 28, 20017 RHO MI
Tel: 0249971 **Fax:** 0249976573
Email: ao-fen@fieramilanoeditore.it **Web site:** http://www.automazioneoggi.it
Freq: Monthly; **Circ:** 11,000
Editor-in-Chief: Corrado Minnella
Profile: Magazine about management and production systems in industrial automation process control, numerical control, robotics, CAD/CAM/CAE/CIM and new materials.
Language(s): Italian
Readership: Aimed at technical management, designers, systems integrators and production specialists.
BUSINESS: COMPUTERS & AUTOMATION: Automation & Instrumentation

APPLICANDO 13191I5C-30
Editorial: c/o Dedamedia Srl - via Venezia 23, 20099 SESTO SAN GIOVANNI MI **Tel:** 0224126817
Email: dedamedia@dedamedia.com **Web site:** http://www.applicando.com
Freq: Monthly; **Circ:** 45,000
Editor-in-Chief: Antonio Greco
Profile: Magazine for users of Macintosh computers.
Language(s): Italian
BUSINESS: COMPUTERS & AUTOMATION: Professional Personal Computers

L' ARCA 13101I4A-5
Editorial: Via Raimondi, 10, 20156 MILANO
Tel: 02 36517220 **Fax:** 02 36517229
Email: pub.arca@arcadata.net **Web site:** http://www.arcadata.com
Freq: Monthly; **Circ:** 42,800
Editor-in-Chief: Cesare Maria Casati
Profile: International magazine about architecture, art, design and visual communications.
Language(s): English; Italian
BUSINESS: ARCHITECTURE & BUILDING: Architecture

ARCHEOLOGIA VIVA 14565I94X-17
Editorial: Via Bolognese 165, 50139 FIRENZE
Tel: 055 5062303 **Fax:** 055 5062298
Email: archeologiaviva@giunti.it **Web site:** http://www.archeologiaviva.it
Freq: 6 issues yearly; **Circ:** 35,000
Editor-in-Chief: Piero Pruneti
Profile: Magazine focusing on land and marine archaeology, also includes articles on national heritage.
Language(s): Italian
Readership: Aimed at students and those with an interest in the field.
CONSUMER: OTHER CLASSIFICATIONS: Miscellaneous

ARCO 14301I75F-251
Editorial: Via Ugo Bassi, 7, 40121 BOLOGNA BO
Tel: 051 223327 **Fax:** 051222946
Email: info@greentime.it **Web site:** http://www.greentime.it
Freq: 6 issues yearly; **Circ:** 46,000
Editor-in-Chief: Valeria Bellagamba
Profile: Magazine about archery, contains news and events.
Language(s): Italian
Readership: Read by archery enthusiasts, members of clubs and retailers of sporting equipment.
CONSUMER: SPORT: Shooting

AREALEGNO 763348I46-10
Editorial: Piazza Agrippa, 1, 20141 MILANO MI
Tel: 02 89546696 **Fax:** 02 89515438
Email: idm@idm.net **Web site:** http://www.editriceidm.it
Freq: 6 issues yearly; **Circ:** 12,000
Editor-in-Chief: Vittorio Scaratti
Profile: Magazine focusing on the wood and timber sector. Provides information on the latest uses of wood for furniture and decoration.
Language(s): Italian
BUSINESS: TIMBER, WOOD & FORESTRY

ARGOS 14438I81B-10
Editorial: Via Torino 51, 20063 CERNUSCO SUL NAVIGLIO MI **Tel:** 02 924321 **Fax:** 02 92432236
Email: argos@sprea.it **Web site:** http://www.sprea.it
Freq: Monthly; **Circ:** 95,000
Profile: Magazine focusing on dogs, cats and other pets.
Language(s): Italian
Readership: Aimed at people with pets.
CONSUMER: ANIMALS & PETS: Dogs

ARMI E MUNIZIONI 14267I75F-125
Editorial: Via Zante, 14, 20138 MILANO
Tel: 0236633301 **Fax:** 0236633339
Email: redazione@armimunizioni.it **Web site:** http://www.armimunizioni.it
Freq: Monthly
Editor-in-Chief: Paolo Romanini
Profile: Magazine focusing on weapons and ammunition, both ancient and modern.
Language(s): Italian
Readership: Read by collectors, antique dealers, arms experts and hunters.
CONSUMER: SPORT: Shooting

ARMI E TIRO 14264I75F-30
Editorial: Via Don Luigi Sturzo 7, 20016 PERO (MI)
Tel: 02 38085262 **Fax:** 02 38010393
Email: armietiro@edisport.it **Web site:** http://www.armietiro.it
Freq: Monthly; **Circ:** 98,000
Editor-in-Chief: Massimo Vallini
Profile: Magazine containing reviews of weapons, hunting and shooting.
Language(s): Italian
CONSUMER: SPORT: Shooting

ARMONIA DI VOCI 14322I76D-30
Editorial: P.zza Ateneo Salesiano 1 c/o Univ. Pontificia, 00139 SALESIANA - ROMA
Tel: 06 87290505 **Fax:** 06 87290505
Email: massimo@ups.urbe.it **Web site:** http://www.elledici.org
Freq: Quarterly; **Circ:** 1,500
Editor-in-Chief: Massimo Palombella
Profile: Publication about Christian liturgical songs.
Language(s): Italian
Readership: Read by the Christian community.
CONSUMER: MUSIC & PERFORMING ARTS: Music

ARPEL 13782I52D-20
Editorial: Via Ippolito Nievo 33, 20145 MILANO
Tel: 02 319121 **Fax:** 02 33611619
Email: arsarpel@arsarpel.it **Web site:** http://www.arsarpel.it
Freq: Quarterly; **Circ:** 29,000
Editor-in-Chief: Stefania Sancini
Profile: International trade and fashion magazine focusing on leather goods and leather garments.
Language(s): English; French; German; Italian; Spanish
Readership: Aimed at people within the leather goods and leather garments industry.
BUSINESS: GIFT TRADE: Leather

ARPEL FUR 13943I64B-11
Editorial: Via Ippolito Nievo, 33, 20145 MILANO MI
Tel: 02 319121 **Fax:** 02 33611619
Email: arsarpel@arsarpel.it **Web site:** http://www.arsarpel.it
Freq: 3 issues yearly; **Circ:** 12,000
Editor-in-Chief: Stefania Sancini
Profile: International magazine containing articles concerning furs and leather garments. Includes details of the fur trade and fashion industry.
Language(s): English; French; German; Italian; Spanish
Readership: Aimed at people within the fashion and fur industry.
BUSINESS: OTHER CLASSIFICATIONS: Fur Trade

L' ARREDAMENTO IN CUCINA 14152I74C-150
Editorial: Via Settembrini, 11, 20124 MILANO MI
Tel: 02 67495261 **Fax:** 02 67495333
Email: belcamino@dibaio.com **Web site:** http://www.dibaio.com
Freq: Half-yearly; **Circ:** 50,000
Editor-in-Chief: Giuseppe Maria Jonghi Lavarini
Profile: Magazine about kitchen fitments, equipment, technology, food and tourism.
Language(s): Italian
CONSUMER: WOMEN'S INTEREST CONSUMER MAGAZINES: Home & Family

ARS SUTORIA 13501I29-10
Editorial: Via Ippolito Nievo, 33, 20145 MILANO
Tel: 02319121 **Fax:** 02 33611603
Email: arsarpel@arsarpel.it **Web site:** http://www.arssutoria.it
Freq: Monthly; **Circ:** 34,000
Editor-in-Chief: Stefania Sancini
Profile: International magazine about footwear. Covers production, materials and fashion.
Language(s): English; French; German; Italian; Spanish
BUSINESS: FOOTWEAR

ART E DOSSIER 14457I84A-75
Editorial: Via Bolognese, 165, 50139 FIRENZE FI
Tel: 055 5062387 **Fax:** 055 5062298
Email: artdoss@giunti.it **Web site:** http://www.artonline.it
Freq: Monthly; **Circ:** 42,000
Editor: Ilaria Ferraris; **Editor-in-Chief:** Claudio Pescio
Profile: European magazine concerning art and the history of art. Includes information about architecture, restorations and exhibitions.
Language(s): Italian
CONSUMER: THE ARTS & LITERARY: Arts

ARTE 14458I84A-90
Editorial: Corso Magenta, 55, 20123 MILANO
Tel: 0243313362 **Fax:** 02 43313932
Email: arte@cairoeditore.it **Web site:** http://www.cairoeditore.it
Freq: Monthly; **Circ:** 45,000
Editor: Mario Pagani; **Editor-in-Chief:** Michele Bonuomo
Profile: Arts and cultural review. Includes reports and information concerning national and international artistic events.
Language(s): Italian
CONSUMER: THE ARTS & LITERARY: Arts

ARTE CRISTIANA RIVISTA INTERNAZIONALE 14459I84A-100
Editorial: Via S. Gimignano, 19, 20146 MILANO MI
Tel: 02 48302854 **Fax:** 02 48301954
Email: bangelic@tin.it **Web site:** http://www.scuolabeatoangelico.it
Freq: 6 issues yearly; **Circ:** 1,000
Editor-in-Chief: Valerio Vigorelli
Profile: International review of art history and liturgical arts.
Language(s): English; French; Italian; Spanish
Readership: Aimed at directors of university, art critics, art students, ecclesiasts public and private museums curators.
CONSUMER: THE ARTS & LITERARY: Arts

L' ARTE IN CUCINA 717805I11A-5
Editorial: Via Zanella 44/7, 20133 MILANO
Tel: 0276115315 **Fax:** 02 76115316
Email: info@cucinaprofessionale.com **Web site:** http://www.cucinaprofessionale.com
Freq: 6 issues yearly
Editor-in-Chief: Carlo Abramo Re
Profile: Magazine containing information on food preparation in hotels, restaurants and catering schools.
Language(s): Italian
Readership: Read by chefs and catering school managers.
BUSINESS: CATERING: Catering, Hotels & Restaurants

ARTICOLI CASALINGHI E DA REGALO 13777I52C-5
Editorial: Viale Coni Zugna 71, 20144 MILANO
Tel: 023451230 **Fax:** 023451231
Email: info@edifis.it **Web site:** http://www.edifis.it
Freq: 6 issues yearly; **Circ:** 14,500
Editor-in-Chief: Andrea Aiello
Profile: Magazine focusing on high quality fancy goods and gift items, cut glass and ceramics.
Language(s): English; Italian
Readership: Read by retailers, wholesalers and manufacturers.
BUSINESS: GIFT TRADE: Fancy Goods

ARTICOLI CASALINGHI ED ELETTROCASALINGHI 13476I25-10
Editorial: Vliale Coni Zugna 71, 20144 MILANO MI
Tel: 023451230 **Fax:** 023451231
Email: articolicasalinghi@edifis.it **Web site:** http://www.edifis.it
Freq: Quarterly; **Circ:** 15,600
Editor-in-Chief: Antonio Savoia
Profile: International magazine about household and electrical goods.
Language(s): English; Italian
Readership: Aimed at retailers, purchasers and distributors of DIY and electrical products.
BUSINESS: HARDWARE

ARTIGIANATO TRA ARTE E DESIGN 13264I12A-82
Editorial: Via Statuto, 10, 20121 MILANO MI
Tel: 02 6572444 **Fax:** 02 6592695
Email: info@fondazionecologni.it **Web site:** http://www.artigianartedesign.it
Freq: Quarterly; **Circ:** 20,000
Editor-in-Chief: Ugo La Pietra
Profile: Magazine covering applied art and crafts, including ceramics, porcelain and modern design.
Language(s): English; Italian
BUSINESS: CERAMICS, POTTERY & GLASS: Ceramics & Pottery

ASIA NEWS 14487I87-5
Editorial: Via Guerrazzi, 11, 00152 ROMA
Tel: 06 58320223 **Fax:** 06 58157756
Email: desk@asianews.it **Web site:** http://www.asianews.it
Freq: Monthly; **Circ:** 5,000
Editor-in-Chief: Bernardo Cervellera
Profile: Publication giving news and information about Asia, particularly covering church and religious news.
Language(s): Italian
Readership: Aimed at those interested in Asian affairs, especially religious news.
CONSUMER: RELIGIOUS

ASSICURA 762855I1D-6
Editorial: Via Pier Luigi da Palestrina 13, 20124 MILANO **Tel:** 02 67101088 **Fax:** 02 67101041
Email: assicura@cardieditore.com **Web site:** http://www.assicuraonline.eu
Freq: Monthly; **Circ:** 10,000
Editor-in-Chief: Mario Salvatori
Profile: Magazine focusing on technical innovations and office automation for the insurance profession.
Language(s): Italian
Readership: Read by office managers in insurance companies.
BUSINESS: FINANCE & ECONOMICS: Insurance

ASSINEWS 13046I1D-12
Editorial: Viale Dante 12, 33170 PORDENONE
Tel: 0434 26136 **Fax:** 0434 20645
Email: info@assinews.it **Web site:** http://www.assinews.it
Freq: Monthly; **Circ:** 4,300
Editor: Mauro Venier
Profile: Magazine containing general, technical and legal information in the insurance field.
Language(s): Italian
Readership: Read by insurance brokers and agents, bankers, risk managers and industry managers.
BUSINESS: FINANCE & ECONOMICS: Insurance

ASTRA 14561I94E-20
Editorial: Via A. Rizzoli 8, 20132 MILANO
Tel: 02 25843045 **Fax:** 02 25843501
Email: astra@rcs.it **Web site:** http://astraincontri.corriere.it
Freq: Monthly; **Circ:** 182,000
Editor-in-Chief: Simona Tedesco
Profile: Magazine about astrology. Includes horoscopes and articles about the body's natural bio-rhythms and yoga.
Language(s): Italian
Readership: Read by those interested in astrology.
CONSUMER: OTHER CLASSIFICATIONS: Paranormal

ASTRELLA 14562I94E-25
Editorial: Viale Platone, 24, 00136 ROMA
Tel: 0639746755 **Fax:** 063231847
Email: astrella@alironda.it **Web site:** http://www.piscopoeditore.it
Freq: Monthly; **Circ:** 120,000
Editor-in-Chief: Ugo Consolazione
Profile: Magazine concerning all aspects of astrology.
Language(s): Italian
Readership: Aimed at astrology enthusiasts.
CONSUMER: OTHER CLASSIFICATIONS: Paranormal

ATELIER BAGNO 713485I23C-7
Editorial: Viale G. Richard, 1, 20143 MILANO MI
Tel: 02 81830648 **Fax:** 0281830414
Email: bagno@reedbusiness.it **Web site:** http://www.reedbusiness.it
Freq: Half-yearly
Editor-in-Chief: Oscar Giorgio Colli
Profile: International magazine containing information about innovations in bathroom styles and accessories.
Language(s): English; French; German; Italian; Spanish
BUSINESS: FURNISHINGS & FURNITURE: Furnishings & Furniture - Kitchens & Bathrooms

AUDIO REVIEW 14395I78A-23
Editorial: Via Olindo Guerrini, 20, 00137 ROMA
Tel: 06 87203321 **Fax:** 06 87139141
Email: rosaria.ferrarese@newmediapro.eu **Web site:** http://www.audioreview.it
Freq: Monthly; **Circ:** 100,000
Editor-in-Chief: Mauro Neri
Profile: Journal concerning electro-acoustics, music and hi-fi products.
Language(s): Italian
CONSUMER: CONSUMER ELECTRONICS: Hi-Fi & Recording

AUGSBURGER ALLGEMEINE ZEITUNG 1829102I73-593
Editorial: Via dell'Umiltà, 83/C, 00187 ROMA
Tel: 06 675911 **Fax:** 066796401
Web site: http://www.augsburger-allgemeine.de
Freq: Daily; **Circ:** 400,000

Language(s): Italian
CONSUMER: NATIONAL & INTERNATIONAL PERIODICALS

AUTO
14342I77A-20
Editorial: Via del Lavoro, 7, 40068 SAN LAZZARO DI SAVENA BO **Tel:** 051 6227111 **Fax:** 051 6258310
Email: laposta@auto-at.it **Web site:** http://www.auto.it
Freq: Monthly; **Circ:** 220,000
Editor-in-Chief: Alberto Sabbatini
Profile: International magazine focusing on all aspects of modern motoring. Includes two sections dedicated to travel, with suggestions for motoring holidays.
Language(s): Italian
Readership: Aimed at the middle to high disposable income earners.
CONSUMER: MOTORING & CYCLING: Motoring

AUTO D'EPOCA
762803I77F-20
Editorial: Villa Torzo - Via Prato Fiera 19, 31100 TREVISO **Tel:** 0422 412727 **Fax:** 0422 541875
Email: autodepoca@edizionipegaso.191.it
Freq: Monthly; **Circ:** 50,000
Editor-in-Chief: Michele Catozzi
Profile: Magazine containing articles on veteran cars, giving dates of events throughout the country.
Language(s): Italian
Readership: Read by vintage car enthusiasts.
CONSUMER: MOTORING & CYCLING: Veteran Cars

AUTO & DESIGN
13510I31A-17
Editorial: Corso Francia, 54, 10143 TORINO
Tel: 011 488225 **Fax:** 011 488120
Email: info@autodesignmagazine.com **Web site:** http://www.autodesignmagazine.com
Freq: 6 issues yearly; **Circ:** 13,000
Editor-in-Chief: Fulvio Cinti
Profile: International magazine covering auto and industrial design and new technology.
Language(s): English; Italian
Readership: Read by designers, engineers, directors of industry and students.
BUSINESS: MOTOR TRADE: Motor Trade Accessories

AUTO & FUORISTRADA
14343I77A-27
Editorial: Viale Sarca 235, 20126 MILANO MI
Tel: 02 66192866 **Fax:** 02 66192651
Email: autofuoristrada@hearst.it
Freq: Monthly; **Circ:** 70,000
Editor-in-Chief: Enrico Violi
Profile: Magazine about all-terrain vehicles.
Language(s): Italian
Readership: Read by people interested in cars, off-the-road motoring and nature.
CONSUMER: MOTORING & CYCLING: Motoring

AUTO TECNICA
13512I31A-40
Editorial: Via Molise, 3, 20085 LOCATE TRIULZI MI
Tel: 02 9048111 **Fax:** 02 904811210
Email: info@editorialecec.it **Web site:** http://www.autotecnica.org
Freq: Monthly; **Circ:** 85,000
Editor-in-Chief: Daniele Cafieri
Profile: Magazine covering automotive technique and technology.
Language(s): Italian
Readership: Aimed at technical engineers, mechanics and people within the automotive sector. Also read by teachers and students at technical schools.
BUSINESS: MOTOR TRADE: Motor Trade Accessories

AUTOBUS
13739I49B-5
Editorial: Via Cassano d'Adda, 20, 20139 MILANO
Tel: 02 55230950 **Fax:** 02 55230592
Email: autobus@vadoetornoedizioni.it **Web site:** http://www.vadoetorno.com
Freq: Monthly; **Circ:** 10,804
Editor-in-Chief: Maurizio Cervetto
Profile: Magazine for the urban transport and tourism sectors, covering technical, economic and cultural news.
Language(s): Italian
BUSINESS: TRANSPORT: Bus & Coach Transport

AUTOCAPITAL
14347I77A-409
Editorial: Via San Giacomo, 8, 26030 MALAGNINO
Tel: 0372 444180 **Fax:** 0372 444180
Email: redazione@autocapitalonline.it
Freq: Monthly; **Circ:** 50,000
Editor-in-Chief: Alberto Franzoni
Profile: Motoring journal covering 4x4 and off-road vehicles.
Language(s): Italian
CONSUMER: MOTORING & CYCLING: Motoring

AUTOMAZIONE E STRUMENTAZIONE
13162I5A-10
Editorial: s.s del Sempione 28, 20017 RHO MILANO
Tel: 0249971 **Fax:** 0249976570
Email: redazione.as@fieramilanoeditore.it **Web site:** http://www.ilb2b.it
Freq: Monthly; **Circ:** 12,500
Profile: Official journal of the Italian Automation Association.
Language(s): Italian
BUSINESS: COMPUTERS & AUTOMATION: Automation & Instrumentation

AUTOMAZIONE INDUSTRIALE
13349I18A-13
Editorial: Via Pisacane 1, 20016 RHO MI
Tel: 0230221
Email: redazione.automazione@ilsole24ore.com **Web site:** http://www.automazioneindustriale.com
Freq: Monthly; **Circ:** 14,000
Editor-in-Chief: Pierantonio Palerma
Profile: Magazine covering marketing, economics and products in the electronics industry and factory and process automation.
Language(s): Italian
Readership: Aimed at professionals in the electronics industry.
BUSINESS: ELECTRONICS

AUTOMAZIONE INTEGRATA
13163I5A-12
Editorial: Via Eritrea, 21, 20157 MILANO
Tel: 02 39090278 **Fax:** 02 39090331
Email: automazione.integrata@tecnichenuove.com
Web site: http://www.tecnichenuove.com
Freq: Monthly; **Circ:** 7,000
Editor-in-Chief: Giuseppe Nardella
Profile: Magazine focusing on advanced automation, robotics, numeric control and flexible working systems.
Language(s): Italian
BUSINESS: COMPUTERS & AUTOMATION: Automation & Instrumentation

AUTOMOBILE CLUB
14348I77A-170
Editorial: Via Cassanese, 224 - Pal. Tiepolo, Milano Oltre, 20090 SEGRATE MI **Tel:** 02 26937500
Fax: 02 26937525
Email: automobile@mondadori.it **Web site:** http://www.aci.it
Freq: Monthly
Editor-in-Chief: Giancarlo Pini
Profile: Magazine contains information about different models of car and also includes advice on exchanging second-hand cars.
Language(s): Italian
CONSUMER: MOTORING & CYCLING: Motoring

AUTOMOBILISMO
14349I77A-110
Editorial: Via Don Luigi Sturzo 7, 20016 PERO MI
Tel: 0238085221 **Fax:** 0238010393
Email: automobilismo@edisport.it **Web site:** http://www.automobilismo.it
Freq: Monthly; **Circ:** 190,000
Editor-in-Chief: Adalberto Falletta
Profile: Motoring magazine containing news items, tests, sport and information about the car market.
Language(s): Italian
CONSUMER: MOTORING & CYCLING: Motoring

AUTORAMA (IL MONDO DEI TRASPORTI)
14350I77A-130
Editorial: Via Ramazzotti, 20, 20052 MONZA PARCO MI **Tel:** 039 493101 **Fax:** 039 493102
Email: info@vegaeditrice.it **Web site:** http://www.vegaeditrice.it
Freq: Monthly; **Circ:** 30,000
Editor-in-Chief: Cristina Altieri
Profile: Motoring magazine containing test reports of new models and new developments.
Language(s): Italian
CONSUMER: MOTORING & CYCLING: Motoring

AUTOSPRINT
14352I77A-160
Editorial: Via del Lavoro 7, 40068 SAN LAZZARO DI SAVENA BO **Tel:** 051 6227111 **Fax:** 051 6258310
Email: segreteria@autosprint.it **Web site:** http://www.autosprint.it
Freq: Weekly; **Circ:** 100,000
Editor: Sergio Remondino; **Editor-in-Chief:** Alberto Sabbatini
Profile: Magazine covering international motor racing. Also includes news reports, comments and road tests carried out by famous racing drivers.
Language(s): Italian
CONSUMER: MOTORING & CYCLING: Motoring

AVVENIRE
13959I65A-15
Editorial: Piazza Carbonari, 3, 20125 MILANO MI
Tel: 02 67801 **Fax:** 02 6780208
Email: lettere@avvenire.it **Web site:** http://www.avvenire.it
Freq: Daily; **Circ:** 126,000
Editor: Francesco Riccardi; **Editor-in-Chief:** Marco Tarquinio
Profile: Broadsheet-sized quality newspaper providing national, international, political, financial and religious news from a Catholic viewpoint.
Language(s): Italian
Readership: Aimed at people with an interest in the Catholic religion.
ADVERTISING RATES:
Full Page Colour .... EUR 81664.00
NATIONAL DAILY & SUNDAY NEWSPAPERS: National Daily Newspapers

AVVENTURE NEL MONDO
14520I89E-301
Editorial: Largo Grigioni, 7, 00152 ROMA
Tel: 06 53293401 **Fax:** 06 53293446
Email: redazione@viaggiavventurenelmondo.it **Web site:** http://www.viaggiavventurenelmondo.it
Freq: Quarterly; **Circ:** 250,000
Editor-in-Chief: Vittorio Kulczycki
Profile: International magazine containing articles about world travel.
Language(s): Italian
CONSUMER: HOLIDAYS & TRAVEL: Holidays

AZ FRANCHISING
1845089I14A-219
Editorial: Via Quarnero, 1, 20146 MILANO
Tel: 02 467781 **Fax:** 02 46778111
Email: info@jrp.it **Web site:** http://www.azfranchising.it
Freq: Monthly; **Circ:** 100,000
Editor-in-Chief: Fabio Pasquali
Language(s): Italian
BUSINESS: COMMERCE, INDUSTRY & MANAGEMENT

AZIENDA & FISCO
13054I1M-2
Editorial: Strada 1 - Palazzo F. 6, 20090 MILANOFIORI ASSAGO MI **Tel:** 02 82476338
Fax: 02 82476800
Email: rivista.aziendaefisco.ipsoa@wki.it **Web site:** http://www.ipsoa.it
Freq: Monthly; **Circ:** 5,000
Editor-in-Chief: Giulietta Lemmi
Profile: Magazine about company tax.
Language(s): Italian
Readership: Read by tax consultants, lawyers, academics, managers in business and banking.
BUSINESS: FINANCE & ECONOMICS: Taxation

AZIENDABANCA
13038I1C-5
Editorial: Via Pier Luigi da Palestrina 13, 20124 MILANO **Tel:** 02 67101088 **Fax:** 02 67101041
Email: aziendabanca@cardieditore.com **Web site:** http://www.aziendabancaonline.eu
Freq: Monthly; **Circ:** 6,500
Editor-in-Chief: Mario Salvatori
Profile: Magazine focusing on innovative technologies and marketing concepts in banking. Also stresses the important role played by hardware and software and the recent developments in information and communication technology in banking, insurance and finance.
Language(s): Italian
Readership: Read by managers and directors in banking, finance and insurance companies.
BUSINESS: FINANCE & ECONOMICS: Banking

BACCHUS
13231I9A-2
Editorial: Via Ciro Menotti, 11/D, 20129 MILANO
Tel: 02 76110303 **Fax:** 02 7496183
Email: redazione@civiltadelbere.com
Freq: Daily; **Circ:** 46,000
Editor-in-Chief: Pino Khail
Profile: International edition of Civiltà del Bere. Contains information concerning the drinks industry and quality control details.
Language(s): German
Readership: Aimed at drinks manufacturers, importers and hotel managers.
BUSINESS: DRINKS & LICENSED TRADE: Drinks, Licensed Trade, Wines & Spirits

BAGNO DESIGN
13471I23C-14
Editorial: Via Eritrea, 21, 20157 MILANO
Tel: 02 39090315 **Fax:** 02 39090331
Email: bagnodesign@tecnichenuove.com **Web site:** http://www.tecnichenuove.com
Freq: 6 issues yearly; **Circ:** 15,000
Editor-in-Chief: Giuseppe Nardella
Profile: Magazine focusing on interior design, furnishing and accessories.
Language(s): Italian
Readership: Aimed at architects and designers, wholesalers, showroom managers and fitters.
BUSINESS: FURNISHINGS & FURNITURE: Furnishings & Furniture - Kitchens & Bathrooms

BAGNO E ACCESSORI
13470I23C-10
Editorial: Via Pisacane 1, 20016 PERO MI
Tel: 0230221
Email: olga.longa@ilsole24ore.com **Web site:** http://www.faenza.com
Freq: 6 issues yearly; **Circ:** 18,000
Editor-in-Chief: Antonio Greco
Profile: Journal containing information about the design, production, marketing and distribution of bathroom products and accessories.
Language(s): English; Italian
BUSINESS: FURNISHINGS & FURNITURE: Furnishings & Furniture - Kitchens & Bathrooms

IL BAGNO OGGI E DOMANI
13472I23C-20
Editorial: Viale G.Richard, 1/A, 20143 MILANO
Tel: 02 81830291 **Fax:** 02 81830413
Email: bagno@reedbusiness.it **Web site:** http://www.reedbusiness.it
Freq: 6 issues yearly; **Circ:** 19,000
Editor-in-Chief: Giovanni Danielli
Profile: International magazine about bathroom design.
Language(s): English; French; German; Italian; Spanish
Readership: Read by designers and architects.
BUSINESS: FURNISHINGS & FURNITURE: Furnishings & Furniture - Kitchens & Bathrooms

BALLETTO OGGI
6801I76G-1
Editorial: Piazza Statuto, 1, 10122 TORINO
Tel: 011 19703356 **Fax:** 011 19703356
Email: info@ballet2000.com **Web site:** http://www.ballet2000.com
Freq: Monthly; **Circ:** 25,000
Editor-in-Chief: Alfio Agostini
Profile: Pan-European dance magazine containing information, reports and opinions about ballet.
Language(s): English; French; Italian
CONSUMER: MUSIC & PERFORMING ARTS: Dance

BAMBI
754457I91D-20
Editorial: Via Sandro Sandri, 1, 20121 MILANO
Tel: 02 290851 **Fax:** 02 29085345
Web site: http://www.disney.it
Freq: Monthly; **Circ:** 47,224
Editor-in-Chief: Marina Migliavacca
Profile: Magazine containing stories, games and Bambi's adventures.
Language(s): Italian
Readership: Aimed at toddlers between the ages of 18 and 36 months.
CONSUMER: RECREATION & LEISURE: Children & Youth

BANCA BORSA E TITOLI DI CREDITO
13634I44-10
Editorial: Via Lanzone, 4 - c/o Studio Portale, 20123 MILANO **Tel:** 02 720881 **Fax:** 02 72088300
Email: studio@portalevisconti.it **Web site:** http://www.giuffre.it
Freq: 6 issues yearly; **Circ:** 4,200
Editor-in-Chief: Federico Martorano
Profile: Legal journal relating to banking, the stock exchange and creditors. Includes details of relevant legislative changes.
Language(s): Italian
Readership: Aimed at professionals in the financial sector and lawyers working on financial matters.
BUSINESS: LEGAL

BANCAFINANZA
13044I1C-50
Editorial: Via Gaetano Negri, 4, 20123 MILANO
Tel: 02 7218701 **Fax:** 02 7218708
Email: bancafinanza@newspapermilano.it **Web site:** http://www.newspapermilano.it
Freq: Monthly; **Circ:** 10,000
Editor-in-Chief: Angela Maria Scullica
Profile: Publication about banking and finance.
Language(s): Italian
BUSINESS: FINANCE & ECONOMICS: Banking

BANCARIA
13041I1C-20
Editorial: Via delle Botteghe Oscure, 54, 00186 ROMA **Tel:** 06 6767465 **Fax:** 06 6767649
Email: redazione@bancariaeditrice.it **Web site:** http://www.bancaria.it
Freq: Monthly; **Circ:** 8,000
Editor-in-Chief: Tancredi Bianchi
Profile: Review of the Italian Banking Association.
Language(s): Italian
Readership: Read by bank managers, banking officials and employees, industrial and commercial companies, cultural institutions and students.
BUSINESS: FINANCE & ECONOMICS: Banking

BARBIE MAGAZINE
1784520I91D-206
Editorial: Centro Direzionale Maciachini, Via B. Crespi 19/C, 20159 MILANO MI **Tel:** 02 699631
Fax: 02 69963699
Email: paola.moretti@mattel.com **Web site:** http://www.barbie.it
Freq: Monthly; **Circ:** 135,000
Editor-in-Chief: Miriam Badalotti
Language(s): Italian
CONSUMER: RECREATION & LEISURE: Children & Youth

BARCHE
14530I91A-32
Editorial: Via Giuseppe Tartini, 13/c, 20158 MILANO
Tel: 02 39359111 **Fax:** 02 39359122

Email: redazione@barcheisp.it **Web site:** http://www.barcheisp.com
Freq: Monthly; **Circ:** 35,000
Editor-in-Chief: Franco Michienzi
Profile: Magazine focusing on boating as a leisure activity. Contains news, technical reports, equipment reviews, results of tests on new boats and information concerning tourism.
Language(s): Italian
Readership: Aimed at boat owners and those interested in sailing for pleasure.
CONSUMER: RECREATION & LEISURE: Boating & Yachting

BARGIORNALE
13248I11A-20
Editorial: Via Pisacane 1, 20016 RHO MI
Tel: 02 30221
Email: redazione.bargiornale@ilsole24ore.com **Web site:** http://www.bargiornale.it
Freq: Monthly; **Circ:** 115,000
Editor: Rossella De Stefano; **Editor-in-Chief:** Mattia Losi
Profile: Magazine covering the technical aspects of food and beverage, catering and the hotel business.
Language(s): Italian
BUSINESS: CATERING: Catering, Hotels & Restaurants

IL BATTELLIERE
13690I45E-10
Editorial: Via Lago Gerundo, 26, 26100 CREMONA CR **Tel:** 348 0561675 0372 25591 **Fax:** 0372 450926
Email: editor@workboats.it **Web site:** http://www.workboats.it
Freq: 6 issues yearly
Editor-in-Chief: Albert Sturlese
Profile: Magazine providing information on marine workboats, ferries and engines. Contains nautical trade news and technical articles.
Language(s): Italian
Readership: Read mainly by port operators, ferry operators, passenger vessel owners and fishermen.
BUSINESS: MARINE & SHIPPING: Boat Trade

BEAT MAGAZINE
1785003I76D-563
Editorial: Via Newton, 4, 20090 ASSAGO MI
Tel: 02 47791858 **Fax:** 02 45713259
Email: redazione@beatpress.it **Web site:** http://www.beatmagazine.it
Freq: Monthly; **Circ:** 180,000
Editor-in-Chief: Marco De Crescenzo
Language(s): Italian
CONSUMER: MUSIC & PERFORMING ARTS: Music

BEAUTYLINE
13316I15A-10
Editorial: Via Eritrea, 21, 20157 MILANO
Tel: 02 390901 **Fax:** 02320391
Email: beauty@tecnichenuove.com **Web site:** http://www.tecnichenuove.com
Freq: 6 issues yearly; **Circ:** 26,500
Editor-in-Chief: Ivo Nardella
Profile: Magazine covering beauty and fashion.
Language(s): Italian
Readership: Aimed at beauticians and hairdressers.
BUSINESS: COSMETICS & HAIRDRESSING: Cosmetics

BELLAUTO
760691I31A-50
Editorial: Via della Liberazione, 1, 20068 PESCHIERA BORROMEO MI **Tel:** 02 55305067 **Fax:** 02 55305068
Email: koster@koster.it **Web site:** http://www.koster.it
Freq: Monthly
Editor-in-Chief: Pierpaolo Bellina
Profile: Magazine containing information about the bodywork, technical aspects and styling of cars.
Language(s): Italian
Readership: Read by coach builders, manufacturers of cars and accessories and car traders.
BUSINESS: MOTOR TRADE: Motor Trade Accessories

BELL'EUROPA
14521I89E-53
Editorial: Corso Magenta, 55, 20123 MILANO
Tel: 02 43313434 **Fax:** 02 43313929
Email: belleuropa@cairoeditore.it **Web site:** http://www.cairoeditore.it
Freq: Monthly; **Circ:** 50,000
Editor: Elisabetta Planca; **Editor-in-Chief:** Emanuela Rosa-Clot
Profile: Magazine concerning travel in Europe.
Language(s): Italian
CONSUMER: HOLIDAYS & TRAVEL: Holidays

BELL'ITALIA
14522I89E-55
Editorial: Corso Magenta 55, 20123 MILANO MI
Tel: 02433131 **Fax:** 02 43313927
Email: bellitalia@cairoeditore.it **Web site:** http://www.cairoeditore.it
Freq: Monthly; **Circ:** 80,000
Editor: Michela Colombo; **Editor-in-Chief:** Emanuela Rosa-Clot
Profile: Magazine about travel in Italy.
Language(s): Italian
Readership: Aimed at tourists in Italy.
CONSUMER: HOLIDAYS & TRAVEL: Holidays

BEST MOVIE
1784893I76A-142
Editorial: Via Donatello, 5/B, 20131 MILANO MI
Tel: 02 277961 **Fax:** 02 27796300
Email: bestmovie@bestmovie.it **Web site:** http://www.bestmovie.it
Freq: Monthly; **Circ:** 173,159
Editor-in-Chief: Vito Sinopoli
Language(s): Italian
CONSUMER: MUSIC & PERFORMING ARTS: Cinema

BIANCO & BRUNO
13624I43A-25
Editorial: c/o Arbe - Via Emilia Ovest 1014, 41123 MODENA **Tel:** 059896957 **Fax:** 059896951
Email: rivista@biancoebruno.it
Freq: 6 issues yearly; **Circ:** 10,000
Editor-in-Chief: Graziano Girotti
Profile: Technical publication covering the domestic electrical appliances trade.
Language(s): Italian
BUSINESS: ELECTRICAL RETAIL TRADE

BIBLIOTECHE OGGI
13915I60B-10
Editorial: Via G. Bergonzoli, 1/5, 20127 MILANO
Tel: 02 28315998 **Fax:** 02 28315906
Email: redazione@bibliotecheoggi.it **Web site:** http://www.bibliotecheoggi.it
Freq: Monthly; **Circ:** 4,000
Editor-in-Chief: Massimo Belotti
Profile: Magazine containing information about library management and news about recent publications.
Language(s): Italian
Readership: Read by library directors and their staff.
BUSINESS: PUBLISHING: Libraries

BICI DA MONTAGNA - MOUNTAIN BIKE WORLD
14376I77C-30
Editorial: Via Della Maratone 66, 00194 ROMA
Tel: 063629021 **Fax:** 06 36309950
Email: mbw@cycling.it **Web site:** http://www.cycling.it
Freq: Monthly; **Circ:** 105,000
Editor-in-Chief: Stefano Garinei
Profile: Magazine about mountain bikes. Includes articles about cycling gear and accessories and technical advice for improving safety.
Language(s): Italian
Readership: Read by mountain bike enthusiasts.
CONSUMER: MOTORING & CYCLING: Cycling

LA BICICLETTA
14377I77C-40
Editorial: Via Della Maratona 66, 00194 ROMA
Tel: 06 3629021 **Fax:** 06 36309950
Email: bicicletta@cycling.it **Web site:** http://www.bicicletta.it
Freq: Monthly; **Circ:** 105,000
Editor-in-Chief: Calogero Cascio
Profile: Magazine about cycling, includes features on racing bikes and mountain biking. Provides technical and medical advice for cyclists. Also contains interviews with celebrities and news about cycling competitions.
Language(s): Italian
Readership: Read by people who enjoy cycling, especially in the country.
CONSUMER: MOTORING & CYCLING: Cycling

BIKERS LIFE
762806I77B-12
Editorial: Via Ciro Di Pers 38, 33030 MAJANO UD
Tel: 0432 948570 **Fax:** 0432 948606
Email: info@bikerslife.com **Web site:** http://www.bikerslife.com
Freq: Monthly; **Circ:** 40,000
Editor-in-Chief: Moreno Persello
Profile: Magazine dedicated entirely to motorcycles, from racing to choppers and tourers, includes events, reunions, the law and tattoos.
Language(s): Italian
CONSUMER: MOTORING & CYCLING: Motorcycling

BIMBISANI & BELLI
14171I74D-28
Editorial: Corso di Porta Nuova 3/a, 20121 MILANO
Tel: 02 63675300 **Fax:** 02 63675519
Email: bimbisani@casaeditriceuniverso.com
Freq: Monthly; **Circ:** 174,000
Editor-in-Chief: Silvia Huen
Profile: Magazine about child care from birth to school age.
Language(s): Italian
CONSUMER: WOMEN'S INTEREST CONSUMER MAGAZINES: Child Care

BIO CASA
718242I4E-30
Editorial: Viale Andrea Doria, 35, 20124 MILANO
Tel: 02 66988188 **Fax:** 02 66988190
Email: redazione@edinterni.it **Web site:** http://www.edinterni.com
Freq: Quarterly; **Circ:** 6,000
Editor-in-Chief: Antonio Vigliante
Profile: Magazine containing information about energy saving house building.
Language(s): Italian
Readership: Aimed at architects, planners and builders.
BUSINESS: ARCHITECTURE & BUILDING: Building

BLU & ROSSO
13473I23C-30
Editorial: Via Lucano 3, 20149 MILANO
Tel: 02 5516109 **Fax:** 02 59902431
Email: claudiamanini@designdiffusion.com **Web site:** http://www.designdiffusion.com
Freq: Monthly; **Circ:** 13,800
Editor-in-Chief: Carlo Ludovico Russo
Profile: Magazine of the National Association of Plumbing Merchants and Bathroom Retailers. Contains information on plumbing, heating, flooring, air-conditioning and bathrooms.
Language(s): Italian
BUSINESS: FURNISHINGS & FURNITURE: Furnishings & Furniture - Kitchens & Bathrooms

BMM
1845294I74B-391
Editorial: Via Magazzini Anteriori, 51, 48100 RAVENNA **Tel:** 0544 590490 **Fax:** 0544 590480
Email: bmm@bmm.cc **Web site:** http://www.bmm.cc
Freq: Quarterly; **Circ:** 100,000
Editor-in-Chief: Piero Cattani
Language(s): Italian
CONSUMER: WOMEN'S INTEREST CONSUMER MAGAZINES: Women's Interest - Fashion

BOLINA MAGAZINE
14531I91A-40
Editorial: Largo Angelicum 6, 00184 ROMA
Tel: 06 6990100 **Fax:** 06 6990137
Email: staff@bolina.it **Web site:** http://www.bolina.it
Freq: Monthly; **Circ:** 45,000
Editor-in-Chief: Alberto Casti
Profile: Magazine for the sailing and boating sector, including news on cruising, racing, chartering, boat building and repairs.
Language(s): Italian
Readership: Read by enthusiasts.
CONSUMER: RECREATION & LEISURE: Boating & Yachting

BOMBONIERA ITALIANA
13778I52C-12
Editorial: Zona Artigianale - Contrada Piano Mulino - Stab. 9, 94010 CATENANUOVA EN **Tel:** 0935 75399
Fax: 0935 545151
Email: redazione@emil.it **Web site:** http://www.emil.it
Freq: Quarterly; **Circ:** 12,000
Editor-in-Chief: Giovanni Mirulla
Profile: International magazine about the manufacture, distribution and sale of sweets, novelty items, presents and giftware.
Language(s): English; Italian
Readership: Aimed at both Italian and foreign buyers also at operators of organisation in the giftware sector.
BUSINESS: GIFT TRADE: Fancy Goods

BONSAI & NEWS
14557I93-81
Editorial: C.so Sempione 35, 20015 PARABIAGO MI
Tel: 0331491440 **Fax:** 0331559410
Email: info@crespieditori.com **Web site:** http://www.crespieditori.it
Freq: 6 issues yearly; **Circ:** 15,000
Editor-in-Chief: Giuseppe Biselli
Profile: Magazine about the cultivation of bonsai trees.
Language(s): Italian
Readership: Read by bonsai enthusiasts and people with a passion for Japanese art, philosophy and gardening.
CONSUMER: GARDENING

BOOK MODA
14118I47A-4_40
Editorial: Via Offienze, 156, 00154 ROMA RM
Tel: 06 83394637 **Fax:** 06 5743052
Email: redazione.roma@bookmoda.com **Web site:** http://www.bookmoda.com
Freq: Half-yearly; **Circ:** 20,000
Editor-in-Chief: Gianluca Lo Vetro
Profile: Magazine focusing on fashion.
Language(s): English; Italian
Readership: Aimed at professionals in the fashion industry.
BUSINESS: CLOTHING & TEXTILES

BOOK MODA UOMO
14483I47A-4_50
Editorial: Via Manzoni, 26, 20089 ROZZANO MI
Tel: 02 8923951 **Fax:** 02 8242644
Email: redazione.milano@bookmoda.com **Web site:** http://www.bookmoda.com
Freq: Half-yearly; **Circ:** 70,000
Editor-in-Chief: Giovanna Roveda
Profile: International magazine covering men's fashion.
Language(s): English; Italian
Readership: Read by professionals in the fashion industry.
BUSINESS: CLOTHING & TEXTILES

BORSA & FINANZA
1645430I1F-51
Editorial: Via Tristano Calco, 2, 20123 MILANO
Tel: 02 303026 1 **Fax:** 02 303026240
Email: redazione@borsaefinanza.it **Web site:** http://www.borsaefinanza.it
Freq: Weekly; **Circ:** 65,000
Editor: Simona Cornaggia; **Editor-in-Chief:** Gianni Gambarotta
Profile: Magazine focusing on stock exchange news and economics. Contains in-depth company analysis.
Language(s): Italian
Readership: Read by bankers and investment brokers.
BUSINESS: FINANCE & ECONOMICS: Investment

BRAVA CASA
14138I74C-50
Editorial: Via A. Rizzoli 8, 20132 MILANO
Tel: 02 25843514 **Fax:** 02 25843572
Email: atredazione@atcasa.it **Web site:** http://www.bravacasa.it
Freq: Monthly; **Circ:** 230,000
Editor: Rita De Angelis; **Editor-in-Chief:** Rosanna Brambilla
Profile: Magazine covering interior design. Also contains articles concerning the garden and electrical appliances.
Language(s): Italian
CONSUMER: WOMEN'S INTEREST CONSUMER MAGAZINES: Home & Family

BRIDGE D'ITALIA
14419I79F-20
Editorial: Via Ciro Menotti 11/C, 20129 MILANO MI
Tel: 02 70000333 **Fax:** 02 70001398
Email: bdi@federbridge.it **Web site:** http://www.federbridge.it
Freq: 6 issues yearly; **Circ:** 25,000
Profile: International journal of the Italian Bridge Federation, including articles on the evolution of the game and information concerning national and international bridge tournaments. Also contains news of the Federation's activities.
Language(s): Italian
Readership: Read by bridge enthusiasts.
CONSUMER: HOBBIES & DIY: Games & Puzzles

BROADCAST & PRODUCTION ITALIA
630479I2D-15
Editorial: S.Felice Strada Prima, 12, 20090 SEGRATE MI **Tel:** 02 92884940 **Fax:** 02 70300211
Email: broadcast@broadcast.it **Web site:** http://www.broadcast.it
Freq: 6 issues yearly; **Circ:** 6,500
Editor-in-Chief: Andrea Rivetta
Profile: Magazine focusing on audio and video technology. Includes news, engineering and production articles, coverage of trade shows, equipment reviews and new products. Also features broadcasting on the Internet .
Language(s): English; Italian
Readership: Read by equipment buyers in the Italian broadcasting, audio and video industry.
BUSINESS: COMMUNICATIONS, ADVERTISING & MARKETING: Broadcasting

BUSINESS
762879I14A-200
Editorial: Via Gaggia 1/A, 20124 MILANO
Tel: 02 6774101 **Fax:** 0267741050
Email: redazione@business-magazine.it **Web site:** http://www.business-magazine.it
Freq: Monthly; **Circ:** 36,000
Editor-in-Chief: Maria Cristina Alfieri
Profile: Magazine containing information on management, communications and logistics.
Language(s): Italian
Readership: Read by managers.
BUSINESS: COMMERCE, INDUSTRY & MANAGEMENT

CACCIA & TIRO
14270I75F-80
Editorial: Via Ugo Bassi 7, 40121 BOLOGNA
Tel: 051223327 **Fax:** 051222946
Email: info@greentime.it **Web site:** http://www.greentime.it
Freq: Monthly; **Circ:** 60,000
Editor-in-Chief: Valeria Bellagamba
Profile: Magazine containing news about hunting, fishing and shooting.
Language(s): Italian
CONSUMER: SPORT: Shooting

IL CAGLIARITANO
13934I63-15
Editorial: Via Sardegna 132, 09124 CAGLIARI
Tel: 070728356 **Fax:** 070728356
Email: giorgioariu@tin.it **Web site:** http://www.giacomunicazione.it
Freq: Monthly; **Circ:** 5,000
Editor-in-Chief: Giorgio Ariu
Profile: Magazine containing articles about culture, environmental issues, politics, economics, law, health, entertainment and sport.
Language(s): Italian
Readership: Read by business executives living in the Cagliari region.
BUSINESS: REGIONAL BUSINESS

IL CAMINO 14139I74C-60
Editorial: Via Settembrini, 11, 20124 MILANO
Tel: 02 67495250 **Fax:** 02 67495333
Email: belcamino@dibaio.com **Web site:** http://www.dibaio.com
Freq: Quarterly; **Circ:** 70,000
Editor-in-Chief: Giuseppe Maria Jonghi Lavarini
Profile: Magazine giving ideas about fires, stoves, fireplaces and surroundings.
Language(s): Italian
CONSUMER: WOMEN'S INTEREST CONSUMER MAGAZINES: Home & Family

CAMPUS 14454I83-20
Editorial: Via Burigozzo, 5, 20122 MILANO MI
Tel: 02582191 **Fax:** 02 58317438
Email: redazione.campus@class.it **Web site:** http://www.campus.it
Freq: Monthly; **Circ:** 80,000
Editor-in-Chief: Paolo Panerai
Profile: University journal covering all aspects of student life and interests.
Language(s): Italian
Readership: Read by students and staff.
CONSUMER: STUDENT PUBLICATIONS

CANI 14439I81B-12
Editorial: Via Enrico Fermi 24 - Località Osmannoro, 50019 SESTO FIORENTINO FI **Tel:** 055 30321
Fax: 055 3032280
Email: cani@edolimpia.it **Web site:** http://www.edolimpia.it
Freq: Monthly; **Circ:** 33,000
Editor-in-Chief: Renato Cacciapuoti
Profile: Magazine containing information about dogs.
Language(s): Italian
Readership: Read by vets, breeders and dog lovers.
CONSUMER: ANIMALS & PETS: Dogs

CANTIERI STRADE COSTRUZIONI 13614I42A-9
Editorial: Viale Coni Zugna, 71, 20144 MILANO
Tel: 023451230 **Fax:** 023451231
Email: csci@edifis.it **Web site:** http://www.edifis.it
Freq: Monthly; **Circ:** 10,000
Editor-in-Chief: Andrea Aiello
Profile: Magazine containing information for the construction and building industry.
Language(s): Italian
Readership: Aimed at professionals in the building and construction trade.
BUSINESS: CONSTRUCTION

CAPITAL 14072I73-28_50
Editorial: Via Burigozzo, 5, 20122 MILANO MI
Tel: 02 58219281 **Fax:** 02 58219920
Email: segreteriacapital@class.it **Web site:** http://www.classcity.it
Freq: Monthly
Editor: Aldo Bolognini Cobianchi
Profile: Magazine containing articles about international business, Italian politics and economy, personal investments, interviews with business personalities, lifestyle, leisure, new trends in culture and fashion.
Language(s): Italian
Readership: Aimed at international business executives.
ADVERTISING RATES:
Full Page Colour .... EUR 30000.00
CONSUMER: NATIONAL & INTERNATIONAL PERIODICALS

CAR AUDIO & FM 14396I78A-45
Editorial: Via Rovereto, 6, 00198 ROMA
Tel: 06 8552649 **Fax:** 06 8558885
Email: eurogest@email.it
Freq: Monthly; **Circ:** 125,000
Editor-in-Chief: Gianni Caserta
Profile: Magazine containing information concerning mobile electronics. Includes details of car hi-fi systems, music, car electronics and satellite systems.
Language(s): English; Italian
Readership: Aimed at young people aged between 18 and 35 years.
CONSUMER: CONSUMER ELECTRONICS: Hi-Fi & Recording

CAR STEREO & FM 14397I78A-50
Editorial: Via Rovereto, 6, 00198 ROMA RM
Tel: 06 8552649 **Fax:** 06 8558885
Email: progeditedi toriale@infinito.it
Freq: Quarterly; **Circ:** 105,000
Editor-in-Chief: Gianni Caserta
Profile: Review of car electronics.
Language(s): Italian
Readership: Read by people interested in car electronics and car stereo enthusiasts.
CONSUMER: CONSUMER ELECTRONICS: Hi-Fi & Recording

IL CARABINIERE 13539I32F-18
Editorial: Piazza San Bernardo 109, 00187 ROMA
Tel: 06483780 **Fax:** 06 48904053
Email: ilcarabiniere@tin.it **Web site:** http://www.carabinieri.it
Freq: Monthly; **Circ:** 50,000
Editor-in-Chief: Roberto Riccardi
Profile: Journal containing news and information for the Italian police force.
Language(s): Italian
Readership: Read by the Italian Police Force.
BUSINESS: LOCAL GOVERNMENT, LEISURE & RECREATION: Police

CARAVAN E CAMPER GRANTURISMO 1785100I50-192
Editorial: Via Eustachi, 31, 20129 MILANO
Tel: 02 20241592 **Fax:** 02 20249336
Email: redazione@caravanecamper.it **Web site:** http://www.caravanecamper.it
Freq: Monthly; **Circ:** 450,000
Editor-in-Chief: Beppe Finello
Language(s): Italian
BUSINESS: TRAVEL & TOURISM

LA CARTOLERIA 13610I41B-23
Editorial: Via della Stradella 14, 20900 MONZA MB
Tel: 039 737312 **Fax:** 039 736547
Email: redazione.lacartoleria@lineacomm.it **Web site:** http://www.lacartoleria.lineacomm.it
Freq: 6 issues yearly; **Circ:** 8,200
Editor-in-Chief: Mario Paleari
Profile: Publication specialising in stationery, books and magazines, toys, educational equipment, giftware and promotions.
Language(s): English; Italian
Readership: Read by manufacturers, wholesalers and retailers.
BUSINESS: PRINTING & STATIONERY: Stationery

CASA CHIC 1828858I74C-321
Editorial: Via Calcare, 15, 00048 NETTUNO RM
Tel: 06452216742 **Fax:** 06 23328541
Email: redazione@lotuspublishing.it **Web site:** http://www.lotuspublishing.it
Freq: Monthly; **Circ:** 100,000
Editor-in-Chief: Maria Letizia Tartaglini
Language(s): Italian
CONSUMER: WOMEN'S INTEREST CONSUMER MAGAZINES: Home & Family

CASA DI 1784928I74C-312
Editorial: Via Lucano 3, 20135 MILANO
Tel: 02 5516109 **Fax:** 025456803
Email: casad@designdiffusion.com **Web site:** http://www.designdiffusion.com
Freq: 6 issues yearly; **Circ:** 120,000
Editor-in-Chief: Carlo Ludovico Russo
Language(s): Italian
CONSUMER: WOMEN'S INTEREST CONSUMER MAGAZINES: Home & Family

CASA FACILE 14142I74C-82_50
Editorial: Palazzo Mondadori, 20090 SEGRATE MI
Tel: 02 75422598 **Fax:** 02 75422708
Email: segreteria.casafacile@mondadori.it **Web site:** http://www.mondadori.it
Freq: Monthly; **Circ:** 250,000
Editor-in-Chief: Giusi Sillighini
Profile: Magazine about furnishing and decorating the home.
Language(s): Italian
CONSUMER: WOMEN'S INTEREST CONSUMER MAGAZINES: Home & Family

CASA GREEN - CASA 99 IDEE 1784595I74C-306
Editorial: Via Settembrini, 11, 20124 MILANO MI
Tel: 02 67495250 **Fax:** 02 67495333
Email: laura.perna@dibaio.com **Web site:** http://www.dibaio.com
Freq: Monthly; **Circ:** 100,000
Language(s): Italian
CONSUMER: WOMEN'S INTEREST CONSUMER MAGAZINES: Home & Family

CASA IN FIORE 624539I93-20
Editorial: Corso di Porta Nuova, 3/a, 20121 MILANO MI **Tel:** 02 63675403 **Fax:** 02 63675515
Freq: Monthly
Editor-in-Chief: Giuliana Maggioni
Profile: Magazine focusing on flowering plants for indoors, terrace and garden.
Language(s): Italian
Readership: Read by amateur gardeners.
CONSUMER: GARDENING

CASA TESSIL REPORTER 13459I23A-11
Editorial: Via XXV Aprile 15, 20020 ARESE MI
Tel: 02 93588188 **Fax:** 02 93588298
Email: info@editeam.com **Web site:** http://www.editeam.com
Freq: 6 issues yearly; **Circ:** 11,000
Editor-in-Chief: Lia Di Clemente
Profile: Magazine containing information about household linens and furnishings.
Language(s): English; Italian
Readership: Aimed at retailers and manufacturers.
BUSINESS: FURNISHINGS & FURNITURE

CASABELLA 13114I4A-113
Editorial: Via Trentacoste, 7, 20134 MILANO MI
Tel: 02 215631 **Fax:** 02 21563260
Email: casabella@mondadori.it **Web site:** http://www.mondadori.it
Freq: Monthly; **Circ:** 40,000
Editor-in-Chief: Roberto Briglia
Profile: International architectural review. Focuses on architecture and design.
Language(s): English; Italian
Readership: Read by architects, planners and designers.
BUSINESS: ARCHITECTURE & BUILDING: Architecture

CASAMICA (CORRIERE DELLA SERA) 1784349I74C-304
Editorial: Via A. Rizzoli 8, 20132 MILANO
Tel: 0225843991 **Fax:** 02 25843693
Email: casamica.designmagazine@rcs.it **Web site:** http://atcasa.it
Freq: 6 issues yearly; **Circ:** 860,000
Editor: Benedetto Marzullo; **Editor-in-Chief:** Pier Luigi Vercesi
Language(s): Italian
CONSUMER: WOMEN'S INTEREST CONSUMER MAGAZINES: Home & Family

CASARREDO & DESIGN 13460I23A-11_20
Editorial: Viale Sarca, 243, 20126 MILANO
Tel: 02 66103539 **Fax:** 02 66103558
Email: redazione@rimaedit.it **Web site:** http://www.rimaedit.it
Freq: Quarterly; **Circ:** 13,000
Editor-in-Chief: Flavio Maestrini
Profile: International magazine focusing on home furnishings.
Language(s): Arabic; English; French; Russian
Readership: Aimed at designers, manufacturers and retailers.
BUSINESS: FURNISHINGS & FURNITURE

CASAVIVA 14144I74C-110
Editorial: Palazzo Mondadori, 20090 SEGRATE MI
Tel: 02 75422463 **Fax:** 02 75422962
Email: casaviva@mondadori.it **Web site:** http://www.mondadori.it
Freq: Monthly; **Circ:** 227,000
Editor-in-Chief: Paola Girardi
Profile: Magazine covering interior design, cooking and leisure.
Language(s): Italian
CONSUMER: WOMEN'S INTEREST CONSUMER MAGAZINES: Home & Family

CASE DA ABITARE 14147I74C-118
Editorial: Via Ventura, 5, 20134 MILANO
Tel: 02210581 **Fax:** 0221058316
Email: redazione@casedaabitare.rcs.it **Web site:** http://atcasa.corriere.it/Casedaabitare
Freq: Monthly; **Circ:** 700,000
Editor: Fabrizio Sarpi; **Editor-in-Chief:** Francesca Taroni
Profile: Magazine focusing on interior design.
Language(s): Italian
Readership: Read by people with a high disposable income and professionals in interior design.
CONSUMER: WOMEN'S INTEREST CONSUMER MAGAZINES: Home & Family

CASE DI CAMPAGNA 14148I74C-120
Editorial: Via Settembrini, 11, 20124 MILANO
Tel: 02 674955250 **Fax:** 02 67495333
Email: casedicampagna@dibaio.com **Web site:** http://www.dibaio.com
Freq: 6 issues yearly; **Circ:** 70,000
Editor-in-Chief: Giuseppe Maria Jonghi Lavarini
Profile: Magazine offering ideas for furnishing and decorating houses in the country.
Language(s): Italian
CONSUMER: WOMEN'S INTEREST CONSUMER MAGAZINES: Home & Family

CASE DI MONTAGNA 14149I74C-140
Editorial: Via Settembrini, 11, 20124 MILANO MI
Tel: 02 67495250 **Fax:** 02 67495333
Email: sara.sperolini@dibaio.com **Web site:** http://www.dibaio.com
Freq: 3 issues yearly; **Circ:** 60,000
Editor-in-Chief: Giuseppe Maria Jonghi Lavarini
Profile: Publication providing ideas for furnishing and repairing properties in the mountains.
Language(s): Italian
CONSUMER: WOMEN'S INTEREST CONSUMER MAGAZINES: Home & Family

CASE & COUNTRY 14145I74C-112
Editorial: Via Burigozzo 5, 20122 MILANO
Tel: 02 582191 **Fax:** 02 58317429
Web site: http://www.classcity.it
Freq: Monthly; **Circ:** 70,000
Editor-in-Chief: Paolo Panerai
Profile: Magazine about country homes and lifestyle.
Language(s): Italian
CONSUMER: WOMEN'S INTEREST CONSUMER MAGAZINES: Home & Family

CAVALLO MAGAZINE & LO SPERONE 763000I81D-1
Editorial: Via Mattei, 106, 40138 BOLOGNA
Tel: 051 6006068 **Fax:** 051 6006657
Email: redazione1@cavallomagazine.it **Web site:** http://www.cavallomagazine.it
Freq: Monthly; **Circ:** 40,000
Editor-in-Chief: Beppe Boni
Profile: Magazine focusing on horse-breeding, equestrian and horse-racing.
Language(s): Italian
CONSUMER: ANIMALS & PETS: Horses & Ponies

CDA - CONDIZIONAMENTO DELL'ARIA 13090I3B-30
Editorial: Vial Olgiati, 26, 20143 MILANO MI
Tel: 02 89151200 **Fax:** 02889151237
Email: cda@shinda.it **Web site:** http://www.shindaedizioni.it
Freq: Monthly; **Circ:** 4,000
Editor-in-Chief: Italo Grifoni
Profile: Journal containing technical news about the installation of air-conditioning plant, ventilation, heating and refrigeration systems.
Language(s): Italian
Readership: Aimed at designers, installers and students.
BUSINESS: HEATING & VENTILATION: Industrial Heating & Ventilation

CELEBRIAMO 14324I76D-561
Editorial: Via Calepio, 4, 24125 BERGAMO
Tel: 035 243618 **Fax:** 035 270298
Email: info@edizionicarrara.it **Web site:** http://www.edizionicarrara.it
Freq: 6 issues yearly; **Circ:** 6,000
Editor-in-Chief: Vittorio Carrara
Profile: Review of liturgical church music.
Language(s): Italian
Readership: Read by members of the religious community.
CONSUMER: MUSIC & PERFORMING ARTS: Music

CER - IL GIORNALE DELLA CERAMICA 13260I12A-30
Editorial: Viale Monte Santo, 40, 41049 SASSUOLO MO **Tel:** 0536 804585 **Fax:** 0536 806510
Email: redazione@confindustriaceramica.it **Web site:** http://www.confindustriaceramica.it
Freq: 6 issues yearly; **Circ:** 10,000
Editor-in-Chief: Franco Manfredini
Profile: Publication about the Italian ceramic industry, includes information on all stages of the ceramic manufacturing process.
Language(s): Italian
Readership: Aimed at entrepreneurs and managers of companies involved in all stages of the ceramic manufacturing process.
BUSINESS: CERAMICS, POTTERY & GLASS: Ceramics & Pottery

CERAMICA INFORMAZIONE 13261I12A-60
Editorial: Via Granarolo 175/3, 48018 FAENZA
Tel: 0546 63781 **Fax:** 0546 660440
Web site: http://www.faenza.com
Freq: Monthly; **Circ:** 4,000
Editor-in-Chief: Antonio Greco
Profile: Official journal of the Italian Ceramics Society.
Language(s): Italian
BUSINESS: CERAMICS, POTTERY & GLASS: Ceramics & Pottery

LA CERAMICA MODERNA & ANTICA 13262I12A-65
Editorial: Via Granarolo 175/3, 48018 FAENZA RA
Tel: 0546 63781 **Fax:** 0546 660440
Email: info.faenza@businessmedia24.com **Web site:** http://www.faenza.com
Freq: Quarterly; **Circ:** 6,000
Editor-in-Chief: Antonio Greco
Profile: Magazine covering the subject of ceramics, including artistic, industrial and artisan products, equipment and rare materials.
Language(s): Italian
Readership: Read by artists, artisans, art critics, students and gallery directors.
BUSINESS: CERAMICS, POTTERY & GLASS: Ceramics & Pottery

CHARTA - COLLEZIONISMO ANTIQUARIATO MERCATI 13224I7-35
Editorial: Via Giudecca, 671, 30133 VENEZIA
Tel: 041 5211204 **Fax:** 041 5208538

Email: charta@novacharta.it **Web site:** http://www.novacharta.it
Freq: 6 issues yearly; **Circ:** 12,000
Editor-in-Chief: Francesco Rapazzini
Profile: Magazine covering antique and collectables books and paper artefacts.
Language(s): Italian
Readership: Read by those interested or involved in the paper world.
BUSINESS: ANTIQUES

CHERIE BIMBI
14123I74B-180
Editorial: Via Gadames, 123, 20151 MILANO MI
Tel: 02 36588435 **Fax:** 0236588222
Email: cheriebimbi@leditore.it **Web site:** http://www.leditore.it
Freq: 6 issues yearly; **Circ:** 60,000
Editor: Giulia Landini; **Editor-in-Chief:** Massimo Bacchetti
Profile: Magazine focusing on fashion trends for babies and young children.
Language(s): Italian
Readership: Aimed at parents of young children.
CONSUMER: WOMEN'S INTEREST CONSUMER MAGAZINES: Women's Interest - Fashion

CHI
14073I74A-414
Editorial: Palazzo Mondadori, 20090 SEGRATE MI
Tel: 02 75421 **Fax:** 02 75423536
Email: chi@mondadori.it **Web site:** http://www.mondadori.it
Freq: Weekly; **Circ:** 800,000
Editor-in-Chief: Alfonso Signorini
Profile: Chi is a women's magazine, featuring stories, interviews, exclusive photographs and prestigious anticipations on the lives of the protagonists from the worlds of television, politics and sport, in a tone that avoids scandal and gossip. It also pays a great deal of attention to the quality of photography and exclusive stories. Chi is one of the groundbreaking editorial formulas of recent years and has a constantly growing circulation. From its launch, Chi established its position thanks to an original formula which, together with personalities in their "natural surroundings", has consistently given space also to fashion and beauty.
Language(s): Italian
CONSUMER: WOMEN'S INTEREST CONSUMER MAGAZINES: Women's Interest

CHI RM
1784416I74A-415
Editorial: Via Sicilia, 136, 00187 ROMA
Tel: 06 47497381 **Fax:** 06 47497414
Email: chiposta@mondadori.it **Web site:** http://www.mondadori.it
Freq: Weekly; **Circ:** 800,000
Profile: Regional office of the publication CHI focussing on gossip.
Language(s): Italian
CONSUMER: WOMEN'S INTEREST CONSUMER MAGAZINES: Women's Interest

CHIESA OGGI - ARCHITETTURA E COMUNICAZIONE
13106I4A-40
Editorial: Via Settembrini 11, 20124 MILANO
Tel: 02 67495263 **Fax:** 02 67495333
Email: chiesaoggi@dibaio.com **Web site:** http://www.dibaio.com
Freq: Monthly; **Circ:** 70,000
Editor-in-Chief: Giuseppe Maria Jonghi Lavarini
Profile: Magazine specialising in international and national church architecture, includes features on conservation, renovation and maintenance.
Language(s): Italian
BUSINESS: ARCHITECTURE & BUILDING: Architecture

LA CHIMICA E L'INDUSTRIA
13275I13-25
Editorial: Via B. De Rolandi, 15, 20156 MILANO MI
Tel: 02 324434 **Fax:** 02 39257668
Email: edichim@tin.it **Web site:** http://www.promediapublishing.it
Freq: Monthly; **Circ:** 6,800
Editor: Alessandro Bignami; **Editor-in-Chief:** Ferruccio Trifiro'
Profile: Journal of RICH (International Chemistry Exhibition) and MAC (Chemical Instrumentation Exhibition) covering chemical instrumentation and laboratory equipment, plant and technology.
Language(s): Italian
BUSINESS: CHEMICALS

CHIMICA OGGI
13274I13-23
Editorial: Viale Brianza, 22, 20127 MILANO
Tel: 02 26809375 **Fax:** 02 2847226
Email: info@teknoscienze.com **Web site:** http://www.teknoscienze.com
Freq: 6 issues yearly; **Circ:** 7,000
Editor: Gayle De Maria; **Editor-in-Chief:** Carla Scesa
Profile: International journal focusing on chemistry, pharmaceuticals, disinfectants, soaps, detergents and biotechnology.
Language(s): English
Readership: Read by managers in biotechnology in the chemical, pharmaceutical and food industry.
BUSINESS: CHEMICALS

CHIP
13169I5B-7
Editorial: Viale Forlanini, 23, 20134 MILANO
Tel: 02 45472867 **Fax:** 02 45472869
Email: chip@playmediacompany.it **Web site:** http://www.playmediacompany.it
Freq: Monthly; **Circ:** 60,000
Editor: Silvia Leoni
Profile: Magazine containing news of developments concerning hard- and software.
Language(s): Italian
ADVERTISING RATES:
Full Page Colour .... EUR 9000.00
BUSINESS: COMPUTERS & AUTOMATION: Data Processing

CHITARRE
14325I76D-70
Editorial: Via Monte Tomatico, 1, 00141 ROMA
Tel: 06 86219922 **Fax:** 06 86219788
Email: redazione.chitarre@gruppoaccordo.it **Web site:** http://www.chitarre.com
Freq: Monthly; **Circ:** 30,000
Editor-in-Chief: Biraghi Alberto
Profile: Magazine focusing on guitars, music and playing techniques.
Language(s): Italian
Readership: Aimed at guitarists aged 15 to 45 years.
CONSUMER: MUSIC & PERFORMING ARTS: Music

CHRONO WORLD
13771I52B-5
Editorial: Circonvallazione Nomentana, 212/214, 00162 ROMA **Tel:** 06 8606129 **Fax:** 06 8606324
Email: chrono@argoeditore.net **Web site:** http://www.argoeditore.net
Freq: Monthly; **Circ:** 60,000
Editor: Fabrizio Giussani; **Editor-in-Chief:** Renato Giussani
Profile: Magazine concentrating on watch and clock marketing, technology and design.
Language(s): Italian
Readership: Aimed at manufacturers, retailers, suppliers and enthusiasts.
BUSINESS: GIFT TRADE: Clocks & Watches

CIAK
14307I76A-23
Editorial: Palazzo Mondadori - Via Mondadori, 1, 20090 SEGRATE MI **Tel:** 02 75423882
Fax: 0275423880
Email: ciak@mondadori.it **Web site:** http://www.mondadori.it
Freq: Monthly; **Circ:** 139,000
Editor-in-Chief: Piera Detassis
Profile: Magazine containing information about the cinema, including new releases and star interviews.
Language(s): Italian
Readership: Read by cinema enthusiasts.
CONSUMER: MUSIC & PERFORMING ARTS: Cinema

CIAK RM
1784782I76A-136
Editorial: Via Sicilia 136, 00187 ROMA
Tel: 06 47497376 **Fax:** 06 47497413
Email: ciak@mondadori.it **Web site:** http://www.mondadori.it
Freq: Monthly; **Circ:** 139,000
Language(s): Italian
CONSUMER: MUSIC & PERFORMING ARTS: Cinema

CICLISMO
14379I77C-48
Editorial: Via Don Luigi Sturzo 7, 20016 PERO MI
Tel: 0238085340 **Fax:** 02 38010393
Email: ciclismo@edisport.it **Web site:** http://www.ciclismo.it
Freq: Monthly; **Circ:** 68,000
Editor-in-Chief: Massimo Vallini
Profile: Magazine covering cycling as a sport and as a hobby, with particular focus on the amateur cyclist and technical innovations.
Language(s): Italian
CONSUMER: MOTORING & CYCLING: Cycling

CICLOTURISMO GRAN FONDO TECNICHE E RAID
14380I77C-50
Editorial: Via Capogrossi, 50, 00155 ROMA RM
Tel: 06 2285728 **Fax:** 06 2285915
Email: redazione@ct-cicloturismo.it **Web site:** http://www.compagniaeditoriale.it
Freq: Monthly; **Circ:** 55,000
Editor-in-Chief: Sergio Neri
Profile: Bicycling magazine with adventure and technical news. Also includes articles covering tourism, ecology and environmental problems.
Language(s): Italian
Readership: Read by young people who enjoy cycling.
CONSUMER: MOTORING & CYCLING: Cycling

CINEFORUM
14308I76A-30
Editorial: Via Pignolo 123, 24121 BERGAMO
Tel: 035361361 **Fax:** 035341255
Email: info@cineforum.it **Web site:** http://www.cineforum.it
Freq: Monthly; **Circ:** 5,000
Editor-in-Chief: Adriano Piccardi
Profile: Magazine published by the Italian Cinema Federation.
Language(s): Italian
CONSUMER: MUSIC & PERFORMING ARTS: Cinema

CIOCCOLATA & C.
14237I74P-60
Editorial: Via Pisacane, 16, 20129 MILANO
Tel: 02 70100135 **Fax:** 02 70102517
Email: info@cioccoweb.it **Web site:** http://www.cioccoweb.it
Freq: Quarterly; **Circ:** 60,000
Editor: Paola Giaculli; **Editor-in-Chief:** Mauro Giaculli
Profile: Magazine covering everything to do with chocolate from art and eroticism to health and the history of chocolate. Also includes classic recipes, the secrets of top celebrity chefs and articles on associated products such as coffee and ice cream.
Language(s): Italian
CONSUMER: WOMEN'S INTEREST CONSUMER MAGAZINES: Food & Cookery

CIOE'
14185I74F-30
Editorial: c/o Emmei - Via Guido Reni 33, 00196 ROMA RM **Tel:** 0645615060
Email: cioe@emmei.info **Web site:** http://www.cioe.it
Freq: Weekly; **Circ:** 150,000
Editor: Linda Maurizi; **Editor-in-Chief:** Marco Iafrate
Profile: Magazine focusing on the world of music and entertainment. Also covers school, family life, love and friendship, and photo stories.
Language(s): Italian
Readership: Aimed at teenagers.
CONSUMER: WOMEN'S INTEREST CONSUMER MAGAZINES: Teenage

CIOE' GIRL
14186I74F-35
Editorial: C/O Emmei - Via Guido Reni 33, 00196 ROMA RM **Tel:** 0645615060
Email: cioe@emmei.info
Freq: 6 issues yearly; **Circ:** 40,000
Editor-in-Chief: Marco Iafrate
Profile: Magazine covering fashion, beauty, love, friendship, school, family matters, music and entertainment.
Language(s): Italian
Readership: Aimed at teenage girls.
CONSUMER: WOMEN'S INTEREST CONSUMER MAGAZINES: Teenage

CITTA' NUOVA
14074I73-42
Editorial: Via degli Scipioni 265, 00192 ROMA
Tel: 06 3203620 **Fax:** 06 3219909
Email: segr.rivista@cittanuova.it **Web site:** http://www.cittanuova.it
Freq: 24 issues yearly; **Circ:** 70,000
Profile: General information magazine containing news, politics, customs, dialogue, art, family and youth sections.
Language(s): Italian
CONSUMER: NATIONAL & INTERNATIONAL PERIODICALS

IL CITTADINO LODI
14039I67B-2200
Editorial: Via Gorini, 34, 26900 LODI
Tel: 0371 544200 **Fax:** 0371 544201
Email: redazione@ilcittadino.it **Web site:** http://www.ilcittadino.it
Freq: Daily; **Circ:** 49,000
Editor-in-Chief: Ferruccio Pallavera
Language(s): Italian
REGIONAL DAILY & SUNDAY NEWSPAPERS: Regional Daily Newspapers

CITY PROJECT
1785275I4A-111
Editorial: Via A. Tadino, 25, 20124 MILANO
Tel: 02 36584135
Email: laura.dellabadia@delettera.it **Web site:** http://www.delettera.it
Freq: 6 issues yearly; **Circ:** 90,000
Editor-in-Chief: Ivan De Lettera
Profile: Magazine focussing on project and planning, architecture and urban design as well as the communication aspect in the sector.
Language(s): Italian
BUSINESS: ARCHITECTURE & BUILDING: Architecture

LA CIVILTA' CATTOLICA
14489I87-30
Editorial: Via di Porta Pinciana 1, 00187 ROMA
Tel: 06 6979201 **Fax:** 06 69792022
Email: civcatt@laciviltacattolica.it **Web site:** http://www.laciviltacattolica.it
Freq: 24 issues yearly; **Circ:** 14,000
Editor-in-Chief: Gianpaolo Salvini
Profile: Catholic publication concerning contemporary religious, cultural, social, political and economical issues.
Language(s): Italian
Readership: Aimed at the Catholic community.
CONSUMER: RELIGIOUS

CIVILTA' DEL BERE
13232I9A-3
Editorial: Via Ciro Menotti 11/D, 20129 MILANO MI
Tel: 02 76110303 **Fax:** 02 7496183
Email: redazione@civiltadelbere.com **Web site:** http://www.civiltadelbere.com
Freq: 6 issues yearly; **Circ:** 50,000
Editor: Alessandro Torcoli
Profile: Journal containing information about the drinks industry. Includes information about quality control.
Language(s): Italian
Readership: Read by drinks manufacturers, importers, bottlers, ADA hotel managers, AIS wine waiters and AIBES barmen.
BUSINESS: DRINKS & LICENSED TRADE: Drinks, Licensed Trade, Wines & Spirits

CLASS
13279I86C-35
Editorial: Via Burigozzo 5, 20122 MILANO
Tel: 02 582191 **Fax:** 02 58317429
Web site: http://www.class.it
Freq: Monthly; **Circ:** 85,000
Editor: Giorgio Angeletti; **Editor-in-Chief:** Paolo Panerai
Profile: Magazine focusing on men's health, travelling, leisure and habits.
Language(s): Italian
Readership: Aimed at men.
ADVERTISING RATES:
Full Page Colour .... EUR 38220.00
CONSUMER: ADULT & GAY MAGAZINES: Men's Lifestyle Magazines

CLEO'
14187I74F-40
Editorial: c/o Emmei - Via Guido Reni 33, 00196 ROMA **Tel:** 0645615060
Email: magazine@emmei.info
Freq: 6 issues yearly; **Circ:** 40,000
Editor-in-Chief: Marco Iafrate
Profile: Magazine covering fashion, health and beauty.
Language(s): Italian
Readership: Aimed at girls aged between 14 and 18 years.
CONSUMER: WOMEN'S INTEREST CONSUMER MAGAZINES: Teenage

LA CLESSIDRA
13772I52B-10
Editorial: Via Pietro Maestri, 3, 00191 ROMA
Tel: 06 3295642 **Fax:** 06 3295624
Email: editorial.office@sothis.net **Web site:** http://www.sothis.net
Freq: 6 issues yearly
Editor-in-Chief: Fabrizio Rinversi
Profile: Official publication of the Italian Association of Watch and Clock Wholesalers.
Language(s): Italian
Readership: Read by wholesalers and retailers.
BUSINESS: GIFT TRADE: Clocks & Watches

CLUB 3 - VIVERE IN ARMONIA
14232I74Q-254
Editorial: Via Giotto, 36, 20145 MILANO
Tel: 02 48010498 **Fax:** 02 48021801
Email: club3@stpauls.it **Web site:** http://www.club3.it
Freq: Monthly; **Circ:** 120,000
Editor-in-Chief: Giuseppe Altamore
Profile: Magazine containing news, information, articles and advice on finance, culture, travel, pastimes and related topics.
Language(s): Italian
Readership: Aimed at middle-aged and elderly people.
CONSUMER: WOMEN'S INTEREST CONSUMER MAGAZINES: Lifestyle

COLLANA CREAIDEE
713451I74E-40
Editorial: Via Fornari, 8, 20146 MILANO
Tel: 02 4073270 **Fax:** 02 4073270
Email: info@idee-on-line.it **Web site:** http://www.idee-on-line.it
Freq: Quarterly; **Circ:** 30,000
Editor-in-Chief: Patrizia Rognoni
Profile: Magazine containing information about creativity and hobbies.
Language(s): English; French; Italian
Readership: Aimed at women.
CONSUMER: WOMEN'S INTEREST CONSUMER MAGAZINES: Crafts

COLLEZIONI TRENDS
1655348I47A-322
Editorial: Strada Curtatona 5/2, 41125 MODENA
Tel: 059412432 **Fax:** 059412623
Email: giulia.bulgarelli@logos.info **Web site:** http://www.collezionionline.com
Freq: Quarterly; **Circ:** 17,000
Profile: Magazine covering fabrics, yarns, knitwear and accessories; includes trends and fashion.
Language(s): English; Italian
Readership: Aimed at people in fashion production and related professions.
BUSINESS: CLOTHING & TEXTILES

COLORE & HOBBY 13323I16A-30
Editorial: Viale Romagna 71, 20161 MILANO
Tel: 02 36524496 **Fax:** 02 70602845
Email: info@contexto.it **Web site:** http://www.edipubblicita.it
Freq: Monthly; **Circ:** 12,500
Editor-in-Chief: Vieri Barsotti
Profile: Magazine concerning painting and decorating, hardware and building materials.
Language(s): Italian
Readership: Aimed at professional decorators, DIY managers and enthusiasts.
BUSINESS: DECORATING & PAINT

COLTURE PROTETTE 13486I26D-10
Editorial: Via Goito, 13, 40126 BOLOGNA
Tel: 051 6575857 **Fax:** 051 6575856
Email: redazione.edagricole@ilsole24ore.com **Web site:** http://www.agricoltura24.com
Freq: Monthly; **Circ:** 7,400
Editor-in-Chief: Elia Zamboni
Profile: Magazine about horticulture and cultivation.
Language(s): Italian
Readership: Aimed at gardening professionals.
BUSINESS: GARDEN TRADE: Garden Trade Horticulture

COME RISTRUTTURARE LA CASA 714849I42A-10
Editorial: Via Giardini 472 Scala L, 41100 MODENA
Tel: 059352324 **Fax:** 059352324
Email: redazione@gardenpictures.it
Freq: 6 issues yearly; **Circ:** 120,000
Editor-in-Chief: Antonio Greco
Profile: Magazine focusing on new ideas and products for home construction.
Language(s): Italian
Readership: Read by architects and project designers.
BUSINESS: CONSTRUCTION

COME STAI 14208I74G-30
Editorial: Corso di Porta Nuova, 3/a, 20121 MILANO
Tel: 0263675300 **Fax:** 02 63675519
Email: comestai@casaeditriceuniverso.com
Freq: Monthly
Editor-in-Chief: Monica Sori
Profile: Magazine giving advice on fitness and health.
Language(s): Italian
CONSUMER: WOMEN'S INTEREST CONSUMER MAGAZINES: Slimming & Health

COMMERCIO IDROTERMOSANITARIO 13089I3B-20
Editorial: Via Eritrea, 21, 20157 MILANO
Tel: 02 39090233 **Fax:** 02 39090331
Email: commercio.its@tecnichenuove.com **Web site:** http://www.tecnichenuove.com
Freq: 6 issues yearly
Editor-in-Chief: Giuseppe Nardella
Profile: Magazine providing information about the heating, sanitation and ventilation industries. Covers production, distribution, operation of appliances and related economic issues and regulations in Europe and throughout the world.
Language(s): Italian
Readership: Aimed at wholesalers, retailers, plumbers and heating and ventilation engineers.
BUSINESS: HEATING & VENTILATION: Industrial Heating & Ventilation

COMMERCIO INTERNAZIONALE 13297I14C-27
Editorial: Strada 1 Palazzo F 6, 20090 MILANOFIORI ASSAGO MI **Tel:** 0282476873 **Fax:** 0282476800
Email: rivista.commerciointernazionale.ipsoa@wki.it
Web site: http://www.ipsoa.it/comintonline
Freq: 24 issues yearly; **Circ:** 14,000
Editor-in-Chief: Giulietta Lemmi
Profile: Magazine focusing on international commerce, finance, contracts, customs, tax and law.
Language(s): Italian
Readership: Read by export and sales managers, accountants, bankers, tax and legal advisers.
BUSINESS: COMMERCE, INDUSTRY & MANAGEMENT: International Commerce

COMPOARREDO 704686I23A-11_50
Editorial: Via G. Rossetti, 9, 20145 MILANO
Tel: 02 48007449 **Fax:** 02 48007493
Email: staffedi@staffedit.it **Web site:** http://www.staffedit.it
Freq: Quarterly; **Circ:** 7,500
Editor-in-Chief: Renato Pisaniello
Profile: International magazine containing information on components and accessories for the furniture industry.
Language(s): English; Italian
BUSINESS: FURNISHINGS & FURNITURE

COMPOLUX 13330I17-20
Editorial: Via G. Rossetti, 9, 20145 MILANO
Tel: 02 48007449 **Fax:** 02 48007493
Email: staffedi@staffedit.it **Web site:** http://www.staffedit.it
Freq: 6 issues yearly; **Circ:** 7,500
Editor-in-Chief: Renato Pisaniello
Profile: International magazine about the lighting industry.
Language(s): Italian
BUSINESS: ELECTRICAL

COMPUTER ARTS 752966I5D-6
Editorial: Via Brescia, 39, 20063 CERNUSCO SUL NAVIGLIO **Tel:** 02 926263172 **Fax:** 02 926263147
Web site: http://www.sprea.it
Freq: Monthly
Profile: Magazine focusing on the graphics facility for PCs.
Language(s): Italian
Readership: Read by home PC owners.
BUSINESS: COMPUTERS & AUTOMATION: Personal Computers

COMPUTER DEALER & VAR 13170I5B-11
Editorial: Via Confalonieri, 36, 20124 MILANO MI
Tel: 025660931 02 56609380 **Fax:** 0256609344
Email: redazione.cdv@matedizioni.it **Web site:** http://www.cdvweb.it
Freq: Monthly
Editor-in-Chief: Roberto Negrini
Profile: Magazine about computer and software retailing.
Language(s): Italian
ADVERTISING RATES:
Full Page Colour .... EUR 4700.00
BUSINESS: COMPUTERS & AUTOMATION: Data Processing

COMPUTER IDEA 628712I5D-12
Editorial: Via Riccardo Lombardi 19/4, 20153 MILANO **Tel:** 02 57429001 **Fax:** 0257429102
Email: redazione@computer-idea.it **Web site:** http://www.computer-idea.it
Freq: 24 issues yearly; **Circ:** 100,000
Editor-in-Chief: Andrea Maselli
Profile: Magazine containing information about PCs.
Language(s): Italian
Readership: Read by people who want to improve their computing skills and by those wanting to purchase a computer for home use.
ADVERTISING RATES:
Full Page Colour .... EUR 9363.00
BUSINESS: COMPUTERS & AUTOMATION: Personal Computers

COMPUTER MAGAZINE 752960I5C-50
Editorial: Via Brescia, 39, 20063 CERNUSCO SUL NAVIGLIO MI **Tel:** 02 926263163 **Fax:** 02 926263147
Email: marcoschiaffino@sprea.it **Web site:** http://www.sprea.it
Freq: Monthly; **Circ:** 110,000
Editor-in-Chief: Luca Sprea
Profile: Magazine containing information on personal computers and DVD applications.
Language(s): Italian
Readership: Aimed at professional users.
ADVERTISING RATES:
Full Page Colour .... EUR 12500.00
BUSINESS: COMPUTERS & AUTOMATION: Professional Personal Computers

COMPUTERWORLD ITALIA 13172I5B-15
Editorial: Via Messina, 47, 20154 MILANO MI
Email: marco_tennyson@cwi.it **Web site:** http://www.cwi.it
Freq: Monthly; **Circ:** 28,000
Editor-in-Chief: Marco Tennyson
Profile: Publication covering hardware, software, personal computer applications and small and medium-sized systems.
Language(s): Italian
Readership: Aimed at professionals within the computing field.
ADVERTISING RATES:
Full Page Colour .... EUR 12100.00
BUSINESS: COMPUTERS & AUTOMATION: Data Processing

COMUNI D'ITALIA 13518I32A-15
Editorial: c/o CPO Rimini - via Coriano, 58, 47900 RIMINI **Tel:** 0541 628111 **Fax:** 0541 622100
Email: abbonamenti@maggioli.it **Web site:** http://www.periodicimaggioli.it
Freq: Monthly; **Circ:** 6,000
Editor-in-Chief: Manlio Maggioli
Profile: Journal containing reference information about municipal policies, administration and legal matters.
Language(s): Italian
Readership: Read by managers and administrators working in local authorities.
BUSINESS: LOCAL GOVERNMENT, LEISURE & RECREATION: Local Government

COMUNICANDO 634468I41A-30
Editorial: Via Stromboli, 18, 20144 MILANO
Tel: 02 48516207 **Fax:** 02 43400509
Email: redazione@comunicandoweb.com **Web site:** http://www.comunicandoweb.com
Freq: Monthly; **Circ:** 12,000
Editor-in-Chief: Susanna Bonati
Profile: Magazine focusing on traditional and digital printing, includes a review of a wide range of materials used for wrapping, packaging and used as containers.
Language(s): Italian
Readership: Read by printing professionals and designers.
BUSINESS: PRINTING & STATIONERY: Printing

CONFEZIONE 13700I47A-12
Editorial: Via Eritrea, 21, 20157 MILANO
Tel: 02 39090297 **Fax:** 02 39090331
Email: confezione@tecnichenuove.com **Web site:** http://www.tecnichenuove.com
Freq: 6 issues yearly; **Circ:** 7,000
Editor-in-Chief: Giuseppe Nardella
Profile: Magazine covering design, manufacture and technology in the clothing and hosiery industries.
Language(s): Italian
Readership: Aimed at manufacturers of clothes, including fashion items, lingerie, work and sports clothes, bridal and evening gowns.
BUSINESS: CLOTHING & TEXTILES

CONFIDENZE 14097I74A-120
Editorial: Palazzo Mondadori, 20090 SEGRATE MI
Tel: 02 75421 **Fax:** 02 75422806
Web site: http://www.mondadori.it
Freq: Weekly
Editor: Angelina Spinoni; **Editor-in-Chief:** Patrizia Avoledo
Profile: Magazine about fashion, beauty, health, cooking and the home.
Language(s): Italian
Readership: Aimed at women.
CONSUMER: WOMEN'S INTEREST CONSUMER MAGAZINES: Women's Interest

CONGRESS TODAY & INCENTIVE TRAVEL 13080I2C-25
Editorial: Via C. Pisacane 26, 20129 MILANO
Tel: 0229419135 **Fax:** 02 29419056
Email: congresstoday@edicip.it **Web site:** http://www.congresstoday.it
Freq: 6 issues yearly; **Circ:** 10,000
Editor-in-Chief: Lanfranco Bonisolli
Profile: Magazine about meetings, congresses and business travel.
Language(s): Italian
BUSINESS: COMMUNICATIONS, ADVERTISING & MARKETING: Conferences & Exhibitions

CONQUISTE DEL LAVORO 13313I14L-30
Editorial: Via Po, 22, 00198 ROMA **Tel:** 06 8473430
Fax: 06 8541233
Email: conquiste_lavoro@cisl.it **Web site:** http://www.conquistedellavoro.it
Freq: Daily; **Circ:** 95,000
Editor-in-Chief: Francesco Guzzardi
Profile: Newspaper of the Italian Workers' Trade Union, with business, industrial and economic news and articles.
Language(s): Italian
ADVERTISING RATES:
Full Page Colour .... EUR 3958.64
BUSINESS: COMMERCE, INDUSTRY & MANAGEMENT: Trade Unions

CONSUMATORI 14150I74C-145
Editorial: Viale Aldo Moro, 16, 40127 BOLOGNA
Tel: 051 6316911 **Fax:** 051 6316908
Email: redazione@consumatori.coop.it **Web site:** http://www.consumatori.e-coop.it
Freq: Monthly; **Circ:** 2,481,645
Editor-in-Chief: Dario Guidi
Profile: Magazine about consumer matters. Includes articles concerning food, health, the environment and the activities of Consumers Cooperative Italia.
Language(s): Italian
Readership: Read by members of the Consumers Cooperative.
CONSUMER: WOMEN'S INTEREST CONSUMER MAGAZINES: Home & Family

CONTATTO ELETTRICO 13331I17-101
Editorial: Via Teocrito, 47, 20128 MILANO
Tel: 02 252071 **Fax:** 02 27000692
Email: contattoelettrico@bema.it **Web site:** http://www.bema.it/contattoelettrico
Freq: Monthly; **Circ:** 12,000
Editor-in-Chief: Gisella Bertini Malgarini
Profile: Magazine about the electrical trade and equipment.
Language(s): Italian
BUSINESS: ELECTRICAL

CONVEGNI INCENTIVE & COMUNICAZIONE 13081I2C-3
Editorial: Via Ezio Biondi, 1, 20154 MILANO MI
Tel: 02 349921 **Fax:** 02 34992290
Email: convegni@convegni.it **Web site:** http://www.convegni.it
Freq: 6 issues yearly; **Circ:** 9,500
Editor-in-Chief: Vittore Castellazzi
Profile: Magazine about congresses, conventions, meetings, venues and incentives.
Language(s): English; Italian
BUSINESS: COMMUNICATIONS, ADVERTISING & MARKETING: Conferences & Exhibitions

CORRERE 14286I75J-40
Editorial: Via Masaccio, 12, 20149 MILANO MI
Tel: 02 4815396 **Fax:** 02 4690907
Email: correre@sportivi.it **Web site:** http://www.correre.it
Freq: Monthly; **Circ:** 70,000
Editor-in-Chief: Orlando Pizzolato
Profile: Magazine about running, both as a pastime and professionally.
Language(s): Italian
CONSUMER: SPORT: Athletics

CORRIERE DEI TRASPORTI 13725I49A-20
Editorial: Piazza S. Silvestro 13 - Sala stampa italiana, 00141 ROMA RM **Tel:** 06 99330133
Fax: 0699330134
Email: redazione@editorialetrasporti.it **Web site:** http://www.corrieredeitrasporti.it
Freq: Weekly; **Circ:** 13,000
Editor-in-Chief: Paolo Li Donni
Profile: Pan-European tabloid newspaper covering land, sea and air communications and transportation logistics.
Language(s): Italian
BUSINESS: TRANSPORT

CORRIERE DELLA SERA 1793257I65A-214
Editorial: Via Solferino 28, 20121 MILANO
Tel: 02 6339 **Fax:** 02 62059668
Email: segretcor@rcs.it **Web site:** http://www.corriere.it
Freq: Daily; **Circ:** 686,813
Editor: Massimo Fracaro; **Editor-in-Chief:** Ferruccio De Bortoli
Profile: Broadsheet-sized evening newspaper containing national and international news and information on finance, economics, culture, society and sport.
Language(s): Italian
Readership: Read by a broad spectrum of the population, over half of whom live in Lombardia.
ADVERTISING RATES:
Full Page Mono .... EUR 113400.00
Full Page Colour .... EUR 147420.00
Mechanical Data: Type Area: 347x478 mm
NATIONAL DAILY & SUNDAY NEWSPAPERS: National Daily Newspapers

CORRIERE DELL'ARTE 1845432I84A-520
Editorial: Piazza Zara 3, 10133 TORINO
Tel: 0116312666 **Fax:** 0116317243
Email: corart@tin.it **Web site:** http://www.corrieredellarte.it
Freq: Weekly; **Circ:** 5,000
Editor-in-Chief: Virginia Colacino
Language(s): Italian
CONSUMER: THE ARTS & LITERARY: Arts

CORRIERE DELLO SPORT-STADIO 13962I65A-30
Editorial: Piazza Indipendenza, 11/B, 00185 ROMA RM **Tel:** 06 49921 **Fax:** 06 4992690
Email: info@corsport.it **Web site:** http://www.corrieredellosport.it
Freq: Daily; **Circ:** 534,000
Editor: Giuliano Riva; **Editor-in-Chief:** Alessandro Vocalelli
Profile: Broadsheet-sized newspaper focusing on all aspects of competitive sport.
Language(s): Italian
Readership: Readership includes a broad range of the Italian society with an interest in sport, half of whom live in the regions of Lazio and Campania.
NATIONAL DAILY & SUNDAY NEWSPAPERS: National Daily Newspapers

CORRIERE ECONOMIA (CORRIERE DELLA SERA) 1645506I74M-13
Editorial: Via Solferino 28, 20121 MILANO
Tel: 026339 **Fax:** 0262827604
Web site: http://www.corriere.it/Primo_Piano/Economia
Freq: Weekly; **Circ:** 860,000
Profile: Magazine focusing on personal finance.
Language(s): Italian
CONSUMER: WOMEN'S INTEREST CONSUMER MAGAZINES: Personal Finance

CORRIERE MEDICO 13808I56A-60
Editorial: Corso Venezia, 6, 20121 MILANO MI
Tel: 02 76003516 **Fax:** 02 76003678
Email: corriere.medico@medweb.it **Web site:** http://www.medweb.it
Freq: Weekly; **Circ:** 36,000
Editor-in-Chief: Silvano Marini
Profile: Journal covering hospital and health policy, social-security matters, medical articles and news.
Language(s): Italian
Readership: Aimed at members of the medical profession especially general practitioners.
BUSINESS: HEALTH & MEDICAL

CORRIERE SALUTE (CORRIERE DELLA SERA) 13982I65H-50
Editorial: Via Solferino, 28, 20121 MILANO
Tel: 02 6339 **Fax:** 02 62827033
Email: galbicoccoli@rcs.it **Web site:** http://www.corriere.it/Rubriche/Salute
Freq: Weekly; **Circ:** 860,000
Editor: Cristina D'Amico
Profile: Magazine concerning health and beauty.
Language(s): Italian
NATIONAL DAILY & SUNDAY NEWSPAPERS: National Colour Supplements

CORRIERE TRIBUTARIO 13055I1M-5
Editorial: Strada 1 Palazzo F. 6, 20090 MILANOFIORI ASSAGO MI **Tel:** 02 82476896 **Fax:** 02 82476600
Email: redazione.corrieretributario.ipsoa@wki.it **Web site:** http://www.ipsoa.it
Freq: Weekly; **Circ:** 20,000
Editor-in-Chief: Donatella Treu
Profile: Magazine containing information about tax and deeds of indemnity for businesses.
Language(s): Italian
Readership: Read by financial consultants, lawyers, magistrates, people working in banking, entrepreneurs and managers in small and large businesses.
BUSINESS: FINANCE & ECONOMICS: Taxation

IL CORRIERE VINICOLO 13433I21H-20
Editorial: Via S.Vittore al Teatro, 3, 20123 MILANO MI **Tel:** 02 7222281 **Fax:** 02 866226
Email: redazione@corrierevinicolo.com **Web site:** http://www.corrierevinicolo.com
Freq: Weekly; **Circ:** 25,000
Editor-in-Chief: Carlo Flamini
Profile: Magazine containing articles and advice about the culture of vines and production of wine.
Language(s): Italian
BUSINESS: AGRICULTURE & FARMING: Vine Growing

LA CORSA 14287I75J-80
Editorial: Via Winckelmann 2, 20146 MILANO
Tel: 0242419 1 **Fax:** 02 48953252
Email: redazione@lacorsa.it **Web site:** http://www.lacorsa.it
Freq: 6 issues yearly; **Circ:** 32,000
Editor-in-Chief: Walter Brambilla
Profile: Sporting publication covering medium and long distance running. Provides articles and reports on important international athletic events.
Language(s): Italian
Readership: Aimed at athletics enthusiasts.
CONSUMER: SPORT: Athletics

CORTEX 13888I56N-10
Editorial: Via Paleocapa, 7, 20121 MILANO
Tel: 02 88184 1 **Fax:** 02 881841302
Web site: http://www.elsevier.com/locate/cortex
Freq: Monthly; **Circ:** 900
Editor-in-Chief: Wubbo Tempel
Profile: International publication of the Association of Neurological Research. Focusing on the study of the relationships between the brain and higher nervous activity.
Language(s): Italian
Readership: Aimed at neurologists and psychologists, also psychiatrists and others interested in the analysis of human behaviour.
BUSINESS: HEALTH & MEDICAL: Mental Health

CORTINA AUTO - IL PIACERE DI GUIDARE 14386I77E-55
Editorial: c/o P.S.E. Srl Via Largo Cairoli, 2, 20121 MILANO **Tel:** 02 72000758 **Fax:** 02 8051429
Email: info@pseeditore.it **Web site:** http://www.pseeditore.it
Freq: Half-yearly; **Circ:** 60,000
Editor-in-Chief: Valerio Alfonzetti
Profile: Magazine concerning the Cortina car.
Language(s): Italian
Readership: Aimed at car enthusiasts.
CONSUMER: MOTORING & CYCLING: Club Cars

CORTINA MAGAZINE 763073I80-49_50
Editorial: Via Seragnoli, 13, 40138 BOLOGNA
Tel: 051 6026111 **Fax:** 051 6026150
Email: redazione@cortinamagazine.it **Web site:** http://www.cortinamagazine.it
Freq: Half-yearly; **Circ:** 80,000
Editor-in-Chief: Francesca Baccolini
Profile: Official magazine of Cortina Turismo containing information concerning the changes which have taken place in the city from past to present, includes regional news and skiing updates.
Language(s): Italian
Readership: Read by holidaymakers and residents.
CONSUMER: RURAL & REGIONAL INTEREST

COSE DI CASA 14151I74C-307
Editorial: Corso di Porta Nuova, 3/a, 20121 MILANO MI **Tel:** 02 63675403 **Fax:** 02 63675515
Email: segreteriared@cose-dicasa.com
Freq: Monthly; **Circ:** 600,000
Editor-in-Chief: Giuliana Maggioni
Profile: Magazine about home furnishings, decor and lifestyle.
Language(s): Italian
CONSUMER: WOMEN'S INTEREST CONSUMER MAGAZINES: Home & Family

COSMOPOLITAN 762778I74A-135
Editorial: Viale Sarca 235, 20126 MILANO
Tel: 0266191 **Fax:** 02 66193071
Email: cosmopolitan@hearst.it **Web site:** http://www.cosmopolitan.it
Freq: Monthly; **Circ:** 237,000
Editor-in-Chief: Annalisa Monfreda
Profile: Magazine covering fashion, beauty, health, travel and work.
Language(s): Italian
Readership: Aimed at young professional women.
ADVERTISING RATES:
Full Page Colour .... EUR 29925.00
CONSUMER: WOMEN'S INTEREST CONSUMER MAGAZINES: Women's Interest

COSTRUIRE 13615I42A-11
Editorial: Via G. Ventura, 5, 20134 MILANO
Tel: 02 21058 1 **Fax:** 02 21058316
Email: redazione@costruire.rcs.it **Web site:** http://www.costruire.it
Freq: Monthly; **Circ:** 24,000
Editor: Pietro Mezzi; **Editor-in-Chief:** Maurizio Favalli
Profile: Journal covering the production, economics and cultural aspects of the construction industry. Also includes articles on European architectural design and urban planning and a section on new products.
Language(s): Italian
BUSINESS: CONSTRUCTION

COSTRUIRE IN LATERIZIO 714848I4E-50
Editorial: Via C. Pisacane 1, 20016 PERO MI
Tel: 0230223002 **Fax:** 0230226025
Freq: 6 issues yearly; **Circ:** 18,000
Editor-in-Chief: Gianfranco Di Cesare
Profile: Magazine containing information and new ideas in lattice construction.
Language(s): Italian
BUSINESS: ARCHITECTURE & BUILDING: Building

COSTRUZIONI 13129I4E-60
Editorial: Via Conca Del Naviglio, 37, 20123 MILANO
Tel: 0289421350 **Fax:** 02 89421484
Email: costruzioni@fiaccola.it **Web site:** http://www.costruzioniweb.com
Freq: Monthly; **Circ:** 18,327
Editor-in-Chief: Lucia Edvige Saronni
Profile: Official journal of the Italian Construction Equipment Manufacturers' Union. Covers machinery, equipment, technology and new developments. Contains articles on the construction and maintenance of infrastructure.
Language(s): Italian
BUSINESS: ARCHITECTURE & BUILDING: Building

CROCEVIA 13540I32F-20
Editorial: c/o CPO Rimini - Via Coriano, 58, 47900 RIMINI **Tel:** 0541 628111 **Fax:** 0541 622778
Email: crocevia@maggioli.it **Web site:** http://www.periodicimaggioli.it
Freq: Monthly; **Circ:** 10,000
Editor-in-Chief: Manlio Maggioli
Profile: Journal of the Italian urban police force, covering administration, roads and health.
Language(s): Italian
BUSINESS: LOCAL GOVERNMENT, LEISURE & RECREATION: Police

CRONACA FILATELICA 14412I79C-70
Editorial: Via E. Fermi 24 - Loc. Osmannoro, 50019 SESTO FIORENTINO FI **Tel:** 05530321
Fax: 0553032250
Email: cfilatelica@edolimpia.it **Web site:** http://www.cronacafilatelica.it
Freq: Monthly; **Circ:** 16,500
Editor-in-Chief: Renato Cacciapuoti
Profile: Magazine about the study and collection of stamps and coins.
Language(s): Italian
Readership: Readership is mainly men aged between 16 and 65 years.
CONSUMER: HOBBIES & DIY: Philately

CRONACA NUMISMATICA 14418I79E-40
Editorial: Via Enrico Fermi 24 - Località Osmannoro, 50019 SESTO FIORENTINO FI **Tel:** 055 30321
Fax: 055 3032280
Email: cnumismatica@edolimpia.it **Web site:** http://www.cronacanumismatica.it
Freq: Monthly; **Circ:** 15,000
Editor-in-Chief: Renato Cacciapuoti
Profile: Magazine concerning coins. Includes information about auctions and exhibitions, expert opinions and news about coin collecting from all over the world.
Language(s): Italian
Readership: Read mainly by men between 16 and 65 years, interested in collecting coins.
CONSUMER: HOBBIES & DIY: Numismatics

LA CUCINA ITALIANA 14238I74P-90
Editorial: Piazza Aspromonte, 13, 20131 MILANO MI
Tel: 02 706421 **Fax:** 0270638544
Email: cucina@quadratum.it **Web site:** http://www.lacucinaitaliana.it
Freq: Monthly; **Circ:** 170,000
Profile: Culinary magazine featuring recipes; includes articles about nutrition.
Language(s): Italian
Readership: Read by people who enjoy experimenting with food.
CONSUMER: WOMEN'S INTEREST CONSUMER MAGAZINES: Food & Cookery

CUCINA LIGHT 1828867I74P-293
Editorial: Via Brescia 39, 20063 CERNUSCO SUL NAVIGLIO MI **Tel:** 02924321 **Fax:** 02 926263147
Web site: http://www.sprea.it
Freq: Monthly; **Circ:** 200,000
Editor-in-Chief: Luca Sprea
Language(s): Italian
CONSUMER: WOMEN'S INTEREST CONSUMER MAGAZINES: Food & Cookery

CUCINA MODERNA 14239I74P-120
Editorial: Palazzo Mondadori, 20090 SEGRATE MI
Tel: 0275422299 **Fax:** 0275422683
Email: cucinamoderna@mondadori.it **Web site:** http://www.mondadori.it
Freq: Monthly; **Circ:** 410,000
Editor-in-Chief: Laura Maragliano
Profile: Magazine focusing on modern cookery with the emphasis on quick and easy recipes.
Language(s): Italian
Readership: Aimed at families who want to spend as little time as possible in the kitchen.
CONSUMER: WOMEN'S INTEREST CONSUMER MAGAZINES: Food & Cookery

CUCINA NATURALE 14241I74P-148
Editorial: Via Eritrea, 21, 20157 MILANO MI
Tel: 02 39090324 **Fax:** 02 39090332
Email: cucina.naturale@tecnichenuove.com **Web site:** http://www.cucina-naturale.it
Freq: Monthly; **Circ:** 38,000
Profile: Magazine about natural food products. Includes reports on quality and safety, also features recipes and expert practical advice on achieving a healthy and balanced diet.
Language(s): Italian
Readership: Aimed at anybody interested in healthy eating.
CONSUMER: WOMEN'S INTEREST CONSUMER MAGAZINES: Food & Cookery

CUCINARE BENE 624548I74P-272
Editorial: Corso di Porta Nuova 3/A, 20121 MILANO MI **Tel:** 02 63675403 **Fax:** 02 63675515
Email: segreteria2@casaeditriceuniverso.com
Freq: Monthly; **Circ:** 400,000
Editor-in-Chief: Angela Costa
Profile: Magazine focusing on all aspects of Italian cookery, providing recipes and suggestions.
Language(s): Italian
Readership: Aimed at those with an interest in cookery.
CONSUMER: WOMEN'S INTEREST CONSUMER MAGAZINES: Food & Cookery

D LA REPUBBLICA DELLE DONNE (LA REPUBBLICA) 1784650I74A-416
Editorial: Via Nervesa 21, 20139 MILANO MI
Tel: 02 480981
Email: dmag@repubblica.it **Web site:** http://d.repubblica.it
Freq: Weekly; **Circ:** 860,000
Editor: Marco Mathieu; **Editor-in-Chief:** Cristina Guarinelli
Language(s): Italian
ADVERTISING RATES:
Full Page Colour .... EUR 55000.00
CONSUMER: WOMEN'S INTEREST CONSUMER MAGAZINES: Women's Interest

DAGENS INDUSTRI 1829039I73-541
Editorial: Via dell'Umiltà, 83/c, 00187 ROMA
Tel: 06675911 **Fax:** 0667591262
Web site: http://www.di.se
Freq: Daily; **Circ:** 400,000
Language(s): Italian
CONSUMER: NATIONAL & INTERNATIONAL PERIODICALS

DAGENS NYHETER 1829087I73-579
Editorial: Via dell'Umiltà 83/c, 00187 ROMA
Tel: 0667591273
Web site: http://www.dn.se
Freq: Daily; **Circ:** 400,000
Language(s): Italian
CONSUMER: NATIONAL & INTERNATIONAL PERIODICALS

D'ARS 14456I84A-60
Editorial: Giardino Aristide Calderini 3 - Via S.Agnese 3, 20123 MILANO **Tel:** 02 860290 **Fax:** 02 865909
Email: redazione@fondazionedars.it **Web site:** http://www.darsmagazine.it
Freq: Quarterly; **Circ:** 10,000
Editor-in-Chief: Grazia Chiesa
Profile: Magazine about contemporary art.
Language(s): Italian
CONSUMER: THE ARTS & LITERARY: Arts

DATA MANAGER 13173I5B-30
Editorial: Via L.B. Alberti, 10, 20149 MILANO
Tel: 02 33101836 **Fax:** 02 3450749
Email: redazione@datamanager.it **Web site:** http://www.datamanager.it
Freq: Monthly; **Circ:** 20,000
Editor-in-Chief: Loris Antonio Belle'
Profile: Magazine about information and communication technology.
Language(s): Italian
Readership: Aimed at IT professionals.
ADVERTISING RATES:
Full Page Colour .... EUR 6000.00
BUSINESS: COMPUTERS & AUTOMATION: Data Processing

DDN - DESIGN DIFFUSION NEWS 13115I4B-100
Editorial: Via Lucano, 3, 20135 MILANO
Tel: 02 5516109 **Fax:** 02 5456803
Email: ddn@designdiffusion.com **Web site:** http://www.designdiffusion.com
Freq: Monthly; **Circ:** 42,000
Editor-in-Chief: Rosa Maria Rinaldi
Profile: International magazine for the interior design field.
Language(s): Italian
BUSINESS: ARCHITECTURE & BUILDING: Interior Design & Flooring

DEBBY PIU' 14189I74F-55
Editorial: c/o Emmei - Via Guido Reni 33, 00196 ROMA RM **Tel:** 0645615060 **Fax:** 0645615232
Email: mgs@emmei.info
Freq: 6 issues yearly; **Circ:** 40,000
Editor-in-Chief: Marco Iafrate
Profile: Teenage magazine covering problems associated with love and sexuality.
Language(s): Italian
Readership: Read by girls aged between 12 and 18 years.
CONSUMER: WOMEN'S INTEREST CONSUMER MAGAZINES: Teenage

DEDALO 13130I4E-65
Editorial: Via San Maurilio, 21, 20123 MILANO MI
Tel: 02 8812951 **Fax:** 02 8056802
Email: dedalo@assimpredilance.it **Web site:** http://www.assimpredilance.it
Freq: 6 issues yearly; **Circ:** 20,000
Editor-in-Chief: Cecilia Bolognesi
Profile: Journal containing economic, social and technical information relevant to the building trade.
Language(s): Italian
BUSINESS: ARCHITECTURE & BUILDING: Building

DENTAL CADMOS 13859I56D-5
Editorial: Via Paleocapa, 7, 20121 MILANO
Tel: 02 881841 **Fax:** 02 88184342
Email: odontoiatria@elsevier.com **Web site:** http://www.elsevier.it
Freq: Monthly; **Circ:** 15,000
Editor-in-Chief: Emile Blomme
Profile: Magazine containing articles about clinical, scientific research and experimental aspects of odontostomatological specialisation. Written by leaders of Italian dentistry.
Language(s): English; Italian
BUSINESS: HEALTH & MEDICAL: Dental

IL DENTISTA MODERNO 13860I56D-20
Editorial: Via Eritrea, 21, 20157 MILANO
Tel: 02 39090341 **Fax:** 02 39090332
Email: ildentistamoderno@tecnichenuove.com **Web site:** http://www.tecnichenuove.com
Freq: Monthly; **Circ:** 20,000

Editor-in-Chief: Giuseppe Nardella
Profile: Publication containing scientific articles on dentistry. Also covers areas of general interest.
Language(s): Italian
Readership: Read by dentists and orthodontists.
BUSINESS: HEALTH & MEDICAL: Dental

DENTRO CASA
1785012I74C-313
Editorial: Via Volturno, 31, 25126 BRESCIA BS
Tel: 030 3730487 **Fax:** 030 3730368
Email: info@dentrocasa.it **Web site:** http://www.dentrocasa.it
Freq: Monthly; **Circ:** 43,500
Editor-in-Chief: GIANPAOLO Natali
Language(s): Italian
CONSUMER: WOMEN'S INTEREST CONSUMER MAGAZINES: Home & Family

DI PIU'
1683469I91E-1
Editorial: Corso Magenta, 55, 20145 MILANO
Tel: 02433131 **Fax:** 02 43313586
Email: settimanaledipiu@cairoeditore.it **Web site:** http://www.cairoeditore.it
Freq: Weekly; **Circ:** 1,000,000
Editor-in-Chief: Sandro Mayer
Profile: General interest magazine including features on fashion, sport, gossip, news and current affairs.
Language(s): Italian
Readership: Read by the general public.
CONSUMER: RECREATION & LEISURE: Lifestyle

DI PIU' - RM
1785127I82-267
Editorial: Via di Villa Emiliani, 46, 00197 ROMA
Tel: 068022544 **Fax:** 06 8022562
Email: fpiccioni@cairoeditore.it **Web site:** http://www.cairoeditore.it
Freq: Weekly; **Circ:** 1,000,000
Language(s): Italian
CONSUMER: CURRENT AFFAIRS & POLITICS

DI PIU' TV
1785181I76C-286
Editorial: Corso Magenta, 55, 20123 MILANO MI
Tel: 02 433131 **Fax:** 02 43313586
Email: settimanaledipiu@cairoeditore.it **Web site:** http://www.cairoeditore.it
Freq: Weekly; **Circ:** 1,000,000
Editor-in-Chief: Sandro Mayer
Language(s): Italian
CONSUMER: MUSIC & PERFORMING ARTS: TV & Radio

DIANA
14266I75F-120
Editorial: Via Enrico Fermi 24 - Località Osmannoro, 50019 SESTO FIORENTINO FI **Tel:** 0553032216
Fax: 0553032280
Email: diana@edolimpia.it **Web site:** http://www.diana.edolimpia.it
Freq: 26 issues yearly; **Circ:** 33,000
Editor-in-Chief: Pasquale Cacciapuoti
Profile: Magazine covering all aspects of hunting in Italy.
Language(s): Italian
Readership: Read by people with a keen interest in hunting.
CONSUMER: SPORT: Shooting

IL DIARIO DEL NORD MILANO
1846406I80-369
Editorial: Piazza Privata Caltagirone 75, 20099 SESTO SAN GIOVANNI **Tel:** 022440579
Fax: 0226263674
Email: redazionediarionm@gmail.com **Web site:** http://www.ainordmilano.com
Freq: 24 issues yearly; **Circ:** 100,000
Editor-in-Chief: Ettore Politi
Language(s): Italian
CONSUMER: RURAL & REGIONAL INTEREST

DIDATTICA DELLE SCIENZE E INFORM.SCUOLA
13925I62B-50
Editorial: Via Cadorna, 11, 25124 BRESCIA
Tel: 030 29931 **Fax:** 030 2993299
Email: dds@lascuola.it **Web site:** http://www.lascuola.it
Freq: Annual; **Circ:** 7,000
Profile: Journal concerning secondary school education.
Language(s): Italian
Readership: Aimed at secondary school science and maths teachers.
BUSINESS: CHURCH & SCHOOL EQUIPMENT & EDUCATION: Education Teachers

DIESEL
13514I19A-15
Editorial: Via Cassano d'Adda, 20, 20139 MILANO
Tel: 02 55230950 **Fax:** 02 55230592
Email: diesel@vadoetorno.com **Web site:** http://www.vadoetorno.com
Freq: Monthly; **Circ:** 11,120
Editor-in-Chief: Maurizio Cervetto
Profile: The only European magazine about the world of diesel engines. Specifically for OEM (original equipment machinery) applications. It includes automotive and driveline features also covers industrial, nautical and agricultural applications.
Language(s): English; French; German; Italian; Spanish
BUSINESS: ENGINEERING & MACHINERY

DIGITAL CAMERA MAGAZINE
1683468I85A-76
Editorial: Via Torino, 51, 20063 CERNUSCO SUL NAVIGLIO MI **Tel:** 02 924321 **Fax:** 02 926263147
Email: andrearotanodari@sprea.it **Web site:** http://www.sprea.it
Freq: Monthly
Editor-in-Chief: Luca Sprea
Profile: Magazine containing infornation and test reports about digital cameras.
Language(s): Italian
Readership: Read by amateur and professional photographers.
CONSUMER: PHOTOGRAPHY & FILM MAKING: Photography

DIGITAL VIDEO HOME THEATER
1637451I78B-351
Editorial: via Montenero 101-103, 00012 GUIDONIA MONTECELIO (RM) **Tel:** 06 872033
Fax: 06 87139141
Email: digitalvideo@newmediapro.eu **Web site:** http://www.digitalvideoht.it
Freq: Monthly
Editor-in-Chief: Mauro Neri
Profile: Magazine focusing on digital equipment and home theatre.
Language(s): Italian
Readership: Aimed at people with an interest in digital technology and potential buyers.
CONSUMER: CONSUMER ELECTRONICS: Video & DVD

DIMAGRIRE
1692645I74G-91
Editorial: Via L. Anelli 1, 20122 MILANO
Tel: 02 5845961 **Fax:** 02 58318162
Email: redazione.dimagrire@riza.it **Web site:** http://www.riza.it
Freq: Monthly; **Circ:** 130,000
Editor-in-Chief: Raffaele Morelli
Profile: Magazine containing information on slimming and health in general.
Language(s): Italian
Readership: Read by women of all ages.
CONSUMER: WOMEN'S INTEREST CONSUMER MAGAZINES: Slimming & Health

DIRIGENTI INDUSTRIA
13935I63-32
Editorial: Via Larga, 31, 20122 MILANO
Tel: 0258376237 **Fax:** 02 58307557
Email: rivista@aldai.it
Freq: Monthly; **Circ:** 26,000
Editor-in-Chief: Renato Garbarini
Profile: Journal of the Lombard Association of Industrial Company Directors.
Language(s): Italian
Readership: Read by managers in industry, employers organisations, advertising companies and political and economic centres in the Lombardy region.
BUSINESS: REGIONAL BUSINESS

DIRITTO DEL COMMERCIO INTERNAZIONALE
13644I44-65
Editorial: Via delle casaccie 1 - c/o Studio Bonelli, 16121 GENOVA **Tel:** 010 84621 **Fax:** 010 813849
Email: silvia.porta@beplex.com **Web site:** http://www.giuffre.it
Freq: Quarterly; **Circ:** 6,800
Editor-in-Chief: Franco Bonelli
Profile: Journal covering international commercial law. Includes details on joint-ventures, banking and financial problems, the protection of investments and EU legislation.
Language(s): Italian
Readership: Aimed at commercial lawyers.
BUSINESS: LEGAL

IL DIRITTO DELL'INFORMAZ. E INFORMATICA
13645I44-69_60
Editorial: Via Boezio 14, 00193 ROMA
Tel: 0632111680 **Fax:** 0632111692
Email: rivista@fondazionecalamandrei.it **Web site:** http://www.fondazionecalamandrei.it
Freq: 6 issues yearly; **Circ:** 1,400
Editor-in-Chief: Luca Boneschi
Profile: Journal about the law relating to mass media and informatics. Includes information on journalistic ethics, advertising laws and the protection of the rights of individuals against media intrusion.
Language(s): Italian
Readership: Aimed at lawyers in the field of media.
BUSINESS: LEGAL

DIRITTO & PRATICA DEL LAVORO
13640I44-60
Editorial: Strada 1 Palazzo F. 6, 20090 MILANOFIORI ASSAGO MI **Tel:** 02 824761 **Fax:** 02 82476436
Web site: http://www.ipsoa.it
Freq: Weekly; **Circ:** 16,000
Editor-in-Chief: Giulietta Lemmi
Profile: Journal about the practice of law relating to the workplace.
Language(s): Italian
BUSINESS: LEGAL

DIRITTO ED ECONOMIA DELL'ASSICURAZIONE
13649I44-72
Editorial: Ania Ari srl Via conservatorio,15, 20122 MILANO **Tel:** 02 723041
Email: giusy.rossi@aniaari.it **Web site:** http://www.irsa.it
Freq: Quarterly; **Circ:** 4,800
Editor-in-Chief: Aldo Frignani
Profile: Journal focusing on insurance legislation, includes articles about management and macroeconomics.
Language(s): Italian
Readership: Read by insurance inspectors, brokers, lawyers, lecturers and students.
BUSINESS: LEGAL

DISCIPLINA DEL COMMERCIO & DEI SERVIZI
13517I14R-12
Editorial: c/o CPO Rimini, Via Coriano, 58, 47900 RIMINI **Tel:** 0541 628111 **Fax:** 0541 622100
Email: servizio.clienti@maggioli.it **Web site:** http://www.periodicimaggioli.it
Freq: Quarterly; **Circ:** 6,000
Editor-in-Chief: Paolo Maggioli
Profile: Publication focusing on commerce, distribution and services.
Language(s): Italian
Readership: Read by commercial managers in regional and local authorities, members of chambers of commerce, police officials, business men and lawyers.
BUSINESS: COMMERCE, INDUSTRY & MANAGEMENT: Commerce Related

DM & COMUNICAZIONE
13063I2A-30
Editorial: Via Spallanzani 10, 20129 MILANO
Tel: 02 7422221 **Fax:** 02 74222223
Email: redazione@dmconline.it **Web site:** http://www.dmconline.it
Freq: 6 issues yearly; **Circ:** 5,000
Editor-in-Chief: Ugo Canonici
Profile: Magazine focusing on direct marketing, communication and technology.
Language(s): Italian
BUSINESS: COMMUNICATIONS, ADVERTISING & MARKETING

DOLCI
1784338I22A-56
Editorial: Strada Curtatona, 5/2, 41125 MODENA MO
Tel: 059 412432 **Fax:** 059 412623
Email: contattaci@dolciedolci.com **Web site:** http://www.dolciedolci.com
Freq: 6 issues yearly; **Circ:** 80,000
Editor-in-Chief: Antonio Vergara Meersohn
Language(s): Italian
BUSINESS: FOOD

DOMENICA QUIZ
1784354I79B-151
Editorial: Via A. Rizzoli 8, 20132 MILANO
Tel: 02 25843568 **Fax:** 02 25843101
Email: michela.gallo@rcs.it **Web site:** http://www.rcs.it
Freq: Weekly; **Circ:** 174,000
Editor-in-Chief: Giorgio Rivieccio
Language(s): Italian
CONSUMER: HOBBIES & DIY: Models & Modelling

DOMUS
13116I4B-110
Editorial: Via Gianni Mazzocchi 1/3, 20089 ROZZANO MI **Tel:** 02824721 **Fax:** 02 82472386
Email: redazione@domusweb.it **Web site:** http://www.domusweb.it
Freq: Monthly; **Circ:** 60,000
Editor-in-Chief: Joseph Grima
Profile: Magazine on international architecture, design, art and communication.
Language(s): English; Italian
BUSINESS: ARCHITECTURE & BUILDING: Interior Design & Flooring

DONNA & MAMMA
14172I74D-30
Editorial: Via Rizzoli, 8, 20132 MILANO
Tel: 02 50366687 **Fax:** 02 50366688
Email: elisabetta.larovere@sfera.rcs.it **Web site:** http://www.quimamme.it
Freq: Monthly; **Circ:** 168,000
Editor: Elisabetta Zocchi; **Editor-in-Chief:** Cristina De Grandis
Profile: Magazine containing articles on motherhood.
Language(s): Italian
CONSUMER: WOMEN'S INTEREST CONSUMER MAGAZINES: Child Care

DONNA IN FORMA (DONNA MODERNA)
1784703I74G-96
Editorial: Palazzo Mondadori, 20090 SEGRATE MI
Tel: 0275423022 **Fax:** 0275423118
Email: donnamoderna@mondadori.it **Web site:** http://www.donnamoderna.com
Freq: Monthly; **Circ:** 492,000
Editor-in-Chief: Patrizia Avoledo
Language(s): Italian
CONSUMER: WOMEN'S INTEREST CONSUMER MAGAZINES: Slimming & Health

DONNA MODERNA
14099I74A-150
Editorial: Palazzo Mondadori, 20090 SEGRATE MI
Tel: 02 75423022 **Fax:** 02 75423118
Email: donnamoderna@mondadori.it **Web site:** http://www.donnamoderna.com
Freq: Weekly; **Circ:** 492,000
Editor: Orsina Baroldi; **Editor-in-Chief:** Patrizia Avoledo
Profile: Magazine covering fashion, beauty, home, cooking, tourism and current affairs.
Language(s): Italian
Readership: Aimed at modern women.
ADVERTISING RATES:
Full Page Colour .... EUR 65650.00
CONSUMER: WOMEN'S INTEREST CONSUMER MAGAZINES: Women's Interest

DOVE
14505I89A-45
Editorial: Via Rizzoli 8, 20132 MILANO
Tel: 02 50956836 **Fax:** 02 50956878
Email: cinzia.bacchetta@rcs.it **Web site:** http://www.rcs.it
Freq: Monthly; **Circ:** 168,500
Editor-in-Chief: Carlo Montanaro
Profile: Magazine covering leisure activities and travel throughout the world.
Language(s): Italian
Readership: Aimed at people aged between 30 and 40 years.
CONSUMER: HOLIDAYS & TRAVEL: Travel

E VAI
14490I87-50
Editorial: Via Mose' Bianchi, 94, 20149 MILANO
Tel: 02 43822317 **Fax:** 02 43822397
Email: segreteriariviste@pimemilano.com **Web site:** http://www.pimemilano.com
Freq: Monthly
Editor-in-Chief: Gian Paolo Gualzetti
Profile: Official magazine of the Papal Institute for Foreign Missions. Includes historical articles, explanations of biblical text and information about missionary work. Also covers ecology and includes comic strips and reviews.
Language(s): Italian
Readership: Read by students aged 7 years and above.
CONSUMER: RELIGIOUS

ECO MOTORI
14353I77A-205
Editorial: Piazza A. Moro 33/A, 70122 BARI
Tel: 080 5242204 **Fax:** 080 5214073
Email: ecomotor@tin.it
Freq: Monthly; **Circ:** 45,000
Editor-in-Chief: Sebastiano Pugliese
Profile: Magazine containing financial, cultural, technical and tourist news covering automobiles, transport, aviation, motorcycling, industrial vehicles and motorboats.
Language(s): Italian
Readership: Aimed at businesses in the transport sector, professionals and directors.
CONSUMER: MOTORING & CYCLING: Motoring

ECONOMIA & MANAGEMENT
13025I1A-60
Editorial: Via Mecenate, 91, 20138 MILANO
Tel: 02 50951 **Fax:** 02 50952309
Email: economiaemanagement@rcs.it **Web site:** http://www.economiaemanagement.it
Freq: 6 issues yearly; **Circ:** 10,000
Editor-in-Chief: Gian Maria Fiameni
Profile: Journal about economics and management.
Language(s): Italian
Readership: Read by company directors and managers, professionals, graduates, university lecturers and researchers.
BUSINESS: FINANCE & ECONOMICS

ECONOMY
1645426I1A-248
Editorial: Palazzo Mondadori, 20090 SEGRATE MI
Tel: 02 7542992 **Fax:** 0275422334
Email: economy@mondadori.it **Web site:** http://www.mondadori.it
Freq: Weekly; **Circ:** 140,000
Editor: Gigi Radice; **Editor-in-Chief:** Giorgio Mule'
Profile: Magazine focusing on current affairs, investment and the economy.
Language(s): Italian
Readership: Aimed at decision makers, opinion formers and investors.
BUSINESS: FINANCE & ECONOMICS

L' EDUCATORE
13921I62A-60
Editorial: Via Mecenate, 91, 20138 MILANO
Tel: 02 50951
Email: educatore@rcs.it **Web site:** http://www.fabbriscuola.it/educatore
Freq: Monthly; **Circ:** 25,000
Editor-in-Chief: Massimiliano Galioni
Profile: Periodical covering pedagogy, didactics and professionalism in primary schools.

Language(s): Italian
BUSINESS: CHURCH & SCHOOL EQUIPMENT & EDUCATION: Education

EI-TECH 13626I43A-40
Editorial: Via Matteo Civitali, 51, 20148 MILANO
Tel: 02 48703201 Fax: 02 48703614
Email: eired@tin.it
Freq: Monthly; Circ: 12,000
Editor-in-Chief: Fiorenza Moradei
Profile: Magazine focusing on consumer electronics.
Language(s): Italian
Readership: Aimed at retailers, dealers and manufacturers.
BUSINESS: ELECTRICAL RETAIL TRADE

ELABORARE 1784659I77A-400
Editorial: Via della Bufalotta, 378, 00139 ROMA RM
Tel: 06 45231502 Fax: 06 45231598
Email: redazione@elaborare.org Web site: http://www.elaborare.com
Freq: Monthly; Circ: 85,000
Editor-in-Chief: Giovanni Mancini
Language(s): Italian
CONSUMER: MOTORING & CYCLING: Motoring

ELETTRIFICAZIONE 13333I17-30
Editorial: Via Lomellina, 33, 20133 MILANO
Tel: 02 70004542 Fax: 02 70005054
Email: info@editorialedelfino.it Web site: http://www.editorialedelfino.it
Freq: Monthly; Circ: 7,000
Editor-in-Chief: Andrea Ferriani
Profile: Journal about all aspects of the electrical industry.
Language(s): Italian
Readership: Aimed at installation engineers, designers and maintenance engineers.
BUSINESS: ELECTRICAL

ELETTRONICA OGGI 13355I18A-40
Editorial: S.S. del Sempione, 28, 20017 RHO - MI
Tel: 02 49976516 Fax: 02 49976570
Email: eo@fieramilanoeditore.it Web site: http://www.eo-web.it
Freq: Monthly; Circ: 7,756
Editor-in-Chief: Corrado Minnella
Profile: Journal about micro-electronics, components and applications. Covers market trends, research and development.
Language(s): Italian
Readership: Aimed at professionals in the electronics trade.
BUSINESS: ELECTRONICS

ELLE 14100I74A-165
Editorial: Viale Sarca, 235, 20126 MILANO MI
Tel: 02 66191 02 66193824 Fax: 02 66193071
Email: elle@hearst.it Web site: http://www.elle.it
Freq: Monthly; Circ: 140,000
Editor: Benedetta Dell'Orto; Editor-in-Chief: Danda Santini
Profile: Magazine containing articles on fashion, beauty, topical news, cinema, theatre, art, travel, cooking and the home.
Language(s): Italian
Readership: Aimed at young women.
CONSUMER: WOMEN'S INTEREST CONSUMER MAGAZINES: Women's Interest

ELLE DECOR 14154I74C-160
Editorial: Viale Sarca, 235, 20126 MILANO
Tel: 02 66191 Fax: 0266193862
Email: rsalvioni@hearst.it
Freq: Monthly; Circ: 81,000
Editor-in-Chief: Livia Peraldo Matton
Profile: Magazine containing prestigious interior design ideas.
Language(s): Italian
Readership: Read by home owners and interior design enthusiasts.
CONSUMER: WOMEN'S INTEREST CONSUMER MAGAZINES: Home & Family

L' ENERGIA ELETTRICA 13334I17-50
Editorial: Via Mauro Macchi 32, 20124 MILANO
Tel: 02 87389960 Fax: 0266989023
Email: redazione@federaeit.it Web site: http://www.federaeit.it
Freq: 6 issues yearly; Circ: 3,000
Editor-in-Chief: Massimo Gallanti
Profile: Publication about the production, transmission, distribution and utilisation of electricity.
Language(s): Italian
Readership: Read by technicians, researchers, utility managers and academics.
BUSINESS: ELECTRICAL

ENJOY 1846476I94X-405
Editorial: Via Pietrasanta, 14 Edificio 2, 20141 MILANO (MI) Tel: 02 55015253 Fax: 0255195851
Email: francescaf@mirata.it Web site: http://www.enjoymagazine.com
Freq: Quarterly; Circ: 200,000
Language(s): Italian
CONSUMER: OTHER CLASSIFICATIONS: Miscellaneous

L' ENOLOGO 13238I21H-25
Editorial: Via Privata Vasto 3, 20121 MILANO
Tel: 02 99785721 Fax: 0299785724
Email: info@assoenologi.it Web site: http://www.assoenologi.it
Freq: Monthly; Circ: 7,150
Editor-in-Chief: Giuseppe Martelli
Profile: Magazine of the Association of Italian Vintage Wine Producers. Provides technical, legal and commercial news.
Language(s): Italian
Readership: Read by winegrowers, producers and oenologists.
BUSINESS: AGRICULTURE & FARMING: Vine Growing

EO NEWS 13352I18A-28
Editorial: S.S. del Sempione, 28, 20017 RHO - MI
Tel: 02 49976516 Fax: 02 49976570
Email: eonews@fieramilanoeditore.it Web site: http://www.eo-news.it
Freq: Monthly
Editor-in-Chief: Corrado Minnella
Profile: News magazine with a broad coverage of the electronics industry. Covers instrumentation, components, PCB production and industrial automation product news.
Language(s): Italian
Readership: Aimed at professionals in the electronics industry.
BUSINESS: ELECTRONICS

L' ERBORISTA 13457I22F-65
Editorial: Via Eritrea, 21, 20157 MILANO
Tel: 02 390901 Fax: 02 39090332
Email: erborista@tecnichenuove.com Web site: http://www.tecnichenuove.com
Freq: Monthly; Circ: 5,000
Editor-in-Chief: Giuseppe Nardella
Profile: Magazine dealing with herbal preparations and by-products, beauty culture and organic food. Also features natural cosmetics.
Language(s): Italian
Readership: Read by herbalists and managers of health food shops.
BUSINESS: FOOD: Health Food

ESPANSIONE 762582I14A-52
Editorial: Via Gaetano Negri, 4, 20123 MILANO
Tel: 02 7218717 Fax: 02 7218724
Email: espansione@newspapermilano.it Web site: http://www.newspapermilano.it
Freq: Monthly; Circ: 250,000
Editor-in-Chief: Marco Gatti
Profile: Magazine focusing on finance and economics, providing information and practical solutions for management.
Language(s): Italian
Readership: Read by managers and financial investors.
BUSINESS: COMMERCE, INDUSTRY & MANAGEMENT

L' ESPRESSO 14444I82-40
Editorial: Via Cristoforo Colombo, 90, 00147 ROMA
Tel: 06 84781 Fax: 06 84787220
Email: espresso@espressoedit.it Web site: http://www.espressonline.it
Freq: Weekly; Circ: 490,000
Editor: Wlodek Goldkorn; Editor-in-Chief: Bruno Manfellotto
Profile: Magazine containing information on current affairs and politics.
Language(s): Italian
ADVERTISING RATES:
Full Page Colour .... EUR 50000.00
CONSUMER: CURRENT AFFAIRS & POLITICS

L' ESPRESSO MI 1784211I82-253
Editorial: Via Nervesa, 21, 20139 MILANO MI
Tel: 02 4818350 Fax: 024817000
Email: espressomilano@espressoedit.it Web site: http://www.espressonline.it
Freq: Weekly; Circ: 490,000
Editor: Enrico Arosio
Profile: Milan office of the publication L'ESPRESSO focussing on news, current affairs and politics.
Language(s): Italian
CONSUMER: CURRENT AFFAIRS & POLITICS

ESSECOME 13793I54C-50
Editorial: Via Pietro Miliani 7, 40132 BOLOGNA
Tel: 051 6419611 Fax: 051 6419620
Email: redazione.edis@securindex.com Web site: http://www.securindex.com
Freq: Monthly; Circ: 6,000
Editor-in-Chief: Monica Bertolo
Profile: Magazine focusing on security systems for buildings.
Language(s): Italian
Readership: Aimed at installers of security systems, wholesalers, insurers, distributors and security personnel in embassies, banks, commercial and industrial sector.
BUSINESS: SAFETY & SECURITY: Security

ESTETICA 13318I15A-50
Editorial: Via Cavour, 50, 10123 TORINO
Tel: 011 83921111 Fax: 011 8125661
Email: redazione.segreteria@estetica.it Web site: http://www.estetica.it
Freq: Monthly; Circ: 276,000
Editor-in-Chief: Roberto Pissimiglia
Profile: Magazine covering beauty, cosmetics and skin treatments.
Language(s): English; French; German; Italian; Spanish
Readership: Aimed at beauticians.
BUSINESS: COSMETICS & HAIRDRESSING: Cosmetics

ETIQUETTE 1845280I74Q-261
Editorial: Via delle Lame, 113 a, 40122 BOLOGNA
Tel: 051 5870750 Fax: 051 5870752
Email: info@etiquette.it Web site: http://www.etiquette.it
Freq: 6 issues yearly; Circ: 100,000
Editor-in-Chief: Simona Artanidi
Language(s): Italian
CONSUMER: WOMEN'S INTEREST CONSUMER MAGAZINES: Lifestyle

EUROSAT 13083I2D-30
Editorial: Via Pisacane 1, 20016 PERO MI
Tel: 02 30223002
Email: redazione.eurosat@ilsole24ore.com Web site: http://www.eurosat-online.it
Freq: Monthly; Circ: 90,000
Editor-in-Chief: Antonio Greco
Profile: Magazine about satellite television broadcasting with an emphasis on European and world markets. Includes reports of forthcoming exhibitions and tests on audio-visual and satellite products.
Language(s): Italian
BUSINESS: COMMUNICATIONS, ADVERTISING & MARKETING: Broadcasting

EVA 3000 14101I74A-417
Editorial: Viale Palermo, 13, 00184 ROMA RM
Tel: 06 48906778 Fax: 06 48907058
Email: eva3000@twistersrl.com
Freq: Weekly; Circ: 180,000
Editor-in-Chief: Luciano Regolo
Profile: Magazine covering the public and private lives of famous people from the world of show business, politics and sport.
Language(s): Italian
CONSUMER: WOMEN'S INTEREST CONSUMER MAGAZINES: Women's Interest

EXECUTIVE.IT 754203I14A-54
Editorial: Via Martiri Oscuri, 3, 20125 MILANO
Tel: 02 26148855 Fax: 02 26149333
Email: executive.it@soiel.it Web site: http://www.soiel.it
Freq: Monthly; Circ: 9,800
Editor-in-Chief: Chiaralba Bollini
Profile: Magazine containing advice and strategies related to IT and ICT.
Language(s): Italian
Readership: Read by managers of small and medium-sized companies.
BUSINESS: COMMERCE, INDUSTRY & MANAGEMENT

EXPORT MAGAZINE 13319I15A-58
Editorial: Via Romolo Gessi, 28, 20146 MILANO
Tel: 02 4239443 Fax: 02 4123405
Email: mteedizi@mteedizioni.it Web site: http://www.mteedizioni.it
Freq: Monthly; Circ: 20,000
Editor-in-Chief: Giuseppe Tirabasso
Profile: International magazine about perfume, cosmetics, costume jewellery, trichology, beauty, equipment and accessories.
Language(s): English
Readership: Aimed at professionals in the beauty and fashion industries. Importers/exporters, wholesalers, manufacturers, distributors and duty free buyers.
BUSINESS: COSMETICS & HAIRDRESSING: Cosmetics

FAI DA TE FACILE 14407I79A-50
Editorial: Via Vallemme 21, 20135 MILANO MI
Tel: 0143645037 Fax: 0143 645049
Email: faidatefacile@edibrico.it Web site: http://www.edibrico.it
Freq: 6 issues yearly; Circ: 250,000
Editor-in-Chief: Nicla De Carolis
Profile: Magazine providing information, advice and articles about DIY.
Language(s): Italian
Readership: Aimed primarily at men aged between 30 and 50 years.
CONSUMER: HOBBIES & DIY

FAMIGLIA CRISTIANA 14155I74C-165
Editorial: Via Giotto 36, 20145 MILANO
Tel: 02 48071 Fax: 02 48072778
Email: famigliacristiana@stpauls.it Web site: http://www.famigliacristiana.it
Freq: Weekly; Circ: 900,000
Editor: Renata Maderna; Editor-in-Chief: Antonio Sciortino
Profile: Publication containing topical news, current affairs and general information from a Christian point of view, includes a TV guide.
Language(s): Italian
Readership: Aimed at Christian families.
ADVERTISING RATES:
Full Page Colour .... EUR 55900.00
CONSUMER: WOMEN'S INTEREST CONSUMER MAGAZINES: Home & Family

FAR DA SE' 14408I79A-60
Editorial: Via Vallemme, 21, 15066 GAVI AL
Tel: 0143 644814 Fax: 0143 645049
Email: fardase@edibrico.it Web site: http://www.edibrico.it
Freq: Monthly; Circ: 132,000
Editor-in-Chief: Nicla De Carolis
Profile: Magazine focusing on DIY and gardening.
Language(s): Italian
Readership: Aimed primarily at men aged between 30 and 50 years.
CONSUMER: HOBBIES & DIY

FARE VELA 14532I91A-55
Editorial: Via del Corso 303, 00186 ROMA
Tel: 0669921143 Fax: 0669921143
Email: info@farevela.net Web site: http://www.farevela.net
Freq: Monthly; Circ: 38,000
Editor-in-Chief: Giovanni Galgani
Profile: Magazine for those interested in sailing for pleasure.
Language(s): Italian
Readership: Aimed at people with a high disposable income.
CONSUMER: RECREATION & LEISURE: Boating & Yachting

FARMA MESE 13572I37-55
Editorial: Piazza della Repubblica 19, 20124 MILANO
Tel: 02 6888775 Fax: 02 6888780
Email: farmamese@giornalidea.it Web site: http://www.farmamese.it
Freq: Monthly; Circ: 17,000
Editor-in-Chief: Lorenzo Verlato
Profile: Magazine containing news about the world of pharmacy.
Language(s): Italian
BUSINESS: PHARMACEUTICAL & CHEMISTS

FARMACIA NEWS 13573I37-60
Editorial: Via Eritrea, 21, 20157 MILANO
Tel: 02 39090 Fax: 02 39090332
Email: farmacianews@tecnichenuove.com Web site: http://www.tecnichenuove.com
Freq: Monthly; Circ: 16,000
Editor-in-Chief: Giuseppe Nardella
Profile: Magazine including scientific information on natural therapies, particularly homeopathy and nutrition.
Language(s): Italian
Readership: Aimed at pharmacists.
BUSINESS: PHARMACEUTICAL & CHEMISTS

IL FARMACISTA 13574I37-116
Editorial: Via Vittore Carpaccio, 18, 00147 ROMA
Tel: 06 594461 Fax: 06 59446228
Email: ilfarmacista@hcom.it Web site: http://www.fofi.it
Freq: 24 issues yearly; Circ: 75,000
Editor-in-Chief: Andrea Mandelli
Profile: Official journal of the Federation of Italian Pharmacists.
Language(s): Italian
Readership: Read by qualified pharmacists.
BUSINESS: PHARMACEUTICAL & CHEMISTS

FASHION 13701I47A-14
Editorial: Piazza Pio XI, 1, 20123 MILANO MI
Tel: 02806201 Fax: 02 80620444
Email: fashion@fashionmagazine.it Web site: http://www.fashionmagazine.it
Freq: Weekly; Circ: 22,000
Editor-in-Chief: Chiara Modini
Profile: Review of the Italian fashion industry and market.
Language(s): Italian
BUSINESS: CLOTHING & TEXTILES

FASHION FILES 767997I74Q-251
Editorial: Via Tirone, 11, 00146 ROMA
Tel: 0645213395 Fax: 0645213301
Email: info@contesticreativi.com Web site: http://www.fashionfiles.it
Freq: Quarterly; Circ: 50,000
Editor-in-Chief: Fabrizio Rinversi
Profile: Magazine focusing on lifestyle and fashion, includes accessories, hair styles, shoes. Focuses on current trends.

Language(s): Italian
CONSUMER: WOMEN'S INTEREST CONSUMER MAGAZINES: Lifestyle

FEDELTA' DEL SUONO
14398I78A-323
Editorial: Via Cavour 65/67, 05100 TERNI
Tel: 0744 441339 Fax: 0744 432018
Email: redazione@fedeltadelsuono.net Web site: http://www.fedeltadelsuono.net
Freq: Monthly; Circ: 32,000
Editor-in-Chief: Andrea Bassanelli
Profile: Magazine about hi-fi stereo systems, music and records.
Language(s): Italian
CONSUMER: CONSUMER ELECTRONICS: Hi-Fi & Recording

FERRAMENTA & CASALINGHI
13478I25-17
Editorial: Via G. Pezzotti 4, 20141 MILANO
Tel: 028372897 Fax: 028373458
Email: ferramenta@netcollins.com Web site: http://www.netcollins.it
Freq: Monthly; Circ: 14,507
Editor-in-Chief: Natascia Giardino
Profile: Journal about ironmongery and domestic items.
Language(s): Italian
BUSINESS: HARDWARE

FILM TV
14312I76C-80
Editorial: Via Settala, 2, 20124 MILANO
Tel: 02 36537800 Fax: 02 36537814
Email: segreteria@film.tv.it Web site: http://www.film.tv.it
Freq: Weekly; Circ: 123,000
Editor-in-Chief: Aldo Fittante
Profile: Magazine containing listings and articles on television, films and theatre.
Language(s): Italian
CONSUMER: MUSIC & PERFORMING ARTS: TV & Radio

FINANZA & FISCO
13028I1A-102
Editorial: Via Cristoforo Colombo, 436, 00145 ROMA RM Tel: 06 5416320 Fax: 06 5415822
Email: redazioneff@tin.it Web site: http://www.finanzaefisco.it
Freq: Weekly; Circ: 12,500
Editor-in-Chief: Eugenio Pompei
Profile: Magazine containing economic and financial news. Also includes information about tax matters.
Language(s): Italian
Readership: Read by businessmen, managers and directors.
BUSINESS: FINANCE & ECONOMICS

FINANZA & MERCATI
1645519I1F-52
Editorial: Via Tristano Calco, 2, 20123 MILANO
Tel: 02 3030261 Fax: 02303026245
Email: redazione@finanzaemercati.it Web site: http://www.finanzaemercati.it
Freq: Daily; Circ: 45,000
Editor: Angelo Ciancarella; Editor-in-Chief: Gianni Gambarotta
Profile: Newspaper focusing on stock exchange news, investment and finance.
Language(s): Italian
BUSINESS: FINANCE & ECONOMICS: Investment

FINANZA MARKETING E PRODUZIONE
13280I14A-60
Editorial: Via Roentgen, 1, 20136 MILANO
Tel: 02 58363706 Fax: 02 58363791
Email: fmp@unibocconi.it Web site: http://www.unibocconi.it
Freq: Quarterly; Circ: 2,000
Editor-in-Chief: Stefano Podesta'
Profile: Magazine covering the problems related to the running of companies, includes a forum for discussion.
Language(s): Italian
Readership: Aimed at managers in the public and private sector and business executives, mainly read by academics.
BUSINESS: COMMERCE, INDUSTRY & MANAGEMENT

FINITURE&COLORE
13324I16A-50
Editorial: Via Teocrito, 47, 20128 MILANO
Tel: 02 252071 Fax: 02 27000692
Email: mara.portesan@bema.it Web site: http://www.ediliziainrete.it
Freq: Monthly; Circ: 8,000
Editor-in-Chief: Gisella Bertini Malgarini
Profile: Magazine about painting, decorating and restoration.
Language(s): Italian
Readership: Aimed at professional painters, decorators and restorers.
BUSINESS: DECORATING & PAINT

FLAIR
1784996I74B-364
Editorial: Palazzo Mondadori, 20090 SEGRATE MI
Tel: 02 75421 Fax: 02 75423206
Email: segreteria.flair@mondadori.it Web site: http://www.mondadori.it
Freq: Monthly; Circ: 200,000
Editor: Paola Salvatore; Editor-in-Chief: Vera Montanari
Language(s): Italian
ADVERTISING RATES:
Full Page Colour .... EUR 46750.00
CONSUMER: WOMEN'S INTEREST CONSUMER MAGAZINES: Women's Interest - Fashion

FLASH ART ITALIA
14463I84A-180
Editorial: Via Carlo Farini, 68, 20159 MILANO MI
Tel: 02 6887341 Fax: 02 66801290
Email: info@flashartonline.com Web site: http://www.flashartonline.com
Freq: Monthly; Circ: 40,000
Editor-in-Chief: Giancarlo Politi
Profile: Review of European art; includes information about Italy's major art exhibitions.
Language(s): Italian
Readership: Read by artists, art collectors, critics and students.
CONSUMER: THE ARTS & LITERARY: Arts

FLORENCE CONCIERGE
1784732I50-178
Editorial: Via Vasco De Gama, 65, 50127 FIRENZE
Tel: 055 412199 Fax: 055 4360111
Email: claudia.manzoni@mega.it Web site: http://www.mega.it
Freq: 6 issues yearly; Circ: 120,000
Language(s): Italian
BUSINESS: TRAVEL & TOURISM

FLORTECNICA
13487I26D-15
Editorial: Viale Europa 4/A, 23870 CERNUSCO LOMBARDONE LC Tel: 0399900545
Fax: 0399718912
Email: info@flortecnica.it Web site: http://www.flortecnica.it
Freq: Monthly; Circ: 6,800
Editor-in-Chief: Arturo Croci
Profile: Magazine covering horticulture and professional gardening, garden centres including floristry.
Language(s): Italian
Readership: Aimed at florists and managers of garden centres.
BUSINESS: GARDEN TRADE: Garden Trade Horticulture

FLUID - TRASMISSIONI DI POTENZA
13380I19D-5
Editorial: Via Eritrea, 21, 20157 MILANO
Tel: 02 390901 Fax: 02 39090331
Email: alessandro.garnero@tecnichenuove.com Web site: http://www.tecnichenuove.com
Freq: 6 issues yearly; Circ: 15,000
Editor-in-Chief: Giuseppe Nardella
Profile: Publication about hydraulic and pneumatic equipment.
Language(s): Italian
BUSINESS: ENGINEERING & MACHINERY: Hydraulic Power

FOCUS
14075I73-130
Editorial: Via Battistotti Sassi 11/a, 20133 MILANO MI Tel: 02 762101 Fax: 02 76013379
Email: redazione@focus.it Web site: http://www.focus.it
Freq: Monthly; Circ: 850,000
Editor-in-Chief: Sandro Boeri
Profile: Magazine covering topics such as medicine, technology, sports and economics with a scientific approach.
Language(s): Italian
ADVERTISING RATES:
Full Page Colour .... EUR 57200.00
CONSUMER: NATIONAL & INTERNATIONAL PERIODICALS

FOOD INDUSTRIA
624660I22C-151
Editorial: Via Giuseppe Mazzini, 132, 56125 PISA
Tel: 050 49490 Fax: 050 49451
Email: segreteriapi@pubblindustria.com Web site: http://www.pubblindustria.info
Freq: 6 issues yearly; Circ: 8,000
Editor-in-Chief: Marco Bindi
Profile: Magazine providing an overview of the food industry, includes raw materials, logistics, packaging, events and fairs, quality control, safety, hygiene and environmental issues.
Language(s): Italian
Readership: Read by people involved in food processing and packaging.
BUSINESS: FOOD: Food Processing & Packaging

FOR MEN MAGAZINE
1785025I86C-185
Editorial: Corso Magenta, 55, 20145 MILANO MI
Tel: 02 43313482 Fax: 02 43313575
Email: annalisabalestrieri@cairoeditore.it Web site: http://www.cairoeditore.it
Freq: Monthly; Circ: 140,000
Editor: Antonela Colicchia; Editor-in-Chief: Andrea Biavardi
Language(s): Italian
ADVERTISING RATES:
Full Page Colour .... EUR 41800.00
CONSUMER: ADULT & GAY MAGAZINES: Men's Lifestyle Magazines

FORZA MILAN!
14251I75B-120
Editorial: Via Eugenio Villoresi, 15, 20143 MILANO MI
Tel: 02 89404021 Fax: 028361182
Email: infoforzamilan@panini.it Web site: http://www.forzamilanonline.com
Freq: Monthly; Circ: 50,000
Editor-in-Chief: Fabrizio Melegari
Profile: Magazine of the football club AC Milan.
Language(s): Italian
Readership: Read by football enthusiasts and AC Milan fans.
CONSUMER: SPORT: Football

FOTO SHOE 15
13502I29-28
Editorial: Via Leonardo Da Vinci 43, 20090 TREZZANO SUL NAVIGLIO MI Tel: 02 4459091
Fax: 02 48402959
Email: info@fotoshoe.com Web site: http://www.fotoshoe.com
Freq: 6 issues yearly; Circ: 8,000
Profile: International journal focusing on technology, machinery, materials, components and accessories for shoe manufacture.
Language(s): English; Italian
BUSINESS: FOOTWEAR

FOTO SHOE 30
13503I29-30
Editorial: Via Leonardo Da Vinci 43, 20090 TREZZANO SUL NAVIGLIO MI Tel: 024459091
Fax: 0248402959
Email: info@fotoshoe.com Web site: http://www.fotoshoe.com
Freq: 6 issues yearly; Circ: 8,000
Editor-in-Chief: Lorenzo Raggi
Profile: International journal focusing on footwear sales and promotion.
Language(s): English; Italian
BUSINESS: FOOTWEAR

FOTOGRAFARE
13583I38-30
Editorial: Via Camerata Picena, 385, 00138 ROMA RM Tel: 068818752 Fax: 068803658
Email: fotografare.novita@fotografare.com Web site: http://www.fotografare.com
Freq: Monthly; Circ: 35,000
Editor-in-Chief: Massimo Marciano
Profile: Magazine containing information about photography.
Language(s): Italian
Readership: Read by professional photographers.
BUSINESS: PHOTOGRAPHIC TRADE

IL FOTOGRAFO
762798I85A-23
Editorial: Via Torino, 51, 20063 CERNUSCO SUL NAVIGLIO MI Tel: 02 924321 Fax: 02 926263147
Email: ilfotografo@sprea.it Web site: http://www.sprea.it
Freq: Monthly; Circ: 47,000
Profile: Magazine focusing on digital photography.
Language(s): Italian
Readership: Aimed at amateur and professional photographers.
CONSUMER: PHOTOGRAPHY & FILM MAKING: Photography

FOTONOTIZIARIO VIDEO NOTIZIARIO
13582I38-25
Editorial: Via M. Melloni, 17, 20129 MILANO
Tel: 02 718341 Fax: 02 714067
Email: redazione@fotonotiziario.it Web site: http://www.fotonotiziario.it
Freq: Weekly; Circ: 14,000
Editor-in-Chief: Virgilio Bernardoni
Profile: Journal focusing on professional photography. Includes articles covering commercial and technical matters concerning the photographers, digital imaging, photofinishing, videomaking and photography trade.
Language(s): Italian
Readership: Aimed at professionals in the photographic market, including professional photographers, cameramen, studio managers, digital imagers, wholesalers, photo/video retailers and those working in photo-labs, photofinishing, minilabs, electronic imaging services, post-production labs and video editing.
BUSINESS: PHOTOGRAPHIC TRADE

FRAMES ARCHITETTURA DEI SERRAMENTI
13134I4A-118
Editorial: Via C. Pisacane 1, 20016 PERO MI
Tel: 0230223002 Fax: 0230226244
Web site: http://www.shopping24.it
Freq: Quarterly; Circ: 20,000
Profile: Journal about door and window architecture.
Language(s): English; Italian
BUSINESS: ARCHITECTURE & BUILDING: Architecture

FUTURA MAGAZINE
13165I5A-30
Editorial: Via Tortona, 14, 20144 MILANO MI
Tel: 0258106415 Fax: 0258106428
Email: letrearance@fastwebnet.it Web site: http://www.letrearance.it
Freq: 6 issues yearly; Circ: 7,000
Editor-in-Chief: Oreste Griotti
Profile: Publication focusing on new technology, science, research and the environment related to computers and automation.
Language(s): Italian
BUSINESS: COMPUTERS & AUTOMATION: Automation & Instrumentation

GAMBERO ROSSO
14506I89A-60
Editorial: Via Enrico Fermi, 161, 00146 ROMA RM
Tel: 06 551121 Fax: 06 55112260
Email: gambero@gamberorosso.it Web site: http://www.gamberorosso.it
Freq: Monthly; Circ: 70,000
Editor-in-Chief: Carlo Ottaviano
Profile: Magazine about travel and tourism, good food and good wine.
Language(s): Italian
CONSUMER: HOLIDAYS & TRAVEL: Travel

THE GAMES MACHINE
14402I78D-50
Editorial: Via Torino, 51, 20063 CERNUSCO SUL NAVIGLIO (MI) Tel: 02 926263173 Fax: 02 926263147
Email: davidetosini@sprea.it Web site: http://www.sprea.it
Freq: Monthly
Profile: Magazine focusing on PC games. Includes news, previews and reviews on the latest hardware and games. Also features articles on online gaming.
Language(s): Italian
Readership: Aimed at young adults aged between 15 and 25 years.
CONSUMER: CONSUMER ELECTRONICS: Games

GARDEN & GRILL
13483I26B-50
Editorial: Piazza San Camillo De Lellis 1, 20124 MILANO Tel: 02 66984880 Fax: 02 6705538
Email: gardengrill@hogaitalia.com
Freq: Monthly; Circ: 8,107
Editor-in-Chief: Roberto Galimberti
Profile: Magazine covering the production and importation of garden products and equipment, leisure and barbecue equipment.
Language(s): Italian
BUSINESS: GARDEN TRADE: Garden Trade Supplies

GARDENIA
14558I93-50
Editorial: Corso Magenta, 55, 20123 MILANO MI
Tel: 02 43313367 Fax: 02 43313931
Email: gardenia@cairoeditore.it Web site: http://www.cairoeditore.it
Freq: Monthly; Circ: 95,000
Editor-in-Chief: Emanuela Rosa-Clot
Profile: Review of flowers, plants, vegetables and gardening. Includes practical advice and features on garden furniture.
Language(s): Italian
Readership: Read by gardening enthusiasts.
CONSUMER: GARDENING

GAZZETTA ANTIQUARIA
13226I7-50
Editorial: Via del Parione, 11, 50123 FIRENZE
Tel: 055 282635 Fax: 055 214831
Email: antiquari@antiquariditalia.it Web site: http://www.antiquariditalia.it
Freq: Half-yearly; Circ: 20,000
Editor-in-Chief: Giovanni Pratesi
Profile: Magazine covering all aspects of the art and antiques trade.
Language(s): Italian
Readership: Read by dealers and collectors of antiques and works of art.
BUSINESS: ANTIQUES

GAZZETTA DELL'ECONOMIA
763959I63-45
Editorial: Via Delle Orchidee, 1 - A.S.I. BARI, 70026 MODUGNO BA Tel: 080 5857444 Fax: 080 5857428
Email: redazione@gazeco.it Web site: http://www.gazeco.it
Freq: Weekly; Circ: 7,919
Editor-in-Chief: Dionisio Ciccarese
Profile: Magazine containing economic and business information.
Language(s): Italian
Readership: Read by members of the local business community in Puglia and Basilicata.
BUSINESS: REGIONAL BUSINESS

LA GAZZETTA DELLO SPORT
13964I65A-192
Editorial: Via Solferino, 28, 20121 MILANO MI
Tel: 02 6339 Fax: 02 62827917

Email: segretgaz@rcs.it Web site: http://www.gazzetta.it
Freq: Daily; Circ: 785,000
Editor: Daniele Redaelli; Editor-in-Chief: Andrea Monti
Profile: Broadsheet-sized newspaper focusing exclusively on sporting events in Italy and around the world.
Language(s): Italian
Readership: Read by a wide range of the general public, over half of whom live in the regions of Lombardia, Veneto and Emilia-Romagna.
ADVERTISING RATES:
Full Page Mono .... EUR 44100.00
Full Page Colour .... EUR 63000.00
NATIONAL DAILY & SUNDAY NEWSPAPERS: National Daily Newspapers

GAZZETTA MEDICA ITALIANA
13854I56C-20
Editorial: C.so Bramante 83, 10126 TORINO
Tel: 011 678282 Fax: 011 674502
Email: minervamedica@minervamedica.it Web site: http://www.minervamedica.it
Freq: 6 issues yearly; Circ: 3,000
Editor-in-Chief: Alberto Oliaro
Profile: Journal focusing on internal medicine and pharmacology.
Language(s): Italian
Readership: Read by academics, students and members of the medical profession.
BUSINESS: HEALTH & MEDICAL: Hospitals

IL GDA GIORNALE DELL'ARREDAMENTO
13117I4B-135
Editorial: Viale Sarca 243, 20126 MILANO
Tel: 02 66103539 Fax: 02 66103558
Email: redazione@rimaedit.it Web site: http://www.rimaedit.it
Freq: Monthly; Circ: 16,700
Editor-in-Chief: Flavio Maestrini
Profile: International magazine covering furniture design.
Language(s): English; Italian
Readership: Aimed at architects, designers and furniture retailers.
BUSINESS: ARCHITECTURE & BUILDING: Interior Design & Flooring

GDOWEEK
13450I22B-25
Editorial: Via Pisacane 1, 20016 PERO MI
Tel: 0230221 Fax: 02 30226637
Email: redazione.gdoweek@ilsole24ore.com Web site: http://www.gdoweek.it
Freq: Weekly; Circ: 26,151
Editor-in-Chief: Mattia Losi
Profile: Publication about distribution and organisation within the food industry.
Language(s): English; Italian
Readership: Aimed at operators and distributors in the food industry.
BUSINESS: FOOD: Cash & Carry

GDOWEEK BLU
13442I22A-10
Editorial: Via Pisacane 1, 20141 PERO MI
Tel: 02 30221 Fax: 0230226637
Email: redazione.gdoweek@ilsole24ore.com Web site: http://www.gdoweek.it
Freq: Monthly; Circ: 48,000
Editor-in-Chief: Cristina Lazzati
Profile: Magazine containing information and topical news for the food trade, includes food stuffs, production costs and new technology.
Language(s): Italian
Readership: Read by wholesalers, distributors and retailers in the food sector.
BUSINESS: FOOD

GDS IL GIORNALE DEL SERRAMENTO
13692I42A-18
Editorial: Via C. Pisacane 1, 20016 MILANO
Tel: 0230223047
Email: nadia.cavagnoli@ilsole24ore.com Web site: http://www.b2b24.ilsole24ore.com
Freq: 6 issues yearly; Circ: 14,500
Editor-in-Chief: Antonio Greco
Profile: Journal about door and window frame manufacturing technology, including information about carpentry and joinery.
Language(s): Italian
BUSINESS: CONSTRUCTION

GEC - IL GIORNALE DEL CARTOLAIO
13611I41B-60
Editorial: Via Eritrea, 21, 20157 MILANO
Tel: 02 39090207 Fax: 02 39090331
Email: gec@tecnichenuove.com Web site: http://www.tecnichenuove.com
Freq: 6 issues yearly; Circ: 7,500
Editor-in-Chief: Giuseppe Nardella
Profile: Magazine with manufacturing, commercial and point of sale news regarding the stationery trade.
Language(s): Italian
Readership: Aimed at the owners and managers of stationery and book shops and producers of stationery items.
BUSINESS: PRINTING & STATIONERY: Stationery

IL GELATIERE ITALIANO
13456I22E-5
Editorial: Viale G. Richard, 1/A, 20143 MILANO MI
Tel: 02818301 Fax: 02 81830424
Email: emanuela.balestrino@reedbusiness.it Web site: http://www.foodclub.it
Freq: Monthly; Circ: 8,500
Profile: Technical journal for Italian Artisanal ice cream.
Language(s): Italian
BUSINESS: FOOD: Frozen Food

GENTE
14076I73-150
Editorial: Viale Sarca 235, 20126 MILANO
Tel: 02 661921 Fax: 02 66192708
Email: gente@hearst.it Web site: http://www.rusconi.it
Freq: Weekly; Circ: 885,000
Editor: Guido Bruschi; Editor-in-Chief: Monica Mosca
Profile: General information magazine with topical, political and cultural news.
Language(s): Italian
ADVERTISING RATES:
Full Page Colour .... EUR 48000.00
CONSUMER: NATIONAL & INTERNATIONAL PERIODICALS

GENTE MOTORI
14354I77A-230
Editorial: Viale Sarca, 235, 20126 MILANO
Tel: 0266192866 Fax: 02 66192651
Web site: http://www.auto-news.it
Freq: Monthly; Circ: 200,000
Editor-in-Chief: Enrico Violi
Profile: Review of motoring and tourism.
Language(s): Italian
Readership: Read by people who want to learn the latest about motoring.
CONSUMER: MOTORING & CYCLING: Motoring

GENTE - RM
1784334I82-256
Editorial: Via Terenzio, 35, 00193 ROMA
Tel: 06 6889981 Fax: 06 68899809
Web site: http://www.rusconi.it
Freq: Weekly; Circ: 885,000
Language(s): Italian
CONSUMER: CURRENT AFFAIRS & POLITICS

GENTLEMAN
14484I86C-50
Editorial: Via Burigozzo, 5, 20122 MILANO MI
Tel: 0258219375 Fax: 02 58317429
Email: segreteriagentleman@class.it Web site: http://www.class.it
Freq: Monthly; Circ: 200,000
Editor-in-Chief: Giulia Pessani
Profile: Magazine containing lifestyle articles. Covers fashion, health, fitness and family issues.
Language(s): Italian
Readership: Aimed at the modern man.
CONSUMER: ADULT & GAY MAGAZINES: Men's Lifestyle Magazines

GIARDINI & AMBIENTE
14559I93-80
Editorial: Strada Curtatona, 5/2, 41125 MODENA
Tel: 059 412507 Fax: 059 412436
Email: giardini@logos.info Web site: http://www.giardini.biz
Freq: 6 issues yearly; Circ: 45,000
Editor-in-Chief: Antonio Vergara
Profile: Magazine concentrating on gardening, includes seasonal information, treatment of plant diseases and reports from gardening shows.
Language(s): Italian
Readership: Read by amateur gardening enthusiasts.
CONSUMER: GARDENING

GIOCHI PER IL MIO COMPUTER
625599I78D-55
Editorial: Via Torino, 51, 20063 CERNUSCO SUL NAVIGLIO MI Tel: 02 92432262 Fax: 02 92432236
Email: pubblicita@sprea.it Web site: http://www.sprea.it
Freq: Monthly; Circ: 80,000
Editor-in-Chief: Luca Sprea
Profile: Magazine containing information about computer games, includes reviews of new products.
Language(s): Italian
ADVERTISING RATES:
Full Page Colour .... EUR 12000.00
CONSUMER: CONSUMER ELECTRONICS: Games

GIOIA
14102I74A-190
Editorial: Viale Sarca, 235, 20126 MILANO MI
Tel: 0266192584 Fax: 02 66192717
Email: rvilla@hearst.it Web site: http://www.gioia.it
Freq: Weekly; Circ: 435,000
Editor: Laura Savini; Editor-in-Chief: Raffaela Carretta
Profile: Magazine covering politics, news, culture, fashion, beauty, cooking and interviews with celebrities and politicians.
Language(s): Italian
Readership: Aimed at women.
ADVERTISING RATES:
Full Page Colour .... EUR 45000.00
CONSUMER: WOMEN'S INTEREST CONSUMER MAGAZINES: Women's Interest

GIOIA BAMBINI (GIOIA)
624137I74D-38
Editorial: Viale Sarca, 235, 20126 MILANO
Tel: 02 66191 Fax: 02 66192717
Web site: http://www.rusconi.it
Freq: 3 issues yearly; Circ: 435,000
Profile: Magazine focusing on the care and upbringing of babies and toddlers.
Language(s): Italian
Readership: Read by parents of children under 5 years.
CONSUMER: WOMEN'S INTEREST CONSUMER MAGAZINES: Child Care

GIOIA CUCINA (GIOIA)
624136I74P-180
Editorial: Viale Sarca, 235, 20126 MILANO MI
Tel: 02 66191 Fax: 02 66192717
Web site: http://www.rusconi.it
Freq: Half-yearly; Circ: 435,000
Profile: Cookery magazine containing seasonal recipes and tips.
Language(s): Italian
CONSUMER: WOMEN'S INTEREST CONSUMER MAGAZINES: Food & Cookery

GIOIA SALUTE (GIOIA)
624138I74G-46
Editorial: Viale Sarca, 235, 20126 MILANO
Tel: 02 66191 66192289 Fax: 02 66192717
Web site: http://www.rusconi.it
Freq: Monthly; Circ: 435,000
Profile: Magazine focusing on health and fitness.
Language(s): Italian
Readership: Aimed at those interested in a healthy lifestyle.
CONSUMER: WOMEN'S INTEREST CONSUMER MAGAZINES: Slimming & Health

IL GIORNALE
13965I65A-50
Editorial: Via Gaetano Negri, 4, 20123 MILANO MI
Tel: 02 85661 Fax: 02 72023880
Email: segreteria@ilgiornale.it Web site: http://www.ilgiornale.it
Freq: Daily; Circ: 328,000
Editor: Gabriele Barberis Vignola; Editor-in-Chief: Alessandro Sallusti
Profile: Broadsheet-sized quality newspaper providing news, financial, economic, political, cultural and sporting information. Also contains events listings.
Language(s): Italian
Readership: Aimed at leaders in the business community, civil servants, university students and office personnel.
ADVERTISING RATES:
Full Page Colour .... EUR 100800.00
NATIONAL DAILY & SUNDAY NEWSPAPERS: National Daily Newspapers

GIORNALE DEL RIVENDITORE EDILE
13135I4E-85
Editorial: Via G. Verga 4, 26831 CASALMAIOCCO LO Tel: 02 4239446 Fax: 02 98175029
Email: redazione@grionieditore.it Web site: http://www.giornaleedilizia.com
Freq: 6 issues yearly; Circ: 8,000
Editor-in-Chief: Samuele Grioni
Profile: Official journal of the National Federation of Building Materials Traders.
Language(s): Italian
BUSINESS: ARCHITECTURE & BUILDING: Building

GIORNALE DELLA LIBRERIA
13911I60A-30
Editorial: Corso di Porta Romana 108, 20122 MILANO Tel: 02 89280802 Fax: 0289280862
Email: redazione@giornaledellalibreria.it Web site: http://www.giornaledellalibreria.it
Freq: Monthly; Circ: 5,000
Editor-in-Chief: Marco Polillo
Profile: Official journal of the Italian Publishing Association.
Language(s): Italian
BUSINESS: PUBLISHING: Publishing & Book Trade

IL GIORNALE DELLA LOGISTICA
760704I10-10
Editorial: Via della Liberazione, 1, 20068 PESCHIERA BORROMEO MI Tel: 02 55305067 Fax: 02 55305068
Email: koster@koster.it Web site: http://www.koster.it
Freq: Monthly; Circ: 18,000
Editor-in-Chief: Pierpaolo Bellina
Profile: Magazine focusing on logistics, including warehousing, transport and automation.
Language(s): Italian
Readership: Read by transport planners and managers.
BUSINESS: MATERIALS HANDLING

GIORNALE DELLA SUBFORNITURA
13305I14B-30
Editorial: Viale G. Richard 1/A, 20143 MILANO
Tel: 02 81830661 Fax: 02 81830414
Email: angelo.grassi@reedbusiness.it Web site: http://www.reedbusiness.it
Freq: Monthly; Circ: 7,000
Profile: Publication about (sub)contracting within the mechanical, textile and electronics industries.
Language(s): German; Italian
Readership: Aimed at managers in the mechanical, textile and electronics industries.
BUSINESS: COMMERCE, INDUSTRY & MANAGEMENT: Industry & Factories

IL GIORNALE DELLA VELA
14533I91A-70
Editorial: Via Quaranta, 52, 20139 MILANO MI
Tel: 02 5358111 Fax: 0256802965
Email: giornaledellavela@panamaeditore.it Web site: http://www.giornaledellavela.com
Freq: Monthly; Circ: 45,000
Editor: Alessandro Mei; Editor-in-Chief: Luca Oriani
Profile: Journal containing information about sailing.
Language(s): Italian
Readership: Aimed at sailing enthusiasts.
CONSUMER: RECREATION & LEISURE: Boating & Yachting

IL GIORNALE DELL'ALBERGATORE
762723I11A-100
Editorial: Via Eritrea, 21, 20157 MILANO
Tel: 02 39090 Fax: 02 39090236
Email: ilgiornaledellalbergatore@tecnichenuove.com
Web site: http://www.tecnichenuove.com
Freq: Quarterly
Editor-in-Chief: Renato Andreoletti
Profile: Magazine for the hotel industry, focusing on the three star category accommodation which represent 50 per cent of the total trade.
Language(s): Italian
BUSINESS: CATERING: Catering, Hotels & Restaurants

IL GIORNALE DELL'ARTE
14465I84A-210
Editorial: Via Mancini, 8, 10131 TORINO TO
Tel: 011 8199111 Fax: 011 8393771
Email: gda.red@allemandi.com Web site: http://www.ilgiornaledellarte.com
Freq: Monthly; Circ: 15,000
Editor: Barbara Antonetto; Editor-in-Chief: Umberto Allemandi
Profile: Journal containing general, cultural and financial news in the field of art.
Language(s): English; French; Greek; Italian; Spanish
Readership: Read by people with a high disposable income.
CONSUMER: THE ARTS & LITERARY: Arts

GIORNALE DELLE ASSICURAZIONI
13047I1D-30
Editorial: Via G. Negri, 4, 20123 MILANO
Tel: 02 7218701 Fax: 02 7218708
Email: assicurazioni@newspapermilano.it
Freq: Monthly; Circ: 15,000
Editor-in-Chief: Angela Maria Scullica
Profile: Journal containing news and information about insurance.
Language(s): Italian
BUSINESS: FINANCE & ECONOMICS: Insurance

IL GIORNALE DELLE BARCHE A MOTORE
14534I91A-75
Editorial: Via Quaranta, 52, 20139 MILANO MI
Tel: 02 5358111 Fax: 02 56802965
Email: barcheamotore@panamaeditore.it Web site: http://www.barcheamotore.com
Freq: Monthly; Circ: 35,000
Editor-in-Chief: Luca Oriani
Profile: Magazine covering news about nautical and leisure-time activities, with an emphasis on motor boats.
Language(s): Italian
CONSUMER: RECREATION & LEISURE: Boating & Yachting

IL GIORNALE DELL'EDILIZIA ITALIANA
13136I4E-87
Editorial: Via G. Verga 4, 26831 CASALMAIOCCO LO Tel: 02 4239446 Fax: 0298175029
Email: redazione@grionieditore.it Web site: http://www.giornaleedilizia.it
Freq: 6 issues yearly; Circ: 20,000
Editor-in-Chief: Samuele Grioni
Profile: Journal providing a review of the building industry.
Language(s): Italian
BUSINESS: ARCHITECTURE & BUILDING: Building

Italy

IL GIORNALE DELL'INFANZIA
14173I74D-40
Editorial: Via Rizzoli, 8, 20132 MILANO **Tel:** 02 50361 **Fax:** 02 50366688
Email: mariella.bertuca@sfera.rcs.it
Freq: Quarterly; **Circ:** 7,700
Editor-in-Chief: Gabriele Melazzini
Profile: Magazine featuring toys and products for babies and toddlers.
Language(s): Italian
CONSUMER: WOMEN'S INTEREST CONSUMER MAGAZINES: Child Care

IL GIORNALE DELL'INSTALLATORE ELETTRICO
13336I17-55
Editorial: Viale G. Richard 1/A, 20143 MILANO MI **Tel:** 02 818301 **Fax:** 02 81830408
Email: gie@reedbusiness.it **Web site:** http://www.elettricoplus.it
Freq: 24 issues yearly; **Circ:** 22,500
Editor-in-Chief: Giovanni Danielli
Profile: Magazine about electrical goods and electrical installation, includes current legislation.
Language(s): Italian
Readership: Aimed at professionals in the electrical industry.
BUSINESS: ELECTRICAL

IL GIORNALE DELL'ODONTOIATRA
13863I56D-25
Editorial: Via Paleocapa, 7, 20121 MILANO **Tel:** 02 881841 **Fax:** 02 88184302
Email: gdo@elsevier.com **Web site:** http://www.elsevier.it
Freq: 24 issues yearly; **Circ:** 19,000
Editor-in-Chief: Emile Blomme
Profile: Newspaper focusing on current issues concerning the dental profession. Provides reports on investigations, news and financial information.
Language(s): Italian
BUSINESS: HEALTH & MEDICAL: Dental

GIORNALE DI ERBA
763723I72-80
Editorial: Corso XXV Aprile, 74/b, 22036 ERBA CO **Tel:** 031 646300 **Fax:** 031 646222
Email: giornale.erba@giornaledierba.it **Web site:** http://www.giornaledierba.it
Freq: Weekly
Editor-in-Chief: Giancarlo Ferrario
Language(s): Italian
LOCAL NEWSPAPERS

IL GIORNALE DI LECCO
762620I72-100
Editorial: Via Aspromonte 52, 23900 LECCO **Tel:** 0341363233 **Fax:** 0341360024
Email: redazione@giornaledilecco.it **Web site:** http://www.giornaledilecco.it
Freq: Weekly; **Circ:** 17,000
Editor-in-Chief: Giancarlo Ferrario
LOCAL NEWSPAPERS

IL GIORNALE DI VIMERCATE
764072I72-210
Editorial: Via Cavour 59, 20059 VIMERCATE MI **Tel:** 039 625151 **Fax:** 039 6853349
Email: redazione@giornaledivimercate.it **Web site:** http://www.giornaledivimercate.it
Freq: Weekly; **Circ:** 10,000
Editor-in-Chief: Angelo Baiguini
Language(s): Italian
LOCAL NEWSPAPERS

IL GIORNALISMO
13072I2B-45
Editorial: Viale Montesanto 7, 20124 MILANO **Tel:** 02 63751 **Fax:** 02 6595842
Email: segreteriaalgmi@assogiornalisti.it **Web site:** http://www.alg.it
Freq: 6 issues yearly; **Circ:** 7,000
Editor-in-Chief: Giovanni Negri
Profile: Bulletin of the Journalists' Association of Lombardy.
Language(s): Italian
BUSINESS: COMMUNICATIONS, ADVERTISING & MARKETING: Press

IL GIORNO
13966I65A-60
Editorial: Via Stradivari, 4, 20131 MILANO **Tel:** 02 277991 **Fax:** 02 27799537
Email: redazione.milano@monrif.net **Web site:** http://www.ilgiorno.it
Freq: Daily; **Circ:** 431,000
Editor: Sandro Neri; **Editor-in-Chief:** Giovanni Morandi
Profile: Broadsheet-sized newspaper covering news, current affairs, politics, economics, sport and entertainment.
Language(s): Italian
Readership: Read by managers, civil servants, office personnel and factory employees, over 80 percent of whom live in Lombardia.
ADVERTISING RATES:
Full Page Mono .... EUR 42000.00
Full Page Colour .... EUR 58800.00
NATIONAL DAILY & SUNDAY NEWSPAPERS: National Daily Newspapers

GIRLFRIEND
1785150I74A-397
Editorial: Via di Santa Cornelia 5A, 00060 FORMELLO RM **Tel:** 0633221250 **Fax:** 0633221235
Email: girlfriend@playmediacompany.it **Web site:** http://www.playmediacompany.it
Freq: Monthly; **Circ:** 180,000
Editor-in-Chief: Alessandro Ferri
Language(s): Italian
CONSUMER: WOMEN'S INTEREST CONSUMER MAGAZINES: Women's Interest

GIUSTIZIA CIVILE
13658I44-83
Editorial: Via Cristoforo Colombo 115, 00147 ROMA **Tel:** 065136691 **Fax:** 065128205
Email: giustciv@giuffre.it **Web site:** http://www.giuffre.it
Freq: Monthly
Editor-in-Chief: Antonio La Torre
Profile: Journal covering civil law and procedure. Includes details on decisions made by the European Court of Justice.
Language(s): Italian
Readership: Aimed at legal professionals.
BUSINESS: LEGAL

GLAMOUR
14222I74H-20
Editorial: Piazza Cadorna 5/7, 20123 MILANO **Tel:** 02 85611 **Fax:** 02 86453259
Email: lcazzaniga@condenast.it **Web site:** http://www.style.it
Freq: Monthly; **Circ:** 150,000
Editor: Edoardo Marchiori; **Editor-in-Chief:** Paola Centomo
Profile: Magazine covering fashion, new beauty products and topical news. Also includes articles concerning society and culture.
Language(s): Italian
Readership: Aimed at women.
ADVERTISING RATES:
Full Page Colour .... EUR 38000.00
Mechanical Data: Type Area: 167x223 mm
CONSUMER: WOMEN'S INTEREST CONSUMER MAGAZINES: Hair & Beauty

GO! ONLINE INTERNET MAGAZINE
71458I5E-35
Editorial: Contrada Lecco, 64 Z.I., 87036 RENDE CS **Tel:** 0984 8319200 **Fax:** 0984 8319225
Email: intmag@edmaster.it **Web site:** http://www.edmaster.it/goonline
Freq: Monthly; **Circ:** 30,000
Editor-in-Chief: Massimo Sesti
Profile: Magazine containing information on the Internet, includes technical information and online applications.
Language(s): Italian
BUSINESS: COMPUTERS & AUTOMATION: Data Transmission

GOLF & TURISMO
14259I75D-100
Editorial: Via Winckelmann, 2, 20146 MILANO **Tel:** 02 424191 **Fax:** 02 48953252
Email: redazione@golfeturismo.it **Web site:** http://www.golfeturismo.it
Freq: Monthly; **Circ:** 28,000
Editor-in-Chief: Nicola Forcignano'
Profile: Magazine containing articles about golfing, including details of courses and competitions.
Language(s): Italian
Readership: Aimed at golfers and tourists.
CONSUMER: SPORT: Golf

IL GOMMONE E LA NAUTICA PER TUTTI
14291I75M-75
Editorial: Via della Liberazione, 1, 20068 PESCHIERA BORROMEO MI **Tel:** 02 55305067 **Fax:** 02 55305068
Email: info@ilgommone.net **Web site:** http://www.ilgommone.net
Freq: Monthly; **Circ:** 30,000
Editor-in-Chief: Pierpaolo Bellina
Profile: Magazine containing articles about water sports, inflatable boats, leisure and tourism.
Language(s): Italian
CONSUMER: SPORT: Water Sports

GOSSIP
1785053I79B-159
Editorial: Via degli Scipioni, 132, 00192 ROMA RM **Tel:** 06 32609760 **Fax:** 06 32609768
Email: gossipmag@tiscali.it
Freq: Monthly; **Circ:** 80,000
Editor-in-Chief: Brunetto Fantauzzi
Language(s): Italian
CONSUMER: HOBBIES & DIY: Models & Modelling

GQ
762590I86C-55
Editorial: Piazza Cadorna, 5, 20123 MILANO **Tel:** 02 85613018 **Fax:** 0285612347
Email: gqitalia@condenast.it **Web site:** http://www.gqitalia.it
Freq: Monthly; **Circ:** 250,000
Editor: Olga Noel Winderling; **Editor-in-Chief:** Gabriele Romagnoli
Profile: Magazine covering men's fashion, lifestyle, politics and culture.
Language(s): Italian
Readership: Aimed at men aged between 20 and 45 years old.
ADVERTISING RATES:
Full Page Colour .... EUR 30000.00
CONSUMER: ADULT & GAY MAGAZINES: Men's Lifestyle Magazines

GRAN FONDO
1784818I77C-112
Editorial: Via Smareglia 7, 20133 MILANO **Tel:** 02714298 **Fax:** 02 7382852
Email: granfondo@edidoss.it **Web site:** http://www.rivistagranfondo.it
Freq: Monthly; **Circ:** 80,000
Editor-in-Chief: Paolo Dossena
Language(s): Italian
CONSUMER: MOTORING & CYCLING: Cycling

GRAND HOTEL
14103I74A-200
Editorial: Corso di Porta Nuova 3/a, 20121 MILANO **Tel:** 02 63675415 **Fax:** 02 63675524
Email: grandhotel@casaeditriceuniverso.com
Freq: Weekly; **Circ:** 425,000
Editor-in-Chief: Orio Buffo
Profile: Magazine containing picture stories, topical news and articles about health, cooking, fashion, gardening, home furnishings and leisure.
Language(s): Italian
Readership: Read by women of all ages.
CONSUMER: WOMEN'S INTEREST CONSUMER MAGAZINES: Women's Interest

GRAZIA
14104I74A-210
Editorial: Palazzo Mondadori - Via Mondadori 1, 20090 SEGRATE MI **Tel:** 02 75421 **Fax:** 02 75422515
Email: grazia@mondadori.it **Web site:** http://www.graziamagazine.it
Freq: Weekly; **Circ:** 382,000
Editor: Stefania Bellinazzo; **Editor-in-Chief:** Vera Montanari
Profile: Women's interest magazine.
Language(s): Italian
ADVERTISING RATES:
Full Page Colour .... EUR 56250.00
Mechanical Data: Type Area: 225x292 mm
CONSUMER: WOMEN'S INTEREST CONSUMER MAGAZINES: Women's Interest

GRAZIA CASA
14158I74C-170
Editorial: Via Trentacoste 7, 20134 MILANO **Tel:** 02215631 **Fax:** 0221563460
Email: segreteria.graziacasa@mondadori.it **Web site:** http://www.mondadori.it
Freq: Monthly; **Circ:** 250,000
Editor-in-Chief: Gilda Bojardi
Profile: Magazine providing articles about home decoration and furnishings.
Language(s): Italian
CONSUMER: WOMEN'S INTEREST CONSUMER MAGAZINES: Home & Family

GT IL GIORNALE DEL TERMOIDRAULICO
13099I3D-50
Editorial: Via Eritrea, 21, 20157 MILANO **Tel:** 02 39090358 **Fax:** 02 3909331
Email: gt@tecnichenuove.com **Web site:** http://www.tecnichenuove.com
Freq: Monthly; **Circ:** 25,000
Profile: Newspaper for wholesalers, retailers and installers of heating, air-conditioning and sanitary systems.
Language(s): Italian
BUSINESS: HEATING & VENTILATION: Heating & Plumbing

GUERIN SPORTIVO
14249I75A-75
Editorial: Via Del Lavoro 7, 40068 SAN LAZZARO BO **Tel:** 051 6227111 **Fax:** 051 6257627
Email: segreteria@guerinsportivo.it **Web site:** http://www.guerinsportivo.it
Freq: Monthly; **Circ:** 60,000
Editor-in-Chief: Matteo Marani
Profile: International magazine about all types of sport, including school and association sport.
Language(s): Italian
CONSUMER: SPORT

GUIDA TV
14313I76C-100
Editorial: Via Mondadori, 1, 20090 SEGRATE **Tel:** 02 75421 **Fax:** 02 75423940
Email: guidatv@mondadori.it **Web site:** http://www.mondadori.it
Freq: Weekly; **Circ:** 400,000
Editor-in-Chief: Giovanni Volpi
Profile: Magazine containing news and information about TV programmes.
Language(s): Italian
CONSUMER: MUSIC & PERFORMING ARTS: TV & Radio

GUIDA VIAGGI
13746I50-8
Editorial: Via San Gregorio, 6, 20124 MILANO MI **Tel:** 02 2020431 **Fax:** 02 20204343
Email: guidaviaggi@givisrl.com **Web site:** http://www.guidaviaggi.it
Freq: Weekly; **Circ:** 9,000
Editor-in-Chief: Paolo Bertagni
Profile: Magazine focusing on travel and tourism.
Language(s): Italian
Readership: Read by travel agents and airline tour operators.
BUSINESS: TRAVEL & TOURISM

GULLIVER
14508I89A-85
Editorial: Via Prati alla Farnesina, 43, 00194 ROMA **Tel:** 06 3331718 **Fax:** 06 3331716
Email: associazione.gulliver@fastwebnet.it
Freq: Monthly; **Circ:** 3,000
Editor-in-Chief: Stefania Brai
Profile: Magazine about holidays and travel. Also includes information on culture, art and lifestyle.
Language(s): Italian
CONSUMER: HOLIDAYS & TRAVEL: Travel

HI-TECH AMBIENTE
13276I57-131
Editorial: Via Giuseppe Mazzini, 132, 56125 PISA **Tel:** 050 49490 **Fax:** 050 49451
Email: segreteriapi@pubblindustria.com **Web site:** http://www.hitechambiente.com
Freq: Monthly; **Circ:** 20,000
Editor-in-Chief: Patrizia Bindi
Profile: Magazine focusing on ecology, environment and and the industrial processing industry. Subjects include marketing, technology, processes, chemical apparatus, analytical methods, new materials, automated systems, logistics and ecological technology.
Language(s): Italian
Readership: Read by ecologists, manufacturers, engineers, public administrators, academics and students.
BUSINESS: ENVIRONMENT & POLLUTION

HOBBY ZOO
13946I64E-50
Editorial: Via E. Fermi 24 - Loc. Osmannoro, 50019 SESTO FIORENTINO FI **Tel:** 05530321 **Fax:** 0553032280
Email: mail@edolimpia.it **Web site:** http://www.edolimpia.it
Freq: Monthly; **Circ:** 15,000
Editor-in-Chief: Renato Cacciapuoti
Profile: International magazine containing articles about products for the care, nutrition and health of pets.
Language(s): English; Italian
Readership: Aimed at distributors, retailers and specialised industry.
BUSINESS: OTHER CLASSIFICATIONS: Pet Trade

HOME HACHETTE
1845437I4B-208
Editorial: Viale Sarca, 235, 20126 MILANO MI **Tel:** 0266192433 **Fax:** 02 66192761
Email: home@hearst.it
Freq: Monthly; **Circ:** 435,000
Editor-in-Chief: Cinzia Felicetti
Language(s): Italian
BUSINESS: ARCHITECTURE & BUILDING: Interior Design & Flooring

HOTEL DOMANI
13747I50-81
Editorial: Via Eritrea, 21, 20157 MILANO **Tel:** 02 390909 **Fax:** 02 39090236
Email: hotel.domani@tecnichenuove.com **Web site:** http://www.tecnichenuove.com
Freq: Monthly; **Circ:** 9,000
Profile: Magazine for the hotel trade. Includes articles on structural and technological aspects, management, staff training, financial and legal matters.
Language(s): Italian
Readership: Aimed at hotel and conference centre managers, financiers, tour operators and architects.
BUSINESS: TRAVEL & TOURISM

HP TRASPORTI CLUB
13728I49A-30
Editorial: Via Cassanese 224 - Pal. Tiepolo - Milano Oltre, 20090 SEGRATE MI **Tel:** 02 26937500 **Fax:** 02 26937525
Email: hptrasporti@mondadori.it **Web site:** http://www.mondadori.it
Freq: Monthly
Editor-in-Chief: Giancarlo Pini
Profile: Magazine focusing on road transport, industrial vehicles and transport policy.
Language(s): English; Italian
BUSINESS: TRANSPORT

HURRIYET
1829068I73-563
Editorial: Via dell'Umiltà, 83/C, 00187 ROMA **Tel:** 06 675911 **Fax:** 06 67591262
Web site: http://www.hurriyet.com.tr
Circ: 600,000
Language(s): Italian
CONSUMER: NATIONAL & INTERNATIONAL PERIODICALS

IA INGEGNERIA AMBIENTALE
13902I57-40
Editorial: Via Andrea Palladio 26, 20135 MILANO
Tel: 02 58301528 **Fax:** 02 58434326
Email: redazione@cipaeditore.it **Web site:** http://www.cipaeditore.it
Freq: 6 issues yearly; **Circ:** 3,000
Editor-in-Chief: Eugenio De Fraja Frangipane
Profile: Journal focusing on waste water treatment and the disposal of solid waste, hygiene and sanitation. Also includes information on environmental protection issues.
Language(s): English; Italian
Readership: Aimed at engineers and managers of waste and water treatment plants, regional, provincial and local administrators, environmental researchers and academics.
BUSINESS: ENVIRONMENT & POLLUTION

ICP-RIVISTA DELL'INDUSTRIA CHIMICA
13277I13-35
Editorial: Via Olgiati, 26, 20143 MILANO MI
Tel: 02 89151200 **Fax:** 0289151237
Email: alessandro.gobbi@shinda.it **Web site:** http://www.shindaedizioni.it
Freq: Monthly; **Circ:** 7,500
Editor: Alessandro Gobbi; **Editor-in-Chief:** Italo Grifoni
Profile: Journal containing articles relating to chemistry and petrology.
Language(s): English; Italian
BUSINESS: CHEMICALS

IDEA TATTOO
1785312I74F-214
Editorial: Via Pier Luigi Nervi, 1/B, 44011 ARGENTA (FE) **Tel:** 0532 852085 **Fax:** 0532 852692
Email: info@ideatattoo.com **Web site:** http://www.ideatattoo.com
Freq: Monthly; **Circ:** 135,000
Editor-in-Chief: Stefano Trentini
Language(s): Italian
CONSUMER: WOMEN'S INTEREST CONSUMER MAGAZINES: Teenage

IDEA WEB
1784930I19J-135
Editorial: Contrada Lecco, 64 Z.I., 87036 RENDE COSENZA **Tel:** 09848319200 **Fax:** 0984 8319225
Email: ideaweb@edmaster.it **Web site:** http://www.edmaster.it/ideaweb
Freq: Monthly; **Circ:** 100,000
Editor-in-Chief: Massimo Sesti
Language(s): Italian
ADVERTISING RATES:
Full Page Colour .... EUR 1300.00
BUSINESS: ENGINEERING & MACHINERY: CAD & CIM (Computer Integrated Manufacture)

ILLUMINOTECNICA
13337I17-60
Editorial: Via F. Albani, 21, 20149 MILANO
Tel: 02 48545811 **Fax:** 0248517108
Email: redazionetecnica@maggioli.it **Web site:** http://www.illuminotecnica.com
Editor-in-Chief: Paolo Maggioli
Profile: International magazine about lighting.
Language(s): English; French; German; Italian; Spanish
Readership: Aimed at lighting designers, importers, exporters, buyers, traders, contractors and retailers.
BUSINESS: ELECTRICAL

IMAGINE
1645457I15A-101
Editorial: Via Rizzoli, 8, 20132 MILANO **Tel:** 02 50361
Fax: 02 50366675
Email: imagine@sfera.rcs.it **Web site:** http://www.sferaeditore.it
Freq: Monthly; **Circ:** 12,000
Editor-in-Chief: Antonella Grua
Profile: Magazine focusing on cosmetics and perfumes. Contains commercial and marketing information.
Language(s): Italian
BUSINESS: COSMETICS & HAIRDRESSING: Cosmetics

IMBOTTIGLIAMENTO
13562I35-40
Editorial: Via Eritrea, 21, 20157 MILANO
Tel: 02 39090280 **Fax:** 02 39090332
Email: imbottigliamento@tecnichenuove.com **Web site:** http://www.tecnichenuove.com
Freq: Monthly; **Circ:** 6,300
Editor-in-Chief: Giuseppe Nardella
Profile: Magazine focusing on the various technologies for the production of alcoholic and non-alcoholic beverages, mineral water and juices, with particular reference to the bottling process for different kinds of containers.
Language(s): Italian
Readership: Aimed at the wine, beverage and bottling industries, research centres and universities.
BUSINESS: PACKAGING & BOTTLING

IMMOBILI & CO.
1784710I1E-2
Editorial: Via Monte Rosa, 18/A, 20030 SENAGO MI
Tel: 02 99055532 **Fax:** 02 99055532
Email: agepmail@tin.it
Freq: Monthly; **Circ:** 100,000
Editor-in-Chief: Antonio Sposari
Profile: Magazine focussing on industrial and commercial property.
Language(s): Italian
BUSINESS: FINANCE & ECONOMICS: Property

L' IMPIANTO ELETTRICO & DOMOTICO
13338I17-63
Editorial: Via Eritrea, 21, 20157 MILANO
Tel: 02 39090350 **Fax:** 02 39090331
Email: impianto.elettrico@tecnichenuove.com **Web site:** http://www.tecnichenuove.com
Freq: Monthly; **Circ:** 9,000
Editor-in-Chief: Giuseppe Nardella
Profile: Magazine focusing on electrical appliances, lighting technology and relevant legislation.
Language(s): Italian
Readership: Aimed at design engineers.
BUSINESS: ELECTRICAL

IMPRESE EDILI
13138I4E-88
Editorial: Via Eritrea, 21, 20157 MILANO
Tel: 02 39090354 **Fax:** 02 39090332
Email: imprese.edili@tecnichenuove.com **Web site:** http://www.tecnichenuove.com
Freq: Monthly; **Circ:** 30,000
Editor-in-Chief: Giuseppe Nardella
Profile: Magazine about all aspects of building and construction including restoration, renovation, special commissions and architectural design.
Language(s): English; Italian
BUSINESS: ARCHITECTURE & BUILDING: Building

IN MOTO
14361I77B-50
Editorial: Via Del Lavoro, 7, 40068 SAN LAZZARO DI SAVENA BO **Tel:** 051 6227111 **Fax:** 051 6227356
Email: posta@inmoto.it **Web site:** http://www.contieditore.it
Freq: Monthly; **Circ:** 115,000
Editor-in-Chief: Stefano Saragoni
Profile: International magazine focusing on all aspects of motorcycling, including articles about vintage bikes, motor-sport news and technology. Also contains complete listings of new and used cars, as well as data of cars tested in the last year.
Language(s): Italian
CONSUMER: MOTORING & CYCLING: Motorcycling

IN SELLA
706996I77B-53
Editorial: Corso di Porta Nuova, 3/a, 20121 MILANO
Tel: 02 63675455 **Fax:** 02 63675523
Email: insella@casaeditriceuniverso.com
Freq: Monthly; **Circ:** 200,000
Editor-in-Chief: Ferdinando Restelli
Profile: Magazine containing information about motorcycles.
Language(s): Italian
Readership: Read by motorcycle enthusiasts.
CONSUMER: MOTORING & CYCLING: Motorcycling

IN TRAVEL
1809699I50-206
Editorial: MILANO
Email: intravel@admmedia.it **Web site:** http://www.infly.it
Freq: Monthly; **Circ:** 80,000
Editor-in-Chief: Armando Siri
Language(s): Italian
BUSINESS: TRAVEL & TOURISM

IN VIAGGIO
718458I89E-300
Editorial: Corso Magenta 55, 20123 MILANO
Tel: 02 43313746 **Fax:** 02 43313928
Email: inviaggio@cairoeditore.it **Web site:** http://www.cairoeditore.it
Freq: Monthly; **Circ:** 70,000
Editor-in-Chief: Andrea Biavardi
Profile: Magazine containing information about locations and ways of travelling to holiday destinations and other places of interest.
Language(s): Italian
CONSUMER: HOLIDAYS & TRAVEL: Holidays

L' INCONTRO
14078I73-200
Editorial: Via Consolata 11, 10122 TORINO
Tel: 011 5212000 **Fax:** 011 5212000
Email: redincontro@gmail.com
Freq: Monthly; **Circ:** 10,000
Editor-in-Chief: Bruno Segre
Profile: General interest magazine, containing articles about politics, anti-racism, religion and culture.
Language(s): Italian
CONSUMER: NATIONAL & INTERNATIONAL PERIODICALS

L' INDUSTRIA DEL MOBILE
13464I23A-25
Editorial: Piazza Agrippa, 1, 20141 MILANO
Tel: 02 89546769 **Fax:** 02 89515438
Email: idm@idm.net **Web site:** http://www.editriceidm.it
Freq: Monthly; **Circ:** 6,000
Editor-in-Chief: Pietro Giovanni Ferrari
Profile: Journal focusing on wood and furniture manufacture, machinery, finishing products, including paint, veneers and glue, tools, plastic materials, upholstery and padding.
Language(s): Italian
Readership: Aimed at furniture manufacturers.
BUSINESS: FURNISHINGS & FURNITURE

L' INDUSTRIA DELLA GOMMA/ ELASTICA
13588I39-60
Editorial: Viale Coni Zugna 71, 20144 MILANO
Tel: 023451230 **Fax:** 023451231
Email: gomma@edifis.it **Web site:** http://www.edifis.it
Freq: Monthly; **Circ:** 3,500
Editor-in-Chief: Eugenio Faiella
Profile: Review of the Italian Association of Rubber, Electric Cables and Related Industries.
Language(s): Italian
BUSINESS: PLASTICS & RUBBER

L' INDUSTRIA DELLE COSTRUZIONI
13142I4E-112
Editorial: Via Guattani, 24, 00161 ROMA
Tel: 0684567403 **Fax:** 0644232981
Email: industria@ance.it **Web site:** http://www.lindustriadellecostruzioni.it
Freq: 6 issues yearly; **Circ:** 23,000
Editor-in-Chief: Giuseppe Nannerini
Profile: Magazine covering architecture, engineering and building.
Language(s): English; Italian
BUSINESS: ARCHITECTURE & BUILDING: Building

L' INDUSTRIA MECCANICA
13373I19A-45
Editorial: Via Scarsellini, 13, 20161 MILANO
Tel: 02 45418500 **Fax:** 02 45418545
Email: anima@anima.it **Web site:** http://www.anima.it
Freq: Monthly; **Circ:** 5,000
Editor-in-Chief: Giuseppe Bonacina
Profile: Magazine of the National Association of Industrial Mechanics. Covers the subjects of industrial mechanics and electro-mechanics.
Language(s): Italian
BUSINESS: ENGINEERING & MACHINERY

INDUSTRIE DELLE BEVANDE
13563I35-50
Editorial: Viale Rimembranza 60, 10064 PINEROLO TO **Tel:** 0121 393127 **Fax:** 0121 794480
Email: info@chiriottieditori.it **Web site:** http://www.chiriottieditori.it
Freq: 6 issues yearly; **Circ:** 5,000
Editor-in-Chief: Giovanni Chiriotti
Profile: International magazine for the beverage industry, with technical, scientific and practical advice, concerning production packaging and legislation.
Language(s): Italian
Readership: Read by managers in the industry.
BUSINESS: PACKAGING & BOTTLING

L' INFORMATORE AGRARIO
13402I21A-230
Editorial: Via Bencivenga-Biondani, 16, 37133 VERONA **Tel:** 045 8057547 **Fax:** 045 597510
Email: segreteria@informatoreagrario.it **Web site:** http://www.informatoreagrario.it/ita/Riviste
Freq: Weekly
Editor-in-Chief: Antonio Boschetti
Profile: Magazine covering the farming practice.
Language(s): Italian
Readership: Read by farmers, breeders, agricultural technicians and students.
BUSINESS: AGRICULTURE & FARMING

INFORMATORE ZOOTECNICO
13419I21D-15
Editorial: Via Goito 13, 40126 BOLOGNA
Tel: 051 65751 **Fax:** 051 6575800
Email: redazione.edagricole@ilsole24ore.com **Web site:** http://www.edagricole.it
Freq: 24 issues yearly; **Circ:** 18,200
Editor-in-Chief: Elia Zamboni
Profile: Publication about animal husbandry, animal feeding, genetic improvement and breeding and reproduction methods.
Language(s): Italian
BUSINESS: AGRICULTURE & FARMING: Livestock

INGREDIENTI ALIMENTARI
13443I22A-40
Editorial: Viale Rimembranza, 60, 10064 PINEROLO TO **Tel:** 0121393127 **Fax:** 0121794480
Email: info@chiriottieditori.it **Web site:** http://www.chiriottieditori.it
Freq: 6 issues yearly; **Circ:** 7,000
Editor-in-Chief: Giovanni Chiriotti
Profile: International magazine containing technological, scientific, economic and legislative information relating to the food industry.
Language(s): Italian
Readership: Read by operators in the food industry.
BUSINESS: FOOD

INQUINAMENTO - TECNOLOGIE AMBIENTE UOMO
13904I57-50
Editorial: s.s del Sempione 28, 20017 RHO MI
Tel: 02 366092520 **Fax:** 02366092525
Email: inquinamento@fieramilanoeditore.it **Web site:** http://www.ilb2b.it\node\22
Freq: Monthly; **Circ:** 6,741
Editor-in-Chief: Alberto Taddei
Profile: Magazine concerning the problems which arise between industry and the environment. Includes information on air pollution, solid waste, noise, recycling, energy saving and environmental conditions.
Language(s): Italian
Readership: Aimed at those in the food, chemical, petro-chemical and mechanical industries, water recycling and treatment consultants.
BUSINESS: ENVIRONMENT & POLLUTION

INSIDE ART
1785182I79B-160
Editorial: Via Archimede, 201, 00197 ROMA RM
Tel: 06 8080099 **Fax:** 06 99700312
Email: redazione@insideitalia.it **Web site:** http://www.insideart.eu
Freq: Monthly; **Circ:** 300,000
Editor-in-Chief: Guido Talarico
Language(s): Italian
CONSUMER: HOBBIES & DIY: Models & Modelling

INSIEME
13546I32G-50
Editorial: Via Rizzoli 8, 20132 MILANO **Tel:** 02 50361
Fax: 02 50366702
Email: insieme@sfera.rcs.it
Freq: Monthly; **Circ:** 176,000
Editor: Luisa Brambilla; **Editor-in-Chief:** Valeria Covini
Profile: Publication for administrators of communal collectives and institutions.
Language(s): Italian
BUSINESS: LOCAL GOVERNMENT, LEISURE & RECREATION: Community Care & Social Services

INTERNAZIONALE
1785137I82-268
Editorial: Viale Regina Margherita, 294, 00198 ROMA
Tel: 06 4417301 **Fax:** 06 44252718
Email: posta@internazionale.it **Web site:** http://www.internazionale.it
Freq: Weekly; **Circ:** 122,000
Editor-in-Chief: Giovanni De Mauro
Language(s): Italian
CONSUMER: CURRENT AFFAIRS & POLITICS

INTERNET.PRO
13210I5E-75
Editorial: Via Eritrea, 21, 20157 MILANO
Tel: 02 39090352 **Fax:** 02 39090302
Email: internet-pro@tecnichenuove.com **Web site:** http://www.internet-pro.it
Freq: Daily
Editor-in-Chief: Giuseppe Nardella
Profile: Magazine containing information about the Internet.
Language(s): Italian
BUSINESS: COMPUTERS & AUTOMATION: Data Transmission

INTERNI
14160I4B-145
Editorial: Via Trentacoste, 7, 20134 MILANO MI
Tel: 0221563320 **Fax:** 0226410847
Email: interni@mondadori.it **Web site:** http://www.internimagazine.it
Freq: Monthly; **Circ:** 50,000
Editor-in-Chief: Gilda Bojardi
Profile: Magazine focusing on interior design and decoration.
Language(s): Italian
Readership: Read by architects, decorators, designers and students.
BUSINESS: ARCHITECTURE & BUILDING: Interior Design & Flooring

INTIMITA'
14105I74A-230
Editorial: Piazza Aspromonte, 13, 20131 MILANO MI
Tel: 02 706421 **Fax:** 02 70642306
Email: intimita@quadratum.it **Web site:** http://www.quadratum.it
Freq: Weekly; **Circ:** 340,000
Editor: Marina Crivelli; **Editor-in-Chief:** Anna Maria Giusti
Profile: Magazine containing articles about family matters. Also covers fashion, health, beauty, knitting, cooking, home furnishings and includes love stories and television programmes.
Language(s): Italian
Readership: Aimed at modern women.
CONSUMER: WOMEN'S INTEREST CONSUMER MAGAZINES: Women's Interest

INTIMO PIU' MARE
13715I47B-18
Editorial: Via Giardini 476/N, 41124 MODENA
Tel: 059342001 **Fax:** 059351290

Italy

Email: info@editorialemoda.com **Web site:** http://www.intimopiumare.com
Freq: Quarterly; **Circ:** 15,000
Editor-in-Chief: Ettore Zanfi
Profile: International magazine covering new fashions and trends in lingerie, hosiery and swimwear. Includes an eight-page English language supplement.
Language(s): English; French; Italian
Readership: Aimed at retailers.
BUSINESS: CLOTHING & TEXTILES: Lingerie, Hosiery/Swimwear

INTOWN MAGAZINE 754232I74Q-230
Editorial: Via Milazzo 6, 20121 MILANO
Tel: 02 36 63 6738 **Fax:** 02 4983358
Email: redazione@publibrands.it **Web site:** http://www.intown-magazine.it
Freq: Quarterly; **Circ:** 65,000
Editor-in-Chief: Edoardo Cela
Profile: Magazine providing a comprehensive view of lifestyle in Milan, Venice, Florence and Rome.
Language(s): English; Italian
CONSUMER: WOMEN'S INTEREST CONSUMER MAGAZINES: Lifestyle

INVESTIRE 14638I1F-50
Editorial: Viale Papiniano 10, 20123 MILANO
Tel: 02 58323055 **Fax:** 02 58318001
Email: investire@ediskipper.it **Web site:** http://www.investireonline.it
Freq: Monthly
Editor-in-Chief: Giulio Palumbo
Profile: Journal focusing on stocks, shares, finance and savings.
Language(s): Italian
Readership: Read by investment advisers.
BUSINESS: FINANCE & ECONOMICS: Investment

IO DONNA (IL CORRIERE DELLA SERA) 762655I74A-145
Editorial: Via Rizzoli 8, 20132 MILANO **Tel:** 02 25841
Fax: 0225843771
Freq: Weekly; **Circ:** 860,000
Editor: Ermanno Lucchini; **Editor-in-Chief:** Diamante D'Alessio
Profile: Magazine focusing on lifestyle, fashion, beauty and health.
Language(s): Italian
Readership: Aimed at women.
ADVERTISING RATES:
Full Page Colour .... EUR 60000.00
CONSUMER: WOMEN'S INTEREST CONSUMER MAGAZINES: Women's Interest

IO E IL MIO BAMBINO 14174I74D-60
Editorial: Via Rizzoli, 8, 20132 MILANO
Tel: 02 50366687 **Fax:** 02 50366688
Email: elisabetta.larovere@sfera.rcs.it
Freq: Monthly; **Circ:** 260,000
Editor-in-Chief: Cristina De Grandis
Profile: Magazine focusing on the care and development of babies in their first year.
Language(s): Italian
Readership: Read by expectant mothers and new parents.
CONSUMER: WOMEN'S INTEREST CONSUMER MAGAZINES: Child Care

L' ISOLA 1785027I61-74
Editorial: Via Sempione, 25, 20016 PERO MI
Tel: 02 3581586
Email: redazione@lisolachenoncera.it **Web site:** http://www.lisolachenoncera.it
Freq: Quarterly; **Circ:** 40,000
Editor-in-Chief: Francesco Paracchini
Language(s): Italian
BUSINESS: MUSIC TRADE

LE ISTITUZIONI DEL FEDERALISMO 13524I32A-70
Editorial: V.le A. Moro, 52, 40127 BOLOGNA
Tel: 051 5275926 **Fax:** 051 6395596
Email: istituzionidelfederalismo@regione.emilia-romagna.it **Web site:** http://www.regione.emilia-romagna.it
Freq: 6 issues yearly; **Circ:** 2,000
Editor-in-Chief: Roberto Bin
Profile: Journal focusing on local and regional government in Italy.
Language(s): Italian
BUSINESS: LOCAL GOVERNMENT, LEISURE & RECREATION: Local Government

ITALIA GRAFICA 13603I41A-40
Editorial: Via Eritrea, 21, 20157 MILANO
Tel: 02 390901 **Fax:** 02 39090302
Email: italia.grafica@tecnichenuove.com **Web site:** http://www.italiagrafica.com
Freq: Monthly; **Circ:** 10,000
Editor-in-Chief: Giuseppe Nardella
Profile: Official journal of the National Italian Association of Graphical Industries, Paper and Board Manufacturers.
Language(s): Italian
BUSINESS: PRINTING & STATIONERY: Printing

ITALIA OGGI 13967I65A-70
Editorial: Via Marco Burigozzo, 5, 20122 MILANO
Tel: 02 582191 **Fax:** 02 58317598
Email: italiaoggi@class.it **Web site:** http://www.italiaoggi.it
Freq: Daily; **Circ:** 104,000
Editor: Gianni Macheda; **Editor-in-Chief:** Paolo Panerai
Profile: Tabloid-sized quality newspaper providing financial, economic, political and legal news.
Language(s): Italian
Readership: Aimed at leaders in the business and financial sectors, senior managers, office personnel and proprietors of small businesses.
ADVERTISING RATES:
Full Page Mono .... EUR 25500.00
Full Page Colour .... EUR 35700.00
NATIONAL DAILY & SUNDAY NEWSPAPERS: National Daily Newspapers

ITALIA OGGI SETTE 1784495I1A-223
Editorial: Via Marco Burigozzo, 5, 20122 MILANO MI
Tel: 02 582191 **Fax:** 02 58317598
Email: italiaoggi@class.it **Web site:** http://www.italiaoggi.it
Freq: Weekly; **Circ:** 60,000
Editor-in-Chief: Paolo Panerai
Language(s): Italian
BUSINESS: FINANCE & ECONOMICS

ITALIA PUBLISHERS MAGAZINE 13912I60A-70
Editorial: Via Stromboli, 18, 20144 MILANO
Tel: 02 48516207 **Fax:** 02 43400509
Email: redazione@italiapublisher.com **Web site:** http://www.italiapublishers.com
Freq: Monthly; **Circ:** 18,000
Editor-in-Chief: Susanna Bonati
Profile: Publication focusing on desktop publishing, digital printing and photography, billposting, imaging, prepress, electronic publishing and the Internet.
Language(s): Italian
Readership: Aimed at publishers, photocopy agencies and business centres, graphic designers, architects, retailers and dealers.
BUSINESS: PUBLISHING: Publishing & Book Trade

ITALIAIMBALLAGGIO 13564I35-52
Editorial: Via B. Crespi, 30/2, 20159 MILANO
Tel: 0269007733 **Fax:** 02 69007664
Email: italiaimballaggio@dativo.it **Web site:** http://www.packmedia.net
Freq: Monthly; **Circ:** 10,500
Editor-in-Chief: Stefano Lavorini
Profile: European magazine containing information about the packaging industry in Italy.
Language(s): English; Italian
BUSINESS: PACKAGING & BOTTLING

ITALIAN BUILDING CONSTRUCTION 13617I42A-14
Editorial: Via Conca del Naviglio, 37, 20123 MILANO
Tel: 02 89421350 **Fax:** 02 89421484
Email: italianbuilding@fiaccola.it **Web site:** http://www.fiaccola.it
Freq: Quarterly; **Circ:** 30,000
Editor-in-Chief: Mauro Nartelli
Profile: International technical review of the Italian construction industry.
Language(s): English
BUSINESS: CONSTRUCTION

ITALIAN FOOD MACHINES 13444I22A-40_5
Editorial: V.le Lunigiana, 14, 20125 MILANO MI
Tel: 02 67100605 **Fax:** 02 67100621
Email: redazione@editricezeus.com **Web site:** http://www.editricezeus.com
Freq: Quarterly; **Circ:** 10,000
Editor-in-Chief: Enrico Maffizzoni
Profile: International magazine focusing on technological machinery used in food production.
Language(s): Chinese; English; Italian; Russian
BUSINESS: FOOD

ITALIAN LIGHTING 13339I17-65
Editorial: Via G. Rossetti, 9, 20145 MILANO
Tel: 02 48007449 **Fax:** 02 48007493
Email: staffedi@staffedit.it **Web site:** http://www.staffedit.it
Freq: 6 issues yearly; **Circ:** 7,500
Editor-in-Chief: Renato Pisaniello
Profile: International journal containing technical information concerning lighting. Includes articles on design and manufacture.
Language(s): Italian
BUSINESS: ELECTRICAL

ITALIAN MAGAZINE FOOD PROCESSING 13452I22C-80
Editorial: V.le Lunigiana, 14, 20125 MILANO MI
Tel: 02 67100605 **Fax:** 02 67100621
Email: info@editricezeus.com **Web site:** http://www.editricezeus.com
Freq: 6 issues yearly; **Circ:** 33,000
Editor-in-Chief: Enrico Maffizzoni
Profile: International magazine focusing on technology for the food and beverage industries.
Language(s): English; French; German; Italian; Spanish
Readership: Read by food industry professionals including manufacturers of technology and systems.
BUSINESS: FOOD: Food Processing & Packaging

ITALY EXPORT 13780I52C-20
Editorial: Via Fieramosca, 31, 20052 MONZA MI
Tel: 039 2620010 **Fax:** 039 834190
Email: info@italyexport.net **Web site:** http://www.italyexport.net
Freq: Quarterly; **Circ:** 9,500
Editor-in-Chief: Daniela Galimberti
Profile: Magazine focusing on Italian goods for export.
Language(s): English; Italian
BUSINESS: GIFT TRADE: Fancy Goods

ITINERARI E LUOGHI 14524I89E-80
Editorial: Via Alessandro Tadino 5, 20124 MILANO
Tel: 02 6570414 **Fax:** 02 6555791
Email: stampa@fiorattieditore.it **Web site:** http://www.itinerarieluoghi.it
Freq: Monthly; **Circ:** 48,000
Editor-in-Chief: Paolo Fioratti
Profile: Publication focusing on tourism, travel and adventure holidays.
Language(s): Italian
CONSUMER: HOLIDAYS & TRAVEL: Holidays

ITP EVENTS INTERNATIONAL TOURIST PRESS 13748I50-90
Editorial: Viale Parioli, 50, 00197 ROMA RM
Tel: 06 8082643 **Fax:** 06 8072844
Email: itpevents@bonelliconsulting.com **Web site:** http://www.bonelliconsulting.com
Freq: Monthly; **Circ:** 10,000
Editor-in-Chief: Luca Patrizio Bonelli
Profile: International magazine containing information about Italian regions and other countries as holiday destinations, also includes hotel information.
Language(s): English; Italian; Spanish
Readership: Read by all involved in the travel and tourism trade, including tour operators, travel agents, managers of hotels and transport companies, also organisers of trade fairs, incentive operators and film location managers.
BUSINESS: TRAVEL & TOURISM

JACK 704431I5R-60
Editorial: Via Battistotti Sassi 11/a, 20133 MILANO
Tel: 02 762101 **Fax:** 02 783153
Email: sanella@gujm.it **Web site:** http://www.jacktech.it
Freq: Monthly; **Circ:** 180,000
Editor: Guido Da Rozze; **Editor-in-Chief:** Jacopo Loredan
Profile: Magazine focusing on information technology and the Internet.
Language(s): Italian
ADVERTISING RATES:
Full Page Colour .... EUR 25000.00
BUSINESS: COMPUTERS & AUTOMATION: Computers Related

JAM VIAGGIO NELLA MUSICA 718466I76D-220
Editorial: Via F.lli Cervi-Residenza Archi, 20090 SEGRATE MI **Tel:** 02 26410457 **Fax:** 0278627501
Email: redazione@jamonline.it **Web site:** http://www.jamonline.it
Freq: Monthly; **Circ:** 45,000
Editor-in-Chief: Roberto Caselli
Profile: Magazine focusing on rock music.
Language(s): Italian
CONSUMER: MUSIC & PERFORMING ARTS: Music

JESUS 14080I73-210
Editorial: Via Giotto, 36, 20145 MILANO
Tel: 02 48071 **Fax:** 02 48072486
Email: jesus@stpauls.it **Web site:** http://www.stpauls.it/jesus/default.htm
Freq: Monthly; **Circ:** 40,000
Editor-in-Chief: Antonio Tarzia
Profile: General interest magazine with a religious perspective.
Language(s): Italian
CONSUMER: NATIONAL & INTERNATIONAL PERIODICALS

JP4 MENSILE DI AERONAUTICA E SPAZIO 13221I6A-101
Editorial: Via XX Settembre 60, 50129 FIRENZE
Tel: 055 4633439 **Fax:** 0554626720
Email: jp4@dueservice.com **Web site:** http://www.edìservice.it
Freq: Monthly; **Circ:** 20,000
Editor-in-Chief: Ugo Passalacqua
Profile: Magazine about aeronautics.
Language(s): English; Italian
BUSINESS: AVIATION & AERONAUTICS

JUTARNJI LIST 1829056I73-554
Editorial: Via Sarnano, 36, 00156 ROMA
Tel: 335 395537 **Fax:** 06 62276298
Web site: http://www.jutarnji.hr
Circ: 130,000
Language(s): Italian
CONSUMER: NATIONAL & INTERNATIONAL PERIODICALS

KOSMETICA 13320I15A-100
Editorial: Via Eritrea, 21, 20157 MILANO
Tel: 02 39090341 **Fax:** 02 39090332
Email: kosmetica@tecnichenuove.com **Web site:** http://www.tecnichenuove.com
Freq: Monthly; **Circ:** 6,000
Editor-in-Chief: Giuseppe Nardella
Profile: Publication concerning all aspects of the cosmetics industry.
Language(s): Italian
Readership: Read by buyers and managers in the cosmetic industry.
ADVERTISING RATES:
Full Page Mono .... EUR 1290.00
Full Page Colour .... EUR 1290.00
Mechanical Data: Type Area: 210x297 mm
BUSINESS: COSMETICS & HAIRDRESSING: Cosmetics

KULT MAGAZINE 706999I74Q-120
Editorial: Via Cadolini 34, 20137 MILANO MI
Tel: 02 89075700 **Fax:** 0236642899
Web site: http://www.kultmagazine.com
Freq: Monthly; **Circ:** 85,000
Editor-in-Chief: Enrico Cammarota
Profile: Magazine focusing on lifestyle. Includes articles on the latest fashion, new styles and trends.
Language(s): Italian
CONSUMER: WOMEN'S INTEREST CONSUMER MAGAZINES: Lifestyle

LABORATORIO 2000 13798I55-16
Editorial: Via Eritrea, 21, 20157 MILANO
Tel: 02 390901 **Fax:** 02 39090332
Email: laboratorio2000@tecnichenuove.com **Web site:** http://www.rivistedigitali.com
Freq: Monthly; **Circ:** 9,000
Editor-in-Chief: Giuseppe Nardella
Profile: Review of chemical and biological research.
Language(s): Italian
BUSINESS: APPLIED SCIENCE & LABORATORIES

LAMIERA 13386I19E-32
Editorial: Via Eritrea, 21, 20157 MILANO MI
Tel: 02 39090356 **Fax:** 02 39090331
Email: lamiera@tecnichenuove.com **Web site:** http://www.tecnichenuove.com
Freq: Monthly; **Circ:** 7,500
Editor-in-Chief: Giuseppe Nardella
Profile: Journal covering sheet metal work from production to metal finishing. Also provides information on new technological achievements, industrial agreements, regulation changes, exhibitions and conventions.
Language(s): Italian
BUSINESS: ENGINEERING & MACHINERY: Machinery, Machine Tools & Metalworking

LARGO CONSUMO 13241I10-16
Editorial: Via Bodoni 2, 20155 MILANO
Tel: 023271646 **Fax:** 02 325190
Email: redazione@largoconsumo.it **Web site:** http://www.largoconsumo.info
Freq: Monthly; **Circ:** 8,832
Editor-in-Chief: Pier Carlo Garosci
Profile: Magazine concerning production and distribution services for the food and non-food sectors. Also includes economic and marketing news.
Language(s): Italian
Readership: Read by managers in production and distribution, agents and representatives.
BUSINESS: MATERIALS HANDLING

LAVORI PUBBLICI 1685626I4F-1
Editorial: Via Principe di Palagonia, 87, 90145 PALERMO PA **Tel:** 091 6823069 **Fax:** 091 6823313
Email: lavoripubblici@lavoripubblici.it **Web site:** http://www.lavoripubblici.it
Freq: Monthly; **Circ:** 1,000
Editor-in-Chief: Paolo Oreto
Profile: Technical magazine regarding public maintenance work, municipal cleaning and refuse collection, also maintenance of roads and parks.
Language(s): Italian
Readership: Aimed at managers in municipal services.
BUSINESS: ARCHITECTURE & BUILDING: Cleaning & Maintenance

LAVORO SICURO - IL SOLE 24 ORE 13790I54B-60
Editorial: Via Monte Rosa 91, 20141 MILANO
Tel: 02 30221 **Fax:** 0230223992
Email: as.tecnologiesoluzioni@ilsole24ore.com **Web site:** http://www.ambientesicurezza.ilsole24ore.com
Freq: 6 issues yearly

Editor-in-Chief: Massimo Cassani
Profile: Journal focusing on accident prevention, includes machine tool safety devices.
Language(s): Italian
BUSINESS: SAFETY & SECURITY: Safety

LEADER FOR CHEMIST HEALTH STRATEGY 13576I37-119
Editorial: Via Olmetto 5, 20123 MILANO
Tel: 02 878397 **Fax:** 02 866576
Email: cesil@cesil.com **Web site:** http://www.cesil.com/leaderforchemist/chemist.htm
Freq: Monthly
Editor-in-Chief: Genina Iacobone
Profile: Magazine containing information about the development of new drugs, legislation affecting pharmacists, technological innovations and articles of general interest.
Language(s): English; Italian
Readership: Aimed at pharmaceutical professionals.
BUSINESS: PHARMACEUTICAL & CHEMISTS

LEADERSHIP MEDICA 1784271I56A-338
Editorial: Via Olmetto 5, 20123 MILANO
Tel: 02 878397 **Fax:** 02 866576
Email: cesil@cesil.com **Web site:** http://www.leadershipmedica.com
Freq: Monthly; **Circ:** 85,000
Editor-in-Chief: Genina Iacobone
Language(s): Italian
BUSINESS: HEALTH & MEDICAL

LED-IN 13351I18A-20
Editorial: Via Console Flaminio 19, 20134 MILANO
Tel: 02 210111250 **Fax:** 02 210111222
Email: redazione@tecnoimprese.it **Web site:** http://www.design-in.tecnoimprese.it
Freq: Monthly; **Circ:** 8,000
Editor-in-Chief: Silvio Baronchelli
Profile: Magazine about the design of micro-electronics products.
Language(s): Italian
Readership: Aimed at professionals in the micro-electronics field.
BUSINESS: ELECTRONICS

LEGEND BIKE 14362I77B-55
Editorial: Via Saliceto 22/e, 40013 BOLOGNA
Tel: 051 0933850 **Fax:** 051 0933869
Email: redazione@legendbike.it
Freq: Monthly; **Circ:** 25,000
Editor-in-Chief: Alessandro Colombo
Profile: Magazine about classic and vintage motorcycles around the world.
Language(s): Italian
Readership: Magazine mainly read by men 20 to 50 years.
CONSUMER: MOTORING & CYCLING: Motorcycling

LEGGERE: TUTTI 1785211I84B-161
Editorial: Via Nomentana, 257, 00199 ROMA
Tel: 06 44254205 **Fax:** 06 44254239
Email: info@agraeditrice.com **Web site:** http://www.agraeditrice.com
Freq: Monthly; **Circ:** 180,000
Editor-in-Chief: Giuseppe Marchetti Tricamo
Language(s): Italian
CONSUMER: THE ARTS & LITERARY: Literary

IL LEGNO 13693I46-30
Editorial: Piazza Agrippa, 1, 20141 MILANO
Tel: 02 89546696 **Fax:** 02 89515438
Email: idm@idm.net **Web site:** http://www.editriceidm.it
Freq: Monthly; **Circ:** 10,000
Editor-in-Chief: Andrea Brega
Profile: Journal covering the import and export of wood, cultivation, ecology, technology, logistics and fabrication.
Language(s): Italian
BUSINESS: TIMBER, WOOD & FORESTRY

LIBERAZIONE - QUOT. PARTITO RIFOND. COMUN. 718467I65A-72
Editorial: Viale del Policlinico, 131, 00161 ROMA RM
Tel: 06 441831 **Fax:** 06 44183254
Email: segreteria@liberazione.it **Web site:** http://www.liberazione.it
Freq: Daily; **Circ:** 45,000
Editor: Carla Cotti; **Editor-in-Chief:** Dino Greco
Profile: Tabloid-size newspaper of the Italian Communist Party. Covers general and political news.
Language(s): Italian
NATIONAL DAILY & SUNDAY NEWSPAPERS: National Daily Newspapers

LIBERETA' 14233I74N-80
Editorial: Via Dei Frentani 4/A, 00185 ROMA
Tel: 06 444291 **Fax:** 06 4469012
Email: redazione@libereta.it **Web site:** http://www.libereta.it
Freq: Monthly; **Circ:** 190,000
Editor-in-Chief: Giorgio Nardinocchi
Profile: Publication for Italian pensioners.
Language(s): Italian
CONSUMER: WOMEN'S INTEREST CONSUMER MAGAZINES: Retirement

LIBERTA' 14052I67B-4700
Editorial: Via Benedettine 68, 29100 PIACENZA
Tel: 0523 393939 **Fax:** 0523 343976
Email: cronaca@liberta.it **Web site:** http://www.liberta.it
Freq: Daily; **Circ:** 38,000
Editor-in-Chief: Gaetano Rizzuto
Language(s): Italian
REGIONAL DAILY & SUNDAY NEWSPAPERS: Regional Daily Newspapers

LA LIBRERIA DELL'AUTOMOBILE MAGAZINE 14390I77F-80
Editorial: Via Claudio Treves, 15/17, 20090 VIMODRONE MI **Tel:** 02 27301126 27301462
Fax: 02 27301454
Email: info@giorgionadaeditore.it **Web site:** http://www.giorgionadaeditore.it
Freq: Half-yearly; **Circ:** 92,000
Editor-in-Chief: Giorgio Nada
Profile: Magazine about classic cars and motorcycles. Covers events and deals with the buying and selling of books on cars.
Language(s): Italian
CONSUMER: MOTORING & CYCLING: Veteran Cars

LIFEGATE.IT 1809680I74G-108
Editorial: Via Manzoni, 18, 22046 MERONE CO
Tel: 031 61803 **Fax:** 031 6180310
Email: redazione@lifegate.it **Web site:** http://www.lifegate.it
Circ: 100,000
Editor-in-Chief: Stefano Carnazzi
Language(s): Italian
CONSUMER: WOMEN'S INTEREST CONSUMER MAGAZINES: Slimming & Health

LIGHTING DESIGN COLLECTION 13340I17-66
Editorial: Via Ferri, 6, 20092 CINISELLO BALSAMO MI **Tel:** 02 66018238 **Fax:** 02 66595846
Email: info@dbcedizioni.it **Web site:** http://www.ediweb.it
Freq: 6 issues yearly; **Circ:** 11,500
Editor-in-Chief: Jacopo Castelfranchi
Profile: Magazine about the lighting trade.
Language(s): English; Italian
Readership: Aimed at professionals in the lighting trade.
BUSINESS: ELECTRICAL

LINEA EDP 13178I5B-43
Editorial: Via F. Confalonieri 36, 20141 MILANO
Tel: 025660931 **Fax:** 0256609344
Email: redazione.lineaedp@matedizioni.it **Web site:** http://www.lineaedp.it
Freq: Weekly; **Circ:** 30,000
Editor-in-Chief: Roberto Negrini
Profile: Magazine focusing on information technology. Covers networks and telecoms, PCs, workgroups, servers and systems within business and industry.
Language(s): Italian
Readership: Aimed at managers, IT personnel, technical assistants and consultants, small business owners, software and hardware retailers.
BUSINESS: COMPUTERS & AUTOMATION: Data Processing

LINEA INTIMA ITALIA 13716I47B-27
Editorial: Via C. Colombo, 1, 20094 CORSICO MI
Tel: 02 89159373 **Fax:** 02 89159349
Email: p.e@intimagroup.com **Web site:** http://www.networkdessous.it
Freq: Monthly; **Circ:** 18,000
Editor-in-Chief: Marco Pisani
Profile: Magazine about underwear, hosiery and swimwear.
Language(s): English; French; Italian; Portuguese; Spanish
Readership: Read by manufacturers and retailers.
BUSINESS: CLOTHING & TEXTILES: Lingerie, Hosiery/Swimwear

LINEAVERDE 13490I26D-70
Editorial: Via La Spezia, 33, 20142 MILANO MI
Tel: 02 89501830 **Fax:** 0289501604
Email: lineaverde@linea-verde.net **Web site:** http://www.linea-verde.net
Freq: Monthly; **Circ:** 6,000
Editor-in-Chief: Massimo Casolaro
Profile: Magazine covering the subject of ornamental plants for parks and gardens.
Language(s): Italian
Readership: Readers include ornamental plant producers and landscape architects.
BUSINESS: GARDEN TRADE: Garden Trade Horticulture

LINUX MAGAZINE 714597I5B-44
Editorial: Contrada Lecco, 64 Z.I., 87030 RENDE COSENZA **Tel:** 09848319200 **Fax:** 0984 319225
Email: linuxmag@edmaster.it **Web site:** http://www.linux-magazine.it
Freq: Monthly; **Circ:** 35,000
Editor-in-Chief: Massimo Sesti
Profile: Official magazine for Linux multimedia.
Language(s): Italian
BUSINESS: COMPUTERS & AUTOMATION: Data Processing

LOCALI TOP 13234I9A-25
Editorial: Via Ercole Oldofredi, 41, 20124 MILANO
Tel: 02 6691692 **Fax:** 02 66711461
Email: tuttopress@tuttopress.it
Freq: Monthly; **Circ:** 99,000
Editor-in-Chief: Silvano Rusmini
Profile: Magazine providing topical news concerning the drinks industry.
Language(s): Italian
Readership: Aimed at bar staff and owners of public houses.
BUSINESS: DRINKS & LICENSED TRADE: Drinks, Licensed Trade, Wines & Spirits

LOGISTICA 13242I10-20
Editorial: Via Eritrea, 21, 20157 MILANO
Tel: 02 390901 **Fax:** 02 39090331
Email: logistica@tecnichenuove.com **Web site:** http://www.tecnichenuove.com
Freq: Monthly; **Circ:** 7,000
Editor-in-Chief: Giuseppe Nardella
Profile: Magazine covering logistics, materials handling, transport and warehousing.
Language(s): Italian
Readership: Aimed at management involved in production, stock movement, transport and packaging.
BUSINESS: MATERIALS HANDLING

LOGISTICA MANAGEMENT 13243I10-30
Editorial: Via Italia 39, 20052 MONZA
Tel: 0392302398 **Fax:** 0392302383
Email: press@editricetemi.it **Web site:** http://www.logisticamanagement.it
Freq: Monthly; **Circ:** 10,000
Editor-in-Chief: Ernesto Salvioli
Profile: Magazine containing information concerning logistics.
Language(s): Italian
Readership: Aimed at directors and managers involved in production and organisation, stock movements, transport and packaging.
BUSINESS: MATERIALS HANDLING

LOMBARD 13030I1A-125
Editorial: Via Burigozzo 5, 20122 MILANO
Tel: 02 582191 **Fax:** 02 58317518
Web site: http://www.classcity.it
Freq: 6 issues yearly; **Circ:** 15,000
Editor-in-Chief: Paolo Panerai
Profile: Journal covering international finance.
Language(s): English; Italian
Readership: Read by presidents and managing directors of major financial institutions.
BUSINESS: FINANCE & ECONOMICS

LOMBARDIA OGGI (LA PREALPINA) 14428I80-150
Editorial: Via IV Novembre 12/A, 21052 BUSTO ARSIZIO MI **Tel:** 0331 327220 **Fax:** 0331 327221
Email: davide@prealpina.it **Web site:** http://www.laprealpina.it
Freq: 26 issues yearly; **Circ:** 35,000
Editor-in-Chief: Giorgio Minazzi
Profile: Magazine containing articles about lifestyle, culture, sport, business and events in Lombardy.
Language(s): Italian
ADVERTISING RATES:
Full Page Mono .... EUR 1057.00
Full Page Colour .... EUR 1427.00
CONSUMER: RURAL & REGIONAL INTEREST

LUCE E DESIGN 13341I17-67
Editorial: Via Eritrea, 21, 20157 MILANO
Tel: 02 39090340 **Fax:** 02 39090331
Email: luceedesign@tecnichenuove.com **Web site:** http://www.tecnichenuove.com
Freq: 6 issues yearly
Editor-in-Chief: Giuseppe Nardella
Profile: Official journal of the Italian Lighting Association, covering technological developments, trends and interviews.
Language(s): Italian
Readership: Aimed at architects, designers, electricians and engineers.
BUSINESS: ELECTRICAL

LUOGHI DELL'INFINITO (AVVENIRE) 1829188I87-270
Editorial: Piazza Carbonari, 3, 20125 MILANO
Tel: 02 6780551 **Fax:** 02 6780347
Email: luoghidellinfinito@avvenire.it **Web site:** http://www.avvenire.it
Freq: Monthly; **Circ:** 100,000
Language(s): Italian
CONSUMER: RELIGIOUS

LUXOS 1846539I74B-405
Editorial: Via Pietrasanta 12, 20141 MILANO MI
Tel: 0287387400 **Fax:** 0287387719
Email: manuela@luxos.com **Web site:** http://www.luxos.com
Freq: Half-yearly; **Circ:** 80,000
Editor-in-Chief: James Gart Hill
Language(s): Italian
CONSUMER: WOMEN'S INTEREST CONSUMER MAGAZINES: Women's Interest - Fashion

LUXURY FILES 767998I74Q-252
Editorial: Via Tirone, 11, 00146 ROMA
Tel: 06 45213395 **Fax:** 06 45213301
Email: info@contesticreativi.com **Web site:** http://www.luxuryfiles.com
Freq: Quarterly; **Circ:** 60,000
Editor-in-Chief: Fabrizio Rinversi
Profile: Magazine dedicated to the ultimate luxuries in life, includes watches, fashion, accessories, holidays and cars.
Language(s): English; Italian
Readership: Aimed at those with a high disposable income.
CONSUMER: WOMEN'S INTEREST CONSUMER MAGAZINES: Lifestyle

M & D - MUSICA E DISCHI 13918I61-50
Editorial: Via De Amicis 47, 20123 MILANO
Tel: 02 89402837 **Fax:** 02 8323843
Email: redazione@musicaedischi.it **Web site:** http://www.musicaedischi.it
Freq: Monthly; **Circ:** 25,000
Editor-in-Chief: Mario De Luigi
Profile: Magazine providing news concerning the international music and record industry. Features information on sales charts and new releases.
Language(s): Italian
Readership: Read by record company and music publishing executives, radio and TV programmers and producers, artists and retailers.
BUSINESS: MUSIC TRADE

MACCHINE UTENSILI 13392I19F-38
Editorial: Via Eritrea, 21, 20157 MILANO
Tel: 02 390901 **Fax:** 02 39090331
Email: macchine.utensili@tecnichenuove.com **Web site:** http://www.tecnichenuove.com
Freq: Monthly; **Circ:** 7,000
Editor-in-Chief: Giuseppe Nardella
Profile: News magazine about modern mechanical engineering.
Language(s): Italian
BUSINESS: ENGINEERING & MACHINERY: Production & Mechanical Engineering

MACPLAS 13590I39-75
Editorial: Milanofiori Palazzo F3, 20090 ASSAGO MI
Tel: 02 82283775 **Fax:** 02 57512490
Email: macplas@macplas.it **Web site:** http://www.macplas.it
Freq: 6 issues yearly; **Circ:** 8,100
Editor-in-Chief: Claudio Celata
Profile: Magazine for the plastics and rubber industry.
Language(s): Arabic; English; Italian; Polish; Spanish
BUSINESS: PLASTICS & RUBBER

MACWORLD ITALIA 13193I5C-145
Editorial: Via Zante, 16/2, 20138 MILANO MI
Tel: 02 580381 **Fax:** 02 58013422
Email: macworld@nuoveperiodici.it **Web site:** http://www.macworld.it
Freq: Monthly; **Circ:** 21,500
Editor-in-Chief: Mario Toffoletti
Profile: Magazine containing information about Macintosh computers, including news and reviews.
Language(s): Italian
Readership: Aimed at users of Macintosh computers.
BUSINESS: COMPUTERS & AUTOMATION: Professional Personal Computers

MADE IN ITALY 13302I14C-55
Editorial: C.so Vittorio Emanuele 15, 20122 MILANO
Tel: 0236560315 **Fax:** 02 561727
Email: info@madeinitaly1946.it **Web site:** http://www.madeinitaly1946.it
Freq: Annual; **Circ:** 30,000
Editor-in-Chief: Marco Polenghi
Profile: Journal of the Italian Chamber of Commerce for Foreign Trade, covers food and drink, fashion, hotel and hospitality equipment, building, furniture and interior decoration.
Language(s): English; Italian

Readership: Aimed at importers, distributors and traders.
BUSINESS: COMMERCE, INDUSTRY & MANAGEMENT: International Commerce

MADRE
14106I74A-258
Editorial: Via Callegari 6, 25121 BRESCIA
Tel: 030 42132 **Fax:** 030 290521
Email: redazione@rivistamadre.it **Web site:** http://www.rivistamadre.it
Freq: Monthly; **Circ:** 50,000
Profile: Magazine covering culture, news, politics and society. Focusing on problems faced by women with families. Also includes practical advice and articles about beauty and cooking.
Language(s): Italian
CONSUMER: WOMEN'S INTEREST CONSUMER MAGAZINES: Women's Interest

MAGLIERIA ITALIANA
13720I47C-30
Editorial: Via Giardini, 476, 41100 MODENA
Tel: 059342001 **Fax:** 059 351290
Email: info@editorialemoda.com **Web site:** http://www.maglieriaitaliana.com
Freq: Quarterly; **Circ:** 10,500
Profile: Magazine covering fashion and trends in the knitwear, wool and knitted garments trade. It also includes a six-page English language section.
Language(s): English; Italian
Readership: Read mainly by manufactures and buyers of knitwear and owners of outlets.
BUSINESS: CLOTHING & TEXTILES: Knitwear

MANI DI FATA
1896469I74E-144
Editorial: Via Vettabbia, 7, 20122 MILANO
Tel: 02 58310413 **Fax:** 0258310536
Email: mdf@manidifata.it **Web site:** http://www.manidifata.it
Freq: Monthly; **Circ:** 116,000
Editor-in-Chief: Vittorio Canetta
Language(s): Italian
CONSUMER: WOMEN'S INTEREST CONSUMER MAGAZINES: Crafts

IL MANIFESTO
13969I65A-75
Editorial: Via Bargoni, 8, 00153 ROMA RM
Tel: 06 687191 **Fax:** 06 68719573
Email: redazione@ilmanifesto.it **Web site:** http://www.ilmanifesto.it
Freq: Daily; **Circ:** 84,000
Editor: Giulia Sbarigia; **Editor-in-Chief:** Norma Rangeri
Profile: Tabloid-sized newspaper covering news, politics, finance, economics, sport and entertainment.
Language(s): Italian
Readership: Aimed at a broad range of the Italian population.
NATIONAL DAILY & SUNDAY NEWSPAPERS: National Daily Newspapers

MARIE CLAIRE
14107I74A-260
Editorial: Viale Sarca, 235, 20126 MILANO
Tel: 02 66193795 **Fax:** 02 66192483
Email: segreteriamarieclaire@hearst.it **Web site:** http://www.marieclaire.it
Freq: Monthly; **Circ:** 220,000
Editor: Antonio Mancinelli; **Editor-in-Chief:** Antonella Antonelli
Profile: Magazine containing articles on fashion, beauty, health, cookery and drink, interiors and worldwide sociopolitical issues.
Language(s): Italian
Readership: Read by women.
ADVERTISING RATES:
Full Page Colour .... EUR 42000.00
CONSUMER: WOMEN'S INTEREST CONSUMER MAGAZINES: Women's Interest

MARK UP
13244I10-60
Editorial: Via Pisacane 1, 20016 PERO MI
Tel: 02 30226194
Email: redazione.markup@ilsole24ore.com **Web site:** http://www.markup.it
Freq: Monthly; **Circ:** 25,000
Editor-in-Chief: Mattia Losi
Profile: Magazine focusing on distribution. Includes information about economics and production.
Language(s): Italian
Readership: Read by directors and managers in the distribution sector and wholesalers.
BUSINESS: MATERIALS HANDLING

MASTER MEETING
14578I2C-150
Editorial: Via San Simpliciano 4, 20121 MILANO
Tel: 02 862327 **Fax:** 02 863856
Email: info@communicationagency.it **Web site:** http://www.communicationagency.it
Freq: Monthly; **Circ:** 7,400
Editor-in-Chief: Manuela Mancini
Profile: Magazine containing information about conferences, exhibitions and meetings.
Language(s): Italian
Readership: Read by conference and convention organisers.
BUSINESS: COMMUNICATIONS, ADVERTISING & MARKETING: Conferences & Exhibitions

MASTER VIAGGI
13760I50-163
Editorial: Via di Sant'Agata De Goti, 2, 00184 ROMA
Tel: 06 6789984 **Fax:** 06 6991260
Email: info@masterviaggi.it **Web site:** http://www.masterviaggi.it
Freq: 6 times a year; **Circ:** 10,000 Unique Users
Editor-in-Chief: Ivano Camponeschi
Profile: International travel trade journal.
Language(s): English; Italian
Readership: Aimed at professionals in the travel industry.
BUSINESS: TRAVEL & TOURISM

MAX
14082I73-280
Editorial: Via A. Rizzoli 8, 20132 MILANO
Tel: 02 25843510 **Fax:** 02 25843683
Email: max@rcs.it **Web site:** http://www.max.rcs.it
Freq: Monthly; **Circ:** 192,000
Editor: Luca Bratina; **Editor-in-Chief:** Andrea Rossi
Profile: General interest magazine containing film reviews, fashion and features.
Language(s): Italian
ADVERTISING RATES:
Full Page Mono .... EUR 22500.00
Full Page Colour .... EUR 22500.00
Mechanical Data: Type Area: 205x287 mm
CONSUMER: NATIONAL & INTERNATIONAL PERIODICALS

MAXIM MAGAZINE
14485I86C-80
Editorial: V.le Sondrio, 7, 20124 MILANO
Tel: 02 89051800 **Fax:** 02 89051814
Email: redazione@maxim.it **Web site:** http://www.maxim.it
Freq: Monthly
Editor: Gianni Passavini; **Editor-in-Chief:** Paolo Gelmi
Profile: Magazine covering general lifestyle issues.
Language(s): Italian
Readership: Aimed at men aged between 20 and 45 years.
ADVERTISING RATES:
Full Page Colour .... EUR 5000.00
CONSUMER: ADULT & GAY MAGAZINES: Men's Lifestyle Magazines

MC MEETING E CONGRESSI
13750I2C-151
Editorial: Via Ripamonti 89, 20141 MILANO
Tel: 0257311532 **Fax:** 02 55231486
Email: mc@ediman.it **Web site:** http://www.mconline.it
Freq: Monthly; **Circ:** 11,000
Editor-in-Chief: Marco Biamonti
Profile: Magazine containing information on organizing conferences, exhibitions, seminars and convents.
Language(s): Italian
Readership: Read by marketing directors, people in the PR industry, organizers of conferences, exhibitions, seminars and convents and business men.
BUSINESS: COMMUNICATIONS, ADVERTISING & MARKETING: Conferences & Exhibitions

M.D. MEDICINAE DOCTOR
13824I56A-130
Editorial: Piazza Duca d'Aosta, 12, 20124 MILANO MI **Tel:** 02 6760681 **Fax:** 02 6702680
Email: medicinae.doctor@passonieditore.it **Web site:** http://www.passonieditore.it
Freq: Weekly; **Circ:** 40,000
Editor-in-Chief: Dario Passoni
Profile: Journal covering the medical profession.
Language(s): Italian
Readership: Read by general practitioners.
BUSINESS: HEALTH & MEDICAL

MDP - LA CONCERIA E LE MANIFATTURE DELLE PELLI
13784I52D-40
Editorial: Via Brisa, 3, 20123 MILANO MI
Tel: 028807711 **Fax:** 02 865732
Email: info@laconceria.it **Web site:** http://www.laconceria.it
Freq: Weekly; **Circ:** 1,500
Editor-in-Chief: Salvatore Mercogliano
Profile: Magazine about the tanning and manufacture of leather goods.
Language(s): English; Italian
Readership: Aimed at tanners, producers of machines, chemists, shoe manufacturers, furniture manufacturers and dealers in leather goods.
BUSINESS: GIFT TRADE: Leather

MEDIA KEY
13065I2A-70
Editorial: Via Arcivescovo Romilli, 20/8, 20139 MILANO **Tel:** 02 5220371 **Fax:** 02 55213037
Email: redazione@mediakey.it **Web site:** http://www.mediakey.tv
Freq: Monthly; **Circ:** 10,500
Editor-in-Chief: Roberto Albano
Profile: Journal about media, marketing and advertising.
Language(s): Italian
ADVERTISING RATES:
Full Page Mono .... EUR 2850.00
Full Page Colour .... EUR 4285.00
Mechanical Data: Type Area: 210x297 mm
BUSINESS: COMMUNICATIONS, ADVERTISING & MARKETING

MEDIAFORUM
13087I2E-60
Editorial: Via Pietrasanta 14, 20141 MILANO
Tel: 02535981 **Fax:** 0253598247
Email: redazione@ediforum.it **Web site:** http://www.ediforum.it
Freq: Weekly; **Circ:** 12,000
Editor-in-Chief: Gianni Quarleri
Profile: Magazine containing news and information concerning global communications and media marketing.
Language(s): Italian
Readership: Read by communications and marketing professionals.
BUSINESS: COMMUNICATIONS, ADVERTISING & MARKETING: Public Relations

MEDIAPLUSNEWS
13066I2A-73
Editorial: Via Capecelatro, 53/2, 20148 MILANO MI
Tel: 02 4039949
Email: paola.pirogalli@fastwebnet.it
Freq: Monthly; **Circ:** 12,000
Editor-in-Chief: Franco Marelli Coppola
Profile: Magazine containing marketing information and cultural and technological news, includes sections on patents, European news and leisure.
Language(s): Italian
BUSINESS: COMMUNICATIONS, ADVERTISING & MARKETING

MEDICINA DELLO SPORT
13827I56A-155
Editorial: C.so Bramante 83/85, 10100 TORINO
Tel: 011 678282 **Fax:** 011 674502
Email: minervamedica@minervamedica.it **Web site:** http://www.minervamedica.it
Freq: Quarterly; **Circ:** 6,000
Editor-in-Chief: Alberto Oliaro
Profile: Journal focusing on sports medicine and traumatology.
Language(s): Italian
Readership: Read by sports physicians, physiotherapists and traumatologists.
BUSINESS: HEALTH & MEDICAL

MEDICINA NATURALE
13825I56A-145
Editorial: Via Eritrea, 21, 20157 MILANO
Tel: 02 39090290 **Fax:** 02 39090332
Email: medicinanaturale@tecnichenuove.com **Web site:** http://www.tecnichenuove.com
Freq: 6 issues yearly; **Circ:** 6,100
Editor-in-Chief: Giuseppe Nardella
Profile: Magazine providing technical and scientific information on all aspects of natural medicine, including nutrition, homeopathy, acupuncture, naturopathy and chiropractics.
Language(s): Italian
BUSINESS: HEALTH & MEDICAL

MEN'S HEALTH
762592I86C-90
Editorial: Via Mondadori, 1, 20090 SEGRATE MI
Tel: 02 75423190 **Fax:** 02 75423193
Email: mens@mondadori.it **Web site:** http://www.menshealth.it
Freq: Monthly; **Circ:** 180,000
Editor: Ezio Genghini; **Editor-in-Chief:** Luigi Grella
Profile: Magazine covering health and fashion issues.
Language(s): Italian
Readership: Aimed at men aged between 20 and 45 years.
ADVERTISING RATES:
Full Page Colour .... EUR 38000.00
CONSUMER: ADULT & GAY MAGAZINES: Men's Lifestyle Magazines

MENU'
13251I11A-150
Editorial: Via Giardini 476/N, 41100 MODENA
Tel: 059342001 **Fax:** 059351290
Email: menu@editorialemoda.com **Web site:** http://www.menu.it
Freq: Quarterly; **Circ:** 33,000
Editor-in-Chief: Maria Muratori Casali
Profile: Review of food specialities for the catering trade. Includes recipes and related items of interest.
Language(s): Italian
Readership: Read by managers in the catering trade.
BUSINESS: CATERING: Catering, Hotels & Restaurants

MERIDIANI
14510I89A-260
Editorial: Via Gianni Mazzocchi 1/3, 20089 ROZZANO MI **Tel:** 02 824721 **Fax:** 02 82472403
Email: redazione@meridiani.com **Web site:** http://www.edidomus.it
Freq: Monthly; **Circ:** 40,000
Editor: Renzo Bassi; **Editor-in-Chief:** Remo Guerrini
Profile: Magazine concerning culture and tourism.
Language(s): Italian
CONSUMER: HOLIDAYS & TRAVEL: Travel

IL MESSAGGERO
13970I65A-80
Editorial: Via Del Tritone 152, 00187 ROMA
Tel: 06 47201 **Fax:** 06 4720665
Email: segreteria.redazione@ilmessaggero.it **Web site:** http://www.ilmessaggero.it
Freq: Daily; **Circ:** 400,000
Editor: Eugenio Malgeri; **Editor-in-Chief:** Mario Orfeo
Profile: Broadsheet-sized quality newspaper providing national and international news and articles on politics, finance, economics, sport and entertainment.
Language(s): Italian
Readership: Read by a wide range of people, predominantly living in the Lazio area.
ADVERTISING RATES:
Full Page Mono .... EUR 129248.00
Full Page Colour .... EUR 193872.00
NATIONAL DAILY & SUNDAY NEWSPAPERS: National Daily Newspapers

MESSAGGERO DEI RAGAZZI
14547I91D-90
Editorial: Via Orto Botanico, 11, 35123 PADOVA
Tel: 049 8225909 **Fax:** 049 8225650
Email: redazione@meraweb.it **Web site:** http://www.meraweb.it
Freq: Monthly; **Circ:** 30,000
Editor-in-Chief: Ugo Sartorio
Profile: European magazine focusing on sport, nature and adventure holidays, religious stories, also contains cartoons and games.
Language(s): English; Italian
Readership: Aimed at young people aged between 14 and 25 years.
CONSUMER: RECREATION & LEISURE: Children & Youth

MESSAGGERO DI S. ANTONIO
14491I87-100
Editorial: Via Orto Botanico, 11, 35123 PADOVA
Tel: 049 8225777 **Fax:** 049 8225650
Email: info@santantonio.org **Web site:** http://www.santantonio.org
Freq: Monthly; **Circ:** 538,310
Editor-in-Chief: Ugo Sartorio
Profile: Journal containing major news stories relating to religious matters concerning the Catholic faith.
Language(s): English; French; German; Portuguese; Romanian; Spanish
CONSUMER: RELIGIOUS

MFF - MAGAZINE FOR FASHION (MF)
762988I74B-175
Editorial: Via Marco Burigozzo, 5, 20122 MILANO MI
Tel: 02 58219696 **Fax:** 0258219609
Email: mffmagazine@class.it **Web site:** http://www.mffashion.it
Freq: 6 issues yearly
Editor-in-Chief: Paolo Panerai
Profile: Magazine containing information on fashion and accessories.
Language(s): Italian
Readership: Read by women.
CONSUMER: WOMEN'S INTEREST CONSUMER MAGAZINES: Women's Interest - Fashion

LA MIA 4X4
1784932I77A-411
Editorial: Via Galileo Galilei, 3, 10023 CHIERI TO
Tel: 011 9470400 **Fax:** 011 9470577
Email: lamia4x4@barberoeditori.it **Web site:** http://www.barberoeditori.it
Freq: Monthly; **Circ:** 120,000
Editor-in-Chief: Riccardo Barbero
Language(s): Italian
CONSUMER: MOTORING & CYCLING: Motoring

LA MIA AUTO
714737I77A-270
Editorial: Via Galileo Galilei 3, 10023 CHIERI TO
Tel: 011 9470400 **Fax:** 011 9470577
Email: lamiaauto@barberoeditori.it **Web site:** http://www.barberoeditori.it
Freq: Monthly; **Circ:** 180,000
Editor-in-Chief: Enrico Artifoni
Profile: Magazine containing reviews, tests and a price guide for new and second hand cars.
Language(s): Italian
CONSUMER: MOTORING & CYCLING: Motoring

MICE - MEETINGS INCENTIVES CONFERENCES EVENTS
13079I2C-20
Editorial: Via Teocrito 47, 20128 MILANO
Tel: 02 252071 **Fax:** 02 27000692
Email: mice@bema.it **Web site:** http://www.bema.it
Freq: 6 issues yearly; **Circ:** 4,704
Editor-in-Chief: Gisella Bertini Malgarini
Profile: Magazine containing information about conferences, exhibitions and congresses for business people. Also includes information concerning the tourism industry.
Language(s): Italian
Readership: Aimed at hoteliers, travel agents and tourist operators.
BUSINESS: COMMUNICATIONS, ADVERTISING & MARKETING: Conferences & Exhibitions

MIGRAZIONE E CACCIA
14269I75F-250
Editorial: Via Enrico Fermi 24 - Località Osmannoro, 50019 SESTO FIORENTINO FI **Tel:** 055 30321
Fax: 055 3032280
Email: segreteria1@edolimpia.it **Web site:** http://www.edolimpia.it
Freq: 6 issues yearly; **Circ:** 30,000
Editor-in-Chief: Pier Luigi Chierici
Profile: Magazine containing articles about the migration of birds and other areas of interest to hunters.
Language(s): Italian
Readership: Aimed at huntsmen.
CONSUMER: SPORT: Shooting

MILANO CASA OGGI MODI DI VIVERE
1784219I74C-301
Editorial: Via Settembrini, 11, 20124 MILANO
Tel: 02 67495250 **Fax:** 02 67495333
Email: traffico@dibaio.com **Web site:** http://www.dibaio.com
Freq: Annual; **Circ:** 80,000
Language(s): Italian
CONSUMER: WOMEN'S INTEREST CONSUMER MAGAZINES: Home & Family

MILANO FINANZA
1784212I1A-216
Editorial: Via Burigozzo, 5, 20122 MILANO MI
Tel: 02 582191 **Fax:** 02 58317509
Email: mf-milanofinanza@class.it **Web site:** http://www.milanofinanza.it
Freq: Weekly; **Circ:** 203,000
Editor: Francesco Allegra; **Editor-in-Chief:** Paolo Panerai
Language(s): Italian
ADVERTISING RATES:
Full Page Colour .... EUR 73000.00
BUSINESS: FINANCE & ECONOMICS

MILANO FINANZA RM
1784482I1A-222
Editorial: Via Santa Maria in Via 12, 00187 ROMA
Tel: 06 6976081 **Fax:** 06 69920373
Email: mf-milanofinanza@class.it **Web site:** http://www.milanofinanza.it
Freq: Weekly; **Circ:** 203,000
Language(s): Italian
BUSINESS: FINANCE & ECONOMICS

MILLECANALI
13084I2D-70
Editorial: Via Pisacane 1, 20016 PERO MI
Tel: 0230226005
Email: redazione.millecanali@ilsole24ore.com **Web site:** http://www.millecanali.it
Freq: Monthly; **Circ:** 18,000
Editor-in-Chief: Antonio Greco
Profile: Magazine about radio and TV broadcasting and communications. Includes product news on audio visual equipment and audiovisual production.
Language(s): Italian
BUSINESS: COMMUNICATIONS, ADVERTISING & MARKETING: Broadcasting

MILLIONAIRE
1784358I1A-240
Editorial: Vai Farnese, 3, 20146 MILANO
Tel: 02 83303433 **Fax:** 02 83303426
Email: segreteria@millionaire.it **Web site:** http://www.millionaire.it
Freq: Monthly; **Circ:** 220,000
Editor: Eleonora Chioda; **Editor-in-Chief:** Virgilio Degiovanni
Profile: Magazine containing information about franchising and related information.
Language(s): Italian
Readership: Aimed at people who want to start their own business.
ADVERTISING RATES:
Full Page Colour .... EUR 24000.00
BUSINESS: FINANCE & ECONOMICS

MINERVA ANESTESIOLOGICA
13857I56C-40
Editorial: C.so Bramante 83, 10126 TORINO
Tel: 011 678282 **Fax:** 011 674502
Email: minervamedica@minervamedica.it **Web site:** http://www.minervamedica.it
Freq: Monthly; **Circ:** 5,000
Editor-in-Chief: Alberto Oliaro
Profile: Official journal of the Italian Society of Anaesthesiology, Analgesia, Resuscitation and Intensive Care.
Language(s): English
Readership: Read by anaesthetists and doctors working in intensive care.
BUSINESS: HEALTH & MEDICAL: Hospitals

MINERVA CARDIOANGIOLOGICA
13831I56A-180
Editorial: C.so Bramante 83, 10126 TORINO
Tel: 011 678282 **Fax:** 011 674502
Email: minervamedica@minervamedica.it **Web site:** http://www.minervamedica.it
Freq: 6 issues yearly; **Circ:** 5,000
Editor-in-Chief: Alberto Oliaro
Profile: Magazine focusing on pathology, ultra-sonics and phlebology. Covers news from the Italian Clinical and Experimental Society.
Language(s): Italian
Readership: Read by specialists in the field.
BUSINESS: HEALTH & MEDICAL

MINERVA CHIRURGICA
13832I56A-182
Editorial: C.so Bramante 83, 10126 TORINO
Tel: 011678282 **Fax:** 011674502
Email: minervamedica@minervamedica.it **Web site:** http://www.minervamedica.it
Freq: 6 issues yearly; **Circ:** 5,000
Editor-in-Chief: Alberto Oliaro
Profile: Journal focusing on surgery, clinical medicine and therapy.
Language(s): Italian
Readership: Read by surgeons.
BUSINESS: HEALTH & MEDICAL

MINERVA GINECOLOGICA
13834I56A-187
Editorial: C.so Bramante 83, 10126 TORINO
Tel: 011 678282 **Fax:** 011 674502
Email: minervamedica@minervamedica.it **Web site:** http://www.minervamedica.it
Freq: 6 issues yearly; **Circ:** 5,000
Editor-in-Chief: Alberto Oliaro
Profile: Journal about obstetrical and gynaecological physiopathology, clinical medicine and therapy.
Language(s): English
Readership: Read by gynaecologists and obstetricians.
BUSINESS: HEALTH & MEDICAL

MINERVA MEDICA
13835I56A-190
Editorial: C.so Bramante 83, 10126 TORINO
Tel: 011 678282 **Fax:** 011 674502
Email: minervamedica@minervamedica.it **Web site:** http://www.minervamedica.it
Freq: 6 issues yearly; **Circ:** 5,000
Editor-in-Chief: Alberto Oliaro
Profile: Journal focusing on internal medicine.
Language(s): Italian
BUSINESS: HEALTH & MEDICAL

MINERVA PEDIATRICA
13837I56A-215_50
Editorial: C.so Bramante 83, 10126 TORINO
Tel: 011 678282 **Fax:** 011 674502
Email: minervamedica@minervamedica.it **Web site:** http://www.minervamedica.it
Freq: 6 issues yearly; **Circ:** 6,000
Editor-in-Chief: Alberto Oliaro
Profile: Journal focusing on paediatrics, neo-natology, adolescent medicine, child and adolescent psychiatry and paediatric surgery.
Language(s): Italian
Readership: Read by paediatricians.
BUSINESS: HEALTH & MEDICAL

MINERVA STOMATOLOGICA
13865I56D-40
Editorial: C.so Bramante 83, 10126 TORINO
Tel: 011 678282 **Fax:** 011 674502
Email: minervamedica@minervamedica.it **Web site:** http://www.minervamedica.it
Freq: Monthly; **Circ:** 4,000
Editor-in-Chief: Alberto Oliaro
Profile: Official journal of the Italian Society of Odontostomatology and Maxillo-Facial Surgery.
Language(s): English
Readership: Read by orthodontists and facial surgeons.
BUSINESS: HEALTH & MEDICAL: Dental

IL MIO COMPUTER
13200I5D-150
Editorial: Via Torino, 51, 20063 CERNUSCO SUL NAVIGLIO MI **Tel:** 02 926263172 **Fax:** 02 926263147
Email: redazione@ilmiocomputer.it **Web site:** http://www.sprea.it
Freq: Monthly
Editor-in-Chief: Luca Sprea
Profile: Magazine focusing on all aspects of personal computing. Contains news and background information about CD-ROM, Windows, the Internet, computer games and accessories. Also includes product reviews and guides to computing and helps in choosing accessories.
Language(s): Italian
Readership: Read by computer owners.
ADVERTISING RATES:
Full Page Colour .... EUR 12500.00
BUSINESS: COMPUTERS & AUTOMATION: Personal Computers

IL MIO VINO
1785019I74P-282
Editorial: Via Feltre, 28/6, 20132 MILANO
Tel: 02 270861 **Fax:** 02 87365819
Email: info@ilmiovino.it **Web site:** http://www.ilmiovino.it
Freq: Monthly; **Circ:** 100,000
Editor-in-Chief: Gaetano Manti
Language(s): Italian
CONSUMER: WOMEN'S INTEREST CONSUMER MAGAZINES: Food & Cookery

MIXER
13235I9A-30
Editorial: Via Ariberto, 21, 20123 MILANO
Tel: 02 58140020 **Fax:** 02 58140021
Email: segreteria@fieramilanoeditore.it **Web site:** http://www.mixable.it
Freq: Monthly; **Circ:** 126,000
Profile: Official journal of the International Bartenders' Association. Covers bar food, drink and tourism.
Language(s): Italian
Readership: Read by members.
BUSINESS: DRINKS & LICENSED TRADE: Drinks, Licensed Trade, Wines & Spirits

MM MAGAZINE
1784629I74B-354
Editorial: Via privata Maria Teresa, 11, 20123 MILANO **Tel:** 02 89015334 **Fax:** 02 86990124
Email: a.carpitella@libero.it **Web site:** http://www.maxmara.com/it/MM-Magazine
Freq: Half-yearly; **Circ:** 550,000
Editor-in-Chief: Riccardo Bertolini
Language(s): Italian
CONSUMER: WOMEN'S INTEREST CONSUMER MAGAZINES: Women's Interest - Fashion

MODA E INDUSTRIA
13717I47B-30
Editorial: Viale Coni Zugna 71, 20144 MILANO
Tel: 023451230 **Fax:** 023451231
Email: modaeindustria@gestoeditore.it **Web site:** http://www.gestoeditore.it
Freq: 6 issues yearly; **Circ:** 7,000
Editor-in-Chief: Eugenio Faiella
Profile: Official journal of the Italian Association of Clothing and Knitwear Manufacturers. Covers lingerie, hosiery and knitwear.
Language(s): Italian
BUSINESS: CLOTHING & TEXTILES: Lingerie, Hosiery/Swimwear

MODULO
13144I4E-140
Editorial: Via Teocrito, 47, 20128 MILANO
Tel: 02252071 **Fax:** 02 27000692
Email: modulo@bema.it **Web site:** http://www.modulo.net
Freq: Monthly; **Circ:** 12,500
Editor-in-Chief: Gisella Bertini Malgarini
Profile: Review of building technology and projects.
Language(s): Italian
BUSINESS: ARCHITECTURE & BUILDING: Building

IL MONDO
14446I82-75
Editorial: Via A. Rizzoli 8, 20132 MILANO
Tel: 02 25841 **Fax:** 02 25843880
Email: ilmondo@rcs.it **Web site:** http://www.ilmondo.rcs.it
Freq: Weekly; **Circ:** 79,000
Editor: Ettore Tamos; **Editor-in-Chief:** Enrico Romagna Manoja
Profile: Magazine covering economics, politics, finance and culture.
Language(s): Italian
Readership: Aimed at managers, graduates and students.
ADVERTISING RATES:
Full Page Colour .... EUR 20000.00
CONSUMER: CURRENT AFFAIRS & POLITICS

MONDO AGRICOLO
13404I21A-250
Editorial: Corso Vittorio Emanuele II, 101, 00186 ROMA **Tel:** 06 6852358 **Fax:** 06 6861726
Email: mondo.agricolo@confagricoltura.it **Web site:** http://www.mondoagricolo.info
Freq: Monthly; **Circ:** 50,000
Editor-in-Chief: Gabriella Bechi
Profile: Official journal of the Italian Confederation of Agriculture.
Language(s): Italian
BUSINESS: AGRICULTURE & FARMING

IL MONDO DEI TRASPORTI
13730I49A-31
Editorial: Via Ramazzotti, 20, 20900 MONZA MI
Tel: 039 493101 **Fax:** 039 493103
Email: info@vegaeditrice.it **Web site:** http://www.vegaeditrice.it
Freq: Monthly; **Circ:** 35,000
Editor-in-Chief: Paolo Altieri
Profile: Magazine covering all aspects of the transport industry.
Language(s): Italian
Readership: Read by managers of transport companies.
BUSINESS: TRANSPORT

IL MONDO DEL GOLF
14261I75D-300
Editorial: Corso Monforte, 36, 20122 MILANO MI
Tel: 02 7788501 **Fax:** 02 76004905
Email: ilmondodelgolf@scode.it **Web site:** http://www.ilmondodelgolf.it
Freq: Monthly; **Circ:** 23,500
Editor-in-Chief: Fulvio Golob
Profile: Review covering golf techniques, competitions and tourism involving golf.
Language(s): Italian
Readership: Read by golf enthusiasts.
CONSUMER: SPORT: Golf

MONDO E MISSIONE
14492I87-120
Editorial: Via Mose' Bianchi, 94, 20149 MILANO
Tel: 02 43822317 **Fax:** 02 43822397
Email: mondoemissione@pimemilano.com **Web site:** http://www.missionline.org
Freq: Monthly; **Circ:** 10,000
Editor-in-Chief: Gian Paolo Gualzetti
Profile: Magazine containing general and cultural news concerning missionary work in the third world.
Language(s): Italian
Readership: Aimed at missionaries and other religious workers.
CONSUMER: RELIGIOUS

MONDO ERRE
14199I74F-145
Editorial: Corso Francia 214, 10090 CASCINE VICA RIVOLI TO **Tel:** 011 9552311 **Fax:** 011 9591095
Email: mondoerre@mondoerre.it **Web site:** http://www.mondoerre.it
Freq: Monthly; **Circ:** 25,000
Editor-in-Chief: Valter Rossi
Profile: Magazine containing topical and cultural news. Covers sport, music, nature, science, history and adventure. Also includes profiles and interviews.
Language(s): Italian
Readership: Aimed at adolescents.
CONSUMER: WOMEN'S INTEREST CONSUMER MAGAZINES: Teenage

MONDO ORTODONTICO
13866I56D-48
Editorial: Via Paleocapa, 7, 20121 MILANO
Tel: 02 881841 **Fax:** 02 88184302
Email: l.fabri@elsevier.com **Web site:** http://www.elsevier.it
Freq: 6 issues yearly; **Circ:** 4,100
Editor-in-Chief: Emile Blomme
Profile: Journal publishing clinical and experimental papers concerning new procedures and the principles underlying orthodontic treatments. Featuring the possibility of implantology in the planning of some treatments that require pre-orthodontic surgery.
Language(s): English; Italian
BUSINESS: HEALTH & MEDICAL: Dental

MONDO SOMMERSO - INTERNATIONAL OCEAN MAGAZINE
14292I75M-120
Editorial: Via E. Fermi 24 - Località Osmannoro, 50019 SESTO FIORENTINO FI **Tel:** 055 30321
Fax: 055 3032280
Email: mondosommerso@edolimpia.it **Web site:** http://www.mondosommerso-online.it
Freq: Monthly; **Circ:** 48,000
Editor-in-Chief: Sabina Cupi
Profile: Magazine covering all aspects of the sea and related topics. Contains articles on scuba diving, science, medicine, photography, archaeology, tourism and the environment.
Language(s): English; Italian
Readership: Read by photographers and diving enthusiasts.
CONSUMER: SPORT: Water Sports

MONITOR RADIO TELEVISIONE
13085I2D-90
Editorial: Via San Michele del Carso, 13, 20144 MILANO MI **Tel:** 02 43910135 **Fax:** 02 43999112
Email: info@monitor-radiotv.com **Web site:** http://www.monitor-radiotv.com
Freq: Monthly; **Circ:** 9,000
Editor-in-Chief: Enrico Callerio
Profile: Magazine concerning broadcasting technology. Includes television, radio and network news, business and technical information.
Language(s): Italian
Readership: Aimed at professionals in the broadcasting industry.
BUSINESS: COMMUNICATIONS, ADVERTISING & MARKETING: Broadcasting

MONOVOLUME & STATION WAGON RADAR
14355I77A-274
Editorial: Via San Fruttuoso 10, 20052 MONZA MI
Tel: 039 736451 **Fax:** 039 736500
Email: radarstudiozeta@tin.it **Web site:** http://www.autoambiente.com
Freq: 6 issues yearly; **Circ:** 40,000
Profile: Magazine containing articles, reviews and news about family cars. Also covers tests and new products.
Language(s): Italian
Readership: Read by people considering purchasing a new vehicle.
CONSUMER: MOTORING & CYCLING: Motoring

MONTEBIANCO 14272I75L-60
Editorial: Via Gadames, 123, 20151 MILANO MI
Tel: 02 365881 **Fax:** 02 36588218
Email: montebianco@leditore.it **Web site:** http://www.montebianco.it
Freq: Monthly; **Circ:** 59,000
Editor-in-Chief: Sara Bovo
Profile: Magazine focusing on travelling in the mountains, includes walking and skiing.
Language(s): Italian
CONSUMER: SPORT: Outdoor

MOTO STORICHE & D' EPOCA 14365I77B-95
Editorial: Via Molise, 3, 20085 LOCATE TRIULZI MI
Tel: 02 9048111 **Fax:** 02 90481120
Email: info@nuoviperiodicimilanesi.com **Web site:** http://www.motostorichedepoca.com
Freq: 6 issues yearly; **Circ:** 40,000
Editor-in-Chief: Daniele Cafieri
Profile: Magazine focusing on motorcycles, bikers and championships from a historical perspective.
Language(s): Italian
Readership: Read by fans of historical and legendary motorcycles, collectors of classic motorcycles and other paraphernalia as well as people who love to visit championships, shows and exhibitions.
CONSUMER: MOTORING & CYCLING: Motorcycling

MOTOCICLISMO 14366I77B-100
Editorial: Via Don Luigi Sturzo 7, 20016 PERO MI
Tel: 02 38085302 **Fax:** 0238010393
Email: motociclismo@edisport.it **Web site:** http://www.motociclismo.it
Freq: Monthly; **Circ:** 200,000
Editor: Federico Aliverti; **Editor-in-Chief:** Adalberto Falletta
Profile: Magazine covering all aspects of motorcycling. Includes articles about classic bikes, new models, technical advice, book and video reviews and tourism. Also contains a section listing new and used bikes for sale.
Language(s): Italian
CONSUMER: MOTORING & CYCLING: Motorcycling

MOTOCICLISMO D'EPOCA 14367I77B-105
Editorial: Via Don Luigi Sturzo 7, 20016 PERO MI
Tel: 02 38085310 **Fax:** 02 38010393
Email: motoepoca@edisport.it **Web site:** http://www.motociclismo.it
Freq: Monthly
Editor-in-Chief: Carlo Perelli
Profile: Magazine containing information about classic bikes.
Language(s): Italian
Readership: Read by motorcycle enthusiasts.
CONSUMER: MOTORING & CYCLING: Motorcycling

MOTOCICLISMO FUORI STRADA 1785031I77A-415
Editorial: Via Don Luigi Sturzo 7, 20016 PERO MI
Tel: 02 380851 **Fax:** 02 38010393
Email: motociclismofuoristrada@edisport.it **Web site:** http://www.motociclismofuoristrada.it
Freq: Monthly; **Circ:** 83,000
Editor-in-Chief: Adalberto Falletta
Language(s): Italian
CONSUMER: MOTORING & CYCLING: Motoring

MOTOCROSS 14368I77B-120
Editorial: Via Cusani, 10, 20121 MILANO MI
Tel: 02809606 **Fax:** 02809609
Email: motocross@motocross.it **Web site:** http://www.motocross.it
Freq: Monthly; **Circ:** 105,000
Editor-in-Chief: Edoardo Pacini
Profile: Motorcycling sport magazine focusing on endurance, motocross, trial, speedway and rally.
Language(s): Italian
Readership: Read by motorcycling enthusiasts.
CONSUMER: MOTORING & CYCLING: Motorcycling

MOTONAUTICA 14536I91A-120
Editorial: Via IV Novembre, 54, 20019 SETTIMO MILANESE (MI) **Tel:** 02 33553234 **Fax:** 02 33513441
Email: info@motonautica.it **Web site:** http://www.motonautica.it
Freq: Monthly; **Circ:** 50,000
Editor-in-Chief: Claudia Muggiani
Profile: International publication covering charter and commercial crafts, yachts, cruisers, sports boats and second-hand boats.
Language(s): English; Italian
Readership: Aimed at motorboat and general boating enthusiasts.
CONSUMER: RECREATION & LEISURE: Boating & Yachting

MOTOR 14356I77A-280
Editorial: Piazza A. Mancini, 4/G, 00196 ROMA
Tel: 06 3233195 **Fax:** 06 3233309
Email: redazione@rivistamotor.com **Web site:** http://www.rivistamotor.it
Freq: Monthly; **Circ:** 65,000
Profile: Motoring magazine covering off-road driving, vintage cars, motorbikes and model-making.
Language(s): Italian
CONSUMER: MOTORING & CYCLING: Motoring

MOTORINEWS 14712I31A-35
Editorial: Via Don Romano Grosso, 45/11, 10060 AIRASCA TO **Tel:** 011 9908841 **Fax:** 011 9908841
Email: info@motorinews.it
Freq: 6 issues yearly; **Circ:** 40,000
Editor-in-Chief: Renato De Giorgis
Profile: Official magazine for AIRA-CNA association covering innovations, legislation and law related business in the car mechanics, tyre repairs, body repairs, car accessories and components sector.
Language(s): Italian
Readership: Read by car mechanics, electricians and car trader management.
BUSINESS: MOTOR TRADE: Motor Trade Accessories

MOTOSPRINT 14369I77B-150
Editorial: Via del Lavoro, 7, 40068 SAN LAZZARO DI SAVENA BO **Tel:** 051 6227111 **Fax:** 051 6256191
Email: motosprint@motosprint.it **Web site:** http://www.motosprint.it
Freq: Weekly; **Circ:** 100,000
Editor-in-Chief: Stefano Saragoni
Profile: Review of national and international motor-sport events, including reports of off-road and motocross championships. Also contains a guide to new models, and information about classic bikes and tourism.
Language(s): Italian
CONSUMER: MOTORING & CYCLING: Motorcycling

MOTOTURISMO 14370I77B-190
Editorial: Piazza Roma, 1, 22070 LURAGO MARINONE CO **Tel:** 031937736 **Fax:** 031937362
Email: redazione@mototurismo.it **Web site:** http://www.mototurismo.it
Freq: Monthly; **Circ:** 35,000
Editor-in-Chief: Tiziano Cantatore
Profile: Magazine about the pleasures of touring by bike. Contains a review of places visited, with additional information regarding history and culture. Also includes articles about food, fashion, photography and leisure.
Language(s): Italian
Readership: Read by motorbike owners who love travel and the open air.
CONSUMER: MOTORING & CYCLING: Motorcycling

MUCCHIO SELVAGGIO 14335I76E-220
Editorial: Via Antonio Silvani, 8 (scala D int. 4), 00139 ROMA **Tel:** 068121374 **Fax:** 06 8108317
Email: redazionespettacoli@ilmucchio.it **Web site:** http://www.ilmucchio.it
Freq: Monthly; **Circ:** 52,000
Editor-in-Chief: Daniela Federico
Profile: Magazine about music and rock culture.
Language(s): Italian
CONSUMER: MUSIC & PERFORMING ARTS: Pop Music

IL MULINO 14447I82-95
Editorial: Strada Maggiore, 37, 40125 BOLOGNA
Tel: 051 222419 **Fax:** 051 6486014
Email: rivistailmulino@mulino.it **Web site:** http://www.rivistailmulino.it
Freq: 6 issues yearly; **Circ:** 12,000
Editor: Bruno Simili; **Editor-in-Chief:** Piero Ignazi
Profile: Journal about culture, politics, change and transformation in contemporary society.
Language(s): Italian
CONSUMER: CURRENT AFFAIRS & POLITICS

MUSICA 14327I76D-300
Editorial: Via Tonale, 60, 21100 VARESE
Tel: 0332 335606 **Fax:** 0332 331013
Email: info@rivistamusica.com **Web site:** http://www.rivistamusica.com
Freq: Monthly; **Circ:** 22,000
Editor-in-Chief: Stephen Hastings
Profile: Magazine about classical music and the recording industry.
Language(s): Italian
CONSUMER: MUSIC & PERFORMING ARTS: Music

NATURAL STYLE 1785050I22A-61
Editorial: Corso Magenta, 55, 20123 MILANO MI
Tel: 02 43313482 **Fax:** 02 43313575
Email: natural@cairoeditore.it **Web site:** http://www.cairoeditore.it
Freq: Monthly; **Circ:** 140,000
Editor: Stefano Negrini; **Editor-in-Chief:** Andrea Biavardi
Language(s): Italian
BUSINESS: FOOD

NAUTICA 14537I91A-130
Editorial: Via Tevere, 44, 00198 ROMA
Tel: 06 8413060 **Fax:** 06 8543653
Email: info@nautica.it **Web site:** http://www.nautica.it
Freq: Monthly; **Circ:** 48,000
Editor: Roberto Giorgi; **Editor-in-Chief:** Luca Sonnino Sorisio
Profile: Magazine about luxury yachts, power cruisers, sailing dinghies and sportsboats.
Language(s): Croatian; Greek; Italian
Readership: Aimed at boating enthusiasts.
CONSUMER: RECREATION & LEISURE: Boating & Yachting

LA NAZIONE 13971I65A-90
Editorial: Viale Giovine Italia, 17, 50122 FIRENZE
Tel: 055 24951 **Fax:** 055 2343646
Email: segreteria.redazione.firenze@monrif.net **Web site:** http://www.lanazione.it
Freq: Daily; **Circ:** 215,000
Editor: Laura Pacciani; **Editor-in-Chief:** Mauro Tedeschini
Profile: Broadsheet-sized newspaper providing regional, national and international news. Also contains articles on finance, economics, sport and entertainment.
Language(s): Italian
Readership: Read predominantly by people living in the Tuscany and Umbria regions.
ADVERTISING RATES:
Full Page Colour .... EUR 105000.00
NATIONAL DAILY & SUNDAY NEWSPAPERS: National Daily Newspapers

NETWORK WORLD ITALIA (COMPUTERWORLD) 76273I5E-150
Editorial: Via Zante, 16/2, 20138 MILANO
Tel: 02 580381 **Fax:** 02 58011670
Web site: http://www.nwi.it
Freq: 6 issues yearly; **Circ:** 13,500
Editor-in-Chief: Alfredo Di Stefano
Profile: Journal about information technology, telecommunications, networking systems and products.
Language(s): Italian
BUSINESS: COMPUTERS & AUTOMATION: Data Transmission

NEXT - STRUMENTI PER L'INNOVAZIONE 14467I84A-310
Editorial: Corso Vittorio Emanuele II, 209, 00186 ROMA **Tel:** 06 68210415 **Fax:** 06 68213114
Email: info@nextonline.it **Web site:** http://www.nextonline.it
Freq: Quarterly; **Circ:** 10,000
Editor-in-Chief: Domenico De Masi
Profile: International magazine focusing on art and culture.
Language(s): English; French; Italian
CONSUMER: THE ARTS & LITERARY: Arts

NOI GENITORI E FIGLI (AVVENIRE) 13123I4C-50
Editorial: Piazza Carbonari 3, 20125 MILANO
Tel: 02 6780465 **Fax:** 02 6780383
Email: noi@avvenire.it **Web site:** http://www.avvenire.it
Freq: Monthly
Profile: Technical magazine published by the College of Surveying for the Milan area.
Language(s): Italian
BUSINESS: ARCHITECTURE & BUILDING: Surveying

NOLEGGIO 712119I42A-14_50
Editorial: Via Eritrea 21, 20157 MILANO
Tel: 02 39090392 **Fax:** 02 39090332
Email: noleggio@tecnichenuove.com **Web site:** http://www.tecnichenuove.com
Freq: 6 issues yearly; **Circ:** 9,000
Editor-in-Chief: Giuseppe Nardella
Profile: Magazine concerning construction, industry and services about machinery hire.
Language(s): Italian
BUSINESS: CONSTRUCTION

NOTIZIARIO MOTORISTICO 14707I31A-110
Editorial: Via G. Pezzotti 4, 20141 MILANO
Tel: 028372897 **Fax:** 0258103891
Email: notiziario@netcollins.com **Web site:** http://www.notiziariomotoristico.com
Freq: Monthly; **Circ:** 17,000
Profile: Journal for the motor trade containing technical, commercial and financial news and information, includes details of trade fairs and motor shows. The magazine promotes exchange of information between countries.
Language(s): English; French; German; Italian
Readership: Read by manufacturers, exporters, importers and suppliers of vehicles and related accessories.
BUSINESS: MOTOR TRADE: Motor Trade Accessories

NOVELLA 2000 14109I74A-290
Editorial: Via A. Rizzoli 8, 20132 MILANO
Tel: 02 25843451 **Fax:** 02 23613906
Email: segreteria.novella@rcs.it **Web site:** http://www.novella2000.it
Freq: Weekly; **Circ:** 265,000
Editor-in-Chief: Franco Bonera
Profile: Magazine covering exclusive stories about famous people.
Language(s): Italian
CONSUMER: WOMEN'S INTEREST CONSUMER MAGAZINES: Women's Interest

NT NATURE TRADE 1846451I15A-102
Editorial: Via Enrico Tellini, 19, 20155 MILANO
Tel: 02 3108121 **Fax:** 02 33611129
Web site: http://www.mediaeris.it
Freq: Monthly
Editor-in-Chief: Aldo Filippo Lotta
Language(s): Italian
BUSINESS: COSMETICS & HAIRDRESSING: Cosmetics

NUOVA DISTRIBUZION& 13446I10-101
Editorial: Via Corfù,50, 25125 BRESCIA
Tel: 030 220261 **Fax:** 030 225868
Email: promodis@promodis.it **Web site:** http://www.promodis.it
Freq: Monthly; **Circ:** 38,000
Editor-in-Chief: Carmelo Lentino
Profile: Magazine covering distribution.
Language(s): Italian
Readership: Aimed at buyers and distributors.
BUSINESS: MATERIALS HANDLING

LA NUOVA ECOLOGIA 1784295I57-133
Editorial: Via Salaria, 403, 00199 ROMA
Tel: 06 86203691 **Fax:** 06 86218474
Email: redazione@lanuovaecologia.it **Web site:** http://www.lanuovaecologia.it
Freq: Monthly; **Circ:** 100,000
Editor-in-Chief: Marco Fratoddi
Language(s): Italian
BUSINESS: ENVIRONMENT & POLLUTION

NUOVA ELETTRAUTO 1668181I31A-124
Editorial: Piazza San Giovanni, 6, 23017 MORBEGNO SO **Tel:** 0342 611979 **Fax:** 0342 611717
Email: info@nuovaelettrauto.com **Web site:** http://www.nuovaelettrauto.com
Freq: Monthly; **Circ:** 18,000
Editor-in-Chief: Maria Luisa Corno
Profile: Magazine focusing on automotive electrics, electronics and technologies. Includes wiring diagrams and diagnostic guidelines.
Language(s): Italian
Readership: Read by car mechanics, technicians and car dealers.
BUSINESS: MOTOR TRADE: Motor Trade Accessories

NUOVA FINESTRA 13145I4E-156
Editorial: Viale G. Richard, 1/A, 20143 MILANO MI
Tel: 02 818301 **Fax:** 02 81830407
Email: finestra@reedbusiness.it **Web site:** http://www.reedbusiness.it
Freq: Monthly; **Circ:** 6,600
Profile: Magazine about new technology in the building industry. Covering metal and components and particularly doors, frames, curtain walls and windows.
Language(s): Italian
Readership: Read by window and door makers, glassmakers, curtain and blind manufacturers, dealers and retailers.
BUSINESS: ARCHITECTURE & BUILDING: Building

NUOVA INFORMAZIONE BIBLIOGRAFICA 14472I84B-110
Editorial: Strada Maggiore 37, 40125 BOLOGNA
Tel: 051 256011 **Fax:** 051 256034
Web site: http://www.mulino.it
Freq: Quarterly
Editor-in-Chief: Pasquale Petrucci
Profile: Magazine focusing on bibliographies.
Language(s): Italian
CONSUMER: THE ARTS & LITERARY: Literary

IL NUOVO CALCIO 14256I75B-220
Editorial: Via Masaccio 12, 20149 MILANO
Tel: 02 4815396 **Fax:** 02 4690907
Email: ilnuovocalcio@sportivi.it **Web site:** http://www.sportivi.it
Freq: Monthly; **Circ:** 90,000
Editor-in-Chief: Michele Di Cesare
Profile: Magazine focusing on all aspects of football. Includes previews, results and interviews.
Language(s): Italian
Readership: Aimed at football enthusiasts.
CONSUMER: SPORT: Football

IL NUOVO CANTIERE 13618I42A-15
Editorial: Via Eritrea, 21, 20157 MILANO
Tel: 02 39090054 **Fax:** 02 39090332
Email: nuovocantiere@tecnichenuove.com **Web site:** http://www.tecnichenuove.com
Freq: Monthly; **Circ:** 9,000
Editor-in-Chief: Giuseppe Nardella
Profile: Magazine covering all aspects of the construction trade.
Language(s): Italian
Readership: Aimed at managers of companies involved in major construction products.
BUSINESS: CONSTRUCTION

NUOVO CONSUMO 1784697I22R-4
Editorial: SS 1 Via Aurelia km 237, 57020 VIGNALE RIOTORTO LI **Tel:** 0565 24720 **Fax:** 0565 24210
Email: nuovoconsumo@unicooptirreno.coop.it **Web site:** http://www.nuovoconsumo.it
Freq: Monthly; **Circ:** 200,000
Editor-in-Chief: Aldo Bassoni
Language(s): Italian
BUSINESS: FOOD: Food Related

NUOVO ORIONE 14568I94X-150
Editorial: Via T. Tasso, 7, 20123 MILANO
Tel: 02 43990124 **Fax:** 02 43910204
Email: redazione@orione.it **Web site:** http://www.astronomianews.it
Freq: Monthly; **Circ:** 30,000
Editor-in-Chief: Paola Dameno
Profile: Magazine about astronomy.
Language(s): Italian
CONSUMER: OTHER CLASSIFICATIONS: Miscellaneous

OASIS 14511I89A-371
Editorial: Via Duccio Galimberti, 7, 12051 ALBA CN
Tel: 0173045250 **Fax:** 0173281280
Email: info@oasisweb.it **Web site:** http://www.oasisweb.it
Freq: 6 issues yearly; **Circ:** 55,000
Editor: Gianfranco Corino
Profile: Magazine containing articles about travel, nature, the countryside and natural environment. Also provides advice on photography.
Language(s): Italian
Readership: Aimed at those who enjoy outdoor activities with an interest in environmental issues.
CONSUMER: HOLIDAYS & TRAVEL: Travel

OFFICE AUTOMATION 13555I34-70
Editorial: Via Martiri Oscuri, 3, 20125 MILANO
Tel: 02 26148855 **Fax:** 02 26149333
Email: office.automation@soiel.it **Web site:** http://www.soiel.it
Freq: Monthly; **Circ:** 17,000
Editor-in-Chief: Grazia Gargiulo
Profile: Magazine containing information about data processing, networking, telecommunications and office systems.
Language(s): Italian
Readership: Aimed at end-users, decision-makers for corporate investment, including network and telecommunications managers, systems integrators, telephone installation firms and dealers.
ADVERTISING RATES:
Full Page Colour .... EUR 4000.00
BUSINESS: OFFICE EQUIPMENT

OFFICE MAGAZINE 62457I65B-48
Editorial: Contrada Lecco, 64 Z.I., 87036 RENDE COSENZA **Tel:** 0984 8319200 **Fax:** 0984 8319225
Email: officemagazine@edmaster.it **Web site:** http://www.edmaster.it/officemagazine
Freq: Monthly; **Circ:** 30,000
Editor-in-Chief: Massimo Sesti
Profile: Magazine containing information about developments in office software, hardware and internet.
Language(s): Italian
Readership: Read by PC users in offices.
BUSINESS: COMPUTERS & AUTOMATION: Data Processing

OFFICELAYOUT 13556I34-80
Editorial: Via Martiri Oscuri, 3, 20125 MILANO
Tel: 02 26148855 **Fax:** 02 26149333
Email: office.layout@soiel.it **Web site:** http://www.soiel.it
Freq: 6 issues yearly; **Circ:** 20,000
Editor-in-Chief: Grazia Gargiulo
Profile: International magazine focusing on the design, organisation and furnishing of office spaces.
Language(s): English; Italian
BUSINESS: OFFICE EQUIPMENT

OGGI 14085I73-300
Editorial: Via Angelo Rizzoli 8, 20132 MILANO
Tel: 02 25841 **Fax:** 02 27201485
Email: oggi@rcs.it **Web site:** http://www.rcs.it
Freq: Weekly; **Circ:** 830,000
Editor: Mario Raffaele Conti; **Editor-in-Chief:** Umberto Brindani
Profile: Magazine containing current affairs and celebrity features. Also covers food, tourism, books, cinema, theatre and music.
Language(s): Italian
CONSUMER: NATIONAL & INTERNATIONAL PERIODICALS

OGGI - RM 1784213I82-254
Editorial: V.le Rossini, 15, 00198 ROMA RM
Tel: 06 84484344 **Fax:** 06 84484361
Email: oggi.roma@rcs.it **Web site:** http://www.rcs.it
Freq: Weekly; **Circ:** 830,000
Editor: Michela Auriti
Language(s): Italian
CONSUMER: CURRENT AFFAIRS & POLITICS

OK LA SALUTE PRIMA DI TUTTO 1692661I74G-92
Editorial: Via A. Rizzoli 8, 20132 MILANO
Tel: 02 25841 **Fax:** 02 25844277
Email: redazione@ok.rcs.it **Web site:** http://ok.corriere.it
Freq: Monthly
Profile: Magazine containing information regarding health and fitness.
Language(s): Italian
Readership: Read by all the family.
CONSUMER: WOMEN'S INTEREST CONSUMER MAGAZINES: Slimming & Health

OLGA E OLIVER 1785102I74F-208
Editorial: Piazzale Baiamonti, 2, 20154 MILANO MI
Tel: 02 653272 **Fax:** 02 87393845
Email: redazione@olgaeoliver.com **Web site:** http://www.olgaeoliver.com
Freq: Monthly; **Circ:** 120,000
Editor-in-Chief: Rosy Calella
Language(s): Italian
CONSUMER: WOMEN'S INTEREST CONSUMER MAGAZINES: Teenage

ON DOMESTIC HI-TECH 1845120I18A-118
Editorial: Via M. Civitali 51, 20148 MILANO MI
Tel: 02 48703201 **Fax:** 02 48703614
Email: eired@tin.it **Web site:** http://www.anes.it
Freq: Monthly; **Circ:** 200,000
Editor-in-Chief: Fiorenza Moradei
Language(s): Italian
BUSINESS: ELECTRONICS

ONBOARD 14273I75G-120
Editorial: Via Winckelmann 2, 20146 MILANO MI
Tel: 02 424191 **Fax:** 02 47710278
Email: info@onboardmag.it **Web site:** http://www.onboardmag.it
Freq: 6 issues yearly; **Circ:** 24,000
Editor-in-Chief: Alessandro Zonca
Profile: Magazine focusing on snowboarding.
Language(s): Italian
Readership: Read by winter sports enthusiasts.
CONSUMER: SPORT: Winter Sports

ONDA VERDE 13620I77E-251
Editorial: ACI Sede Centrale - Via Marsala, 8, 00185 ROMA **Tel:** 06 49982277 **Fax:** 06 49982513
Email: p.benevolo@aci.it **Web site:** http://www.aci.it
Freq: 6 issues yearly; **Circ:** 8,000
Editor-in-Chief: Roberto Miceli
Profile: Journal published by the Automobile Club d'Italia in collaboration with the Italian Association of Traffic Engineers. Contains information on all types of transport, the environment, traffic, roads and communications.
Language(s): Italian
Readership: Aimed at mobility institution managers.
CONSUMER: MOTORING & CYCLING: Club Cars

L' OPERA 14339I76F-90
Editorial: Via Carlo Botta, 4, 20135 MILANO
Tel: 02 55193793 **Fax:** 02 5460154
Email: opera@fastwebnet.it **Web site:** http://www.centralpalc.com
Freq: Monthly; **Circ:** 40,000
Editor: Davide Garattini; **Editor-in-Chief:** Sabino Lenoci
Profile: Magazine about the world of opera.
Language(s): Italian
CONSUMER: MUSIC & PERFORMING ARTS: Opera

L' ORAFO ITALIANO 13767I52A-30
Editorial: Viale Coni Zugna 71, 20144 MILANO MI
Tel: 023451230 **Fax:** 023451231
Email: orafo@edifis.it **Web site:** http://www.edifis.it
Freq: Monthly; **Circ:** 14,000
Editor-in-Chief: Marina Morini
Profile: Magazine focusing on the retail, manufacture and export of gold work, includes new trends, design, communication, exhibitions fairs and technology in Italy and abroad.
Language(s): English; Italian
Readership: Aimed at Italian goldsmiths and jewellers in Italy and worldwide.
BUSINESS: GIFT TRADE: Jewellery

ORGANI DI TRASMISSIONE 13393I19F-40
Editorial: Via Eritrea, 21, 20157 MILANO
Tel: 02 39090300 **Fax:** 02 39090331
Email: organiditrasmissione@tecnichenuove.com
Web site: http://www.tecnichenuove.com
Freq: Monthly; **Circ:** 6,000
Editor-in-Chief: Giuseppe Nardella
Profile: Magazine about the manufacture of power transmission equipment.
Language(s): Italian
Readership: Aimed at manufacturers and engineers.
BUSINESS: ENGINEERING & MACHINERY: Production & Mechanical Engineering

OROLOGI DA POLSO 13774I52B-100
Editorial: Via San Fruttuoso 10, 20090 MONZA MB
Tel: 039 736451 **Fax:** 039 736500
Email: orologidapolso@studiozetasrl.it **Web site:** http://www.polsointernational.com
Freq: 6 issues yearly; **Circ:** 31,000
Editor-in-Chief: Elena Introna
Profile: Magazine about wrist-watches, includes new models, trends and production methods.
Language(s): Chinese; English; French; Italian; Japanese; Portuguese
Readership: Aimed at producers, suppliers and retailers.
BUSINESS: GIFT TRADE: Clocks & Watches

OROLOGI - LE MISURE DEL TEMPO 13773I52B-90
Editorial: Via Giovanni Penta 51, 00157 ROMA
Tel: 06 41735432 **Fax:** 06 62276256
Email: f.bigi@orologi.it **Web site:** http://www.orologi.it
Freq: Monthly; **Circ:** 40,000
Editor-in-Chief: Paola Pujia
Profile: Magazine containing articles about clocks and watches.
Language(s): Italian
Readership: Read mainly by men.
BUSINESS: GIFT TRADE: Clocks & Watches

L' OROLOGIO 13776I74Q-255
Editorial: Circonvallazione Nomentana, 212/214, 00162 ROMA RM **Tel:** 06 8606129 **Fax:** 06 8606324
Email: lorologio@dgedizioni.it **Web site:** http://www.argoeditore.net
Freq: Monthly; **Circ:** 50,000
Editor-in-Chief: Renato Giussani
Profile: Magazine concentrating on watch and clock technology and design.
Language(s): Italian
CONSUMER: WOMEN'S INTEREST CONSUMER MAGAZINES: Lifestyle

OTTICA ITALIANA 13874I56E-30
Editorial: Via Cenisio, 32, 20154 MILANO MI
Tel: 02 33611052 **Fax:** 02 3491374
Email: segreteria.redazione@optoservice.info **Web site:** http://www.federottica.org
Freq: Monthly; **Circ:** 11,000
Editor-in-Chief: Giuliangelo Velati
Profile: Official journal of the National Federation of Opticians. Contains information about technical developments and new equipment used in optometry.
Language(s): Italian
Readership: Circulated to opticians, manufacturers and suppliers of ophthalmic equipment.
BUSINESS: HEALTH & MEDICAL: Optics

PAESAGGIO URBANO - DOSSIER DI CULTURA E PROGETTO 13124I4D-100
Editorial: Via del Carpino, 8, 47822 SANTARCANGELO DI ROMAGNA RN
Tel: 0541 628111 **Fax:** 0541 622020
Email: redazionetecnica@maggioli.it **Web site:** http://www.periodicimaggioli.it
Freq: 6 issues yearly; **Circ:** 15,000
Editor-in-Chief: Amalia Maggioli
Profile: Magazine focusing on town and country planning, design and development, includes information about environmental issues.
Language(s): Italian
Readership: Read by architects and civil engineers.
BUSINESS: ARCHITECTURE & BUILDING: Planning & Housing

PANDA 1784421I81A-3
Editorial: Via Po, 25/c, 00198 ROMA
Tel: 06 84497455 **Fax:** 06 85300612
Email: panda@wwf.it **Web site:** http://www.wwf.it
Freq: 6 issues yearly; **Circ:** 300,000
Editor-in-Chief: Fulco Pratesi
Language(s): Italian
CONSUMER: ANIMALS & PETS: Animals & Pets Protection

IL PANIFICATORE ITALIANO 13227I8A-40
Editorial: Viale G. Richard, 1/a, 20143 MILANO MI
Tel: 02818301 **Fax:** 02 81830424
Web site: http://www.reedbusiness.it
Freq: Monthly; **Circ:** 9,000
Profile: Magazine focusing on baking and confectionery.
Language(s): Italian
BUSINESS: BAKING & CONFECTIONERY: Baking

PANORAMA 14086I73-310
Editorial: Palazzo Mondadori, 20090 SEGRATE MI
Tel: 02 7542 2512 **Fax:** 02 75422769
Email: panorama@mondadori.it **Web site:** http://www.panorama.it
Freq: Weekly; **Circ:** 650,000
Editor: Stefano Scotti; **Editor-in-Chief:** Giorgio Mule'
Profile: Italy's first and leading newsmagazine, both in terms of circulation and readership as well as advertising sales, is an information magazine that is able to provide readers with relevant background and anticipate what's going on in the world. Unique in terms of prestige and authority, every week it covers politics, arts and the economy, as well as lifestyle and leisure.
Language(s): Italian
ADVERTISING RATES:
Full Page Colour .... EUR 65650.00
CONSUMER: NATIONAL & INTERNATIONAL PERIODICALS

PANORAMA DIFESA 13597I40-121
Editorial: Via XX Settembre, 60, 50129 FIRENZE FI
Tel: 055485731 **Fax:** 0554626720
Email: panoramadifesa@dueservice.com **Web site:** http://www.ediservice.it
Freq: Monthly; **Circ:** 33,000
Editor-in-Chief: Ugo Passalacqua
Profile: Magazine focusing on defence, air and ground forces, the navy, space and civil defence.
Language(s): English; Italian
Readership: Read by members of the armed forces and professionals in the defence industry.
BUSINESS: DEFENCE

PANORAMA - RM 1784214I82-255
Editorial: Via Sicilia, 136/138, 00187 ROMA
Tel: 06 47497307 **Fax:** 0647497345
Email: segpanrm@mondadori.it **Web site:** http://www.panorama.it
Freq: Weekly; **Circ:** 920,000
Editor: Fabrizio Paladini
Language(s): Italian
CONSUMER: CURRENT AFFAIRS & POLITICS

PANORAMA TRAVEL 762599I89A-268
Editorial: Pal. Tiepolo - III Piano -Via Cassanese 224, 20090 CENTRO DIR.LE MILANO OLTRE - SEGRATE MI **Tel:** 02269375 00 **Fax:** 02 26937525
Email: patrizia.borroni@mondadori.it **Web site:** http://www.mondadori.it
Freq: Monthly; **Circ:** 100,000
Editor-in-Chief: Giancarlo Pini
Profile: Magazine containing information about travel, accommodation, recreation and how to spend your free time generally.
Language(s): Italian
Readership: Read by the frequent traveller.
CONSUMER: HOLIDAYS & TRAVEL: Travel

PANORAMAUTO 714554I31A-60
Editorial: Via Cassanese, 224 - Pal. Tiepolo, Milano Oltre, 20090 SEGRATE MI **Tel:** 02 26937550
Fax: 02 26937560
Email: cambio@mondadori.it **Web site:** http://www.mondadori.it
Freq: Monthly; **Circ:** 266,000
Editor-in-Chief: Giancarlo Pini
Profile: Magazine containing information and reviews about new and used cars.
Language(s): Italian
BUSINESS: MOTOR TRADE: Motor Trade Accessories

PARTS 13516I31A-123
Editorial: Viale G. Richard, 1/A, 20143 MILANO MI
Tel: 02 81830685 **Fax:** 0281830418
Email: parts@reedbusiness.it **Web site:** http://www.inofficina.it
Freq: Monthly; **Circ:** 6,000
Profile: Magazine focusing on the aftermarket car sector; contains information about components and accessories for cars.
Language(s): Italian
Readership: Read by distributors, installers, mechanics and car electricians.
BUSINESS: MOTOR TRADE: Motor Trade Accessories

PASTICCERIA INTERNAZIONALE 13229I8B-70
Editorial: Viale Rimembranza 60, 10064 PINEROLO TO **Tel:** 0121 393127 **Fax:** 0121 794480
Email: info@pasticceriainternazionale.it **Web site:** http://www.pasticceriainternazionale.it
Freq: Monthly; **Circ:** 12,000
Editor-in-Chief: Emilia Coccolo Chiriotti
Profile: International journal containing articles on raw materials and processing in confectionery, pastry and chocolate manufacture.

Language(s): Italian
Readership: Read by confectioners.
BUSINESS: BAKING & CONFECTIONERY: Confectionery Manufacturing

IL PASTICCIERE ITALIANO
1323018B-100
Editorial: Viale Richard, 1/a, 20143 MILANO MI
Tel: 02 818301 **Fax:** 02 81830405
Email: pasticciere@reedbusiness.it **Web site:** http://www.reedbusiness.it
Freq: Monthly; **Circ:** 8,000
Profile: Magazine focusing on all aspects of pastry making.
Language(s): Italian
BUSINESS: BAKING & CONFECTIONERY: Confectionery Manufacturing

PC MAGAZINE
1320215D-180
Editorial: Via Riccardo Lombardi 19/4, 20153 MILANO **Tel:** 02 57429001 **Fax:** 02 57429102
Email: redazione@pcmagazine.it **Web site:** http://www.pcmag.it
Editor-in-Chief: Lorenzo Zacchetti
Profile: Magazine concerning the digital world, personal computing and the use of the internet.
Language(s): Italian
Readership: Aimed at IT professionals and managers of small and medium-sized companies.
ADVERTISING RATES:
Full Page Mono .... EUR 4130.00
Full Page Colour .... EUR 5783.00
BUSINESS: COMPUTERS & AUTOMATION: Personal Computers

PC PROFESSIONALE
1320515D-220
Editorial: Via Mondadori 1, 20090 SEGRATE MI
Tel: 0275422900 **Fax:** 0275423322
Email: segreteriapcp@mondadori.it **Web site:** http://www.mondadori.it
Freq: Monthly; **Circ:** 150,000
Editor: Mario Pettenghi; **Editor-in-Chief:** Giorgio Panzeri
Profile: Magazine containing information about personal and professional computers. Includes tests of new hard- and software products, accessories and operating systems with particular focus on new trends in technology.
Language(s): Italian
Readership: Aimed at decision makers and purchasers of computing systems.
ADVERTISING RATES:
Full Page Colour .... EUR 13000.00
BUSINESS: COMPUTERS & AUTOMATION: Personal Computers

PC WORLD ITALIA
1320815D-260
Editorial: Viale Majno, 12, 20129 MILANO
Tel: 02 580381 **Fax:** 02 58013422
Email: posta@pcworld.it **Web site:** http://www.pcworld.it
Freq: Monthly; **Circ:** 111,000
Editor-in-Chief: Marco Tennyson
Profile: Magazine for personal computer users with advice on buying and using microcomputers and workstation hardware and software.
Language(s): Italian
Readership: Read by those wishing to purchase new PCs or update existing systems.
ADVERTISING RATES:
Full Page Colour .... EUR 8600.00
BUSINESS: COMPUTERS & AUTOMATION: Personal Computers

PCB MAGAZINE
1335818A-88
Editorial: Via Pisacane 1, 20141 RHO MI
Tel: 02 30226009 **Fax:** 0230226091
Email: redazione.pcb@ilsole24ore.com **Web site:** http://www.elettronicanews.it
Freq: Monthly; **Circ:** 9,000
Editor-in-Chief: Pierantonio Palerma
Profile: Magazine providing information on electronic technology.
Language(s): Italian
BUSINESS: ELECTRONICS

PELLICCE MODA
1394516 4B-65
Editorial: Via Teocrito, 47, 20128 MILANO MI
Tel: 02 252071 **Fax:** 02 27000692
Email: pelliccemoda@bema.it **Web site:** http://www.pelliccemoda.com
Freq: 6 issues yearly; **Circ:** 20,000
Editor-in-Chief: Gisella Bertini Malgarini
Profile: International magazine concerning trends in furs, with information on the fashion industry and fur trade.
Language(s): Chinese; English; Italian; Russian
BUSINESS: OTHER CLASSIFICATIONS: Fur Trade

PENELOPE
1417917 4E-130
Editorial: Via Angelo Maj, 12, 20135 MILANO MI
Tel: 02 55196076 **Fax:** 02 54108521
Email: fracchia@ggfeditore.it
Freq: 3 issues yearly; **Circ:** 30,000
Editor-in-Chief: Patrizia Bonetto
Profile: Magazine about knitting, crochet, sewing and embroidery.
Language(s): Italian
CONSUMER: WOMEN'S INTEREST CONSUMER MAGAZINES: Crafts

PENSIONATI
1784382I14L-81
Editorial: Via Castelfidardo 47, 00185 ROMA
Tel: 06 44881302 **Fax:** 06 4463878
Email: redazione@fnp.cisl.it **Web site:** http://www.conquistepensionati.cisl.it
Freq: 6 issues yearly; **Circ:** 1,780,000
Editor-in-Chief: Gigi Bonfanti
Language(s): Italian
BUSINESS: COMMERCE, INDUSTRY & MANAGEMENT: Trade Unions

PESCA IN MARE
1455119 2-80
Editorial: Via XX Settembre, 60, 50129 FIRENZE FI
Tel: 055485731 **Fax:** 0554626720
Email: pescainmare@ediservice.it
Freq: Monthly; **Circ:** 42,000
Editor-in-Chief: Ugo Passalacqua
Profile: Magazine about sea, river and underwater fishing.
Language(s): Italian
CONSUMER: ANGLING & FISHING

PESCARE MARE
1455519 2-100
Editorial: Via Zante 14, 20138 MILANO
Tel: 0236633301
Email: pescaremare@edolimpia.it **Web site:** http://www.edolimpia.it
Freq: Monthly; **Circ:** 33,000
Editor-in-Chief: Alessandro Cacciapuoti
Profile: Magazine covering all techniques of sea fishing, including information about equipment and fishing boats.
Language(s): Italian
Readership: Read by enthusiasts of sea fishing aged between 8 and 54 years.
CONSUMER: ANGLING & FISHING

IL PESCATORE D'ACQUA DOLCE
1455619 2-130
Editorial: Via Zante 14, 20138 MILANO
Tel: 0236633301 **Fax:** 0236633339
Email: ilpescatore@edolimpia.it **Web site:** http://www.edolimpia.it
Freq: Monthly; **Circ:** 20,000
Editor-in-Chief: Fabrizio Malavasi
Profile: Magazine about freshwater fishing, containing details about angling equipment and accessories. Also includes a guide to attractive fishing spots, with information about how to get there and where to stay.
Language(s): Italian
Readership: Read by fresh water fishermen in the north of Italy, mainly in the Lombardy area.
CONSUMER: ANGLING & FISHING

PIANETA HOTEL
1325211 1A-152
Editorial: Via Pisacane 1, 20016 RHO MI
Tel: 02 30221
Web site: http://www.b2b24.ilsole24ore.com
Freq: 6 issues yearly; **Circ:** 12,000
Editor-in-Chief: Mattia Losi
Profile: Magazine covering the technical management aspects of the hotel business.
Language(s): Italian
BUSINESS: CATERING: Catering, Hotels & Restaurants

LA PISCINA
1416517 4C-234
Editorial: Via Settembrini, 11, 20124 MILANO MI
Tel: 02 67495250 **Fax:** 02 67495333
Email: belcamino@dibaio.com **Web site:** http://www.dibaio.com
Freq: 3 issues yearly; **Circ:** 70,000
Profile: Publication containing information and articles about swimming pools.
Language(s): Italian
CONSUMER: WOMEN'S INTEREST CONSUMER MAGAZINES: Home & Family

PLAST DESIGN
1359313 9-94
Editorial: Via E. Tellini 19, 20155 MILANO
Tel: 02 3108121 **Fax:** 02 33611129
Email: plastdesign@erisprogram.com **Web site:** http://www.erisprogram.it
Freq: Monthly; **Circ:** 6,805
Editor-in-Chief: Aldo Filippo Rotta
Profile: Magazine containing information about the plastics industry. Includes new products and applications for plastic.
Language(s): English; Italian
Readership: Aimed at designers and project managers in plastics application.
BUSINESS: PLASTICS & RUBBER

PLAST - RIVISTA DELLE MATERIE PLASTICHE
1359413 9-95
Editorial: Via G. Richard, 1/A, 20143 MILANO
Tel: 02 818301 **Fax:** 02 81830408
Email: plast@reedbusiness.it **Web site:** http://www.reedbusiness.it
Freq: Monthly; **Circ:** 8,732
Editor-in-Chief: Alessandro Cederle
Profile: Magazine focusing on machinery and equipment for the plastics industry.
Language(s): Italian
BUSINESS: PLASTICS & RUBBER

PLEINAIR
1454319 1B-250
Editorial: P.zza Imerio, 11, 00165 ROMA RM
Tel: 06 6632628 **Fax:** 06 6637266
Web site: http://www.pleinair.it
Freq: Monthly; **Circ:** 92,000
Editor-in-Chief: Lucia Jannucci
Profile: Magazine covering holidays in the open air, hiking, touring, biking and camping. Includes technical information on caravans and motor-caravans.
Language(s): Italian
CONSUMER: RECREATION & LEISURE: Camping & Caravanning

PLUS MAGAZINE
1412617 4B-250
Editorial: Corso Vercelli 53, 20145 MILANO MI
Tel: 02463334 **Fax:** 051 4980526
Email: segreteria@leaderinterservice.com **Web site:** http://www.plusmagazine.it
Freq: 6 issues yearly; **Circ:** 20,000
Editor-in-Chief: Margherita Bertolotti
Profile: Fashion magazine featuring lingerie, swimwear and hosiery.
Language(s): English; Italian
CONSUMER: WOMEN'S INTEREST CONSUMER MAGAZINES: Women's Interest - Fashion

PNEURAMA
1359513 9-100
Editorial: Via A.G. Ragazzi 9, 40011 ANZOLA DELL'EMILIA BO **Tel:** 051 6424004 **Fax:** 051 733008
Email: pneurama@pneurama.com
Freq: 6 issues yearly; **Circ:** 15,000
Editor-in-Chief: Renzo Servadei
Profile: International journal about the production of tyres.
Language(s): English; Italian
Readership: Aimed at tyre specialists and tyre retailers.
BUSINESS: PLASTICS & RUBBER

POCKET
1809692I74B-377
Editorial: Via A. Bertoloni 49, 00197 ROMA RM
Tel: 0680692327 **Fax:** 0680693415
Email: gruppopocket@gruppopocket.com **Web site:** http://www.gruppopocket.com
Freq: Monthly; **Circ:** 310,000
Editor-in-Chief: Pierguido Cavallina
Language(s): Italian
CONSUMER: WOMEN'S INTEREST CONSUMER MAGAZINES: Women's Interest - Fashion

PORTA PORTESE
1784288I2A-104
Editorial: Via Di Porta Maggiore, 95, 00185 ROMA
Tel: 06 70300005 **Fax:** 06 70300007
Email: trepi@portaportese.it **Web site:** http://www.portaportese.it
Freq: 26 issues yearly; **Circ:** 140,000
Editor-in-Chief: Gabriele Caccamo
Language(s): Italian
BUSINESS: COMMUNICATIONS, ADVERTISING & MARKETING

PRESENZA TECNICA IN EDILIZIA
1311114 2A-25
Editorial: Strada Naviglio Alto 46/1, 43100 PARMA
Tel: 0521771818 **Fax:** 0521 773572
Email: info@presenzatecnica.it **Web site:** http://www.edizionipei.it
Freq: Monthly; **Circ:** 15,000
Editor-in-Chief: Carlo Cagozzi
Profile: Magazine covering architecture and environment, design and construction, materials and equipment, restoration and renovation.
Language(s): Italian
BUSINESS: CONSTRUCTION

PRIMA CASA
1896947I4B-212
Editorial: Via Gadames, 123, 20151 MILANO MI
Tel: 02 365881 **Fax:** 02 36588218
Email: primacasa@leditore.it **Web site:** http://www.leditore.it
Freq: Monthly; **Circ:** 150,000
Editor-in-Chief: Massimo Bacchetti
Language(s): Italian
BUSINESS: ARCHITECTURE & BUILDING: Interior Design & Flooring

PRIMA COMUNICAZIONE
1307412B-90
Editorial: Via Vincenzo Monti 15, 20123 MILANO
Tel: 02 48194401 **Fax:** 02 4818658
Email: prima@primaonline.it **Web site:** http://www.primaonline.it
Freq: Monthly; **Circ:** 18,000
Editor-in-Chief: Umberto Brunetti
Profile: Magazine covering the Italian media, with details of new magazines, journalistic problems, TV and radio communication.
Language(s): Italian
Readership: Read by public relations executives, journalists, editors, publishers, advertising managers and opinion leaders.
BUSINESS: COMMUNICATIONS, ADVERTISING & MARKETING: Press

PRIMISSIMA
1431017 6A-130
Editorial: Via Fabio Massimo 107, 00192 ROMA
Tel: 06 45437670 **Fax:** 06 45437670
Email: primissima@primissima.it **Web site:** http://www.primissima.it
Freq: Monthly; **Circ:** 200,000
Editor-in-Chief: Piero Cinelli
Profile: Magazine about new releases and forthcoming films.
Language(s): Italian
Readership: Aimed at moviegoers.
CONSUMER: MUSIC & PERFORMING ARTS: Cinema

PROGETTARE
1338711 9E-80
Editorial: s.s. Sempione n.28, 20017 RHO (MI)
Tel: 02 499761 **Fax:** 0249976570
Email: progettare@fieramilanoeditore.it **Web site:** http://www.fieramilanoeditore.it
Freq: Monthly; **Circ:** 5,445
Editor-in-Chief: Luca Rossi
Profile: Magazine about machinery, metalworking and mechanical engineering.
Language(s): Italian
BUSINESS: ENGINEERING & MACHINERY: Machinery, Machine Tools & Metalworking

PROGETTARE ARCHITETTURA CITTÀ TERRITORIO
7628541 4A-90
Editorial: Via Eritrea 21, 20157 MILANO
Tel: 02 39090361 **Fax:** 02 39090332
Email: progettare@tecnichenuove.com **Web site:** http://www.tecnichenuove.com
Freq: 6 issues yearly
Editor-in-Chief: Giuseppe Nardella
Profile: Magazine focusing on architecture, building and construction. Includes information on renovation, restoration and locations for building.
Language(s): Italian
Readership: Aimed at architects, builders, technical officers and civil engineers.
BUSINESS: ARCHITECTURE & BUILDING: Architecture

PROGETTARE PER LA SANITA'
1384615 6A-264
Editorial: Via Teocrito, 50, 20128 MILANO
Tel: 02 252071 **Fax:** 02 27000692
Email: sanita@bema.it **Web site:** http://www.ediliziainrete.it
Freq: 6 issues yearly; **Circ:** 3,600
Editor-in-Chief: Margherita Carabillo'
Profile: Magazine providing news, information and reports concerning the Italian National Health Service. Reports on international relations and CNETO debates. Also contains articles about hospitals and rehabilitation.
Language(s): Italian
Readership: Read by members of the medical profession.
BUSINESS: HEALTH & MEDICAL

IL PROGETTISTA INDUSTRIALE
1339611 9J-130
Editorial: Via Eritrea, 21, 20157 MILANO MI
Tel: 02 39090351 **Fax:** 02 39090331
Email: ilprogettista.industriale@tecnichenuove.com
Web site: http://www.tecnichenuove.com
Freq: Monthly; **Circ:** 6,500
Editor-in-Chief: Giuseppe Nardella
Profile: Magazine dealing with the varied aspects of industrial planning. Covers the areas of CAD/CAM, materials, components, computer graphics and software.
Language(s): Italian
Readership: Aimed at engineers and technicians in the mechanical, electromechanical, electronic, chemical, pharmaceutical and food industries.
BUSINESS: ENGINEERING & MACHINERY: CAD & CIM (Computer Integrated Manufacture)

PROMETEO
1456919 4X-160
Editorial: Via Sabotino 2, 00195 ROMA
Tel: 06 37515848 **Fax:** 06 3721442
Email: rivprometeo@iol.it **Web site:** http://www.mondadori.it
Freq: Quarterly; **Circ:** 10,000
Editor-in-Chief: Pepa Sparti
Profile: Magazine about science and history.
Language(s): Italian
CONSUMER: OTHER CLASSIFICATIONS: Miscellaneous

PROMOTION MAGAZINE
13068I2A-90
Editorial: P.le Accursio, 14, 20156 MILANO
Tel: 02 3920621 **Fax:** 02 39257050
Email: redazione@ops.it **Web site:** http://www.promotionmagazine.it
Freq: 6 issues yearly; **Circ:** 20,000
Editor: Andrea Demodena; **Editor-in-Chief:** Osvaldo Ponchia
Profile: Publication covering all areas of marketing, promotion and business gifts.
Language(s): English; Italian
BUSINESS: COMMUNICATIONS, ADVERTISING & MARKETING

PUBBLICITA' ITALIA
13069I2A-100
Editorial: Via Gian Battista Vico, 42, 20123 MILANO MI **Tel:** 02 4300001
Email: comunicati@pubblicitaitalia.it **Web site:** http://www.pubblicitaitalia.it
Freq: Monthly; **Circ:** 3,038
Editor-in-Chief: Deborah Baldasarre
Profile: Magazine about advertising, marketing, media and internet communication.
Language(s): Italian
Readership: Aimed at communication professionals, marketing managers and general managers.
BUSINESS: COMMUNICATIONS, ADVERTISING & MARKETING

PUBBLICO
14663I2A-102
Editorial: Via Torino 64, 20123 MILANO
Tel: 02 72000035 **Fax:** 02 89013013
Email: pubblico.today@pubblico-online.it **Web site:** http://www.pubblico-online.it
Freq: Weekly; **Circ:** 10,000
Editor-in-Chief: Valeria Scrivani
Profile: Journal focusing on advertising, publicity, marketing and communication.
Language(s): Italian
BUSINESS: COMMUNICATIONS, ADVERTISING & MARKETING

PUNTO EFFE
1785292I37-121
Editorial: Via Boscovich, 61, 20124 MILANO
Tel: 02 2022941 **Fax:** 02 29513121
Email: info@puntoeffe.it **Web site:** http://www.puntoeffe.it
Freq: 24 issues yearly; **Circ:** 18,800
Editor-in-Chief: LAURA Benfenati
Language(s): Italian
BUSINESS: PHARMACEUTICAL & CHEMISTS

PUPA
14203I74F-162
Editorial: c/o Emmei - Via Guido Reni 33, 00196 ROMA RM **Tel:** 0645615060 **Fax:** 0645615232
Email: mgs@emmei.info
Freq: 6 issues yearly; **Circ:** 50,000
Editor-in-Chief: Marco Iafrate
Profile: Magazine covering love, friendship, school life, family matters and the world of entertainment. Also includes photo stories and fiction.
Language(s): Italian
Readership: Read by girls aged between 12 and 18 years.
CONSUMER: WOMEN'S INTEREST CONSUMER MAGAZINES: Teenage

QN MODA
1829209I74B-380
Editorial: Via Mattei, 106, 40138 BOLOGNA
Tel: 051 6006801 **Fax:** 051 6006266
Email: segreteria.redazione.firenze@monrif.net **Web site:** http://www.quotidiano.net
Freq: Monthly; **Circ:** 500,000
Editor: Eva Desiderio
Language(s): Italian
CONSUMER: WOMEN'S INTEREST CONSUMER MAGAZINES: Women's Interest - Fashion

QUALE COMPUTER
714613I5D-270
Editorial: Contrada Lecco, 64 Z.I., 87036 RENDE COSENZA **Tel:** 0984 8319200 **Fax:** 0984 8319225
Email: qualecomputer@edmaster.it **Web site:** http://www.edmaster.it/qualecomputer
Freq: Monthly; **Circ:** 80,000
Editor-in-Chief: Massimo Sesti
Profile: Magazine containing information on the latest computer hardware, includes test reports.
Language(s): Italian
BUSINESS: COMPUTERS & AUTOMATION: Personal Computers

QUALEIMPRESA
13294I14B-50
Editorial: Viale Dell'Astronomia 30 - c/o Confindustria, 00144 ROMA **Tel:** 0632507379
Fax: 0697656829
Email: oriettasdoja@comunicazione2000.com **Web site:** http://www.giovanimprenditori.org
Freq: 6 issues yearly; **Circ:** 15,000
Profile: Magazine of the Italian Manufacturers' Association, containing information on industrial policy and economics.
Language(s): Italian
Readership: Read by young entrepreneurs and managerial executives who belong to the General Confederation of Italian Industry.
BUSINESS: COMMERCE, INDUSTRY & MANAGEMENT: Industry & Factories

QUALITYTRAVEL DIRECTORY
13751I50-132
Editorial: Via G.Watt, 37, 20143 MILANO MI
Tel: 02 89151814 **Fax:** 02 89151830
Email: promos@qualitytravel.it **Web site:** http://www.qualitytravel.it
Freq: Annual; **Circ:** 9,000
Editor-in-Chief: Roberto Angri
Profile: Magazine containing information on conferences, travel and incentives.
Language(s): English; Italian
Readership: Aimed at business people.
BUSINESS: TRAVEL & TOURISM

QUARRY AND CONSTRUCTION
13508I30-50
Editorial: Strada Naviglio Alto 46/1, 43122 PARMA
Tel: 0521 771818 **Fax:** 0521 773572
Email: info@quarry-construction.it **Web site:** http://www.edizionipei.it
Freq: Monthly; **Circ:** 15,000
Editor-in-Chief: Carlo Cagozzi
Profile: Technical magazine containing information about excavation, explosions, land movement and the construction of buildings and roads, including industrial, public and private constructions.
Language(s): Italian
BUSINESS: MINING & QUARRYING

QUATTRORUOTE
14358I77A-330
Editorial: Via Gianni Mazzocchi 1/3, 20089 ROZZANO MI **Tel:** 02 824721 **Fax:** 02 57500416
Email: redazione@quattroruote.it **Web site:** http://www.quattroruote.it
Freq: Monthly; **Circ:** 581,000
Editor: Emilio Deleidi; **Editor-in-Chief:** Carlo Cavicchi
Profile: Motoring magazine giving information on new car models and road tests.
Language(s): Italian
Readership: Read by motoring enthusiasts.
ADVERTISING RATES:
Full Page Colour .... EUR 30000.00
CONSUMER: MOTORING & CYCLING: Motoring

QUATTRORUOTE AUTOPRO
13511I31A-20
Editorial: Via Gianni Mazzocchi 1/3, 20089 ROZZANO MI **Tel:** 028247 2255 **Fax:** 02 82472519
Email: redazione@autopro.it **Web site:** http://www.autopro.it
Freq: Monthly; **Circ:** 24,000
Editor-in-Chief: Carlo Cavicchi
Profile: Magazine providing news, data, market analysis and technical information concerning the motor trade in Italy.
Language(s): Italian
Readership: Aimed at car dealers, mechanics, tyre repairers and distributors, spare parts dealers, service stations and garages.
BUSINESS: MOTOR TRADE: Motor Trade Accessories

QUATTRORUOTINE
14409I79B-150
Editorial: Via Gianni Mazzocchi 1/3, 20089 ROZZANO MI **Tel:** 02 82472443 **Fax:** 02 82472420
Email: quattroruotine@edidomus.it **Web site:** http://www.quattroruotine.it
Freq: Quarterly; **Circ:** 10,000
Editor-in-Chief: Raffaele Laurenzi
Profile: Magazine focusing on model cars.
Language(s): Italian
Readership: Aimed at model car enthusiasts.
CONSUMER: HOBBIES & DIY: Models & Modelling

QUI TOURING
14525I89E-200
Editorial: Corso Italia, 10, 20122 MILANO
Tel: 02 8526529 **Fax:** 02 8526299
Email: qt.seg@touringclub.it **Web site:** http://www.touringclub.it
Freq: Monthly; **Circ:** 396,939
Profile: International journal of the Italian Touring Club.
Language(s): Italian
CONSUMER: HOLIDAYS & TRAVEL: Holidays

RADIO KIT ELETTRONICA
14416I79D-150
Editorial: Via Naviglio 37/2, 48018 FAENZA RA
Tel: 0546 22112 **Fax:** 0546662046
Email: radiokit@edizionicec.it **Web site:** http://www.edizionicec.it
Freq: Monthly; **Circ:** 20,000
Editor-in-Chief: Nerio Neri
Profile: Magazine containing information about kits for radio and electronic hobbies. Includes technical and construction information.
Language(s): Italian
Readership: Read by people who take a keen interest in electronics and radio communications in their spare time.
CONSUMER: HOBBIES & DIY: Radio Electronics

RAGAZZA MODERNA
1784857I74F-204
Editorial: Via Palermo, 13, 00184 ROMA RM
Tel: 06 48906778 **Fax:** 0648907058
Email: redazione@ragazzamoderna.it **Web site:** http://www.ragazzamoderna.it
Freq: Monthly; **Circ:** 100,000
Editor-in-Chief: Monica Ciccolini
Language(s): Italian
CONSUMER: WOMEN'S INTEREST CONSUMER MAGAZINES: Teenage

RAKAM
14180I74E-140
Editorial: Piazza De Angeli 9, 20146 MILANO
Tel: 0236505607 **Fax:** 02 48110494
Email: segreteria_rakam@edizionimimosa.it **Web site:** http://www.rakaminternet.it
Freq: Monthly; **Circ:** 181,000
Editor-in-Chief: Sandra Rudoni
Profile: Magazine about knitting, handicrafts, cookery, fashion, beauty, house decoration, health and children.
Language(s): Italian
Readership: Aimed at women.
CONSUMER: WOMEN'S INTEREST CONSUMER MAGAZINES: Crafts

RASSEGNA ALIMENTARE
13448I22A-42
Editorial: Viale Lunigiana, 14, 20125 MILANO
Tel: 02 67100605 **Fax:** 02 67100621
Email: redazione@editricezeus.com **Web site:** http://www.editricezeus.com
Freq: 6 issues yearly; **Circ:** 6,000
Editor-in-Chief: Enrico Maffizzoni
Profile: Magazine containing technical information for the food and beverage industry. Covers machines, components and plants.
Language(s): Italian
Readership: Read by food industry and manufacturing professionals.
BUSINESS: FOOD

RCI - RISCALDAMENTO CLIMATIZZAZ. IDRONICA
13093I3B-130
Editorial: Via Eritrea, 21, 20157 MILANO
Tel: 02 39090339 **Fax:** 02 39090331
Email: carlo.cozzi@tecnichenuove.com **Web site:** http://www.tecnichenuove.com
Freq: Monthly; **Circ:** 8,113
Editor-in-Chief: Giuseppe Nardella
Profile: Journal about heating, air-conditioning, insulation and sanitary equipment. Includes details on materials, techniques, research, development and commercial problems.
Language(s): Italian
Readership: Aimed at designers, installers, engineers and architects.
BUSINESS: HEATING & VENTILATION: Industrial Heating & Ventilation

RECUPERO E CONSERVAZIONE
13148I4E-180
Editorial: Via Tadino, 25, 20124 MILANO
Tel: 02 36584135
Email: redazione@delettera.it **Web site:** http://www.delettera.it
Freq: 6 issues yearly; **Circ:** 18,000
Editor-in-Chief: Ivan De Lettera
Profile: Magazine about restoration and renovation.
Language(s): Italian
Readership: Read by architects, specialised companies of restoration, architectural, renovation and diagnostic architecture.
BUSINESS: ARCHITECTURE & BUILDING: Building

LE REGIONI
14431I80-220
Editorial: Strada Maggiore, 37, 40125 BOLOGNA
Tel: 051 256011 **Fax:** 051 256041
Email: riviste@mulino.it **Web site:** http://www.mulino.it
Freq: 6 issues yearly; **Circ:** 3,000
Editor-in-Chief: Giandomenico Falcon
Profile: Magazine concerning local government news.
Language(s): Italian
Readership: Aimed at academics and university students.
CONSUMER: RURAL & REGIONAL INTEREST

LA REPUBBLICA
13973I65A-120
Editorial: Via Cristoforo Colombo, 90, 00147 ROMA RM **Tel:** 06 49821 **Fax:** 06 49822923
Email: larepubblica@repubblica.it **Web site:** http://www.repubblica.it
Freq: Daily; **Circ:** 597,694
Editor: Livio Quagliata; **Editor-in-Chief:** Ezio Mauro
Profile: Tabloid-sized quality newspaper containing national and international news and articles covering politics, economics, finance, culture, entertainment and sport.
Language(s): Italian
Readership: Read by company directors, senior and middle managers, university students and office personnel.
ADVERTISING RATES:
Full Page Mono .... EUR 126000.00
Full Page Colour .... EUR 151000.00
NATIONAL DAILY & SUNDAY NEWSPAPERS: National Daily Newspapers

IL RESTO DEL CARLINO
13974I65A-130
Editorial: Via E. Mattei, 106, 40138 BOLOGNA
Tel: 051 6006111 **Fax:** 051534748
Email: segreteria.redazione.bologna@monrif.net **Web site:** http://www.ilrestodelcarlino.it
Freq: Daily; **Circ:** 307,000
Editor: Aldo Mori; **Editor-in-Chief:** Pierluigi Visci
Profile: Broadsheet-sized newspaper covering regional, national and international news, politics, economics, sport and entertainment.
Language(s): Italian
Readership: Read predominantly by people living in Emilia-Romagna and Marche.
ADVERTISING RATES:
Full Page Colour .... EUR 105000.00
NATIONAL DAILY & SUNDAY NEWSPAPERS: National Daily Newspapers

RI RASSEGNA DELL'IMBALLAGGIO
13567I35-60
Editorial: Via Teocrito, 47, 20128 MILANO
Tel: 02 252071 **Fax:** 02 27000692
Email: rassegnaimballaggio@bema.it **Web site:** http://www.rassegnaimballaggio.it
Freq: Monthly; **Circ:** 9,000
Editor-in-Chief: Gisella Bertini Malgarini
Profile: Review about packing and packaging technology. Also includes information on marketing and sales advice.
Language(s): Italian
BUSINESS: PACKAGING & BOTTLING

RIABITA
13152I4B-196
Editorial: Viale Sarca 243, 20126 MILANO
Tel: 02 66103539 **Fax:** 02 66103558
Email: redazione@rimaedit.it **Web site:** http://www.rimaedit.it
Freq: Monthly; **Circ:** 31,000
Editor-in-Chief: Flavio Maestrini
Profile: Journal about interior restoration.
Language(s): Italian
BUSINESS: ARCHITECTURE & BUILDING: Interior Design & Flooring

RIFINITURE D'INTERNI
718238I74C-240
Editorial: Viale Andrea Doria, 35, 20124 MILANO
Tel: 02 66988188 **Fax:** 02 66988190
Email: redazione@edinterni.it **Web site:** http://www.edinterni.com
Freq: 6 issues yearly; **Circ:** 8,000
Editor-in-Chief: Luisa Buiarelli
Profile: Magazine focusing on home decoration.
Language(s): Italian
CONSUMER: WOMEN'S INTEREST CONSUMER MAGAZINES: Home & Family

RISTORAZIONE COLLETTIVA - CATERING
13254I11A-157
Editorial: Via Pisacane, 1, 20016 RHO MI
Tel: 02 30221
Email: ristorazione.collettiva@ilsole24ore.com **Web site:** http://www.b2b24.it
Freq: 6 issues yearly; **Circ:** 18,000
Editor-in-Chief: Antonio Greco
Profile: Magazine covering the catering trade. Includes information on public catering, canteens, institutional catering (school, university, hospital), wholesaling, importing, design and engineering.
Language(s): English; Italian
Readership: Read by contractors, purchasers, owners and managers within the catering trade.
BUSINESS: CATERING: Catering, Hotels & Restaurants

RIVISTA DEL CLUB ALPINO IT. LO SCARPONE - CAI
1784613I75A-227
Editorial: Via Petrella 19, 20124 MILANO
Tel: 02 2057231 **Fax:** 02 205723201
Email: loscarpone@cai.it **Web site:** http://www.cai.it
Freq: Monthly; **Circ:** 200,000
Editor-in-Chief: Luca Calzolari
Language(s): Italian
CONSUMER: SPORT

RIVISTA DEL CLUB ALPINO ITALIANO - CAI
14289I75L-100
Editorial: Via Petrella 19, 20124 MILANO
Tel: 022057231 **Fax:** 02205723201
Email: larivista@cai.it **Web site:** http://www.cai.it

Freq: 6 issues yearly; **Circ:** 200,000
Editor-in-Chief: Luca Calzolari
Profile: Magazine containing information about alpine sports, includes skiing, mountaineering, caving, trekking and camping.
Language(s): Italian
Readership: Read by members of the Italian Alpine Club.
CONSUMER: SPORT: Outdoor

RIVISTA GIURIDICA DELL'AMBIENTE 13668I44-145
Editorial: Via Cadore 36, 20135 MILANO MI
Tel: 02 541798 **Fax:** 02 54101742
Email: redazione@nespor.it **Web site:** http://www.giuffre.it
Freq: 6 issues yearly; **Circ:** 2,600
Editor-in-Chief: Stefano Nespor
Profile: Journal covering environmental law and legislation. Also includes information on EU regulations and directives.
Language(s): Italian
Readership: Aimed at lawyers specialising in environmental law.
BUSINESS: LEGAL

RIVISTA MILITARE 13599I40-120
Editorial: Via di San Marco, 8, 00186 ROMA RM
Tel: 06 47357373 **Fax:** 0647358139
Email: riv.mil@tiscali.it **Web site:** http://www.esercito.difesa.it
Freq: Quarterly; **Circ:** 10,000
Editor-in-Chief: Marco Ciampini
Profile: Magazine about military developments including reports about science and technology, and improvements in the professional training of military officials.
Language(s): Italian
Readership: Read by military officials, the defence industry and people interested in military problems.
BUSINESS: DEFENCE

RIVISTA TECNO MTB 1784819I77C-113
Editorial: Via Smareglia, 7, 20133 MILANO
Tel: 02714298 **Fax:** 02 7382852
Email: tecnomtb@edidoss.it **Web site:** http://www.rivistatecnomtb.com
Freq: Monthly; **Circ:** 80,000
Editor-in-Chief: Paolo Dossena
Language(s): Italian
CONSUMER: MOTORING & CYCLING: Cycling

RIZA PSICOSOMATICA 14214I74G-58
Editorial: Via Luigi Anelli, 1, 20122 MILANO MI
Tel: 02 5845961 58459648 **Fax:** 02 58318162
Email: rizapsicosomatica@riza.it **Web site:** http://www.riza.it
Freq: Monthly; **Circ:** 75,000
Editor: Giorgio Barbetta; **Editor-in-Chief:** Raffaele Morelli
Profile: Review focusing on physical and mental health.
Language(s): Italian
CONSUMER: WOMEN'S INTEREST CONSUMER MAGAZINES: Slimming & Health

RIZA SCIENZE 14571I74G-60
Editorial: Via Luigi Anelli, 1, 20122 MILANO
Tel: 02 5845961 **Fax:** 0258318162
Email: rizascienze@riza.it **Web site:** http://www.riza.it
Freq: Monthly; **Circ:** 20,000
Editor-in-Chief: Daniela Marafante
Profile: Magazine about science and humanity.
Language(s): Italian
CONSUMER: WOMEN'S INTEREST CONSUMER MAGAZINES: Slimming & Health

RMO - RIVISTA DI MECCANICA OGGI 13394I19F-90
Editorial: s.s. Sempione n.28, 20017 RHO
Tel: 0249971 **Fax:** 0249976570
Email: rmo@fieramilanoeditore.it **Web site:** http://www.edizionifieramilano.it
Freq: Monthly; **Circ:** 7,695
Profile: Journal covering all aspects of mechanical engineering.
Language(s): Italian
Readership: Aimed at mechanical engineers and managers of engineering companies.
BUSINESS: ENGINEERING & MACHINERY: Production & Mechanical Engineering

ROLLING STONE 1785055I76D-565
Editorial: Piazza Aspromonte, 15, 20131 MILANO MI
Tel: 0270642462 **Fax:** 0270642444
Email: rbevivino@rollingstonemagazine.it **Web site:** http://www.rollingstonemagazine.it
Freq: Monthly; **Circ:** 90,000
Editor-in-Chief: Michele Lupi
Language(s): Italian
CONSUMER: MUSIC & PERFORMING ARTS: Music

LA ROMA 14257I75B-221
Editorial: Via di Trigoria Km 3,600 c/o Centro Sportivo F. B, 00128 ROMA **Tel:** 06 5062163
Fax: 06 50651013
Email: redlaroma@asromastore.it **Web site:** http://www.asroma.it
Freq: Monthly; **Circ:** 70,000
Editor-in-Chief: Riccardo Viola
Profile: International official magazine of the Italian football club Roma. Contains news, interviews and profiles of players.
Language(s): Italian
Readership: Aimed at anyone with an interest in Italian football, especially Roma supporters.
CONSUMER: SPORT: Football

RS RIFIUTI SOLIDI 13906I57-55
Editorial: Via Andrea Palladio 26, 20135 MILANO
Tel: 0258301501 **Fax:** 02 58301550
Email: redazione@cipaeditore.it **Web site:** http://www.cipaeditore.it
Freq: 6 issues yearly; **Circ:** 2,000
Editor-in-Chief: Eugenio De Fraja Frangipane
Profile: Magazine focusing on the treatment and disposal of solid waste.
Language(s): Italian
Readership: Read by managers and engineers at treatment plants, administrators in local and provincial authorities, researchers and academics.
BUSINESS: ENVIRONMENT & POLLUTION

RU - RISORSE UMANE NELLA P.A. 13528I14F-1
Editorial: c/o CPO Rimini - Via Coriano, 58, 47900 RIMINI **Tel:** 0541 628111 **Fax:** 0541 622778
Email: asapubblica@maggioli.it **Web site:** http://www.periodicimaggioli.it
Freq: 6 issues yearly; **Circ:** 6,000
Editor-in-Chief: Manlio Maggioli
Profile: Journal concerning management, legislation and jurisprudence relating to local and regional government. Focuses on human resource management.
Language(s): Italian
BUSINESS: COMMERCE, INDUSTRY & MANAGEMENT: Training & Recruitment

RUOTECLASSICHE 14392I77F-200
Editorial: Via Gianni Mazzocchi, 1/3, 20089 ROZZANO MI **Tel:** 02824721 **Fax:** 02 82472420
Email: redazione@ruoteclassiche.it **Web site:** http://www.ruoteclassiche.it
Freq: Monthly; **Circ:** 75,200
Editor: Fulvio Zucco; **Editor-in-Chief:** Raffaele Laurenzi
Profile: Magazine covering the most celebrated cars and motorcycles from the origin of the motoring industry until recent times.
Language(s): Italian
Readership: Aimed at veteran, sports and general car enthusiasts, dealers and restorers.
CONSUMER: MOTORING & CYCLING: Veteran Cars

SALE & PEPE 14245I74P-270
Editorial: Palazzo Mondadori, 20090 SEGRATE MI
Tel: 0275422691 **Fax:** 02 75422683
Web site: http://www.mondadori.it
Freq: Monthly; **Circ:** 145,000
Editor: Livia Fagetti; **Editor-in-Chief:** Laura Maragliano
Profile: Magazine about healthy eating. Focuses on health and the composition of food products and explores new ideas about cooking.
Language(s): Italian
Readership: Read by people who enjoy eating and cooking food.
CONSUMER: WOMEN'S INTEREST CONSUMER MAGAZINES: Food & Cookery

SALUTE NATURALE 712135I74G-65
Editorial: Via Luigi Anelli 1, 20122 MILANO
Tel: 02 5845961 **Fax:** 0258318162
Email: fbonazzi@riza.it **Web site:** http://www.riza.it
Freq: Monthly; **Circ:** 95,000
Editor: Fiammetta Bonazzi; **Editor-in-Chief:** Vittorio Caprioglio
Profile: Magazine containing articles about natural health, includes remedies, lifestyle and comfort.
Language(s): Italian
Readership: Read by people interested in a natural lifestyle.
CONSUMER: WOMEN'S INTEREST CONSUMER MAGAZINES: Slimming & Health

SANITA' PUBBLICA E PRIVATA 13533I32B-90
Editorial: Via Del Carpino, 8, 47829 SANT'ARCANGELO DI ROMAGNA RN
Tel: 0541 628111 **Fax:** 0541 622778
Email: asapubblica@maggioli.it **Web site:** http://www.periodicimaggioli.it
Freq: 6 issues yearly; **Circ:** 6,000
Editor-in-Chief: Manlio Maggioli
Profile: Publication about public health administration.
Language(s): Italian
BUSINESS: LOCAL GOVERNMENT, LEISURE & RECREATION: Public Health & Cleaning

SAPERE 13799I55-19
Editorial: Via Farfa 22-24, 00142 ROMA
Tel: 06 54602121 **Fax:** 06 54602129
Email: sapere@galileonet.it
Freq: 6 issues yearly; **Circ:** 48,000
Editor-in-Chief: Raimondo Coga
Profile: Journal containing articles on science, medicine, environment and engineering technology.
Language(s): Italian
Readership: Mainly read by university students and professors, directors and business leaders.
BUSINESS: APPLIED SCIENCE & LABORATORIES

SAPERE & SALUTE 1784643I74G-95
Editorial: Piazza della Repubblica, 19, 20124 MILANO MI **Tel:** 02 6888775 **Fax:** 02 6888780
Email: sapere.salute@giornaldea.it **Web site:** http://www.farmamese.it
Freq: 6 issues yearly; **Circ:** 750,000
Editor-in-Chief: Giuliano Modesti
Language(s): Italian
CONSUMER: WOMEN'S INTEREST CONSUMER MAGAZINES: Slimming & Health

SCI 14275I75G-170
Editorial: Corso Monforte, 36, 20122 MILANO MI
Tel: 02 7788501 **Fax:** 02 76004905
Email: sci@scode.it **Web site:** http://www.scode.it
Freq: Monthly; **Circ:** 40,000
Editor-in-Chief: Carlo Gandini
Profile: Publication about winter sports and tourism.
Language(s): English; French; Italian
Readership: Aimed at ski and winter sports enthusiasts and mountain lovers.
CONSUMER: SPORT: Winter Sports

SCIARE MAGAZINE 14277I75G-172
Editorial: Via Winckelmann, 2, 20146 MILANO MI
Tel: 02 424191 **Fax:** 0248953252
Email: sciare@sciaremag.it **Web site:** http://www.sciaremag.it
Freq: 24 issues yearly; **Circ:** 42,000
Editor-in-Chief: Marco Di Marco
Profile: Magazine about skiing, winter sports, fashion and tourism.
Language(s): Italian
CONSUMER: SPORT: Winter Sports

LE SCIENZE 13800I55-40
Editorial: Via Cristoforo Colombo, 149, 00147 ROMA RM **Tel:** 06 49823181 **Fax:** 06 49823184
Email: redazione@lescienze.it **Web site:** http://www.lescienze.it
Freq: Monthly; **Circ:** 100,000
Editor-in-Chief: Marco Cattaneo
Profile: Italian edition of Scientific American.
Language(s): Italian
BUSINESS: APPLIED SCIENCE & LABORATORIES

SCIFONDO 14276I75G-173
Editorial: Corso Monforte, 36, 20122 MILANO MI
Tel: 02 7788501 **Fax:** 02 76004905
Email: scifondo@scode.it **Web site:** http://www.scode.it
Freq: Monthly; **Circ:** 18,000
Editor-in-Chief: Carlo Gandini
Profile: Magazine about ski touring, mountain tourism and cross-country skiing races.
Language(s): Italian
Readership: Aimed at skiing and mountain sport enthusiasts, both professionals and amateurs.
CONSUMER: SPORT: Winter Sports

SCOOTER MAGAZINE 762851I77B-220
Editorial: Via Ponte Gardena, 46, 00124 ROMA RM
Tel: 06 50910640 **Fax:** 0645227207
Email: mail@motoresearch.it **Web site:** http://www.scootermag.it
Freq: Monthly; **Circ:** 42,000
Editor-in-Chief: Claudio Molteni
Profile: Magazine focusing on scooters including articles on new models, road tests and price reviews.
Language(s): Italian
Readership: Aimed at scooter owners and enthusiasts.
CONSUMER: MOTORING & CYCLING: Motorcycling

SCUOLA ITALIANA MODERNA 13928I62C-210
Editorial: Via Cadorna 11, 25124 BRESCIA
Tel: 030 29931 **Fax:** 030 2993299
Email: sim@lascuola.it **Web site:** http://www.lascuola.it
Freq: 24 issues yearly; **Circ:** 70,000
Editor-in-Chief: Paolo Calidoni
Profile: Publication focusing on primary school education for children aged between 6 and 11 years.
Language(s): Italian
Readership: Aimed at primary school teachers.
BUSINESS: CHURCH & SCHOOL EQUIPMENT & EDUCATION: Junior Education

SECOLO D'ITALIA 13975I65A-140
Editorial: Via Della Scrofa, 43, 00186 ROMA RM
Tel: 06 68899221 **Fax:** 06 6861598
Email: segreteria@secoloditalia.it **Web site:** http://www.secoloditalia.it
Freq: Daily; **Circ:** 35,000
Editor-in-Chief: Girolamo Fragala'
Profile: Tabloid-sized newspaper containing national and international news and information concerning politics, economics and sport.
Language(s): Italian
Readership: Read by a broad range of the population.
NATIONAL DAILY & SUNDAY NEWSPAPERS: National Daily Newspapers

IL SECOLO XIX 14037I67B-6600
Editorial: Piazza Piccapietra, 21, 16121 GENOVA GE
Tel: 010 53881 **Fax:** 010 5388426
Email: redazione@ilsecoloxix.it **Web site:** http://www.ilsecoloxix.it
Freq: Daily; **Circ:** 127,000
Editor: Nicola Stella; **Editor-in-Chief:** Umberto La Rocca
Language(s): Italian
REGIONAL DAILY & SUNDAY NEWSPAPERS: Regional Daily Newspapers

SEGNO NEL MONDO 1784830I87-267
Editorial: Via Aurelia, 481, 00165 ROMA RM
Tel: 06 661321 **Fax:** 06 66132360
Email: segno@azionecattolica.it **Web site:** http://www.azionecattolica.it
Freq: Monthly; **Circ:** 159,500
Editor-in-Chief: Gianni Borsa
Language(s): Italian
CONSUMER: RELIGIOUS

SELEZIONE DI ELETTRONICA 13360I18A-95
Editorial: Via Pisacane 1, 20016 PERO MI
Tel: 0230226078
Email: redazione.sde@ilsole24ore.com **Web site:** http://www.elettronicanews.it
Freq: Monthly; **Circ:** 10,000
Editor-in-Chief: Pierantonio Palerma
Profile: Magazine focusing on electronic components, applications, industrial automation and instrumentation.
Language(s): Italian
BUSINESS: ELECTRONICS

SELL OUT 624683I53-200
Editorial: Via Donatello, 5/B, 20131 MILANO
Tel: 02277961 **Fax:** 02 27796300
Email: sellout@e-duesse.it **Web site:** http://www.e-duesse.it
Freq: Monthly; **Circ:** 4,859
Editor-in-Chief: Vito Sinopoli
Profile: Magazine focusing on the retail trade in Italy.
Language(s): Italian
Readership: Aimed at buyers in the retail trade.
BUSINESS: RETAILING & WHOLESALING

SERIES 1785325I76C-288
Editorial: Viale Sarca, 235, 20126 MILANO MI
Tel: 02 217681 **Fax:** 0266192622
Email: info@mywaymedia.it **Web site:** http://www.seriesmagazine.it
Freq: Monthly; **Circ:** 100,000
Editor-in-Chief: Dario Tiengo
Language(s): Italian
CONSUMER: MUSIC & PERFORMING ARTS: TV & Radio

SERRAMENTI + DESIGN 13149I4E-185
Editorial: Via Eritrea, 21, 20157 MILANO
Tel: 02 390901 **Fax:** 02 39090332
Email: sec@tecnichenuove.com **Web site:** http://www.edilizianews.com
Freq: Monthly; **Circ:** 7,500
Editor-in-Chief: Ivo Nardella
Profile: Magazine about door and window frames and related components.
Language(s): Italian
Readership: Aimed at builders, architects, fitters and retailers.
BUSINESS: ARCHITECTURE & BUILDING: Building

I SERVIZI DEMOGRAFICI 13522I32A-29
Editorial: Casella Postale 290, 47822 SANTARCANGELO DI ROMAGNA RN
Tel: 0541 628111 **Fax:** 0541 622778
Email: asapubblica@maggioli.it **Web site:** http://www.periodicimaggioli.it
Freq: Monthly; **Circ:** 7,000
Editor-in-Chief: Manlio Maggioli
Profile: Journal focusing on demography.
Language(s): Italian
Readership: Aimed at those involved in the keeping of municipal records and registers.
BUSINESS: LOCAL GOVERNMENT, LEISURE & RECREATION: Local Government

SETTE (CORRIERE DELLA SERA) 13983I65H-80
Editorial: Via Solferino, 28, 20121 MILANO
Tel: 02 6339 **Fax:** 02 29009742
Email: sette@corriere.it **Web site:** http://www.corriere.it
Freq: Weekly; **Circ:** 860,000
Editor: Antonio D'Orrico
Profile: Magazine containing articles about entertainment, fashion, beauty and culture.
Language(s): Italian
NATIONAL DAILY & SUNDAY NEWSPAPERS: National Colour Supplements

LA SETTIMANA VETERINARIA 714603I64H-85
Editorial: Via Medardo Rosso, 11, 20159 MILANO
Tel: 02 6085231 **Fax:** 06 6682866
Email: settimana@pointvet.it **Web site:** http://www.pointvet.it
Freq: Weekly
Editor-in-Chief: Gabriele Lanzarotti
Profile: Magazine featuring current topics and news for the veterinary profession.
Language(s): Italian
Readership: Read by veterinary surgeons and nurses.
BUSINESS: OTHER CLASSIFICATIONS: Veterinary

SICUREZZA 13795I54C-86
Editorial: Via C. Pisacane 1, 20016 PERO MI
Tel: 02 30221
Email: paola.cozzi@ilsole24ore.com **Web site:** http://www.sicurezzamagazine.it
Freq: Monthly; **Circ:** 12,000
Editor-in-Chief: Pierantonio Palerma
Profile: Technical and scientific review on crime prevention, accident prevention and fire-fighting.
Language(s): Italian
BUSINESS: SAFETY & SECURITY: Security

SIKANIA 14435I80-285
Editorial: Piazzatta Scannaserpe 3, 90146 PALERMO
Tel: 091543506 **Fax:** 0916373378
Email: info@sikania.it **Web site:** http://www.sikania.it
Freq: Monthly; **Circ:** 37,450
Editor-in-Chief: Cristina Castellucci M.
Profile: Magazine covering news, culture, nature and tourism in Sicily.
Language(s): English; Italian
Readership: Read by Sicilian residents, people originating from Sicily and particularly those living in the major towns of Brazil and Argentina.
CONSUMER: RURAL & REGIONAL INTEREST

SILHOUETTE DONNA 14112I74A-325
Editorial: Corso di Porta Nuova, 3/a, 20121 MILANO
Tel: 02 636751 **Fax:** 02 63675522
Email: silhouette@casaeditriceuniverso.com
Freq: Monthly; **Circ:** 351,000
Editor: Matilde Perticaroli; **Editor-in-Chief:** Clara Masotti
Profile: Magazine covering health, food and beauty.
Language(s): Italian
CONSUMER: WOMEN'S INTEREST CONSUMER MAGAZINES: Women's Interest

SIPARIO 14311I76B-170
Editorial: Via Rosales 3, 20124 MILANO
Tel: 02653270 **Fax:** 02 29060005
Email: segreteria@sipario.it **Web site:** http://www.sipario.it
Freq: Monthly; **Circ:** 30,000
Editor-in-Chief: Mario Mattia Giorgetti
Profile: International magazine focusing on the arts, shows and cinema.
Language(s): Italian
CONSUMER: MUSIC & PERFORMING ARTS: Theatre

SISTEMI DI TELECOMUNICAZIONI 13367I18B-50
Editorial: Via Taramelli 19, 20124 MILANO
Tel: 0269007179 **Fax:** 02 6072078
Email: info@sistemiditlc.it **Web site:** http://www.sistemiditlc.it
Freq: Monthly; **Circ:** 11,000
Editor-in-Chief: Diletta Casieri
Profile: Magazine covering all aspects of modern telecommunications.
Language(s): Italian
BUSINESS: ELECTRONICS: Telecommunications

SISTEMI & IMPRESA 762943I14A-149_50
Editorial: Via A. Vassallo, 31, 20125 MILANO MI
Tel: 02 91434400 **Fax:** 02 91434424
Email: info@este.it **Web site:** http://www.este.it
Freq: Monthly; **Circ:** 10,000
Editor-in-Chief: Chiara Lupi
Profile: Magazine containing management information, technology, automation and logistics.
Language(s): Italian
Readership: Read by decision makers.
BUSINESS: COMMERCE, INDUSTRY & MANAGEMENT

SNOWBOARDER MAGAZINE 14279I75G-230
Editorial: Via XXIX Maggio, 18, 20025 LEGNANO MI
Tel: 0323 30122 **Fax:** 032330558
Email: info@ambadvertising.it **Web site:** http://www.snowboard.it
Freq: Monthly; **Circ:** 30,000
Editor-in-Chief: Lucia Milvia Maida
Profile: Magazine about snowboarding, contains interviews with celebrities, information about events and travel.
Language(s): English; French; German; Italian
Readership: Read by enthusiasts, mainly aged between 16 and 35 years.
CONSUMER: SPORT: Winter Sports

LE SOCIETA' 13058I1M-90
Editorial: Strada 1 Palazzo F. 6, 20090 MILANOFIORI ASSAGO MI **Tel:** 02 82476005 **Fax:** 02 82476674
Email: redazione.lesocieta.ipsoa@wki.it **Web site:** http://www.ipsoa.it/lesocieta
Freq: Monthly; **Circ:** 12,000
Profile: Journal focusing on tax, book-keeping and legal issues relating to small, medium and large companies.
Language(s): Italian
BUSINESS: FINANCE & ECONOMICS: Taxation

SOLDI & DIRITTI (ALTROCONSUMO) 1784427I44-278
Editorial: Via Valassina 22, 20159 MILANO
Tel: 02668901 **Fax:** 02 66890288
Web site: http://www.altroconsumo.it
Freq: 6 issues yearly; **Circ:** 280,000
Editor-in-Chief: Rosanna Massarenti
Language(s): Italian
BUSINESS: LEGAL

IL SOLE 24 ORE 13976I65A-150
Editorial: Via Monte Rosa, 91, 20149 MILANO
Tel: 02 30221 **Fax:** 02 30222758
Email: gruppoilsole24ore@ilsole24ore.com **Web site:** http://www.ilsole24ore.com
Freq: Daily; **Circ:** 500,000
Editor: Nino Ciravegna; **Editor-in-Chief:** Roberto Napoletano
Profile: Broadsheet-sized quality newspaper providing coverage of national and international news, with particular emphasis on finance and the economy.
Language(s): Italian
Readership: Read by company directors, senior executives, managers, civil servants, university students and academics.
ADVERTISING RATES:
Full Page Colour .... EUR 226560.00
NATIONAL DAILY & SUNDAY NEWSPAPERS: National Daily Newspapers

IL SOLE 24 ORE CENTRONORD - FI 753072I80-295
Editorial: Piazza Dè Peruzzi 4, 50122 FIRENZE
Tel: 0552385223 **Fax:** 055 210400
Email: red.centronord@ilsole24ore.com **Web site:** http://www.ilsole24ore.com
Freq: Weekly
Profile: Magazine containing general interest information for the regions of Emilia-Romagna, Toscana, Marche and Umbria.
Language(s): Italian
CONSUMER: RURAL & REGIONAL INTEREST

IL SOLE 24 ORE EDILIZIA E TERRITORIO 1784669I55-47
Editorial: Piazza dell'Indipendenza, 23 B/C, 00185 ROMA RM **Tel:** 06 30221 **Fax:** 0630227649
Email: edilizia@ilsole24ore.com **Web site:** http://www.ediliziaterritorio.ilsole24ore.com
Freq: Weekly; **Circ:** 500,000
Editor-in-Chief: Elia Zamboni
Language(s): Italian
BUSINESS: APPLIED SCIENCE & LABORATORIES

IL SOLE 24 ORE GUIDA AGLI ENTI LOCALI 1784717I32A-148
Editorial: Piazza Indipendenza, 23/A, 00100 ROMA
Tel: 06 30221 **Fax:** 0630226606
Email: enti.locali@ilsole24ore.com **Web site:** http://www.entilocali.ilsole24ore.com
Freq: Weekly; **Circ:** 500,000
Editor: Agostino Palomba
Language(s): Italian
BUSINESS: LOCAL GOVERNMENT, LEISURE & RECREATION: Local Government

IL SOLE 24 ORE SANITA' 753078I56R-250
Editorial: Piazza dell'Indipendenza 23 B/C, 00142 ROMA **Tel:** 06 30226656 **Fax:** 06 30226484
Email: redazione.sanita@ilsole24ore.com **Web site:** http://www.sanita.ilsole24ore.com
Freq: Weekly
Editor-in-Chief: Elia Zamboni
Profile: Magazine containing articles on management and financial matters regarding health and medical institutions.
Language(s): Italian
Readership: Read by medical and pharmaceutical personnel.
ADVERTISING RATES:
Full Page Mono .... EUR 6600.00
Full Page Colour .... EUR 8900.00
BUSINESS: HEALTH & MEDICAL: Health Medical Related

IL SOLE 24 ORE SCUOLA 753082I62A-250
Editorial: Piazza dell'Indipendenza 23 B/C, 00185 ROMA **Tel:** 0630226656 **Fax:** 06 30227655
Email: scuola@ilsole24ore.com **Web site:** http://www.ilsole24ore.com
Freq: 24 issues yearly
Editor-in-Chief: Elia Zamboni
Profile: Magazine dealing with education laws, legislations, administration, pensions and personnel.
Language(s): Italian
Readership: Read by teachers and school directors in the public and private sector.
BUSINESS: CHURCH & SCHOOL EQUIPMENT & EDUCATION: Education

IL SOLE 24 ORE TRASPORTI 753085I49A-38
Editorial: Piazza dell'Indipendenza, 23 b/c, 00185 ROMA **Tel:** 06 30227632 **Fax:** 06 30227651
Email: trasporti@ilsole24ore.com **Web site:** http://www.gruppo24ore.com
Freq: 24 issues yearly
Editor-in-Chief: Elia Zamboni
Profile: Magazine containing information on transport and logistics.
Language(s): Italian
Readership: Read by directors and managers in the transport industry.
BUSINESS: TRANSPORT

SPECCHIO ECONOMICO 13035I1A-205
Editorial: Via Rasella, 139, 00187 ROMA RM
Tel: 06 4821150 **Fax:** 06 485964
Email: specchioeconomico@iol.it **Web site:** http://www.specchioeconomico.com
Freq: Monthly; **Circ:** 45,000
Editor-in-Chief: Victor Ciuffa
Profile: Journal about economics, finance and politics. Also includes articles on topical news items.
Language(s): Italian
Readership: Read by industrialists, bankers, academics, professionals and entrepreneurs.
BUSINESS: FINANCE & ECONOMICS

SPECIALI DI MOTOCICLISMO 14360I77B-40
Editorial: Via Don Luigi Sturzo, 7, 20016 PERO MI
Tel: 02 38085310 **Fax:** 02 38010393
Email: motospeciali@edisport.it **Web site:** http://www.motociclismo.it
Freq: 6 issues yearly
Editor-in-Chief: Adalberto Falletta
Profile: Magazine containing detailed information on motorcycling, each issue focuses on a specific topic.
Language(s): Italian
Readership: Aimed at motorcycling enthusiasts.
CONSUMER: MOTORING & CYCLING: Motorcycling

SPECIALIZZATA EDILIZIA 13150I4E-210
Editorial: Via Teocrito 47, 20128 MILANO
Tel: 02252071 **Fax:** 02 27000692
Email: specializzata@bema.it **Web site:** http://www.specializzata.it
Freq: Monthly; **Circ:** 10,026
Editor-in-Chief: Gisella Bertini Malgarini
Profile: Magazine about waterproofing, insulation, roofing, flooring, renovation and reconstruction.
Language(s): Italian
BUSINESS: ARCHITECTURE & BUILDING: Building

SPENDIBENE 1784653I94H-3
Editorial: Strada Statale 31, Km 22, 15030 VILLANOVA MONFERRATO AL **Tel:** 0142 338249
Fax: 0142 483907
Email: info@spendibene.it **Web site:** http://www.spendibene.it
Freq: Monthly; **Circ:** 250,000
Editor-in-Chief: Mariarosa Barberis
Language(s): Italian
CONSUMER: OTHER CLASSIFICATIONS: Customer Magazines

SPORT & MEDICINA 13849I56A-325
Editorial: Viale Forlanini, 65, 20134 MILANO
Tel: 02 7021121 **Fax:** 02 70211283
Email: eeinfo@eenet.it **Web site:** http://www.sportemedicina.it
Freq: 6 issues yearly; **Circ:** 20,000
Editor-in-Chief: Raffaele Grandi
Profile: Journal focusing on sports medicine, traumatology and training.
Language(s): Italian
Readership: Read by sports doctors, physiotherapists, cardiologists, traumatologists and masseurs.
BUSINESS: HEALTH & MEDICAL

SPORTIVO 14250I75A-220
Editorial: Via Mauro Macchi, 28, 20124 MILANO
Tel: 02 66714341 **Fax:** 02 66713975
Email: sportivo@publicationspromotion.it **Web site:** http://www.publicationspromotion.it
Freq: Monthly; **Circ:** 36,000
Editor-in-Chief: Natascia Bertoletti
Profile: Magazine containing sports news.
Language(s): English; Italian
Readership: Read by managers in sports and sports federations and sports enthusiasts.
CONSUMER: SPORT

SPORTSWEAR INTERNATIONAL 13708I47A-100
Editorial: Piazza Pio XI, 1, 20123 MILANO
Tel: 02 806 20 1 **Fax:** 02 806 20 333
Email: siww@siww.it **Web site:** http://www.sportswearnet.com
Freq: 6 issues yearly; **Circ:** 30,000
Editor-in-Chief: Klaus Hang
Profile: Fashion magazine for the European jeanswear and sportswear market.
Language(s): English; German; Italian
Readership: Young contemporary fashion executives - retailers, manufacturers, designers or media experts.
BUSINESS: CLOTHING & TEXTILES

SPOSABELLA 14227I74L-50
Editorial: Piazza Castello, 27, 20121 MILANO MI
Tel: 02 85612963 **Fax:** 02 85612974
Web site: http://www.style.it
Freq: 3 issues yearly; **Circ:** 93,000
Editor-in-Chief: Ines Monti
Profile: Magazine focusing on bridal fashion.
Language(s): Italian
CONSUMER: WOMEN'S INTEREST CONSUMER MAGAZINES: Brides

LA STAMPA 13977I65A-160
Editorial: Via Carlo Marenco, 32, 10126 TORINO TO
Tel: 011 6568111 **Fax:** 011 6568924
Email: lettere@lastampa.it **Web site:** http://www.lastampa.it
Freq: Daily; **Circ:** 470,000
Editor: Paolo Mastrolilli; **Editor-in-Chief:** Mario Calabresi
Profile: Tabloid-sized quality newspaper containing national, international and regional news focusing on Piemonte, financial information and articles on society, culture, entertainment and sport.
Language(s): Italian
Readership: Readership includes directors, senior executives, middle managers and office personnel.
ADVERTISING RATES:
Full Page Colour .... EUR 228660.00
NATIONAL DAILY & SUNDAY NEWSPAPERS: National Daily Newspapers

STARBENE 14216I74G-75
Editorial: Palazzo Mondadori, 20090 SEGRATE MI
Tel: 02 75422827 **Fax:** 02 75422086
Email: starbene@mondadori.it **Web site:** http://www.starbene.it
Freq: Monthly; **Circ:** 350,000
Editor: Francesca Pietra; **Editor-in-Chief:** Cristina Merlino
Profile: Magazine covering health and fitness.
Language(s): Italian
CONSUMER: WOMEN'S INTEREST CONSUMER MAGAZINES: Slimming & Health

STOP 14113I73-370
Editorial: Viale Tunisi 21, 20124 MILANO MI
Tel: 0289656612
Email: segreteria@gvssrl.com
Freq: Weekly; **Circ:** 70,000
Editor: Laura Bozzi; **Editor-in-Chief:** Riccardo Signoretti
Profile: Magazine containing topical news and articles on politics, culture, sport and shows.
Language(s): Italian
CONSUMER: NATIONAL & INTERNATIONAL PERIODICALS

LE STRADE 13621I42B-50
Editorial: Via Conca Del Naviglio, 37, 20123 MILANO
Tel: 02 89421350 **Fax:** 02 89421484
Email: lestrade@fiaccola.it **Web site:** http://www.fiaccola.com

Freq: Monthly; **Circ:** 19,325
Editor-in-Chief: Lucia Edvige Saronni
Profile: Magazine providing information about the road construction industry.
Language(s): English; Italian
Readership: Aimed at civil and construction engineers.
BUSINESS: CONSTRUCTION: Roads

STRUCTURAL
13131I4R-501
Editorial: Via Tadino, 25, 20124 MILANO
Tel: 02 36584135
Email: redazione@delettera.it **Web site:** http://www.delettera.it
Freq: 6 issues yearly; **Circ:** 10,500
Editor-in-Chief: Ivan De Lettera
Profile: Journal focusing on structure design, diagnostics, reinforcement, research and advanced materials.
Language(s): Italian
Readership: Read by engineers and contractors.
BUSINESS: ARCHITECTURE & BUILDING: Building Related

STUDI CATTOLICI
14496I87-220
Editorial: Via A. Stradivari 7, 20131 MILANO
Tel: 0229526156 **Fax:** 02 29520163
Email: info@ares.mi.it **Web site:** http://www.ares.mi.it
Freq: Monthly; **Circ:** 10,000
Editor-in-Chief: Cesare Cavalleri
Profile: International religious magazine focusing on the Catholic faith. Includes information on philosophy, history and sociology.
Language(s): Italian
Readership: Read by professors and university students.
CONSUMER: RELIGIOUS

SUB
14294I75M-200
Editorial: Via Comelico 3, 20135 MILANO
Tel: 02 55188494 **Fax:** 02 5464407
Email: redazione@adventuresub.it **Web site:** http://www.adventuresub.it
Freq: Monthly; **Circ:** 31,000
Editor-in-Chief: Guido Pfeiffer
Profile: Magazine about the underwater world and scuba diving.
Language(s): Italian
Readership: Read by people who like diving and the underwater environment.
CONSUMER: SPORT: Water Sports

IL SUBACQUEO
14295I75M-210
Editorial: Via Della Maratona 66, 00194 ROMA
Tel: 06 3629021 **Fax:** 06 36309950
Email: redazione@subacqueo.it **Web site:** http://www.subacqueo.it
Freq: Monthly; **Circ:** 80,000
Editor-in-Chief: Calogero Cascio
Profile: Magazine about scuba diving, includes test results on new equipment.
Language(s): Italian
Readership: Read by scuba diving enthusiasts.
CONSUMER: SPORT: Water Sports

SUITE
13255I11A-162
Editorial: Via Teocrito, 47, 20128 MILANO
Tel: 02252071 **Fax:** 02 27000692
Email: suite@bema.it **Web site:** http://www.mysmarthotel.net
Freq: 6 issues yearly; **Circ:** 14,084
Editor-in-Chief: Gisella Bertini Malgarini
Profile: Magazine about hotel hospitality.
Language(s): English; Italian
Readership: Read by hoteliers in Italy.
BUSINESS: CATERING: Catering, Hotels & Restaurants

SUONO
14399I78A-320
Editorial: Casella Postale18340, 00164 ROMA
Tel: 06 44702611 **Fax:** 06 44702612
Email: segreteria@suono.it **Web site:** http://www.suono.it
Freq: Monthly; **Circ:** 60,000
Editor-in-Chief: Paolo Corciulo
Profile: Magazine containing information concerning hi-fi equipment and music.
Language(s): Italian
CONSUMER: CONSUMER ELECTRONICS: Hi-Fi & Recording

SUPER MOTOTECNICA
14373I77B-230
Editorial: Via Molise, 3, 20085 LOCATE TRIULZI MI
Tel: 02 9048111 **Fax:** 02 90481120
Email: info@nuoviperiodicimilanesi.com **Web site:** http://www.supermototecnica.com
Freq: Monthly; **Circ:** 90,000
Editor-in-Chief: Daniele Cafieri
Profile: International motorcycle magazine concerned with technology. Also includes road tests and information about bike parts and accessories.
Language(s): English; Italian
Readership: Aimed at people with an interest in motorbikes, techniques and technology. Also professionals working in the field.
CONSUMER: MOTORING & CYCLING: Motorcycling

SUPER WHEELS
14374I77B-235
Editorial: Via Don Luigi Sturzo 7, 20016 PERO MI
Tel: 02380851 **Fax:** 0238010393
Email: sw@edisport.it **Web site:** http://www.superwheels.net
Freq: Monthly; **Circ:** 85,000
Editor-in-Chief: Aldo Ballerini
Profile: Magazine covering all aspects of motorcycling, including profiles and reviews of new models, touring, tests, details of equipment, products and exhibitions.
Language(s): Italian
Readership: Aimed at tourists and enthusiasts.
CONSUMER: MOTORING & CYCLING: Motorcycling

SUPERPARTES IN THE WORLD
1829245I50-209
Editorial: Piazzale De Agostini, 3, 20146 MILANO MI
Tel: 02 42297513 **Fax:** 02 99981609
Email: opinioni@superpartesitw.it **Web site:** http://www.superpartesitw.it
Freq: Monthly; **Circ:** 100,000
Editor-in-Chief: Vanni Bolis
Language(s): Italian
BUSINESS: TRAVEL & TOURISM

SURGELATI MAGAZINE
624662I22E-6
Editorial: Via Giuseppe Mazzini, 132, 50125 PISA
Tel: 05049490 **Fax:** 05049451
Email: segreteriapi@pubblindustria.com **Web site:** http://www.surgelatimagazine.com
Freq: 6 issues yearly; **Circ:** 30,000
Editor-in-Chief: Leonardo Bindi
Profile: Magazine focusing on frozen foods.
Language(s): Italian
Readership: Read by producers, suppliers and retailers.
BUSINESS: FOOD: Frozen Food

SVILUPPO & ORGANIZZAZIONE
13289I14A-150
Editorial: Via A. Vassallo 31, 20125 MILANO
Tel: 02 91434400 **Fax:** 02 91434424
Email: info@este.it **Web site:** http://www.este.it
Freq: 6 issues yearly; **Circ:** 6,500
Editor-in-Chief: Gianfranco Rebora
Profile: Publication focusing on work development and organisation.
Language(s): Italian
Readership: Aimed at directors, managers and businessmen.
BUSINESS: COMMERCE, INDUSTRY & MANAGEMENT

LA SVIZZERA
13303I14C-100
Editorial: Via Palestro 2, 20121 MILANO
Tel: 02 7632031 **Fax:** 02 781084
Email: info@ccsi.it **Web site:** http://www.ccsi.it
Freq: Quarterly; **Circ:** 5,000
Editor-in-Chief: Alessandra Modenese Kauffmann
Profile: Magazine covering topics on Italian-Swiss relations.
Language(s): Italian
Readership: Read by members of the Chamber of Commerce, public organisations and ministries.
BUSINESS: COMMERCE, INDUSTRY & MANAGEMENT: International Commerce

SYSTEM I NEWS EDIZIONE ITALIANA
13194I5C-170
Editorial: Via F. Confalonieri 36, 20124 MILANO
Tel: 0256609300 **Fax:** 0257419081
Email: redazione@duke.it **Web site:** http://www.duke.it
Freq: Monthly; **Circ:** 8,000
Editor-in-Chief: Roberto Negrini
Profile: Magazine about IBM and AS/400 computer systems, includes tests and analysis of products and technical information.
Language(s): Italian
Readership: Aimed at IT managers.
BUSINESS: COMPUTERS & AUTOMATION: Professional Personal Computers

TECHNOSHOPPING
1809711I18A-109
Editorial: Via delle Alpi, 13, 00198 ROMA RM
Tel: 06 44202596 **Fax:** 06 44254426
Email: redazione@technoshopping.it **Web site:** http://www.technoshopping.it
Freq: Monthly; **Circ:** 500,000
Editor-in-Chief: Giorgia Vaccari
Language(s): Italian
BUSINESS: ELECTRONICS

TECNICA CALZATURIERA
13506I29-100
Editorial: Via Eritrea, 21, 20157 MILANO
Tel: 02 39090287 **Fax:** 02 39090331
Email: tecnica.calzaturiera@tecnichenuove.com **Web site:** http://www.tecnichenuove.com
Freq: 6 issues yearly; **Circ:** 8,000
Editor-in-Chief: Giuseppe Nardella
Profile: Pan-European journal about the shoe and leather trade, containing technical information, reports and previews, articles on computer science, electronics, production management, quality materials and fashion trends.
Language(s): English; Italian
Readership: Aimed at stylists, buyers and managers in the footwear and leather trade.
BUSINESS: FOOTWEAR

TECNOPLAST
13596I39-130
Editorial: Via Garbiera, 1, 20021 BOLLATE
Tel: 0292865345 **Fax:** 0292865340
Email: redazione@tecnoedizioni.com **Web site:** http://www.tecnoedizioni.com
Freq: Monthly; **Circ:** 6,622
Editor-in-Chief: Riccardo Ampollini
Profile: Magazine about the plastics industry; includes marketing, economic information, technology, materials and components.
Language(s): English; Italian
Readership: Aimed at professionals in the plastics industry.
BUSINESS: PLASTICS & RUBBER

TELESETTE
1784346I76C-283
Editorial: Corso di Porta Nuova 3/a, 20121 MILANO
Tel: 0263675 1 **Fax:** 02 63675525
Email: segreteriadd@casaeditriceuniverso.com
Freq: Weekly; **Circ:** 900,000
Language(s): Italian
CONSUMER: MUSIC & PERFORMING ARTS: TV & Radio

TEMA FARMACIA
13580I37-115
Editorial: Via Eritrea, 21, 20157 MILANO
Tel: 02 39090290 **Fax:** 02 39090332
Email: temafarmacia@tecnichenuove.com **Web site:** http://www.tecnichenuove.com
Freq: Monthly; **Circ:** 16,000
Editor-in-Chief: Giuseppe Nardella
Profile: Publication featuring articles of interest to community pharmacies.
Language(s): Italian
Readership: Aimed at owners of pharmacies.
BUSINESS: PHARMACEUTICAL & CHEMISTS

IL TEMPO
13978I65A-180
Editorial: Piazza Colonna, 366, 00187 ROMA RM
Tel: 06 675881 **Fax:** 06 67588232
Email: segreteria@iltempo.it **Web site:** http://www.iltempo.it
Freq: Daily; **Circ:** 100,000
Editor-in-Chief: Mario Sechi
Profile: Broadsheet-sized newspaper covering regional, national and international news, finance, politics and sport.
Language(s): Italian
Readership: Read predominantly by people living in the Lazio and Abruzzi regions.
ADVERTISING RATES:
Full Page Mono .... EUR 57120.00
Full Page Colour .... EUR 85320.00
NATIONAL DAILY & SUNDAY NEWSPAPERS: National Daily Newspapers

IL TENNIS ITALIANO
14284I75H-210
Editorial: Via Don Luigi Sturzo 7, 20016 PERO MI
Tel: 02 380851 **Fax:** 02 38010393
Email: tennisitaliano@edisport.it **Web site:** http://www.tennisitaliano.it
Freq: Monthly; **Circ:** 49,000
Editor-in-Chief: Piero Bacchetti
Profile: Magazine about tennis in Italy.
Language(s): Italian
CONSUMER: SPORT: Racquet Sports

TENNIS OGGI
14285I75H-220
Editorial: Via Della Balduina 88, 00136 ROMA
Tel: 06 35344859 **Fax:** 06 35454503
Email: redazione@tennis.it **Web site:** http://www.tennis.it
Freq: Monthly; **Circ:** 30,000
Editor-in-Chief: Sergio Rossi
Profile: Magazine covering all aspects of the tennis sport.
Language(s): Italian
CONSUMER: SPORT: Racquet Sports

LA TERMOTECNICA
13095I3B-160
Editorial: Via Lomellina 33, 20133 MILANO
Tel: 02 55181842 **Fax:** 02 55184161
Email: latermotecnica@latermotecnica.net **Web site:** http://www.latermotecnica.net
Freq: Monthly; **Circ:** 7,500
Editor-in-Chief: Pierangelo Andreini
Profile: Official journal of ATI (Italian Thermotechnics Association). Provides information on heating and refrigeration techniques.
Language(s): Italian
Readership: Read by professionals within the thermotechnical field.
BUSINESS: HEATING & VENTILATION: Industrial Heating & Ventilation

TERRA E VITA
13411I21A-350
Editorial: Via Goito, 13, 40126 BOLOGNA
Tel: 051 65751 **Fax:** 051 6575856
Email: redazione.edagricole@ilsole24ore.com **Web site:** http://www.terraevita.it
Freq: Weekly; **Circ:** 33,200
Editor-in-Chief: Elia Zamboni
Profile: Journal covering the politics, economics and technology of farming.
Language(s): Italian
ADVERTISING RATES:
Full Page Mono .... EUR 3070.00
Full Page Colour .... EUR 4530.00
BUSINESS: AGRICULTURE & FARMING

TERZO SETTORE
754198I1P-600
Editorial: c/o Novecento - Via Carlo Tenca 7, 20124 MILANO **Tel:** 0223002401 **Fax:** 0223002411
Email: terzosettore@novecentoweb.it **Web site:** http://www.ilsole24ore.com
Freq: Monthly
Editor-in-Chief: Alberto Bosco
Profile: Magazine focusing on juridical issues for non-profit organisations, providing practical solutions to problems and management tips.
Language(s): Italian
Readership: Read by managers of non-profit organisations.
BUSINESS: FINANCE & ECONOMICS: Fundraising

TEST SALUTE (ALTROCONSUMO)
1784691I56A-346
Editorial: Via Valassina 22, 20159 MILANO MI
Tel: 02668901 **Fax:** 02 66890252
Web site: http://www.altroconsumo.it
Freq: 6 issues yearly; **Circ:** 110,000
Editor-in-Chief: Rosanna Massarenti
Language(s): Italian
BUSINESS: HEALTH & MEDICAL

TEX HOME
13467I23A-75
Editorial: V.le Andrea Doria 35, 20124 MILANO
Tel: 02 66988188 **Fax:** 02 66988190
Email: redazione@edinterni.it **Web site:** http://www.edinterni.com
Freq: Monthly; **Circ:** 8,000
Editor-in-Chief: Luisa Buiarelli
Profile: International magazine containing articles about linen for the home.
Language(s): Italian
Readership: Aimed at those involved in the furnishings industry.
BUSINESS: FURNISHINGS & FURNITURE

TIM-TRADE INTERACTIVE MULTIMEDIA
13217I5F-200
Editorial: Via Donatello, 5/B, 20131 MILANO
Tel: 02277961 **Fax:** 02 27796300
Email: tim@e-duesse.it **Web site:** http://www.e-duesse.it
Freq: Monthly; **Circ:** 5,171
Editor-in-Chief: Vito Sinopoli
Profile: Magazine about interactive multimedia.
Language(s): Italian
BUSINESS: COMPUTERS & AUTOMATION: Multimedia

TIR - LA RIVISTA DELL'AUTOTRASPORTO
624058I49C-70
Editorial: Via Tevere 44, 00198 ROMA
Tel: 0685356494 **Fax:** 0668892416
Email: redazione.tir@tin.it
Freq: Monthly; **Circ:** 163,500
Editor-in-Chief: Fabio Montanaro
Profile: Official magazine of the National Register of Haulage Contractors, contains updates of regulations, information about transport systems and technical developments.
Language(s): Italian
Readership: Read by drivers of small or heavy trucks.
BUSINESS: TRANSPORT: Freight

TIS - IL CORRIERE TERMOIDROSANITARIO
13098I3D-20
Editorial: Via G. Richard 1/A, 20143 MILANO
Tel: 0281830237 **Fax:** 02 81830408
Email: tis@reedbusiness.it **Web site:** http://www.reedbusiness.it
Freq: Monthly; **Circ:** 18,000
Editor-in-Chief: Giovanni Danielli
Profile: Newspaper focusing on heating, plumbing and air-conditioning systems.
Language(s): Italian

Readership: Read by installers.
BUSINESS: HEATING & VENTILATION: Heating & Plumbing

TOOL NEWS
76585915E-251
Editorial: Via V. Monti 23, 27100 PAVIA
Tel: 0382 304985 **Fax:** 0382 303290
Email: toolnews@itware.com **Web site:** http://www.itware.com
Freq: Monthly; **Circ:** 8,000
Editor-in-Chief: Alessandro Giacchino
Profile: Magazine containing information about software solutions for electronic application to business, logistic management and search engines construction for Internet use.
Language(s): English; Italian
Readership: Aimed at computer programmers.
BUSINESS: COMPUTERS & AUTOMATION: Data Transmission

TOP GIRL
14206174F-234
Editorial: c/o Edit. Nord - Piazza De Angeli 9, 20149 MILANO **Tel:** 0287245150 **Fax:** 0287245164
Web site: http://www.topgirl.it
Freq: Monthly; **Circ:** 400,000
Editor-in-Chief: Elisa Alloro
Profile: Magazine containing articles about fashion, beauty, accessories, music, cinema sport, travel and leisure time. Includes problem pages and advice on topical issues relating to young people.
Language(s): Italian
Readership: Aimed at girls aged between 12 and 17 years.
CONSUMER: WOMEN'S INTEREST CONSUMER MAGAZINES: Teenage

TOP SPORT
13724148B-140
Editorial: Via Emilia Ponente 26, 40133 BOLOGNA
Tel: 051 385700 **Fax:** 051 384793
Email: redazione@edizionimiglio.it **Web site:** http://www.topsport.it
Freq: Monthly; **Circ:** 9,000
Editor-in-Chief: Giovanna Glionna
Profile: Magazine for the sports trade about products and events. Contains interviews and profiles.
Language(s): Italian
BUSINESS: TOY TRADE & SPORTS GOODS: Sports Goods

TOP TRADE INFORMATICA
1318815B-70
Editorial: Via F. Confalonieri 36, 20141 MILANO MI
Tel: 0256609380 **Fax:** 0257419081
Email: redazione.toptrade@matedizioni.it **Web site:** http://www.toptrade.it
Freq: Monthly; **Circ:** 15,000
Editor-in-Chief: Roberto Negrini
Profile: Magazine for the IT sector.
Language(s): Italian
BUSINESS: COMPUTERS & AUTOMATION: Data Processing

TOPOLINO
754458191D-200
Editorial: Via Sandro Sandri 1, 20121 MILANO
Tel: 02 290851 **Fax:** 02 29085162
Email: francesca.fagioli@disney.com **Web site:** http://www.disney.it
Freq: Weekly; **Circ:** 630,000
Editor: Santo Scarcella; **Editor-in-Chief:** Valentina De Poli
Profile: Magazine featuring stories based on Walt Disney's characters.
Language(s): Italian
Readership: Aimed at children of all ages.
CONSUMER: RECREATION & LEISURE: Children & Youth

TRADE CONSUMER ELECTRONICS
13361118A-100
Editorial: Via Donatello, 5/B, 20131 MILANO
Tel: 02277961 **Fax:** 02 27796300
Email: tce@e-duesse.it **Web site:** http://www.e-duesse.it
Freq: Monthly; **Circ:** 9,172
Editor-in-Chief: Vito Sinopoli
Profile: Magazine about electronics and electrical consumer goods.
Language(s): Italian
Readership: Aimed at distributors of electrical and electronic consumer goods.
BUSINESS: ELECTRONICS

TRADE HOME ENTERTAINMENT
13630143A-120
Editorial: Via Donatello 5/b, 20131 MILANO
Tel: 02 277961 **Fax:** 02 27796300
Email: the@e-duesse.it **Web site:** http://www.e-duesse.it
Freq: Monthly; **Circ:** 8,499
Editor-in-Chief: Vito Sinopoli
Profile: Journal focusing on the retail trade of televisions, hi-fi systems, video recorders and camera equipment.
Language(s): Italian
Readership: Aimed at owners of music shops, video clubs and those working in the music sector.
BUSINESS: ELECTRICAL RETAIL TRADE

TRASPORTI NEWS
13734149A-55
Editorial: Via B. Eustachi, 47, 20129 MILANO
Tel: 02 6690427 **Fax:** 02 6694185
Email: editrice.trasporti@trasportiweb.it **Web site:** http://www.trasportiweb.it
Freq: Monthly; **Circ:** 11,000
Editor-in-Chief: Marco Girella
Profile: Publication covering all kinds of transport.
Language(s): Italian
BUSINESS: TRANSPORT

TRASPORTI PUBBLICI TP
13735149A-58
Editorial: Piazza Cola Di Rienzo, 80/A, 00192 ROMA
Tel: 06 68603548 **Fax:** 06 3226301
Email: rivista@asstra.it **Web site:** http://www.asstra.it
Freq: Monthly; **Circ:** 5,000
Editor-in-Chief: Paolo Cremonesi
Profile: Magazine about public transport.
Language(s): Italian
BUSINESS: TRANSPORT

TRATTORI
713133121E-53
Editorial: Via Cassano d'Adda, 20, 20139 MILANO
Tel: 02 55230950 **Fax:** 02 55230592
Email: trattori@vadoetornoedizioni.it **Web site:** http://www.vadoetorno.com
Freq: Monthly; **Circ:** 39,720
Editor-in-Chief: Maurizio Cervetto
Profile: Magazine containing technical and market news about agricultural tractors and machinery.
Language(s): English; French; German; Italian; Spanish
Readership: Read by farmers, manufacturers, suppliers and retailers.
BUSINESS: AGRICULTURE & FARMING: Agriculture - Machinery & Plant

TRAVEL QUOTIDIANO
13754150-147
Editorial: Via Merlo, 1, 20122 MILANO MI
Tel: 02 76316846 **Fax:** 02 76013193
Email: redazionemilano@travelquotidiano.com **Web site:** http://www.travelquotidiano.com
Freq: 26 issues yearly; **Circ:** 10,000
Editor-in-Chief: Giuseppe Aloe
Profile: Magazine covering every aspect of the tourism trade nationally and internationally.
Language(s): Italian
BUSINESS: TRAVEL & TOURISM

TRAVELLER
14527189E-242
Editorial: Piazza Castello, 27, 20121 MILANO
Tel: 02 85612696 **Fax:** 02 801117
Email: traveller@condenast.it **Web site:** http://www.menstyle.it/traveller
Freq: Monthly; **Circ:** 120,000
Editor: Eleonora Platania; **Editor-in-Chief:** Roberto Delera
Profile: Magazine focusing on travel, each issue is dedicated to a single destination.
Language(s): Italian
Readership: Aimed at the independent traveller.
CONSUMER: HOLIDAYS & TRAVEL: Holidays

TREND
13755150-148
Editorial: Via Mose Bianchi, 4, 20149 MILANO MI
Tel: 02 48519525 **Fax:** 02 531550
Email: trend@bertaccaservice.191.it **Web site:** http://www.panamaeditore.it
Freq: Weekly; **Circ:** 8,000
Profile: Journal focusing on the tourist trade.
Language(s): Italian
Readership: Read by tour operators and travel agents.
BUSINESS: TRAVEL & TOURISM

TREND AVANTGARDE WAVE
1784222184B-151
Editorial: Via L. B. Alberti, 12, 20149 MILANO
Tel: 02 33600952 **Fax:** 02 3314397
Email: trendclub@trendweb.it **Web site:** http://www.trendweb.it
Freq: Monthly; **Circ:** 120,000
Editor-in-Chief: Raffaele D'Argenzio
Language(s): Italian
CONSUMER: THE ARTS & LITERARY: Literary

TTG ITALIA
13753150-140
Editorial: Via Alberto Nota, 6, 10122 TORINO
Tel: 011 4366300 **Fax:** 011 4366500
Email: redazione@ttgitalia.com **Web site:** http://www.ttgitalia.com
Freq: 26 issues yearly; **Circ:** 11,000
Editor-in-Chief: Remo Vangelista
Profile: Journal focusing on the travel trade.
Language(s): Italian
Readership: Read by travel agents.
BUSINESS: TRAVEL & TOURISM

TU STYLE
762780174A-360
Editorial: Palazzo Mondadori, 20090 SEGRATE MI
Tel: 02 75421 **Fax:** 02 75422509
Email: tustyle@mondadori.it **Web site:** http://www.mondadori.it
Freq: Weekly; **Circ:** 475,000
Editor: Carlotta Marioni; **Editor-in-Chief:** Marisa Deimichei
Profile: Magazine focusing on lifestyle, fashion, beauty and health.
Language(s): Italian
Readership: Aimed at women aged between 25 and 45 years.
ADVERTISING RATES:
Full Page Colour .... EUR 22750.00
CONSUMER: WOMEN'S INTEREST CONSUMER MAGAZINES: Women's Interest

TURISMO D'AFFARI
13757150-153
Editorial: Via Ripamonti, 89, 20141 MILANO MI
Tel: 02 57311511 **Fax:** 02 55231486
Email: tda@ediman.it **Web site:** http://www.ediman.it
Freq: 6 issues yearly; **Circ:** 10,000
Editor-in-Chief: Marco Biamonti
Profile: Magazine covering business travel.
Language(s): Italian
BUSINESS: TRAVEL & TOURISM

TURISMO D'ITALIA
13256111A-180
Editorial: c/o Federalberghi - Via Toscana 1, 00187 ROMA **Tel:** 0642034610 **Fax:** 0246034690
Email: turismoditalia@bema.it **Web site:** http://www.bema.it
Freq: 6 issues yearly; **Circ:** 15,000
Editor-in-Chief: Gisella Bertini Malgarini
Profile: Journal of the Italian Hotel Owners' Association, providing articles on marketing, job training, management and updating of EU recommendations. Also includes information of exhibitions and conventions, regional topics and leisure and tourism in general.
Language(s): Italian
BUSINESS: CATERING: Catering, Hotels & Restaurants

TURISMO E ATTUALITA'
13756150-150
Editorial: Via S. Prisca 16, 00153 ROMA
Tel: 06 5747450 **Fax:** 06 5744154
Email: redazione@turismo-attualita.it **Web site:** http://www.turismo-attualita.it
Freq: Weekly; **Circ:** 10,000
Editor-in-Chief: Ester Ippolito
Profile: Magazine providing information on hotels, executive travel and business venues, excursions for school children, air, land and sea transport and car hire.
Language(s): Italian
Readership: Read by travel agents and tour operators.
BUSINESS: TRAVEL & TOURISM

TUTTI FOTOGRAFI
13586138-90
Editorial: Viale Piceno, 14, 20129 MILANO MI
Tel: 02 70002222 **Fax:** 02 713030
Email: annunci@fotografia.it **Web site:** http://www.fotografia.it
Freq: Monthly; **Circ:** 60,000
Editor-in-Chief: Paolo Namias
Profile: Technical magazine concerning all aspects of photography.
Language(s): Italian
Readership: Read by amateur and professional photographers.
BUSINESS: PHOTOGRAPHIC TRADE

TUTTO FUORISTRADA
14359177A-390
Editorial: Via XXV Aprile, 99, 20068 PESCHIERA BORROMEO MI **Tel:** 02 55300839 **Fax:** 02 55300837
Email: redazione@tuttofuoristrada.it **Web site:** http://www.tuttofuoristrada.it
Freq: Monthly
Editor-in-Chief: Loriano P. Martinoli
Profile: Publication covering news, politics and promotion of cross-country and 4x4 racing, general motoring information and off-road testing results.
Language(s): Italian
Readership: Aimed at cross-country, 4x4 racing and general motoring enthusiasts.
CONSUMER: MOTORING & CYCLING: Motoring

TUTTOBICI
14381177C-110
Editorial: Via Inama, 7, 20133 MILANO MI
Tel: 02 89500028 **Fax:** 02 89512140
Email: info@tuttobiciweb.it **Web site:** http://www.tuttobiciweb.it
Freq: Monthly; **Circ:** 40,000
Editor-in-Chief: Pier Augusto Stagi
Profile: Publication about cycling particularly focusing on great champions of the sport.
Language(s): Italian
Readership: Aimed at mainly men in the 20 to 40 year age bracket.
CONSUMER: MOTORING & CYCLING: Cycling

TUTTORALLY
14384177D-200
Editorial: Via Galileo Galilei, 3, 10023 CHIERI TO
Tel: 011 9470400 **Fax:** 011 9470577
Email: tuttorally@barberoeditori.it **Web site:** http://www.barberoeditori.it
Freq: Monthly; **Circ:** 120,000
Editor-in-Chief: Nanni Barbero
Profile: Magazine about rally sport.
Language(s): Italian
Readership: Aimed at rally sport enthusiasts.
CONSUMER: MOTORING & CYCLING: Motor Sports

TUTTOSCIENZE (LA STAMPA)
1645520194J-2004
Editorial: Via Marenco 32, 10126 TORINO
Tel: 01165681 **Fax:** 011 6568988
Email: tuttoscienze@lastampa.it **Web site:** http://www.lastampa.it/tuttoscienze
Freq: Weekly
Profile: Publication focusing on science and technology.
Language(s): Italian
CONSUMER: OTHER CLASSIFICATIONS: Popular Science

TUTTOSPORT
13979165A-185
Editorial: Corso Svizzera, 185, 10149 TORINO TO
Tel: 011 77731 **Fax:** 011 7773483
Email: posta@tuttosport.com **Web site:** http://www.tuttosport.com
Freq: Daily; **Circ:** 205,000
Editor-in-Chief: Paolo De Paola
Profile: Broadsheet-sized newspaper providing coverage of competitive sport in Italy and throughout the world, with particular emphasis on events in the Turin area.
Language(s): Italian
Readership: Read by a wide range of people interested in sport.
ADVERTISING RATES:
Full Page Mono .... EUR 26768.00
Full Page Colour .... EUR 37475.20
NATIONAL DAILY & SUNDAY NEWSPAPERS: National Daily Newspapers

TUTTOTRASPORTI
13736149A-60
Editorial: Via Gianni Mazzocchi 1/3, 20089 ROZZANO MI **Tel:** 02 82472333 **Fax:** 02 82472287
Email: redazione@tuttotrasporti.it **Web site:** http://www.tuttotrasporti.it
Freq: Monthly; **Circ:** 50,250
Editor-in-Chief: Marcello Minerbi
Profile: Journal containing news and views from the world of transport.
Language(s): English; Italian
BUSINESS: TRANSPORT

TV KEY
1308612D-170
Editorial: Via Arcivescovo Romilli, 20/8, 20139 MILANO **Tel:** 02 5220371 **Fax:** 02 55213037
Email: redazione@mediakey.it **Web site:** http://www.mediakey.tv
Freq: Monthly; **Circ:** 9,500
Editor-in-Chief: Roberto Albano
Profile: Magazine covering creative TV commercials, TV programmes, production and post-production, home video and computer graphics, audience research and innovative technology.
Language(s): Italian
BUSINESS: COMMUNICATIONS, ADVERTISING & MARKETING: Broadcasting

TV SORRISI & CANZONI
14317176C-250
Editorial: Palazzo Mondadori, 20090 SEGRATE
Tel: 02 75421 **Fax:** 0275423960
Email: sorrisi@mondadori.it **Web site:** http://www.sorrisi.com
Freq: Weekly; **Circ:** 1,513,945
Editor: Maurizio Bedini; **Editor-in-Chief:** Alfonso Signorini
Profile: Magazine containing news, articles and information about TV programmes and cinema.
Language(s): Italian
CONSUMER: MUSIC & PERFORMING ARTS: TV & Radio

TV SORRISI E CANZONI RM
1784347176D-555
Editorial: Via Sicilia, 136/138, 00187 ROMA
Tel: 06 474971 **Fax:** 06 47497415
Web site: http://www.sorrisi.com
Freq: Weekly; **Circ:** 1,513,945
Language(s): Italian
CONSUMER: MUSIC & PERFORMING ARTS: Music

TWEENS
1785047174F-206
Editorial: c/o Emmei - Via Guido Reni 33, 00196 ROMA **Tel:** 0645615060 **Fax:** 0645615232
Email: mgs@emmei.info
Freq: Monthly; **Circ:** 40,000
Editor-in-Chief: Marco Iafrate

Language(s): Italian
CONSUMER: WOMEN'S INTEREST CONSUMER MAGAZINES: Teenage

L' UFFICIO TECNICO 13529I42A-28
Editorial: Via del Carpino, 8, 47822 SANTARCANGELO DI ROMAGNA **Tel:** 0541 628111 **Fax:** 0541 622778
Email: redazionetecnica@maggioli.it **Web site:** http://www.periodicimaggioli.it
Freq: Monthly; **Circ:** 12,000
Editor-in-Chief: Manlio Maggioli
Profile: Technical journal focusing on building, urban planning, transport and environmental issues.
Language(s): Italian
Readership: Aimed at people working in public administration, construction professionals, architects, civil engineers and surveyors.
BUSINESS: CONSTRUCTION

L' UNITA' 13980I65A-190
Editorial: Via Ostiense 131/L, 00153 ROMA RM
Tel: 06 585571 **Fax:** 06 58557219
Email: segreteria@unita.it **Web site:** http://www.unita.it
Freq: Daily
Editor: Daniela Amenta; **Editor-in-Chief:** Claudio Sardo
Profile: Broadsheet newspaper covering trade union news throughout Italy. Official organ of the Partito Democratico di Sinistra, providing a forum for readers to express their opinions on a variety of union issues.
Language(s): Italian
Readership: Read by union members and supporters.
ADVERTISING RATES:
Full Page Colour .... EUR 43604.00
Mechanical Data: Type Area: 340 x 492mm
NATIONAL DAILY & SUNDAY NEWSPAPERS: National Daily Newspapers

L' UOMO VOGUE 14486I86C-182
Editorial: Piazza Cadorna 5/7, 20123 MILANO
Tel: 02 85611 **Fax:** 02 8055716
Email: aairaghi@condenast.it **Web site:** http://www.condenast.it
Freq: Monthly; **Circ:** 50,000
Editor-in-Chief: Franca Sozzani
Profile: Men's fashion magazine.
Language(s): Italian
Readership: Aimed at the modern man.
CONSUMER: ADULT & GAY MAGAZINES: Men's Lifestyle Magazines

URBAN 1784858I79B-155
Editorial: Via Rizzoli 8, 20132 MILANO MI
Tel: 02 50951 **Fax:** 0250952120
Email: redazione.urban@rcs.it **Web site:** http://www.urbanmagazine.it
Freq: Monthly; **Circ:** 300,000
Editor-in-Chief: Alberto Coretti
Language(s): Italian
CONSUMER: HOBBIES & DIY: Models & Modelling

US 13557I34-150
Editorial: Via C. Pisacane 1, 20016 PERO MI
Tel: 02 30221 **Fax:** 0230226836
Email: anna.alberti@ilsole24ore.com **Web site:** http://www.ufficiostile-online.it
Freq: Quarterly; **Circ:** 9,000
Editor-in-Chief: Antonio Greco
Profile: International office design magazine, including furnishing, ergonomics, architecture, office automation and advanced technology.
Language(s): Italian
BUSINESS: OFFICE EQUIPMENT

VADO E TORNO 13429I21E-70
Editorial: Via Cassano d'Adda, 20, 20139 MILANO
Tel: 02 55230950 **Fax:** 02 55230592
Email: vadoetorno@vadoetornoedizioni.it **Web site:** http://www.vadoetorno.com
Freq: Monthly; **Circ:** 55,010
Editor-in-Chief: Paolo Scarpat
Profile: Magazine containing technical and market news about tractors, agricultural machinery, components and accessories.
Language(s): English; French; German; Italian; Spanish
Readership: Read by farmers, manufacturers, suppliers and retailers.
BUSINESS: AGRICULTURE & FARMING: Agriculture - Machinery & Plant

VALORI 14437I80-350
Editorial: Via Copernico, 1, 20125 MILANO
Tel: 02 67199099 **Fax:** 02 67491691
Email: redazione@valori.it **Web site:** http://www.valori.it
Freq: Monthly; **Circ:** 10,000
Editor-in-Chief: Andrea Di Stefano
Profile: Periodical covering art, culture and tourism in Naples. Includes details about archaeology, cookery, entertainment, museums and art exhibitions.
Language(s): Italian
Readership: Aimed at visitors to the town.
CONSUMER: RURAL & REGIONAL INTEREST

VANITY FAIR 1785048I74A-394
Editorial: Piazza Cadorna 5, 20123 MILANO
Tel: 02 8561 1 **Fax:** 02 85613100
Email: segreteria@vanityfair.it **Web site:** http://www.vanityfair.it
Freq: Weekly; **Circ:** 270,000
Editor: Francesco Briglia; **Editor-in-Chief:** Luca Dini
Language(s): Italian
ADVERTISING RATES:
Full Page Colour .... EUR 66000.00
CONSUMER: WOMEN'S INTEREST CONSUMER MAGAZINES: Women's Interest

VEDERE ITALIA 13877I56E-40
Editorial: Via Negroli, 51, 20133 MILANO MI
Tel: 02 730091 **Fax:** 02 717346
Email: redazione@vedere.it **Web site:** http://www.vedere.it
Freq: 3 issues yearly; **Circ:** 8,500
Editor-in-Chief: Isabella Morpurgo
Profile: International journal focusing on sight and sun eyewear, sports glasses, protective goggles, lenses, cases, accessories and optical laboratory equipment.
Language(s): English; French; Italian; Spanish
Readership: Aimed at retailers, technicians, manufacturers and distributors.
BUSINESS: HEALTH & MEDICAL: Optics

VELA E MOTORE 14538I91A-200
Editorial: Via Don Luigi Sturzo 7, 20016 PERO MI
Tel: 0238085241 **Fax:** 0238010393
Email: velaemotore@edisport.it **Web site:** http://www.velaemotore.it
Freq: Monthly; **Circ:** 43,000
Editor: Marta Gasparini; **Editor-in-Chief:** Piero Bacchetti
Profile: Magazine containing information on sailing and watersports, includes competitions, boat tests and technical articles.
Language(s): Italian
CONSUMER: RECREATION & LEISURE: Boating & Yachting

IL VENERDI' DI REPUBBLICA (LA REPUBBLICA) 1645433I82-251
Editorial: Via Cristoforo Colombo, 90, 00147 ROMA
Tel: 06 49823128 **Fax:** 06 49823191
Email: segreteria_venerdi@repubblica.it **Web site:** http://www.repubblica.it
Freq: Weekly; **Circ:** 754,000
Editor: Roberta Visco
Profile: Magazine focusing on news, current affairs, culture, leisure and entertainment.
Language(s): Italian
ADVERTISING RATES:
Full Page Colour .... EUR 55000.00
CONSUMER: CURRENT AFFAIRS & POLITICS

VERO 1784672I82-260
Editorial: Viale Tunisia, 21, 20124 MILANO MI
Tel: 0289656612 **Fax:** 0289656614
Email: redazione@settimanalevero.it **Web site:** http://www.settimanalevero.it
Freq: Weekly; **Circ:** 500,000
Editor-in-Chief: Riccardo Signoretti
Language(s): Italian
CONSUMER: CURRENT AFFAIRS & POLITICS

VERO SALUTE (VERO) 1845370I74G-116
Editorial: Viale Tunisia 21, 20124 MILANO
Tel: 0289656612 **Fax:** 0289656614
Email: redazione@settimanalevero.it
Freq: Monthly; **Circ:** 150,000
Editor-in-Chief: Laura Bozzi
Language(s): Italian
CONSUMER: WOMEN'S INTEREST CONSUMER MAGAZINES: Slimming & Health

VETERINARIA - RIVISTA UFFICIALE DELLA SCIVAC 13955I64H-150
Editorial: Palazzo Trecchi, 26100 CREMONA
Tel: 0372 403507 **Fax:** 0372 457091
Email: info@evsrl.it **Web site:** http://www.evsrl.it
Freq: 6 issues yearly; **Circ:** 10,600
Editor-in-Chief: Antonio Manfredi
Profile: Publication covering the veterinary profession.
Language(s): Italian
Readership: Read by veterinary surgeons.
BUSINESS: OTHER CLASSIFICATIONS: Veterinary

VIA! 14389I77E-250
Editorial: Corso Venezia 43, 20121 MILANO
Tel: 02 7745239 **Fax:** 02 7745201
Email: stampa@acimi.it **Web site:** http://www.acimi.it
Freq: 6 issues yearly; **Circ:** 70,000
Editor-in-Chief: Gianfranco Chierchini
Profile: Magazine of the Automobile Club of Milan.
Language(s): Italian
Readership: Read by car enthusiasts in the Milan region.
CONSUMER: MOTORING & CYCLING: Club Cars

VIE & TRASPORTI 13738I49A-100
Editorial: Via Conca del Naviglio, 37, 20123 MILANO
Tel: 02 89421350 **Fax:** 02 89421484
Email: vietrasporti@fiaccola.it **Web site:** http://www.fiaccola.com
Freq: Monthly; **Circ:** 50,000
Editor-in-Chief: Lucia Edvige Saronni
Profile: Magazine reviewing the technical and financial aspects of transport.
Language(s): Italian
BUSINESS: TRANSPORT

VIGNEVINI 13434I21H-100
Editorial: Via Goito, 13, 40126 BOLOGNA
Tel: 051 6575847 **Fax:** 0516575800
Email: redazione.edagricole@ilsole24ore.com **Web site:** http://www.edagricole.it
Freq: Monthly; **Circ:** 8,600
Editor-in-Chief: Elia Zamboni
Profile: Journal covering all aspects of viticulture and oenology.
Language(s): Italian
Readership: Read by professionals involved in the fields of viticulture and oenology.
BUSINESS: AGRICULTURE & FARMING: Vine Growing

VILLE & CASALI 14167I74C-300
Editorial: Via Anton Giulio Bragaglia 33, 00123 ROMA RM **Tel:** 06 96521600 **Fax:** 06 96521622
Email: villeecasali.segreteria@eli.it **Web site:** http://www.villeecasali.com
Freq: Monthly; **Circ:** 96,000
Editor-in-Chief: Enrico Morelli
Profile: Magazine about high quality furnishing and decorative products for the home. Includes articles giving advice on design, building, furnishing and restoration.
Language(s): English; Italian
CONSUMER: WOMEN'S INTEREST CONSUMER MAGAZINES: Home & Family

VILLEGIARDINI 13127I4A-114
Editorial: Via Trentacoste 7, 20134 MILANO
Tel: 02 21563373 **Fax:** 02 21563211
Email: ville_giardini@mondadori.it **Web site:** http://www.mondadori.it
Freq: Monthly; **Circ:** 120,000
Editor-in-Chief: Franco Perfetti
Profile: Magazine specialising in single-family houses, with and without gardens, including related lifestyle articles.
Language(s): Italian
Readership: Read by architects and builders.
BUSINESS: ARCHITECTURE & BUILDING: Architecture

VIP 14111I74A-323
Editorial: Via Palermo, 13, 00184 ROMA
Tel: 06 48906778
Web site: http://www.twistersrl.com
Freq: Weekly
Editor-in-Chief: Luciano Regolo
Profile: Gossip magazine, contains life stories and interviews.
Language(s): Italian
Readership: Read mainly by women.
CONSUMER: WOMEN'S INTEREST CONSUMER MAGAZINES: Women's Interest

VISTO 14090I73-410
Editorial: Via A. Rizzoli 8, 20132 MILANO
Tel: 02 25843962 **Fax:** 02 25843907
Email: visto@rcs.it **Web site:** http://www.vistoblog.it
Freq: Weekly
Editor-in-Chief: Franco Bonera
Profile: Magazine containing news and articles on different issues including tourism, health, cars, legal advice, culture and costumes.
Language(s): Italian
CONSUMER: NATIONAL & INTERNATIONAL PERIODICALS

VITA E SALUTE 14219I74G-90
Editorial: Via Chiantigiana 30 - Falciani, 50023 IMPRUNETA FI **Tel:** 055 2326291 **Fax:** 055 2326241
Email: info@edizioniadv.it **Web site:** http://www.vitaesalute.net
Freq: Monthly; **Circ:** 15,000
Editor-in-Chief: Ennio Battista
Profile: Review of health education and preventive medicine.
Language(s): Italian
CONSUMER: WOMEN'S INTEREST CONSUMER MAGAZINES: Slimming & Health

VITA IN CAMPAGNA 13412I21A-355
Editorial: Via Bencivenga/Biondani, 16, 37133 VERONA **Tel:** 045 8057511 **Fax:** 045 8009240
Email: vitaincampagna@vitaincampagna.it **Web site:** http://www.vitaincampagna.it
Freq: Monthly; **Circ:** 85,000
Editor-in-Chief: Giorgio Vincenzi
Profile: Magazine about small-scale farming, gardening, fruit growing, breeding and nature.
Language(s): Italian
Readership: Read by owners of small farms in Italy.
BUSINESS: AGRICULTURE & FARMING

LA VITA SCOLASTICA 13930I62C-28
Editorial: Via Bolognese, 165, 50139 FIRENZE FI
Tel: 055 5062367 **Fax:** 055 5062351
Email: vitascol@giunti.it **Web site:** http://www.lavitascolastica.it
Freq: 24 issues yearly; **Circ:** 100,000
Editor-in-Chief: Bruno Piazzesi
Profile: Publication about the teaching of children in primary schools.
Language(s): Italian
Readership: Aimed at teachers and directors of schools.
BUSINESS: CHURCH & SCHOOL EQUIPMENT & EDUCATION: Junior Education

VIVIMILANO (CORRIERE DELLA SERA) 13984I65H-100
Editorial: Via Solferino 28, 20121 MILANO
Tel: 02 62827765 **Fax:** 02 29009679
Web site: http://www.vivimilano.it
Freq: Weekly
Editor: Silvia Vedani
Profile: Tabloid-size newspaper containing information about social and cultural matters concerning the city of Milan.
Language(s): Italian
Readership: Read by local residents.
NATIONAL DAILY & SUNDAY NEWSPAPERS: National Colour Supplements

VOCE DEL TABACCAIO 13763I51-50
Editorial: Via Leopoldo Serra, 32, 00153 ROMA
Tel: 06 585501 **Fax:** 06 5809826
Email: vocetabaccaio@tabaccai.it **Web site:** http://www.tabaccai.it
Freq: Weekly; **Circ:** 48,000
Editor-in-Chief: Mara Micalucci
Profile: Official journal of the Italian Federation of Tobacconists.
Language(s): Italian
Readership: Aimed at tobacconists.
BUSINESS: TOBACCO

VOGUE BAMBINI 14131I74B-320
Editorial: Piazza Cadorna 5/7, 20121 MILANO
Tel: 02 85611 **Fax:** 02 85612988
Web site: http://www.voguebambini.it
Freq: 6 issues yearly; **Circ:** 50,000
Editor: Simona Valentini; **Editor-in-Chief:** Giuliana Parabiago
Profile: Magazine about fashion for babies and children.
Language(s): Italian
CONSUMER: WOMEN'S INTEREST CONSUMER MAGAZINES: Women's Interest - Fashion

VOGUE GIOIELLO 14132I74B-325
Editorial: Piazza Cadorna 5/7, 20121 MILANO
Tel: 02 85612840 **Fax:** 02 85612996
Web site: http://www.voguegioiello.net
Freq: 6 issues yearly; **Circ:** 45,000
Editor: Ilaria Danieli; **Editor-in-Chief:** Franca Sozzani
Profile: Magazine about jewellery.
Language(s): Italian
CONSUMER: WOMEN'S INTEREST CONSUMER MAGAZINES: Women's Interest - Fashion

VOGUE ITALIA 14133I74B-330
Editorial: Piazza Cadorna 5/7, 20123 MILANO MI
Tel: 028561 1 **Fax:** 028055716
Web site: http://www.vogue.it
Freq: Monthly; **Circ:** 115,000
Editor: Carlo Ducci; **Editor-in-Chief:** Franca Sozzani
Profile: Italian edition of Vogue, includes articles on fashion, beauty, health and shopping.
Language(s): Italian
Readership: Aimed at modern women.
CONSUMER: WOMEN'S INTEREST CONSUMER MAGAZINES: Women's Interest - Fashion

VOGUE PELLE 14134I74B-340
Editorial: Piazza Castello 21, 20154 MILANO
Tel: 02 85612840 **Fax:** 0285612996
Email: cgirelli@condenast.it **Web site:** http://www.condenast.it
Freq: Quarterly; **Circ:** 30,000
Editor-in-Chief: Franca Sozzani
Profile: Magazine about fashion in leather.
Language(s): Italian
Readership: Aimed at people interested in leather goods and fashion.
CONSUMER: WOMEN'S INTEREST CONSUMER MAGAZINES: Women's Interest - Fashion

VOGUE SPOSA 14228I74L-70
Editorial: Piazza Cadorna 5/7, 20121 MILANO
Tel: 02 85611 **Fax:** 02 85612988
Web site: http://www.iosposa.it
Freq: Quarterly; **Circ:** 65,000
Editor-in-Chief: Giuliana Parabiago

Profile: Magazine for women who are about to get married.
Language(s): Italian
CONSUMER: WOMEN'S INTEREST CONSUMER MAGAZINES: Brides

VOICECOM NEWS 1613896I5B-82
Editorial: Via Rovetta, 18, 20127 MILANO
Tel: 02 2831161 Fax: 02 28311666
Email: voicecomnews@iter.it Web site: http://www.iter.it/vcnews.html
Freq: Quarterly; Circ: 12,000
Editor-in-Chief: Domenico Piazza
Profile: Magazine containing analysis of solutions, applications and profitability of modern technologies in digital offices.
Language(s): Italian
BUSINESS: COMPUTERS & AUTOMATION: Data Processing

VOLARE 13222I6A-100
Editorial: Via Mazzocchi 1/3, 20089 ROZZANO MI
Tel: 02 82472212 Fax: 02 82472665
Email: volare@volare.org Web site: http://www.volare.org
Freq: Monthly; Circ: 45,000
Editor-in-Chief: Giuseppe Braga
Profile: Magazine about flying, including articles on the history of aviation, the air force, private jets, commercial flying, test flights, technology and topical news.
Language(s): Italian
Readership: Read by professionals within the field.
BUSINESS: AVIATION & AERONAUTICS

IL VORTICE 13345I17-95
Editorial: Via Ferri 6, 20092 CINISELLO BALSAMO MI Tel: 02 61294990 Fax: 02 66594914
Email: info@ediweb.it Web site: http://www.ediweb.it
Freq: 6 issues yearly; Circ: 50,000
Editor-in-Chief: Alessandro Poggi
Profile: Magazine covering the electrical industry in Italy.
Language(s): Italian
BUSINESS: ELECTRICAL

WEEKEND & VIAGGI 1784976I50-231
Editorial: c/o Set - Via F. Filzi 27, 20124 MILANO
Tel: 0283121248 Fax: 0283383633
Email: redazioneweekend@edmaster.it Web site: http://www.edmaster.it
Freq: Monthly; Circ: 80,000
Editor-in-Chief: Massimo Sesti
Language(s): Italian
ADVERTISING RATES:
Full Page Colour .... EUR 14000.00
BUSINESS: TRAVEL & TOURISM

WIN MAGAZINE 1845113I5B-95
Editorial: Contrada Lecco, 64 Z.I., 87030 RENDE COSENZA Tel: 0984 8319200 Fax: 0984 8319225
Email: segreteria.ict@edmaster.it Web site: http://www.edmaster.it
Freq: Monthly; Circ: 290,000
Editor-in-Chief: Massimo Sesti
Language(s): Italian
ADVERTISING RATES:
Full Page Colour .... EUR 4000.00
BUSINESS: COMPUTERS & AUTOMATION: Data Processing

WINDOWS & .NET MAGAZINE - ED. ITALIANA 624797I5B-79
Editorial: Via F. Confalonieri 36, 20124 MILANO
Tel: 0256609380 Fax: 0257419081
Email: info@matedizioni.it Web site: http://www.bitmat.it
Freq: Monthly; Circ: 8,000
Editor-in-Chief: Roberto Negrini
Profile: Magazine about the Microsoft Windows 2000 Server computer systems.
Language(s): Italian
Readership: Aimed at MIS managers.
BUSINESS: COMPUTERS & AUTOMATION: Data Processing

WINDSURF ITALIA 14296I75M-300
Editorial: Via Saliceto, 22E, 40013 CASTEL MAGGIORE BO Tel: 02 39820203 051 6328811
Fax: 0239820223
Email: info@windsurf-italia.it Web site: http://www.windsurf-italia.it
Freq: Monthly; Circ: 28,000
Editor-in-Chief: Marzio Bardi
Profile: Magazine focusing on surfing and windsurfing.
Language(s): Italian
Readership: Aimed at surfing enthusiasts.
CONSUMER: SPORT: Water Sports

WIRED 1929591I86C-192
Editorial: Piazza Castello, 27, 20121 MILANO MI
Tel: 0285611 Fax: 0285612377
Web site: http://www.wired.it
Freq: Monthly; Circ: 250,000
Editor-in-Chief: Carlo Antonelli
Language(s): Italian
CONSUMER: ADULT & GAY MAGAZINES: Men's Lifestyle Magazines

XL MAGAZINE (LA REPUBBLICA) 1785263I76D-567
Editorial: Via Cristoforo Colombo, 90, 00147 ROMA
Tel: 0649822205 Fax: 06 49823143
Email: feedback@xelle.it Web site: http://www.xelle.it
Freq: Monthly; Circ: 300,000
Language(s): Italian
ADVERTISING RATES:
Full Page Colour .... EUR 50000.00
CONSUMER: MUSIC & PERFORMING ARTS: Music

Y&S YACHT&SAIL (CORRIERE DELLA SERA) 1809726I91A-230
Editorial: Via Rizzoli 8, 20132 MILANO
Tel: 02 50952713 Fax: 0250952720
Email: yachting@rizzolipublishing.it Web site: http://www.yachtandsail.it
Freq: Monthly; Circ: 80,000
Editor: Maurizio Bertera; Editor-in-Chief: Andrea Brambilla
Language(s): Italian
CONSUMER: RECREATION & LEISURE: Boating & Yachting

YACHT CAPITAL 14539I91A-215
Editorial: Viale Sarca, 235, 20126 MILANO MI
Tel: 02 36609611 Fax: 02 30609631
Email: yachtcapital@hearst.it Web site: http://www.yachtonline.it
Freq: Monthly; Circ: 49,700
Editor-in-Chief: Matteo Zaccagnino
Profile: Magazine focusing on buying and sailing big yachts.
Language(s): English; Italian
Readership: Aimed at boat owners.
CONSUMER: RECREATION & LEISURE: Boating & Yachting

YACHT DIGEST 14540I91A-220
Editorial: Viale Sarca, 235, 20126 MILANO MI
Tel: 02 36609611 Fax: 0236609631
Email: segreteriayc@hearst.it Web site: http://www.yachtonline.it
Freq: Quarterly; Circ: 38,800
Editor: Desiree Sormani; Editor-in-Chief: Matteo Zaccagnino
Profile: Publication about vintage and classic boats, the history of boats and the sailing tradition.
Language(s): Italian
CONSUMER: RECREATION & LEISURE: Boating & Yachting

ZERO 1785177I74F-211
Editorial: Via Orti, 14, 20122 MILANO MI
Tel: 02 5403141 Fax: 0254031450
Email: redazione@edizionizero.com Web site: http://www.edizionizero.com
Freq: 24 issues yearly; Circ: 80,000
Editor-in-Chief: Andrea Amichetti
Language(s): Italian
CONSUMER: WOMEN'S INTEREST CONSUMER MAGAZINES: Teenage

ZERO SOTTO ZERO 13097I3C-200
Editorial: Via Eritrea, 21, 20157 MILANO
Tel: 02 390901 Fax: 02 39090331
Email: zerosottozero@tecnichenuove.com Web site: http://www.tecnichenuove.com
Freq: Monthly; Circ: 4,000
Editor-in-Chief: Giuseppe Nardella
Profile: Publication about the installation and maintenance of refrigerators.
Language(s): Italian
BUSINESS: HEATING & VENTILATION: Refrigeration & Ventilation

ZOOM - LA RIVISTA DELL'IMMAGINE 13587I38-110
Editorial: Viale Piceno 14, 20019 MILANO
Tel: 02 70002222 Fax: 02 713030
Email: info@zoom-net.com Web site: http://www.zoom-net.com
Freq: 3 issues yearly; Circ: 25,000
Editor-in-Chief: Paolo Namias
Profile: International magazine focusing on professional photography and fine art.
Language(s): English; Italian
Readership: Read by amateur and professional photographers.
BUSINESS: PHOTOGRAPHIC TRADE

Latvia

Time Difference: GMT + 2 hrs (EET - Eastern European Time)
National Telephone Code: +371
Continent: Europe
Capital: Riga
Principal Language: Latvian, Lithuanian, Russian
Population: 2270700
Monetary Unit: Lats (LVL)

EMBASSY HIGH COMMISSION: Embassy of the Republic of Latvia: 45 Nottingham Place, London W1U 5LY
Tel: 020 7312 0041
Fax: 020 7312 0042
Email: embassy.uk@mfa.gov.lv/
Website: http://www.mfa.gov.lv/en/london

7 SEKRETOV 1644457LV65J-201
Editorial: Mukusalas Street 41, RIGA LV-1004
Tel: 6 70 68 130 Fax: 6 70 68 131
Email: sekreti@fenster.lv Web site: http://www.fenster.lv
Date Established: 1997; Freq: Weekly - Published on Thursdays; Cover Price: LVL 0.45
Annual Sub.: LVL 25.20; Circ: 34,000
Profile: A weekly for family entertainment containing news in fashion and celebrities' lives.
Language(s): Russian
ADVERTISING RATES:
Full Page Mono .... LVL 1075.59
Full Page Colour .... LVL 1613.39
NATIONAL DAILY & SUNDAY NEWSPAPERS: National Weekly Newspapers

BIZNESS & BALTIJA 762403LV65A-20
Editorial: Kr. Valdemara 149, RIGA LV-1013
Tel: 6 70 33 047 Fax: 6 70 33 040
Email: bb@bb.lv Web site: http://www.bb.lv
Date Established: 1991; Freq: 300 issues yearly - Published Monday - Friday; Cover Price: LVL 0.55; Circ: 12,000
Usual Pagination: 16
Executive Editor: Vera Makromenko
Profile: Full colour broadsheet-sized newspaper focusing on business and finance in the Baltics.
Language(s): Russian
ADVERTISING RATES:
SCC .... LVL 4.99
Mechanical Data: Type Area: A2
Copy instructions: *Copy Date:* 3 days prior to publication date
Supplement(s): Bizness Plius - 4xY, Nedvizimostj & vystavka - 2xY
NATIONAL DAILY & SUNDAY NEWSPAPERS: National Daily Newspapers

BIZNESS PLIUS 1832381LV1A-11
Editorial: Kr. Valdemāra 149, RĪGA LV-1013
Tel: 6 70 33 047 Fax: 6 70 33 040
Email: bb@bb.lv Web site: http://www.bb.lv
Freq: Quarterly; Free to qualifying individuals ; Circ: 20,000
Usual Pagination: 80
Executive Editor: Vera Makromenko; Editor-in-Chief: Jurijs Aleksejevs
Profile: Distributed to subscribers of 'Bizness & Baltija' and separately with 'Double coffee'.
Language(s): Russian
ADVERTISING RATES:
Full Page Colour .... LVL 950.00
Mechanical Data: Type Area: 270 x 380 mm
Supplement to: Bizness & Baltija
BUSINESS: FINANCE & ECONOMICS

CEMODANS 1829959LV50-1
Editorial: Stabu iela 34, RĪGA LV - 1880
Tel: 6 70 06 101 Fax: 6 70 06 111
Email: cemodans@santa.lv Web site: http://www.santa.lv
Freq: 24 issues yearly; Annual Sub.: LVL 11.99; Circ: 19,800
Profile: Monthly magazine about tourism and travelling.
Language(s): Latvian
ADVERTISING RATES:
Full Page Colour .... LVL 840.00
BUSINESS: TRAVEL & TOURISM

CHAS 1500334LV65A-30
Editorial: Peldu 15, RIGA LV-1050 Tel: 70 88 712
Fax: 72 11 067
Email: chas@chas-daily.com Web site: http://www.chas-daily.com
Date Established: 1997; Freq: Daily - Published Monday to Saturday; Annual Sub.: LVL 54.00; Circ: 13,100
Usual Pagination: 12
Editor: Ksenija Zagorovska
Profile: Tabloid-sized newspaper focusing on national and international news, business, politics and sport.
Language(s): Russian
ADVERTISING RATES:
SCC .... LVL 1.77
Mechanical Data: Type Area: A2
NATIONAL DAILY & SUNDAY NEWSPAPERS: National Daily Newspapers

DELOVYE VESTI 1827756LV65H-1
Editorial: (see main outlet for more details)
Tel: 6 70 68 139 Fax: 6 70 68 131
Email: knazeva@fenster.lv
Freq: Daily; Circ: 38,000
Profile: Specialised business supplement to Vesti segodnja and provided information on current situation of Latvian economics and business.
Language(s): Russian
ADVERTISING RATES:
Full Page Mono .... LVL 959.40
Full Page Colour .... LVL 1800.12
Supplement to: Vesti Segodnja
NATIONAL DAILY & SUNDAY NEWSPAPERS: National Colour Supplements

DIENA 1500352LV65A-38
Editorial: Mūkusalas iela 15, RĪGA LV-1004
Tel: 70 63 100 Fax: 70 63 190
Email: diena@diena.lv Web site: http://www.diena.lv
Date Established: 1990; Freq: Daily - Published Monday to Saturday; Cover Price: LVL 0.45; Circ: 55,000
Usual Pagination: 36
Editor-in-Chief: Sarmīte Elerte
Profile: Broadsheet-sized newspaper focusing on national and international news, politics, business, culture and sport.
Language(s): Latvian
ADVERTISING RATES:
Full Page Mono .... LVL 1944.00
Full Page Colour .... LVL 2592.00
Agency Commission: 15%
Mechanical Data: Trim Size: 355 x 253 mm
NATIONAL DAILY & SUNDAY NEWSPAPERS: National Daily Newspapers

DIENAS BIZNESS 762406LV65A-40
Editorial: Terbatas 30, RIGA LV-1011 Tel: 70 84 400
Fax: 70 84 445
Email: editor@db.lv Web site: http://www.db.lv
Date Established: 1992; Freq: 250 issues yearly - Published Monday to Friday; Cover Price: LVL 0.59; Circ: 12,000
Editor-in-Chief: Liga Dzirnekle
Profile: Tabloid-sized newspaper focusing on business, finance and economics. In addition to daily business news and commentary, it publishes regular supplements on construction and real estate, new technologies, education, employment market and cars.
Language(s): Latvian
ADVERTISING RATES:
Full Page Colour .... LVL 2650.00
Agency Commission: 15%
Mechanical Data: Trim Size: 250 x 388 mm, Col Length: 361 mm, Col Widths (Display): 46 mm, No. of Columns (Display): 5, Page Width: 250 mm, Type Area: 255 x 363 mm
Average ad content per issue: 22.7%
NATIONAL DAILY & SUNDAY NEWSPAPERS: National Daily Newspapers

IEVA 762598LV74A-4
Editorial: Stabu iela 34, RĪGA LV-1880
Tel: 6 70 06 102 Fax: 6 70 06 111
Email: ieva@santa.lv
Date Established: 1997; Freq: Weekly - Published on Wednesday; Cover Price: LVL 0.45
Annual Sub.: LVL 19.99; Circ: 68,600
Profile: Magazine focusing on lifestyle, fashion, beauty and health.
Language(s): Latvian
Readership: Aimed at women.
ADVERTISING RATES:
Full Page Colour .... LVL 1500.00
Mechanical Data: Type Area: 215 x 282 mm
CONSUMER: WOMEN'S INTEREST CONSUMER MAGAZINES: Women's Interest

LATVIJAS AVIZE 1644930LV65A-262
Formerly: Lauku Avize
Editorial: AS Lauku Avize, Dzirnavu iela 21, RĪGA LV 1010 Tel: 7 09 66 00 Fax: 7 09 66 45
Email: redakcija@la.lv Web site: http://www2.la.lv
ISSN: 1407-3331
Date Established: 1988; Freq: Daily - Published on Monday - Saturday; Cover Price: LVL 0.39
Annual Sub.: LVL 68.46; Circ: 48,000
News Editor: Guntis Ščerbinskis; Advertising Director: Aigars Stankēvičs

Latvia

Profile: National-conservative newspaper focusing on national and international news, business and economics, politics, culture and sport.
Language(s): Latvian
ADVERTISING RATES:
Full Page Mono .... LVL 480.19
Full Page Colour .... LVL 525.21
Supplement(s): Majas Viesis - 52xY
NATIONAL DAILY & SUNDAY NEWSPAPERS: National Daily Newspapers

LATVIJAS SANTIMS 1828215LV65H-3
Editorial: (see the main outlet for more details)
Tel: 70 68 100 **Fax:** 70 68 101
Freq: Quarterly; **Circ:** 170,000
Profile: Two separate language editions of advertising supplement for TV programma in Russian and Latvian languages.
Language(s): Latvian; Russian
ADVERTISING RATES:
Full Page Mono .... LVL 2032.15
Full Page Colour .... LVL 2246.55
Supplement to: TV programma
NATIONAL DAILY & SUNDAY NEWSPAPERS: National Colour Supplements

LATVIJAS VESTNESIS 762676LV65A-90
Editorial: Bruninieku 36 - 2, RIGA LV-1011
Tel: 7 29 88 33 **Fax:** 7 29 94 10
Email: oskars.gerts@lv.lv **Web site:** http://www.vestnesis.lv
ISSN: 1407-9712
Date Established: 1993; **Freq:** Daily - Published Tuesday to Friday; **Cover Price:** LVL 0.59
Annual Sub.: LVL 60.00; **Circ:** 3,500
Usual Pagination: 48
Editor-in-Chief: Oskars Gerts
Profile: Broadsheet-sized newspaper produced by the Government, containing legislative information, national and international news, politics and economics.
Language(s): Latvian
ADVERTISING RATES:
Full Page Colour .... LVL 770.00
NATIONAL DAILY & SUNDAY NEWSPAPERS: National Daily Newspapers

MAJAS DAKTERIS 1828216LV56A-1
Editorial: Mūkusalas ielā 41, RĪGĀ LV 1004
Tel: 96 06 496 **Fax:** 70 68 131
Freq: 24 issues yearly; **Circ:** 15,000
Advertising Manager: Marina Arhipenko
Profile: Provides advice on healthy way of life, news of medicine and practical usage of biotherapy.
Language(s): Latvian
ADVERTISING RATES:
Full Page Mono .... LVL 648.00
Full Page Colour .... LVL 774.00
BUSINESS: HEALTH & MEDICAL

NEATKARIGA RITA AVIZE 762549LV65A-150
Editorial: Cēsu iela 31 - 2, RIGA **Tel:** 78 86 801
Fax: 78 86 838
Email: redakcija@nra.lv **Web site:** http://www.nra.lv
Date Established: 1991; **Freq:** Mornings - Published Monday to Saturday; **Cover Price:** LVL 0.40; **Circ:** 35,000
Usual Pagination: 40
Editor: Viktors Avotiņš; **Advertising Manager:** Kristīne Sarkane
Profile: Broadsheet-sized newspaper focusing on national and international news, politics, business and sport.
Language(s): Latvian
Readership: Aimed at male and female readers of 25-50 years of age, living in Riga or other big cities in Latvia.
Mechanical Data: Type Area: A3
Supplement(s): Mes - 48xY
NATIONAL DAILY & SUNDAY NEWSPAPERS: National Daily Newspapers

NEDVIZIMOSTJ & DOM 1830974LV1E-3
Editorial: Kr.Valdemāra 149, RĪGA LV-1013
Tel: 70 33 038 **Fax:** 70 33 040
Email: andrey.kovalev@bb.lv
Freq: 6 issues yearly; **Cover Price:** LVL 2.50; **Circ:** 20,000
Usual Pagination: 116
Executive Editor: Andrejs Kovaļevs
Profile: Magazine featuring property market news, interesting projects and modern design solutions.
Language(s): Russian
ADVERTISING RATES:
Full Page Colour .... LVL 950.00
Mechanical Data: Type Area: 211 x 275 mm
BUSINESS: FINANCE & ECONOMICS: Property

NEDVIZIMOSTJ & VYSTAVKA 1832382LV1E-5
Editorial: For all contact details see main record, Bizness & Baltija **Tel:** 6 70 33 047 **Fax:** 6 70 33 040
Email: bb@bb.lv **Web site:** http://www.bb.lv
Freq: Half-yearly; **Cover Price:** Free; **Circ:** 20,000
Usual Pagination: 200
Editor-in-Chief: Andrejs Kovaļevs
Profile: Free for subscribers of 'Bizness & Baltija' and is also distributed by direct mailing and at exhibitions.
Language(s): Russian
ADVERTISING RATES:
Full Page Colour .... LVL 600.00
Mechanical Data: Type Area: 211 x 275 + 5 mm
Supplement to: Bizness & Baltija
BUSINESS: FINANCE & ECONOMICS: Property

PRIVATA DZIVE 1644591LV74A-253
Editorial: Stabu iela 34, RĪGA LV-1880
Tel: 6 70 06 104 **Fax:** 6 70 06 111
Email: pdz@santa.lv
Date Established: 1999; **Freq:** Weekly; **Annual Sub.:** LVL 21.99; **Circ:** 80,300
Profile: Entertainment periodical about celebrities.
Language(s): Latvian
ADVERTISING RATES:
Full Page Colour .... LVL 1560.00
Mechanical Data: Type Area: 205 x 282 mm
CONSUMER: WOMEN'S INTEREST CONSUMER MAGAZINES: Women's Interest

REKLAMA.LV 1828281LV2A-3
Editorial: Peldu iela 15, RIGA LV-1050 **Tel:** 70 88 790
Email: redakcija@reklama.lv
Date Established: 1991; **Freq:** 96 issues yearly - Published on Mondays and Thursdays; **Annual Sub.:** LVL 89.00; **Circ:** 14,000
Profile: Largest personal ads newspaper in Baltic countries. The member of the International Association of Advertising Newspapers ICMA.
Language(s): English; Latvian; Russian
ADVERTISING RATES:
Full Page Colour .... LVL 250.00
BUSINESS: COMMUNICATIONS, ADVERTISING & MARKETING

SUBBOTA 762681LV65J-200
Editorial: Peldu 15, RIGA LV-1050 **Tel:** 70 88 771
Fax: 72 10 203
Email: sub@subbota.com **Web site:** http://www.subbota.com
Date Established: 1994; **Freq:** Weekly - Published on Thursday; **Cover Price:** LVL 0.70
Annual Sub.: LVL 27.00; **Circ:** 46,150
Usual Pagination: 80
Editor: Olga Avdeviča; **Advertising Director:** Oleg Grebnevs
Profile: Newspaper focusing on national and international news, high society, politics, entertainment and culture. The most read weekly edition in Latvia and the largest publication in Russian language in 25 countries of the EU.
Language(s): Russian
ADVERTISING RATES:
SCC .... LVL 2.01
Mechanical Data: Type Area: A3
NATIONAL DAILY & SUNDAY NEWSPAPERS: National Weekly Newspapers

TELEPROGRAMMA S DJADEJ MISHEJ 1828238LV76C-4
Editorial: Peldu 15, RIGA LV-1050 **Tel:** 70 88 765
Email: tvweek@subbota.com **Web site:** http://www.petits.lv
Date Established: 1994; **Freq:** Weekly; **Annual Sub.:** LVL 12.00; **Circ:** 120,000
Usual Pagination: 28
Profile: Contains TV programmes of 57 channels. All materials on movies and television, contests, competitions, crosswords, horoscopes. Provides movies reviews, news of Latvian cultural life.
Language(s): Russian
ADVERTISING RATES:
SCC .... LVL 2.50
CONSUMER: MUSIC & PERFORMING ARTS: TV & Radio

TRANSPORTWEEKLY CHINA 1831390LV49A-4
Editorial: Miera iela 19-22, RIGA LV-1001
Tel: 78 42 444 **Fax:** 78 42 178
Email: info@transportweekly.com **Web site:** http://www.transportweekly.com
Freq: 24 issues yearly; **Annual Sub.:** EUR 108.00; **Circ:** 20,000
Profile: Provides regular updates and analytical information on development of transportation and supply chain market of China and neighbouring countries, covering events, expert opinion and freight rates trends.
Language(s): English
ADVERTISING RATES:
Full Page Colour $3555.00
Mechanical Data: Type Area: A3
BUSINESS: TRANSPORT

TV PROGRAMMA 1828213LV76C-2
Editorial: Mūkusalas ielā 41, RĪGĀ LV 1004
Tel: 70 68 130 **Fax:** 70 68 131
Email: tv@fenster.lv
Freq: Weekly; **Cover Price:** LVL 0.20
Annual Sub.: LVL 11.40; **Circ:** 170,000
Advertising Manager: Marina Arhipenko
Profile: A TV guide for the whole family in Russian language.
Language(s): Russian
ADVERTISING RATES:
Full Page Mono .... LVL 2395.70
Full Page Colour .... LVL 3337.20
Supplement(s): Latvijas santims - 4xY
CONSUMER: MUSIC & PERFORMING ARTS: TV & Radio

VESTI 1828026LV65J-202
Editorial: Mūkusalas ielā 41, RĪGĀ LV 1004
Tel: 70 68 125 **Fax:** 70 68 131
Email: vesty@fenster.lv **Web site:** http://www.ves.lv/vesti
Date Established: 1995; **Freq:** Weekly; **Cover Price:** LVL 0.45
Annual Sub.: LVL 25.20; **Circ:** 36,000
Usual Pagination: 80
Profile: A socio-political weekly in Russian language.
Language(s): Russian
ADVERTISING RATES:
Full Page Mono .... LVL 1447.33
Full Page Colour .... LVL 2026.26
NATIONAL DAILY & SUNDAY NEWSPAPERS: National Weekly Newspapers

VESTI SEGODNJA 762675LV65A-260
Editorial: Mukusalas 3-41, RIGA LV-1004
Tel: 6 70 68 130 **Fax:** 6 70 68 131
Email: sm@fenster.lv **Web site:** http://www.cm.lv
Date Established: 1993; **Freq:** Daily - Published Monday to Saturday; **Cover Price:** LVL 0.30
Annual Sub.: LVL 58.80; **Circ:** 38,000
Profile: Broadsheet-sized newspaper focusing on national and international news, politics, business and sport.
Language(s): Russian
Readership: Aimed at the Russian-speaking community in Latvia.
ADVERTISING RATES:
Full Page Mono .... LVL 2042.70
Full Page Colour .... LVL 3832.69
Supplement(s): Delovye vesti - 365xY, Nedvizimostj i auto - 365xY
NATIONAL DAILY & SUNDAY NEWSPAPERS: National Daily Newspapers

Liechtenstein

Time Difference: GMT + 1 hrs
National Telephone Code: +423
Continent: Europe
Capital: Vaduz
Principal Language: German
Population: 33436
Monetary Unit: Swiss Franc (CHF)

ABC-SCHÜTZEN 1840369LI67H-1
Editorial: Austr. 81, 9490 VADUZ **Tel:** 3 2361616
Fax: 3 2361617
Email: redaktion@vaterland.li **Web site:** http://www.vaterland.li
Freq: Annual
Advertising Manager: Alois Ospelt
Profile: Supplement for children to the newspaper Liechtensteiner Vaterland.
Language(s): German
ADVERTISING RATES:
Full Page Mono .... CHF 1550
Full Page Colour .... CHF 1685
Mechanical Data: Type Area: 285 x 204 mm
REGIONAL DAILY & SUNDAY NEWSPAPERS: Regional Colour Supplements

ASSET MANAGEMENT 1843688LI94H-12
Editorial: Aeulestr. 6, 9490 VADUZ **Tel:** 3 2356969
Fax: 3 2356513
Email: advisory@vpbank.com **Web site:** http://www.vpbank.com
Editor: Hendrik Breitenstein
Language(s): German
CONSUMER: OTHER CLASSIFICATIONS: Customer Magazines

AUTO FRÜHLING 1840375LI65A-20_100
Editorial: Austr. 81, 9490 VADUZ **Tel:** 3 2361616
Fax: 3 2361617
Email: redaktion@vaterland.li **Web site:** http://www.vaterland.li
Freq: Annual; **Circ:** 11,000
Editor: Niki Eder; **Advertising Manager:** Alois Ospelt
Profile: Car magazine.
Language(s): German
ADVERTISING RATES:
Full Page Mono .... CHF 1900
Full Page Colour .... CHF 2035
Mechanical Data: Type Area: 285 x 204 mm
Supplement to: Liechtensteiner Vaterland
NATIONAL DAILY & SUNDAY NEWSPAPERS: National Daily Newspapers

BAUEN WOHNEN 1840377LI65A-20_101
Editorial: Austr. 81, 9490 VADUZ **Tel:** 3 2361616
Fax: 3 2361617
Email: redaktion@vaterland.li **Web site:** http://www.vaterland.li
Freq: 6 issues yearly; **Circ:** 11,000
Editor: Anja Büchel
Profile: Magazine about building and housing.
Language(s): German
ADVERTISING RATES:
Full Page Mono .... CHF 1900
Full Page Colour .... CHF 2035
Mechanical Data: Type Area: 285 x 204 mm
Supplement to: Liechtensteiner Vaterland
NATIONAL DAILY & SUNDAY NEWSPAPERS: National Daily Newspapers

BHZ LIECHTENSTEINER BAU- & HAUSZEITUNG 1843689LI4E-1
Editorial: Städtle 11, 9490 VADUZ **Tel:** 3 2301740
Fax: 3 2375601
Email: bhz@markt.li **Web site:** http://www.bhz.li
Freq: Monthly; **Annual Sub.:** CHF 72,00; **Circ:** 10,000
Editor: Jean-Claude Zurflüh
Profile: Magazine about all aspects of building in Liechtenstein.
Language(s): German
ADVERTISING RATES:
Full Page Mono .... CHF 1415
Mechanical Data: Type Area: 372 x 260 mm, No. of Columns (Display): 4, Col Widths (Display): 65 mm
Copy instructions: *Copy Date:* 20 days prior to publication
BUSINESS: ARCHITECTURE & BUILDING: Building

DORFSPIEGEL TRIESENBERG 725542LI72-20
Editorial: Rathaus, 9497 TRIESENBERG
Tel: 3 2655039 **Fax:** 3 2655011
Email: franz.gassner@triesenberg.li **Web site:** http://www.triesenberg.li
Freq: Quarterly; **Cover Price:** Free; **Circ:** 1,400
Editor: Franz Gassner
Profile: Local official paper.
Language(s): German
LOCAL NEWSPAPERS

EINTRACHT 726046LI80-20
Editorial: Heiligkreuz 19, 9490 VADUZ
Tel: 3 2323439
Web site: http://www.trachten.li
Freq: 3 issues yearly; **Annual Sub.:** CHF 20,00; **Circ:** 3,000
Editor: Adulf Peter Goop
Profile: Magazine about culture and tradition.
Language(s): German
CONSUMER: RURAL & REGIONAL INTEREST

HILTI TEAM 730291LI14L-100
Editorial: Feldkircher Str. 100, 9494 SCHAAN
Tel: 3 2342630 **Fax:** 3 2346630
Email: anja.buechel@hilti.com **Web site:** http://www.hilti.com
Freq: Quarterly; **Circ:** 20,000
Profile: Magazine for employees of Hilti AG.
Language(s): German
BUSINESS: COMMERCE, INDUSTRY & MANAGEMENT: Trade Unions

LIECHTENSTEINER VATERLAND 734166LI65A-20
Editorial: Austr. 81, 9490 VADUZ **Tel:** 3 2361616
Fax: 3 2361617
Email: redaktion@vaterland.li **Web site:** http://www.vaterland.li
Freq: 312 issues yearly; **Annual Sub.:** CHF 259,00; **Circ:** 10,373
Editor: Günther Fritz
Profile: National daily covering politics, economics, sport, travel and the arts.
Language(s): German
ADVERTISING RATES:
SCC .... CHF 24,40
Mechanical Data: Type Area: 440 x 286 mm, No. of Columns (Display): 10, Col Widths (Display): 25 mm
Copy instructions: *Copy Date:* 1 day prior to publication
Supplement(s): auto frühling; bauen wohnen; Liechtensteins Fussball; lifestyle; pe ce; Weihnachten; Wirtschaft regional
NATIONAL DAILY & SUNDAY NEWSPAPERS: National Daily Newspapers

LIECHTENSTEINER VATERLAND 734165LI72-40
Editorial: Austr. 81, 9490 VADUZ **Tel:** 3 2361616
Fax: 3 2361617
Email: redaktion@vaterland.li **Web site:** http://www.vaterland.li
Freq: Weekly; **Cover Price:** Free; **Circ:** 20,145
Editor: Günther Fritz; **Advertising Manager:** Patrick Flammer
Profile: Advertising journal (house-to-house) concentrating on local stories.
Language(s): German
ADVERTISING RATES:
Full Page Mono .... CHF 4250

ull Page Colour .... CHF 5300
echanical Data: Type Area: 440 x 286 mm, No. of olumns (Display): 10, Col Widths (Display): 25 mm
opy instructions: *Copy Date:* 1 day prior to ublication
OCAL NEWSPAPERS

LIECHTENSTEINER VOLKSBLATT
734168LI65A-40
ditorial: Im alten Riet 103, 9494 SCHAAN
el: 3 2375161 **Fax:** 3 2375155
mail: redaktion@volksblatt.li **Web site:** http://www. olksblatt.li
req: 312 issues yearly; **Annual Sub.:** CHF 249,00; **irc:** 9,000
ditor: Heinz Zöchbauer; **Advertising Manager:** atalie Bauer-Schädler
rofile: National daily covering politics, economics, port, travel and the arts.
anguage(s): German
DVERTISING RATES:
CC .... CHF 30,50
echanical Data: Type Area: 440 x 286 mm, No. of olumns (Display): 10, Col Widths (Display): 25 mm
opy instructions: *Copy Date:* 1 day prior to ublication
ATIONAL DAILY & SUNDAY NEWSPAPERS: ational Daily Newspapers

LIECHTENSTEINER VOLKSBLATT
734167LI72-60
ditorial: Im alten Riet 103, 9494 SCHAAN
el: 3 2375161 **Fax:** 3 2375155
mail: redaktion@volksblatt.li **Web site:** http://www. olksblatt.li
req: Weekly; **Cover Price:** Free; **Circ:** 20,000
ditor: Heinz Zöchbauer; **Advertising Manager:** atalie Bauer-Schädler
rofile: Advertising journal (house-to-house) concentrating on local stories.
anguage(s): German
DVERTISING RATES:
ull Page Mono .... CHF 4240
ull Page Colour .... CHF 5300
echanical Data: Type Area: 440 x 286 mm, No. of olumns (Display): 10, Col Widths (Display): 25 mm
opy instructions: *Copy Date:* 1 day prior to ublication
OCAL NEWSPAPERS

LIECHTENSTEINS FUSSBALL
1840434LI65A-20_102
Editorial: Austr. 81, 9490 VADUZ **Tel:** 3 2361616
Fax: 3 2361617
Email: redaktion@vaterland.li **Web site:** http://www. vaterland.li
Freq: Annual
Advertising Manager: Alois Ospelt
Profile: Soccer supplement to the Liechtenstein newspaper Liechtensteiner Vaterland.
Language(s): German
ADVERTISING RATES:
Full Page Mono .... CHF 1550
Full Page Colour .... CHF 1685
Mechanical Data: Type Area: 285 x 204 mm
Supplement to: Liechtensteiner Vaterland
NATIONAL DAILY & SUNDAY NEWSPAPERS: National Daily Newspapers

LIFESTYLE
1840435LI65A-20_103
Editorial: Austr. 81, 9490 VADUZ **Tel:** 3 2361616
Fax: 3 2361617
Email: redaktion@vaterland.li **Web site:** http://www. vaterland.li
Freq: Half-yearly; **Circ:** 11,000
Editor: Andrea Kobler-Kobelt; **Advertising Manager:** Daniela Erne
Profile: Lifestyle magazine.
Language(s): German
ADVERTISING RATES:
Full Page Mono .... CHF 1900
Full Page Colour .... CHF 2035
Mechanical Data: Type Area: 285 x 204 mm
Supplement to: Liechtensteiner Vaterland
NATIONAL DAILY & SUNDAY NEWSPAPERS: National Daily Newspapers

NEUE LIEWO
1647306LI72-101
Editorial: Austr. 81, 9490 VADUZ **Tel:** 3 2361696
Fax: 3 2361699
Email: redaktion@liewo.li **Web site:** http://www. liewo.li
Freq: Weekly; **Cover Price:** Free; **Circ:** 34,230
Editor: Michael Winkler
Profile: Advertising journal (house-to-house) concentrating on local stories.
Language(s): German
ADVERTISING RATES:
Full Page Mono .... CHF 2320
Full Page Colour .... CHF 2900
Mechanical Data: Type Area: 280 x 210 mm, No. of Columns (Display): 6, Col Widths (Display): 33 mm
Copy instructions: *Copy Date:* 3 days prior to publication
LOCAL NEWSPAPERS

OSCAR'S HOTEL & GOURMET MAGAZIN INTERNATIONAL
1850170LI89A-1
Editorial: Industriestr. 753, 9492 ESCHEN
Tel: 3 3750075 **Fax:** 3 3750074
Email: redaktion@oscars.li **Web site:** http://www. oscars.li
Freq: 10 issues yearly; **Cover Price:** CHF 8,00; **Circ:** 21,000
Language(s): German
ADVERTISING RATES:
Full Page Mono .... CHF 3520
Full Page Colour .... CHF 3520
Mechanical Data: Type Area: 265 x 180 mm, No. of Columns (Display): 4, Col Widths (Display): 42 mm
CONSUMER: HOLIDAYS & TRAVEL: Travel

PE CE
1840447LI65A-20_104
Editorial: Austr. 81, 9490 VADUZ **Tel:** 3 2361616
Fax: 3 2361617
Email: redaktion@vaterland.li **Web site:** http://www. vaterland.li
Freq: 6 issues yearly; **Circ:** 11,000
Editor: Niki Eder; **Advertising Manager:** Patrick Flammer
Profile: Magazine about internet, computer, telecommunications and office.
Language(s): German
ADVERTISING RATES:
Full Page Mono .... CHF 1900
Full Page Colour .... CHF 2035
Mechanical Data: Type Area: 285 x 204 mm
Supplement to: Liechtensteiner Vaterland
NATIONAL DAILY & SUNDAY NEWSPAPERS: National Daily Newspapers

STYLE
1753118LI74A-1
Editorial: In der Fina 18, 9494 SCHAAN
Tel: 3 2334381 **Fax:** 3 2334382
Email: andreagreuner@neue-verlagsanstalt.li **Web site:** http://www.neue-verlagsanstalt.li
Freq: Quarterly; **Annual Sub.:** CHF 46,80; **Circ:** 52,099
Editor: Andrea Greuner
Profile: magazine about fashion, society and culture.
Language(s): German
ADVERTISING RATES:
Full Page Mono .... CHF 12990
Full Page Colour .... CHF 12990
Mechanical Data: Type Area: 253 x 190 mm, No. of Columns (Display): 4, Col Widths (Display): 46 mm
CONSUMER: WOMEN'S INTEREST CONSUMER MAGAZINES: Women's Interest

UNTERNEHMER.
764094LI14A-1
Editorial: Zollstr. 23, 9494 SCHAAN **Tel:** 3 2377781
Fax: 3 2377789
Email: i.schaedler@wirtschaftskammer.li **Web site:** http://www.wirtschaftskammer.li
Freq: 10 issues yearly; **Annual Sub.:** CHF 50,00; **Circ:** 4,700
Editor: Isabell Schädler
Language(s): German
Mechanical Data: Type Area: 264 x 178 mm
BUSINESS: COMMERCE, INDUSTRY & MANAGEMENT

WEIHNACHTEN
1840477LI65A-20_105
Editorial: Austr. 81, 9490 VADUZ **Tel:** 3 2361616
Fax: 3 2361617
Email: redaktion@vaterland.li **Web site:** http://www. vaterland.li
Freq: Annual
Advertising Manager: Alois Ospelt
Profile: Christmas supplement to the newspaper Liechtensteiner Vaterland.
Language(s): German
ADVERTISING RATES:
Full Page Mono .... CHF 2300
Full Page Colour .... CHF 2435
Mechanical Data: Type Area: 285 x 204 mm
Supplement to: Liechtensteiner Vaterland
NATIONAL DAILY & SUNDAY NEWSPAPERS: National Daily Newspapers

WIRTSCHAFT REGIONAL
1840480LI65A-20_106
Editorial: Austr. 81, 9490 VADUZ **Tel:** 3 2361616
Fax: 3 2361617
Email: redaktion@vaterland.li **Web site:** http://www. vaterland.li
Freq: Annual
Advertising Manager: Alois Ospelt
Profile: Economy supplement to the newspaper Beilage zur Zeitung Liechtensteiner Vaterland.
Language(s): German
ADVERTISING RATES:
Full Page Mono .... CHF 2100
Full Page Colour .... CHF 2100
Mechanical Data: Type Area: 285 x 204 mm
Supplement to: Liechtensteiner Vaterland
NATIONAL DAILY & SUNDAY NEWSPAPERS: National Daily Newspapers

Lithuania

Time Difference: GMT + 2 hrs (EET - Eastern European Time)
National Telephone Code: +370
Continent: Europe
Capital: Vilnius
Principal Language: Lithuanian
Population: 3369600
Monetary Unit: Litas (LTL)

EMBASSY HIGH COMMISSION: Embassy of the Republic of Lithuania: 84 Gloucester Place, London W1U 6AU /
Tel: 020 7486 6401,
Fax: 020 7468 6403
Website: http://www .lithuanianembassy.co.uk
Email: amb.uk@urm.lt

AKISTATA
711511LT54C-10
Editorial: Žemalės g. 16, LT-48280 KAUNAS
Tel: 37 36 04 22 **Fax:** 37 36 04 26
Email: akistata@kaunas.omnitel.net
Freq: 104 issues yearly - Published Tuesday and Friday; **Cover Price:** LTL 1.50; **Circ:** 16,000
Editor-in-Chief: V. Zutautas
Profile: Periodical reporting on crime, features information about stolen goods, wanted people and a general crime update. Also contains health and travel page.
Language(s): Lithuanian
Readership: Aimed at members of the police force, security officers and members of the general public interested in crime; politicians, artists, doctors.
Supplement(s): Kransklys - 104xY.
BUSINESS: SAFETY & SECURITY: Security

COMPUTER BILD LIETUVA
1827407LT5D-1
Editorial: A.Goštauto g. 8, LT-01108 VILNIUS
Tel: 5 26 49 421 **Fax:** 5 26 22 407
Email: redaktorius@computerbild.lt **Web site:** http:// www.computerbild.lt
Freq: 24 issues yearly; **Cover Price:** LTL 3.80
Annual Sub.: LTL 91.20; **Circ:** 27,000
Usual Pagination: 68
Editor: Salomėja Mise
Profile: Provides information about PCs and its supplements for mass users, software, electronics market news, PC games, Internet, telecommunications, digital hi-fi and cameras equipment.
Language(s): Lithuanian
Readership: Aimed at ordinary PC users in the age group from 12 to 60.
ADVERTISING RATES:
Full Page Colour .... LTL 5100.00
Mechanical Data: Type Area: 215 x 297 mm
BUSINESS: COMPUTERS & AUTOMATION: Personal Computers

COMPUTER BILD PATARAJAS
1827790LT5D-2
Editorial: A.Goštauto g. 8., LT-01108 VILNIUS
Tel: 5 26 49 421 **Fax:** 5 26 22 407
Email: redaktorius@computerbild.lt **Web site:** http:// www.computerbild.lt
Date Established: 2006; **Freq:** 6 issues yearly;
Cover Price: LTL 8.00
Annual Sub.: LTL 42.00; **Circ:** 26,000
Editor: Salomeja Mise
Profile: Presents software tests, practical advises for software and hardware users, digital equipment, prices of computer's parts and equipment.
Language(s): Lithuanian
ADVERTISING RATES:
Full Page Colour .... LTL 5100.00
Mechanical Data: Type Area: 215 x 297 mm
BUSINESS: COMPUTERS & AUTOMATION: Personal Computers

COSMOPOLITAN
711742LT74B-50
Editorial: A.Goštauto g. 12A, LT-01108 VILNIUS
Tel: 5 268 38 40 **Fax:** 5 242 71 27
Email: info@cosmopolitan.lt **Web site:** http://www. cosmopolitan.lt
Date Established: 1998; **Freq:** Monthly; **Cover Price:** LTL 8.00
Annual Sub.: LTL 66.00; **Circ:** 43,000
Editor: Neda Žvybienė; **Advertising Director:** Roma Perepeckiene
Profile: This Lithuanian edition of the international magazine covers beauty, health, fashion, career, travel and relationship issues.
Language(s): Lithuanian
Readership: Aimed at young professional women.
ADVERTISING RATES:
Full Page Colour .... LTL 8000.00
CONSUMER: WOMEN'S INTEREST CONSUMER MAGAZINES: Women's Interest - Fashion

DOMASNYJ DOKTOR V LITVE
1644748LT56A-152
Editorial: Konstitucijos pr. 12, LT-VILNIUS
Tel: 5 27 53 153 **Fax:** 5 27 53 153
Email: obzor@mail.lt **Web site:** http://www.toloka. com/lt/doctor
Freq: 24 issues yearly; **Cover Price:** LTL 1.60
Annual Sub.: LTL 31.20; **Circ:** 21,000
Usual Pagination: 16
Editor-in-Chief: Tatjana Sancuk; **Advertising Manager:** Alla Gorkovaja
Profile: Promotes healthy way of life. features practical advice on home medicine, illness prophylactics and usage of cosmetics.
Language(s): Russian
ADVERTISING RATES:
SCC .... LTL 2.00
Mechanical Data: Type Area: A4
BUSINESS: HEALTH & MEDICAL

EKSPRESS NEDELIA
1644794LT65J-10
Editorial: Laisvės pr. 60-917, LT-2056 VILNIUS
Tel: 5 24 00 816 **Fax:** 5 24 60 622
Email: redakcija@savaite.lt **Web site:** http://www. savaite.lt
Freq: Weekly - Published on Thursdays; **Cover Price:** LTL 1.50; **Circ:** 68,000
Advertising Manager: Januš Skirtun; **Advertising Director:** Loreta Urbonienė
Profile: Features entertainment and social events' articles in Russian language.
Language(s): Russian
ADVERTISING RATES:
Full Page Colour .... LTL 1350.00
SCC .... LTL 6.00
Mechanical Data: Type Area: 205 x 285 mm
NATIONAL DAILY & SUNDAY NEWSPAPERS: National Weekly Newspapers

JI
762693LT74A-125
Editorial: Donelaičio 70-10, LT-3000 KAUNAS
Tel: 37 20 10 51 **Fax:** 37 22 96 39
Email: ji@redakcija.lt **Web site:** http://www.redakcija. lt
Date Established: 1994; **Freq:** Weekly - Published every Monday; **Cover Price:** LTL 2.50; **Circ:** 45,000
Usual Pagination: 64
Editor-in-Chief: Neringa Cerniauskiene; **Advertising Director:** Edita Mielkuvienė
Profile: General interest magazine, covers leisure, fashion, accessories and offers helpful tips and advice.
Language(s): Lithuanian
Readership: Aimed at women between 25-40.
ADVERTISING RATES:
Full Page Colour .... LTL 2500.00
Mechanical Data: Type Area: 235 x 305 mm, Trim Size: 225 x 295 mm
Copy instructions: *Copy Date:* 10 days prior to publication date
CONSUMER: WOMEN'S INTEREST CONSUMER MAGAZINES: Women's Interest

JUMS
1644891LT14R-1
Editorial: Savanorių pr. 287-241, LT-50127 KAUNAS
Tel: 37 40 72 98 **Fax:** 37 31 15 39
Email: jums@dokeda.lt **Web site:** http://www. jumsinfo.lt
Freq: 6 issues yearly; **Cover Price:** Free; **Circ:** 50,000
Profile: Provides business information on Kaunas city, containing popular business news articles, and all information is divided into specialized sectors.
Language(s): Lithuanian
BUSINESS: COMMERCE, INDUSTRY & MANAGEMENT: Commerce Related

LAISVAS LAIKRASTIS
1644932LT65J-7
Editorial: Goštauto g. 12, LT-VILNIUS
Tel: 5 26 24 203
Email: ll@centras.lt **Web site:** http://www. laisvaslaikrastis.lt
Freq: Weekly; **Annual Sub.:** LTL 72.00; **Circ:** 32,400
Editor-in-Chief: Aurimas Drizius
Profile: Weekly newspaper covering politics, economics and entertainment.
Language(s): Lithuanian
NATIONAL DAILY & SUNDAY NEWSPAPERS: National Weekly Newspapers

LIETUVOS RYTAS
1202204LT65A-10
Editorial: Gedimino pr 12 A, LT- 01103 VILNIUS
Tel: 5 27 43 600 **Fax:** 5 27 43 700
Email: daily@lrytas.lt **Web site:** http://www.lrytas.lt
ISSN: 1392-2351
Date Established: 1990; **Freq:** 312 issues yearly;
Cover Price: LTL 3.00
Annual Sub.: LTL 359.00; **Circ:** 165,000

Lithuania

Editor: A. Budrys; **Editor-in-Chief:** Gedvidias Vainauskas; **Advertising Manager:** Rasa Jurkeviciene
Profile: Newspaper featuring lifestyle, gardening, sports, medicine, the home, world news, travel, ecology, art and culture.
Language(s): Lithuanian
ADVERTISING RATES:
SCC .... LTL 19.00
Mechanical Data: Type Area: 370 x 260mm, No. of Columns (Display): 5, Col Length: 370mm, Page Width: 260mm
Supplement(s): TV Antenna - 52xY, Stilius 52xY (Style), Stilius Plus 12xY (Style and Fashion), Krepsinis (Basketball) 52 xY, Temporary Capital Laikinoji sostine 6/week
NATIONAL DAILY & SUNDAY NEWSPAPERS: National Daily Newspapers

LIETUVOS ZINIOS 1615810LT65A-18
Editorial: Kęstučio g. 4/14, LT- 08117 VILNIUS
Tel: 5 249 21 52 **Fax:** 5 275 31 31
Email: red@lzinios.lt **Web site:** http://www.lzinios.lt
Freq: Daily - Published 6 days a week except Sunday; **Cover Price:** LTL 1.00
Annual Sub.: LTL 250.00; **Circ:** 26,900
Usual Pagination: 24
Editor: Rima Razmislevičiūtė; **News Editor:** Raimonda Rameliené; **Advertising Director:** Alma Jakeliūniené
Profile: Newspaper featuring news, current affairs, finance, sport and cultural events. It has got two supplement magazines: LŽ žurnalas and LŽ gidas.
Language(s): Lithuanian
ADVERTISING RATES:
SCC .... LTL 10.00
NATIONAL DAILY & SUNDAY NEWSPAPERS: National Daily Newspapers

LITOVSKIJ KURJER 1615780LT65J-2
Editorial: Ul. Sodu 4, LT- 03211 VILNIUS
Tel: 5 21 20 320 **Fax:** 5 21 20 320
Email: info@kurier.lt **Web site:** http://www.kurier.lt
Date Established: 1760; **Freq:** Weekly - Published on Thursdays; **Cover Price:** LTL 1.60; **Circ:** 30,000
Usual Pagination: 52
Executive Editor: D. Tarasenko; **Editor-in-Chief:** V. Tretyakov; **Advertising Manager:** L. Mechkovskaya
Profile: Newspaper featuring national and regional news, covers current affairs, politics, economics, social issues, culture and sport.
Language(s): Russian
Readership: Aimed at the Russian speaking community.
ADVERTISING RATES:
Full Page Mono .... LTL 4751.00
Full Page Colour .... LTL 6651.00
SCC .... LTL 7.00
Mechanical Data: Type Area: 250 x 370 mm
NATIONAL DAILY & SUNDAY NEWSPAPERS: National Weekly Newspapers

MEDICINA IR DAR KAI KAS VISIEMS 1645029LT56A-155
Editorial: p.d. 2084, LT- KAUNAS **Tel:** 37 20 06 80
Fax: 37 20 06 80
Email: info@medicinavisiems.lt **Web site:** http://www.medicinavisiems.lt
Date Established: 2001; **Freq:** 24 issues yearly; **Cover Price:** LTL 3.99; **Circ:** 20,000
Editor-in-Chief: Gailina Kavaliauskiene; **Advertising Manager:** Neringa Grabauskiené
Profile: Covering all aspects of traditional medicine and prophylactics, beauty and slimming, acupuncture and natural medicine.
Language(s): Lithuanian
BUSINESS: HEALTH & MEDICAL

OBZOR 1645239LT65J-9
Editorial: Konstitucijos pr. 12, LT- VILNIUS
Tel: 5 27 53 153 **Fax:** 5 27 53 153
Email: obzor@mail.lt **Web site:** http://obzor.lt
ISSN: 1392-2688
Date Established: 1997; **Freq:** Weekly - Published on Thursdays; **Cover Price:** LTL 1.50
Annual Sub.: LTL 78.00; **Circ:** 36,000
Editor-in-Chief: Alexander Shakhov
Profile: A weekly independent inter-digest covering international and domestic political, social and business news.
Language(s): Russian
ADVERTISING RATES:
SCC .... LTL 10.00
NATIONAL DAILY & SUNDAY NEWSPAPERS: National Weekly Newspapers

PANELE 762929LT74A-156
Editorial: Ozo g. 10A, LT- 08200 VILNIUS
Tel: 5 24 77 710 **Fax:** 5 24 77 711
Email: magazine@panele.lt **Web site:** http://www.panele.lt
Freq: Monthly; **Cover Price:** LTL 6.00
Annual Sub.: LTL 66.00; **Circ:** 50,000
Editor: Orius Gasanovas; **Editor-in-Chief:** Jurga Baltrukonytė; **Advertising Manager:** Eglė Berželionytė
Profile: Magazine featuring true life stories. Also covers fashion, modern style of living, health, studies, travelling and easy recipes.
Language(s): Lithuanian
Readership: Aimed at readers aged 15-35 years.
ADVERTISING RATES:
Full Page Colour .... LTL 8500.00
Mechanical Data: Print Process: Offset, Type Area: 207 x 280 mm
CONSUMER: WOMEN'S INTEREST CONSUMER MAGAZINES: Women's Interest

RESPUBLIKA 1600417LT65A-15
Editorial: A. Smetonos g. 2, LT-01115 VILNIUS
Tel: 5 21 21 574 **Fax:** 5 21 23 538
Email: press@respublika.lt
ISSN: 1392-5873
Date Established: 1989; **Freq:** Daily - Published Monday to Saturday; **Cover Price:** LTL 2.00; **Circ:** 37,600
Usual Pagination: 32
Advertising Manager: Justas Tontus; **Advertising Director:** Virginija Stabingiene
Profile: National daily newspaper covering politics, economics, business, social issues and entertainment.
Language(s): Lithuanian; Russian
Readership: Aimed at readers aged 16-75.
ADVERTISING RATES:
Full Page Mono .... LTL 6000.00
Full Page Colour .... LTL 6400.00
Mechanical Data: Type Area: 420 x 280 mm
Supplement(s): LAISVALAIKIS, TV PUBLIKA, JULIUS, BRIGITA, TRINTUKAS
NATIONAL DAILY & SUNDAY NEWSPAPERS: National Daily Newspapers

SAVAITE 762402LT76C-200
Editorial: Laisvės pr. 60-917, LT-2056 VILNIUS
Tel: 5 24 60 623 **Fax:** 5 24 60 622
Email: spauda@savaite.lt **Web site:** http://www.savaite.lt
Freq: Weekly - Published on Wednesday; **Cover Price:** LTL 1.30; **Circ:** 89,000
Editor: Sigita Urbonavičiūtė; **Editor-in-Chief:** Asta Jelinskiene; **Advertising Director:** Loreta Urbonienė
Profile: Newspaper containing details about radio and television programmes, also contains features and articles of general interest.
Language(s): Lithuanian
ADVERTISING RATES:
Full Page Colour .... LTL 1350.00
SCC .... LTL 3.00
Mechanical Data: Type Area: 205 x 285 mm
CONSUMER: MUSIC & PERFORMING ARTS: TV & Radio

VAKARO ZINIOS 1642000LT65A-21
Editorial: Jogailos g. 11/2 -11, LT- 01116 VILNIUS
Tel: 5 26 11 544 **Fax:** 5 26 11 544
Email: redakcija@vakarozinios.lt **Web site:** http://www.vakarozinios.lt
Freq: Daily - Published 6 days a week; **Cover Price:** LTL 1.00
Annual Sub.: LTL 179.88; **Circ:** 65,000
News Editor: Raimonda Baublytė
Profile: A tabloid covering politics, news and entertainment.
Language(s): Lithuanian
ADVERTISING RATES:
SCC .... LTL 18.00
NATIONAL DAILY & SUNDAY NEWSPAPERS: National Daily Newspapers

VERSLO KLASE 1828611LT1A-4
Editorial: J. Jasinskio 16A, LT-01112 VILNIUS
Tel: 5 25 26 300 **Fax:** 5 25 26 313
Email: info@verslozinios.lt
Date Established: 2006; **Freq:** Monthly; **Annual Sub.:** LTL 101.32; **Circ:** 25,000
Usual Pagination: 116
Editor: Aurelijus Katkevičius; **Features Editor:** Rytas Staselis; **Advertising Manager:** Brigita Katinauskaitė
Profile: Gives an account on most relevant and interesting business events, economic developments and high-profile figures in global business and in Lithuania.
Language(s): Lithuanian
ADVERTISING RATES:
Full Page Colour .... LTL 9000.00
Mechanical Data: Type Area: 230 x 297 mm
Supplement to: Verslo zinios
BUSINESS: FINANCE & ECONOMICS

ZMONES 762697LT74Q-600
Editorial: J. Jasinskio g. 16 C, LT- 01112 VILNIUS
Tel: 5 25 26 536 **Fax:** 5 25 26 531
Email: zmones@redakcija.lt **Web site:** http://www.redakcija.lt
Date Established: 2001; **Freq:** Weekly - Published every Thursday; **Cover Price:** LTL 2.40
Annual Sub.: LTL 145.00; **Circ:** 145,000
Usual Pagination: 68
Editor-in-Chief: Daina Zemaitytė; **Advertising Director:** Edita Mielkuvienė
Profile: Magazine featuring celebrities, reports and interviews, also covers travel and fashion.
Language(s): Lithuanian
Readership: Aimed at women aged 20-40.
ADVERTISING RATES:
Full Page Colour .... LTL 9460.00
Mechanical Data: Type Area: 235 x 305 mm, Trim Size: 225 x 295 mm
Copy instructions: *Copy Date:* 7 days prior to publication date
CONSUMER: WOMEN'S INTEREST CONSUMER MAGAZINES: Lifestyle

Luxembourg

Time Difference: GMT + 1 hr (CET - Central European Time)
National Telephone Code: +352
Continent: Europe
Capital: Luxembourg
Principal Language: Luxembourgish, French, German
Population: 480222
Monetary Unit: Euro (EUR)
EMBASSY HIGH COMMISSION: Embassy of Luxembourg: 27 Wilton Crescent, London SW1X 8SD
Tel: 020 7235 6961
Fax: 020 7235 9734 Head of Mission: HE Mr Hubert Wurth,
Email: londres.amb@mae.etat.lu

352 LUXEMBOURG NEWS 1892969LU65J-2
Editorial: 21st Century Building, 19, rue de Bitbourg, L-1273 LUXEMBOURG **Tel:** 26 29991 **Fax:** 26299984
Email: info@news352.lu **Web site:** http://www.news352.lu
Freq: Weekly; **Cover Price:** EUR 2.50
Annual Sub.: EUR 75; **Circ:** 5,000
Usual Pagination: 48
Editor-in-Chief: José Campinho; **Publisher:** Pol Wirtz
Language(s): English
Mechanical Data: Type Area: A4
Copy instructions: *Copy Date:* 7 days prior to publication date
NATIONAL DAILY & SUNDAY NEWSPAPERS: National Weekly Newspapers

AGEFI LUXEMBOURG 1157LU1A-5
Editorial: route d'Arlon 111 B, L-8311 LUXEMBOURG **Tel:** 30 57 57 **Fax:** 305601
Email: agefi@agefi.lu **Web site:** http://www.agefi.lu
Date Established: 1988; **Freq:** Monthly - Début du mois; **Cover Price:** EUR 350
Annual Sub.: EUR 35; **Circ:** 10,000
Profile: Financial magazine for private companies, banks and stockbrokers in Belgium and Luxembourg.
Language(s): French
BUSINESS: FINANCE & ECONOMICS

AGENDALUX 1892681LU89C-1
Tel: 42 82 82 23 **Fax:** 42828238
Email: info@agendalux.lu **Web site:** http://www.agendalux.lu
Freq: Monthly - Le 1er du mois; **Cover Price:** Free; **Circ:** 65,000
Usual Pagination: 100
Language(s): French
Mechanical Data: Type Area: 275 x 137
CONSUMER: HOLIDAYS & TRAVEL: Entertainment Guides

AKTUELL 1368LU14L-10
Editorial: 60, bd. J.F. Kennedy, L-4002 ESCH SUR ALZETTE, LUXEMBOURG **Tel:** 54 05 45 1
Fax: 541620
Email: ogbl@ogbl.lu **Web site:** http://www.ogbl.lu
Freq: Monthly - 01 02 03 04 05 06 09 10 12; **Circ:** 60,000
Usual Pagination: 48
Editor-in-Chief: Jacques Delacolette
Profile: Journal for members of the OGBL trade union.
Language(s): French; German
BUSINESS: COMMERCE, INDUSTRY & MANAGEMENT: Trade Unions

ANDY A LUXEMBOURG 1893193LU86C-1
Editorial: BGS Crossmedia, 1, impasse Emile Didderich, L-5616 LUXEMBOURG **Tel:** 35 6877
Email: contact@myofficialstory.com **Web site:** http://www.myofst.com/andy
Freq: Half-yearly - Mai et novembre; **Circ:** 10,000
Usual Pagination: 84
Language(s): French
Copy instructions: *Copy Date:* 31 days prior to publication date
CONSUMER: ADULT & GAY MAGAZINES: Men's Lifestyle Magazines

ARCHITECTURE & BATIMENT 1224LU4A-
Editorial: 171, rue de Luxembourg, L-4940 BASCHARAGE, LUXEMBOURG **Tel:** 23 65 01 75
Fax: 23650174
Email: pyredac@pt.lu **Web site:** http://www.newcom.lu
Date Established: 1996; **Freq:** 6 issues yearly - Le 15; **Annual Sub.:** EUR 35; **Circ:** 2,500
Usual Pagination: 120
Editor-in-Chief: Frédéric Bertinelli
Profile: Publication about architecture, building and the construction industry in Luxembourg.
Language(s): French
Mechanical Data: Type Area: A4
BUSINESS: ARCHITECTURE & BUILDING: Architecture

ATOUT PRIX MAGAZINE 1799190LU74C-1
Editorial: 14 rue Lentz, L-3509 DUDELANGE, LUXEMBOURG **Tel:** 26 52 29 22 **Fax:** 26 52 29 23
Email: dposalski@groupe-peace.com
Freq: 6 issues yearly
Usual Pagination: 58
Language(s): French
CONSUMER: WOMEN'S INTEREST CONSUMER MAGAZINES: Home & Family

AUTO LOISIRS - LUXEMBOURG 2369LU77A-5
Editorial: ZI, 8 Grasbusch, L-3370 LEUDELANGE, LUXEMBOURG **Tel:** 48 45 40 **Fax:** 484566
Email: info@city-image.lu
Freq: Quarterly; **Cover Price:** Free; **Circ:** 20,000
Profile: Motoring magazine for car enthusiasts.
Language(s): French
CONSUMER: MOTORING & CYCLING: Motoring

AUTO MOTO 2370LU77A-10
Editorial: 2, rue Christophe Plantin, L-2988 LUXEMBOURG **Tel:** 49 93 231 **Fax:** 4993757
Email: auto@wort.lu **Web site:** http://www.wort.lu
Freq: Monthly - Luxembourg; **Cover Price:** Free; **Circ:** 81,000
Editor: Claude Feyereisen
Profile: Magazine for car and motorbike owners, includes sport and leisure topics.
Language(s): French; German
CONSUMER: MOTORING & CYCLING: Motoring

AUTO REVUE 2371LU77A-15
Editorial: PO Box 2755, L-1027 LUXEMBOURG
Tel: 49 81 81 **Fax:** 487722
Email: revue@revue.lu **Web site:** http://www.revue.lu
Freq: Monthly - Milieu de mois - Sauf 08; **Cover Price:** EUR 2.30; **Circ:** 30,000
Profile: Magazine for car enthusiasts in Luxembourg.
Language(s): French; German
Copy instructions: *Copy Date:* 21 days prior to publication date
CONSUMER: MOTORING & CYCLING: Motoring

AUTOTOURING 2399LU77E-5
Editorial: 54, route de Longwy, L-8007 BERTRANGE, LUXEMBOURG **Tel:** 45 00 451 **Fax:** 450045620
Email: acl@acl.lu **Web site:** http://www.acl.lu
Freq: Quarterly - 01 04 07 10; **Circ:** 130,000
Usual Pagination: 80
Editor-in-Chief: Daniel Tesch
Profile: Magazine of the Automobile Club of Luxembourg.
Language(s): French; German
Mechanical Data: Type Area: A 4
Copy instructions: *Copy Date:* 42 days prior to publication date
CONSUMER: MOTORING & CYCLING: Club Cars

BULLETIN DE LA SOCIÉTÉ DES SCIENCES MÉDICALES DU GRAND DUCHÉ DE LUXEMBOURG 1668LU56A-5
Editorial: 63 rue de Luxembourg, L-8140 BRIDEL, LUXEMBOURG **Tel:** 33 99 69 **Fax:** 26 330 781
Email: georges.theves@pt.lu **Web site:** http://www.ssm.lu
Date Established: 1864; **Freq:** Half-yearly - 06 11; **Circ:** 1,000
Usual Pagination: 160
Profile: Bulletin of the Luxembourg Society of Medical Science.
Language(s): English; French; German
Readership: Read by doctors, dentists, pharmacists, vets, biologists and chemists.
Mechanical Data: Type Area: 165 x 235
BUSINESS: HEALTH & MEDICAL

BUSINESS REVIEW 1893047LU1A-7
ditorial: 21st Century Building, 19, rue de Bitbourg, -1273 LUXEMBOURG-HAMM **Tel:** 26 29 99 80
ax: 26299984
mail: stephen.evans@business.lu **Web site:** http://www.business.lu
req: Monthly - Sauf juillet et août; **Circ:** 7,000
anguage(s): English; French
USINESS: FINANCE & ECONOMICS

CARRIÈRE 1893068LU74A-6
ditorial: PO Box 2535, L-1025 LUXEMBOURG
el: 85 89 19 **Fax:** 85 89 19
mail: carrieremag@logic.lu **Web site:** http://www.ogic.lu/carriere
ate Established: 1988; **Freq:** Quarterly; **Annual ub.:** EUR 12.40; **Circ:** 8,000
anguage(s): French
CONSUMER: WOMEN'S INTEREST CONSUMER MAGAZINES: Women's Interest

CITY MAGAZINE 1809331LU80-2
Editorial: BP 728, L-2017 BONNEVOIE, LUXEMBOURG **Tel:** 29 66 181 **Fax:** 296619
Email: duncan.roberts@citymag.lu **Web site:** http://citymag.lu
Freq: Monthly - Fin de mois; **Circ:** 35,000
Editor: Mike Koedinger
Profile: Magazine about Luxembourg, providing news and information on leisure and business.
Language(s): French; Luxembourgish
Readership: Aimed at inhabitants, tourists and businessmen.
Mechanical Data: Type Area: 230 x 300
CONSUMER: RURAL & REGIONAL INTEREST

CLC CONNECT 1327LU14A-5
Editorial: 7, rue Alcide de Gasperi, L-2014 LUXEMBOURG **Tel:** 43 94 44 41 **Fax:** 439450
Email: info@clc.lu **Web site:** http://www.clc.lu
Freq: 6 issues yearly; **Circ:** 2,500
Usual Pagination: 32
Managing Director: Yves Gordet
Profile: Official journal of the Luxembourg Trade Confederation providing information about commerce, business, administration, transport, law, publicity and health policy in Luxembourg and Europe.
Language(s): French; German
BUSINESS: COMMERCE, INDUSTRY & MANAGEMENT

CONTACTO 2598LU94D-5
Editorial: 2, Rue Christophe Plantin, L-2988 LUXEMBOURG **Tel:** 49 93 337 **Fax:** 49 93 448
Email: contacto@saint-paul.lu **Web site:** http://www.jornal-contacto.lu
Date Established: 1970; **Freq:** Weekly - Vendredi;
Cover Price: EUR 0.62
Free to qualifying individuals ; **Circ:** 23,500
Profile: Magazine for Portuguese inhabitants of Luxembourg.
Language(s): French; Portuguese
Mechanical Data: Type Area: 270 x 400
CONSUMER: OTHER CLASSIFICATIONS: Expatriates

LE CORPS MEDICAL 1670LU56A-6
Editorial: 29, rue de Vianden, L-2680 LUXEMBOURG
Tel: 44 40 33 **Fax:** 458349
Email: secretariat@ammd.lu **Web site:** http://www.ammd.lu
Freq: 26 issues yearly - Milieu de mois; **Cover Price:** Free; **Circ:** 1,600
Usual Pagination: 35
Editor-in-Chief: Eliane Polfer
Profile: Journal of the Association of Doctors and Dentists of Luxembourg.
Language(s): English; French; German
Mechanical Data: Type Area: A4
Copy instructions: *Copy Date:* 31 days prior to publication date
BUSINESS: HEALTH & MEDICAL

DE LETZEBUERGER BAUER 1436LU21A-5
Editorial: BP 48, L-7501 MERSCH, LUXEMBOURG
Tel: 32 64 64 480 **Fax:** 326464481
Email: letzeburger.bauer@netdsl.lu
Date Established: 1945; **Freq:** Weekly - Le vendredi matin; **Circ:** 4,000
Profile: Magazine containing information on agriculture, viticulture, gardening and horses.
Language(s): French; German
BUSINESS: AGRICULTURE & FARMING

DE LËTZEBUERGER MERKUR 1788LU14A-12
Editorial: 7, rue Alcide de Gasperi, L-2981 LUXEMBOURG **Tel:** 42 39 39 280 **Fax:** 438326
Email: merkur@cc.lu **Web site:** http://www.cc.lu
Freq: Monthly - Milieu de mois; **Annual Sub.:** EUR 15; **Circ:** 33,000
Usual Pagination: 94
Profile: Official journal of the Chamber of Commerce of the Grand Duchy of Luxembourg.
Language(s): English; French; German
Readership: Aimed at heads of companies, executives, political and economic decision makers.
Mechanical Data: Type Area: A 4
Copy instructions: *Copy Date:* 10 days prior to publication date
BUSINESS: COMMERCE, INDUSTRY & MANAGEMENT

DE LËTZEBUERGER ZIICHTE 1446LU21D-5
Editorial: Zone Artisanale & Commerciale, 4, 9085 ETTELBRÜCK, LUXEMBOURG **Tel:** 26 81 200
Fax: 26 81 2012
Email: info@convis.lu **Web site:** http://www.convis.lu
Date Established: 1981; **Freq:** 6 issues yearly - les 1ers : 03 06 09 11 12; **Cover Price:** EUR 2.50; **Circ:** 2,500
Usual Pagination: 80
Profile: Magazine about the breeding and upkeep of cattle, sheep and pigs.
Language(s): French
Mechanical Data: Type Area: A 4
BUSINESS: AGRICULTURE & FARMING: Livestock

DE NEIE FEIERKROP 1893236LU82-17
Editorial: PO Box 1572, L-1015 LUXEMBOURG
Tel: 2643 17 21 **Fax:** 26431723
Email: info@feierkrop.lu **Web site:** http://www.feierkrop.lu
Freq: Weekly - Vendredi; **Cover Price:** EUR 1.50
Annual Sub.: EUR 53.30; **Circ:** 12,000
Language(s): French; German
CONSUMER: CURRENT AFFAIRS & POLITICS

DESIRS 1809326LU74Q-7
Editorial: For all contact details see main record, PaperJam, LUXEMBOURG **Tel:** 29 66 181
Fax: 296619
Web site: http://www.desirsmagazine.com
Date Established: 2004; **Freq:** Quarterly - Variable; **Circ:** 20,000
Usual Pagination: 150
Profile: Lifestyle magazine covering trends, fashion, accessories, interiors and decoration.
Language(s): English; French
Mechanical Data: Type Area: 238 x 300
CONSUMER: WOMEN'S INTEREST CONSUMER MAGAZINES: Lifestyle

D'HANDWIERK 1328LU14A-10
Editorial: PO box 1604, L-1016 LUXEMBOURG
Tel: 42 45 111 **Fax:** 424525
Email: info@fda.lu **Web site:** http://www.fda.lu
Date Established: 1945; **Freq:** Monthly - Dernière semaine du mois; **Annual Sub.:** EUR 1545; **Circ:** 7,500
Managing Editor: Romain Schmit
Profile: Official journal of the Chamber of Crafts and the Federation of Craftsmen of the Grand Duchy of Luxembourg.
Language(s): French; German
Mechanical Data: Type Area: A4
Copy instructions: *Copy Date:* 10 days prior to publication date
BUSINESS: COMMERCE, INDUSTRY & MANAGEMENT

D'LETZEBUERGER LAND 1787LU65J-1
Editorial: BP 2083, L-1020 LUXEMBOURG
Tel: 48 57 57 1 **Fax:** 49 63 09
Email: land@land.lu **Web site:** http://www.land.lu
Freq: Weekly; **Cover Price:** EUR 180
Annual Sub.: EUR 72; **Circ:** 7,500
Profile: Newspaper covering news and current-affairs for Luxembourg and Europe.
Language(s): English; French; German
NATIONAL DAILY & SUNDAY NEWSPAPERS: National Weekly Newspapers

D'WORT (LUXEMBOURG) 1824LU65A-10
Editorial: 2, rue Christophe Plantin, L-2988 LUXEMBOURG **Tel:** 49 93 1 **Fax:** 49 93 726
Email: wort@wort.lu **Web site:** http://www.wort.lu
Date Established: 2001; **Freq:** Daily - Luxembourg;
Annual Sub.: EUR 196; **Circ:** 82,327
Managing Director: Paul Lenert
Profile: Broadsheet-sized quality newspaper containing national and international news, political, economic and financial information.
Language(s): French; German
Readership: Read by decision-makers and business executives, civil servants and university students.
ADVERTISING RATES:
Full Page Mono .... EUR 6823
Full Page Colour .... EUR 9613
NATIONAL DAILY & SUNDAY NEWSPAPERS: National Daily Newspapers

ECHO DES ENTREPRISES 1346LU14B-5
Editorial: PO Box 1304, L-1013 LUXEMBOURG
Tel: 43 53 661 **Fax:** 432328
Email: echo@fedil.lu **Web site:** http://www.fedil.lu
Date Established: 1921; **Freq:** 6 issues yearly - 02 04 06 08 10 11; **Annual Sub.:** EUR 1450; **Circ:** 1,800
Profile: Industry magazine, includes economic and social issues and employment legislation.
Language(s): English; French; German
Copy instructions: *Copy Date:* 15 days prior to publication date
BUSINESS: COMMERCE, INDUSTRY & MANAGEMENT: Industry & Factories

ECOLE & VIE 1759LU62J-5
Editorial: PO Box 2437, BONNEVOIE, LUXEMBOURG **Tel:** 48 11 18 1 **Fax:** 407356
Email: sne@sne.lu **Web site:** http://www.sne.lu
Freq: 6 issues yearly; **Cover Price:** Free; **Circ:** 4,000
Usual Pagination: 44
Profile: Journal of the National Teachers' Union in Belgium.
Language(s): French; German
BUSINESS: CHURCH & SCHOOL EQUIPMENT & EDUCATION: Teachers & Education Management

ECOLOGIQUE 1893218LU57-11
Editorial: Délégué à l'environnement, 30 rue du Laboratoire, L-1911 LUXEMBOURG **Tel:** 47 96 1
Fax: 47 96 55
Email: environnement@vdl.lu **Web site:** http://www.vdl.lu
Date Established: 2008; **Freq:** Quarterly - Fin 03 06 09 12; **Cover Price:** Free; **Circ:** 45,000
Usual Pagination: 20
Managing Director: Norbert Neis
Language(s): French; German
BUSINESS: ENVIRONMENT & POLLUTION

ELAN 2243LU74N-5
Editorial: PO Box 2234, L-1022 LUXEMBOURG
Tel: 40 22 22 **Fax:** 402047
Email: amiperas@pt.lu
Date Established: 1964; **Freq:** Quarterly - Variable; **Circ:** 18,000
Profile: Journal for people who offer products and services to the elderly; includes care, health, gastronomy, leisure and sport.
Language(s): French; German; Luxembourgish
Copy instructions: *Copy Date:* 31 days prior to publication date
CONSUMER: WOMEN'S INTEREST CONSUMER MAGAZINES: Retirement

ENTERPRISES MAGAZINE 1892959LU14A-11
Editorial: 104, rue du Kiem, L-1857 LUXEMBOURG
Tel: 40 84 69 **Fax:** 482078
Email: redaction@entreprisesmagazine.com **Web site:** http://www.entreprisesmagazine.com
Date Established: 2003; **Freq:** 6 issues yearly - 01 03 05 07 09 11
Annual Sub.: EUR 27; **Circ:** 5,000
Usual Pagination: 80
Language(s): French
Mechanical Data: Type Area: A4
BUSINESS: COMMERCE, INDUSTRY & MANAGEMENT

EXCELLENTIA MAGAZINE 1893085LU74A-9
Editorial: 14, rue Lentz, 3509 DUDELANGE, LUXEMBOURG **Tel:** 26 52 29 22 **Fax:** 26 52 29 23
Email: redaction@mixcites.com **Web site:** http://www.mixcites.com
Freq: Quarterly - 03 06 09 12; **Cover Price:** Free; **Circ:** 55,000
Usual Pagination: 88
Language(s): French
Mechanical Data: Type Area: 150 x 170
Copy instructions: *Copy Date:* 15 days prior to publication date
CONSUMER: WOMEN'S INTEREST CONSUMER MAGAZINES: Women's Interest

EXPRESS (ARDENER EXPRESS & LOKAL EXPRESS) 1893263LU67J-1
Editorial: 42, route de Diekirch, L-7220 LUXEMBOURG **Tel:** 2633 05 85 **Fax:** 26330080
Email: info@express.lu **Web site:** http://www.express.lu
Freq: Monthly; **Cover Price:** Free; **Circ:** 52,000
Language(s): French; German
Mechanical Data: Type Area: 210 x 277
REGIONAL DAILY & SUNDAY NEWSPAPERS: Regional Newspapers (excl. dailies)

FEMMES MAGAZINE 1893073LU74A-7
Editorial: 74 rue Ermesinde, L-1469 LUXEMBOURG
Tel: 26 45 85 86 **Fax:** 26 45 84 94
Email: redaction@femmesmagazine.lu **Web site:** http://www.femmesmagazine.lu
Freq: Monthly - Le 1er du mois; **Circ:** 20,200
Editor: Maria Pietrangeli
Language(s): French
CONSUMER: WOMEN'S INTEREST CONSUMER MAGAZINES: Women's Interest

FESCHER, JEER, AN HONDSFREM 1893173LU92-1
Tel: 621 220 935
Email: fjh@flps.lu **Web site:** http://www.flps.lu/fjh.htm
Freq: 6 issues yearly - Mois pairs; **Cover Price:** EUR 2.23
Annual Sub.: EUR 14; **Circ:** 7,000
Usual Pagination: 12
Language(s): French
Mechanical Data: Type Area: A4
Copy instructions: *Copy Date:* 21 days prior to publication date
CONSUMER: ANGLING & FISHING

FLEET EUROPE 1892896LU31-1
Tel: 269 5 85 **Fax:** 26810282
Email: info@mmm.be **Web site:** http://www.fleeteurope.com
Date Established: 2003; **Freq:** Quarterly; **Annual Sub.:** EUR 60; **Circ:** 15,000
Usual Pagination: 52
Language(s): English; French
Mechanical Data: Type Area: A4
BUSINESS: MOTOR TRADE

FLYDOSCOPE 2557LU89D-5
Editorial: BP 728, L-2017 BONNEVOIE, LUXEMBOURG **Tel:** 29 66 181 **Fax:** 296619
Web site: http://www.tempo.lu
Date Established: 1975; **Freq:** 6 issues yearly - Milieu de mois; **Cover Price:** Free; **Circ:** 30,000
Profile: In-flight magazine of Luxair airlines. Contains general information about Luxembourg, articles on holiday destinations, city trips, art and aviation.
Language(s): English; French; German
Mechanical Data: Type Area: 210 x 297
CONSUMER: HOLIDAYS & TRAVEL: In-Flight Magazines

FONCTION COMMUNALE 1499LU32A-5
Editorial: 66, rue Baudouin, L-1218 LUXEMBOURG
Tel: 40 77 20 1 **Fax:** 40772040
Email: fgfc@fgfc.lu **Web site:** http://www.fgfc.lu
Freq: 3 issues yearly - Published in March, June, September and December; **Circ:** 10,000
Usual Pagination: 32
Profile: Official publication of the General Federation of Civil Servants.
Language(s): French; German
Mechanical Data: Type Area: A4
BUSINESS: LOCAL GOVERNMENT, LEISURE & RECREATION: Local Government

GAART AN HEEM 2174LU93-6
Editorial: 97, rue de Bonnevoie, L-1260 LUXEMBOURG **Tel:** 48 01 99 **Fax:** 409798
Email: liguectf@pt.lu **Web site:** http://www.ctf.lu
Freq: 6 issues yearly - Début du mois; **Annual Sub.:** EUR 10; **Circ:** 33,000
Profile: Magazine providing advice and information about gardening.
Language(s): French; German
Copy instructions: *Copy Date:* 10 days prior to publication date
CONSUMER: GARDENING

GALERIE 2535LU88A-1
Editorial: 69, Prinzenberg, L-4650 DIFFERDANGE, LUXEMBOURG **Tel:** 58 70 45 **Fax:** 580275
ISSN: 1012 6716
Date Established: 1982; **Freq:** 3 issues yearly - 03 06 09 12; **Cover Price:** EUR 15
Annual Sub.: EUR 35; **Circ:** 1,000
Usual Pagination: 160
Profile: Educational and cultural journal published by the Cultural Centre of Differdange.
Language(s): English; French; German; Luxembourgish
CONSUMER: EDUCATION

GASTROTOUR 2561LU89E-5
Editorial: BP 48, L-7201 WALFERDANGE, LUXEMBOURG **Tel:** 4213 5 51 **Fax:** 421352299
Freq: 3 issues yearly - even.mill@pt.lu; **Circ:** 5,000
Usual Pagination: 36
Profile: Magazine covering travel and gastronomy.
Language(s): French
CONSUMER: HOLIDAYS & TRAVEL: Holidays

GRAFFITI 1805243LU76A-1
Tel: 49 81 81 1 **Fax:** 487722
Email: revue@revue.lu **Web site:** http://www.revue.lu
Date Established: 1987; **Freq:** Monthly - Milieu du mois; **Circ:** 30,000
Editor-in-Chief: Guy Ludig
Language(s): French; German

Copy instructions: *Copy Date:* 14 days prior to publication date
CONSUMER: MUSIC & PERFORMING ARTS: Cinema

HEMECHT
1892941LU88A-2
Editorial: éditions saint-paul, L-2988 LUXEMBOURG
Tel: 49 93 275 **Fax:** 4993580
Email: editions@editions.lu **Web site:** http://www.editions.lu
ISSN: 0018-0270
Freq: Quarterly; **Cover Price:** EUR 14; **Circ:** 1,000
Usual Pagination: 128
Language(s): French
Mechanical Data: Type Area: 165 x 245
CONSUMER: EDUCATION

LE JEUDI
714153LU82-6
Editorial: 44, rue du Canal, L-4050 ESCH SUR ALZETTE, LUXEMBOURG **Tel:** 22 05 50 **Fax:** 220544
Email: redaction@le-jeudi.lu **Web site:** http://www.le-jeudi.lu
Date Established: 1997; **Freq:** Weekly - Tous les jeudis
Annual Sub.: EUR 77; **Circ:** 12,000
Usual Pagination: 50
Profile: Magazine covering current affairs, finance, culture, lifestyle and travel.
Language(s): French
Mechanical Data: Type Area: Berlinois
CONSUMER: CURRENT AFFAIRS & POLITICS

KEISECKER
1736LU57-5
Editorial: 4, rue Vauban, L-2663 LUXEMBOURG
Tel: 43 90 30 1 **Fax:** 43903043
Email: meco@oeko.lu **Web site:** http://www.oeko.lu
Date Established: 1975; **Freq:** Quarterly - 03 06 09 12; **Annual Sub.:** EUR 40; **Circ:** 4,000
Usual Pagination: 66
Profile: Magazine containing information on ecology; includes background information on environmental politics, new initiatives and developments.
Language(s): French; German
Mechanical Data: Type Area: A4
Copy instructions: *Copy Date:* 21 days prior to publication date
BUSINESS: ENVIRONMENT & POLLUTION

LËTZEBUERGER GEMENGEN
1893244LU82-18
Editorial: 24, rue Michel Rodange, L-4660 LUXEMBOURG **Tel:** 58 45 46 **Fax:** 584919
Email: frederic@euroeditions.lu **Web site:** http://www.gemengen.lu
Freq: Monthly - Début du mois; **Annual Sub.:** EUR 40; **Circ:** 2,500
Language(s): French
CONSUMER: CURRENT AFFAIRS & POLITICS

LËTZEBUERGER JOURNAL
1823LU65A-5
Editorial: BP 2101, L-1021 LUXEMBOURG
Tel: 49 30 331 **Fax:** 49 20 65
Email: journal@journal.lu **Web site:** http://www.journal.lu
Date Established: 1947; **Freq:** Daily - Luxembourg; **Cover Price:** EUR 0.70
Annual Sub.: EUR 112; **Circ:** 8,500
Managing Director: Gusty Graas
Profile: Tabloid-sized quality newspaper providing political, financial and economic coverage.
Language(s): English; French; German
Readership: Read by decision-makers within business and industry, managers, civil servants, university students and investors.
Copy instructions: *Copy Date:* 2 days prior to publication date
NATIONAL DAILY & SUNDAY NEWSPAPERS: National Daily Newspapers

LUXEMBOURG BONJOUR
1893399LU89A-1
Editorial: 30, place Guillaume II, L – 1648 LUXEMBOURG **Tel:** 22 28 09 **Fax:** 467070
Email: touristinfo@lcto.lu **Web site:** http://www.lcto.lu
Freq: Quarterly - Tous les 3 mois; **Cover Price:** Free; **Circ:** 16,000
Language(s): French
CONSUMER: HOLIDAYS & TRAVEL: Travel

LUXEMBOURG FÉMININ
1893082LU74A-8
Editorial: 13 rue Philippe II, L-2340 LUXEMBOURG
Tel: 621 184 082 **Fax:** 46 52 96
Email: contact@luxembourgfeminin.com **Web site:** http://www.luxembourgfeminin.com
Date Established: 2006; **Freq:** Quarterly - 03 05 09 11
Annual Sub.: EUR 16; **Circ:** 20,000
Usual Pagination: 134
Language(s): French
Mechanical Data: Type Area: 23 x 30

Copy instructions: *Copy Date:* 28 days prior to publication date
CONSUMER: WOMEN'S INTEREST CONSUMER MAGAZINES: Women's Interest

LUXEMBOURG TOURISME
1893408LU89A-3
Tel: 8441 10 11 **Fax:** 84412439
Freq: Quarterly; **Annual Sub.:** EUR 10; **Circ:** 5,000
Language(s): French
CONSUMER: HOLIDAYS & TRAVEL: Travel

LUXEMBURGER MARIENKALENDER
1893111LU82-16
Editorial: éditions saint-paul, L-2988 LUXEMBOURG
Tel: 49 93 275 **Fax:** 4993384
Email: editions@editions.lu **Web site:** http://www.editions.lu
Freq: Annual; **Cover Price:** EUR 15; **Circ:** 10,000
Language(s): Luxembourgish
CONSUMER: CURRENT AFFAIRS & POLITICS

LUX-POST
1892973LU65J-4
Tel: 44 44 33 1 **Fax:** 444433555
Email: redaction@lux-post.lu **Web site:** http://www.lux-post.lu
Freq: Weekly; **Cover Price:** Free; **Circ:** 140,000
Editor-in-Chief: Roland Kayser
Language(s): French
NATIONAL DAILY & SUNDAY NEWSPAPERS: National Weekly Newspapers

LUXURIANT
1892949LU74Q-10
Editorial: 42 rue de Hollerich, L-1740 LUXEMBOURG
Tel: 2748 95 21 **Fax:** 27489525
Email: info@luxuriant.lu **Web site:** http://www.luxuriant.lu
Freq: Monthly - variable; **Cover Price:** Free; **Circ:** 20,000
Usual Pagination: 80
Language(s): English; French; Luxembourgish
Mechanical Data: Type Area: A4
Copy instructions: *Copy Date:* 7 days prior to publication date
CONSUMER: WOMEN'S INTEREST CONSUMER MAGAZINES: Lifestyle

MADE IN LUXE
1892868LU74Q-8
Editorial: 19, rue de Bitbourg, L-1273 LUXEMBOURG **Tel:** 2629 99 1 **Fax:** 26299963
Email: contact@madeinluxe.lu **Web site:** http://www.madeinluxe.lu
Freq: Monthly - Mois pairs; **Annual Sub.:** EUR 39.60; **Circ:** 13,500
Editor-in-Chief: Charles Ruppert
Language(s): French
CONSUMER: WOMEN'S INTEREST CONSUMER MAGAZINES: Lifestyle

MAGAZINE HORESCA
1306LU11A-5
Editorial: BP 2524, L-1025 LUXEMBOURG
Tel: 42 13 55 1 **Fax:** 421355299
Email: horesca@pt.lu **Web site:** http://www.horesca.lu
Date Established: 1985; **Freq:** Monthly - 30 du mois
Annual Sub.: EUR 30; **Circ:** 6,000
Profile: Journal of the National Federation of Hoteliers, Restaurateurs and Café Proprietors.
Language(s): French; German
BUSINESS: CATERING: Catering, Hotels & Restaurants

MISERLAND MAGAZINE
1805771LU80-1
Editorial: 23, rue de Trèves, L-6701 GREVENMACHER, LUXEMBOURG **Tel:** 75 01 39
Fax: 758882
Email: info@miselerland.lu **Web site:** http://www.miselerland.lu
Date Established: 2003; **Freq:** Half-yearly - 04 11; **Cover Price:** Free; **Circ:** 17,000
Usual Pagination: 64
Profile: Magazine containing information for people living in the Moselle region.
Language(s): French
CONSUMER: RURAL & REGIONAL INTEREST

NICO
1682021LU74Q-6
Editorial: PO Box 728, L-2017 BONNEVOIE, LUXEMBOURG **Tel:** 29 66 181 **Fax:** 296619
Email: mike@mikekoedinger.com **Web site:** http://www.nicomagazine.com
Freq: Half-yearly - Variable; **Annual Sub.:** EUR 25; **Circ:** 30,000
Profile: Magazine covering fashion, arts, culture, gastronomy, live performances and issues on society.
Language(s): English; French
CONSUMER: WOMEN'S INTEREST CONSUMER MAGAZINES: Lifestyle

NIGHTLIFE
1892698LU89C-2
Tel: 2483 83 1 **Fax:** 24838323
Web site: http://www.nightlife-mag.net
Freq: 6 issues yearly - Première semaine; **Cover Price:** Free; **Circ:** 30,000
Editor: Pierre Thomas; **Editor-in-Chief:** Sébastien Michel
Language(s): French
Mechanical Data: Type Area: A4
CONSUMER: HOLIDAYS & TRAVEL: Entertainment Guides

NOS CAHIERS
1893163LU84B-1
Editorial: éditions saint-paul, L-2988 LUXEMBOURG
Tel: 49 93 275 **Fax:** 4993307
Email: editions@editions.lu **Web site:** http://www.editions.lu
ISSN: 1012-3822
Freq: Quarterly; **Cover Price:** EUR 15; **Circ:** 1,000
Usual Pagination: 128
Language(s): French
Mechanical Data: Type Area: 160 x 225
CONSUMER: THE ARTS & LITERARY: Literary

PAPERJAM
1682019LU1A-6
Editorial: PO Box 728, BONNEVOIE, LUXEMBOURG
Tel: 29 66 18 1 **Fax:** 296619
Email: press@paperjam.lu **Web site:** http://www.paperjam.lu
ISSN: 1608-0432
Date Established: 2000; **Freq:** Monthly - Variable
Annual Sub.: EUR 40; **Circ:** 20,000
Usual Pagination: 240
Profile: Magazine focusing on economic and financial news.
Language(s): English; French
Readership: Aimed at opinion-formers, decision makers and people in business, finance and politics.
Mechanical Data: Type Area: 238 x 300
Copy instructions: *Copy Date:* 15 days prior to publication date
BUSINESS: FINANCE & ECONOMICS

PIZZICATO
2357LU76D-5
Editorial: 129, Mühlenweg, L-2155 LUXEMBOURG
Tel: 49 29 24 **Fax:** 492884
Email: rfranck@pt.lu **Web site:** http://www.pizzicato.lu
Date Established: 1991; **Freq:** Monthly - +/- 27 du mois; **Cover Price:** EUR 380
Annual Sub.: EUR 32; **Circ:** 4,000
Usual Pagination: 60
Profile: Magazine for classical music and opera.
Language(s): English; French; German
Mechanical Data: Type Area: A4
CONSUMER: MUSIC & PERFORMING ARTS: Music

POINT 24
1893368LU65A-23
Editorial: 2 rue Christophe Plantin, L-2988 LUXEMBOURG **Tel:** 49 93 24 24 **Fax:** 49 93 24 25
Email: redaction@point24.lu **Web site:** http://www.point24.lu
Freq: Daily; **Cover Price:** Free; **Circ:** 72,000
Usual Pagination: 24
Language(s): French
Mechanical Data: Type Area: A3
Copy instructions: *Copy Date:* 2 days prior to publication date
NATIONAL DAILY & SUNDAY NEWSPAPERS: National Daily Newspapers

PRINT
1983531LU4A-6
Editorial: 25, avenue de la Gare, L-4131 LUXEMBOURG **Tel:** 2654 11 22 **Fax:** 26532536
Email: info@loft.lu **Web site:** http://www.loft.lu
Date Established: 2006; **Freq:** Half-yearly; **Circ:** 16,000
Usual Pagination: 32
Editor-in-Chief: Fernand Hornung; **Publisher:** Mike Koedinger
Language(s): French
BUSINESS: ARCHITECTURE & BUILDING: Architecture

LE QUOTIDIEN
1804944LU65A-22
Editorial: 44, rue du Canal, L-4050 ESCH SUR ALZETTE, LUXEMBOURG **Tel:** 54 71 31
Fax: 54 71 30
Email: redaction@lequotidien.lu **Web site:** http://www.lequotidien.lu
Date Established: 2001; **Freq:** Daily - Luxembourg; **Circ:** 8,500
Editor-in-Chief: Jean-Marie Martini
Profile: Newspaper providing local, national and international news and current-affairs; includes politics, the economy and sport.
Language(s): French
NATIONAL DAILY & SUNDAY NEWSPAPERS: National Daily Newspapers

RAPPEL
2593LU94A-5
Editorial: PO Box 1424, L-1014 LUXEMBOURG
Tel: 47 82 281 **Fax:** 290039
Date Established: 1946; **Freq:** 3 issues yearly
Annual Sub.: EUR 15; **Circ:** 1,550

Profile: Publication for war veterans and their families.
Language(s): French; German; Luxembourgish
CONSUMER: OTHER CLASSIFICATIONS: War Veterans

REGULUS
1738LU57-1
Editorial: Kraizhaff, route de Luxembourg, L-1899 KOCKELSCHEUER, LUXEMBOURG **Tel:** 29 04 04 1
Fax: 290504
Email: secretariat.commun@luxnatur.lu **Web site:** http://www.lnvl.lu
Date Established: 1920; **Freq:** Quarterly - Fin 03 Début 06 Mi 09 Début 12; **Circ:** 15,000
Usual Pagination: 36
Profile: Journal providing information about the environment and the protection of birds.
Language(s): French; German
Mechanical Data: Type Area: A 4
BUSINESS: ENVIRONMENT & POLLUTION

REVUE
2159LU82-21
Editorial: PO Box 2755, L-1027 LUXEMBOURG
Tel: 49 81 81 **Fax:** 487722
Email: revue@revue.lu **Web site:** http://www.revue.lu
Freq: Weekly - Mercredi; **Cover Price:** EUR 2.50
Annual Sub.: EUR 88.45; **Circ:** 30,421
Editor-in-Chief: Laurent Graff
Profile: Magazine covering current-affairs, politics, culture, social life, entertainment, cooking and television.
Language(s): French; German
CONSUMER: CURRENT AFFAIRS & POLITICS

REVUE MUSICALE
2358LU76D-10
Editorial: 3, route d'Arlon, L-8009 STRASSEN, LUXEMBOURG **Tel:** 46 25 36 1 **Fax:** 471440
Email: revue-musicale@ugda.lu **Web site:** http://www.ugda.lu
Freq: 6 issues yearly - 02 04 07 10 12; **Annual Sub.:** EUR 50; **Circ:** 12,300
Usual Pagination: 32
Editor-in-Chief: Martine Deprez
Profile: Magazine about amateur musical, wind bands, choir and theatrical societies.
Language(s): French; German; Luxembourgish
Readership: Read by members.
Mechanical Data: Type Area: A 4
CONSUMER: MUSIC & PERFORMING ARTS: Music

REVUE TECHNIQUE LUXEMBOURGOISE
1414LU19A-5
Editorial: 7, rue de Gibraltar, L – 1624 LUXEMBOURG **Tel:** 26 11 46 42 **Fax:** 45 09 32
Email: revue@aliai.lu **Web site:** http://www.revue-technique.lu
Freq: Quarterly - 03 06 09 12; **Circ:** 3,000
Usual Pagination: 50
Editor-in-Chief: Sonja Reichert
Profile: Technical journal for engineers, architects and industrialists in Luxembourg.
Language(s): English; French; German
BUSINESS: ENGINEERING & MACHINERY

SAUER ZEIDUNG
1893355LU67J-3
Editorial: PO Box 36, L-6701 GREVENMACHER, LUXEMBOURG **Tel:** 75 87 47 **Fax:** 758432
Email: burton@pt.lu **Web site:** http://www.muselzeidung.lu
Freq: Monthly; **Cover Price:** Free; **Circ:** 14,000
Editor-in-Chief: Ush Burton
Language(s): German
Copy instructions: *Copy Date:* 14 days prior to publication date
REGIONAL DAILY & SUNDAY NEWSPAPERS: Regional Newspapers (excl. dailies)

SEW JOURNAL
1371LU14L-15
Editorial: 1, rue Jean-Pierre Sauvage, L-2514 LUXEMBOURG **Tel:** 26 09 69 1 **Fax:** 26096969
Email: sew@ogbl.lu **Web site:** http://www.sew.lu
Freq: 6 issues yearly - 01 03 06 09 11; **Annual Sub.:** EUR 25; **Circ:** 2,600
Profile: Journal of the trade union of teachers, educators and scientists.
Language(s): English; French; German
Copy instructions: *Copy Date:* 14 days prior to publication date
BUSINESS: COMMERCE, INDUSTRY & MANAGEMENT: Trade Unions

LE SIGNAL
1612LU49A-10
Editorial: 63, rue de Bonnevoie, L-1260 LUXEMBOURG **Tel:** 48 70 441 **Fax:** 488525
Email: lesignal@landesverband.lu **Web site:** http://www.fncttfel.lu
Freq: 26 issues yearly - Début et milieu de mois; **Annual Sub.:** EUR 25; **Circ:** 7,500
Usual Pagination: 12
Profile: Magazine of the FNCTTFEL Landesverband about railway, public service and private transport.
Language(s): French; German
BUSINESS: TRANSPORT

TAGEBLATT - ZEITUNG FIR LETZEBUERG
1825LU65A-15
Editorial: Boîte postale 147, L-4002 ESCH-SUR-ALZETTE, LUXEMBOURG **Tel:** 54 08 84 680 **Fax:** 54 71 30
Email: redaktion@tageblatt.lu **Web site:** http://www.tageblatt.lu
Date Established: 1913; **Freq:** Daily - Luxembourg; **Cover Price:** EUR 1.10
Annual Sub.: EUR 229; **Circ:** 27,000
Editor-in-Chief: Danièle Fonck
Profile: Tabloid-sized quality newspaper providing local, national and international news. Includes articles concerning politics, economics and the stock exchange and coverage of sporting events.
Language(s): French; German
Readership: Aimed at senior executives, managers, university students and office personnel.
NATIONAL DAILY & SUNDAY NEWSPAPERS: National Daily Newspapers

TELECRAN
2347LU76C-5
Editorial: 2 rue Christophe Plantin, L-2988 LUXEMBOURG **Tel:** 49 93 500 **Fax:** 49 93 590
Email: telecran@telecran.lu **Web site:** http://www.telecran.lu
Freq: Weekly - Mercredi
Annual Sub.: EUR 68; **Circ:** 49,500
Managing Director: Roland Arens
Profile: Family television magazine.
Language(s): French; German
CONSUMER: MUSIC & PERFORMING ARTS: TV & Radio

TENDANCES
1892869LU74Q-9
Editorial: éditions saint-paul, L-2988 LUXEMBOURG **Tel:** 49 93 93 **Fax:** 4993477
Email: editions@editions.lu **Web site:** http://www.editions.lu
Freq: Monthly
Annual Sub.: EUR 50; **Circ:** 98,000
Language(s): French
CONSUMER: WOMEN'S INTEREST CONSUMER MAGAZINES: Lifestyle

LA TOQUE BLANCHE
1313LU11A-10
Editorial: PO Box 5, L-7501 MERSCH, LUXEMBOURG **Tel:** 80 24 53 **Fax:** 809897
Email: vatel@pt.lu **Web site:** http://www.vatel.lu
ISSN: 1024-221X
Date Established: 1957; **Freq:** 6 issues yearly - 03/05.07/09/12; **Cover Price:** Free; **Circ:** 5,000
Usual Pagination: 50
Profile: Official publication of the Association of Culinary Professionals.
Language(s): English; French; German
Readership: Aimed at managers in hotels and restaurants and professional caterers.
Mechanical Data: Type Area: 30 X 21
BUSINESS: CATERING: Catering, Hotels & Restaurants

LA VOIX DU LUXEMBOURG
1772664LU65A-21
Editorial: 2 rue Christophe Plantin, L-2988 LUXEMBOURG **Tel:** 49 93 94 00 **Fax:** 49 93 77 3
Email: voix@voix.lu **Web site:** http://www.lavoix.lu
Freq: Daily - Luxembourg; **Circ:** 8,578
Profile: Broadsheet-sized quality newspaper containing national and international news, political, economic and financial information.
Language(s): French
Readership: Read by decision-makers and business executives, civil servants and university students.
Copy instructions: *Copy Date:* 2 days prior to publication date
NATIONAL DAILY & SUNDAY NEWSPAPERS: National Daily Newspapers

WANE - WE ARE NEXT
1983502LU74Q-12
Tel: 62 14 030
Email: contact@wane.lu **Web site:** http://wane.lu
Date Established: 2010; **Freq:** 6 issues yearly - 01 04 06 09; **Cover Price:** Free; **Circ:** 5,000
Language(s): French
Mechanical Data: Type Area: 200 x 260
Copy instructions: *Copy Date:* 10 days prior to publication date
CONSUMER: WOMEN'S INTEREST CONSUMER MAGAZINES: Lifestyle

WOXX
2150LU73-5
Editorial: BP 684, L-2016 LUXEMBOURG **Tel:** 29 79 990 **Fax:** 29 79 79
Email: woxx@woxx.lu **Web site:** http://www.woxx.lu
Date Established: 1988; **Freq:** Weekly - Vendredi;
Annual Sub.: EUR 70; **Circ:** 3,000
Profile: Periodical about current affairs, politics, the economy, ecology, society and culture.
Language(s): French; German; Luxembourgish
ADVERTISING RATES:
Full Page Mono .... EUR 1023
Full Page Colour .... EUR 1713
CONSUMER: NATIONAL & INTERNATIONAL PERIODICALS

WUNNEN MAGAZINE
1892755LU42A-6
Editorial: 275, rue de Luxembourg, L-8077 BERTRANGE, LUXEMBOURG **Tel:** 2638 93 12 **Fax:** 26459550
Email: redaction@wunnen-mag.lu **Web site:** http://www.wunnen-mag.lu
Date Established: 2007; **Freq:** 6 issues yearly - Debut 01 03 05 07 09 11
Annual Sub.: EUR 20; **Circ:** 11,000
Usual Pagination: 86
Language(s): French; German
Mechanical Data: Type Area: A4
Copy instructions: *Copy Date:* 21 days prior to publication date
BUSINESS: CONSTRUCTION

ZLV - ZEITUNG VUM LËTZEBUERGER VOLLEK
1826LU65A-20
Editorial: PO Box 403, L-4005 ESCH-SUR-ALZETTE, LUXEMBOURG **Tel:** 44 60 66 1 **Fax:** 44 60 66 66
Email: info@zlv.lu **Web site:** http://www.zlv.lu
Date Established: 1946; **Freq:** Daily - Luxembourg; **Cover Price:** EUR 77
Annual Sub.: EUR 112; **Circ:** 9,000
Usual Pagination: 12
Profile: Tabloid-sized newspaper providing local, national and international news; includes information on politics and sport. Political outlook: Left wing.
Language(s): French; German; Italian; Portuguese
Mechanical Data: Type Area: Tabloïd
Copy instructions: *Copy Date:* 2 days prior to publication date
NATIONAL DAILY & SUNDAY NEWSPAPERS: National Daily Newspapers

Macedonia

Time Difference: GMT + 1 hr (CET - Central European Time)
National Telephone Code: +389
Continent: Europe
Capital: Skopje
Principal Language: Macedonian, Albanian
Population: 2063122
Monetary Unit: Denar (MKD)
EMBASSY HIGH COMMISSION: Embassy of the Republic of Macedonia: Suites 2.1 & 2.2, Buckingham Court, 75-83 Buckingham Gate, London SW1E 6PE
Tel: 020 7976 0535,
Fax: 020 7976 0539
Email: info@macedonianembassy.org.uk
Website: http://www.macedonianembassy.org.uk/ Head of Mission HE Marija Efremova Ambassador of Republic of Macedonia

DNEVNIK
1500410MK65A-16
Editorial: Teodosij Gologanov 28, 1000 SKOPJE **Tel:** 2 32 36 800 **Fax:** 2 32 36 801
Email: dnevnik@dnevnik.com.mk **Web site:** http://www.dnevnik.com.mk
Date Established: 1996; **Freq:** Daily - Published Monday to Saturday; **Cover Price:** MKD 15.00; **Circ:** 55,000
Editor: Mitko Biljanoski; **Executive Editor:** Katerina Blazevska; **Editor-in-Chief:** Saso Kokalanov
Profile: Newspaper focusing on national and international news, business, politics, culture and sport.
Language(s): Macedonian
ADVERTISING RATES:
Full Page Mono .... EUR 560.00
Full Page Colour .... EUR 770.00
Mechanical Data: Type Area: 262x390mm
Supplement(s): Oglasi - 52xY (Tuesday) Antenna - 52xY (Friday) Weekend - 52xY (Saturday).
NATIONAL DAILY & SUNDAY NEWSPAPERS: National Daily Newspapers

MAKEDONSKI SPORT
1806087MK65A-18
Editorial: 3/6 Lermontova street, 1000 SKOPJE
Tel: 2 32 12 019 **Fax:** 2 32 12 019
Email: sport@on.net.mk **Web site:** http://www.sport.com.mk
ISSN: 1409-7028
Date Established: 1998; **Freq:** Daily; **Cover Price:** MKD 20.00
Free to qualifying individuals ; **Circ:** 12,000
Usual Pagination: 20
Editor: Igor Ivanovski
Profile: Newspaper featuring articles on all types of sport.
Language(s): Macedonian
NATIONAL DAILY & SUNDAY NEWSPAPERS: National Daily Newspapers

MAKEDONSKO SONCE
766848MK82-1
Editorial: Leninova No.79, 1000 SKOPJE
Tel: 2 31 30 137 **Fax:** 2 31 30 377
Email: redakcija@makedonskosonce.com **Web site:** http://www.makedonskosonce.com
ISSN: 1409-5467
Date Established: 1994; **Freq:** Weekly - Published on Friday, Format A4; **Cover Price:** MKD 50.00
Annual Sub.: MKD 2300.00; **Circ:** 40,000
Usual Pagination: 64
Profile: Magazine focusing on current affairs, politics, history, religion and culture.
Language(s): Macedonian
CONSUMER: CURRENT AFFAIRS & POLITICS

NEW BALKAN POLITICS
1616234MK82-2
Editorial: Orce Nikolov 155, 1000 SKOPJE
Tel: 2 30 61 951 **Fax:** 2 30 61 282
Email: maleska@sonet.com.mk **Web site:** http://www.newbalkanpolitics.org.mk
Date Established: 2001; **Freq:** Quarterly; **Cover Price:** Free; **Circ:** 500
Usual Pagination: 215
Profile: Magazine focusing on politics and international, domestic and ethnic issues.
Language(s): Albanian; English; Macedonian
Readership: Aimed at journalists, students, political and NGO activists.
CONSUMER: CURRENT AFFAIRS & POLITICS

NOVA MAKEDONIJA
1500413MK65A-10
Editorial: Naum Ohridski 47, 1000 SKOPJE
Tel: 2 27 36 120 **Fax:** 2 27 36 121
Email: desk@novamakedonija.com.mk **Web site:** http://www.novamakedonija.com.mk
Date Established: 1944; **Freq:** Evenings - Published Monday to Saturday; Free to qualifying individuals
Annual Sub.: EUR 265,00; **Circ:** 15,000
Editor: Marija Tausanska
Profile: Newspaper focusing on national and international news, politics, business and sport.
Language(s): Macedonian
ADVERTISING RATES:
Full Page Mono .... EUR 350.00
Full Page Colour .... EUR 500.00
NATIONAL DAILY & SUNDAY NEWSPAPERS: National Daily Newspapers

UTRINSKI VESNIK
765655MK65A-17
Editorial: Dimitrie Cupovski 11/5, 1000 SKOPJE
Tel: 2 32 36 900 **Fax:** 2 32 36 901
Email: vesnik@utrinski.com.mk **Web site:** http://www.utrinskivesnik.com.mk
Date Established: 1999; **Freq:** Daily; **Cover Price:** MKD 15.00; **Circ:** 25,000
Editor: Lgubco Popovski
Profile: Newspaper focusing on national and international news, business, politics, sport and entertainment and supplements.
Language(s): Macedonian
Readership: Audience: intellectual, cultural, politic, sport audiences.
ADVERTISING RATES:
Full Page Mono .... MKD 27,666.00
Full Page Colour .... MKD 36,403.00
Supplement(s): Advertisments, AUTOBild, Health and Enigmatic, Magazin for TV and Show, Shema - teenagers' supplement, Style and life, TEA - women's supplement
NATIONAL DAILY & SUNDAY NEWSPAPERS: National Daily Newspapers

VECER
1500414MK65A-15
Editorial: Bul. Nikola Vapcarov 2, 1000 SKOPJE
Tel: 2 32 19 650 **Fax:** 2 32 19 651
Email: vecer@vecer.com.mk **Web site:** http://www.vecer.com.mk
Date Established: 1963; **Freq:** Daily - Published Monday to Saturday; **Annual Sub.:** MKD 4680.00; **Circ:** 10,000
Profile: Newspaper focusing on national and international news, politics, business and sport.
Language(s): Macedonian
ADVERTISING RATES:
Full Page Mono .... EUR 660.00
Full Page Colour .... EUR 830.00
Mechanical Data: Type Area: 245x355mm
NATIONAL DAILY & SUNDAY NEWSPAPERS: National Daily Newspapers

Malta

Time Difference: GMT + 1 hr (CET - Central European Time)
National Telephone Code: +356
Continent: Europe
Capital: Valletta
Principal Language: Maltese, English, Italian
Population: 401880
Monetary Unit: Maltese Lira (MIL)
EMBASSY HIGH COMMISSION: Malta High Commission: Malta House, 36/38 Piccadilly, London W1J 0LE
Tel: 020 7292 4800
Fax: 020 7734 1831 Head of Mission: HE Mr. Joseph Zamit Tabona
Email: maltahighcommission.london@gov.mt
Website: http://www.foreign.gov.mt/london

KULLHADD
765051MT65B-3
Editorial: Centru Nazzjonali Laburista, Triq Milend, HAMRUN HMR 1717 **Tel:** 21 23 53 12
Fax: 21 23 82 52
Email: editorial@kullhadd.com **Web site:** http://www.kullhadd.com
Date Established: 1993; **Freq:** Sunday; **Cover Price:** MIL 0.22
Annual Sub.: MIL 11.00; **Circ:** 20,000
Usual Pagination: 48
Executive Editor: Felix Agius; **Advertising Manager:** Philip Schembri
Profile: Tabloid-sized newspaper focusing on national and international news, culture, entertainment and sport.
Language(s): Maltese
ADVERTISING RATES:
Full Page Mono .... EUR 690.05
Full Page Colour .... EUR 947.20
Agency Commission: 15%
Copy instructions: *Copy Date:* Friday at 12 noon
Average ad content per issue: 40%
NATIONAL DAILY & SUNDAY NEWSPAPERS: National Sunday Newspapers

LEHEN IS-SEWWA
1201014MT87-5
Editorial: The Catholic Institute, FLORIANA FRN 1441 **Tel:** 21 22 58 47 **Fax:** 21 22 58 47
Email: lehenissewwa@vol.net.mt
Date Established: 1928; **Freq:** Weekly - Published on Saturday; **Cover Price:** MIL 0.13
Annual Sub.: MIL 8.00; **Circ:** 10,000
Usual Pagination: 24
Editor: John Ciarlo
Profile: Newspaper focusing on religious, political, social and economic issues from a Catholic perspective.
Language(s): Maltese
Readership: Aimed at Catholics.
CONSUMER: RELIGIOUS

THE MALTA INDEPENDENT
1600937MT65A-4
Formerly: The Malta Independent Daily
Editorial: Standard House, Birkirkara Hill, ST JULIANS STJ 1149 **Tel:** 21 34 58 88 **Fax:** 21 34 60 62
Email: tmid@independent.com.mt **Web site:** http://www.independent.com.mt
Date Established: 1997; **Freq:** Daily - Published Monday to Saturday; **Cover Price:** 0.50; **Circ:** 11,000
Editor: Michael Carabott; **Features Editor:** Marie Benoit; **Managing Director:** Noel Azzopardi
Profile: Newspaper focusing on national and international news, politics, business and sport.
Language(s): English
ADVERTISING RATES:
Full Page Mono .... EUR 512.46
Full Page Colour .... EUR 931.75
Supplement(s): I do - 4xY
NATIONAL DAILY & SUNDAY NEWSPAPERS: National Daily Newspapers

THE MALTA INDEPENDENT ON SUNDAY
1201736MT65B-4
Editorial: Standard House, Birkirkara Hill, ST JULIANS STJ 1149 **Tel:** 21 34 58 88 **Fax:** 21 34 60 62
Email: tmis@independent.com.mt **Web site:** http://www.independent.com.mt

Malta

Date Established: 1992; **Freq:** Sunday; **Circ:** 20,000
Editor: Fade Noel Grima; **Features Editor:** Marie Benoit
Profile: Newspaper focusing on national and international news, business, politics and sport.
Language(s): English
ADVERTISING RATES:
Full Page Mono .... EUR 722.11
Full Page Colour .... EUR 1153.04
Supplement(s): First - 12xY, Flair - 6xY, Residence - 6xY, Taste - 7xY
NATIONAL DAILY & SUNDAY NEWSPAPERS: National Sunday Newspapers

IL- MUMENT
1500235MT65B-5
Editorial: Dar Centrali, Herbert Ganado Street, PIETA HMR 08 **Tel:** 21 24 36 41 **Fax:** 21 24 36 40
Email: news@media.link.com.mt **Web site:** http://www.mument.com.mt
Date Established: 1973; **Freq:** Sunday; **Cover Price:** MIL 0.50; **Circ:** 20,000
Usual Pagination: 72
Editor: Victor Camilleri
Profile: Newspaper focusing on national and international news, business, politics, culture and sport.
Language(s): Maltese
ADVERTISING RATES:
Full Page Mono .... EUR 795.00
Full Page Colour .... EUR 1221.00
NATIONAL DAILY & SUNDAY NEWSPAPERS: National Sunday Newspapers

IN- NAZZJON
1500237MT65A-5
Formerly: In-Nazzjon Toghna
Editorial: Dar Centrali, Herbert Ganado Street, PIETA HMR 08 **Tel:** 21 24 36 41 **Fax:** 21 24 36 40
Email: news@media.link.com.mt **Web site:** http://www.media.link.com.mt
Date Established: 1970; **Freq:** Daily - Published Monday to Saturday; **Cover Price:** EUR 0.42; **Circ:** 22,000
Editor: Alex Attard
Profile: Newspaper focusing on national and international news, business, politics, culture and sport.
Language(s): Maltese
NATIONAL DAILY & SUNDAY NEWSPAPERS: National Daily Newspapers

L- ORIZZONT
1500242MT65A-10
Editorial: A41 Marsa Industrial Estate, MARSA LQA 06 **Tel:** 21 242 995 **Fax:** 21 23 84 84
Email: torca@unionprint.com.mt **Web site:** http://www.unionprint.com.mt
Date Established: 1962; **Freq:** Daily - Published Monday to Saturday; **Circ:** 22,000
Advertising Manager: Alfred Anastasi
Profile: Newspaper focusing on national and international news, business, politics and sport.
Language(s): Maltese
ADVERTISING RATES:
Full Page Mono .... MIL 231.00
Full Page Colour .... MIL 431.00
Mechanical Data: Col Length: 370 mm, Col Widths (Display): 450 mm
Supplement(s): Madwarna - 12xY, Roti Magazin - 12xY
NATIONAL DAILY & SUNDAY NEWSPAPERS: National Daily Newspapers

THE SUNDAY TIMES
1500243MT65B-15
Editorial: Strickland House, 341 St Paul Street, VALLETTA VLT 1211 **Tel:** 25 59 41 00
Fax: 25 59 45 10
Email: sunday@timesofmalta.com **Web site:** http://www.timesofmalta.com
Date Established: 1935; **Freq:** Sunday; **Circ:** 40,000
Editor: Steve Mallia; **Advertising Manager:** Edgar Scicluna
Profile: Newspaper focusing on national and international news, business, politics and sport.
Language(s): English
ADVERTISING RATES:
Full Page Mono .... MIL 403.00
Full Page Colour .... MIL 617.00
Supplement(s): Sunday Circle - 12xY
NATIONAL DAILY & SUNDAY NEWSPAPERS: National Sunday Newspapers

THE TIMES
1500244MT65A-15
Editorial: Strickland House, 341 St Paul Street, VALLETTA VLT 1211 **Tel:** 21 24 14 64
Fax: 21 24 79 01
Email: newsroom@timesofmalta.com **Web site:** http://www.timesofmalta.com
Freq: Daily - Published Monday to Saturday; **Cover Price:** EUR 0.60; **Circ:** 21,000
Editor: Raymond Bugeja; **Advertising Manager:** Edgar Scicluna
Profile: Newspaper focusing on national and international news, politics, business and sport.
Language(s): English
ADVERTISING RATES:
Full Page Mono .... MIL 275.00
Full Page Colour .... MIL 504.00
NATIONAL DAILY & SUNDAY NEWSPAPERS: National Daily Newspapers

IT- TORCA
1500238MT65B-10
Editorial: A41 Marsa Industrial Estate, MARSA LQA 06 **Tel:** 21 24 76 87 **Fax:** 21 23 84 84
Email: info@unionprint.com.mt **Web site:** http://www.it-torca.com
Date Established: 1944; **Freq:** Sunday; **Circ:** 30,000
Editor: Aleks Farrugia; **Advertising Manager:** Alfred Anastasi
Profile: Newspaper focusing on national and international news, politics, business and sport.
Language(s): Maltese
ADVERTISING RATES:
Full Page Mono .... MIL 342.00
Full Page Colour .... MIL 527.00
Mechanical Data: Col Length: 370 mm, Col Widths (Display): 45 mm
Supplement(s): MZK Muzayk - 12xY, Wotz Up - 12xY
NATIONAL DAILY & SUNDAY NEWSPAPERS: National Sunday Newspapers

Moldova

Time Difference: GMT + 2 hrs (EET - Eastern European Time)
National Telephone Code: +373
Continent: Europe
Capital: Chisinau, Kishnev
Principal Language: Moldovan, Russian
Population: 4300000
Monetary Unit: Lei (MDL)
EMBASSY HIGH COMMISSION: 5 Dolphin Sqoare, Edensor Road London W4 2ST 020 8995 6818/ the Head of Mission will be appointed on the 1st of September

COMERSANT PLUS
1616122MD65J-3
Editorial: str. Puskin 22, 2012 CHISINAU
Tel: 22 23 33 18 **Fax:** 22 23 33 13
Email: inform@comment.press.md **Web site:** http://www.km.press.md/
Freq: Weekly - Published on Friday; **Circ:** 3,000
Editor: Artem Varenita
Profile: Newspaper focusing on politics, economy and finance.
Language(s): Russian
NATIONAL DAILY & SUNDAY NEWSPAPERS: National Weekly Newspapers

CONTRAFORT
766791MD84B-1
Editorial: Bd. Stefan cel Mare 134, 2012 CHISINAU
Tel: 22 23 24 79 **Fax:** 22 21 06 08
Email: contrafort@moldnet.md **Web site:** http://www.contrafort.md
Freq: Monthly
Editor: Vitalie Ciobanu
Profile: Cultural magazine featuring literary history and criticism, social issues, poetry and book reviews.
Language(s): Romanian
CONSUMER: THE ARTS & LITERARY: Literary

ECONOMICESKOJE OBOZRENIJE
766850MD1A-1
Editorial: Stefan cel Mare 180, 2004 CHISINAU
Tel: 22 23 53 78 **Fax:** 22 23 53 77
Email: red@logos.press.md **Web site:** http://logos.press.md
Freq: Weekly; **Circ:** 10,000
Editor-in-Chief: Sergey Mishin; **Advertising Manager:** Aleksandr Panov
Profile: Newspaper focusing on economics, finance, business and politics.
Language(s): Russian
Readership: Read by managers and executives.
ADVERTISING RATES:
Full Page Mono .... EUR 400.00
BUSINESS: FINANCE & ECONOMICS

JURNAL DE CHIŞINĂU
1633011MD65A-2
Editorial: str. Puskin 22, Casa Presei, 4 etazh, of. 446, 2012 CHISINAU **Tel:** 22 23 40 41
Fax: 22 23 83 31
Email: cotidian@jurnal.md **Web site:** http://www.jurnal.md
Date Established: 1999; **Freq:** 104 issues yearly - Published on Tuesday and Friday; **Cover Price:** MDL 3.00; **Circ:** 15,000
Editor-in-Chief: Val Butnaru; **Advertising Manager:** Mariana Arsene
Profile: Newspaper containing news and reportages, political, economic, cultural and social commentaries, sports and general interest articles.
Language(s): Romanian
Readership: Read by a broad spectrum of the population.
NATIONAL DAILY & SUNDAY NEWSPAPERS: National Daily Newspapers

KISINEVSKY OBOZREVATEL
766749MD65J-4
Editorial: Vlaiku Pyrkelab 45, office 405, 2012 CHISINAU **Tel:** 22 21 02 64 **Fax:** 22 21 02 27
Email: oboz@moldnet.md **Web site:** http://www.ko.md
Date Established: 2000; **Freq:** Weekly - Published on Thursday; **Cover Price:** MDL 3.00; **Circ:** 6,000
Usual Pagination: 24
Editor: Irina Astahova
Profile: Informative-analytical weekly newspaper focusing on politics, culture, economics, sport, regional and general news.
Language(s): Russian
NATIONAL DAILY & SUNDAY NEWSPAPERS: National Weekly Newspapers

MOLDAVSKIE VEDOMOSTI
766598MD65J-1
Editorial: Banulescu-Bodoni st. 21, 2012 CHISINAU
Tel: 22 23 86 18 **Fax:** 22 23 86 18
Email: editor@mv.net.md **Web site:** http://www.vedomosti.md
Date Established: 1995; **Freq:** 96 issues yearly - Published on Wednesday and Friday; **Cover Price:** MDL 2.00; **Circ:** 6,000
Editor: Dumitru Ciubasenco
Profile: Newspaper focusing on politics, business, sport, culture and general news.
Language(s): Russian
Agency Commission: up to 30%
Mechanical Data: Col Length: 450 mm, Col Widths (Display): 45 mm, Page Width: 390 mm
Average ad content per issue: 10%
NATIONAL DAILY & SUNDAY NEWSPAPERS: National Weekly Newspapers

NEZAVISIMAYA MOLDOVA
766597MD65A-1
Editorial: str. Puskin 22, 11052 CHISINAU
Tel: 22 23 31 41 **Fax:** 22 23 31 41
Email: mail@nm.md **Web site:** http://www.nm.md
Date Established: 1994; **Freq:** 250 issues yearly; **Circ:** 17,000
Editor: Yurii Tiscenko
Profile: Newspaper focusing on national and international news, politics, business and sport.
Language(s): Russian
NATIONAL DAILY & SUNDAY NEWSPAPERS: National Daily Newspapers

TIMPUL DE DIMINEAŢA
766869MD65J-2
Formerly: Timpu
Editorial: str. M. Eminescu, 55, 2004 CHISINAU
Tel: 22 29 40 45 **Fax:** 22 29 24 28
Email: timpul@mdl.net **Web site:** http://www.timpul.md
Freq: 104 issues yearly; **Circ:** 19,227
Editor: Constantin Tanase; **Editor-in-Chief:** Sorina Stefarta
Profile: Newspaper focusing on national and international news, culture, society, politics, economics and sport.
Language(s): Romanian
NATIONAL DAILY & SUNDAY NEWSPAPERS: National Weekly Newspapers

WELCOME MOLDOVA
766798MD89A-1
Editorial: PO Box 256, 2012 CHISINAU
Tel: 22 23 42 34 **Fax:** 22 22 51 35
Email: info@welcome-moldova.com **Web site:** http://www.welcome-moldova.com
Cover Price: Paid
Editor: Vlada Popushoi
Profile: E-publication focusing on travelling and sightseeing in Moldova. Features information on history, culture and society.
Language(s): English
Readership: Aimed at foreign visitors to Moldova.
CONSUMER: HOLIDAYS & TRAVEL: Travel

Monaco

Time Difference: GMT + 1 hr (CET - Central European Time)
National Telephone Code: +377
Continent: Europe
Capital: Monaco
Principal Language: French, Monégasque, English, Italian
Population: 32270
Monetary Unit: Euro (EUR)
EMBASSY HIGH COMMISSION: Consulate General of Monaco: 4 Cromwell Place, London, SW7 2JE
Tel: 020 7225 2679
Fax: 020 7581 8161 / Embassy- Email : embassy.uk@gouv.mc 7 Upper Grosvenor Street Mayfair London W1K 2LX Phone : + 44 (0)20 7318 1083 Fax : +44 (0)20 7493 4563 - Lévrier Béatrice Assistant to Mme Eveline Genta, Consul General Email : beatricelevrier@gouv.mc Embassy of Monaco and Chamber of Economic Development Phone : + 44 (0)20 7318 1083 Fax : +44 (0)20 7493 4563 - Roberge Stephan Email : dtc.london@gouv.mc Monaco Government Tourist and Convention Office Phone : +44 (0)20 7491 4264 Fax : +44 (0)20 7408 2487

LA GAZETTE DE MONACO
6974MC80-5
Editorial: 57 rue Grimaldi, Le Panorama - Bloc A-B, 98000 MONACO **Tel:** 9 32 52 03 6 **Fax:** 9 79 80 14 1
Email: lagazette@aip.mc **Web site:** http://www.lagazettedemonaco.com
Date Established: 1977; **Freq:** Monthly; **Cover Price:** EUR 2,75
Annual Sub.: EUR 40; **Circ:** 10,000
Usual Pagination: 48
Editor: Max Poggi
Profile: Magazine for the Monaco - Côte d'Azur area. Includes regional, national, and international news as well as political, economic, sports and fashion items.
Language(s): French
CONSUMER: RURAL & REGIONAL INTEREST

MONACO ECONOMIE
764213MC1A-100
Editorial: Le Soleil d'Or, 20 Boulevard Rainier III, 98000 MONACO **Tel:** 9 21 61 80 2 **Fax:** 9 21 61 80 3
Email: info@davidson.mc **Web site:** http://www.davidson.mc

Date Established: 1995; **Freq:** Quarterly; **Cover Price:** EUR 5
Annual Sub.: EUR 16; **Circ:** 12,000
Usual Pagination: 80
Editor: Liana Caso-Bertaggia
Profile: Magazine focusing on finance and economics.
Language(s): English; French
BUSINESS: FINANCE & ECONOMICS

MONACO HEBDO
764081MC72-200
Editorial: 27 boulevard d'Italie, 98000 MONACO
Tel: 9 35 05 65 2 **Fax:** 9 35 01 92 2
Web site: http://www.monacohebdo.mc
Date Established: 1995; **Freq:** Weekly; **Cover Price:** EUR 1,50
Annual Sub.: EUR 53; **Circ:** 6,000
Usual Pagination: 52
Editor: Roberto Testa
Profile: Regional publication focussing on local news and current affairs including economics, society, culture and sport.
Language(s): French
LOCAL NEWSPAPERS

MONACO-MATIN EDITION MONEGASQUE DE NICE-MATIN
1619616MC67B-1
Editorial: 41 rue Grimaldi, 98000 MONACO
Tel: 9 31 04 39 0 **Fax:** 9 31 04 39 9
Email: monaco@nicematin.fr **Web site:** http://www.nicematin.fr
Freq: Daily - matin; **Cover Price:** EUR 0.85
Annual Sub.: EUR 309
Usual Pagination: 28
Profile: Monaco edition of the regional daily newspaper focussing on news and current affairs including TV guide, sport, real estate, economics and women's interest magazine supplement.
Language(s): French
Mechanical Data: Type Area: A 4
REGIONAL DAILY & SUNDAY NEWSPAPERS: Regional Daily Newspapers

L' OBSERVATEUR DE MONACO
1835184MC67J-1
Editorial: 27 boulevard d'Italie, 98000 MONACO
Tel: 9 79 75 95 9 **Fax:** 9 79 75 95 0
Email: gok@lobservateurdemonaco.mc **Web site:** http://www.lobservateurdemonaco.mc
Date Established: 2005; **Freq:** Monthly; **Cover Price:** EUR 2,50
Annual Sub.: EUR 25; **Circ:** 1,600
Usual Pagination: 90
Editor: Georges-Olivier Kalifa
Profile: Regional newspaper focussing on local news and current affairs including regional interest, health, economics, culture, leisure and cinema.
Language(s): French
REGIONAL DAILY & SUNDAY NEWSPAPERS: Regional Newspapers (excl. dailies)

PASSION PALACES
1853139MC89A-2
Editorial: 'Le Victoria', 13 boulevard Princesse Charlotte, 98000 MONACO **Tel:** 97 70 24 10
Fax: 93 25 54 13
Email: ovmarechal@mediaplus.mc **Web site:** http://www.passion-palaces.com
ISSN: 1998-6181
Freq: 3 issues yearly; **Cover Price:** EUR 6,90
Annual Sub.: EUR 70; **Circ:** 20,000
Usual Pagination: 144
Language(s): French
CONSUMER: HOLIDAYS & TRAVEL: Travel

PNEUMATIQUE MAGAZINE
600954F91A-170
Editorial: Sam Edicom - Le Roqueville, Bât C -20 bd Princesse-Charlotte, 98000 MONACO
Tel: 9 79 70 62 7 **Fax:** 9 79 70 62 8
Email: contact@sam-edicom.com **Web site:** http://www.pneumag.com
ISSN: 1774-8445
Date Established: 1997; **Freq:** 6 issues yearly; **Cover Price:** EUR 6
Annual Sub.: EUR 32; **Circ:** 31,000
Usual Pagination: 116
Editor: Jean-Marc Moréno; **Publisher:** Sabine Toesca
Profile: Boating magazine focusing on inflatable dinghies and boats.
Language(s): French
Readership: Aimed at those interested in inflatable boats and dinghies.
CONSUMER: RECREATION & LEISURE: Boating & Yachting

Netherlands

Time Difference: GMT + 1 hr (CET - Central European Time)
National Telephone Code: +31
Continent: Europe
Capital: Amsterdam
Principal Language: Dutch
Population: 16318199
Monetary Unit: Euro (EUR)

EMBASSY HIGH COMMISSION: Royal Netherlands Embassy: 38 Hyde Park Gate, London SW7 5DP
Tel: 020 7590 3200
Fax: 020 7225 0947
Email: london@netherlands-embassy.org.uk
Website: http://www.netherlands-embassy.org.uk / Head of Mission : H E Pim Waldeck (the Ambasador)

AAN DE HAND
16925N62J-10
Editorial: Emmastraat 18, 8011 AG ZWOLLE
Tel: 13 4662445 **Fax:** 88 2697490
Email: info@inspiritmedia.nl **Web site:** http://www.aandehand.nl
Freq: 8 issues yearly; **Cover Price:** EUR 4,70
Annual Sub.: EUR 32,60; **Circ:** 15,000
Editor: Inge Pauw; **Editor-in-Chief:** P. Kok;
Publisher: Leendert de Jong
Profile: Journal concerning educating from a Christian viewpoint.
Language(s): Dutch
Readership: Aimed at Christian parents and carers.
ADVERTISING RATES:
Full Page Mono .. EUR 1/1: f.c. 1198,-; 1/2: f.c. 698,-; 1/4: f.c. 398,-
Agency Commission: 15%
Mechanical Data: Type Area: 206 x 270mm, Bleed Size: 216 x 280mm
BUSINESS: CHURCH & SCHOOL EQUIPMENT & EDUCATION: Teachers & Education Management

AAN DE SLAG
1636742N94X-438
Editorial: Torenstraat 144b, 2513 BW DEN HAAG
Tel: 23 5566770 **Fax:** 570 614795
Email: info@performa.nl
Date Established: 01-11-2000; **Freq:** 9 issues yearly;
Annual Sub.: EUR 189,50; **Circ:** 2,200
Editor: Hans Delissen; **Publisher:** Hans Delissen
Language(s): Dutch
ADVERTISING RATES:
Full Page Mono EUR 1/1: f.c. 1795,-; b/w 1395,- 1/2: f.c. 990,-; b/w 829,- 1/4: f.c. 595,-; b/w 495,-
Agency Commission: 15%
Mechanical Data: Type Area: 180 x 270mm, Bleed Size: 210 x 297mm
Copy instructions: *Copy Date:* 2 weeks prior to publication date
CONSUMER: OTHER CLASSIFICATIONS: Miscellaneous

AANDRIJFTECHNIEK
16049N19A-5
Editorial: Informaticaweg 3c, 7007 CP DOETINCHEM **Tel:** 53 4842842
Email: industrialmedia@eisma.nl **Web site:** http://www.at-aandrijftechniek.nl
Freq: 10 issues yearly; **Annual Sub.:** EUR 232,-;
Circ: 5,467
Editor: Ad Spijkers; **Editor-in-Chief:** Liedy Bisselink;
Publisher: Henk Meinen
Profile: Magazine supplying information on design, construction, maintenance and use of components and systems for power transmission and their associated control systems as well as ancillary components.
Language(s): Dutch
Readership: Aimed at machine and installation designers.
ADVERTISING RATES:
Full Page Mono .... EUR 1/1: f.c. 4223,-; f.c. color 3175,-; b/w 2217,- 1/2: f.c. 2570,-; f.c. color 2016,-; b/w 1170,- 1/4:
Agency Commission: 15%
Mechanical Data: Type Area: 200 x 275mm, Bleed Size: 235 x 310mm
Copy instructions: *Copy Date:* 3 weeks prior to publication date
BUSINESS: ENGINEERING & MACHINERY

AANNEMER
15667N4E-5
Editorial: Informaticaweg 3c, 7007 CP DOETINCHEM **Tel:** 76 5301715
Date Established: 01-01-1989; **Freq:** 10 issues yearly; **Annual Sub.:** EUR 235,-; **Circ:** 8,000
Editor: Peter de Winter; **Publisher:** Rex Bierlaagh
Profile: Journal providing information on the building trade.
Language(s): Dutch
Readership: Read by building contractors, subcontractors and site supervisors.
ADVERTISING RATES:
Full Page Mono EUR 1/1: f.c. 4722,-; b/w 2992,- 1/2: f.c. 3057,-; b/w 1585,- 1/4: f.c. 2135,-; b/w 840,-
Agency Commission: 15%
Mechanical Data: Type Area: 218 x 298mm, Bleed Size: 240 x 320mm
BUSINESS: ARCHITECTURE & BUILDING: Building

AARDAPPELWERELD MAGAZINE
16199N26C-5
Editorial: Van Stolkweg 31, 2585 JN DEN HAAG
Tel: 314 349422 **Fax:** 30 2643525
Freq: Monthly; **Annual Sub.:** EUR 77,50; **Circ:** 3,000
Editor: Jaap Delleman; **Editor-in-Chief:** Leo Hanse
Profile: Journal about potato-growing.
Language(s): Dutch
Readership: Read by farmers and wholesalers.
ADVERTISING RATES:
Full Page Mono .. EUR 1/1: b/w 1495,- 1/2: b/w 780,- 1/4: b/w 425,-
Agency Commission: 15%
Mechanical Data: Type Area: 184 x 234mm, Bleed Size: 210 x 297mm
Copy instructions: *Copy Date:* 2 weeks prior to publication date
BUSINESS: GARDEN TRADE

AARDSCHOK
17719N76E-5
Editorial: Wilhelminalaan 22, 5691 AZ SON
Tel: 58 2954859 **Fax:** 20 6767728
Date Established: 01-10-1980; **Freq:** 10 issues yearly; **Cover Price:** EUR 4,95
Annual Sub.: EUR 40,-; **Circ:** 19,000
Usual Pagination: 100
Editor: Mike van Rijswijk; **Editor-in-Chief:** Andre Verhuysen; **Publisher:** Mike van Rijswijk
Profile: Magazine about rock and heavy metal music.
Language(s): Dutch
Readership: Aimed at fans.
ADVERTISING RATES:
Full Page Mono EUR 1/1: f.c. 1800,-; b/w 1200,- 1/2: f.c. 1350,-; b/w 700,- 1/4: f.c. 900,-; b/w 400,-
Agency Commission: 15%
Mechanical Data: Type Area: 188 x 266mm, Bleed Size: 206 x 285mm
CONSUMER: MUSIC & PERFORMING ARTS: Pop Music

ABP MAGAZINE
1637161N74N-512
Editorial: Oude Lindestraat 70, 6411 EJ HEERLEN
Tel: 45 5795877 **Fax:** 20 5979614
Email: concern.communicatie@apg.nl
Freq: Half-yearly; **Cover Price:** Free; **Circ:** 1,750,000
Editor: Chris Veerkamp
Language(s): Dutch
Agency Commission: 15%
CONSUMER: WOMEN'S INTEREST CONSUMER MAGAZINES: Retirement

ABP WERELD
15542N1F-90
Editorial: Oude Lindestraat 70, 6411 EJ HEERLEN
Tel: 45 5794251 **Fax:** 229 216416
Email: concern.communicatie@abp.nl
Freq: Quarterly; **Cover Price:** Free; **Circ:** 22,000
Editor: Marcel Vleugels
Profile: Official journal of the ABP, a Dutch company specialising in pensions, insurance, social security and institutional investments. Provides news, articles and information about their activities and business developments.
Language(s): Dutch
Readership: Aimed at investors and people seeking to do business with the company.
Agency Commission: 15%
BUSINESS: FINANCE & ECONOMICS: Investment

ACADEMISCHE BOEKENGIDS
1634250N62R-307
Editorial: Herengracht 221, 1016 BG AMSTERDAM
Tel: 23 5565001 **Fax:** 20 5928600
Email: info@aup.nl **Web site:** http://www.academischeboekengids.nl
Freq: 6 issues yearly; **Cover Price:** EUR 4,50
Annual Sub.: EUR 33,50; **Circ:** 55,000
Editor: Inge van der Bijl; **Editor-in-Chief:** Wardy Poelsta
Language(s): Dutch
ADVERTISING RATES:
Full Page Mono EUR 1/1: b/w 3900,- 1/2: b/w 2400,- 1/3: b/w 1600,-
Agency Commission: 15%
Mechanical Data: Type Area: 246 x 327mm, Bleed Size: 273 x 392mm
Copy instructions: *Copy Date:* 4 weeks prior to publication date
BUSINESS: CHURCH & SCHOOL EQUIPMENT & EDUCATION: Education Related

ACCO.WIJZER
1635980N14R-221
Editorial: Zuidpoolsingel 2, 2408 ZE ALPHEN A/D RIJN **Tel:** 88 2697112 **Fax:** 88 2696983
Email: support@acco.nl
Date Established: 01-01-1993; **Freq:** Annual; **Cover Price:** Free; **Circ:** 25,000
Language(s): Dutch
ADVERTISING RATES:
Full Page Mono .... EUR 1/1: f.c. 2400,-
Agency Commission: 15%
Mechanical Data: Type Area: 193 x 297mm, Bleed Size: 210 x 297mm
BUSINESS: COMMERCE, INDUSTRY & MANAGEMENT: Commerce Related

ACHTERHOEK MAGAZINE
16940N63-4
Editorial: Koopmanslaan 12, 7005 BK DOETINCHEM
Tel: 20 5310161 **Fax:** 20 5302585
Web site: http://www.achterhoekmagazine.nl
Date Established: 28-11-1993; **Freq:** 6 issues yearly;
Annual Sub.: EUR 15,-; **Circ:** 14,500
Usual Pagination: 64
Editor-in-Chief: W. Jansen van Velsen; **Publisher:** W. Jansen van Velsen
Profile: Magazine for businesses in the Achterhoek region.
Language(s): Dutch
ADVERTISING RATES:
Full Page Mono EUR 2/1: f.c. 2680,-; b/w 2365,- 1/1: f.c. 1470,-; b/w 1245,- 1/2: f.c. 900,-; b/w 720,-
Agency Commission: 15%
Mechanical Data: Type Area: 182 x 257mm, Bleed Size: 210 x 297mm
BUSINESS: REGIONAL BUSINESS

ACTIVA
761384N1A-140
Editorial: Rompertdreef 7, 5233 ED 'S-HERTOGENBOSCH **Tel:** 13 4662445
Fax: 88 2697490
Email: noab@noab.nl
Freq: 5 issues yearly; **Annual Sub.:** EUR 45,-; **Circ:** 2,500
Editor: Ed de Vlam
Profile: Official Magazine of NOAB containing information on fiscal, financial and capital administration.
Language(s): Dutch
ADVERTISING RATES:
Full Page Mono EUR 1/1: f.c. 1850,-; 1/2: f.c. 1095,-; 1/4: f.c. 750,-
Agency Commission: 15%
Mechanical Data: Type Area: 185 x 240mm, Bleed Size: 220 x 295mm
Copy instructions: *Copy Date:* 4 weeks prior to publication date
BUSINESS: FINANCE & ECONOMICS

DE ACTUARIS
15513N1D-3
Editorial: Groenewoudsedijk 80, 3528 BK UTRECHT
Tel: 76 5722984 **Fax:** 570 614795
Email: info@ag-ai.nl
Freq: 6 issues yearly; **Annual Sub.:** EUR 75,-; **Circ:** 3,000
Editor: J.D. Berkemeijer; **Editor-in-Chief:** F. van Thooft
Profile: Publication of the Dutch Association of Actuaries.
Language(s): Dutch
ADVERTISING RATES:
Full Page Mono EUR 1/1: f.c. 3515,-; 1/2: f.c. 2585,-; 1/4: f.c. 1645,-
Agency Commission: 15%
Mechanical Data: Type Area: 190 x 250mm, Bleed Size: 210 x 270mm
Copy instructions: *Copy Date:* 3 weeks prior to publication date
BUSINESS: FINANCE & ECONOMICS: Insurance

AD GROENE HART
1634965N67B-7307
Editorial: Raoul Wallenbergplein 9, 2405 CZ ALPHEN A/D RIJN **Tel:** 76 5876329 **Fax:** 0032 34660067
Email: gh.redactie@ad.nl **Web site:** http://www.ad.nl/groenehart
Freq: 312 issues yearly; **Annual Sub.:** EUR 258,50;
Circ: 40,574
Editor: Christiaan Ruesink; **Editor-in-Chief:** Peter Paul Marijnen; **Publisher:** Eric-Paul Dijkhuizen
Language(s): Dutch
ADVERTISING RATES:
Full Page Mono EUR 1/1: b/w 5417,- 1/2: b/w 3683,- 1/4: b/w 1500,- 1/1 ed. za.: b/w 5749,- 1/2 ed. za.: b/w 3909,- 1/4
Agency Commission: 15%
Mechanical Data: Type Area: 266 x 398mm
REGIONAL DAILY & SUNDAY NEWSPAPERS: Regional Daily Newspapers

AD ROTTERDAMS DAGBLAD
17127N67B-6100
Editorial: Westblaak 180, 3012 KN ROTTERDAM
Tel: 10 4004200 **Fax:** 20 6247476
Email: rd.redactie@ad.nl **Web site:** http://www.ad.nl/rotterdam
Freq: 312 issues yearly; **Annual Sub.:** EUR 258,50;
Circ: 125,194
Editor: Bart Verkade; **Editor-in-Chief:** Eddy Nuijten;
Publisher: Eric-Paul Dijkhuizen
Language(s): Dutch

ADVERTISING RATES:
Full Page Mono .... EUR 1/1: b/w 16.746,- 1/2: b/w 11.387,- 1/4: b/w 4637,- 1/1 ed. za.: b/w 17.773,- 1/2 ed. za.: b/w 12.08
Agency Commission: 15%
Mechanical Data: Type Area: 266 x 398mm
REGIONAL DAILY & SUNDAY NEWSPAPERS: Regional Daily Newspapers

AD UTRECHTS NIEUWSBLAD
17119N67B-6550
Editorial: Hengeveldstraat 29, 3572 KH UTRECHT
Tel: 30 6399911 **Fax:** 30 6399937
Web site: http://www.ad.nl/utrecht
Freq: 312 issues yearly; **Annual Sub.:** EUR 258,50; **Circ:** 55,932
Editor: Christiaan Ruesink; **Editor-in-Chief:** Koert Bouwman; **Publisher:** Eric-Paul Dijkhuizen
Language(s): Dutch
ADVERTISING RATES:
Full Page Mono EUR 1/1: b/w 7681,- 1/2: b/w 5223,- 1/4: b/w 2127,- 1/1 ed. za.: b/w 8152,- 1/2 ed. za.: b/ w 5543,- 1/4
Agency Commission: 15%
Mechanical Data: Type Area: 266 x 398mm
REGIONAL DAILY & SUNDAY NEWSPAPERS: Regional Daily Newspapers

AD-VISIE
1636768N14F-184
Editorial: Het Spoor 2, 3994 AK HOUTEN
Tel: 10 4274107 **Fax:** 79 3467846
Freq: 6 issues yearly; **Circ:** 2,705
Editor: Karel Bootsman; **Publisher:** Peter Gijbers
Language(s): Dutch
ADVERTISING RATES:
Full Page Mono EUR 1/1: f.c. 2094,-; b/w 1373,- 1/2: f.c. 1745,-; b/w 1024,- 1/4: f.c. 1458,-; b/w 737,-
Agency Commission: 15%
Mechanical Data: Type Area: 180 x 254mm, Bleed Size: 210 x 297mm
BUSINESS: COMMERCE, INDUSTRY & MANAGEMENT: Training & Recruitment

AFVALFORUM
16285N32B-10
Editorial: Hugo de Grootlaan 39, 5223 LB 'S-HERTOGENBOSCH **Tel:** 30 6383743
Fax: 229 216416
Email: info@verenigingafvalbedrijven.nl
Date Established: 01-02-1997; **Freq:** Quarterly; **Annual Sub.:** EUR 35,-; **Circ:** 2,500
Editor: D.A.C. van Vleuten; **Publisher:** D.A.C. van Vleuten
Profile: Magazine with information on developments in waste disposal and waste policy in the Netherlands and adjoining countries.
Language(s): Dutch
ADVERTISING RATES:
Full Page Mono .. EUR 1/1: b/w 1295,- 1/2: b/w 850,-
Agency Commission: 15%
Mechanical Data: Type Area: 185 x 270mm, Bleed Size: 210 x 297mm
BUSINESS: LOCAL GOVERNMENT, LEISURE & RECREATION: Public Health & Cleaning

AGRAAF
16142N21J-3
Editorial: Handelsweg 2, 7041 GX 'S-HEERENBERG
Tel: 172 466622 **Fax:** 172 440681
Email: info@agrio.nl **Web site:** http://www.agraaf.nl
Date Established: 01-01-1997; **Freq:** 25 issues yearly; **Annual Sub.:** EUR 34,50; **Circ:** 9,250
Editor: R. Ellenkamp; **Publisher:** Ben van Uhm
Profile: Journal concerning farming in West Holland.
Language(s): Dutch
Readership: Read by farmers.
Agency Commission: 15%
Mechanical Data: Type Area: 264 x 390mm, Bleed Size: 290 x 420mm
BUSINESS: AGRICULTURE & FARMING: Agriculture & Farming - Regional

AIOS
16645N56A-2_25
Editorial: Janssoniuslaan 34-36, 3528 AJ UTRECHT
Tel: 30 6702719 **Fax:** 88 7518231
Email: secretariaat@lvag.nl
Date Established: 01-01-1989; **Freq:** Quarterly; **Annual Sub.:** EUR 20,-; **Circ:** 5,400
Editor: Daniël Dresden; **Editor-in-Chief:** Heidi Wals; **Publisher:** Monika Lens-Kerckhoffs
Profile: Official journal of the LVAG - Dutch National Association of Junior Doctors.
Language(s): Dutch
Readership: Read by junior doctors.
ADVERTISING RATES:
Full Page Mono EUR 1/1: f.c. 2125,-; b/w 1417,- 1/2: f.c. 1508,-; b/w 800,- 1/4: f.c. 1208,-; b/w 500,-
Agency Commission: 15%
Mechanical Data: Type Area: 180 x 260mm, Bleed Size: 210 x 297mm
Copy instructions: *Copy Date:* 2 weeks prior to publication date
BUSINESS: HEALTH & MEDICAL

AJAX LIFE
17573N75B-5
Editorial: Mijlweg 61, 3316 BE DORDRECHT
Tel: 88 2696139 **Fax:** 88 2697175
Email: info@zpress-magazines.nl **Web site:** http:// www.ajaxlife.nl
Freq: 20 issues yearly; **Cover Price:** Free; **Circ:** 63,000
Editor: Sander Zeldenrijk
Profile: Magazine of the Association of Ajax Supporters.
Language(s): Dutch
Agency Commission: 15%
Mechanical Data: Bleed Size: 290 x 430mm
CONSUMER: SPORT: Football

ALAN ROGERS CAMPINGGIDSEN
1857813N91B-202
Editorial: Van Boetzelaerlaan 20, 3828 NS HOOGLAND **Tel:** 40 8447611 **Fax:** 53 4842189
Email: info@alanrogers.nl
Freq: Annual; **Circ:** 75,000
Language(s): Dutch
Agency Commission: 15%
Mechanical Data: Type Area: 114 x 216mm, Bleed Size: 149 x 241mm
CONSUMER: RECREATION & LEISURE: Camping & Caravanning

ALMERE VANDAAG
1637281N67B-7312
Editorial: Grote Markt 10, 1315 JG ALMERE
Tel: 36 5485720
Web site: http://www.almerevandaag.nl
Date Established: 04-02-2003; **Freq:** 208 issues yearly; **Cover Price:** Free; **Circ:** 78,153
Language(s): Dutch
Agency Commission: 15%
Mechanical Data: Type Area: 264 x 392mm, Bleed Size: 289 x 415mm
REGIONAL DAILY & SUNDAY NEWSPAPERS: Regional Daily Newspapers

ALPHEN.CC
1704587N67J-1
Editorial: Julianastraat 34, 2405 CH ALPHEN A/D RIJN **Tel:** 314 359940 **Fax:** 314 359978
Web site: http://www.alphen.cc
Freq: 156 issues yearly; **Annual Sub.:** EUR 60,-; **Circ:** 19,241
Language(s): Dutch
ADVERTISING RATES:
Full Page Mono .. EUR 1/1: f.c. 1434,-; 1/2: f.c. 717,-; 1/4: f.c. 359,-
Agency Commission: 15%
Mechanical Data: Type Area: 238 x 392mm
REGIONAL DAILY & SUNDAY NEWSPAPERS: Regional Newspapers (excl. dailies)

ALZHEIMER MAGAZINE
16643N56A-1_25
Editorial: Kosterijland 3, 3981 AJ BUNNIK
Tel: 0032 34660066 **Fax:** 0032 34660067
Email: info@alzheimer-nederland.nl
Date Established: 01-12-1985; **Freq:** Quarterly; **Annual Sub.:** EUR 25,-; **Circ:** 55,000
Profile: Publication about Alzheimer's disease and related disorders. Features include developments in care and research and activities of the Alzheimer's Society.
Language(s): Dutch
Agency Commission: 15%
Mechanical Data: Type Area: 246 x 380mm, Bleed Size: 297 x 420mm
BUSINESS: HEALTH & MEDICAL

AM MAGAZINE
1637158N74Q-286
Editorial: J.J. Viottastraat 50, 1071 JT AMSTERDAM
Tel: 20 5979546 **Fax:** 20 5979614
Email: info@am-media.nl **Web site:** http://www.am-magazine.nl
Freq: 6 issues yearly; **Cover Price:** EUR 5,95; **Circ:** 40,000
Editor: Riek Tawfik; **Editor-in-Chief:** Frederieke van Olffen-Nijenhuis; **Publisher:** Annemarie van Gaal
Language(s): Dutch
ADVERTISING RATES:
Full Page Mono EUR 2/1: f.c. 5750,-; 1/1: f.c. 3450,-; achterpag.: f.c. 4600,-
Agency Commission: 15%
Mechanical Data: Type Area: 195 x 250mm, Bleed Size: 215 x 285mm
CONSUMER: WOMEN'S INTEREST CONSUMER MAGAZINES: Lifestyle

AMBTELIJK CONTACT
18062N87-25
Editorial: W. van Vlietstraat 7, 3262 GM OUD-BEIJERLAND **Tel:** 30 2255065
Date Established: 01-01-1962; **Freq:** 10 issues yearly; **Annual Sub.:** EUR 12,50; **Circ:** 2,550
Editor: J.W. van Pelt; **Editor-in-Chief:** D. Quant
Profile: Magazine for those working in Christian-Reformed churches in the Netherlands.
Language(s): Dutch
Agency Commission: 15%
CONSUMER: RELIGIOUS

AMC MAGAZINE
16638N56A-1
Editorial: Meibergdreef 9, 1105 AZ AMSTERDAM
Tel: 20 6077605 **Fax:** 88 2697490
Email: voorlichting@amc.nl **Web site:** http://www. amc.nl/magazine
Date Established: 01-05-1992; **Freq:** 10 issues yearly; **Annual Sub.:** EUR 22,-; **Circ:** 17,500
Editor: Johan Kortenray; **Editor-in-Chief:** Irene van Elzakker
Profile: Magazine containing research articles from the Academic Medical Centre, covering new developments in medical health care.
Language(s): Dutch
Readership: Aimed at surgeons, doctors and nurses.
ADVERTISING RATES:
Full Page Mono .. EUR 1/1: b/w 1097,- 1/2: b/w 602,- 1/4: b/w 333,-
Agency Commission: 15%
Mechanical Data: Type Area: 208 x 240mm, Bleed Size: 235 x 280mm
Copy instructions: *Copy Date:* 3 weeks prior to publication date
BUSINESS: HEALTH & MEDICAL

DE AMELANDER
18138N89C-61
Editorial: Strandweg 1, 9162 EV BALLUM AMELAND
Tel: 58 2954859 **Fax:** 20 6767728
Email: info@deamelander.nl
Freq: 11 issues yearly; **Annual Sub.:** EUR 41,34; **Circ:** 40,000
Editor: Klaas Touwen; **Publisher:** Klaas Touwen
Language(s): Dutch
Readership: Magazine aimed at tourists of the Dutch island of Ameland.
ADVERTISING RATES:
Full Page Mono EUR 1/1: f.c. 773,-; 1/2: f.c. 387,-; 1/ 4: f.c. 194,-
Agency Commission: 15%
Mechanical Data: Type Area: 270 x 400mm, Bleed Size: 297 x 420mm
CONSUMER: HOLIDAYS & TRAVEL: Entertainment Guides

AMERSFOORT VOOR JOU
1934241N74Q-533
Editorial: Markenhaven 38, 3826 AC AMERSFOORT
Tel: 10 4518007
Web site: http://www.voorjoumagazine.nl
Date Established: 20-11-2009; **Freq:** Monthly; **Cover Price:** Free; **Circ:** 55,000
Editor-in-Chief: Jannes Bijlsma; **Publisher:** Roberto Verhagen
Language(s): Dutch
ADVERTISING RATES:
Full Page Mono EUR 2/1: b/w 3195,- 1/1: b/w 1695,- 1/2: b/w 995,- 1/4: b/w 595,-
Agency Commission: 15%
Mechanical Data: Type Area: 250 x 330mm, Bleed Size: 270 x 350mm
Copy instructions: *Copy Date:* 8 days prior to publication date
CONSUMER: WOMEN'S INTEREST CONSUMER MAGAZINES: Lifestyle

AMNESTY IN ACTIE
706921N82-2
Editorial: Keizersgracht 177, 1016 DR AMSTERDAM
Tel: 88 7518160 **Fax:** 88 7518161
Email: amnesty@amnesty.nl
Date Established: 01-01-2000; **Freq:** 10 issues yearly; **Circ:** 15,000
Usual Pagination: 20
Editor: Saskia Grootegoed; **Publisher:** Ellen Nieuwenhuis
Profile: Magazine containing information about the activities of Amnesty International and its active members.
Language(s): Dutch
Readership: Aimed at members.
Agency Commission: 15%
Mechanical Data: Type Area: 195 x 280mm, Bleed Size: 210 x 297mm
CONSUMER: CURRENT AFFAIRS & POLITICS

AMNESTYNL
1635331N82-224
Editorial: Keizersgracht 177, 1016 DR AMSTERDAM
Tel: 23 5565100 **Fax:** 23 5565105
Email: amnesty@amnesty.nl
Date Established: 01-03-2001; **Freq:** 3 issues yearly; **Circ:** 250,000
Usual Pagination: 8
Editor: M. van Ravenstein; **Editor-in-Chief:** Carolien Cuypers; **Publisher:** Ellen Nieuwenhuis
Language(s): Dutch
Agency Commission: 15%
Mechanical Data: Type Area: 280 x 190mm, Bleed Size: 297 x 210mm
CONSUMER: CURRENT AFFAIRS & POLITICS

AMSTELRING PLUS
1854670N74G-341
Editorial: A. Hofmanweg 5a, 2031 BH HAARLEM
Tel: 40 2336338 **Fax:** 40 2336470
Email: info@brandingmedia.nl
Freq: Quarterly; **Cover Price:** Free; **Circ:** 55,000
Language(s): Dutch
ADVERTISING RATES:
Full Page Mono EUR 1/1: f.c. 1870,-; 1/2: f.c. 1050,-; 1/4: f.c. 580,-
Agency Commission: 15%
Mechanical Data: Type Area: 188 x 275mm, Bleed Size: 210 x 297mm
Copy instructions: *Copy Date:* 4 weeks prior to publication date
CONSUMER: WOMEN'S INTEREST CONSUMER MAGAZINES: Slimming & Health

D' AMSTERDAMSE TRAM
16549N49A-3
Editorial: Varikstraat 77, 1106 CT AMSTERDAM
Tel: 45 5604070
Date Established: 02-09-1967; **Freq:** Weekly; **Annual Sub.:** EUR 20,-; **Circ:** 400
Usual Pagination: 8
Editor: C.J. Vonk
Profile: Magazine containing information concerning public transport in the Netherlands. Includes articles on trams, buses, the metro, timetables, routes and accident statistics.
Language(s): Dutch
Readership: Read by managers of public transport companies.
Agency Commission: 15%
BUSINESS: TRANSPORT

ANBO MAGAZINE
17522N74N-1
Editorial: Kon. Wilhelminalaan 3, 3527 LA UTRECHT
Tel: 76 5876329 **Fax:** 0032 34660067
Email: info@anbo.nl
Freq: 6 issues yearly; **Annual Sub.:** EUR 35,-; **Circ:** 163,603
Editor-in-Chief: Jolande van der Sande
Profile: Publication of the Dutch Society of Senior Citizens.
Language(s): Dutch
Readership: Read by men and women aged 50 years and over.
ADVERTISING RATES:
Full Page Mono EUR 1/1: f.c. 8915,-; 1/2: f.c. 5082,- 1/4: f.c. 2892,-
Agency Commission: 15%
Mechanical Data: Type Area: 179 x 243mm, Bleed Size: 210 x 270mm
Copy instructions: *Copy Date:* 4 weeks prior to publication date
CONSUMER: WOMEN'S INTEREST CONSUMER MAGAZINES: Retirement

ANDO NUCHTER BEKEKEN
16308N32G-3
Editorial: Paviljoenstraat 32, 9001 BR GROUW
Tel: 88 2697183
Email: margalitti.dolfijn@hetnet.nl
Date Established: 01-01-1962; **Freq:** 10 issues yearly; **Annual Sub.:** EUR 12,50; **Circ:** 1,200
Usual Pagination: 12
Editor: Afke Toren; **Editor-in-Chief:** Afke Toren
Profile: Magazine about alcohol, drugs and other dependencies.
Language(s): Dutch
Readership: Read by members of ANDO, social workers and those who help people with all types of dependencies.
Agency Commission: 15%
Mechanical Data: Type Area: 265 x 390mm, Bleed Size: 260 x 430mm
BUSINESS: LOCAL GOVERNMENT, LEISURE & RECREATION: Community Care & Social Services

ANTONIUS MAGAZINE
16644N56A-1_60
Editorial: Graaf Adolfstraat 35b, 8606 BT SNEEK
Tel: 13 4662445 **Fax:** 88 2697490
Email: info@mimicry.nl
Date Established: 10-04-1995; **Freq:** Half-yearly; **Cover Price:** Free; **Circ:** 5,000
Editor: M. Wijnja; **Editor-in-Chief:** M. Wijnja
Profile: Magazine containing information about health care, with an emphasis on hospital care.
Language(s): Dutch
ADVERTISING RATES:
Full Page Mono EUR 1/1: b/w 680,- 1/2: b/w 385,- 1/ 4: b/w 215,-
Agency Commission: 15%
Mechanical Data: Type Area: 183 x 270mm, Bleed Size: 210 x 297mm
Copy instructions: *Copy Date:* 2 weeks prior to publication date
BUSINESS: HEALTH & MEDICAL

ANWB LEDENWIJZER: HANDBOEK FIETSEN
708178N77C-3
Editorial: Wassenaarseweg 220, 2596 EC DEN HAAG **Tel:** 88 2697062 **Fax:** 88 2697659
Freq: Annual; **Circ:** 85,000
Editor: V. de Jong
Profile: Magazine containing information about cycling, including advice on purchase of new models, clothing and accessories, holiday preparation, addresses of places to rent a bicycle in the Netherlands and cycle routes in the Netherlands and Europe.
Language(s): Dutch
Readership: Aimed at the cycling enthusiast.
ADVERTISING RATES:
Full Page Mono .... EUR 1/1: f.c. 2000,-
Agency Commission: 15%
Mechanical Data: Type Area: 118 x 190mm, Bleed Size: 123 x 195mm
CONSUMER: MOTORING & CYCLING: Cycling

ANWB LEDENWIJZER: HANDBOEK KAMPEREN
1647267N91B-185
Editorial: Wassenaarseweg 220, 2596 EC DEN HAAG **Tel:** 88 2697062 **Fax:** 88 2697660
Freq: Annual; **Circ:** 130,000
Editor-in-Chief: D. Polman; **Publisher:** Frank Jacobs
Language(s): Dutch
ADVERTISING RATES:
Full Page Mono .. EUR 1/1: f.c. 3100,-; omslagpag. 2: b/w 3720,- achterpag.: b/w 3720,-

gency Commission: 15%
echanical Data: Type Area: 118 x 190mm, Bleed
ze: 123 x 195mm
ONSUMER: RECREATION & LEISURE: Camping
Caravanning

ANWB LEDENWIJZER: OP STAP N NEDERLAND 708159N89E-206

ditorial: Wassenaarseweg 220, 2596 EC DEN
AAG Tel: 88 2697062 Fax: 88 2697664
eq: Annual; Circ: 155,000
ditor: P. Dam
ofile: Magazine containing information about the
ost famous day attractions in and around the
etherlands and just across the borders in Germany,
elgium and France.
anguage(s): Dutch
eadership: Aimed at those members wishing to go
day trips.
DVERTISING RATES:
ull Page Mono .... EUR 1/1: f.c. 3700,-
gency Commission: 15%
echanical Data: Type Area: 118 x 190mm, Bleed
ze: 123 x 195mm
ONSUMER: HOLIDAYS & TRAVEL: Holidays

ANWB SPECIAL WINTERSPORT 1636513N89A-202

ditorial: Wassenaarseweg 220, 2596 EC DEN
AAG Tel: 88 2696139 Fax: 88 2697175
req: Annual; Circ: 100,000
sual Pagination: 148
ditor: M. de Winter; Publisher: Ben Belt
anguage(s): Dutch
DVERTISING RATES:
ull Page Mono EUR 1/1: f.c. 3990,-; b/w 2859,- 1/2:
c. 1999,-; b/w 1579,- 1/4: f.c. 1009,-; b/w 799,-
gency Commission: 15%
echanical Data: Type Area: 185 x 265mm, Bleed
ize: 215 x 300mm
CONSUMER: HOLIDAYS & TRAVEL: Travel

APOTHEEK & GEZONDHEID 17478N74G-335

Editorial: A. Hofmanweg 11, 2031 BH HAARLEM
Tel: 70 3353535 Fax: 570 504380
Email: info@jdcomm.nl Web site: http://www.
apotheekengezondheid.nl
Date Established: 01-01-1988; Freq: 6 issues yearly;
Cover Price: Free; Circ: 135,000
Usual Pagination: 32
Editor: Jurgen Drieskens
Profile: Magazine concerning family health.
Language(s): Dutch
Readership: Aimed at families.
ADVERTISING RATES:
Full Page Mono EUR 1/1: f.c. 3500,-; 1/2: f.c. 1850,-;
1/4: f.c. 1150,-
Agency Commission: 15%
Mechanical Data: Type Area: 190 x 260mm, Bleed
Size: 210 x 297mm
Copy instructions: *Copy Date:* 3 weeks prior to
publication date
CONSUMER: WOMEN'S INTEREST CONSUMER
MAGAZINES: Slimming & Health

ARBEIDSRECHT 1637181N44-171

Editorial: Staverenstraat 32015, 7418 CJ DEVENTER
Tel: 570 647221 Fax: 570 647803
Email: info@kluwer.nl
Freq: 10 issues yearly; Cover Price: EUR 23,50
Annual Sub.: EUR 184,-; Circ: 1,753
Editor: L.G. Verburg; Editor-in-Chief: A. Baris
Language(s): Dutch
ADVERTISING RATES:
Full Page Mono .. EUR 1/1: b/w 1075,- 1/2: b/w 650,-
1/4: b/w 350,-
Agency Commission: 15%
Mechanical Data: Type Area: 170 x 255mm, Bleed
Size: 210 x 297mm
BUSINESS: LEGAL

ARBO 1635275N14E-107

Editorial: Zuidpoolsingel 2, 2408 ZE ALPHEN A/D
RIJN Tel: 172 466316 Fax: 314 344397
Email: info@kluwer.nl Web site: http://www.
arbo-online.nl
Freq: 10 issues yearly; Cover Price: EUR 24,-
Annual Sub.: EUR 196,-; Circ: 2,873
Editor: Jacqueline Joosten; Publisher: M.N. Lim
Language(s): Dutch
ADVERTISING RATES:
Full Page Mono .. EUR 1/1: b/w 1425,- 1/2: b/w 855,-
1/4: b/w 465,-
Agency Commission: 15%
Mechanical Data: Type Area: 185 x 265mm, Bleed
Size: 210 x 297mm
BUSINESS: COMMERCE, INDUSTRY &
MANAGEMENT: Work Study

ARBO MAGAZINE 1635551N14E-108

Editorial: Oranjesingel 38, 6511 NW NIJMEGEN
Tel: 20 5979500 Fax: 20 5979590
Email: info@ravestein-zwart.nl
Freq: 10 issues yearly; Annual Sub.: EUR 204,75;
Circ: 1,098
Editor: J. Widdershoven; Publisher: Ludo de Boo
Language(s): Dutch
ADVERTISING RATES:
Full Page Mono EUR 1/1: f.c. 1484,-; PMS 1187,-; b/
w 890,- 1/2: f.c. 873,-; PMS 698,-; b/w 524,- 1/4: f.c.
513,-; PMS 4
Agency Commission: 15%
Mechanical Data: Type Area: 180 x 270mm, Bleed
Size: 210 x 297mm
BUSINESS: COMMERCE, INDUSTRY &
MANAGEMENT: Work Study

ARBO RENDEMENT 16309N32G-170

Editorial: Conradstraat 38, 3013 AP ROTTERDAM
Tel: 23 5565135 Fax: 88 5567355
Email: info@rendement.nl Web site: http://www.
arbo-rendement.nl
Date Established: 01-03-1996; Freq: 11 issues
yearly; Cover Price: EUR 27,-
Annual Sub.: EUR 264,-; Circ: 3,150
Publisher: Marnix Hoogerwerf
Profile: Magazine about health and work.
Language(s): Dutch
Readership: Read by HR Managers and directors of
companies.
ADVERTISING RATES:
Full Page Mono .. EUR 1/1: b/w 1415,- 1/2: b/w 850,-
1/4: b/w 510,-
Agency Commission: 15%
Mechanical Data: Bleed Size: 210 x 297mm, Type
Area: 190 x 260mm
Copy instructions: *Copy Date:* 1 month prior to
publication date
BUSINESS: LOCAL GOVERNMENT, LEISURE &
RECREATION: Community Care & Social Services

ARBOUW MAGAZINE 15671N4E-15

Editorial: Ceintuurbaan 2, 3847 LG HARDERWIJK
Tel: 20 5159189 Fax: 314 349037
Email: info@arbouw.nl
Date Established: 10-06-2010; Freq: Quarterly;
Cover Price: Free; Circ: 210,000
Usual Pagination: 24
Editor: Dennis Derksen; Editor-in-Chief: Dennis
Derksen
Profile: General building journal.
Language(s): Dutch
Readership: Read by builders and construction
engineers.
Agency Commission: 15%
BUSINESS: ARCHITECTURE & BUILDING:
Building

ARCHEOLOGIE MAGAZINE 18253N94X-6

Editorial: Storm van 's-Gravesandeweg 8, 2242 JH
WASSENAAR Tel: 88 7518800 Fax: 20 5353696
Web site: http://www.archeologiemagazine.nl
Freq: 6 issues yearly; Annual Sub.: EUR 37,50; Circ:
6,000
Editor: Lou Lichtenberg; Editor-in-Chief: I.
Geraerdts; Publisher: Pepijn Dobbelaer
Profile: Magazine about archeology.
Language(s): Dutch
ADVERTISING RATES:
Full Page Mono EUR 1/1: f.c. 695,-; 1/2: f.c. 395,-; 1/
4: f.c. 225,-
Agency Commission: 15%
Mechanical Data: Type Area: 195 x 265mm, Bleed
Size: 215 x 285mm
CONSUMER: OTHER CLASSIFICATIONS:
Miscellaneous

ARCHIEVENBLAD 16875N60B-10

Editorial: Markt 1, 6811 CG ARNHEM
Tel: 35 6726800 Fax: 35 6726803
Email: bureau@kvan.nl Web site: http://www.
archievenblad.nl
Date Established: 01-01-1896; Freq: 10 issues
yearly; Cover Price: EUR 7,80
Annual Sub.: EUR 76,50; Circ: 1,800
Editor: Hans Berende; Editor-in-Chief: Joris van
Dierendonck
Profile: Magazine dealing with public records.
Language(s): Dutch
Readership: Aimed at archivists, records keepers
and people working in public records offices.
ADVERTISING RATES:
Full Page Mono EUR 1/1: b/w 715,- 1/2: b/w 395,- 1/
4: b/w 225,-
Agency Commission: 15%
Mechanical Data: Type Area: 185 x 270mm, Bleed
Size: 210 x 297mm
BUSINESS: PUBLISHING: Libraries

ARCHITECTUUR EN BOUWEN 15681N4E-76_50

Editorial: Zuidergrachtswal 25, 8933 AE
LEEUWARDEN Tel: 76 5722984 Fax: 570 614795
Email: uhn@planet.nl
Freq: Quarterly; Annual Sub.: EUR 31,50; Circ:
14,000
Editor: H.J. Hendriks; Publisher: H.J. Hendriks
Profile: Magazine about all aspects of the building
trade in the northern part of the Netherlands.
Language(s): Dutch
Readership: Read by architects and building
contractors.
ADVERTISING RATES:
Full Page Mono EUR 1/1: b/w 2595,- 1/2: b/w 1495,-
1/4: b/w 995,-
Agency Commission: 15%
Mechanical Data: Type Area: 185 x 270mm, Bleed
Size: 210 x 297mm
BUSINESS: ARCHITECTURE & BUILDING:
Building

ARKE MAGAZINE 1923881N50-189

Editorial: Jacob Marisstraat 34-2, 1058 JA
AMSTERDAM Tel: 30 6383716
Email: hmpbusiness@gmail.com
Freq: Half-yearly; Cover Price: Free; Circ: 100,000
Editor-in-Chief: Titia Voûte
Language(s): Dutch
ADVERTISING RATES:
Full Page Mono EUR 1/1: f.c. 3300,-; 1/2: f.c. 1925,-;
1/4: f.c. 1050,-
Agency Commission: 15%
BUSINESS: TRAVEL & TOURISM

ARMEX DEFENSIE MAGAZINE 16395N40-20

Editorial: Vogelzand 2311, 1788 GE DEN HELDER
Tel: 20 6077605 Fax: 88 2697490
Email: info@onsleger.nl
Date Established: 01-09-1915; Freq: 6 issues yearly;
Annual Sub.: EUR 25,-; Circ: 2,500
Editor: P.K. Smit; Editor-in-Chief: C. Homan
Profile: Independent journal covering Dutch land
forces, defence policy, arms control and East-West
relations.
Language(s): Dutch
ADVERTISING RATES:
Full Page Mono .... EUR 1/1: f.c. 1575,-; f.c. color
1200,-; b/w 750,-
Agency Commission: 15%
Mechanical Data: Type Area: 185 x 270mm, Bleed
Size: 210 x 297mm
Copy instructions: *Copy Date:* 3 weeks prior to
publication date
BUSINESS: DEFENCE

ARTS EN APOTHEKER 16646N56A-2_28

Editorial: Tweede Jacob van Campenstraat 101,
1073 XP AMSTERDAM Tel: 88 2697112
Fax: 88 2696983
Email: info@mediamedica.nl
Freq: 6 issues yearly; Annual Sub.: EUR 27,50; Circ:
13,520
Publisher: Thomas Kat
Profile: Magazine containing articles about the
integration of conventional and non-conventional
medicine into modern day patient care.
Language(s): Dutch
Readership: Aimed at doctors, pharmacists and food
specialists.
ADVERTISING RATES:
Full Page Mono .. EUR 1/1: f.c. 1795,-; 1/2: f.c. 985,-;
1/4: f.c. 540,-
Agency Commission: 15%
Mechanical Data: Type Area: 185 x 272mm, Bleed
Size: 210 x 297mm
Copy instructions: *Copy Date:* 3 weeks prior to
publication date
BUSINESS: HEALTH & MEDICAL

AS, MAANDBLAD VOOR DE ACTIVITEITENSECTOR 1635526N56R-228

Editorial: Keizersgracht 213, 1016 DT AMSTERDAM
Tel: 76 5722984 Fax: 570 614795
Email: info@y-publicaties.nl
Freq: 10 issues yearly; Cover Price: EUR 9,50
Annual Sub.: EUR 92,-; Circ: 1,853
Editor: Ralf Beekveldt; Publisher: Ben Konings
Language(s): Dutch
ADVERTISING RATES:
Full Page Mono EUR 1/1: f.c. 2930,-; b/w 1121,- 1/2:
f.c. 2393,-; b/w 669,- 1/4: f.c. 1936,-; b/w 403,-
Agency Commission: 15%
Mechanical Data: Type Area: 195 x 265mm, Bleed
Size: 215 x 285mm
BUSINESS: HEALTH & MEDICAL: Health Medical
Related

AUDI MAGAZINE 17796N77E-72

Editorial: Aletta Jacobslaan 7, 1066 BP
AMSTERDAM Tel: 20 5518518 Fax: 20 6269407
Email: info@rhbm.nl
Freq: Quarterly; Cover Price: Free; Circ: 155,000
Usual Pagination: 96
Editor: Hans Verstraaten
Profile: Lifestyle magazine for Audi owners.
Language(s): Dutch
ADVERTISING RATES:
Full Page Mono .... EUR 1/1: f.c. 5460,-
Agency Commission: 15%
Mechanical Data: Bleed Size: 230 x 300mm, Type
Area: 215 x 280mm
Copy instructions: *Copy Date:* 4 weeks prior to
publication date
CONSUMER: MOTORING & CYCLING: Club Cars

AUTO BUSINESS AMSTERDAM 706926N31R-50

Editorial: Essebaan 77, 2908 LJ CAPELLE A/D
IJSSEL Tel: 33 4608953 Fax: 71 3643461
Freq: 5 issues yearly; Circ: 6,000
Editor: Nile van Leeuwen
Profile: Magazine containing information about car
leasing, sales, rentals, new models and tests.
Language(s): Dutch
Readership: Aimed at the managers of local
businesses.
ADVERTISING RATES:
Full Page Mono .. EUR 1/1: b/w 1597,- 1/2: b/w 862,-
1/4: b/w 474,-
Agency Commission: 15%
Mechanical Data: Type Area: 180 x 260mm, Bleed
Size: 210 x 297mm
BUSINESS: MOTOR TRADE: Motor Trade Related

AUTO BUSINESS DEN HAAG 706941N31A-168

Editorial: Essebaan 77, 2908 LJ CAPELLE A/D
IJSSEL Tel: 23 5565370 Fax: 475 551033
Freq: 5 issues yearly; Circ: 5,400
Editor: Nile van Leeuwen
Profile: Magazine giving information about car
leasing, sales, rentals, new models and tests.
Language(s): Dutch
Readership: Aimed at the management of local
businesses.
ADVERTISING RATES:
Full Page Mono .. EUR 1/1: b/w 1484,- 1/2: b/w 799,-
1/4: b/w 439,-
Agency Commission: 15%
Mechanical Data: Type Area: 180 x 260mm, Bleed
Size: 210 x 297mm
BUSINESS: MOTOR TRADE: Motor Trade
Accessories

AUTO BUSINESS DRECHTSTEDEN E.O. 706943N31A-158

Editorial: Essebaan 77, 2908 LJ CAPELLE A/D
IJSSEL Tel: 46 4116600 Fax: 71 3643461
Freq: Monthly; Circ: 4,675
Editor: Nile van Leeuwen
Profile: Magazine giving information about car
leasing, sales, rentals, new models and tests.
Language(s): Dutch
Readership: Aimed at the management of local
businesses.
ADVERTISING RATES:
Full Page Mono .. EUR 1/1: b/w 1277,- 1/2: b/w 686,-
1/4: b/w 381,-
Agency Commission: 15%
Mechanical Data: Type Area: 180 x 260mm, Bleed
Size: 210 x 297mm
BUSINESS: MOTOR TRADE: Motor Trade
Accessories

AUTO BUSINESS HOEKSCHE WAARD 706961N31A-166

Editorial: Essebaan 77, 2908 LJ CAPELLE A/D
IJSSEL Tel: 23 5565370 Fax: 23 5565357
Freq: Quarterly; Circ: 2,500
Editor: Nile van Leeuwen
Profile: Magazine giving information about car
leasing, sales, rentals, new models and tests.
Language(s): Dutch
Readership: Aimed at the management of local
businesses.
ADVERTISING RATES:
Full Page Mono EUR 1/1: b/w 941,- 1/2: b/w 511,- 1/
4: b/w 282,-
Agency Commission: 15%
Mechanical Data: Type Area: 180 x 260mm, Bleed
Size: 210 x 297mm
BUSINESS: MOTOR TRADE: Motor Trade
Accessories

AUTO BUSINESS ROTTERDAM 706997N31A-170

Editorial: Essebaan 77, 2908 LJ CAPELLE A/D
IJSSEL Tel: 23 5565370 Fax: 55 5412288
Freq: 5 issues yearly; Circ: 5,750
Editor: Nile van Leeuwen
Profile: Magazine giving information about car
leasing, sales, rentals, new models and tests.
Language(s): Dutch
Readership: Aimed at the management of local
businesses.
ADVERTISING RATES:
Full Page Mono .. EUR 1/1: b/w 1564,- 1/2: b/w 842,-
1/4: b/w 465,-
Agency Commission: 15%
Mechanical Data: Type Area: 180 x 260mm, Bleed
Size: 210 x 297mm
BUSINESS: MOTOR TRADE: Motor Trade
Accessories

AUTO BUSINESS 'T GOOI 706924N31A-156

Editorial: Essebaan 77, 2908 LJ CAPELLE A/D
IJSSEL Tel: 46 4116600 Fax: 71 3643461
Freq: 5 issues yearly; Circ: 5,640
Editor: Nile van Leeuwen
Profile: Magazine with information about leasing,
sales, renting, tests and new models.
Language(s): Dutch
Readership: Aimed at the management of local
businesses.
ADVERTISING RATES:
Full Page Mono .. EUR 1/1: b/w 1483,- 1/2: b/w 799,-
1/4: b/w 448,-
Agency Commission: 15%

Mechanical Data: Type Area: 180 x 260mm, Bleed Size: 210 x 297mm
BUSINESS: MOTOR TRADE: Motor Trade Accessories

AUTO BUSINESS UTRECHT
707003N31A-155
Editorial: Essebaan 77, 2908 LJ CAPELLE A/D IJSSEL **Tel:** 46 4116600 **Fax:** 46 4116310
Freq: 5 issues yearly; **Circ:** 5,400
Editor: Nile van Leeuwen
Profile: Magazine giving information about car leasing, sales, rentals, new models and tests.
Language(s): Dutch
Readership: Aimed at the management of local businesses.
ADVERTISING RATES:
Full Page Mono .. EUR 1/1: b/w 1453,- 1/2: b/w 781,- 1/4: b/w 430,-
Agency Commission: 15%
Mechanical Data: Type Area: 180 x 260mm, Bleed Size: 210 x 297mm
BUSINESS: MOTOR TRADE: Motor Trade Accessories

AUTO BUSINESS VOORNE PUTTEN
707005N31A-165
Editorial: Essebaan 77, 2908 LJ CAPELLE A/D IJSSEL **Tel:** 23 5565370 **Fax:** 23 5565357
Freq: 5 issues yearly; **Circ:** 3,250
Editor: Nile van Leeuwen
Profile: Magazine giving information about car leasing, sales, rentals, new models and tests.
Language(s): Dutch
Readership: Aimed at the management of local businesses.
ADVERTISING RATES:
Full Page Mono .. EUR 1/1: b/w 1005,- 1/2: b/w 542,- 1/4: b/w 303,-
Agency Commission: 15%
Mechanical Data: Type Area: 180 x 260mm, Bleed Size: 210 x 297mm
BUSINESS: MOTOR TRADE: Motor Trade Accessories

AUTO & MOTOR TECHNIEK
16246N31A-9
Editorial: Hanzestraat 1, 7006 RH DOETINCHEM **Tel:** 314 349540 **Fax:** 314 343991
Email: klantenservice@reedbusiness.nl **Web site:** http://www.amt.nl
Freq: Monthly; **Annual Sub.:** EUR 129,90; **Circ:** 19,734
Editor: Auke Cupédo; **Editor-in-Chief:** Michel Buyvoets; **Publisher:** Geert van den Bosch
Profile: Technical and management journal concerning private and commercial vehicles. Provides organisation news from INNOVAM, ATC and VOC.
Language(s): Dutch
Readership: Aimed at proprietors of motor vehicle companies.
ADVERTISING RATES:
Full Page Mono EUR 1/1: f.c. 4968,-; b/w 2955,- 1/2: f.c. 3157,-; b/w 1563,- 1/4: f.c. 2305,-; b/w 824,-
Agency Commission: 15%
Mechanical Data: Type Area: 187 x 257mm, Bleed Size: 215 x 285mm
Copy instructions: *Copy Date:* 3 weeks prior to publication date
BUSINESS: MOTOR TRADE: Motor Trade Accessories

AUTO IN BEDRIJF
16550N49A-4
Editorial: Aletta Jacobslaan 7, 1066 BP AMSTERDAM **Tel:** 30 2321276 **Fax:** 317 424060
Email: info@rhbm.nl
Freq: 3 issues yearly; **Cover Price:** Free; **Circ:** 30,000
Usual Pagination: 36
Editor: H. Thoma; **Editor-in-Chief:** Nina Knobbe
Profile: Magazine about the management of company cars.
Language(s): Dutch
Readership: Read by car fleet owners.
ADVERTISING RATES:
Full Page Mono .... EUR 1/1: f.c. 2500,-
Agency Commission: 15%
Mechanical Data: Bleed Size: 210 x 297mm
Copy instructions: *Copy Date:* 4 weeks prior to publication date
BUSINESS: TRANSPORT

AUTO IN MINIATUUR
17817N79B-10
Editorial: Postbus 16004, 2301 GA LEIDEN
Tel: 76 5876329
Email: voorzitter@namac.nl
Freq: 6 issues yearly; **Cover Price:** EUR 4,-
Annual Sub.: EUR 24,-; **Circ:** 7,500
Editor: Paul Arets; **Editor-in-Chief:** Albert Gerbel;
Publisher: Otto Snel
Profile: Magazine focusing on model cars.
Language(s): Dutch
Readership: Read by collectors.
ADVERTISING RATES:
Full Page Mono EUR 1/1: b/w 550,- 1/2: b/w 330,- 1/4: b/w 180,-
Agency Commission: 15%
Mechanical Data: Type Area: 190 x 269mm, Bleed Size: 210 x 297mm
Copy instructions: *Copy Date:* 5 weeks prior to publication date
CONSUMER: HOBBIES & DIY: Models & Modelling

AUTO MOTOR KLASSIEK
17800N77F-25
Editorial: Veldstraat 112, 7071 CE ULFT
Tel: 35 6726751 **Fax:** 35 6726752
Email: info@wilberspublishing.nl **Web site:** http://www.amklassiek.nl
Freq: Monthly; **Cover Price:** EUR 3,50
Annual Sub.: EUR 32,50; **Circ:** 19,398
Editor: M.L. Wilbers; **Editor-in-Chief:** Oscar Wilbers
Profile: Magazine for lovers of classic cars and motorcycles.
Language(s): Dutch
ADVERTISING RATES:
Full Page Mono EUR 2/1: f.c. 4800,-; 1/1: f.c. 2675,-; 1/2: f.c. 1350,-
Agency Commission: 15%
Mechanical Data: Type Area: 178 x 249mm, Bleed Size: 213 x 291mm
CONSUMER: MOTORING & CYCLING: Veteran Cars

AUTOGIDS VOOR ROTTERDAM
1634543N77A-262
Editorial: Essebaan 77, 2908 LJ CAPELLE A/D IJSSEL **Tel:** 23 5567955 **Fax:** 23 5567956
Web site: http://www.autogids.nl
Freq: 26 issues yearly; **Cover Price:** Free; **Circ:** 102,551
Editor: Nile van Leeuwen
Language(s): Dutch
Agency Commission: 15%
Mechanical Data: Type Area: 264 x 400mm, Bleed Size: 290 x 420mm
CONSUMER: MOTORING & CYCLING: Motoring

AUTOKOMPAS
16248N31A-15
Editorial: Kon. Wilhelminaplein 30-7, 1062 KR AMSTERDAM **Tel:** 346 577390 **Fax:** 346 577389
Email: info@railangfords.nl **Web site:** http://www.autokompas.nl
Freq: 16 issues yearly; **Cover Price:** EUR 6,-
Annual Sub.: EUR 75,75; **Circ:** 17,845
Editor: Rick Bolt; **Editor-in-Chief:** Emil Peeters;
Publisher: Ron Brokking
Profile: Magazine about all aspects of the motor trade.
Language(s): Dutch
ADVERTISING RATES:
Full Page Mono EUR 1/1: f.c. 2822,-; 1/2: f.c. 1504,-; 1/4: f.c. 802,-
Agency Commission: 15%
Mechanical Data: Type Area: 265 x 380mm, Bleed Size: 289 x 415mm
BUSINESS: MOTOR TRADE: Motor Trade Accessories

HET AUTOMOBIEL KLASSIEKER MAGAZINE
17801N77F-35
Editorial: Veldstraat 112, 7071 CE ULFT
Tel: 30 6383766 **Fax:** 30 6383991
Email: info@wilberspublishing.nl **Web site:** http://www.hetautomobiel.nl
Date Established: 01-04-1980; **Freq:** Monthly;
Cover Price: EUR 4,95
Annual Sub.: EUR 49,50; **Circ:** 15,000
Editor: Oscar Wilbers
Profile: Magazine focusing on popular classic cars.
Language(s): Dutch
Readership: Magazine aimed at lovers of classic cars.
ADVERTISING RATES:
Full Page Mono EUR 2/1: f.c. 3400,-; 1/1: f.c. 1875,-; 1/2: f.c. 950,-
Agency Commission: 15%
Mechanical Data: Type Area: 185 x 268mm, Bleed Size: 213 x 303mm
CONSUMER: MOTORING & CYCLING: Veteran Cars

AUTOMOTIVE
16250N31A-35_50
Editorial: Kon. Wilhelminaplein 30-7, 1062 KR AMSTERDAM **Tel:** 40 2473330 **Fax:** 172 466577
Email: info@railangfords.nl **Web site:** http://www.automotive-online.nl
Freq: 18 issues yearly; **Cover Price:** EUR 4,75
Annual Sub.: EUR 119,-; **Circ:** 10,217
Editor: Jelle Heidstra; **Editor-in-Chief:** B. Kuipers;
Publisher: Ron Brokking
Profile: Journal covering all aspects of the car trade.
Language(s): Dutch
Readership: Aimed at car dealers, managers, importers and distributors.
ADVERTISING RATES:
Full Page Mono EUR 1/1: f.c. 3065,-; 1/2: f.c. 1780,-; 1/4: f.c. 1040,-
Agency Commission: 15%
Mechanical Data: Type Area: 190 x 265mm, Bleed Size: 210 x 285mm
BUSINESS: MOTOR TRADE: Motor Trade Accessories

AUTO-PLUS
1637154N77A-293
Editorial: Akeleiweg 200, 9731 JD GRONINGEN
Tel: 20 5979546 **Fax:** 20 5979614
Web site: http://www.autoplusonline.nl
Date Established: 01-07-2002; **Freq:** 11 issues yearly; **Cover Price:** Free; **Circ:** 152,500
Editor: Evert Flapper; **Publisher:** Evert Flapper
Language(s): Dutch
Agency Commission: 15%
Mechanical Data: Type Area: 264 x 385mm, Bleed Size: 286 x 415mm
Copy instructions: *Copy Date:* 2 weeks prior to publication date
CONSUMER: MOTORING & CYCLING: Motoring

AV&ENTERTAINMENT MAGAZINE
1752563N5F-242
Editorial: Kerkenbos 12-26c, 6546 BE NIJMEGEN
Tel: 20 5310919 **Fax:** 492 371114
Email: info@vanmunstermedia.nl **Web site:** http://www.av-entertainment.nl
Freq: 6 issues yearly; **Annual Sub.:** EUR 39,-; **Circ:** 4,728
Editor: Teun van Thiel
Language(s): Dutch
ADVERTISING RATES:
Full Page Mono .. EUR 1/1: b/w 1791,- 1/2: b/w 949,- 1/4: b/w 499,-
Agency Commission: 15%
Mechanical Data: Type Area: 190 x 260mm, Bleed Size: 215 x 285mm
BUSINESS: COMPUTERS & AUTOMATION: Multimedia

AVANTGARDE
17432N74B-10
Editorial: Joan Muyskenweg 6-6a, 1096 CJ AMSTERDAM **Tel:** 20 5979500 **Fax:** 20 5979590
Email: info@publishing.audax.nl **Web site:** http://www.avantgarde.nl
Freq: 6 issues yearly; **Cover Price:** EUR 4,95
Annual Sub.: EUR 39,60; **Circ:** 40,846
Editor: Robert van der Sanden; **Editor-in-Chief:** Martine Bruynooge
Profile: Magazine about fashion in the Netherlands.
Language(s): Dutch
Readership: Aimed at the modern woman.
ADVERTISING RATES:
Full Page Mono .... EUR 2/1: f.c. 13.500,-; 1/1: f.c. 6750,-; 1/2: f.c. 5065,-
Agency Commission: 15%
Mechanical Data: Type Area: 170 x 244mm, Bleed Size: 205 x 275mm
Copy instructions: *Copy Date:* 4 weeks prior to publication date
CONSUMER: WOMEN'S INTEREST CONSUMER MAGAZINES: Women's Interest - Fashion

AZIË
18160N89E-10
Editorial: Striensestraat 100, 5241 AZ ROSMALEN
Tel: 38 4279423 **Fax:** 38 4279420
Email: boazie@wxs.nl **Web site:** http://www.aziemagazine.nl
Date Established: 01-02-1987; **Freq:** 6 issues yearly;
Annual Sub.: EUR 27,70; **Circ:** 25,000
Usual Pagination: 76
Editor: Eildert de Boer; **Publisher:** Eildert de Boer
Profile: Independent travel magazine.
Language(s): Dutch
ADVERTISING RATES:
Full Page Mono EUR 1/1: b/w 2300,- 1/2: b/w 1250,- 1/4: b/w 650,-
Agency Commission: 15%
Mechanical Data: Type Area: 190 x 260mm, Bleed Size: 215 x 285mm
Copy instructions: *Copy Date:* 3 weeks prior to publication date
CONSUMER: HOLIDAYS & TRAVEL: Holidays

BAAZ
1872923N78E-14
Editorial: Delftweg 147, 2289 BD RIJSWIJK
Tel: 20 6211374 **Fax:** 70 3855505
Email: info@clipboard-publishing.nl **Web site:** http://www.baaz.nl
Freq: Quarterly; **Circ:** 65,000
Editor: Marcel Burger; **Publisher:** Linda Oenema
Language(s): Dutch
ADVERTISING RATES:
Full Page Mono EUR 2/1: b/w 6950,- 1/1: b/w 4395,- 1/2: b/w 2975,-
Agency Commission: 15%
Mechanical Data: Type Area: 215 x 285mm
CONSUMER: CONSUMER ELECTRONICS: Home Computing

BABY WERELD
16547N48C-100
Editorial: Populierenlaantje 2, 1272 CW HUIZEN
Tel: 72 5188825 **Fax:** 20 5159143
Email: ruiters@baby-wereld.nl **Web site:** http://www.baby-wereld.nl
Date Established: 01-09-1991; **Freq:** Quarterly;
Annual Sub.: EUR 17,70; **Circ:** 950
Editor: Carola Siksma-Ruiters; **Editor-in-Chief:** B. Daams; **Publisher:** Carola Siksma-Ruiters
Profile: Trade journal specialised in baby hardware and toddler goods.
Language(s): Dutch
Readership: Aimed at retailers and suppliers.
ADVERTISING RATES:
Full Page Mono .. EUR 1/1: f.c. 1550,-; 1/2: f.c. 850,-; 1/4: f.c. 465,-
Agency Commission: 15%
Mechanical Data: Type Area: 185 x 267mm, Bleed Size: 210 x 297mm
Copy instructions: *Copy Date:* 1 month prior to publication date
BUSINESS: TOY TRADE & SPORTS GOODS: Toy Trade - Baby Goods

BABYGIDS
1748143N74D-16
Editorial: Capellalaan 65, 2132 JL HOOFDDORP
Tel: 10 4066333 **Fax:** 229 216416
Email: info@jongegezinnen.nl **Web site:** http://www.babygids.net
Freq: Annual; **Cover Price:** Free; **Circ:** 100,000
Editor: Carla van Klaveren
Language(s): Dutch
ADVERTISING RATES:
Full Page Mono EUR 1/1: b/w 5500,- 1/2: b/w 3300
Agency Commission: 15%
Mechanical Data: Bleed Size: 133 x 213mm
CONSUMER: WOMEN'S INTEREST CONSUMER MAGAZINES: Child Care

BABY'S EERSTE JAREN
17458N74D-
Editorial: Dorpsstraat 608, 1723 HJ NOORD-SCHARWOUDE **Tel:** 20 6211374
Email: info@positiveresult.nl
Freq: Annual; **Cover Price:** EUR 3,95; **Circ:** 150,000
Editor: Daniëlle van der Lee; **Publisher:** Joanna van Kleef
Profile: Magazine containing articles about the care of babies and toddlers.
Language(s): Dutch
Readership: Aimed at new parents.
ADVERTISING RATES:
Full Page Mono EUR 1/1: b/w 8488,- 1/2: b/w 4988,- 1/4: b/w 3188,-
Agency Commission: 15%
Mechanical Data: Type Area: 187 x 252mm, Bleed Size: 215 x 285mm
Copy instructions: *Copy Date:* 6 weeks prior to publication date
CONSUMER: WOMEN'S INTEREST CONSUMER MAGAZINES: Child Care

BABYSTUF
1742967N74D-165
Editorial: Populierenlaantje 2, 1272 CW HUIZEN
Tel: 20 5612070 **Fax:** 314 343991
Email: info@babystuf.nl **Web site:** http://www.babystuf.nl
Date Established: 22-03-2006; **Freq:** Annual; **Cover Price:** EUR 5,95; **Circ:** 60,000
Usual Pagination: 224
Editor: Carola Siksma-Ruiters; **Publisher:** Carola Siksma-Ruiters
Language(s): Dutch
ADVERTISING RATES:
Full Page Mono EUR 1/1: f.c. 3690,-; 1/2: f.c. 1990,-; 1/4: f.c. 1150,-
Agency Commission: 15%
Mechanical Data: Type Area: 185 x 267mm, Bleed Size: 210 x 290mm
Copy instructions: *Copy Date:* 2 months prior to publication date
CONSUMER: WOMEN'S INTEREST CONSUMER MAGAZINES: Child Care

BAKSTEEN
15670N4E-13
Editorial: Florijnweg 6, 6883 JP VELP
Tel: 23 5344089 **Fax:** 10 4739911
Email: knb@knb-baksteen.nl
Date Established: 01-09-1990; **Freq:** Half-yearly;
Annual Sub.: EUR 14,00; **Circ:** 5,000
Usual Pagination: 24
Editor: E.L.J. van Hal
Profile: Journal of the Royal Association of Dutch Clay Brick Manufacturers.
Language(s): Dutch
Readership: Aimed at architects, builders, wholesalers, suppliers, students and college lecturers.
Agency Commission: 15%
BUSINESS: ARCHITECTURE & BUILDING: Building

BALLONSTOF
17639N75N-50
Editorial: Spechtstraat 16, 1223 NZ HILVERSUM
Tel: 88 2697049
Email: secretariaat@knvvlballonvaren.info
Freq: Quarterly; **Cover Price:** EUR 4,95
Annual Sub.: EUR 13,-; **Circ:** 400
Usual Pagination: 32
Editor: Rutger Coucke; **Editor-in-Chief:** Judith Coucke-Beemer
Profile: Journal of the Dutch Society of Ballooning Enthusiasts.
Language(s): Dutch
Readership: Read by balloonists, officials and flight enthusiasts.
ADVERTISING RATES:
Full Page Mono EUR 1/1: b/w 217,- 1/2: b/w 115,- 1/4: b/w 61,-
Agency Commission: 15%
Mechanical Data: Type Area: 177 x 243mm, Bleed Size: 212 x 299mm
CONSUMER: SPORT: Flight

BANKING REVIEW
15506N1C-20
Editorial: Stationsplein 2, 3112 HJ SCHIEDAM
Tel: 10 4274128 **Fax:** 88 7518231
Email: info@nijgh.nl **Web site:** http://www.bankingreview.nl

eq: 6 issues yearly; **Cover Price:** EUR 15,-
nual Sub.: EUR 185,-; **Circ:** 4,121
itor: Wim Assink; **Editor-in-Chief:** Ingka van
pen; **Publisher:** Rinus Vissers
ofile: Magazine about all aspects of banking and
ancial institutions.
nguage(s): Dutch
adership: Read by managers in the banking and
ance sector.
VERTISING RATES:
Il Page Mono EUR 1/1: f.c. 3600,-; PMS 2900,-; b/
2350,- 1/2: f.c. 2700,-; PMS 1900,-; b/w 1350,- 1/4:
2300,-;
ency Commission: 15%
echanical Data: Type Area: 200 x 255mm, Bleed
:e: 225 x 285mm
py instructions: *Copy Date:* 2 weeks prior to
blication date
SINESS: FINANCE & ECONOMICS: Banking

ASISSCHOOLMANAGEMENT
16923N62J-40
litorial: Zuidpoolsingel 2, 2408 ZE ALPHEN A/D
IJN **Tel:** 172 466539 **Fax:** 172 463270
nail: info@kluwer.nl
ate Established: 01-01-1999; **Freq:** 8 issues yearly;
over Price: EUR 18,-
nual Sub.: EUR 115,-; **Circ:** 4,148
litor-in-Chief: B. de Koning; **Publisher:** Jacqueline
eeburg
ofile: Journal containing news and information for
anagement in primary schools.
nguage(s): Dutch
OVERTISING RATES:
ll Page Mono EUR 1/1: f.c. 2050,-; b/w 1150,- 1/2:
:. 1345,-; b/w 675,- 1/4: f.c. 825,-; b/w 375,-
gency Commission: 15%
echanical Data: Type Area: 185 x 265mm, Bleed
ze: 210 x 297mm
USINESS: CHURCH & SCHOOL EQUIPMENT & DUCATION: Teachers & Education Management

3B BINNENLANDS BESTUUR
16339N32K-30
ditorial: Zuidpoolsingel 2, 2408 ZE ALPHEN A/D
IJN **Tel:** 172 466911 **Fax:** 172 466980
mail: info@kluwer.nl **Web site:** http://www.
innenlandsbestuur.nl
req: 47 issues yearly; **Annual Sub.:** EUR 187,-;
irc: 52,173
ditor: Erik van Zwam; **Editor-in-Chief:** R. Edens;
ublisher: Melle Eijckelhoff
rofile: Journal covering all aspects of civil service
dministration.
anguage(s): Dutch
DVERTISING RATES:
ull Page Mono EUR 1/1: b/w 4965,- 1/2: b/w 2890,-
/4: b/w 1640,-
gency Commission: 15%
lechanical Data: Type Area: 190 x 268mm, Bleed
ize: 210 x 297mm
USINESS: LOCAL GOVERNMENT, LEISURE & ECREATION: Civil Service

BB DIGITAAL BESTUUR
1732830N5E-221
Editorial: Zuidpoolsingel 2, 2408 ZE ALPHEN A/D
RIJN **Tel:** 172 466911 **Fax:** 172 466980
Email: info@kluwer.nl **Web site:** http://www.
digitaalbestuur.nl
Freq: 8 issues yearly; **Annual Sub.:** EUR 72,-; **Circ:**
3,850
Editor: Erik van Zwam
Language(s): Dutch
ADVERTISING RATES:
Full Page Mono EUR 1/1: b/w 2730,- 1/2: b/w 1638,-
1/4: b/w 887,-
Agency Commission: 15%
Mechanical Data: Type Area: 185 x 265mm, Bleed
Size: 210 x 297mm
BUSINESS: COMPUTERS & AUTOMATION: Data Transmission

BD MAGAZINE
1860028N74Q-456
Editorial: Emmaplein 25, 5211 VZ 'S-
HERTOGENBOSCH **Tel:** 35 6256179
Fax: 73 6157171
Circ: 103,727
Editor: Ton Rooms; **Publisher:** Annemieke Besseling
Language(s): Dutch
Agency Commission: 15%
CONSUMER: WOMEN'S INTEREST CONSUMER MAGAZINES: Lifestyle

BEDRIJVIG BOXTEL/ SCHIJNDEL
630293N32A-13
Editorial: Vluchtoord 1, 5406 XP UDEN
Tel: 88 2697183 **Fax:** 88 2697490
Email: contact@dewinter.nl
Date Established: 01-12-1999; **Freq:** Quarterly;
Cover Price: Free; **Circ:** 4,600
Editor: Marco de Jonge Baas; **Editor-in-Chief:**
Edwin Gelissen
Profile: Magazine covering communication between
local municipalities and organisations in both Boxtel
and Schijndel.
Language(s): Dutch
Readership: Aimed at government officials and the
local community.

ADVERTISING RATES:
Full Page Mono EUR 2/1: f.c. 2445,-; 1/1: f.c. 1445,-;
1/2: f.c. 910,-
Agency Commission: 15%
Mechanical Data: Type Area: 186 x 267mm, Bleed
Size: 210 x 297mm
Copy instructions: *Copy Date:* 4 weeks prior to
publication date
BUSINESS: LOCAL GOVERNMENT, LEISURE & RECREATION: Local Government

BEDUMER NIEUWS EN ADVERTENTIEBLAD
626604N72-360
Editorial: Stationsweg 29, 9781 CG BEDUM
Tel: 88 7518380 **Fax:** 88 7518381
Email: info@haan-bedum.nl
Freq: 26 issues yearly; **Cover Price:** Free; **Circ:**
4,600
Editor: H.N. Dool
Language(s): Dutch
Agency Commission: 15%
Mechanical Data: Type Area: 290 x 465mm
LOCAL NEWSPAPERS

DE BEELDENAAR
17832N79E-6
Editorial: Postbus 11, 3500 AA UTRECHT
Tel: 55 5390222 **Fax:** 570 614795
Email: info@debeeldenaar.nl
Date Established: 01-01-1976; **Freq:** 6 issues yearly;
Cover Price: EUR 6,-
Annual Sub.: EUR 25,-; **Circ:** 1,400
Editor: Janjaap Luijt; **Publisher:** Frans Weijer
Profile: Magazine about the collection of coins and
medals.
Language(s): Dutch
Readership: Aimed at coin and medal collectors.
ADVERTISING RATES:
Full Page Mono EUR 1/1: f.c. 236,-; 1/2: f.c. 158,-; 1/
4: f.c. 95,-
Agency Commission: 15%
Mechanical Data: Type Area: 150 x 200mm, Bleed
Size: 168 x 245mm
CONSUMER: HOBBIES & DIY: Numismatics

BEET SPORTVISSERS-MAGAZINE
18202N92-220
Editorial: Takkebijsters 57a, 4817 BL BREDA
Tel: 570 648866 **Fax:** 570 6208980
Email: info@vipmedia.nl **Web site:** http://www.beet.
nl
Date Established: 01-05-1976; **Freq:** Monthly;
Cover Price: EUR 4,95
Annual Sub.: EUR 49,50; **Circ:** 80,000
Editor: Pierre Bronsgeest; **Editor-in-Chief:** P.
Vermeulen; **Publisher:** Jan Diepenbroek
Profile: International sport fishing magazine.
Language(s): Dutch
Readership: Read by sports anglers.
ADVERTISING RATES:
Full Page Mono EUR 1/1: f.c. 2620,-; PMS 2310,-; b/
w 1765,- 1/2: f.c. 1325,-; PMS 1185,-; b/w 915,- 1/4:
f.c. 690,-; PM
Agency Commission: 15%
Mechanical Data: Type Area: 185 x 260mm, Bleed
Size: 215 x 280mm
Copy instructions: *Copy Date:* 4 weeks prior to
publication date
CONSUMER: ANGLING & FISHING

BELONING EN BELASTING
15553N1M-9_50
Editorial: Vonderweg 24, 5616 RM EINDHOVEN
Tel: 229 270002 **Fax:** 20 6208980
Email: info@euroforum-uitgeverij.nl **Web site:** http://
www.beloningenbelasting.nl
Freq: 24 issues yearly; **Annual Sub.:** EUR 489,-
Editor: L. Porsius
Profile: Newsletter about wage taxation and national
insurance.
Language(s): Dutch
Readership: Aimed at wages administrators, HR
managers, controllers, tax advisors and accountants.
Agency Commission: 15%
BUSINESS: FINANCE & ECONOMICS: Taxation

BEM! MAGAZINE
1994118N74G-365
Editorial: Koopmanslaan 3, 7005 BK DOETINCHEM
Tel: 30 2303508
Web site: http://www.bemmagazine.nl
Freq: 5 issues yearly; **Annual Sub.:** EUR 25,-; **Circ:**
80,000
Editor: Roos Schreuder-van der Linden; **Editor-in-Chief:** Anneke van der Linden; **Publisher:** Roos
Schreuder-van der Linden
Language(s): Dutch
ADVERTISING RATES:
Full Page Mono EUR 1/1: b/w 7995,- 1/2: b/w 4797,-
1/4: b/w 2878,-
Agency Commission: 15%
Mechanical Data: Type Area: 190 x 260mm, Bleed
Size: 220 x 290mm
CONSUMER: WOMEN'S INTEREST CONSUMER MAGAZINES: Slimming & Health

DE BERGEN OP ZOOMSE BODE
626607N72-380
Editorial: Sint Catharinaplein 12, 4611 TS BERGEN
OP ZOOM **Tel:** 70 3751758 **Fax:** 15 2126695
Web site: http://www.internetbode.nl

Freq: Weekly; **Circ:** 29,400
Editor: Vif Janssen; **Editor-in-Chief:** Vif Janssen
Language(s): Dutch
Agency Commission: 15%
Mechanical Data: Type Area: 264 x 400mm
LOCAL NEWSPAPERS

DE BERGEN OP ZOOMSE BODE, ED. ZONDAG
749179N72-7531
Editorial: Sint Catharinaplein 12, 4611 TS BERGEN
OP ZOOM **Tel:** 172 466622 **Fax:** 24 3723631
Web site: http://www.internetbode.nl
Freq: Weekly; **Circ:** 29,800
Editor: Vif Janssen; **Editor-in-Chief:** Vif Janssen
Language(s): Dutch
Agency Commission: 15%
Mechanical Data: Type Area: 264 x 400mm
LOCAL NEWSPAPERS

BERICHTEN BUITENLAND
16091N21A-43_25
Editorial: Rotterdamseweg 402d-e, 2629 HH DELFT
Tel: 33 4220082 **Fax:** 20 5465530
Date Established: 01-01-1974; **Freq:** 10 issues
yearly; **Cover Price:** Free; **Circ:** 3,800
Usual Pagination: 28
Editor: J. Rogers
Profile: Magazine containing information about
agricultural trade, projects and markets.
Language(s): Dutch
Readership: Read by professionals in the agricultural
sector.
Agency Commission: 15%
BUSINESS: AGRICULTURE & FARMING

DE BERICHTGEVER
17854N80-3
Editorial: Broeksloot 43, 3474 HS ZEGVELD
Tel: 10 4274102
Date Established: 13-02-1946; **Freq:** 10 issues
yearly; **Cover Price:** Free; **Circ:** 1,100
Editor: G. Ton
Profile: Magazine containing news for the residents
of Zegveld and Meije.
Language(s): Dutch
ADVERTISING RATES:
Full Page Mono EUR 1/1: b/w 205,- 1/2: b/w 105,- 1/
4: b/w 55,-
Agency Commission: 15%
Mechanical Data: Bleed Size: 210 x 297mm
CONSUMER: RURAL & REGIONAL INTEREST

BEROEPENKRANT VMBO/MBO
1637365N14F-194
Editorial: Hugo de Grootlaan 5, 3314 AE
DORDRECHT **Tel:** 30 2738234
Web site: http://www.beroepenkrant.nl
Date Established: 01-09-1973; **Freq:** Half-yearly;
Cover Price: EUR 1,-; **Circ:** 60,000
Editor: Marcel Roemers; **Publisher:** Cees
Blankevoort
Language(s): Dutch
ADVERTISING RATES:
Full Page Mono EUR 1/1: b/w 3200,- 1/2: b/w 1850,-
1/4: b/w 1000,- advertorial: b/w 1500,-
Agency Commission: 15%
Mechanical Data: Type Area: 265 x 385mm, Bleed
Size: 220 x 390mm
BUSINESS: COMMERCE, INDUSTRY & MANAGEMENT: Training & Recruitment

DE BETERE WERELD
1857875N57-151
Editorial: Prinsengracht 675, 1017 JT AMSTERDAM
Tel: 40 8447611 **Fax:** 53 4842189
Email: info@debeterewereld.nl **Web site:** http://www.
debeterewereld.nl
Date Established: 01-01-2007; **Freq:** 6 issues yearly;
Cover Price: Free; **Circ:** 550,000
Editor: Almar Fernhout; **Editor-in-Chief:** Jasper van
der Pol; **Publisher:** Almar Fernhout
Language(s): Dutch
ADVERTISING RATES:
Full Page Mono .... EUR 2/1: b/w 17.995,- 1/1: b/w
9995,- 1/2: b/w 7595,- 1/4: b/w 4995,-
Agency Commission: 15%
Mechanical Data: Type Area: 275 x 395mm, Bleed
Size: 299 x 420mm
BUSINESS: ENVIRONMENT & POLLUTION

BETONVERENIGINGSNIEUWS
16445N42R-5
Editorial: Büchnerweg 3, 2803 GR GOUDA
Tel: 79 3628628 **Fax:** 0032 34660067
Email: info@betonvereniging.nl
Date Established: 01-01-1993; **Freq:** 7 issues yearly;
Circ: 4,750
Editor: Dick Stoelhorst; **Editor-in-Chief:** Bram
Rensen
Profile: Magazine containing information about
construction in concrete and cement, contains details
of trade fairs and exhibitions.
Language(s): Dutch
Readership: Read by directors of construction
companies.
ADVERTISING RATES:
Full Page Mono EUR 1/1: b/w 840,- 1/2: b/w 550,- 1/
4: b/w 315,-
Agency Commission: 15%

Mechanical Data: Bleed Size: 210 x 297mm
BUSINESS: CONSTRUCTION: Construction Related

BEVERPOST
18196N91D-55
Editorial: Larikslaan 5, 3833 AM LEUSDEN
Tel: 15 2617997 **Fax:** 229 216416
Email: info@scouting.nl
Date Established: 24-01-1986; **Freq:** 6 issues yearly;
Annual Sub.: EUR 23,-; **Circ:** 10,000
Editor: R. Groenman
Profile: Magazine for members of Scouting
Nederland.
Language(s): Dutch
Readership: Aimed at all members of the movement
from 5 years up to adult leaders.
Agency Commission: 15%
Mechanical Data: Type Area: 185 x 268mm, Bleed
Size: 200 x 275mm
CONSUMER: RECREATION & LEISURE: Children & Youth

BIBLIOTHEEKBLAD
16876N60B-20
Editorial: Grote Marktstraat 43, 2511 BH DEN HAAG
Tel: 13 4662445 **Fax:** 88 2697490
Freq: 20 issues yearly; **Annual Sub.:** EUR 122,64;
Circ: 2,700
Editor: Eimer Wieldraaijer; **Editor-in-Chief:** Kees
Vreeburg; **Publisher:** André Henderickx
Profile: Magazine published by the Dutch Centre for
Public Libraries and Literature.
Language(s): Dutch
ADVERTISING RATES:
Full Page Mono EUR 1/1: b/w 880,- 1/2: b/w 498,- 1/
4: b/w 295,-
Agency Commission: 15%
Mechanical Data: Type Area: 190 x 274mm, Bleed
Size: 210 x 297mm
BUSINESS: PUBLISHING: Libraries

THE BIG BLACK BOOK
1800428N86C-257
Editorial: Delflandlaan 4, 1062 EB AMSTERDAM
Tel: 314 377831 **Fax:** 314 377839
Email: info@pelicanmags.nl
Freq: Half-yearly; **Cover Price:** EUR 4,95; **Circ:**
80,000
Editor: Carlo Brantsen; **Editor-in-Chief:** Martin van
der Zeeuw; **Publisher:** F.N. Kloppert
Language(s): Dutch
ADVERTISING RATES:
Full Page Mono .... EUR 2/1: f.c. 13.500,-; 1/1: f.c.
6750,-; 1/2: f.c. 5063,-
Agency Commission: 15%
Mechanical Data: Type Area: 210 x 270mm, Bleed
Size: 230 x 297mm
Copy instructions: *Copy Date:* 4 weeks prior to
publication date
CONSUMER: ADULT & GAY MAGAZINES: Men's Lifestyle Magazines

BIGTWIN BIKERLIFESTYLE
17763N77B-20
Editorial: Postbus 256, 4100 AG CULEMBORG
Tel: 20 5302586 **Fax:** 20 5302586
Web site: http://www.bigtwin.nl
Freq: Monthly; **Cover Price:** EUR 5,90
Annual Sub.: EUR 50,-; **Circ:** 30,000
Editor: Gerard van den Akker; **Editor-in-Chief:**
Margot Gerritsen; **Publisher:** Gerard van den Akker
Profile: Magazine containing articles about
motorcycling, includes information about new
models, international events and accessories.
Language(s): Dutch
Readership: Read by motor cyclists.
ADVERTISING RATES:
Full Page Mono EUR 2/1: f.c. 4336,-; PMS 3496,-; b/
w 2510,-** 1/1: f.c. 2430,-; PMS 2000,-; b/w 1460,-**
1/2: f.c. 1333
Agency Commission: 15%
Mechanical Data: Type Area: 210 x 280mm, Bleed
Size: 230 x 300mm
Copy instructions: *Copy Date:* 3 weeks prior to
publication date
CONSUMER: MOTORING & CYCLING: Motorcycling

DE BIJENKORF MAGAZINE
1794842N74Q-347
Editorial: s-Gravenhekje 1a, 1011 TG AMSTERDAM
Tel: 55 5388220 **Fax:** 23 5564588
Web site: http://www.debijenkorf-magazine.nl
Date Established: 01-01-2009; **Freq:** 9 issues yearly;
Cover Price: Free; **Circ:** 500,000
Usual Pagination: 100
Editor: W. Achterberg; **Editor-in-Chief:** J. Ferwerda
Language(s): Dutch
ADVERTISING RATES:
Full Page Mono .... EUR 2/1: f.c. 32.000,-; 1/1: f.c.
18.500,-
Agency Commission: 15%
Mechanical Data: Bleed Size: 222 x 287mm
Copy instructions: *Copy Date:* 5 weeks prior to
publication date
CONSUMER: WOMEN'S INTEREST CONSUMER MAGAZINES: Lifestyle

BIKE EUROPE 16262N31C-20
Editorial: Hanzestraat 1, 7006 RH DOETINCHEM
Tel: 346 577390 **Fax:** 346 577389
Email: klantenservice@reedbusiness.nl **Web site:** http://www.bike-eu.com
Freq: 10 issues yearly; **Annual Sub.:** EUR 257,50; **Circ:** 5,572
Editor: Jack Oortwijn; **Editor-in-Chief:** Jan willem van Schaik; **Publisher:** Geert van den Bosch
Profile: International journal covering the bicycle and scooter industries.
Language(s): Dutch
Readership: Read by importers, manufacturers and component makers.
ADVERTISING RATES:
Full Page Mono EUR 1/1: f.c. 6131,-; b/w 3333,- 1/2: f.c. 4673,-; b/w 1869,- 1/4: f.c. 3848,-; b/w 1052,-
Agency Commission: 15%
Mechanical Data: Type Area: 265 x 383mm, Bleed Size: 300 x 420mm
BUSINESS: MOTOR TRADE: Bicycle Trade

DE BILDTSE POST 627279N72-455
Editorial: Warmoesstraat 49, 9076 ZN ST. ANNAPAROCHIE **Tel:** 20 5208581 **Fax:** 314 349044
Date Established: 01-01-1937; **Freq:** Weekly; **Circ:** 18,600
Editor: G.M. de Jong; **Editor-in-Chief:** D.J. de Jong; **Publisher:** D.J. de Jong
Language(s): Dutch
Agency Commission: 15%
Mechanical Data: Type Area: 392 x 530mm
LOCAL NEWSPAPERS

BINGO! 1634992N79F-92
Editorial: Hogehilweg 13, 1101 CA AMSTERDAM
Tel: 33 4637977 **Fax:** 33 4637976
Email: info@keesing.com
Freq: 18 issues yearly; **Circ:** 50,000
Language(s): Dutch
ADVERTISING RATES:
Full Page Mono EUR 1/1: f.c. 1815,-; 1/2: f.c. 1030,-; 1/4: f.c. 515,-
Agency Commission: 15%
Mechanical Data: Type Area: 210 x 253mm, Bleed Size: 230 x 285mm
Copy instructions: *Copy Date:* 3 weeks prior to publication date
CONSUMER: HOBBIES & DIY: Games & Puzzles

BINK! 1814221N19E-43
Editorial: Treubstraat 1b, 2288 EG RIJSWIJK
Tel: 40 2071162 **Fax:** 20 5852965
Email: info@bpmt.nl
Freq: Half-yearly; **Circ:** 200,000
Editor: Annemieke Biesheuvel
Language(s): Dutch
Agency Commission: 15%
BUSINESS: ENGINEERING & MACHINERY: Machinery, Machine Tools & Metalworking

BIOS SKALA 17606N75H-134
Editorial: Irenestraat 20, 2202 TP NOORDWIJK
Tel: 30 6383743
Freq: 10 issues yearly; **Cover Price:** Free; **Circ:** 275
Editor: R. Koeman
Profile: Journal of the Noordwijk Badminton Society.
Language(s): Dutch
Readership: Aimed at members.
Agency Commission: 15%
CONSUMER: SPORT: Racquet Sports

BIT 17923N81D-20
Editorial: Celsiusweg 41, 8912 AM LEEUWARDEN
Tel: 20 6077605 **Fax:** 88 2697490
Email: businessmedia@eisma.nl **Web site:** http://www.horses.nl/bit
Freq: 8 issues yearly; **Cover Price:** EUR 6,75
Annual Sub.: EUR 59,90; **Circ:** 23,000
Editor: Marjan Tulp; **Editor-in-Chief:** Lonneke Ruesink; **Publisher:** Minne Hovenga
Profile: Magazine giving practical information on the day-to-day care of horses. Includes articles on breeding, care and sport. Also gives medical advice.
Language(s): Dutch
Readership: Aimed at owners and breeders of horses.
ADVERTISING RATES:
Full Page Mono EUR 1/1: f.c. 2069,-; 1/2: f.c. 1251,-; 1/4: f.c. 765,-
Agency Commission: 15%
Mechanical Data: Type Area: 200 x 268mm, Bleed Size: 230 x 297mm
CONSUMER: ANIMALS & PETS: Horses & Ponies

BITS&CHIPS 631509N5C-1_50
Editorial: Snelliusstraat 6, 6533 NV NIJMEGEN
Tel: 10 4274107 **Fax:** 79 3467846
Email: info@techwatch.nl **Web site:** http://www.bits-chips.nl
Date Established: 26-08-1999; **Freq:** 20 issues yearly; **Circ:** 8,000
Editor: Rene Raaijmakers; **Publisher:** Rene Raaijmakers
Profile: Newsletter focusing on new technology and market trends.
Language(s): Dutch
Readership: Aimed at computer engineers and technical managers.
ADVERTISING RATES:
Full Page Mono EUR 2/1: f.c. 6450,-; 1/1: f.c. 3228,-; 1/2: f.c. 2259,-
Agency Commission: 15%
Mechanical Data: Type Area: 184 x 266mm, Bleed Size: 210 x 297mm
BUSINESS: COMPUTERS & AUTOMATION: Professional Personal Computers

BKK BEROEPSKEUZEKRANT, EDITIE HAVO/VWO EN MBO NIVEAU 3 EN 4 1636965N83-197
Editorial: Schoolsteeg 4, 1621 CE HOORN
Tel: 20 5612070
Email: info@beroepskeuzekrant.nl
Freq: 3 issues yearly; **Cover Price:** Free; **Circ:** 54,925
Publisher: Michel Tiepel
Language(s): Dutch
ADVERTISING RATES:
Full Page Mono EUR 2/1: f.c. 3250,-; 1/1: f.c. 1750,-; 1/4: f.c. 950,-
Agency Commission: 15%
Mechanical Data: Type Area: 263 x 398mm, Bleed Size: 296 x 420mm
Copy instructions: *Copy Date:* 2 weeks prior to publication date
CONSUMER: STUDENT PUBLICATIONS

BKK BEROEPSKEUZEKRANT, EDITIE VMBO 19006N88C-10
Editorial: Schoolsteeg 4, 1621 CE HOORN
Tel: 70 3780250
Email: info@beroepskeuzekrant.nl
Date Established: 01-02-1993; **Freq:** Annual; **Cover Price:** Free; **Circ:** 58,719
Editor: Cilia Kersemakers; **Editor-in-Chief:** Michel Tiepel; **Publisher:** Michel Tiepel
Profile: Magazine containing information about career choices and further education.
Language(s): Dutch
Readership: Read by students.
ADVERTISING RATES:
Full Page Mono EUR 1/1: b/w 3250,- 1/2: b/w 1750,- 1/4: b/w 900,-
Agency Commission: 15%
Mechanical Data: Type Area: 263 x 398mm, Bleed Size: 296 x 420mm
Copy instructions: *Copy Date:* 2 weeks prior to publication date
CONSUMER: EDUCATION: Careers

DE BLAUWE GIDS.NL 1636446N94F-269
Editorial: Wilhelminalaan 3, 3743 DB BAARN
Tel: 492 338432 **Fax:** 20 6767728
Email: info@nbav.nl **Web site:** http://www.deblauwegids.nl
Freq: Annual; **Cover Price:** EUR 4,95; **Circ:** 60,000
Editor-in-Chief: A. van Beek
Language(s): Dutch
ADVERTISING RATES:
Full Page Mono EUR 2/1: f.c. 3515,-; 1/1: f.c. 1975,-; 1/2: f.c. 1195,-
Agency Commission: 15%
Mechanical Data: Type Area: 190 x 278mm, Bleed Size: 210 x 297mm
CONSUMER: OTHER CLASSIFICATIONS: Disability

BLOEDSUIKER 1633900N74G-348
Editorial: Meyhorst 91-21, 6537 KJ NIJMEGEN
Tel: 223 650016 **Fax:** 223 650012
Email: info@bloedsuiker.nl **Web site:** http://www.bloedsuiker.nl
Date Established: 01-04-1986; **Freq:** Quarterly; **Annual Sub.:** EUR 5,-; **Circ:** 98,000
Usual Pagination: 28
Editor: V.E.A. Gerdes; **Editor-in-Chief:** I. Seignette
Language(s): Dutch
Agency Commission: 15%
CONSUMER: WOMEN'S INTEREST CONSUMER MAGAZINES: Slimming & Health

BLOEDVERWANT 1637368N74G-285
Editorial: Plesmanlaan 125, 1066 CX AMSTERDAM
Tel: 30 2738234 **Fax:** 30 2738277
Email: bloedverwant@sanquin.nl
Date Established: 01-05-2002; **Freq:** 3 issues yearly; **Cover Price:** Free; **Circ:** 500,000
Editor: Ingeborg van der Heijden
Language(s): Dutch
Agency Commission: 15%
CONSUMER: WOMEN'S INTEREST CONSUMER MAGAZINES: Slimming & Health

BLOEMEN & PLANTEN 18214N93-28
Editorial: Takkebijsters 57a, 4817 BL BREDA
Tel: 76 5301715 **Fax:** 70 3045808
Email: info@vipmedia.nl **Web site:** http://www.bloemenenplanten.nl
Freq: Monthly; **Cover Price:** EUR 6,95
Annual Sub.: EUR 54,95; **Circ:** 85,000
Editor: Jacqueline Leenders; **Editor-in-Chief:** M. van der Voort; **Publisher:** Ed Bruijns
Profile: Magazine about flowers and plants.
Language(s): Dutch
Readership: Read by gardening enthusiasts.
ADVERTISING RATES:
Full Page Mono EUR 1/1: f.c. 3910,-; b/w 2725,- 1/2: f.c. 2010,-; b/w 1400,- 1/4: f.c. 1095,-; b/w 790,-
Agency Commission: 15%
Mechanical Data: Type Area: 198 x 280mm, Bleed Size: 228 x 300mm
Copy instructions: *Copy Date:* 4 weeks prior to publication date
CONSUMER: GARDENING

BLVD MAN 17559N86C-250
Editorial: Vijzelgracht 21-25, 1017 HN AMSTERDAM
Tel: 20 5310161 **Fax:** 20 5302585
Email: creditsmedia@creditsmedia.nl **Web site:** http://www.blvd.nl
Freq: Quarterly; **Cover Price:** EUR 4,95
Annual Sub.: EUR 18,-; **Circ:** 40,112
Editor: Pieter Schol; **Editor-in-Chief:** Mariette van de Sande; **Publisher:** Eugen van de Pas
Profile: Lifestyle, fashion, business and general interest magazine.
Language(s): Dutch
Readership: Aimed at men with a high disposable income.
ADVERTISING RATES:
Full Page Mono EUR 2/1: f.c. 8196,-; 1/1: f.c. 4098,-; 1/2: f.c. 2458,-
Agency Commission: 15%
Mechanical Data: Type Area: 195 x 270mm, Bleed Size: 225 x 300mm
CONSUMER: ADULT & GAY MAGAZINES: Men's Lifestyle Magazines

BMB BOUWMATERIEELBENELUX 15687N4E-85
Editorial: Schootense Dreef 31, 5708 HZ HELMOND
Tel: 492 593162 **Fax:** 30 6383991
Email: service@bouwmaterieel-benelux.nl **Web site:** http://www.bouwmaterieel-benelux.nl
Date Established: 01-02-1992; **Freq:** 11 issues yearly; **Cover Price:** EUR 12,-
Annual Sub.: EUR 36,-; **Circ:** 12,144
Editor: Kees Beijer; **Editor-in-Chief:** Leo van Hoorick; **Publisher:** Leo van Hoorick
Profile: Magazine focusing on equipment and cranes for construction use, also transportation.
Language(s): Dutch
Readership: Read by earthmoving contractors, demolition contractors and crane rental companies.
ADVERTISING RATES:
Full Page Mono ...... EUR 1/1: f.c. 3688,-; PMS 3010,-; f.c. color 3147,-; b/w 2595,- 1/2: f.c. 2318,-; PMS 1767,-; f.c. color
Agency Commission: 15%
Mechanical Data: Type Area: 187 x 257mm, Bleed Size: 215 x 285mm
BUSINESS: ARCHITECTURE & BUILDING: Building

BMW MAGAZINE 1857817N77A-383
Editorial: Aletta Jacobslaan 7, 1066 BP AMSTERDAM **Tel:** 40 8447611 **Fax:** 53 4842189
Email: info@rhbm.nl
Freq: Half-yearly; **Cover Price:** Free; **Circ:** 55,000
Editor: H. Thoma
Language(s): Dutch
ADVERTISING RATES:
Full Page Mono .... EUR 1/1: f.c. 4300,-
Agency Commission: 15%
Mechanical Data: Bleed Size: 215 x 280mm
Copy instructions: *Copy Date:* 4 weeks prior to publication date
CONSUMER: MOTORING & CYCLING: Motoring

BN DESTEM 17104N67B-1450
Editorial: Spinveld 55, 4815 HV BREDA
Tel: 76 5312311 **Fax:** 76 5312520
Web site: http://www.bndestem.nl
Freq: 312 issues yearly; **Annual Sub.:** EUR 277,95; **Circ:** 112,074
Editor: Johan van Uffelen; **Publisher:** A.A.M. Verrest
Language(s): Dutch
ADVERTISING RATES:
Full Page Mono .... EUR W1: b/w 18.381,- W4: b/w 8842,- W8: b/w 6809,- W1 ed. za.: b/w 19.949,- W4 ed. za.: b/w 9595,- W8 ed
Agency Commission: 15%
Mechanical Data: Type Area: 266 x 398mm
REGIONAL DAILY & SUNDAY NEWSPAPERS: Regional Daily Newspapers

BNDR 16092N21A-43_50
Editorial: Bemuurde Weerd Oostzijde 12, 3514 AN UTRECHT **Tel:** 23 5564919 **Fax:** 23 5564911
Email: post@najk.nl
Freq: 5 issues yearly; **Annual Sub.:** EUR 18,-; **Circ:** 9,000
Usual Pagination: 28
Editor: Ellen van den Manacker
Profile: Official journal of the Society of Young Farmers in the Netherlands.
Language(s): Dutch
Readership: Read by young farmers aged between 16 and 36 years.
ADVERTISING RATES:
Full Page Mono EUR 1/1: b/w 1850,- 1/2: b/w 1025,- 1/4: b/w 560,-
Agency Commission: 15%
Mechanical Data: Type Area: 190 x 260mm, Bleed Size: 215 x 285mm
Copy instructions: *Copy Date:* 2 weeks prior to publication date
BUSINESS: AGRICULTURE & FARMING

BODEM 16807N57-10_
Editorial: Zuidpoolsingel 2, 2408 ZE ALPHEN A/D RIJN **Tel:** 172 466792 **Fax:** 172 421702
Email: info@kluwer.nl
Freq: 6 issues yearly; **Cover Price:** EUR 37,-
Annual Sub.: EUR 189,-; **Circ:** 1,425
Editor-in-Chief: Sietske de Boer; **Publisher:** J.W. Ham
Profile: Magazine about soil research and soil polic
Language(s): Dutch
ADVERTISING RATES:
Full Page Mono .. EUR 1/1: b/w 1175,- 1/2: b/w 700 1/4: b/w 375,-
Agency Commission: 15%
Mechanical Data: Type Area: 180 x 262mm, Bleed Size: 210 x 297mm
Copy instructions: *Copy Date:* 4 weeks prior to publication date
BUSINESS: ENVIRONMENT & POLLUTION

BODY BIZ 16539N48B
Editorial: Kasteelstraat 16, 6598 BJ HEIJEN
Tel: 20 5922250 **Fax:** 30 6348909
Email: info@bodybiz.nl **Web site:** http://www.bodybiz.nl
Freq: 11 issues yearly; **Annual Sub.:** EUR 95,-; **Circ:** 2,561
Editor: Jeroen Gerats; **Publisher:** Ben Verhagen
Profile: Publication covering sport and fitness equipment, saunas and physiotherapy.
Language(s): Dutch
Readership: Aimed at fitness instructors.
ADVERTISING RATES:
Full Page Mono EUR 1/1: f.c. 1550,-; 1/2: f.c. 1150, 1/4: f.c. 650,-
Agency Commission: 15%
Mechanical Data: Type Area: 190 x 260mm, Bleed Size: 210 x 280mm
BUSINESS: TOY TRADE & SPORTS GOODS: Sports Goods

BODYMIND OPLEIDINGEN 17481N74G-7_4
Editorial: Eerste Pijnackerstraat 135a, 3035 GS ROTTERDAM **Tel:** 172 466622
Email: info@bodymindopleidingen.nl
Date Established: 01-09-1992; **Freq:** Half-yearly; **Cover Price:** Free; **Circ:** 5,500
Usual Pagination: 20
Editor: H.A. Verschuren
Profile: Magazine about therapies and workshops designed to improve the body, mind and spirit.
Language(s): Dutch
Readership: Read by members of the public interested in alternative medicine.
Agency Commission: 15%
CONSUMER: WOMEN'S INTEREST CONSUMER MAGAZINES: Slimming & Health

BOEKENPOST 18022N84B-2
Editorial: Oerdijk 1c, 7433 AE SCHALKHAAR
Tel: 88 7518070 **Fax:** 30 6076301
Web site: http://www.boekenpost.nl
Freq: 6 issues yearly; **Cover Price:** EUR 6,-
Annual Sub.: EUR 33,-; **Circ:** 2,500
Editor: Janneke van der Veer; **Publisher:** H.J.C. Wechgelaer
Profile: Magazine focusing on antiquarian books, prints, ephemera and comics.
Language(s): Dutch
Agency Commission: 15%
Mechanical Data: Type Area: 185 x 265mm
CONSUMER: THE ARTS & LITERARY: Literary

DE BOEKENWERELD 16870N60A-30
Editorial: Heemstedestraat 51 I, 1059 EA AMSTERDAM **Tel:** 20 5450421
Email: redactie@deboekenwereld.nl **Web site:** http://www.deboekenwereld.nl
Freq: 5 issues yearly; **Cover Price:** EUR 10,-
Annual Sub.: EUR 39,95; **Circ:** 2,000
Editor-in-Chief: Menno Anbeek
Profile: Magazine containing information on old books and prints.
Language(s): Dutch
ADVERTISING RATES:
Full Page Mono EUR 1/1: b/w 280,- 1/2: b/w 150,- 1/4: b/w 92,-
Agency Commission: 15%
Mechanical Data: Type Area: 150 x 220mm, Bleed Size: 175 x 250mm
Copy instructions: *Copy Date:* 4 weeks prior to publication date
BUSINESS: PUBLISHING: Publishing & Book Trade

BOEKIEBOEKIE 629735N91D-6
Editorial: Schiehavenkade 166, 3024 EZ ROTTERDAM **Tel:** 10 4274103
Email: publiciteit@boekie-boekie.nl **Web site:** http://www.boekie-boekie.nl
Date Established: 01-12-1991; **Freq:** Quarterly; **Annual Sub.:** EUR 31,95; **Circ:** 3,500
Editor: Jet Manrho; **Editor-in-Chief:** Pieter van Oudheusden; **Publisher:** Jet Manrho

Profile: Magazine focusing on art and literature. Also contains articles on science.
Language(s): Dutch
Readership: Aimed at children aged between 8 and 12 years.
Agency Commission: 15%
Mechanical Data: Bleed Size: 235 x 320mm
Copy instructions: *Copy Date:* 14 days prior to publication date
CONSUMER: RECREATION & LEISURE: Children & Youth

BONSAI FOCUS
712719N93-31
Editorial: Parallelweg 49b, 4043 KH OPHEUSDEN
Tel: 20 5612070 **Fax:** 570 614795
Email: info@bonsaifocus.com **Web site:** http://www.bonsaifocus.com
Freq: 6 issues yearly; **Cover Price:** EUR 9,50
Annual Sub.: EUR 47,-; **Circ:** 3,000
Editor: F.W. Bloch; **Publisher:** R. Rooswinkel
Profile: Magazine giving a broad view of the world of bonsai.
Language(s): Dutch
Readership: Read by bonsai enthusiasts.
ADVERTISING RATES:
Full Page Mono .... EUR 1/1: f.c. 925,-; b/w 795,- 1/2: f.c. 595,-; b/w 510,- 1/4: f.c. 365,-; b/w 315,-
Agency Commission: 15%
Mechanical Data: Type Area: 190 x 265mm, Bleed Size: 210 x 297mm
CONSUMER: GARDENING

BOODSCHAPPEN
17482N74G-8
Editorial: Doetinchemseweg 59, 7007 CB DOETINCHEM **Tel:** 88 2696670 **Fax:** 88 2696331
Email: info@mcp.nl **Web site:** http://www.boodschappen.nl
Date Established: 01-01-1989; **Freq:** Monthly;
Cover Price: Free; **Circ:** 1,969,054
Editor: Frieda Zieleman
Profile: Magazine about eating and drinking for a healthy lifestyle.
Language(s): Dutch
Readership: Aimed at the general public.
ADVERTISING RATES:
Full Page Mono .... EUR 1/1: f.c. 38.825,-; 1/2: f.c. 25.295,-
Agency Commission: 15%
Mechanical Data: Type Area: 200 x 251mm, Bleed Size: 222 x 285mm
CONSUMER: WOMEN'S INTEREST CONSUMER MAGAZINES: Slimming & Health

BOTEN
1640425N91A-137
Editorial: Sumatrakade 1299, 1019 RM AMSTERDAM **Tel:** 172 440681 **Fax:** 172 422886
Email: info@bohlmedia.nl **Web site:** http://www.botentekoop.nl
Freq: 16 issues yearly; **Cover Price:** EUR 2,50
Annual Sub.: EUR 71,30; **Circ:** 105,000
Editor: Kees Versloot
Language(s): Dutch
ADVERTISING RATES:
Full Page Mono EUR 1/1: b/w 595,- 1/2: b/w 315,- 1/4: b/w 165,-
Agency Commission: 15%
Mechanical Data: Type Area: 230 x 310mm, Bleed Size: 250 x 330mm
Copy instructions: *Copy Date:* 9 days prior to publication date
CONSUMER: RECREATION & LEISURE: Boating & Yachting

BOTEN.NL
1643454N91A-138
Editorial: Keizersgracht 127, 1015 CJ AMSTERDAM
Tel: 23 5565462 **Fax:** 23 5564588
Web site: http://www.boten.nl
Date Established: 09-02-2004; **Freq:** Monthly;
Cover Price: EUR 1,95; **Circ:** 16,520
Language(s): Dutch
ADVERTISING RATES:
Full Page Mono .... EUR 1/1: b/w 600,- 1/2: b/w 325,-
Agency Commission: 15%
Mechanical Data: Type Area: 200 x 275mm, Bleed Size: 210 x 285mm
CONSUMER: RECREATION & LEISURE: Boating & Yachting

BOUW IQ
15696N4E-170
Editorial: Dr. van Helvoortstraat 3, 5281 BJ BOXTEL
Tel: 76 5312311 **Fax:** 76 5312520
Email: mail@aeneas.nl **Web site:** http://www.bouwiqonline.nl
Freq: 6 issues yearly; **Cover Price:** EUR 25,-
Annual Sub.: EUR 135,-; **Circ:** 1,352
Editor: Jos Lichtenberg; **Editor-in-Chief:** Wilbert Leistra; **Publisher:** Æbele Kluwer
Profile: Journal focusing on all aspects of building in relation to the environment.
Language(s): Dutch
ADVERTISING RATES:
Full Page Mono EUR 2/1: f.c. 4305,-; 1/1: f.c. 2580,-; 1/2: f.c. 1420,-
Agency Commission: 15%
Mechanical Data: Type Area: 205 x 277mm, Bleed Size: 225 x 297mm
BUSINESS: ARCHITECTURE & BUILDING: Building

DE BOUWBRIEF
16880N61-5
Editorial: Oude Kraan 72, 6811 LL ARNHEM
Tel: 23 5567955 **Fax:** 23 5567956
Email: info@huismuziek.nl **Web site:** http://www.bouwerskontakt.nl
Date Established: 01-07-1976; **Freq:** Quarterly; **Circ:** 650
Usual Pagination: 32
Editor: Jan Bouterse
Profile: Publication for the makers of musical instruments.
Language(s): Dutch
Agency Commission: 15%
Mechanical Data: Bleed Size: 210 x 297mm
BUSINESS: MUSIC TRADE

BOUWEN
15679N4E-357
Editorial: Ceintuurbaan 2, 3847 LG HARDERWIJK
Tel: 314 349446 **Fax:** 314 344397
Email: info@fundeon.nl
Freq: 6 issues yearly; **Annual Sub.:** EUR 8,60; **Circ:** 175,000
Usual Pagination: 44
Editor: Jolanda de Vries
Profile: Journal containing technical information and news about the building industry.
Language(s): Dutch
Agency Commission: 15%
BUSINESS: ARCHITECTURE & BUILDING: Building

BOUWEN AAN DE ZORG
761191N56B-18
Editorial: Schatbeurderlaan 6, 6002 ED WEERT
Tel: 70 3307156 **Fax:** 70 3602861
Email: info@louwersuitgevers.nl
Freq: 6 issues yearly; **Annual Sub.:** EUR 45,-; **Circ:** 4,500
Editor: Jerry Helmers
Profile: Magazine focusing on hospitals, care institutions and nursing homes for the elderly.
Language(s): Dutch
Readership: Read by government officials associated with care for the elderly and people working in medical institutions.
ADVERTISING RATES:
Full Page Mono EUR 2/1: f.c. 2400,-; 1/1: f.c. 1650,-; 1/2: f.c. 1050,-; 1/4: f.c. 650,-
Agency Commission: 15%
Mechanical Data: Type Area: 197 x 267mm, Bleed Size: 230 x 297mm
BUSINESS: HEALTH & MEDICAL: Nursing

BOUWMARKT
15686N4E-80
Editorial: Hanzestraat 1, 7006 RH DOETINCHEM
Tel: 314 349477 **Fax:** 314 349136
Email: klantenservice@reedbusiness.nl
Date Established: 01-01-1960; **Freq:** 10 issues yearly; **Annual Sub.:** EUR 435,-; **Circ:** 761
Editor: Wil Kuhlmann; **Publisher:** Peter Backx
Profile: Magazine giving details about the economic and financial aspects of the building trade, property and facility management.
Language(s): Dutch
Readership: Aimed at those in the finance departments of building firms, builders, architects, facility managers and building engineers.
ADVERTISING RATES:
Full Page Mono .... EUR 1/1: f.c. 1453,-; f.c. color 1080,-; b/w 748,- 1/2: f.c. 1014,-; f.c. color 695,-; b/w 415,- 1/4: f.c.
Agency Commission: 15%
Mechanical Data: Type Area: 185 x 260mm, Bleed Size: 210 x 297mm
Copy instructions: *Copy Date:* 18 days prior to publication date
BUSINESS: ARCHITECTURE & BUILDING: Building

BOUWSKALA
15690N4E-130
Editorial: Het Var 41, 8939 BJ LEEUWARDEN
Tel: 346 577390 **Fax:** 346 577389
Web site: http://www.bouwskala.nl
Date Established: 01-11-1989; **Freq:** 5 issues yearly; **Circ:** 11,250
Editor: M.P.A. de Baar; **Publisher:** Jaap Bronkhorst
Profile: Magazine about all aspects of professional building.
Language(s): Dutch
Readership: Read by structural engineers and architects.
ADVERTISING RATES:
Full Page Mono .. EUR 1/1: b/w 1120,- 1/2: b/w 660,- 1/4: b/w 410,-
Agency Commission: 15%
Mechanical Data: Type Area: 260 x 380mm
Copy instructions: *Copy Date:* 3 weeks prior to publication date
BUSINESS: ARCHITECTURE & BUILDING: Building

BRABANT BUSINESS MAGAZINE
16949N63-25
Editorial: Steenovenweg 20, 5708 HN HELMOND
Tel: 30 6399911 **Fax:** 30 6399937
Email: publishers@weijmans.com **Web site:** http://www.brabantbusiness.nl
Freq: Quarterly; **Annual Sub.:** EUR 45,-; **Circ:** 15,000
Editor-in-Chief: Antoinette Maas; **Publisher:** Herman Driessen
Profile: Publication covering business and economic issues in Brabant.
Language(s): Dutch
ADVERTISING RATES:
Full Page Mono EUR 1/1: f.c. 1910,-; 1/2: f.c. 1155,-; 1/4: f.c. 720,-
Agency Commission: 15%
Mechanical Data: Bleed Size: 240 x 340mm, Type Area: 210 x 289mm
BUSINESS: REGIONAL BUSINESS

BRABANTS DAGBLAD
17116N67B-1600
Editorial: Emmaplein 25, 5211 VZ 'S-HERTOGENBOSCH **Tel:** 314 349477
Fax: 73 6157171
Web site: http://www.brabantsdagblad.nl
Freq: 312 issues yearly; **Annual Sub.:** EUR 294,15;
Circ: 129,216
Editor: Ton Rooms; **Publisher:** Annemieke Besseling
Language(s): Dutch
ADVERTISING RATES:
Full Page Mono EUR 3/4: b/w 8823,- 1/2: b/w 5882,- 3/4 ed. za.: b/w 9577,- 1/2 ed. za.: b/w 6385,-
Agency Commission: 15%
Mechanical Data: Type Area: 266 x 398mm
REGIONAL DAILY & SUNDAY NEWSPAPERS: Regional Daily Newspapers

BRANDER AFBOUW
15692N4E-140
Editorial: Nieuwe Herengracht 47, 1011 RN AMSTERDAM **Tel:** 35 6726800
Email: media@scripta.nl **Web site:** http://www.brander.nl
Date Established: 01-01-1993; **Freq:** Half-yearly;
Circ: 8,000
Usual Pagination: 12
Editor-in-Chief: Annemieke Wolff
Profile: Magazine with articles on all aspects of plastering and building.
Language(s): Dutch
Readership: Aimed at plasterers and builders.
Agency Commission: 15%
Mechanical Data: Bleed Size: 230 x 270mm
BUSINESS: ARCHITECTURE & BUILDING: Building

BRANDWEER ONTSPANNINGS MAGAZINE
16613N54A-30
Editorial: Muiderweg 4, 3891 DB ZEEWOLDE
Tel: 35 67272103 **Fax:** 20 5159145
Email: info@tolboom.nl
Date Established: 03-05-1993; **Freq:** Quarterly;
Cover Price: Free; **Circ:** 6,000
Usual Pagination: 64
Editor: J.L.H. Labberton; **Editor-in-Chief:** L. Diepeveen; **Publisher:** J.L.H. Labberton
Profile: Magazine providing news and information about the fire brigade. Also includes details of leisure activities, forthcoming events and lifestyle articles.
Language(s): Dutch
ADVERTISING RATES:
Full Page Mono .. EUR 1/1: f.c. 1375,-; 1/2: f.c. 750,-; 1/3: f.c. 525,-
Agency Commission: 15%
Mechanical Data: Type Area: 185 x 265mm, Bleed Size: 210 x 297mm
BUSINESS: SAFETY & SECURITY: Fire Fighting

DE BREDASE BODE
626633N72-540
Editorial: Bredaseweg 26, 4881 DE ZUNDERT
Tel: 76 5722984 **Fax:** 570 614795
Email: zetterij@vorsselmans.nl **Web site:** http://www.internetbode.nl
Freq: Weekly; **Circ:** 74,500
Editor: Vif Janssen; **Editor-in-Chief:** Vif Janssen
Language(s): Dutch
Agency Commission: 15%
Mechanical Data: Type Area: 264 x 400mm
LOCAL NEWSPAPERS

BRIELS NIEUWSLAND
626634N72-550
Editorial: Christiaan Huygensweg 9, 3220 AB HELLEVOETSLUIS **Tel:** 23 5565100 **Fax:** 23 5565105
Web site: http://www.brielsnieuwsland.nl
Freq: Weekly; **Cover Price:** Free; **Circ:** 7,800
Editor: A. Fortuin
Language(s): Dutch
Agency Commission: 15%
Mechanical Data: Type Area: 273 x 350mm
LOCAL NEWSPAPERS

BRIELSE MARE
18244N94X-15
Editorial: J. Matthijssenlaan 10, 3232 ED BRIELLE
Tel: 15 2690256
Email: fteggens@wanadoo.nl
Date Established: 01-04-1991; **Freq:** Half-yearly;
Annual Sub.: EUR 10,-; **Circ:** 440
Editor: Willem Delwel
Profile: Magazine containing articles about the history of the Brielle and Voorne-Putten area.
Language(s): Dutch
ADVERTISING RATES:
Full Page Mono . EUR 1/1: b/w 90,- 1/2: b/w 45,- 1/3: b/w 30,-
Agency Commission: 15%
Mechanical Data: Bleed Size: 148 x 210mm, Type Area: 116 x 168mm
CONSUMER: OTHER CLASSIFICATIONS: Miscellaneous

BRIGHT
1665888N74Q-310
Editorial: Wildenborch 5, 1112 XB DIEMEN
Tel: 70 3307094 **Fax:** 314 359978
Web site: http://www.bright.nl
Freq: 6 issues yearly; **Cover Price:** EUR 5,-
Annual Sub.: EUR 40,-; **Circ:** 8,881
Editor: Erwin van der Zande; **Editor-in-Chief:** Corrie Gerritsma; **Publisher:** Willem de Kok
Language(s): Dutch
ADVERTISING RATES:
Full Page Mono .... EUR 2/1: f.c. 18.995,-; 1/1: f.c. 9995,-; 1/2: f.c. 3595,-
Agency Commission: 15%
Mechanical Data: Bleed Size: 200 x 265mm, Type Area: 179 x 249mm
CONSUMER: WOMEN'S INTEREST CONSUMER MAGAZINES: Lifestyle

THE BRITISH WOMEN'S CLUB MAGAZINE
18230N94D-40
Editorial: Plein 24, 2511 CS DEN HAAG
Tel: 35 6726900
Freq: Monthly; **Circ:** 500
Editor: J. Ballero; **Editor-in-Chief:** L. Osorio;
Publisher: D. van der Elst
Profile: Journal of the British Women's Club in the Netherlands. Contains a programme of club events, articles on gardening, book reviews, a community notice board and small advertisements.
Language(s): Dutch
Agency Commission: 15%
Mechanical Data: Type Area: 130 x 170mm, Bleed Size: 163 x 210mm
Copy instructions: *Copy Date:* 5 days prior to publication date
CONSUMER: OTHER CLASSIFICATIONS: Expatriates

BROADCAST MAGAZINE
15607N2D-20
Editorial: Bussumergrintweg 4, 1217 BP HILVERSUM **Tel:** 13 4627201 **Fax:** 13 5361405
Email: info@fcklap.nl **Web site:** http://www.broadcastmagazine.nl
Freq: 10 issues yearly; **Annual Sub.:** EUR 150,-;
Circ: 10,000
Editor: Jeroen te Nuijl
Profile: Journal giving details about all aspects of broadcasting.
Language(s): Dutch
Readership: Aimed at those in the broadcasting industry.
ADVERTISING RATES:
Full Page Mono EUR 1/1: f.c. 2275,-; 1/2: f.c. 1385,-; 1/4: f.c. 790,-
Agency Commission: 15%
Mechanical Data: Type Area: 210 x 285mm, Bleed Size: 240 x 320mm
Copy instructions: *Copy Date:* 2 weeks prior to publication date
BUSINESS: COMMUNICATIONS, ADVERTISING & MARKETING: Broadcasting

BROCHURE NORTH SEA JAZZ FESTIVAL
1799139N76D-255
Editorial: Noordeinde 19-21, 2611 KE DELFT
Tel: 314 359940
Freq: Annual; **Cover Price:** Free; **Circ:** 300,000
Language(s): Dutch
ADVERTISING RATES:
Full Page Mono . EUR 2/1: f.c. 13.650,-; b/w 11.500,- 1/1: f.c. 7500,-; b/w 6000,- 1/2: f.c. 4500,-; b/w 3500,- 1/4: f.c.
Agency Commission: 15%
Mechanical Data: Type Area: 210 x 285mm, Bleed Size: 195 x 265mm
Copy instructions: *Copy Date:* 4 weeks prior to publication date
CONSUMER: MUSIC & PERFORMING ARTS: Music

BROERSTRAAT 5
17973N83-248
Editorial: Oude Boteringestraat 44, 9712 GL GRONINGEN **Tel:** 570 647730 **Fax:** 13 5078929
Email: alumni@rug.nl
Freq: Quarterly; **Circ:** 69,000
Editor: F.S. Colstee-Wieringa; **Editor-in-Chief:** G. Gritter
Profile: Magazine for students of the University of Groningen.
Language(s): Dutch
Agency Commission: 15%
Mechanical Data: Bleed Size: 230 x 290mm
CONSUMER: STUDENT PUBLICATIONS

BROMFIETS
17765N77B-25
Editorial: Ambachtweg 2, 2841 LZ MOORDRECHT
Tel: 23 5565370 **Fax:** 23 5565357
Email: studio@targetpress.nl **Web site:** http://www.bromfiets.nl
Freq: 6 issues yearly; **Cover Price:** EUR 4,95
Annual Sub.: EUR 27,95; **Circ:** 17,000
Editor: Wout Meppelink; **Editor-in-Chief:** Tom Haanstra; **Publisher:** Lydia de Boorder
Profile: Magazine about classic mopeds.
Language(s): Dutch
ADVERTISING RATES:
Full Page Mono EUR 1/1: b/w 500,- 1/2: b/w 330,- 1/4: b/w 220,-
Agency Commission: 15%

Mechanical Data: Type Area: 185 x 268mm, Bleed Size: 210 x 297mm
Copy instructions: *Copy Date:* 3 weeks prior to publication date
CONSUMER: MOTORING & CYCLING: Motorcycling

BRON VAN CHRISTELIJKE GEEST
1636263N87-2491
Editorial: IJsseldijk 31, 8266 AD KAMPEN
Tel: 23 5344089 **Fax:** 10 2801002
Email: gens@kok.nl
Freq: 56 issues yearly; **Annual Sub.:** EUR 24,16; **Circ:** 105,000
Publisher: F.H. Jonkers
Language(s): Dutch
Agency Commission: 15%
CONSUMER: RELIGIOUS

BROS/OSTEOPOROSE NIEUWS
652148N74G-9
Editorial: Postbus 445, 5240 AK ROSMALEN
Tel: 45 5739390 **Fax:** 20 5233419
Email: info@osteoporosevereniging.nl
Date Established: 01-02-1993; **Freq:** Quarterly; **Annual Sub.:** EUR 14,-; **Circ:** 5,000
Editor: M. van der Zalm-Waterreus; **Publisher:** D.R. Klawer
Profile: Publication containing general medical information about osteoporosis.
Language(s): Dutch
ADVERTISING RATES:
Full Page Mono . EUR 1/1: f.c. 1481,-; 1/2: f.c. 1140,-
Agency Commission: 15%
Mechanical Data: Type Area: 183 x 255mm, Bleed Size: 210 x 297mm
Copy instructions: *Copy Date:* 6 weeks prior to publication date
CONSUMER: WOMEN'S INTEREST CONSUMER MAGAZINES: Slimming & Health

BRUGMEDIA REGIONAAL
626685N80-9_94
Editorial: Constructieweg 41-1, 8263 BC KAMPEN
Tel: 10 4274128 **Fax:** 88 7518231
Email: info@brugmedia.nl
Date Established: 10-10-1995; **Freq:** 26 issues yearly; **Cover Price:** Free; **Circ:** 44,000
Editor-in-Chief: Eric-Jan Berends
Profile: Local newspaper containing information on Kampen and surroundings.
Language(s): Dutch
Readership: Read by local residents.
ADVERTISING RATES:
Full Page Mono EUR 1/1: b/w 875,- 1/2: b/w 525,- 1/4: b/w 315,-
Agency Commission: 15%
Mechanical Data: Type Area: 255 x 389mm
CONSUMER: RURAL & REGIONAL INTEREST

BRUID & BRUIDEGOM MAGAZINE
17505N74L-10
Editorial: Uraniumweg 17e, 3812 RJ AMERSFOORT
Tel: 23 5564590 **Fax:** 20 5159143
Email: info@bruidmedia.nl **Web site:** http://www.huwelijks.net
Date Established: 01-01-1983; **Freq:** Quarterly; **Cover Price:** EUR 6,-
Annual Sub.: EUR 28,-; **Circ:** 39,600
Editor: Susan Lippe-Bernard; **Editor-in-Chief:** Noa Johannes; **Publisher:** Cor Both
Profile: Wedding magazine containing information and articles about wedding organisation, including fashion and accessories.
Language(s): Dutch
Readership: Read by anybody involved in organising a wedding.
ADVERTISING RATES:
Full Page Mono EUR 1/1: f.c. 2930,-; b/w 1735,- 1/2: f.c. 2165,-; b/w 960,- 1/4: f.c. 1115,-; b/w 515,-
Agency Commission: 15%
Mechanical Data: Type Area: 208 x 258mm, Bleed Size: 230 x 300mm
CONSUMER: WOMEN'S INTEREST CONSUMER MAGAZINES: Brides

BUITENLEVEN
1637200N91R-232
Editorial: Wassenaarseweg 220, 2596 EC DEN HAAG **Tel:** 88 2696657 **Fax:** 88 2696887
Web site: http://www.buitenleven.nl
Date Established: 20-12-2002; **Freq:** 8 issues yearly; **Cover Price:** EUR 5,25
Annual Sub.: EUR 37,70; **Circ:** 87,782
Editor: M. Haafkens; **Editor-in-Chief:** H. Zeinstra
Language(s): Dutch
ADVERTISING RATES:
Full Page Mono EUR 2/1: f.c. 9499,-; 1/1: f.c. 4750,-; b/w 3915,- 1/2: f.c. 2850,-; b/w 2349,-
Agency Commission: 15%
Mechanical Data: Type Area: 200 x 270mm, Bleed Size: 230 x 300mm
CONSUMER: RECREATION & LEISURE: Recreation & Leisure Related

BULK
15819N10-8
Editorial: Informaticaweg 3c, 7007 CP DOETINCHEM **Tel:** 348 436599
Email: industrialmedia@eisma.nl **Web site:** http://www.bulkgids.nl
Date Established: 01-10-1993; **Freq:** 8 issues yearly; **Annual Sub.:** EUR 110,-; **Circ:** 5,000
Editor: Jos Verleg; **Publisher:** Henk Meinen
Profile: Logistics magazine focusing on bulk goods. Includes information on the properties of handling, storage and processing of bulk goods. Also has articles on silos, IBCs, transport techniques, enlarging, reducing, mixing, separating, drying, weighing, dosing, opening, sampling, safety and new services and equipment.
Language(s): Dutch
Readership: Aimed at managers in the bulk products processing industry, storage and handling businesses and bulk haulage companies.
ADVERTISING RATES:
Full Page Mono EUR 1/1: f.c. 3624,-; 1/2: f.c. 2165,-; 1/4: f.c. 1332,-
Agency Commission: 15%
Mechanical Data: Type Area: 191 x 265mm, Bleed Size: 230 x 300mm
BUSINESS: MATERIALS HANDLING

DE BUNSCHOTER (H.A.H.)
626642N72-710
Editorial: Broerswetering 10, 3752 AM BUNSCHOTEN-SPAKENBURG **Tel:** 33 2992901
Fax: 229 265738
Email: info@de.bunschoter.nl
Freq: Weekly; **Cover Price:** Free; **Circ:** 7,750
Editor: Abram Muijs; **Publisher:** D. Hartog
Language(s): Dutch
Agency Commission: 15%
Mechanical Data: Type Area: 396 x 540mm
LOCAL NEWSPAPERS

BURGEMEESTERSBLAD
1777317N32A-251
Editorial: Nassaulaan 12, 2514 JS DEN HAAG
Tel: 20 8969530 **Fax:** 24 3723631
Email: info@burgemeesters.nl
Freq: Quarterly; **Cover Price:** EUR 15,-
Annual Sub.: EUR 54,-; **Circ:** 931
Editor: Wim Zielhuis; **Editor-in-Chief:** R. van Bennekom; **Publisher:** Dineke Sonderen
Language(s): Dutch
ADVERTISING RATES:
Full Page Mono .. EUR 1/1: b/w 1540,- 1/2: b/w 920,- 1/4: b/w 510,-
Agency Commission: 15%
Mechanical Data: Type Area: 172 x 262mm, Bleed Size: 210 x 297mm
BUSINESS: LOCAL GOVERNMENT, LEISURE & RECREATION: Local Government

BUSINESS TECHNOLOGY ISSUES
15736N5B-102
Editorial: Weezenhof 32-64, 6536 GL NIJMEGEN
Tel: 20 3467209 **Fax:** 20 6159047
Email: info@marketons.nl **Web site:** http://www.myict.info
Freq: 10 issues yearly; **Annual Sub.:** EUR 249,-; **Circ:** 1,500
Editor: Willem Veldkamp
Profile: Newsletter for the IT and communications industry, specialising in the industry trends and marketing news.
Language(s): Dutch
Readership: Aimed at IT professionals, consultants and employees of venture capital and investment companies.
Agency Commission: 15%
BUSINESS: COMPUTERS & AUTOMATION: Data Processing

BUSY
15865N14A-34_50
Editorial: Oudkerkseweg 3a, 3381 KP GIESSENBURG **Tel:** 184 651558 **Fax:** 570 647815
Web site: http://www.busymagazine.nl
Freq: 6 issues yearly; **Cover Price:** Free; **Circ:** 7,000
Editor: Leo Lanser
Profile: Business to business magazine, covering all aspects of commercial enterprise.
Language(s): Dutch
Readership: Aimed at company directors in the Netherlands.
ADVERTISING RATES:
Full Page Mono EUR 1/1: b/w 795,- 1/2: b/w 495,- 1/4: b/w 295,-
Agency Commission: 15%
Mechanical Data: Type Area: 190 x 260mm
BUSINESS: COMMERCE, INDUSTRY & MANAGEMENT

BUYER'S GUIDE
1634633N75L-378
Editorial: Winthontlaan 200, 3526 KV UTRECHT
Tel: 45 5739390 **Fax:** 20 5233419
Email: maruba@maruba.com **Web site:** http://www.buyersguide.nl
Freq: Half-yearly; **Cover Price:** EUR 3,95; **Circ:** 90,000
Editor: Arjan Kruik
Language(s): Dutch
ADVERTISING RATES:
Full Page Mono EUR 2/1: f.c. 8300,-; 1/1: f.c. 4260,-; 1/2: f.c. 2350,-
Agency Commission: 15%
Mechanical Data: Type Area: 220 x 280mm, Bleed Size: 240 x 300mm
CONSUMER: SPORT: Outdoor

CAD-MAGAZINE
16074N19J-17
Editorial: Postbus 231, 8300 AE EMMELOORD
Tel: 570 648988 **Fax:** 570 614795
Web site: http://www.cadmagazine.nl
Date Established: 01-04-1990; **Freq:** 8 issues yearly; **Annual Sub.:** EUR 79,50; **Circ:** 9,150
Editor-in-Chief: Job van Haaften; **Publisher:** Ruud Groothuis
Profile: Publication containing articles on PC CAD-system, design, visualisation software, hardware and new products.
Language(s): Dutch
Readership: Aimed at engineering agencies, designers and architects.
ADVERTISING RATES:
Full Page Mono EUR 1/1: f.c. 3625,-; 1/2: f.c. 2175,-; 1/4: f.c. 1275,-
Agency Commission: 15%
Mechanical Data: Type Area: 185 x 272mm, Bleed Size: 210 x 297mm
BUSINESS: ENGINEERING & MACHINERY: CAD & CIM (Computer Integrated Manufacture)

CAMERA MAGAZINE
18041N85A-20
Editorial: Amalia van Solmslaan 54, 3708 CP ZEIST
Tel: 88 7518070 **Fax:** 30 6076301
Email: info@janszmedia.nl **Web site:** http://www.cameranet.nl
Date Established: 01-10-1986; **Freq:** 6 issues yearly; **Cover Price:** EUR 6,25
Annual Sub.: EUR 31,50; **Circ:** 11,500
Editor: Fred Jansz; **Publisher:** Fred Jansz
Profile: Magazine about photography and photographic hardware.
Language(s): Dutch
Readership: Read by amateur and professional photographers.
ADVERTISING RATES:
Full Page Mono .. EUR 2/1: f.c. 1765,-; 1/1: f.c. 995,-; 1/2: f.c. 515,-
Agency Commission: 15%
Mechanical Data: Bleed Size: 230 x 297mm
CONSUMER: PHOTOGRAPHY & FILM MAKING: Photography

CAMPERS & CARAVANS
1640429N91B-181
Editorial: Sumatrakade 1299, 1019 RM AMSTERDAM **Tel:** 172 440681 **Fax:** 172 422886
Email: info@bohilmedia.nl **Web site:** http://www.camperscaravans.nl
Freq: 13 issues yearly; **Cover Price:** EUR 1,50
Annual Sub.: EUR 29,05; **Circ:** 55,000
Editor: Baptiste Vermeulen
Language(s): Dutch
Agency Commission: 15%
Mechanical Data: Bleed Size: 250 x 330mm
CONSUMER: RECREATION & LEISURE: Camping & Caravanning

CAMPINGGIDSEN EUROPA
1634689N91B-175
Editorial: Wassenaarseweg 220, 2596 EC DEN HAAG **Tel:** 88 2697183 **Fax:** 88 2697490
Freq: Annual; **Annual Sub.:** EUR 14,95; **Circ:** 53,000
Editor: D. Polman; **Publisher:** Frank Jacobs
Language(s): Dutch
ADVERTISING RATES:
Full Page Mono EUR 1/1: f.c. 3312,-; 1/2: f.c. 2065,-; 1/4: f.c. 1293,-
Agency Commission: 15%
Mechanical Data: Type Area: 125 x 186mm, Bleed Size: 148 x 210mm
CONSUMER: RECREATION & LEISURE: Camping & Caravanning

CARAVANNEN!
18180N91B-40
Editorial: Amstelkade 56, 1427 AN AMSTELHOEK
Tel: 346 577390 **Fax:** 346 577389
Email: info@interdijk.nl **Web site:** http://www.caravanpagina.nl
Date Established: 10-11-1990; **Freq:** Quarterly; **Cover Price:** EUR 5,25
Annual Sub.: EUR 17,95; **Circ:** 40,950
Usual Pagination: 180
Editor: Peter Beving; **Publisher:** Piet van Dijk
Profile: Official magazine of the Caravan Club of the Netherlands.
Language(s): Dutch
ADVERTISING RATES:
Full Page Mono .. EUR 1/1: f.c. 1720,-; 1/2: f.c. 899,-; 1/4: f.c. 478,-
Agency Commission: 15%
Mechanical Data: Type Area: 192 x 273mm, Bleed Size: 220 x 285mm
Copy instructions: *Copy Date:* 1 month prior to publication date
CONSUMER: RECREATION & LEISURE: Camping & Caravanning

HET CARDIOVASCULAIR FORMULARIUM
16656N56A-7
Editorial: Het Spoor 2, 3994 AK HOUTEN
Tel: 58 2954859 **Fax:** 20 6767728
Freq: Annual; **Circ:** 8,500
Editor: L. Nieuwendijk; **Publisher:** L. Nieuwendijk
Profile: Journal covering cardiology. Contains articles, news, debate and research.
Language(s): Dutch
Agency Commission: 15%
Mechanical Data: Bleed Size: 105 x 170mm
BUSINESS: HEALTH & MEDICAL

HET CARRIÈRE JAARBOEK
629827N88C-20
Editorial: Keizersgracht 424, 1016 GC AMSTERDAM
Tel: 45 5739390 **Fax:** 20 5233419
Email: info@memory.nl
Freq: Annual; **Cover Price:** Free; **Circ:** 118,338
Editor: Sandra Veltmaat-Herklots; **Publisher:** Geert Nab
Profile: Publication containing general information on career possibilities.
Language(s): Dutch
Readership: Aimed at technical and economy students and those wishing to further their studies.
ADVERTISING RATES:
Full Page Mono EUR 2/1: b/w 7120,- 1/1: b/w 3990,-
Agency Commission: 15%
Mechanical Data: Type Area: 170 x 230mm, Bleed Size: 195 x 245mm
CONSUMER: EDUCATION: Careers

CARROS MAGAZINE
17752N77A-48_50
Editorial: Delflandlaan 4, 1062 EB AMSTERDAM
Tel: 20 7581000 **Fax:** 20 7581030
Email: info@pelicanmags.nl **Web site:** http://www.carros.nl
Freq: 8 issues yearly; **Cover Price:** EUR 4,95
Annual Sub.: EUR 35,-; **Circ:** 36,085
Editor: Carlo Brantsen; **Editor-in-Chief:** Martin van der Zeeuw; **Publisher:** F.N. Kloppert
Profile: Magazine providing motoring information about luxury cars.
Language(s): Dutch
Readership: Aimed at people interested in luxury cars.
ADVERTISING RATES:
Full Page Mono EUR 1/1: f.c. 4250,-; 1/2: f.c. 3188,-; 1/4: f.c. 1700,-
Agency Commission: 15%
Mechanical Data: Type Area: 200 x 270mm, Bleed Size: 230 x 297mm
Copy instructions: *Copy Date:* 4 weeks prior to publication date
CONSUMER: MOTORING & CYCLING: Motoring

CASCO
1634865N14L-558
Editorial: Houttuinlaan 3, 3447 GM WOERDEN
Tel: 33 2458375 **Fax:** 348 414897
Email: info@fnvbouw.nl
Freq: 8 issues yearly; **Cover Price:** EUR 2,50
Annual Sub.: EUR 20,-; **Circ:** 130,322
Editor: Peter van der Aa
Language(s): Dutch
ADVERTISING RATES:
Full Page Mono EUR 1/1: f.c. 2550,-; 1/2: f.c. 1325,-; 1/4: f.c. 625,-
Agency Commission: 15%
Mechanical Data: Type Area: 210 x 270mm, Bleed Size: 230 x 300mm
Copy instructions: *Copy Date:* 10 days prior to publication date
BUSINESS: COMMERCE, INDUSTRY & MANAGEMENT: Trade Unions

CASH
17509N74M-5
Editorial: Leeuwenveldseweg 3m, 1382 LV WEESP
Tel: 20 6077605 **Fax:** 88 2697490
Email: cash@3xi.nl **Web site:** http://www.cashtoday.nl
Freq: 10 issues yearly; **Cover Price:** EUR 4,95
Annual Sub.: EUR 45,-; **Circ:** 18,916
Publisher: D. Chengadu
Profile: Independent magazine containing advice for the consumer about all aspects of personal financial planning. Covers savings, loans, deposits, mortgages, investments and pensions.
Language(s): Dutch
ADVERTISING RATES:
Full Page Mono EUR 1/1: b/w 4750,- 1/2: b/w 2680,-
Agency Commission: 15%
Mechanical Data: Type Area: 205 x 280mm, Bleed Size: 230 x 300mm
CONSUMER: WOMEN'S INTEREST CONSUMER MAGAZINES: Personal Finance

CATHOLICA MAGAZINE
18086N87-126
Editorial: Dorpsstraat 90, 5735 EG AARLE RIXTEL
Tel: 70 4454149
Web site: http://www.catholica.nl
Date Established: 01-01-1989; **Freq:** 10 issues yearly; **Annual Sub.:** EUR 27,50; **Circ:** 3,000
Usual Pagination: 48
Editor: Angelique van der Horst
Profile: Magazine focusing on church life and the Catholic faith.
Language(s): Dutch
Agency Commission: 15%
Mechanical Data: Type Area: 140 x 205mm, Bleed Size: 170 x 240mm
CONSUMER: RELIGIOUS

CBM (COMPUTER BUSINESS MAGAZINE)
761051N5B-25
Editorial: Bijsterhuizen 31-47, 6604 LV WIJCHEN
Tel: 23 5565370 **Fax:** 55 5412288

Email: magenta@kantoornet.nl **Web site:** http://www.computerweb.nl
Date Established: 01-04-1997; **Freq:** 11 issues yearly; **Annual Sub.:** EUR 60,-; **Circ:** 8,500
Editor-in-Chief: Johan van Leeuwen; **Publisher:** Joost Heessels
Profile: Magazine focusing on computer business, providing information on hardware and software.
Language(s): Dutch
Readership: Aimed at IT professionals.
ADVERTISING RATES:
Full Page Mono EUR 2/1: f.c. 5000,-; 1/1: f.c. 2950,-; 1/2: f.c. 2250,-
Agency Commission: 15%
Mechanical Data: Type Area: 198 x 287mm, Bleed Size: 225 x 318mm
BUSINESS: COMPUTERS & AUTOMATION: Data Processing

CCM
16034N18B-15
Editorial: Europark 24, 4904 SX OOSTERHOUT
Tel: 23 5565370 **Fax:** 55 5412288
Email: info@ccmonline.nl **Web site:** http://www.ccmonline.nl
Freq: 10 issues yearly; **Cover Price:** EUR 15,-
Annual Sub.: EUR 119,-; **Circ:** 8,500
Editor: Mary-Jo van de Velde-de Leeuw
Profile: Magazine about all aspects of call centre management.
Language(s): Dutch
Readership: Read by call centre managers, senior management, consultants, telecom and ICT specialists.
ADVERTISING RATES:
Full Page Mono EUR 2/1: b/w 2550,- 1/1: b/w 2130,- 1/2: b/w 1250,-
Agency Commission: 15%
Mechanical Data: Type Area: 185 x 270mm, Bleed Size: 210 x 297mm
Copy instructions: *Copy Date:* 2 weeks prior to publication date
BUSINESS: ELECTRONICS: Telecommunications

CHANNELCONNECT
15733N5B-85
Editorial: Mgr. Dr. H. Poelslaan 140, 1187 BE AMSTELVEEN **Tel:** 88 7518800 **Fax:** 20 5353696
Email: info@connexie.nl **Web site:** http://www.channelconnect.nl
Freq: 9 issues yearly; **Cover Price:** EUR 4,95
Annual Sub.: EUR 84,-; **Circ:** 7,118
Editor: Hans Peter van Tilburg; **Publisher:** Fred Schuit
Profile: Magazine providing news and information concerning all aspects of the IT trade.
Language(s): Dutch
Readership: Aimed at IT directors, managers, consultants and other professionals involved in the field.
ADVERTISING RATES:
Full Page Mono EUR 2/1: b/w 7895,- 1/1: b/w 5195,- 1/2: b/w 3115,-
Agency Commission: 15%
Mechanical Data: Type Area: 184 x 260mm, Bleed Size: 210 x 285mm
BUSINESS: COMPUTERS & AUTOMATION: Data Processing

CHAPEAU! MAGAZINE
17858N80-430
Editorial: Het Bat 8, 6211 EX MAASTRICHT
Tel: 70 3789880 **Fax:** 70 3789783
Web site: http://www.chapeaumagazine.com
Date Established: 01-01-1997; **Freq:** 6 issues yearly; **Cover Price:** EUR 5,95
Annual Sub.: EUR 22,50; **Circ:** 19,209
Editor: Jo Cortenraedt
Profile: General interest magazine about life in Limburg.
Language(s): Dutch
ADVERTISING RATES:
Full Page Mono EUR 2/1: f.c. 4295,-; 1/1: f.c. 2225,-; 1/2: f.c. 1295,-
Agency Commission: 15%
Mechanical Data: Type Area: 215 x 287mm, Bleed Size: 225 x 297mm
CONSUMER: RURAL & REGIONAL INTEREST

CHECKPOINT
1775301N94A-1
Editorial: Energieweg 40, 6541 CX NIJMEGEN
Tel: 113 274014 **Fax:** 24 3723631
Email: checkpoint@veteranen.nl
Date Established: 01-01-2000; **Freq:** 10 issues yearly; **Annual Sub.:** EUR 18,50; **Circ:** 82,000
Editor: Fred Lardenoye; **Editor-in-Chief:** J.R. Rozemuller; **Publisher:** J. Schoeman
Language(s): Dutch
ADVERTISING RATES:
Full Page Mono EUR 1/1: f.c. 3770,-; b/w 2900,- 1/2: f.c. 2094,-; b/w 1611,- 1/4: f.c. 1164,-; b/w 895,-
Agency Commission: 15%
Mechanical Data: Type Area: 190 x 270mm, Bleed Size: 210 x 297mm
CONSUMER: OTHER CLASSIFICATIONS: War Veterans

CHEMIE AKTUEEL
15854N13-25
Editorial: De Moeshof 9, 5258 ER BERLICUM
Tel: 35 6726900
Email: info@chemieaktueel.nl
Date Established: 01-01-1988; **Freq:** 3 issues yearly; **Annual Sub.:** EUR 40,-; **Circ:** 1,000
Usual Pagination: 72
Editor: Miek Scheffers-Sap; **Editor-in-Chief:** Toon de Valk
Profile: Magazine covering about chemistry education.
Language(s): Dutch
ADVERTISING RATES:
Full Page Mono EUR 1/1: b/w 454,- 1/2: b/w 227,- 1/4: b/w 136,-
Agency Commission: 15%
Mechanical Data: Type Area: 127 x 237mm, Bleed Size: 210 x 297mm
BUSINESS: CHEMICALS

CHEMIE MAGAZINE
15857N13-80
Editorial: Loire 150, 2941 AK DEN HAAG
Tel: 20 5159172 **Fax:** 20 5159145
Email: info@vnci.nl
Freq: 11 issues yearly; **Circ:** 3,000
Editor: I. Znidarsic; **Editor-in-Chief:** Jos de Gruiter
Profile: Pan-European official journal of the Association of the Dutch Chemical Industry.
Language(s): Dutch
Readership: Read by managers and stakeholders of The Netherlands operating chemical companies.
ADVERTISING RATES:
Full Page Mono .. EUR 1/1: f.c. 1425,-; 1/2: f.c. 780,-; 1/4: f.c. 435,-
Agency Commission: 15%
Mechanical Data: Type Area: 185 x 267mm, Bleed Size: 210 x 297mm
BUSINESS: CHEMICALS

CHILDREN'S RELIEF MAGAZINE
16685N56A-9
Editorial: Tiendweg 9, 2931 LC KRIMPEN A/D LEK
Tel: 20 5979500 **Fax:** 20 5979590
Email: info@childrensrelief.nl
Freq: Quarterly; **Cover Price:** Free; **Circ:** 8,000
Editor: Silvia Hafkamp; **Editor-in-Chief:** A. Drease
Profile: Magazine about medical relief aid in Eastern Europe.
Language(s): Dutch
Agency Commission: 15%
BUSINESS: HEALTH & MEDICAL

CHIP
1637168N5D-235
Editorial: Meyhorst 60-10, 6537 KT NIJMEGEN
Tel: 45 5795877 **Fax:** 24 3723631
Email: fnl@fnl.nl **Web site:** http://www.chip.nl
Freq: 10 issues yearly; **Cover Price:** EUR 4,75
Annual Sub.: EUR 42,50; **Circ:** 13,498
Editor: Pieter van Megen; **Editor-in-Chief:** Mark van Sommeren
Language(s): Dutch
ADVERTISING RATES:
Full Page Mono EUR 2/1: f.c. 5000,-; 1/1: f.c. 2950,-; 1/2: f.c. 2250,-
Agency Commission: 15%
Mechanical Data: Bleed Size: 210 x 297mm
BUSINESS: COMPUTERS & AUTOMATION: Personal Computers

CHIP FOTO-VIDEO DIGITAAL
1643999N85A-28
Editorial: Meyhorst 60-10, 6537 KT NIJMEGEN
Tel: 23 5565462 **Fax:** 23 5564588
Email: fnl@fnl.nl **Web site:** http://www.chipfotovideo.nl
Freq: 8 issues yearly; **Cover Price:** EUR 3,75
Annual Sub.: EUR 27,-; **Circ:** 15,473
Usual Pagination: 100
Editor: Pieter van Megen; **Editor-in-Chief:** Joeri Folman
Language(s): Dutch
ADVERTISING RATES:
Full Page Mono EUR 2/1: f.c. 5000,-; 1/1: f.c. 2950,-; 1/2: f.c. 2250,-; 1/4: f.c. 1550,-
Agency Commission: 15%
Mechanical Data: Type Area: 190 x 239mm, Bleed Size: 230 x 300mm
CONSUMER: PHOTOGRAPHY & FILM MAKING: Photography

CHRISTELIJK WEEKBLAD
18068N87-58
Editorial: Reviusstraat 1, 8913 HT LEEUWARDEN
Tel: 23 5564565 **Fax:** 23 5564575
Date Established: 01-01-1952; **Freq:** Weekly; **Annual Sub.:** EUR 59,-; **Circ:** 3,600
Editor: Theo Klein; **Editor-in-Chief:** Ineke Evink
Profile: Magazine focusing on religious news and views.
Language(s): Dutch
ADVERTISING RATES:
Full Page Mono .. EUR 1/1: b/w 1059,- 1/2: b/w 582,- 1/4: b/w 320,-
Agency Commission: 15%
Mechanical Data: Type Area: 242 x 370mm, Bleed Size: 280 x 395mm
CONSUMER: RELIGIOUS

CICERO
16728N56C-10
Editorial: Postbus 9600, 2300 RC LEIDEN
Tel: 23 5564565 **Fax:** 23 5564575
Web site: http://www.lumc.nl/cicero
Date Established: 17-01-1986; **Freq:** 10 issues yearly; **Annual Sub.:** EUR 25,-; **Circ:** 9,000
Editor: G.J.M. van Baarsel; **Editor-in-Chief:** Diana de Veld
Profile: Magazine containing information from the University Medical Centre of Leiden (Research, teaching and hospital).
Language(s): Dutch
Agency Commission: 15%
Mechanical Data: Type Area: 217 x 302mm, Bleed Size: 245 x 335mm
BUSINESS: HEALTH & MEDICAL: Hospitals

CJP MAGAZINE
629470N89C-143
Editorial: Westerstraat 187, 1015 MA AMSTERDAM
Email: cjp@cjp.nl
Date Established: 04-04-2003; **Freq:** 6 issues yearly; **Annual Sub.:** EUR 9,90; **Circ:** 100,000
Editor: Arne van Terphoven
Profile: Magazine providing information on cultural events, concerts and exhibitions in Rotterdam, including travel and festivals, also features profiles of artistes.
Language(s): Dutch
Readership: Aimed at people aged between 18 and 20 years.
ADVERTISING RATES:
Full Page Mono EUR 2/1: f.c. 6990,-; 1/1: f.c. 3750,-; 1/2: f.c. 2500,-
Agency Commission: 15%
Mechanical Data: Type Area: 128 x 190mm, Bleed Size: 148 x 210mm
CONSUMER: HOLIDAYS & TRAVEL: Entertainment Guides

CLOU
15591N2A-58_50
Editorial: Arlandaweg 92, 1043 EX AMSTERDAM
Tel: 255 530577 **Fax:** 223 650011
Email: info@moaweb.nl
Freq: 6 issues yearly; **Cover Price:** Free; **Circ:** 9,500
Editor: Jan Roekens; **Editor-in-Chief:** Jan Roekens
Profile: Official publication of MOA - the Market Research Association. Contains society news, interviews and trade views.
Language(s): Dutch
Readership: Read by marketing analysts and market researchers.
ADVERTISING RATES:
Full Page Mono EUR 2/1: f.c. 2500,-; 1/1: f.c. 1950,-; 1/2: f.c. 1000,-
Agency Commission: 15%
Mechanical Data: Type Area: 190 x 275mm, Bleed Size: 210 x 297mm
Copy instructions: *Copy Date:* 3 weeks prior to publication date
BUSINESS: COMMUNICATIONS, ADVERTISING & MARKETING

CLUBGREEN JAARMAGAZINE
1900596N57-217
Editorial: Baarsjesweg 311, 1058 AH AMSTERDAM
Tel: 30 6383716 **Fax:** 73 6157171
Email: info@clubgreen.nl **Web site:** http://www.clubgreen.nl
Freq: Annual; **Cover Price:** EUR 4,95; **Circ:** 100,000
Editor-in-Chief: Lysanne Horsten; **Publisher:** Jeannot Tuijnman
Language(s): Dutch
ADVERTISING RATES:
Full Page Mono EUR 2/1: b/w 4690,- 1/1: b/w 3250,-
Agency Commission: 15%
Mechanical Data: Bleed Size: 185 x 255mm
BUSINESS: ENVIRONMENT & POLLUTION

COC ZWOLLE MAGAZINE
18052N86B-17
Editorial: Kamperstraat 17, 8011 LJ ZWOLLE
Tel: 20 5159722 **Fax:** 71 3643461
Email: info@coczwolle.nl
Date Established: 01-07-1995; **Freq:** Quarterly; **Cover Price:** Free; **Circ:** 700
Usual Pagination: 24
Editor: Hanneke Gerritsen
Profile: Publication of the COC - the Netherlands Association for Integration of Homosexuality. Focuses on the district of Zwolle.
Language(s): Dutch
ADVERTISING RATES:
Full Page Mono ..... EUR 3x 1/1: f.c. 570,-; 3x 1/2: f.c. 270,-
Agency Commission: 15%
CONSUMER: ADULT & GAY MAGAZINES: Gay & Lesbian Magazines

COIFFURE GENERATION
624026N15B-101
Editorial: Stationsplein 2, 3112 HJ SCHIEDAM
Tel: 172 466539 **Fax:** 10 4521797
Email: itsabc@itsamazing.nl **Web site:** http://www.coiffure.nl
Freq: Half-yearly; **Cover Price:** EUR 15,20; **Circ:** 4,343
Editor: Danielle Sant; **Editor-in-Chief:** Anouk Oudkerk Pool; **Publisher:** Rinus Vissers
Profile: Magazine focusing on hairdressing styles and trends.
Language(s): Dutch
Readership: Read by hairdressers.
ADVERTISING RATES:
Full Page Mono .... EUR 1/1: f.c. 1495,-
Agency Commission: 15%
Mechanical Data: Bleed Size: 170 x 230mm
Copy instructions: *Copy Date:* 14 days prior to publication date
BUSINESS: COSMETICS & HAIRDRESSING: Hairdressing

THE COINHUNTER MAGAZINE
17833N79E-10
Editorial: Dollard 147, 8032 KD ZWOLLE
Tel: 20 5159703
Web site: http://www.thecoinhunter.com
Freq: Quarterly; **Annual Sub.:** EUR 17,02; **Circ:** 1,750
Editor: Henk Hasselt; **Publisher:** Henk Hasselt
Profile: Magazine providing information about old coins.
Language(s): Dutch
Readership: Aimed at coin collectors and people who enjoy metal detecting.
Agency Commission: 15%
Mechanical Data: Bleed Size: 210 x 297mm
CONSUMER: HOBBIES & DIY: Numismatics

COLLECT
1634439N79C-103
Editorial: Postbus 30250, 2500 GG DEN HAAG
Tel: 570 647102 **Fax:** 570 647533
Freq: Quarterly; **Cover Price:** EUR 2,50; **Circ:** 200,000
Language(s): Dutch
ADVERTISING RATES:
Full Page Mono .... EUR 1/1: f.c. 9450,-
Agency Commission: 15%
Mechanical Data: Type Area: 180 x 260mm, Bleed Size: 200 x 280mm
Copy instructions: *Copy Date:* 2 months prior to publication date
CONSUMER: HOBBIES & DIY: Philately

COLLECTEKRANT
1637198N1P-8
Editorial: Utrechtseweg 1b, 3811 NA AMERSFOORT
Tel: 570 647659 **Fax:** 570 647803
Email: info@ango.nl **Web site:** http://www.handicap.nl
Freq: Annual; **Cover Price:** Free; **Circ:** 1,000,000
Language(s): Dutch
Agency Commission: 15%
Mechanical Data: Bleed Size: 290 x 420mm
BUSINESS: FINANCE & ECONOMICS: Fundraising

COLOR STUDIO
2009545N74C-392
Editorial: Singel 468, 1017 AW AMSTERDAM
Tel: 88 2697112 **Fax:** 88 2696983
Email: singel@hearstmagazines.nl
Date Established: 01-05-2010; **Freq:** Annual; **Cover Price:** Free; **Circ:** 300,000
Usual Pagination: 36
Editor: A. Vlasblom; **Editor-in-Chief:** Annelies Kooijman; **Publisher:** Luc van Os
Language(s): Dutch
Agency Commission: 15%
CONSUMER: WOMEN'S INTEREST CONSUMER MAGAZINES: Home & Family

COMMON MARKET LAW REVIEW
16465N44-15
Editorial: Zuidpoolsingel 2, 2408 ZE ALPHEN A/D RIJN **Tel:** 70 3780250 **Fax:** 70 7999866
Freq: 6 issues yearly; **Annual Sub.:** EUR 682,-; **Circ:** 1,600
Editor: A. McDonnell
Profile: Pan-European publication concerning law in the European Union.
Language(s): Dutch
Readership: Aimed at academic lawyers and judiciary personnel.
ADVERTISING RATES:
Full Page Mono .... EUR 1/1: f.c. 715,-
Agency Commission: 15%
BUSINESS: LEGAL

COMMUNICATIE
625280N2A-34
Editorial: Kon. Wilhelminaplein 30, 1062 KR AMSTERDAM **Tel:** 20 3467209 **Fax:** 20 6159047
Web site: http://www.communicatie-online.nl
Date Established: 01-01-1994; **Freq:** 10 issues yearly; **Cover Price:** EUR 17,-
Annual Sub.: EUR 144,50; **Circ:** 4,941
Editor: Rocco Mooij; **Editor-in-Chief:** E. Elsinghorst; **Publisher:** Antje Bosscher
Profile: Magazine focusing on mass-communication and communication management.
Language(s): Dutch
Readership: Aimed at communications professionals.
ADVERTISING RATES:
Full Page Mono EUR 1/1: b/w 1850,- 1/2: b/w 1250,- 1/4: b/w 800,-
Agency Commission: 15%
Mechanical Data: Type Area: 190 x 268mm, Bleed Size: 210 x 297mm
BUSINESS: COMMUNICATIONS, ADVERTISING & MARKETING

COMPUTER EASY
761201N5D-13
Editorial: Meyhorst 60-10, 6537 KT NIJMEGEN
Tel: 20 5612070 **Fax:** 24 3723631
Email: fnl@fnl.nl **Web site:** http://www.computereasy.nl
Freq: 10 issues yearly; **Cover Price:** EUR 2,95
Annual Sub.: EUR 21,25; **Circ:** 35,707
Editor: P.J.J. Gerrits
Profile: Magazine providing information and advice for computer beginners.
Language(s): Dutch
Readership: Aimed at computer beginners, including members of the computer banking clubs.

ADVERTISING RATES:
Full Page Mono EUR 2/1: f.c. 5000,-; 1/1: f.c. 2950,-; 1/2: f.c. 2250,-
Agency Commission: 15%
Mechanical Data: Type Area: 183 x 248mm, Bleed Size: 210 x 297mm
BUSINESS: COMPUTERS & AUTOMATION: Personal Computers

COMPUTER EXPRESS 15731N5B-45
Editorial: John F. Kennedylaan 8, WBC C0.44, 7314 PS APELDOORN **Tel:** 88 2697364 **Fax:** 88 2697490
Email: secretariaat@pvcf.nl
Freq: 6 issues yearly; **Circ:** 15,500
Editor: Otto Slijkhuis; **Editor-in-Chief:** Otto Slijkhuis
Profile: Computer magazine containing product reviews and specifications, information on software and hardware and news about developments in the IT industry.
Language(s): Dutch
Readership: Aimed at members of the PVCF club.
Agency Commission: 15%
Mechanical Data: Type Area: 210 x 280mm
BUSINESS: COMPUTERS & AUTOMATION: Data Processing

COMPUTER IDEE 15765N5D-15
Editorial: Prof. Eijkmanlaan 2, 2035 XB HAARLEM
Tel: 23 5565370 **Fax:** 23 5565357
Email: info@hub.nl **Web site:** http://www.computeridee.nl
Freq: 26 issues yearly; **Cover Price:** EUR 2,50
Annual Sub.: EUR 55,-; **Circ:** 60,079
Editor: Rob Coenraads; **Publisher:** Martin Smelt
Profile: Magazine providing information on personal computers, peripherals, telecommunications, software and applications.
Language(s): Dutch
Readership: Aimed at people of all ages using a PC at home, work or school.
ADVERTISING RATES:
Full Page Mono .... EUR 2/1: f.c. 12.383,-; 1/1: f.c. 6318,-; 1/2: f.c. 4411,-
Agency Commission: 15%
Mechanical Data: Type Area: 192 x 252mm, Bleed Size: 215 x 285mm
Copy instructions: *Copy Date:* 4 weeks prior to publication date
BUSINESS: COMPUTERS & AUTOMATION: Personal Computers

COMPUTER!TOTAAL 15767N5D-22
Editorial: Transformatorweg 80, 1014 AK AMSTERDAM **Tel:** 23 5461122
Email: info@idg.nl **Web site:** http://www.computertotaal.nl
Freq: Monthly; **Cover Price:** EUR 4,95
Annual Sub.: EUR 46,85; **Circ:** 95,451
Editor: Volkert Deen
Profile: Official journal of the Hobby Computer Club, providing an insight and survey of hard- and software.
Language(s): Dutch
Readership: Aimed at small business management and home PC users.
ADVERTISING RATES:
Full Page Mono .... EUR 2/1: f.c. 13.399,-; 1/1: f.c. 7875,-; 1/2: f.c. 4925,-
Agency Commission: 15%
Mechanical Data: Type Area: 217 x 290mm, Bleed Size: 230 x 300mm
BUSINESS: COMPUTERS & AUTOMATION: Personal Computers

CONNECT 17475N74F-95
Editorial: Provincialeweg 70, 3329 KP DORDRECHT
Tel: 33 4220082 **Fax:** 24 3723631
Email: info@dehoop.org **Web site:** http://www.cnct.nl
Freq: 6 issues yearly; **Cover Price:** Free; **Circ:** 18,000
Editor: Teun Stortenbeker; **Editor-in-Chief:** Diana Langerak
Profile: Magazine containing information about free time, music and drug abuse.
Language(s): Dutch
Readership: Read by children aged 12 years and over.
Agency Commission: 15%
CONSUMER: WOMEN'S INTEREST CONSUMER MAGAZINES: Teenage

CONNEXIE 16035N18B-30
Editorial: Mgr. Dr. H. Poelslaan 140, 1187 BE AMSTELVEEN **Tel:** 79 6366208 **Fax:** 79 3636262
Email: info@connexie.nl **Web site:** http://www.connexie.nl
Date Established: 01-09-1997; **Freq:** 10 issues yearly; **Cover Price:** EUR 4,50
Annual Sub.: EUR 65,-; **Circ:** 5,500
Usual Pagination: 112
Editor: Hans Peter van Tilburg; **Editor-in-Chief:** Marco Mekenkamp; **Publisher:** Fred Schuit
Profile: Practical magazine about telecommunications, with special attention to mobile communications.
Language(s): Dutch
Readership: Aimed at ICT managers and telecommunications purchasers.
ADVERTISING RATES:
Full Page Mono EUR 2/1: f.c. 4247,-; 1/1: f.c. 2741,-; 1/2: f.c. 1780,-; 1/4: f.c. 1150,-
Agency Commission: 15%
Mechanical Data: Type Area: 192 x 279mm, Bleed Size: 210 x 297mm
Copy instructions: *Copy Date:* 17 days prior to publication date
BUSINESS: ELECTRONICS: Telecommunications

CONSUMENTENGIDS 704428N74C-13
Editorial: Enthovenplein 1, 2521 DA DEN HAAG
Tel: 70 4454149 **Fax:** 70 7999866
Freq: 11 issues yearly; **Circ:** 420,000
Editor: Mark Friederichs; **Editor-in-Chief:** M. van Burk; **Publisher:** Gerjan Huis in 't Veld
Profile: Magazine containing information about products, includes tests and reports on new products.
Language(s): Dutch
Readership: Read by prospective purchasers.
Agency Commission: 15%
CONSUMER: WOMEN'S INTEREST CONSUMER MAGAZINES: Home & Family

'T CONTACT 626648N72-770
Editorial: Kerkstraat 2a, 5711 GV SOMEREN
Tel: 70 3307094 **Fax:** 226 333555
Email: info@hetcontact.nl **Web site:** http://www.hetcontact.nl
Date Established: 01-08-1955; **Freq:** Weekly; **Circ:** 14,500
Editor: Annemie Urlings; **Publisher:** R. Weijmans
Language(s): Dutch
Agency Commission: 15%
Mechanical Data: Type Area: 289 x 450mm, Bleed Size: 315 x 495mm
LOCAL NEWSPAPERS

CONTACT VSN 704420N74G-11
Editorial: Lt. Generaal van Heutszlaan 6, 3743 JN BAARN **Tel:** 314 349884 **Fax:** 314 349037
Email: vsn@vsn.nl **Web site:** http://www.vsn.nl/leden/contact
Date Established: 01-01-1967; **Freq:** 6 issues yearly; **Annual Sub.:** EUR 35,-; **Circ:** 10,000
Editor: Erik van Uden; **Editor-in-Chief:** M. Meijer
Profile: Magazine containing information for patients with neuromuscular disease.
Language(s): Dutch
Readership: Aimed at patients and members of the VSN organisation.
ADVERTISING RATES:
Full Page Mono EUR 1/1: b/w 770,- 1/2: b/w 440,- 1/4: b/w 255,-
Agency Commission: 15%
Mechanical Data: Type Area: 185 x 270mm, Bleed Size: 210 x 297mm
Copy instructions: *Copy Date:* 5 weeks prior to publication date
CONSUMER: WOMEN'S INTEREST CONSUMER MAGAZINES: Slimming & Health

CONTOUR AMSTERDAM 18125N89A-150
Editorial: De Ruyterkade 5, 1013 AA AMSTERDAM
Tel: 20 5922250 **Fax:** 20 5465530
Email: info@atcb.nl
Freq: Quarterly; **Cover Price:** Free; **Circ:** 2,000
Editor: H. ter Balkt
Profile: Magazine containing news and background information about tourism in Amsterdam.
Language(s): Dutch
Agency Commission: 15%
CONSUMER: HOLIDAYS & TRAVEL: Travel

CONTROLLERS JOURNAAL 15866N14A-45
Editorial: Vlierbeek 6, 3772 SW BARNEVELD
Web site: http://www.controllersjournaal.nl
Freq: 24 issues yearly; **Annual Sub.:** EUR 419,-
Editor: J.C.H. Speel; **Publisher:** M.F. Moons
Profile: Publication for business administrators and controllers.
Language(s): Dutch
Agency Commission: 15%
BUSINESS: COMMERCE, INDUSTRY & MANAGEMENT

CONTROLLERS MAGAZINE 15469N1A-19
Editorial: Utrechtseweg 31a, 3812 NA AMERSFOORT **Tel:** 33 4220082 **Fax:** 30 6383991
Email: info@ivbnetworks.nl **Web site:** http://www.controllersmagazine.nl
Date Established: 01-10-1986; **Freq:** 8 issues yearly; **Cover Price:** EUR 21,08
Annual Sub.: EUR 168,60; **Circ:** 2,816
Editor: R. Vahl; **Publisher:** Heleen Kooistra
Profile: Magazine providing financial information and advice.
Language(s): Dutch
Readership: Aimed at controllers, credit managers, treasurers and financial directors.
ADVERTISING RATES:
Full Page Mono EUR 1/1: f.c. 3396,-; b/w 2203,- 1/2: f.c. 2253,-; b/w 1272,- 1/4: f.c. 1493,-; b/w 747,-
Agency Commission: 15%
Mechanical Data: Type Area: 183 x 242mm, Bleed Size: 215 x 285mm
BUSINESS: FINANCE & ECONOMICS

CONVERSE AGENDA 1641559N88R-79
Editorial: Reaal 2b, 2353 TL LEIDERDORP
Tel: 314 349562 **Fax:** 314 340515
Email: info@stationeryteam.nl
Freq: Annual; **Cover Price:** EUR 11,95; **Circ:** 70,000
Publisher: M. Leguijt
Language(s): Dutch
Agency Commission: 15%
Mechanical Data: Bleed Size: 140 x 188mm
CONSUMER: EDUCATION: Education Related

CORDARES-POST 15708N4E-283_50
Editorial: Basisweg 10, 1043 AP AMSTERDAM
Tel: 20 5833451 **Fax:** 20 5159145
Email: info@cordares.nl
Date Established: 01-12-1969; **Freq:** 6 issues yearly; **Cover Price:** Free; **Circ:** 20,000
Editor-in-Chief: Frank de Carpentier
Profile: Magazine containing information for employees in the building trade.
Language(s): Dutch
Agency Commission: 15%
BUSINESS: ARCHITECTURE & BUILDING: Building

CORDIAAL 16714N56B-13
Editorial: Postbus 2087, 3440 DB WOERDEN
Tel: 523 285330
Email: secretariaat@nvhvv.nl
Freq: 5 issues yearly; **Circ:** 1,800
Profile: Official journal of the Society of Nurses in the Field of Cardiology.
Language(s): Dutch
ADVERTISING RATES:
Full Page Mono .. EUR 1/1: f.c. color 800,-[0] 1/2; b/w [1][1]500,- 1/4: b/w 0,-
Agency Commission: 15%
Mechanical Data: Type Area: 185 x 268mm, Bleed Size: 210 x 297mm
Copy instructions: *Copy Date:* 1 month prior to publication date
BUSINESS: HEALTH & MEDICAL: Nursing

COS (COMPUTERS OP SCHOOL) 15734N5B-93
Editorial: Niels Bohrweg 3, 3542 CA UTRECHT
Tel: 88 2697112 **Fax:** 88 2696983
Email: ess@ess.nl **Web site:** http://www.cos-online.nl
Date Established: 01-01-1988; **Freq:** 10 issues yearly; **Annual Sub.:** EUR 45,-; **Circ:** 4,300
Usual Pagination: 36
Editor: Theo Louwers; **Editor-in-Chief:** Albert Lubberink
Profile: Magazine about computers used in schools.
Language(s): Dutch
Readership: Read by teachers and students.
ADVERTISING RATES:
Full Page Mono EUR 2/1: f.c. 1885,-; 1/1: f.c. 1075,-; 1/2: f.c. 595,-
Agency Commission: 15%
Mechanical Data: Type Area: 209 x 284mm, Bleed Size: 225 x 300mm
Copy instructions: *Copy Date:* 4 weeks prior to publication date
BUSINESS: COMPUTERS & AUTOMATION: Data Processing

COSMOGIRL! 1637370N74Q-282
Editorial: Delflandlaan 4, 1062 EB AMSTERDAM
Tel: 30 2738234 **Fax:** 30 2738277
Email: info@pelicanmags.nl **Web site:** http://www.cosmogirl.nl
Freq: 13 issues yearly; **Cover Price:** EUR 3,95
Annual Sub.: EUR 51,35; **Circ:** 100,385
Publisher: F.N. Kloppert
Language(s): Dutch
ADVERTISING RATES:
Full Page Mono EUR 1/1: f.c. 6824,-; 1/2: f.c. 5118,-; 1/4: f.c. 2730,-
Agency Commission: 15%
Mechanical Data: Type Area: 174 x 252mm, Bleed Size: 206 x 275mm
CONSUMER: WOMEN'S INTEREST CONSUMER MAGAZINES: Lifestyle

COSMOPOLITAN 17413N74A-40
Editorial: Capellalaan 65, 2132 JL HOOFDDORP
Tel: 23 5565280 **Fax:** 23 5565251
Web site: http://www.cosmopolitan.nl
Date Established: 01-01-1982; **Freq:** Monthly; **Cover Price:** EUR 4,95
Annual Sub.: EUR 58,20; **Circ:** 120,691
Editor: Claudia Straatmans; **Publisher:** Sanne Visser
Profile: Magazine containing articles on fashion, beauty, travel, homes, leisure, employment and current-affairs.
Language(s): Dutch
Readership: Aimed at the modern woman.
ADVERTISING RATES:
Full Page Mono .... EUR 2/1: f.c. 23.900,-; 1/1: f.c. 11.950,-; 1/2: f.c. 7170,-
Agency Commission: 15%
Mechanical Data: Type Area: 178 x 252mm, Bleed Size: 210 x 280mm
CONSUMER: WOMEN'S INTEREST CONSUMER MAGAZINES: Women's Interest

COUNTRY LIFE MAGAZINE 17550N74Q-24
Editorial: Ekselerbrink 84, 7812 VM EMMEN
Tel: 70 3780250
Web site: http://www.gocountry.nl
Freq: Quarterly; **Annual Sub.:** EUR 18,50; **Circ:** 12,500
Editor: K. Stulen; **Publisher:** K. Stulen
Profile: Magazine focusing on articles about Dutch country life and social history. Includes features on country music and line dancing.
Language(s): Dutch
Agency Commission: 15%
Mechanical Data: Bleed Size: 210 x 275mm
CONSUMER: WOMEN'S INTEREST CONSUMER MAGAZINES: Lifestyle

CREATIE 1660387N2A-131
Editorial: Kon. Wilhelminaplein 30, 1062 KR AMSTERDAM **Tel:** 23 5430090 **Fax:** 30 6383839
Web site: http://www.creatie.nl
Date Established: 22-11-2004; **Freq:** 6 issues yearly; **Cover Price:** EUR 27,50
Annual Sub.: EUR 125,-; **Circ:** 2,043
Editor: Astrid Prummel; **Editor-in-Chief:** Ton Goedknegt; **Publisher:** Jelske Gerritsma
Language(s): Dutch
ADVERTISING RATES:
Full Page Mono EUR 1/1: b/w 1850,- 1/2: b/w 1050,- 1/4: b/w 650,-
Agency Commission: 15%
Mechanical Data: Type Area: 190 x 268mm, Bleed Size: 210 x 297mm
BUSINESS: COMMUNICATIONS, ADVERTISING & MARKETING

CREDO 18071N87-70
Editorial: Oranjestraat 29, 6741 CV LUNTEREN
Tel: 30 6399911
Date Established: 01-01-1974; **Freq:** 9 issues yearly; **Annual Sub.:** EUR 18,-; **Circ:** 3,000
Editor: W.J.W. Scheltens
Profile: Calvinist magazine.
Language(s): Dutch
Readership: Aimed at members of the Reformed Church.
Agency Commission: 15%
CONSUMER: RELIGIOUS

CRITICAL CARE 1664544N56A-428
Editorial: Het Spoor 2, 3994 AK HOUTEN
Tel: 30 6383838 **Fax:** 30 6383839
Web site: http://www.criticalcare.nl
Freq: 6 issues yearly; **Annual Sub.:** EUR 46,95; **Circ:** 1,194
Editor: Irma Spaans; **Editor-in-Chief:** Mireille van Brussel; **Publisher:** Karin Linden
Language(s): Dutch
ADVERTISING RATES:
Full Page Mono .. EUR 1/1: f.c. 2281,-; b/w 964,- 1/2: f.c. 1893,-; b/w 576,- 1/4: f.c. 1674,-; b/w 330,-
Agency Commission: 15%
Mechanical Data: Type Area: 170 x 256mm, Bleed Size: 210 x 297mm
BUSINESS: HEALTH & MEDICAL

CROSSOVER 1903426N77A-404
Editorial: Beechavenue 101, 1119 RB SCHIPHOL-RIJK **Tel:** 30 6383716 **Fax:** 73 6157171
Email: marketing@atp.nl
Freq: Quarterly; **Circ:** 70,000
Editor: Ron Bongers
Language(s): Dutch
ADVERTISING RATES:
Full Page Mono .... EUR 2/1: b/w 10.000,- 1/1: b/w 7000,- 1/2: b/w 4000,-
Agency Commission: 15%
Mechanical Data: Type Area: 95 x 200mm, Bleed Size: 105 x 210mm
Copy instructions: *Copy Date:* 4 weeks prior to publication date
CONSUMER: MOTORING & CYCLING: Motoring

CROW ET CETERA 16431N42B-100
Editorial: Galvanistraat 1, 6716 AE EDE
Tel: 570 648901 **Fax:** 20 5979505
Email: crow@crow.nl **Web site:** http://www.crow.nl/etcetera
Freq: 8 issues yearly; **Cover Price:** Free; **Circ:** 6,800
Editor: Tim Oosten; **Editor-in-Chief:** Tim Oosten
Profile: Journal of the Technology Centre for Transport and Infrastructure of the Dutch Committee in the World Road Association. Includes details on traffic, hydraulic engineering and road construction.
Language(s): Dutch
Readership: Read by the committee members.
ADVERTISING RATES:
Full Page Mono EUR 1/1: f.c. 1900,-; 1/2: f.c. 1120,-; 1/4: f.c. 660,-
Agency Commission: 15%
Mechanical Data: Type Area: 190 x 270mm, Bleed Size: 210 x 297mm
Copy instructions: *Copy Date:* 3 weeks prior to publication date
BUSINESS: CONSTRUCTION: Roads

C'T MAGAZINE VOOR COMPUTER TECHNIEK
15758N5C-2

Editorial: Meyhorst 60-10, 6537 KT NIJMEGEN
Tel: 172 466622 **Fax:** 24 3723631
Email: fnl@fnl.nl **Web site:** http://www.ct.nl
Freq: 10 issues yearly; **Cover Price:** EUR 5,99
Annual Sub.: EUR 51,-; **Circ:** 22,375
Editor: Patrick Smits; **Editor-in-Chief:** Ton Heijnen
Profile: Magazine covering all aspects of computing. Includes information about Macintosh, Windows, OS/2 and Unix systems. Also provides articles on hard- and software, product tests and tips and the Internet.
Language(s): Dutch
Readership: Aimed at experienced and business users.
ADVERTISING RATES:
Full Page Mono EUR 2/1: f.c. 5000,-; 1/1: f.c. 2950,-; 1/2: f.c. 2250,-
Agency Commission: 15%
Mechanical Data: Type Area: 185 x 247mm, Bleed Size: 210 x 297mm
BUSINESS: COMPUTERS & AUTOMATION: Professional Personal Computers

CTR/DE POLDERBODE
626651N72-840

Editorial: Smidsweg 59, 1761 BH ANNA PAULOWNA
Web site: http://www.polderbode.nl
Freq: Weekly; **Circ:** 7,850
Language(s): Dutch
Agency Commission: 15%
Mechanical Data: Type Area: 260 x 390mm
LOCAL NEWSPAPERS

LA CUCINA ITALIANA
1637299N74P-222

Editorial: Meyhorst 60-10, 6537 KT NIJMEGEN
Tel: 70 3789880 **Fax:** 70 3789783
Email: fnl@fnl.nl **Web site:** http://www.cucinait.nl
Freq: Monthly; **Cover Price:** EUR 4,99
Annual Sub.: EUR 54,-; **Circ:** 9,970
Editor: Joachim Hilhorst; **Publisher:** P. Lemmens
Language(s): Dutch
ADVERTISING RATES:
Full Page Mono EUR 1/1: b/w 2000,- 1/2: b/w 1400,- 1/4: b/w 850,-
Agency Commission: 15%
Mechanical Data: Bleed Size: 220 x 276mm
CONSUMER: WOMEN'S INTEREST CONSUMER MAGAZINES: Food & Cookery

CULTOURA
18116N89A-182

Editorial: Prinsengracht 783-785, 1017 JZ AMSTERDAM **Tel:** 30 6383743 **Fax:** 229 216416
Email: info@academischereizen.nl **Web site:** http://www.cultoura.nl
Freq: Quarterly; **Annual Sub.:** EUR 25,-; **Circ:** 4,500
Editor: Marijke Dessing
Profile: Magazine about cultural travel, archaeology, art and music.
Language(s): Dutch
Agency Commission: 15%
Mechanical Data: Bleed Size: 210 x 279mm
CONSUMER: HOLIDAYS & TRAVEL: Travel

CURSOR
629701N83-13_10

Editorial: Postbus 513, 5600 MB EINDHOVEN
Tel: 35 6726900 **Fax:** 20 5854158
Web site: http://www.tue.nl/cursor
Date Established: 01-01-1958; **Freq:** 40 issues yearly; **Annual Sub.:** EUR 47,50; **Circ:** 8,000
Editor: J.L. Konings; **Editor-in-Chief:** B.E.M. Span
Profile: E-zine containing information about university life and events. Includes research news.
Language(s): Dutch
Readership: Read by students and personnel of the Technical University of Eindhoven.
Agency Commission: 15%
Mechanical Data: Type Area: 266 x 390mm, Bleed Size: 300 x 420mm
CONSUMER: STUDENT PUBLICATIONS

CURSUSGIDS
1634452N84A-409

Editorial: Raadhuisplein 7, 2132 TZ HOOFDDORP
Tel: 20 5512208 **Fax:** 570 647533
Email: info@pier-k.nl
Freq: Annual; **Cover Price:** Free; **Circ:** 60,000
Editor: Ineke de Vries; **Editor-in-Chief:** Ineke de Vries
Language(s): Dutch
ADVERTISING RATES:
Full Page Mono EUR 1/1: f.c. 2175,-; b/w 1375,- 1/2: f.c. 1095,-; b/w 795,- 1/3: f.c. 920,-; b/w 670,-
Agency Commission: 15%
Mechanical Data: Type Area: 185 x 275mm, Bleed Size: 210 x 297mm
CONSUMER: THE ARTS & LITERARY: Arts

DA BEAUTÉ
17498N74H-43

Editorial: Vijverweg 18, 2061 GX BLOEMENDAAL
Tel: 172 575581 **Fax:** 23 5565136
Email: info@vdbj.nl
Freq: Quarterly; **Cover Price:** Free; **Circ:** 140,000
Editor: Suzanne Bodegraven
Profile: Magazine containing consumer information about DA chemists and perfumeries with an emphasis on luxury cosmetics.
Language(s): Dutch
ADVERTISING RATES:
Full Page Mono .... EUR 2/1: f.c. 22.000,-; 1/1: f.c. 12.500,-
Agency Commission: 15%
Mechanical Data: Type Area: 210 x 285mm, Bleed Size: 210 x 285mm
CONSUMER: WOMEN'S INTEREST CONSUMER MAGAZINES: Hair & Beauty

DAARBUITEN
1635179N89A-183

Editorial: Timorplein 21a, 1094 CC AMSTERDAM
Tel: 23 5566770 **Fax:** 23 5565155
Freq: 3 issues yearly; **Circ:** 60,000
Language(s): Dutch
ADVERTISING RATES:
Full Page Mono EUR 2/1: f.c. 6300,-; 1/1: f.c. 3950,-; 1/2: f.c. 2550,-
Agency Commission: 15%
Mechanical Data: Bleed Size: 210 x 277mm, Type Area: 210 x 273mm
CONSUMER: HOLIDAYS & TRAVEL: Travel

DADA
18004N84A-40

Editorial: Dommelstraat 4, 5611 CK EINDHOVEN
Tel: 88 2944819 **Fax:** 30 6383991
Email: informatie@plint.nl
Date Established: 01-10-1995; **Freq:** Quarterly; **Annual Sub.:** EUR 20,-; **Circ:** 9,000
Editor: Mia Goes; **Editor-in-Chief:** Mia Goes
Profile: Magazine focusing on art.
Language(s): Dutch
Readership: Aimed at people of all ages who enjoy art.
Agency Commission: 15%
CONSUMER: THE ARTS & LITERARY: Arts

DAGBLAD DE LIMBURGER
17124N67B-1750

Editorial: Mercator 3, 6135 KW SITTARD
Tel: 46 4116300 **Fax:** 314 372706
Web site: http://www.limburger.nl
Freq: 312 issues yearly; **Annual Sub.:** EUR 294,95; **Circ:** 129,172
Editor: H. Paulissen
Language(s): Dutch
ADVERTISING RATES:
Full Page Mono . EUR C2: b/w 8149,- C7: b/w 4075,- C2, ed. za.: b/w 8838,- C7, ed. za.: b/w 4419,-
Agency Commission: 15%
Mechanical Data: Type Area: 266 x 398mm
REGIONAL DAILY & SUNDAY NEWSPAPERS: Regional Daily Newspapers

DAGBLAD DE PERS
1799049N65A-73

Editorial: Anthony Fokkerweg 61, 1059 CP AMSTERDAM **Tel:** 172 469050 **Fax:** 118 434059
Email: info@depers.nl **Web site:** http://www.depers.nl
Date Established: 01-01-2007; **Freq:** 260 issues yearly; **Cover Price:** Free; **Circ:** 244,138
Editor: Jan-Jaap Heij; **Editor-in-Chief:** Caroline Griep; **Publisher:** Ben Rogmans
Language(s): Dutch
ADVERTISING RATES:
Full Page Mono .... EUR 2/1: b/w 28.500,- 1/1: b/w 19.000,- 1/2: b/w 9500,-
Agency Commission: 15%
Mechanical Data: Type Area: 266 x 398mm
NATIONAL DAILY & SUNDAY NEWSPAPERS: National Daily Newspapers

DAGBLAD VAN HET NOORDEN
17111N67B-5050

Editorial: Lübeckweg 2, 9723 HE GRONINGEN
Tel: 50 5844205 **Fax:** 70 3602861
Email: info@ndcmediagroep.nl **Web site:** http://www.dvhn.nl
Freq: 312 issues yearly; **Annual Sub.:** EUR 274,50; **Circ:** 137,813
Editor: P. Sijpersma
Language(s): Dutch
ADVERTISING RATES:
Full Page Mono .... EUR 2/1: b/w 52.704,- 1/1: b/w 26.352,- 1/2: b/w 13.176,- 2/1 ed. za.: b/w 57.744,- 1/1 ed. za.: b/w 28.
Agency Commission: 15%
Mechanical Data: Type Area: 266 x 398mm
REGIONAL DAILY & SUNDAY NEWSPAPERS: Regional Daily Newspapers

DAK+BOUW
15694N4E-155_50

Editorial: Beursplein 37, 3001 AA ROTTERDAM
Tel: 45 5739390 **Fax:** 299 666645
Freq: 3 issues yearly; **Circ:** 12,000
Editor: Jan Oeij; **Editor-in-Chief:** Patricia van Boven; **Publisher:** Dirk Lahuis
Profile: Journal for those in the building and roofing industry.
Language(s): Dutch
ADVERTISING RATES:
Full Page Mono EUR 2/1: f.c. 5600,-; 1/1: f.c. 3350,-; 1/2: f.c. 2550,-
Agency Commission: 15%
Mechanical Data: Type Area: 200 x 255mm, Bleed Size: 220 x 275mm
Copy instructions: *Copy Date:* 3 weeks prior to publication date
BUSINESS: ARCHITECTURE & BUILDING: Building

DAKENRAAD
15695N4E-160

Editorial: Oude Zeedijk 7, 4271 BD DUSSEN
Tel: 30 6399911 **Fax:** 30 6399937
Email: info@dakenraad.nl
Freq: 6 issues yearly; **Cover Price:** EUR 11,-
Annual Sub.: EUR 61,-; **Circ:** 6,000
Editor: A.F. van den Hout; **Editor-in-Chief:** Ankh Brandt; **Publisher:** Ankh Brandt
Profile: Magazine containing information about roofing, including design, building, restoration and maintenance.
Language(s): Dutch
Readership: Aimed at roofers, architects, builders and suppliers of materials.
ADVERTISING RATES:
Full Page Mono EUR 1/1: f.c. 2650,-; 1/2: f.c. 1600,-; 1/4: f.c. 950,-
Agency Commission: 15%
Mechanical Data: Type Area: 190 x 277mm, Bleed Size: 210 x 297mm
BUSINESS: ARCHITECTURE & BUILDING: Building

DE DALFSER MARSKRAMER
626918N72-3170

Editorial: Postbus 61, 7710 AB NIEUWLEUSEN
Tel: 492 338432 **Fax:** 20 6767728
Web site: http://www.dedalfsermarskramer.nl
Date Established: 01-01-1962; **Freq:** Weekly; **Cover Price:** Free; **Circ:** 22,000
Editor: J. Hilbrink; **Editor-in-Chief:** J. Hilbrink
Language(s): Dutch
Agency Commission: 15%
Mechanical Data: Type Area: 265 x 388mm, Bleed Size: 290 x 400mm
LOCAL NEWSPAPERS

DE DANSMEESTER
17737N76G-15

Editorial: Marathonlaan 71, 1183 VC AMSTELVEEN
Tel: 570 647102 **Fax:** 570 647533
Date Established: 01-01-1922; **Freq:** Quarterly; **Cover Price:** Free; **Circ:** 400
Editor: David Simon; **Publisher:** David Simon
Profile: Magazine focusing on the teaching of dance at both amateur and professional levels.
Language(s): Dutch
Readership: Aimed at dance teachers and their pupils.
ADVERTISING RATES:
Full Page Mono .. EUR 1/1: f.c. 685,-; b/w 455,-** 1/2: b/w 350,-** 1/4: b/w 230,-
Agency Commission: 15%
Mechanical Data: Bleed Size: 210 x 297mm
CONSUMER: MUSIC & PERFORMING ARTS: Dance

DATABASE MAGAZINE
15737N5B-105

Editorial: Lemelerberg 19-23, 2402 ZN ALPHEN A/D RIJN **Tel:** 172 469050 **Fax:** 20 6159047
Email: array@array.nl **Web site:** http://www.dbm.nl
Freq: 8 issues yearly; **Cover Price:** EUR 13,50
Annual Sub.: EUR 96,30; **Circ:** 4,000
Editor: Hans Lamboo; **Editor-in-Chief:** Bart Plooij; **Publisher:** Werner Schoots
Profile: Journal for professionals involved with business intelligence and database management systems.
Language(s): Dutch
Readership: Aimed at business intelligence and database management systems professionals.
ADVERTISING RATES:
Full Page Mono EUR 1/1: b/w 2485,- 1/2: b/w 1460,- 1/4: b/w 855,-
Agency Commission: 15%
Mechanical Data: Type Area: 190 x 265mm, Bleed Size: 210 x 285mm
Copy instructions: *Copy Date:* 4 weeks prior to publication date
BUSINESS: COMPUTERS & AUTOMATION: Data Processing

DEALER INFO
15738N5B-105_75

Editorial: Weesperstraat 180, 1018 DN AMSTERDAM
Web site: http://www.dealerinfo.nl
Date Established: 01-01-1989; **Freq:** 9 issues yearly; **Annual Sub.:** EUR 45,-; **Circ:** 8,000
Editor: Luc Sala; **Editor-in-Chief:** S. Crone
Profile: Newsletter providing information on new products and IT services available in the Netherlands.
Language(s): Dutch
Readership: Aimed at computer retailers.
ADVERTISING RATES:
Full Page Mono EUR 1/1: f.c. 2500,-; b/w 1750,- 1/2: f.c. 1250,-; b/w 875,- 1/4: f.c. 625,-; b/w 450,-
Agency Commission: 15%
Mechanical Data: Type Area: 210 x 297mm, Bleed Size: 216 x 303mm
Copy instructions: *Copy Date:* 14 days prior to publication date
BUSINESS: COMPUTERS & AUTOMATION: Data Processing

DEFENSIEKRANT
16396N40-35

Editorial: Kalvermarkt 38, 2511 CB DEN HAAG
Tel: 35 5480900 **Fax:** 35 5417272
Freq: Weekly; **Annual Sub.:** EUR 13,61; **Circ:** 50,000
Usual Pagination: 12
Editor: Ellen Eggink-Scheurkogel; **Editor-in-Chief:** Wiebren Tabak
Profile: Magazine focusing on defence policy and actual issues concerning defence.
Language(s): Dutch
Agency Commission: 15%
Mechanical Data: Type Area: 266 x 370mm
BUSINESS: DEFENCE

DELA KRONIEK
1633552N64L-79

Editorial: Postbus 522, 5600 AM EINDHOVEN
Tel: 570 647730 **Fax:** 570 647815
Email: info@dela.nl **Web site:** http://www.dela.nl/kroniek
Freq: Half-yearly; **Cover Price:** Free; **Circ:** 1,300,000
Usual Pagination: 28
Editor: Yvonne van Bruggen; **Editor-in-Chief:** C. Klijn
Language(s): Dutch
Agency Commission: 15%
Mechanical Data: Type Area: 200 x 200mm, Bleed Size: 230 x 230mm
BUSINESS: OTHER CLASSIFICATIONS: Funeral Directors, Cemeteries & Crematoria

DEN HAAG AGENDA
18132N89C-31

Editorial: Prinsegracht 166a, 2512 GE DEN HAAG
Tel: 15 2564718 **Fax:** 70 3364640
Email: uitgeverij@rooduijn.com **Web site:** http://www.denhaagagenda.nl
Date Established: 01-01-1969; **Freq:** Monthly; **Circ:** 20,000
Usual Pagination: 48
Editor: Els van Weezenbeek
Profile: Events magazine distributed in hotels, restaurants, conference centres and tourist offices.
Language(s): Dutch
Readership: Aimed at business travellers and tourists visiting The Hague.
ADVERTISING RATES:
Full Page Mono EUR 1/1: b/w 658,- 1/2: b/w 364,- 1/4: b/w 200,- 1/8: b/w 109,-
Agency Commission: 15%
Mechanical Data: Type Area: 155 x 224mm, Bleed Size: 165 x 240mm
Copy instructions: *Copy Date:* 3 weeks prior to publication date
CONSUMER: HOLIDAYS & TRAVEL: Entertainment Guides

DEN HAAG INFORMATIEGIDS
1636458N89A-200

Editorial: Grote Marktstraat 43, 2511 BH DEN HAAG
Tel: 70 3342179 **Fax:** 20 5979490
Email: info@denhaag.com
Freq: 3 issues yearly; **Cover Price:** Free; **Circ:** 50,000
Editor: A.J. de Jager
Language(s): Dutch
ADVERTISING RATES:
Full Page Mono EUR 1/1: f.c. 2700,-; 1/2: f.c. 1500,-; achterpag.: f.c. 3200,-
Agency Commission: 15%
Mechanical Data: Bleed Size: 200 x 265mm, Type Area: 180 x 245mm
Copy instructions: *Copy Date:* 1 month prior to publication date
CONSUMER: HOLIDAYS & TRAVEL: Travel

DENKSPORT PUZZELBLADEN
1633876N79F-125

Editorial: Hogehilweg 13, 1101 CA AMSTERDAM
Tel: 223 650016 **Fax:** 223 650012
Email: info@keesing.com **Web site:** http://www.denksport.nl
Freq: 26 issues yearly; **Circ:** 1,500,000
Language(s): Dutch
ADVERTISING RATES:
Full Page Mono ...... EUR omslagpag. 2: f.c. 16.440,-; omslagpag. 3: f.c. 14.615,-; achterpag.: f.c. 23.760,-
Agency Commission: 15%
Copy instructions: *Copy Date:* 7 weeks prior to publication date
CONSUMER: HOBBIES & DIY: Games & Puzzles

DERIVATIVES AND FINANCIAL INSTRUMENTS
760709N1A-19_3

Editorial: Postbus 20237, 1000 HE AMSTERDAM
Tel: 570 648902 **Fax:** 570 614795
Email: info@ibfd.org
Date Established: 01-01-1999; **Freq:** 6 issues yearly; **Annual Sub.:** EUR 460,-; **Circ:** 700
Usual Pagination: 20
Editor: C. Rotondaro
Profile: Journal providing the latest information and analyses of the financial market.
Language(s): Dutch
Readership: Read by tax professionals and financial market experts.
ADVERTISING RATES:
Full Page Mono .. EUR 1/1: b/w 595,-** 1/2: b/w 395,-
Agency Commission: 15%
Mechanical Data: Type Area: 186 x 243mm, Bleed Size: 212 x 275mm
BUSINESS: FINANCE & ECONOMICS

DHZ MARKT
16190N25-10

Editorial: Julianaweg 31, 2042 NZ ZANDVOORT
Tel: 570 667835 **Fax:** 570 686404
Email: info@vvpbv.nl **Web site:** http://www.dhzmarkt.nl

Date Established: 01-01-1959; **Freq:** 11 issues yearly; **Cover Price:** EUR 6,20
Annual Sub.: EUR 58,80; **Circ:** 3,810
Editor: Els Langmar-van den Berg
Profile: Hardware trade magazine including news about tools, ironmongery, building, paints and varnish.
Language(s): Dutch
ADVERTISING RATES:
Full Page Mono .. EUR 1/1: b/w 1225,- 1/2: b/w 660,- 1/4: b/w 360,-
Agency Commission: 15%
Mechanical Data: Type Area: 185 x 270mm, Bleed Size: 210 x 297mm
Copy instructions: *Copy Date:* 14 days prior to publication date
BUSINESS: HARDWARE

DIAGNED MAGAZINE
761234N56A-11_10
Editorial: Postbus 84098, 2508 AB DEN HAAG
Tel: 70 3378124 **Fax:** 40 2060165
Email: betacom@planet.nl **Web site:** http://www.diagned.nl
Freq: Half-yearly; **Circ:** 7,500
Editor: Marian van Opstal
Profile: Magazine focusing on invitro diagnostics in health medicine.
Language(s): Dutch
Agency Commission: 15%
Mechanical Data: Bleed Size: 210 x 297mm
BUSINESS: HEALTH & MEDICAL

DIDAKTIEF
16924N62J-80
Editorial: Molukkenstraat 200, 1098 TW AMSTERDAM **Tel:** 70 3780541 **Fax:** 70 3789783
Web site: http://www.didaktief.nl
Freq: 9 issues yearly; **Cover Price:** EUR 6,20
Annual Sub.: EUR 42,50; **Circ:** 10,280
Usual Pagination: 64
Editor: S. Barneveld; **Editor-in-Chief:** L. Welther
Profile: Journal about educational development.
Language(s): Dutch
Readership: Read by parent-teacher associations, school governors and other educational professionals.
ADVERTISING RATES:
Full Page Mono EUR 1/1: b/w 930,- 1/2: b/w 520,- 1/4: b/w 300,-
Agency Commission: 15%
Mechanical Data: Type Area: 185 x 270mm, Bleed Size: 210 x 297mm
Copy instructions: *Copy Date:* 3 weeks prior to publication date
BUSINESS: CHURCH & SCHOOL EQUIPMENT & EDUCATION: Teachers & Education Management

DIER
17900N81A-183
Editorial: Scheveningseweg 58, 2517 KW DEN HAAG **Tel:** 570 667835 **Fax:** 570 686404
Email: info@dierenbescherming.nl
Freq: Quarterly; **Circ:** 130,000
Editor-in-Chief: Jairo van Lunteren
Profile: Magazine of the Society for the Protection of Animals in the Netherlands.
Language(s): Dutch
Readership: Aimed at members of the Society and public libraries.
ADVERTISING RATES:
Full Page Mono EUR 1/1: f.c. 3451,-; 1/2: f.c. 2410,-; 1/4: f.c. 1708,-
Agency Commission: 15%
Mechanical Data: Type Area: 185 x 255mm, Bleed Size: 205 x 275mm
Copy instructions: *Copy Date:* 4 weeks prior to publication date
CONSUMER: ANIMALS & PETS: Animals & Pets Protection

DIER EN MILIEU
17908N81A-159
Editorial: Sparrenlaan 26, 7642 VC WIERDEN
Tel: 314 349422 **Fax:** 33 4626063
Email: secr@politiedierenenmilieu.nl
Freq: 6 issues yearly; **Annual Sub.:** EUR 25,-; **Circ:** 2,500
Editor: K. Kasemir; **Editor-in-Chief:** K. Kasemir
Profile: Magazine about laws protecting animals and their natural environment as well as related green issues.
Language(s): Dutch
ADVERTISING RATES:
Full Page Mono EUR 1/1: b/w 885,- 1/2: b/w 460,- 1/4: b/w 130,-
Agency Commission: 15%
Mechanical Data: Type Area: 185 x 260mm, Bleed Size: 210 x 296mm
CONSUMER: ANIMALS & PETS: Animals & Pets Protection

DIER & VRIEND
17941N81X-26
Editorial: Postbus 32, 5100 AA DONGEN
Tel: 172 466622
Email: info@horse-power.nl
Date Established: 01-01-2000; **Freq:** Quarterly;
Cover Price: EUR 3,25
Annual Sub.: EUR 8,25; **Circ:** 125,000
Editor: Janine Verschure
Profile: Magazine containing news, information and articles about the care of animals.
Language(s): Dutch
Readership: Aimed at pet owners.
ADVERTISING RATES:
Full Page Mono EUR 1/1: f.c. 3328,-; b/w 2828,- 1/2: f.c. 1794,-; b/w 1526,- 1/4: f.c. 931,-; b/w 791,-
Agency Commission: 15%
Mechanical Data: Type Area: 187 x 272mm, Bleed Size: 210 x 297mm
CONSUMER: ANIMALS & PETS

DIERENPRAKTIJKEN
17902N81A-27
Editorial: Kromstraat 15, 5341 JB OSS
Tel: 35 6726880 **Fax:** 23 5564911
Email: info@maasland.com
Freq: Quarterly; **Annual Sub.:** EUR 12,50; **Circ:** 25,000
Editor: Peter van Riel; **Publisher:** Peter van Riel
Profile: Magazine about the care and protection of animals.
Language(s): Dutch
Readership: Aimed at animal lovers.
ADVERTISING RATES:
Full Page Mono EUR 1/1: f.c. 2150,-; 1/2: f.c. 1250,-; 1/4: f.c. 750,-
Agency Commission: 15%
Mechanical Data: Type Area: 180 x 230mm, Bleed Size: 210 x 260mm
CONSUMER: ANIMALS & PETS: Animals & Pets Protection

DIERPLAGEN INFORMATIE
16287N32B-20
Editorial: Vadaring 81, 6702 EA WAGENINGEN
Tel: 70 3780232 **Fax:** 314 344397
Email: info@kad.nl
Date Established: 01-02-1998; **Freq:** Quarterly;
Cover Price: EUR 12,50
Annual Sub.: EUR 46,-; **Circ:** 2,750
Editor: J.I. Duurland; **Editor-in-Chief:** N.A.H.W. Vonk
Profile: Magazine about pest control in the surroundings of buildings.
Language(s): Dutch
Readership: Aimed at managers in the food industry, building industry, pest control agencies and local councils.
ADVERTISING RATES:
Full Page Mono EUR 1/1: f.c. 1290,-; b/w 1145,- 1/2: f.c. 743,-; b/w 620,- 1/4: f.c. 410,-; b/w 340,-
Agency Commission: 15%
Mechanical Data: Type Area: 165 x 265mm, Bleed Size: 210 x 297mm
Copy instructions: *Copy Date:* 3 weeks prior to publication date
BUSINESS: LOCAL GOVERNMENT, LEISURE & RECREATION: Public Health & Cleaning

DIGIFOTO PRO MAGAZINE
1873038N85A-40
Editorial: Delftweg 147, 2289 BD RIJSWIJK
Tel: 70 3789880 **Fax:** 70 3789783
Email: info@clipboard-publishing.nl **Web site:** http://www.digifotopro.nl
Freq: Quarterly; **Annual Sub.:** EUR 15,-; **Circ:** 62,500
Editor: Raymond Luijbregts; **Editor-in-Chief:** Julian Huijbregts; **Publisher:** Linda Oenema
Language(s): Dutch
ADVERTISING RATES:
Full Page Mono EUR 2/1: f.c. 7450,-; 1/1: f.c. 3950,-; 1/2: f.c. 2750,-
Agency Commission: 15%
Mechanical Data: Bleed Size: 230 x 300mm, Type Area: 210 x 280mm
CONSUMER: PHOTOGRAPHY & FILM MAKING: Photography

DIGITAALGIDS
1637045N5D-234
Editorial: Enthovenplein 1, 2521 DA DEN HAAG
Tel: 50 5844205 **Fax:** 70 3602861
Freq: 6 issues yearly; **Circ:** 60,000
Usual Pagination: 52
Editor: V. van Amerongen; **Editor-in-Chief:** R. Schleiffert; **Publisher:** Gerjan Huis in 't Veld
Language(s): Dutch
Agency Commission: 15%
BUSINESS: COMPUTERS & AUTOMATION: Personal Computers

DITJES & DATJES
17437N74C-362
Editorial: Rhijngeesterstraatweg 40n, 2341 BV OEGSTGEEST **Tel:** 20 5512208 **Fax:** 570 647533
Email: info@buurmultimedia.nl **Web site:** http://www.ditjesendatjes.com
Date Established: 01-03-1995; **Freq:** Monthly;
Cover Price: Free; **Circ:** 650,000
Editor-in-Chief: Francine van Egmond
Profile: Family magazine concerning new consumer products and services. Available from Dutch supermarkets, chemists and travel agencies.
Language(s): Dutch
Readership: Aimed at families.
ADVERTISING RATES:
Full Page Mono .... EUR 1/1: f.c. 9650,-
Agency Commission: 15%
Mechanical Data: Type Area: 160 x 255mm, Bleed Size: 170 x 265mm
Copy instructions: *Copy Date:* 4 weeks prior to publication date
CONSUMER: WOMEN'S INTEREST CONSUMER MAGAZINES: Home & Family

DOCENTENAGENDA
1635729N88R-49
Editorial: Niels Bohrweg 123, 3542 CA UTRECHT
Tel: 523 285330 **Fax:** 30 6348909
Email: info@edg.nl
Freq: Annual; **Cover Price:** Free; **Circ:** 57,804
Publisher: Marjolein Nadorp
Language(s): Dutch
ADVERTISING RATES:
Full Page Mono .... EUR 1/1: f.c. 7669,-
Agency Commission: 15%
Mechanical Data: Type Area: 95 x 180mm, Bleed Size: 120 x 190mm
Copy instructions: *Copy Date:* 7 weeks prior to publication date
CONSUMER: EDUCATION: Education Related

DOE EEN WENSKRANT
761189N74F-10
Editorial: Polanerbaan 13m, 3447 GN WOERDEN
Tel: 70 3378124 **Fax:** 40 2060165
Email: info@doe-een-wens.org
Date Established: 01-01-1994; **Freq:** Quarterly;
Cover Price: Free; **Circ:** 25,000
Usual Pagination: 12
Profile: Magazine focusing on fulfilling wishes for terminally ill young people.
Language(s): Dutch
Readership: Aimed at girls and boys aged between 3 and 18 years.
Agency Commission: 15%
CONSUMER: WOMEN'S INTEREST CONSUMER MAGAZINES: Teenage

DE DOKTER
16669N56A-29
Editorial: Mercatorlaan 1200, 3528 BL UTRECHT
Tel: 10 4274128 **Fax:** 35 6474569
Freq: 9 issues yearly; **Annual Sub.:** EUR 97,-; **Circ:** 12,000
Editor: Charlotte Vermeulen; **Editor-in-Chief:** Marieke ten Dam
Profile: Magazine containing news about developments in the health care sector, focusing on general practice.
Language(s): Dutch
Readership: Read by general practitioners and hospital managers.
ADVERTISING RATES:
Full Page Mono .. EUR 1/1: b/w 1800,- 1/2: b/w 990,- 1/4: b/w 545,-
Agency Commission: 15%
Mechanical Data: Type Area: 180 x 260mm, Bleed Size: 210 x 285mm
BUSINESS: HEALTH & MEDICAL

DE DOKTERSASSISTENT
16802N56R-35
Editorial: Othellodreef 91-93, 3561 GT UTRECHT
Tel: 492 338432 **Fax:** 492 338421
Freq: 6 issues yearly; **Annual Sub.:** EUR 55,-; **Circ:** 6,000
Editor: J. Hoppenbrouwer; **Editor-in-Chief:** J. Hoppenbrouwer
Profile: Magazine featuring medical and social information including articles from the association for doctors' assistants and news about developments regarding the profession.
Language(s): Dutch
Readership: Read by doctors' assistants.
ADVERTISING RATES:
Full Page Mono EUR 1/1: f.c. 2350,-; b/w 1500,- 1/2: f.c. 1800,-; b/w 950,- 1/4: f.c. 1345,-; b/w 495,-
Agency Commission: 15%
Mechanical Data: Type Area: 185 x 260mm, Bleed Size: 210 x 297mm
Copy instructions: *Copy Date:* 3 weeks prior to publication date
BUSINESS: HEALTH & MEDICAL: Health Medical Related

DONALD
2002267N86C-278
Editorial: Capellalaan 65, 2132 JL HOOFDDORP
Tel: 30 2303508 **Fax:** 314 373646
Freq: Half-yearly; **Circ:** 90,000
Editor: Thom Roep
Language(s): Dutch
ADVERTISING RATES:
Full Page Mono .... EUR 1/1: b/w 6500,-
Agency Commission: 15%
Copy instructions: *Copy Date:* 2 months prior to publication date
CONSUMER: ADULT & GAY MAGAZINES: Men's Lifestyle Magazines

DONALD DUCK EXTRA
1636189N91D-123
Editorial: Capellalaan 65, 2132 JL HOOFDDORP
Tel: 77 3556160 **Fax:** 77 3556152
Web site: http://www.donaldduckextra.nl
Freq: 13 issues yearly; **Cover Price:** EUR 2,35
Annual Sub.: EUR 27,95; **Circ:** 61,752
Editor: Thom Roep; **Publisher:** Suzan Schouten
Language(s): Dutch
ADVERTISING RATES:
Full Page Mono . EUR 1/1: f.c. 4200,-; achterpag.: f.c. 5250,-
Agency Commission: 15%
Mechanical Data: Type Area: 160 x 230mm, Bleed Size: 180 x 260mm
CONSUMER: RECREATION & LEISURE: Children & Youth

DORPSKLANKEN
626672N72-1000
Editorial: Prins Bernhardlaan 8, 9765 AK PATERSWOLDE **Tel:** 20 5518406 **Fax:** 20 5518646
Web site: http://www.dorpsklanken.nl
Date Established: 01-05-1946; **Freq:** Weekly;
Annual Sub.: EUR 32,50; **Circ:** 4,500
Editor: Nico Harms
Language(s): Dutch
Agency Commission: 15%
Mechanical Data: Type Area: 260 x 395mm, Bleed Size: 290 x 420mm
LOCAL NEWSPAPERS

DOUANE UPDATE
16340N32K-50
Editorial: Postbus 11620, 2502 AP DEN HAAG
Tel: 10 4274128
Date Established: 26-09-1996; **Freq:** 24 issues yearly; **Annual Sub.:** EUR 619,-
Usual Pagination: 24
Profile: Newsletter focusing on customs matters in the European Union.
Language(s): Dutch
Readership: Aimed at importers, exporters, solicitors and customs advisers.
Agency Commission: 15%
BUSINESS: LOCAL GOVERNMENT, LEISURE & RECREATION: Civil Service

DOWN TO EARTH
16834N57-30
Editorial: Nieuwe Looiersstraat 31, 1017 VA AMSTERDAM **Tel:** 25 2564718 **Fax:** 70 3364640
Email: service@milieudefensie.nl
Date Established: 01-01-1972; **Freq:** 6 issues yearly;
Cover Price: EUR 2,20
Annual Sub.: EUR 30,-; **Circ:** 19,000
Editor: Annemarie Opmeer; **Editor-in-Chief:** Freek Kallenberg
Profile: Magazine of the Friends of the Earth.
Language(s): Dutch
Readership: Read by environmentalists.
ADVERTISING RATES:
Full Page Mono .. EUR 1/1: b/w 1370,- 1/2: b/w 719,- 1/4: b/w 395,-
Agency Commission: 15%
Mechanical Data: Type Area: 190 x 250mm, Bleed Size: 210 x 275mm
BUSINESS: ENVIRONMENT & POLLUTION

DR. YEP
2001122N56A-537
Editorial: Florijn 1j, 9251 MP BERGUM
Tel: 33 4220082
Freq: Annual; **Cover Price:** EUR 12,50; **Circ:** 60,000
Editor-in-Chief: Ronald Hofstede
Language(s): Dutch
ADVERTISING RATES:
Full Page Mono . EUR 1/1: f.c. 3600,-; 1/2: f.c. 1980,-
Agency Commission: 15%
Mechanical Data: Type Area: 190 x 257mm, Bleed Size: 230 x 297mm
BUSINESS: HEALTH & MEDICAL

DRAF & RENSPORT
17594N75E-10
Editorial: Esp 101, 5633 AA EINDHOVEN
Tel: 70 3780541 **Fax:** 70 3789783
Email: bcm@bcm.nl
Freq: Weekly; **Cover Price:** EUR 3,70
Annual Sub.: EUR 165,-; **Circ:** 8,500
Editor: D.P. Frerichs; **Publisher:** Eric Brüger
Profile: Official publication of the Dutch Horse Racing Association.
Language(s): Dutch
ADVERTISING RATES:
Full Page Mono EUR 1/1: f.c. 757,-; 1/2: f.c. 397,-; 1/4: f.c. 208,-
Agency Commission: 15%
Mechanical Data: Type Area: 213 x 300mm, Bleed Size: 233 x 320mm
CONSUMER: SPORT: Horse Racing

DRINKS ONLY!
1813726N9A-154
Editorial: Van Breestraat 57, 1071 ZG AMSTERDAM
Tel: 40 2071162
Web site: http://www.drinksonly.nl
Date Established: 20-11-2006; **Freq:** Half-yearly;
Cover Price: EUR 3,95; **Circ:** 80,000
Editor: Frank van Paridon
Language(s): Dutch
ADVERTISING RATES:
Full Page Mono EUR 1/1: f.c. 5950,-; 1/2: f.c. 3750,-; 1/4: f.c. 1875,-
Agency Commission: 15%
Mechanical Data: Type Area: 194 x 277mm, Bleed Size: 210 x 297mm
Copy instructions: *Copy Date:* 4 weeks prior to publication date
BUSINESS: DRINKS & LICENSED TRADE: Drinks, Licensed Trade, Wines & Spirits

DRINKS SLIJTERSVAKBLAD
15813N9A-150
Editorial: De Mossel 9, 1723 HZ NOORD-SCHARWOUDE **Tel:** 76 5301715 **Fax:** 70 3045808
Web site: http://www.slijtersvakblad.nl
Freq: 9 issues yearly; **Cover Price:** EUR 8,45
Annual Sub.: EUR 69,50; **Circ:** 1,765
Publisher: Michael Davidson
Profile: Magazine containing information about soft drinks, beer, wine and spirits trade.
Language(s): Dutch

Readership: Read by wholesalers and retailers.
ADVERTISING RATES:
Full Page Mono .. EUR 1/1: b/w 1070,- 1/2: b/w 595,- 1/4: b/w 360,-
Agency Commission: 15%
Mechanical Data: Type Area: 190 x 260mm, Bleed Size: 210 x 285mm
Copy instructions: *Copy Date:* 2 weeks prior to publication date
BUSINESS: DRINKS & LICENSED TRADE: Drinks, Licensed Trade, Wines & Spirits

DRUK DOENDE 17823N79C-15
Editorial: p/a Florastraat 34a, 1695 BK BLOKKER
Tel: 20 5853045
Freq: 3 issues yearly; **Annual Sub.:** EUR 10,-; **Circ:** 150
Editor: Ton Cornet
Profile: Magazine covering aspects of stamp collection.
Language(s): Dutch
Readership: Aimed at stamp collectors in the Netherlands and Belgium.
Agency Commission: 15%
Mechanical Data: Type Area: 122 x 183mm, Bleed Size: 147 x 210mm
CONSUMER: HOBBIES & DIY: Philately

DUEMILA 17785N77E-35
Editorial: Dorpstraat 4a, 5504 HH VELDHOVEN
Tel: 23 5461122 **Fax:** 23 5561177
Email: info@varln.nl
Date Established: 01-01-1986; **Freq:** Quarterly;
Cover Price: EUR 7,-
Annual Sub.: EUR 27,50; **Circ:** 1,000
Editor: P.J. van Zanten; **Editor-in-Chief:** P. Erhardt
Profile: Magazine for owners of Alfa Romeo cars.
Language(s): Dutch
ADVERTISING RATES:
Full Page Mono .. EUR 1/1: f.c. 225,-; 1/2: f.c. 87,-; 1/4: f.c. 70,-
Agency Commission: 15%
Mechanical Data: Type Area: 180 x 265mm, Bleed Size: 210 x 297mm
CONSUMER: MOTORING & CYCLING: Club Cars

DUIKEN 17628N75M-30
Editorial: Takkebijsters 57a, 4817 BL BREDA
Tel: 76 5722984 **Fax:** 570 614795
Email: info@vipmedia.nl **Web site:** http://www.duiken.nl
Date Established: 01-04-1986; **Freq:** Monthly;
Cover Price: EUR 4,95
Annual Sub.: EUR 54,45; **Circ:** 22,000
Editor: R. Lipmann; **Editor-in-Chief:** Judith Rietveld;
Publisher: Jan Diepenbroek
Profile: Magazine dealing with diving for sport and the underwater environment.
Language(s): Dutch
Readership: Aimed at sports divers.
ADVERTISING RATES:
Full Page Mono . EUR 1/1: f.c. 2755,-; PMS 2250,-; b/w 1650,- 1/2: f.c. 1435,-; PMS 1185,-; b/w 840,- 1/4: f.c. 735,-; PM
Agency Commission: 15%
Mechanical Data: Type Area: 185 x 260mm, Bleed Size: 215 x 280mm
Copy instructions: *Copy Date:* 4 weeks prior to publication date
CONSUMER: SPORT: Water Sports

DUTCH BIRDING 17932N81F-15
Editorial: Postbus 75611, 1070 AP AMSTERDAM
Tel: 88 6022707
Date Established: 21-04-1979; **Freq:** 6 issues yearly;
Annual Sub.: EUR 39,50; **Circ:** 2,500
Editor: Arnoud van den Berg; **Editor-in-Chief:** André van Loon
Profile: Journal of the Dutch Bird Association, publishing articles and news on the occurrence and distribution of birds in the Benelux, European, Palaearctic and Asian-Pacific regions.
Language(s): Dutch
ADVERTISING RATES:
Full Page Mono EUR 1/1: b/w 226,- 1/2: b/w 147,- 1/4: b/w 100,-
Agency Commission: 15%
Mechanical Data: Type Area: 140 x 210mm, Bleed Size: 170 x 235mm
CONSUMER: ANIMALS & PETS: Birds

DYNAMISCH PERSPECTIEF
16095N21A-361
Editorial: Wisentweg 12, 8251 PC DRONTEN
Tel: 0032 34660066 **Fax:** 0032 34660067
Email: info@bdvereniging.nl
Freq: 5 issues yearly; **Circ:** 2,400
Editor: Onno Bakker
Profile: Journal covering environmentally friendly agriculture.
Language(s): Dutch
Agency Commission: 15%
Mechanical Data: Bleed Size: 210 x 200mm
BUSINESS: AGRICULTURE & FARMING

EADV-MAGAZINE 629739N56A-11_20
Editorial: Het Spoor 2, 3994 AK HOUTEN
Tel: 30 2991929 **Fax:** 77 3556140
Freq: Quarterly; **Cover Price:** EUR 6,81; **Circ:** 1,877
Editor: Stéphanie Korpershoek; **Publisher:** Frans Luyendijk
Profile: Journal providing information about diabetes.
Language(s): Dutch
Readership: Read by members of the Association of Diabetes, including nurses, general practitioners, pharmacists, clients and physiotherapists.
ADVERTISING RATES:
Full Page Mono EUR 1/1: f.c. 1748,-; b/w 1065,- 1/2: f.c. 1290,-; b/w 607,- 1/4: f.c. 1033,-; b/w 350,-
Agency Commission: 15%
Mechanical Data: Type Area: 186 x 275mm, Bleed Size: 210 x 297mm
Copy instructions: *Copy Date:* 6 weeks prior to publication date
BUSINESS: HEALTH & MEDICAL

ECLAIRE 15472N1A-19_50
Editorial: Burg. Oudlaan 50, Kamer CB-03, 3062 PA ROTTERDAM **Tel:** 33 2458375 **Fax:** 348 414897
Email: secretaris@efr.nl **Web site:** http://www.eclaire.nl
Freq: 6 issues yearly; **Annual Sub.:** EUR 29,-; **Circ:** 6,000
Profile: Magazine containing articles on business and economics.
Language(s): Dutch
Readership: Read by those in the field of business and economics.
Agency Commission: 15%
Mechanical Data: Type Area: 185 x 280mm, Bleed Size: 210 x 297mm
BUSINESS: FINANCE & ECONOMICS

ECOLOGIE EN ONTWIKKELING
16811N57-14_30
Editorial: Plantage Middenlaan 2k, 1018 DD AMSTERDAM **Tel:** 523 285330 **Fax:** 20 5690137
Email: mail@iucn.nl
Freq: Quarterly; **Annual Sub.:** EUR 20,-; **Circ:** 1,000
Editor: Cas Besselink; **Editor-in-Chief:** M. Ligtelijn
Profile: Journal focusing on international ecology, covering nature conservation and other topical issues.
Language(s): Dutch
Readership: Read by decision makers within parliament and conservation groups.
Agency Commission: 15%
Mechanical Data: Bleed Size: 210 x 297mm
BUSINESS: ENVIRONMENT & POLLUTION

ED 17108N67B-2800
Editorial: Begijnenhof 4-6, 5611 EL EINDHOVEN
Tel: 40 2336338 **Fax:** 40 2336470
Web site: http://www.ed.nl
Freq: 312 issues yearly; **Annual Sub.:** EUR 286,55;
Circ: 107,804
Editor: John van den Oetelaar
Language(s): Dutch
ADVERTISING RATES:
Full Page Mono EUR 3/4: b/w 7161,- 1/2: b/w 4774,- 3/4 ed. za.: b/w 7759,- 1/2 ed. za.: b/w 5173,-
Agency Commission: 15%
Mechanical Data: Type Area: 266 x 398mm
REGIONAL DAILY & SUNDAY NEWSPAPERS: Regional Daily Newspapers

DE EEMSLANDER 626703N72-1150
Editorial: Oude Schans 7, 9934 CM DELFZIJL
Tel: 20 5518518 **Fax:** 20 6269407
Email: eemslander@noordpers.nl
Date Established: 01-01-1980; **Freq:** Weekly; **Cover Price:** Free; **Circ:** 33,000
Editor: Peter Mönnichmann; **Editor-in-Chief:** Peter Mönnichmann; **Publisher:** M. Hielkema
Language(s): Dutch
Agency Commission: 15%
Mechanical Data: Type Area: 374 x 520mm, Bleed Size: 400 x 580mm
LOCAL NEWSPAPERS

EÉN JAAR! 1635635N74D-155
Editorial: Veermanskade 2, 1621 AN HOORN
Tel: 88 2944819 **Fax:** 30 6383991
Email: info@wij.nl
Freq: Annual; **Circ:** 145,000
Editor: P. Remmers; **Publisher:** R. van Vroenhoven
Language(s): Dutch
ADVERTISING RATES:
Full Page Mono .... EUR 2/1: f.c. 16.190,-; 1/1: f.c. 8095,-; 1/2: f.c. 5145,-
Agency Commission: 15%
Mechanical Data: Type Area: 185 x 252mm, Bleed Size: 215 x 282mm
Copy instructions: *Copy Date:* 4 weeks prior to publication date
CONSUMER: WOMEN'S INTEREST CONSUMER MAGAZINES: Child Care

EENDRACHT MAGAZINE
16492N45A-30
Editorial: Lloydstraat 300, 3024 EA ROTTERDAM
Tel: 75 6813545 **Fax:** 71 3643461
Email: info@eendracht.nl
Freq: Half-yearly; **Annual Sub.:** EUR 42,-; **Circ:** 10,000
Editor: Maureen Overdevest
Profile: Magazine containing information about the Eendracht, a sailing ship in the Netherlands.
Language(s): Dutch
Readership: Aimed at those involved in the maritime trade and people with a specialist interest in ships.
Agency Commission: 15%
Mechanical Data: Type Area: 180 x 252mm, Bleed Size: 210 x 297mm
Copy instructions: *Copy Date:* 4 weeks prior to publication date
BUSINESS: MARINE & SHIPPING

EENDRACHTBODE, DE THOOLSE COURANT 627291N72-1160
Editorial: Nieuwstraat 4, 4697 CC ST. ANNALAND
Tel: 23 7523919 **Fax:** 318 696179
Date Established: 01-11-1944; **Freq:** Weekly; **Cover Price:** EUR 1,-
Annual Sub.: EUR 29,-; **Circ:** 7,000
Editor: W. Heijboer; **Editor-in-Chief:** A.M. de Vliet;
Publisher: W. Heijboer
Language(s): Dutch
Agency Commission: 15%
Mechanical Data: Type Area: 395 x 550mm
LOCAL NEWSPAPERS

EÉN-EÉN-TWEE 16614N54A-150
Editorial: Diephuisstraat 124, 3053 TC ROTTERDAM
Tel: 172 466911 **Fax:** 229 216416
Email: een-een-twee@brandweer.org
Date Established: 01-08-1979; **Freq:** 6 issues yearly;
Cover Price: EUR 3,75
Annual Sub.: EUR 21,50; **Circ:** 2,700
Editor: A.P. van Eijsden; **Editor-in-Chief:** Pieter Hoving
Profile: Magazine about the fire brigade and emergency services.
Language(s): Dutch
ADVERTISING RATES:
Full Page Mono EUR 1/1: b/w 500,- 1/2: b/w 295,- 1/4: b/w 169,-
Agency Commission: 15%
Mechanical Data: Type Area: 189 x 271mm, Bleed Size: 210 x 297mm
BUSINESS: SAFETY & SECURITY: Fire Fighting

EERST LEZEN DAN FIETSEN
18117N89A-38
Editorial: Buiksloterweg 7a, 1031 CC AMSTERDAM
Tel: 33 4637977 **Fax:** 229 216416
Email: info@cycletours.nl
Freq: 15 issues yearly; **Cover Price:** Free; **Circ:** 25,000
Editor: E. van den Bemd; **Publisher:** R. Snoek
Profile: Publication containing articles about cycling holidays.
Language(s): Dutch
Agency Commission: 15%
CONSUMER: HOLIDAYS & TRAVEL: Travel

EIGEN BEDRIJF 1634049N63-459
Editorial: Watermolenlaan 1, 3447 GT WOERDEN
Tel: 70 3789184 **Fax:** 70 7999878
Freq: 6 issues yearly; **Cover Price:** Free; **Circ:** 793,819
Editor: Jan Portegijs
Language(s): Dutch
ADVERTISING RATES:
Full Page Mono .... EUR 1/1: f.c. 36.050,-; 1/2: f.c. 18.926,-; 1/4: f.c. 9936,-
Agency Commission: 15%
Mechanical Data: Bleed Size: 210 x 280mm
Copy instructions: *Copy Date:* 6 weeks prior to publication date
BUSINESS: REGIONAL BUSINESS

EIGEN BEDRIJF, REGIO AMSTERDAM 1857922N14H-239
Editorial: Watermolenlaan 1, 3447 GT WOERDEN
Tel: 0032 34660066 **Fax:** 0032 34660067
Date Established: 25-02-2010; **Freq:** 6 issues yearly;
Cover Price: Free; **Circ:** 96,741
Editor: Jan Portegijs; **Editor-in-Chief:** Anke Hoets
Language(s): Dutch
ADVERTISING RATES:
Full Page Mono EUR 1/1: f.c. 8207,-; 1/2: f.c. 4309,-; 1/4: f.c. 2262,-
Agency Commission: 15%
Mechanical Data: Bleed Size: 210 x 280mm
Copy instructions: *Copy Date:* 6 weeks prior to publication date
BUSINESS: COMMERCE, INDUSTRY & MANAGEMENT: Small Business

EIGEN BEDRIJF, REGIO BRABANT 1857918N14H-235
Editorial: Watermolenlaan 1, 3447 GT WOERDEN
Tel: 0032 34660066 **Fax:** 0032 34660067
Date Established: 25-02-2010; **Freq:** 6 issues yearly;
Cover Price: Free; **Circ:** 92,449
Editor: Jan Portegijs; **Editor-in-Chief:** Lisette van der Swaluw
Language(s): Dutch
ADVERTISING RATES:
Full Page Mono EUR 1/1: f.c. 7667,-; 1/2: f.c. 4025,-; 1/4: f.c. 2113,-
Agency Commission: 15%
Mechanical Data: Bleed Size: 210 x 280mm
Copy instructions: *Copy Date:* 6 weeks prior to publication date
BUSINESS: COMMERCE, INDUSTRY & MANAGEMENT: Small Business

EIGEN BEDRIJF, REGIO CENTRAAL GELDERLAND
1857913N14H-231
Editorial: Watermolenlaan 1, 3447 GT WOERDEN
Tel: 0032 34660066 **Fax:** 0032 34660067
Date Established: 25-02-2010; **Freq:** 6 issues yearly;
Cover Price: Free; **Circ:** 52,315
Editor: Jan Portegijs; **Editor-in-Chief:** Chantal Gerritsen
Language(s): Dutch
ADVERTISING RATES:
Full Page Mono EUR 1/1: f.c. 4311,-; 1/2: f.c. 2263,-; 1/4: f.c. 1188,-
Agency Commission: 15%
Mechanical Data: Bleed Size: 210 x 280mm
Copy instructions: *Copy Date:* 6 weeks prior to publication date
BUSINESS: COMMERCE, INDUSTRY & MANAGEMENT: Small Business

EIGEN BEDRIJF, REGIO DEN HAAG 1857921N14H-238
Editorial: Watermolenlaan 1, 3447 GT WOERDEN
Tel: 0032 34660066 **Fax:** 0032 34660067
Date Established: 25-02-2010; **Freq:** 6 issues yearly;
Cover Price: Free; **Circ:** 77,358
Editor: Jan Portegijs; **Editor-in-Chief:** Margot Kuiper-van der Stap
Language(s): Dutch
ADVERTISING RATES:
Full Page Mono EUR 1/1: f.c. 6422,-; 1/2: f.c. 3372,-; 1/4: f.c. 1770,-
Agency Commission: 15%
Mechanical Data: Bleed Size: 210 x 280mm
Copy instructions: *Copy Date:* 6 weeks prior to publication date
BUSINESS: COMMERCE, INDUSTRY & MANAGEMENT: Small Business

EIGEN BEDRIJF, REGIO FRIESLAND 1857910N14H-229
Editorial: Watermolenlaan 1, 3447 GT WOERDEN
Tel: 0032 34660066 **Fax:** 0032 34660067
Date Established: 25-02-2010; **Freq:** 6 issues yearly;
Cover Price: Free; **Circ:** 26,590
Editor: Jan Portegijs; **Editor-in-Chief:** Nynke Dijkstra
Language(s): Dutch
ADVERTISING RATES:
Full Page Mono EUR 1/1: f.c. 2225,-; 1/2: f.c. 1168,-; 1/4: f.c. 613,-
Agency Commission: 15%
Mechanical Data: Bleed Size: 210 x 280mm
Copy instructions: *Copy Date:* 6 weeks prior to publication date
BUSINESS: COMMERCE, INDUSTRY & MANAGEMENT: Small Business

EIGEN BEDRIJF, REGIO GOOI-, EEM- EN FLEVOLAND
1857915N14H-233
Editorial: Watermolenlaan 1, 3447 GT WOERDEN
Tel: 0032 34660066 **Fax:** 0032 34660067
Date Established: 25-02-2010; **Freq:** 6 issues yearly;
Cover Price: Free; **Circ:** 54,183
Editor: Jan Portegijs; **Editor-in-Chief:** Sylvia Valk
Language(s): Dutch
ADVERTISING RATES:
Full Page Mono EUR 1/1: f.c. 4556,-; 1/2: f.c. 2392,-; 1/4: f.c. 1256,-
Agency Commission: 15%
Mechanical Data: Bleed Size: 210 x 280mm
Copy instructions: *Copy Date:* 6 weeks prior to publication date
BUSINESS: COMMERCE, INDUSTRY & MANAGEMENT: Small Business

EIGEN BEDRIJF, REGIO MIDDEN-NEDERLAND
1857916N14H-234
Editorial: Watermolenlaan 1, 3447 GT WOERDEN
Tel: 0032 34660066 **Fax:** 0032 34660067
Date Established: 25-02-2010; **Freq:** 6 issues yearly;
Cover Price: Free; **Circ:** 70,769
Editor: Jan Portegijs; **Editor-in-Chief:** Mariska Smolders
Language(s): Dutch
ADVERTISING RATES:
Full Page Mono EUR 1/1: f.c. 5939,-; 1/2: f.c. 3118,-; 1/4: f.c. 1637,-
Agency Commission: 15%
Mechanical Data: Bleed Size: 210 x 280mm
Copy instructions: *Copy Date:* 6 weeks prior to publication date
BUSINESS: COMMERCE, INDUSTRY & MANAGEMENT: Small Business

EIGEN BEDRIJF, REGIO NOORD EN MIDDEN LIMBURG
1857914N14H-232
Editorial: Watermolenlaan 1, 3447 GT WOERDEN
Tel: 0032 34660066 **Fax:** 0032 34660067

Date Established: 25-02-2010; **Freq:** 6 issues yearly; **Cover Price:** Free; **Circ:** 19,577
Editor: Jan Portegijs; **Editor-in-Chief:** Monique Joosten-Janssen
Language(s): Dutch
ADVERTISING RATES:
Full Page Mono .. EUR 1/1: f.c. 1650,-; 1/2: f.c. 866,-; 1/4: f.c. 455,-
Agency Commission: 15%
Mechanical Data: Bleed Size: 210 x 280mm
Copy instructions: *Copy Date:* 6 weeks prior to publication date
BUSINESS: COMMERCE, INDUSTRY & MANAGEMENT: Small Business

EIGEN BEDRIJF, REGIO OOST-NEDERLAND
1857911N14H-230
Editorial: Watermolenlaan 1, 3447 GT WOERDEN
Tel: 0032 34660066 **Fax:** 0032 34660067
Date Established: 25-02-2010; **Freq:** 6 issues yearly; **Cover Price:** Free; **Circ:** 73,613
Editor: Jan Portegijs; **Editor-in-Chief:** Karin Lubs
Language(s): Dutch
ADVERTISING RATES:
Full Page Mono EUR 1/1: f.c. 6179,-; 1/2: f.c. 3244,-; 1/4: f.c. 1703,-
Agency Commission: 15%
Mechanical Data: Bleed Size: 210 x 280mm
Copy instructions: *Copy Date:* 6 weeks prior to publication date
BUSINESS: COMMERCE, INDUSTRY & MANAGEMENT: Small Business

EIGEN BEDRIJF, REGIO ROTTERDAM
1857920N14H-237
Editorial: Watermolenlaan 1, 3447 GT WOERDEN
Tel: 0032 34660066 **Fax:** 0032 34660067
Date Established: 25-02-2010; **Freq:** 6 issues yearly; **Cover Price:** Free; **Circ:** 75,870
Editor: Jan Portegijs; **Editor-in-Chief:** Antoinette Kranenburg
Language(s): Dutch
ADVERTISING RATES:
Full Page Mono EUR 1/1: f.c. 6642,-; 1/2: f.c. 3487,-; 1/4: f.c. 1831,-
Agency Commission: 15%
Mechanical Data: Bleed Size: 210 x 280mm
Copy instructions: *Copy Date:* 6 weeks prior to publication date
BUSINESS: COMMERCE, INDUSTRY & MANAGEMENT: Small Business

EIGEN HUIS MAGAZINE
17457N74C-17
Editorial: Displayweg 1, 3821 BT AMERSFOORT
Tel: 33 4507674 **Fax:** 24 3723631
Freq: 11 issues yearly; **Cover Price:** EUR 0; **Circ:** 695,177
Editor: Andrea Hollebeek; **Editor-in-Chief:** Albert van der Horst; **Publisher:** M. Neeleman
Profile: Publication providing information and advice for home-owners.
Language(s): Dutch
Readership: Aimed at home-owners in the Netherlands.
ADVERTISING RATES:
Full Page Mono .... EUR 1/1: f.c. 14.370,-; 1/2: f.c. 8600,-; 1/4: f.c. 4490,-
Agency Commission: 15%
Mechanical Data: Type Area: 165 x 233mm, Bleed Size: 200 x 265mm
CONSUMER: WOMEN'S INTEREST CONSUMER MAGAZINES: Home & Family

EIGEN TIJD
1636690N56B-173
Editorial: Postbus 2014, 3700 CA ZEIST
Tel: 570 648902 **Fax:** 570 614795
Email: info@pggm.nl **Web site:** http://www.pfzw.nl/Particulieren/[VA]eigen_tijd/eigen_tijd.asp
Freq: 3 issues yearly; **Cover Price:** Free; **Circ:** 1,200,000
Editor-in-Chief: Leontina Burgers
Language(s): Dutch
ADVERTISING RATES:
Full Page Mono . EUR 1/1: f.c. 10.474,-; b/w 10.133,- 1/2: f.c. 5408,-; b/w 5093,-
Agency Commission: 15%
Mechanical Data: Type Area: 195 x 245mm, Bleed Size: 225 x 275mm
BUSINESS: HEALTH & MEDICAL: Nursing

EIGENWIJS
1748151N74Q-331
Editorial: Churchillaan 11, 3527 GV UTRECHT
Tel: 10 4066333 **Fax:** 492 371114
Email: info@pgb.nl
Date Established: 01-09-2005; **Freq:** 6 issues yearly; **Circ:** 16,339
Editor-in-Chief: Kees Dijkman; **Publisher:** J. Verbeek
Language(s): Dutch
ADVERTISING RATES:
Full Page Mono EUR 1/1: f.c. 2010,-; b/w 1320,- 1/2: f.c. 1225,-; b/w 795,- 1/4: f.c. 735,-; b/w 495,-
Agency Commission: 15%
Mechanical Data: Type Area: 185 x 270mm, Bleed Size: 210 x 297mm
CONSUMER: WOMEN'S INTEREST CONSUMER MAGAZINES: Lifestyle

EINDHOVEN BUSINESS
18984N63-422
Editorial: Paradijslaan 40a, 5611 KP EINDHOVEN
Tel: 88 8002010 **Fax:** 226 333555
Email: info@uitgeverijpion.nl **Web site:** http://www.eindhovenbusiness.nl
Freq: 6 issues yearly; **Annual Sub.:** EUR 40,-; **Circ:** 5,000
Editor: Edwin van de Ven; **Publisher:** P.H.M. Steeg
Profile: Magazine about business in the Eindhoven region.
Language(s): Dutch
ADVERTISING RATES:
Full Page Mono .. EUR 1/1: f.c. 1300,-; 1/2: f.c. 700,-; 1/4: f.c. 350,-
Agency Commission: 15%
Mechanical Data: Type Area: 220 x 320mm, Bleed Size: 240 x 340mm
BUSINESS: REGIONAL BUSINESS

EISMA VOEDINGSMIDDELEN-INDUSTRIE
1636859N22A-149
Editorial: Celsiusweg 41, 8912 AM LEEUWARDEN
Tel: 70 3378124 **Fax:** 70 3455302
Email: businessmedia@eisma.nl **Web site:** http://www.evmi.nl
Date Established: 01-12-2000; **Freq:** 10 issues yearly; **Cover Price:** EUR 20,-
Annual Sub.: EUR 179,-; **Circ:** 2,500
Editor: Jacqueline Wijbenga; **Editor-in-Chief:** Tom van der Meer; **Publisher:** Minne Hovenga
Language(s): Dutch
ADVERTISING RATES:
Full Page Mono EUR 1/1: f.c. 3071,-; 1/2: f.c. 1999,-; 1/4: f.c. 1249,-
Agency Commission: 15%
Mechanical Data: Type Area: 191 x 265mm, Bleed Size: 230 x 300mm
Copy instructions: *Copy Date:* 3 days prior to publication date
BUSINESS: FOOD

EKOLAND
16096N21A-65_5
Editorial: Regenboog 25, 3742 ZA BAARN
Tel: 20 6211374 **Fax:** 20 6752709
Email: uvw@vwg.net **Web site:** http://www.ekoland.vwg.net
Freq: 11 issues yearly; **Cover Price:** EUR 7,95
Annual Sub.: EUR 77,50; **Circ:** 2,200
Editor: Kees van Veluw; **Editor-in-Chief:** Ellen Driessen; **Publisher:** Bart van Ommeren
Profile: Magazine focusing on ecological farming, including information on horticulture, fruitgrowing, agriculture and livestock. Also covers health food retail and marketing.
Language(s): Dutch
ADVERTISING RATES:
Full Page Mono EUR 1/1: f.c. 2035,-; 1/2: f.c. 1045,-; 1/4: f.c. 550,-
Agency Commission: 15%
Mechanical Data: Type Area: 187 x 258mm, Bleed Size: 210 x 285mm
Copy instructions: *Copy Date:* 3 weeks prior to publication date
BUSINESS: AGRICULTURE & FARMING

ELEKTOR
16028N18A-52
Editorial: Allee 1, 6141 AV LIMBRICHT
Tel: 40 2336338 **Fax:** 40 2336470
Freq: 11 issues yearly; **Cover Price:** EUR 8,20
Annual Sub.: EUR 79,50; **Circ:** 14,626
Editor: H. Baggen; **Publisher:** P. Snakkers
Profile: Journal containing news from the world of electronics, computers and communications. Includes articles on audio, hi-fi, micro-processors, electrophonics, radio, TV, video, testing equipment, Internet and robotics.
Language(s): Dutch
Readership: Read by professionals and amateurs interested in electronics and computer technology.
ADVERTISING RATES:
Full Page Mono EUR 1/1: f.c. 3381,-; b/w 2460,- 1/2: f.c. 2221,-; b/w 1509,- 1/3: f.c. 1874,-; b/w 1250,-
Agency Commission: 15%
Mechanical Data: Type Area: 185 x 265mm, Bleed Size: 210 x 297mm
Copy instructions: *Copy Date:* 2 weeks prior to publication date
BUSINESS: ELECTRONICS

ELEKTRO-DATA
16026N18A-20
Editorial: Mr. H.F. de Boerlaan 28, 7417 DA DEVENTER **Tel:** 314 349422 **Fax:** 30 2643525
Email: info@mybusinessmedia.nl
Freq: 10 issues yearly; **Cover Price:** EUR 13,75
Annual Sub.: EUR 101,75; **Circ:** 10,706
Editor: Henk de Vries; **Editor-in-Chief:** J. Pot; **Publisher:** Elsbeth Lamfers
Profile: Magazine covering industrial automation and electronics.
Language(s): Dutch
Readership: Read by designers and electrical engineers.
ADVERTISING RATES:
Full Page Mono EUR 1/1: f.c. 2820,-; 1/2: f.c. 1730,-; 1/4: f.c. 945,-
Agency Commission: 15%
Mechanical Data: Type Area: 201 x 270mm, Bleed Size: 230 x 325mm
BUSINESS: ELECTRONICS

ELEKTRONICA
16027N18A-30
Editorial: Mr. H.F. de Boerlaan 28, 7417 DA DEVENTER **Tel:** 23 5565370 **Fax:** 23 5565357
Email: info@mybusinessmedia.nl
Freq: 10 issues yearly; **Cover Price:** EUR 20,50
Annual Sub.: EUR 159,75; **Circ:** 4,182
Editor: Henk de Vries; **Editor-in-Chief:** J. Pot; **Publisher:** Elsbeth Lamfers
Profile: Technical magazine about electronic designs and computer engineering.
Language(s): Dutch
Readership: Read by electronic design, production, test and service engineers.
ADVERTISING RATES:
Full Page Mono EUR 1/1: f.c. 2120,-; 1/2: f.c. 1140,-; 1/4: f.c. 640,-
Agency Commission: 15%
Mechanical Data: Type Area: 185 x 259mm, Bleed Size: 210 x 297mm
BUSINESS: ELECTRONICS

ELF VOETBAL
17575N75B-15
Editorial: Neuhuyskade 9, 2596 XZ DEN HAAG
Tel: 23 5344089 **Fax:** 10 2801002
Email: info@elfvoetbal.nl
Freq: 11 issues yearly; **Cover Price:** EUR 4,75
Annual Sub.: EUR 49,-; **Circ:** 75,385
Editor: Jan-Hermen de Bruijn; **Editor-in-Chief:** P.M.M. Leemans; **Publisher:** Jan-Hermen de Bruijn
Profile: International football magazine.
Language(s): Dutch
ADVERTISING RATES:
Full Page Mono EUR 1/1: f.c. 4500,-; 1/2: f.c. 2850,-; 1/4: f.c. 1495,-
Agency Commission: 15%
Mechanical Data: Type Area: 190 x 280mm, Bleed Size: 210 x 297mm
CONSUMER: SPORT: Football

ELLE
17417N74A-55
Editorial: Singel 468, 1017 AW AMSTERDAM
Tel: 570 647064 **Fax:** 20 5353696
Email: singel@hearstmagazines.nl **Web site:** http://www.elle.nl
Freq: Monthly; **Cover Price:** EUR 5,25
Annual Sub.: EUR 55,-; **Circ:** 90,824
Editor: Cécile Narinx; **Publisher:** Luc van Os
Profile: Magazine containing articles on current-affairs, lifestyle, health, beauty, fashion, food, homes, relationships, sex, travel and leisure.
Language(s): Dutch
Readership: Aimed at the modern woman.
ADVERTISING RATES:
Full Page Mono .... EUR 2/1: f.c. 20.500,-; 1/1: f.c. 10.250,-; 1/2: f.c. 7690,-
Agency Commission: 15%
Mechanical Data: Type Area: 198 x 260mm, Bleed Size: 220 x 284mm
CONSUMER: WOMEN'S INTEREST CONSUMER MAGAZINES: Women's Interest

ELLE ETEN
624130N74P-23
Editorial: Singel 468, 1017 AW AMSTERDAM
Tel: 70 3789880 **Fax:** 70 3789783
Email: singel@hearstmagazines.nl **Web site:** http://www.elle.nl/eten
Freq: 6 issues yearly; **Cover Price:** EUR 4,99
Annual Sub.: EUR 29,95; **Circ:** 62,876
Editor: Edine Russel; **Publisher:** Luc van Os
Profile: Cookery magazine containing recipes and tips.
Language(s): Dutch
ADVERTISING RATES:
Full Page Mono .... EUR 2/1: f.c. 12.300,-; 1/1: f.c. 6150,-; 1/2: f.c. 4615,-
Agency Commission: 15%
Mechanical Data: Type Area: 190 x 253mm, Bleed Size: 210 x 273mm
Copy instructions: *Copy Date:* 5 weeks prior to publication date
CONSUMER: WOMEN'S INTEREST CONSUMER MAGAZINES: Food & Cookery

ELLIOTT
18577N1A-343
Editorial: Postbus 27, 7670 AA VRIEZENVEEN
Tel: 492 338432 **Fax:** 492 338421
Email: fibonacci-press@xs4all.nl
Date Established: 01-01-1987; **Freq:** 10 issues yearly; **Annual Sub.:** EUR 279,-; **Circ:** 500
Editor: H.L.M. Hulsbergen; **Publisher:** H.L.M. Hulsbergen
Profile: Journal containing analyses of trends in the financial markets.
Language(s): Dutch
Readership: Read by investors.
Agency Commission: 15%
BUSINESS: FINANCE & ECONOMICS

ELNA
626720N72-1190
Editorial: Nieuwstad 30, 7251 AH VORDEN
Tel: 10 2894018 **Fax:** 172 493270
Email: info@weevers.nl **Web site:** http://www.elna.nl
Date Established: 01-01-1935; **Freq:** Weekly; **Cover Price:** Free; **Circ:** 8,900
Editor: L.G. Weevers; **Editor-in-Chief:** J. Oonk
Language(s): Dutch
Agency Commission: 15%
Mechanical Data: Bleed Size: 290 x 405mm
LOCAL NEWSPAPERS

ELSEVIER BELASTING ALMANAK
1636397N1M-118
Editorial: Radarweg 29, 1043 NX AMSTERDAM
Tel: 58 2954859 **Fax:** 20 6767728
Email: info@reedbusiness.nl
Date Established: 01-01-1945; **Freq:** Annual;
Annual Sub.: EUR 25,95; **Circ:** 107,360
Editor-in-Chief: K.M. Beukers; **Publisher:** Sander de Groot
Language(s): Dutch
Agency Commission: 15%
Mechanical Data: Type Area: 150 x 240mm, Bleed Size: 182 x 281mm
BUSINESS: FINANCE & ECONOMICS: Taxation

ELSEVIER SALARISMAGAZINE
15490N1B-5
Editorial: Radarweg 29, 1043 NX AMSTERDAM
Tel: 570 673344 **Fax:** 20 5159143
Email: info@reedbusiness.nl **Web site:** http://www.salarisnet.nl
Date Established: 01-01-1989; **Freq:** 10 issues yearly; **Annual Sub.:** EUR 267,75; **Circ:** 2,781
Editor: H.T. Kuipers; **Publisher:** Ludo de Boo
Profile: Publication about the administration of wages and salaries.
Language(s): Dutch
Readership: Aimed at consultants dealing with the payroll.
ADVERTISING RATES:
Full Page Mono EUR 1/1: f.c. 2461,-; PMS 1969,-; b/w 1477,- 1/2: f.c. 1448,-; PMS 1158,-; b/w 869,- 1/4: f.c. 852,-; PM
Agency Commission: 15%
Mechanical Data: Type Area: 180 x 270mm, Bleed Size: 210 x 297mm
BUSINESS: FINANCE & ECONOMICS: Accountancy

EN FRANCE
629730N94X-28
Editorial: Delflandlaan 4, 1062 EB AMSTERDAM
Tel: 71 5239058 **Fax:** 20 5159145
Email: info@pelicanmags.nl **Web site:** http://www.enfrance.nl
Freq: Quarterly; **Cover Price:** EUR 4,75
Annual Sub.: EUR 16,-; **Circ:** 36,161
Editor: N. Bouwmeester; **Editor-in-Chief:** Vanno Jobse; **Publisher:** F.N. Kloppert
Profile: Publication featuring articles and background information on the various facets of French culture.
Language(s): Dutch
ADVERTISING RATES:
Full Page Mono EUR 1/1: f.c. 4980,-; 1/2: f.c. 3735,-; 1/4: f.c. 1992,-
Agency Commission: 15%
Mechanical Data: Type Area: 210 x 270mm, Bleed Size: 230 x 297mm
Copy instructions: *Copy Date:* 4 weeks prior to publication date
CONSUMER: OTHER CLASSIFICATIONS: Miscellaneous

ENERGIE+
16857N58-8
Editorial: Dr. van Helvoortstraat 3, 5281 BJ BOXTEL
Tel: 20 5159172 **Fax:** 20 5159145
Email: mail@aeneas.nl **Web site:** http://www.energieplus.nl
Freq: 6 issues yearly; **Cover Price:** EUR 19,50
Annual Sub.: EUR 97,-; **Circ:** 1,428
Editor: Ad Brogtrop; **Editor-in-Chief:** Peter de Koning; **Publisher:** Æbele Kluwer
Profile: Magazine about alternative forms of sustainable energy, such as solar, wind and water power.
Language(s): Dutch
ADVERTISING RATES:
Full Page Mono EUR 2/1: f.c. 4220,-; 1/1: f.c. 2530,-; 1/2: f.c. 1390,-
Agency Commission: 15%
Mechanical Data: Type Area: 206 x 277mm, Bleed Size: 225 x 297mm
BUSINESS: ENERGY, FUEL & NUCLEAR

ENTOURAGE
1634472N74C-363
Editorial: Postbus 262, 3760 AG SOEST
Tel: 23 5564240
Web site: http://www.entourage.nl
Date Established: 01-10-1990; **Freq:** Annual; **Cover Price:** Free; **Circ:** 2,000,000
Usual Pagination: 32
Publisher: R. Krijgsman
Language(s): Dutch
ADVERTISING RATES:
Full Page Mono .... EUR 1/1: f.c. 15.000,-
Agency Commission: 15%
Mechanical Data: Bleed Size: 210 x 270mm
Copy instructions: *Copy Date:* 9 weeks prior to publication date
CONSUMER: WOMEN'S INTEREST CONSUMER MAGAZINES: Home & Family

ERASMUS MAGAZINE
17978N83-13_50
Editorial: Burg. Oudlaan 50, 3062 PA ROTTERDAM
Tel: 23 5565370 **Fax:** 23 5565357
Web site: http://www.erasmusmagazine.nl
Freq: 20 issues yearly; **Annual Sub.:** EUR 30,-; **Circ:** 11,500
Editor: Wieneke Gunneweg-Kok; **Editor-in-Chief:** Gert van der Ende

Profile: Magazine publishing information and opinions about the University of Rotterdam by tutors, students and university personnel.
Language(s): Dutch
ADVERTISING RATES:
Full Page Mono EUR 2/1: f.c. 4496,-; PMS 3592,-; b/w 3247,- 1/1: f.c. 2901,-; PMS 1997,-; b/w 1652,- 1/2: f.c. 2201,-;
Agency Commission: 15%
Mechanical Data: Type Area: 201 x 270mm, Bleed Size: 230 x 297mm
Copy instructions: *Copy Date:* 9 days prior to publication date
CONSUMER: STUDENT PUBLICATIONS

EREDIENSTVAARDIG 18074N87-73
Editorial: Kettingweg 1-6, 3743 HN BAARN
Tel: 77 3556160
Date Established: 01-02-1985; **Freq:** 5 issues yearly; **Annual Sub.:** EUR 28,50; **Circ:** 1,500
Editor: Ekkehard Muth; **Editor-in-Chief:** Jan Marten de Vries
Profile: Journal about liturgy and church music.
Language(s): Dutch
Readership: Aimed at professional and amateur church musicians, clergy and laity.
ADVERTISING RATES:
Full Page Mono EUR 1/1: b/w 325,- 1/2: b/w 190,- 1/4: b/w 115,-
Agency Commission: 15%
Mechanical Data: Type Area: 170 x 225mm, Bleed Size: 200 x 260mm
Copy instructions: *Copy Date:* 5 weeks prior to publication date
CONSUMER: RELIGIOUS

ERGOTHERAPIE 761596N56L-98_20
Editorial: Kaap Hoorndreef 56b, 3563 AV UTRECHT
Tel: 35 6726800 **Fax:** 30 6076301
Freq: 8 issues yearly; **Cover Price:** EUR 11,-
Annual Sub.: EUR 59,-; **Circ:** 4,000
Editor-in-Chief: Suzanne de Boer
Profile: Magazine focusing on occupational therapy, includes retraining of muscle movement.
Language(s): Dutch
Readership: Read by physicians, specialists in muscle movement and patients affected by muscle malfunction.
ADVERTISING RATES:
Full Page Mono .. EUR 1/1: f.c. 1268,-; 1/2: f.c. 764,-; 1/4: f.c. 467,-
Agency Commission: 15%
Mechanical Data: Type Area: 185 x 268mm, Bleed Size: 210 x 297mm
BUSINESS: HEALTH & MEDICAL: Disability & Rehabilitation

ESQUIRE 18058N86C-100
Editorial: H.J.E. Wenckebachweg 200, 1096 AS AMSTERDAM **Tel:** 70 3342179 **Fax:** 20 5979490
Email: info@freemediagroup.nl **Web site:** http://www.esquire.nl
Freq: 10 issues yearly; **Cover Price:** EUR 5,95
Annual Sub.: EUR 47,75; **Circ:** 24,894
Editor: Arno Kantelberg; **Publisher:** Arno Kantelberg
Profile: Lifestyle magazine for men.
Language(s): Dutch
ADVERTISING RATES:
Full Page Mono EUR 1/1: b/w 4916,- 1/2: b/w 3687,- 1/4: b/w 1965,-
Agency Commission: 15%
Mechanical Data: Type Area: 199 x 261mm, Bleed Size: 213 x 275mm
CONSUMER: ADULT & GAY MAGAZINES: Men's Lifestyle Magazines

ESTA 1643430N74A-226
Editorial: Capellalaan 65, 2132 JL HOOFDDORP
Tel: 23 5567830 **Fax:** 23 5567831
Web site: http://www.esta-online.nl
Date Established: 14-06-2004; **Freq:** 26 issues yearly; **Cover Price:** EUR 3,95
Annual Sub.: EUR 89,96; **Circ:** 65,219
Editor: Ellen de Jong; **Editor-in-Chief:** Nicole van Borkulo; **Publisher:** Sandra Dol
Language(s): Dutch
ADVERTISING RATES:
Full Page Mono .... EUR 2/1: f.c. 11.300,-; 1/1: f.c. 5650,-; 1/2: f.c. 3390,-
Agency Commission: 15%
Mechanical Data: Type Area: 204 x 254mm, Bleed Size: 221 x 274mm
CONSUMER: WOMEN'S INTEREST CONSUMER MAGAZINES: Women's Interest

DE ETTEN-LEURSE BODE 626722N72-1220
Editorial: Bredaseweg 26, 4881 DE ZUNDERT
Tel: 88 2697049 **Fax:** 70 3544642
Email: zetterij@vorsselmans.nl **Web site:** http://www.internetbode.nl
Freq: 104 issues yearly; **Circ:** 18,700
Editor: Vif Janssen; **Editor-in-Chief:** Vif Janssen
Language(s): Dutch
Agency Commission: 15%
Mechanical Data: Type Area: 264 x 400mm
LOCAL NEWSPAPERS

EUROPEAN FOREIGN AFFAIRS REVIEW 15913N14C-32
Editorial: Zuidpoolsingel 2, 2408 ZE ALPHEN A/D RIJN **Tel:** 23 5564919 **Fax:** 23 5564911
Freq: Quarterly; **Annual Sub.:** EUR 349,-; **Circ:** 350
Editor: D. O'Keefe; **Editor-in-Chief:** G. Wisman;
Publisher: Karel van der Linde
Profile: Journal providing information on European trade, developments and industry.
Language(s): Dutch
ADVERTISING RATES:
Full Page Mono .... EUR 1/1: f.c. 715,-
Agency Commission: 15%
BUSINESS: COMMERCE, INDUSTRY & MANAGEMENT: International Commerce

EUROPEAN JOURNAL OF HEALTH LAW 16470N44-127
Editorial: Plantijnstraat 2, 2321 JC LEIDEN
Tel: 88 8002010 **Fax:** 226 333555
Email: cs@brill.nl **Web site:** http://www.brill.nl/ejhl
Freq: Quarterly; **Annual Sub.:** EUR 119,-
Editor: J.K.M. Gevers; **Publisher:** P. Bushman
Profile: Journal containing articles about the development of health law in Europe.
Language(s): Dutch; English
Readership: Read by European lawyers, health workers and students.
Agency Commission: 15%
BUSINESS: LEGAL

EUROPEAN REVIEW OF PRIVATE LAW 16471N44-33
Editorial: Zuidpoolsingel 2, 2408 ZE ALPHEN A/D RIJN **Tel:** 15 2617997 **Fax:** 229 216416
Freq: 6 issues yearly; **Annual Sub.:** EUR 568,-; **Circ:** 400
Editor: E. Hondius
Profile: Journal focusing on the importance of national privacy laws.
Language(s): Dutch
Readership: Read by members of the legal profession and students.
ADVERTISING RATES:
Full Page Mono .... EUR 1/1: f.c. 715,-
Agency Commission: 15%
BUSINESS: LEGAL

EVA 17552N74Q-50
Editorial: Oude Amersfoortseweg 79, 1213 AC HILVERSUM **Tel:** 10 4274128 **Fax:** 35 6474569
Email: eo@eo.nl **Web site:** http://www.eo.nl/eva
Freq: 10 issues yearly; **Cover Price:** EUR 3,95
Annual Sub.: EUR 41,50; **Circ:** 43,405
Editor: N. Westerbeek; **Editor-in-Chief:** M. Medema
Profile: Christian women's magazine.
Language(s): Dutch
ADVERTISING RATES:
Full Page Mono EUR 2/1: f.c. 5564,-; b/w 3790,- 1/1: f.c. 2784,-; b/w 1896,- 1/2: f.c. 1423,-; b/w 970,-
Agency Commission: 15%
Mechanical Data: Type Area: 183 x 250mm, Bleed Size: 210 x 275mm
Copy instructions: *Copy Date:* 2 weeks prior to publication date
CONSUMER: WOMEN'S INTEREST CONSUMER MAGAZINES: Lifestyle

EVENTS 15603N2C-70
Editorial: Dukatenburg 82, 3437 AE NIEUWEGEIN
Tel: 172 466622 **Fax:** 24 3723631
Email: info@highprofile.nl
Date Established: 01-11-1997; **Freq:** Quarterly;
Annual Sub.: EUR 37,50; **Circ:** 11,000
Editor: Jan Jacobs; **Editor-in-Chief:** Jan Jacobs;
Publisher: R. Küchler
Profile: Magazine providing information about high profile events, career, fairs and exhibitions.
Language(s): Dutch
ADVERTISING RATES:
Full Page Mono EUR 2/1: f.c. 3795,-; 1/1: f.c. 2795,-; 1/2: f.c. 1590,-; 1/4: f.c. 965,-
Agency Commission: 15%
Mechanical Data: Type Area: 199 x 261mm, Bleed Size: 225 x 297mm
BUSINESS: COMMUNICATIONS, ADVERTISING & MARKETING: Conferences & Exhibitions

EVO LOGISTIEK 718042N10-70
Editorial: Signaalrood 60, 2718 SG ZOETERMEER
Tel: 33 4507674 **Fax:** 24 3723631
Email: evo@evo.nl
Date Established: 13-03-2002; **Freq:** 8 issues yearly;
Annual Sub.: EUR 95,-; **Circ:** 5,305
Editor: Judy van Vuurde
Profile: Magazine containing information about the latest developments in logistics worldwide, such as modes of transport, laws concerning transport in different countries, import and export streaming. Also warehousing, ICT, transport of dangerous goods.
Language(s): Dutch
Readership: Aimed at specialists in logistics, managers of logistic companies and the owners of smaller logistic firms.
ADVERTISING RATES:
Full Page Mono EUR 1/1: f.c. 2704,-; 1/2: f.c. 1622,-; 1/4: f.c. 979,-
Agency Commission: 15%
Mechanical Data: Type Area: 270 x 380mm, Bleed Size: 297 x 420mm
BUSINESS: MATERIALS HANDLING

EVO MAGAZINE 16551N49A-5
Editorial: Signaalrood 60, 2718 SG ZOETERMEER
Tel: 10 4274107 **Fax:** 79 3467846
Email: evo@evo.nl
Freq: 11 issues yearly; **Annual Sub.:** EUR 207,-;
Circ: 29,973
Editor: Judy van Vuurde
Profile: Magazine focusing on logistics and transport of goods for trade, industry, building and agricultural enterprises.
Language(s): Dutch
Readership: Read by transport and warehousing managers in small and medium sized companies.
ADVERTISING RATES:
Full Page Mono EUR 1/1: f.c. 4634,-; 1/2: f.c. 2782,-; 1/4: f.c. 1666,-
Agency Commission: 15%
Mechanical Data: Type Area: 185 x 269mm, Bleed Size: 210 x 297mm
BUSINESS: TRANSPORT

EXPOSÉ 1634540N1M-103
Editorial: Sarphatistraat 500, 1018 AV AMSTERDAM
Tel: 88 7518160 **Fax:** 88 7518161
Email: nob@nob.net
Freq: 5 issues yearly; **Cover Price:** EUR 10,-; **Circ:** 4,958
Editor: H. Bergman; **Editor-in-Chief:** H. Bergman
Language(s): Dutch
ADVERTISING RATES:
Full Page Mono EUR 1/1: b/w 1705,- 1/2: b/w 1056,- 1/4: b/w 614,-
Agency Commission: 15%
Mechanical Data: Type Area: 160 x 243mm, Bleed Size: 210 x 297mm
BUSINESS: FINANCE & ECONOMICS: Taxation

EXTRA 630261N72-1270
Editorial: Kanaalweg 72, 8861 KG HARLINGEN
Tel: 172 447345 **Fax:** 30 6383991
Email: info@fh.nl
Date Established: 01-01-1979; **Freq:** Weekly; **Cover Price:** Free; **Circ:** 22,500
Editor-in-Chief: Renate Huisman
Language(s): Dutch
Agency Commission: 15%
Mechanical Data: Type Area: 260 x 380mm, Bleed Size: 290 x 420mm
LOCAL NEWSPAPERS

EYELINE 16743N56E-15
Editorial: Stieltjesweg 4, 6827 BV ARNHEM
Tel: 20 5245524 **Fax:** 20 5159040
Web site: http://www.eyeline-magazine.nl
Freq: Quarterly; **Cover Price:** EUR 12,50
Annual Sub.: EUR 38,50; **Circ:** 2,850
Editor: Loes Brussen; **Editor-in-Chief:** Anneke Pastoor
Profile: Magazine covering the latest trends, developments and fashion in the field of spectacles and contact lenses.
Language(s): Dutch
ADVERTISING RATES:
Full Page Mono EUR 1/1: f.c. 1892,-; b/w 1495,- 1/2: f.c. 1055,-; b/w 798,- 1/4: f.c. 599,-; b/w 415,-
Agency Commission: 15%
Mechanical Data: Type Area: 185 x 273mm, Bleed Size: 210 x 297mm
Copy instructions: *Copy Date:* 3 weeks prior to publication date
BUSINESS: HEALTH & MEDICAL: Optics

F & O 1638046N14A-433
Editorial: Burgemeester Haspelslaan 63, 1181 NB AMSTELVEEN **Tel:** 314 349562 **Fax:** 314 340515
Email: info@cxomedia.nl **Web site:** http://www.feno.nl
Freq: 10 issues yearly; **Annual Sub.:** EUR 245,-;
Circ: 1,000
Editor: Michiel Rohlof; **Publisher:** A. van Groningen
Language(s): Dutch
ADVERTISING RATES:
Full Page Mono EUR 1/1: b/w 1500,- 1/2: b/w 1000,-
Agency Commission: 15%
Mechanical Data: Type Area: 185 x 250mm, Bleed Size: 215 x 285mm
Copy instructions: *Copy Date:* 2 weeks prior to publication date
BUSINESS: COMMERCE, INDUSTRY & MANAGEMENT

FA RENDEMENT 15486N1A-36
Editorial: Conradstraat 38, 3013 AP ROTTERDAM
Tel: 570 648902 **Fax:** 570 614795
Email: info@rendement.nl **Web site:** http://www.rendement.nl/fa
Date Established: 01-10-2000; **Freq:** 11 issues yearly; **Cover Price:** EUR 27,-
Annual Sub.: EUR 264,-; **Circ:** 9,000
Publisher: Marnix Hoogerwerf
Profile: Magazine providing information on financial matters.
Language(s): Dutch
Readership: Read by financial directors.
ADVERTISING RATES:
Full Page Mono EUR 1/1: b/w 2080,- 1/2: b/w 1250,- 1/4: b/w 750,-
Agency Commission: 15%
Mechanical Data: Type Area: 190 x 260mm, Bleed Size: 210 x 297mm

Copy instructions: *Copy Date:* 3 weeks prior to publication date
BUSINESS: FINANCE & ECONOMICS

FACILITY MANAGEMENT INFORMATIE 1635045N4F-102
Editorial: Gooimeer 4, 1411 DC NAARDEN
Tel: 76 5301715 **Fax:** 70 3045808
Email: info@appr.nl
Date Established: 20-01-1994; **Freq:** 11 issues yearly; **Circ:** 3,971
Editor: Joan Koele; **Publisher:** Joan Koele
Language(s): Dutch
ADVERTISING RATES:
Full Page Mono EUR 1/1: f.c. 2642,-; 1/2: f.c. 1985,-; 1/4: f.c. 1418,-
Agency Commission: 15%
Mechanical Data: Type Area: 190 x 275mm, Bleed Size: 210 x 297mm
BUSINESS: ARCHITECTURE & BUILDING: Cleaning & Maintenance

FACTO MAGAZINE 15717N4R-22
Editorial: Zuidpoolsingel 2, 2408 ZE ALPHEN A/D RIJN **Tel:** 172 466622 **Fax:** 172 440681
Email: info@kluwer.nl **Web site:** http://www.factomagazine.nl
Freq: 10 issues yearly; **Cover Price:** EUR 17,-
Annual Sub.: EUR 135,-; **Circ:** 4,573
Editor: Gerard Dessing
Profile: Journal containing practical information concerning total facility management. Includes articles on the cleaning and maintenance of office buildings and the ordering of office equipment.
Language(s): Dutch
ADVERTISING RATES:
Full Page Mono .. EUR 1/1: b/w 1650,- 1/2: b/w 975,- 1/4: b/w 575,-
Agency Commission: 15%
Mechanical Data: Type Area: 185 x 265mm, Bleed Size: 210 x 297mm
BUSINESS: ARCHITECTURE & BUILDING: Building Related

FANCY 17473N74F-20
Editorial: Capellalaan 65, 2132 JL HOOFDDORP
Tel: 23 5565135 **Fax:** 23 5565116
Web site: http://www.fancy.nl
Freq: Monthly; **Cover Price:** EUR 3,45
Annual Sub.: EUR 44,85; **Circ:** 60,150
Editor: Katalijn Verel; **Publisher:** Anneliese Bergman
Profile: Magazine containing features on fashion, beauty, shopping and celebrities.
Language(s): Dutch
Readership: Aimed at teenage girls.
ADVERTISING RATES:
Full Page Mono EUR 2/1: b/w 9500,- 1/1: b/w 4750,- 1/2: b/w 2850,-
Agency Commission: 15%
Mechanical Data: Bleed Size: 185 x 245mm, Type Area: 155 x 215mm
CONSUMER: WOMEN'S INTEREST CONSUMER MAGAZINES: Teenage

FARMACOTHERAPEUTISCH KOMPAS 1635733N56A-364
Editorial: Eekholt 4, 1112 XH DIEMEN
Tel: 523 285330 **Fax:** 30 6348909
Email: info@cvz.nl
Freq: Annual; **Cover Price:** EUR 31,76; **Circ:** 62,000
Editor: J.M.A. Sitsen
Language(s): Dutch
Agency Commission: 15%
BUSINESS: HEALTH & MEDICAL

FAVORITES 1638183N91R-234
Editorial: Postbus 355, 2130 AJ HOOFDDORP
Date Established: 01-01-2002; **Freq:** Quarterly; **Circ:** 200,000
Editor: R. Meerkerk
Language(s): Dutch
ADVERTISING RATES:
Full Page Mono .... EUR 1/1: f.c. 3950,-
Agency Commission: 15%
Mechanical Data: Bleed Size: 215 x 275mm
CONSUMER: RECREATION & LEISURE: Recreation & Leisure Related

FD OUTLOOK 1634243N14A-581
Editorial: Prins Bernhardplein 173, 1097 BL AMSTERDAM **Tel:** 23 5565001 **Fax:** 20 5928600
Email: info@fd.nl **Web site:** http://www.fd.nl/fdoutlook
Date Established: 15-12-1999; **Freq:** 6 issues yearly;
Cover Price: EUR 7,95
Annual Sub.: EUR 30,-; **Circ:** 70,000
Usual Pagination: 72
Editor: Jan Fred van Wijnen; **Publisher:** A. van den Berg
Language(s): Dutch
ADVERTISING RATES:
Full Page Mono .... EUR 2/1: b/w 18.325,- 1/1: b/w 10.995,-
Agency Commission: 15%
Mechanical Data: Type Area: 190 x 260mm, Bleed Size: 205 x 275mm
BUSINESS: COMMERCE, INDUSTRY & MANAGEMENT

FD PERSOONLIJK 1697964N74M-266
Editorial: Prins Bernhardplein 173, 1097 BL AMSTERDAM **Tel:** 20 5721643 **Fax:** 20 5928700
Email: info@fd.nl **Web site:** http://www.fd.nl/persoonlijk
Freq: Weekly; **Circ:** 67,571
Publisher: A. van den Berg
Language(s): Dutch
ADVERTISING RATES:
Full Page Mono .... EUR 2/1: b/w 18.870,- 1/1: b/w 11.320,- 1/2: b/w 5940,-
Agency Commission: 15%
Mechanical Data: Type Area: 260 x 378mm, Bleed Size: 280 x 395mm
CONSUMER: WOMEN'S INTEREST CONSUMER MAGAZINES: Personal Finance

FELIKAT MAGAZINE 17920N81C-10
Editorial: Elsa Brandstromstraat 60, 2037 LS HAARLEM
Email: fmredactie@felicat.com
Freq: 5 issues yearly; **Annual Sub.:** EUR 25,-; **Circ:** 3,000
Profile: Official journal of the Netherlands Society of Breeders and Lovers of Cats.
Language(s): Dutch
ADVERTISING RATES:
Full Page Mono EUR 1/1: f.c. 210,-; 1/2: f.c. 165,-; 1/4: f.c. 140,-
Agency Commission: 15%
Mechanical Data: Type Area: 185 x 270mm, Bleed Size: 210 x 297mm
CONSUMER: ANIMALS & PETS: Cats

FHM (FOR HIM MAGAZINE) 629357N86C-110
Editorial: H.J.E. Wenckebachweg 200, 1096 AS AMSTERDAM **Tel:** 314 349422 **Fax:** 33 4626063
Email: info@freemediagroup.nl **Web site:** http://www.fhm.nl
Freq: 10 issues yearly; **Cover Price:** EUR 5,40
Annual Sub.: EUR 47,50; **Circ:** 47,873
Editor: Sander Kersten; **Editor-in-Chief:** Sander Kersten; **Publisher:** Arno Kantelberg
Profile: Magazine containing articles about fashion, women, food, drink and travel.
Language(s): Dutch
Readership: Read by men.
ADVERTISING RATES:
Full Page Mono EUR 1/1: f.c. 4752,-; 1/2: f.c. 3565,-; 1/4: f.c. 1901,-
Agency Commission: 15%
Mechanical Data: Type Area: 202 x 280mm, Bleed Size: 222 x 300mm
Copy instructions: *Copy Date:* 3 weeks prior to publication date
CONSUMER: ADULT & GAY MAGAZINES: Men's Lifestyle Magazines

FIAT MAGAZINE 17786N77E-40
Editorial: Aletta Jacobslaan 7, 1066 BP AMSTERDAM **Tel:** 495 538247 **Fax:** 475 551033
Email: info@rhbm.nl
Freq: Half-yearly; **Cover Price:** Free; **Circ:** 125,000
Editor: Hans Verstraaten; **Publisher:** Hans Vervoorn
Profile: Magazine containing articles and information about Fiat cars.
Language(s): Dutch
Readership: Aimed at Fiat owners.
ADVERTISING RATES:
Full Page Mono .... EUR 1/1: f.c. 4550,-
Agency Commission: 15%
Mechanical Data: Bleed Size: 230 x 300mm
Copy instructions: *Copy Date:* 4 weeks prior to publication date
CONSUMER: MOTORING & CYCLING: Club Cars

FIETS 16263N77C-15
Editorial: Capellalaan 65, 2132 JL HOOFDDORP **Tel:** 88 7518070 **Fax:** 88 7518061
Web site: http://www.fiets.nl
Freq: Monthly; **Cover Price:** EUR 4,95
Annual Sub.: EUR 59,54; **Circ:** 36,306
Editor: Rodrick de Munnik; **Editor-in-Chief:** P. van de Gaag; **Publisher:** Jan Paul de Wildt
Profile: Magazine focusing on cycling, includes tests of new models, interviews with racing stars, reports from race events and tourism.
Language(s): Dutch
Readership: Read by cycling enthusiasts.
ADVERTISING RATES:
Full Page Mono EUR 2/1: f.c. 7500,-; b/w 4690,- 1/1: f.c. 3750,-; b/w 2345,- 1/2: f.c. 2470,-; b/w 1275,-
Agency Commission: 15%
Mechanical Data: Type Area: 195 x 265mm, Bleed Size: 215 x 285mm
CONSUMER: MOTORING & CYCLING: Cycling

FIETS ACTIEF 17773N77C-20
Editorial: Capellalaan 65, 2132 JL HOOFDDORP **Tel:** 88 7518070 **Fax:** 30 6076301
Web site: http://www.fietsactief.nl
Freq: 6 issues yearly; **Cover Price:** EUR 5,10
Annual Sub.: EUR 29,04; **Circ:** 30,394
Editor: Rodrick de Munnik; **Editor-in-Chief:** M. Schaap; **Publisher:** Jan Paul de Wildt
Profile: Cycling magazine containing articles on new products, the latest equipment, cycle routes and places to visit in the Netherlands.
Language(s): Dutch
Readership: Aimed at cycling enthusiasts and tourists.
ADVERTISING RATES:
Full Page Mono EUR 2/1: f.c. 6460,-; b/w 4030,- 1/1: f.c. 3230,-; b/w 2015,- 1/2: f.c. 1980,-; b/w 1165,-
Agency Commission: 15%
Mechanical Data: Type Area: 195 x 265mm, Bleed Size: 215 x 285mm
CONSUMER: MOTORING & CYCLING: Cycling

FILATELIE 17826N79C-80
Editorial: Katrien Duckstraat 9, 1336 ZH ALMERE
Tel: 35 6726800
Email: redactie@defilatelie.nl
Date Established: 15-01-1922; **Freq:** 11 issues yearly; **Annual Sub.:** EUR 31,-; **Circ:** 29,500
Editor: Frits Njio; **Publisher:** S.W.D. Veenstra
Profile: Magazine focusing on collecting stamps and other philatelic material.
Language(s): Dutch
Readership: Read by stamp collectors.
ADVERTISING RATES:
Full Page Mono EUR 1/1: f.c. 1445,-; b/w 1135,- 1/2: f.c. 890,-; b/w 640,- 1/4: f.c. 535,-; b/w 350,-
Agency Commission: 15%
Mechanical Data: Type Area: 183 x 275mm, Bleed Size: 210 x 297mm
Copy instructions: *Copy Date:* 4 weeks prior to publication date
CONSUMER: HOBBIES & DIY: Philately

FILM1 SPORT1 MAGAZINE 17669N76C-26
Editorial: Kon. Wilhelminaplein 2-4, 1062 HK AMSTERDAM **Tel:** 10 4004200
Freq: Monthly; **Cover Price:** EUR 2,50
Annual Sub.: EUR 22,95; **Circ:** 504,980
Editor-in-Chief: A. Nauta
Profile: Programme guide for the television channel Canal+.
Language(s): Dutch
ADVERTISING RATES:
Full Page Mono .... EUR 2/1: f.c. 11.990,-; 1/1: f.c. 5995,-; 1/2: f.c. 3595,-
Agency Commission: 15%
Mechanical Data: Bleed Size: 196 x 271mm, Type Area: 196 x 271mm
CONSUMER: MUSIC & PERFORMING ARTS: TV & Radio

DE FILMKRANT 17662N76A-10
Editorial: Prinsengracht 770/4e etage, 1017 LE AMSTERDAM **Tel:** 70 3780250
Email: info@filmkrant.nl **Web site:** http://www.filmkrant.nl
Freq: 11 issues yearly; **Cover Price:** Free; **Circ:** 32,000
Editor: Dana Linssen; **Editor-in-Chief:** M. Graveland; **Publisher:** H. Rabbers
Profile: Magazine providing news on current cinema releases in the Netherlands.
Language(s): Dutch
ADVERTISING RATES:
Full Page Mono EUR 1/1: f.c. 2118,-; 1/2: f.c. 1165,-; 1/4: f.c. 741,-
Agency Commission: 15%
Mechanical Data: Type Area: 270 x 370mm, Bleed Size: 280 x 380mm
Copy instructions: *Copy Date:* 8 days prior to publication date
CONSUMER: MUSIC & PERFORMING ARTS: Cinema

FILOSOFIE MAGAZINE 18246N94X-40
Editorial: Wildenborch 5, 1112 XB DIEMEN
Tel: 20 5310970 **Fax:** 20 5159145
Web site: http://www.filosofiemagazine.nl
Freq: 10 issues yearly; **Cover Price:** EUR 7,50
Annual Sub.: EUR 71,50; **Circ:** 21,358
Editor: Daan Roovers; **Editor-in-Chief:** F. van Rootslaar; **Publisher:** Hans van Vloten
Profile: Journal about philosophy.
Language(s): Dutch
ADVERTISING RATES:
Full Page Mono EUR 2/1: f.c. 4790,-; PMS 3735,-; b/w 3195,- 1/1: f.c. 2660,-; PMS 1955,-; b/w 1595,- 1/2: f.c. 1725,-
Agency Commission: 15%
Mechanical Data: Type Area: 185 x 255mm, Bleed Size: 210 x 280mm
Copy instructions: *Copy Date:* 3 weeks prior to publication date
CONSUMER: OTHER CLASSIFICATIONS: Miscellaneous

FINANCE & CONTROL 1636999N1A-359
Editorial: Staverenstraat 32015, 7418 CJ DEVENTER
Tel: 20 5612070 **Fax:** 570 614795
Email: info@kluwer.nl
Date Established: 01-01-2002; **Freq:** 6 issues yearly; **Annual Sub.:** EUR 470,-; **Circ:** 2,042
Editor: Eduard Loedeman; **Publisher:** Freek Talsma
Language(s): Dutch
ADVERTISING RATES:
Full Page Mono EUR 1/1: f.c. 2200,-; b/w 1400,- 1/2: f.c. 1300,-; b/w 800,- 1/4: f.c. 725,-; b/w 450,-
Agency Commission: 15%
Mechanical Data: Type Area: 180 x 260mm, Bleed Size: 210 x 297mm
BUSINESS: FINANCE & ECONOMICS

FINANCIËLE & MONETAIRE STUDIES 760724N1A-48
Editorial: Prinses Beatrixlaan 116, 2595 AL DEN HAAG **Tel:** 70 4161339 **Fax:** 20 5159145
Email: sdu@sdu.nl
Date Established: 01-01-1982; **Freq:** Quarterly;
Cover Price: EUR 19,50
Annual Sub.: EUR 48,-; **Circ:** 600
Profile: Magazine containing stock exchange news, articles on banking and other general financial news.
Language(s): Dutch
Agency Commission: 15%
BUSINESS: FINANCE & ECONOMICS

FINANZIEN 760776N14L-110
Editorial: Strevelsweg 700/305, 3083 AS ROTTERDAM **Tel:** 70 3780586 **Fax:** 30 6076301
Email: info@ncfned.nl
Date Established: 01-07-1997; **Freq:** 8 issues yearly; **Circ:** 6,000
Usual Pagination: 12
Editor: Anke Groeneboom
Profile: Magazine focusing on trade union matters in the finance industry.
Language(s): Dutch
Readership: Read by trade union members.
Agency Commission: 15%
BUSINESS: COMMERCE, INDUSTRY & MANAGEMENT: Trade Unions

FISCAAL ADVIES 15557N1M-30
Editorial: Utrechtseweg 31a, 3812 NA AMERSFOORT **Tel:** 20 5922250 **Fax:** 30 6348909
Email: info@lvbnetworks.nl
Date Established: 01-01-1989; **Freq:** 6 issues yearly;
Cover Price: EUR 11,98
Annual Sub.: EUR 59,62; **Circ:** 12,793
Editor: Günther Robben; **Publisher:** Heleen Kooistra
Profile: Magazine covering all aspects of taxation.
Language(s): Dutch
Readership: Read by tax inspectors and accountants.
ADVERTISING RATES:
Full Page Mono EUR 1/1: f.c. 5408,-; 1/2: f.c. 4012,-; 1/4: f.c. 3071,-
Agency Commission: 15%
Mechanical Data: Type Area: 185 x 250mm, Bleed Size: 215 x 285mm
BUSINESS: FINANCE & ECONOMICS: Taxation

FISCAAL RENDEMENT 760718N1A-50
Editorial: Conradstraat 38, 3013 AP ROTTERDAM
Tel: 570 648902 **Fax:** 570 614795
Email: info@rendement.nl **Web site:** http://www.rendement.nl/fiscaal
Date Established: 01-11-1989; **Freq:** 11 issues yearly; **Cover Price:** EUR 27,-
Annual Sub.: EUR 264,-; **Circ:** 6,300
Editor: Nicole Slagboom; **Publisher:** Marnix Hoogerwerf
Profile: Magazine containing advice and information on financial matters.
Language(s): Dutch
ADVERTISING RATES:
Full Page Mono EUR 1/1: b/w 1670,- 1/2: b/w 1005,- 1/4: b/w 685,-
Agency Commission: 15%
Mechanical Data: Type Area: 190 x 260mm, Bleed Size: 210 x 297mm
Copy instructions: *Copy Date:* 3 weeks prior to publication date
BUSINESS: FINANCE & ECONOMICS

FISCALERT 1636885N74M-259
Editorial: Max Euweplein 42, 1017 MB AMSTERDAM
Tel: 570 648931 **Fax:** 570 637533
Email: info@fiscalert.nl
Date Established: 01-04-1995; **Freq:** 10 issues yearly; **Circ:** 70,000
Editor: M.J. Piket; **Editor-in-Chief:** L. Matter; **Publisher:** Luc van Os
Language(s): Dutch
ADVERTISING RATES:
Full Page Mono EUR 2/1: f.c. 8900,-; 1/1: f.c. 4450,-; 1/2: f.c. 3340,-
Agency Commission: 15%
Mechanical Data: Type Area: 185 x 250mm, Bleed Size: 210 x 273mm
Copy instructions: *Copy Date:* 3 weeks prior to publication date
CONSUMER: WOMEN'S INTEREST CONSUMER MAGAZINES: Personal Finance

FISCOLOOG 18727N1M-37
Editorial: Bezuidenhoutseweg 1, 2594 AB DEN HAAG **Tel:** 348 436599 **Fax:** 88 2697490
Web site: http://www.fiscoloog.nl
Freq: 22 issues yearly; **Annual Sub.:** EUR 255,-
Editor: Sandra Ligtenberg
Profile: Newsletter focusing on all aspects of finance and taxation.
Language(s): Dutch
Agency Commission: 15%
BUSINESS: FINANCE & ECONOMICS: Taxation

FIT MET VOEDING 19114N74G-22
Editorial: Anholtseweg 36, 7081 CM GENDRINGEN
Tel: 20 7150600 **Fax:** 10 4521797
Email: ortho@orthoeurope.com **Web site:** http://www.fitmetvoeding.nl
Date Established: 01-01-1993; **Freq:** 8 issues yearly;
Annual Sub.: EUR 32,25; **Circ:** 10,000
Editor: Gert Schuitemaker; **Editor-in-Chief:** Jac van Dongen; **Publisher:** Gert Schuitemaker
Profile: Magazine containing information about health, nutrition and fitness.
Language(s): Dutch
Readership: Aimed at people interested in a healthy lifestyle, also read by professionals.
ADVERTISING RATES:
Full Page Mono EUR 1/1: f.c. 1765,-; 1/2: f.c. 1173,-; 1/4: f.c. 561,-
Agency Commission: 15%
Mechanical Data: Type Area: 176 x 252mm, Bleed Size: 210 x 280mm
CONSUMER: WOMEN'S INTEREST CONSUMER MAGAZINES: Slimming & Health

FLAIR 629460N74A-60
Editorial: Capellalaan 65, 2132 JL HOOFDDORP
Tel: 23 5565551 **Fax:** 23 5565136
Web site: http://www.flaironline.nl
Date Established: 01-01-1986; **Freq:** Weekly; **Cover Price:** EUR 2,40
Annual Sub.: EUR 122,20; **Circ:** 111,381
Editor: Carlein Kieboom; **Publisher:** Anneliese Bergman
Profile: Magazine containing articles on lifestyle, trends, relationships and leisure.
Language(s): Dutch
Readership: Aimed at women aged between 24 and 40 years old.
ADVERTISING RATES:
Full Page Mono .... EUR 2/1: b/w 18.600,- 1/1: b/w 9300,- 1/2: b/w 5580,-
Agency Commission: 15%
Mechanical Data: Type Area: 204 x 254mm, Bleed Size: 221 x 274mm
CONSUMER: WOMEN'S INTEREST CONSUMER MAGAZINES: Women's Interest

DE FLEANENDE KRIE 18075N87-80
Editorial: Tjalling H. Haismastraat 26, 9251 AV BERGUM **Tel:** 45 5739390
Date Established: 03-02-1954; **Freq:** 3 issues yearly; **Circ:** 4,000
Editor: J. Jongsma; **Editor-in-Chief:** J. Jongsma
Profile: Christian magazine about culture and literature in Frisia. Distributed among the Frisian population within the Netherlands.
Language(s): Dutch
Agency Commission: 15%
CONSUMER: RELIGIOUS

FLEETMOTIVE 1637309N49A-114
Editorial: Kon. Wilhelminaplein 30-7, 1062 KR AMSTERDAM **Tel:** 70 3789880 **Fax:** 58 2987505
Email: info@railangfords.nl
Freq: Quarterly; **Cover Price:** EUR 8,90
Annual Sub.: EUR 30,-; **Circ:** 6,407
Editor: Jelle Heidstra; **Editor-in-Chief:** B. Kuipers; **Publisher:** Ron Brokking
Language(s): Dutch
ADVERTISING RATES:
Full Page Mono EUR 2/1: f.c. 6065,-; 1/1: f.c. 3350,-; 1/2: f.c. 2015,-
Agency Commission: 15%
Mechanical Data: Type Area: 190 x 265mm, Bleed Size: 210 x 285mm
BUSINESS: TRANSPORT

FLEVOLAND BUSINESS 18759N63-424
Editorial: Houtsaachmole 1, 8531 WC LEMMER
Tel: 10 2435550 **Fax:** 10 2435565
Email: info@businesscompany.nl
Freq: 6 issues yearly; **Annual Sub.:** EUR 55,-; **Circ:** 4,500
Editor: G. Voorn; **Publisher:** Remco Voorn
Profile: Business magazine for the province of Flevoland.
Language(s): Dutch
ADVERTISING RATES:
Full Page Mono .. EUR 1/1: f.c. 1700,-; 1/2: f.c. 925,-; 1/4: f.c. 495,-
Agency Commission: 15%
Mechanical Data: Type Area: 190 x 260mm, Bleed Size: 215 x 285mm
BUSINESS: REGIONAL BUSINESS

FLORE MAGAZINE 1753359N94H-17
Editorial: Geestbrugkade 35, 2281 CX RIJSWIJK
Tel: 70 3780551
Email: flore@florence-zorg.nl
Date Established: 01-06-2005; **Freq:** 3 issues yearly; **Cover Price:** Free; **Circ:** 275,000
Editor: E.R. van der Sluis
Language(s): Dutch
Agency Commission: 15%
CONSUMER: OTHER CLASSIFICATIONS: Customer Magazines

FLOW 1858834N74Q-450
Editorial: Capellalaan 65, 2132 JL HOOFDDORP
Tel: 40 2336262 **Fax:** 570 677062
Web site: http://www.flowmagazine.nl
Freq: 8 issues yearly; **Cover Price:** EUR 6,95
Annual Sub.: EUR 55,60; **Circ:** 65,665

Editor: Astrid van der Hulst; **Publisher:** Wouter Verkennis
Language(s): Dutch
ADVERTISING RATES:
Full Page Mono .... EUR 2/1: b/w 14.200,- 1/1: b/w 7100,- 1/2: b/w 4260,-
Agency Commission: 15%
Mechanical Data: Type Area: 185 x 250mm, Bleed Size: 225 x 280mm
CONSUMER: WOMEN'S INTEREST CONSUMER MAGAZINES: Lifestyle

FLYING DUTCHMAN 18158N89D-25
Editorial: Olympia 10, 1213 NP HILVERSUM
Tel: 20 7150600 **Fax:** 20 4521797
Email: mail@hemels.com
Freq: Quarterly; **Circ:** 165,335
Editor: Karen Wikart; **Editor-in-Chief:** Anja Speelman
Profile: KLM magazine featuring the latest news and business travel features.
Language(s): Dutch
Readership: Read by frequent travellers with KLM.
ADVERTISING RATES:
Full Page Mono .... EUR 2/1: f.c. 19.055,-; 1/1: f.c. 9528,-
Agency Commission: 15%
Mechanical Data: Bleed Size: 210 x 280mm
CONSUMER: HOLIDAYS & TRAVEL: In-Flight Magazines

FM FOTOMARKT 16382N38-38
Editorial: Hendrik Figeeweg 1z, 2031 BJ HAARLEM
Tel: 75 6813545 **Fax:** 75 6813535
Email: fotomarkt@focusmedia.nl
Freq: 10 issues yearly; **Cover Price:** EUR 5,-; **Circ:** 2,000
Editor: Remco de Graaf; **Publisher:** Remco de Graaf
Profile: Magazine covering photograph retail and photofinishing.
Language(s): Dutch
Readership: Aimed at professional photographers and developers.
ADVERTISING RATES:
Full Page Mono EUR 2/1: f.c. 3700,-; 1/1: f.c. 2700,-; 1/2: f.c. 1600,-
Agency Commission: 15%
Mechanical Data: Type Area: 210 x 280mm, Bleed Size: 230 x 300mm
Copy instructions: *Copy Date:* 8 days prior to publication date
BUSINESS: PHOTOGRAPHIC TRADE

FNVB MAGAZINE 1637349N14L-569
Editorial: Varrolaan 100, 3584 BW UTRECHT
Tel: 30 2738234 **Fax:** 30 2738277
Freq: 6 issues yearly; **Circ:** 466,955
Editor: Eldert Kuiken; **Editor-in-Chief:** Peter Beekman
Language(s): Dutch
ADVERTISING RATES:
Full Page Mono EUR 1/1: f.c. 8200,-; b/w 6700,- 1/2: f.c. 5150,-; b/w 3650,- 1/4: f.c. 3450,-; b/w 2000,-
Agency Commission: 15%
Mechanical Data: Type Area: 190 x 260mm, Bleed Size: 210 x 282mm
BUSINESS: COMMERCE, INDUSTRY & MANAGEMENT: Trade Unions

FONDSENWERVING 15568N1P-20
Editorial: Bosboom Toussaintlaan 78b, 2103 SN HEEMSTEDE **Tel:** 88 7518160 **Fax:** 88 7518161
Date Established: 01-03-1998; **Freq:** 6 issues yearly; **Annual Sub.:** EUR 99,50; **Circ:** 5,500
Editor: Jaap Zeekant; **Editor-in-Chief:** Marianne Zeekant; **Publisher:** Jan Krol
Profile: Publication covering all aspects of fundraising and not-for-profit marketing.
Language(s): Dutch
Readership: Aimed at fundraising managers, chief executives and charity trustees.
ADVERTISING RATES:
Full Page Mono EUR 1/1: b/w 2650,- 1/2: b/w 1640,- 1/4: b/w 980,-
Agency Commission: 15%
Mechanical Data: Bleed Size: 210 x 285mm, Type Area: 190 x 265mm
BUSINESS: FINANCE & ECONOMICS: Fundraising

FOODNOTE NIEUWS 1637218N11A-160
Editorial: Postbus 70, 3454 ZH DE MEERN
Tel: 88 2696657 **Fax:** 88 2696887
Email: info@albron.nl
Freq: Quarterly; **Cover Price:** Free; **Circ:** 45,000
Language(s): Dutch
ADVERTISING RATES:
Full Page Mono .... EUR 1/1: f.c. 2900,-
Agency Commission: 15%
Mechanical Data: Type Area: 274 x 396mm
BUSINESS: CATERING: Catering, Hotels & Restaurants

FOODPERSONALITY 16157N22A-29
Editorial: Molenveldlaan 104, 6523 RN NIJMEGEN
Tel: 161 457342 **Fax:** 20 5159145
Web site: http://www.foodpersonality.nl
Freq: Monthly; **Cover Price:** EUR 10,-
Annual Sub.: EUR 130,-; **Circ:** 5,525
Editor: G.F.M. Lommen; **Publisher:** Dave van Loon
Profile: Journal focusing on food retailing with emphasis on retail management.
Language(s): Dutch
Readership: Read by supermarket managers and professionals working in the food industry.
ADVERTISING RATES:
Full Page Mono EUR 2/1: f.c. 6880,-; 1/1: f.c. 4300,-; 1/2: f.c. 2700,-
Agency Commission: 15%
Mechanical Data: Type Area: 240 x 340mm, Bleed Size: 240 x 340mm
BUSINESS: FOOD

FORMULE1.NL 17777N77D-20
Editorial: Capellalaan 65, 2132 JL HOOFDDORP
Tel: 33 2471104 **Fax:** 522 257664
Web site: http://www.formule1.nl
Date Established: 01-12-1994; **Freq:** 19 issues yearly; **Cover Price:** EUR 4,75
Annual Sub.: EUR 92,10; **Circ:** 19,969
Editor: Arjen van Vliet; **Editor-in-Chief:** Diederik Plug; **Publisher:** Sander Stallinga
Profile: Magazine about Formula One racing.
Language(s): Dutch
Readership: Aimed at men aged between 15 and 40 years.
ADVERTISING RATES:
Full Page Mono EUR 2/1: b/w 5900,- 1/1: b/w 2950,- 1/2: b/w 1770,-
Agency Commission: 15%
Mechanical Data: Type Area: 190 x 255mm, Bleed Size: 210 x 275mm
CONSUMER: MOTORING & CYCLING: Motor Sports

DE FOTOGRAAF 16384N38-45
Editorial: Postbus 16, 7160 AA NEEDE
Tel: 88 7518070 **Fax:** 30 6076301
Email: info@artned.com **Web site:** http://www.de-fotograaf.nl
Freq: 6 issues yearly; **Annual Sub.:** EUR 45,-; **Circ:** 8,500
Editor: J. Nijkerk; **Publisher:** Waldo te Kloeze
Profile: Photographic journal.
Language(s): Dutch
Readership: Aimed at professional photographers.
ADVERTISING RATES:
Full Page Mono .. EUR 1/1: b/w 1295,- 1/2: b/w 715,- 1/4: b/w 395,-
Agency Commission: 15%
Mechanical Data: Type Area: 188 x 277mm, Bleed Size: 210 x 297mm
Copy instructions: *Copy Date:* 3 weeks prior to publication date
BUSINESS: PHOTOGRAPHIC TRADE

FOTOGRAFIE 18042N85A-24
Editorial: Straatweg 28, 3604 BB MAARSSEN
Tel: 71 5273515 **Fax:** 20 5302585
Email: info@blauwmedia.com
Freq: 11 issues yearly; **Annual Sub.:** EUR 49,95; **Circ:** 4,359
Publisher: Henk Louwmans
Profile: Magazine covering the photographic sector.
Language(s): Dutch
ADVERTISING RATES:
Full Page Mono EUR 2/1: f.c. 4300,-; 1/1: f.c. 2390,-; 1/2: f.c. 1315,-
Agency Commission: 15%
Mechanical Data: Type Area: 220 x 300mm, Bleed Size: 235 x 322mm
CONSUMER: PHOTOGRAPHY & FILM MAKING: Photography

FOTOGRAFISCH GEHEUGEN 16387N38-70
Editorial: Rhenanialaan 10, 2406 GS ALPHEN A/D RIJN **Tel:** 172 466539
Email: nieuwsbrief@fotogenootschap.nl
Date Established: 01-01-2008; **Freq:** Quarterly;
Cover Price: EUR 9,-
Annual Sub.: EUR 35,-; **Circ:** 500
Editor: Okke Groot
Profile: Magazine of the Dutch Photographers' Society.
Language(s): Dutch
Readership: Aimed at those who collect photographs for museums, organisations and their own interest, also read by researchers.
ADVERTISING RATES:
Full Page Mono EUR 1/1: f.c. 240,-; 1/2: f.c. 120,-; 1/4: f.c. 60,-
Agency Commission: 15%
Mechanical Data: Type Area: 170 x 250mm, Bleed Size: 214 x 297mm
BUSINESS: PHOTOGRAPHIC TRADE

FOTOVISIE 16383N38-40
Editorial: Straatweg 28, 3604 BB MAARSSEN
Tel: 45 5739390 **Fax:** 314 349023
Email: info@blauwmedia.com
Freq: 10 issues yearly; **Annual Sub.:** EUR 39,95; **Circ:** 3,000
Editor-in-Chief: Diana Bokje; **Publisher:** Henk Louwmans
Profile: Magazine covering the photographic trade.
Language(s): Dutch
Readership: Aimed at people in the photographic industry.
ADVERTISING RATES:
Full Page Mono EUR 2/1: f.c. 4125,-; 1/1: f.c. 2290,-; 1/2: f.c. 1260,-
Agency Commission: 15%
Mechanical Data: Type Area: 220 x 300mm, Bleed Size: 235 x 322mm
Copy instructions: *Copy Date:* 9 days prior to publication date
BUSINESS: PHOTOGRAPHIC TRADE

FOXY 1636842N86A-58
Editorial: Postbus 925, 1000 AX AMSTERDAM
Tel: 70 3378124 **Fax:** 40 2060165
Email: info@foxymagazine.nl **Web site:** http://www.foxymagazine.nl
Date Established: 25-05-2001; **Freq:** Monthly;
Annual Sub.: EUR 39,-; **Circ:** 70,000
Editor: P.J. Muller; **Editor-in-Chief:** W.C. van der Linden; **Publisher:** P.J. Muller
Language(s): Dutch
ADVERTISING RATES:
Full Page Mono EUR 1/1: f.c. 1825,-; b/w 1325,- 1/1: f.c. 1077,-; b/w 730,- 1/4: f.c. 645,-; b/w 540,-
Agency Commission: 15%
Mechanical Data: Type Area: 190 x 275mm, Bleed Size: 210 x 295mm
CONSUMER: ADULT & GAY MAGAZINES: Adult Magazines

FRAME 15647N4B-25
Editorial: Laan der Hesperiden 68, 1076 DX AMSTERDAM **Tel:** 172 466622 **Fax:** 24 3723631
Web site: http://www.framemag.com
Date Established: 01-12-1997; **Freq:** 6 issues yearly;
Cover Price: EUR 19,95; **Circ:** 35,497
Editor: R. Thiemann; **Publisher:** Peter Huiberts
Profile: International magazine of interior architecture and design.
Language(s): Dutch
Readership: Aimed at interior architects and designers.
ADVERTISING RATES:
Full Page Mono . EUR 2/1: f.c. 9940,-; 1/1: f.c. 5170,-
Agency Commission: 15%
Mechanical Data: Type Area: 180 x 250mm, Bleed Size: 230 x 297mm
Copy instructions: *Copy Date:* 3 weeks prior to publication date
BUSINESS: ARCHITECTURE & BUILDING: Interior Design & Flooring

FRANCHISE PLUS 630136N14A-86
Editorial: Eemnesserweg 79, 3743 AG BAARN
Tel: 314 349422 **Fax:** 33 4626063
Email: info@franchiseplus.nl
Date Established: 01-05-1993; **Freq:** 6 issues yearly;
Cover Price: EUR 7,-
Annual Sub.: EUR 36,-; **Circ:** 8,500
Editor: Jan Bezemer; **Editor-in-Chief:** Nicolette Vervat; **Publisher:** Guido van der Horst
Profile: Magazine containing information about setting up and operating franchises.
Language(s): Dutch
Readership: Read by people interested in taking out a franchise.
ADVERTISING RATES:
Full Page Mono .. EUR 1/1: b/w 1795,- 1/2: b/w 995,- 1/4: b/w 555,-
Agency Commission: 15%
Mechanical Data: Type Area: 182 x 270mm, Bleed Size: 210 x 297mm
BUSINESS: COMMERCE, INDUSTRY & MANAGEMENT

FRET MAGAZINE 629728N76E-27
Editorial: Rokin 111, 1012 KN AMSTERDAM
Tel: 20 5629444 **Fax:** 20 6680389
Email: info@mcn.nl **Web site:** http://www.fretmagazine.nl
Freq: 6 issues yearly; **Annual Sub.:** EUR 19,95; **Circ:** 20,000
Editor: Tiemen Koopman; **Editor-in-Chief:** Tiemen Koopman; **Publisher:** Janneke van der Wijk
Profile: Music magazine featuring local and international rock, pop and dance music.
Language(s): Dutch
Readership: Aimed at music lovers.
ADVERTISING RATES:
Full Page Mono .. EUR 1/1: b/w 1040,- 1/2: b/w 590,- 1/4: b/w 325,-
Agency Commission: 15%
Mechanical Data: Type Area: 185 x 262mm, Bleed Size: 205 x 280mm
CONSUMER: MUSIC & PERFORMING ARTS: Pop Music

FRIEDENSSTIMME CONTACT 18192N87-84
Editorial: Kampenringweg 21, 2803 PE GOUDA
Tel: 0032 34660066 **Fax:** 0032 34660067
Email: info@friedensstimme.nl
Freq: 6 issues yearly; **Cover Price:** Free; **Circ:** 22,000
Editor: M.J. Uijl; **Editor-in-Chief:** P.J. van den Dool
Profile: Magazine containing information on Christian organisations in all of the former Russian states.
Language(s): Dutch
Readership: Read by people who wish to help or donate.
Agency Commission: 15%
CONSUMER: RELIGIOUS

FRIENDS IN BUSINESS 16953N63-110
Editorial: Prins Hendrikkade 16a, 3071 KB ROTTERDAM **Tel:** 88 2697112 **Fax:** 88 2696983
Email: digidesk@puntuitmedia.nl **Web site:** http://www.friendsinbusiness.info
Date Established: 01-10-1987; **Freq:** Quarterly;
Annual Sub.: EUR 23,-; **Circ:** 10,000
Editor: Aad Wagenaar; **Editor-in-Chief:** Aad Wagenaar
Profile: Business magazine for Rotterdam.
Language(s): Dutch
ADVERTISING RATES:
Full Page Mono EUR 2/1: f.c. 3798,-; 1/1: f.c. 1995,-; 1/2: f.c. 1130,-
Agency Commission: 15%
Mechanical Data: Type Area: 190 x 277mm, Bleed Size: 210 x 297mm
Copy instructions: *Copy Date:* 3 weeks prior to publication date
BUSINESS: REGIONAL BUSINESS

FRIESLAND HOLLAND VAKANTIEMAGAZINE 18135N89C-54
Editorial: Hoofdstraat West 38, 8471 HV WOLVEGA
Tel: 35 67272103 **Fax:** 20 5159145
Email: info@frieslandholland.nl
Date Established: 01-01-1996; **Freq:** Quarterly;
Cover Price: Free; **Circ:** 100,000
Usual Pagination: 128
Editor: Albert Hendriks; **Publisher:** Albert Hendriks
Profile: Entertainment guide focusing on the province of Friesland.
Language(s): Dutch
Readership: Read by tourists.
ADVERTISING RATES:
Full Page Mono . EUR 1/1: f.c. 7552,-; 1/2: f.c. 4012,-
Agency Commission: 15%
Mechanical Data: Type Area: 190 x 277mm, Bleed Size: 210 x 297mm
CONSUMER: HOLIDAYS & TRAVEL: Entertainment Guides

FRUCTUS 16207N26C-26_40
Editorial: Postbus 83, 6980 AB DOESBURG
Email: fructus@scarlet.nl
Freq: Quarterly; **Annual Sub.:** EUR 25,-; **Circ:** 1,000
Editor: B.J. Giesen
Profile: Journal focusing on fruit cultivation.
Language(s): Dutch
ADVERTISING RATES:
Full Page Mono .... EUR 1/1: f.c. 900,-; b/w 450,-
Agency Commission: 15%
Mechanical Data: Type Area: 210 x 297mm
BUSINESS: GARDEN TRADE

FUNDAMENT 15704N4E-291
Editorial: Ceintuurbaan 2, 3847 LG HARDERWIJK
Tel: 35 6726751 **Fax:** 35 6726752
Email: info@fundeon.nl
Freq: 6 issues yearly; **Cover Price:** Free; **Circ:** 28,000
Editor: Jolanda de Vries; **Editor-in-Chief:** Jolanda de Vries
Profile: Newsletter concerning training and courses for the building trade.
Language(s): Dutch
Agency Commission: 15%
Mechanical Data: Type Area: 185 x 270mm, Bleed Size: 210 x 297mm
BUSINESS: ARCHITECTURE & BUILDING: Building

FYSIOPRAXIS 1635077N56R-219
Editorial: Het Spoor 2, 3994 AK HOUTEN
Tel: 30 6383743 **Fax:** 20 5159700
Freq: Monthly; **Annual Sub.:** EUR 106,-; **Circ:** 22,811
Editor: Eline van Dijk; **Editor-in-Chief:** Suzet Hoevers
Language(s): Dutch
ADVERTISING RATES:
Full Page Mono EUR 1/1: f.c. 3472,-; b/w 2161,- 1/2: f.c. 1998,-; b/w 1345,- 1/4: f.c. 1136,-; b/w 811,-
Agency Commission: 15%
Mechanical Data: Type Area: 185 x 268mm, Bleed Size: 210 x 297mm
BUSINESS: HEALTH & MEDICAL: Health Medical Related

GAAF GOED 16178N23A-15
Editorial: Nijenburg 2h, 1081 GG AMSTERDAM
Tel: 45 5739390 **Fax:** 20 5233419
Web site: http://www.gaafgoed.com
Date Established: 01-01-1988; **Freq:** 6 issues yearly;
Annual Sub.: EUR 55,-; **Circ:** 3,500
Editor: Hans Huitenga; **Publisher:** Hans Huitenga
Profile: European journal containing articles on furnishings, interior design and floor coverings.
Language(s): Dutch
Readership: Aimed at professional interior decorators.
ADVERTISING RATES:
Full Page Mono EUR 1/1: f.c. 2310,-; b/w 2050,- 1/2: f.c. 1455,-; b/w 1195,- 1/4: f.c. 865,-; b/w 660,-
Agency Commission: 15%
Mechanical Data: Bleed Size: 230 x 285mm
Copy instructions: *Copy Date:* 3 weeks prior to publication date
BUSINESS: FURNISHINGS & FURNITURE

GALERIE GIDS 717814N84A-339
Editorial: Wildenborch 5, 1112 XB DIEMEN
Tel: 30 2417045 **Fax:** 79 3467846
Date Established: 01-12-1999; **Freq:** Annual; **Annual Sub.:** EUR 9,95; **Circ:** 20,000
Editor: Roos van Put; **Editor-in-Chief:** Raymond Frencken; **Publisher:** Hans van Vloten
Profile: Magazine focusing on art galleries.
Language(s): Dutch
ADVERTISING RATES:
Full Page Mono EUR 2/1: f.c. 1965,-; 1/1: f.c. 1090,-; 1/2: f.c. 545,-
Agency Commission: 15%
Mechanical Data: Type Area: 105 x 150mm, Bleed Size: 120 x 165mm
CONSUMER: THE ARTS & LITERARY: Arts

GAMES GUIDE 1873466N78D-104
Editorial: Capellalaan 65, 2132 JL HOOFDDORP
Tel: 20 6211374 **Fax:** 70 3855505
Web site: http://www.gamesguide.nl
Freq: 10 issues yearly; **Cover Price:** Free; **Circ:** 150,000
Editor: Simon Zijlemans
Language(s): Dutch
ADVERTISING RATES:
Full Page Mono EUR 2/1: b/w 9500,- 1/1: b/w 5450,- 1/2: b/w 3270,-
Agency Commission: 15%
Mechanical Data: Bleed Size: 210 x 297mm
CONSUMER: CONSUMER ELECTRONICS: Games

GASWIJS 16188N24-35
Editorial: Postbus 20127, 7302 HC APELDOORN
Tel: 45 5739390 **Fax:** 20 5233419
Email: info@sterkin.nl
Freq: Quarterly; **Annual Sub.:** EUR 30,-; **Circ:** 6,000
Editor: J. Pronk; **Editor-in-Chief:** M. Oomens; **Publisher:** Albert Janssen
Profile: Publication containing information on technical aspects of gas installations.
Language(s): Dutch
Readership: Aimed at recognised technical installers.
Agency Commission: 15%
BUSINESS: GAS

GAWALO 15629N3D-20
Editorial: Prinses Beatrixlaan 116, 2595 AL DEN HAAG **Tel:** 70 3780586 **Fax:** 30 6076301
Email: sdu@sdu.nl
Freq: 10 issues yearly; **Cover Price:** EUR 19,-
Annual Sub.: EUR 125,-; **Circ:** 6,364
Editor: Piet Voorter; **Publisher:** Johan Schot
Profile: Magazine focusing on plumbing and central heating, contains information about new products and techniques.
Language(s): Dutch
Readership: Aimed at technicians, installers and builders.
ADVERTISING RATES:
Full Page Mono EUR 2/1: f.c. 3670,-; PMS 2920,-; b/w 2170,- 1/1: f.c. 2570,-; PMS 2070,-; b/w 1570,- 1/2: f.c. 1570,-;
Agency Commission: 15%
Mechanical Data: Type Area: 185 x 268mm, Bleed Size: 210 x 297mm
Copy instructions: *Copy Date:* 2 weeks prior to publication date
BUSINESS: HEATING & VENTILATION: Heating & Plumbing

GAY & NIGHT 629820N86B-14
Editorial: Keizersgracht 205, 1016 DS AMSTERDAM
Tel: 88 7518380 **Fax:** 88 7518381
Email: info@outmedia.nl **Web site:** http://www.gay-night.nl
Date Established: 01-07-1997; **Freq:** 11 issues yearly; **Annual Sub.:** EUR 31,50; **Circ:** 20,000
Editor: F. van den Bosch; **Editor-in-Chief:** L. Verhoeven; **Publisher:** Rob Doms
Profile: Lifestyle magazine for the gay community.
Language(s): Dutch
Readership: Read by homosexuals.
ADVERTISING RATES:
Full Page Mono .. EUR 1/1: b/w 1200,- 1/2: b/w 775,- 1/4: b/w 500,-
Agency Commission: 15%
Mechanical Data: Type Area: 204,5 x 284mm, Bleed Size: 210 x 300mm
Copy instructions: *Copy Date:* 2 weeks prior to publication date
CONSUMER: ADULT & GAY MAGAZINES: Gay & Lesbian Magazines

GAY NEWS 18051N86B-16
Editorial: Postbus 76609, 1070 HE AMSTERDAM
Tel: 70 3789880 **Fax:** 70 3789783
Web site: http://www.gaynews.nl
Date Established: 25-04-1991; **Freq:** Monthly;
Cover Price: EUR 3,75
Annual Sub.: EUR 25,-; **Circ:** 20,000
Editor: Hans Hafkamp; **Publisher:** Jasper van Capelle
Profile: Magazine containing information for the gay population in Amsterdam.
Language(s): Dutch
ADVERTISING RATES:
Full Page Mono .... EUR 1/1: f.c. 980,-; b/w 865,- 1/2: f.c. 635,-; b/w 520,- 1/4: f.c. 390,-; b/w 275,-
Agency Commission: 15%
Mechanical Data: Type Area: 210 x 280mm, Bleed Size: 230 x 300mm
CONSUMER: ADULT & GAY MAGAZINES: Gay & Lesbian Magazines

GEA 19119N94J-301
Editorial: Rietspinner 15, 3831 DP LEUSDEN
Tel: 20 5159703
Date Established: 01-09-1968; **Freq:** Quarterly;
Annual Sub.: EUR 21,-; **Circ:** 2,100
Usual Pagination: 44
Editor-in-Chief: J. Stemvers-van Bemmel;
Publisher: W.R. Moorer
Profile: Journal for amateurs and those interested in geology, mineralogy, palaeontology and lapidary.
Language(s): Dutch
Agency Commission: 15%
CONSUMER: OTHER CLASSIFICATIONS: Popular Science

GEBOORTE 1636057N74D-160
Editorial: Veermanskade 2, 1621 AN HOORN
Tel: 543 493705 **Fax:** 15 2158918
Email: info@wij.nl
Freq: Annual; **Cover Price:** Free; **Circ:** 160,000
Editor: P. Remmers; **Publisher:** R. van Vroenhoven
Language(s): Dutch
ADVERTISING RATES:
Full Page Mono .... EUR 2/1: f.c. 16.390,-; 1/1: f.c. 8195,-; 1/2: f.c. 5190,-
Agency Commission: 15%
Mechanical Data: Type Area: 185 x 252mm, Bleed Size: 215 x 282mm
Copy instructions: *Copy Date:* 5 weeks prior to publication date
CONSUMER: WOMEN'S INTEREST CONSUMER MAGAZINES: Child Care

GEBOUWBEHEER 15718N4R-25
Editorial: Celsiusweg 41, 8912 AM LEEUWARDEN
Tel: 58 2954859 **Fax:** 20 6767728
Email: businessmedia@eisma.nl **Web site:** http://www.gebouwbeheer.nu
Date Established: 01-01-1989; **Freq:** 6 issues yearly; **Circ:** 2,700
Editor: Trees van der Wal; **Publisher:** Rex Bierlaagh
Profile: Journal about the management and maintenance of property. Assists officials in purchasing and using products and services for management and maintenance of buildings and dwellings.
Language(s): Dutch
ADVERTISING RATES:
Full Page Mono EUR 1/1: f.c. 2295,-; 1/2: f.c. 1505,-; 1/4: f.c. 1053,-
Agency Commission: 15%
Mechanical Data: Type Area: 185 x 262mm, Bleed Size: 230 x 310mm
BUSINESS: ARCHITECTURE & BUILDING: Building Related

GELD & BELEGGEN 17512N74M-30
Editorial: Herengracht 493, 1017 BT AMSTERDAM
Tel: 88 2944822 **Fax:** 88 2944870
Email: info@wijs.nl **Web site:** http://www.geldenbeleggen.nl
Date Established: 01-10-1993; **Freq:** Quarterly;
Annual Sub.: EUR 29,75; **Circ:** 30,000
Editor: H. de Ruijter; **Publisher:** R. Gribbroek
Profile: Magazine about personal finance and savings.
Language(s): Dutch
ADVERTISING RATES:
Full Page Mono EUR 2/1: f.c. 8500,-; 1/1: f.c. 4500,-; 1/2: f.c. 2500,-
Agency Commission: 15%
Mechanical Data: Type Area: 200 x 285mm, Bleed Size: 210 x 297mm
Copy instructions: *Copy Date:* 4 weeks prior to publication date
CONSUMER: WOMEN'S INTEREST CONSUMER MAGAZINES: Personal Finance

DE GELDERBLOM 18247N94X-55
Editorial: Arij Koplaan 65, 3123 CA SCHIEDAM
Tel: 88 8002010
Email: degelderblom@planet.nl
Date Established: 01-01-1974; **Freq:** Quarterly; **Circ:** 250
Usual Pagination: 16
Editor: P. van Oordt
Profile: Genealogy news bulletin.
Language(s): Dutch
Agency Commission: 15%
Mechanical Data: Bleed Size: 210 x 297mm
CONSUMER: OTHER CLASSIFICATIONS: Miscellaneous

DE GELDERLANDER 17126N67B-3100
Editorial: Winselingseweg 10, 6541 AK NIJMEGEN
Tel: 20 5159703 **Fax:** 24 3650479
Web site: http://www.dg.nl
Date Established: 01-01-1848; **Freq:** 312 issues yearly; **Annual Sub.:** EUR 286,-; **Circ:** 148,592
Editor: Kees Pijnappels; **Publisher:** Stef Rietbergen
Language(s): Dutch
ADVERTISING RATES:
Full Page Mono .... EUR 3/4: b/w 11.395,- 1/2: b/w 7596,- 1/4: b/w 3799,- 3/4 ed. za.: b/w 12.658,- 1/2 ed. za.: b/w 8439,-
Agency Commission: 15%
Mechanical Data: Type Area: 266 x 398mm
REGIONAL DAILY & SUNDAY NEWSPAPERS: Regional Daily Newspapers

GELDGIDS 17510N74M-10
Editorial: Enthovenplein 1, 2521 DA DEN HAAG
Tel: 70 4454149 **Fax:** 30 2759930
Date Established: 01-10-1981; **Freq:** 8 issues yearly; **Circ:** 70,000
Usual Pagination: 52
Editor: R. van der Heijden; **Editor-in-Chief:** W. Nijdam; **Publisher:** Gerjan Huis in 't Veld
Profile: Magazine about personal finance planning, savings, insurance, investment, taxation and legal matters.
Language(s): Dutch
Agency Commission: 15%
CONSUMER: WOMEN'S INTEREST CONSUMER MAGAZINES: Personal Finance

GEMEENTEREINIGING & AFVALMANAGEMENT 18561N32B-81
Editorial: Kroonpark 2, 6831 GV ARNHEM
Tel: 20 5310161 **Fax:** 20 5302585
Email: post@nvrd.nl
Freq: 11 issues yearly; **Cover Price:** EUR 11,50
Annual Sub.: EUR 92,50; **Circ:** 2,300
Editor: Henk Klösters; **Editor-in-Chief:** Karin Hegeman
Profile: Magazine about recycling and waste management.
Language(s): Dutch
ADVERTISING RATES:
Full Page Mono EUR 1/1: f.c. 1695,-; PMS 1272,-; b/w 927,- 1/2: f.c. 937,-; PMS 757,-; b/w 525,- 1/4: f.c. 601,-; PMS 4
Agency Commission: 15%
Mechanical Data: Type Area: 190 x 270mm, Bleed Size: 210 x 297mm
Copy instructions: *Copy Date:* 3 weeks prior to publication date
BUSINESS: LOCAL GOVERNMENT, LEISURE & RECREATION: Public Health & Cleaning

GENEESMIDDELENBULLETIN 16663N56A-19_5
Editorial: Mercatorlaan 1200, 3528 BL UTRECHT
Tel: 20 5922250 **Fax:** 30 6348909
Email: gebu@fed.knmg.nl **Web site:** http://www.geneesmiddelenbulletin.nl
Freq: Monthly; **Annual Sub.:** EUR 39,-; **Circ:** 58,000
Editor: Dick Bijl
Profile: Netherlands drug information bulletin, contains unbiased information about drug treatment as well as news about new drugs and their side effects.
Language(s): Dutch
Agency Commission: 15%
BUSINESS: HEALTH & MEDICAL

GENOEG 17514N74M-45
Editorial: Swammerdamstraat 60hs, 1091 RW AMSTERDAM **Tel:** 10 4274102
Email: redactie@genoeg.nl
Date Established: 15-03-1997; **Freq:** 6 issues yearly;
Cover Price: EUR 3,95
Annual Sub.: EUR 22,50; **Circ:** 11,000
Editor: Mar Oomen; **Editor-in-Chief:** Roos van der Sanden; **Publisher:** Heleen van der Sanden
Profile: Magazine about personal finance with an emphasis on money-saving ideas for individual households.
Language(s): Dutch
ADVERTISING RATES:
Full Page Mono .. EUR 1/1: f.c. 1500,-; 1/2: f.c. 750,-; 1/4: f.c. 375,-
Agency Commission: 15%
Mechanical Data: Type Area: 195 x 250mm, Bleed Size: 230 x 285mm
Copy instructions: *Copy Date:* 3 weeks prior to publication date
CONSUMER: WOMEN'S INTEREST CONSUMER MAGAZINES: Personal Finance

GEOGRAFIE 16905N62B-80
Editorial: Ganzenmarkt 6, 3512 GD UTRECHT
Tel: 38 4279423 **Fax:** 38 4279420
Email: info@knag.nl **Web site:** http://www.geografie.nl
Date Established: 01-01-1992; **Freq:** 9 issues yearly;
Annual Sub.: EUR 91,-; **Circ:** 3,800
Editor: R.H. Kranenburg; **Editor-in-Chief:** Gemmeke van Kempen
Profile: Magazine for geography teachers, urban and regional planners.
Language(s): Dutch
ADVERTISING RATES:
Full Page Mono EUR 1/1: f.c. 1650,-; PMS 1235,-; b/w 825,- 1/2: f.c. 945,-; PMS 705,-; b/w 470,- 1/4: f.c. 595,-; PMS 4
Agency Commission: 15%
Mechanical Data: Type Area: 183 x 268mm, Bleed Size: 210 x 297mm
BUSINESS: CHURCH & SCHOOL EQUIPMENT & EDUCATION: Education Teachers

GEOINFORMATICS 1643839N5E-215
Editorial: Postbus 231, 8300 AE EMMELOORD
Tel: 50 5445815 **Fax:** 527 620984
Web site: http://www.geoinformatics.com
Freq: 8 issues yearly; **Annual Sub.:** EUR 85,-; **Circ:** 8,000
Editor: Eric Rees; **Editor-in-Chief:** Eric Rees
Language(s): Dutch
ADVERTISING RATES:
Full Page Mono EUR 1/1: f.c. 2700,-; 1/2: f.c. 1850,-; 1/4: f.c. 980,-
Agency Commission: 15%
Mechanical Data: Type Area: 185 x 272mm, Bleed Size: 210 x 297mm
BUSINESS: COMPUTERS & AUTOMATION: Data Transmission

GEVAARLIJKE LADING 15820N10-30
Editorial: Prinses Beatrixlaan 116, 2595 AL DEN HAAG **Tel:** 172 466622 **Fax:** 172 440681
Email: sdu@sdu.nl **Web site:** http://www.gevaarlijke-lading.nl
Freq: 6 issues yearly; **Annual Sub.:** EUR 102,50; **Circ:** 1,254
Editor: Sandra Bergman
Profile: Magazine concerning the handling and transport of dangerous materials. Includes information on storage, transportation by air, land, rail and water and legal aspects of transportation.
Language(s): Dutch
Readership: Read by professionals in the transport and logistics field.
ADVERTISING RATES:
Full Page Mono EUR 1/1: f.c. 2735,-; 1/2: f.c. 1460,-; 1/4: f.c. 780,-
Agency Commission: 15%
Mechanical Data: Type Area: 185 x 267mm, Bleed Size: 210 x 297mm
BUSINESS: MATERIALS HANDLING

GEVELBOUW 1659856N4E-316
Editorial: Schatbeurderlaan 6, 6002 ED WEERT
Tel: 30 6383838 **Fax:** 30 6383839
Email: info@louwersuitgevers.nl
Freq: Quarterly; **Annual Sub.:** EUR 45,-; **Circ:** 5,000
Editor: Willem Ruyters
Language(s): Dutch
ADVERTISING RATES:
Full Page Mono EUR 2/1: b/w 1995,- 1/1: b/w 1350,- 1/2: b/w 975,-
Agency Commission: 15%
Mechanical Data: Type Area: 190 x 270mm, Bleed Size: 210 x 297mm
Copy instructions: *Copy Date:* 5 weeks prior to publication date
BUSINESS: ARCHITECTURE & BUILDING: Building

GEZOND BOUWEN & WONEN 15644N4A-30
Editorial: Regenboog 25, 3742 ZA BAARN
Tel: 23 5344089 **Fax:** 10 2801002
Email: uvw@vwg.net **Web site:** http://www.gezondbouwenenwonen.nl
Freq: Quarterly; **Cover Price:** EUR 17,50
Annual Sub.: EUR 59,50; **Circ:** 2,500
Editor: Anne Ubbels; **Editor-in-Chief:** Elzemarie Karsdorp; **Publisher:** Bart van Ommeren
Profile: Special interest magazine about biological and ecological architecture, with particular attention to environmentally friendly building designs,.
Language(s): Dutch
ADVERTISING RATES:
Full Page Mono .. EUR 1/1: f.c. 1850,-; 1/2: f.c. 950,-; 1/4: f.c. 500,-
Agency Commission: 15%
Mechanical Data: Type Area: 180 x 255mm, Bleed Size: 210 x 285mm
Copy instructions: *Copy Date:* 3 weeks prior to publication date
BUSINESS: ARCHITECTURE & BUILDING: Architecture

GEZOND THUIS 1857825N32G-334
Editorial: Lt. Generaal van Heutszlaan 4, 3743 JN BAARN **Tel:** 40 8447611 **Fax:** 53 4842189
Email: informatie@axioma.nl
Freq: 3 issues yearly; **Cover Price:** Free; **Circ:** 82,000
Editor: Peter Bierhaus
Language(s): Dutch
ADVERTISING RATES:
Full Page Mono EUR 2/1: f.c. 4182,-; 1/1: f.c. 2200,-; 1/2: f.c. 1320,-
Agency Commission: 15%
Mechanical Data: Type Area: 185 x 243mm
BUSINESS: LOCAL GOVERNMENT, LEISURE & RECREATION: Community Care & Social Services

GEZOND VGZ MAGAZINE 1634071N74G-243
Editorial: Postbus 30374, 6503 HZ NIJMEGEN
Tel: 88 2944900 **Fax:** 35 6728834
Date Established: 01-06-1980; **Freq:** 3 issues yearly; **Circ:** 650,000
Usual Pagination: 24
Editor-in-Chief: Roel Willems
Language(s): Dutch
Agency Commission: 15%
CONSUMER: WOMEN'S INTEREST CONSUMER MAGAZINES: Slimming & Health

GEZONDGIDS
1637082N74G-279
Editorial: Enthovenplein 1, 2521 DA DEN HAAG
Tel: 43 3561490 **Fax:** 182 543500
Freq: 10 issues yearly; **Annual Sub.:** EUR 50,-; **Circ:** 52,000
Editor: M. Bijleveld; **Editor-in-Chief:** E. Brenninkmeijer; **Publisher:** Gerjan Huis in 't Veld
Language(s): Dutch
Agency Commission: 15%
CONSUMER: WOMEN'S INTEREST CONSUMER MAGAZINES: Slimming & Health

GEZONDHEID! SAMEN DELEN
1634485N1P-87
Editorial: Lutherse Burgwal 10, 2512 CB DEN HAAG
Tel: 33 2471104 **Fax:** 23 5564241
Email: info@cordaidmemisa.nl
Date Established: 01-01-1983; **Freq:** Quarterly; **Cover Price:** Free; **Circ:** 170,000
Usual Pagination: 16
Editor: Jacqueline Bal
Language(s): Dutch
Agency Commission: 15%
Mechanical Data: Type Area: 200 x 290mm, Bleed Size: 215 x 305mm
BUSINESS: FINANCE & ECONOMICS: Fundraising

GEZONDHEIDPLUS
634029N74G-160
Editorial: Terborgseweg 47, 7064 AB SILVOLDE
Tel: 20 5612070 **Fax:** 70 3364640
Web site: http://www.gezondheidplus.nl
Freq: 6 issues yearly; **Annual Sub.:** EUR 25,-; **Circ:** 50,000
Editor: E. Schoorel; **Publisher:** Jan Olthof
Profile: Magazine containing information about vitamins, diet, health and lifestyle.
Language(s): Dutch
Readership: Read mainly by women over 35 years.
ADVERTISING RATES:
Full Page Mono . EUR 1/1: f.c. 2500,-; 1/2: f.c. 1350,-
Agency Commission: 15%
Mechanical Data: Type Area: 190 x 277mm, Bleed Size: 210 x 297mm
Copy instructions: *Copy Date:* 4 weeks prior to publication date
CONSUMER: WOMEN'S INTEREST CONSUMER MAGAZINES: Slimming & Health

GEZZOND
1637099N74G-281
Editorial: Haagse Schouwweg 12, 2332 KG LEIDEN
Tel: 71 5825159 **Fax:** 88 2696946
Date Established: 01-09-2007; **Freq:** Quarterly; **Circ:** 250,000
Usual Pagination: 20
Language(s): Dutch
Agency Commission: 15%
CONSUMER: WOMEN'S INTEREST CONSUMER MAGAZINES: Slimming & Health

GIRLZ!
1637144N74F-138
Editorial: Joan Muyskenweg 6-6a, 1096 CJ AMSTERDAM **Tel:** 20 5979546 **Fax:** 20 5979614
Email: info@publishing.audax.nl **Web site:** http://www.girlz-online.nl
Freq: 13 issues yearly; **Cover Price:** EUR 3,95
Annual Sub.: EUR 42,35; **Circ:** 104,704
Editor: Robert van der Sanden; **Editor-in-Chief:** Renée Brouwer
Language(s): Dutch
ADVERTISING RATES:
Full Page Mono .... EUR 2/1: b/w 12.500,- 1/1: b/w 6250,- 1/2: b/w 4690,-
Agency Commission: 15%
Mechanical Data: Type Area: 179 x 230mm, Bleed Size: 210 x 270mm
Copy instructions: *Copy Date:* 4 weeks prior to publication date
CONSUMER: WOMEN'S INTEREST CONSUMER MAGAZINES: Teenage

GIS-MAGAZINE
1637362N14R-252
Editorial: Postbus 231, 8300 AE EMMELOORD
Tel: 30 2738234 **Fax:** 30 2738277
Web site: http://www.gismagazine.nl
Date Established: 01-01-2003; **Freq:** 8 issues yearly; **Annual Sub.:** EUR 69,-; **Circ:** 5,000
Editor: Remco Takken; **Publisher:** Ruud Groothuis
Language(s): Dutch
ADVERTISING RATES:
Full Page Mono EUR 1/1: f.c. 2575,-; 1/2: f.c. 1550,-; 1/4: f.c. 900,-
Agency Commission: 15%
Mechanical Data: Type Area: 185 x 272mm, Bleed Size: 210 x 297mm
BUSINESS: COMMERCE, INDUSTRY & MANAGEMENT: Commerce Related

GITARIST
17693N76D-45
Editorial: Rozenstraat 206, 1016 PA AMSTERDAM
Tel: 70 3342179 **Fax:** 20 5979490
Web site: http://www.gitarist.nl
Date Established: 01-01-1991; **Freq:** Monthly; **Cover Price:** EUR 5,90
Annual Sub.: EUR 59,-; **Circ:** 11,500
Editor: Mark van Schaick; **Publisher:** Erk Willemsen
Profile: Magazine for lead and bass guitarists.
Language(s): Dutch
ADVERTISING RATES:
Full Page Mono EUR 1/1: f.c. 1840,-; 1/2: f.c. 1000,-; 1/4: f.c. 540,-
Agency Commission: 15%
Mechanical Data: Type Area: 190 x 270mm, Bleed Size: 210 x 297mm
Copy instructions: *Copy Date:* 2 weeks prior to publication date
CONSUMER: MUSIC & PERFORMING ARTS: Music

GLAMOUR
1667166N74A-230
Editorial: Dalsteindreef 82-92, 1112 XC DIEMEN
Tel: 20 5244510 **Fax:** 314 359978
Email: info@genj.nl **Web site:** http://www.glamour.nl
Date Established: 01-09-2005; **Freq:** Monthly; **Cover Price:** EUR 2,95
Annual Sub.: EUR 32,50; **Circ:** 152,556
Editor: Karin Swerink; **Editor-in-Chief:** Evelyn van Driel; **Publisher:** E. Blok
Language(s): Dutch
ADVERTISING RATES:
Full Page Mono .... EUR 2/1: f.c. 22.400,-; 1/1: f.c. 11.800,-; 1/2: f.c. 7100,-
Agency Commission: 15%
Mechanical Data: Type Area: 147 x 203mm, Bleed Size: 167 x 223mm
CONSUMER: WOMEN'S INTEREST CONSUMER MAGAZINES: Women's Interest

GLAMPING MAGAZINE
2009265N91B-207
Editorial: Wassenaarseweg 220, 2596 EC DEN HAAG **Tel:** 88 2697112 **Fax:** 88 2696983
Date Established: 14-12-2010; **Freq:** Annual; **Cover Price:** Free; **Circ:** 100,000
Usual Pagination: 164
Editor: Gerard-Paul Wisgerhof
Language(s): Dutch
ADVERTISING RATES:
Full Page Mono EUR 1/1: f.c. 2700,-; 1/2: f.c. 1620,-; 1/4: f.c. 972,-
Agency Commission: 15%
Mechanical Data: Type Area: 190 x 236mm, Bleed Size: 200 x 250mm
Copy instructions: *Copy Date:* 50 days prior to publication date
CONSUMER: RECREATION & LEISURE: Camping & Caravanning

GLAS IN BEELD
15851N12B-8
Editorial: Informaticaweg 3c, 7007 CP DOETINCHEM **Tel:** 20 5922250
Web site: http://www.glasinbeeld.nl
Freq: 6 issues yearly; **Circ:** 4,500
Editor: Marco Groothoff; **Editor-in-Chief:** Arno Verbaas; **Publisher:** Rex Bierlaagh
Profile: Journal about the glass trade and the use of glass in building applications.
Language(s): Dutch
Readership: Aimed at builders and glass traders.
ADVERTISING RATES:
Full Page Mono EUR 1/1: f.c. 3368,-; 1/2: f.c. 1894,-; 1/4: f.c. 1055,-
Agency Commission: 15%
Mechanical Data: Type Area: 185 x 262mm, Bleed Size: 230 x 310mm
BUSINESS: CERAMICS, POTTERY & GLASS: Glass

GOAL! MAGAZINE
1658926N91D-160
Editorial: Mijlweg 61, 3316 BE DORDRECHT
Tel: 45 5792379 **Fax:** 88 2697660
Email: info@zpress-magazines.nl **Web site:** http://www.goalmagazine.nl
Freq: Monthly; **Cover Price:** EUR 3,10
Annual Sub.: EUR 34,95; **Circ:** 29,878
Editor-in-Chief: Joeri Donsu; **Publisher:** Robert van Ginhoven
Language(s): Dutch
ADVERTISING RATES:
Full Page Mono . EUR 2/1: f.c. 5000,-; 1/1: f.c. 2950,-
Agency Commission: 15%
Mechanical Data: Type Area: 190 x 277mm, Bleed Size: 210 x 297mm
CONSUMER: RECREATION & LEISURE: Children & Youth

GOLFERS MAGAZINE
17588N75D-90
Editorial: Capellalaan 65, 2132 JL HOOFDDORP
Tel: 30 6399911 **Fax:** 30 6399937
Freq: 10 issues yearly; **Cover Price:** EUR 6,50
Annual Sub.: EUR 75,35; **Circ:** 22,698
Editor: Jan Kees van der Velden; **Editor-in-Chief:** Angela Houdijk; **Publisher:** Jan Paul de Wildt
Profile: Publication covering all aspects of golf, including clothing and equipment.
Language(s): Dutch
Readership: Aimed at golfers.
ADVERTISING RATES:
Full Page Mono EUR 1/1: b/w 4410,- 1/2: b/w 3050,- 1/4: b/w 2060,-
Agency Commission: 15%
Mechanical Data: Type Area: 180 x 252mm, Bleed Size: 210 x 275mm
CONSUMER: SPORT: Golf

GOLFJOURNAAL
17587N75D-70
Editorial: Capellalaan 65, 2132 JL HOOFDDORP
Tel: 20 5922250 **Fax:** 30 6348909
Freq: 10 issues yearly; **Annual Sub.:** EUR 31,50; **Circ:** 166,665
Editor: Jan Kees van der Velden; **Editor-in-Chief:** Angela Houdijk; **Publisher:** Jan Paul de Wildt
Profile: Journal of the Dutch Golf Federation.
Language(s): Dutch
ADVERTISING RATES:
Full Page Mono .... EUR 1/1: f.c. 10.990,-; 1/2: f.c. 7364,-; 1/4: f.c. 4614,-
Agency Commission: 15%
Mechanical Data: Type Area: 188 x 275mm, Bleed Size: 210 x 297mm
CONSUMER: SPORT: Golf

GOOI- EN EEMLAND BUSINESS
16955N63-122
Editorial: Houtsaachmole 1, 8531 WC LEMMER
Tel: 88 8002010 **Fax:** 226 333555
Email: info@businesscompany.nl **Web site:** http://www.gooieneemland-business.nl
Date Established: 01-01-1985; **Freq:** 6 issues yearly; **Annual Sub.:** EUR 55,-; **Circ:** 4,500
Editor: G. Voorn; **Publisher:** Remco Voorn
Profile: Business magazine for the Gooi and Eemland regions.
Language(s): Dutch
Readership: Aimed at managers and directors.
ADVERTISING RATES:
Full Page Mono .. EUR 1/1: b/w 1700,- 1/2: b/w 925,- 1/4: b/w 495,-
Agency Commission: 15%
Mechanical Data: Type Area: 190 x 260mm, Bleed Size: 215 x 285mm
Copy instructions: *Copy Date:* 2 weeks prior to publication date
BUSINESS: REGIONAL BUSINESS

GREENPEACE
16817N57-21_50
Editorial: Jollemanhof 15-17, 1019 GW AMSTERDAM **Tel:** 20 5159743 **Fax:** 20 6752709
Email: info@greenpeace.nl
Freq: Quarterly; **Circ:** 500,000
Editor: Annemiek van Bentem
Profile: Magazine of the Greenpeace organisation in the Netherlands. Includes updates and background on the campaigns of Greenpeace and articles on subjects connected to their work.
Language(s): Dutch
Readership: Read by supporters of Greenpeace.
Agency Commission: 15%
Mechanical Data: Bleed Size: 210 x 297mm
BUSINESS: ENVIRONMENT & POLLUTION

GROEN
16818N57-22_50
Editorial: Achtergracht 71, 1381 BL WEESP
Tel: 35 6256180
Web site: http://www.vakbladgroen.nl
Date Established: 01-01-1944; **Freq:** 11 issues yearly; **Annual Sub.:** EUR 80,-; **Circ:** 2,000
Editor-in-Chief: Noortje Krikhaar
Profile: Journal focusing on urban and environmentally green planning, design, construction and management.
Language(s): Dutch
Readership: Aimed at environmentalists, town planners, architects and designers.
ADVERTISING RATES:
Full Page Mono EUR 1/1: b/w 770,- 1/2: b/w 470,- 1/4: b/w 300,-
Agency Commission: 15%
Mechanical Data: Type Area: 185 x 260mm, Bleed Size: 210 x 290mm
Copy instructions: *Copy Date:* 3 weeks prior to publication date
BUSINESS: ENVIRONMENT & POLLUTION

GROEN LINKS MAGAZINE
17953N82-35
Editorial: Oude Gracht 312, 3511 PK UTRECHT
Tel: 23 5565135 **Fax:** 88 5567355
Email: info@groenlinks.nl
Freq: 6 issues yearly; **Annual Sub.:** EUR 17,50; **Circ:** 27,000
Editor: A. de Kruijf; **Editor-in-Chief:** M. van Dijck
Profile: Newspaper published by the Green Party.
Language(s): Dutch
ADVERTISING RATES:
Full Page Mono .. EUR 1/1: b/w 1370,- 1/2: b/w 719,- 1/4: b/w 395,-
Agency Commission: 15%
Mechanical Data: Type Area: 190 x 260mm, Bleed Size: 210 x 290mm
CONSUMER: CURRENT AFFAIRS & POLITICS

GRONINGER STUDENTENKRANT
17991N83-70
Editorial: Sint Walburgstraat 22c, 9712 HX GRONINGEN
Email: bestuur@studentenkrant.org **Web site:** http://www.studentenkrant.org
Date Established: 01-02-1983; **Freq:** 11 issues yearly; **Cover Price:** Free; **Circ:** 8,000
Editor: Randy Martens
Profile: Magazine for students in the city of Groningen.
Language(s): Dutch
ADVERTISING RATES:
Full Page Mono EUR 1/1: f.c. 450,-; b/w 300,- 1/2: f.c. 250,-; b/w 150,- 1/4: f.c. 125,-; b/w 75,-
Agency Commission: 15%
Mechanical Data: Type Area: 260 x 380mm, Bleed Size: 300 x 420mm
CONSUMER: STUDENT PUBLICATIONS

GROOMERS EUROPE
16997N64E-40
Editorial: Booldersdijk 29, 6031 PK NEDERWEERT
Tel: 70 3342179 **Fax:** 20 5979490
Email: jetty@worldonline.nl
Freq: 6 issues yearly; **Annual Sub.:** EUR 24,03; **Circ:** 3,000
Editor: Jetty van der Hulst
Profile: Magazine covering dog grooming, includes information concerning boarding kennels.
Language(s): Dutch
Readership: Aimed at professional dog groomers.
ADVERTISING RATES:
Full Page Mono .. EUR 1/1: f.c. 987,-; b/w 476,-** 1/2: f.c. 633,-; b/w 293,-** 1/4: f.c. 470,-; b/w 4213-
Agency Commission: 15%
Mechanical Data: Type Area: 185 x 275mm, Bleed Size: 210 x 297mm
Copy instructions: *Copy Date:* 3 weeks prior to publication date
BUSINESS: OTHER CLASSIFICATIONS: Pet Trade

GROOT HELLEVOET
630265N72-1720
Editorial: Christiaan Huygensweg 9, 3220 AB HELLEVOETSLUIS **Tel:** 23 5567955 **Fax:** 23 5567956
Web site: http://www.groothellevoet.nl
Date Established: 01-01-1977; **Freq:** Weekly; **Cover Price:** Free; **Circ:** 20,500
Editor: L. Blok
Language(s): Dutch
Agency Commission: 15%
Mechanical Data: Type Area: 273 x 350mm
LOCAL NEWSPAPERS

GROOT WESTLAND
626831N72-1740
Editorial: Dreesplein 4, 2672 EA NAALDWIJK
Tel: 161 457342 **Fax:** 20 5159145
Freq: Weekly; **Cover Price:** Free; **Circ:** 47,000
Editor: M. van Amerongen; **Editor-in-Chief:** J. Wageveld
Language(s): Dutch
Agency Commission: 15%
Mechanical Data: Type Area: 273 x 350mm
LOCAL NEWSPAPERS

GROTER GROEIEN
17460N74D-25
Editorial: Capellalaan 65, 2132 JL HOOFDDORP
Tel: 23 5565135 **Fax:** 88 5567355
Web site: http://www.grotergroeien.nl
Freq: 13 issues yearly; **Cover Price:** EUR 4,50
Annual Sub.: EUR 55,25; **Circ:** 75,168
Editor: Nancy Berendsen; **Publisher:** Stefan Hutten
Profile: Magazine containing information on parenthood and child care and development.
Language(s): Dutch
Readership: Aimed at parents with children aged between 0 and 8 years.
ADVERTISING RATES:
Full Page Mono .... EUR 2/1: b/w 11.600,- 1/1: b/w 5800,- 1/2: b/w 3480,-
Agency Commission: 15%
Mechanical Data: Type Area: 185 x 250mm, Bleed Size: 210 x 285mm
CONSUMER: WOMEN'S INTEREST CONSUMER MAGAZINES: Child Care

GSUS AGENDA
1637046N83-198
Editorial: Reaal 2b, 2353 TL LEIDERDORP
Tel: 50 5844205 **Fax:** 70 3602861
Email: info@stationeryteam.nl
Freq: Annual; **Cover Price:** EUR 13,50; **Circ:** 70,000
Publisher: M. Leguijt
Language(s): Dutch
Agency Commission: 15%
Mechanical Data: Bleed Size: 140 x 188mm
CONSUMER: STUDENT PUBLICATIONS

HA DIE PUP!
1644000N81B-83
Editorial: Dahliastraat 36, 4702 CJ ROOSENDAAL
Tel: 23 5565462
Email: info@kynotrain.nl
Date Established: 01-01-1995; **Freq:** Annual; **Cover Price:** EUR 5,95; **Circ:** 55,000
Editor: Peter Beekman
Language(s): Dutch
ADVERTISING RATES:
Full Page Mono .... EUR 1/1: f.c. 2500,-
Agency Commission: 15%
Mechanical Data: Bleed Size: 210 x 297mm
CONSUMER: ANIMALS & PETS: Dogs

DE HAARLEMMER
626856N72-1820
Editorial: Boekerslootlaan 49, 2201 BT NOORDWIJK
Tel: 570 647207 **Fax:** 71 3643461
Email: info@buijzepers.nl
Freq: Weekly; **Cover Price:** Free; **Circ:** 76,000
Language(s): Dutch
Agency Commission: 15%
Mechanical Data: Type Area: 270 x 410mm, Bleed Size: 290 x 440mm
LOCAL NEWSPAPERS

Netherlands

DE HALDERBERGSE BODE
626859N72-1850
Editorial: Bredaseweg 26, 4881 DE ZUNDERT
Tel: 88 2697049 **Fax:** 70 3544642
Email: zetterij@vorsselmans.nl **Web site:** http://www.internetbode.nl
Freq: Weekly; **Circ:** 13,500
Editor: Vif Janssen; **Editor-in-Chief:** Vif Janssen
Language(s): Dutch
Agency Commission: 15%
Mechanical Data: Type Area: 264 x 400mm
LOCAL NEWSPAPERS

HAND IN HAND
1636075N56R-233
Editorial: Weltevreden 4a, 3731 AL DE BILT
Tel: 20 5159172 **Fax:** 20 5159145
Email: info@kinderfonds.nl
Freq: Half-yearly; **Cover Price:** Free; **Circ:** 70,000
Editor: G.J. Nederlof
Language(s): Dutch
Agency Commission: 15%
BUSINESS: HEALTH & MEDICAL: Health Medical Related

HANDBOEKBINDEN
16874N60A-200
Editorial: Postbus 50076, 1305 AB ALMERE
Tel: 58 2954859
Email: secretariaat@stichting-handboekbinden.nl
Freq: Quarterly; **Annual Sub.:** EUR 25,-; **Circ:** 1,500
Usual Pagination: 36
Editor: Karin Cox
Profile: Publication about the book-binding trade.
Language(s): Dutch
Agency Commission: 15%
BUSINESS: PUBLISHING: Publishing & Book Trade

HANDSCHRIFT
17971N82-42
Editorial: Puntenburgerlaan 91, 3812 CC AMERSFOORT **Tel:** 88 2697183 **Fax:** 88 2697490
Email: bureau@christenunie.nl
Date Established: 30-09-2000; **Freq:** 5 issues yearly; **Circ:** 26,000
Editor: Shahied Badoella; **Editor-in-Chief:** Hermen Ridderikhof; **Publisher:** Shahied Badoella
Profile: Publication of the Christen Unie Federation.
Language(s): Dutch
ADVERTISING RATES:
Full Page Mono .. EUR 1/1: f.c. 1190,-; 1/2: f.c. 649,-; 1/4: f.c. 378,-
Agency Commission: 15%
Mechanical Data: Type Area: 185 x 270mm, Bleed Size: 210 x 297mm
CONSUMER: CURRENT AFFAIRS & POLITICS

HANZEMAG
18103N88A-29
Editorial: Zernikeplein 7, 9747 AS GRONINGEN
Tel: 229 216416 **Fax:** 229 265738
Email: hanzemag@org.hanze.nl
Freq: 11 issues yearly; **Annual Sub.:** EUR 60,-; **Circ:** 8,500
Editor: C.F. Wind; **Editor-in-Chief:** J.B.M. Otten
Profile: Publication of Hanzehogeschool in Groningen.
Language(s): Dutch
Readership: Read by teachers and pupils.
ADVERTISING RATES:
Full Page Mono EUR 1/1: f.c. 1700,-; 1/2: f.c. 1000,-; 1/4: f.c. 580,-
Agency Commission: 15%
Mechanical Data: Type Area: 215 x 305mm, Bleed Size: 240 x 335mm
CONSUMER: EDUCATION

HAPPINEZ
1640453N94X-457
Editorial: Cattenhagestraat 8a, 1411 CT NAARDEN
Tel: 172 440681 **Fax:** 172 422886
Email: info@happinez.nl **Web site:** http://www.happinez.nl
Freq: 8 issues yearly; **Cover Price:** EUR 5,95
Annual Sub.: EUR 42,50; **Circ:** 193,563
Editor: Marije de Jong; **Editor-in-Chief:** Roos Tesselaar; **Publisher:** Lim Olsthoorn
Language(s): Dutch
ADVERTISING RATES:
Full Page Mono .... EUR 2/1: f.c. 21.600,-; 1/1: f.c. 10.800,-; 1/2: f.c. 6480,-
Agency Commission: 15%
Mechanical Data: Type Area: 200 x 265mm, Bleed Size: 230 x 297mm
CONSUMER: OTHER CLASSIFICATIONS: Miscellaneous

HART BULLETIN
629358N56A-24_30
Editorial: Het Spoor 2, 3994 AK HOUTEN
Tel: 35 6726900 **Fax:** 20 5854158
Freq: 6 issues yearly; **Circ:** 10,485
Editor: H.W. Vliegen
Profile: Journal focusing on latest developments in the field of cardiovascular diseases. Includes review articles, care reports and case studies.
Language(s): Dutch
Readership: Read by members of the Dutch Heart Foundation, general practitioners, cardiologists, internists, neurologists, pharmacists, traumatologists and students.
ADVERTISING RATES:
Full Page Mono EUR 1/1: f.c. 3880,-; b/w 2089,- 1/2: f.c. 2428,-; b/w 1309,- 1/4: f.c. 1374,-; b/w 742,-
Agency Commission: 15%
Mechanical Data: Type Area: 180 x 228mm, Bleed Size: 210 x 280mm
Copy instructions: *Copy Date:* 5 weeks prior to publication date
BUSINESS: HEALTH & MEDICAL

HART VOOR DIEREN
17903N81A-30
Editorial: Takkebijsters 57a, 4817 BL BREDA
Tel: 23 5344089 **Fax:** 10 2801002
Email: info@vipmedia.nl **Web site:** http://www.hartvoordieren.nl
Date Established: 01-03-1988; **Freq:** Monthly;
Cover Price: EUR 3,95
Annual Sub.: EUR 39,95; **Circ:** 81,000
Editor: Nique Hanskamp; **Publisher:** Jan Diepenbroek
Profile: Magazine for animal lovers.
Language(s): Dutch
ADVERTISING RATES:
Full Page Mono EUR 1/1: f.c. 3630,-; PMS 3175,-; b/w 2625,- 1/2: f.c. 1955,-; PMS 1675,-; b/w 1415,- 1/4: f.c. 925,-; P
Agency Commission: 15%
Mechanical Data: Type Area: 185 x 260mm, Bleed Size: 215 x 280mm
Copy instructions: *Copy Date:* 4 weeks prior to publication date
CONSUMER: ANIMALS & PETS: Animals & Pets Protection

HARTBRUG MAGAZINE
16665N56A-512
Editorial: Postbus 1002, 6040 KA ROERMOND
Tel: 10 4274101 **Fax:** 10 4739911
Email: roermond@hartpatienten.nl
Date Established: 01-07-1970; **Freq:** 6 issues yearly;
Annual Sub.: EUR 17,50; **Circ:** 120,000
Editor: J.M. van Overveld
Profile: Magazine about heart diseases and their treatment.
Language(s): Dutch
Agency Commission: 15%
Mechanical Data: Type Area: 170 x 250mm, Bleed Size: 180 x 270mm
BUSINESS: HEALTH & MEDICAL

HARTSLAG
629456N74G-28_50
Editorial: Bordewijklaan 3, 2591 XR DEN HAAG
Tel: 30 2536321 **Fax:** 30 6007595
Email: info@hartstichting.nl
Freq: Quarterly; **Cover Price:** Free; **Circ:** 40,000
Editor: Chantal Lamens; **Editor-in-Chief:** Chantal Lamens
Profile: Magazine of the Dutch Heart Foundation, contains news of treatments, prevention, healthy lifestyle and general interest.
Language(s): Dutch
Readership: Read by heart patients, supporters of the charity and those concerned with health issues.
Agency Commission: 15%
Mechanical Data: Type Area: 210 x 277mm, Bleed Size: 230 x 297mm
CONSUMER: WOMEN'S INTEREST CONSUMER MAGAZINES: Slimming & Health

HEEMSTEEDSE COURANT
761163N72-2075
Editorial: Tempeliersstraat 67, 2012 EC HAARLEM
Web site: http://www.heemsteedsecourant.nl
Date Established: 01-03-1992; **Freq:** Weekly; **Cover Price:** Free; **Circ:** 27,645
Language(s): Dutch
Agency Commission: 15%
Mechanical Data: Type Area: 260 x 390mm
LOCAL NEWSPAPERS

HEILS- EN STRIJDZANGEN
16882N61-11
Editorial: Spoordreef 10, 1315 GN ALMERE
Tel: 36 5398291 **Fax:** 36 5398167
Freq: 3 issues yearly; **Annual Sub.:** EUR 12,50; **Circ:** 1,100
Editor: R. van Kesteren
Profile: Magazine focusing on the Salvation Army in the Netherlands, includes gospel songs.
Language(s): Dutch
Agency Commission: 15%
BUSINESS: MUSIC TRADE

HELDEN
1866334N75A-474
Editorial: Capellalaan 65, 2132 JL HOOFDDORP
Tel: 10 2092609 **Fax:** 88 2696983
Web site: http://www.heldenmagazine.nl
Date Established: 14-05-2009; **Freq:** Quarterly;
Cover Price: EUR 5,95
Annual Sub.: EUR 19,50; **Circ:** 60,000
Usual Pagination: 164
Editor: Frits Barend
Language(s): Dutch
ADVERTISING RATES:
Full Page Mono . EUR 2/1: f.c. 6600,-; 1/1: f.c. 3495,-
Agency Commission: 15%
Mechanical Data: Type Area: 190 x 267mm, Bleed Size: 210 x 275mm
CONSUMER: SPORT

HELPEN
1636315N56R-239
Editorial: Vijverweg 18, 2061 GX BLOEMENDAAL
Tel: 570 647207 **Fax:** 73 6210512
Email: info@vdbj.nl
Freq: Quarterly; **Cover Price:** Free; **Circ:** 280,000
Editor: Marleen Spoor
Language(s): Dutch
ADVERTISING RATES:
Full Page Mono .... EUR 1/1: b/w 12.000,- 1/2: b/w 6000,- 1/4: b/w 3000,-
Agency Commission: 15%
Mechanical Data: Bleed Size: 210 x 240mm
BUSINESS: HEALTH & MEDICAL: Health Medical Related

HELSINKI MONITOR
17956N82-44
Editorial: Bezuidenhoutseweg 331, 2594 AR DEN HAAG **Tel:** 88 2697183 **Fax:** 88 2697490
Email: office@nhc.nl **Web site:** http://www.brill.nl/hels
Date Established: 01-01-1990; **Freq:** Quarterly;
Annual Sub.: EUR 44,-
Usual Pagination: 100
Editor: Arie Bloed; **Editor-in-Chief:** Julia Koster
Profile: Journal about international law, human rights, security and co-operation in Europe.
Language(s): Dutch
Agency Commission: 15%
Mechanical Data: Type Area: 165 x 240mm
CONSUMER: CURRENT AFFAIRS & POLITICS

DE HERAUT
627166N72-2150
Editorial: Condorweg 1, 2651 WN BERKEL EN RODENRIJS **Tel:** 172 466539 **Fax:** 10 4521797
Web site: http://www.heraut-online.nl
Freq: Weekly; **Cover Price:** Free; **Circ:** 22,500
Editor-in-Chief: Annet Docter
Language(s): Dutch
Agency Commission: 15%
Mechanical Data: Type Area: 264 x 390mm, Bleed Size: 280 x 410mm
LOCAL NEWSPAPERS

HI, HYDRO INTERNATIONAL
16516N45R-50
Editorial: Nieuwedijk 43, 8531 HK LEMMER
Tel: 229 216416 **Fax:** 229 265738
Email: info@geomares.nl **Web site:** http://www.hydro-international.com
Date Established: 01-02-1997; **Freq:** 6 issues yearly;
Annual Sub.: EUR 100,-; **Circ:** 9,840
Publisher: Durk Haarsma
Profile: Magazine focusing on hydrography.
Language(s): Dutch
Readership: Read by industry managers.
ADVERTISING RATES:
Full Page Mono EUR 2/1: b/w 6890,- 1/1: b/w 3970,- 1/2: b/w 2385,-
Agency Commission: 15%
Mechanical Data: Type Area: 189 x 269,5mm, Bleed Size: 210 x 297mm
BUSINESS: MARINE & SHIPPING: Marine Related

HISTORISCH NIEUWSBLAD
708121N94X-92
Editorial: Wildenborch 5, 1112 XB DIEMEN
Tel: 20 5310960 **Fax:** 20 5310971
Web site: http://www.historischnieuwsblad.nl
Freq: 10 issues yearly; **Cover Price:** EUR 7,75
Annual Sub.: EUR 71,50; **Circ:** 23,623
Editor: Frans Smits; **Publisher:** Leo Schaap
Profile: Magazine about history.
Language(s): Dutch
Readership: Read by lecturers and the general public.
ADVERTISING RATES:
Full Page Mono EUR 2/1: f.c. 4985,-; PMS 3685,-; b/w 3020,- 1/1: f.c. 2875,-; PMS 2010,-; b/w 1570,- 1/2: f.c. 1845,-;
Agency Commission: 15%
Mechanical Data: Type Area: 174 x 242mm, Bleed Size: 210 x 265mm
CONSUMER: OTHER CLASSIFICATIONS: Miscellaneous

HISWA-MAGAZINE
16494N45A-45
Editorial: Hoofdstraat 82, 3972 LB DRIEBERGEN
Tel: 79 6366208 **Fax:** 79 3636262
Email: communicatie@hiswa.nl
Freq: 8 issues yearly; **Annual Sub.:** EUR 49,50; **Circ:** 5,000
Editor: Linda Jansen; **Publisher:** Farouk Nefzi
Profile: Magazine for the nautical industry.
Language(s): Dutch
ADVERTISING RATES:
Full Page Mono EUR 2/1: f.c. 3375,-; 1/1: f.c. 1725,-; 1/2: f.c. 915,-
Agency Commission: 15%
Mechanical Data: Type Area: 210 x 280mm, Bleed Size: 230 x 300mm
Copy instructions: *Copy Date:* 2 weeks prior to publication date
BUSINESS: MARINE & SHIPPING

DE HOEKSE KRANT
761359N72-2250
Editorial: Herckenrathstraat 52, 2681 DG MONSTER
Tel: 30 6383743 **Fax:** 229 216416
Web site: http://www.dehoeksekrant.nl
Date Established: 27-08-1998; **Freq:** Weekly; **Cover Price:** Free; **Circ:** 6,000
Editor: T. van Ooyen; **Publisher:** P.C. de Groot
Language(s): Dutch
Agency Commission: 15%
Mechanical Data: Type Area: 260 x 400mm, Bleed Size: 290 x 440mm
LOCAL NEWSPAPERS

HOFFMANN STATISTIEK
1635824N14A-386
Editorial: Luidsprekerstraat 10, 1322 AX ALMERE
Tel: 20 7150600 **Fax:** 10 4521797
Email: info@hoffmannbv.nl
Freq: Annual; **Cover Price:** Free; **Circ:** 70,000
Editor: G. Hoffmann
Language(s): Dutch
Agency Commission: 15%
BUSINESS: COMMERCE, INDUSTRY & MANAGEMENT

HOFPOORT INFO
652201N80-19
Editorial: Graaf Adolfstraat 36d, 8606 BT SNEEK
Tel: 23 5567955 **Fax:** 23 5567956
Email: bcuitgevers@planet.nl
Freq: Quarterly; **Cover Price:** Free; **Circ:** 3,500
Editor: M. van Rijn
Profile: Magazine about Hofpoort hospital.
Language(s): Dutch
Readership: Aimed at patients and local residents.
Agency Commission: 15%
Mechanical Data: Bleed Size: 210 x 297mm, Type Area: 184 x 270mm
CONSUMER: RURAL & REGIONAL INTEREST

HOLLAND
17864N80-18_50
Editorial: Torenlaan 25, 1211 JA HILVERSUM
Tel: 10 2894026 **Fax:** 88 2697490
Email: info@verloren.nl
Date Established: 01-03-1968; **Freq:** 5 issues yearly;
Cover Price: EUR 15,-
Annual Sub.: EUR 35,-; **Circ:** 1,200
Editor-in-Chief: Marieke Anema; **Publisher:** Thijs Verloren van Themaat
Profile: Magazine about the local history of North and South Holland.
Language(s): Dutch
Agency Commission: 15%
Mechanical Data: Type Area: 105 x 195mm, Bleed Size: 160 x 240mm
CONSUMER: RURAL & REGIONAL INTEREST

HOLLAND HERALD
18159N89D-1
Editorial: Stroombaan 4, 1181 VX AMSTELVEEN
Tel: 20 5979409 **Fax:** 20 5979505
Email: info@mediapartners.nl
Date Established: 01-01-1966; **Freq:** Monthly;
Cover Price: Free; **Circ:** 155,000
Editor: Mike Cooper; **Editor-in-Chief:** B. Jones
Profile: International in-flight magazine for KLM.
Language(s): Dutch
ADVERTISING RATES:
Full Page Mono .... EUR 2/1: f.c. 27.855,-; 1/1: f.c. 15.425,-; 1/2: f.c. 8050,-
Agency Commission: 15%
Mechanical Data: Type Area: 180 x 230mm, Bleed Size: 210 x 260mm
CONSUMER: HOLIDAYS & TRAVEL: In-Flight Magazines

HOLLAND HIGHLIGHTS
1799044N89A-238
Editorial: Hoofdstraat West 38, 8471 HV WOLVEGA
Tel: 172 469050 **Fax:** 118 434059
Email: info@frieslandholland.nl **Web site:** http://www.holland-highlights.nl
Date Established: 30-04-2008
Cover Price: Free; **Circ:** 100,000
Usual Pagination: 96
Editor: Albert Hendriks; **Publisher:** Albert Hendriks
Language(s): Dutch; English; French; German
ADVERTISING RATES:
Full Page Mono EUR 1/1: b/w 6336,- 1/16: b/w 495,-
Agency Commission: 15%
Mechanical Data: Type Area: 190 x 277mm, Bleed Size: 210 x 297mm
CONSUMER: HOLIDAYS & TRAVEL: Travel

HOLLAND MANAGEMENT REVIEW
1635905N14A-388
Editorial: Pelmolenlaan 1m, 3447 GW WOERDEN
Tel: 492 338432 **Fax:** 492 338421
Email: klantenservice@bbp.nl **Web site:** http://www.hmr.nl
Date Established: 01-01-1984; **Freq:** 6 issues yearly;
Cover Price: EUR 45,-
Annual Sub.: EUR 245,-; **Circ:** 2,500
Editor: Peter Schramade; **Editor-in-Chief:** Friso Liesker; **Publisher:** Maarten Timmers Verhoeven
Language(s): Dutch
ADVERTISING RATES:
Full Page Mono EUR 2/1: f.c. 6652,-; 1/1: f.c. 3501,-; 1/2: f.c. 2043,-
Agency Commission: 15%
Mechanical Data: Type Area: 180 x 250mm, Bleed Size: 210 x 280mm
BUSINESS: COMMERCE, INDUSTRY & MANAGEMENT

THE HOLLAND TIMES
1800593N94D-183
Editorial: Westerdreef 9, 2151 BR NIEUW-VENNEP
Tel: 20 5310919 **Fax:** 492 371114
Web site: http://www.thehollandtimes.nl
Date Established: 19-09-2003; **Freq:** Monthly; **Circ:** 120,000
Editor: Laura Owings; **Editor-in-Chief:** Alex Balcombe; **Publisher:** A. Makau
Language(s): Dutch
ADVERTISING RATES:
Full Page Mono EUR 1/1: f.c. 4020,-; 1/2: f.c. 2250,-; 1/4: f.c. 1290–
Agency Commission: 15%
Mechanical Data: Type Area: 265 x 398mm, Bleed Size: 288 x 417mm
Copy instructions: *Copy Date:* 9 days prior to publication date
CONSUMER: OTHER CLASSIFICATIONS: Expatriates

HOME & LIVING
717822N74C-21
Editorial: J.C. van Markenlaan 3, 2285 VL RIJSWIJK
Tel: 78 6133223 **Fax:** 70 3364640
Email: uitgeverij@lakerveld.nl **Web site:** http://www.homeandliving.nl
Date Established: 01-09-2001; **Freq:** 8 issues yearly; **Cover Price:** EUR 7,-
Annual Sub.: EUR 34,-; **Circ:** 6,450
Editor: Rieneke Kok; **Publisher:** Ad van Gaalen
Profile: Magazine covering information and all aspects on home decorating and furnishing.
Language(s): Dutch
ADVERTISING RATES:
Full Page Mono .. EUR 1/1: b/w 1390,- 1/2: b/w 735,- 1/4: b/w 415,-
Agency Commission: 15%
Mechanical Data: Type Area: 185 x 268mm, Bleed Size: 210 x 297mm
CONSUMER: WOMEN'S INTEREST CONSUMER MAGAZINES: Home & Family

HONDENSPORT EN SPORTHONDEN
17914N81B-29
Editorial: Kamplaan 2, 9462 TS GASSELTE
Tel: 13 4662445 **Fax:** 88 2697490
Email: topaaz@wxs.nl **Web site:** http://www.hondensport.nl
Freq: 6 issues yearly; **Annual Sub.:** EUR 27,95; **Circ:** 12,500
Editor: T.F.B. Dijkman; **Editor-in-Chief:** M. Dijkman-Kluger; **Publisher:** T.F.B. Dijkman
Profile: Magazine containing articles about dogs and sport, includes dog training, police and guard dogs, sniffer and rescue dogs, also gives details of competitions. Includes interviews with top trainers, also health and breeding tips.
Language(s): Dutch
ADVERTISING RATES:
Full Page Mono EUR 1/1: f.c. 654,-; 1/2: f.c. 415,-; 1/4: f.c. 222,-
Agency Commission: 15%
Mechanical Data: Type Area: 183 x 262mm, Bleed Size: 210 x 297mm
CONSUMER: ANIMALS & PETS: Dogs

HOOFDLIJNEN
16666N56A-25
Editorial: Verl. Bonedijkestraat 287, 4383 BC VLISSINGEN **Tel:** 20 5922250
Email: hoofdlijnen@nvlknf.nl
Date Established: 01-01-1965; **Freq:** Quarterly; **Circ:** 700
Editor: Yvonne van den Bogaard
Profile: Magazine of the Dutch Society of Laboratory Workers and Clinical Neurophysiologists.
Language(s): Dutch
Agency Commission: 15%
Mechanical Data: Bleed Size: 148 x 210mm
Copy instructions: *Copy Date:* 6 weeks prior to publication date
BUSINESS: HEALTH & MEDICAL

HOOGEVEENSCHE COURANT
627326N72-2295
Editorial: Hoofdstraat 83-87, 7902 EC HOOGEVEEN
Tel: 30 2971119 **Fax:** 20 5159143
Date Established: 01-01-1857; **Freq:** 104 issues yearly; **Circ:** 10,300
Editor: J.T. Koers
Language(s): Dutch
Agency Commission: 15%
Mechanical Data: Type Area: 416 x 550mm, Bleed Size: 450 x 600mm
LOCAL NEWSPAPERS

HOOR!
1809299N56R-270
Editorial: Stroombaan 4, 1181 VX AMSTELVEEN
Tel: 20 5473633 **Fax:** 20 5852965
Email: info@mediapartners.nl
Freq: 3 issues yearly; **Cover Price:** Free; **Circ:** 340,000
Language(s): Dutch
ADVERTISING RATES:
Full Page Mono EUR 1/1: f.c. 6250,-; 1/2: f.c. 3475,-; 1/4: f.c. 1975,-
Agency Commission: 15%
Mechanical Data: Type Area: 195 x 270mm, Bleed Size: 210 x 285mm
BUSINESS: HEALTH & MEDICAL: Health Medical Related

HOREN
16766N56L-47
Editorial: De Molen 89a, 3995 AW HOUTEN
Tel: 113 820203 **Fax:** 20 5159145
Email: info@nvvs.nl
Freq: 6 issues yearly; **Annual Sub.:** EUR 28,-; **Circ:** 9,000
Editor: Nic van Son
Profile: Magazine covering issues concerning the hard of hearing.
Language(s): Dutch
Readership: Read by people with hearing difficulties.
ADVERTISING RATES:
Full Page Mono EUR 1/1: b/w 851,- 1/2: b/w 472,- 1/4: b/w 249,-
Agency Commission: 15%
Mechanical Data: Type Area: 185 x 270mm, Bleed Size: 210 x 297mm
Copy instructions: *Copy Date:* 2 weeks prior to publication date
BUSINESS: HEALTH & MEDICAL: Disability & Rehabilitation

HORSE INTERNATIONAL
17925N81D-77
Editorial: Esp 101, 5633 AA EINDHOVEN
Tel: 23 5564919 **Fax:** 23 5564911
Email: bcm@bcm.nl
Freq: 9 issues yearly; **Annual Sub.:** EUR 82,50; **Circ:** 19,000
Editor: P. Young; **Publisher:** Eric Brüger
Profile: Magazine focusing on top level show jumping, dressage, trials and driving. Contains news, features, reports and previews from around the world. Includes interviews with top competition riders. It is the official news carrier of the Fédération Equestre International.
Language(s): Dutch
ADVERTISING RATES:
Full Page Mono EUR 1/1: f.c. 2818,-; b/w 2395,- 1/2: f.c. 1479,-; b/w 1257,- 1/4: f.c. 775,-; b/w 659,-
Agency Commission: 15%
Mechanical Data: Type Area: 210 x 290mm, Bleed Size: 233 x 320mm
CONSUMER: ANIMALS & PETS: Horses & Ponies

HOSPITALITY MANAGEMENT
15841N11A-65
Editorial: Leyenseweg 111f, 3721 BC BLITHOVEN
Tel: 70 3780436 **Fax:** 70 7999815
Email: info@uitgeverijps.nl
Date Established: 20-03-1991; **Freq:** 6 issues yearly; **Annual Sub.:** EUR 52,50; **Circ:** 4,065
Editor: Frank Lindner; **Publisher:** Paul Sprakel
Profile: Magazine for managers in hotels, restaurants and other branches of the hospitality trade.
Language(s): Dutch
ADVERTISING RATES:
Full Page Mono EUR 1/1: f.c. 2110,-; b/w 1360,- 1/2: f.c. 1135,-; b/w 750,- 1/4: f.c. 795,-; b/w 410,-
Agency Commission: 15%
Mechanical Data: Type Area: 186 x 273mm, Bleed Size: 210 x 297mm
Copy instructions: *Copy Date:* 2 weeks prior to publication date
BUSINESS: CATERING: Catering, Hotels & Restaurants

HOTELLO
15846N11A-150
Editorial: Zocherstraat 35, 1815 VE ALKMAAR
Tel: 229 270002 **Fax:** 20 6208980
Date Established: 01-01-1976; **Freq:** 6 issues yearly; **Circ:** 2,000
Editor: B.B. Berlijn
Profile: Journal of the Society of Graduates of Recognised Higher Hotel Schools.
Language(s): Dutch
ADVERTISING RATES:
Full Page Mono .... EUR 1/1: b/w 340,- 1/2: b/w 205,-
Agency Commission: 15%
Mechanical Data: Type Area: 90 x 275mm, Bleed Size: 105 x 297mm
BUSINESS: CATERING: Catering, Hotels & Restaurants

HOTSPOTS
1859441N74Q-452
Editorial: Molenstraat 3a, 3882 AC PUTTEN
Tel: 40 2336262 **Fax:** 570 677062
Email: info@qcreators.nl **Web site:** http://www.hotspotsmagazine.nl
Freq: 6 issues yearly; **Cover Price:** Free; **Circ:** 55,000
Editor: Esmeralda van der Mee; **Editor-in-Chief:** Robert van der Mee
Language(s): Dutch
ADVERTISING RATES:
Full Page Mono .. EUR 1/1: f.c. 1395,-; 1/2: f.c. 795,-; 1/3: f.c. 570,-
Agency Commission: 15%
Mechanical Data: Type Area: 190 x 267mm, Bleed Size: 210 x 297mm
CONSUMER: WOMEN'S INTEREST CONSUMER MAGAZINES: Lifestyle

HET HOUTBLAD
16520N46-37
Editorial: Essebaan 63, 2908 LJ CAPELLE AAN DEN IJSSEL **Tel:** 58 2954859 **Fax:** 20 6767728
Email: info@mybusinessmedia.nl **Web site:** http://www.houtblad.nl
Freq: 8 issues yearly; **Cover Price:** EUR 23,05
Annual Sub.: EUR 147,50; **Circ:** 4,889
Editor: Kees de Vries; **Publisher:** J. Verbeek
Profile: Journal focusing on the timber trade and timber building industry including timber architecture.
Language(s): Dutch
ADVERTISING RATES:
Full Page Mono EUR 1/1: f.c. 3525,-; 1/2: f.c. 2000,-; 1/4: f.c. 1115,-
Agency Commission: 15%
Mechanical Data: Type Area: 185 x 259mm, Bleed Size: 210 x 297mm
BUSINESS: TIMBER, WOOD & FORESTRY

HUIS AAN HUIS
626695N72-2320
Editorial: Velserduinweg 330, 1971 ZK IJMUIDEN
Tel: 20 5688440 **Fax:** 20 6159047
Email: info@weekbladhuisaanhuis.nl **Web site:** http://www.weekbladhuisaanhuis.nl
Freq: Weekly; **Cover Price:** Free; **Circ:** 36,000
Editor: Dorien Veldman
Language(s): Dutch
ADVERTISING RATES:
Full Page Mono EUR 1/1: b/w 510,- 1/2: b/w 275,- 1/4: b/w 155,-
Agency Commission: 15%
Mechanical Data: Type Area: 265 x 395mm, Bleed Size: 285 x 415mm
LOCAL NEWSPAPERS

HUISARTS EN WETENSCHAP (H&W)
16667N56A-330
Editorial: Lomanlaan 103, 3526 XD UTRECHT
Tel: 88 2944900 **Fax:** 35 6728834
Email: info@nhg.org **Web site:** http://www.henw.org
Freq: 13 issues yearly; **Annual Sub.:** EUR 157,-; **Circ:** 12,479
Editor: Henk van Weert
Profile: Publication of the Nederlandse Huisartsen Genootschap (NHG) Netherlands College of General Practitioners. Contains scientific articles about family medicine.
Language(s): Dutch
Readership: Aimed at general practitioners.
ADVERTISING RATES:
Full Page Mono EUR 1/1: f.c. 4051,-; b/w 1747,- 1/2: f.c. 3396,-; b/w 1093,- 1/4: f.c. 2958,-; b/w 655,-
Agency Commission: 15%
Mechanical Data: Type Area: 185 x 244mm, Bleed Size: 210 x 280mm
BUSINESS: HEALTH & MEDICAL

HUISHOUD ELECTRO
16450N43A-70
Editorial: De Trompet 2148b, 1967 DC HEEMSKERK
Tel: 20 5310161
Freq: 6 issues yearly; **Cover Price:** EUR 7,-
Annual Sub.: EUR 38,-; **Circ:** 3,150
Editor: Nelleke Vogel; **Editor-in-Chief:** H. Goddijn; **Publisher:** J.M. Haak
Profile: International magazine focusing on the domestic electrical appliance trade.
Language(s): Dutch
Readership: Read by retailers and manufacturers of electrical appliances.
ADVERTISING RATES:
Full Page Mono .. EUR 1/1: b/w 1505,- 1/2: b/w 910,- 1/4: b/w 535,-
Agency Commission: 15%
Mechanical Data: Type Area: 205 x 255mm, Bleed Size: 230 x 300mm
BUSINESS: ELECTRICAL RETAIL TRADE

HUISMUZIEK NIEUWSBRIEF
16883N61-12
Editorial: Oude Kraan 72, 6811 LL ARNHEM
Tel: 23 5344089 **Fax:** 10 2801002
Email: info@huismuziek.nl
Date Established: 01-10-1951; **Freq:** 5 issues yearly; **Circ:** 2,500
Editor-in-Chief: Chris Eken
Profile: Publication of Huismuziek - the Association for Music and Instrument Making, includes articles about the development of music and instruments and details of concerts.
Language(s): Dutch
Readership: Read by association members.
ADVERTISING RATES:
Full Page Mono ..... EUR 1/4: f.c. 495,-; 1/8: f.c. 240,-
Agency Commission: 15%
Mechanical Data: Type Area: 270 x 125mm, Bleed Size: 295 x 208mm
Copy instructions: *Copy Date:* 5 weeks prior to publication date
BUSINESS: MUSIC TRADE

HUISSTIJL
1976439N74C-380
Editorial: Velperbinnensingel 5, 6811 BP ARNHEM
Tel: 10 4518007 **Fax:** 314 349041
Email: info@lbl.nl **Web site:** http://www.huisstijlmagazine.nl
Freq: Quarterly; **Annual Sub.:** EUR 9,95; **Circ:** 100,000
Usual Pagination: 84
Editor: Jeannette van Dooren
Language(s): Dutch
Agency Commission: 15%
CONSUMER: WOMEN'S INTEREST CONSUMER MAGAZINES: Home & Family

HULPPOST
1633710N1P-82
Editorial: Plantage Middenlaan 18, 1018 DD AMSTERDAM **Tel:** 46 4775555 **Fax:** 46 4775455
Email: info@artsenzondergrenzen.nl
Date Established: 01-06-1985; **Freq:** 5 issues yearly; **Circ:** 500,000
Usual Pagination: 16
Editor: Celine The
Language(s): Dutch
Agency Commission: 15%
BUSINESS: FINANCE & ECONOMICS: Fundraising

HUWELIJK IN...
760715N74L-40
Editorial: Tijnjedijk 89, 8936 AC LEEUWARDEN
Tel: 30 2417045 **Fax:** 79 3467846
Email: info@wardmedia.nl **Web site:** http://www.huwelijk.nl
Freq: Annual; **Cover Price:** EUR 4,70; **Circ:** 8,500
Editor: Jan Dijkstra
Profile: Bridal magazine containing wedding preparations, includes features on beauty, fashion and travel.
Language(s): Dutch
Readership: Read by brides.
ADVERTISING RATES:
Full Page Mono .. EUR 1/1: f.c. 1195,-; 1/2: f.c. 625,-; 1/4: f.c. 325,-
Agency Commission: 15%
Mechanical Data: Type Area: 190 x 267mm, Bleed Size: 220 x 297mm
CONSUMER: WOMEN'S INTEREST CONSUMER MAGAZINES: Brides

DE HUWELIJKSDATA GIDS
1633366N74L-161
Editorial: Industrieweg 58, 1521 NE WORMERVEER
Tel: 70 3780436 **Fax:** 172 422804
Email: info@huwelijksdatagids.nl
Date Established: 01-01-1994; **Freq:** Annual; **Circ:** 128,700
Publisher: Edwin Bos
Language(s): Dutch
Agency Commission: 15%
Mechanical Data: Type Area: 95 x 275mm
CONSUMER: WOMEN'S INTEREST CONSUMER MAGAZINES: Brides

HVT
17699N78B-88
Editorial: Kerkenbos 10-33, 6546 BB NIJMEGEN
Tel: 24 3722911 **Fax:** 76 5312520
Date Established: 01-11-1972; **Freq:** 11 issues yearly; **Annual Sub.:** EUR 49,95; **Circ:** 13,500
Usual Pagination: 84
Editor: Theo Wubbolts
Profile: Journal containing reviews and articles on audio-video, hi-fi equipment and CD/DVD, also features interviews with musicians.
Language(s): Dutch
ADVERTISING RATES:
Full Page Mono .. EUR 1/1: f.c. 1480,-; 1/2: f.c. 765,-; 1/4: f.c. 390,-; 1/2: f.c. 245,-
Agency Commission: 15%
Mechanical Data: Type Area: 195 x 250mm, Bleed Size: 220 x 285mm
CONSUMER: CONSUMER ELECTRONICS: Video & DVD

DE HYPOTHEEKADVISEUR
1667168N1A-371
Editorial: Staverenstraat 32015, 7418 CJ DEVENTER
Tel: 570 647730 **Fax:** 570 637533
Email: info@kluwer.nl **Web site:** http://www.vakbladdehypotheek[VA]adviseur.nl
Date Established: 25-02-2005; **Freq:** 6 issues yearly; **Cover Price:** EUR 26,95
Annual Sub.: EUR 132,50; **Circ:** 1,605
Editor: Harrie-Jan van Nunen; **Publisher:** Karin Sok
Language(s): Dutch
ADVERTISING RATES:
Full Page Mono EUR 1/1: b/w 899,- 1/2: b/w 539,- 1/4: b/w 292,-
Agency Commission: 15%
Mechanical Data: Type Area: 180 x 267mm, Bleed Size: 210 x 297mm
BUSINESS: FINANCE & ECONOMICS

HYPOTHEEKSHOP MAGAZINE
1648451N74K-233
Editorial: A. Hofmanweg 5a, 2031 BH HAARLEM
Tel: 45 5792379 **Fax:** 88 2697660
Email: info@brandingmedia.nl
Freq: Half-yearly; **Cover Price:** Free; **Circ:** 60,000
Editor: Carla Person
Language(s): Dutch
ADVERTISING RATES:
Full Page Mono EUR 1/1: f.c. 3950,-; 1/2: f.c. 2175,-; 1/4: f.c. 1200,-
Agency Commission: 15%
Mechanical Data: Type Area: 193 x 263mm, Bleed Size: 215 x 285mm
Copy instructions: *Copy Date:* 2 weeks prior to publication date
CONSUMER: WOMEN'S INTEREST CONSUMER MAGAZINES: Home Purchase

ICT CONSULTANCY GUIDE
760614N5R-55
Editorial: Mt. Lincolnweg 40, 1033 SN AMSTERDAM
Tel: 172 466728 **Fax:** 172 494044
Email: info@vnumedia.nl
Freq: Annual; **Circ:** 30,000

Editor-in-Chief: Jolein de Rooij
Profile: Publication providing an overview for those who are looking for the right ICT advisor. Presents over 600 businesses in the Netherlands and Belgium.
Language(s): Dutch
Readership: Aimed at IT decision-makers employed at leading companies in the Netherlands and Belgium.
ADVERTISING RATES:
Full Page Mono .... EUR 2/1: f.c. 14.450,-; 1/1: f.c. 7225,-
Agency Commission: 15%
Mechanical Data: Type Area: 190 x 264mm, Bleed Size: 210 x 285mm
Copy instructions: *Copy Date:* 3 weeks prior to publication date
BUSINESS: COMPUTERS & AUTOMATION: Computers Related

ICT ZORG 1635076N5A-205
Editorial: Radarweg 29, 1043 NX AMSTERDAM
Tel: 70 3307094 **Fax:** 20 5159700
Email: info@reedbusiness.nl **Web site:** http://www.ictzorg.com
Freq: 6 issues yearly; **Annual Sub.:** EUR 140,-; **Circ:** 3,188
Editor: Mario Gibbels; **Publisher:** Ben Konings
Language(s): Dutch
ADVERTISING RATES:
Full Page Mono EUR 1/1: f.c. 4059,-; b/w 2727,- 1/2: f.c. 2822,-; b/w 1728,- 1/4: f.c. 2172,-; b/w 1053,-
Agency Commission: 15%
Mechanical Data: Type Area: 188 x 260mm, Bleed Size: 215 x 285mm
BUSINESS: COMPUTERS & AUTOMATION: Automation & Instrumentation

IDEE MAGAZINE 1640450N74Q-287
Editorial: Vluchtoord 1, 5406 XP UDEN
Tel: 172 440681 **Fax:** 172 422886
Email: contact@dewinter.nl **Web site:** http://www.ideemagazine.nl
Date Established: 18-09-2002; **Freq:** Half-yearly; **Cover Price:** EUR 2,95; **Circ:** 100,000
Editor-in-Chief: Anke Langelaar
Language(s): Dutch
ADVERTISING RATES:
Full Page Mono EUR 2/1: f.c. 2300,-; 1/1: f.c. 1450,-; 1/2: f.c. 750,-
Agency Commission: 15%
Mechanical Data: Type Area: 210 x 273mm, Bleed Size: 230 x 297mm
CONSUMER: WOMEN'S INTEREST CONSUMER MAGAZINES: Lifestyle

IJMUIDER COURANT 17121N67B-4000
Editorial: Marktplein 1, 1972 GA IJMUIDEN
Tel: 20 5218938 **Fax:** 30 6922233
Email: redactie@ijmuidercourant.nl **Web site:** http://www.ijmuidercourant.nl
Freq: 312 issues yearly; **Annual Sub.:** EUR 262,75; **Circ:** 6,918
Editor: Geert ten Dam
Language(s): Dutch
Agency Commission: 15%
Mechanical Data: Type Area: 398 x 550mm
REGIONAL DAILY & SUNDAY NEWSPAPERS: Regional Daily Newspapers

DE IJSSELBODE 629924N72-7438
Editorial: Noorder-Kerkstraat 4, 3421 AX OUDEWATER **Tel:** 23 5565370 **Fax:** 55 5412288
Email: heno@ijsselbode.nl **Web site:** http://www.ijsselbode.nl
Freq: Weekly; **Circ:** 24,000
Editor-in-Chief: Mieke van Uden
Language(s): Dutch
Agency Commission: 15%
Mechanical Data: Type Area: 265 x 435mm
LOCAL NEWSPAPERS

IJSSELHAMMER 626771N80-21_40
Editorial: Binnenpad 28, 8355 BR GIETHOORN
Tel: 521 362556 **Fax:** 348 414897
Email: info@wiedenenweerribben.nl
Date Established: 01-01-1971; **Freq:** 24 issues yearly; **Annual Sub.:** EUR 45,-; **Circ:** 8,000
Editor-in-Chief: Gerrit Mol; **Publisher:** Gerrit Mol
Language(s): Dutch
Agency Commission: 15%
Mechanical Data: Type Area: 261 x 388mm, Bleed Size: 320 x 460mm
CONSUMER: RURAL & REGIONAL INTEREST

IKAZIA MAGAZINE 18856N80-21_50
Editorial: Graaf Adolfstraat 36d, 8606 BT SNEEK
Tel: 172 466622 **Fax:** 172 440681
Email: bcuitgevers@planet.nl
Freq: Quarterly; **Cover Price:** Free; **Circ:** 9,000
Editor: T. Schutrups
Profile: Magazine containing information about the Ikazia Hospital in Rotterdam.
Language(s): Dutch
Readership: Read by patients, staff and local business people.
Agency Commission: 15%
Mechanical Data: Bleed Size: 210 x 297mm, Type Area: 184 x 270mm
CONSUMER: RURAL & REGIONAL INTEREST

IKGAWERKEN.NL 1903310N14L-591
Editorial: Achterwerf 303a, 1357 DD ALMERE
Tel: 30 6383716 **Fax:** 73 6157171
Email: info@jeugdenwerk.nl **Web site:** http://www.ikgawerken.nl
Date Established: 01-01-2000; **Freq:** Annual; **Cover Price:** Free; **Circ:** 50,000
Editor: Corry Puts
Language(s): Dutch
ADVERTISING RATES:
Full Page Mono EUR 1/1: b/w 2495,- 1/2: b/w 1495,- 1/4: b/w 795,-
Agency Commission: 15%
Mechanical Data: Type Area: 185 x 270mm, Bleed Size: 210 x 297mm
BUSINESS: COMMERCE, INDUSTRY & MANAGEMENT: Trade Unions

ILLUSTER 1635961N83-184
Editorial: Heidelberglaan 8, 3584 CS UTRECHT
Tel: 30 2539300 **Fax:** 0032 34660067
Date Established: 01-12-1995; **Freq:** Quarterly; **Cover Price:** Free; **Circ:** 73,000
Editor: C.F. Hamerslag; **Editor-in-Chief:** C.F. Hamerslag
Language(s): Dutch
Agency Commission: 15%
CONSUMER: STUDENT PUBLICATIONS

IMAINTAIN 1638657N4F-106
Editorial: Veembroederhof 7, 1019 HD AMSTERDAM
Tel: 314 349562 **Fax:** 314 340515
Email: info@industrielinqs.nl **Web site:** http://www.industrialmaintenance-[VA]vakblad.nl
Date Established: 01-01-2003; **Freq:** 10 issues yearly; **Cover Price:** EUR 13,90
Annual Sub.: EUR 83,35; **Circ:** 4,160
Editor: Mark Oosterveer; **Publisher:** Wim Raaijen
Language(s): Dutch
ADVERTISING RATES:
Full Page Mono EUR 1/1: f.c. 2442,-; PMS 2051,-; b/w 1700,- 1/2: f.c. 1429,-; PMS 1283,-; b/w 929,- 1/4: f.c. 898,-; PM
Agency Commission: 15%
Mechanical Data: Type Area: 185 x 267mm, Bleed Size: 210 x 297mm
BUSINESS: ARCHITECTURE & BUILDING: Cleaning & Maintenance

IN DIT VERBAND 16798N56R-32
Editorial: Bas Pauuwestraat 116, 3077 MP ROTTERDAM **Tel:** 172 466622
Date Established: 01-01-1991; **Freq:** Quarterly; **Annual Sub.:** EUR 18,50; **Circ:** 2,000
Editor: Cor Gersen; **Editor-in-Chief:** Cor Gersen; **Publisher:** J. van Oene
Profile: Publication about medical casting and splinting, application and removal, plaster and synthetic casting materials, devices and artificial limbs.
Language(s): Dutch
Readership: Aimed at orthopaedic technologists.
Agency Commission: 15%
Mechanical Data: Type Area: 185 x 259mm, Bleed Size: 210 x 297mm
BUSINESS: HEALTH & MEDICAL: Health Medical Related

INCOMPANY 1699330N14A-472
Editorial: Cornelis Schuytstraat 2, 1071 JH AMSTERDAM **Tel:** 172 466911 **Fax:** 40 8447611
Email: info@vondelpublications.nl **Web site:** http://www.incompany.eu
Freq: 3 issues yearly; **Cover Price:** EUR 8,95
Annual Sub.: EUR 22,50; **Circ:** 70,000
Editor: R. Gerhardus; **Editor-in-Chief:** Rianne van Boxtel
Language(s): Dutch
ADVERTISING RATES:
Full Page Mono .... EUR 2/1: f.c. 11.995,-; 1/1: f.c. 6500,-; 1/2: f.c. 3995,-
Agency Commission: 15%
Mechanical Data: Type Area: 185 x 255mm, Bleed Size: 210 x 285mm
BUSINESS: COMMERCE, INDUSTRY & MANAGEMENT

INDISCH ANDERS 1808946N90-125
Editorial: Bezuidenhoutseweg 331, 2594 AR DEN HAAG **Tel:** 20 5855333 **Fax:** 20 5852965
Email: info@tongtong.nl
Date Established: 01-01-2006; **Freq:** Annual; **Cover Price:** Free; **Circ:** 50,000
Editor: Siem Boon
Language(s): Dutch
ADVERTISING RATES:
Full Page Mono EUR 1/1: b/w 2950,- 1/2: b/w 1550,- 1/4: b/w 835,-
Agency Commission: 15%
Mechanical Data: Type Area: 240 x 340mm, Bleed Size: 260 x 360mm
Copy instructions: *Copy Date:* 1 month prior to publication date
CONSUMER: ETHNIC

INFINANCE 714856N1A-106
Editorial: Leeuwenveldseweg 3m, 1382 LV WEESP
Tel: 342 494848 **Fax:** 172 539171
Email: infinance@3xi.nl **Web site:** http://www.infinance.nl
Freq: 18 issues yearly; **Cover Price:** EUR 19,25
Annual Sub.: EUR 260,-; **Circ:** 16,069
Editor: Echardt Dulfer; **Editor-in-Chief:** P. Firet
Profile: Magazine containing articles focusing on finance.
Language(s): Dutch
Readership: Read by finance professionals, stockbrokers, insurance agents and accountants.
ADVERTISING RATES:
Full Page Mono EUR 1/1: f.c. 3986,-; 1/2: f.c. 2266,-; 1/4: f.c. 1329,-
Agency Commission: 15%
Mechanical Data: Type Area: 180 x 256mm, Bleed Size: 210 x 297mm
BUSINESS: FINANCE & ECONOMICS

INFO AIDS FONDS 16671N56A-515
Editorial: Keizersgracht 390-394, 1016 GB AMSTERDAM **Tel:** 30 2971119 **Fax:** 314 349237
Email: aidsfonds@aidsfonds.nl
Freq: Half-yearly; **Cover Price:** Free; **Circ:** 105,000
Usual Pagination: 8
Editor: Caspar Brinkman
Profile: Newsletter with information about the Aids Fonds activities especially for donors.
Language(s): Dutch
Agency Commission: 15%
BUSINESS: HEALTH & MEDICAL

INFORMATIE PROFESSIONAL 16878N60R-150
Editorial: Herengracht 416, 1017 BZ AMSTERDAM
Tel: 20 4276583 **Fax:** 418 572601
Email: info@cram.nl **Web site:** http://www.informatieprofessional.nl
Circ: 3,600
Editor: Bram Donkers; **Editor-in-Chief:** Ronald de Nijs; **Publisher:** Otto Cramwinckel
Profile: Journal for anyone involved in the search for or selection, structuring, provision and publishing of information. Also covers news of interactive information systems.
Language(s): Dutch
Readership: Aimed at information specialists, librarians, literature and on-line searchers.
ADVERTISING RATES:
Full Page Mono EUR 1/1: f.c. 1920,-; 1/2: f.c. 1145,-; 1/4: f.c. 620,-
Agency Commission: 15%
Mechanical Data: Type Area: 182 x 265mm, Bleed Size: 210 x 297mm
BUSINESS: PUBLISHING: Publishing Related

INFORMATIEGIDS STAD AMSTERDAM 1635848N80-373
Editorial: Deimoslaan 3, 1702 CK HEERHUGOWAARD **Tel:** 10 2894015
Fax: 20 6159047
Email: maypress@maypress.nl **Web site:** http://www.infowebamsterdam.nl
Date Established: 01-01-1984; **Freq:** Half-yearly; **Cover Price:** Free; **Circ:** 105,000
Editor: Jol Riemsma
Language(s): Dutch
ADVERTISING RATES:
Full Page Mono EUR 1/1: f.c. 2995,-; 1/2: f.c. 1750,-; 1/4: f.c. 899,-
Agency Commission: 15%
Mechanical Data: Type Area: 180 x 240mm, Bleed Size: 200 x 280mm
CONSUMER: RURAL & REGIONAL INTEREST

INFORMATION SERVICES & USE 1645999N5E-216
Editorial: Postbus 688, 3800 AR AMERSFOORT
Freq: Quarterly; **Annual Sub.:** EUR 371,-; **Circ:** 400
Editor: E.R. Siegel
Language(s): Dutch
Agency Commission: 15%
Mechanical Data: Type Area: 192 x 262mm
BUSINESS: COMPUTERS & AUTOMATION: Data Transmission

DE INGENIEUR 16051N19A-40
Editorial: Wildenborch 5, 1112 XB DIEMEN
Tel: 20 5310919 **Fax:** 20 5159700
Web site: http://www.deingenieur.nl
Date Established: 01-01-1888; **Freq:** 21 issues yearly; **Cover Price:** EUR 7,50; **Circ:** 25,626
Editor: Erwin van den Brink; **Editor-in-Chief:** J. Oomen; **Publisher:** Hans van Vloten
Profile: Magazine of the Royal Institution of Engineers in the Netherlands and the Dutch Association of Engineers.
Language(s): Dutch
Readership: Read by people interested in new technology.
ADVERTISING RATES:
Full Page Mono EUR 2/1: f.c. 9725,-; PMS 8310,-; b/w 7360,- 1/1: f.c. 5620,-; PMS 4680,-; b/w 4040,- 1/2: f.c. 3670,-;
Agency Commission: 15%
Mechanical Data: Type Area: 209 x 271mm, Bleed Size: 230 x 300mm
Copy instructions: *Copy Date:* 1 week prior to publication date
BUSINESS: ENGINEERING & MACHINERY

INSITE 1634295N74F-151
Editorial: Oude Amersfoortseweg 79, 1213 AC HILVERSUM **Tel:** 10 4274149 **Fax:** 35 6474444
Email: eo@eo.nl **Web site:** http://www.ronduit.nl/insite
Date Established: 01-01-1989; **Freq:** 6 issues yearly; **Annual Sub.:** EUR 12,-; **Circ:** 57,000
Editor: Ellen Danhof; **Editor-in-Chief:** J. Alberts
Language(s): Dutch
ADVERTISING RATES:
Full Page Mono .. EUR 1/1: b/w 1869,- 1/2: b/w 953,- 1/4: b/w 489,-
Agency Commission: 15%
Mechanical Data: Type Area: 183 x 250mm, Bleed Size: 210 x 275mm
Copy instructions: *Copy Date:* 3 weeks prior to publication date
CONSUMER: WOMEN'S INTEREST CONSUMER MAGAZINES: Teenage

INSPIRATIE MAGAZINE 18082N87-106
Editorial: Jan Heinsstraat 26, 5211 TD 'S-HERTOGENBOSCH **Tel:** 10 2894015
Fax: 20 6159047
Web site: http://www.inspiratiemagazine.nl
Date Established: 01-01-1996; **Freq:** 7 issues yearly; **Annual Sub.:** EUR 25,-; **Circ:** 10,000
Usual Pagination: 32
Editor: A. Kruse
Profile: Catholic magazine, containing articles encouraging people to continue their religious beliefs, attempts to provide answers to questions and reconcile doubts.
Language(s): Dutch
Readership: Read mainly by people considering leaving the Catholic faith.
ADVERTISING RATES:
Full Page Mono .. EUR 1/1: b/w 1590,- 1/2: b/w 840,- 1/4: b/w 440,-
Agency Commission: 15%
Mechanical Data: Type Area: 175 x 244mm, Bleed Size: 210 x 285mm
Copy instructions: *Copy Date:* 4 weeks prior to publication date
CONSUMER: RELIGIOUS

INSTALLATIE JOURNAAL 16022N17-45
Editorial: Prinses Beatrixlaan 116, 2595 AL DEN HAAG **Tel:** 492 338432 **Fax:** 492 338421
Email: sdu@sdu.nl
Freq: 10 issues yearly; **Cover Price:** EUR 19,-
Annual Sub.: EUR 167,-; **Circ:** 5,798
Editor: Marjolein Eilander; **Publisher:** Johan Schot
Profile: Trade magazine for the electrical installer.
Language(s): Dutch
ADVERTISING RATES:
Full Page Mono EUR 2/1: f.c. 4120,-; PMS 3370,-; b/w 2620,- 1/1: f.c. 2820,-; PMS 2320,-; b/w 1820,- 1/2: f.c. 1720,-;
Agency Commission: 15%
Mechanical Data: Type Area: 185 x 268mm, Bleed Size: 210 x 297mm
BUSINESS: ELECTRICAL

INSTORE 629816N53-60
Editorial: Nonnenmate 41, 7006 CN DOETINCHEM
Tel: 45 5762897 **Fax:** 172 493270
Email: redactie@instore-online.nl **Web site:** http://www.instore-online.nl
Freq: 6 issues yearly; **Annual Sub.:** EUR 45,-; **Circ:** 4,500
Editor: Koos van Reesch
Profile: Magazine focusing on national and international developments in the retail scene, instore management and marketing.
Language(s): Dutch
Readership: Read by marketeers, retailers, store designers and shop fitters.
ADVERTISING RATES:
Full Page Mono EUR 1/1: f.c. 1900,-; 1/2: f.c. 1325,-; 1/4: f.c. 1050,-
Agency Commission: 15%
Mechanical Data: Type Area: 197 x 267mm, Bleed Size: 230 x 297mm
BUSINESS: RETAILING & WHOLESALING

INTERCOM 18081N87-102
Editorial: Spoordreef 10, 1315 GN ALMERE
Tel: 30 2991929 **Fax:** 77 3556140
Freq: 10 issues yearly; **Annual Sub.:** EUR 12,50; **Circ:** 7,600
Editor: Ruud Tinga
Profile: Magazine published by the Salvation Army in the Netherlands.
Language(s): Dutch
Readership: Read by members and people interested in the Salvation Army Organisation.
ADVERTISING RATES:
Full Page Mono EUR 1/1: b/w 464,- 1/2: b/w 249,- 1/4: b/w 153,-
Agency Commission: 15%
Mechanical Data: Type Area: 170 x 256mm, Bleed Size: 210 x 297mm
Copy instructions: *Copy Date:* 6 weeks prior to publication date
CONSUMER: RELIGIOUS

INTERMEDIAIRPW 15932N14F-82
Editorial: Mt. Lincolnweg 40, 1033 SN AMSTERDAM
Tel: 570 673344 **Fax:** 20 5159143

Email: info@vnumedia.nl **Web site:** http://www.intermediairpw.nl
Freq: 26 issues yearly; **Cover Price:** EUR 8,90
Annual Sub.: EUR 160,-; **Circ:** 9,416
Editor: H. Roelofs; **Editor-in-Chief:** N. de Winter;
Publisher: Masha Kodden
Profile: Magazine about human resources and personnel management.
Language(s): Dutch
ADVERTISING RATES:
Full Page Mono EUR 2/1: b/w 4307,- 1/1: b/w 2537,- 1/2: b/w 1391,-
Agency Commission: 15%
Mechanical Data: Type Area: 200 x 270mm, Bleed Size: 215 x 285mm
BUSINESS: COMMERCE, INDUSTRY & MANAGEMENT: Training & Recruitment

INTERNATIONAL JEANS CULT
16529N47A-35
Editorial: Achterwetering 3c, 2871 RK SCHOONHOVEN **Tel:** 492 338432 **Fax:** 20 6767728
Web site: http://www.jeanscult.nl
Date Established: 01-01-1990; **Freq:** 8 issues yearly;
Cover Price: EUR 9,00
Annual Sub.: EUR 57,50; **Circ:** 4,300
Usual Pagination: 36
Editor: Michelle van Kampen; **Editor-in-Chief:** Annelies Spaan; **Publisher:** Rien Hartelust
Profile: Journal covering the retail and manufacture of jeans and casual wear.
Language(s): Dutch
ADVERTISING RATES:
Full Page Mono EUR 2/1: f.c. 6000,-; b/w 4750,- 1/1: f.c. 3400,-; b/w 2800,- 1/2: f.c. 2500,-; b/w 1800,- 1/4: f.c. 130
Agency Commission: 15%
Mechanical Data: Type Area: 277 x 400mm, Bleed Size: 297 x 420mm
BUSINESS: CLOTHING & TEXTILES

INTERNATIONAL PHARMACY JOURNAL
16367N37-185
Editorial: Andries Bickerweg 5, 2517 JP DEN HAAG
Tel: 20 5159172 **Fax:** 20 5159145
Email: publications@fip.org
Freq: Half-yearly; **Circ:** 4,000
Editor: Myriah Lesko
Profile: Official journal of the International Pharmaceutical Federation.
Language(s): Dutch
Agency Commission: 15%
Mechanical Data: Bleed Size: 210 x 297mm
BUSINESS: PHARMACEUTICAL & CHEMISTS

INTERNATIONALE SAMENWERKING-IS
1634082N82-485
Editorial: Mauritskade 63, 1092 AD AMSTERDAM
Tel: 88 2944900 **Fax:** 35 6728834
Email: info@ncdo.nl **Web site:** http://www.isonline.nl
Freq: 10 issues yearly; **Cover Price:** Free; **Circ:** 124,000
Editor: Hans Ariëns; **Editor-in-Chief:** Lonneke van Genugten
Language(s): Dutch
Agency Commission: 15%
CONSUMER: CURRENT AFFAIRS & POLITICS

INTERNE COMMUNICATIE
761870N2A-41
Editorial: POSTBUS
Web site: http://www.communicatie-online.nl
Date Established: 01-01-2002; **Freq:** 6 issues yearly;
Cover Price: EUR 13,-
Annual Sub.: EUR 71,-; **Circ:** 2,000
Editor: Rocco Mooij; **Editor-in-Chief:** E. Elsinghorst;
Publisher: Antje Bosscher
Profile: Magazine covering internal communications within companies. Special attention is paid to the importance of Intranet systems.
Language(s): Dutch
Readership: Aimed at professionals dealing with internal and external communications, as well as organisation advisors and HRM-managers.
ADVERTISING RATES:
Full Page Mono .... EUR 1/1: b/w 1000,-
Agency Commission: 15%
Mechanical Data: Type Area: 190 x 268mm, Bleed Size: 210 x 297mm
BUSINESS: COMMUNICATIONS, ADVERTISING & MARKETING

INTERTAX
15562N1M-42
Editorial: Claude Debussylaan 54, 1032 MD AMSTERDAM **Tel:** 88 2944900 **Fax:** 35 6728834
Freq: Monthly; **Annual Sub.:** EUR 901,-; **Circ:** 650
Editor: Fred de Hosson; **Publisher:** Lou Rolla
Profile: Journal concerning both direct and indirect taxation giving reviews of international taxation developments.
Language(s): Dutch
Readership: Aimed at those involved with all aspects of taxation.
ADVERTISING RATES:
Full Page Mono .... EUR 1/1: b/w 715,-
Agency Commission: 15%
Mechanical Data: Type Area: 170 x 255mm, Bleed Size: 210 x 297mm
BUSINESS: FINANCE & ECONOMICS: Taxation

INTIEM
761401N74A-75
Editorial: Burg. Krollaan 14, 5126 PT GILZE
Tel: 70 3342179 **Fax:** 20 5979490
Web site: http://www.tijdschrift-intiem.nl
Freq: 8 issues yearly; **Cover Price:** EUR 2,95
Annual Sub.: EUR 19,-; **Circ:** 21,155
Profile: Magazine containing interviews with readers, covering a broad spectrum of problems offering practical solutions.
Language(s): Dutch
Readership: Read predominantly by women under 30 years.
ADVERTISING RATES:
Full Page Mono EUR 1/1: f.c. 1950,-; 1/2: f.c. 1465,-; 1/4: f.c. 875,-
Agency Commission: 15%
Mechanical Data: Type Area: 181 x 240mm, Bleed Size: 209 x 269mm
Copy instructions: *Copy Date:* 3 weeks prior to publication date
CONSUMER: WOMEN'S INTEREST CONSUMER MAGAZINES: Women's Interest

INZINE
18104N88A-40
Editorial: Bijdorplaan 15, 2015 CE HAARLEM
Tel: 50 5844205
Freq: 8 issues yearly; **Circ:** 14,500
Editor: Peter de Brock
Profile: Publication for students and personnel of Hogeschool Holland and the Amsterdam Academy, giving general information about the Hogeschool and Academy and career advice.
Language(s): Dutch
ADVERTISING RATES:
Full Page Mono EUR 1/1: f.c. 1765,-; 1/2: f.c. 1000,-; 1/4: f.c. 580,-
Agency Commission: 15%
Mechanical Data: Bleed Size: 170 x 240mm
Copy instructions: *Copy Date:* 8 days prior to publication date
CONSUMER: EDUCATION

IPO MILIEUWERK
16836N57-34_75
Editorial: Postbus 158, 1600 AD ENKHUIZEN
Tel: 20 5253370 **Fax:** 20 6767728
Email: graafcom@wxs.nl
Freq: Quarterly; **Cover Price:** Free; **Circ:** 2,000
Editor: J. de Graaf
Profile: Magazine about the execution of the interprovincial environmental policy of the twelve Dutch provinces.
Language(s): Dutch
Agency Commission: 15%
BUSINESS: ENVIRONMENT & POLLUTION

ISOLATIE MAGAZINE
1636193N4R-104
Editorial: Essebaan 63, 2908 LJ CAPELLE AAN DEN IJSSEL **Tel:** 77 3556160 **Fax:** 77 3556152
Email: info@mybusinessmedia.nl
Date Established: 01-01-1998; **Freq:** Quarterly;
Cover Price: Free; **Circ:** 2,362
Editor: L.J. de Ridder; **Editor-in-Chief:** M. van der Ende; **Publisher:** Elsbeth Lamfers
Language(s): Dutch
ADVERTISING RATES:
Full Page Mono EUR 1/1: f.c. 1610,-; 1/2: f.c. 1045,-; 1/4: f.c. 680,-
Agency Commission: 15%
Mechanical Data: Type Area: 190 x 260mm, Bleed Size: 210 x 297mm
Copy instructions: *Copy Date:* 2 weeks prior to publication date
BUSINESS: ARCHITECTURE & BUILDING: Building Related

ISRAËL AKTUEEL
1634005N87-2651
Editorial: Patroonstraat 1, 3861 RN NIJKERK
Tel: 10 4274160 **Fax:** 229 216416
Email: info@christenenvoorisrael.nl
Freq: 10 issues yearly; **Circ:** 65,000
Editor: Pim van der Hoff; **Editor-in-Chief:** Marijke Terlouw
Language(s): Dutch
ADVERTISING RATES:
Full Page Mono EUR 1/1: b/w 2241,- 1/2: b/w 1230,- 1/4: b/w 615,-
Agency Commission: 15%
Mechanical Data: Type Area: 256 x 384mm, Bleed Size: 290 x 420mm
Copy instructions: *Copy Date:* 2 weeks prior to publication date
CONSUMER: RELIGIOUS

DE IT-AUDITOR
712832N5R-22
Editorial: Utrechtseweg 31a, 3812 NA AMERSFOORT **Tel:** 172 466539 **Fax:** 10 4521797
Email: info@lvbnetworks.nl
Date Established: 01-01-1991; **Freq:** Quarterly;
Cover Price: EUR 31,50
Annual Sub.: EUR 112,04; **Circ:** 2,269
Editor: G.J. van der Pijl; **Publisher:** Heleen Kooistra
Profile: Publication containing information about EDP and IT auditing, includes effectiveness, efficiency, integrity and security of IT systems within organisations.
Language(s): Dutch
Readership: Aimed at the members of the NOREA (Nederlandse Orde van Register EDP Auditors).
ADVERTISING RATES:
Full Page Mono EUR 1/1: f.c. 2844,-; b/w 1404,- 1/2: f.c. 1971,-; b/w 801,- 1/4: f.c. 1363,-; b/w 480,-
Agency Commission: 15%
Mechanical Data: Type Area: 185 x 250mm, Bleed Size: 215 x 285mm
BUSINESS: COMPUTERS & AUTOMATION: Computers Related

IT-INFRA
15743N5B-120
Editorial: Binckhorstlaan 403, 2516 BC DEN HAAG
Tel: 172 466622 **Fax:** 24 3723631
Email: sdu@sdu.nl **Web site:** http://www.itbeheermagazine.nl
Freq: 10 issues yearly; **Annual Sub.:** EUR 192,50;
Circ: 3,828
Editor: Wijnand Westerveld; **Publisher:** Mels Dees
Profile: Magazine focusing on the structure of IT management.
Language(s): Dutch
Readership: Read by IT service managers and consultants.
ADVERTISING RATES:
Full Page Mono .. EUR 1/1: b/w 1674,- 1/2: b/w 922,- 1/4: b/w 479,-
Agency Commission: 15%
Mechanical Data: Type Area: 192 x 252mm, Bleed Size: 210 x 275mm
BUSINESS: COMPUTERS & AUTOMATION: Data Processing

JAARBOEKJE ROTTERDAMPAS
1637185N80-458
Editorial: Hoogstraat 110, 3011 PV ROTTERDAM
Tel: 570 647221 **Fax:** 570 647803
Email: info@rotterdampas.nl
Freq: Annual; **Circ:** 100,000
Editor: Annemieke van Wegen-Delhaas
Language(s): Dutch
ADVERTISING RATES:
Full Page Mono ... EUR 1/1: f.c. 2250,-; omslagpag. 2 of 3: f.c. 2650,-
Agency Commission: 15%
Mechanical Data: Type Area: 115 x 165mm, Bleed Size: 115 x 166mm
CONSUMER: RURAL & REGIONAL INTEREST

JACHT & BEHEER
17595N75F-28
Editorial: Postbus 72, 7480 AB HAAKSBERGEN
Tel: 70 3789880 **Fax:** 70 3789783
Email: nojg@planet.nl
Freq: 6 issues yearly; **Circ:** 3,000
Publisher: J. ten Thije-Asbroek
Profile: Magazine about hunting and land management.
Language(s): Dutch
Readership: Aimed at landowners and hunters.
ADVERTISING RATES:
Full Page Mono EUR 1/1: f.c. 250,-; 1/2: f.c. 210,-; 1/4: f.c. 145,-
Agency Commission: 15%
Mechanical Data: Type Area: 185 x 268mm, Bleed Size: 210 x 297mm
CONSUMER: SPORT: Shooting

JACKIE
1643423N74A-225
Editorial: De Cuserstraat 93, 1081 CN AMSTERDAM
Tel: 50 5445815 **Fax:** 20 3011701
Email: info@gmg.nl **Web site:** http://www.jackieonline.nl
Date Established: 01-12-2003; **Freq:** 8 issues yearly;
Cover Price: EUR 4,95; **Circ:** 55,000
Editor: Eva Hoeke; **Editor-in-Chief:** Liselot Rijsdijk;
Publisher: Y.M.A. Gijrath
Language(s): Dutch
ADVERTISING RATES:
Full Page Mono .... EUR 2/1: f.c. 12.000,-; 1/1: f.c. 6500,-
Agency Commission: 15%
Mechanical Data: Bleed Size: 202 x 276mm
CONSUMER: WOMEN'S INTEREST CONSUMER MAGAZINES: Women's Interest

JACKIE BUSINESS
1861803N74A-276
Editorial: De Cuserstraat 93, 1081 CN AMSTERDAM
Tel: 35 6256179 **Fax:** 73 6157171
Email: info@gmg.nl
Date Established: 02-10-2008; **Freq:** Annual; **Cover Price:** EUR 5,95; **Circ:** 55,000
Usual Pagination: 164
Publisher: Y.M.A. Gijrath
Language(s): Dutch
ADVERTISING RATES:
Full Page Mono .... EUR 2/1: f.c. 12.900,-; 1/1: f.c. 6500,-
Agency Commission: 15%
Mechanical Data: Type Area: 226 x 290mm, Bleed Size: 220 x 284mm
Copy instructions: *Copy Date:* 3 weeks prior to publication date
CONSUMER: WOMEN'S INTEREST CONSUMER MAGAZINES: Women's Interest

JAMES
1857658N74B-165
Editorial: Capellalaan 65, 2132 JL HOOFDDORP
Tel: 88 7518486 **Fax:** 88 7518481
Web site: http://www.james-magazine.nl
Date Established: 14-09-2007; **Freq:** Annual; **Cover Price:** EUR 2,50; **Circ:** 75,000
Usual Pagination: 116
Editor: Jan Heemskerk; **Editor-in-Chief:** Marcel Langedijk
Language(s): Dutch
ADVERTISING RATES:
Full Page Mono .... EUR 1/1: f.c. 7500,-
Agency Commission: 15%
Mechanical Data: Type Area: 194 x 266mm, Bleed Size: 210 x 275mm
Copy instructions: *Copy Date:* 1 month prior to publication date
CONSUMER: WOMEN'S INTEREST CONSUMER MAGAZINES: Women's Interest - Fashion

JAN
1704589N74Q-324
Editorial: Keizersgracht 182, 1016 DW AMSTERDAM
Web site: http://www.jan-magazine.nl
Date Established: 22-09-2005; **Freq:** 11 issues yearly; **Cover Price:** EUR 4,95
Annual Sub.: EUR 49,50; **Circ:** 68,593
Editor: Esther Goedegebuure
Language(s): Dutch
ADVERTISING RATES:
Full Page Mono .... EUR 2/1: f.c. 17.000,-; 1/1: f.c. 8500,-
Agency Commission: 15%
Mechanical Data: Type Area: 180 x 250mm, Bleed Size: 230 x 297mm
CONSUMER: WOMEN'S INTEREST CONSUMER MAGAZINES: Lifestyle

JANSEN
2009404N74Q-559
Editorial: Prof. Eijkmanlaan 2, 2035 XB HAARLEM
Tel: 88 2697112 **Fax:** 88 2696983
Email: info@hub.nl **Web site:** http://www.nietrijkwelsmaak.nl
Date Established: 18-11-2010; **Freq:** 6 issues yearly;
Cover Price: EUR 4,95; **Circ:** 60,000
Usual Pagination: 100
Editor: Mat Heffels
Language(s): Dutch
ADVERTISING RATES:
Full Page Mono .... EUR 2/1: f.c. 12.155,-; 1/1: f.c. 7150,-; 1/2: f.c. 4290,-; 1/4: f.c. 2574,-
Agency Commission: 15%
Mechanical Data: Type Area: 190 x 260mm, Bleed Size: 210 x 280mm
CONSUMER: WOMEN'S INTEREST CONSUMER MAGAZINES: Lifestyle

JEUGDBELEID
16317N32G-120
Editorial: Vrijthof 8, 5081 CA HILVARENBEEK
Tel: 570 647207 **Fax:** 73 6210512
Email: jeugdbeleid@xs4all.nl
Freq: Quarterly; **Annual Sub.:** EUR 75,50; **Circ:** 1,400
Editor: R. Clarijs; **Publisher:** N. van Hoorn
Profile: Magazine about the care and social welfare of young people.
Language(s): Dutch
Readership: Aimed at social workers.
ADVERTISING RATES:
Full Page Mono ... EUR 1/1: f.c. 2084,-; b/w 798,- 1/2: f.c. 1292,-; b/w 501,- 1/4: f.c. 775,-; b/w 303,-
Agency Commission: 15%
Mechanical Data: Type Area: 148 x 213mm, Bleed Size: 168 x 242mm
BUSINESS: LOCAL GOVERNMENT, LEISURE & RECREATION: Community Care & Social Services

JEUGDLITERATUUR IN PRAKTIJK
18024N84B-35
Editorial: Veursestraatweg 280, 2265 CL LEIDSCHENDAM **Tel:** 172 466622 **Fax:** 24 3723631
Freq: Quarterly; **Cover Price:** EUR 10,15
Annual Sub.: EUR 36,80; **Circ:** 800
Editor: Ger van Hoek; **Editor-in-Chief:** R. Saris;
Publisher: André Henderickx
Profile: Magazine about books and literature for children and young people.
Language(s): Dutch
Agency Commission: 15%
Mechanical Data: Type Area: 185 x 265mm, Bleed Size: 210 x 297mm
CONSUMER: THE ARTS & LITERARY: Literary

JEUGDVERKEERSKRANT
1634100N62R-306
Editorial: Stationsstraat 79a, 3811 MH AMERSFOORT **Tel:** 20 5310960
Email: info@vvn.nl **Web site:** http://www.vvn.nl/jvk
Freq: 8 issues yearly; **Annual Sub.:** EUR 3,44; **Circ:** 179,000
Language(s): Dutch
Agency Commission: 15%
Mechanical Data: Type Area: 182 x 261mm, Bleed Size: 210 x 297mm
BUSINESS: CHURCH & SCHOOL EQUIPMENT & EDUCATION: Education Related

JGZ, TIJDSCHRIFT VOOR JEUGDGEZONDHEIDSZORG
16675N56A-46
Editorial: Het Spoor 2, 3994 AK HOUTEN
Tel: 88 2944900 **Fax:** 35 6728834
Freq: 6 issues yearly; **Annual Sub.:** EUR 59,06; **Circ:** 1,229
Editor: R.A. Hira Sing; **Publisher:** Paul Dijkstra
Profile: Magazine about health and medical care for young people.
Language(s): Dutch
ADVERTISING RATES:
Full Page Mono .. EUR 1/1: f.c. 2610,-; b/w 962,- 1/2: f.c. 1633,-; b/w 603,- 1/4: f.c. 976,-; b/w 361,-

Agency Commission: 15%
Mechanical Data: Type Area: 185 x 268mm, Bleed Size: 210 x 297mm
BUSINESS: HEALTH & MEDICAL

J/M
17462N74D-29_50
Editorial: Raamgracht 4, 1011 KK AMSTERDAM
Tel: 20 5518406 **Fax:** 20 5518646
Web site: http://www.jmvoorouders.nl
Freq: 11 issues yearly; **Cover Price:** EUR 4,35
Annual Sub.: EUR 47,-; **Circ:** 51,504
Editor: Evert de Vos; **Editor-in-Chief:** M. Montanus; **Publisher:** Femke Leemeijer
Profile: Magazine focusing on child development and childcare.
Language(s): Dutch
Readership: Read by parents with children aged between 4 and 14 years.
ADVERTISING RATES:
Full Page Mono EUR 2/1: f.c. 9170,-; 1/1: f.c. 4585,-; 1/2: f.c. 2751,-
Agency Commission: 15%
Mechanical Data: Type Area: 180 x 240mm, Bleed Size: 210 x 275mm
Copy instructions: *Copy Date:* 3 weeks prior to publication date
CONSUMER: WOMEN'S INTEREST CONSUMER MAGAZINES: Child Care

JOB IN DE REGIO, ED. REGIO HAAGLANDEN
1636589N14F-181
Editorial: Anjerstraat 57, 2461 TG TER AAR
Tel: 172 466622 **Fax:** 24 3723631
Web site: http://www.jobinderegio.nl
Date Established: 26-08-1997; **Freq:** 26 issues yearly; **Cover Price:** Free; **Circ:** 70,000
Editor: H. van Beusichem; **Editor-in-Chief:** H. van Beusichem; **Publisher:** M.C. de Jong
Language(s): Dutch
Agency Commission: 15%
Mechanical Data: Type Area: 260 x 390mm, Bleed Size: 290 x 420mm
BUSINESS: COMMERCE, INDUSTRY & MANAGEMENT: Training & Recruitment

JOIE DE VIVRE
1637278N74Q-279
Editorial: Vijzelgracht 21-25, 1017 HN AMSTERDAM
Tel: 20 5310161 **Fax:** 30 6383990
Email: creditsmedia@creditsmedia.nl **Web site:** http://www.joiedevivre-magazine.nl
Freq: Quarterly; **Cover Price:** EUR 4,95
Annual Sub.: EUR 18,-; **Circ:** 35,000
Editor: P. van Eijndhoven; **Editor-in-Chief:** Mariette van de Sande; **Publisher:** Eugen van de Pas
Language(s): Dutch
ADVERTISING RATES:
Full Page Mono EUR 2/1: f.c. 8930,-; 1/1: f.c. 4465,-; 1/2: f.c. 2680,-
Agency Commission: 15%
Mechanical Data: Type Area: 210 x 277mm, Bleed Size: 230 x 297mm
CONSUMER: WOMEN'S INTEREST CONSUMER MAGAZINES: Lifestyle

JOURNAL OF EMPIRICAL THEOLOGY
18954N87-2492
Editorial: Erasmusplein 1, 6525 HT NIJMEGEN
Tel: 570 647064
Email: jet@theo.ru.nl **Web site:** http://www.brill.nl/jet
Freq: Half-yearly; **Annual Sub.:** EUR 37,-
Editor: C.A.M. Hermans
Profile: Journal concerning all aspects of theology.
Language(s): Dutch
Agency Commission: 15%
CONSUMER: RELIGIOUS

JOURNAL OF WORLD TRADE
15919N14C-70
Editorial: Zuidpoolsingel 2, 2408 ZE ALPHEN A/D RIJN **Tel:** 58 2954859 **Fax:** 20 6767728
Freq: 6 issues yearly; **Annual Sub.:** EUR 844,-; **Circ:** 1,250
Editor: Edwin Vermulst; **Publisher:** Lou Rolla
Profile: International journal providing news and information concerning commerce.
Language(s): Dutch
Readership: Read by students.
ADVERTISING RATES:
Full Page Mono .... EUR 1/1: f.c. 715,-
Agency Commission: 15%
BUSINESS: COMMERCE, INDUSTRY & MANAGEMENT: International Commerce

JUDO VISIE
1633410N75Q-196
Editorial: Postbus 1016, 4801 BA BREDA
Tel: 10 4274103 **Fax:** 10 4739911
Email: info@hartstudio.nl
Date Established: 01-03-2001; **Freq:** Quarterly; **Circ:** 50,000
Usual Pagination: 32
Editor: Annelies 't Hart
Language(s): Dutch
ADVERTISING RATES:
Full Page Mono EUR 1/1: b/w 1500,-** 1/2: b/w 800,-** 1/4: b/w 450,-
Agency Commission: 15%
Mechanical Data: Type Area: 190 x 277mm, Bleed Size: 210 x 297mm
CONSUMER: SPORT: Combat Sports

JUMBO MAGAZINE
1640468N74A-224
Editorial: Velperbinnensingel 5, 6811 BP ARNHEM
Tel: 26 8450860 **Fax:** 172 422886
Email: info@lbl.nl
Freq: 13 issues yearly; **Circ:** 2,500,000
Editor-in-Chief: L. Heisen
Language(s): Dutch
Agency Commission: 15%
CONSUMER: WOMEN'S INTEREST CONSUMER MAGAZINES: Women's Interest

DE KALVERHOUDER
16168N22D-2_90
Editorial: Postweg 8, 7963 PD RUINEN
Tel: 23 5565100 **Fax:** 23 5565105
Web site: http://www.dekalverhouder.nl
Freq: 6 issues yearly; **Annual Sub.:** EUR 75,-; **Circ:** 1,700
Editor: Bert Loseman; **Publisher:** Bert Loseman
Profile: Journal about veal production.
Language(s): Dutch
ADVERTISING RATES:
Full Page Mono EUR 1/1: b/w 988,- 1/2: b/w 533,- 1/4: b/w 314,-
Agency Commission: 15%
Mechanical Data: Type Area: 190 x 277mm, Bleed Size: 210 x 297mm
Copy instructions: *Copy Date:* 4 weeks prior to publication date
BUSINESS: FOOD: Meat Trade

KAMPEERAUTO
18182N91B-100
Editorial: Amersfoortsestraat 124b, 3769 AN SOESTERBERG **Tel:** 223 650017 **Fax:** 223 650011
Email: secretariaat@kampeerauto.nl
Freq: 9 issues yearly; **Circ:** 22,079
Editor: Ilse Uijlenbroek
Profile: Official magazine of the Camper Van Club of the Netherlands.
Language(s): Dutch
ADVERTISING RATES:
Full Page Mono EUR 1/1: f.c. 1940,-; b/w 1285,- 1/2: f.c. 1180,-; b/w 685,- 1/4: f.c. 685,-; b/w 360,-
Agency Commission: 15%
Mechanical Data: Type Area: 187 x 257mm, Bleed Size: 215 x 285mm
CONSUMER: RECREATION & LEISURE: Camping & Caravanning

KANOSPORT
19153N75M-297
Editorial: Wattbaan 31-49, 3439 ML NIEUWEGEIN
Tel: 20 5922250 **Fax:** 30 6348909
Email: info@nkb.nl
Date Established: 01-01-1983; **Freq:** Quarterly;
Annual Sub.: EUR 36,50; **Circ:** 6,000
Editor: R. Burger
Profile: Magazine about canoeing.
Language(s): Dutch
ADVERTISING RATES:
Full Page Mono .... EUR 1/1: f.c. 665,-; b/w 610,- 1/2: f.c. 380,-; b/w 355,- 1/4: f.c. 250,-; b/w 220,-
Agency Commission: 15%
Mechanical Data: Type Area: 185 x 270mm, Bleed Size: 210 x 297mm
CONSUMER: SPORT: Water Sports

DE KARPERWERELD
18204N92-72
Editorial: Postbus 3187, 3760 DD SOEST
Tel: 172 466622 **Fax:** 24 3723631
Email: mediapub@wxs.nl **Web site:** http://www.dekarperwereld.nl
Date Established: 15-11-1997; **Freq:** 6 issues yearly;
Cover Price: EUR 8,75
Annual Sub.: EUR 45,-; **Circ:** 17,500
Editor: Peter Dohmen; **Publisher:** H. te Kloeze
Profile: International magazine about carp fishing.
Language(s): Dutch
ADVERTISING RATES:
Full Page Mono EUR 1/1: b/w 775,- 1/2: b/w 420,- 1/4: b/w 240,-
Agency Commission: 15%
Mechanical Data: Type Area: 184 x 252mm, Bleed Size: 210 x 280mm
CONSUMER: ANGLING & FISHING

KATRIEN
1687069N91D-168
Editorial: Capellalaan 65, 2132 JL HOOFDDORP
Tel: 23 5564660 **Fax:** 314 359978
Web site: http://www.katrienduck.nl
Freq: 6 issues yearly; **Cover Price:** EUR 2,75
Annual Sub.: EUR 15,90; **Circ:** 23,532
Editor: Thom Roep; **Editor-in-Chief:** Mariella Manfré; **Publisher:** Suzan Schouten
Language(s): Dutch
ADVERTISING RATES:
Full Page Mono .... EUR 1/1: f.c. 2750,-
Agency Commission: 15%
Mechanical Data: Type Area: 172 x 247mm, Bleed Size: 192 x 277mm
CONSUMER: RECREATION & LEISURE: Children & Youth

KATTEN KATERN
17921N81C-25
Editorial: Postbus 85686, 2508 CJ DEN HAAG
Tel: 20 5922250
Email: secretariaat@kattenzorg-denhaag.nl
Freq: 3 issues yearly; **Circ:** 6,000
Editor-in-Chief: Marjolein Dekker
Profile: Publication of the Association of Cat Care, concentrating on stray cats in The Hague region.
Language(s): Dutch
Readership: Read by cat lovers.
Agency Commission: 15%
CONSUMER: ANIMALS & PETS: Cats

KATTENMANIEREN
761710N81C-40
Editorial: Postbus 111, 5750 AC DEURNE
Tel: 88 7518380 **Fax:** 88 7518381
Email: administratie@compassmedia.nl **Web site:** http://www.kattenmanieren.com
Date Established: 01-09-1999; **Freq:** 6 issues yearly;
Annual Sub.: EUR 19,50; **Circ:** 9,000
Editor: Annemiek van Zwol; **Publisher:** H. Kroon
Profile: Magazine focusing on cat behaviour and the relationship between felines and humans.
Language(s): Dutch
Readership: Read by cat lovers.
ADVERTISING RATES:
Full Page Mono .. EUR 1/1: f.c. 1097,-; b/w 711,- 1/2: f.c. 833,-; b/w 446,- 1/4: f.c. 634,-; b/w 248,-
Agency Commission: 15%
Mechanical Data: Type Area: 195 x 265mm, Bleed Size: 210 x 297mm
Copy instructions: *Copy Date:* 3 weeks prior to publication date
CONSUMER: ANIMALS & PETS: Cats

KATWIJK SPECIAAL
629911N72-7371
Editorial: Ambachtsweg 7a, 2222 AH KATWIJK
Tel: 45 5739390 **Fax:** 314 349023
Web site: http://www.katwijkspeciaal.nl
Freq: Weekly; **Circ:** 18,000
Editor: Esdor van Elten; **Editor-in-Chief:** Cor de Mooij; **Publisher:** G. Verhagen
Language(s): Dutch
Agency Commission: 15%
Mechanical Data: Type Area: 378 x 550mm, Bleed Size: 400 x 577mm
LOCAL NEWSPAPERS

DE KATWIJKSCHE POST
627235N72-2420
Editorial: Ambachtsweg 7a, 2222 AH KATWIJK
Tel: 15 2153232 **Fax:** 314 349035
Web site: http://www.katwijkschepost.nl
Date Established: 01-01-1922; **Freq:** Weekly;
Annual Sub.: EUR 27,20; **Circ:** 8,300
Editor: Esdor van Elten; **Editor-in-Chief:** Paul van de Putte
Language(s): Dutch
Agency Commission: 15%
Mechanical Data: Type Area: 378 x 550mm, Bleed Size: 400 x 577mm
LOCAL NEWSPAPERS

KBM (KANTOOR BUSINESSMAGAZINE)
16348N34-25
Editorial: Bijsterhuizen 31-47, 6604 LV WIJCHEN
Tel: 172 466539 **Fax:** 10 4521797
Email: magenta@kantoornet.nl **Web site:** http://www.kantoornet.nl
Date Established: 01-02-1918; **Freq:** Monthly;
Annual Sub.: EUR 85,-; **Circ:** 3,800
Editor: Emiel te Walvaart; **Publisher:** Joost Heessels
Profile: Magazine about office supplies, computer supplies, distribution and layout.
Language(s): Dutch
ADVERTISING RATES:
Full Page Mono EUR 2/1: f.c. 3950,-; 1/1: f.c. 2450,-; 1/2: f.c. 1550,-
Agency Commission: 15%
Mechanical Data: Type Area: 185 x 268mm, Bleed Size: 210 x 297mm
BUSINESS: OFFICE EQUIPMENT

KBO-WEGWIJZER
17526N74N-63
Editorial: Julianaplein 2, 5211 BC 'S-HERTOGENBOSCH **Tel:** 314 349629
Fax: 314 360699
Email: info@uniekbo.nl
Freq: 17 issues yearly; **Annual Sub.:** EUR 34,-; **Circ:** 2,200
Editor: A. Heltzel; **Editor-in-Chief:** S. Smets
Profile: Bulletin of the Union of Catholic Associations of the Elderly.
Language(s): Dutch
Agency Commission: 15%
Mechanical Data: Bleed Size: 210 x 297mm
CONSUMER: WOMEN'S INTEREST CONSUMER MAGAZINES: Retirement

KEK MAMA
1606542N91D-86
Editorial: Capellalaan 65, 2132 JL HOOFDDORP
Tel: 88 5567250 **Fax:** 24 3723631
Web site: http://www.kekmama.nl
Freq: Monthly; **Cover Price:** EUR 4,95
Annual Sub.: EUR 59,40; **Circ:** 41,384
Editor: Brigitte Donders; **Publisher:** Stefan Hutten
Profile: Magazine providing a guide to fashion, style and trends for children. Also includes information on holidays, sport and leisure.
Language(s): Dutch
Readership: Aimed at parents of children aged 4 to 12 years.
ADVERTISING RATES:
Full Page Mono .... EUR 2/1: b/w 10.200,- 1/1: b/w 5100,- 1/2: b/w 3060,-
Agency Commission: 15%
Mechanical Data: Type Area: 185 x 243mm, Bleed Size: 230 x 298mm
Copy instructions: *Copy Date:* 4 weeks prior to publication date
CONSUMER: RECREATION & LEISURE: Children & Youth

KENMERK
1635529N55-272
Editorial: Industrieweg 41b, 2382 NT ZOETERWOUDE **Tel:** 76 5722984 **Fax:** 570 614795
Email: info@zorn.nl **Web site:** http://www.kenmerk.nl
Freq: 20 issues yearly; **Cover Price:** Free; **Circ:** 70,000
Editor: Cees Noordegraaf
Language(s): Dutch
Agency Commission: 15%
Mechanical Data: Type Area: 152 x 224mm
BUSINESS: APPLIED SCIENCE & LABORATORIES

KENNISNETINDRUK PO
1637315N62A-190
Editorial: Paletsingel 32, 2718 NT ZOETERMEER
Tel: 70 3789880 **Fax:** 58 2987505
Email: info@kennisnet.nl **Web site:** http://www.kennisnet.nl/po
Date Established: 27-11-2002; **Freq:** Quarterly;
Cover Price: Free; **Circ:** 50,000
Editor: Alexandra Myk; **Editor-in-Chief:** J. Teske
Language(s): Dutch
Agency Commission: 15%
BUSINESS: CHURCH & SCHOOL EQUIPMENT & EDUCATION: Education

KERK EN MUZIEK
16886N87-132
Editorial: Welhorst 25, 3332 RP ZWIJNDRECHT
Tel: 20 5159743
Web site: http://www.kerkenmuziek.nl
Freq: 6 issues yearly; **Annual Sub.:** EUR 37,50; **Circ:** 750
Editor: Okke Dijkhuizen
Profile: Journal about traditional church music.
Language(s): Dutch
Agency Commission: 15%
CONSUMER: RELIGIOUS

KEUKEN EN BAD TECHNIEK
16186N23C-40
Editorial: De Trompet 2148b, 1967 DC HEEMSKERK
Tel: 0032 34660066
Web site: http://www.keukenenbadtechniek.nl
Freq: 6 issues yearly; **Cover Price:** EUR 4,60
Annual Sub.: EUR 21,-; **Circ:** 4,600
Editor: Maarten Zegstroo; **Publisher:** J.M. Haak
Profile: Magazine focusing on fixtures, fittings and furniture for kitchens and bathrooms.
Language(s): Dutch
Readership: Aimed at kitchen specialists, sanitary shops and interior architects.
ADVERTISING RATES:
Full Page Mono .. EUR 1/1: b/w 1180,- 1/2: b/w 665,- 1/4: b/w 380,-
Agency Commission: 15%
Mechanical Data: Type Area: 205 x 255mm, Bleed Size: 230 x 300mm
BUSINESS: FURNISHINGS & FURNITURE: Furnishings & Furniture - Kitchens & Bathrooms

KEUKEN STUDIO
17444N74C-357
Editorial: Walburgstraete III, Dreef 6h, 7202 AG ZUTPHEN **Tel:** 10 4274101 **Fax:** 10 4739911
Email: info@qumedia.nl **Web site:** http://www.keukenstudio.com
Date Established: 01-01-1988; **Freq:** Half-yearly;
Cover Price: EUR 5,95; **Circ:** 50,000
Editor: P. Besselink; **Editor-in-Chief:** G. Hilferink; **Publisher:** Arnold Jansen
Profile: Magazine containing details about kitchen design and appliances.
Language(s): Dutch
Readership: Aimed at those wishing to buy a kitchen.
ADVERTISING RATES:
Full Page Mono EUR 2/1: b/w 7024,- 1/1: b/w 3697,- 1/2: b/w 2218,-
Agency Commission: 15%
Mechanical Data: Type Area: 200 x 277mm, Bleed Size: 220 x 297mm
CONSUMER: WOMEN'S INTEREST CONSUMER MAGAZINES: Home & Family

KIDS FOR ANIMALS
17904N81A-50
Editorial: Scheveningseweg 58, 2517 KW DEN HAAG **Tel:** 20 5042829 **Fax:** 20 5159143
Email: info@dierenbescherming.nl **Web site:** http://www.kidsforanimals.nl
Freq: 6 issues yearly; **Annual Sub.:** EUR 12,-; **Circ:** 30,000
Editor: Paul van der Valk; **Editor-in-Chief:** Maartje Mulckhuyse
Profile: Magazine for children about the care and protection of animals.
Language(s): Dutch
Readership: Read by children from 7-12 years old.
Agency Commission: 15%
Mechanical Data: Type Area: 185 x 260mm, Bleed Size: 215 x 285mm
CONSUMER: ANIMALS & PETS: Animals & Pets Protection

KIJK
717768N74F-31
Editorial: Capellalaan 65, 2132 JL HOOFDDORP
Tel: 88 7518320 **Fax:** 35 6474444
Web site: http://www.kijk.nl
Freq: 13 issues yearly; **Cover Price:** EUR 4,99
Annual Sub.: EUR 59,-; **Circ:** 54,522
Editor: Vivianne Bendermacher; **Editor-in-Chief:** I. Fraters; **Publisher:** Wouter Verkennis
Profile: Magazine featuring articles on popular science.
Language(s): Dutch
Readership: Read by young people aged 15 to 25 years.
ADVERTISING RATES:
Full Page Mono .... EUR 2/1: b/w 15.000,- 1/1: b/w 7500,- 1/2: b/w 4500,-
Agency Commission: 15%
Mechanical Data: Type Area: 178 x 254mm, Bleed Size: 210 x 285mm
CONSUMER: WOMEN'S INTEREST CONSUMER MAGAZINES: Teenage

KIJK OP OOST-NEDERLAND
18994N63-423
Editorial: Bruchterweg 108, 7772 BJ HARDENBERG
Tel: 523 285330 **Fax:** 30 6348909
Email: info@periodiekenpartners.nl **Web site:** http://www.kijkopoostnederland.nl
Freq: 8 issues yearly; **Cover Price:** EUR 5,70
Annual Sub.: EUR 42,85; **Circ:** 16,000
Editor: K. Koolhoven; **Editor-in-Chief:** Guus Wiggerts; **Publisher:** A.J. Giethoorn
Profile: Magazine about trade and industry in East Holland.
Language(s): Dutch
ADVERTISING RATES:
Full Page Mono EUR 1/1: f.c. 1700,-; 1/2: f.c. 1010,-; 1/4: f.c. 560,-
Agency Commission: 15%
Mechanical Data: Type Area: 198 x 266mm, Bleed Size: 225 x 297mm
Copy instructions: *Copy Date:* 5 weeks prior to publication date
BUSINESS: REGIONAL BUSINESS

KIJKKEZ
1634279N88A-133
Editorial: Deimoslaan 3, 1702 CK HEERHUGOWAARD **Tel:** 348 487067
Fax: 45 5762766
Email: maypress@maypress.nl **Web site:** http://www.kijkkez.nl
Date Established: 01-11-1984; **Freq:** 6 issues yearly;
Cover Price: Free; **Circ:** 600,000
Usual Pagination: 32
Editor: Jol Riemsma; **Editor-in-Chief:** Jol Riemsma
Language(s): Dutch
ADVERTISING RATES:
Full Page Mono EUR 1/1: f.c. 5458,-; 1/2: f.c. 3280,-; 1/4: f.c. 2200,-
Agency Commission: 15%
Mechanical Data: Type Area: 250 x 328mm, Bleed Size: 265 x 360mm
CONSUMER: EDUCATION

KIJKKEZ GEZONDHEIDSZORG
16713N56A-310
Editorial: Deimoslaan 3, 1702 CK HEERHUGOWAARD **Tel:** 570 673344
Fax: 20 5159143
Email: maypress@maypress.nl
Date Established: 01-05-2006; **Freq:** Half-yearly;
Cover Price: Free; **Circ:** 56,000
Editor: Jol Riemsma; **Editor-in-Chief:** Jol Riemsma
Profile: Magazine about work and developments within healthcare.
Language(s): Dutch
ADVERTISING RATES:
Full Page Mono EUR 1/1: f.c. 2442,-; 1/2: f.c. 1474,-; 1/4: f.c. 939,-
Agency Commission: 15%
Mechanical Data: Type Area: 250 x 328mm, Bleed Size: 265 x 360mm
BUSINESS: HEALTH & MEDICAL

KIND EN ADOLESCENT
16679N56A-60_25
Editorial: Kruisweg 16bis, 3513 CT UTRECHT
Tel: 20 5159172 **Fax:** 229 216416
Web site: http://www.kindenadolescent.nl
Freq: Quarterly; **Circ:** 1,630
Editor: Gerda Vlieger-Smid; **Publisher:** N. van Hoorn
Profile: Journal containing news about child development. Covers psychiatry and psychology.
Language(s): Dutch
Readership: Aimed at medical specialists within the field, university students and lecturers.
ADVERTISING RATES:
Full Page Mono .... EUR 1/1: b/w 850,- 1/2: b/w 534,-
Agency Commission: 15%
Mechanical Data: Type Area: 118 x 210mm, Bleed Size: 168 x 242mm
Copy instructions: *Copy Date:* 4 weeks prior to publication date
BUSINESS: HEALTH & MEDICAL

KINDER PUZZEL & KLEURBOEK
1637389N91D-150
Editorial: Hoofdstraat 208a, 7311 BG APELDOORN
Tel: 70 7890630 **Fax:** 20 3728277
Email: info@goodwill.nl **Web site:** http://www.kinderkleurboek.nl
Date Established: 01-04-1992; **Freq:** Monthly;
Cover Price: Free; **Circ:** 1,250
Editor: H.A. van Telgen; **Publisher:** H.A. van Telgen
Language(s): Dutch
ADVERTISING RATES:
Full Page Mono EUR 1/1: f.c. 2500,-; b/w 1095,- 1/2: f.c. 1250,-; b/w 650,- 1/4: f.c. 995,-; b/w 435,-
Agency Commission: 15%
Mechanical Data: Type Area: 190 x 270mm, Bleed Size: 210 x 297mm
CONSUMER: RECREATION & LEISURE: Children & Youth

DE KINDERPOSTZEGEL KRANT
1634367N91D-242
Editorial: Schipholweg 73-75, 2316 ZL LEIDEN
Tel: 23 5564000 **Fax:** 71 5356415
Email: info@kinderpostzegels.nl
Freq: Annual; **Cover Price:** Free; **Circ:** 275,000
Editor: Anne Jacobs
Language(s): Dutch
Agency Commission: 15%
CONSUMER: RECREATION & LEISURE: Children & Youth

KINDSCHAP GODS
18093N87-146
Editorial: Hereweg 46, 6373 VJ LANDGRAAF
Tel: 172 466405 **Fax:** 492 371114
Freq: Quarterly; **Circ:** 2,500
Editor: J.A.A. Leechburch Auwers
Profile: Religious publication.
Language(s): Dutch
Agency Commission: 15%
CONSUMER: RELIGIOUS

KLASSIEKE ZAKEN
704751N76D-89
Editorial: Arendstraat 53, 1223 RE HILVERSUM
Tel: 70 3789880 **Fax:** 70 3789783
Email: info@imediate.nl **Web site:** http://www.klassiekezaken.nl
Date Established: 15-01-1999; **Freq:** 6 issues yearly;
Cover Price: Free; **Circ:** 50,000
Editor: Bela Luttmer; **Editor-in-Chief:** Bela Luttmer;
Publisher: Henriette Zrour
Profile: Magazine containing articles about classical music, includes reviews, interviews and discussions about CDs.
Language(s): Dutch
Readership: Aimed at the members of the Klassieke Zaken Vereniging and people with an interest in classical music.
ADVERTISING RATES:
Full Page Mono EUR 1/1: f.c. 2750,-; 1/2: f.c. 2125,-; 1/4: f.c. 1500,-
Agency Commission: 15%
Mechanical Data: Type Area: 186 x 252mm, Bleed Size: 210 x 285mm
CONSUMER: MUSIC & PERFORMING ARTS: Music

DE KLEPPER
1634360N1P-85
Editorial: Wibautstraat 137k, 1097 DN AMSTERDAM
Tel: 71 5356356 **Fax:** 71 5356415
Email: info@leprastichting.nl
Date Established: 01-01-1969; **Freq:** Quarterly;
Cover Price: Free; **Circ:** 190,000
Editor: J. van Berkel; **Editor-in-Chief:** R. van Haeften
Language(s): Dutch
Agency Commission: 15%
Mechanical Data: Type Area: 195 x 265mm
BUSINESS: FINANCE & ECONOMICS: Fundraising

KLEUR
16762N56L-33
Editorial: Maliebaan 71m, 3581 CG UTRECHT
Tel: 172 466539 **Fax:** 10 4521797
Email: info@ditkoningskind.nl
Freq: Quarterly; **Annual Sub.:** EUR 23,-; **Circ:** 17,000
Editor: Mariska van Bergen
Profile: Magazine focusing on all aspects of disability.
Language(s): Dutch
Readership: Aimed at people with a disability, their family and friends.
Agency Commission: 15%
BUSINESS: HEALTH & MEDICAL: Disability & Rehabilitation

DE KLINKER
17866N80-23
Editorial: Raadhuisplein 2, 2922 AD KRIMPEN A/D IJSSEL **Tel:** 172 466622 **Fax:** 24 3723631
Email: gemeente@krimpenaandenijssel.nl
Date Established: 01-01-1972; **Freq:** 6 issues yearly;
Cover Price: Free; **Circ:** 12,000
Usual Pagination: 20
Editor: Leendert Vermeulen
Profile: Magazine for the population of Krimpen a/d IJssel.
Language(s): Dutch
ADVERTISING RATES:
Full Page Mono EUR 1/1: b/w 550,- 1/2: b/w 300,- 1/4: b/w 160,-
Agency Commission: 15%
Mechanical Data: Bleed Size: 210 x 297mm
Copy instructions: *Copy Date:* 3 weeks prior to publication date
CONSUMER: RURAL & REGIONAL INTEREST

KNTV-MAGAZINE
16885N61-12_50
Editorial: Grote Bickersstraat 50a, 1013 KS AMSTERDAM **Tel:** 10 2894015 **Fax:** 20 6159047
Email: office@kntv.nl
Date Established: 01-01-1998; **Freq:** 6 issues yearly;
Circ: 4,000
Usual Pagination: 28
Editor: Gaston ten Horn; **Editor-in-Chief:** Gaston ten Horn
Profile: Journal of the Royal Union of Dutch Musicians.
Language(s): Dutch
Readership: Aimed at professional musicians and policymakers.
ADVERTISING RATES:
Full Page Mono EUR 1/1: b/w 675,- 1/2: b/w 350,- 1/4: b/w 225,- 1/8: b/w 125,-
Agency Commission: 15%
Mechanical Data: Bleed Size: 210 x 297mm, Type Area: 184 x 271mm
BUSINESS: MUSIC TRADE

DE KOGGENLANDER
627076N72-2630
Editorial: Randweg 11, 1671 GG MEDEMBLIK
Tel: 88 7518380 **Fax:** 88 7518381
Email: drukkerij@idemadruk.nl
Date Established: 01-01-1905; **Freq:** Weekly; **Cover Price:** Free; **Circ:** 4,965
Editor: R.C.M. Koomen
Language(s): Dutch
Agency Commission: 15%
Mechanical Data: Type Area: 398 x 540mm, Bleed Size: 410 x 580mm
LOCAL NEWSPAPERS

DE KOMEET
16989N64A-40
Editorial: Oudegracht 186, 1811 CP ALKMAAR
Tel: 30 2539300 **Fax:** 0032 34660067
Email: nkbalkmaar@hetnet.nl
Freq: 26 issues yearly; **Annual Sub.:** EUR 175,-;
Circ: 1,500
Usual Pagination: 752
Editor: J. Boots
Profile: Magazine covering the amusement trade, focusing on fairs and recreation parks.
Language(s): Dutch
Agency Commission: 15%
BUSINESS: OTHER CLASSIFICATIONS: Amusement Trade

KRAAMSUPPORT
634841N56B-25
Editorial: Keizersgracht 213, 1016 DT AMSTERDAM
Tel: 70 3780541 **Fax:** 70 3789783
Email: info@y-publicaties.nl **Web site:** http://www.kraamsupportonline.nl
Freq: 8 issues yearly; **Cover Price:** EUR 8,-
Annual Sub.: EUR 50,95; **Circ:** 2,925
Editor: Maartje van der Zedde; **Publisher:** Ralf Beekveldt
Profile: Magazine focusing on maternity care.
Language(s): Dutch
Readership: Read by midwives, nurses and specialists.
ADVERTISING RATES:
Full Page Mono EUR 1/1: f.c. 2755,-; b/w 1766,- 1/2: f.c. 1985,-; b/w 1189,- 1/4: f.c. 1367,-; b/w 578,-
Agency Commission: 15%
Mechanical Data: Type Area: 185 x 264mm, Bleed Size: 215 x 285mm
BUSINESS: HEALTH & MEDICAL: Nursing

KRAAMZORG
1635127N56B-159
Editorial: Barentzplein 6b, 1013 NJ AMSTERDAM
Tel: 24 3722911
Email: info@reclamij.nl **Web site:** http://www.vakbladkraamzorg.nl
Freq: 6 issues yearly; **Cover Price:** Free; **Circ:** 7,531
Editor: Lara Geeurickx; **Publisher:** Carin Derks
Language(s): Dutch
ADVERTISING RATES:
Full Page Mono .... EUR 1/1: f.c. 3995,-
Agency Commission: 15%
Mechanical Data: Type Area: 180 x 180mm, Bleed Size: 210 x 210mm
Copy instructions: *Copy Date:* 8 weeks prior to publication date
BUSINESS: HEALTH & MEDICAL: Nursing

KRACHT
1857933N56J-52
Editorial: Delflandlaan 17, 1062 EA AMSTERDAM
Tel: 0032 34660066 **Fax:** 0032 34660067
Email: info@kwfkankerbestrijding.nl
Freq: Quarterly; **Cover Price:** Free; **Circ:** 65,000
Editor: Stan Termeer; **Editor-in-Chief:** Resi Lankester
Language(s): Dutch
Agency Commission: 15%
BUSINESS: HEALTH & MEDICAL: Radiography

KRANT VAN DE AARDE
1857696N57-149
Editorial: Amaliastraat 5, 1052 GM AMSTERDAM
Tel: 70 3789685
Email: redactie@krantvandeaarde.nl **Web site:** http://www.krantvandeaarde.nl
Freq: 6 issues yearly; **Cover Price:** Free; **Circ:** 125,000
Editor: Ilse Eggenkamp; **Editor-in-Chief:** Petra van der Veer
Language(s): Dutch
ADVERTISING RATES:
Full Page Mono EUR 1/1: f.c. 3500,-; 1/2: f.c. 1875,-; 1/4: f.c. 1000,-
Agency Commission: 15%
Mechanical Data: Type Area: 202 x 284mm, Bleed Size: 230 x 310mm
BUSINESS: ENVIRONMENT & POLLUTION

KREAVAK
16609N53-70
Editorial: Noordenseweg 1, 2421 XW NIEUWKOOP
Tel: 172 575581 **Fax:** 23 5565136
Email: info@asws.nl
Freq: 5 issues yearly; **Annual Sub.:** EUR 23,40; **Circ:** 3,000
Usual Pagination: 52
Editor: R.J.G. Waldhober; **Editor-in-Chief:** R.J.G. Waldhober; **Publisher:** R.J.G. Waldhober
Profile: Journal covering the retail trade.
Language(s): Dutch
ADVERTISING RATES:
Full Page Mono .. EUR 1/1: f.c. 1415,-; 1/2: f.c. 920,-; 1/4: f.c. 519,-
Agency Commission: 15%
Mechanical Data: Type Area: 183 x 263mm, Bleed Size: 210 x 297mm
BUSINESS: RETAILING & WHOLESALING

KRITIEK
16791N56P-50
Editorial: Postbus 13141, 3507 LC UTRECHT
Tel: 543 493705 **Fax:** 15 2158918
Email: info@kritiek.org
Date Established: 01-01-1991; **Freq:** 6 issues yearly;
Annual Sub.: EUR 33,-; **Circ:** 4,000
Editor: B. de Lange; **Editor-in-Chief:** B. de Lange
Profile: Magazine focusing on the care of patients in intensive care.
Language(s): Dutch
Readership: Aimed at those working in intensive care departments.
ADVERTISING RATES:
Full Page Mono .... EUR 1/1: b/w 1380,-
Agency Commission: 15%
Mechanical Data: Bleed Size: 210 x 297mm
Copy instructions: *Copy Date:* 1 month prior to publication date
BUSINESS: HEALTH & MEDICAL: Casualty & Emergency

KRO MAGAZINE
17676N76C-100
Editorial: Marathon 1, 1213 PA HILVERSUM
Tel: 35 6726880 **Fax:** 23 5564911
Web site: http://www.kromagazine.nl
Date Established: 01-05-1925; **Freq:** Weekly; **Cover Price:** EUR 1,20
Annual Sub.: EUR 57,85; **Circ:** 134,718
Editor-in-Chief: Marco Entrop; **Publisher:** Barbara van der Veen
Profile: TV and radio magazine of the KRO - Catholic Radio Broadcasting Association.
Language(s): Dutch
ADVERTISING RATES:
Full Page Mono EUR 2/1: f.c. 8840,-; 1/1: f.c. 4420,-; 1/2: f.c. 3094,-
Agency Commission: 15%
Mechanical Data: Type Area: 172 x 215mm, Bleed Size: 202 x 245mm
CONSUMER: MUSIC & PERFORMING ARTS: TV & Radio

KRÖDDE
18026N84B-40
Editorial: Walta 34, 9202 JN DRACHTEN
Tel: 76 5876329
Email: info@krodde.nl
Date Established: 01-04-1982; **Freq:** Quarterly;
Cover Price: EUR 4,-
Annual Sub.: EUR 15,-; **Circ:** 350
Usual Pagination: 48
Editor: J. Glas; **Editor-in-Chief:** W. Hartholt
Profile: Magazine about Groninger and Ostfrisian literature.
Language(s): Dutch
Agency Commission: 15%
Mechanical Data: Type Area: 115 x 175mm, Bleed Size: 150 x 210mm
CONSUMER: THE ARTS & LITERARY: Literary

KR@SH MAGAZINE
1994023N74F-184
Editorial: Mijlweg 61, 3316 BE DORDRECHT
Tel: 30 2303508 **Fax:** 46 4116281
Email: info@zpress-magazines.nl **Web site:** http://www.krash.nl
Date Established: 16-02-2010; **Freq:** 11 issues yearly; **Cover Price:** EUR 3,45
Annual Sub.: EUR 39,95; **Circ:** 60,000
Editor-in-Chief: Joeri Donsu; **Publisher:** Robert van Ginhoven
Language(s): Dutch
ADVERTISING RATES:
Full Page Mono . EUR 2/1: f.c. 5000,-; 1/1: f.c. 2950,-
Agency Commission: 15%
Mechanical Data: Type Area: 190 x 277mm, Bleed Size: 210 x 297mm
CONSUMER: WOMEN'S INTEREST CONSUMER MAGAZINES: Teenage

KUNST EN KLASSIEK MAGAZINE
1638039N84A-344
Editorial: 's-Gravelandseweg 80, 1217 EW HILVERSUM **Tel:** 30 6383873 **Fax:** 30 6383998

Freq: Quarterly; **Annual Sub.:** EUR 6,-; **Circ:** 55,000
Editor: W. Weijland; **Editor-in-Chief:** Christien Blanken
Language(s): Dutch
ADVERTISING RATES:
Full Page Mono . EUR 1/1: f.c. 4500,-; achterpag.: f.c. 3500,-
Agency Commission: 15%
Mechanical Data: Type Area: 185 x 230mm, Bleed Size: 210 x 260mm
CONSUMER: THE ARTS & LITERARY: Arts

KUNST EN WETENSCHAP
18007N84A-100
Editorial: Smidstraat 12, 8746 NG SCHRAARD
Tel: 23 5565370 **Fax:** 475 551033
Email: kunstenwetenschap@planet.nl **Web site:** http://www.kunstenwetenschap.nl
Date Established: 01-03-1992; **Freq:** Quarterly;
Cover Price: EUR 4,75
Annual Sub.: EUR 14,-; **Circ:** 5,000
Editor: Pieter Bakker; **Publisher:** Pieter Bakker
Profile: Magazine for art students and teachers.
Language(s): Dutch
ADVERTISING RATES:
Full Page Mono EUR 1/1: f.c. 1950,-; b/w 1200,- 1/2: b/w 625,- 1/4: b/w 350,-
Agency Commission: 15%
Mechanical Data: Type Area: 185 x 250mm, Bleed Size: 215 x 285mm
Copy instructions: *Copy Date:* 4 weeks prior to publication date
CONSUMER: THE ARTS & LITERARY: Arts

KUNSTBEELD
18008N84A-120
Editorial: Wildenborch 5, 1112 XB DIEMEN
Tel: 88 8002915 **Fax:** 35 6474444
Web site: http://www.kunstbeeld.nl
Date Established: 01-10-1976; **Freq:** 10 issues yearly; **Cover Price:** EUR 10,75
Annual Sub.: EUR 89,-; **Circ:** 8,545
Editor: Roos van Put; **Editor-in-Chief:** Judith van Meeuwen; **Publisher:** Hans van Vloten
Profile: Magazine about modern art.
Language(s): Dutch
Readership: Read by art lovers and buyers.
ADVERTISING RATES:
Full Page Mono EUR 2/1: f.c. 3975,-; PMS 2885,-; b/w 2390,- 1/1: f.c. 2360,-; PMS 1750,-; b/w 1420,- 1/2: f.c. 1340,-;
Agency Commission: 15%
Mechanical Data: Type Area: 215 x 292mm, Bleed Size: 235 x 312mm
Copy instructions: *Copy Date:* 3 weeks prior to publication date
CONSUMER: THE ARTS & LITERARY: Arts

KUNSTSCHRIFT
629724N84A-155
Editorial: Oudezijds Achterburgwal 119, 1012 DE AMSTERDAM **Tel:** 314 349446 **Fax:** 314 344397
Web site: http://www.kunstschrift.nl
Date Established: 01-01-1956; **Freq:** 6 issues yearly;
Cover Price: EUR 9,50
Annual Sub.: EUR 51,00; **Circ:** 10,000
Editor: Mariëtte Haveman; **Editor-in-Chief:** A. Overbeek; **Publisher:** Mariëtte Haveman
Profile: Magazine featuring art in general.
Language(s): Dutch
Readership: Aimed at students, artists and those with a passion for art.
ADVERTISING RATES:
Full Page Mono .. EUR 1/1: f.c. 1200,-; 1/2: f.c. 625,-; 1/4: f.c. 350,-
Agency Commission: 15%
Mechanical Data: Type Area: 200 x 260mm, Bleed Size: 220 x 280mm
CONSUMER: THE ARTS & LITERARY: Arts

KUNSTSTOF EN RUBBER
16392N39-80
Editorial: Essebaan 63, 2908 LJ CAPELLE AAN DEN IJSSEL **Tel:** 10 2894026 **Fax:** 88 2697490
Email: info@mybusinessmedia.nl **Web site:** http://www.kunststofonline.nl
Freq: 9 issues yearly; **Cover Price:** EUR 20,63
Annual Sub.: EUR 181,50; **Circ:** 1,865
Editor: L.J. de Ridder; **Publisher:** Elsbeth Lamfers
Profile: Journal for the plastics and rubber industry.
Language(s): Dutch
Readership: Aimed at managers and suppliers in the plastics and rubber industry.
ADVERTISING RATES:
Full Page Mono EUR 1/1: b/w 2680,- 1/2: b/w 1450,- 1/4: b/w 820,-
Agency Commission: 15%
Mechanical Data: Bleed Size: 210 x 297mm, Type Area: 185 x 267mm
Copy instructions: *Copy Date:* 3 weeks prior to publication date
BUSINESS: PLASTICS & RUBBER

KUNSTSTOF MAGAZINE
16391N39-70
Editorial: Hettenheuvelweg 41-43, 1101 BM AMSTERDAM **Tel:** 58 2954859 **Fax:** 20 6767728
Email: info@koggeschip-vakbladen.nl **Web site:** http://www.kunststof-magazine.nl
Date Established: 01-01-1990; **Freq:** 9 issues yearly;
Cover Price: EUR 15,-
Annual Sub.: EUR 126,75; **Circ:** 3,376
Editor: Hugo van der Horst; **Publisher:** Anthony van Trigt
Profile: Magazine providing technical application-related information on raw materials, machinery, tools and the associated operations.
Language(s): Dutch
Readership: Aimed at people working in the plastics industry.
ADVERTISING RATES:
Full Page Mono EUR 1/1: f.c. 3165,-; b/w 1870,- 1/2: f.c. 1895,-; b/w 1030,- 1/4: f.c. 1135,-; b/w 560,-
Agency Commission: 15%
Mechanical Data: Type Area: 185 x 270mm, Bleed Size: 210 x 297mm
Copy instructions: *Copy Date:* 2 weeks prior to publication date
BUSINESS: PLASTICS & RUBBER

KUST & ZEEGIDS
1748163N81A-182
Editorial: Breestraat 89a, 2311 CK LEIDEN
Tel: 26 4452725 **Fax:** 492 311114
Email: admin@eucc.net **Web site:** http://www.kustgids.nl
Freq: Annual; **Cover Price:** Free; **Circ:** 100,000
Editor: Elsbeth Lamme
Language(s): Dutch
ADVERTISING RATES:
Full Page Mono .... EUR 1/1: f.c. 3000,-
Agency Commission: 15%
Mechanical Data: Type Area: 185 x 275mm, Bleed Size: 210 x 297mm
CONSUMER: ANIMALS & PETS: Animals & Pets Protection

KVGO-KERNNIEUWS
16412N41A-50
Editorial: Startbaan 10, 1181 XR AMSTELVEEN
Tel: 23 5565370 **Fax:** 55 5412288
Email: info@kvgo.nl
Freq: Monthly; **Annual Sub.:** EUR 30,-; **Circ:** 3,500
Editor: W. Gielissen
Profile: Official journal of the Dutch Association of Printing and Allied Industries.
Language(s): Dutch
Agency Commission: 15%
Mechanical Data: Bleed Size: 210 x 297mm
BUSINESS: PRINTING & STATIONERY: Printing

LAAT LEVEN
1634149N94X-590
Editorial: Arnhemseweg 23, 3811 NN AMERSFOORT
Tel: 226 333577
Email: info@vbok.nl
Date Established: 01-09-1971; **Freq:** Quarterly;
Annual Sub.: EUR 15,-; **Circ:** 100,000
Editor: J.J. van Veelen; **Editor-in-Chief:** Mirjam Velthuis
Language(s): Dutch
Agency Commission: 15%
CONSUMER: OTHER CLASSIFICATIONS: Miscellaneous

LAN MAGAZINE
15774N5E-33
Editorial: Lemelerberg 19-23, 2402 ZN ALPHEN A/D RIJN **Tel:** 172 469050 **Fax:** 35 6563174
Email: array@array.nl **Web site:** http://www.lanmagazine.nl
Freq: 10 issues yearly; **Cover Price:** EUR 13,50
Annual Sub.: EUR 112,75; **Circ:** 4,489
Editor: Dick Schievels; **Publisher:** Werner Schoots
Profile: Magazine focusing on networking. Contains tests on hard- and software, product information and technical background articles. Also covers the Internet.
Language(s): Dutch
Readership: Aimed at IT, systems and network managers.
ADVERTISING RATES:
Full Page Mono EUR 1/1: b/w 3650,- 1/2: b/w 2295,- 1/4: b/w 1335,-
Agency Commission: 15%
Mechanical Data: Type Area: 190 x 265mm, Bleed Size: 210 x 285mm
BUSINESS: COMPUTERS & AUTOMATION: Data Transmission

LAND + WATER
16434N42C-43
Editorial: Adrianus van Driellaan 30, 2493 BR DEN HAAG **Tel:** 20 5518518
Web site: http://www.landwater.nl
Date Established: 01-03-1957; **Freq:** 10 issues yearly; **Annual Sub.:** EUR 121,15; **Circ:** 3,925
Editor: Bas Keijts; **Editor-in-Chief:** B. Dijkhuizen
Profile: Journal containing information on projects and studies regarding road and hydraulic engineering and environmental technology.
Language(s): Dutch
Readership: Aimed at civil engineers, architects and students.
ADVERTISING RATES:
Full Page Mono EUR 1/1: f.c. 2648,-; PMS 2197,-; b/w 1661,- 1/2: f.c. 1850,-; PMS 1469,-; b/w 1013,- 1/4: f.c. 1333,-;
Agency Commission: 15%
Mechanical Data: Type Area: 180 x 262mm, Bleed Size: 210 x 297mm
BUSINESS: CONSTRUCTION: Water Engineering

LANDELIJK WANDEL PROGRAMMA
1636592N75L-382
Editorial: Edisonbaan 14f, 3439 MN NIEUWEGEIN
Tel: 172 466622 **Fax:** 24 3723631
Email: info@sportsmedia.nl
Freq: Annual; **Cover Price:** EUR 6,95; **Circ:** 75,000
Usual Pagination: 500
Language(s): Dutch
ADVERTISING RATES:
Full Page Mono EUR 1/1: f.c. 3251,-; b/w 2121,- 1/2: f.c. 1714,-; b/w 1152,-
Agency Commission: 15%
Mechanical Data: Bleed Size: 148 x 148mm, Type Area: 128 x 128mm
CONSUMER: SPORT: Outdoor

LANDGRAAF KOERIER
17867N80-23_50
Editorial: Kerkplein 39, 6372 EZ LANDGRAAF
Tel: 35 6726751 **Fax:** 35 6726752
Email: stichting@landgraagkoerier.nl **Web site:** http://www.landgraafkoerier.nl
Date Established: 01-08-1997; **Freq:** Weekly; **Cover Price:** Free; **Circ:** 22,000
Editor: Sante Brun
Profile: Magazine containing cultural, political and general information about the Landgraaf and Eygelshoven areas.
Language(s): Dutch
Agency Commission: 15%
Mechanical Data: Type Area: 265 x 400mm, Bleed Size: 290 x 430mm
CONSUMER: RURAL & REGIONAL INTEREST

LANDMACHT
16398N40-40
Editorial: Mineurslaan 500, 3521 AG UTRECHT
Tel: 88 2697856 **Fax:** 58 2845419
Date Established: 01-01-1947; **Freq:** 10 issues yearly; **Annual Sub.:** EUR 17,-; **Circ:** 50,000
Editor: J. Evertse; **Editor-in-Chief:** C.M.J. Dalebout
Profile: Information magazine for the Dutch Army.
Language(s): Dutch
Agency Commission: 15%
Mechanical Data: Bleed Size: 210 x 285mm
BUSINESS: DEFENCE

DE LANDPACHTER
16104N21A-178_50
Editorial: Hoofdweg 1, 9621 AA SLOCHTEREN
Tel: 88 2697856 **Fax:** 70 3364601
Web site: http://www.landpachter.nl
Freq: Monthly; **Annual Sub.:** EUR 38,50; **Circ:** 2,000
Editor: J. Wierenga
Profile: Journal of the Association of Land Lessors in the Netherlands.
Language(s): Dutch
Readership: Aimed at the Association's members.
Agency Commission: 15%
BUSINESS: AGRICULTURE & FARMING

LANDSCHAP
16822N57-24
Editorial: Postbus 80123, 3508 TC UTRECHT
Tel: 71 5239058 **Fax:** 20 5159145
Email: wlo@knag.nl **Web site:** http://www.landschap.nl
Date Established: 01-01-1984; **Freq:** Quarterly;
Annual Sub.: EUR 45,-; **Circ:** 1,100
Editor: J. Vermaat
Profile: Journal concerning landscape ecology and environmental protection.
Language(s): Dutch
ADVERTISING RATES:
Full Page Mono .... EUR 1/1: b/w 500,- 1/2: b/w 300,-
Agency Commission: 15%
BUSINESS: ENVIRONMENT & POLLUTION

LANDSCHAP NOORD-HOLLAND
17873N80-640
Editorial: Rechte Hondsbosschelaan 24a, 1851 HM HEILOO **Tel:** 20 5159703 **Fax:** 314 366503
Email: info@landschapnoordholland.nl
Date Established: 01-05-1988; **Freq:** Quarterly;
Annual Sub.: EUR 22,-; **Circ:** 50,000
Editor: Johan Stuart; **Editor-in-Chief:** Frans Buissink
Profile: Magazine focusing on rural North Holland.
Language(s): Dutch
ADVERTISING RATES:
Full Page Mono EUR 1/1: f.c. 2485,-; 1/2: f.c. 1395,-; 1/4: f.c. 825,-
Agency Commission: 15%
Mechanical Data: Type Area: 185 x 267mm, Bleed Size: 215 x 297mm
Copy instructions: *Copy Date:* 3 weeks prior to publication date
CONSUMER: RURAL & REGIONAL INTEREST

LAUWERSMEER KOERIER
1634557N80-297
Editorial: Schoolstraat 6, 9974 RL ZOUTKAMP
Tel: 342 494848 **Fax:** 172 539171
Email: seal.productions@planet.nl **Web site:** http://www.lauwersmeerkoerier.nl
Date Established: 01-04-1999; **Freq:** Quarterly;
Cover Price: Free; **Circ:** 50,000
Usual Pagination: 48
Editor: G.K. Bakker; **Publisher:** G.K. Bakker
Language(s): Dutch
ADVERTISING RATES:
Full Page Mono EUR 1/1: f.c. 1288,-; b/w 859,-** 1/2: f.c. 677,-; b/w 452,-** 1/4: f.c. 391,-; b/w 261,-** 1/8: f.c. 20
Agency Commission: 15%
Mechanical Data: Type Area: 260 x 385mm, Bleed Size: 290 x 400mm
CONSUMER: RURAL & REGIONAL INTEREST

LAVA LITERAIR TIJDSCHRIFT
18027N84B-48
Editorial: Lange Leidsedwarsstraat 22a, 1017 NL AMSTERDAM
Email: info@lavaliterair.nl
Freq: 3 issues yearly; **Cover Price:** EUR 15,-
Annual Sub.: EUR 30,-; **Circ:** 250
Profile: Magazine publishing work from upcoming authors and occasionally also reviews, essays and interviews.
Language(s): Dutch
Agency Commission: 15%
CONSUMER: THE ARTS & LITERARY: Literary

LAWINE NIEUWSBRIEF
17564N74R-50
Editorial: Postbus 56690, 1040 AR AMSTERDAM
Tel: 20 4276583
Email: st.lawine@worldonline.nl
Date Established: 01-11-1998; **Freq:** Quarterly; **Circ:** 175
Usual Pagination: 16
Profile: Information magazine for Dutch women with foreign partners.
Language(s): Dutch
Agency Commission: 15%
CONSUMER: WOMEN'S INTEREST CONSUMER MAGAZINES: Women's Interest Related

LEASEPLAN DRIVE
1719582N1K-2
Editorial: Aletta Jacobslaan 7, 1066 BP AMSTERDAM **Tel:** 20 5721643 **Fax:** 20 5721521
Email: info@rhbm.nl
Freq: Half-yearly; **Circ:** 110,000
Usual Pagination: 64
Editor: M.J.J. van den Heuvel; **Editor-in-Chief:** W. Klaasse
Language(s): Dutch
ADVERTISING RATES:
Full Page Mono . EUR 1/1: f.c. 7800,-; 1/2: f.c. 3200,-
Agency Commission: 15%
Mechanical Data: Bleed Size: 215 x 280mm, Type Area: 186 x 265mm
Copy instructions: *Copy Date:* 4 weeks prior to publication date
BUSINESS: FINANCE & ECONOMICS: Rental Leasing

LEIDERDORPS WEEKBLAD
629913N72-7398
Editorial: Ambachtsweg 7a, 2222 AH KATWIJK
Tel: 88 2697856 **Fax:** 58 2845419
Web site: http://www.leiderdorpsweekblad.nl
Freq: Weekly; **Circ:** 17,000
Editor: Esdor van Elten; **Editor-in-Chief:** Corrie van der Laan; **Publisher:** G. Verhagen
Language(s): Dutch
Agency Commission: 15%
Mechanical Data: Type Area: 378 x 550mm, Bleed Size: 400 x 577mm
LOCAL NEWSPAPERS

LEIDRAAD
17982N83-243
Editorial: Postbus 9500, 2300 RA LEIDEN
Tel: 35 5480900 **Fax:** 35 5417272
Email: contact@leidraad.leidenuniv.nl
Freq: 3 issues yearly; **Cover Price:** Free; **Circ:** 55,000
Editor: Yoeri Albrecht; **Publisher:** Renee Merkx
Profile: Magazine for alumni of Leiden University.
Language(s): Dutch
Agency Commission: 15%
CONSUMER: STUDENT PUBLICATIONS

LEIDS KWARTIER
16927N88A-47
Editorial: Postbus 9500, 2300 RA LEIDEN
Tel: 20 5852111 **Fax:** 20 5854158
Email: contact@leidraad.leidenuniv.nl **Web site:** http://www.leidskwartier.nl
Date Established: 01-11-1993; **Freq:** 3 issues yearly;
Cover Price: Free; **Circ:** 16,000
Usual Pagination: 32
Editor: J. Tio
Profile: Magazine concerning education and lifestyle.
Language(s): Dutch
Readership: Aimed at secondary school students.
Agency Commission: 15%
CONSUMER: EDUCATION

LEIDS NIEUWSBLAD WEEKEND
629921N72-7444
Editorial: Boekerslootlaan 49, 2201 BT NOORDWIJK
Tel: 15 2617997 **Fax:** 71 3643461
Email: info@buijzepers.nl
Freq: Weekly; **Cover Price:** Free; **Circ:** 94,550
Language(s): Dutch
Agency Commission: 15%
Mechanical Data: Type Area: 270 x 410mm, Bleed Size: 290 x 440mm
LOCAL NEWSPAPERS

LEKKER
1634541N94G-81
Editorial: Capellalaan 65, 2132 JL HOOFDDORP
Tel: 23 5567955 **Fax:** 23 5567956
Web site: http://www.lekker.nl
Freq: Annual; **Cover Price:** EUR 9,95; **Circ:** 71,787

Editor: Makkie Mulder; **Editor-in-Chief:** Mara Grimm; **Publisher:** Anneliese Bergman
Language(s): Dutch
ADVERTISING RATES:
Full Page Mono EUR 1/1: b/w 7400,- 1/2: b/w 4425,- 1/4: b/w 2225,-
Agency Commission: 15%
Mechanical Data: Type Area: 185 x 267mm, Bleed Size: 210 x 287mm
CONSUMER: OTHER CLASSIFICATIONS: Restaurant Guides

LEVE JE LIJF-BLAD
17497N74H-214
Editorial: Vijverweg 18, 2061 GX BLOEMENDAAL
Tel: 570 647730 **Fax:** 570 647815
Email: info@vdbj.nl
Date Established: 02-02-2004; **Freq:** 5 issues yearly; **Cover Price:** Free; **Circ:** 500,000
Profile: Magazine containing information about products sold in chemists and perfumeries.
Language(s): Dutch
ADVERTISING RATES:
Full Page Mono EUR 2/1: f.c. 22.000; 1/1: f.c. 12.500
Agency Commission: 15%
Mechanical Data: Bleed Size: 173 x 224mm
CONSUMER: WOMEN'S INTEREST CONSUMER MAGAZINES: Hair & Beauty

DE LEVENDE NATUUR
17905N57-24_25
Editorial: Lekkumerweg 87, 9081 AK LEKKUM
Tel: 20 5159172 **Fax:** 20 5159145
Email: bestuur@delevendenatuur.nl **Web site:** http://www.delevendenatuur.nl
Date Established: 01-03-1896; **Freq:** 6 issues yearly; **Annual Sub.:** EUR 29,50; **Circ:** 2,400
Editor: B.F. van Tooren; **Editor-in-Chief:** Isa Schimmel-ten Kate
Profile: Magazine covering nature protection, nature development, nature conservation and management.
Language(s): Dutch
Readership: Aimed at those with an interest in protecting the natural environment, in particular managers and policy makers.
ADVERTISING RATES:
Full Page Mono EUR 1/1: f.c. 904,-; 1/2: f.c. 641,-; 1/4: f.c. 510,-
Agency Commission: 15%
Mechanical Data: Type Area: 188 x 264mm, Bleed Size: 210 x 297mm
Copy instructions: *Copy Date:* 8 weeks prior to publication date
BUSINESS: ENVIRONMENT & POLLUTION

LEVENSMIDDELENKRANT
16162N22A-55
Editorial: Anne Hendrik Kooistrastraat 140, 2441 CP NIEUWVEEN **Tel:** 58 2954859 **Fax:** 172 539171
Web site: http://www.levensmiddelenkrant.nl
Freq: 26 issues yearly; **Annual Sub.:** EUR 136,-; **Circ:** 10,142
Usual Pagination: 20
Editor: Willem-Paul de Mooij; **Editor-in-Chief:** Ruth Eppink; **Publisher:** Katja Riethof
Profile: Magazine containing news about food retailing and products.
Language(s): Dutch
Readership: Aimed at decision makers and personnel in the food retail industry.
ADVERTISING RATES:
Full Page Mono EUR 2/1: f.c. 6950,-; 1/1: f.c. 5350,-; 1/2: f.c. 3950,-
Agency Commission: 15%
Mechanical Data: Type Area: 280 x 410mm, Bleed Size: 300 x 440mm
BUSINESS: FOOD

LEVENSSTROOM
1634064N87-2656
Editorial: Elisabethhof 5, 2353 EW LEIDERDORP
Tel: 88 2944900 **Fax:** 35 6728834
Email: info@levensstroom.nl
Date Established: 01-09-1992; **Freq:** Quarterly; **Annual Sub.:** EUR 7,50; **Circ:** 100,000
Usual Pagination: 48
Editor: J.P.H. Zijlstra; **Editor-in-Chief:** J.P.H. Zijlstra
Language(s): Dutch
Agency Commission: 15%
Mechanical Data: Type Area: 183 x 256mm, Bleed Size: 210 x 297mm
CONSUMER: RELIGIOUS

LIEF!
1896836N74Q-501
Editorial: Buiten Molenstraat 7, 4101 CJ CULEMBORG **Tel:** 30 6383716
Email: redactie@kolkengeense.nl **Web site:** http://www.liefmagazine.nl
Freq: Quarterly; **Cover Price:** EUR 4,95
Annual Sub.: EUR 19,35; **Circ:** 50,000
Editor: Marijke Kolk; **Publisher:** Marijke Kolk
Language(s): Dutch
ADVERTISING RATES:
Full Page Mono EUR 2/1: f.c. 8500,-; 1/1: f.c. 5000,-; 1/2: f.c. 2950,-
Agency Commission: 15%
Mechanical Data: Type Area: 195 x 257mm, Bleed Size: 225 x 287mm
CONSUMER: WOMEN'S INTEREST CONSUMER MAGAZINES: Lifestyle

LIFE AND STUDY IN HOLLAND
18108N88B-130
Editorial: Kortenaerkade 11, 2518 AX DEN HAAG
Tel: 75 6813545 **Fax:** 75 6813535
Email: nuffic@nuffic.nl **Web site:** http://www.studyinholland.nl
Date Established: 01-01-1995; **Freq:** Annual; **Cover Price:** Free; **Circ:** 30,000
Profile: Journal containing information about studying in the Netherlands.
Language(s): Dutch
Readership: Aimed at foreign students.
Agency Commission: 15%
Mechanical Data: Type Area: 130 x 180mm, Bleed Size: 148 x 210mm
CONSUMER: EDUCATION: Adult Education

LIFELINE
18096N87-153
Editorial: Postbus 1505, 1300 BM ALMERE
Tel: 20 5206064
Email: info@lifeblad.nl **Web site:** http://www.lifeblad.nl
Freq: Quarterly; **Cover Price:** Free; **Circ:** 6,800
Editor: F.T.J. Danenberg; **Editor-in-Chief:** F.T.J. Danenberg
Profile: Evangelical magazine containing articles on religion, world news, science, social and political issues.
Language(s): Dutch
Agency Commission: 15%
CONSUMER: RELIGIOUS

LIFESTYLE MAGAZINE
629533N74C-52
Editorial: Bedrijvenpark Eschendael, Haarweg 15, 7651 KE TUBBERGEN **Tel:** 20 5245524
Fax: 20 5159040
Web site: http://www.lifestyle.nl
Date Established: 01-12-1994; **Freq:** Quarterly; **Cover Price:** EUR 4,25
Annual Sub.: EUR 17,-; **Circ:** 51,000
Editor: Anette Ripolli; **Editor-in-Chief:** Martin Paalhaar; **Publisher:** Hans Bake
Profile: Magazine focusing on the family. Includes travel, recreation and fashion.
Language(s): Dutch
Readership: Read by men and women aged between 25 and 45 years.
ADVERTISING RATES:
Full Page Mono EUR 2/1: b/w 3905,- 1/1: b/w 2485,- 1/2: b/w 1339,-
Agency Commission: 15%
Mechanical Data: Type Area: 203 x 276mm, Bleed Size: 230 x 300mm
Copy instructions: *Copy Date:* 3 weeks prior to publication date
CONSUMER: WOMEN'S INTEREST CONSUMER MAGAZINES: Home & Family

LIFT MAGAZINE
17623N75L-250
Editorial: Winthontlaan 200, 3526 KV UTRECHT
Tel: 23 5461122 **Fax:** 23 5561177
Email: maruba@maruba.com
Freq: 8 issues yearly; **Cover Price:** EUR 3,95
Annual Sub.: EUR 29,-; **Circ:** 35,000
Editor: Arjan Kruik
Profile: Magazine covering outdoor sports such as mountaineering, walking, trekking, climbing, lightweight camping and rafting as well as adventurous travelling and holidays.
Language(s): Dutch
Readership: Aimed at enthusiasts of outdoor activities.
ADVERTISING RATES:
Full Page Mono EUR 2/1: f.c. 7800,-; 1/1: f.c. 4000,-; 1/2: f.c. 2200,-
Agency Commission: 15%
Mechanical Data: Type Area: 220 x 280mm, Bleed Size: 240 x 300mm
Copy instructions: *Copy Date:* 3 weeks prior to publication date
CONSUMER: SPORT: Outdoor

LIFTINSTITUUT-MAGAZINE
16053N19A-53
Editorial: Buikslotermeerplein 381, 1025 XE AMSTERDAM **Tel:** 30 6383766 **Fax:** 30 6383991
Email: info@liftinstituut.nl
Freq: Quarterly; **Annual Sub.:** EUR 22,95; **Circ:** 3,200
Usual Pagination: 36
Editor: Koos van Lindenberg; **Editor-in-Chief:** E. Jelierse
Profile: Journal focusing on the lift industry, with special reference to safety measures for lifts and escalators.
Language(s): Dutch
Agency Commission: 15%
BUSINESS: ENGINEERING & MACHINERY

LIJF & LEVEN
1857846N32G-336
Editorial: Lt. Generaal van Heutszlaan 4, 3743 JN BAARN **Tel:** 40 8447611 **Fax:** 53 4842189
Email: informatie@axioma.nl
Freq: 3 issues yearly; **Cover Price:** Free; **Circ:** 83,000
Editor: Peter Bierhaus
Language(s): Dutch
ADVERTISING RATES:
Full Page Mono .... EUR 2/1: f.c. 3983,-; ** 1/1: f.c. 2096,-; ** 1/2: f.c. 1258,-; ** 1/4: f.c. 755,-
Agency Commission: 15%

Mechanical Data: Type Area: 185 x 243mm, Bleed Size: 210 x 274mm
BUSINESS: LOCAL GOVERNMENT, LEISURE & RECREATION: Community Care & Social Services

LIMBURGS DAGBLAD
17115N67B-4750
Editorial: Mercator 3, 6135 KW SITTARD
Tel: 46 4116600 **Fax:** 46 4116310
Web site: http://www.ld.nl
Date Established: 26-10-1918; **Freq:** 312 issues yearly; **Annual Sub.:** EUR 259,95; **Circ:** 43,730
Editor: H. Paulissen
Language(s): Dutch
ADVERTISING RATES:
Full Page Mono EUR 1/2: b/w 8149,- 1/4: b/w 4075,- ed. za. 1/2: b/w 8838,- ed. za. 1/4: b/w 4419,-
Agency Commission: 15%
Mechanical Data: Type Area: 266 x 395mm
REGIONAL DAILY & SUNDAY NEWSPAPERS: Regional Daily Newspapers

LIMOSA
17935N81F-30
Editorial: Posthoornsteeg 1c, 8911 AS LEEUWARDEN **Tel:** 46 4116600
Freq: Quarterly; **Annual Sub.:** EUR 19,-; **Circ:** 2,100
Editor: Romke Kleefstra; **Editor-in-Chief:** Kees Koffijberg
Profile: Publication of the Netherlands Ornithology Society and SOVON - the Society of Bird Research in the Netherlands.
Language(s): Dutch
Readership: Read by biologists with special interest in birds.
Agency Commission: 15%
Mechanical Data: Bleed Size: 198 x 270mm
CONSUMER: ANIMALS & PETS: Birds

LINDA
1643650N74A-227
Editorial: Adriaan Dortsmanplein 3, 1411 RC NAARDEN **Tel:** 23 5565462 **Fax:** 23 5564588
Email: info@moodformagazines.nl **Web site:** http://www.lindamagazine.nl
Date Established: 01-01-2003; **Freq:** Monthly; **Cover Price:** EUR 5,50
Annual Sub.: EUR 66,-; **Circ:** 168,905
Editor: Jildou van der Bijl; **Editor-in-Chief:** Margot Jamnisek; **Publisher:** Rozemarijn de Witte
Language(s): Dutch
ADVERTISING RATES:
Full Page Mono .... EUR 1/1: f.c. 11.535,-
Agency Commission: 15%
Mechanical Data: Type Area: 195 x 241mm, Bleed Size: 230 x 275mm
CONSUMER: WOMEN'S INTEREST CONSUMER MAGAZINES: Women's Interest

LINDA.MAN
1776523N86C-254
Editorial: Adriaan Dortsmanplein 3, 1411 RC NAARDEN **Tel:** 35 7999333 **Fax:** 24 3723631
Email: info@moodformagazines.nl
Date Established: 23-05-2006; **Freq:** Annual; **Cover Price:** EUR 5,25; **Circ:** 76,989
Editor: Rozemarijn de Witte; **Editor-in-Chief:** M. Bleeker; **Publisher:** Rozemarijn de Witte
Language(s): Dutch
ADVERTISING RATES:
Full Page Mono .... EUR 1/1: f.c. 7920,-
Agency Commission: 15%
Mechanical Data: Type Area: 195 x 241mm, Bleed Size: 230 x 275mm
Copy instructions: *Copy Date:* 4 weeks prior to publication date
CONSUMER: ADULT & GAY MAGAZINES: Men's Lifestyle Magazines

LINDA.WONEN.
1776524N74A-233
Editorial: Adriaan Dortsmanplein 3, 1411 RC NAARDEN **Tel:** 35 7999333 **Fax:** 24 3723631
Email: info@moodformagazines.nl
Date Established: 21-09-2006; **Freq:** Annual; **Cover Price:** EUR 5,25; **Circ:** 57,825
Editor: Linda de Mol; **Editor-in-Chief:** M. Bleeker; **Publisher:** Rozemarijn de Witte
Language(s): Dutch
ADVERTISING RATES:
Full Page Mono .... EUR 1/1: f.c. 7920,-
Agency Commission: 15%
Mechanical Data: Type Area: 195 x 241mm, Bleed Size: 230 x 275mm
Copy instructions: *Copy Date:* 4 weeks prior to publication date
CONSUMER: WOMEN'S INTEREST CONSUMER MAGAZINES: Women's Interest

LINK MODEVAKBLAD
708166N47A-38
Editorial: Haarlemmermeerstraat 26, 1058 KA AMSTERDAM **Tel:** 172 466622 **Fax:** 24 3723631
Web site: http://www.linkmag.nl
Freq: Quarterly; **Cover Price:** EUR 9,95
Annual Sub.: EUR 40,-; **Circ:** 6,760
Editor: Esther van Maurik; **Publisher:** Esther van Maurik
Profile: Magazine featuring the latest developments in the fashion world.
Language(s): Dutch
Readership: Aimed at professionals in the fashion industry.

ADVERTISING RATES:
Full Page Mono EUR 2/1: f.c. 6950,-; 1/1: f.c. 3770,-; 1/2: f.c. 2630,-
Agency Commission: 15%
Mechanical Data: Type Area: 216 x 286mm, Bleed Size: 230 x 300mm
BUSINESS: CLOTHING & TEXTILES

LIV
1635322N77A-294
Editorial: Stationsweg 2, 4153 RD BEESD
Tel: 20 5629222 **Fax:** 20 5626289
Freq: 3 issues yearly; **Cover Price:** Free; **Circ:** 125,000
Usual Pagination: 48
Editor: M.J.J. van den Heuvel; **Editor-in-Chief:** Nina Knobbe
Language(s): Dutch
ADVERTISING RATES:
Full Page Mono .... EUR 1/1: b/w 4800,-
Agency Commission: 15%
Mechanical Data: Type Area: 190 x 259mm, Bleed Size: 220 x 280mm
CONSUMER: MOTORING & CYCLING: Motoring

LIVECOMM
15601N2C-20
Editorial: Schatbeurderlaan 6, 6002 ED WEERT
Tel: 30 6383743 **Fax:** 229 216416
Email: info@louwersuitgevers.nl **Web site:** http://www.livecomm.nl
Freq: 6 issues yearly; **Annual Sub.:** EUR 45,-; **Circ:** 4,500
Editor: Ted Wesselius
Profile: Magazine focusing on exhibitions and conferences throughout the Netherlands.
Language(s): Dutch
Readership: Aimed at event organisers and personnel and marketing managers.
ADVERTISING RATES:
Full Page Mono EUR 1/1: f.c. 1650,-; 1/2: f.c. 1050,-; 1/4: f.c. 650,-
Agency Commission: 15%
Mechanical Data: Type Area: 197 x 267mm, Bleed Size: 230 x 297mm
Copy instructions: *Copy Date:* 4 weeks prior to publication date
BUSINESS: COMMUNICATIONS, ADVERTISING & MARKETING: Conferences & Exhibitions

LIVEXS
629759N76E-40
Editorial: Nachtwachtlaan 155, 1058 EE AMSTERDAM **Tel:** 76 5301715 **Fax:** 70 3045808
Email: info@livexs.nl **Web site:** http://www.livexs.nl
Date Established: 01-09-1998; **Freq:** 10 issues yearly; **Annual Sub.:** EUR 24,99; **Circ:** 50,000
Editor: Anton Slotboom; **Editor-in-Chief:** Patrick Oxsener
Profile: Pop magazine covering news, interviews and music festivals in Netherlands.
Language(s): Dutch
Readership: Aimed at music fans of all ages.
ADVERTISING RATES:
Full Page Mono EUR 2/1: f.c. 7580,-; b/w 5500,- 1/1: f.c. 3790,-; b/w 2750,- 1/2: f.c. 2550,-; b/w 1520,-
Agency Commission: 15%
Mechanical Data: Bleed Size: 210 x 280mm, Type Area: 190 x 260mm
Copy instructions: *Copy Date:* 2 weeks prior to publication date
CONSUMER: MUSIC & PERFORMING ARTS: Pop Music

LOKALE POST
1634901N80-311
Editorial: Paaldijk 95, 1689 WE ZWAAG
Tel: 23 5565370 **Fax:** 23 5565357
Email: deatlas@cs.com
Date Established: 01-01-1977; **Freq:** Quarterly; **Cover Price:** Free; **Circ:** 249,000
Language(s): Dutch
ADVERTISING RATES:
Full Page Mono ..... EUR 1/1: f.c. 595,-; 1/2: f.c. 380,-
Agency Commission: 15%
Mechanical Data: Type Area: 266 x 390mm, Bleed Size: 290 x 415mm
CONSUMER: RURAL & REGIONAL INTEREST

LOONEY TUNES AGENDA
1634567N88R-39
Editorial: Reaal 2b, 2353 TL LEIDERDORP
Tel: 35 6726800 **Fax:** 35 6726803
Email: info@stationeryteam.nl
Freq: Annual; **Cover Price:** EUR 9,95; **Circ:** 50,000
Publisher: M. Leguijt
Language(s): Dutch
Agency Commission: 15%
Mechanical Data: Bleed Size: 140 x 188mm
CONSUMER: EDUCATION: Education Related

LOS MAGAZINE
1900598N74Q-509
Editorial: Maresingel 6, 2316 HA LEIDEN
Tel: 30 6383716 **Fax:** 73 6157171
Email: contact@v6k.eu **Web site:** http://www.los-online.nl
Freq: Monthly; **Cover Price:** Free; **Circ:** 60,000
Editor: Richard Post
Language(s): Dutch
ADVERTISING RATES:
Full Page Mono .. EUR 1/1: b/w 1395,- 1/2: b/w 795,- 1/4: b/w 495,-
Agency Commission: 15%

Mechanical Data: Type Area: 194 x 267mm
CONSUMER: WOMEN'S INTEREST CONSUMER MAGAZINES: Lifestyle

LOURENS J.C. 1635636N80-359
Editorial: Keienbergweg 81, 1101 GE AMSTERDAM
Tel: 88 2944819 **Fax:** 30 6383991
Web site: http://www.lourens.nl
Date Established: 01-01-1989; **Freq:** Quarterly;
Cover Price: Free; **Circ:** 135,000
Editor: Mirjam Dijkstra
Language(s): Dutch
ADVERTISING RATES:
Full Page Mono EUR 2/1: f.c. 2250,-; 1/1: f.c. 1525,-; 1/2: f.c. 925,-
Agency Commission: 15%
Mechanical Data: Type Area: 182 x 262mm, Bleed Size: 225 x 297mm
Copy instructions: *Copy Date:* 5 weeks prior to publication date
CONSUMER: RURAL & REGIONAL INTEREST

LUCHTVRACHT 15789N6A-60
Editorial: Minervaplein 22-3, 1077 TR AMSTERDAM
Tel: 46 4116600 **Fax:** 71 3643461
Date Established: 01-01-1969; **Freq:** Quarterly;
Annual Sub.: EUR 35,-; **Circ:** 4,500
Editor: M. Ouwendijk; **Publisher:** C.G. Hundepool
Profile: Magazine focusing on the air freight industry and logistic services.
Language(s): Dutch
Readership: Aimed at shippers, forwarders and others involved in the air cargo industry.
ADVERTISING RATES:
Full Page Mono EUR 1/1: b/w 1750,- 1/2: b/w 1225,- 1/4: b/w 790,-
Agency Commission: 15%
Mechanical Data: Type Area: 190 x 252mm, Bleed Size: 210 x 297mm
Copy instructions: *Copy Date:* 3 weeks prior to publication date
BUSINESS: AVIATION & AERONAUTICS

LUCIFER 18251N94X-100
Editorial: De Ruijterstraat 74, 2518 AV DEN HAAG
Tel: 20 5159743 **Fax:** 20 6272709
Email: luciferred@stichtingisis.org
Date Established: 21-03-1979; **Freq:** 6 issues yearly;
Annual Sub.: EUR 25,-; **Circ:** 800
Usual Pagination: 32
Editor: H.C. Vermeulen; **Editor-in-Chief:** B. Voorham
Profile: Theosophical magazine.
Language(s): Dutch
Agency Commission: 15%
Mechanical Data: Type Area: 214 x 280mm, Bleed Size: 165 x 216mm
CONSUMER: OTHER CLASSIFICATIONS: Miscellaneous

MAARTEN! 1899447N82-580
Editorial: Wildenborch 5, 1112 XB DIEMEN
Tel: 30 6383716 **Fax:** 73 6157171
Freq: 6 issues yearly; **Cover Price:** EUR 6,95
Annual Sub.: EUR 39,50; **Circ:** 23,778
Editor: Maarten van Rossem; **Publisher:** Hans van Vloten
Language(s): Dutch
ADVERTISING RATES:
Full Page Mono EUR 2/1: f.c. 9390,-; PMS 8395,-; b/w 7875,- 1/1: f.c. 4950,-; PMS 4275,-; b/w 3935,- 1/2: f.c. 2750,-;
Agency Commission: 15%
Mechanical Data: Type Area: 175 x 255mm, Bleed Size: 210 x 280mm
Copy instructions: *Copy Date:* 3 weeks prior to publication date
CONSUMER: CURRENT AFFAIRS & POLITICS

MAASTRICHT: STADSGIDS 1633251N89A-267
Editorial: Kleine Staat 1, 6211 ED MAASTRICHT
Tel: 45 5604070 **Fax:** 70 3839840
Email: info@vvvmaastricht.nl
Date Established: 01-01-1984; **Freq:** Annual; **Cover Price:** Free; **Circ:** 100,000
Editor: Laura Damoiseaux; **Editor-in-Chief:** Laura Damoiseaux
Language(s): Dutch
ADVERTISING RATES:
Full Page Mono .. EUR 1/1: f.c. 1625,-; 1/2: f.c. 825,-; 1/4: f.c. 445,-
Agency Commission: 15%
Mechanical Data: Type Area: 150 x 193mm, Bleed Size: 150 x 193mm
CONSUMER: HOLIDAYS & TRAVEL: Travel

MAATWERK 17790N32G-90
Editorial: Het Spoor 2, 3994 AK HOUTEN
Tel: 172 575581 **Fax:** 23 5565136
Freq: 6 issues yearly; **Annual Sub.:** EUR 58,95; **Circ:** 5,100
Profile: Magazine covering all aspects of the profession of a social worker.
Language(s): Dutch
Readership: Aimed at social workers.
ADVERTISING RATES:
Full Page Mono .. EUR 1/1: f.c. 2185,-; b/w 821,- 1/2: f.c. 1367,-; b/w 514,- 1/4: f.c. 815,-; b/w 307,-
Agency Commission: 15%

Mechanical Data: Type Area: 172 x 260mm, Bleed Size: 210 x 297mm
BUSINESS: LOCAL GOVERNMENT, LEISURE & RECREATION: Community Care & Social Services

---

MACFAN 15760N5C-60
Editorial: Cyclaamrood 2, 2718 SE ZOETERMEER
Tel: 10 2894015 **Fax:** 20 6159047
Email: info@divo.nl **Web site:** http://www.macfan.nl
Date Established: 01-05-1995; **Freq:** 6 issues yearly;
Cover Price: EUR 7,95
Annual Sub.: EUR 40,-; **Circ:** 20,700
Usual Pagination: 84
Editor: Miro Lucassen; **Publisher:** Jan van Die
Profile: Magazine about Apple Macintosh computers.
Language(s): Dutch
ADVERTISING RATES:
Full Page Mono EUR 1/1: f.c. 1750,-; b/w 1400,- 1/2: f.c. 900,-; b/w 750,- 1/4: f.c. 475,-; b/w 400,-
Agency Commission: 15%
Mechanical Data: Type Area: 185 x 270mm, Bleed Size: 210 x 297mm
BUSINESS: COMPUTERS & AUTOMATION: Professional Personal Computers

---

MAF LUCHTPOST 1635981N87-2468
Editorial: Van Leeuwenhoekstraat 20-1, 3846 CB HARDERWIJK **Tel:** 88 2697112 **Fax:** 88 2696983
Email: info@maf.nl
Date Established: 01-12-1987; **Freq:** Quarterly;
Cover Price: Free; **Circ:** 34,000
Usual Pagination: 12
Editor-in-Chief: C. Zwanenburg
Language(s): Dutch
Agency Commission: 15%
CONSUMER: RELIGIOUS

LE MAGAZINE 1809300N74Q-360
Editorial: Europalaan 30, 3526 KS UTRECHT
Tel: 20 5473633
Date Established: 01-11-2006; **Freq:** 6 issues yearly;
Cover Price: Free; **Circ:** 250,000
Editor: Ico van Rheenen; **Editor-in-Chief:** J. van Haastert
Language(s): Dutch
ADVERTISING RATES:
Full Page Mono .... EUR 1/1: f.c. 6500,-
Agency Commission: 15%
Mechanical Data: Bleed Size: 225 x 280mm
CONSUMER: WOMEN'S INTEREST CONSUMER MAGAZINES: Lifestyle

MAGAZINE VROUWEN EN GEZONDHEID 16684N56A-64_14
Editorial: Meibergdreef 15, 1105 AZ AMSTERDAM
Tel: 20 5159743
Freq: Half-yearly; **Circ:** 70
Editor: C.J. Moerman
Profile: Official publication of the Dutch Foundation of Women and Health Research.
Language(s): Dutch
Readership: Read by women's policy makers and health care providers.
Agency Commission: 15%
BUSINESS: HEALTH & MEDICAL

MAIL! 1636457N14R-233
Editorial: Prinses Beatrixlaan 23, 2595 AK DEN HAAG **Tel:** 70 3342179 **Fax:** 20 5979490
Email: mail@tntpost.nl
Freq: 16 issues yearly; **Cover Price:** Free; **Circ:** 85,000
Editor-in-Chief: Lotte van Doorn
Language(s): Dutch
Agency Commission: 15%
Mechanical Data: Bleed Size: 410 x 290mm
BUSINESS: COMMERCE, INDUSTRY & MANAGEMENT: Commerce Related

MAINLINE 16800N56R-33
Editorial: Postbus 58303, 1040 HH AMSTERDAM
Tel: 33 4220082 **Fax:** 20 5465530
Email: info@mainline.nl
Freq: Quarterly; **Annual Sub.:** EUR 27,50; **Circ:** 12,000
Editor: J. Schupp
Profile: Magazine focusing on health and the effects of drugs.
Language(s): Dutch
Agency Commission: 15%
BUSINESS: HEALTH & MEDICAL: Health Medical Related

DE MAKELAAR 15530N1E-55
Editorial: Leidse Rijn 7, 3454 PZ DE MEERN
Tel: 412 452331 **Fax:** 20 6269407
Email: info@wegenermedia.nl
Date Established: 01-01-1981; **Freq:** Monthly; **Circ:** 217,000
Editor: Mart Jochemsen; **Editor-in-Chief:** Frank Kuijpers
Profile: Magazine containing articles about the property trade, includes information about properties for sale in the Utrecht region.
Language(s): Dutch

ADVERTISING RATES:
Full Page Mono EUR 1/1: f.c. 4870,-; 1/2: f.c. 2647,-; 1/4: f.c. 1415,-
Agency Commission: 15%
Mechanical Data: Type Area: 264 x 398mm
BUSINESS: FINANCE & ECONOMICS: Property

MAKRO GASTVRIJ 1637431N11A-162
Editorial: Doetinchemseweg 59, 7007 CB DOETINCHEM **Tel:** 30 6383767 **Fax:** 314 340515
Email: info@mcp.nl
Date Established: 01-01-2003; **Freq:** Quarterly;
Cover Price: Free; **Circ:** 50,000
Usual Pagination: 40
Editor: Ad van der Salm; **Editor-in-Chief:** E. Knoppert
Language(s): Dutch
ADVERTISING RATES:
Full Page Mono EUR 1/1: b/w 6975,- 1/2: b/w 3900,- 1/4: b/w 2290,-
Agency Commission: 15%
Mechanical Data: Type Area: 204 x 270mm, Bleed Size: 230 x 300mm
BUSINESS: CATERING: Catering, Hotels & Restaurants

MAL & MASKER 16413N41A-142
Editorial: Postbus 6118, 5600 HC EINDHOVEN
Tel: 20 5922250 **Fax:** 30 6348909
Email: info@poost.nl **Web site:** http://www.poost.nl/malmasker
Freq: Quarterly; **Cover Price:** Free; **Circ:** 150
Editor: R. Paré
Profile: Journal about graphic design, multimedia, digital imaging, photography, art and printing.
Language(s): Dutch
Readership: Read by professionals in the graphic design industry.
ADVERTISING RATES:
Full Page Mono .... EUR 1/1: f.c. 250,-; b/w 150,-
Agency Commission: 15%
Mechanical Data: Bleed Size: 210 x 297mm
BUSINESS: PRINTING & STATIONERY: Printing

MAMMAZONE 17488N74G-38
Editorial: Churchilllaan 11-2, 3527 GV UTRECHT
Tel: 30 2321276 **Fax:** 317 424060
Email: info@borstkankervereniging.nl
Date Established: 01-03-1981; **Freq:** Quarterly;
Annual Sub.: EUR 25,-; **Circ:** 6,500
Usual Pagination: 28
Editor: S. Brendel; **Editor-in-Chief:** N.J. Ekama-van Dorsten
Profile: Magazine about the treatment of breast cancer.
Language(s): Dutch
Readership: Aimed at those with, or who have had breast cancer as well as people who belong to a genetically at risk group.
Agency Commission: 15%
CONSUMER: WOMEN'S INTEREST CONSUMER MAGAZINES: Slimming & Health

---

MANAGEMENT CONTROL & ACCOUNTING (MCA) 15499N1B-51
Editorial: Staverenstraat 32015, 7418 CJ DEVENTER
Tel: 570 647698 **Fax:** 570 614795
Email: info@kluwer.nl
Date Established: 01-01-1997; **Freq:** 6 issues yearly;
Annual Sub.: EUR 164,-; **Circ:** 8,887
Editor: Eddy Vaassen; **Editor-in-Chief:** Frieda Crince le Roy
Profile: Journal containing articles and information for financial executives and controllers.
Language(s): Dutch
ADVERTISING RATES:
Full Page Mono EUR 1/1: f.c. 3350,-; b/w 2100,- 1/2: f.c. 2150,-; b/w 1350,- 1/4: f.c. 1250,-; b/w 775,-
Agency Commission: 15%
Mechanical Data: Type Area: 180 x 260mm, Bleed Size: 210 x 297mm
BUSINESS: FINANCE & ECONOMICS: Accountancy

MANAGEMENT EN LITERATUUR 1634434N14R-139
Editorial: Jan van Galenstraat 7, 3115 JG SCHIEDAM **Tel:** 570 647102 **Fax:** 570 647533
Web site: http://www.managementenliteratuur.nl
Date Established: 01-09-1995; **Freq:** 11 issues yearly; **Annual Sub.:** EUR 19,50; **Circ:** 75,000
Editor: Pierre Pieterse; **Editor-in-Chief:** Justin van Lopik
Language(s): Dutch
ADVERTISING RATES:
Full Page Mono EUR 1/1: f.c. 3750,-; 1/2: f.c. 1975,-; 1/4: f.c. 1050,-
Agency Commission: 15%
Mechanical Data: Type Area: 297 x 420mm, Bleed Size: 267 x 375mm
BUSINESS: COMMERCE, INDUSTRY & MANAGEMENT: Commerce Related

MANAGEMENT INFO 15878N14A-120
Editorial: Bedrijvenpark Eschendael, Haarweg 15, 7651 KE TUBBERGEN **Tel:** 35 6726880
Fax: 23 5564911
Web site: http://www.management-info.nl

Date Established: 01-01-1985; **Freq:** Quarterly;
Annual Sub.: EUR 17,47; **Circ:** 51,000
Editor: Bart Luteijn; **Publisher:** Hans Bake
Profile: Magazine covering all aspects of business management.
Language(s): Dutch
ADVERTISING RATES:
Full Page Mono EUR 1/1: b/w 3857,- 1/2: b/w 2700,- 1/4: b/w 1361,-
Agency Commission: 15%
Mechanical Data: Type Area: 235 x 338mm, Bleed Size: 265 x 360mm
BUSINESS: COMMERCE, INDUSTRY & MANAGEMENT

MANAGEMENT KINDEROPVANG 16314N32G-100
Editorial: Radarweg 29, 1043 NX AMSTERDAM
Tel: 20 5159726 **Fax:** 20 5159814
Email: info@reedbusiness.nl
Freq: 10 issues yearly; **Cover Price:** EUR 15,-
Annual Sub.: EUR 145,-; **Circ:** 2,166
Editor: Marike Vroom; **Publisher:** Ben Konings
Profile: Publication focusing on childcare management.
Language(s): Dutch
ADVERTISING RATES:
Full Page Mono EUR 1/1: f.c. 2243,-; b/w 1155,- 1/2: f.c. 1551,-; b/w 647,- 1/4: f.c. 1108,-; b/w 352,-
Agency Commission: 15%
Mechanical Data: Type Area: 185 x 270mm, Bleed Size: 210 x 297mm
BUSINESS: LOCAL GOVERNMENT, LEISURE & RECREATION: Community Care & Social Services

---

MANAGEMENT SCOPE 15879N14A-123
Editorial: Kerkstraat 54, 1191 JD OUDERKERK A/D AMSTEL **Tel:** 20 3113797 **Fax:** 30 6007595
Email: info@scopebusinessmedia.nl **Web site:** http://www.managementscope.nl
Freq: 10 issues yearly; **Cover Price:** EUR 9,45
Annual Sub.: EUR 94,50; **Circ:** 52,641
Editor-in-Chief: Nicole Gommers; **Publisher:** Walter Vesters
Profile: Business and management magazine covering interviews and debate articles. Top managers and directors are interviewed by colleagues and topics discussed include leadership, business strategy, innovations, training, marketing, finance and taxation issues, human resource management, legal matters and media communication.
Language(s): Dutch
Readership: Aimed at senior managers of medium sized and large companies and organisations.
ADVERTISING RATES:
Full Page Mono EUR 1/1: f.c. 7450,-; 1/2: f.c. 4475,-; 1/4: f.c. 2425,-
Agency Commission: 15%
Mechanical Data: Type Area: 175 x 239mm, Bleed Size: 210 x 276mm
Copy instructions: *Copy Date:* 2 weeks prior to publication date
BUSINESS: COMMERCE, INDUSTRY & MANAGEMENT

MANNENMODE 16530N47A-50
Editorial: Straatweg 28, 3604 BB MAARSSEN
Tel: 30 6383743 **Fax:** 20 5159700
Email: info@blauwmedia.com **Web site:** http://www.vakbladmannenmode.nl
Freq: Quarterly; **Annual Sub.:** EUR 48,60; **Circ:** 2,264
Publisher: Henk Louwmans
Profile: Magazine covering the men's clothing trade.
Language(s): Dutch
Readership: Aimed at people involved in the retail and wholesale industry in men's clothing in The Netherlands.
ADVERTISING RATES:
Full Page Mono EUR 2/1: f.c. 4600,-; 1/1: f.c. 2875,-; 1/2: f.c. 1580,-
Agency Commission: 15%
Mechanical Data: Type Area: 220 x 300mm, Bleed Size: 235 x 322mm
BUSINESS: CLOTHING & TEXTILES

DE MANTELZORGER 1799367N74G-298
Editorial: J.F. Kennedylaan 99, 3981 GB BUNNIK
Tel: 314 359940
Email: info@mezzo.nl **Web site:** http://www.mantelzorg.nl
Freq: Annual; **Cover Price:** Free; **Circ:** 110,000
Editor-in-Chief: Fleur Kusters
Language(s): Dutch
ADVERTISING RATES:
Full Page Mono EUR 1/1: f.c. 5000,-; b/w 4500,- 1/2: f.c. 3000,-; b/w 2700,- 1/4: f.c. 1800,-; b/w 1650,-
Agency Commission: 15%
CONSUMER: WOMEN'S INTEREST CONSUMER MAGAZINES: Slimming & Health

---

MARIE CLAIRE 17421N74A-120
Editorial: Capellalaan 65, 2132 JL HOOFDDORP
Tel: 23 5565330 **Fax:** 23 5565319
Web site: http://www.marieclaire.nl
Date Established: 01-01-1990; **Freq:** Monthly;
Cover Price: EUR 4,75
Annual Sub.: EUR 54,-; **Circ:** 86,187
Editor: May-Britt Mobach; **Publisher:** Sanne Visser

Profile: Magazine containing articles on homes, fashion, beauty, travel, leisure and also human interest stories.
Language(s): Dutch
Readership: Aimed at women.
ADVERTISING RATES:
Full Page Mono .... EUR 2/1: f.c. 18.400,-; 1/1: f.c. 9200,-; 1/2: f.c. 5520,-
Agency Commission: 15%
Mechanical Data: Type Area: 180 x 232mm, Bleed Size: 213 x 268mm
CONSUMER: WOMEN'S INTEREST CONSUMER MAGAZINES: Women's Interest

MARITIEM NEDERLAND
16498N45A-73
Editorial: Rijswijkseweg 60, 2516 DEN HAAG
Tel: 75 6813545
Email: info@betapublishers.nl **Web site:** http://www.maritiemnederland.nl
Freq: 10 issues yearly; **Annual Sub.:** EUR 76,50; **Circ:** 5,597
Editor: J. Spoelstra; **Editor-in-Chief:** A. Bosman; **Publisher:** Roeland Dobbelaer
Profile: Magazine with articles on naval history, shipping, modern warships and merchant ships, heavy transport, machinery, vessels and technical and industrial news. Also covers harbours, fisheries, offshore and inland shipping.
Language(s): Dutch
ADVERTISING RATES:
Full Page Mono EUR 1/1: f.c. 2150,-; PMS 1750,-; b/w 1550,- 1/2: f.c. 1290,-; PMS 1050,-; b/w 930,- 1/4: f.c. 775,-; PM
Agency Commission: 15%
Mechanical Data: Type Area: 190 x 259mm, Bleed Size: 210 x 297mm
BUSINESS: MARINE & SHIPPING

MARKANT
760705N2A-45
Editorial: Landleven 5, 9747 AD GRONINGEN
Tel: 229 216416
Email: info@marug.nl
Freq: Quarterly; **Annual Sub.:** EUR 8,-; **Circ:** 1,750
Editor: Hanneke Poelman; **Editor-in-Chief:** Arthur van Zanten
Profile: Magazine focusing on advertising and marketing. Written by the marketing students of the Groningen university.
Language(s): Dutch
Readership: Aimed at marketing managers and students.
ADVERTISING RATES:
Full Page Mono ..... EUR 1/1: f.c. 695,-; 1/2: f.c. 495,-
Agency Commission: 15%
Mechanical Data: Type Area: 190 x 277mm, Bleed Size: 210 x 297mm
BUSINESS: COMMUNICATIONS, ADVERTISING & MARKETING

MARKANT
16767N56L-87
Editorial: Oudlaan 4, 3515 GA UTRECHT
Tel: 76 5876329 **Fax:** 0032 34660067
Email: markant@vgn.org **Web site:** http://www.tijdschriftmarkant.nl
Freq: 10 issues yearly; **Cover Price:** EUR 7,90
Annual Sub.: EUR 61,95; **Circ:** 4,500
Editor: Johan de Koning; **Editor-in-Chief:** Lia Bruin
Profile: Journal for middle and higher management working with people with learning disabilities and physical disabilities.
Language(s): Dutch
ADVERTISING RATES:
Full Page Mono EUR 1/1: f.c. 1858,-; PMS 1429,-; b/w 823,- 1/2: f.c. 1294,-; PMS 979,-; b/w 485,- 1/4: f.c. 912,-; PMS
Agency Commission: 15%
Mechanical Data: Type Area: 176 x 250mm, Bleed Size: 210 x 297mm
Copy instructions: *Copy Date:* 3 weeks prior to publication date
BUSINESS: HEALTH & MEDICAL: Disability & Rehabilitation

MARKETHINGS
15580N2A-47
Editorial: Warandelaan 2e-101, 5037 AB TILBURG
Tel: 20 5733686 **Fax:** 20 6752709
Email: info@ma-tilburg.nl
Date Established: 01-01-1987; **Freq:** Quarterly;
Cover Price: EUR 5,-
Annual Sub.: EUR 20,-; **Circ:** 1,000
Editor: C.C.P.M. Denissen; **Editor-in-Chief:** B.J. Harpers
Profile: Official journal of the Dutch Marketing Association.
Language(s): Dutch
Readership: Read by the members of the marketing students group at the Katholiek Universiteit of Brabant.
ADVERTISING RATES:
Full Page Mono .... EUR 1/1: f.c. 650,-
Agency Commission: 15%
Mechanical Data: Bleed Size: 210 x 297mm
Copy instructions: *Copy Date:* 3 weeks prior to publication date
BUSINESS: COMMUNICATIONS, ADVERTISING & MARKETING

MARKETINGRSLT
15618N2F-10
Editorial: Kon. Wilhelminaplein 30, 1062 KR AMSTERDAM **Tel:** 20 5688440 **Fax:** 20 6159047
Freq: Quarterly; **Cover Price:** EUR 17,-
Annual Sub.: EUR 144,50; **Circ:** 11,335
Editor: Theo van Vugt; **Editor-in-Chief:** Kari-Anne Fygi; **Publisher:** Rogier Mulder
Profile: News journal about direct marketing and sales promotion.
Language(s): Dutch
Readership: Aimed at sales and marketing managers.
ADVERTISING RATES:
Full Page Mono EUR 1/1: b/w 2400,- 1/2: b/w 1400,- 1/4: b/w 800,-
Agency Commission: 15%
Mechanical Data: Bleed Size: 210 x 297mm, Type Area: 190 x 268mm
BUSINESS: COMMUNICATIONS, ADVERTISING & MARKETING: Selling

MARKT & MEDEDINGING
1636633N14R-238
Editorial: Amaliastraat 9, 2514 JC DEN HAAG
Tel: 70 3789880 **Fax:** 70 3789783
Email: info@bju.nl
Date Established: 26-02-1998; **Freq:** 6 issues yearly;
Cover Price: EUR 30,-
Annual Sub.: EUR 235,-; **Circ:** 450
Language(s): Dutch
ADVERTISING RATES:
Full Page Mono .... EUR 1/1: f.c. 2775,-; f.c. color 1946,-; b/w 1243,- 1/2: f.c. 2221,-; f.c. color 1389,-; b/w 687,-
Agency Commission: 15%
Mechanical Data: Type Area: 180 x 270mm, Bleed Size: 210 x 297mm
BUSINESS: COMMERCE, INDUSTRY & MANAGEMENT: Commerce Related

MARKTVISIE
15586N2A-52_15
Editorial: Postbus 4032, 5604 EA EINDHOVEN
Tel: 70 3490165
Email: info@matue.nl
Date Established: 01-04-1990; **Freq:** 3 issues yearly;
Cover Price: EUR 9,95
Annual Sub.: EUR 15,-; **Circ:** 500
Profile: Magazine focusing on marketing issues.
Language(s): Dutch
Readership: Read by marketing managers and students.
ADVERTISING RATES:
Full Page Mono .... EUR 1/1: b/w 595,- 1/2: b/w 375,-
Agency Commission: 15%
Mechanical Data: Type Area: 175 x 272mm, Bleed Size: 210 x 297mm
BUSINESS: COMMUNICATIONS, ADVERTISING & MARKETING

MARNE-INFO
17577N75B-40
Editorial: Schoolstraat 6, 9974 RL ZOUTKAMP
Tel: 0032 34660066 **Fax:** 0032 34660067
Email: seal.productions@planet.nl **Web site:** http://www.marne.info
Date Established: 01-11-2003; **Freq:** 10 issues yearly; **Cover Price:** Free; **Circ:** 6,000
Usual Pagination: 24
Publisher: G.K. Bakker
Profile: Football magazine focusing on the Leeuwarden football club.
Language(s): Dutch
Agency Commission: 15%
Mechanical Data: Type Area: 255 x 370mm, Bleed Size: 290 x 400mm
CONSUMER: SPORT: Football

MATRIX
17984N83-36
Editorial: Postbus 513, 5600 MB EINDHOVEN
Tel: 40 2473330 **Fax:** 172 466577
Freq: Quarterly; **Cover Price:** Free; **Circ:** 22,000
Editor: J.L. Konings
Profile: Magazine for graduates from the University of Eindhoven, providing information on courses, activities and social functions.
Language(s): Dutch
ADVERTISING RATES:
Full Page Mono EUR 1/1: f.c. 1500,-; PMS 1250,-; b/w 1000,- 1/2: f.c. 975,-; PMS 813,-; b/w 650,-
Agency Commission: 15%
Mechanical Data: Type Area: 185 x 282mm, Bleed Size: 210 x 297mm
CONSUMER: STUDENT PUBLICATIONS

MAX MAGAZINE
1808585N76C-140
Editorial: Amalialaan 126, 3743 KJ BAARN
Tel: 20 5855333 **Fax:** 20 5852965
Email: info@spn.nl **Web site:** http://www.maxmagazine.nl
Freq: Quarterly; **Circ:** 250,000
Editor: Sylvia Aué
Language(s): Dutch
ADVERTISING RATES:
Full Page Mono . EUR 1/1: f.c. 8000,-; 1/2: f.c. 5000,-
Agency Commission: 15%
Mechanical Data: Type Area: 179 x 243mm, Bleed Size: 210 x 270mm
Copy instructions: *Copy Date:* 5 weeks prior to publication date
CONSUMER: MUSIC & PERFORMING ARTS: TV & Radio

MBO&HBO COURANT
1636595N83-192
Editorial: Edisonweg 22, 1821 BN ALKMAAR
Tel: 172 466622 **Fax:** 24 3723631
Email: mailbox@mbo-hbo.nl **Web site:** http://www.mbo-hbo.nl
Date Established: 01-01-1994; **Freq:** 13 issues yearly; **Cover Price:** Free; **Circ:** 150,000
Language(s): Dutch
Agency Commission: 15%
Mechanical Data: Type Area: 263 x 385mm, Bleed Size: 289 x 420mm
Copy instructions: *Copy Date:* 3 days prior to publication date
CONSUMER: STUDENT PUBLICATIONS

MCL JOURNAAL
16730N56C-45
Editorial: Graaf Adolfstraat 35b, 8606 BT SNEEK
Tel: 20 5302586 **Fax:** 23 5564575
Email: info@mimicry.nl
Date Established: 01-07-1991; **Freq:** 6 issues yearly;
Annual Sub.: EUR 27,23; **Circ:** 5,000
Editor: F.J. Mostert; **Editor-in-Chief:** F.J. Mostert
Profile: Magazine of the medical centre of Leeuwarden.
Language(s): Dutch
Readership: Read by patients and visitors to the hospital.
ADVERTISING RATES:
Full Page Mono EUR 1/1: b/w 725,- 1/2: b/w 400,- 1/4: b/w 225,-
Agency Commission: 15%
Mechanical Data: Type Area: 183 x 269mm, Bleed Size: 210 x 297mm
BUSINESS: HEALTH & MEDICAL: Hospitals

MEDEMBLIKKER COURANT
626922N72-3180
Editorial: Randweg 11, 1671 GG MEDEMBLIK
Tel: 23 5567955 **Fax:** 23 5567956
Email: drukkerij@idemadruk.nl
Date Established: 01-01-1905; **Freq:** Weekly; **Cover Price:** Free; **Circ:** 18,130
Editor: R.C.M. Koomen
Language(s): Dutch
Agency Commission: 15%
Mechanical Data: Type Area: 398 x 540mm, Bleed Size: 410 x 580mm
LOCAL NEWSPAPERS

MEDIA UPDATE
15781N5F-40
Editorial: Feestlan 15, 8408 JK LIPPENHUIZEN
Tel: 513 466162 **Fax:** 35 6712552
Email: info@media-update.nl **Web site:** http://www.media-update.nl
Date Established: 01-11-1995; **Freq:** 156 issues yearly; **Annual Sub.:** EUR 395,-; **Circ:** 2,000
Editor: H. Sleurink; **Publisher:** D. Mooij
Profile: Newsletter delivering national and international news for decision makers in the ICT and multimedia industries.
Language(s): Dutch
Readership: Aimed at multimedia managers and decision makers in the government and consultant organisations.
Agency Commission: 15%
BUSINESS: COMPUTERS & AUTOMATION: Multimedia

MEDIAFACTS
1636598N60A-208
Editorial: Joan Muyskenweg 22, 1096 CJ AMSTERDAM **Tel:** 33 4220082 **Fax:** 24 3723631
Web site: http://www.mediafacts.nl
Freq: 6 issues yearly; **Cover Price:** EUR 23,-
Annual Sub.: EUR 115,-; **Circ:** 1,765
Editor: Wim Danhof; **Publisher:** Lise van de Kamp
Language(s): Dutch
ADVERTISING RATES:
Full Page Mono EUR 1/1: f.c. 2850,-; 1/2: f.c. 1850,-; 1/4: f.c. 1300,-
Agency Commission: 15%
Mechanical Data: Type Area: 210 x 280mm, Bleed Size: 230 x 300mm
BUSINESS: PUBLISHING: Publishing & Book Trade

MEDIAFORUM
15587N2A-52_50
Editorial: Korte Spinhuissteeg 3, 1012 CG AMSTERDAM **Tel:** 20 5253370 **Fax:** 20 6767728
Email: ivir@ivir.nl **Web site:** http://www.mediaforum.nl
Date Established: 01-10-1988; **Freq:** 10 issues yearly; **Annual Sub.:** EUR 105,-; **Circ:** 1,000
Editor: A.W. Hins; **Publisher:** Otto Cramwinckel
Profile: Publication about the law relating to the media, press and broadcasting, telecommunications and related matters.
Language(s): Dutch
ADVERTISING RATES:
Full Page Mono EUR 1/1: b/w 600,- 1/2: b/w 375,- 1/4: b/w 235,-
Agency Commission: 15%
Mechanical Data: Type Area: 165 x 262mm, Bleed Size: 210 x 297mm
BUSINESS: COMMUNICATIONS, ADVERTISING & MARKETING

MEDISCHE ONCOLOGIE
761575N56A-66_7
Editorial: Arena Boulevard 61-75, 1101 DL AMSTERDAM **Tel:** 492 338432 **Fax:** 20 6767728
Freq: 6 issues yearly; **Annual Sub.:** EUR 108,-; **Circ:** 3,100
Editor-in-Chief: Henri Neuvel
Profile: Magazine focusing on all medical diseases.
Language(s): Dutch
Readership: Read by doctors and medical researchers.
ADVERTISING RATES:
Full Page Mono EUR 2/1: f.c. 4275,-; 1/1: f.c. 2935,-; 1/2: f.c. 1878,-
Agency Commission: 15%
Mechanical Data: Type Area: 190 x 277mm, Bleed Size: 210 x 297mm
Copy instructions: *Copy Date:* 3 weeks prior to publication date
BUSINESS: HEALTH & MEDICAL

MEDNET MAGAZINE
1643434N56A-425
Editorial: Het Spoor 2, 3994 AK HOUTEN
Tel: 30 6383873 **Fax:** 30 6383998
Web site: http://www.mednet.nl
Freq: Monthly; **Circ:** 16,636
Editor: Marjan Enzlin
Language(s): Dutch
ADVERTISING RATES:
Full Page Mono EUR 1/1: f.c. 4111,-; b/w 1962,- 1/2: f.c. 2462,-; b/w 1177,- 1/4: f.c. 1435,-; b/w 686,-
Agency Commission: 15%
Mechanical Data: Type Area: 179 x 259mm, Bleed Size: 215 x 285mm
BUSINESS: HEALTH & MEDICAL

MEELEVEN
16801N56R-34
Editorial: Droogbak 1d, 1013 GE AMSTERDAM
Tel: 172 466539 **Fax:** 10 4521797
Date Established: 01-12-1977; **Freq:** Quarterly;
Cover Price: Free; **Circ:** 9,000
Editor: Carole Leblond
Profile: Publication about drug abuse prevention and help for users.
Language(s): Dutch
Readership: Aimed at members of the medical profession, carers, social workers and patients.
Agency Commission: 15%
Mechanical Data: Bleed Size: 340 x 470mm
BUSINESS: HEALTH & MEDICAL: Health Medical Related

MEETING MAGAZINE.NL
1748133N14R-270
Editorial: Kerkenbos 12-26c, 6546 BE NIJMEGEN
Tel: 10 4066333 **Fax:** 229 216416
Email: info@vanmunstermedia.nl **Web site:** http://www.meetingmagazine.nl
Date Established: 01-11-2005; **Freq:** 6 issues yearly;
Annual Sub.: EUR 39,95; **Circ:** 5,500
Editor: Astrid Enderman; **Publisher:** Michael van Munster
Language(s): Dutch
ADVERTISING RATES:
Full Page Mono .. EUR 1/1: b/w 1865,- 1/2: b/w 990,- 1/4: b/w 510,-
Agency Commission: 15%
Mechanical Data: Type Area: 190 x 260mm, Bleed Size: 215 x 285mm
BUSINESS: COMMERCE, INDUSTRY & MANAGEMENT: Commerce Related

MEIDENMAGAZINE
1693175N91D-173
Editorial: Mijlweg 61, 3316 BE DORDRECHT
Tel: 20 6275453 **Fax:** 78 6397078
Email: info@zpress-magazines.nl **Web site:** http://www.meidenmagazine.nl
Freq: 13 issues yearly; **Cover Price:** EUR 3,25
Annual Sub.: EUR 39,95; **Circ:** 53,108
Editor-in-Chief: Maaike Wierckx; **Publisher:** Robert van Ginhoven
Language(s): Dutch
ADVERTISING RATES:
Full Page Mono . EUR 2/1: f.c. 7400,-; 1/1: f.c. 3950,-
Agency Commission: 15%
Mechanical Data: Type Area: 190 x 250mm, Bleed Size: 210 x 270mm
CONSUMER: RECREATION & LEISURE: Children & Youth

MEMORY MAGAZINE
629531N14A-130
Editorial: Keizersgracht 424, 1016 GC AMSTERDAM
Tel: 172 466539 **Fax:** 10 4521797
Email: info@memory.nl
Freq: 6 issues yearly; **Annual Sub.:** EUR 12,-; **Circ:** 140,423
Editor: Sandra Veltmaat-Herklots; **Editor-in-Chief:** Renske van Bers; **Publisher:** Geert Nab
Profile: Magazine containing information about company affairs, including market trends and company reports.
Language(s): Dutch
Readership: Read by managers, economists and business students.
Agency Commission: 15%
Mechanical Data: Bleed Size: 210 x 283mm
BUSINESS: COMMERCE, INDUSTRY & MANAGEMENT

Netherlands

MENS & MOLECULE 1667432N55-333
Editorial: Rijswijkseweg 60, 2516 DEN HAAG
Tel: 570 647730
Email: info@betapublishers.nl
Freq: 9 issues yearly; **Annual Sub.:** EUR 92,-; **Circ:** 3,665
Editor: Arno van 't Hoog; **Publisher:** Roeland Dobbelaer
Language(s): Dutch
ADVERTISING RATES:
Full Page Mono EUR 1/1: f.c. 1745,-; PMS 1360,-; b/w 1155,- 1/2: f.c. 1050,-; PMS 825,-; b/w 695,- 1/4: f.c. 635,-; PMS
Agency Commission: 15%
Mechanical Data: Type Area: 190 x 259mm, Bleed Size: 210 x 297mm
BUSINESS: APPLIED SCIENCE & LABORATORIES

MEN'S HEALTH 629464N86C-180
Editorial: Raamgracht 4, 1011 KK AMSTERDAM
Tel: 10 4274128 **Fax:** 20 5853598
Web site: http://www.menshealth.nl
Freq: 10 issues yearly; **Cover Price:** EUR 5,50
Annual Sub.: EUR 52,50; **Circ:** 46,988
Editor: Jan Peter Jansen; **Publisher:** Femke Leemeijer
Profile: Magazine focusing on men's health and fitness.
Language(s): Dutch
ADVERTISING RATES:
Full Page Mono .... EUR 2/1: f.c. 10.230,-; 1/1: f.c. 5115,-; 1/2: f.c. 3080,-
Agency Commission: 15%
Mechanical Data: Type Area: 190 x 265mm, Bleed Size: 215 x 280mm
Copy instructions: *Copy Date:* 3 weeks prior to publication date
CONSUMER: ADULT & GAY MAGAZINES: Men's Lifestyle Magazines

MENSEN 1634738N74G-251
Editorial: Postbus 30470, 2500 GL DEN HAAG
Tel: 172 466327 **Fax:** 172 493270
Email: info@msvn.nl
Date Established: 01-02-1993; **Freq:** 6 issues yearly;
Annual Sub.: EUR 20,-; **Circ:** 12,000
Language(s): Dutch
ADVERTISING RATES:
Full Page Mono .. EUR 1/1: b/w 1400,- 1/2: b/w 840,- 1/4: b/w 504,-
Agency Commission: 15%
Mechanical Data: Type Area: 185 x 268mm, Bleed Size: 210 x 297mm
CONSUMER: WOMEN'S INTEREST CONSUMER MAGAZINES: Slimming & Health

MENSEN IN NOOD NIEUWS
1633491N1P-80
Editorial: Lutherse Burgwal 10, 2512 CB DEN HAAG
Tel: 20 5302586 **Fax:** 23 5564575
Email: info@cordaidmenseninnood.nl
Date Established: 01-01-1963; **Freq:** 3 issues yearly;
Cover Price: Free; **Circ:** 250,000
Usual Pagination: 16
Editor-in-Chief: Judith Maat
Language(s): Dutch
Agency Commission: 15%
BUSINESS: FINANCE & ECONOMICS: Fundraising

MENSPORT 17593N75E-30
Editorial: Postbus 154, 7240 AD LOCHEM
Web site: http://www.mensport.nl
Freq: 9 issues yearly; **Cover Price:** EUR 4,75; **Circ:** 13,000
Editor: Meike Merks; **Editor-in-Chief:** Marjet Bosma;
Publisher: Rob Mekelenkamp
Profile: Magazine about horse racing and other sports.
Language(s): Dutch
ADVERTISING RATES:
Full Page Mono .. EUR 1/1: f.c. 1044,-; b/w 820,- 1/2: f.c. 590,-; b/w 471,- 1/4: f.c. 331,-; b/w 270,-
Agency Commission: 15%
Mechanical Data: Type Area: 185 x 250mm, Bleed Size: 230 x 297mm
Copy instructions: *Copy Date:* 4 weeks prior to publication date
CONSUMER: SPORT: Horse Racing

MERCEDES MAGAZINE
1636337N77A-279
Editorial: Olympia 10, 1213 NP HILVERSUM
Tel: 13 4662445 **Fax:** 88 2697490
Email: mail@hemels.com
Freq: Quarterly; **Annual Sub.:** EUR 20,-; **Circ:** 106,067
Editor: H. Dubbelman; **Publisher:** Wilfred Mons
Language(s): Dutch
ADVERTISING RATES:
Full Page Mono .... EUR 2/1: f.c. 14.729,-; 1/1: f.c. 7365,-
Agency Commission: 15%
Mechanical Data: Type Area: 176 x 242mm, Bleed Size: 216 x 280mm
CONSUMER: MOTORING & CYCLING: Motoring

MERIDIAN TRAVEL! 18164N89E-60
Editorial: Heemstederweg 64, 1902 RP CASTRICUM
Tel: 23 5565135 **Fax:** 23 5565116
Email: info@dorizon.nl **Web site:** http://www.meridiantravel.nl
Freq: 6 issues yearly; **Cover Price:** EUR 4,25
Annual Sub.: EUR 24,50; **Circ:** 20,000
Publisher: Harald Kolkman
Profile: International magazine about worldwide travel.
Language(s): Dutch
Readership: Aimed at men and women aged between 25 and 55 years.
ADVERTISING RATES:
Full Page Mono .... EUR 1/1: f.c. 2450,-; ** 1/2: f.c. 1350,-; ** 1/4: f.c. 750,-
Agency Commission: 15%
Mechanical Data: Type Area: 210 x 277mm, Bleed Size: 230 x 297mm
Copy instructions: *Copy Date:* 3 weeks prior to publication date
CONSUMER: HOLIDAYS & TRAVEL: Holidays

MESO MAGAZINE 1634733N62J-305
Editorial: Zuidpoolsingel 2, 2408 ZE ALPHEN A/D RIJN **Tel:** 172 466327 **Fax:** 172 493270
Email: info@kluwer.nl
Freq: 6 issues yearly; **Cover Price:** EUR 18,-
Annual Sub.: EUR 98,-; **Circ:** 1,213
Editor: A. Olthof; **Publisher:** Jacqueline Vreeburg
Language(s): Dutch
ADVERTISING RATES:
Full Page Mono .. EUR 1/1: b/w 1025,- 1/2: b/w 625,- 1/4: b/w 325,-
Agency Commission: 15%
Mechanical Data: Type Area: 185 x 265mm, Bleed Size: 210 x 297mm
BUSINESS: CHURCH & SCHOOL EQUIPMENT & EDUCATION: Teachers & Education Management

METAAL & TECHNIEK 16064N19E-30
Editorial: Essebaan 63, 2908 LJ CAPELLE AAN DEN IJSSEL **Tel:** 33 2471104 **Fax:** 522 257664
Email: info@mybusinessmedia.nl
Date Established: 01-01-1955; **Freq:** 11 issues yearly; **Cover Price:** EUR 13,80
Annual Sub.: EUR 102,-; **Circ:** 12,648
Editor: Kees de Vries; **Editor-in-Chief:** Astrid Mol
Profile: Trade journal for small or medium-sized companies in the metalworking industry. Official journal of the Metal Association.
Language(s): Dutch
ADVERTISING RATES:
Full Page Mono EUR 1/1: f.c. 3225,-; b/w 1955,- 1/2: f.c. 1930,-; b/w 1075,- 1/4: f.c. 1160,-; b/w 595,-
Agency Commission: 15%
Mechanical Data: Type Area: 205 x 255mm, Bleed Size: 230 x 280mm
BUSINESS: ENGINEERING & MACHINERY: Machinery, Machine Tools & Metalworking

METAAL MAGAZINE 16063N19E-25
Editorial: Informaticaweg 3c, 7007 CP DOETINCHEM **Tel:** 33 2471104
Email: industrialmedia@eisma.nl **Web site:** http://www.metaalmagazine.nl
Freq: 11 issues yearly; **Annual Sub.:** EUR 232,-; **Circ:** 5,000
Editor: Reinold Tomberg; **Editor-in-Chief:** Liedy Bisselink; **Publisher:** Henk Meinen
Profile: Practice-orientated technical journal for the whole metalworking industry which deals with practically every aspect of metal working and processing.
Language(s): Dutch
ADVERTISING RATES:
Full Page Mono EUR 1/1: f.c. 4128,-; PMS 3244,-; b/w 2317,- 1/2: f.c. 2485,-; PMS 2042,-; b/w 1227,- 1/4: f.c. 1543,-;
Agency Commission: 15%
Mechanical Data: Type Area: 191 x 265mm, Bleed Size: 230 x 300mm
BUSINESS: ENGINEERING & MACHINERY: Machinery, Machine Tools & Metalworking

METAALJOURNAAL 1900800N27-73
Editorial: Frankrijklaan 10, 2391 PX HAZERSWOUDE-DORP **Tel:** 30 6383716
Fax: 73 6157171
Email: info@oom.nl **Web site:** http://www.metaaljournaal.nl
Freq: Quarterly; **Cover Price:** Free; **Circ:** 165,000
Usual Pagination: 24
Editor: Michel Revet
Language(s): Dutch
Agency Commission: 15%
BUSINESS: METAL, IRON & STEEL

METAALNIEUWS 1640463N27-60
Editorial: Prinsenweide 26, 7317 BB APELDOORN
Tel: 172 440681 **Fax:** 172 422886
Email: info@udr-media.nl **Web site:** http://www.metaalnieuws.nl
Freq: 22 issues yearly; **Cover Price:** Free; **Circ:** 16,534
Editor: Eric Weustink; **Publisher:** Peter de Ruygt
Language(s): Dutch
Agency Commission: 15%
Mechanical Data: Type Area: 278 x 380mm, Bleed Size: 300 x 420mm
BUSINESS: METAL, IRON & STEEL

METEOROLOGICA 17032N64N-25
Editorial: Postbus 464, 6700 AL WAGENINGEN
Tel: 20 5629222
Freq: Quarterly; **Annual Sub.:** EUR 34,-; **Circ:** 450
Editor: Leo Kroon
Profile: Official journal of the Dutch Association of Meteorology.
Language(s): Dutch
ADVERTISING RATES:
Full Page Mono .... EUR 1/1: f.c. 250,-; b/w 375,-
Agency Commission: 15%
BUSINESS: OTHER CLASSIFICATIONS: Weather

METROPOLIS M 18012N84A-180
Editorial: Doelenstraat 30, 3512 XJ UTRECHT
Tel: 229 284949 **Fax:** 229 284999
Email: info@metropol.nl
Date Established: 01-01-1979; **Freq:** 6 issues yearly;
Cover Price: EUR 10,-
Annual Sub.: EUR 55,-; **Circ:** 5,000
Editor: D. Ruyters; **Editor-in-Chief:** Saskia van der Kroef
Profile: Magazine about contemporary visual art.
Language(s): Dutch
ADVERTISING RATES:
Full Page Mono EUR 1/1: b/w 895,- 1/2: b/w 505,- 1/4: b/w 305,-
Agency Commission: 15%
Mechanical Data: Type Area: 184 x 244mm, Bleed Size: 204 x 268mm
Copy instructions: *Copy Date:* 5 weeks prior to publication date
CONSUMER: THE ARTS & LITERARY: Arts

MIDDEN NEDERLAND MAGAZINE 1894318N4D-192
Editorial: Molenstraat 3a, 3882 AC PUTTEN
Tel: 70 3307094 **Fax:** 70 3855505
Email: info@qcreators.nl
Date Established: 01-01-2002; **Freq:** 3 issues yearly;
Cover Price: Free; **Circ:** 65,000
Editor: Esmeralda van der Mee; **Editor-in-Chief:** Robert van der Mee
Language(s): Dutch
ADVERTISING RATES:
Full Page Mono .. EUR 1/1: b/w 1695,- 1/2: b/w 795,- 1/4: b/w 395,-
Agency Commission: 15%
Mechanical Data: Type Area: 190 x 267mm, Bleed Size: 210 x 297mm
Copy instructions: *Copy Date:* 4 weeks prior to publication date
BUSINESS: ARCHITECTURE & BUILDING: Planning & Housing

DE MIDDENSTANDER
626951N72-3223
Editorial: Zesstedenweg 165, 1613 JD GROOTEBROEK **Tel:** 20 5629444 **Fax:** 20 6680389
Email: info@rosier.nl **Web site:** http://www.middenstander.nl
Date Established: 01-01-1913; **Freq:** Weekly; **Cover Price:** Free; **Circ:** 31,000
Language(s): Dutch
ADVERTISING RATES:
Full Page Mono EUR 1/1: b/w 688,- 1/2: b/w 344,- 1/4: b/w 172,-
Agency Commission: 15%
Mechanical Data: Type Area: 258 x 398mm, Bleed Size: 290 x 430mm
LOCAL NEWSPAPERS

MIJN VAKBOND.NL 1634758N82-210
Editorial: Carnegielaan 1, 2517 KH DEN HAAG
Tel: 20 5518525 **Fax:** 70 4160636
Email: publiciteit@cnvpubliekezaak.nl **Web site:** http://www.mijnvakbond.nl
Date Established: 23-01-1986; **Freq:** Quarterly;
Annual Sub.: EUR 41,64; **Circ:** 80,000
Editor-in-Chief: J. Spijk
Language(s): Dutch
Agency Commission: 15%
CONSUMER: CURRENT AFFAIRS & POLITICS

MILIEU 16824N57-4
Editorial: Postbus 158, 1600 AD ENKHUIZEN
Tel: 570 648902 **Fax:** 570 614795
Email: graafcom@wxs.nl
Freq: 8 issues yearly; **Annual Sub.:** EUR 110,-; **Circ:** 2,500
Editor: J. de Graaf
Profile: Magazine on developments in environmental research, information and policy; includes air pollution topics.
Language(s): Dutch
Readership: Read by environmental professionals in industry, government, interest groups, scientific research and consultancy.
ADVERTISING RATES:
Full Page Mono EUR 2/1: f.c. 2175,-; b/w 1990,- 1/1: f.c. 1180,-; b/w 995,- 1/2: f.c. 880,-; b/w 695,-
Agency Commission: 15%
Mechanical Data: Type Area: 180 x 270mm, Bleed Size: 210 x 297mm
Copy instructions: *Copy Date:* 3 weeks prior to publication date
BUSINESS: ENVIRONMENT & POLLUTION

MILIEUMAGAZINE 16833N57-29_80
Editorial: Zuidpoolsingel 2, 2408 ZE ALPHEN A/D RIJN **Tel:** 10 4274128 **Fax:** 35 6474569
Email: info@kluwer.nl **Web site:** http://www.milieumagazine.nl
Freq: 8 issues yearly; **Cover Price:** EUR 29,-
Annual Sub.: EUR 195,-; **Circ:** 2,361
Editor: Jos van der Schot; **Publisher:** Sietske de Boer
Profile: Journal focusing on environmental management and planning.
Language(s): Dutch
Readership: Aimed at environmental professionals.
ADVERTISING RATES:
Full Page Mono .. EUR 1/1: b/w 1275,- 1/2: b/w 765,- 1/4: b/w 414,-
Agency Commission: 15%
Mechanical Data: Type Area: 175 x 262mm, Bleed Size: 210 x 297mm
Copy instructions: *Copy Date:* 2 weeks prior to publication date
BUSINESS: ENVIRONMENT & POLLUTION

MILITAIRE SPECTATOR
16401N40-80
Editorial: Van Alkemadelaan 357, 2597 BA DEN HAAG **Tel:** 15 2564718 **Fax:** 70 3364640
Email: info@kvbk.nl
Date Established: 29-01-1832; **Freq:** Monthly;
Annual Sub.: EUR 22,50; **Circ:** 13,000
Editor: J.M.J. Bosch; **Editor-in-Chief:** Astrid Kool
Profile: Journal containing technical, scientific, historical and managerial articles about war history and defence.
Language(s): Dutch
Readership: Readership includes all active serving officers of the Dutch Army and Air Force, high ranking civil servants in the Ministry of Defense and members of the Royal Society for Military Art and Science.
ADVERTISING RATES:
Full Page Mono .... EUR 1/1: b/w 575,- 1/2: b/w 295,-
Agency Commission: 15%
Mechanical Data: Type Area: 158 x 224mm, Bleed Size: 190 x 267mm
BUSINESS: DEFENCE

MIX 1635247N25-71
Editorial: Jagersbosstraat 6, 5241 JT ROSMALEN
Tel: 30 6399911 **Fax:** 30 6399937
Freq: 11 issues yearly; **Cover Price:** EUR 7,50
Annual Sub.: EUR 61,-; **Circ:** 5,743
Editor: Bert Hoogeland; **Publisher:** Marc Nelissen
Language(s): Dutch
ADVERTISING RATES:
Full Page Mono .. EUR 1/1: b/w 1607,- 1/2: b/w 870,- 1/4: b/w 481,-
Agency Commission: 15%
Mechanical Data: Type Area: 187 x 257mm, Bleed Size: 215 x 285mm
Copy instructions: *Copy Date:* 3 days prior to publication date
BUSINESS: HARDWARE

MMNIEUWS 17035N64P-33
Editorial: Planciusstraat 13b, 1013 MD AMSTERDAM
Tel: 30 2539300
Email: info@buromennoheling.nl **Web site:** http://www.mmnieuws.nl
Freq: 6 issues yearly; **Annual Sub.:** EUR 135,-; **Circ:** 1,200
Editor: Menno Heling; **Editor-in-Chief:** Pieter de Nijs;
Publisher: Menno Heling
Profile: Journal focusing on marketing and management in museums, theatres, cultural and leisure establishments throughout the Netherlands.
Language(s): Dutch
Readership: Aimed at managers and directors.
ADVERTISING RATES:
Full Page Mono EUR 1/1: b/w 745,- 1/2: b/w 430,- 1/4: b/w 255,-
Agency Commission: 15%
Mechanical Data: Type Area: 186 x 244mm, Bleed Size: 210 x 297mm
Copy instructions: *Copy Date:* 4 weeks prior to publication date
BUSINESS: OTHER CLASSIFICATIONS: Museums

MOBILIA INTERIEURTEXTIEL
16180N23A-26
Editorial: Isaac Titsingkade 107, 1018 LL AMSTERDAM **Tel:** 15 2564718 **Fax:** 70 3364640
Email: mobilia@interieur.net **Web site:** http://www.mobilia-interieurtextiel.nl
Freq: 6 issues yearly; **Cover Price:** EUR 8,50; **Circ:** 5,500
Editor: Peter Vorstenbosch; **Editor-in-Chief:** Pascal Thole; **Publisher:** Ton Roskam
Profile: Magazine focusing on interior textiles.
Language(s): Dutch
Readership: Aimed at interior designers, project and facility managers.
ADVERTISING RATES:
Full Page Mono .. EUR 1/1: b/w 1251,- 1/2: b/w 666,- 1/4: b/w 374,-
Agency Commission: 15%
Mechanical Data: Type Area: 185 x 261mm, Bleed Size: 230 x 285mm
Copy instructions: *Copy Date:* 4 weeks prior to publication date
BUSINESS: FURNISHINGS & FURNITURE

MOBILIA VLOEREN 16014N4B-122
Editorial: Isaac Titsingkade 107, 1018 LL AMSTERDAM **Tel:** 23 5344089 **Fax:** 10 2801002
Email: mobilia@interieur.net **Web site:** http://www.mobiliavloeren.nl
Freq: 6 issues yearly; **Cover Price:** EUR 8,70; **Circ:** 5,500
Editor: Peter Vorstenbosch; **Editor-in-Chief:** Ingmar van der Hoek; **Publisher:** Ton Roskam
Profile: Magazine covering decorating, design and furnishing. Also provides information on flooring.
Language(s): Dutch
ADVERTISING RATES:
Full Page Mono .. EUR 1/1: b/w 1251,- 1/2: b/w 666,- 1/4: b/w 374,-
Agency Commission: 15%
Mechanical Data: Type Area: 185 x 261mm, Bleed Size: 230 x 285mm
Copy instructions: *Copy Date:* 4 weeks prior to publication date
BUSINESS: ARCHITECTURE & BUILDING: Interior Design & Flooring

MODELAUTO 17845N79K-50
Editorial: Postbus 26, 7200 AA ZUTPHEN
Tel: 161 457342 **Fax:** 20 5159145
Email: modelauto@planet.nl
Date Established: 01-04-1984; **Freq:** 6 issues yearly; **Cover Price:** EUR 5,95
Annual Sub.: EUR 35,-; **Circ:** 7,500
Editor: R. Boswinkel; **Editor-in-Chief:** R. Boswinkel
Profile: Magazine containing information and advice about collecting model cars.
Language(s): Dutch
Readership: Read by model car collectors.
ADVERTISING RATES:
Full Page Mono .. EUR 1/1: f.c. 656,-; b/w 606,- 1/2: f.c. 377,-; b/w 327,- 1/4: f.c. 230,-; b/w 180,-
Agency Commission: 15%
Mechanical Data: Type Area: 185 x 268mm, Bleed Size: 230 x 297mm
Copy instructions: *Copy Date:* 4 weeks prior to publication date
CONSUMER: HOBBIES & DIY: Collectors Magazines

MODELBOUW IN PLASTIC
17820N79B-102
Editorial: Eefsebeek 35, 1509 ER ZAANDAM
Tel: 30 6399911
Email: bestuur@imps.nl
Freq: 5 issues yearly; **Annual Sub.:** EUR 32,-; **Circ:** 1,000
Profile: Magazine devoted to all forms of plastic modelling.
Language(s): Dutch
Readership: Aimed at those interested in modelling with plastic.
Agency Commission: 15%
Mechanical Data: Type Area: 185 x 261mm, Bleed Size: 210 x 297mm
CONSUMER: HOBBIES & DIY: Models & Modelling

DE MODELBOUWER 17821N79B-55
Editorial: Postbus 26, 4697 ZG ST. ANNALAND
Date Established: 01-12-1936; **Freq:** 10 issues yearly; **Annual Sub.:** EUR 49,-; **Circ:** 3,100
Usual Pagination: 72
Editor-in-Chief: A.P.A. Ros
Profile: Hobby magazine published by the Netherlands Modelmakers' Association, contains articles on traditional modelling.
Language(s): Dutch
ADVERTISING RATES:
Full Page Mono EUR 1/1: b/w 545,- 1/2: b/w 295,- 1/4: b/w 159,-
Agency Commission: 15%
Mechanical Data: Type Area: 185 x 268mm, Bleed Size: 210 x 297mm
Copy instructions: *Copy Date:* 3 weeks prior to publication date
CONSUMER: HOBBIES & DIY: Models & Modelling

MODERN MEDICINE 16689N56A-80
Editorial: Henri Dunantweg 40a, 2697 NR ALPHEN A/D RIJN **Tel:** 58 2954859 **Fax:** 172 539171
Email: zuiden@zuidencom.nl
Freq: 11 issues yearly; **Annual Sub.:** EUR 105,-; **Circ:** 6,675
Usual Pagination: 80
Publisher: D. Mackay
Profile: Journal covering all aspects of modern medicine.
Language(s): Dutch
Readership: Read by GPs, physicians, chemists and pharmacists.
ADVERTISING RATES:
Full Page Mono .... EUR 1/1: f.c. 3420,-
Agency Commission: 15%
Mechanical Data: Type Area: 165 x 268mm, Bleed Size: 210 x 297mm
Copy instructions: *Copy Date:* 4 weeks prior to publication date
BUSINESS: HEALTH & MEDICAL

MONSTERSE COURANT
626983N72-3300
Editorial: Herckenrathstraat 52, 2681 DG MONSTER
Tel: 88 2944822 **Fax:** 88 2944870
Email: info@thuisbladen.nl
Date Established: 01-01-1939; **Freq:** Weekly; **Cover Price:** Free; **Circ:** 9,500
Editor: M. Domech; **Editor-in-Chief:** Rob de Voogd; **Publisher:** P.C. de Groot
Language(s): Dutch
Agency Commission: 15%
Mechanical Data: Type Area: 260 x 400mm, Bleed Size: 290 x 440mm
LOCAL NEWSPAPERS

MONTFERLAND NIEUWS
626986N72-3310
Editorial: Plantenstraat 24, 7001 EZ DOETINCHEM
Tel: 20 3467209 **Fax:** 10 4521797
Email: info@wcgo.nl
Date Established: 01-03-1988; **Freq:** Weekly; **Cover Price:** EUR 1,80; **Circ:** 17,900
Editor-in-Chief: B. Engelen; **Publisher:** P.V. Janssen
Language(s): Dutch
ADVERTISING RATES:
Full Page Mono .... EUR 1/1: b/w 1215,- 1/2: b/w 627,- 1/4: b/w 323,-
Agency Commission: 15%
Mechanical Data: Type Area: 318 x 490mm, Bleed Size: 290 x 420mm
LOCAL NEWSPAPERS

MONUMENTEN MAGAZINE
1857836N84A-382
Editorial: Van der Does de Willeboissingel 2, 5211 CA 'S-HERTOGENBOSCH **Tel:** 40 8447611
Fax: 53 4842189
Email: info@damenromijn.nl
Freq: Annual; **Cover Price:** Free; **Circ:** 64,000
Editor: Miriam Verstappen
Language(s): Dutch
Agency Commission: 15%
CONSUMER: THE ARTS & LITERARY: Arts

MOOI 712980N74H-70
Editorial: Provincialeweg 11, 1506 MA ZAANDAM
Tel: 73 6136424 **Fax:** 20 6238538
Freq: 5 issues yearly; **Cover Price:** Free; **Circ:** 455,162
Profile: Magazine focusing on health and beauty.
Language(s): Dutch
Readership: Read by customers of Etos.
Agency Commission: 15%
CONSUMER: WOMEN'S INTEREST CONSUMER MAGAZINES: Hair & Beauty

MORE THAN CLASSIC
707865N74Q-100
Editorial: Capellalaan 65, 2132 JL HOOFDDORP
Tel: 23 5566770 **Fax:** 570 614795
Freq: 6 issues yearly; **Cover Price:** EUR 6,45
Annual Sub.: EUR 38,50; **Circ:** 51,531
Editor: Mary Hessing; **Publisher:** Ard Siekerman
Profile: Magazine containing articles about international living and lifestyle, including interiors, hotels and antiques.
Language(s): Dutch
Readership: Aimed at those with a high disposable income, wanting to invest in property.
ADVERTISING RATES:
Full Page Mono .... EUR 2/1: b/w 11.600,- 1/1: b/w 5800,- 1/2: b/w 3480,-
Agency Commission: 15%
Mechanical Data: Type Area: 201 x 266mm, Bleed Size: 230 x 297mm
CONSUMER: WOMEN'S INTEREST CONSUMER MAGAZINES: Lifestyle

MOTO 73 17778N77D-150
Editorial: Capellalaan 65, 2132 JL HOOFDDORP
Tel: 88 7518148 **Fax:** 88 7518141
Web site: http://www.moto73.nl
Freq: 26 issues yearly; **Cover Price:** EUR 3,95
Annual Sub.: EUR 79,65; **Circ:** 25,748
Editor: Arie Blokland; **Editor-in-Chief:** Jan Boer; **Publisher:** Sander Stallinga
Profile: Magazine about motorcycle sports and motorcycles. Includes information on tests, technical features, racing reports and motorcycle tourism.
Language(s): Dutch
ADVERTISING RATES:
Full Page Mono EUR 2/1: f.c. 6340,-; b/w 3170,- 1/1: f.c. 3370,-; b/w 1685,- 1/2: f.c. 1900,-; b/w 950,-
Agency Commission: 15%
Mechanical Data: Type Area: 210 x 280mm, Bleed Size: 230 x 300mm
CONSUMER: MOTORING & CYCLING: Motor Sports

MOTOR 17772N77B-160
Editorial: Capellalaan 65, 2132 JL HOOFDDORP
Tel: 88 7518160 **Fax:** 88 7518161
Web site: http://www.motor.nl
Freq: 26 issues yearly; **Cover Price:** EUR 4,25
Annual Sub.: EUR 76,70; **Circ:** 28,709
Editor: Arie Blokland; **Publisher:** Sander Stallinga
Profile: Official journal of the KNMV - the Royal Dutch Motorcycle Association. Contains product reviews, reports on competitions, technical tips and touring and travelling information.
Language(s): Dutch
Readership: Aimed at motorcycle enthusiasts.
ADVERTISING RATES:
Full Page Mono EUR 2/1: f.c. 6040,-; b/w 3020,- 1/1: f.c. 3210,-; b/w 1605,- 1/2: f.c. 1810,-; b/w 850,-
Agency Commission: 15%
Mechanical Data: Type Area: 210 x 280mm, Bleed Size: 230 x 300mm
CONSUMER: MOTORING & CYCLING: Motorcycling

MOTORBOOT 18172N91A-45
Editorial: Isaac Titsinghkade 107, 1018 LL AMSTERDAM **Tel:** 30 2539300 **Fax:** 0032 34660067
Email: motorboot@bdu.nl **Web site:** http://www.motorboot.com
Freq: Monthly; **Cover Price:** EUR 5,50
Annual Sub.: EUR 52,-; **Circ:** 21,450
Editor: H. Papenburg; **Editor-in-Chief:** Y. Zwaan
Profile: Magazine containing news about engines, accessories, navigation and communication equipment, regulations, shows and exhibitions.
Language(s): Dutch
Readership: Aimed at owners of powerboats and cruisers, for both coastal and inland use.
ADVERTISING RATES:
Full Page Mono .. EUR 1/1: b/w 1455,- 1/2: b/w 940,- 1/4: b/w 535,-
Agency Commission: 15%
Mechanical Data: Type Area: 198 x 284mm, Bleed Size: 230 x 310mm
Copy instructions: *Copy Date:* 5 weeks prior to publication date
CONSUMER: RECREATION & LEISURE: Boating & Yachting

HET MOTORRIJWIEL 17767N77B-60
Editorial: Snelliusstraat 11, 2517 RG DEN HAAG
Tel: 20 5629444 **Fax:** 20 6680389
Email: info@motorrijwiel.nu **Web site:** http://www.motorrijwiel.nu
Date Established: 01-01-1993; **Freq:** 6 issues yearly; **Cover Price:** EUR 5,25
Annual Sub.: EUR 26,-; **Circ:** 20,000
Usual Pagination: 92
Editor: Hans van Dissel; **Editor-in-Chief:** E. Kil; **Publisher:** Hans van Dissel
Profile: Publication focusing on classic bikes, scooters and mopeds, includes technical information, background and lifestyle.
Language(s): Dutch
Readership: Read by classic bike lovers.
ADVERTISING RATES:
Full Page Mono .. EUR 1/1: f.c. 1120,-; b/w 560,- 1/2: f.c. 560,-; b/w 280,- 1/4: f.c. 308,-; b/w 154,-
Agency Commission: 15%
Mechanical Data: Type Area: 184 x 249mm, Bleed Size: 210 x 297mm
CONSUMER: MOTORING & CYCLING: Motorcycling

MUNTKOERIER 17834N79E-40
Editorial: Asselsestraat 104, 7311 ER APELDOORN
Tel: 88 7518160 **Fax:** 88 7518161
Email: omni-trading@planet.nl **Web site:** http://www.muntkoerier.com
Date Established: 01-01-1972; **Freq:** 11 issues yearly; **Cover Price:** EUR 5,50
Annual Sub.: EUR 47,90; **Circ:** 4,500
Editor: Tom Passon
Profile: Magazine concerning coins, medals, bank-notes, precious metals and collectables.
Language(s): Dutch
Readership: Aimed at investors and coin collectors.
ADVERTISING RATES:
Full Page Mono .... EUR 1/1: f.c. 943,-; b/w 727,- 1/2: f.c. 501,-; b/w 415,- 1/4: f.c. 294,-; b/w 254,-
Agency Commission: 15%
Mechanical Data: Type Area: 179 x 259mm, Bleed Size: 204 x 292mm
Copy instructions: *Copy Date:* 1 month prior to publication date
CONSUMER: HOBBIES & DIY: Numismatics

MUNTPERS 17835N79E-50
Editorial: Leidseweg 90, 3531 BG UTRECHT
Tel: 30 2910465 **Fax:** 30 2946179
Email: info@coins.nl
Date Established: 01-03-1989; **Freq:** Quarterly; **Cover Price:** Free; **Circ:** 80,000
Usual Pagination: 8
Editor: A.W. de Groot
Profile: Magazine for coin collectors.
Language(s): Dutch
Agency Commission: 15%
CONSUMER: HOBBIES & DIY: Numismatics

MUSEUMGIDS NOORD-BRABANT 1635021N64P-56
Editorial: Parade 18, 5211 KL 'S-HERTOGENBOSCH
Tel: 15 2617997 **Fax:** 229 216416
Email: info@erfgoedbrabant.nl
Date Established: 01-01-1993; **Freq:** Annual; **Cover Price:** Free; **Circ:** 100,000
Usual Pagination: 60
Editor: Petra Bakker
Language(s): Dutch
ADVERTISING RATES:
Full Page Mono .... EUR 1/1: f.c. 1950,-
Agency Commission: 15%
Mechanical Data: Bleed Size: 210 x 148mm, Type Area: 190 x 130mm
Copy instructions: *Copy Date:* 1 month prior to publication date
BUSINESS: OTHER CLASSIFICATIONS: Museums

MUSEUMVISIE 17034N64P-35
Editorial: Rapenburgerstraat 123, 1011 VL AMSTERDAM **Tel:** 88 7518160 **Fax:** 88 7518161
Email: info@museumvereniging.nl
Freq: Quarterly; **Cover Price:** EUR 12,50
Annual Sub.: EUR 45,-; **Circ:** 2,100
Editor: Chris Reinewald; **Editor-in-Chief:** Carlo Keijzer
Profile: Magazine focusing on news, trends, best practice, plans, book reviews, information on products, training, events and features on museum politics in the Netherlands. Each issue contains English summaries of the main articles.
Language(s): Dutch
Readership: Aimed at staff in Dutch museums.
ADVERTISING RATES:
Full Page Mono .. EUR 1/1: f.c. 1300,-; 1/2: f.c. 650,-; 1/4: f.c. 350,-
Agency Commission: 15%
Mechanical Data: Bleed Size: 220 x 290mm, Type Area: 195 x 270mm
Copy instructions: *Copy Date:* 5 weeks prior to publication date
BUSINESS: OTHER CLASSIFICATIONS: Museums

MUSIC EMOTION 1772928N78A-74
Editorial: Palinggracht 13, 6642 EE BEUNINGEN
Tel: 20 5310921 **Fax:** 492 371114
Email: info@vdgeld.nl **Web site:** http://www.music-emotion.nl
Freq: 11 issues yearly; **Annual Sub.:** EUR 39,95; **Circ:** 8,000
Editor: Ivo van den Broek; **Publisher:** Rene van der Geld
Language(s): Dutch
ADVERTISING RATES:
Full Page Mono .. EUR 1/1: f.c. 1190,-; 1/2: f.c. 723,-; 1/4: f.c. 419,-
Agency Commission: 15%
Mechanical Data: Type Area: 190 x 260mm, Bleed Size: 215 x 285mm
CONSUMER: CONSUMER ELECTRONICS: Hi-Fi & Recording

MUSIC POST JUST FOR YOU
17730N76E-55
Editorial: Joke Smitlaan 20, 2104 TG HEEMSTEDE
Tel: 0032 34660066
Email: music-master@zonnet.nl
Date Established: 28-08-1978; **Freq:** Half-yearly; **Annual Sub.:** EUR 13,61; **Circ:** 750
Editor: Christiaan Vrolijk; **Publisher:** Christiaan Vrolijk
Profile: Pop music magazine with details on old and new records, music memorabilia and music publications. Also includes interviews with pop stars.
Language(s): Dutch
Readership: Aimed at pop music enthusiasts.
Agency Commission: 15%
Mechanical Data: Type Area: 180 x 265mm, Bleed Size: 210 x 297mm
CONSUMER: MUSIC & PERFORMING ARTS: Pop Music

MUSICMAKER 16890N61-25
Editorial: Parkstraat 31, 6828 JC ARNHEM
Tel: 88 7518160
Web site: http://www.musicmaker.nl
Date Established: 01-11-1977; **Freq:** Monthly; **Annual Sub.:** EUR 65,-; **Circ:** 9,500
Editor: Mark Postema; **Publisher:** Mark Postema
Profile: Journal focusing on the music profession.
Language(s): Dutch
Readership: Read by amateur, semi-professional and professional musicians.
ADVERTISING RATES:
Full Page Mono EUR 1/1: f.c. 1900,-; 1/2: f.c. 1000,-; 1/4: f.c. 500,-
Agency Commission: 15%
Mechanical Data: Type Area: 205 x 265mm, Bleed Size: 225 x 285mm
Copy instructions: *Copy Date:* 2 weeks prior to publication date
BUSINESS: MUSIC TRADE

MUZIEK&LITURGIE 16896N61-75
Editorial: Postbus 1091, 1000 BB AMSTERDAM
Tel: 58 2954859 **Fax:** 20 6767728
Web site: http://www.muziekenliturgie.nl
Freq: 6 issues yearly; **Cover Price:** EUR 4,50; **Circ:** 1,300
Editor-in-Chief: Peter Ouwerkerk
Profile: Official journal of the Dutch Society of Church Organists.
Language(s): Dutch
ADVERTISING RATES:
Full Page Mono EUR 1/1: b/w 312,- 1/2: b/w 156,- 1/4: b/w 83,-
Agency Commission: 15%
Mechanical Data: Type Area: 180 x 270mm, Bleed Size: 210 x 297mm
BUSINESS: MUSIC TRADE

DE MUZIEKHANDEL 16893N61-50
Editorial: Stationslaan 117-5, 3844 GC HARDERWIJK **Tel:** 23 5567955 **Fax:** 23 5567956
Email: info@vmn.nl
Date Established: 01-01-1950; **Freq:** Quarterly; **Cover Price:** Free; **Circ:** 400
Usual Pagination: 16
Editor: F.J.P. de Wit
Profile: Journal about music publishing and sheet music.

Language(s): Dutch
Readership: Aimed at music publishers and distributors.
Agency Commission: 15%
Mechanical Data: Type Area: 172 x 239mm, Bleed Size: 190 x 270mm
BUSINESS: MUSIC TRADE

MUZIEKWERELD 16894N61-53
Editorial: Keizersgracht 317, 1016 EE AMSTERDAM
Tel: 23 5567955 **Fax:** 23 5567956
Email: info@ntb.nl
Date Established: 01-01-1919; **Freq:** Quarterly; **Annual Sub.:** EUR 20,-; **Circ:** 4,000
Editor: E. Angad-Gaur; **Editor-in-Chief:** R. Zinzen
Profile: Official publication of the Dutch Musicians' Union.
Language(s): Dutch
Readership: Read by members of the union.
ADVERTISING RATES:
Full Page Mono EUR 1/1: f.c. 500,-; 1/2: f.c. 300,-; 1/4: f.c. 180,-
Agency Commission: 15%
Mechanical Data: Bleed Size: 205 x 255mm
BUSINESS: MUSIC TRADE

MY TOYOTA 1857709N77A-378
Editorial: Olympia 10, 1213 NP HILVERSUM
Tel: 70 3789685 **Fax:** 70 3705372
Email: mail@hemels.com
Freq: Quarterly; **Cover Price:** Free; **Circ:** 240,000
Editor: Marlies van Steenoven; **Publisher:** Wilfred Mons
Language(s): Dutch
ADVERTISING RATES:
Full Page Mono .... EUR 2/1: f.c. 20.435,-; 1/1: f.c. 10.218,-
Agency Commission: 15%
Mechanical Data: Bleed Size: 210 x 265mm
Copy instructions: *Copy Date:* 6 weeks prior to publication date
CONSUMER: MOTORING & CYCLING: Motoring

MYCAMPINA MAGAZINE 16117N21C-20
Editorial: Postbus 2100, 5300 CC ZALTBOMMEL
Tel: 33 2471104 **Fax:** 23 5564241
Date Established: 01-11-1991; **Freq:** 13 issues yearly; **Annual Sub.:** EUR 28,-; **Circ:** 12,000
Usual Pagination: 16
Editor: G. Zeissink
Profile: Publication with information for members of Campina Milk Union and dairy cattle farmers.
Language(s): Dutch
Readership: Read by members of Campina Milk Union and dairy cattle farmers.
Agency Commission: 15%
BUSINESS: AGRICULTURE & FARMING: Dairy Farming

NATIONAL GEOGRAPHIC 707287N73-105
Editorial: Dalsteindreef 82-92, 1112 XC DIEMEN
Tel: 23 5566770 **Fax:** 570 614795
Email: info@genj.nl **Web site:** http://www.nationalgeographic.nl
Freq: Monthly; **Cover Price:** EUR 4,95
Annual Sub.: EUR 54,45; **Circ:** 119,427
Editor: Aart Aarsbergen
Profile: Magazine providing geographic information, articles concerning natural history and society. Also includes news of general interest from around the world.
Language(s): Dutch
ADVERTISING RATES:
Full Page Mono .... EUR 2/1: f.c. 19.950,-; 1/1: f.c. 10.625,-; 1/2: f.c. 6300,-
Agency Commission: 15%
Mechanical Data: Type Area: 142 x 224mm, Bleed Size: 175 x 254mm
Copy instructions: *Copy Date:* 4 weeks prior to publication date
CONSUMER: NATIONAL & INTERNATIONAL PERIODICALS

NATIONAL GEOGRAPHIC TRAVELER 1643432N89A-219
Editorial: Dalsteindreef 82-92, 1112 XC DIEMEN
Tel: 15 2690180 **Fax:** 15 2690287
Email: info@genj.nl **Web site:** http://www.ngmag.nl/traveler
Freq: Quarterly; **Cover Price:** EUR 4,95
Annual Sub.: EUR 19,95; **Circ:** 42,446
Editor: Aart Aarsbergen; **Publisher:** E. Blok
Language(s): Dutch
ADVERTISING RATES:
Full Page Mono EUR 2/1: f.c. 8075,-; 1/1: f.c. 4295,-; 1/2: f.c. 2550,-
Agency Commission: 15%
Mechanical Data: Type Area: 188 x 247mm, Bleed Size: 208 x 267mm
Copy instructions: *Copy Date:* 4 weeks prior to publication date
CONSUMER: HOLIDAYS & TRAVEL: Travel

NATIONALE KIDSKRANT 1637077N91D-140
Editorial: Asterweg 20c, 1031 HN AMSTERDAM
Tel: 53 4871543 **Fax:** 182 543500
Web site: http://www.nationalekinderkrant.nl
Freq: 8 issues yearly; **Annual Sub.:** EUR 139,95; **Circ:** 100,000
Editor: Marieke Rikken
Language(s): Dutch
ADVERTISING RATES:
Full Page Mono EUR 1/1: f.c. 5250,-; 1/2: f.c. 2750,-
Agency Commission: 15%
Mechanical Data: Type Area: 261 x 383mm, Bleed Size: 290 x 420mm
Copy instructions: *Copy Date:* 4 weeks prior to publication date
CONSUMER: RECREATION & LEISURE: Children & Youth

NATURAL BODY 17642N75P-150
Editorial: A. Hofmanweg 11, 2031 BH HAARLEM
Tel: 15 2126695 **Fax:** 15 2126695
Email: info@jdcomm.nl **Web site:** http://www.nbody.nl
Freq: 6 issues yearly; **Cover Price:** EUR 3,95
Annual Sub.: EUR 15,-; **Circ:** 31,702
Editor: Jurgen Drieskens; **Editor-in-Chief:** M. Veenstra; **Publisher:** Jurgen Drieskens
Profile: Magazine about aerobics, fitness and healthy eating.
Language(s): Dutch
Readership: Aimed at fitness and health enthusiasts.
ADVERTISING RATES:
Full Page Mono EUR 2/1: f.c. 7250,-; 1/1: f.c. 4250,-; b/w 2950,- 1/2: f.c. 2450,-; b/w 1750,-
Agency Commission: 15%
Mechanical Data: Type Area: 180 x 266mm, Bleed Size: 210 x 297mm
Copy instructions: *Copy Date:* 6 weeks prior to publication date
CONSUMER: SPORT: Fitness/Bodybuilding

NATUURBEHOUD 16840N57-47
Editorial: Noordereinde 60, 1243 JJ 'S-GRAVELAND
Tel: 23 5567955 **Fax:** 23 5567956
Freq: Quarterly; **Annual Sub.:** EUR 20,-; **Circ:** 850,000
Editor: Jeroen van de Koppel; **Editor-in-Chief:** Frans Bosscher
Profile: Publication about the preservation of nature reserves and monuments in the Netherlands.
Language(s): Dutch
Agency Commission: 15%
BUSINESS: ENVIRONMENT & POLLUTION

NATUUREILAND TEXEL 1899523N57-215
Editorial: Ruijslaan 90, 1796 AZ DE KOOG
Tel: 30 6383716
Date Established: 01-05-2004; **Freq:** Half-yearly; **Cover Price:** Free; **Circ:** 60,000
Editor-in-Chief: Johan Bos
Language(s): Dutch
Agency Commission: 15%
BUSINESS: ENVIRONMENT & POLLUTION

DE NATUURGIDS 16841N57-48
Editorial: Pergamijndonk 16, 6218 GV MAASTRICHT
Tel: 23 5567955 **Fax:** 23 5567956
Web site: http://www.denatuurgids.nl
Freq: 8 issues yearly; **Annual Sub.:** EUR 17,50; **Circ:** 5,000
Editor-in-Chief: J.W. Bonten
Profile: Magazine about nature and the environment in Limburg.
Language(s): Dutch
Agency Commission: 15%
BUSINESS: ENVIRONMENT & POLLUTION

NATUURHISTORISCH MAANDBLAD 16842N81A-125
Editorial: Godsweerderstraat 2, 6041 GH ROERMOND **Tel:** 23 5567955
Email: kantoor@nhgl.nl
Freq: Monthly; **Annual Sub.:** EUR 27,50; **Circ:** 1,400
Usual Pagination: 24
Editor: G. Verschoor
Profile: Magazine containing information about nature, the landscape and geology in Limburg.
Language(s): Dutch
Readership: Aimed at all nature lovers and birdwatchers.
Agency Commission: 15%
Mechanical Data: Type Area: 170 x 240mm, Bleed Size: 205 x 290mm
CONSUMER: ANIMALS & PETS: Animals & Pets Protection

NATUURSTEEN 1634556N4E-290
Editorial: Marconistraat 33, 3771 AM BARNEVELD
Tel: 342 494848 **Fax:** 342 494299
Email: i@bdu.nl **Web site:** http://www.vakbladnatuursteen.nl
Date Established: 01-01-1948; **Freq:** 11 issues yearly; **Annual Sub.:** EUR 65,81; **Circ:** 1,729
Editor: Sandra van der Horst; **Publisher:** Ton Roskam
Language(s): Dutch
ADVERTISING RATES:
Full Page Mono EUR 1/1: b/w 723,- 1/2: b/w 402,- 1/4: b/w 286,-
Agency Commission: 15%
Mechanical Data: Type Area: 180 x 262mm, Bleed Size: 210 x 297mm
Copy instructions: *Copy Date:* 3 weeks prior to publication date
BUSINESS: ARCHITECTURE & BUILDING: Building

NAUTIQUE MAGAZINE 18173N91A-50
Editorial: Delflandlaan 4, 1062 EB AMSTERDAM
Tel: 20 3113797 **Fax:** 30 6007595
Email: info@pelicanmags.nl **Web site:** http://www.nautique.nl
Date Established: 01-01-1995; **Freq:** Quarterly;
Cover Price: EUR 6,50
Annual Sub.: EUR 19,50; **Circ:** 14,176
Editor: Arthur van 't Hof; **Editor-in-Chief:** Marike Popma; **Publisher:** F.N. Kloppert
Profile: Yachting magazine.
Language(s): Dutch
ADVERTISING RATES:
Full Page Mono EUR 1/1: f.c. 3970,-; 1/2: f.c. 2978,-; 1/4: f.c. 1588,-
Agency Commission: 15%
Mechanical Data: Type Area: 210 x 270mm, Bleed Size: 230 x 297mm
Copy instructions: *Copy Date:* 4 weeks prior to publication date
CONSUMER: RECREATION & LEISURE: Boating & Yachting

NAVENANT 1660715N74Q-301
Editorial: Kraanpoort 10, 6041 EG ROERMOND
Tel: 20 8969520 **Fax:** 30 6383839
Email: info@holbox.nl **Web site:** http://www.navenant.nl
Freq: 6 issues yearly; **Cover Price:** EUR 4,50
Annual Sub.: EUR 12,50; **Circ:** 16,954
Editor: A. Oomen
Language(s): Dutch
ADVERTISING RATES:
Full Page Mono EUR 2/1: f.c. 2850,-; 1/1: f.c. 1650,-; 1/2: f.c. 950,-
Agency Commission: 15%
Mechanical Data: Type Area: 190 x 255mm, Bleed Size: 200 x 265mm
CONSUMER: WOMEN'S INTEREST CONSUMER MAGAZINES: Lifestyle

NCRV-GIDS 1634562N76C-126
Editorial: 's-Gravelandseweg 80, 1217 EW HILVERSUM **Tel:** 35 6726800 **Fax:** 35 6726803
Web site: http://www.ncrvgids.nl
Date Established: 06-01-1925; **Freq:** Weekly; **Cover Price:** EUR 1,30
Annual Sub.: EUR 55,25; **Circ:** 233,066
Editor: Saskia de Jong; **Editor-in-Chief:** W. Hekhuis; **Publisher:** Saskia de Jong
Language(s): Dutch
ADVERTISING RATES:
Full Page Mono .... EUR 2/1: f.c. 15.380,-; 1/1: f.c. 7690,-; 1/2: f.c. 5383,-
Agency Commission: 15%
Mechanical Data: Type Area: 172 x 215mm, Bleed Size: 202 x 245mm
CONSUMER: MUSIC & PERFORMING ARTS: TV & Radio

NEDERLANDS DAGBLAD 17041N65A-35
Editorial: Hermesweg 20, 3771 ND BARNEVELD
Tel: 35 6726800 **Fax:** 35 6726803
Email: info@nd.nl **Web site:** http://www.nd.nl
Freq: 312 issues yearly; **Annual Sub.:** EUR 315,-; **Circ:** 30,150
Editor: Peter Bergwerff; **Editor-in-Chief:** C. Dorland
Profile: Broadsheet-sized newspaper covering news, politics, current affairs, culture, leisure and religion from a Christian viewpoint.
Language(s): Dutch
Readership: Aimed at people with an active interest in the Christian religion.
ADVERTISING RATES:
Full Page Mono EUR 2/1: f.c. 9390,-; b/w 6260,- 1/1: f.c. 4755,-; b/w 3170,- 1/2: f.c. 2400,-; b/w 1600,-
Agency Commission: 15%
Mechanical Data: Type Area: 266 x 398mm, Bleed Size: 315 x 470mm
NATIONAL DAILY & SUNDAY NEWSPAPERS: National Daily Newspapers

NEDERLANDS MILITAIR GENEESKUNDIG TIJDSCHRIFT 16690N56A-115
Editorial: Binckhorstlaan 135, 2516 BA DEN HAAG
Tel: 35 6726800 **Fax:** 35 6726803
Date Established: 01-12-1947; **Freq:** 6 issues yearly; **Cover Price:** Free; **Circ:** 12,000
Editor: R.P. van der Meulen; **Editor-in-Chief:** A.H.M. de Bok
Profile: Official military medical review for the Dutch armed forces and for those out of active service.
Language(s): Dutch
ADVERTISING RATES:
Full Page Mono EUR 1/1: f.c. 1550,-; 1/2: f.c. 1090,-
Agency Commission: 15%
Mechanical Data: Type Area: 180 x 265mm, Bleed Size: 210 x 297mm
Copy instructions: *Copy Date:* 4 weeks prior to publication date
BUSINESS: HEALTH & MEDICAL

NEDERLANDS TIJDSCHRIFT VOOR ANESTHESIOLOGIE 16692N56A-118_50
Editorial: Postbus 5800, 6202 AZ MAASTRICHT
Tel: 20 5629444 **Fax:** 20 6680389
Email: ntva@sane.azm.nl
Freq: 5 issues yearly; **Cover Price:** EUR 19,50; **Circ:** 2,015
Editor: Marco Marcus
Profile: Journal about anaesthesiology.
Language(s): Dutch
ADVERTISING RATES:
Full Page Mono EUR 1/1: f.c. 2400,-; 1/2: f.c. 1500,-; 1/4: f.c. 1150,-
Agency Commission: 15%
Mechanical Data: Type Area: 205 x 277mm, Bleed Size: 190 x 260mm
BUSINESS: HEALTH & MEDICAL

NEDERLANDS TIJDSCHRIFT VOOR DERMATOLOGIE & VENEREOLOGIE 16693N56A-119_50
Editorial: Postbus 9101, 6500 HB NIJMEGEN
Tel: 161 457342 **Fax:** 20 5159145
Email: redactiesecretariaat@derma.umcn.nl
Date Established: 01-01-1990; **Freq:** 10 issues yearly; **Cover Price:** EUR 25,-
Annual Sub.: EUR 180,-; **Circ:** 1,200
Editor: P.G.M. van der Valk; **Editor-in-Chief:** Laura Fritschy
Profile: Journal containing articles on the treatment of skin disorders and venereal disease.
Language(s): Dutch
Agency Commission: 15%
Mechanical Data: Bleed Size: 210 x 297mm
BUSINESS: HEALTH & MEDICAL

NEDERLANDS TIJDSCHRIFT VOOR FYSIOTHERAPIE 16768N56L-95
Editorial: Stadsring 159b, 3817 BA AMERSFOORT
Tel: 35 6726800 **Fax:** 30 6076301
Email: hoofdkantoor@kngf.nl
Freq: Quarterly; **Annual Sub.:** EUR 65,-; **Circ:** 19,500
Editor: Paul Helders; **Editor-in-Chief:** Sjoerd Olthof
Profile: Magazine about physiotherapy. Covers new methods and research.
Language(s): Dutch
Readership: Aimed at paramedics and physiotherapists.
ADVERTISING RATES:
Full Page Mono EUR 1/1: f.c. 2526,-; b/w 1497,- 1/2: f.c. 1452,-; b/w 934,- 1/4: f.c. 822,-; b/w 562,-
Agency Commission: 15%
Mechanical Data: Type Area: 167 x 230mm, Bleed Size: 195 x 265mm
BUSINESS: HEALTH & MEDICAL: Disability & Rehabilitation

NEDERLANDS TIJDSCHRIFT VOOR HEELKUNDE 16696N56A-122
Editorial: Mercatorlaan 12, 3528 BL UTRECHT
Tel: 342 494848 **Fax:** 342 494299
Email: nvvh@nvvh.knmg.nl
Date Established: 01-01-1992; **Freq:** 9 issues yearly;
Annual Sub.: EUR 45,65; **Circ:** 2,085
Editor-in-Chief: C. Kramer; **Publisher:** Ben Konings
Profile: Journal for specialists in surgery.
Language(s): Dutch
ADVERTISING RATES:
Full Page Mono EUR 1/1: f.c. 2835,-; 1/2: f.c. 2158,-; 1/4: f.c. 1739,-
Agency Commission: 15%
Mechanical Data: Type Area: 185 x 268mm, Bleed Size: 210 x 297mm
BUSINESS: HEALTH & MEDICAL

NEDERLANDS TIJDSCHRIFT VOOR TANDHEELKUNDE (NTVT) 16738N56D-40
Editorial: Postbus 1378, 3430 BJ NIEUWEGEIN
Tel: 35 6726800 **Fax:** 30 6076301
Email: ntvtred@planet.nl **Web site:** http://www.ntvt.nl
Freq: 11 issues yearly; **Circ:** 4,735
Editor: Cees de Baat; **Editor-in-Chief:** J.S. van der Vos
Profile: Magazine about all aspects of dentistry.
Language(s): Dutch
Readership: Read by dental practitioners, dental nurses and students.
ADVERTISING RATES:
Full Page Mono EUR 1/1: f.c. 2600,-; PMS 1800,-; b/w 1325,- 1/2: f.c. 1470,-; PMS 1190,-; b/w 795,- 1/4: f.c. 970,-; PM
Agency Commission: 15%
Mechanical Data: Type Area: 185 x 267mm, Bleed Size: 210 x 297mm
Copy instructions: *Copy Date:* 1 month prior to publication date
BUSINESS: HEALTH & MEDICAL: Dental

NEDERLANDS TIJDSCHRIFT VOOR TRAUMATOLOGIE 16698N56A-123_30
Editorial: Het Spoor 2, 3994 AK HOUTEN
Tel: 172 466539 **Fax:** 10 4521797
Freq: 6 issues yearly; **Annual Sub.:** EUR 61,85; **Circ:** 1,144

Editor: J. Biert
Profile: Journal covering research and developments in the treatment of injury or wounds.
Language(s): Dutch
Readership: Read by those involved in treatment of traumas.
ADVERTISING RATES:
Full Page Mono EUR 1/1: f.c. 3533,-; b/w 1687,- 1/2: f.c. 1273,-; b/w 1052,- 1/4: f.c. 1321,-; b/w 633,-
Agency Commission: 15%
Mechanical Data: Type Area: 184 x 272mm, Bleed Size: 210 x 297mm
BUSINESS: HEALTH & MEDICAL

NEDERLANDS TIJDSCHRIFT VOOR VOEDING & DIËTETIEK
16803N56R-213
Editorial: De Molen 93, 3995 AW HOUTEN
Tel: 35 6726800 **Fax:** 30 6076301
Web site: http://www.nvdietist.nl
Freq: 6 issues yearly; **Annual Sub.:** EUR 63,-; **Circ:** 3,008
Editor: Evelien Adriaan; **Editor-in-Chief:** W. van Koningsbruggen; **Publisher:** P. van Mameren
Profile: Official journal of the Dutch Dieticians' Association, containing medical and scientific information, book reviews, useful web-pages and training advice.
Language(s): Dutch
Readership: Read by nutritional experts and hospital dieticians.
ADVERTISING RATES:
Full Page Mono EUR 1/1: f.c. 2241,-; PMS 1495,-; b/w 1241,- 1/2: f.c. 1786,-; PMS 1043,-; b/w 729,- 1/4: f.c. 1297,-; P
Agency Commission: 15%
Mechanical Data: Type Area: 185 x 268mm, Bleed Size: 210 x 297mm
Copy instructions: *Copy Date:* 11 days prior to publication date
BUSINESS: HEALTH & MEDICAL: Health Medical Related

NEDERLANDS VERVOER
16552N49A-14
Editorial: Spui 188, 2511 BW DEN HAAG
Tel: 35 6726800 **Fax:** 30 6076301
Email: knvmedia@knv.nl
Date Established: 05-05-1949; **Freq:** 10 issues yearly; **Annual Sub.:** EUR 72,-; **Circ:** 2,799
Editor: Jos Haas
Profile: Journal providing information on public transport in the Netherlands. Focuses on taxis and touring coaches, taxi branches and touring car branches.
Language(s): Dutch
Readership: Aimed at entrepreneurs, managers of taxi firms and coach companies and owners of public transport companies.
ADVERTISING RATES:
Full Page Mono .. EUR 1/1: b/w 1404,- 1/2: b/w 771,- 1/4: b/w 424,-
Agency Commission: 15%
Mechanical Data: Type Area: 185 x 270mm, Bleed Size: 210 x 297mm
Copy instructions: *Copy Date:* 10 days prior to publication date
BUSINESS: TRANSPORT

DE NEDERLANDSCHE LEEUW
18252N94X-120
Editorial: Prins Willem-Alexanderhof 22, 2595 BE DEN HAAG
Email: redactie@knggw.nl
Date Established: 01-01-1883; **Freq:** 5 issues yearly; **Cover Price:** EUR 15,-
Annual Sub.: EUR 55,-; **Circ:** 900
Editor-in-Chief: P.M. Kernkamp
Profile: Magazine about genealogy and heraldry.
Language(s): Dutch
Readership: Aimed at all those interested in heraldry and genealogy.
ADVERTISING RATES:
Full Page Mono EUR 1/1: b/w 300,- 1/2: b/w 175,- 1/4: b/w 100,-
Agency Commission: 15%
Mechanical Data: Type Area: 155 x 240mm
CONSUMER: OTHER CLASSIFICATIONS: Miscellaneous

HET NEDERLANDSE BOEK
18031N84B-70
Editorial: De Lairessestraat 108, 1071 PK AMSTERDAM **Tel:** 35 6726800
Date Established: 01-01-1961; **Freq:** 6 issues yearly; **Annual Sub.:** EUR 10,-; **Circ:** 12,000
Usual Pagination: 24
Editor: J.G. Waldorp; **Publisher:** J.G. Waldorp
Profile: Magazine for book lovers.
Language(s): Dutch
Agency Commission: 15%
CONSUMER: THE ARTS & LITERARY: Literary

DE NEDERLANDSE VLIEGVISSER
18206N92-90
Editorial: Nieuwe Gracht 78, 3512 LV UTRECHT
Tel: 172 466911 **Fax:** 229 216416
Date Established: 01-01-1986; **Freq:** Quarterly; **Cover Price:** EUR 7,50
Annual Sub.: EUR 25,-; **Circ:** 5,000
Editor: H. Spruijt; **Editor-in-Chief:** Hyppo Wanders
Profile: Magazine about flyfishing, the environment, the biology of fish and the conservation of their habitat.
Language(s): Dutch
Readership: Read by anglers.
ADVERTISING RATES:
Full Page Mono .... EUR 1/1: f.c. 715,-; b/w 445,- 1/2: f.c. 465,-; b/w 255,- 1/4: f.c. 310,-; b/w 170,-
Agency Commission: 15%
Mechanical Data: Type Area: 210 x 267mm, Bleed Size: 230 x 297mm
Copy instructions: *Copy Date:* 7 weeks prior to publication date
CONSUMER: ANGLING & FISHING

NETHERLANDS HEART JOURNAL
16655N56A-110
Editorial: Het Spoor 2, 3994 AK HOUTEN
Tel: 30 6383838 **Fax:** 30 6383839
Freq: 11 issues yearly; **Circ:** 2,359
Editor: E.E. van der Wall
Profile: Journal focusing on cardiac treatment.
Language(s): Dutch
Readership: Read by specialists in cardiology.
ADVERTISING RATES:
Full Page Mono EUR 1/1: f.c. 3880,-; b/w 2089,- 1/2: f.c. 3097,-; b/w 1306,- 1/4: f.c. 2532,-; b/w 742,-
Agency Commission: 15%
Mechanical Data: Type Area: 180 x 228mm, Bleed Size: 210 x 280mm
BUSINESS: HEALTH & MEDICAL

THE NETHERLANDS JOURNAL OF MEDICINE
16700N56A-124
Editorial: Postbus 9101, 6500 HB NIJMEGEN
Tel: 70 3780586 **Fax:** 30 6076301
Freq: 11 issues yearly; **Annual Sub.:** EUR 670,-; **Circ:** 2,800
Usual Pagination: 48
Editor: Marcel Levi; **Editor-in-Chief:** J.P.H. Drenth
Profile: Journal about internal medicine. Includes articles about endocrinology/metabolism, oncology, nephrology, gastroenterology, haematology, infectious, respiratory and cardiovascular diseases and pharmacology.
Language(s): Dutch
Readership: Aimed at medical specialists.
ADVERTISING RATES:
Full Page Mono .... EUR 1/1: f.c. 2935,-
Agency Commission: 15%
Mechanical Data: Type Area: 165 x 268mm, Bleed Size: 210 x 297mm
BUSINESS: HEALTH & MEDICAL

NEUROPRAXIS
16781N56N-65
Editorial: Het Spoor 2, 3994 AK HOUTEN
Tel: 172 466622 **Fax:** 24 3723631
Freq: 6 issues yearly; **Annual Sub.:** EUR 74,70; **Circ:** 1,340
Profile: Publication focusing on neuroscience and practice.
Language(s): Dutch
ADVERTISING RATES:
Full Page Mono .. EUR 1/1: f.c. 2071,-; b/w 786,- 1/2: f.c. 1304,-; b/w 494,- 1/4: f.c. 782,-; b/w 297,-
Agency Commission: 15%
Mechanical Data: Type Area: 165 x 240mm, Bleed Size: 205 x 275mm
BUSINESS: HEALTH & MEDICAL: Mental Health

NEVAC BLAD
16635N55-30
Editorial: Nijenborgh 4, 9747 AG GRONINGEN
Tel: 35 6726800
Web site: http://www.nevac.nl
Date Established: 01-01-1962; **Freq:** Quarterly; **Annual Sub.:** EUR 25,-; **Circ:** 400
Usual Pagination: 32
Editor: Bart Kooi; **Publisher:** Ben Mobach
Profile: Journal focusing on vacuum science, technology and applications.
Language(s): Dutch
Readership: Aimed at technicians and scientists working with vacuum systems and related products.
ADVERTISING RATES:
Full Page Mono ..... EUR 1/1: f.c. 500,-; 1/2: f.c. 250,-
Agency Commission: 15%
Mechanical Data: Type Area: 170 x 225mm, Bleed Size: 210 x 297mm
Copy instructions: *Copy Date:* 2 weeks prior to publication date
BUSINESS: APPLIED SCIENCE & LABORATORIES

NEW FOLKSOUNDS
17704N76D-105
Editorial: Postbus 1022, 4388 ZG OOST-SOUBURG
Tel: 88 2944900 **Fax:** 35 6728834
Web site: http://www.newfolksounds.nl
Freq: 6 issues yearly; **Cover Price:** EUR 4,25
Annual Sub.: EUR 23,75; **Circ:** 1,000
Editor: L. Zevenbergen; **Editor-in-Chief:** M. Pol
Profile: Magazine focusing on folk, world and roots music.
Language(s): Dutch
Readership: Aimed at those interested in folk, world and alternative music.
ADVERTISING RATES:
Full Page Mono EUR 1/1: b/w 270,- 1/2: b/w 165,- 1/3: b/w 130,-
Agency Commission: 15%
Mechanical Data: Type Area: 190 x 255mm, Bleed Size: 209 x 297mm
Copy instructions: *Copy Date:* 6 weeks prior to publication date
CONSUMER: MUSIC & PERFORMING ARTS: Music

NIEUW LEVEN
19224N87-2281
Editorial: Apeldoornselaan 2, 2573 LM DEN HAAG
Tel: 70 3780586 **Fax:** 30 6076301
Email: info@maasbach.com
Date Established: 01-03-1963; **Freq:** Monthly; **Annual Sub.:** EUR 10,-; **Circ:** 20,000
Usual Pagination: 36
Editor: D. Maasbach; **Editor-in-Chief:** D. Maasbach; **Publisher:** D. Maasbach
Profile: Evangelical journal.
Language(s): Dutch
Agency Commission: 15%
Mechanical Data: Type Area: 180 x 230mm, Bleed Size: 210 x 297mm
CONSUMER: RELIGIOUS

DE NIEUWE SCHAKEL
627029N72-3460
Editorial: Torenhoekstraat 15, 5056 AM BERKEL-ENSCHOT **Tel:** 73 6136424
Email: info@denieuweschakel.nl **Web site:** http://www.denieuweschakel.nl
Date Established: 01-07-1965; **Freq:** Weekly; **Cover Price:** Free; **Circ:** 4,400
Usual Pagination: 40
Editor: Marcel Panis; **Publisher:** Marcel Panis
Language(s): Dutch
ADVERTISING RATES:
Full Page Mono EUR 2/1: b/w 221,- 1/1: b/w 120,- 1/2: b/w 78,-
Agency Commission: 15%
Mechanical Data: Type Area: 135 x 178mm, Bleed Size: 150 x 215mm
LOCAL NEWSPAPERS

NIEUWS OOSTEUROPA ZENDING
18099N87-172
Editorial: Tiendweg 9, 2931 LC KRIMPEN A/D LEK
Tel: 172 466539 **Fax:** 172 463270
Freq: Monthly; **Cover Price:** Free; **Circ:** 12,000
Editor: M.J. van der Weide
Profile: Magazine focusing on missions in East Europe.
Language(s): Dutch
Readership: Read by evangelical Christians, in particular people interested in undertaking and/or financially supporting mission work.
Agency Commission: 15%
CONSUMER: RELIGIOUS

NIEUWSBLAD RODE KRUIS UTRECHT MIDDEN
16793N56P-100
Editorial: Koningsweg 2, 3582 GE UTRECHT
Tel: 20 5922250 **Fax:** 30 6348909
Email: info@rodekruisutrechtmidden.nl
Date Established: 01-01-1980; **Freq:** 6 issues yearly; **Cover Price:** Free; **Circ:** 2,500
Usual Pagination: 16
Editor: M. van de Ven
Profile: Journal focusing on the work of the Utrecht Red Cross Society.
Language(s): Dutch
Readership: Read by the Society's members and both internal and external volunteers.
Agency Commission: 15%
BUSINESS: HEALTH & MEDICAL: Casualty & Emergency

NIEUWSBLAD VAN NOORD-OOST FRIESLAND
626719N72-3620
Editorial: Sixmastraat 15, 8932 PA LEEUWARDEN
Tel: 88 7518380 **Fax:** 511 452931
Email: info@ndcmediagroep.nl **Web site:** http://www.nieuwsbladnof.nl
Date Established: 02-08-1880; **Freq:** 104 issues yearly; **Cover Price:** EUR 0,85; **Circ:** 7,500
Editor: Roel Muskee
Language(s): Dutch
ADVERTISING RATES:
Full Page Mono EUR 2/1: b/w 4032,- 1/1: b/w 2016,- 1/2: b/w 1008,-
Agency Commission: 15%
Mechanical Data: Type Area: 262 x 397mm
Copy instructions: *Copy Date:* 1 day prior to publication date
LOCAL NEWSPAPERS

NIEUWSBLAD VOOR CASTRICUM
626981N72-3630
Editorial: Spoorsingel 26c, 1941 JM BEVERWIJK
Tel: 88 7518380 **Fax:** 511 452931
Web site: http://www.nieuwsbladcastricum.nl
Freq: Weekly; **Cover Price:** Free; **Circ:** 17,500
Language(s): Dutch
Agency Commission: 15%
Mechanical Data: Type Area: 260 x 390mm
LOCAL NEWSPAPERS

NIEUWSBRIEF BOND VOOR MATERIALENKENNIS
16054N19R-120
Editorial: Postbus 359, 5600 AJ EINDHOVEN
Tel: 10 2894015 **Fax:** 20 6159047
Email: info@materialenkennis.nl
Date Established: 01-01-2003; **Freq:** Quarterly; **Circ:** 1,750
Usual Pagination: 8
Editor-in-Chief: Eddy Brinkman
Profile: Official journal of the Organisation for Materials Engineering.
Language(s): Dutch
Readership: Aimed at production companies, engineers and students in higher education.
Agency Commission: 15%
Mechanical Data: Type Area: 190 x 270mm, Bleed Size: 210 x 297mm
BUSINESS: ENGINEERING & MACHINERY: Engineering Related

NIEUWSBRIEF VOEDSELVEILIGHEID
16164N22A-70
Editorial: Essebaan 63, 2908 LJ CAPELLE AAN DEN IJSSEL **Tel:** 10 2894018 **Fax:** 24 3723631
Email: info@mybusinessmedia.nl
Date Established: 01-01-1995; **Freq:** 11 issues yearly; **Cover Price:** EUR 9,90
Annual Sub.: EUR 95,65; **Circ:** 900
Editor: Martin Michels; **Editor-in-Chief:** A.C.M. Weber; **Publisher:** P.T. Both
Profile: Magazine about all aspects of food safety.
Language(s): Dutch
ADVERTISING RATES:
Full Page Mono ..... EUR 1/2: b/w 440,- 1/4: b/w 242,-
Agency Commission: 15%
Mechanical Data: Type Area: 155 x 255mm, Bleed Size: 210 x 297mm
BUSINESS: FOOD

NIEUWSBRIEF ZACCO (VOORHEEN SCHIELDMARK)
15589N2A-58_25
Editorial: Nachtwachtlaan 20, 1058 EA AMSTERDAM
Tel: 70 3780586 **Fax:** 30 6076301
Email: info.amsterdam@zacco.com
Freq: Quarterly; **Cover Price:** Free; **Circ:** 40,000
Editor: Esthel Douwstra-van Onselen
Profile: Magazine containing news and information relating to brands and laws in business and marketing.
Language(s): Dutch
Readership: Aimed at general and marketing managers and company lawyers.
Agency Commission: 15%
BUSINESS: COMMUNICATIONS, ADVERTISING & MARKETING

NIEUWSPOORT NIEUWS
15595N2B-40
Editorial: Lange Poten 10, 2511 CL DEN HAAG
Tel: 45 5739390 **Fax:** 20 5233419
Date Established: 06-03-1962; **Freq:** 10 issues yearly; **Circ:** 2,400
Usual Pagination: 28
Editor: Milja de Zwart
Profile: Magazine focusing on journalism, media, publicity and public relations.
Language(s): Dutch
Readership: Read by members of the International press centre Nieuwspoort.
ADVERTISING RATES:
Full Page Mono EUR 2/1: b/w 1250,- 1/1: f.c. 1895,-; b/w 640,-
Agency Commission: 15%
Mechanical Data: Type Area: 185 x 265mm, Bleed Size: 213 x 291mm
BUSINESS: COMMUNICATIONS, ADVERTISING & MARKETING: Press

NIGHTLIFE MAGAZINE
16992N64C-7
Editorial: Oostergrachtswal 95, 8921 AB LEEUWARDEN **Tel:** 46 4116600 **Fax:** 71 3643461
Web site: http://www.nightlifemagazine.nl
Freq: 6 issues yearly; **Annual Sub.:** EUR 49,50; **Circ:** 4,058
Editor: Jacco Bijlsma; **Publisher:** Jacco Bijlsma
Profile: Magazine with information about discos, nightclubs and dance pubs in Belgium and the Netherlands.
Language(s): Dutch
Readership: Aimed at the managers of these establishments.
ADVERTISING RATES:
Full Page Mono EUR 2/1: f.c. 2595,-; 1/1: f.c. 1695,-; 1/2: f.c. 995,-
Agency Commission: 15%
Mechanical Data: Type Area: 182 x 257mm, Bleed Size: 210 x 297mm
Copy instructions: *Copy Date:* 10 days prior to publication date
BUSINESS: OTHER CLASSIFICATIONS: Clubs

DE NIJMEEGSE STADSKRANT
17872N80-85
Editorial: Tweede Walstraat 19/21, 6511 LN NIJMEGEN **Tel:** 88 2697112
Email: nsk@antenna.nl **Web site:** http://www.antenna.nl/nsk
Date Established: 20-01-1981; **Freq:** 6 issues yearly; **Circ:** 12,500

Netherlands

Usual Pagination: 12
Editor-in-Chief: Max van Wel
Profile: Magazine for Nijmegen.
Language(s): Dutch
ADVERTISING RATES:
Full Page Mono .. EUR 1/1: f.c. 930,-; PMS 865,-; b/w 800,- 1/2: f.c. 530,-; PMS 465,-; b/w 400,- 1/4: f.c. 330,-; PMS 265
Agency Commission: 15%
Mechanical Data: Type Area: 255 x 370mm, Bleed Size: 290 x 420mm
Copy instructions: *Copy Date:* 3 days prior to publication date
CONSUMER: RURAL & REGIONAL INTEREST

NIJMEGEN BUSINESS 16964N63-197
Editorial: St. Annastraat 61, 6524 EH NIJMEGEN
Tel: 30 6383743 **Fax:** 229 216416
Email: info@eberson-nijhof.nl
Freq: 7 issues yearly; **Annual Sub.:** EUR 53,-; **Circ:** 5,500
Editor: Hans Eberson; **Editor-in-Chief:** Rico van Kranen; **Publisher:** Hans Eberson
Profile: Business magazine for the Nijmegen area.
Language(s): Dutch
ADVERTISING RATES:
Full Page Mono .. EUR 2/1: f.c. 2340,-; b/w 1875,- 1/1: f.c. 1500,-; b/w 1200,- 1/2: f.c. 960,-; b/w 770,- 1/4: f.c. 600,-
Agency Commission: 15%
Mechanical Data: Type Area: 190 x 260mm, Bleed Size: 215 x 285mm
BUSINESS: REGIONAL BUSINESS

NIVEAU EUREGIOMAGAZINE 1637079N94X-448
Editorial: Molensingel 73, 6229 PC MAASTRICHT
Tel: 43 3561490 **Fax:** 182 543500
Email: info@niveaumagazine.nl **Web site:** http://www.niveaumagazine.nl
Freq: Half-yearly; **Cover Price:** EUR 7,50; **Circ:** 20,500
Editor: Guy van Grinsven; **Publisher:** Guy van Grinsven
Language(s): Dutch
ADVERTISING RATES:
Full Page Mono .... EUR 1/1: f.c. 1500,-
Agency Commission: 15%
Mechanical Data: Type Area: 208 x 263mm, Bleed Size: 228 x 295mm
CONSUMER: OTHER CLASSIFICATIONS: Miscellaneous

NL 1634720N1A-336
Editorial: Stroombaan 4, 1181 VX AMSTELVEEN
Tel: 20 6077605 **Fax:** 88 2697490
Email: info@mediapartners.nl
Date Established: 01-01-1999; **Freq:** Quarterly; **Circ:** 1,300,000
Usual Pagination: 44
Editor: R. Meerkerk; **Editor-in-Chief:** Y. Rengers
Language(s): Dutch
Agency Commission: 15%
Mechanical Data: Type Area: 204 x 233mm, Bleed Size: 230 x 272mm
Copy instructions: *Copy Date:* 2 months prior to publication date
BUSINESS: FINANCE & ECONOMICS

100% NL MAGAZINE 1902581N74Q-510
Editorial: Morseweg 2, 1131 PK VOLENDAM
Tel: 30 6383716 **Fax:** 73 6157171
Email: info@100pmagazine.nl **Web site:** http://www.100pmagazine.nl
Date Established: 16-06-2009; **Freq:** 10 issues yearly; **Cover Price:** EUR 3,95
Annual Sub.: EUR 25,-; **Circ:** 105,226
Editor: Wilma van de Ven
Language(s): Dutch
ADVERTISING RATES:
Full Page Mono .... EUR 2/1: f.c. 11.250,-; 1/1: f.c. 6500,-; 1/2: f.c. 4000,-
Agency Commission: 15%
Copy instructions: *Copy Date:* 4 weeks prior to publication date
CONSUMER: WOMEN'S INTEREST CONSUMER MAGAZINES: Lifestyle

NOBILES JURISTENGIDS 1637074N44-169
Editorial: Herengracht 208, 1016 BS AMSTERDAM
Tel: 53 4871543 **Fax:** 182 543500
Email: info@nobiles.nl **Web site:** http://www.nobiles.nl
Freq: Annual; **Circ:** 7,890
Editor: Hilde Tholen
Language(s): Dutch
ADVERTISING RATES:
Full Page Mono ... EUR bedr.pres. 2 pag.: b/w 4250,- bedr.pres. 4 pag.: b/w 5100,-
Agency Commission: 15%
Mechanical Data: Type Area: 130 x 210mm, Bleed Size: 170 x 245mm
BUSINESS: LEGAL

NOBILES MAGAZINE 1636219N83-186
Editorial: Herengracht 208, 1016 BS AMSTERDAM
Tel: 20 5042829 **Fax:** 346 577389
Email: info@nobiles.nl
Freq: 6 issues yearly; **Annual Sub.:** EUR 10,-; **Circ:** 65,210
Editor: Hilde Tholen; **Editor-in-Chief:** Angelique Roozen; **Publisher:** M.L. van Grieken
Language(s): Dutch
ADVERTISING RATES:
Full Page Mono .... EUR 2/1: b/w 11.900,- 1/1: b/w 6700,-
Agency Commission: 15%
Mechanical Data: Type Area: 180 x 270mm, Bleed Size: 210 x 297mm
CONSUMER: STUDENT PUBLICATIONS

NOBILES MASTERGIDS 1776503N88A-118
Editorial: Herengracht 208, 1016 BS AMSTERDAM
Tel: 20 8969530 **Fax:** 24 3723631
Email: info@nobiles.nl **Web site:** http://www.mastergids.nl
Freq: Annual; **Circ:** 19,740
Editor: Inge Nieuweboer; **Publisher:** P. van der Linden
Language(s): Dutch
ADVERTISING RATES:
Full Page Mono ... EUR bedr.pres. 2 pag.: b/w 2200,- bedr.pres. 4 pag.: b/w 3100,- bedr.pres. 6 pag.: b/w 3750,-
Agency Commission: 15%
Mechanical Data: Type Area: 130 x 210mm, Bleed Size: 170 x 245mm
CONSUMER: EDUCATION

NOORDERBREEDTE 16844N57-58
Editorial: Westerkade 2, 9718 AN GRONINGEN
Tel: 45 5739390 **Fax:** 299 666645
Email: stichting@noorderbreedte.nl
Date Established: 01-05-1977; **Freq:** 5 issues yearly; **Annual Sub.:** EUR 32,50; **Circ:** 7,500
Editor: Annemarie Kok; **Editor-in-Chief:** T. Haartsen
Profile: Magazine about nature, cultural history, the environment and the landscape in Groningen, Friesland and Drenthe.
Language(s): Dutch
Readership: Aimed at politicians, managers, landscape architects, teachers and local council employees.
ADVERTISING RATES:
Full Page Mono .... EUR 1/1: f.c. 1375,-
Agency Commission: 15%
Mechanical Data: Type Area: 210 x 210mm, Bleed Size: 230 x 230mm
BUSINESS: ENVIRONMENT & POLLUTION

HET NOORDERLICHT 17825N79C-50
Editorial: Laarstraat 6a, 5664 BM GELDROP
Tel: 58 2954859
Date Established: 01-10-1964; **Freq:** Quarterly; **Annual Sub.:** EUR 27,50; **Circ:** 600
Usual Pagination: 36
Editor: A. Steenbakkers; **Editor-in-Chief:** A. Steenbakkers
Profile: Magazine about Scandinavian stamp collecting.
Language(s): Dutch
Readership: Read by collectors and professionals of Scandinavian stamp collecting.
ADVERTISING RATES:
Full Page Mono . EUR 1/1: b/w 55,- 1/2: b/w 33,- 1/4: b/w 23,-
Agency Commission: 15%
Mechanical Data: Type Area: 135 x 179mm, Bleed Size: 170 x 214mm
Copy instructions: *Copy Date:* 6 weeks prior to publication date
CONSUMER: HOBBIES & DIY: Philately

DE NOORDOOSTPOLDER 626755N72-3840
Editorial: Lübeckweg 2, 9723 HE GRONINGEN
Tel: 76 5722984 **Fax:** 570 614795
Email: info@ndcmediagroep.nl **Web site:** http://www.denoordoostpolder.nl
Date Established: 01-06-1945; **Freq:** Weekly; **Cover Price:** Free; **Circ:** 61,400
Editor: Roel Muskee; **Publisher:** Peter Idema
Language(s): Dutch
ADVERTISING RATES:
Full Page Mono EUR ed. di. 2/1: b/w 3008,- ed. di. 1/1: b/w 1504,- ed. di. 1/2: b/w 752,- ed. do. 2/1: b/w 3264,- ed. d
Agency Commission: 15%
Mechanical Data: Type Area: 262 x 397mm
LOCAL NEWSPAPERS

NOORDWIJKERHOUTS WEEKBLAD 629914N72-7361
Editorial: Ambachtsweg 7a, 2222 AH KATWIJK
Tel: 23 5564565 **Fax:** 23 5564575
Web site: http://www.noordwijkerhoutsweekblad.nl
Freq: Weekly; **Circ:** 7,000
Editor: Esdor van Elten; **Editor-in-Chief:** Thea ter Heide-Vrolijk; **Publisher:** G. Verhagen
Language(s): Dutch
Agency Commission: 15%
Mechanical Data: Type Area: 264 x 375mm, Bleed Size: 288,5 x 403mm
LOCAL NEWSPAPERS

NORDIC MAGAZINE 629447N89A-60
Editorial: Kromstraat 15, 5341 JB OSS
Tel: 30 2539300 **Fax:** 0032 34660067
Email: info@maasland.com **Web site:** http://www.nordview.nl/nordic
Date Established: 01-12-1995; **Freq:** Quarterly;
Cover Price: EUR 5,95
Annual Sub.: EUR 21,50; **Circ:** 15,000
Editor: Jaap van Splunter; **Publisher:** Hans Kuilder
Profile: Magazine containing information and articles about Denmark, Norway, Sweden, Finland and Iceland.
Language(s): Dutch
Readership: Read by people wishing to visit these countries and members of the expatriate community.
ADVERTISING RATES:
Full Page Mono .. EUR 1/1: f.c. 1550,-; 1/2: f.c. 825,-; 1/4: f.c. 525,-
Agency Commission: 15%
Mechanical Data: Type Area: 210 x 277mm, Bleed Size: 230 x 297mm
CONSUMER: HOLIDAYS & TRAVEL: Travel

NORMALISATIENIEUWS 15947N14K-150
Editorial: Vlinderweg 6, 2623 AX DELFT
Tel: 15 2690256 **Fax:** 15 2690652
Email: info@nen.nl
Date Established: 01-01-1916; **Freq:** 10 issues yearly; **Cover Price:** Free; **Circ:** 3,600
Editor-in-Chief: Nicolette Drop
Profile: Journal of the NEN - Netherlands Standardisation Institute. Contains reports on NEN activities, news and background information concerning standardisation and certification in general.
Language(s): Dutch
Agency Commission: 15%
Mechanical Data: Type Area: 185 x 259mm, Bleed Size: 210 x 297mm
BUSINESS: COMMERCE, INDUSTRY & MANAGEMENT: Quality Assurance

NOTARIAAT MAGAZINE 1636809N44-165
Editorial: Spui 184, 2511 BW DEN HAAG
Tel: 70 3307156 **Fax:** 70 3602861
Email: communicatie@knb.nl
Date Established: 25-01-2001; **Freq:** 11 issues yearly; **Cover Price:** EUR 17,50
Annual Sub.: EUR 89,25; **Circ:** 5,166
Editor: M.J.H.H. Berkers; **Publisher:** Maaike Jonker
Language(s): Dutch
ADVERTISING RATES:
Full Page Mono .. EUR 1/1: b/w 1545,- 1/2: b/w 917,- 1/4: b/w 556,-
Agency Commission: 15%
Mechanical Data: Type Area: 178 x 239mm, Bleed Size: 220 x 297mm
BUSINESS: LEGAL

NOUVEAU 17423N74A-130
Editorial: Capellalaan 65, 2132 JL HOOFDDORP
Tel: 23 5565370 **Fax:** 23 5565357
Web site: http://www.nouveau.nl
Freq: Monthly; **Cover Price:** EUR 4,99
Annual Sub.: EUR 59,88; **Circ:** 60,785
Editor: Brigitte Speekman; **Editor-in-Chief:** Mariska Vermeulen; **Publisher:** Sanne Visser
Profile: Magazine containing articles on homes, fashion, cookery, travel, beauty, leisure and also human interest stories.
Language(s): Dutch
Readership: Aimed at women.
ADVERTISING RATES:
Full Page Mono .... EUR 2/1: b/w 17.000,- 1/1: b/w 8500,- 1/2: b/w 5100,-
Agency Commission: 15%
Mechanical Data: Type Area: 200 x 261mm, Bleed Size: 230 x 285mm
CONSUMER: WOMEN'S INTEREST CONSUMER MAGAZINES: Women's Interest

NPT PROCESTECHNOLOGIE 16056N19A-81
Editorial: Argonweg 7-11, 3812 RB AMERSFOORT
Tel: 33 4637977 **Fax:** 33 4637976
Email: info@indpers.com **Web site:** http://www.nptprocestechnologie.nl
Date Established: 01-01-1994; **Freq:** Quarterly;
Cover Price: EUR 13,50
Annual Sub.: EUR 91,-; **Circ:** 2,750
Editor-in-Chief: Peter van Nierop; **Publisher:** Peter van Nierop
Profile: Magazine containing articles on process and control systems, industrial maintenance, water treatment, process equipment, industrial automation and process efficiency.
Language(s): Dutch
Readership: Read by members of engineering associations and process managers in the chemical, petrochemical, food, water and engineering sectors.
ADVERTISING RATES:
Full Page Mono EUR 1/1: f.c. 2250,-; 1/2: f.c. 1290,-; 1/4: f.c. 735,-
Agency Commission: 15%
Mechanical Data: Type Area: 182 x 247mm, Bleed Size: 210 x 297mm
Copy instructions: *Copy Date:* 1 month prior to publication date
BUSINESS: ENGINEERING & MACHINERY

NRC HANDELSBLAD 17040N65A-30
Editorial: Marten Meesweg 35, 3068 AV ROTTERDAM **Tel:** 10 4066333 **Fax:** 10 4066306
Web site: http://www.nrc.nl
Freq: 312 issues yearly; **Annual Sub.:** EUR 339,-; **Circ:** 200,723
Editor: Peter Vandermeersch; **Editor-in-Chief:** W. op den Brouw; **Publisher:** Hans Nijenhuis
Profile: Broadsheet-sized quality evening newspaper providing in-depth political and economic coverage.
Language(s): Dutch
Readership: Aimed at business leaders.
ADVERTISING RATES:
Full Page Mono .... EUR ed. ma. t/m vr. 1/1: b/w 29.571,- ed. ma. t/m vr. 1/2S: b/w 20.700,- ed. ma. t/m vr. 1/4: b/w 8.576,
Agency Commission: 15%
Mechanical Data: Type Area: 266 x 398mm
NATIONAL DAILY & SUNDAY NEWSPAPERS: National Daily Newspapers

NRC WEEKBLAD 1896300N65H-2
Editorial: Marten Meesweg 35, 3068 AV ROTTERDAM **Tel:** 30 6383716 **Fax:** 73 6157171
Freq: Weekly; **Circ:** 229,285
Editor-in-Chief: Rinskje Koelewijn
Language(s): Dutch
Agency Commission: 15%
Mechanical Data: Bleed Size: 251 x 334mm
NATIONAL DAILY & SUNDAY NEWSPAPERS: National Colour Supplements

NRK NETWERK 16532N47A-80
Editorial: Postbus 420, 2260 AK LEIDSCHENDAM
Tel: 88 7518380 **Fax:** 88 7518381
Email: info@nrk.nl
Freq: 5 issues yearly; **Circ:** 1,450
Editor: W.F. de Ruijter
Profile: Journal concerning the production of synthetics and other materials.
Language(s): Dutch
Agency Commission: 15%
BUSINESS: CLOTHING & TEXTILES

NTI-STUDIEGIDS 1636501N62F-154
Editorial: Schipholweg 101, 2316 XC LEIDEN
Tel: 346 577390 **Fax:** 346 577389
Email: info@nti.nl
Freq: Half-yearly; **Cover Price:** Free; **Circ:** 150,000
Language(s): Dutch
Agency Commission: 15%
Mechanical Data: Bleed Size: 200 x 280mm
BUSINESS: CHURCH & SCHOOL EQUIPMENT & EDUCATION: Adult Education

NUMMER 1 1636024N74C-220
Editorial: Dorpstraat 136, 6122 CC BUCHTEN
Tel: 223 650019 **Fax:** 223 650011
Email: info@nummer1.nl **Web site:** http://www.nummer1.nl
Freq: 10 issues yearly; **Cover Price:** Free; **Circ:** 125,035
Editor-in-Chief: A. Pibiri; **Publisher:** A. Boerman
Language(s): Dutch
ADVERTISING RATES:
Full Page Mono ..... EUR 2/1: f.c. 8305,-; PMS 7397,-; f.c. color 6444,-; b/w 5582,- 1/1: f.c. 4311,-; PMS 3858,-; f.c. color
Agency Commission: 15%
Mechanical Data: Type Area: 204 x 254mm, Bleed Size: 221 x 274mm
CONSUMER: WOMEN'S INTEREST CONSUMER MAGAZINES: Home & Family

NUON SEIZOENGIDS 1637157N57-119
Editorial: Spaklerweg 20, 1096 BA AMSTERDAM
Tel: 20 5979546 **Fax:** 20 5979614
Freq: Quarterly; **Cover Price:** Free; **Circ:** 2,200,000
Language(s): Dutch
Agency Commission: 15%
BUSINESS: ENVIRONMENT & POLLUTION

NURSING 16718N56B-31
Editorial: Radarweg 29, 1043 NX AMSTERDAM
Tel: 343 535753 **Fax:** 20 5159577
Email: info@reedbusiness.nl **Web site:** http://www.nursing.nl
Freq: 11 issues yearly; **Cover Price:** EUR 7,-
Annual Sub.: EUR 73,-; **Circ:** 20,637
Editor: Alexia Hageman; **Editor-in-Chief:** Dorien te Voortwis; **Publisher:** Ben Konings
Profile: Publication providing current news and medical information.
Language(s): Dutch
Readership: Aimed at nurses in the Netherlands and Belgium.
ADVERTISING RATES:
Full Page Mono EUR 1/1: f.c. 3981,-; b/w 3555,- 1/2: f.c. 3069,-; b/w 2197,- 1/4: f.c. 2252,-; b/w 1467,-
Agency Commission: 15%
Mechanical Data: Type Area: 188 x 260mm, Bleed Size: 215 x 285mm
Copy instructions: *Copy Date:* 3 weeks prior to publication date
BUSINESS: HEALTH & MEDICAL: Nursing

NWT NATUURWETENSCHAP & TECHNIEK 16839N57-45
Editorial: Wildenborch 5, 1112 XB DIEMEN
Tel: 23 5567955 **Fax:** 23 5567956
Web site: http://www.nwtonline.nl
Freq: 11 issues yearly; **Cover Price:** EUR 7,95
Annual Sub.: EUR 86,25; **Circ:** 18,618
Editor: Irene de Bel; **Editor-in-Chief:** A. Jaspers;
Publisher: Hans van Vloten
Profile: General journal about technical, computer, physical, medical, life, earth and environmental sciences.
Language(s): Dutch
Readership: Read by students, scientists, physicians and technicians.
ADVERTISING RATES:
Full Page Mono EUR 2/1: f.c. 6040,-; PMS 5070,-; b/w 4135,- 1/1: f.c. 3435,-; PMS 2785,-; b/w 2165,- 1/2: f.c. 2075,-;
Agency Commission: 15%
Mechanical Data: Type Area: 175 x 255mm, Bleed Size: 210 x 280mm
BUSINESS: ENVIRONMENT & POLLUTION

NY SMELLINGHE NIEUWS 652120N80-93
Editorial: Graaf Adolfstraat 35b, 8606 BT SNEEK
Tel: 20 5253370 **Fax:** 20 6767728
Email: info@mimicry.nl
Date Established: 15-03-1993; **Freq:** Quarterly;
Cover Price: Free; **Circ:** 3,500
Usual Pagination: 24
Editor: C. Visscher; **Editor-in-Chief:** C. Visscher
Profile: Magazine containing information about the NY Smellinge hospital.
Language(s): Dutch
Readership: Aimed at patients, medical and ancillary and people interested in the hospital.
ADVERTISING RATES:
Full Page Mono EUR 1/1: b/w 635,- 1/2: b/w 390,- 1/4: b/w 225,- 1/8: b/w 135,-
Agency Commission: 15%
Mechanical Data: Type Area: 183 x 269mm, Bleed Size: 210 x 297mm
CONSUMER: RURAL & REGIONAL INTEREST

OAK 1775292N74C-274
Editorial: Postbus 374, 3960 BJ WIJK BIJ DUURSTEDE **Tel:** 20 5721643
Email: info@lime-c.nl
Freq: Half-yearly; **Cover Price:** Free; **Circ:** 100,000
Editor: Astrid Warntjes; **Editor-in-Chief:** R. Cornelissen
Language(s): Dutch
Agency Commission: 15%
Mechanical Data: Bleed Size: 210 x 297mm
CONSUMER: WOMEN'S INTEREST CONSUMER MAGAZINES: Home & Family

OASE 15659N4D-35
Editorial: Prins Frederik Hendrikstraat 107, 3051 ER ROTTERDAM
Web site: http://www.oase.archined.nl
Freq: 3 issues yearly; **Annual Sub.:** EUR 55,-; **Circ:** 1,500
Profile: Journal about research in the field of architecture and town planning.
Language(s): Dutch
Readership: Read by students of architecture and people involved in town planning.
Agency Commission: 15%
Mechanical Data: Bleed Size: 170 x 240mm
BUSINESS: ARCHITECTURE & BUILDING: Planning & Housing

OCULUS 16745N56E-40
Editorial: Jaap Bijzerweg 21a, 3446 CR WOERDEN
Tel: 348 436599 **Fax:** 88 2697490
Email: info@nuvo.nl
Date Established: 01-09-1938; **Freq:** 10 issues yearly; **Annual Sub.:** EUR 75,80; **Circ:** 1,866
Editor-in-Chief: Myrthe Blazis; **Publisher:** B.J.M. de Wieman-de Wit
Profile: Magazine for the optical trade.
Language(s): Dutch
ADVERTISING RATES:
Full Page Mono EUR 1/1: f.c. 1715,-; 1/2: f.c. 1000,-; 1/4: f.c. 555,-
Agency Commission: 15%
Mechanical Data: Type Area: 188 x 267mm, Bleed Size: 210 x 297mm
BUSINESS: HEALTH & MEDICAL: Optics

OD (OVERHEIDSDOCUMENTATIE) 1634770N32A-220
Editorial: Prinses Beatrixlaan 116, 2595 AL DEN HAAG **Tel:** 70 3780541 **Fax:** 70 3789783
Email: sdu@sdu.nl
Freq: 11 issues yearly; **Circ:** 1,644
Editor: G.J.M. de Graaf; **Editor-in-Chief:** Tom Kooiman; **Publisher:** A.H.G. Oldeman
Language(s): Dutch
ADVERTISING RATES:
Full Page Mono .. EUR 1/1: b/w 1225,- 1/2: b/w 760,- 1/4: b/w 505,-
Agency Commission: 15%
Mechanical Data: Type Area: 185 x 270mm, Bleed Size: 210 x 297mm
BUSINESS: LOCAL GOVERNMENT, LEISURE & RECREATION: Local Government

ODE 1634886N73-300
Editorial: Willem Buytewechstraat 45, 3024 BK ROTTERDAM **Tel:** 23 5565370
Email: ode@ode.nl **Web site:** http://www.ode.nl
Freq: 10 issues yearly; **Cover Price:** EUR 7,75
Annual Sub.: EUR 72,50; **Circ:** 16,041
Editor: Jurriaan Kamp; **Editor-in-Chief:** M. Visscher;
Publisher: H. Hogerheijde
Language(s): Dutch
ADVERTISING RATES:
Full Page Mono EUR 1/1: f.c. 3750,-; 1/2: f.c. 2280,-; 1/4: f.c. 1300,-
Agency Commission: 15%
Mechanical Data: Type Area: 180 x 245mm, Bleed Size: 207 x 273mm
CONSUMER: NATIONAL & INTERNATIONAL PERIODICALS

OF 16971N63-212
Editorial: Tussendiepen 21, 9206 AA DRACHTEN
Tel: 20 7150600 **Fax:** 10 4521797
Email: drachten@novema.nl **Web site:** http://www.of.nl
Freq: 13 issues yearly; **Annual Sub.:** EUR 35,-; **Circ:** 7,500
Editor: Menno Bakker
Profile: Business-to-business magazine for the Friesland area.
Language(s): Dutch
ADVERTISING RATES:
Full Page Mono EUR 1/1: f.c. 995,-; 1/2: f.c. 565,-; 1/4: f.c. 315,-
Agency Commission: 15%
Mechanical Data: Type Area: 170 x 233mm, Bleed Size: 210 x 260mm
BUSINESS: REGIONAL BUSINESS

OFF THE RECORD 1857797N89C-131
Editorial: Esp 101, 5633 AA EINDHOVEN
Tel: 40 8447611 **Fax:** 53 4842189
Email: bcm@bcm.nl **Web site:** http://www.offtherecord.nl
Freq: Quarterly; **Cover Price:** EUR 3,95
Annual Sub.: EUR 13,30; **Circ:** 55,000
Editor: Jean Paul Heck; **Editor-in-Chief:** Marlies Strik
Language(s): Dutch
ADVERTISING RATES:
Full Page Mono EUR 1/1: b/w 3000,- 1/2: b/w 1750,-
Agency Commission: 15%
Mechanical Data: Bleed Size: 230 x 300mm
Copy instructions: *Copy Date:* 3 weeks prior to publication date
CONSUMER: HOLIDAYS & TRAVEL: Entertainment Guides

OFFICE MAGAZINE.NL 1749781N34-70
Editorial: Kerkenbos 12-26c, 6546 BE NIJMEGEN
Tel: 20 5310919 **Fax:** 492 371114
Email: info@vanmunstermedia.nl **Web site:** http://www.officemagazine.nl
Date Established: 04-12-2005; **Freq:** 6 issues yearly;
Annual Sub.: EUR 48,-; **Circ:** 5,626
Editor: Hans Hooft; **Publisher:** Michael van Munster
Language(s): Dutch
ADVERTISING RATES:
Full Page Mono .. EUR 1/1: b/w 1800,- 1/2: b/w 950,-
Agency Commission: 15%
Mechanical Data: Type Area: 210 x 286mm, Bleed Size: 235 x 310mm
BUSINESS: OFFICE EQUIPMENT

THE OFFICIAL DUTCH BAYWATCH AND DAVID HASSELHOFF FANCLUB 712243N91D-27
Editorial: Joke Smitlaan 20, 2104 TG HEEMSTEDE
Tel: 15 2126695
Date Established: 01-07-1995; **Freq:** Quarterly;
Annual Sub.: EUR 15,-; **Circ:** 300
Usual Pagination: 40
Editor: Christiaan Vrolijk; **Publisher:** Christiaan Vrolijk
Profile: Magazine containing articles about Baywatch and David Hasselhoff.
Language(s): Dutch
Readership: Read by fans.
Agency Commission: 15%
Mechanical Data: Type Area: 180 x 265mm, Bleed Size: 210 x 297mm
CONSUMER: RECREATION & LEISURE: Children & Youth

OFFSHORE VISIE 16345N33-90
Editorial: Willebrordstraat 82-84, 1971 DE IJMUIDEN
Tel: 255 530577 **Fax:** 223 650011
Email: tridens@practica.nl **Web site:** http://www.offshorevisie.nl
Date Established: 08-06-1984; **Freq:** 6 issues yearly;
Cover Price: EUR 5,75
Annual Sub.: EUR 26,-; **Circ:** 2,500
Editor: Han Heilig; **Publisher:** Han Heilig
Profile: International newsletter for executives and engineers in the Dutch and Belgian offshore oil and gas exploration industries and the petrochemical industry.
Language(s): Dutch
Readership: Aimed at people working in research institutes.
ADVERTISING RATES:
Full Page Mono .. EUR 1/1: b/w 1415,- 1/2: b/w 825,- 1/4: b/w 500,-
Agency Commission: 15%
Mechanical Data: Type Area: 183 x 254mm, Bleed Size: 210 x 297mm
Copy instructions: *Copy Date:* 2 weeks prior to publication date
BUSINESS: OIL & PETROLEUM

OK OPERATIONEEL 761604N56B-35
Editorial: Keizersgracht 213, 1016 DT AMSTERDAM
Tel: 70 3751758 **Fax:** 15 2126695
Email: info@y-publicaties.nl
Freq: 8 issues yearly; **Cover Price:** EUR 8,50
Annual Sub.: EUR 59,50; **Circ:** 6,000
Profile: Magazine focusing on care and assistance during medical operations.
Language(s): Dutch
Readership: Aimed at nurses and anaesthetists.
ADVERTISING RATES:
Full Page Mono EUR 1/1: f.c. 3875,-; b/w 2915,- 1/2: f.c. 2775,-; b/w 1895,- 1/4: f.c. 2095,-; b/w 1225,-
Agency Commission: 15%
Mechanical Data: Type Area: 185 x 255mm, Bleed Size: 215 x 285mm
BUSINESS: HEALTH & MEDICAL: Nursing

OKEE-KRANT 16771N94F-274
Editorial: Keizersgracht 213, 1016 DT AMSTERDAM
Tel: 88 2697183 **Fax:** 88 2697490
Email: info@eenvoudigcommuniceren.nl
Date Established: 01-01-1994; **Freq:** 10 issues yearly; **Annual Sub.:** EUR 35,-; **Circ:** 2,071
Editor: Ralf Beekveldt; **Editor-in-Chief:** N. Oost-Lievense; **Publisher:** Ralf Beekveldt
Profile: Magazine focusing on the needs of people with learning disabilities and special needs.
Language(s): Dutch
Agency Commission: 15%
CONSUMER: OTHER CLASSIFICATIONS: Disability

OKKI 1634674N91D-107
Editorial: Koningsweg 66, 5211 BN 'S-HERTOGENBOSCH **Tel:** 348 436599
Fax: 88 2697490
Web site: http://www.okki.nl
Freq: 26 issues yearly; **Cover Price:** EUR 1,95
Annual Sub.: EUR 43,95; **Circ:** 30,000
Usual Pagination: 24
Editor-in-Chief: Ineke van Kasteren; **Publisher:** Dieneke Kuijpers
Language(s): Dutch
ADVERTISING RATES:
Full Page Mono EUR 2/1: f.c. 6000,-; 1/1: f.c. 3000,-; 1/2: f.c. 1500,-
Agency Commission: 15%
Mechanical Data: Bleed Size: 210 x 270mm
CONSUMER: RECREATION & LEISURE: Children & Youth

DE OLDAMBTSTER 19243N32A-228
Editorial: Johan Modastraat 6, 9671 CD WINSCHOTEN **Tel:** 20 4276583 **Fax:** 418 572601
Email: info@gemeente-oldambt.nl
Freq: 10 issues yearly; **Cover Price:** Free; **Circ:** 23,000
Usual Pagination: 32
Editor: Jan-Kees Dommisse; **Publisher:** Jan-Kees Dommisse
Profile: Municipal information magazine.
Language(s): Dutch
ADVERTISING RATES:
Full Page Mono .... EUR 1/1: f.c. 630,-; b/w 504,- 1/2: f.c. 315,-; b/w 252,- 1/4: f.c. 126,-; b/w 158,-
Agency Commission: 15%
Mechanical Data: Type Area: 264 x 387mm, Bleed Size: 288 x 420mm
BUSINESS: LOCAL GOVERNMENT, LEISURE & RECREATION: Local Government

DE OLIFANT 17906N81A-135
Editorial: Hoofdweg 120, 1433 JW KUDELSTAART
Tel: 88 2697183
Email: info@olifanten.org **Web site:** http://www.olifanten.org
Date Established: 01-05-1994; **Freq:** Quarterly;
Annual Sub.: EUR 15,-; **Circ:** 10,000
Editor: R. Faber; **Editor-in-Chief:** M. van Ham
Profile: Publication about elephants.
Language(s): Dutch
Readership: Aimed at members of the Friends of the Elephant Foundation, supporters of Elephant Protection Organisations and people who want to know more about elephants.
ADVERTISING RATES:
Full Page Mono EUR 1/1: f.c. 700,-; 1/2: f.c. 400,-; 1/4: f.c. 250,-
Agency Commission: 15%
Mechanical Data: Type Area: 152 x 222mm, Bleed Size: 170 x 240mm
Copy instructions: *Copy Date:* 3 weeks prior to publication date
CONSUMER: ANIMALS & PETS: Animals & Pets Protection

OMEGA 18193N91D-28
Editorial: Postbus 19005, 3501 DA UTRECHT
Tel: 492 338432
Email: info@wkj.nl **Web site:** http://www.omega-magazine.nl
Freq: Quarterly; **Annual Sub.:** EUR 16,-; **Circ:** 1,000
Editor-in-Chief: Caroline Tax
Profile: Catholic magazine for young people.
Language(s): Dutch
Readership: Aimed at young people between the ages of 16 and 26 years, looking for inspiration in their lives.
ADVERTISING RATES:
Full Page Mono EUR 1/1: b/w 510,- 1/2: b/w 305,- 1/4: b/w 178,-
Agency Commission: 15%
Mechanical Data: Type Area: 170 x 256mm, Bleed Size: 210 x 297mm
CONSUMER: RECREATION & LEISURE: Children & Youth

ONDER DOKTERS 629450N56A-135
Editorial: Graaf Adolfstraat 35b, 8606 BT SNEEK
Tel: 20 5245524 **Fax:** 20 5159040
Email: info@mimicry.nl
Date Established: 02-12-1999; **Freq:** Half-yearly;
Cover Price: Free; **Circ:** 7,700
Usual Pagination: 32
Editor: F.J. Mostert
Profile: Medical magazine for the region of Friesland.
Language(s): Dutch
Readership: Read by general practitioners and specialists.
ADVERTISING RATES:
Full Page Mono .. EUR 1/1: b/w 1500,- 1/2: b/w 800,- 1/4: b/w 450,-
Agency Commission: 15%
Mechanical Data: Type Area: 183 x 270mm, Bleed Size: 210 x 297mm
BUSINESS: HEALTH & MEDICAL

ONDERNEMEN! 15890N14A-145
Editorial: Kerkstraat 54, 1191 JD OUDERKERK A/D AMSTEL **Tel:** 20 5206064 **Fax:** 71 3643461
Email: info@scopebusinessmedia.nl
Freq: 10 issues yearly; **Cover Price:** EUR 7,50
Annual Sub.: EUR 66,50; **Circ:** 105,842
Publisher: Walter Vesters
Profile: Official journal of the Dutch Business Association.
Language(s): Dutch
ADVERTISING RATES:
Full Page Mono .. EUR 1/1: f.c. 11.075,-; PMS 1150,-; b/w 7975,- 1/2: b/w 4800,- 1/4: b/w 2625,-
Agency Commission: 15%
Mechanical Data: Type Area: 175 x 239mm, Bleed Size: 210 x 276mm
Copy instructions: *Copy Date:* 2 weeks prior to publication date
BUSINESS: COMMERCE, INDUSTRY & MANAGEMENT

HET ONDERNEMERSBELANG 1636689N14A-400
Editorial: Weegbree 1, 9861 ES GROOTEGAST
Tel: 570 648902 **Fax:** 570 614795
Email: info@novema.nl **Web site:** http://www.hetondernemersbelang.nl
Date Established: 01-01-2001; **Freq:** 5 issues yearly;
Circ: 193,500
Editor: J. van Caulil; **Editor-in-Chief:** Myra Eeken-Hermans
Language(s): Dutch
ADVERTISING RATES:
Full Page Mono .. EUR 1/1: b/w 1400,- 1/2: b/w 725,- 1/3: b/w 475,- 2/1 (landelijk): b/w 15.000,- 1/1 (landelijk): b/w 890
Agency Commission: 15%
Mechanical Data: Type Area: 210 x 315mm, Bleed Size: 240 x 335mm
BUSINESS: COMMERCE, INDUSTRY & MANAGEMENT

ONDERNEMING & FINANCIERING (O&F) 15496N1B-30
Editorial: Amaliastraat 9, 2514 JC DEN HAAG
Tel: 570 647064 **Fax:** 570 637533
Email: info@bju.nl
Freq: Quarterly; **Cover Price:** EUR 33,-
Annual Sub.: EUR 176,-; **Circ:** 600
Profile: Journal about finance and law, each issue has a themed topic.
Language(s): Dutch
Readership: Read by accountants, financial directors, lawyers, tax advisers and managers.
ADVERTISING RATES:
Full Page Mono .... EUR 1/1: f.c. 3092,-; f.c. color 2367,-; b/w 1641,- 1/2: f.c. 2437,-; f.c. color 1712,-; b/w 986,- 1/4:
Agency Commission: 15%
Mechanical Data: Type Area: 180 x 270mm, Bleed Size: 210 x 297mm
Copy instructions: *Copy Date:* 1 month prior to publication date
BUSINESS: FINANCE & ECONOMICS: Accountancy

ONDERWATERSPORT 17630N75M-175
Editorial: Landjuweel 62, 3905 PH VEENENDAAL
Tel: 43 4077490 **Fax:** 43 4077480
Email: info@onderwatersport.org
Freq: 10 issues yearly; **Circ:** 18,000
Editor: P. Onvlee

Profile: Journal of the NOB - Dutch Diving Association.
Language(s): Dutch
Readership: Aimed at diving enthusiasts.
ADVERTISING RATES:
Full Page Mono EUR 1/1: f.c. 1480,-; 1/2: f.c. 1055,-; 1/4: f.c. 585,-
Agency Commission: 15%
Mechanical Data: Type Area: 185 x 278mm, Bleed Size: 210 x 297mm
CONSUMER: SPORT: Water Sports

ONDERWIJS EN GEZONDHEIDSZORG 16752N56F-100
Editorial: Het Spoor 2, 3994 AK HOUTEN
Tel: 30 2539300 **Fax:** 0032 34660067
Freq: 7 issues yearly; **Annual Sub.:** EUR 58,-; **Circ:** 1,550
Profile: Journal covering developments in healthcare education.
Language(s): Dutch
ADVERTISING RATES:
Full Page Mono .. EUR 1/1: f.c. 2272,-; b/w 909,- 1/2: f.c. 1409,-; b/w 571,- 1/4: f.c. 1085,-; b/w 445,-
Agency Commission: 15%
Mechanical Data: Type Area: 190 x 280mm, Bleed Size: 210 x 297mm
Copy instructions: *Copy Date:* 3 weeks prior to publication date
BUSINESS: HEALTH & MEDICAL: Health Education

O'NEILL AGENDA 1634093N88R-113
Editorial: Reaal 2b, 2353 TL LEIDERDORP
Tel: 88 2944900 **Fax:** 35 6728834
Email: info@stationeryteam.nl
Freq: Annual; **Cover Price:** EUR 12,95; **Circ:** 76,937
Publisher: M. Leguijt
Language(s): Dutch
ADVERTISING RATES:
Full Page Mono .... EUR 1/1: b/w 4400,-
Agency Commission: 15%
Mechanical Data: Bleed Size: 157 x 202mm
CONSUMER: EDUCATION: Education Related

ONS 1799152N74M-270
Editorial: A. Luthulilaan 10, 5231 HV 'S-HERTOGENBOSCH **Tel:** 314 359940
Fax: 314 359978
Email: info@kbo-brabant.nl
Freq: 10 issues yearly; **Circ:** 113,500
Editor-in-Chief: Ruud Kamphoven
Language(s): Dutch
ADVERTISING RATES:
Full Page Mono EUR 1/1: f.c. 3020,-; b/w 2150,- 1/2: f.c. 1170,-; b/w 1170,- 1/4: f.c. 680,-; b/w 680,-
Agency Commission: 15%
Mechanical Data: Type Area: 185 x 230mm, Bleed Size: 210 x 260mm
CONSUMER: WOMEN'S INTEREST CONSUMER MAGAZINES: Personal Finance

ONS AMSTERDAM 17874N80-95
Editorial: Hillegomstraat 12-14, 1058 LS AMSTERDAM **Tel:** 88 2697183 **Fax:** 88 2697490
Date Established: 01-01-1948; **Freq:** 10 issues yearly; **Cover Price:** EUR 4,95
Annual Sub.: EUR 46,50; **Circ:** 11,000
Editor: Peter-Paul de Baar; **Editor-in-Chief:** Arie Vestering; **Publisher:** Pepijn Dobbelaer
Profile: Historical magazine about Amsterdam.
Language(s): Dutch
ADVERTISING RATES:
Full Page Mono EUR 2/1: f.c. 2900,-; 1/1: f.c. 1575,-; 1/2: f.c. 875,-
Agency Commission: 15%
Mechanical Data: Type Area: 185 x 272mm, Bleed Size: 205 x 290mm
CONSUMER: RURAL & REGIONAL INTEREST

ONS HUIS 16181N23A-30
Editorial: Biltstraat 443, 3572 AW UTRECHT
Tel: 20 5159722 **Fax:** 71 3643461
Email: info@onshuis.nl
Freq: 11 issues yearly; **Cover Price:** EUR 9,50
Annual Sub.: EUR 67,50; **Circ:** 5,000
Usual Pagination: 48
Publisher: Michiel de Brabander
Profile: Magazine covering furniture and home furnishings.
Language(s): Dutch
Readership: Aimed at retailers, interior designers, manufacturers and distributors.
ADVERTISING RATES:
Full Page Mono EUR 2/1: f.c. 3050,-; b/w 2280,- 1/1: f.c. 2110,-; b/w 1340,- 1/2: f.c. 1170,-; b/w 700,- 1/4: f.c. 640,
Agency Commission: 15%
Mechanical Data: Type Area: 205 x 267mm, Bleed Size: 235 x 297mm
Copy instructions: *Copy Date:* 2 weeks prior to publication date
BUSINESS: FURNISHINGS & FURNITURE

ONS WEEKBLAD 627226N72-7428
Editorial: Posthoornstraat 69, 6219 NV MAASTRICHT **Tel:** 20 6077605 **Fax:** 88 2697490
Email: info@meestersmedia.com
Date Established: 01-01-1938; **Freq:** Weekly; **Cover Price:** Free; **Circ:** 12,000
Editor: Roger Meesters; **Editor-in-Chief:** Roger Meesters; **Publisher:** Roger Meesters
Language(s): Dutch
Agency Commission: 15%
Mechanical Data: Type Area: 265 x 380mm, Bleed Size: 290 x 430mm
LOCAL NEWSPAPERS

ONVERWACHT NEDERLAND 1633473N91R-244
Editorial: Princenhof Park 1, 3972 NG DRIEBERGEN
Tel: 23 5564565 **Fax:** 23 5564575
Email: info@staatsbosbeheer.nl
Date Established: 21-03-1998; **Freq:** Quarterly;
Annual Sub.: EUR 12,50; **Circ:** 60,000
Editor: K. Goedemondt
Language(s): Dutch
Agency Commission: 15%
Mechanical Data: Bleed Size: 210 x 230mm
CONSUMER: RECREATION & LEISURE: Recreation & Leisure Related

ONZE BOSTONS 17917N81B-40
Editorial: Hoogte Kadijk 176, 1018 BW AMSTERDAM
Tel: 348 436599
Freq: Quarterly; **Circ:** 300
Usual Pagination: 20
Editor: M. Bergen
Profile: Publication of the Dutch Boston Terrier Club.
Language(s): Dutch
Agency Commission: 15%
CONSUMER: ANIMALS & PETS: Dogs

ONZE HOND 17918N81B-50
Editorial: Esp 101, 5633 AA EINDHOVEN
Tel: 20 6077605 **Fax:** 88 2697490
Email: bcm@bcm.nl **Web site:** http://www.onzehond.nl
Date Established: 01-01-1975; **Freq:** Monthly;
Cover Price: EUR 4,65
Annual Sub.: EUR 43,75; **Circ:** 30,000
Editor: R. Haak; **Editor-in-Chief:** Marlies Strik;
Publisher: Eric Brüger
Profile: Magazine containing information about different breeds of dogs.
Language(s): Dutch
ADVERTISING RATES:
Full Page Mono EUR 1/1: f.c. 1377,-; b/w 1170,- 1/2: f.c. 723,-; b/w 615,- 1/4: f.c. 377,-; b/w 321,-
Agency Commission: 15%
Mechanical Data: Type Area: 185 x 248mm, Bleed Size: 215 x 285mm
CONSUMER: ANIMALS & PETS: Dogs

ONZE VOGELS 17936N81F-40
Editorial: Aletta Jacobsstraat 4, 4623 ZB BERGEN OP ZOOM **Tel:** 30 2964469 **Fax:** 475 551033
Email: info@nbvv.nl
Freq: Monthly; **Annual Sub.:** EUR 25,-; **Circ:** 32,000
Editor: Hans van der Stroom; **Editor-in-Chief:** Tino Simons
Profile: Magazine containing articles and information about birds.
Language(s): Dutch
ADVERTISING RATES:
Full Page Mono .... EUR 1/1: f.c. 900,-
Agency Commission: 15%
Mechanical Data: Type Area: 180 x 262mm
CONSUMER: ANIMALS & PETS: Birds

ONZEEIGENTUIN 18222N93-150
Editorial: Amstel 157, 1018 ER AMSTERDAM
Tel: 20 6077605 **Fax:** 88 2697490
Web site: http://www.onzeeigentuin.nl
Freq: Quarterly; **Cover Price:** EUR 6,20
Annual Sub.: EUR 22,25; **Circ:** 15,000
Editor-in-Chief: Leo den Dulk
Profile: Magazine covering all aspects of garden design and landscaping.
Language(s): Dutch
Readership: Magazine aiming at garden and plant lovers.
ADVERTISING RATES:
Full Page Mono .. EUR 1/1: b/w 1165,- 1/2: b/w 660,- 1/4: b/w 370,-
Agency Commission: 15%
Mechanical Data: Type Area: 210 x 284mm, Bleed Size: 240 x 320mm
Copy instructions: *Copy Date:* 6 weeks prior to publication date
CONSUMER: GARDENING

ONZEWERELD 17408N73-120
Editorial: Spuistraat 239d, 1012 VP AMSTERDAM
Tel: 30 2964469 **Fax:** 475 551033
Email: administratie@globalvillagemedia.nl **Web site:** http://www.onzewereld.nl
Date Established: 01-01-1957; **Freq:** 10 issues yearly; **Cover Price:** EUR 5,95
Annual Sub.: EUR 49,50; **Circ:** 19,299
Editor: Peter van Lier; **Publisher:** Peter van Lier
Profile: Publication of the NOVIB - the Netherlands Organisation for International Developments Co-operation.
Language(s): Dutch
Readership: Read by all those interested in international affairs and non-Western culture.
ADVERTISING RATES:
Full Page Mono EUR 1/1: f.c. 2995,-; 1/2: f.c. 2100,-; 1/4: f.c. 1650,-
Agency Commission: 15%
Mechanical Data: Type Area: 180 x 260mm, Bleed Size: 210 x 297mm
CONSUMER: NATIONAL & INTERNATIONAL PERIODICALS

DE OOGST 16109N21A-220
Editorial: Oudezijds Voorburgwal 241, 1012 EZ AMSTERDAM **Tel:** 30 2964469 **Fax:** 475 551033
Email: info@deoogst.nl
Freq: Monthly; **Annual Sub.:** EUR 22,50; **Circ:** 8,000
Editor: H.J. van Rhee; **Editor-in-Chief:** de Jong
Profile: Magazine containing news and information concerning all aspects of agriculture.
Language(s): Dutch
Readership: Aimed at farmers in the Netherlands.
Agency Commission: 15%
BUSINESS: AGRICULTURE & FARMING

OOIT 17025N64L-78
Editorial: Van Stolkweg 29a, 2585 JN DEN HAAG
Tel: 343 535753 **Fax:** 70 7999866
Email: info@facultatieve-verzekeringen.nl
Freq: Quarterly; **Circ:** 60,000
Editor: Theo de Natris
Profile: Publication covering funeral insurance and news concerning the funeral trade.
Language(s): Dutch
Readership: Aimed at funeral directors.
Agency Commission: 15%
BUSINESS: OTHER CLASSIFICATIONS: Funeral Directors, Cemeteries & Crematoria

OOK 1643458N74C-254
Editorial: Capellalaan 65, 2132 JL HOOFDDORP
Tel: 23 5565462 **Fax:** 23 5564588
Email: info@jongegezinnen.nl **Web site:** http://www.tijdschriftook.nl
Freq: Monthly; **Cover Price:** EUR 3,99
Annual Sub.: EUR 45,-; **Circ:** 46,473
Editor: Carla van Klaveren; **Editor-in-Chief:** Anita de Jager; **Publisher:** Stefan Hutten
Language(s): Dutch
ADVERTISING RATES:
Full Page Mono EUR 2/1: b/w 8400,- 1/1: b/w 4200,- 1/2: b/w 2520,-
Agency Commission: 15%
Mechanical Data: Type Area: 195 x 255mm, Bleed Size: 215 x 282mm
CONSUMER: WOMEN'S INTEREST CONSUMER MAGAZINES: Home & Family

OOR 16895N61-55
Editorial: Westerdreef 9, 2151 BR NIEUW-VENNEP
Tel: 23 5567955 **Fax:** 23 5567956
Web site: http://www.oor.nl
Date Established: 01-04-1971; **Freq:** Monthly;
Cover Price: EUR 6,50
Annual Sub.: EUR 66,95; **Circ:** 15,710
Editor: E. van den Berg; **Editor-in-Chief:** Koen Poolman; **Publisher:** P. Evers
Profile: Magazine covering all aspects of the music trade.
Language(s): Dutch
ADVERTISING RATES:
Full Page Mono EUR 2/1: f.c. 7400,-; 1/1: f.c. 4355,-; 1/2: f.c. 2560,-
Agency Commission: 15%
Mechanical Data: Type Area: 216 x 286mm, Bleed Size: 230 x 300mm
BUSINESS: MUSIC TRADE

OOST EUROPA FILATELIE 19136N79C-105
Editorial: Grotestraat 37, 7478 AB DIEPENHEIM
Tel: 30 6383766
Email: redactie@fcoe.nl
Date Established: 01-01-1982; **Freq:** Quarterly;
Annual Sub.: EUR 25,-; **Circ:** 180
Editor: G.R.J. Jansen
Profile: Magazine of the Philately Group of East Europe.
Language(s): Dutch
ADVERTISING RATES:
Full Page Mono .... EUR 1/1: b/w 50,- 1/2: b/w 25,-
Agency Commission: 15%
Mechanical Data: Type Area: 120 x 180mm, Bleed Size: 147 x 208mm
Copy instructions: *Copy Date:* 4 weeks prior to publication date
CONSUMER: HOBBIES & DIY: Philately

OOSTERSCHELDE MAGAZINE 18918N80-97
Editorial: Graaf Adolfstraat 36d, 8606 BT SNEEK
Tel: 172 466622 **Fax:** 172 440681
Email: bcuitgevers@planet.nl
Freq: Quarterly; **Cover Price:** Free; **Circ:** 3,500
Editor: M.C. van de Kreeke
Profile: Magazine about the Oosterschelde hospital.
Language(s): Dutch
Readership: Aimed at patients and local residents.
Agency Commission: 15%
Mechanical Data: Bleed Size: 210 x 297mm, Type Area: 184 x 270mm
CONSUMER: RURAL & REGIONAL INTEREST

OP DE BOK 15791N6A-90
Editorial: Dellaertlaan 61, 1171 KZ BADHOEVEDORP
Tel: 30 2964469 **Fax:** 172 539171
Date Established: 01-01-1959; **Freq:** Monthly; **Circ:** 5,100
Editor: Francis van Haaff; **Editor-in-Chief:** Herma Flipsen-Persoon
Profile: Magazine containing information of interest to airline pilots in the Netherlands.
Language(s): Dutch
ADVERTISING RATES:
Full Page Mono .. EUR 1/1: f.c. 1100,-; 1/2: f.c. 610,-; 1/4: f.c. 345,-
Agency Commission: 15%
Mechanical Data: Type Area: 190 x 230mm, Bleed Size: 200 x 280mm
Copy instructions: *Copy Date:* 3 weeks prior to publication date
BUSINESS: AVIATION & AERONAUTICS

OP DE RAILS 16573N79J-50
Editorial: De Savornin Lohmanplantsoen 34, 2253 VP VOORSCHOTEN
Email: secretariaat@nvbs.com
Freq: Monthly; **Annual Sub.:** EUR 56,-; **Circ:** 5,150
Editor: H.P. van Keulen; **Editor-in-Chief:** P.B.L. Wissenraad
Profile: Publication providing information about rail transport.
Language(s): Dutch
Readership: Aimed at rail enthusiasts.
ADVERTISING RATES:
Full Page Mono EUR 1/1: f.c. 800,-; 1/2: f.c. 400,-; 1/3: f.c. 285,-
Agency Commission: 15%
CONSUMER: HOBBIES & DIY: Rail Enthusiasts

OP KOERS 652196N80-98
Editorial: Graaf Adolfstraat 36d, 8606 BT SNEEK
Tel: 172 466622 **Fax:** 172 440681
Email: bcuitgevers@planet.nl
Freq: Quarterly; **Cover Price:** Free; **Circ:** 3,500
Editor: J. Groothuis
Profile: Magazine giving information about the local hospital.
Language(s): Dutch
Readership: Aimed at patients and local residents.
Agency Commission: 15%
Mechanical Data: Bleed Size: 210 x 297mm, Type Area: 184 x 270mm
CONSUMER: RURAL & REGIONAL INTEREST

OP LEMEN VOETEN 17622N75L-210
Editorial: Postbus 10542, 1001 EM AMSTERDAM
Tel: 88 2697183 **Fax:** 88 2697490
Email: redactie@oplemenvoeten.nl
Date Established: 01-06-1979; **Freq:** 5 issues yearly;
Annual Sub.: EUR 24,-; **Circ:** 8,000
Editor: J.E.J.M. Burger; **Editor-in-Chief:** E. Smit;
Publisher: J.E.J.M. Burger
Profile: Magazine covering hiking and country walking focusing on landscapes and landscape history.
Language(s): Dutch
Readership: Aimed at walking and landscape enthusiasts.
Agency Commission: 15%
Mechanical Data: Type Area: 182 x 260mm
CONSUMER: SPORT: Outdoor

OP OUDE RAILS 16579N49F-55
Editorial: Erfvoort 32, 2211 DE NOORDWIJKERHOUT **Tel:** 172 466327
Email: post@tramwegstichting.nl
Date Established: 01-01-1965; **Freq:** Quarterly;
Annual Sub.: EUR 18,-; **Circ:** 1,400
Editor: Paul Hekking; **Editor-in-Chief:** Paul Hekking
Profile: Magazine providing information about Dutch tramways.
Language(s): Dutch
Agency Commission: 15%
Mechanical Data: Type Area: 190 x 270mm, Bleed Size: 210 x 297mm
BUSINESS: TRANSPORT: Electric Vehicles

OP PAD 18120N89A-70
Editorial: Wassenaarseweg 220, 2596 EC DEN HAAG **Tel:** 88 2697112 **Fax:** 88 2696983
Web site: http://www.oppad.nl
Freq: 8 issues yearly; **Cover Price:** EUR 5,60
Annual Sub.: EUR 44,-; **Circ:** 33,496
Editor: B. Gorissen; **Editor-in-Chief:** S. Janssen;
Publisher: Ben Belt
Profile: Magazine focusing on outdoor and activity holidays.
Language(s): Dutch
Readership: Aimed at readers aged between 25 and 55 years of age.
ADVERTISING RATES:
Full Page Mono EUR 2/1: f.c. 9996,-; 1/1: f.c. 4998,-; 1/2: f.c. 2999,-
Agency Commission: 15%
Mechanical Data: Type Area: 195 x 280mm, Bleed Size: 215 x 300mm
CONSUMER: HOLIDAYS & TRAVEL: Travel

OP VOETEN EN FIETSEN
1634735N62A-156
Editorial: Stationsstraat 79a, 3811 MH AMERSFOORT **Tel:** 172 466327
Email: info@vvn.nl **Web site:** http://www.veiligverkeernederland.nl/[VA]ovef
Freq: 8 issues yearly; **Annual Sub.:** EUR 3,28; **Circ:** 187,000
Language(s): Dutch
Agency Commission: 15%
Mechanical Data: Type Area: 182 x 261mm, Bleed Size: 120 x 297mm
BUSINESS: CHURCH & SCHOOL EQUIPMENT & EDUCATION: Education

HET OP ZONDAG
761165N72-2160
Editorial: Rooseveltstraat 12, 2321 BM LEIDEN
Tel: 76 5301715 **Fax:** 70 3045808
Web site: http://www.hetopzondag.nl
Date Established: 01-01-1992; **Freq:** Weekly; **Cover Price:** Free; **Circ:** 107,000
Language(s): Dutch
Agency Commission: 15%
Mechanical Data: Type Area: 260 x 390mm
LOCAL NEWSPAPERS

OPENBAAR BESTUUR
16275N32A-57
Editorial: Zuidpoolsingel 2, 2408 ZE ALPHEN A/D RIJN **Tel:** 172 466405 **Fax:** 172 466577
Email: info@kluwer.nl
Freq: 11 issues yearly; **Annual Sub.:** EUR 150,50; **Circ:** 1,250
Editor: J.H.J. van den Heuvel; **Editor-in-Chief:** R.H. Roelen; **Publisher:** Marjolein Vogel
Profile: Journal about the management of central, provincial and local government.
Language(s): Dutch
ADVERTISING RATES:
Full Page Mono EUR 1/1: b/w 700,- 1/2: b/w 450,- 1/4: b/w 230,-
Agency Commission: 15%
Mechanical Data: Type Area: 190 x 268mm, Bleed Size: 210 x 297mm
BUSINESS: LOCAL GOVERNMENT, LEISURE & RECREATION: Local Government

OPLEIDING & ONTWIKKELING
15931N14F-80
Editorial: Radarweg 29, 1043 NX AMSTERDAM
Tel: 20 5042829 **Fax:** 20 5159143
Email: info@reedbusiness.nl **Web site:** http://www.opleidingnet.nl
Freq: 6 issues yearly; **Annual Sub.:** EUR 215,25; **Circ:** 1,398
Editor: Jan Stavenga-de Jong; **Editor-in-Chief:** Heiny van den Ham; **Publisher:** Ben Konings
Profile: Magazine about in-house training and human resource development.
Language(s): Dutch
ADVERTISING RATES:
Full Page Mono .... EUR 1/1: f.c. 2183,-; f.c. color 1746,-; b/w 1310,- 1/2: f.c. 1284,-; f.c. color 1027,-; b/w 770,- 1/4:
Agency Commission: 15%
Mechanical Data: Type Area: 180 x 270mm, Bleed Size: 210 x 297mm
Copy instructions: *Copy Date:* 2 weeks prior to publication date
BUSINESS: COMMERCE, INDUSTRY & MANAGEMENT: Training & Recruitment

OPTIMA FARMA
629782N37-183
Editorial: Waterweg 120, 3731 HP DE BILT
Tel: 20 5733686
Freq: 11 issues yearly; **Annual Sub.:** EUR 70,-; **Circ:** 14,500
Profile: Magazine focusing on the pharmaceutical industry.
Language(s): Dutch
Readership: Read by pharmacists.
ADVERTISING RATES:
Full Page Mono EUR 1/1: b/w 2525,- 1/2: b/w 1350,- 1/4: b/w 695,-
Agency Commission: 15%
Mechanical Data: Type Area: 190 x 272mm, Bleed Size: 210 x 297mm
Copy instructions: *Copy Date:* 3 weeks prior to publication date
BUSINESS: PHARMACEUTICAL & CHEMISTS

OPTIMIZE
626390N5C-105
Editorial: Lemelerberg 19-23, 2402 ZN ALPHEN A/D RIJN **Tel:** 70 3751728 **Fax:** 24 3723631
Email: array@array.nl **Web site:** http://www.optimize.nl
Freq: 6 issues yearly; **Cover Price:** EUR 13,50
Annual Sub.: EUR 73,50; **Circ:** 3,500
Editor: Robert de Ruiter; **Editor-in-Chief:** Arjen van den Berg; **Publisher:** Werner Schoots
Profile: Magazine focusing on the IT industry. Contains news, views and information on new software and hardware.
Language(s): Dutch
Readership: Aimed at IT professionals.
ADVERTISING RATES:
Full Page Mono EUR 1/1: b/w 2485,- 1/2: b/w 1460,- 1/4: b/w 855,-
Agency Commission: 15%
Mechanical Data: Type Area: 190 x 265mm, Bleed Size: 210 x 285mm
Copy instructions: *Copy Date:* 4 weeks prior to publication date
BUSINESS: COMPUTERS & AUTOMATION: Professional Personal Computers

OPZIJ
17557N74Q-125
Editorial: Raamgracht 4, 1011 KK AMSTERDAM
Tel: 20 5518525 **Fax:** 20 6227265
Web site: http://www.opzij.nl
Date Established: 01-11-1972; **Freq:** 11 issues yearly; **Cover Price:** EUR 4,95
Annual Sub.: EUR 48,50; **Circ:** 61,980
Editor: Margriet van der Linden; **Editor-in-Chief:** Martha van Buuren; **Publisher:** Karin van Gilst
Profile: Magazine with articles on law, society, current-affairs, health and leisure, arts, music, literature, work and working climate. All articles are from a woman's viewpoint.
Language(s): Dutch
Readership: Aimed at the general public, especially women.
ADVERTISING RATES:
Full Page Mono .... EUR 2/1: f.c. 15.330,-; 1/1: f.c. 7665,-; 1/2: f.c. 4599,-
Agency Commission: 15%
Mechanical Data: Type Area: 185 x 250mm, Bleed Size: 215 x 285mm
CONSUMER: WOMEN'S INTEREST CONSUMER MAGAZINES: Lifestyle

OR INFORMATIE
1634762N14R-160
Editorial: Zuidpoolsingel 2, 2408 ZE ALPHEN A/D RIJN **Tel:** 172 466728 **Fax:** 172 494044
Email: info@kluwer.nl **Web site:** http://www.or-informatie.nl
Date Established: 01-01-1974; **Freq:** 10 issues yearly; **Cover Price:** EUR 19,50
Annual Sub.: EUR 150,-; **Circ:** 4,232
Editor: Marion Winnink; **Editor-in-Chief:** Joukje Sanders; **Publisher:** Henriëtte Emmelot
Language(s): Dutch
ADVERTISING RATES:
Full Page Mono EUR 1/1: b/w 1750,- 1/2: b/w 1050,- 1/4: b/w 575,-
Agency Commission: 15%
Mechanical Data: Type Area: 185 x 265mm, Bleed Size: 210 x 297mm
BUSINESS: COMMERCE, INDUSTRY & MANAGEMENT: Commerce Related

HET ORAKEL
17987N83-46
Editorial: Leeghwaterstraat 42, 2628 CA DELFT
Tel: 20 5518525 **Fax:** 20 6227265
Email: bestuur@vssd.nl
Freq: 7 issues yearly; **Annual Sub.:** EUR 7,95; **Circ:** 3,000
Editor: Renske van Slooten
Profile: Journal of the Students' Union at the Technical University of Delft.
Language(s): Dutch
ADVERTISING RATES:
Full Page Mono EUR 1/1: f.c. 600,-; 1/2: f.c. 350,-; 1/4: f.c. 225,-
Agency Commission: 15%
Mechanical Data: Bleed Size: 205 x 205mm
CONSUMER: STUDENT PUBLICATIONS

ORANJE BOVEN
1637233N74A-222
Editorial: Rhijngeesterstraatweg 40n, 2341 BV OEGSTGEEST **Tel:** 88 2696657 **Fax:** 88 2696887
Email: info@buurmultimedia.nl **Web site:** http://www.oranje-boven.com
Freq: 3 issues yearly; **Cover Price:** Free; **Circ:** 450,000
Language(s): Dutch
ADVERTISING RATES:
Full Page Mono .... EUR 2/1: f.c. 14.630,-; 1/1: f.c. 7350,-; 1/2: f.c. 3780,-
Agency Commission: 15%
Mechanical Data: Type Area: 160 x 225mm, Bleed Size: 170 x 265mm
CONSUMER: WOMEN'S INTEREST CONSUMER MAGAZINES: Women's Interest

ORCHIDEEËN
16212N26C-60
Editorial: Madameperenlaan 7, 3452 EN VLEUTEN
Tel: 20 5518525
Freq: 6 issues yearly; **Annual Sub.:** EUR 30,-; **Circ:** 1,500
Editor: Gab van Winkel; **Editor-in-Chief:** Marja Lutgerink
Profile: Official journal of the Netherlands Orchid Society. Covers all aspects of orchid growing, including light and temperature conditions, diseases and fertilisation.
Language(s): Dutch
Readership: Read by members of the society.
ADVERTISING RATES:
Full Page Mono .... EUR 1/4: b/w 90,- 1/8: b/w 53,-
Agency Commission: 15%
BUSINESS: GARDEN TRADE

HET ORGEL
17707N76D-110
Editorial: H. van Steenwijckstraat 10, 8331 KK STEENWIJK **Tel:** 10 4274107
Web site: http://www.hetorgel.nl
Date Established: 01-03-1886; **Freq:** 6 issues yearly; **Annual Sub.:** EUR 60,-; **Circ:** 1,800
Editor: Jan Smelik; **Publisher:** H. Beek
Profile: Official journal of the Royal Dutch Association of Organists.
Language(s): Dutch
Readership: Read by professional and amateur organists.
ADVERTISING RATES:
Full Page Mono EUR 1/1: b/w 481,- 1/2: b/w 262,- 1/4: b/w 143,-
Agency Commission: 15%
Mechanical Data: Type Area: 180 x 245mm, Bleed Size: 214 x 279mm
CONSUMER: MUSIC & PERFORMING ARTS: Music

DE ORGELVRIEND
17709N76D-120
Editorial: Zandvoortweg 13, 3741 BA BAARN
Tel: 10 4274107
Email: orgelvriend@wanadoo.nl
Date Established: 01-01-1958; **Freq:** 11 issues yearly; **Cover Price:** EUR 7,50
Annual Sub.: EUR 50,50; **Circ:** 3,500
Editor-in-Chief: G.A. Schaap
Profile: Magazine covering all aspects of organs and organ music.
Language(s): Dutch
Readership: Aimed at people who enjoy organ music.
ADVERTISING RATES:
Full Page Mono .... EUR 1/1: f.c. 535,-; b/w 435,- 1/2: f.c. 355,-; b/w 277,- 1/4: f.c. 260,-; b/w 195,-
Agency Commission: 15%
Mechanical Data: Type Area: 190 x 277mm, Bleed Size: 210 x 297mm
CONSUMER: MUSIC & PERFORMING ARTS: Music

ORIGINE
15802N7-80
Editorial: Frankestraat 37, 2011 HT HAARLEM
Tel: 88 2697049
Web site: http://www.origine.nl
Date Established: 01-01-1992; **Freq:** 6 issues yearly; **Cover Price:** EUR 7,95
Annual Sub.: EUR 39,50; **Circ:** 4,150
Editor: A.K.J. van der Gulik; **Publisher:** A.K.J. van der Gulik
Profile: Magazine about art, antiques and historical interiors.
Language(s): Dutch
ADVERTISING RATES:
Full Page Mono .. EUR 1/1: f.c. 1500,-; 1/2: f.c. 775,-; 1/4: f.c. 425,-
Agency Commission: 15%
Mechanical Data: Type Area: 202 x 278mm, Bleed Size: 230 x 310mm
Copy instructions: *Copy Date:* 2 weeks prior to publication date
BUSINESS: ANTIQUES

ORTHO
17490N74G-47
Editorial: Anholtseweg 36, 7081 CM GENDRINGEN
Tel: 88 2697112 **Fax:** 88 2696983
Email: ortho@orthoeurope.com
Date Established: 01-03-1983; **Freq:** 6 issues yearly; **Cover Price:** EUR 17,50
Annual Sub.: EUR 81,25; **Circ:** 5,000
Usual Pagination: 192
Editor: Gert Schuitemaker; **Editor-in-Chief:** Jac van Dongen; **Publisher:** Gert Schuitemaker
Profile: Magazine containing information on nutrition and science.
Language(s): Dutch
Readership: Read by people interested in a healthy lifestyle.
ADVERTISING RATES:
Full Page Mono . EUR 1/1: f.c. 1846,-; 1/2: f.c. 1079,-
Agency Commission: 15%
Mechanical Data: Type Area: 176 x 252mm, Bleed Size: 210 x 280mm
CONSUMER: WOMEN'S INTEREST CONSUMER MAGAZINES: Slimming & Health

OUDERS & COO MAGAZINE
18106N88A-90
Editorial: Rijksstraatweg 150, 3956 CT LEERSUM
Tel: 0032 34660066 **Fax:** 0032 34660067
Email: info@ouders.net
Date Established: 01-01-1992; **Freq:** Quarterly; **Annual Sub.:** EUR 14,95; **Circ:** 40,000
Editor: W.J.V. van Katwijk; **Editor-in-Chief:** Saskia Hankins
Profile: Magazine for parents and teachers about Protestant-Christian education. Featuring summer camps and out-of-school activities for children.
Language(s): Dutch
Agency Commission: 15%
Mechanical Data: Type Area: 193 x 243mm, Bleed Size: 220 x 275mm
CONSUMER: EDUCATION

OUDERS VAN NU
17464N74D-70
Editorial: Capellalaan 65, 2132 JL HOOFDDORP
Tel: 172 466728 **Fax:** 172 494044
Web site: http://www.oudersvannu.nl
Freq: 13 issues yearly; **Cover Price:** EUR 4,50
Annual Sub.: EUR 53,30; **Circ:** 68,343
Editor: Nancy Berendsen; **Editor-in-Chief:** Marieta van Driel; **Publisher:** Stefan Hutten
Profile: Magazine for new parents covering all aspects of raising and caring for children.
Language(s): Dutch
Readership: Aimed at parents with young children up to the age of 5 years.
ADVERTISING RATES:
Full Page Mono .... EUR 2/1: b/w 13.000,- 1/1: b/w 6500,- 1/2: b/w 3900,-
Agency Commission: 15%
Mechanical Data: Type Area: 185 x 252mm, Bleed Size: 215 x 282mm
CONSUMER: WOMEN'S INTEREST CONSUMER MAGAZINES: Child Care

DE OUD-HAGENAAR
1897006N94X-656
Editorial: Koningsplein 28, 2518 JG DEN HAAG
Tel: 30 6383716
Web site: http://www.deoud-hagenaar.nl
Date Established: 03-02-2009; **Freq:** 26 issues yearly; **Circ:** 50,000
Usual Pagination: 16
Editor: Frans Hoynck van Papendrecht; **Publisher:** Constant Martini
Language(s): Dutch
ADVERTISING RATES:
Full Page Mono .. EUR 1/1: b/w 1650,- 1/2: b/w 850,- 1/4: b/w 450,- 1/8: b/w 250,-
Agency Commission: 15%
Mechanical Data: Type Area: 255 x 367mm, Bleed Size: 367 x 530mm
CONSUMER: OTHER CLASSIFICATIONS: Miscellaneous

OUD-UTRECHT
17875N80-110
Editorial: Alexander Numankade 199, 3572 KW UTRECHT **Tel:** 172 466728
Email: redactie.tijdschrift@oud-utrecht.nl
Date Established: 01-01-1926; **Freq:** 6 issues yearly; **Circ:** 2,100
Editor-in-Chief: Maurice van Lieshout
Profile: Historical magazine about the city and province of Utrecht.
Language(s): Dutch
ADVERTISING RATES:
Full Page Mono EUR 1/1: f.c. 2400,-; 1/2: f.c. 1200,-; 1/3: f.c. 800,-
Agency Commission: 15%
CONSUMER: RURAL & REGIONAL INTEREST

OUT.OF.HOME-SHOPS
760707N22R-500
Editorial: Anne Hendrik Kooistrastraat 140, 2441 CP NIEUWVEEN **Tel:** 342 494848 **Fax:** 172 539171
Web site: http://www.outofhome-shops.nl
Date Established: 01-09-1999; **Freq:** Monthly; **Annual Sub.:** EUR 136,-; **Circ:** 28,077
Editor: Steffen van Beek; **Editor-in-Chief:** Paul Blonk; **Publisher:** Katja Riethof
Profile: Magazine containing information on the eating trends of people on the move.
Language(s): Dutch
Readership: Aimed at petrol stations managers, supermarkets managers and fast food producers.
Agency Commission: 15%
Mechanical Data: Type Area: 280 x 410mm, Bleed Size: 300 x 440mm
BUSINESS: FOOD: Food Related

OVER DIEREN
17944N81X-75
Editorial: Stationsweg 9, 9989 BT WARFFUM
Tel: 88 2696670 **Fax:** 88 2696331
Email: welzo.media@worldonline.nl **Web site:** http://www.overdieren.nl
Date Established: 01-09-1988; **Freq:** Quarterly; **Annual Sub.:** EUR 7,95; **Circ:** 260,000
Editor: Henk van Welzen; **Editor-in-Chief:** Jessika Mastebroek; **Publisher:** Henk van Welzen
Profile: Magazine about pets.
Language(s): Dutch
Readership: Read by pet owners.
ADVERTISING RATES:
Full Page Mono EUR 1/1: f.c. 6750,-; PMS 5600,-; b/w 4850,- 1/2: f.c. 3525,-; PMS 3000,-; b/w 2500,-
Agency Commission: 15%
Mechanical Data: Type Area: 190 x 264mm, Bleed Size: 210 x 284mm
CONSUMER: ANIMALS & PETS

OVER MULTATULI
18034N84B-85
Editorial: Buiten Dommerstraat 11hs, 1013 HW AMSTERDAM
Freq: Half-yearly; **Annual Sub.:** EUR 16,50; **Circ:** 750
Editor: G. Leerdam; **Editor-in-Chief:** J. Grave; **Publisher:** B. Lubberhuizen
Profile: Literary magazine about the author Multatuli.
Language(s): Dutch
Readership: Read by men and women of all ages.
ADVERTISING RATES:
Full Page Mono ...... EUR 1/1: b/w 150,- 1/2: b/w 75,-
Agency Commission: 15%
CONSUMER: THE ARTS & LITERARY: Literary

DE OVERSCHIESE KRANT
627218N72-7431
Editorial: Singel 55, 2992 BN BARENDRECHT
Tel: 70 3780541 **Fax:** 70 3789783
Email: info@baruitgeverij.nl **Web site:** http://www.overschiesekrant.nl
Date Established: 01-08-1955; **Freq:** Weekly; **Annual Sub.:** EUR 91,-; **Circ:** 12,800
Language(s): Dutch
Agency Commission: 15%

Mechanical Data: Type Area: 400 x 540mm, Bleed Size: 420 x 560mm
LOCAL NEWSPAPERS

OVERTOOM, ZO GEREGELD
1633638N14A-574
Editorial: Postbus 2, 3734 ZG DEN DOLDER **Tel:** 40 2336338 **Fax:** 40 2336470
Email: info@overtoom.nl
Freq: 10 issues yearly; **Cover Price:** Free; **Circ:** 100,000
Editor: Derk Jan Dales
Language(s): Dutch
Agency Commission: 15%
Mechanical Data: Bleed Size: 210 x 297mm
BUSINESS: COMMERCE, INDUSTRY & MANAGEMENT

OXFAM NOVIB NIEUWS
1635849N1P-62
Editorial: Mauritskade 9, 2514 HD DEN HAAG **Tel:** 10 2894015 **Fax:** 20 6159047
Email: info@oxfamnovib.nl
Date Established: 01-06-1992; **Freq:** 3 issues yearly; **Circ:** 160,000
Editor: Robbert Bodegraven; **Editor-in-Chief:** Paul Vieveen
Language(s): Dutch
Agency Commission: 15%
BUSINESS: FINANCE & ECONOMICS: Fundraising

P&OACTUEEL
1637240N14F-189
Editorial: Radarweg 29, 1043 NX AMSTERDAM **Tel:** 88 2696657 **Fax:** 20 5159143
Email: info@reedbusiness.nl **Web site:** http://www.penoactueel.nl
Freq: 10 issues yearly; **Cover Price:** EUR 25,- **Annual Sub.:** EUR 115,-; **Circ:** 13,658
Editor: Yolanda Stil; **Publisher:** Ben Konings
Language(s): Dutch
ADVERTISING RATES:
Full Page Mono .... EUR 1/1: f.c. 3003,-; f.c. color 2402,-; b/w 1802,- 1/2: f.c. 1766,-; f.c. color 1413,-; b/w 1059,- 1/4:
Agency Commission: 15%
Mechanical Data: Type Area: 180 x 270mm, Bleed Size: 210 x 297mm
BUSINESS: COMMERCE, INDUSTRY & MANAGEMENT: Training & Recruitment

PADDESTOELEN
1636512N64F-289
Editorial: Looierslaan 107, 2272 BJ VOORBURG
Freq: 6 issues yearly; **Annual Sub.:** EUR 170,50; **Circ:** 1,073
Editor: Roel Dreve; **Publisher:** Roel Dreve
Language(s): Dutch
ADVERTISING RATES:
Full Page Mono .. EUR 1/1: f.c. 1339,-; b/w 671,- 1/2: f.c. 953,-; b/w 365,- 1/4: f.c. 697,-; b/w 198,-
Agency Commission: 15%
Mechanical Data: Type Area: 185 x 270mm, Bleed Size: 210 x 297mm
BUSINESS: OTHER CLASSIFICATIONS: Biology

PALLIUM
1636419N56B-171
Editorial: Het Spoor 2, 3994 AK HOUTEN
Tel: 492 338432 **Fax:** 492 338421
Date Established: 28-01-1999; **Freq:** 5 issues yearly; **Annual Sub.:** EUR 66,-; **Circ:** 1,450
Language(s): Dutch
ADVERTISING RATES:
Full Page Mono .. EUR 1/1: f.c. 2053,-; b/w 878,- 1/2: f.c. 1293,-; b/w 555,- 1/4: f.c. 930,-; b/w 405,-
Agency Commission: 15%
Mechanical Data: Type Area: 190 x 250mm, Bleed Size: 215 x 285mm
BUSINESS: HEALTH & MEDICAL: Nursing

PANDA
1634775N81A-166
Editorial: Velperbinnensingel 5, 6811 BP ARNHEM
Tel: 70 3780541 **Fax:** 70 3789783
Email: info@lbl.nl **Web site:** http://www.wnf.nl/panda
Freq: Quarterly; **Circ:** 700,000
Usual Pagination: 20
Editor: W.A. Vierdag
Language(s): Dutch
Agency Commission: 15%
Mechanical Data: Type Area: 190 x 260mm, Bleed Size: 205 x 280mm
CONSUMER: ANIMALS & PETS: Animals & Pets Protection

PARAVISIE
18236N94E-100
Editorial: Oude Enghweg 24, 1217 JD HILVERSUM
Tel: 20 5629222 **Fax:** 20 5626289
Freq: Monthly; **Cover Price:** EUR 4,75
Annual Sub.: EUR 46,75; **Circ:** 30,000
Editor: Pepita de Jager; **Editor-in-Chief:** Niels Brummelman
Profile: Magazine about supernatural phenomena and alternative ways of healing.
Language(s): Dutch
ADVERTISING RATES:
Full Page Mono .. EUR 1/1: b/w 1085,- 1/2: b/w 652,- 1/4: b/w 357,-
Agency Commission: 15%
Mechanical Data: Type Area: 185 x 257mm, Bleed Size: 215 x 285mm
CONSUMER: OTHER CLASSIFICATIONS: Paranormal

PARKEER
1699328N49R-94
Editorial: Admiraliteitslaan 818, 5224 ET 'S-HERTOGENBOSCH **Tel:** 172 466911
Email: parkeer@jbcv.nl **Web site:** http://www.parkeermagazine.nl
Freq: 6 issues yearly; **Annual Sub.:** EUR 60,-; **Circ:** 6,289
Editor: Jan van den Broek
Language(s): Dutch
ADVERTISING RATES:
Full Page Mono EUR 2/1: f.c. 4490,-; 1/1: f.c. 2295,-; 1/2: f.c. 1480,-
Agency Commission: 15%
Mechanical Data: Type Area: 200 x 267mm, Bleed Size: 230 x 297mm
BUSINESS: TRANSPORT: Transport Related

PARMENTIER
18035N84B-90
Editorial: Postbus 1084, 6501 BB NIJMEGEN
Email: info@literairtijdschriftparmentier.nl **Web site:** http://www.literairtijdschriftparmentier.nl
Date Established: 01-10-1989; **Freq:** Quarterly;
Cover Price: EUR 9,-
Annual Sub.: EUR 25,-; **Circ:** 300
Usual Pagination: 100
Editor: Arnoud van Adrichem
Profile: Magazine containing articles on all aspects of literature and philosophy.
Language(s): Dutch
Readership: Aimed at all those interested in literature.
ADVERTISING RATES:
Full Page Mono .... EUR 1/1: b/w 125,-
Agency Commission: 15%
CONSUMER: THE ARTS & LITERARY: Literary

HET PAROOL
17100N67B-7318
Editorial: Jacob Bontiusplaats 9, 1018 LL AMSTERDAM **Tel:** 20 5584300 **Fax:** 20 5584301
Web site: http://www.parool.nl
Date Established: 25-07-1940; **Freq:** 312 issues yearly; **Annual Sub.:** EUR 271,50; **Circ:** 87,658
Editor: Barbara van Beukering; **Editor-in-Chief:** Peter van den Berg
Language(s): Dutch
ADVERTISING RATES:
Full Page Mono .... EUR ed. ma. t/m vr. 2/1: b/w 17.760,- ed. ma. t/m vr. 1/1: b/w 10.635,- ed. ma. t/m vr. 1/2: b/w 7232,-
Agency Commission: 15%
Mechanical Data: Type Area: 264 x 396mm
REGIONAL DAILY & SUNDAY NEWSPAPERS: Regional Daily Newspapers

PASARKRANT
1636090N94X-408
Editorial: Bezuidenhoutseweg 331, 2594 AR DEN HAAG **Tel:** 113 820203 **Fax:** 20 5159145
Email: info@tongtong.nl
Date Established: 01-05-1985; **Freq:** Annual; **Cover Price:** Free; **Circ:** 185,000
Editor: Florine Koning; **Editor-in-Chief:** Siem Boon; **Publisher:** Siem Boon
Language(s): Dutch
ADVERTISING RATES:
Full Page Mono EUR 1/1: f.c. 4675,-; 1/2: f.c. 2500,-; 1/4: f.c. 1320,-
Agency Commission: 15%
Mechanical Data: Type Area: 198 x 285mm, Bleed Size: 210 x 297mm
CONSUMER: OTHER CLASSIFICATIONS: Miscellaneous

PASSIE
18060N86C-275
Editorial: Anna van Renesseplein 8, 1911 KN UITGEEST **Tel:** 88 2944900 **Fax:** 35 6728834
Web site: http://www.passie.nl
Date Established: 01-02-1996; **Freq:** Monthly;
Cover Price: EUR 4,20
Annual Sub.: EUR 40,-; **Circ:** 60,000
Editor: Ilja Gernandt; **Publisher:** Sandy Wenderhold-van de Sanden
Profile: Lifestyle magazine for men.
Language(s): Dutch
ADVERTISING RATES:
Full Page Mono EUR 2/1: f.c. 5790,-; 1/1: f.c. 3120,-; 1/2: f.c. 2150,-
Agency Commission: 15%
Mechanical Data: Type Area: 193 x 246mm, Bleed Size: 215 x 272mm
CONSUMER: ADULT & GAY MAGAZINES: Men's Lifestyle Magazines

PAULUSWERK
16323N32G-152
Editorial: Hang 7, 3011 GG ROTTERDAM
Tel: 70 3789880 **Fax:** 70 3789783
Email: info@stichtingksa.nl
Date Established: 01-01-1997; **Freq:** Quarterly;
Cover Price: Free; **Circ:** 1,000
Usual Pagination: 8
Editor: W.J. Lammers; **Editor-in-Chief:** W.J. Lammers
Profile: Magazine for members, friends and those interested in the work of Pauluskerk.
Language(s): Dutch
Agency Commission: 15%
BUSINESS: LOCAL GOVERNMENT, LEISURE & RECREATION: Community Care & Social Services

PAUZE MAGAZINE
18194N91D-240
Editorial: Haarlemmerdijk 159, 1013 KH AMSTERDAM **Tel:** 88 2697856
Web site: http://www.pauze.nl
Date Established: 01-01-1987; **Freq:** 6 issues yearly; **Circ:** 175,000
Editor: Esther Kollmann; **Editor-in-Chief:** Nanneke Koning; **Publisher:** Pim Hermeling
Profile: Magazine for young people aged between 12 and 19 years.
Language(s): Dutch
ADVERTISING RATES:
Full Page Mono .... EUR 2/1: b/w 12.900,- 1/1: b/w 6900,- 1/4: b/w 1950,-
Agency Commission: 15%
Mechanical Data: Type Area: 190 x 260mm, Bleed Size: 202 x 270mm
Copy instructions: *Copy Date:* 3 weeks prior to publication date
CONSUMER: RECREATION & LEISURE: Children & Youth

PAYROLL
761386N1A-155
Editorial: Geldropseweg 26, 5611 SJ EINDHOVEN
Tel: 45 5739390 **Fax:** 20 5233419
Email: administratie@2xplain.nl **Web site:** http://www.payrollmagazine.nl
Date Established: 01-01-1998; **Freq:** 11 issues yearly; **Cover Price:** Free; **Circ:** 1,200
Usual Pagination: 28
Editor: J. van Weert; **Editor-in-Chief:** F.C. la Poutré; **Publisher:** F.C. la Poutré
Profile: Magazine focusing on payroll management and administration.
Language(s): Dutch
Readership: Aimed at payroll managers, accountants and human resources managers.
ADVERTISING RATES:
Full Page Mono EUR 1/1: b/w 589,- 1/2: b/w 324,- 1/4: b/w 181,-
Agency Commission: 15%
Mechanical Data: Type Area: 186 x 265mm, Bleed Size: 210 x 297mm
Copy instructions: *Copy Date:* 3 weeks prior to publication date
BUSINESS: FINANCE & ECONOMICS

PC-ACTIVE
15762N5C-120
Editorial: Prof. Eijkmanlaan 2, 2035 XB HAARLEM
Tel: 23 5565370 **Fax:** 23 5565357
Email: info@hub.nl **Web site:** http://www.pc-active.nl
Date Established: 01-10-1989; **Freq:** 11 issues yearly; **Cover Price:** EUR 6,99
Annual Sub.: EUR 66,-; **Circ:** 25,000
Editor: Rob Coenraads; **Publisher:** Martin Smelt
Profile: Magazine providing information on IBM-compatible PCs, running DOS, Windows and Linux. Contains reviews of hard- and software and in-depth technical articles.
Language(s): Dutch
Readership: Aimed at IT professionals.
ADVERTISING RATES:
Full Page Mono EUR 2/1: b/w 3240,- 1/1: b/w 1800,- 1/2: b/w 1080,-
Agency Commission: 15%
Mechanical Data: Type Area: 190 x 280mm, Bleed Size: 210 x 297mm
BUSINESS: COMPUTERS & AUTOMATION: Professional Personal Computers

PEDDELPRAAT
17631N75M-180
Editorial: Duivenkamp 726, 3607 VD MAARSSEN
Email: redactie@peddelpraat.nl
Freq: 6 issues yearly; **Annual Sub.:** EUR 23,-; **Circ:** 700
Editor: Ine Dost-Huetink
Profile: Magazine focusing on canoe activities, includes equipment reviews, holidays and competitions.
Language(s): Dutch
Readership: Aimed at canoeists.
Agency Commission: 15%
Mechanical Data: Type Area: 120 x 170mm
CONSUMER: SPORT: Water Sports

PEEL EN MAAS
627246N72-4130
Editorial: Keizersveld 19, 5803 AM VENRAY
Tel: 35 6726751 **Fax:** 35 6726752
Email: info@vandenmunckhof.nl **Web site:** http://www.peelenmaasonline.nl
Date Established: 27-03-1880; **Freq:** Weekly;
Annual Sub.: EUR 21,95; **Circ:** 13,000
Editor: C. van den Munckhof; **Editor-in-Chief:** R. Koenen; **Publisher:** C. van den Munckhof
Language(s): Dutch
Agency Commission: 15%
Mechanical Data: Type Area: 396 x 540mm, Bleed Size: 416 x 570mm
LOCAL NEWSPAPERS

DE PELSDIERENHOUDER
16990N64B-60
Editorial: Molenweg 7, 6612 AE NEDERASSELT
Tel: 88 2697049 **Fax:** 88 2697356
Email: info@nfe.nl
Freq: 10 issues yearly; **Annual Sub.:** EUR 65,-; **Circ:** 850
Editor: W.P.A.M. Verhagen; **Editor-in-Chief:** Dorine Cornelissen-Bulkens
Profile: Magazine covering the breeding of animals for fur.
Language(s): Dutch
ADVERTISING RATES:
Full Page Mono EUR 2/1: b/w 570,- 1/1: b/w 285,- 1/2: b/w 176,-
Agency Commission: 15%
Mechanical Data: Type Area: 185 x 275mm, Bleed Size: 210 x 297mm
BUSINESS: OTHER CLASSIFICATIONS: Fur Trade

PENNY
1857653N81D-278
Editorial: Theo van Doesburgweg 4, 1703 DL HEERHUGOWAARD **Tel:** 40 2071162
Fax: 23 5519544
Freq: Monthly; **Annual Sub.:** EUR 38,-; **Circ:** 50,000
Editor: Anneke Smit
Language(s): Dutch
ADVERTISING RATES:
Full Page Mono EUR 1/1: f.c. 3740,-; 1/2: f.c. 2244,-; 1/4: f.c. 1122,-
Agency Commission: 15%
Mechanical Data: Type Area: 200 x 270mm, Bleed Size: 210 x 280mm
CONSUMER: ANIMALS & PETS: Horses & Ponies

PENSIOEN & PRAKTIJK
15546N1H-100
Editorial: Utrechtseweg 31a, 3812 NA AMERSFOORT **Tel:** 33 4220082 **Fax:** 24 3723631
Email: info@lvbnetworks.nl
Date Established: 01-01-1990; **Freq:** 10 issues yearly; **Cover Price:** EUR 22,72
Annual Sub.: EUR 208,80; **Circ:** 1,064
Editor: E. Lutjens; **Publisher:** Heleen Kooistra
Profile: Magazine providing informative articles and advice on pensions.
Language(s): Dutch
Readership: Aimed at financial advisors, bank managers, insurance brokers and financial directors.
ADVERTISING RATES:
Full Page Mono EUR 1/1: f.c. 2988,-; b/w 1589,- 1/2: f.c. 2080,-; b/w 942,- 1/4: f.c. 1380,-; b/w 517,-
Agency Commission: 15%
Mechanical Data: Type Area: 171 x 270mm, Bleed Size: 210 x 297mm
BUSINESS: FINANCE & ECONOMICS: Pensions

PENSIOEN JOURNAAL
1640466N74N-514
Editorial: Treubstraat 1b, 2288 EG RIJSWIJK
Tel: 172 440681 **Fax:** 172 422886
Email: info@bpmt.nl
Freq: Quarterly; **Cover Price:** Free; **Circ:** 600,000
Usual Pagination: 8
Editor: Annemieke Biesheuvel
Language(s): Dutch
Agency Commission: 15%
CONSUMER: WOMEN'S INTEREST CONSUMER MAGAZINES: Retirement

PENSIOEN MAGAZINE
15549N1H-110
Editorial: Staverenstraat 32015, 7418 CJ DEVENTER
Tel: 570 647064 **Fax:** 570 637533
Email: info@kluwer.nl
Freq: 10 issues yearly; **Cover Price:** EUR 23,95
Annual Sub.: EUR 192,95; **Circ:** 823
Editor: G.J.B. Dietvorst; **Publisher:** G.P.K. Sok
Profile: Magazine containing information about taxation, civil and social aspects of pensions.
Language(s): Dutch
Readership: Read by pensions advisors.
ADVERTISING RATES:
Full Page Mono EUR 1/1: b/w 899,- 1/2: b/w 539,- 1/4: b/w 292,-
Agency Commission: 15%
Mechanical Data: Type Area: 170 x 255mm, Bleed Size: 210 x 297mm
BUSINESS: FINANCE & ECONOMICS: Pensions

PENSIOENBELANGEN
15550N1H-115
Editorial: Scheveningseweg 7, 2517 KS DEN HAAG
Tel: 23 5564600 **Fax:** 23 5564626
Email: info@pensioenbelangen.nl
Freq: 6 issues yearly; **Annual Sub.:** EUR 36,-; **Circ:** 14,985
Editor-in-Chief: Carien Rövekamp
Profile: Official journal of the NBP - the Netherlands Society of Pension Advisors.
Language(s): Dutch
Readership: Read by members and financial directors.
ADVERTISING RATES:
Full Page Mono EUR 1/1: f.c. 1850,-; b/w 1125,- 1/2: f.c. 1200,-; b/w 680,- 1/4: f.c. 840,-; b/w 335,-
Agency Commission: 15%
Mechanical Data: Type Area: 185 x 267mm, Bleed Size: 210 x 285mm
Copy instructions: *Copy Date:* 3 weeks prior to publication date
BUSINESS: FINANCE & ECONOMICS: Pensions

DE PENSIOENSPECIAL
15522N1D-80
Editorial: Kloosterberg 3, 6436 CV AMSTENRADE
Tel: 20 5979500 **Fax:** 20 5979590

Freq: Annual; **Annual Sub.:** EUR 25,50; **Circ:** 10,500
Publisher: M.T. Meijers
Profile: Magazine covering all aspects of the insurance trade.
Language(s): Dutch
Readership: Aimed at insurance brokers and agents.
ADVERTISING RATES:
Full Page Mono .. EUR 1/1: b/w 1495,- 1/2: b/w 795,-
Agency Commission: 15%
Mechanical Data: Type Area: 185 x 267mm, Bleed Size: 210 x 297mm
BUSINESS: FINANCE & ECONOMICS: Insurance

PENTHOUSE 18045N86A-40
Editorial: Busitel 1, Orlyplein 85, 1043 DS AMSTERDAM **Tel:** 70 3751758 **Fax:** 15 2126695
Email: info@mediaventura.nl
Freq: Monthly; **Cover Price:** EUR 6,95
Annual Sub.: EUR 55,-; **Circ:** 10,413
Editor: Harmen Lustig
Profile: Magazine containing adult photography and articles, celebrity interviews, music and book reviews, also details of restaurants and night life.
Language(s): Dutch
Readership: Aimed at men.
ADVERTISING RATES:
Full Page Mono EUR 2/1: f.c. 6120,-; 1/1: f.c. 3060,-; 1/2: f.c. 1912,-
Agency Commission: 15%
Mechanical Data: Type Area: 176 x 256mm, Bleed Size: 210 x 275mm
CONSUMER: ADULT & GAY MAGAZINES: Adult Magazines

PERSONEELBELEID 15933N14F-90
Editorial: Veldweg 28, 1404 CV BUSSUM
Tel: 38 4279423 **Fax:** 38 4279420
Email: info@hetnri.nl
Freq: 11 issues yearly; **Cover Price:** EUR 19,-
Annual Sub.: EUR 179,-; **Circ:** 6,933
Editor: Henk Vlaming; **Editor-in-Chief:** M. Nijessen; **Publisher:** Harry Schram
Profile: Journal of the Dutch Association for Human Resources Management, covering news, recent developments and legal issues.
Language(s): Dutch
Readership: Read mainly by personnel managers.
ADVERTISING RATES:
Full Page Mono .. EUR 1/1: b/w 1695,- 1/2: b/w 995,- 1/4: b/w 595,-
Agency Commission: 15%
Mechanical Data: Type Area: 192 x 281mm, Bleed Size: 210 x 297mm
Copy instructions: *Copy Date:* 2 weeks prior to publication date
BUSINESS: COMMERCE, INDUSTRY & MANAGEMENT: Training & Recruitment

PERSPECTIEF 713733N74N-528
Editorial: Blijmarkt 12, 8011 NE ZWOLLE
Tel: 72 5188825 **Fax:** 20 5159143
Email: info@pcob.nl
Date Established: 01-11-1960; **Freq:** 10 issues yearly; **Annual Sub.:** EUR 32,-; **Circ:** 92,000
Editor: Hans van Ronkel
Profile: Magazine containing background and human interest articles for the elderly. Also includes information and up to date facts, news, tips and visions on the treatment of the elderly population.
Language(s): Dutch
Readership: Aimed at those aged over 50 years.
ADVERTISING RATES:
Full Page Mono EUR 1/1: f.c. 2810,-; b/w 2045,- 1/2: f.c. 1825,-; b/w 1115,- 1/4: f.c. 1275,-; b/w 650,-
Agency Commission: 15%
Mechanical Data: Type Area: 185 x 267mm, Bleed Size: 210 x 297mm
Copy instructions: *Copy Date:* 3 weeks prior to publication date
CONSUMER: WOMEN'S INTEREST CONSUMER MAGAZINES: Retirement

PETROCHEM 16346N33-120
Editorial: Veemboerhof 7, 1019 HD AMSTERDAM
Tel: 492 338432 **Fax:** 492 338421
Email: info@industrielinqs.nl **Web site:** http://www.petrochem.nl
Freq: 11 issues yearly; **Cover Price:** EUR 18,45
Annual Sub.: EUR 148,90; **Circ:** 4,109
Editor: Wim Raaijen; **Editor-in-Chief:** L. Schipper
Profile: Management magazine for the petrochemical industry.
Language(s): Dutch
Readership: Aimed at managers in the petrochemical industry, contractors and sub-contractors.
ADVERTISING RATES:
Full Page Mono EUR 2/1: f.c. 4753,-; 1/1: f.c. 3183,-; PMS 2553,-; b/w 2073,- 1/2: f.c. 2148,-; PMS 1756,-; b/w 1276,-
Agency Commission: 15%
Mechanical Data: Type Area: 185 x 267mm, Bleed Size: 210 x 297mm
BUSINESS: OIL & PETROLEUM

PETS INTERNATIONAL MAGAZINE 16998N64E-100
Editorial: Prinses Marielaan 12, 3818 HM AMERSFOORT **Tel:** 20 3467209 **Fax:** 20 6159047
Web site: http://www.petsinfo.net/magazine[VA]online.html
Freq: 7 issues yearly; **Cover Price:** EUR 16,-
Annual Sub.: EUR 89,-; **Circ:** 10,500
Editor: Corine van Winden
Profile: International business-to-business marketing magazine for the pet industry and trade.
Language(s): Dutch
Readership: Read by wholesalers, retailers, importers, exporters, buyers, manufacturers, agents and supermarket managers.
ADVERTISING RATES:
Full Page Mono EUR 1/1: f.c. 3220,-; 1/2: f.c. 2360,-; 1/4: f.c. 1350,-
Agency Commission: 15%
Mechanical Data: Type Area: 185 x 270mm, Bleed Size: 210 x 297mm
Copy instructions: *Copy Date:* 3 weeks prior to publication date
BUSINESS: OTHER CLASSIFICATIONS: Pet Trade

PHARMACEUTISCH WEEKBLAD 16374N37-90
Editorial: Alexanderstraat 11, 2514 JL DEN HAAG
Tel: 88 2697183 **Fax:** 88 2697490
Web site: http://www.pw.nl
Freq: 40 issues yearly; **Cover Price:** EUR 10,50
Annual Sub.: EUR 202,-; **Circ:** 10,108
Profile: Journal published by the Royal Dutch Association for Advancement of Pharmacy. Covers developments in pharmaceutical sciences and pharmacy practice.
Language(s): Dutch
Readership: Aimed at pharmacists.
ADVERTISING RATES:
Full Page Mono EUR 1/1: f.c. 3310,-; 1/2: f.c. 1820,-; 1/4: f.c. 995,-
Agency Commission: 15%
Mechanical Data: Type Area: 190 x 272mm, Bleed Size: 210 x 297mm
BUSINESS: PHARMACEUTICAL & CHEMISTS

PI, PROJEKT & INTERIEUR 16182N23A-50
Editorial: Burg. Haspelslaan 23, 1181 NB AMSTELVEEN **Tel:** 88 7518800 **Fax:** 20 5353696
Web site: http://www.pi-online.nl
Freq: 6 issues yearly; **Annual Sub.:** EUR 65,25; **Circ:** 9,017
Editor: Rutger van Oldenbeek; **Publisher:** Ton Roskam
Profile: Magazine containing information on the furniture trade.
Language(s): Dutch
Readership: Aimed at interior and institutional designers, decorators and architects.
ADVERTISING RATES:
Full Page Mono EUR 2/1: b/w 4069,- 1/1: b/w 2307,- 1/2: b/w 1293,-
Agency Commission: 15%
Mechanical Data: Type Area: 185 x 261mm, Bleed Size: 240 x 290mm
Copy instructions: *Copy Date:* 17 days prior to publication date
BUSINESS: FURNISHINGS & FURNITURE

PIANO BULLETIN 17711N76D-130
Editorial: Broerhuisstraat 44, 2611 GD DELFT
Tel: 15 2126695 **Fax:** 15 2126695
Date Established: 01-03-1982; **Freq:** 3 issues yearly;
Cover Price: EUR 8,50
Annual Sub.: EUR 29,80; **Circ:** 1,200
Editor: Christo Lelie; **Editor-in-Chief:** Bert Mooiman
Language(s): Dutch
Readership: Magazine read by professional pianists, piano teachers and their pupils.
ADVERTISING RATES:
Full Page Mono EUR 1/1: b/w 265,- 1/2: b/w 190,- 1/4: b/w 135,-
Agency Commission: 15%
Mechanical Data: Type Area: 148 x 220mm, Bleed Size: 168 x 240mm
CONSUMER: MUSIC & PERFORMING ARTS: Music

PIANOWERELD 16897N61-100
Editorial: Herenstraat 105, 1406 PC BUSSUM
Tel: 71 5239058 **Fax:** 20 5159145
Web site: http://www.pianowereld.nl
Date Established: 01-10-1984; **Freq:** 6 issues yearly;
Cover Price: EUR 7,45
Annual Sub.: EUR 43,45; **Circ:** 2,750
Editor: Hans Goddijn; **Editor-in-Chief:** Elger Niels
Profile: Music magazine about pianos, digital pianos and professional artists.
Language(s): Dutch
Readership: Read by piano lovers, piano tuners and piano players.
Agency Commission: 15%
Mechanical Data: Type Area: 190 x 270mm, Bleed Size: 210 x 297mm
BUSINESS: MUSIC TRADE

PINK 18053N86B-40
Editorial: In de Betouwstraat 9, 6511 GA NIJMEGEN
Tel: 314 349446 **Fax:** 314 344397
Email: info@cocnijmegen.nl
Freq: 5 issues yearly; **Annual Sub.:** EUR 10,-; **Circ:** 1,000
Profile: Magazine focusing on issues of interest to lesbians and gay men.
Language(s): Dutch
Readership: Read by members of the gay community.
Agency Commission: 15%
Mechanical Data: Bleed Size: 297 x 420mm
CONSUMER: ADULT & GAY MAGAZINES: Gay & Lesbian Magazines

PLAFOND EN WAND.INFO 15705N4E-274
Editorial: Marconistraat 33, 3771 AM BARNEVELD
Tel: 342 494848 **Fax:** 342 494299
Email: i@bdu.nl **Web site:** http://www.plafondenwand.info
Date Established: 01-01-1987; **Freq:** 6 issues yearly;
Circ: 8,906
Editor: Sandra van der Horst; **Publisher:** Ton Roskam
Profile: Journal about ceilings and walls.
Language(s): Dutch
Readership: Aimed at architects, interior designers and builders.
ADVERTISING RATES:
Full Page Mono EUR 1/1: b/w 1788,- 1/2: b/w 1059,- 1/4: b/w 540,-
Agency Commission: 15%
Mechanical Data: Type Area: 190 x 270mm, Bleed Size: 230 x 310mm
Copy instructions: *Copy Date:* 3 weeks prior to publication date
BUSINESS: ARCHITECTURE & BUILDING: Building

PLATFORM A 15949N14L-576
Editorial: Boerhaavelaan 1, 2713 HA ZOETERMEER
Tel: 0032 34660066 **Fax:** 314 349049
Web site: http://www.abvakabofnv.nl/aaneen
Freq: 6 issues yearly; **Annual Sub.:** EUR 18,15; **Circ:** 356,170
Profile: Trade union magazine.
Language(s): Dutch
Readership: Read by members.
ADVERTISING RATES:
Full Page Mono EUR 1/1: f.c. 6090,-; b/w 5060,- 1/2: f.c. 4430,-; b/w 2880,- 1/4: f.c. 2760,-; b/w 1590,-
Agency Commission: 15%
Mechanical Data: Type Area: 187 x 251mm, Bleed Size: 215 x 280mm
Copy instructions: *Copy Date:* 24 days prior to publication date
BUSINESS: COMMERCE, INDUSTRY & MANAGEMENT: Trade Unions

PLATTELANDSPOST 16111N21A-250
Editorial: Celsiusweg 41, 8912 AM LEEUWARDEN
Tel: 23 5565135 **Fax:** 88 5567355
Email: businessmedia@eisma.nl **Web site:** http://www.plattelandspost.nl
Date Established: 01-01-1970; **Freq:** 10 issues yearly; **Annual Sub.:** EUR 62,-; **Circ:** 7,784
Editor: Jacqueline Wijbenga; **Editor-in-Chief:** Durkje Hietkamp; **Publisher:** Minne Hovenga
Profile: Publication containing information about agriculture.
Language(s): Dutch
Readership: Read by farmers and suppliers.
ADVERTISING RATES:
Full Page Mono EUR 1/1: f.c. 894,-; 1/2: f.c. 492,-; 1/4: f.c. 272,-
Agency Commission: 15%
Mechanical Data: Type Area: 210 x 280mm, Bleed Size: 230 x 300mm
Copy instructions: *Copy Date:* 3 days prior to publication date
BUSINESS: AGRICULTURE & FARMING

PLAYBOY 18046N86A-50
Editorial: Capellalaan 65, 2132 JL HOOFDDORP
Tel: 88 7518480 **Fax:** 88 7518481
Web site: http://www.playboy.nl
Freq: Monthly; **Cover Price:** EUR 5,95
Annual Sub.: EUR 68,-; **Circ:** 54,211
Editor: Jan Heemskerk; **Publisher:** Wouter Verkennis
Profile: Adult magazine for men.
Language(s): Dutch
ADVERTISING RATES:
Full Page Mono .... EUR 2/1: b/w 17.200,- 1/1: b/w 8600,- 1/2: b/w 5160,-
Agency Commission: 15%
Mechanical Data: Type Area: 178 x 252mm, Bleed Size: 210 x 280mm
CONSUMER: ADULT & GAY MAGAZINES: Adult Magazines

PLEEGCONTACT 16324N32G-160
Editorial: Postbus 1139, 3500 BC UTRECHT
Tel: 23 5565370 **Fax:** 23 5565357
Email: info@denvp.nl
Freq: Quarterly; **Circ:** 1,750
Profile: Magazine focusing on fostercare.
Language(s): Dutch
Agency Commission: 15%
Mechanical Data: Bleed Size: 210 x 298mm
BUSINESS: LOCAL GOVERNMENT, LEISURE & RECREATION: Community Care & Social Services

PLUIMVEEHOUDERIJ 16139N21F-40
Editorial: Hanzestraat 1, 7006 RH DOETINCHEM
Tel: 314 349422 **Fax:** 314 360699
Email: klantenservice@reedbusiness.nl
Annual Sub.: EUR 192,85; **Circ:** 3,621
Editor: Fabian Brockotter; **Editor-in-Chief:** A. Papenburg; **Publisher:** Aart Freriks
Profile: Magazine covering the poultry industry, containing technical and financial information plus market and price developments in poultry keeping.
Language(s): Dutch
ADVERTISING RATES:
Full Page Mono EUR 1/1: f.c. 3282,-; b/w 2163,- 1/2: f.c. 1939,-; b/w 1158,- 1/4: f.c. 1272,-; b/w 604,-
Agency Commission: 15%
Mechanical Data: Type Area: 194 x 257mm, Bleed Size: 215 x 285mm
BUSINESS: AGRICULTURE & FARMING: Poultry

PLUS MAGAZINE 17533N74N-80
Editorial: Amalialaan 126, 3743 KJ BAARN
Tel: 13 4662445 **Fax:** 88 2697490
Email: info@spn.nl **Web site:** http://www.plusonline.nl
Date Established: 01-04-1990
Cover Price: EUR 4,50
Annual Sub.: EUR 46,-; **Circ:** 282,484
Editor-in-Chief: Ida Aguado; **Publisher:** Tjangja Galdeij
Profile: Magazine for active people over 50 years of age.
Language(s): Dutch
ADVERTISING RATES:
Full Page Mono .... EUR 1/1: f.c. 12.967,-; 1/2: f.c. 8435,-; 1/4: f.c. 5665,-
Agency Commission: 15%
Mechanical Data: Type Area: 179 x 243mm, Bleed Size: 210 x 270mm
CONSUMER: WOMEN'S INTEREST CONSUMER MAGAZINES: Retirement

PLUSPUNT 16774N56L-99
Editorial: Maliebaan 71h, 3581 CG UTRECHT
Tel: 23 5565370 **Fax:** 23 5565357
Email: info@kansplus.nl
Date Established: 01-09-1976; **Freq:** 5 issues yearly;
Annual Sub.: EUR 29,-; **Circ:** 15,000
Editor: Amina Lamrini
Profile: Magazine about the care of mentally handicapped children.
Language(s): Dutch
Readership: Read by carers, medical staff and parents.
Agency Commission: 15%
Mechanical Data: Bleed Size: 170 x 240mm
BUSINESS: HEALTH & MEDICAL: Disability & Rehabilitation

PODOSOPHIA 16759N56K-60
Editorial: Het Spoor 2, 3994 AK HOUTEN
Tel: 223 650019 **Fax:** 223 650011
Web site: http://www.podosophia.nl
Date Established: 01-09-1993; **Freq:** 6 issues yearly;
Annual Sub.: EUR 51,25; **Circ:** 1,034
Editor-in-Chief: John Frijters; **Publisher:** Karin Linden
Profile: Journal about chiropody and foot care.
Language(s): Dutch
ADVERTISING RATES:
Full Page Mono .. EUR 1/1: f.c. 1205,-; b/w 931,- 1/2: f.c. 708,-; b/w 556,- 1/4: f.c. 421,-; b/w 339,-
Agency Commission: 15%
Mechanical Data: Type Area: 192 x 258mm, Bleed Size: 215 x 285mm
BUSINESS: HEALTH & MEDICAL: Chiropody

DE POEZENKRANT 19126N81C-43
Editorial: Postbus 70053, 1007 KB AMSTERDAM
Email: info@poezenkrant.com
Date Established: 01-02-1974
Circ: 4,000
Usual Pagination: 24
Editor: P.E. Schreuders; **Publisher:** P.E. Schreuders
Profile: Cat magazine.
Language(s): Dutch
Agency Commission: 15%
CONSUMER: ANIMALS & PETS: Cats

DE POLITIE 18526N32F-67
Editorial: Steinhagenseweg 2d, 3446 GP WOERDEN
Tel: 314 349422 **Fax:** 33 4626063
Email: info@politiebond.nl
Freq: 11 issues yearly; **Annual Sub.:** EUR 19,06;
Circ: 25,000
Editor: T.J.M. Harte
Profile: Official journal of the Dutch Police Association.
Language(s): Dutch
ADVERTISING RATES:
Full Page Mono EUR 1/1: f.c. 1995,-; b/w 1195,- 1/2: f.c. 1040,-; b/w 640,- 1/4: f.c. 560,-; b/w 340,-
Agency Commission: 15%
Mechanical Data: Type Area: 180 x 277mm, Bleed Size: 210 x 297mm
Copy instructions: *Copy Date:* 15 days prior to publication date
BUSINESS: LOCAL GOVERNMENT, LEISURE & RECREATION: Police

DE POLITIEHOND 16303N32F-68
Editorial: Liendertseweg 108, 3815 BJ AMERSFOORT **Tel:** 314 349422 **Fax:** 33 4626063
Email: bureau-knpv@planet.nl
Freq: 10 issues yearly; **Cover Price:** Free; **Circ:** 7,000
Editor: B.B.L. de Winter

Profile: Magazine focusing on the training of police dogs.
Language(s): Dutch
Readership: Read by members.
Agency Commission: 15%
Mechanical Data: Bleed Size: 210 x 297mm
BUSINESS: LOCAL GOVERNMENT, LEISURE & RECREATION: Police

POLSSLAG
16402N40-100
Editorial: Postbus 109, 3769 ZJ SOESTERBERG
Tel: 314 349422 **Fax:** 30 2643525
Freq: Half-yearly; **Annual Sub.:** EUR 30,-; **Circ:** 500
Editor: Jos van 't Root; **Editor-in-Chief:** Henk Jonker
Profile: Official journal of VOGD - the Association of Officers in Medical Services.
Language(s): Dutch
ADVERTISING RATES:
Full Page Mono .... EUR 1/1: b/w 430,- 1/2: b/w 239,-
Agency Commission: 15%
Mechanical Data: Type Area: 180 x 265mm, Bleed Size: 210 x 297mm
BUSINESS: DEFENCE

POMPSHOP
16256N31A-80
Editorial: J.C. van Markenlaan 3, 2285 VL RIJSWIJK
Tel: 23 5344089 **Fax:** 10 2801002
Email: uitgeverij@lakerveld.nl **Web site:** http://www.pompshop.com
Freq: 11 issues yearly; **Cover Price:** EUR 7,-
Annual Sub.: EUR 61,60; **Circ:** 2,041
Editor: Jiri Hartog; **Publisher:** Ad van Gaalen
Profile: Magazine concerning petrol stations and car washes.
Language(s): Dutch
ADVERTISING RATES:
Full Page Mono .. EUR 1/1: b/w 1595,- 1/2: b/w 930,- 1/4: b/w 555,-
Agency Commission: 15%
Mechanical Data: Type Area: 185 x 268mm, Bleed Size: 210 x 297mm
Copy instructions: *Copy Date:* 3 weeks prior to publication date
BUSINESS: MOTOR TRADE: Motor Trade Accessories

DE POOK
16213N26C-80
Editorial: Wolfswei 5, 6118 CR NIEUWSTADT
Tel: 314 349422 **Fax:** 30 2643525
Email: info@tpk-media.nl
Freq: 6 issues yearly; **Cover Price:** EUR 12,-
Annual Sub.: EUR 62,-; **Circ:** 5,000
Editor: K. Verdonschot; **Editor-in-Chief:** Amaury Stroux; **Publisher:** Tjeerd Posthumus
Profile: Magazine covering all aspects of floristry, including cultivation and arranging techniques.
Language(s): Dutch
ADVERTISING RATES:
Full Page Mono EUR 1/1: f.c. 1965,-; PMS 1600,-; b/w 1170,- 1/2: f.c. 1033,-; PMS 850,-; b/w 635,- 1/4: b/w 359,-
Agency Commission: 15%
Mechanical Data: Type Area: 207 x 266mm, Bleed Size: 235 x 300mm
BUSINESS: GARDEN TRADE

PORTS AND DREDGING
16515N45D-16
Editorial: Molendijk 94, 3361 EP SLIEDRECHT
Tel: 23 5565135 **Fax:** 23 5567355
Email: info@ihcmerwede.com
Date Established: 01-01-1951; **Freq:** 3 issues yearly;
Cover Price: Free; **Circ:** 8,500
Usual Pagination: 40
Editor: Katja Jansen; **Editor-in-Chief:** Katja Jansen; **Publisher:** Katja Jansen
Profile: Journal covering developments in dredging technology, vessels and equipment.
Language(s): Dutch
Agency Commission: 15%
BUSINESS: MARINE & SHIPPING: Marine Engineering Equipment

POST VAN PORTAAL
1637270N74C-248
Editorial: Javalaan 3, 3743 HE BAARN
Tel: 26 3898821 **Fax:** 229 216416
Email: info@portaal.nl
Date Established: 23-03-2005; **Freq:** Quarterly;
Cover Price: Free; **Circ:** 57,000
Editor-in-Chief: Stefan Gradisen
Language(s): Dutch
Agency Commission: 15%
Mechanical Data: Type Area: 210 x 210mm
CONSUMER: WOMEN'S INTEREST CONSUMER MAGAZINES: Home & Family

DE POSTILJON, EDITIE ALEXANDERPOLDER E.O.
627238N72-7497
Editorial: Basisweg 30, 1043 AP AMSTERDAM
Tel: 543 493705 **Fax:** 223 650011
Email: info@hollandcombinatie.nl **Web site:** http://www.postiljon-online.nl
Date Established: 01-01-1996; **Freq:** Weekly; **Cover Price:** Free; **Circ:** 45,000
Language(s): Dutch
Agency Commission: 15%
Mechanical Data: Type Area: 260 x 390mm
LOCAL NEWSPAPERS

DE POSTILJON, EDITIE ZOETERMEER
1636103N72-7503
Editorial: Basisweg 30, 1043 AP AMSTERDAM
Tel: 161 457342 **Fax:** 20 5159145
Email: info@hollandcombinatie.nl **Web site:** http://www.postiljon-online.nl
Date Established: 01-01-1991; **Freq:** Weekly; **Cover Price:** Free; **Circ:** 68,000
Language(s): Dutch
Agency Commission: 15%
Mechanical Data: Type Area: 260 x 390mm
LOCAL NEWSPAPERS

DE POSTZAK
19162N79C-104
Editorial: Oude Hoflaan 11, 9751 BK HAREN
Tel: 23 5565135
Date Established: 01-01-1946; **Freq:** 3 issues yearly; **Circ:** 800
Usual Pagination: 36
Editor: E.W. Flentge
Profile: Journal of the Dutch Society of Postmark Collectors. Also covers postal stationery and postal history.
Language(s): Dutch
Agency Commission: 15%
Mechanical Data: Type Area: 145 x 215mm
CONSUMER: HOBBIES & DIY: Philately

POUR VOUS
17500N74H-213
Editorial: Amsterdamsestraatweg 37, 3744 MA BAARN **Tel:** 20 5302586 **Fax:** 20 5302586
Email: info@pourvous.nl
Freq: Quarterly; **Cover Price:** Free; **Circ:** 162,517
Editor: Leontine Kraan; **Publisher:** P.S.A. Ruiter
Profile: Magazine containing articles about cosmetics.
Language(s): Dutch
Readership: Aimed at women.
ADVERTISING RATES:
Full Page Mono .... EUR 2/1 : f.c. 14.900,-; 1/1 : f.c. 7450,-
Agency Commission: 15%
Mechanical Data: Type Area: 190 x 277mm, Bleed Size: 210 x 297mm
CONSUMER: WOMEN'S INTEREST CONSUMER MAGAZINES: Hair & Beauty

PRAGMATICS & COGNITION
1500478N94X-432
Editorial: Klaprozenweg 75g, 1033 NN AMSTERDAM
Tel: 88 2696139 **Fax:** 88 2697175
Email: customer.services@benjamins.nl
Freq: 3 issues yearly; **Annual Sub.:** EUR 438,-
Editor: M. Dascal
Profile: Journal seeking to bring together such disciplines as philosophy, linguistics, semiotics, cognitive science, neuroscience, artificial intelligence, ethology and cognitive anthropology, by focusing on the relationship between linguistic activity and mental activity.
Language(s): Dutch
Readership: Aimed at researchers in the above disciplines, as well as education, psychology, and history of ideas.
Agency Commission: 15%
CONSUMER: OTHER CLASSIFICATIONS: Miscellaneous

PRAKTIJKBLAD SALARISADMINISTRATIE
761387N1A-157
Editorial: Staverenstraat 32015, 7418 CJ DEVENTER
Tel: 570 648988 **Fax:** 570 614795
Email: info@kluwer.nl **Web site:** http://www.kluwersalaris[VA]administratie.nl
Freq: 16 issues yearly; **Cover Price:** EUR 10,-
Annual Sub.: EUR 145,-; **Circ:** 1,800
Editor: Anja Jalink; **Editor-in-Chief:** Caroline Jansen; **Publisher:** Freek Talsma
Profile: Magazine containing advice and information on salary administration.
Language(s): Dutch
Readership: Aimed at payroll managers, accountants and human resources managers.
ADVERTISING RATES:
Full Page Mono EUR 1/1: b/w 875,- 1/2: b/w 600,- 1/4: b/w 425,-
Agency Commission: 15%
Mechanical Data: Type Area: 180 x 275mm, Bleed Size: 210 x 297mm
BUSINESS: FINANCE & ECONOMICS

PREDIKANT EN SAMENLEVING
18100N87-250
Editorial: Cornelis Houtmanstraat 2, 3572 LV UTRECHT **Tel:** 20 5518525 **Fax:** 70 4160636
Email: bnp@predikanten.nl
Freq: 6 issues yearly; **Annual Sub.:** EUR 33,40; **Circ:** 3,700
Editor: F.T. Bos
Profile: Publication of the Society of Chaplains in the Netherlands.
Language(s): Dutch
Readership: Aimed at preachers.
ADVERTISING RATES:
Full Page Mono .... EUR 1/1: f.c. 925,-; b/w 775,- 1/2: f.c. 550,-; b/w 425,- 1/4: f.c. 350,-; b/w 250,-
Agency Commission: 15%
Mechanical Data: Type Area: 190 x 275mm, Bleed Size: 210 x 297mm
CONSUMER: RELIGIOUS

PRELUDIUM
629749N76D-133
Editorial: Postbus 78098, 1070 LP AMSTERDAM
Tel: 23 5565135 **Fax:** 88 5567355
Email: info@concertgebouworkest.nl
Freq: 10 issues yearly; **Cover Price:** EUR 4,00
Annual Sub.: EUR 39,50; **Circ:** 12,000
Editor: C. Tausch; **Editor-in-Chief:** J. Boeser
Profile: Magazine covering concerts and musical programmes.
Language(s): Dutch
Readership: Aimed at those interested in attending musical performances at the Concertgebouw.
ADVERTISING RATES:
Full Page Mono EUR 1/1: f.c. 2325,-; 1/2: f.c. 1325,-; 1/4: f.c. 750,-
Agency Commission: 15%
Mechanical Data: Bleed Size: 170 x 240mm, Type Area: 150 x 220mm
CONSUMER: MUSIC & PERFORMING ARTS: Music

PRÉNATAL MAGAZINE
1635833N74D-158
Editorial: Vlotbrugweg 10, 1332 AH ALMERE
Tel: 20 3467209 **Fax:** 10 4521797
Email: info@prenatal.nl
Freq: Annual; **Cover Price:** Free; **Circ:** 250,000
Editor: Irma Gros
Language(s): Dutch
ADVERTISING RATES:
Full Page Mono .... EUR 2/1: f.c. 22.250,-; 1/1: f.c. 11.750,-; 1/2: f.c. 7000,-
Agency Commission: 15%
Mechanical Data: Type Area: 252 x 185mm
CONSUMER: WOMEN'S INTEREST CONSUMER MAGAZINES: Child Care

PRETTIG WEEKEND
627201N72-7385
Editorial: De Zarken 20, 1141 BL MONNICKENDAM
Tel: 20 5310960
Web site: http://www.prettig-weekend.nl
Date Established: 06-01-1990; **Freq:** Weekly; **Cover Price:** Free; **Circ:** 22,500
Editor: Riet Cerpentier; **Publisher:** Riet Cerpentier
Language(s): Dutch
ADVERTISING RATES:
Full Page Mono ..... EUR 1/1: f.c. 425,-; 1/2: f.c. 220,-
Agency Commission: 15%
Mechanical Data: Type Area: 180 x 255mm
LOCAL NEWSPAPERS

PREVIEW
17663N76A-50
Editorial: Wilgenweg 14a, 1031 HV AMSTERDAM
Tel: 0032 34660066 **Fax:** 0032 34660067
Email: info@boomerang.nl
Freq: 8 issues yearly; **Cover Price:** Free; **Circ:** 200,000
Editor: Mick Boskamp
Profile: Magazine focusing on films.
Language(s): Dutch
Readership: Read by cinema-goers.
ADVERTISING RATES:
Full Page Mono .... EUR 2/1: f.c. 12.900,-; 1/1: f.c. 6900,-; 1/2: f.c. 3900,-
Agency Commission: 15%
Mechanical Data: Bleed Size: 210 x 297mm
CONSUMER: MUSIC & PERFORMING ARTS: Cinema

PRIMAONDERWIJS.NL
1857673N62A-222
Editorial: Niels Bohrweg 123, 3542 CA UTRECHT
Tel: 70 3789685 **Fax:** 70 7999840
Email: info@edg.nl
Freq: 6 issues yearly; **Circ:** 180,000
Editor: Pauline de Pater; **Editor-in-Chief:** Caroline Broeijer; **Publisher:** Erik Trimp
Language(s): Dutch
ADVERTISING RATES:
Full Page Mono EUR 1/1: b/w 3850,- 1/2: b/w 2050,- 1/4: b/w 1150,-
Agency Commission: 15%
Mechanical Data: Type Area: 172 x 265mm, Bleed Size: 192 x 285mm
Copy instructions: *Copy Date:* 5 weeks prior to publication date
BUSINESS: CHURCH & SCHOOL EQUIPMENT & EDUCATION: Education

PRIMAOUDERS.NL
1615351N74D-151
Editorial: Niels Bohrweg 123, 3542 CA UTRECHT
Tel: 30 2417045 **Fax:** 79 3467846
Email: info@edg.nl **Web site:** http://www.primaouders.nl
Freq: 6 issues yearly; **Cover Price:** Free; **Circ:** 345,000
Editor-in-Chief: Cindy Curré; **Publisher:** Erik Trimp
Profile: Newspaper containing information about the care of children who go to day care centres.
Language(s): Dutch
Readership: Aimed at parents and carers of children aged 0 to 4 years.
ADVERTISING RATES:
Full Page Mono EUR 1/1: f.c. 7750,-; 1/2: f.c. 4250,-; 1/4: f.c. 2500,-
Agency Commission: 15%
Mechanical Data: Type Area: 172 x 265mm, Bleed Size: 192 x 285mm
Copy instructions: *Copy Date:* 4 weeks prior to publication date
CONSUMER: WOMEN'S INTEREST CONSUMER MAGAZINES: Child Care

PRINT BUYER
16416N41A-61_80
Editorial: 3e Binnenvestgracht 23s, 2312 NR LEIDEN
Tel: 70 3780541 **Fax:** 70 3789783
Email: info@uitgeverijcompres.nl **Web site:** http://www.printbuyer.nl
Date Established: 01-01-1989; **Freq:** 10 issues yearly; **Cover Price:** EUR 15,-
Annual Sub.: EUR 135,-; **Circ:** 3,227
Editor: Hanneke Jelles; **Editor-in-Chief:** Marco den Engelsman; **Publisher:** Wim Findhammer
Profile: Journal containing information on developments in print buying, includes technical aspects.
Language(s): Dutch
Readership: Read by print buyers, traffic managers of advertising agencies and buyers of publishing companies and graphics companies.
ADVERTISING RATES:
Full Page Mono EUR 1/1: b/w 2105,- 1/2: b/w 1135,- 1/4: b/w 630,-
Agency Commission: 15%
Mechanical Data: Type Area: 185 x 265mm, Bleed Size: 200 x 283mm
BUSINESS: PRINTING & STATIONERY: Printing

PRIVÉ
17424N74A-140
Editorial: Basisweg 30, 1043 AP AMSTERDAM
Tel: 20 5853375 **Fax:** 20 5854225
Email: tijdschriften@telegraafmedia.nl **Web site:** http://www.prive.nl
Freq: Weekly; **Cover Price:** EUR 2,25
Annual Sub.: EUR 96,-; **Circ:** 194,838
Editor: Evert Santegoeds; **Editor-in-Chief:** Matthieu van Winsen; **Publisher:** Petra Lubbers
Profile: Magazine containing features on television, celebrities, films, shopping, beauty, cookery and health.
Language(s): Dutch
Readership: Aimed at women.
ADVERTISING RATES:
Full Page Mono .... EUR 1/1: f.c. 10.720,-; 1/2: f.c. 8040,-; 1/4: f.c. 4288,-
Agency Commission: 15%
Mechanical Data: Type Area: 208 x 258mm, Bleed Size: 240 x 285mm
CONSUMER: WOMEN'S INTEREST CONSUMER MAGAZINES: Women's Interest

PRIVIUM UPDATE
1894173N6A-166
Editorial: Postbus 7501, 1118 ZG SCHIPHOL
Tel: 0032 34660066
Email: privium@schiphol.nl
Freq: Quarterly; **Circ:** 55,000
Editor-in-Chief: Jojo Oomes; **Publisher:** Luc van Os
Language(s): Dutch
ADVERTISING RATES:
Full Page Mono . EUR 2/1: f.c. 9500,-; 1/1: f.c. 5000,-
Agency Commission: 15%
Mechanical Data: Bleed Size: 220 x 265mm
BUSINESS: AVIATION & AERONAUTICS

PROAUDIOVIDEO
16455N43B-58
Editorial: Hulsterstraat 16, 4116 EZ BUREN
Tel: 543 493705 **Fax:** 15 2158918
Web site: http://www.proaudiovideo.info
Freq: 11 issues yearly; **Cover Price:** EUR 6,10
Annual Sub.: EUR 58,75; **Circ:** 4,600
Editor: Hans Beekhuyzen; **Publisher:** Hans Beekhuyzen
Profile: Trade magazine for the professional audio-visual trade.
Language(s): Dutch
ADVERTISING RATES:
Full Page Mono EUR 2/1: b/w 2565,- 1/1: b/w 1365,- 1/2: b/w 818,-
Agency Commission: 15%
Mechanical Data: Type Area: 175 x 261mm, Bleed Size: 210 x 297mm
BUSINESS: ELECTRICAL RETAIL TRADE: Radio & Hi-Fi

PRODUCT
15906N14B-82
Editorial: Essebaan 63, 2908 LJ CAPELLE AAN DEN IJSSEL **Tel:** 20 5159743 **Fax:** 20 6752709
Email: info@mybusinessmedia.nl **Web site:** http://www.productmagazine.nl
Freq: 6 issues yearly; **Cover Price:** EUR 23,95
Annual Sub.: EUR 114,95; **Circ:** 1,378
Editor-in-Chief: Astrid Mol; **Publisher:** S. Wanders
Profile: Journal focusing on industrial product development.
Language(s): Dutch
ADVERTISING RATES:
Full Page Mono EUR 1/1: f.c. 2635,-; 1/2: f.c. 1580,-; 1/4: f.c. 945,-
Agency Commission: 15%
Mechanical Data: Type Area: 185 x 267mm, Bleed Size: 210 x 297mm

Copy instructions: *Copy Date:* 2 weeks prior to publication date
BUSINESS: COMMERCE, INDUSTRY & MANAGEMENT: Industry & Factories

PROEF... 17538N74P-253
Editorial: Biezenkamp 3a, 3831 JA LEUSDEN
Tel: 33 4220082 **Fax:** 20 5465530
Email: info@keurslager.nl
Freq: 8 issues yearly; **Annual Sub.:** EUR 39,-; **Circ:** 230,000
Editor-in-Chief: J. Klaver; **Publisher:** J. van Sluiters
Profile: Magazine covering all aspects of food and drink, with an emphasis on meat and meat products. Contains recipes and product information.
Language(s): Dutch
Readership: Read by anybody who likes cooking.
Agency Commission: 15%
Mechanical Data: Bleed Size: 215 x 275mm
CONSUMER: WOMEN'S INTEREST CONSUMER MAGAZINES: Food & Cookery

PROEF& 1857851N9A-159
Editorial: Provincialeweg 11, 1506 MA ZAANDAM
Tel: 40 8447611
Email: info@gall.nl
Freq: 11 issues yearly; **Cover Price:** Free; **Circ:** 300,000
Usual Pagination: 52
Language(s): Dutch
Agency Commission: 15%
Mechanical Data: Bleed Size: 200 x 250mm, Type Area: 188 x 238mm
BUSINESS: DRINKS & LICENSED TRADE: Drinks, Licensed Trade, Wines & Spirits

PROEFDIERVRIJ MAGAZINE 1635228N81A-160
Editorial: Groot Hertoginnelaan 201, 2517 ES DEN HAAG **Tel:** 20 5159743 **Fax:** 20 6752709
Email: info@proefdiervrij.nl **Web site:** http://www.proefdiervrij.nl
Freq: Quarterly; **Annual Sub.:** EUR 20,-; **Circ:** 50,000
Usual Pagination: 16
Editor: P.J. de Leu
Language(s): Dutch
Agency Commission: 15%
CONSUMER: ANIMALS & PETS: Animals & Pets Protection

PROEFSCHRIFT-WINE & FOOD PROFESSIONAL 17543N74P-80
Editorial: Winkeldijk 12a, 1391 HL ABCOUDE
Tel: 70 3789880 **Fax:** 70 3789783
Email: info@thewinesite.nl
Freq: 6 issues yearly; **Circ:** 6,000
Editor: Jan van Lissum; **Editor-in-Chief:** P. Bijpost
Profile: Newspaper containing information about wine, spirits, liqueurs and other drinks.
Language(s): Dutch
Readership: Aimed at the general public.
ADVERTISING RATES:
Full Page Mono . EUR 1/1: f.c. 2175,-; 1/2: f.c. 1610,-
Agency Commission: 15%
Mechanical Data: Type Area: 210 x 297mm, Bleed Size: 213 x 303mm
Copy instructions: *Copy Date:* 3 weeks prior to publication date
CONSUMER: WOMEN'S INTEREST CONSUMER MAGAZINES: Food & Cookery

PROF NAIL 16004N15A-47
Editorial: Hettenheuvelweg 41-43, 1101 BM AMSTERDAM **Tel:** 20 5159172 **Fax:** 20 5159700
Email: info@koggeschip-vakbladen.nl **Web site:** http://www.prof-nail.nl
Freq: 10 issues yearly; **Cover Price:** EUR 11,-
Annual Sub.: EUR 74,-; **Circ:** 7,039
Editor: Marco Jouret; **Publisher:** Anthony van Trigt
Profile: Magazine concerning professional hand and nail care.
Language(s): Dutch
Readership: Read by nailstylists, manicurists and beauticians.
ADVERTISING RATES:
Full Page Mono EUR 1/1: f.c. 2540,-; 1/2: f.c. 1510,-; 1/4: f.c. 925,-
Agency Commission: 15%
Mechanical Data: Type Area: 185 x 270mm, Bleed Size: 210 x 297mm
Copy instructions: *Copy Date:* 2 weeks prior to publication date
BUSINESS: COSMETICS & HAIRDRESSING: Cosmetics

PROFESSIONEEL SCHOONMAKEN 1637241N4F-105
Editorial: Gooimeer 4, 1411 DC NAARDEN
Tel: 88 2696657 **Fax:** 20 5159143
Email: info@appr.nl **Web site:** http://www.professioneelschoonmaken.nl
Freq: 10 issues yearly; **Cover Price:** Free; **Circ:** 4,856
Editor: Joan Koele; **Publisher:** Joan Koele
Language(s): Dutch
ADVERTISING RATES:
Full Page Mono EUR 1/1: f.c. 2561,-; 1/2: f.c. 1846,-; 1/4: f.c. 1126,-
Agency Commission: 15%
Mechanical Data: Type Area: 190 x 275mm, Bleed Size: 210 x 297mm
BUSINESS: ARCHITECTURE & BUILDING: Cleaning & Maintenance

PROGRAMMABOEK OPEN DAGEN KONINKLIJKE LUCHTMACHT 1633822N40-182
Editorial: Kalvermarkt 38, 2511 CB DEN HAAG
Tel: 35 6256180 **Fax:** 20 5584301
Freq: Annual; **Cover Price:** Free; **Circ:** 200,000
Language(s): Dutch
Agency Commission: 15%
BUSINESS: DEFENCE

PROOST! 1637398N9A-153
Editorial: Kon. Wilhelminaplein 30-7, 1062 KR AMSTERDAM **Tel:** 20 8944900 **Fax:** 88 2944998
Email: info@railangfords.nl **Web site:** http://www.proostmagazine.nl
Freq: 10 issues yearly; **Cover Price:** EUR 3,25
Annual Sub.: EUR 45,-; **Circ:** 16,768
Editor: Marjon Prummel; **Editor-in-Chief:** Emil Peeters; **Publisher:** Luuk Aleva
Language(s): Dutch
ADVERTISING RATES:
Full Page Mono EUR 2/1: f.c. 5910,-; 1/1: f.c. 3170,-; 1/2: f.c. 1825,-
Agency Commission: 15%
Mechanical Data: Type Area: 190 x 277mm, Bleed Size: 210 x 297mm
Copy instructions: *Copy Date:* 3 weeks prior to publication date
BUSINESS: DRINKS & LICENSED TRADE: Drinks, Licensed Trade, Wines & Spirits

PROPRIA CURES 17988N83-50
Editorial: Vendelstraat 2, 1012 XX AMSTERDAM
Tel: 33 2458375 **Fax:** 348 414897
Email: propriacures@knoware.nl **Web site:** http://www.propriacures.nl
Date Established: 01-01-1890; **Freq:** 26 issues yearly; **Cover Price:** EUR 1,50
Annual Sub.: EUR 45,-; **Circ:** 3,400
Editor-in-Chief: Jurg van Ginkel
Profile: Satirical magazine for students studying in Amsterdam.
Language(s): Dutch
ADVERTISING RATES:
Full Page Mono EUR 1/1: b/w 672,- 1/2: b/w 350,- 1/4: b/w 187,-
Agency Commission: 15%
Mechanical Data: Type Area: 231 x 328mm, Bleed Size: 251 x 350mm
CONSUMER: STUDENT PUBLICATIONS

PROVINCIALE ZEEUWSE COURANT 17128N67B-5650
Editorial: Park Veldzigt 35, 4336 DR MIDDELBURG
Tel: 521 362556 **Fax:** 348 414897
Email: redactie@pzc.nl **Web site:** http://www.pzc.nl
Date Established: 01-04-1758; **Freq:** 312 issues yearly; **Annual Sub.:** EUR 274,95; **Circ:** 54,570
Editor: P. Jansen; **Publisher:** A.A.M. Verrest
Language(s): Dutch
ADVERTISING RATES:
Full Page Mono EUR 3/4: b/w 2829,- 1/2: b/w 1886,- 1/4: b/w 943,- 3/4 ed. za.: b/w 3058,- 1/2 ed. za.: b/w 2038,- 1/4 e
Agency Commission: 15%
Mechanical Data: Type Area: 266 x 398mm
REGIONAL DAILY & SUNDAY NEWSPAPERS: Regional Daily Newspapers

PROVINCIE EN GEMEENTE 17970N82-105
Editorial: Vinkenborghlaan 15, 2265 GG LEIDSCHENDAM **Tel:** 30 6383766 **Fax:** 30 6383991
Email: info@saffierpr.nl
Date Established: 15-07-1950; **Freq:** 9 issues yearly; **Annual Sub.:** EUR 40,17; **Circ:** 2,800
Editor: Wim Schoevers; **Editor-in-Chief:** Wim Schoevers
Profile: Magazine about politics in the Netherlands.
Language(s): Dutch
Readership: Read by liberal members of local and regional councils and water authorities.
ADVERTISING RATES:
Full Page Mono EUR 1/1: b/w 2100,- 1/2: b/w 1450,- 1/4: b/w 750,-
Agency Commission: 15%
Mechanical Data: Type Area: 260 x 400mm, Bleed Size: 297 x 420mm
CONSUMER: CURRENT AFFAIRS & POLITICS

PSV INSIDE 718315N75B-60
Editorial: Postbus 886, 5600 AW EINDHOVEN
Tel: 70 3789880 **Fax:** 70 3789783
Email: media@psv.nl
Date Established: 01-08-1996; **Freq:** 5 issues yearly; **Circ:** 30,000
Editor: Jeroen van den Berk; **Publisher:** Peter Kentie
Profile: Magazine focusing on PSV Eindhoven football club.
Language(s): Dutch
Readership: Aimed at PSV Eindhoven supporters.
ADVERTISING RATES:
Full Page Mono EUR 2/1: f.c. 4400,-; 1/1: f.c. 2200,-; 1/2: f.c. 1300,-
Agency Commission: 15%
Mechanical Data: Type Area: 220 x 287mm, Bleed Size: 230 x 297mm
CONSUMER: SPORT: Football

DE PSYCHIATER 719327N56N-80
Editorial: Arena Boulevard 61-75, 1101 DL AMSTERDAM **Tel:** 20 7150600 **Fax:** 10 4521797
Date Established: 01-04-1994; **Freq:** 10 issues yearly; **Annual Sub.:** EUR 76,-; **Circ:** 3,700
Editor: Patrick Knapen; **Editor-in-Chief:** Wijnand van Dijk
Profile: Magazine containing information for the members of the Nederlandse Vereniging voor Psychiatry.
Language(s): Dutch
Readership: Aimed at the members of the NVvP and anyone else involved with mental healthcare.
ADVERTISING RATES:
Full Page Mono EUR 2/1: f.c. 4238,-; 1/1: f.c. 3190,-; 1/2: f.c. 2035,-
Agency Commission: 15%
Mechanical Data: Type Area: 190 x 277mm, Bleed Size: 210 x 297mm
Copy instructions: *Copy Date:* 3 weeks prior to publication date
BUSINESS: HEALTH & MEDICAL: Mental Health

PSYCHOLOGIE & GEZONDHEID 16661N56A-384
Editorial: Drift 10, 3512 BS UTRECHT
Tel: 70 3342179 **Fax:** 20 5979490
Email: tvg@let.uu.nl
Date Established: 01-01-1972; **Freq:** 5 issues yearly; **Annual Sub.:** EUR 83,-; **Circ:** 480
Editor: H.A.W. Schut; **Editor-in-Chief:** M. Bloemendaal
Profile: Magazine about psychology and health.
Language(s): Dutch
ADVERTISING RATES:
Full Page Mono .... EUR 1/1: b/w 551,- 1/2: b/w 348,-
Agency Commission: 15%
Mechanical Data: Type Area: 130 x 210mm, Bleed Size: 168 x 242mm
BUSINESS: HEALTH & MEDICAL

PSYCHOLOGIE MAGAZINE 1635858N74G-262
Editorial: Raamgracht 4, 1011 KK AMSTERDAM
Tel: 20 5518518 **Fax:** 20 6269407
Web site: http://www.psychologiemagazine.nl
Freq: 11 issues yearly; **Cover Price:** EUR 5,45
Annual Sub.: EUR 59,90; **Circ:** 123,343
Editor: Sterre van Leer
Language(s): Dutch
ADVERTISING RATES:
Full Page Mono .... EUR 2/1: f.c. 19.000,-; 1/1: f.c. 9500,-; 1/2: f.c. 5700,-
Agency Commission: 15%
Mechanical Data: Type Area: 180 x 250mm, Bleed Size: 210 x 280mm
CONSUMER: WOMEN'S INTEREST CONSUMER MAGAZINES: Slimming & Health

DE PSYCHOLOOG 1634871N56N-157
Editorial: Nieuwekade 1-5, 3511 RV UTRECHT
Tel: 570 673344 **Fax:** 20 5159143
Email: info@psynip.nl
Freq: 11 issues yearly; **Cover Price:** EUR 9,25
Annual Sub.: EUR 61,-; **Circ:** 14,000
Editor: W. Zeegers; **Editor-in-Chief:** W. Zeegers
Language(s): Dutch
ADVERTISING RATES:
Full Page Mono EUR 1/1: f.c. 2990,-; b/w 1495,- 1/2: f.c. 1704,-; b/w 852,- 1/4: f.c. 987,-; b/w 494,-
Agency Commission: 15%
Mechanical Data: Type Area: 170 x 230mm, Bleed Size: 205 x 275mm
BUSINESS: HEALTH & MEDICAL: Mental Health

PT INDUSTRIEEL MANAGEMENT 1635036N14A-379
Editorial: Binckhorstlaan 403, 2516 BC DEN HAAG
Tel: 570 648988 **Fax:** 70 3045808
Email: sdu@sdu.nl
Freq: 9 issues yearly; **Annual Sub.:** EUR 239,-; **Circ:** 4,122
Editor: Maarten Legius; **Editor-in-Chief:** A. Schilderman; **Publisher:** Ted den Bieman
Language(s): Dutch
ADVERTISING RATES:
Full Page Mono .. EUR 1/1: b/w 1700,- 1/2: b/w 895,- 1/4: b/w 575,-
Agency Commission: 15%
Mechanical Data: Type Area: 185 x 259mm, Bleed Size: 210 x 297mm
Copy instructions: *Copy Date:* 2 weeks prior to publication date
BUSINESS: COMMERCE, INDUSTRY & MANAGEMENT

PUBLISH 15783N5F-241
Editorial: Emmastraat 61, 1213 AK HILVERSUM
Tel: 172 469050 **Fax:** 35 6563174
Email: info@managementmedia.nl **Web site:** http://www.publish.nl
Freq: 6 issues yearly; **Cover Price:** EUR 12,95
Annual Sub.: EUR 65,-; **Circ:** 3,736
Editor: Alex Kunst; **Editor-in-Chief:** Jasper van Laar; **Publisher:** Mike Velleman
Profile: Magazine focusing on all aspects of information technology. Includes articles on Windows NT, digital communications and photography, video, multimedia, the Internet and web design.
Language(s): Dutch
ADVERTISING RATES:
Full Page Mono EUR 1/1: f.c. 3035,-; 1/2: f.c. 1850,-; 1/4: f.c. 1195,-
Agency Commission: 15%
Mechanical Data: Type Area: 210 x 268mm, Bleed Size: 230 x 280mm
BUSINESS: COMPUTERS & AUTOMATION: Multimedia

DE PYRAMIDE 16912N62B-170
Editorial: Cornelisgracht 38, 8355 CH GIETHOORN
Tel: 570 673344
Freq: 5 issues yearly; **Circ:** 2,500
Editor: Jan de Vuijst; **Editor-in-Chief:** Eleonore Riksen
Profile: Magazine focusing on music education.
Language(s): Dutch
Readership: Read by school teachers.
ADVERTISING RATES:
Full Page Mono EUR 1/1: f.c. 750,-; 1/2: f.c. 395,-; 1/4: f.c. 230,-
Agency Commission: 15%
Mechanical Data: Type Area: 210 x 260mm, Bleed Size: 230 x 280mm
Copy instructions: *Copy Date:* 4 weeks prior to publication date
BUSINESS: CHURCH & SCHOOL EQUIPMENT & EDUCATION: Education Teachers

QAVIAAR 1934309N74Q-535
Editorial: Brielselaan 14d, 3081 LB ROTTERDAM
Tel: 10 4518007
Web site: http://www.qaviaar.nl
Freq: 6 issues yearly; **Cover Price:** EUR 6,45; **Circ:** 158,531
Usual Pagination: 72
Publisher: Ton Kluver
Language(s): Dutch
ADVERTISING RATES:
Full Page Mono EUR 2/1: f.c. 6650,-; 1/1: f.c. 3950,-; 1/2: f.c. 2150,-; 1/4: f.c. 1200,-
Agency Commission: 15%
CONSUMER: WOMEN'S INTEREST CONSUMER MAGAZINES: Lifestyle

QM, QUALITY IN MEETINGS 15604N2C-160
Editorial: Veerdijk 40i, 1531 MS WORMER
Tel: 172 466911 **Fax:** 229 216416
Email: info@hetportaal.com **Web site:** http://www.qualityinmeetings.nl
Date Established: 01-01-1998; **Freq:** Quarterly; **Annual Sub.:** EUR 81,90; **Circ:** 7,000
Usual Pagination: 100
Editor: Edwin Nunnink; **Publisher:** Edwin Nunnink
Profile: Magazine covering business events and congresses.
Language(s): Dutch
Readership: Aimed at event organisers and marketing companies.
ADVERTISING RATES:
Full Page Mono EUR 2/1: f.c. 2900,-; 1/1: f.c. 1906,-; 1/2: f.c. 1250,-
Agency Commission: 15%
Mechanical Data: Type Area: 185 x 262mm, Bleed Size: 230 x 297mm
BUSINESS: COMMUNICATIONS, ADVERTISING & MARKETING: Conferences & Exhibitions

QUAERENDO 16873N60A-120
Editorial: Singel 425, 1012 WP AMSTERDAM
Web site: http://www.brill.nl/qua
Freq: Quarterly; **Annual Sub.:** EUR 49,-
Usual Pagination: 80
Editor: A.R.A. Croiset van Uchelen
Profile: Journal publishing articles, notes and news on the science of manuscripts and books.
Language(s): Dutch
Readership: Read by scientists, lecturers, students and researchers.
Agency Commission: 15%
Mechanical Data: Bleed Size: 122 x 198mm
BUSINESS: PUBLISHING: Publishing & Book Trade

QUEST 1643448N85A-27
Editorial: Dalsteindreef 82-92, 1112 XC DIEMEN
Tel: 23 5565462 **Fax:** 23 5564588
Email: info@genj.nl **Web site:** http://www.questmagazine.nl
Freq: Monthly; **Cover Price:** EUR 4,95
Annual Sub.: EUR 54,45; **Circ:** 198,270
Editor: Thomas Hendriks; **Publisher:** E. Blok
Language(s): Dutch
ADVERTISING RATES:
Full Page Mono .... EUR 2/1: f.c. 22.325,-; 1/1: f.c. 11.750,-; 1/2: f.c. 7050,-
Agency Commission: 15%
Mechanical Data: Type Area: 195 x 255mm, Bleed Size: 224 x 285mm
CONSUMER: PHOTOGRAPHY & FILM MAKING: Photography

Netherlands

QUEST HISTORIE
1894341N94X-654

Editorial: Dalsteindreef 82-92, 1112 XC DIEMEN **Tel:** 70 3307094 **Fax:** 70 3855505
Email: info@genj.nl
Date Established: 05-03-2009; **Freq:** Quarterly; **Annual Sub.:** EUR 25,-; **Circ:** 80,000
Usual Pagination: 116
Editor: Monique Kitzen; **Publisher:** E. Blok
Language(s): Dutch
ADVERTISING RATES:
Full Page Mono .... EUR 1/1: b/w 5000,-
Agency Commission: 15%
CONSUMER: OTHER CLASSIFICATIONS: Miscellaneous

QUEST PSYCHOLOGIE
1994519N94J-314

Editorial: Dalsteindreef 82-92, 1112 XC DIEMEN **Tel:** 30 2303508 **Fax:** 314 373646
Email: info@genj.nl
Date Established: 01-04-2010; **Freq:** Quarterly; **Annual Sub.:** EUR 25,-; **Circ:** 70,000
Language(s): Dutch
ADVERTISING RATES:
Full Page Mono .... EUR 1/1: b/w 5000,-
Agency Commission: 15%
Mechanical Data: Type Area: 195 x 255mm, Bleed Size: 224 x 285mm
CONSUMER: OTHER CLASSIFICATIONS: Popular Science

QUOTE
15895N14A-228

Editorial: Singel 468, 1017 AW AMSTERDAM **Tel:** 73 6136424 **Fax:** 20 6238538
Email: singel@hearstmagazines.nl **Web site:** http://www.quotenet.nl
Freq: Monthly; **Cover Price:** EUR 6,95
Annual Sub.: EUR 87,95; **Circ:** 51,896
Editor: Sjoerd van Stokkum; **Editor-in-Chief:** Ben Kuenen; **Publisher:** Luc van Os
Profile: Magazine about management, finance and investment, including interviews.
Language(s): Dutch
Readership: Read by directors and senior managers.
ADVERTISING RATES:
Full Page Mono .... EUR 2/1: f.c. 13.500,-; 1/1: f.c. 6750,-; 1/2: f.c. 5065,-
Agency Commission: 15%
Mechanical Data: Type Area: 185 x 250mm, Bleed Size: 215 x 285mm
Copy instructions: *Copy Date:* 4 weeks prior to publication date
BUSINESS: COMMERCE, INDUSTRY & MANAGEMENT

RAALTE KOERIER
626791N80-113

Editorial: L.J. Costerstraat 11, 8141 GN HEINO **Tel:** 23 5565370 **Fax:** 23 5565357
Email: info@sonodruk.nl
Freq: Monthly; **Cover Price:** Free; **Circ:** 16,000
Editor-in-Chief: D. Ramaker; **Publisher:** F.B.M. Zwerink
Profile: Newspaper containing information about Heino.
Language(s): Dutch
Readership: Read by local residents.
ADVERTISING RATES:
Full Page Mono .... EUR 1/1: f.c. 766,-; b/w 505,- 1/2: f.c. 428,-; b/w 280,- 1/4: f.c. 252,-; b/w 177,-
Agency Commission: 15%
Mechanical Data: Type Area: 190 x 276mm, Bleed Size: 210 x 297mm
CONSUMER: RURAL & REGIONAL INTEREST

RAI VOORRANG
16257N31A-90

Editorial: Kon. Wilhelminaplein 30-7, 1062 KR AMSTERDAM **Tel:** 23 5565370 **Fax:** 23 5565357
Email: info@railangfords.nl
Date Established: 12-03-1997; **Freq:** 26 issues yearly; **Annual Sub.:** EUR 79,50; **Circ:** 2,500
Editor: M.F. Timmer
Profile: Official publication of the Dutch Bicycle and Automobile Industry Association.
Language(s): Dutch
Agency Commission: 15%
BUSINESS: MOTOR TRADE: Motor Trade Accessories

RAIL MAGAZINE
17842N79J-60

Editorial: Postbus 211, 3340 AE HENDRIK-IDO-AMBACHT **Tel:** 172 466616 **Fax:** 172 422892
Web site: http://www.railmagazine.nl
Freq: 10 issues yearly; **Cover Price:** EUR 6,10
Annual Sub.: EUR 53,-; **Circ:** 15,000
Editor: H.A. de Jager; **Editor-in-Chief:** L. de Vries; **Publisher:** E. van Werkhoven
Profile: Magazine about railways and model railways.
Language(s): Dutch
Readership: Aimed at those interested in railways and model railways.
ADVERTISING RATES:
Full Page Mono .... EUR 1/1: f.c. 723,-; b/w 634,- 1/2: f.c. 508,-; b/w 349,- 1/4: f.c. 389,-; b/w 190,-
Agency Commission: 15%
Mechanical Data: Type Area: 199 x 273mm, Bleed Size: 230 x 297mm
CONSUMER: HOBBIES & DIY: Rail Enthusiasts

READER'S DIGEST, HET BESTE
1633331N73-291

Editorial: Hogehilweg 17, 1101 CB AMSTERDAM **Tel:** 20 5678377 **Fax:** 20 5678378
Freq: Monthly; **Cover Price:** EUR 4,45
Annual Sub.: EUR 44,50; **Circ:** 110,495
Editor: Oele Steenks; **Editor-in-Chief:** Titske Schwering; **Publisher:** Oele Steenks
Language(s): Dutch
ADVERTISING RATES:
Full Page Mono .... EUR 2/1: f.c. 10.950,-; 1/1: f.c. 7300,-
Agency Commission: 15%
Mechanical Data: Type Area: 110 x 157mm, Bleed Size: 134 x 184mm
CONSUMER: NATIONAL & INTERNATIONAL PERIODICALS

REAL ESTATE MAGAZINE
1636006N1E-95

Editorial: Amsterdamsestraatweg 869, 3555 HL UTRECHT **Tel:** 223 650019 **Fax:** 223 650011
Email: info@vriesco.nl **Web site:** http://www.realestatemagazine.nl
Date Established: 01-06-1998; **Freq:** 6 issues yearly; **Cover Price:** EUR 28,50
Annual Sub.: EUR 136,-; **Circ:** 2,519
Editor-in-Chief: Peter Bekkering; **Publisher:** Arend Jan Kornet
Profile: This publication provides information and analysis on residential and commercial properties.
Language(s): Dutch
ADVERTISING RATES:
Full Page Mono EUR 2/1: f.c. 5560,-; 1/1: f.c. 3620,-; 1/2: f.c. 2715,-
Agency Commission: 15%
Mechanical Data: Type Area: 175 x 248mm, Bleed Size: 195 x 280mm
BUSINESS: FINANCE & ECONOMICS: Property

RECHERCHETIPS VOOR HET BEDRIJFSLEVEN
1633946N32F-84

Editorial: Luidsprekerstraat 10, 1322 AX ALMERE **Tel:** 20 5979409 **Fax:** 20 5979505
Email: info@hoffmannbv.nl
Date Established: 01-06-1976; **Freq:** 5 issues yearly; **Cover Price:** Free; **Circ:** 75,000
Editor: G. Hoffmann; **Editor-in-Chief:** J. van der Ploeg
Language(s): Dutch
Agency Commission: 15%
BUSINESS: LOCAL GOVERNMENT, LEISURE & RECREATION: Police

RECHTSPOOR
15995N14L-450

Editorial: Varrolaan 100, 3584 BW UTRECHT **Tel:** 23 5565370 **Fax:** 229 216416
Freq: 6 issues yearly; **Circ:** 7,000
Editor-in-Chief: Ronald de Kreij
Profile: Journal of the Federation of Railway Trade Unions.
Language(s): Dutch
Agency Commission: 15%
Mechanical Data: Type Area: 190 x 265mm
BUSINESS: COMMERCE, INDUSTRY & MANAGEMENT: Trade Unions

RECREATIE & TOERISME
16589N50-18

Editorial: Edisonbaan 14f, 3439 MN NIEUWEGEIN **Tel:** 23 5565370 **Fax:** 475 551033
Email: info@sportsmedia.nl **Web site:** http://www.recreatie-toerisme.nl
Freq: 6 issues yearly; **Cover Price:** EUR 31,50
Annual Sub.: EUR 165,-; **Circ:** 941
Editor: M. Gerlings; **Publisher:** M.J. van Troost
Profile: Journal of the Organisation of Dutch Recreation Businesses focusing on management and marketing in respect of recreation, tourism and environmental issues.
Language(s): Dutch
ADVERTISING RATES:
Full Page Mono EUR 2/1: f.c. 3940,-; b/w 3260,- 1/1: f.c. 2345,-; b/w 1665,- 1/2: f.c. 1600,-; b/w 920,-
Agency Commission: 15%
Mechanical Data: Type Area: 185 x 270mm, Bleed Size: 210 x 297mm
BUSINESS: TRAVEL & TOURISM

RECREATIEKRANT VELUWE
1635180N80-325

Editorial: Getfertsingel 41, 7513 GA ENSCHEDE **Tel:** 23 5566770 **Fax:** 23 5565155
Email: info@wegenermedia.nl
Date Established: 12-01-1970; **Freq:** Monthly; **Cover Price:** Free; **Circ:** 60,000
Editor: Mart Jochemsen; **Editor-in-Chief:** Peter Koehorst
Language(s): Dutch
ADVERTISING RATES:
Full Page Mono EUR 1/1: b/w 2064,- 1/2: b/w 1085,- 1/4: b/w 608,-
Agency Commission: 15%
Mechanical Data: Type Area: 264 x 398mm, Bleed Size: 300 x 420mm
Copy instructions: *Copy Date:* 5 days prior to publication date
CONSUMER: RURAL & REGIONAL INTEREST

RECYCLING MAGAZINE BENELUX
16825N57-25_50

Editorial: Informaticaweg 3c, 7007 CP DOETINCHEM **Tel:** 33 4220082
Email: industrialmedia@eisma.nl **Web site:** http://www.recyclingmagazine.nl
Date Established: 01-02-1967; **Freq:** 8 issues yearly; **Cover Price:** EUR 15,-
Annual Sub.: EUR 116,-; **Circ:** 2,350
Editor: Henk Meinen; **Publisher:** Henk Meinen
Profile: International magazine providing information on the recovery and recycling industry in the Benelux countries with reports, market forecasts, prices and techniques.
Language(s): Dutch
ADVERTISING RATES:
Full Page Mono EUR 1/1: f.c. 2803,-; b/w 1312,- 1/2: f.c. 1942,-; b/w 848,- 1/4: f.c. 1308,-; b/w 526,-
Agency Commission: 15%
Mechanical Data: Type Area: 191 x 265mm, Bleed Size: 230 x 300mm
BUSINESS: ENVIRONMENT & POLLUTION

RED
1658944N74Q-298

Editorial: Singel 468, 1017 AW AMSTERDAM **Tel:** 20 5353952 **Fax:** 88 2697660
Email: singel@hearstmagazines.nl **Web site:** http://www.redmagazine.nl
Date Established: 14-10-2004; **Freq:** Monthly; **Cover Price:** EUR 4,99
Annual Sub.: EUR 49,95; **Circ:** 56,970
Editor: Marte Kau; **Publisher:** Luc van Os
Language(s): Dutch
ADVERTISING RATES:
Full Page Mono .... EUR 2/1: f.c. 15.000,-; 1/1: f.c. 7500,-; 1/2: f.c. 5625,-
Agency Commission: 15%
Mechanical Data: Type Area: 193 x 256mm, Bleed Size: 220 x 284mm
CONSUMER: WOMEN'S INTEREST CONSUMER MAGAZINES: Lifestyle

DE REDDINGBOOT
16623N54R-151

Editorial: Stroombaan 4, 1181 VX AMSTELVEEN **Tel:** 23 5565370 **Fax:** 475 551033
Email: info@mediapartners.nl
Date Established: 01-01-1911; **Freq:** Quarterly; **Circ:** 80,000
Editor-in-Chief: Janneke Stokroos
Profile: Magazine about emergency lifeboats and sea rescue.
Language(s): Dutch
Agency Commission: 15%
Mechanical Data: Bleed Size: 210 x 240mm
BUSINESS: SAFETY & SECURITY: Safety Related

REFLEXZONE
16804N56R-46_50

Editorial: Het Spoor 2, 3994 AK HOUTEN **Tel:** 184 651558 **Fax:** 20 6767728
Email: info@springermedia.nl **Web site:** http://www.reflexzone.nl
Date Established: 01-04-1994; **Freq:** 6 issues yearly; **Cover Price:** EUR 7,-
Annual Sub.: EUR 34,50; **Circ:** 1,852
Editor: John Frijters; **Editor-in-Chief:** Ingrid Helmink; **Publisher:** Karin Linden
Profile: Journal about reflexology and other alternative treatments.
Language(s): Dutch
ADVERTISING RATES:
Full Page Mono .. EUR 1/1: f.c. 1147,-; b/w 872,- 1/2: f.c. 649,-; b/w 497,- 1/4: f.c. 369,-; b/w 287,-
Agency Commission: 15%
Mechanical Data: Type Area: 180 x 240mm, Bleed Size: 215 x 285mm
Copy instructions: *Copy Date:* 22 days prior to publication date
BUSINESS: HEALTH & MEDICAL: Health Medical Related

REFORMATORISCH DAGBLAD
17102N67B-5950

Editorial: Laan van Westenenk 12, 7336 AZ APELDOORN **Tel:** 23 5565370 **Fax:** 55 5412288
Email: directie@refdag.nl **Web site:** http://www.refdag.nl
Freq: 312 issues yearly; **Annual Sub.:** EUR 287,-; **Circ:** 53,629
Editor: W.B. Kranendonk
Language(s): Dutch
Agency Commission: 15%
Mechanical Data: Type Area: 398 x 550mm
REGIONAL DAILY & SUNDAY NEWSPAPERS: Regional Daily Newspapers

REGELINGEN ONDERWIJS
1705231N62A-202

Editorial: Prinses Beatrixlaan 116, 2595 AL DEN HAAG **Tel:** 70 3780551 **Fax:** 70 7999816
Email: sdu@sdu.nl
Date Established: 01-09-2005; **Freq:** Monthly; **Cover Price:** EUR 7,-
Annual Sub.: EUR 99,-; **Circ:** 4,414
Editor: J.L. de Vriend; **Publisher:** Roel Langelaar
Language(s): Dutch
ADVERTISING RATES:
Full Page Mono EUR 1/1: b/w 1751,- 1/2: b/w 1009,- 1/4: b/w 504,-
Agency Commission: 15%
Mechanical Data: Type Area: 190 x 270mm, Bleed Size: 210 x 297mm
BUSINESS: CHURCH & SCHOOL EQUIPMENT & EDUCATION: Education

REGIOJOURNAAL, EDITIE BERGEN OP ZOOM/ ROOSENDAAL
1911306N74Q-515

Editorial: Heemraadssingel 199, 3023 CB ROTTERDAM **Tel:** 30 6383716 **Fax:** 73 6157171
Email: info@trichis.nl **Web site:** http://www.regiojournaal.nl
Freq: 6 issues yearly; **Cover Price:** Free; **Circ:** 85,000
Editor-in-Chief: Marina Besselink
Language(s): Dutch
ADVERTISING RATES:
Full Page Mono EUR 2/1: f.c. 2750,-; 1/1: f.c. 1450,-; 1/2: f.c. 775,-; 1/4: f.c. 395,-
Agency Commission: 15%
Mechanical Data: Bleed Size: 230 x 300mm
CONSUMER: WOMEN'S INTEREST CONSUMER MAGAZINES: Lifestyle

REGIOJOURNAAL, EDITIE BREDA/OOSTERHOUT
1911308N74Q-516

Editorial: Heemraadssingel 199, 3023 CB ROTTERDAM **Tel:** 30 6383716 **Fax:** 73 6157171
Email: info@trichis.nl **Web site:** http://www.regiojournaal.nl
Freq: 9 issues yearly; **Cover Price:** Free; **Circ:** 85,000
Editor-in-Chief: Marina Besselink
Language(s): Dutch
ADVERTISING RATES:
Full Page Mono EUR 2/1: f.c. 2900,-; 1/1: f.c. 1595,-; 1/2: f.c. 850,-; 1/4: f.c. 435,-
Agency Commission: 15%
Mechanical Data: Bleed Size: 230 x 300mm
CONSUMER: WOMEN'S INTEREST CONSUMER MAGAZINES: Lifestyle

REIZEN MAGAZINE
18121N89A-100

Editorial: Wassenaarseweg 220, 2596 EC DEN HAAG **Tel:** 88 2696670 **Fax:** 88 2696331
Web site: http://www.reizen.nl
Freq: 11 issues yearly; **Cover Price:** EUR 6,35
Annual Sub.: EUR 67,35; **Circ:** 47,812
Editor: M. de Winter; **Editor-in-Chief:** J. van der Linden; **Publisher:** Ben Belt
Profile: Magazine about travel, holidays, recreational and weekend activities.
Language(s): Dutch
Readership: Read by the general public.
ADVERTISING RATES:
Full Page Mono EUR 2/1: f.c. 8700,-; b/w 6338,- 1/1: f.c. 4350,-; b/w 3202,- 1/2: f.c. 2179,-; b/w 1768,-
Agency Commission: 15%
Mechanical Data: Type Area: 200 x 270mm, Bleed Size: 230 x 300mm
CONSUMER: HOLIDAYS & TRAVEL: Travel

REKELS
1660711N74C-262

Editorial: Archangelkade 47, 1013 BE AMSTERDAM **Tel:** 23 5430090 **Fax:** 30 6383839
Date Established: 01-10-2006; **Freq:** Quarterly; **Cover Price:** EUR 0,99; **Circ:** 50,000
Editor: Sharon van Minden; **Publisher:** Frank Meijer
Language(s): Dutch
ADVERTISING RATES:
Full Page Mono EUR 2/1: f.c. 6000,-; 1/1: f.c. 3250,-; 1/2: f.c. 1750,-
Agency Commission: 15%
Mechanical Data: Type Area: 147 x 203mm, Bleed Size: 167 x 223mm
CONSUMER: WOMEN'S INTEREST CONSUMER MAGAZINES: Home & Family

REKREAVAKKRANT
16995N64D-80

Editorial: Terborgseweg 47, 7064 AB SILVOLDE **Tel:** 70 3789880 **Fax:** 70 3789783
Web site: http://www.rvk.nl
Freq: 8 issues yearly; **Cover Price:** EUR 8,50; **Circ:** 7,467
Editor: Jan Olthof; **Publisher:** Jan Olthof
Profile: Magazine covering the leisure industry.
Language(s): Dutch
Readership: Read by campsite owners, owners of boat marinas and other leisure operators.
ADVERTISING RATES:
Full Page Mono .. EUR 1/1: b/w 1365,- 1/2: b/w 754,- 1/4: b/w 397,-
Agency Commission: 15%
Mechanical Data: Type Area: 292 x 392mm, Bleed Size: 297 x 420mm
Copy instructions: *Copy Date:* 4 weeks prior to publication date
BUSINESS: OTHER CLASSIFICATIONS: Course Maintenance

RELATIE MENS EN DIER
17909N81A-150

Editorial: Leonard Bramerstraat 18, 1816 TR ALKMAAR **Tel:** 72 5922250 **Fax:** 229 216416
Email: boerveenrvawl@chello.nl
Freq: Quarterly; **Circ:** 1,000
Editor: E. de Boer

Profile: Magazine about animal rights.
Language(s): Dutch
Agency Commission: 15%
CONSUMER: ANIMALS & PETS: Animals & Pets Protection

RELEASE 15754N5B-192
Editorial: Lemelerberg 19-23, 2402 ZN ALPHEN A/D RIJN **Tel:** 20 5922250 **Fax:** 30 6348909
Email: array@array.nl **Web site:** http://www.release.nl
Freq: Quarterly; **Cover Price:** EUR 13,50
Annual Sub.: EUR 45,50; **Circ:** 4,100
Editor: Robert de Ruiter; **Editor-in-Chief:** Arjen van den Berg; **Publisher:** Werner Schoots
Profile: Journal focusing on the latest software developments for businesses.
Language(s): Dutch
Readership: Aimed at IT professionals.
ADVERTISING RATES:
Full Page Mono EUR 1/1: b/w 2845,- 1/2: b/w 1460,- 1/4: b/w 855,-
Agency Commission: 15%
Mechanical Data: Type Area: 190 x 265mm, Bleed Size: 210 x 285mm
Copy instructions: *Copy Date:* 4 weeks prior to publication date
BUSINESS: COMPUTERS & AUTOMATION: Data Processing

RELEVANT 1634310N94X-592
Editorial: Leidsegracht 103, 1017 ND AMSTERDAM
Tel: 88 8002915 **Fax:** 35 6474444
Freq: Quarterly; **Annual Sub.:** EUR 10,-; **Circ:** 105,000
Editor: Walburg de Jong; **Editor-in-Chief:** Janneke Vonkeman
Language(s): Dutch
ADVERTISING RATES:
Full Page Mono EUR 1/1: f.c. 3375,-; 1/2: f.c. 2025,-; 1/4: f.c. 1095,-
Agency Commission: 15%
Mechanical Data: Type Area: 185 x 275mm, Bleed Size: 210 x 297mm
CONSUMER: OTHER CLASSIFICATIONS: Miscellaneous

RELOAD 629824N86C-120
Editorial: Kon. Wilhelminaplein 1, 1062 HG AMSTERDAM **Tel:** 70 3780586 **Fax:** 30 6076301
Web site: http://www.reload.nl
Date Established: 04-04-1998; **Freq:** Quarterly; **Cover Price:** EUR 4,95; **Circ:** 25,000
Editor: Jeroen Smeets; **Publisher:** Peter van Rhoon
Profile: Lifestyle magazine containing information on boardsports (snowboarding, surfing, skateboarding), music and upmarket clothing.
Language(s): Dutch
Readership: Aimed at sports enthusiasts, in general for the younger generation.
ADVERTISING RATES:
Full Page Mono EUR 2/1: f.c. 4950,-; 1/1: f.c. 2950,-; 1/2: f.c. 1750,-
Agency Commission: 15%
Mechanical Data: Bleed Size: 244 x 305mm
Copy instructions: *Copy Date:* 4 weeks prior to publication date
CONSUMER: ADULT & GAY MAGAZINES: Men's Lifestyle Magazines

DE RESERVE OFFICIER 16403N40-130
Editorial: Postbus 95395, 2509 CJ DEN HAAG
Tel: 23 5565370 **Fax:** 55 5412288
Email: pr-werving@kvnro.nl
Date Established: 01-01-1917; **Freq:** 6 issues yearly; **Annual Sub.:** EUR 17,50; **Circ:** 1,700
Usual Pagination: 20
Editor: M.C.J.B. Daverveldt
Profile: Journal of the Dutch Reserve Officers' Association.
Language(s): Dutch
Agency Commission: 15%
Mechanical Data: Type Area: 210 x 297mm
BUSINESS: DEFENCE

RESIDENCE 17448N74C-59
Editorial: Delflandlaan 4, 1062 EB AMSTERDAM
Tel: 79 6366208 **Fax:** 79 3636262
Email: info@pelicanmags.nl **Web site:** http://www.residence.nl
Freq: 11 issues yearly; **Cover Price:** EUR 6,25
Annual Sub.: EUR 64,50; **Circ:** 30,826
Publisher: F.N. Kloppert
Profile: Magazine about home improvements, decorating and lifestyle.
Language(s): Dutch
ADVERTISING RATES:
Full Page Mono EUR 1/1: f.c. 5800,-; 1/2: f.c. 4350,-; 1/4: f.c. 2320,-
Agency Commission: 15%
Mechanical Data: Type Area: 210 x 277mm, Bleed Size: 230 x 297mm
Copy instructions: *Copy Date:* 4 weeks prior to publication date
CONSUMER: WOMEN'S INTEREST CONSUMER MAGAZINES: Home & Family

RESOURCE 18111N88C-351
Editorial: Costerweg 50, 6701 BH WAGENINGEN
Tel: 317 484020 **Fax:** 317 424060
Email: wageningen.world@wur.nl **Web site:** http://www.resource.wur.nl
Date Established: 01-01-1999; **Freq:** 26 issues yearly; **Annual Sub.:** EUR 58,-; **Circ:** 12,000
Editor: Gaby van Caulil; **Editor-in-Chief:** Rob Goossens
Profile: Magazine containing information on the study and career opportunities open to those at the Wageningen Agricultural University.
Language(s): Dutch
Readership: Aimed at students and researchers at the university.
ADVERTISING RATES:
Full Page Mono EUR 1/1: b/w 2145,- 1/2: b/w 1127,- 1/4: b/w 564,-
Agency Commission: 15%
Mechanical Data: Type Area: 200 x 258mm, Bleed Size: 230 x 300mm
Copy instructions: *Copy Date:* 7 days prior to publication date
CONSUMER: EDUCATION: Careers

RETAILTRENDS 1667172N53-139
Editorial: Lindelaan 8, 6721 VC BENNEKOM
Tel: 570 647730 **Fax:** 570 637533
Email: info@retailtrends.nl
Date Established: 09-09-2004; **Freq:** Monthly; **Annual Sub.:** EUR 215,-; **Circ:** 5,410
Editor: Marcel ten Holte; **Editor-in-Chief:** Marjolein Veen; **Publisher:** Marcel ten Holte
Language(s): Dutch
ADVERTISING RATES:
Full Page Mono EUR 2/1: b/w 4800,- 1/1: b/w 3000,- 1/2: b/w 1800,-
Agency Commission: 15%
Mechanical Data: Type Area: 185 x 267mm, Bleed Size: 210 x 297mm
BUSINESS: RETAILING & WHOLESALING

REVALIDATIE MAGAZINE 16775N56L-105
Editorial: Het Spoor 2, 3994 AK HOUTEN
Tel: 30 6383766 **Fax:** 30 6383991
Freq: Quarterly; **Annual Sub.:** EUR 30,-; **Circ:** 8,000
Editor: S.J. Vegter; **Editor-in-Chief:** A. van Lonkhuyzen; **Publisher:** Karin Linden
Profile: Journal of the VRIN - the Association of Dutch Institutions for Rehabilitation.
Language(s): Dutch
Readership: Aimed at medical professionals dealing with rehabilitation.
ADVERTISING RATES:
Full Page Mono .. EUR 1/1: b/w 1443,- 1/2: b/w 796,- 1/4: b/w 440,-
Agency Commission: 15%
Mechanical Data: Type Area: 191 x 246mm, Bleed Size: 215 x 270mm
BUSINESS: HEALTH & MEDICAL: Disability & Rehabilitation

DE REVISOR 18037N84B-110
Editorial: Singel 262, 1016 AC AMSTERDAM
Tel: 23 5565370 **Fax:** 55 5412288
Email: info@revisor.nl **Web site:** http://www.revisor.nl
Freq: 6 issues yearly; **Cover Price:** EUR 11,-
Annual Sub.: EUR 53,-; **Circ:** 700
Editor: Menno Lievers; **Editor-in-Chief:** Manon Uphoff
Profile: Magazine focusing on literature.
Language(s): Dutch
Agency Commission: 15%
Mechanical Data: Type Area: 204 x 260mm
CONSUMER: THE ARTS & LITERARY: Literary

RICHE 714857N1A-19_4
Editorial: Leeuwenveldseweg 3m, 1382 LV WEESP
Tel: 222 362620 **Fax:** 222 323000
Email: dfp@3xi.nl
Date Established: 01-01-1998; **Freq:** Quarterly; **Cover Price:** EUR 4,95; **Circ:** 65,000
Editor: L. Chengadu; **Publisher:** D. Chengadu
Profile: Magazine containing information and articles focusing on finance.
Language(s): Dutch
Readership: Read by finance professionals, stockbrokers, insurance agents and accountants.
ADVERTISING RATES:
Full Page Mono .... EUR 1/1: b/w 5000,-
Agency Commission: 15%
Mechanical Data: Type Area: 185 x 272mm, Bleed Size: 210 x 297mm
Copy instructions: *Copy Date:* 4 weeks prior to publication date
BUSINESS: FINANCE & ECONOMICS

HET RICHTSNOER 18611N56B-163
Editorial: Plesmanstraat 68, 3905 KZ VEENENDAAL
Tel: 88 2944819 **Fax:** 30 6383991
Email: info@rmu.org
Freq: 5 issues yearly; **Circ:** 3,000
Usual Pagination: 16
Profile: Nursing review.
Language(s): Dutch
Agency Commission: 15%
Mechanical Data: Type Area: 180 x 274mm, Bleed Size: 210 x 296mm
BUSINESS: HEALTH & MEDICAL: Nursing

RIJ-INSTRUCTIE 18634N31D-26
Editorial: Van Cappellestraat 15, 7001 ZA DOETINCHEM **Tel:** 76 5876329
Email: rij-instructie@sdu.nl
Freq: 11 issues yearly; **Cover Price:** EUR 8,25
Annual Sub.: EUR 70,75; **Circ:** 2,057
Editor: Hans Peijs; **Publisher:** Roel Roos
Profile: Independent magazine about all forms of driving instruction.
Language(s): Dutch
ADVERTISING RATES:
Full Page Mono .. EUR 1/1: b/w 1360,- 1/2: b/w 726,- 1/4: b/w 453,-
Agency Commission: 15%
Mechanical Data: Type Area: 185 x 260mm, Bleed Size: 210 x 297mm
BUSINESS: MOTOR TRADE: Driving Schools

RIJNMOND BUSINESS 16975N63-245
Editorial: Bourgondischelaan 30m, 2983 SH RIDDERKERK **Tel:** 30 6383743 **Fax:** 229 216416
Email: bpr@rijnmondbusiness.nl
Freq: 10 issues yearly; **Annual Sub.:** EUR 58,50; **Circ:** 7,500
Editor: Bas den Otter; **Editor-in-Chief:** Kees van 't Zelfde; **Publisher:** Kees van 't Zelfde
Profile: Magazine about business in the Rijnmond area.
Language(s): Dutch
ADVERTISING RATES:
Full Page Mono EUR 1/1: f.c. 1950,-; 1/2: f.c. 1200,-; 1/4: f.c. 700,-
Agency Commission: 15%
Mechanical Data: Type Area: 190 x 260mm, Bleed Size: 215 x 285mm
Copy instructions: *Copy Date:* 2 weeks prior to publication date
BUSINESS: REGIONAL BUSINESS

RIJNSTREEK BUSINESS 16976N63-246
Editorial: Vliet Noord Zijde 37, 2231 GN RIJNSBURG
Tel: 30 6383743 **Fax:** 229 216416
Email: info@rijnstreekbusiness.nl **Web site:** http://www.rijnstreekbusiness.nl
Freq: 6 issues yearly; **Circ:** 5,000
Publisher: H. de Reus
Profile: Magazine about business in the Rijnstreek region.
Language(s): Dutch
Agency Commission: 15%
Mechanical Data: Bleed Size: 215 x 285mm
BUSINESS: REGIONAL BUSINESS

RIJSSENS NIEUWSBLAD 627143N72-4570
Editorial: Elsenerstraat 30a, 7461 DN RIJSSEN
Tel: 20 5159172 **Fax:** 20 5159145
Email: redactie.rijssensnieuwsblad@wcgo.nl
Date Established: 15-02-1995; **Freq:** Weekly; **Cover Price:** Free; **Circ:** 31,800
Editor: F. Nijholt-de Haan; **Editor-in-Chief:** E. Spit
Language(s): Dutch
ADVERTISING RATES:
Full Page Mono .. EUR 1/1: b/w 1372,- 1/2: b/w 744,- 1/4: b/w 382,-
Agency Commission: 15%
Mechanical Data: Type Area: 490 x 320mm, Bleed Size: 520 x 350mm
LOCAL NEWSPAPERS

RIOLERING 16289N32B-68
Editorial: Kluizerdijk 1, 5554 XA VALKENSWAARD
Tel: 10 4274128 **Fax:** 88 7518231
Email: info@holapress.com **Web site:** http://www.vakbladriolering.nl
Freq: 10 issues yearly; **Cover Price:** EUR 10,-
Annual Sub.: EUR 149,-; **Circ:** 3,000
Editor: Rob van der Velde; **Editor-in-Chief:** Frank van de Ven; **Publisher:** K. Pattyn
Profile: Journal containing articles about sewage and waste disposal.
Language(s): Dutch
ADVERTISING RATES:
Full Page Mono .. EUR 1/1: b/w 1279,- 1/2: b/w 778,- 1/4: b/w 467,-
Agency Commission: 15%
Mechanical Data: Type Area: 190 x 272mm, Bleed Size: 210 x 297mm
BUSINESS: LOCAL GOVERNMENT, LEISURE & RECREATION: Public Health & Cleaning

RIVIERENLAND BUSINESS 16977N63-250
Editorial: Kerkenbos 12-26c, 6546 BE NIJMEGEN
Tel: 30 6383743 **Fax:** 229 216416
Email: info@vanmunstermedia.nl **Web site:** http://www.rivierenland-business.nl
Freq: 6 issues yearly; **Annual Sub.:** EUR 53,50; **Circ:** 4,600
Editor: Jessica Scheffers; **Publisher:** Michael van Munster
Profile: Regional business magazine.
Language(s): Dutch
Readership: Read by local business managers and executives.
ADVERTISING RATES:
Full Page Mono .. EUR 1/1: f.c. 1234,-; 1/2: f.c. 683,-; 1/4: f.c. 410,-
Agency Commission: 15%
Mechanical Data: Type Area: 190 x 260mm, Bleed Size: 215 x 285mm
Copy instructions: *Copy Date:* 2 weeks prior to publication date
BUSINESS: REGIONAL BUSINESS

RIVIERENLAND VISIE 17887N80-129
Editorial: Panovenweg 10, 4004 JE TIEL
Tel: 570 647207
Email: info@primamedia.nl **Web site:** http://www.rivierenlandvisie.nl
Freq: Quarterly; **Cover Price:** Free; **Circ:** 70,000
Editor: A.J.F. de Jong; **Publisher:** A.J.F. de Jong
Profile: Magazine for the Tiel region, including information on leisure and culture.
Language(s): Dutch
Readership: Aimed at local residents and those wishing to move to the region.
ADVERTISING RATES:
Full Page Mono .... EUR 1/1: f.c. 2940,-
Agency Commission: 15%
Mechanical Data: Bleed Size: 210 x 297mm
CONSUMER: RURAL & REGIONAL INTEREST

ROEIEN 17632N75M-190
Editorial: Bosbaan 6, 1182 AG AMSTELVEEN
Tel: 23 5565370 **Fax:** 55 5412288
Email: info@knrb.nl
Freq: 11 issues yearly; **Annual Sub.:** EUR 27,50; **Circ:** 6,200
Editor: Leo van de Ruit
Profile: Magazine focusing on rowing.
Language(s): Dutch
Readership: Read by members of the Royal Dutch Rowing Club.
ADVERTISING RATES:
Full Page Mono EUR 1/1: f.c. 975,-; 1/2: f.c. 585,-; 1/4: f.c. 350,-
Agency Commission: 15%
Mechanical Data: Type Area: 183 x 279mm, Bleed Size: 210 x 297mm
Copy instructions: *Copy Date:* 3 weeks prior to publication date
CONSUMER: SPORT: Water Sports

ROESTVAST STAAL 16233N27-40
Editorial: De Laat de Kanterstraat 27a, 2313 JS LEIDEN **Tel:** 35 67272103 **Fax:** 20 5159145
Web site: http://www.alurvs.nl
Date Established: 01-01-1984; **Freq:** 10 issues yearly; **Annual Sub.:** EUR 120,-; **Circ:** 4,000
Profile: Journal containing information about stainless steel and other high quality alloys.
Language(s): Dutch
ADVERTISING RATES:
Full Page Mono .. EUR 1/1: b/w 1529,- 1/2: b/w 839,- 1/4: b/w 460,-
Agency Commission: 15%
Mechanical Data: Type Area: 190 x 265mm, Bleed Size: 210 x 297mm
BUSINESS: METAL, IRON & STEEL

ROND REUMA 1634917N74G-254
Editorial: Dr. Jan van Breemenstraat 4, 1056 AB AMSTERDAM **Tel:** 23 5565370 **Fax:** 55 5412288
Email: info@reumafonds.nl
Freq: Quarterly; **Circ:** 115,000
Language(s): Dutch
ADVERTISING RATES:
Full Page Mono . EUR 1/1: f.c. 2936,-; 1/2: f.c. 1761,-
Agency Commission: 15%
Mechanical Data: Bleed Size: 210 x 297mm, Type Area: 177 x 259mm
Copy instructions: *Copy Date:* 4 weeks prior to publication date
CONSUMER: WOMEN'S INTEREST CONSUMER MAGAZINES: Slimming & Health

ROOD 1634448N82-492
Editorial: Herengracht 54, 1015 BN AMSTERDAM
Tel: 20 5512208 **Fax:** 570 647533
Email: rood@pvda.nl
Freq: 8 issues yearly; **Annual Sub.:** EUR 15,88; **Circ:** 63,000
Usual Pagination: 28
Editor: Ottolien van Rossem; **Editor-in-Chief:** Jurjen Fedde Wiersma
Language(s): Dutch
Agency Commission: 15%
Mechanical Data: Type Area: 200 x 250mm, Bleed Size: 223 x 275mm
CONSUMER: CURRENT AFFAIRS & POLITICS

ROOFS 15707N4E-282_50
Editorial: Salomonstraat 24, 1812 PA ALKMAAR
Tel: 70 3490165 **Fax:** 70 3490181
Email: info@lumail.nl
Freq: 11 issues yearly; **Cover Price:** EUR 7,-
Annual Sub.: EUR 73,-; **Circ:** 12,613
Editor: Edwin Fagel; **Publisher:** D. Lindeman
Profile: Publication about the construction of sloping roofs.
Language(s): Dutch
Readership: Read by builders and architects.
ADVERTISING RATES:
Full Page Mono EUR 1/1: f.c. 3520,-; b/w 2195,- 1/2: f.c. 2150,-; b/w 1215,- 1/4: f.c. 1335,-; b/w 670,-
Agency Commission: 15%

Mechanical Data: Type Area: 195 x 265mm, Bleed Size: 230 x 300mm
BUSINESS: ARCHITECTURE & BUILDING: Building

ROOFS HANDBOEK VOOR DE DAKBRANCHE
18945N4E-289
Editorial: Salomonstraat 24, 1812 PA ALKMAAR
Tel: 88 7518160 **Fax:** 88 7518161
Email: info@lumail.nl
Date Established: 20-01-1993; **Freq:** Annual; **Cover Price:** EUR 12,-; **Circ:** 14,000
Usual Pagination: 340
Language(s): Dutch
Readership: Read by professional roofers and architects.
Agency Commission: 15%
Mechanical Data: Type Area: 125 x 185mm, Bleed Size: 148 x 210mm
BUSINESS: ARCHITECTURE & BUILDING: Building

DE ROOFVIS
18208N92-126
Editorial: Postbus 85027, 3508 AA UTRECHT
Tel: 70 3751728 **Fax:** 24 3723631
Web site: http://www.deroofvis.nl
Date Established: 26-02-1997; **Freq:** 6 issues yearly; **Cover Price:** EUR 8,75
Annual Sub.: EUR 45,-; **Circ:** 12,500
Editor: S. Meijers; **Editor-in-Chief:** Peter Dohmen; **Publisher:** H. te Kloeze
Profile: International magazine about predatory fish, including salt and fresh-water fish.
Language(s): Dutch
Readership: Read by angling enthusiasts.
ADVERTISING RATES:
Full Page Mono EUR 1/1: b/w 775,- 1/2: b/w 420,- 1/4: b/w 240,-
Agency Commission: 15%
Mechanical Data: Type Area: 184 x 252mm, Bleed Size: 210 x 280mm
Copy instructions: *Copy Date:* 2 weeks prior to publication date
CONSUMER: ANGLING & FISHING

DE ROOSENDAALSE BODE
627126N72-4470
Editorial: Sint Catharinaplein 12, 4611 TS BERGEN OP ZOOM **Tel:** 70 3751758 **Fax:** 15 2126695
Web site: http://www.internetbode.nl
Freq: Weekly; **Circ:** 35,000
Editor: Vif Janssen; **Editor-in-Chief:** Vif Janssen
Language(s): Dutch
Agency Commission: 15%
Mechanical Data: Type Area: 264 x 400mm
LOCAL NEWSPAPERS

DE ROOSENDAALSE BODE, ED. ZONDAG
629962N72-7533
Editorial: Sint Catharinaplein 12, 4611 TS BERGEN OP ZOOM **Tel:** 172 466622 **Fax:** 24 3723631
Web site: http://www.internetbode.nl
Freq: Weekly; **Circ:** 35,000
Editor: Vif Janssen; **Editor-in-Chief:** Vif Janssen
Language(s): Dutch
Agency Commission: 15%
Mechanical Data: Type Area: 264 x 400mm
LOCAL NEWSPAPERS

ROOTS
17861N80-15
Editorial: Capellalaan 65, 2132 JL HOOFDDORP
Tel: 88 7518110 **Fax:** 342 494299
Web site: http://www.grasduinen.nl
Date Established: 01-01-1979; **Freq:** Monthly;
Cover Price: EUR 5,30
Annual Sub.: EUR 60,68; **Circ:** 24,084
Usual Pagination: 124
Editor: Fanny Glazenburg; **Editor-in-Chief:** Paul Böhre
Profile: Magazine about nature in Holland. Each issue also has a feature on one other European country.
Language(s): Dutch
Readership: Educated people age 35+, interested in photography, walking, travel and reading.
ADVERTISING RATES:
Full Page Mono EUR 2/1: b/w 7500,- 1/1: b/w 3750,- 1/2: b/w 2250,-
Agency Commission: 15%
Mechanical Data: Type Area: 204 x 253mm, Bleed Size: 223 x 285mm
CONSUMER: RURAL & REGIONAL INTEREST

DE ROSKAM
627300N72-4480
Editorial: Haven Noordzijde 55a, 7607 ES ALMELO
Tel: 70 3780586 **Fax:** 30 6076301
Email: info@roskam.nl
Freq: Weekly; **Annual Sub.:** EUR 56,72; **Circ:** 10,000
Editor: H. Pape
Language(s): Dutch
ADVERTISING RATES:
Full Page Mono .. EUR 1/1: b/w 1600,- 1/2: b/w 850,- 1/4: b/w 450,-
Agency Commission: 15%
Mechanical Data: Type Area: 257 x 398mm, Bleed Size: 289 x 420mm
LOCAL NEWSPAPERS

ROTTERDAM PUNT UIT
18142N89C-70
Editorial: Prins Hendrikkade 16a, 3071 KB ROTTERDAM **Tel:** 342 494848 **Fax:** 342 494299
Email: digidesk@puntuitmedia.nl
Date Established: 01-06-1985; **Freq:** 6 issues yearly;
Cover Price: EUR 4,30
Annual Sub.: EUR 22,95; **Circ:** 10,000
Editor: N. van Huët
Profile: Magazine focusing on lifestyle and entertainment in Rotterdam.
Language(s): Dutch
Readership: Read by the general public.
ADVERTISING RATES:
Full Page Mono .. EUR 1/1: f.c. 1400,-; 1/2: f.c. 790,-; 1/4: f.c. 425,-
Agency Commission: 15%
Mechanical Data: Type Area: 218 x 277mm, Bleed Size: 238 x 297mm
Copy instructions: *Copy Date:* 3 weeks prior to publication date
CONSUMER: HOLIDAYS & TRAVEL: Entertainment Guides

ROTTERDAMPAS
1633636N80-637
Editorial: Hoogstraat 110, 3011 PV ROTTERDAM
Tel: 40 2336338 **Fax:** 40 2336470
Email: info@rotterdampas.nl
Date Established: 01-04-1996; **Freq:** Quarterly;
Cover Price: Free; **Circ:** 100,000
Editor: Ina Schoorl
Language(s): Dutch
ADVERTISING RATES:
Full Page Mono ... EUR 1/1: b/w 2350,- omslagpag. 2 of 3: b/w 2850,- achterpag.: b/w 3350,-
Agency Commission: 15%
Mechanical Data: Bleed Size: 210 x 280mm
Copy instructions: *Copy Date:* 3 weeks prior to publication date
CONSUMER: RURAL & REGIONAL INTEREST

ROUTIERS
16570N49D-50
Editorial: Pieter Zeemanstraat 3, 6603 AV WIJCHEN
Tel: 0032 34660066 **Fax:** 0032 34660067
Email: routiers@routiers.nl **Web site:** http://www.routiers.nl
Date Established: 01-01-1980; **Freq:** 6 issues yearly;
Cover Price: EUR 5,-
Annual Sub.: EUR 39,-; **Circ:** 11,000
Usual Pagination: 48
Editor: Rick Ohm; **Editor-in-Chief:** Rick Ohm
Profile: Publication covering all aspects of road transport.
Language(s): Dutch
Agency Commission: 15%
Mechanical Data: Type Area: 185 x 270mm, Bleed Size: 210 x 297mm
BUSINESS: TRANSPORT: Commercial Vehicles

ROZENBURGSE COURANT DE SCHAKEL
627136N72-4510
Editorial: Dr. Kuyperkade 28, 3142 GC MAASSLUIS
Tel: 0032 34660066 **Fax:** 0032 34660067
Email: info@thuisbladen.nl
Freq: Weekly; **Cover Price:** Free; **Circ:** 7,000
Editor: P.C. de Groot; **Publisher:** P.C. de Groot
Language(s): Dutch
Agency Commission: 15%
Mechanical Data: Type Area: 260 x 400mm, Bleed Size: 290 x 440mm
LOCAL NEWSPAPERS

RTL GP
1812941N77A-335
Editorial: Lijndenweg 25a, 1948 ND BEVERWIJK
Tel: 20 5518418 **Fax:** 20 5852965
Email: info@formula-once.nl
Date Established: 05-04-2007; **Freq:** 6 issues yearly;
Cover Price: EUR 6,95
Annual Sub.: EUR 35,-; **Circ:** 42,000
Editor: Mark Koense; **Publisher:** Mark Koense
Language(s): Dutch
ADVERTISING RATES:
Full Page Mono EUR 2/1: f.c. 4800,-; 1/1: f.c. 2500,-; 1/2: f.c. 1500,-
Agency Commission: 15%
Mechanical Data: Bleed Size: 230 x 297mm
Copy instructions: *Copy Date:* 18 days prior to publication date
CONSUMER: MOTORING & CYCLING: Motoring

DE RUCPHENSE BODE
627140N72-4530
Editorial: Bredaseweg 26, 4881 DE ZUNDERT
Tel: 88 2697049 **Fax:** 70 3544642
Email: zetterij@vorsselmans.nl **Web site:** http://www.internetbode.nl
Freq: Weekly; **Circ:** 10,500
Editor: Vif Janssen; **Editor-in-Chief:** Vif Janssen
Language(s): Dutch
Agency Commission: 15%
Mechanical Data: Type Area: 264 x 400mm
LOCAL NEWSPAPERS

RUN2DAY MAGAZINE
1927954N75L-407
Editorial: Koningin Wilhelminaplein 1, 1062 HG AMSTERDAM **Tel:** 10 4518007 **Fax:** 70 7999889
Date Established: 22-09-2009; **Freq:** Half-yearly;
Cover Price: EUR 4,95; **Circ:** 50,000
Publisher: Peter van Rhoon
Language(s): Dutch
ADVERTISING RATES:
Full Page Mono EUR 2/1: b/w 6950,- 1/1: b/w 3950,- 1/2: b/w 2250,-
Agency Commission: 15%
Mechanical Data: Bleed Size: 285 x 230mm
Copy instructions: *Copy Date:* 4 weeks prior to publication date
CONSUMER: SPORT: Outdoor

RUNDVEEHOUDERIJ - VAKDEEL VAN BOERDERIJ
1635272N21D-105
Editorial: Hanzestraat 1, 7006 RH DOETINCHEM
Tel: 314 349446 **Fax:** 314 344397
Email: klantenservice@reedbusiness.nl **Web site:** http://www.boerderij.nl/rundvee[VA]houderij.htm
Freq: 13 issues yearly; **Annual Sub.:** EUR 363,75;
Circ: 27,445
Editor: Geert Hekkert
Language(s): Dutch
ADVERTISING RATES:
Full Page Mono .... EUR 1/1: f.c. 5332,-; f.c. color 5046,-; b/w 3910,- 1/2: f.c. 3081,-; f.c. color 2881,-; b/w 2088,- 1/4:
Agency Commission: 15%
Mechanical Data: Type Area: 194 x 260mm, Bleed Size: 215 x 285mm
BUSINESS: AGRICULTURE & FARMING: Livestock

RUNNER'S WORLD
17616N75J-300
Editorial: Raamgracht 4, 1011 KK AMSTERDAM
Tel: 20 5518601 **Fax:** 20 5518567
Web site: http://www.runnersweb.nl
Date Established: 01-01-1983; **Freq:** 11 issues yearly; **Cover Price:** EUR 5,45
Annual Sub.: EUR 53,-; **Circ:** 41,757
Editor: Olivier Heimel; **Publisher:** Femke Leemeijer
Profile: Magazine featuring racing, marathons, equipment, news, interviews with runners and reports from different marathons.
Language(s): Dutch
Readership: Read by athletes.
ADVERTISING RATES:
Full Page Mono EUR 2/1: f.c. 6970,-; 1/1: f.c. 3485,-; 1/4: f.c. 1653,-
Agency Commission: 15%
Mechanical Data: Type Area: 174 x 241mm, Bleed Size: 200 x 267mm
CONSUMER: SPORT: Athletics

RUSH ON AMSTERDAM
18130N89B-200
Editorial: De Opgang 2, 9203 GD DRACHTEN
Tel: 58 2954859 **Fax:** 20 6767728
Email: info@rush.nl
Freq: Quarterly; **Cover Price:** EUR 4,50
Annual Sub.: EUR 14,-; **Circ:** 26,000
Editor: Andries Jonker
Profile: Magazine distributed in 4 and 5 star hotels in Amsterdam, covering lifestyle issues as well as entertainment and business news.
Language(s): Dutch
ADVERTISING RATES:
Full Page Mono EUR 2/1: b/w 5700,- 1/1: b/w 3200,- 1/2: b/w 1750,-
Agency Commission: 15%
Mechanical Data: Type Area: 180 x 245mm, Bleed Size: 210 x 280mm
CONSUMER: HOLIDAYS & TRAVEL: Hotel Magazines

RUWAARD VAN PUTTEN INFO
652202N80-121
Editorial: Graaf Adolfstraat 36d, 8606 BT SNEEK
Tel: 172 466622 **Fax:** 172 440681
Email: bcuitgevers@planet.nl
Freq: Quarterly; **Cover Price:** Free; **Circ:** 3,500
Editor: E. Kruik
Profile: Magazine containing information about the local hospital.
Language(s): Dutch
Readership: Aimed at patients and the local residents.
Agency Commission: 15%
Mechanical Data: Bleed Size: 210 x 297mm, Type Area: 184 x 270mm
CONSUMER: RURAL & REGIONAL INTEREST

S+RO
15662N4D-60
Editorial: Binckhorstlaan 36, 2516 BE DEN HAAG
Tel: 30 6383743 **Fax:** 229 216416
Email: info@nirov.nl **Web site:** http://www.s-ro.nl
Freq: 6 issues yearly; **Annual Sub.:** EUR 90,-; **Circ:** 2,450
Editor-in-Chief: D.P. Vrolijk
Profile: Journal covering urban development, public housing, physical planning and environmental policy.
Language(s): Dutch
ADVERTISING RATES:
Full Page Mono .. EUR 1/1: b/w 1255,- 1/2: b/w 875,-
Agency Commission: 15%
Mechanical Data: Type Area: 185 x 250mm, Bleed Size: 200 x 265mm
BUSINESS: ARCHITECTURE & BUILDING: Planning & Housing

SALES MANAGEMENT
15621N2F-200
Editorial: Postbus 2, 7400 AA DEVENTER
Tel: 77 3556160 **Fax:** 77 3556152
Email: eindredsales@mybusinessmedia.nl **Web site:** http://www.sales-online.nl
Date Established: 01-01-1994; **Freq:** 9 issues yearly;
Cover Price: EUR 25,-
Annual Sub.: EUR 150,-; **Circ:** 1,924
Editor: B. Rittger; **Publisher:** M.F.J. Mathijssen
Profile: Magazine about sales and sales management. Includes articles on database marketing, sales leads, call centres, telemarketing and marketing sales and communication.
Language(s): Dutch
Readership: Aimed at sales managers.
ADVERTISING RATES:
Full Page Mono EUR 1/1: f.c. 3280,-; 1/2: f.c. 2000,-; 1/4: f.c. 1230,-
Agency Commission: 15%
Mechanical Data: Type Area: 190 x 268mm, Bleed Size: 210 x 297mm
BUSINESS: COMMUNICATIONS, ADVERTISING & MARKETING: Selling

LE SALON
16009N15B-80
Editorial: Hettenheuvelweg 41-43, 1101 BM AMSTERDAM **Tel:** 88 7518380 **Fax:** 88 7518381
Email: info@koggeschip-vakbladen.nl **Web site:** http://www.le-salon.nl
Date Established: 01-01-1992; **Freq:** 8 issues yearly;
Cover Price: EUR 11,-
Annual Sub.: EUR 62,-; **Circ:** 4,826
Editor: Marco Jouret; **Editor-in-Chief:** Jacha Rootlieb; **Publisher:** Anthony van Trigt
Profile: Magazine concerning hair fashions and styling techniques.
Language(s): Dutch
Readership: Read by hairdressers and stylists.
ADVERTISING RATES:
Full Page Mono EUR 1/1: f.c. 2540,-; 1/2: f.c. 1510,-; 1/4: f.c. 925,-
Agency Commission: 15%
Mechanical Data: Type Area: 185 x 270mm, Bleed Size: 210 x 297mm
Copy instructions: *Copy Date:* 2 weeks prior to publication date
BUSINESS: COSMETICS & HAIRDRESSING: Hairdressing

SAMEN OP VAKANTIE MET BABY'S, PEUTERS EN KLEUTERS
1634979N89A-181
Editorial: Van Breestraat 57, 1071 ZG AMSTERDAM
Tel: 76 5876329
Web site: http://www.samenopvakantie.nl
Freq: Half-yearly; **Cover Price:** EUR 3,95; **Circ:** 79,945
Editor: Marlou van Paridon; **Publisher:** Marlou van Paridon
Language(s): Dutch
ADVERTISING RATES:
Full Page Mono EUR 1/1: f.c. 6950,-; 1/2: f.c. 4380,-; 1/4: f.c. 2350,-
Agency Commission: 15%
Mechanical Data: Type Area: 199 x 267mm, Bleed Size: 215 x 285mm
CONSUMER: HOLIDAYS & TRAVEL: Travel

SAMSAM
1634983N94X-319
Editorial: Mauritskade 63, 1092 AD AMSTERDAM
Tel: 20 5688440 **Fax:** 229 216416
Email: info@ncdo.nl **Web site:** http://www.samsam.net
Date Established: 01-01-1975; **Freq:** 7 issues yearly;
Cover Price: Free; **Circ:** 475,000
Usual Pagination: 24
Editor: L. Schouten; **Editor-in-Chief:** J.T. Serrarens
Language(s): Dutch
Agency Commission: 15%
CONSUMER: OTHER CLASSIFICATIONS: Miscellaneous

SAM-WAPENMAGAZINE
16404N40-140
Editorial: Postbus 446, 6800 AK ARNHEM
Tel: 172 466911 **Fax:** 229 216416
Email: info@samwapenmagazine.nl
Date Established: 01-01-1982; **Freq:** 6 issues yearly;
Annual Sub.: EUR 32,-; **Circ:** 16,500
Editor: B.J. Martens
Profile: Magazine containing information on weapons.
Language(s): Dutch
Readership: Read by shooting enthusiasts, hunters, police and soldiers.
ADVERTISING RATES:
Full Page Mono EUR 1/1: b/w 655,- 1/2: b/w 345,- 1/4: b/w 190,-
Agency Commission: 15%
Mechanical Data: Type Area: 185 x 262mm, Bleed Size: 210 x 297mm
Copy instructions: *Copy Date:* 4 weeks prior to publication date
BUSINESS: DEFENCE

SANITAIR REGISTER
18964N4F-103
Editorial: Bredewater 20, 2715 CA ZOETERMEER
Tel: 20 5629444 **Fax:** 20 6680389
Email: info@uneto-vni.nl
Date Established: 01-01-1988; **Freq:** Annual; **Cover Price:** EUR 75,-; **Circ:** 2,500

Usual Pagination: 552
Editor: John Warnas; **Publisher:** John Warnas
Profile: Journal concerning sanitation.
Language(s): Dutch
ADVERTISING RATES:
Full Page Mono EUR 1/1: f.c. 2295,-; b/w 1545,- 1/2: f.c. 1295,-; b/w 825,- 1/4: f.c. 795,-; b/w 555,-
Agency Commission: 15%
Mechanical Data: Bleed Size: 210 x 297mm
BUSINESS: ARCHITECTURE & BUILDING: Cleaning & Maintenance

SANTÉ
17492N74G-65
Editorial: Singel 468, 1017 AW AMSTERDAM
Tel: 20 6245673 **Fax:** 10 2801002
Email: singel@hearstmagazines.nl **Web site:** http://www.santeonline.nl
Freq: Monthly; **Cover Price:** EUR 3,95
Annual Sub.: EUR 39,95; **Circ:** 66,797
Editor: Jose Bernaerts; **Publisher:** Luc van Os
Profile: Magazine focusing on health issues relevant to women.
Language(s): Dutch
ADVERTISING RATES:
Full Page Mono EUR 2/1: f.c. 14.250,-; 1/1: f.c. 7125,-; 1/2: f.c. 5345,-
Agency Commission: 15%
Mechanical Data: Type Area: 177,5 x 252mm, Bleed Size: 220 x 284mm
Copy instructions: *Copy Date:* 4 weeks prior to publication date
CONSUMER: WOMEN'S INTEREST CONSUMER MAGAZINES: Slimming & Health

SAWN STJERREN NIJS
627156N80-121_60
Editorial: Jipperdastraat 17, 9074 CW HALLUM
Tel: 20 5688440 **Fax:** 20 6159047
Cover Price: Free; **Circ:** 5,400
Editor: Bram Buruma
Profile: Newspaper containing information for people living in and around Ferwerderadeel.
Language(s): Dutch
Readership: Read by residents.
Agency Commission: 15%
Mechanical Data: Type Area: 250 x 360mm
Copy instructions: *Copy Date:* 2 weeks prior to publication date
CONSUMER: RURAL & REGIONAL INTEREST

SCHAAK MAGAZINE
17838N79F-85
Editorial: Frans Halsplein 5, 2021 DL HAARLEM
Tel: 33 4637977 **Fax:** 33 4637976
Email: bondsbureau@schaakbond.nl
Date Established: 01-01-1893; **Freq:** 6 issues yearly;
Cover Price: EUR 2,95
Annual Sub.: EUR 44,46; **Circ:** 17,000
Editor: Minze bij de Weg
Profile: Magazine of the Dutch Chess Association.
Language(s): Dutch
ADVERTISING RATES:
Full Page Mono EUR 1/1: f.c. 1975,-; 1/2: f.c. 1100,-; 1/4: f.c. 650,-
Agency Commission: 15%
Mechanical Data: Type Area: 190 x 277mm, Bleed Size: 215 x 285mm
CONSUMER: HOBBIES & DIY: Games & Puzzles

HET SCHAAP
16129N21D-55
Editorial: Informaticaweg 3c, 7007 CP DOETINCHEM **Tel:** 88 2944978
Freq: 10 issues yearly; **Annual Sub.:** EUR 85,85;
Circ: 8,700
Editor: Jacqueline Wijbenga; **Editor-in-Chief:** Jacqueline van Onna; **Publisher:** Minne Hovenga
Profile: Trade magazine focusing on sheep farming in the Netherlands.
Language(s): Dutch
Readership: Read by sheep farmers and breeders, vets, veterinary researchers and slaughter houses.
ADVERTISING RATES:
Full Page Mono .... EUR 1/1: f.c. 2506,-; f.c. color 2141,-; b/w 1457,- 1/2: f.c. 1522,-; f.c. color 1266,-; b/w 787,- 1/4:
Agency Commission: 15%
Mechanical Data: Type Area: 194 x 257mm, Bleed Size: 215 x 285mm
BUSINESS: AGRICULTURE & FARMING: Livestock

SCHAAPSKOOI
761219N72-3710
Editorial: Dorpsstraat 55, 8181 HN HEERDE
Tel: 23 5566770 **Fax:** 570 614795
Web site: http://www.schaapskooi-kabelkrant.nl
Freq: Weekly; **Cover Price:** Free; **Circ:** 28,250
Editor: R. Kloekke
Language(s): Dutch
ADVERTISING RATES:
Full Page Mono EUR 1/1: b/w 492,- 1/2: b/w 246,- 1/4: b/w 123,-
Agency Commission: 15%
Mechanical Data: Type Area: 255 x 390mm
LOCAL NEWSPAPERS

SCHAATSMARATHON
17658N75X-146
Editorial: Jipperdastraat 17, 9074 CW HALLUM
Tel: 33 4220082 **Fax:** 24 3723631
Freq: 6 issues yearly; **Circ:** 5,000
Editor-in-Chief: Ard Alderts; **Publisher:** Ying Mellema
Profile: Magazine about speed skating on natural ice, at ice-rinks and marathon ice-skating.
Language(s): Dutch
ADVERTISING RATES:
Full Page Mono .. EUR 1/1: f.c. 1015,-; 1/2: f.c. 535,-; 1/4: f.c. 295,-
Agency Commission: 15%
Mechanical Data: Type Area: 183 x 269mm, Bleed Size: 210 x 297mm
CONSUMER: SPORT: Other Sport

SCHAGEN OP ZONDAG
627161N72-7512
Editorial: Broeker Werf 8, 1721 PC BROEK OP LANGEDIJK **Tel:** 10 4274102 **Fax:** 10 4739911
Email: rodimedia@rodi.nl **Web site:** http://www.schagenopzondag.nl
Freq: Weekly; **Cover Price:** Free; **Circ:** 37,800
Editor: Donald Esser
Language(s): Dutch
Agency Commission: 15%
Mechanical Data: Type Area: 265 x 395mm, Bleed Size: 281 x 405mm
LOCAL NEWSPAPERS

HET SCHAGER WEEKBLAD
627164N72-4640
Editorial: Smidsweg 59, 1761 BH ANNA PAULOWNA
Web site: http://www.schagerweekblad.nl
Freq: Weekly; **Cover Price:** Free; **Circ:** 30,500
Language(s): Dutch
Agency Commission: 15%
Mechanical Data: Type Area: 260 x 390mm
LOCAL NEWSPAPERS

DE SCHELDEPOST
627041N72-4730
Editorial: Kloosterweg 20, 4421 PV KAPELLE
Tel: 33 4637977 **Fax:** 229 216416
Email: info@herselman.nl **Web site:** http://www.scheldepost.nl
Date Established: 01-01-1945; **Freq:** Weekly; **Cover Price:** Free; **Circ:** 5,500
Editor: D.C.F. Herselman
Language(s): Dutch
Agency Commission: 15%
Mechanical Data: Type Area: 264 x 440mm, Bleed Size: 460 x 570mm
LOCAL NEWSPAPERS

SCHIETSPORT
17597N75F-50
Editorial: Landweg 235, 3833 VH LEUSDEN
Tel: 33 4637977 **Fax:** 229 216416
Email: info@knsa.nl
Freq: 5 issues yearly; **Annual Sub.:** EUR 17,50; **Circ:** 40,000
Editor: S. Duisterhof
Profile: Publication of the Royal Dutch Shooting Association.
Language(s): Dutch
Agency Commission: 15%
Mechanical Data: Bleed Size: 210 x 297mm
CONSUMER: SPORT: Shooting

SCHILDERSVAKKRANT
16016N16B-20
Editorial: Informaticaweg 3c, 7007 CP DOETINCHEM **Tel:** 20 5979500
Web site: http://www.schildersvakkrant.nl
Date Established: 01-09-1996; **Freq:** 14 issues yearly; **Annual Sub.:** EUR 138,-; **Circ:** 6,066
Editor: Jan Maurits Schouten; **Editor-in-Chief:** Hein van Gennip; **Publisher:** Rex Bierlaagh
Profile: Journal about maintenance, finishing and glazing in the building industry.
Language(s): Dutch
Readership: Aimed at professional painters and decorators, manufacturers, suppliers and retailers of paint and equipment.
ADVERTISING RATES:
Full Page Mono EUR 1/1: f.c. 2816,-; PMS 2177,-; b/w 1833,- 1/2: f.c. 1951,-; PMS 1310,-; b/w 970,- 1/4: f.c. 1492,-; P
Agency Commission: 15%
Mechanical Data: Type Area: 280 x 400mm, Bleed Size: 300 x 420mm
BUSINESS: DECORATING & PAINT: Paint - Technical Manufacture

SCHIPHOLLAND
15794N6B-50
Editorial: Postbus 7501, 1118 ZG SCHIPHOL
Tel: 15 2617997 **Fax:** 229 216416
Email: schipholland@schiphol.nl **Web site:** http://www.schiphol.nl/schipholland
Date Established: 01-01-1978; **Freq:** Quarterly; **Circ:** 700,000
Editor: Inge Kerssens
Profile: Journal about Schiphol Airport. Features include environmental issues, health and safety at work, recreation and forthcoming events relating to the airport.
Language(s): Dutch
Agency Commission: 15%
Mechanical Data: Type Area: 258 x 383mm, Bleed Size: 300 x 410mm
BUSINESS: AVIATION & AERONAUTICS: Airports

SCHOENVISIE
16239N29-10
Editorial: Joan Muyskenweg 22, 1096 CJ AMSTERDAM **Tel:** 33 4637977 **Fax:** 229 216416
Web site: http://www.schoenvisie.nl
Freq: 11 issues yearly; **Annual Sub.:** EUR 111,35;
Circ: 1,963
Editor: Rosanne Loffeld
Profile: Journal providing information on new shoes and trends, product news, industry bulletins and marketing opinions.
Language(s): Dutch
Readership: Aimed at shoe retailers.
ADVERTISING RATES:
Full Page Mono EUR 2/1: f.c. 3950,-; 1/1: f.c. 2750,-; 1/2: f.c. 1650,-
Agency Commission: 15%
Mechanical Data: Type Area: 202 x 268mm, Bleed Size: 230 x 300mm
BUSINESS: FOOTWEAR

SCHOKKEND NIEUWS
17849N79L-190
Editorial: Trompenburgstraat 20-3, 1079 TX AMSTERDAM **Tel:** 172 469050 **Fax:** 35 6563174
Email: info@schokkendnieuws.nl **Web site:** http://www.schokkendnieuws.nl
Freq: 6 issues yearly; **Cover Price:** EUR 4,50
Annual Sub.: EUR 15,-; **Circ:** 4,000
Editor: Phil van Tongeren; **Editor-in-Chief:** Bart Oosterhoorn
Profile: Magazine about sci-fi, horror and fantasy films.
Language(s): Dutch
ADVERTISING RATES:
Full Page Mono .. EUR 2/1: f.c. 1100,-; 1/1: f.c. 715,-; 1/2: f.c. 450,-
Agency Commission: 15%
Mechanical Data: Type Area: 192 x 252mm, Bleed Size: 210 x 275mm
Copy instructions: *Copy Date:* 3 weeks prior to publication date
CONSUMER: HOBBIES & DIY: Fantasy Games & Science Fiction

SCHOOLBESTUUR
18921N62J-309
Editorial: Houttuinlaan 5a, 3447 GM WOERDEN
Tel: 15 2617997 **Fax:** 229 216416
Email: info@bkonet.nl
Date Established: 01-01-1980; **Freq:** 7 issues yearly;
Annual Sub.: EUR 27,-; **Circ:** 4,000
Editor-in-Chief: G.J. Meulenbeld
Profile: Journal for governors involved in education from infants to pre-university students.
Language(s): Dutch
ADVERTISING RATES:
Full Page Mono .. EUR 1/1: b/w 1095,- 1/2: b/w 625,- 1/4: b/w 395,-
Agency Commission: 15%
Mechanical Data: Bleed Size: 230 x 297mm, Type Area: 200 x 265mm
Copy instructions: *Copy Date:* 4 weeks prior to publication date
BUSINESS: CHURCH & SCHOOL EQUIPMENT & EDUCATION: Teachers & Education Management

SCHOOLFACILITIES
15843N11A-97
Editorial: Dollemansstraat 3, 7223 KG BAAK
Tel: 20 6077605 **Fax:** 88 2697490
Email: info@schoolfacilities.nl **Web site:** http://www.schoolfacilities.nl
Freq: 9 issues yearly; **Annual Sub.:** EUR 75,-; **Circ:** 8,000
Editor: F.G. Wolters; **Publisher:** F.G. Wolters
Profile: Journal about canteen and catering management at educational establishments.
Language(s): Dutch
ADVERTISING RATES:
Full Page Mono EUR 1/1: b/w 1760,- 1/2: b/w 1030,- 1/4: b/w 720,-
Agency Commission: 15%
Mechanical Data: Type Area: 190 x 277mm, Bleed Size: 210 x 297mm
BUSINESS: CATERING: Catering, Hotels & Restaurants

SCHOOLJOURNAAL
15996N14L-582
Editorial: Tiberdreef 4, 3561 GG UTRECHT
Tel: 15 2153232 **Fax:** 314 349035
Email: algemeen@cnvo.nl
Freq: 26 issues yearly; **Annual Sub.:** EUR 144,-;
Circ: 55,000
Usual Pagination: 32
Editor-in-Chief: Peter Magnee
Profile: Official journal of the CNV Trade Union for Education.
Language(s): Dutch
ADVERTISING RATES:
Full Page Mono EUR 1/1: b/w 2416,- 1/2: b/w 1246,- 1/4: b/w 661,-
Agency Commission: 15%
Mechanical Data: Type Area: 190 x 264mm, Bleed Size: 210 x 297mm
Copy instructions: *Copy Date:* 10 days prior to publication date
BUSINESS: COMMERCE, INDUSTRY & MANAGEMENT: Trade Unions

SCHOOLMAGAZINE
1697394N83-207
Editorial: Westerstraat 187, 1015 MA AMSTERDAM
Email: cjp@cjp.nl **Web site:** http://www.schoolmagazine.nl
Freq: 8 issues yearly; **Cover Price:** Free; **Circ:** 600,000
Editor: Arne van Terphoven; **Editor-in-Chief:** René van der Meer; **Publisher:** Edwin Teljeur
Language(s): Dutch
ADVERTISING RATES:
Full Page Mono .... EUR 1/1: f.c. 11.900,-; 1/2: f.c. 7500,-
Agency Commission: 15%
Mechanical Data: Type Area: 132 x 200mm, Bleed Size: 142 x 210mm
CONSUMER: STUDENT PUBLICATIONS

SCHOOLSCHRIFT
1635016N62R-248
Editorial: Postbus 1492, 3800 BL AMERSFOORT
Tel: 15 2617997 **Fax:** 229 216416
Email: info@edukans.nl
Freq: Quarterly; **Cover Price:** Free; **Circ:** 60,000
Editor: Jantine Willemsen; **Editor-in-Chief:** Karlijne Brouwer
Language(s): Dutch
Agency Commission: 15%
BUSINESS: CHURCH & SCHOOL EQUIPMENT & EDUCATION: Education Related

SCHOON SCHIP 93
19220N84B-220
Editorial: De Vallei 42, 9405 KK ASSEN
Tel: 75 6813545 **Fax:** 75 6813535
Email: ebijma@planet.nl
Freq: Quarterly; **Annual Sub.:** EUR 22,50; **Circ:** 150
Editor: R. ten Berge; **Publisher:** R. ten Berge
Profile: Literature magazine.
Language(s): Dutch
Agency Commission: 15%
CONSUMER: THE ARTS & LITERARY: Literary

SCHRIJVEN MAGAZINE
630800N84B-113
Editorial: Godfried van Seijstlaan 53, 3703 BR ZEIST
Tel: 229 270002 **Fax:** 20 6767728
Email: info@virtumedia.nl **Web site:** http://www.schrijvenonline.org
Date Established: 01-01-1997; **Freq:** 6 issues yearly;
Cover Price: EUR 6,-
Annual Sub.: EUR 32,50; **Circ:** 6,500
Editor: Louis Stiller; **Publisher:** Pepijn Dobbelaer
Profile: Magazine focusing on all forms of creative writing.
Language(s): Dutch
Readership: Aimed at amateur and potential writers.
ADVERTISING RATES:
Full Page Mono EUR 1/1: f.c. 600,-; 1/2: f.c. 350,-; 1/4: f.c. 250,-
Agency Commission: 15%
Mechanical Data: Type Area: 195 x 265mm, Bleed Size: 215 x 285mm
Copy instructions: *Copy Date:* 3 weeks prior to publication date
CONSUMER: THE ARTS & LITERARY: Literary

SCIENTIFIC AMERICAN
1695393N55-334
Editorial: Joan Muyskenweg 6-6a, 1096 CJ AMSTERDAM **Tel:** 20 5721643 **Fax:** 20 5721521
Email: info@publishing.audax.nl
Freq: 6 issues yearly; **Cover Price:** EUR 5,90
Annual Sub.: EUR 30,-; **Circ:** 8,326
Editor: Ed Croonenberg; **Publisher:** L. Verpoort
Language(s): Dutch
ADVERTISING RATES:
Full Page Mono EUR 1/1: f.c. 2950,-; 1/2: f.c. 1855,-; 1/4: f.c. 1120,-
Agency Commission: 15%
Mechanical Data: Type Area: 190 x 252mm, Bleed Size: 215 x 285mm
BUSINESS: APPLIED SCIENCE & LABORATORIES

SCOUTING NIEUWSBRIEF
19143N91D-121
Editorial: Larikslaan 5, 3833 AM LEUSDEN
Tel: 71 5239058 **Fax:** 20 5159145
Email: info@scouting.nl
Date Established: 01-09-1991; **Freq:** Quarterly;
Cover Price: Free; **Circ:** 2,000
Profile: Publication about developments and highlights within the Youth Scouting Association of the Netherlands.
Language(s): Dutch
Agency Commission: 15%
Mechanical Data: Type Area: 186 x 270mm
CONSUMER: RECREATION & LEISURE: Children & Youth

SECURITY MANAGEMENT
16617N54B-200
Editorial: Zuidpoolsingel 2, 2408 ZE ALPHEN A/D RIJN **Tel:** 172 466622 **Fax:** 172 440681
Email: info@kluwer.nl **Web site:** http://www.securitymanagement.nl
Freq: 10 issues yearly; **Cover Price:** EUR 17,-
Annual Sub.: EUR 125,-; **Circ:** 3,110
Editor: Arjen de Kort
Profile: Journal about fire, accident crime prevention, risk and safety management.
Language(s): Dutch
Readership: Aimed at security managers and facility managers.

ADVERTISING RATES:
Full Page Mono .. EUR 1/1: b/w 1225,- 1/2: b/w 750,- 1/4: b/w 450,-
Agency Commission: 15%
Mechanical Data: Type Area: 185 x 265mm, Bleed Size: 210 x 297mm
Copy instructions: *Copy Date:* 3 weeks prior to publication date
BUSINESS: SAFETY & SECURITY: Safety

SEIZOENSBROCHURE SCHOUWBURG HET PARK
1634289N76B-125
Editorial: Westerdijk 4, 1621 LE HOORN
Tel: 10 4274149 **Fax:** 45 5762766
Email: info@parkhoorn.nl
Freq: Annual; **Cover Price:** Free; **Circ:** 50,000
Editor: Astrid Honing
Language(s): Dutch
Agency Commission: 15%
CONSUMER: MUSIC & PERFORMING ARTS: Theatre

SEKSOA
16704N56A-215
Editorial: Keizersgracht 390-394, 1016 GB AMSTERDAM **Tel:** 45 5762897 **Fax:** 172 493270
Email: info@soaaids.nl **Web site:** http://www.soaaidsmagazine.nl
Date Established: 01-03-1979; **Freq:** Quarterly; **Cover Price:** EUR 4,50
Annual Sub.: EUR 20,-; **Circ:** 15,500
Editor-in-Chief: R.P. Vlasblom
Profile: Medical journal dealing specifically with HIV and AIDS and sexually transmitted diseases.
Language(s): Dutch
Readership: Read by doctors and carers.
Agency Commission: 15%
Mechanical Data: Type Area: 195 x 268mm, Bleed Size: 220 x 297mm
BUSINESS: HEALTH & MEDICAL

SENZ
1813970N56R-274
Editorial: A. Hofmanweg 5a, 2031 BH HAARLEM
Tel: 40 2071162 **Fax:** 20 5852965
Email: info@brandingmedia.nl
Freq: 3 issues yearly; **Cover Price:** Free; **Circ:** 55,000
Usual Pagination: 24
Editor: Carla Person
Language(s): Dutch
Agency Commission: 15%
BUSINESS: HEALTH & MEDICAL: Health Medical Related

SESAMSTRAAT MAGAZINE
1636100N91D-119
Editorial: Mijlweg 61, 3316 BE DORDRECHT
Tel: 161 457342 **Fax:** 20 5159145
Email: info@zpress-magazines.nl **Web site:** http://www.sesamstraatmagazine.nl
Date Established: 01-01-1991; **Freq:** Monthly; **Cover Price:** EUR 3,45; **Circ:** 20,000
Editor: Barbara Niemantsverdriet; **Publisher:** Robert van Ginhoven
Language(s): Dutch
Agency Commission: 15%
Mechanical Data: Type Area: 190 x 280mm, Bleed Size: 210 x 300mm
CONSUMER: RECREATION & LEISURE: Children & Youth

SGJ NIEUWS
1636943N87-2515
Editorial: Puntenburgerlaan 91, 3812 CC AMERSFOORT **Tel:** 20 5612070 **Fax:** 70 3364640
Email: info@sgj.nl
Freq: Half-yearly; **Cover Price:** Free; **Circ:** 79,000
Usual Pagination: 8
Editor: Nelleke Hegeman; **Editor-in-Chief:** Nelleke Hegeman
Language(s): Dutch
Agency Commission: 15%
CONSUMER: RELIGIOUS

DE SHETLAND PONY
17928N81D-160
Editorial: Nieuwstad 89, 7201 NM ZUTPHEN
Tel: 71 5239058 **Fax:** 20 5159145
Email: info@shetlandponystamboek.nl
Date Established: 15-07-1952; **Freq:** Monthly;
Annual Sub.: EUR 62,-; **Circ:** 4,000
Editor: Betteke van Eijk
Profile: Official journal of the Dutch Shetland Pony Stud-Book Society.
Language(s): Dutch
Readership: Read by Shetland pony breeders.
ADVERTISING RATES:
Full Page Mono EUR 1/1: f.c. 410,-; 1/2: f.c. 215,-; 1/4: f.c. 155,-
Agency Commission: 15%
Mechanical Data: Type Area: 184 x 254mm, Bleed Size: 210 x 280mm
Copy instructions: *Copy Date:* 3 weeks prior to publication date
CONSUMER: ANIMALS & PETS: Horses & Ponies

SI GIDS
1637164N83-204
Editorial: Arlandaweg 14, 1043 EW AMSTERDAM
Tel: 45 5795877 **Fax:** 20 5979614
Email: info@mediadam.nl **Web site:** http://www.sigids.nl
Freq: Annual; **Cover Price:** EUR 7,95; **Circ:** 100,000
Editor: Martine van den Houten; **Editor-in-Chief:** Angelo Grooten
Language(s): Dutch
ADVERTISING RATES:
Full Page Mono .... EUR 2/1: f.c. 17.850,-; 1/1: f.c. 10.275,-; 1/2: f.c. 6375,-
Agency Commission: 15%
Mechanical Data: Bleed Size: 120 x 210mm
CONSUMER: STUDENT PUBLICATIONS

SIGMA
15948N14K-200
Editorial: Staverenstraat 32015, 7418 CJ DEVENTER
Tel: 570 648988 **Fax:** 570 614795
Email: info@kluwer.nl **Web site:** http://www.sigma-online.nl
Date Established: 01-01-1956; **Freq:** 6 issues yearly;
Annual Sub.: EUR 210,-; **Circ:** 1,387
Editor: Marjan Hoogendijk; **Publisher:** Anneke van Dijk
Profile: Publication focusing on quality assurance and control and total quality management.
Language(s): Dutch
Readership: Read by quality control managers, CEOs and management consultants.
ADVERTISING RATES:
Full Page Mono .. EUR 1/1: b/w 1100,- 1/2: b/w 650,- 1/4: b/w 350,-
Agency Commission: 15%
Mechanical Data: Type Area: 185 x 267mm, Bleed Size: 210 x 297mm
Copy instructions: *Copy Date:* 3 weeks prior to publication date
BUSINESS: COMMERCE, INDUSTRY & MANAGEMENT: Quality Assurance

SIGMAFOON
16018N16B-30
Editorial: Nieuwe Herengracht 47, 1011 RN AMSTERDAM **Tel:** 570 648988
Email: media@scripta.nl
Date Established: 01-01-1962; **Freq:** 3 issues yearly; **Circ:** 21,075
Editor-in-Chief: Jan Bakker
Profile: Publication about paint and maintenance.
Language(s): Dutch
Readership: Aimed at architects, building corporations, builders and plasterers.
Agency Commission: 15%
Mechanical Data: Bleed Size: 245 x 283mm
BUSINESS: DECORATING & PAINT: Paint - Technical Manufacture

SIGN+ MAGAZINE
15623N2R-100
Editorial: Celsiusweg 41, 8912 AM LEEUWARDEN
Tel: 20 5042829 **Fax:** 20 5159143
Email: businessmedia@eisma.nl **Web site:** http://www.sign.nl
Date Established: 01-01-1988; **Freq:** 8 issues yearly;
Annual Sub.: EUR 134,-; **Circ:** 4,100
Editor: Wouter Mooij; **Editor-in-Chief:** Marijke Kuypers; **Publisher:** Minne Hovenga
Profile: Journal providing information about fleet marketing, route indication, displays and illuminated signs.
Language(s): Dutch
Readership: Aimed at producers and users of visual communication media.
ADVERTISING RATES:
Full Page Mono EUR 1/1: f.c. 2052,-; 1/2: f.c. 1109,-; 1/4: f.c. 579,-
Agency Commission: 15%
Mechanical Data: Type Area: 202 x 268mm, Bleed Size: 230 x 300mm
BUSINESS: COMMUNICATIONS, ADVERTISING & MARKETING: Communications Related

SIGNPRO BENELUX
1636849N60A-209
Editorial: Weegschaalstraat 3, 5632 CW EINDHOVEN **Tel:** 70 3378124 **Fax:** 70 3455302
Email: publimoremedia@chello.nl **Web site:** http://www.signpro.nl
Date Established: 01-06-2000; **Freq:** 6 issues yearly;
Annual Sub.: EUR 59,-; **Circ:** 4,505
Editor: H. Hartman; **Publisher:** A.J.C. ter Meer
Language(s): Dutch
ADVERTISING RATES:
Full Page Mono EUR 1/1: b/w 1925,- 1/2: b/w 1020,- 1/4: b/w 560,-
Agency Commission: 15%
Mechanical Data: Type Area: 220 x 310mm, Bleed Size: 240 x 330mm
BUSINESS: PUBLISHING: Publishing & Book Trade

SIGNS
17700N76D-100
Editorial: Robert Kochplaats 342, 3068 JD ROTTERDAM **Tel:** 76 5301715 **Fax:** 70 3045808
Freq: 6 issues yearly; **Annual Sub.:** EUR 68,-; **Circ:** 1,800
Editor: Jacqueline la Rivière; **Editor-in-Chief:** B. Scholten
Profile: Guide to Christian music, the arts and theatre.
Language(s): Dutch
Readership: Read by members.
ADVERTISING RATES:
Full Page Mono .... EUR 1/1: f.c. 663,-; b/w 510,- 1/2: f.c. 383,-; b/w 296,- 1/4: f.c. 179,-; b/w 153,-
Agency Commission: 15%
Mechanical Data: Type Area: 172 x 262mm, Bleed Size: 210 x 297mm
CONSUMER: MUSIC & PERFORMING ARTS: Music

SIMIOLUS
18015N84A-210
Editorial: p/a Drift 10, 3512 BS UTRECHT
Tel: 76 5301715 **Fax:** 70 3045808
Freq: Quarterly; **Annual Sub.:** EUR 55,-; **Circ:** 900
Editor: Peter Hecht
Profile: Magazine about the history of art.
Language(s): Dutch
ADVERTISING RATES:
Full Page Mono .... EUR 1/1: b/w 295,-
Agency Commission: 15%
Mechanical Data: Type Area: 160 x 210mm, Bleed Size: 190 x 240mm
Copy instructions: *Copy Date:* 4 weeks prior to publication date
CONSUMER: THE ARTS & LITERARY: Arts

SINT
1934238N74C-391
Editorial: Esp 101, 5633 AA EINDHOVEN
Tel: 10 4518007 **Fax:** 70 7999889
Email: bcm@bcm.nl **Web site:** http://www.sint-magazine.nl
Date Established: 23-10-2009; **Freq:** Annual; **Cover Price:** EUR 6,95; **Circ:** 60,000
Usual Pagination: 180
Editor: Marlies Strik; **Publisher:** Eric Brüger
Language(s): Dutch
ADVERTISING RATES:
Full Page Mono EUR 2/1: f.c. 5450,-; b/w 4050,- 1/1: f.c. 2755,-; b/w 2055,-
Agency Commission: 15%
Mechanical Data: Type Area: 230 x 300mm
Copy instructions: *Copy Date:* 1 month prior to publication date
CONSUMER: WOMEN'S INTEREST CONSUMER MAGAZINES: Home & Family

SINTE BARBARA
16405N40-191
Editorial: Eperweg 149, 8084 HE 'T HARDE
Date Established: 01-11-1948; **Freq:** 6 issues yearly;
Annual Sub.: EUR 27,-; **Circ:** 1,650
Usual Pagination: 40
Editor: H.J.M. van Rijssen; **Editor-in-Chief:** P. Fröling
Profile: Journal of the Society of Artillery Officers.
Language(s): Dutch
ADVERTISING RATES:
Full Page Mono .. EUR 1/1: f.c. 500,-; b/w 300,-** 1/2: f.c. 450,-; b/w 275,-** omslagpag. 2 of 3: f.c. 600,-; ** achterpa
Agency Commission: 15%
Mechanical Data: Type Area: 184 x 265mm, Bleed Size: 210 x 297mm
BUSINESS: DEFENCE

SIONSBERG MAGAZINE
652209N80-123
Editorial: Graaf Adolfstraat 35b, 8606 BT SNEEK
Tel: 492 338432 **Fax:** 492 338421
Email: info@mimicry.nl
Date Established: 06-04-1993; **Freq:** Half-yearly;
Cover Price: Free; **Circ:** 8,500
Usual Pagination: 32
Editor: J. Alkema; **Editor-in-Chief:** J. Alkema
Profile: Magazine about the local hospital.
Language(s): Dutch
Readership: Aimed at patients and local residents.
ADVERTISING RATES:
Full Page Mono EUR 1/1: b/w 680,- 1/2: b/w 385,- 1/4: b/w 215,- 1/8: b/w 135,-
Agency Commission: 15%
Mechanical Data: Type Area: 183 x 269mm, Bleed Size: 210 x 297mm
CONSUMER: RURAL & REGIONAL INTEREST

SKIKANTEN
17601N75G-35
Editorial: St. Annastraat 4, 1381 XR WEESP
Tel: 58 2954859 **Fax:** 172 539171
Email: nvvski@xs4all.nl
Freq: 3 issues yearly; **Annual Sub.:** EUR 30,-; **Circ:** 750
Editor: F. Luiten
Profile: Magazine for ski, cross country and snowboard instructors.
Language(s): Dutch
Agency Commission: 15%
Mechanical Data: Type Area: 185 x 261mm, Bleed Size: 210 x 297mm
CONSUMER: SPORT: Winter Sports

SLAGWERKKRANT
17715N76D-145
Editorial: Rozenstraat 206, 1016 PA AMSTERDAM
Tel: 543 493705 **Fax:** 223 650011
Email: office@k18.nl
Date Established: 01-01-1983; **Freq:** 6 issues yearly;
Cover Price: EUR 5,90
Annual Sub.: EUR 29,50; **Circ:** 11,500
Usual Pagination: 72
Editor: Mark van Schaick; **Editor-in-Chief:** Bouke Bijlsma; **Publisher:** Erk Willemsen
Profile: Music magazine focusing on drums and percussion.
Language(s): Dutch
Readership: Aimed at percussionists and drummers.
ADVERTISING RATES:
Full Page Mono EUR 1/1: f.c. 1840,-; 1/2: f.c. 1000,-; 1/4: f.c. 540,-
Agency Commission: 15%
Mechanical Data: Type Area: 190 x 270mm, Bleed Size: 210 x 297mm
Copy instructions: *Copy Date:* 3 weeks prior to publication date
CONSUMER: MUSIC & PERFORMING ARTS: Music

SLEEP & DUWVAART
16502N45A-110
Editorial: Postbus 190, 1520 AD WORMERVEER
Email: basmbehoud@xs4all.nl **Web site:** http://www.sleepduwvaart.nl
Date Established: 01-02-1986; **Freq:** 6 issues yearly;
Annual Sub.: EUR 44,-; **Circ:** 1,150
Usual Pagination: 80
Editor: M. Boer; **Editor-in-Chief:** M. Boer
Profile: Publication containing articles on pushboats, tugs and steamboats in inland waterways. Includes information on ship launches and maritime history.
Language(s): Dutch
Agency Commission: 15%
Mechanical Data: Bleed Size: 210 x 297mm
BUSINESS: MARINE & SHIPPING

DE SMAAK VAN ITALIË
1640499N74Q-290
Editorial: Korte Prinsengracht 44, 1013 GT AMSTERDAM **Tel:** 26 8450860 **Fax:** 35 5425772
Email: info@dsvmedia.nl **Web site:** http://www.desmaakvanitalie.nl
Freq: 6 issues yearly; **Cover Price:** EUR 5,50
Annual Sub.: EUR 31,-; **Circ:** 31,087
Editor: M. Molenbeek; **Editor-in-Chief:** M. Bosmans; **Publisher:** M. Molenbeek
Language(s): Dutch
ADVERTISING RATES:
Full Page Mono EUR 2/1: b/w 4950,- 1/1: b/w 2950,- 1/2: b/w 1775,-
Agency Commission: 15%
Mechanical Data: Type Area: 195 x 265mm, Bleed Size: 215 x 285mm
Copy instructions: *Copy Date:* 4 weeks prior to publication date
CONSUMER: WOMEN'S INTEREST CONSUMER MAGAZINES: Lifestyle

SMAAKMAKEND
17546N74P-148
Editorial: Herculesplein 269, 3584 AA UTRECHT
Tel: 492 338432 **Fax:** 492 338421
Email: info@bionext.nl **Web site:** http://www.smaakmakend.nl
Date Established: 01-04-1993; **Freq:** 6 issues yearly;
Annual Sub.: EUR 22,-; **Circ:** 70,000
Editor: Anneke Ammerlaan; **Editor-in-Chief:** Hans Moltzer
Profile: Magazine covering organic food, health and the environment.
Language(s): Dutch
ADVERTISING RATES:
Full Page Mono EUR 2/1: f.c. 8410,-; 1/1: f.c. 4785,-; 1/2: f.c. 2640,-
Agency Commission: 15%
Mechanical Data: Type Area: 200 x 265mm, Bleed Size: 210 x 275mm
Copy instructions: *Copy Date:* 4 weeks prior to publication date
CONSUMER: WOMEN'S INTEREST CONSUMER MAGAZINES: Food & Cookery

SNACKKOERIER
15844N11A-100
Editorial: Hanzestraat 1, 7006 RH DOETINCHEM
Tel: 314 349591 **Fax:** 314 349797
Email: klantenservice@reedbusiness.nl **Web site:** http://www.snackkoerier.nl
Freq: 26 issues yearly; **Annual Sub.:** EUR 164,95; **Circ:** 5,660
Editor: Peter Garstenveld; **Publisher:** Hans Hondtong
Profile: Newspaper containing information about the fast food industry.
Language(s): Dutch
Readership: Read by snack, fast food and ice-cream sellers.
ADVERTISING RATES:
Full Page Mono EUR 1/1: f.c. 7144,-; b/w 4764,- 1/2: f.c. 3721,-; b/w 2482,- 1/4: f.c. 1938,-; b/w 1294,-
Agency Commission: 15%
Mechanical Data: Type Area: 272 x 380mm, Bleed Size: 297 x 420mm
Copy instructions: *Copy Date:* 10 days prior to publication date
BUSINESS: CATERING: Catering, Hotels & Restaurants

SNEEKER NIEUWSBLAD
627035N72-4800
Editorial: Martiniplein 15b, 8601 EG SNEEK
Tel: 88 8002010 **Fax:** 226 333555
Email: verkoop@hoekstra-uitgeverij.nl **Web site:** http://www.sneekernieuwsblad.nl
Date Established: 03-01-1846; **Freq:** Weekly; **Circ:** 3,200
Usual Pagination: 16
Editor: F. Nijholt-de Haan; **Publisher:** Peter Idema
Language(s): Dutch
Agency Commission: 15%

Mechanical Data: Type Area: 264 x 397mm
LOCAL NEWSPAPERS

SNOWBOARDER MAGAZINE
17629N75M-60
Editorial: Winthontlaan 200, 3526 KV UTRECHT
Tel: 88 2944819 **Fax:** 30 6383991
Email: maruba@maruba.com **Web site:** http://www.snowboardermagazine.com
Date Established: 01-10-1989; **Freq:** Quarterly;
Cover Price: EUR 3,95
Annual Sub.: EUR 14,50; **Circ:** 26,000
Editor: Arjan Kruik; **Publisher:** Maas van Drie
Profile: Sports magazine focusing on snowboarding.
Language(s): Dutch
Readership: Aimed at snowboarding enthusiasts.
ADVERTISING RATES:
Full Page Mono EUR 2/1: f.c. 7800,-; 1/1: f.c. 4000,-; 1/2: f.c. 2200,-
Agency Commission: 15%
Mechanical Data: Type Area: 205 x 255mm, Bleed Size: 210 x 260mm
Copy instructions: *Copy Date:* 4 weeks prior to publication date
CONSUMER: SPORT: Water Sports

SOCIALE PSYCHIATRIE
16785N56N-120
Editorial: Hosingenhof 5, 5625 NJ EINDHOVEN
Tel: 23 5564800 **Fax:** 23 5564810
Freq: Quarterly; **Annual Sub.:** EUR 29,-; **Circ:** 1,975
Editor: G. Lohuis; **Publisher:** F. van Vugt
Profile: Journal about all aspects of social psychiatric nursing.
Language(s): Dutch
ADVERTISING RATES:
Full Page Mono .... EUR 1/1: b/w 175,-
Agency Commission: 15%
BUSINESS: HEALTH & MEDICAL: Mental Health

SOS-BULLETIN
1634219N1P-84
Editorial: Kon. Wilhelminaplein 30, 1062 KR AMSTERDAM **Tel:** 0032 34660066
Fax: 0032 34660067
Email: info@soskinderdorpen.nl
Freq: Quarterly; **Annual Sub.:** EUR 15,-; **Circ:** 140,000
Usual Pagination: 8
Language(s): Dutch
Agency Commission: 15%
BUSINESS: FINANCE & ECONOMICS: Fundraising

SPAARMOTIEF
1643457N94H-16
Editorial: Alexanderstraat 28, 2514 JM DEN HAAG
Tel: 23 5565462 **Fax:** 23 5564588
Email: informatie@asnbank.nl
Freq: 5 issues yearly; **Cover Price:** Free; **Circ:** 270,000
Editor: Marianne Bodenstaff
Language(s): Dutch
Agency Commission: 15%
CONSUMER: OTHER CLASSIFICATIONS: Customer Magazines

SPECIALBITE JAARGIDS
1637249N94G-84
Editorial: Wildenborch 5, 1112 XB DIEMEN
Tel: 88 2696657 **Fax:** 20 5159143
Email: info@specialbite.com
Freq: Annual; **Annual Sub.:** EUR 9,95; **Circ:** 65,000
Editor: Anouk Turkenburg
Language(s): Dutch
ADVERTISING RATES:
Full Page Mono EUR 2/1: f.c. 9000,-; 1/1: f.c. 5750,-; 1/2: f.c. 3150,-
Agency Commission: 15%
Mechanical Data: Bleed Size: 230 x 285mm, Type Area: 220 x 275mm
CONSUMER: OTHER CLASSIFICATIONS: Restaurant Guides

SPEELGOED EN HOBBY
16538N48A-8
Editorial: Ierlandlaan 2, 2713 HL ZOETERMEER
Tel: 30 6383743 **Fax:** 20 5159700
Email: stiva@gebra.nl **Web site:** http://www.speelgoedenhobby.nl
Date Established: 01-09-1975; **Freq:** 11 issues yearly; **Annual Sub.:** EUR 54,95; **Circ:** 1,547
Editor: Jan Sinke
Profile: International magazine focusing on the toy and hobby equipment trade.
Language(s): Dutch
Readership: Read by managers of toyshops and hobbyshops, toy manufacturers and wholesalers.
ADVERTISING RATES:
Full Page Mono .. EUR 2/1: f.c. 1645,-; 1/1: f.c. 925,-; 1/2: f.c. 510,-
Agency Commission: 15%
Mechanical Data: Type Area: 177 x 257mm, Bleed Size: 210 x 297mm
Copy instructions: *Copy Date:* 3 weeks prior to publication date
BUSINESS: TOY TRADE & SPORTS GOODS: Toy Trade

SPIEGEL DER ZEILVAART
18174N91A-60
Editorial: Van Oosten de Bruijnstraat 13, 2014 VL HAARLEM **Tel:** 30 6383743 **Fax:** 229 216416
Email: spiegelderzeilvaart@gmail.com
Freq: 10 issues yearly; **Cover Price:** EUR 4,50
Annual Sub.: EUR 41,-; **Circ:** 10,300
Editor: Wim de Bruijn; **Publisher:** Wim de Bruijn
Profile: Magazine about charter and commercial vessels and traditional and classic yachts. Also includes information about the building and restoration of vessels.
Language(s): Dutch
Readership: Aimed at sailing and boating enthusiasts.
ADVERTISING RATES:
Full Page Mono .. EUR 1/1: f.c. 1125,-; b/w 925,- 1/2: f.c. 585,-; b/w 485,- 1/4: f.c. 295,-; b/w 265,-
Agency Commission: 15%
Mechanical Data: Type Area: 196 x 256,5mm, Bleed Size: 215 x 280mm
Copy instructions: *Copy Date:* 3 weeks prior to publication date
CONSUMER: RECREATION & LEISURE: Boating & Yachting

SPITS
627261N65A-45
Editorial: Basisweg 30, 1043 AP AMSTERDAM
Tel: 20 5853045 **Fax:** 20 5853065
Web site: http://www.spitsnieuws.nl
Date Established: 21-06-1999; **Freq:** 260 issues yearly; **Cover Price:** Free; **Circ:** 382,273
Editor: Willem Schouten; **Editor-in-Chief:** Daniëlle Kool; **Publisher:** M.C.A. Roos
Profile: Tabloid-sized newspaper covering national and international news, finance, business, music, culture and sport.
Language(s): Dutch
Readership: Aimed at managers, office and factory workers, also students. Read mainly by people aged 25 to 40 years.
ADVERTISING RATES:
Full Page Mono .... EUR 2/1: b/w 48.410,- 1/1: b/w 24.205,- 1/2: b/w 12.105,-
Agency Commission: 15%
Mechanical Data: Type Area: 264 x 398mm
NATIONAL DAILY & SUNDAY NEWSPAPERS: National Daily Newspapers

SPITZ
1860025N76G-168
Editorial: Eendrachtsstraat 8, 3012 XL ROTTERDAM
Tel: 88 5567321 **Fax:** 20 4853249
Email: info@scapinoballet.nl
Freq: 5 issues yearly; **Cover Price:** Free; **Circ:** 200,000
Editor: Maureen Hol
Language(s): Dutch
Agency Commission: 15%
Mechanical Data: Bleed Size: 289 x 415mm
CONSUMER: MUSIC & PERFORMING ARTS: Dance

SPONSORTRIBUNE
627304N2R-101
Editorial: Pelmolenlaan 1m, 3447 GW WOERDEN
Tel: 88 7518800 **Fax:** 20 5353696
Email: klantenservice@bbp.nl **Web site:** http://www.sponsortribune.nl
Freq: 6 issues yearly; **Annual Sub.:** EUR 225,-; **Circ:** 1,500
Editor: Ad Maatjens; **Publisher:** Ad Maatjens
Profile: Magazine covering international trends and developments in the field of sponsoring.
Language(s): Dutch
Readership: Aimed at directors of major companies giving sponsorship.
ADVERTISING RATES:
Full Page Mono EUR 2/1: b/w 3500,- 1/1: b/w 1800,- 1/2: b/w 1250,-
Agency Commission: 15%
Mechanical Data: Type Area: 185 x 252mm, Bleed Size: 210 x 297mm
BUSINESS: COMMUNICATIONS, ADVERTISING & MARKETING: Communications Related

SPOOR
1635801N94H-13
Editorial: Laan van Puntenburg 100, 3511 ER UTRECHT **Tel:** 172 466539 **Fax:** 10 4521797
Date Established: 01-12-2001; **Freq:** Quarterly; **Circ:** 1,235,393
Editor: Bonita van Lier
Language(s): Dutch
ADVERTISING RATES:
Full Page Mono .... EUR 1/1: f.c. 18.800,-
Agency Commission: 15%
Mechanical Data: Type Area: 180 x 233mm, Bleed Size: 210 x 269mm
CONSUMER: OTHER CLASSIFICATIONS: Customer Magazines

SPORT PARTNER
623989N48B-20
Editorial: Winthontlaan 200, 3526 KV UTRECHT
Tel: 10 4274102 **Fax:** 10 4739911
Email: maruba@maruba.com **Web site:** http://www.sportpartner.info
Date Established: 01-01-1988; **Freq:** 10 issues yearly; **Annual Sub.:** EUR 77,50; **Circ:** 2,300
Editor: H. Broekhof; **Editor-in-Chief:** T. de Boer;
Publisher: Maas van Drie
Profile: Magazine containing information concerning the sports retail trade in the Benelux countries.
Language(s): Dutch
Readership: Read by managers at sports retailers and suppliers.
ADVERTISING RATES:
Full Page Mono EUR 2/1: f.c. 6275,-; 1/1: f.c. 3225,-; 1/2: f.c. 1800,-
Agency Commission: 15%
Mechanical Data: Type Area: 220 x 280mm, Bleed Size: 240 x 300mm
Copy instructions: *Copy Date:* 3 weeks prior to publication date
BUSINESS: TOY TRADE & SPORTS GOODS: Sports Goods

SPORTACCOM
16542N48B-25
Editorial: Postbus 302, 6800 AH ARNHEM
Tel: 71 5239058 **Fax:** 20 5159145
Web site: http://www.sportaccom.nl
Freq: 6 issues yearly; **Cover Price:** EUR 14,25
Annual Sub.: EUR 85,-; **Circ:** 1,332
Editor: Thea van Setten; **Editor-in-Chief:** Nicole Eyssen; **Publisher:** M.J. van Troost
Profile: Magazine about sports facilities, equipment and venues. Includes articles on management and finance.
Language(s): Dutch
ADVERTISING RATES:
Full Page Mono EUR 2/1: f.c. 4620,-; b/w 3745,- 1/1: f.c. 2850,-; b/w 1975,- 1/2: f.c. 1970,-; b/w 1095,-
Agency Commission: 15%
Mechanical Data: Type Area: 185 x 270mm, Bleed Size: 210 x 297mm
BUSINESS: TOY TRADE & SPORTS GOODS: Sports Goods

SPORTCULT
16541N48B-12
Editorial: Joan Muyskenweg 22, 1096 CJ AMSTERDAM **Tel:** 0032 34660066
Fax: 0032 34660067
Web site: http://www.sportcult.nl
Date Established: 01-05-2003; **Freq:** 6 issues yearly;
Annual Sub.: EUR 48,75; **Circ:** 2,350
Usual Pagination: 48
Editor: Veronique van der Waal
Profile: Magazine focusing on the international sports trade.
Language(s): Dutch
Readership: Aimed at sport retailers and wholesalers.
ADVERTISING RATES:
Full Page Mono EUR 2/1: f.c. 3580,-; 1/1: f.c. 2100,-; 1/2: f.c. 1500,-
Agency Commission: 15%
Mechanical Data: Type Area: 241 x 351mm, Bleed Size: 265 x 375mm
BUSINESS: TOY TRADE & SPORTS GOODS: Sports Goods

DE SPORTFISKER
18209N92-135
Editorial: Fugelsang 8, 8403 BA JONKERSLAN
Email: info@sportfisker.nl
Date Established: 01-03-1996; **Freq:** Quarterly; **Circ:** 13,000
Editor: Pyt Achenbach
Profile: Magazine containing information about fishing.
Language(s): Dutch
Readership: Read by anglers of 6 fishing clubs in Friesland (Leeuwarden, Drachten, Wolvega, Heerenveen, Jubbega and Kootstertille).
ADVERTISING RATES:
Full Page Mono .... EUR 1/2: f.c. 175,-
Agency Commission: 15%
Mechanical Data: Type Area: 118 x 190mm, Bleed Size: 210 x 260mm
CONSUMER: ANGLING & FISHING

SPORTLOKAAL
16337N32H-150
Editorial: Past. Bruggemanlaan 33, 6861 GR OOSTERBEEK **Tel:** 70 4161339 **Fax:** 20 5159145
Email: info@sportengemeenten.nl
Freq: 6 issues yearly; **Annual Sub.:** EUR 66,80; **Circ:** 1,500
Usual Pagination: 52
Editor: P.F. Coppes; **Editor-in-Chief:** Kitty Potman
Profile: Official journal of the Society for Local Government Promotion of Physical Exercise, Sports, Recreation and Swimming Pools.
Language(s): Dutch
ADVERTISING RATES:
Full Page Mono EUR 1/1: f.c. 2150,-; PMS 1830,-; b/w 1450,- 1/2: f.c. 1500,-; PMS 1180,-; b/w 810,- 1/4: f.c. 1130,-; P
Agency Commission: 15%
Mechanical Data: Type Area: 200 x 260mm, Bleed Size: 220 x 280mm
BUSINESS: LOCAL GOVERNMENT, LEISURE & RECREATION: Leisure, Recreation & Entertainment

SPORTMASSAGE
1635099N75A-394
Editorial: Het Spoor 2, 3994 AK HOUTEN
Tel: 30 6383743 **Fax:** 229 216416
Email: info@springermedia.nl
Freq: 10 issues yearly; **Circ:** 8,081
Editor: C. Vollebergh; **Editor-in-Chief:** Suzet Hoevers
Language(s): Dutch
ADVERTISING RATES:
Full Page Mono EUR 1/1: f.c. 1800,-; b/w 1126,- 1/2: f.c. 1026,-; b/w 642,- 1/4: f.c. 558,-; b/w 349,-
Agency Commission: 15%
Mechanical Data: Type Area: 180 x 270mm, Bleed Size: 210 x 297mm
CONSUMER: SPORT

SPROUT
1695373N14A-469
Editorial: Paul van Vlissingenstraat 10e, 1096 BK AMSTERDAM **Tel:** 15 2690416 **Fax:** 15 2690766
Email: info@mtmediagroep.nl **Web site:** http://www.sprout.nl
Freq: 9 issues yearly; **Cover Price:** EUR 5,45
Annual Sub.: EUR 39,-; **Circ:** 96,905
Editor: Ewald Smits; **Editor-in-Chief:** Karin Husslage; **Publisher:** Berend Jan Veldkamp
Language(s): Dutch
ADVERTISING RATES:
Full Page Mono .... EUR 2/1: f.c. 18.219,-; PMS 15.486,-; b/w 12.753,- 1/1: f.c. 10.122,-; PMS 8603,-; b/w 7085,- 1/2: f.c.
Agency Commission: 15%
Mechanical Data: Type Area: 190 x 264mm, Bleed Size: 215 x 285mm
Copy instructions: *Copy Date:* 3 weeks prior to publication date
BUSINESS: COMMERCE, INDUSTRY & MANAGEMENT

SPUI
1635012N83-165
Editorial: Spui 21, 1012 WX AMSTERDAM
Tel: 15 2617997 **Fax:** 229 216416
Email: alumni@uva.nl **Web site:** http://www.uva-alumni.nl/spui
Freq: 3 issues yearly; **Circ:** 85,000
Editor: A.W. Goutbeek; **Publisher:** A.W. Goutbeek
Language(s): Dutch
Agency Commission: 15%
CONSUMER: STUDENT PUBLICATIONS

DE STADSKRANT
627033N72-4930
Editorial: Grote Kerkstraat 24b, 1135 BD EDAM
Tel: 570 647207 **Fax:** 73 6210512
Email: stadskrant@wxs.nl **Web site:** http://www.stadskrant-edam.nl
Date Established: 01-05-1990; **Freq:** 26 issues yearly; **Cover Price:** Free; **Circ:** 13,500
Editor: Luc van den Berg; **Publisher:** Luc van den Berg
Language(s): Dutch
ADVERTISING RATES:
Full Page Mono EUR 1/1: b/w 640,- 1/2: b/w 325,- 1/4: b/w 174,-
Agency Commission: 15%
Mechanical Data: Type Area: 265 x 380mm, Bleed Size: 270 x 400mm
LOCAL NEWSPAPERS

STADSKRANT VEGHEL
627078N72-4940
Editorial: Hoofdstraat 1a, 5461 JC VEGHEL
Tel: 20 5979500 **Fax:** 20 5979590
Email: stadskrant@stadskrantveghel.nl
Date Established: 01-05-1992; **Freq:** Weekly; **Cover Price:** Free; **Circ:** 46,675
Editor: Philip van den Brand; **Editor-in-Chief:** Annemieke van der Aa
Language(s): Dutch
Agency Commission: 15%
Mechanical Data: Type Area: 278 x 415mm, Bleed Size: 290 x 420mm
LOCAL NEWSPAPERS

STADSNIEUWS
626998N72-4980
Editorial: Ringbaan Noord 179, 5046 AA TILBURG
Tel: 13 4627201 **Fax:** 13 5361405
Email: info@wegenermedia.nl **Web site:** http://www.stadsnieuws.nl
Date Established: 01-01-1981; **Freq:** 104 issues yearly; **Cover Price:** Free; **Circ:** 109,500
Editor: Mart Jochemsen; **Editor-in-Chief:** Ruud Spoor
Language(s): Dutch
ADVERTISING RATES:
Full Page Mono EUR 1/1: b/w 2303,- 1/2: b/w 1218,- 1/4: b/w 641,-
Agency Commission: 15%
Mechanical Data: Type Area: 264 x 398mm
LOCAL NEWSPAPERS

STAL & AKKER
16146N21J-75
Editorial: Handelsweg 2, 7041 GX 'S-HEERENBERG
Tel: 492 338432 **Fax:** 20 6767728
Email: info@agrio.nl **Web site:** http://www.stal-en-akker.nl
Date Established: 01-01-1993; **Freq:** 30 issues yearly; **Annual Sub.:** EUR 45,95; **Circ:** 13,750
Editor: R. Ellenkamp; **Publisher:** Ben van Uhm
Profile: Magazine covering all aspects of agriculture in Noord-Braband, Limburg and Zeeland.
Language(s): Dutch
Readership: Read by farmers in South Holland.
Agency Commission: 15%
Mechanical Data: Type Area: 264 x 390mm, Bleed Size: 290 x 420mm
BUSINESS: AGRICULTURE & FARMING: Agriculture & Farming - Regional

STALLENBOUW 18260N21A-366
Editorial: Langpoort 2, 6001 CL WEERT
Tel: 70 3789780 **Fax:** 70 3789783
Email: info@ugaatbouwen.nl **Web site:** http://www.stallenbouw.info
Date Established: 01-07-1997; **Freq:** Half-yearly; **Cover Price:** Free; **Circ:** 3,500
Editor: Twan van Gent
Profile: Building magazine focusing on the agricultural sector.
Language(s): Dutch
ADVERTISING RATES:
Full Page Mono EUR 1/1: f.c. 1850,-; 1/2: f.c. 1150,-; 1/4: f.c. 800,-
Agency Commission: 15%
Mechanical Data: Type Area: 180 x 271mm, Bleed Size: 216 x 303mm
BUSINESS: AGRICULTURE & FARMING

STANDBY 16739N56D-52
Editorial: Het Spoor 2, 3994 AK HOUTEN
Tel: 70 3789184 **Fax:** 70 7999878
Freq: 6 issues yearly; **Annual Sub.:** EUR 67,95; **Circ:** 1,836
Editor: Maria Jansma-de Vries
Profile: Magazine containing articles and information about dental care and dentistry.
Language(s): Dutch
Readership: Aimed at dental assistants.
ADVERTISING RATES:
Full Page Mono EUR 1/1: f.c. 3010,-; b/w 1351,- 1/2: f.c. 1667,-; b/w 749,- 1/4: f.c. 879,-; b/w 440,-
Agency Commission: 15%
Mechanical Data: Type Area: 185 x 267mm, Bleed Size: 210 x 297mm
BUSINESS: HEALTH & MEDICAL: Dental

STARS 1695395N74Q-318
Editorial: Joan Muyskenweg 6-6a, 1096 CJ AMSTERDAM **Tel:** 20 5721643 **Fax:** 20 5721521
Email: info@publishing.audax.nl **Web site:** http://www.stars-online.nl
Date Established: 07-07-2005; **Freq:** 10 issues yearly; **Cover Price:** EUR 2,95
Annual Sub.: EUR 29,50; **Circ:** 69,477
Editor: W.G. Schaap
Language(s): Dutch
ADVERTISING RATES:
Full Page Mono EUR 1/1: b/w 3250,- 1/2: b/w 2440,- 1/4: b/w 1465,-
Agency Commission: 15%
Mechanical Data: Type Area: 152 x 203mm, Bleed Size: 172 x 233mm
Copy instructions: *Copy Date:* 4 weeks prior to publication date
CONSUMER: WOMEN'S INTEREST CONSUMER MAGAZINES: Lifestyle

START 711720N77D-250
Editorial: Vliet 24, 5422 VV GEMERT **Tel:** 543 493705 **Fax:** 223 650011
Email: uitgeverij@vanhelvoortgroep.nl **Web site:** http://www.startautosportmagazine.nl
Freq: Monthly; **Annual Sub.:** EUR 66,-; **Circ:** 10,000
Editor: Henk de Winter; **Editor-in-Chief:** Bart-Jan Keizer
Profile: Autosports magazine, containing information about events, the latest models, tests and drivers.
Language(s): Dutch
Readership: Aimed at motor sport enthusiasts.
ADVERTISING RATES:
Full Page Mono .. EUR 1/1: f.c. 1000,-; 1/2: f.c. 550,-; 1/4: f.c. 300,-
Agency Commission: 15%
Mechanical Data: Type Area: 195 x 257mm, Bleed Size: 225 x 287mm
Copy instructions: *Copy Date:* 3 weeks prior to publication date
CONSUMER: MOTORING & CYCLING: Motor Sports

STARTERSMAGAZINE 1635515N14H-206
Editorial: Postbus 191, 3440 AD WOERDEN
Freq: Annual; **Cover Price:** Free; **Circ:** 100,000
Language(s): Dutch
ADVERTISING RATES:
Full Page Mono .... EUR 1/1: b/w 19.055,- 1/2: b/w 11.433,- 1/4: b/w 6860,-
Agency Commission: 15%
Mechanical Data: Type Area: 190 x 265mm, Bleed Size: 210 x 280mm
BUSINESS: COMMERCE, INDUSTRY & MANAGEMENT: Small Business

DE STATUS 1857833N14H-228
Editorial: Hunzebos 2a, 1447 TX PURMEREND
Tel: 40 8447611 **Fax:** 53 4842189
Email: info@klocks.nl **Web site:** http://www.destatus.nl
Freq: 6 issues yearly; **Cover Price:** Free; **Circ:** 104,700
Publisher: Marco Klockenbrink
Language(s): Dutch
ADVERTISING RATES:
Full Page Mono EUR 1/1: f.c. 8195,-; 1/2: f.c. 4505,-; 1/4: f.c. 2475,-
Agency Commission: 15%
Mechanical Data: Type Area: 190 x 275mm, Bleed Size: 210 x 297mm
BUSINESS: COMMERCE, INDUSTRY & MANAGEMENT: Small Business

STEDEBOUW & ARCHITECTUUR 15661N4D-50
Editorial: Zekeringstraat 21, 1014 BM AMSTERDAM
Tel: 10 2894015 **Fax:** 20 6159047
Email: info@weka.nl **Web site:** http://www.stedebouwarchitectuur.nl
Date Established: 01-01-1984; **Freq:** 10 issues yearly; **Cover Price:** EUR 20,-
Annual Sub.: EUR 105,-; **Circ:** 6,949
Editor: Wijnand Beemster; **Editor-in-Chief:** Peter Bekkering; **Publisher:** Arend Jan Kornet
Profile: Magazine focusing on town planning, architecture and building.
Language(s): Dutch
Readership: Read by builders, architects, developers and town planners.
ADVERTISING RATES:
Full Page Mono EUR 1/1: f.c. 3180,-; 1/2: f.c. 2295,-; 1/4: f.c. 1350,-
Agency Commission: 15%
Mechanical Data: Type Area: 226 x 297mm, Bleed Size: 243 x 318mm
BUSINESS: ARCHITECTURE & BUILDING: Planning & Housing

STEDENBOUW 15663N4D-70
Editorial: Schatbeurderlaan 6, 6002 ED WEERT
Tel: 30 6383743 **Fax:** 229 216416
Email: info@louwersuitgevers.nl
Annual Sub.: EUR 75,-; **Circ:** 5,000
Editor: Willem Ruyters
Profile: Journal about town planning, architecture and building practice.
Language(s): Dutch
Readership: Read by architects, builders and suppliers.
ADVERTISING RATES:
Full Page Mono EUR 2/1: f.c. 2495,-; 1/1: f.c. 1810,-; 1/2: f.c. 1427,-
Agency Commission: 15%
Mechanical Data: Type Area: 197 x 267mm, Bleed Size: 230 x 297mm
Copy instructions: *Copy Date:* 5 weeks prior to publication date
BUSINESS: ARCHITECTURE & BUILDING: Planning & Housing

DE STEM IN DE WOESTIJN 1635122N87-2350
Editorial: Postbus 3605, 6019 ZG WESSEM
Tel: 76 5312311 **Fax:** 76 5312520
Email: heroldverlag@t-online.de
Date Established: 01-01-1961; **Freq:** Monthly;
Annual Sub.: EUR 5,-; **Circ:** 65,000
Usual Pagination: 8
Editor: W. Gerstenberg
Language(s): Dutch
Agency Commission: 15%
CONSUMER: RELIGIOUS

DE STEM VAN GRAVE 16720N56B-158
Editorial: St. Elisabethstraat 4, 5361 HK GRAVE
Tel: 76 5312311 **Fax:** 76 5312520
Email: info@ksbs.nl
Date Established: 01-01-1950; **Freq:** Quarterly; **Circ:** 17,000
Usual Pagination: 8
Editor: Marianne van Duijnhoven
Profile: Publication about the care of blind and partially-sighted people.
Language(s): Dutch
Readership: Aimed at nursing staff in hospitals and homes for the elderly.
Agency Commission: 15%
Mechanical Data: Bleed Size: 295 x 430mm
BUSINESS: HEALTH & MEDICAL: Nursing

DE STENTOR 1793864N67B-7315
Editorial: Laan van Westenenk 6, 7336 AZ APELDOORN **Tel:** 55 5388220
Freq: 312 issues yearly; **Annual Sub.:** EUR 268,20; **Circ:** 130,828
Editor: A. Engbers
Language(s): Dutch
ADVERTISING RATES:
Full Page Mono EUR 3/4: b/w 9797,- 1/2: b/w 6532,- 1/4: b/w 3266,- 3/4 ed. za.: b/w 10.841,- 1/2 ed. za.: b/w 7228,- 1/
Agency Commission: 15%
Mechanical Data: Type Area: 266 x 398mm, Bleed Size: 290 x 415mm
REGIONAL DAILY & SUNDAY NEWSPAPERS: Regional Daily Newspapers

STEUNPUNTSGEWIJS 18233N94D-170
Editorial: Biltstraat 95, 3572 AL UTRECHT
Tel: 223 650017 **Fax:** 223 650011
Email: info@lsem.nl
Date Established: 01-03-1998; **Freq:** Half-yearly;
Cover Price: Free; **Circ:** 1,000
Usual Pagination: 4
Editor: O. Rahantoknam
Profile: Newsletter focusing on culture and education for the Moluccan (Indonesian) community in the Netherlands.
Language(s): Dutch
Agency Commission: 15%
CONSUMER: OTHER CLASSIFICATIONS: Expatriates

STIBANS BULLETIN 16577N49E-40
Editorial: Landweg 7, 7041 VS 'S-HEERENBERG
Tel: 23 5565370
Email: secretariaat@stibans.nl
Date Established: 01-01-1979; **Freq:** Half-yearly; **Circ:** 550
Usual Pagination: 36
Editor: P. van der Meer; **Editor-in-Chief:** P.P.A. de Winter
Profile: Journal covering developments related to the preservation of railway rolling stock, in particular restoration projects carried out by members of STIBANS (Society for the Preservation of Dutch Railway Stock).
Language(s): Dutch
Agency Commission: 15%
BUSINESS: TRANSPORT: Railways

STITCH & PRINT INTERNATIONAL 17467N47A-24
Editorial: Celsiusweg 41, 8912 AM LEEUWARDEN
Tel: 88 2944819 **Fax:** 30 6383991
Email: businessmedia@eisma.nl **Web site:** http://www.stitchprint.eu
Date Established: 01-02-1993; **Freq:** Quarterly; **Circ:** 10,271
Editor: Marijke Kuypers; **Publisher:** Minne Hovenga
Profile: Magazine focusing on embroidery and the textile printing industry.
Language(s): Dutch
Readership: Read by designers, manufacturers, buyers and sales representatives.
ADVERTISING RATES:
Full Page Mono EUR 2/1: f.c. 4115,-; 1/1: f.c. 2436,-; 1/2: f.c. 1339,-
Agency Commission: 15%
Mechanical Data: Type Area: 202 x 268mm, Bleed Size: 230 x 300mm
Copy instructions: *Copy Date:* 2 weeks prior to publication date
BUSINESS: CLOTHING & TEXTILES

STOER! 1996210N74F-185
Editorial: Assendelftstraat 13, 1013 SN AMSTERDAM
Email: info@jellyhood.com
Freq: Quarterly; **Cover Price:** EUR 2,-; **Circ:** 65,000
Editor: Arthur Geraerts; **Publisher:** Frank Beentjes
Language(s): Dutch
ADVERTISING RATES:
Full Page Mono EUR 2/1: b/w 5500,- 1/1: b/w 3250,-
Agency Commission: 15%
Mechanical Data: Type Area: 190 x 277mm, Bleed Size: 210 x 207mm
CONSUMER: WOMEN'S INTEREST CONSUMER MAGAZINES: Teenage

STORY 17425N74A-160
Editorial: Capellalaan 65, 2132 JL HOOFDDORP
Tel: 23 5564919 **Fax:** 23 5564911
Web site: http://www.story.nl
Freq: Weekly; **Cover Price:** EUR 2,10
Annual Sub.: EUR 99,32; **Circ:** 129,186
Editor: Matthieu Slee; **Publisher:** Anneliese Bergman
Profile: Magazine containing articles on television, celebrities and films.
Language(s): Dutch
Readership: Read mainly by women over 20 years.
ADVERTISING RATES:
Full Page Mono .... EUR 2/1: b/w 12.800,- 1/1: b/w 6400,- 1/2: b/w 3840,-
Agency Commission: 15%
Mechanical Data: Type Area: 204 x 265mm, Bleed Size: 221 x 285mm
CONSUMER: WOMEN'S INTEREST CONSUMER MAGAZINES: Women's Interest

STRAAT MAGAZINE 17883N80-126
Editorial: Mauritsplaats 24, 3012 CD ROTTERDAM
Tel: 172 466622
Email: straatkrant@hotmail.com **Web site:** http://www.straatmagazine.nl
Freq: 24 issues yearly; **Cover Price:** EUR 1,50; **Circ:** 70,000
Editor: Sander de Kramer; **Editor-in-Chief:** J. Post
Profile: Magazine about lifestyle, social trends and developments in Limburg, Utrecht, Dordrecht and Rotterdam.
Language(s): Dutch
ADVERTISING RATES:
Full Page Mono EUR 2/1: f.c. 4538,-; b/w 2723,- 1/1: f.c. 2269,-; b/w 1361,- 1/2: f.c. 1588,-; b/w 953,-
Agency Commission: 15%
Mechanical Data: Type Area: 210 x 285mm, Bleed Size: 210 x 285mm
Copy instructions: *Copy Date:* 5 days prior to publication date
CONSUMER: RURAL & REGIONAL INTEREST

STREEKPOST AMSTELVEEN 17885N80-127
Editorial: De Factorij 47g, 1689 AK ZWAAG
Tel: 30 2964469 **Fax:** 475 551033
Email: rodiaddvice@rodi.nl
Date Established: 01-03-1998; **Freq:** 6 issues yearly; **Cover Price:** Free; **Circ:** 45,500
Profile: Magazine containing information on the Amstelveen area.
Language(s): Dutch
Readership: Read by local residents.
Agency Commission: 15%

Mechanical Data: Type Area: 264 x 398mm
CONSUMER: RURAL & REGIONAL INTEREST

STRUINEN 16850N57-66_50
Editorial: Vogelenzangseweg 21, 2114 BA VOGELENZANG **Tel:** 13 4662926
Email: struinen@waternet.nl
Freq: Quarterly; **Cover Price:** Free; **Circ:** 10,000
Editor: Miranda Kok
Profile: Publication focusing on the environmental issues rising from management of the water supply extracted from the dunes around Amsterdam.
Language(s): Dutch
Agency Commission: 15%
BUSINESS: ENVIRONMENT & POLLUTION

STUDIE AGENDA 1635410N88R-46
Editorial: Reaal 2b, 2353 TL LEIDERDORP
Tel: 20 5159172 **Fax:** 229 216416
Email: info@stationeryteam.nl
Freq: Annual; **Cover Price:** EUR 4,95; **Circ:** 50,000
Language(s): Dutch
Agency Commission: 15%
CONSUMER: EDUCATION: Education Related

STYLE CITY MAGAZINE ZEEUWS-VLAANDEREN 1800599N80-546
Editorial: Axelsestraat 16, 4537 AK TERNEUZEN
Tel: 23 5565462 **Fax:** 23 5564588
Email: zvm@zvm.eu
Date Established: 01-10-1996; **Freq:** 11 issues yearly; **Cover Price:** Free; **Circ:** 51,100
Editor: Peter Verdurmen
Language(s): Dutch
Agency Commission: 15%
Mechanical Data: Type Area: 240 x 340mm, Bleed Size: 260 x 360mm
CONSUMER: RURAL & REGIONAL INTEREST

THE STYLE MAGAZINE 1931384N74Q-529
Editorial: Buiten Molenstraat 7, 4101 CJ CULEMBORG **Tel:** 10 4518007
Email: redactie@kolkengeense.nl
Date Established: 22-10-2009; **Freq:** Half-yearly; **Cover Price:** EUR 4,95; **Circ:** 100,000
Editor: Marijke Kolk
Language(s): Dutch
ADVERTISING RATES:
Full Page Mono .... EUR 1/1: b/w 3500,-
Agency Commission: 15%
CONSUMER: WOMEN'S INTEREST CONSUMER MAGAZINES: Lifestyle

SUCCULENTA 18223N93-200
Editorial: Brinklaan 31, 7261 JH RUURLO
Tel: 35 6726880
Web site: http://www.succulenta.nl
Date Established: 19-06-1919; **Freq:** 6 issues yearly;
Annual Sub.: EUR 27,-; **Circ:** 1,800
Usual Pagination: 64
Editor: H.W. Viscaal
Profile: Magazine containing articles about cacti and other succulent plants.
Language(s): Dutch
ADVERTISING RATES:
Full Page Mono .. EUR 1/1: b/w 125,- 1/2: b/w 73,- 1/4: b/w 46,-
Agency Commission: 15%
Mechanical Data: Type Area: 145 x 200mm, Bleed Size: 170 x 240mm
CONSUMER: GARDENING

SUM 17993N83-72
Editorial: Utrechtseweg 101, 3702 AB ZEIST
Tel: 346 577390 **Fax:** 346 577389
Email: info@stiptomedia.nl **Web site:** http://www.sum.nl
Date Established: 10-03-1991; **Freq:** 8 issues yearly; **Cover Price:** Free; **Circ:** 80,000
Editor: Remko Allertz
Profile: Magazine containing articles and information about university life.
Language(s): Dutch
Readership: Read by university students.
ADVERTISING RATES:
Full Page Mono EUR 1/1: b/w 7200,- 1/2: b/w 4100,-
Agency Commission: 15%
Mechanical Data: Type Area: 190 x 277mm, Bleed Size: 210 x 297mm
CONSUMER: STUDENT PUBLICATIONS

SUM HOGESCHOOL AGENDA 1636277N88R-57
Editorial: Utrechtseweg 101, 3702 AB ZEIST
Tel: 23 5344089 **Fax:** 10 2801002
Email: info@stiptomedia.nl **Web site:** http://www.sum.nl
Freq: Annual; **Cover Price:** Free; **Circ:** 151,515
Editor: Remko Allertz
Language(s): Dutch
ADVERTISING RATES:
Full Page Mono . EUR 1/1: f.c. 14.750,-; b/w 16.700,-
Agency Commission: 15%

Mechanical Data: Type Area: 100 x 180mm, Bleed Size: 115 x 190mm
CONSUMER: EDUCATION: Education Related

SUM UNIVERSITEITS AGENDA
1636198N88R-54
Editorial: Utrechtseweg 101, 3702 AB ZEIST **Tel:** 23 5565551 **Fax:** 23 5565136
Email: info@stiptomedia.nl **Web site:** http://www.sum.nl
Freq: Annual; **Cover Price:** Free; **Circ:** 117,457
Editor: Remko Allertz
Language(s): Dutch
ADVERTISING RATES:
Full Page Mono .... EUR 1/1: f.c. 11.900,-; b/w 9950,-
Agency Commission: 15%
Mechanical Data: Type Area: 70 x 125mm, Bleed Size: 85 x 135mm
CONSUMER: EDUCATION: Education Related

SUPERMARKT ACTUEEL
16611N53-125
Editorial: Sint Agnetenweg 56, 6545 AW NIJMEGEN
Tel: 33 4637977
Email: info@t-en-s-productions.nl **Web site:** http://www.supermarktactueel.nl
Date Established: 01-01-1992; **Freq:** 26 issues yearly; **Annual Sub.:** EUR 119,25; **Circ:** 6,500
Editor: Lianne Kooistra; **Editor-in-Chief:** Marloes Kleijer; **Publisher:** Tom van Apeldoorn
Profile: Magazine containing articles about trends and developments in supermarket retailing.
Language(s): Dutch
Readership: Read by supermarket managers.
ADVERTISING RATES:
Full Page Mono EUR 2/1: f.c. 3650,-; 1/1: f.c. 2250,-; 1/2: f.c. 1100,-
Agency Commission: 15%
Mechanical Data: Type Area: 190 x 269mm, Bleed Size: 210 x 298mm
BUSINESS: RETAILING & WHOLESALING

SUPPORT MAGAZINE
1637089N94F-272
Editorial: J.C. van Markenlaan 3, 2285 VL RIJSWIJK
Tel: 43 3561490 **Fax:** 182 543500
Email: uitgeverij@lakerveld.nl **Web site:** http://www.supportmagazine.nl
Freq: 7 issues yearly; **Cover Price:** EUR 7,-
Annual Sub.: EUR 24,20; **Circ:** 8,484
Editor: Joeri van der Kloet; **Publisher:** Ad van Gaalen
Language(s): Dutch
ADVERTISING RATES:
Full Page Mono EUR 1/1: b/w 2070,- 1/2: b/w 1100,- 1/4: b/w 580,-
Agency Commission: 15%
Mechanical Data: Type Area: 185 x 268mm, Bleed Size: 210 x 297mm
CONSUMER: OTHER CLASSIFICATIONS: Disability

SURF MAGAZINE
1643651N75M-307
Editorial: Stettinweg 15, 9723 HD GRONINGEN
Tel: 23 5565462 **Fax:** 23 5564588
Email: info@pijpermedia.nl **Web site:** http://www.surfmagazine.nl
Freq: 6 issues yearly; **Cover Price:** EUR 5,50
Annual Sub.: EUR 30,-; **Circ:** 18,500
Editor: Stefan Grolleman; **Editor-in-Chief:** Jeroen Aerts; **Publisher:** Anton Pijper
Language(s): Dutch
ADVERTISING RATES:
Full Page Mono EUR 2/1: f.c. 1800,-; 1/1: f.c. 1400,-; 1/2: f.c. 700,-
Agency Commission: 15%
Mechanical Data: Type Area: 210 x 277mm, Bleed Size: 230 x 297mm
CONSUMER: SPORT: Water Sports

SWZ MARITIME
16512N45C-50
Editorial: Mathenesserlaan 185, 3014 HA ROTTERDAM **Tel:** 33 4637977 **Fax:** 229 216416
Email: swz.rotterdam@planet.nl **Web site:** http://www.swzonline.nl
Freq: 11 issues yearly; **Cover Price:** EUR 17,50
Annual Sub.: EUR 102,75; **Circ:** 4,313
Editor: H Boonstra; **Editor-in-Chief:** M. Buitendijk-Pijl; **Publisher:** J. Verbeek
Profile: Journal about marine technology.
Language(s): Dutch
ADVERTISING RATES:
Full Page Mono EUR 1/1: b/w 2045,- 1/2: b/w 1230,- 1/4: b/w 695,-
Agency Commission: 15%
Mechanical Data: Bleed Size: 225 x 297mm, Type Area: 195 x 255mm
BUSINESS: MARINE & SHIPPING: Maritime Freight

SYNAPS
634094N32G-198
Editorial: De Boelelaan 1118, 1081 HV AMSTERDAM
Tel: 30 6383838 **Fax:** 30 6383839
Email: communicatie@vumc.nl **Web site:** http://www.vumc.nl/synaps
Freq: 5 issues yearly; **Cover Price:** Free; **Circ:** 10,000
Usual Pagination: 24
Editor: M. Bolluijt; **Editor-in-Chief:** Caroline Arps
Profile: Magazine focusing on work and health issues.
Language(s): Dutch
Readership: Read by social workers and general practitioners.
Agency Commission: 15%
BUSINESS: LOCAL GOVERNMENT, LEISURE & RECREATION: Community Care & Social Services

SYNTHESHIS
1637246N56A-412
Editorial: Waterpoortweg 391, 1051 PX AMSTERDAM **Tel:** 88 2696657 **Fax:** 20 5159143
Freq: Quarterly; **Annual Sub.:** EUR 52,45; **Circ:** 4,718
Editor: Jeroen van der Lugt
Language(s): Dutch
ADVERTISING RATES:
Full Page Mono EUR 1/1: f.c. 2557,-; b/w 1120,- 1/2: f.c. 1406,-; b/w 626,- 1/4: f.c. 857,-; b/w 383,-
Agency Commission: 15%
Mechanical Data: Type Area: 180 x 254mm, Bleed Size: 210 x 297mm
BUSINESS: HEALTH & MEDICAL

TABAK & GEMAK
15808N8C-100
Editorial: Dorpsweg 198, 3738 CL MAARTENSDIJK
Tel: 20 5159722 **Fax:** 30 6007595
Email: info@vanvlaardingen.nl
Date Established: 01-01-1942; **Freq:** 10 issues yearly; **Annual Sub.:** EUR 27,50; **Circ:** 3,500
Editor: Dick van Vlaardingen; **Editor-in-Chief:** Lorette van Vlaardingen; **Publisher:** Dick van Vlaardingen
Profile: Retailing magazine covering tobacco ware, newspapers, magazines and confectionery. Also includes articles on retail management and marketing.
Language(s): Dutch
Readership: Aimed at people in the tobacco industry, including retailers and wholesalers.
ADVERTISING RATES:
Full Page Mono EUR 1/1: f.c. 1810,-; b/w 1290,- 1/2: f.c. 1205,-; b/w 685,-
Agency Commission: 15%
Mechanical Data: Type Area: 145 x 200mm, Bleed Size: 165 x 230mm
Copy instructions: *Copy Date:* 1 month prior to publication date
BUSINESS: BAKING & CONFECTIONERY: Confectioners & Tobacconists

TAFERELEN
18018N84A-250
Editorial: Keizersgracht 258, 1016 EV AMSTERDAM
Tel: 88 2944819 **Fax:** 30 6383991
Email: post@vrijeacademie.nl
Date Established: 01-08-1995; **Freq:** 3 issues yearly; **Cover Price:** Free; **Circ:** 40,000
Editor: A.D. Doevendans; **Editor-in-Chief:** P.A. van Duinen
Profile: Journal about plastic art, culture and the history of art.
Language(s): Dutch
Readership: Read by adults who are attending art courses and interested in museum activities.
ADVERTISING RATES:
Full Page Mono EUR 1/2: b/w 794,- 1/4: b/w 408,- 1/8: b/w 227,-
Agency Commission: 15%
CONSUMER: THE ARTS & LITERARY: Arts

TAIKO
17646N75Q-190
Editorial: Eisenhowerlaan 198-202, 3527 HK UTRECHT **Tel:** 570 673344 **Fax:** 20 5159143
Email: info@kbn.nl
Freq: Quarterly; **Circ:** 10,000
Editor-in-Chief: Diana Pluut
Profile: Official journal of the Dutch Karate-Do Organisation.
Language(s): Dutch
ADVERTISING RATES:
Full Page Mono EUR 1/1: f.c. 700,-; 1/2: f.c. 400,-; 1/4: f.c. 250,-
Agency Commission: 15%
Mechanical Data: Bleed Size: 210 x 297mm, Type Area: 185 x 270mm
CONSUMER: SPORT: Combat Sports

TALENT & PASSION
18036N84B-100
Editorial: Pastoor van der Voortlaan 16, 5591 JB HEEZE **Tel:** 320 265083 **Fax:** 342 494299
Email: info@jre.eu
Freq: Half-yearly; **Cover Price:** EUR 5,95
Annual Sub.: EUR 16,-; **Circ:** 100,000
Profile: Magazine about Dutch and international literature. Contains reviews about new books, magazines and newspapers.
Language(s): Dutch
ADVERTISING RATES:
Full Page Mono EUR 2/1: b/w 7000,- 1/1: b/w 4000,- 1/2: b/w 2500,-
Agency Commission: 15%
Mechanical Data: Type Area: 210 x 295mm, Bleed Size: 210 x 295mm
CONSUMER: THE ARTS & LITERARY: Literary

TALKIES MAGAZINE
627271N74A-280
Editorial: Schieweg 93, 2627 AT DELFT
Tel: 23 5565001 **Fax:** 20 5928600
Email: info@talkiesmagazine.nl **Web site:** http://www.talkiesmagazine.nl
Date Established: 01-01-1994; **Freq:** 6 issues yearly; **Cover Price:** EUR 4,95
Annual Sub.: EUR 25,-; **Circ:** 50,000
Editor-in-Chief: M. van de Kerkhof
Profile: Magazine containing articles on health, beauty, cosmetics, leisure and general women's issues.
Language(s): Dutch
Readership: Read mainly by women over 30 years.
ADVERTISING RATES:
Full Page Mono EUR 2/1: f.c. 9250,-; 1/1: f.c. 4950,-
Agency Commission: 15%
Mechanical Data: Type Area: 170 x 240mm, Bleed Size: 220 x 280mm
Copy instructions: *Copy Date:* 4 weeks prior to publication date
CONSUMER: WOMEN'S INTEREST CONSUMER MAGAZINES: Women's Interest

TAMTAM
1635153N91D-114
Editorial: Driebergseweg 10, 3708 JB ZEIST
Freq: 10 issues yearly; **Circ:** 110,000
Language(s): Dutch
Agency Commission: 15%
CONSUMER: RECREATION & LEISURE: Children & Youth

TANDARTSPRAKTIJK (TP)
16740N56D-55
Editorial: Pieter Calandlaan 35, 1065 KJ AMSTERDAM **Tel:** 492 338432 **Fax:** 492 338421
Web site: http://www.tandartspraktijk.nl
Freq: Monthly; **Annual Sub.:** EUR 119,95; **Circ:** 4,861
Editor: M.J.H. de Cleen; **Publisher:** P. Kalker
Profile: Practical dentistry journal.
Language(s): Dutch
Readership: Aimed at dentists.
ADVERTISING RATES:
Full Page Mono EUR 1/1: f.c. 2623,-; b/w 1339,- 1/2: f.c. 1481,-; b/w 756,- 1/4: f.c. 865,-; b/w 442,-
Agency Commission: 15%
Mechanical Data: Type Area: 185 x 267mm, Bleed Size: 210 x 297mm
BUSINESS: HEALTH & MEDICAL: Dental

TANDTECHNISCH MAGAZINE
16741N56D-60
Editorial: Postbus 658, 3700 AR ZEIST
Tel: 77 3556160 **Fax:** 77 3556152
Email: info@stpublicaffairs.nl **Web site:** http://www.tandtechnischmagazine.nl
Freq: 6 issues yearly; **Annual Sub.:** EUR 63,60; **Circ:** 9,000
Editor: J.M.C. Spijker; **Editor-in-Chief:** N.J.C. Eikmans; **Publisher:** N.J.C. Eikmans
Profile: Magazine covering all aspects of dentistry, emphasising technical aspects.
Language(s): Dutch
Readership: Aimed at dental surgeons, researchers and students.
ADVERTISING RATES:
Full Page Mono .... EUR 1/1: PMS 1179,-; 1/2: PMS 666,-; 1/4: PMS 443,-
Agency Commission: 15%
Mechanical Data: Type Area: 185 x 265mm, Bleed Size: 210 x 297mm
Copy instructions: *Copy Date:* 3 weeks prior to publication date
BUSINESS: HEALTH & MEDICAL: Dental

TECHNI-SHOW MAGAZINE
717897N27-22
Editorial: Postbus 262, 1860 AG BERGEN
Tel: 492 338432 **Fax:** 492 338421
Email: memo@euronet.nl **Web site:** http://www.technishowonline.nl
Freq: 6 issues yearly; **Annual Sub.:** EUR 26,41; **Circ:** 14,225
Editor: M. Bakker; **Editor-in-Chief:** P. van Dijk; **Publisher:** Harry Steunenberg
Profile: Newspaper containing the latest news in the metal industry about new business, jobs, events diary and new products.
Language(s): Dutch
Readership: Aimed at managers.
ADVERTISING RATES:
Full Page Mono EUR 1/1: f.c. 2900,-; 1/2: f.c. 1608,-; 1/4: f.c. 963,-
Agency Commission: 15%
Mechanical Data: Type Area: 240 x 340mm
BUSINESS: METAL, IRON & STEEL

TEGELTOTAAL
1659572N12A-86
Editorial: Marconistraat 33, 3771 AM BARNEVELD
Tel: 342 494848 **Fax:** 342 494299
Email: i@bdu.nl **Web site:** http://www.vakbladtegeltotaal.nl
Freq: 6 issues yearly; **Annual Sub.:** EUR 30,68; **Circ:** 3,761
Editor: Peter Vorstenbosch; **Editor-in-Chief:** Ingmar van der Hoek; **Publisher:** Ton Roskam
Language(s): Dutch
ADVERTISING RATES:
Full Page Mono EUR 1/1: b/w 1958,- 1/2: b/w 1173,- 1/4: b/w 702,-
Agency Commission: 15%
Mechanical Data: Type Area: 190 x 270mm, Bleed Size: 230 x 310mm
BUSINESS: CERAMICS, POTTERY & GLASS: Ceramics & Pottery

TELECOMMAGAZINE
16046N18B-240
Editorial: Lemelerberg 19-23, 2402 ZN ALPHEN A/D RIJN **Tel:** 23 5567955 **Fax:** 23 5567956
Email: array@array.nl **Web site:** http://www.telecommagazine.nl
Freq: 10 issues yearly; **Cover Price:** EUR 13,50
Annual Sub.: EUR 87,50; **Circ:** 4,621
Editor: Eric van der Steen; **Editor-in-Chief:** Rob Zandvliet; **Publisher:** Werner Schoots
Profile: Magazine covering data and telecommunications, system integration, EDI, VANs, ISDN and cabling.
Language(s): Dutch
Readership: Aimed at telecommunications managers.
ADVERTISING RATES:
Full Page Mono EUR 1/1: b/w 3650,- 1/2: b/w 2295,- 1/4: b/w 1335,-
Agency Commission: 15%
Mechanical Data: Type Area: 190 x 265mm, Bleed Size: 210 x 285mm
BUSINESS: ELECTRONICS: Telecommunications

TELECOMMERCE
16044N18B-250
Editorial: Pelmolenlaan 1m, 3447 GW WOERDEN
Tel: 348 485080 **Fax:** 79 3467846
Email: klantenservice@bbp.nl **Web site:** http://www.telecommerce.nl
Date Established: 10-04-2001; **Freq:** 11 issues yearly; **Annual Sub.:** EUR 99,-; **Circ:** 10,760
Editor: Maxim Renders; **Editor-in-Chief:** E. van der Bij; **Publisher:** Paul Petermeijer
Profile: Magazine covering the latest developments in interactive direct media for particular use in client contact, networking, marketing and service. Includes CRM, e-commerce, telecommunications, mobile commerce, database-marketing, e-mail marketing, datawarehousing, customer service and helpdesk, direct marketing and loyalties.
Language(s): Dutch
Readership: Aimed at managers, middle managers and marketing executives.
ADVERTISING RATES:
Full Page Mono EUR 1/1: f.c. 3385,-; 1/2: f.c. 2380,-
Agency Commission: 15%
Mechanical Data: Type Area: 180 x 240mm, Bleed Size: 210 x 285mm
BUSINESS: ELECTRONICS: Telecommunications

DE TELEFOONGIDS
1635379N94X-356
Editorial: Condensatorweg 54, 1014 AX AMSTERDAM **Tel:** 88 2697049 **Fax:** 70 3544642
Web site: http://www.detelefoongids.nl
Freq: Annual; **Cover Price:** Free; **Circ:** 8,300,000
Language(s): Dutch
Agency Commission: 15%
CONSUMER: OTHER CLASSIFICATIONS: Miscellaneous

DE TELEGRAAF
17042N65A-50
Editorial: Basisweg 30, 1043 AP AMSTERDAM
Tel: 20 5852111 **Fax:** 20 5854158
Web site: http://www.telegraaf.nl
Freq: 312 issues yearly; **Annual Sub.:** EUR 277,-; **Circ:** 648,958
Editor: Sjuul Paradijs; **Editor-in-Chief:** Jessica Kolenberg
Profile: Broadsheet-sized newspaper providing national and international news. Includes financial, cultural, political and social information and opinion.
Language(s): Dutch
Readership: Aimed at a broad sector of society, including public sector employees and students.
Agency Commission: 15%
Mechanical Data: Type Area: 398 x 550mm
NATIONAL DAILY & SUNDAY NEWSPAPERS: National Daily Newspapers

TENNIS MAGAZINE
17612N75H-75
Editorial: Het Spoor 2, 3994 AK HOUTEN
Tel: 35 6726900 **Fax:** 20 5854158
Email: info@springermedia.nl **Web site:** http://www.tennismagazine.nl
Freq: 8 issues yearly; **Annual Sub.:** EUR 32,50; **Circ:** 70,199
Editor: Karianne van der Zant
Profile: Official journal of the Dutch Lawn Tennis Association.
Language(s): Dutch
ADVERTISING RATES:
Full Page Mono EUR 1/1: f.c. 4773,-; 1/2: f.c. 2545,-; 1/4: f.c. 1377,-
Agency Commission: 15%
Mechanical Data: Type Area: 190 x 260mm, Bleed Size: 210 x 280mm
Copy instructions: *Copy Date:* 1 month prior to publication date
CONSUMER: SPORT: Racquet Sports

TERDEGE
18101N87-500
Editorial: Laan van Westenenk 12, 7336 AZ APELDOORN **Tel:** 55 5390222 **Fax:** 570 614795
Email: info@terburg.nl **Web site:** http://www.terdege.nl
Freq: 26 issues yearly; **Annual Sub.:** EUR 71,50; **Circ:** 28,842
Editor: W.B. Kranendonk; **Editor-in-Chief:** W.A.F. Lemstra
Profile: Christian magazine focusing on family issues.
Language(s): Dutch
Readership: Aimed at Christian families.

ADVERTISING RATES:
Full Page Mono EUR 2/1: f.c. 4745,-; 1/1: f.c. 2835,-; b/w 1390,- 1/2: f.c. 1420,-; b/w 745,-
Agency Commission: 15%
Mechanical Data: Type Area: 180 x 267mm, Bleed Size: 210 x 297mm
CONSUMER: RELIGIOUS

TERRE MAGAZINE
1635165N1P-68
Editorial: Zoutmanstraat 42-44, 2518 GS DEN HAAG
Tel: 35 6726900 **Fax:** 20 5854158
Email: info@tdh.nl
Freq: 3 issues yearly; **Circ:** 80,000
Usual Pagination: 20
Editor: Taco van der Mark
Language(s): Dutch
Agency Commission: 15%
BUSINESS: FINANCE & ECONOMICS: Fundraising

TEXELNU
1899336N50-183
Editorial: Burgwal 37, 1791 AH DEN BURG
Tel: 30 6383716 **Fax:** 73 6157171
Email: info@ziltezaken.nl **Web site:** http://www.texelnu.nl
Freq: Quarterly; **Cover Price:** Free; **Circ:** 50,000
Usual Pagination: 40
Language(s): Dutch
ADVERTISING RATES:
Full Page Mono EUR 1/1 per jaar: b/w 3225,- 1/2 per jaar: b/w 2040,- 1/3 per jaar: b/w 1425,-
Agency Commission: 15%
Mechanical Data: Type Area: 261 x 383mm
BUSINESS: TRAVEL & TOURISM

TEXPRESS
16533N47A-110
Editorial: Nijenburg 2h, 1081 GG AMSTERDAM
Tel: 35 6726900 **Fax:** 20 5854158
Web site: http://www.texpress.nl
Date Established: 01-01-1957; **Freq:** Monthly; **Annual Sub.:** EUR 172,50; **Circ:** 891
Editor: Hans Huitenga; **Publisher:** Hans Huitenga
Profile: Magazine providing technical and economic news on the textile and clothing industries.
Language(s): Dutch
ADVERTISING RATES:
Full Page Mono .... EUR 1/1: f.c. 2310,-; f.c. color 2050,-; b/w 1845,- 1/2: f.c. 1455,-; f.c. color 1195,-; b/w 990,- 1/4:
Agency Commission: 15%
Mechanical Data: Type Area: 210 x 290mm, Bleed Size: 240 x 320mm
BUSINESS: CLOTHING & TEXTILES

TEXTIELBEHEER
16237N28-30
Editorial: Molenstraat 29, 4061 AB OPHEMERT
Tel: 77 3556160 **Fax:** 77 3556152
Email: menp@menp.nl **Web site:** http://www.textielbeheer.nl
Freq: 8 issues yearly; **Annual Sub.:** EUR 123,-; **Circ:** 1,650
Usual Pagination: 40
Editor: P.N.M. Wennekes; **Publisher:** P.N.M. Wennekes
Profile: Magazine containing articles about laundries, chemical cleaning and the environment.
Language(s): Dutch
Readership: Readers include managers and directors in the textile care, cleaning and rental industries.
ADVERTISING RATES:
Full Page Mono EUR 1/1: b/w 890,- 1/2: b/w 518,- 1/4: b/w 347,-
Agency Commission: 15%
Mechanical Data: Type Area: 186 x 267mm, Bleed Size: 210 x 297mm
Copy instructions: *Copy Date:* 3 weeks prior to publication date
BUSINESS: LAUNDRY & DRY CLEANING

TEXTILIA
16535N47A-170
Editorial: Joan Muyskenweg 22, 1096 CJ AMSTERDAM **Tel:** 35 6726900 **Fax:** 20 5854158
Web site: http://www.textilia.nl
Date Established: 01-01-1921; **Freq:** 24 issues yearly; **Cover Price:** EUR 3,22
Annual Sub.: EUR 150,80; **Circ:** 5,191
Editor: Rosanne Loffeld; **Editor-in-Chief:** Ellen den Berg
Profile: Publication covering textiles and ready-to-wear fashion.
Language(s): Dutch
ADVERTISING RATES:
Full Page Mono EUR 2/1: b/w 8150,- 1/1: b/w 5080,- 1/2: b/w 2650,-
Agency Commission: 15%
Mechanical Data: Type Area: 202 x 268mm, Bleed Size: 230 x 300mm
BUSINESS: CLOTHING & TEXTILES

THEMA - NVTF
17829N79C-100
Editorial: Amalia van Solmslaan 13, 9602 GM HOOGEZAND **Tel:** 570 648866
Date Established: 01-02-1988; **Freq:** 5 issues yearly; **Annual Sub.:** EUR 28,-; **Circ:** 1,000
Editor: F. Warmenhoven
Profile: Official journal of the NVTF - the Dutch Society of Thematic Philately.
Language(s): Dutch
Readership: Read by stamp collectors.
ADVERTISING RATES:
Full Page Mono .. EUR 1/1: b/w 134,- 1/2: b/w 71,- 1/4: b/w 40,-
Agency Commission: 15%
Mechanical Data: Type Area: 184 x 262mm, Bleed Size: 210 x 297mm
CONSUMER: HOBBIES & DIY: Philately

THERMIEK
17641N75N-250
Editorial: Papendallaan 50, 6816 VD ARNHEM
Tel: 35 6726900 **Fax:** 20 5854158
Email: knvvlth@xs4all.nl
Freq: Quarterly; **Annual Sub.:** EUR 20,-; **Circ:** 4,250
Editor: Frits Snijder; **Editor-in-Chief:** Frits Snijder
Profile: Magazine focusing on all aspects of gliding, including training, new developments and safety.
Language(s): Dutch
Readership: Aimed at glider pilots in The Netherlands and members of the Royal Netherlands Aeronautical Association.
Agency Commission: 15%
Mechanical Data: Bleed Size: 210 x 297mm
CONSUMER: SPORT: Flight

THERMISCH VERZINKEN
16234N27-55
Editorial: Smederijstraat 2, 4814 DB BREDA
Tel: 570 647730 **Fax:** 570 647815
Web site: http://www.thermisch-verzinken.nl
Freq: Quarterly; **Cover Price:** Free; **Circ:** 4,000
Usual Pagination: 64
Editor: Gerard Reimerink; **Publisher:** Gerard Reimerink
Profile: Publication with technical information concerning hot dip galvanising.
Language(s): Dutch
Readership: Aimed at professionals in the metal industry and architects.
Agency Commission: 15%
BUSINESS: METAL, IRON & STEEL

' THUIS MAGAZINE
1637193N74Q-276
Editorial: Postmastraat 50, 4105 DW CULEMBORG
Tel: 570 647659 **Fax:** 570 647803
Email: info@alivra.nl **Web site:** http://www.thuisselect.nl
Date Established: 01-09-2001; **Freq:** Quarterly; **Cover Price:** EUR 4,75; **Circ:** 97,880
Editor: J. de Vreugd
Language(s): Dutch
ADVERTISING RATES:
Full Page Mono EUR 2/1: f.c. 6500,-; 1/1: f.c. 3750,-; 1/2: f.c. 2250,-
Agency Commission: 15%
Mechanical Data: Type Area: 190 x 264mm, Bleed Size: 210 x 297mm
CONSUMER: WOMEN'S INTEREST CONSUMER MAGAZINES: Lifestyle

TIJDSCHRIFT ADMINISTRATIE
16282N32A-134
Editorial: Staverenstraat 32015, 7418 CJ DEVENTER
Tel: 570 648902 **Fax:** 570 614795
Email: info@kluwer.nl
Freq: 10 issues yearly; **Annual Sub.:** EUR 155,66; **Circ:** 3,515
Editor-in-Chief: Marjorie Berghuis; **Publisher:** Freek Talsma
Profile: Magazine covering all aspects of financial management at administration level within companies and government.
Language(s): Dutch
Readership: Aimed at company managers and government administrators.
ADVERTISING RATES:
Full Page Mono EUR 1/1: f.c. 2700,-; b/w 1600,- 1/2: f.c. 1600,-; b/w 1000,- 1/4: f.c. 925,-; b/w 600,-
Agency Commission: 15%
Mechanical Data: Type Area: 180 x 260mm, Bleed Size: 210 x 297mm
BUSINESS: LOCAL GOVERNMENT, LEISURE & RECREATION: Local Government

TIJDSCHRIFT CONTROLLING
15501N1B-55
Editorial: Staverenstraat 32015, 7418 CJ DEVENTER
Tel: 570 648953 **Fax:** 570 614795
Email: info@kluwer.nl
Freq: 10 issues yearly; **Annual Sub.:** EUR 168,87; **Circ:** 2,406
Editor: Anja Jalink; **Publisher:** Freek Talsma
Profile: Official journal of the NGA - the Society of Finance Administration Managers in the Netherlands.
Language(s): Dutch
ADVERTISING RATES:
Full Page Mono EUR 1/1: f.c. 2900,-; b/w 1800,- 1/2: f.c. 1750,-; b/w 1100,- 1/4: f.c. 950,-; b/w 600,-
Agency Commission: 15%
Mechanical Data: Type Area: 180 x 260mm, Bleed Size: 210 x 297mm
BUSINESS: FINANCE & ECONOMICS: Accountancy

TIJDSCHRIFT OUDE MUZIEK
16899N61-150
Editorial: Mariaplaats 23, 3511 LK UTRECHT
Tel: 10 2435550 **Fax:** 10 2435565
Email: info@oudemuziek.nl
Date Established: 01-01-1985; **Freq:** Quarterly; **Annual Sub.:** EUR 30,-; **Circ:** 5,000
Editor: J. van der Klis; **Editor-in-Chief:** J. van der Klis
Profile: Trade journal about early and classical music. Contains interviews, news and information concerning the history of music.
Language(s): Dutch
Readership: Professionals and amateurs interested in this music.
ADVERTISING RATES:
Full Page Mono .... EUR 1/1: f.c. 885,-; b/w 500,- 1/2: f.c. 500,-; b/w 380,-
Agency Commission: 15%
Mechanical Data: Type Area: 145 x 220mm, Bleed Size: 170 x 240mm
BUSINESS: MUSIC TRADE

TIJDSCHRIFT VOOR AGRARISCH RECHT
16086N21A-16
Editorial: Postbus 245, 6700 AE WAGENINGEN
Tel: 70 3780541 **Fax:** 70 3789783
Email: info@iar.nl
Freq: Monthly; **Annual Sub.:** EUR 358,-; **Circ:** 600
Editor: G.M.F. Snijders; **Editor-in-Chief:** D.W. Bruil
Profile: Journal about the law relating to agriculture.
Language(s): Dutch
ADVERTISING RATES:
Full Page Mono .... EUR 1/1: b/w 1040,-
Agency Commission: 15%
Mechanical Data: Type Area: 180 x 270mm, Bleed Size: 210 x 297mm
BUSINESS: AGRICULTURE & FARMING

TIJDSCHRIFT VOOR BEDRIJFS- EN VERZEKERINGS-GENEESKUNDE
15518N1D-58
Editorial: Het Spoor 2, 3994 AK HOUTEN
Tel: 172 466539 **Fax:** 172 463270
Freq: 10 issues yearly; **Annual Sub.:** EUR 99,75; **Circ:** 2,917
Editor: Nico Croon; **Publisher:** Karin Verhoeven
Profile: Journal about medical insurance and occupational health.
Language(s): Dutch
ADVERTISING RATES:
Full Page Mono EUR 1/1: f.c. 2533,-; b/w 1095,- 1/2: f.c. 1512,-; b/w 655,- 1/1: f.c. 861,-; b/w 373,-
Agency Commission: 15%
Mechanical Data: Type Area: 180 x 254mm, Bleed Size: 210 x 297mm
BUSINESS: FINANCE & ECONOMICS: Insurance

TIJDSCHRIFT VOOR DE POLITIE
16305N32F-60
Editorial: Radarweg 29, 1043 NX AMSTERDAM
Tel: 20 5159189 **Fax:** 314 349037
Email: info@reedbusiness.nl **Web site:** http://www.tijdschriftvoordepolitie.nl
Freq: 10 issues yearly; **Cover Price:** EUR 30,45
Annual Sub.: EUR 170,10; **Circ:** 3,679
Editor: B. Wijbenga; **Editor-in-Chief:** Max Rozenboom; **Publisher:** Heleen Kooistra
Profile: Independent journal covering policing, public order, security and law enforcement. Also contains features on new developments in police management in the Netherlands.
Language(s): Dutch
ADVERTISING RATES:
Full Page Mono .... EUR 1/1: f.c. 2298,-; f.c. color 1613,-; b/w 957,- 1/2: f.c. 1898,-; f.c. color 1214,-; b/w 559,- 1/4: f
Agency Commission: 15%
Mechanical Data: Type Area: 195,5 x 299mm, Bleed Size: 220 x 320mm
Copy instructions: *Copy Date:* 2 weeks prior to publication date
BUSINESS: LOCAL GOVERNMENT, LEISURE & RECREATION: Police

TIJDSCHRIFT VOOR DE VOLKSHUISVESTING
15665N4D-127
Editorial: Binckhorstlaan 36, 2516 BE DEN HAAG
Tel: 570 673344 **Fax:** 570 677062
Email: info@nirov.nl **Web site:** http://www.nirov.nl/tvv
Freq: 6 issues yearly; **Annual Sub.:** EUR 90,-; **Circ:** 1,800
Editor: Marja Elsinga; **Editor-in-Chief:** Eduard Herkes
Profile: Housing and planning magazine.
Language(s): Dutch
Readership: Read by accountants, members of councils and housing associations.
ADVERTISING RATES:
Full Page Mono .. EUR 1/1: b/w 1025,- 1/2: b/w 625,-
Agency Commission: 15%
Mechanical Data: Type Area: 190 x 277mm, Bleed Size: 210 x 297mm
BUSINESS: ARCHITECTURE & BUILDING: Planning & Housing

TIJDSCHRIFT VOOR DIERGENEESKUNDE
17008N64H-50
Editorial: De Molen 77, 3995 AW HOUTEN
Tel: 20 5159189 **Fax:** 314 349037
Email: info@knmvd.nl
Freq: 24 issues yearly; **Cover Price:** EUR 7,95
Annual Sub.: EUR 175,-; **Circ:** 5,500
Editor: H. Geertsen; **Editor-in-Chief:** Miel Bingen
Profile: Magazine about all aspects of veterinary science.
Language(s): Dutch
ADVERTISING RATES:
Full Page Mono EUR 1/1: f.c. 2170,-; b/w 1525,- 1/2 f.c. 1410,-; b/w 995,- 1/4: f.c. 915,-; b/w 635,-
Agency Commission: 15%
Mechanical Data: Type Area: 174 x 256mm, Bleed Size: 210 x 297mm
Copy instructions: *Copy Date:* 3 weeks prior to publication date
BUSINESS: OTHER CLASSIFICATIONS: Veterinary

TIJDSCHRIFT VOOR ERGONOMIE
15923N14E-100
Editorial: Luytelaer 20, 5632 BG EINDHOVEN
Tel: 88 2697049 **Fax:** 70 3544642
Email: nvve@planet.nl
Date Established: 01-01-1976; **Freq:** Quarterly; **Annual Sub.:** EUR 75,-; **Circ:** 800
Editor: Ingeborg Griffioen
Profile: Journal containing information on all aspects of ergonomics.
Language(s): Dutch
Readership: Aimed at professionals in the ergonomics field.
ADVERTISING RATES:
Full Page Mono EUR 1/1: b/w 735,- 1/2: b/w 515,- 1/4: b/w 405,-
Agency Commission: 15%
Mechanical Data: Type Area: 190 x 275mm, Bleed Size: 210 x 297mm
BUSINESS: COMMERCE, INDUSTRY & MANAGEMENT: Work Study

TIJDSCHRIFT VOOR GERONTOLOGIE EN GERIATRIE
768346N56A-311
Editorial: Het Spoor 2, 3994 AK HOUTEN
Tel: 10 4274128 **Fax:** 88 7518231
Date Established: 01-01-1969; **Freq:** 6 issues yearly; **Annual Sub.:** EUR 92,-; **Circ:** 1,070
Profile: Magazine covering ageing and geriatric medicine.
Language(s): Dutch
ADVERTISING RATES:
Full Page Mono .. EUR 1/1: b/w 1249,- 1/2: b/w 635,- 1/4: b/w 383,-
Agency Commission: 15%
Mechanical Data: Type Area: 170 x 270mm, Bleed Size: 210 x 297mm
BUSINESS: HEALTH & MEDICAL

TIJDSCHRIFT VOOR KINDERGENEESKUNDE
1635211N56A-355
Editorial: Het Spoor 2, 3994 AK HOUTEN
Tel: 30 6383838 **Fax:** 30 6383839
Freq: 6 issues yearly; **Annual Sub.:** EUR 107,10; **Circ:** 2,443
Editor: J.M.T. Draaisma
Language(s): Dutch
ADVERTISING RATES:
Full Page Mono .. EUR 1/1: f.c. 2610,-; b/w 962,- 1/2: f.c. 2252,-; b/w 605,- 1/4: f.c. 2015,-; b/w 367,-
Agency Commission: 15%
Mechanical Data: Type Area: 167 x 230mm, Bleed Size: 195 x 265mm
Copy instructions: *Copy Date:* 4 weeks prior to publication date
BUSINESS: HEALTH & MEDICAL

TIJDSCHRIFT VOOR MANAGEMENT DEVELOPMENT
15899N14A-247
Editorial: Naarderstraat 296, 1272 NT HUIZEN
Tel: 23 5564919 **Fax:** 23 5564911
Email: mail@emdcentre.com **Web site:** http://www.emdcentre.com/MD.aspx
Date Established: 01-06-1993; **Freq:** Quarterly; **Annual Sub.:** EUR 82,-; **Circ:** 800
Usual Pagination: 44
Editor: Rino Schreuder; **Publisher:** Yvonne Kuijsters
Profile: Publication of the European Management Development Centre.
Language(s): Dutch
ADVERTISING RATES:
Full Page Mono .... EUR 1/1: b/w 595,- 1/2: b/w 350,-
Agency Commission: 15%
Mechanical Data: Type Area: 165 x 200mm, Bleed Size: 200 x 230mm
BUSINESS: COMMERCE, INDUSTRY & MANAGEMENT

TIJDSCHRIFT VOOR MARKETING
15593N2A-80
Editorial: Kon. Wilhelminaplein 30, 1062 KR AMSTERDAM **Tel:** 20 5733686 **Fax:** 20 6752709
Web site: http://www.marketing-online.nl
Date Established: 01-01-1967; **Freq:** 11 issues yearly; **Cover Price:** EUR 17,-
Annual Sub.: EUR 147,50; **Circ:** 11,364
Editor: Theo van Vugt; **Editor-in-Chief:** Kari-Anne Fygi; **Publisher:** Rogier Mulder
Profile: Official journal of the Netherlands Marketing Institute. Contains technical articles, company reports, essays and interviews.
Language(s): Dutch
Readership: Read by marketing managers.

ADVERTISING RATES:
Full Page Mono EUR 1/1: b/w 2400,- 1/2: b/w 1400,- 1/4: b/w 800,-
Agency Commission: 15%
Mechanical Data: Type Area: 190 x 268mm, Bleed Size: 210 x 297mm
Copy instructions: *Copy Date:* 3 weeks prior to publication date
BUSINESS: COMMUNICATIONS, ADVERTISING & MARKETING

TIJDSCHRIFT VOOR NUCLEAIRE GENEESKUNDE
16708N56A-237
Editorial: Napoleonsweg 128a, 6086 AJ NEER
Tel: 172 575581 **Fax:** 23 5565136
Email: info@kloosterhof.nl
Freq: Quarterly; **Cover Price:** EUR 13,50
Annual Sub.: EUR 45,-; **Circ:** 1,500
Profile: Journal covering nuclear medicine.
Language(s): Dutch
Readership: Read by nuclear medical scientists, academics involved with nuclear medical science and other nuclear medical workers.
ADVERTISING RATES:
Full Page Mono .. EUR 1/1: b/w 1050,- 1/2: b/w 550,- 1/4: b/w 345,-
Agency Commission: 15%
Mechanical Data: Type Area: 185 x 270mm, Bleed Size: 210 x 297mm
BUSINESS: HEALTH & MEDICAL

TIJDSCHRIFT VOOR ORTHOMOLECULAIRE GENEESKUNDE
633790N56A-141
Editorial: Wormerweg 1, 1311 XA ALMERE
Tel: 88 7518800 **Fax:** 20 5353696
Email: secretariaat@soe.nl
Freq: 6 issues yearly; **Cover Price:** EUR 7,65
Annual Sub.: EUR 36,60; **Circ:** 2,200
Editor: Wolfgang Diekstra
Profile: Publication focusing on healing with vitamins and minerals, called orthomolecular healing.
Language(s): Dutch
Readership: Read by doctors and therapists.
ADVERTISING RATES:
Full Page Mono .. EUR 1/1: f.c. 1110,-; 1/2: f.c. 625,-; 1/4: f.c. 370,-
Agency Commission: 15%
Mechanical Data: Type Area: 185 x 265mm, Bleed Size: 210 x 295mm
BUSINESS: HEALTH & MEDICAL

TIJDSCHRIFT VOOR OUDERENGENEESKUNDE
1636372N56B-169
Editorial: Mercatorlaan 1200, 3502 LB UTRECHT
Tel: 70 3480719 **Fax:** 35 6474569
Email: redactie@verpleeghuisartsen.nl
Freq: 6 issues yearly; **Annual Sub.:** EUR 51,50; **Circ:** 1,798
Editor: J.W.P.M. Konings; **Publisher:** Gina Doedens
Language(s): Dutch
ADVERTISING RATES:
Full Page Mono EUR 1/1: f.c. 1941,-; b/w 1374,- 1/2: f.c. 993,-; b/w 704,- 1/4: f.c. 597,-; b/w 424,-
Agency Commission: 15%
Mechanical Data: Type Area: 185 x 270mm, Bleed Size: 210 x 297mm
BUSINESS: HEALTH & MEDICAL: Nursing

TIJDSCHRIFT VOOR PSYCHIATRIE
719358N56N-160
Editorial: Postbus 20062, 3502 LB UTRECHT
Tel: 20 5733686 **Fax:** 20 6752709
Email: info@tijdschriftvoorpsychiatrie.nl **Web site:** http://www.tijdschriftvoorpsychiatrie.nl
Freq: Monthly; **Annual Sub.:** EUR 129,50; **Circ:** 4,404
Editor: P.N. van Harten; **Editor-in-Chief:** M. Kabos; **Publisher:** N.F. van 't Zet
Profile: Scientific publication focusing on studies and research into Psychiatry.
Language(s): Dutch
Readership: Read by psychiatrists and psychologists.
ADVERTISING RATES:
Full Page Mono EUR 1/1: b/w 948,- 1/2: b/w 525,- 1/4: b/w 330,-
Agency Commission: 15%
Mechanical Data: Type Area: 155 x 225mm, Bleed Size: 195 x 265mm
Copy instructions: *Copy Date:* 3 weeks prior to publication date
BUSINESS: HEALTH & MEDICAL: Mental Health

TIJDSCHRIFT VOOR REMEDIAL TEACHING
16922N62G-150
Editorial: Kosterijland 7a, 3981 AJ BUNNIK
Tel: 229 270002 **Fax:** 20 6767728
Email: bureau@lbrt.nl
Date Established: 21-03-1993; **Freq:** 5 issues yearly; **Annual Sub.:** EUR 47,50; **Circ:** 6,400
Editor: Petra van Ree
Profile: Journal focusing on special needs children and children with learning disabilities.
Language(s): Dutch
Readership: Read predominantly by remedial teachers.
ADVERTISING RATES:
Full Page Mono EUR 1/1: b/w 935,- 1/2: b/w 515,- 1/4: b/w 285,-
Agency Commission: 15%
Mechanical Data: Bleed Size: 210 x 297mm, Type Area: 184 x 263mm
Copy instructions: *Copy Date:* 3 weeks prior to publication date
BUSINESS: CHURCH & SCHOOL EQUIPMENT & EDUCATION: Special Needs Education

TIJDSCHRIFT VOOR UROLOGIE
16699N56A-123_50
Editorial: Het Spoor 2, 3994 AK HOUTEN
Tel: 88 2696139 **Fax:** 88 2697175
Freq: 8 issues yearly; **Cover Price:** EUR 14,10
Annual Sub.: EUR 58,90; **Circ:** 1,061
Editor: H.G. van der Poel
Profile: Journal covering all aspects of urology.
Language(s): Dutch
Readership: Read by specialists and members of the medical profession.
ADVERTISING RATES:
Full Page Mono EUR 1/1: f.c. 3503,-; b/w 1693,- 1/2: f.c. 2881,-; b/w 969,- 1/4: f.c. 2435,-; b/w 521,-
Agency Commission: 15%
Mechanical Data: Type Area: 184 x 272mm, Bleed Size: 210 x 297mm
BUSINESS: HEALTH & MEDICAL

TIMMERFABRIKANT
16524N46-70
Editorial: Marconistraat 33, 3771 AM BARNEVELD
Tel: 342 494848 **Fax:** 13 4668385
Email: i@bdu.nl **Web site:** http://www.timmerfabrikant.nl
Freq: 11 issues yearly; **Annual Sub.:** EUR 69,46; **Circ:** 1,133
Editor: Albert Schuurman; **Publisher:** Ton Roskam
Profile: Publication of the NBvT - the Association of Joinery Manufacturers.
Language(s): Dutch
ADVERTISING RATES:
Full Page Mono EUR 1/1: b/w 998,- 1/2: b/w 567,- 1/4: b/w 353,-
Agency Commission: 15%
Mechanical Data: Type Area: 180 x 262mm, Bleed Size: 210 x 297mm
Copy instructions: *Copy Date:* 3 weeks prior to publication date
BUSINESS: TIMBER, WOOD & FORESTRY

TINA
627268N91D-72_80
Editorial: Capellalaan 65, 2132 JL HOOFDDORP
Tel: 23 5566770 **Fax:** 23 5565155
Web site: http://www.tina.nl
Freq: Weekly; **Cover Price:** EUR 2,30
Annual Sub.: EUR 109,20; **Circ:** 45,751
Editor: Joan Lommen; **Publisher:** Suzan Schouten
Profile: Magazine containing articles about pop stars, beauty and fashion.
Language(s): Dutch
Readership: Read by girls aged 10 to 14 years.
ADVERTISING RATES:
Full Page Mono EUR 2/1: b/w 7500,- 1/1: b/w 3750,- 1/2: b/w 2250,-
Agency Commission: 15%
Mechanical Data: Type Area: 190 x 240mm, Bleed Size: 210 x 260mm
CONSUMER: RECREATION & LEISURE: Children & Youth

TIPS & TRUCS
760565N5D-230
Editorial: Transformatorweg 80, 1014 AK AMSTERDAM **Tel:** 23 5461122
Email: info@idg.nl **Web site:** http://www.tipsentrucs.nl
Freq: 11 issues yearly; **Cover Price:** EUR 3,45
Annual Sub.: EUR 42,95; **Circ:** 55,857
Editor: Jeroen de Jager; **Editor-in-Chief:** J. Wensink
Profile: Magazine featuring information concerning the practical application of computer hardware and software. Provides useful information on installing a new computer as well as tips on the optimal use of Windows and other software applications.
Language(s): Dutch
Readership: Aimed at computer users.
ADVERTISING RATES:
Full Page Mono EUR 2/1: f.c. 6899,-; 1/1: f.c. 3825,-; 1/2: f.c. 2295,-
Agency Commission: 15%
Mechanical Data: Type Area: 184 x 260mm, Bleed Size: 210 x 285mm
BUSINESS: COMPUTERS & AUTOMATION: Personal Computers

TOBE
1857905N84A-385
Editorial: Doetinchemseweg 59, 7007 CB DOETINCHEM **Tel:** 0032 34660066
Web site: http://www.tobemagazine.nl
Date Established: 15-09-2008; **Freq:** Half-yearly; **Cover Price:** EUR 4,95; **Circ:** 60,000
Editor: Wim Huijser; **Publisher:** Ad van der Salm
Language(s): Dutch
ADVERTISING RATES:
Full Page Mono EUR 1/1: f.c. 6640,-; 1/2: f.c. 3745,-; 1/4: f.c. 2135,-
Agency Commission: 15%
Mechanical Data: Type Area: 204 x 273mm, Bleed Size: 230 x 285mm
Copy instructions: *Copy Date:* 3 weeks prior to publication date
CONSUMER: THE ARTS & LITERARY: Arts

TOEN & NU '40-'45
17840N79H-80
Editorial: Postbus 188, 6800 AD OOSTERBEEK
Tel: 30 2531826 **Fax:** 23 5565319
Email: si@sipublicaties.nl
Freq: Quarterly; **Annual Sub.:** EUR 21,25; **Circ:** 9,000
Editor: K. Margry; **Publisher:** J. Boissevain
Profile: Military history magazine, particularly concerned with articles connected with World War II.
Language(s): Dutch
Agency Commission: 15%
CONSUMER: HOBBIES & DIY: Military History

TOERACTIEF
1637095N77C-79
Editorial: Wassenaarseweg 220, 2596 EC DEN HAAG **Tel:** 88 2696665 **Fax:** 88 2696946
Web site: http://www.toeractief.nl
Freq: 6 issues yearly; **Cover Price:** EUR 5,65
Annual Sub.: EUR 46,35; **Circ:** 52,276
Editor: B. Gorissen; **Editor-in-Chief:** O. Visser; **Publisher:** Vincent van der Meys
Language(s): Dutch
ADVERTISING RATES:
Full Page Mono EUR 2/1: f.c. 6708,-; 1/1: f.c. 3354,-; 1/2: f.c. 2011,-
Agency Commission: 15%
Mechanical Data: Type Area: 176 x 250mm, Bleed Size: 215 x 285mm
CONSUMER: MOTORING & CYCLING: Cycling

TOETS
16821N57-22_75
Editorial: Kapteijnstraat 32, 2313 RN LEIDEN
Tel: 70 3780586
Email: toets@aeneas.nl
Freq: Quarterly; **Cover Price:** EUR 37,-
Annual Sub.: EUR 120,-; **Circ:** 745
Editor: Diederik Bel; **Editor-in-Chief:** Janneke Klunder; **Publisher:** Æbele Kluwer
Profile: Magazine containing news and information about campaigns to protect the environment.
Language(s): Dutch
ADVERTISING RATES:
Full Page Mono EUR 2/1: f.c. 4305,-; 1/1: f.c. 2580,-; 1/2: f.c. 1420,-
Agency Commission: 15%
Mechanical Data: Type Area: 206 x 277mm, Bleed Size: 225 x 297mm
Copy instructions: *Copy Date:* 3 weeks prior to publication date
BUSINESS: ENVIRONMENT & POLLUTION

TON
1703297N49A-118
Editorial: Maliebaan 9, 3581 CA UTRECHT
Tel: 23 5425105 **Fax:** 23 5519544
Email: info@boss-wijnhoven.nl **Web site:** http://www.tonmagazine.nl
Date Established: 25-08-2005; **Freq:** 6 issues yearly; **Annual Sub.:** EUR 22,50; **Circ:** 140,200
Usual Pagination: 52
Editor: G. Wijnhoven; **Editor-in-Chief:** Marlies Lolkema; **Publisher:** G. Wijnhoven
Language(s): Dutch
ADVERTISING RATES:
Full Page Mono .... EUR 2/1: f.c. 11.201,-; 1/1: f.c. 5850,-; 1/2: f.c. 3550,-
Agency Commission: 15%
Mechanical Data: Type Area: 200 x 240mm, Bleed Size: 230 x 270mm
Copy instructions: *Copy Date:* 3 weeks prior to publication date
BUSINESS: TRANSPORT

TONEELSCHUUR/ FILMSCHUUR
17021N64K-90
Editorial: Lange Begijnestraat 9, 2011 HH HAARLEM
Tel: 20 5159172 **Fax:** 20 5159145
Email: informatie@toneelschuur.nl **Web site:** http://www.toneelschuur.nl
Freq: 6 issues yearly; **Annual Sub.:** EUR 20,-; **Circ:** 15,000
Editor: Kirsten Bootsma
Profile: Magazine focusing on the entertainment industry, with particular emphasis on theatre and cinema.
Language(s): Dutch
Agency Commission: 15%
BUSINESS: OTHER CLASSIFICATIONS: Cinema Entertainment

TOP HAIR BENELUX
16010N15B-100
Editorial: Spinneweil 30, 1251 DB LAREN
Tel: 172 466405 **Fax:** 172 466577
Email: info@tophair.nl **Web site:** http://www.tophair.nl
Freq: 11 issues yearly; **Cover Price:** EUR 10,50
Annual Sub.: EUR 93,-; **Circ:** 4,500
Editor: Wolfgang Peppmeier; **Publisher:** Aldert Faassen
Profile: Magazine covering all aspects of the hairdressing trade.
Language(s): Dutch
Readership: Aimed at hairdressers.
ADVERTISING RATES:
Full Page Mono .. EUR 1/1: b/w 1095,- 1/2: b/w 570,- 1/4: b/w 290,-
Agency Commission: 15%
Mechanical Data: Type Area: 199 x 284mm, Bleed Size: 220 x 297mm
Copy instructions: *Copy Date:* 4 weeks prior to publication date
BUSINESS: COSMETICS & HAIRDRESSING: Hairdressing

DE TOREN
626834N72-5320
Editorial: Burg. Bramerstraat 59, 7772 CD HARDENBERG **Tel:** 418 572641 **Fax:** 418 572601
Email: info@detoren.net
Date Established: 03-05-1956; **Freq:** Weekly; **Circ:** 52,000
Editor-in-Chief: Grietje Grendelman; **Publisher:** Margret Ticheler
Language(s): Dutch
Agency Commission: 15%
Mechanical Data: Type Area: 266 x 382mm, Bleed Size: 289 x 415mm
LOCAL NEWSPAPERS

TORTUCA
18039N84B-123
Editorial: Postbus 23267, 3001 KG ROTTERDAM
Tel: 20 5853045
Date Established: 01-12-1996; **Freq:** 3 issues yearly; **Annual Sub.:** EUR 21,-; **Circ:** 600
Editor: Rob Streevelaar; **Editor-in-Chief:** Kees van de Ven
Profile: Magazine focusing on art and literature.
Language(s): Dutch
Agency Commission: 15%
CONSUMER: THE ARTS & LITERARY: Literary

TOUR MAGAZINE
16557N49A-22
Editorial: Spui 188, 2511 BW DEN HAAG
Tel: 70 3751728 **Fax:** 24 3723631
Email: knvmedia@knv.nl
Date Established: 01-06-1995; **Freq:** Quarterly; **Annual Sub.:** EUR 15,50; **Circ:** 8,000
Editor: Jos Haas; **Publisher:** N.J.J. Zethof
Profile: Magazine about touring vehicles and touring car branches in the Netherlands.
Language(s): Dutch
ADVERTISING RATES:
Full Page Mono .. EUR 1/1: b/w 1160,- 1/2: b/w 602,- 1/4: b/w 348,-
Agency Commission: 15%
Mechanical Data: Type Area: 185 x 270mm, Bleed Size: 210 x 297mm
Copy instructions: *Copy Date:* 10 days prior to publication date
BUSINESS: TRANSPORT

TRANSPORTVISIE
16567N49C-20
Editorial: Spui 188, 2511 BW DEN HAAG
Tel: 70 3751758 **Fax:** 15 2126695
Email: knvmedia@knv.nl
Date Established: 01-02-1993; **Freq:** 6 issues yearly; **Cover Price:** EUR 7,95
Annual Sub.: EUR 30,85; **Circ:** 7,000
Editor: Jos Haas
Profile: Magazine covering all aspects of the transportation of goods.
Language(s): Dutch
ADVERTISING RATES:
Full Page Mono .. EUR 1/1: b/w 1453,- 1/2: b/w 747,- 1/4: b/w 405,-
Agency Commission: 15%
Mechanical Data: Type Area: 185 x 270mm, Bleed Size: 210 x 297mm
Copy instructions: *Copy Date:* 10 days prior to publication date
BUSINESS: TRANSPORT: Freight

TRED
16241N29-40
Editorial: Straatweg 28, 3604 BB MAARSSEN
Tel: 30 2743551 **Fax:** 30 2744409
Email: info@blauwmedia.com
Freq: Monthly; **Annual Sub.:** EUR 92,24; **Circ:** 2,425
Publisher: Henk Louwmans
Profile: Journal covering the shoe trade.
Language(s): Dutch
Readership: Read by wholesalers and retailers.
ADVERTISING RATES:
Full Page Mono EUR 2/1: f.c. 4545,-; 1/1: f.c. 2840,-; 1/2: f.c. 1560,-
Agency Commission: 15%
Mechanical Data: Type Area: 220 x 300mm, Bleed Size: 235 x 322mm
BUSINESS: FOOTWEAR

TREKKER
16136N21E-60
Editorial: Hanzestraat 1, 7006 RH DOETINCHEM
Tel: 314 349629 **Fax:** 314 360699
Email: klantenservice@reedbusiness.nl **Web site:** http://www.trekkermagazine.nl
Freq: 11 issues yearly; **Annual Sub.:** EUR 104,50; **Circ:** 14,296
Editor: Geert Hekkert; **Editor-in-Chief:** W. Vorselman; **Publisher:** Aart Freriks
Profile: Publication containing information on tractors and farm machinery. It provides information on new models, developments and inventions.
Language(s): Dutch
ADVERTISING RATES:
Full Page Mono EUR 1/1: f.c. 2888,-; b/w 1891,- 1/2: f.c. 1681,-; b/w 985,- 1/4: f.c. 1100,-; b/w 503,-
Agency Commission: 15%
Mechanical Data: Type Area: 200 x 270mm, Bleed Size: 230 x 295mm
Copy instructions: *Copy Date:* 11 days prior to publication date
BUSINESS: AGRICULTURE & FARMING: Agriculture - Machinery & Plant

TREMA 1637336N44-176
Editorial: Prinses Beatrixlaan 116, 2595 AL DEN HAAG **Tel:** 70 3789880 **Fax:** 70 3789783
Email: sdu@sdu.nl
Freq: 10 issues yearly; **Annual Sub.:** EUR 125,-; **Circ:** 3,700
Editor-in-Chief: A. Koelma; **Publisher:** Gert Jan Schinkel
Language(s): Dutch
ADVERTISING RATES:
Full Page Mono EUR 1/1: b/w 1515,- 1/2: b/w 1010,- 1/4: b/w 505,-
Agency Commission: 15%
Mechanical Data: Type Area: 170 x 270mm, Bleed Size: 210 x 290mm
BUSINESS: LEGAL

TREND 15852N12B-50
Editorial: Van Hogendorplaan 51, 7003 CM DOETINCHEM **Tel:** 20 4276583 **Fax:** 418 572601
Email: trend@trendcrossmedia.nl
Date Established: 01-01-1974; **Freq:** 8 issues yearly; **Cover Price:** EUR 5,50
Annual Sub.: EUR 36,-; **Circ:** 2,506
Editor: J. Kuypers; **Publisher:** G.J.B. Pas
Profile: Journal for contemporary entrepreneurs in glass, porcelain, ceramic, luxury goods, household ware, industrial arts and gifts.
Language(s): Dutch
ADVERTISING RATES:
Full Page Mono ... EUR 1/1: f.c. 1590,-; 1/2: f.c. 835,-
Agency Commission: 15%
Mechanical Data: Type Area: 220 x 300mm, Bleed Size: 235 x 322mm
Copy instructions: *Copy Date:* 2 weeks prior to publication date
BUSINESS: CERAMICS, POTTERY & GLASS: Glass

TREND BOUTIQUE 16536N47A-200
Editorial: Straatweg 28, 3604 BB MAARSSEN
Tel: 10 2894026 **Fax:** 88 2697490
Email: info@blauwmedia.com
Freq: 6 issues yearly; **Annual Sub.:** EUR 53,05; **Circ:** 1,949
Publisher: Henk Louwmans
Profile: Magazine about leather goods, luggage and fashion accessories.
Language(s): Dutch
Readership: Read by retailers, suppliers and importers.
ADVERTISING RATES:
Full Page Mono EUR 2/1: f.c. 3310,-; 1/1: f.c. 2070,-; 1/2: f.c. 1140,-
Agency Commission: 15%
Mechanical Data: Type Area: 220 x 300mm, Bleed Size: 235 x 322mm
BUSINESS: CLOTHING & TEXTILES

TRIATHLON SPORT 17617N75J-350
Editorial: Coranthijnestraat 22, 9715 RH GRONINGEN **Tel:** 23 5344089 **Fax:** 10 2801002
Email: roelkerkhof@home.nl
Date Established: 01-01-1988; **Freq:** Monthly; **Annual Sub.:** EUR 33,-; **Circ:** 5,600
Editor: Roel Kerkhof
Profile: Magazine focusing on all aspects of diathlon and triathlon sports.
Language(s): Dutch
Readership: Aimed at diathlon and triathlon athletes.
ADVERTISING RATES:
Full Page Mono EUR 1/1: f.c. 995,-; 1/2: f.c. 525,-; 1/4: f.c. 289,-
Agency Commission: 15%
Mechanical Data: Type Area: 183 x 269mm, Bleed Size: 210 x 297mm
CONSUMER: SPORT: Athletics

TRIBUNE 1636179N82-251
Editorial: Vijverhofstraat 65, 3032 SC ROTTERDAM
Tel: 10 2435550 **Fax:** 10 2435565
Email: sp@sp.nl **Web site:** http://www.sp.nl/nieuws/tribune
Date Established: 01-01-1964; **Freq:** Monthly; **Cover Price:** EUR 1,75
Annual Sub.: EUR 24,-; **Circ:** 55,000
Usual Pagination: 32
Editor: D. de Jongh; **Editor-in-Chief:** Jurgen van den Hout
Language(s): Dutch
Agency Commission: 15%
Mechanical Data: Type Area: 186 x 274mm, Bleed Size: 210 x 297mm
CONSUMER: CURRENT AFFAIRS & POLITICS

TRIVIZIER 16406N40-150
Editorial: Postbus 93037, 2509 AA DEN HAAG
Tel: 492 338432 **Fax:** 70 3839840
Email: vbmnov@vbmnov.nl
Freq: 10 issues yearly; **Annual Sub.:** EUR 40,-; **Circ:** 33,500
Editor: Henri Lansink; **Editor-in-Chief:** Henri Lansink
Profile: Publication containing information about defence and the welfare of soldiers.
Language(s): Dutch
ADVERTISING RATES:
Full Page Mono .. EUR 2/1: b/w 1270,- 1/1: b/w 925,- 1/2: b/w 508,-
Agency Commission: 15%
Mechanical Data: Type Area: 183 x 262mm, Bleed Size: 210 x 297mm
BUSINESS: DEFENCE

TROMPETTER ROERMOND WEEKEND 629991N72-5377
Editorial: Nassaustraat 102, 6043 EE ROERMOND
Tel: 30 2964469 **Fax:** 475 551033
Email: info@aencmedia.nl
Date Established: 01-01-1977; **Freq:** Weekly; **Cover Price:** Free; **Circ:** 69,500
Language(s): Dutch
Agency Commission: 15%
Mechanical Data: Type Area: 267 x 390mm, Bleed Size: 289 x 420mm
LOCAL NEWSPAPERS

TROUW 17043N65A-60
Editorial: Jacob Bontiusplaats 9, 1018 LL AMSTERDAM **Tel:** 20 5629444
Web site: http://www.trouw.nl
Freq: 312 issues yearly; **Annual Sub.:** EUR 299,45; **Circ:** 106,440
Editor: Willem Schoonen; **Editor-in-Chief:** Onno Havermans; **Publisher:** Frits Campagne
Profile: Broadsheet-sized quality newspaper placing particular emphasis on religion, ethics, philosophy, education, health care and the environment.
Language(s): Dutch
Readership: Read particularly by academics, health care workers, students and politicians, the majority of whom are Protestants.
ADVERTISING RATES:
Full Page Mono .... EUR ed. ma. t/m vr. 1/1: b/w 10.578,- ed. ma. t/m vr. 1/2: b/w 7193,- ed. ma. t/m vr. 1/4: b/w 2929,- ed
Agency Commission: 15%
Mechanical Data: Type Area: 238 x 387mm, Bleed Size: 265 x 398mm
NATIONAL DAILY & SUNDAY NEWSPAPERS: National Daily Newspapers

TROUWEN 17506N74L-100
Editorial: Postbus 84081, 3009 CB ROTTERDAM
Tel: 10 4274128 **Fax:** 35 6474569
Email: info@trouwen.nl **Web site:** http://www.trouwen.nl
Freq: Quarterly; **Cover Price:** EUR 6,-; **Circ:** 30,000
Usual Pagination: 500
Editor: K. van de Mark
Profile: Magazine concerning the planning and organisation of weddings.
Language(s): Dutch
Readership: Aimed at women planning to get married.
ADVERTISING RATES:
Full Page Mono EUR 2/1: f.c. 4250,-; PMS 3590,-; b/w 2885,- 1/1: f.c. 2310,-; PMS 1940,-; b/w 1575,- 1/2: f.c. 1470,-;
Agency Commission: 15%
Mechanical Data: Type Area: 200 x 260mm, Bleed Size: 230 x 300mm
Copy instructions: *Copy Date:* 6 weeks prior to publication date
CONSUMER: WOMEN'S INTEREST CONSUMER MAGAZINES: Brides

TRUCKSTAR 16568N49C-25
Editorial: Capellalaan 65, 2132 JL HOOFDDORP
Tel: 88 7518190 **Fax:** 30 6383991
Web site: http://www.truckstar.nl
Freq: 13 issues yearly; **Cover Price:** EUR 4,75
Annual Sub.: EUR 62,-; **Circ:** 41,818
Editor: Arjen van Vliet; **Editor-in-Chief:** B. Mateboer; **Publisher:** Sander Stallinga
Profile: Magazine covering all aspects of the freight industry.
Language(s): Dutch
ADVERTISING RATES:
Full Page Mono EUR 2/1: f.c. 9140,-; b/w 4570,- 1/1: f.c. 4570,-; b/w 2285,- 1/2: f.c. 2590,-; b/w 1295,-
Agency Commission: 15%
Mechanical Data: Type Area: 210 x 280mm, Bleed Size: 230 x 300mm
BUSINESS: TRANSPORT: Freight

TSJAKKA! 1634819N74C-201
Editorial: Doetinchemseweg 59, 7007 CB DOETINCHEM **Tel:** 88 2697183 **Fax:** 88 2697490
Email: info@mcp.nl **Web site:** http://www.tsjakka.nl
Date Established: 15-01-1995; **Freq:** Monthly; **Cover Price:** Free; **Circ:** 2,000,000
Editor: Jasper Bosman
Language(s): Dutch
ADVERTISING RATES:
Full Page Mono .... EUR 1/1: f.c. 21.175,-; 1/2: f.c. 14.120,-
Agency Commission: 15%
Mechanical Data: Type Area: 160 x 230mm, Bleed Size: 180 x 260mm
CONSUMER: WOMEN'S INTEREST CONSUMER MAGAZINES: Home & Family

TT CIRCUIT ASSEN 1664117N77D-256
Editorial: De Haar 9, 9405 TE ASSEN
Tel: 314 359940 **Fax:** 314 359978
Email: info@tt-assen.com
Date Established: 03-02-2005; **Freq:** Annual; **Cover Price:** Free; **Circ:** 150,000
Editor: P. Schorer
Language(s): Dutch
ADVERTISING RATES:
Full Page Mono .... EUR 1/1: f.c. 4400,-
Agency Commission: 15%
Mechanical Data: Type Area: 190 x 260mm, Bleed Size: 210 x 280mm
CONSUMER: MOTORING & CYCLING: Motor Sports

TTM (TRUCK & TRANSPORT MANAGEMENT) 16571N49D-80
Editorial: Informaticaweg 3c, 7007 CP DOETINCHEM **Tel:** 113 820203
Email: industrialmedia@eisma.nl **Web site:** http://www.ttm.nl
Freq: Monthly; **Annual Sub.:** EUR 197,50; **Circ:** 10,124
Editor: Pieter Wieman; **Editor-in-Chief:** Arjan Velthoven; **Publisher:** Henk Meinen
Profile: Magazine containing information on commercial vehicles and trailers in the form of tests, news reports and product summaries. Also covers national and international road transport.
Language(s): Dutch
Readership: Read by road transport operators.
ADVERTISING RATES:
Full Page Mono EUR 1/1: f.c. 4800,-; b/w 3106,- 1/2: f.c. 2980,-; b/w 1641,- 1/4: f.c. 2108,-; b/w 865,-
Agency Commission: 15%
Mechanical Data: Type Area: 187 x 257mm, Bleed Size: 215 x 285mm
BUSINESS: TRANSPORT: Commercial Vehicles

TUINIDEEKRANT 1857720N32H-241
Editorial: Terborgseweg 47, 7064 AB SILVOLDE
Tel: 570 648891 **Fax:** 570 614795
Freq: Quarterly; **Cover Price:** Free; **Circ:** 100,000
Editor-in-Chief: Wendy Venhorst; **Publisher:** Jan Olthof
Language(s): Dutch
ADVERTISING RATES:
Full Page Mono EUR 2/1: f.c. 9000,-; 1/1: f.c. 4950,-; 1/2: f.c. 2950,-
Agency Commission: 15%
Mechanical Data: Type Area: 280 x 395mm, Bleed Size: 297 x 420mm
Copy instructions: *Copy Date:* 4 weeks prior to publication date
BUSINESS: LOCAL GOVERNMENT, LEISURE & RECREATION: Leisure, Recreation & Entertainment

TUINONTWERP 1857810N32H-243
Editorial: Takkebijsters 57a, 4817 BL BREDA
Tel: 40 8447611 **Fax:** 53 4842189
Email: info@vipmedia.nl
Date Established: 06-03-2008; **Freq:** 3 issues yearly; **Cover Price:** EUR 6,95; **Circ:** 55,000
Editor: Jacqueline Leenders
Language(s): Dutch
ADVERTISING RATES:
Full Page Mono EUR 1/1: f.c. 2050,-; b/w 1515,- 1/2: f.c. 1200,-; b/w 815,- 1/4: f.c. 675,-; b/w 450,-
Agency Commission: 15%
Mechanical Data: Type Area: 198 x 280mm, Bleed Size: 228 x 300mm
BUSINESS: LOCAL GOVERNMENT, LEISURE & RECREATION: Leisure, Recreation & Entertainment

TUINPLUS 1857811N32H-244
Editorial: Takkebijsters 57a, 4817 BL BREDA
Tel: 40 8447611 **Fax:** 53 4842189
Email: info@vipmedia.nl
Date Established: 27-03-2008; **Freq:** Half-yearly; **Cover Price:** EUR 6,95; **Circ:** 55,000
Editor: Jacqueline Leenders
Language(s): Dutch
ADVERTISING RATES:
Full Page Mono EUR 1/1: f.c. 2050,-; b/w 1515,- 1/2: f.c. 1200,-; b/w 815,- 1/4: f.c. 675,-; b/w 450,-
Agency Commission: 15%
Mechanical Data: Type Area: 198 x 280mm, Bleed Size: 228 x 300mm
BUSINESS: LOCAL GOVERNMENT, LEISURE & RECREATION: Leisure, Recreation & Entertainment

TUINZAKEN 16197N26B-120
Editorial: Wolfswei 5, 6118 CR NIEUWSTADT
Tel: 570 648988 **Fax:** 570 614795
Email: info@tpk-media.nl
Date Established: 01-02-1996; **Freq:** Monthly; **Annual Sub.:** EUR 82,50; **Circ:** 3,221
Editor: K. Verdonschot; **Editor-in-Chief:** Amaury Stroux; **Publisher:** Tjeerd Posthumus
Profile: Journal about the management of garden centres and the retail of garden equipment.
Language(s): Dutch
Readership: Aimed at retailers of garden equipment and managers of garden centres and DIY outlets.
ADVERTISING RATES:
Full Page Mono .. EUR 1/1: b/w 1345,- 1/2: b/w 795,- 1/4: b/w 440,-
Agency Commission: 15%
Mechanical Data: Type Area: 185 x 268mm, Bleed Size: 210 x 297mm
Copy instructions: *Copy Date:* 3 weeks prior to publication date
BUSINESS: GARDEN TRADE: Garden Trade Supplies

TVB ZORG 16328N32G-19
Editorial: Spacelab 2, 3824 MR AMERSFOORT
Tel: 20 5159722 **Fax:** 30 6007595
Email: info@aprgroep.nl **Web site:** http://www.tijdschriftvoorverzorging[VA]enbeheer.nl
Date Established: 01-01-1971; **Freq:** 6 issues yearly; **Cover Price:** EUR 10,-
Annual Sub.: EUR 57,50; **Circ:** 8,100
Editor: Charlotte Maassen; **Editor-in-Chief:** Jaco Otto; **Publisher:** Jaco Otto
Profile: Magazine focusing on the care of the elderly in institutions and home care.
Language(s): Dutch
Readership: Read by managers and care staff.
ADVERTISING RATES:
Full Page Mono EUR 1/1: f.c. 3090,-; PMS 2490,-; b/w 2290,-
Agency Commission: 15%
Mechanical Data: Type Area: 190 x 270mm, Bleed Size: 210 x 297mm
BUSINESS: LOCAL GOVERNMENT, LEISURE & RECREATION: Community Care & Social Services

TVV, TIJDSCHRIFT VOOR VERZORGENDEN 16721N56B-45
Editorial: Keizersgracht 213, 1016 DT AMSTERDAM
Tel: 314 349884 **Fax:** 314 349037
Email: info@y-publicaties.nl **Web site:** http://www.tvvonline.nl
Freq: 10 issues yearly; **Annual Sub.:** EUR 68,-; **Circ:** 6,343
Editor: Ralph Beekveldt; **Publisher:** Ben Konings
Profile: Journal focusing on maternity care, the care of the elderly and the physically handicapped.
Language(s): Dutch
Readership: Aimed at carers in hospitals, nursing homes and at home.
ADVERTISING RATES:
Full Page Mono EUR 1/1: f.c. 2316,-; b/w 1638,- 1/2: f.c. 1660,-; b/w 1055,- 1/4: f.c. 1330,-; b/w 715,-
Agency Commission: 15%
Mechanical Data: Type Area: 185 x 264mm, Bleed Size: 215 x 285mm
Copy instructions: *Copy Date:* 2 weeks prior to publication date
BUSINESS: HEALTH & MEDICAL: Nursing

TVZ, TIJDSCHRIFT VOOR VERPLEEGKUNDIGEN 16722N56B-50
Editorial: Radarweg 29, 1043 NX AMSTERDAM
Tel: 20 5159743 **Fax:** 20 6752709
Email: info@reedbusiness.nl **Web site:** http://www.tvzdirect.nl
Freq: 10 issues yearly; **Cover Price:** EUR 14,95
Annual Sub.: EUR 122,-; **Circ:** 3,617
Editor: Tonny van de Pasch; **Publisher:** Ben Konings
Profile: Magazine containing articles about the nursing profession, education, research and developments in nursing and healthcare.
Language(s): Dutch
Readership: Aimed at registered nurses and nurses in training.
ADVERTISING RATES:
Full Page Mono EUR 1/1: f.c. 3072,-; b/w 1947,- 1/2: f.c. 2339,-; b/w 1282,- 1/4: f.c. 1917,-; b/w 833,-
Agency Commission: 15%
Mechanical Data: Type Area: 188 x 258mm, Bleed Size: 215 x 285mm
BUSINESS: HEALTH & MEDICAL: Nursing

DE TWAALF AMBACHTEN/ NIEUWSBRIEF 16851N57-111
Editorial: Mezenlaan 2, 5282 HB BOXTEL
Tel: 20 5159172 **Fax:** 20 5159700
Email: info@de12ambachten.nl **Web site:** http://www.de12ambachten.nl
Freq: Quarterly; **Circ:** 100
Editor: Sietz Leeflang; **Editor-in-Chief:** Lieselot Leeflang
Profile: Magazine providing information on environmental issues within all industry sectors.
Language(s): Dutch
Agency Commission: 15%
BUSINESS: ENVIRONMENT & POLLUTION

HET TWEEDE HUIS 18183N91B-135
Editorial: Amstelkade 56, 1427 AN AMSTELHOEK
Tel: 20 6077605 **Fax:** 88 2697490
Email: info@interdijk.nl **Web site:** http://www.het-tweede-huis.nl
Date Established: 01-11-1992; **Freq:** 6 issues yearly; **Cover Price:** EUR 5,45; **Circ:** 14,800
Usual Pagination: 164
Editor: Peter Beving
Profile: Magazine about caravans, holiday chalets, camping sites and camping equipment.
Language(s): Dutch
Readership: Aimed at families.
ADVERTISING RATES:
Full Page Mono .. EUR 1/1: b/w 1286,- 1/2: b/w 672,- 1/4: b/w 377,- 1/8: b/w 200,-
Agency Commission: 15%
Mechanical Data: Type Area: 200 x 280mm, Bleed Size: 230 x 297mm
Copy instructions: *Copy Date:* 1 month prior to publication date
CONSUMER: RECREATION & LEISURE: Camping & Caravanning

TWEEWIELER 16261N31B-60
Editorial: Hanzestraat 1, 7006 RH DOETINCHEM
Tel: 314 349884 **Fax:** 314 349037
Email: klantenservice@reedbusiness.nl **Web site:** http://www.tweewieler.nl
Freq: 11 issues yearly; **Annual Sub.:** EUR 145,-; **Circ:** 4,395
Editor: Jack Oortwijn; **Publisher:** Geert van den Bosch
Profile: Official journal of the retailers' federations BOVAG, NCBRM and the BTE giving information on the two-wheeler trade.
Language(s): Dutch
Readership: Aimed at retailers of motorcycles.
ADVERTISING RATES:
Full Page Mono EUR 1/1: f.c. 5395,-; b/w 2966,- 1/2: f.c. 3336,-; b/w 1643,- 1/4: f.c. 2450,-; b/w 891,-
Agency Commission: 15%
Mechanical Data: Type Area: 211 x 268mm, Bleed Size: 230 x 300mm
BUSINESS: MOTOR TRADE: Motorcycle Trade

TYREZONE 1857773N77A-380
Editorial: Gouverneurlaan 4, 6002 EC WEERT
Tel: 53 4842274 **Fax:** 53 4842189
Email: info@fkmedia.nl **Web site:** http://www.tyrezone.nl
Freq: 3 issues yearly; **Cover Price:** EUR 4,95
Annual Sub.: EUR 8,-; **Circ:** 75,000
Editor: R. Duivis
Language(s): Dutch
ADVERTISING RATES:
Full Page Mono EUR 2/1: f.c. 4500,-; 1/1: f.c. 2500,-; 1/2: f.c. 1500,-
Agency Commission: 15%
Mechanical Data: Type Area: 210 x 277mm, Bleed Size: 230 x 297mm
Copy instructions: *Copy Date:* 3 weeks prior to publication date
CONSUMER: MOTORING & CYCLING: Motoring

U EN UW BABY 1635222N74D-154
Editorial: Brahmslaan 24, 2253 CK VOORSCHOTEN
Tel: 20 5159743 **Fax:** 20 6752709
Email: jjproductions@familyproductions.nl
Date Established: 01-11-1970; **Freq:** Annual; **Cover Price:** Free; **Circ:** 125,000
Usual Pagination: 100
Editor: H. Westerneng; **Publisher:** J.W.J. Overgaauw
Language(s): Dutch
ADVERTISING RATES:
Full Page Mono .... EUR 1/1: f.c. 6200,-; b/w 4750,-
Agency Commission: 15%
Mechanical Data: Type Area: 188 x 258mm, Bleed Size: 220 x 297mm
CONSUMER: WOMEN'S INTEREST CONSUMER MAGAZINES: Child Care

UDENS WEEKBLAD 626896N72-5560
Editorial: Oranjestraat 9, 5401 CB UDEN
Tel: 20 5159743 **Fax:** 20 6752709
Email: udensweekblad@udensweekblad.nl
Date Established: 01-01-1951; **Freq:** Weekly; **Cover Price:** Free; **Circ:** 95,375
Editor: Philip van den Brand; **Editor-in-Chief:** S. van Berkel
Language(s): Dutch
Agency Commission: 15%
Mechanical Data: Type Area: 400 x 550mm, Bleed Size: 420 x 578mm
LOCAL NEWSPAPERS

UIT AGENDA 18140N89C-67
Editorial: Stationsplein 45, 3013 AK ROTTERDAM
Tel: 172 447345 **Fax:** 30 6383991
Email: info@rotterdamfestivals.nl
Freq: 10 issues yearly; **Annual Sub.:** EUR 21,-; **Circ:** 75,000
Editor: Helmut de Hoogh
Profile: Guide to entertainment, art, culture and events in Rotterdam.
Language(s): Dutch
Readership: Read by local people, visitors and tourists.
ADVERTISING RATES:
Full Page Mono EUR 1/1: b/w 2095,- 1/2: b/w 1235,- 1/4: b/w 655,-
Agency Commission: 15%
Mechanical Data: Type Area: 180 x 267mm, Bleed Size: 210 x 297mm
Copy instructions: *Copy Date:* 3 weeks prior to publication date
CONSUMER: HOLIDAYS & TRAVEL: Entertainment Guides

UITDAGING 1635674N87-2432
Editorial: Emmastraat 18, 8011 AG ZWOLLE
Tel: 20 5922250 **Fax:** 20 5465530
Email: info@inspiritmedia.nl **Web site:** http://www.uitdagingonline.nl
Date Established: 01-03-1973; **Freq:** 8 issues yearly; **Cover Price:** EUR 2,75
Annual Sub.: EUR 29,90; **Circ:** 6,500
Editor: R. Koops; **Publisher:** Leendert de Jong
Language(s): Dutch
ADVERTISING RATES:
Full Page Mono .. EUR 1/1: f.c. 1120,-; 1/2: f.c. 616,-; 1/4: f.c. 374,-
Agency Commission: 15%
Mechanical Data: Type Area: 255 x 390mm, Bleed Size: 286 x 420mm
CONSUMER: RELIGIOUS

UITGIDS 629467N76B-126
Editorial: Kleine-Gartmanplantsoen 21, 1017 RP AMSTERDAM **Tel:** 10 4274149 **Fax:** 35 6474444
Email: receptie@aub.nl
Freq: Annual; **Cover Price:** Free; **Circ:** 60,000
Editor: Jacques Oirbons; **Editor-in-Chief:** Jacques Oirbons
Profile: Magazine providing information on the theatre season in Amsterdam, including opera and music cabaret.
Language(s): Dutch
ADVERTISING RATES:
Full Page Mono EUR 1/1: f.c. 3700,-; 1/2: f.c. 2300,-; 1/4: f.c. 1500,-
Agency Commission: 15%
Mechanical Data: Type Area: 180 x 267mm, Bleed Size: 210 x 297mm
Copy instructions: *Copy Date:* 4 weeks prior to publication date
CONSUMER: MUSIC & PERFORMING ARTS: Theatre

UITKRANT 629758N76B-100
Editorial: Kleine-Gartmanplantsoen 21, 1017 RP AMSTERDAM **Tel:** 20 6211374 **Fax:** 20 6752709
Email: receptie@aub.nl
Freq: 11 issues yearly; **Annual Sub.:** EUR 24,95; **Circ:** 80,000
Editor: Bart van Oosterhout
Profile: Magazine containing information on theatre, entertainment, music, bands and films.
Language(s): Dutch
Readership: Aimed at people who enjoy concerts, music and the arts.
ADVERTISING RATES:
Full Page Mono EUR 2/1: f.c. 8000,-; 1/1: f.c. 4500,-; 1/2: f.c. 2500,-
Agency Commission: 15%
Mechanical Data: Type Area: 182 x 269mm, Bleed Size: 210 x 297mm
Copy instructions: *Copy Date:* 4 weeks prior to publication date
CONSUMER: MUSIC & PERFORMING ARTS: Theatre

UITKRANT HAARLEM 19128N89C-120
Editorial: Nassaulaan 46, 2011 PD HAARLEM
Tel: 70 3342179 **Fax:** 20 5979490
Date Established: 01-10-1987; **Freq:** 11 issues yearly; **Annual Sub.:** EUR 15,88; **Circ:** 35,000
Usual Pagination: 24
Editor: Marcel Schmidt; **Publisher:** Marcel Schmidt
Profile: Entertainment guide to Haarlem, Amsterdam, Zaanstreek, Wijk aan Zee, Beverwijk and Zandvoort.
Language(s): Dutch
ADVERTISING RATES:
Full Page Mono .. EUR 1/1: f.c. 1500,-; 1/2: f.c. 850,-; 1/4: f.c. 600,-
Agency Commission: 15%
Mechanical Data: Bleed Size: 297 x 420mm
CONSUMER: HOLIDAYS & TRAVEL: Entertainment Guides

UITMARKT 1896657N84A-419
Editorial: Kleine-Gartmanplantsoen 21, 1017 RP AMSTERDAM **Tel:** 20 6211374 **Fax:** 70 3855505
Email: receptie@aub.nl
Freq: Annual; **Cover Price:** Free; **Circ:** 100,000
Editor: Bart van Oosterhout; **Editor-in-Chief:** H. Greebe
Language(s): Dutch
ADVERTISING RATES:
Full Page Mono EUR 1/1: f.c. 4500,-; 1/2: f.c. 2400,-; 1/4: f.c. 1400,-
Agency Commission: 15%
Mechanical Data: Type Area: 160 x 240mm, Bleed Size: 180 x 260mm
Copy instructions: *Copy Date:* 4 weeks prior to publication date
CONSUMER: THE ARTS & LITERARY: Arts

HET UITVAARTWEZEN 17026N64L-60
Editorial: Veerweg 40, 6991 GP RHEDEN
Tel: 20 6211374
Email: redactie@hetuitvaartwezen.nl **Web site:** http://www.hetuitvaartwezen.nl
Freq: 10 issues yearly; **Annual Sub.:** EUR 79,50; **Circ:** 817
Editor: Marjon Weijzen; **Editor-in-Chief:** Femke van den Berg; **Publisher:** Theo de Natris
Profile: Journal of the NUVU - the Dutch Society of Recognized Undertakers.
Language(s): Dutch
ADVERTISING RATES:
Full Page Mono EUR 1/1: b/w 650,- 1/2: b/w 390,- 1/4: b/w 235,-
Agency Commission: 15%
Mechanical Data: Type Area: 185 x 270mm, Bleed Size: 210 x 297mm
BUSINESS: OTHER CLASSIFICATIONS: Funeral Directors, Cemeteries & Crematoria

UITWAAIER 629742N84A-96
Editorial: Bergerweg 1, 1815 AC ALKMAAR
Tel: 20 5922250
Email: info@kcnh.nl **Web site:** http://www.uitwaaier.nl
Date Established: 01-04-2001; **Freq:** Annual; **Annual Sub.:** EUR 1,75; **Circ:** 260,000
Editor: Carla Voorendonk; **Editor-in-Chief:** José Bernard
Profile: Magazine focusing on art, culture and tourism in North Holland.
Language(s): Dutch
ADVERTISING RATES:
Full Page Mono EUR 1/1: f.c. 4500,-; 1/2: f.c. 2750,-; 1/4: f.c. 1500,-
Agency Commission: 15%
Mechanical Data: Type Area: 238 x 392mm
CONSUMER: THE ARTS & LITERARY: Arts

UNICEF MAGAZINE 1635236N82-221
Editorial: Jacob van den Eyndestraat 73, 2274 XA VOORBURG **Tel:** 20 6211374 **Fax:** 20 6752709
Email: info@unicef.nl
Date Established: 01-02-1999; **Freq:** Half-yearly; **Annual Sub.:** EUR 10,-; **Circ:** 250,000
Editor: J. Jansma; **Editor-in-Chief:** D. Groenendijk
Language(s): Dutch
Agency Commission: 15%
CONSUMER: CURRENT AFFAIRS & POLITICS

UNIENFTO-TIJDSCHRIFT 16920N62F-145
Editorial: Boschweg 6, 4105 DL CULEMBORG
Tel: 20 5159172 **Fax:** 20 5159145
Email: info@unienfto.nl
Date Established: 01-01-1874; **Freq:** 10 issues yearly; **Annual Sub.:** EUR 34,03; **Circ:** 5,000
Editor: Jan van den Dries; **Editor-in-Chief:** Jan van den Dries
Profile: Magazine focusing on middle and higher education.
Language(s): Dutch
ADVERTISING RATES:
Full Page Mono .. EUR 1/1: b/w 1200,- 1/2: b/w 800,- 1/4: b/w 500,-
Agency Commission: 15%
Mechanical Data: Type Area: 180 x 255mm, Bleed Size: 185 x 287mm
BUSINESS: CHURCH & SCHOOL EQUIPMENT & EDUCATION: Adult Education

UNIVERSITEITSKRANT GRONINGEN 17995N83-100
Editorial: Oude Kijk in 't Jatstraat 28, 9712 EK GRONINGEN **Tel:** 20 5450421 **Fax:** 20 6752709
Email: uk@rug.nl **Web site:** http://www.universiteitskrant.nl
Freq: 38 issues yearly; **Annual Sub.:** EUR 30,-; **Circ:** 19,000
Editor: J.F. Boonstra; **Editor-in-Chief:** Christien Boomsma
Profile: Magazine for students and tutors at the University of Groningen.
Language(s): Dutch
Agency Commission: 15%
Mechanical Data: Type Area: 264 x 398mm, Bleed Size: 289 x 420mm
CONSUMER: STUDENT PUBLICATIONS

UTILITIES 623856N58-83
Editorial: Veembroederhof 7, 1019 HD AMSTERDAM
Tel: 10 2894026 **Fax:** 88 2697490
Email: info@industrielinqs.nl **Web site:** http://www.utilities.nl
Freq: 10 issues yearly; **Cover Price:** EUR 16,40
Annual Sub.: EUR 119,05; **Circ:** 4,122
Editor: David van Baarle; **Publisher:** Wim Raaijen
Profile: Magazine focusing on energy, water and gas industrial processes.
Language(s): Dutch
Readership: Aimed at managers within the industry.
ADVERTISING RATES:
Full Page Mono EUR 1/1: f.c. 2768,-; PMS 2195,-; b/w 1855,- 1/2: f.c. 1793,-; PMS 1450,-; b/w 1110,- 1/4: f.c. 1134,-;
Agency Commission: 15%
Mechanical Data: Type Area: 185 x 267mm, Bleed Size: 210 x 297mm
BUSINESS: ENERGY, FUEL & NUCLEAR

UT-NIEUWS 17994N83-90
Editorial: Drienerlolaan 5, 7522 NB ENSCHEDE
Tel: 35 6726900 **Fax:** 20 5854158
Web site: http://www.utnws.utwente.nl/utnieuws
Date Established: 01-01-1963; **Freq:** 40 issues yearly; **Annual Sub.:** EUR 30,-; **Circ:** 9,000
Editor: B. Groenman
Profile: Magazine of the University of Twente.
Language(s): Dutch
Agency Commission: 15%
Mechanical Data: Type Area: 260 x 390mm, Bleed Size: 290 x 415mm
CONSUMER: STUDENT PUBLICATIONS

UTRECHT BUSINESS 16979N63-265
Editorial: Mecklenburglaan 16, 3581 NW UTRECHT
Tel: 23 5565370 **Fax:** 23 5565357
Email: ub@wxs.nl **Web site:** http://www.utrechtbusiness.nl
Date Established: 10-05-1986; **Freq:** 6 issues yearly; **Annual Sub.:** EUR 55,-; **Circ:** 7,000
Editor: M. Rienstra; **Publisher:** Hans Hajeé
Profile: Business magazine for the Utrecht region.
Language(s): Dutch
Readership: Read by business company managers.
ADVERTISING RATES:
Full Page Mono EUR 1/1: f.c. 1995,-; b/w 1265,- 1/2: f.c. 1065,-; b/w 680,- 1/4: f.c. 760,-; b/w 370,-
Agency Commission: 15%
Mechanical Data: Type Area: 190 x 260mm, Bleed Size: 215 x 285mm
Copy instructions: *Copy Date:* 2 weeks prior to publication date
BUSINESS: REGIONAL BUSINESS

UWMAGAZINE 15991N14L-584
Editorial: Multatulilaan 12, 4103 NM CULEMBORG
Tel: 33 2471104 **Fax:** 23 5564241
Email: info@unie.nl
Freq: Quarterly; **Circ:** 20,000
Usual Pagination: 60
Editor: Mariëtte van de Rest
Profile: Official journal of the Unie - the Trade Union for Administration, Technical and Commercial Personnel.
Language(s): Dutch
ADVERTISING RATES:
Full Page Mono . EUR 1/1: f.c. 4500,-; 1/2: f.c. 2250,-
Agency Commission: 15%
Mechanical Data: Type Area: 185 x 268mm, Bleed Size: 210 x 297mm
Copy instructions: *Copy Date:* 4 weeks prior to publication date
BUSINESS: COMMERCE, INDUSTRY & MANAGEMENT: Trade Unions

UWV PERSPECTIEF 1636463N32G-322
Editorial: La Guardiaweg 68, 1043 DK AMSTERDAM
Tel: 70 3342179
Freq: Quarterly; **Cover Price:** Free; **Circ:** 510,000
Usual Pagination: 8
Editor: Kees Diamant
Language(s): Dutch
Agency Commission: 15%
BUSINESS: LOCAL GOVERNMENT, LEISURE & RECREATION: Community Care & Social Services

VA MAGAZINE (VRUCHTBARE AARDE) 18950N21A-359
Editorial: Wg-Plein 380, 1054 SG AMSTERDAM
Tel: 513 466162 **Fax:** 35 6712552
Email: va@xs4all.nl **Web site:** http://www.va-magazine.nl
Freq: Quarterly; **Cover Price:** EUR 4,85
Annual Sub.: EUR 19,20; **Circ:** 5,000
Editor: Bart Hommersen; **Publisher:** Bart Hommersen
Profile: Journal covering biological farming methods and the nature and quality of food.
Language(s): Dutch
ADVERTISING RATES:
Full Page Mono EUR 1/1: f.c. 955,-; 1/2: f.c. 555,-; 1/4: f.c. 330,-
Agency Commission: 15%
Mechanical Data: Type Area: 185 x 275mm, Bleed Size: 210 x 297mm
Copy instructions: *Copy Date:* 3 weeks prior to publication date
BUSINESS: AGRICULTURE & FARMING

VADEMECUM MONDHYGIËNISTEN 1637412N56D-65
Editorial: Het Spoor 2, 3994 AK HOUTEN
Tel: 30 6383767 **Fax:** 314 340515
Freq: 16 issues yearly; **Circ:** 2,267
Language(s): Dutch
ADVERTISING RATES:
Full Page Mono EUR 1/1: f.c. 2544,-; b/w 1178,- 1/2: f.c. 1580,-; b/w 737,- 1/4: f.c. 900,-; b/w 421,-
Agency Commission: 15%
Mechanical Data: Type Area: 185 x 267mm, Bleed Size: 210 x 297mm
Copy instructions: *Copy Date:* 2 weeks prior to publication date
BUSINESS: HEALTH & MEDICAL: Dental

VAK M 1998537N14L-595
Editorial: Tiberdreef 4, 3561 GG UTRECHT
Tel: 30 2303508 **Fax:** 314 373646
Web site: http://www.cnvvakmensen.nl/vakm
Freq: 8 issues yearly; **Circ:** 135,000
Language(s): Dutch
ADVERTISING RATES:
Full Page Mono EUR 1/1: f.c. 4675,-; b/w 3800,- 1/2: f.c. 2985,-; b/w 2100,-
Agency Commission: 15%
Mechanical Data: Type Area: 195 x 235mm, Bleed Size: 230 x 280mm
BUSINESS: COMMERCE, INDUSTRY & MANAGEMENT: Trade Unions

VAKANTIEDELUXE 1857821N50-172
Editorial: Stationsplein 3, 1211 EX HILVERSUM
Tel: 40 8447611 **Fax:** 53 4842189
Email: info@reisrevue.nl **Web site:** http://www.vakantiedeluxe.nl
Freq: Annual; **Cover Price:** EUR 4,95; **Circ:** 60,000
Editor: Jan Lokhoff; **Publisher:** Martine de Knoop
Language(s): Dutch
ADVERTISING RATES:
Full Page Mono EUR 2/1: f.c. 6250,-; 1/1: f.c. 3625,-; 1/2: f.c. 1975,-
Agency Commission: 15%
Mechanical Data: Type Area: 185 x 270mm, Bleed Size: 210 x 297mm

Copy instructions: *Copy Date:* 2 weeks prior to publication date
BUSINESS: TRAVEL & TOURISM

VAKANTIEJOURNAAL
1740507N89A-230
Editorial: Sint Agnetenweg 56, 6545 AW NIJMEGEN
Tel: 493 671060
Email: info@digiscript.nl
Date Established: 01-01-2005; **Freq:** Half-yearly;
Cover Price: Free; **Circ:** 1,000,000
Editor: René Tanchette; **Publisher:** René Tanchette
Language(s): Dutch
Agency Commission: 15%
Mechanical Data: Type Area: 255 x 385mm, Bleed Size: 289 x 420mm
Copy instructions: *Copy Date:* 1 month prior to publication date
CONSUMER: HOLIDAYS & TRAVEL: Travel

DE VAKANTIEKRANT
1936288N50-191
Editorial: Markerkant 1382, 1314 AN ALMERE
Tel: 10 4518007 **Fax:** 70 7999889
Web site: http://www.vakantiekrant.nl
Date Established: 04-01-2010; **Freq:** Monthly;
Cover Price: Free; **Circ:** 1,000,000
Editor: Marvin Struisvlugt
Language(s): Dutch
ADVERTISING RATES:
Full Page Mono .... EUR 1/1: f.c. 10.900,-
Agency Commission: 15%
Mechanical Data: Type Area: 265 x 420mm, Bleed Size: 290 x 420mm
BUSINESS: TRAVEL & TOURISM

VAKANTIEMAGAZINE
761559N89E-79_10
Editorial: Stationsplein 3, 1211 EX HILVERSUM
Tel: 10 2435550 **Fax:** 10 2435565
Email: info@reisrevue.nl **Web site:** http://www.vakantiemagazineonline.nl
Date Established: 01-01-1999; **Freq:** Half-yearly;
Cover Price: EUR 4,50; **Circ:** 75,000
Usual Pagination: 100
Editor: Jan Lokhoff; **Publisher:** Martine de Knoop
Profile: Magazine containing information on several holiday destinations throughout Europe.
Language(s): Dutch
ADVERTISING RATES:
Full Page Mono EUR 2/1: f.c. 5710,-; 1/1: f.c. 3250,-; 1/2: f.c. 1850,-; 1/4: f.c. 995,-
Agency Commission: 15%
Mechanical Data: Type Area: 197 x 260mm, Bleed Size: 215 x 285mm
CONSUMER: HOLIDAYS & TRAVEL: Holidays

VAKBLAD FINANCIËLE PLANNING
15489N1A-351
Editorial: Staverenstraat 32015, 7418 CJ DEVENTER
Tel: 570 647207 **Fax:** 20 5353696
Email: info@kluwer.nl
Freq: 11 issues yearly; **Cover Price:** EUR 32,-
Annual Sub.: EUR 225,75; **Circ:** 868
Editor: J.E. van den Berg; **Publisher:** G.P.K. Sok
Profile: Magazine about financial planning and relevant legislation.
Language(s): Dutch
Readership: Read by financial advisers, lawyers and insurers.
ADVERTISING RATES:
Full Page Mono EUR 1/1: b/w 950,- 1/2: b/w 570,- 1/4: b/w 309,-
Agency Commission: 15%
Mechanical Data: Type Area: 170 x 255mm, Bleed Size: 210 x 297mm
Copy instructions: *Copy Date:* 3 weeks prior to publication date
BUSINESS: FINANCE & ECONOMICS

VAKBLAD NATUUR BOS LANDSCHAP
16526N46-110
Editorial: Postbus 618, 6700 AP WAGENINGEN
Tel: 15 2617997 **Fax:** 229 216416
Email: vakblad@vakbladnbl.nl **Web site:** http://www.vakbladnatuurbosland[VA]schap.nl
Date Established: 01-01-2004; **Freq:** 10 issues yearly; **Annual Sub.:** EUR 50,-; **Circ:** 2,500
Editor: Ido Borkent; **Editor-in-Chief:** Koen Moons
Profile: Journal containing information concerning carpentry.
Language(s): Dutch
ADVERTISING RATES:
Full Page Mono EUR 1/1: f.c. 880,-; 1/2: f.c. 478,-; 1/4: f.c. 282,-
Agency Commission: 15%
Mechanical Data: Bleed Size: 220 x 280mm
Copy instructions: *Copy Date:* 2 weeks prior to publication date
BUSINESS: TIMBER, WOOD & FORESTRY

VALK MAGAZINE
1635855N89B-201
Editorial: Gouverneurlaan 4, 6002 EC WEERT
Tel: 10 2894015 **Fax:** 20 6159047
Email: info@fkmedia.nl
Date Established: 01-01-1983; **Freq:** Quarterly;
Annual Sub.: EUR 8,-; **Circ:** 160,000
Editor-in-Chief: Eva van Meijl
Language(s): Dutch
ADVERTISING RATES:
Full Page Mono EUR 2/1: f.c. 4000,-; 1/1: f.c. 2100,-; 1/2: f.c. 1100,-
Agency Commission: 15%
Mechanical Data: Type Area: 205 x 265mm, Bleed Size: 225 x 285mm
CONSUMER: HOLIDAYS & TRAVEL: Hotel Magazines

VANDAAR
1635257N87-2372
Editorial: Joseph Haydnlaan 2a, 3533 AE UTRECHT
Tel: 30 6399911 **Fax:** 30 6399937
Email: servicedesk@kerkinactie.nl
Date Established: 01-01-1885; **Freq:** Quarterly; **Circ:** 60,000
Editor-in-Chief: Paula van Cuilenburg
Language(s): Dutch
Agency Commission: 15%
Mechanical Data: Type Area: 190 x 250mm, Bleed Size: 215 x 283mm
CONSUMER: RELIGIOUS

VARKENSHOUDERIJ - VAKDEEL VAN BOERDERIJ
16131N21D-59
Editorial: Hanzestraat 1, 7006 RH DOETINCHEM
Tel: 314 349446 **Fax:** 314 344397
Email: klantenservice@reedbusiness.nl **Web site:** http://www.boerderij.nl/varkens[VA]houderij.shtml
Freq: 13 issues yearly; **Circ:** 6,288
Editor: Geert Hekkert
Profile: Magazine containing information for the specialist pig farmer.
Language(s): Dutch
ADVERTISING RATES:
Full Page Mono .... EUR 1/1: f.c. 3998,-; f.c. color 3594,-; b/w 2585,- 1/2: f.c. 2363,-; f.c. color 2079,-; b/w 1373,- 1/4:
Agency Commission: 15%
Mechanical Data: Type Area: 194 x 260mm, Bleed Size: 215 x 285mm
BUSINESS: AGRICULTURE & FARMING: Livestock

VASTGOED
1635268N1E-91
Editorial: Kronenburgsingel 515, 6831 GM ARNHEM
Tel: 314 344446 **Fax:** 314 344397
Email: info@hoogte80.com **Web site:** http://www.vastgoedactueel.nl
Date Established: 01-01-1925; **Freq:** 10 issues yearly; **Annual Sub.:** EUR 145,-; **Circ:** 6,150
Editor-in-Chief: Susanne Mullenders
Profile: Publication focusing on real estate market.
Language(s): Dutch
Readership: Aimed at realty professionals.
ADVERTISING RATES:
Full Page Mono EUR 2/1: f.c. 5040,-; b/w 3600,- 1/1: f.c. 2975,-; b/w 2055,- 1/2: f.c. 1515,-; b/w 1045,- 1/4: f.c. 790
Agency Commission: 15%
Mechanical Data: Type Area: 194 x 264mm, Bleed Size: 228 x 295mm
Copy instructions: *Copy Date:* 3 weeks prior to publication date
BUSINESS: FINANCE & ECONOMICS: Property

VASTGOEDMARKT
15531N1E-85
Editorial: Binckhorstlaan 403, 2516 BC DEN HAAG
Tel: 70 3780232 **Fax:** 314 344397
Email: sdu@sdu.nl **Web site:** http://www.vastgoedmarkt.nl
Date Established: 01-01-1974; **Freq:** Monthly;
Cover Price: EUR 59,-
Annual Sub.: EUR 562,-; **Circ:** 9,300
Editor: Mels Dees; **Editor-in-Chief:** Nel Meeder
Profile: Journal about the property and real estate market. Includes construction, maintenance, legal, security and sales information.
Language(s): Dutch
Readership: Read by developers, real estate agents and builders.
Agency Commission: 15%
Mechanical Data: Type Area: 278 x 397mm, Bleed Size: 300 x 420mm
BUSINESS: FINANCE & ECONOMICS: Property

VASTGOEDPERSONALITY
1660716N32A-250
Editorial: Thomas R. Malthusstraat 3c, 1066 JR AMSTERDAM **Tel:** 20 8969520
Email: info@vastgoedpersonality.nl
Freq: Half-yearly; **Cover Price:** EUR 6,95; **Circ:** 1,300
Publisher: Erwin Asselman
Language(s): Dutch
ADVERTISING RATES:
Full Page Mono EUR 1/1: b/w 3950,- 1/2: b/w 5750,-
Agency Commission: 15%
Mechanical Data: Type Area: 210 x 275mm, Bleed Size: 210 x 275mm
BUSINESS: LOCAL GOVERNMENT, LEISURE & RECREATION: Local Government

VB CONTACT
713078N1H-220
Editorial: Prinses Margrietplantsoen 90, 2595 BR DEN HAAG **Tel:** 23 5564600
Email: info@pensioenfederatie.nl
Freq: Quarterly; **Cover Price:** Free; **Circ:** 3,500
Editor: Marjolein Zaal; **Editor-in-Chief:** J. van Klaveren
Profile: Publication containing information about pension funds and relevant legislation.
Language(s): Dutch
Readership: Aimed at pension fund administrators and interested individuals.
Agency Commission: 15%
Mechanical Data: Bleed Size: 200 x 297mm
BUSINESS: FINANCE & ECONOMICS: Pensions

VEE EN VLEES
16172N22D-38
Editorial: Postbus 251, 2700 AG ZOETERMEER
Tel: 70 3780232 **Fax:** 314 344397
Email: info@nbhv.nl
Freq: 26 issues yearly; **Annual Sub.:** EUR 45,-; **Circ:** 1,800
Usual Pagination: 16
Editor: Tamara Flippo
Profile: Journal covering livestock and the meat trade.
Language(s): Dutch
Readership: Read by cattle farmers and meat traders.
ADVERTISING RATES:
Full Page Mono EUR 1/1: b/w 700,- 1/2: b/w 350,- 1/3: b/w 230,-
Agency Commission: 15%
Mechanical Data: Type Area: 170 x 252mm, Bleed Size: 210 x 285mm
Copy instructions: *Copy Date:* 7 days prior to publication date
BUSINESS: FOOD: Meat Trade

VEEHOUDER & DIERENARTS, ED. RUNDVEEHOUDERIJ
17009N64H-130
Editorial: Binnenhaven 1, 6709 PD WAGENINGEN
Tel: 23 5344089 **Fax:** 10 2801002
Email: mail@agrimedia.info
Date Established: 01-01-1986; **Freq:** Quarterly;
Annual Sub.: EUR 11,59; **Circ:** 6,000
Editor-in-Chief: Miel Bingen
Profile: Journal about veterinary science and general pet care.
Language(s): Dutch
Readership: Read by veterinary surgeons and assistants.
ADVERTISING RATES:
Full Page Mono EUR 1/1: f.c. 2030,-; 1/2: f.c. 1220,-; 1/4: f.c. 660,-
Agency Commission: 15%
Mechanical Data: Type Area: 180 x 264mm, Bleed Size: 210 x 295mm
Copy instructions: *Copy Date:* 2 weeks prior to publication date
BUSINESS: OTHER CLASSIFICATIONS: Veterinary

VEEHOUDERIJ TECHNIEK
16119N21C-67
Editorial: Binnenhaven 1, 6709 PD WAGENINGEN
Tel: 77 3556160 **Fax:** 77 3556152
Email: mail@agrimedia.info **Web site:** http://www.veehouderijtechniek.nl
Freq: 6 issues yearly; **Annual Sub.:** EUR 46,75; **Circ:** 4,000
Editor: Gertjan Zevenbergen; **Editor-in-Chief:** Willem van den Broek; **Publisher:** F.J.M. Visser
Profile: Journal focusing on the care of dairy cattle, includes details of new technology and developments.
Language(s): Dutch
Readership: Read by dairy farmers and suppliers.
ADVERTISING RATES:
Full Page Mono EUR 1/1: f.c. 2268,-; b/w 1428,- 1/2: f.c. 1228,-; b/w 785,- 1/4: f.c. 705,-; b/w 471,-
Agency Commission: 15%
Mechanical Data: Type Area: 200 x 254mm, Bleed Size: 230 x 295mm
Copy instructions: *Copy Date:* 3 weeks prior to publication date
BUSINESS: AGRICULTURE & FARMING: Dairy Farming

VEETEELT
16121N21C-69
Editorial: Wassenaarweg 20, 6843 NW ARNHEM
Tel: 20 7581000 **Fax:** 26 3898839
Web site: http://www.veeteelt.nl
Date Established: 15-01-1984; **Freq:** 20 issues yearly; **Circ:** 30,633
Editor: Jaap van der Knaap; **Editor-in-Chief:** Mirjam Braam; **Publisher:** Rochus Kingmans
Profile: Official journal of CR Delta. Includes information about the improvement of dairy farming, with articles on breeding, food and nutrition and farm management.
Language(s): Dutch
Readership: Read by dairy farmers.
ADVERTISING RATES:
Full Page Mono EUR 1/1: b/w 2796,- 1/2: b/w 1613,- 1/4: b/w 937,-
Agency Commission: 15%
Mechanical Data: Type Area: 180 x 256mm, Bleed Size: 210 x 297mm
Copy instructions: *Copy Date:* 6 days prior to publication date
BUSINESS: AGRICULTURE & FARMING: Dairy Farming

VEETEELTVLEES
1637259N21D-111
Editorial: Wassenaarweg 20, 6843 NW ARNHEM
Tel: 26 3898821 **Fax:** 26 3898839
Web site: http://www.veeteeltvlees.nl
Freq: Monthly; **Circ:** 6,083
Editor: Jaap van der Knaap; **Editor-in-Chief:** Mirjam Braam; **Publisher:** Rochus Kingmans
Language(s): Dutch
ADVERTISING RATES:
Full Page Mono EUR 1/1: b/w 750,- 1/2: b/w 413,- 1/4: b/w 206,-
Agency Commission: 15%
Mechanical Data: Type Area: 180 x 256mm, Bleed Size: 210 x 297mm
Copy instructions: *Copy Date:* 8 days prior to publication date
BUSINESS: AGRICULTURE & FARMING: Livestock

VEILIG VLIEGEN
15793N6A-150
Editorial: Luchtmachtplein 1, 4822 ZB BREDA
Tel: 314 349446 **Fax:** 314 344397
Email: avkam@mindef.nl
Date Established: 01-07-1954; **Freq:** 6 issues yearly; **Circ:** 14,000
Usual Pagination: 32
Editor: R.C. van den Heuvel; **Editor-in-Chief:** R.C. van den Heuvel
Profile: Magazine about safety in connection with the KLU - Dutch Royal Airforce.
Language(s): Dutch
Readership: Internal magazine read by members of the Dutch Royal Airforce.
Agency Commission: 15%
BUSINESS: AVIATION & AERONAUTICS

VEILIGHEID VOOROP
629445N49A-98
Editorial: Stationsstraat 79a, 3811 MH AMERSFOORT **Tel:** 570 648901
Email: info@vvn.nl
Freq: Quarterly; **Annual Sub.:** EUR 15,-; **Circ:** 65,000
Editor: Joyce Bierlee; **Editor-in-Chief:** Femke Rethans
Profile: Magazine focusing on transport safety.
Language(s): Dutch
Readership: Read by members of VVVO and transport associations.
Agency Commission: 15%
BUSINESS: TRANSPORT

VEILIGHEIDSNIEUWS
622635N54B-208
Editorial: Postbus 86, 3300 AB DORDRECHT
Tel: 20 3467209 **Fax:** 20 6159047
Email: info@intersafe-groeneveld.nl
Date Established: 01-05-1968; **Freq:** Quarterly; **Circ:** 15,000
Editor: K. Swieb
Profile: Magazine containing articles, news and information about safe work environments and the prevention of work-induced accidents and illnesses.
Language(s): Dutch
Readership: Read mainly by managers, supervisors and safety engineers within industry.
Agency Commission: 15%
BUSINESS: SAFETY & SECURITY: Safety

VELDPOST
16149N21J-98
Editorial: Handelsweg 2, 7041 GX 'S-HEERENBERG
Tel: 40 2473330 **Fax:** 172 466577
Email: info@agrio.nl **Web site:** http://www.veld-post.nl
Freq: 35 issues yearly; **Annual Sub.:** EUR 47,95; **Circ:** 12,750
Editor: R. Ellenkamp; **Publisher:** Ben van Uhm
Profile: Regional agricultural magazine.
Language(s): Dutch
Readership: Read by farmers in North Holland.
Agency Commission: 15%
Mechanical Data: Type Area: 264 x 390mm, Bleed Size: 290 x 420mm
BUSINESS: AGRICULTURE & FARMING: Agriculture & Farming - Regional

VERBOUWBLAD
1693605N74C-272
Editorial: Kronenburgsingel 515, 6831 GM ARNHEM
Tel: 15 2690416 **Fax:** 15 2690766
Email: info@hoogte80.com **Web site:** http://www.verbouwblad.nl
Date Established: 15-08-2005; **Freq:** Annual; **Cover Price:** Free; **Circ:** 150,000
Publisher: R. de Groot
Language(s): Dutch
ADVERTISING RATES:
Full Page Mono .... EUR 1/1: f.c. 3995,-
Agency Commission: 15%
Mechanical Data: Bleed Size: 210 x 297mm
CONSUMER: WOMEN'S INTEREST CONSUMER MAGAZINES: Home & Family

VERHUIZEN
16569N49R-92
Editorial: Boris Pasternaklaan 22, 2719 DA ZOETERMEER **Tel:** 79 6366208 **Fax:** 79 3636262
Email: info@tln.nl
Date Established: 01-01-1984; **Freq:** 8 issues yearly;
Annual Sub.: EUR 100,-; **Circ:** 1,000
Editor: Rick Ohm; **Editor-in-Chief:** T. van der Heijden
Profile: Magazine concerning the Dutch removals industry. Includes news on all aspects and developments in the trade.
Language(s): Dutch
Readership: Read by owners and managers in the removal industry.

ADVERTISING RATES:
Full Page Mono EUR 1/1: b/w 427,- 1/2: b/w 273,- 1/4: b/w 171,-
Agency Commission: 15%
Mechanical Data: Type Area: 185 x 276mm, Bleed Size: 210 x 297mm
Copy instructions: *Copy Date:* 2 weeks prior to publication date
BUSINESS: TRANSPORT: Transport Related

VERKEERSKUNDE 16582N49R-70
Editorial: Wassenaarseweg 220, 2596 EC DEN HAAG **Tel:** 79 6366208 **Fax:** 79 3636262
Web site: http://www.verkeerskunde.nl
Freq: 8 issues yearly; **Cover Price:** EUR 13,-
Annual Sub.: EUR 108,-; **Circ:** 1,515
Editor: Nettie Bakker; **Editor-in-Chief:** Jacques Lorsheijd; **Publisher:** J. Verbeek
Profile: Magazine containing news and information on road traffic and transportation.
Language(s): Dutch
Readership: Read by managers of transport companies.
ADVERTISING RATES:
Full Page Mono .. EUR 1/1: b/w 1180,- 1/2: b/w 710,- 1/4: b/w 385,-
Agency Commission: 15%
Mechanical Data: Type Area: 193 x 255mm, Bleed Size: 220 x 285mm
BUSINESS: TRANSPORT: Transport Related

VERKEERSRECHT 16583N49R-90
Editorial: Wassenaarseweg 220, 2596 EC DEN HAAG **Tel:** 79 6366208 **Fax:** 79 3636262
Email: verkeersrecht@anwb.nl **Web site:** http://www.verkeersrecht.nl
Freq: 11 issues yearly; **Cover Price:** EUR 14,-
Annual Sub.: EUR 132,-; **Circ:** 1,100
Editor: N. Frenk; **Editor-in-Chief:** Machteld Donkerlo
Profile: Journal about traffic law.
Language(s): Dutch
Readership: Read by insurance agents and brokers.
ADVERTISING RATES:
Full Page Mono EUR 1/1: b/w 850,- 1/2: b/w 425,- 1/4: b/w 250,-
Agency Commission: 15%
Mechanical Data: Type Area: 175 x 260mm, Bleed Size: 210 x 297mm
BUSINESS: TRANSPORT: Transport Related

VERPAKKEN 16356N35-60
Editorial: Emmastraat 61, 1213 AK HILVERSUM
Tel: 70 3780541 **Fax:** 70 3789783
Email: info@managementmedia.nl
Date Established: 01-01-1985; **Freq:** Quarterly;
Annual Sub.: EUR 95,-; **Circ:** 4,625
Editor: Gerard Molenaar; **Editor-in-Chief:** Kristi Houtkamp; **Publisher:** Mike Velleman
Profile: Journal containing information about packaging.
Language(s): Dutch
Readership: Read by senior managers in the packaging, design and associated sectors.
ADVERTISING RATES:
Full Page Mono EUR 1/1: f.c. 3180,-; 1/2: f.c. 1860,-; 1/4: f.c. 1010,-
Agency Commission: 15%
Mechanical Data: Bleed Size: 230 x 280mm, Type Area: 210 x 268mm
Copy instructions: *Copy Date:* 3 weeks prior to publication date
BUSINESS: PACKAGING & BOTTLING

VERPAKKINGSMANAGEMENT 16358N35-80
Editorial: Emmastraat 61, 1213 AK HILVERSUM
Tel: 172 466539 **Fax:** 10 4521797
Email: info@managementmedia.nl **Web site:** http://www.verpakkingsmanagement.nl
Date Established: 01-03-1985; **Freq:** 11 issues yearly; **Annual Sub.:** EUR 146,-; **Circ:** 7,349
Editor: Gerard Molenaar; **Editor-in-Chief:** Harry van Deursen; **Publisher:** Mike Velleman
Profile: Magazine focusing on the national and international packaging and logistics sector. Includes new products, systems, technological developments, distribution and marketing, also interviews and company profiles.
Language(s): Dutch
Readership: Read by managers in the chemical, pharmaceutical, cosmetics, packaging, metal, graphics, transport and textile sectors.
ADVERTISING RATES:
Full Page Mono EUR 1/1: f.c. 4725,-; 1/2: f.c. 2755,-; 1/4: f.c. 1635,-
Agency Commission: 15%
Mechanical Data: Type Area: 280 x 358mm, Bleed Size: 307 x 378mm
BUSINESS: PACKAGING & BOTTLING

VERPLEEGKUNDE 16723N56B-70
Editorial: Keizersgracht 213, 1016 DT AMSTERDAM
Tel: 20 5206064 **Fax:** 71 3643461
Email: info@y-publicaties.nl **Web site:** http://www.tijdschriftverpleegkunde.com
Freq: Quarterly; **Cover Price:** EUR 10,-
Annual Sub.: EUR 79,50; **Circ:** 1,000
Editor: M. Goosen; **Editor-in-Chief:** A. Maseland
Profile: Scientific publication focusing on national and international news about health-care, patient-care, education and management in the field of nursing.
Language(s): Dutch
Agency Commission: 15%
Mechanical Data: Type Area: 150 x 210mm, Bleed Size: 170 x 240mm
BUSINESS: HEALTH & MEDICAL: Nursing

VERWARMING VENTILATIE + 15627N3B-130
Editorial: Bredewater 20, 2715 CA ZOETERMEER
Tel: 79 6366208 **Fax:** 79 3250665
Email: info@uneto-vni.nl
Freq: 11 issues yearly; **Cover Price:** EUR 15,25
Annual Sub.: EUR 90,-; **Circ:** 4,155
Editor: Wally Keyzer-Broers; **Editor-in-Chief:** Stéphanie Korpershoek
Profile: Magazine about heating, ventilation, energy conservation and domestic installations. Includes installation techniques in addition to environmental and technical developments.
Language(s): Dutch
Readership: Read by installation engineers, manufacturers, wholesalers, retailers, importers and students.
ADVERTISING RATES:
Full Page Mono EUR 1/1: f.c. 2720,-; 1/2: f.c. 1510,-; 1/4: f.c. 1110,-
Agency Commission: 15%
Mechanical Data: Type Area: 190 x 265mm, Bleed Size: 210 x 297mm
Copy instructions: *Copy Date:* 4 weeks prior to publication date
BUSINESS: HEATING & VENTILATION: Industrial Heating & Ventilation

VIDEO EMOTION 17808N78B-50
Editorial: Postbus 6808, 6503 GH NIJMEGEN
Tel: 33 4220082 **Fax:** 24 3723631
Freq: 6 issues yearly; **Annual Sub.:** EUR 29,75; **Circ:** 7,000
Editor: Ivo van den Broek; **Publisher:** Rene van der Geld
Profile: Magazine covering all aspects of film making, with information on the latest products, trends and developments in the home video industry.
Language(s): Dutch
ADVERTISING RATES:
Full Page Mono EUR 1/1: b/w 952,- 1/2: b/w 586,- 1/4: b/w 335,-
Agency Commission: 15%
Mechanical Data: Type Area: 190 x 260mm, Bleed Size: 215 x 285mm
Copy instructions: *Copy Date:* 2 weeks prior to publication date
CONSUMER: CONSUMER ELECTRONICS: Video & DVD

VIECURI 652212N80-222
Editorial: Tegelseweg 210, 5912 BL VENLO
Tel: 88 7518510
Freq: Quarterly; **Cover Price:** Free; **Circ:** 5,500
Editor: M. Esselman
Profile: Magazine about the local hospital.
Language(s): Dutch
Readership: Aimed at patients and local residents.
Agency Commission: 15%
Mechanical Data: Bleed Size: 210 x 297mm, Type Area: 183 x 269mm
CONSUMER: RURAL & REGIONAL INTEREST

VILLA D'ARTE 17999N84A-398
Editorial: Westerdreef 9, 2151 BR NIEUW-VENNEP
Tel: 72 5188825 **Fax:** 20 5159143
Web site: http://www.villadarte.nl
Freq: 6 issues yearly; **Cover Price:** EUR 3,25
Annual Sub.: EUR 19,50; **Circ:** 479,680
Editor: Claudia Koopman; **Publisher:** P. Evers
Profile: Magazine about lifestyle, travelling, interior decoration and art.
Language(s): Dutch
Readership: Read by men and women aged 35 to 50 years.
ADVERTISING RATES:
Full Page Mono .... EUR 2/1: f.c. 23.900,-; 1/1: f.c. 14.900,-; 1/2: f.c. 8625,-
Agency Commission: 15%
Mechanical Data: Type Area: 216 x 286mm, Bleed Size: 230 x 300mm
CONSUMER: THE ARTS & LITERARY: Arts

VIP/DOC 713333N14A-55
Editorial: Pelmolenlaan 1m, 3447 GW WOERDEN
Tel: 43 4077490 **Fax:** 43 4077480
Email: klantenservice@bbp.nl **Web site:** http://www.vipdoc.nl
Freq: 8 issues yearly; **Annual Sub.:** EUR 125,-; **Circ:** 8,273
Usual Pagination: 44
Editor: Jan Kloeze
Profile: Business to business magazine containing information focusing on latest trends, developments and software for documentation management.
Language(s): Dutch
Readership: Read by documentation managers.
ADVERTISING RATES:
Full Page Mono EUR 2/1: f.c. 4675,-; 1/1: f.c. 2850,-; 1/2: f.c. 1925,-
Agency Commission: 15%
Mechanical Data: Bleed Size: 210 x 297mm, Type Area: 185 x 285mm
Copy instructions: *Copy Date:* 3 weeks prior to publication date
BUSINESS: COMMERCE, INDUSTRY & MANAGEMENT

VIS MAGAZINE 16506N45B-18
Editorial: Celsiusweg 41, 8912 AM LEEUWARDEN
Tel: 88 2697112 **Fax:** 88 2696983
Web site: http://www.vismagazine.nl
Freq: 10 issues yearly; **Annual Sub.:** EUR 135,-;
Circ: 2,000
Editor: Lieneke Schuitemaker; **Editor-in-Chief:** Petra Hermans-Taekema; **Publisher:** Roland Klaverstijn
Profile: Official journal of the Association of Dutch Fish Retailers.
Language(s): Dutch
Readership: Read by fishmongers, fishermen and supermarket managers.
ADVERTISING RATES:
Full Page Mono EUR 1/1: f.c. 2000,-; 1/2: f.c. 1000,-; 1/4: f.c. 600,-
Agency Commission: 15%
Mechanical Data: Type Area: 205 x 275mm, Bleed Size: 230 x 300mm
BUSINESS: MARINE & SHIPPING: Commercial Fishing

VISAGIE 16006N15A-80
Editorial: Hettenheuvelweg 41-43, 1101 BM AMSTERDAM **Tel:** 70 4161339 **Fax:** 20 5159145
Email: info@koggeschip-vakbladen.nl **Web site:** http://www.visagie.nl
Date Established: 28-02-1998; **Freq:** 8 issues yearly;
Cover Price: EUR 13,-
Annual Sub.: EUR 74,50; **Circ:** 5,222
Editor: Marco Jouret; **Editor-in-Chief:** Sarah den Boef; **Publisher:** Anthony van Trigt
Profile: Magazine focusing on make-up, bodypainting, fashion and styling.
Language(s): Dutch
Readership: Read by make-up artists, hairdressers and beauticians.
ADVERTISING RATES:
Full Page Mono EUR 1/1: f.c. 2540,-; 1/2: f.c. 1510,-; 1/4: f.c. 925,-
Agency Commission: 15%
Mechanical Data: Type Area: 185 x 270mm, Bleed Size: 210 x 297mm
Copy instructions: *Copy Date:* 2 weeks prior to publication date
BUSINESS: COSMETICS & HAIRDRESSING: Cosmetics

HET VISBLAD 18210N92-223
Editorial: Leijenseweg 115, 3721 BC BILTHOVEN
Tel: 223 650016 **Fax:** 223 650012
Email: info@sportvisserijnederland.nl
Date Established: 01-01-1974; **Freq:** Monthly;
Cover Price: EUR 2,50
Annual Sub.: EUR 13,45; **Circ:** 90,000
Editor: Joran Bal; **Editor-in-Chief:** O. Terlouw;
Publisher: H. te Kloeze
Profile: Magazine of the Dutch Sport-Fishing Association.
Language(s): Dutch
ADVERTISING RATES:
Full Page Mono EUR 1/1: b/w 1750,- 1/2: b/w 1050,- 1/4: b/w 630,-
Agency Commission: 15%
Mechanical Data: Type Area: 210 x 297mm, Bleed Size: 188 x 276mm
Copy instructions: *Copy Date:* 4 weeks prior to publication date
CONSUMER: ANGLING & FISHING

VISSEN 18211N92-200
Editorial: Beethovenstraat 178, 1077 JX AMSTERDAM **Tel:** 184 651558 **Fax:** 570 647815
Email: ahv@ahv.nl
Freq: 6 issues yearly; **Cover Price:** EUR 4,-; **Circ:** 17,000
Editor: A. Kempen
Profile: Magazine of the Amsterdam Angling Association.
Language(s): Dutch
ADVERTISING RATES:
Full Page Mono EUR 1/1: b/w 710,- 1/2: b/w 375,- 1/4: b/w 200,-
Agency Commission: 15%
Mechanical Data: Type Area: 184 x 252mm, Bleed Size: 210 x 280mm
CONSUMER: ANGLING & FISHING

VISUS 16750N56E-140
Editorial: Postbus 10417, 6000 GK WEERT
Tel: 23 5344089 **Fax:** 10 2801002
Email: info@optometrie.nl
Freq: Quarterly; **Annual Sub.:** EUR 55,90; **Circ:** 1,150
Editor: M.F. Blokdijk
Profile: Professional journal containing information on ophthalmic optometry and contact lenses.
Language(s): Dutch
ADVERTISING RATES:
Full Page Mono EUR 1/1: f.c. 950,-; 1/2: f.c. 575,-; 1/4: f.c. 310,-
Agency Commission: 15%
Mechanical Data: Type Area: 188 x 267mm, Bleed Size: 210 x 297mm
Copy instructions: *Copy Date:* 3 weeks prior to publication date
BUSINESS: HEALTH & MEDICAL: Optics

VITALE STAD 15666N4D-140
Editorial: Stadsring 2, 3811 HR AMERSFOORT
Tel: 314 349422 **Fax:** 33 4626063
Email: info@elbamedia.nl **Web site:** http://www.vitalestad.nl
Freq: 10 issues yearly; **Cover Price:** EUR 18,50
Annual Sub.: EUR 146,-; **Circ:** 4,000
Editor: Peter de Bois; **Editor-in-Chief:** Rudi Engel;
Publisher: Edgar van Eekelen
Profile: Construction magazine focusing on the renovation of towns and cities.
Language(s): Dutch
Readership: Read by architects, planners and council officials.
ADVERTISING RATES:
Full Page Mono EUR 1/1: f.c. 2053,-; 1/2: f.c. 1736,-; 1/4: f.c. 1590,-
Agency Commission: 15%
Mechanical Data: Type Area: 185 x 272mm, Bleed Size: 210 x 297mm
BUSINESS: ARCHITECTURE & BUILDING: Planning & Housing

VITRAS/CMD BIJ U THUIS 1634579N74G-249
Editorial: Lt. Generaal van Heutszlaan 4, 3743 JN BAARN **Tel:** 35 6726800 **Fax:** 30 6076301
Email: informatie@axioma.nl
Date Established: 18-01-2000; **Freq:** Half-yearly;
Circ: 50,000
Language(s): Dutch
Agency Commission: 15%
CONSUMER: WOMEN'S INTEREST CONSUMER MAGAZINES: Slimming & Health

VIVA 17426N74A-180
Editorial: Capellalaan 65, 2132 JL HOOFDDORP
Tel: 23 5565165 **Fax:** 20 6767728
Web site: http://www.viva.nl
Freq: Weekly; **Cover Price:** EUR 2,40
Annual Sub.: EUR 127,40; **Circ:** 89,663
Editor: Corinne van Duin; **Publisher:** Anneliese Bergman
Profile: Magazine for young women with articles on fashion, beauty, health, leisure and lifestyle.
Language(s): Dutch
Readership: Aimed at women aged between 18 and 35 years.
ADVERTISING RATES:
Full Page Mono .... EUR 2/1: b/w 16.300,- 1/1: b/w 8150,- 1/2: b/w 4890,-
Agency Commission: 15%
Mechanical Data: Type Area: 204 x 254mm, Bleed Size: 221 x 274mm
CONSUMER: WOMEN'S INTEREST CONSUMER MAGAZINES: Women's Interest

VIVACE MAGAZINE 1637267N74Q-278
Editorial: Essebaan 77, 2908 LJ CAPELLE A/D IJSSEL **Tel:** 26 3898821 **Fax:** 26 3898839
Email: info@vivacemedia.nl **Web site:** http://www.vivacemagazine.nl
Freq: Quarterly; **Annual Sub.:** EUR 22,-; **Circ:** 56,000
Editor: S. Provoost; **Publisher:** Stefan Louwerse
Language(s): Dutch
ADVERTISING RATES:
Full Page Mono EUR 1/1: b/w 1985,- 1/2: b/w 1045,- 1/4: b/w 545,-
Agency Commission: 15%
Mechanical Data: Type Area: 206 x 265mm, Bleed Size: 230 x 297mm
Copy instructions: *Copy Date:* 3 weeks prior to publication date
CONSUMER: WOMEN'S INTEREST CONSUMER MAGAZINES: Lifestyle

VIVES WEBBOEKJE 1659573N62R-270
Editorial: Prof. Eijkmanlaan 2, 2035 XB HAARLEM
Tel: 30 6383838 **Fax:** 30 6383839
Email: info@vives.nl
Freq: Annual; **Circ:** 50,000
Usual Pagination: 84
Editor: Maaike Neuteboom; **Editor-in-Chief:** Sandra Evers
Language(s): Dutch
ADVERTISING RATES:
Full Page Mono .... EUR 1/1: f.c. 1510,-
Agency Commission: 15%
Mechanical Data: Bleed Size: 148 x 210mm
BUSINESS: CHURCH & SCHOOL EQUIPMENT & EDUCATION: Education Related

VLIETLAND MAGAZINE 652204N80-147
Editorial: Graaf Adolfstraat 36d, 8606 BT SNEEK
Tel: 35 6726900 **Fax:** 20 5854158
Email: bcuitgevers@planet.nl
Freq: Quarterly; **Cover Price:** Free; **Circ:** 4,000
Editor: I. Donkersloot; **Editor-in-Chief:** B. Terpstra
Profile: Magazine about the local hospital.
Language(s): Dutch
Readership: Aimed at patients and local residents.
Agency Commission: 15%
Mechanical Data: Bleed Size: 210 x 297mm, Type Area: 183 x 269mm
CONSUMER: RURAL & REGIONAL INTEREST

VLINDERS
17947N81X-150

Editorial: Mennonietenweg 10, 6702 AD WAGENINGEN **Tel:** 23 5344089
Email: info@vlinderstichting.nl
Date Established: 01-01-1986; **Freq:** Quarterly;
Annual Sub.: EUR 25,-; **Circ:** 7,000
Editor: Liesbeth van Agt
Profile: Magazine containing articles about butterflies, damselflies and dragonflies. Includes information about endangered species, habitat destruction and conservation measures.
Language(s): Dutch
ADVERTISING RATES:
Full Page Mono EUR 1/1: f.c. 690,-; 1/2: f.c. 410,-; 1/4: f.c. 220,-
Agency Commission: 15%
Mechanical Data: Type Area: 190 x 242mm, Bleed Size: 210 x 297mm
CONSUMER: ANIMALS & PETS

VNG MAGAZINE
16274N32A-185

Editorial: Prinses Beatrixlaan 116, 2595 AL DEN HAAG **Tel:** 70 3780586 **Fax:** 30 6076301
Email: sdu@sdu.nl
Freq: 24 issues yearly; **Cover Price:** EUR 9,75
Annual Sub.: EUR 105; **Circ:** 27,613
Editor: Simon Kooistra; **Publisher:** Dineke Sonderen
Profile: Magazine containing information from the VNG about the management of local government departments.
Language(s): Dutch
Readership: Read by local government officials.
ADVERTISING RATES:
Full Page Mono EUR 1/1: b/w 2995,- 1/2: b/w 1775,- 1/4: b/w 865,-
Agency Commission: 15%
Mechanical Data: Bleed Size: 210 x 270mm, Type Area: 186 x 255mm
BUSINESS: LOCAL GOVERNMENT, LEISURE & RECREATION: Local Government

VOEDING & VISIE
652182N22A-2

Editorial: De Breide 17, 6983 HG DOESBURG
Tel: 23 5565551 **Fax:** 23 5565136
Email: info@academicjournals.nl **Web site:** http://www.voeding-visie.nl
Freq: Annual; **Cover Price:** Free; **Circ:** 12,500
Editor: M. Former-Boon; **Editor-in-Chief:** K. Lassche
Profile: Publication containing information about nutritional values and their effect on the human body.
Language(s): Dutch
Readership: Aimed at the members of the medical profession, nutritionists and dietitians.
Agency Commission: 15%
Mechanical Data: Type Area: 180 x 260mm, Bleed Size: 210 x 280mm
BUSINESS: FOOD

VOEDING NU
16165N22A-130

Editorial: Essebaan 63, 2908 LJ CAPELLE AAN DEN IJSSEL **Tel:** 229 270002 **Fax:** 20 6767728
Email: info@mybusinessmedia.nl **Web site:** http://www.voedingnu.nl
Freq: 9 issues yearly; **Cover Price:** EUR 7,50
Annual Sub.: EUR 61,50; **Circ:** 4,061
Editor: Hans Kraak; **Editor-in-Chief:** Marjolein Spek;
Publisher: S. Wanders
Profile: Journal covering all aspects of nutrition research.
Language(s): Dutch
Readership: Read by food advisers and managers of professional kitchens.
ADVERTISING RATES:
Full Page Mono EUR 1/1: f.c. 2755,-; 1/2: f.c. 1855,-; 1/4: f.c. 1145,-
Agency Commission: 15%
Mechanical Data: Type Area: 188 x 258mm, Bleed Size: 215 x 285mm
BUSINESS: FOOD

VOEDINGSINDUSTRIE
16176N22D-120

Editorial: Markweg 11, 6883 JL VELP
Tel: 35 67272103 **Fax:** 20 5159145
Email: info@proca-mpp.com
Date Established: 01-03-1995; **Freq:** 8 issues yearly;
Annual Sub.: EUR 78,-; **Circ:** 4,000
Editor: Judith Witte; **Publisher:** Klaas Dijkstra
Profile: Journal for the meat and convenience food industry.
Language(s): Dutch
Readership: Read by managers of manufacturing companies in the meat, poultry, convenience and food industries as well as managers of companies supplying meat and food sector manufacturers.
ADVERTISING RATES:
Full Page Mono .. EUR 1/1: f.c. 1600,-; 1/2: f.c. 925,-; 1/4: f.c. 475,-
Agency Commission: 15%
Mechanical Data: Type Area: 205 x 275mm, Bleed Size: 230 x 300mm
BUSINESS: FOOD: Meat Trade

VOEDINGSMAGAZINE
16711N56A-270

Editorial: Louis Braillelaan 80, 2719 EK ZOETERMEER **Tel:** 20 5310161 **Fax:** 20 5302585
Email: info@nzo.nl **Web site:** http://www.voedingsmagazine.nl
Date Established: 01-06-1988; **Freq:** 6 issues yearly;
Cover Price: Free; **Circ:** 30,000
Usual Pagination: 24
Editor: Gert Jan Hiddink; **Editor-in-Chief:** M.J.C. van de Pol
Profile: Official journal of the Dutch Dairy Foundation for Nutrition and Health.
Language(s): Dutch
Readership: Read by doctors and dieticians.
Agency Commission: 15%
BUSINESS: HEALTH & MEDICAL

VOETBAL MAGAZINE
17580N75B-177

Editorial: Esp 101, 5633 AA EINDHOVEN
Tel: 172 575581 **Fax:** 23 5565136
Email: bcm@bcm.nl **Web site:** http://www.voetbalmagazine.nl
Freq: 11 issues yearly; **Cover Price:** EUR 4,65
Annual Sub.: EUR 38,-; **Circ:** 85,000
Editor: S. Kooijman; **Editor-in-Chief:** P. Heyblom;
Publisher: Eric Brüger
Profile: Magazine of the Royal Dutch Football Association.
Language(s): Dutch
ADVERTISING RATES:
Full Page Mono . EUR 1/1: f.c. 5041,-; 1/2: f.c. 2646,-
Agency Commission: 15%
Mechanical Data: Type Area: 202 x 280mm, Bleed Size: 222 x 300mm
CONSUMER: SPORT: Football

DE VOETBALTRAINER
17582N75B-185

Editorial: Tolhutterweg 7, 7261 KS RUURLO
Tel: 20 5979500 **Fax:** 35 6728848
Email: devoetbaltrainer@wxs.nl **Web site:** http://www.voetbaltrainer.nl
Freq: 8 issues yearly; **Circ:** 5,500
Editor: Paul Geerars; **Publisher:** Minne Hovenga
Profile: Magazine providing news, information and features about football.
Language(s): Dutch
Readership: Magazine read by football trainers and managers.
ADVERTISING RATES:
Full Page Mono .. EUR 1/1: b/w 1875,- 1/2: b/w 970,- 1/4: b/w 504,-
Agency Commission: 15%
Mechanical Data: Type Area: 185 x 262mm, Bleed Size: 210 x 297mm
Copy instructions: *Copy Date:* 2 weeks prior to publication date
CONSUMER: SPORT: Football

VOETVAK+
1637258N56K-61

Editorial: Hettenheuvelweg 41-43, 1101 BM AMSTERDAM **Tel:** 70 4415257 **Fax:** 20 5159143
Email: info@koggeschip-vakbladen.nl **Web site:** http://www.voetvakplus.nl
Date Established: 01-01-2003; **Freq:** 8 issues yearly;
Cover Price: EUR 12,-
Annual Sub.: EUR 66,75; **Circ:** 5,605
Editor: Marco Jouret; **Editor-in-Chief:** Yvonne de Leeuw; **Publisher:** Anthony van Trigt
Language(s): Dutch
ADVERTISING RATES:
Full Page Mono EUR 1/1: f.c. 1725,-; 1/2: f.c. 1085,-; 1/4: f.c. 650,-
Agency Commission: 15%
Mechanical Data: Type Area: 185 x 270mm, Bleed Size: 210 x 297mm
Copy instructions: *Copy Date:* 2 weeks prior to publication date
BUSINESS: HEALTH & MEDICAL: Chiropody

HET VOGELJAAR
17940N81F-55

Editorial: Postbus 65, 3750 GB BUNSCHOTEN
Tel: 229 270002
Email: redactie@vogeljaar.nl
Freq: 6 issues yearly; **Cover Price:** EUR 3,40
Annual Sub.: EUR 13,50; **Circ:** 4,600
Editor: Rob Kole
Profile: Magazine about bird research and the protection of wild birds.
Language(s): Dutch
Readership: Aimed at bird breeders and enthusiasts.
ADVERTISING RATES:
Full Page Mono EUR 1/1: f.c. 910,-; 1/2: f.c. 525,-; 1/4: f.c. 295,-
Agency Commission: 15%
Mechanical Data: Type Area: 125 x 210mm, Bleed Size: 155 x 240mm
CONSUMER: ANIMALS & PETS: Birds

VOGELS
19134N81F-66

Editorial: Boulevard 12, 3707 BM ZEIST
Tel: 71 5356356 **Fax:** 71 5356415
Email: info@vogelbescherming.nl
Freq: 5 issues yearly; **Circ:** 165,000
Editor: Hans Peeters
Profile: Magazine about the protection of birds.
Language(s): Dutch
ADVERTISING RATES:
Full Page Mono . EUR 1/1: f.c. 4690,-; 1/2: f.c. 2580,-
Agency Commission: 15%
Mechanical Data: Type Area: 173 x 270mm, Bleed Size: 210 x 297mm
CONSUMER: ANIMALS & PETS: Birds

VOGELVRIJE FIETSER
17774N77C-65

Editorial: Kanaalweg 50, 3526 KM UTRECHT
Tel: 229 270002 **Fax:** 20 6208980
Email: info@fietsersbond.nl **Web site:** http://www.vogelvrijefietser.nl
Date Established: 01-10-1975; **Freq:** 6 issues yearly;
Circ: 35,000
Usual Pagination: 48
Editor: Michiel Slütter
Profile: Official journal of the Dutch Cyclists' Association.
Language(s): Dutch
ADVERTISING RATES:
Full Page Mono .. EUR 1/1: f.c. 1253,-; 1/2: f.c. 686,-; 1/4: f.c. 421,-
Agency Commission: 15%
Mechanical Data: Type Area: 185 x 270mm, Bleed Size: 210 x 297mm
CONSUMER: MOTORING & CYCLING: Cycling

VOLGENS
1996415N84B-303

Editorial: Wildenborch 5, 1112 XB DIEMEN
Tel: 30 2303508 **Fax:** 314 373646
Freq: Half-yearly; **Cover Price:** EUR 6,95
Annual Sub.: EUR 12,50; **Circ:** 60,000
Publisher: Willem de Kok
Language(s): Dutch
ADVERTISING RATES:
Full Page Mono EUR 2/1: f.c. 9390,-; PMS 8395,-; b/w 7875,- 1/1: f.c. 4950,-; PMS 4275,-; b/w 3935,- 1/2: f.c. 2750,-;
Agency Commission: 15%
Mechanical Data: Type Area: 174 x 242mm, Bleed Size: 210 x 265mm
Copy instructions: *Copy Date:* 3 weeks prior to publication date
CONSUMER: THE ARTS & LITERARY: Literary

DE VOLKSKRANT
17044N65A-70

Editorial: Jacob Bontiusplaats 9, 1018 LL AMSTERDAM **Tel:** 20 5629222
Web site: http://www.vk.nl
Freq: 312 issues yearly; **Annual Sub.:** EUR 291,90;
Circ: 262,183
Editor: Philippe Remarque; **Editor-in-Chief:** Anneke Teunissen; **Publisher:** Frits Campagne
Profile: Broadsheet-sized quality newspaper providing national and international news, political, financial and cultural information.
Language(s): Dutch
Readership: Read by a broad spectrum of the population.
ADVERTISING RATES:
Full Page Mono .... EUR ed. ma. t/m vr. 2/1: b/w 49.017,- ed. ma. t/m vr. 1/1: b/w 29.352,- ed. ma. t/m vr. 1/2: b/w 19.959,
Agency Commission: 15%
Mechanical Data: Type Area: 266 x 398mm
NATIONAL DAILY & SUNDAY NEWSPAPERS: National Daily Newspapers

VOLKSWAGEN MAGAZINE
17799N77E-1

Editorial: Aletta Jacobslaan 7, 1066 BP AMSTERDAM **Tel:** 20 5245753 **Fax:** 20 5242228
Email: info@rhbm.nl
Freq: Quarterly; **Cover Price:** Free; **Circ:** 200,000
Editor: Hans Verstraaten
Profile: Magazine providing articles for owners of Volkswagen cars.
Language(s): Dutch
ADVERTISING RATES:
Full Page Mono .... EUR 1/1: f.c. 5050,-
Agency Commission: 15%
Mechanical Data: Type Area: 190 x 260mm, Bleed Size: 210 x 297mm
Copy instructions: *Copy Date:* 4 weeks prior to publication date
CONSUMER: MOTORING & CYCLING: Club Cars

VOLUME
1646329N4A-33

Editorial: Tolhuisweg 1, 1031 CL AMSTERDAM
Tel: 23 5565462 **Fax:** 23 5564588
Email: info@archis.org **Web site:** http://www.volumeproject.org
Date Established: 01-01-2005; **Freq:** Quarterly;
Cover Price: EUR 19,50
Annual Sub.: EUR 75,-; **Circ:** 6,000
Usual Pagination: 164
Editor: A. Oosterman; **Publisher:** A. Oosterman
Language(s): Dutch
ADVERTISING RATES:
Full Page Mono . EUR 1/1: f.c. 2000,-; 1/2: f.c. 1000,-
Agency Commission: 15%
Mechanical Data: Type Area: 200 x 267mm, Bleed Size: 200 x 267mm
Copy instructions: *Copy Date:* 4 weeks prior to publication date
BUSINESS: ARCHITECTURE & BUILDING: Architecture

VOORSTER NIEUWS
627179N72-5920

Editorial: Stationsstraat 7, 7391 EG TWELLO
Tel: 10 2435550 **Fax:** 10 2435565
Email: info@voorsternieuws.nl **Web site:** http://www.voorsternieuws.nl
Date Established: 01-08-1986; **Freq:** Weekly; **Cover Price:** Free; **Circ:** 13,500
Editor: G.M. Jacobs; **Publisher:** G.M. Jacobs
Language(s): Dutch
Agency Commission: 15%
Mechanical Data: Type Area: 265 x 395mm
LOCAL NEWSPAPERS

VORMBERICHTEN
16058N19B-100

Editorial: Danzigerkade 8a, 1013 AP AMSTERDAM
Tel: 88 2697183 **Fax:** 88 2697490
Email: bno@bno.nl **Web site:** http://www.bno.nl/vormberichten
Freq: 8 issues yearly; **Circ:** 4,250
Editor: Freek Kroesbergen; **Editor-in-Chief:** Floor van Essen
Profile: Journal containing news about the Association of Industrial Designers and developments in two and three-dimensional design.
Language(s): Dutch
Readership: Aimed at members of the Association of Industrial Designers and those in the field of industrial design.
ADVERTISING RATES:
Full Page Mono EUR 1/1: f.c. 1720,-; b/w 1295,- 1/2: f.c. 1140,-; b/w 715,- 1/4: f.c. 920,-; b/w 495,-
Agency Commission: 15%
Mechanical Data: Bleed Size: 230 x 320mm, Type Area: 216 x 306mm
Copy instructions: *Copy Date:* 2 weeks prior to publication date
BUSINESS: ENGINEERING & MACHINERY: Engineering - Design

VORMEN UIT VUUR
15849N12A-80

Editorial: Lampongstraat 6 II, 1094 AT AMSTERDAM
Web site: http://www.vormenuitvuur.nl
Circ: 1,000
Editor: J.W. Put; **Editor-in-Chief:** T. Vugts
Profile: Magazine covering ceramic art and glass history.
Language(s): Dutch
ADVERTISING RATES:
Full Page Mono EUR 1/1: b/w 350,- 1/2: b/w 175,- 1/4: b/w 100,-
Agency Commission: 15%
Mechanical Data: Type Area: 160 x 225mm, Bleed Size: 190 x 260mm
BUSINESS: CERAMICS, POTTERY & GLASS: Ceramics & Pottery

VORSTEN ROYALE
711629N74Q-242

Editorial: Capellalaan 65, 2132 JL HOOFDDORP
Tel: 23 5565100 **Fax:** 23 5565105
Web site: http://www.vorsten.nl
Freq: 13 issues yearly; **Cover Price:** EUR 4,95
Annual Sub.: EUR 72,93; **Circ:** 35,283
Editor: Marianne de Groot; **Publisher:** Anneliese Bergman
Profile: Magazine containing information and interviews about the Dutch royal family, includes other royal people across the world.
Language(s): Dutch
Readership: Read mainly by women.
ADVERTISING RATES:
Full Page Mono EUR 2/1: b/w 7000,- 1/1: b/w 3500,- 1/2: b/w 2100,-
Agency Commission: 15%
Mechanical Data: Type Area: 200 x 252mm, Bleed Size: 230 x 285mm
CONSUMER: WOMEN'S INTEREST CONSUMER MAGAZINES: Lifestyle

DE VRIEND VAN OUD EN JONG
18102N87-2005

Editorial: Marktweg 73a, 8444 AB HEERENVEEN
Tel: 50 3636743
Freq: 26 issues yearly; **Annual Sub.:** EUR 34,-; **Circ:** 2,000
Editor: T.M.E. Aangeenbrug-van der Maas; **Editor-in-Chief:** D.L. Aangeenbrug; **Publisher:** D.L. Aangeenbrug
Profile: Christian family magazine.
Language(s): Dutch
Readership: Read by Christians.
Agency Commission: 15%
CONSUMER: RELIGIOUS

VRIJ NEDERLAND
17409N73-290

Editorial: Raamgracht 4, 1011 KK AMSTERDAM
Tel: 20 5518442 **Fax:** 20 6247476
Web site: http://www.vrijnederland.nl
Freq: 47 issues yearly; **Cover Price:** EUR 4,50
Annual Sub.: EUR 171,-; **Circ:** 50,792
Editor: Frits van Exter; **Editor-in-Chief:** J. Berkhout;
Publisher: Karin van Gilst
Profile: Magazine giving the opportunity for political and cultural debate in the Netherlands.
Language(s): Dutch
ADVERTISING RATES:
Full Page Mono .... EUR 2/1: b/w 12.460,- 1/1: b/w 6230,- 1/2: b/w 3738,-
Agency Commission: 15%
Mechanical Data: Type Area: 202 x 264mm, Bleed Size: 230 x 297mm
CONSUMER: NATIONAL & INTERNATIONAL PERIODICALS

VROUWEN VAN NU
1634825N74A-208

Editorial: Jan van Nassaustraat 63, 2596 BP DEN HAAG **Tel:** 10 2894026 **Fax:** 88 2697490
Email: bureau@nbvp.nl
Date Established: 01-01-1930; **Freq:** 6 issues yearly;
Annual Sub.: EUR 10,80; **Circ:** 53,000
Editor: B.J.A. Leferink
Language(s): Dutch
ADVERTISING RATES:
Full Page Mono EUR 1/1: f.c. 2920,-; b/w 2265,- 1/2: f.c. 1620,-; b/w 1185,- 1/4: f.c. 950,-; b/w 620,-
Agency Commission: 15%

Mechanical Data: Type Area: 195 x 265mm, Bleed Size: 205 x 275mm
Copy instructions: *Copy Date:* 3 weeks prior to publication date
CONSUMER: WOMEN'S INTEREST CONSUMER MAGAZINES: Women's Interest

VT WONEN 15650N74C-180
Editorial: Capellalaan 65, 2132 JL HOOFDDORP
Tel: 23 5564600 **Fax:** 23 5564626
Web site: http://www.vtwonen.nl
Freq: Monthly; **Cover Price:** EUR 5,65
Annual Sub.: EUR 66,-; **Circ:** 141,023
Editor: Monique de Ruiter; **Publisher:** Ard Siekerman
Profile: Magazine containing information on homes and interiors .
Language(s): Dutch
Readership: Read by people with an interest in home decorating.
ADVERTISING RATES:
Full Page Mono .... EUR 2/1: b/w 23.600,- 1/1: b/w 11.800,- 1/2: b/w 7080,-
Agency Commission: 15%
Mechanical Data: Type Area: 206 x 258mm, Bleed Size: 228 x 283mm
CONSUMER: WOMEN'S INTEREST CONSUMER MAGAZINES: Home & Family

VU MAGAZINE 1806181N62R-278
Editorial: De Boelelaan 1091, kamer OE-60, 1081 HV AMSTERDAM **Tel:** 20 5855333
Freq: Quarterly; **Cover Price:** Free; **Circ:** 50,000
Editor: Marieke Schilp; **Editor-in-Chief:** Rianne Lindhout
Language(s): Dutch
ADVERTISING RATES:
Full Page Mono EUR 1/1: f.c. 3350,-; 1/2: f.c. 1850,-; 1/4: f.c. 995,-
Agency Commission: 15%
Mechanical Data: Type Area: 180 x 260mm
BUSINESS: CHURCH & SCHOOL EQUIPMENT & EDUCATION: Education Related

VVA MAGAZINE 16525N46-80
Editorial: Handelsweg 2, 7041 GX 'S-HEERENBERG
Tel: 23 5344089 **Fax:** 10 4739911
Email: info@agrio.nl
Freq: 6 issues yearly; **Circ:** 3,800
Editor: Reinout Burgers
Profile: Journal of the Society for Graduates of Larenstein University. Covers agricultural and related subjects including management of wood and nature and garden design.
Language(s): Dutch
ADVERTISING RATES:
Full Page Mono .. EUR 1/1: b/w 1230,- 1/2: b/w 780,- 1/4: b/w 435,-
Agency Commission: 15%
Mechanical Data: Type Area: 263 x 400mm, Bleed Size: 285 x 430mm
Copy instructions: *Copy Date:* 2 weeks prior to publication date
BUSINESS: TIMBER, WOOD & FORESTRY

VVV UITKRANT GRONINGEN, FRIESLAND, DRENTHE 1634976N89A-180
Editorial: Nijbracht 120, 7821 CE EMMEN
Tel: 76 5876329 **Fax:** 0032 34660067
Email: info@menzenmedia.nl
Freq: 9 issues yearly; **Annual Sub.:** EUR 13,61
Publisher: Henk Kroezen
Language(s): Dutch
ADVERTISING RATES:
Full Page Mono .. EUR 1/1: b/w 1372,- 1/2: b/w 690,- 1/4: b/w 347,-
Agency Commission: 15%
Mechanical Data: Type Area: 260 x 375mm
CONSUMER: HOLIDAYS & TRAVEL: Travel

WAAR PANNENKOEKEN ETEN? 1636930N94G-83
Editorial: Postbus 566, 3440 AN WOERDEN
Tel: 78 6133223 **Fax:** 70 3364640
Email: vep@horeca.org
Date Established: 01-03-2002; **Freq:** Annual; **Cover Price:** Free; **Circ:** 80,000
Language(s): Dutch
ADVERTISING RATES:
Full Page Mono EUR 1/1: f.c. 1995,-; 1/2: f.c. 1200,-; 1/4: f.c. 325,-
Agency Commission: 15%
Mechanical Data: Type Area: 148 x 210mm
CONSUMER: OTHER CLASSIFICATIONS: Restaurant Guides

WADDENMAGAZINE 16853N57-69_50
Editorial: Droogstraat 3, 8861 SR HARLINGEN
Tel: 23 5564600 **Fax:** 23 5564626
Email: magazine@waddenvereniging.nl
Freq: Quarterly; **Cover Price:** EUR 2,50
Annual Sub.: EUR 23,-; **Circ:** 35,000
Editor: Hans Revier; **Editor-in-Chief:** Kees Loogman
Profile: Information magazine about nature preservation of the Dutch, German and Danish shallows, tidal flats, coasts and islands.
Language(s): Dutch
ADVERTISING RATES:
Full Page Mono EUR 1/1: f.c. 2850,-; 1/2: f.c. 1530,-; 1/4: f.c. 815,-
Agency Commission: 15%
Mechanical Data: Type Area: 200 x 240mm, Bleed Size: 220 x 260mm
BUSINESS: ENVIRONMENT & POLLUTION

WADDENREISGIDS 1633773N89A-270
Editorial: Willem Barentszkade 19a, 8881 BC TERSCHELLING WEST **Tel:** 172 466405
Fax: 342 494299
Email: info@vvvterschelling.nl
Freq: Annual; **Cover Price:** Free; **Circ:** 210,000
Usual Pagination: 100
Editor: Mathijs van Walsum
Language(s): Dutch
Agency Commission: 15%
Mechanical Data: Type Area: 185 x 265mm, Bleed Size: 210 x 297mm
CONSUMER: HOLIDAYS & TRAVEL: Travel

HET WANDELSPORTMAGAZINE 17621N75L-200
Editorial: Berg en Dalseweg 125, 6522 BE NIJMEGEN **Tel:** 172 466327 **Fax:** 172 493270
Email: info@wandel.nl
Freq: 6 issues yearly; **Cover Price:** EUR 3,50
Annual Sub.: EUR 21,50; **Circ:** 27,336
Editor: Bob Gaster
Profile: Official publication of the Walking Association in the Netherlands.
Language(s): Dutch
Readership: Read mainly by members.
ADVERTISING RATES:
Full Page Mono EUR 2/1: f.c. 3631,-; b/w 2019,- 1/1: f.c. 2137,-; b/w 1178,- 1/2: f.c. 1226,-; b/w 680,-
Agency Commission: 15%
Mechanical Data: Type Area: 195 x 255mm, Bleed Size: 215 x 285mm
Copy instructions: *Copy Date:* 4 weeks prior to publication date
CONSUMER: SPORT: Outdoor

WANTIJ 17892N80-306
Editorial: Ravelijn de Groene Jager 5, 4461 DJ GOES
Tel: 172 466327 **Fax:** 172 493270
Email: info@zmf.nl
Date Established: 01-01-1984; **Freq:** 3 issues yearly; **Cover Price:** EUR 1,15; **Circ:** 1,200
Usual Pagination: 24
Editor: Willem de Weert; **Editor-in-Chief:** Willem de Weert
Profile: Magazine containing information, articles, opinions and comments concerning the development of nature, landscape and environment in the Zeeland region.
Language(s): Dutch
ADVERTISING RATES:
Full Page Mono EUR 1/1: b/w 400,- 1/2: b/w 200,- 1/4: b/w 100,-
Agency Commission: 15%
Mechanical Data: Bleed Size: 210 x 297mm
CONSUMER: RURAL & REGIONAL INTEREST

DE WASSENAARDER 627038N72-6010
Editorial: Ambachtsweg 7a, 2222 AH KATWIJK
Tel: 30 2321276 **Fax:** 317 424060
Web site: http://www.dewassenaarder.nl
Freq: Weekly; **Circ:** 14,000
Editor: Esdor van Elten; **Publisher:** G. Verhagen
Language(s): Dutch
Agency Commission: 15%
Mechanical Data: Type Area: 374 x 550mm, Bleed Size: 400 x 577mm
LOCAL NEWSPAPERS

WATCHING 17434N74B-150
Editorial: Regenboog 25, 3742 ZA BAARN
Tel: 76 5722984 **Fax:** 570 614795
Email: uvw@vwg.net **Web site:** http://www.watching.nl
Date Established: 03-12-1995; **Freq:** Quarterly; **Cover Price:** EUR 4,95
Annual Sub.: EUR 18,95; **Circ:** 21,000
Editor: Jaap van Westering; **Editor-in-Chief:** Elzemarie Karsdorp; **Publisher:** Jaap van Westering
Profile: Magazine focusing on wrist watches, including articles on new innovations and celebrities.
Language(s): Dutch
Readership: Aimed at people with an interest in watches.
ADVERTISING RATES:
Full Page Mono EUR 2/1: f.c. 5250,-; 1/1: f.c. 3250,-; 1/2: f.c. 1750,-
Agency Commission: 15%
Mechanical Data: Type Area: 210 x 277mm, Bleed Size: 230 x 297mm
Copy instructions: *Copy Date:* 3 weeks prior to publication date
CONSUMER: WOMEN'S INTEREST CONSUMER MAGAZINES: Women's Interest - Fashion

WATER & LAND 17893N80-155
Editorial: Dijkwater 177, 1025 CW AMSTERDAM
Tel: 76 5722984
Date Established: 01-01-1972; **Freq:** Half-yearly; **Annual Sub.:** EUR 14,-; **Circ:** 600
Editor: R. van den Hoek
Profile: Publication focusing on the preservation of the Waterland area.
Language(s): Dutch
Readership: Read by residents of the Waterland region.
Agency Commission: 15%
Mechanical Data: Type Area: 180 x 180mm, Bleed Size: 210 x 210mm
CONSUMER: RURAL & REGIONAL INTEREST

WATERKAMPIOEN 17634N75M-275
Editorial: Wassenaarseweg 220, 2596 EC DEN HAAG **Tel:** 88 2697049 **Fax:** 88 2697356
Web site: http://www.waterkampioen.nl
Date Established: 01-01-1927; **Freq:** 20 issues yearly; **Cover Price:** EUR 4,95
Annual Sub.: EUR 89,95; **Circ:** 36,790
Editor: A. Beuken; **Publisher:** J. Rosier
Profile: Magazine covering all water sports.
Language(s): Dutch
ADVERTISING RATES:
Full Page Mono EUR 2/1: f.c. 9790,-; b/w 7333,- 1/1: f.c. 4895,-; b/w 3667,- 1/2: f.c. 2937,-; b/w 2199,-
Agency Commission: 15%
Mechanical Data: Type Area: 185 x 265mm, Bleed Size: 215 x 300mm
CONSUMER: SPORT: Water Sports

DE WATERKRANT 17453N74C-361
Editorial: Kronenburgsingel 515, 6831 GM ARNHEM
Tel: 88 8002915 **Fax:** 35 6474444
Email: info@hoogte80.com **Web site:** http://www.dewaterkrant.nl
Date Established: 01-01-1995; **Freq:** 3 issues yearly; **Cover Price:** Free; **Circ:** 500,000
Editor-in-Chief: Marjo Lodewikus
Profile: Magazine containing information about water quality and efficiency, health and hygiene.
Language(s): Dutch
Readership: Distributed to all customers of Dutch water companies.
Agency Commission: 15%
CONSUMER: WOMEN'S INTEREST CONSUMER MAGAZINES: Home & Family

WATERLAND WELZIJN 627163N72-6040
Editorial: Gorslaan 60b, 1441 RG PURMEREND
Tel: 20 5253370 **Fax:** 20 6767728
Email: info@webregiomedia.nl **Web site:** http://www.waterlandwelzijn.nl
Date Established: 01-07-1992; **Freq:** 8 issues yearly; **Cover Price:** Free; **Circ:** 51,000
Editor: Mark Klein; **Editor-in-Chief:** Mark Klein
Language(s): Dutch
ADVERTISING RATES:
Full Page Mono EUR 1/1: b/w 830,- 1/2: b/w 494,- 1/4: b/w 279,-
Agency Commission: 15%
Mechanical Data: Type Area: 262 x 390mm, Bleed Size: 289 x 415mm
Copy instructions: *Copy Date:* 3 weeks prior to publication date
LOCAL NEWSPAPERS

HET WATERSCHAP 16443N42C-70
Editorial: Prinses Beatrixlaan 116, 2595 AL DEN HAAG **Tel:** 88 2697049 **Fax:** 70 3544642
Email: sdu@sdu.nl
Freq: 11 issues yearly; **Cover Price:** EUR 13,25
Annual Sub.: EUR 104,50; **Circ:** 4,951
Editor: Kees Meijer; **Editor-in-Chief:** Bert Nijveld; **Publisher:** Dineke Sonderen
Profile: Magazine providing information on water management and the maintenance of waterways.
Language(s): Dutch
Readership: Read by water engineers and workers.
ADVERTISING RATES:
Full Page Mono .. EUR 1/1: b/w 1494,- 1/2: b/w 819,- 1/4: b/w 463,-
Agency Commission: 15%
Mechanical Data: Type Area: 185 x 280mm, Bleed Size: 210 x 297mm
Copy instructions: *Copy Date:* 2 weeks prior to publication date
BUSINESS: CONSTRUCTION: Water Engineering

WAVIN INFO 16071N19G-100
Editorial: J.C. Kellerlaan 8, 7772 SG HARDENBERG
Tel: 23 5565370 **Fax:** 55 5412288
Email: info@wavin.nl
Date Established: 01-03-1986; **Freq:** Quarterly; **Circ:** 7,500
Usual Pagination: 8
Profile: Magazine focusing on engineering pipelines.
Language(s): Dutch
Agency Commission: 15%
BUSINESS: ENGINEERING & MACHINERY: Pipelines

4 WD AUTO-MAGAZINE 17741N77A-3
Editorial: Kon. Wilhelminaweg 441, 3737 BE GROENEKAN **Tel:** 543 493705 **Fax:** 223 650011
Web site: http://www.4wdautomagazine.nl
Date Established: 30-05-1984; **Freq:** 11 issues yearly; **Cover Price:** EUR 4,20
Annual Sub.: EUR 39,-; **Circ:** 25,000
Editor: Dick van Zijl
Profile: Magazine containing reviews of new vehicle models, information about driving courses and holidays.
Language(s): Dutch
Readership: Aimed at owners of 4 wheel drive vehicles.
ADVERTISING RATES:
Full Page Mono EUR 1/1: f.c. 2045,-; b/w 1316,- 1/2: f.c. 1051,-; b/w 689,- 1/4: f.c. 543,-; b/w 363,-
Agency Commission: 15%
Mechanical Data: Type Area: 184 x 265mm, Bleed Size: 210 x 297mm
Copy instructions: *Copy Date:* 4 weeks prior to publication date
CONSUMER: MOTORING & CYCLING: Motoring

WEEKBLAD REGIO OSS 626768N72-6130
Editorial: Hooghuisstraat 34, 5341 CE OSS
Tel: 88 2944819 **Fax:** 30 6383991
Email: regiooss@weekbladregiooss.nl
Date Established: 19-03-1980; **Freq:** Weekly; **Cover Price:** Free; **Circ:** 49,300
Editor: Philip van den Brand; **Editor-in-Chief:** E. van de Pol-van de Ven
Language(s): Dutch
Agency Commission: 15%
Mechanical Data: Type Area: 278 x 415mm, Bleed Size: 290 x 420mm
LOCAL NEWSPAPERS

WEEKBLAD SPIJKENISSE 755524N72-6135
Editorial: Hoefsmitstraat 41, 3194 AA HOOGVLIET
Tel: 88 7518110 **Fax:** 20 5584301
Web site: http://www.weekbladspijkenisse.nl
Date Established: 13-03-1999; **Freq:** Weekly; **Cover Price:** Free; **Circ:** 44,000
Publisher: W. Fortuin
Language(s): Dutch
Agency Commission: 15%
Mechanical Data: Type Area: 273 x 350mm, Bleed Size: 287 x 380mm
LOCAL NEWSPAPERS

WEG EN WAGEN 16561N49A-60
Editorial: Hofweg 33, 2631 XD DEN HAAG
Tel: 23 5344089 **Fax:** 10 2801002
Email: info@beurtvaartadres.nl
Date Established: 01-05-1987; **Freq:** 3 issues yearly; **Annual Sub.:** EUR 15,-; **Circ:** 1,600
Usual Pagination: 4
Editor: R.G. Bruijne
Profile: Journal covering the law relating to road transport.
Language(s): Dutch
Agency Commission: 15%
BUSINESS: TRANSPORT

WEGWIJS 1795193N74M-268
Editorial: Spuiboulevard 196, 3311 GR DORDRECHT
Tel: 55 5388220 **Fax:** 23 5564588
Email: info@thuredrecht.nl **Web site:** http://www.wegwijs.nl
Freq: Half-yearly; **Cover Price:** EUR 4,95; **Circ:** 417,200
Usual Pagination: 76
Editor: O.C. Geysendorpher; **Editor-in-Chief:** B. Lou
Profile: Consumer magazine focusing on residential properties market, mortgages, investments, insurances and retiring pensions.
Language(s): Dutch
ADVERTISING RATES:
Full Page Mono ...... EUR 1/1: f.c. 12.500,-; ** 1/2: f.c. 7000,-; ** 1/4: f.c. 4000,-
Agency Commission: 15%
Mechanical Data: Bleed Size: 210 x 279mm
CONSUMER: WOMEN'S INTEREST CONSUMER MAGAZINES: Personal Finance

WEIGHTWATCHERS MAGAZINE 1644001N74G-287
Editorial: Kaldenkerkerweg 223, 5915 PP VENLO
Tel: 23 5565462 **Fax:** 23 5564588
Email: info@uitgeverijmarken.nl
Freq: 6 issues yearly; **Cover Price:** EUR 3,50; **Circ:** 55,000
Usual Pagination: 100
Editor: Marcel Hogenhuis
Language(s): Dutch
ADVERTISING RATES:
Full Page Mono EUR 1/1: f.c. 4750,-; 1/2: f.c. 2660,-; 1/4: f.c. 1450,-
Agency Commission: 15%
Mechanical Data: Type Area: 175 x 250mm, Bleed Size: 205 x 297mm
CONSUMER: WOMEN'S INTEREST CONSUMER MAGAZINES: Slimming & Health

WEL THUIS 760990N56R-200
Editorial: Van der Does de Willeboissingel 2, 5211 CA 'S-HERTOGENBOSCH **Tel:** 45 5739390
Fax: 299 666645
Email: info@damenromijn.nl
Date Established: 01-05-1999; **Freq:** 3 issues yearly; **Circ:** 232,535
Profile: Magazine focusing on health and welfare issues.

Language(s): Dutch
ADVERTISING RATES:
Full Page Mono . EUR 1/1: f.c. 4850,-; 1/2: f.c. 2850,-
Agency Commission: 15%
Mechanical Data: Type Area: 210 x 295mm, Bleed Size: 210 x 295mm
BUSINESS: HEALTH & MEDICAL: Health Medical Related

WELEDA BERICHTEN
1635393N14R-200
Editorial: Platinastraat 161, 2718 SR ZOETERMEER
Tel: 88 7518480 **Fax:** 88 7518481
Email: info@weleda.nl
Date Established: 01-01-1932; **Freq:** Quarterly; **Cover Price:** Free; **Circ:** 195,000
Editor: Sandra Vlot; **Publisher:** M. Niemeijer
Language(s): Dutch
Agency Commission: 15%
BUSINESS: COMMERCE, INDUSTRY & MANAGEMENT: Commerce Related

WELKE WONEN
16565N74K-260
Editorial: Grasweg 63-65, 1031 HX AMSTERDAM
Tel: 53 4842842 **Fax:** 53 4842706
Email: info@mediamij.nl **Web site:** http://www.welke.nl
Freq: Quarterly; **Cover Price:** EUR 3,95; **Circ:** 120,000
Editor: Rogier Swagerman; **Publisher:** Jan Jaap van der Klei
Profile: Journal covering all aspects of moving accommodation, including finance and interiors.
Language(s): Dutch
Readership: Aimed at people who are interesting in information about moving house.
ADVERTISING RATES:
Full Page Mono .... EUR 2/1: f.c. 15.800,-; 1/1: f.c. 8550,-; 1/2: f.c. 5750,-
Agency Commission: 15%
Mechanical Data: Type Area: 185 x 250mm, Bleed Size: 215 x 285mm
CONSUMER: WOMEN'S INTEREST CONSUMER MAGAZINES: Home Purchase

WELLNESS LIFE
1857682N74G-326
Editorial: Meeleweg 26, 7711 EM NIEUWLEUSEN
Tel: 70 3789685 **Fax:** 70 7999840
Email: info@hmseuro.com
Freq: Quarterly; **Annual Sub.:** EUR 30,-; **Circ:** 65,000
Editor: Guido Willemsen
Language(s): Dutch
Agency Commission: 15%
Mechanical Data: Bleed Size: 210 x 297mm
CONSUMER: WOMEN'S INTEREST CONSUMER MAGAZINES: Slimming & Health

DE WELSH SPRINGER
17919N81B-75
Editorial: Aarweg 3. 01, 8071 WV NUNSPEET
Tel: 88 7518380
Date Established: 01-04-1976; **Freq:** 6 issues yearly; **Circ:** 1,050
Editor: R. Hörter
Profile: Magazine about Welsh Springer Spaniels.
Language(s): Dutch
Agency Commission: 15%
Mechanical Data: Type Area: 125 x 180mm, Bleed Size: 145 x 215mm
CONSUMER: ANIMALS & PETS: Dogs

DE WERELD VAN HET JONGE KIND (HJK)
16916N62C-180
Editorial: Smallepad 30, 3811 MG AMERSFOORT
Tel: 20 5159172 **Fax:** 20 5159700
Web site: http://www.hjk-online.nl
Freq: 10 issues yearly; **Cover Price:** EUR 8,-
Annual Sub.: EUR 58,95; **Circ:** 5,823
Editor-in-Chief: Iris van den Berg
Profile: Publication covering the development, upbringing and education of children.
Language(s): Dutch
Readership: Aimed at teachers of children aged between 4 and 8 years.
ADVERTISING RATES:
Full Page Mono .. EUR 1/1: b/w 1315,- 1/2: b/w 695,- 1/4: b/w 385,-
Agency Commission: 15%
Mechanical Data: Type Area: 170 x 257mm, Bleed Size: 210 x 297mm
Copy instructions: *Copy Date:* 3 weeks prior to publication date
BUSINESS: CHURCH & SCHOOL EQUIPMENT & EDUCATION: Junior Education

DE WERELDFIETSER
17775N77C-68
Editorial: Postbus 94005, 1090 GA AMSTERDAM
Tel: 23 5565135 **Fax:** 88 5567355
Web site: http://www.wereldfietser.nl
Freq: Quarterly; **Cover Price:** EUR 4,95
Annual Sub.: EUR 22,-; **Circ:** 5,000
Editor: Monique van Klaveren; **Publisher:** Theo Jorna
Profile: Magazine covering cycling holidays and travel by bicycle worldwide.
Language(s): Dutch
ADVERTISING RATES:
Full Page Mono EUR 1/1: f.c. 250,-; 1/2: f.c. 148,-; 1/4: f.c. 84,-
Agency Commission: 15%
Mechanical Data: Type Area: 188 x 228mm, Bleed Size: 220 x 275mm
Copy instructions: *Copy Date:* 3 weeks prior to publication date
CONSUMER: MOTORING & CYCLING: Cycling

WERELDKINDEREN
16331N32G-199_75
Editorial: Riouwstraat 191, 2585 HT DEN HAAG
Tel: 523 285330 **Fax:** 30 6348909
Email: info@wereldkinderen.nl **Web site:** http://www.wereldkinderen.nl
Freq: 6 issues yearly; **Circ:** 8,600
Usual Pagination: 32
Editor: Martien Miedema
Profile: Magazine about international adoption, child sponsorship and project help, seen from a Dutch perspective.
Language(s): Dutch
Agency Commission: 15%
BUSINESS: LOCAL GOVERNMENT, LEISURE & RECREATION: Community Care & Social Services

WERELDS
1808942N89A-242
Editorial: Jacob Marisstraat 34-2, 1058 JA AMSTERDAM **Tel:** 20 5855333
Email: hmpbusiness@gmail.com
Freq: Half-yearly; **Cover Price:** Free; **Circ:** 200,000
Editor-in-Chief: Titia Voûte
Language(s): Dutch
ADVERTISING RATES:
Full Page Mono EUR 1/1: f.c. 3300,-; 1/2: f.c. 1925,-; 1/4: f.c. 1050,-
Agency Commission: 15%
Mechanical Data: Bleed Size: 210 x 265mm
CONSUMER: HOLIDAYS & TRAVEL: Travel

WERKBLAD
1753367N14F-202
Editorial: Vijverweg 18, 2061 GX BLOEMENDAAL
Tel: 113 274014 **Fax:** 24 3723631
Email: info@vdbj.nl
Freq: Half-yearly; **Cover Price:** Free; **Circ:** 200,000
Language(s): Dutch
Agency Commission: 15%
Mechanical Data: Bleed Size: 210 x 297mm
BUSINESS: COMMERCE, INDUSTRY & MANAGEMENT: Training & Recruitment

WERK!NAMSTERDAM.NL
1800431N80-545
Editorial: Edisonweg 22, 1821 BN ALKMAAR
Tel: 314 377831 **Fax:** 314 377839
Email: info@werk-in.nl **Web site:** http://www.werkinamsterdam.nl
Freq: 13 issues yearly; **Cover Price:** Free; **Circ:** 420,000
Language(s): Dutch
Agency Commission: 15%
Mechanical Data: Type Area: 263 x 375mm, Bleed Size: 290 x 420mm
CONSUMER: RURAL & REGIONAL INTEREST

DE WERKPOCKET
1633725N14F-159
Editorial: Postbus 12600, 1100 AP AMSTERDAM
Tel: 342 494848 **Fax:** 314 349023
Email: contentmanagement@nl.randstad.com
Date Established: 01-01-1976; **Freq:** Annual; **Cover Price:** Free; **Circ:** 65,000
Language(s): Dutch
Agency Commission: 15%
BUSINESS: COMMERCE, INDUSTRY & MANAGEMENT: Training & Recruitment

WERKWOORD
1634333N32G-337
Editorial: Weesperstraat 113, 1018 VN AMSTERDAM
Tel: 88 2697856 **Fax:** 70 3364601
Email: info@dwi.amsterdam.nl
Freq: Monthly; **Cover Price:** Free; **Circ:** 51,500
Editor: Carmen Westra
Language(s): Dutch
Agency Commission: 15%
Mechanical Data: Type Area: 140 x 270mm, Bleed Size: 170 x 300mm
BUSINESS: LOCAL GOVERNMENT, LEISURE & RECREATION: Community Care & Social Services

DE WESSANER
19241N80-428
Editorial: Middel 165, 1551 SV WESTZAAN
Tel: 229 216416
Email: wessaner@gmail.com
Date Established: 01-11-1984; **Freq:** 11 issues yearly; **Circ:** 2,600
Editor: P. Huisman; **Editor-in-Chief:** P. Huisman
Profile: Regional newspaper covering all aspects of the Westzaan area.
Language(s): Dutch
ADVERTISING RATES:
Full Page Mono EUR 1/1: b/w 240,- 1/1: b/w 120,- 1/4: b/w 60,-
Agency Commission: 15%
CONSUMER: RURAL & REGIONAL INTEREST

WEST
15517N1D-40
Editorial: Stadsring 201, 3817 BA AMERSFOORT
Tel: 23 5565370 **Fax:** 475 551033
Email: info@nva.nl
Freq: 11 issues yearly; **Cover Price:** EUR 17,50
Annual Sub.: EUR 82,50; **Circ:** 1,790
Editor: R. Andriessen; **Publisher:** J. Verbeek
Profile: Publication of the NVA - the Netherlands Association of Assurance Advisers.
Language(s): Dutch
Readership: Aimed at insurance agents and brokers.
ADVERTISING RATES:
Full Page Mono EUR 1/1: b/w 2855,- 1/2: b/w 1855,- 1/4: b/w 1185,-
Agency Commission: 15%
Mechanical Data: Bleed Size: 210 x 280mm, Type Area: 165 x 233mm
BUSINESS: FINANCE & ECONOMICS: Insurance

WESTFRIES WEEKBLAD
626742N72-6350
Editorial: Dr. C.J.K. van Aalstweg 8r, 1625 NV HOORN **Tel:** 20 5159172 **Fax:** 229 216416
Email: redactie@westfriesweekblad.nl **Web site:** http://www.westfriesweekblad.nl
Freq: Weekly; **Cover Price:** Free; **Circ:** 86,120
Language(s): Dutch
Agency Commission: 15%
Mechanical Data: Type Area: 260 x 390mm
LOCAL NEWSPAPERS

WESTVOORNSE COURANT
626793N72-6370
Editorial: Dr. Kuyperkade 28, 3142 GC MAASSLUIS
Tel: 35 67272103 **Fax:** 20 5159145
Email: info@thuisbladen.nl
Date Established: 01-01-1981; **Freq:** Weekly; **Cover Price:** Free; **Circ:** 14,000
Editor: P.C. de Groot; **Publisher:** P.C. de Groot
Language(s): Dutch
Agency Commission: 15%
Mechanical Data: Type Area: 260 x 400mm, Bleed Size: 290 x 440mm
LOCAL NEWSPAPERS

WHY'S IN DE KRAAMTIJD
1866139N56M-1
Editorial: Barentzplein 6b, 1013 NJ AMSTERDAM
Tel: 314 349446
Email: info@reclamij.nl
Freq: Annual; **Cover Price:** Free; **Circ:** 100,000
Editor: Lara Geeurickx; **Publisher:** Carin Derks
Language(s): Dutch
ADVERTISING RATES:
Full Page Mono ... EUR 1/1: f.c. 3525,-; 1/4: f.c. 590,-
Agency Commission: 15%
Mechanical Data: Type Area: 160 x 195mm, Bleed Size: 160 x 195mm
BUSINESS: HEALTH & MEDICAL: Family Planning

WHY'S IN VERWACHTING
1637202N74D-162
Editorial: Barentzplein 6b, 1013 NJ AMSTERDAM
Tel: 88 2696657
Email: info@reclamij.nl
Freq: Half-yearly; **Cover Price:** Free; **Circ:** 187,647
Editor: Carla Blaauw; **Publisher:** Carin Derks
Language(s): Dutch
ADVERTISING RATES:
Full Page Mono . EUR 1/1: f.c. 7060,-; 1/2: f.c. 3530,-
Agency Commission: 15%
Mechanical Data: Type Area: 160 x 195mm, Bleed Size: 160 x 195mm
CONSUMER: WOMEN'S INTEREST CONSUMER MAGAZINES: Child Care

WHY'S MET KLEINTJES
1702912N74P-226
Editorial: Barentzplein 6b, 1013 NJ AMSTERDAM
Tel: 23 5425105
Email: info@reclamij.nl
Freq: Half-yearly; **Cover Price:** Free; **Circ:** 50,000
Editor: Laura Jansma; **Publisher:** Carin Derks
Language(s): Dutch
ADVERTISING RATES:
Full Page Mono .... EUR 1/1: f.c. 3000,-
Agency Commission: 15%
Mechanical Data: Type Area: 160 x 195mm
CONSUMER: WOMEN'S INTEREST CONSUMER MAGAZINES: Food & Cookery

WIERINGER COURANT
627253N72-6385
Editorial: Smidsweg 59, 1761 BH ANNA PAULOWNA
Web site: http://www.wieringercourant.nl
Freq: 104 issues yearly; **Circ:** 5,400
Language(s): Dutch
Agency Commission: 15%
Mechanical Data: Type Area: 260 x 390mm
LOCAL NEWSPAPERS

WIJ IN WIJCHEN, DUKENBURG EN LINDENHOLT
17895N80-162
Editorial: Startvenseweg 69, 6601 EL WIJCHEN
Tel: 20 5310161 **Fax:** 20 5302585
Email: reflex-nieuws@online.nl **Web site:** http://www.wijchensnieuws.nl
Freq: 26 issues yearly; **Cover Price:** Free; **Circ:** 35,500
Editor: J. Vrolijks
Profile: Magazine containing information for the Dukenburg area.
Language(s): Dutch
Readership: Read by local residents.
ADVERTISING RATES:
Full Page Mono .... EUR 12x 1/1 (per plaatsing): f.c. 650,-; 12x 1/2 (per plaatsing): f.c. 330,-; 12x 1/4 (per plaatsing):
Agency Commission: 15%
Mechanical Data: Type Area: 260 x 380mm
CONSUMER: RURAL & REGIONAL INTEREST

WIJ JONGE OUDERS
17466N74D-150
Editorial: Veermanskade 2, 1621 AN HOORN
Tel: 20 5310161 **Fax:** 20 5302585
Email: info@wij.nl
Freq: 10 issues yearly; **Cover Price:** Free; **Circ:** 239,260
Editor: P. Remmers; **Publisher:** R. van Vroenhoven
Profile: Magazine for young parents and parents-to-be.
Language(s): Dutch
ADVERTISING RATES:
Full Page Mono .... EUR 2/1: f.c. 19.580,-; 1/1: f.c. 9790,-; 1/2: f.c. 6490,-
Agency Commission: 15%
Mechanical Data: Type Area: 185 x 252mm, Bleed Size: 215 x 282mm
Copy instructions: *Copy Date:* 4 weeks prior to publication date
CONSUMER: WOMEN'S INTEREST CONSUMER MAGAZINES: Child Care

WIJN AAN TAFEL
15818N9C-110
Editorial: Wilhelminakanaal Noord 2a, 4902 VR OOSTERHOUT **Tel:** 45 5739390
Date Established: 01-01-1985; **Freq:** 3 issues yearly; **Annual Sub.:** EUR 9,-; **Circ:** 4,000
Editor: Joke Holster
Profile: Magazine containing culinary and wine news.
Language(s): Dutch
Readership: Aimed at restaurateurs and wine retailers.
Agency Commission: 15%
Mechanical Data: Type Area: 185 x 260mm, Bleed Size: 210 x 297mm
BUSINESS: DRINKS & LICENSED TRADE: Licensed Trade, Wines & Spirits

DE WINDMOLEN
16864N58-85
Editorial: Cornelis de Vriendtstraat 17, 50411 GL TILBURG
Date Established: 01-12-1975; **Freq:** Quarterly; **Circ:** 350
Usual Pagination: 56
Editor: Michel Dellebeke
Profile: Magazine about windmills in the province of Zeeland.
Language(s): Dutch
Agency Commission: 15%
BUSINESS: ENERGY, FUEL & NUCLEAR

WINDNIEUWS
16865N58-88
Editorial: Briljant 82, 1703 GS HEERHUGOWAARD
Tel: 20 5159172
Date Established: 01-03-1988; **Freq:** 6 issues yearly; **Cover Price:** EUR 10,-
Annual Sub.: EUR 42,-; **Circ:** 1,200
Editor: Cees Bakker; **Editor-in-Chief:** Huub Halsema
Profile: Journal containing information about windmills and wind power.
Language(s): Dutch
ADVERTISING RATES:
Full Page Mono .... EUR 1/1: f.c. 1450,-; ** 1/2: f.c. 850,-; ** 1/4: f.c. 250,-
Agency Commission: 15%
Mechanical Data: Type Area: 180 x 269mm, Bleed Size: 213 x 303mm
BUSINESS: ENERGY, FUEL & NUCLEAR

WINMAG PRO MAGAZINE
15757N5B-285
Editorial: Delftweg 147, 2289 BD RIJSWIJK
Tel: 15 2153232 **Fax:** 314 349035
Email: info@clipboard-publishing.nl **Web site:** http://www.winmag.nl
Freq: 6 issues yearly; **Circ:** 49,500
Editor: Raymond Luijbregts; **Publisher:** Linda Oenema
Profile: Magazine containing information about Windows.
Language(s): Dutch
Readership: Aimed at IT professionals.
ADVERTISING RATES:
Full Page Mono EUR 2/1: f.c. 6250,-; 1/1: f.c. 3895,-; 1/2: f.c. 2650,-
Agency Commission: 15%
Mechanical Data: Type Area: 185 x 250mm, Bleed Size: 215 x 285mm
BUSINESS: COMPUTERS & AUTOMATION: Data Processing

WINTERSPORT MAGAZINE
17604N75G-222
Editorial: Aletta Jacobslaan 7, 1066 BP AMSTERDAM **Tel:** 23 7523919 **Fax:** 318 696179
Email: info@rhbm.nl
Freq: 5 issues yearly; **Cover Price:** EUR 4,80; **Circ:** 60,000
Editor: Fleur Breitbarth
Profile: Magazine of the Dutch Snowboarding and Skiing Association.
Language(s): Dutch
Readership: Aimed at winter sports enthusiasts.
ADVERTISING RATES:
Full Page Mono EUR 2/1: f.c. 9995,-; 1/1: f.c. 5250,-; 1/2: f.c. 3700,-
Agency Commission: 15%
Mechanical Data: Bleed Size: 175 x 255mm
Copy instructions: *Copy Date:* 4 weeks prior to publication date
CONSUMER: SPORT: Winter Sports

WINTERVAKANTIEMAGAZINE
761363N89E-100
Editorial: Kronkelbaan 11, 1157 LH ABBEKERK
Tel: 492 338432 **Fax:** 70 3839840
Email: info@globe-advertising.nl
Freq: Annual; **Cover Price:** Free; **Circ:** 1,200,000
Editor: Gunther Gagg; **Publisher:** Gunther Gagg
Profile: Magazine covering news and information on winter holidays abroad.
Language(s): Dutch
Agency Commission: 15%
Mechanical Data: Type Area: 190 x 255mm, Bleed Size: 200 x 272mm
CONSUMER: HOLIDAYS & TRAVEL: Holidays

WITTE WEEKBLAD EDITIE BADHOEVEDORP E.O.
630257N72-7493
Editorial: Luzernestraat 19, 2153 GM NIEUW-VENNEP **Tel:** 88 2697112 **Fax:** 88 2696983
Date Established: 01-08-1983; **Freq:** Weekly; **Cover Price:** Free; **Circ:** 7,500
Language(s): Dutch
Agency Commission: 15%
Mechanical Data: Type Area: 260 x 390mm
LOCAL NEWSPAPERS

WITTE WEEKBLAD EDITIE HILLEGOM E.O.
627008N72-6450
Editorial: Luzernestraat 19, 2153 GM NIEUW-VENNEP **Tel:** 570 647064 **Fax:** 570 637533
Date Established: 06-01-1994; **Freq:** Weekly; **Cover Price:** Free; **Circ:** 11,300
Language(s): Dutch
Agency Commission: 15%
Mechanical Data: Type Area: 260 x 390mm
LOCAL NEWSPAPERS

WITTE WEEKBLAD EDITIE TEYLINGEN & NOORDWIJKERHOUT
629861N72-7519
Editorial: Basisweg 30, 1043 AP AMSTERDAM
Tel: 23 5344089 **Fax:** 10 2801002
Email: info@hollandcombinatie.nl
Date Established: 06-01-1994; **Freq:** Weekly; **Cover Price:** Free; **Circ:** 19,925
Language(s): Dutch
Agency Commission: 15%
Mechanical Data: Type Area: 260 x 390mm
LOCAL NEWSPAPERS

WITTE WEEKBLAD EDITIE ZWANENBURG E.O.
630008N72-7492
Editorial: Luzernestraat 19, 2153 GM NIEUW-VENNEP **Tel:** 88 2697112 **Fax:** 88 2696983
Date Established: 01-08-1983; **Freq:** Weekly; **Cover Price:** Free; **Circ:** 7,350
Language(s): Dutch
Agency Commission: 15%
Mechanical Data: Type Area: 260 x 390mm
LOCAL NEWSPAPERS

WITVIS TOTAAL
765757N92-211
Editorial: Keppelseweg 28, 7001 CG DOETINCHEM
Tel: 20 5979546 **Fax:** 20 5979614
Email: info@publishinghouse.nl **Web site:** http://www.witvistotaal.nl
Date Established: 24-05-2002; **Freq:** 6 issues yearly; **Cover Price:** EUR 6,60
Annual Sub.: EUR 35,-; **Circ:** 12,500
Editor: Peter Dohmen; **Publisher:** H. te Kloeze
Profile: Magazine about coarse fishing.
Language(s): Dutch
Readership: Read by angling enthusiasts.
ADVERTISING RATES:
Full Page Mono EUR 1/1: b/w 775,- 1/2: b/w 420,- 1/4: b/w 240,-
Agency Commission: 15%
Mechanical Data: Type Area: 184 x 252mm, Bleed Size: 210 x 280mm
CONSUMER: ANGLING & FISHING

WMO MAGAZINE
16765N56L-40
Editorial: Keizersgracht 213, 1016 DT AMSTERDAM
Tel: 23 5565370 **Fax:** 55 5412288
Email: info@y-publicaties.nl
Freq: 6 issues yearly; **Annual Sub.:** EUR 85,50; **Circ:** 1,500
Editor: Stan Verhaag; **Publisher:** Ralf Beekveldt
Profile: Magazine about policy making on care and support of people with disabilities.
Language(s): Dutch
Readership: Policy makers, service providers and people who work with people with disabilities.
ADVERTISING RATES:
Full Page Mono EUR 1/1: f.c. 1980,-; b/w 1286,- 1/2: f.c. 1368,-; b/w 743,- 1/4: f.c. 964,-; b/w 409,-
Agency Commission: 15%
Mechanical Data: Bleed Size: 210 x 297mm, Type Area: 179 x 265mm
Copy instructions: *Copy Date:* 3 weeks prior to publication date
BUSINESS: HEALTH & MEDICAL: Disability & Rehabilitation

DE WOENSDRECHTSE BODE
629929N72-7534
Editorial: Sint Catharinaplein 12, 4611 TS BERGEN OP ZOOM **Tel:** 172 466622 **Fax:** 24 3723631
Web site: http://www.internetbode.nl
Freq: Weekly; **Circ:** 9,800
Editor: Vif Janssen; **Editor-in-Chief:** Vif Janssen
Language(s): Dutch
Agency Commission: 15%
Mechanical Data: Type Area: 264 x 400mm
LOCAL NEWSPAPERS

WOLKENRIDDER MAGAZINE
15798N6F-16
Editorial: Amsterdamseweg 55, 1182 GP AMSTELVEEN **Tel:** 223 650017
Date Established: 05-10-1946; **Freq:** 10 issues yearly; **Annual Sub.:** EUR 27,27; **Circ:** 43,000
Usual Pagination: 24
Editor: Elsbeth Ketting
Profile: Magazine for staff of KLM Royal Dutch Airlines.
Language(s): Dutch
Agency Commission: 15%
Mechanical Data: Bleed Size: 215 x 279mm
BUSINESS: AVIATION & AERONAUTICS: Airlines

WOMEN'S GLOBAL NETWORK FOR REPRODUCTIVE RIGHTS NEWSLETTER
17563N74Q-255
Editorial: Vrolikstraat 453d, 1092 TJ AMSTERDAM
Tel: 23 5564919 **Fax:** 23 5564911
Email: office@wgnrr.nl
Date Established: 01-01-1984; **Freq:** Half-yearly; **Annual Sub.:** EUR 41,-; **Circ:** 2,200
Usual Pagination: 36
Editor: Zelda Soriano
Profile: Publication focusing on international issues related to women's health and reproductive rights.
Language(s): Dutch
Agency Commission: 15%
CONSUMER: WOMEN'S INTEREST CONSUMER MAGAZINES: Lifestyle

247 WONEN
1640486N74K-231
Editorial: Keurenplein 53, 1069 CD AMSTERDAM
Tel: 26 8450860 **Fax:** 172 422886
Email: office@dcmp.nl **Web site:** http://www.247wonen.nl
Date Established: 01-05-2000; **Freq:** Monthly; **Cover Price:** Free; **Circ:** 50,000
Profile: Publication focusing on owner occupied and vacant properties within the Greater Amsterdam area.
Language(s): Dutch
ADVERTISING RATES:
Full Page Mono EUR 1/1: b/w 2080,- 1/2: b/w 1134,-
Agency Commission: 15%
Mechanical Data: Type Area: 240 x 310mm, Bleed Size: 260 x 330mm
CONSUMER: WOMEN'S INTEREST CONSUMER MAGAZINES: Home Purchase

WONEN-DOE-JE-ZO.NL
1986293N4D-203
Editorial: Lijnbaan 17a, 3231 AE BRIELLE
Tel: 30 2303508 **Fax:** 46 4116281
Email: info@cubicmedia.nl **Web site:** http://www.wonen-doe-je-zo.nl
Date Established: 23-03-2010; **Freq:** 6 issues yearly; **Circ:** 180,000
Editor: Gerrit van Loon
Language(s): Dutch
ADVERTISING RATES:
Full Page Mono .... EUR 1/1: f.c. 9000,-
Agency Commission: 15%
Mechanical Data: Bleed Size: 255 x 385mm
BUSINESS: ARCHITECTURE & BUILDING: Planning & Housing

WONENWONEN.NL
1731997N74C-271
Editorial: Eindsestraat 37a, 5105 AA DONGEN
Tel: 172 469050 **Fax:** 23 5565511
Email: info@wonenwonen.nl **Web site:** http://www.wonenwonen.nl
Date Established: 01-05-2001; **Freq:** Half-yearly; **Cover Price:** EUR 2,45; **Circ:** 370,000
Language(s): Dutch
ADVERTISING RATES:
Full Page Mono .... EUR 1/1: b/w 2995,-
Agency Commission: 15%
Mechanical Data: Type Area: 260 x 375mm, Bleed Size: 289 x 400mm
CONSUMER: WOMEN'S INTEREST CONSUMER MAGAZINES: Home & Family

DE WOONBODE 'T GOOI
718621N72-6593
Editorial: Seinstraat 14, 1223 DA HILVERSUM
Tel: 223 650017 **Fax:** 35 6254567
Freq: Weekly; **Cover Price:** Free; **Circ:** 138,020
Language(s): Dutch
Agency Commission: 15%
Mechanical Data: Type Area: 260 x 390mm
LOCAL NEWSPAPERS

WOONBOOT MAGAZINE
18175N91A-120
Editorial: Postbus 8192, 3503 RD UTRECHT
Tel: 23 5344089 **Fax:** 10 4739911
Email: lwo@lwoorg.nl **Web site:** http://www.woonbootmagazine.nl
Freq: 6 issues yearly; **Cover Price:** EUR 3,80
Annual Sub.: EUR 39,50; **Circ:** 2,500
Profile: Magazine containing articles about houseboats and water culture worldwide.
Language(s): Dutch
ADVERTISING RATES:
Full Page Mono .... EUR 1/1: f.c. 700,-; b/w 524,- 1/2: f.c. 400,-; b/w 286,- 1/4: f.c. 250,-; b/w 167,-
Agency Commission: 15%
Mechanical Data: Type Area: 185 x 270mm, Bleed Size: 210 x 297mm
CONSUMER: RECREATION & LEISURE: Boating & Yachting

WOONSTIJL
1665215N74K-235
Editorial: Havendijk 6, 4201 XA GORINCHEM
Tel: 20 8969520
Email: info@mediamikx.nl
Date Established: 01-10-2001; **Freq:** 8 issues yearly; **Cover Price:** Free; **Circ:** 192,500
Editor-in-Chief: G. Peeters; **Publisher:** J.H. van der Meijden
Profile: Publication focusing on residential real estate properties.
Language(s): Dutch
Agency Commission: 15%
Mechanical Data: Type Area: 190 x 272mm, Bleed Size: 230 x 300mm
CONSUMER: WOMEN'S INTEREST CONSUMER MAGAZINES: Home Purchase

WOONWEST
1799048N74Q-350
Editorial: Pieter Calandlaan 323, 1068 NH AMSTERDAM **Tel:** 172 469050 **Fax:** 118 434059
Web site: http://www.woonwest.nl
Freq: Monthly; **Cover Price:** Free; **Circ:** 80,000
Editor-in-Chief: René Kater; **Publisher:** J.J. Kater
Language(s): Dutch
ADVERTISING RATES:
Full Page Mono .. EUR 1/1: b/w 1670,- 1/2: b/w 840,- 1/4: b/w 475,-
Agency Commission: 15%
Mechanical Data: Type Area: 264,8 x 395mm, Bleed Size: 280,8 x 405mm
CONSUMER: WOMEN'S INTEREST CONSUMER MAGAZINES: Lifestyle

WPNR
1637024N44-167
Editorial: Spui 184, 2511 BW DEN HAAG
Tel: 70 3307156 **Fax:** 70 3602861
Email: communicatie@knb.nl **Web site:** http://www.wpnr.nl
Freq: 44 issues yearly; **Cover Price:** EUR 7,08
Annual Sub.: EUR 154,48; **Circ:** 4,938
Publisher: Maaike Jonker
Language(s): Dutch
ADVERTISING RATES:
Full Page Mono .. EUR 1/1: b/w 1478,- 1/2: b/w 860,- 1/4: b/w 490,-
Agency Commission: 15%
Mechanical Data: Type Area: 172 x 262mm, Bleed Size: 210 x 297mm
Copy instructions: *Copy Date:* 10 days prior to publication date
BUSINESS: LEGAL

WRITTEN LANGUAGE AND LITERACY
18973N84B-241
Editorial: Klaprozenweg 75g, 1033 NN AMSTERDAM
Tel: 229 216416 **Fax:** 229 265738
Email: customer.services@benjamins.nl
Freq: Half-yearly; **Annual Sub.:** EUR 200,-
Profile: Professional journal focusing on written language and literacy.
Language(s): Dutch
Agency Commission: 15%
CONSUMER: THE ARTS & LITERARY: Literary

XIST IN CHRIST
1703300N87-2522
Editorial: Emmastraat 18, 8011 AG ZWOLLE
Tel: 23 5425105 **Fax:** 23 5519544
Email: info@inspiritmedia.nl **Web site:** http://www.xistinchrist.nl
Freq: 8 issues yearly; **Cover Price:** EUR 3,50
Annual Sub.: EUR 31,95; **Circ:** 5,000
Editor: Hanna Smallenbroek; **Editor-in-Chief:** Wilfred Hermans; **Publisher:** Leendert de Jong
Language(s): Dutch
ADVERTISING RATES:
Full Page Mono EUR 1/1: f.c. 635,-; 1/2: f.c. 370,-; 1/4: f.c. 215,-
Agency Commission: 15%
Mechanical Data: Type Area: 190 x 277mm, Bleed Size: 210 x 297mm
CONSUMER: RELIGIOUS

YINX MAGAZINE
2000799N15A-98
Editorial: Galopstraat 44, 1326 RR ALMERE
Email: mediaemotions@me.com
Freq: 6 issues yearly; **Cover Price:** Free; **Circ:** 100,000
Usual Pagination: 52
Editor: Mike Kepel
Language(s): Dutch
ADVERTISING RATES:
Full Page Mono EUR 1/1: b/w 3000,- 1/2: b/w 2000,-
Agency Commission: 15%
Mechanical Data: Bleed Size: 210 x 297mm
BUSINESS: COSMETICS & HAIRDRESSING: Cosmetics

YPSILON NIEUWS
16787N56N-150
Editorial: Prins Bernhardlaan 177, 2273 DP VOORBURG **Tel:** 45 5739390 **Fax:** 20 5233419
Email: ypsilon@ypsilon.org **Web site:** http://www.ypsilon.org/yn
Date Established: 01-02-1994; **Freq:** 6 issues yearly; **Annual Sub.:** EUR 40,-; **Circ:** 6,500
Usual Pagination: 36
Editor: Bert Stavenuiter; **Editor-in-Chief:** A.M.B. de Kruif
Profile: Journal focusing on the effects of schizophrenia. Covers new drugs available, research developments and provides articles on care, health and treatments.
Language(s): Dutch
Readership: Aimed at nurses, carers, families, counsellors, doctors and psychiatrists.
Agency Commission: 15%
Mechanical Data: Bleed Size: 210 x 297mm
BUSINESS: HEALTH & MEDICAL: Mental Health

Z & R
16184N23A-100
Editorial: Mariadal 1, 5916 SL VENLO
Tel: 0032 34660066
Email: redactie@zenronline.nl **Web site:** http://www.zenrvaktijdschrift.nl
Date Established: 23-05-1997; **Freq:** 8 issues yearly; **Annual Sub.:** EUR 53,77; **Circ:** 3,250
Editor-in-Chief: Thijs Pubben
Profile: Journal about blinds and shutters.
Language(s): Dutch
ADVERTISING RATES:
Full Page Mono EUR 2/1: f.c. 2200,-; 1/1: f.c. 1500,-; 1/2: f.c. 1150,-
Agency Commission: 15%
Mechanical Data: Type Area: 197 x 267mm, Bleed Size: 230 x 297mm
BUSINESS: FURNISHINGS & FURNITURE

ZAAD & VOER MAGAZINE
16113N21A-350
Editorial: Stationsstraat 40, 6515 AB NIJMEGEN
Tel: 20 5159172 **Fax:** 20 5159700
Email: info@barenbrug.nl
Freq: Half-yearly; **Cover Price:** Free; **Circ:** 27,500
Usual Pagination: 16
Editor: Astrid van den Brink
Profile: Journal containing information on utilisation of pasture and growing of maize, clovers, alfalfa and fodderbeet.
Language(s): Dutch
Readership: Read by growers and retailers of agricultural seeds, advisers and teachers in agricultural colleges and dairy farmers.
Agency Commission: 15%
BUSINESS: AGRICULTURE & FARMING

ZAANSTREEK OP ZONDAG
629880N72-7421
Editorial: Broeker Werf 8, 1721 PC BROEK OP LANGEDIJK **Tel:** 45 5739390 **Fax:** 299 666645
Email: rodimedia@rodi.nl **Web site:** http://www.zaanstreekopzondag.nl
Freq: Weekly; **Cover Price:** Free; **Circ:** 74,900
Editor: Donald Esser
Language(s): Dutch
Agency Commission: 15%
Mechanical Data: Type Area: 265 x 395mm, Bleed Size: 281 x 405mm
LOCAL NEWSPAPERS

ZAKELIJK
16952N63-73
Editorial: Driezeeg 4, 5258 LE BERLICUM
Tel: 348 436599 **Fax:** 88 2697490
Email: info@toppers.nl

Date Established: 01-09-1994; **Freq:** 6 issues yearly; **Cover Price:** EUR 4,25; **Circ:** 8,000
Editor: M. van Diessen; **Editor-in-Chief:** S. Kagie
Profile: Business-to-business publication for industry and wholesale trade in the Eindhoven and Helmond regions.
Language(s): Dutch
Readership: Aimed at managers.
ADVERTISING RATES:
Full Page Mono .. EUR 1/1: f.c. 1425,-; 1/2: f.c. 825,-; 1/4: f.c. 495,-
Agency Commission: 15%
Mechanical Data: Type Area: 190 x 270mm, Bleed Size: 212 x 290mm
BUSINESS: REGIONAL BUSINESS

ZAKENBLAD REGIO WEERT
718322N63-235
Editorial: Gouverneurlaan 4, 6002 EC WEERT
Tel: 492 338432 **Fax:** 492 338421
Email: info@fkmedia.nl **Web site:** http://www.weertzakenblad.nl
Freq: Quarterly; **Annual Sub.:** EUR 18,-; **Circ:** 6,500
Editor: Maikel Deben; **Publisher:** Frank Kerkhofs
Profile: Magazine focusing on regional business in the Weert area.
Language(s): Dutch
Readership: Aimed at local businessmen.
ADVERTISING RATES:
Full Page Mono .. EUR 1/1: f.c. 1615,-; 1/2: f.c. 865,-; 1/4: f.c. 440,-
Agency Commission: 15%
Mechanical Data: Type Area: 210 x 277mm, Bleed Size: 230 x 297mm
BUSINESS: REGIONAL BUSINESS

ZAKENNIEUWS VOOR HAAGLANDEN & RIJNLAND
16985N63-300
Editorial: Hoofdstraat 275, 2171 BE SASSENHEIM
Tel: 75 6813545 **Fax:** 75 6813535
Email: leeuwenbergh@planet.nl
Date Established: 20-10-1966; **Freq:** 11 issues yearly; **Annual Sub.:** EUR 23,75; **Circ:** 5,150
Editor: J.L. Klint; **Editor-in-Chief:** Bob den Haring; **Publisher:** Bob den Haring
Profile: Journal containing business news relevant to The Hague and the western part of the Netherlands.
Language(s): Dutch
ADVERTISING RATES:
Full Page Mono EUR 1/1: f.c. 825,-; 1/2: f.c. 460,-; 1/4: f.c. 300,-
Agency Commission: 15%
Mechanical Data: Type Area: 140 x 215mm, Bleed Size: 170 x 240mm
BUSINESS: REGIONAL BUSINESS

ZAKENPOST
1635248N14H-205
Editorial: Rietlandpark 301, 1019 DW AMSTERDAM
Tel: 30 6399911 **Fax:** 30 6399937
Freq: 6 issues yearly; **Circ:** 85,000
Editor: Gusta Winnubst
Language(s): Dutch
Agency Commission: 15%
Mechanical Data: Bleed Size: 210 x 210mm
BUSINESS: COMMERCE, INDUSTRY & MANAGEMENT: Small Business

ZAKENREIS
16601N50-150
Editorial: Minervaplein 22-3, 1077 TR AMSTERDAM
Tel: 75 6813545 **Fax:** 75 6813535
Web site: http://www.zakenreis.nl
Date Established: 01-01-1967; **Freq:** 10 issues yearly; **Annual Sub.:** EUR 35,-; **Circ:** 7,000
Editor: M.J.C. Hundepool; **Publisher:** M.J.C. Hundepool
Profile: Magazine focusing on the frequent traveller and the business travel industry.
Language(s): Dutch
Readership: Aimed at travel industry professionals.
ADVERTISING RATES:
Full Page Mono EUR 1/1: b/w 2050,- 1/2: b/w 1230,- 1/4: b/w 720,-
Agency Commission: 15%
Mechanical Data: Type Area: 184 x 257mm, Bleed Size: 210 x 297mm
BUSINESS: TRAVEL & TOURISM

ZAMIKRANT
17431N90-100
Editorial: VEC, Bijlmerdreef 1301, 1103 TV AMSTERDAM **Tel:** 492 338432
Email: info@zami.nl
Date Established: 01-03-1992; **Freq:** Annual; **Circ:** 500
Usual Pagination: 8
Editor: A. Runs; **Editor-in-Chief:** M.H. Esajas
Profile: Journal covering political and cultural issues concerning migrant women in the Netherlands.
Language(s): Dutch
Readership: Aimed at female refugees, women within the black community and other ethnic minority groups in the Netherlands.
Agency Commission: 15%
CONSUMER: ETHNIC

DE ZEEKANT
629923N72-7466
Editorial: Boekerslootlaan 49, 2201 BT NOORDWIJK
Tel: 75 6813545 **Fax:** 71 3643461
Email: info@buijzepers.nl
Freq: Weekly; **Cover Price:** Free; **Circ:** 11,350
Language(s): Dutch
Agency Commission: 15%
Mechanical Data: Type Area: 270 x 410mm, Bleed Size: 290 x 440mm
LOCAL NEWSPAPERS

ZEEUWS VLAANDEREN MAGAZINE
18852N80-21
Editorial: Graaf Adolfstraat 36d, 8606 BT SNEEK
Tel: 172 466622 **Fax:** 172 440681
Email: bcuitgevers@planet.nl
Freq: Quarterly; **Cover Price:** Free; **Circ:** 3,500
Editor: E. Minderhout
Profile: Magazine about the local hospital.
Language(s): Dutch
Readership: Aimed at patients and local residents.
Agency Commission: 15%
Mechanical Data: Bleed Size: 210 x 297mm, Type Area: 184 x 270mm
CONSUMER: RURAL & REGIONAL INTEREST

ZEILEN
18177N91A-130
Editorial: Capellalaan 65, 2132 JL HOOFDDORP
Tel: 184 651558 **Fax:** 570 647815
Web site: http://www.zeilen.nl
Date Established: 01-01-1985; **Freq:** Monthly;
Cover Price: EUR 6,25
Annual Sub.: EUR 59,88; **Circ:** 25,891
Editor: Cees van Dijk
Profile: Magazine about yachting in the Netherlands and Belgium.
Language(s): Dutch
Readership: Aimed at cruise yachtsmen.
ADVERTISING RATES:
Full Page Mono EUR 1/1: f.c. 2940,-; b/w 1940,- 1/2: f.c. 1535,-; b/w 1035,- 1/4: f.c. 795,-; b/w 545,-
Agency Commission: 15%
Mechanical Data: Type Area: 203 x 275mm, Bleed Size: 229 x 298mm
CONSUMER: RECREATION & LEISURE: Boating & Yachting

ZELDZAAM HUISDIER
17948N81X-200
Editorial: Runderweg 6, 8219 PK LELYSTAD
Email: szh@planet.nl
Freq: Quarterly; **Circ:** 2,200
Editor: Henk Jansen
Profile: Publication of the Society of Rare Animal Breeds. Focuses on rare breeds originating as farm animals which are no longer profitable to keep and therefore threatened with extinction.
Language(s): Dutch
ADVERTISING RATES:
Full Page Mono EUR 1/1: b/w 250,- 1/2: b/w 130,- 1/4: b/w 70,-
Agency Commission: 15%
Mechanical Data: Type Area: 120 x 210mm, Bleed Size: 155 x 240mm
Copy instructions: *Copy Date:* 2 weeks prior to publication date
CONSUMER: ANIMALS & PETS

DE ZELFKAZER
16122N21C-70
Editorial: Binnenhaven 1, 6709 PD WAGENINGEN
Tel: 20 5206064 **Fax:** 71 3643461
Email: mail@agrimedia.info
Freq: 6 issues yearly; **Annual Sub.:** EUR 40,12; **Circ:** 650
Editor: Geesje Rotgers; **Editor-in-Chief:** Henk ten Have; **Publisher:** F.J.M. Visser
Profile: Journal about the preparation of dairy products at farms.
Language(s): Dutch
ADVERTISING RATES:
Full Page Mono EUR 1/1: f.c. 780,-; 1/2: f.c. 449,-; 1/4: f.c. 259,-
Agency Commission: 15%
Mechanical Data: Type Area: 230 x 295mm, Bleed Size: 200 x 254mm
BUSINESS: AGRICULTURE & FARMING: Dairy Farming

ZENIT
18255N94X-220
Editorial: Zonnenburg 2, 3512 NL UTRECHT
Tel: 20 5206064 **Fax:** 71 3643461
Email: info@dekoepel.nl **Web site:** http://www.sterrenkunde.nl/zenit
Freq: 11 issues yearly; **Cover Price:** EUR 5,65
Annual Sub.: EUR 57,50; **Circ:** 4,800
Editor: F. Hissink; **Publisher:** Edwin Mathlener
Profile: Magazine containing articles on astronomy and meteorology.
Language(s): Dutch
Readership: Aimed at amateur astronomers and those interested in astronomy.
ADVERTISING RATES:
Full Page Mono .. EUR 2/1: b/w 1830,- 1/1: b/w 915,- 1/2: b/w 455,-
Agency Commission: 15%
Mechanical Data: Type Area: 185 x 260mm, Bleed Size: 207 x 294mm
CONSUMER: OTHER CLASSIFICATIONS: Miscellaneous

ZICHTLIJNEN
17022N64K-150
Editorial: Funenpark 1, 1018 AK AMSTERDAM
Tel: 10 4274128 **Fax:** 35 6474569
Email: secretariaat@vpt.nl **Web site:** http://www.zichtlijnen.nl
Freq: 6 issues yearly; **Annual Sub.:** EUR 73,15; **Circ:** 2,350
Editor: Jos van de Haterd
Profile: Journal about theatre technology and theatre management.
Language(s): Dutch
ADVERTISING RATES:
Full Page Mono EUR 1/1: b/w 618,- 1/2: b/w 381,- 1/4: b/w 257,-
Agency Commission: 15%
Mechanical Data: Type Area: 170 x 264mm, Bleed Size: 210 x 297mm
BUSINESS: OTHER CLASSIFICATIONS: Cinema Entertainment

ZIE
1931410N5F-247
Editorial: Aletta Jacobslaan 7, 1066 BP AMSTERDAM **Tel:** 10 4518007 **Fax:** 70 7999889
Email: info@rhbm.nl **Web site:** http://www.ziemagazine.nl
Freq: Quarterly; **Circ:** 3,400,000
Editor: Lieke Lemmens; **Editor-in-Chief:** Nina Knobbe
Language(s): Dutch
ADVERTISING RATES:
Full Page Mono .... EUR 1/1: f.c. 10.500,-
Agency Commission: 15%
Mechanical Data: Bleed Size: 210 x 275mm
Copy instructions: *Copy Date:* 4 weeks prior to publication date
BUSINESS: COMPUTERS & AUTOMATION: Multimedia

ZIEZO
1857912N79A-27
Editorial: Storkstraat 2, 3833 LB LEUSDEN
Tel: 0032 34660066 **Fax:** 0032 34660067
Freq: Quarterly; **Cover Price:** Free; **Circ:** 500,000
Usual Pagination: 60
Editor-in-Chief: Marlou Hermans
Language(s): Dutch
ADVERTISING RATES:
Full Page Mono ...... EUR 1/1: f.c. 18.000,-; ** 1/2: f.c. 10.000,-; ** omslagpag. 2: f.c. 20.000,-; ** achterpag.: f.c. 23.00
Agency Commission: 15%
Mechanical Data: Type Area: 210 x 260mm
CONSUMER: HOBBIES & DIY

ZIN
1687073N74Q-315
Editorial: Capellalaan 65, 2132 JL HOOFDDORP
Tel: 23 5565971 **Fax:** 23 5565511
Web site: http://www.zin.nl
Freq: Monthly; **Cover Price:** EUR 4,95
Annual Sub.: EUR 55,20; **Circ:** 95,693
Editor: Karen Kroonstuiver; **Editor-in-Chief:** Joep Zijp; **Publisher:** Sandra Dol
Language(s): Dutch
ADVERTISING RATES:
Full Page Mono .... EUR 2/1: b/w 11.000,- 1/1: b/w 5500,- 1/2: b/w 3300,-
Agency Commission: 15%
Mechanical Data: Type Area: 180 x 230mm, Bleed Size: 210 x 280mm
CONSUMER: WOMEN'S INTEREST CONSUMER MAGAZINES: Lifestyle

ZING MAGAZINE
17718N76D-185
Editorial: Rozenstraat 206, 1016 PA AMSTERDAM
Tel: 70 3789880 **Fax:** 70 3789783
Web site: http://www.zingmagazine.nl
Freq: 6 issues yearly; **Cover Price:** EUR 5,90
Annual Sub.: EUR 32,50; **Circ:** 7,600
Editor: Claar Urbanus; **Publisher:** G. Graafland
Profile: Music magazine about Dutch choirs.
Language(s): Dutch
ADVERTISING RATES:
Full Page Mono EUR 1/1: b/w 750,- 1/2: b/w 450,- 1/4: b/w 250,-
Agency Commission: 15%
Mechanical Data: Type Area: 190 x 270mm, Bleed Size: 210 x 297mm
CONSUMER: MUSIC & PERFORMING ARTS: Music

ZM - MAGAZINE
1635846N56A-366
Editorial: Essebaan 63, 2908 LJ CAPELLE AAN DEN IJSSEL **Tel:** 10 2894015 **Fax:** 20 6159047
Email: info@mybusinessmedia.nl **Web site:** http://www.zmmagazine.nl
Freq: 11 issues yearly; **Cover Price:** EUR 17,61
Annual Sub.: EUR 155,-; **Circ:** 4,931
Editor: T. Brouwer; **Editor-in-Chief:** M. Kroef; **Publisher:** S. Wanders
Language(s): Dutch
ADVERTISING RATES:
Full Page Mono EUR 1/1: f.c. 2970,-; b/w 1835,- 1/2: f.c. 2195,-; b/w 1105,- 1/4: f.c. 1710,-; b/w 670,-
Agency Commission: 15%
Mechanical Data: Type Area: 185 x 267mm, Bleed Size: 210 x 297mm
BUSINESS: HEALTH & MEDICAL

ZOMERVAKANTIEMAGAZINE
761362N89E-200
Editorial: Kronkelbaan 11, 1157 LH ABBEKERK
Tel: 492 338432 **Fax:** 492 338421
Email: info@globe-advertising.nl
Freq: Annual; **Cover Price:** Free; **Circ:** 1,200,000
Editor: Gunther Gagg; **Publisher:** Gunther Gagg
Profile: Magazine covering news and information on summer holidays abroad.
Language(s): Dutch
Agency Commission: 15%
Mechanical Data: Type Area: 190 x 255mm, Bleed Size: 200 x 272mm
Copy instructions: *Copy Date:* 2 months prior to publication date
CONSUMER: HOLIDAYS & TRAVEL: Holidays

DE ZONDAG VIEREN
1635458N87-2411
Editorial: Postbus 60, 5473 ZH HEESWIJK
Tel: 20 5159722 **Fax:** 71 3643461
Freq: 60 issues yearly; **Annual Sub.:** EUR 14,-; **Circ:** 93,000
Editor: Martin Hoondert; **Publisher:** Martin Hoondert
Language(s): Dutch
Agency Commission: 15%
Mechanical Data: Type Area: 100 x 190mm, Bleed Size: 118 x 200mm
CONSUMER: RELIGIOUS

ZONDAG, WEEKBLAD VOOR WEST-FRIESLAND
627083N72-6910
Editorial: Geldelozeweg 33, 1625 NW HOORN
Tel: 23 5344089 **Fax:** 10 2801002
Email: info@weekbladzondag.nl **Web site:** http://www.weekbladzondag.nl
Date Established: 01-03-1983; **Freq:** Weekly; **Cover Price:** Free; **Circ:** 85,400
Editor: G. Venverloo; **Publisher:** H. van Amstel
Language(s): Dutch
Agency Commission: 15%
Mechanical Data: Type Area: 267,5 x 397mm, Bleed Size: 290 x 415mm
LOCAL NEWSPAPERS

ZONDAGOCHTENDBLAD BEVERWIJK/HEEMSKERK
626734N72-7000
Editorial: Spoorsingel 26c, 1941 JM BEVERWIJK
Tel: 10 2894018 **Fax:** 172 493270
Freq: Weekly; **Cover Price:** Free; **Circ:** 37,900
Language(s): Dutch
Agency Commission: 15%
Mechanical Data: Type Area: 260 x 390mm
LOCAL NEWSPAPERS

ZONDAGOCHTENDBLAD HEILOO/CASTRICUM
626764N72-7040
Editorial: Basisweg 30, 1043 AP AMSTERDAM
Tel: 348 436599 **Fax:** 88 2697490
Email: info@hollandcombinatie.nl
Freq: Weekly; **Cover Price:** Free; **Circ:** 31,700
Language(s): Dutch
Agency Commission: 15%
Mechanical Data: Type Area: 260 x 390mm
LOCAL NEWSPAPERS

ZONNEBLOEM
16779N56L-160
Editorial: Postbus 2100, 4800 CC BREDA
Tel: 20 5159722 **Fax:** 71 3643461
Email: info@zonnebloem.nl
Freq: Quarterly; **Circ:** 162,500
Editor: Eleonora Bakker; **Editor-in-Chief:** R. Rijkers
Profile: Magazine focusing on disability within all age groups, in particular the elderly.
Language(s): Dutch
Readership: Read by social workers, carers, nursing home managers and hospital workers as well as those with a disability.
ADVERTISING RATES:
Full Page Mono EUR 1/1: f.c. 3510,-; b/w 2965,- 1/2: f.c. 1980,-; b/w 1660,- 1/4: f.c. 1150,-; b/w 925,-
Agency Commission: 15%
Mechanical Data: Type Area: 185 x 267mm, Bleed Size: 210 x 297mm
Copy instructions: *Copy Date:* 5 weeks prior to publication date
BUSINESS: HEALTH & MEDICAL: Disability & Rehabilitation

ZONVAK MAGAZINE
15720N4R-100
Editorial: Walburgstaete III, Dreef 6h, 7202 AG ZUTPHEN **Tel:** 76 5876329 **Fax:** 0032 34660067
Email: info@qumedia.nl **Web site:** http://www.zonvak.nl
Freq: 8 issues yearly; **Annual Sub.:** EUR 79,80; **Circ:** 1,133
Editor: P. Besselink; **Editor-in-Chief:** G. Hilferink; **Publisher:** Arnold Jansen
Profile: Journal for the sun blind and roller shutter industry. Contains information about products and new collections, management aspects, sales promotion, customer service and staff policy.
Language(s): Dutch
ADVERTISING RATES:
Full Page Mono EUR 2/1: b/w 2859,- 1/1: b/w 1505,- 1/2: b/w 903,-
Agency Commission: 15%
Mechanical Data: Type Area: 190 x 277mm, Bleed Size: 210 x 297mm
BUSINESS: ARCHITECTURE & BUILDING: Building Related

ZOOM.NL
1637442N85A-26
Editorial: Transformatorweg 80, 1014 AK AMSTERDAM **Tel:** 23 5461122
Email: info@idg.nl **Web site:** http://www.zoom.nl
Freq: Monthly; **Cover Price:** EUR 4,95
Annual Sub.: EUR 25,95; **Circ:** 53,571
Editor: Robert Theunissen; **Editor-in-Chief:** Hans Kluppel
Language(s): Dutch
ADVERTISING RATES:
Full Page Mono EUR 2/1: f.c. 5385,-; 1/1: f.c. 3169,-; 1/2: f.c. 2065,-
Agency Commission: 15%
Mechanical Data: Type Area: 210 x 280mm, Bleed Size: 230 x 300mm
CONSUMER: PHOTOGRAPHY & FILM MAKING: Photography

ZORG ANNO NU
16725N56B-120
Editorial: Bernadottelaan 11, 3527 GA UTRECHT
Tel: 20 5922250 **Fax:** 30 6348909
Email: nu91@nu91.nl
Date Established: 01-01-1991; **Freq:** 6 issues yearly;
Annual Sub.: EUR 40,-; **Circ:** 22,000
Editor: Yvonne Sturkenboom; **Editor-in-Chief:** Yvonne Sturkenboom
Profile: Magazine with all the latest news from the world of nursing.
Language(s): Dutch
Readership: Members of the professional nursing organisation "Nieuwe Unie '91".
ADVERTISING RATES:
Full Page Mono . EUR 1/1: f.c. 2350,-; 1/2: f.c. 1620,-
Agency Commission: 15%
Mechanical Data: Type Area: 198 x 262mm, Bleed Size: 215 x 285mm
Copy instructions: *Copy Date:* 3 weeks prior to publication date
BUSINESS: HEALTH & MEDICAL: Nursing

ZORG, CARE IN DEVELOPMENT
16334N32G-275
Editorial: Lopikerweg Oost 54, 3411 JH LOPIK
Tel: 23 5565370 **Fax:** 55 5412288
Email: sbb-bureau@planet.nl
Freq: Half-yearly; **Circ:** 1,500
Editor: J.N. Broeders
Profile: Newsletter about community care in developing countries.
Language(s): Dutch
Agency Commission: 15%
BUSINESS: LOCAL GOVERNMENT, LEISURE & RECREATION: Community Care & Social Services

ZORG + WELZIJN
16333N32G-310
Editorial: Radarweg 29, 1043 NX AMSTERDAM
Tel: 20 5159172 **Fax:** 20 5159700
Email: info@reedbusiness.nl **Web site:** http://www.zorgwelzijn.nl
Freq: 11 issues yearly; **Annual Sub.:** EUR 110,29;
Circ: 4,950
Editor: Martin Zuithof; **Editor-in-Chief:** Hedwig Neggers; **Publisher:** Ludo de Boo
Profile: Journal focusing on social welfare.
Language(s): Dutch
ADVERTISING RATES:
Full Page Mono .... EUR 1/1: f.c. 2625,-; f.c. color 2035,-; b/w 1249,- 1/2: f.c. 1791,-; f.c. color 1316,-; b/w 688,- 1/4:
Agency Commission: 15%
Mechanical Data: Type Area: 206 x 265mm, Bleed Size: 232 x 297mm
BUSINESS: LOCAL GOVERNMENT, LEISURE & RECREATION: Community Care & Social Services

ZORGALERT
760607N1H-20
Editorial: Nieuwe Herengracht 47, 1011 RN AMSTERDAM **Tel:** 20 6275453
Email: media@scripta.nl
Date Established: 01-04-1999; **Freq:** 3 issues yearly;
Cover Price: Free; **Circ:** 6,000
Editor-in-Chief: Annelies Bakker; **Publisher:** S.G. van de Vusse
Profile: Magazine covering finance and pension matters.
Language(s): Dutch
Readership: Read by managers of pension suppliers and financial advisers.
Agency Commission: 15%
Mechanical Data: Bleed Size: 225 x 285mm
BUSINESS: FINANCE & ECONOMICS: Pensions

ZORGSAAM
16727N56B-140
Editorial: Zwolseweg 290, 7315 GZ APELDOORN
Tel: 570 648901 **Fax:** 20 5979505
Email: info@zorgsaam.nl
Date Established: 01-01-1996; **Freq:** 3 issues yearly;
Cover Price: Free; **Circ:** 40,000
Editor: Mariska Teunissen
Profile: Magazine for members of care organisations in the East Veluwe area (around Apeldoorn).
Language(s): Dutch
Agency Commission: 15%
Mechanical Data: Type Area: 190 x 267mm, Bleed Size: 210 x 297mm
BUSINESS: HEALTH & MEDICAL: Nursing

ZORGVISIE
16733N56C-150
Editorial: Radarweg 29, 1043 NX AMSTERDAM
Tel: 20 5159722 **Fax:** 71 3643461
Email: info@reedbusiness.nl **Web site:** http://www.zorgvisie.nl
Freq: Monthly; **Annual Sub.:** EUR 361,20; **Circ:** 7,725
Editor: Eric Bassant; **Publisher:** Ben Konings
Profile: Magazine containing news and opinion articles about cure and care matter.
Language(s): Dutch
Readership: Aimed at hospital and care managers and policymakers.
ADVERTISING RATES:
Full Page Mono EUR 1/1: f.c. 4060,-; b/w 3201,- 1/2: f.c. 2800,-; b/w 1800,- 1/4: f.c. 2029,-; b/w 1041,-
Agency Commission: 15%
Mechanical Data: Type Area: 184 x 265mm, Bleed Size: 210 x 297mm
BUSINESS: HEALTH & MEDICAL: Hospitals

ZOZITDAT
1636295N55-303
Editorial: Capellalaan 65, 2132 JL HOOFDDORP
Tel: 88 7518800 **Fax:** 20 5353696
Web site: http://www.zozitdat.nl
Freq: Monthly; **Cover Price:** EUR 3,50
Annual Sub.: EUR 46,80; **Circ:** 38,190
Editor: Renske Lamers
Language(s): Dutch
ADVERTISING RATES:
Full Page Mono EUR 2/1: b/w 6540,- 1/1: b/w 3270,- 1/2: b/w 1962,-
Agency Commission: 15%
Mechanical Data: Type Area: 195 x 267mm, Bleed Size: 205 x 277mm
BUSINESS: APPLIED SCIENCE & LABORATORIES

Z@PPMAGAZINE
1933452N74F-178
Editorial: Bussumergrintweg 4, 1217 BP HILVERSUM **Tel:** 10 4518007 **Fax:** 70 7999889
Email: info@fcklap.nl
Freq: 6 issues yearly; **Cover Price:** EUR 3,45; **Circ:** 50,000
Editor: Kim Hopmans
Language(s): Dutch
ADVERTISING RATES:
Full Page Mono EUR 1/1: b/w 2750,- 1/2: b/w 1600,- 1/4: b/w 1000,-
Agency Commission: 15%
Mechanical Data: Bleed Size: 200 x 280mm
CONSUMER: WOMEN'S INTEREST CONSUMER MAGAZINES: Teenage

ZUID-HOLLANDS LANDSCHAP
16855N57-100
Editorial: Nesserdijk 368, 3063 NE ROTTERDAM
Tel: 523 285330 **Fax:** 30 6348909
Email: zhl@zuidhollandslandschap.nl
Date Established: 01-01-1977; **Freq:** Quarterly;
Annual Sub.: EUR 17,50; **Circ:** 60,000
Editor: M.R. Houtzagers; **Publisher:** M.R. Houtzagers
Profile: Journal about the landscape and environment in the province of South Holland.
Language(s): Dutch
ADVERTISING RATES:
Full Page Mono EUR 1/1: b/w 2695,- 1/2: b/w 1495,- 1/4: b/w 855,-
Agency Commission: 15%
Mechanical Data: Type Area: 185 x 275mm, Bleed Size: 210 x 297mm
BUSINESS: ENVIRONMENT & POLLUTION

ZUIDKRANT
17898N80-230
Editorial: De Kuiperij 27, 7437 CW BATHMEN
Tel: 70 3378124 **Fax:** 70 3455302
Email: katern@katern.nl
Date Established: 31-01-1998; **Freq:** 11 issues yearly; **Cover Price:** Free; **Circ:** 12,750
Editor: Henk ten Katen; **Publisher:** Henk ten Katen
Profile: Local newspaper for the Bathmen and Apeldoorn area.
Language(s): Dutch
Agency Commission: 15%
Mechanical Data: Type Area: 264 x 385mm, Bleed Size: 290 x 420mm
CONSUMER: RURAL & REGIONAL INTEREST

DE ZUNDERTSE BODE
627211N72-7330
Editorial: Bredaseweg 26, 4881 DE ZUNDERT
Tel: 88 2697049 **Fax:** 70 3544642
Email: zetterij@vorsselmans.nl **Web site:** http://www.internetbode.nl
Freq: Weekly; **Circ:** 9,300
Editor: Vif Janssen; **Editor-in-Chief:** Vif Janssen
Language(s): Dutch
Agency Commission: 15%
Mechanical Data: Type Area: 264 x 400mm
LOCAL NEWSPAPERS

ZWANGER!
1636869N74C-238
Editorial: Veermanskade 2, 1621 AN HOORN
Tel: 70 3378124 **Fax:** 70 3455302
Email: info@wij.nl
Freq: Annual; **Cover Price:** EUR 4,50; **Circ:** 180,000
Editor: P. Remmers; **Editor-in-Chief:** I. van Dijk;
Publisher: R. van Vroenhoven
Language(s): Dutch
ADVERTISING RATES:
Full Page Mono .... EUR 2/1: f.c. 15.150,-; 1/1: f.c. 7575,-; 1/2: f.c. 4785,-; 1/4: f.c. 2580,-
Agency Commission: 15%
Mechanical Data: Type Area: 185 x 252mm, Bleed Size: 215 x 282mm
Copy instructions: *Copy Date:* 5 weeks prior to publication date
CONSUMER: WOMEN'S INTEREST CONSUMER MAGAZINES: Home & Family

ZWANGER
1634030N74D-185
Editorial: Capellalaan 65, 2132 JL HOOFDDORP
Tel: 88 5567306 **Fax:** 70 3999853
Web site: http://www.zwanger.nl
Freq: Annual; **Cover Price:** EUR 4,50; **Circ:** 235,000
Editor: Yolande de Best-Meijer; **Editor-in-Chief:** Marieta van Driel
Language(s): Dutch
ADVERTISING RATES:
Full Page Mono .... EUR 2/1: b/w 29.990,- 1/1: b/w 14.995,- 1/2: b/w 8997,-
Agency Commission: 15%
Mechanical Data: Type Area: 192 x 255mm, Bleed Size: 215 x 282mm
CONSUMER: WOMEN'S INTEREST CONSUMER MAGAZINES: Child Care

ZWANGER & ZO
1633540N74D-183
Editorial: Capellalaan 65, 2132 JL HOOFDDORP
Tel: 343 535753 **Fax:** 53 4842706
Date Established: 01-12-1993; **Freq:** Annual; **Cover Price:** EUR 4,95; **Circ:** 185,000
Editor: Carla van Klaveren; **Publisher:** Stefan Hutten
Language(s): Dutch
ADVERTISING RATES:
Full Page Mono .... EUR 2/1: b/w 25.990,- 1/1: b/w 12.995,- 1/2: b/w 7797,-
Agency Commission: 15%
Mechanical Data: Type Area: 192 x 255mm, Bleed Size: 215 x 282mm
CONSUMER: WOMEN'S INTEREST CONSUMER MAGAZINES: Child Care

ZWARTSLUIZER REKLAMEBLAD
627215N72-7350
Editorial: Westeinde 17, 8064 AJ ZWARTSLUIS
Tel: 20 5159172 **Fax:** 20 5159700
Email: info@drukkerijkuiper.nl
Date Established: 01-04-1951; **Freq:** Weekly; **Cover Price:** Free; **Circ:** 2,425
Usual Pagination: 12
Editor: J. van der Stouwe
Language(s): Dutch
Agency Commission: 15%
Mechanical Data: Type Area: 257 x 385mm, Bleed Size: 290 x 400mm
LOCAL NEWSPAPERS

Norway

Time Difference: GMT + 1 hr (CET - Central European Time)
National Telephone Code: +47
Continent: Europe
Capital: Oslo
Principal Language: Norwegian, Danish, Swedish, English, German
Population: 4290000
Monetary Unit: Norwegian Krone (NOK)

EMBASSY HIGH

COMMISSION: Royal Norwegian Embassy: 25 Belgrave Sq, London, SW1X 8QD
Tel: 020 7591 5500
Fax: 020 7245 6993
Email: emb.london@mfa.no
Website: http://www.norway.org.uk Head of Mission: HE (Mr) Kim Traavik

101 BLADET
1624869R40-34
Editorial: NTL Forsvaret, Pb 8788 Youngstorget, 0028 OSLO **Tel:** 22 41 04 00
Email: ntl101@online.no **Web site:** http://medlem.ntl.no/forsvaret
Freq: Quarterly; **Circ:** 6,500
Language(s): Norwegian
BUSINESS: DEFENCE

1LOGOS
1740820R90-204
Editorial: Pb. 9285 Grønland, 0134 OSLO
Tel: 22 99 29 69 **Fax:** 22 99 29 60
Email: logos@bibelleseringen.no **Web site:** http://www.bibelleseringen.no
Freq: Quarterly
Language(s): Norwegian
CONSUMER: ETHNIC

=OSLO
1697382R56L-102
Editorial: Skippergata 14, 0152 OSLO
Tel: 22 42 16 70
Email: anlov@erlikoslo.no **Web site:** http://erlikoslo.wordpress.com
Freq: Monthly
Language(s): Norwegian
BUSINESS: HEALTH & MEDICAL: Disability & Rehabilitation

ABBL NYTT
1624960R14H-47
Editorial: P.B 385, 1301 SANDVIKA **Tel:** 67574000
Email: post@abbl.no **Web site:** http://www.abbl.no
Freq: Quarterly; **Circ:** 25,000
Editor: Irene Nøbben
Language(s): Norwegian
BUSINESS: COMMERCE, INDUSTRY & MANAGEMENT: Small Business

ABELIA.NO
1863940R5E-8
Editorial: PB 5490, Majorstuen, 0305 OSLO
Tel: 23088070 **Fax:** 23088071
Email: post@abelia.no **Web site:** http://www.abelia.no
Freq: Daily; **Cover Price:** Free; **Circ:** 2,500 Unique Users
Language(s): Norwegian
BUSINESS: COMPUTERS & AUTOMATION: Data Transmission

ADRESSEAVISEN
31804R67B-2500
Editorial: Industriveien 13, 7003 TRONDHEIM
Tel: 07 20 0 **Fax:** 72 50 15 00
Email: redaksjon@adresseavisen.no **Web site:** http://www.adressa.no
Freq: Daily; **Circ:** 75,835
Language(s): Norwegian
ADVERTISING RATES:
Full Page Colour .... NOK 71294
REGIONAL DAILY & SUNDAY NEWSPAPERS: Regional Daily Newspapers

ADVOKATBLADET
31562R44-15
Editorial: Advokatforeningen, Kristian Augustsgate 9, 0164 OSLO **Tel:** 22035050 **Fax:** 22115325
Email: advokatbladet@jus.no **Web site:** http://www.advokatbladet.no
Freq: Monthly - 11 ganger i året; **Circ:** 8,290
Editor: Marit Aschehoug
Profile: Journal of the Society of Lawyers and Judges.
Language(s): Norwegian
ADVERTISING RATES:
Full Page Colour .... NOK 17500
BUSINESS: LEGAL

ADVOKATBLADET; ADVOKATBLADET.NO
1971387R44-112
Editorial: kr. Augustsgate 9, 0164 OSLO
Tel: 22035132 **Fax:** 22115325
Email: advokatbladet@jus.no **Web site:** http://www.advokatbladet.no
Freq: Daily
Editor: Marit Aschehoug
Language(s): Norwegian
BUSINESS: LEGAL

ÆSCULAP
31633R56A-3
Editorial: Nye Studentpaviljongen, Ullevål Sykehus, 0407 OSLO **Tel:** 22117854 **Fax:** 22117854
Email: k.j.tunheim@studmed.uio.no **Web site:** http://www.aesculap.no
Date Established: 1920; **Freq:** Quarterly - 5 ganger i året
Profile: Magazine containing articles, information and news of interest to medical students and academics.
Language(s): Norwegian
BUSINESS: HEALTH & MEDICAL

AFGHANISTAN-NYTT
32341R90-50
Editorial: Osterhausgate 27, 0183 OSLO
Tel: 22989315 **Fax:** 22989301
Email: ain@afghanistan.no **Web site:** http://www.afghanistan.no
Freq: Half-yearly; **Circ:** 1,600
Profile: Magazine containing articles, news and information from and about Afghanistan.
Language(s): Norwegian
CONSUMER: ETHNIC

Norway

AFRICA NEWS UPDATE
1624519R82-306
Editorial: Osterhausgata 27, 0183 OSLO
Tel: 22 98 93 11 **Fax:** 22 98 93 01
Email: editor@afrika.no **Web site:** http://www.afrika.no
Freq: 208 times a year; **Cover Price:** Paid; **Circ:** 4,400 Unique Users
Language(s): Norwegian
CONSUMER: CURRENT AFFAIRS & POLITICS

AFTENPOSTEN A-MAGASINET
1740762R73-156
Editorial: Pb. 1 Sentrum, 0051 OSLO
Tel: 22 86 40 40
Email: amagasinet@aftenposten.no **Web site:** http://www.aftenposten.no/amagasinet
Freq: Daily; **Circ:** 250,179
Editor: Kjersti Løken Stavrum
Language(s): Norwegian
CONSUMER: NATIONAL & INTERNATIONAL PERIODICALS

AFTENPOSTEN; DEBATTREDAKSJONEN
31736R65A-10
Editorial: Pb. 1 Sentrum, 0051 OSLO
Tel: 22 86 36 66 **Fax:** 22863684
Email: debatt@aftenposten.no **Web site:** http://www.aftenposten.no
Date Established: 1860; **Freq:** Daily - Akershus; **Circ:** 250,179
Editor: Knut Olav Åmås
Profile: Broadsheet-sized morning newspaper covering national and international news, culture, finance and sports. Also publish a tabloid-sized evening edition.
Language(s): Norwegian
Readership: Read by professional people.
Editions:
Aftenposten (UK Office)
NATIONAL DAILY & SUNDAY NEWSPAPERS: National Daily Newspapers

AFTENPOSTEN; HYTTE MAGASINET
1800781R74C-84
Editorial: Pb. 1, 0185 OSLO **Tel:** 22863000
Email: hyttemagasinet@aftenposten.no **Web site:** http://www.hyttemag.no
Freq: Monthly; **Circ:** 180,000
Editor: Pål Berg
Language(s): Norwegian
Copy instructions: *Copy Date:* 21 days prior to publication date
CONSUMER: WOMEN'S INTEREST CONSUMER MAGAZINES: Home & Family

AFTENPOSTEN INNSIKT
1840848R82-363
Editorial: Pb. 1, 0051 OSLO **Tel:** 22863000
Email: innsikt@aftenposteninnsikt.no **Web site:** http://www.aftenposteninnsikt.no
Freq: Monthly - 11 ganger i året; **Circ:** 28,000
Editor: Tine Skarland
Language(s): Norwegian
CONSUMER: CURRENT AFFAIRS & POLITICS

AFTENPOSTEN; LEVE
1873245R74C-95
Editorial: Pb. 1 Sentrum, 0051 OSLO
Tel: 22 86 40 40
Email: leve@aftenposten.no **Web site:** http://www.aftenposten.no/leve
Freq: Weekly
Language(s): Norwegian
CONSUMER: WOMEN'S INTEREST CONSUMER MAGAZINES: Home & Family

AFTENPOSTEN; MAMMA
1656531R74D-78
Editorial: Pb. 1, 0051 OSLO **Tel:** 23 36 19 70
Email: mamma@mamma.no **Web site:** http://www.mamma.no
Freq: Monthly; **Circ:** 20,000
Language(s): Norwegian
ADVERTISING RATES:
SCC .... NOK 316.67
Copy instructions: *Copy Date:* 30 days prior to publication date
CONSUMER: WOMEN'S INTEREST CONSUMER MAGAZINES: Child Care

AFTENPOSTEN; SPORTSREDAKSJONEN
1623960R75A-201
Editorial: Pb. 1 Sentrum, 0051 OSLO
Tel: 22 86 44 01 **Fax:** 22864084
Email: sporten@aftenposten.no **Web site:** http://www.aftenposten.no
Freq: Daily; **Circ:** 250,179
Language(s): Norwegian
CONSUMER: SPORT

AFTENPOSTEN; UTENRIKSREDAKSJONEN
1936771R82-488
Editorial: Pb. 1, 0051 OSLO **Tel:** 22 86 39 42
Fax: 22428967
Email: utenriks@aftenposten.no **Web site:** http://www.aftenposten.no
Language(s): Norwegian
CONSUMER: CURRENT AFFAIRS & POLITICS

AGDER; AVISENAGDER.NO
1624700R82-318
Editorial: Pb 40, 4401 FLEKKEFJORD
Tel: 38 32 03 00 **Fax:** 38 32 45 60
Email: administrasjon@avisenagder.no **Web site:** http://www.avisenagder.no
Cover Price: Paid
Language(s): Norwegian
CONSUMER: CURRENT AFFAIRS & POLITICS

AGDERPOSTEN
31748R67B-2550
Editorial: Pb. 8, 4801 ARENDAL **Tel:** 37 00 37 00
Fax: 37 00 37 17
Email: redaksjonen@agderposten.no **Web site:** http://www.agderposten.no
Date Established: 1874; **Freq:** Daily; **Circ:** 23,329 Unique Users
Language(s): Norwegian
REGIONAL DAILY & SUNDAY NEWSPAPERS: Regional Daily Newspapers

AGI NORSK GRAFISK TIDSSKRIFT
1624951R41A-76
Editorial: Norske Media AS, c/o Olsvold & co AS, Postboks 34, 1483 SKYTTA **Tel:** 90882518
Email: lasse@agi.no **Web site:** http://www.agi.no
Freq: Monthly - 11 ganger i året; **Circ:** 3,414
Language(s): Norwegian
ADVERTISING RATES:
SCC .... NOK 132
Copy instructions: *Copy Date:* 21 days prior to publication date
BUSINESS: PRINTING & STATIONERY: Printing

AGORA
1660261R84A-119
Editorial: H. Aschehoug & Co, Pb. 363 Sentrum, 0102 OSLO **Tel:** 22 40 04 00
Email: kaja.s.mollerin@aschehoug.no **Web site:** http://www.aschehoug.no/om/tidsskrift
Freq: Half-yearly; **Circ:** 1,100
Editor: Geir O. Rønning
Language(s): Norwegian
CONSUMER: THE ARTS & LITERARY: Arts

AKAM.NO
1935268R78R-8
Editorial: Tek.no, c/o Edda Digital. Postboks 428 Sentrum, 0103 OSLO **Tel:** 920 53683
Fax: 21 56 97 01
Email: erik@akam.no **Web site:** http://akam.no
Cover Price: Paid
Language(s): Norwegian
CONSUMER: CONSUMER ELECTRONICS: Consumer Electronics Related

AKERSHUS AMTSTIDENDE
31761R67B-2600
Editorial: Pb. 12, 1440 DRØBAK **Tel:** 64 90 54 00
Email: redaksjon@amta.no **Web site:** http://www.amta.no
Freq: Daily; **Circ:** 8,621
Editor: Terje Lundefaret
Language(s): Norwegian
ADVERTISING RATES:
Full Page Colour .... NOK 35802
SCC .... NOK 179.01
REGIONAL DAILY & SUNDAY NEWSPAPERS: Regional Daily Newspapers

AKERSHUS AMTSTIDENDE~AVD. NESODDEN
1810302R82-359
Editorial: Postboks 12, 1440 DRØBAK
Tel: 64 90 54 00
Email: nesodden-kontor@amta.no **Web site:** http://www.amta.no
Freq: Daily; **Circ:** 8,621
Language(s): Norwegian
CONSUMER: CURRENT AFFAIRS & POLITICS

AKSJONÆREN
1624656R1F-2
Editorial: Pb. 1963 Vika, 0125 OSLO **Tel:** 24 11 78 62
Fax: 24 11 78 61
Email: post@aksjonaerforeningen.no **Web site:** http://www.aksjonaerforeningen.no
Freq: Quarterly; **Circ:** 5,000
Language(s): Norwegian
BUSINESS: FINANCE & ECONOMICS: Investment

AKTIV LIVSSTIL - AKTIVLIVSSTIL.NO
32178R75A-25
Editorial: Norges Bedriftsidrettsforbund, Ullevål Stadion, Sognsveien 75, 0840 OSLO **Tel:** 21 02 94 68
Fax: 21 02 94 51
Email: aktivlivsstil@bedriftsidrett.no **Web site:** http://www.aktivlivsstil.no
Freq: Daily; **Cover Price:** Paid; **Circ:** 2,500 Unique Users
Editor: Ingunn Haavi Finstad
Profile: Publication of the Norwegian Company Sports Federation.
Language(s): Norwegian
Readership: Aimed at people who enjoy sport.
CONSUMER: SPORT

AKTIVITET
32353R91D-10
Editorial: 4H Norge, Pb 113, 2026 SKJETTEN
Tel: 64 83 21 00 **Fax:** 64 83 21 19
Email: 4hnorge@4h.no **Web site:** http://www.n4h.no
Freq: Quarterly
Profile: Newspaper for children and young people in the 4H Club.
Language(s): Norwegian
CONSUMER: RECREATION & LEISURE: Children & Youth

AKTIVITØREN
1624240R56A-201
Editorial: Aktivitørenes Landsforbund v/ Karina Sandnes, Krakelivegen 237, 6490 EIDE
Tel: 48251202
Email: alf@kfo.no **Web site:** http://www.delta.no/alf/Fagbladet+Aktivitoren
Freq: Quarterly; **Circ:** 2,500
Language(s): Norwegian
BUSINESS: HEALTH & MEDICAL

AKTUELL SIKKERHET
31627R54C-30
Editorial: Pb. 130, 2261 KIRKENAER **Tel:** 91123330
Email: even@askmedia.no **Web site:** http://www.askmedia.no
Date Established: 1997; **Freq:** 6 issues yearly; **Circ:** 3,821
Editor: Even Rise
Profile: Magazine containing information, articles and news of interest to people working in the security trade.
Language(s): Norwegian
ADVERTISING RATES:
Full Page Colour .... NOK 17500
Copy instructions: *Copy Date:* 22 days prior to publication date
BUSINESS: SAFETY & SECURITY: Security

AKTUELT FRA NASJONALFORENINGEN
1624319R56A-203
Editorial: Pb 7139 Majorstuen, 0307 OSLO
Tel: 23120000 **Fax:** 23120001
Email: post@nasjonalforeningen.no **Web site:** http://www.nasjonalforeningen.no
Freq: Quarterly
Language(s): Norwegian
BUSINESS: HEALTH & MEDICAL

ALLERGI I PRAKSIS
1660590R56R-166
Editorial: Pb. 2603 St. Hanshaugen, 0131 OSLO
Tel: 23353535 **Fax:** 23353530
Email: nina@naaf.no **Web site:** http://www.naaf.no/no/Tjenester/Fagbladet_Allergi_i_Praksis
Freq: Quarterly; **Circ:** 17,124
Editor: Nina Brun
Language(s): Norwegian
BUSINESS: HEALTH & MEDICAL: Health Medical Related

ALLERS
32142R74C-10
Editorial: Pb. 1169 Sentrum, 0107 OSLO
Tel: 21301000 **Fax:** 21301204
Email: redaksjonen@allers.no **Web site:** http://www.allers.no
Freq: Weekly - 52; **Circ:** 69,259
Editor: Aud Dalsegg
Profile: Home and family magazine.
Language(s): Norwegian
ADVERTISING RATES:
Full Page Colour .... NOK 41500
SCC .... NOK 337.50
CONSUMER: WOMEN'S INTEREST CONSUMER MAGAZINES: Home & Family

ALT OM FISKE
32368R92-10
Editorial: Sandakerveien 116, 0441 OSLO
Tel: 22585000 **Fax:** 22585239
Email: fiske@egmonthm.no **Web site:** http://www.altomfiske.no
Date Established: 1986; **Freq:** 6 issues yearly - 10; **Circ:** 16,430
Profile: Magazine for those interested in all types of fishing.
Language(s): Norwegian
ADVERTISING RATES:
Full Page Colour .... NOK 23800
CONSUMER: ANGLING & FISHING

ALTAPOSTEN
31747R67B-2650
Editorial: Labyrinten 5, 9510 ALTA **Tel:** 78 45 67 00
Fax: 78 45 67 40
Email: redaksjonen@altaposten.no **Web site:** http://www.altaposten.no
Date Established: 1969; **Freq:** Daily; **Circ:** 5,505
Language(s): Norwegian
ADVERTISING RATES:
Full Page Colour .... NOK 49029
SCC .... NOK 245.14
REGIONAL DAILY & SUNDAY NEWSPAPERS: Regional Daily Newspapers

AMATØRRADIO
32234R79D-10
Editorial: Pb 20 Haugenstua, 0915 OSLO
Tel: 22213790 **Fax:** 22213791
Email: nrrl@nrrl.no **Web site:** http://www.nrrl.no
Freq: Monthly
Profile: Magazine for amateur radio enthusiasts.
Language(s): Norwegian
CONSUMER: HOBBIES & DIY: Radio Electronics

AMBIS
31712R61-85
Editorial: Pb. 674 Sentrum, 5807 BERGEN
Tel: 815 56 777 **Fax:** 40 00 17 07
Email: nmf@musikkorps.no **Web site:** http://www.musikkorps.no
Freq: Quarterly; **Circ:** 60,000
Profile: Publication about all kinds of bands, including brass bands, school bands, marching bands, wind bands and concert bands. Also includes information on music teaching.
Language(s): Norwegian
BUSINESS: MUSIC TRADE

AMBULANSEFORUM
31676R56P-10
Editorial: Nardoveien 4b, 7430 TRONDHEIM
Tel: 73964434
Email: einar@ambulanseforum.no **Web site:** http://www.ambulanseforum.no
Date Established: 1975; **Freq:** 6 issues yearly; **Circ:** 2,000
Profile: Journal about the Norwegian Ambulance Service.
Language(s): Norwegian
BUSINESS: HEALTH & MEDICAL: Casualty & Emergency

AMBULANSEFORUM; AMBULANSEFORUM.NO
1938351R56A-229
Editorial: Nardoveien 4b, 7430 TRONDHEIM
Tel: 73 96 44 34
Email: einar@ambulanseforum.no **Web site:** http://www.ambulanseforum.no
Cover Price: Paid
Language(s): Norwegian
BUSINESS: HEALTH & MEDICAL

AMCAR
32219R77A-30
Editorial: Pb. 6006, 7434 TRONDHEIM
Tel: 72896000 **Fax:** 72896020
Email: amcar@amcar.no **Web site:** http://www.amcar.no
Date Established: 1976; **Freq:** Monthly - 10 ganger i året
Profile: Magazine of the American Car Club of Norway. Contains information about US cars of all makes both new and old.
Language(s): Norwegian
Readership: Read by enthusiasts and prospective purchasers.
CONSUMER: MOTORING & CYCLING: Motoring

AMNYTT MAGAZINE
1645124R5A-4
Editorial: Pb. 2352 Strømsø, 3003 DRAMMEN
Tel: 99798302
Email: jan.eirik@amnytt.no **Web site:** http://www.amnytt.no
Freq: 6 issues yearly - 6 ganger i året; **Circ:** 4,200
Language(s): Norwegian
BUSINESS: COMPUTERS & AUTOMATION: Automation & Instrumentation

AMNYTT MAGAZINE; AMNYTT.NO
1863334R58-114
Editorial: Pb. 2352 Strømsø, 3003 DRAMMEN
Tel: 997 98 302
Email: jan.eirik@amnytt.no **Web site:** http://www.amnytt.no
Freq: Daily; **Cover Price:** Free; **Circ:** 2,500 Unique Users
Language(s): Norwegian
BUSINESS: ENERGY, FUEL & NUCLEAR

AMOBIL.NO
1866757R5E-13
Editorial: c/o Edda Digital, Postboks 428 Sentrum, 0103 OSLO **Tel:** 55 31 93 55 **Fax:** 55 31 93 56
Email: presse@amobil.no **Web site:** http://www.amobil.no
Circ: 6,000

Language(s): Norwegian
BUSINESS: COMPUTERS & AUTOMATION: Data Transmission

ANALYSEN
31363R2A-1
Editorial: Pb. 5077 Majorstuen, 0301 OSLO
Tel: 22 60 16 77
Email: nmf@nmf-org.no **Web site:** http://www.markedsanalyse.org
Freq: Quarterly
Profile: Official publication of the Norwegian Market Research Association.
Language(s): Norwegian
Readership: Read by marketing managers, planners, product managers and marketing consultants.
ADVERTISING RATES:
Full Page Colour .... NOK 8000
BUSINESS: COMMUNICATIONS, ADVERTISING & MARKETING

ANLEGG & TRANSPORT
31414R10-50
Editorial: Pb 11, 1411 KOLBOTN **Tel:** 66822121
Fax: 66822120
Email: bjorgu@bjorgu.no **Web site:** http://www.anlegg-transport.no
Date Established: 1984; **Freq:** Monthly; **Circ:** 16,500
Editor: Ingebrigt Vaagland
Profile: Magazine about construction and transport machinery, including on and off highway vehicles, also materials handling and personnel movers.
Language(s): Norwegian
ADVERTISING RATES:
SCC .... NOK 162.50
BUSINESS: MATERIALS HANDLING

ANLEGGSMAGASINET
31595R49A-4
Editorial: Pb. 67, Bryn, 0611 OSLO **Tel:** 22757500
Fax: 22757521
Email: knut.viggen@hm-fagmedia.no **Web site:** http://www.tungt.no/tungt/redaksjon
Freq: 6 issues yearly; **Circ:** 22,150
Profile: Magazine containing articles, product news and trade information for the transport, building and construction industries.
Language(s): Norwegian
ADVERTISING RATES:
Full Page Colour .... NOK 16950
BUSINESS: TRANSPORT

ANLEGGSMASKINEN
31556R42A-10
Editorial: Fred Olsens gate 3, 0152 OSLO
Tel: 22404190
Email: sem@mef.no **Web site:** http://www.mef.no/index.asp?strUrl=1004573i
Date Established: 1960; **Freq:** Monthly - 10 ganger i året; **Circ:** 5,452
Profile: Journal about construction machinery, private works and forestry.
Language(s): Norwegian
ADVERTISING RATES:
Full Page Colour .... NOK 16890
BUSINESS: CONSTRUCTION

ANLEGGSMASKINEN; MEF.NO
1863348R4E-111
Editorial: Fred Olsensgate 3, 0152 OSLO
Tel: 22404190
Email: sem@mef.no **Web site:** http://www.mef.no
Freq: Daily; **Circ:** 2,500 Unique Users
Language(s): Norwegian
BUSINESS: ARCHITECTURE & BUILDING: Building

ANTIRASISTEN
1624652R82-314
Editorial: Pb. 7073 St. Olavsplass, 0166 OSLO
Tel: 23353200 **Fax:** 23353201
Email: au@sos-rasisme.no **Web site:** http://www.sos-rasisme.no/antirasisten
Freq: Quarterly; **Circ:** 30,000
Language(s): Norwegian
CONSUMER: CURRENT AFFAIRS & POLITICS

APÉRITIF
32404R11A-2
Editorial: Furuveien 39c, 0678 OSLO **Tel:** 2219 0075
Fax: 22671477
Email: aperitif@aperitif.no **Web site:** http://www.aperitif.no
Date Established: 1995; **Freq:** Monthly - 9 ganger i året; **Circ:** 4,514
Editor: Jan H. Amundsen
Profile: Magazine covering all aspects of food and drink. Contains product news and tests, advice, recipes, interviews, surveys and articles.
Language(s): Norwegian
Readership: Aimed at professionals within the catering trade and restaurant owners.
ADVERTISING RATES:
Full Page Colour .... NOK 19800
Copy instructions: *Copy Date:* 21 days prior to publication date
BUSINESS: CATERING: Catering, Hotels & Restaurants

APÈRITIF; APERITIF.NO
1863346R74P-208
Editorial: Rosenkrantz' gate 11 b, 0678 OSLO
Tel: 22 98 86 00 **Fax:** 22 99 47 81
Email: aperitif@aperitif.no **Web site:** http://www.aperitif.no
Freq: Daily; **Cover Price:** Free; **Circ:** 2,500 Unique Users
Language(s): Norwegian
CONSUMER: WOMEN'S INTEREST CONSUMER MAGAZINES: Food & Cookery

APPELL
1624472R32G-151
Editorial: Pb 8844 Youngstorget, 0028 OSLO
Tel: 22037700 **Fax:** 22200870
Email: norsk.folkehjelp@npaid.org **Web site:** http://www.folkehjelp.no
Freq: Quarterly; **Circ:** 39,000
Language(s): Norwegian
BUSINESS: LOCAL GOVERNMENT, LEISURE & RECREATION: Community Care & Social Services

APPETITT
1740825R22A-170
Editorial: Tømmerbakkeveien 19, 1453 BJØRNEMYR
Tel: 66918163
Email: hilde@appetitt.no **Web site:** http://www.appetitt.no
Freq: 6 issues yearly; **Circ:** 8,500
Language(s): Norwegian
ADVERTISING RATES:
Full Page Colour .... NOK 25500
BUSINESS: FOOD

ARBEIDERVERN
31432R14F-30
Editorial: Direktoratet for Arbeidstilsynet, Statens Hus, 7468 TRONDHEIM **Tel:** 97 40 70 73
Fax: 73 19 97 01
Email: arbeidervern@arbeidstilsynet.no **Web site:** http://www.arbeidstilsynet.no/publikasjoner/arbeidervern.html
Freq: 6 issues yearly; **Circ:** 9,000
Editor: Torstein Kvakland
Profile: Magazine covering employment issues. Contains articles and information about workers' rights, work environment and related legal matters.
Language(s): Norwegian
Readership: Aimed at professionals working with the improvement of work conditions for employees in the public as well as the private sector.
ADVERTISING RATES:
Full Page Colour .... NOK 12000
BUSINESS: COMMERCE, INDUSTRY & MANAGEMENT: Training & Recruitment

ARBEIDETS RETT; RETTEN.NO
1863339R73-184
Editorial: Postboks 24, 7361 RØROS
Tel: 72 40 64 00
Email: redaksjonen@retten.no **Web site:** http://www.retten.no
Freq: Daily; **Cover Price:** Free; **Circ:** 48,000
Language(s): Norwegian
CONSUMER: NATIONAL & INTERNATIONAL PERIODICALS

ARBEIDSLIV
32248R82-45
Editorial: Storgata 33a, 0184 OSLO **Tel:** 22 86 84 00
Fax: 22 86 84 01
Email: kari.solholm@fn.no **Web site:** http://www.ilo.no
Freq: Quarterly
Profile: Magazine covering national and international articles about human rights, equality in the labour market and work opportunities.
Language(s): Norwegian
CONSUMER: CURRENT AFFAIRS & POLITICS

ARBEIDSMANDEN
31436R14L-16
Editorial: Pb 231 Sentrum, 0103 OSLO
Tel: 23063371 **Fax:** 23061111
Email: ane.borrud@lomedia.no **Web site:** http://www.arbeidsmanden.no
Date Established: 1898; **Freq:** Monthly - 10 ganger i året
Profile: Publication about trade unions and their members.
Language(s): Norwegian
ADVERTISING RATES:
Full Page Colour .... NOK 16400
BUSINESS: COMMERCE, INDUSTRY & MANAGEMENT: Trade Unions

ARBEIDSMILJØ
31625R54B-10
Editorial: Pb. 9326 Grønland, 0135 OSLO
Tel: 81 55 97 50 **Fax:** 22 05 78 39
Email: paul@arbeidsmiljo.no **Web site:** http://www.arbeidsmiljo.no
Freq: 6 issues yearly; **Circ:** 7,512
Profile: Journal about industrial accident prevention and working environment safety.
Language(s): Norwegian
ADVERTISING RATES:
Full Page Colour .... NOK 15500
BUSINESS: SAFETY & SECURITY: Safety

ARBEIDSMILJØ; ARBEIDSMILJO.NO
1863345R14A-236
Editorial: Postboks 9326, Grønland, 0135 OSLO
Tel: 815 59 750 **Fax:** 22 05 78 39
Email: paul@arbeidsmiljo.no **Web site:** http://www.arbeidsmiljo.no
Freq: Daily; **Cover Price:** Free; **Circ:** 2,500 Unique Users
Language(s): Norwegian
BUSINESS: COMMERCE, INDUSTRY & MANAGEMENT

ARENDALS-TIDENDE.NO
1863340R73-185
Editorial: Arendal stasjon, Møllebakken 15, 4841 ARENDAL **Tel:** 37 00 62 60
Email: post@at-avis.no **Web site:** http://www.arendals-tidende.no
Freq: Daily; **Cover Price:** Free; **Circ:** 550 Unique Users
Language(s): Norwegian
CONSUMER: NATIONAL & INTERNATIONAL PERIODICALS

ARGUMENT STUDENTTIDSSKRIFT
2010141R62A-251
Editorial: Chateau Neuf, Slemdalsveien 15, 0369 OSLO **Tel:** 97 18 25 23
Email: argument-redaksjon@studorg.uio.no **Web site:** http://argument-tidsskrift.blogspot.com
Freq: 6 issues yearly - 5 ganger i året; **Circ:** 5,000
Language(s): Norwegian
BUSINESS: CHURCH & SCHOOL EQUIPMENT & EDUCATION: Education

ARISTOKATT
1645184R81C-1
Editorial: NRR - Østre Strandvei 70, 3482 TOFTE
Tel: 924 47 217
Email: efogas@online.no **Web site:** http://www.nrr.no/Aristokatt
Freq: Quarterly
Language(s): Norwegian
CONSUMER: ANIMALS & PETS: Cats

ARKITEKTNYTT
31382R4A-20
Editorial: Josefinesgate 34, 0351 OSLO
Tel: 23 33 25 45 **Fax:** 23 33 25 50
Email: arkitektnytt@arkitektnytt.no **Web site:** http://www.arkitektnytt.no
Freq: 6 issues yearly; **Circ:** 5,637
Editor: Grete Kristin Hennissen
Profile: Magazine for architects, engineers, interior designers and landscape architects. Also includes two pages of trade union news and information.
Language(s): Norwegian
ADVERTISING RATES:
Full Page Colour .... NOK 24800
BUSINESS: ARCHITECTURE & BUILDING: Architecture

ARKITEKTNYTT; ARKITEKTNYTT.NO
1863338R4A-24
Editorial: Josefines gate 34, 0351 OSLO
Tel: 23332500 **Fax:** 23332550
Email: arkitektnytt@arkitektnytt.no **Web site:** http://www.arkitektnytt.no
Freq: Daily; **Cover Price:** Free; **Circ:** 2,500 Unique Users
Editor: Grete Kristin Hennissen
Language(s): Norwegian
BUSINESS: ARCHITECTURE & BUILDING: Architecture

ARKITEKTUR N
31390R4E-50
Editorial: Josefines gate 34, 0351 OSLO
Tel: 23332500 **Fax:** 23332550
Email: redaksjon@arkitektur-n.no **Web site:** http://www.arkitektur.no/?nid=5734
Date Established: 1918; **Freq:** 6 issues yearly; **Circ:** 6,396
Editor: Ingerid Helsing Almaas
Profile: Publication about the building industry.
Language(s): Norwegian
Readership: Read by contractors, architects, engineers, central and local government, machine owners and users.
ADVERTISING RATES:
Full Page Colour .... NOK 24800
BUSINESS: ARCHITECTURE & BUILDING: Building

ARR - IDEHISTORISK TIDSSKRIFT
1645178R14L-108
Editorial: Huitfeldts Gate 15, 0253 OSLO
Tel: 22 44 87 76
Email: redaksjonen@arrvev.com **Web site:** http://www.arrvev.com
Language(s): Norwegian
BUSINESS: COMMERCE, INDUSTRY & MANAGEMENT: Trade Unions

ASTMA ALLERGI
31635R56A-10
Editorial: Pb. 2603 St. Hanshaugen, 0131 OSLO
Tel: 23353535 **Fax:** 23353530
Email: tonje@naaf.no **Web site:** http://www.naaf.no/no/Tjenester/AstmaAllergi-bladet
Freq: 6 issues yearly - 6 ganger i året; **Circ:** 16,500
Profile: Journal about asthma and other allergies.
Language(s): Norwegian
Readership: Read by members of the Norwegian Asthma and Allergy Society.
ADVERTISING RATES:
Full Page Colour .... NOK 36900
BUSINESS: HEALTH & MEDICAL

ASTROLOGISK FORUM
32373R94E-15
Editorial: Pb 1432 Vika, 0115 OSLO **Tel:** 93 43 31 35
Email: astrologiskforum@gmail.com **Web site:** http://www.astrologiskforening.no
Freq: Quarterly
Editor: Rita G. Wilhelmsen
Profile: Magazine concerning all aspects of astrology.
Language(s): Norwegian
Readership: Aimed at people interested in astrology and practising astrologers.
CONSUMER: OTHER CLASSIFICATIONS: Paranormal

AUDIOGRAFEN
31560R43B-40
Editorial: Monica Rolandsen, Krystallveien 2, 8410 9481 HARSTAD LØDINGEN **Tel:** 951 62 367
Email: redaksjon@audiograf.no **Web site:** http://www.audiograf.no
Freq: Quarterly
Editor: Hanne Ingeborg Berg
Profile: Magazine containing information, articles and news of interest to sound technicians and other professionals working with audio systems and audio technology.
Language(s): Norwegian
BUSINESS: ELECTRICAL RETAIL TRADE: Radio & Hi-Fi

AUDIOVISUELT.NO
1935267R78R-7
Editorial: Tek.no c/o Edda Digital, Postboks 428 Sentrum, 0103 OSLO **Tel:** 920 53683
Fax: 21 56 97 01
Email: havard@tek.no **Web site:** http://audiovisuelt.no
Cover Price: Paid
Language(s): Norwegian
CONSUMER: CONSUMER ELECTRONICS: Consumer Electronics Related

AUTOFIL
1625212R77A-215
Editorial: Pb. 1169 Sentrum, 0107 OSLO
Tel: 21301000 **Fax:** 21301201
Email: espen.autofil@aller.no **Web site:** http://www.aller.no/Autofil.hTL99TVVp2Z–231D7A_xENi9zm2tVPL28nMhPLZB9MtlY05hRjUXV.ips
Freq: Monthly - 10 ganger i året; **Circ:** 30,352
Language(s): Norwegian
ADVERTISING RATES:
SCC .... NOK 366.67
CONSUMER: MOTORING & CYCLING: Motoring

AUTOMATISERING
1656537R5A-3
Editorial: TU Industri AS, Pb. 5844 Majorstuen, 0308 OSLO **Tel:** 23199300
Email: even.fladberg@tu.no **Web site:** http://www.tecpress.no
Freq: 6 issues yearly; **Circ:** 6,000
Language(s): Norwegian
BUSINESS: COMPUTERS & AUTOMATION: Automation & Instrumentation

AUTOMATISERING; AUTOMATISERING.ORG
1865437R33-85
Editorial: TU Industri as, Postboks 5844, Majorstuen, 0134 OSLO **Tel:** 46 81 44 83
Email: even.fladberg@tu.no **Web site:** http://www.tecpress.no
Freq: Daily; **Cover Price:** Free; **Circ:** 2,500 Unique Users
Language(s): Norwegian
BUSINESS: OIL & PETROLEUM

BABY, HOBBY & LEKETØY
707520R48A-5
Editorial: c/o Press Telegraph A/S, Postboks 3004 Elisenberg, 0207 OSLO **Tel:** 22 44 05 06
Fax: 22 56 08 61
Email: pnl@leketoy.org **Web site:** http://www.leketoy.org
Date Established: 1992; **Freq:** Quarterly; **Circ:** 2,200
Profile: Journal containing information about toys, children's hobbies and baby equipment, including events and trade fairs.
Language(s): Norwegian

Norway

Readership: Read by manufacturers and owners of retail outlets.
BUSINESS: TOY TRADE & SPORTS GOODS: Toy Trade

BABYLON 1645179R82-333
Editorial: Institutt for kulturstudier og orientalske språk, Pb 1010 Blindern, 0315 OSLO **Tel:** 22 85 45 49
Email: babylon-redaksjon@ikos.uio.no **Web site:** http://www.tidsskriftet-babylon.com
Freq: Half-yearly; **Circ:** 1,200
Editor: Jørgen Jensehaugen
Language(s): Norwegian
CONSUMER: CURRENT AFFAIRS & POLITICS

BADETEKNISK FORUM 31514R32E-20
Editorial: Pb 153, 2302 HAMAR **Tel:** 950 68 540
Fax: 62519971
Email: badeteknisk@badeteknisk.no **Web site:** http://www.badeteknisk.no
Date Established: 1985; **Freq:** Quarterly
Editor: Bo Norseng
Profile: Magazine containing articles and information about the construction and maintenance of swimming pools.
Language(s): Norwegian
BUSINESS: LOCAL GOVERNMENT, LEISURE & RECREATION: Swimming Pools

BAKER OG KONDITOR 31413R8A-10
Editorial: Vest Vind Media AS, Bruhagen, Sentrumsbygg, 6530 AVERØY **Tel:** 71513470
Fax: 71513473
Email: fagblad@vvm.no **Web site:** http://www.bakeri.net
Date Established: 1898; **Freq:** Monthly - 10 ganger i året; **Circ:** 1,435
Editor: Oddbjørn Roksvåg
Profile: Magazine concerning confectionery and baking.
Language(s): Norwegian
Readership: Aimed at confectioners and bakers.
ADVERTISING RATES:
Full Page Colour .... NOK 15400
BUSINESS: BAKING & CONFECTIONERY: Baking

BALLADE.NO 1645170R76D-276
Editorial: Pb. 2674 Solli, 0203 OSLO **Tel:** 23 27 63 00
Fax: 23 27 63 01
Email: ballade@mic.no **Web site:** http://www.ballade.no
Freq: Daily; **Cover Price:** Paid
Editor: Tellef Øgrim
Language(s): Norwegian
CONSUMER: MUSIC & PERFORMING ARTS: Music

BAR APÉRITIF 1803793R11A-70
Editorial: Furuveien 39c, 0678 OSLO **Tel:** 22190075
Fax: 22671477
Email: aperitif@aperitif.no **Web site:** http://www.aperitif.no
Freq: Quarterly; **Circ:** 4,936
Editor: Jan H. Amundsen
Language(s): Norwegian
BUSINESS: CATERING: Catering, Hotels & Restaurants

BARNEBOKKRITIKK.NO 1803787R62R-1
Editorial: Barnebokkritikk.no, c/o Sævareid, Minister Ditleffsvei 5 A, 0862 OSLO
Email: redaksjonen@barnebokkritikk.no **Web site:** http://www.barnebokkritikk.no
Cover Price: Paid; **Circ:** 2,500 Unique Users
Editor: Heidi Sævareid
Language(s): Norwegian
BUSINESS: CHURCH & SCHOOL EQUIPMENT & EDUCATION: Education Related

BARNEHAGE 1663400R62A-221
Editorial: Private Barnehagers Landsforbund, Pb. 23 Stormyra, 8088 BODØ **Tel:** 75 54 16 90
Fax: 75 54 16 91
Email: red@pbl.no **Web site:** http://www.barnehage.no
Freq: 6 issues yearly; **Circ:** 9,781
Editor: Frode Antonsen
Language(s): Norwegian
ADVERTISING RATES:
Full Page Colour .... NOK 15000
BUSINESS: CHURCH & SCHOOL EQUIPMENT & EDUCATION: Education

BARNIMAGEN.COM 1692823R74D-81
Editorial: Gullhaugveien 1, 0441 OSLO
Tel: 22 58 50 00
Email: firmapost@babymedia.no **Web site:** http://www.barnimagen.com
Language(s): Norwegian
CONSUMER: WOMEN'S INTEREST CONSUMER MAGAZINES: Child Care

BASSETPOSTEN 1625232R81B-204
Editorial: Bjørn Sønsteby, Sandbakken Veldresagvegen 370, 2380 BRUMUNDDAL
Tel: 62 35 64 13
Email: webmaster@norskbassetklubb.no **Web site:** http://www.norskbassetklubb.no
Freq: Quarterly; **Circ:** 700
Editor: Bjørn Sønsteby
Language(s): Norwegian
CONSUMER: ANIMALS & PETS: Dogs

BÅTAVISA.NO 1863748R91A-210
Editorial: Skolmar 11, 3232 SANDEFJORD
Tel: 33 44 72 20
Email: joyce@batavisa.no **Web site:** http://www.baatavisa.no
Freq: Daily; **Cover Price:** Free; **Circ:** 2,500 Unique Users
Language(s): Norwegian
CONSUMER: RECREATION & LEISURE: Boating & Yachting

BÅTGUIDEN 32345R91A-20
Editorial: Leangbukta 40, 1392 VETTRE
Tel: 66764950 **Fax:** 66764951
Web site: http://www.batguiden.no
Freq: Annual
Editor: Tor-Kristian Øines
Profile: Magazine containing information, news and articles about boats. Covers product news, interviews, tests, facts and technical information.
Language(s): Norwegian
Readership: Aimed at people interested in boats and boating.
CONSUMER: RECREATION & LEISURE: Boating & Yachting

BÅTLIV; BATLIV.COM 1863496R91A-209
Editorial: Norsk Maritimt Forlag A/S, Leangbuka 40, 1392 VETTRE **Tel:** 66 76 49 50 **Fax:** 66 76 49 51
Email: frode@batliv.com **Web site:** http://www.batliv.com/wip4
Freq: Daily; **Cover Price:** Free; **Circ:** 2,500 Unique Users
Language(s): Norwegian
CONSUMER: RECREATION & LEISURE: Boating & Yachting

BÅTMAGASINET 32581R91A-40
Editorial: Pb. 1169 Sentrum, 0107 OSLO
Tel: 21301000 **Fax:** 21301259
Email: hans.due@aller.no **Web site:** http://www.batmagasinet.no
Freq: Monthly; **Circ:** 25,505
Profile: Boating magazine including articles about commercial craft, luxury boats, power cruisers, sportsboats, sportsfishing, electronics and navigational equipment. Also contains information about different harbours.
Language(s): Norwegian
Readership: Read by boating enthusiasts.
ADVERTISING RATES:
Full Page Colour .... NOK 22300
CONSUMER: RECREATION & LEISURE: Boating & Yachting

BÅTMAGASINET; BATMAGASINET.NO 1863446R91A-208
Editorial: Postboks 1169 Sentrum, 0107 OSLO
Tel: 21 30 10 00 **Fax:** 21 30 12 59
Email: hans.due@aller.no **Web site:** http://www.batmagasinet.no
Freq: Daily; **Cover Price:** Free; **Circ:** 2,500 Unique Users
Language(s): Norwegian
CONSUMER: RECREATION & LEISURE: Boating & Yachting

BEDRE GARDSDRIFT 31460R21A-10
Editorial: Pb. 130, 2261 KIRKENÆR **Tel:** 95 75 01 04
Email: bo@askmedia.no **Web site:** http://www.gardsdrift.no
Freq: Monthly
Profile: Magazine about tractors and agricultural machinery.
Language(s): Norwegian
ADVERTISING RATES:
Full Page Colour .... NOK 15900
SCC .... NOK 200
BUSINESS: AGRICULTURE & FARMING

BEDRE HELSE 32160R74G-20
Editorial: Gullhaugveien 1, 0441 OSLO
Tel: 22585000
Email: bedre-helse@egmonthm.no **Web site:** http://www.klikk.no/bedrehelse
Freq: Monthly - 9 ganger i året; **Circ:** 27,238
Editor: Grethe Rønningen
Profile: Magazine about achieving better health and fitness, including information about alternative health remedies.
Language(s): Norwegian
ADVERTISING RATES:
SCC .... NOK 195.83
CONSUMER: WOMEN'S INTEREST CONSUMER MAGAZINES: Slimming & Health

BEDRE SKOLE 1624689R62B-201
Editorial: Pb. 9191 Grønland, 0134 OSLO
Tel: 24 14 20 00 **Fax:** 22 00 21 50
Email: bedreskole@utdanningsakademiet.no **Web site:** http://old.utdanningsforbundet.no/no/Akademiet/~Bedre-Skole
Freq: Quarterly
Editor: Ragnhild Midtbø
Language(s): Norwegian
ADVERTISING RATES:
Full Page Colour .... NOK 28000
BUSINESS: CHURCH & SCHOOL EQUIPMENT & EDUCATION: Education Teachers

BEDRIFTSIDRETT I OSLO 1624890R75X-92
Editorial: Ekebergveien 101, 1178 OSLO
Tel: 22 57 97 73
Email: tore@obik.no **Web site:** http://www.obik.no
Freq: 6 issues yearly; **Circ:** 3,500
Language(s): Norwegian
CONSUMER: SPORT: Other Sport

BEFALSBLADET 31541R40-5
Editorial: Møllergata 10, 0179 OSLO **Tel:** 98 28 33 10
Fax: 23 06 15 77
Email: befalsbladet@norgesoffisersforbund.no **Web site:** http://www.milnytt.no
Freq: Quarterly; **Circ:** 7,500
Editor: Staale I. Reiten
Profile: Magazine for commissioned and non-commissioned officers.
Language(s): Norwegian
BUSINESS: DEFENCE

BEKHTEREVER'N 1624993R56A-206
Editorial: Pb 2653 Solli, 0203 OSLO **Tel:** 482 53 810
Email: redaksjon@bekhterevern.no **Web site:** http://www.bekhterev.no
Freq: Quarterly
Language(s): Norwegian
BUSINESS: HEALTH & MEDICAL

BELLONA.NO 31686R57-15
Editorial: Pb 2141 Grünerløkka, 0505 OSLO
Tel: 23 23 46 00 **Fax:** 22 38 38 62
Email: info@bellona.no **Web site:** http://www.bellona.no
Cover Price: Paid
Profile: Internet magazine concerning environmental issues.
Language(s): Norwegian
BUSINESS: ENVIRONMENT & POLLUTION

BENSINFORHANDLEREN 1645190R14A-209
Editorial: Pb 183, 1377 BILLINGSTAD **Tel:** 66983860
Fax: 66983869
Email: frank@williksen.no **Web site:** http://www.bensinforhandlerne.no
Freq: 6 issues yearly
Language(s): Norwegian
BUSINESS: COMMERCE, INDUSTRY & MANAGEMENT

BERGENS TIDENDE 31750R67B-2750
Editorial: Krinkelkroken 1, Postboks 7240, 5020 BERGEN **Tel:** 05 50 0
Email: nyhet@bt.no **Web site:** http://www.bt.no
Freq: Daily; **Circ:** 83,086
Language(s): Norwegian
ADVERTISING RATES:
Full Page Colour .... NOK 78500
SCC .... NOK 392.50
REGIONAL DAILY & SUNDAY NEWSPAPERS: Regional Daily Newspapers

BERGENSAVISEN; DEBATT 1832699R84A-131
Editorial: Pb. 824, Sentrum, 5807 BERGEN
Tel: 55 23 50 00 **Fax:** 55310030
Email: debatt@ba.no **Web site:** http://www.ba.no
Circ: 29,311
Editor: Kjell-Eirik Mikkelsen
Language(s): Norwegian
CONSUMER: THE ARTS & LITERARY: Arts

BERGENSAVISEN; MEG & DEG-REDAKSJONEN 1832700R74A-74
Editorial: Pb 824 Sentrum, 5807 BERGEN
Tel: 55 23 50 00 **Fax:** 55231736
Email: meg.deg@ba.no **Web site:** http://www.ba.no
Circ: 29,311
Language(s): Norwegian
CONSUMER: WOMEN'S INTEREST CONSUMER MAGAZINES: Women's Interest

DET BESTE 1624378R82-304
Editorial: Vakåsveien 9, 1395 HVALSTAD
Tel: 66 98 11 56
Email: redaksjon@detbeste.no **Web site:** http://www.detbeste.no
Freq: Monthly
Language(s): Norwegian
CONSUMER: CURRENT AFFAIRS & POLITICS

BETA - TIDSSKRIFT FOR BEDRIFTSØKONOMI 1624926R1A-124
Editorial: NHH, Helleveien 30, 5045 BERGEN
Tel: 55 95 94 89
Email: odd.nordhaug@nhh.no **Web site:** http://www.universitetsforlaget.no/beta
Freq: Half-yearly; **Cover Price:** Paid
Language(s): Norwegian
BUSINESS: FINANCE & ECONOMICS

BEVIS - KRIMINALTEKNISK FORUM 1660594R32F-51
Editorial: Pb. 240, 4001 STAVANGER
Tel: 51 89 92 98
Email: redaksjonen@bevis.no **Web site:** http://www.bevis.no
Freq: Quarterly
Language(s): Norwegian
BUSINESS: LOCAL GOVERNMENT, LEISURE & RECREATION: Police

BIBLIOTEKAREN 31704R60B-20
Editorial: Runnen 4, 6800 FØRDE **Tel:** 91 31 80 01
Fax: 94 76 22 12
Email: erling.bergan@bibforb.no **Web site:** http://www.bibforb.no
Freq: Monthly
Editor: Erling Bergan
Profile: Journal covering information, news and articles of interest to librarians.
Language(s): Norwegian
BUSINESS: PUBLISHING: Libraries

BIBLIOTEKFORUM 31705R60B-40
Editorial: Postboks 6540, 0606 OSLO
Tel: 23 24 34 30 **Fax:** 22 67 23 68
Email: bibliotekforum@norskbibliotekforening.no
Web site: http://www.norskbibliotekforening.no
Freq: Monthly; **Circ:** 3,326
Editor: Ingrid Stephensen
Profile: Official journal of the Norwegian Library Association.
Language(s): Norwegian
BUSINESS: PUBLISHING: Libraries

BIKE 1625106R77B-152
Editorial: Smalvollveien 63 Etg 2, 0667 OSLO
Tel: 23401030 **Fax:** 23401034
Email: info@bike.no **Web site:** http://www.bike.no/start
Language(s): Norwegian
CONSUMER: MOTORING & CYCLING: Motorcycling

BIKE.NO 1645159R77B-154
Editorial: Smalvollveien 63 Etg 2, 0667 OSLO
Tel: 23 40 10 30 **Fax:** 23 40 10 34
Email: info@bike.no **Web site:** http://www.bike.no
Freq: Daily; **Cover Price:** Paid
Language(s): Norwegian
CONSUMER: MOTORING & CYCLING: Motorcycling

BIL 32220R77A-50
Editorial: Postboks 63 Skøyen, 0134 OSLO
Tel: 23036600 **Fax:** 23036640
Email: bil@bilforlaget.no **Web site:** http://www.bilnorge.no/bil
Date Established: 1975; **Freq:** Monthly - 10 utgaver i året; **Circ:** 45,423
Editor: Jon Winding-Sørensen
Profile: Motoring magazine covering new cars, testing of cars and car-related equipment, caravans, motorcycles and motorsport. Includes four pages of news from the Royal Norwegian Automobile Club.
Language(s): Norwegian
Readership: Read by club members.
ADVERTISING RATES:
Full Page Colour .... NOK 42900
CONSUMER: MOTORING & CYCLING: Motoring

BILBRANSJEN 31501R31A-10
Editorial: Norges Bilbransjeforbunds servicekontor, Pb. 2804 Solli, 0204 OSLO **Tel:** 22 54 21 00
Fax: 22 44 10 56
Email: bilbransjen@nbf.no **Web site:** http://www.nbf.no
Freq: Monthly; **Circ:** 7,072

Editor: Svein-Erik Tosterud
Profile: Official publication of the Norwegian Association of Motor Dealers and Service Organisations.
Language(s): Norwegian
ADVERTISING RATES:
SCC .... NOK 170.83
BUSINESS: MOTOR TRADE: Motor Trade Accessories

BILLISTEN.NO 1853252R77A-236
Editorial: Pb 9 Kokstad, 5863 BERGEN
Tel: 51 82 02 00 **Fax:** 51 82 02 05
Email: redaksjon@billisten.no **Web site:** http://www.billisten.no
Freq: Daily; **Cover Price:** Paid
Language(s): Norwegian
CONSUMER: MOTORING & CYCLING: Motoring

BILMAGASINET 1625046R77D-101
Editorial: Vækerøveien 203, 0751 BILLINGSTAD
Tel: 22500737
Email: redaksjon@bilmagasinet.no **Web site:** http://www.bilmagasinet.net
Freq: Monthly; **Circ:** 40,000
Editor: Sven Furuly
Language(s): Norwegian
CONSUMER: MOTORING & CYCLING: Motor Sports

BILMAGASINET; BILMAGASINET.NET
1865566R77A-238
Editorial: Vækerøveien 203, 0751 OSLO
Tel: 22 50 07 37 **Fax:** 22 52 17 02
Email: redaksjon@bilmagasinet.no **Web site:** http://www.bilmagasinet.net
Cover Price: Paid
Editor: Sven Furly
Language(s): Norwegian
CONSUMER: MOTORING & CYCLING: Motoring

BILNORGE.NO 1658779R77A-220
Editorial: Hovfaret 17b Skøyen, 0212 OSLO
Tel: 23 03 66 00 **Fax:** 23 03 66 40
Email: bil@bilforlaget.no **Web site:** http://www.bilnorge.no
Freq: Daily
Language(s): Norwegian
CONSUMER: MOTORING & CYCLING: Motoring

BILNYTT.NO 1692460R32A-155
Editorial: Postboks 63 Skøyen, 0212 OSLO
Tel: 23 03 66 00 **Fax:** 23 03 66 40
Email: bilnytt@bilnytt.no **Web site:** http://www.bilnytt.no
Language(s): Norwegian
BUSINESS: LOCAL GOVERNMENT, LEISURE & RECREATION: Local Government

BILREVYEN.NO 1658782R77A-222
Web site: http://www.bilrevyen.no
Cover Price: Paid; **Circ:** 2,500 Unique Users
Language(s): Norwegian
CONSUMER: MOTORING & CYCLING: Motoring

BIOINGENIØREN 31660R56H-10
Editorial: NITO - Norges Ingeniør- og Teknologorganisasjon, Postboks 9100 Grønland, 0133 OSLO **Tel:** 22 05 35 00 **Fax:** 22 17 24 80
Email: epost@nito.no **Web site:** http://www.nito.no/organisasjon/Bioingeniorfaglig-institutt/Bioingenioren
Date Established: 1965; **Freq:** Monthly - 11 ganger i året; **Circ:** 6,290
Profile: Official publication of the Norwegian Institute of Medical Laboratory Technology. Contents include medical technology, health in Norway and abroad, the administration of hospitals and laboratories and further education for medical laboratory technologists.
Language(s): Norwegian
Readership: Aimed at biomedical scientists, medical laboratory technologists, specialists in laboratory medicine, laboratory managers and health administrators.
ADVERTISING RATES:
Full Page Colour .... NOK 15900
BUSINESS: HEALTH & MEDICAL: Medical Engineering Technology

BIRKEBEINER'N 32185R75G-50
Editorial: Rakkestadveien 1, 1814 ASKIM
Tel: 69 81 97 00 **Fax:** 69 88 94 33
Email: kristin.roset@sportmedia.no **Web site:** http://www.sportmedia.no
Freq: 6 issues yearly
Editor: Kristin Roset
Profile: Skiing magazine.
Language(s): Norwegian
CONSUMER: SPORT: Winter Sports

BIRKEBEINER'N; BIRKEBEINER.NO 1865902R75A-235
Editorial: Elvegata 19, 2609 LILLEHAMMER
Tel: 41 77 29 00 **Fax:** 62 44 07 35
Email: info@birkebeiner.no **Web site:** http://birkebeiner.no
Cover Price: Paid
Editor: Ingunn Rønningen Kleven
Language(s): Norwegian
CONSUMER: SPORT

BIRØKTEREN 32566R81G-50
Editorial: Dyrskuevegen 20, 2040 KLØFTA
Tel: 63 94 20 80
Email: post@norbi.no **Web site:** http://www.norbi.no
Date Established: 1885; **Freq:** Monthly; **Circ:** 4,100
Profile: Magazine containing articles and information about beekeeping. Covers honey and wax production, practical advice, interviews and news.
Language(s): Norwegian
Readership: Aimed at professional and amateur beekeepers.
CONSUMER: ANIMALS & PETS: Bees

BISTANDSAKTUELT 625067R1P-30
Editorial: Pb 8034 Dep, 0030 OSLO **Tel:** 22242040
Fax: 22242066
Email: gunnar.zachrisen@norad.no **Web site:** http://www.bistandsaktuelt.no
Date Established: 1998; **Freq:** Monthly - 10 utgaver per år; **Circ:** 17,600
Editor: Thore Hem
Profile: Magazine covering Norwegian and international development aid.
Language(s): Norwegian
Readership: Read by private and public development aid staff.
ADVERTISING RATES:
Full Page Colour .... NOK 16000
SCC .... NOK 150
BUSINESS: FINANCE & ECONOMICS: Fundraising

BISTANDSAKTUELT.NO
1837660R82-362
Editorial: Pb 8034 Dep, 0030 OSLO **Tel:** 22 24 20 40
Fax: 22 24 05 72
Email: jasp@norad.no **Web site:** http://www.bistandsaktuelt.no
Freq: Daily; **Cover Price:** Paid; **Circ:** 2,500 Unique Users
Language(s): Norwegian
ADVERTISING RATES:
SCC .... NOK 19.2
CONSUMER: CURRENT AFFAIRS & POLITICS

BIVIRKNINGSBLADET
1660595R56R-167
Editorial: Bivirkningsgruppen, Årstadveien 17, 5009 BERGEN **Tel:** 55586271 **Fax:** 55589862
Email: bivirkningsgruppen@uib.no **Web site:** http://www.uib.no/bivirkningsgruppen
Freq: Half-yearly - 1-2 ganger i året ved behov
Language(s): Norwegian
BUSINESS: HEALTH & MEDICAL: Health Medical Related

BLADET FOLKEMUSIKK
32754R61-200
Editorial: Tyinvegen 27, 2900 FAGERNES
Tel: 907 68 797 **Fax:** 61 35 99 01
Email: knut@folkemusikk.no **Web site:** http://www.folkemusikk.no
Date Established: 1941; **Freq:** 6 issues yearly
Profile: Magazine focusing on folk music, includes interviews, profiles of musicians and dancers, album reviews and events.
Language(s): Norwegian
Readership: Read by managers of clubs and event organisers.
BUSINESS: MUSIC TRADE

BLADET FORSKNING 1624972R55-102
Editorial: Norges Forskningsråd, Pb 2700 St.Hanshaugen, 0131 OSLO **Tel:** 22 03 70 82
Fax: 22 03 71 66
Email: forskning@forskningsradet.no **Web site:** http://www.forskningsradet.no/forskning
Freq: Quarterly
Language(s): Norwegian
BUSINESS: APPLIED SCIENCE & LABORATORIES

BLADET VESTERÅLEN; BLV.NO
1826300R73-173
Editorial: Pb. 33, 8401 SORTLAND **Tel:** 76 11 09 00
Fax: 76110891
Email: red@blv.no **Web site:** http://www.blv.no
Circ: 6,000 Unique Users
Language(s): Norwegian
CONSUMER: NATIONAL & INTERNATIONAL PERIODICALS

BLIKK 1624565R32G-155
Editorial: Pb 8875 Youngstorget, 0028 OSLO
Tel: 22 33 44 55 **Fax:** 22 33 66 37
Email: redaksjonen@blikk.no **Web site:** http://www.blikk.no
Freq: Monthly
Editor: Erna Bøyum
Language(s): Norwegian
BUSINESS: LOCAL GOVERNMENT, LEISURE & RECREATION: Community Care & Social Services

BLINDESAKEN 31662R56L-5
Editorial: Pb 5900 Majorstuen, 0308 OSLO
Tel: 23 21 50 00 **Fax:** 23 21 50 72
Email: info@blindeforbundet.no **Web site:** http://www.blindeforbundet.no
Freq: Quarterly; **Circ:** 12,000
Editor: Mia Jacobsen
Profile: Journal of the Norwegian Society for the Blind and Partially-Sighted.
Language(s): Norwegian
BUSINESS: HEALTH & MEDICAL: Disability & Rehabilitation

BLOMSTER 31494R26C-10
Editorial: Billingstadsletta 13, 1396 BILLINGSTAD
Tel: 66857500 **Fax:** 66857575
Email: berit.bakke@interflora.no **Web site:** http://www.interflora.no
Freq: Monthly - 10 ganger i året; **Circ:** 1,643
Profile: Magazine covering all aspects of the flower trade. Published by the Interflora Organisation.
Language(s): Norwegian
ADVERTISING RATES:
Full Page Colour .... NOK 8600
BUSINESS: GARDEN TRADE

BLYTTIA 1624927R93-102
Editorial: NHM, Pb. 1172 Blindern, 0318 OSLO
Tel: 22 85 17 01 **Fax:** 22 85 18 35
Email: blyttia@nhm.uio.no **Web site:** http://www.nhm.uio.no/botanisk/nbf/blyttia
Freq: Quarterly
Language(s): Norwegian
CONSUMER: GARDENING

BO BEDRE 1645147R74C-60
Editorial: Kirkegaten 20, 0153 OSLO **Tel:** 22 40 12 00
Fax: 22401201
Email: post@bobedrenorge.no **Web site:** http://www.bobedrenorge.no
Freq: Monthly; **Circ:** 32,625
Language(s): Norwegian
ADVERTISING RATES:
SCC .... NOK 300.83
Copy instructions: *Copy Date:* 30 days prior to publication date
CONSUMER: WOMEN'S INTEREST CONSUMER MAGAZINES: Home & Family

BO BEDRE; BOBEDRENORGE.NO 1839818R4A-23
Editorial: Kirkegaten 20, 0103 OSLO **Tel:** 22 40 12 00
Fax: 22 40 12 01
Email: post@bobedrenorge.no **Web site:** http://www.bobedrenorge.no
Freq: Daily; **Cover Price:** Paid; **Circ:** 42,200 Unique Users
Language(s): Norwegian
BUSINESS: ARCHITECTURE & BUILDING: Architecture

BO BYGG OG BOLIG 1624564R74C-52
Editorial: HM Fagmedia AS, avd. Markedskontakt, Redaksjonen Bo Bygg og Bolig, Postboks 24, 1485 HAKADAL **Tel:** 67 06 46 02 **Fax:** 67064611
Email: mail@bbbas.no **Web site:** http://www.bbbas.no
Freq: Quarterly; **Circ:** 80,000
Editor: Iril Kolle
Language(s): Norwegian
CONSUMER: WOMEN'S INTEREST CONSUMER MAGAZINES: Home & Family

BOARDING.NO 1660598R50-154
Editorial: Pb. 557, 4055 STAVANGER LUFTHAVN SOLA **Tel:** 40 85 41 37 **Fax:** 51 65 25 11
Email: posten@boarding.no **Web site:** http://www.boarding.no
Cover Price: Paid; **Circ:** 2,500 Unique Users
Editor: Bjørn Ingolf Søreng
Language(s): Norwegian
BUSINESS: TRAVEL & TOURISM

BOBIL & CARAVAN 1810298R89A-183
Editorial: Rakkestadveien 1, 1814 ASKIM
Tel: 69 81 97 00 **Fax:** 69 88 94 33
Email: anja.guerrera@sportmedia.no **Web site:** http://www.sportmedia.no
Freq: 6 issues yearly; **Circ:** 13,000
Editor: Anja Aarsrud Guerrera
Language(s): Norwegian
ADVERTISING RATES:
Full Page Colour .... NOK 15700
CONSUMER: HOLIDAYS & TRAVEL: Travel

BOINFORM 31358R1J-20
Editorial: Pb 88 Sentrum, 4001 STAVANGER
Tel: 51849500 **Fax:** 51849505
Email: tms@stavanger.bbl.no **Web site:** http://ny.boligbyggelaget.no/boinform.shtml
Freq: Quarterly
Profile: Magazine for members of the Building Association in Norway, interested in buying or renting houses and apartments designed, built and managed by the Association.
Language(s): Norwegian
BUSINESS: FINANCE & ECONOMICS: Building Societies

BOING 1645035R75B-123
Editorial: Pb 8054, 4068 STAVANGER
Tel: 51 84 54 54 **Fax:** 51 84 54 90
Email: boing@stabenfeldt.no **Web site:** http://www.boing-klubben.com
Freq: Monthly
Editor: Trond Hadland
Language(s): Norwegian
CONSUMER: SPORT: Football

BOK OG BIBLIOTEK 31706R60B-50
Editorial: Pb. 4, St. Olavsplass, 0130 OSLO
Tel: 41 33 77 86
Email: odd.letnes@bokogbibliotek.no **Web site:** http://www.bokogbibliotek.no
Freq: 6 issues yearly
Profile: Magazine about books and libraries.
Language(s): Norwegian
BUSINESS: PUBLISHING: Libraries

BOK OG SAMFUNN 31703R60A-50
Editorial: Øvre Vollgt 15, 0158 OSLO
Tel: 22 40 45 40
Email: post@bokogsamfunn.no **Web site:** http://www.bokogsamfunn.no
Freq: 26 issues yearly; **Circ:** 1,882
Profile: Magazine of the Norwegian Book Traders' Association.
Language(s): Norwegian
Readership: Aimed at booksellers, publishers and librarians.
ADVERTISING RATES:
SCC .... NOK 110.83
BUSINESS: PUBLISHING: Publishing & Book Trade

BOK OG SAMFUNN; BOKOGSAMFUNN.NO
1863344R84B-252
Editorial: Øvre Vollgate 15, 0158 OSLO
Tel: 22 40 45 40
Email: post@bokogsamfunn.no **Web site:** http://www.bokogsamfunn.no
Freq: Daily; **Cover Price:** Free; **Circ:** 1,026 Unique Users
Language(s): Norwegian
CONSUMER: THE ARTS & LITERARY: Literary

BOKAVISEN.NO 1803852R74C-86
Editorial: Christiesgate 28, 0557 OSLO
Tel: 40001957
Email: bokavisen@bokavisen.no **Web site:** http://www.bokavisen.no
Cover Price: Paid; **Circ:** 2,500 Unique Users
Editor: Bent Mosfjell
Language(s): Norwegian
CONSUMER: WOMEN'S INTEREST CONSUMER MAGAZINES: Home & Family

BOKNETT.NO 1863942R84B-253
Editorial: c/o Den norske Bokdatabasen AS, Grensen 12, 0159 OSLO **Tel:** 23 35 89 50 **Fax:** 23 35 89 51
Email: boknett@boknett.no **Web site:** http://www.boknett.no
Freq: Daily; **Cover Price:** Free; **Circ:** 2,500 Unique Users
Language(s): Norwegian
CONSUMER: THE ARTS & LITERARY: Literary

BOKSING.NO 1852044R75A-228
Editorial: Serviceboks 1, 0840 OSLO **Tel:** 926 63 633
Email: fwalstad@c2i.net **Web site:** http://www.boksing.no
Freq: Daily; **Cover Price:** Paid
Language(s): Norwegian
CONSUMER: SPORT

BOKVENNEN 32289R84B-25
Editorial: Postboks 6794 St. Olavs plass, 0130 OSLO
Tel: 22 19 14 25 **Fax:** 22 19 14 26
Email: post@vidarforlaget.no **Web site:** http://www.blm.no
Freq: Quarterly

Editor: Gabriel Vosgraff Michael Moro
Profile: Literary journal covering debate, reviews, articles and news.
Language(s): Norwegian
CONSUMER: THE ARTS & LITERARY: Literary

BOLIG I UTLANDET 1692446R74C-85
Editorial: Pb. 1169 Sentrum, 0107 OSLO
Tel: 22912222
Email: boligiutlandet@aller.no **Web site:** http://www.boligiutlandet.com
Freq: 6 issues yearly; **Circ:** 34,000
Language(s): Norwegian
ADVERTISING RATES:
Full Page Colour .... NOK 24500
CONSUMER: WOMEN'S INTEREST CONSUMER MAGAZINES: Home & Family

BOLIG & MILJØ 31383R4D-20
Editorial: Pb 6666 St. Olavs Pl., 0129 OSLO
Tel: 22 86 82 19
Email: eddie.chr.thomas@obos.no **Web site:** http://www.obos.no
Date Established: 1979; **Freq:** 6 issues yearly
Editor: Eddie Chr. Thomas
Profile: Magazine about housing and the surrounding environment.
Language(s): Norwegian
BUSINESS: ARCHITECTURE & BUILDING: Planning & Housing

BOLIGAKTØREN 1645113R74C-68
Editorial: Pb. 630, 4305 SANDNES **Tel:** 51 68 31 00
Fax: 51 68 31 40
Email: post@sbbl.no **Web site:** http://www.sbbl.no
Freq: Quarterly; **Circ:** 10,000
Editor: Marianne Slaughter
Language(s): Norwegian
CONSUMER: WOMEN'S INTEREST CONSUMER MAGAZINES: Home & Family

BOLIGPLUSS 1827078R74C-91
Editorial: Bonnier Media AS, Postboks 1010 Sentrum, 0104 OSLO **Tel:** 22407000
Email: redaksjonen@boligpluss.com **Web site:** http://www.boligpluss.com
Freq: Monthly; **Circ:** 40,612
Language(s): Norwegian
Copy instructions: *Copy Date:* 30 days prior to publication date
CONSUMER: WOMEN'S INTEREST CONSUMER MAGAZINES: Home & Family

BOMAGASINET 1624411R74C-51
Editorial: Pb. 473, 6414 MOLDE **Tel:** 71 20 12 00
Fax: 71 20 12 01
Email: bomagasinet@tibe.no **Web site:** http://www.bomagasinet.no
Freq: 6 issues yearly
Language(s): Norwegian
CONSUMER: WOMEN'S INTEREST CONSUMER MAGAZINES: Home & Family

BONDE OG SMÅBRUKER 31461R21A-12
Editorial: Solfjellsjøen, 8820 DØNNA **Tel:** 48 25 37 00
Email: leonid@smabrukarlaget.no **Web site:** http://www.smabrukarlaget.no
Freq: Monthly - 10 utgaver i året; **Circ:** 8,036
Editor: Leonid Rødsten
Profile: Publication about agricultural smallholdings.
Language(s): Norwegian
ADVERTISING RATES:
Full Page Colour .... NOK 15000
BUSINESS: AGRICULTURE & FARMING

BONDEBLADET 31462R21A-15
Editorial: Tun Media, Pb. 9303 Grønland, 0135 OSLO
Tel: 21 31 44 00 **Fax:** 21 31 44 01
Email: redaksjon@bondebladet.no **Web site:** http://www.bondebladet.no
Date Established: 1974; **Freq:** Weekly - 45 utgaver i året; **Circ:** 72,393
Profile: Magazine about all aspects of farming.
Language(s): Norwegian
Readership: Aimed at Norwegian farmers.
ADVERTISING RATES:
Full Page Colour .... NOK 46400
SCC .... NOK 359.17
BUSINESS: AGRICULTURE & FARMING

BONYTT 32144R74C-24
Editorial: Gullhaugveien 1, 0441 OSLO
Tel: 22585000 **Fax:** 22585829
Email: bonytt@hm-media.no **Web site:** http://www.klikk.no/bonytt
Freq: Monthly - 14 ganger i året; **Circ:** 59,829
Editor: Kriss Daatland
Profile: Magazine about furniture, furnishings, interior decoration, design and architecture.
Language(s): Norwegian
Readership: Read by people wishing to improve their home surroundings.
ADVERTISING RATES:
SCC .... NOK 404.17
CONSUMER: WOMEN'S INTEREST CONSUMER MAGAZINES: Home & Family

BONYTT; BONYTT.NO 1977545R74C-98
Editorial: Bonytt Redaksjonen, 0441 OSLO
Tel: 22 58 50 00 **Fax:** 22 58 58 29
Email: bonytt@hm-media.no **Web site:** http://www.klikk.no/bonytt
Freq: Daily; **Cover Price:** Paid
Editor: Anne Kolberg
Language(s): Norwegian
CONSUMER: WOMEN'S INTEREST CONSUMER MAGAZINES: Home & Family

BRANN & SIKKERHET 31622R54A-50
Editorial: Stiftelsen Norsk brannvernforening, Pb. 6754, Etterstad, 0609 OSLO **Tel:** 23 15 71 00
Fax: 23 15 71 01
Email: syh@brannvernforeningen.no **Web site:** http://www.brannvernforeningen.no/Tjenester/Tidsskriftet-Brann-Sikkerhet
Freq: 6 issues yearly; **Circ:** 6,189
Profile: Publication about fire prevention, fire-fighting techniques and safety equipment.
Language(s): Norwegian
Readership: Read by fire-fighters, manufacturers and suppliers of equipment.
ADVERTISING RATES:
Full Page Colour .... NOK 10100
BUSINESS: SAFETY & SECURITY: Fire Fighting

BRANNMANNEN 31624R54A-70
Editorial: Arne Garborgs Plass 1, 0179 OSLO
Tel: 928 00 378
Email: post@brannmannen.no **Web site:** http://www.brannmannen.no
Freq: 6 issues yearly
Profile: Journal for Norwegian fire fighters.
Language(s): Norwegian
BUSINESS: SAFETY & SECURITY: Fire Fighting

BREPOSTEN 32197R75L-20
Editorial: DNT Fjellsport Oslo, Pb 7 Sentrum, 0101 OSLO **Tel:** 22 82 28 42 **Fax:** 22 82 29 00
Email: fjellsportoslo@dntoslo.no **Web site:** http://www.turistforeningen.no/jotunheimstien/index.php?fo_id=3355
Freq: Half-yearly
Profile: Mountaineering journal.
Language(s): Norwegian
CONSUMER: SPORT: Outdoor

BRIDGE I NORGE 32572R79F-20
Editorial: Nesgaten 25, 4400 FLEKKEFJORD
Tel: 38 32 10 60 **Fax:** 38 32 10 61
Email: bridge@bin.no **Web site:** http://www.bin.no
Freq: 6 issues yearly
Profile: Games magazine focusing on bridge.
Language(s): Norwegian
Readership: Read by all those who are interested in playing bridge.
CONSUMER: HOBBIES & DIY: Games & Puzzles

BRUKTNYTT 31596R49A-10
Editorial: Hjemmet Mortensen Fagmedia AS/BruktNytt, Postboks 67, Bryn, 0611 OSLO
Tel: 22757520 **Fax:** 22757521
Email: petter.vemo@hm-fagmedia.no **Web site:** http://www.bruktnytt.no
Freq: Monthly; **Circ:** 21,000
Profile: Magazine containing news and information about the world of transport.
Language(s): Norwegian
BUSINESS: TRANSPORT

BRYLLUPSMAGASINET 1624694R74H-1
Editorial: Trykkeriveien 6, 1653 SELLEBAKK
Tel: 69351800 **Fax:** 69351809
Email: info@bryllupsmagasinet.no **Web site:** http://www.bryllupsmagasinet.no
Freq: Half-yearly
Language(s): Norwegian
CONSUMER: WOMEN'S INTEREST CONSUMER MAGAZINES: Hair & Beauty

BRYTING.NO 1852430R75A-229
Editorial: Norges Bryteforbund, Serviceboks 1, 0840 OSLO **Tel:** 922 41 690
Email: bryting@nif.idrett.no **Web site:** http://www.bryting.no
Freq: Daily; **Cover Price:** Paid
Language(s): Norwegian
CONSUMER: SPORT

BUD OG HILSEN 625086R87-25
Editorial: Sjømannskirken, Pb 2007, 5817 BERGEN
Tel: 55 55 22 55
Email: inge.morland@sjomannskirken.no **Web site:** http://www.sjomannskirken.no
Date Established: 1864; **Freq:** 6 issues yearly
Editor: Inge Mørland
Profile: Magazine covering religion and questions about the challenges of living abroad.
Language(s): Norwegian
Readership: Read by Norwegians abroad and church-goers in Norway.
CONSUMER: RELIGIOUS

BUDSTIKKA 31753R67B-2700
Editorial: Pb 133, 1376 BILLINGSTAD
Tel: 66 77 00 00 **Fax:** 66 77 00 60
Email: redaksjonen@budstikka.no **Web site:** http://www.budstikka.no
Freq: Daily; **Circ:** 28,264
Language(s): Norwegian
ADVERTISING RATES:
Full Page Colour .... NOK 28855
REGIONAL DAILY & SUNDAY NEWSPAPERS: Regional Daily Newspapers

BUESTIKKA 32206R75X-17
Editorial: Serviceboks 1, 0840 OSLO
Tel: 21 02 97 85 **Fax:** 21 02 90 03
Email: bue@nif.idrett.no **Web site:** http://www.bueskyting.no
Date Established: 1974; **Freq:** Monthly; **Circ:** 1,350
Profile: Archery magazine.
Language(s): Norwegian
Readership: Read by archery enthusiasts.
CONSUMER: SPORT: Other Sport

BUSINESS Q4 SØRLANDET 1810272R14A-222
Editorial: Pb. 51, 4854 NEDENES **Tel:** 909 23 795
Email: tips@bq4.no **Web site:** http://www.bq4.no
Freq: Quarterly; **Circ:** 5,000
Language(s): Norwegian
BUSINESS: COMMERCE, INDUSTRY & MANAGEMENT

BUSINESS Q4 SØRLANDET; BQ4.NO 1863443R86C-163
Editorial: Postboks 51, 4854 NEDENES
Tel: 909 23 795
Email: tips@bq4.no **Web site:** http://www.bq4.no
Freq: Daily; **Cover Price:** Free; **Circ:** 2,500 Unique Users
Language(s): Norwegian
CONSUMER: ADULT & GAY MAGAZINES: Men's Lifestyle Magazines

BUSKAP 31474R21D-10
Editorial: Holsetgata 22, 2326 HAMAR
Tel: 62 52 06 00
Email: buskap@geno.no **Web site:** http://www.buskap.no
Freq: 6 issues yearly; **Circ:** 15,298
Profile: Journal about cattle breeding.
Language(s): Norwegian
ADVERTISING RATES:
Full Page Colour .... NOK 17650
BUSINESS: AGRICULTURE & FARMING: Livestock

BYENS NÆRINGSLIV 1692459R63-3
Editorial: Norsk Avisdrift AS, 7032 TRONDHEIM
Tel: 73 95 49 00
Email: post@norskavisdrift.no **Web site:** http://www.byavisa.no/bn
Freq: Monthly; **Circ:** 90,000
Language(s): Norwegian
ADVERTISING RATES:
Full Page Colour .... NOK 23000
BUSINESS: REGIONAL BUSINESS

BYGDEBLADET.NO 1863444R73-191
Editorial: Postboks 94, 4096 RANDABERG
Tel: 51 41 46 66
Email: tips@bygdebladet.no **Web site:** http://www.bygdebladet.no
Freq: Daily; **Cover Price:** Free; **Circ:** 2,600 Unique Users
Language(s): Norwegian
CONSUMER: NATIONAL & INTERNATIONAL PERIODICALS

BYGDEPOSTEN.NO 1863448R73-192
Editorial: Postboks 53, 3371 VIKERSUND
Tel: 32 78 34 40 **Fax:** 32783441
Email: redaksjon@bygdeposten.no **Web site:** http://www.bygdeposten.no
Freq: Daily; **Cover Price:** Free; **Circ:** 4,400 Unique Users
Language(s): Norwegian
CONSUMER: NATIONAL & INTERNATIONAL PERIODICALS

BYGG & HANDEL 1624963R46-102
Editorial: Trelast- og byggevarehandelens Fellesorganisasjon, Vollsveien 13H, 1366 LYSAKER
Tel: 67 20 41 40 **Fax:** 67204141
Email: tsm@tbf.no **Web site:** http://www.tbf.no
Freq: 6 issues yearly - 5 ganger i året
Language(s): Norwegian
BUSINESS: TIMBER, WOOD & FORESTRY

BYGGAKTUELT 31387R4E-25
Editorial: Pb. 1024, 1510 MOSS **Tel:** 69 91 24 00
Fax: 69 91 24 04
Email: red@byggaktuelt.no **Web site:** http://www.byggaktuelt.no
Freq: Monthly; **Circ:** 13,572
Editor: Anton Granhus
Profile: Magazine containing news and information about the building and construction trade.
Language(s): Norwegian
ADVERTISING RATES:
Full Page Colour .... NOK 25100
SCC .... NOK 209.17
BUSINESS: ARCHITECTURE & BUILDING: Building

BYGGAKTUELT; BYGGAKTUELT.NO 1863445R4E-112
Editorial: Postbks 1024, 1510 MOSS
Tel: 69 91 24 00
Email: info@byggaktuelt.no **Web site:** http://www.byggaktuelt.no
Freq: Daily; **Cover Price:** Free; **Circ:** 7,108 Unique Users
Editor: Anton Granhus
Language(s): Norwegian
BUSINESS: ARCHITECTURE & BUILDING: Building

BYGGEINDUSTRIEN 31388R4E-40
Editorial: Pb. 6831 St. Olavs plass, 0130 OSLO
Tel: 23 70 95 00 **Fax:** 23 70 95 01
Email: ab@bygg.no **Web site:** http://www.bygg.no
Date Established: 1968; **Freq:** Monthly; **Circ:** 14,235
Editor: Arve Brekkhus
Profile: Journal covering all aspects of the building industry.
Language(s): Norwegian
ADVERTISING RATES:
Full Page Colour .... NOK 28200
SCC .... NOK 220
BUSINESS: ARCHITECTURE & BUILDING: Building

BYGGEINDUSTRIEN; BYGG.NO 1740801R3D-5
Editorial: Postboks 6831 St. Olavs plass, 0130 OSLO
Tel: 23 70 95 00 **Fax:** 23 70 95 01
Email: ab@bygg.no **Web site:** http://www.bygg.no
Freq: Daily; **Circ:** 11,000 Unique Users
Language(s): Norwegian
BUSINESS: HEATING & VENTILATION: Heating & Plumbing

BYGGENYTT 31391R4E-60
Editorial: Pb 5023 Majorstua, 0301 OSLO
Tel: 22 87 12 00 **Fax:** 22 87 12 01
Email: post@byggenytt.no **Web site:** http://www.byggenytt.no
Freq: Monthly; **Circ:** 7,000
Profile: Magazine containing news and information concerning the building industry.
Language(s): Norwegian
ADVERTISING RATES:
Full Page Colour .... NOK 29000

BYGGFAGBLADET 1624389R14L-102
Editorial: Grønland 12, 0188 OSLO **Tel:** 22 99 28 70
Fax: 22992871
Email: post@byggfag.org **Web site:** http://www.byggfag.org
Freq: Quarterly
Language(s): Norwegian
BUSINESS: COMMERCE, INDUSTRY & MANAGEMENT: Trade Unions

BYGGMESTEREN 31393R4E-70
Editorial: Pb. 5475 Majorstuen, 0305 OSLO
Tel: 23087500 **Fax:** 23087550
Email: post@byggmesteren.as **Web site:** http://www.byggmesteren.as
Date Established: 1926; **Freq:** Monthly - 10 ganger i året; **Circ:** 6,637
Profile: Magazine for and about master builders.
Language(s): Norwegian
ADVERTISING RATES:
Full Page Colour .... NOK 20300
Copy instructions: *Copy Date:* 14 days prior to publication date

BYGGMESTEREN; BYGGMESTEREN.AS 1863447R4A-25
Editorial: Postboks 5475 Majostuen, 0305 OSLO
Tel: 23 08 75 00 **Fax:** 23 08 75 50

Email: post@byggmesteren.as **Web site:** http://www.byggmesteren.as
Freq: Daily; **Cover Price:** Free; **Circ:** 2,500 Unique Users
Language(s): Norwegian
BUSINESS: ARCHITECTURE & BUILDING: Architecture

C!
1645189R82-332
Editorial: Magasinet C!, 0441 OSLO **Tel:** 22 58 50 00
Fax: 22 58 50 25
Email: c@egmonthm.no **Web site:** http://www.egmonthm.no
Freq: Monthly; **Circ:** 25,095
Language(s): Norwegian
ADVERTISING RATES:
Full Page Colour .... NOK 27000
SCC .... NOK 165.83
CONSUMER: CURRENT AFFAIRS & POLITICS

CAMPUS
1810339R62A-240
Editorial: Youngstorget 4, 0181 OSLO
Tel: 909 32 807 **Fax:** 24 20 15 94
Email: post@studenttorget.no **Web site:** http://www.studenttorget.no
Freq: Quarterly; **Circ:** 20,000
Editor: Tor Hernan Floor
Language(s): Norwegian
BUSINESS: CHURCH & SCHOOL EQUIPMENT & EDUCATION: Education

CANIS
1645153R81B-205
Editorial: Canis AS, Mediahuset Vestre Rosten 78, 7075 TILLER **Tel:** 72 87 86 50 **Fax:** 72 87 86 55
Email: canis@canis.no **Web site:** http://www.canis.no
Cover Price: Paid
Language(s): Norwegian
CONSUMER: ANIMALS & PETS: Dogs

CARAVAN
32352R91B-20
Editorial: Pb 104, 1921 SØRUMSAND **Tel:** 63829990
Fax: 63829999
Email: caravan@nocc.no **Web site:** http://www.norskcaravanclub.no
Date Established: 1962; **Freq:** Quarterly; **Circ:** 29,000
Profile: Publication of the Norwegian Caravan Club.
Language(s): Norwegian
Readership: Aimed at those interested in camping and caravanning.
ADVERTISING RATES:
Full Page Colour .... NOK 25020
CONSUMER: RECREATION & LEISURE: Camping & Caravanning

CIVINORD
32374R94F-100
Editorial: Pb. 18, 4701 VENNESLA **Tel:** 38 15 50 80
Email: civinord@civitan.no **Web site:** http://www.civitan.no
Date Established: 1972; **Freq:** Quarterly
Profile: Magazine containing information and articles about Civitan, an international humanitarian organisation working to improving the well-being and the quality of life for people who are mentally retarded or affected by development disabilities.
Language(s): Norwegian
CONSUMER: OTHER CLASSIFICATIONS: Disability

CØLIAKI-NYTT
1936410R56A-227
Editorial: Boks 4725 Nydalen, 0421 OSLO
Tel: 22799170 **Fax:** 22799395
Email: post@ncf.no **Web site:** http://www.ncf.no
Freq: Quarterly; **Circ:** 9,900
Language(s): Norwegian
ADVERTISING RATES:
Full Page Colour .... NOK 11600
BUSINESS: HEALTH & MEDICAL

COLOR CLUB MAGASIN
32338R89E-30
Editorial: Color Line AS - Color Club, Postboks 2090, 3202 SANDEFJORD **Tel:** 24 11 71 00
Fax: 24 11 71 01
Email: ccmagasin@colorline.no **Web site:** http://www.colorline.no/color_club
Freq: Half-yearly
Profile: Passenger magazine available on board Color Line ships, which sail between Norway, England, Denmark and Germany.
Language(s): Norwegian
CONSUMER: HOLIDAYS & TRAVEL: Holidays

COMPUTERWORLD
31398R5B-5
Editorial: IDG Magazines Norge, Postboks 9090, Grønland, 0133 OSLO **Tel:** 22053000 **Fax:** 22053051
Email: redaksjonen@computerworld.no **Web site:** http://www.idg.no/computerworld
Freq: Weekly; **Circ:** 15,000
Editor: Michael Oreld
Profile: Newspaper containing articles about computers and data processing in Norway.
Language(s): Norwegian
ADVERTISING RATES:
Full Page Colour .... NOK 63200
SCC .... NOK 491.67
Copy instructions: *Copy Date:* 30 days prior to publication date
BUSINESS: COMPUTERS & AUTOMATION: Data Processing

COMPUTERWORLD.NO
1837367R5E-5
Editorial: Pb. 9090 Grønland, 0133 OSLO
Tel: 22 05 30 00
Email: redaksjonen@computerworld.no **Web site:** http://www.idg.no/computerworld
Freq: Daily; **Cover Price:** Paid
Language(s): Norwegian
BUSINESS: COMPUTERS & AUTOMATION: Data Transmission

CONPOT
1624955R74Q-72
Editorial: Prinsensgate 46, 7011 TRONDHEIM
Tel: 992 89 500 **Fax:** 73 51 65 50
Email: conpotnorge@conpot.com **Web site:** http://www.conpot.com/no
Freq: Monthly - 15 ganger i året
Language(s): Norwegian
CONSUMER: WOMEN'S INTEREST CONSUMER MAGAZINES: Lifestyle

COSMOPOLITAN
1692444R74B-54
Editorial: Pb. 1169 Sentrum, 0107 OSLO
Tel: 21301000
Email: redaksjonen@cosmopolitan.no **Web site:** http://www.cosmopolitan.no
Freq: Monthly; **Circ:** 28,790
Language(s): Norwegian
ADVERTISING RATES:
SCC .... NOK 375
CONSUMER: WOMEN'S INTEREST CONSUMER MAGAZINES: Women's Interest - Fashion

COSTUME
1803747R74G-167
Editorial: Pb. 1010, Sentrum, 0104 OSLO
Tel: 22401200 **Fax:** 22401241
Email: mail@costume.no **Web site:** http://www.costume.no
Freq: Monthly; **Circ:** 37,058
Editor: Randi Helene Svendsen
Language(s): Norwegian
ADVERTISING RATES:
Full Page Colour .... NOK 49000
SCC .... NOK 341.67
Copy instructions: *Copy Date:* 25 days prior to publication date
CONSUMER: WOMEN'S INTEREST CONSUMER MAGAZINES: Slimming & Health

COSTUME.NO
1873302R74A-80
Editorial: Pb. 1010, Sentrum, 0104 OSLO
Tel: 22 40 12 40 **Fax:** 22 40 12 41
Email: mail@costume.no **Web site:** http://www.costume.no
Freq: Daily; **Cover Price:** Paid
Language(s): Norwegian
CONSUMER: WOMEN'S INTEREST CONSUMER MAGAZINES: Women's Interest

CP-BLADET
1936406R56L-104
Editorial: Bergsalleen 21, 0854 OSLO **Tel:** 22599900
Fax: 22599901
Email: solveig@cp.no **Web site:** http://www.cp.no
Freq: Quarterly
Editor: Solveig Espeland Ertresvaag
Language(s): Norwegian
ADVERTISING RATES:
Full Page Colour .... NOK 8000
BUSINESS: HEALTH & MEDICAL: Disability & Rehabilitation

CRESCENDO
1803742R56L-103
Editorial: Emma Hjorths vei 50, 1336 SANDVIKA
Tel: 67 17 48 80 **Fax:** 67 13 16 10
Email: post@dissimilis.no **Web site:** http://www.dissimilis.no/index.php/om-dissimilis/crescendo-medlemsblad
Freq: Quarterly
Editor: Øyvind Risvik
Language(s): Norwegian
BUSINESS: HEALTH & MEDICAL: Disability & Rehabilitation

CUBA-NYTT
31459R20-20
Editorial: Pb. 8708 Youngstorget, 0028 OSLO
Tel: 2217 2900 **Fax:** 2217 2902
Email: kontakt@cubaforeningen.no **Web site:** http://www.cubaforeningen.no/cubanytt.htm
Date Established: 1964; **Freq:** Quarterly; **Circ:** 1,500
Editor: Terje Enger
Profile: Magazine published by the Norwegian-Cuban Association.
Language(s): Norwegian
BUSINESS: IMPORT & EXPORT

D!
1645192R74C-66
Editorial: Pb. 1164 Sentrum, 0107 OSLO
Tel: 22 91 22 00
Email: d-postkassen@aller.no **Web site:** http://www.aller.no
Freq: Monthly; **Circ:** 20,380
Language(s): Norwegian
ADVERTISING RATES:
SCC .... NOK 208.33
CONSUMER: WOMEN'S INTEREST CONSUMER MAGAZINES: Home & Family

D2
1826773R14A-235
Editorial: Pb. 1182 Sentrum, 0107 OSLO
Tel: 22001190
Email: annab.jenssen@d2.no **Web site:** http://www.d2.no
Freq: Weekly; **Circ:** 81,391
Language(s): Norwegian
BUSINESS: COMMERCE, INDUSTRY & MANAGEMENT

DAG OG TID
32251R82-50
Editorial: Pb. 7044 St. Olavs plass, 0130 OSLO
Tel: 21 50 47 47 **Fax:** 21 50 47 49
Email: redaksjonen@dagogtid.no **Web site:** http://www.dagogtid.no
Freq: Weekly; **Circ:** 7,233
Profile: Magazine focusing on cultural, environmental and political matters.
Language(s): Norwegian
ADVERTISING RATES:
Full Page Colour .... NOK 64438
SCC .... NOK 536.98
CONSUMER: CURRENT AFFAIRS & POLITICS

DAG OG TID; DAGOGTID.NO
1863494R74Q-84
Editorial: Postboks 7044 St. Olavs plass, 0130 OSLO
Tel: 21 50 47 47
Email: redaksjonen@dagogtid.no **Web site:** http://www.dagogtid.no
Freq: Daily; **Cover Price:** Free
Language(s): Norwegian
CONSUMER: WOMEN'S INTEREST CONSUMER MAGAZINES: Lifestyle

DAGBLADET; NYHETSREDAKSJONEN
31737R65A-30
Editorial: Pb. 1184 Sentrum, 0150 OSLO
Tel: 24 00 10 00 **Fax:** 22 42 95 48
Email: nyhet@dagbladet.no **Web site:** http://www.dagbladet.no
Freq: Daily; **Circ:** 123,383
Profile: Broadsheet-sized newspaper covering national and international news, politics and culture. Political outlook: Independent.
Language(s): Norwegian
Readership: Read by a broad range of the population.
NATIONAL DAILY & SUNDAY NEWSPAPERS: National Daily Newspapers

DAGBLADET; SØNDAGSMAGASIN
1818386R14A-229
Editorial: Pb. 1184 Sentrum, 0150 OSLO
Tel: 24001000
Email: sondag@dagbladet.no **Web site:** http://www.dagbladet.no
Freq: Weekly; **Circ:** 106,561
Language(s): Norwegian
BUSINESS: COMMERCE, INDUSTRY & MANAGEMENT

DAGBLADET.NO- KJENDIS.NO
1803785R74Q-78
Editorial: Postboks 1184, Sentrum, 0150 OSLO
Tel: 24 00 10 00
Email: 2400@dagbladet.no **Web site:** http://www.kjendis.no
Language(s): Norwegian
CONSUMER: WOMEN'S INTEREST CONSUMER MAGAZINES: Lifestyle

DAGEN
31752R67B-2900
Editorial: Pb. 2394, Solheimsviken, 5824 BERGEN
Tel: 55 55 97 25 **Fax:** 55 55 97 20
Email: redaksjonen@dagenmagazinet.no **Web site:** http://www.dagenmagazinet.no
Date Established: 1919; **Freq:** Daily; **Circ:** 10,842
Language(s): Norwegian
REGIONAL DAILY & SUNDAY NEWSPAPERS: Regional Daily Newspapers

DAGENS MEDISIN; DAGENSMEDISIN.NO
1839822R56A-213
Editorial: Pb 6970, St. Olav's Plass, 0130 OSLO
Tel: 934 30 200 **Fax:** 24 14 68 81
Email: post@dagensmedisin.no **Web site:** http://www.dagensmedisin.no
Freq: Daily; **Cover Price:** Paid; **Circ:** 5,950 Unique Users
Language(s): Norwegian
BUSINESS: HEALTH & MEDICAL

DAGENS NÆRINGSLIV
31738R65A-35
Editorial: Pb. 1182 Sentrum, 0107 OSLO
Tel: 22001000 **Fax:** 22001110
Email: redaksjonen@dn.no **Web site:** http://www.dn.no
Date Established: 1890; **Freq:** Daily - Norway; **Circ:** 81,391
Features Editor: Gry Egenes
Profile: Tabloid-sized quality newspaper providing in-depth coverage of national and international business news, politics, finance and economics.
Language(s): Norwegian
Readership: Read by the business community, academics, politicians, business managers and financial executives.
ADVERTISING RATES:
Full Page Colour .... NOK 98222
SCC .... NOK 491.11
NATIONAL DAILY & SUNDAY NEWSPAPERS: National Daily Newspapers

DAGENSIT.NO
1853153R18A-106
Editorial: Pb. 1182, Sentrum, 0107 OSLO
Tel: 22 00 10 00
Email: dagensit@dagensit.no **Web site:** http://www.dagensit.no
Freq: Daily; **Cover Price:** Paid; **Circ:** 2,500 Unique Users
Language(s): Norwegian
BUSINESS: ELECTRONICS

DAGLIGVAREHANDELEN
32419R22A-20
Editorial: Rosenholmveien 20, 1252 OSLO
Tel: 22629190 **Fax:** 22629199
Email: company@dagligvarehandelen.com **Web site:** http://www.dagligvarehandelen.com
Date Established: 1993; **Freq:** Weekly; **Circ:** 17,625
Profile: Magazine covering the grocery trade.
Language(s): Norwegian
Readership: Read by owners and employees of grocery outlets.
ADVERTISING RATES:
Full Page Colour .... NOK 39800
SCC .... NOK 290.83
Copy instructions: *Copy Date:* 10 days prior to publication date
BUSINESS: FOOD

DAGSAVISEN
31739R65A-36
Editorial: Pb. 1183 Sentrum, 0107 OSLO
Tel: 22998000 **Fax:** 22998252
Email: tipset@dagsavisen.no **Web site:** http://www.dagsavisen.no
Date Established: 1884; **Freq:** Daily; **Circ:** 29,041
Profile: Tabloid-sized newspaper covering news, politics, events, entertainment and culture.
Language(s): Norwegian
Readership: Read by the general public.
ADVERTISING RATES:
Full Page Colour .... NOK 108044
SCC .... NOK 540.22
NATIONAL DAILY & SUNDAY NEWSPAPERS: National Daily Newspapers

DALANE TIDENDE
31762R67B-2950
Editorial: Pb. 68, 4379 EGERSUND **Tel:** 51 46 11 00
Fax: 51 46 11 01
Email: redaksjon@dalane-tidende.no **Web site:** http://www.dalane-tidende.no
Freq: 156 issues yearly; **Circ:** 8,418
Language(s): Norwegian
ADVERTISING RATES:
Full Page Colour .... NOK 39923
SCC .... NOK 199.62
REGIONAL DAILY & SUNDAY NEWSPAPERS: Regional Daily Newspapers

DE DANSEGLADE
1740660R76D-299
Editorial: Høilundhagen 4, 1440 DRØBAK
Tel: 64 98 89 10
Email: post@dd.no **Web site:** http://www.dans.no
Freq: 6 issues yearly
Language(s): Norwegian
CONSUMER: MUSIC & PERFORMING ARTS: Music

DECOR-MAGASINET
1977751R74C-100
Editorial: Bygdøy allé 64 a, 0265 OSLO
Tel: 94872363 **Fax:** 22443552
Email: post@decor-magasinet.no **Web site:** http://www.decor-magasinet.no
Editor: Margrete Tennfjord
Language(s): Norwegian
CONSUMER: WOMEN'S INTEREST CONSUMER MAGAZINES: Home & Family

DEMOKRATEN; KULTURREDAKSJONEN
1835160R84A-138
Editorial: Pb. 82, 1601 FREDRIKSTAD
Tel: 69 36 80 00
Email: kultur@demokraten.no **Web site:** http://www.demokraten.no
Circ: 8,670
Language(s): Norwegian
CONSUMER: THE ARTS & LITERARY: Arts

DEMOKRATEN; SPORTSREDAKSJONEN
1835161R75A-220
Editorial: Pb. 82, 1601 FREDRIKSTAD
Tel: 69 36 80 00
Email: sport@demokraten.no **Web site:** http://www.demokraten.no
Circ: 8,670
Language(s): Norwegian
CONSUMER: SPORT

DESENTRALIST
32790R82-285
Editorial: Senterungdommen, Postboks 1191 Sentrum, 0107 OSLO **Tel:** 23690100 **Fax:** 23690101
Email: senterungdommen@senterpartiet.no **Web site:** http://www.senterungdommen.no
Freq: Half-yearly
Profile: Magazine of the Youth Centre Party in Norway.
Language(s): Norwegian
Readership: Aimed at members.
CONSUMER: CURRENT AFFAIRS & POLITICS

DESIGN:INTERIØR
1625043R4B-2
Editorial: Pb. 6974, St.Olavs plass, 0130 OSLO
Tel: 24 14 69 40
Email: mhj@designinterior.no **Web site:** http://www.designinterior.no
Freq: 6 issues yearly; **Circ:** 10,000
Language(s): Norwegian
ADVERTISING RATES:
Full Page Colour .... NOK 26900
BUSINESS: ARCHITECTURE & BUILDING: Interior Design & Flooring

DEVELOPMENT TODAY
2010142R82-501
Editorial: Box 140, 1371 ASKER **Tel:** 66902660
Email: devtoday@devtoday.no **Web site:** http://www.development-today.com
Language(s): Norwegian
CONSUMER: CURRENT AFFAIRS & POLITICS

DIABETES
31637R56A-12
Editorial: Pb 6442 Etterstad, 0605 OSLO
Tel: 23051800 **Fax:** 23051801
Email: diabetes@diabetes.no **Web site:** http://www.diabetes.no
Freq: 6 issues yearly - 7 ganger i året; **Circ:** 39,786
Profile: Official journal of the Norwegian Diabetics' Association.
Language(s): Norwegian
ADVERTISING RATES:
SCC .... NOK 229.17
BUSINESS: HEALTH & MEDICAL

DIABETESFORUM
31636R56A-15
Editorial: Pb 6442 Etterstad, 0605 OSLO
Tel: 23051800 **Fax:** 23051801
Email: diabetes@diabetes.no **Web site:** http://www.diabetes.no/Fagbladet+Diabetesforum.9UFRnG50.ips
Freq: Quarterly
Profile: Journal containing information, news and articles about diabetes.
Language(s): Norwegian
Readership: Aimed at professionals within the medical field.
BUSINESS: HEALTH & MEDICAL

DIGI.NO
1624643R5F-1
Editorial: Stenersgata 8, 0184 OSLO **Tel:** 40 60 10 30
Email: redaksjon@digi.no **Web site:** http://www.digi.no
Editor: Eirik Rossen
Language(s): Norwegian
BUSINESS: COMPUTERS & AUTOMATION: Multimedia

DIGITAL FOTO
1645120R85A-258
Editorial: Torvgt. 15 B, 2000 LILLESTRØM
Tel: 63883807
Email: redaksjonen@digital-foto.no **Web site:** http://www.digital-foto.no
Freq: Monthly; **Circ:** 11,726
Editor: Ronny Sennerud
Language(s): Norwegian
ADVERTISING RATES:
SCC .... NOK 460
CONSUMER: PHOTOGRAPHY & FILM MAKING: Photography

DIGIT.NO
1656526R85A-254
Editorial: PB 9025 Grønland, 0133 OSLO
Tel: 21 00 60 00 **Fax:** 22 20 21 11
Email: marte@teknofil.no **Web site:** http://www.digit.no
Cover Price: Paid; **Circ:** 2,500 Unique Users
Language(s): Norwegian
CONSUMER: PHOTOGRAPHY & FILM MAKING: Photography

DIN HØRSEL
31663R56L-10
Editorial: Pb 6652 Etterstad, 0609 OSLO
Tel: 22639900
Email: tor.slette.johansen@hlf.no **Web site:** http://www.hlf.no/Om-HLF/Medlemsbladet-Din-Horsel
Date Established: 1947; **Freq:** 6 issues yearly; **Circ:** 55,000
Profile: Magazine containing information about deafness.
Language(s): Norwegian
Readership: Read by those who are deaf or hard of hearing and also members of the medical profession specialising in this field.
ADVERTISING RATES:
Full Page Colour .... NOK 18000
BUSINESS: HEALTH & MEDICAL: Disability & Rehabilitation

DINBABY.COM
1692824R74D-82
Editorial: NO-0277 OSLO **Tel:** 45 25 25 48
Email: firmapost@babymedia.no **Web site:** http://www.dinbaby.com
Language(s): Norwegian
CONSUMER: WOMEN'S INTEREST CONSUMER MAGAZINES: Child Care

DINE PENGER
32170R74M-50
Editorial: Postboks 1185 sentrum, 0277 OSLO
Tel: 22 00 00 50 **Fax:** 22 00 00 60
Email: dinepenger@dinepenger.no **Web site:** http://www.dinepenger.no
Freq: Monthly - 11 ganger i året; **Circ:** 55,813
Profile: Magazine covering many different aspects of personal finance including savings, investment, shares, pensions and general finance news.
Language(s): Norwegian
ADVERTISING RATES:
SCC .... NOK 466.67
CONSUMER: WOMEN'S INTEREST CONSUMER MAGAZINES: Personal Finance

DINEPENGER.NO
1740630R74M-211
Editorial: Postboks 1185 sentrum, 0107 OSLO
Tel: 22 00 00 50 **Fax:** 22000060
Email: dpo@dinepenger.no **Web site:** http://www.dinepenger.no
Freq: Daily; **Circ:** 76,600 Unique Users
Language(s): Norwegian
CONSUMER: WOMEN'S INTEREST CONSUMER MAGAZINES: Personal Finance

DINGZ.NO
1803792R78R-1
Editorial: Stenersgt 2-8, 0184 OSLO **Tel:** 40 60 20 80
Email: oyvind@dingz.no **Web site:** http://www.dingz.no
Editor: Øyvind Paulsen
Language(s): Norwegian
CONSUMER: CONSUMER ELECTRONICS: Consumer Electronics Related

DINSIDE
1625044R74Q-73
Editorial: Postboks 1169, 0107 OSLO **Tel:** 4060 1000
Fax: 2103 2052
Email: tips@dinside.no **Web site:** http://www.dinside.no
Editor: Karoline Brubæk
Language(s): Norwegian
CONSUMER: WOMEN'S INTEREST CONSUMER MAGAZINES: Lifestyle

DINSIDE; BOLIG
1935935R74C-97
Editorial: Postboks 1169, 0107 OSLO **Tel:** 4060 1000
Fax: 2103 2052
Email: tips@dinside.no **Web site:** http://www.dinside.no/bolig
Freq: Daily; **Cover Price:** Paid
Language(s): Norwegian
CONSUMER: WOMEN'S INTEREST CONSUMER MAGAZINES: Home & Family

DINSIDE; DATA
1740636R5E-2
Tel: 4060 1000 **Fax:** 2103 2052
Email: data@dinside.no
Cover Price: Paid
Language(s): Norwegian
BUSINESS: COMPUTERS & AUTOMATION: Data Transmission

DINSIDE; MOTOR
1740637R77A-235
Tel: 4060 1000
Email: motor@dinside.no **Web site:** http://www.dinside.no
Cover Price: Paid
Language(s): Norwegian
CONSUMER: MOTORING & CYCLING: Motoring

DINSIDE; ØKONOMI
1740635R1A-130
Tel: 4060 1000
Email: okonomi@dinside.no **Web site:** http://www.dinside.no
Cover Price: Paid
Language(s): Norwegian
BUSINESS: FINANCE & ECONOMICS

DINSIDE; REISE
1740638R89A-182
Tel: 4060 1000
Email: reise@dinside.no **Web site:** http://www.dinside.no
Cover Price: Paid
Language(s): Norwegian
CONSUMER: HOLIDAYS & TRAVEL: Travel

DISTRIKTSINFO (RØDE KORS)
1624483R32G-153
Editorial: Pb 3 Grønland, 0133 OSLO **Tel:** 22992330
Email: kontakt.oslo@rodekors.no **Web site:** http://www.oslo.redcross.no
Freq: Half-yearly; **Circ:** 120,000
Language(s): Norwegian
BUSINESS: LOCAL GOVERNMENT, LEISURE & RECREATION: Community Care & Social Services

DITT DYR
1740794R81A-44
Editorial: Postboks 9386 Grønland, 0323 OSLO
Tel: 2100 6000 **Fax:** 2257 0942
Email: thomas.witso-bjolmer@nettavisen.no **Web site:** http://www.nettavisen.no/dyr
Freq: 6 issues yearly; **Circ:** 8,000
Editor: Thomas N. Witsø-Bjølmer
Language(s): Norwegian
CONSUMER: ANIMALS & PETS: Animals & Pets Protection

DITT HUS
1645156R74C-70
Editorial: Pb. 1266 Majorstuveien 17, 0367 OSLO
Tel: 22 43 80 10
Email: redaksjon@ditthus.no **Web site:** http://www.ditthus.no
Freq: 6 issues yearly - 5 ganger i året
Editor: Arne-Harald Hanssen
Language(s): Norwegian
Copy instructions: *Copy Date:* 14 days prior to publication date
CONSUMER: WOMEN'S INTEREST CONSUMER MAGAZINES: Home & Family

DN.NO
1624655R1F-1
Editorial: Pb 1182 Sentrum, 0107 OSLO
Tel: 22001000 **Fax:** 22 00 12 33
Email: dn.no@dn.no **Web site:** http://www.dn.no
Freq: Daily
Language(s): Norwegian
BUSINESS: FINANCE & ECONOMICS: Investment

DOKTORONLINE.NO
1657599R56R-158
Editorial: Doktor Online AS, Gullhaugveien 1, 0441 OSLO **Tel:** 22 58 50 00
Email: redaksjon@doktoronline.no **Web site:** http://www.doktoronline.no
Circ: 15,100 Unique Users
Editor: Trude Susegg
Language(s): Norwegian
BUSINESS: HEALTH & MEDICAL: Health Medical Related

DØLEN; DOLEN.NO
1863497R73-197
Editorial: Lomoen, 2640 VINSTRA **Tel:** 61 29 24 80
Email: post@dolen.no **Web site:** http://www.dolen.no
Freq: Daily; **Cover Price:** Free; **Circ:** 527 Unique Users
Editor: Tor Larsen
Language(s): Norwegian
CONSUMER: NATIONAL & INTERNATIONAL PERIODICALS

DØVBLINDES UKEBLAD
31664R56L-12
Editorial: Pb 354, 4803 ARENDAL **Tel:** 37 02 11 47
Email: fndbred@online.no **Web site:** http://www.fndb.no
Date Established: 1957; **Freq:** Weekly
Profile: Magazine containing articles and information about people who are deaf and blind.
Language(s): Norwegian
Readership: Aimed at politicians, medical personnel, administrators, disabled people and their families.
BUSINESS: HEALTH & MEDICAL: Disability & Rehabilitation

DØVES BLAD
31665R56L-14
Editorial: Døveprosten i Norge, Fagerborggaten 12, 0360 OSLO **Tel:** 70 11 45 66 **Fax:** 70 11 45 68
Email: ebe@ebe-data.com **Web site:** http://www.dovekirken.no
Freq: 6 issues yearly
Profile: Magazine focusing on hearing problems.
Language(s): Norwegian
Readership: Aimed at the deaf and members of the medical profession.
BUSINESS: HEALTH & MEDICAL: Disability & Rehabilitation

DØVES TIDSSKRIFT
1624383R94F-101
Editorial: Grensen 9, 0159 OSLO **Tel:** 23 31 06 30
Fax: 23 31 06 40
Email: helge.herland@doveforbundet.no **Web site:** http://www.doveforbundet.no
Freq: Monthly
Editor: Helge Herland
Language(s): Norwegian
CONSUMER: OTHER CLASSIFICATIONS: Disability

DRAMA-NORDISK DRAMAPEDAGOGISK TIDSSKRIFT
31734R64K-15
Editorial: co. Hedda Fredly, Kongensgate 16, 0153 OSLO **Tel:** 97 66 63 61
Email: redaksjon@dramaiskolen.no **Web site:** http://www.dramaiskolen.no
Date Established: 1963; **Freq:** Quarterly; **Circ:** 1,500
Profile: Publication for students and teachers of drama.
Language(s): Norwegian
BUSINESS: OTHER CLASSIFICATIONS: Cinema Entertainment

DYSLEKTIKEREN
31666R56L-20
Editorial: Pb. 8731 Youngstorget, 0028 OSLO
Tel: 22 47 44 50 **Fax:** 22 42 95 54
Email: hs-hal@online.no **Web site:** http://www.dysleksiforbundet.no
Freq: Quarterly
Editor: Helge Svein Halvorsen
Profile: Publication about dyslexia.
Language(s): Norwegian
BUSINESS: HEALTH & MEDICAL: Disability & Rehabilitation

E24 NÆRINGSLIV
1803798R1A-129
Editorial: Postboks 1185, 0051 0107 OSLO OSLO OSLO OSLO **Tel:** 22 86 40 25 **Fax:** 22 86 43 77
Email: nyhetssjefer@e24.no **Web site:** http://www.e24.no
Freq: Daily
Language(s): Norwegian
BUSINESS: FINANCE & ECONOMICS

EBL FORUM
1624965R58-102
Editorial: Pb 7184 Majorstua, 0307 OSLO
Tel: 23088900 **Fax:** 23088901
Email: forum@ebl.no **Web site:** http://www.ebl.no
Freq: Monthly
Editor: Therese Manus Hønningstad
Language(s): Norwegian
BUSINESS: ENERGY, FUEL & NUCLEAR

EDDA
32290R84B-50
Editorial: v/ Gerd Granhaug, Høllingsbakken, 2340 LØTEN **Tel:** 24 14 75 00 **Fax:** 24 14 75 01
Email: edda@hum.uit.no **Web site:** http://www.universitetsforlaget.no/edda
Date Established: 1914; **Freq:** Quarterly
Editor: Ole Karlsen
Profile: Magazine concerning international literature in general, with a main focus on literary research in the Nordic countries.
Language(s): Norwegian
Readership: Aimed at people with a general interest in literature as well as teachers, students and academics.
CONSUMER: THE ARTS & LITERARY: Literary

EIKER AVIS
1625249R74C-58
Editorial: Pb. 55, 3301 HOKKSUND **Tel:** 32 25 39 50
Fax: 32 25 36 51
Email: redaksjonen@eikeravis.no **Web site:** http://www.eikeravis.no
Freq: Weekly; **Cover Price:** Free; **Circ:** 2,141
Language(s): Norwegian
CONSUMER: WOMEN'S INTEREST CONSUMER MAGAZINES: Home & Family

EIKER AVIS; EIKERAVIS.NO
1863495R73-196
Editorial: Postboks 55, 3301 HOKKSUND
Tel: 32 25 39 50 **Fax:** 32 25 36 51
Email: redaksjonen@eikeravis.no **Web site:** http://www.eikeravis.no
Freq: Daily; **Cover Price:** Free; **Circ:** 2,500 Unique Users

Language(s): Norwegian
CONSUMER: NATIONAL & INTERNATIONAL PERIODICALS

EKSPORTUTVALGET FOR FISK - GODFISK
1657804R74P-206
Editorial: Pb. 6176, 9291 TROMSØ **Tel:** 77 60 33 33 **Fax:** 77 68 00 12
Email: editor@seafood.no **Web site:** http://www.godfisk.no
Cover Price: Paid
Language(s): Norwegian
CONSUMER: WOMEN'S INTEREST CONSUMER MAGAZINES: Food & Cookery

ELEKTRONIKK
31451R18A-20
Editorial: Elektronikkforlaget AS, Pb 570, 1337 SANDVIKA **Tel:** 67804280 **Fax:** 67804290
Email: elektronikk@elektronikkforlaget.no **Web site:** http://www.elektronikknett.no
Freq: Monthly - 11 ganger i året; **Circ:** 7,500
Editor: Einar Karlsen
Profile: Magazine concerning professional electronics, components, design, manufacture and instrumentation as well as computer technology.
Language(s): Norwegian
ADVERTISING RATES:
Full Page Colour .... NOK 27300
SCC .... NOK 216.67
Copy instructions: *Copy Date:* 21 days prior to publication date
BUSINESS: ELECTRONICS

ELEKTRONIKK; ELEKTRONIKKNETT.NO
1839960R18A-104
Editorial: Postboks 570, 1337 SANDVIIKA
Tel: 67 80 42 80 **Fax:** 67 80 42 90
Email: elektronikk@elektronikkforlaget.no **Web site:** http://www.elektronikknett.no
Freq: Daily; **Cover Price:** Paid; **Circ:** 2,500 Unique Users
Language(s): Norwegian
ADVERTISING RATES:
SCC .... NOK 43.4
BUSINESS: ELECTRONICS

ELEKTRONIKKBRANSJEN
31561R43B-70
Editorial: Pb. 6640 Etterstad, 0607 OSLO
Tel: 23060707 **Fax:** 23060700
Email: ss@elektronikkbransjen.no **Web site:** http://www.elektronikkbransjen.no
Date Established: 1938; **Freq:** Monthly - 10 ganger i året; **Circ:** 5,758
Profile: Magazine about consumer electronics.
Language(s): Norwegian
Readership: Read by consumer electronics retailers and their employees. Also manufacturers, importers and agencies of consumer electronics, photo, video, mobile phones, telematics, computers, cable networks, white goods and small electrical appliances.
ADVERTISING RATES:
Full Page Colour .... NOK 20100
SCC .... NOK 133.33
Copy instructions: *Copy Date:* 16 days prior to publication date
BUSINESS: ELECTRICAL RETAIL TRADE: Radio & Hi-Fi

ELLE
32597R74A-10_50
Editorial: Pb. 5134 Majorstua, 0302 OSLO
Tel: 23 36 98 00 **Fax:** 23 36 98 01
Email: post@elle.no **Web site:** http://www.elle.no
Date Established: 1997; **Freq:** Monthly; **Circ:** 34,528
Editor: Petra Middelthon
Profile: Women's interest magazine covering shopping, fashion, health, beauty, current affairs, human interest stories and travel.
Language(s): Norwegian
ADVERTISING RATES:
SCC .... NOK 442
CONSUMER: WOMEN'S INTEREST CONSUMER MAGAZINES: Women's Interest

ELLE INTERIØR
1624624R74C-53
Editorial: Pb. 5134 Majorstua, 0302 OSLO
Tel: 23369800 **Fax:** 22369801
Email: cecilie@elle.no **Web site:** http://www.elle.no/elle/elle_interior/elle_interior.shtml
Freq: 6 issues yearly; **Circ:** 20,741
Language(s): Norwegian
ADVERTISING RATES:
SCC .... NOK 441.67
Copy instructions: *Copy Date:* 30 days prior to publication date
CONSUMER: WOMEN'S INTEREST CONSUMER MAGAZINES: Home & Family

ELLE.NO
1839958R74A-76
Editorial: Pb. 5134 Majorstua, 0302 OSLO
Tel: 23 36 98 00 **Fax:** 23 36 98 01
Email: live@elle.no **Web site:** http://www.elle.no
Freq: Daily; **Cover Price:** Paid
Language(s): Norwegian
CONSUMER: WOMEN'S INTEREST CONSUMER MAGAZINES: Women's Interest

ELMAGASINET
1624247R17-171
Editorial: Pb. 5467 Majorstua, 0305 OSLO
Tel: 23087700
Email: bjorn@elmagasinet.no **Web site:** http://www.elmagasinet.no
Freq: Monthly; **Circ:** 7,500
Language(s): Norwegian
BUSINESS: ELECTRICAL

ELMAGASINET; ELMAGASINET.NO
1863751R58-116
Editorial: Postboks 5467 Majorstua, 0305 OSLO
Tel: 23 08 77 00
Email: bjorn@elmagasinet.no **Web site:** http://www.elmagasinet.no
Freq: Daily; **Cover Price:** Free; **Circ:** 2,500 Unique Users
Language(s): Norwegian
BUSINESS: ENERGY, FUEL & NUCLEAR

ENERGI
1624992R58-103
Editorial: Pb. 1182, Sentrum, 0107 OSLO
Email: ola.nedrelid@energi-nett.no **Web site:** http://www.energi-nett.no
Freq: Monthly; **Circ:** 6,000
Language(s): Norwegian
ADVERTISING RATES:
Full Page Colour .... NOK 21420
SCC .... NOK 170
BUSINESS: ENERGY, FUEL & NUCLEAR

ENERGI; ENERGI-NETT.NO
1936027R58-125
Editorial: Pb. 1182, Sentrum, 0107 OSLO
Fax: 22 00 10 83
Email: ola.nedrelid@energi-nett.no **Web site:** http://www.energi-nett.no
Freq: Daily; **Cover Price:** Paid
Language(s): Norwegian
BUSINESS: ENERGY, FUEL & NUCLEAR

ENERGI & LEDELSE
31698R58-50
Editorial: Oksenøyvn. 14, 1366 LYSAKER
Tel: 67512333 **Fax:** 67512335
Email: hs@lederforeningen.no **Web site:** http://www.lederforeningen.no
Freq: 6 issues yearly; **Circ:** 2,000
Profile: Journal for electricity board managers and engineers.
Language(s): Norwegian
BUSINESS: ENERGY, FUEL & NUCLEAR

ENERGITEKNIKK
1660605R58-108
Editorial: Energiteknikk, Postboks 4, 1371 ASKER
Tel: 66787535 **Fax:** 66 78 14 45
Email: sab@elektronett.no **Web site:** http://www.elektronett.no
Freq: Monthly; **Circ:** 6,505
Language(s): Norwegian
ADVERTISING RATES:
SCC .... NOK 164.83
BUSINESS: ENERGY, FUEL & NUCLEAR

ENERGITEKNIKK; ELEKTRONETT.NO
1839959R58-111
Editorial: Postboks 4, 1371 ASKER **Tel:** 66 78 75 35
Fax: 66 78 14 45
Email: sab@energibransjen.no **Web site:** http://ELEKTRONETT.NO
Freq: Daily; **Cover Price:** Paid; **Circ:** 2,500 Unique Users
Editor: Stein Arne Bakken
Language(s): Norwegian
BUSINESS: ENERGY, FUEL & NUCLEAR

ENKELT
1740795R14H-48
Editorial: Pb. 784, 7651 VERDAL **Tel:** 924 43 987
Email: redaksjonen@enkelt.cc **Web site:** http://www.enkelt.cc
Freq: Quarterly
Editor: Pål Stavrum
Language(s): Norwegian
BUSINESS: COMMERCE, INDUSTRY & MANAGEMENT: Small Business

EPILEPSI NYTT
1624606R94F-107
Editorial: Karl Johansgt. 7, 0154 OSLO
Tel: 22 47 66 00 **Fax:** 23 35 31 01
Email: nef@epilepsi.no **Web site:** http://www.epilepsi.no
Freq: Quarterly
Language(s): Norwegian
CONSUMER: OTHER CLASSIFICATIONS: Disability

ERGOSTART
1813254R14A-228
Editorial: Solar Media AS, Postboks 217, 2381 BRUMUNDDAL **Tel:** 41177953
Email: mail@ergostart.com **Web site:** http://www.ergostart.no
Freq: 6 issues yearly; **Circ:** 5,000
Language(s): Norwegian
BUSINESS: COMMERCE, INDUSTRY & MANAGEMENT

ERGOTERAPEUTEN
31431R14E-100
Editorial: Lakkegata 21, 0187 OSLO **Tel:** 22059900
Fax: 22059901
Email: ergoterapeuten@netf.no **Web site:** http://www.ergoterapeuten.no
Freq: Monthly; **Circ:** 3,600
Profile: Magazine containing articles and information about ergonomics.
Language(s): Norwegian
ADVERTISING RATES:
Full Page Colour .... NOK 12500
BUSINESS: COMMERCE, INDUSTRY & MANAGEMENT: Work Study

ESTATE MAGASIN
1934364R1E-4
Editorial: Estate Media AS.Holbergsgate 21, 0166 OSLO **Tel:** 21951000 **Fax:** 21951001
Email: thor@estatemedia.no **Web site:** http://www.estatemedia.no
Freq: 6 issues yearly
Language(s): Norwegian
BUSINESS: FINANCE & ECONOMICS: Property

ESTHETIQUE
32134R74A-11
Editorial: Pb 6137 Etterstad, 0602 OSLO
Tel: 22576900 **Fax:** 22576901
Email: kundeservice@esthetique.no **Web site:** http://www.esthetique.no
Freq: Quarterly
Profile: Magazine containing interviews, articles, reviews and information about fashion, health, beauty, travel, careers, sports and current affairs.
Language(s): Norwegian
Readership: Aimed at women over 25 years with an above average disposable income.
CONSUMER: WOMEN'S INTEREST CONSUMER MAGAZINES: Women's Interest

ESTRATEGI.NO
1625094R5A-2
Editorial: Grønvoldvegen 7, 3830 ULEFOSS
Tel: 90192708
Email: post@estrategi.no **Web site:** http://www.estrategi.no
Cover Price: Paid
Language(s): Norwegian
BUSINESS: COMPUTERS & AUTOMATION: Automation & Instrumentation

ET BARN FOR LITE
1645129R94J-6
Editorial: Foreningen "Vi som har et barn for lite", Pb. 4730 Nydalen, 0421 OSLO **Tel:** 81 54 85 01
Email: foreningen@etbarnforlite.no **Web site:** http://www.etbarnforlite.no
Freq: Half-yearly; **Circ:** 600
Language(s): Norwegian
CONSUMER: OTHER CLASSIFICATIONS: Popular Science

EUROPAVEGEN
1660609R62A-219
Editorial: Pb 1093, 5811 BERGEN **Tel:** 55 30 38 00
Fax: 55 30 88 01
Email: siu@siu.no **Web site:** http://siu.no/vev.nsf/O/SOKRATES-Comenius-Publikasjonar-Europavegen
Freq: Annual
Language(s): Norwegian
BUSINESS: CHURCH & SCHOOL EQUIPMENT & EDUCATION: Education

EUROPOWER
1625372R18A-102
Editorial: Pb 1182 Sentrum, 0107 OSLO
Tel: 22 00 11 50 **Fax:** 22 00 10 83
Email: news@europower.com **Web site:** http://www.europower.com
Language(s): Norwegian
ADVERTISING RATES:
SCC .... NOK 333.33
BUSINESS: ELECTRONICS

EUROPOWER; EUROPOWER.COM
1863746R58-115
Editorial: Posboks 1182 Sentrum, 0170 OSLO
Tel: 22 00 11 50
Email: news@europower.com **Web site:** http://www.europower.com
Freq: Daily; **Cover Price:** Free; **Circ:** 2,100 Unique Users
Language(s): Norwegian
BUSINESS: ENERGY, FUEL & NUCLEAR

EXACT
625122R76A-80
Editorial: Postboks 454, 2305 HAMAR **Tel:** 62519630
Fax: 62519631
Email: red@exact24.no **Web site:** http://www.exact24.no
Date Established: 1995; **Freq:** Monthly; **Cover Price:** Free
Profile: Magazine containing information and news about music, films and general culture.
Language(s): Norwegian
Readership: Aimed at people aged 18 to 35 years.
CONSUMER: MUSIC & PERFORMING ARTS: Cinema

F - FORSVARETS FORUM
31544R40-8
Editorial: Forsvarsforum Oslo Mil/ Akershus, 0015 OSLO **Tel:** 23 09 20 40
Email: tips@fofo.no **Web site:** http://www.fofo.no
Freq: Monthly; **Circ:** 80,000
Editor: Erling Eikli
Profile: Magazine for the military, civilian employers and reserve officers.
Language(s): Norwegian
BUSINESS: DEFENCE

F - FORSVARETS FORUM; FOFO.NO
1977074R40-50
Editorial: F - Forsvarets forum, Oslo mil/Akershus, 0015 OSLO **Tel:** 2309 2040
Email: tips@fofo.no **Web site:** http://www.fofo.no
Freq: Daily; **Cover Price:** Paid
Language(s): Norwegian
BUSINESS: DEFENCE

F- FORSVARETS FORUM~BARDUFOSS
1840332R40-48
Editorial: Pb. 1103, 9326 BARDUFOSS
Tel: 77 89 60 30
Email: tl@fofo.no **Web site:** http://www.fofo.no
Freq: Monthly; **Circ:** 80,000
Language(s): Norwegian
BUSINESS: DEFENCE

FÆDRELANDSVENNEN
31779R67B-3100
Editorial: Pb 369, 4664 KRISTIANSAND S
Tel: 38113000 **Fax:** 38113001
Email: 03811@fvn.no **Web site:** http://www.fedrelandsvennen.no
Freq: Daily - Norway; **Circ:** 41,326
Language(s): Norwegian
ADVERTISING RATES:
Full Page Colour .... NOK 27893
REGIONAL DAILY & SUNDAY NEWSPAPERS: Regional Daily Newspapers

FAGBLADET
1660606R32A-154
Editorial: Pb. 7003 St. Olavs plass, 0130 OSLO
Tel: 23 06 40 00 **Fax:** 23 06 44 07
Email: tips@fagforbundet.no **Web site:** http://www.frifagbevegelse.no/fagbladet
Freq: Monthly - 11 ganger i året; **Circ:** 313,623
Language(s): Norwegian
ADVERTISING RATES:
Full Page Colour .... NOK 60000
BUSINESS: LOCAL GOVERNMENT, LEISURE & RECREATION: Local Government

FAGBLADET CREDITINFORM
31357R1G-50
Editorial: Pb. 5275 Majorstuen, 0303 OSLO
Tel: 81 55 54 54 **Fax:** 22 93 20 80
Email: redaksjonen@no.experian.com **Web site:** http://www.experian.no
Freq: Monthly
Editor: Hanne Broen
Profile: Publication covering all aspects of credit trading.
Language(s): Norwegian
BUSINESS: FINANCE & ECONOMICS: Credit Trading

FAGBLADET; FAGBLADET.NO
1863753R32A-158
Editorial: Postboks 7003 St. Olavs plass, 0130 OSLO
Tel: 23 06 40 00 **Fax:** 23064407
Email: tips@fagforbundet.no **Web site:** http://www.fagbladet.no
Freq: Daily; **Cover Price:** Free; **Circ:** 2,500 Unique Users
Language(s): Norwegian
BUSINESS: LOCAL GOVERNMENT, LEISURE & RECREATION: Local Government

FAGPRESSENYTT.NO
1624571R60A-51
Editorial: Akersgata 43, 0158 OSLO **Tel:** 24 14 61 00
Fax: 24 14 61 10
Email: bn@fagpressen.no **Web site:** http://www.fagpressenytt.no
Cover Price: Paid; **Circ:** 2,500 Unique Users
Language(s): Norwegian
BUSINESS: PUBLISHING: Publishing & Book Trade

FAGSENTERET FOR KJØTT - ANIMALIA; ANIMALIA.NO
1864047R21A-155
Editorial: Postboks 396, Økern, 0153 OSLO
Tel: 22 09 23 00 **Fax:** 22 22 00 16
Email: animalia@animalia.no **Web site:** http://www.animalia.no
Freq: Daily; **Cover Price:** Free; **Circ:** 2,500 Unique Users
Language(s): Norwegian
BUSINESS: AGRICULTURE & FARMING

FAMILIEN
32145R74C-30
Editorial: Gullhaugveien 1, 0441 OSLO
Tel: 22585000
Email: familien@egmonthm.no **Web site:** http://www.familien.no
Date Established: 1939; **Freq:** 26 issues yearly; **Circ:** 129,367
Profile: Home and family magazine.
Language(s): Norwegian
Readership: Read by people interested in family life and the home.
ADVERTISING RATES:
SCC .... NOK 345.83
CONSUMER: WOMEN'S INTEREST CONSUMER MAGAZINES: Home & Family

FARGEMAGASINET
1660607R74C-65
Editorial: IFI - Informasjonskontoret for farge og interiør, Hamang terrasse 63, 1336 SANDVIKA
Tel: 67 55 46 80 **Fax:** 67554681
Email: ifi@ifi.no **Web site:** http://www.ifi.no
Freq: 6 issues yearly
Language(s): Norwegian
CONSUMER: WOMEN'S INTEREST CONSUMER MAGAZINES: Home & Family

FARMASILIV
31535R37-10
Editorial: Farmasiforbundet, Hegdehaugsveien 8, 0167 OSLO **Tel:** 22992660 **Fax:** 22201301
Email: vetle.daler@farmasiforbundet.no **Web site:** http://www.farmasiforbundet.no/?template=medlemsbladet
Freq: Monthly - 9 ganger i året; **Circ:** 4,900
Profile: Journal about the pharmaceutical and medical industry.
Language(s): Norwegian
BUSINESS: PHARMACEUTICAL & CHEMISTS

FARSUNDS AVIS
31765R67B-3150
Editorial: Pb. 23, 4551 FARSUND **Tel:** 38 39 50 00
Fax: 38 39 20 86
Email: redaksjon@favis.no **Web site:** http://www.farsunds-avis.no
Freq: Daily; **Circ:** 6,103
Editor: Steinar Spjelkaviknes
Language(s): Norwegian
ADVERTISING RATES:
Full Page Colour .... NOK 21694
SCC .... NOK 108.47
REGIONAL DAILY & SUNDAY NEWSPAPERS: Regional Daily Newspapers

FASTFOOD
1624617R22-1
Editorial: Postboks 130, 2261 KIRKENAER
Tel: 90962490
Email: odd@askmedia.no **Web site:** http://www.askmedia.no/id/30273
Freq: 6 issues yearly; **Circ:** 2,830
Editor: Odd H. Vanebo
Language(s): Norwegian
Copy instructions: *Copy Date:* 45 days prior to publication date
BUSINESS: FOOD

FAUNA
31732R64H-30
Editorial: Norsk Zoologisk Forening, Postboks 102 Blindern, 0314 OSLO **Tel:** 22261131
Email: fauna@zoologi.no **Web site:** http://www.zoologi.no/fauna.htm
Date Established: 1948; **Freq:** Quarterly
Profile: Publication of the Norwegian Zoological Association.
Language(s): Norwegian
BUSINESS: OTHER CLASSIFICATIONS: Veterinary

FAUNA NORVEGICA
1624855R57-305
Editorial: NTNU, Vitenskapsmuseet, Seksjon for naturhistorie, 2, 7491 TRONDHEIM **Tel:** 73592382
Fax: 73592295
Email: torkild.bakken@vm.ntnu.no **Web site:** http://www.vm.ntnu.no/faunanorvegica
Freq: Annual
Language(s): Norwegian
BUSINESS: ENVIRONMENT & POLLUTION

FAVN (EX. KPF-KONTAKTEN)
1624440R62A-203
Editorial: Kristent Pedagogisk Forum, Colletts gt 43, 01456 OSLO **Tel:** 954 564 22
Email: post@kpf.no **Web site:** http://www.kpf.no
Freq: Quarterly; **Circ:** 3,000
Language(s): Norwegian
BUSINESS: CHURCH & SCHOOL EQUIPMENT & EDUCATION: Education

FDV - FORVALTNING, DRIFT OG VEDLIKEHOLD
1800759R4E-110
Editorial: Skarland Press AS, Postboks 2843, Tøyen, 0608 OSLO **Tel:** 22 70 83 00 **Fax:** 22 70 83 01
Email: fdv@skarland.no **Web site:** http://www.driftogvedlikehold.no
Freq: 6 issues yearly; **Circ:** 4,000
Editor: Jan Erik Røine
Language(s): Norwegian
ADVERTISING RATES:
Full Page Colour .... NOK 17900
BUSINESS: ARCHITECTURE & BUILDING: Building

FETT - FEMINISTISK TIDSSKRIFT
1656970R74A-66
Editorial: Osterhausgata 27, 0183 OSLO
Tel: 95 13 90 06
Email: post@fett.no **Web site:** http://www.fett.no
Freq: Quarterly
Language(s): Norwegian
ADVERTISING RATES:
Full Page Colour .... NOK 10000
CONSUMER: WOMEN'S INTEREST CONSUMER MAGAZINES: Women's Interest

FHM
1656530R86C-151
Editorial: Pb. 1010 Sentrum, 0104 OSLO
Tel: 22401240 **Fax:** 22401241
Email: post@fhm.no **Web site:** http://www.fhm.no
Freq: Monthly; **Circ:** 47,721
Editor: John Ødegård Jensen
Language(s): Norwegian
ADVERTISING RATES:
Full Page Colour .... NOK 57000
SCC .... NOK 366.67
CONSUMER: ADULT & GAY MAGAZINES: Men's Lifestyle Magazines

FHM.NO
1840344R78R-3
Editorial: Pb. 1010 Sentrum, 0104 OSLO
Tel: 22 40 12 40 **Fax:** 22 40 12 41
Email: espens@fhm.no **Web site:** http://www.fhm.no
Freq: Daily; **Cover Price:** Paid
Language(s): Norwegian
CONSUMER: CONSUMER ELECTRONICS: Consumer Electronics Related

FIDELITY
1645191R43A-4
Editorial: Halvdan Svartes Gt. 8, 0268 OSLO
Tel: 905 40 974
Email: knuvadse@online.no **Web site:** http://www.audiofidelity.no
Freq: 6 issues yearly
Language(s): Norwegian
BUSINESS: ELECTRICAL RETAIL TRADE

FILM & KINO
31735R64K-20
Editorial: Pb 446 Sentrum, 0104 OSLO
Tel: 22 47 46 28 **Fax:** 22 47 46 98
Email: geir@kino.no **Web site:** http://www.filmweb.no/tidsskriftet
Date Established: 1930; **Freq:** Monthly
Profile: Magazine about the film and cinema industry.
Language(s): Norwegian
BUSINESS: OTHER CLASSIFICATIONS: Cinema Entertainment

FILMGUIDEN.NO
1864048R76C-77
Editorial: Oxo Media, Avdeling filmguiden.no, Litledalsveien 17B, 5521 HAUGESUND
Tel: 48 03 26 35
Email: redaksjon@filmguiden.no **Web site:** http://www.filmguiden.no
Freq: Daily; **Cover Price:** Free; **Circ:** 2,500 Unique Users
Language(s): Norwegian
CONSUMER: MUSIC & PERFORMING ARTS: TV & Radio

FILMMAGASINET
32211R76A-100
Editorial: Gjerdrumsvei 19, 0484 OSLO
Tel: 21 50 80 00 **Fax:** 21 50 80 84
Email: post@filmmagasinet.no **Web site:** http://www.filmmagasinet.no
Freq: 6 issues yearly; **Cover Price:** Free; **Circ:** 80,000
Profile: Magazine containing film and celebrity news, including music and interviews.
Language(s): Norwegian
Readership: Aimed mainly at people aged 23 to 49 years.
ADVERTISING RATES:
SCC .... NOK 331.67
CONSUMER: MUSIC & PERFORMING ARTS: Cinema

FILMMAGASINET; FILMMAGASINET.NO
1863741R76C-75
Editorial: Gjerdrumsvei 19, 0484 OSLO
Tel: 21 50 80 00 **Fax:** 21 50 80 84
Email: post@filmmagasinet.no **Web site:** http://www.filmmagasinet.no
Freq: Daily; **Cover Price:** Free; **Circ:** 49,200 Unique Users
Language(s): Norwegian
CONSUMER: MUSIC & PERFORMING ARTS: TV & Radio

FILOLOGEN
2010143R84B-254
Editorial: P.B. 106 Blindern, 0314 OSLO
Email: filologen@filologiskforening.no **Web site:** http://www.filologen.no
Editor: Torunn Johansen
Language(s): Norwegian
CONSUMER: THE ARTS & LITERARY: Literary

FINANSAVISEN
31341R1A-50
Editorial: Pb 724 Skøyen, 0214 OSLO
Tel: 2329 63 00 **Fax:** 2329 63 01
Email: vaktsjef@finansavisen.no **Web site:** http://www.hegnar.no/finansavisen
Freq: Daily; **Circ:** 24,856
Editor: Steinar Grini
Profile: Financial newspaper.
Language(s): Norwegian
ADVERTISING RATES:
Full Page Colour .... NOK 45176
SCC .... NOK 225.88
BUSINESS: FINANCE & ECONOMICS

FINANSFOKUS
31342R1A-52
Editorial: Pb 9234 Grønland, 0134 OSLO
Tel: 22056300 **Fax:** 22170690
Email: post@finansforbundet.no **Web site:** http://www.finansforbundet.no
Date Established: 2000; **Freq:** Monthly - 8 ganger i året; **Circ:** 37,691
Profile: Magazine concerning all aspects of finance.
Language(s): Norwegian
Readership: Aimed at financial organisations.
ADVERTISING RATES:
Full Page Colour .... NOK 18000
SCC .... NOK 150
BUSINESS: FINANCE & ECONOMICS

FINNMARK DAGBLAD
31772R67B-3200
Editorial: Pb. 293, 9615 HAMMERFEST
Tel: 78 42 86 00 **Fax:** 78 42 86 39
Email: redaksjonen@fd.no **Web site:** http://www.finnmarkdagblad.no
Freq: Daily; **Circ:** 8,813
Editor: Svein G. Jørstad
Language(s): Norwegian
ADVERTISING RATES:
Full Page Colour .... NOK 23059
SCC .... NOK 115.3
REGIONAL DAILY & SUNDAY NEWSPAPERS: Regional Daily Newspapers

FINNMARK DAGBLAD; KULTUR
2000230R84A-168
Editorial: Pb. 293, 9615 HAMMERFEST
Tel: 78 42 86 00 **Fax:** 78428639
Email: kultur@fd.no **Web site:** http://www.finnmarkdagblad.no
Circ: 8,813
Language(s): Norwegian
CONSUMER: THE ARTS & LITERARY: Arts

FINNMARKEN
31805R67B-3250
Editorial: Pb. 616, 9811 VADSØ **Tel:** 78 95 55 00
Fax: 78 95 55 60
Email: desk@finnmarken.no **Web site:** http://www.finnmarken.no
Freq: Daily; **Circ:** 7,060
Language(s): Norwegian
ADVERTISING RATES:
Full Page Colour .... NOK 18811
SCC .... NOK 94.06
REGIONAL DAILY & SUNDAY NEWSPAPERS: Regional Daily Newspapers

FIRDA
31766R67B-3300
Editorial: Firda Media AS, Pb. 160, 6801 FØRDE
Tel: 57 83 33 00 **Fax:** 57 20 53 11
Email: redaksjon@firda.no **Web site:** http://www.firda.no
Date Established: 1918; **Freq:** Daily; **Circ:** 13,875
Language(s): Norwegian
ADVERTISING RATES:
Full Page Colour .... NOK 23969
SCC .... NOK 119.85
REGIONAL DAILY & SUNDAY NEWSPAPERS: Regional Daily Newspapers

FIRDA TIDEND; FIRDATIDEND.NO
1863745R73-204
Editorial: Postboks 38, 6821 SANDANE
Tel: 57 86 87 90 **Fax:** 57 86 87 99
Email: redaksjon@firdatidend.no **Web site:** http://www.firdatidend.no
Freq: Daily; **Cover Price:** Free; **Circ:** 2,400 Unique Users
Language(s): Norwegian
CONSUMER: NATIONAL & INTERNATIONAL PERIODICALS

FISK - INDUSTRI & MARKED
31576R45B-9
Editorial: Skarland Press AS, Pb.2843 Tøyen, 0608 9481 HARSTAD OSLO **Tel:** 22708300 **Fax:** 22708301
Email: per@skarland.no **Web site:** http://www.netfisk.no
Date Established: 1990; **Freq:** Monthly - 9 ganger i året; **Circ:** 1,615
Profile: Publication covering topics related to the fish processing industry.
Language(s): Norwegian
ADVERTISING RATES:
SCC .... NOK 90
BUSINESS: MARINE & SHIPPING: Commercial Fishing

FISK - INDUSTRI OG MARKED; NETFISK.NO
1863738R92-55
Editorial: Postboks 2843 Tøyen, 0608 OSLO
Tel: 22 70 83 00 **Fax:** 22 70 83 01
Email: fisk@netfisk.no **Web site:** http://www.netfisk.no
Freq: Daily; **Cover Price:** Free; **Circ:** 2,500 Unique Users
Language(s): Norwegian
CONSUMER: ANGLING & FISHING

FISKEBÅT-MAGASINET
1624394R22G-2
Editorial: Pb 67, 6001 ÅLESUND **Tel:** 70 10 14 60
Fax: 70 10 14 80
Email: fiskebat@fiskebat.no **Web site:** http://www.fiskebat.no
Freq: 6 issues yearly
Language(s): Norwegian
BUSINESS: FOOD: Fish Trade

FISKEGUIDEN.NO
1657814R92-53
Editorial: Jølstramuseet, 6847 VASSENDEN
Email: eivind.fossheim@fiskeguiden.no **Web site:** http://www.fiskeguiden.no
Cover Price: Paid; **Circ:** 500 Unique Users
Language(s): Norwegian
CONSUMER: ANGLING & FISHING

FISKERIBLADETFISKAREN- AVD. BERGEN
31577R45B-10
Editorial: Bontelabo 2, 5003 BERGEN
Tel: 55 21 33 00
Email: redaksjonen@fbfi.no **Web site:** http://www.fiskeribladetfiskaren.no
Date Established: 1923; **Freq:** 156 issues yearly; **Circ:** 9,500
Profile: Newspaper containing information and articles about the fishing industry. Also covers aquaculture and shipping.
Language(s): Norwegian
Readership: Aimed at owners of fishing vessels and those in related industries.
ADVERTISING RATES:
Full Page Colour .... NOK 59250
BUSINESS: MARINE & SHIPPING: Commercial Fishing

FISKERIBLADETFISKAREN- HARSTAD
31578R45B-20
Tel: 77 05 90 00
Email: redaksjonen@fbfi.no **Web site:** http://fiskeribladetfiskaren.no
Date Established: 1946; **Freq:** Monthly; **Circ:** 9,500
Profile: Magazine covering all aspects of the fishing industry.
Language(s): Norwegian
ADVERTISING RATES:
Full Page Colour .... NOK 59250
BUSINESS: MARINE & SHIPPING: Commercial Fishing

FISKERIBLADETFISKAREN.NO
1624749R45C-51
Editorial: Bontelabo 2, 5003 BERGEN
Tel: 55 21 33 00
Email: redaksjonen@fbfi.no **Web site:** http://www.fiskeribladetfiskaren.no
Freq: Daily; **Cover Price:** Paid; **Circ:** 2,500 Unique Users
Language(s): Norwegian
ADVERTISING RATES:
SCC .... NOK 40
BUSINESS: MARINE & SHIPPING: Maritime Freight

FISKETSGANG.NO 1863759R92-56
Editorial: Fiskeridirektoratet, Postboks 185 Sentrum, 5817 BERGEN **Tel:** 90 88 74 03 **Fax:** 55 23 80 72
Email: info@fiskeridir.no **Web site:** http://www.fisketsgang.no
Freq: Daily; **Cover Price:** Free; **Circ:** 2,500 Unique Users
Language(s): Norwegian
CONSUMER: ANGLING & FISHING

FITNESSBLOGGEN 1938270R75A-237
Email: robertoleh@hotmail.com **Web site:** http://fitnessbloggen.no
Cover Price: Paid
Language(s): Norwegian
CONSUMER: SPORT

FJÆRBLADET 1624331R77A-201
Editorial: Bernt Erik Olsen, Astrids vei 2, 4633 KRISTIANSAND **Tel:** 38097489 **Fax:** 38090964
Email: berneol@online.no **Web site:** http://www.a-m-k.net/fjaerbladet.html
Freq: Monthly - 9 ganger i året
Editor: Bernt Erik Olsen
Language(s): Norwegian
CONSUMER: MOTORING & CYCLING: Motoring

FJELL OG VIDDE 32198R75L-50
Editorial: Den Norske Turistforening, DNT Youngstorget 1, 0181 OSLO **Tel:** 4000 1868
Fax: 22 82 28 01
Email: ha@turistforeningen.no **Web site:** http://www.turistforeningen.no
Freq: 6 issues yearly
Profile: Magazine for members of the Norwegian Mountain Touring Association.
Language(s): Norwegian
ADVERTISING RATES:
Full Page Colour .... NOK 45000
CONSUMER: SPORT: Outdoor

FJELL-LJOM.NO 1863744R73-199
Editorial: Postboks 204, 7361 RØROS
Tel: 72 40 65 90 **Fax:** 72 40 65 91
Email: redaksjonen@fjell-ljom.no **Web site:** http://www.fjell-ljom.no
Freq: Daily; **Cover Price:** Free; **Circ:** 658 Unique Users
Language(s): Norwegian
CONSUMER: NATIONAL & INTERNATIONAL PERIODICALS

FJORD 1 MAGASINET 1810350R14L-110
Editorial: Pb. 354, 6901 FLORØ **Tel:** 957 51 992
Email: geir@inmedia.no **Web site:** http://www.fjord1.no
Freq: Quarterly
Language(s): Norwegian
BUSINESS: COMMERCE, INDUSTRY & MANAGEMENT: Trade Unions

FJORDABALDET; SPORTSREDAKSJONEN 1835554R75A-226
Editorial: Pb. 74, 6771 NORDFJORD
Tel: 57 88 53 10 **Fax:** 57885111
Email: sporten@fjordabladet.no **Web site:** http://www.fjordabladet.no
Circ: 2,729
Language(s): Norwegian
CONSUMER: SPORT

FJORDABLADET.NO 1863752R73-200
Editorial: Postboks 74, 6770 NORDFJORDEID
Tel: 57 88 53 10
Email: redaksjon@fjordabladet.no **Web site:** http://www.fjordabladet.no
Freq: Daily; **Cover Price:** Free; **Circ:** 2,000 Unique Users
Language(s): Norwegian
CONSUMER: NATIONAL & INTERNATIONAL PERIODICALS

FJORDENES TIDENDE; FJT.NO 1863750R73-193
Editorial: Postboks 55, 6701 MÅLØY
Tel: 57 84 00 00
Email: fjordenes.tidende@fjt.no **Web site:** http://www.fjt.no
Freq: Daily; **Cover Price:** Free; **Circ:** 4,000 Unique Users
Language(s): Norwegian
CONSUMER: NATIONAL & INTERNATIONAL PERIODICALS

FJORDHESTEN 1624834R75E-2
Editorial: Løken, 6770 NORDFJORDEID
Tel: 952 16 161 **Fax:** 57864801
Email: bladet@fjordhest.no **Web site:** http://www.fjordhest.no
Freq: Quarterly
Language(s): Norwegian
CONSUMER: SPORT: Horse Racing

FJORDINGEN.NO 1863758R73-188
Editorial: Postboks 248, 6781 STRYN
Tel: 57 87 45 00
Email: redaksjon@fjordingen.no **Web site:** http://www.fjordingen.no
Freq: Daily; **Cover Price:** Free; **Circ:** 3,200 Unique Users
Language(s): Norwegian
CONSUMER: NATIONAL & INTERNATIONAL PERIODICALS

FJORDS MAGAZINE 1645175R89A-180
Editorial: Pb 2164 Grünerløkka, 0505 OSLO
Tel: 900 67 660
Email: pauline@fjordsmagazine.com **Web site:** http://www.screenplay.no/fjords/main.htm
Freq: Quarterly
Editor: Marius Jøntvedt
Language(s): Norwegian
CONSUMER: HOLIDAYS & TRAVEL: Travel

FJØRFE 31478R21F-10
Editorial: Lørenveien 38, 0585 OSLO **Tel:** 22090712
Fax: 22090710
Email: nfl@nfl.no **Web site:** http://www.nfl.no
Freq: Monthly; **Circ:** 1,200
Profile: Magazine about poultry farming and poultry breeding.
Language(s): Norwegian
BUSINESS: AGRICULTURE & FARMING: Poultry

FLASHMAGAZINE 1656534R5F-5
Editorial: Grønland 18, 0188 OSLO **Tel:** 906 91 786
Email: feedus@flashmagazine.com **Web site:** http://www.flashmagazine.com
Freq: Daily; **Cover Price:** Paid
Language(s): Norwegian
BUSINESS: COMPUTERS & AUTOMATION: Multimedia

FLYNYTT 31411R6A-20
Editorial: Flynytt, NLF, Pb. 383 Sentrum, 0102 OSLO
Tel: 23 01 04 50 **Fax:** 23 01 04 51
Email: flynytt@nlf.no **Web site:** http://www.flynytt.no
Date Established: 1956; **Freq:** 6 issues yearly; **Circ:** 6,600
Profile: Journal covering articles, news and information about aircraft, air sports and airports.
Language(s): Norwegian
Readership: Read by airline pilots and and aircraft personnel.
ADVERTISING RATES:
SCC .... NOK 65
BUSINESS: AVIATION & AERONAUTICS

FN-SAMBANDET - FN.NO 32403R88A-16
Editorial: Storgata 33 A, 0184 OSLO **Tel:** 22 86 84 00
Fax: 22 86 84 01
Email: fn-sambandet@fn.no **Web site:** http://www.fn.no
Profile: Magazine containing articles concerning all aspects of education, both nationally and internationally.
Language(s): Norwegian
Readership: Aimed at teachers and parents of students in primary and lower-secondary education.
CONSUMER: EDUCATION

FOKUS PÅ FAMILIEN 31681R56R-50
Editorial: Redaksjonen, v/ Siv Nordang, Aker familiekontor, Smedgaten 49, 0651 OSLO
Tel: 24 14 75 00 **Fax:** 24 14 75 01
Email: fokus.familien@gmail.com **Web site:** http://www.universitetsforlaget.no/fokus
Date Established: 1973; **Freq:** Quarterly
Editor: Anne Øfsti
Profile: Family therapy journal. Covers theoretical and practical psychiatry and nursing, family counselling, sociology, education and politics.
Language(s): Norwegian
Readership: Read by psychologists, psychiatrists and academics.
BUSINESS: HEALTH & MEDICAL: Health Medical Related

FOLK OG FORSVAR 31543R40-7
Editorial: Arbeidersamfunnets Pl. 1 C, 0181 OSLO
Tel: 22 98 83 60 **Fax:** 22 98 83 61
Email: post@folkogforsvar.no **Web site:** http://www.folkogforsvar.no
Freq: Quarterly
Profile: Magazine containing articles and information about civil defence.
Language(s): Norwegian
BUSINESS: DEFENCE

FOLKEHØGSKOLEN 31714R62A-60
Editorial: Pb. 420 Sentrum, 0103 OSLO
Tel: 22 47 43 00
Email: redaktor@folkehogskole.no **Web site:** https://folkehogskolene.net
Date Established: 1904; **Freq:** Monthly
Editor: Øyvind Krabberød
Profile: Journal about Norwegian Folk High schools.
Language(s): Norwegian
Readership: Read by Union members.
BUSINESS: CHURCH & SCHOOL EQUIPMENT & EDUCATION: Education

FOLKEVETT 31687R57-40
Editorial: Fredensborgveien 24g, 0177 OSLO
Tel: 22033150 **Fax:** 22033151
Email: folkevett@framtiden.no **Web site:** http://www.folkevett.no
Freq: 6 issues yearly; **Circ:** 18,500
Profile: Magazine concerning the environment and third world issues.
Language(s): Norwegian
BUSINESS: ENVIRONMENT & POLLUTION

FOLLDALS MARKED 1663835R80-162
Editorial: 2580 FOLLDAL **Tel:** 62 49 05 55
Fax: 62 49 05 63
Email: post@infotek.as **Web site:** http://www.folldalsmarked.no
Freq: Monthly; **Circ:** 1,289
Language(s): Norwegian
CONSUMER: RURAL & REGIONAL INTEREST

FONTENE 31439R14L-40
Editorial: Pb. 231, Sentrum, 0103 OSLO
Tel: 23061170 **Fax:** 23061111
Email: solfrid.rod@lomedia.no **Web site:** http://www.frifagbevegelse.no/fontene
Freq: Monthly - 14 ganger i året
Profile: Magazine about social welfare and trade union matters.
Language(s): Norwegian
BUSINESS: COMMERCE, INDUSTRY & MANAGEMENT: Trade Unions

FORBRUKER.NO 1695421R32A-157
Editorial: Pb. 1 Sentrum, 0051 OSLO
Tel: 22 86 30 00 **Fax:** 22 86 41 30
Email: redaksjonen@forbruker.no **Web site:** http://www.forbruker.no
Cover Price: Paid; **Circ:** 2,500 Unique Users
Editor: Arild Kveldstad
Language(s): Norwegian
BUSINESS: LOCAL GOVERNMENT, LEISURE & RECREATION: Local Government

FORBRUKERRAPPORTEN 32146R74C-35
Editorial: Pb 4594 Nydalen, 0404 OSLO
Tel: 23 40 05 00 **Fax:** 23 42 39 61
Email: fr-rapport@forbrukerradet.no **Web site:** http://forbrukerportalen.no/Emner/forbrukerrapporten
Freq: Monthly; **Circ:** 32,000
Profile: Magazine published by the Consumers' Council.
Language(s): Norwegian
CONSUMER: WOMEN'S INTEREST CONSUMER MAGAZINES: Home & Family

FORELDRE & BARN 32154R74D-50
Editorial: Foreldre & Barn, 0441 OSLO
Tel: 22 58 54 33 **Fax:** 22 58 58 79
Email: foreldreogbarn@egmonthm.no **Web site:** http://www.foreldreogbarn.no
Freq: Monthly; **Circ:** 52,506
Profile: Magazine containing articles and information about the education, health and development of young children, includes holidays, kindergartens, equipment, food and nutrition.
Language(s): Norwegian
Readership: Read by parents of children up to the age of seven years.
ADVERTISING RATES:
SCC .... NOK 340
CONSUMER: WOMEN'S INTEREST CONSUMER MAGAZINES: Child Care

FORSKERFORUM 31630R55-50
Editorial: Pb. 1025 Sentrum, 0104 OSLO
Tel: 21 02 34 00 **Fax:** 21 02 34 01
Email: redaksjonen@forskerforum.no **Web site:** http://www.forskerforum.no
Freq: Monthly
Profile: Magazine containing articles and information about modern science and methods of research.
Language(s): Norwegian
Readership: Read by scientists, politicians, civil servants and the media.
BUSINESS: APPLIED SCIENCE & LABORATORIES

FORSKERFORUM.NO 1858597R62A-246
Editorial: Pb. 1025 Sentrum, 0104 OSLO
Tel: 21 02 34 00 **Fax:** 21 02 34 01
Email: redaksjonen@forskerforum.no **Web site:** http://www.forskerforum.no
Freq: Daily; **Cover Price:** Paid
Editor: Unn Rognmo
Language(s): Norwegian
BUSINESS: CHURCH & SCHOOL EQUIPMENT & EDUCATION: Education

FORSKNING.NO 1657787R55-104
Editorial: pb. 5 Torshov, 0412 OSLO **Tel:** 22 80 98 90
Fax: 22 80 98 99
Email: epost@forskning.no **Web site:** http://www.forskning.no
Cover Price: Paid; **Circ:** 2,500 Unique Users
Language(s): Norwegian
BUSINESS: APPLIED SCIENCE & LABORATORIES

FORSKNINGSETIKK 707527R32A-30
Editorial: Pb 522 Sentrum, 0105 OSLO
Tel: 23 31 83 00 **Fax:** 23 31 83 01
Email: post@etikkom.no **Web site:** http://www.etikkom.no
Date Established: 1992; **Freq:** Quarterly
Profile: Journal for the Danish National Committee of Research Ethics in Science and Technology.
Language(s): Norwegian
Readership: Read by local and national government officials.
BUSINESS: LOCAL GOVERNMENT, LEISURE & RECREATION: Local Government

FORSKNINGSPOLITIKK 32434R62A-80
Editorial: Wergelandsveien 7, 0167 OSLO
Tel: 22 59 51 00 **Fax:** 22 59 51 01
Email: fpol@nifustep.no **Web site:** http://www.fpol.no/Forskningspolitikk
Date Established: 1978; **Freq:** Quarterly; **Circ:** 8,800
Profile: Journal containing articles and information about the studies of research and higher education.
Language(s): Norwegian
Readership: Read by academics, researchers, scientists, lecturers, PhD students, policy advisors and politicians.
BUSINESS: CHURCH & SCHOOL EQUIPMENT & EDUCATION: Education

FØRSTERADEN 1624937R88D-1
Editorial: Ungdommens Sjakkforbund, Sandakerveien 24D, 0473 OSLO **Tel:** 924 09 376
Email: forsteraden@gmail.com **Web site:** http://www.sjakk.no/usf/forsidelenker/forsteraden.html
Freq: 6 issues yearly; **Circ:** 3,500
Editor: Torstein Bae
Language(s): Norwegian
CONSUMER: EDUCATION: Crafts

FORTID 2010144R94J-20
Editorial: Universitetet i Oslo, IAKH, Fortid, Pb. 1008 Blindern, 0315 OSLO
Email: redaksjonen@fortid.no **Web site:** http://www.fortid.no
Editor: Nina Maria Rud
Language(s): Norwegian
CONSUMER: OTHER CLASSIFICATIONS: Popular Science

FORTIDSVERN 32610R94B-80
Editorial: Dronningens gt. 11, 0152 OSLO
Tel: 23 31 70 71 **Fax:** 23 31 70 50
Email: silja@fortidsminneforeningen.no **Web site:** http://www.fortidsminneforeningen.no/fortidsvern
Date Established: 1974; **Freq:** Quarterly
Editor: Silja Selfors
Profile: Magazine concerning the preservation of ancient monuments and Norwegian national heritage.
Language(s): Norwegian
CONSUMER: OTHER CLASSIFICATIONS: Historic Buildings

FORUM FOR DEVELOPMENT STUDIES 32256R82-67
Editorial: Pb 8159 Dep, 0033 OSLO **Tel:** 22 99 40 00
Fax: 22 36 21 82
Email: olav.stokke@nupi.no **Web site:** http://www.nupi.no
Date Established: 1973; **Freq:** Half-yearly
Editor: Axel Borchgrevink
Profile: Journal containing information and debate articles concerning aid assistance, Third World issues and development studies.
Language(s): Norwegian
CONSUMER: CURRENT AFFAIRS & POLITICS

FORUT-NYTT 32254R82-62_50
Editorial: Pb 300, 2803 GJØVIK **Tel:** 61187400
Fax: 61187401
Email: forut@forut.no **Web site:** http://www.forut.no
Date Established: 1982; **Freq:** Quarterly
Profile: Journal containing articles and information about North/South issues, modern politics, international current affairs and aid projects.
Language(s): Norwegian

Readership: Read by members of owner organisations, preschool teachers, donors, mayors, newspaper editors and individual subscribers.
CONSUMER: CURRENT AFFAIRS & POLITICS

FOSNA-FOLKET 31758R67B-3350
Editorial: Pb. 205, 7129 BREKSTAD **Tel:** 72 51 57 00 **Fax:** 72 51 57 01
Email: firmapost@fosna-folket.no **Web site:** http://www.fosna-folket.no
Date Established: 1964; **Freq:** 156 issues yearly; **Circ:** 7,570
Language(s): Norwegian
ADVERTISING RATES:
Full Page Colour .... NOK 18144
SCC .... NOK 90.72
REGIONAL DAILY & SUNDAY NEWSPAPERS: Regional Daily Newspapers

FOSTERHJEMSKONTAKT 1624475R32G-152
Editorial: Storgata 10a, 0155 OSLO **Tel:** 23 31 54 00 **Fax:** 23 31 54 01
Email: redaksjon@fosterhjemsforening.no **Web site:** http://www.fosterhjemsforening.no
Freq: 6 issues yearly
Language(s): Norwegian
BUSINESS: LOCAL GOVERNMENT, LEISURE & RECREATION: Community Care & Social Services

FOTBALLMAGASINET.NO 1740709R75B-131
Editorial: Sentrumsbygget, 3145 TJØME
Tel: 40 04 04 04
Email: per@fotballmagasinet.no **Web site:** http://www.fotballmagasinet.no
Editor: Mats Nordgård
Language(s): Norwegian
CONSUMER: SPORT: Football

FOTOGRAFI 32435R38-25
Editorial: Postboks 703, Skøyen, 0214 OSLO
Tel: 67120610
Email: red@fotografi.no **Web site:** http://www.fotografi.no
Freq: 6 issues yearly; **Circ:** 12,000
Profile: Magazine containing information about photography, includes tests of new models, information about trade fairs and discussion of new techniques.
Language(s): Norwegian
Readership: Read by professional photographers.
ADVERTISING RATES:
Full Page Colour .... NOK 24500
SCC .... NOK 200
BUSINESS: PHOTOGRAPHIC TRADE

FOTOGRAFI; FOTOGRAFI.NO 1840346R19A-103
Editorial: Kjelsåsveien 145, 0491 OSLO
Tel: 22 15 17 63
Email: redweb@fotografi.no **Web site:** http://www.fotografi.no
Freq: Daily; **Cover Price:** Paid
Language(s): Norwegian
BUSINESS: ENGINEERING & MACHINERY

FOTO.NO 1657808R85A-256
Editorial: Østerdalsgata 1K, 0658 OSLO
Email: red@foto.no **Web site:** http://www.foto.no
Cover Price: Paid; **Circ:** 6,750 Unique Users
Language(s): Norwegian
CONSUMER: PHOTOGRAPHY & FILM MAKING: Photography

FOTTERAPEUTEN 1625005R56A-207
Editorial: Pb 9202 Grønland, 0134 OSLO
Tel: 99450090
Email: ann.beate@grasdalen.no **Web site:** http://www.fotterapeutene.no
Freq: Quarterly
Editor: Ann Beate Grasdalen
Language(s): Norwegian
BUSINESS: HEALTH & MEDICAL

FRAKTEMANN 1624403R45A-71
Editorial: Pb 2020 Nordnes, 5817 BERGEN
Tel: 55 55 16 20 **Fax:** 55 55 16 21
Email: sh@fraktefartoyene.no **Web site:** http://www.fraktefartoyene.no/?page_id=61
Freq: Quarterly; **Circ:** 600
Language(s): Norwegian
BUSINESS: MARINE & SHIPPING

FRED OG FRIHET 32257R82-69
Editorial: Pb 8810 Youngstorget, 0028 OSLO
Tel: 23010340 **Fax:** 23010301
Email: ikff@online.no **Web site:** http://www.ikff.no
Date Established: 1940; **Freq:** Quarterly; **Circ:** 750
Editor: Lillian Angelo
Profile: Magazine covering international politics, peace policies, current affairs, justice and legal matters concerning women.
Language(s): Norwegian
CONSUMER: CURRENT AFFAIRS & POLITICS

FREDRIKKE 1624253R56A-202
Editorial: Munthes gate 33, 0260 OSLO
Tel: 24 11 56 20 **Fax:** 22 44 76 21
Email: mjs@sanitetskvinnene.no **Web site:** http://www.sanitetskvinnene.no
Freq: Quarterly; **Circ:** 60,000
Editor: Marianne J. Seip
Language(s): Norwegian
BUSINESS: HEALTH & MEDICAL

FREDRIKSSTAD BLAD 31768R67B-3400
Editorial: Postboks 143, 1601 FREDRIKSTAD
Tel: 46 80 77 77
Email: tips@f-b.no **Web site:** http://www.f-b.no
Freq: Daily; **Circ:** 22,883
Editor: Øivind Lågbu
Language(s): Norwegian
ADVERTISING RATES:
Full Page Colour .... NOK 32644
SCC .... NOK 163.22
REGIONAL DAILY & SUNDAY NEWSPAPERS: Regional Daily Newspapers

FREDRIKSSTAD BLAD; SPORTEN 1996211R75A-239
Editorial: Postboks 143, 1601 FREDRIKSTAD
Tel: 69388000
Email: sporten@f-b.no **Web site:** http://www.f-b.no
Language(s): Norwegian
CONSUMER: SPORT

FREMOVER 31791R67B-3500
Editorial: Pb. 324, 8504 NARVIK **Tel:** 76 95 00 00
Fax: 76 95 00 30
Email: redaksjon@fremover.no **Web site:** http://www.fremover.no
Date Established: 1902; **Freq:** Daily; **Circ:** 8,835
Language(s): Norwegian
ADVERTISING RATES:
Full Page Colour .... NOK 19819
SCC .... NOK 99.10
REGIONAL DAILY & SUNDAY NEWSPAPERS: Regional Daily Newspapers

FRI FLYT 1624645R91R-3
Editorial: Mølleparken 6, 0459 OSLO
Tel: 22 04 46 00 **Fax:** 22 04 46 09
Email: nett@friflyt.no **Web site:** http://www.friflyt.no
Freq: 6 issues yearly; **Circ:** 11,686
Editor: Christian Nerdrum
Language(s): Norwegian
ADVERTISING RATES:
Full Page Colour .... NOK 28000
CONSUMER: RECREATION & LEISURE: Recreation & Leisure Related

FRI TANKE 32380R94X-90
Editorial: Pb 6744 St. Olavs Plass, 0130 OSLO
Tel: 23 15 60 00 **Fax:** 23 15 60 21
Email: fri.tanke@human.no **Web site:** http://www.human.no/fritanke
Freq: 6 issues yearly; **Circ:** 53,000
Profile: Magazine containing articles on ethics and moral issues. Covers human rights and related topics.
Language(s): Norwegian
CONSUMER: OTHER CLASSIFICATIONS: Miscellaneous

FRIFAGBEVEGELSE.NO 1864049R14L-113
Editorial: Postboks 231, Sentrum, 0103 OSLO
Tel: 23 06 33 59
Email: frifagbevegelse@lo-media.no **Web site:** http://www.frifagbevegelse.no
Freq: Daily; **Cover Price:** Free; **Circ:** 2,500 Unique Users
Language(s): Norwegian
BUSINESS: COMMERCE, INDUSTRY & MANAGEMENT: Trade Unions

FRIHETEN; FRIHETEN.NO 1863947R73-205
Editorial: Postboks 9286, Grønland, 0553 OSLO
Tel: 22 71 60 44 **Fax:** 22 71 79 07
Web site: http://www.friheten.no
Freq: Daily; **Cover Price:** Free; **Circ:** 2,500 Unique Users
Language(s): Norwegian
CONSUMER: NATIONAL & INTERNATIONAL PERIODICALS

FRIIDRETT 32194R75J-40
Editorial: Rakkestadveien 1, 1814 ASKIM
Tel: 69 81 97 00 **Fax:** 69 88 94 33
Email: jon.wiik@sportmedia.no **Web site:** http://www.sportmedia.no
Freq: 6 issues yearly; **Circ:** 4,600
Editor: Jon Wiik
Profile: Journal of the Norwegian Athletics Association.
Language(s): Norwegian
CONSUMER: SPORT: Athletics

FRIKANALEN 1935711R73-177
Editorial: FORENINGEN FRIKANALEN, Pb 4743 NYDALEN, 0421 OSLO
Email: post@frikanalen.no **Web site:** http://WWW.FRIKANALEN.NO
Language(s): Norwegian
CONSUMER: NATIONAL & INTERNATIONAL PERIODICALS

FRILUFTSLIV MULTIMEDIA 1625023R91R-4
Editorial: Postboks 3, 7221 MELHUS
Tel: 92 44 76 45
Email: redaksjonen@friluftsliv.no **Web site:** http://www.friluftsliv.no
Freq: 6 issues yearly; **Circ:** 13,000
Language(s): Norwegian
CONSUMER: RECREATION & LEISURE: Recreation & Leisure Related

FRILUFTSMAGASINET UTE 1625234R75A-205
Editorial: Mølleparken 6, 0459 OSLO
Tel: 22 04 46 00 **Fax:** 22 04 46 09
Email: nett@friflyt.no **Web site:** http://www.utemagasinet.no
Freq: 6 issues yearly
Language(s): Norwegian
CONSUMER: SPORT

FRIMURERBLADET 1624376R63-1
Editorial: Nedre Vollgate 19, 0158 OSLO
Tel: 92 05 05 05
Email: frimurerbladet@dnfo.no **Web site:** http://www.frimurer.no
Freq: Quarterly; **Circ:** 18,000
Language(s): Norwegian
BUSINESS: REGIONAL BUSINESS

FRISK SOM EN FISK 1938274R74G-171
Web site: http://frisksomenfisk.blogg.no/blogg.html
Cover Price: Paid
Language(s): Norwegian
CONSUMER: WOMEN'S INTEREST CONSUMER MAGAZINES: Slimming & Health

FRISØR 31445R15B-10
Editorial: Pb 7017 Majorstua, 0306 OSLO
Tel: 23 08 79 60 **Fax:** 23 08 79 70
Email: post@nfvb.no **Web site:** http://www.nfvb.no
Date Established: 1904; **Freq:** 6 issues yearly
Profile: Official magazine of the Norwegian Hairdressers' Association.
Language(s): Norwegian
BUSINESS: COSMETICS & HAIRDRESSING: Hairdressing

FRITANKE.NO 1998538R94J-19
Editorial: Pb 6744, St. Olavs plass, 0130 OSLO
Tel: 23156020 **Fax:** 23156021
Email: bergh@human.no **Web site:** http://www.fritanke.no
Cover Price: Paid
Editor: Kirsti Bergh
Language(s): Norwegian
CONSUMER: OTHER CLASSIFICATIONS: Popular Science

FRITT FALL 32208R75X-65
Editorial: C/O Kitt Grønningsæter, Furuvegen 15, 3560 HEMSEDAL **Tel:** 90 12 71 54
Email: kitt@frittfall.org **Web site:** http://www.frittfall.org
Date Established: 1972; **Freq:** Quarterly
Profile: Scandinavian magazine containing articles and information about parachuting and sky-diving.
Language(s): Norwegian
Readership: Aimed at members of the Norwegian Federation for Air Sports and people interested in parachuting.
CONSUMER: SPORT: Other Sport

FROSTINGEN.NO 1863950R73-202
Editorial: Banken, 7633 FROSTA **Tel:** 74 80 88 35
Fax: 74 80 88 39
Email: frostingen@frostingen.no **Web site:** http://frostingen.no
Freq: Daily; **Cover Price:** Free; **Circ:** 399 Unique Users
Language(s): Norwegian
CONSUMER: NATIONAL & INTERNATIONAL PERIODICALS

FUGLAR I HORDALAND 1624856R64F-21
Editorial: Norsk Ornitologisk Forening, Avdeling Hordaland, Boks 280, 5751 ODDA **Tel:** 53 64 29 37
Email: nof@fuglar.no **Web site:** http://www.fuglar.no
Freq: Quarterly; **Circ:** 500
Language(s): Norwegian
BUSINESS: OTHER CLASSIFICATIONS: Biology

FYSIOTERAPEUTEN 31639R56A-30
Editorial: Pb 2704 St.Hanshaugen, 0131 OSLO
Tel: 22933050 **Fax:** 22565825
Email: fysioterapeuten@fysio.no **Web site:** http://www.fysioterapeuten.no
Date Established: 1934; **Freq:** Monthly; **Circ:** 8,312
Profile: Publication covering health and physiotherapy.
Language(s): Norwegian
ADVERTISING RATES:
Full Page Colour .... NOK 17300
BUSINESS: HEALTH & MEDICAL

FYSIOTERAPEUTEN.NO 1936031R56A-222
Editorial: Pb 2704 St.Hanshaugen, 0131
Tel: 22 93 30 50
Email: fysioterapeuten@fysio.no **Web site:** http://www.fysioterapeuten.no
Freq: Daily; **Cover Price:** Paid
Editor: Heidi Johnsen
Language(s): Norwegian
BUSINESS: HEALTH & MEDICAL

FYSIOTERAPI I PRIVAT PRAKSIS 31667R56L-25
Editorial: Schwartzgt. 2, 3043 DRAMMEN
Tel: 32893719
Email: pff@fysioterapi.org **Web site:** http://www.fysioterapi.org
Date Established: 1992; **Freq:** 6 issues yearly; **Circ:** 2,500
Editor: Hilde Stette
Profile: Journal containing articles and information about physiotherapy.
Language(s): Norwegian
Readership: Read by physiotherapists, medical students, politicians, hospital personnel and other professionals dealing with health issues.
Copy instructions: *Copy Date:* 30 days prior to publication date
BUSINESS: HEALTH & MEDICAL: Disability & Rehabilitation

GAMEPAD.NO 1865443R78R-5
Email: redaksjon@gamepad.no **Web site:** http://gamepad.no
Freq: Daily; **Cover Price:** Free; **Circ:** 2,500 Unique Users
Language(s): Norwegian
CONSUMER: CONSUMER ELECTRONICS: Consumer Electronics Related

GAMEREACTOR 1740752R5F-16
Editorial: Gamez Publishing Nuf, Postboks 479 Sentrum, 0105 OSLO **Tel:** 47026909
Email: redaksjonen@gamereactor.no **Web site:** http://www.gamereactor.no
Freq: Monthly
Language(s): Norwegian
BUSINESS: COMPUTERS & AUTOMATION: Multimedia

GAMEREACTOR; GAMEREACTOR.NO 1864564R5E-9
Editorial: Gamez Publishing Nuf, Postboks 479 Sentrum, 0105 OSLO **Tel:** 47 02 69 09
Email: redaksjonen@gamereactor.no **Web site:** http://www.gamereactor.no
Freq: Daily; **Cover Price:** Free; **Circ:** 2,500 Unique Users
Editor: Kristian Nymoen
Language(s): Norwegian
BUSINESS: COMPUTERS & AUTOMATION: Data Transmission

GAMER.NO 1657997R78D-1
Editorial: C/O Mediehuset Tek, Postboks 1314 Vika, 0110 OSLO **Tel:** 22 82 32 36 **Fax:** 22 82 32 33
Email: mail@gamer.no **Web site:** http://gamer.no
Editor: Tor-Steinar Tangedal
Language(s): Norwegian
CONSUMER: CONSUMER ELECTRONICS: Games

GAMERSWEB.NO 1810313R73-160
Editorial: V/Roger Evensen, Riskestien 7, 1529 MOSS **Tel:** 90033545

Email: roger@gamersweb.no **Web site:** http://www.gamersweb.no
Cover Price: Paid; **Circ:** 2,500 Unique Users
Editor: Roger Evensen
Language(s): Norwegian
CONSUMER: NATIONAL & INTERNATIONAL PERIODICALS

GAMLE HUS & HAGER
1985730R74C-101
Editorial: Postboks 10, 1851 0164 OSLO MYSEN
Tel: 922 58 954
Email: redaksjon@gamlehusoghager.no **Web site:** http://www.gamlehusoghager.no
Freq: 6 issues yearly; **Circ:** 27,500
Language(s): Norwegian
ADVERTISING RATES:
Full Page Colour .... NOK 15500
Copy instructions: *Copy Date:* 43 days prior to publication date
CONSUMER: WOMEN'S INTEREST CONSUMER MAGAZINES: Home & Family

GARDISTEN
31545R40-8_50
Editorial: HM Kongens Garde, Pb 7 Røa, 0701 OSLO
Tel: 23 09 80 00 **Fax:** 23 09 72 78
Email: info@garden.no **Web site:** http://www.mil.no/haren/hmkg
Freq: Quarterly
Profile: Magazine containing articles and information for and about the Norwegian Royal Guard.
Language(s): Norwegian
BUSINESS: DEFENCE

GARDSPLASSEN.NO
1864565R21A-156
Editorial: Stokmoveien 1, 7500 STJØRDAL
Tel: 901 26 963
Email: ole@ostkil.no **Web site:** http://www.gardsplassen.no
Freq: Daily; **Cover Price:** Free; **Circ:** 2,500 Unique Users
Language(s): Norwegian
BUSINESS: AGRICULTURE & FARMING

GARTNERYRKET
31495R26C-20
Editorial: Schweigaardsgate 34 F, 0191 OSLO
Tel: 23 15 93 50 **Fax:** 23 15 93 51
Email: gartneryrket@gartnerforbundet.no **Web site:** http://www.gartnerforbundet.no
Date Established: 1910; **Freq:** Monthly; **Circ:** 2,093
Profile: Magazine about fruit, vegetable and flower production.
Language(s): Norwegian
BUSINESS: GARDEN TRADE

GASSMAGASINET
1625049R58-104
Editorial: Skarland Press AS, Postboks 2843T øyen, 0608 OSLO **Tel:** 22 70 83 00 **Fax:** 22 70 83 01
Email: per@skarland.no **Web site:** http://www.gassmagasinet.no
Freq: 6 issues yearly; **Circ:** 3,000
Language(s): Norwegian
ADVERTISING RATES:
SCC .... NOK 166.67
BUSINESS: ENERGY, FUEL & NUCLEAR

GATEAVISA
1624406R82-305
Editorial: Hjelmsgate 3, 0355 OSLO **Tel:** 22466896
Email: gateavisa@gateavisa.no **Web site:** http://www.gateavisa.no
Freq: Half-yearly
Language(s): Norwegian
CONSUMER: CURRENT AFFAIRS & POLITICS

GATEBIL MAGAZINE
1740818R86C-162
Editorial: Postboks 783, 0107 OSLO **Tel:** 21301220
Fax: 21301213
Email: post@gatebil.no **Web site:** http://www.gatebil.no
Freq: 6 issues yearly; **Circ:** 24,166
Editor: Rune Nesheim
Language(s): Norwegian
CONSUMER: ADULT & GAY MAGAZINES: Men's Lifestyle Magazines

GAUSDØL'N - LOKALAVISA FOR GAUSDAL
1660644R80-161
Editorial: 2653 VESTRE GAUSDAL **Tel:** 61 22 34 23
Fax: 61 22 35 30
Email: firmapost@gausdolen.no **Web site:** http://www.gausdolen.no
Freq: Monthly; **Circ:** 950
Language(s): Norwegian
CONSUMER: RURAL & REGIONAL INTEREST

GAVE OG INTERIØR
1819153R74C-88
Editorial: Ask Media, Pb 130, 2261 KIRKENAER
Tel: 92258431
Email: geir@askmedia.no **Web site:** http://www.gaveoginterior.no
Freq: 6 issues yearly; **Circ:** 2,683
Editor: Geir Nøsterud
Language(s): Norwegian
CONSUMER: WOMEN'S INTEREST CONSUMER MAGAZINES: Home & Family

GAVLEN
1624898R84A-107
Editorial: Sunnmøre Museum, Borgundgavlen, 6015 ÅLESUND **Tel:** 70 17 40 00 **Fax:** 70 17 40 01
Email: museum@sunnmore.museum.no **Web site:** http://www.sunnmore.museum.no
Freq: Half-yearly; **Circ:** 1,000
Language(s): Norwegian
CONSUMER: THE ARTS & LITERARY: Arts

GEMINI
1645034R56R-157
Editorial: 7465 TRONDHEIM **Tel:** 73592476
Email: ase.dragland@sintef.no **Web site:** http://www.ntnu.no/gemini
Freq: Quarterly - Samt 1. utg. i året på engelsk
Editor: Åse Dragland
Language(s): Norwegian
BUSINESS: HEALTH & MEDICAL: Health Medical Related

GENEALOGEN
1747631R74C-83
Editorial: Norsk Slektshistorisk Forening, Lakkegata 21, 0187 OSLO
Email: genealogen@genealogi.no **Web site:** http://www.genealogi.no/Genealogen/Genealogen.htm
Freq: Half-yearly
Editor: Are S. Gustavsen
Language(s): Norwegian
CONSUMER: WOMEN'S INTEREST CONSUMER MAGAZINES: Home & Family

GENEALOGI.NO
1859290R94J-18
Editorial: Norsk Slektshistorisk Forening, Lakkegata 21, 0187 OSLO **Tel:** 22 05 90 00
Email: webredaksjon@genealogi.no **Web site:** http://www.genealogi.no
Freq: Daily
Language(s): Norwegian
CONSUMER: OTHER CLASSIFICATIONS: Popular Science

GEN-I-ALT
1660645R56R-169
Editorial: Pb. 522 Sentrum, 0105 OSLO
Tel: 24 15 60 20 **Fax:** 24 15 60 29
Email: bion@bion.no **Web site:** http://www.bion.no
Freq: Quarterly; **Cover Price:** Free
Editor: Norunn Torheim
Language(s): Norwegian
BUSINESS: HEALTH & MEDICAL: Health Medical Related

GEO
1657825R94J-4
Editorial: GeoPublishing co/NGU, Postboks 6315 Sluppen, 7491 TRONDHEIM **Tel:** 73904090
Fax: 73921620
Email: halfdan@geoaktuelt.no **Web site:** http://www.geoaktuelt.no
Freq: 6 issues yearly
Language(s): Norwegian
CONSUMER: OTHER CLASSIFICATIONS: Popular Science

GJENGANGEREN
31775R67B-3650
Editorial: Pb. 85, 3191 HORTEN **Tel:** 33 02 00 00
Fax: 33 02 00 30
Email: redaksjonen@gjengangeren.no **Web site:** http://www.gjengangeren.no
Date Established: 1851; **Freq:** Daily; **Circ:** 6,173
Language(s): Norwegian
ADVERTISING RATES:
Full Page Colour .... NOK 18174
SCC .... NOK 90.87
REGIONAL DAILY & SUNDAY NEWSPAPERS: Regional Daily Newspapers

GJESDALBUEN.NO
1864561R73-198
Editorial: Postboks 13, 4339 ÅLGÅRD
Tel: 51 61 28 50 **Fax:** 51 61 99 50
Email: redaksjonen@gjesdalbuen.no **Web site:** http://www.gjesdalbuen.no
Freq: Daily; **Cover Price:** Free; **Circ:** 2,400 Unique Users
Language(s): Norwegian
CONSUMER: NATIONAL & INTERNATIONAL PERIODICALS

GJØR DET SELV
1624470R79A-3
Editorial: Glåmstadvegen 8, 2213 KONGSVINGER
Email: geir@gjoerdetselv.com **Web site:** http://www.gjoerdetselv.com
Freq: Monthly; **Circ:** 25,775
Editor: Geir Nøsterud
Language(s): Norwegian
Copy instructions: *Copy Date:* 25 days prior to publication date
CONSUMER: HOBBIES & DIY

GLAD I MAT
1624567R74Q-71
Editorial: Kristian Augusts gate 14, 0164 OSLO
Tel: 23358330
Email: gladimat@teft.no **Web site:** http://www.gladimat.no
Freq: 6 issues yearly; **Cover Price:** Free
Language(s): Norwegian
CONSUMER: WOMEN'S INTEREST CONSUMER MAGAZINES: Lifestyle

GLADE BARN I BARNEHAGEN
1803803R32G-165
Editorial: C/O Barnemagasinet, 0441 OSLO
Tel: 23 00 81 83 **Fax:** 22 58 05 85
Email: monica.eriksen@bam.no **Web site:** http://www.gladebarn.com
Freq: Annual; **Circ:** 100,000
Editor: Monica Eriksen
Language(s): Norwegian
BUSINESS: LOCAL GOVERNMENT, LEISURE & RECREATION: Community Care & Social Services

GLÅMDALEN
31777R67B-3700
Editorial: PB 757, 2204 KONGSVINGER
Tel: 62 88 25 00 **Fax:** 62 88 25 70
Email: redaksjon@glomdalen.no **Web site:** http://www.glomdalen.no
Date Established: 1982; **Freq:** Daily; **Circ:** 19,370
Language(s): Norwegian
ADVERTISING RATES:
Full Page Colour .... NOK 29729
SCC .... NOK 148.64
REGIONAL DAILY & SUNDAY NEWSPAPERS: Regional Daily Newspapers

GLASS & FASADE
31422R12B-5
Editorial: Glass og Fasadeforeningen, Fridtjof Nansens vei 19, 0369 OSLO **Tel:** 47 47 47 05
Email: post@gffn.no **Web site:** http://www.glassportal.no
Freq: Quarterly; **Circ:** 5,518
Editor: Arne Eidal
Profile: Magazine for glaziers and those in the glass industry.
Language(s): Norwegian
ADVERTISING RATES:
Full Page Colour .... NOK 18000
BUSINESS: CERAMICS, POTTERY & GLASS: Glass

GOLFEREN.NO
1660018R75D-103
Editorial: Postboks 2814 Solli, 0204 OSLO
Tel: 400 02 254
Email: golferen@papaya.no **Web site:** http://www.golferen.no
Freq: Daily; **Cover Price:** Paid
Language(s): Norwegian
CONSUMER: SPORT: Golf

GOLF.NO
1658230R75D-102
Editorial: Pb. 1, 0051 OSLO **Tel:** 22 86 42 96
Fax: 22 86 32 73
Email: s@golf.no **Web site:** http://www.golf.no
Freq: Daily; **Cover Price:** Paid
Language(s): Norwegian
CONSUMER: SPORT: Golf

GO'MØRNING
32442R22D-7
Editorial: Pb 396 Økern, 0513 OSLO **Tel:** 22 09 23 00
Fax: 22 22 00 16
Email: animalia@animalia.no **Web site:** http://www.animalia.no
Date Established: 1989; **Freq:** Quarterly - 5 ganger i året
Profile: Journal concerning the meat industry.
Language(s): Norwegian
BUSINESS: FOOD: Meat Trade

GRAMART - GRAMMOFONARTISTENES FORENING
1657502R76D-264
Editorial: Kirkegata 5, 0153 OSLO **Fax:** 22 00 56 51
Email: gramart@gramart.no **Web site:** http://www.gramart.no
Cover Price: Paid
Language(s): Norwegian
CONSUMER: MUSIC & PERFORMING ARTS: Music

GRAVID
32629R74D-60
Editorial: Foreldre og Barn, 0441 OSLO
Tel: 22 58 54 33 **Fax:** 22 58 58 79
Email: foreldreogbarn@egmonthm.no **Web site:** http://www.barnimagen.com
Freq: 6 issues yearly; **Circ:** 14,772
Profile: Magazine containing articles about pregnancy and childcare.
Language(s): Norwegian
Readership: Aimed at expectant mothers and new parents.
CONSUMER: WOMEN'S INTEREST CONSUMER MAGAZINES: Child Care

GRENDA.NO
1864560R73-201
Editorial: postboks 100, 5470 ROSENDAL
Tel: 53 47 71 00
Email: post@grenda.no **Web site:** http://www.grenda.no
Freq: Daily; **Cover Price:** Free; **Circ:** 2,186 Unique Users
Editor: Håvard Sætrevik
Language(s): Norwegian
CONSUMER: NATIONAL & INTERNATIONAL PERIODICALS

GREVLINGEN
1624814R57-304
Editorial: Naturvernforbundet i Oslo og Akershus, Maridalsveien 120, 0461 OSLO **Tel:** 22383520
Email: noa@noa.no **Web site:** http://www.noa.no
Freq: Quarterly
Editor: Frithjof Funder
Language(s): Norwegian
BUSINESS: ENVIRONMENT & POLLUTION

GRØNN HVERDAG MAGASIN
1660646R57-309
Editorial: Grensen 9B, 0159 OSLO **Tel:** 23109550
Fax: 23109551
Email: post@gronnhverdag.no **Web site:** http://www.gronnhverdag.no
Freq: 6 issues yearly
Editor: Håkon Lindahl
Language(s): Norwegian
BUSINESS: ENVIRONMENT & POLLUTION

GRONNHVERDAG.NO
1859772R57-312
Editorial: Grensen 9B, 0159 OSLO **Tel:** 23 10 95 50
Fax: 23 10 95 51
Email: post@gronnhverdag.no **Web site:** http://www.gronnhverdag.no
Freq: Daily
Editor: Håkon Lindahl
Language(s): Norwegian
BUSINESS: ENVIRONMENT & POLLUTION

GROOVE.NO
1800778R76D-308
Email: oyvind.adde@groove.no **Web site:** http://www.groove.no
Cover Price: Paid
Language(s): Norwegian
CONSUMER: MUSIC & PERFORMING ARTS: Music

GRÜNDER ØKONOMISK RAPPORT
1657818R74M-201
Editorial: Pb. 1180 Sentrum, 0107 OSLO
Tel: 22 31 02 20 **Fax:** 22 31 02 25
Email: redaksjon@orapp.no **Web site:** http://www.grunder.no
Freq: Monthly; **Circ:** 7,000
Editor: Terje Aurdal
Language(s): Norwegian
ADVERTISING RATES:
SCC .... NOK 165.83
CONSUMER: WOMEN'S INTEREST CONSUMER MAGAZINES: Personal Finance

GRÜNDER ØKONOMISK RAPPORT; GRUNDER.NO
1864559R14A-237
Editorial: Postboks 1180 Sentrum, 0107 OSLO
Tel: 22 31 02 20
Email: redaksjon@orapp.no **Web site:** http://www.grunder.no
Freq: Daily; **Cover Price:** Free; **Circ:** 5,000 Unique Users
Language(s): Norwegian
BUSINESS: COMMERCE, INDUSTRY & MANAGEMENT

GUDBRANDSDØLEN DAGNINGEN
31781R67B-3750
Editorial: Pb. 954, 2604 LILLEHAMMER
Tel: 61 22 10 00 **Fax:** 61 25 09 20
Email: redaksjonen@gd.no **Web site:** http://www.gd.no
Date Established: 1837; **Freq:** Daily; **Circ:** 26,458
Editor: Gunnar Tore Larsen
Language(s): Norwegian
ADVERTISING RATES:
Full Page Colour .... NOK 30603
SCC .... NOK 153.02
REGIONAL DAILY & SUNDAY NEWSPAPERS: Regional Daily Newspapers

GULL & UR
31617R52A-10

Editorial: Storgt. 14, 0184 OSLO **Tel:** 22348900
Fax: 22348919
Email: gullogur@gullsmed.no **Web site:** http://www.gullsmed.no
Freq: Monthly - 9 ganger i året
Profile: Magazine of the Norwegian Association for Gold and Silversmiths.
Language(s): Norwegian
BUSINESS: GIFT TRADE: Jewellery

GYM & TURN
31592R48B-8

Editorial: Norges Gymnastikk- og Turnforbund, 0840 OSLO **Tel:** 21 02 96 16 **Fax:** 21 02 96 11
Email: hermod.buttedahl@nif.idrett.no **Web site:** http://www.gymogturn.no
Date Established: 1947; **Freq:** 6 issues yearly; **Circ:** 4,000
Editor: Hermod Buttedahl
Profile: Magazine about sports equipment and goods.
Language(s): Norwegian
BUSINESS: TOY TRADE & SPORTS GOODS: Sports Goods

HADELAND
31757R67B-3800

Editorial: Pb. 227, 2711 GRAN **Tel:** 61 31 31 32
Fax: 61 31 31 01
Email: desken@hadeland.net **Web site:** http://www.hadeland.net
Freq: Daily; **Circ:** 7,487
Language(s): Norwegian
ADVERTISING RATES:
SCC .... NOK 238.14
REGIONAL DAILY & SUNDAY NEWSPAPERS: Regional Daily Newspapers

HADELAND.NET
1864558R73-194

Editorial: Postboks 227, 2711 GRAN
Tel: 61 31 31 32
Email: desken@hadeland.net **Web site:** http://www.hadeland.net
Freq: Daily; **Cover Price:** Free; **Circ:** 4,000 Unique Users
Language(s): Norwegian
CONSUMER: NATIONAL & INTERNATIONAL PERIODICALS

HAGEN FOR ALLE
32371R93-50

Editorial: C/O Bonnier Publications International AS, Pb. 433 sentrum, 0103 OSLO **Tel:** 22 40 12 00
Email: post@hagenforalle.no **Web site:** http://www.hagenforalle.no
Date Established: 1993; **Freq:** Monthly - 15 ganger i året
Editor: Arild Sandgren
Profile: Magazine containing practical advice and information for the gardening enthusiast.
Language(s): Norwegian
Copy instructions: *Copy Date:* 30 days prior to publication date
CONSUMER: GARDENING

HALDEN ARBEIDERBLAD
31770R67B-3850

Editorial: Pb. 113, 1751 HALDEN **Tel:** 69 21 56 00
Fax: 69 21 56 01
Email: redaksjonen@ha-halden.no **Web site:** http://www.ha-halden.no
Freq: Daily; **Circ:** 8,533
Editor: Bjørn Ystrøm
Language(s): Norwegian
ADVERTISING RATES:
SCC .... NOK 121.36
REGIONAL DAILY & SUNDAY NEWSPAPERS: Regional Daily Newspapers

HAMAR ARBEIDERBLAD
31771R67B-3900

Editorial: Pb. 262, 2302 HAMAR **Fax:** 62 51 95 55
Email: red@h-a.no **Web site:** http://www.h-a.no
Date Established: 1925; **Freq:** Daily; **Circ:** 26,677
Language(s): Norwegian
ADVERTISING RATES:
Full Page Colour .... NOK 34392
SCC .... NOK 343.92
REGIONAL DAILY & SUNDAY NEWSPAPERS: Regional Daily Newspapers

HAMAR ARBEIDERBLAD; SAMFUNNSREDAKSJONEN
1995205R82-500

Editorial: Postboks 262, 2302 HAMAR
Email: red@h-a.no **Web site:** http://h-a.no
Language(s): Norwegian
CONSUMER: CURRENT AFFAIRS & POLITICS

HÅNDBALLMAGASINET
32648R75X-70

Editorial: Norges Håndballforbund, 0840 OSLO
Tel: 21 02 90 00 **Fax:** 21 02 99 51
Email: nhf@handball.no **Web site:** http://www.handball.no
Date Established: 1998; **Freq:** Quarterly; **Circ:** 35,000
Profile: Sports magazine focusing on handball.
Language(s): Norwegian
CONSUMER: SPORT: Other Sport

HANDELSBLADET FK
1624256R22A-153

Editorial: Pb. 793, Sentrum, 0106 OSLO
Tel: 22348760 **Fax:** 22348761
Email: ak@handelsbladet.no **Web site:** http://www.handelsbladet.no
Freq: Weekly; **Circ:** 17,182
Language(s): Norwegian
ADVERTISING RATES:
Full Page Colour .... NOK 36000
SCC .... NOK 278.33
BUSINESS: FOOD

HANDELSBLADET FK; HANDELSBLADETFK.NO
1864556R53-20

Editorial: Postboks 793, Sentrum, 0106 OSLO
Tel: 22 34 87 60 **Fax:** 22 34 87 61
Email: lsh@handelsbladet.no **Web site:** http://www.handelsbladetfk.no
Freq: Daily; **Cover Price:** Free; **Circ:** 9,335 Unique Users
Language(s): Norwegian
BUSINESS: RETAILING & WHOLESALING

HANDIKAPNYTT
31668R56L-30

Editorial: Pb 9217 Grønland, 0134 OSLO
Tel: 24 10 24 00 **Fax:** 24 10 24 99
Email: handikapnytt@nhf.no **Web site:** http://www.handikapnytt.no
Freq: Monthly - 8 ganger i året; **Circ:** 23,000
Editor: Ivar Kvistum
Profile: Official magazine of the Norwegian Association for the Disabled.
Language(s): Norwegian
ADVERTISING RATES:
Full Page Colour .... NOK 20100
SCC .... NOK 143.33
Copy instructions: *Copy Date:* 9 days prior to publication date
BUSINESS: HEALTH & MEDICAL: Disability & Rehabilitation

HANGAR.NO
1864563R89A-185

Editorial: Postboks 35, 1410 KOLBOTN
Tel: 481 801 06 **Fax:** 66 80 52 55
Email: post@hangar.no **Web site:** http://www.hangar.no
Freq: Daily; **Cover Price:** Free; **Circ:** 2,500 Unique Users
Language(s): Norwegian
CONSUMER: HOLIDAYS & TRAVEL: Travel

HARDANGER-FOLKEBLAD.NO
1835222R76B-5

Editorial: Pb. 374, 5750 ODDA **Tel:** 53 65 06 00
Fax: 53 65 06 21
Email: redaksjon@hardanger-folkeblad.no **Web site:** http://www.hardanger-folkeblad.no
Freq: Daily; **Cover Price:** Paid; **Circ:** 3,000 Unique Users
Language(s): Norwegian
ADVERTISING RATES:
SCC .... NOK 18.6
CONSUMER: MUSIC & PERFORMING ARTS: Theatre

HARDWARE.NO
1657596R5F-6

Editorial: Hardware.no c/o Mediehuset Tek, Postboks 1314 Vika, 0112 OSLO **Tel:** 21 56 97 66
Fax: 21 56 97 01
Email: rolf@hardware.no **Web site:** http://www.hardware.no
Circ: 80,000 Unique Users
Language(s): Norwegian
BUSINESS: COMPUTERS & AUTOMATION: Multimedia

HARSTAD TIDENDE
31773R67B-3950

Editorial: Pb. 85, 9481 HARSTAD **Tel:** 77 01 80 00
Fax: 77 01 80 05
Email: redaksjonen@ht.no **Web site:** http://www.ht.no
Freq: Daily; **Circ:** 13,173
Language(s): Norwegian
ADVERTISING RATES:
SCC .... NOK 105.65
REGIONAL DAILY & SUNDAY NEWSPAPERS: Regional Daily Newspapers

HARSTAD TIDENDE; KULTURREDAKSJONEN
1833134R84A-133

Editorial: Pb. 85, 9481 HARSTAD **Tel:** 77 01 80 00
Fax: 77018005
Email: kultur@ht.no **Web site:** http://www.ht.no/kultur
Circ: 13,503
Language(s): Norwegian
CONSUMER: THE ARTS & LITERARY: Arts

HARSTAD TIDENDE; SPORTREDAKSJONEN
1833133R75A-215

Editorial: Pb. 85, 9481 HARSTAD **Tel:** 77018001
Fax: 77 01 80 05
Email: sport@ht.no **Web site:** http://www.ht.no
Circ: 13,173
Language(s): Norwegian
CONSUMER: SPORT

HAUGESUNDS AVIS
31774R67B-4000

Editorial: Pb. 2024 Postterminalen, 5504 HAUGESUND **Tel:** 52 72 00 00 **Fax:** 52 72 04 44
Email: redaksjonen@haugesunds-avis.no **Web site:** http://www.haugesunds-avis.no
Date Established: 1895; **Freq:** Daily; **Circ:** 31,907
Language(s): Norwegian
ADVERTISING RATES:
SCC .... NOK 154.47
REGIONAL DAILY & SUNDAY NEWSPAPERS: Regional Daily Newspapers

HEGNAR ONLINE
625171R1A-70

Editorial: Pb. 724 Skøyen, 0214 OSLO
Tel: 23 29 64 86 **Fax:** 23 29 64 87
Email: tips@hegnar.no **Web site:** http://www.hegnar.no
Editor: Stein Ove Haugen
Profile: E-zine focusing on financial news, both national and international. Features news about stock markets, economy and currency.
Language(s): Norwegian
Readership: Read by leaders at companies involved in finance and other interested individuals.
BUSINESS: FINANCE & ECONOMICS

HELGELAND ARBEIDERBLAD
31788R67B-4050

Editorial: 8654 MOSJØEN **Tel:** 75 11 36 00
Fax: 75113630
Email: vaktsjef@helgeland-arbeiderblad.no **Web site:** http://www.helgeland-arbeiderblad.no
Freq: Daily; **Circ:** 8,939
Language(s): Norwegian
ADVERTISING RATES:
SCC .... NOK 104.34
REGIONAL DAILY & SUNDAY NEWSPAPERS: Regional Daily Newspapers

HELGELANDS BLAD; HBLAD.NO
1864644R73-195

Editorial: Postboks 174, 8801 SANDNESSJØEN
Tel: 75 07 03 00 **Fax:** 75 04 39 78
Email: red@hblad.no **Web site:** http://www.hblad.no
Freq: Daily; **Cover Price:** Free; **Circ:** 3,200 Unique Users
Language(s): Norwegian
CONSUMER: NATIONAL & INTERNATIONAL PERIODICALS

HELSENETT.NO
1657773R74G-157

Editorial: Helsenett AS, P.T. Mallingsvei 40d, 0286 OSLO
Email: kontakt@helsenett.no **Web site:** http://www.helsenett.no
Cover Price: Paid
Language(s): Norwegian
CONSUMER: WOMEN'S INTEREST CONSUMER MAGAZINES: Slimming & Health

HELSENYHETER
1938276R56A-228

Web site: http://helsenyheter.blogspot.com
Cover Price: Paid
Language(s): Norwegian
BUSINESS: HEALTH & MEDICAL

HELSESEKRETÆREN
31682R56R-54

Editorial: Norsk Helsesekretærforbund, Pb 9202 Grønland, 0134 OSLO **Tel:** 21 01 36 00
Fax: 21 01 36 60
Email: nhsf@delta.no **Web site:** http://www.nhsf.no
Freq: 6 issues yearly; **Circ:** 3,692
Profile: Journal of the Norwegian Association of Medical Secretaries.
Language(s): Norwegian
Copy instructions: *Copy Date:* 20 days prior to publication date
BUSINESS: HEALTH & MEDICAL: Health Medical Related

HELSETILSYNET
1657605R56R-160

Editorial: Pb. 8128 Dep, 0032 OSLO **Tel:** 21 52 99 00
Fax: 21 52 99 99
Email: nettredaksjonen@helsetilsynet.no **Web site:** http://www.helsetilsynet.no
Cover Price: Paid
Language(s): Norwegian
BUSINESS: HEALTH & MEDICAL: Health Medical Related

HENNE
32139R74B-30

Editorial: Pb. 1169 Sentrum, 0107 OSLO
Tel: 21301000 **Fax:** 21301216
Email: redaksjonen@henne.no **Web site:** http://www.henne.no
Freq: Monthly; **Circ:** 39,318
Profile: Fashion and lifestyle magazine.
Language(s): Norwegian
ADVERTISING RATES:
SCC .... NOK 441.67
CONSUMER: WOMEN'S INTEREST CONSUMER MAGAZINES: Women's Interest - Fashion

HENNE.NO
1810290R73-159

Editorial: Pb. 1169 Sentrum, 0107 OSLO
Tel: 21 30 10 00
Email: nettredaksjonen@henne.no **Web site:** http://www.henne.no
Freq: Daily; **Circ:** 46,600 Unique Users
Editor: Hilde Elisabeth Håve
Language(s): Norwegian
CONSUMER: NATIONAL & INTERNATIONAL PERIODICALS

HERBA
1625071R21A-154

Editorial: Biologisk-dynamisk forening, Skonhovedveien 149, 2318 HAMAR **Tel:** 61 18 44 50
Fax: 61 18 44 51
Email: redaksjon@biodynamisk.no **Web site:** http://www.biodynamisk.no
Freq: Quarterly; **Circ:** 800
Language(s): Norwegian
BUSINESS: AGRICULTURE & FARMING

HERØYNYTT
1660647R45A-75

Editorial: Pb. 187, 6099 FOSNAVÅG **Tel:** 9910 6090
Email: redaksjon@heroynytt.no **Web site:** http://www.heroynytt.no
Cover Price: Paid; **Circ:** 2,500 Unique Users
Language(s): Norwegian
BUSINESS: MARINE & SHIPPING

HESTEGUIDEN.COM
1658788R81D-104

Editorial: Pb. 386 Økern, NO-0513 OSLO
Email: nina@hesteguiden.com **Web site:** http://www.hesteguiden.com
Cover Price: Paid
Language(s): Norwegian
CONSUMER: ANIMALS & PETS: Horses & Ponies

HESTELIV
1803744R81D-106

Editorial: Rakkestadveien 1, 1814 ASKIM
Tel: 69 81 97 00
Email: anja.guerrera@sportmedia.no **Web site:** http://www.sportmedia.no
Freq: 6 issues yearly
Editor: Anja Aarsrud Guerrera
Language(s): Norwegian
CONSUMER: ANIMALS & PETS: Horses & Ponies

HESTESPORT
32637R81D-100

Editorial: Norges Rytterforbund, Serviceboks 1 Ullevål Stadion, 0840 OSLO **Tel:** 21 02 96 50
Fax: 21 02 96 51
Email: redaksjon@hestesport.no **Web site:** http://www.hestesport.no
Date Established: 1962; **Freq:** 6 issues yearly; **Circ:** 17,000
Editor: Anne L. Buvik
Profile: Magazine covering all aspects of equestrian sports.
Language(s): Norwegian
Readership: Aimed at all people interested in horses and riding.
ADVERTISING RATES:
Full Page Colour .... NOK 14150
CONSUMER: ANIMALS & PETS: Horses & Ponies

HEST.NO
1657809R81D-102

Editorial: Klebervn 3, 1540 VETSBY **Tel:** 64 98 51 40
Fax: 64 98 51 49
Email: post@hest.no **Web site:** http://www.hest.no
Cover Price: Paid
Editor: Knut Houge
Language(s): Norwegian
CONSUMER: ANIMALS & PETS: Horses & Ponies

HIFO-NYTT
1740809R62A-236

Editorial: HIFO, AHKR, Postboks 7805, 5020 BERGEN **Tel:** 55 58 32 60 **Fax:** 55 58 96 54

Email: runar.jordaen@ahkr.uib.no **Web site:** http://uit.no/152/5828
Freq: 6 issues yearly
Editor: Runar Jordåen
Language(s): Norwegian
BUSINESS: CHURCH & SCHOOL EQUIPMENT & EDUCATION: Education

HJEM & SKOLE 32155R74D-70
Editorial: PEDLEX Norsk Skoleinformasjon, Postboks 6611, St. Olavs plas, 0129 OSLO **Tel:** 23 35 47 00
Fax: 23 35 47 01
Email: info@lex.no **Web site:** http://www.hjemogskole.no
Date Established: 1985; **Freq:** Quarterly; **Circ:** 8,000
Editor: Kristin Green Nicolaysen
Profile: Magazine containing articles and information about education, learning and child care.
Language(s): Norwegian
Readership: Aimed at parents and teachers.
CONSUMER: WOMEN'S INTEREST CONSUMER MAGAZINES: Child Care

HJEMME-PC 31406R5D-75
Editorial: 0441 OSLO **Tel:** 22585000
Email: hjemmepc@egmonthm.no **Web site:** http://www.hjemmepc.no
Freq: Monthly; **Circ:** 29,670
Profile: Magazine containing information and articles of interest to home PC users.
Language(s): Norwegian
ADVERTISING RATES:
SCC .... NOK 290.83
BUSINESS: COMPUTERS & AUTOMATION: Personal Computers

HJEMME-PC; HJEMMEPC.NO 1864643R5E-10
Editorial: Gullhaugveien 1, 0441 OSLO
Tel: 22 58 50 00
Email: hjemmepc@hm-media.no **Web site:** http://www.hjemmepc.no
Freq: Daily; **Cover Price:** Free; **Circ:** 26,200 Unique Users
Language(s): Norwegian
BUSINESS: COMPUTERS & AUTOMATION: Data Transmission

HJEMMET 32147R74C-40
Editorial: 0441 OSLO **Tel:** 22 58 54 00
Fax: 22 58 05 70
Web site: http://www.klikk.no/hjemmet
Freq: Weekly; **Circ:** 206,543
Editor: Lise Hansen
Profile: Family magazine, includes articles on home decoration, interiors, food, health, fashion and beauty.
Language(s): Norwegian
Readership: Aimed at career women between 25 and 55 years.
ADVERTISING RATES:
SCC .... NOK 662.50
CONSUMER: WOMEN'S INTEREST CONSUMER MAGAZINES: Home & Family

HJEMMETS HOBBY KRYSS 1624417R79F-22
Editorial: Fridtjof Nansensvei 14, 0369 OSLO
Tel: 24 05 13 00
Email: hojara@egmont.no
Freq: Monthly; **Circ:** 25,000
Language(s): Norwegian
CONSUMER: HOBBIES & DIY: Games & Puzzles

HJERTEBARNET 1800785R56A-211
Editorial: Postboks 4535 Nydalen, 0103 OSLO
Tel: 22799450 **Fax:** 22799451
Email: ffhb@ffhb.no **Web site:** http://www.ffhb.no
Freq: Quarterly; **Circ:** 19,500
Editor: Hanni Winsvold Petersen
Language(s): Norwegian
BUSINESS: HEALTH & MEDICAL

HK-NYTT 31531R34-10
Editorial: Pb. 231, Sentrum, 0103 OSLO
Tel: 23 06 33 80 **Fax:** 23 06 11 11
Email: hk-nytt@lo-media.no **Web site:** http://www.hk-nytt.no
Date Established: 1906; **Freq:** Monthly; **Circ:** 61,367
Profile: Magazine covering issues of interest to administrative and office personnel.
Language(s): Norwegian
BUSINESS: OFFICE EQUIPMENT

HMS MAGASINET 1624662R34-31
Editorial: Pb 130, 2261 KIRKENAER **Tel:** 91123330
Email: jan@askmedia.no **Web site:** http://www.hmsmagasinet.no
Freq: 6 issues yearly
Language(s): Norwegian
Copy instructions: *Copy Date:* 14 days prior to publication date
BUSINESS: OFFICE EQUIPMENT

HMT - HELSE MEDISIN TEKNIKK 32445R56A-34
Editorial: Pb 9178 Grønland, 0134 OSLO
Tel: 69308830 **Fax:** 22172508
Email: hmt@amundsen-informasjon.no **Web site:** http://www.helsemedisinteknikk.no
Date Established: 1957; **Freq:** 6 issues yearly
Profile: Journal containing articles, news and information about medical technology and public health. Also covers management, administration and financial issues relating to the medical field.
Language(s): Norwegian
Readership: Read by health and medical professionals, politicians and suppliers of medical equipment.
BUSINESS: HEALTH & MEDICAL

HOLD PUSTEN 31661R56J-20
Editorial: Rådhusgata 4 A, 1051 OSLO
Tel: 23100470 **Fax:** 23100480
Email: firmapost@amundsen-informasjon.no **Web site:** http://www.radiograf.no/modules/module_123/proxy.asp?D=2&C=12&I=58&mids=33
Date Established: 1973; **Freq:** Monthly - 9 ganger i året
Editor: Tone Stidahl
Profile: Publication of the Norwegian Association of Radiographers.
Language(s): Norwegian
BUSINESS: HEALTH & MEDICAL: Radiography

HOLMGANG 1624362R74F-121
Editorial: Pb 451 Madla, 4090 HAFRSFJORD
Tel: 51 55 95 15 **Fax:** 51 55 95 16
Email: bul.stav@gmail.com **Web site:** http://www.bul-stavanger.no
Freq: Quarterly; **Circ:** 350
Language(s): Norwegian
CONSUMER: WOMEN'S INTEREST CONSUMER MAGAZINES: Teenage

HOMØOPATISK TIDSSKRIFT 1692465R56R-170
Editorial: Kjøpmannsgt. 51, 7404 TRONDHEIM
Tel: 235223 07 **Fax:** 73522307
Email: post@nhpf.no **Web site:** http://www.nhpf.no
Freq: Quarterly; **Circ:** 1,800
Language(s): Norwegian
BUSINESS: HEALTH & MEDICAL: Health Medical Related

HORECA 31415R11A-20
Editorial: Pb. 130, 2261 KIRKENÆR **Tel:** 99 52 79 02
Email: morten@askmedia.no **Web site:** http://www.askmedia.no
Freq: Monthly; **Circ:** 5,212
Editor: Morten Holt
Profile: Magazine about catering in business and institutional kitchens.
Language(s): Norwegian
Readership: Read by chefs and executive managers.
ADVERTISING RATES:
SCC .... NOK 137.5
BUSINESS: CATERING: Catering, Hotels & Restaurants

HORECA STORKJØKKEN; HORECANYTT.NO 1864640R74P-209
Editorial: Postboks 130, 2261 KIRKENÆR
Tel: 99 52 79 02
Email: morten@askmedia.no **Web site:** http://www.horecanytt.no
Freq: Daily; **Cover Price:** Free; **Circ:** 2,678 Unique Users
Editor: MORTEN Holt
Language(s): Norwegian
CONSUMER: WOMEN'S INTEREST CONSUMER MAGAZINES: Food & Cookery

HØRELUREN 1624423R94F-102
Editorial: Inkognitogt. 12, 0258 OSLO
Tel: 22 55 73 58
Email: post@hlfoslo.no **Web site:** http://www.hlfoslo.no
Freq: 6 issues yearly; **Circ:** 1,800
Language(s): Norwegian
CONSUMER: OTHER CLASSIFICATIONS: Disability

HOTELL, RESTAURANT & REISELIV 31416R11A-60
Editorial: Øvre Slottsgate 12, 0157 OSLO
Tel: 22 41 71 18 **Fax:** 22 41 71 99
Email: hrr@travelmart.no **Web site:** http://www.hr-r.no
Freq: 6 issues yearly; **Circ:** 3,000
Profile: Magazine about hotels, restaurants, guest houses and fast food.
Language(s): Norwegian
ADVERTISING RATES:
Full Page Colour .... NOK 19000
BUSINESS: CATERING: Catering, Hotels & Restaurants

HOTELL, RESTAURANT & REISELIV; HR-R.NO 1864639R50-156
Editorial: Øvre Slottsgate 12, 0157 OSLO
Tel: 22 41 71 18 **Fax:** 22 41 71 99
Email: hrr@travelmart.no **Web site:** http://www.hr-r.no
Freq: Daily; **Cover Price:** Free; **Circ:** 2,500 Unique Users
Language(s): Norwegian
BUSINESS: TRAVEL & TOURISM

HOTELLMAGASINET; HOTELLMAGASINET.NO 1864637R50-155
Editorial: Byggfakta Docu AS, postboks 1024, 1510 MOSS **Tel:** 69 91 24 00
Email: red@byggfaktamedia.no **Web site:** http://www.hotellmagasinet.no
Freq: Daily; **Cover Price:** Free; **Circ:** 2,500 Unique Users
Language(s): Norwegian
BUSINESS: TRAVEL & TOURISM

HUBRO 31719R62A-200
Editorial: Pb. 7800, 5020 BERGEN **Tel:** 55 58 69 00
Email: hubro@uib.no **Web site:** http://www.hubro.uib.no
Date Established: 1965; **Freq:** Quarterly; **Circ:** 8,750
Editor: Elin F. Styve
Profile: Journal containing articles and information about research at the University of Bergen.
Language(s): Norwegian
Readership: Aimed at teachers, politicians, academics, researchers and the media.
BUSINESS: CHURCH & SCHOOL EQUIPMENT & EDUCATION: Education

HUND & FRITID 625187R81B-53
Editorial: Godtfredsensvei 4, 1617 FREDRIKSTAD
Tel: 92 09 51 22 **Fax:** 69 39 70 11
Email: pal@nkf.as **Web site:** http://www.hundfritid.no
Date Established: 1999; **Freq:** 6 issues yearly; **Circ:** 15,000
Profile: Magazine covering all aspects of training and breeding of working and pet dogs.
Language(s): Norwegian
Readership: Aimed at owners.
CONSUMER: ANIMALS & PETS: Dogs

HUNDEKJØRING 32209R75X-75
Editorial: v/Monica Celius, Skimten Søndre, 2090 Hurdal, 2090 HURDAL **Tel:** 90 98 32 16
Email: post@hundekjoring.no **Web site:** http://www.hundekjoring.no
Freq: Quarterly; **Circ:** 1,100
Editor: Monica Celius
Profile: Magazine containing articles, news and information concerning sled dog racing.
Language(s): Norwegian
CONSUMER: SPORT: Other Sport

HUNDEN VÅR 1624449R81B-201
Editorial: Norges Hunder Landsforbund, Postboks 880, 3007 DRAMMEN
Email: hundenvaar@norgeshunder.no **Web site:** http://www.norgeshunder.no
Freq: 6 issues yearly; **Circ:** 600
Editor: Mari Møller
Language(s): Norwegian
CONSUMER: ANIMALS & PETS: Dogs

HUNDESPORT 32240R81B-50
Editorial: Pb 163 Bryn, 0611 OSLO **Tel:** 21 60 09 00
Fax: 21 60 09 01
Email: hundesport@nkk.no **Web site:** http://www.nkk.no
Date Established: 1900; **Freq:** Monthly; **Circ:** 75,000
Profile: Magazine about dogs and dog-related sports including hunting and racing.
Language(s): Norwegian
ADVERTISING RATES:
Full Page Colour .... NOK 28000
CONSUMER: ANIMALS & PETS: Dogs

HUS & BOLIG 32168R74K-80
Editorial: Fred Olsens Gt. 5, 0152 OSLO
Tel: 22 47 75 00 **Fax:** 22 41 19 90
Email: husogbolig@huseierne.no **Web site:** http://www.huseierne.no/Hus-Bolig
Date Established: 1909; **Freq:** 6 issues yearly; **Circ:** 171,380
Editor: Nina Granlund Sæther
Profile: Magazine containing political and economic news, technical and practical DIY articles and other property news.
Language(s): Norwegian
Readership: Read by housing association members.
ADVERTISING RATES:
Full Page Colour .... NOK 37500
Copy instructions: *Copy Date:* 25 days prior to publication date
CONSUMER: WOMEN'S INTEREST CONSUMER MAGAZINES: Home Purchase

HUSBYGGEREN; HUSBYGGEREN.NO 1657779R74C-63
Editorial: Fagaktuelt AS - Pb. 1, 7701 STEINKJER
Tel: 90 74 67 52
Email: post@husbyggeren.no **Web site:** http://www.husbyggeren.no
Cover Price: Paid; **Circ:** 13,000 Unique Users
Language(s): Norwegian
CONSUMER: WOMEN'S INTEREST CONSUMER MAGAZINES: Home & Family

HUSEIER 1624591R4D-102
Editorial: Øvregaten 21, 5003 BERGEN
Tel: 55 31 69 16 **Fax:** 55234154
Email: info@huseierforening.no **Web site:** http://www.huseierforening.no
Freq: Quarterly; **Circ:** 3,500
Editor: Terje Haahjem Dahl
Language(s): Norwegian
BUSINESS: ARCHITECTURE & BUILDING: Planning & Housing

HUSEIERINFO 1624346R4D-101
Editorial: Norges Huseierforbund, Universitetsgaten 20, 0162 OSLO **Tel:** 22 42 17 90 **Fax:** 22 42 76 51
Email: post@huseierforbundet.no **Web site:** http://www.huseierforbundet.no
Freq: Quarterly; **Circ:** 8,000
Language(s): Norwegian
BUSINESS: ARCHITECTURE & BUILDING: Planning & Housing

HV-BLADET 32444R40-8_60
Editorial: Oslo mil/Akershus festning, 0015 OSLO
Tel: 23 09 81 23 **Fax:** 23 09 81 24
Email: redaktor@hvbladet.no **Web site:** http://www.mil.no/hv/start/aktuelt/HV-bladet
Freq: 6 issues yearly; **Circ:** 80,000
Profile: Military publication concerning voluntary defence services.
Language(s): Norwegian
BUSINESS: DEFENCE

DET HVITE BÅND 1624877R32G-158
Editorial: Torggt. 1, 0181 OSLO **Tel:** 23 21 45 37
Fax: 23 21 45 01
Email: landskontoret@hviteband.no **Web site:** http://www.hviteband.no
Freq: 6 issues yearly
Editor: Brita Nilssen
Language(s): Norwegian
BUSINESS: LOCAL GOVERNMENT, LEISURE & RECREATION: Community Care & Social Services

HVOR HENDER DET? 32646R82-69_50
Editorial: Norsk Utenrikspolitisk Institutt - NUPI, Postboks 8159 Dep., 0033 OSLO **Tel:** 22994000
Fax: 22362182
Email: info@nupi.no **Web site:** http://hvorhenderdet.nupi.no
Date Established: 1962; **Freq:** 26 issues yearly; **Circ:** 4,500
Profile: Journal containing background articles and information concerning international relations and current affairs. Covers analysis of the current political situation within states as well as internationally.
Language(s): Norwegian
Readership: Aimed at students and teachers in high schools, lower grade university students, bureaucrats and other interested people.
CONSUMER: CURRENT AFFAIRS & POLITICS

HYTTA VÅR 1657817R91R-5
Editorial: Sundrev. 81, 3570 ÅL **Tel:** 32 08 21 33
Fax: 32 08 12 65
Email: post@hyttavaar.no **Web site:** http://www.hyttavaar.no
Freq: Quarterly; **Circ:** 22,000
Editor: Christian Snare
Language(s): Norwegian
ADVERTISING RATES:
Full Page Colour .... NOK 19900
CONSUMER: RECREATION & LEISURE: Recreation & Leisure Related

HYTTE INFORMASJON 1625052R4D-104
Editorial: Pb 14 Røa, 0701 OSLO **Tel:** 23 25 32 32
Fax: 22 52 24 80
Email: erik@kobo.no **Web site:** http://www.kobo.no/hytte.html
Freq: Annual; **Circ:** 75,000
Editor: Jan Tangen
Language(s): Norwegian
ADVERTISING RATES:
Full Page Colour .... NOK 40000
BUSINESS: ARCHITECTURE & BUILDING: Planning & Housing

HYTTE & FRITID 1645157R74C-61
Editorial: Arbinsgt. 1, 0253 OSLO **Tel:** 23 27 37 60
Fax: 23 27 37 61
Email: tove@hytteforbund.no **Web site:** http://www.hytteforbund.no

Freq: Quarterly; **Circ:** 3,300
Editor: Tove Helen Selbæk
Language(s): Norwegian
CONSUMER: WOMEN'S INTEREST CONSUMER MAGAZINES: Home & Family

HYTTEAVISEN.NO
1836509R74C-93
Editorial: Edda Vestfold, Postboks 2003, 3103 TØNSBERG **Tel:** 33 37 30 00 **Fax:** 33 37 30 32
Email: post@hytteavisen.no **Web site:** http://www.hytteavisen.no
Freq: Daily
Editor: Jan Erik Hvidsten
Language(s): Norwegian
CONSUMER: WOMEN'S INTEREST CONSUMER MAGAZINES: Home & Family

HYTTELIV
32169R74K-90
Editorial: Hytteliv, 0441 OSLO **Tel:** 22585000
Fax: 22585859
Email: hytteliv@hm-media.no **Web site:** http://www.klikk.no/hytteliv
Date Established: 1971; **Freq:** Monthly; **Circ:** 61,043
Profile: Magazine for the owners of holiday homes and weekend cottages.
Language(s): Norwegian
CONSUMER: WOMEN'S INTEREST CONSUMER MAGAZINES: Home Purchase

I CARE
1645126R82-338
Editorial: Universitetsgata 12, 0164 OSLO
Tel: 22 99 26 00 **Fax:** 22 99 26 01
Email: care@care.no **Web site:** http://www.care.no
Freq: Quarterly; **Circ:** 12,000
Editor: Ida Sem Fossvik
Language(s): Norwegian
CONSUMER: CURRENT AFFAIRS & POLITICS

I FORM
1624471R75L-151
Editorial: Dronningens gt. 28, 0154 OSLO
Tel: 21 44 75 81
Email: eli.stangvik@iform.nu **Web site:** http://www.iform.nu
Freq: Monthly; **Circ:** 29,599
Editor: Eli Stangvik
Language(s): Norwegian
ADVERTISING RATES:
Full Page Colour .... NOK 39000
SCC .... NOK 26.67
CONSUMER: SPORT: Outdoor

I SKOLEN
31725R62J-70
Editorial: Keysersgt 15, 0130 OSLO **Tel:** 23 06 40 00
Fax: 23 06 40 07
Email: sidsel.valum@fagforbundet.no **Web site:** http://www.skoleneslandsforbund.no
Freq: Monthly; **Circ:** 5,750
Profile: Publication of the Norwegian Teachers' Trade Union.
Language(s): Norwegian
BUSINESS: CHURCH & SCHOOL EQUIPMENT & EDUCATION: Teachers & Education Management

I USE THIS
1937965R5E-15
Editorial: Nordaaker Ltd, Lindebergåsen 23b, 1071 OSLO
Email: feedback@iusethis.com **Web site:** http://iphone.iusethis.com
Cover Price: Paid
Language(s): Norwegian
BUSINESS: COMPUTERS & AUTOMATION: Data Transmission

IDG MAGAZINES
1936029R18A-111
Editorial: Postboks 9090 Grønland, 0133 OSLO
Tel: 22053000
Email: idg@kundetjeneste.no **Web site:** http://www.idg.no/omidg
Language(s): Norwegian
BUSINESS: ELECTRONICS

IDG.NO
1810320R5E-3
Editorial: Pb. 9090 Grønland, 0133 OSLO
Tel: 22053000
Email: online@idg.no **Web site:** http://www.idg.no
Freq: Daily
Editor: Morten Kristiansen
Language(s): Norwegian
BUSINESS: COMPUTERS & AUTOMATION: Data Transmission

IDRETT & ANLEGG
31513R32D-20
Editorial: SPORTMEDIA AS, Rakkestadveien 1, 1814 ASKIM **Tel:** 69 81 97 00 **Fax:** 69889433
Email: harald.aase@sportmedia.no **Web site:** http://www.sportmedia.no
Date Established: 1988; **Freq:** 6 issues yearly; **Circ:** 3,000
Profile: Magazine about the construction, maintenance and equipping of sports and leisure centres, stadiums, tracks and golf clubs.
Language(s): Norwegian
BUSINESS: LOCAL GOVERNMENT, LEISURE & RECREATION: Parks

IFORM.NO
1658786R75P-2
Editorial: Trim.no AS, 6789 LOEN **Tel:** 913 85 926
Email: redaksjonen@trim.no **Web site:** http://www.iform.no
Cover Price: Paid; **Circ:** 1,000,000 Unique Users
Editor: Geir Tverdal
Language(s): Norwegian
CONSUMER: SPORT: Fitness/Bodybuilding

ILLUSTRERT VITENSKAP
707398R94X-110
Editorial: Sandakerveien 24d, 0473 OSLO
Tel: 23232200 **Fax:** 22421595
Email: ane.thurid.brudi@eunet.no **Web site:** http://www.illustrertvitenskap.com
Date Established: 1984; **Freq:** Monthly; **Circ:** 76,113
Editor: Ane Thurid Brudi
Profile: Magazine covering popular science subjects, such as medicine, astronomy, archaeology, anthropology, biology and geography.
Language(s): Norwegian
Readership: Read by all those with an interest in learning about everything that surrounds us.
CONSUMER: OTHER CLASSIFICATIONS: Miscellaneous

IMPULS-TIDSSKRIFT FOR PSYKOLOGI
31671R56N-10
Editorial: Pb 1094 Blindern, 0317 OSLO
Tel: 22845030
Email: redimpuls@psykologi.uio.no **Web site:** http://www.psykologi.uio.no/studentliv/foreninger/impuls
Date Established: 1950; **Freq:** Half-yearly; **Circ:** 1,000
Profile: Magazine containing articles, news and information about psychology.
Language(s): Norwegian
Readership: Aimed at medical students and psychologists.
BUSINESS: HEALTH & MEDICAL: Mental Health

INDRE AKERSHUS BLAD
31754R67B-4100
Editorial: Pb. 68, 1941 BJØRKELANGEN
Tel: 63 85 48 00 **Fax:** 63855590
Email: redaksjon@iablad.no **Web site:** http://www.indre.no
Date Established: 1909; **Freq:** 104 issues yearly - Norway; **Circ:** 7,457
Language(s): Norwegian
ADVERTISING RATES:
Full Page Colour .... NOK 17598
SCC .... NOK 175.98
REGIONAL DAILY & SUNDAY NEWSPAPERS: Regional Daily Newspapers

INDUSTRIEN
1666591R19A-102
Editorial: Postboks 5844, Majorstuen, 0308 OSLO
Tel: 95749469 **Fax:** 23199301
Email: hugo.ryvik@tu.no **Web site:** http://www.prosessindustrien.no
Freq: Monthly - 10 ganger i året; **Circ:** 5,091
Language(s): Norwegian
ADVERTISING RATES:
SCC .... NOK 125
BUSINESS: ENGINEERING & MACHINERY

INDUSTRIEN
1852270R27-52
Editorial: Postboks 5844, Majorstuen, 0308 OSLO
Tel: 90868254 **Fax:** 23199301
Email: anders.steensen@industrien.no **Web site:** http://www.industrien.no
Freq: Monthly - 10 ganger i året; **Circ:** 8,115
Editor: Anders J. Steensen
Language(s): Norwegian
ADVERTISING RATES:
Full Page Colour .... NOK 24500
BUSINESS: METAL, IRON & STEEL

INGENIØRNYTT
31455R19A-20
Editorial: Pb. 164, 1332 ØSTERÅS **Tel:** 67 16 34 99
Fax: 67 16 34 55
Email: redaksjonen@ingeniornytt.no **Web site:** http://www.ingeniornytt.no
Freq: Monthly; **Circ:** 55,000
Profile: Tabloid-sized newspaper covering technical and industrial news, and including interviews, articles on product and process development, financial surveys and feature articles on specific technical and engineering subjects.
Language(s): Norwegian
ADVERTISING RATES:
Full Page Colour .... NOK 28000
SCC .... NOK 333.33
Copy instructions: *Copy Date:* 12 days prior to publication date
BUSINESS: ENGINEERING & MACHINERY

INGENIØRNYTT; INGENIORNYTT.NO
1864634R19A-104
Editorial: Postboks 164, 1332 ØSTERÅS
Tel: 67 16 34 99 **Fax:** 67163455
Email: redaksjonen@ingeniornytt.no **Web site:** http://www.ingeniornytt.no
Freq: Daily; **Cover Price:** Free; **Circ:** 22,173 Unique Users
Language(s): Norwegian
BUSINESS: ENGINEERING & MACHINERY

INNSIKT
2010146R56A-230
Editorial: Oslo universitetssykehus HF, Ullevål, Postboks 4956 Nydalen, 0424 NYDALEN
Tel: 23016030
Email: redaksjon@innsikt.org **Web site:** http://www.innsikt.org
Circ: 3,500
Language(s): Norwegian
BUSINESS: HEALTH & MEDICAL

IN-PUBLISH
31554R41A-15
Editorial: Pb. 524, 1401 SKI **Tel:** 22 20 80 90
Email: news@in-publish.no **Web site:** http://www.in-publish.no
Date Established: 1988; **Freq:** Monthly; **Circ:** 3,000
Profile: Magazine covering graphics, printing, publishing and repro-scanning.
Language(s): Norwegian
Readership: Aimed at publishers, printers and graphic designers.
ADVERTISING RATES:
SCC .... NOK 132.5
BUSINESS: PRINTING & STATIONERY: Printing

IN-PUBLISH.NO
1625198R41A-77
Editorial: Pb. 524, 1401 SKI **Tel:** 22208090
Email: news@in-publish.no **Web site:** http://www.in-publish.no
Freq: Weekly; **Circ:** 2,500 Unique Users
Language(s): Norwegian
BUSINESS: PRINTING & STATIONERY: Printing

INSEKT-NYTT
32325R88A-20
Editorial: Pb 386, 4002 STAVANGER **Tel:** 994 50 917
Email: insektnytt@gmail.com **Web site:** http://www.entomologi.no
Date Established: 1975; **Freq:** Quarterly; **Circ:** 1,000
Editor: Anders Endrestøl
Profile: Journal containing articles and information about entomology.
Language(s): Norwegian
Readership: Aimed at entomologists and people interested in zoology and related topics.
CONSUMER: EDUCATION

INSIDE 24 - STUDENTAVISEN PÅ BI
32357R91D-30
Editorial: Nydalsveien 15, 0484 OSLO
Tel: 464 10 931
Email: inside24@inside24.no **Web site:** http://www.inside24.no
Freq: 6 issues yearly; **Circ:** 11,000
Profile: Magazine containing articles and information of interest to girls aged between 15 and 20 years old.
Language(s): Norwegian
CONSUMER: RECREATION & LEISURE: Children & Youth

INSPIRASJON
1624621R4B-1
Editorial: Hamang terrasse 63, 1336 SANDVIKA
Tel: 67554680 **Fax:** 67554681
Email: ifi@ifi.no **Web site:** http://www.ifi.no
Freq: Half-yearly - 2 ganger i året; **Circ:** 300,000
Editor: Kristian Owren
Language(s): Norwegian
ADVERTISING RATES:
Full Page Colour .... NOK 65940
Copy instructions: *Copy Date:* 30 days prior to publication date
BUSINESS: ARCHITECTURE & BUILDING: Interior Design & Flooring

INTERIØR MAGASINET
32148R74C-41_50
Editorial: Pb. 724 Skøyen, 0377 OSLO
Tel: 23296516 **Fax:** 23296543
Web site: http://www.hegnar.no/publikasjoner/interior
Freq: 6 issues yearly; **Circ:** 65,000
Profile: Magazine about homes and interiors.
Language(s): Norwegian
ADVERTISING RATES:
Full Page Colour .... NOK 42000
SCC .... NOK 329.17
CONSUMER: WOMEN'S INTEREST CONSUMER MAGAZINES: Home & Family

INTERIØRMAGASINET MAISON
1624796R74C-56
Editorial: Pb 6974, St.Olavs Plass, 0130 OSLO
Tel: 24 14 69 40
Email: redaksjonen@maison.no **Web site:** http://www.maison.no
Freq: 6 issues yearly; **Circ:** 27,780
Language(s): Norwegian
CONSUMER: WOMEN'S INTEREST CONSUMER MAGAZINES: Home & Family

INTERNASJONAL POLITIKK
32258R82-70
Editorial: Pb 8159 Dep, 0033 OSLO **Tel:** 22994000
Email: ip@nupi.no **Web site:** http://www.nupi.no/publikasjoner/tidsskrifter/internasjonal_politikk
Date Established: 1937; **Freq:** Quarterly; **Circ:** 1,800
Editor: Benjamin de Carvalho
Profile: Magazine containing information and articles about international current affairs and politics.
Language(s): Norwegian
Readership: Read by academics, media workers, decision makers and the interested public at large.
CONSUMER: CURRENT AFFAIRS & POLITICS

INTRAFISH.NO
1625225R22G-5
Editorial: Bontelabo 2, 5003 BERGEN
Tel: 55 21 33 00 **Fax:** 55 21 33 40
Email: redaksjonen@intrafish.com **Web site:** http://www.intrafish.no
Cover Price: Paid
Language(s): Norwegian
BUSINESS: FOOD: Fish Trade

ISF SAMMENDRAG
1660720R32G-163
Editorial: Pb. 3233 Elisenberg, 0208 OSLO
Tel: 23 08 61 00 **Fax:** 23 08 61 01
Email: isf-info@samfunnsforskning.no **Web site:** http://www.samfunnsforskning.no/nor/Tidsskrifter/ISF-Sammendrag
Freq: Quarterly
Editor: Johanne Severinsen
Language(s): Norwegian
BUSINESS: LOCAL GOVERNMENT, LEISURE & RECREATION: Community Care & Social Services

ITAVISEN.NO
1625027R5D-77
Editorial: Stenersgt 2-8, 0184 OSLO **Tel:** 4060 1080
Fax: 2340 7301
Email: red@itavisen.no **Web site:** http://www.itavisen.no
Circ: 597,298 Unique Users
Editor: Tore Neset
Language(s): Norwegian
BUSINESS: COMPUTERS & AUTOMATION: Personal Computers

IT-BRANSJEN
1625042R5C-53
Editorial: IDG Magazines Norge AS, Pb 9090 Grønland, 0133 OSLO **Tel:** 22 05 30 20
Fax: 22 05 30 21
Email: charles.williamsen@idg.no **Web site:** http://www.idg.no/itbransjen
Freq: Monthly; **Circ:** 10,000
Editor: Charles Williamsen
Language(s): Norwegian
ADVERTISING RATES:
Full Page Colour .... NOK 51700
SCC .... NOK 365
BUSINESS: COMPUTERS & AUTOMATION: Professional Personal Computers

IT-BRANSJEN - NETT
1936030R18A-112
Editorial: IDG Magazines Norge AS, Pb 9090 Grønland, 0133 OSLO **Tel:** 22 05 30 21
Fax: 22 05 30 20
Email: charles.williamsen@idg.no **Web site:** http://www.idg.no/itbransjen
Cover Price: Paid
Language(s): Norwegian
BUSINESS: ELECTRONICS

IT-KARRIERE
1625219R5D-78
Editorial: Pb 9090 Grønland, 0133 OSLO
Tel: 22053000
Email: nard@idg.no **Web site:** http://www.idg.no/computerworld/karriere
Freq: 6 issues yearly; **Circ:** 27,500
Editor: Nard Schreurs
Language(s): Norwegian
ADVERTISING RATES:
Full Page Colour .... NOK 39000
BUSINESS: COMPUTERS & AUTOMATION: Personal Computers

ITPRO.NO
1657597R5F-7
Editorial: Tormods gate 3b, 7030 TRONDHEIM
Tel: 46446624
Email: red@itpro.no **Web site:** http://itpro.no
Circ: 32,500 Unique Users
Language(s): Norwegian
BUSINESS: COMPUTERS & AUTOMATION: Multimedia

ITROMSØ; SPORTEN
2010597R75A-246
Editorial: Pb. 1028, Strandveien 144, 9620 TROMSØ
Tel: 77 64 06 00 **Fax:** 77 64 06 01
Email: sporten@itromso.no **Web site:** http://itromso.no
Circ: 9,858
Language(s): Norwegian
CONSUMER: SPORT

ITRO.NO
1814185R73-170
Editorial: Sinsenveien 25, 0572 OSLO
Tel: 22 00 72 00 **Fax:** 22 00 72 03
Email: itro@nlm.no **Web site:** http://www.dittparadis.no
Cover Price: Paid; **Circ:** 2,200 Unique Users
Language(s): Norwegian
CONSUMER: NATIONAL & INTERNATIONAL PERIODICALS

JAKT & FISKE
32370R92-50
Editorial: Hvalstadåsen 5, Postboks 94, 1378 OSLO
Tel: 66 79 22 00 **Fax:** 66 90 15 87
Email: jaktogfiske@njff.org **Web site:** http://www.jaktogfiske.info
Freq: Monthly; **Circ:** 88,377
Editor: Leif Øystein Haug
Profile: Magazine published by the Norwegian Hunting and Fishing Association containing articles, news, information, practical advice and interviews. Also covers equipment and product tests.
Language(s): Norwegian
Readership: Aimed at people interested in hunting, fishing, wildlife and outdoor activities.
CONSUMER: ANGLING & FISHING

JARLSBERG AVIS; JARLSBERGAVIS.NO
1864642R73-189
Editorial: Postboks 303, 3081 HOLMESTRAND
Tel: 33 09 90 00
Email: redaksjonen@jarlsbergavis.no **Web site:** http://www.jarlsbergavis.no
Freq: Daily; **Cover Price:** Free; **Circ:** 2,200 Unique Users
Language(s): Norwegian
CONSUMER: NATIONAL & INTERNATIONAL PERIODICALS

JAZZNYTT
32215R76D-75
Editorial: Pb. 440, Sentrum, 0103 OSLO
Tel: 22 00 56 66
Email: jan@jazzforum.no **Web site:** http://jazznytt.no
Date Established: 1965; **Freq:** 6 issues yearly; **Circ:** 5,000
Profile: Magazine containing articles, news, information, reviews and events.
Language(s): Norwegian
Readership: Read by jazz lovers.
CONSUMER: MUSIC & PERFORMING ARTS: Music

JEGER, HUND & VÅPEN
32655R75F-100
Editorial: Pb. 1164 Sentrum, 0107 OSLO
Tel: 22 91 22 22 **Fax:** 22 91 21 24
Email: kvp@jeger.no **Web site:** http://www.jeger.no
Date Established: 1996; **Freq:** Monthly; **Circ:** 18,384
Profile: Magazine covering all aspects of hunting. Contains articles on hunting dogs, weapons and wildlife.
Language(s): Norwegian
Readership: Aimed at hunters and owners of hunting dogs.
CONSUMER: SPORT: Shooting

JENTER I SKOGBRUKET
1645130R46-103
Editorial: Serviceboks 606, 4809 ARENDAL
Tel: 37 01 75 17
Email: jis@fmaa.no **Web site:** http://www.jenteriskogbruket.no
Freq: Quarterly; **Circ:** 800
Language(s): Norwegian
BUSINESS: TIMBER, WOOD & FORESTRY

JOURNALISTEN
31368R2B-15
Editorial: Pb 8793 Youngstorget, 0028 OSLO
Tel: 4000 4888
Email: journalisten@journalisten.no **Web site:** http://www.journalisten.no
Freq: 26 issues yearly; **Circ:** 10,380
Profile: Magazine for editors and journalists.
Language(s): Norwegian
ADVERTISING RATES:
Full Page Colour .... NOK 25000
SCC .... NOK 191.67
BUSINESS: COMMUNICATIONS, ADVERTISING & MARKETING: Press

JOURNALISTEN; JOURNALISTEN.NO
1864636R2E-106
Editorial: Postboks 8793 Youngstorget, 0028 OSLO
Tel: 4000 4888
Email: journalisten@journalisten.no **Web site:** http://www.journalisten.no
Freq: Daily; **Cover Price:** Free; **Circ:** 5,480 Unique Users
Language(s): Norwegian
BUSINESS: COMMUNICATIONS, ADVERTISING & MARKETING: Public Relations

JURISTKONTAKT
31563R44-40
Editorial: Juristenes Hus, K. Augustsgate 9, 0164 OSLO **Tel:** 22 03 50 50 **Fax:** 22 03 50 30
Email: omg@jus.no **Web site:** http://www.juristkontakt.no
Freq: 6 issues yearly; **Circ:** 15,451
Profile: Journal of the Norwegian Lawyers' Association.
Language(s): Norwegian
BUSINESS: LEGAL

KABB-NYTT
1624946R94F-110
Editorial: Pb 333, 1802 ASKIM **Tel:** 69 81 69 81
Fax: 69 88 57 66
Email: turid.kind.ekroll@kabb.no **Web site:** http://www.kabb.no/publikasjoner/kabbnytt
Freq: 6 issues yearly; **Circ:** 7,300
Language(s): Norwegian
CONSUMER: OTHER CLASSIFICATIONS: Disability

KAMILLE
1740813R74B-70
Editorial: Hjemmet Mortensen A/S, 0441 OSLO
Tel: 22585800 **Fax:** 22580585
Email: kjersti.mo@egmonthm.no **Web site:** http://www.kamille.no
Freq: 26 issues yearly; **Circ:** 46,213
Language(s): Norwegian
ADVERTISING RATES:
SCC .... NOK 341.67
CONSUMER: WOMEN'S INTEREST CONSUMER MAGAZINES: Women's Interest - Fashion

KAMILLE.NO
1837514R74A-75
Editorial: Hjemmet Mortensen A/S, 0441 OSLO
Tel: 22 58 50 00
Email: kamille@hm-media.no **Web site:** http://www.kamille.no
Freq: Daily; **Cover Price:** Paid; **Circ:** 3,600 Unique Users
Language(s): Norwegian
ADVERTISING RATES:
SCC .... NOK 68.4
CONSUMER: WOMEN'S INTEREST CONSUMER MAGAZINES: Women's Interest

KAMPANJE
31365R2A-5
Editorial: Kampanje Forlag AS, Prinsens gate 22, 0157 OSLO **Tel:** 22 33 31 00
Email: kampanje@kampanje.com **Web site:** http://www.kampanje.com
Freq: Monthly; **Circ:** 7,445
Profile: Publication about marketing, media, sales and administration.
Language(s): Norwegian
ADVERTISING RATES:
SCC .... NOK 220.83
BUSINESS: COMMUNICATIONS, ADVERTISING & MARKETING

KAMPANJE.COM
1625170R2E-102
Editorial: Prinsens gate 22, 0157 OSLO
Tel: 22 33 31 00
Email: kampanje@kampanje.com **Web site:** http://www.kampanje.com
Freq: Daily
Language(s): Norwegian
BUSINESS: COMMUNICATIONS, ADVERTISING & MARKETING: Public Relations

KAPITAL
31343R1A-90
Editorial: Pb 724 Skøyen, 0377 OSLO
Tel: 23 29 65 50 **Fax:** 23 29 65 51
Web site: http://www.hegnar.no
Freq: 26 issues yearly; **Circ:** 38,000
Profile: Journal about financial business management.
Language(s): Norwegian
Copy instructions: *Copy Date:* 9 days prior to publication date
BUSINESS: FINANCE & ECONOMICS

KARMØYBLADET; KARMOYBLADET.NO
1864702R73-206
Editorial: Strandaveien 9, 4296 ÅKREHAMN
Tel: 52 81 80 00
Email: red@karmoybladet.no **Web site:** http://www.karmoybladet.no
Freq: Daily; **Cover Price:** Free; **Circ:** 335 Unique Users
Language(s): Norwegian
CONSUMER: NATIONAL & INTERNATIONAL PERIODICALS

KARRIEREMAGASINET KALEIDOSKOPET
1692461R62A-222
Editorial: Markveien 55, 1337 SANDVIKA
Tel: 67 57 53 00
Email: post@kaleidoskopet.no **Web site:** http://www.karrieremagasinet.no
Freq: Half-yearly; **Circ:** 40,000
Language(s): Norwegian
BUSINESS: CHURCH & SCHOOL EQUIPMENT & EDUCATION: Education

KART OG PLAN
31384R4D-60
Editorial: Institutt for matematiske realfag og teknologi, Pb 5003, 1432 ÅS **Tel:** 64 96 54 72
Fax: 64 96 54 01
Email: inge.revhaug@umb.no **Web site:** http://njkf.no/kart-og-plan
Date Established: 1908; **Freq:** Quarterly; **Circ:** 3,300
Profile: European journal published by The Norwegian Association of Chartered Surveyors and GeoForum covering mapping sciences, land use planning and law, geodesy, photogrammetry and hydrography.
Language(s): Norwegian
BUSINESS: ARCHITECTURE & BUILDING: Planning & Housing

KF UKESLUTT
1624660R2E-103
Editorial: Fredensborgvn. 24 M, 0177 OSLO
Tel: 22 03 30 00 **Fax:** 22 03 30 01
Email: redaksjonen@kreativtforum.no **Web site:** http://www.kreativt-forum.no
Circ: 1,400
Language(s): Norwegian
BUSINESS: COMMUNICATIONS, ADVERTISING & MARKETING: Public Relations

KILDEN - INFORMASJONSSENTER FOR KJØNNSFORSKNING
1971359R74A-81
Tel: 22 03 80 80
Email: post@kilden.forskningsradet.no
Cover Price: Paid
Language(s): Norwegian
CONSUMER: WOMEN'S INTEREST CONSUMER MAGAZINES: Women's Interest

KINA OG VI
32259R82-73
Editorial: Pb 320, 1301 SANDVIKA **Tel:** 22382243
Fax: 22382243
Email: norge.kina@gmail.com **Web site:** http://home.online.no/~rolf.odd
Date Established: 1952; **Freq:** Quarterly; **Circ:** 600
Profile: Magazine covering international relations in general and the relation between Norway and China in particular. Contains articles and information about politics, current affairs and culture.
Language(s): Norwegian
Readership: Read by people interested in China.
CONSUMER: CURRENT AFFAIRS & POLITICS

KIRKEAKTUELT
32310R87-60
Editorial: Pb. 799 Sentrum, 0106 OSLO
Tel: 23 08 12 00 **Fax:** 23 08 12 01
Email: post.kirkeradet@kirken.no **Web site:** http://www.kirken.no
Freq: Quarterly; **Circ:** 19,000
Editor: Vidar Kristensen
Profile: Magazine about all aspects of church life in Norway.
Language(s): Norwegian
CONSUMER: RELIGIOUS

KIRKEGÅRDEN
1645095R94J-1
Editorial: Neslandsvatn, 3750 DRANGEDAL
Tel: 35 99 45 74 **Fax:** 35 99 45 73
Email: kirkegaarden@kirkegaardskultur.no **Web site:** http://www.kirkegaardskultur.no
Freq: Quarterly; **Circ:** 1,300
Language(s): Norwegian
CONSUMER: OTHER CLASSIFICATIONS: Popular Science

KIRKENS NØDHJELP MAGASINET
1624430R40-30
Editorial: Pb 7100, St.Olavs Plass, 0130 OSLO
Tel: 22092700 **Fax:** 22092720
Email: nca-oslo@nca.no **Web site:** http://www.kirkensnodhjelp.no
Freq: Quarterly; **Circ:** 80,000
Editor: Unni Grevestad
Language(s): Norwegian
BUSINESS: DEFENCE

KITE.NO
1659354R75X-94
Editorial: Fluid Net AS, Kirkeveien 157, 0451 OSLO
Email: mail@fluid.no **Web site:** http://www.kite.no
Cover Price: Paid; **Circ:** 10,000 Unique Users
Editor: Morten Gjerstad
Language(s): Norwegian
CONSUMER: SPORT: Other Sport

KJÆLEDYRBLADET
32245R81X-25
Editorial: Klæbuveien 196 B, 2etg, 7037 TRONDHEIM **Tel:** 98 29 71 00 **Fax:** 73 95 17 55
Email: sverre@tropegruppen.no **Web site:** http://www.tropehagen-zoo.no/comweb.asp?ID=9&segment=1
Freq: 6 issues yearly; **Circ:** 30,000
Profile: Magazine covering all aspects of interest to pet owners.
Language(s): Norwegian
CONSUMER: ANIMALS & PETS

KJEDEMAGASINET
1840547R53-18
Editorial: Vestre Rosten 78, 7075 TILLER
Tel: 72450095
Email: redaksjon@kjedemagasinet.no **Web site:** http://www.kjedemagasinet.no
Freq: Monthly - 11 ganger i året; **Circ:** 4,000
Language(s): Norwegian
ADVERTISING RATES:
SCC .... NOK 114.58
BUSINESS: RETAILING & WHOLESALING

KJEMI
31423R13-40
Editorial: Media Oslo AS, Boks 119 Manglerud, 0612 OSLO **Tel:** 23 15 85 00
Email: kjemi@online.no **Web site:** http://www.kjemi.com
Date Established: 1940; **Freq:** Monthly; **Circ:** 3,000
Profile: Journal covering the chemical industry.
Language(s): Norwegian
Readership: Read by graduate engineers and scientists within management, production, consulting, research and development.
BUSINESS: CHEMICALS

KJETIL LØSET - I MAKTENS KORRIDORER
1995104R82-494
Email: kjetilloset@tv2blogg.no **Web site:** http://kjetilloset.tv2blogg.no
Cover Price: Paid
Language(s): Norwegian
CONSUMER: CURRENT AFFAIRS & POLITICS

KJØKKENSJEFEN
31418R11A-65
Editorial: Norges Kokkemesteres Landsforening, Pb 8034, 4068 STAVANGER **Tel:** 51 83 37 95
Email: post@nkl.no **Web site:** http://www.norgeskokker.no
Date Established: 1925; **Freq:** 6 issues yearly; **Circ:** 2,500
Profile: Magazine of the Norwegian Association of Master Chefs.
Language(s): Norwegian
Readership: Read by all professionals within the food and catering industry.
BUSINESS: CATERING: Catering, Hotels & Restaurants

KJØKKENSKRIVEREN
31419R11A-66
Editorial: Kost- og ernæringsforbundet, Pb 9202 Grønland, 0134 OSLO **Tel:** 21013600
Email: elisabeth.strom@delta.no **Web site:** http://www.kjokkenskriveren.no
Date Established: 1962; **Freq:** 6 issues yearly; **Circ:** 2,497
Editor: Elisabeth Strøm
Profile: Magazine giving general information about the food sector as well as specific information for the institutional catering sector.
Language(s): Norwegian
Readership: Read by chefs, cooks and others within institutional catering.
BUSINESS: CATERING: Catering, Hotels & Restaurants

KJØTTBRANSJEN
31488R22D-10
Editorial: Fred Olsens gate 5, 0152 OSLO
Tel: 23244470 **Fax:** 23244480
Email: pas@kjottbransjen.no **Web site:** http://www.kjottbransjen.no
Freq: Monthly; **Circ:** 3,928
Profile: Official magazine of the Norwegian Independent Meat Association.
Language(s): Norwegian
BUSINESS: FOOD: Meat Trade

KK
32135R74A-12
Editorial: Pb. 1169 Sentrum, 0107 OSLO
Tel: 21 30 10 00 **Fax:** 21301206
Email: redaksjonen@kk.no **Web site:** http://www.kk.no
Freq: Weekly; **Circ:** 71,297
Editor: Hilde Beate Berg
Profile: Magazine for women aged between 20 and 49 years old.
Language(s): Norwegian
CONSUMER: WOMEN'S INTEREST CONSUMER MAGAZINES: Women's Interest

KLASSISK MUSIKKMAGASIN
1645155R76D-277
Editorial: Pb. 11, 3201 SANDEFJORD
Tel: 33 42 15 75

Email: klassisk@mezzomedia.no Web site: http://www.mezzomedia.no
Language(s): Norwegian
CONSUMER: MUSIC & PERFORMING ARTS: Music

KLATRING 1645139R75J-101
Editorial: Fri Flyt AS, Mølleparken 6, 0459 OSLO
Tel: 22 04 06 00 Fax: 22 04 06 09
Email: post@norsk-klatring.no Web site: http://www.norsk-klatring.no
Freq: 6 issues yearly; Circ: 4,692
Language(s): Norwegian
ADVERTISING RATES:
Full Page Colour .... NOK 15500
CONSUMER: SPORT: Athletics

KLIKK.NO 1895543R74C-96
Editorial: Gullhaugveien 1, 0441 OSLO
Tel: 22 58 50 00
Email: jan.thoresen@egmonthm.no Web site: http://www.klikk.no
Freq: Daily; Cover Price: Paid
Language(s): Norwegian
CONSUMER: WOMEN'S INTEREST CONSUMER MAGAZINES: Home & Family

KLIMA 1819078R14A-230
Editorial: CICERO Senter for klimaforskning, Pb. 1129 Blindern, 0318 OSLO Tel: 22858750
Fax: 22858751
Email: admin@cicero.uio.no Web site: http://www.cicero.uio.no/klima
Freq: 6 issues yearly; Circ: 6,000
Language(s): Norwegian
BUSINESS: COMMERCE, INDUSTRY & MANAGEMENT

KLIMAKLUBBEN.NO 1859771R57-311
Editorial: Grensen 9B, 0159 OSLO Tel: 23 10 95 50
Fax: 23 10 95 51
Email: post@gronnhverdag.no Web site: http://www.klimaklubben.no
Freq: Daily
Editor: Håkon Mella
Language(s): Norwegian
BUSINESS: ENVIRONMENT & POLLUTION

KNUTEPUNKT 1800786R45A-76
Editorial: Postboks 6479, Tonstad, 7497 TRONDHEIM Tel: 40 85 29 14
Email: knutepunkt@dbpartner.no Web site: http://www.knutepunkt.no
Freq: Monthly; Circ: 3,500
Language(s): Norwegian
BUSINESS: MARINE & SHIPPING

KOLONIHAGEN 32662R89A-90
Editorial: Møllerveien 2, 0182 OSLO Tel: 22 11 00 90
Email: forbundet@kolonihager.no Web site: http://www.kolonihager.no
Freq: Quarterly; Circ: 5,000
Profile: Magazine containing information on holiday and summer homes.
Language(s): Norwegian
CONSUMER: HOLIDAYS & TRAVEL: Travel

KOMMUNAL ØKONOMI 1624454R1A-117
Editorial: NKK Kommunaløkonomisk forlag, Henrik Ibsensgt. 20, 0255 OSLO Tel: 22 94 76 93
Email: asbjorn.o.pedersen@nkkf.no Web site: http://www.nkkf.no
Freq: Monthly; Circ: 1,800
Language(s): Norwegian
BUSINESS: FINANCE & ECONOMICS

KOMMUNAL RAPPORT 31505R32A-45
Editorial: Pb. 1940 Vika, 0125 OSLO Tel: 24 13 64 50
Fax: 22 83 23 72
Email: redaksjon@kommunal-rapport.no Web site: http://www.kommunal-rapport.no
Freq: Weekly; Circ: 11,551
Editor: Ragnhild Sved
Profile: Newspaper of the Association of Municipal Administration.
Language(s): Norwegian
ADVERTISING RATES:
Full Page Colour .... NOK 37000
SCC .... NOK 282.92
BUSINESS: LOCAL GOVERNMENT, LEISURE & RECREATION: Local Government

KOMMUNAL RAPPORT; KOMMUNAL-RAPPORT.NO 1864703R32A-159
Editorial: Postboks 1940 Vika, 0125 OSLO
Tel: 24 13 64 50 Fax: 22 83 23 72
Email: redaksjon@kommunal-rapport.no Web site: http://www.kommunal-rapport.no
Freq: Daily; Cover Price: Free; Circ: 27,400 Unique Users
Editor: Ragnhild Sved
Language(s): Norwegian
BUSINESS: LOCAL GOVERNMENT, LEISURE & RECREATION: Local Government

KOMMUNALTEKNIKK 31506R32A-48
Editorial: Norsk Kommunalteknisk Forening, Pb. 1905 Vika, 0124 OSLO Tel: 22 04 81 40
Fax: 22 04 81 49
Email: astrid.oygard@kommunalteknikk.no Web site: http://www.kommunalteknikk.no
Freq: Monthly; Circ: 7,100
Editor: Astrid Øygard
Profile: Publication for engineers and architects involved in community and municipal maintenance work.
Language(s): Norwegian
ADVERTISING RATES:
Full Page Colour .... NOK 15900
BUSINESS: LOCAL GOVERNMENT, LEISURE & RECREATION: Local Government

KOMMUNEREVISOREN 32457R1B-50
Editorial: Trondheim Kommunerevisjon, 7004 TRONDHEIM
Email: per-olav.nilsen@trondheim.kommune.no Web site: http://tidsskrift.nkrf.prosjektweb.net/siste
Freq: 6 issues yearly; Circ: 3,300
Profile: Magazine containing articles, news and information concerning accountancy.
Language(s): Norwegian
Readership: Read by accountants and financial executives.
BUSINESS: FINANCE & ECONOMICS: Accountancy

KOMMUNIKASJON 32449R2E-100
Editorial: Norsk kommunikasjonsforening, Postboks 333 Sentrum, 0153 OSLO Tel: 23315900
Fax: 23315909
Email: post@kommunikasjon.no Web site: http://www.kommunikasjon.no
Freq: 6 issues yearly; Circ: 3,100
Profile: Magazine concerning the PR and communication sector.
Language(s): Norwegian
Readership: Aimed at PR and communication professionals.
ADVERTISING RATES:
SCC .... NOK 71.67
BUSINESS: COMMUNICATIONS, ADVERTISING & MARKETING: Public Relations

KOMMUNIKÉ 31507R32A-50
Editorial: Postboks 9202 Grønland, 0134 OSLO
Tel: 21 01 36 00 Fax: 21 01 36 50
Email: post@delta.no Web site: http://www.kommunike.no
Date Established: 1948; Freq: 6 issues yearly; Circ: 62,064
Profile: Journal for municipal employees.
Language(s): Norwegian
BUSINESS: LOCAL GOVERNMENT, LEISURE & RECREATION: Local Government

KOMMUNIKÉ; KOMMUNIKE.NO 1977750R32A-163
Editorial: Postboks 9202 Grønland, 0134 OSLO
Tel: 21 01 36 00 Fax: 21 01 36 50
Email: audun.hopland@kfo.no Web site: http://www.kommunike.no
Freq: Daily; Cover Price: Paid
Language(s): Norwegian
BUSINESS: LOCAL GOVERNMENT, LEISURE & RECREATION: Local Government

KOMPUTER FOR ALLE 1624620R5D-76
Editorial: Komputer for alle, Kirkegaten 20, 0153 OSLO Tel: 23068705 Fax: 23068730
Email: red@komputer.no Web site: http://www.komputer.no
Freq: 18 ganger i året; Circ: 16,159
Editor: Atle Bjørge
Language(s): Norwegian
ADVERTISING RATES:
Full Page Colour .... NOK 18000
SCC .... NOK 244.17
BUSINESS: COMPUTERS & AUTOMATION: Personal Computers

KONDIS 32195R75J-70
Editorial: Dovregata 2, 0170 OSLO Tel: 22 60 94 70
Fax: 22 60 90 67
Email: kondis@kondis.no Web site: http://www.kondis.no
Date Established: 1969; Freq: 6 issues yearly; Circ: 11,000
Editor: Kjell Vigestad
Profile: Magazine containing information, articles and news about running and related activities.
Language(s): Norwegian
Readership: Aimed at runners on all levels.
CONSUMER: SPORT: Athletics

KONTURTIDSSKRIFT 1660319R82-335
Email: info@konturtidsskrift.no Web site: http://www.konturtidsskrift.no
Freq: Quarterly; Circ: 1,000
Language(s): Norwegian
CONSUMER: CURRENT AFFAIRS & POLITICS

KORBLADET 31709R61-35
Editorial: Nedre Vollgate 3, 0158 OSLO
Tel: 22 39 68 50 Fax: 22 39 68 51
Email: ina@korforbundet.no Web site: http://www.kor.no
Freq: Quarterly; Circ: 30,000
Profile: Magazine containing articles, information and news about choral music.
Language(s): Norwegian
ADVERTISING RATES:
Full Page Colour .... NOK 11100
BUSINESS: MUSIC TRADE

KOSMETIKA 1624949R15A-26
Editorial: Brekkelia 57, 3153 TOLVSRØD
Tel: 91556068 Fax: 33019954
Email: post@nkhf.no Web site: http://www.nkhf.no
Freq: Quarterly; Circ: 1,200
Language(s): Norwegian
BUSINESS: COSMETICS & HAIRDRESSING: Cosmetics

KREATIVT FORUM 31366R2A-15
Editorial: Fredensborgvn.24 M, 0177 OSLO
Tel: 22 03 30 00 Fax: 22 03 30 01
Email: redaksjonen@kreativtforum.no Web site: http://www.kreativt-forum.no
Freq: 6 issues yearly; Circ: 3,500
Editor: Harald Grenne
Profile: Journal covering creative advertising and marketing.
Language(s): Norwegian
ADVERTISING RATES:
Full Page Colour .... NOK 39000
BUSINESS: COMMUNICATIONS, ADVERTISING & MARKETING

KREATIVT FORUM; KREATIVT-FORUM.NO 1864707R2E-107
Editorial: Fredensborgvn. 24 M, 0177 OSLO
Tel: 22 03 30 00 Fax: 22 03 30 01
Email: redaksjonen@kreativtforum.no Web site: http://www.kreativt-forum.no
Freq: Daily; Cover Price: Free; Circ: 2,500 Unique Users
Language(s): Norwegian
BUSINESS: COMMUNICATIONS, ADVERTISING & MARKETING: Public Relations

KRETSLØPET 32461R57-50
Editorial: Boks 541 Sentrum, 015 OSLO
Tel: 92433582
Email: johs.bjorndal@norsas.no Web site: http://www.norsas.no
Date Established: 1995; Freq: 6 issues yearly; Circ: 1,682
Editor: Johs Bjørndal
Profile: Environmental magazine focusing on recycling waste.
Language(s): Norwegian
BUSINESS: ENVIRONMENT & POLLUTION

KRIGSINVALIDEN 1624436R94F-103
Editorial: Pb 749 Sentrum, 0106 OSLO
Tel: 23 09 50 12 Fax: 23 09 50 11
Email: krigsi@oslo.mil.no Web site: http://krigsinvalideforbundet.net
Freq: Quarterly; Circ: 2,200
Editor: Finn Pettersen
Language(s): Norwegian
CONSUMER: OTHER CLASSIFICATIONS: Disability

KRISTEN FOLKEHØGSKOLE 32326R88A-40
Editorial: Noregs Kristelege Folkehøgskolelag, Postboks 420 Sentrum, 0103 OSLO Tel: 22 47 43 00
Email: ikf@ikf.no Web site: http://nkf.folkehogskole.no/nkf/blad.php
Freq: 6 issues yearly; Circ: 1,100
Profile: Magazine containing articles and information regarding ecclesiastical education and Norwegian Folk High Schools.
Language(s): Norwegian
CONSUMER: EDUCATION

KROPPSØVING 32462R62B-15
Editorial: Landslaget Fysisk Fostring i Skolen, Møllegaten 10, 3111 TØNSBERG Tel: 33 31 53 00
Fax: 33 31 52 66
Email: lff@lff.no Web site: http://www.lff.no
Date Established: 1950; Freq: 6 issues yearly; Circ: 2,200
Profile: Magazine focusing on physical education activities.
Language(s): Norwegian
Readership: Aimed at teachers of physical education.
BUSINESS: CHURCH & SCHOOL EQUIPMENT & EDUCATION: Education Teachers

KSLMATMERK.NO 1936028R22C-102
Editorial: Pb 487 Sentrum, 0105 OSLO
Tel: 24 14 83 00 Fax: 24 14 83 13
Email: post@kslmatmerk.no Web site: http://www.kslmatmerk.no
Freq: Daily; Cover Price: Paid
Language(s): Norwegian
BUSINESS: FOOD: Food Processing & Packaging

KS.NO 1624559R32A-152
Editorial: Haakon VIIs gate 9, 0161 OSLO
Tel: 24 13 28 33
Email: web-red@ks.no Web site: http://www.ks.no
Cover Price: Paid
Language(s): Norwegian
BUSINESS: LOCAL GOVERNMENT, LEISURE & RECREATION: Local Government

KULDE SKANDINAVIA 31380R3C-100
Editorial: Marielundsveien 5, 1358 JAR
Tel: 67 12 06 59 Fax: 67121790
Email: postmaster@kulde.biz Web site: http://www.kulde.biz
Date Established: 1984; Freq: 6 issues yearly; Circ: 4,150
Profile: Scandinavian journal about the refrigeration and freezing field.
Language(s): Norwegian
Readership: Read by consultants, contractors and service engineers within the refrigeration and freezing field.
BUSINESS: HEATING & VENTILATION: Refrigeration & Ventilation

KULTMAG 1624442R84A-102
Editorial: Postboks 1180, Sentrum, 0330 OSLO
Tel: 23 31 02 39
Email: post@kultmag.no Web site: http://www.kultmag.no
Freq: 6 issues yearly; Circ: 8,000
Editor: Esben Hoff
Language(s): Norwegian
CONSUMER: THE ARTS & LITERARY: Arts

KULTURARVEN 1740815R84A-130
Editorial: Vågåvegen 35, 2680 VÅGÅ
Tel: 61 21 77 20 Fax: 61 21 77 01
Email: post@kulturarv.no Web site: http://www.kulturarv.no/kulturarven
Freq: Quarterly; Circ: 7,000
Editor: Grete Horntvedt
Language(s): Norwegian
CONSUMER: THE ARTS & LITERARY: Arts

KULTURAVISA - BREIDABLIKK 1660599R76D-275
Editorial: Kjerkgata 48, 7374 0130 OSLO RØROS
Tel: 72 41 27 86 Fax: 850 37 701
Email: post@breidablikk.net Web site: http://www.breidablikk.net
Freq: 6 issues yearly; Circ: 18,000
Language(s): Norwegian
CONSUMER: MUSIC & PERFORMING ARTS: Music

KULTURSPEILET 1657826R84B-232
Editorial: K. Moe Schweigaardsgt. 94 D, 0656 OSLO
Tel: 2268 8516
Email: kulturspeilet@pluto.no Web site: http://www.pluto.no/KulturSpeilet
Cover Price: Paid; Circ: 2,500 Unique Users
Language(s): Norwegian
CONSUMER: THE ARTS & LITERARY: Literary

KUNDEFOKUS 31371R2F-50
Editorial: Idéforlaget Nydalen Allé 23, 0484 OSLO
Tel: 92 23 95 96 Fax: 22 22 02 22
Email: mette.malka@ideforlaget.no Web site: http://www.ideforlaget.no
Date Established: 1997; Freq: Monthly; Circ: 500
Profile: Magazine containing information, articles and news. Contains advice, market research and debate articles.
Language(s): Norwegian
Readership: Read by sales and marketing personnel.
BUSINESS: COMMUNICATIONS, ADVERTISING & MARKETING: Selling

KUNST OG KULTUR 32286R84A-70
Editorial: Nasjonalmuseet for kunst, arkitektur og design, Boks 7014 St. Olavs plass, 0130 OSLO
Tel: 21 98 20 00
Email: birgitte.sauge@nasjonalmuseet.no **Web site:** http://www.universitetsforlaget.no/kunst
Date Established: 1911; **Freq:** Quarterly; **Circ:** 800
Editor: Birgitte Sauge
Profile: Magazine about art, culture, architecture and handicrafts.
Language(s): Norwegian
CONSUMER: THE ARTS & LITERARY: Arts

KUNSTHÅNDVERK 32157R74E-50
Editorial: Rådhusgt. 20, 0151 OSLO **Tel:** 22 91 02 60
Fax: 22 91 02 61
Email: khv@kunsthandverk.no **Web site:** http://www.kunsthandverk.no
Date Established: 1980; **Freq:** Quarterly; **Circ:** 2,400
Editor: Christer Dynna
Profile: Arts and crafts magazine.
Language(s): Norwegian
CONSUMER: WOMEN'S INTEREST CONSUMER MAGAZINES: Crafts

KVINNEGUIDEN.NO 1657603R74A-67
Editorial: Postboks 428 Sentrum, 0106 OSLO
Tel: 21 56 97 10 **Fax:** 21 56 97 11
Email: post@kvinneguiden.no **Web site:** http://www.kvinneguiden.no
Editor: Hilde Aasnæs
Language(s): Norwegian
CONSUMER: WOMEN'S INTEREST CONSUMER MAGAZINES: Women's Interest

KVINNER & FAMILIE 32137R74A-20
Editorial: Øvre Slottsgate 6, 0157 OSLO
Tel: 22 47 83 80 **Fax:** 22478399
Web site: http://www.kvinnerogfamilie.no
Freq: Quarterly; **Circ:** 7,500
Profile: Women's interest magazine.
Language(s): Norwegian
Readership: Read mainly by housewives.
CONSUMER: WOMEN'S INTEREST CONSUMER MAGAZINES: Women's Interest

KVINNER SAMMEN 1661728R74A-68
Editorial: Storg. 11, 0155 OSLO **Tel:** 23 01 03 00
Fax: 23010301
Email: fokus@fokuskvinner.no **Web site:** http://www.fokuskvinner.no
Freq: Quarterly
Editor: Trine Tandberg
Language(s): Norwegian
CONSUMER: WOMEN'S INTEREST CONSUMER MAGAZINES: Women's Interest

KVINNFORSKS SKRIFTSERIE 1625053R62F-172
Editorial: KVINNEFORSK-Senter For Kvinne- og kjønnsforsk - UiT, 9037 TROMSØ **Tel:** 77 64 52 40
Fax: 77 64 64 20
Email: kvinnforsk@skk.uit.no **Web site:** http://www.skk.uit.no
Freq: Annual; **Circ:** 300
Language(s): Norwegian
BUSINESS: CHURCH & SCHOOL EQUIPMENT & EDUCATION: Adult Education

KYSTEN 32671R80-55
Editorial: v/Bente Foldvik, Djupvikveien 27, 9519 KVIBY **Tel:** 78440833
Email: tidsskriftet@kysten.no **Web site:** http://www.kysten.no
Date Established: 1979; **Freq:** Quarterly; **Circ:** 8,500
Profile: Magazine containing articles and information about people who live by the coast and their way of life. Covers cultural as well as practical issues.
Language(s): Norwegian
Readership: Aimed at people who live by the coast and in the countryside.
CONSUMER: RURAL & REGIONAL INTEREST

KYSTMAGASINET 31570R45A-13
Editorial: Skuteviksboder 11, 5035 BERGEN
Tel: 55 30 48 60
Email: edmund@atlanticforlag.no **Web site:** http://www.atlanticforlag.no
Freq: Monthly; **Circ:** 3,200
Profile: Magazine containing information, articles and news for the maritime trade. Covers product news, fishing, transport and different boat types.
Language(s): Norwegian
ADVERTISING RATES:
SCC .... NOK 125
BUSINESS: MARINE & SHIPPING

KYSTNYTT.NO 1864705R45A-77
Editorial: Lårbåten 95, 1614 FREDRIKSTAD
Tel: 69 50 53 36
Email: tove@kystnytt.no **Web site:** http://www.kystnytt.no
Freq: Daily; **Cover Price:** Free; **Circ:** 2,500 Unique Users
Language(s): Norwegian
BUSINESS: MARINE & SHIPPING

LAAGENDALSPOSTEN 31776R67B-4250
Editorial: Pb. 480, 3605 KONGSBERG
Tel: 32 77 10 00
Email: redaksjonen@laagendalsposten.no **Web site:** http://www.laagendalsposten.no
Date Established: 1903; **Freq:** Daily; **Circ:** 10,217
Language(s): Norwegian
ADVERTISING RATES:
Full Page Colour .... NOK 19115
SCC .... NOK 191,15
REGIONAL DAILY & SUNDAY NEWSPAPERS: Regional Daily Newspapers

LABYRINT 1831505R55-107
Editorial: Labyrint, Avdeling for kommunikasjon og samfunnskontakt, Universitetet i Tromsø, 9037 TROMSØ **Tel:** 77 64 40 00
Email: labyrint-kommentar@uit.no **Web site:** http://uit.no/labyrint
Freq: Quarterly; **Cover Price:** Free
Language(s): Norwegian
BUSINESS: APPLIED SCIENCE & LABORATORIES

LANDBRUKSTIDENDE 31468R21A-40
Editorial: Landbrukstidende, 7500 STJØRDAL
Tel: 90 12 69 63
Email: ole@ostkil.no **Web site:** http://www.gardsplassen.no
Date Established: 1895; **Freq:** 26 issues yearly; **Circ:** 25,000
Profile: Farming and forestry magazine.
Language(s): Norwegian
BUSINESS: AGRICULTURE & FARMING

LATINAMERIKA 1624788R90-201
Editorial: LAG Norge, Osterhausgate 27, 0183 OSLO
Tel: 22 98 93 20 **Fax:** 55 58 99 11
Email: info@latin-amerikagruppene.no **Web site:** http://www.latin-amerikagruppene.no
Freq: Quarterly; **Circ:** 700
Editor: Reidun Blehr Lånkan
Language(s): Norwegian
CONSUMER: ETHNIC

LEDELSE OG TEKNIKK 31428R14A-100
Editorial: Pb 8906 Youngstorget, 0028 OSLO
Tel: 23061029 **Fax:** 23061017
Email: astor.larsen@flt.no **Web site:** http://www.flt.no
Freq: Monthly; **Circ:** 20,500
Editor: Astor Larsen
Profile: Publication for technical employees and supervisors.
Language(s): Norwegian
BUSINESS: COMMERCE, INDUSTRY & MANAGEMENT

LEDERNE 1624320R14A-207
Editorial: Pb. 2523 Solli, 0202 OSLO **Tel:** 22 54 51 50
Fax: 22 55 65 48
Email: tor.haehre@lederne.no **Web site:** http://www.lederne.no
Freq: Quarterly; **Circ:** 20,000
Editor: Sverre Simen Hov
Language(s): Norwegian
BUSINESS: COMMERCE, INDUSTRY & MANAGEMENT

LEDERNYTT 1657330R14D-1
Editorial: Box 4335 Nydalen, 0402 OSLO
Tel: 920 22 199 **Fax:** 2155 55 62
Email: redaksjon@bullmediaconsulting.no **Web site:** http://www.ledernytt.no
Freq: 6 issues yearly; **Circ:** 70,000
Language(s): Norwegian
BUSINESS: COMMERCE, INDUSTRY & MANAGEMENT: Purchasing

LENES OPPSKRIFTER 1934358R74P-212
Email: nuftenoft@gmail.com **Web site:** http://nuftenoft.wordpress.com
Freq: Daily; **Cover Price:** Paid
Language(s): Norwegian
CONSUMER: WOMEN'S INTEREST CONSUMER MAGAZINES: Food & Cookery

LEVANGER-AVISA; SPORT 1999461R75A-241
Editorial: Pb. 14, 7601 LEVANGER **Tel:** 93 83 44 44
Fax: 74019001
Email: sport@levangeravisa.no **Web site:** http://www.levangeravisa.no
Language(s): Norwegian
CONSUMER: SPORT

LEVLANDLIG 1693452R80A-1
Editorial: Tun Media AS, Pb. 9303 Grønland, 0135 OSLO **Tel:** 21314400 **Fax:** 21314491
Email: levlandlig@tunmedia.no **Web site:** http://www.levlandlig.no
Freq: 6 issues yearly
Language(s): Norwegian
Copy instructions: *Copy Date:* 34 days prior to publication date
CONSUMER: RURAL & REGIONAL INTEREST: Rural Interest

LIBERALEREN.NO 1865441R82-368
Email: pleym@liberaleren.no **Web site:** http://www.liberaleren.no
Freq: Daily; **Cover Price:** Free; **Circ:** 2,500 Unique Users
Language(s): Norwegian
CONSUMER: CURRENT AFFAIRS & POLITICS

LIERPOSTEN.NO 1864701R73-187
Editorial: Vestsideveien 9c, 3400 LIER
Tel: 32 24 07 60
Email: redaksjonen@lierposten.no **Web site:** http://www.lierposten.no
Freq: Daily; **Cover Price:** Free; **Circ:** 882 Unique Users
Language(s): Norwegian
CONSUMER: NATIONAL & INTERNATIONAL PERIODICALS

LINDESNES AVIS 1625247R63-2
Editorial: Pb. 41, 4501 MANDAL **Tel:** 38 27 10 00
Fax: 38 27 10 01
Email: redaksjon@l-a.no **Web site:** http://www.lindesnes-avis.no
Freq: Daily; **Circ:** 6,422
Language(s): Norwegian
ADVERTISING RATES:
SCC .... NOK 125.92
BUSINESS: REGIONAL BUSINESS

LINE MARION 1938278R74G-173
Web site: http://www.linemarion.no
Cover Price: Paid
Language(s): Norwegian
CONSUMER: WOMEN'S INTEREST CONSUMER MAGAZINES: Slimming & Health

LINUXMAGASINET 634403R5C-25
Editorial: Lizacom DA, Pb. 123, 2150 ÅRNES
Tel: 63 90 37 10
Email: redaksjonen@linmag.org **Web site:** http://www.linmag.no
Freq: Daily; **Cover Price:** Paid
Profile: Magazine providing information about Linux computerware.
Language(s): Norwegian
BUSINESS: COMPUTERS & AUTOMATION: Professional Personal Computers

LITEN STORM PÅ KYSTEN (ANNONSESAMKJØRING) 1645219R91E-4
Editorial: Pb. 100, 7970 KOLVEREID **Tel:** 74 39 60 50
Fax: 74 39 60 51
Email: frode@ba-avis.no **Web site:** http://www.litenstormpaakysten.no
Freq: Daily; **Circ:** 13,584
Language(s): Norwegian
CONSUMER: RECREATION & LEISURE: Lifestyle

LIVET 1624441R94F-104
Editorial: Pb 333, 1802 ASKIM **Tel:** 69 81 69 81
Fax: 69885766
Email: turid.kind.ekroll@kabb.no **Web site:** http://www.kabb.no
Freq: Monthly; **Circ:** 155
Language(s): Norwegian
CONSUMER: OTHER CLASSIFICATIONS: Disability

LNT-NYTT 32162R74G-60
Editorial: Pb 6727 Etterstad, 0609 OSLO
Tel: 23 05 45 50 **Fax:** 23 05 45 51
Email: post@lnt.no **Web site:** http://www.lnt.no
Freq: Quarterly; **Circ:** 3,300
Profile: Magazine containing information and articles for patients who have had an organ transplantation or a kidney-related disease.
Language(s): Norwegian
CONSUMER: WOMEN'S INTEREST CONSUMER MAGAZINES: Slimming & Health

LO-AKTUELT 31440R14L-66_50
Editorial: Postboks 231 Sentrum, 0103 OSLO
Tel: 23063359
Email: red.lo-aktuelt@lo-media.no **Web site:** http://www.frifagbevegelse.no
Freq: 26 issues yearly; **Circ:** 32,368
Profile: Magazine of the Norwegian Confederation of Free Trade Unions. Includes coverage of economic and political developments, stock exchange, social and cultural information.
Language(s): Norwegian
ADVERTISING RATES:
SCC .... NOK 175
BUSINESS: COMMERCE, INDUSTRY & MANAGEMENT: Trade Unions

LOFOTPOSTEN 31800R67B-4350
Editorial: Avisgata 15, 8305 SVOLVÆR
Tel: 76 06 78 00 **Fax:** 76 07 00 09
Email: red@lofotposten.no **Web site:** http://www.lofotposten.no
Date Established: 1896; **Freq:** Daily; **Circ:** 7,133
Editor: Jan Eivind Fredly
Language(s): Norwegian
ADVERTISING RATES:
SCC .... NOK 102.86
REGIONAL DAILY & SUNDAY NEWSPAPERS: Regional Daily Newspapers

LOGISTIKK NETTVERK 31597R49A-25
Editorial: Schenker AS, Erling Sæther, Pb 223 Økern, 0510 OSLO **Tel:** 22 72 74 44 **Fax:** 22 72 74 60
Email: einar.spurkeland@schenker.com **Web site:** http://www.schenker.no/media&information/publication/index.html
Freq: Quarterly; **Circ:** 8,000
Profile: Magazine covering logistics and transport.
Language(s): Norwegian
BUSINESS: TRANSPORT

LOGISTIKK & LEDELSE 32471R10-100
Editorial: Pb. 130, 1306 BÆRUM POSTTERMINAL
Tel: 67 55 54 30 **Fax:** 67 55 54 31
Email: info@logistikk-ledelse.no **Web site:** http://www.logistikk-ledelse.no
Date Established: 1988; **Freq:** Monthly; **Circ:** 7,517
Profile: Magazine focusing on logistics management.
Language(s): Norwegian
Readership: Aimed at logistics managers.
ADVERTISING RATES:
Full Page Colour .... NOK 24000
SCC .... NOK 170
BUSINESS: MATERIALS HANDLING

LOKALAVISA NORDSALTEN; NORD-SALTEN.NO 1864710R73-203
Editorial: Postboks 94, 8260 INNHAVET
Tel: 75 77 24 50 **Fax:** 75 77 24 51
Email: lokalavisa@nord-salten.no **Web site:** http://www.nord-salten.no
Freq: Daily; **Cover Price:** Free; **Circ:** 1,600 Unique Users
Language(s): Norwegian
CONSUMER: NATIONAL & INTERNATIONAL PERIODICALS

LOKALAVISA.NO 1864706R73-183
Editorial: Storgata 15, 2408 ELVERUM
Web site: http://www.lokal-avisa.no
Freq: Daily; **Cover Price:** Free; **Circ:** 2,500 Unique Users
Language(s): Norwegian
CONSUMER: NATIONAL & INTERNATIONAL PERIODICALS

LOKALAVISEN FROGNER - ST.HANSHAUGEN 1656540R80-155
Editorial: Postboks 79, Bryn, 0345 OSLO
Tel: 23 20 56 00
Email: redaksjon.fs@lokalavisen.no **Web site:** http://www.lokalavisenfrogner.no
Freq: Monthly; **Circ:** 30,000
Language(s): Norwegian
CONSUMER: RURAL & REGIONAL INTEREST

LOKALRADIOPOSTEN 32504R2D-120
Editorial: Skippergata 14, 6413 MOLDE
Tel: 22 40 27 20 **Fax:** 22 40 27 30
Email: ef@lokalradio.no **Web site:** http://www.nlrf.no
Freq: 6 times a year; **Cover Price:** Paid; **Circ:** 740 Unique Users
Profile: Magazine containing articles about local radio stations in Norway.
Language(s): Norwegian
Readership: Read by those working in radio stations.
BUSINESS: COMMUNICATIONS, ADVERTISING & MARKETING: Broadcasting

LOMMELEGEN.NO 1657608R74G-156
Editorial: Lommelegen AS, Stenersgt 2-8, 0184 OSLO **Tel:** 40 60 20 70 **Fax:** 23407301
Email: redaksjon@lommelegen.no **Web site:** http://www.lommelegen.no
Editor: Ine Thereze Gransæter
Language(s): Norwegian
CONSUMER: WOMEN'S INTEREST CONSUMER MAGAZINES: Slimming & Health

LOTTEBLADET 1624459R40-33
Editorial: Pb 908 Sentrum, 0104 OSLO
Tel: 22 47 82 52 **Fax:** 22 33 27 23
Email: lottebladet@lottene.no **Web site:** http://www.lottene.no
Freq: 6 issues yearly; **Circ:** 2,500
Editor: Anne-Jorunn Bech
Language(s): Norwegian
BUSINESS: DEFENCE

LOV & DATA 1624432R5R-1
Editorial: Postboks 2016 Vika, 0125 OSLO
Tel: 23 11 83 00 **Fax:** 23118301
Email: lov&data@lovdata.no **Web site:** http://www.lovdata.no
Freq: Quarterly; **Circ:** 2,000
Language(s): Norwegian
BUSINESS: COMPUTERS & AUTOMATION: Computers Related

LOV OG RETT 31565R44-45
Editorial: Inst for privatrett. UiO, PB 6706 St Olavs plass, 0130 OSLO **Tel:** 24 14 75 00 **Fax:** 22859620
Email: kare.lilleholt@jus.uio.no **Web site:** http://www.universitetsforlaget.no/lovogrett
Date Established: 1962; **Freq:** Monthly; **Circ:** 2,500
Profile: Legal journal.
Language(s): Norwegian
Readership: Aimed at lawyers and students.
BUSINESS: LEGAL

LYD & BILDE 1624938R43A-3
Editorial: Billingstadsletta 19 B, 1396 BILLINGSTAD
Tel: 81573510 **Fax:** 81573511
Email: redaksjon@lydogbilde.no **Web site:** http://www.lydogbilde.no
Freq: Monthly; **Circ:** 23,000
Language(s): Norwegian
ADVERTISING RATES:
Full Page Colour .... NOK 44900
SCC .... NOK 325
BUSINESS: ELECTRICAL RETAIL TRADE

LYDOGBILDE.NO 1895551R78R-6
Editorial: Billingstadsletta 19 B, 1396 BILLINGSTAD
Tel: 815 73 510 **Fax:** 815 73 511
Email: redaksjon@publish.no **Web site:** http://www.lydogbilde.no
Freq: Daily; **Cover Price:** Paid
Editor: Lasse Svendsen
Language(s): Norwegian
CONSUMER: CONSUMER ELECTRONICS: Consumer Electronics Related

LYKKELIG SOM LITEN 1938275R74D-83
Email: dr.klm@lykkeligsomliten.no **Web site:** http://www.lykkeligsomliten.no/blogg
Cover Price: Paid
Editor: Kari Løvendahl Mogstad
Language(s): Norwegian
CONSUMER: WOMEN'S INTEREST CONSUMER MAGAZINES: Child Care

MAAL OG MINNE 32472R88A-70
Editorial: Pb 4672 Sofienberg, 0506 OSLO
Tel: 22 70 78 00 **Fax:** 22 68 75 02
Email: k.brudevoll@samlaget.no **Web site:** http://www.samlaget.no/maalogminne/index.html
Date Established: 1909; **Freq:** Half-yearly; **Circ:** 400
Editor: Lars S. Vikør
Profile: Magazine focusing on linguistics and related subjects.
Language(s): Norwegian
Readership: Aimed at all those interested in linguistics.
CONSUMER: EDUCATION

MAG 32360R91D-52
Editorial: Pb. 481 Sentrum, 0105 OSLO
Tel: 22912200
Email: mening@mag.no **Web site:** http://www.mag.no
Freq: Monthly; **Circ:** 36,092
Profile: Magazine containing articles and information of interest to young people.
Language(s): Norwegian
Readership: Aimed at girls aged between 15 and 20 years old.
ADVERTISING RATES:
SCC .... NOK 254.17
CONSUMER: RECREATION & LEISURE: Children & Youth

MAGASINET AKTUELL 32453R32K-40
Editorial: Møllergata 10, 0179 OSLO **Tel:** 23 06 15 61
Fax: 23062271
Email: post@aktuell.no **Web site:** http://www.aktuell.no
Freq: Monthly; **Circ:** 155,000
Profile: Magazine containing news, articles and information concerning the public sector. Covers infrastructure, defence, public health and state administration.
Language(s): Norwegian
Readership: Read mainly by civil servants and people employed by public institutions and government bodies.
BUSINESS: LOCAL GOVERNMENT, LEISURE & RECREATION: Civil Service

MAGASINET AKTUELL FOR NORSK FENGSELS- OG FRIOMSORGSF 31525R32R-50
Editorial: Møllergata 10, 0179 OSLO **Tel:** 23 06 15 92
Fax: 23 06 22 71
Email: jan.erik.ostlie@aktuell.no **Web site:** http://www.aktuell.no/aktuell_for_nff
Freq: Monthly; **Circ:** 3,900
Profile: Journal about the prison service.
Language(s): Norwegian
BUSINESS: LOCAL GOVERNMENT, LEISURE & RECREATION: Local Government Related

MAGASINET AKTUELL FOR NORSK JERNBANEFORBUND 1624480R49A-101
Editorial: Postboks 231 Sentrum, 0179 OSLO
Tel: 23 06 33 59 **Fax:** 23062271
Email: frifagbevegelse@lo-media.no **Web site:** http://www.frifagbevegelse.no/aktuell/kontakt
Freq: Monthly; **Circ:** 14,400
Language(s): Norwegian
BUSINESS: TRANSPORT

MAGASINET DET GODE LIV 1625181R74Q-74
Editorial: Postboks 123 Bogstadveien, 0323 OSLO
Tel: 23204450
Email: edda.espeland@dgl.no **Web site:** http://www.dgl.no
Freq: 6 issues yearly; **Circ:** 23,000
Language(s): Norwegian
ADVERTISING RATES:
SCC .... NOK 140.83
CONSUMER: WOMEN'S INTEREST CONSUMER MAGAZINES: Lifestyle

MAGASINET FOR FAGORGANISERTE 1624551R42-1
Editorial: Pb. 231 Sentrum, 0103 OSLO
Tel: 23 06 33 91 **Fax:** 23 06 33 94
Email: magasinet@lomedia.no **Web site:** http://www.magasinett.org
Freq: 6 issues yearly; **Circ:** 132,098
Language(s): Norwegian
BUSINESS: CONSTRUCTION

MAGASINET IDÉ 1803749R14F-33
Editorial: KrF v/Idéredaksjonen, Pb. 478 Sentrum, 0105 OSLO **Tel:** 23 10 28 00 **Fax:** 23 10 28 10
Email: ide@krf.no **Web site:** http://www.krf.no/ikbViewer/page/krf/nyheter/ide-krfs-medlemsmagasin
Freq: Quarterly; **Circ:** 34,000
Editor: Erik Lunde
Language(s): Norwegian
BUSINESS: COMMERCE, INDUSTRY & MANAGEMENT: Training & Recruitment

MAGASINET KUNST 1692464R84A-125
Editorial: Postboks 2644 St.Hanshaugen, 0175 OSLO **Tel:** 22 99 54 18
Email: mette@fineart.no **Web site:** http://www.kunstklubben.no
Freq: Monthly; **Circ:** 10,000
Language(s): Norwegian
CONSUMER: THE ARTS & LITERARY: Arts

MAGASINET REDD BARNA 32506R32G-67
Editorial: Postboks 6902 St.Olavsplass, 0130 OSLO
Tel: 22990900 **Fax:** 22990850
Email: post@reddbarna.no **Web site:** http://www.reddbarna.no/default.asp?V_ITEM_ID=86
Freq: 5 ed. pr. year; **Circ:** 11,000
Editor: Elin Toft
Profile: Magazine containing information and news about children's rights.
Language(s): Norwegian
Readership: Read by social workers, journalists and students.
BUSINESS: LOCAL GOVERNMENT, LEISURE & RECREATION: Community Care & Social Services

MAGASINET TEKNA 1624325R4A-21
Editorial: Pb 2312 Solli, 0201 OSLO **Tel:** 22947500
Fax: 22947501
Email: magasinet@tekna.no **Web site:** http://www.teknamag.no
Freq: Monthly; **Circ:** 42,000
Language(s): Norwegian
BUSINESS: ARCHITECTURE & BUILDING: Architecture

MAGASINET TREINDUSTRIEN 31491R23A-30
Editorial: Postboks 130, 2261 KIRKENAER
Tel: 46941000 **Fax:** 62948705
Email: even@askmedia.no **Web site:** http://www.magasinet-treindustrien.no
Date Established: 1969; **Freq:** Monthly - 10 ganger i året; **Circ:** 3,700
Editor: Pål Sønsteli
Profile: Journal about the furniture industry and door and window manufacture.
Language(s): Norwegian
Readership: Read by furniture industry manufacturers and door and window manufacturers.
ADVERTISING RATES:
Full Page Colour .... NOK 13900
SCC .... NOK 140.83
BUSINESS: FURNISHINGS & FURNITURE

MAGASINET VFB 32575R32G-10
Editorial: Organisasjonen voksne for barn, Stortorvet 10, 0155 OSLO **Tel:** 23 10 06 10 **Fax:** 23 10 06 11
Email: vfb@vfb.no **Web site:** http://www.vfb.no
Freq: Quarterly
Editor: Ingeborg Vea
Profile: Magazine focusing on children in crisis and their needs.
Language(s): Norwegian
Readership: Read by social workers and parents of children who have problems.
BUSINESS: LOCAL GOVERNMENT, LEISURE & RECREATION: Community Care & Social Services

MAGASINETT.NO 1657827R84A-118
Editorial: Næringsbedet i Vatlandsvåg, 4235 HEBNES **Tel:** 52 79 04 89 **Fax:** 52790481
Email: post@magasinett.no **Web site:** http://www.magasinett.no
Circ: 2,500 Unique Users
Language(s): Norwegian
CONSUMER: THE ARTS & LITERARY: Arts

MAGMA 31345R1A-93_50
Editorial: Stortingsgata 22, Postboks 1869 Vika, 0124 OSLO **Tel:** 22 82 80 00
Email: charlotte.hartvigsen.lem@fagbokforlaget.no
Web site: http://www.sivilokonomene.no/?nid=104827
Date Established: 1998; **Freq:** 6 issues yearly
Editor: Charlotte Hartvigsen Lem
Profile: Business magazine providing financial news and articles concerning management. Covers debate, research and practice.
Language(s): Norwegian
BUSINESS: FINANCE & ECONOMICS

MAISON MAT & VIN 1656536R74P-201
Editorial: Pb. 6975, St.Olavs plass, 0130 OSLO
Tel: 24 14 69 40 **Fax:** 24 14 69 41
Email: post@matvin.no **Web site:** http://www.matvin.no
Circ: 20,000
Editor: Cecilie Louise Berg
Language(s): Norwegian
ADVERTISING RATES:
Full Page Colour .... NOK 32900
CONSUMER: WOMEN'S INTEREST CONSUMER MAGAZINES: Food & Cookery

MALEREN 1624270R16A-11
Editorial: Skarland Press AS, Pb 2843 Tøyen, 0608 OSLO **Tel:** 22708300 **Fax:** 22708301
Email: forlaget@maleren.no **Web site:** http://www.maleren.no
Freq: Monthly - 10 ganger i året; **Circ:** 2,500
Language(s): Norwegian
ADVERTISING RATES:
Full Page Colour .... NOK 14900
BUSINESS: DECORATING & PAINT

MALVIK-BLADET; MB.NO 1864863R73-179
Editorial: Postboks 130, 7551 HOMMELVIK
Tel: 73 98 00 80
Email: redaksjonen@mb.no **Web site:** http://www.mb.no
Freq: Daily; **Cover Price:** Free; **Circ:** 2,400 Unique Users
Language(s): Norwegian
CONSUMER: NATIONAL & INTERNATIONAL PERIODICALS

MAMMANETT.NO 1657601R74D-77
Editorial: Mathias Blilies vei 9, 2843 EINA
Tel: 614 21 781 **Fax:** 614 21 773
Email: post@mammanett.no **Web site:** http://www.mammanett.no
Cover Price: Paid
Language(s): Norwegian
CONSUMER: WOMEN'S INTEREST CONSUMER MAGAZINES: Child Care

MANDAG MORGEN 1645165R32G-164
Editorial: Postboks 1180 Sentrum, 0181 OSLO
Tel: 22 99 18 18 **Fax:** 22 99 18 10
Email: redaksjonen@mandagmorgen.no **Web site:** http://www.mandagmorgen.no
Freq: Weekly; **Cover Price:** Paid; **Circ:** 3,000 Unique Users
Editor: Knut Petter Rønne
Language(s): Norwegian
ADVERTISING RATES:
Full Page Colour .... NOK 15000
SCC .... NOK 100
BUSINESS: LOCAL GOVERNMENT, LEISURE & RECREATION: Community Care & Social Services

MANDAG MORGEN; MANDAGMORGEN.NO 1864862R14A-238
Editorial: Postboks 1180 Sentrum, 0181 OSLO
Tel: 22 99 18 18 **Fax:** 22 99 18 10
Email: redaksjonen@mandagmorgen.no **Web site:** http://www.mandagmorgen.no
Freq: Daily; **Cover Price:** Free; **Circ:** 2,500 Unique Users
Editor: Knut Petter Rønne
Language(s): Norwegian
BUSINESS: COMMERCE, INDUSTRY & MANAGEMENT

MANN 32298R86C-150
Editorial: Gullhaugveien 1, 0441 OSLO
Tel: 22 58 50 00 **Fax:** 22 58 05 69
Email: post@mann.no **Web site:** http://www.klikk.no/mann
Date Established: 1996; **Freq:** Monthly; **Circ:** 15,348
Editor: Jan Thoresen
Profile: Magazine for modern men containing articles about fashion, motoring, career issues, health and fitness, sports and travel.
Language(s): Norwegian
ADVERTISING RATES:
SCC .... NOK 307.5
CONSUMER: ADULT & GAY MAGAZINES: Men's Lifestyle Magazines

MARG - NOTATER FRA RANDSONEN 1813126R14A-227
Editorial: Strandveien 95, 9006 TROMSØ
Tel: 77 60 04 23
Email: margbok@gmail.com **Web site:** http://www.margmedia.no
Freq: Quarterly; **Circ:** 2,000
Language(s): Norwegian
BUSINESS: COMMERCE, INDUSTRY & MANAGEMENT

MARINE BIOLOGY RESEARCH 1624921R55-101
Editorial: Pb. 12 Posthuset, 0051 OSLO
Tel: 23 10 34 60 **Fax:** 23 10 34 61
Email: journals@tandf.no **Web site:** http://www.tandf.no/marinebiology
Freq: 6 issues yearly; **Circ:** 700
Language(s): Norwegian
BUSINESS: APPLIED SCIENCE & LABORATORIES

MARINTEK REVIEW 1624846R58-101
Editorial: Pb 4125 Valentinlyst, 7450 TRONDHEIM
Tel: 73595500 **Fax:** 73595776
Email: marintek@marintek.sintef.no **Web site:** http://www.marintek.sintef.no
Circ: 3,000
Language(s): Norwegian
BUSINESS: ENERGY, FUEL & NUCLEAR

MARITIMT MAGASIN 1645161R45A-74
Editorial: Postboks 44, 6282 BRATTVÅG
Tel: 70 20 78 65
Email: redaksjon@maritimt.com **Web site:** http://www.maritimt.com
Freq: 6 issues yearly
Language(s): Norwegian
BUSINESS: MARINE & SHIPPING

MASKINREGISTERET 1624800R19R-1
Editorial: Pb. 67 Bryn, 0611 OSLO **Tel:** 22 75 75 10
Fax: 22 75 75 21
Email: mr@mediaoslo.no **Web site:** http://www.maskinregisteret.no
Freq: Monthly; **Circ:** 12,000
Editor: Karl Jørgen Gurandsrud
Language(s): Norwegian
BUSINESS: ENGINEERING & MACHINERY: Engineering Related

MAT & HELSE 1625240R74G-152
Editorial: Tun Media AS, Postboks 9309 Grønland, 0135 OSLO **Tel:** 21314408
Email: anne.paulsen@tunmedia.no **Web site:** http://www.matoghelse.no
Freq: Monthly; **Circ:** 18,000
Language(s): Norwegian

ADVERTISING RATES:
Full Page Colour .... NOK 33000
SCC .... NOK 275
CONSUMER: WOMEN'S INTEREST CONSUMER MAGAZINES: Slimming & Health

MATAVISEN.NO 1985729R74P-214
Editorial: Microenta Media Group AS, Kingos gate 15, 0457 OSLO **Tel:** 92 89 93 05
Email: kontakt@matavisen.no **Web site:** http://www.matavisen.no
Freq: Daily; **Cover Price:** Paid
Editor: Rubina Olsen
Language(s): Norwegian
CONSUMER: WOMEN'S INTEREST CONSUMER MAGAZINES: Food & Cookery

MATERIALISTEN 1645180R55-105
Editorial: Sagveien 10, 0459 OSLO
Email: redaksjonen@materialisten.no **Web site:** http://www.materialisten.no
Freq: Quarterly; **Circ:** 750
Editor: Jane Dullum
Language(s): Norwegian
BUSINESS: APPLIED SCIENCE & LABORATORIES

MATINDUSTRIEN 31486R22C-100
Editorial: Pb 2843, Tøyen, 0608 OSLO **Tel:** 22708324 **Fax:** 22708301
Email: vebjorg@skarland.no **Web site:** http://www.matindustrien.no
Date Established: 1947; **Freq:** Monthly; **Circ:** 3,172
Editor: Vebjørg Skjelmerud
Profile: Magazine about food and beverage processing, packaging, laboratories and quality management.
Language(s): Norwegian
Readership: Read by people working within management, product development, food analysis and quality control or being in charge of the technical aspects of processing food.
ADVERTISING RATES:
SCC .... NOK 143.33
BUSINESS: FOOD: Food Processing & Packaging

MATINDUSTRIEN; MATINDUSTRIEN.NO 1864866R74P-210
Editorial: Postboks 2843 Tøyen, 0608 OSLO
Tel: 22 70 83 24 **Fax:** 22 70 83 01
Email: vebjorg@skarland.no **Web site:** http://www.matindustrien.no
Freq: Daily; **Cover Price:** Free; **Circ:** 1,913 Unique Users
Editor: Vebjørg Skjelmerud
Language(s): Norwegian
CONSUMER: WOMEN'S INTEREST CONSUMER MAGAZINES: Food & Cookery

MAT.NO 1656700R22A-156
Editorial: P. b. 395 Økern, 0513 OSLO
Tel: 22 09 25 60
Email: post@mat.no **Web site:** http://www.mat.no
Circ: 2,500 Unique Users
Language(s): Norwegian
BUSINESS: FOOD

MATNYTTIG 1624795R22C-101
Editorial: Muninbakken 9-13, Breivika, 9291 TROMSØ **Tel:** 77629000 **Fax:** 77629100
Email: mette.risbrathe@nofima.no **Web site:** http://www.nofima.no/matnyttig
Freq: Quarterly; **Circ:** 3,000
Editor: Mette Risbråthe
Language(s): Norwegian
BUSINESS: FOOD: Food Processing & Packaging

MATOGDRIKKE.NO 1864875R74P-211
Editorial: Postboks 40 Kjelsås, 0411 OSLO
Tel: 900 85 134
Email: redaksjon@matogdrikke.no **Web site:** http://www.matogdrikke.no
Freq: Daily; **Cover Price:** Free; **Circ:** 2,500 Unique Users
Editor: Jesper Jørgensen
Language(s): Norwegian
CONSUMER: WOMEN'S INTEREST CONSUMER MAGAZINES: Food & Cookery

MATOPPSKRIFT.NO 1656701R22A-157
Editorial: DatabaseSør v/ Knut Pettersen, Pb. 1638, 4688 KRISTIANSAND **Tel:** 47 26 09 97
Email: matoppskrift@gmail.com **Web site:** http://www.matoppskrift.no
Cover Price: Paid
Language(s): Norwegian
BUSINESS: FOOD

MATPORTALEN 1645119R22A-154
Editorial: Pb. 383, 2381 BRUMUNDDAL
Tel: 23 21 66 32 **Fax:** 23 21 70 01
Email: redaksjon@matportalen.no **Web site:** http://matportalen.no
Freq: Daily
Editor: Hanne Røvig Schjold
Language(s): Norwegian
BUSINESS: FOOD

MATSIDEN.NO 1656699R22A-155
Editorial: PSD, Skotselvveien 741, 3330 SKOTSELV
Email: post@matsiden.no **Web site:** http://www.matsiden.no
Language(s): Norwegian
BUSINESS: FOOD

MATTILSYNET 1657800R81X-51
Editorial: Pb. 383, 2381 BRUMUNDDAL
Tel: 23 21 68 00 **Fax:** 23 21 68 01
Email: redaksjon@mattilsynet.no **Web site:** http://www.mattilsynet.no
Cover Price: Paid
Language(s): Norwegian
CONSUMER: ANIMALS & PETS

MC-AVISA 32224R77B-150
Editorial: Box 3009, 4392 SANDNES **Tel:** 51675300 **Fax:** 51672326
Email: post@mc-avisa.no **Web site:** http://www.mc-avisa.no
Date Established: 1983; **Freq:** Monthly; **Circ:** 8,500
Profile: Newspaper containing articles and information about motorcycles. Covers practical advice, travel, maintenance, buying and selling and product news.
Language(s): Norwegian
ADVERTISING RATES:
Full Page Colour .... NOK 12190
CONSUMER: MOTORING & CYCLING: Motorcycling

MC-AVISA; MC-AVISA.NO 1740651R77B-160
Editorial: MC-avisa, Box 3009, 4392 SANDNES
Tel: 51675300 **Fax:** 51672326
Email: post@mc-avisa.no **Web site:** http://www.mc-avisa.no
Cover Price: Paid
Language(s): Norwegian
CONSUMER: MOTORING & CYCLING: Motorcycling

MC-BLADET 1624848R77A-208
Editorial: Pb 351, 1502 MOSS **Tel:** 90837374 **Fax:** 69240809
Email: bjorn@mcnu.org **Web site:** http://nmcu.org/mc-bladet
Freq: Quarterly; **Circ:** 11,500
Language(s): Norwegian
CONSUMER: MOTORING & CYCLING: Motoring

MC-BØRSEN 1625107R77A-214
Editorial: Hjemmet Mortensen AS, 0441 OSLO
Tel: 22585000
Email: annonse@autoborsen.no **Web site:** http://www.autoborsen.no
Circ: 6,559
Language(s): Norwegian
CONSUMER: MOTORING & CYCLING: Motoring

MEDISINSK INFORMASJON 31644R56A-55
Editorial: MEDLEX Norsk Helseinformasjon, Pb 6611 St.Olavsplass, 0129 OSLO **Tel:** 23354700 **Fax:** 23354701
Email: info@lex.no **Web site:** http://www.medisinskinformasjon.no
Date Established: 1986; **Freq:** Quarterly; **Circ:** 5,000
Profile: Magazine containing articles and information about the medical profession. Covers also general news and the latest research and developments from the medical field.
Language(s): Norwegian
Readership: Read by members of the medical profession.
BUSINESS: HEALTH & MEDICAL

MEDLEMSAVISEN FREMSKRITT 32274R82-280
Editorial: 0159 OSLO **Tel:** 23135450 **Fax:** 23135451
Email: bos@frp.no **Web site:** http://www.frp.no
Date Established: 1973; **Freq:** Daily; **Circ:** 15,000
Editor: Børge Sandnes
Profile: Magazine covering the activities of the Norwegian Progress Party.
Language(s): Norwegian
Readership: Read by members of the party.
CONSUMER: CURRENT AFFAIRS & POLITICS

MEDLEMSBLADET PARAT 1666035R14L-107
Editorial: Pb 9029 Grønland, 0133 OSLO
Tel: 21 01 36 00 **Fax:** 21 01 38 00
Email: post@parat.com **Web site:** http://www.parat.com
Freq: Quarterly; **Circ:** 27,000
Editor: Trygve Bergsland
Language(s): Norwegian
BUSINESS: COMMERCE, INDUSTRY & MANAGEMENT: Trade Unions

MEGAFON 2010151R14A-241
Editorial: Sverres gate 3, 5057 BERGEN
Tel: 55 54 66 55
Email: post@megafon.no **Web site:** http://www.megafon.no
Freq: Monthly
Language(s): Norwegian
BUSINESS: COMMERCE, INDUSTRY & MANAGEMENT

MEIERIPOSTEN 31473R21C-50
Editorial: Postboks 9370, Grønland, 0135 OSLO
Tel: 23002710
Email: meieriposten@nml.no **Web site:** http://www.nml.no
Date Established: 1911; **Freq:** Monthly; **Circ:** 1,900
Editor: Jostein Kolberg
Profile: Journal for the dairy and food industries.
Language(s): Norwegian
BUSINESS: AGRICULTURE & FARMING: Dairy Farming

MENNESKERETTIGHETS-MAGASINET MR 1936404R82-487
Editorial: Kirkegata 5, 0153 OSLO **Tel:** 22 47 92 02 **Fax:** 22 41 60 76
Email: lindeman@nhc.no **Web site:** http://www.nhc.no
Freq: Half-yearly
Language(s): Norwegian
CONSUMER: CURRENT AFFAIRS & POLITICS

MENNESKEVENNEN 32691R74G-63
Editorial: Det Norske Totalavholdsselskap, Pb 8885 Youngstorget, 0028 OSLO **Tel:** 23 21 45 70 **Fax:** 23 21 45 51
Email: menneskevennen@dnt.no **Web site:** http://www.dnt.no/menneskevennen
Freq: 6 issues yearly; **Circ:** 2,600
Profile: Magazine focusing on the activities of DNT, contains articles about drug free social activities.
Language(s): Norwegian
CONSUMER: WOMEN'S INTEREST CONSUMER MAGAZINES: Slimming & Health

MENTOR 1625102R14A-206
Tel: 95 26 00 00
Email: jens-erik.huneide@no.pwc.com **Web site:** http://www.pwc.com/no/no/mentor/index.jhtml
Freq: Quarterly; **Circ:** 11,500
Language(s): Norwegian
BUSINESS: COMMERCE, INDUSTRY & MANAGEMENT

MERKBART 1625221R22A-152
Editorial: KSL Matmerk, Postboks 487 - Sentrum, 0158 OSLO **Tel:** 24148300 **Fax:** 24148313
Email: post@kslmatmerk.no **Web site:** http://www.matmerk.no
Freq: Half-yearly; **Circ:** 8,000
Editor: Mette Sørensen
Language(s): Norwegian
BUSINESS: FOOD

MICROSOFT MAGAZINE 1645039R5F-4
Editorial: Pb. 43, Lilleaker, 0216 OSLO
Tel: 22022500 **Fax:** 22950664
Email: norge@microsoft.com
Freq: Half-yearly; **Circ:** 50,000
Language(s): Norwegian
BUSINESS: COMPUTERS & AUTOMATION: Multimedia

MIDTØSTEN I FOKUS 1624802R82-323
Editorial: Pb 9101, 3006 DRAMMEN **Tel:** 41176780
Email: post@miff.no **Web site:** http://www.miff.no/moif/index.htm
Freq: Quarterly; **Circ:** 3,400
Language(s): Norwegian
CONSUMER: CURRENT AFFAIRS & POLITICS

MILITÆRTEKNIKK 31546R40-9
Editorial: Fred Olsens gate 1, 0303 OSLO
Tel: 22416077 **Fax:** 22416011
Email: b.josefsen@mil-tek.no **Web site:** http://www.mil-tek.no
Date Established: 1995; **Freq:** Quarterly; **Circ:** 4,500
Profile: Military magazine covering Navy, Army and Airforce. Comprehensive articles about military technology, defence material and military contracts. Press releases about military contracts, new products and general news. Articles and press releases about both the armed forces and defence industry.
Language(s): Norwegian
Readership: Read by officers, professionals and leaders in the armed forces in Norway, Sweden, Finland and Denmark. Also leaders and professionals in defence industry in Scandinavia and political authorities in the Nordic countries. Magazine favoured by personnel in positions of making decisions concerning purchasing for the armed forces and defence industry in the Scandinavian countries.
BUSINESS: DEFENCE

MILJØ & HELSE 31689R57-90
Editorial: Forum for miljø og helse c/o Svein Kvakland, Molde kommune, Rådhusplassen 1, 6413 MOLDE **Tel:** 71111245
Email: fmh@fmh.no **Web site:** http://www.fmh.no
Date Established: 1982; **Freq:** Quarterly - 4 ganger i året
Profile: Magazine covering articles and information concerning links between health and the environment.
Language(s): Norwegian
ADVERTISING RATES:
Full Page Colour .... NOK 5000
BUSINESS: ENVIRONMENT & POLLUTION

MILJØKRIM 1663295R57-310
Editorial: Økokrim, Pb. 8193 Dep., 0034 OSLO
Tel: 23291000 **Fax:** 23291001
Email: miljokrim@okokrim.no **Web site:** http://www.miljokrim.no
Freq: Quarterly
Language(s): Norwegian
BUSINESS: ENVIRONMENT & POLLUTION

MILJØMAGASINET 1624616R57-302
Editorial: Pb.593, 5806 BERGEN **Tel:** 55 30 67 00 **Fax:** 55 30 67 01
Email: nmf@nmf.no **Web site:** http://www.miljovernforbundet.no
Freq: Quarterly; **Circ:** 3,000
Editor: Snorre Sletvold
Language(s): Norwegian
BUSINESS: ENVIRONMENT & POLLUTION

MILJØSTRATEGI 31690R57-100
Editorial: Findexa Forlag, Pb. 457 Sentrum, 0104 OSLO **Tel:** 21508020
Email: jan.bjerk@findexaforlag.no **Web site:** http://www.miljostrategi.no
Freq: Monthly - 8 ganger i året; **Circ:** 4,103
Profile: Magazine containing topical articles on new technology in the field of environmental protection and pollution problems, their prevention and solution.
Language(s): Norwegian
ADVERTISING RATES:
SCC .... NOK 107.92
BUSINESS: ENVIRONMENT & POLLUTION

MINERVA 1660320R82-336
Editorial: Akersgaten 20, 0158 OSLO
Tel: 92 89 85 71 **Fax:** 22 82 90 92
Email: magnus.thue@minerva.as **Web site:** http://www.minerva.as
Freq: Quarterly; **Circ:** 1,500
Editor: Nils August Andresen
Language(s): Norwegian
CONSUMER: CURRENT AFFAIRS & POLITICS

MJ-BLADET 32696R79J-100
Editorial: Modelljernbaneforeningen i Norge, Pb. 467 Skøyen, 0213 OSLO **Tel:** 994 18 736
Email: mj-bladet@mjf.no **Web site:** http://www.mj-bladet.no
Freq: Quarterly; **Circ:** 2,500
Editor: Morten Pelle Korsmo
Profile: Magazine containing articles and information published by the Model Railway Association of Norway.
Language(s): Norwegian
Readership: Aimed at railway enthusiasts.
CONSUMER: HOBBIES & DIY: Rail Enthusiasts

MØBEL & INTERIØR 31490R23A-20
Editorial: Skarland Press AS, Postboks 2843 TØYEN, 0608 OSLO **Tel:** 22708300 **Fax:** 22708301
Email: firmapost@skarland.no **Web site:** http://www.mobelogiinterior.no
Date Established: 1929; **Freq:** Monthly - 8 ganger i året; **Circ:** 2,000
Profile: Magazine about furniture retail and design.
Language(s): Norwegian
ADVERTISING RATES:
Full Page Colour .... NOK 14700
SCC .... NOK 115.83
BUSINESS: FURNISHINGS & FURNITURE

MOBILEN.NO 1740764R18B-305
Editorial: PB 9025 Grønland, 0133 FORNEBU
Tel: 99452000 **Fax:** 22420120
Email: redaksjon@mobilen.no **Web site:** http://www.mobilen.no

Language(s): Norwegian
BUSINESS: ELECTRONICS: Telecommunications

MODERNE PRODUKSJON
31430R14B-90
Editorial: Pb. 163, 1332 ØSTERÅS Tel: 671634 00
Fax: 67163410
Email: redaksjonen@moderneproduksjon.com Web site: http://www.moderneproduksjon.com
ISSN: 0803-0502
Date Established: 1990; Freq: 26 issues yearly - 16 ganger i året; Circ: 45,000
Usual Pagination: 40
Profile: Newspaper covering the latest developments in the industrial world in Norway and other countries. Contains articles about automation, electronics, technology, logistics and industrial computing, research and development, raw materials, mechanical industry and process industry.
Language(s): Norwegian
Readership: Aimed at those in the mechanical and engineering industries.
ADVERTISING RATES:
SCC .... NOK 218.59
Mechanical Data: Type Area: 365 x 255mm, Trim Size: 270 x 199mm
Copy instructions: *Copy Date:* 20 days prior to publication date
BUSINESS: COMMERCE, INDUSTRY & MANAGEMENT: Industry & Factories

MODERNE TRANSPORT
31606R49C-30
Editorial: Pb. 11, 1411 KOLBOTN Tel: 66 82 21 21
Fax: 66 82 21 20
Email: bjorgu@bjorgu.no Web site: http://www.bjorgu.no/MT.aspx
Date Established: 1970; Freq: Monthly; Circ: 6,000
Editor: Glenn-Frode Lund
Profile: Magazine focusing on transport and logistics. Covers road, rail, sea and air transport, forwarding, warehousing, materials handling and packaging.
Language(s): Norwegian
ADVERTISING RATES:
Full Page Colour .... NOK 16900
SCC .... NOK 160.83
BUSINESS: TRANSPORT: Freight

LE MONDE DIPLOMATIQUE
1645132R82-334
Editorial: Pb. 1180 Sentrum, 0170 OSLO
Tel: 22 31 0 224 Fax: 22 31 03 05
Email: redaksjon@lmd.no Web site: http://www.lmd.no
Freq: Monthly; Circ: 18,000
Language(s): Norwegian
CONSUMER: CURRENT AFFAIRS & POLITICS

LE MONDE DIPLOMATIQUE; LMD.NO
1864704R82-365
Editorial: Postboks 1180 Sentrum, 0107 OSLO
Tel: 22 31 03 10
Email: redaksjon@lmd.no Web site: http://www.lmd.no
Freq: Daily; Cover Price: Free; Circ: 2,500 Unique Users
Language(s): Norwegian
CONSUMER: CURRENT AFFAIRS & POLITICS

MONITOR
32408R2D-10
Editorial: Postb. 33, 3209 SANDEFJORD
Tel: 22 11 24 55 Fax: 94770442
Email: post@monitormagasin.no Web site: http://www.monitormagasin.no
Freq: Quarterly; Circ: 5,056
Profile: Magazine concerning the audio, video and broadcasting industry. Contains technical information and articles on new products and equipment.
Language(s): Norwegian
Readership: Aimed at users and producers of audio equipment.
BUSINESS: COMMUNICATIONS, ADVERTISING & MARKETING: Broadcasting

MORGENBLADET
31743R82-85
Editorial: Karl Johansgt 25, 0159 OSLO
Tel: 21006300 Fax: 21006301
Email: redaksjon@morgenbladet.no Web site: http://www.morgenbladet.no
Date Established: 1819; Freq: Weekly; Circ: 21,442
Profile: Newspaper covering current affairs, cultural and religious issues, debate articles and literature.
Language(s): Norwegian
Readership: Aimed at people interested in up-to-date cultural information.
ADVERTISING RATES:
SCC .... NOK 158.33
CONSUMER: CURRENT AFFAIRS & POLITICS

MORGENBLADET; MORGENBLADET.NO
1864865R84A-150
Editorial: Karl Johansgate 25, 0159 OSLO
Tel: 21006300 Fax: 21006301
Email: redaksjon@morgenbladet.no Web site: http://www.morgenbladet.no
Freq: Daily; Cover Price: Free; Circ: 15,000 Unique Users
Language(s): Norwegian
CONSUMER: THE ARTS & LITERARY: Arts

MOSS AVIS
31789R67B-4400
Editorial: Pb. 248/250, 1501 MOSS Tel: 69 20 50 00
Email: desken@moss-avis.no Web site: http://www.moss-avis.no
Date Established: 1876; Freq: Daily; Circ: 14,983
Language(s): Norwegian
ADVERTISING RATES:
SCC .... NOK 125.92
REGIONAL DAILY & SUNDAY NEWSPAPERS: Regional Daily Newspapers

MOSS AVIS; KULTURREDAKSJONEN
1833159R84A-132
Editorial: Pb. 250, 1501 MOSS Tel: 46907777
Email: eva.fretheim@moss-avis.no Web site: http://www.moss-avis.no
Circ: 14,983
Language(s): Norwegian
CONSUMER: THE ARTS & LITERARY: Arts

MOT RUSGIFT
1657828R56R-163
Editorial: Forbundet Mot Rusgift, Torggata 1, 0181 OSLO Tel: 23 21 45 26 Fax: 23 21 45 01
Email: post@fmr.no Web site: http://www.fmr.no
Freq: Quarterly
Language(s): Norwegian
BUSINESS: HEALTH & MEDICAL: Health Medical Related

MOT STOFF
1624987R32G-160
Editorial: Grønland 12, 0188 OSLO Tel: 23 08 05 50
Fax: 23 08 05 51
Email: stoffmisbruk@motstoff.no Web site: http://www.motstoff.no
Freq: Quarterly; Circ: 9,000
Language(s): Norwegian
BUSINESS: LOCAL GOVERNMENT, LEISURE & RECREATION: Community Care & Social Services

MOTMÆLE
32330R88R-100
Editorial: Pb 285 Sentrum, 0103 OSLO
Tel: 23 00 29 40 Fax: 23 00 29 31
Web site: http://nmu.s0.no/organisasjon/motmaele
Freq: Quarterly; Circ: 2,500
Editor: Kristian Weibye
Profile: Magazine containing information, news and articles about Nynorsk, which is one of two official languages in Norway.
Language(s): Norwegian
CONSUMER: EDUCATION: Education Related

MOTOR
32221R77A-100
Editorial: Østensjøveien 14 på Helsfyr, 0441 OSLO
Tel: 22 58 50 00 Fax: 22 58 59 59
Email: redaksjon@motor.no Web site: http://www.naf.no/kontakt-oss/Medlemsbladet-MOTOR
Freq: 8 ganger i året; Circ: 436,935
Profile: Special-interest magazine about motoring, travel and leisure. Published by the Norwegian Automobile Association.
Language(s): Norwegian
ADVERTISING RATES:
SCC .... NOK 579.17
Copy instructions: *Copy Date:* 20 days prior to publication date
CONSUMER: MOTORING & CYCLING: Motoring

MOTORBRANSJEN
1624391R77A-203
Editorial: Pb. 63 Skøyen, 0212 OSLO
Tel: 23 03 66 00 Fax: 23 03 66 40
Email: trygve.larsen@bilforlaget.no Web site: http://www.motorbransjen.no
Freq: Monthly; Circ: 14,977
Language(s): Norwegian
ADVERTISING RATES:
SCC .... NOK 315.83
CONSUMER: MOTORING & CYCLING: Motoring

MOTORFØREREN
1624685R77A-207
Editorial: Pb 80 Alnabru, 0614 OSLO Tel: 22956969
Fax: 22956968
Email: motorfoereren@ma-norge.no Web site: http://www.ma-norge.no
Freq: 6 issues yearly; Circ: 12,806
Language(s): Norwegian
CONSUMER: MOTORING & CYCLING: Motoring

MOTORSPORTAVISEN.NO
1659359R77D-105
Editorial: Gullveien 3, 4629 KRISTIANSAND
Tel: 38 03 37 15 Fax: 380 33996
Email: post@motorsportavisen.no Web site: http://www.motorsportavisen.no
Language(s): Norwegian
CONSUMER: MOTORING & CYCLING: Motor Sports

MOTORSPORT.NO
1625237R75A-206
Editorial: SPORTMEDIA AS, Rakkestadveien 1, 1814 ASKIM Tel: 69 81 97 19
Email: kari@sportmedia.no Web site: http://www.motorsport.no
Cover Price: Paid; Circ: 2,500 Unique Users
Editor: Kari Nilsen
Language(s): Norwegian
CONSUMER: SPORT

MOTORSPORT.NO
1658232R77D-104
Editorial: SPORTMEDIA AS, Rakkestadveien 1, 1814 ASKIM Tel: 69 81 97 00 Fax: 69 88 99 80
Email: kari.nilsen@sportmedia.no Web site: http://www.motorsport.no
Cover Price: Paid
Editor: Kari Nilsen
Language(s): Norwegian
CONSUMER: MOTORING & CYCLING: Motor Sports

MS-BLADET
1624808R56D-78
Editorial: Tollbugata 35, 0157 OSLO Tel: 22477992
Fax: 22477991
Email: olav@ms.no Web site: http://www.ms.no
Freq: Quarterly; Circ: 7,000
Language(s): Norwegian
BUSINESS: HEALTH & MEDICAL: Dental

MUNNPLEIEN
1624867R56D-79
Editorial: Norsk Tannvern, Pb 9341 Grønland, 0135 OSLO Tel: 22113440 Fax: 22113441
Email: tannvern@tannvern.no Web site: http://www.tannvern.no/sider/munnpleien.html
Freq: Half-yearly; Circ: 4,000
Language(s): Norwegian
BUSINESS: HEALTH & MEDICAL: Dental

MUR+BETONG
31394R4E-75
Editorial: Pb. 102 Lilleaker, 0216 OSLO
Tel: 22 87 84 21 Fax: 22 87 84 01
Email: post@murbetong.no Web site: http://www.murbetong.no
Date Established: 1976; Freq: Quarterly; Circ: 2,400
Profile: Journal covering masonry building and architecture.
Language(s): Norwegian
Readership: Read by architects, construction engineers, contractors, researchers and teachers in the building sector.
BUSINESS: ARCHITECTURE & BUILDING: Building

MURMESTEREN
31395R4E-80
Editorial: Per Christian Berg, Bjerkelundsveien 5, 1358 JAR Tel: 92043200
Email: berg@teglhus.no Web site: http://www.norskemurmestre.no/murmesteren
Date Established: 1903; Freq: 6 issues yearly; Circ: 1,450
Editor: Per Christian Berg
Profile: Journal containing information about the building trade.
Language(s): Norwegian
Readership: Read by master builders.
BUSINESS: ARCHITECTURE & BUILDING: Building

MUSEUMSNYTT
1936400R84A-162
Editorial: Ullevålsvn. 11, 0165 OSLO Tel: 22 20 14 02
Fax: 22 99 31 31
Email: post@museumsnytt.no Web site: http://www.museumsnytt.no
Freq: 5 ganger i året; Circ: 2,000
Editor: Signy Norendal
Language(s): Norwegian
CONSUMER: THE ARTS & LITERARY: Arts

MUSIKK-KULTUR
31710R61-50
Editorial: Postboks 9246 Grønland, 0134 OSLO
Tel: 22 05 28 20 Fax: 22 05 28 21
Email: redaksjon@musikk-kultur.no Web site: http://www.musikk-kultur.no
Freq: Monthly; Circ: 8,200
Editor: Geir Storli
Profile: Magazine covering all aspects of the music industry.
Language(s): Norwegian
BUSINESS: MUSIC TRADE

MUSIKK-KULTUR; MUSIKK-KULTUR.NO
1864871R76D-312
Editorial: Postboks 9246 Grønland, 0134 OSLO
Tel: 22 05 28 20 Fax: 22 05 28 21
Email: redaksjon@musikk-kultur.no Web site: http://www.musikk-kultur.no
Freq: Daily; Cover Price: Free; Circ: 2,500 Unique Users
Editor: Geir Storli
Language(s): Norwegian
CONSUMER: MUSIC & PERFORMING ARTS: Music

MUSIKK.NO
1624771R76D-253
Editorial: Pstboks 4651, Sofienberg, 0506 OSLO
Tel: 22 00 56 00 Fax: 22 00 56 01
Email: nmr@musikk.no Web site: http://www.musikk.no
Cover Price: Paid
Language(s): Norwegian
CONSUMER: MUSIC & PERFORMING ARTS: Music

MUSIKKNYHETER.NO
1803861R76D-311
Editorial: Calmeyersgate 4, 0183 OSLO
Email: post@musikknyheter.no Web site: http://www.musikknyheter.no
Cover Price: Paid
Language(s): Norwegian
CONSUMER: MUSIC & PERFORMING ARTS: Music

MUSIKKPRAKSIS
31711R61-55
Editorial: Niels Juels gate 5, 0242 OSLO
Tel: 975 17 980
Email: nyheter@musikkpraksis.no Web site: http://www.musikkweb.no
Freq: 6 issues yearly; Circ: 12,000
Profile: Magazine covering all aspects of the music trade. Includes information on musicians, instruments, studio equipment and installation, broadcasting and music videos.
Language(s): Norwegian
BUSINESS: MUSIC TRADE

MUSIKKTERAPI
1740663R76D-302
Editorial: Pb 4727 Sofienberg, 0103 OSLO
Tel: 22 00 56 45
Email: redaksjon@musikkterapi.no Web site: http://www.musikkterapi.no
Freq: Quarterly
Editor: Tor Olav Heldal
Language(s): Norwegian
CONSUMER: MUSIC & PERFORMING ARTS: Music

MUSIQ
1625222R76D-261
Editorial: Co / Geir Atle Ellingsen, Tøane 11, 4760 BIRKELAND
Email: red@musiq.no Web site: http://www.musiq.no
Cover Price: Paid
Language(s): Norwegian
CONSUMER: MUSIC & PERFORMING ARTS: Music

MUSKELNYTT
1624649R56C-1
Editorial: Foreningen for Muskelsyke, Brynsveien 96, 1352 KOLSÅS Tel: 51113938
Email: muskelnytt@ffm.no Web site: http://www.ffm.no
Freq: Quarterly
Language(s): Norwegian
BUSINESS: HEALTH & MEDICAL: Hospitals

NA24.NO
1740689R74M-208
Editorial: Postboks 9386 Grønland, 0135 OSLO
Tel: 400 13 500
Email: alle@na24.no Web site: http://www.na24.no
Circ: 470,000 Unique Users
Language(s): Norwegian
CONSUMER: WOMEN'S INTEREST CONSUMER MAGAZINES: Personal Finance

NA24.NO; FINANS
1829608R1A-131
Editorial: Postboks 9386 Grønland, 0135 OSLO
Tel: 400 13 500
Email: alle@na24.no Web site: http://www.na24.no
Freq: Daily
Language(s): Norwegian
BUSINESS: FINANCE & ECONOMICS

NA24.NO; PROPAGANDA
1625164R2A-54
Editorial: Postboks 9386 Grønland, 0135 OSLO
Tel: 400 13 500
Email: propaganda@na24.no Web site: http://www.na24.no/propaganda
Language(s): Norwegian
BUSINESS: COMMUNICATIONS, ADVERTISING & MARKETING

NÆRINGSAVISEN
1624675R1A-121
Editorial: Løvenskioldsgate 10, 3916 PORSGRUNN
Tel: 915 74 756
Email: kjartan@hkf.no Web site: http://www.naeringsavisen.com

Circ: 15,000 Unique Users
Language(s): Norwegian
BUSINESS: FINANCE & ECONOMICS

NÆRINGSAVISEN; NAERINGSAVISEN.COM
1864867R14A-239
Editorial: Løvenskioldsgate 10, 3916 PORSGRUNN
Tel: 915 74 756
Email: kjartan@hkf.no **Web site:** http://www.naeringsavisen.com
Freq: Daily; **Cover Price:** Free; **Circ:** 2,500 Unique Users
Language(s): Norwegian
BUSINESS: COMMERCE, INDUSTRY & MANAGEMENT

NÆRINGSEIENDOM
1624385R1E-2
Editorial: Pb 2374 Solli, 0201 OSLO **Tel:** 23115600
Fax: 23115601
Email: post@ne.no **Web site:** http://www.ne.no
Freq: Monthly - 11 ganger i året; **Circ:** 50,000
Language(s): Norwegian
ADVERTISING RATES:
Full Page Colour .... NOK 27000
SCC .... NOK 196.92
BUSINESS: FINANCE & ECONOMICS: Property

NÆRINGSLIVET I TELEMARK
1625018R14A-208
Editorial: Luksefjellveien 186, 3721 SKIEN
Tel: 35 59 49 00 **Fax:** 35 59 00 80
Email: kent@observer.org **Web site:** http://watchtower.tripod.com/index1.htm
Freq: 6 issues yearly; **Circ:** 5,300
Language(s): Norwegian
BUSINESS: COMMERCE, INDUSTRY & MANAGEMENT

NÆRINGSRAPPORT
1624889R27-51
Editorial: Pb 1166, 9262 TROMSØ **Tel:** 40052883
Fax: 77639051
Email: post@nrapp.no **Web site:** http://www.nrapp.no
Freq: 6 issues yearly; **Circ:** 7,000
Language(s): Norwegian
ADVERTISING RATES:
SCC .... NOK 197.71
BUSINESS: METAL, IRON & STEEL

NÅR MAT GJØR DEG FRISK
1938272R74G-170
Web site: http://24022.vgb.no
Cover Price: Paid
Language(s): Norwegian
CONSUMER: WOMEN'S INTEREST CONSUMER MAGAZINES: Slimming & Health

NATIONAL GEOGRAPHIC
1624678R73-151
Editorial: Bonnier Media A/S, 0158 OSLO
Tel: 22 04 70 00
Email: redaksjonen@nationalgeographic.no **Web site:** http://www.nationalgeographic.no
Freq: Monthly; **Circ:** 16,851
Editor: Gunnar Falkum
Language(s): Norwegian
CONSUMER: NATIONAL & INTERNATIONAL PERIODICALS

NATIONEN
31740R65A-50
Editorial: Pb. 9390 Grønland, 0135 OSLO
Tel: 21310000
Email: tips@nationen.no **Web site:** http://www.nationen.no
Date Established: 1918; **Freq:** Daily; **Circ:** 15,670
Profile: Broadsheet-sized newspaper covering national news, politics and finance.
Language(s): Norwegian
Readership: Read predominantly by those living in the countryside.
ADVERTISING RATES:
SCC .... NOK 124.40
NATIONAL DAILY & SUNDAY NEWSPAPERS: National Daily Newspapers

NATT&DAG
32332R89C-100
Editorial: Innovation Media avd Oslo, PB 266 Sentrum, 0103 OSLO **Tel:** 22419441
Email: redaksjon@nattogdag.no **Web site:** http://www.nattogdag.no
Date Established: 1988; **Freq:** Monthly; **Cover Price:** Free
Editor: Eirik Kydland
Profile: Magazine focusing on fashionable clubs and restaurants, music, cinema, bands, fashion and travel.
Language(s): Norwegian
Readership: Read by men and women aged between 18 and 35 years.
Copy instructions: *Copy Date:* 30 days prior to publication date
CONSUMER: HOLIDAYS & TRAVEL: Entertainment Guides

NATT&DAG; NATTOGDAG.NO
1859642R76C-74
Editorial: Innovation Media AS, PB 266 Sentrum, 0103 OSLO **Tel:** 22 41 94 41
Email: redaksjon@nattogdag.no **Web site:** http://www.nattogdag.no
Freq: Daily
Language(s): Norwegian
CONSUMER: MUSIC & PERFORMING ARTS: TV & Radio

NATUR & MILJØ
31691R57-165
Editorial: Grensen 9b, 0101 OSLO **Tel:** 23 10 96 10
Fax: 23 10 96 11
Email: redaksjonen@miljojournalen.no **Web site:** http://www.miljojournalen.no
Date Established: 1916; **Freq:** Monthly; **Circ:** 16,772
Profile: Nature and environmental bulletin published by the Norwegian branch of Friends of the Earth.
Language(s): Norwegian
ADVERTISING RATES:
Full Page Colour .... NOK 33 000
SCC .... NOK 275
BUSINESS: ENVIRONMENT & POLLUTION

NATURTERAPEUTEN
1624589R76D-251
Editorial: Postboks 9397 Grønland, 0136 OSLO
Tel: 21013700 **Fax:** 21013705
Email: redaksjon@nnh.no **Web site:** http://www.nnh.no/article.aspx?id=16
Freq: Quarterly; **Circ:** 3,000
Language(s): Norwegian
CONSUMER: MUSIC & PERFORMING ARTS: Music

NATURVITEREN
31469R21A-50
Editorial: Keysers Gt. 5, 0165 OSLO **Tel:** 22033400
Fax: 22033401
Email: post@naturviterne.no **Web site:** http://www.naturviterforbundet.no
Freq: Quarterly; **Circ:** 5,050
Profile: Official publication of the Norwegian Association of Agricultural Graduates. Includes information on agriculture, dairy farming, food technology, land consolidation, surveying and natural resource conservation.
Language(s): Norwegian
BUSINESS: AGRICULTURE & FARMING

NAVIGARE
32479R45A-22
Editorial: Postboks 2222, N-5509 HAUGESUND
Tel: 52745000 **Fax:** 52745001
Email: bam@sjofartsdir.no **Web site:** http://www.sjofartsdir.no/no/Publikasjoner/Navigare
Date Established: 1994; **Freq:** Quarterly; **Circ:** 15,000
Editor: Bente Amandussen
Profile: Magazine containing articles, news and information about shipping, in particular safety at sea.
Language(s): Norwegian
Readership: Aimed at all professionals within the field.
BUSINESS: MARINE & SHIPPING

NBS-NYTT
32480R55-73
Tel: 64965257 **Fax:** 41337230
Email: tore.skotland@rr-research.no **Web site:** http://www.biokjemisk.com
Freq: Quarterly; **Circ:** 1,703
Profile: Publication concerning the field of bio-chemistry.
Language(s): Norwegian
BUSINESS: APPLIED SCIENCE & LABORATORIES

NEA RADIO; NEARADIO.NO
1864859R84A-149
Editorial: Postboks 60, 7581 SELBU **Tel:** 73 81 74 00
Email: nr-selbu@nearadio.no **Web site:** http://www.nearadio.no
Freq: Daily; **Cover Price:** Free; **Circ:** 2,500 Unique Users
Language(s): Norwegian
CONSUMER: THE ARTS & LITERARY: Arts

NEGOTIA MAGASIN
1624257R74J-1
Editorial: Pb 9187 Grønland, 0134 OSLO
Tel: 21 01 36 00 **Fax:** 21 01 37 50
Email: post@negotia.no **Web site:** http://www.negotia.no
Freq: Quarterly; **Circ:** 16,842
Language(s): Norwegian
CONSUMER: WOMEN'S INTEREST CONSUMER MAGAZINES: Secretary & PA

NETTAVISEN
624625R73-176
Editorial: Pb. 9386 Grønland, 0135 OSLO
Tel: 21 00 60 00 **Fax:** 22570942
Email: redaksjonen@nettavisen.no **Web site:** http://www.nettavisen.no
Freq: Daily; **Circ:** 577,000 Unique Users
Profile: Internet magazine with articles on all general-interest subjects.
Language(s): Norwegian
Readership: Aimed at the general public.
CONSUMER: NATIONAL & INTERNATIONAL PERIODICALS

NETTAVISEN; SIDE2.NO
1692442R82-364
Editorial: Pb. 9386 Grønland, 0135 OSLO
Tel: 21 00 60 00 **Fax:** 22570942
Email: redaksjonen@nettavisen.no **Web site:** http://www.side2.no
Freq: Daily
Editor: Gaute Tyssebotn
Language(s): Norwegian
CONSUMER: CURRENT AFFAIRS & POLITICS

NETTAVISEN; SPORTREDAKSJONEN
1740750R75A-214
Editorial: Pb. 9386 Grønland, 0135 **Tel:** 21 00 60 00
Fax: 22570942
Email: anders.skjerdingstad@nettavisen.no **Web site:** http://www.nettavisen.no/sport
Freq: Daily
Language(s): Norwegian
CONSUMER: SPORT

NETTVERK
31453R18B-200
Editorial: Pb. 231 Sentrum, 0103 OSLO
Tel: 23063381
Email: anette.hobaek.ravnsborg@lomedia.no **Web site:** http://www.frifagbevegelse.no/nettverk
Freq: Monthly; **Circ:** 37,800
Profile: Official journal of the Telecommunications, Information Technology and Electricians' Union.
Language(s): Norwegian
ADVERTISING RATES:
Full Page Colour .... NOK 22100
BUSINESS: ELECTRONICS: Telecommunications

NETTVERK & KOMMUNIKASJON
625264R5C-51
Editorial: Pb 9090 Grønland, 0133 OSLO
Tel: 22053000
Web site: http://nettverk.idg.no
Freq: 6 issues yearly; **Circ:** 20,000
Editor: Stig-Roar Martinsen
Profile: Magazine focusing on system and network management, new technology and telecommunications.
Language(s): Norwegian
Readership: Read by network, systems and IT managers.
ADVERTISING RATES:
SCC .... NOK 450
BUSINESS: COMPUTERS & AUTOMATION: Professional Personal Computers

NFF-BULLETIN
1663398R84B-238
Editorial: Norsk faglitterær forfatter- og oversetterforening, Uranienborgveien 2, 0258 OSLO
Tel: 22 12 11 40 **Fax:** 22 12 11 50
Email: magnus.holm@nffo.no **Web site:** http://www.nffo.no
Freq: 6 issues yearly; **Circ:** 5,000
Editor: Magnus Holm
Language(s): Norwegian
CONSUMER: THE ARTS & LITERARY: Literary

NHH - BULETTIN
1657788R14R-2
Editorial: NHH, Helleveien 30, 5045 BERGEN
Tel: 55 95 97 02
Email: bulletin@nhh.no **Web site:** http://www.nhh.no/silhuetten
Freq: Quarterly; **Circ:** 10,700
Editor: Sigrid Folkestad
Language(s): Norwegian
BUSINESS: COMMERCE, INDUSTRY & MANAGEMENT: Commerce Related

NITO REFLEKS
1663399R19R-2
Editorial: Pb. 9100 Grønland, 0133 OSLO
Tel: 22 05 35 25 **Fax:** 22 17 24 80
Email: hh@nito.no **Web site:** http://www.nito.no
Freq: 6 issues yearly
Language(s): Norwegian
BUSINESS: ENGINEERING & MACHINERY: Engineering Related

NOFIMA.NO
1657806R22A-159
Editorial: Postboks 6122, 9291 TROMSÆ
Tel: 77 62 90 00 **Fax:** 77 62 91 00
Email: nofima@nofima.no **Web site:** http://nofima.no
Freq: Daily; **Cover Price:** Paid
Language(s): Norwegian
BUSINESS: FOOD

NØKKELEN
32718R88R-125
Editorial: Tøyengata 26, 0190 OSLO **Tel:** 22 68 22 06
Fax: 22 68 78 31
Email: hovden@folkeakademiet.no **Web site:** http://www.folkeakademiet.no
Date Established: 1980; **Freq:** Quarterly; **Circ:** 3,300
Editor: Lina Bjelland
Profile: Magazine containing articles about cultural activities and related issues. Includes musical events, children's programmes and details of educational grants.
Language(s): Norwegian
CONSUMER: EDUCATION: Education Related

NOPA-NYTT
1740675R76D-304
Editorial: Kongensgt. 4, 0153 OSLO **Tel:** 22 47 30 00
Fax: 22 17 25 60
Email: post@nopa.no **Web site:** http://www.nopa.no
Freq: Annual
Language(s): Norwegian
CONSUMER: MUSIC & PERFORMING ARTS: Music

NORAFORUM
1625019R56A-208
Editorial: P.B. 1045 Sentrum, 0104 OSLO
Tel: 23034513 **Fax:** 24101221
Email: gunnar.sandbaek@medisin.uio.no **Web site:** http://www.radiologforeningen.no
Freq: Quarterly; **Circ:** 700
Language(s): Norwegian
BUSINESS: HEALTH & MEDICAL

NORDENS NYHETER
31346R1A-93_75
Editorial: Postboks 76 Smestad, 0309 OSLO
Tel: 22741498
Email: post@nordensnyheter.no **Web site:** http://www.nordensnyheter.no
Date Established: 1989; **Freq:** Monthly; **Circ:** 104,714
Profile: Magazine covering business and financial news and articles about management and current affairs.
Language(s): Norwegian
Readership: Aimed at managers, directors, politicians and financial executives at companies throughout the Nordic countries.
BUSINESS: FINANCE & ECONOMICS

NORDIC JOURNAL OF PSYCHIATRY
31672R56N-20
Editorial: Pb. 12 Posthuset, 0051 OSLO
Tel: 23103460 **Fax:** 23103461
Email: post@tandf.no **Web site:** http://www.tandf.no/psychiatry
Date Established: 1947; **Freq:** 6 issues yearly; **Circ:** 6,000
Profile: Journal containing articles and information on current psychiatry in the Nordic countries and related fields.
Language(s): Norwegian
Readership: Read by psychiatrists, psychologists and social workers.
BUSINESS: HEALTH & MEDICAL: Mental Health

NORDINA
1740819R62A-237
Editorial: Pb. 1099 Blindern, 0317 OSLO
Fax: 22 85 44 09
Email: anders.isnes@naturfagsenteret.no **Web site:** http://www.naturfagsenteret.no/tidsskrift/nordina.html
Freq: Half-yearly
Language(s): Norwegian
BUSINESS: CHURCH & SCHOOL EQUIPMENT & EDUCATION: Education

NORDISK DOMSSAMLING
1624931R44-102
Editorial: Inst. for privatrett, PB 6706 St. Olavs plass, 0130 OSLO **Tel:** 22859386 **Fax:** 22859720
Email: janicke.wiggen@jus.uio.no **Web site:** http://www.universitetsforlaget.no/tidsskrifter/juss/article.jhtml?articleID=181
Freq: Half-yearly; **Circ:** 1,600
Language(s): Norwegian
BUSINESS: LEGAL

NORDISK ØSTFORUM
32343R90-150
Editorial: Norsk Utenrikspolitisk Institutt, Pb 8159 Dep., 0033 OSLO **Tel:** 22 99 40 00 **Fax:** 24 36 21 82
Email: nof@nupi.no **Web site:** http://www.universitetsforlaget.no
Date Established: 1987; **Freq:** Quarterly; **Circ:** 1,000
Profile: Magazine covering politics, culture, society and social issues in Eastern Europe, Russia and the newly independent States.
Language(s): Norwegian
Readership: Read by researchers, students and other people with a special interest in Eastern Europe and the former Soviet Union.
CONSUMER: ETHNIC

NORDLYS 31802R67B-4600
Editorial: Pb. 2515, 9272 TROMSØ **Fax:** 77 62 35 01
Email: nyheter@nordlys.no **Web site:** http://www.nordlys.no
Date Established: 1902; **Freq:** Daily; **Circ:** 26,714
Language(s): Norwegian
ADVERTISING RATES:
SCC .... NOK 161.76
REGIONAL DAILY & SUNDAY NEWSPAPERS: Regional Daily Newspapers

NORDNORSK MAGASIN 1624816R84A-106
Editorial: Bankbygget, 9392 STONGLANDSEIDET
Tel: 77 85 46 10
Email: karin@nordnorsk-magasin.no **Web site:** http://www.nordnorsk-magasin.no
Freq: Quarterly; **Circ:** 3,000
Language(s): Norwegian
CONSUMER: THE ARTS & LITERARY: Arts

NORDRE AKER BUDSTIKKE 1659357R80-159
Editorial: Postboks 79, Bryn, 0611 OSLO
Tel: 23 20 56 60 **Fax:** 22 13 30 29
Email: redaksjon@nordreakerbudstikke.no **Web site:** http://www.nordreakerbudstikke.no
Freq: Weekly; **Circ:** 22,200
Language(s): Norwegian
CONSUMER: RURAL & REGIONAL INTEREST

NORDSTRANDS BLAD; NOBLAD.NO 1864869R73-186
Editorial: Postboks 79, Bryn, 0611 OSLO
Tel: 22 63 91 00
Email: redaksjon@noblad.no **Web site:** http://www.noblad.no
Freq: Daily; **Cover Price:** Free; **Circ:** 11,200 Unique Users
Language(s): Norwegian
CONSUMER: NATIONAL & INTERNATIONAL PERIODICALS

NORGE I DAG 1625250R91A-204
Editorial: Fjøsangerveien 28, 5054 BERGEN
Tel: 55 92 29 00 **Fax:** 55 29 55 00
Email: redaksjonen@idag.no **Web site:** http://www.idag.no
Freq: Weekly; **Circ:** 10,293
Language(s): Norwegian
ADVERTISING RATES:
SCC .... NOK 40
CONSUMER: RECREATION & LEISURE: Boating & Yachting

NORGES BARNEVERN 31519R32G-55
Editorial: Storgata 10 A, 1055 OSLO **Tel:** 22 41 74 46
Email: redaksjon@barnevernsambandet.no **Web site:** http://www.barnevernsambandet.no
Freq: Quarterly; **Circ:** 1,800
Profile: Magazine containing information and articles about the protection of children's rights and aid to children in need.
Language(s): Norwegian
Readership: Read by people working for the social welfare of children in Norway.
BUSINESS: LOCAL GOVERNMENT, LEISURE & RECREATION: Community Care & Social Services

NORGES BLINDE 1624818R94F-109
Editorial: Norges Blindeforbund, Pb 5900 Majorstuen, 0308 OSLO **Tel:** 23 21 50 00
Fax: 23 21 50 72
Email: info@blindeforbundet.no **Web site:** http://www.blindeforbundet.no
Freq: 26 issues yearly; **Circ:** 5,000
Editor: Karianne Havsberg
Language(s): Norwegian
CONSUMER: OTHER CLASSIFICATIONS: Disability

NORGES FORSVAR 31547R40-10
Editorial: Nordengveien 39, 0755 OSLO
Tel: 22 52 59 96
Email: dt-olsen@online.no **Web site:** http://www.forsvarsforening.no
Date Established: 1918; **Freq:** Monthly; **Circ:** 10,000
Editor: Dag Tangen Olsen
Profile: Journal covering defence matters, also includes political and security implications.
Language(s): Norwegian
Readership: Read by key people in government, armed forces, parliament and the media. January edition also circulated to officials and decision-makers in NATO member countries and to embassies.
ADVERTISING RATES:
SCC .... NOK 208.33
BUSINESS: DEFENCE

NORILCO-NYTT 1625078R56A-209
Editorial: NORILCO. Pb. 4, Sentrum, 0102 OSLO
Tel: 93420838
Email: norilco-nytt@vidar-haagensen.no **Web site:** http://www.norilco.no
Freq: 6 issues yearly; **Circ:** 6,000
Language(s): Norwegian
BUSINESS: HEALTH & MEDICAL

THE NORSEMAN 1624552R84A-104
Editorial: Nordmanns-Forbundet, Rådhusgata 23 B, 0158 OSLO **Tel:** 23 35 71 70 **Fax:** 23 35 71 75
Email: norseman@norseman.no **Web site:** http://www.norseman.no
Freq: Quarterly; **Circ:** 5,300
Editor: Harry T.Cleven
Language(s): Norwegian
CONSUMER: THE ARTS & LITERARY: Arts

NORSK ANTROPOLOGISK TIDSSKRIFT 32486R62B-20
Editorial: Att: Mari D. Bergseth, Sosialantropologisk institutt, Pb 1091 Blindern, 0317 OSLO
Fax: 22854502
Email: nat-redaksjon@sai.uio.no **Web site:** http://www.universitetsforlaget.no/nat
Freq: Quarterly; **Circ:** 700
Editor: Christian Krohn-Hansen
Profile: Journal covering current research within the field of anthropology.
Language(s): Norwegian
Readership: Read mainly by students, teachers and people interested in anthropology, sociology and cultural studies.
BUSINESS: CHURCH & SCHOOL EQUIPMENT & EDUCATION: Education Teachers

NORSK BARNEHAGENYTT 1740643R32G-166
Editorial: Pb. 6611 St. Olavs plass, 0129 OSLO
Tel: 23 35 47 00 **Fax:** 23 35 47 01
Email: info@lex.no **Web site:** http://salg.lex.no
Freq: Quarterly
Language(s): Norwegian
BUSINESS: LOCAL GOVERNMENT, LEISURE & RECREATION: Community Care & Social Services

NORSK BORDTENNIS 32210R75X-90
Editorial: Serviceboks, Ullevål Stadion, 0840 OSLO
Tel: 21 02 97 82
Email: svenn-erik.nordby@bordtennis.no **Web site:** http://www.bordtennis.no
Freq: Quarterly; **Circ:** 2,000
Profile: Publication of the Norwegian Table Tennis Association.
Language(s): Norwegian
CONSUMER: SPORT: Other Sport

NORSK BRIDGE 1624577R91R-2
Editorial: Serviceboks 1 Ullevaal Stadion, 0840 OSLO **Tel:** 21 02 90 00 **Fax:** 21 02 91 45
Email: bridge@bridge.no **Web site:** http://www.bridgefederation.no
Freq: Quarterly; **Circ:** 11,500
Editor: Vegard Brekke
Language(s): Norwegian
CONSUMER: RECREATION & LEISURE: Recreation & Leisure Related

NORSK ENERGI 31700R58-100
Editorial: Pb 27 Skøyen, 0212 OSLO **Tel:** 22061800
Fax: 22061890
Email: hans.borchsenius@energi.no **Web site:** http://www.energi.no
Date Established: 1923; **Freq:** Quarterly; **Circ:** 3,000
Profile: Magazine containing information about energy efficiency in Norwegian industry.
Language(s): Norwegian
Readership: Read by industry personnel.
BUSINESS: ENERGY, FUEL & NUCLEAR

NORSK FAMILIEØKONOMI 32707R74M-200
Editorial: Pb 184, 4349 BRYNE **Fax:** 51 77 50 01
Email: gisle.hoyland@norskfamilie.no **Web site:** http://www.norskfamilie.no
Freq: 6 issues yearly; **Circ:** 24,207
Profile: Magazine covering all aspects of personal finance and investments.
Language(s): Norwegian
ADVERTISING RATES:
SCC .... NOK 245.83
CONSUMER: WOMEN'S INTEREST CONSUMER MAGAZINES: Personal Finance

NORSK FARMACEUTISK TIDSSKRIFT 31537R37-30
Editorial: Tollbugata 35, 0157 OSLO **Tel:** 21023352
Fax: 21023350
Email: nft@farmaceutene.no **Web site:** http://www.farmaceutene.no/id/3514
Freq: Monthly; **Circ:** 3,065
Profile: Journal of the Norwegian Pharmaceutical Association.
Language(s): Norwegian
BUSINESS: PHARMACEUTICAL & CHEMISTS

NORSK FILOSOFISK TIDSSKRIFT 32709R82-92
Editorial: Universitetet i Tromsø, Institutt for filosofi, NTNU Dragvoll, 9037 TROMSØ **Tel:** 77 64 91 76
Email: kjersti.fjortoft@nit.no **Web site:** http://www.universitetsforlaget.no/filosofisk
Freq: Quarterly; **Circ:** 350
Editor: Ingebjørg Seip
Profile: Magazine covering political and philosophical matters in Norway.
Language(s): Norwegian
Readership: Aimed at students, university lecturers and those with an interest in current affairs.
CONSUMER: CURRENT AFFAIRS & POLITICS

NORSK FISKEOPPDRETT 31581R45B-100
Editorial: Pb 4084 Dreggen, 5835 BERGEN
Tel: 55 54 13 00 **Fax:** 55 54 13 01
Email: redaksjon@kyst.no **Web site:** http://www.kyst.no
Freq: Monthly; **Circ:** 2,200
Editor: Pål Mugaas Jensen
Profile: Journal about the Norwegian fish-farming industry.
Language(s): Norwegian
ADVERTISING RATES:
SCC .... NOK 114.17
BUSINESS: MARINE & SHIPPING: Commercial Fishing

NORSK FISKERINÆRING 31582R45B-150
Editorial: Pb. 244, 2071 RÅHOLT **Tel:** 63 95 90 90
Email: post@norskfisk.no **Web site:** http://www.norskfisk.no
Freq: Monthly; **Circ:** 2,208
Profile: Magazine containing articles, information and news from the fishing trade.
Language(s): Norwegian
ADVERTISING RATES:
SCC .... NOK 83.33
BUSINESS: MARINE & SHIPPING: Commercial Fishing

NORSK GOLF 32183R75D-100
Editorial: Norges Golfforbund, 0855 OSLO
Tel: 69 81 97 00 **Fax:** 69 88 94 33
Email: redaksjon@norskgolf.no **Web site:** http://www.norskgolf.no
Freq: 6 issues yearly - 8 ganger i året; **Circ:** 75,626
Editor: Tom Erik Andersen
Profile: Magazine containing articles and news concerning golf.
Language(s): Norwegian
CONSUMER: SPORT: Golf

NORSK HAGETIDEND 31493R26B-60
Editorial: Pb 53 Manglerud, 0612 OSLO
Tel: 23031600 **Fax:** 23031601
Email: postkasse@hageselskapet.no **Web site:** http://www.hagetidend.no
Date Established: 1884; **Freq:** Monthly; **Circ:** 30,000
Profile: Magazine published by the Horticultural Society of Norway.
Language(s): Norwegian
Readership: Read by garden owners, professionals and nurserymen.
ADVERTISING RATES:
Full Page Colour .... NOK 23800
Copy instructions: *Copy Date:* 28 days prior to publication date
BUSINESS: GARDEN TRADE: Garden Trade Supplies

NORSK HUSFLID 32158R74E-90
Editorial: Øvre Slottsgate 2B, 0157 OSLO
Tel: 22 00 87 00 **Fax:** 22 00 87 50
Email: berit@husflid.no **Web site:** http://www.husflid.no
Freq: 6 issues yearly; **Circ:** 27,350
Editor: Berit Solhaug
Profile: Magazine about Norwegian handicrafts, such as knitting, weaving, embroidery, carving and knifemaking.
Language(s): Norwegian
ADVERTISING RATES:
Full Page Colour .... NOK 17400
CONSUMER: WOMEN'S INTEREST CONSUMER MAGAZINES: Crafts

NORSK JAZZFORUM 1657555R76D-270
Editorial: Pb. 440, 0103 OSLO **Tel:** 22 00 56 60
Fax: 22 00 56 61
Email: norsk@jazzforum.no **Web site:** http://www.jazzforum.no
Cover Price: Paid
Language(s): Norwegian
CONSUMER: MUSIC & PERFORMING ARTS: Music

NORSK LANDBRUK 31470R21A-70
Editorial: Pb 9303 Grønland, 0135 OSLO
Tel: 21 31 44 00 **Fax:** 21 31 44 92
Email: norsk.landbruk@tunmedia.no **Web site:** http://www.norsklandbruk.no
Freq: Monthly; **Circ:** 14,500
Profile: Journal about farming and forestry. Covers new agricultural methods and resources, economic issues, industrial policies and production techniques.
Language(s): Norwegian
ADVERTISING RATES:
Full Page Colour .... NOK 18450
BUSINESS: AGRICULTURE & FARMING

NORSK LITTERATURVITENSKAPELIG TIDSSKRIFT 1624623R62F-171
Editorial: Institutt for nordistikk og litteraturvitenskap NTNU, 7491 TRONDHEIM
Email: britt.andersen@hf.ntnu.no **Web site:** http://www.universitetsforlaget.no/nlvt
Freq: Half-yearly; **Circ:** 650
Language(s): Norwegian
BUSINESS: CHURCH & SCHOOL EQUIPMENT & EDUCATION: Adult Education

NORSK LUFTAMBULANSE MAGASIN 1624838R56R-153
Editorial: Pb 94, 1441 DRØBAK **Tel:** 64904444
Fax: 64904445
Email: info@snla.no **Web site:** http://www.norskluftambulanse.no
Freq: Quarterly; **Circ:** 410,000
Editor: Marte Ramborg
Language(s): Norwegian
BUSINESS: HEALTH & MEDICAL: Health Medical Related

NORSK LYSINGSBLAD PÅ NETT 1692825R32A-156
Editorial: Norsk lysingsblad, Skrivarvegen 2, 6863 LEIKANGER **Tel:** 800 30 301 **Fax:** 57 65 50 55
Email: lysingsbladet@norge.no **Web site:** http://www.norsk.lysingsblad.no
Language(s): Norwegian
BUSINESS: LOCAL GOVERNMENT, LEISURE & RECREATION: Local Government

NORSK MEDIETIDSSKRIFT 1663296R2B-19
Editorial: v/ Lars Nyre, Institutt for informasjons- og medievitenskap, Universitetet i Bergen, Pb. 7802, 5020 BERGEN **Tel:** 55 58 91 00 **Fax:** 55 58 91 49
Email: lars.nyre@infomedia.uib.no **Web site:** http://www.universitetsforlaget.no/tidsskrift/vaare/mediefag
Freq: Quarterly
Language(s): Norwegian
BUSINESS: COMMUNICATIONS, ADVERTISING & MARKETING: Press

NORSK MILITÆRT TIDSSKRIFT 31548R40-20
Editorial: Tollbugata 10, 0152 OSLO **Tel:** 22 33 62 33
Fax: 22 42 87 87
Email: rednmt@gmail.com **Web site:** http://www.nor-miltids.com
Freq: Monthly; **Circ:** 2,700
Editor: Tor Jørgen Melien
Profile: Journal about Norwegian military and national security matters.
Language(s): Norwegian
Readership: Read by senior managers in the defence and armaments industries and academics.
BUSINESS: DEFENCE

NORSK MOTORVETERAN 1624609R77A-205
Editorial: Pb. 67 Bryn Senter, 0667 OSLO
Tel: 22757500 **Fax:** 22757501
Email: norskmo@online.no **Web site:** http://www.norskmo.no
Freq: Monthly - 10 ganger i året
Editor: Tor Ivar Volla
Language(s): Norwegian
CONSUMER: MOTORING & CYCLING: Motoring

NORSK ØKONOMISK TIDSSKRIFT 1740690R1R-2
Editorial: Pb. 8872 Youngstorget, 0028 OSLO
Tel: 22 31 79 90 **Fax:** 22 31 79 91
Email: sekretariatet@samfunnsokonomene.no **Web site:** http://www.samfunnsokonomene.no
Freq: Half-yearly
Editor: Annegrete Bruvoll
Language(s): Norwegian
BUSINESS: FINANCE & ECONOMICS: Financial Related

NORSK PEDAGOGISK TIDSSKRIFT 31715R62A-110
Editorial: Pedagogisk forskningsinstitutt, UIO, Boks 1092, 0317 OSLO
Email: norskpedagogisktidsskrift@gmail.com **Web site:** http://www.universitetsforlaget.no/npt

Date Established: 1916; **Freq:** 6 issues yearly; **Circ:** 2,800
Profile: Norwegian journal of education and teaching.
Language(s): Norwegian
BUSINESS: CHURCH & SCHOOL EQUIPMENT & EDUCATION: Education

NORSK PELSDYRBLAD
31728R64B-10
Editorial: Pb 175 Økern, 0509 OSLO **Tel:** 23 25 81 00 **Fax:** 22 64 35 91
Web site: http://www.norpels.no
Date Established: 1926; **Freq:** 6 issues yearly; **Circ:** 1,800
Editor: Ingebjørg Myrstad-Nilsen
Profile: Publication concerning fur farming.
Language(s): Norwegian
Readership: Read by fur farmers.
BUSINESS: OTHER CLASSIFICATIONS: Fur Trade

NORSK POLARINSTITUTTS RAPPORTSERIE
31693R57-200
Editorial: Polarmiljøsenteret, 9296 TROMSØ
Tel: 77 75 05 00 **Fax:** 77 75 05 01
Email: jaklin@npolar.no **Web site:** http://www.npolar.no
Freq: Half-yearly; **Circ:** 500
Profile: Journal containing reports and articles from the Norwegian Institute of Polar Research. Covers biology, geology and geophysics.
Language(s): Norwegian
BUSINESS: ENVIRONMENT & POLLUTION

NORSK SHAKESPEARE OG TEATER-TIDSSKRIFT
1645149R84B-240
Editorial: Litteraturhuset, Wergelandsveien 29, 0167 OSLO **Tel:** 22 44 69 28
Email: redaksjon@shakespearetidsskrift.no **Web site:** http://www.shakespearetidsskrift.no
Language(s): Norwegian
CONSUMER: THE ARTS & LITERARY: Literary

NORSK SJAKKBLAD
1624460R79A-2
Editorial: Sandakerveien 24 D, 0473 OSLO
Tel: 21 01 98 11
Email: nsb@sjakk.no **Web site:** http://www.sjakk.no/NSF/nsb_index.html
Freq: 6 issues yearly
Editor: Torstein Bae
Language(s): Norwegian
CONSUMER: HOBBIES & DIY

NORSK SJØMAT
31583R45B-200
Editorial: Norske Sjømatbedrifters Landsforening, Pb 639 Sentrum, 7406 TRONDHEIM **Tel:** 73 84 14 00
Fax: 73 84 14 01
Email: norsk.sjomat@nsl.no **Web site:** http://www.nsl.no
Freq: 6 issues yearly; **Circ:** 3,500
Editor: Svein Reppe
Profile: Magazine covering the fishing and seafood trade.
Language(s): Norwegian
BUSINESS: MARINE & SHIPPING: Commercial Fishing

NORSK SKIPSFART OG FISKERI AKTUELT
1624644R45A-73
Editorial: Pb 224 Nyborg, 5871 BERGEN
Tel: 55 19 77 70 **Fax:** 55 19 77 80
Email: redaksjonen@norsk-skipsfart.no **Web site:** http://www.norsk-skipsfart.no
Freq: Monthly; **Circ:** 4,000
Editor: Stig Ottesen
Language(s): Norwegian
BUSINESS: MARINE & SHIPPING

NORSK SKOGBRUK
31586R46-20
Editorial: Wergelandsveien 23 B, 0167 OSLO
Tel: 23 36 58 60 **Fax:** 22 60 41 89
Email: post@norsk-skogbruk.no **Web site:** http://www.norsk-skogbruk.no
Date Established: 1956; **Freq:** Monthly; **Circ:** 6,035
Editor: Johs Bjørndal
Profile: Journal of the Norwegian Forestry Society.
Language(s): Norwegian
Readership: Aimed at all professional foresters.
ADVERTISING RATES:
SCC .... NOK 62.5
BUSINESS: TIMBER, WOOD & FORESTRY

NORSK SKYTTERTIDENDE
1800783R75A-212
Editorial: Pb. 298, Økern, 0511 OSLO
Tel: 911 77 680 **Fax:** 23 17 21 01
Email: nst@dfs.no **Web site:** http://www.dfs.no/no/Om_DFS/Skytterkontoret/Norsk_Skyttertidende
Freq: 6 issues yearly; **Circ:** 10,000
Editor: Viktor Storsveen
Language(s): Norwegian
CONSUMER: SPORT

NORSK SOKKEL
1800776R58-110
Editorial: Oljedirektoratet, Pb. 600, 4003 STAVANGER **Tel:** 51876000 **Fax:** 51551571
Email: postboks@npd.no **Web site:** http://www.npd.no/no/Publikasjoner/Norsk-sokkel
Freq: Half-yearly; **Circ:** 9,000
Editor: Bjørn Rasen
Language(s): Norwegian
BUSINESS: ENERGY, FUEL & NUCLEAR

NORSK STATSVITENSKAPELIG TIDSSKRIFT
31508R32A-90
Editorial: Institutt for statsvitenskap, Postboks 1097 Blindern, 0317 OSLO
Email: marit.brochmann@stv.uio.no **Web site:** http://www.universitetsforlaget.no/nst
Freq: Quarterly; **Circ:** 1,000
Editor: Håvard Hegre
Profile: Political and public administration journal.
Language(s): Norwegian
BUSINESS: LOCAL GOVERNMENT, LEISURE & RECREATION: Local Government

NORSK TEOLOGISK TIDSSKRIFT
31720R62B-50
Editorial: Det teologiske fakultet, Boks 1023 – Blindern, 0315 OSLO **Tel:** 22 85 03 00
Email: tarald.rasmussen@teologi.uio.no **Web site:** http://www.universitetsforlaget.no/teologisk
Date Established: 1900; **Freq:** Quarterly; **Circ:** 500
Profile: Journal covering the study of theology.
Language(s): Norwegian
Readership: Aimed at academics and priests.
BUSINESS: CHURCH & SCHOOL EQUIPMENT & EDUCATION: Education Teachers

NORSK TIDEND
32262R82-95
Editorial: Pb 474 Sentrum, 0105 OSLO
Tel: 23 00 29 30 **Fax:** 23 00 29 31
Email: kjartan.helleve@nm.no **Web site:** http://www.nm.no
Freq: Quarterly; **Circ:** 13,000
Editor: Kjartan Helleve
Profile: Journal containing information, news and articles about culture, linguistic communication and politics.
Language(s): Norwegian
CONSUMER: CURRENT AFFAIRS & POLITICS

NORSK TIDSSKRIFT FOR MIGRASJONSFORSKNING (NTM)
1660585R32A-153
Editorial: v. Thor Indset, NAKMI, Søsterhjemmet, Ullevål Universitetssykehus, 0407 OSLO
Tel: 23 01 60 64
Email: thor.indseth@nakmi.no **Web site:** http://www.tapirforlag.no/migrasjonsforskning
Freq: Half-yearly
Editor: Hakan G. Sicakkan
Language(s): Norwegian
BUSINESS: LOCAL GOVERNMENT, LEISURE & RECREATION: Local Government

NORSK TIDSSKRIFT FOR MISJONSVITENSKAP
31549R40-25
Editorial: Egede Instituttet, Postboks 5144 Majorstua, 0302 OSLO **Tel:** 22 59 06 91
Fax: 22 59 05 30
Email: egede@mf.no
Date Established: 1882; **Freq:** Quarterly; **Circ:** 500
Editor: Kristin Norseth
Profile: Journal of maritime defence.
Language(s): Norwegian
BUSINESS: DEFENCE

NORSK TIDSSKRIFT FOR SJØVESEN
1625208R40-36
Editorial: Sjømilitære Samfund, Jens Jørgen Jensen, Harald Sæverudsv 103, 5239 RÅDAL **Tel:** 92691877
Email: redaksjon@ntfs.no **Web site:** http://www.sms1835.no
Freq: 6 issues yearly; **Circ:** 2,728
Editor: Jens-Jørgen Jensen
Language(s): Norwegian
BUSINESS: DEFENCE

NORSK TOLLBLAD
1624873R54C-101
Editorial: Pb 8122 Dep., 0032 OSLO **Tel:** 22 86 03 00
Email: nina.johansen.bullock@toll.no **Web site:** http://www.norsktollerforbund.no
Freq: 6 issues yearly; **Circ:** 2,700
Editor: Steinar Myhre Knutsen
Language(s): Norwegian
BUSINESS: SAFETY & SECURITY: Security

NORSK TRANSPORT
31605R49C-20
Editorial: Pb 7134, St.Olavs plass, 0130 OSLO
Tel: 22 03 32 00 **Fax:** 22 20 56 15
Email: post@lastebil.no **Web site:** http://www.lastebil.no
Freq: Monthly; **Circ:** 14,000
Profile: Truck Owners' Society journal.
Language(s): Norwegian
ADVERTISING RATES:
SCC .... NOK 155.75
BUSINESS: TRANSPORT: Freight

NORSK UKEBLAD
32150R74C-50
Editorial: Gullhaugveien 1, Nydalen, 0441 OSLO
Tel: 22 58 50 00 **Fax:** 22 58 05 69
Email: nu-tips@egmonthm.no **Web site:** http://www.norskukeblad.no
Freq: Weekly; **Circ:** 126,591
Profile: Home and family journal, includes articles about health, fashion, beauty and food.
Language(s): Norwegian
Readership: Aimed at career women between 20 and 50 years, who have a family.
ADVERTISING RATES:
SCC .... NOK 541.67
CONSUMER: WOMEN'S INTEREST CONSUMER MAGAZINES: Home & Family

NORSK VETERINÆRTIDSSKRIFT
31733R64H-50
Editorial: Pb 6781 St. Olavs plass, 0130 OSLO
Tel: 22 99 46 00 **Fax:** 22 99 46 01
Email: nvt@vetnett.no **Web site:** http://www.vetnett.no
Date Established: 1888; **Freq:** 6 issues yearly; **Circ:** 2,400
Editor: Steinar Tessem
Profile: Journal published by the Norwegian Veterinary Association.
Language(s): Norwegian
Readership: Aimed at veterinarians and veterinary students in Norway and abroad, pharmacists and those involved with public health, hygiene and meat control.
BUSINESS: OTHER CLASSIFICATIONS: Veterinary

NORSK VVS
31376R3B-20
Editorial: Pb 2843 Tøyen, 0608 OSLO **Tel:** 22708300
Fax: 22708301
Email: norskvvs@skarland.no **Web site:** http://www.norsk-vvs.no
Freq: Monthly; **Circ:** 4,129
Profile: Journal of the Norwegian Association of Heating, Ventilation and Sanitation Engineers.
Language(s): Norwegian
ADVERTISING RATES:
SCC .... NOK 146.67
BUSINESS: HEATING & VENTILATION: Industrial Heating & Ventilation

NORSKDESIGN.NO
1657778R4A-22
Editorial: Hausmanns gate 16, 0182 OSLO
Tel: 23 29 25 50 **Fax:** 23 29 25 51
Email: firmapost@norskdesign.no **Web site:** http://www.norskdesign.no
Cover Price: Paid
Language(s): Norwegian
BUSINESS: ARCHITECTURE & BUILDING: Architecture

DEN NORSKE TANNLEGEFOR. TIDENDE
1624546R56D-76
Editorial: Pb 3063 Elisenberg, 0207 OSLO
Tel: 22547400
Email: tidende@tannlegeforeningen.no **Web site:** http://www.tannlegetidende.no
Freq: Monthly - 15 ganger i året; **Circ:** 5,598
Language(s): Norwegian
ADVERTISING RATES:
Full Page Colour .... NOK 17250
BUSINESS: HEALTH & MEDICAL: Dental

NORSKLÆRAREN/ NORSKLÆREREN
1624448R62A-204
Editorial: Astrid Elisabeth Kleiveland, Kastellhagen 6a, 1176 OSLO **Tel:** 92 68 37 21
Email: astridkleiveland@gmail.com **Web site:** http://www.fagbokforlaget.no
Freq: Quarterly; **Circ:** 2,800
Language(s): Norwegian
BUSINESS: CHURCH & SCHOOL EQUIPMENT & EDUCATION: Education

NORTRADE.COM
1740735R14A-217
Editorial: Findexa Forlag AS, Pb 457 sentrum, 0609 OSLO **Tel:** 21 50 80 00 **Fax:** 21 50 80 01
Email: nortrade@nortrade.com **Web site:** http://www.nortrade.com
Cover Price: Paid
Editor: Jørgen Fodstad
Language(s): Norwegian
BUSINESS: COMMERCE, INDUSTRY & MANAGEMENT

NORWATCH.NO
1657996R14C-1
Editorial: Fredensborgveien 24 G, 0177 OSLO
Tel: 222 03 31 62
Freq: Daily
Language(s): Norwegian
BUSINESS: COMMERCE, INDUSTRY & MANAGEMENT: International Commerce

NORWAY EXPORTS
1740736R14C-2
Editorial: Findexa Forlag AS, Pb 457 sentrum, 0104 OSLO **Tel:** 21508000 **Fax:** 21508001
Email: nortrade@nortrade.com **Web site:** http://www.nortrade.com
Editor: Robert Moses
Profile: Magazine covering Norwegian export companies abroad, and a wide range of industries.
Language(s): Norwegian
Readership: Distributed to Norwegian foreign missions, a good number of international trade fairs and through our cooperative partners to mention a few distribution channels.
BUSINESS: COMMERCE, INDUSTRY & MANAGEMENT: International Commerce

THE NORWAY POST
1624777R82-321
Editorial: P.O.Box 25, Ringeriksveien 243, 1340 BÆRUM **Tel:** 67176850 **Fax:** 67176851
Email: editor@norwaypost.no **Web site:** http://www.norwaypost.no
Cover Price: Paid; **Circ:** 2,500 Unique Users
Language(s): Norwegian
CONSUMER: CURRENT AFFAIRS & POLITICS

NORWEGIAN
1810353R14L-111
Editorial: Pb. 115, NO-1330 FORNEBU
Tel: 67 59 30 43 **Fax:** 67 59 30 01
Email: magasinet@norwegian.no **Web site:** http://www.norwegian.no
Language(s): Norwegian
BUSINESS: COMMERCE, INDUSTRY & MANAGEMENT: Trade Unions

NOTABENE
1624495R94F-106
Editorial: Statens råd for likestilling av, Postboks 7075 St. Olavs plass, 0130 OSLO **Tel:** 81 02 00 50
Fax: 24 16 30 04
Email: ordbua@online.no **Web site:** http://www.helsedirektoratet.no/srff/notabene
Freq: Quarterly; **Circ:** 4,500
Language(s): Norwegian
CONSUMER: OTHER CLASSIFICATIONS: Disability

NRK
1814100R2D-121
Editorial: NRK, 0340 OSLO **Tel:** 22 04 70 00
Fax: 23047575
Email: info@nrk.no **Web site:** http://www.nrk.no
Circ: 1,187,614 Unique Users
Language(s): Norwegian
BUSINESS: COMMUNICATIONS, ADVERTISING & MARKETING: Broadcasting

NRK 1; SOMMERMORGEN
1656636R80-156
Email: sommermorgen@nrk.no
Language(s): Norwegian
CONSUMER: RURAL & REGIONAL INTEREST

NRK GULL (KANAL)
1994354R76C-89
Editorial: Bj. Bjørnsons Plass 1, 0340 OSLO
Tel: 23 04 70 00
Email: gull@nrk.no **Web site:** http://www.nrk.no/gull
Editor: Ivar Johannessen
Language(s): Norwegian
CONSUMER: MUSIC & PERFORMING ARTS: TV & Radio

NUMER
2010150R84A-171
Editorial: Tegnerforbundet, Rådhusgata 17, 0158 OSLO **Tel:** 22 42 38 06
Email: numer@tegnerforbundet.no **Web site:** http://www.tegnerforbundet.no
Circ: 800
Editor: Anne Schäffer
Language(s): Norwegian
CONSUMER: THE ARTS & LITERARY: Arts

NY TEKNIKK
32490R14A-120
Editorial: Hausmannsgt. 6, 0186 OSLO
Tel: 22997620 **Fax:** 22116151
Email: info@nyteknikk.no **Web site:** http://www.nyteknikk.no
Freq: Monthly - 11 ganger i året; **Circ:** 30,000
Profile: Magazine providing information about technical and industrial developments.
Language(s): Norwegian
Readership: Read by managers and executives.
ADVERTISING RATES:
SCC .... NOK 341.67
Copy instructions: *Copy Date:* 7 days prior to publication date
BUSINESS: COMMERCE, INDUSTRY & MANAGEMENT

Norway

NY TEKNIKK; NYTEKNIKK.NO
1864954R18A-107
Editorial: Hausmannsgate 6, 0186 OSLO
Tel: 22 99 76 20 **Fax:** 22 11 61 51
Email: per@nyteknikk.no **Web site:** http://www.nyteknikk.no
Freq: Daily; **Cover Price:** Free; **Circ:** 2,500 Unique Users
Language(s): Norwegian
BUSINESS: ELECTRONICS

NY TID
32264R82-102
Editorial: Pb 50 Økern, 0107 OSLO **Tel:** 22 31 04 70
Fax: 22 31 02 25
Email: post@nytid.no **Web site:** http://www.nytid.no
Freq: Weekly; **Circ:** 4,811
Editor: Dag Herbjørnsrud
Profile: Political newspaper of the Socialist Left with emphasis on the environment and foreign affairs.
Language(s): Norwegian
ADVERTISING RATES:
SCC .... NOK 120
CONSUMER: CURRENT AFFAIRS & POLITICS

DET NYE
1624388R74F-122
Editorial: Gullhaugveien 1, 0441 OSLO
Tel: 22 58 50 00 **Fax:** 22 58 58 09
Email: detnye@egmonthm.no **Web site:** http://www.klikk.no/detnye
Freq: Monthly; **Circ:** 62,284
Editor: Mari Midtstigen
Language(s): Norwegian
ADVERTISING RATES:
SCC .... NOK 460
CONSUMER: WOMEN'S INTEREST CONSUMER MAGAZINES: Teenage

NYE TROMS; SPORTSREDAKSJONEN
1836254R75A-240
Editorial: Boks 44, 9329 MOEN **Tel:** 778 37 913
Email: sporten@nye-troms.no **Web site:** http://www.nye-troms.no
Language(s): Norwegian
CONSUMER: SPORT

NYTID.NO
1864948R84A-151
Editorial: Postboks 1180 Sentrum, 0107 OSLO
Tel: 22 31 04 70 **Fax:** 22 31 02 25
Email: post@nytid.no **Web site:** http://www.nytid.no
Freq: Daily; **Cover Price:** Free; **Circ:** 2,500 Unique Users
Editor: Dag Herbjørnsrud
Language(s): Norwegian
CONSUMER: THE ARTS & LITERARY: Arts

NYTT FRA NORGES VEKTLØFTERFORBUND
1624463R75X-91
Editorial: Serviceboks 1, 0840 OSLO
Tel: 21 02 98 65 **Fax:** 21 02 90 03
Email: vektlofting@nif.idrett.no **Web site:** http://www.vektlofting.no
Freq: Quarterly; **Circ:** 350
Language(s): Norwegian
CONSUMER: SPORT: Other Sport

NYTT NORSK TIDSSKRIFT
32266R82-104
Editorial: Pb 508 Sentrum, 0105 OSLO
Tel: 24147500
Email: joakim.caspersen@universitetsforlaget.no
Web site: http://www.universitetsforlaget.no/nnt
Date Established: 1984; **Freq:** Quarterly
Profile: Politics and current affairs journal.
Language(s): Norwegian
CONSUMER: CURRENT AFFAIRS & POLITICS

NYTT OM BIL
32222R77A-150
Editorial: Pb 183, 1377 BILLINGSTAD **Tel:** 66854460
Fax: 66981408
Email: frank@williksen.no **Web site:** http://www.nyttombil.no
Date Established: 1989; **Freq:** Monthly; **Circ:** 500,000
Profile: Magazine containing information, articles and news about cars and related issues. Covers maintenance, technical facts, events, practical advice and the buying and selling of cars.
Language(s): Norwegian
CONSUMER: MOTORING & CYCLING: Motoring

DET NYTTER
1624948R56R-154
Editorial: Pb 4375 Nydalen, 0402 OSLO
Tel: 22799300 **Fax:** 22223811
Email: moj@lhl.no **Web site:** http://www.lhl.no
Freq: 6 issues yearly - 5 ganger i året
Editor: Mona Johansen
Language(s): Norwegian
BUSINESS: HEALTH & MEDICAL: Health Medical Related

OBOS BLADET
31359R1J-100
Editorial: Pb. 6666 St. Olavs Plass, 0129 OSLO
Tel: 22865785 **Fax:** 22868210
Email: obosbladet@obos.no **Web site:** http://www.obos.no
Freq: 6 issues yearly
Profile: Magazine for members of the Oslo Building and Housing Association.
Language(s): Norwegian
Copy instructions: *Copy Date:* 27 days prior to publication date
BUSINESS: FINANCE & ECONOMICS: Building Societies

OBSERVATOR
1624531R1A-119
Editorial: Pb 1095 Blindern, 0317 OSLO
Tel: 22 85 59 42 **Fax:** 22 85 50 35
Email: tidsskrift.observator@gmail.com **Web site:** http://foreninger.uio.no/observator
Freq: Quarterly; **Circ:** 600
Language(s): Norwegian
BUSINESS: FINANCE & ECONOMICS

OFFENTLIG DRIFT
1936397R32A-162
Editorial: Boks 1024, 1510 MOSS **Tel:** 69 91 24 00
Fax: 69 91 24 02
Email: post@byggfaktamedia.no **Web site:** http://www.offentligdrift.no
Circ: 4,600
Language(s): Norwegian
BUSINESS: LOCAL GOVERNMENT, LEISURE & RECREATION: Local Government

OFFENTLIG HANDEL
1645167R2A-55
Editorial: Stenholtsvei 15a, 1738 BORGENHAUGEN
Tel: 69 35 40 90 **Fax:** 69 35 40 98
Email: kan@offentlighandel.no **Web site:** http://www.offentlighandel.no
Freq: 6 issues yearly; **Circ:** 2,000
Language(s): Norwegian
BUSINESS: COMMUNICATIONS, ADVERTISING & MARKETING

OFFISERSBLADET
31550R40-28
Editorial: Pb 501, Sentrum, 0105 OSLO
Tel: 23 10 02 42 **Fax:** 23 10 02 25
Email: holst.clausen@bfo.no **Web site:** http://offisersbladet.no
Freq: 6 issues yearly; **Circ:** 10,500
Profile: Military magazine covering the army, navy, the airforce and international defence and security politics.
Language(s): Norwegian
BUSINESS: DEFENCE

OFFSHORE ENGINEER
1624500R33-72
Editorial: Lisbeth Lødner, Media Call A/S, 1358 JAR
Tel: 67156290 **Fax:** 67156291
Email: lisbeth@mediacall.no **Web site:** http://www.oilonline.com/Magazines/OffshoreEngineer.aspx
Freq: Monthly; **Circ:** 32,000
Language(s): Norwegian
BUSINESS: OIL & PETROLEUM

OFFSHORE & ENERGY
31528R33-35
Editorial: Trollhaugsmyra 15, 5353 STRAUME
Tel: 56314020 **Fax:** 56314030
Email: redaksjonen@offshore.no **Web site:** http://www.offshore.no
Date Established: 1982; **Freq:** Quarterly; **Circ:** 10,800
Editor: Stein Tjelta
Profile: Magazine focusing on Norway's offshore and energy industries.
Language(s): Norwegian
ADVERTISING RATES:
SCC .... NOK 175
BUSINESS: OIL & PETROLEUM

OFFSHORE & ENERGY; OFFSHORE.NO
1625242R33-75
Editorial: Trollhaugsmyra 15, 5353 STRAUME
Tel: 56 31 40 20 **Fax:** 56 31 40 30
Email: redaksjonen@offshore.no **Web site:** http://www.offshore.no
Freq: Daily; **Cover Price:** Paid; **Circ:** 2,500 Unique Users
Language(s): Norwegian
ADVERTISING RATES:
SCC .... NOK 35
BUSINESS: OIL & PETROLEUM

ØKOLOGISK LANDBRUK
31471R21A-100
Editorial: Reddalsveien 215, 4886 GRIMSTAD
Tel: 91 87 08 93 **Fax:** 37257739
Email: okologisk.landbruk@lfr.no **Web site:** http://okologisk.lfr.no
Freq: Quarterly; **Circ:** 2,800
Profile: Magazine containing articles and information about ecological farming.
Language(s): Norwegian
Readership: Aimed at farmers.
Copy instructions: *Copy Date:* 30 days prior to publication date
BUSINESS: AGRICULTURE & FARMING

ØKONOMISKE ANALYSER
32547R1A-94_50
Editorial: Statistisk sentralbyrå, Forskningsavdelingen, Pb 8131 Dep, 0033 OSLO
Tel: 21090000 **Fax:** 21090040
Email: auw@ssb.no **Web site:** http://www.ssb.no/oa
Date Established: 1982; **Freq:** 6 issues yearly; **Circ:** 1,400
Profile: Magazine containing debate articles analysing the economy and the private and public sectors. Also covers financial reports, economic forecasts, surveys and developments in the international economy.
Language(s): Norwegian
Readership: Read by academics, politicians, financial executives and statisticians.
BUSINESS: FINANCE & ECONOMICS

OMSORG
1625074R56R-156
Editorial: Kirurgisk Serviceklinikk Etg 3, Haukeland Universite, 5021 BERGEN **Tel:** 55976894
Fax: 55976898
Email: tove.langeland@haukeland.no **Web site:** http://www.fagbokforlaget.no/omsorg
Freq: Quarterly; **Circ:** 4,000
Language(s): Norwegian
BUSINESS: HEALTH & MEDICAL: Health Medical Related

ONLINEMAGASINET
1657781R86C-154
Editorial: Fjellborgveien 6, Våle, 3178 OSLO
Tel: 91 77 33 66
Email: arne@onlinemagasinet.no **Web site:** http://www.onlinemagasinet.no
Circ: 120,000 Unique Users
Editor: Arne Daniel Skalmeraas
Language(s): Norwegian
CONSUMER: ADULT & GAY MAGAZINES: Men's Lifestyle Magazines

OPP
1625246R1E-3
Editorial: Inge Krokanns vei 11, 7340 OPPDAL
Tel: 72 42 40 04 **Fax:** 72 42 25 25
Email: perroar@opp.no **Web site:** http://www.opp.no
Freq: Weekly; **Circ:** 2,329
Language(s): Norwegian
ADVERTISING RATES:
SCC .... NOK 29.8
BUSINESS: FINANCE & ECONOMICS: Property

OPPLAND ARBEIDERBLAD
31769R67B-4650
Editorial: Pb 24, 2801 GJØVIK **Tel:** 61 18 93 00
Fax: 61 17 07 25
Email: redaksjonen@oa.no **Web site:** http://www.oa.no
Freq: Daily; **Circ:** 26,578
Editor: Tonje Sagstuen Andersen; **Features Editor:** Anne Marit Sletten
Language(s): Norwegian
ADVERTISING RATES:
SCC .... NOK 164.68
REGIONAL DAILY & SUNDAY NEWSPAPERS: Regional Daily Newspapers

OPPLYSNINGSKONTORET FOR EGG OG HVITT KJØTT
1657801R74P-205
Editorial: Postboks 395 Økern, 0513 OSLO
Tel: 22 09 23 00 **Fax:** 22 15 02 20
Email: post@egg.no **Web site:** http://www.egg.no
Cover Price: Paid
Language(s): Norwegian
CONSUMER: WOMEN'S INTEREST CONSUMER MAGAZINES: Food & Cookery

OPTIKEREN
31659R56E-50
Editorial: Norges Optikerforbund, Øvre Slottsgt. 18/20, 0157 OSLO **Tel:** 23 35 54 50 **Fax:** 23 35 54 40
Email: synsinfo@optikerforbund.no **Web site:** http://www.synsinformasjon.no/Optikeren
Date Established: 1980; **Freq:** 6 issues yearly; **Circ:** 1,660
Profile: Official journal of the Norwegian Optometrists' Association. Covers all aspects of the optical industry.
Language(s): Norwegian
Readership: Distributed to all opticians and optometrists in Norway.
BUSINESS: HEALTH & MEDICAL: Optics

ORDET
32331R88R-150
Editorial: Rosenborggaten 3, 0256 OSLO
Tel: 22 60 88 59 **Fax:** 22 60 03 74
Email: ordet@riksmalsforbundet.no **Web site:** http://www.riksmalsforbundet.no/Ordet.aspx
Freq: Quarterly; **Circ:** 5,500
Profile: Magazine covering in-depth analysis of the Norwegian language containing debate articles and guidelines on the proper use of words and grammar. Also covers literature, art, music, theatre, film and general cultural issues.
Language(s): Norwegian
Readership: Aimed at people interested in the study of language and culture. Read also by authors, students, journalists and philologists.
CONSUMER: EDUCATION: Education Related

ORNIS NORVEGICA
1625199R81F-101
Editorial: Sandgata 30 B, 7012 TRONDHEIM
Tel: 73 84 16 40 **Fax:** 73 52 40 90
Email: nof@birdlife.no **Web site:** http://www.birdlife.no
Freq: Half-yearly; **Circ:** 1,000
Language(s): Norwegian
CONSUMER: ANIMALS & PETS: Birds

OSLO BØRS - OSLOBORS.NO
1864956R1A-134
Editorial: Postboks 460 Sentrum, 0105 OSLO
Tel: 22 34 17 00
Email: guro.steine@oslobors.no **Web site:** http://www.oslobors.no
Freq: Daily; **Cover Price:** Paid; **Circ:** 2,500 Unique Users
Language(s): Norwegian
BUSINESS: FINANCE & ECONOMICS

OSLOIDRETT
32196R75J-100
Editorial: Oslo Idrettskrets, Ekebergveien 101, 1178 OSLO **Tel:** 22 57 97 00 **Fax:** 22 57 97 01
Email: ivar.glomstein@nif.idrett.no **Web site:** http://www.osloidrettskrets.no
Freq: Quarterly; **Circ:** 3,500
Profile: Magazine about athletics in Oslo.
Language(s): Norwegian
CONSUMER: SPORT: Athletics

OSS FORELDRE I MELLOM
1625220R74D-76
Editorial: Landsforeningen uventet barneded, Ole Fladagers gt. 1 A, 0353 OSLO **Tel:** 22 54 52 00
Fax: 22 54 52 01
Email: post@lub.no **Web site:** http://www.lub.no
Freq: Quarterly; **Circ:** 5,200
Editor: Line Schrader
Language(s): Norwegian
CONSUMER: WOMEN'S INTEREST CONSUMER MAGAZINES: Child Care

ØSTFOLDAVISEN
32238R80-150
Editorial: Pb 73, 1720 GREÅKER **Tel:** 69 12 75 00
Fax: 69127501
Email: post@ostfoldavisen.no **Web site:** http://www.ostfoldavisen.no
Freq: Monthly; **Cover Price:** Free; **Circ:** 93,000
Profile: Magazine containing news and information about the region of Østfold.
Language(s): Norwegian
CONSUMER: RURAL & REGIONAL INTEREST

ØSTKANTAVISA
1659358R80-160
Editorial: Postboks 79, Bryn, 0611 OSLO
Tel: 23 20 56 30 **Fax:** 23205601
Email: redaksjon@ostkantavisa.no **Web site:** http://www.ostkantavisa.no
Freq: Weekly; **Circ:** 70,000
Language(s): Norwegian
CONSUMER: RURAL & REGIONAL INTEREST

ØSTLANDS-POSTEN
31780R67B-4700
Editorial: Postboks 5, 3285 LARVIK **Tel:** 33 16 30 00
Fax: 33 16 30 01
Email: redaksjon@op.no **Web site:** http://www.op.no
Freq: Daily; **Circ:** 13,932
Editor: Per Marvin Tennum
Language(s): Norwegian
ADVERTISING RATES:
SCC .... NOK 75.09
REGIONAL DAILY & SUNDAY NEWSPAPERS: Regional Daily Newspapers

ØSTLENDINGEN
31763R67B-4750
Editorial: Pb 231, 2402 ELVERUM **Tel:** 62 43 25 00
Email: redaksjonen@ostlendingen.no **Web site:** http://www.ostlendingen.no
Freq: Daily; **Circ:** 19,142
Language(s): Norwegian
ADVERTISING RATES:
Full Page Colour .... NOK 28976
SCC .... NOK 289.76
REGIONAL DAILY & SUNDAY NEWSPAPERS: Regional Daily Newspapers

OYENE.NO
1865445R73-190
Editorial: Postboks 124 Teie, 3106 NØTTERØY
Tel: 33 34 57 77

Email: red@oyene.no Web site: http://www.oyene.no
Freq: Daily; Cover Price: Free; Circ: 3,400 Unique Users
Language(s): Norwegian
CONSUMER: NATIONAL & INTERNATIONAL PERIODICALS

P4 RADIO; MICHAEL DIREKTE
1985625R74Q-89
Editorial: Serviceboks, LILLEHAMMER 2626 LILLEHAMMER
Email: mikke@p4.no Web site: http://www.p4.no/programmer/homepage.aspx?id=36
Language(s): Norwegian
CONSUMER: WOMEN'S INTEREST CONSUMER MAGAZINES: Lifestyle

P4 RADIO; OSS MEGGER IMELLOM
1985732R74Q-90
Email: megge@p4.no Web site: http://www.p4.no/programmer/homepage.aspx?id=607
Language(s): Norwegian
CONSUMER: WOMEN'S INTEREST CONSUMER MAGAZINES: Lifestyle

P4 RADIO; P4S HELGEFROKOST
1985628R89C-101
Editorial: Serviceboks, 2626 LILLEHAMMER
Email: helg@p4.no Web site: http://www.p4.no/programmer/homepage.aspx?id=616
Language(s): Norwegian
CONSUMER: HOLIDAYS & TRAVEL: Entertainment Guides

PÅ BØLGELENGDE
32727R87-87
Editorial: Skjenet 2, 5353 STRAUME Tel: 56 31 40 50 Fax: 56314051
Email: post@fom.no Web site: http://www.fom.no
Freq: Quarterly; Circ: 18,500
Editor: Linda Askeland
Profile: Magazine focusing on religious television and radio broadcasting and related subjects.
Language(s): Norwegian
Readership: Aimed at people interested in religious issues.
CONSUMER: RELIGIOUS

PÅ SYKKEL
32226R77C-50
Editorial: Pb 8883 Youngstorget, 0028 OSLO
Tel: 22 47 30 30 Fax: 22 47 30 31
Email: post@syklistene.no Web site: http://www.slf.no
Date Established: 1947; Freq: Quarterly; Circ: 13,335
Editor: Olav Rokseth
Profile: Magazine containing articles about bicycles and cycling.
Language(s): Norwegian
Readership: Read by family cycling enthusiasts.
CONSUMER: MOTORING & CYCLING: Cycling

PÅ TV
1826642R74C-90
Editorial: Pb. 1169 Sentrum, 0107 OSLO
Tel: 21 30 10 00
Email: patv@aller.no Web site: http://www.aller.no/Allergruppen/Kontakt/Redaksjonene
Freq: Weekly; Circ: 43,564
Language(s): Norwegian
CONSUMER: WOMEN'S INTEREST CONSUMER MAGAZINES: Home & Family

PACKNEWS
31533R35-10
Editorial: Pb 2843 Tøyen, 0608 OSLO Tel: 22708323 Fax: 22708301
Email: per@skarland.no Web site: http://www.packnews.no
Date Established: 1969; Freq: 6 times a year; Circ: 2,630 Unique Users
Editor: Per Øyvind Nordberg
Profile: Magazine focusing on packaging.
Language(s): Norwegian
Readership: Read by professionals within the food industry, non-food consumer goods producers, suppliers and manufacturers of packaging equipment, retailers and designers.
BUSINESS: PACKAGING & BOTTLING

PACKNEWS; PACKNEWS.NO
1864952R35-13
Editorial: Postboks 2843 Tøyen, 0608 OSLO
Tel: 22 70 83 23 Fax: 22 70 83 01
Email: per@skarland.no Web site: http://www.packnews.no
Freq: Daily; Cover Price: Free; Circ: 1,529 Unique Users
Editor: Per Øyvind Nordberg
Language(s): Norwegian
BUSINESS: PACKAGING & BOTTLING

PANORAMA.NO
1645117R76E-201
Editorial: Henning Poulsen, øvrefoss 4b, 0555 OSLO
Tel: 22 60 69 30
Email: panorama@panorama.no Web site: http://www.panorama.no
Cover Price: Paid; Circ: 6,000 Unique Users
Language(s): Norwegian
CONSUMER: MUSIC & PERFORMING ARTS: Pop Music

PARFYMERIET
31444R15A-25
Editorial: Pb 3004 Elisenberg, 0207 OSLO
Tel: 22440506 Fax: 22560861
Date Established: 1956; Freq: Quarterly; Circ: 2,250
Profile: Official journal of the Norwegian Association of Perfume Wholesalers and Retailers.
Language(s): Norwegian
BUSINESS: COSMETICS & HAIRDRESSING: Cosmetics

PARK & ANLEGG
1740734R26C-21
Editorial: Schweigaardsgt. 34 F, 0191 OSLO
Tel: 23 15 93 50 Fax: 23 15 93 51
Email: asbjorgr@gartnerforbundet.no Web site: http://www.gartnerforbundet.no
Freq: Monthly
Editor: Asbjørg Røneid-Hansen
Language(s): Norwegian
BUSINESS: GARDEN TRADE

PC WORLD NORGE
31405R5C-50
Editorial: PB 9090 Grønland, 0133 OSLO
Tel: 22 05 30 00 Fax: 22053021
Email: pressemelding@pcworld.no Web site: http://www.idg.no/pcworld
Freq: Monthly; Circ: 230,000
Editor: Bjørn Unnersaker
Profile: Magazine containing news and information about PCs.
Language(s): Norwegian
ADVERTISING RATES:
SCC .... NOK 494.17
Copy instructions: *Copy Date:* 14 days prior to publication date
BUSINESS: COMPUTERS & AUTOMATION: Professional Personal Computers

PC WORLD ONLINE
1841102R5E-7
Editorial: Pb. 9090 Grønland, 0133 OSLO
Tel: 22 05 30 00 Fax: 22 05 30 21
Email: bjorn.unnersaker@idg.no Web site: http://www.idg.no/pcworld
Freq: Daily; Cover Price: Paid
Editor: Bjørn Unnersaker
Language(s): Norwegian
BUSINESS: COMPUTERS & AUTOMATION: Data Transmission

PEAK MAGAZINE
31452R18A-100
Editorial: Pb. 122, 1300 SANDVIKA Tel: 67559555 Fax: 67559556
Email: post@peakmagazine.no Web site: http://www.peakmag.no
Date Established: 1995; Freq: 6 issues yearly; Circ: 6,581
Profile: Magazine covering all aspects of electronics including components, telecommunications, computers, data processing, testing, measurement and instrumentation.
Language(s): Norwegian
Readership: Aimed at electricians, engineers and technicians.
ADVERTISING RATES:
Full Page Colour .... NOK 15350
BUSINESS: ELECTRONICS

PEAK MAGAZINE; PEAKMAGAZINE.NO
1864950R58-118
Editorial: Postboks 122, 1300 SANDVIKA
Tel: 24115707
Email: post@peakmagazine.no Web site: http://www.peakmagazine.no
Freq: Daily; Cover Price: Free; Circ: 2,500 Unique Users
Language(s): Norwegian
BUSINESS: ENERGY, FUEL & NUCLEAR

PENSJONISTEN
32173R74N-100
Editorial: Lilletorget 1, 0184 OSLO Tel: 22 98 17 70 Fax: 22348783
Email: npf@pensjonistforbundet.no Web site: http://npfportal.pensjonistforbundet.no/portal/page/portal/npf/pensjonisten
Freq: 6 issues yearly; Circ: 148,000
Editor: Marianne Næss
Profile: Magazine containing articles, news and information of interest to retired people, includes information about holidays and organised travel, entertainment, medical issues, financial and legal advice.
Language(s): Norwegian
Readership: Read by retired people.
CONSUMER: WOMEN'S INTEREST CONSUMER MAGAZINES: Retirement

PEPPERKVERNA
1934359R74P-213
Tel: 92024605
Email: hege@ordsmia.no Web site: http://pepperkverna.blogspot.com
Freq: Daily; Cover Price: Paid
Editor: Hege Johansen
Language(s): Norwegian
CONSUMER: WOMEN'S INTEREST CONSUMER MAGAZINES: Food & Cookery

PERSONAL OG LEDELSE
1624555R14R-1
Editorial: v. Ole Alvik, Postboks 9231 Grønland, 0134 OSLO Tel: 97 68 92
Email: ole@askmedia.no Web site: http://www.ledernett.no
Freq: 6 issues yearly
Editor: Ole Alvik
Language(s): Norwegian
BUSINESS: COMMERCE, INDUSTRY & MANAGEMENT: Commerce Related

PERSONAL OG LEDELSE; LEDERNETT.NO
1698325R14A-212
Editorial: v. Ole Alvik, Postboks 9231 Grønland, 0134 OSLO Tel: 976 89 264
Email: ole@askmedia.no Web site: http://www.ledernett.no
Freq: Daily; Cover Price: Paid
Editor: Ole Alvik
Language(s): Norwegian
BUSINESS: COMMERCE, INDUSTRY & MANAGEMENT

PERSPEKTIV - WIDERØES FLYMAGASIN
1624400R89A-176
Editorial: Universitetsgaten 14, 0164 OSLO
Tel: 21 60 81 90
Email: cecilie.larvaag@dgcom.no Web site: http://www.wideroe.no/perspektiv
Freq: 6 issues yearly; Circ: 14,000
Editor: Cecilie Larvåg
Language(s): Norwegian
CONSUMER: HOLIDAYS & TRAVEL: Travel

PETRONEWS
1695148R33-81
Editorial: Lagårdsveien 77-81, co Vaalandsbakken7, 4010 STAVANGER Tel: 51 91 76 50 Fax: 51 91 76 51
Email: post@oilinfo.no Web site: http://www.oilinfo.no
Freq: Half-yearly
Editor: Magnus Birkenes
Language(s): Norwegian
ADVERTISING RATES:
Full Page Colour .... NOK 32000
Copy instructions: *Copy Date:* 20 days prior to publication date
BUSINESS: OIL & PETROLEUM

PETRONEWS; OILINFO.NO
1666590R33-80
Editorial: Lagårdsveien 77-81, v/Vålandsbakken 5, 4010 STAVANGER Tel: 51 91 76 50 Fax: 51 91 76 51
Email: post@oilinfo.no Web site: http://www.oilinfo.no
Freq: Quarterly; Cover Price: Paid
Language(s): Norwegian
BUSINESS: OIL & PETROLEUM

PETRO.NO
1864946R58-117
Editorial: Lagårdsveien 77-81, 4010 STAVANGER
Tel: 51 84 36 36 Fax: 51 84 36 37
Email: redaksjon@petro.no Web site: http://www.petro.no
Freq: Daily; Cover Price: Free; Circ: 6,755 Unique Users
Language(s): Norwegian
BUSINESS: ENERGY, FUEL & NUCLEAR

PLAN
31385R4D-100
Editorial: Pb. 508 Sentrum, 0105 OSLO
Tel: 24 14 75 00 Fax: 24 14 75 01
Web site: http://www.universitetsforlaget.no
Freq: 6 issues yearly; Circ: 2,500
Profile: Magazine about town planning and community development.
Language(s): Norwegian
BUSINESS: ARCHITECTURE & BUILDING: Planning & Housing

PLASTFORUM
1624650R39-1
Editorial: Pb 9178 Grønland, 0134 OSLO
Tel: 92055852 Fax: 22172508
Email: asle@askmedia.no Web site: http://www.plastforum.no
Freq: Monthly - 10 gangeri året; Circ: 2,165
Language(s): Norwegian
ADVERTISING RATES:
SCC .... NOK 124.17
Copy instructions: *Copy Date:* 20 days prior to publication date
BUSINESS: PLASTICS & RUBBER

PLASTFORUM; PLASTFORUM.NO
1864953R35-14
Editorial: Postboks 9231, Grønland, 0134 OSLO
Tel: 920 55 852
Email: asle@askmedia.no Web site: http://www.plastforum.no
Freq: Daily; Cover Price: Free; Circ: 1,287 Unique Users
Language(s): Norwegian
BUSINESS: PACKAGING & BOTTLING

PLAYBOARD MAGAZINE
1645127R75J-104
Editorial: Nesflåtveien 18, 4018 STAVANGER
Tel: 51 58 03 03
Email: post@playboard.no Web site: http://www.playboard.no
Freq: Quarterly; Circ: 15,000
Language(s): Norwegian
CONSUMER: SPORT: Athletics

POINTCARBON.COM
1852606R58-113
Editorial: Pb. 7120 St.Olavs plass, 0130 OSLO
Tel: 22 40 53 40 Fax: 22 40 53 41
Email: contact@pointcarbon.com Web site: http://www.pointcarbon.com
Freq: Daily; Cover Price: Paid
Language(s): Norwegian
BUSINESS: ENERGY, FUEL & NUCLEAR

POLAR RESEARCH
31695R57-250
Editorial: Norsk Polarinstitutt, 9296 TROMSØ
Tel: 77 75 06 18 Fax: 77750501
Email: goldman@npolar.no Web site: http://www.npolar.no/PolarResearch
Date Established: 1982; Freq: Half-yearly; Circ: 600
Profile: Journal published by the Norwegian Polar Institute. Contains scientific articles and information about the polar environment.
Language(s): Norwegian
Readership: Read primarily by scientists and environmental managers.
BUSINESS: ENVIRONMENT & POLLUTION

POLITIFORUM
31516R32F-50
Editorial: Møllergata 39, 0184 OSLO Tel: 23 16 31 00 Fax: 23 16 31 40
Email: redaktor@pf.no Web site: http://www.politiforum.no
Freq: Monthly; Circ: 12,000
Profile: Publication for members of the Norwegian Police Association.
Language(s): Norwegian
BUSINESS: LOCAL GOVERNMENT, LEISURE & RECREATION: Police

POSISJON
32501R4C-150
Editorial: GeoForum, Kvernberggata 5, 3510 HØNEFOSS Tel: 32 12 31 66 Fax: 32 12 06 16
Email: geoforum@geoforum.no Web site: http://www.geoforum.no
Date Established: 1993; Freq: 6 issues yearly; Circ: 2,700
Editor: Marianne Meinich
Profile: Magazine focusing on GIS, cartography, satellite and digital mapping, aerial and groundsurveying and related subjects.
Language(s): Norwegian
Readership: Read by those involved in the production and handling of maps and geo-information systems both in private industry, municipalities and by members of government departments.
BUSINESS: ARCHITECTURE & BUILDING: Surveying

POSITIV
1657776R56R-161
Editorial: Christian Krohgs gate 34, 0186 OSLO
Tel: 21314580 Fax: 21314581
Web site: http://www.hivnorge.no
Freq: 6 issues yearly
Language(s): Norwegian
BUSINESS: HEALTH & MEDICAL: Health Medical Related

POST & BRINGAVISEN
1624941R14L-106
Editorial: Posten Norge AS, 0001 OSLO
Tel: 23 14 84 10 Fax: 23 14 80 25
Email: redaksjonen@posten.no Web site: http://www.postennorge.no/Forside/Kundemagasiner+og+publikasjoner
Freq: 26 issues yearly; Circ: 25,000
Editor: Mads Yngve Storvik
Language(s): Norwegian
BUSINESS: COMMERCE, INDUSTRY & MANAGEMENT: Trade Unions

POSTHORNET
31509R32A-110
Editorial: Møllergata 10, 0179 OSLO Tel: 23061561 Fax: 23062271
Email: post@aktuell.no Web site: http://www.aktuell.no

Freq: Monthly; **Circ:** 22,500
Profile: Magazine of the Norwegian Postal Organisation and the Norwegian Union of Postal Employees.
Language(s): Norwegian
ADVERTISING RATES:
Full Page Colour .... NOK 16000
BUSINESS: LOCAL GOVERNMENT, LEISURE & RECREATION: Local Government

PRAKTISK ØKONOMI & FINANS
1624693R1A-122
Editorial: Pb 508 Sentrum, 0105 OSLO
Tel: 95 92 51 05
Email: tstavik@broadpark.no **Web site:** http://www.universitetsforlaget.no/?marketplaceId=200&languageId=1&siteNodeId=697825
Freq: Quarterly
Editor: Frode Sættem
Language(s): Norwegian
BUSINESS: FINANCE & ECONOMICS

PRINT & PUBLISERING
1826643R14A-232
Editorial: Boks 9231 Grønland, 0134 OSLO
Tel: 92201214 **Fax:** 22172508
Email: marit.gullien@agi.no
Freq: Quarterly; **Circ:** 5,000
Language(s): Norwegian
BUSINESS: COMMERCE, INDUSTRY & MANAGEMENT

PRISMET
31721R62B-140
Editorial: IKO – Kirkelig pedagogisk senter, Pb. 2623, St. Hanshaugen, 0103 OSLO **Tel:** 22 59 53 00
Fax: 22 59 53 01
Email: lena.skattum@iko.no **Web site:** http://www.iko.no
Freq: Quarterly; **Circ:** 500
Editor: Birgitte Lerheim
Profile: Magazine about Christian and religious teaching.
Language(s): Norwegian
BUSINESS: CHURCH & SCHOOL EQUIPMENT & EDUCATION: Education Teachers

PROFFEN
1656533R94H-1
Editorial: PO:MEDIA:AS, v. Per Olav BErg, Strøket 5, 1383 ASKER **Tel:** 90858532
Email: po@pob.as **Web site:** http://www.byggmakker.no/?module=Articles
Freq: Quarterly; **Circ:** 1,000
Editor: Per Olav Berg
Language(s): Norwegian
CONSUMER: OTHER CLASSIFICATIONS: Customer Magazines

PROGRAMBLADET
32213R76C-70
Editorial: Pb. 1151 Sentrum, 0107 OSLO
Tel: 22 31 03 10 **Fax:** 22 31 04 55
Email: trudeh@tv-guiden.no **Web site:** http://www.programbladet.no
Date Established: 1946; **Freq:** Weekly; **Circ:** 25,894
Profile: Magazine about the latest TV and radio programmes in Norway.
Language(s): Norwegian
CONSUMER: MUSIC & PERFORMING ARTS: TV & Radio

PROPATRIA/VÅRT VERN
1624437R40-31
Editorial: Postboks 908 Sentrum, 0104 OSLO
Tel: 22 47 82 50 **Fax:** 22 33 27 23
Email: pro.patria@nrof.no **Web site:** http://www.nrof.no
Freq: 6 issues yearly; **Circ:** 9,555
Language(s): Norwegian
BUSINESS: DEFENCE

PROSA, FAGLITTERÆRT TIDSSKRIFT
1645138R84B-234
Editorial: PROSA, Uranienborgveien 2, 0258 OSLO
Tel: 22 12 11 40 **Fax:** 22 12 11 50
Email: kbg@prosa.no **Web site:** http://www.prosa.no
Freq: 6 issues yearly; **Circ:** 6,800
Language(s): Norwegian
CONSUMER: THE ARTS & LITERARY: Literary

PROSOPOPEIA
1660322R84B-236
Editorial: Sydnesplass 7, 5007
Email: proso@uib.no **Web site:** http://prosopopeia.b.uib.no
Freq: Half-yearly; **Circ:** 400
Language(s): Norwegian
CONSUMER: THE ARTS & LITERARY: Literary

PSYKISK HELSE
31673R56N-40
Editorial: Postboks 817 Sentrum, 0104 OSLO
Tel: 23103880 **Fax:** 23103881
Email: redaksjonen@psykiskhelse.no **Web site:** http://www.bladet.psykiskhelse.no
Freq: 6 issues yearly; **Circ:** 11,430
Editor: Cathrine Th. Paulsen
Profile: Magazine containing articles, news and information about mental health and psychology.
Language(s): Norwegian
BUSINESS: HEALTH & MEDICAL: Mental Health

PSYKISK HELSE; PSYKISKHELSE.NO
1864944R56A-220
Editorial: Postboks 817 Sentrum, 0104 OSLO
Tel: 23 10 38 80 **Fax:** 23 10 38 81
Email: redaksjonen@psykiskhelse.no **Web site:** http://www.psykiskhelse.no
Freq: Daily; **Cover Price:** Free; **Circ:** 2,500 Unique Users
Language(s): Norwegian
BUSINESS: HEALTH & MEDICAL

PSYKOLOGISK TIDSSKRIFT
1625059R56R-155
Editorial: Psykologisk Institutt, Svt-fakultetet, Ntnu, 7491 TRONDHEIM **Tel:** 73550737 **Fax:** 73591920
Email: pt@svt.ntnu.no **Web site:** http://www.svt.ntnu.no/psy/pt
Freq: Half-yearly; **Circ:** 600
Editor: Øyvind T. Heidenstrøm
Language(s): Norwegian
BUSINESS: HEALTH & MEDICAL: Health Medical Related

PUDDELPOSTEN
32241R81B-100
Editorial: Norsk Puddelklubb, Pb. 932, 0104 OSLO
Email: puddel@klubb.nkk.no **Web site:** http://www.puddelklubb.no
Freq: Quarterly; **Circ:** 1,000
Editor: Anita Byklum
Profile: Magazine containing information, articles and news about the care of poodles.
Language(s): Norwegian
Readership: Read by dog owners in general and poodle owners in particular.
CONSUMER: ANIMALS & PETS: Dogs

PULP NEWS
1625169R32H-3
Editorial: Bentsebrugt. 13 B, 0476 OSLO
Tel: 22 09 88 40 **Fax:** 22 09 88 46
Email: nsbf@nsbf.no **Web site:** http://www.nsbf.no
Freq: Quarterly; **Circ:** 15,000
Editor: Dagfrid Forberg
Language(s): Norwegian
BUSINESS: LOCAL GOVERNMENT, LEISURE & RECREATION: Leisure, Recreation & Entertainment

PULS
1625176R76D-258
Editorial: Eilert Sundts gt. 41, 0355 OSLO
Tel: 91 55 11 11
Email: redaksjonen@puls.no **Web site:** http://www.puls.no
Freq: 6 issues yearly; **Circ:** 10,000
Language(s): Norwegian
CONSUMER: MUSIC & PERFORMING ARTS: Music

PULS.NO
1624648R76D-252
Editorial: Eilert Sundts gt. 41, 0355 OSLO
Tel: 930 49 178
Email: redaksjonen@puls.no **Web site:** http://www.puls.no
Freq: 6 times a year; **Cover Price:** Paid; **Circ:** 10,000 Unique Users
Language(s): Norwegian
CONSUMER: MUSIC & PERFORMING ARTS: Music

PUTSJ
1624813R57-303
Editorial: Pb 4783 Sofienberg, 0506 OSLO
Tel: 23327400 **Fax:** 23327429
Email: putsj@nu.no **Web site:** http://www.putsj.no
Freq: Quarterly; **Circ:** 7,000
Language(s): Norwegian
BUSINESS: ENVIRONMENT & POLLUTION

QUILTEMAGASINET
1625168R79A-4
Editorial: Quilteforlaget AS, Mulvadsgate 14, 1610 FREDRIKSTAD **Tel:** 69 31 59 26
Email: bevoldk@online.no **Web site:** http://www.quilteforlaget.no
Freq: 6 issues yearly; **Circ:** 6,000
Language(s): Norwegian
CONSUMER: HOBBIES & DIY

RACING
32228R77D-100
Editorial: Rakkestadveien 1, 1814 ASKIM
Tel: 69819700 **Fax:** 69889433
Email: kari.nilsen@sportmedia.no **Web site:** http://www.sportmedia.no
Freq: 26 issues yearly; **Circ:** 6,300
Profile: Motor racing journal.
Language(s): Norwegian
CONSUMER: MOTORING & CYCLING: Motor Sports

RÅDGIVERNYTT
31716R62A-120
Editorial: Pb. 574, 3412 LIERSTRANDA
Tel: 32 22 06 12 **Fax:** 32 22 06 00
Email: ranveig.myrmo@skole.bfk.no **Web site:** http://www.srl.no
Freq: Quarterly; **Circ:** 2,100
Profile: Newspaper providing information about educational matters in general and vocational training in particular.
Language(s): Norwegian
ADVERTISING RATES:
Full Page Colour .... NOK 7000
BUSINESS: CHURCH & SCHOOL EQUIPMENT & EDUCATION: Education

RADIO 3 BODØ; RADIO3.NO
1865020R76D-317
Editorial: Storgata 38, 8002 BODØ **Tel:** 75 52 50 00
Email: epost@radio3.no **Web site:** http://radio3.no
Freq: Daily; **Cover Price:** Free; **Circ:** 2,500 Unique Users
Language(s): Norwegian
CONSUMER: MUSIC & PERFORMING ARTS: Music

RADIO CITY; RADIOCITY.NO
1865016R76D-316
Editorial: Trøgstadveien 1, 1830 ASKIM
Tel: 47 64 99 99
Web site: http://www.radiocity.no
Freq: Daily; **Cover Price:** Free; **Circ:** 2,500 Unique Users
Language(s): Norwegian
CONSUMER: MUSIC & PERFORMING ARTS: Music

RADIO LØDINGEN: LODINGEN.COM
1865014R76D-315
Editorial: Rådhusvn. 8, 8411 LØDINGEN
Tel: 76 93 23 00 **Fax:** 76932210
Email: radio@lodingen.com **Web site:** http://www.lodingen.com
Freq: Daily; **Cover Price:** Free; **Circ:** 2,500 Unique Users
Language(s): Norwegian
CONSUMER: MUSIC & PERFORMING ARTS: Music

RADIO NORDKAPP; RADIONORDKAPP.NO
1865013R76D-314
Editorial: Storgata 9, 9750 HONNINGSVÅG
Tel: 78 47 70 80 **Fax:** 78 47 70 81
Email: kontakt@radionordkapp.no **Web site:** http://www.radionordkapp.no
Freq: Daily; **Cover Price:** Free; **Circ:** 2,500 Unique Users
Language(s): Norwegian
CONSUMER: MUSIC & PERFORMING ARTS: Music

RADIO ØST; RADIOEAST.NU
1865024R84A-154
Editorial: Postboks 14, 1641 RÅDE **Tel:** 69 29 42 42
Email: redaksjonen@radio-ost.no **Web site:** http://www.radio-ost.no
Freq: Daily; **Cover Price:** Free; **Circ:** 2,500 Unique Users
Language(s): Norwegian
CONSUMER: THE ARTS & LITERARY: Arts

RADIO TOTEN; RADIOTOTEN.NO
1865011R76D-313
Editorial: Postboks 102, 2830 RAUFOSS
Tel: 61 19 48 00
Email: radtoten@online.no **Web site:** http://www.radiototen.no
Freq: Daily; **Cover Price:** Free; **Circ:** 2,500 Unique Users
Language(s): Norwegian
CONSUMER: MUSIC & PERFORMING ARTS: Music

RADIO UNG; RADIOUNG.NO
1865008R84A-152
Editorial: Postboks 721, 4666 KRISTIANSAND
Tel: 38 00 64 04 **Fax:** 38 00 64 48
Email: studio@radiosor.no **Web site:** http://www.radioung.no
Freq: Daily; **Cover Price:** Free; **Circ:** 2,500 Unique Users
Language(s): Norwegian
CONSUMER: THE ARTS & LITERARY: Arts

RATATOSK
2010145R84B-255
Editorial: RATATOSK v/ Guri Sørumgård Botheim, 2665 LESJA **Tel:** 970 31 624
Email: guri@ratatosknett.org **Web site:** http://www.ratatosknett.org
Editor: Kjersti Rognes Solbu
Language(s): Norwegian
CONSUMER: THE ARTS & LITERARY: Literary

RAUMNES; RAUMNES.NO
1865019R84A-153
Editorial: Postboks 44, 2151 ÅRNES **Tel:** 63 91 18 14
Fax: 63 91 18 22
Email: redaksjon@raumnes.no **Web site:** http://www.raumnes.no
Freq: Daily; **Cover Price:** Free; **Circ:** 2,400 Unique Users
Editor: Terje Smith
Language(s): Norwegian
CONSUMER: THE ARTS & LITERARY: Arts

RECHARGE AS
1897677R58-124
Editorial: PO Box 1182 Sentrum, NO-0107 OSLO
Tel: 24101700 **Fax:** 24101710
Email: editorial@rechargenews.com **Web site:** http://www.rechargenews.com
Freq: Weekly; **Circ:** 300
Editor: Paul Berrill
Language(s): Norwegian
BUSINESS: ENERGY, FUEL & NUCLEAR

RECHARGE AS – HOUSTON
1897669R58-121
Editorial: 5151 San Felipe, Suite 1440, TX 77056 HOUSTON
Email: editorial@rechargenews.com **Web site:** http://www.rechargenews.com
Freq: Weekly; **Circ:** 300
Language(s): Norwegian
BUSINESS: ENERGY, FUEL & NUCLEAR

RECHARGE AS– LONDON
1897657R58-122
Editorial: Eldon House, 2 Eldon Street, EC2M 7LS LONDON **Tel:** 0207 650 1060
Email: editorial@rechargenews.com **Web site:** http://www.rechargenews.com
Freq: Weekly; **Circ:** 300
Language(s): Norwegian
BUSINESS: ENERGY, FUEL & NUCLEAR

RECHARGE AS– STAVANGER
1897667R58-123
Editorial: PO Box 419, 4001 STAVANGER
Tel: 51 93 87 80 **Fax:** 51 93 87 81
Email: editorial@rechargenews.com **Web site:** http://www.rechargenews.com
Freq: Weekly; **Circ:** 300
Language(s): Norwegian
BUSINESS: ENERGY, FUEL & NUCLEAR

RECHARGE AS–RIO DE JANEIRO
1897678R58-120
Editorial: Rua do Russel 300 - 601 Gloria, 22210-010 RIO DE JANEIRO **Tel:** 21 2285 9217
Fax: 21 2265 5062
Email: editorial@rechargenews.com **Web site:** http://www.rechargenews.com
Freq: Weekly; **Circ:** 300
Language(s): Norwegian
BUSINESS: ENERGY, FUEL & NUCLEAR

RECHARGE AS–SINGAPORE
1897655R58-119
Editorial: The Riverwalk #04-04, 20 Upper Circular Road, 058416 SINGAPORE **Fax:** 6557 0222
Email: editorial@rechargenews.com **Web site:** http://www.rechargenews.com
Freq: Weekly; **Circ:** 300
Language(s): Norwegian
BUSINESS: ENERGY, FUEL & NUCLEAR

REGNSKAP & ØKONOMI
1624881R1A-123
Editorial: Pb. 99 Sentrum, 0101 OSLO
Tel: 23 35 69 00 **Fax:** 23 35 69 20
Email: post@narf.no **Web site:** http://www.narf.no
Freq: Quarterly; **Circ:** 16,500
Language(s): Norwegian
BUSINESS: FINANCE & ECONOMICS

REIS
1624696R89A-177
Editorial: Reis, PB. 265 Øker, 0510 OSLO
Tel: 92827551
Email: stein@reis.no **Web site:** http://www.reis.no
Freq: 6 issues yearly; **Circ:** 101,000
Language(s): Norwegian
CONSUMER: HOLIDAYS & TRAVEL: Travel

REISELIV 1624570R89E-121
Editorial: Postboks 2050 Vika, 0125 OSLO
Tel: 23 38 82 50
Email: redaksjon@reiseliv.no **Web site:** http://www.reiseliv.no
Freq: Daily; **Circ:** 30,000
Language(s): Norwegian
CONSUMER: HOLIDAYS & TRAVEL: Holidays

REISELIV; REISELIV.NO
1865015R89A-187
Editorial: Postboks 2050 Vika, 0125 OSLO
Tel: 23 38 82 50
Email: redaksjon@reiseliv.no **Web site:** http://www.reiseliv.no
Freq: Daily; **Cover Price:** Free; **Circ:** 2,500 Unique Users
Language(s): Norwegian
CONSUMER: HOLIDAYS & TRAVEL: Travel

REISER & FERIE 1624990R89A-178
Editorial: Postboks 1110, 0104 OSLO
Tel: 22 40 30 20 **Fax:** 22 40 30 21
Email: bjorn.moholdt@reiserogferie.no **Web site:** http://www.reiserogferie.no
Freq: Monthly; **Circ:** 30,000
Language(s): Norwegian
ADVERTISING RATES:
Full Page Colour .... NOK 29000
SCC .... NOK 241.67
CONSUMER: HOLIDAYS & TRAVEL: Travel

REISER & FERIE; REISEROGFERIE.NO
1865012R89A-186
Editorial: Postboks 1110, 0104 OSLO
Tel: 22 40 30 20 **Fax:** 22 40 30 21
Email: post@reiserogferie.no **Web site:** http://www.reiserogferie.no
Freq: Daily; **Cover Price:** Free; **Circ:** 26,800 Unique Users
Language(s): Norwegian
CONSUMER: HOLIDAYS & TRAVEL: Travel

RELEASE 1624806R43A-2
Editorial: JB Forlag, Drammensveien 70 C, 0271 OSLO **Tel:** 22 43 10 07 **Fax:** 22 44 99 11
Email: john.berge@release.no **Web site:** http://www.release.no
Freq: Monthly; **Circ:** 4,800
Editor: John Berge
Language(s): Norwegian
BUSINESS: ELECTRICAL RETAIL TRADE

REN MAT 31465R21A-32_50
Editorial: Ren Mat c/o OIKOS, Grensen 9b, 0159 OSLO **Tel:** 38095278 **Fax:** 23109641
Email: renmat@oikos.no **Web site:** http://www.oikos.no/renmat
Date Established: 1971; **Freq:** 6 issues yearly; **Circ:** 2,350
Profile: Journal containing information, articles and news about ecological farming.
Language(s): Norwegian
Copy instructions: *Copy Date:* 21 days prior to publication date
BUSINESS: AGRICULTURE & FARMING

RENHOLDSNYTT 31397R4F-100
Editorial: Pb 130, 2260 3061 SVELVIK KIRKENÆR
Tel: 469 41 000
Email: pal@askmedia.no **Web site:** http://www.askmedia.no
Freq: 6 issues yearly
Editor: Pål Sønsteli
Profile: Magazine about all aspects of cleaning and maintenance.
Language(s): Norwegian
BUSINESS: ARCHITECTURE & BUILDING: Cleaning & Maintenance

RETT OG PLIKT I ARBEIDSLIVET 1624424R44-101
Editorial: Info Forlag AS, Postboks 1113, 1705 SARPSBORG **Tel:** 69971790 **Fax:** 69971717
Email: info@infotjenester.no **Web site:** http://www.infotjenester.no
Freq: Quarterly; **Circ:** 3,000
Language(s): Norwegian
BUSINESS: LEGAL

REVISJON OG REGNSKAP
31351R1B-100
Editorial: Den norske Revisorforening, Postboks 2914 Solli, 0230 OSLO **Tel:** 23 36 52 00
Fax: 23 36 52 02
Email: alf.asklund@revisornett.no **Web site:** http://www.revisorforeningen.no/d9358620/Revisjon-og-Regnskap-7-2007
Date Established: 1931; **Freq:** 6 issues yearly; **Circ:** 8,000
Profile: Journal covering auditing, accounting, tax and the economy.
Language(s): Norwegian
BUSINESS: FINANCE & ECONOMICS: Accountancy

REVMATIKEREN 31669R56L-100
Editorial: Pb 2653 Solli, 0203 OSLO **Tel:** 22547600
Fax: 22431251
Email: ra@revmatiker.no **Web site:** http://www.revmatiker.no/Organisasjonen/Medlemsbladet
Freq: 6 issues yearly; **Circ:** 40,000
Profile: Journal of the Physiotherapy Association of Norway.
Language(s): Norwegian
BUSINESS: HEALTH & MEDICAL: Disability & Rehabilitation

RICA MAGASIN 1624590R89B-1
Tel: 21608190
Email: kristian.roise.dahl@rica.no **Web site:** http://www.dgmedia.no
Freq: Quarterly; **Circ:** 35,000
Language(s): Norwegian
CONSUMER: HOLIDAYS & TRAVEL: Hotel Magazines

RIGHTS.NO 1831509R32G-167
Editorial: Møllergata 9, 0179 OSLO **Tel:** 22 33 80 00
Email: post@rights.no **Web site:** http://www.rights.no
Freq: Daily; **Cover Price:** Paid
Editor: Hege Storhaug
Language(s): Norwegian
BUSINESS: LOCAL GOVERNMENT, LEISURE & RECREATION: Community Care & Social Services

RIMFROST MAGAZINE
1645133R91E-3
Editorial: c/o Darklands, Henrik Wergelandsgt. 47, 4612 KRISTIANSAND **Tel:** 47 29 85 20
Email: rimfrost@gothic.no **Web site:** http://www.gothic.no
Freq: Quarterly; **Circ:** 500
Language(s): Norwegian
CONSUMER: RECREATION & LEISURE: Lifestyle

RØDE KORS MAGASINET
31678R56P-100
Editorial: Pb 1 Grønland, 0133 OSLO
Tel: 22 05 40 00 **Fax:** 22 05 40 40
Email: jon.martin.larsen@rodekors.no **Web site:** http://www.rodekors.no/nyheter/rode-kors-magasinet
Freq: Quarterly; **Circ:** 170,000
Editor: Jon Martin Larsen
Profile: Magazine of the Norwegian Red Cross.
Language(s): Norwegian
BUSINESS: HEALTH & MEDICAL: Casualty & Emergency

RØDT! 32270R82-210
Editorial: Pb 124 Sentrum, 3251 LARVIK
Email: roedt@marxisme.no **Web site:** http://www.akp.no/roedt
Freq: Quarterly; **Circ:** 800
Profile: Radical left-wing magazine covering political news and current affairs.
Language(s): Norwegian
Readership: Read mainly by members of the Norwegian Workers' Communist Party.
CONSUMER: CURRENT AFFAIRS & POLITICS

RØDT & HVITT VINMAGASIN
1625082R22A-151
Editorial: Hausmannsgate 6, 0186 OSLO
Tel: 97494427
Email: vin@rodtoghvitt.no **Web site:** http://www.rodtoghvitt.no
Freq: 6 issues yearly; **Circ:** 9,000
Language(s): Norwegian
BUSINESS: FOOD

RØDT PRESS 32271R82-215
Editorial: Sosialistisk Ungdom, Akersgt. 35, 0158 OSLO **Tel:** 21933350 **Fax:** 21933301
Email: rp@su.no **Web site:** http://www.su.no/rp
Freq: Quarterly; **Circ:** 4,000
Profile: Socialist political magazine containing social, cultural and current affairs information.
Language(s): Norwegian
Readership: Aimed at those in the Socialist Youth League.
CONSUMER: CURRENT AFFAIRS & POLITICS

ROGALANDS AVIS 31797R67B-5050
Editorial: Pb 233, 4001 STAVANGER
Tel: 51 82 20 00 **Fax:** 51822140
Email: redaksjon@rogalandsavis.no **Web site:** http://www.rogalandsavis.no
Freq: Daily - Norway; **Circ:** 12,452
Editor: Torun Fanuelsen
Language(s): Norwegian
ADVERTISING RATES:
SCC .... NOK 32.40
REGIONAL DAILY & SUNDAY NEWSPAPERS: Regional Daily Newspapers

ROGALANDS AVIS; PULSREDAKSJONEN
1833378R84A-134
Editorial: Pb. 233, 4001 STAVANGER
Tel: 51 82 20 00 **Fax:** 51822150
Email: ekj@rogalandsavis.no **Web site:** http://www.rogalandsavis.no
Circ: 12,452
Language(s): Norwegian
CONSUMER: THE ARTS & LITERARY: Arts

ROM123 1810312R94H-2
Editorial: Gullhaugveien 1, 0441 OSLO
Tel: 22585000
Email: rom123@hm-media.no **Web site:** http://www.rom123.no
Freq: Monthly; **Circ:** 32,477
Language(s): Norwegian
CONSUMER: OTHER CLASSIFICATIONS: Customer Magazines

ROMERIKES BLAD 31782R67B-5100
Editorial: Pb 235, 2001 LILLESTRØM
Tel: 63 80 50 50 **Fax:** 63 80 48 70
Email: redaksjonen@rb.no **Web site:** http://www.rb.no
Date Established: 1902; **Freq:** Daily; **Circ:** 37,659
Language(s): Norwegian
ADVERTISING RATES:
Full Page Colour .... NOK 38764
SCC .... NOK 387,64
REGIONAL DAILY & SUNDAY NEWSPAPERS: Regional Daily Newspapers

ROMSDALS BUDSTIKKE
31787R67B-5150
Editorial: Pb. 2100, 6402 MOLDE **Tel:** 71 25 00 00
Fax: 71 25 00 14
Email: redaksjon@r-b.no **Web site:** http://www.rbnett.no
Freq: Daily; **Circ:** 18,167
Editor: Jan Inge Tomren
Language(s): Norwegian
ADVERTISING RATES:
SCC .... NOK 106.19
REGIONAL DAILY & SUNDAY NEWSPAPERS: Regional Daily Newspapers

RØRFAG 31377R3B-30
Editorial: Skarland Press AS, Pb. 2843, Tøyen, 0608 OSLO **Tel:** 22 70 83 00 **Fax:** 22 70 83 01
Email: jorn.soderholm@skarland.no **Web site:** http://www.rorfag.no
Date Established: 1936; **Freq:** Monthly; **Circ:** 3,191
Profile: Magazine for the plumbing, gas-fitting and heating trades.
Language(s): Norwegian
Readership: Read by master plumbers, plumbers, plumbing wholesalers, HVAC consultants, copper and tinsmiths and co-workers in supplier and wholesales firms. Along with others involved in the plumbing industry, the magazine is also read by practitioners in the areas of heating and ventilation systems.
ADVERTISING RATES:
SCC .... NOK 137.5
BUSINESS: HEATING & VENTILATION: Industrial Heating & Ventilation

ROSENKILDEN - NÆRINGSLIVSMAGASINET
1645108R14E-101
Editorial: Pb. 182, 4001 STAVANGER
Tel: 51 51 08 80 **Fax:** 51 51 08 81
Web site: http://www.stavanger-chamber.no
Freq: Monthly; **Circ:** 17,100
Language(s): Norwegian
BUSINESS: COMMERCE, INDUSTRY & MANAGEMENT: Work Study

RØYKFRITT.NO 32513R74G-70
Editorial: Pb. 8701 Youngstorget, 0028 OSLO
Tel: 22 65 35 79
Email: roykfritt@roykfritt.no **Web site:** http://www.roykfritt.no
Freq: Quarterly; **Cover Price:** Paid; **Circ:** 2,500 Unique Users
Profile: Magazine containing articles about the dangers of smoking.
Language(s): Norwegian
CONSUMER: WOMEN'S INTEREST CONSUMER MAGAZINES: Slimming & Health

RØYNDA 1624631R62A-209
Editorial: Studentsamfunnet i Sogndal, Pb. 230, 6856 SOGNDAL **Tel:** 57 67 69 30 **Fax:** 57 67 69 31
Email: roynda@meieriet.no **Web site:** http://www.meieriet.no
Freq: 6 issues yearly; **Circ:** 4,000
Editor: Ingve Lende
Language(s): Norwegian
BUSINESS: CHURCH & SCHOOL EQUIPMENT & EDUCATION: Education

RUS & SAMFUNN 31520R32G-70
Editorial: Universitetsforlaget, Postboks 508 Sentrum, 0105 OSLO **Tel:** 22 85 02 20
Email: astrid.renland@rus.no **Web site:** http://www.rus.no
Freq: 6 issues yearly; **Circ:** 2,500
Editor: Astrid Renland
Profile: Magazine for health workers specialising in the field of drug abuse.
Language(s): Norwegian
BUSINESS: LOCAL GOVERNMENT, LEISURE & RECREATION: Community Care & Social Services

RUSFRI 32377R94F-50
Editorial: Pb 4793 Sofienberg, 0506 OSLO
Tel: 22 03 27 40 **Fax:** 22 03 27 41
Email: steinar.glimsdal@blakors.no **Web site:** http://www.blakors.no
Date Established: 1915; **Freq:** Quarterly
Profile: Newspaper for members of the Blue Cross. Covers alcohol and drug-related problems, rehabilitation, also Christian theology.
Language(s): Norwegian
CONSUMER: OTHER CLASSIFICATIONS: Disability

RUSH PRINT 1624493R43A-1
Editorial: Dronningensgate 16, 0152 OSLO
Tel: 22 47 46 43 **Fax:** 22 82 24 22
Email: redaksjon@rushprint.no **Web site:** http://www.rushprint.no
Freq: 6 issues yearly; **Circ:** 2,500
Language(s): Norwegian
BUSINESS: ELECTRICAL RETAIL TRADE

RYKOGREIS.NO 1976347R73-178
Editorial: Byggfakta Docu AS, postboks 1024, 1510 MOSS **Tel:** 69 91 24 00
Email: info@byggaktuelt.no **Web site:** http://www.rykogreis.no
Language(s): Norwegian
CONSUMER: NATIONAL & INTERNATIONAL PERIODICALS

SAFEMAGASINET 1624959R33-73
Editorial: Postboks 145 Sentrum, 4001 STAVANGER
Tel: 51843900 **Fax:** 51843940
Email: safe@safe.no **Web site:** http://www.safe.no
Freq: Quarterly
Editor: Mette Møllerop
Language(s): Norwegian
BUSINESS: OIL & PETROLEUM

SAFEMAGASINET; SAFE.NO
1865007R33-84
Editorial: Postboks 145 Sentrum, 4001 STAVANGER
Tel: 51 84 39 00 **Fax:** 51 84 39 40
Email: safe@safe.no **Web site:** http://www.safe.no
Freq: Daily; **Cover Price:** Free; **Circ:** 2,500 Unique Users
Editor: Mette Møllerop
Language(s): Norwegian
BUSINESS: OIL & PETROLEUM

SALGSIMPULS 31372R2F-75
Editorial: Nydalen Allé 23, 0103 OSLO
Tel: 92 23 95 96
Email: mette.malka@ideforlaget.no **Web site:** http://www.ideforlaget.no
Freq: Monthly; **Circ:** 1,000
Profile: Magazine containing articles, news and information about sales and marketing.
Language(s): Norwegian
BUSINESS: COMMUNICATIONS, ADVERTISING & MARKETING: Selling

SALGSLEDELSE 31373R2F-80
Editorial: Nydalen Allé 23, 0484 OSLO
Tel: 92 23 95 96
Email: mette.malka@ideforlaget.no **Web site:** http://www.ideforlaget.no
Freq: Monthly; **Circ:** 1,000
Profile: Magazine containing articles, information and news about sales and marketing.
Language(s): Norwegian
Readership: Aimed at managers, executives and decision makers.
BUSINESS: COMMUNICATIONS, ADVERTISING & MARKETING: Selling

SAMENES VENN 32739R90-200
Editorial: Norges Samemisjon, Vestre Kanalkai 20, 7010 TRONDHEIM **Tel:** 47 47 61 61 **Fax:** 73 51 25 05

Email: samenes.venn@samemisjonen.no **Web site:** http://www.samemisjonen.no
Date Established: 1925; **Freq:** Monthly; **Circ:** 2,500
Editor: Jon Amundal
Profile: Magazine covering articles, news and information about the native Scandinavians, the Saamis, and their way of life. Covers political and legal matters as well as cultural and human rights issues.
Language(s): Norwegian
Readership: Aimed at Saamis and people who are working towards the preservation of national heritage and rights for ethnic minority groups.
CONSUMER: ETHNIC

SAMFERDSEL
31599R49A-50
Editorial: Gaustadalléen 21, 0349 OSLO
Tel: 22 57 38 00 **Fax:** 22609200
Email: are.wormnes@toi.no **Web site:** http://samferdsel.toi.no
Freq: Monthly; **Circ:** 2,067
Profile: Magazine covering all transport matters, including road construction and transport research.
Language(s): Norwegian
BUSINESS: TRANSPORT

SAMFUNN FOR ALLE
1624473R94F-105
Editorial: Norsk forbund for utiklingshemmede, Pb. 8953, Youngstorget, 0028 OSLO **Tel:** 22 39 60 50
Fax: 22 39 60 60
Email: helene@nfunorge.org **Web site:** http://www.nfunorge.org/view.cgi?&link_id=0.1046.1078
Freq: 6 issues yearly; **Circ:** 7,500
Language(s): Norwegian
CONSUMER: OTHER CLASSIFICATIONS: Disability

SAMFUNNSMAGASINET
1625055R53-17
Editorial: Pb 1118, 1787 BERG I ØSTFOLD
Email: sfm@sfm.no **Web site:** http://www.sfm.no
Freq: Monthly; **Cover Price:** Paid
Language(s): Norwegian
BUSINESS: RETAILING & WHOLESALING

SAMFUNNSØKONOMEN
1624520R1A-118
Editorial: Pb 8872 Youngstorget, 0028 OSLO
Tel: 22 31 79 90 **Fax:** 22 31 79 91
Email: sekretariatet@samfunnsokonomene.no **Web site:** http://www.samfunnsokonomene.no
Freq: 6 issues yearly
Editor: Annegrete Bruvoll
Language(s): Norwegian
BUSINESS: FINANCE & ECONOMICS

SAMFUNNSSPEILET
31510R32A-130
Editorial: Pb 8131 Dep, 0033 OSLO **Tel:** 21 09 00 00
Fax: 21 09 44 04
Email: dae@ssb.no **Web site:** http://www.ssb.no/ssp
Date Established: 1987; **Freq:** 6 issues yearly; **Circ:** 2,100
Editor: Natasza P. Sandbu
Profile: Magazine containing articles and information about education, development, public administration, social matters and issues concerning society as a whole.
Language(s): Norwegian
BUSINESS: LOCAL GOVERNMENT, LEISURE & RECREATION: Local Government

SAMMEN MOT KREFT
32163R74G-75
Editorial: Pb. 4 Sentrum, 0101 OSLO **Tel:** 07877
Fax: 22866610
Email: servicetorget@kreftforeningen.no **Web site:** http://www.kreftforeningen.no
Freq: Quarterly; **Circ:** 138,000
Profile: Magazine containing information and articles about cancer and related health issues.
Language(s): Norwegian
Readership: Aimed at people suffering from cancer and their families.
CONSUMER: WOMEN'S INTEREST CONSUMER MAGAZINES: Slimming & Health

SAMORA MAGASIN
1624554R84A-105
Editorial: Pløens gt. 4, 0182 OSLO **Tel:** 22209690
Fax: 22209691
Email: samora@samora.no **Web site:** http://www.samora.no
Freq: 6 issues yearly; **Circ:** 1,500
Language(s): Norwegian
CONSUMER: THE ARTS & LITERARY: Arts

SAMORA MAGASIN; SAMORA.NO
1865026R84A-156
Editorial: Pløens gt. 4, 0103 OSLO **Tel:** 22 20 96 90
Fax: 22 20 96 91
Email: samora@samora.no **Web site:** http://www.samora.no
Freq: Daily; **Cover Price:** Free; **Circ:** 2,500 Unique Users
Language(s): Norwegian
CONSUMER: THE ARTS & LITERARY: Arts

SAMTIDEN
32272R82-220
Editorial: Pb 363, Sentrum, 0102 OSLO
Tel: 22400406 **Fax:** 22206395
Email: cathrine.sandnes@aschehoug.no **Web site:** http://www.samtiden.no
Freq: Quarterly; **Circ:** 6,500
Profile: Journal covering culture, politics and literature.
Language(s): Norwegian
ADVERTISING RATES:
SCC .... NOK 25
CONSUMER: CURRENT AFFAIRS & POLITICS

SAMVIRKE
31472R21A-120
Editorial: Felleskjøpet Agri, Postboks 469 Sentrum, 0105 OSLO **Tel:** 22 86 10 04 **Fax:** 22 86 10 01
Email: oddrun.karlstad@felleskjopet.no **Web site:** http://www.fka.no/om-oss/sider/samvirke.aspx
Freq: Monthly; **Circ:** 35,000
Editor: Oddrun Karlstad
Profile: Magazine containing articles and information about farming and agriculture.
Language(s): Norwegian
BUSINESS: AGRICULTURE & FARMING

SANDEFJORDS BLAD
31793R67B-5200
Editorial: Pb. 143, 3201 SANDEFJORD
Tel: 33422000 **Fax:** 33422011
Email: redaksjonen@sb.no **Web site:** http://www.sb.no
Freq: Daily - Norway; **Circ:** 14,260
Language(s): Norwegian
ADVERTISING RATES:
SCC .... NOK 129.70
REGIONAL DAILY & SUNDAY NEWSPAPERS: Regional Daily Newspapers

SARPSBORG ARBEIDERBLAD
31794R67B-5250
Editorial: Pb. 83, 1701 SARPSBORG
Tel: 69 11 11 11 **Fax:** 69 11 10 74
Email: redaksjonen@sa.no **Web site:** http://www.sa.no
Date Established: 1929; **Freq:** Daily; **Circ:** 14,578
Language(s): Norwegian
ADVERTISING RATES:
SCC .... NOK 167.59
REGIONAL DAILY & SUNDAY NEWSPAPERS: Regional Daily Newspapers

SARPSBORG ARBEIDERBLAD; SPORTSREDAKSJONEN
1833444R75A-217
Editorial: Pb. 83, 1701 SARPSBORG
Tel: 69 11 11 11 **Fax:** 69 11 11 00
Email: sporten@sa.no **Web site:** http://www.sa.no
Circ: 14,578
Language(s): Norwegian
CONSUMER: SPORT

SAU OG GEIT
31475R21D-60
Editorial: Postboks 104, 1431 Ås, 0201 OSLO
Tel: 23 08 47 70 **Fax:** 22 43 16 60
Email: arne.flatebo@nsg.no **Web site:** http://www.nsg.no
Freq: 6 issues yearly; **Circ:** 14,000
Profile: Agricultural magazine giving information on sheep and goat breeding, management of rams' cycles and training of sheep dogs.
Language(s): Norwegian
BUSINESS: AGRICULTURE & FARMING: Livestock

SCANDINAVIAN JOURNAL OF TRAUMA, RESUSCIATION AND EMERGENCY MEDICINE (SJTREM)
1853536R56A-218
Editorial: Idse, 4102 IDSE **Tel:** 51 74 14 80
Fax: 51 74 14 81
Email: editorial@sjtrem.com
Freq: Daily; **Cover Price:** Paid
Language(s): Norwegian
BUSINESS: HEALTH & MEDICAL

SCANDINAVIAN OIL-GAS MAGAZINE
31529R33-60
Editorial: Pb 6865 St.Olavs Plass, 0130 OSLO
Tel: 22447270 **Fax:** 22447287
Email: magazine@scandoil.com **Web site:** http://www.scandoil.com
Date Established: 1973; **Freq:** 6 issues yearly; **Circ:** 11,000
Profile: International publication about the Scandinavian oil and gas industry. Provides in-depth articles and analyses trends in the trade.
Language(s): Norwegian
Readership: Read by decision makers in oil and oil-supply companies, local government and authority personnel and research institutions.
ADVERTISING RATES:
SCC .... NOK 183.33
Copy instructions: *Copy Date:* 30 days prior to publication date
BUSINESS: OIL & PETROLEUM

SCANDINAVIAN OIL-GAS MAGAZINE; SCANDOIL.COM
1841141R33-82
Editorial: Pb 6865 St.Olavs Plass, 0130 OSLO
Tel: 22 44 72 70 **Fax:** 22 44 72 87
Email: editor@scandoil.no **Web site:** http://www.scandoil.com
Freq: Daily; **Cover Price:** Paid; **Circ:** 7,000 Unique Users
Language(s): Norwegian
ADVERTISING RATES:
SCC .... NOK 36.6
BUSINESS: OIL & PETROLEUM

SCENEKUNST.NO
1657556R76B-3
Editorial: Storgt. 10B, 0155 OSLO **Tel:** 23 29 29 00
Email: chris@scenekunst.no **Web site:** http://www2.scenekunst.no
Cover Price: Paid
Editor: Chris Erichsen
Profile: Website Scenekunst.no is a news service and information channel for performing arts, with daily news updates and reviews from Norway and abroad. The website is run by Norwegian Association for Performing Arts (NAPA) in collaboration with Association of Norwegian Theatres and Orchestras (NTO).
Language(s): Norwegian
CONSUMER: MUSIC & PERFORMING ARTS: Theatre

SCOOTERNORGE.NO
1657816R77B-156
Editorial: Postboks 2123, 9507 ALTA
Tel: 78 44 06 70 **Fax:** 78442508
Email: post@motomedia.no **Web site:** http://www.scooternorge.no
Freq: 6 times a year; **Circ:** 10,000 Unique Users
Editor: Øystein Løland
Language(s): Norwegian
CONSUMER: MOTORING & CYCLING: Motorcycling

SE OG HØR
32132R73-150
Editorial: Pb. 1164 Sentrum, 0107 OSLO
Tel: 22 91 22 22 **Fax:** 22 91 21 7
Email: seher@seher.no **Web site:** http://www.seher.no
Freq: 104 issues yearly; **Circ:** 235,695
Editor: Trond Stensåsen
Profile: News magazine including radio and television programme listings.
Language(s): Norwegian
ADVERTISING RATES:
SCC .... NOK 766.67
CONSUMER: NATIONAL & INTERNATIONAL PERIODICALS

SEHER.NO
1800766R74Q-77
Editorial: Postboks 1164, Sentrum, 0184 OSLO
Tel: 40 60 10 00 **Fax:** 23 40 73 71
Email: seher@seher.no **Web site:** http://www.seher.no
Freq: Daily; **Circ:** 237,800 Unique Users
Editor: David Stenerud
Language(s): Norwegian
CONSUMER: WOMEN'S INTEREST CONSUMER MAGAZINES: Lifestyle

SEILAS
32348R91A-130
Editorial: Leangbukta 40, 1392 VETTRE
Tel: 66764950 **Fax:** 66764951
Email: post@seilas.no **Web site:** http://www.seilas.no
Date Established: 1906; **Freq:** 6 issues yearly; **Circ:** 15,000
Editor: Mikkel Thommesen
Profile: Magazine of the Royal Norwegian Yacht Club and the Norwegian Yacht Racing Union.
Language(s): Norwegian
Copy instructions: *Copy Date:* 20 days prior to publication date
CONSUMER: RECREATION & LEISURE: Boating & Yachting

SEILAS; SEILAS.NO
1865162R91A-211
Editorial: Leangbukta 40, 1392 VETTRE
Tel: 66 76 49 50 **Fax:** 66 76 49 51
Email: post@seilas.no **Web site:** http://www.seilas.no
Freq: Daily; **Cover Price:** Free; **Circ:** 2,500 Unique Users
Language(s): Norwegian
CONSUMER: RECREATION & LEISURE: Boating & Yachting

SEILFLYSPORT
32203R75N-100
Editorial: Pb 383 Sentrum, 0102 OSLO
Tel: 23 01 04 50 **Fax:** 23 01 04 51
Email: seilflysport@nak.no **Web site:** http://www.nak.no/seilfly
Freq: Quarterly; **Circ:** 2,200
Profile: Magazine for gliding and soaring enthusiasts and members of aviation clubs.
Language(s): Norwegian
CONSUMER: SPORT: Flight

SEILMAGASINET
32346R91A-155
Editorial: Gartnerveien 1, 1394 NESBRU
Tel: 21377790 **Fax:** 66774061
Email: post@seilmagasinet.no **Web site:** http://www.seilmagasinet.no
Date Established: 1975; **Freq:** Monthly; **Circ:** 14,000
Profile: Publication about charter and luxury yachts, sailing boats, dinghies and sports boats.
Language(s): Norwegian
CONSUMER: RECREATION & LEISURE: Boating & Yachting

SENIORPOLITIKK.NO
1660588R82-337
Editorial: Senter for seniorpolitikk, St. Olavs plass 3, 0165 OSLO **Tel:** 23 15 65 50
Email: ssp@seniorpolitikk.no **Web site:** http://www.seniorpolitikk.no
Freq: 6 times a year; **Cover Price:** Paid; **Circ:** 8,848 Unique Users
Language(s): Norwegian
CONSUMER: CURRENT AFFAIRS & POLITICS

SESAM
1800764R14A-218
Editorial: Media Solution AS, Postboks 9393, Grønland, 0134 OSLO **Tel:** 905 85 639
Email: trygve@sesamnett.no **Web site:** http://www.selgerforbundet.no
Freq: 6 issues yearly
Editor: Trygve Bergsland
Language(s): Norwegian
BUSINESS: COMMERCE, INDUSTRY & MANAGEMENT

SHAPE-UP
1624371R74A-62
Editorial: Gullhaugveien 1, 0441 OSLO
Tel: 22585000 **Fax:** 22585879
Email: detnye-shapeup@hm-media.no **Web site:** http://www.shapeup.no
Freq: Monthly; **Circ:** 22,833
Language(s): Norwegian
ADVERTISING RATES:
SCC .... NOK 212.50
CONSUMER: WOMEN'S INTEREST CONSUMER MAGAZINES: Women's Interest

SIKKERHET
1624265R14A-201
Editorial: Pb 5468 Majorstua, 0305 OSLO
Tel: 23 08 85 30 **Fax:** 23 08 85 50
Email: sikkerhet@nso.no **Web site:** http://www.nso.no
Freq: 6 issues yearly; **Circ:** 5,500
Editor: Gisle Havstein
Language(s): Norwegian
BUSINESS: COMMERCE, INDUSTRY & MANAGEMENT

SJEKKPOSTEN
1692822R40-37
Editorial: Pb 1635 Vika, 0119 OSLO **Tel:** 23 09 35 49
Email: kbjerkli@nvio.no **Web site:** http://www.nvio.no/?show=sjekkposten
Freq: 6 issues yearly; **Circ:** 9,000
Editor: Kristin Bjerkli
Language(s): Norwegian
BUSINESS: DEFENCE

SKATTEBETALEREN
31361R1M-70
Editorial: Pb. 213 Sentrum, 0103 OSLO
Tel: 22 97 97 04
Email: stig.flesland@skattebetaleren.no **Web site:** http://www.skattebetaleren.no
Freq: 6 issues yearly; **Circ:** 19,000
Editor: Stig Flesland
Profile: Journal of the Norwegian Taxpayers' Association.
Language(s): Norwegian
ADVERTISING RATES:
Full Page Colour .... NOK 20000
BUSINESS: FINANCE & ECONOMICS: Taxation

SKATTERETT
31362R1M-100
Editorial: Skattelovavdelingen, Finansdepartementet, PB 8008 Dep, 0030 OSLO **Tel:** 24 14 75 00
Fax: 22 85 94 20
Email: hilde.widerberg@finans.dep.no **Web site:** http://www.universitetsforlaget.no
Date Established: 1982; **Freq:** Quarterly; **Circ:** 1,700
Profile: Publication about taxation. Covers related legal and political matters.
Language(s): Norwegian
BUSINESS: FINANCE & ECONOMICS: Taxation

SKEPSIS 1657998R94J-3
Editorial: St. Olavs gt. 27, 0166 OSLO
Email: kontakt@skepsis.no **Web site:** http://www.skepsis.no
Editor: Asbjørn Dyrendal
Language(s): Norwegian
CONSUMER: OTHER CLASSIFICATIONS: Popular Science

SKIER 1858404R75A-231
Editorial: Maridalsv. 87, 0461 OSLO **Tel:** 22 04 06 00
Email: post@skier.no **Web site:** http://www.skier.no
Freq: Monthly
Language(s): Norwegian
CONSUMER: SPORT

SKIGUIDEN 32188R75G-120
Editorial: Pb. 6, 0855 OSLO **Tel:** 67 13 46 46
Fax: 67 13 46 47
Email: skisport@skisport.no **Web site:** http://www.skisport.no
Freq: Annual; **Circ:** 12,000
Editor: Ellen Aabech
Profile: Magazine containing the raceprogramme for all national ski events includes alpine, telemark, cross country, jumping and combined. Also includes statistical results for all last seasons national championships and world cups.
Language(s): Norwegian
Readership: Read by people at all the skiclubs in Norway and all volunteers in clubs and the Norwegian Ski Association.
CONSUMER: SPORT: Winter Sports

SKIPSMEGLEREN.NO 31584R45C-50
Editorial: Postboks 1895 Vika, 0124 OSLO
Tel: 22 20 14 85
Email: mail@shipbroker.no **Web site:** http://www.skipsmegleren.no
Cover Price: Paid
Profile: Magazine for ship brokers.
Language(s): Norwegian
BUSINESS: MARINE & SHIPPING: Maritime Freight

SKIPSREVYEN 31585R45D-70
Editorial: Boks 2613, Liamyrane, 5828 BERGEN
Tel: 55 19 77 70 **Fax:** 55 19 77 80
Email: post@skipsrevyen.no **Web site:** http://www.skipsrevyen.no
Date Established: 1971; **Freq:** 6 issues yearly; **Circ:** 10,000
Editor: Jan Einar Zachariassen
Profile: Journal providing total coverage of the shipbuilding, shipping and marine engineering industry, including new technology, safety at sea and the maritime section of the offshore oil industry.
Language(s): Norwegian
ADVERTISING RATES:
SCC .... NOK 197.5
BUSINESS: MARINE & SHIPPING: Marine Engineering Equipment

SKIPSREVYEN; SKIPSREVYEN.NO 1841163R33-83
Editorial: Boks 2613, Liamyrane, 5871 BERGEN
Tel: 55 19 77 70 **Fax:** 55 19 77 80
Email: post@skipsrevyen.no **Web site:** http://www.skipsrevyen.no
Freq: Daily; **Cover Price:** Paid; **Circ:** 9,900 Unique Users
Editor: Jan Einar Zachariassen
Language(s): Norwegian
ADVERTISING RATES:
SCC .... NOK 39.6
BUSINESS: OIL & PETROLEUM

SKISPORT 32189R75G-150
Editorial: Sognsveien 75 E, 0855 OSLO
Tel: 69 81 97 00
Email: allan.aabech@sportmedia.no **Web site:** http://www.skisport.no
Date Established: 1948; **Freq:** 6 issues yearly; **Circ:** 12,000
Editor: Allan Aabech
Profile: Magazine covering all ski disciplines. Official magazine of the Norwegian Ski Association.
Language(s): Norwegian
CONSUMER: SPORT: Winter Sports

SKO 31499R29-20
Editorial: Fredrik Selmers vei 2, 0663 OSLO
Tel: 22653941 **Fax:** 22657353
Email: skoforlaget@skoforlaget.no **Web site:** http://www.skoforlaget.no
Date Established: 1954; **Freq:** 6 issues yearly; **Circ:** 1,068
Profile: Magazine about the shoe and leather industry. Published by the Norwegian Shoe Council.
Language(s): Norwegian
BUSINESS: FOOTWEAR

SKOGEIEREN 31587R46-70
Editorial: Pb. 1438 Vika, 0115 OSLO **Tel:** 23 00 07 50
Fax: 22 42 16 90
Email: skogeier@skog.no **Web site:** http://www.skog.no
Freq: Monthly; **Circ:** 39,800
Editor: Anders Hals
Profile: Journal about forestry and research.
Language(s): Norwegian
Readership: Aimed at forest owners, forest engineers and professionals within the industry.
ADVERTISING RATES:
Full Page Colour .... NOK 13800
BUSINESS: TIMBER, WOOD & FORESTRY

SKOGINDUSTRI 31588R46-90
Editorial: Media Oslo AS, Boks 119 Manglerud, 0102 OSLO **Tel:** 23158500 **Fax:** 22171279
Email: karljorgen.gurandsrud@mediaoslo.no
Date Established: 1947; **Freq:** 6 issues yearly; **Circ:** 1,145
Profile: International journal focusing on the timber, pulp and paper industry.
Language(s): Norwegian
ADVERTISING RATES:
Full Page Colour .... NOK 13000
Copy instructions: *Copy Date:* 11 days prior to publication date
BUSINESS: TIMBER, WOOD & FORESTRY

SKOGINDUSTRI; SKOGINDUSTRI.NO 1938677R46-104
Editorial: Media Oslo AS, Boks 119 Manglerud, NO-0612 OSLO **Tel:** 23 15 85 00
Email: karljorgen.gurandsrud@mediaoslo.no **Web site:** http://www.skogindustri.no
Cover Price: Paid
Editor: Karl Jørgen Gurandsrud
Language(s): Norwegian
BUSINESS: TIMBER, WOOD & FORESTRY

SKOLELEDEREN 1624863R62A-211
Editorial: Lakkegata 21, 0187 OSLO **Tel:** 24 10 19 16
Fax: 24 10 19 10
Email: tsm@nslf.no **Web site:** http://www.nslf.no
Freq: Monthly; **Circ:** 5,550
Editor: Tormod Smedstad
Language(s): Norwegian
BUSINESS: CHURCH & SCHOOL EQUIPMENT & EDUCATION: Education

SKOLEMAGASINET 31717R62A-150
Editorial: Avisen SkoleMagasinet, co Redaktør Per Rune Eknes, Postboks 301, 1379 NESBRU
Tel: 92 23 48 47 **Fax:** 62 53 53 94
Email: per.rune@skolemagasinet.no **Web site:** http://www.skolemagasinet.no
Date Established: 1990; **Freq:** 6 issues yearly; **Circ:** 5,064
Profile: Magazine containing information, news and articles about the Norwegian educational system and the integration of information and communications technology into education on all levels.
Language(s): Norwegian
Readership: Aimed at Headteachers and those responsible for information technology in schools.
ADVERTISING RATES:
SCC .... NOK 114.17
BUSINESS: CHURCH & SCHOOL EQUIPMENT & EDUCATION: Education

SKOLEPSYKOLOGI 1624688R56R-152
Editorial: Pb. 165, 2711 GRAN **Tel:** 61 33 16 16
Fax: 61 33 01 07
Email: j-moss@online.no **Web site:** http://www.skolepsykologer.no/skolepsykologi/index.shtml
Freq: 6 issues yearly; **Circ:** 1,597
Language(s): Norwegian
BUSINESS: HEALTH & MEDICAL: Health Medical Related

SMAALENENES AVIS; SPORTSREDAKSJONEN 1835237R75A-222
Editorial: Pb. B, 1801 ASKIM **Tel:** 69 81 61 56
Fax: 69 88 95 84
Email: sporten@smaalenene.no **Web site:** http://www.smaalenene.no
Freq: Daily; **Circ:** 13,305
Language(s): Norwegian
CONSUMER: SPORT

SNITT 31555R41A-75
Editorial: Skovveien 20, 0505 OSLO **Tel:** 22 12 82 00
Email: grafill@grafill.no **Web site:** http://www.grafill.no/snitt
Date Established: 1991; **Freq:** 6 issues yearly; **Circ:** 1,722
Profile: Magazine of the Association of Norwegian Graphic Designers and Illustrators.
Language(s): Norwegian
BUSINESS: PRINTING & STATIONERY: Printing

SNØ & SKI 32190R75G-160
Editorial: Kongeveien 5, 0787 OSLO **Tel:** 22 92 32 00
Fax: 22 92 32 50
Email: redaksjon@skiforeningen.no **Web site:** http://www.skiforeningen.no/medlem/medlemsbladet_snoe_ski_og_skiforeningen_no
Freq: Quarterly; **Circ:** 36,375
Profile: Magazine about skiing and other winter sports.
Language(s): Norwegian
CONSUMER: SPORT: Winter Sports

SOLVEIGS SMIL 1938277R74G-172
Web site: http://www.solveigs-smil.blogspot.com
Cover Price: Paid
Language(s): Norwegian
CONSUMER: WOMEN'S INTEREST CONSUMER MAGAZINES: Slimming & Health

SØRØY-SAMKJØRINGEN 1625482R2A-30
Editorial: Pb. 44, 6090 FOSNAVÅG **Tel:** 70 08 44 00
Fax: 70 08 44 01
Email: annonse@vestlandsnytt.no
Freq: 208 issues yearly; **Circ:** 10,000
Language(s): Norwegian
BUSINESS: COMMUNICATIONS, ADVERTISING & MARKETING

SOS-BARNEBYER 32752R91D-63
Editorial: Pb 733 Sentrum, 0105 OSLO
Tel: 23353900 **Fax:** 23353901
Email: sos@sos-barnebyer.no **Web site:** http://www.sos-barnebyer.no
Date Established: 1964; **Freq:** Quarterly; **Circ:** 140,000
Editor: Camilla Gilje Thommessen
Profile: Magazine concerning the activities of the organisation SOS Barneby which provides help for children all over the world.
Language(s): Norwegian
Readership: Read by sponsors and supporters of the organisation SOS Barneby.
CONSUMER: RECREATION & LEISURE: Children & Youth

SPAREBANKBLADET 31352R1C-120
Editorial: Pb 6772 St. Olavs Plass, 0130 OSLO
Tel: 22 11 00 75 **Fax:** 22 36 25 33
Email: ragnar.falck@sparebankforeningen.no **Web site:** http://www.sparebankbladet.no
Freq: Monthly; **Circ:** 5,482
Profile: Journal about savings banks.
Language(s): Norwegian
ADVERTISING RATES:
SCC .... NOK 120
BUSINESS: FINANCE & ECONOMICS: Banking

SPEAKER.NO 1657791R75J-102
Editorial: Akersgt. 28 A, 0158 OSLO **Tel:** 21 56 98 00
Email: redaksjonen@speaker.no **Web site:** http://www.speaker.no
Cover Price: Paid
Language(s): Norwegian
CONSUMER: SPORT: Athletics

SPEIDERBLADET 1624665R32H-2
Editorial: Pb 6810 St.Olavspl., 0130 OSLO
Tel: 22 99 15 50 **Fax:** 22 99 15 51
Email: post@kfuk-kfum-speiderne.no **Web site:** http://www.kfuk-kfum-speiderne.no
Freq: Quarterly; **Circ:** 13,500
Editor: Magnus Holm
Language(s): Norwegian
BUSINESS: LOCAL GOVERNMENT, LEISURE & RECREATION: Leisure, Recreation & Entertainment

SPEIDEREN 32363R91D-80
Editorial: Postboks 6910, 0130 OSLO
Tel: 22 99 22 30 **Fax:** 22 86 20 50
Email: speideren@scout.no **Web site:** http://www.speiding.no
Freq: Quarterly; **Circ:** 22,500
Profile: Magazine of the Norwegian Guide and Scout Association.
Language(s): Norwegian
CONSUMER: RECREATION & LEISURE: Children & Youth

SPESIALPEDAGOGIKK 1624292R62A-201
Editorial: Pb. 9191, Grønland, 0134 OSLO
Tel: 24 14 20 00 **Fax:** 24 14 21 57
Email: redaksjonen@spesialpedagogikk.no **Web site:** http://www.spesialpedagogikk.no
Freq: Monthly; **Circ:** 6,015
Language(s): Norwegian
BUSINESS: CHURCH & SCHOOL EQUIPMENT & EDUCATION: Education

SPILLVERKET.NO 1935269R5E-14
Editorial: Tek.no c/o Edda Digital, Postboks 428 Sentrum, 0103 OSLO **Tel:** 920 53683
Fax: 21 56 97 01
Email: lars.lager@eddamedia.no **Web site:** http://spillverket.no
Cover Price: Paid
Language(s): Norwegian
BUSINESS: COMPUTERS & AUTOMATION: Data Transmission

SPIRIT 32365R91D-105
Editorial: Henrik Ibsensgt 28, 0175 OSLO
Tel: 21 56 90 00 **Fax:** 21569001
Email: spirit@chilipublications.no **Web site:** http://www.spirit.no
Date Established: 1994; **Freq:** 6 issues yearly;
Cover Price: Free; **Circ:** 55,000
Editor: Pål Kaalaas
Profile: Magazine containing articles of interest to people aged between 15-25 years.
Language(s): Norwegian
CONSUMER: RECREATION & LEISURE: Children & Youth

SPIS BEDRE 1740787R22A-168
Editorial: Bonnier Blader AS, Øvre Vollgate 6, 0158 OSLO **Tel:** 22401200 **Fax:** 22401201
Email: redaksjonen@spisbedre.no **Web site:** http://www.spisbedre.no
Freq: Monthly; **Circ:** 14,041
Editor: Cecilie Espensen
Language(s): Norwegian
BUSINESS: FOOD

SPOR 1740793R56R-207
Editorial: KoRus-Nord, Pb. 385, 8505 NARVIK
Tel: 76966500 **Fax:** 76966879
Email: post@korusnord.no **Web site:** http://www.korusnord.no
Circ: 3,000
Language(s): Norwegian
BUSINESS: HEALTH & MEDICAL: Health Medical Related

SPORT 31593R48B-10
Editorial: SPORTSBRANSJEN AS, Sjølyst Plass 3, 0278 OSLO **Tel:** 23 00 15 33 **Fax:** 23 00 15 32
Email: morten.dahl@sportsbransjen.no **Web site:** http://www.sportsbransjen.no
Freq: 6 issues yearly; **Circ:** 3,000
Profile: Magazine about sports equipment manufacture, import and trade.
Language(s): Norwegian
ADVERTISING RATES:
SCC .... NOK 132.5
BUSINESS: TOY TRADE & SPORTS GOODS: Sports Goods

SPORTFISKER'N 1624382R92-51
Editorial: Drammens Sportsfiskere, Pb. 335, 3001 DRAMMEN **Tel:** 32 82 09 31
Email: redaksjonen@drammenssportsfiskere.no **Web site:** http://www.drammenssportsfiskere.com
Freq: Quarterly; **Circ:** 600
Editor: Tor Andreassen
Language(s): Norwegian
CONSUMER: ANGLING & FISHING

SPORTMEDIA 1935738R14A-240
Editorial: Rakkestadveien 1, 1814 ASKIM
Tel: 69 81 97 00 **Fax:** 69 88 94 33
Email: erik.unaas@sportmedia.no
Language(s): Norwegian
BUSINESS: COMMERCE, INDUSTRY & MANAGEMENT

SPRÅKNYTT 1624865R60B-201
Editorial: Pb. 8107, Dep., 0032 OSLO
Tel: 22 54 19 50
Email: post@sprakradet.no **Web site:** http://www.sprakradet.no
Freq: Quarterly; **Circ:** 25,500
Editor: Svein Nestor
Language(s): Norwegian
BUSINESS: PUBLISHING: Libraries

ST. HALLVARD 1624953R84A-108
Editorial: Militærhospitalet, Grev Wedels Plass 1, 0151 OSLO **Tel:** 22 40 50 90 **Fax:** 22 40 50 91
Email: post@oslobyesvel.no **Web site:** http://www.oslobyesvel.no
Freq: Quarterly; **Circ:** 4,300
Language(s): Norwegian
CONSUMER: THE ARTS & LITERARY: Arts

STALLSKRIKET 1624999R81D-101
Editorial: Pb. 2385, 3003 DRAMMEN STRØMSØ
Tel: 32 20 56 00
Email: cloevaas@online.no **Web site:** http://www.stallskriket.no
Freq: 104 issues yearly; **Circ:** 2,869

Editor: Knut Håvåg
Language(s): Norwegian
CONSUMER: ANIMALS & PETS: Horses & Ponies

STAMPOSTEN
1645134R79C-102
Editorial: Postboks 31, 2860 HOV **Tel:** 61129611
Email: nifs@stamming.no **Web site:** http://www.stamming.no
Freq: Quarterly
Editor: Arne Hope
Language(s): Norwegian
CONSUMER: HOBBIES & DIY: Philately

STAT & STYRING
31511R32A-150
Editorial: Universitetsforlaget, Postboks 508 Sentrum, 0105 OSLO **Tel:** 24 14 75 00
Fax: 24 14 75 01
Email: redaksjon@statogstyring.no **Web site:** http://www.universitetsforlaget.no/tidsskrift/vaare/samfunnsvitenskap/zacv_stat_og_styring
Freq: Quarterly; **Circ:** 3,700
Editor: Jan Erik Grindheim
Profile: Magazine about governmental and public leadership, published in cooperation with the Norwegian Directorate of Organisation and Management.
Language(s): Norwegian
BUSINESS: LOCAL GOVERNMENT, LEISURE & RECREATION: Local Government

STATISTISK SENTRALBYRÅ - SSB.NO
1624560R14A-203
Editorial: Pb 8131 Dep, 0033 OSLO **Tel:** 21 09 00 00
Email: webgruppa@ssb.no **Web site:** http://www.ssb.no
Cover Price: Paid
Language(s): Norwegian
BUSINESS: COMMERCE, INDUSTRY & MANAGEMENT

STATSBYGG
1657789R3D-1
Editorial: Pb. 8106 Dep, 0032 OSLO **Tel:** 815 55 045
Email: postmottak@statsbygg.no **Web site:** http://www.statsbygg.no
Language(s): Norwegian
BUSINESS: HEATING & VENTILATION: Heating & Plumbing

STATSSPRÅK
1625108R32R-54
Editorial: Språkrådet, Pb 8107 Dep, 0032 OSLO
Tel: 22 54 19 50
Email: torunn.reksten@sprakradet.no **Web site:** http://www.sprakrad.no
Freq: Quarterly; **Circ:** 17,000
Editor: Torunn Reksten
Language(s): Norwegian
BUSINESS: LOCAL GOVERNMENT, LEISURE & RECREATION: Local Government Related

STAVANGER AFTENBLAD
31798R67B-5350
Editorial: Pb. 229, 4001 STAVANGER **Tel:** 0515 0
Fax: 51893005
Email: vaktsjef@aftenbladet.no **Web site:** http://www.aftenbladet.no
Freq: Daily - Norway; **Circ:** 68,010
Editor: Tarald Aano
Language(s): Norwegian
ADVERTISING RATES:
Full Page Colour .... NOK 32177
SCC .... NOK 321.77
REGIONAL DAILY & SUNDAY NEWSPAPERS: Regional Daily Newspapers

STEMMER
2010149R84B-256
Editorial: STEMMER, Strandvn. 2, 3186 HORTEN
Tel: 33 04 97 15
Email: unn-c@online.no **Web site:** http://www.stemmer.no
Language(s): Norwegian
CONSUMER: THE ARTS & LITERARY: Literary

STI OG VARDE
1624347R91R-1
Editorial: Tverrgaten 4-6, 5017 BERGEN
Tel: 55 33 58 10 **Fax:** 55 33 58 29
Email: post@bergen-turlag.no **Web site:** http://www.bergen-turlag.no
Freq: Quarterly; **Circ:** 13,000
Language(s): Norwegian
CONSUMER: RECREATION & LEISURE: Recreation & Leisure Related

STOCKLINK
1657595R1F-4
Editorial: Thunesvei 2, 0203 OSLO **Tel:** 21 07 50 08
Email: tips@stocklink.no **Web site:** http://www.stocklink.no
Circ: 2,500 Unique Users
Language(s): Norwegian
BUSINESS: FINANCE & ECONOMICS: Investment

STREK
1819079R14A-231
Editorial: Strek Media AS, St. Olavsgt. 24, 0166 OSLO **Tel:** 22 310 335
Email: tips@strekmag.no **Web site:** http://www.strekmag.no
Freq: Quarterly
Language(s): Norwegian
BUSINESS: COMMERCE, INDUSTRY & MANAGEMENT

STUDENTTORGET.NO
1996366R62A-250
Editorial: Youngstorget 4 / Pløensgate 4, 0181 OSLO
Tel: 24 20 04 12 **Fax:** 24 20 15 94
Email: post@studenttorget.no **Web site:** http://www.studenttorget.no
Cover Price: Paid
Language(s): Norwegian
BUSINESS: CHURCH & SCHOOL EQUIPMENT & EDUCATION: Education

STUDIA MUSICOLOGICA NORVEGICA
1624935R76D-256
Editorial: Studia Musicologica Norvegica, Universitetet i Bergen, Griegakademiet, Lars Hilles gt. 3, 5015 BERGEN
Email: petter.stigar@grieg.hib.no **Web site:** http://www.universitetsforlaget.no/studmus
Freq: Annual; **Circ:** 400
Language(s): Norwegian
CONSUMER: MUSIC & PERFORMING ARTS: Music

STUD.JUR
1624629R62A-207
Editorial: Karl Johansgt. 47, 0162 OSLO
Tel: 22 85 98 25 **Fax:** 22 85 98 02
Email: studjur-mail@jus.uio.no **Web site:** http://www.juristforeningen.no/studjur_nettutgave
Freq: 6 issues yearly; **Circ:** 5,500
Language(s): Norwegian
BUSINESS: CHURCH & SCHOOL EQUIPMENT & EDUCATION: Education

STUDVEST
32328R88A-150
Editorial: Parkveien 1, 5007 BERGEN
Tel: 55 54 52 06 **Fax:** 55 32 84 05
Email: studvest@uib.no **Web site:** http://www.studvest.no
Freq: Weekly; **Circ:** 7,000
Profile: Magazine containing information and news concerning the University of Bergen and the Norwegian School of Business.
Language(s): Norwegian
ADVERTISING RATES:
SCC .... NOK 87.25
CONSUMER: EDUCATION

STUFF
1837366R18A-103
Editorial: Østre Akervei 22, 0581 OSLO
Tel: 22659555
Email: post@hl-media.no **Web site:** http://www.stuffmagazine.no
Freq: Monthly - 11 ganger i året; **Circ:** 25,000
Language(s): Norwegian
BUSINESS: ELECTRONICS

SUNNHETSBLADET
31647R74G-125
Editorial: Norsk Bokforlag, Pb. 103, 3529 RØYSE
Tel: 32161550 **Fax:** 32161551
Email: post@sunnhetsbladet.no **Web site:** http://www.sunnhetsbladet.no
Freq: Monthly - 9 times a year; **Circ:** 7,793
Editor: Svanhild G. Stølen
Profile: Health magazine.
Language(s): Norwegian
Readership: Read by women aged 30 to 60 years.
ADVERTISING RATES:
Full Page Colour .... NOK 5000
CONSUMER: WOMEN'S INTEREST CONSUMER MAGAZINES: Slimming & Health

SUNNHETSBLOGGEN
1938271R74G-169
Web site: http://sunnhet.wordpress.com
Cover Price: Paid
Language(s): Norwegian
CONSUMER: WOMEN'S INTEREST CONSUMER MAGAZINES: Slimming & Health

SUNNMØRSPOSTEN
31746R67B-5400
Editorial: Pb. 123, 6001 ÅLESUND **Tel:** 70 12 00 00
Fax: 70 12 46 42
Email: redaksjonen@smp.no **Web site:** http://www.smp.no
Date Established: 1882; **Freq:** Daily; **Circ:** 32,667
Language(s): Norwegian
ADVERTISING RATES:
SCC .... NOK 239.65
REGIONAL DAILY & SUNDAY NEWSPAPERS: Regional Daily Newspapers

SVIN
1624297R21A-151
Editorial: Pb 504, Norsvinsenteret, Hamar, 2304 HAMAR **Tel:** 62 51 01 00 **Fax:** 62 51 01 01
Email: svin@norsvin.no **Web site:** http://www.norsvin.no
Freq: Monthly; **Circ:** 2,730
Language(s): Norwegian
BUSINESS: AGRICULTURE & FARMING

SYKEPLEIEN
31656R56B-70
Editorial: Postboks 456 Sentrum, 0104 OSLO
Tel: 22043304
Email: redaksjonen@sykepleien.no **Web site:** http://www.sykepleien.no
Freq: Monthly; **Circ:** 77,000
Profile: Magazine about all aspects of nursing and health politics. Published by the Norwegian Nurses' Association.
Language(s): Norwegian
BUSINESS: HEALTH & MEDICAL: Nursing

SYKKELMAGASINET
1624550R75A-202
Editorial: Postboks 20, Grefsen, 0409 OSLO
Tel: 23058100 **Fax:** 23058101
Email: post@sykkelmagasinet.no **Web site:** http://www.sykkelmagasinet.no
Freq: Monthly; **Circ:** 10,500
Language(s): Norwegian
CONSUMER: SPORT

SYN OG SEGN
32762R82-283
Editorial: Pb 4672 Sofienberg, 0506 OSLO
Tel: 22 70 78 00 **Fax:** 22 68 75 02
Email: syn.og.segn@samlaget.no **Web site:** http://www.synogsegn.no
Date Established: 1894; **Freq:** Quarterly; **Circ:** 3,400
Editor: Bente Riise
Profile: Magazine covering political and social matters, human interest stories and human rights issues, also Norwegian history.
Language(s): Norwegian
Readership: Aimed mainly at students but also read by the general public.
CONSUMER: CURRENT AFFAIRS & POLITICS

TANNSTIKKA
1624603R56D-77
Editorial: Pb. 9202 Grønland, 0134 OSLO
Tel: 21013600
Email: ntpf@kfo.no **Web site:** http://www.tannpleier.no
Freq: 6 issues yearly; **Circ:** 950
Editor: Anniken Schiøll
Language(s): Norwegian
BUSINESS: HEALTH & MEDICAL: Dental

TARA
1692443R74A-70
Editorial: Bonnier Media, Tara, Pb. 61, 0158 OSLO
Tel: 22 04 70 00
Email: redaksjon@tara.no **Web site:** http://www.tara.no
Freq: Monthly; **Circ:** 31,328
Language(s): Norwegian
ADVERTISING RATES:
SCC .... NOK 341.67
Copy instructions: *Copy Date:* 30 days prior to publication date
CONSUMER: WOMEN'S INTEREST CONSUMER MAGAZINES: Women's Interest

TAXI
31731R64G-10
Editorial: Pb. 6754 Rodeløkka, 0503 OSLO
Tel: 22 38 95 00 **Fax:** 22 38 95 01
Email: post@nortaxi.no **Web site:** http://www.taxiforbundet.no
Freq: Monthly; **Circ:** 6,150
Profile: Norwegian Taxi Association journal.
Language(s): Norwegian
BUSINESS: OTHER CLASSIFICATIONS: Taxi Trade

TEATERNETT
1657557R76B-4
Editorial: Emil Nordbysveg 43, 2312 OTTESTAD
Tel: 992 35 393
Email: teaternett@teaternett.no **Web site:** http://www.teaternett.no
Cover Price: Paid
Language(s): Norwegian
CONSUMER: MUSIC & PERFORMING ARTS: Theatre

TECHNETT.NO
1935317R18A-109
Editorial: NEDRE GOKSTADVEI 48 **Tel:** 400 08 020
Email: red@itpro.no **Web site:** http://technett.no
Cover Price: Paid
Editor: Frank Aune
Language(s): Norwegian
BUSINESS: ELECTRONICS

TEKNISK UKEBLAD
31456R19A-100
Editorial: Pb 5844 Majorstua, 0308 OSLO
Tel: 23 19 93 00 **Fax:** 23 19 93 01
Email: redaksjonen@tu.no **Web site:** http://www.tu.no
Freq: Weekly; **Circ:** 93,542
Profile: Journal of the Norwegian Society of Professional Engineers, the Association of Norwegian Engineers and Industry (NITO) and the Polytechnical Association.
Language(s): Norwegian
ADVERTISING RATES:
SCC .... NOK 377.50
Copy instructions: *Copy Date:* 8 days prior to publication date
BUSINESS: ENGINEERING & MACHINERY

TEK.NO
1935266R18A-108
Editorial: c/o Edda Digital. Postboks 428 Sentrum, 0103 OSLO **Tel:** 920 53683 **Fax:** 21569701
Email: desk@tek.no **Web site:** http://tek.no
Language(s): Norwegian
BUSINESS: ELECTRONICS

TEKNOFIL
1935931R18A-110
Editorial: Pb. 9025 grønland, Urtegata 9, 0133 OSLO
Tel: 21006000 **Fax:** 22191020
Email: post@teknofil.no **Web site:** http://www.teknofil.no
Freq: 6 issues yearly - Åtte utgaver pr. år
Editor: Marte Ottemo
Language(s): Norwegian
BUSINESS: ELECTRONICS

TEKNOFIL.NO
1840846R5E-6
Editorial: Pb. 9025 grønland, 0133 OSLO
Tel: 21006000 **Fax:** 22191020
Email: post@teknofil.no **Web site:** http://www.teknofil.no
Freq: Daily
Editor: Marte Ottemo
Language(s): Norwegian
BUSINESS: COMPUTERS & AUTOMATION: Data Transmission

TEKSTILFORUM
31590R47A-20
Editorial: Sjølyst Plass 3, 0278 OSLO **Tel:** 46941000
Fax: 62948705
Email: post@tekstilforum.no **Web site:** http://www.tekstilforum.no
Date Established: 1931; **Freq:** Monthly - 11 ganger i året; **Circ:** 3,384
Editor: Ove Hansrud
Profile: Magazine about the fashion trade.
Language(s): Norwegian
Readership: Read by shopkeepers, managers, decision makers, textile agents, wholesalers and people interested in the textile trade.
ADVERTISING RATES:
SCC .... NOK 154.17
Copy instructions: *Copy Date:* 20 days prior to publication date
BUSINESS: CLOTHING & TEXTILES

TEKSTILFORUM.NO
1841139R74B-71
Editorial: Sjølyst Plass 3, 0278 OSLO
Tel: 46 94 10 00 **Fax:** 62 94 87 05
Email: post@tekstilforum.no **Web site:** http://www.tekstilforum.no
Freq: Daily; **Cover Price:** Paid
Language(s): Norwegian
CONSUMER: WOMEN'S INTEREST CONSUMER MAGAZINES: Women's Interest - Fashion

TELEPENSJONISTEN
1624902R74N-203
Editorial: Telepensjonistenes Landsforbund, Kirkegata 9, 1331 FORNEBU **Tel:** 22776952
Fax: 22776955
Email: kon.telepensjonistene@telenor.com **Web site:** http://www.telepensjonistene.no
Freq: Quarterly; **Circ:** 4,200
Editor: Viggo Bj. Kristiansen
Language(s): Norwegian
CONSUMER: WOMEN'S INTEREST CONSUMER MAGAZINES: Retirement

TENNER I FOKUS
31658R56D-75
Editorial: Pb. 244, 2901 FAGERNES **Tel:** 61366900
Fax: 61366901
Email: tif@tannteknikerforbundet.no **Web site:** http://www.tannteknikerforbundet.no
Date Established: 1940; **Freq:** Quarterly; **Circ:** 600
Profile: Magazine containing information, articles and news about all aspects of dentistry.
Language(s): Norwegian
Readership: Aimed at dentists, dental technicians and health personnel.
BUSINESS: HEALTH & MEDICAL: Dental

TENNER & HELSE
32166R74G-130
Editorial: Forbundet Tenner og Helse, Postboks 6416, Etterstad, 0605 OSLO **Tel:** 23054565
Email: post@tenneroghelse.no **Web site:** http://www.tenneroghelse.no
Freq: Quarterly; **Circ:** 2,500
Editor: Anne-Grethe Storvik

Profile: Magazine containing articles and information about biological dentistry and toxicology. Also covers general related health issues. The publication is the official journal of the Norwegian Dental Patients' Association.
Language(s): Norwegian
Readership: Read mainly by dental patients and members of the association, but also by dentists and doctors.
CONSUMER: WOMEN'S INTEREST CONSUMER MAGAZINES: Slimming & Health

TERRENGSYKKEL 1803851R77C-51
Editorial: Mølleparken 6, 0459 OSLO
Tel: 22 04 46 00 **Fax:** 22 04 46 09
Email: redaksjon@terrengsykkel.no **Web site:** http://terrengsykkel.no
Freq: Quarterly; **Circ:** 7,117
Editor: Øyvind Aas
Language(s): Norwegian
ADVERTISING RATES:
Full Page Colour .... NOK 18000
CONSUMER: MOTORING & CYCLING: Cycling

TERRIER-BLADET 1624536R81B-202
Editorial: Norsk Terrier Klubb, Postboks 90 Økern, 0580 OSLO **Tel:** 974 74 944
Email: tb@ntk.org **Web site:** http://www.ntk.org
Freq: Quarterly; **Circ:** 2,100
Language(s): Norwegian
CONSUMER: ANIMALS & PETS: Dogs

TIDENS KRAV 31778R67B-5500
Editorial: Pb. 8, 6501 KRISTIANSUND N
Tel: 71 57 00 00 **Fax:** 71570002
Email: redaksjonen@tidenskrav.no **Web site:** http://www.tk.no
Date Established: 1906; **Freq:** Daily - Norway; **Circ:** 15,412
Language(s): Norwegian
ADVERTISING RATES:
SCC .... NOK 273.16
REGIONAL DAILY & SUNDAY NEWSPAPERS: Regional Daily Newspapers

TIDENS KRAV; SPORTSREDAKSJONEN 1833493R75A-218
Editorial: Pb. 8, 6501 KRISTANSUND N
Tel: 71 57 00 30 **Fax:** 71570001
Email: sporten@tidenskrav.no **Web site:** http://www.tk.no
Circ: 15,412
Language(s): Norwegian
CONSUMER: SPORT

TIDSSKRIFT FOR DEN NORSKE LEGEFORENING 31649R56A-80
Editorial: Pb 1152 Sentrum, 0107 OSLO
Tel: 23109050 **Fax:** 23109090
Email: tidsskriftet@legeforeningen.no **Web site:** http://www.tidsskriftet.no
Freq: 26 issues yearly; **Circ:** 24,684
Profile: Periodical of the Norwegian Medical Association.
Language(s): Norwegian
ADVERTISING RATES:
Full Page Colour .... NOK 29800
BUSINESS: HEALTH & MEDICAL

TIDSSKRIFT FOR JORDMØDRE 31655R56B-60
Editorial: Den norske jordmorforening, Tollbugata 35, 0157 OSLO **Tel:** 21023372 **Fax:** 21023377
Email: eddyg@online.no **Web site:** http://www.jordmorforeningen.no
Freq: 6 issues yearly; **Circ:** 2,234
Editor: Eddy Grønset
Profile: Magazine containing articles, information and news for midwives.
Language(s): Norwegian
Readership: Read by members of Norwegian Association of Midwives, any other midwives, other related health professionals, health policy makers and interested persons.
ADVERTISING RATES:
Full Page Colour .... NOK 8400
BUSINESS: HEALTH & MEDICAL: Nursing

TIDSSKRIFT FOR KANINAVL 1624452R21D-71
Editorial: Bjørn Egeland, Frøyerv. 46, 4328 SANDNES **Tel:** 51 67 19 00
Email: redaktor@kanin-nkf.net **Web site:** http://www.kanin-nkf.net
Freq: Monthly; **Circ:** 1,500
Language(s): Norwegian
BUSINESS: AGRICULTURE & FARMING: Livestock

TIDSSKRIFT FOR KJØNNSFORSKNING 32463R74Q-70
Editorial: Grensen 5, 0159 OSLO **Tel:** 24 05 59 95
Fax: 24 05 59 60
Email: post@kilden.forskningsradet.no **Web site:** http://kilden.forskningsradet.no/index.html
Date Established: 1977; **Freq:** Quarterly; **Circ:** 1,400
Editor: Hilde Danielsen
Profile: Magazine containing articles relating to women's studies and gender research.
Language(s): Norwegian
Readership: Read by researchers and the general public.
CONSUMER: WOMEN'S INTEREST CONSUMER MAGAZINES: Lifestyle

TIDSSKRIFT FOR NORSK PSYKOLOGFORENING 31675R56N-90
Editorial: Postboks 419 Sentrum, 0103 OSLO
Tel: 23103130 **Fax:** 22424292
Email: tidsskrift@psykologforeningen.no **Web site:** http://www.psykologforeningen.no
Freq: Monthly; **Circ:** 7,047
Profile: Journal containing articles and information about mental health and psychology. Published by the Norwegian Psychological Association.
Language(s): Norwegian
Readership: Read mainly by members.
ADVERTISING RATES:
Full Page Colour .... NOK 14900
BUSINESS: HEALTH & MEDICAL: Mental Health

TIDSSKRIFT FOR PSYKISK HELSEARBEID 1645142R56R-164
Editorial: Boks 508 Sentrum, 0105 OSLO
Email: nina@linguafil.no **Web site:** http://www.universitetsforlaget.no/tph
Freq: Quarterly
Editor: Anders J.W. Andersen
Language(s): Norwegian
BUSINESS: HEALTH & MEDICAL: Health Medical Related

TIDSSKRIFT FOR RETTSVITENSKAP 31568R44-100
Editorial: Inst for privatrett, UiO, Pb. 6706 St. Olavs plass, 0130 OSLO **Tel:** 24 14 75 00 **Fax:** 24 14 75 01
Email: are.stenvik@jus.uio.no **Web site:** http://www.universitetsforlaget.no
Freq: Quarterly; **Circ:** 1,600
Profile: Journal about law and legal matters.
Language(s): Norwegian
Readership: Read by law students, teachers and lawyers.
BUSINESS: LEGAL

TIDSSKRIFT FOR SAMFUNNSFORSKNING 31722R62B-200
Editorial: Pb. 3233 Elisenberg, 0208 OSLO
Tel: 24147500
Email: tfs@samfunnsforskning.no **Web site:** http://www.universitetsforlaget.no/tfs
Date Established: 1960; **Freq:** Quarterly; **Circ:** 1,000
Editor: Jo Saglie
Profile: Magazine containing information, news and articles about the study of history, anthropology, sociology, political science and civics.
Language(s): Norwegian
Readership: Aimed at teachers, researchers and students.
BUSINESS: CHURCH & SCHOOL EQUIPMENT & EDUCATION: Education Teachers

TIDSSKRIFT FOR VELFERDSFORSKNING 1625045R62A-216
Editorial: Nygårdsgaten 5, 5015 BERGEN
Tel: 55 58 97 10 **Fax:** 55 58 97 11
Email: velferd@rokkan.uib.no **Web site:** http://www.fagbokforlaget.no/tidsskrift/?artikkelid=62
Freq: Quarterly; **Circ:** 300
Language(s): Norwegian
BUSINESS: CHURCH & SCHOOL EQUIPMENT & EDUCATION: Education

TIDSSKRIFTET 2 FORELDRE 1625090R74C-57
Editorial: Postboks 9924, 7079 TRONDHEIM
Tel: 88 00 88 45 **Fax:** 6487 3954
Email: redaksjon@f2f.no **Web site:** http://www.f2f.no
Freq: Half-yearly; **Circ:** 2,500
Editor: Ketil Petersen
Language(s): Norwegian
CONSUMER: WOMEN'S INTEREST CONSUMER MAGAZINES: Home & Family

TIDSSKRIFTET FORM 1624447R74E-91
Editorial: Kunst og Design i skolen, Postboks 4703, 0506 OSLO **Tel:** 24 14 11 90
Email: hilde.degerud@c2i.net **Web site:** http://www.kunstogdesign.no
Freq: Quarterly; **Circ:** 1,900
Language(s): Norwegian
CONSUMER: WOMEN'S INTEREST CONSUMER MAGAZINES: Crafts

TIDSSKRIFTET SYKEPLEIEN; SYKEPLEIEN.NO 1865438R56A-221
Editorial: Postboks 456 Sentrum, 0104 OSLO
Tel: 22043304
Email: redaksjonen@sykepleien.no **Web site:** http://www.sykepleien.no
Freq: Daily; **Cover Price:** Free; **Circ:** 2,500 Unique Users
Language(s): Norwegian
BUSINESS: HEALTH & MEDICAL

TIDSSKRIFTET.NO 1841161R56A-214
Editorial: Pb 1152 Sentrum, 0107 OSLO
Tel: 23 10 90 50 **Fax:** 23 10 90 40
Email: tidsskriftet@legeforeningen.no **Web site:** http://www.tidsskrift.no
Freq: Daily; **Cover Price:** Paid
Language(s): Norwegian
BUSINESS: HEALTH & MEDICAL

TJENESTEMANNSBLADET 1624872R14L-105
Editorial: Møllergata 10, 0179 OSLO **Tel:** 23061561
Fax: 23062271
Email: anne.grete.lossius@aktuell.no **Web site:** http://www.aktuell.no
Freq: Monthly; **Circ:** 47,500
Language(s): Norwegian
BUSINESS: COMMERCE, INDUSTRY & MANAGEMENT: Trade Unions

TONENS MAKT 1740677R76D-306
Editorial: Norsk Sangerforbund, Samfunnshuset, 0181 OSLO **Tel:** 22 20 51 42
Email: ingunnwe@online.no **Web site:** http://www.korsang.org
Freq: Quarterly
Editor: Ingunn Wesenlund Lia
Language(s): Norwegian
CONSUMER: MUSIC & PERFORMING ARTS: Music

TONO-NYTT 1740678R14R-7
Editorial: Pb. 9171, Grønland, 0134 OSLO
Tel: 22 05 72 00 **Fax:** 22 05 72 50
Email: tono@tono.no **Web site:** http://www.tono.no
Freq: Quarterly; **Circ:** 12,000
Language(s): Norwegian
BUSINESS: COMMERCE, INDUSTRY & MANAGEMENT: Commerce Related

TOPP 32218R76E-200
Editorial: Pb. 481 Sentrum, 0107 OSLO
Tel: 21 30 10 00
Email: hillevi@topp.no **Web site:** http://www.topp.no
Freq: Monthly; **Cover Price:** Paid; **Circ:** 43,941 Unique Users
Editor: Hillevi Forsman
Profile: Pop and rock magazine.
Language(s): Norwegian
Readership: Read by young people aged between 10 and 19 years.
CONSUMER: MUSIC & PERFORMING ARTS: Pop Music

TOPP.NO 1841164R74Q-81
Editorial: Pb. 481 Sentrum, 0107 OSLO
Tel: 21 30 10 00
Email: webred@topp.no **Web site:** http://www.topp.no
Freq: Daily
Editor: Ine Thereze Gransæter
Language(s): Norwegian
CONSUMER: WOMEN'S INTEREST CONSUMER MAGAZINES: Lifestyle

TRADEWINDS 31575R45A-70
Editorial: Christian Krohgs gate 16, 0186 OSLO
Tel: 22001200 **Fax:** 22001210
Email: trond.lillestolen@tradewinds.no **Web site:** http://www.tradewinds.no
Freq: Weekly; **Circ:** 8,000
Profile: Magazine concerning all aspects of shipping.
Language(s): Norwegian
ADVERTISING RATES:
SCC .... NOK 927.50
BUSINESS: MARINE & SHIPPING

TRAFIKKSKOLEN 31504R31D-250
Editorial: Autoriserte Trafikkskolers Landsforbund, Pb. 144 Manglerud, 0612 OSLO **Tel:** 22 62 60 80
Fax: 22 62 60 81
Email: atl@atl.no **Web site:** http://www.atl.no
Date Established: 1986; **Freq:** Quarterly; **Circ:** 2,200
Profile: Magazine containing articles, news and information about driving schools and training.
Language(s): Norwegian
Readership: Read by driving instructors.
BUSINESS: MOTOR TRADE: Driving Schools

TRAIDING CARBON MAGAZINE 1852605R58-112
Editorial: Pb. 7120 St.Olavs plass, 0130 OSLO
Tel: 22405340 **Fax:** 22405341
Email: contact@pointcarbon.com **Web site:** http://www.pointcarbon.com
Freq: Monthly - 10 ganger i året; **Cover Price:** Free
Language(s): Norwegian
BUSINESS: ENERGY, FUEL & NUCLEAR

TRAKTOR 1697479R77R-1
Editorial: Pb. 9303 Grønland, 0191 OSLO
Tel: 21 31 44 00 **Fax:** 21 31 44 92
Email: marianne.rohme@tunmedia.no **Web site:** http://www.traktor.no
Language(s): Norwegian
CONSUMER: MOTORING & CYCLING: Motoring & Cycling Related

TRANSPORT INSIDE 1645121R49C-31
Editorial: Pb. 11, 1411 KOLBOTN **Tel:** 66822121
Fax: 66822120
Email: bjorgu@bjorgu.no **Web site:** http://www.bjorgu.no
Freq: 26 issues yearly; **Circ:** 1,000
Editor: Per Dagfinn Wolden
Language(s): Norwegian
BUSINESS: TRANSPORT: Freight

TRANSPORTARBEIDEREN 1803804R10-102
Editorial: Hammersborg Torg 3, 0179 OSLO
Tel: 40 64 64 64 **Fax:** 22 20 50 89
Email: ntf@transportarbeider.no **Web site:** http://www.transportarbeider.no
Freq: 6 issues yearly; **Circ:** 16,000
Editor: Vegard Holm
Language(s): Norwegian
BUSINESS: MATERIALS HANDLING

TRANSPORTFORUM 31603R49B-40
Editorial: Pb. 5477 Majorstua, 0305 OSLO
Tel: 23 08 86 00 **Fax:** 23 08 86 01
Email: transportforum@transport.no **Web site:** http://www.transportforum.no
Date Established: 1930; **Freq:** Monthly; **Circ:** 4,000
Editor: Marit Grøttheim
Profile: Magazine for transport companies in Norway.
Language(s): Norwegian
Readership: Read by employees in bus, coach, rail and ferryboat services, freight companies, tourism and public administration.
ADVERTISING RATES:
Full Page Colour .... NOK 15850
SCC .... NOK 129.17
BUSINESS: TRANSPORT: Bus & Coach Transport

TRANSPORTMAGASINET 31607R49D-50
Editorial: Pb. 67 Bryn, 0611 OSLO **Tel:** 22 75 75 00
Email: redaksjonen@transportmagasinet.no **Web site:** http://www.transportmagasinet.no
Freq: Monthly; **Circ:** 22,500
Profile: Magazine containing articles and information about commercial road vehicles and the transport trade in general.
Language(s): Norwegian
ADVERTISING RATES:
SCC .... NOK 182.50
BUSINESS: TRANSPORT: Commercial Vehicles

TRAV OG GALOPP-NYTT 1624910R75E-3
Editorial: Pb 10, Årvoll, 0515 OSLO **Tel:** 22 88 30 00
Fax: 22 88 30 10
Email: tgn@tgn.no **Web site:** http://www.tgn.no
Freq: 104 issues yearly; **Circ:** 13,000
Language(s): Norwegian
ADVERTISING RATES:
Full Page Colour .... NOK 10650
CONSUMER: SPORT: Horse Racing

TRAVEL NEWS 31614R50-120
Editorial: Findexa Forlag, Gjerdrumsvei 19, 0484 OSLO **Tel:** 21 50 80 00
Email: sa@travelnews.no **Web site:** http://www.travelnews.no
Date Established: 1995; **Freq:** Monthly; **Circ:** 3,814
Editor: Stein Arild Iglebæk
Profile: Travel trade magazine.
Language(s): Norwegian
Readership: Read by travel agents, tour operators and their suppliers.
ADVERTISING RATES:
SCC .... NOK 163.33
BUSINESS: TRAVEL & TOURISM

Norway

TREKKSPILLNYTT 32217R76D-200
Editorial: co Per J. Grøthe, Einerveien 11, 3092 SUNDBYFOSS **Tel:** 906 44 927
Email: per-jog@online.no **Web site:** http://www.trekkspillforbundet.no/trekkspillnytt
Date Established: 1972; **Freq:** Quarterly; **Circ:** 3,500
Editor: Per J. Grøthe
Profile: Magazine containing articles and information about accordions and related musical instruments.
Language(s): Norwegian
CONSUMER: MUSIC & PERFORMING ARTS: Music

TRENINGSFORUM.NO 1658787R75P-3
Editorial: Grønlivegen 9, 3922 PORSGRUNN
Tel: 47 37 51 27
Email: post@treningsforum.no **Web site:** http://www.treningsforum.no
Cover Price: Paid
Language(s): Norwegian
CONSUMER: SPORT: Fitness/Bodybuilding

TRIM.NO 1657775R75P-1
Editorial: Trim.no AS, 6789 LOEN **Tel:** 913 85 926
Email: redaksjonen@trim.no **Web site:** http://www.trim.no
Language(s): Norwegian
CONSUMER: SPORT: Fitness/Bodybuilding

TRIVSEL.NET 1657796R74G-160
Email: post@trivsel.net **Web site:** http://www.trivsel.net
Cover Price: Paid
Language(s): Norwegian
CONSUMER: WOMEN'S INTEREST CONSUMER MAGAZINES: Slimming & Health

TROMS FOLKEBLAD; SPORTSREDAKSJONEN 1835426R75A-225
Editorial: Pb. 308, 9305 FINNSNES **Tel:** 77 85 20 60
Fax: 77 85 20 30
Email: sporten@folkebladet.no **Web site:** http://www.folkebladet.no/sport
Circ: 7,779
Language(s): Norwegian
CONSUMER: SPORT

TRØNDELAGSPAKKEN 1645220R35-11
Editorial: Trøndelagspakken AS, Postboks 3200, Sluppen, 7003 HEIMDAL **Tel:** 406 03 070
Fax: 72 50 16 17
Email: post@trondelagspakken.no **Web site:** http://www.trondelagspakken.no
Freq: Daily; **Circ:** 140,767
Language(s): Norwegian
BUSINESS: PACKAGING & BOTTLING

TRYGG HAVN 1624375R22G-1
Editorial: Postboks 1904 Damsgård, 5828 BERGEN
Tel: 55349310 **Fax:** 55349311
Email: tryggh@online.no **Web site:** http://www.dism.no/hXGXBT3lHGZV.22.idium
Freq: Monthly; **Circ:** 3,500
Language(s): Norwegian
BUSINESS: FOOD: Fish Trade

TRYGG PÅ SJØEN 1899497R91A-212
Editorial: Redningsselskapet, Postboks 500, 1323 HØVIK **Tel:** 67577777
Email: post@nssr.no **Web site:** http://www.nssr.no/Medlemskap/Medlemsblad
Freq: Quarterly; **Circ:** 70,000
Editor: Ingvar Johnsen
Language(s): Norwegian
CONSUMER: RECREATION & LEISURE: Boating & Yachting

TRYGGE SAMFUNN 1624443R40-32
Editorial: Pb. 796 Sentrum, 0106 OSLO
Tel: 22 42 49 12 **Fax:** 22 42 85 52
Email: kfb@kfb.no **Web site:** http://www.kfb.no
Freq: Quarterly; **Circ:** 8,300
Editor: Jan Erik Thoresen
Language(s): Norwegian
BUSINESS: DEFENCE

TRYGGTRAFIKK.NO 1625050R77A-212
Editorial: Pb 2610 St.Hanshaugen, 0131 OSLO
Tel: 22 40 40 40 **Fax:** 22 40 40 70
Email: oyen@tryggtrafikk.no **Web site:** http://www.tryggtrafikk.no
Cover Price: Paid
Language(s): Norwegian
CONSUMER: MOTORING & CYCLING: Motoring

TS AVISEN; TS-AVISEN.NO 1865156R14F-34
Editorial: Industritoppen 4A, 4848 ARENDAL
Tel: 37 06 39 00 **Fax:** 37 06 39 01
Email: post@ts-avisen.no **Web site:** http://www.ts-avisen.no
Freq: Daily; **Cover Price:** Free; **Circ:** 2,500 Unique Users
Language(s): Norwegian
BUSINESS: COMMERCE, INDUSTRY & MANAGEMENT: Training & Recruitment

TU.NO 1841140R13-41
Editorial: Pb 5844 Majorstua, 0308 OSLO
Tel: 23 19 93 00 **Fax:** 23 19 93 01
Email: nettdesk@tu.no **Web site:** http://www.tu.no
Freq: Daily; **Circ:** 17,000 Unique Users
Language(s): Norwegian
BUSINESS: CHEMICALS

TUNTREET 1624630R62A-208
Editorial: Pb 1211, 1432 ÅS **Tel:** 64 96 63 63
Fax: 64 94 73 73
Email: tuntreet@samfunnetiaas.no **Web site:** http://tuntreet.umb.no
Freq: 26 issues yearly; **Circ:** 3,000
Editor: Mari Eskerud
Language(s): Norwegian
BUSINESS: CHURCH & SCHOOL EQUIPMENT & EDUCATION: Education

TURMARSJNYTT 32201R75L-17
Editorial: Norges Folkesportforbund, Pb. 147, 1471 LØRENSKOG **Tel:** 67 90 55 36 **Fax:** 67 90 91 44
Email: nff@turmarsjforbundet.no **Web site:** http://www.folkesport.no/bladet/bladet.htm
Date Established: 1979; **Freq:** Quarterly
Profile: Magazine containing information, articles and news for people who enjoy walking.
Language(s): Norwegian
CONSUMER: SPORT: Outdoor

TV 2 HJELPER DEG 1863347R74C-94
Editorial: Postboks 2 Grünerløkka, 0505 OSLO
Email: hjelperdeg@tv2.no **Web site:** http://www.tv2underholdning.no/hjelperdeg
Freq: Weekly; **Cover Price:** Free; **Circ:** 410,000
Editor: Nils Ketil Andresen
Language(s): Norwegian
CONSUMER: WOMEN'S INTEREST CONSUMER MAGAZINES: Home & Family

TV2 INTERAKTIV 1624597R82-310
Editorial: Pb. 2 Sentrum, NO-0101 OSLO
Tel: 02 25 5 **Fax:** 21 00 60 03
Email: pressemelding@tv2.no **Web site:** http://www.tv2.no
Cover Price: Paid
Editor: Rune Indrøy
Language(s): Norwegian
CONSUMER: CURRENT AFFAIRS & POLITICS

TVILLINGNYTT 1645136R74C-69
Editorial: Stortorvet 10, 0155 OSLO **Tel:** 22 33 14 22
Fax: 22 33 14 24
Email: post@tvilling.no **Web site:** http://www.tvilling.no
Freq: Quarterly
Language(s): Norwegian
CONSUMER: WOMEN'S INTEREST CONSUMER MAGAZINES: Home & Family

UKEAVISEN LEDELSE 1624241R80-151
Editorial: Pb. 1180 Sentrum, 0107 OSLO
Tel: 22 31 02 10 **Fax:** 22 31 02 15
Email: red@adfontesmedier.no **Web site:** http://www.ukeavisenledelse.no
Freq: Weekly; **Circ:** 15,000
Language(s): Norwegian
ADVERTISING RATES:
SCC .... NOK 191.67
CONSUMER: RURAL & REGIONAL INTEREST

UKEAVISENLEDELSE.NO 1810322R73-165
Editorial: Pb. 1180 Sentrum, 0107 OSLO
Tel: 22 31 02 10 **Fax:** 22 31 02 15
Email: red@adfontesmedier.no **Web site:** http://www.ukeavisenledelse.no
Freq: Daily; **Cover Price:** Paid; **Circ:** 5,200 Unique Users
Language(s): Norwegian
ADVERTISING RATES:
SCC .... NOK 38.4
CONSUMER: NATIONAL & INTERNATIONAL PERIODICALS

UNDER DUSKEN; UNDERDUSKEN.NO 1837123R62A-241
Editorial: Elgesetergt. 1, 7030 TRONDHEIM
Tel: 73 53 18 13
Email: ud@underdusken.no **Web site:** http://www.underdusken.no
Freq: Daily; **Cover Price:** Paid
Language(s): Norwegian
BUSINESS: CHURCH & SCHOOL EQUIPMENT & EDUCATION: Education

UNGFOTEN 1624917R50-153
Editorial: Pb. 7 Sentrum, 0101 OSLO **Tel:** 22822841
Email: ung@dntoslo.no **Web site:** http://www.dntung.no/oslo/index.php?fo_id=142
Freq: Quarterly; **Circ:** 5,300
Editor: Kjersti Magnussen
Language(s): Norwegian
BUSINESS: TRAVEL & TOURISM

UNIKUM 1625224R62A-218
Editorial: Serviceboks 422, 4604 KRISTIANSAND S
Tel: 38 14 21 95
Email: red@unikumnett.no **Web site:** http://www.unikumnett.no
Freq: 6 issues yearly; **Circ:** 3,000
Editor: Tone Marie Jørgensen
Language(s): Norwegian
BUSINESS: CHURCH & SCHOOL EQUIPMENT & EDUCATION: Education

UNINYTT 1657821R55-106
Editorial: UNINETT - Abels gate 5 - Teknobyen, 7465 TRONDHEIM **Tel:** 73 55 79 00 **Fax:** 73 55 79 01
Email: info@uninett.no **Web site:** http://www.uninett.no/uninytt
Cover Price: Paid
Language(s): Norwegian
BUSINESS: APPLIED SCIENCE & LABORATORIES

UNITED SUPPORTEREN 32182R75B-100
Editorial: Pb 1992, Nordnes, 5817 BERGEN
Tel: 69 16 63 94 **Fax:** 55962033
Email: redaksjonen@muscsb.no **Web site:** http://www.united.no
Freq: 6 issues yearly; **Circ:** 23,770
Profile: Magazine containing information about Manchester United Football Club.
Language(s): Norwegian
Readership: Read by members of the Manchester United Supporters Club in Norway, Sweden and Denmark.
CONSUMER: SPORT: Football

UNIVERSITAS; UNIVERSITAS.NO 1865163R62A-247
Editorial: Postboks 89 Blindern, 0134 OSLO
Tel: 22 85 33 36
Email: universitas@studorg.uio.no **Web site:** http://www.universitas.no
Freq: Daily; **Cover Price:** Free
Language(s): Norwegian
BUSINESS: CHURCH & SCHOOL EQUIPMENT & EDUCATION: Education

UNIVERSITETSAVISA.NO 1624634R62A-210
Editorial: NTNU - Informasjonsavdelingen, 7491 TRONDHEIM **Tel:** 73 59 55 40 **Fax:** 73 59 54 37
Email: tips@universitetsavisa.no **Web site:** http://www.universitetsavisa.no
Cover Price: Paid
Editor: Tore Oksholen
Language(s): Norwegian
BUSINESS: CHURCH & SCHOOL EQUIPMENT & EDUCATION: Education

UPSTREAM 1625037R33-74
Editorial: Pb. 1182 Sentrum, 0107 OSLO
Tel: 22001300 **Fax:** 22001305
Email: editorial@upstreamonline.com **Web site:** http://www.upstreamonline.com
Freq: Weekly; **Circ:** 5,700
Language(s): Norwegian
ADVERTISING RATES:
SCC .... NOK 808.13
BUSINESS: OIL & PETROLEUM

UPSTREAM ONLINE 1936053R58-126
Editorial: Pb. 1182 Sentrum, 0107 OSLO
Tel: 22 00 13 05 **Fax:** 22 00 13 00
Email: editorial@upstreamonline.com **Web site:** http://www.upstreamonline.com
Freq: Daily; **Cover Price:** Paid
Language(s): Norwegian
BUSINESS: ENERGY, FUEL & NUCLEAR

USBL-NYTT 1624345R4E-10
Editorial: Pb 4764 Sofienberg, 0506 OSLO
Tel: 22983800 **Fax:** 22983893
Email: info@usbl.no **Web site:** http://www.usbl.no/Medlemskap/Usbl-nytt.aspx
Freq: 6 issues yearly; **Circ:** 25,000
Language(s): Norwegian
Copy instructions: *Copy Date:* 45 days prior to publication date
BUSINESS: ARCHITECTURE & BUILDING: Building

UT 1881547R89A-188
Editorial: Den Norske Turistforening, Youngsgt. 1, 0181 OSLO **Tel:** 400 01 868
Email: hallgrim.rogn@turistforeningen.no **Web site:** http://www.turistforeningen.no
Freq: Half-yearly; **Circ:** 25,000
Language(s): Norwegian
CONSUMER: HOLIDAYS & TRAVEL: Travel

UTDANNING 1625210R62B-203
Editorial: Pb. 9191 Grønland, 0134 0101 OSLO OSLO **Tel:** 24 14 20 00 **Fax:** 24 14 22 85
Email: redaksjonen@utdanningsnytt.no **Web site:** http://www.utdanningsnytt.no
Freq: 26 issues yearly; **Circ:** 130,000
Editor: Knut Hovland
Language(s): Norwegian
BUSINESS: CHURCH & SCHOOL EQUIPMENT & EDUCATION: Education Teachers

UTDANNING.NO 1625211R62B-204
Editorial: Postboks 9191 Grønland, 0134 OSLO
Tel: 24 14 20 00 **Fax:** 24 14 22 85
Email: redaksjonen@utdanningsnytt.no **Web site:** http://www.utdanning.ws
Language(s): Norwegian
BUSINESS: CHURCH & SCHOOL EQUIPMENT & EDUCATION: Education Teachers

UTEMILJØ 1645146R57-308
Editorial: Postboks 9178, Grønland, 0134 OSLO
Tel: 69308830 **Fax:** 22 17 25 08
Email: firmapost@amundsen-informasjon.no **Web site:** http://www.utemiljonytt.no
Freq: 6 issues yearly; **Circ:** 2,905
Editor: Ola Jacob Amundsen
Language(s): Norwegian
BUSINESS: ENVIRONMENT & POLLUTION

UTFLUKT 1645186R84A-121
Editorial: Pb. 4757 Sofienberg, 0506 OSLO
Email: redaksjonen@utflukt.no **Web site:** http://www.utflukt.no
Freq: Quarterly; **Circ:** 1,000
Language(s): Norwegian
CONSUMER: THE ARTS & LITERARY: Arts

UTPOSTEN/FOR ALLMENN- OG SAMFUNNSMEDISIN 31650R56A-100
Editorial: RMR/UTPOSTEN v/Tove Rutle, Sjøbergveien 32, 2050 JESSHEIM **Tel:** 63 97 32 22
Fax: 63 97 16 25
Email: rmrtove@online.no **Web site:** http://www.uib.no/isf/utposten/utposten.htm
Freq: Monthly; **Circ:** 2,000
Editor: Jannike Reymert
Profile: Journal for GPs and family doctors.
Language(s): Norwegian
BUSINESS: HEALTH & MEDICAL

UTROPIA - STUDENTAVISA I TROMSØ 1625111R62A-217
Editorial: Hovedgården - Universitetet i Tromsø, 9037 TROMSØ **Tel:** 776 45 901
Email: redaktor@utropia.no **Web site:** http://www.utropia.no
Freq: Monthly; **Circ:** 5,000
Language(s): Norwegian
BUSINESS: CHURCH & SCHOOL EQUIPMENT & EDUCATION: Education

UTROP.NO 1865167R84A-158
Editorial: Postboks 8962 Youngstorget, 0028 OSLO
Tel: 22 04 14 61
Email: tips@utrop.no **Web site:** http://www.utrop.no
Freq: Daily; **Cover Price:** Free; **Circ:** 2,500 Unique Users
Editor: Saroj Chumber
Language(s): Norwegian
CONSUMER: THE ARTS & LITERARY: Arts

UTSYN 32324R87-170
Editorial: Sinsenvn. 25, 0572 OSLO **Tel:** 22 00 72 00
Fax: 22 00 72 03
Email: utsyn@nlm.no **Web site:** http://www.utsyn.no
Date Established: 1891; **Freq:** 26 issues yearly; **Circ:** 17,000

Profile: Magazine about religious and missionary work in Norway, Africa, South America and the Far East.
Language(s): Norwegian
CONSUMER: RELIGIOUS

UTVEIER 1660587R32G-162
Editorial: Solidaritetshuset, Osterhausgate 27, 0183 OSLO **Tel:** 22 98 93 04
Email: terje@attac.no **Web site:** http://utveier.attac.no/nr3/index.html
Freq: Quarterly
Editor: Terje Karlsen
Language(s): Norwegian
BUSINESS: LOCAL GOVERNMENT, LEISURE & RECREATION: Community Care & Social Services

VAGABOND 32340R89E-120
Editorial: Sagveien 21 A, 0459 OSLO
Tel: 23 23 05 50
Email: post@vagabond.no **Web site:** http://www.vagabond.no
Date Established: 1994; **Freq:** 6 issues yearly; **Circ:** 11,119
Editor: Helge Baardseth
Profile: Consumer travel publication.
Language(s): Norwegian
CONSUMER: HOLIDAYS & TRAVEL: Holidays

VAGANT 32793R84B-200
Editorial: Nygårdsgt. 2 A, 5015 BERGEN
Tel: 55 36 84 36 **Fax:** 55 36 84 36
Email: redaksjon@vagant.no **Web site:** http://www.vagant.no
Date Established: 1988; **Freq:** Quarterly; **Circ:** 1,400
Editor: Audun Lindholm
Profile: Magazine covering general literature and literary issues.
Language(s): Norwegian
Readership: Read by people interested in literature and literary criticism.
CONSUMER: THE ARTS & LITERARY: Literary

VAKRE HJEM OG INTERIØR 1810343R14A-224
Editorial: 2743 HARESTUA **Tel:** 33390220
Fax: 33390221
Email: mail@vakrehjem.com **Web site:** http://www.vakrehjem.com
Freq: 6 issues yearly; **Circ:** 37,000
Language(s): Norwegian
Copy instructions: *Copy Date:* 30 days prior to publication date
BUSINESS: COMMERCE, INDUSTRY & MANAGEMENT

VALDRES 31764R67B-5750
Editorial: Pb. 54, 2901 FAGERNES **Tel:** 61 36 42 00
Email: redaksjonen@avisa-valdres.no **Web site:** http://www.avisa-valdres.no
Date Established: 1903; **Freq:** Daily; **Circ:** 9,342 Unique Users
Language(s): Norwegian
REGIONAL DAILY & SUNDAY NEWSPAPERS: Regional Daily Newspapers

VÅL'ENGA MAGASIN 1645181R75B-125
Editorial: PB 6064 Etterstad, 6064 ETTERSTAD
Tel: 23 24 78 00 **Fax:** 23 24 78 01
Email: graff@vif.no **Web site:** http://www.vif-fotball.no
Freq: 6 issues yearly; **Circ:** 7,000
Editor: SVEIN Graff
Language(s): Norwegian
CONSUMER: SPORT: Football

VANN 31559R42C-100
Editorial: Norsk Vannforening, Postboks 2312 Solli, 0201 OSLO **Tel:** 22 94 75 75
Email: post@vannforeningen.no **Web site:** http://www.vannforeningen.no
Date Established: 1964; **Freq:** Quarterly; **Circ:** 2,200
Editor: John Mikal Raaheim
Profile: Journal of interest to Norwegian water engineers.
Language(s): Norwegian
BUSINESS: CONSTRUCTION: Water Engineering

VÅR ENERGI 31449R17-170
Editorial: Pb. 1182, Sentrum, 0107 OSLO
Tel: 22001150 **Fax:** 22001083
Email: energi@energi-nett.no **Web site:** http://www.energi-nett.no
Freq: Half-yearly; **Circ:** 250,000
Profile: Magazine containing information about the electrical industry.
Language(s): Norwegian
ADVERTISING RATES:
Full Page Colour .... NOK 15000
BUSINESS: ELECTRICAL

VÅR FUGLEFAUNA 32244R81F-100
Editorial: Norsk ornitologisk forening, Sandgata 30b, 7012 TRONDHEIM **Tel:** 73 84 16 40 **Fax:** 73 52 40 90
Email: vf@birdlife.no **Web site:** http://www.birdlife.no
Date Established: 1978; **Freq:** Quarterly; **Circ:** 3,500
Profile: International magazine containing articles about birds in Norway.
Language(s): Norwegian
Readership: Aimed at ornithologists and bird lovers.
CONSUMER: ANIMALS & PETS: Birds

VARDEN 31796R67B-5800
Editorial: Pb. 2873, Kjørbekk, 3702 SKIEN
Tel: 35 54 30 00 **Fax:** 35 54 30 85
Email: redaksjonen@varden.no **Web site:** http://www.varden.no
Date Established: 1874; **Freq:** Daily; **Circ:** 26,091
Language(s): Norwegian
ADVERTISING RATES:
SCC .... NOK 168.32
REGIONAL DAILY & SUNDAY NEWSPAPERS: Regional Daily Newspapers

VÅRE BARN 1625076R94F-112
Editorial: Pb. 4 Sentrum, 0101 OSLO **Tel:** 02099
Email: skb@kreftforeningen.no **Web site:** http://www.kreftsyke-barn.no
Freq: Quarterly; **Circ:** 9,000
Language(s): Norwegian
CONSUMER: OTHER CLASSIFICATIONS: Disability

VÅRE VEGER 31558R42B-20
Editorial: Pb. 5844 Majorstua, 0308 OSLO
Tel: 23 19 93 60 **Fax:** 23 19 93 02
Email: jarle.skoglund@tu.no **Web site:** http://www.vareveger.no
Freq: Monthly; **Circ:** 15,000
Profile: Journal about road planning, road engineering and construction machines.
Language(s): Norwegian
ADVERTISING RATES:
Full Page Colour .... NOK 20600
BUSINESS: CONSTRUCTION: Roads

VÅRE VEGER; VAREVEGER.NO 1865148R49A-103
Editorial: Postboks 5488 Majorstuen, 0308 OSLO
Tel: 23 19 93 60 **Fax:** 23 19 93 02
Email: jarle.skoglund@tu.no **Web site:** http://www.vareveger.no
Freq: Daily; **Cover Price:** Free; **Circ:** 2,500 Unique Users
Language(s): Norwegian
BUSINESS: TRANSPORT

VARMENYTT 31375R3A-100
Editorial: Breivikskjenet 29, 5179 GODVIK
Tel: 55509760 **Fax:** 55509768
Email: pg-alfh@online.no **Web site:** http://varmenytt.no
Date Established: 1977; **Freq:** Quarterly; **Circ:** 2,250
Profile: Magazine containing articles and information about home heating. Covers product news and modern technology.
Language(s): Norwegian
BUSINESS: HEATING & VENTILATION: Domestic Heating & Ventilation

VÅRT LAND 31742R65A-90
Editorial: Pb. 1180 Sentrum, 0107 OSLO
Tel: 22310310 **Fax:** 22310 05
Email: tips@vl.no **Web site:** http://www.vl.no
Date Established: 1945; **Freq:** Daily; **Circ:** 26,344
Features Editor: Une Bratberg
Profile: Tabloid-sized quality newspaper covering national news, features, sports and finance from a Christian viewpoint.
Language(s): Norwegian
Readership: Read predominantly by Christian people throughout Norway.
ADVERTISING RATES:
SCC .... NOK 179.01
Copy instructions: *Copy Date:* 30 days prior to publication date
NATIONAL DAILY & SUNDAY NEWSPAPERS: National Daily Newspapers

VÅRT SYN 1625097R94F-113
Editorial: Enebakkveien 457, 1290 OSLO
Tel: 22 61 60 60 **Fax:** 22 61 60 68
Email: vaart-syn@svaksynte.org **Web site:** http://www.svaksynte.org
Freq: Quarterly
Editor: Ulf Bjaaland
Language(s): Norwegian
CONSUMER: OTHER CLASSIFICATIONS: Disability

VEGEN OG VI 1624534R49A-102
Editorial: Pb 8142 Dep, 0033 OSLO **Tel:** 22 07 36 92
Fax: 22 07 35 11
Email: vegenogvi@vegvesen.no **Web site:** http://www.vegvesen.no/vegenogvi
Freq: 26 issues yearly; **Circ:** 16,000
Language(s): Norwegian
BUSINESS: TRANSPORT

VEIVALG 1624387R32H-1
Editorial: Rakkestadveien 1, 1814 ASKIM
Tel: 69 81 97 00 **Fax:** 69 88 94 33
Email: jensolav.klovrud@sportmedia.no **Web site:** http://www.sportmedia.no
Freq: 6 issues yearly; **Circ:** 4,000
Editor: Jens Olav Kløvrud
Language(s): Norwegian
BUSINESS: LOCAL GOVERNMENT, LEISURE & RECREATION: Leisure, Recreation & Entertainment

VELFERD 31521R32G-150
Editorial: Hegdehaugsveien 36 A, 0352 OSLO
Tel: 22850770 **Fax:** 22850771
Email: velferd@velferd.no **Web site:** http://www.velferd.no
Freq: 6 issues yearly; **Circ:** 3,000
Profile: Journal about social security matters.
Language(s): Norwegian
BUSINESS: LOCAL GOVERNMENT, LEISURE & RECREATION: Community Care & Social Services

VENSTRE OM 32796R82-295
Editorial: Akersgata 35, 0158 OSLO **Tel:** 21933300
Fax: 21933301
Email: post@sv.no **Web site:** http://www.sv.no/content/view/full/481
Freq: 6 issues yearly; **Circ:** 9,000
Editor: Arun Ghosh
Profile: Political journal focusing on socialist issues.
Language(s): Norwegian
CONSUMER: CURRENT AFFAIRS & POLITICS

VENTUS NETT 1852033R62A-244
Editorial: Høgskolen i Bodø, 8049 BODØ
Tel: 900 67 019
Email: redaksjon@ventusmedia.no **Web site:** http://www.ventusmedia.no
Freq: Daily; **Cover Price:** Paid
Language(s): Norwegian
BUSINESS: CHURCH & SCHOOL EQUIPMENT & EDUCATION: Education

VERDENS NATUR (WWF) 1624402R81A-41
Editorial: Pb. 6784 St. Olavs Plass, 0130 OSLO
Tel: 22036500 **Fax:** 22200666
Email: info@wwf.no **Web site:** http://www.wwf.no/bibliotek/fantastisk/verdens_natur
Freq: Quarterly; **Circ:** 8,000
Editor: Signe Prøis
Language(s): Norwegian
CONSUMER: ANIMALS & PETS: Animals & Pets Protection

VERDENSMAGASINET X 1624518R32G-154
Editorial: Osterhausgata 27, 0183 OSLO
Tel: 22989332
Email: redaktor@xmag.no **Web site:** http://www.verdensmagasinetx.no
Freq: 6 issues yearly; **Circ:** 4,000
Language(s): Norwegian
BUSINESS: LOCAL GOVERNMENT, LEISURE & RECREATION: Community Care & Social Services

VERDENSMAGASINET X; VERDENSMAGASINETX.NO 1865155R82-367
Editorial: Osterhausgata 27, 0183 OSLO
Tel: 22989332
Email: redaktor@xmag.no **Web site:** http://www.verdensmagasinetx.no
Freq: Daily; **Cover Price:** Free; **Circ:** 2,500 Unique Users
Language(s): Norwegian
CONSUMER: CURRENT AFFAIRS & POLITICS

VESTBO-INFO 1624308R32A-151
Editorial: Pb 1947 Nordnes, 5817 BERGEN
Tel: 55 30 96 00
Email: sissel.urdal@vestbo.no **Web site:** http://www.vestbo.no
Freq: Quarterly; **Circ:** 19,500
Language(s): Norwegian
BUSINESS: LOCAL GOVERNMENT, LEISURE & RECREATION: Local Government

VETERAN & SPORTSBIL 32231R77F-100
Editorial: Ryensvingen 15, 0680 OSLO
Tel: 90623492 **Fax:** 22682965
Email: lasse@veteran-sportsbil.no **Web site:** http://www.veteran-sportsbil.no
Freq: 6 issues yearly; **Circ:** 7,500
Profile: Magazine about veteran cars and classic sports cars.
Language(s): Norwegian
CONSUMER: MOTORING & CYCLING: Veteran Cars

VG 31741R65A-70
Editorial: Pb 1185 Sentrum, 0107 OSLO
Tel: 22 00 00 00 **Fax:** 22 42 75 04
Email: pressemeldinger@vg.no **Web site:** http://www.vg.no
Date Established: 1945; **Freq:** Daily; **Circ:** 284,414
Editor: Torry Pedersen
Profile: Tabloid-sized newspaper covering national and international news, events, sports, entertainment, politics and culture. Political outlook: Independent.
Language(s): Norwegian
Readership: Read by a broad range of the population.
ADVERTISING RATES:
Full Page Colour .... NOK 141358
SCC .... NOK 1413.58
NATIONAL DAILY & SUNDAY NEWSPAPERS: National Daily Newspapers

VG - HELG 1740763R73-157
Editorial: Pb 1185 Sentrum, 0107 OSLO
Tel: 22 00 06 04 **Fax:** 22427504
Email: reportasjen@vg.no **Web site:** http://vg.no
Circ: 309,610
Language(s): Norwegian
CONSUMER: NATIONAL & INTERNATIONAL PERIODICALS

VG; VEKTKLUBB.NO 1740797R74G-166
Editorial: VG Multimedia, Pb. 1185 Sentrum, 0107 OSLO **Tel:** 22 00 00 00
Email: vektklubb@vg.no **Web site:** http://www.vektklubb.no
Cover Price: Paid
Language(s): Norwegian
CONSUMER: WOMEN'S INTEREST CONSUMER MAGAZINES: Slimming & Health

VI ER MANGE 32275R82-300
Editorial: Osterhausgt 27, 0183 OSLO
Tel: 22 20 64 00
Email: kvinnefronten@online.no **Web site:** http://www.kvinnefronten.no
Date Established: 1974; **Freq:** Monthly; **Circ:** 300
Profile: Magazine containing articles and news about current affairs, culture and politics concerning women.
Language(s): Norwegian
Readership: Read by members of Kvinnefronten.
CONSUMER: CURRENT AFFAIRS & POLITICS

VI I VILLA 1624659R74C-54
Editorial: Pb. 797 Sentrum, 0106 OSLO
Tel: 22047400 **Fax:** 23310301
Email: post@viivilla.no **Web site:** http://www.viivilla.no
Freq: 6 issues yearly; **Cover Price:** Free; **Circ:** 1,200,000
Editor: Lisbeth Fosser
Language(s): Norwegian
Copy instructions: *Copy Date:* 32 days prior to publication date
CONSUMER: WOMEN'S INTEREST CONSUMER MAGAZINES: Home & Family

VI MENN 32295R86A-60
Editorial: 0441 OSLO **Tel:** 22585000
Email: vimenn@egmonthm.no **Web site:** http://www.vimenn.no
Freq: Weekly; **Circ:** 96,827
Editor: Reidar Martinsen
Profile: Magazine for men. Covers lifestyle, popular science, technology, motorsports, health, travel, personal finance, food and drink and current affairs. Also contains erotic pictures and short stories.
Language(s): Norwegian
Readership: Aimed at men aged between 25-50 years with a high disposable income.
ADVERTISING RATES:
SCC .... NOK 495.83
CONSUMER: ADULT & GAY MAGAZINES: Adult Magazines

VI MENN BÅT 1692449R91A-207
Editorial: vimenn.no / HMI Hjemmet Mortensen, 0441 OSLO **Tel:** 22585000 **Fax:** 22580571
Email: vimenn@egmonthm.no **Web site:** http://www.vimenn.no
Freq: 6 issues yearly - 7 ganger i året; **Circ:** 9,391
Language(s): Norwegian
CONSUMER: RECREATION & LEISURE: Boating & Yachting

VI MENN BIL 32223R77A-200
Editorial: 0441 OSLO **Tel:** 22585000 **Fax:** 22580571
Email: vimenn@egmonthm.no **Web site:** http://www.klikk.no/vimenn
Freq: Monthly - 8 gangeri året; **Circ:** 93,827

Profile: Car and motoring magazine.
Language(s): Norwegian
CONSUMER: MOTORING & CYCLING: Motoring

VI MENN FOTBALL 1624414R75B-121
Editorial: 0441 OSLO **Tel:** 22 58 50 00
Fax: 22580571
Email: fotball@hm-media.no **Web site:** http://www.hm-media.no
Freq: Annual; **Circ:** 96,827
Editor: Øyvind Steen-Jensen
Language(s): Norwegian
CONSUMER: SPORT: Football

VI OVER 60 32174R74N-200
Editorial: Pb 287 Sentrum, 5012 BERGEN
Tel: 55 21 31 00 **Fax:** 55213140
Email: post@viover60.no **Web site:** http://www.viover60.no
Freq: Monthly; **Circ:** 82,028
Profile: Magazine containing interviews and articles, also practical information on topics such as health, pensions and legal advice.
Language(s): Norwegian
Readership: Aimed at people over 60 years.
CONSUMER: WOMEN'S INTEREST CONSUMER MAGAZINES: Retirement

VI OVER 60; VIOVER60.NO 1977747R74C-99
Editorial: Valkendorfsgaten 1A, 5012 BERGEN
Tel: 55 21 31 00
Email: post@viover60.no **Web site:** http://viover60.no
Freq: Daily; **Cover Price:** Paid
Language(s): Norwegian
CONSUMER: WOMEN'S INTEREST CONSUMER MAGAZINES: Home & Family

VIIVILLA.NO 1624786R4D-103
Editorial: Pb. 797 Sentrum, 0106 OSLO
Tel: 22 04 74 00 **Fax:** 23 31 03 01
Email: post@viivilla.no **Web site:** http://www.viivilla.no
Language(s): Norwegian
BUSINESS: ARCHITECTURE & BUILDING: Planning & Housing

VILLMARKSLIV 32246R81X-50
Editorial: Villmarksliv, 0441 OSLO, 0441 OSLO
Tel: 22 58 50 00
Email: knut.brevik@egmonthm.no **Web site:** http://www.klikk.no/villmarksliv
Freq: Monthly; **Circ:** 43,800
Editor: Britt Pedersen
Profile: Magazine about wildlife, fishing and hunting.
Language(s): Norwegian
CONSUMER: ANIMALS & PETS

VIMENN.NO 1810887R73-168
Editorial: vimenn.no/HMI Hjemmet Mortensen 0441 Oslo, 0441 OSLO **Tel:** 22 58 50 00
Email: vimenn@hm-media.no **Web site:** http://www.vimenn.no
Freq: Daily; **Cover Price:** Paid; **Circ:** 15,350 Unique Users
Language(s): Norwegian
ADVERTISING RATES:
SCC .... NOK 99.2
CONSUMER: NATIONAL & INTERNATIONAL PERIODICALS

VINDUET 32802R84B-230
Editorial: Gyldendal Akademisk, Pb. 6860 St. Olavs Plass, 0130 OSLO **Tel:** 22 03 42 71 **Fax:** 22 03 41 05
Email: vinduet@vinduet.no **Web site:** http://www.vinduet.no
Freq: Quarterly; **Circ:** 4,000
Profile: Magazine featuring articles, essays, and poetry mainly encouraging new writters.
Language(s): Norwegian
Readership: Read by those interested in literature.
CONSUMER: THE ARTS & LITERARY: Literary

VINFORUM 32177R74P-200
Editorial: Pedicel AS, Postboks 3130 Elisenberg, 0207 OSLO **Tel:** 23086846
Email: redaksjonen@vinforum.no **Web site:** http://www.vinforum.no
Freq: Quarterly; **Circ:** 4,509
Editor: Ola Dybvik
Profile: Magazine containing articles, news, tests, recipes and information about food, wine and related topics.
Language(s): Norwegian
CONSUMER: WOMEN'S INTEREST CONSUMER MAGAZINES: Food & Cookery

VISER.NO 1624876R76D-262
Editorial: Norsk Viseforum, Postb. 4647, 0506 OSLO
Tel: 22 00 56 30 **Fax:** 22 00 56 01
Email: post@viseforum.no **Web site:** http://www.viseforum.no
Freq: Half-yearly; **Circ:** 1,500
Editor: Øyvind Rauset
Language(s): Norwegian
CONSUMER: MUSIC & PERFORMING ARTS: Music

VISJON 32553R74G-5
Editorial: Øvre Slottsgt. 7, 0157 OSLO
Tel: 22 33 84 04 **Fax:** 22 33 84 09
Email: redaksjon@altnett.no **Web site:** http://www.altnett.no
Date Established: 1992; **Freq:** 6 issues yearly; **Circ:** 15,000
Editor: Eirik Svenke Solum
Profile: Magazine covering alternative medicine, personal growth, spirituality and ecology.
Language(s): Norwegian
Readership: Read by people with an interest in alternative medicine and lifestyle.
CONSUMER: WOMEN'S INTEREST CONSUMER MAGAZINES: Slimming & Health

VOLKSWAGEN MAGASINET 1624681R77A-206
Editorial: Pb. 46 Kjelsås, 0411 OSLO
Tel: 22 95 33 00 **Fax:** 22 95 33 90
Email: vw-magasinet@moller.no **Web site:** http://wip.volkswagen.no/wip4/magasinet
Freq: Half-yearly; **Circ:** 170,000
Language(s): Norwegian
CONSUMER: MOTORING & CYCLING: Motoring

VOLT 1660604R58-107
Editorial: Postboks A – Bygdøy, 0211 OSLO
Tel: 24115707
Email: tor@voltmag.no **Web site:** http://www.voltmag.no
Freq: 6 issues yearly; **Circ:** 8,180
Language(s): Norwegian
BUSINESS: ENERGY, FUEL & NUCLEAR

VOLVAT DOKTOR 1624490R56A-205
Editorial: Pb. 5280 Majorstua, 0303 OSLO
Tel: 22957500 **Fax:** 22957635
Email: katrine.ruthgerson@volvat.no **Web site:** http://www.volvat.no
Freq: Quarterly; **Circ:** 28,000
Language(s): Norwegian
BUSINESS: HEALTH & MEDICAL

VRENG 1660584R32G-161
Editorial: Adbusters v/ Hausmania, Hausmannsgate 34, 0187 OSLO
Email: magasinet@adbusters.no **Web site:** http://www.adbusters.no
Freq: Quarterly
Language(s): Norwegian
BUSINESS: LOCAL GOVERNMENT, LEISURE & RECREATION: Community Care & Social Services

VVS AKTUELT 31379R3B-150
Editorial: Tørkoppveien 10, 1570 DILLING
Tel: 69700570 **Fax:** 69700550
Email: obo@byggfaktamedia.no **Web site:** http://www.vvsaktuelt.no
Freq: 6 issues yearly; **Circ:** 7,000
Profile: Journal containing information, articles and news concerning heating, ventilating and water engineering.
Language(s): Norwegian
Copy instructions: *Copy Date:* 21 days prior to publication date
BUSINESS: HEATING & VENTILATION: Industrial Heating & Ventilation

VVS AKTUELT; VVSAKTUELT.NO 1936026R73-180
Editorial: Tørkoppveien 10, 1570 DILLING
Tel: 69 70 05 70 **Fax:** 69 70 05 50
Email: post@linc.no **Web site:** http://www.vvsaktuelt.no
Freq: Daily; **Cover Price:** Paid
Language(s): Norwegian
CONSUMER: NATIONAL & INTERNATIONAL PERIODICALS

WEB MAGASIN 1826641R78R-2
Editorial: Postboks 41 Sentrum, Pb. 41 Sentrum, 0101 OSLO **Tel:** 454 75 000
Email: post@webmagasin.no **Web site:** http://www.webmagasin.no
Circ: 4,000
Editor: Lise Andresen
Language(s): Norwegian
CONSUMER: CONSUMER ELECTRONICS: Consumer Electronics Related

WOMAN 1663836R74A-69
Editorial: Bonnier Media - Kirkegata 20, 0153 OSLO
Tel: 22047000 **Fax:** 23068730
Email: woman@woman.no **Web site:** http://www.woman.no
Freq: Monthly; **Circ:** 30,999
Editor: Karoline Hestenes
Language(s): Norwegian
ADVERTISING RATES:
Full Page Colour .... NOK 42500
SCC .... NOK 391.67
Copy instructions: *Copy Date:* 30 days prior to publication date
CONSUMER: WOMEN'S INTEREST CONSUMER MAGAZINES: Women's Interest

WOMAN.NO 1841162R74A-79
Editorial: Pb. 1010 Sentrum, 0104 OSLO
Tel: 23 06 87 19
Email: web@woman.no **Web site:** http://www.woman.no
Freq: Daily; **Cover Price:** Paid
Language(s): Norwegian
CONSUMER: WOMEN'S INTEREST CONSUMER MAGAZINES: Women's Interest

YGGDRASIL 1740691R62A-238
Editorial: Pb. 2110, 6402 MOLDE **Tel:** 71 19 59 73
Email: yggdrasil@himolde.no **Web site:** http://www.ymag.no
Editor: Jaran S. Kjellmo
Language(s): Norwegian
BUSINESS: CHURCH & SCHOOL EQUIPMENT & EDUCATION: Education

YLF-FORUM 32544R56A-200
Editorial: Yngre legers forening, postboks 1152 Sentrum, 0107 OSLO **Tel:** 23109000 **Fax:** 23109150
Email: ylf.redaktor@legeforeningen.no **Web site:** http://www.legeforeningen.no/ylf
Freq: 6 issues yearly; **Circ:** 6,500
Editor: Marit Tveito
Profile: Magazine of the Association of Junior Doctors containing news of the association and general medical information.
Language(s): Norwegian
Readership: Aimed at junior doctors.
BUSINESS: HEALTH & MEDICAL

YRKESBIL 31608R49D-90
Editorial: Postboks 63 Skøyen, 0212 OSLO
Tel: 23 03 66 00 **Fax:** 23 03 66 40
Email: yrkesbil@bilforlaget.no **Web site:** http://www.bilnorge.no
Date Established: 1980; **Freq:** Monthly; **Circ:** 29,011
Profile: Magazine covering new vehicles, testing of vans, trucks, buses, technical articles, national and international news from the truck, bus and van industry.
Language(s): Norwegian
Readership: Read by managers of transport companies.
ADVERTISING RATES:
Full Page Colour .... NOK 51750
SCC .... NOK 395.83
BUSINESS: TRANSPORT: Commercial Vehicles

YRKESTRAFIKK 31604R49B-70
Editorial: Pb. 9175 Grønland, 0134 OSLO
Tel: 932 40011 **Fax:** 21 01 38 51
Email: anne@ytf.no **Web site:** http://www.yrkestrafikk.no
Freq: 6 issues yearly; **Circ:** 11,476
Profile: Transport journal giving news and information about trucks and buses.
Language(s): Norwegian
ADVERTISING RATES:
Full Page Colour .... NOK 12750
BUSINESS: TRANSPORT: Bus & Coach Transport

Z FILMTIDSSKRIFT 32212R76A-200
Editorial: Filmens Hus, Dronningens Gate 16, 0157 OSLO **Tel:** 22 47 46 80 **Fax:** 22 47 46 92
Email: zred@filmklubb.no **Web site:** http://www.znett.com
Freq: Quarterly; **Circ:** 1,000
Profile: Magazine of the Norwegian Film Society.
Language(s): Norwegian
CONSUMER: MUSIC & PERFORMING ARTS: Cinema

ZINE TRAVEL 1800762R89A-181
Editorial: Bispegata 16, 0191 OSLO **Tel:** 901 22 242
Email: info@zinetravel.no **Web site:** http://www.zinetravel.no
Freq: 6 issues yearly; **Circ:** 20,000
Language(s): Norwegian
CONSUMER: HOLIDAYS & TRAVEL: Travel

Poland

Time Difference: GMT + 1 hr (CET - Central European Time)
National Telephone Code: +48
Continent: Europe
Capital: Warsaw
Principal Language: Polish
Population: 38633912
Monetary Unit: New Zloty (PLN)

EMBASSY HIGH COMMISSION: Embassy of the Republic of Poland: 47 Portland Place, London, W1B 1JH
Tel: 0207 291 35 20
Fax: 020 72 91 35 75
Email: londyn@msz.gov.pl / **Website:** http://www.london.polemb.net
Head of Mission : HE Barbara Tuge-Eracinska

.PSD 1796127PL5C-7
Editorial: ul. Bokserska, 1, 02-682 WARSZAWA
Tel: 22 427 35 33 **Fax:** 22 22 244 24 59
Email: psd@psdmag.org **Web site:** http://www.psdmag.org
ISSN: 1732-2200
Date Established: 1995; **Freq:** Monthly; **Circ:** 8,000
Usual Pagination: 84
Managing Director: Ewa Łozowicka; **Advertising Director:** Anna Adamczyk
Profile: For users of Adobe Photoshop and other graphic programs, usage instruction films on 2 CDs in each copy.
Language(s): Polish
Mechanical Data: Type Area: A4
BUSINESS: COMPUTERS & AUTOMATION: Professional Personal Computers

100% WNĘTRZA 1796164PL4B-6
Editorial: ul. Andersa, 38, 15-113 BIAŁYSTOK
Tel: 85 653 90 00 **Fax:** 85 653 98 56
Email: poczta@publikator.com.pl **Web site:** http://www.publikator.com.pl
ISSN: 1734-848X
Date Established: 2005; **Freq:** Half-yearly; **Circ:** 26,000
Usual Pagination: 160
Managing Director: Anita Frank; **Advertising Director:** Agnieszka Panasewicz
Profile: Magazine about interior design of living rooms, bedrooms, bathrooms and kitchens.
Language(s): Polish
Mechanical Data: Type Area: 230 x 297 mm
BUSINESS: ARCHITECTURE & BUILDING: Interior Design & Flooring

2+3D GRAFIKA PLUS PRODUKT 1928843PL41A-5
Editorial: ul. Smoleńsk 9, 31-108 KRAKÓW
Tel: 12 292 62 12 **Fax:** 12 422 34 44
Email: redakcja@2plus3d.pl **Web site:** http://www.2plus3d.pl
ISSN: 1642-7602
Date Established: 2001; **Freq:** Quarterly; **Circ:** 7,300
Usual Pagination: 104
Profile: Professional magazine dedicated to graphic design, logos, packaging design, products 3D projects.
Language(s): Polish
Mechanical Data: Type Area: 210 x 280 mm
BUSINESS: PRINTING & STATIONERY: Printing

A4 MAGAZYN 1796206PL14J-1
Editorial: ul. Wiktorska, 14, 17, 02-587 WARSZAWA
Tel: 22 848 02 82 **Fax:** 22 848 02 82
Email: box@a4mag.com **Web site:** http://www.a4mag.com
ISSN: 1731-1454
Date Established: 2003; **Freq:** 6 issues yearly; **Circ:** 15,000
Usual Pagination: 190
Profile: Features fashion, culture, art and design.
Language(s): Polish
Mechanical Data: Type Area: A4
BUSINESS: COMMERCE, INDUSTRY & MANAGEMENT: Commercial Design

AGD-RTV 1708732PL43A-1
Editorial: ul. Dzika, 4, 00-194 WARSZAWA
Tel: 22 635 73 70 **Fax:** 22 635 74 62

mail: p.krzysica@ppwp.pl **Web site:** http://www.ppwp.pl
SSN: 1429-317X
ate Established: 1997; **Freq:** Monthly; **Circ:** 8,000
sual Pagination: 150
anaging Director: Paweł Krzysica
rofile: Magazine dedicated to home appliances and tensils.
anguage(s): Polish
DVERTISING RATES:
ull Page Colour .... PLN 7700.00
echanical Data: Type Area: A4
USINESS: ELECTRICAL RETAIL TRADE

AGRO SERWIS 1928878PL21R-2
ditorial: ul. Świętokrzyska, 20, p. 302,322, 00-002 WARSZAWA **Tel:** 22 827 24 01 **Fax:** 22 827 24 01
mail: agroserwis@agroserwis.pol.pl **Web site:** ttp://www.agroserwis.pol.pl
SSN: 1230-1825
ate Established: 1992; **Freq:** 26 issues yearly
Jsual Pagination: 60
dvertising Director: Agnieszka Kozłowska
Profile: Professional magazine dedicated to agricultural business, providing information concerning current situation in Polish agriculture and agricultural technology (which includes machinery eature, application technology, irrigation special, agricultural equipment).
Language(s): Polish
Readership: It is addressed to farmers, businessmen and companies that act in agriculture sector.
Mechanical Data: Type Area: A4
BUSINESS: AGRICULTURE & FARMING: Agriculture & Farming Related

AGROMECHANIKA 1796149PL21E-1
Editorial: ul. Kaliska, 1, 8, 02-316 WARSZAWA
Tel: 22 883 39 52 **Fax:** 22 822 66 49
Email: agromechanika@oikos.net.pl **Web site:** http://www.agromechanika.net.pl
ISSN: 1895-5029
Date Established: 2006; **Freq:** Monthly; **Circ:** 10,000
Usual Pagination: 64
Profile: Magazine focused on agro news regarding new machines and new technologies; advice on maintenance and repairing of agricultural machines; testing and new methods.
Language(s): Polish
ADVERTISING RATES:
Full Page Mono .... PLN 3600.00
Mechanical Data: Type Area: 205 x 286 mm
BUSINESS: AGRICULTURE & FARMING: Agriculture - Machinery & Plant

AKADEMIA KURTA SCHELLERA 1709003PL74P-6
Editorial: ul. Garażowa, 7, 02-651 WARSZAWA
Tel: 22 607 77 71 **Fax:** 22 848 22 66
Email: proszynskimedia@proszynskimedia.pl
Date Established: 2003
Circ: 20,000
Usual Pagination: 96
Profile: Original cuisine recipes of chef Kurt Scheller.
Language(s): Polish
Mechanical Data: Type Area: 166x225 mm
CONSUMER: WOMEN'S INTEREST CONSUMER MAGAZINES: Food & Cookery

AKCENT 1709059PL84A-12
Editorial: ul. Grodzka, 3, 20-112 LUBLIN
Tel: 81 532 74 69 **Fax:** 81 532 74 69
Email: akcent_pismo@gazeta.pl **Web site:** http://www.akcent.glt.pl
ISSN: 0208-6220
Date Established: 1980; **Freq:** Quarterly; **Circ:** 1,000
Usual Pagination: 176
Profile: A magazine dedicated to literature, arts and social science.
Language(s): Polish
Mechanical Data: Type Area: 140 x 275 mm
CONSUMER: THE ARTS & LITERARY: Arts

AKTIVIST 1708926PL72J-4
Editorial: ul. Elbląska, 15/17, 01-747 WARSZAWA
Tel: 22 639 85 67 **Fax:** 22 639 85 69
Email: amichalak@valkea.com **Web site:** http://www.aktivist.pl
ISSN: 1640-8152
Date Established: 2000; **Freq:** Monthly; **Cover Price:** Free; **Circ:** 110,000
Usual Pagination: 48
Managing Director: Monika Stawicka; **Advertising Director:** Zuzanna Partyka
Profile: Focused on nightlife, city culture, new trends and events.
Language(s): Polish
ADVERTISING RATES:
Full Page Mono .... PLN 37500.00
Mechanical Data: Type Area: 230 x 297 mm
LOCAL NEWSPAPERS: Community Newsletters

AMBIENTE 1796214PL4B-9
Editorial: ul. Stępińska, 22/30, 00-739 WARSZAWA
Tel: 22 559 39 61 **Fax:** 22 559 39 62
Email: biuro@promedia.biz.pl **Web site:** http://www.promedia.biz.pl
Date Established: 2002; **Freq:** Quarterly; **Circ:** 3,000
Profile: Provides information on interior design and decoration.
Language(s): Polish
Mechanical Data: Type Area: A4
BUSINESS: ARCHITECTURE & BUILDING: Interior Design & Flooring

ANGORA 1708640PL82-65
Editorial: ul. Piotrkowska, 94, 90-103 ŁÓDŹ
Tel: 42 632 61 79 **Fax:** 42 632 07 59
Email: redakcja@angora.com.pl **Web site:** http://www.angora.com.pl
ISSN: 0867-8162
Date Established: 1990; **Freq:** Weekly; **Circ:** 450,000
Usual Pagination: 72
Profile: Presents overview of the most interesting articles of foreign and national press.
Language(s): Polish
Mechanical Data: Type Area: 220 x 288 mm
CONSUMER: CURRENT AFFAIRS & POLITICS

ANTYKI 1819629PL79K-1
Editorial: ul. Okrzei, 1a, 03-715 WARSZAWA
Tel: 22 333 80 00 **Fax:** 22 333 88 99
Email: redakcja@magazynantyki.pl
Date Established: 2005; **Freq:** 6 issues yearly; **Circ:** 8,000
Usual Pagination: 80
Managing Director: Joanna Waszkiewicz
Profile: Magazine on antiques, arts, market overview and collectors' investments.
Language(s): Polish
CONSUMER: HOBBIES & DIY: Collectors Magazines

APARTAMENTY I MIESZKANIA 1796101PL1E-3
Editorial: ul. Tytoniowa, 20, 04-228 WARSZAWA
Tel: 22 515 01 87 **Fax:** 22 613 25 84
Email: apartamenty@migutmedia.pl **Web site:** http://www.migutmedia.pl
Date Established: 2005
Circ: 15,000
Usual Pagination: 96
Advertising Director: Magdalena Kiedrowska
Profile: Magazine about property and interior design, presents developers' offers.
Language(s): Polish
Mechanical Data: Type Area: 225 x 295 mm
BUSINESS: FINANCE & ECONOMICS: Property

ARCHITEKTURA I BIZNES 1835742PL4A-31
Editorial: ul. Świętokrzyska 12, p. 512, 516, 30-015 KRAKÓW **Tel:** 12 632 88 67 **Fax:** 12 632 69 30
Email: redakcja@architekturaibiznes.com.pl **Web site:** http://www.architekturaibiznes.com.pl
Date Established: 1992; **Freq:** 11 issues yearly; **Cover Price:** PLN 12.00
Annual Sub.: PLN 120.00; **Circ:** 15,000
Usual Pagination: 140
News Editor: Magda Broniatowska; **Editor-in-Chief:** Sylwia Ratajczyk; **Advertising Director:** Renata Kiepura
Profile: Professional magazine focused on architecture, urbanization projects, newest industrial and commercial designs, building materials, interior designs and modern technologies.
Language(s): Polish
Readership: Aimed at architects, design office technologists, engineers and building specialists.
ADVERTISING RATES:
Full Page Colour .... PLN 10800.00
Mechanical Data: Type Area: 240 x 330mm
BUSINESS: ARCHITECTURE & BUILDING: Architecture

ARCHITEKTURA - MURATOR 1795613PL4A-22
Editorial: ul. Kamionkowska, 45, 03-812 WARSZAWA **Tel:** 22 590 50 26 **Fax:** 22 590 52 89
Email: architektura@murator.com.pl **Web site:** http://www.architektura-murator.pl
ISSN: 1232-6372
Date Established: 1994; **Freq:** Monthly; **Circ:** 8,500
Usual Pagination: 116
Managing Director: Renata Krzewska; **Advertising Director:** Anna Dygasiewicz-Piwko
Profile: Presents overview of the newest Polish urban and architecture projects; architectonic events in the world: competitions, exhibitions, conferences, presentations, etc; modern technical solutions and history and theory of architecture.
Language(s): Polish
Mechanical Data: Type Area: 230 x 310 mm
BUSINESS: ARCHITECTURE & BUILDING: Architecture

ARCHIVES OF MEDICAL SCIENCE 1796193PL56R-1
Editorial: ul. Żeromskiego, 113, 90-549 ŁÓDŹ
Tel: 42 639 34 65 **Fax:** 42 639 34 65
Email: maciej.banach@kardiolog.pl **Web site:** http://www.ams.termedia.pl
ISSN: 1734-1922
Circ: 1,000
Usual Pagination: 70
Managing Director: Andrzej Kordas
Profile: Publishes high quality original medical articles, case reports and reviews in experimental and clinical medicine aiming at young medical scientists and doctors.
Language(s): English; Polish
Mechanical Data: Type Area: A4
BUSINESS: HEALTH & MEDICAL: Health Medical Related

ARCHIVOLTA 1708716PL4A-10
Editorial: C12, 23, 32-086 WĘGRZCE
Tel: 12 285 73 25 **Fax:** 12 285 73 25
Email: archivolta@archivolta.com.pl **Web site:** http://www.archivolta.com.pl
ISSN: 1506-5928
Date Established: 1999; **Freq:** Quarterly; **Circ:** 8,000
Usual Pagination: 96
Profile: Professional magazine about architecture, interior design, new technologies and building materials.
Language(s): Polish
Mechanical Data: Type Area: 203 x 285 mm
BUSINESS: ARCHITECTURE & BUILDING: Architecture

ARSENAŁ 1709026PL75F-2
Editorial: ul. Marconich 3, 02-954 WARSZAWA
Tel: 22 858 20 40 **Fax:** 22 858 28 98
Email: redakcja@dvc.pl **Web site:** http://www.arsenal.dvc.pl
ISSN: 1731-190X
Date Established: 2003; **Freq:** Monthly; **Circ:** 10,500
Usual Pagination: 74
Editor: Paweł Kalisz; **Advertising Director:** Adam Głuszcz
Profile: The Shooters Review ARSENAL is a color illustrated magazine entirely devoted to shooting. As distinguished from others which are directed to narrow hermetic groups of gun owners like hunters or collectors, Arsenal comprises concerning access, possession and operational use of small arms.
Language(s): Polish
Readership: Addressed to people who practice shooting: private gun owners, huntsmen, police and army forces, collectors and all those who want to hold guns legally.
Mechanical Data: Type Area: 205x293 mm
CONSUMER: SPORT: Shooting

ART & LIFE 1708799PL84A-4
Editorial: ul. Bohomolca, 17, 1, 01-613 WARSZAWA
Tel: 22 865 67 41 **Fax:** 22 865 67 41
Email: redakcja@orbiplus.pl
Date Established: 2006
Circ: 8,000
Usual Pagination: 132
Profile: Academic arts, practical and business arts, arts in private life, life as an art.
Language(s): Polish
Mechanical Data: Type Area: A4
CONSUMER: THE ARTS & LITERARY: Arts

ARTEON 1795911PL84A-14
Editorial: ul. Grunwaldzka, 104, 60-307 POZNAŃ
Tel: 61 869 91 77 **Fax:** 61 865 99 09
Email: arteon@kruszona.pl **Web site:** http://www.arteon.pl
ISSN: 1508-3454
Date Established: 1999; **Freq:** Monthly; **Circ:** 3,000
Usual Pagination: 56
Profile: Covers modern arts, arts news, talks with artists, archives of art pieces.
Language(s): Polish
Mechanical Data: Type Area: A4
CONSUMER: THE ARTS & LITERARY: Arts

ARTLUK 1813204PL84A-16
Editorial: ul. Nowy Świat, 7, 6, 00-496 WARSZAWA
Tel: 692 439 567 **Fax:** 22 621 01 37
Email: redakcja@artluk.com **Web site:** http://www.artluk.com
ISSN: 1896-3676
Date Established: 2006; **Freq:** Quarterly; **Circ:** 1,000
Usual Pagination: 108
Advertising Director: Marzena Karcz
Profile: News from various fields of art: painters, sculptors, graphic artists, designers, conservators.
Language(s): Polish
Mechanical Data: Type Area: A4
CONSUMER: THE ARTS & LITERARY: Arts

AUDIO 1819523PL78A-1
Editorial: ul. Leszczynowa, 11, 03-197 WARSZAWA
Tel: 22 257 84 30 **Fax:** 22 257 84 44
Email: news@audio.com.pl **Web site:** http://audio.com.pl
Date Established: 1995; **Freq:** Monthly; **Circ:** 20,000
Usual Pagination: 132
Advertising Director: Krystyna Bogdan
Profile: Magazine on home audio sound systems, Hi-Fi, home cinema.
Language(s): Polish
ADVERTISING RATES:
Full Page Colour .... PLN 5500.00
Mechanical Data: Type Area: 220 x 290 mm
CONSUMER: CONSUMER ELECTRONICS: Hi-Fi & Recording

AUDIO VIDEO 1708910PL5B-10
Editorial: ul. Tytoniowa, 20, 04-228 WARSZAWA
Tel: 22 515 00 17 **Fax:** 22 613 25 84
Email: f.kulpa@migutmedia.pl **Web site:** http://www.av.com.pl
ISSN: 1230-395X
Date Established: 1984; **Freq:** Monthly; **Circ:** 15,000
Usual Pagination: 100
Advertising Director: Ewa Majerska
Profile: Magazine focused on audio and video equipment and its testing.
Language(s): Polish
Mechanical Data: Type Area: A4
BUSINESS: COMPUTERS & AUTOMATION: Data Processing

AUTO FIRMOWE 1804100PL31R-1
Editorial: ul. Racławicka, 15/19, 53-149 WROCŁAW
Tel: 71 783 51 00 **Fax:** 71 783 51 01
Email: redakcja@e-ipm.pl **Web site:** http://www.autofirmowe.pl
ISSN: 1733-991X
Date Established: 2005; **Freq:** Monthly; **Cover Price:** Free; **Circ:** 10,000
Usual Pagination: 48
Advertising Director: Robert Zieliński
Profile: Magazine dedicated to car advising and business-motoring issues.
Language(s): Polish
Mechanical Data: Type Area: 230x297 mm
BUSINESS: MOTOR TRADE: Motor Trade Related

AUTO MOTO 1623041PL77A-12
Editorial: al. Stanów Zjednoczonych, 61a, 04-028 WARSZAWA **Tel:** 22 516 34 81 **Fax:** 22 516 34 80
Email: redakcja@automoto.bauer.pl **Web site:** http://www.reklama.bauer.pl
ISSN: 0208-7863
Date Established: 1997; **Freq:** Monthly; **Circ:** 70,000
Usual Pagination: 100
Advertising Director: Marcin Warych
Profile: Magazine containing reports and tests of latest models, tips and advice on purchasing new or used cars and new technology.
Language(s): Polish
Readership: Read by men aged 25 and 44 years.
ADVERTISING RATES:
Full Page Colour .... PLN 23000.00
Mechanical Data: Type Area: 225 x 285 mm
CONSUMER: MOTORING & CYCLING: Motoring

AUTO MOTO SERWIS 1708932PL77A-45
Editorial: al. Komisji Edukacji Narodowej, 95, 02-777 WARSZAWA **Tel:** 22 678 64 90 **Fax:** 22 679 71 01
Email: r.polit@automotoserwis.com.pl **Web site:** http://www.automotoserwis.com.pl
ISSN: 1231-0131
Date Established: 1993; **Freq:** Monthly; **Circ:** 7,000
Usual Pagination: 56
Profile: Magazine containing articles on car repair, servicing and general motoring issues.
Language(s): English
Mechanical Data: Type Area: A4
CONSUMER: MOTORING & CYCLING: Motoring

AUTO MOTOR I SPORT 1201735PL31A-5
Editorial: ul. Ostrowskiego, 7, 53-238 WROCŁAW
Tel: 71 780 66 11 **Fax:** 71 780 66 12
Email: redakcja@mpp.pl **Web site:** http://www.auto-motor-i-sport.pl
ISSN: 1426-6385
Date Established: 1994
Circ: 73,000
Usual Pagination: 108
Profile: Magazine giving practical tips and comparative tests, technical explanations, car sporting events, all the latest news.
Language(s): Polish
Mechanical Data: Type Area: 225 x 285 mm
BUSINESS: MOTOR TRADE: Motor Trade Accessories

AUTO ŚWIAT 1201734PL77A-5
Editorial: ul. Suwak, 3, 02-676 WARSZAWA
Tel: 22 232 08 00 **Fax:** 22 232 55 02
Email: redakcja@auto-swiat.pl **Web site:** http://www.auto-swiat.pl
ISSN: 1234-0294
Date Established: 1995; **Freq:** Weekly
Usual Pagination: 52
Managing Director: Małgorzata Barankiewicz; **Advertising Director:** Marek Drzewiecki
Profile: Magazine focusing on motoring market in Poland and worldwide, includes tests on new models, reports, legal and expert advice for car users, second-hand and racing sections.
Language(s): Polish
Readership: Aimed at those interested in cars.
Mechanical Data: Type Area: 225 x 295 mm
CONSUMER: MOTORING & CYCLING: Motoring

AUTO TUNING ŚWIAT 1810954PL77A-42
Editorial: ul. Krakowskie Przedmieście, 58, 14, 20-076 LUBLIN **Tel:** 81 534 44 29 **Fax:** 81 534 44 29
Email: kasia@grupac2.pl **Web site:** http://www.autotuningswiat.pl

ISSN: 1643-2002
Date Established: 1999; **Freq:** Monthly; **Circ:** 37,000
Usual Pagination: 148
Advertising Director: Robert Nogaj
Profile: Magazine dedicated to car tuning, car audio systems, car market news and experts' advice.
Language(s): Polish
Mechanical Data: Type Area: 205x295 mm
CONSUMER: MOTORING & CYCLING: Motoring

AUTO-BIT
1810899PL77A-36
Editorial: al. Pokoju, 3, 31-548 KRAKÓW
Tel: 12 430 41 31 **Fax:** 12 412 80 06
Email: glepak@trader.pl **Web site:** http://www.trader.pl
ISSN: 1731-5514
Date Established: 2000; **Freq:** Weekly; **Circ:** 19,100
Usual Pagination: 96
Advertising Director: Sławomir Smoliński
Profile: Magazine containing cars' ads, info on new and used cars and accessories, financial and legal advice.
Language(s): Polish
Mechanical Data: Type Area: A3
CONSUMER: MOTORING & CYCLING: Motoring

AUTOBIZNES OGŁOSZENIA
1810910PL77A-37
Editorial: ul. Towarowa, 22, 00-839 WARSZAWA
Tel: 22 455 33 00 **Fax:** 22 455 33 01
Email: autobiznes@trader.pl **Web site:** http://www.trader.pl
ISSN: 1425-5324
Date Established: 1992; **Freq:** Weekly; **Circ:** 17,500
Usual Pagination: 60
Advertising Director: Krzysztof Dzięgielewski
Profile: Magazine containing cars' ads, info on new and used cars and accessories, financial and legal advice.
Language(s): Polish
Mechanical Data: Type Area: 257x370 mm
CONSUMER: MOTORING & CYCLING: Motoring

AUTOEXPERT
1708696PL77A-16
Editorial: ul. Grabiszyńska, 163, 53-439 WROCŁAW
Tel: 71 782 31 80 **Fax:** 71 782 31 84
Email: autoexpert@vogel.pl **Web site:** http://www.autoexpert.pl
ISSN: 1234-480X
Date Established: 1995; **Freq:** Monthly; **Cover Price:** Free; **Circ:** 10,000
Usual Pagination: 76
Advertising Director: Krzysztof Faściszewski
Profile: Information about car mechanics, car tools and accessories and practical advice on running car-servicing business.
Language(s): Polish
Mechanical Data: Type Area: 205 x 290 mm
CONSUMER: MOTORING & CYCLING: Motoring

AUTOMATYKA, PODZESPOŁY, APLIKACJE
1819633PL5A-27
Editorial: ul. Leszczynowa, 11, 03-197 WARSZAWA
Tel: 22 257 84 65 **Fax:** 22 257 84 67
Email: marketing@automatykab2b.pl **Web site:** http://www.automatykab2b.pl
Date Established: 2006; **Freq:** Monthly; **Circ:** 10,000
Usual Pagination: 100
Advertising Director: Katarzyna Wiśniewska
Profile: Professional magazine about industrial automation, production managing, components, applications and integration systems equipment.
Language(s): Polish
ADVERTISING RATES:
Full Page Colour .... PLN 4200.00
Mechanical Data: Type Area: A4
BUSINESS: COMPUTERS & AUTOMATION: Automation & Instrumentation

AVANTI
1709022PL74A-1021
Editorial: ul. Czerska, 8/10, 00-732 WARSZAWA
Tel: 22 555 66 53 **Fax:** 22 555 47 80
Email: avanti@agora.pl **Web site:** http://www.avantimoda.pl
ISSN: 1732-0305
Date Established: 2004; **Freq:** Monthly; **Circ:** 199,929
Usual Pagination: 156
Advertising Director: Paulina Skorwider
Profile: Magazine dedicated to fashion, cosmetics, hairdos and make-up.
Language(s): Polish
Mechanical Data: Type Area: 203 x 257 mm
CONSUMER: WOMEN'S INTEREST CONSUMER MAGAZINES: Women's Interest

BANK
1810982PL1C-1
Editorial: ul. Solec, 101, 5, 00-382 WARSZAWA
Tel: 22 629 18 77 **Fax:** 22 629 18 72
Email: biuro@wydawnictwocpb.pl **Web site:** http://www.alebank.pl
ISSN: 1230-9125
Date Established: 1992; **Freq:** Monthly; **Circ:** 2,000
Usual Pagination: 80
Editor: Jan Osiecki; **Managing Director:** Waldemar Zbytek
Profile: Professional magazine about banking, finance and financial institutions.
Language(s): Polish

ADVERTISING RATES:
Full Page Colour .... PLN 11600.00
Mechanical Data: Type Area: 220 x 280 mm
BUSINESS: FINANCE & ECONOMICS: Banking

BELLA RELAKS
1795897PL74R-4
Editorial: ul. Motorowa, 1, 04-035 WARSZAWA
Tel: 22 517 02 49 **Fax:** 22 517 03 17
Email: bella-relaks@bauer.pl **Web site:** http://www.reklama.bauer.pl
ISSN: 1730-4253
Date Established: 2003; **Freq:** Weekly; **Circ:** 199,000
Usual Pagination: 32
Advertising Director: Ewa Kozłowska
Profile: Magazine containing information on health, recipes and crosswords.
Language(s): Polish
ADVERTISING RATES:
Full Page Colour .... PLN 11900.00
Mechanical Data: Type Area: 210 x 280 mm
CONSUMER: WOMEN'S INTEREST CONSUMER MAGAZINES: Women's Interest Related

BIBLIOTEKA W SZKOLE
1708760PL62A-3
Editorial: skr. poczt. 109, 00-950 WARSZAWA
Tel: 22 832 36 12 **Fax:** 22 832 36 12
Email: sukurs@sukurs.edu.pl **Web site:** http://www.bibliotekawszkole.pl
ISSN: 0867-5600
Date Established: 1990; **Freq:** Monthly; **Circ:** 11,000
Usual Pagination: 32
Profile: Library materials and instructions for teachers and school administration.
Language(s): Polish
Mechanical Data: Type Area: A4
BUSINESS: CHURCH & SCHOOL EQUIPMENT & EDUCATION: Education

BIEGANIE
1810989PL75A-23
Editorial: ul. Grochowska, 316/320, 03-839 WARSZAWA **Tel:** 22 353 85 32 **Fax:** 22 353 85 33
Email: sekretariat@bieganie.com.pl **Web site:** http://www.bieganie.com.pl
ISSN: 1895-4707
Date Established: 2005; **Freq:** Monthly; **Circ:** 10,000
Usual Pagination: 72
Profile: Magazine focused on running and training, running equipment, health, sports events and information on other sports: fitness, adventure racing, triathlon.
Language(s): Polish
Mechanical Data: Type Area: 275x210 mm
CONSUMER: SPORT

BIKE ACTION
1709027PL75A-16
Editorial: ul. Wolności, 179, 58-560 JELENIA GÓRA
Tel: 75 755 98 88 **Fax:** 75 755 98 89
Email: bike@bikeaction.pl **Web site:** http://www.bikeaction.pl
ISSN: 1426-0735
Date Established: 1996
Circ: 20,000
Usual Pagination: 84
Advertising Director: Krzysztof Grabiński
Profile: Magazine dedicated to bicycles and equipment, bike accessories and new trends.
Language(s): Polish
Mechanical Data: Type Area: 205 x 275 mm
CONSUMER: SPORT

BIKEBOARD
1708724PL77C-5
Editorial: ul. Praska, 4, 30-328 KRAKÓW
Tel: 12 431 22 80 **Fax:** 12 259 00 22
Email: redakcja@bikeboard.pl **Web site:** http://www.bikeboard.pl
ISSN: 1427-1672
Date Established: 1995
Circ: 25,000
Usual Pagination: 96
Advertising Director: Katarzyna Kędracka
Profile: Bicycles.
Language(s): Polish
Mechanical Data: Type Area: 212 x 285 mm
CONSUMER: MOTORING & CYCLING: Cycling

BIULETYN PODATKÓW DOCHODOWYCH
1795857PL1M-3
Editorial: ul. Okopowa, 58/72, 01-042 WARSZAWA
Tel: 22 530 41 75 **Fax:** 22 530 42 22
Email: bok@infor.pl **Web site:** http://www.bpd.infor.pl
ISSN: 1734-7254
Date Established: 2005; **Freq:** Monthly
Usual Pagination: 84
Managing Director: Mariusz Drozdowicz; **Advertising Director:** Michał Sądowicz
Profile: Focused on taxation problems' solutions addressed to companies and individuals.
Language(s): Polish
Mechanical Data: Type Area: B5mm
BUSINESS: FINANCE & ECONOMICS: Taxation

BIULETYN RACHUNKOWOŚCI
1795603PL1B-14
Editorial: ul. Okopowa, 58/72, 01-042 WARSZAWA
Tel: 22 530 41 75 **Fax:** 22 530 42 22
Web site: http://www.br.infor.pl
ISSN: 1898-6455
Date Established: 2006; **Freq:** 26 issues yearly
Usual Pagination: 66
Managing Director: Mariusz Drozdowicz
Profile: Provides practical advice on accountancy and company's finances.
Language(s): Polish
Mechanical Data: Type Area: B5mm
BUSINESS: FINANCE & ECONOMICS: Accountancy

BIULETYN VAT
1796028PL1M-6
Editorial: ul. Okopowa, 58/72, 01-042 WARSZAWA
Tel: 22 530 41 75 **Fax:** 22 530 42 22
Web site: http://www.bv.infor.pl
ISSN: 1733-0882
Date Established: 2004; **Freq:** 26 issues yearly
Usual Pagination: 66
Managing Director: Mariusz Drozdowicz
Profile: Experts' advice on how to deal with a company's VAT.
Language(s): Polish
Mechanical Data: Type Area: B5mm
BUSINESS: FINANCE & ECONOMICS: Taxation

BIZNES POZNAŃSKI
1709093PL14A-61
Editorial: ul. Roosevelta, 18, 60-829 POZNAŃ
Tel: 61 845 10 13 **Fax:** 61 845 10 14
Email: mwelyczko@biznespolska.pl **Web site:** http://www.biznespolska.pl
ISSN: 1733-9677
Date Established: 2007; **Freq:** 26 issues yearly; **Circ:** 2,000
Usual Pagination: 16
Advertising Director: Thompson Barnhardt
Profile: Provides information about business in Poznan region, investments, new technologies and news on property market.
Language(s): Polish
Mechanical Data: Type Area: 290x380 mm
BUSINESS: COMMERCE, INDUSTRY & MANAGEMENT

BIZPOLAND
1708966PL1F-9
Editorial: ul. Św. Bonifacego 92 lok. 13/18, 02-920 WARSZAWA **Tel:** 22 437 97 00 **Fax:** 22 437 97 01
Email: barnhardt@biznespolska.pl **Web site:** http://www.bizpoland.pl
Date Established: 2008; **Freq:** Monthly; **Annual Sub.:** PLN 500.00; **Circ:** 10,000
Profile: Poland's Business Magazine for Foreign Investors and the International Business Community, with business feature stories, news, coverage ofkey industries, and regional business news from more than 8 Polish cities.
Language(s): English
Readership: In English-language only, the magazine targets Poland's foreign business community, foreign investors – both resident in Poland, and based abroad with current or future business interest in Poland, expatriate business executives currently living in Poland, high-end International Polish executives.business responsibilities.
ADVERTISING RATES:
Full Page Colour .... PLN 9500.00
Mechanical Data: Type Area: 210x297mm
BUSINESS: FINANCE & ECONOMICS: Investment

BOSTON IT SECURITY REVIEW
1811025PL5B-54
Editorial: ul. Bokserska 1, 02-682 WARSZAWA
Tel: 22 427 37 11 **Fax:** 22 244 24 59
Email: boston@software.com.pl **Web site:** http://www.boston-review.com
ISSN: 1896-5032
Date Established: 1995; **Freq:** 6 issues yearly; **Cover Price:** Free; **Circ:** 7,000
Usual Pagination: 60
Advertising Director: Katarzyna Czajkowska
Profile: Focused on IT technologies – security of information, the latest software and antivirus tools on the market.
Language(s): Polish
Readership: Targets managers, administrators and programmers responsible for the security of IT systems within the company.
ADVERTISING RATES:
Full Page Colour .... PLN 6000.00
Mechanical Data: Type Area: 210 x 297 + 5 mm spady
BUSINESS: COMPUTERS & AUTOMATION: Data Processing

BOUTIQUE
1708769PL74B-110
Editorial: ul. Marii Konopnickiej, 6, 00-491 WARSZAWA **Tel:** 22 628 97 65 **Fax:** 22 625 59 24
Email: redakcja@boutique.com.pl **Web site:** http://boutique.com.pl
ISSN: 1733-1951
Date Established: 1992; **Freq:** Monthly; **Circ:** 55,000
Usual Pagination: 100
Advertising Director: Małgorzata Pisula; **Publisher:** Wieńczysław Zaczek
Profile: Magazine focused on fashion, beauty and celebrities.
Language(s): Polish

Mechanical Data: Type Area: 210 x 265 mm
CONSUMER: WOMEN'S INTEREST CONSUMER MAGAZINES: Women's Interest - Fashion

BRAĆ ŁOWIECKA
1708649PL75F-
Editorial: ul. Kaliska, 1, 9, 02-316 WARSZAWA
Tel: 22 824 57 28 **Fax:** 22 822 66 49
Email: braclowiecka@oikos.net.pl **Web site:** http://www.braclowiecka.net.pl
ISSN: 1429-7698
Date Established: 1998; **Freq:** Monthly; **Circ:** 23,000
Usual Pagination: 84
Advertising Director: Paweł Szustkiewicz
Profile: Magazine on ammunition, guns and hunting, hunting dogs and jeeps for hunting.
Language(s): Polish
Mechanical Data: Type Area: A4
CONSUMER: SPORT: Shooting

BRAIN DAMAGE
1708933PL84A-1
Editorial: ul. Miączyńska, 57a, 02-637 WARSZAWA
Tel: 22 898 04 15 **Fax:** 22 898 04 21
Email: igor@bd.pl **Web site:** http://www.bd.pl
ISSN: 1509-2135
Date Established: 1997; **Freq:** Quarterly; **Circ:** 10,000
Usual Pagination: 100
Profile: Wall galleries, Street Art, modern CITY art.
Language(s): Polish
CONSUMER: THE ARTS & LITERARY: Arts

BRAVO SPORT
1622990PL75A-1
Editorial: ul. Motorowa, 1, 04-035 WARSZAWA
Tel: 22 517 05 69 **Fax:** 22 517 02 43
Email: bsport@bauer.pl **Web site:** http://www.bravo.pl
ISSN: 1428-1791
Date Established: 1997; **Freq:** 26 issues yearly; **Circ:** 151,000
Usual Pagination: 40
Managing Director: Monika Maciąg; **Advertising Director:** Małgorzata Dominik
Profile: Magazine featuring football, basketball, volleyball, water and motor sports.
Language(s): Polish
Readership: Aimed at youths aged 15 to 19 years.
ADVERTISING RATES:
Full Page Colour .... PLN 13600.00
Mechanical Data: Type Area: 210 x 280 mm
CONSUMER: SPORT

BRIEF
1708711PL2A-6
Editorial: ul. Zdrojowa, 38, 02-927 WARSZAWA
Tel: 22 424 04 45-48 **Fax:** 22 642 86 86
Email: brief@brief.pl **Web site:** http://www.brief.pl
ISSN: 1508-5406
Date Established: 1999; **Freq:** Monthly; **Circ:** 9,000
Usual Pagination: 98
Profile: Magazine on marketing and sales, ads and PR, sales promotion.
Language(s): Polish
ADVERTISING RATES:
Full Page Colour .... PLN 29200.00
Mechanical Data: Type Area: 205 x 280 mm
BUSINESS: COMMUNICATIONS, ADVERTISING & MARKETING

BUDOWLANIEC
1796181PL4E-8
Editorial: ul. Łucka, 15, 1907, 00-842 WARSZAWA
Tel: 22 635 41 08
Email: marcin.sikora@ardo.pl **Web site:** http://www.budowlaniec.org
ISSN: 1895-6300
Date Established: 2005; **Freq:** Quarterly; **Cover Price:** Free; **Circ:** 15,000
Usual Pagination: 48
Advertising Director: Marcin Sikora
Profile: Provides practical advice for specialists and building firms.
Language(s): Polish
Mechanical Data: Type Area: 200 x 283 mm
BUSINESS: ARCHITECTURE & BUILDING: Building

BUDUJEMY DOM
1796219PL4E-9
Editorial: ul. Leszczynowa, 11, 03-197 WARSZAWA
Tel: 22 257 84 72 **Fax:** 22 257 84 77
Email: ernest@budujemydom.pl **Web site:** http://www.budujemydom.pl
ISSN: 1429-8783
Date Established: 1999; **Freq:** Monthly; **Circ:** 50,000
Usual Pagination: 210
Managing Director: Ernest Jagodziński; **Advertising Director:** Iza Konikowska
Profile: Magazine dedicated to family house building.
Language(s): Polish
Mechanical Data: Type Area: 202 x 290 mm
BUSINESS: ARCHITECTURE & BUILDING: Building

BUILDER (D. KALEJDOSKOP BUDOWLANY)
1796220PL4E-7
Editorial: ul. Rolna, 155, 1, 02-729 WARSZAWA
Tel: 22 853 06 87 **Fax:** 22 853 06 86
Email: suwinski@pwbmedia.pl **Web site:** http://www.ebuilder.pl
ISSN: 1896-0642

ate Established: 1997; **Freq:** Monthly; **Circ:** 10,000
sual Pagination: 100
dvertising Director: Dominik Suwiński
ofile: Professional magazine focused on nstriction technologies, building materials, systems d building equipment, international building andards and safety.
nguage(s): Polish
eadership: Aimed at building managers, designers, gineers and technical construction specialists.
echanical Data: Type Area: A4
USINESS: ARCHITECTURE & BUILDING: uilding

UKIETY 1201733PL26D-5
ditorial: ul. Czerska, 8/10, 00-732 WARSZAWA
el: 22 555 66 09 **Fax:** 22 555 66 68
nail: bukiety@agora.pl **Web site:** http://www.ukiety.pl
SN: 1505-7453
ate Established: 1998; **Freq:** Quarterly; **Circ:** ,000
sual Pagination: 68
dvertising Director: Elżbieta Kaiser
rofile: Magazine featuring flower arranging, aditional and contemporary compositions, advice of orists.
anguage(s): Polish
eadership: Read by professionals and all those terested in floral arrangements.
echanical Data: Type Area: 205 x 272 mm
USINESS: GARDEN TRADE: Garden Trade orticulture

UNNY HOP 1708862PL77C-1
ditorial: ul. Pilchowicka, 16a, 02-175 WARSZAWA
el: 22 886 85 60 **Fax:** 22 886 85 60
mail: bunnyhop@poczta.onet.pl
SN: 1642-3100
ate Established: 2002; **Freq:** Quarterly; **Circ:** 5,000
sual Pagination: 40
rofile: bmx magazine.
anguage(s): Polish
CONSUMER: MOTORING & CYCLING: Cycling

URDA 1708657PL74A-1011
ditorial: ul. Ostrowskiego, 7, 53-238 WROCŁAW
el: 71 376 28 46-47 **Fax:** 71 376 28 47
mail: moda@burdamedia.pl **Web site:** http://www.urdamedia.pl
SSN: 0867-387X
Date Established: 1989; **Freq:** Monthly; **Circ:** 54,000
Usual Pagination: 100
Managing Director: Justyna Namięta, 071 376 28 00 Małgorzata Węgierek, 022 448 83 27; **Advertising Director:** Barbara Ożóg
Profile: Magazine featuring information on fashion, health and beauty.
Language(s): Polish
Mechanical Data: Type Area: 215 x 267 mm
CONSUMER: WOMEN'S INTEREST CONSUMER MAGAZINES: Women's Interest

BUSINES APPLICATIONS REVIEW 1811024PL14A-90
Editorial: ul. Bokserska, 1, 02-682 WARSZAWA
Tel: 22 887 14 66 **Fax:** 22 887 10 11
Email: bar@software.com.pl **Web site:** http://www.app-review.com
ISSN: 1896-8902
Date Established: 1995; **Freq:** 6 issues yearly; **Cover Price:** Free; **Circ:** 7,000
Usual Pagination: 32
Advertising Director: Małgorzata Bladowska
Profile: Focuses on IT technology in business and marketing.
Language(s): Polish
Mechanical Data: Type Area: 225x297 + 5 mm na spady
BUSINESS: COMMERCE, INDUSTRY & MANAGEMENT

BUSINESS ENGLISH MAGAZINE 1928841PL88R-5
Editorial: ul. Lednicka, 23, 60-413 POZNAŃ
Tel: 61 833 63 28 **Fax:** 61 833 63 28
Email: colorful@colorfulmedia.pl **Web site:** http://www.business-english.com.pl
ISSN: 1897-0796
Date Established: 2003; **Freq:** 6 issues yearly; **Circ:** 7,500
Usual Pagination: 72
Managing Director: Piotr Olejniczak; **Advertising Director:** Agnieszka Bułajewska
Profile: Magazine dedicated to learning of business English, with some economic information from Europe and the world.
Language(s): English; Polish
Readership: Targets managers and office workers learning business English for their work.
Mechanical Data: Type Area: 210 x 280mm
CONSUMER: EDUCATION: Education Related

BUSINESS & LIFE 1811078PL14A-94
Editorial: ul. Bohomolca, 17, 1, 01-613 WARSZAWA
Tel: 22 865 67 41 **Fax:** 22 834 74 85
Email: biuro@orbiplus.pl
Date Established: 2007; **Freq:** 6 issues yearly; **Circ:** 15,000
Usual Pagination: 130
Profile: Covers business connected with the life, business life, images of managers, marketing, law, finance, recreation, hobbies.
Language(s): English; Polish
Readership: Aimed at investors, businessmen and managers.
Mechanical Data: Type Area: 215 x 280 mm
BUSINESS: COMMERCE, INDUSTRY & MANAGEMENT

BUSINESS MEDIA 1708651PL2A-20
Editorial: ul. Kochanowskiego, 10, 5, 40-035 KATOWICE **Tel:** 32 206 76 77 **Fax:** 32 253 99 96
Email: redakcja@business-media.pl **Web site:** http://www.business-media.pl
ISSN: 1644-7131
Date Established: 2002; **Freq:** 6 issues yearly; **Circ:** 8,000
Usual Pagination: 40
Profile: Professional magazine on media, marketing and advertising, media events.
Language(s): Polish
ADVERTISING RATES:
Full Page Colour .... PLN 4500.00
Mechanical Data: Type Area: 228 x 296 mm
BUSINESS: COMMUNICATIONS, ADVERTISING & MARKETING

BUSINESS TRUCK 1811021PL77A-43
Editorial: al. Pokoju, 3, 31-548 KRAKÓW
Tel: 12 430 41 31 **Fax:** 12 412 80 06
Email: slawomir.smolinski@trader.pl **Web site:** http://www.trader.pl/pl/gazety/truck/info.asp
ISSN: 1897-1067
Date Established: 2007; **Freq:** 26 issues yearly; **Circ:** 27,000
Usual Pagination: 80
Advertising Director: Sławomir Smoliński
Profile: 'Sell and buy' ads for trucks, vans and news in the market of delivery cars.
Language(s): Polish
Mechanical Data: Type Area: A3
CONSUMER: MOTORING & CYCLING: Motoring

BUSINESSMAN.PL 1834599PL1A-75
Tel: 22 511 50 00 **Fax:** 22 613 25 84
Email: redakcja@businessman.pl **Web site:** http://www.businessman.pl
ISSN: 1898-3162
Date Established: 2007; **Freq:** Monthly; **Circ:** 50,000
Usual Pagination: 132
Profile: A modern business magazine directed at a specific group of readers: businessmen who make most important decisions regarding business investments, expenses and finance.
Language(s): Polish
Readership: Aimed at Polish businessmen, top management, company owners, presidents and vice-presidents of companies, directors responsible for managing departments of enterprises: finance, marketing, production, HR, sale and administration.
ADVERTISING RATES:
Full Page Colour .... PLN 29500.00
Mechanical Data: Type Area: A4
BUSINESS: FINANCE & ECONOMICS

CABINES 1709025PL74G-13
Editorial: ul. Powstańców Śl., 32a, 1, 45-087 OPOLE
Tel: 77 402 52 52 **Fax:** 77 423 14 27
Email: kryniewski@pressmedia.pl **Web site:** http://www.cabines.pl
ISSN: 1897-1032
Date Established: 2003; **Freq:** 6 issues yearly; **Cover Price:** Free; **Circ:** 7,000
Usual Pagination: 132
Advertising Director: Marzena Szklanny
Profile: Cosmetics products and news on beauty surgeries, manicure, pedicure, healthy lifestyle, wellness, spa, sauna, massage.
Language(s): Polish
Mechanical Data: Type Area: 205x280 mm
CONSUMER: WOMEN'S INTEREST CONSUMER MAGAZINES: Slimming & Health

CANAL+ CYFROWY 1821046PL2D-6
Editorial: ul. Kawalerii, 5, 00-468 WARSZAWA
Tel: 22 657 07 01 **Fax:** 22 657 07 50
Web site: http://www.canalpluscyfrowy.pl
Date Established: 1995 -
Managing Director: Jacques Aymar de Roquefeuil
Language(s): Polish
BUSINESS: COMMUNICATIONS, ADVERTISING & MARKETING: Broadcasting

CD ACTION 1623037PL78D-4
Editorial: ul. Sukiennice, 6, 50-107 WROCŁAW
Tel: 71 341 20 83 **Fax:** 71 341 99 11
Email: cdaction@cdaction.com.pl **Web site:** http://www.cdaction.com.pl
ISSN: 1426-2916
Date Established: 1996; **Freq:** Monthly; **Circ:** 83,680
Usual Pagination: 128
Advertising Director: Magdalena Milewska
Profile: Magazine covering reviews, previews and features on computer games.
Language(s): Polish
Readership: Read by computer games' enthusiasts.
ADVERTISING RATES:
Full Page Colour .... PLN 12000.00
Mechanical Data: Type Area: 214 x 297 mm
CONSUMER: CONSUMER ELECTRONICS: Games

CEE PACKAGING 1851126PL35-2
Editorial: ul. Zwyciezcow 42 -1, 03-938 WARSZAWA
Tel: 22 21 95 466
Email: alan@ceepackaging.com **Web site:** http://www.ceepackaging.com
Freq: 8 issues yearly - Electronic newsletter distributed daily to 30000 subscribers; **Annual Sub.:** EUR 400.00; **Circ:** 5,000
Usual Pagination: 60
Editor-in-Chief: Alan Heath
Profile: Focused on most rapidly expanding packaging markets, latest innovations, trends, design, branding, legislation, news of products, technology, analysis of the sector and environmental issues with in-depth profiles of major industry achievers.
Language(s): English
Readership: Targets managers in packaging industry, buyers and sellers of packaging products.
ADVERTISING RATES:
Full Page Colour .... EUR 4800.00
Mechanical Data: Type Area: 210x285mm
BUSINESS: PACKAGING & BOTTLING

CENTRAL EASTERN EUROPEAN REAL ESTATE GUIDE 1796218PL1E-5
Editorial: ul. Łucka, 15, 313, 00-842 WARSZAWA
Tel: 22 586 30 14 **Fax:** 22 586 30 11
Email: anna@europaproperty.com **Web site:** http://www.europaproperty.com
Date Established: 2000; **Freq:** Quarterly; **Cover Price:** Free
Profile: Presents news and investments on the real-estate market.
Language(s): English
Mechanical Data: Type Area: A4
BUSINESS: FINANCE & ECONOMICS: Property

CENTRAL EUROPEAN JOURNAL OF IMMUNOLOGY 1709010PL56A-19
Editorial: ul. Wenedów, 9/1, 61-614 POZNAŃ
Tel: 61 822 77 81 **Fax:** 61 822 77 81
Email: zpatiir@warman.com.pl **Web site:** http://www.immunologia.termedia.pl
ISSN: 1426-3912
Date Established: 2000
Circ: 900
Usual Pagination: 60
Managing Director: Andrzej Kordas
Language(s): English; Polish
Readership: Information included in the journal is intended for physicians, pharmacists, medicine and pharmacy students, and biomedicine scientists.
Mechanical Data: Type Area: A4
BUSINESS: HEALTH & MEDICAL

CEO 1796009PL14A-72
Editorial: ul. Jordanowska, 12, 04-204 WARSZAWA
Tel: 22 321 78 00 **Fax:** 22 321 78 88
Email: redakcjaceo@idg.com.pl **Web site:** http://www.magazynceo.pl
ISSN: 1734-9478
Date Established: 2001; **Freq:** Monthly; **Circ:** 2,000
Usual Pagination: 72
Advertising Director: Agnieszka Busz
Profile: Covering practice and theory of management, experts' advice and comments, news on current trends in management.
Language(s): Polish
ADVERTISING RATES:
Full Page Colour .... PLN 17400.00
Mechanical Data: Type Area: 225 x 275 mm
BUSINESS: COMMERCE, INDUSTRY & MANAGEMENT

CEO MOTO 1810940PL77A-40
Editorial: ul. Jordanowska, 12, 04-204 WARSZAWA
Tel: 22 321 78 00 **Fax:** 22 321 78 88
Email: redakcjaceo@idg.com.pl **Web site:** http://www.magazynceo.pl
Date Established: 2006; **Freq:** Half-yearly; **Circ:** 6,500
Usual Pagination: 68
Advertising Director: Aneta Woźniak
Profile: Cars' market, luxury cars and finance, automobile hobbies.
Language(s): Polish
Mechanical Data: Type Area: 225x275 mm
CONSUMER: MOTORING & CYCLING: Motoring

CFO 1709062PL14A-56
Editorial: ul. Jordanowska, 12, 04-204 WARSZAWA
Tel: 22 321 78 00 **Fax:** 22 321 78 88
Email: redakcjacfo@idg.com.pl **Web site:** http://www.magazyncfo.pl
ISSN: 1732-5617
Date Established: 2004; **Freq:** 6 issues yearly; **Circ:** 2,000
Usual Pagination: 44
Profile: Featuring professional comments and news, trends in financial strategy management, usage of IT technologies.
Language(s): Polish
Mechanical Data: Type Area: 225 x 275 mm
BUSINESS: COMMERCE, INDUSTRY & MANAGEMENT

CHARAKTERY 1708967PL94J-302
Editorial: ul. Warszawska, 6, 25-512 KIELCE
Tel: 41 343 28 40 **Fax:** 41 343 28 40
Email: charaktery@charaktery.com.pl **Web site:** http://www.charaktery.eu
Date Established: 1997; **Freq:** Monthly; **Circ:** 70,000
Usual Pagination: 116
Advertising Director: Marek Malarz
Profile: Psychology and human behaviour.
Language(s): Polish
Mechanical Data: Type Area: 205 x 280 mm
CONSUMER: OTHER CLASSIFICATIONS: Popular Science

CHIC LUXURY LIFESTYLE MAGAZINE 1929114PL74Q-22
Editorial: ul. Grażyny, 13, 02-548 WARSZAWA
Tel: 22 465 99 47 **Fax:** 22 469 93 30
Email: redakcja@chicmagazine.pl **Web site:** http://www.chicmagazine.pl
ISSN: 1689-3174
Date Established: 2008; **Freq:** Quarterly; **Cover Price:** Free; **Circ:** 10,000
Advertising Director: Gabriela Sobiech
Profile: Lifestyle magazine presenting luxury goods from the whole world.
Language(s): Polish
ADVERTISING RATES:
Full Page Colour .... PLN 20000.00
Mechanical Data: Type Area: 230 x 300 mm
CONSUMER: WOMEN'S INTEREST CONSUMER MAGAZINES: Lifestyle

CHIP 1500205PL5C-17
Editorial: ul. Topiel, 23, 00-342 WARSZAWA
Tel: 22 320 19 00 **Fax:** 22 320 19 01
Email: redakcja@chip.pl **Web site:** http://www.chip.pl
Date Established: 1994; **Freq:** Monthly; **Circ:** 37,521
Usual Pagination: 164
Managing Director: Małgorzata Węgierek Justyna Namięta; **Advertising Director:** Cezary Żelazowski
Profile: Magazine covering computer news, software news, HW and SW testing, applications and devices.
Language(s): Polish
ADVERTISING RATES:
Full Page Colour .... PLN 14200.00
Mechanical Data: Type Area: A4
BUSINESS: COMPUTERS & AUTOMATION: Professional Personal Computers

CHIP FOTO-VIDEO DIGITAL 1709094PL78R-6
Email: listy@fvd.pl **Web site:** http://www.fvd.pl
ISSN: 1732-7938
Date Established: 2004; **Freq:** Monthly; **Circ:** 37,500
Usual Pagination: 124
Profile: Magazine on digital cameras and video equipment.
Language(s): Polish
CONSUMER: CONSUMER ELECTRONICS: Consumer Electronics Related

CHIP KOMPUTER TEST 1709102PL78E-2
Email: listy@komputertest.pl **Web site:** http://www.komputertest.pl
ISSN: 1733-9499
Date Established: 2005; **Freq:** Monthly; **Circ:** 100,000
Usual Pagination: 76
Language(s): Polish
CONSUMER: CONSUMER ELECTRONICS: Home Computing

CHŁODNICTWO 1811041PL3C-1
Editorial: ul. Ratuszowa, 11, 743a, 03-450 WARSZAWA **Tel:** 22 818 65 21 **Fax:** 22 818 65 21
Email: chlodnictwo@sigma-not.pl **Web site:** http://sigma-not.pl
ISSN: 0009-4919
Date Established: 1966; **Freq:** Monthly
Usual Pagination: 48
Profile: Focused on freezing and cooling, ventilation and air-conditioning, heating pumps, building and exploitation of machines, installations and equipment.
Language(s): Polish
ADVERTISING RATES:
Full Page Mono .... PLN 1200.00
Full Page Colour .... PLN 2760.00
Mechanical Data: Type Area: 205 x 290 mm
BUSINESS: HEATING & VENTILATION: Refrigeration & Ventilation

CHŁODNICTWO & KLIMATYZACJA 754592PL3C-2
Editorial: al. Komisji Edukacji Narodowej, 95, 02-777 WARSZAWA **Tel:** 22 678 66 09 **Fax:** 22 678 54 21
Email: chlodnictwo@chlodnictwoiklimatyzacja.pl
Web site: http://www.chlodnictwoiklimatyzacja.pl
ISSN: 1425-9796
Date Established: 1996; **Freq:** Monthly; **Circ:** 4,000

Usual Pagination: 80
Profile: Provides practical know-how in the scope of designing, installing and exploitation of refrigerating, ventilating and air-conditioning devices.
Language(s): Polish
Readership: Aimed at food industry professionals and specialists of the refrigerating, air-conditioning and ventilation sector.
ADVERTISING RATES:
Full Page Colour .... EUR 1250.00
Mechanical Data: Type Area: A4
BUSINESS: HEATING & VENTILATION: Refrigeration & Ventilation

CHŁOPSKA DROGA 1796022PL21A-1
Editorial: ul. Górnośląska, 14, 00-432 WARSZAWA
Tel: 22 628 25 58 **Fax:** 22 628 76 69
Email: reklama@media500.pl **Web site:** http://www.chlopskadroga.pl
ISSN: 0137-9070
Date Established: 1943; **Freq:** Weekly; **Circ:** 30,000
Usual Pagination: 24
Profile: Newspaper on agriculture, agro business and food sales.
Language(s): Polish
ADVERTISING RATES:
Full Page Mono .... PLN 5600.00
Mechanical Data: Type Area: 300x400 mm
BUSINESS: AGRICULTURE & FARMING

CHRONOS 1795672PL52B-1
Editorial: ul. Kierbedzia, 4, 00-728 WARSZAWA
Tel: 22 320 15 00 **Fax:** 22 320 15 50
Email: chronos@unit.com.pl **Web site:** http://www.chronos-zegarki.pl
ISSN: 1895-6351
Date Established: 2004; **Freq:** Quarterly; **Circ:** 10,000
Usual Pagination: 88
Advertising Director: Joanna Pratzer
Profile: Magazine about watches: exclusive and the newest models and their testing.
Language(s): Polish
ADVERTISING RATES:
Full Page Colour .... PLN 5400.00
Mechanical Data: Type Area: 230 x 300 mm
BUSINESS: GIFT TRADE: Clocks & Watches

CHWILA DLA CIEBIE
1622949PL74A-1040
Editorial: ul. Motorowa, 1, 04-035 WARSZAWA
Tel: 22 517 01 36 **Fax:** 22 517 04 64
Email: chwila@bauer.pl **Web site:** http://www.reklama.bauer.pl
ISSN: 1234-3129
Date Established: 1995; **Freq:** Weekly; **Circ:** 446,000
Usual Pagination: 64
Advertising Director: Ewa Kozłowska
Profile: Magazine containing news on fashion and beauty and general women's interest features: health tips, cooking, dieting, legal advice, interior design, psychology, puzzles, real life stories.
Language(s): Polish
Readership: Aimed at women in age group between 25 and 50 years.
ADVERTISING RATES:
Full Page Colour .... PLN 43000.00
Mechanical Data: Type Area: 210 x 280 mm
CONSUMER: WOMEN'S INTEREST CONSUMER MAGAZINES: Women's Interest

---

CIENIE I BLASKI 765847PL74A-1002
Editorial: ul. Wiejska 19, 00-480 WARSZAWA
Tel: 22 58 42 200 **Fax:** 22 58 42 201
Email: ewa.siniarska@edipresse.pl
Date Established: 1995; **Freq:** Monthly; **Circ:** 183,000
Usual Pagination: 48
Profile: Women's interest magazine containing short stories, professional advice, cosmetic and health sections.
Language(s): Polish
Mechanical Data: Type Area: 205x295 mm
CONSUMER: WOMEN'S INTEREST CONSUMER MAGAZINES: Women's Interest

---

CIEPŁOWNICTWO, OGRZEWNICTWO, WENTYLACJA 1811043PL3B-4
Editorial: ul. Czackiego, 3/5, 216, 00-043 WARSZAWA **Tel:** 22 828 27 26 **Fax:** 22 828 27 26
Email: cieploogrzewwent@sigma-not.pl **Web site:** http://www.cieplowent.pl
ISSN: 0137-3676
Date Established: 1969; **Freq:** Monthly
Usual Pagination: 40
Profile: Writes about sources of energy, heating installations, central heating, ventilation, air-conditioning, etc.
Language(s): Polish
ADVERTISING RATES:
Full Page Mono .... PLN 1700.00
Full Page Colour .... PLN 3630.00
Mechanical Data: Type Area: 205 x 290 mm
BUSINESS: HEATING & VENTILATION: Industrial Heating & Ventilation

---

CIĘŻARÓWKI I AUTOBUSY
1709042PL77A-26
Editorial: ul. Ostrowskiego, 7, 52-238 WROCŁAW
Tel: 71 780 66 11 **Fax:** 71 780 66 12
Email: redakcja@mpp.pl
ISSN: 1734-0527
Date Established: 2005
Circ: 6,000
Usual Pagination: 78
Profile: Magazine about buses, trucks, vans, testing, accessories, servicing and motoring news.
Language(s): Polish
Mechanical Data: Type Area: 210 x 297 mm
CONSUMER: MOTORING & CYCLING: Motoring

CIO 1709061PL14A-55
Editorial: ul. Jordanowska, 12, 04-204 WARSZAWA
Tel: 22 321 78 00 **Fax:** 22 321 78 88
Email: redakcjacio@idg.com.pl **Web site:** http://www.magazyncio.pl
ISSN: 1733-6651
Date Established: 2002; **Freq:** Monthly; **Circ:** 2,000
Usual Pagination: 64
Advertising Director: Aneta Woźniak
Profile: Magazine on management, IT knowledge, business latest technologies in project management, innovative solutions and their practice in Europe, the USA and Poland.
Language(s): Polish
Mechanical Data: Type Area: 225 x 275 mm
BUSINESS: COMMERCE, INDUSTRY & MANAGEMENT

CITY MAX 1819401PL89C-21
Editorial: ul. Zgoda, 9, 81-361 GDYNIA
Tel: 58 622 63 00 **Fax:** 58 622 63 00
Email: maxicon@maxicon.pl **Web site:** http://www.maxmagazine.pl
Date Established: 1999; **Freq:** 26 issues yearly; **Cover Price:** Free; **Circ:** 90,000
Usual Pagination: 8
Profile: City newsletter providing cultural-entertaining information, concerts, performances reviews and schedules.
Language(s): Polish
Mechanical Data: Type Area: A4
CONSUMER: HOLIDAYS & TRAVEL: Entertainment Guides

CKM 1500394PL86C-5
Editorial: ul. Wilcza, 50/52, 00-679 WARSZAWA
Tel: 22 421 12 46 **Fax:** 22 421 12 00
Email: ckm@ckm.pl **Web site:** http://www.ckm.pl
ISSN: 1505-6562
Date Established: 1998; **Freq:** Monthly; **Circ:** 130,000
Usual Pagination: 140
Advertising Director: Monika Ruszkowska
Profile: Magazine covering lifestyle, relationships, sport and fashion. Features glamour photography and articles on sex issues.
Language(s): Polish
Readership: Aimed at men aged 20 to 40 years.
ADVERTISING RATES:
Full Page Colour .... PLN 49000.00
Mechanical Data: Type Area: 210 x 273mm
CONSUMER: ADULT & GAY MAGAZINES: Men's Lifestyle Magazines

CLAUDIA 1500210PL74A-5
Editorial: ul. Wynalazek, 4, 02-677 WARSZAWA
Tel: 22 607 02 84/86 **Fax:** 22 607 02 90
Email: claudia@claudia.pl **Web site:** http://www.kobieta.pl
ISSN: 1230-8609
Date Established: 1993; **Freq:** Monthly; **Circ:** 697,000
Usual Pagination: 180
Managing Director: Michał Brudzyński; **Advertising Director:** Beata Bartczak
Profile: Women's magazine covering beauty, health, culture, lifestyle, fashion, psychology, law, home finance and cooking.
Language(s): Polish
Mechanical Data: Type Area: 220 x 280 mm, 176 x 224 mm
CONSUMER: WOMEN'S INTEREST CONSUMER MAGAZINES: Women's Interest

---

CLICK 1708755PL78E-5
Editorial: ul. Sukiennice, 6, 50-107 WROCŁAW
Tel: 71 341 20 83 **Fax:** 71 341 99 11
Email: click@click.pl **Web site:** http://www.click.pl
ISSN: 1509-0558
Date Established: 2000; **Freq:** Monthly; **Circ:** 97,500
Usual Pagination: 64
Managing Director: Jerzy Szulwic; **Advertising Director:** Magdalena Milewska
Profile: Provides information on world of computing, Internet and computer games.
Language(s): Polish
ADVERTISING RATES:
Full Page Colour .... PLN 7000.00
Mechanical Data: Type Area: 225x285 mm
CONSUMER: CONSUMER ELECTRONICS: Home Computing

COMPERIA.PL 1967449PL1A-98
Editorial: ul. Płaskowickiej Filipiny 46/33, 02-778 WARSZAWA **Tel:** 22 642 91 19 **Fax:** 22 642 91 19
Email: media@comperia.pl **Web site:** http://www.comperia.pl
Freq: Daily; **Circ:** 282,739 Unique Users
Profile: Comperia.pl is the first website in Poland, providing a comprehensive search of financial products. Contains a tool section: mortgage loans comparison, cash, cars, credit cards, bank deposits and investment funds.
Language(s): Polish
BUSINESS: FINANCE & ECONOMICS

COMPUTERWORLD 1708630PL5C-19
Editorial: ul. Jordanowska, 12, 04-204 WARSZAWA
Tel: 22 321 78 00 **Fax:** 22 321 78 88
Email: cw@idg.com.pl **Web site:** http://www.computerworld.pl
ISSN: 08672334
Date Established: 1990; **Freq:** Weekly; **Circ:** 5,000
Usual Pagination: 40
Advertising Director: Joanna Tarnowska
Profile: Informative investments and strategies in companies, banks, financial institutions. Programming and latest trends in computing solutions.
Language(s): Polish
ADVERTISING RATES:
Full Page Colour .... PLN 12600.00
Mechanical Data: Type Area: 235 x 297 mm
BUSINESS: COMPUTERS & AUTOMATION: Professional Personal Computers

---

CONFERENCE & BUSINESS
1708987PL14A-48
Editorial: ul. Rakietników, 27/29, 10, 02-495 WARSZAWA **Tel:** 22 882 37 33 **Fax:** 22 882 37 66
Email: redakcja@e-conference.pl **Web site:** http://e-conference.pl
ISSN: 1731-1403
Date Established: 2001; **Freq:** Quarterly; **Circ:** 15,000
Usual Pagination: 64
Profile: Magazine containing information on training, hotel business and business meetings and conferences.
Language(s): Polish
Mechanical Data: Type Area: 220x285 mm
BUSINESS: COMMERCE, INDUSTRY & MANAGEMENT

CONTACT INTERNATIONAL BUSINESS VOICE 1835438PL1A-76
Editorial: ul. Fabryczna 16/22, 00-446 WARSZAWA
Tel: 22 320 01 00 **Fax:** 22 621 19 37
Email: editor@bpcc.org.pl **Web site:** http://bpcc.org.pl
Date Established: 1993; **Freq:** 6 issues yearly; **Circ:** 4,000
Usual Pagination: 52
Profile: The magazine's mission is to be a platform for the exchange of business experiences in Poland, increase mutual understanding of potential partners, contribute to strengthening British-Polish trade links.
Language(s): English
ADVERTISING RATES:
Full Page Colour .... PLN 9100.00
Mechanical Data: Type Area: 202 x 272mm
BUSINESS: FINANCE & ECONOMICS

CONTROLLING I RACHUNKOWOŚĆ ZARZĄDCZA
1708876PL14A-38
Editorial: ul. Okopowa, 58/72, 01-042 WARSZAWA
Tel: 22 530 41 73 **Fax:** 22 530 42 22
Email: czytelnicy.controlling@infor.pl **Web site:** http://www.controlling.infor.pl
ISSN: 1428-8117
Date Established: 1999; **Freq:** Monthly
Usual Pagination: 52
Managing Director: Mariusz Drozdowicz
Profile: Magazine focused on controlling, accounting and management, financial analyzing, balance scorecard and Value Based Management.
Language(s): Polish
Mechanical Data: Type Area: A4
BUSINESS: COMMERCE, INDUSTRY & MANAGEMENT

COSMOPOLITAN 754775PL74A-20
Editorial: ul. Wilcza, 50/52, 00-679 WARSZAWA
Tel: 22 421 10 00 **Fax:** 22 421 11 11
Email: cosmo@cosmo.pl **Web site:** http://www.cosmo.pl
ISSN: 1428-2542
Date Established: 1997; **Freq:** Monthly; **Circ:** 177,000
Usual Pagination: 154
Managing Director: Beata Milewska; **Advertising Director:** Julita Ziółkowska
Profile: Magazine covering fashion, beauty, health, travel and work issues.
Language(s): Polish
Readership: Aimed at young, professional women.
ADVERTISING RATES:
Full Page Colour .... PLN 58000.00
Mechanical Data: Type Area: 190 x 253 mm
CONSUMER: WOMEN'S INTEREST CONSUMER MAGAZINES: Women's Interest

---

CRN COMPUTER RESELLER NEWS POLSKA 1708709PL5B-
Editorial: ul. Topiel, 23, 00-342 WARSZAWA
Tel: 22 320 19 00 **Fax:** 22 320 19 01
Email: redakcja@crn.pl **Web site:** http://www.crn.pl
ISSN: 1429-8945
Date Established: 1998; **Freq:** 26 issues yearly; **Cover Price:** Free; **Circ:** 9,000
Usual Pagination: 64
Managing Director: Małgorzata Węgierek Justyna Namięta; **Advertising Director:** Cezary Żelazowski
Profile: Magazine with news in tele-informative industry and IT branch.
Language(s): Polish
Mechanical Data: Type Area: 225 x 320 mm
BUSINESS: COMPUTERS & AUTOMATION: Data Processing

CSO 1796089PL14A-7
Editorial: ul. Jordanowska, 12, 04-204 WARSZAWA
Tel: 22 321 79 96 **Fax:** 22 321 78 88
Email: redakcjacso@idg.com.pl **Web site:** http://www.magazyncso.pl
ISSN: 1734-946X
Date Established: 2005; **Freq:** Quarterly; **Circ:** 4,000
Usual Pagination: 60
Advertising Director: Małgorzata Brudniak
Profile: Magazine on security of business and information.
Language(s): Polish
ADVERTISING RATES:
Full Page Colour .... PLN 12000.0
Mechanical Data: Type Area: 225x275 mm
BUSINESS: COMMERCE, INDUSTRY & MANAGEMENT

CUKIERNICTWO I PIEKARSTWO 1811008PL8A-
Editorial: al. Roździeńskiego, 188, 40-203 KATOWICE **Tel:** 32 788 51 69 **Fax:** 32 788 51 64
Email: cukiernictwo@elamed.pl **Web site:** http://www.cukiernictwo.elamed.pl
ISSN: 1643-9988
Date Established: 1997; **Freq:** Monthly
Usual Pagination: 90
Advertising Director: Barbara Zając
Profile: Focuses on production and new technologies in baking, products and processes, new equipment, recipes, hygiene and safety and introduction of HACCP.
Language(s): Polish
Mechanical Data: Type Area: 204 x 290 mm
BUSINESS: BAKING & CONFECTIONERY: Baking

CZTERY KĄTY 1708661PL74C-20
Editorial: ul. Czerska, 8/10, 00-732 WARSZAWA
Tel: 22 555 68 50 **Fax:** 22 555 66 72
Email: czterykaty@agora.pl **Web site:** http://www.czterykaty.pl
ISSN: 0867-7298
Date Established: 1991; **Freq:** Monthly; **Circ:** 159,000
Usual Pagination: 130
Advertising Director: Elżbieta Kaiser
Profile: Design and interior of flats and houses and modern arrangements.
Language(s): Polish
Mechanical Data: Type Area: 230 x 295 mm
CONSUMER: WOMEN'S INTEREST CONSUMER MAGAZINES: Home & Family

CZYSTA ENERGIA 1811006PL58-4
Editorial: ul. Daleka, 33, 60-124 POZNAŃ
Tel: 61 655 81 50 **Fax:** 61 655 81 01
Email: redakcja@czystaenergia.pl **Web site:** http://www.czystaenergia.pl
Date Established: 2001; **Freq:** Monthly; **Circ:** 6,700
Usual Pagination: 44
Profile: Magazine on energy and environment, alternative sources of energy, new technologies friendly to environment, energy saving issues.
Language(s): Polish
ADVERTISING RATES:
Full Page Colour .... PLN 3300.00
Mechanical Data: Type Area: A4
BUSINESS: ENERGY, FUEL & NUCLEAR

DARMOWE PROGRAMY
1811081PL5D-6
Editorial: ul. Mangalia, 4, 02-758 WARSZAWA
Tel: 22 742 14 55 **Fax:** 22 642 70 05
Email: info@darmowe-programy.com **Web site:** http://www.darmowe-programy.com
ISSN: 1896-955X
Date Established: 2006; **Freq:** Quarterly; **Circ:** 10,000
Profile: Magazine on computing, software and freeware applications.
Language(s): Polish
Mechanical Data: Type Area: 210x297 mm
BUSINESS: COMPUTERS & AUTOMATION: Personal Computers

DECISION MAKER 1708999PL14A-49
Editorial: ul. ks. J. Popiełuszki, 19/21, 01-595 WARSZAWA **Tel:** 22 833 14 07 **Fax:** 22 833 14 07
Email: editor@decisionmaker.pl **Web site:** http://www.decisionmaker.pl
ISSN: 1731-2051

ate Established: 2004
over Price: Free; Circ: 5,000
sual Pagination: 32
rofile: Focuses on Polish lobbying in Europe and orldwide, promotion of Poland, its regions and its chievements.
anguage(s): Polish
Mechanical Data: Type Area: A4
BUSINESS: COMMERCE, INDUSTRY & MANAGEMENT

DECYDENT
1708673PL14A-12
Editorial: ul. ks. J. Popiełuszki, 19/21, 01-595 WARSZAWA **Tel:** 22 833 14 07 **Fax:** 22 833 14 07
Email: decydent@decydent.pl **Web site:** http://www.decydent.pl
ISSN: 1508-5635
Date Established: 1999
Cover Price: Free; **Circ:** 5,000
Usual Pagination: 32
Profile: Focuses on political and economical lobbying, public affairs, PR, advertising brand campaigns.
Language(s): Polish
Mechanical Data: Type Area: A4
BUSINESS: COMMERCE, INDUSTRY & MANAGEMENT

DEDAL
1708882PL84A-8
Editorial: ul. Zbożowa, 4, 25-416 KIELCE
Tel: 41 344 38 77 **Fax:** 41 344 38 77
Email: redakcja@dedal.info.pl **Web site:** http://www.dedal.info.pl
ISSN: 1732-6478
Date Established: 2004
Circ: 1,000
Usual Pagination: 80
Profile: Cultural magazine with aspects on regional arts, music, crafts, literature and history.
Language(s): Polish
Mechanical Data: Type Area: A4
CONSUMER: THE ARTS & LITERARY: Arts

DEKARZ I CIEŚLA
1810911PL42A-6
Editorial: ul. Łucka, 15, 1907, 00-842 WARSZAWA
Tel: 515 251 052
Email: dekarz@ardo.pl **Web site:** http://www.fachowydekarz.pl
ISSN: 1898-1534
Date Established: 2007; **Freq:** Quarterly; **Cover Price:** Free; **Circ:** 5,000
Usual Pagination: 48
Advertising Director: Marcin Sikora
Language(s): Polish
Readership: Magazine aimed at carpenters and roof-building workers.
Mechanical Data: Type Area: 200 x 283 mm
BUSINESS: CONSTRUCTION

DESIGN NEWS POLSKA
1835844PL19J-1
Editorial: ul. Wita Stwosza 59a, 02-661 WARSZAWA
Tel: 22 852 44 15 **Fax:** 22 899 29 48
Email: redakcja@designnews.pl **Web site:** http://www.designnews.pl
Freq: Monthly; **Circ:** 5,000
Editor-in-Chief: Krzysztof Ziemkiewicz
Profile: Professional magazine covering engineering design and constructions industry. Delivers critical technical information about technologies, solutions and products including CAD, CAM, CAx, mechanics, electronics, materials, fastening & assembly, hydraulics & pneumatics, power transmission.
Language(s): Polish
Readership: Aimed at engineers who design and engineer products for a range of industries and at management staff from manufacturing companies.
ADVERTISING RATES:
Full Page Colour .... PLN 3940.00
Mechanical Data: Type Area: 212 x 276mm
BUSINESS: ENGINEERING & MACHINERY: CAD & CIM (Computer Integrated Manufacture)

DETAL DZISIAJ
1708761PL53-7
Editorial: ul. Puławska 405, 16, 02-801 WARSZAWA
Tel: 22 257 06 00 **Fax:** 22 257 06 01
Email: redakcjadd@detaldzisiaj.com.pl **Web site:** http://www.detaldzisiaj.com.pl
ISSN: 1640-0909
Freq: 26 issues yearly - dwutygodnik; **Circ:** 83,000
Usual Pagination: 32
Editor: Łukasz Izakowski; **Editor-in-Chief:** Robert Szewczyk; **Advertising Director:** Tomasz Chrzanowski
Profile: Magazine focused on problems of retail sector.
Language(s): Polish
ADVERTISING RATES:
Full Page Colour .... PLN 52000
Mechanical Data: Type Area: 277 x 390 mm, Col Length: 350mm
BUSINESS: RETAILING & WHOLESALING

DIABETOLOGIA DOŚWIADCZALNA I KLINICZNA
1709015PL56A-50
Editorial: ul. Świętokrzyska 73, 80-180 GDAŃSK
Tel: 58 320 94 94 **Fax:** 58 320 94 60
Email: marketing@viamedica.pl **Web site:** http://www.viamedica.pl
Freq: 6 issues yearly; **Circ:** 2,500
Advertising Director: Krzysztof Słomiński
Profile: Journal of the Polish Diabetes Association offers original papers by Poland's most recognized specialists and in part also review articles presenting the latest developments in the field of diabetology. It also aims at presenting the most active diabetological centres in Poland.
Language(s): English; Polish
BUSINESS: HEALTH & MEDICAL

DIABETOLOGIA PRAKTYCZNA
1796154PL56A-24
Editorial: ul. Świętokrzyska 73, 80-180 GDAŃSK
Tel: 58 320 94 94 **Fax:** 58 320 94 60
Email: marketing@viamedica.pl **Web site:** http://www.viamedica.pl
ISSN: 1640-8497
Freq: 6 issues yearly; **Circ:** 2,000
Usual Pagination: 42
Managing Director: Łuczyńska; **Advertising Director:** Krzysztof Słomiński
Profile: Educational and scientific journal of Polish Diabetes Association aimed primarily at general practitioners. Contains editorials, original articles, reviews, commentaries, letters to Editor and translated articles from leading journals of the American Diabetes Association.
Language(s): Polish
ADVERTISING RATES:
Full Page Colour .... PLN 6000.00
BUSINESS: HEALTH & MEDICAL

DIGITAL FOTO VIDEO
1929046PL85A-5
Editorial: ul. Tytoniowa, 20, 04-228 WARSZAWA
Tel: 22 515 02 91 **Fax:** 22 613 25 84
Email: t.kulas@dfv.pl **Web site:** http://www.dfv.pl
Date Established: 2007; **Freq:** Monthly; **Circ:** 20,000
Advertising Director: Ewa Majerska
Profile: Magazine dedicated to digital photography and digital video.
Language(s): Polish
ADVERTISING RATES:
Full Page Colour .... PLN 11550.00
CONSUMER: PHOTOGRAPHY & FILM MAKING: Photography

DLACZEGO
1708740PL83-5
Editorial: Al. Jerozolimskie, 146c, 02-305 WARSZAWA **Tel:** 22 347 50 00 **Fax:** 22 347 50 01
Email: redakcja@dlaczego.korba.pl **Web site:** http://www.dlaczego.korba.pl
ISSN: 1429-8252
Date Established: 1998; **Freq:** Monthly; **Cover Price:** PLN 5.99; **Circ:** 70,000
Usual Pagination: 116
Profile: Magazine featuring information on job career, university studies, money, lifestyle and culture.
Language(s): Polish
Mechanical Data: Type Area: 215 x 280 mm
CONSUMER: STUDENT PUBLICATIONS

DLATEGO
1819626PL83-7
Editorial: Al. Jerozolimskie, 146c, 02-305 WARSZAWA **Tel:** 22 347 50 00 **Fax:** 22 347 50 01
Email: redakcja@dlaczego.korba.pl **Web site:** http://www.dlaczego.korba.pl
Freq: Annual; **Cover Price:** Free; **Circ:** 300,000
Usual Pagination: 48
Managing Director: Robert Pstrokoński; **Advertising Director:** Ewa Szczegielniak
Profile: Presents students' life overview, holidays reviews, fashion calendar, newest models, testing of holidays equipment.
Language(s): Polish
Mechanical Data: Type Area: A3
CONSUMER: STUDENT PUBLICATIONS

DOBRE RADY
1708656PL74A-1010
Editorial: ul. Warecka, 11a, 00-034 WARSZAWA
Tel: 22 448 83 35 **Fax:** 22 448 80 01
Email: dobrerady@burda.pl **Web site:** http://www.burdamedia.pl
ISSN: 1643-8264
Date Established: 2002; **Freq:** Monthly; **Circ:** 236,000
Usual Pagination: 116
Managing Director: Justyna Namięta, 071 376 28 00 Małgorzata Węgierek, 022 44 88 327; **Advertising Director:** Barbara Ożóg
Profile: Advice on every day life: health and beauty, fashion and cooking, job career and family relations.
Language(s): Polish
Mechanical Data: Type Area: 210 x 270 mm
CONSUMER: WOMEN'S INTEREST CONSUMER MAGAZINES: Women's Interest

DOBRE WNĘTRZE
1616344PL4B-1
Editorial: ul. Kamionkowska, 45, 03-812 WARSZAWA **Tel:** 22 590 50 29 **Fax:** 22 590 54 55
Email: dobre_wnetrze@murator.com.pl **Web site:** http://www.dobrewnetrze.pl
ISSN: 1429-3226
Date Established: 1998; **Freq:** Monthly; **Circ:** 38,000
Usual Pagination: 168
Managing Director: Katarzyna Białek; **Advertising Director:** Anna Dygasiewicz-Piwko
Profile: Magazine about interior design, modern patterns and designs, newest trends.
Language(s): Polish
Mechanical Data: Type Area: 230 x 295 mm
BUSINESS: ARCHITECTURE & BUILDING: Interior Design & Flooring

DOBRE WNĘTRZE NUMER SPECJALNY
1796074PL4B-4
Editorial: ul. Kamionkowska, 45, 03-812 WARSZAWA **Tel:** 22 590 50 29 **Fax:** 22 590 51 35
Email: dobre_wnetrze@murator.com.pl **Web site:** http://www.dobrewnetrze.pl
ISSN: 1733-5396
Date Established: 2004; **Freq:** Half-yearly; **Circ:** 28,000
Usual Pagination: 144
Managing Director: Katarzyna Białek; **Advertising Director:** Anna Dygasiewicz-Piwko
Profile: Magazine about interior design in living rooms, bathrooms and kitchens and newest trends.
Language(s): Polish
Mechanical Data: Type Area: 230 x 295 mm
BUSINESS: ARCHITECTURE & BUILDING: Interior Design & Flooring

DOKUMENTACJA KADROWA
1810916PL14F-7
Editorial: ul. Łotewska, 9a, 03-918 WARSZAWA
Tel: 22 518 29 29 **Fax:** 22 617 60 10
Email: dokumentacjakadrowa@wip.pl **Web site:** http://www.dokumentacjakadrowa.pl
Date Established: 1999
Usual Pagination: 500
Profile: Magazine presenting human resources knowledge, changes in work law, templates how to prepare HR documents.
Language(s): Polish
Mechanical Data: Type Area: segregator A5, CD-ROM
BUSINESS: COMMERCE, INDUSTRY & MANAGEMENT: Training & Recruitment

DOM DLA POCZĄTKUJĄCYCH
1796165PL4E-6
Editorial: ul. Andersa, 38, 15-113 BIAŁYSTOK
Tel: 85 653 90 00 **Fax:** 85 653 98 56
Email: dom@publikator.com.pl **Web site:** http://www.publikator.com.pl
ISSN: 1895-4251
Date Established: 2006; **Freq:** Monthly; **Circ:** 20,000
Usual Pagination: 128
Managing Director: Anita Frank; **Advertising Director:** Alicja Klimowicz
Profile: Magazine on building a house, materials and renovations.
Language(s): Polish
Mechanical Data: Type Area: 230 x 297 mm
BUSINESS: ARCHITECTURE & BUILDING: Building

DOM & WNĘTRZE
1708923PL4A-21
Editorial: ul. Wiejska, 19, 00-480 WARSZAWA
Tel: 22 584 22 00 **Fax:** 22 584 23 18
Email: info@domiwnetrze.pl **Web site:** http://www.domiwnetrze.pl
ISSN: 0867-2105
Date Established: 1996; **Freq:** Monthly; **Circ:** 40,000
Usual Pagination: 141
Managing Director: Alicja Modzelewska; **Advertising Director:** Małgorzata Pędzich
Profile: Magazine on interior design and architecture.
Language(s): Polish
Mechanical Data: Type Area: 225 x 290 mm
BUSINESS: ARCHITECTURE & BUILDING: Architecture

DOM POLSKI
1796217PL4E-10
Editorial: ul. Leszczynowa, 11, 03-197 WARSZAWA
Tel: 22 257 84 72 **Fax:** 22 568 99 77
Email: ernest@budujemydom.pl **Web site:** http://www.budujemydom.pl
ISSN: 1734-6207
Date Established: 2005; **Freq:** Annual; **Cover Price:** PLN 15.00; **Circ:** 40,000
Usual Pagination: 300
Managing Director: Ernest Jagodziński; **Advertising Director:** Iza Konikowska
Profile: Magazine on building a house according to a particular project, new technologies and estimated costs.
Language(s): Polish
Mechanical Data: Type Area: 202 x 290 mm
BUSINESS: ARCHITECTURE & BUILDING: Building

DOMY JEDNORODZINNE
1708712PL4A-8
Editorial: ul. Stokrotek, 51, 43-384 JAWORZE
Tel: 33 817 38 79 **Fax:** 33 817 36 31
Email: karolina.polinska@kwiecinski.pl **Web site:** http://www.kwiecinski.pl
ISSN: 1234-1401
Date Established: 1996; **Freq:** Monthly
Usual Pagination: 56
Advertising Director: Karolina Polińska
Profile: Magazine focused on architecture, building, interior design and projects.
Language(s): Polish
Mechanical Data: Type Area: 222x290 mm
BUSINESS: ARCHITECTURE & BUILDING: Architecture

DORADCA ENERGETYCZNY
1819569PL58-3
Editorial: al. Komisji Edukacji Narodowej, 95, 02-777 WARSZAWA **Tel:** 22 678 35 92 **Fax:** 22 678 32 52
Email: de@doradcaenergetyczny.pl **Web site:** http://www.doradcaenergetyczny.pl
ISSN: 1897-6204
Date Established: 2007; **Freq:** Monthly; **Circ:** 6,000
Usual Pagination: 52
Editor: Jerzy Wierzbowski
Profile: Informative-practical magazine with news in energy sector, effectiveness of energy -saving building and recycling sources of energy.
Language(s): Polish
Mechanical Data: Type Area: A4
BUSINESS: ENERGY, FUEL & NUCLEAR

DORADCA PODATNIKA
1708858PL1M-9
Editorial: ul. Okrzei, 1a, 03-715 WARSZAWA
Tel: 22 333 80 00 **Fax:** 22 333 88 99
Email: w.moczydlowska@wtrendy.pl **Web site:** http://www.e-podatnik.pl
ISSN: 1231-3084
Date Established: 1993; **Freq:** Weekly; **Circ:** 4,000
Usual Pagination: 80
Managing Director: Windorbski; **Advertising Director:** Małgorzata Skrobiszewska
Profile: Providing practical information on taxation, VAT, insurance and financial legal issues.
Language(s): Polish
BUSINESS: FINANCE & ECONOMICS: Taxation

DOZÓR TECHNICZNY
1811045PL19A-8
Editorial: ul. Szczęśliwicka, 34, 02-353 WARSZAWA
Tel: 22 527 21 15 **Fax:** 22 822 72 09
Email: dozortechniczny@sigma-not.pl **Web site:** http://sigma-not.pl
ISSN: 0209-1763
Date Established: 1969; **Freq:** 6 issues yearly
Usual Pagination: 24
Profile: Technical surveillance of technical devices and machines, their production and exploitation.
ADVERTISING RATES:
Full Page Mono .... PLN 1700.00
Full Page Colour .... PLN 3400.00
Mechanical Data: Type Area: 205 x 290 mm
BUSINESS: ENGINEERING & MACHINERY

DRWAL
1709063PL46-1
Editorial: ul. Kaliska, 1, 8, 02-316 WARSZAWA
Tel: 22 822 10 26 **Fax:** 22 822 66 49
Email: drwal@oikos.net.pl **Web site:** http://drwal.net.pl
ISSN: 1733-4578
Date Established: 2004; **Freq:** Monthly; **Circ:** 2,000
Usual Pagination: 44
Profile: Contains practical advice on usage of forestry machines and tools, new forestry technologies.
Language(s): Polish
Mechanical Data: Type Area: 205 x 286 mm
BUSINESS: TIMBER, WOOD & FORESTRY

DZIECKO
1626018PL74D-2
Editorial: ul. Czerska, 8/10, 00-732 WARSZAWA
Tel: 22 555 68 84 **Fax:** 22 555 66 69
Email: dziecko@agora.pl **Web site:** http://www.edziecko.pl
ISSN: 1233-2984
Date Established: 1995; **Freq:** Monthly; **Circ:** 156,000
Usual Pagination: 96
Advertising Director: Beata Remjasz
Profile: Magazine covering all aspects of parenthood, including education, activities, information and health updates.
Language(s): Polish
Readership: Read by parents of young children.
Mechanical Data: Type Area: 213 x 272 mm
CONSUMER: WOMEN'S INTEREST CONSUMER MAGAZINES: Child Care

DZIENNIK GAZETA PRAWNA
1795587PL65A-40
Formerly: Dziennik
Editorial: ul.Okopowa 58/72, 01-042 WARSZAWA
Tel: 22 531 48 00 **Fax:** 22 530 40 39
Email: dziennik@dziennik.pl **Web site:** http://www.dziennik.pl
Date Established: 2006; **Freq:** Daily; **Circ:** 126,093
Usual Pagination: 40
Managing Director: Michał Zgorzelski; **Publisher:** Michał Zgorzelski
Profile: A serious opinion -creating daily newspaper covering politics, economics, business, law and social issues.
Language(s): Polish
ADVERTISING RATES:
Full Page Mono .... PLN 39330.00
Full Page Colour .... PLN 51130.00

Mechanical Data: Type Area: 252x339 mm
NATIONAL DAILY & SUNDAY NEWSPAPERS: National Daily Newspapers

DZIENNIK ŁÓDZKI - WIADOMOŚCI DNIA 1201438PL67B-1
Editorial: ul. ks. I. Skorupki, 17/19, 90-532 ŁÓDŹ
Tel: 42 665 91 04 **Fax:** 42 665 91 01
Email: dziennik@dziennik.lodz.pl **Web site:** http://www.dziennik.lodz.pl
ISSN: 0208-7707
Date Established: 1884; **Freq:** Daily; **Circ:** 43,836
Usual Pagination: 32
Advertising Director: Michał Frontczak
Profile: A socio-political daily newspaper covering national and regional news.
Language(s): Polish
ADVERTISING RATES:
Full Page Colour .... PLN 18200.00
Mechanical Data: Type Area: 289 x 390 mm
REGIONAL DAILY & SUNDAY NEWSPAPERS: Regional Daily Newspapers

DZIENNIK POLSKI 1795588PL67B-40
Editorial: ul. Wielopole, 1, 31-072 KRAKÓW
Tel: 12 619 92 00 **Fax:** 12 619 92 75
Email: redakcja@dziennik.krakow.pl **Web site:** http://dziennik.krakow.pl
ISSN: 0137-9089
Date Established: 1945; **Freq:** Daily; **Circ:** 42,376
Usual Pagination: 48
News Editor: Marek Halberda; **Managing Director:** Tomasz Maciejowski; **Advertising Director:** Renata Tracz
Profile: Regional newspaper covering national and regional news, social issues, culture, sports, economics and business.
Language(s): Polish
ADVERTISING RATES:
Full Page Colour .... PLN 19000.00
Mechanical Data: Type Area: A3
REGIONAL DAILY & SUNDAY NEWSPAPERS: Regional Daily Newspapers

EASYLINUX 1810900PL5C-12
Editorial: ul. Mangalia, 4, 02-758 WARSZAWA
Tel: 22 742 14 55 **Fax:** 22 642 70 05
Email: info@easylinux.pl **Web site:** http://www.easylinux.pl
Date Established: 2005
Circ: 10,000
Usual Pagination: 24
Profile: Magazine about computing and computer software.
Language(s): Polish
Mechanical Data: Type Area: A4
BUSINESS: COMPUTERS & AUTOMATION: Professional Personal Computers

ECHO MIASTA KRAKÓW
1819718PL72I-1
Editorial: ul. Dietla, 50/6, 31-039 KRAKÓW
Tel: 12 428 76 03 **Fax:** 12 376 45 81
Email: redakcja.krakow@echomiasta.pl **Web site:** http://www.echomiasta.pl
ISSN: 1734-6037
Date Established: 2005
Usual Pagination: 16
Advertising Director: Aneta Sarga
Profile: Newspaper covering regional and local news.
Language(s): Polish
Mechanical Data: Type Area: A3
LOCAL NEWSPAPERS: Regional Weekly Newspapers

EDEN 1709098PL74G-17
Editorial: ul. Marii Konopnickiej, 6, 00-491 WARSZAWA **Tel:** 22 625 59 24 **Fax:** 22 625 59 24
Email: eden@vimedia.com.pl **Web site:** http://www.spaeden.pl
ISSN: 1734-5456
Date Established: 2005; **Freq:** Monthly; **Circ:** 22,000
Usual Pagination: 68
Advertising Director: Marzena Szczecińska
Profile: Magazine focused on beauty, spa, home & wellness.
Language(s): Polish
Mechanical Data: Type Area: 210 x 275 mm
CONSUMER: WOMEN'S INTEREST CONSUMER MAGAZINES: Slimming & Health

EDUKACJA I DIALOG 1929226PL88R-4
Editorial: ul. Nowy Świat, 39, 00-029 WARSZAWA
Tel: 22 826 78 64 **Fax:** 22 826 78 64
Email: witold.kolodziejczyk@eid.edu.pl **Web site:** http://www.eid.edu.pl
Date Established: 1985; **Freq:** Monthly
Usual Pagination: 80
Advertising Director: Piotr Woźniak
Profile: Magazine covering aspects of pedagogics, psychology, IT technology at schools, teaching methods and didactics.
Language(s): Polish
ADVERTISING RATES:
Full Page Colour .... PLN 1000.00
Mechanical Data: Type Area: A4
CONSUMER: EDUCATION: Education Related

EDUKACJA PRAWNICZA
1708841PL44-4
Editorial: ul. Bonifraterska, 17, 00-203 WARSZAWA
Tel: 22 337 76 00 **Fax:** 22 337 74 91
Email: edukacjaprawnicza@beck.pl **Web site:** http://www.edukacjaprawnicza.pl
ISSN: 1231-0336
Date Established: 1997
Circ: 6,000
Usual Pagination: 48
Profile: Magazine containing legal advice, educational materials for lawyers exams, legal documentation overview and information on law and courts.
Language(s): Polish
Mechanical Data: Type Area: 204 x 287 mm
BUSINESS: LEGAL

EKOLOGIA 1810969PL57-6
Editorial: ul. Porcelanowa, 11c, 40-246 KATOWICE
Tel: 32 730 32 32 **Fax:** 32 258 16 45
Email: ekologia@grupainfomax.com **Web site:** http://www.ekologia-info.pl
Date Established: 1992; **Freq:** Quarterly; **Circ:** 5,000
Usual Pagination: 52
Managing Director: Jacek Szczęsny
Profile: Magazine on environment and industries, communal news, legal advice and latest research and innovations.
Language(s): Polish
Mechanical Data: Type Area: 213x305 mm
BUSINESS: ENVIRONMENT & POLLUTION

EKSPERT BUDOWLANY
1929123PL4E-37
Editorial: ul. Karczewska, 18, 04-112 WARSZAWA
Tel: 22 810 23 18 **Fax:** 22 810 27 42
Email: redakcja@ekspertbudowlany.pl **Web site:** http://www.ekspertbudowlany.pl
ISSN: 1730-1904
Date Established: 2003; **Freq:** Quarterly; **Cover Price:** Free; **Circ:** 55,000
Usual Pagination: 100
Advertising Director: Joanna Grabek
Profile: Professional magazine dedicated to building, installations, interiors and gardens.
Language(s): Polish
Mechanical Data: Type Area: 205 x 295 mm
BUSINESS: ARCHITECTURE & BUILDING: Building

ELEKTRO.INFO 1929116PL17-3
Editorial: ul. Karczewska, 18, 04-112 WARSZAWA
Tel: 22 810 65 61 **Fax:** 22 810 27 42
Email: redakcja@elektro.info.pl **Web site:** http://www.elektro.info.pl
ISSN: 1642-8722
Date Established: 2001; **Freq:** Monthly; **Circ:** 15,000
Usual Pagination: 80
Advertising Director: Joanna Grabek
Profile: Magazine dedicated to electro industry, electrical technologies, electro energy and its distribution.
Language(s): Polish
Readership: Aimed at designers, electricians, installators and technicians.
Mechanical Data: Type Area: 210 x 297 mm
BUSINESS: ELECTRICAL

ELEKTROINSTALATOR
766101PL19A-1
Editorial: al. Komisji Edukacji Narodowej, 95, 02-777 WARSZAWA **Tel:** 22 678 37 47 **Fax:** 22 678 61 38
Email: ei@elektroinstalator.com.pl **Web site:** http://elektroinstalator.com.pl
ISSN: 1231-2355
Date Established: 1994; **Freq:** Monthly; **Circ:** 9,000
Usual Pagination: 90
Advertising Director: Sławomir Zalewski
Profile: Magazine focusing on electrical engineering, machinery and installation equipment.
Language(s): Polish
Readership: Read by electrical engineers and installation engineers.
Mechanical Data: Type Area: A4
BUSINESS: ENGINEERING & MACHINERY

ELEKTRONIK 1796223PL18A-116
Editorial: ul. Leszczynowa, 11, 03-197 WARSZAWA
Tel: 22 257 84 65 **Fax:** 22 257 84 67
Email: elektronik@elektronik.com.pl **Web site:** http://www.elektronikab2b.pl
ISSN: 1248-4030
Date Established: 1997; **Freq:** Monthly; **Circ:** 10,000
Usual Pagination: 100
Advertising Director: Katarzyna Wiśniewska
Profile: Professional magazine on electronics and new technologies.
Language(s): Polish
Mechanical Data: Type Area: 205 x 290 mm
BUSINESS: ELECTRONICS

ELEKTRONIKA DLA WSZYSTKICH
708210PL18A-110
Editorial: ul. Leszczynowa, 11, 03-197 WARSZAWA
Tel: 22 786 26 58 **Fax:** 22 257 84 00
Email: edw@elportal.pl **Web site:** http://www.elportal.pl
Date Established: 1996; **Freq:** Monthly; **Circ:** 40,000
Usual Pagination: 84
Profile: Magazine providing in-depth coverage on a variety of aspects from the world of electronics.
Language(s): Polish
Readership: Aimed at all involved in the electronics sector from professional engineers to amateur enthusiasts.
Mechanical Data: Type Area: A4
BUSINESS: ELECTRONICS

ELEKTRONIKA - KONSTRUKCJE, TECHNOLOGIE, ZASTOSOWANIA 1811046PL18A-118
Editorial: ul. Chmielna, 6, 6, 00-020 WARSZAWA
Tel: 22 827 38 79 **Fax:** 22 827 38 79
Email: elektronika@red.pl.pl **Web site:** http://elektronika.orf.pl
ISSN: 0033-2089
Date Established: 1960; **Freq:** Monthly
Usual Pagination: 68
Profile: Magazine on electronic technologies, microelectronics, testing and electromagnetic compatibility, IT - technologies.
Language(s): Polish
ADVERTISING RATES:
Full Page Mono .... PLN 900.00
Full Page Colour .... PLN 1950.00
Mechanical Data: Type Area: 205 x 290 mm
BUSINESS: ELECTRONICS

ELEKTRONIKA PRAKTYCZNA
634319PL18A-115
Editorial: ul. Leszczynowa, 11, 03-197 WARSZAWA
Tel: 22 257 84 65 **Fax:** 22 257 84 67
Email: redakcja@ep.com.pl **Web site:** http://www.ep.com.pl
Date Established: 1993; **Freq:** Monthly; **Circ:** 29,000
Usual Pagination: 160
Advertising Director: Katarzyna Wiśniewska
Profile: Magazine focusing on electronic design, construction and automation.
Language(s): Polish
Readership: Aimed at electronic engineers and designers.
Mechanical Data: Type Area: A4
BUSINESS: ELECTRONICS

ELLE 749729PL74B-107
Editorial: ul. Warecka, 11a, 00-034 WARSZAWA
Tel: 22 448 83 14 **Fax:** 22 448 80 01
Email: bozena.kiszczak@elle.com.pl **Web site:** http://www.burdamedia.pl
ISSN: 1232-8308
Date Established: 1994; **Freq:** Monthly; **Circ:** 146,000
Usual Pagination: 188
Managing Director: Justyna Namięta, 071 37 62 800 Małgorzata Węgierek, 022 44 88 327; **Advertising Director:** Ewa Kudasiewicz-Winkler
Profile: Magazine featuring fashion, beauty, health and articles on women's issues.
Language(s): Polish
ADVERTISING RATES:
Full Page Colour .... PLN 48900.00
Mechanical Data: Type Area: 210 x 280 mm
CONSUMER: WOMEN'S INTEREST CONSUMER MAGAZINES: Women's Interest - Fashion

ELLE DECORATION 1795644PL4B-3
Editorial: ul. Warecka, 11a, 00-034 WARSZAWA
Tel: 22 448 83 15 **Fax:** 22 448 80 01
Email: anna.chwalinska@elledeco.com.pl **Web site:** http://www.burdamedia.pl
ISSN: 1640-9027
Date Established: 2000; **Freq:** Monthly; **Circ:** 28,000
Usual Pagination: 124
Managing Director: Justyna Namięta, 071 37 62 800 Małgorzata Węgierek, 022 44 88 327; **Advertising Director:** Anna Zabłocka
Profile: Magazine focused on interior design and interior arrangements.
Language(s): Polish
Mechanical Data: Type Area: 230 x 285 mm
BUSINESS: ARCHITECTURE & BUILDING: Interior Design & Flooring

ENERGIA & PRZEMYSŁ
1810917PL58-5
Editorial: ul. Tytoniowa, 20, 04-228 WARSZAWA
Tel: 22 515 00 53 **Fax:** 22 613 25 84
Email: d.zielinska@migutmedia.pl **Web site:** http://www.energiaiprzemysl.pl
ISSN: 1896-5814
Date Established: 2002; **Freq:** Monthly; **Circ:** 10,000
Usual Pagination: 48
Advertising Director: Magda Mroczek
Profile: Magazine containing articles about energy market and gas and petrol industry.
Language(s): Polish
Mechanical Data: Type Area: A4
BUSINESS: ENERGY, FUEL & NUCLEAR

ESTRADA I STUDIO 1708720PL78R-2
Editorial: ul. Leszczynowa, 11, 03-197 WARSZAWA
Tel: 22 257 84 99 **Fax:** 22 257 84 32
Email: info@eis.com.pl **Web site:** http://www.eis.com.pl
ISSN: 1427-0404
Date Established: 1996; **Freq:** Monthly; **Circ:** 12,00
Usual Pagination: 172
Profile: Modern technologies in music, instruments and equipment, sound technologies, interviews with experts, stage sounding and lightning.
Language(s): Polish
Mechanical Data: Type Area: 205 x 275 mm
CONSUMER: CONSUMER ELECTRONICS: Consumer Electronics Related

EUROBUILD 1835770PL1E-1
Editorial: Al. Jerozolimskie 53, 00-697 WARSZAWA
Tel: 22 356 25 00 **Fax:** 22 356 25 01
Email: eurobuild@eurobuildcee.com **Web site:** http://www.eurobuild.pl
Freq: Monthly; **Annual Sub.:** EUR 150.00; **Circ:** 70,000
Editor: Magda Konstantynowicz; **Managing Director:** Ernest Kiruja
Profile: Provides information on Polish property, real estate and construction market with news, analyses, forecasts and regulations. Supplies information on major projects and mergers, and most vital business contacts.
Language(s): English; Polish
Readership: Aimed at investors, construction companies and property firms on Polish market.
ADVERTISING RATES:
Full Page Colour .... PLN 4235.0
Mechanical Data: Type Area: 210 x 297 +5 mm
BUSINESS: FINANCE & ECONOMICS: Property

EUROPEJSKI DORADCA SAMORZĄDOWY 1811091PL44-17
Editorial: ul. Solec, 101, 5, 00-382 WARSZAWA
Tel: 22 629 18 76 **Fax:** 22 629 18 72
Email: redakcja@doradcasamorzadowy.pl **Web site:** http://www.doradcasamorzadowy.pl
ISSN: 1897-7456
Date Established: 2006; **Freq:** Quarterly; **Circ:** 3,000
Usual Pagination: 104
Managing Director: Waldemar Zbytek
Profile: Magazine on EU funds for local governments, other sources of funding and development of the regional councils.
Language(s): Polish
Mechanical Data: Type Area: 205 x 287 mm
BUSINESS: LEGAL

EXKLUSIV XMAGAZYN
1795988PL74Q-23
Editorial: ul. Elbląska, 15/17, 01-747 WARSZAWA
Tel: 22 639 85 67/68 **Fax:** 22 639 85 69
Email: zziomecka@valkea.com **Web site:** http://www.x-mag.pl
ISSN: 1731-6642
Date Established: 2003; **Freq:** Monthly; **Circ:** 65,000
Usual Pagination: 96
Managing Director: Monika Stawicka; **Advertising Director:** Zuzanna Partyka
Profile: Controversial opinions, gossip and interviews.
Language(s): Polish
Mechanical Data: Type Area: 230 x 297 mm
CONSUMER: WOMEN'S INTEREST CONSUMER MAGAZINES: Lifestyle

EXPRESS ILUSTROWANY
765504PL67B-2
Editorial: ul. ks. I. Skorupki, 17/19, 90-532 ŁÓDŹ
Tel: 42 665 92 03 **Fax:** 42 665 92 06
Email: express@express.lodz.pl **Web site:** http://www.express.lodz.pl
ISSN: 0137-9097
Date Established: 1923; **Freq:** Daily; **Circ:** 50,891
Usual Pagination: 28
Advertising Director: Michał Frontczak
Profile: Provides domestic information and from abroad, regional news, politics, entertainment and sports.
Language(s): Polish
ADVERTISING RATES:
Full Page Mono .... PLN 900.00
Mechanical Data: Type Area: 289 x 390 mm
REGIONAL DAILY & SUNDAY NEWSPAPERS: Regional Daily Newspapers

F1 RACING 1708689PL77D-1
Editorial: ul. Piotrkowska, 94, 90-103 ŁÓDŹ
Tel: 42 632 61 79 **Fax:** 42 632 07 59
Email: turski@f1racing.pl **Web site:** http://www.f1racing.pl
ISSN: 1732-7032
Date Established: 2004; **Freq:** Monthly; **Circ:** 15,000
Usual Pagination: 100
Advertising Director: Agnieszka Borzym
Profile: Formula 1: people and money.
Language(s): Polish
Mechanical Data: Type Area: 205 x 275 mm
CONSUMER: MOTORING & CYCLING: Motor Sports

FACHOWY ELEKTRYK
1796177PL17-1
Editorial: ul. Łucka, 15, 1907, 00-842 WARSZAWA
Tel: 22 635 41 08

Web site: http://www.fachowyelektryk.pl
ISSN: 1643-7209
Date Established: 2004; Freq: 6 issues yearly;
Cover Price: Free; Circ: 5,000
Usual Pagination: 60
Advertising Director: Robert Karwowski
Profile: Contains professional advice for electro installation specialists.
Language(s): Polish
Mechanical Data: Type Area: 200 x 283 mm
BUSINESS: ELECTRICAL

FACHOWY INSTALATOR
1796182PL3D-2
Editorial: ul. Łucka, 15, 1907, 00-842 WARSZAWA
Tel: 22 635 41 08
Web site: http://www.fachowyinstalator.pl
Date Established: 2006; Freq: 6 issues yearly;
Cover Price: Free; Circ: 6,000
Usual Pagination: 40
Advertising Director: Robert Karwowski
Profile: Providing professional advice for electro installation specialists.
Language(s): Polish
Mechanical Data: Type Area: 200 x 283 mm
BUSINESS: HEATING & VENTILATION: Heating & Plumbing

FAKT
1640035PL65A-30
Editorial: ul. Domaniewska, 52, 02-672 WARSZAWA
Tel: 22 232 02 00 Fax: 22 232 55 11
Email: redakcja@efakt.pl Web site: http://www.eFakt.pl
ISSN: 1731-7118
Date Established: 2003; Freq: Daily; Circ: 443,427
Usual Pagination: 24
Managing Director: Marcin Biegluk
Profile: National newspaper covering current affairs, national and international news, politics and economy.
Language(s): Polish
Mechanical Data: Type Area: 252 x 339 mm
NATIONAL DAILY & SUNDAY NEWSPAPERS: National Daily Newspapers

FAKTY
1796129PL1R-4
Editorial: ul. Korfantego 75, 01-496 WARSZAWA
Tel: 22 832 42 51 Fax: 22 832 24 99
Email: fakty@maxmedia.org.pl Web site: http://www.magazynfakty.pl
ISSN: 1644-3055
Date Established: 2002; Freq: 6 issues yearly; Circ: 15,000
Usual Pagination: 120
Profile: A prestigious magazine touching on main aspects of Polish economic and political life. The close cooperation with ministries, economic, trade and business chambers lets it follow the most important issues of Polish economy.
Language(s): Polish
Readership: Businessmen, managers of big companies in Poland, representatives of local authorities and political groups are their main readers.
ADVERTISING RATES:
Full Page Colour .... PLN 5000.00
Mechanical Data: Type Area: A4
BUSINESS: FINANCE & ECONOMICS: Financial Related

FARMACJA I JA
1709067PL37-5
Editorial: ul. Puławska 118 A, 16, 02-620 WARSZAWA Tel: 22 846 82 43 Fax: 22 868 13 87
Email: farmacjaija@xxlmedia.pl Web site: http://www.farmacjaija.pl
ISSN: 1733-5256
Date Established: 2004; Freq: Monthly; Cover Price: Free; Circ: 30,000
Usual Pagination: 44
Managing Director: Kwiatek
Profile: Provides advice on pharmaceuticals, on healthy way of life.
Language(s): Polish
BUSINESS: PHARMACEUTICAL & CHEMISTS

FASHION MAGAZINE
1796081PL74B-102
Editorial: ul. Słupska, 6a, 02-495 WARSZAWA
Tel: 22 867 04 64/65 Fax: 22 867 04 64
Email: redakcja@fashionmagazine.pl Web site: http://www.fashionmagazine.pl
ISSN: 1640-4378
Date Established: 2000; Freq: Quarterly; Circ: 30,000
Usual Pagination: 248
Profile: Magazine covering fashion trends and lifestyle, beauty and cosmetics, fashion shows and fashion news.
Language(s): Polish
ADVERTISING RATES:
Full Page Colour .... PLN 30000.00
Mechanical Data: Type Area: 230 x 297 mm
CONSUMER: WOMEN'S INTEREST CONSUMER MAGAZINES: Women's Interest - Fashion

FILM
766122PL76A-2
Editorial: Al. Jerozolimskie, 146c, 02-305 WARSZAWA Tel: 22 347 50 00 Fax: 22 347 50 01
Email: film@film.com.pl Web site: http://www.film.com.pl
Date Established: 1946; Freq: Monthly; Circ: 65,000
Usual Pagination: 100
Profile: Magazine containing information on new film releases, actor profiles, interviews and behind-the-scenes news.
Language(s): Polish
Readership: Aimed at film enthusiasts.
Mechanical Data: Type Area: 210 x 280 mm
CONSUMER: MUSIC & PERFORMING ARTS: Cinema

FILM & TV KAMERA
1708851PL85B-1
Editorial: ul. Kierbedzia, 4, 00-728 WARSZAWA
Tel: 22 320 15 26 Fax: 22 320 15 40
Email: kamera@unit.com.pl Web site: http://www.unit.com.pl
ISSN: 1642-9966
Date Established: 2001; Freq: Quarterly; Circ: 7,000
Usual Pagination: 98
Advertising Director: Małgorzata Aiston
Profile: Film analysis of stylistic tools, film and TV productions, interviews with film crews, animation films, film education and news.
Language(s): Polish
Mechanical Data: Type Area: 162 x 230 mm
CONSUMER: PHOTOGRAPHY & FILM MAKING: Film Making

FILMWEB.PL
1860836PL89C-24
Editorial: ul. Bukowińska, 22b, 02-703 WARSZAWA
Tel: 22 380 13 00 Fax: 22 380 13 14
Email: redakcja@filmweb.pl Web site: http://www.filmweb.pl
Date Established: 1998
Circ: 3,531,108 Unique Users
Advertising Director: Wojciech Przybylski
Language(s): Polish
CONSUMER: HOLIDAYS & TRAVEL: Entertainment Guides

FINANSE PUBLICZNE
1811035PL1A-74
Editorial: ul. Tadeusza Kościuszki, 29, 2, 50-011 WROCŁAW Tel: 71 797 28 46 Fax: 71 797 28 16
Email: redakcja@finansepubliczne.pl Web site: http://www.finansepubliczne.pl
ISSN: 1896-5717
Date Established: 2006; Freq: Monthly; Circ: 3,000
Usual Pagination: 68
Managing Director: Arkadiusz Karasek
Profile: Magazine about accountancy, taxation, budget, insurance, EU funding, audit and control.
Language(s): Polish
Mechanical Data: Type Area: 210 x 280 mm
BUSINESS: FINANCE & ECONOMICS

FINANSOWANIE NIERUCHOMOŚCI
1810998PL1E-14
Editorial: ul. Solec, 101, 5, 00-382 WARSZAWA
Tel: 22 629 18 72 Fax: 22 629 18 72
Email: redakcja@kwartalnikfn.pl Web site: http://www.kwartalnikfn.pl
ISSN: 1733-4217
Date Established: 2004; Freq: Quarterly; Circ: 2,000
Usual Pagination: 112
Managing Director: Waldemar Zbytek
Profile: Magazine with analysis and forecast on financing properties, mortgage market.
Language(s): Polish
Mechanical Data: Type Area: 205 x 297 mm
BUSINESS: FINANCE & ECONOMICS: Property

FISKUS
1708857PL1B-5
Editorial: ul. Okrzei, 1a, 03-715 WARSZAWA
Tel: 22 333 80 00 Fax: 22 333 88 99
Email: m.abramczyk@wtrendy.pl Web site: http://www.e-podatnik.pl
ISSN: 0867-3748
Date Established: 1991; Freq: 26 issues yearly; Circ: 2,000
Usual Pagination: 32
Managing Director: Windorbski; Advertising Director: Małgorzata Skrobiszewska
Profile: Magazine giving practical advice on taxation and changes in legal financial services.
Language(s): Polish
BUSINESS: FINANCE & ECONOMICS: Accountancy

FLOTA
1708981PL31R-5
Editorial: ul. Racławicka, 15/19, 53-149 WROCŁAW
Tel: 71 783 52 05 Fax: 22 783 51 01
Email: kontakt@forum-press.pl Web site: http://www.flota.com.pl
ISSN: 1643-9112
Date Established: 2001; Freq: Monthly; Circ: 6,000
Usual Pagination: 96
Advertising Director: Krzysztof Turczak
Profile: Magazine focused on analysis on the car market, finance and law, tools and technologies supporting management of car fleet, service and safety.
Language(s): Polish
Mechanical Data: Type Area: 213x290 mm
BUSINESS: MOTOR TRADE: Motor Trade Related

FLUID
1708860PL84A-7
Editorial: ul. Pilchowicka, 16a, 02-185 WARSZAWA
Tel: 22 886 85 60 Fax: 22 886 85 60
Email: dinn@fluid.com.pl Web site: http://www.fluid.com.pl
ISSN: 1641-1978
Date Established: 2000; Freq: Monthly; Circ: 50,000
Usual Pagination: 96
Language(s): Polish
CONSUMER: THE ARTS & LITERARY: Arts

FOCUS
1795820PL94J-304
Editorial: ul. Wynalazek, 4, 02-677 WARSZAWA
Tel: 22 607 02 73/74 Fax: 22 607 02 76
Email: focus@focus.pl Web site: http://www.focus.pl
ISSN: 1234-9992
Date Established: 1995; Freq: Monthly; Circ: 174,000
Usual Pagination: 108
Managing Director: Michał Brudzyński; Advertising Director: Katarzyna Składowska
Profile: Popular science magazine providing miscellaneous information on civilizations, technologies, adventures, animals and entertainment.
Language(s): Polish
ADVERTISING RATES:
Full Page Colour .... PLN 36200.00
Mechanical Data: Type Area: 210 x 284 mm
CONSUMER: OTHER CLASSIFICATIONS: Popular Science

FOLIA NEUROPATHOLOGICA
1796194PL56A-28
Editorial: ul. Pawińskiego, 5, 02-106 WARSZAWA
Tel: 22 608 65 43 Fax: 22 668 55 32
Email: folia@cmdik.pan.pl Web site: http://www.folianeuro.termedia.pl
ISSN: 1641-4640
Date Established: 2005; Freq: Quarterly; Circ: 500
Usual Pagination: 90
Managing Director: Andrzej Kordas; Advertising Manager: Marcin Miedzianow
Profile: Professional magazine with academic articles on Neuropathology.
Language(s): English
Readership: English-language quarterly aimed at neuropathologists.
Mechanical Data: Type Area: A4
Official Journal of: Polish Association of Neuropathologists
BUSINESS: HEALTH & MEDICAL

FOOD SERVICE
765615PL22A-501
Editorial: ul. Jadźwingów, 14, 02-692 WARSZAWA
Tel: 22 853 67 03 Fax: 22 853 67 03
Email: fsp@pwf.com.pl Web site: http://pwf.com.pl
ISSN: 1231-2274
Date Established: 1994; Freq: 6 issues yearly; Circ: 5,000
Usual Pagination: 40
Advertising Director: Maria Gościeta
Profile: Magazine focusing on new products, trends in food and catering equipment technology and consumption patterns in the market, acts also as a source of specialist knowledge for owners, managers and personnel of restaurants, hotels and catering facilities of all levels.
Language(s): Polish
Readership: Aimed at restaurants, catering and hotel trade professionals.
ADVERTISING RATES:
Full Page Mono .... PLN 4600.00
Full Page Colour .... PLN 7000.00
Mechanical Data: Type Area: 210 x 297 mm
BUSINESS: FOOD

FORBES
1709045PL14A-53
Editorial: ul. Domaniewska, 52, 02-672 WARSZAWA
Tel: 22 232 11 50 Fax: 22 232 55 28
Email: forbes@axelspringer.pl Web site: http://www.forbes.pl
ISSN: 1733-7291
Freq: Monthly
Managing Director: Małgorzata Barankiewicz; Advertising Director: Hanna Szymańska
Profile: Presents current financial and economic news, business - advice and reports, job and career, lifestyle.
Language(s): Polish
ADVERTISING RATES:
Full Page Colour .... PLN 47500.00
Mechanical Data: Type Area: 205 x 265 mm
BUSINESS: COMMERCE, INDUSTRY & MANAGEMENT

FORUM
1625760PL82-116
Editorial: ul. Słupecka, 6, 02-309 WARSZAWA
Tel: 22 451 60 96 Fax: 22 451 61 64
Email: redakcja@tygodnikforum.pl Web site: http://www.tygodnikforum.pl
ISSN: 0015-8402
Date Established: 1965; Freq: Weekly; Circ: 34,000
Usual Pagination: 64
Managing Director: Jadwiga Kucharczyk; Advertising Director: Krystyna Jarosz
Profile: Magazine focused on current affairs, politics, economy and culture, includes articles from foreign e-media such as: The Financial Times, The Economist, Der Spiegel, Time, Le Figaro, The New York Times, El Pais.
Language(s): Polish
ADVERTISING RATES:
Full Page Colour .... PLN 15000.00
Mechanical Data: Type Area: 215 x 275 mm
CONSUMER: CURRENT AFFAIRS & POLITICS

FORUM MLECZARSKIE
1796026PL21C-1
Editorial: św. Bonifacego, 92, 13/18, 02-940 WARSZAWA Tel: 22 642 43 12 Fax: 22 642 36 25
Email: redakcja@nathusius.pl Web site: http://www.nathusius.pl
ISSN: 1731-4372
Freq: 6 issues yearly; Cover Price: Free
Profile: Provides newest information on the trade of dairy products and margarine.
Language(s): Polish
Mechanical Data: Type Area: A4
BUSINESS: AGRICULTURE & FARMING: Dairy Farming

FORUM PRZEMYSŁU DRZEWNEGO
1796094PL46-2
Editorial: ul. Dzika, 4, 00-194 WARSZAWA
Tel: 22 635 29 30 Fax: 22 635 73 70
Email: ppwp@ppwp.pl Web site: http://www.ppwp.pl
ISSN: 1734-9567
Date Established: 1996; Freq: 6 issues yearly; Circ: 7,000
Usual Pagination: 84
Managing Director: Paweł Krzysica
Profile: Features timber industry news, professional trades and trade events.
Language(s): Polish
ADVERTISING RATES:
Full Page Colour .... PLN 5900.00
Mechanical Data: Type Area: A4
BUSINESS: TIMBER, WOOD & FORESTRY

FORUM SŁODKO-SŁONE
1796085PL8B-1
Editorial: św. Bonifacego, 92, 13/18, 02-940 WARSZAWA Tel: 22 642 43 12 Fax: 22 642 36 25
Email: redakcja@nathusius.pl Web site: http://www.nathusius.pl
ISSN: 1733-6317
Freq: 6 issues yearly; Cover Price: Free
Managing Director: Krzysztof Lorenc
Profile: Presents current news on sweets' and sour snacks' sales.
Language(s): Polish
Mechanical Data: Type Area: A4
BUSINESS: BAKING & CONFECTIONERY: Confectionery Manufacturing

FOTO KURIER
1796131PL85A-2
Editorial: ul. Rzędzińska, 23, 01-368 WARSZAWA
Tel: 22 665 24 33 Fax: 22 665 41 79
Email: redakcja@foto-kurier.pl Web site: http://www.foto-kurier.pl
ISSN: 0867-6151
Date Established: 1991; Freq: Monthly; Circ: 8,000
Usual Pagination: 118
Advertising Director: Aleksander Holak
Profile: Magazine on regular and digital cameras, printers and multi-functional equipment.
Language(s): Polish
Mechanical Data: Type Area: 190 x 270 mm
CONSUMER: PHOTOGRAPHY & FILM MAKING: Photography

FRAZPC.PL
1860847PL5B-61
Editorial: ul. Dróżnicza, 37, 52-129 WROCŁAW
Email: redakcja@frazpc.pl Web site: http://www.frazpc.pl
Date Established: 2000
Circ: 1,075,648 Unique Users
Managing Director: Krzysztof Krutul; Advertising Director: Rafał Karczewski
Profile: Portal about computing, IT technologies, and software and hardware.
Language(s): Polish
BUSINESS: COMPUTERS & AUTOMATION: Data Processing

FUNDUSZE EUROPEJSKIE
1819399PL14A-98
Editorial: os. Na Murawie, 7, 4, 61-655 POZNAŃ
Tel: 61 825 30 47 Fax: 61 825 30 47
Email: redakcja@fundusze-europejskie.pl Web site: http://fundusze-europejskie.pl
Date Established: 2003; Freq: 6 issues yearly; Circ: 10,000
Usual Pagination: 82
Profile: Provides information on EU funding, ways of its usage and examples of applications for receiving EU funds, experts' advice.
Language(s): Polish
Mechanical Data: Type Area: 205 x 265 mm
BUSINESS: COMMERCE, INDUSTRY & MANAGEMENT

FUTU MAGAZINE
1796111PL85A-1
Editorial: ul. Odolańska, 60, 02 - 562 WARSZAWA
Tel: 22 880 04 65 Fax: 22 880 04 66

Email: info@futumag.com Web site: http://www.futumag.com
ISSN: 1989-6374
Date Established: 2006
Cover Price: Free; Circ: 6,000
Usual Pagination: 240
Advertising Director: Wojciech Ponikowski
Profile: Magazine focused on lifestyle, design, architecture, interior design, art projects and creative people presented in the form of an album.
Language(s): English; Polish
Mechanical Data: Type Area: 230 x 280 mm
CONSUMER: PHOTOGRAPHY & FILM MAKING: Photography

GALA 1795821PL91E-11
Editorial: ul. Wynalazek, 4, 02-677 WARSZAWA
Tel: 22 607 02 77/82 Fax: 22 607 02 83
Email: gala@gala.pl Web site: http://www.gala.pl
ISSN: 1642-5626
Date Established: 2001; Freq: Weekly; Circ: 237,000
Usual Pagination: 108
Managing Director: Michał Brudzyński; Advertising Director: Renata Bogusz
Profile: Presents interviews with famous people, news on celebrities, fashion and health tips and lifestyle and events reportages.
Language(s): Polish
ADVERTISING RATES:
Full Page Colour .... PLN 47900.00
Mechanical Data: Type Area: 230 x 297 mm
CONSUMER: RECREATION & LEISURE: Lifestyle

GAZ, WODA I TECHNIKA SANITARNA 1811048PL42C-1
Editorial: ul. Czackiego, 3/5, 404, 00-043 WARSZAWA Tel: 22 827 02 49 Fax: 22 336 14 07
Email: gazwoda@sigma-not.pl Web site: http://www.cieplogaz.com.pl
ISSN: 0016-5352
Date Established: 1921; Freq: Monthly
Usual Pagination: 40
Profile: Gas and water pipelines, water and sewages protection and their filtration, environment and air protection, noise reductions and keeping cities clean, industry rubbish utilisation.
Language(s): Polish
ADVERTISING RATES:
Full Page Mono .... PLN 1700.00
Full Page Colour .... PLN 3630.00
Mechanical Data: Type Area: 205 x 290 mm
BUSINESS: CONSTRUCTION: Water Engineering

GAZETA BANKOWA 1708856PL1C-3
Editorial: ul. Pilotów 21, 80-460 GDAŃSK
Tel: 58 550 97 20 Fax: 58 550 97 02
Email: redakcja@gb.pl Web site: http://www.gazetabankowa.pl
ISSN: 0860-7613
Date Established: 1988; Freq: Monthly; Cover Price: PLN 29.00; Circ: 7,500
Usual Pagination: 130
Managing Director: Tomasz Przybek; Advertising Director: Jarosław Dotka
Profile: National magazine focused on banking and finance, insurance and local councils.
Language(s): Polish
ADVERTISING RATES:
Full Page Colour .... PLN 11900.00
Mechanical Data: Type Area: 220x290mm
BUSINESS: FINANCE & ECONOMICS: Banking

GAZETA CUKROWNICZA 1811049PL21R-1
Editorial: ul. Ratuszowa, 11, 743, 03-450 WARSZAWA Tel: 22 818 72 13 Fax: 22 818 72 13
Email: gazetacukrownicza@sigma-not.pl Web site: http://sigma-not.pl
ISSN: 0016-5395
Date Established: 1893; Freq: Monthly
Usual Pagination: 32
Profile: Magazine covering sugar beetroot and its cultivation, technological values of it, technologies and sugar production, equipment and progress in the industry, new technologies.
Language(s): Polish
ADVERTISING RATES:
Full Page Mono .... PLN 1370.00
Full Page Colour .... PLN 3020.00
Mechanical Data: Type Area: 205 x 290 mm
BUSINESS: AGRICULTURE & FARMING: Agriculture & Farming Related

GAZETA FINANSOWA 1708634PL1A-94
Editorial: Al. Jerozolimskie, 123a, 02-017 WARSZAWA Tel: 22 438 87 76 Fax: 22 438 87 64
Email: gazeta@gazetafinansowa.pl Web site: http://www.gazetafinansowa.pl
ISSN: 1506-0985
Date Established: 1998; Freq: Weekly; Circ: 15,000
Usual Pagination: 40
Profile: A newspaper covering banking and finance, insurance, marketing and management.
Language(s): Polish
ADVERTISING RATES:
Full Page Colour .... PLN 13500.00
Mechanical Data: Type Area: 321 x 506 mm
BUSINESS: FINANCE & ECONOMICS

GAZETA LUBUSKA 1614543PL67B-28
Editorial: al. Niepodległości, 25, 65-042 ZIELONA GÓRA Tel: 68 324 88 00/02 Fax: 68 324 88 72
Email: redakcja@gazetalubuska.pl Web site: http://www.gazetalubuska.pl
ISSN: 0137-9518
Date Established: 1952; Freq: Daily; Circ: 42,342
Usual Pagination: 24
Managing Director: Grzegorz Widenka; Advertising Director: Joanna Butora; Publisher: Cezary Siciński
Profile: A regional newspaper covering political, economic, cultural events and sports.
Language(s): Polish
Mechanical Data: Type Area: A3
REGIONAL DAILY & SUNDAY NEWSPAPERS: Regional Daily Newspapers

GAZETA MAŁYCH I ŚREDNICH PRZEDSIĘBIORSTW 1708688PL14H-3
Editorial: ul. Tużycka, 16, 03-683 WARSZAWA
Tel: 22 678 79 83 Fax: 22 678 01 67
Email: redakcja@gazeta-msp.pl Web site: http://www.gazeta-msp.pl
ISSN: 1643-8639
Date Established: 2002; Freq: Monthly; Circ: 20,000
Usual Pagination: 80
Managing Director: Tomasz Peplak; Advertising Director: Krzysztof Kowalówczany
Profile: Economics monthly with informative-educational profile supporting small companies in their management.
Language(s): Polish
ADVERTISING RATES:
Full Page Colour .... PLN 10800.00
Mechanical Data: Type Area: A4 (210x297 mm)
BUSINESS: COMMERCE, INDUSTRY & MANAGEMENT: Small Business

GAZETA OLSZTYŃSKA/ DZIENNIK ELBLĄSKI 1614414PL67B-24
Editorial: ul. Tracka, 5, 10-364 OLSZTYN
Tel: 89 539 77 00 Fax: 89 539 75 11
Email: redakcja@gazetaolsztynska.pl Web site: http://www.gazetaolsztynska.pl
ISSN: 0137-9127
Date Established: 1886; Freq: Daily
Advertising Director: Beata Tokarczyk
Profile: Regional newspaper from Eastern Poland featuring regional information and news.
Language(s): Polish
ADVERTISING RATES:
Full Page Mono .... PLN 1900.00
Mechanical Data: Type Area: A3
REGIONAL DAILY & SUNDAY NEWSPAPERS: Regional Daily Newspapers

GAZETA PODATKOWA 1795589PL1M-17
Editorial: ul. Owocowa, 8, 66-400 GORZÓW WLKP.
Tel: 95 720 85 40 Fax: 95 720 85 60
Email: marketing@gofin.pl Web site: http://www.gazetapodatkowa.pl
ISSN: 1731-9447
Date Established: 2004; Freq: 104 issues yearly; Circ: 35,162
Usual Pagination: 28
Advertising Director: Iwona Sałgut-Szerechowicz
Profile: Newspaper providing information on taxation and VAT, insurance, rents, accountancy, legal aspects at work, business activities and EU legal system.
Language(s): Polish
ADVERTISING RATES:
Full Page Mono .... PLN 8000.00
Full Page Colour .... PLN 27000.00
Mechanical Data: Type Area: A3
BUSINESS: FINANCE & ECONOMICS: Taxation

GAZETA POMORSKA (GAZETA KUJAWSKA) 1614405PL67B-7
Editorial: ul. Zamoyskiego, 2, 85-063 BYDGOSZCZ
Tel: 52 326 31 64/00 Fax: 52 322 10 31
Email: gp.redakcja@pomorska.pl Web site: http://www.pomorska.pl
ISSN: 0867-4965
Date Established: 1948; Freq: Daily; Circ: 77,980
Usual Pagination: 20
Managing Director: Tomasz Niski; Advertising Director: Przemysław Wacławski
Profile: Regional newspaper of informative-publicizing character.
Language(s): Polish
ADVERTISING RATES:
Full Page Mono .... PLN 9240.00
Full Page Colour .... PLN 12012.00
Mechanical Data: Type Area: 315 x 470 mm
REGIONAL DAILY & SUNDAY NEWSPAPERS: Regional Daily Newspapers

GAZETA POZNAŃSKA 1614508PL67B-14
Editorial: ul. Grunwaldzka, 19, 60-782 POZNAŃ
Tel: 61 860 60 00 Fax: 61 860 60 69
Email: gazeta@poczta.gp.pl Web site: http://www.gp.pl
Date Established: 1948; Freq: Daily
Usual Pagination: 40
Advertising Director: Elżbieta Wrońska
Language(s): Polish
REGIONAL DAILY & SUNDAY NEWSPAPERS: Regional Daily Newspapers

GAZETA PRAWNA 1614186PL44-20
Editorial: ul. Okopowa, 58/72, 01-042 WARSZAWA
Tel: 22 530 40 40 Fax: 22 530 40 39
Email: gp@infor.pl Web site: http://www.gazetaprawna.pl
ISSN: 1232-6712
Date Established: 1994; Freq: Daily
Managing Director: Dariusz Piekarski; Advertising Director: Jacek Szczęsny
Profile: Daily newspaper covering the financial and insurance market, law, business and economics issues.
Language(s): Polish
ADVERTISING RATES:
Full Page Mono .... PLN 29700.00
Full Page Colour .... PLN 35750.00
Mechanical Data: Type Area: A3
BUSINESS: LEGAL

GAZETA PRAWNA 1873625PL44-30
Editorial: ul.Okopowa 58/72, 01-042 WARSZAWA
Tel: 22 531 48 00 Fax: 22 530 40 39
Email: gp@infor.pl Web site: http://www.gazetaprawna.pl
Freq: Daily; Circ: 906,849 Unique Users
Profile: Website covering topics related to labor law, social insurance, taxation, accounting, criminal law, family and consumer law.
Language(s): Polish
BUSINESS: LEGAL

GAZETA REGIONALNA 1796172PL72I-13
Editorial: ul. Chopina, 24, 68-200 ŻARY
Tel: 68 470 07 00 Fax: 68 470 07 17
Email: redakcja@regionalna.pl Web site: http://www.regionalna.pl
ISSN: 1642-4360
Date Established: 2001; Freq: Weekly; Circ: 28,000
Usual Pagination: 40
Profile: A regional weekly covering news on politics, economics, culture, sports and society.
Language(s): Polish
ADVERTISING RATES:
Full Page Mono .... PLN 1788.00
Full Page Colour .... PLN 3570.00
Mechanical Data: Type Area: A3
LOCAL NEWSPAPERS: Regional Weekly Newspapers

GAZETA STUDENCKA 1708832PL83-2
Editorial: ul. Krakowskie Przedmieście, 24, 203, 00-927 WARSZAWA Tel: 22 552 02 29
Fax: 22 552 02 29
Email: redakcja@studencka.pl Web site: http://www.studencka.pl
ISSN: 1427-2601
Date Established: 1996; Freq: Monthly; Cover Price: Free; Circ: 105,000
Usual Pagination: 36
Language(s): Polish
Mechanical Data: Type Area: A4
CONSUMER: STUDENT PUBLICATIONS

GAZETA SZKOLNA 1620673PL62R-1
Editorial: ul. Felińskiego, 44, 01-563 WARSZAWA
Tel: 22 839 32 44 Fax: 22 839 32 44
Email: gazeta.szkolna@tworzywo.org.pl Web site: http://gazetaszkolna.edu.pl
ISSN: 1508-6593
Date Established: 1999; Freq: Weekly; Circ: 12,600
Usual Pagination: 32
Profile: Magazine focusing on educational issues in schools up to higher level. Includes latest teaching methods, administration news and reports.
Language(s): Polish
Readership: Aimed at academics, teachers and all professionals involved in the education sector.
BUSINESS: CHURCH & SCHOOL EQUIPMENT & EDUCATION: Education Related

GAZETA WSPÓŁCZESNA 1819656PL67B-42
Editorial: ul. św. Mikołaja, 1, 15-419 BIAŁYSTOK
Tel: 85 748 74 00 Fax: 85 748 74 01
Email: redakcja@wspolczesna.pl Web site: http://www.wspolczesna.pl
ISSN: 0137-9488
Date Established: 1956
Usual Pagination: 28
Managing Director: Krzysztof Paliński; Advertising Director: Dariusz Gilewski
Profile: Contains local news and sports, supplements: real estate, homes, jobs, cars, small adverts in the region.
Language(s): Polish
Mechanical Data: Type Area: A3
REGIONAL DAILY & SUNDAY NEWSPAPERS: Regional Daily Newspapers

GAZETA WYBORCZA 1500349PL65A-10
Editorial: ul. Czerska, 8/10, 00-732 WARSZAWA
Tel: 22 555 60 00 Fax: 22 841 69 20
Email: listydogazety@gazeta.pl Web site: http://www.wyborcza.pl
ISSN: 0860-908X
Date Established: 1989; Freq: Daily; Circ: 355,565
Usual Pagination: 117
Managing Director: Stanisław Turnau; Advertising Director: Marek Tretyn
Profile: Tabloid-sized newspaper covering national and international news with features on business and finance, education, appointments, lifestyle, entertainment and sport.
Language(s): Polish
ADVERTISING RATES:
Full Page Mono .... PLN 129900.00
Full Page Colour .... PLN 129900.00
Mechanical Data: Type Area: 280 x 410 mm
NATIONAL DAILY & SUNDAY NEWSPAPERS: National Daily Newspapers

GAZETAPRACA.PL 1835914PL14F-6
Editorial: ul. Czerska, 8/10, 00-732 WARSZAWA
Tel: 22 555 49 90 Fax: 22 555 48 70
Email: redakcja-praca@agora.pl Web site: http://www.gazetapraca.pl
Circ: 1,088,591 Unique Users
Managing Director: Anna Podkowińska; Advertising Director: Przemysław Bartkowiak
Profile: Offers new job positions, provides information about jobs and careers available abroad and information for employers.
Language(s): Polish
BUSINESS: COMMERCE, INDUSTRY & MANAGEMENT: Training & Recruitment

GENTLEMAN 1708633PL74Q-6
Editorial: ul. Stawki, 2, 00-193 WARSZAWA
Tel: 22 860 63 12 Fax: 22 860 63 09
Email: gentleman@numedia.pl Web site: http://numedia.pl
ISSN: 1427-0420
Date Established: 1996; Freq: Monthly; Circ: 15,000
Usual Pagination: 148
Advertising Director: Consuella Pujszo
Profile: Focused on the world of show-business, politics, fashion, culture and careers of VIP persons.
Language(s): Polish
ADVERTISING RATES:
Full Page Colour .... PLN 16000.00
Mechanical Data: Type Area: 225 x 300 mm
CONSUMER: WOMEN'S INTEREST CONSUMER MAGAZINES: Lifestyle

GEODETA 1835745PL55-9
Editorial: ul. Narbutta 40/20, 02-541 WARSZAWA
Tel: 22 849 41 63 Fax: 22 646 87 44
Email: redakcja@geoforum.pl Web site: http://www.geoforum.pl
Date Established: 1995; Freq: Monthly; Circ: 3,000
Editor-in-Chief: Katarzyna Pakuła-Kwiecińska
Profile: Scientific magazine focused on geodesy, cartography, GIS and photogram science, satellite navigation and mapping.
Language(s): Polish
ADVERTISING RATES:
Full Page Colour .... PLN 3450.00
Mechanical Data: Type Area: 207 x 294mm
BUSINESS: APPLIED SCIENCE & LABORATORIES

GIFTS JOURNAL 1804099PL52-1
Editorial: ul. Podbiałowa, 11, 61-680 POZNAŃ
Tel: 61 825 73 22 Fax: 61 825 84 85
Email: magda.konieczna@gjc.pl Web site: http://www.giftsjournal.pl
ISSN: 1640-7415
Date Established: 2000; Freq: Quarterly; Cover Price: Free; Circ: 5,000
Editor: Inga Królikowska
Profile: Gifts Journal is a quarterly periodical devoted to topics of advertising gifts and gadgets.
Language(s): Polish
Readership: targets group of customers - companies operating in the advertising industry, suppliers, importers and producers of advertising gifts, as well as the marketing departments of large and medium-sized businesses.
ADVERTISING RATES:
Full Page Colour .... PLN 2600.00
Mechanical Data: Type Area: A4
BUSINESS: GIFT TRADE

GINEKOLOGIA PRAKTYCZNA 1708796PL56M-3
Editorial: ul. Wenedów, 9/1, 61-614 POZNAŃ
Tel: 61 822 77 81 Fax: 61 822 77 81
Email: m.jadwizak@termedia.pl Web site: http://www.ginekologia.termedia.pl
ISSN: 1231-6407
Date Established: 1993; Freq: Quarterly; Circ: 3,000
Usual Pagination: 54
Managing Director: Andrzej Kordas
Profile: Practical advice on genecology and new-born baby care.
Language(s): Polish
Readership: Practical Gynecology is a quarterly scientific journal addressed to gynecologists.
Mechanical Data: Type Area: 210 x 297 mm
BUSINESS: HEALTH & MEDICAL: Family Planning

GLAMOUR
1708645PL74B-111
Editorial: ul. Wynalazek, 4, 02-677 WARSZAWA
Tel: 22 640 07 21/22 **Fax:** 22 640 07 23
Email: skrzynkanalisty@glamour.com.pl **Web site:** http://www.glamour.pl
ISSN: 1730-2781
Date Established: 2003; **Freq:** Monthly; **Circ:** 238,000
Usual Pagination: 220
Managing Director: Michał Brudzyński; **Advertising Director:** Anna Niewodzka
Profile: Covering news in fashion, lifestyle and celebrities.
Language(s): Polish
ADVERTISING RATES:
Full Page Colour .... PLN 55900.00
Mechanical Data: Type Area: 170 x 225 mm
CONSUMER: WOMEN'S INTEREST CONSUMER MAGAZINES: Women's Interest - Fashion

GLOBTROTER
1796116PL50-3
Editorial: ul. Łąkowa 27, 32-082 BOLECHOWICE
Tel: 12 632 04 60 **Fax:** 12 632 04 60
Email: redakcja@globtroter.tv **Web site:** http://www.globtroter.tv
ISSN: 1895-6440
Date Established: 2006; **Freq:** 6 issues yearly; **Annual Sub.:** PLN 40.00; **Circ:** 10,000
Usual Pagination: 112
Advertising Director: Krzysztof Śmiałek
Profile: Focused on travelling and tourism, actively spent holidays, reportages from the furthest corners of our world, places less known, interviews with famous globetrotters, advice on safe travelling.
Language(s): Polish
Mechanical Data: Type Area: 160x233 mm
BUSINESS: TRAVEL & TOURISM

GŁOS POMORZA
1614644PL67B-25
Editorial: Ul. Henryka Pobożnego 19, 76-200 SŁUPSK **Tel:** 59 8488100 **Fax:** 59 8488104
Email: red@glos-pomorza.pl **Web site:** http://www.gp24.pl/apps/pbcs.dll/frontpage
Date Established: 1952; **Freq:** 312 issues yearly; **Circ:** 43,340
Usual Pagination: 16
Advertising Director: Anna Pruszak
Profile: Providing regional news and reports from the Northern region of Poland close to the Baltic sea.
Language(s): Polish
ADVERTISING RATES:
Full Page Mono .... PLN 32650.00
REGIONAL DAILY & SUNDAY NEWSPAPERS: Regional Daily Newspapers

GOLDENLINE
1929273PL14A-163
Editorial: ul. Skrzetuskiego, 17, a, 02-726 WARSZAWA **Tel:** 22 203 51 43
Email: reklama@goldenline.pl **Web site:** http://www.goldenline.pl
Date Established: 2005; **Freq:** Daily; **Circ:** 1,255,196 Unique Users
Advertising Director: Roman Cieślik
Profile: GoldenLine is a community focused on career development and professional life. It helps you meet people, exist in the industry and monitor the labor market.
Language(s): Polish
BUSINESS: COMMERCE, INDUSTRY & MANAGEMENT

GOLF & LIFE
1708636PL75D-2
Editorial: ul. Bohomolca, 17, 01-613 WARSZAWA
Tel: 22 865 67 41 **Fax:** 22 865 67 41
Email: redakcja@orbiplus.pl **Web site:** http://www.golfandlife.pl
ISSN: 1730-0576
Date Established: 2003; **Freq:** Monthly; **Circ:** 25,000
Usual Pagination: 230
Profile: Magazine about golf and everything with it related: travelling, lifestyle, culture and socio-political issues.
Language(s): Polish
Mechanical Data: Type Area: 215 x 280 mm
CONSUMER: SPORT: Golf

GOLF VADEMECUM
1708635PL75D-1
Editorial: ul. Bohomolca, 17, 1, 01-613 WARSZAWA
Tel: 22 865 67 41 **Fax:** 22 865 67 41
Email: redakcja@orbiplus.pl **Web site:** http://orbiplus.pl
ISSN: 1730-0568
Date Established: 2002; **Freq:** Annual; **Circ:** 15,000
Usual Pagination: 256
Profile: Everything about golf and Polish golf courses.
Language(s): Polish
Mechanical Data: Type Area: 210 x 200 mm
CONSUMER: SPORT: Golf

GÓRY
1708671PL75A-5
Editorial: ul. Bajana, 4, 11, 31-465 KRAKÓW
Tel: 12 421 14 82 **Fax:** 12 421 14 82
Email: gory@wyd.pl **Web site:** http://www.goryonline.com
ISSN: 0867-8324
Date Established: 1991; **Freq:** Monthly; **Circ:** 10,000
Usual Pagination: 80
Advertising Director: Marek Obara
Profile: Polish mountaineering and climbing magazine.
Language(s): Polish
CONSUMER: SPORT

GOSPODARKA MATERIAŁOWA I LOGISTYKA
1708687PL14A-13
Editorial: ul. Canaletta, 4, 00-099 WARSZAWA
Tel: 22 827 80 01 **Fax:** 22 827 55 67
Email: gmil@pwe.com.pl **Web site:** http://www.gmil.pl
ISSN: 1231-2037
Date Established: 1948; **Freq:** Monthly; **Circ:** 2,000
Usual Pagination: 40
Managing Director: Mariola Rozmus
Profile: Professional magazine covering logistics and integrated deliveries' management, new technologies and management of recycling, work organization and e-business.
Language(s): Polish
Readership: Targets managers creating and implementing business strategies that enable cost reduction, streamlining processes, shortening delivery periods, improving customer service.
ADVERTISING RATES:
Full Page Colour .... PLN 1650.00
Mechanical Data: Type Area: 205 x 287 mm
BUSINESS: COMMERCE, INDUSTRY & MANAGEMENT

GOSPODARKA MIĘSNA
1811051PL22C-1
Editorial: ul. Rakowiecka, 36, 13b, 02-532 WARSZAWA **Tel:** 22 606 36 16 **Fax:** 22 606 36 16
Email: gospodarkamiesna@sigma-not.pl **Web site:** http://sigma-not.pl
ISSN: 0367-4916
Date Established: 1949; **Freq:** Monthly
Usual Pagination: 76
Profile: Professional magazine covering new technologies in meat storage, its smoking and processing, quality control, advertising and marketing of meat-processing industry, packaging machines, safety and hygiene on working place.
Language(s): Polish
ADVERTISING RATES:
Full Page Mono .... PLN 1700.00
Full Page Colour .... PLN 3000.00
Mechanical Data: Type Area: 205 x 290 mm
BUSINESS: FOOD: Food Processing & Packaging

GOSPODARKA WODNA
1811052PL57-2
Editorial: ul. Ratuszowa, 11, 718, 03-450 WARSZAWA **Tel:** 22 619 20 15
Email: gospodarkawodna@sigma-not.pl **Web site:** http://sigma-not.pl
ISSN: 0017-2448
Date Established: 1935; **Freq:** Monthly
Usual Pagination: 44
Profile: Magazine on water management, hydrology and environmental issues, hydrogeology and water administration, water deficit, river regulation and flood protection, hydro-energy.
Language(s): Polish
ADVERTISING RATES:
Full Page Mono .... PLN 1500.00
Full Page Colour .... PLN 3300.00
Mechanical Data: Type Area: 205 x 290 mm
BUSINESS: ENVIRONMENT & POLLUTION

GRACZ
1929196PL91R-2
Editorial: Dobrego Pasterza, 31a, 31-416 KRAKÓW
Tel: 12 442 48 01 **Fax:** 12 442 48 02
Email: redakcja@miesiecznikgracz.pl **Web site:** http://www.miesiecznikgracz.pl
Date Established: 2009; **Freq:** Monthly; **Circ:** 40,000
Usual Pagination: 68
Advertising Director: Tomasz Kamiński
Profile: Magazine about bookmakers' shops in Poland.
Language(s): Polish
Mechanical Data: Type Area: 195 mm x 263 mm
CONSUMER: RECREATION & LEISURE: Recreation & Leisure Related

GT
1709057PL77A-28
Editorial: ul. Heroldów, 6, 01-991 WARSZAWA
Tel: 22 569 98 99 **Fax:** 22 569 98 96
Email: gt@gt-online.pl **Web site:** http://www.gt-online.pl
ISSN: 1505-9960
Date Established: 1998; **Freq:** Monthly; **Circ:** 55,000
Usual Pagination: 148
Profile: Focused on motoring industry, sport cars, auto tuning and car audio equipment.
Language(s): Polish
Mechanical Data: Type Area: 220 x 280 mm
CONSUMER: MOTORING & CYCLING: Motoring

H2O
1810961PL75M-7
Editorial: ul. Krakowskie Przedmieście, 79, 401, 00-079 WARSZAWA **Tel:** 22 394 84 66
Fax: 22 829 21 90
Email: h2o@h2o-magazyn.pl **Web site:** http://www.h2o-magazyn.pl
ISSN: 1896-1738
Date Established: 2006; **Freq:** Monthly; **Circ:** 18,000
Usual Pagination: 100
Profile: Dedicated to water sports and tourism.
Language(s): Polish
Mechanical Data: Type Area: A4
CONSUMER: SPORT: Water Sports

HAKIN9
1796118PL5C-3
Formerly: Haking
Editorial: ul. Bokserska, 1, 02-682 WARSZAWA
Tel: 22 427 36 77 **Fax:** 22 244 24 59
Email: hakin9@software.com.pl **Web site:** http://www.hakin9.org
ISSN: 1731-7150
Date Established: 1995; **Freq:** Monthly; **Cover Price:** Paid; **Circ:** 43,000 Unique Users
Usual Pagination: 82
Profile: Digital magazine covering latest methods of IT protection, most recent hacking and protection techniques and tools, latest trends in IT Security and pursuing consumers' tests.
Language(s): English; French; German; Polish
Readership: Targets everyone interested in securing and hacking – both professionals (security officers, system administrators) and hobbyists.
ADVERTISING RATES:
Full Page Colour $1000.00
Mechanical Data: Type Area: 203 x 293 mm
BUSINESS: COMPUTERS & AUTOMATION: Professional Personal Computers

HANDEL
1201761PL53-5
Editorial: ul. Jadźwingów, 14, 02-692 WARSZAWA
Tel: 22 847 61 45 **Fax:** 22 847 61 45
Email: handel.redakcja@pwf.com.pl **Web site:** http://www.handel.pwf.com.pl
ISSN: 1230-9664
Date Established: 1993; **Freq:** 26 issues yearly; **Circ:** 70,000
Usual Pagination: 48
Advertising Director: Rafał Krzycki
Profile: Magazine focusing on the Polish wholesale and retail trade. Includes information on the current situation in the sector, discussion and analysis of development trends, practical hints in marketing, commercial law and product knowledge.
Language(s): Polish
Readership: Read by managers in medium and large food stores, drugstores, super- and hypermarkets and wholesale stores. Also by decision-makers in headquarters of national, regional and local networks.
ADVERTISING RATES:
Full Page Colour .... PLN 37900.00
Mechanical Data: Type Area: 215 x 280 mm
BUSINESS: RETAILING & WHOLESALING

HANDLOWIEC
1796093PL2F-3
Editorial: ul. Garbary, 106/108, 61-757 POZNAŃ
Tel: 61 852 08 94 **Fax:** 61 851 92 41
Email: redakcja@poradnikhandlowca.com.pl **Web site:** http://www.handlowiec-generalczyk.com.pl
ISSN: 1734-4972
Date Established: 2005; **Freq:** Monthly; **Cover Price:** Free; **Circ:** 10,000
Advertising Director: Wojtek Generalczyk
Profile: Dedicated to trade and sales issues.
Language(s): Polish
ADVERTISING RATES:
Full Page Colour .... PLN 7900.00
Mechanical Data: Type Area: A4
BUSINESS: COMMUNICATIONS, ADVERTISING & MARKETING: Selling

HARVARD BUSINESS REVIEW POLSKA
1796226PL14A-80
Editorial: Al. Jerozolimskie, 65/79, 00-697 WARSZAWA **Tel:** 22 630 66 87 **Fax:** 22 630 66 85
Email: redakcja@hbrp.pl **Web site:** http://www.hbrp.pl
Date Established: 2003; **Freq:** Monthly; **Circ:** 8,700
Usual Pagination: 140
Managing Director: Andrzej Jacaszek; **Advertising Director:** Beata Micialkiewicz
Profile: Focused on motivation and strategic decisions, marketing and client relations, finance, analysis and advice on business management.
Language(s): Polish
ADVERTISING RATES:
Full Page Colour .... PLN 34600.00
Mechanical Data: Type Area: 208 x 273 mm
BUSINESS: COMMERCE, INDUSTRY & MANAGEMENT

HEREDITARY CANCER IN CLINICAL PRACTICE
1709011PL56A-20
Editorial: ul. Połabska, 4, 70-115 SZCZECIN
Tel: 91 466 15 32 **Fax:** 91 466 15 33
Email: lubinski@sci.pam.szczecin.pl **Web site:** http://www.termedia.pl/magazine.php?magazine_id=14&magazine_subpage=CURRENT
ISSN: 1731-2302
Date Established: 2003
Circ: 1,000
Usual Pagination: 70
Managing Director: Andrzej Kordas
Profile: Presents information, critical analyses of opinions and elaboration of basis for scientifically verified protocols of diagnosis, prevention and treatment of hereditary cancer in clinical genetics.
Language(s): English
Readership: Intended for physicians, pharmacists, medicine and pharmacy students, and biomedicine scientists.
Mechanical Data: Type Area: A4
BUSINESS: HEALTH & MEDICAL

HI-FI
1810905PL78R-4
Editorial: ul. Blokowa, 24, 03-641 WARSZAWA
Tel: 22 679 56 42 **Fax:** 22 679 52 17
Email: redakcja@hfm.pl **Web site:** http://www.hfm.pl
ISSN: 1234-2173
Date Established: 1995; **Freq:** Monthly; **Circ:** 5,000
Usual Pagination: 112
Managing Director: Maciej Stryjecki; **Advertising Director:** Maciej Stryjecki
Profile: Featuring articles on Hi-Fi equipment, home cinema and new music releases.
Language(s): Polish
ADVERTISING RATES:
Full Page Colour .... PLN 12078.00
Mechanical Data: Type Area: A4
CONSUMER: CONSUMER ELECTRONICS: Consumer Electronics Related

HIP HOP ARCHIWUM
1709020PL76D-6
Editorial: ul. Marii Konopnickiej, 6, 00-491 WARSZAWA **Tel:** 22 625 59 24 **Fax:** 22 625 49 95
Email: biuro@vimedia.com.pl **Web site:** http://vimedia.com.pl
ISSN: 1732-0887
Date Established: 2004; **Freq:** Monthly; **Circ:** 35,000
Usual Pagination: 32
Language(s): Polish
CONSUMER: MUSIC & PERFORMING ARTS: Music

HIP HOP RGB
1796124PL76D-3
Editorial: ul. Kochanowskiego, 25, 31-127 KRAKÓW
Tel: 12 633 99 01 **Fax:** 12 633 90 01
Email: redakcja@magazynhiphop.pl **Web site:** http://www.magazynhiphop.pl
ISSN: 1644-2407
Date Established: 2002; **Freq:** Monthly; **Circ:** 6,000
Usual Pagination: 96
Advertising Director: Krzysztof Śmiałek
Language(s): English
Mechanical Data: Type Area: 205x295 mm
CONSUMER: MUSIC & PERFORMING ARTS: Music

HIRO
1708719PL76D-4
Editorial: ul. Chmielna, 7, 14, 00-021 WARSZAWA
Tel: 22 826 29 92 **Fax:** 22 890 98 55
Email: halo@hiro.pl **Web site:** http://www.hiro.pl
ISSN: 1642-9745
Date Established: 2001; **Freq:** Monthly; **Circ:** 20,000
Usual Pagination: 96
Advertising Director: Krzysztof Grabań
Profile: Features articles on music, extreme sports, photography and graphic design.
Language(s): Polish
Mechanical Data: Type Area: 274 x 205 mm (format poziomy)
CONSUMER: MUSIC & PERFORMING ARTS: Music

HOME & MARKET
1708632PL1A-97
Editorial: Aleje Jerozolimskie 101/14, 02-011 WARSZAWA **Tel:** 22 628 02 23
Email: homemarket@numedia.pl **Web site:** http://www.homemarket.com.pl
ISSN: 1734-302X
Date Established: 1992; **Freq:** Monthly; **Circ:** 15,000
Usual Pagination: 148
Editor: Dominika Górska - Szymańka; **Advertising Director:** Emilia Socha
Profile: Features economic-financial information: finance, marketing and management, analysis of changes in Polish economy.
Language(s): Polish
ADVERTISING RATES:
Full Page Colour .... PLN 15000.00
Mechanical Data: Type Area: 205 x 280 mm
BUSINESS: FINANCE & ECONOMICS

HOT WHEELS
1796086PL77A-31
Editorial: ul. Dzielna, 60, 01-029 WARSZAWA
Tel: 22 838 41 00 **Fax:** 22 838 42 00
Email: hotwheels@egmont.pl **Web site:** http://www.egmont.pl
ISSN: 1895-4391
Date Established: 2006; **Freq:** Monthly; **Circ:** 55,000
Usual Pagination: 32
Profile: Magazine on cars for boys at the age of 12.
Language(s): Polish
ADVERTISING RATES:
Full Page Colour .... PLN 7500.00
Mechanical Data: Type Area: 215 x 290 mm
CONSUMER: MOTORING & CYCLING: Motoring

HOTELARZ
1819396PL11A-11
Editorial: ul. Okrzei, 1a, 03-715 WARSZAWA
Tel: 22 333 80 00 **Fax:** 22 333 88 82
Email: hotelarz@pws-promedia.pl **Web site:** http://www.e-hotelarz.pl
ISSN: 0137-7612
Date Established: 1962; **Freq:** Monthly; **Circ:** 4,000
Usual Pagination: 52
Advertising Director: Katarzyna Chmal

Poland

Profile: Provides practical advice in hotel management and presents newest trends on hotel market.
Language(s): Polish
Mechanical Data: Type Area: A4
Supplement(s): Raport z rynku hotelarskiego w Polsce - 1xY
BUSINESS: CATERING: Catering, Hotels & Restaurants

HUTNIK - WIADOMOŚCI HUTNICZE
1811053PL27-1
Editorial: ul. Krasińskiego, 13, 40-019 KATOWICE
Tel: 32 256 17 77 **Fax:** 32 256 17 77
Web site: http://sigma-not.pl
ISSN: 1230-3534
Date Established: 1929; **Freq:** Monthly
Usual Pagination: 44
Profile: Focuses on technologies and machines for metal produce, forming of steel, scientific and technical presentations, automation and mechanization of processes.
Language(s): Polish
ADVERTISING RATES:
Full Page Mono .... PLN 1200.00
Full Page Colour .... PLN 2000.00
Mechanical Data: Type Area: 204 x 287 mm
BUSINESS: METAL, IRON & STEEL

IDG.PL
1839867PL5F-1
Editorial: ul. Jordanowska 12, 04-204 WARSZAWA
Tel: 22 321 78 00 **Fax:** 22 321 78 88
Email: idg@idg.com.pl **Web site:** http://www.idg.pl
Circ: 2,474,086 Unique Users
Profile: Web site about computing news, computer games, Internet and computer software.
Language(s): Polish
BUSINESS: COMPUTERS & AUTOMATION: Multimedia

IMPERIUM TV
1795660PL76C-18
Editorial: ul. Motorowa, 1, 04-035 WARSZAWA
Tel: 22 517 01 64 **Fax:** 22 517 03 52
Email: imperiumtv@bauer.pl **Web site:** http://www.reklama.bauer.pl
ISSN: 1427-2202
Date Established: 1997; **Freq:** Weekly; **Circ:** 226,000
Usual Pagination: 64
Advertising Director: Izabela Sarnecka
Profile: TV guide covering latest news in media world, films and cinema.
Language(s): Polish
ADVERTISING RATES:
Full Page Colour .... PLN 11600.00
Mechanical Data: Type Area: 210 x 280 mm
CONSUMER: MUSIC & PERFORMING ARTS: TV & Radio

IMPULS
1819400PL72J-7
Editorial: ul. Wąwozowa 7B, 75-339 KOSZALIN
Tel: 94 716 22 86 **Fax:** 94 347 31 87
Email: biuro@rhemapress.pl **Web site:** http://www.rhemapress.pl
Date Established: 2001; **Freq:** Monthly; **Cover Price:** Free; **Circ:** 10,000
Usual Pagination: 16
Profile: Contains information on city life and cultural events.
Language(s): Polish
Mechanical Data: Type Area: 205 x 295 mm
LOCAL NEWSPAPERS: Community Newsletters

INFOMARKET - MAGAZYN AGD I RTV
1929158PL43A-4
Editorial: ul. Trylogii, 2/16, 50, 01-982 WARSZAWA
Tel: 22 835 19 17 **Fax:** 22 835 19 17
Email: redakcja@infomarket.edu.pl **Web site:** http://www.infomarket.edu.pl
Date Established: 2009; **Freq:** Monthly; **Cover Price:** Free
Usual Pagination: 48
Managing Director: Piotr Krakowiak
Profile: Magazine about home appliances and home electronic devices.
Language(s): Polish
Mechanical Data: Type Area: 240 x 325 mm
BUSINESS: ELECTRICAL RETAIL TRADE

INFORMATOR BCC - FIRMY DORADCZE I KANCELARIE PRAWNICZE
1796001PL44-18
Editorial: pl. Żelaznej Bramy, 10, 01-318 WARSZAWA **Tel:** 22 625 30 37 **Fax:** 22 582 61 67
Email: wydawca@bcc.org.pl **Web site:** http://www.bcc.org.pl
Date Established: 1991
Cover Price: Free; **Circ:** 4,000
Usual Pagination: 52
Profile: Contains legal advice and information on notary solicitors.
Language(s): Polish
Mechanical Data: Type Area: A5
BUSINESS: LEGAL

INNE OBLICZA HISTORII
1928877PL94J-318
Editorial: ul. Kościuszki 51 B, 87-100 TORUŃ
Email: redakcja@ioh.pl **Web site:** http://www.ioh.pl
ISSN: 0137-8929
Date Established: 2004; **Freq:** Quarterly; **Circ:** 25,000
Usual Pagination: 84
Profile: Magazine dedicated entirely to history and historic issues, culture and society.
Language(s): Polish
Mechanical Data: Type Area: 205 x 272 mm
CONSUMER: OTHER CLASSIFICATIONS: Popular Science

INTEGRACJA
1708831PL56L-1
Editorial: ul. Sapieżyńska, 10a, 00-215 WARSZAWA
Tel: 22 635 13 30 **Fax:** 22 635 11 82
Email: redakcja@integracja.org **Web site:** http://www.integracja.org
ISSN: 12328510
Date Established: 1994; **Freq:** 6 issues yearly;
Cover Price: Free; **Circ:** 50,000
Usual Pagination: 92
Profile: Dedicated to disabled people and informs on their rights, legal issues, health and society.
Language(s): Polish
Mechanical Data: Type Area: 203 x 275 mm
BUSINESS: HEALTH & MEDICAL: Disability & Rehabilitation

INTERNET MAKER
1796224PL5C-8
Editorial: ul. Leszczynowa, 11, 03-197 WARSZAWA
Tel: 22 257 84 99 **Fax:** 22 257 84 00
Email: avt@avt.com.pl **Web site:** http://www.internetmaker.pl
Date Established: 2006; **Freq:** Daily; **Cover Price:** Paid
Advertising Director: Bożena Krzykawska;
Publisher: Szymon Narożniak
Profile: Focuses on web mastering, software and programs writing and web graphics.
Language(s): Polish
BUSINESS: COMPUTERS & AUTOMATION: Professional Personal Computers

INŻYNIERIA MATERIAŁOWA
1811054PL19A-2
Editorial: ul. Krasińskiego, 8, 40-017 KATOWICE
Tel: 32 603 44 22 **Fax:** 32 603 44 32
Email: i.mat@o2.pl **Web site:** http://sigma-not.pl
ISSN: 0208-6247
Date Established: 1980; **Freq:** 6 issues yearly
Usual Pagination: 38
Profile: Focuses on projects on metal and ceramic-metal production, composites and polymers, development of new materials and technologies, engineering and popularization of new methods of testing, etc.
Language(s): Polish
ADVERTISING RATES:
Full Page Mono .... PLN 2000.00
Full Page Colour .... PLN 2600.00
Mechanical Data: Type Area: 204 x 290 mm
BUSINESS: ENGINEERING & MACHINERY

INŻYNIERIA I UTRZYMANIE RUCHU ZAKŁADÓW PRZEMYSŁOWYCH
1837263PL19A-7
Editorial: ul. Wita Stwosza 59a, 02-661 WARSZAWA
Tel: 22 852 44 15 **Fax:** 22 899 29 48
Email: redakcja@utrzymanieruchu.pl **Web site:** http://utrzymanieruchu.pl
Freq: Monthly; **Circ:** 5,000
Editor-in-Chief: Tomasz Kurzacz
Profile: Contains information on latest techniques, tools and trends, automation and diagnostics, maintenance and management, production logistic solutions. Electronic version of magazine also includes interactive presentations, animation, sound and videos.
Language(s): Polish
ADVERTISING RATES:
Full Page Mono .... PLN 3750.00
Mechanical Data: Type Area: 200 x 267mm
BUSINESS: ENGINEERING & MACHINERY

IT RESELLER
1708909PL5B-48
Editorial: ul. Tytoniowa, 20, 04-228 WARSZAWA
Tel: 22 515 00 67 **Fax:** 22 613 25 84
Email: redakcja@itreseller.pl **Web site:** http://www.itreseller.pl
Date Established: 2002; **Freq:** 26 issues yearly;
Cover Price: Free; **Circ:** 9,000
Usual Pagination: 48
Advertising Director: Anna Jelińska
Profile: Contains informative-educational articles on IT industry, general information on products, new technologies, legal aspects and clients service.
Language(s): Polish
ADVERTISING RATES:
Full Page Colour .... PLN 12000.00
Mechanical Data: Type Area: 235 x 297 mm
BUSINESS: COMPUTERS & AUTOMATION: Data Processing

IZOLACJE
1929131PL4R-2
Editorial: ul. Karczewska, 18, 04-112 WARSZAWA
Tel: 22 810 58 09 **Fax:** 22 810 27 42
Email: redakcja@izolacje.com.pl **Web site:** http://www.izolacje.com.pl
ISSN: 1427-6682
Date Established: 1996; **Freq:** Monthly; **Circ:** 9,000
Usual Pagination: 100
Advertising Director: Joanna Grabek
Profile: Specialized magazine dedicated to various kinds of insulation used in construction.
Language(s): Polish
Mechanical Data: Type Area: 210 x 297 mm
BUSINESS: ARCHITECTURE & BUILDING: Building Related

JACHTING
1709089PL91A-6
Editorial: ul. Saska, 9a, 03-968 WARSZAWA
Tel: 22 616 16 04 **Fax:** 22 616 15 24
Email: jachting@jachting.pl **Web site:** http://www.jachting.pl
ISSN: 0867-4337
Freq: Monthly; **Circ:** 16,000
Usual Pagination: 116
Profile: Featuring useful articles about techniques and practices at sea best tips, tests of new yachts and boats, reviews and descriptions of exotic trips, interviews, columns and sea stories.
Language(s): Polish
ADVERTISING RATES:
Full Page Colour .... PLN 12000.00
Mechanical Data: Type Area: 220 x 275 mm
CONSUMER: RECREATION & LEISURE: Boating & Yachting

JEANS & SPORTSWEAR
1796114PL47A-254
Editorial: ul. Stępińska, 22/30, 00-739 WARSZAWA
Tel: 22 559 39 61 **Fax:** 22 559 39 62
Email: biuro@promedia.biz.pl **Web site:** http://www.promedia.biz.pl
Date Established: 1999; **Freq:** Quarterly; **Circ:** 3,000
Profile: Provides information on youth clothing: sports, jeans and outdoor clothes.
Language(s): Polish
Mechanical Data: Type Area: A4
BUSINESS: CLOTHING & TEXTILES

KALEJDOSKOP LOSÓW
1708813PL74A-1046
Editorial: ul. św. Antoniego, 7, 50-073 WROCŁAW
Tel: 71 344 77 75 **Fax:** 71 346 01 74
Email: kl@phoenix.pl **Web site:** http://www.phoenix.pl
ISSN: 1428-5274
Date Established: 1997; **Freq:** Monthly; **Circ:** 95,000
Usual Pagination: 48
Profile: Magazine featuring love stories, specialists' advice and crosswords.
Language(s): Polish
ADVERTISING RATES:
Full Page Colour .... PLN 3500.00
Mechanical Data: Type Area: 205 x 280 mm
CONSUMER: WOMEN'S INTEREST CONSUMER MAGAZINES: Women's Interest

KARDIOCHIRURGIA I TORAKOCHIRURGIA POLSKA
1796195PL56A-29
Editorial: ul. Szpitalna, 2, 41-800 ZABRZE
Tel: 32 278 43 34 **Fax:** 32 278 43 34
Email: wokedit@infomed.slam.katowice.pl **Web site:** http://www.termedia.pl/magazine.php?magazine_id=40&magazine_subpage=CURRENT
ISSN: 1731-5530
Date Established: 2006; **Freq:** Quarterly; **Circ:** 1,000
Usual Pagination: 100
Managing Director: Andrzej Kordas
Profile: Informs on atrial fibrillation, cardiomyopathy, heart failure, transplantation and pulmonary issues.
Language(s): Polish
Mechanical Data: Type Area: A4
BUSINESS: HEALTH & MEDICAL

KARDIOLOGIA POLSKA
1796196PL56A-30
Editorial: ul. Stawki, 3a, 3, 00-193 WARSZAWA
Tel: 22 887 20 56/7 **Fax:** 22 887 20 58
Email: kardiologiapolska@ptkardio.pl **Web site:** http://www.kardiologiapolska.pl
ISSN: 0022-9032
Date Established: 2005; **Freq:** Monthly; **Circ:** 5,000
Usual Pagination: 150
Managing Director: Andrzej Kordas
Profile: Focused on Polish cardiology.
Language(s): Polish
Mechanical Data: Type Area: A4
BUSINESS: HEALTH & MEDICAL

KINO
1708984PL76A-4
Editorial: ul. Chełmska, 21 bud. 4, 28, 00-724 WARSZAWA **Tel:** 22 841 68 43 **Fax:** 22 841 90 57
Email: kino@kino.org.pl **Web site:** http://www.kino.org.pl
ISSN: 0023-1673
Date Established: 1966; **Freq:** Monthly; **Circ:** 10,000
Usual Pagination: 88
Advertising Director: Jacek Cegiełka
Profile: A magazine dedicated to films and audiovisual multimedia.
Language(s): Polish
Mechanical Data: Type Area: 200 x 275 mm
CONSUMER: MUSIC & PERFORMING ARTS: Cinema

KINO DOMOWE
1708627PL76A-3
Editorial: ul. Jordanowska, 12, 04-204 WARSZAWA
Tel: 22 321 78 00 **Fax:** 22 321 78 88
Email: kino_domowe@idg.com.pl **Web site:** http://www.kinodomowe.idg.pl
Date Established: 1999; **Freq:** Monthly; **Circ:** 25,000
Usual Pagination: 68
Advertising Director: Włodzimierz Duszyk;
Publisher: Maciej Obuchowicz
Profile: Focused on DVD technologies, DVD equipment available on Polish market, DVD film reviews and entertainment news.
Language(s): Polish
ADVERTISING RATES:
Full Page Mono .... PLN 9000.00
Mechanical Data: Type Area: 225 x 275 mm
CONSUMER: MUSIC & PERFORMING ARTS: Cinema

KOBIETA I ŻYCIE
1929140PL74A-1042
Editorial: ul. Motorowa 1, 04-035 WARSZAWA
Tel: 22 517 52 64
Email: redakcja@kobietaizycie.com.pl **Web site:** http://www.reklama.bauer.pl
ISSN: 0023-2548
Date Established: 2008; **Freq:** Monthly; **Circ:** 620,000
Usual Pagination: 100
Managing Director: Monika Krokiewicz; **Advertising Director:** Ewa Kozłowska
Profile: Magazine covering celebrities, fashion, beauty, culinary recipes, interiors, health, entertainment, etc.
Language(s): Polish
ADVERTISING RATES:
Full Page Colour .... PLN 47250.00
Mechanical Data: Type Area: 210 x 280 mm
CONSUMER: WOMEN'S INTEREST CONSUMER MAGAZINES: Women's Interest

KOMPUTER ŚWIAT
765855PL5D-1
Editorial: ul. Domaniewska, 52, 02-672 WARSZAWA
Tel: 22 232 00 78 **Fax:** 22 232 55 05
Email: redakcja@komputerswiat.pl **Web site:** http://www.komputerswiat.pl
ISSN: 1506-4026
Date Established: 1998; **Freq:** 26 issues yearly; **Circ:** 48,437
Managing Director: Małgorzata Barankiewicz;
Advertising Director: Paweł Stano
Profile: Magazine containing articles on new products and technology for computers and multimedia in general.
Language(s): Polish
Readership: Aimed at beginners and advanced computer users.
ADVERTISING RATES:
Full Page Colour .... PLN 19000.00
Mechanical Data: Type Area: 230 x 297 mm
BUSINESS: COMPUTERS & AUTOMATION: Personal Computers

KOMPUTER ŚWIAT BIBLIOTECZKA
1708782PL5D-7
Editorial: ul. Domaniewska, 52, 02-672 WARSZAWA
Tel: 22 232 00 78 **Fax:** 22 232 55 05
Email: redakcja@komputerswiat.pl **Web site:** http://www.komputerswiat.pl
Date Established: 1999
Usual Pagination: 116
Managing Director: Małgorzata Barankiewicz;
Advertising Director: Paweł Stano
Profile: Magazine for beginners and intermediate computer users - learning, multimedia, advice on computer usage.
Language(s): Polish
Mechanical Data: Type Area: 140x187 mm
BUSINESS: COMPUTERS & AUTOMATION: Personal Computers

KOMPUTER ŚWIAT EKSPERT
1708781PL5C-15
Editorial: ul. Domaniewska, 52, 02-672 WARSZAWA
Tel: 22 232 00 78 **Fax:** 22 232 55 05
Email: redakcja@ks-ekspert.pl **Web site:** http://www.ks-ekspert.pl
Date Established: 2002; **Freq:** Monthly
Usual Pagination: 84
Managing Director: Małgorzata Barankiewicz;
Advertising Director: Paweł Stano
Profile: Featuring advice on computer's software and program's usage, tips for programmers, webmasters and system administrators.
Language(s): Polish
Mechanical Data: Type Area: 215 x 297 mm
BUSINESS: COMPUTERS & AUTOMATION: Professional Personal Computers

KOMPUTER ŚWIAT TWÓJ NIEZBĘDNIK
1708779PL5D-10
Editorial: ul. Domaniewska, 52, 02-672 WARSZAWA
Tel: 22 232 00 78 **Fax:** 22 232 55 05
Email: redakcja@komputerswiat.pl **Web site:** http://www.komputerswiat.pl
ISSN: 1640-2332
Date Established: 2000; **Freq:** 6 issues yearly
Advertising Director: Paweł Stano
Profile: Magazine on computer programs, multimedia and computing entertainment.
Language(s): Polish
ADVERTISING RATES:
Full Page Colour .... PLN 19000.00
Mechanical Data: Type Area: 215 x 297 mm
BUSINESS: COMPUTERS & AUTOMATION: Personal Computers

KOŃ POLSKI
1708659PL81D-1
Editorial: ul. Wał Miedzeszyński, 872, 4, 03-917 WARSZAWA **Tel:** 22 869 93 18
Email: konpolski@konpolski.pl **Web site:** http://www.konpolski.pl
ISSN: 0137-1487
Date Established: 1965; **Freq:** Monthly; **Circ:** 12,000
Usual Pagination: 80
Profile: Featuring information on horses: breeding, veterinary advice and recreation.
Language(s): Polish
ADVERTISING RATES:
Full Page Mono .... PLN 1480.00
Full Page Colour .... PLN 2200.00
Mechanical Data: Type Area: 204 x 286 mm
CONSUMER: ANIMALS & PETS: Horses & Ponies

KOSMETYKI
1796158PL15A-5
Editorial: ul. Śmiała, 26, 01-523 WARSZAWA
Tel: 22 327 16 82 **Fax:** 22 327 16 87
Email: llewandowska@mediadirect.pl **Web site:** http://www.magazynkosmetyki.pl
ISSN: 1234-4575
Date Established: 2005; **Freq:** Monthly; **Circ:** 10,000
Usual Pagination: 60
Advertising Director: Beata Kwaśny
Profile: Featuring information on new products and trade names, news and trends in cosmetics, reports on cosmetics' development, opinions of retail sellers and producers.
Language(s): Polish
ADVERTISING RATES:
Full Page Colour .... PLN 17000.00
Mechanical Data: Type Area: 205x275 mm
BUSINESS: COSMETICS & HAIRDRESSING: Cosmetics

KUCHNIA
1626020PL74P-2
Editorial: ul. Czerska, 8/10, 00-732 WARSZAWA
Tel: 22 555 66 06 **Fax:** 22 555 66 68
Email: kuchnia@agora.pl **Web site:** http://www.ugotujto.pl
ISSN: 1233-2976
Date Established: 1995; **Freq:** Monthly; **Circ:** 39,000
Usual Pagination: 92
Advertising Director: Beata Remjasz
Profile: Cookery magazine containing recipes and articles on home cooking and baking.
Language(s): Polish
Mechanical Data: Type Area: 203 x 272 mm
CONSUMER: WOMEN'S INTEREST CONSUMER MAGAZINES: Food & Cookery

KULTURYSTYKA I FITNESS
1709109PL75P-1
Editorial: ul. Ostrzycka, 2/4, 04-035 WARSZAWA
Tel: 22 673 77 95 **Fax:** 22 870 78 08
Email: redakcja@kif.pl **Web site:** http://www.kif.pl
ISSN: 1429-5156
Date Established: 1997; **Freq:** Monthly; **Circ:** 25,000
Usual Pagination: 134
Profile: Magazine about body-building and fitness in Poland and abroad with practical advice.
Language(s): Polish
CONSUMER: SPORT: Fitness/Bodybuilding

KUP AUTO
1810897PL77A-35
Editorial: ul. Giżycka, 4, 60-348 POZNAŃ
Tel: 61 8656 38 60 **Fax:** 61 656 38 88
Email: darek.misiorny@tdm.com.pl **Web site:** http://www.tdm.com.pl
ISSN: 1231-8884
Date Established: 1991; **Freq:** Weekly; **Cover Price:** Free; **Circ:** 10,000
Usual Pagination: 32
Profile: Focused on interesting facts from automobile industry, contains car industry ads and from individuals.
Language(s): Polish
Mechanical Data: Type Area: A4
CONSUMER: MOTORING & CYCLING: Motoring

KUP DOM
1810898PL4A-24
Editorial: ul. Giżycka, 4, POZNAŃ **Tel:** 61 656 38 60
Fax: 61 656 38 88
Email: halina.lipinska@tdm.com.pl **Web site:** http://www.tdm.com.pl
ISSN: 1231-8914
Date Established: 1993; **Freq:** Weekly; **Cover Price:** Free; **Circ:** 10,000
Usual Pagination: 32
Profile: Contains advice and offers on interior design and décor, house building news, properties and developer companies, bank housing mortgage offers and professional tips.
Language(s): Polish
Mechanical Data: Type Area: A4
BUSINESS: ARCHITECTURE & BUILDING: Architecture

KURIER FINANSOWY
1810996PL74M-1
Editorial: ul. Solec, 101, 5, 00-382 WARSZAWA
Tel: 22 629 18 77 **Fax:** 22 629 18 72
Email: redakcja@kurier-finansowy.pl **Web site:** http://www.alebank.pl
ISSN: 1897-032X
Date Established: 2006; **Freq:** 6 issues yearly; **Circ:** 4,000
Usual Pagination: 56
Managing Director: Waldemar Zbytek
Profile: Contains news on personal financing and investments.
Language(s): Polish
ADVERTISING RATES:
Full Page Colour .... PLN 11600.00
Mechanical Data: Type Area: 220 x 280 mm
CONSUMER: WOMEN'S INTEREST CONSUMER MAGAZINES: Personal Finance

KURIER LUBELSKI
1839886PL67B-47
Editorial: ul. 3 Maja 14, 20-078 LUBLIN
Tel: 81 532 66 34 **Fax:** 81 532 68 35
Email: redakcja@kurierlubelski.pl **Web site:** http://www.kurierlubelski.pl
ISSN: 0137-9224
Date Established: 1957; **Freq:** Daily; **Circ:** 10,884
Advertising Director: Agnieszka Kulik
Profile: Regional newspaper covering regional political and economical news, culture and social issues.
Language(s): Polish
ADVERTISING RATES:
Full Page Mono .... PLN 7200.00
Full Page Colour .... PLN 11000.00
Mechanical Data: Type Area: 180 x 258mm
REGIONAL DAILY & SUNDAY NEWSPAPERS: Regional Daily Newspapers

KURIER MEDYCYNY
1819581PL56A-45
Editorial: ul. Kubickiego, 7, 13, 02-954 WARSZAWA
Tel: 22 550 61 23 **Fax:** 22 550 61 25
Email: redakcja@kurier-medycyny.com **Web site:** http://www.kurier-medycyny.eu/km_cms
ISSN: 1896-7434
Date Established: 2006; **Freq:** Monthly; **Cover Price:** Free
Usual Pagination: 40
Profile: Focuses on health issues, health protection and national health service in Poland and worldwide.
Language(s): Polish
ADVERTISING RATES:
Full Page Colour .... PLN 13000.00
Mechanical Data: Type Area: A4
BUSINESS: HEALTH & MEDICAL

KURIER PORANNY
1819655PL67B-41
Editorial: ul. św. Mikołaja, 1, 15-419 BIAŁYSTOK
Tel: 85 748 96 13 **Fax:** 85 748 96 20
Email: redakcja@poranny.pl **Web site:** http://www.poranny.pl
ISSN: 0866-9511
Date Established: 1989; **Freq:** Mornings
Usual Pagination: 32
Editor: Piotr Wąsikowski; **Managing Director:** Krzysztof Paliński; **Advertising Director:** Jacek Romanowski; **Publisher:** Barbara Likowska-Matys
Profile: Informative regional newspaper with business news, ranking the best and biggest companies in Podlasie.
Language(s): Polish
Mechanical Data: Type Area: A3
REGIONAL DAILY & SUNDAY NEWSPAPERS: Regional Daily Newspapers

KURIER SZCZECIŃSKI DZIENNIK POMORZA ZACHODNIEGO
1614561PL67B-17
Editorial: pl. Hołdu Pruskiego, 8, 70-550 SZCZECIN
Tel: 91 442 91 00/01 **Fax:** 91 442 91 05
Email: redakcja@kurier.szczecin.pl **Web site:** http://www.kurier.szczecin.pl
ISSN: 0137-9240
Date Established: 1945; **Freq:** Daily
Usual Pagination: 24
Managing Director: Tomasz Kowlaczyk; **Advertising Director:** Andrzej Szymkiewicz
Profile: A socio-informative regional newspaper covering all kinds of news.
Language(s): Polish
Mechanical Data: Type Area: A3 (31,5 x 42)
REGIONAL DAILY & SUNDAY NEWSPAPERS: Regional Daily Newspapers

KURIER TV
1622904PL76C-2
Editorial: ul. Motorowa, 1, 04-035 WARSZAWA
Tel: 22 517 03 93 **Fax:** 22 517 05 27
Email: kuriertv@bauer.pl **Web site:** http://www.reklama.bauer.pl
ISSN: 1644-7522
Date Established: 2002; **Freq:** Weekly; **Circ:** 451,000
Usual Pagination: 48
Advertising Director: Izabela Sarnecka
Profile: Magazine containing a guide to television programmes, covering news and stories on films, programmes and actors.
Language(s): Polish
ADVERTISING RATES:
Full Page Colour .... PLN 18900.00
Mechanical Data: Type Area: 225 x 285 mm
CONSUMER: MUSIC & PERFORMING ARTS: TV & Radio

KWIETNIK
1202194PL93-5
Editorial: ul. Czerska, 8/10, 00-732 WARSZAWA
Tel: 22 555 68 79 **Fax:** 22 555 66 74
Email: kwietnik@agora.pl **Web site:** http://www.kwietnik.pl
ISSN: 1233-3808
Date Established: 1995; **Freq:** Monthly; **Circ:** 83,000
Usual Pagination: 60
Advertising Director: Elżbieta Kaiser
Profile: Magazine providing practical advice for plant lovers.
Language(s): Polish
Readership: Aimed at women aged 25 to 54 years.
Mechanical Data: Type Area: 205 x 272 mm
CONSUMER: GARDENING

LABORATORIUM - PRZEGLĄD OGÓLNOPOLSKI
1810971PL55-8
Editorial: al. Rożdzieńskiego, 188, 40-203 KATOWICE **Tel:** 32 788 51 40 **Fax:** 32 203 93 56
Email: laboratorium@elamed.pl **Web site:** http://www.laboratorium.elamed.pl
ISSN: 1643-7381
Date Established: 2001; **Freq:** Monthly
Usual Pagination: 70
Profile: Presents scientific laboratories news, testing of laboratory products and equipment.
Language(s): Polish
Mechanical Data: Type Area: 204 x 290 mm
BUSINESS: APPLIED SCIENCE & LABORATORIES

ŁADNY DOM
1201732PL4E-5
Editorial: ul. Czerska, 8/10, 00-732 WARSZAWA
Tel: 22 555 68 56 **Fax:** 22 555 66 71
Email: ladnydom@agora.pl **Web site:** http://www.ladnydom.pl
ISSN: 1506-3267
Date Established: 1998; **Freq:** Monthly; **Circ:** 90,000
Usual Pagination: 160
Advertising Director: Elżbieta Kaiser
Profile: Magazine providing advice and features on building, renovating, converting, extensions and interior design. Includes photos of houses and gardens.
Language(s): Polish
Readership: Aimed at active self-builders, architects, designers and home owners.
ADVERTISING RATES:
Full Page Colour .... PLN 24600.00
Mechanical Data: Type Area: 203 x 272 mm
BUSINESS: ARCHITECTURE & BUILDING: Building

LAIF
1708865PL76E-4
Editorial: ul. Locci, 30, 02-928 WARSZAWA
Tel: 22 852 17 31 **Fax:** 22 899 29 45
Email: przemek@laif.pl **Web site:** http://www.laif.pl
ISSN: 1642-4220
Date Established: 2001; **Freq:** Monthly; **Circ:** 55,000
Usual Pagination: 80
Managing Director: Anna Rozwadowska
Profile: Provides information on pop and rock music, clubbing, lifestyle.
Language(s): Polish
Mechanical Data: Type Area: 232 x 290 mm
Supplement(s): Laifstyle - 6xY
CONSUMER: MUSIC & PERFORMING ARTS: Pop Music

LAIFSTYLE
1708973PL91E-1
Editorial: For all contact details see main record, Laif
Tel: 22 637 54 23 **Fax:** 22 637 54 23
Email: redakcja@laif.pl
Freq: 6 issues yearly; **Circ:** 55,000
Usual Pagination: 114
Managing Director: Kicińska; **Advertising Director:** Anna Orłowska
Language(s): Polish
Supplement to: Laif
CONSUMER: RECREATION & LEISURE: Lifestyle

LAKIERNICTWO PRZEMYSŁOWE
1708743PL16B-1
Editorial: ul. Armii Krajowej, 86, 83-110 TCZEW
Tel: 58 777 01 25 **Fax:** 58 777 01 25
Email: lakiernictwo@goldnet.pl **Web site:** http://www.lakiernictwo.net
ISSN: 1508-7514
Date Established: 1999; **Freq:** 6 issues yearly; **Cover Price:** Free; **Circ:** 6,000
Usual Pagination: 66
Profile: Contains articles on industrial paintwork and varnishing, equipment and various techniques.
Language(s): Polish
Mechanical Data: Type Area: A4
BUSINESS: DECORATING & PAINT: Paint - Technical Manufacture

LAMPA
1708986PL84A-11
Editorial: ul. Hoża, 42, 8, 00-516 WARSZAWA
Tel: 22 622 10 09
Email: redakcja@lampa.art.pl **Web site:** http://www.lampa.art.pl
ISSN: 1732-4661
Date Established: 2004; **Freq:** Monthly; **Annual Sub.:** PLN 90.00; **Circ:** 3,300
Usual Pagination: 88
Advertising Director: Marek Włodarski
Profile: Magazine on city art and modern arts.
Language(s): Polish
ADVERTISING RATES:
Full Page Mono .... PLN 1200.00
Full Page Colour .... PLN 2000.00
CONSUMER: THE ARTS & LITERARY: Arts

LAPTOP MAGAZYN
1795948PL5D-4
Editorial: ul. Rakietników, 27, 10, 02-495 WARSZAWA **Tel:** 22 882 37 33 **Fax:** 22 882 37 66
Email: tomasz.cieslak@laptopmag.pl **Web site:** http://www.laptopmag.pl
Date Established: 2001; **Freq:** 6 issues yearly; **Circ:** 20,000
Usual Pagination: 60
Editor: Tomasz Cieślak; **Managing Director:** Tomasz Cieślak
Profile: Features news on laptops, software, testing and accessories.
Language(s): Polish
Mechanical Data: Type Area: 205x285 mm
BUSINESS: COMPUTERS & AUTOMATION: Personal Computers

LAS POLSKI
1708648PL46-3
Editorial: ul. Kaliska, 1, 7, 02-316 WARSZAWA
Tel: 22 822 03 34 **Fax:** 22 822 66 49
Email: laspolski@oikos.net.pl **Web site:** http://www.laspolski.net.pl
ISSN: 0023-8538
Date Established: 1921; **Freq:** 26 issues yearly; **Circ:** 7,000
Usual Pagination: 36
Profile: Contains articles on forestry: new technologies, tools and machines used in forestry industry.
Language(s): Polish
ADVERTISING RATES:
Full Page Colour .... PLN 3200.00
Mechanical Data: Type Area: A4
BUSINESS: TIMBER, WOOD & FORESTRY

ŁAZIENKA
1860648PL23C-3
Editorial: ul. Andersa, 38, 15-113 BIAŁYSTOK
Tel: 85 653 90 00 **Fax:** 85 653 98 56
Email: redakcja@lazienka.com.pl **Web site:** http://www.lazienka.com.pl
ISSN: 1426-0700
Date Established: 1996; **Freq:** Monthly; **Circ:** 8,000
Usual Pagination: 64
Managing Director: Anita Frank; **Advertising Director:** Ewa Kuryłowicz
Profile: Providing information on sanitary and bathroom equipment, new technologies and ideas for bathroom modification.
Language(s): Polish
Mechanical Data: Type Area: 230 x 310 mm
BUSINESS: FURNISHINGS & FURNITURE: Furnishings & Furniture - Kitchens & Bathrooms

LEKARZ
1810986PL56A-40
Editorial: al. Rożdzieńskiego, 188, 40-203 KATOWICE **Tel:** 32 788 51 44 **Fax:** 322039356
Email: lekarz@elamed.pl **Web site:** http://www.lekarz.elamed.pl
ISSN: 1896-2920
Date Established: 1997; **Freq:** Monthly - miesięcznik
Usual Pagination: 110
Editor-in-Chief: Anna Bętkowska-Bielach
Profile: Presents medical news and events, pharmaceutical news, equipment and description of clinical illnesses, review of medical press.
Language(s): Polish
Mechanical Data: Type Area: 170 x 248 mm
BUSINESS: HEALTH & MEDICAL

LEKI WSPÓŁCZESNEJ TERAPII
1708730PL37-3
Editorial: ul. Dzika, 4, 00-194 WARSZAWA
Tel: 22 635 73 70 **Fax:** 22 635 64 72
Email: r.zoltowski@ppwp.pl **Web site:** http://ppwp.pl
ISSN: 1427-2660
Date Established: 1996; **Freq:** 6 issues yearly; **Circ:** 11,000
Usual Pagination: 80
Managing Director: Paweł Krzysica
Profile: Provides information on new medicine and gives medical advice.
Language(s): Polish
ADVERTISING RATES:
Full Page Colour .... PLN 4700.00
Mechanical Data: Type Area: A4
BUSINESS: PHARMACEUTICAL & CHEMISTS

Poland

LICZ I BUDUJ
1708889PL4E-12
Editorial: ul. Migdałowa, 4, 02-796 WARSZAWA
Tel: 22 242 54 39 **Fax:** 22 242 54 45
Email: lib@sekocenbud.pl **Web site:** http://www.liczibuduj.pl
ISSN: 1425-7254
Date Established: 1996; **Freq:** Monthly; **Circ:** 5,500
Usual Pagination: 40
Advertising Director: Marzena Kasprzak
Profile: Focused on economics in building: prices and costs, law and finance, latest technologies.
Language(s): Polish
Mechanical Data: Type Area: 200 x 290 mm
BUSINESS: ARCHITECTURE & BUILDING: Building

LINUX+
1796121PL5C-6
Editorial: ul. Bokserska, 1, 02-682 WARSZAWA
Tel: 917 338 3631 **Fax:** 22 887 10 11
Email: editors@lpmagazine.org **Web site:** http://www.lpmagazine.org
ISSN: 1732-3681
Date Established: 1997; **Freq:** Quarterly; **Circ:** 10,000
Usual Pagination: 84
Advertising Director: Andrzej Jankowski
Profile: Providing information on Linux, Open Source and solutions for companies. Linux+ is directed to individual Linux users, IT specialists, technicians and professionals, but also to those, who are looking for an alternative for MS Windows. The readers are interested in current news from the world of Linux, new projects and latest distributions and events.
Language(s): English; Polish
Readership: Read by professional network and database administrators, system programmers, webmasters and all those who believe in the power of Open Source software.
ADVERTISING RATES:
Full Page Colour $1500.00
Mechanical Data: Type Area: A4
BUSINESS: COMPUTERS & AUTOMATION: Professional Personal Computers

LINUX+EXTRA
1796112PL5C-2
Editorial: ul. Bokserska, 1, 02-682 WARSZAWA
Tel: 22 887 13 45 **Fax:** 22 887 10 11
Email: redakcja@lpmagazine.org **Web site:** http://www.lpmagazine.org
ISSN: 1508-8618
Date Established: 1995
Circ: 5,000
Usual Pagination: 32
Advertising Director: Patrycja Wądołowski
Profile: Magazine providing information on OpenSuse, Debian, BSD, Open Office, Slackaware, Ubuntu.
Language(s): Polish
Mechanical Data: Type Area: A4
BUSINESS: COMPUTERS & AUTOMATION: Professional Personal Computers

LINUX MAGAZINE
1810927PL5B-49
Editorial: ul. Mangalia, 4, 02-758 WARSZAWA
Tel: 22 742 14 55 **Fax:** 22 642 70 05
Email: info@linux-magazine.pl **Web site:** http://www.linux-magazine.pl
ISSN: 1732-1263
Date Established: 2004; **Freq:** Monthly; **Cover Price:** PLN 24.90; **Circ:** 10,000
Usual Pagination: 100
Profile: Providing information on computing, solutions "real life" and technologies Open Source and Linux.
Language(s): Polish
ADVERTISING RATES:
Full Page Colour .... PLN 5000.00
Mechanical Data: Type Area: A4
BUSINESS: COMPUTERS & AUTOMATION: Data Processing

LIST
1708842PL87-5
Editorial: ul. Dominikańska, 3, 12, 31-043 KRAKÓW
Tel: 12 429 54 79 **Fax:** 12 429 54 79
Email: stow@list.media.pl **Web site:** http://www.list.media.pl
ISSN: 0867-2342
Date Established: 1985; **Freq:** Monthly; **Circ:** 20,000
Usual Pagination: 56
Language(s): Polish
ADVERTISING RATES:
Full Page Colour .... PLN 1600.00
Mechanical Data: Type Area: A4
CONSUMER: RELIGIOUS

LOGO
1709048PL86C-11
Editorial: ul. Czerska, 8/10, 00-732 WARSZAWA
Tel: 22 555 66 30 **Fax:** 22 555 68 10
Email: logo@agora.pl **Web site:** http://www.logo24.pl
ISSN: 1734-1566
Date Established: 2005; **Freq:** Monthly; **Circ:** 118,000
Usual Pagination: 132
Advertising Director: Paulina Skorwider
Profile: Features new trends in men's fashion, newest sport and electronics equipment, new gadgets and cars.
Language(s): Polish
ADVERTISING RATES:
Full Page Colour .... PLN 31000.00
Mechanical Data: Type Area: 218 x 285 mm
CONSUMER: ADULT & GAY MAGAZINES: Men's Lifestyle Magazines

ŁOWIEC POLSKI
1708683PL75F-3
Editorial: ul. Nowy Świat, 35, 00-029 WARSZAWA
Tel: 22 556 82 80 **Fax:** 22 556 82 99
Email: poczta@lowiec.pl **Web site:** http://www.lowiecpolski.pl
ISSN: 0137-1266
Date Established: 1899; **Freq:** Monthly; **Circ:** 40,000
Usual Pagination: 116
Managing Director: Bogdan Bronowski
Profile: Largest hunter-nature magazine in Poland.
Language(s): Polish
ADVERTISING RATES:
Full Page Colour .... PLN 15000.00
Mechanical Data: Type Area: A4
CONSUMER: SPORT: Shooting

LUBIĘ GOTOWAĆ
1626026PL74P-1
Editorial: ul. Czerska, 8/10, 00-732 WARSZAWA
Tel: 22 555 66 06 **Fax:** 22 555 66 67
Email: lubiegotowac@agora.pl **Web site:** http://www.lubiegotowac.pl
ISSN: 1429-2866
Date Established: 1997; **Freq:** Monthly; **Circ:** 52,000
Usual Pagination: 36
Advertising Director: Beata Remjasz
Profile: Cookery magazine featuring recipes and tips. Each issue has a different seasonal theme.
Language(s): Polish
Readership: Read by cookery enthusiasts.
Mechanical Data: Type Area: 134 x 202 mm
CONSUMER: WOMEN'S INTEREST CONSUMER MAGAZINES: Food & Cookery

M JAK MAMA
1819402PL56M-1
Editorial: ul. Kamionkowska, 45, 03-812 WARSZAWA **Tel:** 22 590 50 00 **Fax:** 22 590 54 44
Email: redakcja@miesiecznikmjakmam.pl **Web site:** http://www.miesiecznikmjakmama.pl
ISSN: 1897-2071
Date Established: 2007; **Freq:** Monthly; **Circ:** 89,143
Usual Pagination: 96
Managing Director: Katarzyna Białek; **Advertising Director:** Anna Dygasiewicz-Piwko
Profile: Magazine covering news from gynaecology, provides practical advice on giving birth, baby care.
Language(s): Polish
Mechanical Data: Type Area: 210 x 280 mm
BUSINESS: HEALTH & MEDICAL: Family Planning

M JAK MIESZKANIE
1708669PL4E-13
Editorial: ul. Kamionkowska, 45, 03-812 WARSZAWA **Tel:** 22 590 51 09 **Fax:** 22 590 51 35
Email: mieszkanie@murator.com.pl **Web site:** http://www.mjakmieszkanie.pl
ISSN: 1508-2083
Date Established: 2000; **Freq:** Monthly; **Circ:** 128,000
Usual Pagination: 144
Managing Director: Katarzyna Białek; **Advertising Director:** Anna Dygasiewicz-Piwko
Profile: Providing information on flat renovations, practical advice on interior design, tools and house fixing, projects and house interior arrangements.
Language(s): Polish
Mechanical Data: Type Area: 210 x 280 mm
BUSINESS: ARCHITECTURE & BUILDING: Building

M JAK MIESZKANIE POLECA
1819444PL1E-8
Editorial: ul. Kamionkowska, 45, 03-812 WARSZAWA **Tel:** 22 590 51 09 **Fax:** 22 590 51 35
Email: mieszkanie@murator.com.pl **Web site:** http://www.mjakmieszkanie.pl
ISSN: 1733-2362
Date Established: 2006
Circ: 50,000
Usual Pagination: 96
Managing Director: Katarzyna Białek; **Advertising Director:** Anna Dygasiewicz-Piwko
Profile: Contains detailed and sufficient information on real-estate market, tips on buying property, advice on paperwork done while buying a house, interior design advice and practical tips on property renovation.
Language(s): Polish
Mechanical Data: Type Area: 210 x 280 mm
BUSINESS: FINANCE & ECONOMICS: Property

MACHINA
1795858PL76E-5
Editorial: Al. Jerozolimskie, 146c, 02-305 WARSZAWA **Tel:** 22 347 50 00 **Fax:** 22 347 50 01
Email: redakcja@machina.net.pl **Web site:** http://www.machina.net.pl
ISSN: 1426-2312
Date Established: 1995; **Freq:** Monthly; **Circ:** 100,000
Usual Pagination: 132
Profile: Magazine on pop culture, music and entertainment.
Language(s): Polish
Mechanical Data: Type Area: 210 x 280 mm
CONSUMER: MUSIC & PERFORMING ARTS: Pop Music

MAGAZYN AUTOSTRADY
1811001PL42B-2
Editorial: al. Roździeńskiego, 188, 40-203 KATOWICE **Tel:** 32 788 52 53 **Fax:** 32 203 93 56
Email: autostrady@elamed.pl **Web site:** http://www.autostrady.elamed.pl
ISSN: 1730-0703
Date Established: 2002; **Freq:** Monthly
Usual Pagination: 80
Editor: Sabina Szczerbak; **Advertising Director:** Justyna Ścibska
Profile: Focused on design, building of motorways and bridges, technologies and materials for modern road building.
Language(s): Polish
ADVERTISING RATES:
Full Page Colour .... EUR 1180.00
Mechanical Data: Type Area: 204 x 290 mm
BUSINESS: CONSTRUCTION: Roads

MAGAZYN BCC (W MIESIĘCZNIKU BUSINESSMAN.PL)
1795640PL14A-68
Editorial: pl. Żelaznej Bramy, 10, 00-136 WARSZAWA **Tel:** 22 625 30 37 **Fax:** 22 621 84 20
Email: magazyn@bcc.org.pl **Web site:** http://www.bcc.org.pl
Date Established: 1992
Cover Price: Free; **Circ:** 50,000
Usual Pagination: 16
Advertising Director: Małgorzata Matulka
Profile: Features information on clubbing (BCC), lobbing, business and lifestyle.
Language(s): Polish
Mechanical Data: Type Area: A4
BUSINESS: COMMERCE, INDUSTRY & MANAGEMENT

MAGAZYN GÓRSKI
1709017PL75A-15
Editorial: ul. Głowackiego, 10b, 26, 30-085 KRAKÓW
Tel: 12 638 25 93 **Fax:** 12 638 25 93
Email: ski@alpinmedia.com.pl **Web site:** http://www.alpinmedia.com.pl
ISSN: 1641-9421
Date Established: 2001
Circ: 12,000
Usual Pagination: 84
Profile: Contains information on travelling and mountaineering: trekking, rock climbing, equipment advice, events and competitions.
Language(s): Polish
Mechanical Data: Type Area: 284 x 204 mm
CONSUMER: SPORT

MAGAZYN INSTALATORA
1616244PL3B-3
Editorial: ul. marsz. F. Focha, 7, 4, 80-156 GDAŃSK
Tel: 58 306 29 27 **Fax:** 58 306 29 27
Email: redakcja-mi@instalator.pl **Web site:** http://www.instalator.pl
ISSN: 1505-8336
Date Established: 1998; **Freq:** Monthly; **Cover Price:** Free; **Circ:** 15,000
Usual Pagination: 76
Profile: Magazine focusing on plumbing, heating and ventilation technology.
Language(s): Polish
Readership: Read by fitters and engineers.
Mechanical Data: Type Area: 207 x 293 mm
BUSINESS: HEATING & VENTILATION: Industrial Heating & Ventilation

MAGAZYN INTERNET
1796222PL5C-9
Editorial: ul. Leszczynowa, 11, 03-197 WARSZAWA
Tel: 22 257 84 46 **Fax:** 22 257 84 00
Email: redakcja@mi.com.pl **Web site:** http://www.magazyninternet.pl
Date Established: 1995; **Freq:** Daily; **Cover Price:** Free
Advertising Director: Marta Zaczek
Profile: Educational online magazine with practical advice for all Internet users.
Language(s): Polish
BUSINESS: COMPUTERS & AUTOMATION: Professional Personal Computers

MAGAZYN MŁODEJ KULTURY SLAJD
1929156PL74Q-21
Editorial: ul. Rewolucji 1905 r., 52, 90-213 ŁÓDŹ
Tel: 42 631 59 40 **Fax:** 42 631 59 77
Email: slajd@wshe.lodz.pl **Web site:** http://www.klubslajd.pl
Date Established: 2006; **Freq:** Monthly; **Cover Price:** Free; **Circ:** 90,000
Usual Pagination: 48
Advertising Director: Renata Gralak
Profile: Magazine dedicated to culture, society, cultural trends, fashion, with interviews. Distributed for free in 6 biggest cities in Poland.
Language(s): Polish
Readership: Targets young people in the age group 17-28.
ADVERTISING RATES:
Full Page Colour .... PLN 4000.00
Mechanical Data: Type Area: 160 x 190 mm
CONSUMER: WOMEN'S INTEREST CONSUMER MAGAZINES: Lifestyle

MAGAZYN PRZEMYSŁU MIĘSNEGO
1810958PL22D-202
Editorial: al. Roździeńskiego, 188, 40-203 KATOWICE **Tel:** 32 788 51 20 **Fax:** 32 788 51 21
Email: mpm@elamed.pl **Web site:** http://www.mpm.elamed.pl
ISSN: 1643-7306
Date Established: 2000; **Freq:** Monthly
Usual Pagination: 60
Advertising Director: Beata Sitarz
Profile: Magazine on meat industry providing information on meat processing, newest technologies on keeping it fresh and gives practical advice how to run a meat processing factory.
Language(s): Polish
Mechanical Data: Type Area: 204 x 290 mm
BUSINESS: FOOD: Meat Trade

MAGAZYN ROWEROWY
1708798PL75A-11
Editorial: ul. Bacciarellego, 54 bud. C, 51-649 WROCŁAW **Tel:** 71 347 83 88 **Fax:** 71 347 83 87
Email: redakcja@magazynrowerowy.pl **Web site:** http://www.magazynrowerowy.pl
ISSN: 1643-8744
Date Established: 2002
Circ: 40,000
Usual Pagination: 100
Advertising Director: Paweł Urbaniak
Profile: Features information on equipment, cycling, places and people.
Language(s): Polish
Mechanical Data: Type Area: 215 x 280 mm
CONSUMER: SPORT

MAGAZYN WETERYNARYJNY
1708928PL64H-1
Editorial: ul. 29 Listopada, 10, 00-465 WARSZAWA
Tel: 22 444 24 00 **Fax:** 22 832 10 77
Email: h.zientek@medical-tribune.pl **Web site:** http://www.magwet.pl
ISSN: 1230-4425
Freq: Monthly; **Circ:** 5,000
Usual Pagination: 72
Profile: Featuring diagnosing and treatment of animal diseases.
Language(s): Polish
Mechanical Data: Type Area: A4
BUSINESS: OTHER CLASSIFICATIONS: Veterinary

MAGIEL
1804101PL83-3
Editorial: al. Niepodległości, 162, 66a, 02-554 WARSZAWA **Tel:** 22 564 97 57 **Fax:** 22 849 53 12
Email: magiel@magiel.waw.pl **Web site:** http://www.magiel.waw.pl
ISSN: 1505-1714
Date Established: 1996; **Freq:** Monthly; **Cover Price:** Free; **Circ:** 3,000
Usual Pagination: 52
Advertising Director: Piotr Robaczewski
Profile: Provides information concerning Warsaw School of Economics, students' organisations and students' hobbies, concerts, performances, books and students' life in Warsaw.
Language(s): Polish
Mechanical Data: Type Area: A4
CONSUMER: STUDENT PUBLICATIONS

MAJSTER
1810979PL79A-25
Editorial: ul. Garażowa, 7, 02-651 WARSZAWA
Tel: 22 607 78 19 **Fax:** 22 848 22 66
Email: bartosznowacki@proszynskimedia.pl **Web site:** http://www.diy-majster.pl
ISSN: 0946-2503
Date Established: 1991; **Freq:** Monthly; **Annual Sub.:** PLN 48.00; **Circ:** 55,000
Usual Pagination: 68
Profile: Original projects and ideas for DIY on furniture renovation, house minor repairs and garden work.
Language(s): Polish
ADVERTISING RATES:
Full Page Colour .... PLN 15000.00
Mechanical Data: Type Area: 223 x 295 mm
CONSUMER: HOBBIES & DIY

MAM DZIECKO
1616624PL74D-1
Editorial: ul. Motorowa, 1, 04-035 WARSZAWA
Tel: 22 517 03 86 **Fax:** 22 517 04 95
Email: redakcja@mamdziecko.pl **Web site:** http://www.reklama.bauer.pl
ISSN: 1731-1020
Date Established: 2002; **Freq:** Monthly; **Circ:** 163,745
Usual Pagination: 94
Managing Director: Monika Krokiewicz; **Advertising Director:** Ewa Kozłowska
Profile: Magazine focusing on pregnancy and parenthood.
Language(s): Polish
Readership: Read by expectant mothers and new parents.
ADVERTISING RATES:
Full Page Colour .... PLN 25300.00
Mechanical Data: Type Area: 210 x 280 mm
CONSUMER: WOMEN'S INTEREST CONSUMER MAGAZINES: Child Care

MAMO, TO JA 1623254PL74D-3
Editorial: ul. Wiejska, 19, 00-480 WARSZAWA
Tel: 22 584 23 35 **Fax:** 22 584 23 36
Email: kontakt@mamotoja.pl **Web site:** http://www.mamotoja.pl
ISSN: 1233-7366
Date Established: 1995; **Freq:** Monthly; **Circ:** 179,000
Usual Pagination: 152
Managing Director: Alicja Modzelewska;
Advertising Director: Krystyna Kurmanowska
Profile: Magazine covering parental, health and baby care issues.
Language(s): Polish
Mechanical Data: Type Area: 205 x 270 mm
CONSUMER: WOMEN'S INTEREST CONSUMER MAGAZINES: Child Care

MARKETING I RYNEK 1708624PL2A-3
Editorial: ul. Canaletta, 4, 00-099 WARSZAWA
Tel: 22 827 80 01 **Fax:** 22 827 55 67
Email: mir@pwe.com.pl **Web site:** http://www.marketingirynek.pl
ISSN: 1231-7853
Date Established: 1994; **Freq:** Monthly; **Circ:** 2,000
Usual Pagination: 40
Managing Director: Mariola Rozmus
Profile: Presents theoretical views and newest trends in marketing and functioning of markets, news on Polish companies and practical advice how to organise marketing campaign.
Language(s): Polish
ADVERTISING RATES:
Full Page Mono .... PLN 2500.00
Full Page Colour .... PLN 3500.00
Mechanical Data: Type Area: A4
BUSINESS: COMMUNICATIONS, ADVERTISING & MARKETING

MARKETING W PRAKTYCE
1620678PL2A-2
Editorial: Sady Żoliborskie 13/16, 01-772 WARSZAWA **Tel:** 22 353 25 11 **Fax:** 22 435 51 21
Email: redakcja@marketing.org.pl **Web site:** http://www.marketing.org.pl
ISSN: 1425-8315
Date Established: 1996; **Freq:** Monthly - miesięcznik; **Circ:** 6,100
Usual Pagination: 96
Profile: Magazine focusing on marketing and advertising, newest trends and solutions in marketing.
Language(s): Polish
ADVERTISING RATES:
Full Page Colour .... PLN 9000
Mechanical Data: Type Area: 220 x 280 mm
BUSINESS: COMMUNICATIONS, ADVERTISING & MARKETING

MASZYNY BUDOWLANE
1709046PL19A-9
Editorial: ul. Pasaż Ursynowski 1/45, 02-784 WARSZAWA **Tel:** 22 859 19 65 **Fax:** 22 859 19 67
Email: baranski@posbud.pl **Web site:** http://posbud.com.pl
Freq: Quarterly; **Cover Price:** Free; **Circ:** 3,000
Advertising Manager: Katarzyna Janasiewicz;
Advertising Director: Magdalena Ziemkiewicz
Profile: Professional magazine on construction machines, their repairs and spare parts.
Language(s): Polish
ADVERTISING RATES:
Full Page Colour .... PLN 4000.00
Mechanical Data: Type Area: 175 x 250mm
BUSINESS: ENGINEERING & MACHINERY

MASZYNY, TECHNOLOGIE, MATERIAŁY - TECHNIKA ZAGRANICZNA 1811055PL19A-10
Editorial: ul. Ku Wiśle, 7, 00-950 WARSZAWA
Tel: 22 827 03 71 **Fax:** 22 827 03 71
Email: mwitak@op.pl **Web site:** http://sigma-not.pl
ISSN: 0137-3730
Date Established: 1972; **Freq:** 6 issues yearly
Usual Pagination: 32
Profile: Provides information on management, various analyses, contracts concluded by foreign companies in Poland, electronics, telecommunication, control and automation, news on technology and industry.
Language(s): Polish
ADVERTISING RATES:
Full Page Mono .... PLN 900.00
Full Page Colour .... PLN 1850.00
Mechanical Data: Type Area: 205 x 289 mm
BUSINESS: ENGINEERING & MACHINERY

MATERIAŁY BUDOWLANE
1811056PL4E-24
Editorial: ul. Świętokrzyska, 14a, 00-049 WARSZAWA **Tel:** 22 826 20 27 **Fax:** 22 827 52 55
Email: materbud@sigma-not.pl **Web site:** http://materialybudowlane.info.pl
ISSN: 0137-2971
Date Established: 1947; **Freq:** Monthly
Usual Pagination: 104
Profile: Professional magazine on building materials and newest technologies applied in construction, presents news of Polish building market and legal documentation.
Language(s): Polish
ADVERTISING RATES:
Full Page Mono .... PLN 3000.00
Full Page Colour .... PLN 6000.00
Mechanical Data: Type Area: 205 x 290 mm
BUSINESS: ARCHITECTURE & BUILDING: Building

MAX - PRZEWODNIK DLA INWESTORA 1708718PL42A-10
Editorial: ul. Rolna, 155, 1, 02-729 WARSZAWA
Tel: 22 853 06 87 **Fax:** 22 853 06 86
Email: suwinski@pwbmedia.pl **Web site:** http://www.builderonline.pl
Date Established: 1998; **Freq:** Half-yearly; **Cover Price:** Free
Usual Pagination: 100
Advertising Director: Dominik Suwiński
Profile: Professional magazine on construction, building investments, road construction, management of building investments and European construction funding schemes.
Language(s): Polish
Mechanical Data: Type Area: A4
BUSINESS: CONSTRUCTION

MAXI TUNING 1709041PL77A-25
Editorial: ul. Ostrowskiego, 7, 53-238 WROCŁAW
Tel: 71 780 66 11 **Fax:** 71 780 66 12
Email: redakcja.maxituning@mpp.pl **Web site:** http://www.maxituning.pl
ISSN: 1733-1668
Date Established: 2004
Circ: 33,000
Usual Pagination: 132
Profile: Focused on car tuning, car audio systems and tuning events.
Language(s): Polish
Mechanical Data: Type Area: 215x280 mm
CONSUMER: MOTORING & CYCLING: Motoring

MAXMAGAZINE 1819393PL91E-10
Editorial: ul. Zgoda, 9, 81-361 GDYNIA
Tel: 58 622 63 00 **Fax:** 58 622 63 00
Email: redakcja@maxmagazine.pl **Web site:** http://www.maxmagazine.pl
Date Established: 1999; **Freq:** Monthly; **Cover Price:** Free; **Circ:** 95,000
Usual Pagination: 24
Managing Director: Hanna Kolasińska
Profile: Presents cultural-entertaining information: clubbing, photo reportages, cultural events, films, music, fashion, literature.
Language(s): Polish
Mechanical Data: Type Area: B4mm
CONSUMER: RECREATION & LEISURE: Lifestyle

MEBLE PLUS 1708918PL23A-3
Editorial: ul. Andersa, 38, 15-113 BIAŁYSTOK
Tel: 85 653 90 00 **Fax:** 85 653 98 56
Email: redakcja@meble.com.pl **Web site:** http://www.meble.com.pl
ISSN: 1428-4693
Date Established: 1997; **Freq:** Monthly; **Circ:** 8,000
Usual Pagination: 64
Managing Director: Anita Frank; **Advertising Director:** Katarzyna Pawłowska
Profile: Focused on furniture industry and interior design, promotion of new designs in furniture and market news.
Language(s): Polish
Mechanical Data: Type Area: 230 x 310 mm
BUSINESS: FURNISHINGS & FURNITURE

MEBLE.COM.PL 1796062PL23A-2
Editorial: ul. Andersa, 38, 15-113 BIAŁYSTOK
Tel: 85 653 90 00 **Fax:** 85 653 98 56
Email: webpublikator.com.pl **Web site:** http://www.meble.com.pl
Editor-in-Chief: Marek Hryniewicki; **Managing Director:** Anita Frank; **Advertising Director:** Katarzyna Pawłowska
Profile: Web site on furniture trade, furniture market news and reports, analysis and design, aiming at furniture salespeople and ordinary people.
Language(s): Polish
Mechanical Data: Type Area: 230x310 mm
BUSINESS: FURNISHINGS & FURNITURE

MECHANIK 1835842PL19F-1
Editorial: ul. Świętokrzyska 14A V p. pok. 534, 00-050 WARSZAWA **Tel:** 22 827 16 37
Fax: 22 33 61 476
Email: mechanik@wa.onet.pl **Web site:** http://www.mechanik.media.pl
ISSN: 0025-6552
Date Established: 1909; **Freq:** Monthly; **Cover Price:** PLN 14.50
Annual Sub.: PLN 174.00; **Circ:** 5,000
Editor: Krzysztof Janus; **Editor-in-Chief:** Kazimierz E. Oczoś
Profile: Scientific technical monthly covering design, tool engineering, workshop practice, usage of machine tools and production equipment, abrasive machining, electro erosive machining and plastic forming, plastics processing, metrology, materials science, production organization, hydraulic and pneumatic drives and controls, computer techniques in engineering practice.
Language(s): Polish
Readership: Aimed at design and production engineers, contractors, manufacturers and students of technical secondary schools and colleges.
ADVERTISING RATES:
Full Page Mono .... EUR 697.00
Full Page Colour .... EUR 1066.00
Mechanical Data: Type Area: 210 x 297mm
BUSINESS: ENGINEERING & MACHINERY: Production & Mechanical Engineering

MED INFO 1796160PL56C-1
Editorial: ul. Krzywickiego, 34, 02-078 WARSZAWA
Tel: 22 521 20 00 **Fax:** 22 521 20 20
Email: brog@brog.pl **Web site:** http://www.brog.pl
ISSN: 1733-0521
Date Established: 2004; **Freq:** Monthly; **Circ:** 5,000
Usual Pagination: 48
Managing Director: Radosław Rybiński; **Advertising Director:** Anna Stypińska
Profile: A magazine for medical managers on latest management methods and financing, legal advice and medical equipment.
Language(s): Polish
ADVERTISING RATES:
Full Page Colour .... PLN 5390.00
Mechanical Data: Type Area: 230x297 mm
BUSINESS: HEALTH & MEDICAL: Hospitals

MEDIA2.PL 1977652PL2A-38
Editorial: Kłopotowskiego 22, 03-717 WARSZAWA
Tel: 40 670 26 40 **Fax:** 40 244 26 90
Email: redakcja@media2.pl **Web site:** http://media2.pl
Freq: Daily; **Circ:** 524,786 Unique Users
Profile: Media2.pl covering topics related to media, internet, advertising and PR, as well as new technologies and research. Every day presents latest information, live coverage of press conferences and the current statistics of the media industry.
Readership: Readers are mainly professionals from the media industry, telecommunications, public relations and IT.
BUSINESS: COMMUNICATIONS, ADVERTISING & MARKETING

MEDIA & MARKETING POLSKA
1708927PL2A-7
Editorial: ul. Wał Miedzeszyński, 630, 03-994 WARSZAWA **Tel:** 22 514 65 00 **Fax:** 22 740 50 55
Email: redakcja@media.com.pl **Web site:** http://www.media.com.pl
ISSN: 1507-174X
Date Established: 1999; **Freq:** Weekly; **Circ:** 10,000
Usual Pagination: 28
Advertising Director: Agnieszka Wrembel
Profile: Features latest news from marketing industry, media and advertising, client and ad agencies' relations.
Language(s): Polish
ADVERTISING RATES:
Full Page Colour .... PLN 22000.00
Mechanical Data: Type Area: 228 x 296 mm
BUSINESS: COMMUNICATIONS, ADVERTISING & MARKETING

MEDICAL TRIBUNE 1819406PL56A-44
Editorial: ul. 29 Listopada, 10, 00-465 WARSZAWA
Tel: 22 444 24 00 **Fax:** 22 832 10 77
Email: m-t@m-t.pl **Web site:** http://www.medical-tribune.pl
ISSN: 1895-5754
Date Established: 2006; **Freq:** 26 issues yearly; **Circ:** 20,000
Usual Pagination: 32
Profile: Presents news on Health service and current state of medicine in Poland.
Language(s): Polish
Mechanical Data: Type Area: 273 x 370 mm
BUSINESS: HEALTH & MEDICAL

MEDYCYNA PO DYPLOMIE
1819404PL56A-43
Editorial: ul. 29 Listopada, 10, 00-465 WARSZAWA
Tel: 22 444 24 00 **Fax:** 22 832 10 77
Email: m-t@medical-tribune.pl **Web site:** http://www.medical-tribune.pl
ISSN: 1231-1812
Date Established: 1991; **Freq:** Monthly; **Circ:** 30,000
Usual Pagination: 180
Profile: Contains medical educational articles and reviews of different aspects of medical treatment.
Language(s): Polish
ADVERTISING RATES:
Full Page Colour .... PLN 16900.00
Mechanical Data: Type Area: 209 x 286 mm
BUSINESS: HEALTH & MEDICAL

MEDYCYNA PRAKTYCZNA
1708702PL56A-5
Editorial: ul. Skawińska, 8, 31-066 KRAKÓW
Tel: 12 293 40 20 **Fax:** 12 293 40 30
Email: listy@mp.pl **Web site:** http://www.mp.pl
Date Established: 1991; **Freq:** Monthly; **Circ:** 30,000
Usual Pagination: 200
Advertising Director: Małgorzata Gajewska
Profile: Provides selected articles from the most reputable medical journals in the world, with significant impact on medical practice, most of them are developed by scientific societies and international teams of experts, the current recommendations for diagnostic and therapeutic procedures.
Language(s): Polish
Readership: Aimed at doctors of first contact, therapists and surgeries.
ADVERTISING RATES:
Full Page Mono .... PLN 9000.00
Full Page Colour .... PLN 16000.00
Mechanical Data: Type Area: 205 x 285 mm
BUSINESS: HEALTH & MEDICAL

MEDYCYNA PRAKTYCZNA - CHIRURGIA 1708701PL56A-4
Editorial: ul. Krakowska, 41, 31-066 KRAKÓW
Tel: 12 293 40 70 **Fax:** 12 293 40 10
Email: listy@mp.pl **Web site:** http://www.mp.pl
ISSN: 1507-5230
Date Established: 1997; **Freq:** 6 issues yearly; **Circ:** 5,000
Usual Pagination: 150
Advertising Director: Monika Potocka
Profile: Provides information on diagnosis and treatment in work of surgeons.
Language(s): Polish
ADVERTISING RATES:
Full Page Mono .... PLN 4300.00
Full Page Colour .... PLN 8100.00
Mechanical Data: Type Area: 205 x 285 mm
BUSINESS: HEALTH & MEDICAL

MEDYCYNA PRAKTYCZNA - GINEKOLOGIA I POŁOŻNICTWO
1708699PL56A-2
Editorial: ul. Krakowska, 41, 31-066 KRAKÓW
Tel: 12 293 40 00 **Fax:** 12 293 40 10
Email: ginekologia.redakcja@mp.pl **Web site:** http://www.mp.pl
ISSN: 1507-5230
Date Established: 1999; **Freq:** 6 issues yearly; **Circ:** 4,000
Usual Pagination: 100
Profile: Magazine on gynaecology and parturition.
Language(s): Polish
Readership: Targets gynecologists who are interested in translations of interesting articles from reputable journals in Gynecological - maternity.
ADVERTISING RATES:
Full Page Mono .... PLN 4300.00
Full Page Colour .... PLN 8100.00
Mechanical Data: Type Area: 205 x 285 mm
BUSINESS: HEALTH & MEDICAL

MEDYCYNA PRAKTYCZNA - PEDIATRIA 1708698PL56A-1
Editorial: ul. Krakowska, 41, 31-066 KRAKÓW
Tel: 12 293 40 00 **Fax:** 12 293 40 10
Email: listy@mp.pl **Web site:** http://www.mp.pl
ISSN: 1507-2134
Date Established: 1999; **Freq:** 6 issues yearly; **Circ:** 8,000
Usual Pagination: 160
Advertising Director: Wojciech Strojny
Profile: Magazine featuring latest achievements and news in paediatrics.
Language(s): Polish
ADVERTISING RATES:
Full Page Mono .... PLN 5800.00
Full Page Colour .... PLN 9800.00
Mechanical Data: Type Area: 205 x 295 mm
BUSINESS: HEALTH & MEDICAL

MEDYCYNA WIEKU ROZWOJOWEGO 1929224PL56M-2
Editorial: ul. Niedźwiedzia, 12a, 02-737 WARSZAWA
Tel: 22 853 73 72 **Fax:** 22 853 73 72
Email: mwr@medi-press.pl **Web site:** http://www.mwr.resmedica.pl
Date Established: 1997; **Freq:** Quarterly; **Circ:** 2,000
Usual Pagination: 200
Managing Director: Dorota Świderska; **Advertising Director:** Anna Harazińska
Profile: Professional magazine dedicated to aspects of medicine dealing with pregnancy and babies.
Language(s): Polish
Mechanical Data: Type Area: A4
BUSINESS: HEALTH & MEDICAL: Family Planning

MENEDŻER ZDROWIA
1708795PL56A-12
Editorial: ul. Wenedów, 9/1, 61-614 POZNAŃ
Tel: 61 822 77 81 **Fax:** 61 822 77 81
Email: termedia@termedia.pl **Web site:** http://www.menedzer.termedia.pl
ISSN: 1730-2935
Date Established: 1999
Circ: 5,000
Usual Pagination: 80
Managing Director: Andrzej Kordas
Profile: Features modern methods of management in health services, economics and legal advice.
Language(s): Polish
Mechanical Data: Type Area: 210 x 297 mm
BUSINESS: HEALTH & MEDICAL

MEN'S HEALTH 1708830PL86C-9
Editorial: ul. Ostrowskiego, 7, 53-238 WROCŁAW
Tel: 71 780 66 11 **Fax:** 71 780 66 12

Email: menshealth@mpp.pl **Web site:** http://www.menshealth.pl
ISSN: 1731-8173
Date Established: 2004; **Freq:** Monthly; **Circ:** 106,000
Usual Pagination: 132
Profile: Featuring information on lifestyle, sex and partnership, job career, fashion and beauty, diets and food, cars and latest technical accessories.
Language(s): Polish
ADVERTISING RATES:
Full Page Colour .... PLN 42000.00
Mechanical Data: Type Area: 210 x 280 mm
CONSUMER: ADULT & GAY MAGAZINES: Men's Lifestyle Magazines

METRO
1819719PL65A-41
Editorial: ul. Czerska, 8/10, 00-732 WARSZAWA
Tel: 22 555 50 19 **Fax:** 22 555 77 07
Email: metro@agora.pl **Web site:** http://www.emetro.pl
ISSN: 1642-8684
Date Established: 1998; **Freq:** Daily; **Circ:** 446,347
Usual Pagination: 12
Managing Director: Joanna Parczyńska; **Advertising Director:** Ewa Budzińska
Profile: National daily covering international and national news, culture, entertainment, lifestyle and sports.
Language(s): Polish
ADVERTISING RATES:
Full Page Colour .... PLN 67500.00
Mechanical Data: Type Area: A3
NATIONAL DAILY & SUNDAY NEWSPAPERS: National Daily Newspapers

MIĘDZY NAMI CAFE
1708834PL85A-3
Editorial: ul. Bagno, 3, 165, 00-112 WARSZAWA
Tel: 601 203 411 **Fax:** 22 828 54 17
Email: info@miedzynamicafe.com **Web site:** http://www.miedzynamicafe.com
Date Established: 1996
Circ: 5,000
Usual Pagination: 46
Profile: Magazine dedicated to photography.
Language(s): Polish
CONSUMER: PHOTOGRAPHY & FILM MAKING: Photography

MŁODY TECHNIK
1796225PL94J-305
Editorial: ul. Leszczynowa, 11, 03-197 WARSZAWA
Tel: 22 257 84 10 **Fax:** 22 257 84 11
Email: mt@mt.com.pl **Web site:** http://www.mt.com.pl
ISSN: 0462-9760
Date Established: 1932; **Freq:** Monthly; **Circ:** 40,000
Usual Pagination: 100
Profile: Popular science magazine featuring news from chemistry, astronomy, physics and including information on tools and technical approaches.
Language(s): Polish
Mechanical Data: Type Area: B5mm
CONSUMER: OTHER CLASSIFICATIONS: Popular Science

MM MAGAZYN PRZEMYSŁOWY
1708695PL14A-15
Formerly: MM
Editorial: ul. Grabiszyńska, 163, 53-439 WROCŁAW
Tel: 71 782 31 94 **Fax:** 71 782 31 84
Email: magazynprzemyslowy@vogel.pl **Web site:** http://www.magazynprzemyslowy.pl
ISSN: 0945-5485
Date Established: 1993; **Freq:** Monthly; **Cover Price:** Free
Usual Pagination: 76
Advertising Director: Agnieszka Tyc
Profile: Covering latest achievements in industry technologies, investments in industries and economies, engineering knowledge, investment decisions, comparison of Polish companies vs. international corporations.
Language(s): Polish
Readership: Aimed at managers and engineers of Polish industries.
ADVERTISING RATES:
Full Page Colour .... PLN 10200.00
Mechanical Data: Type Area: 210 x 297 mm
BUSINESS: COMMERCE, INDUSTRY & MANAGEMENT

MOBILITY
1708979PL18B-4
Editorial: ul. Rakietników, 27/29, 10, 02-495 WARSZAWA **Tel:** 22 882 37 33 **Fax:** 22 882 37 33
Email: redakcja@mobility.com.pl **Web site:** http://mobility.com.pl
ISSN: 1733-2214
Date Established: 2001; **Freq:** Monthly; **Circ:** 30,000
Usual Pagination: 80
Profile: Contains information on mobile phone technologies, laptops, palmtops, satellite navigation, testing and comparison of mobile network operators.
Language(s): Polish
Mechanical Data: Type Area: 205 x 285 mm
BUSINESS: ELECTRONICS: Telecommunications

MODA DAMSKA
1796211PL47A-256
Editorial: ul. Stępińska, 22/30, 00-739 WARSZAWA
Tel: 22 559 39 61 **Fax:** 22 559 39 62
Email: biuro@promedia.biz.pl **Web site:** http://www.promedia.biz.pl
Date Established: 2002; **Freq:** Half-yearly; **Circ:** 5,000
Profile: Professional magazine on women's fashion, clothes, accessories and lingerie.
Language(s): Polish
Mechanical Data: Type Area: A4
BUSINESS: CLOTHING & TEXTILES

MODA & STYL
1796123PL74B-103
Editorial: ul. Toruńska, 6/8, 95-200 PABIANICE
Tel: 42 214 91 16 **Fax:** 42 214 91 18
Email: info@bestsellergroup.pl **Web site:** http://bestsellergroup.pl
Date Established: 2003; **Freq:** Quarterly; **Circ:** 20,000
Usual Pagination: 150
Managing Director: Anna Szpetkowska
Profile: Focused on fashion, culture and arts.
Language(s): Polish
Mechanical Data: Type Area: B4mm
CONSUMER: WOMEN'S INTEREST CONSUMER MAGAZINES: Women's Interest - Fashion

MODA MĘSKA
1796212PL47A-257
Editorial: ul. Stępińska, 22/30, 00-739 WARSZAWA
Tel: 22 559 39 61 **Fax:** 22 559 39 62
Email: biuro@promedia.biz.pl **Web site:** http://www.promedia.biz.pl
Date Established: 1998; **Freq:** Quarterly; **Circ:** 4,000
Profile: Professional magazine on men's fashion: clothes, accessories and underwear.
Language(s): Polish
Mechanical Data: Type Area: A4
BUSINESS: CLOTHING & TEXTILES

MODA NA FARMACJĘ
1810915PL37-1
Editorial: ul. Krakowiaków, 16, 02-255 WARSZAWA
Tel: 22 356 85 00/01 **Fax:** 22 356 85 02
Email: modanafarmacje@modanafarmacje.pl **Web site:** http://www.modanafarmacje.pl
ISSN: 1897-6255
Date Established: 2007; **Freq:** Monthly; **Circ:** 20,000
Usual Pagination: 100
Advertising Director: Katarzyna Smolaga
Profile: Focused on pharmacological medicine and dermatological cosmetics.
Language(s): Polish
ADVERTISING RATES:
Full Page Colour .... PLN 13500.00
Mechanical Data: Type Area: 210 x 275 mm
BUSINESS: PHARMACEUTICAL & CHEMISTS

MODA NA ZDROWIE
1709005PL74G-11
Editorial: ul. Krakowiaków, 16, 02-255 WARSZAWA
Tel: 22 356 85 00 **Fax:** 22 356 85 02
Email: modanazdrowie@modanazdrowie.pl **Web site:** http://www.modanazdrowie.pl
ISSN: 1730-9034
Date Established: 2003; **Freq:** Monthly; **Circ:** 428,000
Usual Pagination: 100
Advertising Director: Katarzyna Smolaga
Profile: Magazine focused on illness prophylactics and health issues, fitness and beauty, psychology and healthy eating.
Language(s): Polish
ADVERTISING RATES:
Full Page Colour .... PLN 42000.00
Mechanical Data: Type Area: 210 x 275 mm
CONSUMER: WOMEN'S INTEREST CONSUMER MAGAZINES: Slimming & Health

MÓJ DOM
1708890PL4E-29
Editorial: Aleja W. Korfantego 195, 40-153 KATOWICE **Tel:** 32 730 23 65 **Fax:** 32 730 31 51
Email: poczta@mojdom.pub.pl **Web site:** http://www.mojdom.pub.pl
Date Established: 1997; **Freq:** 6 issues yearly;
Cover Price: PLN 3.20
Annual Sub.: PLN 19.00; **Circ:** 50,000
Usual Pagination: 52
Editor: A. Miller; **Advertising Director:** Michał Majewski
Profile: Professional magazine on building, maintaining and renovation your house, gives practical advice on interior design.
Language(s): Polish
ADVERTISING RATES:
Full Page Colour .... PLN 6900.00
Mechanical Data: Type Area: 210 x 280 mm
BUSINESS: ARCHITECTURE & BUILDING: Building

MÓJ PIĘKNY DOM
1796070PL74C-21
Editorial: ul. Warecka, 11a, 00-034 WARSZAWA
Tel: 22 448 83 15 **Fax:** 22 448 80 01
Email: mpd@burdamedia.pl **Web site:** http://www.burdamedia.pl
Date Established: 2005
Circ: 63,000
Usual Pagination: 96
Managing Director: Justyna Namięta, 071 376 28 01 Małgorzata Węgierek, 022 448 83 27
Profile: Contains advice on interior design and decorations.
Language(s): Polish
Mechanical Data: Type Area: 210 x 275 mm
CONSUMER: WOMEN'S INTEREST CONSUMER MAGAZINES: Home & Family

MÓJ PIĘKNY OGRÓD
1708654PL93-8
Editorial: ul. Ostrowskiego, 7, 53-238 WROCŁAW
Tel: 71 376 28 42 **Fax:** 71 376 28 02
Email: ogrod@burdamedia.pl **Web site:** http://www.burdamedia.pl
ISSN: 1426-6334
Date Established: 1996; **Freq:** Monthly; **Circ:** 99,000
Usual Pagination: 68
Managing Director: Justyna Namięta, 071 376 28 00 Małgorzata Węgierek, 022 448 83 27; **Advertising Director:** Anna Zabłocka
Profile: Features examples of garden decoration and ideas for garden arrangements.
Language(s): Polish
ADVERTISING RATES:
Full Page Colour .... PLN 13500.00
Mechanical Data: Type Area: 210 x 275 mm
CONSUMER: GARDENING

MÓJ PIĘKNY OGRÓD - EKSTRA
1708653PL93-7
Editorial: ul. Ostrowskiego, 7, 53-238 WROCŁAW
Tel: 71 376 28 42 **Fax:** 71 376 28 02
Email: ogrod@burda.pl **Web site:** http://www.burda.pl
Date Established: 1996
Circ: 35,000
Usual Pagination: 100
Profile: Features examples of garden decoration and ideas for garden arrangements.
Language(s): Polish
ADVERTISING RATES:
Full Page Colour .... PLN 13500.00
Mechanical Data: Type Area: 230x285 mm
CONSUMER: GARDENING

MÓJ PIES
1708924PL81B-2
Editorial: ul. Domaniewska, 39a Horizon Plaza, 02-672 WARSZAWA **Tel:** 22 529 11 00
Fax: 22 529 11 90
Email: mojpies@wprost.pl **Web site:** http://www.psy.pl
ISSN: 0867-2822
Date Established: 1989; **Freq:** Monthly; **Circ:** 44,000
Usual Pagination: 88
Profile: Features information for dog-owners on dog-breeding, training and feeding.
Language(s): Polish
Mechanical Data: Type Area: 205 x 288 mm
CONSUMER: ANIMALS & PETS: Dogs

MOJE GOTOWANIE
1708644PL74P-3
Editorial: ul. Wynalazek, 4, 02-677 WARSZAWA
Tel: 22 607 02 65/69 **Fax:** 22 607 02 72
Email: mojegotowanie@gjpoland.com.pl **Web site:** http://www.mojegotowanie.pl
ISSN: 1233-4847
Date Established: 1994; **Freq:** Monthly; **Circ:** 73,000
Usual Pagination: 52
Managing Director: Michał Brudzyński; **Advertising Director:** Agnieszka Całka
Profile: Recipes and practical advice on quick and cheap cooking.
Language(s): Polish
Mechanical Data: Type Area: 210 x 275 mm
CONSUMER: WOMEN'S INTEREST CONSUMER MAGAZINES: Food & Cookery

MOJE MIESZKANIE
1929133PL4B-28
Editorial: ul. Kamionkowska, 45, 03-812 WARSZAWA **Tel:** 22 590 67 35 **Fax:** 22 590 54 44
Email: mojemieszkanie@murator.com.pl **Web site:** http://www.mojemieszkanie.pl
ISSN: 0945-5310
Freq: Monthly; **Circ:** 121,000
Usual Pagination: 100
Managing Director: Katarzyna Białek; **Advertising Director:** Anna Dygasiewicz-Piwko
Profile: Popular magazine about interior design, home interiors, new trends and products in decoration, with tips and advice.
Language(s): Polish
ADVERTISING RATES:
Full Page Colour .... PLN 21700.00
Mechanical Data: Type Area: 210 x 280 mm
BUSINESS: ARCHITECTURE & BUILDING: Interior Design & Flooring

MONEY.PL
1835886PL1A-79
Editorial: ul. Kościuszki, 29, 50-011 WROCŁAW
Tel: 71 337 42 60 **Fax:** 71 337 42 70
Email: firma@money.pl **Web site:** http://www.money.pl
Date Established: 2000
Circ: 2,025,180 Unique Users
Advertising Director: Tomasz Pudlis
Profile: Focused on general financial, banking, insurance, pensions and taxation issues.
Language(s): Polish
BUSINESS: FINANCE & ECONOMICS

MONITOR KSIĘGOWEGO
1708874PL1B-9
Editorial: ul. Okopowa, 58/72, 01-042 WARSZAWA
Tel: 22 530 41 75 **Fax:** 22 530 42 22
Email: mk@infor.pl **Web site:** http://www.mk.infor.pl
ISSN: 1731-5786
Date Established: 2003; **Freq:** 26 issues yearly
Usual Pagination: 96
Managing Director: Mariusz Drozdowicz
Profile: Contains practical advice on accountancy issues and tax calculations.
Language(s): Polish
Mechanical Data: Type Area: B5mm
BUSINESS: FINANCE & ECONOMICS: Accountancy

MONITOR PODATKOWY
1708840PL1M-11
Editorial: ul. Bonifraterska, 17, 00-203 WARSZAWA
Tel: 22 337 76 00 **Fax:** 22 337 76 02
Email: iwona.kordjak@beck.pl **Web site:** http://www.monitorpodatkowy.pl
ISSN: 1231-1855
Date Established: 1994; **Freq:** Monthly; **Circ:** 5,000
Usual Pagination: 56
Profile: Magazine dedicated to taxation and economics legal issues, accountancy and gives legal business advice.
Language(s): Polish
Mechanical Data: Type Area: 204 x 287 mm
BUSINESS: FINANCE & ECONOMICS: Taxation

MONITOR PRAWA PRACY
1708839PL44-3
Editorial: ul. Bonifraterska, 17, 00-203 WARSZAWA
Tel: 22 337 76 00 **Fax:** 22 337 74 91
Email: mopr@beck.pl **Web site:** http://www.monitorprawapracy.pl
ISSN: 1731-8165
Date Established: 2004; **Freq:** Monthly; **Circ:** 4,000
Usual Pagination: 58
Profile: Polish and EU work related legal issues and insurance, information on job market.
Language(s): Polish
Mechanical Data: Type Area: 204 x 287 mm
BUSINESS: LEGAL

MONITOR PRAWA PRACY I UBEZPIECZEŃ
1795904PL1D-2
Editorial: ul. Okopowa, 58/72, 01-042 WARSZAWA
Tel: 22 530 44 56 **Fax:** 22 530 42 22
Email: mp@infor.pl **Web site:** http://www.mp.infor.pl
Date Established: 2004; **Freq:** 26 issues yearly
Usual Pagination: 80
Managing Director: Mariusz Drozdowicz
Profile: Provides advise on job related legal issues and health and social insurance.
Language(s): Polish
Mechanical Data: Type Area: B5mm
BUSINESS: FINANCE & ECONOMICS: Insurance

MONITOR PRAWNICZY
1708838PL44-2
Editorial: ul. Bonifraterska, 17, 00-203 WARSZAWA
Tel: 22 337 76 00 **Fax:** 22 337 74 91
Email: monitorprawniczy@beck.pl **Web site:** http://www.monitorprawniczy.pl
ISSN: 1230-6509
Date Established: 1993; **Freq:** 26 issues yearly; **Circ:** 8,000
Usual Pagination: 56
Profile: Contains professional analysis and legal advice on civil law, economic and HR issues, legal news.
Language(s): Polish
Mechanical Data: Type Area: 204 x 287 mm
BUSINESS: LEGAL

MONITOR RACHUNKOWOŚCI I FINANSÓW
1708837PL1B-3
Editorial: ul. gen. Zajączka, 9, 01-518 WARSZAWA
Tel: 22 337 76 00 **Fax:** 22 337 76 02
Email: redakcja@beck.pl **Web site:** http://www.mrf.pl
ISSN: 1506-932X
Date Established: 1999; **Freq:** Monthly; **Circ:** 3,000
Usual Pagination: 56
Profile: Professional publication on accountancy, taxes, company finance and financial management.
Language(s): Polish
Mechanical Data: Type Area: 204x287 mm
BUSINESS: FINANCE & ECONOMICS: Accountancy

MOSTY
1810974PL42A-3
Editorial: al. Roździeńskiego, 188, 40-203 KATOWICE **Tel:** 32 788 52 53 **Fax:** 32 203 93 56
Email: mosty@elamed.pl **Web site:** http://www.mosty.elamed.pl
ISSN: 1896-7663
Date Established: 2006; **Freq:** Quarterly
Usual Pagination: 60
Editor: Sabina Szczerbak; **Advertising Director:** Justyna Ścibska
Profile: Magazine about design, building and maintenance of bridges and their engineering objects, new technologies and materials used in bridges' construction.
Language(s): Polish

ADVERTISING RATES:
Full Page Colour .... EUR 3900.00
Mechanical Data: Type Area: 238 x 336 mm
BUSINESS: CONSTRUCTION

MOTO EXPRESS 1810929PL77A-39
Editorial: ul. Domaniewska, 41, 02-672 WARSZAWA
Tel: 22 201 40 27 **Fax:** 22 201 40 30
Email: redakcja@motoexpress.pl **Web site:** http://www.motoexpress.pl
ISSN: 0867-7948
Date Established: 1991; **Freq:** Weekly; **Circ:** 30,000
Usual Pagination: 48
Advertising Director: Krystyna Dzwonkowska
Language(s): Polish
Mechanical Data: Type Area: 275 x 365 mm
CONSUMER: MOTORING & CYCLING: Motoring

MOTOCYKL 1625939PL77B-2
Editorial: ul. Ostrowskiego, 7, 53-238 WROCŁAW
Tel: 71 780 66 11 **Fax:** 71 780 66 12
Email: motocykl@mpp.pl **Web site:** http://www.motocykl-online.pl
ISSN: 1230-767X
Date Established: 1994
Circ: 48,000
Usual Pagination: 132
Profile: Magazine focusing on motorcycling world, features new technologies, tests, news and practical advice.
Language(s): Polish
Mechanical Data: Type Area: 215 x 280 mm
CONSUMER: MOTORING & CYCLING: Motorcycling

MOTOCYKLE ŚWIATA 1795905PL31B-1
Editorial: ul. Czerska, 8/10, 00-732 WARSZAWA
Tel: 22 555 67 94 **Fax:** 22 555 68 10
Email: swiat-motocykli@agora.pl
ISSN: 1234-6470
Date Established: 1992; **Freq:** Annual; **Circ:** 25,000
Usual Pagination: 124
Advertising Director: Beata Remjasz
Profile: Provides information on motorbikes and scooters produced in all countries, their technical data, prices and testing.
Language(s): Polish
Mechanical Data: Type Area: 218 x 285 mm
BUSINESS: MOTOR TRADE: Motorcycle Trade

MOTOR 1708753PL77A-20
Editorial: al. Stanów Zjednoczonych, 61a, 04-028 WARSZAWA **Tel:** 22 516 35 51 **Fax:** 22 516 35 85
Email: redakcja@motor.com.pl **Web site:** http://www.reklama.bauer.pl
ISSN: 0580-0447
Date Established: 1952; **Freq:** Weekly; **Circ:** 171,000
Usual Pagination: 52
Advertising Director: Marcin Warych
Profile: Features presentation of new cars, testing and advice for car users.
Language(s): Polish
ADVERTISING RATES:
Full Page Colour .... PLN 27000.00
Mechanical Data: Type Area: 225 x 285 mm
CONSUMER: MOTORING & CYCLING: Motoring

MOTORYZACYJNY RAPORT SPECJALNY 1709101PL31A-7
Editorial: ul. Racławicka, 15/19, 53-149 WROCŁAW
Tel: 71 783 51 16 **Fax:** 71 783 51 00
Email: arkadiusz.czarkowski@e-ipm.pl **Web site:** http://www.flota.com.pl
ISSN: 1733-3784
Date Established: 2004; **Freq:** Quarterly; **Cover Price:** Free; **Circ:** 2,000
Usual Pagination: 60
Advertising Director: Krzysztof Turczak
Profile: Provides information on car producers, car market analysis, car sales reports and news on car insurances, repairs and import-export issues.
Language(s): Polish
Mechanical Data: Type Area: 213x290 mm
BUSINESS: MOTOR TRADE: Motor Trade Accessories

MSI POLSKA 1836211PL5A-26
Editorial: ul. Wita Stwosza 59a, 02-661 WARSZAWA
Tel: 22 852 44 15 **Fax:** 22 899 29 48
Email: redakcja@msipolska.pl **Web site:** http://www.msipolska.pl
Freq: Monthly; **Circ:** 5,000
Editor: Adam Majczak; **Editor-in-Chief:** Elżbieta Jaworska; **Publisher:** Michael J. Majchrzak
Profile: Professional publication about IT management of industrial companies addressed to managers of industrial sectors and manufacturing executives.
Language(s): Polish
ADVERTISING RATES:
Full Page Colour .... PLN 5000.00
Mechanical Data: Type Area: 200 x 267mm
BUSINESS: COMPUTERS & AUTOMATION: Automation & Instrumentation

---

MURATOR 1708668PL4E-25
Editorial: ul. Kamionkowska, 45, 03-812 WARSZAWA **Tel:** 22 590 52 96 **Fax:** 22 590 54 22
Email: murator@murator.com.pl **Web site:** http://www.murator.pl
ISSN: 0239-6866
Date Established: 1983; **Freq:** Monthly; **Circ:** 155,000
Usual Pagination: 224
Managing Director: Renata Krzewska; **Advertising Director:** Anna Dygasiewicz-Piwko
Profile: Features specialists' advice on all works related to building a house or renovating it, new technologies and new materials used in building.
Language(s): Polish
ADVERTISING RATES:
Full Page Colour .... PLN 29600.00
Mechanical Data: Type Area: 203 x 275 mm
BUSINESS: ARCHITECTURE & BUILDING: Building

MURATOR NUMER SPECJALNY 1708667PL4E-26
Editorial: ul. Kamionkowska, 45, 03-812 WARSZAWA **Tel:** 22 590 54 11 **Fax:** 22 590 54 22
Email: murator@murator.com.pl **Web site:** http://www.murator.pl
ISSN: 1429-8198
Date Established: 1999
Circ: 30,000
Usual Pagination: 150
Managing Director: Renata Krzewska; **Advertising Director:** Anna Dygasiewicz-Piwko
Profile: Provides information on all aspects of building a house, building materials and renovation.
Language(s): Polish
ADVERTISING RATES:
Full Page Colour .... PLN 8600.00
Mechanical Data: Type Area: 203 x 275 mm
BUSINESS: ARCHITECTURE & BUILDING: Building

MURATOR - WYDANIE SPECJALNE 1860761PL4E-31
Editorial: ul. Kamionkowska, 45, 03-812 WARSZAWA **Tel:** 22 590 52 96 **Fax:** 22 590 54 22
Email: murator@murator.com.pl **Web site:** http://www.murator.pl
ISSN: 1899-136X
Date Established: 2006
Cover Price: Free; **Circ:** 1,000,000
Usual Pagination: 32
Managing Director: Renata Krzewska; **Advertising Director:** Anna Dygasiewicz-Piwko
Profile: Provides practical advice with house renovation, house insulation, newest technologies and solutions.
Language(s): Polish
ADVERTISING RATES:
Full Page Colour .... PLN 8600.00
Mechanical Data: Type Area: 203x275 mm
BUSINESS: ARCHITECTURE & BUILDING: Building

NA ŚCIEŻKACH ŻYCIA 1708812PL74A-1027
Editorial: ul. św. Antoniego, 7, 50-073 WROCŁAW
Tel: 71 344 77 75 **Fax:** 71 346 01 74
Email: nsz@phoenix.pl **Web site:** http://www.phoenix.pl
ISSN: 1429-8139
Date Established: 1998; **Freq:** Monthly; **Circ:** 96,000
Usual Pagination: 48
Profile: Contains 4 real life stories for women, horoscope, crosswords, specialists' advice on health and beauty, and readers' letters.
Language(s): Polish
ADVERTISING RATES:
Full Page Colour .... PLN 4000.00
Mechanical Data: Type Area: 205 x 275 mm
CONSUMER: WOMEN'S INTEREST CONSUMER MAGAZINES: Women's Interest

---

NA ZDROWIE. DOSTĘPNE BEZ RECEPTY 1795949PL74G-19
Editorial: ul. Jaracza, 2, 00-378 WARSZAWA
Tel: 22 622 98 34 **Fax:** 22 622 98 34
Web site: http://www.nazdrowie.pl
ISSN: 1733-9294
Date Established: 2005; **Freq:** Quarterly; **Cover Price:** Free; **Circ:** 200,000
Usual Pagination: 80
Advertising Director: Agata Kosińska
Profile: Focused on health and beauty issues, provides information on dermatology and skin cosmetics.
Language(s): Polish
Mechanical Data: Type Area: A4
CONSUMER: WOMEN'S INTEREST CONSUMER MAGAZINES: Slimming & Health

---

NA ZDROWIE. MANAGER APTEKI 1796170PL37-2
Editorial: ul. Jaracza, 2, 00-378 WARSZAWA
Tel: 22 622 98 34 **Fax:** 22 622 98 34
Email: marta.figielska@mediatv.com.pl **Web site:** http://www.nazdrowie.pl
ISSN: 1895-1333
Date Established: 2005; **Freq:** Monthly; **Cover Price:** Free; **Circ:** 10,000
Usual Pagination: 90
Advertising Director: Agata Kosińska
Profile: Provides information on chemists' marketing, scientific news in pharmacology and medicine.
Language(s): Polish
Mechanical Data: Type Area: A4
BUSINESS: PHARMACEUTICAL & CHEMISTS

NAJ 1708642PL74A-1008
Editorial: ul. Wynalazek, 4, 02-677 WARSZAWA
Tel: 22 607 02 65/70 **Fax:** 22 607 02 71
Email: naj@naj.pl **Web site:** http://www.kobieta.pl
ISSN: 1232-7654
Date Established: 1994; **Freq:** Weekly; **Circ:** 474,000
Usual Pagination: 52
Managing Director: Michał Brudzyński; **Advertising Director:** Karina Dąbska
Profile: Focused on fashion and beauty, lifestyle and practical advice.
Language(s): Polish
ADVERTISING RATES:
Full Page Colour .... PLN 60000.00
Mechanical Data: Type Area: 210 x 287 mm
CONSUMER: WOMEN'S INTEREST CONSUMER MAGAZINES: Women's Interest

---

NARZĘDZIA I ELEKTRONARZĘDZIA 1708729PL19E-1
Editorial: ul. Dzika, 4, 00-194 WARSZAWA
Tel: 22 635 73 70 **Fax:** 22 635 29 30
Email: ppwp@ppwp.pl **Web site:** http://ppwp.pl
ISSN: 1505-2486
Date Established: 1998; **Freq:** 6 issues yearly; **Circ:** 8,000
Usual Pagination: 150
Editor: Dariusz Świnarski; **Advertising Director:** Beatrycze Góral
Profile: Provided information on tools and electric tools, presenting the full range tools and power tools and accessories, available on the Polish market, with descriptions to facilitate choice. It also contains expert advice.
Language(s): Polish
Readership: Targets professionals, individual investors planning or carrying out the construction, renovation or modernization, and all interested in tools and power tools of high quality.
ADVERTISING RATES:
Full Page Colour .... PLN 7700.00
Mechanical Data: Type Area: A4
BUSINESS: ENGINEERING & MACHINERY: Machinery, Machine Tools & Metalworking

---

NASZ DZIENNIK 708016PL65A-18
Editorial: ul. Żeligowskiego, 16/20, 04-476 WARSZAWA **Tel:** 22 515 77 77 **Fax:** 22 515 77 78
Email: redakcja@naszdziennik.pl **Web site:** http://www.naszdziennik.pl
ISSN: 1429-4834
Date Established: 1998; **Freq:** Daily
Usual Pagination: 16
Profile: Newspaper covering politics, religion, news, sport, culture, public affairs and entertainment from the position of Catholic Church.
Language(s): Polish
Readership: Aimed at the general public.
Mechanical Data: Type Area: A3
NATIONAL DAILY & SUNDAY NEWSPAPERS: National Daily Newspapers

---

NASZ OLSZTYNIAK 1819720PL72-25
Editorial: ul. Tracka, 7, 10-364 OLSZTYN
Tel: 89 539 77 30 **Fax:** 89 539 77 34
Email: poczta@naszolsztyniak.pl **Web site:** http://www.naszolsztyniak.pl
ISSN: 1642-9079
Date Established: 2001; **Freq:** 104 issues yearly; **Cover Price:** Free; **Circ:** 15,000
Usual Pagination: 12
Editor: Przemysław Pawłowski; **Advertising Director:** Beata Tokarczyk
Profile: Newspaper covering events and news from Olsztyn and its region.
Language(s): Polish
ADVERTISING RATES:
Full Page Colour .... PLN 2688.00
Mechanical Data: Type Area: A3
LOCAL NEWSPAPERS

NASZA MIERZEJA 1819733PL80A-6
Editorial: ul. Rybacka, 29a, 82-300 ELBLĄG
Tel: 55 611 46 00 **Fax:** 55 235 10 77
Email: redakcjane@naszelblag.pl
Date Established: 2007; **Freq:** Monthly; **Circ:** 15,000
Usual Pagination: 24
Advertising Director: Beata Tokarczyk
Profile: A regional guide on cultural events, sports and interesting historical places.
Language(s): Polish
ADVERTISING RATES:
Full Page Colour .... PLN 1945.00
Mechanical Data: Type Area: A3
CONSUMER: RURAL & REGIONAL INTEREST: Rural Interest

NASZE INSPIRACJE 1708737PL74C-15
Editorial: ul. 3 Maja, 14, 43-450 USTROŃ
Tel: 33 854 45 22 **Fax:** 33 854 18 14
Email: inspiracje@misja.org.pl **Web site:** http://www.inspiracje.misja.org.pl
ISSN: 1429-0367
Date Established: 1995; **Freq:** Quarterly; **Circ:** 4,500
Usual Pagination: 68
Advertising Director: Estera Wieja
Profile: Magazine about physical health, human relations, soul and mind states, Catholic religion.
Language(s): Polish
ADVERTISING RATES:
Full Page Colour .... PLN 1600.00
Mechanical Data: Type Area: 200x260 mm
CONSUMER: WOMEN'S INTEREST CONSUMER MAGAZINES: Home & Family

NASZEMIASTO.PL 1944948PL80A-7
Email: redakcja@naszemiasto.pl **Web site:** http://www.naszemiasto.pl
Freq: Daily; **Circ:** 1,154,812 Unique Users
Language(s): Polish
CONSUMER: RURAL & REGIONAL INTEREST: Rural Interest

NATIONAL GEOGRAPHIC POLSKA 1708714PL89A-5
Editorial: ul. Wynalazek, 4, 02-677 WARSZAWA
Tel: 22 607 02 56/57 **Fax:** 22 607 02 61
Email: ngm@nationalgeographic.pl **Web site:** http://www.national-geographic.pl
ISSN: 1507-5966
Date Established: 1999; **Freq:** Monthly; **Circ:** 82,000
Usual Pagination: 160
Managing Director: Michał Brudzyński
Profile: Focused on travelling, different cultures, remote places and photography.
Language(s): Polish
ADVERTISING RATES:
Full Page Colour .... RUR 50000.00
Mechanical Data: Type Area: 175 x 254 mm
CONSUMER: HOLIDAYS & TRAVEL: Travel

NATIONAL GEOGRAPHIC TRAVELER 1796040PL89A-20
Editorial: ul. Wynalazek, 4, 02-677 WARSZAWA
Tel: 22 607 02 56 **Fax:** 22 607 02 61
Email: ngm@nationalgeographic.pl **Web site:** http://www.national-geographic.pl
ISSN: 1507-5966
Date Established: 2004; **Freq:** 6 issues yearly; **Circ:** 50,000
Usual Pagination: 144
Managing Director: Michał Brudzyński; **Advertising Director:** Małgorzata Pawłowska-Babut
Profile: Focused on travelling, culture and traditions and tourism.
Language(s): Polish
ADVERTISING RATES:
Full Page Colour .... PLN 29900.00
Mechanical Data: Type Area: 205 x 265 mm
CONSUMER: HOLIDAYS & TRAVEL: Travel

NETWORLD 1708626PL18B-9
Editorial: ul. Jordanowska, 12, 04-204 WARSZAWA
Tel: 22 321 78 00 **Fax:** 22 321 78 88
Email: networld@idg.com.pl **Web site:** http://www.networld.pl
ISSN: 1232-8723
Date Established: 1994; **Freq:** Monthly; **Circ:** 4,000
Usual Pagination: 80
Profile: Dedicated to applications of computer networks, telecommunication systems and tele-informative infrastructure.
Language(s): Polish
ADVERTISING RATES:
Full Page Mono .... PLN 4900.00
Full Page Colour .... PLN 7500.00
Mechanical Data: Type Area: 203 x 288 mm
BUSINESS: ELECTRONICS: Telecommunications

NEUROLOGIA I NEUROCHIRURGIA POLSKA 1708886PL56A-14
Editorial: ul. Botaniczna, 3, 31-503 KRAKÓW
Tel: 12 424 86 33 **Fax:** 12 424 86 32
Email: neurologia@termedia.pl **Web site:** http://www.neurologia.termedia.pl
ISSN: 0028-3843
Date Established: 2004; **Freq:** 6 issues yearly; **Circ:** 4,000
Usual Pagination: 90
Managing Director: Andrzej Kordas
Profile: Contains original articles and reviews on neurology and neurosurgery.
Language(s): Polish
Mechanical Data: Type Area: A4
BUSINESS: HEALTH & MEDICAL

NEUROLOGY 1708700PL56A-3
Editorial: ul. Krakowska, 41, 31-066 KRAKÓW
Tel: 12 293 40 00 **Fax:** 12 293 40 10
Email: neurologia@mp.pl **Web site:** http://www.mp.pl
ISSN: 1644-5589
Date Established: 2003; **Freq:** 6 issues yearly; **Circ:** 2,000

Usual Pagination: 110
Advertising Director: Sylwester Marszał
Profile: Professional publication on neurology.
Language(s): Polish
ADVERTISING RATES:
Full Page Colour .... PLN 6800.00
Mechanical Data: Type Area: 205 x 276 mm
BUSINESS: HEALTH & MEDICAL

NEWSWEEK POLSKA 765911PL82-63
Editorial: ul. Domaniewska, 52, 02-672 WARSZAWA
Tel: 22 232 10 62 **Fax:** 22 232 55 26
Email: redakcja@newsweek.pl **Web site:** http://www.newsweek.pl
ISSN: 1642-5685
Date Established: 2001; **Freq:** Weekly; **Circ:** 184,047
Usual Pagination: 112
Managing Director: Małgorzata Barankiewicz; **Advertising Director:** Mariusz Szynalik
Profile: Magazine covering news, politics, business analysis, comments and current affairs.
Language(s): Polish
ADVERTISING RATES:
Full Page Colour .... PLN 75500.00
Mechanical Data: Type Area: 205 x 270 mm
CONSUMER: CURRENT AFFAIRS & POLITICS

NIERUCHOMOŚCI CH BECK
1708836PL1E-2
Editorial: ul. Bonifraterska, 17, 00-203 WARSZAWA
Tel: 22 337 76 00 **Fax:** 22 337 74 91
Email: nieruchomosci@beck.pl **Web site:** http://www.nieruchomosci.beck.pl
ISSN: 1506-2899
Date Established: 1998; **Freq:** Monthly; **Circ:** 8,000
Usual Pagination: 48
Profile: Features news on property market in Poland and abroad.
Language(s): Polish
Mechanical Data: Type Area: 204 x 287 mm
BUSINESS: FINANCE & ECONOMICS: Property

NIERUCHOMOŚCI WARSZAWA I OKOLICE 1810909PL1E-6
Editorial: ul. Towarowa, 22, 00-839 WARSZAWA
Tel: 22 455 33 00 **Fax:** 22 455 33 01
Email: autobiznes@trader.pl **Web site:** http://www.trader.pl
ISSN: 1643-8248
Date Established: 2002; **Freq:** 24 issues yearly; **Circ:** 18,000
Usual Pagination: 66
Advertising Director: Krzysztof Dzięgielewski
Profile: Focused on property market in Poland, building investments, bank mortgage and developers' offers.
Language(s): Polish
ADVERTISING RATES:
Full Page Colour .... PLN 2500.00
Mechanical Data: Type Area: A3
BUSINESS: FINANCE & ECONOMICS: Property

NOWA FANTASTYKA
1202190PL79L-10
Editorial: ul. Garażowa, 7, 02-651 WARSZAWA
Tel: 22 607 77 90 **Fax:** 22 848 22 66
Email: nowafantastyka@fantastyka.pl **Web site:** http://www.fantastyka.pl
Date Established: 1982; **Freq:** Monthly; **Circ:** 26,000
Usual Pagination: 80
Profile: Magazine featuring science fiction literature, film reviews and relevant graphic art.
Language(s): Polish
Mechanical Data: Type Area: 200 x 285 mm
CONSUMER: HOBBIES & DIY: Fantasy Games & Science Fiction

NOWA TRYBUNA OPOLSKA
1614573PL67B-21
Editorial: ul. Powstańców Śląskich, 9, 45-086 OPOLE **Tel:** 77 443 25 00 **Fax:** 77 443 25 15
Email: nto@nto.pl **Web site:** http://nto.pl
ISSN: 1230-6134
Date Established: 1993; **Freq:** Daily; **Circ:** 29,492
Usual Pagination: 20
Profile: A socio-publicizing regional newspaper.
Language(s): Polish
Mechanical Data: Type Area: A3
REGIONAL DAILY & SUNDAY NEWSPAPERS: Regional Daily Newspapers

NOWE PAŃSTWO 1708672PL82-66
Editorial: Al. Jerozolimskie, 125/127, 02-017 WARSZAWA **Tel:** 22 699 72 22 **Fax:** 22 628 76 73
Email: np@nowe-panstwo.pl **Web site:** http://www.nowe-panstwo.pl
ISSN: 1231-4765
Date Established: 1995; **Freq:** Quarterly; **Circ:** 5,000
Usual Pagination: 122
Profile: Focused on history, civilizations and politics.
Language(s): Polish
ADVERTISING RATES:
Full Page Colour .... PLN 3000.00
Mechanical Data: Type Area: A4
CONSUMER: CURRENT AFFAIRS & POLITICS

NOWOCZESNE HALE 1929191PL14J-2
Editorial: al. Roździeńskiego, 188, 40-203 KATOWICE **Tel:** 32 788 51 83 **Fax:** 32 203 93 56
Email: nowoczesnehale@elamed.pl **Web site:** http://www.nowoczesnehale.elamed.pl
ISSN: 1899-8224
Date Established: 2008; **Freq:** 6 issues yearly
Usual Pagination: 60
Profile: Magazine dedicated to projects and construction of warehouses, new technologies, investments.
Language(s): Polish
Mechanical Data: Type Area: 204 x 290 mm
BUSINESS: COMMERCE, INDUSTRY & MANAGEMENT: Commercial Design

NOWOCZESNY BANK SPÓŁDZIELCZY 1811030PL1C-2
Editorial: ul. Solec, 101, 5, 00-382 WARSZAWA
Tel: 22 629 18 72 **Fax:** 22 629 18 72
Email: redakcja@miesiecznikbs.pl **Web site:** http://www.miesiecznikbs.pl
ISSN: 1644-5325
Date Established: 2002; **Freq:** Monthly; **Circ:** 2,000
Usual Pagination: 48
Managing Director: Waldemar Zbytek
Profile: Professional magazine on banking, communities banks, property market and finance.
Language(s): Polish
ADVERTISING RATES:
Full Page Colour .... PLN 6800.00
Mechanical Data: Type Area: 220 x 280 mm
BUSINESS: FINANCE & ECONOMICS: Banking

NOWOCZESNY TECHNIK DENTYSTYCZNY 1810991PL56D-3
Editorial: al. Roździeńskiego, 188, 40-203 KATOWICE **Tel:** 32 788 52 54 **Fax:** 32 788 51 65
Email: stomatologia@elamed.pl **Web site:** http://www.technik.elamed.pl
ISSN: 1733-6546
Date Established: 2002; **Freq:** 6 issues yearly
Usual Pagination: 70
Profile: Presents newest dental technologies, practical advice for dental technicians and dental news.
Language(s): Polish
Mechanical Data: Type Area: 204 x 290 mm
BUSINESS: HEALTH & MEDICAL: Dental

NOWOŚCI GASTRONOMICZNE
1708828PL11A-4
Editorial: ul. Krzywickiego 34, 02-078 WARSZAWA
Tel: 22521 20 00 **Fax:** 22 521 20 20
Email: brog@brog.com.pl **Web site:** http://www.brog.pl
ISSN: 1730-525X
Date Established: 2003; **Freq:** 6 issues yearly; **Circ:** 4,000
Usual Pagination: 48
Managing Director: Radosław Rybiński; **Advertising Director:** Beata Wołek
Profile: Featuring analysis of problems in gastronomic sector of services in Poland.
Language(s): Polish
Readership: Aimed at owners and managerial staff of restaurants, bars, mass catering establishments, catering firms, producers of fittings, suppliers of services and goods for the food service business.
ADVERTISING RATES:
Full Page Colour .... PLN 4290.00
Mechanical Data: Type Area: 230x297 mm
BUSINESS: CATERING: Catering, Hotels & Restaurants

NOWY PRZEMYSŁ 1708835PL14A-24
Editorial: ul. Jana Matejki, 3, 40-077 KATOWICE
Tel: 32 209 10 42 **Fax:** 32 782 13 10
Email: np@wnp.pl **Web site:** http://www.wnp.pl
Date Established: 1998; **Freq:** Monthly; **Circ:** 15,000
Usual Pagination: 100
Editor: Oskar Filipowicz
Profile: Featuring news on enterprise strategies, investments, finance, marketing and new technologies.
Language(s): Polish
Mechanical Data: Type Area: 205 x 275 mm
BUSINESS: COMMERCE, INDUSTRY & MANAGEMENT

N.P.M. 1708853PL89A-6
Editorial: ul. Grunwaldzka, 104, 60-307 POZNAŃ
Tel: 61 869 91 77 **Fax:** 61 865 99 09
Email: redakcja@npm.pl **Web site:** http://www.npm.pl
ISSN: 1641-8050
Date Established: 2001; **Freq:** Monthly; **Circ:** 9,000
Usual Pagination: 68
Profile: Focused on mountain tourism.
Language(s): Polish
Mechanical Data: Type Area: A4
CONSUMER: HOLIDAYS & TRAVEL: Travel

NURKOWANIE 1796203PL75M-3
Editorial: ul. Kolumba, 86, 70-035 SZCZECIN
Tel: 91 489 22 83 **Fax:** 91 482 68 08
Email: redakcja@nurkowanie.v.pl **Web site:** http://www.nurkowanie.v.pl
ISSN: 1425-3100
Date Established: 1995; **Freq:** Monthly; **Circ:** 8,000
Usual Pagination: 76
Profile: Magazine on diving and diving equipment, underwater photography and shipwrecks.
Language(s): Polish
Mechanical Data: Type Area: 202x290 mm
CONSUMER: SPORT: Water Sports

O2.PL 1835873PL89C-19
Editorial: ul. Jutrzenki, 177, 02-231 WARSZAWA
Tel: 22 398 88 88 **Fax:** 22 398 80 99
Email: info@firma.o2.pl **Web site:** http://www.o2.pl
Date Established: 1999; **Freq:** Daily; **Circ:** 7,799,338 Unique Users
Advertising Director: Karol Suchenek
Profile: Provides general entertainment information with celebrities gossip.
Language(s): Polish
CONSUMER: HOLIDAYS & TRAVEL: Entertainment Guides

OBUWIE I GALANTERIA
1796216PL29-2
Editorial: ul. Stępińska, 22/30, 00-739 WARSZAWA
Tel: 22 559 39 61 **Fax:** 22 559 39 62
Email: biura@promedia.biz.pl **Web site:** http://www.promedia.biz.pl
Date Established: 2008; **Freq:** Half-yearly; **Circ:** 5,000
Profile: Magazine on shoes and accessories.
Language(s): Polish
Mechanical Data: Type Area: A4
BUSINESS: FOOTWEAR

OCHRONA MIENIA I INFORMACJI 1708676PL54C-2
Editorial: al. Komisji Edukacji Narodowej, 95, 02-777 WARSZAWA **Tel:** 22 678 84 94 **Fax:** 22 678 54 21
Email: ochrona@euro-media.pl **Web site:** http://www.ochrona-mienia.pl
ISSN: 1732-5951
Date Established: 1998; **Freq:** 6 issues yearly; **Circ:** 4,000
Usual Pagination: 52
Advertising Director: Sławomir Zalewski
Profile: Covering procedures of protecting people, property and information.
Language(s): Polish
ADVERTISING RATES:
Full Page Colour .... PLN 4200.00
Mechanical Data: Type Area: A4
BUSINESS: SAFETY & SECURITY: Security

OCHRONA PRZED KOROZJĄ
1811057PL27-2
Editorial: ul. Jana Pawła II, 13, 44-100 GLIWICE
Tel: 32 302 06 44 **Fax:** 32 231 02 24
Email: redakcja@ochronaprzedkorozja.pl **Web site:** http://www.ochronaprzedkorozja.pl
ISSN: 0473-7733
Date Established: 1957; **Freq:** Monthly
Usual Pagination: 28
Profile: Professional magazine on corrosion, metal protection with paints and synthetical materials.
Language(s): Polish
ADVERTISING RATES:
Full Page Mono .... PLN 1600.00
Full Page Colour .... PLN 3300.00
Mechanical Data: Type Area: 210 x 297 mm
BUSINESS: METAL, IRON & STEEL

OFFICE WORLD 1819572PL14A-102
Editorial: ul. Tytoniowa, 20, 04-228 WARSZAWA
Tel: 22 515 00 00 **Fax:** 22 613 25 84
Email: a.koziejowska@migutmedia.pl **Web site:** http://www.migutmedia.pl
Date Established: 2006; **Freq:** Monthly; **Cover Price:** Free; **Circ:** 50,000
Usual Pagination: 80
Profile: Magazine on office interiors, office equipment and office furniture.
Language(s): Polish
ADVERTISING RATES:
Full Page Colour .... PLN 11500.00
Mechanical Data: Type Area: A3
BUSINESS: COMMERCE, INDUSTRY & MANAGEMENT

OFF-ROAD PL MAGAZYN 4 X 4
1709044PL77A-27
Editorial: ul. Konecznego, 6, 9u, 31-216 KRAKÓW
Tel: 12 412 26 57 **Fax:** 12 412 26 57
Email: redakcja@off-road.pl **Web site:** http://www.off-road.pl
ISSN: 1508-8324
Date Established: 1999; **Freq:** Monthly; **Circ:** 35,000
Usual Pagination: 84
Managing Director: Grzegorz Surowiec
Profile: Provides information on 4 wheel drive cars, their testing, spare parts and accessories, car events in Poland and abroad.
Language(s): Polish
Mechanical Data: Type Area: A4
CONSUMER: MOTORING & CYCLING: Motoring

OGRODY, OGRÓDKI, ZIELEŃCE
765708PL93-6
Editorial: ul. Czerska, 8/10, 00-732 WARSZAWA
Tel: 22 555 68 78 **Fax:** 22 555 66 74
Email: ogrody@agora.pl **Web site:** http://www.e-ogrody.pl
ISSN: 1507-4161
Date Established: 1999; **Freq:** Monthly; **Circ:** 45,000
Usual Pagination: 84
Advertising Director: Elżbieta Kaiser
Profile: Magazine containing gardening hints and tips, including articles on the history of gardening, creative ideas, people and their gardens as well as regular news from gardening experts.
Language(s): Polish
Readership: Read by hobby gardeners and professionals.
Mechanical Data: Type Area: 218 x 272 mm
CONSUMER: GARDENING

OLIVIA 1860767PL74B-113
Editorial: ul. Wilcza, 50/52, 00-679 WARSZAWA
Tel: 22 421 11 44 **Fax:** 22 421 10 11
Email: olivia@olivia.pl **Web site:** http://www.olivia.pl
ISSN: 1429-6950
Date Established: 1998; **Freq:** Monthly; **Circ:** 525,000
Usual Pagination: 184
Advertising Director: Paulina Wrzesińska
Profile: Women's magazine about fashion, beauty, health, cooking, relationships, travel, etc.
Language(s): Polish
ADVERTISING RATES:
Full Page Colour .... PLN 75900.00
Mechanical Data: Type Area: 210 x 273 mm
CONSUMER: WOMEN'S INTEREST CONSUMER MAGAZINES: Women's Interest - Fashion

OOH MAGAZINE 1929145PL2A-27
Editorial: ul. Kochanowskiego, 10, 5, 40-035 KATOWICE **Tel:** 32 206 76 77 **Fax:** 32 253 99 96
Email: redakcja@oohmagazine.pl **Web site:** http://www.oohmagazine.pl
ISSN: 1689-7358
Date Established: 2009 -; **Freq:** Monthly
Usual Pagination: 80
Advertising Director: Marzena Ziarkowska
Profile: Contains information on out-of-home, outdoor and indoor media, ambient media, visual advertising and marketing, guerrilla marketing and field marketing.
Language(s): Polish
Mechanical Data: Type Area: 205 x 265 mm
BUSINESS: COMMUNICATIONS, ADVERTISING & MARKETING

OPAKOWANIE 1811059PL35-1
Editorial: ul. Mazowiecka, 12, 00-048 WARSZAWA
Tel: 22 826 61 31 **Fax:** 22 826 61 31
Email: opakowanie@sigma-not.pl **Web site:** http://www.opakowanie.net
ISSN: 0030-3348
Date Established: 1955; **Freq:** Monthly
Usual Pagination: 84
Profile: Covering research, production and usage of packaging materials and machines, marketing and international cooperation in the packaging business.
Language(s): Polish
ADVERTISING RATES:
Full Page Mono .... PLN 1700.00
Full Page Colour .... PLN 3200.00
Mechanical Data: Type Area: 205 x 290 mm
BUSINESS: PACKAGING & BOTTLING

OPM - OGÓLNOPOLSKI PRZEGLĄD MEDYCZNY
1811011PL56A-42
Editorial: al. Roździeńskiego, 188, 40-203 KATOWICE **Tel:** 32 788 51 13 **Fax:** 32 788 51 09
Email: medyczny@elamed.pl **Web site:** http://www.medyczny.elamed.pl
ISSN: 1641-7348
Date Established: 1992; **Freq:** Monthly
Usual Pagination: 70
Advertising Director: Dagmara Pochłopień
Profile: Focused on newest medicine techniques, management of health service hospitals, general medical news.
Language(s): Polish
ADVERTISING RATES:
Full Page Colour .... PLN 4000.00
Mechanical Data: Type Area: 204 x 290 mm
BUSINESS: HEALTH & MEDICAL

OUTSOURCING MAGAZINE
1709100PL14A-63
Editorial: ul. Racławicka, 15/19, 53-149 WARSZAWA
Tel: 71 783 51 00 **Fax:** 71 783 51 01
Email: redakcja@flota.com.pl **Web site:** http://www.outsourcing.com.pl
ISSN: 1733-005X
Date Established: 2004; **Freq:** Quarterly; **Circ:** 4,500
Usual Pagination: 96
Managing Director: Marcin Hutnik; **Advertising Director:** Tomasz Łyszega
Profile: Covering all aspects where outsourcing is applicable (complex accountancy and financial services, controlling marketing, HR and documentation management.
Language(s): Polish

ADVERTISING RATES:
Full Page Colour .... PLN 8400.00
Mechanical Data: Type Area: A4
BUSINESS: COMMERCE, INDUSTRY & MANAGEMENT

PANI
754776PL74A-200
Editorial: al. Stanów Zjednoczonych, 61a, 04-028 WARSZAWA **Tel:** 22 516 31 90 **Fax:** 22 516 31 14
Email: listy.pani@bauer.pl **Web site:** http://www.styl.pl/pani
ISSN: 1230-8293
Date Established: 1989; **Freq:** Monthly; **Circ:** 137,000
Usual Pagination: 192
Managing Director: Monika Krokiewicz; **Advertising Director:** Beata Madeja
Profile: Magazine covering fashion, beauty, health and lifestyle issues.
Language(s): Polish
Readership: Aimed at affluent women over 30 years of age.
ADVERTISING RATES:
Full Page Colour .... PLN 42900.00
Mechanical Data: Type Area: 220 x 280 mm
CONSUMER: WOMEN'S INTEREST CONSUMER MAGAZINES: Women's Interest

PANI DOMU
1860766PL74A-1035
Editorial: ul. Wiejska 19, 00-480 WARSZAWA
Tel: 22 584 24 38 **Fax:** 22 584 24 36
Email: panidomu@edipresse.pl **Web site:** http://polki.pl/panidomu.html
Date Established: 1994; **Freq:** Weekly; **Circ:** 473,000
Usual Pagination: 54
Advertising Director: Agnieszka Bieniek
Profile: Magazine featuring articles on lifestyle, interior design, travel, cookery, fashion and cosmetics.
Language(s): Polish
Readership: Read mainly by women aged between 24 and 54 years.
ADVERTISING RATES:
Full Page Colour .... PLN 69000.00
Mechanical Data: Type Area: 215 x 285 mm
CONSUMER: WOMEN'S INTEREST CONSUMER MAGAZINES: Women's Interest

PANI DOMU POLECA
1708773PL74P-5
Editorial: ul. Wiejska 19, 00-480 WARSZAWA
Tel: 22 58 42 200 **Fax:** 22 58 42 201
Email: panidomu@edipresse.pl
Date Established: 1996
Circ: 103,000
Usual Pagination: 96
Profile: Contains cookery recipes.
Language(s): Polish
Mechanical Data: Type Area: 170x225 mm
CONSUMER: WOMEN'S INTEREST CONSUMER MAGAZINES: Food & Cookery

PAPIERNICZY ŚWIAT
1708849PL36-1
Editorial: ul. Kierbedzia, 4, 00-728 WARSZAWA
Tel: 22 320 15 36 **Fax:** 22 320 15 40
Email: papiernik@unit.com.pl **Web site:** http://www.unit.com.pl
ISSN: 1426-1456
Date Established: 1996; **Freq:** 8 issues yearly; **Circ:** 4,000
Usual Pagination: 56
Advertising Director: Justyna Szwak
Profile: Provides various information and news from paper industry.
Language(s): Polish
ADVERTISING RATES:
Full Page Colour .... PLN 4750.00
Mechanical Data: Type Area: 210 x 297 mm
BUSINESS: PAPER

PARKIET - GAZETA GIEŁDY
1614219PL1F-1
Editorial: ul. Prosta, 51, 00-838 WARSZAWA
Tel: 22 463 06 00 **Fax:** 22 463 05 10
Email: redakcja@parkiet.com **Web site:** http://www.parkiet.com
ISSN: 1231-2207
Date Established: 1994; **Freq:** Daily; **Circ:** 9,072
Usual Pagination: 28
Advertising Director: Adrian Grabiński
Profile: Newspaper focusing on political and legal issues, information on the stock exchange, business and economic reports and also in-depth analysis of the financial markets.
Language(s): Polish
Readership: Read by investment managers.
ADVERTISING RATES:
Full Page Mono .... PLN 13300.00
Full Page Colour .... PLN 15600.00
Mechanical Data: Type Area: 249x329,6mm
BUSINESS: FINANCE & ECONOMICS: Investment

PARTY
1860651PL74Q-16
Editorial: ul. Wiejska, 16, 00-480 WARSZAWA
Tel: 22 584 25 78
Email: party@edipresse.pl **Web site:** http://www.partynews.pl
ISSN: 1898-2883
Date Established: 2007; **Freq:** 26 issues yearly; **Circ:** 563,000
Usual Pagination: 92
Managing Director: Alicja Modzelewska;
Advertising Director: Małgorzata Szumigaj
Profile: Magazine about celebrities and lifestyle.
Language(s): Polish
Mechanical Data: Type Area: 230 x 300 mm
CONSUMER: WOMEN'S INTEREST CONSUMER MAGAZINES: Lifestyle

PC FORMAT
1623038PL5D-2
Editorial: al. Stanów Zjednoczonych, 61a, 04-028 WARSZAWA **Tel:** 22 516 36 30 **Fax:** 22 516 36 37
Email: redakcja@pcformat.pl **Web site:** http://www.pcformat.pl
ISSN: 1640-7776
Date Established: 2000; **Freq:** Monthly; **Circ:** 90,159
Usual Pagination: 112
Advertising Director: Magdalena Milewska
Profile: Magazine focusing on use of basic computer software and the Internet.
Language(s): Polish
Readership: Read mainly by men aged between 15 and 24 years interested in latest computer applications.
ADVERTISING RATES:
Full Page Colour .... PLN 19500.00
Mechanical Data: Type Area: 225 x 300 mm
BUSINESS: COMPUTERS & AUTOMATION: Personal Computers

PC WORLD KOMPUTER
1600646PL5C-1
Editorial: ul. Jordanowska, 12, 04-204 WARSZAWA
Tel: 22 321 78 00 **Fax:** 22 321 78 88
Email: pcwk@idg.com.pl **Web site:** http://www.pcworld.pl
ISSN: 1232-3004
Date Established: 1986; **Freq:** Monthly; **Circ:** 46,629
Usual Pagination: 146
Advertising Director: Włodzimierz Duszyk
Profile: Publication features computer news, product reviews, purchasing guides and products' information.
Language(s): Polish
Readership: Aimed at volume buyers of PCs and related products.
ADVERTISING RATES:
Full Page Colour .... PLN 14900.00
Mechanical Data: Type Area: 210 x 297 mm
BUSINESS: COMPUTERS & AUTOMATION: Professional Personal Computers

PERKUSISTA
1928959PL76E-2
Editorial: ul. Leszczynowa, 11, 03-197 WARSZAWA
Tel: 22 257 84 99 **Fax:** 22 257 84 32
Email: redakcja@magazynperkusista.pl **Web site:** http://www.magazynperkusista.pl
ISSN: 1899-7732
Date Established: 2008; **Freq:** 6 issues yearly; **Circ:** 9,000
Usual Pagination: 120
Profile: Magazine entirely dedicated to drumming and drummer kits.
Language(s): Polish
Mechanical Data: Type Area: 220 x 290 mm
CONSUMER: MUSIC & PERFORMING ARTS: Pop Music

PERSONEL I ZARZĄDZANIE
1620684PL14F-1
Editorial: ul. Okopowa 58/72, 01-042 WARSZAWA
Tel: 22 530 42 52 **Fax:** 22 530 42 51
Email: personel@infor.pl **Web site:** http://www.personel.infor.pl
ISSN: 1641-0793
Date Established: 1994; **Freq:** Monthly
Usual Pagination: 120
Managing Director: Mariusz Drozdowicz
Profile: Magazine covering latest trends in HR management and HR issues.
Language(s): Polish
Readership: Aimed at HR managers.
Mechanical Data: Type Area: A4
BUSINESS: COMMERCE, INDUSTRY & MANAGEMENT: Training & Recruitment

PERSONEL PLUS
1929152PL14F-9
Editorial: ul. Gilarska, 58, 03-589 WARSZAWA
Tel: 22 394 54 32 **Fax:** 22 435 70 49
Email: redakcja@personelplus.pl **Web site:** http://www.personelplus.pl
ISSN: 1899-2412
Date Established: 2000; **Freq:** Monthly; **Circ:** 9,000
Usual Pagination: 104
Managing Director: Bartłomiej Ślusarczyk
Profile: Magazine about HR management, job legal issues, recruitment, HR training, etc.
Language(s): Polish
Mechanical Data: Type Area: 205 x 280 mm
BUSINESS: COMMERCE, INDUSTRY & MANAGEMENT: Training & Recruitment

PESO PERFECTO
1929143PL74G-29
Editorial: ul. Puławska, 118a, 02-620 WARSZAWA
Tel: 22 843 49 83 **Fax:** 22 353 94 38
Email: pesoperfecto@aude.pl
Date Established: 2008; **Freq:** Quarterly; **Circ:** 30,000
Usual Pagination: 64
Profile: Magazine covering wellness, fitness, health aspects, beauty, psychology.
Language(s): Polish
Mechanical Data: Type Area: A4
CONSUMER: WOMEN'S INTEREST CONSUMER MAGAZINES: Slimming & Health

PHP SOLUTIONS
1796119PL5C-4
Editorial: ul. Bokserska, 1, 02-682 WARSZAWA
Tel: 22 427 36 51 **Fax:** 22 244 24 59
Email: phpsolutions@software.com.pl **Web site:** http://www.phpsolmag.org
ISSN: 1731-2922
Date Established: 2004; **Freq:** 6 times a year; **Cover Price:** Paid; **Circ:** 6,000 Unique Users
Usual Pagination: 82
Editor: Magdalena Sobiś; **Advertising Director:** Patrycja Wądołowska
Profile: Digital magazine covering Internet applications and databases, web developing.
Language(s): Polish
Mechanical Data: Type Area: A4
BUSINESS: COMPUTERS & AUTOMATION: Professional Personal Computers

PIAR.PL
1796008PL2E-1
Editorial: ul. Zeylanda, 4, 6, 60-808 POZNAŃ
Tel: 61 855 14 55 **Fax:** 61 851 99 54
Email: redakcja@piar.pl **Web site:** http://www.piar.pl
ISSN: 1733-7488
Date Established: 2005
Circ: 5,000
Usual Pagination: 100
Profile: Magazine covering PR in theory and practice, political marketing and lobbing.
Language(s): Polish
ADVERTISING RATES:
Full Page Colour .... PLN 10800.00
Mechanical Data: Type Area: 290x205 mm
BUSINESS: COMMUNICATIONS, ADVERTISING & MARKETING: Public Relations

PIELĘGNIARSTWO XXI WIEKU
1811000PL56B-1
Editorial: Al. Racławickie 1, 20-059 LUBLIN
Tel: 81 532 27 47
Email: bdob10@wp.pl **Web site:** http://www.czelej.com.pl
ISSN: 1730-1912
Freq: Quarterly; **Cover Price:** PLN 8.00; **Circ:** 1,000
Usual Pagination: 76
Profile: Quarterly magazine which aims to facilitate the exchange of ideas, research results and analysis of faculty members of nursing and midwifery and to bring the problems of nursing practice.
Language(s): Polish
Readership: Aimed at nurses, midwives and National Health service offices.
Mechanical Data: Type Area: 200 x 280 mm
BUSINESS: HEALTH & MEDICAL: Nursing

PIŁKA NOŻNA
1708679PL75B-3
Editorial: ul. Stawki, 2, 00-193 WARSZAWA
Tel: 22 536 92 81/82 **Fax:** 22 536 92 83
Email: redakcja@pilkanozna.pl **Web site:** http://www.pilkanozna.pl
ISSN: 0137-4710
Date Established: 1956; **Freq:** Weekly; **Circ:** 58,000
Usual Pagination: 48
Managing Director: Gabriela Profus; **Advertising Director:** Aleksandra Trojnar
Profile: Magazine dedicated to football.
Language(s): Polish
Mechanical Data: Type Area: 213 x 272 mm
CONSUMER: SPORT: Football

PIŁKA NOŻNA PLUS
1795930PL75B-1
Editorial: ul. Stawki, 2, 00-193 WARSZAWA
Tel: 22 536 92 81/82 **Fax:** 22 536 92 83
Email: redakcja@pilkanozna.pl **Web site:** http://www.pilkanozna.pl
ISSN: 1230-9737
Date Established: 1986; **Freq:** Monthly; **Circ:** 42,000
Usual Pagination: 68
Managing Director: Gabriela Profus; **Advertising Director:** Aleksandra Trojnar
Profile: Magazine covering all aspects of football, sports medicine and other team games.
Language(s): Polish
Mechanical Data: Type Area: 210 x 275 mm
CONSUMER: SPORT: Football

PILOT CLUB MAGAZINE
1796126PL6A-1
Editorial: ul. Dobra 56/66, 00-920 WARSZAWA
Tel: 22 826 20 09 **Fax:** 22 427 83 65
Email: redakcja@pilotclub.pl **Web site:** http://www.pilotclub.pl
ISSN: 1734-4638
Date Established: 2005; **Freq:** Monthly; **Annual Sub.:** PLN 89.00; **Circ:** 9,000
Usual Pagination: 102
Profile: Stylish and trendy magazine related exclusively to General Aviation in Poland.
Language(s): Polish
Readership: Aimed at pilots, airplanes owners, pilot-students, managers and businessmen starting to think about new challenge and passion and all GA enthusiasts.
ADVERTISING RATES:
Full Page Colour .... EUR 2400.00
Mechanical Data: Type Area: 205x280 mm
Copy instructions: *Copy Date:* 15th of the previous month due to the publication
BUSINESS: AVIATION & AERONAUTICS

PLAYBOY
1708694PL86C-8
Editorial: ul. Wilcza, 50/52, 00-679 WARSZAWA
Tel: 22 421 12 72 **Fax:** 22 421 11 11
Email: redakcja@playboy.pl **Web site:** http://marquardmedia.pl
ISSN: 1230-2724
Date Established: 1992/93; **Freq:** Monthly; **Circ:** 105,000
Usual Pagination: 154
Advertising Director: Monika Ruszkowska
Profile: Men's magazine covering all aspects of life of modern men, culture, automotive, technology and gadgets, style (fashion, trends, beauty, travel, cuisine).
Language(s): Polish
ADVERTISING RATES:
Full Page Colour .... PLN 44500.00
Mechanical Data: Type Area: 210 x 273 mm
CONSUMER: ADULT & GAY MAGAZINES: Men's Lifestyle Magazines

PODATKI DOCHODOWE W PRAKTYCE
1709065PL1M-10
Formerly: Poradnik Podatnika
Editorial: ul. Łotewska, 9a, 03-918 WARSZAWA
Tel: 22 518 27 27 **Fax:** 22 518 27 50
Email: podatki@wip.pl **Web site:** http://www.poradnikpodatnika.pl
Date Established: 1998
Usual Pagination: 600
Editor: Iwona Kryśpiak
Profile: Informs about taxation issues, tax calculations and changes in taxation documentation.
Language(s): Polish
BUSINESS: FINANCE & ECONOMICS: Taxation

PODŁOGI I ŚCIANY
1708917PL23B-2
Editorial: ul. Andersa, 38, 15-113 BIAŁYSTOK
Tel: 85 653 90 00 **Fax:** 85 653 98 56
Email: redakcja@podlogi-sciany.pl **Web site:** http://www.podlogi-sciany.pl
ISSN: 1644-9606
Date Established: 2000
Circ: 12,000
Usual Pagination: 64
Managing Director: Anita Frank; **Advertising Director:** Alicja Klimowicz
Profile: Contains information on material used for floors, walls and ceilings' finishing, informs on the new technologies, designs and patterns used in this branch.
Language(s): Polish
Mechanical Data: Type Area: 225 x 290 mm
BUSINESS: FURNISHINGS & FURNITURE: Furnishings, Carpets & Flooring

PODRÓŻE
1709105PL89A-8
Editorial: ul. Kamionkowska, 45, 03-812 WARSZAWA **Tel:** 22 590 51 19 **Fax:** 22 590 54 44
Email: podroze@murator.com.pl **Web site:** http://www.podroze.pl
ISSN: 1505-3601
Date Established: 1998; **Freq:** Monthly; **Circ:** 31,000
Usual Pagination: 112
Managing Director: Ewa P. Porębska; **Advertising Director:** Anna Dygasiewicz-Piwko
Profile: Featuring tourism for everyone and inspires people for fulfilling their travel dreams and advises on their realization.
Language(s): Polish
Mechanical Data: Type Area: 230 x 270 mm
CONSUMER: HOLIDAYS & TRAVEL: Travel

POLAND MONTHLY
1796171PL82-78
Editorial: ul. Łucka, 15, 3 p., 00-842 WARSZAWA
Tel: 22 586 30 00 **Fax:** 22 586 30 01
Email: letters@polandmonthly.pl **Web site:** http://www.polandmonthly.pl
ISSN: 1643-742X
Date Established: 2002; **Freq:** Monthly; **Circ:** 7,000
Advertising Director: Aneta Kłodaś
Profile: English-language publication specializing in business news and insight, politics, and lifestyle issues in Poland.
Language(s): English
ADVERTISING RATES:
Full Page Colour .... PLN 12000.00
CONSUMER: CURRENT AFFAIRS & POLITICS

POLIGRAFIKA
1796078PL41A-2
Editorial: ul. Pańska, 97, 00-834 WARSZAWA
Tel: 22 654 93 22 **Fax:** 22 654 50 84
Email: poligrafika@poligrafika.pl **Web site:** http://www.poligrafika.pl
Date Established: 1947; **Freq:** Monthly; **Circ:** 2,500
Usual Pagination: 88
Profile: Covering all the information connected with printing: digital technologies, offset and flexography, printing functions and materials.
Language(s): Polish
Mechanical Data: Type Area: A4
BUSINESS: PRINTING & STATIONERY: Printing

POLISH CONSTRUCTION REVIEW
1835719PL42A-1
Editorial: ul. Supniewskiego 9, 31-527, 31-527, KRAKÓW **Tel:** 12 618 90 00 **Fax:** 12 618 90 08
Email: info@pmrpublications.com **Web site:** http://www.pmrpublications.com
Freq: 60 issues yearly; **Annual Sub.:** EUR 760.00; **Circ:** 1,000
Profile: A monthly report for construction professionals with most recent statistics on the Polish construction market, comprehensive ongoing analysis of the situation in residential, non-residential and civil engineering and summary of the present situation on the Polish construction market.
Language(s): English; Polish
BUSINESS: CONSTRUCTION

POLISH MARKET
708049PL1A-70
Editorial: ul. Elektoralna, 13, 4, 00-137 WARSZAWA
Tel: 22 620 31 42 **Fax:** 22 620 31 37
Email: info@polishmarket.com.pl **Web site:** http://www.polishmarket.com.pl
ISSN: 1427-0978
Date Established: 1996; **Freq:** Monthly; **Circ:** 8,000
Usual Pagination: 84
Advertising Director: Natalia Suhoveeva
Profile: Newsletter covering analysis of trends, regional reports, economical and financial forecasts, foreign investment, demographics, also legal and taxation issues.
Language(s): English; Polish
Readership: Aimed at business executives, managers and investors.
Mechanical Data: Type Area: 230x295 mm
BUSINESS: FINANCE & ECONOMICS

POLISH MARKET REVIEW
1835779PL1F-3
Editorial: ul. Supniewskiego 9, 31-527, KRAKÓW
Tel: 12 618 90 00 **Fax:** 12 618 90 08
Email: info@pmrpublications.com **Web site:** https://www.pmrpublications.com
Date Established: 1995; **Freq:** 60 issues yearly; **Annual Sub.:** EUR 720.00; **Circ:** 1,000
Managing Editor: Joanna Rybak
Profile: English language information service for business professionals who invest in Poland, providing information on Polish economy through macroeconomic indicators, managing investments, changes in tax regulations and marketing products on Polish market.
Language(s): English
BUSINESS: FINANCE & ECONOMICS: Investment

POLITYKA
1500365PL82-83
Editorial: ul. Słupecka, 6, 02-309 WARSZAWA
Tel: 22 451 61 33/34/35 **Fax:** 22 451 61 35
Email: polityka@polityka.com.pl **Web site:** http://www.polityka.pl
ISSN: 0032-3500
Date Established: 1957; **Freq:** Weekly; **Circ:** 198,713
Usual Pagination: 96
Managing Director: Jadwiga Kucharczyk; **Advertising Director:** Krystyna Jarosz
Profile: Magazine covering current affairs, latest events in Poland and abroad, economics and social news.
Language(s): Polish
Readership: Aimed at those interested in politics.
ADVERTISING RATES:
Full Page Colour .... PLN 83000.00
Mechanical Data: Type Area: 215 x 286 mm
CONSUMER: CURRENT AFFAIRS & POLITICS

POLSKA DZIENNIK BAŁTYCKI
1614418PL67B-9
Editorial: ul. Targ Drzewny, 9/11, 80-894 GDAŃSK
Tel: 58 300 33 00 **Fax:** 58 300 33 03
Email: redakcja@prasa.gda.pl **Web site:** http://www.dziennikbaltycki.pl
Date Established: 1945; **Freq:** Daily; **Circ:** 47,353
Usual Pagination: 20
Advertising Director: Justyna Bizewska
Profile: An informative-publicity newspaper covering news from Pomeranian region: political, scientific, cultural and sports.
Language(s): Polish
ADVERTISING RATES:
Full Page Mono .... PLN 14900.00
Mechanical Data: Type Area: A3
REGIONAL DAILY & SUNDAY NEWSPAPERS: Regional Daily Newspapers

POLSKA DZIENNIK ZACHODNI
1614450PL67B-10
Editorial: ul. Młyńska, 1, 40-954 KATOWICE
Tel: 32 358 21 04 **Fax:** 32 358 31 04
Email: redakcja@dz.com.pl **Web site:** http://www.dz.com.pl
ISSN: 0137-9038
Date Established: 1945; **Freq:** Daily; **Circ:** 78,923
Usual Pagination: 40
Advertising Director: Magdalena Kopka
Profile: An informative-publicizing regional newspaper.
Language(s): Polish
ADVERTISING RATES:
Full Page Mono .... PLN 15780.00
Mechanical Data: Type Area: A3
REGIONAL DAILY & SUNDAY NEWSPAPERS: Regional Daily Newspapers

POLSKA GAZETA KRAKOWSKA
1614468PL67B-12
Editorial: al. Pokoju, 3, 31-548 KRAKÓW
Tel: 12 688 80 00 **Fax:** 12 688 81 09
Email: sekretariat@gk.pl **Web site:** http://www.gazetakrakowska.pl
ISSN: 1898-3138
Date Established: 1949; **Freq:** Daily; **Circ:** 30,995
Usual Pagination: 32
Advertising Director: Marcin Zięciak
Profile: Regional newspaper resenting views on economics and society.
Language(s): Polish
ADVERTISING RATES:
Full Page Colour .... PLN 12000.00
Mechanical Data: Type Area: A3
REGIONAL DAILY & SUNDAY NEWSPAPERS: Regional Daily Newspapers

POLSKA GAZETA TRANSPORTOWA
765840PL49A-1
Editorial: ul. Miedziana, 3a, 21, 00-814 WARSZAWA
Tel: 22 620 92 23 **Fax:** 22 890 98 32
Email: k.bachulski@pgt.pl **Web site:** http://pgt.pl
ISSN: 1230-7599
Date Established: 1993; **Freq:** Weekly; **Circ:** 4,000
Usual Pagination: 10
Editor: Elżbieta Haber
Profile: Newspaper focusing on all aspects of heavy goods transport. Includes air, rail and sea transportation.
Language(s): Polish
Readership: Read by exporters, manufacturers, hauliers, suppliers and importers.
ADVERTISING RATES:
Full Page Mono .... PLN 10900.00
Full Page Colour .... PLN 19100.00
Mechanical Data: Type Area: A3
BUSINESS: TRANSPORT

POLSKA GAZETA WROCŁAWSKA
1614530PL67B-15
Editorial: ul. Strzegomska, 42a, 53-611 WROCŁAW
Tel: 71 374 81 00 **Fax:** 71 374 81 75
Email: sekretariat@gazeta.wroc.pl **Web site:** http://www.gazetawroclawska.pl
ISSN: 1732-5102
Date Established: 2003; **Freq:** Daily
Usual Pagination: 40
Advertising Director: Magdalena Przygodzka
Profile: Regional newspaper covering international, national and local news, events in Wroclaw city and south of Poland.
Language(s): Polish
ADVERTISING RATES:
Full Page Colour .... PLN 11150.00
Mechanical Data: Type Area: A3
REGIONAL DAILY & SUNDAY NEWSPAPERS: Regional Daily Newspapers

POLSKA GŁOS WIELKOPOLSKI
1614570PL67B-20
Editorial: ul. Grunwaldzka, 19, 60-782 POZNAŃ
Tel: 61 869 41 00 **Fax:** 61 860 61 15
Email: redakcja@glos.com **Web site:** http://www.gloswielkopolski.pl
ISSN: 0137-9186
Date Established: 1945; **Freq:** Daily; **Circ:** 49,233
Usual Pagination: 40
Advertising Director: Natasza Szymczak
Profile: Covering local events, politics, sports, cars, computers, health, family and entertainment.
Language(s): Polish
ADVERTISING RATES:
Full Page Mono .... PLN 17600.00
Mechanical Data: Type Area: 251 x 347 mm
REGIONAL DAILY & SUNDAY NEWSPAPERS: Regional Daily Newspapers

POLSKA (METROPOLIA WARSZAWSKA)
1835768PL65K-1
Editorial: ul. Domaniewska 41, budynek Saturn, II piętro, 02-696 WARSZAWA **Tel:** 22 201 42 00
Fax: 22 201 42 01
Email: a.wiater@polskapresse.pl **Web site:** http://www.polskatimes.pl
Freq: Daily; **Circ:** 15,561
Usual Pagination: 40
Editor-in-Chief: Paweł Fąfara
Profile: Metropolitan newspaper covering news, political events, cultural and social issues.
Language(s): Polish
ADVERTISING RATES:
Full Page Colour .... PLN 18780.00
Mechanical Data: Type Area: 263 x335mm
NATIONAL DAILY & SUNDAY NEWSPAPERS: Metropolitan Daily Newspapers

POLSKI CARAVANING
1796088PL91B-1
Editorial: ul. Armii Krajowej, 86, 83-110 TCZEW
Tel: 58 777 01 25 **Fax:** 58 777 01 25
Email: redakcja@polskicaravaning.pl **Web site:** http://www.polskicaravaning.pl
ISSN: 1734-9311
Date Established: 2005; **Freq:** 6 issues yearly; **Circ:** 5,000
Usual Pagination: 64
Editor: Janusz Czerwiński
Profile: Covering news in caravanning, tourism and travel, camping and active recreation.
Language(s): Polish
Mechanical Data: Type Area: A4 (205x290 mm)
CONSUMER: RECREATION & LEISURE: Camping & Caravanning

POLSKI INSTALATOR
766096PL3A-1
Editorial: al. Komisji Edukacji Narodowej, 95, 02-777 WARSZAWA **Tel:** 22 678 37 60 **Fax:** 22 679 52 03
Email: pi@polskiinstalator.com.pl **Web site:** http://www.polskiinstalator.com.pl
ISSN: 1231-2428
Date Established: 1991; **Freq:** Monthly; **Circ:** 8,000
Usual Pagination: 80
Advertising Director: Sławomir Zalewski
Profile: Trade magazine dedicated to all kind of interior building installations, includes information on the latest technology and new products.
Language(s): Polish
Mechanical Data: Type Area: A4
BUSINESS: HEATING & VENTILATION: Domestic Heating & Ventilation

POLSKI JUBILER
1819398PL52A-2
Editorial: ul. Okrzei 1a, 03-715 WARSZAWA
Tel: 22 333 80 00 **Fax:** 22 333 88 82
Email: polskijubiler@pws-promedia.pl **Web site:** http://www.polskijubiler.pl
ISSN: 1429-3773
Date Established: 1991; **Freq:** Monthly; **Circ:** 4,000
Usual Pagination: 40
Advertising Director: Monika Rybitwa
Profile: Professional magazine on jewellery production and precious stones, watches and clocks, design and news. Polish Jeweler enjoys being the leading source of information and promotion for new products, showcase of jewelry designs, supplies and services in the jewelry and watch fields.
Language(s): Polish
Readership: Targets professional buyers and consumers in Poland.
ADVERTISING RATES:
Full Page Mono .... PLN 1800.00
Full Page Colour .... PLN 3300.00
Mechanical Data: Type Area: A4
BUSINESS: GIFT TRADE: Jewellery

POLSKIE DOMY - PRZEWODNIK PO PROJEKTACH
1811090PL4A-29
Editorial: ul. Andersa, 38, 15-113 BIAŁYSTOK
Tel: 85 653 90 00 **Fax:** 85 653 98 56
Email: projekty@publikator.com.pl **Web site:** http://www.publikator.com.pl
Freq: Annual; **Circ:** 20,000
Usual Pagination: 208
Managing Director: Anita Frank; **Advertising Director:** Alicja Klimowicz
Profile: Contains 120 projects for detached houses helping to select and appropriate one and assisting with all house and garden arrangements.
Language(s): Polish
Mechanical Data: Type Area: 230 x 297 mm
BUSINESS: ARCHITECTURE & BUILDING: Architecture

POLSKIE DROGI
1835778PL42B-1
Editorial: ul. Dobrowoja 17/11, 03-403 WARSZAWA
Tel: 22 81 04 382 **Fax:** 22 87 06 041
Email: redakcja@polskiedrogi.com.pl **Web site:** http://www.polskiedrogi.com.pl
Freq: Monthly; **Annual Sub.:** PLN 240.00; **Circ:** 5,000
Editor: Adam K. Spiechowicz; **Advertising Director:** Jarosław Chałka
Profile: Focuses on construction of roads and motorways in Poland, new technologies, materials and investments.
Language(s): Polish
ADVERTISING RATES:
Full Page Mono .... PLN 2000.00
Full Page Colour .... PLN 3500.00
Mechanical Data: Type Area: 216 x 296mm
BUSINESS: CONSTRUCTION: Roads

PORADNIK DOMOWY
1201737PL74C-10
Editorial: ul. Czerska, 8/10, 00-732 WARSZAWA
Tel: 22 555 68 90 **Fax:** 22 555 66 67
Email: poradnik@agora.pl **Web site:** http://www.poradnikdomowy.pl
ISSN: 0867-2229
Date Established: 1990; **Freq:** Monthly; **Circ:** 626,000
Usual Pagination: 124
Advertising Director: Paulina Skorwider
Profile: Magazine featuring ideas for family homes, health, fashion, beauty, psychology, work, law and finance, travel, recipes, images of modern women, caring for family, etc.
Language(s): Polish
Mechanical Data: Type Area: 213 x 282 mm
CONSUMER: WOMEN'S INTEREST CONSUMER MAGAZINES: Home & Family

PORADNIK GAZETY PRAWNEJ
1620679PL1M-1
Editorial: ul. Okopowa, 58/72, 01-042 WARSZAWA
Tel: 22 530 40 06 **Fax:** 22 530 40 12
Email: pgp@infor.pl **Web site:** http://www.pgp.infor.pl
ISSN: 1234-5695
Date Established: 1995; **Freq:** Weekly
Usual Pagination: 48
Managing Director: Mariusz Drozdowicz
Profile: Magazine focusing on tax, insurance and employment legislation issues.
Language(s): Polish
Readership: Read by financial advisors.
Mechanical Data: Type Area: A4
BUSINESS: FINANCE & ECONOMICS: Taxation

PORADNIK HANDLOWCA
1708859PL53-6
Editorial: ul. Garbary, 106/108, 61-757 POZNAŃ
Tel: 61 852 08 94 **Fax:** 61 851 92 41
Email: redakcja@poradnikhandlowca.com.pl **Web site:** http://www.poradnikhandlowca.com.pl
ISSN: 1231-1545
Freq: Monthly; **Cover Price:** Free; **Circ:** 65,000
Advertising Director: Wojtek Generalczyk
Profile: Monthly national magazine for warehouse managers and retailers selling groceries and household chemicals.
Language(s): Polish
Readership: Aimed at managing staff in chain stores, managers and owners of stores and retail and wholesale shops selling groceries, household chemicals and cosmetics.
ADVERTISING RATES:
Full Page Colour .... PLN 26000.00
Mechanical Data: Type Area: A4
BUSINESS: RETAILING & WHOLESALING

PORADNIK ORGANIZACJI NON-PROFIT
1708971PL1B-10
Editorial: ul. Okopowa, 58/72, 01-042 WARSZAWA
Tel: 22 530 41 71 **Fax:** 22 530 42 22
Web site: http://www.nonprofit.infor.pl
ISSN: 1899-9026
Date Established: 2003; **Freq:** Monthly
Usual Pagination: 48
Managing Director: Mariusz Drozdowicz
Profile: Dedicated to various issues of accountancy and taxation for non-profit institutions.
Language(s): Polish
Mechanical Data: Type Area: A4
BUSINESS: FINANCE & ECONOMICS: Accountancy

PORADNIK PRZEDSIĘBIORCY BUDOWLANEGO
1708920PL4E-27
Editorial: ul. Łotewska, 9a, 03-918 WARSZAWA
Tel: 22 429 40 00 **Fax:** 22 518 27 50
Email: budowlaniec@wip.pl **Web site:** http://www.poradnikbudowlany.pl
Date Established: 2003; **Freq:** Monthly
Usual Pagination: 500
Profile: Provides practical information how to run a building company.
Language(s): Polish
BUSINESS: ARCHITECTURE & BUILDING: Building

PORADNIK RESTAURATORA
1708705PL11A-1
Editorial: ul. Garbary, 106/108, 61-757 POZNAŃ
Tel: 61 852 08 94 **Fax:** 61 852 51 41
Email: redakcja@poradnikrestauratora.com.pl **Web site:** http://www.poradnikrestauratora.com.pl
ISSN: 1508-6194
Date Established: 1999; **Freq:** Monthly; **Cover Price:** Free; **Circ:** 10,000
Advertising Director: Wojtek Generalczyk
Profile: National trade magazine on gastronomy. Since the beginning in September 1991, the magazine has been dynamically developing, which found its results in independent researches. „Poradnik Restauratora" is a professional advisory-informational magazine featuring both analysis of gastronomy market in Poland, as well as its development trends all over the world, interviews with celebrities.
Language(s): Polish
ADVERTISING RATES:
Full Page Colour .... PLN 7900.00
Mechanical Data: Type Area: A4
BUSINESS: CATERING: Catering, Hotels & Restaurants

PORADNIK STOMATOLOGICZNY
1796151PL56D-1
Editorial: ul. Niedźwiedzia, 12a, 02-737 WARSZAWA
Tel: 22 853 73 72 **Fax:** 22 853 73 72
Email: sekretariat.bielsko@medi-press.pl **Web site:** http://poradnik-stomatologiczny.pl
ISSN: 1428-1716
Date Established: 2000; **Freq:** Monthly; **Circ:** 7,000
Usual Pagination: 60
Managing Director: Anna Łuczyńska; **Advertising Director:** Anna Grzesiowska
Profile: Professional magazine dedicated to all aspects of dental treatments.
Language(s): Polish

Mechanical Data: Type Area: A4
BUSINESS: HEALTH & MEDICAL: Dental

PORADNIK VAT
1929199PL1M-14
Editorial: ul. Owocowa, 8, 66-400 GORZÓW WLKP.
Tel: 95 720 85 40 **Fax:** 95 720 85 60
Email: poradnik@gofin.pl **Web site:** http://www.gofin.pl
ISSN: 1429-3978
Date Established: 1998; **Freq:** 26 issues yearly; **Circ:** 20,000
Usual Pagination: 68
Profile: Publication dedicated to VAT taxation and taxation procedures with calculations.
Language(s): Polish
ADVERTISING RATES:
Full Page Colour .... PLN 2500.00
Mechanical Data: Type Area: 170 x 240 mm
BUSINESS: FINANCE & ECONOMICS: Taxation

PORADNIK ZDROWIA Z KALENDARZEM
1709095PL74G-16
Editorial: ul. Niedźwiedzia, 12a, 02-737 WARSZAWA
Tel: 22 853 73 72 **Fax:** 22 853 73 72
Email: redakcja.zyjmydluzej@medi-press.pl **Web site:** http://www.medigo.pl
Date Established: 2003; **Freq:** Annual; **Circ:** 15,000
Usual Pagination: 224
Profile: Contains health advice and medical tests and vaccination tables.
Language(s): Polish
Mechanical Data: Type Area: A5
CONSUMER: WOMEN'S INTEREST CONSUMER MAGAZINES: Slimming & Health

POSTĘPY DERMATOLOGII I ALERGOLOGII
1708794PL56A-11
Editorial: ul. Wenedów, 9/1, 61-614 POZNAŃ
Tel: 61 822 77 81 **Fax:** 61 822 77 81
Email: termedia@termedia.pl **Web site:** http://www.dermatologia.termedia.pl
Date Established: 2001; **Freq:** 6 issues yearly; **Circ:** 4,000
Usual Pagination: 60
Managing Director: Andrzej Kordas
Profile: Features articles on achievements in dermatology and allergology.
Language(s): Polish
Mechanical Data: Type Area: 210 x 297 mm
BUSINESS: HEALTH & MEDICAL

POSTĘPY W CHIRURGII GŁOWY I SZYI
1709009PL56A-18
Editorial: ul. Przybyszewskiego, 49, 60-355 POZNAŃ
Tel: 61 869 13 87 **Fax:** 61 869 16 90
Email: dabpio@poczta.wprost.pl **Web site:** http://www.chirurgia.termedia.pl
ISSN: 1643-9279
Date Established: 2002; **Freq:** 6 issues yearly; **Circ:** 1,500
Usual Pagination: 32
Managing Director: Andrzej Kordas
Profile: Magazine dedicated to aspects of modern surgery of head, neck and otolaryngology.
Language(s): Polish
Mechanical Data: Type Area: A4
BUSINESS: HEALTH & MEDICAL

POSTĘPY W KARDIOLOGII INTERWENCYJNEJ
1796200PL56A-34
Editorial: ul. Alpejska, 42, 04-628 WARSZAWA
Tel: 22 343 46 16 **Fax:** 22 812 13 46
Email: onínko@yahoo.com **Web site:** http://www.kardiologiainterwencyjna.termedia.pl
ISSN: 1734-9338
Date Established: 2005; **Freq:** Quarterly; **Circ:** 1,500
Usual Pagination: 70
Managing Director: Andrzej Kordas
Profile: Provides information on modern cardio surgery and preventive and intervene methods of treatment of heart illnesses.
Language(s): Polish
Mechanical Data: Type Area: A4
BUSINESS: HEALTH & MEDICAL

POZNAJ ŚWIAT
1709031PL89A-7
Editorial: ul. Walecznych 40 lok. 5, 03-916 WARSZAWA **Tel:** 696 492 170 **Fax:** 22 616 40 08
Email: redakcja@poznajswiat.com.pl **Web site:** http://www.poznajswiat.com.pl
ISSN: 0032-6143
Date Established: 1948; **Freq:** Monthly; **Annual Sub.:** PLN 90.00; **Circ:** 30,000
Usual Pagination: 100
Profile: Travel magazine covering trips to different corners of the world.
Language(s): Polish
CONSUMER: HOLIDAYS & TRAVEL: Travel

POZNAŃ PO GODZIANCH
1798846PL89C-22
Editorial: ul. Bukowska 12, 60-810 POZNAŃ
Tel: 61 865 38 90 **Fax:** 61 866 61 34
Email: gazeta@wtc-poznan.com.pl **Web site:** http://www.wtc-poznan.com.pl
ISSN: 0137-9550
Date Established: 2006; **Freq:** Half-yearly; **Cover Price:** Free; **Circ:** 3,000
Usual Pagination: 24
Editor: Monika Gałka
Profile: Information on Poznan city, its hotels, restaurants, pubs, cultural and entertainment events.
Language(s): Polish
Mechanical Data: Type Area: A4
CONSUMER: HOLIDAYS & TRAVEL: Entertainment Guides

POŚREDNIK BUDOWLANY
1810956PL42A-9
Editorial: ul. Pasaż Ursynowski 1/45, 02-784 WARSZAWA **Tel:** 22 859 19 66 **Fax:** 22 859 19 67
Email: baranski@posbud.pl **Web site:** http://posbud.com.pl
Date Established: 1996; **Freq:** 6 issues yearly; **Circ:** 7,500
Advertising Manager: Katarzyna Janasiewicz; **Advertising Director:** Magdalena Ziemkiewicz
Profile: Professional magazine about building machines, tools and equipment in Poland and abroad.
Language(s): Polish
ADVERTISING RATES:
Full Page Mono .... PLN 6000.00
Full Page Colour .... PLN 7000.00
Mechanical Data: Type Area: 182 x 260mm
Official Journal of: Construction middleman
BUSINESS: CONSTRUCTION

PRACA I ZABEZPIECZENIE SPOŁECZNE
1708892PL14L-2
Editorial: ul. Canaletta, 4, 00-099 WARSZAWA
Tel: 22 827 80 01 **Fax:** 22 827 55 67
Email: pizs@pwe.com.pl **Web site:** http://www.pizs.pl
ISSN: 0032-6186
Date Established: 1959; **Freq:** Monthly; **Circ:** 4,000
Usual Pagination: 48
Managing Director: Mariola Rozmus
Profile: Magazine covering social benefits and insurance, HR management, payments and working conditions.
Language(s): Polish
Mechanical Data: Type Area: A4
BUSINESS: COMMERCE, INDUSTRY & MANAGEMENT: Trade Unions

PRACA I ŻYCIE ZA GRANICĄ
1929150PL94K-2
Editorial: ul. Dobrego Pasterza, 31a, 31-416 KRAKÓW **Tel:** 12 442 48 01 **Fax:** 12 442 48 02
Email: redakcja@pracaizycie.pl **Web site:** http://www.pracaizycie.pl
Date Established: 2005; **Freq:** 26 issues yearly; **Circ:** 35,000
Usual Pagination: 52
Advertising Director: Konrad Niedziela
Profile: Magazine with job offers abroad, job markets in EU, with tips and language corner.
Language(s): Polish
ADVERTISING RATES:
Full Page Colour .... PLN 9000.00
Mechanical Data: Type Area: 195 x 263 mm
CONSUMER: OTHER CLASSIFICATIONS: Job Seekers

PRAKTYKA LEKARSKA
1708895PL56A-16
Editorial: ul. Wawelska, 78, 30, 02-034 WARSZAWA
Tel: 22 822 20 16 **Fax:** 22 823 78 83
Email: lekarska@praktykalekarska.com **Web site:** http://www.eurosys.pl/prawo/start.html
ISSN: 1640-2189
Date Established: 1999; **Freq:** Monthly; **Cover Price:** Free; **Circ:** 30,000
Usual Pagination: 36
Advertising Director: Jagoda Walczak
Profile: Journal is designed for general practitioners, doctors of all types of specialties, physicians with private practice and health service managers. Includes information about new diagnostic methods and contemporary treatment techniques in illnesses.
Language(s): Polish
ADVERTISING RATES:
Full Page Colour .... PLN 8200.00
Mechanical Data: Type Area: A4+
BUSINESS: HEALTH & MEDICAL

PRAWO I PODATKI
1796192PL1M-8
Editorial: ul. Łotewska, 9a, 03-918 WARSZAWA
Tel: 22 429 42 99 **Fax:** 22 617 60 10
Email: prawoipodatki@opp.com.pl **Web site:** http://www.prawoipodatki.com.pl
Date Established: 2005; **Freq:** Monthly; **Cover Price:** PLN 49.00
Profile: Magazine providing thorough analysis of taxation system, news and experts' comments.
Language(s): Polish
Mechanical Data: Type Area: A4
BUSINESS: FINANCE & ECONOMICS: Taxation

PRAWO PRZEDSIĘBIORCY
1620682PL14A-117
Editorial: ul. Okopowa 58/72, 01-042 WARSZAWA
Tel: 22 530 42 75 **Fax:** 22 530 41 30
Email: prawoprzedsiebiorcy@infor.pl **Web site:** http://www.prawoprzedsiebiorcy.infor.pl
Date Established: 1991; **Freq:** Weekly; **Cover Price:** Paid
Managing Director: Mariusz Drozdowicz
Profile: Weekly e-zine focusing on all issues relevant to employment, including work law, accountancy, insurance and tax advice.
Language(s): Polish
Readership: Aimed at employers, accountants and human resource managers.
BUSINESS: COMMERCE, INDUSTRY & MANAGEMENT

PRAWO SPÓŁEK
1708871PL44-7
Editorial: ul. Okopowa 58/72, 01-042 WARSZAWA
Tel: 22 530 41 57 **Fax:** 22 530 41 30
Email: julita.karas@infor.pl **Web site:** http://www.ps.infor.pl
ISSN: 1426-2878
Date Established: 1996; **Freq:** Monthly
Usual Pagination: 60
Managing Director: Mariusz Drozdowicz
Profile: Focused on civil, banking and trade law applied to company management.
Language(s): Polish
Mechanical Data: Type Area: A4
BUSINESS: LEGAL

PRAWO TELEINFORMATYCZNE
1819508PL44-19
Editorial: ul. Tytoniowa, 20, 04-228 WARSZAWA
Tel: 22 515 00 47
Email: d.chelstowski@migutmedia.pl
Date Established: 2006; **Freq:** Quarterly; **Circ:** 1,000
Usual Pagination: 100
Profile: Focused on legal aspects of IT and telecommunication, covering law on electronic signatures, telecommunications, the Law on Personal Data Protection, Law on Copyright, Act on Electronic Services, the Law on protection of databases, and changes, amendments to other Acts.
Language(s): Polish
Mechanical Data: Type Area: A4
BUSINESS: LEGAL

PRESS
1708637PL2B-3
Editorial: ul. Płocka, 5a, 01-231WARSZAWA
Tel: 22 334 83 33 **Fax:** 22 334 83 00
Email: wawa@press.pl **Web site:** http://www.press.pl
ISSN: 1425-9818
Date Established: 1996; **Freq:** Monthly; **Circ:** 9,000
Usual Pagination: 124
Managing Director: Krzysztof Kwiatkowski
Profile: Magazine covering media, advertising and PR.
Language(s): Polish
ADVERTISING RATES:
Full Page Colour .... PLN 25800.00
Mechanical Data: Type Area: 218 x 297 mm
BUSINESS: COMMUNICATIONS, ADVERTISING & MARKETING: Press

PRESTIGE HOUSE
1819505PL74C-22
Editorial: ul. Elbląska, 15/17, 01-747 WARSZAWA
Tel: 22 346 32 62 **Fax:** 22 639 85 69
Email: ejagalska@valkea.com **Web site:** http://www.prestigehouse.pl
ISSN: 1734-3291
Date Established: 2005; **Freq:** 10 issues yearly; **Cover Price:** Free; **Circ:** 18,000
Usual Pagination: 72
Managing Director: Monika Stawicka; **Advertising Director:** Karol Kosiorek
Profile: Presents reviews of newest trends in interior design, architecture, property and modern technologies, inspiring its readers in furnishing, renovating, equipping and improving their houses or apartments.
Language(s): Polish
ADVERTISING RATES:
Full Page Colour .... PLN 11500.00
Mechanical Data: Type Area: A3
CONSUMER: WOMEN'S INTEREST CONSUMER MAGAZINES: Home & Family

PRESTIGE MAGAZINE
1929165PL74Q-20
Editorial: ul. Wichrowa, 20, 30-438 KRAKÓW
Tel: 12 262 22 44 **Fax:** 12 262 22 44
Email: redakcja@prestigemagazine.com.pl **Web site:** http://prestigemagazine.com.pl
ISSN: 1644-7905
Freq: Quarterly; **Circ:** 11,000
Advertising Director: Marta Skorupska
Profile: Exclusive quarterly magazine presenting the profiles of people with influence on the course of current affairs in Poland and worldwide. The magazine presents the most distinguished world authorities while magazine columns are made available to celebrities for whom the magazine is an excellent forum for presenting their activity, interests and points of view.
Language(s): English; Polish
ADVERTISING RATES:
Full Page Colour .... PLN 15000.00
CONSUMER: WOMEN'S INTEREST CONSUMER MAGAZINES: Lifestyle

PRINT PARTNER
1796180PL41A-3
Editorial: ul. Sokratesa, 15, 01-909 WARSZAWA
Tel: 22 834 80 35 **Fax:** 22 834 80 34
Email: printpartner@vidart.com.pl **Web site:** http://www.vidart.com.pl
ISSN: 1734-5987
Date Established: 2005; **Freq:** Quarterly; **Circ:** 3,000
Usual Pagination: 120
Managing Director: Andrzej Tuka
Profile: Professional magazine on printing industry, providing practical information and advice.
Language(s): Polish
ADVERTISING RATES:
Full Page Colour .... PLN 3500.00
Mechanical Data: Type Area: A4
BUSINESS: PRINTING & STATIONERY: Printing

PROBLEMY JAKOŚCI
1811060PL14K-1
Editorial: ul. Chmielna, 98, 36, 00-801 WARSZAWA
Tel: 22 654 96 89 **Fax:** 22 620 69 64
Email: projak@op.pl **Web site:** http://sigma-not.pl
ISSN: 0137-8651
Date Established: 1968; **Freq:** Monthly
Usual Pagination: 52
Profile: Scientific magazine with an extensive section dedicated to practice, appropriate organization and management of goods and services manufacturing processes, management of know-how, company's and staff's potential and resources.
Language(s): Polish
Readership: Aimed at company owners, management, executives of firms of various branches of industry.
ADVERTISING RATES:
Full Page Mono .... PLN 1400.00
Full Page Colour .... PLN 3050.00
Mechanical Data: Type Area: 205 x 290 mm
BUSINESS: COMMERCE, INDUSTRY & MANAGEMENT: Quality Assurance

PRODUCENT ODZIEŻY
1796215PL47A-259
Editorial: ul. Stępińska, 22/30, 00-739 WARSZAWA
Tel: 22 559 39 61 **Fax:** 22 559 39 62
Email: biuro@promedia.biz.pl **Web site:** http://www.promedia.biz.pl
Date Established: 2005; **Freq:** Half-yearly; **Circ:** 4,000
Profile: Provides information on technological innovations in clothing industry: collections' design, production process, fabrics and sewing accessories, textiles storage and transport.
Language(s): Polish
Mechanical Data: Type Area: A4
BUSINESS: CLOTHING & TEXTILES

PRODUKCJA MEBLI
1796061PL23A-1
Editorial: ul. Andersa, 38, 15-113 BIAŁYSTOK
Tel: 85 653 90 00 **Fax:** 85 653 98 56
Email: produkcja@publikator.com.pl **Web site:** http://www.publikator.com.pl
ISSN: 1733-2869
Date Established: 2004; **Freq:** 6 issues yearly; **Circ:** 6,000
Usual Pagination: 64
Managing Director: Anita Frank; **Advertising Director:** Katarzyna Pawłowska
Profile: A trade magazine covering news in furniture industry, materials and accessories used in furniture produce. Introduces latest technologies and tools.
Language(s): Polish
Mechanical Data: Type Area: 230 x 310 mm
BUSINESS: FURNISHINGS & FURNITURE

PROJEKTORY I EKRANY
1811036PL18A-119
Editorial: Skr. Pocz. 16, 00-920 WARSZAWA 43
Tel: 22 438 86 49 **Fax:** 22 438 86 47
Email: redakcja@projektoryiekrany.pl **Web site:** http://www.projektoryiekrany.pl
ISSN: 1896-4125
Date Established: 2006; **Freq:** Half-yearly
Usual Pagination: 132
Advertising Director: Wanda Owczarek
Profile: Magazine on audiovisual technologies for home and office: Presentation projectors, Projectors Screens, AV equipment, DLP&LCD Technologies, etc.
Language(s): Polish
Mechanical Data: Type Area: 205x290 mm
BUSINESS: ELECTRONICS

PROJEKTOWANIE I KONSTRUKCJE INŻYNIERSKIE
1835767PL19A-3
Editorial: ul. Pilicka 22, 02-613 WARSZAWA
Tel: 22 402 36 10 **Fax:** 22 402 36 11
Email: redakcja@konstrukcjeinzynierskie.pl **Web site:** http://www.konstrukcjeinzynierskie.pl
Freq: Monthly; **Circ:** 2,000
Usual Pagination: 72
Editor-in-Chief: Maciej Stanisławski
Profile: Focuses on designing area, CAx systems, solutions to resolve problems during designing.
Language(s): Polish
Readership: Magazine for engineers and decision-makers who design machines, equipment, mechanical devices and industrial products.
ADVERTISING RATES:
Full Page Mono .... PLN 3400.00

Mechanical Data: Type Area: 210 x 297mm
BUSINESS: ENGINEERING & MACHINERY

PROMOTOR
1811009PL54B-3
Editorial: al. Roździeńskiego, 188, 40-203 KATOWICE **Tel:** 32 788 51 06 **Fax:** 32 203 93 56
Email: promotor@elamed.pl **Web site:** http://www.promotor.elamed.pl
ISSN: 1426-6660
Date Established: 1996; **Freq:** Monthly
Usual Pagination: 68
Advertising Director: Magdalena Ciemnołońska
Profile: Covering all kinds of safety procedures at work: legal aspects and innovations, products and ergonometric procedures.
Language(s): Polish
Mechanical Data: Type Area: 204 x 290 mm
BUSINESS: SAFETY & SECURITY: Safety

PRO-TEST
1708930PL94H-2
Formerly: Świat Konsumenta
Editorial: ul. Filtrowa 67/109, 02-055 WARSZAWA
Tel: 22 825 51 26
Email: redakcja@pro-test.pl **Web site:** http://www.pro-test.pl
Date Established: 2001; **Freq:** Monthly; **Cover Price:** PLN 7.99; **Circ:** 25,000
Usual Pagination: 48
Advertising Director: Amanda Potocka
Profile: Magazine informing consumers on food tests, electronic equipment and cosmetics tests and on product quality.
Language(s): Polish
ADVERTISING RATES:
Full Page Colour .... PLN 11000.00
Mechanical Data: Type Area: 205,8x291,06 mm
CONSUMER: OTHER CLASSIFICATIONS: Customer Magazines

PRZEGLĄD
1810936PL82-81
Editorial: ul. Szara, 10a, 00-420 WARSZAWA
Tel: 22 635 84 10 **Fax:** 22 635 62 85
Email: przeglad@przeglad-tygodnik.pl **Web site:** http://przeglad-tygodnik.pl
ISSN: 1509-3115
Date Established: 1999; **Freq:** Weekly; **Circ:** 70,000
Usual Pagination: 68
Profile: Features articles on politics, economics, social and cultural events.
Language(s): Polish
ADVERTISING RATES:
Full Page Colour .... PLN 13000.00
Mechanical Data: Type Area: 210 x 285 mm
CONSUMER: CURRENT AFFAIRS & POLITICS

PRZEGLĄD ELEKTROTECHNICZNY
1811061PL43A-2
Editorial: ul. Ratuszowa, 11, 737, 03-450 WARSZAWA **Tel:** 22 827 25 09 **Fax:** 22 827 25 09
Email: red.pe@sigma-not.pl **Web site:** http://red.pe.org.pl
Date Established: 1919; **Freq:** Monthly
Usual Pagination: 56
Profile: Writes about scientific and professional achievements of Polish engineers, electricians and reports on branch events, all aspects concerning all fields of the electro-technology: electricity theory, electro-power generation, power electronics, traction, measurements, light technique, machines, apparatus and transformers, electro-thermal aspects, electric material science.
Language(s): Polish
Readership: Aimed at contactors of electronic equipment, constructors, designers and machinery exploiters, designers of appliances, electrical systems and transmission lines.
ADVERTISING RATES:
Full Page Mono .... PLN 1260.00
Full Page Colour .... PLN 2520.00
Mechanical Data: Type Area: 205 x 290 mm
BUSINESS: ELECTRICAL RETAIL TRADE

PRZEGLĄD GASTROENTEROLOGICZNY
1796197PL56A-31
Editorial: ul. Wenedów, 9, 1, 61-614 POZNAŃ
Tel: 61 822 77 81 **Fax:** 61 822 77 81
Email: m.miedzianow@termedia.pl **Web site:** http://www.gastroenterologia.termedia.pl
ISSN: 1895-5770
Date Established: 2006
Circ: 2,000
Usual Pagination: 60
Managing Director: Andrzej Kordas
Profile: Professional magazine on gastroenterology and gastrointestinal disorders.
Language(s): Polish
Mechanical Data: Type Area: A4
BUSINESS: HEALTH & MEDICAL

PRZEGLĄD GASTRONOMICZNY
1811062PL11A-10
Editorial: ul. Rakowiecka, 36, 32, 02-532 WARSZAWA **Tel:** 22 849 19 24 **Fax:** 22 849 19 24
Email: przegast@przeglad-gastronomiczny.pl **Web site:** http://przeglad-gastronomiczny.pl
ISSN: 0033-2119
Date Established: 1946; **Freq:** Monthly
Usual Pagination: 48
Profile: Presents theory and practice of eating habits in Poland, gastronomy, modern kitchen equipment and machines, marketing, news on gastronomy, professional advice.
Language(s): Polish
ADVERTISING RATES:
Full Page Mono .... PLN 2000.00
Full Page Colour .... PLN 4400.00
Mechanical Data: Type Area: 205 x 290 mm
BUSINESS: CATERING: Catering, Hotels & Restaurants

PRZEGLĄD GEODEZYJNY
1811063PL55-12
Editorial: ul. Ratuszowa, 11, 309, 03-450 WARSZAWA **Tel:** 22 619 19 95 **Fax:** 22 619 19 95
Email: p.geo@neostrada.pl **Web site:** http://sigma-not.pl
ISSN: 0033-2127
Date Established: 1924; **Freq:** Monthly
Usual Pagination: 32
Profile: Focuses on practice and theory concerning the geodesy, photogrammetry, tele-detection, real estate appraisal and the application of the geodesy in the construction industry, agriculture, geology and environmental protection.
Language(s): Polish
Readership: Aimed at geodesic enterprises, employees of geodesic departments in districts and province offices, universities, schools, estates experts.
ADVERTISING RATES:
Full Page Mono .... PLN 900.00
Full Page Colour .... PLN 1850.00
Mechanical Data: Type Area: 205 x 290 mm
BUSINESS: APPLIED SCIENCE & LABORATORIES

PRZEGLĄD KOMUNALNY
1810965PL57-4
Editorial: ul. Daleka, 33, 60-124 POZNAŃ
Tel: 61 655 81 37 **Fax:** 61 655 81 01
Email: redakcja@abrys.pl **Web site:** http://www.abrys.pl
Date Established: 1991; **Freq:** Monthly; **Circ:** 9,000
Usual Pagination: 86
Profile: Focused on communal services and environment.
Language(s): Polish
Mechanical Data: Type Area: A4
BUSINESS: ENVIRONMENT & POLLUTION

PRZEGLĄD LOTNICZY AVIATION REVUE
1709023PL6A-2
Editorial: ul. Zamoyskiego, 4, 03-801 WARSZAWA
Tel: 22 670 06 08 **Fax:** 22 670 06 08
Email: plar@plar.pl **Web site:** http://www.plar.pl
ISSN: 1231-9328
Date Established: 1993; **Freq:** Monthly; **Circ:** 9,000
Usual Pagination: 80
Advertising Director: Roman Peczka
Profile: Covers general and sport aviation.
Language(s): Polish
Readership: Aimed at pilots, plane owners and aviation companies.
Mechanical Data: Type Area: 205 x 292 mm
BUSINESS: AVIATION & AERONAUTICS

PRZEGLĄD MENOPAUZALNY
1708793PL56A-10
Editorial: ul. Wenedów, 9/1, 61-614 POZNAŃ
Tel: 61 822 77 81 **Fax:** 61 822 77 81
Email: m.jadwizak@termedia.pl **Web site:** http://www.menopauza.termedia.pl
ISSN: 1643-8876
Date Established: 2002
Circ: 5,000
Usual Pagination: 74
Managing Director: Andrzej Kordas
Profile: Provides information on general genecology and menopause issues.
Language(s): Polish
Mechanical Data: Type Area: 210 x 297 mm
BUSINESS: HEALTH & MEDICAL

PRZEGLĄD PAPIERNICZY
1811064PL36-3
Editorial: pl. Komuny Paryskiej, 5a, 90-950 ŁÓDŹ
Tel: 42 633 54 23 **Fax:** 42 633 54 23
Email: przegl.pap@t-system.com.pl **Web site:** http://przegl.pap.com.pl
ISSN: 0033-2291
Date Established: 1945; **Freq:** Monthly
Usual Pagination: 64
Profile: A specialized magazine covering all range of paper industry interests: companies' profiles, interviews with decision-makers, expert analysis, research results, machinery and technology updates.
Language(s): English; Polish
ADVERTISING RATES:
Full Page Mono .... PLN 1200.00
Full Page Colour .... PLN 2640.00
Mechanical Data: Type Area: 205 x 290 mm
BUSINESS: PAPER

PRZEGLĄD PIEKARSKI I CUKIERNICZY
1811065PL8A-2
Editorial: ul. Rakowiecka, 36, 251, 02-532 WARSZAWA **Tel:** 22 606 37 64 **Fax:** 22 606 37 64
Email: ppic@ppic.pl **Web site:** http://ppic.pl
ISSN: 0033-2313
Date Established: 1953; **Freq:** Monthly
Usual Pagination: 120
Profile: Professional magazine on baking and confectionary, ice cream and chocolate production technologies, equipment and produce methods.
Language(s): Polish
ADVERTISING RATES:
Full Page Mono .... PLN 2100.00
Full Page Colour .... PLN 4700.00
Mechanical Data: Type Area: 205 x 290 mm
BUSINESS: BAKING & CONFECTIONERY: Baking

PRZEGLĄD PODATKU DOCHODOWEGO
1929201PL1M-15
Editorial: ul. Owocowa, 8, 66-400 GORZÓW WLKP.
Tel: 95 720 85 40 **Fax:** 95 720 85 60
Email: przeglad@gofin.pl **Web site:** http://www.gofin.pl
ISSN: 1429-3986
Date Established: 1998; **Freq:** 26 issues yearly; **Circ:** 18,000
Usual Pagination: 70
Profile: Publication dedicated to individual taxation of physical people.
Language(s): Polish
ADVERTISING RATES:
Full Page Colour .... PLN 2500.00
Mechanical Data: Type Area: 170 x 240 mm
BUSINESS: FINANCE & ECONOMICS: Taxation

PRZEGLĄD POŻARNICZY
1709021PL54A-1
Editorial: ul. Podchorążych, 38, 00-463 WARSZAWA
Tel: 22 523 33 06/08 **Fax:** 22 523 33 05
Email: pp@kgpsp.gov.pl **Web site:** http://www.ppoz.pl
ISSN: 0137-8910
Date Established: 1912; **Freq:** Monthly; **Circ:** 7,000
Usual Pagination: 56
Profile: Provides information on all aspects of fire safety and issues of protecting people.
Language(s): Polish
Mechanical Data: Type Area: A4
BUSINESS: SAFETY & SECURITY: Fire Fighting

PRZEGLĄD PSZCZELARSKI
1819532PL21A-4
Editorial: Al. Jerozolimskie, 107, 02-011 WARSZAWA
Tel: 22 429 24 36 **Fax:** 22 429 25 90
Web site: http://www.przegladpszczelarski.pl
ISSN: 1733-9030
Date Established: 2005; **Freq:** Quarterly; **Circ:** 1,000
Usual Pagination: 68
Profile: Professional magazine on bees and their cultivation, honey production and entomology.
Language(s): Polish
Mechanical Data: Type Area: 230x290 mm
BUSINESS: AGRICULTURE & FARMING

PRZEGLĄD SPORTOWY
1795467PL75A-26
Editorial: ul. Domaniewska, 52, 02-672 WARSZAWA
Tel: 22 232 05 03 **Fax:** 22 232 55 23
Email: redakcja@przeglad.com.pl **Web site:** http://www.sports.pl
ISSN: 0137-9267
Date Established: 1921; **Freq:** Daily; **Circ:** 61,263
Usual Pagination: 16
Managing Director: Bogdan Mróz; **Advertising Director:** Jacek Makowski
Language(s): Polish
ADVERTISING RATES:
Full Page Colour .... PLN 37000.00
Mechanical Data: Type Area: 280 x 410 mm
CONSUMER: SPORT

PRZEGLĄD TECHNICZNY. GAZETA INŻYNIERSKA
1811066PL19A-11
Editorial: ul. Czackiego, 3/5, 00-043 WARSZAWA
Tel: 22 651 00 68 **Fax:** 22 651 00 68
Email: emc@vip.wp.pl **Web site:** http://przeglad-techniczny.pl
ISSN: 0137-8783
Date Established: 1866; **Freq:** 26 issues yearly
Usual Pagination: 40
Profile: Contains information about all areas of technology and related economic aspects, state and perspectives of implementation of technical progress in various field of economy, stressing the role of a engineer.
Language(s): Polish
Readership: Aimed at engineers and technicians, owners of small and medium enterprises.
ADVERTISING RATES:
Full Page Mono .... PLN 3450.00
Full Page Colour .... PLN 4050.00
Mechanical Data: Type Area: 204 x 298 mm
BUSINESS: ENGINEERING & MACHINERY

PRZEGLĄD TELEKOMUNIKACYJNY - WIADOMOŚCI TELEKOMUNIKACYJNE
1811067PL18B-11
Editorial: ul. Ratuszowa, 11, 637, 03-450 WARSZAWA **Tel:** 22 619 86 99 **Fax:** 22 619 86 99
Email: przeg.tel@interia.pl **Web site:** http://ptiwtel.neostrada.pl
ISSN: 1230-3496
Date Established: 1928; **Freq:** Monthly; **Circ:** 5,000
Profile: Presents technical and scientific views on electronics, radio communication, TV and multimedia, testing, servicing, legal and economic advice.
Language(s): Polish
ADVERTISING RATES:
Full Page Mono .... PLN 2000.00
Full Page Colour .... PLN 3200.00
Mechanical Data: Type Area: 205 x 290 mm
BUSINESS: ELECTRONICS: Telecommunications

PRZEGLĄD USTAWODAWSTWA GOSPODARCZEGO
1708891PL44-10
Editorial: ul. Canaletta, 4, 00-099 WARSZAWA
Tel: 22 827 80 01 **Fax:** 22 827 55 67
Email: pug@pwe.com.pl **Web site:** http://www.pug.pl
ISSN: 0137-5490
Date Established: 1947; **Freq:** Monthly; **Circ:** 2,000
Usual Pagination: 32
Managing Director: Mariola Rozmus
Profile: Presents changes in economic law, legal aspects of civil, industrial and trade issues, comments and newest legal official documentation.
Language(s): Polish
ADVERTISING RATES:
Full Page Colour .... PLN 2500.00
Mechanical Data: Type Area: A4
BUSINESS: LEGAL

PRZEGLĄD WŁÓKIENNICZY - WŁÓKNO, ODZIEŻ, SKÓRA
1811068PL47A-262
Editorial: pl. Komuny Paryskiej, 5a, 90-950 ŁÓDŹ
Tel: 42 632 31 30 **Fax:** 42 630 64 87
Email: pewos@op.pl **Web site:** http://sigma-not.pl
ISSN: 1731-8645
Date Established: 1947; **Freq:** Monthly
Usual Pagination: 60
Profile: Presents issues concerning textile, equipment and leather technologies, finishing and imprinting, dyes and accessories, assessments of products, raw materials and metrology, economics, work organization, environmental protection, machines and equipment.
Language(s): Polish
Readership: Targets managers, engineers and technicians of textile, leather and garments industry and also employees of wholesales and retails firms, students.
ADVERTISING RATES:
Full Page Mono .... PLN 2000.00
Full Page Colour .... PLN 4180.00
Mechanical Data: Type Area: 205 x 290 mm
BUSINESS: CLOTHING & TEXTILES

PRZEGLĄD ZBOŻOWO-MŁYNARSKI
1811069PL21A-5
Editorial: ul. Rakowiecka, 36, 258, 02-532 WARSZAWA **Tel:** 22 849 92 51 **Fax:** 22 849 92 51
Email: pzmlyn@post.pl **Web site:** http://sigma-not.pl
ISSN: 0033-2461
Date Established: 1886; **Freq:** Monthly
Usual Pagination: 40
Profile: Presents latest developments in grain processing techniques and technologies, grain storage, milling, cereals, oatmeal, production of pasta and industrial fodder, economics related to grain processing companies, standardization and quality control, marketing information and information about the grain and grain products market, information and reports on important conferences, symposia, trade fairs and exhibitions organized in Poland and abroad.
Language(s): Polish
Readership: Targets managers, owners of grain processing companies, employees of machines, grain stores, mills, pasta producers, food companies.
ADVERTISING RATES:
Full Page Mono .... PLN 1500.00
Full Page Colour .... PLN 3300.00
Mechanical Data: Type Area: 205 x 290 mm
BUSINESS: AGRICULTURE & FARMING

PRZEGLĄD BUDOWLANY
1836392PL42A-4
Editorial: ul. Świętokrzyska 14 A, pok. 201, 00-050 WARSZAWA **Tel:** 22 828 27 20 **Fax:** 22 826 67 00
Email: biuro@przegladbudowlany.pl **Web site:** http://www.przegladbudowlany.pl
Date Established: 1929; **Freq:** Monthly; **Annual Sub.:** PLN 180.00; **Circ:** 12,500
Editor-in-Chief: Agnieszka Stachecka-Rodziewicz; **Advertising Director:** Grażyna Furmańczyk
Profile: Presents and reviews new building technologies, specialist articles devoted to recent solutions and research results in general construction field, information on new products, construction materials and technologies. The magazine is published by Polish Association of Engineers and Construction Technologists.
Language(s): Polish

Readership: Addressed to engineers active in the construction field, investors, architects, building materials producing factories and developer companies.
ADVERTISING RATES:
Full Page Colour .... PLN 4000.00
BUSINESS: CONSTRUCTION

PRZEGLĄD MECHANICZNY
1835836PL19A-4
Editorial: IMBiGS, ul. Racjonalizacji 6/8, 02-673 WARSZAWA **Tel:** 22 843 02 01 **Fax:** 22 853 81 13
Email: pmech@imbigs.org.pl **Web site:** http://www.przegladmechaniczny.pl
Date Established: 1935; **Freq:** Monthly; **Annual Sub.:** PLN 216.00; **Circ:** 1,000
Editor: Martyna Jachimowicz; **Editor-in-Chief:** Jan Szlagowski; **Advertising Manager:** Małgorzata Jaskulska; **Publisher:** Ryszard Kwiecień
Profile: Scientific and technical monthly magazine about design, testing and operation of machines and equipment, CAD/CAM issues, material engineering, new manufacturing techniques, organization of production, diagnostic methods, reliability issues and standards and patents reviews.
Language(s): Polish
Readership: Aimed at engineering and managerial staff of industrial plants, private enterprises, companies and trade agencies, specialist of research and development centres and scientific research institutes.
ADVERTISING RATES:
Full Page Mono .... EUR 300.00
Full Page Colour .... EUR 422.00
Mechanical Data: Type Area: 167 x 255mm
BUSINESS: ENGINEERING & MACHINERY

PRZEKRÓJ
1623177PL82-64
Editorial: ul. Nowogrodzka 47a, IV p., 00-695 WARSZAWA **Tel:** 22 525 99 33 **Fax:** 22 525 99 88
Email: redakcja@przekroj.pl **Web site:** http://www.przekroj.pl
ISSN: 0033-2488
Date Established: 1945; **Freq:** Weekly; **Circ:** 131,000
Usual Pagination: 76
Managing Director: Alicja Modzelewska; **Advertising Director:** Małgorzata Golba
Profile: Magazine covering current social and political issues, includes articles on culture and history.
Language(s): Polish
ADVERTISING RATES:
Full Page Colour .... PLN 44500.00
Mechanical Data: Type Area: 205 x 290 mm
CONSUMER: CURRENT AFFAIRS & POLITICS

PRZEMYSŁ CHEMICZNY
1811070PL13-6
Editorial: ul. Ratuszowa, 11, 711, 03-450 WARSZAWA **Tel:** 22 818 51 71 **Fax:** 22 818 51 71
Email: przemyslchemiczny@sigma-not.pl **Web site:** http://sigma-not.pl
ISSN: 0033-2496
Date Established: 1917; **Freq:** Monthly
Usual Pagination: 80
Profile: Focuses on development, economics, and organisation of chemical industry, chemical aspects of the national economy, raw material base of chemical industry, waste management. scientific and technical articles concerning the technology of organic and inorganic chemistry, processing of plastics, pharmaceutical technologies, catalysis, flotation, electrochemistry, chemical equipment and engineering. Aspects of the environmental protection from the point of view of chemical industry.
Language(s): Polish
Readership: Targets managers, engineers and technicians of different industry companies, students and staff of different chemical institutes.
ADVERTISING RATES:
Full Page Mono .... PLN 1500.00
Full Page Colour .... PLN 3400.00
Mechanical Data: Type Area: 205 x 290 mm
BUSINESS: CHEMICALS

PRZEMYSŁ FERMENTACYJNY I OWOCOWO-WARZYWNY
1811071PL21A-6
Editorial: ul. Ratuszowa, 11, 215/3, 03-450 WARSZAWA **Tel:** 22 818 62 63 **Fax:** 22 818 62 63
Email: pfiow@sigma-not.pl **Web site:** http://sigma-not.pl
ISSN: 0137-2645
Date Established: 1956; **Freq:** Monthly
Usual Pagination: 44
Profile: Focuses on brewery, distilling of alcohol, spirit, wine, yeast, fruit and vegetable, fruit and vegetable juices, condensed juices, alcohol-free drinks, mineral waters - technological innovations, market analyses, forecasts, directions of the branches, development, marketing, repercussions of changes in the EU regulations for activities of companies, aid funds especially for small and medium-size enterprises, environmental protection, packaging, activities of branch organisations in Poland and the EU, fairs and exhibitions.
Language(s): Polish
ADVERTISING RATES:
Full Page Mono .... PLN 1800.00
Full Page Colour .... PLN 3600.00
Mechanical Data: Type Area: 205 x 290 mm
BUSINESS: AGRICULTURE & FARMING

PRZEMYSŁ SPOŻYWCZY
1811072PL22A-502
Editorial: ul. Rakowiecka, 36, 255, 02-532 WARSZAWA **Tel:** 22 849 53 33 **Fax:** 22 849 53 33
Email: przemspozywczy@sigma-not.pl **Web site:** http://sigma-not.pl
Date Established: 1946; **Freq:** Monthly; **Annual Sub.:** PLN 234.00
Usual Pagination: 48
Profile: Focused on aspects of the food sector, information on technical, technological, and product innovations in the food branch. Economics, organisation, marketing and management of food enterprises, restructuring and ownership transformations. Presentation of new technologies and techniques of packing and storage in the food industry, tendencies in the food market.
Language(s): Polish
Readership: Targets process engineers and management teams in food processing plants of all types, representatives of foreign companies, trading companies, food wholesalers, central agencies, pest control staff, universities, vocational schools and research institutes.
ADVERTISING RATES:
Full Page Mono .... PLN 1500.00
Full Page Colour .... PLN 3150.00
Mechanical Data: Type Area: 205 x 290 mm
BUSINESS: FOOD

PRZEMYSŁ I ŚRODOWISKO
1860705PL14B-1
Formerly: Kwartalnik o jakości i zarządzaniu
Editorial: ul. Trylogii 2/16, 01-982 WARSZAWA
Tel: 22 353 58 43 **Fax:** 22 865 24 91
Email: m.szczepanik@ekopartner.com.pl **Web site:** http://www.przemyslisrodowisko.pl
ISSN: 1897-4481
Date Established: 2007; **Freq:** Quarterly; **Cover Price:** Free; **Circ:** 10,000
Usual Pagination: 56
Managing Editor: Iwona Czech; **Advertising Director:** Jacek Markowski
Profile: The quarterly journal is a specialist business operating in the area of industry, environment and management systems.Issues related to the economy and the environment brought together about the quality of products and services. Appropriate management of a company, all aspects related to this is the way to achieve high quality and market position in accordance with the principles of sustainable development.
Language(s): Polish
Mechanical Data: Type Area: A4
BUSINESS: COMMERCE, INDUSTRY & MANAGEMENT: Industry & Factories

PRZETARGI PUBLICZNE
1796230PL1R-5
Editorial: ul. Tadeusza Kościuszki, 29, 2, 50-011 WROCŁAW **Tel:** 71 797 28 46 **Fax:** 71 797 28 16
Email: redakcja@przetargipubliczne.pl **Web site:** http://www.przetargipubliczne.pl
ISSN: 1895-0825
Date Established: 2005; **Freq:** Monthly; **Circ:** 4,000
Usual Pagination: 68
Managing Director: Arkadiusz Karasek; **Advertising Director:** Mikołaj Marzec
Profile: Magazine about public bidding, legal documentation and public offers.
Language(s): Polish
Mechanical Data: Type Area: 210 x 280 mm
BUSINESS: FINANCE & ECONOMICS: Financial Related

PRZEWODNIK BUDOWLANY
1708663PL4E-28
Editorial: ul. Katowicka, 19, 03-932 WARSZAWA
Tel: 22 616 10 88 **Fax:** 22 616 10 89
Email: redakcja@przewodnik-budowlany.com.pl
Web site: http://www.przewodnik-budowlany.com.pl
ISSN: 1426-8264
Date Established: 1996; **Freq:** Monthly; **Circ:** 50,000
Usual Pagination: 100
Advertising Director: Ryszard Piotrowski
Profile: Provides practical and professional advice for those building or renovating houses.
Language(s): Polish
BUSINESS: ARCHITECTURE & BUILDING: Building

PRZEWODNIK LEKARZA
1708792PL56A-9
Editorial: ul. Wenedów, 9/1, 61-614 POZNAŃ
Tel: 61 822 77 81 **Fax:** 61 822 77 81
Email: termedia@termedia.pl **Web site:** http://www.lekarz.termedia.pl
ISSN: 1505-8409
Date Established: 1998
Circ: 14,000
Usual Pagination: 120
Managing Director: Andrzej Kordas
Profile: Provides information for therapists and doctors of first contact.
Language(s): Polish
Mechanical Data: Type Area: 210 x 297 mm
BUSINESS: HEALTH & MEDICAL

PRZEWODNIK ŚLUBNY
1708922PL74L-2
Formerly: Ślubnik
Editorial: ul. Henryka Sienkiewicza 4 lok. 6, 90-113 ŁÓDŹ **Tel:** 42 638 09 00 **Fax:** 42 638 09 11
Email: slubwlodzi@lupomedia.com **Web site:** http://www.slubwlodzi.pl
ISSN: 1644-4728
Date Established: 2002; **Freq:** Annual; **Circ:** 20,000
Usual Pagination: 128
Advertising Director: Sławomir Wilk
Profile: Covering love and wedding: wedding planning, fashion and beauty, accessories, wedding presents, etc.
Language(s): Polish
Mechanical Data: Type Area: 205x285 mm
CONSUMER: WOMEN'S INTEREST CONSUMER MAGAZINES: Brides

PRZYJACIÓŁKA
1623310PL74A-1018
Editorial: ul. Wiejska, 19, 00-480 WARSZAWA
Tel: 22 584 24 38 **Fax:** 22 584 24 36
Email: redakcja@przyjaciolka.pl **Web site:** http://www.przyjaciolka.pl
ISSN: 0033-2534
Date Established: 1948; **Freq:** 26 issues yearly; **Circ:** 683,000
Usual Pagination: 84
Managing Director: Alicja Modzelewska; **Advertising Director:** Edyta Kordowska
Profile: Magazine featuring articles on fashion, real life stories and celebrity features as well as advice on health, relationships and career problems.
Language(s): English
Mechanical Data: Type Area: 230 x 287 mm
CONSUMER: WOMEN'S INTEREST CONSUMER MAGAZINES: Women's Interest

PSYCHOLOGIA W SZKOLE
1811016PL94J-312
Editorial: ul. Warszawska, 6, 25-512 KIELCE
Tel: 41 343 28 64 **Fax:** 41 343 28 49
Email: pws@charaktery.com.pl
Freq: Quarterly; **Circ:** 6,000
Usual Pagination: 162
Advertising Director: Marek Malarz
Profile: Magazine dedicated to psychology.
Language(s): Polish
Mechanical Data: Type Area: B5mm
CONSUMER: OTHER CLASSIFICATIONS: Popular Science

PULS
1709029PL56A-21
Editorial: ul. Kozia, 3/5, 31, 00-070 WARSZAWA
Tel: 22 828 36 39 **Fax:** 22 828 36 39
Email: puls@warszawa.oil.org.pl **Web site:** http://www.warszawa.oil.org.pl
Date Established: 1993; **Freq:** Monthly; **Cover Price:** Free; **Circ:** 26,400
Usual Pagination: 48
Profile: Features articles an medical law, all aspects of treatment, provides advice for doctors of all specialities.
Language(s): Polish
ADVERTISING RATES:
Full Page Colour .... PLN 3300.00
BUSINESS: HEALTH & MEDICAL

PULS BIZNESU
1614326PL14A-116
Editorial: ul. Kijowska, 1, 03-738 WARSZAWA
Tel: 22 333 99 99 **Fax:** 22 333 99 98
Email: puls@pb.pl **Web site:** http://www.pb.pl
ISSN: 1427-6852
Date Established: 1997; **Freq:** Daily; **Circ:** 17,941
Usual Pagination: 24
News Editor: Tadeusz Markiewicz; **Advertising Director:** Krzysztof Zarzeczny
Profile: National newspaper containing detailed coverage of national and international financial, banking and corporate news.
Language(s): Polish
ADVERTISING RATES:
Full Page Colour .... PLN 27500.00
Mechanical Data: Type Area: A3
BUSINESS: COMMERCE, INDUSTRY & MANAGEMENT

QUALITY NEWS
1795741PL14R-1
Editorial: Królów Polskich 13, 02-496 WARSZAWA
Tel: 22 478 55 11 **Fax:** 22 478 55 10
Email: biuro@qualitynews.com.pl **Web site:** http://www.qualitynews.com.pl
Freq: 6 issues yearly; **Circ:** 14,000
Profile: Professional magazine on quality in business and industry, environment and safety.
Language(s): Polish
ADVERTISING RATES:
Full Page Colour .... PLN 2900.00
BUSINESS: COMMERCE, INDUSTRY & MANAGEMENT: Commerce Related

RACHUNKOWOŚĆ BUDŻETOWA
1620688PL1B-1
Editorial: ul. Okopowa, 58/72, 01-042 WARSZAWA
Tel: 22 530 41 72 **Fax:** 22 530 42 22
Web site: http://www.rb.infor.pl
ISSN: 1428-8176
Date Established: 1999; **Freq:** 26 issues yearly
Usual Pagination: 40
Managing Director: Mariusz Drozdowicz
Profile: Magazine covering the public finance sector, accountancy, taxation, public orders, insurance issues.
Language(s): Polish
Readership: Aimed at finance professionals.
Mechanical Data: Type Area: A4
BUSINESS: FINANCE & ECONOMICS: Accountancy

RACHUNKOWOŚĆ BUDŻETOWA. PORADNIK KSIĘGOWEGO, PERSONEL OD A DO Z
1709073PL1B-16
Editorial: ul. Łotewska, 9a, 03-918 WARSZAWA
Tel: 22 429 41 30 **Fax:** 22 617 60 10
Email: rb@wip.pl **Web site:** http://www.rachunkowoscbudzetowa.pl
Date Established: 2004; **Freq:** Monthly; **Circ:** 5,000
Usual Pagination: 100
Publisher: Łukasz Sadura
Profile: Provides practical advice for accountancy depts. of public financial institutions.
Language(s): Polish
BUSINESS: FINANCE & ECONOMICS: Accountancy

RACHUNKOWOŚĆ DLA PRAKTYKÓW
1709066PL1B-24
Formerly: Poradnik Finansowo-Księgowy
Editorial: ul. Łotewska, 9a, 03-918 WARSZAWA
Tel: 22 518 27 27 **Fax:** 22 518 27 50
Email: rdp@wip.pl **Web site:** http://rachunkowoscdlapraktykow.pl
Date Established: 1999; **Freq:** Monthly
Usual Pagination: 600
Profile: Provides information on accountancy issues, taxation and financial reports.
Language(s): Polish
BUSINESS: FINANCE & ECONOMICS: Accountancy

RADIO-LIDER, TV-LIDER
1709076PL76C-17
Editorial: ul. Żywiczna, 17, 05-092 ŁOMIANKI
Tel: 22 751 31 29 **Fax:** 22 751 94 54
Email: redakcja@radiolider.pl **Web site:** http://www.radiolider.pl
ISSN: 1234-2122
Date Established: 1995; **Freq:** 6 issues yearly; **Circ:** 2,500
Usual Pagination: 64
Profile: Informs on work of radio and TV journalists, TV and radio engineering and equipment, news about broadcast branch.
Language(s): Polish
Mechanical Data: Type Area: 205x290 mm
CONSUMER: MUSIC & PERFORMING ARTS: TV & Radio

RAPORT BRANŻOWY
1708681PL36-2
Editorial: ul. Przemysłowa, 3, 40-020 KATOWICE
Tel: 32 757 24 01 **Fax:** 32 757 24 02
Email: raport@madin.com.pl **Web site:** http://www.madin.com.pl/rb.htm
ISSN: 1426-3084
Date Established: 1996
Cover Price: Free; **Circ:** 5,000
Profile: Provides information on paper industry, office and school stationary news.
Language(s): Polish
ADVERTISING RATES:
Full Page Mono .... PLN 3500.00
Full Page Colour .... PLN 4800.00
Mechanical Data: Type Area: A4
BUSINESS: PAPER

RAPORT TELEINFO
1708906PL5B-56
Editorial: ul. Tytoniowa, 20, 04-228 WARSZAWA
Tel: 22 515 00 00 **Fax:** 22 812 47 40
Email: a.wisniewska@migutmedia.pl **Web site:** http://www.migutmedia.pl
Date Established: 1997
Circ: 12,000
Usual Pagination: 40
Profile: Magazine on IT in business, opinions of experts and achievements of Polish companies in teleinformative technologies.
Language(s): Polish
ADVERTISING RATES:
Full Page Mono .... PLN 8300.00
Mechanical Data: Type Area: A4
BUSINESS: COMPUTERS & AUTOMATION: Data Processing

READER'S DIGEST EDYCJA POLSKA
1708968PL94J-303
Editorial: ul. Taśmowa, 7, 02-677 WARSZAWA
Tel: 22 319 32 00 **Fax:** 22 319 32 99
Email: info@digest.com.pl **Web site:** http://digest.com.pl
ISSN: 1233-5649
Date Established: 1995; **Freq:** Monthly; **Circ:** 150,000
Usual Pagination: 160
Managing Director: Bożena Chmielarczyk; **Advertising Director:** Jolanta Gajewska

Profile: Provides tips, news and medical research, descriptions of events, extraordinary stories of the people, reviews of the interesting parts of the world.
Language(s): English
Mechanical Data: Type Area: 134 x 184 mm
CONSUMER: OTHER CLASSIFICATIONS: Popular Science

RECYKLING 1810987PL57-5
Editorial: ul. Daleka, 33, 60-124 POZNAŃ
Tel: 61 655 81 42 **Fax:** 61 655 81 01
Email: recykling@abrys.pl **Web site:** http://www.abrys.pl
Date Established: 2001; **Freq:** Monthly; **Circ:** 5,000
Usual Pagination: 36
Editor: Katarzyna Matuszak
Profile: Magazine focused on recycling of garbage, latest developments and trends in the waste industry.
Language(s): Polish
ADVERTISING RATES:
Full Page Colour .... PLN 3000.00
Mechanical Data: Type Area: A4
BUSINESS: ENVIRONMENT & POLLUTION

RES PUBLICA NOWA 1708680PL84B-5
Editorial: ul. Gałczyńskiego 5, 00-362 WARSZAWA
Tel: 22 826 05 66 **Fax:** 22 343 08 33
Email: redakcja@res.publica.pl **Web site:** http://www.res.publica.pl
ISSN: 1230-2155
Date Established: 1987; **Freq:** Quarterly; **Circ:** 3,600
Usual Pagination: 164
Publisher: Wojciech Przybylski
Profile: Res Publica became famous with the publication of the articles of Polish intellectuals and other countries, such as H. Arendt, I. Berlin, M. Oakeshott, and many others who as a result of censorship, were then known to Polish readers. In the decades it has published articles in various fields, including philosophy, political science, sociology, literature and art.
Language(s): English
CONSUMER: THE ARTS & LITERARY: Literary

RESTAURATOR 1796185PL11A-9
Editorial: ul. Andersa, 38, 15-113 BIAŁYSTOK
Tel: 85 653 90 00 **Fax:** 85 653 98 56
Email: restaurator@publikator.com.pl **Web site:** http://www.restaurator.com.pl
ISSN: 1733-8255
Date Established: 1992; **Freq:** Monthly; **Circ:** 7,000
Usual Pagination: 64
Managing Director: Anita Frank; **Advertising Director:** Ewa Kuryłowicz
Profile: Provides professional news, recipes, market newest technologies and products.
Language(s): Polish
Mechanical Data: Type Area: A4 ekstra
BUSINESS: CATERING: Catering, Hotels & Restaurants

REUMATOLOGIA 1796198PL56A-32
Editorial: ul. Spartańska, 1, 02-637 WARSZAWA
Tel: 22 844 42 41
Email: red_reumat@ir.ids.pl **Web site:** http://www.reumatologia.termedia.pl
ISSN: 0034-6233
Circ: 2,000
Usual Pagination: 60
Managing Director: Andrzej Kordas
Profile: Official journal of the Institute of Rheumatology and the Polish Rheumatologic Society with news in treatment.
Language(s): Polish
Mechanical Data: Type Area: A4
BUSINESS: HEALTH & MEDICAL

REWIA 1708972PL74Q-9
Editorial: al. Stanów Zjednoczonych, 61a, 04-028 WARSZAWA **Tel:** 22 516 36 80 **Fax:** 22 516 36 62
Web site: http://www.reklama.bauer.pl
Date Established: 2004; **Freq:** Weekly; **Circ:** 422,000
Usual Pagination: 40
Advertising Director: Ewa Kozłowska
Profile: News on celebrities, entertainment and practical advice.
Language(s): Polish
ADVERTISING RATES:
Full Page Colour .... PLN 26000.00
Mechanical Data: Type Area: 225 x 285 mm
CONSUMER: WOMEN'S INTEREST CONSUMER MAGAZINES: Lifestyle

REZYDENCJE 1708631PL4A-1
Editorial: ul. Bora-Komorowskiego, 35, 161, 03-982 WARSZAWA **Tel:** 22 406 39 14 **Fax:** 22 406 39 15
ISSN: 1427-0439
Date Established: 1997; **Freq:** 6 issues yearly; **Circ:** 12,000
Usual Pagination: 148
Profile: Magazine on architecture, luxury interior design and luxury palaces.
Language(s): Polish
Mechanical Data: Type Area: 230 x 275 mm
BUSINESS: ARCHITECTURE & BUILDING: Architecture

RODZICE 1708641PL74D-18
Editorial: ul. Wynalazek, 4, 02-677 WARSZAWA
Tel: 22 607 00 20 **Fax:** 22 607 02 90
Email: rodzice@gjpoland.com.pl **Web site:** http://www.rodzice.pl
ISSN: 1506-9796
Date Established: 1996; **Freq:** Monthly; **Circ:** 157,000
Usual Pagination: 100
Managing Director: Michał Brudzyński; **Advertising Director:** Agnieszka Całka
Profile: Provides tips for women during pregnancy, infant care, psychology, education of children 0-6, parental expertise.
Language(s): Polish
ADVERTISING RATES:
Full Page Colour .... PLN 23000.00
Mechanical Data: Type Area: 210 x 284 mm
CONSUMER: WOMEN'S INTEREST CONSUMER MAGAZINES: Child Care

ROLNICZE ABC 1811088PL21B-1
Editorial: ul. Tracka, 5, 10-364 OLSZTYN
Tel: 89 539 74 73 **Fax:** 89 539 74 44
Email: a.uranowska@rolniczeabc.pl
Date Established: 1971; **Freq:** Monthly; **Circ:** 3,000
Usual Pagination: 28
Profile: Professional publication on agriculture and agricultural produce.
Language(s): Polish
Mechanical Data: Type Area: A4
BUSINESS: AGRICULTURE & FARMING: Agriculture - Supplies & Services

RUDY I METALE NIEŻELAZNE 1811073PL27-3
Editorial: ul. Krasińskiego, 13, 40-019 KATOWICE
Tel: 32 256 17 77 **Fax:** 32 256 17 77
Email: sekretariat@sigma-not.pl **Web site:** http://sigma-not.pl
ISSN: 0035-9696
Date Established: 1956; **Freq:** Monthly
Usual Pagination: 50
Profile: Presents news on mining and processing of ores, metallurgy and processing of nonferrous metals, problems of machines and equipment connected with it, economic aspects, organisation and management, environmental protection, analyses of ores and metals.
Language(s): Polish
Readership: Aimed at managers, engineers and technicians design engineers of non-ferrous metals industry, scientific workers of research institutes.
ADVERTISING RATES:
Full Page Mono .... PLN 1550.00
Full Page Colour .... RUR 3410.00
Mechanical Data: Type Area: 204 x 287 mm
BUSINESS: METAL, IRON & STEEL

RYNEK GAZOWY 1708827PL24-1
Editorial: ul. Krzywickiego 34, 02-078 WARSZAWA
Tel: 22 521 20 00 **Fax:** 22 521 20 20
Email: brog@brog.pl **Web site:** http://www.brog.pl
ISSN: 1507-1952
Date Established: 1996; **Freq:** Quarterly; **Circ:** 2,500
Usual Pagination: 44
Managing Director: Radosław Rybiński; **Advertising Director:** Norbert Rodziejczak
Profile: Provides information on house gas installations, car gas tanks, gas services and workshops.
Language(s): Polish
ADVERTISING RATES:
Full Page Colour .... PLN 3790.00
Mechanical Data: Type Area: 230x297 mm
BUSINESS: GAS

RYNEK KONFERENCJI I SZKOLEŃ 1929154PL14F-10
Editorial: ul. Gilarska, 58, 03-589 WARSZAWA
Tel: 22 435 70 48 **Fax:** 22 435 70 49
Email: ewa.wosk@topmedia.com.pl **Web site:** http://www.topmedia.com.pl
Date Established: 2000; **Freq:** Quarterly; **Cover Price:** Free; **Circ:** 50,000
Usual Pagination: 48
Managing Director: Bartłomiej Ślusarczyk
Profile: Magazine about work training, conferences, events organization, team building, work integration.
Language(s): Polish
Mechanical Data: Type Area: 205 x 280 mm
BUSINESS: COMMERCE, INDUSTRY & MANAGEMENT: Training & Recruitment

RYNEK PODRÓŻY 1709053PL50-4
Editorial: ul. Robotnicza, 20, 05-850 OŻARÓW MAZ.
Tel: 22 721 10 15 **Fax:** 22 721 10 15
Email: reklama@rynekpodrozy.com.pl **Web site:** http://www.rynekpodrozy.com.pl
Date Established: 2004; **Freq:** 6 issues yearly;
Cover Price: PLN 12.00
Annual Sub.: PLN 60.00; **Circ:** 6,000
Usual Pagination: 52
Advertising Director: Anna Olszewska
Profile: Trade news from Poland, Europe and the world; events, problems of the tourism in Poland and in the world; advertising and commercial information; promotion of countries and regions.
Language(s): Polish
Readership: It is addressed to professionals, managers and employees of the firms which are operating in three main sectors of the tourist economy.
ADVERTISING RATES:
Full Page Mono .... EUR 950.00
Mechanical Data: Type Area: A4
BUSINESS: TRAVEL & TOURISM

RYNEK TURYSTYCZNY 1819397PL89A-12
Editorial: ul. Okrzei 1a, 03-715 WARSZAWA
Tel: 22 333 80 00 **Fax:** 22 333 88 82
Email: rynekturystyczny@pws-promedia.pl **Web site:** http://www.rynekturystyczny.pl
ISSN: 1230-2716
Date Established: 1992; **Freq:** Monthly; **Circ:** 3,000
Usual Pagination: 48
Advertising Director: Magdalena Kłusek
Profile: Provides information, analysis, presentations regards tourist market in Poland and abroad.
Language(s): Polish
Mechanical Data: Type Area: 203 x 275 mm
CONSUMER: HOLIDAYS & TRAVEL: Travel

RYNEK ZDROWIA 1709047PL56A-22
Editorial: ul. Jana Matejki, 3, 40-077 KATOWICE
Tel: 32 209 10 43 **Fax:** 32 782 13 10
Email: redakcja@rynekzdrowia.pl **Web site:** http://www.rynekzdrowia.pl
ISSN: 1733-7917
Date Established: 2004; **Freq:** Monthly; **Circ:** 20,000
Usual Pagination: 92
Advertising Director: Tomasz Ruszkowski
Profile: Provides information on Polish NHS financial issues, pharmacy and new investigations, law and marketing of medical service.
Language(s): Polish
Mechanical Data: Type Area: 205 x 275 mm
BUSINESS: HEALTH & MEDICAL

RYNKI ALKOHOLOWE 1708738PL9A-1
Editorial: ul. Szosa Bydgoska, 56, 87-100 TORUŃ
Tel: 56 660 31 60 **Fax:** 56 660 31 61
Email: redakcja@rynki.pl **Web site:** http://www.rynki.pl
ISSN: 1233-8818
Date Established: 1995; **Freq:** Monthly; **Circ:** 12,000
Usual Pagination: 60
Advertising Director: Lidia Potwardowska
Profile: Covers news of industry and promotes brand alcoholic products, high quality spirits products, advertisements of products and services in alcohol-producing branch, market, trade, legal and marketing issues.
Language(s): Polish
ADVERTISING RATES:
Full Page Mono .... PLN 6000.00
Full Page Colour .... PLN 9400.00
Mechanical Data: Type Area: A4
BUSINESS: DRINKS & LICENSED TRADE: Drinks, Licensed Trade, Wines & Spirits

RZECZPOSPOLITA 1201435PL65A-20
Editorial: ul. Prosta, 51, 00-838 WARSZAWA
Tel: 22 628 34 01-09 **Fax:** 22 628 05 88
Email: listy@rp.pl **Web site:** http://rzeczpospolita.pl
ISSN: 0208-9130
Date Established: 1982; **Freq:** Daily; **Circ:** 138,869
Usual Pagination: 90
Advertising Director: Tomasz Dąbrowski
Profile: Broadsheet-sized quality newspaper providing in-depth national and international news, with political and financial coverage, social issues, media, education, IT, travel, arts, sport and entertainment. Also includes features on legislation and personal finance.
Language(s): Polish
Readership: Read by senior managers, decision-makers, civil servants, university students and academics.
ADVERTISING RATES:
Full Page Mono .... PLN 69600.00
Full Page Colour .... PLN 108710.00
Mechanical Data: Type Area: 249 x 329 mm
NATIONAL DAILY & SUNDAY NEWSPAPERS: National Daily Newspapers

RZECZPOSPOLITA 1929253PL65A-43
Formerly: rp.pl
Editorial: ul. Prosta, 51, 00-838 WARSZAWA
Tel: 22 622 09 33
Email: serwisinformacyjny@rp.pl **Web site:** http://www.rzeczpospolita.pl
Freq: Daily; **Circ:** 1,064,510 Unique Users
Advertising Director: Tomasz Dąbrowski
Profile: Website of a national newspaper covering world and national affairs, opinions, law, economics, money issues, jobs, Real Estate, sports, science, culture, style, and travel.
Language(s): Polish
NATIONAL DAILY & SUNDAY NEWSPAPERS: National Daily Newspapers

SAILNEWS.PL 1796134PL45E-1
Editorial: ul. Bosmańska 23b/20, 75-257 KOSZALIN
Email: sailnews@sailnews.pl **Web site:** http://www.sailnews.pl
Freq: Daily; **Cover Price:** Paid
Editor-in-Chief: Paweł Maksymiuk
Profile: Web site dedicated to sailing and provides news on competitions and gives practical advice.
Language(s): Polish
BUSINESS: MARINE & SHIPPING: Boat Trade

SALON I ELEGANCJA 1708965PL15A-3
Editorial: ul. Księcia Janusza, 64, 01-452 WARSZAWA **Tel:** 22 335 97 00/41 **Fax:** 22 335 97 10
Email: joanna.kwiatkowska@warsawvoice.pl
ISSN: 1230-9656
Date Established: 1993; **Freq:** Monthly; **Circ:** 15,000
Usual Pagination: 76
Profile: Contains professional articles and beauty information, reports, interviews, descriptions of new products and worldwide correspondence interesting to cosmeticians and hairdressers.
Language(s): Polish
Readership: Targets cosmetic and dermatological centres, hairdressers, cosmetics wholesalers, cosmetic producers and distributors throughout Poland.
Mechanical Data: Type Area: A4
BUSINESS: COSMETICS & HAIRDRESSING: Cosmetics

SALON I SYPIALNIA 1708915PL4B-2
Editorial: ul. Andersa, 38, 15-113 BIAŁYSTOK
Tel: 85 653 90 00 **Fax:** 85 653 98 56
Email: salon@publikator.com.pl **Web site:** http://www.publikator.com.pl
Date Established: 2001; **Freq:** Monthly; **Circ:** 27,000
Usual Pagination: 144
Managing Director: Anita Frank; **Advertising Director:** Agnieszka Panasewicz
Profile: Magazine on interior design with original and stylistic project offers, modern solutions and newest trends.
Language(s): Polish
Mechanical Data: Type Area: 230 x 297 mm
BUSINESS: ARCHITECTURE & BUILDING: Interior Design & Flooring

SAMO ZDROWIE 766127PL74G-1
Editorial: ul. Warecka, 11a, 00-035 WARSZAWA
Tel: 22 448 83 00 **Fax:** 22 448 80 01
Email: samo-zdrowie@samo-zdrowie.com.pl **Web site:** http://www.burdamedia.pl
ISSN: 1429-1568
Date Established: 1997; **Freq:** Monthly; **Circ:** 117,000
Usual Pagination: 84
Managing Director: Justyna Namięta; **Advertising Director:** Barbara Ożóg
Profile: Magazine focusing on different aspects of health includes sections on fitness, diet, beauty, sex and psychology.
Language(s): Polish
ADVERTISING RATES:
Full Page Colour .... PLN 22900.00
Mechanical Data: Type Area: 195 x 255 mm
CONSUMER: WOMEN'S INTEREST CONSUMER MAGAZINES: Slimming & Health

SAMOCHODY UŻYTKOWE 1796184PL31R-4
Editorial: ul. Polska 13, 60-595 POZNAŃ
Tel: 61 66 55 800 **Fax:** 61 66 55 888
Email: kontakt@forum-press.pl **Web site:** http://www.flota.com.pl
ISSN: 1644-8634
Date Established: 2002; **Freq:** Quarterly; Free to qualifying individuals
Annual Sub.: PLN 160.50; **Circ:** 4,000
Usual Pagination: 68
Advertising Director: Małgorzata Prościak
Profile: Magazine covering problems of modern fleets of commercial vehicles, informing on most important products and services in the automotive industry, financial, legal, environmental, safety and the latest technical and technological solutions.
Language(s): English
Mechanical Data: Type Area: 230x297 mm
BUSINESS: MOTOR TRADE: Motor Trade Related

SEKRETARIAT 1708868PL14G-1
Editorial: ul. Okopowa, 58/72, 01-402 WARSZAWA
Tel: 22 530 42 14 **Fax:** 22 530 40 12
Email: redakcja.sekretariat@infor.pl **Web site:** http://www.sekretariat.infor.pl
ISSN: 1425-5782
Date Established: 1996; **Freq:** Monthly
Usual Pagination: 48
Managing Director: Mariusz Drozdowicz
Profile: Professional magazine on office and administrative work, office procedures and work organization.
Language(s): Polish
Mechanical Data: Type Area: A4
BUSINESS: COMMERCE, INDUSTRY & MANAGEMENT: Company Secretaries

SEKRETY I NAMIĘTNOŚCI 1708810PL74A-1026
Editorial: ul. św. Antoniego, 7, 50-073 WROCŁAW
Tel: 71 344 77 75 **Fax:** 71 346 01 74
Email: sin@phoenix.pl **Web site:** http://www.phoenix.pl
ISSN: 1643-9767
Date Established: 2002; **Freq:** Monthly; **Circ:** 79,000
Usual Pagination: 48
Profile: Magazine of 'real life stories' kind featuring realistic stories of contemporary Polish women.

Distinguishing element introduced during re-launch of the title is a special emphasis on participation of readers in the creation of this monthly.
Language(s): English
ADVERTISING RATES:
Full Page Colour .... PLN 3500.00
Mechanical Data: Type Area: 215 x 295 mm
CONSUMER: WOMEN'S INTEREST CONSUMER MAGAZINES: Women's Interest

---

SERIA INFO 1796157PL56A-26
Editorial: ul. Niedźwiedzia, 12a, 02-737 WARSZAWA
Tel: 22 853 73 72 **Fax:** 22 853 73 72
Email: sekretariat@medi-press.pl **Web site:** http://www.resmedica.pl
Circ: 3,000
Usual Pagination: 42
Managing Director: Anna Łuczyńska
Profile: Professional articles on pneumology, oncology, contagious diseases, cardiology and allergies.
Language(s): Polish
Mechanical Data: Type Area: A4
BUSINESS: HEALTH & MEDICAL

SERWIS PRAWNO-PRACOWNICZY 1708866PL44-5
Editorial: ul. Okopowa, 58/72, 01-042 WARSZAWA
Tel: 22 530 43 56 **Fax:** 22 530 43 64
Email: serwispp@infor.pl **Web site:** http://www.serwispp.infor.pl
ISSN: 1234-8325
Date Established: 1995; **Freq:** Weekly
Usual Pagination: 56
Managing Director: Mariusz Drozdowicz
Profile: Focuses on legal aspects of employment, social and health insurance, payments.
Language(s): Polish
Mechanical Data: Type Area: A4
BUSINESS: LEGAL

SHAPE 766108PL74G-30
Editorial: ul. Wilcza, 50/52, 00-679 WARSZAWA
Tel: 22 421 10 00 **Fax:** 22 421 11 11
Email: shape@shape.pl **Web site:** http://www.shape.pl
ISSN: 1509-8834
Date Established: 2000; **Freq:** Monthly; **Circ:** 50,000
Usual Pagination: 130
Managing Director: Beata Milewska; **Advertising Director:** Monika Wdowiak
Profile: Magazine covering all aspects of lifestyle includes sections on fitness, health, diet and alternative medicine, psychology, beauty, fashion and culture.
Language(s): Polish
Readership: Read mostly by educated, modern women.
ADVERTISING RATES:
Full Page Colour .... PLN 21500.00
Mechanical Data: Type Area: 190 x 253 mm
CONSUMER: WOMEN'S INTEREST CONSUMER MAGAZINES: Slimming & Health

---

SHOPPING CENTER POLAND 1796161PL14A-79
Editorial: ul. Krzywickiego, 34, 02-078 WARSZAWA
Tel: 22 521 20 00 **Fax:** 22 521 20 20
Email: brog@brog.pl **Web site:** http://www.brog.pl
ISSN: 1734-7599
Date Established: 2005; **Freq:** Quarterly; **Circ:** 2,500
Usual Pagination: 44
Managing Director: Radosław Rybiński; **Advertising Director:** Cezary Goss
Profile: Provides information for investors and owners of shopping centres.
Language(s): Polish
ADVERTISING RATES:
Full Page Colour .... PLN 4740.00
Mechanical Data: Type Area: 230x297 mm
BUSINESS: COMMERCE, INDUSTRY & MANAGEMENT

SHOW 1929137PL74Q-19
Editorial: ul. Motorowa, 1, 04-028 WARSZAWA
Tel: 22 517 08 09
Email: anna.zaleska@bauer.pl **Web site:** http://www.reklama.bauer.pl
ISSN: 1899-6574
Date Established: 2008; **Freq:** 26 issues yearly; **Circ:** 582,000
Usual Pagination: 88
Managing Director: Monika Krokiewicz; **Advertising Director:** Beata Madeja
Profile: Magazine dedicated to celebrities, lifestyle, fashion, beauty and health issues.
Language(s): Polish
ADVERTISING RATES:
Full Page Colour .... PLN 43000.00
Mechanical Data: Type Area: 225 x 285 mm
CONSUMER: WOMEN'S INTEREST CONSUMER MAGAZINES: Lifestyle

SKI MAGAZYN 1709016PL75G-1
Editorial: ul. Głowackiego, 10b, 26, 30-085 KRAKÓW
Tel: 12 623 13 52 **Fax:** 12 638 25 93
Email: ski@alpinmedia.com.pl **Web site:** http://www.alpinmedia.com.pl
ISSN: 1641-1579
Date Established: 2000; **Freq:** 5 issues yearly; **Circ:** 20,000
Usual Pagination: 80
Profile: Provided practical advice on equipment and skiing techniques, ski events and competitions.
Language(s): Polish
Mechanical Data: Type Area: 284 x 204 mm
CONSUMER: SPORT: Winter Sports

ŚLUB JAK Z BAJKI 1708974PL74L-1
Editorial: ul. Czerska, 8/10, 00-732 WARSZAWA
Tel: 22 555 68 90 **Fax:** 22 555 66 67
Email: slub@agora.pl **Web site:** http://kobieta.gazeta.pl/slub/0,0.html
ISSN: 1732-9701
Date Established: 2004; **Freq:** Half-yearly; **Circ:** 23,000
Usual Pagination: 130
Profile: Advice on wedding clothing, make-up, hairdo, flower decorations, etc.
Language(s): Polish
ADVERTISING RATES:
Full Page Colour .... PLN 30000.00
Mechanical Data: Type Area: 218x285 mm
CONSUMER: WOMEN'S INTEREST CONSUMER MAGAZINES: Brides

SNOW IT! 1810912PL75G-2
Editorial: ul. Świeradowska, 44a, 02-662 WARSZAWA **Tel:** 22 898 04 15 **Fax:** 22 898 04 21
Email: redakcja@surfit.pl **Web site:** http://www.surfit.pl
ISSN: 1733-7208
Date Established: 2004
Circ: 20,000
Usual Pagination: 100
Language(s): Polish
Mechanical Data: Type Area: 219x275 mm
CONSUMER: SPORT: Winter Sports

SOFTWARE DEVELOPERS JOURNAL 1796120PL5C-5
Editorial: ul. Bokserska, 1, 02-682 WARSZAWA
Tel: 22 427 36 91 **Fax:** 22 244 24 59
Email: sdj@software.com.pl **Web site:** http://www.sdjournal.org
ISSN: 1734-3917
Date Established: 1995; **Freq:** Monthly; **Circ:** 6,000
Usual Pagination: 84
Advertising Director: Sylwia Pogroszewska
Profile: Professional magazine on IT technologies and computer software.
Language(s): Polish
Mechanical Data: Type Area: A4
BUSINESS: COMPUTERS & AUTOMATION: Professional Personal Computers

---

SÓL I PIEPRZ 1708652PL74P-4
Editorial: ul. Ostrowskiego, 7, 53-238 WROCŁAW
Tel: 71 376 28 32 **Fax:** 71 376 28 02
Email: kulinaria@burdamedia.pl **Web site:** http://www.burdamedia.pl
ISSN: 1427-406X
Date Established: 1996; **Freq:** Monthly; **Circ:** 45,000
Usual Pagination: 52
Managing Director: Justyna Namięta; **Advertising Director:** Barbara Ożóg
Profile: Magazine providing original recipes, practical tips and culinary news from around the world.
Language(s): English
ADVERTISING RATES:
Full Page Colour .... PLN 10900.00
Mechanical Data: Type Area: 210 x 267 mm
CONSUMER: WOMEN'S INTEREST CONSUMER MAGAZINES: Food & Cookery

---

SOLARIUM 1709024PL15R-1
Editorial: ul. Powstańców Śl., 32a, 1, 45-087 OPOLE
Tel: 77 402 52 52 **Fax:** 77 423 14 27
Email: info@solarium.pl **Web site:** http://www.solarium.info.pl
ISSN: 1508-1265
Date Established: 1999; **Freq:** 6 issues yearly; **Cover Price:** Free; **Circ:** 7,000
Usual Pagination: 132
Profile: Magazine covering wellness, information on technology used in solariums, marketing, medicine and hygiene, a review of the market for equipment and professional tanning preparations, sunburns, saunas, beauty equipment.
Language(s): English
ADVERTISING RATES:
Full Page Colour .... PLN 4850.00
Mechanical Data: Type Area: 205x280 mm
BUSINESS: COSMETICS & HAIRDRESSING: Cosmetics & Hairdressing Related

---

SPA BUSINESS 1810908PL74G-23
Formerly: Spa Busines
Editorial: ul. Andersa, 38, 15-113 BIAŁYSTOK
Tel: 85 653 90 00 **Fax:** 85 653 98 56
Email: spabusiness@publikator.com.pl **Web site:** http://www.publikator.com.pl
ISSN: 1896-5881
Date Established: 1992; **Freq:** 6 issues yearly; **Circ:** 3,000
Usual Pagination: 64
Managing Director: Anita Frank; **Advertising Director:** Ewa Kuryłowicz
Profile: Provides analytical information and experts advice, marketing organization in beauty parlours and spa objects, newest trends in beauty and recreation industry.
Language(s): Polish
Mechanical Data: Type Area: 230 x 310 mm
CONSUMER: WOMEN'S INTEREST CONSUMER MAGAZINES: Slimming & Health

---

SPEDYCJA TRANSPORT LOGISTYKA 1708727PL49C-1
Editorial: ul. Dzika, 4, 00-194 WARSZAWA
Tel: 22 635 29 30 **Fax:** 22 635 73 70
Email: ppwp@ppwp.pl **Web site:** http://ppwp.pl
ISSN: 1640-7903
Date Established: 2000; **Freq:** Monthly; **Circ:** 8,000
Usual Pagination: 100
Advertising Director: Beatrycze Góral
Profile: Focused on transportation and logistics, machines and equipment, courier companies.
Language(s): Polish
ADVERTISING RATES:
Full Page Colour .... PLN 6600.00
Mechanical Data: Type Area: A4
BUSINESS: TRANSPORT: Freight

SPORTPLUS 1804104PL4R-1
Editorial: ul. Rolna, 155, 1, 02-729 WARSZAWA
Tel: 22 853 06 87 **Fax:** 22 853 06 86
Email: suwinski@pwbmedia.pl **Web site:** http://www.esportplus.pl
ISSN: 1734-6142
Date Established: 1997; **Freq:** Monthly; **Circ:** 8,000
Usual Pagination: 100
Editor: Paweł Kociel; **Advertising Director:** Dominik Suwiński
Profile: Dedicated to designing, constriction, infrastructure, maintenance and management of sports and recreation objects.
Language(s): Polish
Readership: It is addressed to institutions supporting and influencing creation of conditions which help to develop this segment of building sector, to state investors (cities, towns, districts), to private investors, but also to designers, producers of materials, suppliers of technologies and machines, contractors, sports facilities administrators.
Mechanical Data: Type Area: A4
BUSINESS: ARCHITECTURE & BUILDING: Building Related

STACJA BENZYNOWA 1708826PL58-2
Editorial: ul. Krzywickiego, 34, 02-078 WARSZAWA
Tel: 22 521 20 00 **Fax:** 22 521 20 20
Email: brog@brog.pl **Web site:** http://www.brog.pl
ISSN: 1429-7914
Date Established: 1998; **Freq:** Monthly; **Circ:** 4,500
Usual Pagination: 48
Managing Director: Radosław Rybiński; **Advertising Director:** Norbert Rodziejczak
Profile: A professional B2B monthly addressed to the fuel business. Themagazine presents major problems of the sector of retail and bulk distribution of fuels and FMCG, offering practical advice on running modern filling stations, Cstore and carwash operations. It provides information in the area of managing and fitting stations.
Language(s): Polish
ADVERTISING RATES:
Full Page Colour .... PLN 4990.00
Mechanical Data: Type Area: 230x297 mm
BUSINESS: ENERGY, FUEL & NUCLEAR

STAL METALE & NOWE TECHNOLOGIE 1811077PL27-4
Editorial: al. Roździeńskiego, 188, 40-203 KATOWICE **Tel:** 32 788 51 98 **Fax:** 32 203 93 56
Email: stal@elamed.pl **Web site:** http://www.stal.elamed.pl
ISSN: 1895-6408
Date Established: 2006; **Freq:** 6 issues yearly
Usual Pagination: 60
Advertising Director: Agnieszka Szutenberg
Profile: Professional magazine on production, distribution, machining, assembly, surface protection, measurements, design and norms in latest technologies related to market of steel and non-ferrous metals.
Language(s): Polish
Mechanical Data: Type Area: 204 x 290 mm
BUSINESS: METAL, IRON & STEEL

STOSUNKI MIĘDZYNARODOWE 1796174PL82-79
Editorial: ul. Ordynacka, 11, 5, 00-364 WARSZAWA
Tel: 22 498 15 37 **Fax:** 22 644 63 70
Email: redakcja@stosunki.pl **Web site:** http://www.stosunki.pl
ISSN: 1509-3077
Date Established: 1999; **Freq:** Monthly; **Circ:** 6,000
Usual Pagination: 64
Advertising Director: Michał Sierpiński
Profile: Covering international relations, diplomacy, foreign affairs, international law and international trade.
Language(s): Polish
Mechanical Data: Type Area: A4
CONSUMER: CURRENT AFFAIRS & POLITICS

STREET XTREME 1796147PL31R-2
Editorial: ul. 10 Lutego, 5, 7, 81-366 GDYNIA
Tel: 58 612 15 51 **Fax:** 58 620 47 51
Email: fabas@fabas.pl **Web site:** http://www.streetxtreme.pl
ISSN: 1733-3644
Date Established: 2000
Circ: 30,000
Usual Pagination: 64
Managing Director: Aleksandra Zielińska
Profile: Focuses on international tuning trends, styling, car audio systems, international car events.
Language(s): Polish
Mechanical Data: Type Area: 212x300 mm
BUSINESS: MOTOR TRADE: Motor Trade Related

STUDENT NEWS 1708800PL83-4
Editorial: ul. Laurowa, 37, 10, 03-197 WARSZAWA
Tel: 22 747 07 00 **Fax:** 22 747 07 01
Email: studentnews@studentnews.pl **Web site:** http://www.studentnews.pl
ISSN: 1644-5287
Date Established: 2002
Cover Price: Free; **Circ:** 100,000
Usual Pagination: 44
Profile: Student life, interviews, competitions, films, music, fashion and beauty.
Language(s): Polish
Mechanical Data: Type Area: 201x272 mm
CONSUMER: STUDENT PUBLICATIONS

STUDIOWAĆ 1819635PL83-9
Editorial: ul. Bruna, 16, 11, 02-781 WARSZAWA
Tel: 22 875 29 05 **Fax:** 22 825 28 78
Email: grazyna.wroblewska@aromedia.pl **Web site:** http://www.studiowac.pl
ISSN: 1896-9798
Date Established: 2006; **Freq:** Quarterly; **Cover Price:** Free; **Circ:** 100,000
Usual Pagination: 32
Profile: Magazine on studying at universities and colleges in Poland and abroad.
Language(s): Polish
Mechanical Data: Type Area: A4
CONSUMER: STUDENT PUBLICATIONS

STYLE I CHARAKTERY 1811015PL94J-311
Editorial: ul. Warszawska, 6, 25-512 KIELCE
Tel: 41 343 28 40 **Fax:** 41 343 28 40
Email: style@charaktery.com.pl
ISSN: 1897-0745
Freq: Quarterly; **Circ:** 15,000
Usual Pagination: 76
Advertising Director: Marek Malarz
Language(s): English
Mechanical Data: Type Area: 215 x 280 mm
CONSUMER: OTHER CLASSIFICATIONS: Popular Science

SUKCESY I PORAŻKI. WYDANIE SPECJALNE 1709077PL74A-1023
Editorial: ul. św. Antoniego, 7, 50-073 WROCŁAW
Tel: 71 344 77 75 **Fax:** 71 346 01 74
Email: sip@phoenix.pl **Web site:** http://www.phoenix.pl
Date Established: 1996
Circ: 136,000
Usual Pagination: 48
Profile: Magazine covering real life stories for women, culinary recipes, health and diet advice.
Language(s): Polish
ADVERTISING RATES:
Full Page Colour .... PLN 3000.00
Mechanical Data: Type Area: 205 x 280 mm
CONSUMER: WOMEN'S INTEREST CONSUMER MAGAZINES: Women's Interest

---

SUPER EXPRESS 707995PL65A-23
Editorial: ul. Jubilerska, 10, 00-939 WARSZAWA
Tel: 22 515 91 00 **Fax:** 22 515 91 10
Email: listy@superexpress.pl **Web site:** http://www.se.pl
ISSN: 0867-8723
Date Established: 1991; **Freq:** Daily; **Circ:** 182,741
Usual Pagination: 28
Managing Director: Małgorzata Golińska; **Advertising Director:** Marek Białek
Profile: Newspaper concentrating on national and international politics, finance, business, public issues, culture and entertainment.
Language(s): English
Readership: Aimed at the general public.
ADVERTISING RATES:
Full Page Colour .... PLN 75000.00
Mechanical Data: Type Area: A3
NATIONAL DAILY & SUNDAY NEWSPAPERS: National Daily Newspapers

---

SUPER LINIA 1708623PL74G-3
Editorial: ul. Niedźwiedzia, 12a, 02-737 WARSZAWA
Tel: 22 853 73 72 **Fax:** 22 853 73 72
Email: superlinia@medi-press.pl **Web site:** http://www.superlinia.pl
ISSN: 1231-5710
Date Established: 1994
Circ: 110,000
Managing Director: Dorota Świderska; **Advertising Director:** Agnieszka Jackowska

Profile: Magazine on dieting, figure-shaping, health, slimming, beauty.
Language(s): Polish
Mechanical Data: Type Area: A4
CONSUMER: WOMEN'S INTEREST CONSUMER MAGAZINES: Slimming & Health

SUPER LINIA - WYDANIE SPECJALNE 1796150PL74G-20
Editorial: ul. Niedźwiedzia, 12a, 02-737 WARSZAWA
Tel: 22 853 73 72 **Fax:** 22 853 73 72
Email: superlinia@medi-press.pl **Web site:** http://www.superlinia.pl
ISSN: 1427-4973
Date Established: 1994
Circ: 60,000
Usual Pagination: 84
Managing Director: Dorota Świderska; **Advertising Director:** Agnieszka Jackowska
Language(s): English
Mechanical Data: Type Area: A5
CONSUMER: WOMEN'S INTEREST CONSUMER MAGAZINES: Slimming & Health

SUPER TELE 1708746PL76C-7
Editorial: ul. Domaniewska, 41, 02-672 WARSZAWA
Tel: 22 201 41 00 **Fax:** 22 201 41 99
Email: reklama@polskapresse.pl **Web site:** http://www.polskapresse.pl/reklama
ISSN: 1230-9796
Date Established: 1991; **Freq:** Weekly; **Cover Price:** Free; **Circ:** 251,500
Usual Pagination: 16
Advertising Director: Małgorzata Cetera-Bulka
Language(s): Polish
Mechanical Data: Type Area: 215x280 mm
CONSUMER: MUSIC & PERFORMING ARTS: TV & Radio

SUPER TV 1622906PL76C-3
Editorial: ul. Motorowa, 1, 04-035 WARSZAWA
Tel: 22 517 01 64 **Fax:** 22 517 03 52
Email: supertv@bauer.pl **Web site:** http://www.reklama.bauer.pl
ISSN: 1230-9788
Date Established: 2001; **Freq:** Weekly; **Circ:** 428,000
Usual Pagination: 48
Advertising Director: Izabela Sarnecka
Profile: Guide to cable television programmes, includes news, celebrity profiles, interviews and gossip.
Language(s): Polish
ADVERTISING RATES:
Full Page Colour .... PLN 16800.00
Mechanical Data: Type Area: 225 x 285 mm
CONSUMER: MUSIC & PERFORMING ARTS: TV & Radio

SUPERMARKET POLSKA 1708825PL53-8
Editorial: ul. Krzywickiego, 34, 02-078 WARSZAWA
Tel: 22 521 20 00 **Fax:** 22 521 20 20
Email: brog@brog.pl **Web site:** http://www.brog.pl
ISSN: 1508-8510
Date Established: 1999; **Freq:** Monthly; **Circ:** 8,000
Usual Pagination: 48
Managing Director: Radosław Rybiński; **Advertising Director:** Cezary Goss
Profile: Magazine focused on marketing, merchandising and technologies and equipment in retail outlets.
Language(s): Polish
ADVERTISING RATES:
Full Page Colour .... PLN 7990.00
Mechanical Data: Type Area: 230x297 mm
BUSINESS: RETAILING & WHOLESALING

SURF IT! 1709054PL75M-5
Editorial: ul. Świeradowska, 44a, 02-662 WARSZAWA **Tel:** 22 898 04 16 **Fax:** 22 898 04 21
Email: redakcja@surfit.pl **Web site:** http://www.surfit.pl
ISSN: 1733-7208
Date Established: 2004
Circ: 20,000
Usual Pagination: 100
Language(s): Polish
Mechanical Data: Type Area: 219x275 mm
CONSUMER: SPORT: Water Sports

ŚWIAT ALKOHOLI 1708912PL9A-2
Editorial: ul. Andersa, 38, 15-113 BIAŁYSTOK
Tel: 85 653 90 00 **Fax:** 85 653 98 56
Email: redakcja@swiat-alkoholi.pl **Web site:** http://www.swiat-alkoholi.pl
ISSN: 1644-6844
Date Established: 1992; **Freq:** Monthly; **Circ:** 8,000
Usual Pagination: 72
Advertising Director: Aneta Purta-Stankiewicz
Profile: Professional magazine on spirits market in Poland, reports and advice on spirits and fortified wines.
Language(s): Polish
Mechanical Data: Type Area: A4 ekstra
BUSINESS: DRINKS & LICENSED TRADE: Drinks, Licensed Trade, Wines & Spirits

ŚWIAT BUTÓW 1708847PL29-1
Editorial: ul. Kierbedzia, 4, 00-728 WARSZAWA
Tel: 22 320 15 28 **Fax:** 22 320 15 40
Email: jbanakiewicz@unit.com.pl **Web site:** http://www.swiatbutow.eu
ISSN: 1428-3905
Date Established: 1997
Circ: 6,000
Usual Pagination: 56
Profile: Leading and only Polish shoe trade magazine.
Language(s): Polish
Readership: Addressed to managers and employees of Polish industry, wholesalers and retailers working in Polish shoe branch.
ADVERTISING RATES:
Full Page Colour .... PLN 4900.00
Mechanical Data: Type Area: 210 x 297 mm
BUSINESS: FOOTWEAR

ŚWIAT DRUKU 1795892PL41A-1
Editorial: ul. Obywatelska, 115, 94-104 ŁÓDŹ
Tel: 42 687 12 92 **Fax:** 42 687 12 99
Email: biuro@swiatdruku.com.pl **Web site:** http://www.swiatdruku.com.pl
ISSN: 1230-5316
Date Established: 1993
Circ: 3,000
Usual Pagination: 80
Managing Director: Jolanta Ziemniak-Ronke
Profile: Covering various aspects of printing industry: printing technologies, machines and materials for the printing industry as well as scientific research results, presentations of various products, interviews, accounts of visits at companies and branch events.
Language(s): Polish
Readership: It is read by companies' proprietors, printing house employees, graphic studios, advertising agencies and suppliers of new technologies.
ADVERTISING RATES:
Full Page Mono .... EUR 935.00
Full Page Colour .... EUR 1310.00
Mechanical Data: Type Area: 205 x 286 mm
BUSINESS: PRINTING & STATIONERY: Printing

ŚWIAT ELIT 1796176PL82-80
Editorial: al. Solidarności, 104, 01-016 WARSZAWA
Tel: 22 632 29 29 **Fax:** 22 862 91 32
Email: redakcja@swiatelit.com.pl **Web site:** http://www.swiatelit.com.pl
ISSN: 1643-5729
Date Established: 2001; **Freq:** Monthly; **Circ:** 10,000
Usual Pagination: 120
Profile: Presents interviews with politicians of different political views and of success, articles of ambassadors, national security issues, security in Europe and worldwide, defense and development strategies, military and police forces, promoting the cultural texts of outstanding Polish artists of outstanding creative achievements and international fame, celebrities of the world culture and science, columns and reports, information on prestigious events and banquets, guest wizards of social life, people's views on various political issues.
Language(s): Polish
Mechanical Data: Type Area: A4
CONSUMER: CURRENT AFFAIRS & POLITICS

ŚWIAT FRYZJERSTWA 1708726PL15B-1
Editorial: ul. Dzika, 4, 00-194 WARSZAWA
Tel: 22 635 73 70 **Fax:** 22 635 29 30
Email: ppwp@ppwp.pl **Web site:** http://swiatfryzjerstwa.pl
ISSN: 1426-7101
Date Established: 1996
Circ: 10,000
Usual Pagination: 100
Managing Director: Paweł Krzysica
Profile: Magazine focused on hairdressing and hair cosmetics, with news of from hairdressing and cosmetics industries, technical advances, presentations, interviews, reports from trade fairs.
Language(s): Polish
ADVERTISING RATES:
Full Page Colour .... PLN 7700.00
Mechanical Data: Type Area: A4
BUSINESS: COSMETICS & HAIRDRESSING: Hairdressing

ŚWIAT HOTELI 1708824PL11A-3
Editorial: ul. Krzywickiego, 34, 02-078 WARSZAWA
Tel: 22 521 20 00 **Fax:** 22 521 20 20
Email: brog@brog.pl **Web site:** http://www.brog.pl
ISSN: 1642-6460
Date Established: 2001; **Freq:** Monthly; **Circ:** 4,000
Usual Pagination: 48
Managing Director: Radosław Rybiński; **Advertising Director:** Beata Wołek
Profile: Analyzes problems of hotel management and smooth hotel running in Poland.
Language(s): Polish
ADVERTISING RATES:
Full Page Colour .... PLN 4290.00
Mechanical Data: Type Area: 230x297 mm
BUSINESS: CATERING: Catering, Hotels & Restaurants

ŚWIAT & LUDZIE 1810904PL74Q-11
Editorial: al. Stanów Zjednoczonych, 61a, 04-028 WARSZAWA **Tel:** 22 516 36 64 **Fax:** 22 516 36 61
Email: swiatiludzie@bauer.pl **Web site:** http://www.reklama.bauer.pl
ISSN: 1896-5792
Date Established: 2006; **Freq:** Weekly; **Circ:** 318,000
Usual Pagination: 48
Advertising Director: Ewa Kozłowska
Profile: Featuring stories about celebrities, travelling tips, practical advice on beauty and cookery, crosswords.
Language(s): Polish
ADVERTISING RATES:
Full Page Colour .... PLN 19000.00
Mechanical Data: Type Area: 225 x 285 mm
CONSUMER: WOMEN'S INTEREST CONSUMER MAGAZINES: Lifestyle

ŚWIAT KOBIETY 1616476PL74A-1004
Editorial: ul. Motorowa, 1, 04-035 WARSZAWA
Tel: 22 517 01 11 **Fax:** 22 517 03 13
Email: skobiety@bauer.pl **Web site:** http://www.reklama.bauer.pl
ISSN: 1230-7920
Date Established: 1993; **Freq:** Monthly; **Circ:** 639,000
Usual Pagination: 144
Managing Director: Monika Krokiewicz; **Advertising Director:** Ewa Kozłowska
Profile: Women's interest magazine covering health, beauty, fashion, fitness and related issues.
Language(s): Polish
Readership: Read mainly by women aged between 20 and 45 years of age.
ADVERTISING RATES:
Full Page Colour .... PLN 70350.00
Mechanical Data: Type Area: 210 x 280 mm
CONSUMER: WOMEN'S INTEREST CONSUMER MAGAZINES: Women's Interest

ŚWIAT KOMINKÓW 1796173PL4B-7
Editorial: ul. Roztocze, 5, 5, 20-722 LUBLIN
Tel: 81 743 65 91 **Fax:** 81 535 09 69
Email: redakcja@swiatkominkow.pl **Web site:** http://www.ihz.pl/sk
ISSN: 1644-6054
Date Established: 2001; **Freq:** Quarterly; **Circ:** 25,000
Usual Pagination: 164
Advertising Director: Małgorzata Bogdanowicz
Profile: Magazine on building and exploitation of chimneys and fire places.
Language(s): Polish
ADVERTISING RATES:
Full Page Colour .... PLN 6900.00
Mechanical Data: Type Area: 216x282 mm
BUSINESS: ARCHITECTURE & BUILDING: Interior Design & Flooring

ŚWIAT ŁAZIENEK I KUCHNI 1708913PL23C-1
Editorial: ul. Andersa 38, 15-113 BIAŁYSTOK
Tel: 85 653 90 00 **Fax:** 85 653 98 56
Email: swiat@publikator.com.pl **Web site:** http://www.publikator.com.pl
ISSN: 1509-0671
Date Established: 1992
Circ: 30,000
Usual Pagination: 128
Managing Director: Anita Frank; **Advertising Director:** Agnieszka Panasewicz
Profile: Magazine on interior design of kitchen and bathroom presenting newest designs and practical advice.
Language(s): Polish
Mechanical Data: Type Area: 230 x 297 mm
BUSINESS: FURNISHINGS & FURNITURE: Furnishings & Furniture - Kitchens & Bathrooms

ŚWIAT MOTOCYKLI 1626031PL77B-1
Editorial: ul. Czerska, 8/10, 00-732 WARSZAWA
Tel: 22 555 67 94 **Fax:** 22 555 68 10
Email: swiat-motocykli@agora.pl **Web site:** http://www.swiatmotocykli.pl
ISSN: 1230-9397
Date Established: 1993; **Freq:** Monthly; **Circ:** 57,000
Usual Pagination: 108
Advertising Director: Beata Remjasz
Profile: Magazine focusing on mopeds and scooters. Includes model tests and discussion of the use of mopeds in cities.
Language(s): English
Readership: Read by enthusiasts.
Mechanical Data: Type Area: 220 x 285 mm
CONSUMER: MOTORING & CYCLING: Motorcycling

ŚWIAT MOTORYZACJI 1708902PL77A-22
Editorial: ul. Tytoniowa, 20, 04-228 WARSZAWA
Tel: 22 515 00 31 **Fax:** 22 613 25 84
Email: k.rybarski@migutmedia.pl **Web site:** http://www.swiatmotoryzacji.com.pl
ISSN: 1731-5468
Date Established: 2003; **Freq:** Monthly; **Cover Price:** Free; **Circ:** 18,000
Usual Pagination: 60
Profile: Professional magazine on motoring issues and car-servicing.
Language(s): English
ADVERTISING RATES:
Full Page Colour .... PLN 8000.00
Mechanical Data: Type Area: A4
CONSUMER: MOTORING & CYCLING: Motoring

ŚWIAT NAUKI 1201742PL94J-200
Editorial: ul. Garażowa, 7, 02-651 WARSZAWA
Tel: 22 607 77 71 **Fax:** 22 848 22 66
Email: swiatnauki@proszynskimedia.pl **Web site:** http://www.swiatnauki.pl
ISSN: 0867-6380
Date Established: 1991; **Freq:** Monthly; **Circ:** 35,000
Usual Pagination: 88
Profile: Polish-language edition of Scientific American.
Language(s): English
Readership: Aimed at students, scientists, teachers, engineers and medical doctors.
Mechanical Data: Type Area: 205 x 275 mm
CONSUMER: OTHER CLASSIFICATIONS: Popular Science

ŚWIAT POLIGRAFII 1833996PL41A-4
Editorial: ul. Karabeli 2 E lok. 3, 01-313 WARSZAWA
Tel: 22 424 47 57 **Fax:** 22 723 41 25
Email: info@swiatpoligrafii.pl **Web site:** http://swiatpoligrafii.pl
Freq: Monthly - www.swiatpoligrafii.pl -700,000 page views a month; **Annual Sub.:** PLN 100.00; **Circ:** 3,500
Usual Pagination: 76
Editor: Tomasz Krawczak; **Editor-in-Chief:** Mirosław Pawliński
Profile: Provides information about printing markets and materials, prepress and digit print, new technologies and news in printing industry. In each issue there are special few pages section in English entitled "Review" for international readers.
Language(s): Polish
Readership: Aimed at publishers, printing houses, advertising agencies and polygraph equipment producers.
ADVERTISING RATES:
Full Page Colour .... PLN 3800.00
Mechanical Data: Type Area: 220 x 290mm, Print Process: Offset
BUSINESS: PRINTING & STATIONERY: Printing

ŚWIAT RADIO 1819528PL18A-120
Editorial: ul. Leszczynowa, 11, 03-197 WARSZAWA
Tel: 22 257 84 60 **Fax:** 22 257 84 44
Email: swiatradio@swiatradio.com.pl **Web site:** http://www.swiatradio.pl
ISSN: 1425-1701
Date Established: 1995; **Freq:** Monthly; **Circ:** 14,000
Usual Pagination: 92
Advertising Director: Grzegorz Krzykawski
Profile: Focused on radio equipment, newest technologies and achievements, information from professional exhibitions.
Language(s): Polish
ADVERTISING RATES:
Full Page Colour .... PLN 3000.00
Mechanical Data: Type Area: 205 x 295 mm
BUSINESS: ELECTRONICS

ŚWIAT REZYDENCJI WNĘTRZ I OGRODÓW 1929087PL4A-58
Editorial: ul. Watykańska, 13, 15-638 BIAŁYSTOK
Tel: 85 743 82 10 **Fax:** 85 653 90 03
Email: redakcja@koncept-wydawnictwo.pl **Web site:** http://www.swiatrezydencji.pl
ISSN: 1897-3108
Date Established: 2006; **Freq:** 6 issues yearly; **Circ:** 20,000
Usual Pagination: 160
Advertising Director: Elżbieta Michalczuk
Profile: Magazine presenting projects of houses, interiors and gardens, offices and architectural projects.
Language(s): Polish
Mechanical Data: Type Area: 215 x 300 mm
BUSINESS: ARCHITECTURE & BUILDING: Architecture

ŚWIAT SERIALI 1622951PL76C-11
Editorial: ul. Motorowa, 1, 04-035 WARSZAWA
Tel: 22 517 03 93 **Fax:** 22 517 05 27
Email: sseriali@bauer.pl **Web site:** http://www.reklama.bauer.pl
ISSN: 1640-2294
Date Established: 2000; **Freq:** 26 issues yearly; **Circ:** 311,000
Usual Pagination: 56
Advertising Director: Izabela Sarnecka
Profile: Television soap opera magazine covering series' news, film features and interviews.
Language(s): Polish
Readership: Aimed at women aged 25 to 55 years.
ADVERTISING RATES:
Full Page Colour .... PLN 8500.00
Mechanical Data: Type Area: 210 x 280 mm
CONSUMER: MUSIC & PERFORMING ARTS: TV & Radio

ŚWIAT SKÓR 1796146PL47A-255
Editorial: ul. Kierbedzia, 4, 00-728 WARSZAWA
Tel: 22 320 15 28 **Fax:** 22 320 15 40
Email: jbanakiewicz@unit.com.pl **Web site:** http://www.unit.com.pl
ISSN: 1733-0122

Date Established: 2004; **Freq:** Half-yearly; **Circ:** 2,000
Usual Pagination: 24
Profile: Leading branch magazine for the polish leather industry, highlighting information about tanneries, leather, components, machines, accessories and leather clothes and products.
Language(s): Polish
ADVERTISING RATES:
Full Page Colour .... EUR 600.00
Mechanical Data: Type Area: 210 x 297 mm
BUSINESS: CLOTHING & TEXTILES

ŚWIAT SZKŁA 1708675PL12B-2
Editorial: al. Komisji Edukacji Narodowej, 95, 02-777 WARSZAWA **Tel:** 22 678 35 60 **Fax:** 22 678 54 21
Email: szklo@euro-media.pl **Web site:** http://www.swiat-szkla.pl
ISSN: 1426-5494
Date Established: 1996; **Freq:** Monthly; **Circ:** 4,000
Usual Pagination: 80
Advertising Director: Sławomir Zalewski
Profile: Professional magazine on glass -windows business, production, processing, market of windows, doors and accessories, buildings' facades, winter gardens, chemicals, machinery and tools for glass processing and other equipment used in glass industry.
Language(s): Polish
ADVERTISING RATES:
Full Page Colour .... PLN 4400.00
Mechanical Data: Type Area: A4
BUSINESS: CERAMICS, POTTERY & GLASS: Glass

SZKŁO I CERAMIKA 1811074PL12A-1
Editorial: ul. Postępu, 9, 02-676 WARSZAWA
Tel: 22 843 74 21 **Fax:** 22 843 17 89
Email: info@isic.neostrada.pl **Web site:** http://sigma-not.pl
ISSN: 0039-8144
Date Established: 1935; **Freq:** 6 issues yearly
Usual Pagination: 48
Profile: Presents scientific and technical achievements of domestic and international glass and ceramics industries, review of patents and discoveries in glass and ceramics industry in Poland and abroad, ceramics plants and glass works, schedule of industry trade fairs and exhibitions.
Language(s): Polish
Readership: Targets middle and top inspection staff at industrial plants, employees of scientific institutions and universities students.
ADVERTISING RATES:
Full Page Mono .... PLN 1200.00
Full Page Colour .... PLN 2700.00
Mechanical Data: Type Area: 206 x 290 mm
BUSINESS: CERAMICS, POTTERY & GLASS: Ceramics & Pottery

SŁUŻBA ZDROWIA 1846242PL56A-51
Editorial: ul. Jana Brożka 4, 02-482 WARSZAWA
Tel: 22 836 77 77 **Fax:** 22 877 44 01
Email: redakcja@sluzbazdrowia.com.pl **Web site:** http://www.sluzbazdrowia.com.pl
Date Established: 2000; **Freq:** 24 issues yearly; **Annual Sub.:** PLN 195.52; **Circ:** 10,000
Editor: Tomasz Sienkiewicz; **Editor-in-Chief:** Aleksandra Gielewska; **Advertising Manager:** Monika Drozdowska; **Advertising Director:** Beata Binienda-Muszyńska
Profile: Focused on health care management, health insurance, medical law and finance.
Language(s): Polish
Readership: Targets GP's, specialists, pharmacists, health care managers and politicians, pharmaceutical companies and equipment manufactures.
ADVERTISING RATES:
Full Page Colour .... PLN 4000.00
Mechanical Data: Type Area: A4
BUSINESS: HEALTH & MEDICAL

T3 1931399PL78R-9
Editorial: ul. Leszczynowa 11, 03-197 WARSZAWA
Tel: 22 257 84 99 **Fax:** 22 257 84 00
Email: paulina.stepien@avt.pl **Web site:** http://www.magazynt3.pl
Freq: 6 issues yearly; **Cover Price:** PLN 9.80
Annual Sub.: PLN 39.20
Usual Pagination: 120
Profile: Magazine covering latest models of mobile phones, digital cameras, audio equipment and HD.
Language(s): Polish
CONSUMER: CONSUMER ELECTRONICS: Consumer Electronics Related

TAK MIESZKAM 1709013PL4B-11
Editorial: ul. Garażowa, 7, 02-651 WARSZAWA
Tel: 22 607 77 71 **Fax:** 22 848 22 66
Email: takmieszkam@proszynskimedia.pl **Web site:** http://www.takmieszkam.pl
ISSN: 1731-6545
Date Established: 2004; **Freq:** 6 issues yearly; **Circ:** 53,000
Usual Pagination: 100
Profile: Magazine on interior design, home renovations and decorations.
Language(s): Polish
Mechanical Data: Type Area: 230 x 285 mm
BUSINESS: ARCHITECTURE & BUILDING: Interior Design & Flooring

TAKIE JEST ŻYCIE 1622952PL74R-2
Editorial: ul. Motorowa, 1, 04-035 WARSZAWA
Tel: 22 517 03 68 **Fax:** 22 517 02 45
Email: takiejestzycie@bauer.pl **Web site:** http://www.reklama.bauer.pl
ISSN: 1641-1706
Date Established: 2001; **Freq:** Weekly; **Circ:** 214,000
Usual Pagination: 40
Advertising Director: Ewa Kozłowska
Profile: Magazine featuring mainly life stories and family issues, includes articles on fashion and contains culinary tips and recipes.
Language(s): Polish
Readership: Read by women in the age group from 25 to 55.
ADVERTISING RATES:
Full Page Colour .... PLN 9900.00
Mechanical Data: Type Area: 210 x 280 mm
CONSUMER: WOMEN'S INTEREST CONSUMER MAGAZINES: Women's Interest Related

TATRY 1811028PL94J-313
Editorial: ul. Chałubińskiego, 42a, 34-500 ZAKOPANE **Tel:** 18 202 32 26 **Fax:** 18 202 32 50
Email: tatry@tpn.pl **Web site:** http://www.tatry.tpn.pl
ISSN: 0867-4531
Date Established: 1991; **Freq:** Quarterly; **Circ:** 6,700
Usual Pagination: 116
Profile: Magazine on Tatry and Carpathian mountains: ecology, history, nature and culture.
Language(s): English; Polish
Mechanical Data: Type Area: 210x272 mm
CONSUMER: OTHER CLASSIFICATIONS: Popular Science

TECHNIKA W DOMU 1708725PL78R-3
Editorial: ul. Dzika, 4, 00-194 WARSZAWA
Tel: 22 635 73 70 **Fax:** 22 635 48 47
Web site: http://ppwp.pl
Date Established: 2004; **Freq:** Annual; **Circ:** 20,000
Usual Pagination: 300
Managing Director: Paweł Krzysica
Profile: Catalogue presenting various equipment, home appliances and special tools.
Language(s): Polish
ADVERTISING RATES:
Full Page Colour .... PLN 11000.00
Mechanical Data: Type Area: 215 x 295 mm
CONSUMER: CONSUMER ELECTRONICS: Consumer Electronics Related

TEKSTYLIA W DOMU 1796213PL47A-258
Editorial: ul. Stępińska, 22/30, 00-739 WARSZAWA
Tel: 22 559 39 61 **Fax:** 22 559 39 62
Email: biuro@promedia.biz.pl **Web site:** http://www.promedia.biz.pl
Date Established: 2000; **Freq:** Quarterly; **Circ:** 3,000
Profile: Features information on home textiles and indoor decoration.
Language(s): Polish
Mechanical Data: Type Area: A4
BUSINESS: CLOTHING & TEXTILES

TELE MAGAZYN 1708745PL76C-6
Editorial: ul. Domaniewska, 41, 02-672 WARSZAWA
Tel: 22 201 41 02 **Fax:** 22 201 41 01
Email: telemagazyn@polskapresse.pl **Web site:** http://www.telemagazyn.pl
ISSN: 1231-6830
Date Established: 1991; **Freq:** Weekly; **Cover Price:** Free; **Circ:** 1,100,000
Usual Pagination: 64
Managing Director: Dorota Pacocha; **Advertising Director:** Małgorzata Cetera-Bulka
Profile: TV guide on 41 most popular TV stations plus entertainment.
Language(s): Polish
Mechanical Data: Type Area: 215x280 mm
CONSUMER: MUSIC & PERFORMING ARTS: TV & Radio

TELE MAX 1622943PL76C-1
Editorial: ul. Motorowa, 1, 04-035 WARSZAWA
Tel: 22 517 01 64 **Fax:** 22 517 03 52
Email: telemax@bauer.pl **Web site:** http://www.reklama.bauer.pl
ISSN: 1730-0673
Date Established: 2002; **Freq:** Weekly; **Circ:** 436,000
Usual Pagination: 48
Advertising Director: Izabela Sarnecka
Profile: Magazine containing TV guide and film reviews, DVD releases, celebrities and entertainment.
Language(s): Polish
Readership: Aimed at young readers aged between 12 and 18 years.
ADVERTISING RATES:
Full Page Colour .... PLN 16000.00
Mechanical Data: Type Area: 225 x 285 mm
CONSUMER: MUSIC & PERFORMING ARTS: TV & Radio

TELE ŚWIAT 1622944PL76C-10
Editorial: ul. Motorowa, 1, 04-035 WARSZAWA
Tel: 22 517 03 93 **Fax:** 22 517 05 27
Email: teleswiat@bauer.pl **Web site:** http://www.reklama.bauer.pl
ISSN: 1234-267X
Date Established: 1995; **Freq:** Weekly; **Circ:** 360,000
Usual Pagination: 96
Advertising Director: Izabela Sarnecka
Profile: Magazine containing TV films' and programmes' reviews.
Language(s): Polish
ADVERTISING RATES:
Full Page Colour .... PLN 38000.00
Mechanical Data: Type Area: 225 x 285 mm
CONSUMER: MUSIC & PERFORMING ARTS: TV & Radio

TELE TYDZIEŃ 1708750PL76C-9
Editorial: ul. Motorowa, 1, 04-035 WARSZAWA
Tel: 22 517 01 54 **Fax:** 22 517 03 53
Email: teletydz@bauer.pl **Web site:** http://www.reklama.bauer.pl
ISSN: 1230-7912
Date Established: 1993; **Freq:** Weekly; **Circ:** 1,474,606
Usual Pagination: 96
Advertising Director: Izabela Sarnecka
Profile: TV stations' guide presenting film descriptions, reportages and interviews.
Language(s): Polish
ADVERTISING RATES:
Full Page Colour .... PLN 110250.00
Mechanical Data: Type Area: 225 x 285 mm
CONSUMER: MUSIC & PERFORMING ARTS: TV & Radio

TELEINFO 1708903PL18B-10
Editorial: ul. Tytoniowa, 20, 04-228 WARSZAWA
Tel: 22 515 00 41 **Fax:** 22 812 46 77
Email: teleinfo@teleinfo.com.pl **Web site:** http://www.teleinfo.com.pl
ISSN: 1425-4999
Date Established: 1995; **Freq:** 26 issues yearly; **Circ:** 9,000
Usual Pagination: 48
Advertising Director: Ewa Kazimierska-Wiewiórska
Profile: Magazine containing news on events in the IT and telecommunication's market abroad and in Poland.
Language(s): Polish
ADVERTISING RATES:
Full Page Colour .... PLN 6000.00
Mechanical Data: Type Area: 275x235 mm
BUSINESS: ELECTRONICS: Telecommunications

TELEPROGRAM 1708879PL76C-13
Editorial: ul. Okrężna, 9, 02-916 WARSZAWA
Tel: 22 671 50 00 **Fax:** 22 671 48 88
Email: teleprogram@teleprogram.net.pl **Web site:** http://www.teleprogram.net.pl
ISSN: 1505-5442
Date Established: 1993; **Freq:** Weekly; **Cover Price:** Free; **Circ:** 1,228,291
Usual Pagination: 16
Advertising Director: Arek Gębicz
Profile: TV guide with film reviews, interviews and interesting entertainment facts.
Language(s): Polish
ADVERTISING RATES:
Full Page Colour .... PLN 73000.00
Mechanical Data: Type Area: 205 x 290, 195 x 290, 210 x 280 mm
CONSUMER: MUSIC & PERFORMING ARTS: TV & Radio

TELEWIZJA POLSAT SA 1798726PL2D-1
Editorial: ul. Ostrobramska 77, 04-175 WARSZAWA
Tel: 22 514 40 00 **Fax:** 22 514 55 50
Email: biuro@polsat.com.pl **Web site:** http://polsat.com.pl
Date Established: 1992
Language(s): Polish
BUSINESS: COMMUNICATIONS, ADVERTISING & MARKETING: Broadcasting

TELEWIZJA POLSKA SA 1798725PL2D-2
Editorial: ul. J.P. Woronicza, 17, 00-999 WARSZAWA
Tel: 22 547 80 00
Email: widzowie@tvp.pl **Web site:** http://www.tvp.pl
Date Established: 1952
Language(s): Polish
BUSINESS: COMMUNICATIONS, ADVERTISING & MARKETING: Broadcasting

TELEWIZJA PULS 1798728PL2D-3
Editorial: Chełmska, 21, 22, 00-724 WARSZAWA
Tel: 22 559 35 01 **Fax:** 22 559 35 02
Email: kontakt@pulstv.pl **Web site:** http://www.pulstv.pl
Date Established: 2004
Language(s): Polish
BUSINESS: COMMUNICATIONS, ADVERTISING & MARKETING: Broadcasting

TENISKLUB 1811033PL75H-2
Editorial: al. KEN, 21, 86, 02-722 WARSZAWA
Tel: 22 855 62 72 **Fax:** 22 641 70 15
Email: redakcja@tenisklub.pl **Web site:** http://www.tenisklub.pl
ISSN: 1734-9850
Date Established: 2005; **Freq:** 11 issues yearly; **Annual Sub.:** PLN 90.00; **Circ:** 9,500
Usual Pagination: 100
Managing Director: Magdalena Rejniak-Romer
Profile: A magazine dedicated to tennis events abroad and in Poland.
Language(s): Polish
Mechanical Data: Type Area: 210x275 mm
CONSUMER: SPORT: Racquet Sports

TERAPIA 1708887PL56A-15
Editorial: ul. Księcia Janusza, 64, 01-452 WARSZAWA **Tel:** 22 335 97 43/44 **Fax:** 22 335 97 10/50
Email: terapia@warsawvoice.pl **Web site:** http://www.terapia.com.pl
ISSN: 1230-3917
Date Established: 1993; **Freq:** Monthly; **Circ:** 14,000
Usual Pagination: 64
Advertising Director: Barbara Milczarek
Profile: Professional magazine on therapy and treatment aiming at all GPs.
Language(s): Polish
ADVERTISING RATES:
Full Page Mono .... PLN 9400.00
Mechanical Data: Type Area: 202 x 288 mm
BUSINESS: HEALTH & MEDICAL

TERAZ DOM 1811005PL4A-28
Editorial: ul. Straży Ludowej, 9, 60-465 POZNAŃ
Tel: 61 842 29 89 **Fax:** 61 842 25 59
Email: biuro@terazdom.info **Web site:** http://www.terazdom.info/go.live.php
Date Established: 2004; **Freq:** Weekly; **Cover Price:** Free; **Circ:** 10,000
Usual Pagination: 16
Advertising Director: Ilona Królikowska
Profile: Dedicated to housing issues: interior design and architecture, building, market of residential property, practical advice and professional articles written by specialists.
Language(s): Polish
ADVERTISING RATES:
Full Page Mono .... PLN 2000.00
Mechanical Data: Type Area: A4; pełnokolorowe, papier kredowy
BUSINESS: ARCHITECTURE & BUILDING: Architecture

TERAZ ROCK 1708990PL76E-1
Editorial: ul. Cedrowa, 34, 04-533 WARSZAWA
Tel: 22 517 13 60 **Fax:** 22 517 13 61
Email: redakcja@terazrock.pl **Web site:** http://www.terazrock.pl
Date Established: 1991; **Freq:** Monthly; **Circ:** 52,000
Usual Pagination: 116
Managing Director: Leszek Jastrzębski
Profile: Over the years 'Teraz/Tylko Rock' has hosted monthly articles written by the most important Polish musicians such as Czeslaw Niemen, Kazik Staszewski, Lech Janerka, Tomasz Budzynski and the members of Myslovitz band.
Language(s): Polish
Mechanical Data: Type Area: 205 x 285 mm
CONSUMER: MUSIC & PERFORMING ARTS: Pop Music

TEXTILWIRTSCHAFT MODA FORUM 1708845PL47A-253
Editorial: ul. Kierbedzia, 4, 00-728 WARSZAWA
Tel: 22 320 15 33 **Fax:** 22 320 15 40
Email: mlesinska@unit.pl **Web site:** http://www.unit.com.pl
ISSN: 1506-2805
Date Established: 1998
Circ: 6,000
Usual Pagination: 44
Advertising Director: Paulina Siódmak
Profile: Poland's leading trade magazine for fashion and textile business, features regularly international fashion trends from important fashion shows, reports about national and international fairs and highlights Polish fashion.
Language(s): Polish
ADVERTISING RATES:
Full Page Colour .... PLN 5900.00
Mechanical Data: Type Area: 234 x 331 mm
BUSINESS: CLOTHING & TEXTILES

TINA 1616511PL74A-1006
Editorial: ul. Motorowa, 1, 04-035 WARSZAWA
Tel: 22 517 01 37 **Fax:** 22 517 01 19
Email: tina@bauer.pl **Web site:** http://www.reklama.bauer.pl
ISSN: 1230-3372
Date Established: 1992; **Freq:** 26 issues yearly; **Circ:** 484,000
Usual Pagination: 84
Managing Director: Monika Krokiewicz; **Advertising Director:** Ewa Kozłowska
Profile: Magazine focusing on beauty, health, natural medicine, interior design, gardening and cooking.
Language(s): Polish
Readership: Aimed at women between 24 and 54 years.
ADVERTISING RATES:
Full Page Colour .... PLN 58700.00

Mechanical Data: Type Area: 225 x 285 mm
CONSUMER: WOMEN'S INTEREST CONSUMER MAGAZINES: Women's Interest

TO & OWO
1622945PL76C-8
Editorial: ul. Wrocławska, 20, 91-310 ŁÓDŹ
Tel: 42 676 04 19 **Fax:** 42 676 05 92
Email: toiowo@bauer.pl **Web site:** http://www.reklama.bauer.pl
ISSN: 1230-8331
Date Established: 1989; **Freq:** Weekly; **Circ:** 669,000
Usual Pagination: 96
Advertising Director: Izabela Sarnecka
Profile: Guide on satellite television programmes and includes interviews and gossip.
Language(s): Polish
Readership: Read mainly by women aged 25 to 44 years.
ADVERTISING RATES:
Full Page Colour .... PLN 27500.00
Mechanical Data: Type Area: 210 x 280 mm
CONSUMER: MUSIC & PERFORMING ARTS: TV & Radio

TO LUBIĘ!
1929120PL74A-1041
Editorial: ul. św. Antoniego, 7, 50-073 WROCŁAW
Tel: 71 344 77 75 **Fax:** 71 346 01 74
Email: tolubie@phoenix.pl **Web site:** http://www.phoenix.pl
ISSN: 1730-2714
Date Established: 2008; **Freq:** Monthly; **Circ:** 300,000
Usual Pagination: 32
Profile: Women's interest magazine covering health, slimming, beauty, fashion, celebrities, cooking, travel.
Language(s): Polish
Mechanical Data: Type Area: 215 x 305 mm
CONSUMER: WOMEN'S INTEREST CONSUMER MAGAZINES: Women's Interest

TOP CLASS
1795678PL91E-3
Editorial: ul. Kierbedzia, 4, 00-728 WARSZAWA
Tel: 22 320 15 25 **Fax:** 22 320 15 40
Email: info@unit.com.pl **Web site:** http://www.unit.com.pl
ISSN: 1429-0898
Date Established: 1997; **Freq:** Quarterly; **Circ:** 15,000
Usual Pagination: 88
Advertising Director: Joanna Pratzer
Profile: Magazine with information on luxury and beautiful goods.
Language(s): English
ADVERTISING RATES:
Full Page Colour .... PLN 9500.00
Mechanical Data: Type Area: 210 x 297 mm
CONSUMER: RECREATION & LEISURE: Lifestyle

TOPSPEED
1796079PL77D-2
Editorial: ul. Cedrowa, 34, 04-533 WARSZAWA
Tel: 22 517 13 76 **Fax:** 22 517 13 70
Email: topspeed@topspeed.pl **Web site:** http://www.topspeed.pl
ISSN: 1734-8285
Date Established: 2005
Circ: 30,000
Usual Pagination: 84
Language(s): English
Mechanical Data: Type Area: 205 x 285 mm
CONSUMER: MOTORING & CYCLING: Motor Sports

TPS - TWÓJ PRZEGLĄD STOMATOLOGICZNY
1810952PL56D-2
Editorial: al. Rożdzieńskiego, 188, 40-203 KATOWICE **Tel:** 32 788 52 54 **Fax:** 32 788 51 65
Email: stomatologia@elamed.pl **Web site:** http://www.tps.elamed.pl
ISSN: 1426-2789
Date Established: 1997; **Freq:** Monthly
Usual Pagination: 80
Profile: A magazine focused on dental clinical advice in treatment, materials and equipment.
Language(s): Polish
Mechanical Data: Type Area: 204 x 290 mm
BUSINESS: HEALTH & MEDICAL: Dental

TRAILER MAGAZINE
1709058PL77A-29
Editorial: ul. 10 Lutego, 5, 4, 81-366 GDYNIA
Tel: 58 621 15 51 **Fax:** 58 620 47 51
Email: fabas@fabas.pl **Web site:** http://www.trailer.pl
ISSN: 1644-0439
Date Established: 2002
Circ: 15,000
Usual Pagination: 64
Managing Director: Aleksandra Zielińska
Profile: A magazine on truck transport: interesting reportages, news on truck tests, truck tuning, etc.
Language(s): Polish
Mechanical Data: Type Area: 212x298 mm
CONSUMER: MOTORING & CYCLING: Motoring

TV-SAT MAGAZYN
1708888PL76C-14
Editorial: ul. Traugutta, 25, 90-113 ŁÓDŹ
Tel: 42 632 99 12 **Fax:** 42 639 78 83
Email: redakcja@tvsat.pl **Web site:** http://www.tvsat.pl
ISSN: 0860-9349
Date Established: 1989; **Freq:** Monthly; **Circ:** 80,000
Usual Pagination: 48
Language(s): English
Mechanical Data: Type Area: 205 x 285 mm
CONSUMER: MUSIC & PERFORMING ARTS: TV & Radio

TWÓJ BIZNES
1819429PL14A-99
Editorial: ul. Okopowa, 58/72, 01-042 WARSZAWA
Tel: 22 530 43 66 **Fax:** 22 530 43 39
Email: twojbiznes@infor.pl **Web site:** http://www.twojbiznes.infor.pl
ISSN: 1427-5112
Date Established: 2006; **Freq:** Monthly
Usual Pagination: 80
Managing Director: Mariusz Drozdowicz; **Advertising Director:** Wioletta Biała
Profile: Contains practical information and business advice for small and medium-sized companies.
Language(s): Polish
ADVERTISING RATES:
Full Page Mono .... PLN 20000.00
Mechanical Data: Type Area: A4
BUSINESS: COMMERCE, INDUSTRY & MANAGEMENT

TWÓJ STYL
754774PL74B-100
Editorial: al. Stanów Zjednoczonych, 61a, 04-028 WARSZAWA **Tel:** 22 516 34 34 **Fax:** 22 516 34 60
Email: redakcja@twojstyl.com.pl **Web site:** http://www.twojstyl.pl
ISSN: 0867-1826
Date Established: 1990; **Freq:** Monthly; **Circ:** 286,374
Usual Pagination: 196
Managing Director: Monika Krokiewicz; **Advertising Director:** Beata Madeja
Profile: Women's magazine featuring articles on fashion, health and beauty, family issues, careers and lifestyle.
Language(s): Polish
Readership: Aimed at women of all ages.
ADVERTISING RATES:
Full Page Colour .... PLN 78500.00
Mechanical Data: Type Area: 230 x 295 mm
CONSUMER: WOMEN'S INTEREST CONSUMER MAGAZINES: Women's Interest - Fashion

TWÓJ WEEKEND
1796136PL86A-1
Editorial: ul. św. Antoniego, 15, 50-049 WROCŁAW
Tel: 71 335 21 60 **Fax:** 71 335 21 61
Email: redakcja@twojweekend.pl **Web site:** http://www.twojweekend.pl
ISSN: 1230-8706
Date Established: 1992; **Freq:** 26 issues yearly; **Circ:** 87,400
Usual Pagination: 48
Profile: Men's magazine covering entertainment, erotica, sex advice, sports, cars.
Language(s): Polish
Mechanical Data: Type Area: 210x297 mm
CONSUMER: ADULT & GAY MAGAZINES: Adult Magazines

TWOJA KOMÓRKA
1839885PL18B-7
Editorial: ul. Porannej Bryzy 8, 03-284 WARSZAWA
Tel: 22 864 16 83 **Fax:** 22 864 27 17
Email: redakcja@t-k.pl **Web site:** http://www.t-k.pl
Date Established: 1998; **Freq:** Daily; **Cover Price:** Paid; **Circ:** 15,000 Unique Users
Editor-in-Chief: Piotr Rabiej; **Advertising Manager:** Piotr Szczypiór
Profile: Website containing everything about mobile phones: tests, news and advice, games and software.
Language(s): Polish
BUSINESS: ELECTRONICS: Telecommunications

TWOJE DZIECKO
1623258PL74D-4
Editorial: ul. Wiejska, 19, 00-480 WARSZAWA
Tel: 22 584 23 35 **Fax:** 22 584 23 36
Email: info@twojedziecko.pl **Web site:** http://www.twojedziecko.pl
ISSN: 0137-7256
Date Established: 1952; **Freq:** Monthly; **Circ:** 137,000
Usual Pagination: 132
Managing Director: Alicja Modzelewska; **Advertising Director:** Krystyna Kurmanowska
Profile: Magazine focusing on parenting issues and all aspects of childcare.
Language(s): English
Readership: Read by parents of babies and toddlers.
ADVERTISING RATES:
Full Page Colour .... PLN 24750.00
Mechanical Data: Type Area: 205 x 270 mm
CONSUMER: WOMEN'S INTEREST CONSUMER MAGAZINES: Child Care

TWOJE IMPERIUM
1622954PL74Q-5
Editorial: ul. Motorowa, 1, 04-035 WARSZAWA
Tel: 22 517 02 95 **Fax:** 22 517 04 15
Email: timp@bauer.pl **Web site:** http://www.reklama.bauer.pl
ISSN: 1234-6918
Date Established: 1995; **Freq:** Weekly; **Circ:** 457,000
Usual Pagination: 48
Advertising Director: Ewa Kozłowska
Profile: Lifestyle magazine focusing on TV, cinema and pop stars.
Language(s): Polish
Readership: Read mainly by women aged 25 to 55 years.
ADVERTISING RATES:
Full Page Colour .... PLN 27000.00
Mechanical Data: Type Area: 225 x 285 mm
CONSUMER: WOMEN'S INTEREST CONSUMER MAGAZINES: Lifestyle

TYGODNIK PODHALAŃSKI
1929166PL67J-4
Editorial: ul. Kościuszki, 3, 34-500 ZAKOPANE
Tel: 18 200 00 00 **Fax:** 18 200 00 01
Email: tp@tygodnikpodhalanski.pl **Web site:** http://www.tygodnikpodhalanski.pl
ISSN: 1231-5818
Date Established: 1989; **Freq:** Weekly; **Circ:** 22,000
Usual Pagination: 68
Profile: Regional weekly newspaper covering events from Podhale region.
Language(s): Polish
Mechanical Data: Type Area: A3
REGIONAL DAILY & SUNDAY NEWSPAPERS: Regional Newspapers (excl. dailies)

TYGODNIK POWSZECHNY
1614310PL65J-3
Editorial: ul. Wiślna, 12, 31-007 KRAKÓW
Tel: 12 422 25 18 **Fax:** 12 421 67 31
Email: redakcja@tygodnik.com.pl **Web site:** http://www.tygodnik.onet.pl
ISSN: 0041-4808
Date Established: 1945; **Freq:** Weekly; **Circ:** 40,000
Usual Pagination: 48
Advertising Director: Rafał Rudziarczyk
Profile: Catholic newspaper focusing on national and international news, politics, religion, society and culture.
Language(s): English
Mechanical Data: Type Area: 274 x 358 mm
NATIONAL DAILY & SUNDAY NEWSPAPERS: National Weekly Newspapers

UBEZPIECZENIA I PRAWO PRACY
1929198PL1D-4
Editorial: ul. Owocowa, 8, 66-400 GORZÓW WLKP.
Tel: 95 720 85 40 **Fax:** 95 720 85 60
Email: ubezpieczenia@gofin.pl **Web site:** http://www.gofin.pl
ISSN: 1507-6962
Date Established: 1999; **Freq:** 26 issues yearly; **Circ:** 29,000
Usual Pagination: 70
Profile: Publication dedicated to social insurance, health insurance and sick leaves payments, job legal aspects of workers.
Language(s): Polish
ADVERTISING RATES:
Full Page Colour .... PLN 2500.00
Mechanical Data: Type Area: 170 x 240 mm
BUSINESS: FINANCE & ECONOMICS: Insurance

ULTRAMARYNA
1708715PL72J-1
Editorial: pl. Sejmu Śląskiego, 2, 40-032 KATOWICE
Tel: 32 785 77 77 **Fax:** 32 785 77 88
Email: poczta@ultramaryna.pl **Web site:** http://www.ultramaryna.pl
ISSN: 1642-3437
Date Established: 2001; **Freq:** Monthly; **Cover Price:** Free; **Circ:** 10,000
Usual Pagination: 32
Profile: Cultural-entertaining, Silesian news.
Language(s): English
Mechanical Data: Type Area: 165 x 210 mm
LOCAL NEWSPAPERS: Community Newsletters

URODA
754786PL74A-1000
Editorial: ul. Wiejska, 19, 00-480 WARSZAWA
Tel: 22 584 22 00 **Fax:** 22 584 25 00
Email: uroda.redakcja@edipresse.pl **Web site:** http://www.uroda.pl
ISSN: 0500-7194
Date Established: 1957; **Freq:** Monthly; **Circ:** 132,000
Usual Pagination: 148
Managing Director: Alicja Modzelewska; **Advertising Director:** Iwona Czapran
Profile: Magazine focusing on health and beauty, family issues, fashion, travel and careers.
Language(s): Polish
Readership: Aimed at professional women.
ADVERTISING RATES:
Full Page Colour .... PLN 28000.00
Mechanical Data: Type Area: 203 x 257 mm
CONSUMER: WOMEN'S INTEREST CONSUMER MAGAZINES: Women's Interest

VIDEO MIX
1708908PL78R-5
Editorial: ul. Tytoniowa, 20, 04-228 WARSZAWA
Tel: 22 515 00 13 **Fax:** 22 613 25 84
Email: e.sucharzewska@migutmedia.pl **Web site:** http://www.migutmedia.pl
ISSN: 1730-4660
Date Established: 1991
Circ: 15,000
Usual Pagination: 98
Profile: A magazine featuring latest home electronics' equipment.
Language(s): Polish
Mechanical Data: Type Area: A4
CONSUMER: CONSUMER ELECTRONICS: Consumer Electronics Related

VILLA
1708901PL4A-15
Editorial: ul. Tytoniowa, 20, 04-228 WARSZAWA
Tel: 22 515 00 00 **Fax:** 22 613 25 84
Email: villa@migutmedia.pl **Web site:** http://www.villa.net.pl
ISSN: 1730-4911
Date Established: 2003; **Freq:** Monthly; **Circ:** 26,000
Usual Pagination: 144
Advertising Director: Katarzyna Łobejko
Profile: Presents stylish interiors - houses, mansions and apartments, lifestyle, travel, interviews with leading designers and stories featuring most prestigious trademarks or companies.
Language(s): Polish
Readership: Targets educated, wealthy and active homeowners, who appreciate and enjoy beautiful interiors, furniture and accessories.
ADVERTISING RATES:
Full Page Colour .... PLN 16900.00
Mechanical Data: Type Area: 225 x 295 mm
BUSINESS: ARCHITECTURE & BUILDING: Architecture

VIP POLITYKA PRAWO GOSPODARKA
1796130PL14A-118
Editorial: ul. Korfantego, 75, 01-496 WARSZAWA
Tel: 22 832 24 53 **Fax:** 22 832 24 99
Email: vip@maxmedia.org.pl **Web site:** http://www.magazynvip.pl
ISSN: 1732-9361
Date Established: 2003; **Freq:** Quarterly; **Circ:** 15,000
Usual Pagination: 120
Profile: Magazine on business, politics, culture and events review.
Language(s): Polish
ADVERTISING RATES:
Full Page Colour .... PLN 5000.00
Mechanical Data: Type Area: A4
BUSINESS: COMMERCE, INDUSTRY & MANAGEMENT

VISUAL COMMUNICATION
1928985PL2A-26
Editorial: ul. Fredry, 1, 18, 61-701 POZNAŃ
Tel: 61 855 19 90 **Fax:** 61 855 19 90
Email: redakcja.vc@printernet.pl **Web site:** http://www.visualcommunication.pl
Freq: Monthly; **Circ:** 5,000
Usual Pagination: 68
Profile: Specialized magazine dedicated to visual communications, outdoor and indoor advertising, lighting systems, design.
Language(s): Polish
ADVERTISING RATES:
Full Page Colour .... PLN 6500.00
BUSINESS: COMMUNICATIONS, ADVERTISING & MARKETING

VITA
1623260PL74G-2
Editorial: ul. Wiejska, 19, 00-480 WARSZAWA
Tel: 22 584 22 00 **Fax:** 22 584 24 10
Email: info@vita.pl **Web site:** http://www.vita.pl
ISSN: 1505-9294
Date Established: 1998; **Freq:** Monthly; **Circ:** 166,000
Usual Pagination: 100
Managing Director: Alicja Modzelewska; **Advertising Director:** Edyta Kordowska
Profile: Magazine focusing on health and beauty issues, promoting a healthy diet and lifestyle.
Language(s): Polish
ADVERTISING RATES:
Full Page Colour .... PLN 25500.00
Mechanical Data: Type Area: 147 x 208 mm
CONSUMER: WOMEN'S INTEREST CONSUMER MAGAZINES: Slimming & Health

VIVA!
1623179PL74Q-4
Editorial: ul. Wiejska, 19, 00-480 WARSZAWA
Tel: 22 584 23 57 **Fax:** 22 584 23 56
Web site: http://www.viva.pl
ISSN: 1426-9554
Date Established: 1997; **Freq:** 26 issues yearly; **Circ:** 341,000
Usual Pagination: 140
Managing Director: Alicja Modzelewska; **Advertising Director:** Agnieszka Cwalina
Profile: Magazine covering lifestyle features, includes interviews with famous people, articles on travel, history, events and beauty.
Language(s): Polish
Readership: Aimed at women aged between 20 and 40 years.
ADVERTISING RATES:
Full Page Colour .... PLN 55000.00
Mechanical Data: Type Area: 230 x 287 mm
CONSUMER: WOMEN'S INTEREST CONSUMER MAGAZINES: Lifestyle

VOYAGE
1708693PL89A-4

Editorial: ul. Wilcza, 50/52, 00-679 WARSZAWA
Tel: 22 421 10 00 **Fax:** 22 421 11 11
Email: redakcja@voyage.pl **Web site:** http://www.marquard.pl/voyage.html
ISSN: 1505-0882
Date Established: 1998; **Freq:** Monthly; **Circ:** 42,000
Usual Pagination: 134
Advertising Director: Monika Wdowiak
Profile: Travel magazine for those keen on opening forgotten or exclusive corners of the world, a practical guide to the most interesting and beautiful parts of Poland and the world.
Language(s): Polish
Readership: targets those who travel a lot and are looking for inspiration for his next expedition, and the dreamers who are just exploring the world through him.
ADVERTISING RATES:
Full Page Colour .... PLN 22000.00
Mechanical Data: Type Area: 220 x 285 mm
CONSUMER: HOLIDAYS & TRAVEL: Travel

W AKCJI
1810972PL54A-2

Editorial: al. Roździeńskiego, 188, 40-203 KATOWICE **Tel:** 32 788 52 58 **Fax:** 32 788 51 68
Email: wakcji@elamed.pl **Web site:** http://www.wakcji.elamed.pl
ISSN: 1643-7373
Date Established: 2001; **Freq:** 6 issues yearly
Usual Pagination: 70
Profile: Dedicated to fire prevention, strategies in fire protection and fire fighting, analysis of fire fighting actions.
Language(s): Polish
ADVERTISING RATES:
Full Page Mono .... PLN 1600.00
Full Page Colour .... PLN 2100.00
Mechanical Data: Type Area: 170 x 248 mm
BUSINESS: SAFETY & SECURITY: Fire Fighting

W DRODZE
1810901PL87-7

Editorial: ul. Kościuszki, 99, 60-920 POZNAŃ
Tel: 61 850 47 22 **Fax:** 61 850 17 82
Email: miesiecznik@wdrodze.pl **Web site:** http://www.mateusz.pl/wdrodze
ISSN: 0137-480X
Date Established: 1973; **Freq:** Monthly; **Circ:** 2,500
Usual Pagination: 128
Advertising Director: Agnieszka Kaczmarek
Profile: Christian magazine about Church problems, Bible solutions, social issues and society.
Language(s): English
Mechanical Data: Type Area: A5
CONSUMER: RELIGIOUS

WARSAW BUSINESS JOURNAL
1614364PL14A-6

Editorial: ul. Elbląska, 15/17, 01-747 WARSZAWA
Tel: 22 639 85 68 **Fax:** 22 639 85 69
Email: wbj@wbj.pl **Web site:** http://www.wbj.pl
ISSN: 1233-7889
Date Established: 1994; **Freq:** Weekly; **Circ:** 22,500
Usual Pagination: 24
Managing Director: Monika Stawicka; **Advertising Director:** Agnieszka Brejwo
Profile: Journal featuring investigative articles concerning all latest business news and issues. Includes up-to-date information on all leading companies and business executives.
Language(s): English
Readership: Aimed at managers, executives and decision makers.
ADVERTISING RATES:
Full Page Colour .... PLN 10480.00
Mechanical Data: Type Area: 290x410 mm
BUSINESS: COMMERCE, INDUSTRY & MANAGEMENT

WARSAW INSIDER
1709070PL89C-30

Editorial: ul. Elbląska 15/17, 01-747 WARSZAWA
Tel: 22 639 85 67 **Fax:** 22 639 85 69
Email: warsawinsider@warsawinsider.pl **Web site:** http://www.warsawinsider.pl
ISSN: 1643-1723
Date Established: 1996; **Freq:** Monthly; **Circ:** 20,000
Usual Pagination: 96
Managing Director: Monika Stawicka
Profile: Comprehensive monthly guide to good living and fast times in Poland's capital. Entertainment, information, culture, travel, food and drink in a compact glossy magazine.
Language(s): English
ADVERTISING RATES:
Full Page Colour .... PLN 7150.00
Mechanical Data: Type Area: B5mm
CONSUMER: HOLIDAYS & TRAVEL: Entertainment Guides

THE WARSAW VOICE
1614374PL65J-4

Editorial: ul. Księcia Janusza, 64, 01-452 WARSZAWA **Tel:** 22 335 97 00/01 **Fax:** 22 335 97 10
Email: voice@warsawvoice.pl **Web site:** http://www.warsawvoice.pl
ISSN: 0860-7591
Date Established: 1988; **Freq:** Weekly; **Circ:** 10,500
Usual Pagination: 40
News Editor: Witold Żygulski; **Managing Editor:** Leszek Żmijewski
Profile: Newspaper focusing on national and international news, politics, business, culture and entertainment.
Language(s): English
Readership: Read mainly by foreign business people living and working in Poland, professionals, diplomats, academics, teachers and students.
Mechanical Data: Type Area: A4
NATIONAL DAILY & SUNDAY NEWSPAPERS: National Weekly Newspapers

WĘDKARSKI ŚWIAT
1708757PL92-1

Editorial: ul. Miedziana, 11, 00-835 WARSZAWA
Tel: 22 652 19 21 **Fax:** 22 652 15 15
Email: redakcja@wedkarskiswiat.pl **Web site:** http://www.wedkarskiswiat.pl
ISSN: 1425-719X
Date Established: 1996; **Freq:** Monthly; **Circ:** 60,000
Usual Pagination: 96
Profile: Magazine covering angling, active tourism and ecological issues.
Language(s): Polish
Mechanical Data: Type Area: A4
CONSUMER: ANGLING & FISHING

WĘDKARSTWO MOJE HOBBY
1709038PL92-2

Editorial: ul. Saska, 9a, 03-968 WARSZAWA
Tel: 22 616 16 20 **Fax:** 22 616 15 24
Email: gazeta@wedkarstwomojehobby.pl **Web site:** http://www.wmh.pl
Date Established: 2002; **Freq:** Monthly; **Circ:** 40,000
Usual Pagination: 96
Profile: Magazine dedicated to recreational angling in Poland and abroad.
Language(s): Polish
ADVERTISING RATES:
Full Page Colour .... PLN 11000.00
Mechanical Data: Type Area: 220 x 275 mm
CONSUMER: ANGLING & FISHING

WĘDKARZ POLSKI
1708717PL92-3

Editorial: ul. Łódzka, 19, 50-521 WROCŁAW
Tel: 71 791 30 14 **Fax:** 71 791 30 15
Email: redakcja@wedkarz.pl **Web site:** http://www.wedkarz.pl
ISSN: 0867-3195
Date Established: 1990; **Freq:** Monthly; **Cover Price:** PLN 8.50; **Circ:** 92,000
Usual Pagination: 84
Profile: A magazine dedicated to fishing and angling.
Language(s): Polish
Mechanical Data: Type Area: 275x205 mm
CONSUMER: ANGLING & FISHING

WEGETARIAŃSKI ŚWIAT
1708650PL74G-4

Editorial: ul. Bruna, 34, 02-594 WARSZAWA
Tel: 22 825 25 00 **Fax:** 22 849 86 00
Email: redakcja@ws.most.org.pl **Web site:** http://www.wegetarianski.pl
ISSN: 1231-0271
Date Established: 1994; **Freq:** Monthly; **Circ:** 24,000
Usual Pagination: 48
Language(s): English
Mechanical Data: Type Area: A4
CONSUMER: WOMEN'S INTEREST CONSUMER MAGAZINES: Slimming & Health

WERANDA
1708765PL4A-11

Editorial: ul. Malczewskiego, 19, 02-612 WARSZAWA **Tel:** 22 854 14 14 **Fax:** 22 854 14 49
Email: beata@weranda.pl **Web site:** http://www.weranda.pl
ISSN: 1641-1382
Date Established: 2001; **Freq:** Monthly; **Circ:** 38,000
Usual Pagination: 194
Advertising Director: Jolanta Otrębska
Profile: Presents Polish houses, residential palaces and gardens, interior design.
Language(s): Polish
Mechanical Data: Type Area: 225 x 295 mm
BUSINESS: ARCHITECTURE & BUILDING: Architecture

WETERYNARIA W PRAKTYCE
1810963PL64H-2

Editorial: al. Roździeńskiego, 188, 40-203 KATOWICE **Tel:** 32 788 51 51 **Fax:** 32 203 93 56
Email: weterynaria@elamed.pl **Web site:** http://www.weterynaria.elamed.pl
ISSN: 1732-1999
Date Established: 2004; **Freq:** 6 issues yearly
Usual Pagination: 80
Advertising Director: Honorata Guzik
Profile: Professional magazine on veterinary with clinic description of animals treatment, practical advice and vet news.
Language(s): Polish
ADVERTISING RATES:
Full Page Mono .... PLN 3000.00
Full Page Colour .... PLN 4000.00
Mechanical Data: Type Area: 204 x 290 mm
BUSINESS: OTHER CLASSIFICATIONS: Veterinary

WHAT'S UP IN WARSAW
1708976PL89C-28

Editorial: al. 3 Maja, 12, 411, 00-391 WARSZAWA
Tel: 22 625 78 79 **Fax:** 22 625 78 79
Email: redakcja@whatsup.pl **Web site:** http://www.whatsup.pl
ISSN: 1644-7182
Date Established: 2002; **Freq:** Quarterly; **Cover Price:** Free; **Circ:** 10,000
Usual Pagination: 32
Profile: Capital city guide on hotels, business centres, tourist information points, airports, embassies, restaurants, with articles concerning new trends in art, essential economic and social matters, lifestyle, health and sport.
Language(s): English
Mechanical Data: Type Area: 205x275 mm
CONSUMER: HOLIDAYS & TRAVEL: Entertainment Guides

WIADOMOŚCI ELEKTROTECHNICZNE
1811075PL17-2

Editorial: ul. Ratuszowa, 11, 739, 03-450 WARSZAWA **Tel:** 22 619 43 60 **Fax:** 22 619 43 60
Email: red.we@sigma-not.pl **Web site:** http://sigma-not.pl
ISSN: 0043-5112
Date Established: 1933; **Freq:** Monthly
Profile: Focused on contemporary strong power electro-technologies: batteries and cells, equipment, automatics, testing and certification, work safety, industrial electronics, electric general usage appliances, power generation, power-electronics, electro-installations, cables and conduits, machines and transformers, materials and technologies, measurement, electric drive, standardization and regulations, lightning and electric shock protection, electro-power networks, lighting technologies.
Language(s): Polish
Readership: Aimed at design engineers and users of power machinery, equipment and systems, power transmission lines, distribution equipment and electrical installations, staff of technical universities and electrical vocational schools.
ADVERTISING RATES:
Full Page Mono .... PLN 1400.00
Full Page Colour .... PLN 2800.00
BUSINESS: ELECTRICAL

WIADOMOŚCI HANDLOWE
1795999PL14R-3

Editorial: ul. Wałbrzyska, 11, 254, 02-739 WARSZAWA **Tel:** 22 549 94 50 **Fax:** 22 549 94 50
Email: info@wiadomoscihandlowe.com.pl **Web site:** http://wiadomoscihandlowe.com.pl
ISSN: 1643-8787
Date Established: 2002; **Freq:** Monthly; **Cover Price:** Free; **Circ:** 65,000
Usual Pagination: 52
Editor: Anna Krężlewicz; **Advertising Director:** Iwona Szwan
Profile: Professional publication on developments of commerce and trade markets, FMCG branch market news.
Language(s): Polish
ADVERTISING RATES:
Full Page Colour .... PLN 29800.00
Mechanical Data: Type Area: 287 x 370 mm
BUSINESS: COMMERCE, INDUSTRY & MANAGEMENT: Commerce Related

WIADOMOŚCI KOSMETYCZNE
1796108PL15A-4

Editorial: ul. Wałbrzyska, 11, 254, 02-793 WARSZAWA **Tel:** 22 549 94 60 **Fax:** 22 549 94 50
Email: redaktor@wiadomoscikosmetyczne.pl **Web site:** http://www.wiadomoscikosmetyczne.pl
ISSN: 1895-3948
Date Established: 2002; **Freq:** Monthly; **Cover Price:** Free; **Circ:** 13,000
Usual Pagination: 40
Editor: Anna Klichowska; **Advertising Director:** Bożena Graczyk
Profile: Magazine covering news form cosmetics trade and industry, providing reliable information about trends in this market and articles concerning cosmetics managers in stores, reviewing current legislation, covering new products and equipment associated with the department stores.
Language(s): Polish
ADVERTISING RATES:
Full Page Colour .... PLN 14900.00
Mechanical Data: Type Area: A4
BUSINESS: COSMETICS & HAIRDRESSING: Cosmetics

WIADOMOŚCI TURYSTYCZNE
1696189PL50-5

Editorial: ul. Wawelska, 78, 30, 02-034 WARSZAWA
Tel: 22 822 20 16 **Fax:** 22 817 63 39
Email: wt@wiadomosciturystyczne.pl **Web site:** http://www.wiadomosciturystyczne.pl
ISSN: 1641-2451
Date Established: 2000; **Freq:** 26 issues yearly; **Circ:** 6,000
Usual Pagination: 20
Advertising Director: Jagoda Walczak
Profile: Journal of the Polish tourism industry. Features tourist events taking place in Poland and abroad.
Language(s): Polish
Readership: Aimed at tourists.
ADVERTISING RATES:
Full Page Colour .... PLN 6200.00
Mechanical Data: Type Area: A3
BUSINESS: TRAVEL & TOURISM

WIDEOCHIRURGIA I INNE TECHNIKI MAŁOINWAZYJNE
1796199PL56A-33

Editorial: ul. Banacha, 1a, 02-097 WARSZAWA
Tel: 22 599 25 43 **Fax:** 22 599 15 45
Email: office@videosurgeryjournal.com **Web site:** http://www.termedia.pl/magazine.php?magazine_id=42&magazine_subpage=CURRENT
ISSN: 1895-4588
Date Established: 2006; **Freq:** Quarterly; **Circ:** 1,000
Usual Pagination: 80
Managing Director: Andrzej Kordas
Profile: Professional publication about general surgery, gynaecology surgery, urology surgery and neurosurgery, laparoscopy and endoscopic surgery.
Language(s): Polish
Mechanical Data: Type Area: A4
BUSINESS: HEALTH & MEDICAL

WIEDZA I ŻYCIE
1201744PL94J-300

Editorial: ul. Garażowa, 7, 02-651 WARSZAWA
Tel: 22 607 77 71 **Fax:** 22 848 22 66
Email: wiedzaizycie@proszynskimedia.pl **Web site:** http://www.wiedzaizycie.pl
ISSN: 0137-8929
Date Established: 1926; **Freq:** Monthly; **Circ:** 70,000
Usual Pagination: 80
Profile: Magazine focusing on popular science. Includes articles on astronomy, biology, physics, medicine and archaeology.
Language(s): Polish
Readership: Aimed at students, teachers and scholars.
Mechanical Data: Type Area: 205 x 275 mm
CONSUMER: OTHER CLASSIFICATIONS: Popular Science

WIELKI BŁĘKIT
1811034PL75M-6

Editorial: ul. Ogrodowa, 28/30, 00-896 WARSZAWA
Tel: 22 620 01 68 **Fax:** 22 620 01 68
Email: redakcja@wielkiblekit.pl **Web site:** http://www.wielkiblekit.pl
ISSN: 1732-9116
Date Established: 2004; **Freq:** 6 issues yearly; **Circ:** 8,000
Usual Pagination: 76
Profile: A magazine dedicated to travelling and diving.
Language(s): Polish
Mechanical Data: Type Area: 215x280 mm
CONSUMER: SPORT: Water Sports

WIĘŹ
1708964PL87-9

Editorial: ul. Trębacka, 3, 00-074 WARSZAWA
Tel: 22 827 29 17 **Fax:** 22 827 29 17
Email: wiez@wiez.com.pl **Web site:** http://www.wiez.com.pl
ISSN: 0511-9405
Date Established: 1958; **Freq:** Monthly; **Circ:** 3,000
Usual Pagination: 162
Profile: Covers most important problems of religious, social and political life, culture and history.
Language(s): Polish
Mechanical Data: Type Area: A5
CONSUMER: RELIGIOUS

WIK
1795986PL89C-34

Editorial: ul. Postępu, 18b, 02-676 WARSZAWA
Tel: 22 874 51 44 **Fax:** 22 606 05 48
Email: redakcja@wik.com.pl **Web site:** http://www.wik.com.pl
Freq: Weekly; **Cover Price:** Free
Editor: Karolina Keller
Profile: Magazine providing information about the most interesting events in the capital, premieres at cinemas and theaters, and TV programs; Warsaw restaurants and clubs offer trips on weekends and active leisure time.
Language(s): English
Supplement to: Wprost
CONSUMER: HOLIDAYS & TRAVEL: Entertainment Guides

WIRTUALNEMEDIA.PL
1878064PL2A-37

Editorial: ul. Dąbrowszczaków 24A / 95, GDAŃSK 80-365 **Fax:** 58 7181250
Email: redakcja@wirtualnemedia.pl **Web site:** http://www.wirtualnemedia.pl
Freq: Daily; **Circ:** 626,450 Unique Users
Profile: Wirtualnemedia.pl is the largest Polish media website, devoted to television, radio, newspapers, internet, advertising, telecommunications, public relations, marketing research and the economy. Wirtualnemedia.pl is updated daily with latest information.
Language(s): Polish
BUSINESS: COMMUNICATIONS, ADVERTISING & MARKETING

WŁASNY BIZNES FRANCHISING
1796117PL14A-77

Editorial: ul. Brązownicza, 16, 01-929 WARSZAWA
Tel: 22 560 80 20 **Fax:** 22 560 80 21
Email: redakcja@franchising.pl **Web site:** http://www.wlasnybiznes.com
ISSN: 1730-3109
Date Established: 2003; **Freq:** Monthly; **Circ:** 12,000

Usual Pagination: 100
Managing Director: Michał Wiśniewski; **Advertising Director:** Małgorzata Boruń
Profile: Magazine on business setup, business strategies, economic and financial news.
Language(s): Polish
Mechanical Data: Type Area: 210x282 mm
BUSINESS: COMMERCE, INDUSTRY & MANAGEMENT

WŁASNY DOM Z KONCEPTEM
1708797PL4A-12
Editorial: ul. Bacciarellego, 54 bud. C, 51-649 WROCŁAW **Tel:** 71 348 22 14 **Fax:** 71 347 83 87
Email: redakcja@wlasnydom.pl **Web site:** http://www.wlasnydom.pl
ISSN: 1509-3042
Date Established: 1998; **Freq:** Monthly; **Circ:** 25,000
Usual Pagination: 112
Advertising Director: Paweł Jasiński
Profile: Provides practical advice for those building or renovating own house presenting ready projects for detached houses.
Language(s): Polish
Mechanical Data: Type Area: 215 x 300 mm
BUSINESS: ARCHITECTURE & BUILDING: Architecture

WNĘTRZA
1796210PL4B-8
Editorial: ul. Burleska, 9, 01-939 WARSZAWA
Tel: 22 568 99 82 **Fax:** 22 568 99 77
Email: dorota@irbj.pl
ISSN: 1733-5477
Date Established: 2004
Circ: 40,000
Usual Pagination: 290
Managing Director: Ernest Jagodziński; **Advertising Director:** Iza Konikowska
Profile: A-Z information on interiors and interior design.
Language(s): Polish
Mechanical Data: Type Area: 220 x 290 mm
BUSINESS: ARCHITECTURE & BUILDING: Interior Design & Flooring

WODOCIĄGI-KANALIZACJA
1811003PL32B-1
Editorial: ul. Daleka, 33, 60-124 POZNAŃ
Tel: 61 655 81 65 **Fax:** 61 655 81 01
Email: wodkan@abrys.pl **Web site:** http://www.abrys.pl
Date Established: 2003; **Freq:** Monthly; **Circ:** 5,000
Usual Pagination: 32
Profile: A magazine dedicated to latest technological achievements in water piping and sewage piping and to management and exploitation of water and sewage cleaning plants.
Language(s): Polish
ADVERTISING RATES:
Full Page Colour .... PLN 3450.00
Mechanical Data: Type Area: A4
BUSINESS: LOCAL GOVERNMENT, LEISURE & RECREATION: Public Health & Cleaning

WOKÓŁ ENERGETYKI
1708791PL58-6
Editorial: ul. Wenedów, 9/1, 61-614 POZNAŃ
Tel: 61 822 77 81 **Fax:** 61 822 77 81
Email: m.olejniczak@termedia.pl **Web site:** http://www.energetyka.termedia.pl
Date Established: 2001
Circ: 3,000
Usual Pagination: 60
Managing Director: Andrzej Kordas
Profile: Professional publication on electro energy, gas an heat energy, their management.
Language(s): Polish
Mechanical Data: Type Area: 205 x 297 mm
BUSINESS: ENERGY, FUEL & NUCLEAR

WOKÓŁ PŁYTEK CERAMICZNYCH
1811076PL4B-13
Editorial: ul. Świętokrzyska, 14a, 00-049 WARSZAWA **Tel:** 22 826 20 27 **Fax:** 22 827 52 55
Email: wpc@sigma-not.pl **Web site:** http://plytkiceramiczne.info.pl
ISSN: 1429-9089
Date Established: 1998; **Freq:** Quarterly
Usual Pagination: 72
Profile: Presents news on ceramics tiles market in Poland and abroad, newest technologies and market developments.
Language(s): Polish
ADVERTISING RATES:
Full Page Colour .... PLN 6400.00
Mechanical Data: Type Area: 210 x 297 mm
BUSINESS: ARCHITECTURE & BUILDING: Interior Design & Flooring

WOLIERA
1811027PL81F-1
Editorial: ul. Zastawie, 12, 05-074 HALINÓW
Tel: 22 760 41 67 **Fax:** 22 783 66 82
Email: redakcja@woliera.com **Web site:** http://www.woliera.pl
ISSN: 1644-7832
Date Established: 2002; **Freq:** 6 issues yearly; **Circ:** 3,000
Usual Pagination: 100
Profile: Magazine on ornithology, exotic and common birds, bird watching.
Language(s): Polish
ADVERTISING RATES:
Full Page Colour .... PLN 2000.00
Mechanical Data: Type Area: A4
CONSUMER: ANIMALS & PETS: Birds

WPROST
1201730PL82-61
Editorial: ul. Domaniewska, 39a Horizon Plaza, 02-672 WARSZAWA **Tel:** 22 529 11 00
Fax: 22 529 11 90
Email: redakcja@wprost.pl **Web site:** http://www.wprost24.pl
ISSN: 0209-1747
Date Established: 1982; **Freq:** Weekly; **Circ:** 213,000
Usual Pagination: 112
Publisher: Katarzyna Kozłowska
Profile: Magazine focusing on current affairs, economics, politics and social issues.
Language(s): Polish
ADVERTISING RATES:
Full Page Colour .... PLN 77000.00
Mechanical Data: Type Area: 210 x 272 mm
Supplement(s): WiK - 52xY
CONSUMER: CURRENT AFFAIRS & POLITICS

WRC MAGAZYN RAJDOWY
1708703PL77A-17
Editorial: ul. Kochanowskiego, 16, 11, 40-035 KATOWICE **Tel:** 32 251 70 86 **Fax:** 32 251 70 86
Email: wrc@wrc.net.pl **Web site:** http://www.wrc.net.pl
ISSN: 1643-3785
Date Established: 2001; **Freq:** Monthly; **Circ:** 17,000
Usual Pagination: 84
Managing Director: Maciej Partyka; **Advertising Director:** Renata Niezbecka
Profile: Magazine about car rallies, sports cars, automotive engineering, automotive tips, announcements of rally events.
Language(s): English
ADVERTISING RATES:
Full Page Colour .... PLN 6200.00
Mechanical Data: Type Area: 205x275 mm
CONSUMER: MOTORING & CYCLING: Motoring

WRÓŻKA
1708764PL74A-1013
Editorial: ul. Malczewskiego, 19, 02-612 WARSZAWA **Tel:** 22 854 14 30 **Fax:** 22 854 14 39
Email: wrozka@wrozka.com.pl **Web site:** http://www.wrozka.com.pl
ISSN: 1231-2983
Date Established: 1994; **Freq:** Monthly; **Circ:** 140,000
Usual Pagination: 130
Advertising Director: Jolanta Otrębska
Profile: A magazine featuring reportages and interviews with interesting people, articles on health and beauty, unusual real stories.
Language(s): Polish
Mechanical Data: Type Area: 215 x 278 mm
CONSUMER: WOMEN'S INTEREST CONSUMER MAGAZINES: Women's Interest

WSPÓŁCZESNA ONKOLOGIA
1708790PL56A-8
Editorial: ul. Wenedów, 9/1, 61-614 POZNAŃ
Tel: 61 822 77 81 **Fax:** 61 822 77 81
Email: andrzej.mackiewicz@wco.pl **Web site:** http://www.onkologia.termedia.pl
ISSN: 1428-2526
Date Established: 1997
Circ: 2,000
Usual Pagination: 70
Managing Director: Andrzej Kordas
Profile: Professional magazine on oncology and cancer treatments.
Language(s): Polish
Mechanical Data: Type Area: 210 x 297 mm
BUSINESS: HEALTH & MEDICAL

WWW.ABC.COM.PL
1860852PL14A-149
Editorial: Płocka, 5a, 01-231 WARSZAWA
Tel: 22 535 80 00 **Fax:** 22 535 80 01
Email: abc@wolterskluwer.pl **Web site:** http://www.abc.com.pl
Date Established: 1996; **Freq:** Daily; **Circ:** 511,703 Unique Users
Advertising Director: Tomasz Sokół
Profile: Website containing information on business legislation, service tax, service personnel, service construction, environmental services, educational services, banking services.
Language(s): Polish
BUSINESS: COMMERCE, INDUSTRY & MANAGEMENT

WWW.MAXMAGAZINE.PL
1835903PL86C-15
Editorial: ul. Zgoda, 9, 81-361 GDYNIA
Tel: 58 622 63 00 **Fax:** 58 622 63 00
Email: max@maxmagazine.pl **Web site:** http://www.maxmagazine.pl
Date Established: 1999; **Freq:** Daily; **Circ:** 896,000 Unique Users
Managing Director: Hanna Kolasinska; **Advertising Director:** Piotr Małyszczyk
Profile: Online city lifestyle and cultural-entertaining magazine for men.
Language(s): Polish
CONSUMER: ADULT & GAY MAGAZINES: Men's Lifestyle Magazines

WWW.WNP.PL
1860857PL14A-150
Formerly: Wirtualny Nowy Przemysł
Editorial: ul. J. Matejki, 3, 40-077 KATOWICE
Tel: 32 209 10 42 **Fax:** 32 782 13 10
Email: internet@wnp.pl **Web site:** http://www.wnp.pl
Date Established: 2005; **Freq:** Daily; **Circ:** 524,000 Unique Users
Advertising Director: Tomasz Ruszkowski
Profile: Business portal with news in oil, gas, mining, construction, chemical industries IT, logistics and finance.
Language(s): Polish
BUSINESS: COMMERCE, INDUSTRY & MANAGEMENT

WWW.WYMARZONYOGROD.PL
1860866PL93-12
Editorial: ul. Kamionkowska, 45, 03-812 WARSZAWA **Tel:** 22 590 55 73 **Fax:** 22 590 54 44
Email: mmichalak@murator.com.pl **Web site:** http://www.wymarzonyogrod.pl
Date Established: 2008
Circ: 1,211,137 Unique Users
Managing Director: Katarzyna Białek
Profile: Dedicated to all aspects of gardening.
Language(s): Polish
CONSUMER: GARDENING

WYKAŃCZAMY DOM
1804097PL4B-14
Editorial: ul. Kamionkowska 45, 03-812 WARSZAWA
Tel: 22 590 52 96
Email: murator@murator.com.pl **Web site:** http://www.publikator.com.pl
Freq: Quarterly; **Cover Price:** PLN 15.00; **Circ:** 5,000
Usual Pagination: 72
Editor-in-Chief: Anna Kamińska
Profile: Professional publication on interior design news and technologies for specialists and ordinary people refurbishing their houses.
Language(s): Polish
ADVERTISING RATES:
Full Page Colour .... PLN 12500.00
BUSINESS: ARCHITECTURE & BUILDING: Interior Design & Flooring

Z ŻYCIA WZIĘTE. WYDANIE SPECJALNE
1709078PL74A-1024
Editorial: ul. św. Antoniego, 7, 50-073 WROCŁAW
Tel: 71 344 77 75 **Fax:** 71 346 01 74
Email: zzw@phoenix.pl **Web site:** http://www.phoenix.pl
ISSN: 1429-2696
Date Established: 1996
Circ: 292,000
Usual Pagination: 48
Profile: Special edition of the magazine "Life Stories", which in addition to prominent portion of life stories, publishes a main topic - most frequently in the form of a guide. Topics discussed in the edition are the following: a guidance on preparing a successful adoption, the art of dressing, the secrets of wise parenting or esoteric, etc.
Language(s): English
ADVERTISING RATES:
Full Page Colour .... PLN 8000.00
Mechanical Data: Type Area: 205 x 297 mm
CONSUMER: WOMEN'S INTEREST CONSUMER MAGAZINES: Women's Interest

ZABYTKI
1795849PL4A-23
Editorial: Al. Jerozolimskie, 107, 02-011 WARSZAWA
Tel: 22 429 24 45 **Fax:** 22 429 25 90
Email: zabytki@pwrsa.pl **Web site:** http://www.magazynzabytki.pl
ISSN: 1640-0194
Date Established: 2000; **Freq:** Monthly; **Circ:** 4,000
Usual Pagination: 96
Profile: Comprehensive source of information about the material culture and industrial heritage, historical monuments and historical architecture or industrial objects.
Language(s): Polish
Readership: Targets wide range of readers, both enthusiasts of and people interested in historical monuments and their condition, history of art, archaeology and protection of cultural heritage, people professionally involved in the subject who would like to invest in protection of national heritage in Poland.
Mechanical Data: Type Area: 230x290 mm
BUSINESS: ARCHITECTURE & BUILDING: Architecture

ŻAGLE
1708664PL91A-8
Editorial: ul. Kamionkowska, 45, 03-812 WARSZAWA **Tel:** 22 590 51 75 **Fax:** 22 590 54 44
Email: zagle@murator.com.pl **Web site:** http://www.zagle.com.pl
ISSN: 0860-2670
Date Established: 1959; **Freq:** Monthly; **Circ:** 81,000
Usual Pagination: 104
Managing Director: Ewa P. Porębska; **Advertising Director:** Anna Dygasiewicz-Piwko
Profile: A magazine dedicated to sailing and water sports. Focused on international and national events and competitions.
Language(s): Polish
Mechanical Data: Type Area: 215 x 290 mm
CONSUMER: RECREATION & LEISURE: Boating & Yachting

ZARZĄDZANIE JAKOŚCIĄ W PRAKTYCE. NORMY ISO SERII 9000
1811083PL14A-95
Editorial: ul. Łotewska, 9a, 03-918 WARSZAWA
Tel: 22 429 41 00 **Fax:** 22 518 27 50
Email: iso@wip.pl **Web site:** http://www.isowpraktyce.pl
Date Established: 1997; **Freq:** Monthly
Usual Pagination: 500
Profile: Focused on introduction and implementation of ISO certificate.
Language(s): Polish
Mechanical Data: Type Area: A5
BUSINESS: COMMERCE, INDUSTRY & MANAGEMENT

ZARZĄDZANIE PRODUKCJĄ W PRAKTYCE
1796110PL14A-76
Editorial: ul. Łotewska, 9a, 03-918 WARSZAWA
Tel: 22 518 29 29 **Fax:** 22 617 60 10
Email: cok@wip.pl **Web site:** http://www.firmaprodukcyjna.pl
Usual Pagination: 350
Publisher: Mariusz Miętusiewicz
Profile: Provides practical information on production management, quality control, work related safety, logistics and warehouse issues.
Language(s): Polish
Mechanical Data: Type Area: A5
BUSINESS: COMMERCE, INDUSTRY & MANAGEMENT

ZBUDUJ DOM
1708666PL4E-14
Editorial: ul. Kamionkowska, 45, 03-812 WARSZAWA **Tel:** 22 590 50 00 **Fax:** 22 590 54 22
Email: redakcja@zbuduj.pl **Web site:** http://www.zbuduj.pl
ISSN: 1731-5921
Date Established: 2003; **Freq:** Monthly; **Circ:** 49,000
Usual Pagination: 120
Managing Director: Renata Krzewska; **Advertising Director:** Anna Dygasiewicz-Piwko
Profile: A magazine focused on all aspects of building a house, practical advice and ready design projects, functional and interesting solutions, smart indoor arrangements.
Language(s): Polish
ADVERTISING RATES:
Full Page Colour .... PLN 9200.00
Mechanical Data: Type Area: 210 x 278 mm
BUSINESS: ARCHITECTURE & BUILDING: Building

ZDROWIE
1708665PL74G-5
Editorial: ul. Kamionkowska, 45, 03-812 WARSZAWA **Tel:** 22 590 50 00 **Fax:** 22 590 54 44
Email: zdrowie@murator.com.pl **Web site:** http://www.poradnikzdrowie.pl
ISSN: 0137-8066
Date Established: 1885; **Freq:** Monthly; **Circ:** 81,000
Usual Pagination: 108
Managing Director: Katarzyna Białek; **Advertising Director:** Anna Dygasiewicz-Piwko
Profile: A magazine advising on how to maintain good health and shape.
Language(s): Polish
Mechanical Data: Type Area: 180 x 232 mm
CONSUMER: WOMEN'S INTEREST CONSUMER MAGAZINES: Slimming & Health

ZEGARKI & BIŻUTERIA
1708843PL52A-1
Editorial: ul. Kierbedzia, 4, 00-728 WARSZAWA
Tel: 22 320 15 30 **Fax:** 22 320 15 40
Email: ebromberkowska@unit.pl **Web site:** http://www.zegarkibizuteria.pl
ISSN: 1427-3799
Date Established: 1997
Circ: 3,000
Usual Pagination: 40
Advertising Director: Joanna Pratzer
Profile: Leading Polish watch and jewellery trade magazine addressed to polish wholesalers and retailers, as well as producers, operating in the watch and jewellery business.
Language(s): Polish
ADVERTISING RATES:
Full Page Colour .... PLN 4200.00
Mechanical Data: Type Area: 210 x 297 mm
BUSINESS: GIFT TRADE: Jewellery

ZESZYTY METODYCZNE RACHUNKOWOŚCI
1929200PL1B-18
Editorial: ul. Owocowa, 8, 66-400 GORZÓW WLKP.
Tel: 95 720 85 40 **Fax:** 95 720 85 60
Email: zeszyty@gofin.pl **Web site:** http://www.gofin.pl
Date Established: 1998; **Freq:** 26 issues yearly; **Circ:** 19,000
Usual Pagination: 70

Profile: Professional magazine dedicated to accountancy, account books filing, financial reporting.
Language(s): Polish
Readership: Targets accountants.
ADVERTISING RATES:
Full Page Colour .... PLN 2500.00
Mechanical Data: Type Area: 170 x 240 mm
BUSINESS: FINANCE & ECONOMICS: Accountancy

ZIELEŃ MIEJSKA 1810976PL32A-2

Editorial: ul. Daleka, 33, 60-124 POZNAŃ
Tel: 61 655 81 32 **Fax:** 61 655 81 01
Email: zielen@abrys.pl **Web site:** http://www.abrys.pl
Date Established: 2006; **Freq:** Monthly; **Circ:** 6,000
Usual Pagination: 32
Profile: A magazine focused on trees' preservation in big cities and how to make cities greener with examples of investments, guidelines on cultivation and preservation of greenery. Presents projects and designs of green areas, maintenance and restoration of gardens and parks, city planting.
Language(s): Polish
Readership: Targets municipality offices, building societies, Social Construction Associations, management and greenery maintenance companies, landscape designers.
ADVERTISING RATES:
Full Page Colour .... EUR 3300.00
Mechanical Data: Type Area: A4
BUSINESS: LOCAL GOVERNMENT, LEISURE & RECREATION: Local Government

ZNAK 1810902PL87-8

Editorial: ul. Kościuszki, 37, 30-105 KRAKÓW
Tel: 12 619 95 30 **Fax:** 12 619 95 02
Email: miesiecznik@znak.com.pl **Web site:** http://www.miesiecznik.znak.com.pl
ISSN: 0044-488X
Date Established: 1946; **Freq:** Monthly; **Circ:** 2,400
Usual Pagination: 168
Profile: Magazine on religion aspects in politics, society and culture.
Language(s): Polish
Mechanical Data: Type Area: A5
CONSUMER: RELIGIOUS

ZWIERCIADŁO 1708697PL74A-1012

Editorial: ul. Karowa, 31a, 00-324 WARSZAWA
Tel: 22 312 37 12 **Fax:** 22 312 37 21
Email: sekretariat@zwierciadlo.pl **Web site:** http://www.zwierciadlo.pl
ISSN: 0514-0994
Date Established: 1957; **Freq:** Monthly; **Circ:** 130,000
Usual Pagination: 186
Advertising Director: Agata Przonek
Profile: Provides information on culture and arts, includes practical advice on beauty and health, interviews with famous people and cookery recipes.
Language(s): Polish
ADVERTISING RATES:
Full Page Colour .... PLN 34500.00
Mechanical Data: Type Area: 215 x 280 mm
CONSUMER: WOMEN'S INTEREST CONSUMER MAGAZINES: Women's Interest

ŻYCIE HANDLOWE 1796128PL14A-78

Editorial: ul. Młynarska, 7, 01-205 WARSZAWA
Tel: 22 539 59 40 **Fax:** 22 539 59 50
Email: redakcja@mediadirect.pl **Web site:** http://www.portalfmcg.pl
ISSN: 1231-2010
Date Established: 2005; **Freq:** Monthly; **Circ:** 90,000
Usual Pagination: 52
Managing Director: Beata Farmus
Profile: Features latest market news, information on products advertising campaigns and trade events.
Language(s): Polish
ADVERTISING RATES:
Full Page Colour .... PLN 28500.00
Mechanical Data: Type Area: 235 x 335 mm
BUSINESS: COMMERCE, INDUSTRY & MANAGEMENT

ŻYCIE NA GORĄCO 1622987PL74Q-8

Editorial: ul. Motorowa, 1, 04-035 WARSZAWA
Tel: 22 517 02 23 **Fax:** 22 517 03 31
Email: zng@bauer.pl **Web site:** http://www.reklama.bauer.pl
ISSN: 1232-8944
Date Established: 1994; **Freq:** Weekly; **Circ:** 844,000
Usual Pagination: 64
Advertising Director: Ewa Kozłowska
Profile: Contains latest information on celebrities, health advice, beauty and cookery tips.
Language(s): Polish
ADVERTISING RATES:
Full Page Colour .... PLN 67000.00
Mechanical Data: Type Area: 225 x 285 mm
CONSUMER: WOMEN'S INTEREST CONSUMER MAGAZINES: Lifestyle

ŻYCIE WARSZAWY 1500358PL67B-3

Editorial: ul. Prosta, 51, 00-838 WARSZAWA
Tel: 22 628 34 01
Email: redakcjaonline@zw.com.pl **Web site:** http://www.zw.com.pl
ISSN: 0137-943X
Date Established: 2000
Usual Pagination: 28
News Editor: Zofia Krajewska; **Advertising Director:** Paweł Brudnicki
Profile: Covering international and Polish political news, business news and reviews, information on cultural and sports events.
Language(s): Polish
ADVERTISING RATES:
Full Page Mono .... PLN 21880.00
Full Page Colour .... PLN 28420.00
Mechanical Data: Type Area: kompaktmm
REGIONAL DAILY & SUNDAY NEWSPAPERS: Regional Daily Newspapers

ŻYJMY DŁUŻEJ 1709043PL74G-14

Editorial: ul. Niedźwiedzia, 12a, 02-737 WARSZAWA
Tel: 22 853 73 72 **Fax:** 22 853 73 72
Email: redakcja.zyjmydluzej@medi-press.pl **Web site:** http://www.medigo.pl
Date Established: 1958; **Freq:** Monthly; **Circ:** 60,000
Usual Pagination: 86
Managing Director: Dorota Świderska
Profile: Focused on heath problems, diagnosing testing, treatments and medical achievements.
Language(s): Polish
ADVERTISING RATES:
Full Page Colour .... PLN 10700.00
CONSUMER: WOMEN'S INTEREST CONSUMER MAGAZINES: Slimming & Health

Portugal

Time Difference: GMT
National Telephone Code: +351
Continent: Europe
Capital: Lisbon
Principal Language: Portuguese
Population: 10524145
Monetary Unit: Euro (EUR)

EMBASSY HIGH COMMISSION: Portuguese Embassy: 11 Belgrave Sq, London, SW1X 8PP
Tel: 020 7235 5331
Fax: 020 7245 1287
Email: london@portembassy.co.uk
Website: http://www.portembassy.gla.ac.uk/
Head of Mission : H E Antonio Santana-Carlos

1000 MAIORES EMPRESAS (DE) 1779896P14A-187

Editorial: R. Vieira da Silva, 45, 1350-342 LISBOA
Tel: 213 236 700 **Fax:** 213 236 701
Email: deconomico@economico.pt **Web site:** http://economico.pt
Freq: Annual; **Cover Price:** Free; **Circ:** 23,147
Profile: Published with: Diário Económico.
Language(s): Portuguese
Readership: National.
ADVERTISING RATES:
Full Page Colour .... EUR 5490
Mechanical Data: Trim Size: 210 x 280 mm

1000 MAIORES EMPRESAS (DN + JN) 1934825P14A-276

Editorial: Edifício Diário de Notícias, Av. da Liberdade, 266, 1250-149 LISBOA **Tel:** 213 187 500
Fax: 213 187 516
Email: dnot@dn.pt **Web site:** http://www.dn.pt
Date Established: 2009; **Freq:** Annual; **Cover Price:** Free; **Circ:** 150,180
Usual Pagination: 84
Profile: Published with: Jornal de Notícias; Diário de Notícias.
Language(s): Portuguese
Readership: National.
ADVERTISING RATES:
Full Page Colour .... EUR 2900
Mechanical Data: Trim Size: 215 x 290 mm, Type Area: 185 x 260 mm

1000 MAIORES EMPRESAS (E) 1820350P14A-132

Editorial: Edifício S. Francisco de Sales, R. Calvet de Magalhães, 242, 2770-022 PAÇO DE ARCOS
Tel: 214 544 000 **Fax:** 214 435 349
Email: director@expresso.impresa.pt
Date Established: 2006; **Freq:** Annual; **Circ:** 136,500
Usual Pagination: 68
Profile: Published with: Expresso.
Language(s): Portuguese
Readership: National.
ADVERTISING RATES:
Full Page Colour .... EUR 5150
Mechanical Data: Trim Size: 225 x 297 mm, Type Area: 199 x 270 mm
BUSINESS: COMMERCE, INDUSTRY & MANAGEMENT

100% JOVEM 623647P74F-5

Editorial: R. da Impala, N° 33 A - Abrunheira, S. Pedro de Penaferrim, 2710-070 SINTRA
Tel: 219 238 166 **Fax:** 219 238 040
Email: 100jovem@impala.pt **Web site:** http://www.impala.pt
ISSN: 0873-4801
Date Established: 1983; **Freq:** Monthly; **Cover Price:** EUR 1,9; **Circ:** 30,000
Managing Director: Gisela Cristina Régio Martins
Profile: Magazine containing articles about youth culture, includes pop star interviews, reviews of new CDs, cinema, fashion and beauty.
Language(s): Portuguese
Readership: National. Aimed for teenagers and young adults.
ADVERTISING RATES:
Full Page Colour .... EUR 3000
Mechanical Data: Type Area: 180 x 245 mm, Trim Size: 210 x 280 mm
CONSUMER: WOMEN'S INTEREST CONSUMER MAGAZINES: Teenage

100% NATURAL 1820349P56A-182

Editorial: R. dos Bem Lembrados, 141, Manique, 2645-471 ALCABIDECHE **Tel:** 214 449 688
Fax: 214 449 691
Email: naturalmedia@mail.telepac.pt
ISSN: 1646-6438
Date Established: 2007; **Freq:** Occasional; **Cover Price:** EUR 1,5; **Circ:** 60,000
Usual Pagination: 68
Profile: 100% Natural is a free magazine focused on natural health and the advantages of a healthy diet in illnesses prevention.
Language(s): Portuguese
Readership: National.
ADVERTISING RATES:
Full Page Colour .... EUR 1950
Mechanical Data: Type Area: 200 x 287 mm, Trim Size: 216 x 303 mm

250 MAIORES EMPRESAS (JL + P) 1820354P14A-133

Editorial: R. Comandante João Belo, N° 31, Apartado 1098, 2401-801 LEIRIA **Tel:** 244 800 400
Fax: 244 800 405
Email: geral@jornaldeleiria.pt **Web site:** http://www.jornaldeleiria.pt
Date Established: 2006; **Freq:** Annual; **Cover Price:** Free; **Circ:** 65,283
Usual Pagination: 124
Profile: Published with: Jornal de Leiria; Público.
Language(s): Portuguese
Readership: National.
ADVERTISING RATES:
Full Page Colour .... EUR 1500
Mechanical Data: Type Area: 176 x 235 mm, Trim Size: 206 x 280 mm

250 MAIORES EMPRESAS (JL + P) 1820354P14A-249

Editorial: R. Comandante João Belo, N° 31, Apartado 1098, 2401-801 LEIRIA **Tel:** 244 800 400
Fax: 244 800 405
Email: geral@jornaldeleiria.pt **Web site:** http://www.jornaldeleiria.pt
Date Established: 2006; **Freq:** Annual; **Cover Price:** Free; **Circ:** 65,283
Usual Pagination: 124
Profile: Published with: Jornal de Leiria; Público.
Language(s): Portuguese
Readership: National.
ADVERTISING RATES:
Full Page Colour .... EUR 1500
Mechanical Data: Type Area: 176 x 235 mm, Trim Size: 206 x 280 mm

AÇORES 1779983P65A-50_100

Editorial: Av. João Crisóstomo, 72, 1069-043 LISBOA **Tel:** 213 185 462 **Fax:** 213 540 695
Email: geral@correiomanha.pt **Web site:** http://www.cmjornal.pt
Freq: Annual; **Cover Price:** Free; **Circ:** 155,480
Usual Pagination: 48
Profile: Special edition about Açores' island.
Language(s): Portuguese
Readership: National.
ADVERTISING RATES:
Full Page Colour .... EUR 4250
Mechanical Data: Trim Size: 205 x 275 mm, Type Area: 180 x 253 mm
Section of: Correio da Manhã
NATIONAL DAILY & SUNDAY NEWSPAPERS: Unabhängiges konservatives MdEP

AÇORES 1779983P65A-50_100

Editorial: Av. João Crisóstomo, 72, 1069-043 LISBOA **Tel:** 213 185 462 **Fax:** 213 540 695
Email: geral@correiomanha.pt **Web site:** http://www.cmjornal.pt
Freq: Annual; **Cover Price:** Free; **Circ:** 155,480
Usual Pagination: 48
Profile: Special edition about Açores' island.
Language(s): Portuguese
Readership: National.
ADVERTISING RATES:
Full Page Colour .... EUR 4250
Mechanical Data: Trim Size: 205 x 275 mm, Type Area: 180 x 253 mm
Section of: Correio da Manhã
NATIONAL DAILY & SUNDAY NEWSPAPERS: Unabhängiges konservatives MdEP

AÇORIANÍSSIMA 634762P94D-7

Editorial: R. Dr. João Francisco de Sousa, 14, 9500-187 PONTA DELGADA **Tel:** 296 201 060
Fax: 296 286 119
Email: jornal@correiodosacores.net **Web site:** http://www.correiodosacores.net
Freq: Quarterly; **Cover Price:** EUR 2,5; **Circ:** 2,600
Usual Pagination: 82
Editor: Ana Coelho
Profile: Magazine with cultural and social news regarding Açores' island.
Language(s): Portuguese
Readership: Read by Açores population.
ADVERTISING RATES:
Full Page Mono .... EUR 600
Full Page Colour .... EUR 950
Mechanical Data: Trim Size: 225 x 305 mm, Type Area: 205 x 288 mm
CONSUMER: OTHER CLASSIFICATIONS: Expatriates

AÇORIANO ORIENTAL 19484P67B-600

Editorial: R. Dr. Bruno Tavares Carreiro, 34/36, 9500-055 PONTA DELGADA **Tel:** 296 202 800
Fax: 296 202 825
Email: acorianooriental@acorianooriental.pt **Web site:** http://www.acorianooriental.pt
ISSN: 0874-8705
Date Established: 1835; **Freq:** Daily; **Cover Price:** EUR 0,8; **Circ:** 5,015
Usual Pagination: 40
Editor: Nuno Galopim; **Executive Editor:** Leonídio Paulo Ferreira; **Managing Director:** Paulo Simões
Profile: Daily regional newspaper containing information about Açores' island. Current affairs, politics, society, sport, entertainment and events are some of the main themes.
Language(s): Portuguese
Readership: Read by the population of Açores.
ADVERTISING RATES:
Full Page Mono .... EUR 1250
Full Page Colour .... EUR 2250
Mechanical Data: Type Area: 253 x 360 mm, Trim Size: 277 x 400 mm
REGIONAL DAILY & SUNDAY NEWSPAPERS: Regional Daily Newspapers

ACTIVA 19689P74A-15

Editorial: Edifício S. Francisco de Sales, R. Calvet de Magalhães, 242, 2770-022 PAÇO DE ARCOS
Tel: 214 544 000 **Fax:** 214 435 310
Email: bbettencourt@activa.impresa.pt **Web site:** http://aeiou.activa.pt
ISSN: 0874-0453
Date Established: 1987; **Freq:** Monthly; **Cover Price:** EUR 2,9; **Circ:** 75,900
Editor: Isabel Vidal; **Executive Editor:** Rosária Barreto; **Managing Director:** Clara Marques
Profile: Women's magazine featuring fashion, beauty, cooking, money and home decoration.
Language(s): Portuguese
Readership: Mainland.
ADVERTISING RATES:
Full Page Colour .... EUR 5950
Mechanical Data: Type Area: 194 x 260 mm, Trim Size: 230 x 297 mm
Series owner and contact point for the following titles, see individual entries:
Cabelos
Cabelos
Saúde & Beleza
CONSUMER: WOMEN'S INTEREST CONSUMER MAGAZINES: Women's Interest

ACTIVA - NOIVAS 1779993P74L-4

Editorial: Edifício S. Francisco de Sales, R. Calvet de Magalhães, 242, 2770-022 PAÇO DE ARCOS
Tel: 214 544 000 **Fax:** 214 435 310
Email: bbettencourt@activa.impresa.pt **Web site:** http://activa.aeiou.pt/artigo.aspx?contentid=1E1FEB1D-CCD6-4DE2-B28E-34B6E50C8DC5&channelid=6638A5B0
ISSN: 0874-0453
Freq: Annual; **Cover Price:** EUR 3,5; **Circ:** 12,800
Usual Pagination: 124
Editor: Isabel Vidal; **Executive Editor:** Rosária Barreto; **Managing Director:** Clara Marques
Profile: Magazine that serves as a guide for the wedding day. New trends on brides dresses, hair, make up, suggestions on how to receive the guests and so on.
Language(s): Portuguese
Readership: National.
Mechanical Data: Trim Size: 230 x 295 mm

ACTUALIDAD€ - ECONOMIA IBÉRICA 1780002P1A-163

Editorial: Av. Marquês de Tomar, N° 2 - 7°, 1050-155 LISBOA **Tel:** 213 509 310 **Fax:** 213 526 333

Email: ccile@ccile.org **Web site:** http://www.portugalespanha.org
Freq: Monthly; **Cover Price:** EUR 2,5; **Circ:** 6,000
Usual Pagination: 76
Profile: Magazine dedicated to Iberian themes.
Language(s): Portuguese
Readership: Mainland.
ADVERTISING RATES:
Full Page Colour .... EUR 978.5
Mechanical Data: Trim Size: 200 x 270 mm

AGENDA
1821082P75A-316
Editorial: Av. Conde de Valbom, 30 - 4°/5°, 1050-068 LISBOA **Tel:** 210 124 900 **Fax:** 213 151 315
Email: antoniomagalhaes@record.pt **Web site:** http://www.record.xl.pt
Date Established: 2007; **Freq:** Occasional; **Cover Price:** Free; **Circ:** 101,873
Usual Pagination: 8
Profile: The most important sport events of the year.
Language(s): Portuguese
Readership: Mainland.
Mechanical Data: Type Area: 257 x 338 mm, Trim Size: 280 x 370 mm
Part of Series, see entry for: Record
CONSUMER: SPORT

ÁGORA
1821111P65A-181_110
Editorial: Instituto Superior da Maia, Av. Carlos Oliveira Campos, 4475-690 AVIOSO S. PEDRO
Tel: 213 187 500 **Fax:** 213 187 506
Email: info@ismai.pt **Web site:** http://www.ismai.pt
ISSN: 0874-1352
Date Established: 2007; **Freq:** Occasional; **Cover Price:** Free; **Circ:** 116,688
Usual Pagination: 12
Language(s): Portuguese
Readership: National.
ADVERTISING RATES:
Full Page Mono .... EUR 2700
Full Page Colour .... EUR 3780
Mechanical Data: Type Area: 260 x 330 mm, Trim Size: 288 x 365 mm
Section of: Jornal de Notícias
NATIONAL DAILY & SUNDAY NEWSPAPERS: National Daily Newspapers

ÁGUA & AMBIENTE
1780021P57-62
Editorial: R. da Madalena, 191 - 4°, 1100-319 LISBOA **Tel:** 218 806 123 **Fax:** 218 111 300
Email: aboutnet@about.pt **Web site:** http://aguaeambiente.ambienteonline.pt
Date Established: 1998; **Freq:** Monthly; **Cover Price:** EUR 10; **Circ:** 2,500
Usual Pagination: 80
Editor-in-Chief: Joana Filipe; **Managing Director:** Fernando Santana
Profile: Monthly newspaper with information about the environment. Studies, projects, legislation, opinions and so on.
Language(s): Portuguese
Readership: National.
ADVERTISING RATES:
Full Page Colour .... EUR 1730
Mechanical Data: Trim Size: 246 x 341 mm, Type Area: 240 x 335 mm

AICEP PORTUGAL GLOBAL
1860358P14A-234
Editorial: Agência para o Investimento e Comércio Externo de Portugal, EPE, Av. 5 de Outubro, 101, 1050-051 LISBOA **Tel:** 217 909 500 **Fax:** 217 909 578
Email: revista@portugalglobal.pt **Web site:** http://www.portugalglobal.pt
Freq: Monthly; **Cover Price:** Free; **Circ:** 8,000
Usual Pagination: 58
Managing Director: Ana de Carvalho
Profile: Magazine of analysis and information markets.
Language(s): English; Portuguese
Readership: National.
ADVERTISING RATES:
Full Page Colour .... EUR 600
Mechanical Data: Type Area: 170 x 247 mm, Trim Size: 210 x 297 mm

ALGARVE
1821149P65A-50_112
Editorial: Av. João Crisóstomo, 72, 1069-043 LISBOA **Tel:** 213 185 462 **Fax:** 213 540 695
Email: geral@correiomanha.pt **Web site:** http://www.cmjornal.pt
Freq: Daily; **Cover Price:** Free; **Circ:** 160,521
Usual Pagination: 52
Language(s): Portuguese
Readership: Aimed at south Portugal population.
ADVERTISING RATES:
Full Page Mono .... EUR 2020
Full Page Colour .... EUR 3030
Mechanical Data: Type Area: 257 x 338 mm, Trim Size: 273 x 370 mm
Section of: Correio da Manhã
NATIONAL DAILY & SUNDAY NEWSPAPERS: National Daily Newspapers

ALGARVE MAIS
1642511P80-196
Editorial: R. José Prudêncio Vieira, Lote 3 - 1° R/C, Apartado 28, 8365-909 ARMAÇÃO DE PÊRA
Tel: 282 310 720 **Fax:** 282 310 729
Email: algarvemais@algarvemais.pt **Web site:** http://www.algarvemais.pt
Date Established: 1993; **Freq:** Monthly; **Cover Price:** EUR 3; **Circ:** 8,000
Usual Pagination: 164
Editor: João Pina
Language(s): Portuguese
Readership: Aimed at Faro locals.
ADVERTISING RATES:
Full Page Colour .... EUR 1250
Mechanical Data: Trim Size: 225 x 300 mm
CONSUMER: RURAL & REGIONAL INTEREST

O ALMEIRINENSE
1642973P80-197
Editorial: Santa Casa da Misericórdia, R. Almirante Reis, N° 32, 2080-060 ALMEIRIM **Tel:** 243 594 360
Fax: 243 594 368
Email: redaccao@almeirinense.com **Web site:** http://www.almeirinense.com
Date Established: 1955; **Freq:** 26 issues yearly; **Cover Price:** EUR 0,5; **Circ:** 2,900
Usual Pagination: 20
Editor: Filipe Rego
Language(s): Portuguese
Readership: Aimed at Santarém locals.
ADVERTISING RATES:
Full Page Mono .... EUR 240
Full Page Colour .... EUR 360
Mechanical Data: Trim Size: 302 x 424 mm, Type Area: 264 x 370 mm
CONSUMER: RURAL & REGIONAL INTEREST

O ALMONDA
1642974P67B-6006
Editorial: Travessa da Cerca, N° 35, 2354-909 TORRES NOVAS **Tel:** 249 812 499 **Fax:** 249 812 446
Email: geral@oalmonda.net **Web site:** http://oalmonda.net
Date Established: 1918; **Freq:** Weekly; **Cover Price:** EUR 0,5; **Circ:** 4,900
Managing Director: Carlos Alberto Ramos Dias
Language(s): Portuguese
Readership: Aimed at the population of Torres Novas.
ADVERTISING RATES:
Full Page Mono .... EUR 280
Full Page Colour .... EUR 450
Mechanical Data: Trim Size: 295 x 415 mm, Type Area: 265 x 364 mm
REGIONAL DAILY & SUNDAY NEWSPAPERS: Regional Daily Newspapers

ALVORADA
1642516P65B-1
Editorial: Centro Pastoral de Santo António, 2530-120 LOURINHÃ **Tel:** 261 416 171 **Fax:** 261 416 174
Email: jornal@alvorada.pt **Web site:** http://www.alvorada.pt
Date Established: 1960; **Freq:** 26 issues yearly; **Cover Price:** EUR 0,6; **Circ:** 4,600
Usual Pagination: 32
Editor-in-Chief: Paulo Ribeiro; **Managing Director:** Ricardo Miguel Sousa Franco; **Advertising Manager:** Genoveva Maria Pereira da Cunha
Profile: Fortnightly newspaper with information about Lourinhã. Politics, current affairs, society, sport, entertainment and events.
Language(s): Portuguese
Readership: Read by Lourinhã locals.
ADVERTISING RATES:
Full Page Mono .... EUR 293
Full Page Colour .... EUR 737
Mechanical Data: Trim Size: 290 x 410 mm, Type Area: 245 x 340 mm
NATIONAL DAILY & SUNDAY NEWSPAPERS: National Sunday Newspapers

AMBIENTE (DN + JN)
1936057P57-177
Editorial: Edifício Diário de Notícias, Av. da Liberdade, 266, 1250-149 LISBOA **Tel:** 213 187 500
Fax: 213 187 516
Email: dnot@dn.pt **Web site:** http://www.dn.pt
Date Established: 2009; **Freq:** Occasional; **Cover Price:** Free; **Circ:** 168,106
Usual Pagination: 8
Profile: Published with: Jornal de Notícias; Diário de Notícias.
Language(s): Portuguese
Readership: National.
Mechanical Data: Type Area: 253 x 334 mm, Trim Size: 290 x 370 mm

AMBIENTE MAGAZINE
19445P57-6
Editorial: Av. Infante Santo, 343 - R/C Esq., 1350-177 LISBOA **Tel:** 213 954 110 **Fax:** 213 953 070
Email: ambientemagazine@mail.telepac.pt **Web site:** http://www.ambientemagazine.com
Date Established: 1993; **Freq:** 3 issues yearly; **Cover Price:** EUR 7,5; **Circ:** 5,000
Usual Pagination: 42
Editor: Pedro Chenrim
Profile: Publication about the environment.
Language(s): Portuguese
Readership: National.
ADVERTISING RATES:
Full Page Colour .... EUR 1212
Mechanical Data: Trim Size: 210 x 290 mm, Type Area: 175 x 250 mm
BUSINESS: ENVIRONMENT & POLLUTION

AMBIENTE PISCINAS
1642518P32E-1
Editorial: Parque Industrial de Sobreposta, R. da Piscina, 70, 4715-553 BRAGA **Tel:** 253 689 040
Fax: 253 689 049
Email: info@ambientepiscinas.com **Web site:** http://www.ambientepiscinas.com
ISSN: 1645-3956
Date Established: 2002; **Freq:** Half-yearly; **Cover Price:** EUR 5; **Circ:** 20,000
Usual Pagination: 66
Language(s): Portuguese
Readership: Mainland.
ADVERTISING RATES:
Full Page Colour .... EUR 2800
Mechanical Data: Trim Size: 220 x 297 mm, Type Area: 208 x 283 mm
BUSINESS: LOCAL GOVERNMENT, LEISURE & RECREATION: Swimming Pools

AMBIENTES DE FESTA
1642519P2C-51
Editorial: R. Alexandre Herculano, 341 - 4°, Sala14, 4000-055 PORTO **Tel:** 222 073 040 **Fax:** 222 073 044
Email: info@pronupcias.pt **Web site:** http://www.ambientesdefesta.com
ISSN: 0874-9450
Date Established: 2000; **Freq:** Half-yearly; **Cover Price:** EUR 5; **Circ:** 25,000
Managing Director: Ana Paula Ribeiro
Language(s): Portuguese
Readership: National.
ADVERTISING RATES:
Full Page Colour .... EUR 1500
Mechanical Data: Trim Size: 220 x 290 mm
BUSINESS: COMMUNICATIONS, ADVERTISING & MARKETING: Conferences & Exhibitions

AMBITUR
19446P57-8
Editorial: Av. Infante Santo, 343 - R/C Esq., 1350-177 LISBOA **Tel:** 213 954 110 **Fax:** 213 953 070
Email: atm.ambitur@mail.telepac.pt **Web site:** http://www.ambitur.pt
ISSN: 0872-2714
Date Established: 1991; **Freq:** Monthly; **Cover Price:** EUR 7,5; **Circ:** 5,500
Usual Pagination: 60
Managing Director: Pedro Chenrim
Profile: Magazine containing articles about tourism and environmental concerns.
Language(s): Portuguese
Readership: National.
ADVERTISING RATES:
Full Page Colour .... EUR 1250
Mechanical Data: Trim Size: 240 x 320 mm, Type Area: 210 x 285 mm
BUSINESS: ENVIRONMENT & POLLUTION

AMI NOTÍCIAS
1642520P32G-7
Editorial: Pátio Manuel Guerreiro, R. José do Patrocínio, 49 - Marvila, 1949-008 LISBOA
Tel: 218 362 100 **Fax:** 218 362 199
Email: fundacao-ami@mail.telepac.pt **Web site:** http://www.fundacao-ami.org/ami/seccao.asp?cod_seccao=54325
Date Established: 1994; **Freq:** Quarterly; **Cover Price:** Free; **Circ:** 120,000
Usual Pagination: 24
Managing Director: Fernando José de La Vieter Ribeiro Nobre
Profile: Official magazine of AMI - International Medical Assistance - portuguese foundation.
Language(s): Portuguese
Readership: National.
Mechanical Data: Type Area: 163 x 254 mm, Trim Size: 194 x 270 mm
BUSINESS: LOCAL GOVERNMENT, LEISURE & RECREATION: Community Care & Social Services

ANA
622991P74A-17
Editorial: R. da Impala, N° 33 A - Abrunheira, S. Pedro de Penaferrim, 2710-070 SINTRA
Tel: 219 238 400 **Fax:** 219 238 462
Email: impala.editora@impala.pt **Web site:** http://www.impala.pt
Date Established: 1983; **Freq:** Weekly; **Cover Price:** EUR 0,65; **Circ:** 67,750
Usual Pagination: 98
Advertising Manager: Luís Monteiro Pereira
Profile: Magazine containing celebrity interviews, news items and features on fashion and beauty.
Language(s): Portuguese
Readership: National.
ADVERTISING RATES:
Full Page Colour .... EUR 2290
Mechanical Data: Trim Size: 150 x 220 mm
CONSUMER: WOMEN'S INTEREST CONSUMER MAGAZINES: Women's Interest

ANECRA REVISTA
19365P31A-5
Editorial: R. Luis de Camões, 118-A, 1300-362 LISBOA **Tel:** 213 929 030 **Fax:** 213 978 504
Email: lisboa@anecra.pt **Web site:** http://www.anecra.pt
Freq: 6 issues yearly; **Cover Price:** EUR 2,5; **Circ:** 7,500
Usual Pagination: 116
Profile: Official journal of the Portuguese Society of Garages and Car Repair Businesses.
Language(s): Portuguese
Readership: National.
ADVERTISING RATES:
Full Page Mono .... EUR 950
Full Page Colour .... EUR 1100
Mechanical Data: Trim Size: 210 x 297 mm, Type Area: 180 x 270 mm
BUSINESS: MOTOR TRADE: Motor Trade Accessories

ANIVERSÁRIO
1820983P57-91
Editorial: R. da Madalena, 191 - 4°, 1100-319 LISBOA **Tel:** 218 806 123 **Fax:** 218 111 300
Email: aboutnet@about.pt **Web site:** http://aguaeambiente.ambienteonline.pt/noticias
Date Established: 2007; **Freq:** Occasional; **Cover Price:** Free; **Circ:** 4,000
Usual Pagination: 64
Profile: Suplemento de comemoração da 100ª edição do Água & Ambiente, com exemplos ilustrativos da evolução do jornal.
Language(s): Portuguese
Readership: National.
ADVERTISING RATES:
Full Page Colour .... EUR 1640
Mechanical Data: Trim Size: 246 x 341 mm

ANIVERSÁRIO
1820983P57-149
Editorial: R. da Madalena, 191 - 4°, 1100-319 LISBOA **Tel:** 218 806 123 **Fax:** 218 111 300
Email: aboutnet@about.pt **Web site:** http://aguaeambiente.ambienteonline.pt/noticias
Date Established: 2007; **Freq:** Occasional; **Cover Price:** Free; **Circ:** 4,000
Usual Pagination: 64
Profile: Suplemento de comemoração da 100ª edição do Água & Ambiente, com exemplos ilustrativos da evolução do jornal:
Language(s): Portuguese
Readership: National.
ADVERTISING RATES:
Full Page Colour .... EUR 1640
Mechanical Data: Trim Size: 246 x 341 mm

ANIVERSÁRIO
1781382P65A-20_101
Editorial: Travessa da Queimada, 23 - R/C, 1° e 2°, 1249-113 LISBOA **Tel:** 213 463 981 **Fax:** 213 464 503
Web site: http://www.abola.pt
Date Established: 2005; **Freq:** Annual; **Cover Price:** Free; **Circ:** 130,000
Usual Pagination: 16
Profile: Special anniversary edition.
Language(s): Portuguese
Readership: National. Read by a broad range of the population, mainly man, with a particular interest in sporting events.
Mechanical Data: Type Area: 259 x 348 mm, Trim Size: 281 x 400 mm
Section of: A Bola
NATIONAL DAILY & SUNDAY NEWSPAPERS: Unabhängiges konservatives MdEP

ANUÁRIO DE SUSTENTABILIDADE
1780105P1A-164
Editorial: Edifício Capitólio, Av. de França, 256 - E, Sala 3.1, 4050-276 PORTO **Tel:** 228 349 580
Fax: 228 349 589
Email: geral@biorumo.com **Web site:** http://www.biorumo.com
Freq: Annual; **Cover Price:** EUR 10; **Circ:** 10,000
Usual Pagination: 114
Profile: Magazine focused on sustainable economic development.
Language(s): Portuguese
Readership: National.
ADVERTISING RATES:
Full Page Colour .... EUR 2500
Mechanical Data: Type Area: 205 x 275 mm, Trim Size: 230 x 297 mm

ARQ & DESIGN
2093352P4-164
Editorial: Praça Paulo Vidal, 34 A, S. Victor, 4715-245 BRAGA **Tel:** 215 466 **Fax:** 215 468
Email: info@jpjeditora.pt
Date Established: 2011; **Freq:** 6 issues yearly; **Cover Price:** EUR 4,5; **Circ:** 14,500
Usual Pagination: 100
Managing Director: Sofia Pires
Profile: Magazine about architecture and design.
Language(s): Portuguese
Readership: National.
Mechanical Data: Trim Size: 230 x 320 mm

ARQUITECTOS INFORMAÇÃO
1642578P4A-102
Editorial: Travessa do Carvalho, 23, 1249-003 LISBOA **Tel:** 213 241 100 **Fax:** 213 241 101
Email: cdn@ordemdosarquitectos.pt **Web site:** http://www.arquitectos.pt
ISSN: 0872-4415
Freq: Monthly; **Cover Price:** Free; **Circ:** 17,200
Usual Pagination: 8
Profile: Architecture magazine with the latest news, laws and ideas on the subject.
Language(s): Portuguese
Readership: National. Aimed at architects, designers, town planners and architecture students.
ADVERTISING RATES:
Full Page Colour .... EUR 2490
Mechanical Data: Trim Size: 297 x 380 mm, Type Area: 163 x 249 mm

ARQUITECTURA 21 1606425P4A-101
Editorial: Av. das Robineas, 10, Rinchoa, 2635-545 RIO DE MOURO **Tel:** 219 198 210 **Fax:** 219 171 053
Email: geral@beprofit.pt **Web site:** http://www.beprofit.pt
Freq: Monthly; **Cover Price:** EUR 2,3; **Circ:** 15,000
Usual Pagination: 96
Managing Director: José Romano
Profile: Magazine focusing on architecture and design featuring detailed information on structure.
Language(s): Portuguese
Readership: Mainland.
ADVERTISING RATES:
Full Page Colour .... EUR 2200
Mechanical Data: Trim Size: 210 x 270 mm

ARQUITECTURA 21 1606425P4A-112
Editorial: Av. das Robineas, 10, Rinchoa, 2635-545 RIO DE MOURO **Tel:** 219 198 210 **Fax:** 219 171 053
Email: geral@beprofit.pt **Web site:** http://www.beprofit.pt
Freq: Monthly; **Cover Price:** EUR 2,3; **Circ:** 15,000
Usual Pagination: 96
Managing Director: José Romano
Profile: Magazine focusing on architecture and design featuring detailed information on structure.
Language(s): Portuguese
Readership: Mainland.
ADVERTISING RATES:
Full Page Colour .... EUR 2200
Mechanical Data: Trim Size: 210 x 270 mm

ARTE & CONSTRUÇÃO 19380P42A-5
Editorial: Centro Empresarial Tejo, R. de Xabregas, 20 - 2°, Sala 10, 1900-440 LISBOA **Tel:** 218 650 070
Fax: 218 650 079
Email: geral@mtg.pt **Web site:** http://www.arteconstrucao.com
ISSN: 0873-5271
Date Established: 1990; **Freq:** Monthly; **Cover Price:** EUR 3,5; **Circ:** 10,500
Usual Pagination: 72
Advertising Manager: Duarte Mourato
Profile: Magazine specializing in modern construction techniques and new materials.
Language(s): Portuguese
Readership: National.
ADVERTISING RATES:
Full Page Colour .... EUR 2100
Mechanical Data: Type Area: 200 x 265 mm, Trim Size: 230 x 297 mm
BUSINESS: CONSTRUCTION

ATLÂNTICO EXPRESSO 1642549P80-199
Editorial: R. Dr. João Francisco de Sousa, 14, 9500-187 PONTA DELGADA **Tel:** 296 201 060
Fax: 296 286 119
Email: atlanticoexpresso@correiodosacores.net
Date Established: 1990; **Freq:** Weekly; **Cover Price:** EUR 0,9; **Circ:** 6,650
Usual Pagination: 28
Editor-in-Chief: Ana Coelho; **Managing Director:** Américo Natalino Viveiros
Profile: Weekly regional newspaper with information about Açores. Politics, current affairs, society, religion, sport, entertainment and events.
Language(s): Portuguese
Readership: Read in Açores.
ADVERTISING RATES:
Full Page Mono .... EUR 340
Full Page Colour .... EUR 500
Mechanical Data: Trim Size: 280 x 400 mm, Type Area: 254 x 345 mm
CONSUMER: RURAL & REGIONAL INTEREST

ATUAL 1779996P94X-212
Editorial: Edifício S. Francisco de Sales, R. Calvet de Magalhães, 242, 2770-022 PAÇO DE ARCOS
Tel: 214 544 000 **Fax:** 214 435 310
Email: atual@expresso.impresa.pt **Web site:** http://www.expresso.pt
Freq: Weekly; **Cover Price:** Free; **Circ:** 126,575
Usual Pagination: 80
Editor-in-Chief: Jorge Leitão Ramos
Language(s): Portuguese
Readership: National.
ADVERTISING RATES:
Full Page Mono .... EUR 2520
Full Page Colour .... EUR 3360
Mechanical Data: Trim Size: 260 x 340 mm, Type Area: 234 x 314 mm
Part of Series, see entry for: Expresso
CONSUMER: OTHER CLASSIFICATIONS: Miscellaneous

ÁUDIO & CINEMA EM CASA 1744883P78B-3
Editorial: R. D.João V, 6 - R/C Esq., 1250-090 LISBOA **Tel:** 213 190 650 **Fax:** 213 190 659
Email: geral@audiopt.com **Web site:** http://www.audio.online.pt
Date Established: 1989; **Freq:** 6 issues yearly; **Cover Price:** EUR 4; **Circ:** 10,000
Usual Pagination: 140
Language(s): Portuguese
Readership: National.
ADVERTISING RATES:
Full Page Colour .... EUR 2200
Mechanical Data: Trim Size: 205 x 285 mm, Type Area: 173 x 253 mm
CONSUMER: CONSUMER ELECTRONICS: Video & DVD

AURI NEGRA 1642552P80-200
Editorial: Praça Florindo José Frota, 17, Apartado 79, 3061-906 FEBRES **Tel:** 231 469 090
Fax: 231 469 092
Email: jornal.aurinegra@gmail.com **Web site:** http://www.aurinegra.com
Date Established: 2002; **Freq:** 26 issues yearly; **Cover Price:** EUR 0,75; **Circ:** 2,500
Usual Pagination: 24
Managing Director: António Fresco
Language(s): Portuguese
Readership: Read by Coimbra locals.
ADVERTISING RATES:
Full Page Mono .... EUR 390
Full Page Colour .... EUR 565
Mechanical Data: Trim Size: 295 x 431 mm, Type Area: 252 x 365 mm
CONSUMER: RURAL & REGIONAL INTEREST

AUTO 1934840P65A-181_106
Editorial: R. de Gonçalo Cristóvão 195-219, 4049-011 PORTO **Tel:** 222 096 100 **Fax:** 222 096 140
Email: dpe@jn.pt **Web site:** http://www.jn.pt
ISSN: 0874-1352
Date Established: 2009; **Freq:** Occasional; **Cover Price:** Free; **Circ:** 106,688
Usual Pagination: 24
Profile: Publication dedicated to the mobile industry and market.
Language(s): Portuguese
Readership: National.
ADVERTISING RATES:
Full Page Mono .... EUR 2700
Full Page Colour .... EUR 3780
Mechanical Data: Type Area: 253 x 358 mm, Trim Size: 290 x 400 mm
Section of: Jornal de Notícias
NATIONAL DAILY & SUNDAY NEWSPAPERS: Unabhängiges konservatives MdEP

AUTO 1934840P65A-181_113
Editorial: R. de Gonçalo Cristóvão 195-219, 4049-011 PORTO **Tel:** 222 096 100 **Fax:** 222 096 140
Email: dpe@jn.pt **Web site:** http://www.jn.pt
ISSN: 0874-1352
Date Established: 2009; **Freq:** Occasional; **Cover Price:** Free; **Circ:** 106,688
Usual Pagination: 24
Profile: Publication dedicated to the mobile industry and market.
Language(s): Portuguese
Readership: National.
ADVERTISING RATES:
Full Page Mono .... EUR 2700
Full Page Colour .... EUR 3780
Mechanical Data: Type Area: 253 x 358 mm, Trim Size: 290 x 400 mm
Section of: Jornal de Notícias
NATIONAL DAILY & SUNDAY NEWSPAPERS: Unabhängiges konservatives MdEP

AUTO 1642553P77A-260
Editorial: R. Bernardo Lima, 35 - 4° A/B, 1150-075 LISBOA **Tel:** 213 570 418 **Fax:** 213 142 767
Email: revista.auto@netcabo.pt
Date Established: 2006; **Freq:** Occasional; **Cover Price:** EUR 4; **Circ:** 30,000
Usual Pagination: 116
Editor-in-Chief: António Vieira; **Managing Director:** Francisco Paulo de Oliveira Vieira; **Advertising Manager:** Luísa Moreira
Language(s): Portuguese
Readership: Mainland.
ADVERTISING RATES:
Full Page Colour .... EUR 3000
Mechanical Data: Trim Size: 230 x 275 mm, Type Area: 205 x 240 mm
CONSUMER: MOTORING & CYCLING: Motoring

AUTO COMPRA & VENDA 1606442P77A-255
Editorial: Largo do Cruzeiro, Nogueira, Apartado 2157, 4715-177 BRAGA **Tel:** 253 204 180
Fax: 253 204 185
Email: geral@pdc.pt **Web site:** http://www.portalacv.com
Date Established: 1992; **Freq:** Monthly; **Cover Price:** EUR 3,8; **Circ:** 20,000
Usual Pagination: 196
Advertising Manager: Cristina Costa
Profile: Magazine focusing on new and second hand cars, offering all the latest news and reviews, prices and comparisons. Also contains information on upcoming sporting events.
Language(s): Portuguese
Readership: Mainland. Aimed at potential car buyers and others interested in cars.
ADVERTISING RATES:
Full Page Colour .... EUR 750
Mechanical Data: Trim Size: 218 x 288 mm, Type Area: 180 x 250 mm
CONSUMER: MOTORING & CYCLING: Motoring

AUTO FOCO 1606439P77A-254
Editorial: Travessa da Queimada, 23, 4°, 1249-113 LISBOA **Tel:** 213 232 148 **Fax:** 213 232 154
Email: geral@autofoco.pt
ISSN: 0874-8667
Date Established: 2000; **Freq:** Weekly; **Cover Price:** EUR 1,5; **Circ:** 30,000
Usual Pagination: 84
Editor: Ricardo Jorge Costa; **Managing Director:** José Caetano
Profile: Magazine about cars. New models, tests, analyses, new technologies and environment are some of the themes of each edition.
Language(s): Portuguese
Readership: National. Aimed at males aged between 30 and 54 years.
ADVERTISING RATES:
Full Page Colour .... EUR 3190
Mechanical Data: Trim Size: 230 x 300 mm, Type Area: 213 x 280 mm
CONSUMER: MOTORING & CYCLING: Motoring

AUTO HOJE 19736P77A-80
Editorial: R. Policarpo Anjos, 4, 1495-742 CRUZ QUEBRADA/DAFUNDO **Tel:** 214 154 500
Fax: 214 154 504
Email: autohoje@motorpress.pt **Web site:** http://www.autohoje.com
Date Established: 1989; **Freq:** Weekly; **Cover Price:** EUR 1,75; **Circ:** 29,500
Usual Pagination: 132
Editor: José Ribeiro; **Managing Director:** Sandro Mêda
Profile: Publication about the latest cars, also contains information about road tests and manufacturers.
Language(s): Portuguese
Readership: Mainland. Aimed at men aged between 18 and 44 years old.
ADVERTISING RATES:
Full Page Colour .... EUR 3380
Mechanical Data: Trim Size: 230 x 300 mm, Type Area: 212 x 277 mm
CONSUMER: MOTORING & CYCLING: Motoring

AUTO MOTOR 19740P77A-120
Editorial: Av. João Crisóstomo, 72 - Galeria, 1069-043 LISBOA **Tel:** 213 307 700 **Fax:** 213 540 695
Email: jmg@mediafin.pt **Web site:** http://www.automotor.pt
Date Established: 1989; **Freq:** Monthly; **Cover Price:** EUR 3,3; **Circ:** 40,000
Executive Editor: Jorge Flores; **Managing Director:** António de Sousa Pereira
Profile: Magazine for car enthusiasts.
Language(s): Portuguese
Readership: Mainland.
ADVERTISING RATES:
Full Page Colour .... EUR 5500
Mechanical Data: Trim Size: 230 x 297 mm, Type Area: 206 x 275 mm
CONSUMER: MOTORING & CYCLING: Motoring

AUTO SPORT 19746P77D-40
Editorial: Edifício S. Francisco de Sales, R. Calvet de Magalhães, 242, 2770-022 PAÇO DE ARCOS
Tel: 214 544 184 **Fax:** 214 697 121
Email: autosport@autosport.impresa.pt **Web site:** http://www.autosport.pt
Date Established: 1977; **Freq:** Weekly; **Cover Price:** EUR 1,95; **Circ:** 17,650
Usual Pagination: 76
Managing Director: Rui Pelejão; **Advertising Manager:** Ricardo Miranda
Profile: Newspaper containing news and information on motor sports.
Language(s): Portuguese
Readership: Mainland.
ADVERTISING RATES:
Full Page Colour .... EUR 3100
Mechanical Data: Trim Size: 210 x 297 mm, Type Area: 185 x 266 mm
CONSUMER: MOTORING & CYCLING: Motor Sports

O AVEIRO 1642976P72-6
Editorial: R. 31 de Janeiro - Edifício de Sta. Catarina, 19 - 1° G/H, Apartado 328, 3811-759 AVEIRO
Tel: 234 400 090 **Fax:** 234 400 099
Email: info@oaveiro.pt **Web site:** http://www.portugal-linha.pt/oaveiro/index.html
Date Established: 1991; **Freq:** Monthly; **Cover Price:** Free; **Circ:** 10,000
Usual Pagination: 36
Managing Director: António Granjeia
Language(s): Portuguese
Readership: Read in Aveiro region.
ADVERTISING RATES:
Full Page Colour .... EUR 700
Mechanical Data: Trim Size: 280 x 395 mm, Type Area: 255 x 340 mm
LOCAL NEWSPAPERS

A AVEZINHA 1642466P74A-106
Editorial: R. Miguel Bombarda, 67/69, 8200-855 PADERNE/ALBUFEIRA **Tel:** 289 367 288
Fax: 289 367 488
Email: avezinha@mail.telepac.pt **Web site:** http://www.jornalavezinha.com
Date Established: 1924; **Freq:** 26 issues yearly; **Cover Price:** EUR 0,7; **Circ:** 3,200
Usual Pagination: 24
Language(s): Portuguese
Readership: Read in Faro region.
ADVERTISING RATES:
Full Page Mono .... EUR 650
Full Page Colour .... EUR 910
Mechanical Data: Trim Size: 287 x 403 mm, Type Area: 260 x 355 mm
CONSUMER: WOMEN'S INTEREST CONSUMER MAGAZINES: Women's Interest

BACALHAU 1830494P74P-302
Editorial: Cascais Office, Rotunda das Tojas, 2° E, 2645-901 ALCABIDECHE **Tel:** 214 606 100
Fax: 214 606 119
Email: receitassucesso@presspeople.pt **Web site:** http://presspeople.pt
Date Established: 2007; **Freq:** Occasional; **Cover Price:** EUR 1,2
Free to qualifying individuals ; **Circ:** 50,000
Usual Pagination: 36
Profile: Revista com variadas receitas à base de bacalhau.
Language(s): Portuguese
Readership: Mainland. Aimed mainly at women with 25 to 44 years old. C1 and C2.
ADVERTISING RATES:
Full Page Colour .... EUR 900
Mechanical Data: Type Area: 131 x 185 mm, Trim Size: 148 x 210 mm
Part of Series, see entry for: Receitas de Sucesso

BACALHAU 1830496P74P-304
Editorial: Cascais Office, Rotunda das Tojas, 2° E, 2645-091 ALCABIDECHE **Tel:** 214 606 100
Fax: 214 606 119
Email: cozinhasucesso@presspeople.pt **Web site:** http://presspeople.pt
Date Established: 2007; **Freq:** Occasional; **Cover Price:** Free; **Circ:** 50,000
Usual Pagination: 52
Profile: Revista ocasional que contém receitas especiais à base de bacalhau.
Language(s): Portuguese
Readership: Mainland.
ADVERTISING RATES:
Full Page Colour .... EUR 2100
Mechanical Data: Type Area: 182 x 254 mm, Trim Size: 210 x 275 mm
Part of Series, see entry for: Cozinha Prática de Sucesso

BACALHAU 1830496P74P-334
Editorial: Cascais Office, Rotunda das Tojas, 2° E, 2645-091 ALCABIDECHE **Tel:** 214 606 100
Fax: 214 606 119
Email: cozinhasucesso@presspeople.pt **Web site:** http://presspeople.pt
Date Established: 2007; **Freq:** Occasional; **Cover Price:** Free; **Circ:** 50,000
Usual Pagination: 52
Profile: Revista ocasional que contém receitas especiais à base de bacalhau.
Language(s): Portuguese
Readership: Mainland.
ADVERTISING RATES:
Full Page Colour .... EUR 2100
Mechanical Data: Type Area: 182 x 254 mm, Trim Size: 210 x 275 mm
Part of Series, see entry for: Cozinha Prática de Sucesso

BACALHAU 1830494P74P-335
Editorial: Cascais Office, Rotunda das Tojas, 2° E, 2645-901 ALCABIDECHE **Tel:** 214 606 100
Fax: 214 606 119
Email: receitassucesso@presspeople.pt **Web site:** http://presspeople.pt
Date Established: 2007; **Freq:** Occasional; **Cover Price:** EUR 1,2
Free to qualifying individuals ; **Circ:** 50,000
Usual Pagination: 36
Profile: Revista com variadas receitas à base de bacalhau.
Language(s): Portuguese
Readership: Mainland. Aimed mainly at women with 25 to 44 years old. C1 and C2.
ADVERTISING RATES:
Full Page Colour .... EUR 900
Mechanical Data: Type Area: 131 x 185 mm, Trim Size: 148 x 210 mm
Part of Series, see entry for: Receitas de Sucesso

BADALADAS 1642824P72I-27
Editorial: Praça 25 Abril, 6 - 1° Esq., 2561-311 TORRES VEDRAS **Tel:** 261 335 476 **Fax:** 261 315 170
Email: geral@badaladas.pt **Web site:** http://www.badaladas.pt
Date Established: 1947; **Freq:** Weekly; **Cover Price:** EUR 0,65; **Circ:** 11,000
Usual Pagination: 36
Managing Director: Fernando Miguel Silva
Profile: Tabloid-sized newspaper featuring the latest news, entertainment and sport from the region.
Language(s): Portuguese
Readership: Read in Lisboa region.
ADVERTISING RATES:
Full Page Mono .... EUR 700
Full Page Colour .... EUR 895
Mechanical Data: Trim Size: 280 x 400 mm, Type Area: 260 x 358 mm
LOCAL NEWSPAPERS: Regional Weekly Newspapers

BAIRRO ALTO & PRÍNCIPE REAL 1821286P89C-21
Editorial: R. do Loreto, 16 - 2° Dto., 1200-242 LISBOA **Tel:** 213 408 090 **Fax:** 213 256 809
Email: email@convida.pt **Web site:** http://www.convida.pt
Date Established: 2003; **Freq:** Half-yearly; **Cover Price:** Free; **Circ:** 70,000
Usual Pagination: 60
Language(s): English
ADVERTISING RATES:
Full Page Colour .... EUR 1950
Mechanical Data: Trim Size: 148 x 210 mm
Part of Series, see entry for: Convida
CONSUMER: HOLIDAYS & TRAVEL: Entertainment Guides

BAIXA & CHIADO 1821287P89C-22
Editorial: R. do Loreto, 16 - 2° Dto., 1200-242 LISBOA **Tel:** 213 408 090 **Fax:** 213 256 809
Email: email@convida.pt **Web site:** http://www.convida.pt
Date Established: 2003; **Freq:** Half-yearly; **Cover Price:** Free; **Circ:** 75,000
Usual Pagination: 60
Language(s): English
ADVERTISING RATES:
Full Page Colour .... EUR 1950
Mechanical Data: Trim Size: 148 x 210 mm
Part of Series, see entry for: Convida
CONSUMER: HOLIDAYS & TRAVEL: Entertainment Guides

BANCA ON-LINE 1780230P1C-13
Editorial: R. da Oliveira ao Carmo, 8, 1249-111 LISBOA **Tel:** 213 236 711 **Fax:** 213 236 701
Email: deconomico@economico.pt **Web site:** http://www.diarioeconomico.com
Freq: Occasional; **Cover Price:** Free; **Circ:** 20,102
Profile: Broadsheet-sized quality newspaper providing in-depth coverage of politics, economics, financial and business news. Includes reports on the stock exchange, taxation, updates of national and European affairs, relevant conferences and exhibitions, world market developments, opinion and technology.
Language(s): Portuguese
Readership: National. Aimed at leaders within business and industry, financial directors, public and private investors.
Mechanical Data: Type Area: 250 x 360 mm, Trim Size: 280 x 394 mm

BARBEIROS & CABELEIREIROS 1642561P15R-1
Editorial: R. dos Fanqueiros, 135 - 2°, 1100-227 LISBOA **Tel:** 218 820 840 **Fax:** 218 877 264
Email: apcib@netnovis.pt
Freq: Occasional; **Cover Price:** EUR 17,5; **Circ:** 8,500
Usual Pagination: 54
Language(s): Portuguese
Readership: National.
Mechanical Data: Trim Size: 220 x 280 mm, Type Area: 195 x 240 mm
BUSINESS: COSMETICS & HAIRDRESSING: Cosmetics & Hairdressing Related

BARCELOS POPULAR 1642565P67B-6007
Editorial: Av. João Paulo II, 355, 4750-304 BARCELOS **Tel:** 253 813 585 **Fax:** 253 823 362
Email: geral@barcelos-popular.pt **Web site:** http://www.barcelos-popular.pt
Date Established: 1975; **Freq:** Weekly; **Cover Price:** EUR 0,7; **Circ:** 9,000
Managing Director: José Santos Alves
Language(s): Portuguese
Readership: Read in Barcelos region.
ADVERTISING RATES:
Full Page Mono .... EUR 502
Full Page Colour .... EUR 552
Mechanical Data: Trim Size: 275 x 400 mm, Type Area: 245 x 352 mm
REGIONAL DAILY & SUNDAY NEWSPAPERS: Regional Daily Newspapers

BARLAVENTO 1642566P72I-26
Editorial: Edifício Pátio da Rocha, Loja 46 - Piso 0 BA, Praia da Rocha, Apartado 168, 8501-911 PORTIMÃO **Tel:** 282 480 220 **Fax:** 282 480 221
Email: barlavento@mail.telepac.pt **Web site:** http://www.barlavento.online.pt
Freq: Weekly; **Cover Price:** EUR 1; **Circ:** 7,500
Usual Pagination: 40
Editor-in-Chief: Elisabete Rodrigues; **Managing Director:** Hélder Nunes
Profile: Weekly regional newspaper with information about Faro region. Politics, current affairs, society, religion, sport, entertainment and events.
Language(s): Portuguese
Readership: Aimed at Algarve's windward locals. Read mainly by upper to middle classed people, aged from 26 to 54 years old.
ADVERTISING RATES:
Full Page Mono .... EUR 1200
Full Page Colour .... EUR 1500
Mechanical Data: Trim Size: 290 x 410 mm, Type Area: 260 x 345 mm
LOCAL NEWSPAPERS: Regional Weekly Newspapers

BEBÉ D'HOJE 622786P74D-20
Editorial: R. Policarpo Anjos, 4, 1495-742 CRUZ QUEBRADA/DAFUNDO **Tel:** 214 154 500
Fax: 214 154 504
Email: bebedhoje@motorpress.pt **Web site:** http://www.mpl.pt
Date Established: 1997; **Freq:** Monthly; **Cover Price:** EUR 2,95; **Circ:** 20,000
Managing Director: Helena Gatinho
Profile: Magazine with pre-natal information for parents-to-be and information about childhood matters.
Language(s): Portuguese
Readership: National. Aimed at young parents and parents-to-be.
ADVERTISING RATES:
Full Page Colour .... EUR 4490
Mechanical Data: Trim Size: 185 x 248 mm
CONSUMER: WOMEN'S INTEREST CONSUMER MAGAZINES: Child Care

BEBÉ SAÚDE 1642569P91D-145
Editorial: R. General Ferreira Martins, N° 10 - 6° B, Miraflores, 1495-137 ALGÉS **Tel:** 219 959 510
Fax: 219 959 515
Email: promercado@promercado.pt **Web site:** http://www.promercado.pt/bbSaude.htm
Date Established: 2000; **Freq:** Monthly; **Cover Price:** EUR 2; **Circ:** 18,000
Usual Pagination: 52
Language(s): Portuguese
Readership: National.
ADVERTISING RATES:
Full Page Colour .... EUR 1600
Mechanical Data: Type Area: 180 x 297 mm, Trim Size: 210 x 297 mm
CONSUMER: RECREATION & LEISURE: Children & Youth

BGAMER 1606541P78D-3
Editorial: Av. Infante D. Henrique, 306 - Lote 6 R/C, 1950-421 LISBOA **Tel:** 218 621 530 **Fax:** 218 621 540
Email: bgamer@goody.pt **Web site:** http://www.bgamer.pt
Date Established: 1997; **Freq:** Monthly; **Cover Price:** EUR 4,99; **Circ:** 15,000
Usual Pagination: 100
Editor: Jorge Daniel Lopes; **Managing Director:** Bruno Mendonça
Profile: Magazine focusing on PC and console games features information on new releases and helpful hints and tips.
Language(s): Portuguese
Readership: Mainland. Aimed at computer games enthusiasts' aged 15 to 25 years.
ADVERTISING RATES:
Full Page Colour .... EUR 5900
Mechanical Data: Trim Size: 230 x 300 mm, Type Area: 205 x 265 mm
CONSUMER: CONSUMER ELECTRONICS: Games

BIKE MAGAZINE 19745P77C-50
Editorial: R. Policarpo Anjos, 4, 1495-742 CRUZ QUEBRADA/DAFUNDO **Tel:** 214 154 500
Fax: 214 154 504
Email: bikemagazine@motorpress.pt **Web site:** http://www.bikemagazine.pt
Date Established: 1994; **Freq:** Monthly; **Cover Price:** EUR 3,5; **Circ:** 16,833
Usual Pagination: 116
Editor-in-Chief: Carlos Almeida Pinto; **Managing Director:** Alexandre Silva; **Advertising Manager:** Pedro Portas
Profile: Magazine about bikes: the news and events.
Language(s): Portuguese
Readership: Mainland.
ADVERTISING RATES:
Full Page Colour .... EUR 2400
Mechanical Data: Trim Size: 210 x 284 mm, Type Area: 185 x 252 mm
CONSUMER: MOTORING & CYCLING: Cycling

BIT 714058P5C-54
Editorial: Av. dos Maristas, 82 A, 2775-241 PAREDE
Tel: 211 545 910 **Fax:** 211 545 919
Email: geral@bit.pt **Web site:** http://www.bit.pt
ISSN: 0874-3223
Date Established: 1997; **Freq:** Monthly; **Cover Price:** EUR 3,95; **Circ:** 30,000
Usual Pagination: 84
Profile: Magazine focusing on computer science. Features all the latest news on the IT market, information on new technologies, reviews and previews of hardware and software, articles on IT events, expert advice and step-by-step guides, reviews of games and Internet sites.
Language(s): Portuguese
Readership: National. Read by IT managers, IT technicians, IT end-users, game players, web explorers and others who need information and answers for their IT problems.
ADVERTISING RATES:
Full Page Colour .... EUR 1500
Mechanical Data: Trim Size: 200 x 280 mm
BUSINESS: COMPUTERS & AUTOMATION: Professional Personal Computers

BLITZ 19733P76D-50
Editorial: Edifício S. Francisco de Sales, R. Calvet de Magalhães, 242, 2770-022 PAÇO DE ARCOS
Tel: 214 698 000 **Fax:** 214 698 533
Email: blitz@aeiou.pt **Web site:** http://blitz.pt
Date Established: 1983; **Freq:** Monthly; **Cover Price:** EUR 2,5; **Circ:** 26,400
Editor: Luís Guerra; **Managing Director:** Miguel Francisco Cadete
Profile: Magazine about music, dance, theatre and shows. News, interviews and fait-divers.
Language(s): Portuguese
Readership: Mainland.
ADVERTISING RATES:
Full Page Colour .... EUR 3000
Mechanical Data: Trim Size: 220 x 280 mm, Type Area: 220 x 280 mm
CONSUMER: MUSIC & PERFORMING ARTS: Music

BLUE COOKING 1780276P74P-225
Editorial: R. Vera Lagoa, 12, 1649-012 LISBOA
Tel: 217 203 340 **Fax:** 217 203 349
Email: blue@blue.com.pt **Web site:** http://www.blue.com.pt
Date Established: 2005; **Freq:** 6 issues yearly; **Cover Price:** EUR 3,2; **Circ:** 20,000
Usual Pagination: 100
Managing Director: Margarida Magalhães
Profile: Magazine containing articles related to food and drink. Recipes, tricks and tips to use in the kitchen or in the dining-room and suggestions on interior design and consumer electronics. Also available in pocket size, for 1,80€.
Language(s): Portuguese
Readership: National.
ADVERTISING RATES:
Full Page Colour .... EUR 2400
Mechanical Data: Type Area: 220 x 265 mm, Trim Size: 230 x 275 mm

BLUE TRAVEL 1780279P50-96
Editorial: R. Vera Lagoa, 12, 1649-012 LISBOA
Tel: 217 203 340 **Fax:** 217 203 349
Email: blue@blue.com.pt **Web site:** http://www.blue.com.pt
Date Established: 2003; **Freq:** Monthly; **Cover Price:** EUR 3,95; **Circ:** 20,000
Editor: Rosário Sá Coutinho
Profile: Magazine about tourism and traveling. The people, the food, the pleasures, the nature, the landscape, the enchanting places that transform a trip into a life memory.
Language(s): Portuguese
Readership: National.
ADVERTISING RATES:
Full Page Colour .... EUR 4000
Mechanical Data: Type Area: 220 x 265 mm, Trim Size: 230 x 275 mm

BOA MESA 1780281P74P-339
Editorial: R. Calvet de Magalhães, 242, Laveiras, 2770-022 PAÇO DE ARCOS **Tel:** 214 698 000
Fax: 214 698 500
Email: boamesa@edimpresa.pt **Web site:** http://pub.edimpresa.pt/index.asp?revista=boa_mesa&lang=pt
Freq: Monthly; **Cover Price:** EUR 1,75; **Circ:** 92,000
Usual Pagination: 52
Managing Director: Rita Sena Lino
Profile: Monthly magazine containing recipes.
Language(s): Portuguese
Readership: National.
ADVERTISING RATES:
Full Page Colour .... EUR 5650
Mechanical Data: Type Area: 182 x 247 mm, Trim Size: 205 x 275 mm

A BOLA 622945P65A-20
Editorial: Travessa da Queimada, 23 - R/C, 1° e 2°, 1249-113 LISBOA **Tel:** 213 463 981 **Fax:** 213 464 503
Email: publicidag@abola.pt **Web site:** http://www.abola.pt
Date Established: 1945; **Freq:** Daily; **Cover Price:** EUR 0,8; **Circ:** 120,000
Usual Pagination: 48
Executive Editor: Nuno Perestrelo; **Managing Director:** Vítor Hugo dos Santos Serpa
Profile: Tabloid-sized newspaper focusing on all aspects of competitive sport in Portugal and throughout the world.
Language(s): Portuguese
Readership: Sold in Portugal and in some cities in Brazil, USA and Canada. Read by a broad range of the population, mainly man, with a particular interest in sporting events.
ADVERTISING RATES:
Full Page Colour .... EUR 8215
Mechanical Data: Type Area: 259 x 350 mm, Trim Size: 281 x 400 mm
Sections:
Aniversário
Cadernos de Futebol
Modalidades
NATIONAL DAILY & SUNDAY NEWSPAPERS: National Daily Newspapers

BOLOS E TORTAS 1831588P74P-311
Editorial: Cascais Office, Rotunda das Tojas, 2° E, 2645-901 ALCABIDECHE **Tel:** 214 606 100
Fax: 214 606 119
Email: receitassucesso@presspeople.pt **Web site:** http://presspeople.pt
Date Established: 2008; **Freq:** Occasional; **Cover Price:** EUR 1,2; **Circ:** 50,000
Usual Pagination: 36
Profile: Receitas e sugestões dos mais variados bolos e tortas: salgadas, com chocolate, fruta, doce de ovos, etc.
Language(s): Portuguese
Readership: Mainland. Aimed mainly at women with 25 to 44 years old. C1 and C2.
ADVERTISING RATES:
Full Page Colour .... EUR 900
Mechanical Data: Type Area: 131 x 185 mm, Trim Size: 148 x 210 mm
Part of Series, see entry for: Receitas de Sucesso

BOLOS E TORTAS 1831588P74P-337
Editorial: Cascais Office, Rotunda das Tojas, 2° E, 2645-901 ALCABIDECHE **Tel:** 214 606 100
Fax: 214 606 119
Email: receitassucesso@presspeople.pt **Web site:** http://presspeople.pt
Date Established: 2008; **Freq:** Occasional; **Cover Price:** EUR 1,2; **Circ:** 50,000
Usual Pagination: 36
Profile: Receitas e sugestões dos mais variados bolos e tortas: salgadas, com chocolate, fruta, doce de ovos, etc.
Language(s): Portuguese
Readership: Mainland. Aimed mainly at women with 25 to 44 years old. C1 and C2.
ADVERTISING RATES:
Full Page Colour .... EUR 900
Mechanical Data: Type Area: 131 x 185 mm, Trim Size: 148 x 210 mm
Part of Series, see entry for: Receitas de Sucesso

BOLSA DE TURISMO DE LISBOA 1937714P50-272
Editorial: R. Gonçalo Cristóvão, 111 - 6°, 4049-037 PORTO **Tel:** 223 399 404 **Fax:** 222 058 098
Email: redaccao@vidaeconomica.pt **Web site:** http://www.vidaeconomica.pt
ISSN: 0871-4320
Date Established: 2010; **Freq:** Occasional; **Cover Price:** Free; **Circ:** 21,700
Usual Pagination: 8
Profile: Supplement with information regarding the 22.nd Edition of the International Tourism Fair of Lisbon-BTL 2010.
Language(s): Portuguese
Readership: National. Aimed at managers and directors in business, finance and industry and politicians.
ADVERTISING RATES:
Full Page Mono .... EUR 1800
Full Page Colour .... EUR 2335
Mechanical Data: Type Area: 256 x 388 mm, Trim Size: 288 x 416 mm
Part of Series, see entry for: Vida Económica

A BOLSA M.I.A. 1642467P21A-82
Editorial: R. Nelson Pereira Neves, Lojas 1 e 2, 2670-338 LOURES **Tel:** 219 830 130 **Fax:** 219 833 359
Email: abolsamia@abolsamia.pt **Web site:** http://www.abolsamia.pt/home_agricola.php
Date Established: 2008; **Freq:** 6 issues yearly; **Cover Price:** EUR 6; **Circ:** 15,000
Usual Pagination: 172
Managing Director: Nuno de Gusmão
Profile: Online magazine focused on agriculture and related machinery such as tractors. Importers and manufacturers, agriculturist's events and products, companies and products, awarded agricultural produts, adds, weather report and image gallery, characterize this web site.
Language(s): Portuguese
Readership: National.
ADVERTISING RATES:
Full Page Colour .... EUR 1550
Mechanical Data: Trim Size: 228 x 285 mm

BRAVO 1606441P74F-101
Editorial: R. Joaquim António de Aguiar, 35 - 3° Esq., 1070-149 LISBOA **Tel:** 213 839 580 **Fax:** 213 839 581
Email: revistabravo@portugalmail.pt **Web site:** http://www.bravopt.com
ISSN: 0874-3401
Date Established: 1998; **Freq:** 26 issues yearly; **Cover Price:** EUR 1,8; **Circ:** 60,000
Usual Pagination: 64
Editor-in-Chief: Elsa Prata
Profile: Magazine containing the latest music and film news and reviews as well as celebrity gossip. Also offers advice on teenage issues.
Language(s): Portuguese
Readership: Mainland. Aimed at teenagers.
ADVERTISING RATES:
Full Page Colour .... EUR 3870
Mechanical Data: Trim Size: 210 x 280 mm, Type Area: 210 x 280 mm
CONSUMER: WOMEN'S INTEREST CONSUMER MAGAZINES: Teenage

BRIEFING 19292P2A-101
Editorial: Edifício Lisboa Oriente, Av. Infante D. Henrique, 333 H, Esc. 44, 1800-282 LISBOA
Tel: 218 504 060 **Fax:** 210 435 935
Email: briefing@briefing.pt **Web site:** http://www.briefing.pt
Date Established: 1988; **Freq:** Monthly; **Cover Price:** EUR 3,5; **Circ:** 2,500
Editor: António Barradinhas; **Executive Editor:** Fátima de Sousa; **Managing Director:** Hermínio Santos; **Advertising Manager:** Maria Luís
Profile: Journal focusing on advertisement and marketing.
Language(s): Portuguese
Readership: Mainland. Aimed at PR professionals.

ADVERTISING RATES:
Full Page Colour .... EUR 2900
Mechanical Data: Type Area: 220 x 310 mm, Trim Size: 240 x 335 mm
BUSINESS: COMMUNICATIONS, ADVERTISING & MARKETING

BTL
1937450P50-271
Editorial: Edifício Diário de Notícias, Av. da Liberdade, 266, 1250-149 LISBOA **Tel:** 213 187 500 **Fax:** 213 187 516
Email: dnot@dn.pt **Web site:** http://www.dn.pt
Date Established: 2010; **Freq:** Occasional; **Cover Price:** Free; **Circ:** 81,061
Profile: Tourism. Published with: Diário de Notícias; 24 Horas.
Language(s): Portuguese
Readership: National.
Mechanical Data: Trim Size: 246 x 348 mm
Series owner and contact point for the following titles, see individual entries:
BTL
Part of Series, see entry for: BTL

CABELOS
1780356P74B-64
Editorial: Edifício S. Francisco de Sales, R. Calvet de Magalhães, 242, 2770-022 PAÇO DE ARCOS
Tel: 214 544 000 **Fax:** 214 435 310
Email: rbarreto@activa.impresa.pt **Web site:** http://activa.aeiou.pt
ISSN: 0874-0453
Freq: Occasional; **Cover Price:** Free; **Circ:** 96,600
Profile: Special supplement about haird and hairdressing.
Language(s): Portuguese
Readership: Mainland.
ADVERTISING RATES:
Full Page Colour .... EUR 5950
Mechanical Data: Trim Size: 230 x 297 mm, Type Area: 194 x 260 mm
Part of Series, see entry for: Activa

CABELOS
1780356P74B-165
Editorial: Edifício S. Francisco de Sales, R. Calvet de Magalhães, 242, 2770-022 PAÇO DE ARCOS
Tel: 214 544 000 **Fax:** 214 435 310
Email: rbarreto@activa.impresa.pt **Web site:** http://activa.aeiou.pt
ISSN: 0874-0453
Freq: Occasional; **Cover Price:** Free; **Circ:** 96,600
Profile: Special supplement about haird and hairdressing.
Language(s): Portuguese
Readership: Mainland.
ADVERTISING RATES:
Full Page Colour .... EUR 5950
Mechanical Data: Trim Size: 230 x 297 mm, Type Area: 194 x 260 mm
Part of Series, see entry for: Activa

CAÇA & CÃES DE CAÇA
1642589P91R-2
Editorial: Av. Infante D. Henrique, 306, 1900-717 LISBOA **Tel:** 218 310 920 **Fax:** 218 310 939
Email: redaccao.caca@grupov.com **Web site:** http://www.grupov.com
Freq: Monthly; **Cover Price:** EUR 4,95; **Circ:** 17,500
Usual Pagination: 100
Editor-in-Chief: Ana Raquel Matos; **Managing Director:** Pedro Vitorino
Language(s): Portuguese
Readership: National. 16 - 65. A, B, C1, C2.
ADVERTISING RATES:
Full Page Colour .... EUR 1550
Mechanical Data: Trim Size: 210 x 285 mm
CONSUMER: RECREATION & LEISURE: Recreation & Leisure Related

CADERNOS DE FUTEBOL
1780291P65A-20_103
Editorial: Travessa da Queimada, 23 - R/C, 1° e 2°, 1249-113 LISBOA **Tel:** 213 463 981 **Fax:** 213 464 503
Web site: http://www.abola.pt
Freq: Annual; **Cover Price:** EUR 3; **Circ:** 100,000
Usual Pagination: 228
Language(s): Portuguese
Readership: National.
ADVERTISING RATES:
Full Page Colour .... EUR 3350
Mechanical Data: Trim Size: 208 x 295 mm, Type Area: 195 x 265 mm
Section of: A Bola
NATIONAL DAILY & SUNDAY NEWSPAPERS: National Daily Newspapers

---

CÃES & COMPANHIA
1642593P91R-3
Editorial: Av. Infante D. Henique, N° 306, 1900-717 LISBOA **Tel:** 218 310 920 **Fax:** 218 310 939
Email: redaccao.caes@grupov.com **Web site:** http://www.grupov.com
Freq: Monthly; **Cover Price:** EUR 3; **Circ:** 10,000
Usual Pagination: 100
Managing Director: Marta Manta
Language(s): Portuguese
Readership: National. 13 - 55. A, B, C1.
ADVERTISING RATES:
Full Page Colour .... EUR 1500
Mechanical Data: Trim Size: 210 x 285 mm
CONSUMER: RECREATION & LEISURE: Recreation & Leisure Related

CÂMARAS VERDES
1642595P57-51
Editorial: R. Sampaio Pina, 58 - 2° Dto., 1070-250 LISBOA **Tel:** 213 825 610 **Fax:** 213 825 619
Email: design@companhiadascores.com **Web site:** http://www.camarasverdes.pt
Date Established: 1994; **Freq:** Monthly; **Cover Price:** EUR 12
Free to qualifying individuals ; **Circ:** 5,000
Usual Pagination: 12
Language(s): Portuguese
Readership: Read in Lisboa region.
ADVERTISING RATES:
Full Page Mono .... EUR 1000
Mechanical Data: Trim Size: 196 x 330 mm, Type Area: 170 x 300 mm
BUSINESS: ENVIRONMENT & POLLUTION

O CAMINHENSE
1642978P80-201
Editorial: R. da Corredoura, 117, 4910-133 CAMINHA **Tel:** 258 921 754 **Fax:** 258 721 041
Email: geral@caminhense.com **Web site:** http://www.caminhense.com
Date Established: 1971; **Freq:** Weekly; **Cover Price:** EUR 0,8; **Circ:** 4,100
Usual Pagination: 24
Editor-in-Chief: Cidália Cacais Aldeia
Language(s): Portuguese
Readership: Read in Viana do Castelo region.
ADVERTISING RATES:
Full Page Mono .... EUR 200
Full Page Colour .... EUR 325
Mechanical Data: Trim Size: 290 x 410 mm, Type Area: 345 x 390 mm
CONSUMER: RURAL & REGIONAL INTEREST

CAMPEÃO DAS PROVÍNCIAS
1642597P72I-33
Editorial: R. Adriano Lucas, 216 Az. D, Eiras, 3020-430 COIMBRA **Tel:** 239 497 750 **Fax:** 239 497 759
Email: jornalcp@mail.telepac.pt **Web site:** http://campeaoprovincias.com
ISSN: 0874-3622
Date Established: 1999; **Freq:** Weekly; **Cover Price:** EUR 0,75; **Circ:** 9,000
Usual Pagination: 20
Editor: Luís Santos; **Editor-in-Chief:** José Fidalgo; **Managing Director:** Lino Augusto Vinhal; **Advertising Manager:** Adelaide Pinto
Language(s): Portuguese
Readership: Read by Coimbra locals.
ADVERTISING RATES:
Full Page Mono .... EUR 687
Full Page Colour .... EUR 893.1
Mechanical Data: Trim Size: 290 x 410 mm, Type Area: 260 x 360 mm
LOCAL NEWSPAPERS: Regional Weekly Newspapers

CARAS
19690P74Q-102
Editorial: Edifício S. Francisco de Sales, R. Calvet de Magalhães, 242, 2770-022 PAÇO DE ARCOS
Tel: 214 544 000 **Fax:** 214 435 310
Email: ipublishing@impresa.pt **Web site:** http://aeiou.caras.pt
ISSN: 0874-017X
Date Established: 1987; **Freq:** Weekly; **Cover Price:** EUR 1,35; **Circ:** 103,060
Usual Pagination: 16
Editor: Pedro Amante; **Executive Editor:** Natalina de Almeida; **Managing Director:** Fernanda Dias
Profile: Magazine containing interviews and latest news about celebrities. Contains travel, fashion and cookery tips.
Language(s): Portuguese
Readership: Mainland.
ADVERTISING RATES:
Full Page Colour .... EUR 5250
Mechanical Data: Type Area: 207 x 272 mm, Trim Size: 230 x 297 mm
CONSUMER: WOMEN'S INTEREST CONSUMER MAGAZINES: Lifestyle

CARAS DECORAÇÃO
623602P74C-86
Editorial: Edifício S. Francisco de Sales, R. Calvet de Magalhães, 242, 2770-022 PAÇO DE ARCOS
Tel: 214 544 000 **Fax:** 214 435 310
Email: cdecor@impresa.pt **Web site:** http://aeiou.caras.pt/decoracao=s25088?mid1=cr.menus/1&m2=7revista=caras_decoracao&lang=pt
ISSN: 0874-0488
Freq: Monthly; **Cover Price:** EUR 2,8; **Circ:** 26,700
Usual Pagination: 124
Executive Editor: Teresa Mafalda
Profile: Magazine featuring displays of personalised interior decorating plans, advice and ideas from decorators and designers as well as information on new products and trends in both the portuguese and the international market.
Language(s): Portuguese
Readership: Mainland. Aimed at those interested in home decoration and interior design.
ADVERTISING RATES:
Full Page Colour .... EUR 4000
Mechanical Data: Type Area: 202 x 261 mm, Trim Size: 230 x 297 mm
CONSUMER: WOMEN'S INTEREST CONSUMER MAGAZINES: Home & Family

CARGO
1642600P49C-11
Editorial: Edifício Rocha Conde d'Óbidos, 1° A, Cais de Alcântara, 1350-352 LISBOA **Tel:** 213 973 968 **Fax:** 213 973 984
Email: cargo@cargoedicoes.pt **Web site:** http://www.cargoedicoes.pt
Freq: Monthly; **Cover Price:** EUR 4,5; **Circ:** 8,000
Usual Pagination: 36
Editor-in-Chief: Raquel Sales Pontes Ferreira e Amaral; **Managing Director:** Luís Filipe Duarte
Language(s): Portuguese
Readership: National.
ADVERTISING RATES:
Full Page Colour .... EUR 1360
Mechanical Data: Trim Size: 210 x 297 mm, Type Area: 174 x 263 mm
BUSINESS: TRANSPORT: Freight

O CARRILHÃO
1642979P80-204
Editorial: R. Serafim Paz Medeiros, Centro Comercial de Mafra, Loja 16, 2640-533 MAFRA
Tel: 261 815 848 **Fax:** 261 815 848
Email: carrilhao@sapo.pt **Web site:** http://www.jornal-o-carrilhao.com
Date Established: 1981; **Freq:** 26 issues yearly; **Cover Price:** EUR 0,8; **Circ:** 3,600
Usual Pagination: 24
Language(s): Portuguese
Readership: Read by Mafra locals.
ADVERTISING RATES:
Full Page Mono .... EUR 210
Full Page Colour .... EUR 480
Mechanical Data: Trim Size: 298 x 425 mm, Type Area: 270 x 365 mm
CONSUMER: RURAL & REGIONAL INTEREST

CARTEIA
1642826P67B-6014
Editorial: Av. de Ceuta, Urbanização A Nora, Bloco 6 - Loja Carteia, 8125-116 QUARTEIRA
Tel: 289 315 560 **Fax:** 289 389 756
Email: jornal.carteia@citymap.pt **Web site:** http://www.citymap.pt
Freq: 26 issues yearly; **Cover Price:** EUR 0,5; **Circ:** 4,500
Usual Pagination: 32
Managing Director: Vaz dos Santos; **Advertising Manager:** Vanessa Santos
Language(s): Portuguese
Readership: Read in Faro region.
ADVERTISING RATES:
Full Page Colour .... EUR 840
Mechanical Data: Type Area: 260 x 345 mm, Trim Size: 314 x 403 mm
REGIONAL DAILY & SUNDAY NEWSPAPERS: Regional Daily Newspapers

---

CASA CLÁUDIA
1642602P74C-89
Editorial: Edifício S. Francisco de Sales, R. Calvet de Magalhães, 242, 2770-022 PAÇO DE ARCOS
Tel: 214 544 000 **Fax:** 214 435 310
Email: cmonteiro@edimpresa.pt **Web site:** http://activa.aeiou.pt/tema.aspx?channelid=B9A017AF-7E4-449C-8E66-AF561408A541
ISSN: 0874-050X
Date Established: 1988; **Freq:** Monthly; **Cover Price:** EUR 3,3; **Circ:** 18,800
Editor: Petra Alves; **Managing Director:** Isabel Pilar Figueiredo
Language(s): Portuguese
Readership: Mainland.
ADVERTISING RATES:
Full Page Colour .... EUR 3650
Mechanical Data: Type Area: 202 x 261 mm, Trim Size: 230 x 297 mm
CONSUMER: WOMEN'S INTEREST CONSUMER MAGAZINES: Home & Family

CASAMENTO & LUA DE MEL
1780459P74L-5
Editorial: Av. João Crisóstomo, 72, 1069-043 LISBOA **Tel:** 213 307 706 **Fax:** 213 540 695
Email: lauratorres@maxima.investec.pt
ISSN: 0874-6931
Freq: Annual; **Cover Price:** Free; **Circ:** 106,000
Usual Pagination: 124
Profile: Magazine about wedding preparations. Published with: Máxima; Máxima Interiores; Rotas & Destinos.
Language(s): Portuguese
Readership: National.
ADVERTISING RATES:
Full Page Colour .... EUR 4950
Mechanical Data: Trim Size: 180 x 225 mm, Type Area: 156 x 198 mm

---

CASAMENTO & LUA DE MEL
1780459P74L-28
Editorial: Av. João Crisóstomo, 72, 1069-043 LISBOA **Tel:** 213 307 706 **Fax:** 213 540 695
Email: lauratorres@maxima.investec.pt
ISSN: 0874-6931
Freq: Annual; **Cover Price:** Free; **Circ:** 106,000
Usual Pagination: 124
Profile: Magazine about wedding preparations. Published with: Máxima; Máxima Interiores; Rotas & Destinos.
Language(s): Portuguese
Readership: National.
ADVERTISING RATES:
Full Page Colour .... EUR 4950
Mechanical Data: Trim Size: 180 x 225 mm, Type Area: 156 x 198 mm

---

CASAS DE PORTUGAL
1606428P74K-1
Editorial: R. General Firmino Miguel, 3 - Torre 2, 3°, 1600-100 LISBOA **Tel:** 210 410 324 **Fax:** 210 410 306
Email: casasdeportugaleditorial@gmail.com
Date Established: 1995; **Freq:** 6 issues yearly; **Cover Price:** EUR 4; **Circ:** 16,000
Usual Pagination: 108
Advertising Manager: Paula Vasconcelos
Profile: Magazine focusing on property. Includes information and advice on mortgages and surveys as well as listings of homes for sale. Includes articles on home design and tourism.
Language(s): Portuguese
Readership: Mainland. Aimed at those interested in purchasing a house, mainly people between 25 and 54 years old of A, B and C1 social classes.
ADVERTISING RATES:
Full Page Colour .... EUR 2200
Mechanical Data: Trim Size: 230 x 297 mm, Type Area: 205 x 270 mm
CONSUMER: WOMEN'S INTEREST CONSUMER MAGAZINES: Home Purchase

CATÁLOGO
1834910P77B-74
Editorial: R. Policarpo Anjos, 4, 1495-742 CRUZ QUEBRADA/DAFUNDO **Tel:** 214 154 500
Fax: 214 154 501
Email: motociclismo@motorpress.pt **Web site:** http://www.motociclismo.pt
Freq: Annual; **Cover Price:** EUR 5; **Circ:** 18,000
Usual Pagination: 100
Profile: Magazine covering the motorcycle trade.
Language(s): Portuguese
Readership: Mainland. Aimed at motorcycle enthusiasts.
ADVERTISING RATES:
Full Page Colour .... EUR 2670
Mechanical Data: Trim Size: 215 x 280 mm

CERTA
1780493P94H-2
Editorial: Edifício S. Francisco de Sales, R. Calvet de Magalhães, 242, 2770-022 PAÇO DE ARCOS
Tel: 214 544 000 **Fax:** 214 698 542
Email: enova@impresa.pt **Web site:** http://www.edimpresa.pt
Freq: Monthly; **Circ:** 1,282,610
Usual Pagination: 60
Profile: Free magazine of the supermarket Continente containing some entertainment and leisure articles but mainly refering to it's products and prices.
Language(s): Portuguese
Readership: Distributed in the portuguese continent.
ADVERTISING RATES:
Full Page Colour .... EUR 3250
Mechanical Data: Type Area: 160 x 235 mm, Trim Size: 190 x 270 mm
CONSUMER: OTHER CLASSIFICATIONS: Customer Magazines

CHICK - INTIMATE CULT
1642607P74A-102
Editorial: Global Chick, Publicações, Lda., R. dos Cafés, 24 Sobreloja, 4490-595 PÓVOA DE VARZIM
Tel: 252 637 570 **Fax:** 252 637 570
Email: chick@chick-pt.com **Web site:** http://chickintimate.wordpress.com
ISSN: 1645-3719
Date Established: 1989; **Freq:** Half-yearly; **Cover Price:** EUR 10; **Circ:** 3,000
Usual Pagination: 138
Managing Director: Monserrat Camell Rafols
Language(s): Portuguese
Readership: National.
ADVERTISING RATES:
Full Page Colour .... EUR 2200
Mechanical Data: Trim Size: 210 x 290 mm, Type Area: 175 x 237 mm
CONSUMER: WOMEN'S INTEREST CONSUMER MAGAZINES: Women's Interest

---

CIDADE DE TOMAR
1642827P72I-45
Editorial: Praça da República, N° 27, 1°, Apartado 62, 2304-909 TOMAR **Tel:** 249 324 041
Fax: 249 323 898
Email: redaccao@cidadetomar.pt **Web site:** http://www.cidadetomar.pt
Date Established: 1934; **Freq:** Weekly; **Cover Price:** EUR 0,7; **Circ:** 6,000
Usual Pagination: 40
Editor-in-Chief: Mário Cobra; **Managing Director:** António Cândido Lopes Madureira
Language(s): Portuguese
Readership: Read by Tomar locals.
ADVERTISING RATES:
Full Page Mono .... EUR 550
Full Page Colour .... EUR 750
Mechanical Data: Type Area: 252 x 358 mm, Trim Size: 280 x 400 mm
LOCAL NEWSPAPERS: Regional Weekly Newspapers

CIDADE HOJE
1642612P74Q-91
Editorial: R. 5 de Outubro, Edifício Vilarminda - Loja 204, Apartado 218, 4764-976 VILA NOVA DE FAMALICÃO **Tel:** 252 301 780 **Fax:** 252 301 789
Email: jornal@cidadehoje.pt **Web site:** http://www.cidadehoje.pt
Date Established: 1985; **Freq:** Weekly; **Cover Price:** EUR 0,7; **Circ:** 5,500
Usual Pagination: 40

Managing Director: Rui Lima
Language(s): Portuguese
Readership: Aimed at Braga locals.
ADVERTISING RATES:
Full Page Mono .... EUR 300
Full Page Colour .... EUR 390
Mechanical Data: Trim Size: 280 x 410 mm, Type Area: 260 x 360 mm
CONSUMER: WOMEN'S INTEREST CONSUMER MAGAZINES: Lifestyle

CINEMA 1820958P76A-54

Editorial: Edifício Impala, Ranholas, 2710-460 SINTRA **Tel:** 219 238 120 **Fax:** 219 238 195
Email: tv7dias@impala.pt **Web site:** http://www.impala.pt
Freq: Occasional; **Cover Price:** EUR 1,25; **Circ:** 210,000
Usual Pagination: 66
Language(s): Portuguese
Readership: National.
ADVERTISING RATES:
Full Page Colour .... EUR 4370
Mechanical Data: Type Area: 172 x 242 mm, Trim Size: 205 x 275 mm
Part of Series, see entry for: TV 7 Dias
CONSUMER: MUSIC & PERFORMING ARTS: Cinema

CLÁSSICOS DA TV 2094343P74P-366

Editorial: Cascais Office, Rotunda das Tojas, 2° E, 2645-091 ALCABIDECHE **Tel:** 214 606 100
Fax: 214 606 119
Email: cozinhasucesso@presspeople.pt **Web site:** http://presspeople.pt
Date Established: 2011; **Freq:** Occasional; **Cover Price:** Free; **Circ:** 50,000
Profile: Cooking.
Language(s): Portuguese
Readership: National.
Mechanical Data: Trim Size: 210 x 275 mm
Part of Series, see entry for: Mariana Culinária

CLASSIFICADOS 1780537P65A-50_101

Editorial: Av. João Crisóstomo, 72, 1069-043 LISBOA **Tel:** 213 185 462 **Fax:** 213 540 695
Email: geral@correiomanha.pt **Web site:** http://www.cmjornal.pt
Freq: Daily; **Cover Price:** Free; **Circ:** 160,521
Usual Pagination: 28
Profile: Newspaper supplement with classified advertisement, arranged according to specific categories or classifications. The three major headings are employment, real estate, and automotive, although there are additional categories (e.g., business opportunities, pets, personal ads and legal notices).
Language(s): Portuguese
Readership: National. Read predominantly by public sector employees and those seeking employment of northern Portugal.
ADVERTISING RATES:
Full Page Mono .... EUR 2160
Full Page Colour .... EUR 3240
Mechanical Data: Trim Size: 280 x 370 mm, Type Area: 257 x 340 mm
Section of: Correio da Manhã
NATIONAL DAILY & SUNDAY NEWSPAPERS: National Daily Newspapers

CLASSIFICADOS TUTI

1780536P65A-90_102
Editorial: Av. da Liberdade, 266 - 1°, 1250-149 LISBOA **Tel:** 213 187 500 **Fax:** 213 187 515
Email: master@tuti.pt **Web site:** http://www.tuti.pt
ISSN: 0870-1954
Freq: Daily; **Cover Price:** Free; **Circ:** 57,850
Usual Pagination: 20
Profile: Newspaper supplement with classified advertisement, arranged according to specific categories or classifications. The three major headings are employment, real estate, and automotive, although there are additional categories (e.g., business opportunities, pets, personal ads and legal notices).
Language(s): Portuguese
Readership: National.
ADVERTISING RATES:
Full Page Mono .... EUR 1408
Full Page Colour .... EUR 1971.2
Mechanical Data: Trim Size: 294 x 370 mm, Type Area: 266 x 355 mm
Section of: Diário de Notícias
NATIONAL DAILY & SUNDAY NEWSPAPERS: Unabhängiges konservatives MdEP

CLASSIFICADOS TUTI

1782181P65A-181_103
Editorial: Av. da Liberdade, 266 - 1°, 1250-149 LISBOA **Tel:** 213 187 500 **Fax:** 213 187 515
Email: master@tuti.pt **Web site:** http://www.tuti.pt
ISSN: 0874-1352
Freq: Daily; **Cover Price:** Free; **Circ:** 122,218
Usual Pagination: 32
Profile: Newspaper supplement with classified advertisement. The three major headings are employment, real estate, and automotive, although there are additional categories (e.g., business opportunities, personals, and legal notices).
Language(s): Portuguese
Readership: National. General population.

ADVERTISING RATES:
Full Page Mono .... EUR 2400
Full Page Colour .... EUR 3360
Mechanical Data: Trim Size: 288 x 370 mm, Type Area: 252 x 334 mm
Section of: Jornal de Notícias
NATIONAL DAILY & SUNDAY NEWSPAPERS: National Daily Newspapers

CLIMATIZAÇÃO 1849903P3-719

Editorial: R. da Piedade, N° 15 C, 1495-104 ALGÉS
Tel: 214 118 360 **Fax:** 214 118 369
Email: climatizacao@medialine.pt **Web site:** http://www.climatizacao.pt
Freq: 6 issues yearly; **Cover Price:** EUR 5; **Circ:** 5,000
Usual Pagination: 98
Managing Director: Rita Ascenso
Profile: Magazine about air conditioning: heating, ventilation, buildings, energy and renewable energy.
Language(s): Portuguese
Readership: National.
ADVERTISING RATES:
Full Page Colour .... EUR 1380
Mechanical Data: Trim Size: 210 x 297 mm

A COMARCA 19753P80-17

Editorial: R. Dr. António José de Almeida, 41, 3260-420 FGUEIRÓ DOS VINHOS **Tel:** 236 553 669
Fax: 236 553 692
Email: acomarca.jornal@gmail.com
Date Established: 1977; **Freq:** 6 issues yearly; **Cover Price:** EUR 0,6; **Circ:** 5,000
Usual Pagination: 20
Language(s): Portuguese
Readership: Read by Leiria locals.
ADVERTISING RATES:
Full Page Mono .... EUR 450
Full Page Colour .... EUR 475
Mechanical Data: Trim Size: 280 x 370 mm, Type Area: 246 x 336 mm
CONSUMER: RURAL & REGIONAL INTEREST

O COMÉRCIO DA PÓVOA DE VARZIM 1642982P74E-47

Editorial: R. da Caverneira, 18 - 1°, 4490-500 PÓVOA DE VARZIM **Tel:** 252 626 921
Fax: 252 626 921
Email: ocomerciopv@sapo.pt
Date Established: 1903; **Freq:** Weekly; **Cover Price:** EUR 0,75; **Circ:** 3,000
Usual Pagination: 16
Managing Director: Manuel Frasco
Language(s): Portuguese
Readership: Read by Póvoa do Varzim locals.
ADVERTISING RATES:
Full Page Mono .... EUR 250
Full Page Colour .... EUR 500
Mechanical Data: Trim Size: 302 x 402 mm, Type Area: 275 x 346 mm
CONSUMER: WOMEN'S INTEREST CONSUMER MAGAZINES: Crafts

COMÉRCIO DE GONDOMAR

1642983P80-208
Editorial: R. da Guiné, 18, Apartado 72, 4420-159 PORTO **Tel:** 224 644 902 **Fax:** 224 644 902
Email: comercigondomar@gmail.com **Web site:** http://www.ocomerciodegondomar.com
Date Established: 1960; **Freq:** 6 issues yearly; **Cover Price:** EUR 0,75; **Circ:** 3,000
Usual Pagination: 20
Profile: Newspaper containing local information for the Gondomar area.
Language(s): Portuguese
Readership: Read by Gondomar locals.
ADVERTISING RATES:
Full Page Mono .... EUR 500
Full Page Colour .... EUR 750
Mechanical Data: Trim Size: 280 x 400 mm
CONSUMER: RURAL & REGIONAL INTEREST

O COMÉRCIO DE GUIMARÃES

1642984P67B-6009
Editorial: R. Dr. José Sampaio, 264, Apartado 485, 4810-275 GUIMARÃES **Tel:** 253 421 700
Fax: 253 421 709
Email: geral@guimaraesdigital.com **Web site:** http://www.guimaraesdigital.com
Date Established: 1884; **Freq:** Weekly; **Cover Price:** EUR 0,7; **Circ:** 5,000
Usual Pagination: 20
Editor-in-Chief: Elisabete Pinto; **Managing Director:** Joaquim A. Fernandes
Language(s): Portuguese
Readership: Read by Guimarães locals.
ADVERTISING RATES:
Full Page Mono .... EUR 495
Full Page Colour .... EUR 770
Mechanical Data: Trim Size: 284 x 423 mm, Type Area: 260 x 370 mm
REGIONAL DAILY & SUNDAY NEWSPAPERS: Regional Daily Newspapers

COMUNICAÇÕES 19343P18B-15

Editorial: R. Tomás Ribeiro, 41 - 8°, 1050-225 LISBOA **Tel:** 213 129 670 **Fax:** 213 129 688
Email: apdc@apdc.pt **Web site:** http://www.apdc.pt
ISSN: 0870-4449

Date Established: 1985; **Freq:** Occasional; **Cover Price:** EUR 3,25; **Circ:** 4,000
Usual Pagination: 180
Editor-in-Chief: Isabel Travessa; **Managing Director:** Paulo Neves
Profile: Electronic communications and new technologies journal.
Language(s): Portuguese
Readership: National.
ADVERTISING RATES:
Full Page Colour .... EUR 2100
Mechanical Data: Trim Size: 210 x 297 mm
BUSINESS: ELECTRONICS: Telecommunications

CONFERÊNCIAS 1821513P1A-572

Editorial: R. Vieira da Silva, 45, 1350-342 LISBOA
Tel: 213 236 800 **Fax:** 213 236 801
Email: deconomico@economico.pt **Web site:** http://economico.pt
Date Established: 2007; **Freq:** Occasional; **Cover Price:** Free; **Circ:** 19,403
Usual Pagination: 8
Profile: Publication dedicated to the CGD-DE Conference.
Language(s): Portuguese
Readership: National. Aimed at leaders within business and industry, financial directors, public and private investors.
Mechanical Data: Type Area: 250 x 360 mm, Trim Size: 280 x 403 mm

O CONQUISTADOR 1642986P72-10

Editorial: R. Santa Maria, 6, 4810-248 GUIMARÃES
Tel: 253 416 144 **Fax:** 253 416 113
Email: jornal@oconquistador.com **Web site:** http://www.oconquistador.com
Date Established: 1950; **Freq:** 26 issues yearly; **Cover Price:** EUR 0,4; **Circ:** 1,550
Language(s): Portuguese
Readership: Read by Braga locals.
ADVERTISING RATES:
Full Page Mono .... EUR 226.95
Mechanical Data: Trim Size: 300 x 415 mm
LOCAL NEWSPAPERS

CONSTRUÇÃO E IMOBILIÁRIA

1783760P4E-3
Editorial: Praça do Almada, 10 1°, 4490-438 PÓVOA DE VARZIM **Tel:** 252 615 198 **Fax:** 252 627 636
Email: povoasemanario@povoasemanario.pt **Web site:** http://www.povoasemanario.pt
ISSN: 1646-2904
Freq: Occasional; **Cover Price:** Free; **Circ:** 3,300
Profile: Publication focused on local and regional building construction and real estate market.
Language(s): Portuguese
Readership: Read by Póvoa do Varzim locals.
Mechanical Data: Trim Size: 285 x 400 mm
Part of Series, see entry for: Póvoa Semanário

CONVIDA 1820552P89C-19

Editorial: R. do Loreto, 16 - 2° Dto., 1200-242 LISBOA **Tel:** 213 408 090 **Fax:** 213 256 809
Email: email@convida.pt **Web site:** http://www.convida.pt
Date Established: 2003; **Freq:** Half-yearly; **Cover Price:** Free; **Circ:** 560,000
Usual Pagination: 60
Advertising Manager: Vera Abecassis
Language(s): Portuguese
ADVERTISING RATES:
Full Page Colour .... EUR 1950
Mechanical Data: Trim Size: 148 x 210 mm
Series owner and contact point for the following titles, see individual entries:
Bairro Alto & Príncipe Real
Baixa & Chiado
Roma & Alvalade
Santos
CONSUMER: HOLIDAYS & TRAVEL: Entertainment Guides

O CORREIO DA LINHA 1642811P72-39

Editorial: R. Prof. Mota Pinto, Loja 4, Bairro do Pombal, 2780-275 OEIRAS **Tel:** 214 430 095
Fax: 214 422 531
Email: jornal.c.linha@sapo.pt **Web site:** http://www.ocorreiodalinha.pt
Date Established: 1989; **Freq:** Monthly; **Cover Price:** EUR 1,25; **Circ:** 15,000
Usual Pagination: 24
Managing Director: Paulo Pimenta
Profile: Tabloid-sized regional newspaper with information regarding Lisboa region. Politics, current affairs, society, religion, sport, entertainment and events.
Language(s): Portuguese
Readership: Read by Lisboa, Cascais, Amadora and Oeiras population.
ADVERTISING RATES:
Full Page Colour .... EUR 1701
Mechanical Data: Trim Size: 240 x 340 mm, Type Area: 220 x 320 mm
LOCAL NEWSPAPERS

CORREIO DA MANHÃ 19469P65A-50

Editorial: Av. João Crisóstomo, 72, 1069-043 LISBOA **Tel:** 213 185 462 **Fax:** 213 540 695
Email: geral@correiomanha.pt **Web site:** http://www.cmjornal.pt

Date Established: 1979; **Freq:** Daily; **Cover Price:** EUR 0,9; **Circ:** 160,521
Usual Pagination: 52
Editor: José Rodrigues; **Executive Editor:** Miguel Alexandre Ganhão; **Managing Director:** Octávio Ribeiro; **Advertising Manager:** Sónia Jordão
Profile: Tabloid-sized newspaper providing coverage of national news, events and current affairs. Contains political, economical and international news, interviews and information concerning the environment and current events. Particular emphasis is placed upon advertising, recruitment, entertainment, motoring and sport.
Language(s): Portuguese
Readership: National.
ADVERTISING RATES:
Full Page Mono .... EUR 6795
Full Page Colour .... EUR 10170
Mechanical Data: Type Area: 257 x 336 mm, Trim Size: 280 x 370 mm
Sections:
Açores
Açores
Algarve
Classificados
Domingo
Edição de Natal
Festas
Futebol
Futebol
Guia de Gestão do Condomínio
Natal
Norte
Primeiro Emprego
Santarém
Sport
TV
NATIONAL DAILY & SUNDAY NEWSPAPERS: National Daily Newspapers

CORREIO DE AZEMÉIS

1642630P72I-1
Editorial: Edifício Rainha - 8° Piso, 3720-232 OLIVEIRA DE AZEMÉIS **Tel:** 256 661 460
Fax: 256 673 861
Email: geral@correiodeazemeis.pt **Web site:** http://www.correiodeazemeis.pt
Date Established: 1922; **Freq:** Weekly; **Cover Price:** EUR 0,5; **Circ:** 6,500
Usual Pagination: 40
Managing Director: António Magalhães
Profile: Weekly regional newspaper with information about Oliveira de Azeméis (Aveiro). Politics, current affairs, society, religion, sport, entertainment and events.
Language(s): Portuguese
Readership: Read in Aveiro region.
ADVERTISING RATES:
Full Page Mono .... EUR 598
Full Page Colour .... EUR 698
Mechanical Data: Trim Size: 290 x 370 mm, Type Area: 260 x 330 mm
LOCAL NEWSPAPERS: Regional Weekly Newspapers

CORREIO DE FAFE 1642631P72I-16

Editorial: Largo de Portugal, 17, Apartado 41, 4824-909 FAFE **Tel:** 253 490 820 **Fax:** 253 490 829
Email: correiodefafe@rcfafe.com **Web site:** http://www.correiodefafe.com
ISSN: 1645-3808
Freq: Weekly; **Cover Price:** EUR 0,75; **Circ:** 3,000
Usual Pagination: 20
Editor: António Ferreira Leite
Profile: Weekly regional newspaper with information about Fafe (Braga). Politics, current affairs, society, religion, sport, entertainment and events.
Language(s): Portuguese
Readership: Read by Fafe locals.
ADVERTISING RATES:
Full Page Mono .... EUR 300
Full Page Colour .... EUR 400
Mechanical Data: Trim Size: 290 x 410 mm, Type Area: 252 x 357 mm
LOCAL NEWSPAPERS: Regional Weekly Newspapers

O CORREIO DE POMBAL

1642633P72-14
Editorial: R. de Ansião, 33, Apartado 111, 3100-474 POMBAL **Tel:** 236 207 460 **Fax:** 236 219 542
Email: geral@ocorreiodepombal.net **Web site:** http://www.ocorreiodepombal.net
Date Established: 1990; **Freq:** Weekly; **Cover Price:** EUR 0,7; **Circ:** 5,100
Usual Pagination: 32
Managing Director: Prates Miguel
Profile: Weekly regional newspaper with information about Pombal (Leiria). Politics, current affairs, society, religion, sport, entertainment and events.
Language(s): Portuguese
Readership: Read by Pombal locals.
ADVERTISING RATES:
Full Page Mono .... EUR 500
Full Page Colour .... EUR 700
Mechanical Data: Trim Size: 300 x 402 mm, Type Area: 260 x 370 mm
LOCAL NEWSPAPERS

CORREIO DO MINHO

1642635P67B-6036
Editorial: Praceta do Magistério, 34, Maximinos, 4700-236 BRAGA **Tel:** 253 309 500 **Fax:** 253 309 525
Email: administracao@correiodominho.pt **Web site:** http://www.correiodominho.pt

Date Established: 1926; **Freq:** Daily; **Cover Price:** EUR 0,7; **Circ:** 8,000
Usual Pagination: 40
Editor: Paulo Machado; **Editor-in-Chief:** Rui Alberto Sequeira; **Managing Director:** Paulo Monteiro
Profile: Daily regional newspaper with information about Braga and Viana do Castelo. Politics, current affairs, society, religion, sport, entertainment and events.
Language(s): Portuguese
Readership: Read in Braga and Viana do Castelo regions.
ADVERTISING RATES:
Full Page Mono .... EUR 550
Full Page Colour .... EUR 650
Mechanical Data: Trim Size: 290 x 395 mm, Type Area: 250 x 357 mm
REGIONAL DAILY & SUNDAY NEWSPAPERS: Regional Daily Newspapers

CORREIO DO RIBATEJO
1642636P72I-23
Editorial: R. Serpa Pinto, 98/104, Apartado 323, 2000-046 SANTARÉM **Tel:** 243 333 116
Fax: 243 333 258
Email: correiodoribatejo@mail.telepac.pt **Web site:** http://www.correiodoribatejo.com
Date Established: 1889; **Freq:** Weekly; **Cover Price:** EUR 0,6; **Circ:** 5,000
Usual Pagination: 32
Managing Director: João Paulo Narciso
Profile: Weekly regional newspaper with information about Ribatejo region. Politics, current affairs, society, religion, sport, entertainment and events.
Language(s): Portuguese
Readership: Read in Santarém region.
ADVERTISING RATES:
Full Page Mono .... EUR 800
Full Page Colour .... EUR 1000
Mechanical Data: Trim Size: 290 x 410 mm, Type Area: 260 x 350 mm
LOCAL NEWSPAPERS: Regional Weekly Newspapers

CORREIO DOS AÇORES
19486P67B-1000
Editorial: R. Dr. João Francisco de Sousa, 14, 9500-187 PONTA DELGADA **Tel:** 296 201 060
Fax: 296 286 119
Email: jornal@correiodosacores.net **Web site:** http://www.correiodosacores.net
Date Established: 1920; **Freq:** Daily; **Cover Price:** EUR 0,6; **Circ:** 4,600
Usual Pagination: 36
Editor-in-Chief: Nélia Câmara; **Managing Director:** Américo Natalino Viveiros
Profile: Daily regional newspaper with information about Açores. Politics, current affairs, society, religion, sport, entertainment and events.
Language(s): Portuguese
Readership: Aimed at Açores residents.
ADVERTISING RATES:
Full Page Mono .... EUR 1008
Full Page Colour .... EUR 1814
Mechanical Data: Trim Size: 280 x 400 mm, Type Area: 254 x 345 mm
REGIONAL DAILY & SUNDAY NEWSPAPERS: Regional Daily Newspapers

COSMOBELEZA
1780651P74B-73
Editorial: Edifício S. Francisco de Sales, R. Calvet de Magalhães, 242, 2770-022 PAÇO DE ARCOS
Tel: 214 544 000 **Fax:** 214 435 310
Email: cosmopolitan@edimpresa.pt **Web site:** http://cosmopolitan.chilltime.com/home
ISSN: 0874-0518
Freq: Annual; **Cover Price:** Free; **Circ:** 51,800
Usual Pagination: 36
Language(s): Portuguese
Readership: National.
Mechanical Data: Trim Size: 213 x 275 mm, Type Area: 193 x 255 mm
CONSUMER: WOMEN'S INTEREST CONSUMER MAGAZINES: Women's Interest - Fashion

COSMOPOLITAN
19691P74A-25
Editorial: R. Policarpo Anjos, 4, 1495-742 CRUZ QUEBRADA/DAFUNDO **Tel:** 214 154 560
Fax: 214 154 504
Email: smauricio@gjportugal.pt **Web site:** http://www.cosmopolitan.com
ISSN: 0874-0518
Date Established: 1992; **Freq:** Monthly; **Cover Price:** EUR 2,9; **Circ:** 57,100
Usual Pagination: 124
Editor: Ana Passos; **Editor-in-Chief:** Carmen Saraiva; **Managing Director:** Sandra Maurício
Profile: Women magazine covering fashion, beauty, health, lifestyle advice, sex, relationships, travel and work.
Language(s): Portuguese
Readership: National. Aimed at young, professional women.
ADVERTISING RATES:
Full Page Colour .... EUR 5100
Mechanical Data: Type Area: 175 x 237 mm, Trim Size: 213 x 277 mm
CONSUMER: WOMEN'S INTEREST CONSUMER MAGAZINES: Women's Interest

COZINHA PORTUGUESA
1780661P94X-291
Editorial: Av. João Crisóstomo, 72 - 4°, 1069-043 LISBOA **Tel:** 213 185 460 **Fax:** 213 540 695
Email: mjcoelho@tvguia.cofina.pt
ISSN: 0871-7362
Freq: Weekly; **Cover Price:** Free; **Circ:** 118,000
Language(s): Portuguese
Readership: Mainland.
Mechanical Data: Trim Size: 230 x 297 mm, Type Area: 190 x 257 mm
Part of Series, see entry for: TV Guia
CONSUMER: OTHER CLASSIFICATIONS: Miscellaneous

O CRIME
1642995P80-209
Editorial: R. Alexandre Herculano, N° 1 - 2° Dto., 1150-005 LISBOA **Tel:** 210 962 060 **Fax:** 213 553 235
Email: jornalcrime@gmail.com
Date Established: 1984; **Freq:** Weekly; **Cover Price:** EUR 1,3; **Circ:** 25,000
Usual Pagination: 16
Managing Director: Carlos Saraiva
Profile: Weekly national newspaper covering crime stories.
Language(s): Portuguese
Readership: National.
ADVERTISING RATES:
Full Page Mono .... EUR 1200
Full Page Colour .... EUR 1500
Mechanical Data: Trim Size: 288 x 368 mm, Type Area: 262 x 335 mm
CONSUMER: RURAL & REGIONAL INTEREST

CULINÁRIA
1821654P74P-281
Editorial: Edifício S. Francisco de Sales, R. Calvet de Magalhães, 242, 2770-022 PAÇO DE ARCOS
Tel: 214 544 000 **Fax:** 214 698 542
Email: tvmais@edimpresa.pt **Web site:** http://www.edimpresa.pt
ISSN: 0872-3559
Freq: Weekly; **Cover Price:** Free; **Circ:** 82,904
Usual Pagination: 8
Language(s): Portuguese
Readership: National.
Mechanical Data: Type Area: 182 x 267 mm, Trim Size: 205 x 295 mm
Part of Series, see entry for: TV Mais
CONSUMER: WOMEN'S INTEREST CONSUMER MAGAZINES: Food & Cookery

DANCE CLUB
1642645P76D-76
Editorial: Av. David Mourão Ferreira, Lote 15.5 C - Esc. B, 1750-209 LISBOA **Tel:** 217 530 710
Fax: 217 530 719
Email: info@danceclub.pt **Web site:** http://www.danceclub.pt
Date Established: 1996; **Freq:** Monthly; **Cover Price:** EUR 4,95; **Circ:** 10,000
Editor: Sónia Silvestre; **Managing Director:** Nuno Rodrigues
Language(s): Portuguese
Readership: National.
ADVERTISING RATES:
Full Page Colour .... EUR 2250
Mechanical Data: Trim Size: 230 x 297 mm, Type Area: 230 x 275 mm
CONSUMER: MUSIC & PERFORMING ARTS: Music

A DEFESA
1642471P87-202
Editorial: R. da Misericórdia, 9-13, Apartado 28, 7002-501 ÉVORA **Tel:** 266 750 550 **Fax:** 266 750 559
Email: geral@adefesa.org **Web site:** http://www.adefesa.org
Freq: Weekly; **Cover Price:** EUR 0,5; **Circ:** 5,000
Usual Pagination: 12
Managing Director: António Salvador dos Santos
Profile: Weekly newspaper with information about Évora Region. Politics, current affairs, society, religion, sport, entertainment and events.
Language(s): Portuguese
Readership: Read in Évora region.
ADVERTISING RATES:
Full Page Mono .... EUR 600
Full Page Colour .... EUR 900
Mechanical Data: Trim Size: 305 x 428 mm, Type Area: 265 x 375 mm
CONSUMER: RELIGIOUS

DEFESA DA BEIRA
1642646P80-210
Editorial: R. Pinheiro de Ázere, 7, 3440-000 SANTA COMBA DÃO **Tel:** 231 922 667 **Fax:** 231 922 667
Email: defesadabeira@sapo.pt
Date Established: 1941; **Freq:** Weekly; **Cover Price:** EUR 1; **Circ:** 4,000
Profile: Weekly newspaper with information about Mortágua, Santa Comba Dão and Carregal do Sal. Politics, current affairs, society, religion, sport, entertainment and events.
Language(s): Portuguese
Readership: Read in Mortágua, Santa Comba Dão and Carregal do Sal regions.
Mechanical Data: Trim Size: 282 x 390 mm
CONSUMER: RURAL & REGIONAL INTEREST

DEFESA DE ESPINHO
1642648P80-212
Editorial: Av. 8, 456 - 1°, Sala R, Centro Comercial Solverde 1, Apartado 39, 4501-853 ESPINHO
Tel: 227 341 525 **Fax:** 227 319 911
Email: defesadeespinho@mail.telepac.pt **Web site:** http://defesadeespinho.no.sapo.pt
Date Established: 1932; **Freq:** Weekly; **Cover Price:** EUR 0,65; **Circ:** 3,700
Usual Pagination: 40
Profile: Weekly newspaper with information about Espinho. Politics, current affairs, society, religion, sport, entertainment and events.
Language(s): Portuguese
Readership: Read by Espinho locals.
ADVERTISING RATES:
Full Page Mono .... EUR 680
Full Page Colour .... EUR 820
Mechanical Data: Trim Size: 290 x 400 mm, Type Area: 260 x 343 mm
CONSUMER: RURAL & REGIONAL INTEREST

DESAFIOS
1642649P14A-91
Editorial: Av. bernardo Pimenta, Ed. NERLEI, 2403-010 LEIRIA **Tel:** 244 890 200 **Fax:** 244 890 210
Email: nerlei@nerlei.pt **Web site:** http://www.nerlei.pt
Freq: Quarterly; **Cover Price:** EUR 0,3
Free to qualifying individuals ; **Circ:** 1,500
Editor: Célia Santos; **Managing Director:** José Ribeiro Vieira
Language(s): Portuguese
Readership: Read in Leiria region.
ADVERTISING RATES:
Full Page Colour .... EUR 500
Mechanical Data: Trim Size: 205 x 270 mm, Type Area: 175 x 240 mm
BUSINESS: COMMERCE, INDUSTRY & MANAGEMENT

O DESPERTAR
1642996P80-213
Editorial: R. Pedro Rocha, 27-31, 3000-330 COIMBRA **Tel:** 239 852 710 **Fax:** 239 497 759
Email: jornaldespertar@mail.telepac.pt **Web site:** http://www.odespertar.com
Date Established: 1917; **Freq:** Weekly; **Cover Price:** EUR 0,75; **Circ:** 3,500
Usual Pagination: 24
Managing Director: Zilda Monteiro
Profile: Weekly newspaper with information about Coimbra region. Politics, current affairs, society, religion, sport, entertainment and events.
Language(s): Portuguese
Readership: Read by Coimbra locals.
ADVERTISING RATES:
Full Page Mono .... EUR 750
Full Page Colour .... EUR 1000
Mechanical Data: Trim Size: 305 x 420 mm, Type Area: 260 x 347 mm
CONSUMER: RURAL & REGIONAL INTEREST

DESPERTAR DO ZÊZERE
1642865P72-81
Editorial: R. Pé da Costa Baixo, 26 - A, 2300-000 TOMAR **Tel:** 249 312 615 **Fax:** 249 312 615
Email: dzezere@gmail.com
Freq: 26 issues yearly; **Cover Price:** EUR 0,75; **Circ:** 3,815
Usual Pagination: 16
Profile: Fortnightly newspaper with information about Tomar, Ferreira do Zêzere, Vila de Rei, Constância and Sardoal. Politics, current affairs, society, religion, sport, entertainment and events.
Language(s): Portuguese
Readership: Read by Tomar, Ferreira do Zêzere, Vila de Rei, Constância and Sardoal locals.
ADVERTISING RATES:
Full Page Mono .... EUR 300
Full Page Colour .... EUR 400
Mechanical Data: Trim Size: 295 x 420 mm, Type Area: 263 x 386 mm
LOCAL NEWSPAPERS

DESPORTIVO DE GUIMARÃES
1642997P75A-219
Editorial: R. Dr. José Sampaio, 264, Apartado 485, 4801-850 GUIMARÃES **Tel:** 253 421 700
Fax: 253 421 709
Email: desporto@guimaraesdigital.com **Web site:** http://www.guimaraesdigital.com
ISSN: 0872-0800
Date Established: 1992; **Freq:** Weekly; **Cover Price:** EUR 0,7; **Circ:** 3,000
Managing Director: Abel Sousa
Language(s): Portuguese
Readership: Aimed at Guimarães locals. Read in Braga region.
ADVERTISING RATES:
Full Page Mono .... EUR 300
Full Page Colour .... EUR 440
Mechanical Data: Trim Size: 284 x 423 mm, Type Area: 260 x 370 mm
CONSUMER: SPORT

DESPORTO
1780779P65A-181_116
Editorial: R. de Gonçalo Cristóvão, 195-219, 4049-011 PORTO **Tel:** 222 096 100 **Fax:** 222 096 140
Email: desporto@jn.pt **Web site:** http://www.jn.pt
ISSN: 0874-1352
Freq: Occasional; **Cover Price:** Free; **Circ:** 111,762
Profile: Supplement about sports, specially about the national football championship. Sports news, events and interviews.
Language(s): Portuguese
Readership: National.
ADVERTISING RATES:
Full Page Mono .... EUR 2700
Full Page Colour .... EUR 3780
Mechanical Data: Trim Size: 288 x 370 mm, Type Area: 253 x 358 mm
Section of: Jornal de Notícias
NATIONAL DAILY & SUNDAY NEWSPAPERS: Unabhängiges konservatives MdEP

DESTAK
1642653P82-402
Editorial: Estrada da Outurela, 118, Parque Holanda - Edifício Holanda, 2790-114 CARNAXIDE
Tel: 214 169 210 **Fax:** 214 169 228
Email: destak@destak.pt **Web site:** http://www.destak.pt
Date Established: 2001; **Freq:** Daily; **Cover Price:** Free; **Circ:** 135,000
Usual Pagination: 28
Executive Editor: João Moniz
Language(s): Portuguese
Readership: Read in Aveiro, Braga, Coimbra, Leiria, Lisboa, Porto and Setúbal districts.
ADVERTISING RATES:
Full Page Mono .... EUR 9200
Full Page Colour .... EUR 9200
Mechanical Data: Type Area: 260 x 316 mm, Trim Size: 290 x 370 mm
Series owner and contact point for the following titles, see individual entries:
Destak Lisboa
CONSUMER: CURRENT AFFAIRS & POLITICS

DESTAK LISBOA
1780873P67B-6055
Editorial: Estrada da Outurela, 118, Parque Holanda - Edifício Holanda, 2790-114 CARNAXIDE
Tel: 214 169 210 **Fax:** 214 169 228
Email: destak@destak.pt **Web site:** http://www.destak.pt
Date Established: 2001; **Freq:** Daily; **Cover Price:** Free; **Circ:** 90,000
Usual Pagination: 28
Profile: Free newspaper.
Language(s): Portuguese
Readership: Aimed at subway users from Lisboa and Setúbal.
ADVERTISING RATES:
Full Page Mono .... EUR 6440
Full Page Colour .... EUR 6440
Mechanical Data: Trim Size: 290 x 370 mm, Type Area: 260 x 316 mm
Part of Series, see entry for: Destak
REGIONAL DAILY & SUNDAY NEWSPAPERS: Regional Daily Newspapers

DIABETES
1823239P8-1034
Editorial: R. da Impala, N° 33 A - Abrunheira, S. Pedro de Penaferrim, 2710-070 SINTRA
Tel: 219 238 033 **Fax:** 219 238 044
Email: mmc@impala.pt **Web site:** http://www.impala.pt
Date Established: 2007; **Freq:** Occasional; **Cover Price:** EUR 1,95; **Circ:** 45,000
Usual Pagination: 66
Language(s): Portuguese
Readership: National. Aimed at women.
ADVERTISING RATES:
Full Page Colour .... EUR 3080
Mechanical Data: Type Area: 180 x 237 mm, Trim Size: 210 x 273 mm
Part of Series, see entry for: Mulher Moderna na Cozinha
BUSINESS: BAKING & CONFECTIONERY

O DIABO
19680P73-20
Editorial: R. Alexandre Herculano, 1 - 2° Dto., 1150-005 LISBOA **Tel:** 210 962 060 **Fax:** 213 553 235
Email: jornalodiabo@gmail.com **Web site:** http://jornalodiabo.blogspot.com
Date Established: 1975; **Freq:** Weekly; **Cover Price:** EUR 1,8; **Circ:** 25,000
Editor-in-Chief: Alfredo Miranda
Profile: Newspaper containing political interviews and opinion articles.
Language(s): Portuguese
Readership: National.
ADVERTISING RATES:
Full Page Colour .... EUR 1750
Mechanical Data: Trim Size: 260 x 330 mm
CONSUMER: NATIONAL & INTERNATIONAL PERIODICALS

DIÁRIO AS BEIRAS
1642547P67B-6008
Editorial: R. Abel Dias Urbano, 4, 2°, 3000-001 COIMBRA **Tel:** 239 980 280 **Fax:** 239 980 281
Email: beirastexto@asbeiras.pt **Web site:** http://www.asbeiras.pt
Date Established: 1994; **Freq:** Daily; **Cover Price:** EUR 0,8; **Circ:** 12,000
Usual Pagination: 48
Editor-in-Chief: Dora Loureiro; **Managing Director:** Agostinho Franklin
Profile: Daily newspaper with information about Aveiro, Coimbra, Leiria, Viseu, Guarda and Castelo Branco regions. Politics, current affairs, society, religion, sport, entertainment and events.
Language(s): Portuguese

Readership: Read in Aveiro, Castelo Branco, Coimbra, Guarda, Leiria and Viseu but also in Lisboa and Porto regions.
ADVERTISING RATES:
Full Page Mono .... EUR 1500
Full Page Colour .... EUR 1850
Mechanical Data: Trim Size: 247 x 348 mm, Type Area: 225 x 325 mm
REGIONAL DAILY & SUNDAY NEWSPAPERS: Regional Daily Newspapers

DIÁRIO DE AVEIRO 19482P67B-1100
Editorial: Av. Dr. Lourenço Peixinho, 15 - 1° G, 3800-801 AVEIRO **Tel:** 234 000 030 **Fax:** 234 000 033
Email: diarioaveiro@diarioaveiro.pt **Web site:** http://www.diarioaveiro.pt
Freq: Daily; **Cover Price:** EUR 0,7; **Circ:** 7,014
Usual Pagination: 12
Editor-in-Chief: José Manuel Rodrigues Silva
Profile: Daily magazine with information about Aveiro region. Politics, current affairs, society, sport, entertainment and events.
Language(s): Portuguese
Readership: Read by the population of Aveiro.
ADVERTISING RATES:
Full Page Mono .... EUR 971.97
Full Page Colour .... EUR 1295.96
Mechanical Data: Trim Size: 290 x 370 mm, Type Area: 262 x 346 mm
REGIONAL DAILY & SUNDAY NEWSPAPERS: Regional Daily Newspapers

DIÁRIO DE COIMBRA 19494P67B-1200
Editorial: R. Adriano Lucas, Apartado 542, 3020-264 COIMBRA **Tel:** 239 499 900 **Fax:** 239 499 912
Email: redac@diariocoimbra.pt **Web site:** http://www.diariocoimbra.pt
Date Established: 1930; **Freq:** Daily; **Cover Price:** EUR 0,8; **Circ:** 10,624
Usual Pagination: 32
Executive Editor: Manuela Ventura; **Editor-in-Chief:** António Manuel Rodrigues; **Advertising Manager:** Mário Rasteiro
Profile: Daily regional newspaper with information about the center region of Portugal. Politics, current affairs, society, religion, sport, entertainment and events.
Language(s): Portuguese
Readership: Aimed mainly for Coimbra population, but also distributed in Aveiro, Castelo Branco, Guarda, Lisboa, Porto and Viseu.
ADVERTISING RATES:
Full Page Mono .... EUR 1600
Full Page Colour .... EUR 2080
Mechanical Data: Trim Size: 290 x 370 mm, Type Area: 262 x 346 mm
REGIONAL DAILY & SUNDAY NEWSPAPERS: Regional Daily Newspapers

DIÁRIO DE LEIRIA 19493P67B-1300
Editorial: Edifício Maringá, R. S. Francisco, 7 - 4° Esq., 2400-000 LEIRIA **Tel:** 244 000 030
Fax: 244 000 032
Email: diarioleiria@diarioleiria.pt **Web site:** http://www.diarioleiria.pt
Date Established: 1987; **Freq:** Daily; **Cover Price:** EUR 0,65; **Circ:** 3,722
Editor-in-Chief: José Carlos Salgueiro
Profile: Daily regional newspaper with information about Leiria. Politics, current affairs, society, religion, sport, entertainment and events.
Language(s): Portuguese
Readership: Read in Leiria region.
ADVERTISING RATES:
Full Page Mono .... EUR 998.8
Mechanical Data: Trim Size: 290 x 374 mm, Type Area: 262 x 346 mm
REGIONAL DAILY & SUNDAY NEWSPAPERS: Regional Daily Newspapers

DIÁRIO DE NOTÍCIAS 19472P65A-90
Editorial: Edifício Diário de Notícias, Av. da Liberdade, 266, 1250-149 LISBOA **Tel:** 213 187 500
Fax: 213 187 515
Email: dnot@dn.pt **Web site:** http://www.dn.pt
ISSN: 0870-1954
Date Established: 1864; **Freq:** Daily; **Cover Price:** EUR 1,1; **Circ:** 57,850
Usual Pagination: 64
Editor: Nuno Galopim; **Managing Director:** João Marcelino
Profile: Tabloid-sized quality newspaper covering regional, national and international news, events and current affairs. Includes business, stock market and investment information, opinion and culture. Also provides information on sport, society, property, recruitment, motoring and the arts.
Language(s): Portuguese
Readership: National. Read by decision-makers within business, managers, executives, university students, civil servants and office personnel, half of whom live in Lisbon.
ADVERTISING RATES:
Full Page Mono .... EUR 3400
Full Page Colour .... EUR 4760
Mechanical Data: Trim Size: 294 x 370 mm, Type Area: 253 x 351 mm
Sections:
Classificados Tuti
DN Emprego
Dossier Saúde
Dossier Saúde
Edição Norte
Medicina Veterinária
NATIONAL DAILY & SUNDAY NEWSPAPERS: National Daily Newspapers

DIÁRIO DE NOTÍCIAS DA MADEIRA 19495P67B-1400
Editorial: R. Dr. Fernão de Ornelas, 56 - 3°, 9054-514 FUNCHAL **Tel:** 291 202 300 **Fax:** 291 202 305
Email: secretariado@dnoticias.pt **Web site:** http://www.dnoticias.pt
Date Established: 1876; **Freq:** Daily; **Cover Price:** EUR 0,7; **Circ:** 13,775
Usual Pagination: 40
Managing Director: Ricardo Miguel de Oliveira; **Advertising Manager:** Luís Carlos Gouveia
Language(s): Portuguese
Readership: Read by Madeira population.
ADVERTISING RATES:
Full Page Mono .... EUR 1122
Full Page Colour .... EUR 1683
Mechanical Data: Trim Size: 292 x 394 mm, Type Area: 260 x 366 mm
REGIONAL DAILY & SUNDAY NEWSPAPERS: Regional Daily Newspapers

DIÁRIO DE VISEU 1642661P67B-6012
Editorial: R. Alexandre Herculano, 198 - 2° Dto., 3510-033 VISEU **Tel:** 232 000 031 **Fax:** 232 000 032
Email: diarioviseu@diariodeviseu.pt **Web site:** http://www.diariodeviseu.pt
Date Established: 1997; **Freq:** Daily; **Cover Price:** EUR 0,65; **Circ:** 2,327
Usual Pagination: 20
Advertising Manager: Daniela Homem Pinto
Profile: Daily regional newspaper with information about Viseu region. Politics, current affairs, society, religion, sport, entertainment and events.
Language(s): Portuguese
Readership: Read in Viseu region.
ADVERTISING RATES:
Full Page Mono .... EUR 510
Full Page Colour .... EUR 600
Mechanical Data: Trim Size: 290 x 370 mm, Type Area: 262 x 346 mm
REGIONAL DAILY & SUNDAY NEWSPAPERS: Regional Daily Newspapers

DIÁRIO DO ALENTEJO 19489P72I-17
Editorial: Praça da República, 12, 7800-427 BEJA
Tel: 284 310 165 **Fax:** 284 240 881
Email: jornal@diariodoalentejo.pt **Web site:** http://www.diariodoalentejo.pt
Date Established: 1932; **Freq:** Weekly; **Cover Price:** EUR 0,9; **Circ:** 6,000
Usual Pagination: 16
Managing Director: Paulo Barriga
Profile: Weekly newspaper providing information about Alentejo region. Politics, current affairs, society, religion, sport, entertainment and events.
Language(s): Portuguese
Readership: Read by Beja, Évora and Portalegre locals.
ADVERTISING RATES:
Full Page Mono .... EUR 759
Full Page Colour .... EUR 958
Mechanical Data: Trim Size: 282 x 400 mm, Type Area: 254 x 360 mm
LOCAL NEWSPAPERS: Regional Weekly Newspapers

DIÁRIO DO MINHO 19491P67B-1500
Editorial: R. de Santa Margarida, 4 A, 4710-306 BRAGA **Tel:** 253 609 460 **Fax:** 253 609 465
Email: redaccao@diariodominho.pt **Web site:** http://www.diariodominho.pt
Date Established: 1919; **Freq:** Daily; **Cover Price:** EUR 0,75; **Circ:** 8,500
Usual Pagination: 40
Editor-in-Chief: Damião Pereira; **Managing Director:** Fernando da Silva Pereira
Profile: Daily regional newspaper with information about the north region of Portugal. Politics, current affairs, society, religion, sport, entertainment and events.
Language(s): Portuguese
Readership: Read in Braga and Viana do Castelo regions.
ADVERTISING RATES:
Full Page Mono .... EUR 550
Full Page Colour .... EUR 750
Mechanical Data: Trim Size: 290 x 420 mm, Type Area: 260 x 357 mm
REGIONAL DAILY & SUNDAY NEWSPAPERS: Regional Daily Newspapers

DIÁRIO DO SUL 1642659P65A-172
Editorial: Travessa de Santo André, 6 - 8, Apartado 2037, 7000-951 ÉVORA **Tel:** 266 744 444
Fax: 266 741 252
Email: administracao@diariodosul.com.pt **Web site:** http://www.diariodosul.com.pt
Date Established: 1969; **Freq:** Daily; **Cover Price:** EUR 0,5; **Circ:** 7,000
Usual Pagination: 28
Executive Editor: Paulo Jorge M. Piçarra; **Managing Director:** Manuel Madeira Piçarra
Profile: Daily regional newspaper with information about the south region of Portugal. Politics, current affairs, society, religion, sport, entertainment and events.
Language(s): Portuguese
Readership: Read in Beja, Évora, Faro, Lisboa, Portalegre and Setúbal.
ADVERTISING RATES:
Full Page Mono .... EUR 700
Full Page Colour .... EUR 2000
Mechanical Data: Trim Size: 304 x 400 mm, Type Area: 285 x 355 mm
NATIONAL DAILY & SUNDAY NEWSPAPERS: National Daily Newspapers

DIÁRIO DOS AÇORES 19488P67B-6001
Editorial: R. Dr. João Francisco de Sousa, 16, 9500-187 PONTA DELGADA **Tel:** 296 284 355
Fax: 296 284 840
Email: jornal@diariodosacores.pt **Web site:** http://www.diariodosacores.pt
Date Established: 1870; **Freq:** Daily; **Cover Price:** EUR 0,5; **Circ:** 3,630
Profile: Daily regional newspaper with information about Açores region. Politics, current affairs, society, religion, sport, entertainment and events.
Language(s): Portuguese
Readership: Read by Açores population.
ADVERTISING RATES:
Full Page Mono .... EUR 936
Full Page Colour .... EUR 1638
Mechanical Data: Trim Size: 280 x 400 mm, Type Area: 254 x 345 mm
REGIONAL DAILY & SUNDAY NEWSPAPERS: Regional Daily Newspapers

DIÁRIO ECONÓMICO 19471P65A-70
Editorial: R. Vieira da Silva, 45, 1350-342 LISBOA
Tel: 213 236 800 **Fax:** 213 236 801
Email: deconomico@economico.pt **Web site:** http://economico.pt
Freq: Daily; **Cover Price:** EUR 1,6; **Circ:** 19,667
Usual Pagination: 48
Editor: Isabel Lucas; **Executive Editor:** Renato Santos; **Advertising Manager:** Elsa Gil Sobral
Profile: Broadsheet-sized quality newspaper providing in-depth coverage of politics, economics, financial and business news. Includes reports on the stock exchange, taxation, updates of national and European affairs, relevant conferences and exhibitions, world market developments, opinion and technology.
Language(s): Portuguese
Readership: National. Aimed at leaders within business and industry, financial directors, public and private investors.
ADVERTISING RATES:
Full Page Colour .... EUR 5600
Mechanical Data: Type Area: 250 x 360 mm, Trim Size: 280 x 394 mm
NATIONAL DAILY & SUNDAY NEWSPAPERS: National Daily Newspapers

DIÁRIO INSULAR 19487P67B-6002
Editorial: Av. Infante D. Henrique, I, 9700-098 ANGRA DO HEROÍSMO **Tel:** 295 401 050
Fax: 295 214 246
Email: diarioins@mail.telepac.pt **Web site:** http://www.diarioinsular.com
Date Established: 1946; **Freq:** Daily; **Cover Price:** EUR 0,55; **Circ:** 3,500
Usual Pagination: 16
Editor-in-Chief: Armando Mendes
Profile: Daily newspaper with information about Açores region. Politics, current affairs, society, religion, sport, entertainment and events.
Language(s): Portuguese
Readership: Read by Açores population.
ADVERTISING RATES:
Full Page Mono .... EUR 524
Full Page Colour .... EUR 1310
Mechanical Data: Trim Size: 300 x 425 mm, Type Area: 280 x 380 mm
REGIONAL DAILY & SUNDAY NEWSPAPERS: Regional Daily Newspapers

DINHEIRO & DIREITOS 1642666P1A-158
Editorial: Av. Engenheiro Arantes e Oliveira, 13 - 1° B, Olaias, 1900-221 LISBOA **Tel:** 218 410 800
Fax: 218 410 802
Email: sga@edideco.pt **Web site:** http://www.deco.proteste.pt
ISSN: 0873-8793
Date Established: 1993; **Freq:** 6 issues yearly; **Cover Price:** EUR 7,5; **Circ:** 420,000
Usual Pagination: 48
Managing Director: Pedro Moreira
Language(s): Portuguese
Readership: National.
Mechanical Data: Trim Size: 210 x 285 mm, Type Area: 181 x 237 mm
BUSINESS: FINANCE & ECONOMICS

DIRHOTEL 19313P11-55
Editorial: Pr. de Alvalade, 6 - 10° Esq., 1700-036 LISBOA **Tel:** 217 986 759 **Fax:** 217 986 764
Email: info@artecomum.com **Web site:** http://www.artecomum.com
Freq: 6 issues yearly; **Cover Price:** EUR 3,5; **Circ:** 10,000
Usual Pagination: 62
Profile: Magazine of the Portuguese Association of Hotel Managers.
Language(s): Portuguese
Readership: National.
ADVERTISING RATES:
Full Page Colour .... EUR 1440
Mechanical Data: Trim Size: 230 x 270 mm

DIRHOTEL 19313P11-61
Editorial: Pr. de Alvalade, 6 - 10° Esq., 1700-036 LISBOA **Tel:** 217 986 759 **Fax:** 217 986 764
Email: info@artecomum.com **Web site:** http://www.artecomum.com
Freq: 6 issues yearly; **Cover Price:** EUR 3,5; **Circ:** 10,000
Usual Pagination: 62
Profile: Magazine of the Portuguese Association of Hotel Managers.
Language(s): Portuguese
Readership: National.
ADVERTISING RATES:
Full Page Colour .... EUR 1440
Mechanical Data: Trim Size: 230 x 270 mm

DIRIGIR 1642675P62B-1
Editorial: R. de Xabregas, 52, 1949-003 LISBOA
Tel: 218 614 100 **Fax:** 218 614 621
Email: dirigir@iefp.pt **Web site:** http://www.iefp.pt
ISSN: 0871-7354
Date Established: 1987; **Freq:** Quarterly; **Cover Price:** EUR 2,5; **Circ:** 21,000
Managing Director: Francisco Caneira Madelino
Language(s): Portuguese
Readership: National.
Mechanical Data: Trim Size: 209 x 275 mm
BUSINESS: CHURCH & SCHOOL EQUIPMENT & EDUCATION: Education Teachers

DISTRIBUIÇÃO HOJE 19415P53-30
Editorial: R. Basílio Teles, 35 - 1° Dto., 1070-020 LISBOA **Tel:** 210 033 800 **Fax:** 210 033 888
Email: geral@ife.pt **Web site:** http://www.distribuicaohoje.com
ISSN: 0873-5298
Date Established: 1986; **Freq:** Monthly; **Cover Price:** EUR 5,4; **Circ:** 4,000
Usual Pagination: 64
Editor: Joana Correia; **Advertising Manager:** Sónia Albuquerque
Profile: Magazine specialising in modern production and distribution, with particular emphasis on supermarkets.
Language(s): Portuguese
Readership: National. Read by supermarket sales and distribution directors, general distributors, manufacturers and shopkeepers.
ADVERTISING RATES:
Full Page Colour .... EUR 2480
Mechanical Data: Type Area: 200 x 260 mm, Trim Size: 216 x 270 mm
BUSINESS: RETAILING & WHOLESALING

DN EMPREGO 1781026P65A-90_125
Editorial: Edifício Diário de Notícias, Av. da Liberdade, 266, 1250-149 LISBOA **Tel:** 213 187 500
Fax: 213 187 515
Email: dnot@dn.pt **Web site:** http://www.dn.pt
ISSN: 0870-1954
Freq: Weekly; **Cover Price:** Free; **Circ:** 43,943
Profile: Newspaper supplement with articles about Employment and Business Opportunities.
Language(s): Portuguese
Readership: National.
ADVERTISING RATES:
Full Page Mono .... EUR 4600
SCC .... EUR 0.04
Mechanical Data: Trim Size: 252 x 415 mm
Section of: Diário de Notícias
NATIONAL DAILY & SUNDAY NEWSPAPERS: Unabhängiges konservatives MdEP

DOMINGO 1781044P65A-50_103
Editorial: Av. João Crisóstomo, 72, 1069-043 LISBOA **Tel:** 213 185 462 **Fax:** 213 540 695
Email: geral@correiomanha.pt **Web site:** http://www.cmjornal.pt
Freq: Weekly; **Cover Price:** Free; **Circ:** 160,521
Usual Pagination: 76
Editor: Fernanda Cachão
Profile: General interest magazine containing articles about fashion, celebrities, arts, fait divers, new technologies, tourism and entertainment guides.
Language(s): Portuguese
Readership: National.
ADVERTISING RATES:
Full Page Colour .... EUR 5185
Mechanical Data: Type Area: 180 x 253 mm, Trim Size: 205 x 275 mm
Section of: Correio da Manhã
NATIONAL DAILY & SUNDAY NEWSPAPERS: National Daily Newspapers

DOSSIER SAÚDE 1781070P56A-284
Editorial: Edifício Diário de Notícias, Av. da Liberdade, 266, 1250-149 LISBOA **Tel:** 213 187 500
Fax: 213 187 516
Email: dnot@dn.pt **Web site:** http://www.globalnoticias.pt
Freq: Occasional; **Cover Price:** Free; **Circ:** 178,542
Usual Pagination: 16
Profile: Published with: Jornal de Notícias; Diário de Notícias.
Language(s): Portuguese
Readership: National.
Mechanical Data: Trim Size: 215 x 290 mm

DOSSIER SAÚDE 1781070P56A-297
Editorial: Edifício Diário de Notícias, Av. da Liberdade, 266, 1250-149 LISBOA **Tel:** 213 187 500 **Fax:** 213 187 516
Email: dnot@dn.pt **Web site:** http://www.globalnoticias.pt
Freq: Occasional; **Cover Price:** Free; **Circ:** 178,542
Usual Pagination: 16
Profile: Published with: Jornal de Notícias; Diário de Notícias.
Language(s): Portuguese
Readership: National.
Mechanical Data: Trim Size: 215 x 290 mm

DOSSIER SAÚDE 1781071P65A-90_108
Editorial: Edifício Diário de Notícias, Av. da Liberdade, 266, 1250-149 LISBOA **Tel:** 213 187 500 **Fax:** 213 187 515
Email: dnot@dn.pt **Web site:** http://www.dn.pt
ISSN: 0870-1954
Freq: Occasional; **Cover Price:** Free; **Circ:** 51,040
Usual Pagination: 16
Profile: Magazine about health issues.
Language(s): Portuguese
Readership: National.
Mechanical Data: Type Area: 182 x 260 mm, Trim Size: 215 x 290 mm
Section of: Diário de Notícias
NATIONAL DAILY & SUNDAY NEWSPAPERS: Unabhängiges konservatives MdEP

DOSSIER SAÚDE 1781071P65A-90_109
Editorial: Edifício Diário de Notícias, Av. da Liberdade, 266, 1250-149 LISBOA **Tel:** 213 187 500 **Fax:** 213 187 515
Email: dnot@dn.pt **Web site:** http://www.dn.pt
ISSN: 0870-1954
Freq: Occasional; **Cover Price:** Free; **Circ:** 51,040
Usual Pagination: 16
Profile: Magazine about health issues.
Language(s): Portuguese
Readership: National.
Mechanical Data: Type Area: 182 x 260 mm, Trim Size: 215 x 290 mm
Section of: Diário de Notícias
NATIONAL DAILY & SUNDAY NEWSPAPERS: Unabhängiges konservatives MdEP

DOURO HOJE 1642896P72I-6
Editorial: R. de S. João, Urbanização da Ortigosa, Bloco 21 - Sub-Cave Dto., Apartado 40, 5100-909 LAMEGO **Tel:** 254 613 930 **Fax:** 254 655 508
Email: dourohoje@gmail.com **Web site:** http://www.dourohoje.com
Date Established: 1987; **Freq:** Weekly; **Cover Price:** EUR 0,6; **Circ:** 6,000
Usual Pagination: 28
Editor-in-Chief: Iolanda Vilar; **Managing Director:** Ermelinda Osório
Profile: Weekly newspaper with information about lamego. Politics, current affairs, society, sport, entertainment and events.
Language(s): Portuguese
Readership: Read by Lamego locals.
ADVERTISING RATES:
Full Page Mono .... EUR 400
Full Page Colour .... EUR 500
Mechanical Data: Type Area: 255 x 340 mm, Trim Size: 300 x 400 mm
LOCAL NEWSPAPERS: Regional Weekly Newspapers

ECO REGIONAL 1642689P72-27
Editorial: R. da Atalaia, 67 - 3° Esq., 1200-037 LISBOA **Tel:** 213 430 236 **Fax:** 213 476 770
Email: ecoregional@sapo.pt **Web site:** http://turispress.net
Date Established: 1992; **Freq:** Monthly; **Cover Price:** EUR 0,65; **Circ:** 5,000
Language(s): Portuguese
Readership: Read in Lisboa region.
ADVERTISING RATES:
Full Page Mono .... EUR 885
Full Page Colour .... EUR 1150
Mechanical Data: Trim Size: 295 x 390 mm, Type Area: 260 x 340 mm
LOCAL NEWSPAPERS

ECONOMIA 1781095P1A-189
Editorial: Edifício S. Francisco de Sales, R. Calvet de Magalhães, 242, 2770-022 PAÇO DE ARCOS
Tel: 214 544 000 **Fax:** 214 435 310
Email: economia@expresso.impresa.pt **Web site:** http://www.expresso.pt
Freq: Weekly; **Cover Price:** Free; **Circ:** 126,575
Usual Pagination: 32
Profile: Magazine containing the latest news about national and international economy. Interviews and opinions of famous economists or business people.
Language(s): Portuguese
Readership: National.
ADVERTISING RATES:
Full Page Mono .... EUR 13005
Full Page Colour .... EUR 17340
Mechanical Data: Trim Size: 330 x 500 mm, Type Area: 300 x 460 mm
Part of Series, see entry for: Expresso
BUSINESS: FINANCE & ECONOMICS

O ECONOMISTA 1820588P1A-346
Editorial: POLIMEIOS - Produção de Meios, Lda., R. Francisco Rodrigues Lobo, 2 - R/C Dto., 1070-134 LISBOA **Tel:** 213 859 950 **Fax:** 213 851 430
Email: c.economia@mail.telepac.pt **Web site:** http://www.cadernoseconomia.com.pt
Date Established: 1987; **Freq:** Annual; **Cover Price:** EUR 12,5; **Circ:** 18,000
Usual Pagination: 290
Profile: Official magazine of the Ordem dos Economistas association, containing an annual report of the portuguese economy.
Language(s): Portuguese
Readership: National.
ADVERTISING RATES:
Full Page Mono .... EUR 4075
Full Page Colour .... EUR 5040
Mechanical Data: Type Area: 165 x 250 mm, Trim Size: 205 x 290 mm

ECOS DE BASTO 1642694P72-29
Editorial: R. Antunes Basto, Refojos, 4860-000 CABECEIRAS DE BASTO **Tel:** 253 661 601 **Fax:** 253 666 156
Email: adib.ecos@sapo.pt **Web site:** http://www.ecosdebasto.com
Freq: Monthly; **Cover Price:** EUR 0,8; **Circ:** 2,750
Profile: Newspaper with information about Cabeceiras de Basto region. Politics, current affairs, society, religion, sport, entertainment and events.
Language(s): Portuguese
Readership: Read in Braga region.
ADVERTISING RATES:
Full Page Mono .... EUR 300
Full Page Colour .... EUR 400
Mechanical Data: Trim Size: 305 x 425 mm
LOCAL NEWSPAPERS

EDIÇÃO DE NATAL
1781125P65A-50_107
Editorial: Av. João Crisóstomo, 72, 1069-043 LISBOA **Tel:** 213 185 462 **Fax:** 213 540 695
Email: geral@correiomanha.pt **Web site:** http://www.cmjornal.pt
Freq: Annual; **Cover Price:** Free; **Circ:** 158,796
Usual Pagination: 100
Profile: Christmas' special edition.
Language(s): Portuguese
Readership: National.
ADVERTISING RATES:
Full Page Mono .... EUR 2020
Full Page Colour .... EUR 3030
Mechanical Data: Type Area: 177 x 264 mm, Trim Size: 205 x 275 mm
Section of: Correio da Manhã
NATIONAL DAILY & SUNDAY NEWSPAPERS: Unabhängiges konservatives MdEP

EDIÇÃO NORTE 1781024P65A-90_114
Editorial: R. Gonçalo Cristóvão, 195 - 5°, 4000-269 PORTO **Tel:** 222 096 480 **Fax:** 222 096 483
Email: dnot@dn.pt **Web site:** http://www.dn.pt
ISSN: 0870-1954
Freq: Daily; **Cover Price:** EUR 0,9; **Circ:** 44,743
Profile: Tabloid-sized quality newspaper covering regional, national and international news, events and current affairs. Includes business, stock market and investment information, opinion and culture. Also provides information on sport, society, property, recruitment, motoring and the arts.
Language(s): Portuguese
Readership: Sold in north Portugal. Read by decision-makers within business, managers, executives, university students, civil servants and office personnel.
Mechanical Data: Type Area: 253 x 355 mm, Trim Size: 294 x 400 mm
Section of: Diário de Notícias
NATIONAL DAILY & SUNDAY NEWSPAPERS: Unabhängiges konservatives MdEP

O ELECTRICISTA 1643001P58-6
Editorial: Praça da Corujeira, 38, Apartado 3825, 4300-144 PORTO **Tel:** 225 899 620 **Fax:** 225 899 629
Email: geral@publindustria.pt **Web site:** http://www.oelectricista.pt
Freq: Quarterly; **Cover Price:** EUR 9,5; **Circ:** 7,000
Usual Pagination: 140
Editor-in-Chief: Helena Paulino; **Managing Director:** Custódio Dias; **Advertising Manager:** Júlio Almeida
Profile: Business magazine about Telecommunications, Security and Energy.
Language(s): Portuguese
Readership: National.
ADVERTISING RATES:
Full Page Colour .... EUR 1146
Mechanical Data: Trim Size: 210 x 297 mm, Type Area: 180 x 267 mm

ELEKTOR ELECTRÓNICA
19342P18A-40
Editorial: Edifício Central Park, R. Alexandre Herculano, 3 - 3° B, 2795-240 LINDA-A-VELHA
Tel: 214 131 600 **Fax:** 214 131 601
Email: elektor@editorialbolina.com **Web site:** http://www.elektor.com.pt
ISSN: 0870-1407
Freq: Monthly; **Cover Price:** EUR 4,6; **Circ:** 10,000
Usual Pagination: 64
Editor-in-Chief: Ana Rita Soares Dinis
Profile: International magazine covering the aspects of electronics and computer technology.
Language(s): Portuguese
Readership: Mainland. Aimed at electronic professionals.
ADVERTISING RATES:
Full Page Colour .... EUR 1340
Mechanical Data: Trim Size: 205 x 285 mm
BUSINESS: ELECTRONICS

ELES & ELAS 1642701P74Q-93
Editorial: Praça Luís de Camões, 36 - 2° Dto., 1200-243 LISBOA **Tel:** 213 224 660 **Fax:** 213 224 679
Email: rp@gabinete1.pt **Web site:** http://www.gabinete1.pt
ISSN: 0820-8932
Date Established: 1982; **Freq:** Monthly; **Cover Price:** EUR 2,5; **Circ:** 60,000
Usual Pagination: 100
Managing Director: Maria da Luz de Bragança
Language(s): English; Portuguese
Readership: National.
ADVERTISING RATES:
Full Page Colour .... EUR 3616
Mechanical Data: Trim Size: 210 x 297 mm
CONSUMER: WOMEN'S INTEREST CONSUMER MAGAZINES: Lifestyle

ELITE NEGÓCIOS & LIFESTYLE
1782783P1A-271
Editorial: Av. Tomás Ribeiro, 129 - Salas 11 e 12, Edifício Quinta Jamor, 2790-466 QUEIJAS
Tel: 211 919 835 **Fax:** 211 911 605
Email: geral@eliterevista.com **Web site:** http://www.eliterevista.com
Date Established: 2005; **Freq:** Monthly; **Cover Price:** EUR 4; **Circ:** 20,000
Usual Pagination: 100
Editor-in-Chief: Simone Costa Carvalho; **Managing Director:** Alfredo Lavrador
Profile: Lifestyle magazine covering art, literature, politics, business, cigars, wine, gastronomy, travel, holidays and sport.
Language(s): Portuguese
Readership: National.
ADVERTISING RATES:
Full Page Colour .... EUR 4500
Mechanical Data: Trim Size: 230 x 320 mm

ELLE 19692P74A-30
Editorial: R. Filipe Folque, N° 40 - 4° Andar, 1069-124 LISBOA **Tel:** 213 164 200 **Fax:** 213 164 205
Email: redaccao@rbarevistas.pt
Freq: Monthly; **Cover Price:** EUR 3,5; **Circ:** 73,682
Usual Pagination: 148
Advertising Manager: Maria João Dias
Profile: Magazine about fashion, beauty, health and lifestyle.
Language(s): Portuguese
Readership: Mainland. Mainly women in the ages of 24/54.
ADVERTISING RATES:
Full Page Colour .... EUR 6050
Mechanical Data: Trim Size: 225 x 297 mm, Type Area: 190 x 252 mm
CONSUMER: WOMEN'S INTEREST CONSUMER MAGAZINES: Women's Interest

O EMIGRANTE - MUNDO PORTUGUÊS 1643002P80-216
Editorial: Av. Elias Garcia, 57 7°, 1049-017 LISBOA
Tel: 217 957 668 **Fax:** 217 957 665
Email: redaccao@mundoportugues.org **Web site:** http://www.mundoportugues.org
Freq: Weekly; **Cover Price:** EUR 1,3; **Circ:** 29,739
Profile: National newspaper that covers all the major news about Portugal.
Language(s): Portuguese
Readership: Aimed at Portuguese communities living abroad.
ADVERTISING RATES:
Full Page Mono .... EUR 3115
Full Page Colour .... EUR 4049
Mechanical Data: Trim Size: 290 x 375 mm, Type Area: 340 x 260 mm
CONSUMER: RURAL & REGIONAL INTEREST

EMPREGO 1781173P94X-341
Editorial: Edifício S. Francisco de Sales, R. Calvet de Magalhães, 242, 2770-022 PAÇO DE ARCOS
Tel: 214 544 000 **Fax:** 214 435 310
Email: ipublishing@impresa.pt **Web site:** http://www.expresso.pt
Freq: Weekly; **Cover Price:** Free; **Circ:** 126,575
Usual Pagination: 40
Language(s): Portuguese
Readership: National.
ADVERTISING RATES:
Full Page Colour .... EUR 6000
Mechanical Data: Trim Size: 260 x 340 mm, Type Area: 237 x 309 mm
Part of Series, see entry for: Expresso
CONSUMER: OTHER CLASSIFICATIONS: Miscellaneous

ENSINO SUPERIOR 1821894P88A-103
Editorial: Av. João Crisóstomo, 72, Galeria, 1069-043 LISBOA **Tel:** 213 185 321 **Fax:** 213 540 392
Email: publicidade@sabado.cofina.pt **Web site:** http://www.sabado.pt
Date Established: 2007; **Freq:** Occasional; **Cover Price:** Free; **Circ:** 110,900
Usual Pagination: 36
Language(s): Portuguese
Readership: National.
ADVERTISING RATES:
Full Page Colour .... EUR 3475
Mechanical Data: Type Area: 180 x 253 mm, Trim Size: 205 x 275 mm
Part of Series, see entry for: Sábado
CONSUMER: EDUCATION

ENSINO SUPERIOR 1821895P88A-104
Editorial: Edifício São Francisco de Sales, R. Calvet de Magalhães, 242, 2770-022 PAÇO DE ARCOS
Tel: 214 544 000 **Fax:** 214 698 547
Email: visao@edimpresa.pt **Web site:** http://www.visao.pt
ISSN: 0872-3540
Date Established: 2007; **Freq:** Occasional; **Cover Price:** Free; **Circ:** 107,000
Usual Pagination: 52
Language(s): Portuguese
ADVERTISING RATES:
Full Page Colour .... EUR 6550
Mechanical Data: Type Area: 185 x 221 mm, Trim Size: 210 x 260 mm
CONSUMER: EDUCATION

EPICUR 1642708P50-84
Editorial: R. Poeta Bocage, 2 C, 1600-233 LISBOA
Tel: 217 271 564 **Fax:** 217 162 597
Email: epicur@epicur.pt **Web site:** http://www.epicur.pt
Date Established: 1998; **Freq:** 6 issues yearly; **Cover Price:** EUR 5; **Circ:** 3,000
Usual Pagination: 132
Editor: Eduardo Miragaia; **Managing Director:** Rui Manuel Dias José
Profile: Lifestyle magazine covering cigars, wine, food and drink, travel, holidays, art, literature, politics and sport.
Language(s): Portuguese
Readership: National. Aimed at high and medium classed people that enjoy the pleasures of life.
ADVERTISING RATES:
Full Page Colour .... EUR 2400
Mechanical Data: Trim Size: 230 x 280 mm, Type Area: 210 x 260 mm
BUSINESS: TRAVEL & TOURISM

ESCOLHAS 1820602P88A-81
Editorial: R. dos Anjos, 66 - 3°, 1150-039 LISBOA
Tel: 218 103 060 **Fax:** 218 103 079
Email: escolhas@programaescolhas.pt **Web site:** http://www.programaescolhas.pt
Freq: Quarterly; **Cover Price:** Free; **Circ:** 112,000
Usual Pagination: 42
Managing Director: Rosário Farmhouse; **Advertising Manager:** Sandra Mateus
Language(s): Portuguese
Readership: National. Aimed to children, teenagers and young people between 6 and 24 years old with social or economical problems. Also aimed for their families and teachers.
Mechanical Data: Type Area: 189 x 273 mm, Trim Size: 210 x 298 mm
CONSUMER: EDUCATION

ESPAÇOS & CASAS 1781236P94X-350
Editorial: Edifício S. Francisco de Sales, R. Calvet de Magalhães, 242, 2770-022 PAÇO DE ARCOS
Tel: 214 544 000 **Fax:** 214 435 310
Email: ipublishing@impresa.pt **Web site:** http://www.expresso.pt
Freq: Weekly; **Cover Price:** Free; **Circ:** 126,575
Usual Pagination: 40
Language(s): Portuguese
Readership: National.
ADVERTISING RATES:
Full Page Mono .... EUR 5350
Full Page Colour .... EUR 7490
Mechanical Data: Trim Size: 260 x 334 mm, Type Area: 237 x 309 mm
Part of Series, see entry for: Expresso
CONSUMER: OTHER CLASSIFICATIONS: Miscellaneous

ESPIRAL DO TEMPO 1606551P52B-151
Editorial: Av. Almirante Reis, 39, 1169-039 LISBOA
Tel: 218 110 896
Email: espiraldotempo@torresdistrib.com **Web site:** http://www.espiraldotempo.com
Freq: 3 issues yearly; **Cover Price:** EUR 5; **Circ:** 20,000
Usual Pagination: 164
Editor: Paulo Costa Dias; **Managing Director:** Hubert de Haro
Profile: Magazine focusing on luxury watch-making. Includes technical details and information on the latest trends and developments.
Language(s): Portuguese
Readership: National. Aimed at retailers and suppliers.
ADVERTISING RATES:
Full Page Colour .... EUR 3570
Mechanical Data: Trim Size: 230 x 297 mm, Type Area: 209 x 275 mm
BUSINESS: GIFT TRADE: Clocks & Watches

ESPIRAL DO TEMPO 1821945P74-287
Editorial: R. Filipe Folque, N° 40 - 4° Andar, 1069-124 LISBOA **Tel:** 213 164 200 **Fax:** 213 164 205
Email: redaccao@rbarevistas.pt
Date Established: 2006; **Freq:** Occasional; **Cover Price:** Free; **Circ:** 73,682
Language(s): Portuguese
Readership: Mainland.
ADVERTISING RATES:
Full Page Colour .... EUR 3570
Mechanical Data: Trim Size: 183 x 219 mm, Type Area: 240 x 300 mm
CONSUMER: WOMEN'S INTEREST CONSUMER MAGAZINES

ESTAÇÕES 1821951P8-863
Editorial: R. da Impala, N° 33 A - Abrunheira, S. Pedro de Penaferrim, 2710-070 SINTRA
Tel: 219 238 033 **Fax:** 219 238 044
Email: mmc@impala.pt **Web site:** http://www.impala.pt
Date Established: 2007; **Freq:** Seasonal; **Cover Price:** EUR 1,95; **Circ:** 66,417
Usual Pagination: 66
Language(s): Portuguese
Readership: National. Aimed at women.
ADVERTISING RATES:
Full Page Colour .... EUR 3080
Mechanical Data: Type Area: 180 x 237 mm, Trim Size: 210 x 273 mm
Part of Series, see entry for: Mulher Moderna na Cozinha
BUSINESS: BAKING & CONFECTIONERY

ESTÉTICA PORTUGAL 1642714P15R-3
Editorial: Av. das Forças Armadas, 4 S/L ou 4 B, 1600-082 LISBOA **Tel:** 217 614 500 **Fax:** 217 614 520
Email: contactos@cabelosonline.com **Web site:** http://www.cabelosonline.com
Date Established: 2001; **Freq:** Quarterly; **Cover Price:** EUR 6,25; **Circ:** 3,000
Usual Pagination: 132
Editor: Roberto Pissimiglia; **Advertising Manager:** Isabel Romano
Language(s): Portuguese
Readership: National. Aimed at professionals from hairdressers and beauty-saloons.
ADVERTISING RATES:
Full Page Colour .... EUR 1500
Mechanical Data: Trim Size: 216 x 288 mm, Type Area: 209 x 296 mm
BUSINESS: COSMETICS & HAIRDRESSING: Cosmetics & Hairdressing Related

ESTÉTICA VIVA 1642715P74H-3
Editorial: Av. Miguel Bombarda, 42 - 3° D, 1050-166 LISBOA **Tel:** 217 971 683 **Fax:** 218 280 295
Email: geral@esteticaviva.com **Web site:** http://www.esteticaviva.com
Date Established: 1997; **Freq:** Quarterly; **Cover Price:** EUR 7,9; **Circ:** 10,000
Usual Pagination: 132
Editor-in-Chief: Stela Martins; **Managing Director:** Patrícia Bandeira; **Advertising Manager:** Emília Moita
Language(s): Portuguese
Readership: National.
ADVERTISING RATES:
Full Page Colour .... EUR 2000
Mechanical Data: Trim Size: 230 x 300 mm, Type Area: 210 x 260 mm
CONSUMER: WOMEN'S INTEREST CONSUMER MAGAZINES: Hair & Beauty

EVASÕES 1606547P89A-124
Editorial: R. João da Silva, 20, 1900-271 LISBOA
Tel: 218 440 700 **Fax:** 218 440 753
Email: ana.carla@ci-media.pt
Freq: Monthly; **Cover Price:** EUR 3,7; **Circ:** 11,930
Editor: Paulo Rolão; **Executive Editor:** Paulo Farinha; **Managing Director:** José Jaime Costa
Profile: Magazine providing a guide to the various tourist destinations within Portugal.
Language(s): Portuguese
Readership: National.
ADVERTISING RATES:
Full Page Colour .... EUR 4310
Mechanical Data: Trim Size: 218 x 280 mm, Type Area: 190 x 250 mm
CONSUMER: HOLIDAYS & TRAVEL: Travel

EXAME 19865P1A-43
Editorial: Edifício S. Francisco de Sales, R. Calvet de Magalhães, 242, 2770-022 PAÇO DE ARCOS
Tel: 214 544 000 **Fax:** 214 698 500
Email: exame@edimpresa.pt **Web site:** http://www.exame.expresso.pt
Date Established: 1989; **Freq:** Monthly; **Cover Price:** EUR 3,5; **Circ:** 23,100
Usual Pagination: 138
Editor: Rosália Amorim; **Managing Director:** Isabel Canha
Profile: Magazine containing information on economic issues, business, companies and financial issues, also contains articles on leisure and hobbies for business people.
Language(s): Portuguese
Readership: National. Aimed at decision makers within business and industry, investors, financial directors and managers.
ADVERTISING RATES:
Full Page Colour .... EUR 4990
Mechanical Data: Type Area: 190 x 245 mm, Trim Size: 220 x 280 mm
BUSINESS: FINANCE & ECONOMICS

EXAME INFORMÁTICA 19300P5B-30
Editorial: Edifício S. Francisco de Sales, R. Calvet de Magalhães, 242, 2770-022 PAÇO DE ARCOS
Tel: 214 544 000 **Fax:** 214 698 500
Email: exame.informatica@edimpresa.pt **Web site:** http://www.exameinformatica.pt
ISSN: 0873-4798
Date Established: 1995; **Freq:** Monthly; **Cover Price:** EUR 2,95; **Circ:** 34,100
Editor: Hugo Séneca; **Editor-in-Chief:** Sérgio Magno; **Managing Director:** Pedro Miguel Oliveira
Profile: Magazine about information technology.
Language(s): Portuguese
Readership: Mainland.
ADVERTISING RATES:
Full Page Colour .... EUR 3700
Mechanical Data: Type Area: 185 x 276 mm, Trim Size: 205 x 295 mm
BUSINESS: COMPUTERS & AUTOMATION: Data Processing

EXECUTIVE DIGEST 19325P14A-18
Editorial: R. Basílio Teles, 36 - 6° Dto., 1070-020 LISBOA **Tel:** 210 123 400 **Fax:** 210 123 444
Email: geral@multipublicacoes.pt **Web site:** http://www.executivedigest.pt
ISSN: 0874-0526
Freq: Monthly; **Cover Price:** EUR 2,75; **Circ:** 19,000
Usual Pagination: 100
Managing Director: Paulo Carmona
Profile: Monthly magazine about management and business.
Language(s): Portuguese
Readership: National.
ADVERTISING RATES:
Full Page Colour .... EUR 4250
Mechanical Data: Trim Size: 220 x 280 mm
BUSINESS: COMMERCE, INDUSTRY & MANAGEMENT

EXPRESSO 19681P65J-6
Editorial: Edifício S. Francisco de Sales, R. Calvet de Magalhães, 242, 2770-022 PAÇO DE ARCOS
Tel: 214 544 000 **Fax:** 214 435 349
Email: ipublishing@impresa.pt **Web site:** http://www.expresso.pt
Date Established: 1973; **Freq:** Weekly; **Cover Price:** EUR 3; **Circ:** 126,575
Usual Pagination: 44
Editor: Miguel Martins; **Managing Director:** Ricardo Costa; **Advertising Manager:** Manuela Batle Y Font
Profile: Berliner-sized national newspaper providing coverage of national and international current affairs and in-depth information concerning finance, economics, business and industry. Also covers society, culture, media, sports, fashion, lifestyle and television.
Language(s): Portuguese
Readership: National.
ADVERTISING RATES:
Full Page Mono .... EUR 13545
Full Page Colour .... EUR 18060
Mechanical Data: Type Area: 300 x 460 mm, Trim Size: 330 x 500 mm
Sections:
Atual
Economia
Emprego
Espaços & Casas
Férias e Viagens
Inovação & Tecnologia
Mamãs & Bebés
Nauticampo
Revista Única
Saúde Pública
NATIONAL DAILY & SUNDAY NEWSPAPERS: National Weekly Newspapers

FAMÍLIA CRISTÃ 19779P87-50
Editorial: R. D. Pedro de Cristo, 10, 1749-092 LISBOA **Tel:** 218 437 620 **Fax:** 218 437 629
Email: familiacrista@paulus.pt **Web site:** http://www.familiacrista.com
ISSN: 1646-3498
Date Established: 1954; **Freq:** Monthly; **Cover Price:** EUR 3,5; **Circ:** 16,000
Usual Pagination: 100
Editor-in-Chief: Silvia Júlio; **Managing Director:** José Carlos Nunes
Profile: Magazine focusing on religion and family issues from a Christian point of view. Includes articles on personal finance, culture, politics and current affairs.
Language(s): Portuguese
Readership: National. Aimed at Christian families.
ADVERTISING RATES:
Full Page Colour .... EUR 800
Mechanical Data: Trim Size: 148 x 238 mm
CONSUMER: RELIGIOUS

FARMÁCIA DISTRIBUIÇÃO 19340P37-15
Editorial: R. Barão de Sabrosa, 165 - A, 1900-088 LISBOA **Tel:** 218 110 130
Email: fd@netfarma.pt **Web site:** http://www.netfarma.pt
ISSN: 0873-5301
Date Established: 1991; **Freq:** Monthly; **Cover Price:** EUR 5; **Circ:** 6,000
Usual Pagination: 88
Advertising Manager: Nuno Costa
Profile: Magazine focusing on the pharmaceutical industry.
Language(s): Portuguese
Readership: National. Read by pharmacists and pharmaceutical students.
ADVERTISING RATES:
Full Page Colour .... EUR 2065
Mechanical Data: Type Area: 190 x 242 mm, Trim Size: 213 x 270 mm
BUSINESS: PHARMACEUTICAL & CHEMISTS

FARMÁCIA SAÚDE 1642724P74G-75
Editorial: Edifício Lisboa Oriente, Av. Infante D. Henrique, 333H - Escritório 49, 1800-282 LISBOA
Tel: 218 508 110 **Fax:** 218 530 426
Email: farmaciasaude@lpmcom.pt **Web site:** http://www.anf.pt
ISSN: 0873-5468
Date Established: 1996; **Freq:** Monthly; **Cover Price:** EUR 10
Free to qualifying individuals ; **Circ:** 165,000
Usual Pagination: 64
Managing Director: Luís Matias
Profile: Free magazine distributed in pharmacies.
Language(s): Portuguese
Readership: National.
ADVERTISING RATES:
Full Page Colour .... EUR 4500
Mechanical Data: Trim Size: 210 x 280 mm, Type Area: 180 x 250 mm
CONSUMER: WOMEN'S INTEREST CONSUMER MAGAZINES: Slimming & Health

FÉRIAS E VIAGENS 1822059P50-156
Editorial: Edifício S. Francisco de Sales, R. Calvet de Magalhães, 242, 2770-022 PAÇO DE ARCOS
Tel: 214 544 000 **Fax:** 214 435 310
Email: ipublishing@impresa.pt **Web site:** http://www.expresso.pt
Date Established: 2007; **Freq:** Occasional; **Cover Price:** Free; **Circ:** 133,340
Usual Pagination: 45
Language(s): Portuguese
Readership: National.
ADVERTISING RATES:
Full Page Colour .... EUR 4900
Mechanical Data: Type Area: 199 x 270 mm, Trim Size: 225 x 297 mm
Part of Series, see entry for: Expresso
BUSINESS: TRAVEL & TOURISM

FESTAS 1822093P65A-50_121
Editorial: Av. João Crisóstomo, 72, 1069-043 LISBOA **Tel:** 213 185 462 **Fax:** 213 540 695
Email: geral@correiomanha.pt **Web site:** http://www.cmjornal.pt
Date Established: 2007; **Freq:** Occasional; **Cover Price:** Free; **Circ:** 171,395
Usual Pagination: 8
Language(s): Portuguese
Readership: National.
ADVERTISING RATES:
Full Page Mono .... EUR 2020
Full Page Colour .... EUR 3030
Mechanical Data: Type Area: 257 x 338 mm, Trim Size: 280 x 370 mm
Section of: Correio da Manhã
NATIONAL DAILY & SUNDAY NEWSPAPERS: National Daily Newspapers

FIBRA 2093812P2A-219
Editorial: Av. Infante D. Henrique, 333 H - 44, 1800-282 LISBOA **Tel:** 218 504 060 **Fax:** 210 435 935
Email: fibra@briefing.pt **Web site:** http://www.fibra.pt
Date Established: 2011; **Freq:** Monthly; **Cover Price:** EUR 8; **Circ:** 2,500
Usual Pagination: 48
Editor: António Barradinhas; **Executive Editor:** Hermínio Santos
Profile: Magazine dedicated to the communication sector.
Language(s): Portuguese
Readership: National. Aimed at communication's professionals.
ADVERTISING RATES:
Full Page Colour .... EUR 2900
Mechanical Data: Trim Size: 210 x 297 mm

O FIGUEIRENSE 1643003P72I-44
Editorial: R. de O Figueirense N°14, 3080-059 FIGUEIRA DA FOZ **Tel:** 233 402 930
Fax: 233 402 931
Email: jornal@ofigueirense.com **Web site:** http://www.ofigueirense.com
Date Established: 1919; **Freq:** Weekly; **Cover Price:** EUR 1,1; **Circ:** 4,500
Usual Pagination: 28
Editor-in-Chief: Jorge Lemos; **Managing Director:** Joaquim Gil
Profile: Weekly newspaper with information about Figueira da Foz region. Politics, current affairs, society, religion, sport, entertainment and events.
Language(s): Portuguese
Readership: Read by Figueira da Foz locals.
ADVERTISING RATES:
Full Page Mono .... EUR 350
Full Page Colour .... EUR 450
Mechanical Data: Trim Size: 282 x 410 mm, Type Area: 255 x 364 mm
LOCAL NEWSPAPERS: Regional Weekly Newspapers

FITO+SAÚDE 1820624P56A-196
Editorial: R. dos Bem-Lembrados, 141, Manique, 2645-471 ALCABIDECHE **Tel:** 214 449 660
Fax: 214 449 651
Email: apoio.cliente@distrifa.pt **Web site:** http://www.distrifa.pt
Freq: Half-yearly; **Cover Price:** Free; **Circ:** 80,000
Usual Pagination: 36
Language(s): Portuguese
Readership: National.
Mechanical Data: Trim Size: 148 x 210 mm
BUSINESS: HEALTH & MEDICAL

FLASH 1642728P74A-110
Editorial: Av. João Crisóstomo, 72 - 4°, 1069-043 LISBOA **Tel:** 213 185 287 **Fax:** 213 540 380
Email: correio@flash.cofina.pt
ISSN: 0871-7362
Date Established: 2003; **Freq:** Weekly; **Cover Price:** EUR 1,25; **Circ:** 85,000
Editor: Hélder Ramalho; **Editor-in-Chief:** Rita Marques; **Managing Director:** Luísa Jeremias; **Advertising Manager:** Elsa Madeira
Language(s): Portuguese
Readership: National.
ADVERTISING RATES:
Full Page Colour .... EUR 4100
Mechanical Data: Trim Size: 230 x 297 mm, Type Area: 190 x 257 mm
CONSUMER: WOMEN'S INTEREST CONSUMER MAGAZINES: Women's Interest

FOCUS 622973P73-85
Editorial: R. da Impala, 33 A - Abrunheira, S. Pedro de Penaferrim, 2710-070 SINTRA **Tel:** 219 238 400
Fax: 219 238 496
Email: geral@focus-online.net **Web site:** http://www.impala.pt
Date Established: 1983; **Freq:** Weekly; **Cover Price:** EUR 2,75; **Circ:** 30,000
Usual Pagination: 130
Editor: Carlos Correia; **Editor-in-Chief:** Vítor Crisóstomo; **Managing Director:** Humberto Simões; **Advertising Manager:** Luís Monteiro Pereira
Profile: Magazine providing coverage of national and international news. Includes articles on worldwide politics, economics, science and technology, along with features on society and cultural trends.
Language(s): Portuguese
Readership: Mainland.
ADVERTISING RATES:
Full Page Colour .... EUR 5010
Mechanical Data: Type Area: 185 x 237 mm, Trim Size: 215 x 267 mm
CONSUMER: NATIONAL & INTERNATIONAL PERIODICALS

FOLHA DE PORTUGAL 1781641P65J-4
Editorial: Alameda D. Afonso Henriques, 35, 1000-123 LISBOA **Tel:** 210 300 097 **Fax:** 210 300 999
Email: claudia.publicidade@folhadeportugal.com
Web site: http://www.folhadeportugal.com
Date Established: 2003; **Freq:** Weekly; **Cover Price:** Free; **Circ:** 50,000
Usual Pagination: 16
Managing Director: João Filipe
Profile: Free weekly newspaper covering national and international news about society, health, sport, science and religion (evangelic).
Language(s): Portuguese
Readership: National.
Mechanical Data: Type Area: 250 x 340 mm, Trim Size: 270 x 380 mm
NATIONAL DAILY & SUNDAY NEWSPAPERS: Grünes MdEP

FOLHA DE SANTA CLARA 1642473P80-217
Editorial: Largo da Portagem, 18 - 2° Dto., 3000-337 COIMBRA **Tel:** 239 832 264
Email: jornalfolha@net.novis.pt
Date Established: 1994; **Freq:** Monthly; **Cover Price:** EUR 0,5; **Circ:** 2,000
Usual Pagination: 16
Managing Director: Rosa Cabeças Simão
Profile: Diocesan newspaper.
Language(s): Portuguese
Readership: Read by Coimbra locals.
ADVERTISING RATES:
Full Page Mono .... EUR 500
Mechanical Data: Trim Size: 280 x 372 mm, Type Area: 255 x 335 mm
CONSUMER: RURAL & REGIONAL INTEREST

FOLHA DO DOMINGO 1642730P74Q-96
Editorial: R. do Município, 14 - 1° Dto., 8000-398 FARO **Tel:** 289 822 319 **Fax:** 289 821 529
Email: folha.domingo@diocese-algarve.pt **Web site:** http://folhadodomingo.diocese-algarve.pt/site/index.php
Date Established: 1964; **Freq:** Weekly; **Cover Price:** EUR 0,5; **Circ:** 4,000

Usual Pagination: 12
Managing Director: Samuel Mendonça
Language(s): Portuguese
Readership: Read in Faro region.
Mechanical Data: Trim Size: 290 x 418 mm, Type Area: 268 x 370 mm
CONSUMER: WOMEN'S INTEREST CONSUMER MAGAZINES: Lifestyle

FOLLOW ME
1642732P89A-126
Editorial: R. do Arsenal, N° 15, 1100-038 LISBOA Tel: 210 312 717 Fax: 210 312 899
Email: atl@visitlisboa.com Web site: http://www.visitlisboa.com
Freq: Monthly; Cover Price: Free; Circ: 65,000
Usual Pagination: 68
Advertising Manager: Leonilde Rodrigues
Profile: Magazine guide with Lisboa's events. Written in english and in spanish.
Language(s): English; Portuguese; Spanish
Readership: Read in Lisboa region. Aimed mainly for turists.
ADVERTISING RATES:
Full Page Colour .... EUR 2450
Mechanical Data: Trim Size: 148 x 207 mm, Type Area: 128 x 187 mm
CONSUMER: HOLIDAYS & TRAVEL: Travel

FORA DE SÉRIE
1781648P74Q-110
Editorial: R. Vieira da Silva, 45, 1350-342 LISBOA Tel: 213 236 700 Fax: 213 236 801
Email: deconomico@economico.pt Web site: http://economico.pt
Freq: Monthly; Cover Price: EUR 2,5; Circ: 34,000
Usual Pagination: 76
Editor: Rita Ibérico Nogueira; Managing Director: António Costa
Profile: Monthly magazine with lifestyle related articles. On each edition a special theme is approached. Published with: Diário Económico.
Language(s): Portuguese
Readership: National. Aimed at businessmen.
ADVERTISING RATES:
Full Page Colour .... EUR 5500
Mechanical Data: Trim Size: 290 x 390 mm

FOREIGN POLICY
1924998P14A-270
Editorial: Av. do Restelo, 14, 1400-315 LISBOA Tel: 213 011 390 Fax: 213 011 423
Email: fp.portugal@fp-portugal.com Web site: http://www.fp-portugal.com
Freq: 6 issues yearly; Cover Price: EUR 5; Circ: 10,000
Usual Pagination: 100
Executive Editor: Luís Fonseca; Managing Director: Filipe Coelho
Profile: Bimonthly magazine dedicated to the general nature of current national and international affairs, focusing on several areas of interest such as economy, politics, society and cultural events.
Language(s): Portuguese
Readership: National.
ADVERTISING RATES:
Full Page Colour .... EUR 5000
Mechanical Data: Type Area: 175 x 245 mm, Trim Size: 205 x 275 mm

FÓRUM EMPRESARIAL
1781671P1A-532
Editorial: Av. João Crisóstomo, 72 - 1°, 1069-043 LISBOA Tel: 213 180 900 Fax: 213 540 361
Email: info@negocios.pt Web site: http://www.jornaldenegocios.pt
ISSN: 0874-1360
Date Established: 1997; Freq: Occasional; Cover Price: Free; Circ: 21,141
Usual Pagination: 8
Profile: Magazine covering business, finance, investment and politics.
Language(s): Portuguese
Readership: National. Aimed at businessmen and investors.
Mechanical Data: Type Area: 257 x 336 mm, Trim Size: 280 x 370 mm
Part of Series, see entry for: Jornal de Negócios

FÓRUM ESTUDANTE
1642736P91D-147
Editorial: Travessa das Pedras Negras, 1 - 4° Andar, 1100-404 LISBOA Tel: 218 854 730 Fax: 218 877 666
Email: rfe@forum.pt Web site: http://www.forum.pt
Date Established: 1991; Freq: Monthly; Cover Price: EUR 4,99; Circ: 70,000
Usual Pagination: 48
Language(s): Portuguese
Readership: National.
ADVERTISING RATES:
Full Page Colour .... EUR 3620
Mechanical Data: Trim Size: 230 x 297 mm, Type Area: 210 x 277 mm
CONSUMER: RECREATION & LEISURE: Children & Youth

FRANCHISING (DN + JN)
1988410P1J-1
Editorial: Edifício Diário de Notícias, Av. da Liberdade, 266, 1250-149 LISBOA Tel: 213 187 500 Fax: 213 187 516
Email: dnot@dn.pt Web site: http://www.dn.pt
Date Established: 2010; Freq: Occasional; Cover Price: Free; Circ: 165,912
Profile: Published with: Diário de Notícias; Jornal de Notícias.
Language(s): Portuguese
Readership: National.
Mechanical Data: Type Area: 148 x 208 mm, Trim Size: 148 x 208 mm

FUNDIÇÃO
19360P4-121
Editorial: APF - Associação Portuguesa de Fundição, R. do Campo Alegre, 672 - 2° Esq., 4150-171 PORTO Tel: 226 090 675 Fax: 226 000 764
Email: info@apf.com.pt Web site: http://www.publindustria.pt
Freq: Quarterly; Cover Price: EUR 15; Circ: 1,000
Usual Pagination: 50
Advertising Manager: Júlio Almeida
Profile: Journal focusing on the Portuguese foundry industry.
Language(s): Portuguese
Readership: Aimed at engineers, technicians and executives in the foundry sector.
ADVERTISING RATES:
Full Page Colour .... EUR 700
Mechanical Data: Type Area: 180 x 267 mm, Trim Size: 210 x 297 mm

FUTEBOL
1841876P65A-50_102
Editorial: Av. João Crisóstomo, 72 - 6°, 1069-043 LISBOA Tel: 213 185 200 Fax: 213 185 377
Email: geral@correiomanha.pt Web site: http://www.cmjornal.pt
Date Established: 2008; Freq: Occasional; Cover Price: Free; Circ: 165,562
Usual Pagination: 52
Profile: Edição especial sobre o Campeonato da Europa de Futebol.
Language(s): Portuguese
Readership: National.
Mechanical Data: Type Area: 200 x 272 mm, Trim Size: 202 x 274 mm
Section of: Correio da Manhã
NATIONAL DAILY & SUNDAY NEWSPAPERS: Unabhängiges konservatives MdEP

FUTEBOL
1841876P65A-50_108
Editorial: Av. João Crisóstomo, 72 - 6°, 1069-043 LISBOA Tel: 213 185 200 Fax: 213 185 377
Email: geral@correiomanha.pt Web site: http://www.cmjornal.pt
Date Established: 2008; Freq: Occasional; Cover Price: Free; Circ: 165,562
Usual Pagination: 52
Profile: Edição especial sobre o Campeonato da Europa de Futebol.
Language(s): Portuguese
Readership: National.
Mechanical Data: Type Area: 200 x 272 mm, Trim Size: 202 x 274 mm
Section of: Correio da Manhã
NATIONAL DAILY & SUNDAY NEWSPAPERS: Unabhängiges konservatives MdEP

GAZETA DA BEIRA
1642743P74Q-97
Editorial: R. dos Bombeiros Voluntários, 37, Apartado 40, São Pedro do Sul, 3660-502 VISEU Tel: 232 723 408 Fax: 232 712 150
Email: gazetadabeira@oninet.pt
Freq: 26 issues yearly; Cover Price: EUR 0,5; Circ: 1,600
Managing Director: Carmo Bica
Profile: Fortnightly newspaper with information about S. Pedro do Sul, Vouzela, Oliveira de Frades and Castro Daire regions (Viseu). Politics, current affairs, society, religion, sport, entertainment and events.
Language(s): Portuguese
Readership: Read in Viseu region, mainly in S. Pedro do Sul, Vouzela, Oliveira de Frades and Castro Daire.
ADVERTISING RATES:
Full Page Mono .... EUR 180
Full Page Colour .... EUR 240
Mechanical Data: Trim Size: 275 x 352 mm
CONSUMER: WOMEN'S INTEREST CONSUMER MAGAZINES: Lifestyle

GAZETA DE LAGOA
1642745P74Q-99
Editorial: Largo Alves Roçadas, 8 - A, 8400-313 LAGOA Tel: 282 341 512 Fax: 282 341 512
Email: gazetadelagoa@gmail.com
Date Established: 1989; Freq: Weekly; Cover Price: EUR 1; Circ: 2,500
Usual Pagination: 12
Profile: Weekly newspaper with information about Lagoa. Politics, current affairs, society, religion, sport, entertainment and events.
Language(s): Portuguese
Readership: Read by Lagoa locals.
ADVERTISING RATES:
Full Page Mono .... EUR 700
Full Page Colour .... EUR 920
Mechanical Data: Trim Size: 300 x 400 mm, Type Area: 260 x 340 mm
CONSUMER: WOMEN'S INTEREST CONSUMER MAGAZINES: Lifestyle

GAZETA DO INTERIOR
1642872P72-87
Editorial: Av. 1° de Maio, 39 - 1° Dto., 6000-086 CASTELO BRANCO Tel: 272 320 090 Fax: 272 320 091
Email: gazeta.interior@netvisao.pt Web site: http://www.gazetadointerior.pt
Date Established: 1988; Freq: Weekly; Cover Price: EUR 0,6; Circ: 5,000
Usual Pagination: 36
Editor-in-Chief: Célia Domingues; Managing Director: Leopoldo Rodrigues
Profile: Weekly newspaper with information about Castelo Branco region. Politics, current affairs, society, religion, sport, entertainment and events.
Language(s): Portuguese
Readership: Read in Castelo Branco region.
ADVERTISING RATES:
Full Page Mono .... EUR 710
Full Page Colour .... EUR 1070
Mechanical Data: Trim Size: 289 x 410 mm, Type Area: 263 x 357 mm
LOCAL NEWSPAPERS

GENTLEMEN MAGAZINE
1933922P86C-29
Editorial: R. Bernardo Lima, 47 - 2° Esq., 1150-078 LISBOA Tel: 213 149 025
Email: redaccao@presscoast.com.pt Web site: http://www.presscoast.com.pt
Date Established: 2009; Freq: Monthly; Cover Price: EUR 3,5; Circ: 30,000
Usual Pagination: 116
Managing Director: Paula Martin
Profile: Men's magazine on fashion, cosmetics and perfumes, health, gadgets, motor, social behavior, among others.
Language(s): Portuguese
Readership: Mainland.
ADVERTISING RATES:
Full Page Colour .... EUR 5650
Mechanical Data: Type Area: 190 x 265 mm, Trim Size: 230 x 297 mm

GENTLEMEN MAGAZINE
1933922P86C-32
Editorial: R. Bernardo Lima, 47 - 2° Esq., 1150-078 LISBOA Tel: 213 149 025
Email: redaccao@presscoast.com.pt Web site: http://www.presscoast.com.pt
Date Established: 2009; Freq: Monthly; Cover Price: EUR 3,5; Circ: 30,000
Usual Pagination: 116
Managing Director: Paula Martin
Profile: Men's magazine on fashion, cosmetics and perfumes, health, gadgets, motor, social behavior, among others.
Language(s): Portuguese
Readership: Mainland.
ADVERTISING RATES:
Full Page Colour .... EUR 5650
Mechanical Data: Type Area: 190 x 265 mm, Trim Size: 230 x 297 mm

GENTLEMEN MAGAZINE
1933922P86C-34
Editorial: R. Bernardo Lima, 47 - 2° Esq., 1150-078 LISBOA Tel: 213 149 025
Email: redaccao@presscoast.com.pt Web site: http://www.presscoast.com.pt
Date Established: 2009; Freq: Monthly; Cover Price: EUR 3,5; Circ: 30,000
Usual Pagination: 116
Managing Director: Paula Martin
Profile: Men's magazine on fashion, cosmetics and perfumes, health, gadgets, motor, social behavior, among others.
Language(s): Portuguese
Readership: Mainland.
ADVERTISING RATES:
Full Page Colour .... EUR 5650
Mechanical Data: Type Area: 190 x 265 mm, Trim Size: 230 x 297 mm

GESTÃO DE FROTAS (AH + VC)
1857285P49D-4
Editorial: R. Policarpo Anjos, 4, 1495-742 CRUZ QUEBRADA/DAFUNDO Tel: 214 154 500 Fax: 214 154 504
Email: autohoje@motorpress.pt Web site: http://www.autohoje.com
Freq: Occasional; Cover Price: Free; Circ: 49,500
Usual Pagination: 32
Profile: Published with: Auto Hoje; Veículos Comerciais.
Language(s): Portuguese
Readership: Mainland.
ADVERTISING RATES:
Full Page Colour .... EUR 3320
Mechanical Data: Trim Size: 209 x 284 mm

GESTÃO DE FROTAS (AH + VC)
1857285P49D-6
Editorial: R. Policarpo Anjos, 4, 1495-742 CRUZ QUEBRADA/DAFUNDO Tel: 214 154 500 Fax: 214 154 504
Email: autohoje@motorpress.pt Web site: http://www.autohoje.com
Freq: Occasional; Cover Price: Free; Circ: 49,500
Usual Pagination: 32
Profile: Published with: Auto Hoje; Veículos Comerciais.
Language(s): Portuguese
Readership: Mainland.
ADVERTISING RATES:
Full Page Colour .... EUR 3320
Mechanical Data: Trim Size: 209 x 284 mm

GOLF DIGEST
1642749P75D-1
Editorial: Alameda das Linhas de Torres, 179, 1750-142 LISBOA Tel: 217 541 450 Fax: 217 541 458
Email: geral@golfpress.pt Web site: http://www.mediagolf.pt
ISSN: 1645-0787
Date Established: 1993; Freq: 6 issues yearly; Cover Price: EUR 4; Circ: 15,100
Managing Director: Manuel Agrellos
Profile: Magazine containing lessons and tips from the world best golf players and articles about equipment, golf courses and trips.
Language(s): Portuguese
Readership: National. Aimed for golf players and affectionates. Class A, B. Men 80%.
ADVERTISING RATES:
Full Page Colour .... EUR 2950
Mechanical Data: Type Area: 177 x 230 mm, Trim Size: 203 x 267 mm
CONSUMER: SPORT: Golf

GQ
1642751P86C-2
Editorial: Av. João Crisóstomo, 72 - Galeria, 1069-043 LISBOA Tel: 213 307 700 Fax: 213 540 695
Email: leonorpatrone@gq.cofina.pt Web site: http://revistagq.no.sapo.pt
Date Established: 2001; Freq: Monthly; Cover Price: EUR 3,5; Circ: 24,000
Editor: Miguel Szymanski; Managing Director: Domingos Freitas do Amaral
Language(s): Portuguese
Readership: Mainland.
ADVERTISING RATES:
Full Page Colour .... EUR 5400
Mechanical Data: Trim Size: 220 x 285 mm
CONSUMER: ADULT & GAY MAGAZINES: Men's Lifestyle Magazines

A GUARDA
1642474P72I-30
Editorial: R. Marquês de Pombal, 55/61, 6300-728 GUARDA Tel: 271 222 105 Fax: 271 208 387
Email: a.guarda.veritas@mail.telepac.pt Web site: http://www.jornalaguarda.com
Date Established: 1904; Freq: Weekly; Cover Price: EUR 0,65; Circ: 22,000
Usual Pagination: 26
Managing Director: Eugénio da Cunha Sério
Profile: Weekly newspaper with information about Guarda region. Politics, current affairs, society, religion, sport, entertainment and events.
Language(s): Portuguese
Readership: Read in Guarda region.
ADVERTISING RATES:
Full Page Mono .... EUR 300
Full Page Colour .... EUR 450
Mechanical Data: Type Area: 265 x 360 mm, Trim Size: 300 x 423 mm
LOCAL NEWSPAPERS: Regional Weekly Newspapers

GUIA DE EMPRESAS CERTIFICADAS
1820649P14A-145
Editorial: Av. Almirante Reis, 114 - 2° C, 1150-023 LISBOA Tel: 218 141 574 Fax: 218 142 664
Email: geral@cempalavras.pt Web site: http://www.cempalavras.pt
Freq: Annual; Cover Price: Free; Circ: 20,000
Usual Pagination: 162
Profile: Guide for certified Companies.
Language(s): English; Portuguese
Readership: National.
ADVERTISING RATES:
Full Page Colour .... EUR 1100
Mechanical Data: Type Area: 200 x 200 mm, Trim Size: 220 x 220 mm

GUIA DE ESTILO
1781938P86C-11
Editorial: R. Policarpo Anjos, 4, 1495-742 CRUZ QUEBRADA/DAFUNDO Tel: 214 154 500 Fax: 214 154 501
Email: menshealth@motorpress.pt Web site: http://www.menshealth.com.pt
Freq: Occasional; Cover Price: Free; Circ: 38,000
Profile: Men's fashion magazine.
Language(s): Portuguese
Readership: Mainland.
Mechanical Data: Trim Size: 220 x 280 mm

GUIA DE FUTEBOL
1783346P75B-10
Editorial: Av. Conde de Valbom, 30 - 4° e 5°, 1050-068 LISBOA Tel: 210 124 900 Fax: 213 151 315
Email: antoniomagalhaes@record.pt Web site: http://www.record.xl.pt
Freq: Annual; Cover Price: EUR 3; Circ: 90,000
Language(s): Portuguese
Readership: Mainland.
ADVERTISING RATES:
Full Page Colour .... EUR 3030
Mechanical Data: Trim Size: 230 x 295 mm, Type Area: 205 x 268 mm
Part of Series, see entry for: Record
CONSUMER: SPORT: Football

GUIA DE GESTÃO DO CONDOMÍNIO 1822262P65A-50_124
Editorial: Av. João Crisóstomo, 72, 1069-043 LISBOA **Tel:** 213 185 462 **Fax:** 213 540 695
Email: geral@correiomanha.pt **Web site:** http://www.cmjornal.pt
Date Established: 2007; **Freq:** Occasional; **Cover Price:** Free; **Circ:** 166,657
Usual Pagination: 48
Language(s): Portuguese
Readership: National.
ADVERTISING RATES:
Full Page Colour .... EUR 2655
Mechanical Data: Type Area: 96 x 169 mm, Trim Size: 115 x 190 mm
Section of: Correio da Manhã
NATIONAL DAILY & SUNDAY NEWSPAPERS: National Daily Newspapers

GUIA DO ALGARVE 1820651P80-397
Editorial: Av. 5 de Outubro, 18, 8000-076 FARO
Tel: 289 800 400 **Fax:** 289 800 489
Email: edicoes@turismodoalgarve.pt **Web site:** http://www.visitalgarve.pt
Freq: Monthly; **Cover Price:** Free; **Circ:** 80,000
Usual Pagination: 32
Language(s): English
ADVERTISING RATES:
Full Page Colour .... EUR 1200
Mechanical Data: Type Area: 135 x 170 mm, Trim Size: 148 x 210 mm
CONSUMER: RURAL & REGIONAL INTEREST

GUIA DO AUTOMÓVEL
1605946P77A-251
Editorial: R. Policarpo Anjos, 4, 1495-742 CRUZ QUEBRADA/DAFUNDO **Tel:** 214 154 500
Fax: 214 154 501
Email: guiadoautomovel@motorpress.pt **Web site:** http://www.guiadoautomovel.pt
Date Established: 1985; **Freq:** Monthly; **Cover Price:** EUR 2,4; **Circ:** 46,583
Usual Pagination: 292
Managing Director: Alexandre Rodrigues;
Advertising Manager: Rita Vidreiro
Profile: Magazine focusing on new and old cars includes vehicle tests and comparisons, expert advice and price lists.
Language(s): Portuguese
Readership: Mainland. Aimed at potential buyers and motoring enthusiasts.
ADVERTISING RATES:
Full Page Colour .... EUR 2400
Mechanical Data: Trim Size: 145 x 215 mm, Type Area: 123 x 195 mm
CONSUMER: MOTORING & CYCLING: Motoring

HAPPY WOMAN 1782001P74B-93
Editorial: Av. António Augusto Aguiar, 11 - 1° Esq., 1050-010 LISBOA **Tel:** 213 103 370 **Fax:** 213 153 115
Email: ruben.casimiro@baleskapress.pt
Date Established: 2006; **Freq:** Monthly; **Cover Price:** EUR 2,2; **Circ:** 136,000
Usual Pagination: 132
Advertising Manager: Rúben Casimiro
Language(s): Portuguese
Readership: National.
ADVERTISING RATES:
Full Page Colour .... EUR 6000
Mechanical Data: Trim Size: 230 x 297 mm, Type Area: 190 x 263 mm
CONSUMER: WOMEN'S INTEREST CONSUMER MAGAZINES: Women's Interest - Fashion

HEALTH & BEAUTY 2094501P56A-370
Editorial: Parque Empresarial do Algarve, 7, Apartado 59, 8401-901 LAGOA **Tel:** 282 341 333
Fax: 282 341 360
Email: essential.algarve@open-media.net **Web site:** http://www.essential-portugal.com
Date Established: 2011; **Freq:** Occasional; **Cover Price:** Free; **Circ:** 15,000
Profile: Health & Beauty.
Language(s): Portuguese
Readership: National.
Mechanical Data: Type Area: 200 x 290 mm, Trim Size: 230 x 320 mm
Part of Series, see entry for: Essential Algarve

HORÓSCOPO 1780346P91D-154
Editorial: R. Joaquim António de Aguiar, 35 - 3° Esq., 1070-149 LISBOA **Tel:** 213 839 580 **Fax:** 213 839 581
Email: revistabravo@portugalmail.pt **Web site:** http://www.bravopt.com
ISSN: 1136-1239
Freq: Annual; **Cover Price:** EUR 1,85; **Circ:** 100,000
Usual Pagination: 52
Language(s): Portuguese
Readership: National. Aimed at teenagers.
ADVERTISING RATES:
Full Page Colour .... EUR 1550
Mechanical Data: Trim Size: 212 x 278 mm
CONSUMER: RECREATION & LEISURE: Children & Youth

IMEDIATO 1642784P80-220
Editorial: Alameda do Mosteiro, Loja 2, N° 52, 4590-909 PAÇOS DE FERREIRA **Tel:** 255 860 960
Fax: 255 860 969
Email: imediato@imediato.pt **Web site:** http://www.imediato.pt
ISSN: 1646-8538
Date Established: 1994; **Freq:** 26 issues yearly;
Cover Price: EUR 0,8; **Circ:** 4,200
Usual Pagination: 24
Profile: Fortnightly newspaper with information about Paços de Ferreira. Politics, current affairs, society, sport, entertainment and events.
Language(s): Portuguese
Readership: Read in Paços de Ferreira.
ADVERTISING RATES:
Full Page Mono .... EUR 325
Full Page Colour .... EUR 425
Mechanical Data: Type Area: 260 x 350 mm, Trim Size: 290 x 400 mm
CONSUMER: RURAL & REGIONAL INTEREST

IMOBILIÁRIA 19287P1E-40
Editorial: Edifício Atrium Saldanha, Praça Duque de Saldanha, 1 - 11° A, 1069-970 LISBOA
Tel: 213 170 850 **Fax:** 213 160 297
Email: imobiliaria@lusosinal.pt **Web site:** http://www.revistaimobiliaria.com.pt
ISSN: 1645-8640
Date Established: 1991; **Freq:** Monthly; **Cover Price:** EUR 4,5; **Circ:** 3,000
Usual Pagination: 84
Editor: Carla Celestino; **Managing Director:** Acácio Pinheiro
Language(s): Portuguese
Readership: National. Aimed at estate agents, investors and people interested in the property market.
ADVERTISING RATES:
Full Page Colour .... EUR 1750
Mechanical Data: Type Area: 210 x 280 mm, Trim Size: 230 x 300 mm
BUSINESS: FINANCE & ECONOMICS: Property

INDEPENDENTE DE CANTANHEDE 1643004P72-37
Editorial: Praça Marquês de Marialva, N° 6, Sala 6, 1°, 3060-133 CANTANHEDE **Tel:** 231 429 499
Fax: 231 423 613
Email: indcantanhede@mail.telepac.pt **Web site:** http://www.independentedecantanhede.com
Date Established: 1994; **Freq:** Weekly; **Cover Price:** EUR 0,6; **Circ:** 3,000
Usual Pagination: 20
Managing Director: Américo Guimaro
Profile: Weekly newspaper with information about Cantanhede. Politics, current affairs, society, religion, sport, entertainment and events.
Language(s): Portuguese
Readership: Read by Cantanhede locals.
ADVERTISING RATES:
Full Page Mono .... EUR 413
Full Page Colour .... EUR 620
Mechanical Data: Trim Size: 287 x 410 mm, Type Area: 260 x 360 mm
LOCAL NEWSPAPERS

INDÚSTRIA 1642786P37-63
Editorial: BLEED - Soc. Editorial e Organização de Eventos, Lda., Campo Grande, 30 - 9° C, 1700-093 LISBOA **Tel:** 217 957 045 **Fax:** 217 957 047
Email: bleed@netcabo.pt **Web site:** http://www.cip.org.pt
Date Established: 1984; **Freq:** 6 issues yearly;
Cover Price: EUR 3,5; **Circ:** 10,000
Usual Pagination: 60
Managing Director: António Saraiva
Language(s): Portuguese
Readership: National.
ADVERTISING RATES:
Full Page Colour .... EUR 1500
Mechanical Data: Trim Size: 210 x 295 mm, Type Area: 185 x 280 mm
BUSINESS: PHARMACEUTICAL & CHEMISTS

INDÚSTRIA FARMACÊUTICA
1830668P56A-249
Editorial: R. Gonçalo Cristóvão, 111 - 6°, 4049-037 PORTO **Tel:** 223 399 404 **Fax:** 222 058 098
Email: redaccao@vidaeconomica.pt **Web site:** http://www.vidaeconomica.pt
ISSN: 0871-4320
Date Established: 2007; **Freq:** Occasional; **Cover Price:** Free; **Circ:** 21,900
Usual Pagination: 8
Profile: Suplemento sobre a indústria farmacêutica: as marcas, congressos, novidades, etc.
Language(s): Portuguese
Readership: National.
ADVERTISING RATES:
Full Page Mono .... EUR 1800
Full Page Colour .... EUR 2335
Mechanical Data: Type Area: 257 x 390 mm, Trim Size: 290 x 418 mm
Part of Series, see entry for: Vida Económica

INDÚSTRIA FARMACÊUTICA
1830668P56A-296
Editorial: R. Gonçalo Cristóvão, 111 - 6°, 4049-037 PORTO **Tel:** 223 399 404 **Fax:** 222 058 098
Email: redaccao@vidaeconomica.pt **Web site:** http://www.vidaeconomica.pt
ISSN: 0871-4320
Date Established: 2007; **Freq:** Occasional; **Cover Price:** Free; **Circ:** 21,900
Usual Pagination: 8
Profile: Suplemento sobre a indústria farmacêutica: as marcas, congressos, novidades, etc.
Language(s): Portuguese
Readership: National.
ADVERTISING RATES:
Full Page Mono .... EUR 1800
Full Page Colour .... EUR 2335
Mechanical Data: Type Area: 257 x 390 mm, Trim Size: 290 x 418 mm
Part of Series, see entry for: Vida Económica

INGENIUM 19344P19A-45
Editorial: Av. António Augusto de Aguiar, N° 3 Dto., 1069-030 LISBOA **Tel:** 213 132 600 **Fax:** 213 524 632
Email: gabinete.comunicacao@ordemdosengenheiros.pt **Web site:** http://www.ordemengenheiros.pt
ISSN: 0870-5968
Freq: 6 issues yearly; **Cover Price:** EUR 3; **Circ:** 48,500
Profile: Official publication of the Portuguese Association of Engineers focusing on new engineering technology.
Language(s): Portuguese
Readership: National. Read by engineers, technologists and the general public.
ADVERTISING RATES:
Full Page Colour .... EUR 3180
Mechanical Data: Trim Size: 207 x 297 mm
BUSINESS: ENGINEERING & MACHINERY

INOVAÇÃO 1822415P1A-384
Editorial: R. Gonçalo Cristóvão, 111 - 6°, 4049-037 PORTO **Tel:** 223 399 400 **Fax:** 222 058 098
Email: ve@vidaeconomica.pt **Web site:** http://www.vidaeconomica.pt
ISSN: 0871-4320
Date Established: 2007; **Freq:** Occasional; **Cover Price:** Free; **Circ:** 20,900
Usual Pagination: 8
Profile: Suplemento dedicado aos investidores portugueses.
Language(s): Portuguese
Readership: National.
ADVERTISING RATES:
Full Page Mono .... EUR 1750
Full Page Colour .... EUR 2270
Mechanical Data: Type Area: 257 x 390 mm, Trim Size: 290 x 418 mm
Part of Series, see entry for: Vida Económica

INOVAÇÃO 1822415P1A-615
Editorial: R. Gonçalo Cristóvão, 111 - 6°, 4049-037 PORTO **Tel:** 223 399 400 **Fax:** 222 058 098
Email: ve@vidaeconomica.pt **Web site:** http://www.vidaeconomica.pt
ISSN: 0871-4320
Date Established: 2007; **Freq:** Occasional; **Cover Price:** Free; **Circ:** 20,900
Usual Pagination: 8
Profile: Suplemento dedicado aos investidores portugueses.
Language(s): Portuguese
Readership: National.
ADVERTISING RATES:
Full Page Mono .... EUR 1750
Full Page Colour .... EUR 2270
Mechanical Data: Type Area: 257 x 390 mm, Trim Size: 290 x 418 mm
Part of Series, see entry for: Vida Económica

INOVAÇÃO BES 1782125P1A-238
Editorial: R. da Oliveira ao Carmo, 8, 1249-111 LISBOA **Tel:** 213 236 711 **Fax:** 213 236 701
Email: deconomico@economico.pt **Web site:** http://economico.pt
Freq: Monthly; **Cover Price:** Free; **Circ:** 19,667
Profile: Published with: Diário Económico.
Language(s): Portuguese
Readership: National. Aimed at leaders within business and industry, financial directors, public and private investors.
Mechanical Data: Trim Size: 280 x 394 mm, Type Area: 250 x 360 mm

INOVAÇÃO BES 1782125P1A-616
Editorial: R. da Oliveira ao Carmo, 8, 1249-111 LISBOA **Tel:** 213 236 711 **Fax:** 213 236 701
Email: deconomico@economico.pt **Web site:** http://economico.pt
Freq: Monthly; **Cover Price:** Free; **Circ:** 19,667
Profile: Published with: Diário Económico.
Language(s): Portuguese
Readership: National. Aimed at leaders within business and industry, financial directors, public and private investors.
Mechanical Data: Trim Size: 280 x 394 mm, Type Area: 250 x 360 mm

INOVAÇÃO & TECNOLOGIA
1788044P5-229
Editorial: Edifício S. Francisco de Sales, R. Calvet de Magalhães, 242, 2770-022 PAÇO DE ARCOS
Tel: 214 544 000 **Fax:** 214 435 310
Email: ipublishing@impresa.pt **Web site:** http://www.expresso.pt
Date Established: 2006; **Freq:** Occasional; **Cover Price:** Free; **Circ:** 133,425
Usual Pagination: 12
Language(s): Portuguese
Readership: National.
ADVERTISING RATES:
Full Page Colour .... EUR 5800
Mechanical Data: Type Area: 237 x 307 mm, Trim Size: 260 x 330 mm
Part of Series, see entry for: Expresso
BUSINESS: COMPUTERS & AUTOMATION

O INSTALADOR 1643006P57-138
Editorial: R. do Alecrim, 53 - R/C Ftr., 1200-014 LISBOA **Tel:** 218 820 160 **Fax:** 218 820 169
Email: oinstalador@gmail.com **Web site:** http://www.oinstalador.pt
Date Established: 1996; **Freq:** Monthly; **Cover Price:** EUR 5,22; **Circ:** 7,000
Usual Pagination: 138
Managing Director: Isabel Fonseca
Profile: Technical magazine about technology developments and business sectors related to air conditioning, heating and ventilation, electricity, construction, architecture, energy and environment.
Language(s): Portuguese
Readership: National.
ADVERTISING RATES:
Full Page Colour .... EUR 930
Mechanical Data: Trim Size: 210 x 297 mm, Type Area: 180 x 270 mm

INTER MAGAZINE 19317P11A-50
Editorial: Av. Padre Manuel de Nóbrega, 9 R/C Esq., 1000-223 LISBOA **Tel:** 218 822 993 **Fax:** 218 884 504
Email: inter@e-gosto.com **Web site:** http://www.inter-magazine.com
ISSN: 0873-531X
Date Established: 1989; **Freq:** Monthly; **Cover Price:** EUR 3,5; **Circ:** 4,000
Usual Pagination: 60
Managing Director: Paulo Amado
Profile: Magazine focusing on the hotel, catering and food service trades.
Language(s): Portuguese
Readership: National. Read by hotel, restaurant and catering management.
ADVERTISING RATES:
Full Page Colour .... EUR 1800
Mechanical Data: Trim Size: 220 x 270 mm
BUSINESS: CATERING: Catering, Hotels & Restaurants

INTER.FACE - ADMINISTRAÇÃO PÚBLICA 1642796P5C-58
Editorial: R. Alexandre Herculano, 2 - 2° Dto., 1150-006 LISBOA **Tel:** 218 823 300 **Fax:** 211 204 349
Email: geral@algebrica.pt **Web site:** http://www.algebrica.pt
Freq: 6 issues yearly; **Cover Price:** EUR 7,5; **Circ:** 25,000
Usual Pagination: 56
Editor: Hugo Jorge; **Advertising Manager:** Patrícia Lopes
Language(s): Portuguese
Readership: National.
ADVERTISING RATES:
Full Page Colour .... EUR 500
Mechanical Data: Type Area: 175 x 245 mm, Trim Size: 205 x 285 mm
BUSINESS: COMPUTERS & AUTOMATION: Professional Personal Computers

INTER.FACE - BANCA & SEGUROS 1642797P5C-59
Editorial: R. Alexandre Herculano, 2 - 2° Dto., 1150-006 LISBOA **Tel:** 218 823 300 **Fax:** 218 851 559
Email: geral@algebrica.pt **Web site:** http://www.algebrica.pt
Freq: 3 issues yearly; **Cover Price:** EUR 7,5; **Circ:** 25,000
Usual Pagination: 52
Editor: Cristina Guedes; **Advertising Manager:** Patrícia Lopes
Language(s): Portuguese
Readership: National.
ADVERTISING RATES:
Full Page Colour .... EUR 1850
Mechanical Data: Type Area: 175 x 245 mm, Trim Size: 205 x 285 mm
BUSINESS: COMPUTERS & AUTOMATION: Professional Personal Computers

INTER.FACE - SAÚDE
1642798P74G-76
Editorial: R. Alexandre Herculano, 2 - 2° Dto., 1150-006 LISBOA **Tel:** 218 823 300 **Fax:** 218 851 559
Email: geral@algebrica.pt **Web site:** http://www.algebrica.pt/i_s
Freq: Annual; **Cover Price:** EUR 7,5; **Circ:** 25,000
Usual Pagination: 68
Advertising Manager: Patrícia Lopes
Language(s): Portuguese
Readership: National.
ADVERTISING RATES:
Full Page Colour .... EUR 1850
Mechanical Data: Type Area: 175 x 245 mm, Trim Size: 205 x 285 mm
CONSUMER: WOMEN'S INTEREST CONSUMER MAGAZINES: Slimming & Health

INTERNACIONAL CANETAS
1642802P41B-1
Editorial: Av. Almirante Gago Coutinho, 128, Edifício Posterior, 1700-033 LISBOA **Tel:** 213 472 127
Fax: 213 421 490
Email: geral@homemmagazine.com
ISSN: 0874-0372
Date Established: 1997; **Freq:** Seasonal; **Cover Price:** EUR 5; **Circ:** 12,500
Usual Pagination: 92
Language(s): Portuguese
Readership: National.
ADVERTISING RATES:
Full Page Mono .... EUR 2440
Full Page Colour .... EUR 3250
Mechanical Data: Trim Size: 210 x 270 mm, Type Area: 175 x 240 mm
BUSINESS: PRINTING & STATIONERY: Stationery

INVEST
1782149P1F-2
Editorial: Largo Rainha Santa Isabel, 1 - 1° Esq., 2410-165 LEIRIA **Tel:** 244 811 205 **Fax:** 244 838 549
Email: geral@revistainvest.pt **Web site:** http://www.revistainvest.pt
Date Established: 2005; **Freq:** Monthly; **Cover Price:** EUR 3; **Circ:** 3,000
Managing Director: João Paulo Leonardo
Profile: Magazine regarding the economic and regional development of Leiria, Santarém, Coimbra and Aveiro districts. Contains also national and international economic information.
Language(s): Portuguese
Readership: Aimed mainly for Leiria district, but also regarding Santarém, Coimbra and Aveiro districts.
ADVERTISING RATES:
Full Page Colour .... EUR 950
Mechanical Data: Trim Size: 225 x 286 mm

JADA
1931468P56A-316
Editorial: Al. António Sérgio, 22 - 4° B, Edifício Amadeo de Souza-Cardoso, Miraflores, 1495-132 ALGÉS **Tel:** 214 123 105 **Fax:** 214 121 146
Email: revisfarma@mail.telepac.pt
Freq: 6 issues yearly; **Cover Price:** EUR 34
Free to qualifying individuals ; **Circ:** 4,500
Editor: Manuel Magalhães; **Managing Director:** Paulo Melo
Profile: Portuguese edition of The Journal of the American Dental Association.
Language(s): Portuguese
Readership: National.
ADVERTISING RATES:
Full Page Colour .... EUR 1330
Mechanical Data: Trim Size: 207 x 280 mm

JARDINS
1642807P74C-93
Editorial: R. Joaquim António de Aguiar, 45 - 2° Dto., 1070-150 LISBOA **Tel:** 213 804 010 **Fax:** 213 804 011
Email: geral@entusiasmomedia.pt **Web site:** http://www.jardins.com.pt
Freq: Monthly; **Cover Price:** EUR 3,5; **Circ:** 15,000
Usual Pagination: 68
Managing Director: Luís Melo
Profile: Magazine about garden architecture, decorative gardening and related events.
Language(s): Portuguese
Readership: Mainland.
ADVERTISING RATES:
Full Page Colour .... EUR 2660
Mechanical Data: Type Area: 170 x 250 mm, Trim Size: 210 x 275 mm
CONSUMER: WOMEN'S INTEREST CONSUMER MAGAZINES: Home & Family

JN NEGÓCIOS
1782184P65A-181_104
Editorial: R. de Gonçalo Cristóvão, 195-219, 4049-011 PORTO **Tel:** 222 096 100 **Fax:** 222 096 140
Email: dpe@jn.pt **Web site:** http://www.jn.pt
ISSN: 0874-1352
Freq: Weekly; **Cover Price:** Free; **Circ:** 112,738
Profile: Newspaper supplement containing a Portuguese adaptation of the Wall Street Journal.
Language(s): Portuguese
Readership: National. Individuals with special interest in the economical and financial business areas.
ADVERTISING RATES:
Full Page Mono .... EUR 8000
Full Page Colour .... EUR 11200
Mechanical Data: Trim Size: 290 x 400 mm, Type Area: 253 x 358 mm
Section of: Jornal de Notícias
NATIONAL DAILY & SUNDAY NEWSPAPERS: National Daily Newspapers

JOÃO SEMANA
1642809P72-38
Editorial: Av. do Bom Reitor, 3880-110 OVAR
Tel: 256 574 173 **Fax:** 256 588 545
Email: jornaljoaosemana@sapo.pt
Freq: 6 issues yearly; **Cover Price:** EUR 0,5; **Circ:** 1,330
Usual Pagination: 8
Profile: Fortnightly newspaper with information about Ovar. Politics, current affairs, society, religion, sport, entertainment and events.
Language(s): Portuguese
Readership: Read by Ovar locals.
ADVERTISING RATES:
Full Page Mono .... EUR 150
Mechanical Data: Type Area: 260 x 365 mm, Trim Size: 286 x 410 mm
LOCAL NEWSPAPERS

O JOGO
19473P65A-110
Editorial: R. Gonçalo Cristóvão, 195, 4000-269 PORTO **Tel:** 222 096 147 **Fax:** 222 096 127
Email: ojogo@mail.telepac.pt **Web site:** http://www.ojogo.pt
ISSN: 0872-2811
Date Established: 1985; **Freq:** Daily; **Cover Price:** EUR 0,8; **Circ:** 51,910
Usual Pagination: 48
Editor-in-Chief: Sérgio Krithinas; **Managing Director:** João Marcelino
Profile: Tabloid-sized newspaper containing in-depth sporting news, information and opinion. Focuses predominantly on football, providing interviews, statistics, player profiles and team reports. Also covers international sporting events and includes articles on hockey, basketball, athletics, swimming, cycling and motor sports. Contains comic strips and game puzzles.
Language(s): Portuguese
Readership: National. Aimed at people with a keen interest in sport, specially football.
ADVERTISING RATES:
Full Page Mono .... EUR 3020
Full Page Colour .... EUR 4250
Mechanical Data: Trim Size: 290 x 372 mm, Type Area: 253 x 325 mm
NATIONAL DAILY & SUNDAY NEWSPAPERS: National Daily Newspapers

JOGO DA BOLSA
1822440P1A-387
Editorial: Av. João Crisóstomo, 72 - 1°, 1069-043 LISBOA **Tel:** 213 180 900 **Fax:** 213 540 361
Email: info@negocios.pt **Web site:** http://www.jornaldenegocios.pt
ISSN: 0874-1360
Date Established: 2007; **Freq:** Occasional; **Cover Price:** Free; **Circ:** 17,944
Usual Pagination: 16
Profile: Suplemento com o resultado do Jogo da Bolsa. A classificação geral, suas cotações e valorizações.
Language(s): Portuguese
Readership: National.
Mechanical Data: Trim Size: 280 x 370 mm
Part of Series, see entry for: Jornal de Negócios

JOGO DA BOLSA
1822440P1A-501
Editorial: Av. João Crisóstomo, 72 - 1°, 1069-043 LISBOA **Tel:** 213 180 900 **Fax:** 213 540 361
Email: info@negocios.pt **Web site:** http://www.jornaldenegocios.pt
ISSN: 0874-1360
Date Established: 2007; **Freq:** Occasional; **Cover Price:** Free; **Circ:** 17,944
Usual Pagination: 16
Profile: Suplemento com o resultado do Jogo da Bolsa. A classificação geral, suas cotações e valorizações.
Language(s): Portuguese
Readership: National.
Mechanical Data: Trim Size: 280 x 370 mm
Part of Series, see entry for: Jornal de Negócios

JORNAL 1X2
1642812P91D-148
Editorial: Apartado 148, 2801-997 ALMADA
Tel: 212 760 511 **Fax:** 212 743 421
Email: geral@jornal1x2.com **Web site:** http://www.jornal1x2.com
Date Established: 1979; **Freq:** Weekly; **Cover Price:** EUR 1; **Circ:** 30,000
Language(s): Portuguese
Readership: National.
Mechanical Data: Trim Size: 300 x 370 mm
CONSUMER: RECREATION & LEISURE: Children & Youth

JORNAL ARQUITECTOS
19296P4A-104
Editorial: Edifício Banhos de São Paulo, Travessa do Carvalho, 21/23, 1249-003 LISBOA **Tel:** 213 241 110
Fax: 213 241 101
Email: jornalarquitectos@ordemdosarquitectos.pt
Web site: http://www.jornalarquitectos.pt
ISSN: 0870-1504
Freq: Quarterly; **Cover Price:** EUR 10; **Circ:** 15,000
Usual Pagination: 146
Advertising Manager: Maria Miguel
Profile: Publication of the Association of Professional Portuguese Architects. Contains news and articles on design and architecture.
Language(s): English; Portuguese
Readership: National. Aimed at architects, designers, town planners and students.
ADVERTISING RATES:
Full Page Colour .... EUR 1950
Mechanical Data: Trim Size: 245 x 310 mm

JORNAL DA AMADORA
1642830P72-46
Editorial: Estrada da Falagueira, 8-B, 2700-362 AMADORA **Tel:** 214 989 780 **Fax:** 214 989 788
Email: jornal.amadora@mail.telepac.pt **Web site:** http://www.noticiasdaamadora.com.pt
Date Established: 1977; **Freq:** Weekly; **Cover Price:** EUR 0,5; **Circ:** 4,000
Usual Pagination: 8
Profile: Weekly regional newspaper with information about Amadora (Lisboa). Politics, current affairs, society, religion, sport, entertainment and events.
Language(s): Portuguese
Readership: Read by Amadora locals.
ADVERTISING RATES:
Full Page Mono .... EUR 419.73
Full Page Colour .... EUR 629.59
Mechanical Data: Trim Size: 295 x 420 mm, Type Area: 267 x 370 mm
LOCAL NEWSPAPERS

JORNAL DA BAIRRADA
1642831P72I-28
Editorial: Urbanização O Adro, Bloco 5 N° 25, Apartado 121, 3770-909 OLIVEIRA DO BAIRRO
Tel: 234 740 390 **Fax:** 234 740 399
Email: jb@jb.pt **Web site:** http://www.jb.pt
Date Established: 1951; **Freq:** Weekly; **Cover Price:** EUR 0,8; **Circ:** 10,875
Usual Pagination: 56
Managing Director: António Granjeia
Profile: Weekly regional newspaper with information about Bairrada region. Politics, current affairs, society, religion, sport, entertainment and events.
Language(s): Portuguese
Readership: Read by Anadia, Mealhada, Cantanhede, Oliveira do Bairro and Águeda locals.
ADVERTISING RATES:
Full Page Mono .... EUR 776
Full Page Colour .... EUR 970
Mechanical Data: Trim Size: 280 x 350 mm, Type Area: 255 x 340 mm
LOCAL NEWSPAPERS: Regional Weekly Newspapers

JORNAL DA BATALHA
1642832P72-48
Editorial: R. Infante D. Fernando, Lote 2, Porta 2 B, Apartado 81, 2440-901 BATALHA **Tel:** 244 767 583
Fax: 244 767 739
Email: info@jornaldabatalha.pt **Web site:** http://www.jornaldabatalha.pt
Date Established: 1989; **Freq:** Monthly; **Cover Price:** EUR 1; **Circ:** 3,000
Usual Pagination: 24
Profile: Monthly regional newspaper with information about Batalha (Leiria). Politics, current affairs, society, religion, sport, entertainment and events.
Language(s): Portuguese
Readership: Aimed for Batalha locals.
ADVERTISING RATES:
Full Page Mono .... EUR 440
Full Page Colour .... EUR 550
Mechanical Data: Trim Size: 282 x 393 mm, Type Area: 255 x 340 mm
LOCAL NEWSPAPERS

JORNAL DA CONSTRUÇÃO
19388P42A-70
Editorial: Praça de Alvalade, 6 - 6° Fte., 1700-036 LISBOA **Tel:** 213 110 200 **Fax:** 213 554 810
Email: jc@aecops.pt **Web site:** http://www.aecops.pt
Date Established: 1995; **Freq:** 26 issues yearly; **Cover Price:** EUR 1,5; **Circ:** 15,000
Usual Pagination: 16
Editor-in-Chief: Isabel Travassos; **Managing Director:** José Tomaz Gomes
Profile: Official journal of the Portuguese Association of Construction and Public Works.
Language(s): Portuguese
Readership: Aimed at managers and high-profile employers of construction companies.
ADVERTISING RATES:
Full Page Colour .... EUR 1180
Mechanical Data: Trim Size: 290 x 370 mm, Type Area: 255 x 322 mm
BUSINESS: CONSTRUCTION

JORNAL DA MADEIRA
19497P67B-3500
Editorial: R. Dr. Fernão de Ornelas, 35, 9001-905 FUNCHAL **Tel:** 291 210 400 **Fax:** 291 210 401
Email: secretariado@jornaldamadeira.pt **Web site:** http://www.jornaldamadeira.pt
Date Established: 1932; **Freq:** Daily; **Cover Price:** EUR 0,1; **Circ:** 6,500
Usual Pagination: 48
Editor: Miguel Ângelo; **Editor-in-Chief:** Marsílio Aguiar; **Managing Director:** João Henrique Pinto Correia
Profile: Daily regional newspaper with information about Madeira region. Politics, current affairs, society, religion, sport, entertainment and events.
Language(s): Portuguese
Readership: Read by Madeira population.
ADVERTISING RATES:
Full Page Mono .... EUR 750
Full Page Colour .... EUR 1150
Mechanical Data: Type Area: 260 x 351 mm, Trim Size: 290 x 396 mm
REGIONAL DAILY & SUNDAY NEWSPAPERS: Regional Daily Newspapers

JORNAL DA MARINHA GRANDE
1642834P72I-47
Editorial: Travessa Vieira de Leiria, 9, Apartado 102, 2430-902 MARINHA GRANDE **Tel:** 244 502 628
Fax: 244 569 093
Email: jmg@jornaldamarinha.pt **Web site:** http://www.jornaldamarinha.pt
Freq: Weekly; **Cover Price:** EUR 1; **Circ:** 14,000
Profile: Weekly regional newspaper with information about Marinha Grande (Leiria). Politics, current affairs, society, religion, sport, entertainment and events.
Language(s): Portuguese
Readership: Read by Marinha Grande locals.
ADVERTISING RATES:
Full Page Mono .... EUR 700
Mechanical Data: Trim Size: 286 x 405 mm, Type Area: 260 x 363 mm
LOCAL NEWSPAPERS: Regional Weekly Newspapers

JORNAL DA MEALHADA
1642835P72-51
Editorial: R. das Escolas Novas, 36, Apartado 30, 3050-901 MEALHADA **Tel:** 231 203 167
Fax: 231 203 167
Email: geral@jornaldamealhada.com **Web site:** http://www.jornaldamealhada.com
Date Established: 1985; **Freq:** Weekly; **Cover Price:** EUR 0,7; **Circ:** 4,200
Usual Pagination: 24
Managing Director: Nuno Castela Canilho
Profile: Weekly regional newspaper with information about Mealhada (Aveiro). Politics, current affairs, society, religion, sport, entertainment and events.
Language(s): Portuguese
Readership: Read by Mealhada locals.
ADVERTISING RATES:
Full Page Mono .... EUR 250
Full Page Colour .... EUR 350
Mechanical Data: Trim Size: 290 x 410 mm, Type Area: 260 x 350 mm
LOCAL NEWSPAPERS

JORNAL DA REGIÃO
1606575P72I-22
Editorial: Al. António Sérgio, 7 - 1° D, 2799-531 LINDA-A-VELHA **Tel:** 214 157 200 **Fax:** 214 150 781
Email: jr-editor@jornaldaregiao.pt **Web site:** http://www.jornaldaregiao.pt
Date Established: 1996; **Freq:** Weekly; **Cover Price:** Free; **Circ:** 225,000
Editor-in-Chief: João Carlos Sebastião
Profile: Free weekly regional newspaper with information about Lisboa. Politics, current affairs, society, religion, sport, entertainment and events.
Language(s): Portuguese
Readership: Read in Cascais, Sintra, Oeiras, Amadora e Almada.
ADVERTISING RATES:
Full Page Mono .... EUR 4990
Full Page Colour .... EUR 6487
Mechanical Data: Trim Size: 289 x 420 mm, Type Area: 262 x 391 mm
LOCAL NEWSPAPERS: Regional Weekly Newspapers

JORNAL DAS CALDAS
1642840P72-56
Editorial: R. Heróis da Grande Guerra, 84 - 1°, Apartado 122, 2501-216 CALDAS DA RAINHA
Tel: 262 844 443 **Fax:** 262 844 022
Email: jornal@jornaldascaldas.com **Web site:** http://www.jornaldascaldas.com
Date Established: 1991; **Freq:** Weekly; **Cover Price:** EUR 0,5; **Circ:** 11,000
Usual Pagination: 40
Editor-in-Chief: Francisco Gomes; **Managing Director:** Jaime Duarte Costa
Profile: Weekly regional newspaper with information about Caldas da Rainha. Politics, current affairs, society, religion, sport, entertainment and events.
Language(s): Portuguese
Readership: Read by Caldas da Rainha locals.
ADVERTISING RATES:
Full Page Mono .... EUR 459
Full Page Colour .... EUR 800
Mechanical Data: Trim Size: 290 x 410 mm, Type Area: 260 x 370 mm
LOCAL NEWSPAPERS

JORNAL DE AMARANTE
1643007P72-63
Editorial: Largo de S. Pedro, 2° C, Apartado 75, 4600-036 AMARANTE **Tel:** 255 432 914
Email: jornaldeamarante@iol.pt
Date Established: 1983; **Freq:** Weekly; **Cover Price:** EUR 0,8; **Circ:** 3,500
Usual Pagination: 12
Managing Director: Maria José Cunha
Profile: Weekly regional newspaper with information about Amarante (Porto). Politics, current affairs, society, religion, sport, entertainment and events.
Language(s): Portuguese
Readership: Read by Amarante locals.
ADVERTISING RATES:
Full Page Mono .... EUR 230
Full Page Colour .... EUR 300
Mechanical Data: Trim Size: 300 x 430 mm, Type Area: 265 x 380 mm
LOCAL NEWSPAPERS

JORNAL DE ARGANIL
1642847P72-64
Editorial: R. Dr. Veiga Simões, 1 e 3, Apartado 48, 3300-048 ARGANIL **Tel:** 235 202 432
Fax: 235 204 364
Email: mail@jornaldearganil.net **Web site:** http://www.jornaldearganil.net
Date Established: 1926; **Freq:** Weekly; **Cover Price:** EUR 0,6; **Circ:** 4,951
Usual Pagination: 20
Profile: Regional newspaper with information about Arganil (Coimbra). Politics, current affairs, society, sport, entertainment and events.
Language(s): Portuguese

Readership: Read by Arganil, Góis, Oliveira Hospital, Pampilhosa da Serra, Penacova, Tábua, Covilhã, Vila Nova de Poiares, Lousã and Pedrógão Grande locals.
ADVERTISING RATES:
Full Page Mono .... EUR 350
Full Page Colour .... EUR 500
Mechanical Data: Trim Size: 305 x 430 mm, Type Area: 265 x 380 mm
LOCAL NEWSPAPERS

JORNAL DE ESTARREJA

1643008P72-67
Editorial: R. dos Bombeiros Voluntários de Estarreja, 65 - 2° Esq., Apartado 65, 3860-001 ESTARREJA
Tel: 234 849 713 **Fax:** 234 849 713
Email: geral@jornalestarreja.com **Web site:** http://www.jornalestarreja.com
Date Established: 1883; **Freq:** Weekly; **Cover Price:** EUR 0,6; **Circ:** 3,000
Usual Pagination: 16
Editor-in-Chief: Andreia Tavares
Profile: Weekly regional newspaper with information about Estarreja (Aveiro). Politics, current affairs, society, religion, sport, entertainment and events.
Language(s): Portuguese
Readership: Read by Estarreja locals.
ADVERTISING RATES:
Full Page Mono .... EUR 350
Full Page Colour .... EUR 550
Mechanical Data: Trim Size: 286 x 408 mm
LOCAL NEWSPAPERS

JORNAL DE LEIRIA

1642850P72I-21
Editorial: R. Comandante João Belo, 31, Apartado 1098, 2401-801 LEIRIA **Tel:** 244 800 400
Fax: 244 800 401
Email: geral@jornaldeleiria.pt **Web site:** http://www.jornaldeleiria.pt
Date Established: 1988; **Freq:** Weekly; **Cover Price:** EUR 1; **Circ:** 15,000
Usual Pagination: 40
Managing Director: José Ribeiro Vieira
Profile: Regional newspaper with information about Leiria. Politics, current affairs, society, religion, sport, entertainment and events.
Language(s): Portuguese
Readership: Read in Leiria region mainly by urbane and active population with medium or high degree of education.
ADVERTISING RATES:
Full Page Colour .... EUR 1400
Mechanical Data: Type Area: 248 x 345 mm, Trim Size: 284 x 400 mm
Series owner and contact point for the following titles, see individual entries:
Leiria Global
Leiria Global
LOCAL NEWSPAPERS: Regional Weekly Newspapers

JORNAL DE MATOSINHOS

1642852P72I-3
Editorial: Av. Joaquim Neves dos Santos, (Traseiras do Cemitério de Sendim), Apartado 2201, 4451-901 MATOSINHOS **Tel:** 229 516 880 **Fax:** 229 516 719
Email: geral@jornaldematosinhos.com **Web site:** http://www.jornaldematosinhos.com
Date Established: 1980; **Freq:** Weekly; **Cover Price:** EUR 1; **Circ:** 4,000
Profile: Weekly regional newspaper with information about Matosinhos (Porto). Politics, current affairs, society, religion, sport, entertainment and events.
Language(s): Portuguese
Readership: Read by Matosinhos locals.
ADVERTISING RATES:
Full Page Mono .... EUR 748
Full Page Colour .... EUR 900
Mechanical Data: Trim Size: 305 x 410 mm, Type Area: 256 x 356 mm
LOCAL NEWSPAPERS: Regional Weekly Newspapers

JORNAL DE NEGÓCIOS

622956P14A-50
Editorial: Av. João Crisóstomo, 72 - 1°, 1069-043 LISBOA **Tel:** 213 180 900 **Fax:** 213 540 361
Email: info@negocios.pt **Web site:** http://www.jornaldenegocios.pt
ISSN: 0874-1360
Date Established: 2003; **Freq:** Daily; **Cover Price:** EUR 1,6; **Circ:** 18,381
Usual Pagination: 40
Editor: Ricardo Domingos; **Executive Editor:** Celso Filipe; **Managing Director:** Pedro Santos Guerreiro
Profile: Newspaper covering business, finance, investment and politics.
Language(s): Portuguese
Readership: National. Aimed at businessmen and investors.
ADVERTISING RATES:
Full Page Mono .... EUR 4030
Full Page Colour .... EUR 5040
Mechanical Data: Type Area: 257 x 336 mm, Trim Size: 280 x 370 mm
Series owner and contact point for the following titles, see individual entries:
Fórum Empresarial
Jogo da Bolsa
Jogo da Bolsa
MBA
Saúde
Weekend
BUSINESS: COMMERCE, INDUSTRY & MANAGEMENT

JORNAL DE NOTÍCIAS

1782276P65A-181
Editorial: R. de Gonçalo Cristovão, 195, 4049-011 PORTO **Tel:** 213 187 500 **Fax:** 222 096 140
Email: secdir@jn.pt **Web site:** http://www.jn.pt
ISSN: 0874-1352
Date Established: 1888; **Freq:** Daily; **Cover Price:** EUR 0,9; **Circ:** 122,218
Usual Pagination: 52
Editor: Manuel Molinos; **Executive Editor:** Couto Soares; **Editor-in-Chief:** Paulo Martins; **Managing Director:** Manuel Tavares
Profile: National newspaper providing regional, national and international news, political coverage and in-depth information concerning finance, economics and new technologies. Also covers society, culture, the media, sport and television. Contains comic strips, game puzzles and fait-divers.
Language(s): Portuguese
Readership: National.
ADVERTISING RATES:
Full Page Mono .... EUR 7740
Full Page Colour .... EUR 10836
Mechanical Data: Type Area: 252 x 315 mm, Trim Size: 288 x 370 mm
Sections:
Ágora
Auto
Auto
Classificados Tuti
Desporto
JN Negócios
Porto
Revista da Queima das Fitas
Roteiros Gastronómicos
NATIONAL DAILY & SUNDAY NEWSPAPERS: National Daily Newspapers

JORNAL DE NOTÍCIAS - NORTE

1782180P67B-6024
Editorial: R. Gonçalo Cristóvão, 195-219, 4049-011 PORTO **Tel:** 222 096 100 **Fax:** 222 096 140
Email: dpe@jn.pt **Web site:** http://www.jn.pt
ISSN: 0870-2020
Freq: Daily; **Cover Price:** EUR 0,8; **Circ:** 109,520
Editor: Dora Mota; **Editor-in-Chief:** Rafael Barbosa
Profile: National newspaper providing regional, national and international news, political coverage and in-depth information concerning finance, economics and new technologies. Also covers society, culture, the media, sport and television. Contains comic strips, game puzzles and fait-divers. Local news regarding the north region of Portugal. Publication that is a part of the newspaper Jornal de Notícias.
Language(s): Portuguese
Readership: Aimed at northern Portugal readers.
ADVERTISING RATES:
Full Page Mono .... EUR 2340
Full Page Colour .... EUR 3276
Mechanical Data: Type Area: 253 x 358 mm, Trim Size: 290 x 397 mm
REGIONAL DAILY & SUNDAY NEWSPAPERS: Regional Daily Newspapers

JORNAL DE SETÚBAL

1642860P72-76
Editorial: Av. Luísa Todi, 408 - 1°, 2900 SETÚBAL
Tel: 265 520 716 **Fax:** 265 520 717
Email: jornaldesetubal@gmail.com
Freq: Weekly; **Cover Price:** EUR 0,01
Free to qualifying individuals ; **Circ:** 15,000
Usual Pagination: 16
Profile: Free weekly regional newspaper with information about Setúbal. Politics, current affairs, society, sport, entertainment and events.
Language(s): Portuguese
Readership: Read in Setúbal region.
ADVERTISING RATES:
Full Page Mono .... EUR 740
Full Page Colour .... EUR 1100
Mechanical Data: Type Area: 260 x 325 mm, Trim Size: 298 x 370 mm
LOCAL NEWSPAPERS

JORNAL DE SINTRA

1642861P72-77
Editorial: Av. Heliodoro Salgado, 6, 2710-572 SINTRA **Tel:** 219 106 831 **Fax:** 219 106 837
Email: jornalsintra.redac@mail.telepac.pt **Web site:** http://www.jornaldesintra.com
Date Established: 1934; **Freq:** Weekly; **Cover Price:** EUR 0,6; **Circ:** 12,000
Usual Pagination: 16
Editor: António Afonso Faias; **Managing Director:** Idalina Grácio de Andrade
Profile: Weekly newspaper with information about Sintra. Politics, current affairs, society, sport, entertainment and events.
Language(s): Portuguese
Readership: Read by Sintra locals.
ADVERTISING RATES:
Full Page Mono .... EUR 800
Mechanical Data: Trim Size: 292 x 400 mm, Type Area: 260 x 340 mm
LOCAL NEWSPAPERS

JORNAL DE TONDELA

1642862P72-78
Editorial: R. Dr. Marques da Costa, Apartado 97, 3460-000 TONDELA **Tel:** 232 822 137
Fax: 232 821 118
Email: jornaldetondela@mail.telepac.pt **Web site:** http://jornaldetondela.com.sapo.pt
Date Established: 1989; **Freq:** Weekly; **Cover Price:** EUR 0,6; **Circ:** 3,000
Usual Pagination: 24
Managing Director: Manuel Ventura da Costa
Profile: Weekly newspaper with information about Tondela. Politics, current affairs, society, sport, entertainment and events.
Language(s): Portuguese
Readership: Read by Tondela locals.
ADVERTISING RATES:
Full Page Mono .... EUR 350
Full Page Colour .... EUR 455
Mechanical Data: Type Area: 260 x 352 mm, Trim Size: 290 x 410 mm
LOCAL NEWSPAPERS

JORNAL DO ALGARVE

1642866P72-82
Editorial: R. Jornal do Algarve, 46, Apartado 23, 8900-000 VILA REAL DE SANTO ANTÓNIO
Tel: 281 511 955 **Fax:** 281 511 958
Email: geral@jornaldoalgarve.pt **Web site:** http://www.jornaldoalgarve.pt
ISSN: 0870-6433
Freq: Weekly; **Cover Price:** EUR 1; **Circ:** 11,500
Usual Pagination: 28
Editor: Luísa Travassos; **Managing Director:** Fernando Reis
Profile: Weekly newspaper with information about Algarve region. Politics, current affairs, society, religion, sport, entertainment and events.
Language(s): Portuguese
Readership: Read in Algarve region.
ADVERTISING RATES:
Full Page Mono .... EUR 1700
Full Page Colour .... EUR 2100
Mechanical Data: Trim Size: 280 x 405 mm, Type Area: 250 x 335 mm
LOCAL NEWSPAPERS

JORNAL DO CENTRO

1642867P72I-4
Editorial: Bairro S. João da Carreira, R. D. Maria Gracinda Torres Vasconcelos, Lote 10 - R/C, 3500-187 VISEU **Tel:** 232 437 461 **Fax:** 232 431 225
Email: redaccao@jornaldocentro.pt **Web site:** http://www.jornaldocentro.pt
Date Established: 2002; **Freq:** Weekly; **Cover Price:** EUR 1; **Circ:** 6,000
Usual Pagination: 40
Managing Director: Paulo Neto
Profile: Weekly regional newspaper with information about Viseu. Politics, current affairs, society, religion, sport, entertainment and events.
Language(s): Portuguese
Readership: Read by Viseu locals.
ADVERTISING RATES:
Full Page Mono .... EUR 900
Full Page Colour .... EUR 1050
Mechanical Data: Type Area: 255 x 340 mm, Trim Size: 282 x 400 mm
LOCAL NEWSPAPERS: Regional Weekly Newspapers

JORNAL DO CENTRO DE SAÚDE

1820712P56A-201
Editorial: Beloura Office Park, Edifício 4, Escritório 1.2, 2710-693 SINTRA **Tel:** 219 247 670
Fax: 219 247 679
Email: redaccao@jornaldocentrodesaude.pt **Web site:** http://www.jornaldocentrodesaude.pt
Date Established: 2004; **Freq:** Monthly; **Cover Price:** Free; **Circ:** 46,000
Usual Pagination: 24
Editor: Sofia Filipe; **Managing Director:** Rui Moreira de Sá; **Advertising Manager:** Carla Gonçalves
Profile: Elaborated by the Carnaxide health center, Jornal do Centro de Saúde is a free newspaper foccused on public health and the connection between health center professionals and the patients.
Language(s): Portuguese
Readership: National.
ADVERTISING RATES:
Full Page Colour .... EUR 2950
Mechanical Data: Type Area: 257 x 339 mm, Trim Size: 283 x 400 mm

JORNAL DO FUNDÃO

1606548P80-183
Editorial: R. Jornal do Fundão, 4/6, 6231-406 FUNDÃO **Tel:** 275 779 350 **Fax:** 275 779 369
Email: redaccao@jornaldofundao.pt **Web site:** http://www.jornaldofundao.pt
Date Established: 1946; **Freq:** Weekly; **Cover Price:** EUR 0,7; **Circ:** 3,285
Usual Pagination: 48
Managing Director: Fernando Manuel Paulouro Serrasqueiro das Neves
Profile: Newspaper covering the latest news, politics, sport and culture for the region.
Language(s): Portuguese
Readership: Read in Castelo Branco and Guarda regions.
ADVERTISING RATES:
Full Page Mono .... EUR 810
Full Page Colour .... EUR 1215
Mechanical Data: Trim Size: 290 x 400 mm, Type Area: 260 x 361 mm
CONSUMER: RURAL & REGIONAL INTEREST

JORNAL DO NORTE

1642869P72-85
Editorial: R. Dr. Roque da Silveira, 57 - 1°, Apartado 156, 5000-630 VILA REAL **Tel:** 259 321 772
Fax: 259 322 079
Email: jornaldonorte@net.novis.pt
Date Established: 1985; **Freq:** 26 issues yearly; **Cover Price:** EUR 0,5; **Circ:** 250
Usual Pagination: 8
Profile: Newspaper with information about the north region. Politics, current affairs, society, religion, sport, entertainment and events.
Language(s): Portuguese
Readership: Read in Vila Real region.
ADVERTISING RATES:
Full Page Mono .... EUR 170
Mechanical Data: Trim Size: 222 x 324 mm, Type Area: 190 x 270 mm
LOCAL NEWSPAPERS

JORNAL DO TÉNIS

1782315P75-389
Editorial: Av. Conde de Valbom, 30 - 4°/5°, 1050-068 LISBOA **Tel:** 210 124 900 **Fax:** 213 151 315
Email: antoniomagalhaes@record.pt **Web site:** http://www.record.xl.pt
Freq: 26 issues yearly; **Cover Price:** Free; **Circ:** 101,429
Usual Pagination: 8
Profile: Newspaper containing national and international news regarding tennis.
Language(s): Portuguese
Readership: Mainland.
Mechanical Data: Trim Size: 280 x 370 mm, Type Area: 257 x 338 mm
Part of Series, see entry for: Record
CONSUMER: SPORT

LABOR.PT

1642895P72-100
Editorial: R. Camilo Castelo Branco, 200 A, Apartado 104, 3701-910 S. JOÃO DA MADEIRA
Tel: 256 202 600 **Fax:** 256 202 609
Email: geral@labor.pt **Web site:** http://www.labor.pt
Date Established: 1987; **Freq:** Weekly; **Cover Price:** EUR 0,5; **Circ:** 3,000
Usual Pagination: 24
Managing Director: Pedro Ferreira da Silva
Profile: Weekly newspaper with information about S. João da Madeira. Politics, current affairs, society, religion, sport, entertainment and events.
Language(s): Portuguese
Readership: Read in S. João da Madeira region.
ADVERTISING RATES:
Full Page Mono .... EUR 600
Mechanical Data: Trim Size: 290 x 370 mm, Type Area: 257 x 329 mm
LOCAL NEWSPAPERS

LEIRIA GLOBAL

1782363P14A-130
Editorial: R. Comandante João Belo, 31, Apartado 1098, 2401-801 LEIRIA **Tel:** 244 800 400
Fax: 244 800 401
Email: geral@jornaldeleiria.pt **Web site:** http://www.jornaldeleiria.pt
Freq: Annual; **Cover Price:** Free; **Circ:** 15,000
Usual Pagination: 60
Profile: Special edition focused mainly on the region of Leiria. It's industry, potential of exportation and resources. Contains also information regarding the international market.
Language(s): Portuguese
Readership: Read in Leiria region mainly by urbane and active population with medium or high degree of education.
ADVERTISING RATES:
Full Page Colour .... EUR 1500
Mechanical Data: Trim Size: 205 x 280 mm, Type Area: 170 x 240 mm
Part of Series, see entry for: Jornal de Leiria

LEIRIA GLOBAL

1782363P14A-186
Editorial: R. Comandante João Belo, 31, Apartado 1098, 2401-801 LEIRIA **Tel:** 244 800 400
Fax: 244 800 401
Email: geral@jornaldeleiria.pt **Web site:** http://www.jornaldeleiria.pt
Freq: Annual; **Cover Price:** Free; **Circ:** 15,000
Usual Pagination: 60
Profile: Special edition focused mainly on the region of Leiria. It's industry, potential of exportation and resources. Contains also information regarding the international market.
Language(s): Portuguese
Readership: Read in Leiria region mainly by urbane and active population with medium or high degree of education.
ADVERTISING RATES:
Full Page Colour .... EUR 1500
Mechanical Data: Trim Size: 205 x 280 mm, Type Area: 170 x 240 mm
Part of Series, see entry for: Jornal de Leiria

O LEME

1643009P72-102
Editorial: Bairro Azul, Colectiva B1, Apartado 6, 7500-999 VILA NOVA DE SANTO ANDRÉ
Tel: 269 752 205 **Fax:** 269 084 307
Email: jornal@o-leme.com **Web site:** http://www.o-leme.blogspot.com
Date Established: 1984; **Freq:** 26 issues yearly; **Cover Price:** EUR 0,5; **Circ:** 3,000
Usual Pagination: 16
Editor: Fátima Lychnos Moita; **Managing Director:** António Novais Pereira
Profile: Fortnightly newspaper with information about Setúbal region. Politics, current affairs, society, religion, entertainment and events.
Language(s): Portuguese
Readership: Read in Setúbal region.
ADVERTISING RATES:
Full Page Mono .... EUR 400

Full Page Colour .... EUR 700
Mechanical Data: Trim Size: 300 x 430 mm, Type Area: 260 x 380 mm
LOCAL NEWSPAPERS

LEZÍRIA TEJO 1643011P72I-5
Editorial: R. 31 de Janeiro, 22, Apartado 389, 2005-188 SANTARÉM **Tel:** 243 305 080 **Fax:** 243 305 081
Email: omirante@omirante.pt **Web site:** http://www.omirante.pt
Freq: Weekly; **Cover Price:** EUR 0,6; **Circ:** 35,000
Usual Pagination: 16
Profile: Weekly newspaper with information about Santarém region. Politics, current affairs, society, sport, entertainment and events.
Language(s): Portuguese
Readership: Read in Santarém region.
ADVERTISING RATES:
Full Page Mono .... EUR 1279
Full Page Colour .... EUR 1589
Mechanical Data: Type Area: 230 x 305 mm, Trim Size: 254 x 344 mm
LOCAL NEWSPAPERS: Regional Weekly Newspapers

LINHAS DE ELVAS 1642897P72-103
Editorial: R. Alfredo Mirante, 10 B, 7350-154 ELVAS
Tel: 268 622 697 **Fax:** 268 620 192
Email: linhasdeelvas@mail.telepac.pt **Web site:** http://www.linhasdeelvas.net
Date Established: 1950; **Freq:** Weekly; **Cover Price:** EUR 0,85; **Circ:** 4,300
Usual Pagination: 24
Managing Director: João Manuel Laureano Alves e Almeida
Profile: Weekly newspaper with information about Elvas. Politics, current affairs, society, religion, sport, entertainment and events.
Language(s): Portuguese
Readership: Read by Elvas locals.
ADVERTISING RATES:
Full Page Mono .... EUR 485
Full Page Colour .... EUR 770
Mechanical Data: Trim Size: 288 x 410 mm, Type Area: 260 x 345 mm
LOCAL NEWSPAPERS

LOGÍSTICA & TRANSPORTES HOJE 19312P10-60
Editorial: R. Basílio Teles, 35 - 1° Dto., 1070-020 LISBOA **Tel:** 210 033 800 **Fax:** 210 033 888
Email: geral@ife.pt **Web site:** http://www.logisticahoje.com
Date Established: 1996; **Freq:** 6 issues yearly; **Cover Price:** EUR 6; **Circ:** 4,000
Usual Pagination: 52
Profile: Magazine providing news and information concerning all aspects of logistics. Includes articles on transportation in Portugal and other countries.
Language(s): Portuguese
Readership: National.
ADVERTISING RATES:
Full Page Colour .... EUR 2060
Mechanical Data: Type Area: 200 x 260 mm, Trim Size: 220 x 280 mm
BUSINESS: MATERIALS HANDLING

LOGÍSTICA MODERNA 1642902P10-61
Editorial: Alameda do Grupo Desportivo Alcochetense, 133 - 137, 2890-110 ALCOCHETE
Tel: 212 348 450 **Fax:** 214 043 506
Email: geral@logisticamoderna.com **Web site:** http://www.logisticamoderna.com
Date Established: 2002; **Freq:** Monthly; **Cover Price:** EUR 4; **Circ:** 9,000
Usual Pagination: 44
Editor: Dora Assis; **Managing Director:** Ferreira Simões
Language(s): Portuguese
Readership: National.
ADVERTISING RATES:
Full Page Colour .... EUR 1885
Mechanical Data: Trim Size: 240 x 335 mm, Type Area: 220 x 315 mm
BUSINESS: MATERIALS HANDLING

LUX 1606845P74A-101
Editorial: R. Mário Castelhano, 40, Queluz de Baixo, 2734-502 BARCARENA **Tel:** 214 369 616
Fax: 214 369 539
Email: luxonline@lux.iol.pt **Web site:** http://www.lux.pt
Date Established: 2000; **Freq:** Weekly; **Cover Price:** EUR 1,35; **Circ:** 90,000
Managing Director: Felipa Garnel; **Advertising Manager:** Carmen Mello
Profile: Magazine covering lifestyle, fashion and beauty, health and culture. Includes TV listings.
Language(s): Portuguese
Readership: Mainland. Aimed at women with 24-54 years old. B, C1, C2.
ADVERTISING RATES:
Full Page Colour .... EUR 4500
Mechanical Data: Trim Size: 230 x 297 mm, Type Area: 195 x 273 mm
CONSUMER: WOMEN'S INTEREST CONSUMER MAGAZINES: Women's Interest

LUX DECORAÇÃO 1606843P16-5
Editorial: R. Mário Castelhano, 40, Queluz de Baixo, 2749-502 BARCARENA **Tel:** 214 369 616
Fax: 214 369 539
Email: mguimaraes@lux.iol.pt **Web site:** http://www.lux.pt
Freq: Occasional; **Cover Price:** EUR 2,5; **Circ:** 70,000
Usual Pagination: 148
Editor: Marina Ribeiro
Profile: Magazine focusing on home design, style and decoration.
Language(s): Portuguese
Readership: Mainland. Aimed at individuals looking for ideas on improving their homes.
Mechanical Data: Type Area: 197 x 262 mm, Trim Size: 228 x 295 mm
BUSINESS: DECORATING & PAINT

LUX WOMAN 1606844P74B-56
Editorial: R. Mário Castelhano, 40, Queluz de Baixo, 2734-502 BARCARENA **Tel:** 214 349 149
Fax: 214 369 460
Email: beverlo@lux.iol.pt
Date Established: 2001; **Freq:** Monthly; **Cover Price:** EUR 2,5; **Circ:** 70,000
Usual Pagination: 172
Editor: Anett Bohme; **Managing Director:** Rita Machado; **Advertising Manager:** Carmen Mello
Profile: Magazine focusing on the latest trends in fashion, beauty and style.
Language(s): Portuguese
Readership: Mainland. Aimed at women with 24-54 years old. B, C1, C2.
ADVERTISING RATES:
Full Page Colour .... EUR 6000
Mechanical Data: Trim Size: 230 x 297 mm, Type Area: 195 x 273 mm
CONSUMER: WOMEN'S INTEREST CONSUMER MAGAZINES: Women's Interest - Fashion

MADEIRA MOTOR SPORT 1782454P77A-340
Editorial: R. Dr. Francisco Peres, Edifício Jardins do Caniço, Loja 18, 9125-014 CANIÇO/MADEIRA
Tel: 291 934 930 **Fax:** 291 934 930
Email: madeiramotorsport@gmail.com **Web site:** http://www.madeiramotorsport.com
ISSN: 0874-5153
Date Established: 1999; **Freq:** Monthly; **Cover Price:** EUR 2,5; **Circ:** 10,000
Usual Pagination: 72
Editor-in-Chief: Juan Santos; **Managing Director:** Márcia Santos
Profile: Regional magazine about rally, karting, classic cars, motorcycling, formula 1 and cross-country racing. Interviews and news articles about events and related issues.
Language(s): Portuguese
Readership: Read in Madeira island.
ADVERTISING RATES:
Full Page Colour .... EUR 435
Mechanical Data: Trim Size: 230 x 297 mm, Type Area: 205 x 264 mm

MÃE IDEAL 1642904P74A-103
Editorial: R. General Ferreira Martins, 10 - 6° B, Miraflores, 1495-137 ALGÉS **Tel:** 219 959 510
Fax: 219 959 515
Email: promercado@promercado.pt **Web site:** http://www.promercado.pt/Maeideal.htm
Date Established: 2000; **Freq:** Monthly; **Cover Price:** EUR 2,7; **Circ:** 22,000
Usual Pagination: 100
Editor-in-Chief: Cláudia Pinto; **Managing Director:** Isabel Santos
Language(s): Portuguese
Readership: National.
ADVERTISING RATES:
Full Page Colour .... EUR 2500
Mechanical Data: Type Area: 200 x 270 mm, Trim Size: 225 x 295 mm
CONSUMER: WOMEN'S INTEREST CONSUMER MAGAZINES: Women's Interest

MAMÃS & BEBÉS 1822596P74D-43
Editorial: Edifício S. Francisco de Sales, R. Calvet de Magalhães, 242, 2770-022 PAÇO DE ARCOS
Tel: 214 544 000 **Fax:** 214 435 310
Email: ipublishing@impresa.pt **Web site:** http://www.expresso.pt
Date Established: 2007; **Freq:** Occasional; **Cover Price:** Free; **Circ:** 133,425
Usual Pagination: 24
Language(s): Portuguese
Readership: National.
ADVERTISING RATES:
Full Page Colour .... EUR 4900
Mechanical Data: Type Area: 199 x 270 mm, Trim Size: 225 x 297 mm
Part of Series, see entry for: Expresso
CONSUMER: WOMEN'S INTEREST CONSUMER MAGAZINES: Child Care

MARCAS HISTÓRICAS 1934485P14A-275
Editorial: Edifício Diário de Notícias, Av. da Liberdade, 266, 1250-149 LISBOA **Tel:** 213 187 500
Fax: 213 187 516
Email: dnot@dn.pt **Web site:** http://www.dn.sapo.pt
Date Established: 2009; **Freq:** Occasional; **Cover Price:** Free; **Circ:** 147,970
Usual Pagination: 16
Profile: Published with: Diário de Notícias; Jornal de Notícias.
Language(s): Portuguese
Readership: National.
Mechanical Data: Trim Size: 213 x 290 mm

MARIA 19694P74A-60
Editorial: R. da Impala, N° 33 A - Abrunheira, S. Pedro de Penaferrim, 2710-070 SINTRA
Tel: 219 238 100 **Fax:** 219 238 193
Email: maria@impala.pt **Web site:** http://www.impala.pt
Freq: Weekly; **Cover Price:** EUR 0,65; **Circ:** 241,250
Editor-in-Chief: Carla Santos; **Managing Director:** Anabela Colaço
Profile: Magazine including features on fashion and beauty, home decor, cookery and careers.
Language(s): Portuguese
Readership: National.
ADVERTISING RATES:
Full Page Colour .... EUR 4880
Mechanical Data: Trim Size: 147 x 194 mm
CONSUMER: WOMEN'S INTEREST CONSUMER MAGAZINES: Women's Interest

MARIANA 1782527P74B-102
Editorial: Cascais Office, Rotunda das Tojas, 2° E, 2645-091 ALCABIDECHE **Tel:** 214 606 100
Fax: 214 606 119
Email: geral@presspeople.pt **Web site:** http://presspeople.pt
Freq: Weekly; **Cover Price:** EUR 0,65; **Circ:** 50,000
Usual Pagination: 100
Managing Director: Manuela Bica
Profile: Magazine focused on fashion, health and beauty and lifestyle.
Language(s): Portuguese
Readership: National.
ADVERTISING RATES:
Full Page Colour .... EUR 1300
Mechanical Data: Trim Size: 148 x 210 mm
CONSUMER: WOMEN'S INTEREST CONSUMER MAGAZINES: Women's Interest - Fashion

MARIANA CULINÁRIA 1848713P74P-326
Editorial: Cascais Office, Rotunda das Tojas, 2° E, 2645-091 ALCABIDECHE **Tel:** 214 606 100
Fax: 214 606 119
Email: cozinhasucesso@presspeople.pt **Web site:** http://presspeople.pt
Date Established: 2008; **Freq:** Monthly; **Cover Price:** EUR 2,5; **Circ:** 50,000
Usual Pagination: 48
Managing Director: Manuela Bica
Profile: Cooking.
Language(s): Portuguese
Readership: National.
ADVERTISING RATES:
Full Page Colour .... EUR 2100
Mechanical Data: Trim Size: 210 x 275 mm
Series owner and contact point for the following titles, see individual entries:
Clássicos da TV

MARKET REPORT 1782532P2A-111
Editorial: R. Cidade de Bolama, Lote 17 - 7° B, 1800-079 LISBOA **Tel:** 218 537 812 **Fax:** 218 537 807
Email: casimiro.santos.insat@gmail.com **Web site:** http://www.insat.pt
ISSN: 1645-6092
Date Established: 1991; **Freq:** 26 issues yearly; **Cover Price:** EUR 175; **Circ:** 3,000
Managing Director: Casimiro Santos; **Advertising Manager:** Ana Gonçalves
Profile: Newspaper about the national market - studies and statistics.
Language(s): Portuguese
Readership: National. Companies and market analysts.
ADVERTISING RATES:
Full Page Colour .... EUR 1200
Mechanical Data: Trim Size: 210 x 295 mm

MARKETEER 622995P2A-30
Editorial: R. Basílio Teles, 35 - 6° Dto., 1070-020 LISBOA **Tel:** 210 123 400 **Fax:** 210 123 444
Email: marketeer@marketeer.pt **Web site:** http://www.marketeer.pt
Date Established: 1996; **Freq:** Monthly; **Cover Price:** EUR 3,3; **Circ:** 19,500
Usual Pagination: 132
Profile: Magazine specialised in marketing.
Language(s): Portuguese
Readership: National. Aimed at marketing managers and university students.
ADVERTISING RATES:
Full Page Colour .... EUR 4250
Mechanical Data: Type Area: 220 x 280 mm, Trim Size: 220 x 280 mm
BUSINESS: COMMUNICATIONS, ADVERTISING & MARKETING

MÁXIMA 19700P74B-50
Editorial: Av. João Crisóstomo, 72 - 3°, 1069-043 LISBOA **Tel:** 213 309 400 **Fax:** 213 540 410
Email: lauratorres@maxima.cofina.pt **Web site:** http://www.maxima.xl.pt
ISSN: 0874-6931
Date Established: 1988; **Freq:** Monthly; **Cover Price:** EUR 3; **Circ:** 83,000
Editor: Helena Assédio Maltez; **Editor-in-Chief:** Pilar Diogo
Profile: Women magazine about fashion, trends and accessories.
Language(s): Portuguese
Readership: Mainland. Aimed generally at women aged 18 to 35 years.
ADVERTISING RATES:
Full Page Colour .... EUR 6350
Mechanical Data: Trim Size: 230 x 297 mm, Type Area: 206 x 275 mm
CONSUMER: WOMEN'S INTEREST CONSUMER MAGAZINES: Women's Interest - Fashion

MÁXIMA INTERIORES 1606850P74C-88
Editorial: Av. João Crisóstomo, 72, Galeria, 1069-043 LISBOA **Tel:** 213 540 410 **Fax:** 213 309 400
Email: cristinabelo@minteriores.cofina.pt **Web site:** http://www.maximainteriores.pt
Freq: Monthly; **Cover Price:** EUR 3,3; **Circ:** 23,000
Usual Pagination: 132
Editor-in-Chief: Carla Macedo; **Advertising Manager:** Beatriz Pinto
Profile: Magazine focusing on home decoration and design.
Language(s): Portuguese
Readership: Mainland. Aimed at people interested in home improvements.
ADVERTISING RATES:
Full Page Colour .... EUR 3850
Mechanical Data: Trim Size: 230 x 297 mm, Type Area: 190 x 275 mm
CONSUMER: WOMEN'S INTEREST CONSUMER MAGAZINES: Home & Family

MBA 1782551P1A-261
Editorial: Av. João Crisóstomo, 72 - 1°, 1069-043 LISBOA **Tel:** 213 180 900 **Fax:** 213 540 361
Email: info@negocios.pt **Web site:** http://www.jornaldenegocios.pt
ISSN: 0874-1360
Freq: Annual; **Cover Price:** Free; **Circ:** 16,528
Profile: Newspaper covering business, finance, investment and politics.
Language(s): Portuguese
Readership: National. Aimed at businessmen and investors.
ADVERTISING RATES:
Full Page Mono .... EUR 2505
Mechanical Data: Type Area: 257 x 336 mm, Trim Size: 280 x 370 mm
Part of Series, see entry for: Jornal de Negócios

MEDIA XXI 1642911P88A-43
Editorial: R. Dr. Egas Moniz, 11 - Loja A, 2675-341 ODIVELAS **Tel:** 217 573 459 **Fax:** 217 576 316
Email: geralmediaxxi@formalpress.com **Web site:** http://www.mediaxxi.com
Date Established: 1995; **Freq:** 3 issues yearly; **Cover Price:** EUR 12; **Circ:** 4,000
Usual Pagination: 140
Editor: Guilherme Pires
Language(s): Portuguese
Readership: National.
ADVERTISING RATES:
Full Page Colour .... EUR 1380
Mechanical Data: Trim Size: 160 x 230 mm
CONSUMER: EDUCATION

MEDICINA VETERINÁRIA 1936062P65A-90_131
Editorial: Edifício Diário de Notícias, Av. da Liberdade, 266, 1250-149 LISBOA **Tel:** 213 187 500
Fax: 213 187 515
Email: dnot@dn.pt **Web site:** http://www.dn.pt
ISSN: 0870-1954
Date Established: 2009; **Freq:** Occasional; **Cover Price:** Free; **Circ:** 43,325
Usual Pagination: 8
Profile: Suplement about Veterinary, new products, services and equipment.
Language(s): Portuguese
Readership: National.
Mechanical Data: Type Area: 253 x 370 mm, Trim Size: 292 x 400 mm
Section of: Diário de Notícias
NATIONAL DAILY & SUNDAY NEWSPAPERS: Unabhängiges konservatives MdEP

MÉDICO DE FAMÍLIA 1642914P56A-203
Editorial: Ed. Lisboa Oriente Office, Av. Infante D. Henrique, 333 - H, 4°, Sala 45, 1800-282 LISBOA
Tel: 218 532 916 **Fax:** 218 532 918
Email: jmfamilia@vfbm.com **Web site:** http://www.jmfamilia.com
ISSN: 0871-763X
Date Established: 1988; **Freq:** 6 issues yearly; **Cover Price:** EUR 2; **Circ:** 15,000
Managing Director: Miguel Múrias Mauritti
Profile: Medical and general information.
Language(s): Portuguese
Readership: National.
ADVERTISING RATES:
Full Page Colour .... EUR 1650
Mechanical Data: Trim Size: 255 x 400 mm, Type Area: 255 x 345 mm

MEIOS & PUBLICIDADE
622996P2A-40
Editorial: R. General Firmino Miguel, 3 - Torre 2, 3°, 1600-100 LISBOA **Tel:** 210 410 300 **Fax:** 210 410 306
Email: geral@workmedia.pt **Web site:** http://www.meiosepublicidade.pt
Date Established: 1998; **Freq:** Weekly; **Cover Price:** EUR 5; **Circ:** 2,500
Usual Pagination: 40
Editor: Maria João Lima; **Managing Director:** Carla Borges Ferreira; **Advertising Manager:** João Paulo Pereira
Profile: Publication providing information on communications, marketing strategies, studies of trends and advertising especially relating to the media.
Language(s): Portuguese
Readership: National. Aimed at people working in the advertising and media sectors.
ADVERTISING RATES:
Full Page Colour .... EUR 1315
Mechanical Data: Type Area: 220 x 300 mm, Trim Size: 240 x 335 mm
BUSINESS: COMMUNICATIONS, ADVERTISING & MARKETING

MEN'S HEALTH
718425P86C-1
Editorial: R. Policarpo Anjos, 4, 1495-742 CRUZ QUEBRADA/DAFUNDO **Tel:** 214 154 500
Fax: 214 154 501
Email: menshealth@motorpress.pt **Web site:** http://www.menshealth.com.pt
Date Established: 2001; **Freq:** Monthly; **Cover Price:** EUR 3,2; **Circ:** 38,000
Usual Pagination: 132
Editor: Bárbara Correia; **Managing Director:** Pedro Lucas; **Advertising Manager:** Paulo Santos
Profile: Magazine focusing on fitness and health aimed to improve the personal, physical and mental welfare of men.
Language(s): Portuguese
Readership: Mainland. Aimed at men aged between 25 and 45 years.
ADVERTISING RATES:
Full Page Colour .... EUR 5460
Mechanical Data: Trim Size: 220 x 280 mm
CONSUMER: ADULT & GAY MAGAZINES: Men's Lifestyle Magazines

MENSAGEIRO DE BRAGANÇA
1642918P72-106
Editorial: R. Dr. Herculano da Conceição, Apartado 77, 5301-901 BRAGANÇA **Tel:** 273 323 367
Fax: 273 329 176
Email: geral@mensageironoticias.pt **Web site:** http://www.mensageironoticias.pt
Date Established: 1940; **Freq:** Weekly; **Cover Price:** EUR 0,8; **Circ:** 5,000
Usual Pagination: 24
Managing Director: Octávio Sobrinho
Profile: Weekly newspaper with information about Bragança region. Politics, current affairs, society, religion, sport, entertainment and events.
Language(s): Portuguese
Readership: Read in Trás-os-Montes e Alto Douro regions.
ADVERTISING RATES:
Full Page Mono .... EUR 480
Full Page Colour .... EUR 660
Mechanical Data: Trim Size: 305 x 430 mm, Type Area: 263 x 365 mm
LOCAL NEWSPAPERS

MERCADO IMOBILIÁRIO
1642919P1E-155
Editorial: Av. Eng. Arantes e Oliveira, 1 - R/C D, 1900-221 LISBOA **Tel:** 218 453 340 **Fax:** 218 453 345
Email: geral@imomercado.com
Freq: Weekly; **Circ:** 200,000
Language(s): Portuguese
Readership: National.
BUSINESS: FINANCE & ECONOMICS: Property

METRO CASA
1782603P94X-741
Editorial: Estrada da Outurela, 118, Parque Holanda - Edifício Holanda, 2790-114 CARNAXIDE
Tel: 214 169 210 **Fax:** 213 894 240
Email: metrocasa@metroportugal.com **Web site:** http://www.readmetro.com
Freq: Occasional; **Cover Price:** Free; **Circ:** 130,000
Usual Pagination: 12
Profile: Tips on home decorating, the latest style on home fashion tendencies, articles and interviews with well-known interior designers, news on the real estate market and the suggested best places where can acquire a property.
Language(s): Portuguese
Readership: Distributed in the most populous areas (like public transports) in the cities of Aveiro, Braga, Coimbra, Évora, Faro, Leiria, Lisboa and Porto.
ADVERTISING RATES:
Full Page Colour .... EUR 4500
Mechanical Data: Trim Size: 280 x 400 mm, Type Area: 247 x 335 mm
Part of Series, see entry for: Metro Portugal
CONSUMER: OTHER CLASSIFICATIONS: Miscellaneous

METRO LISBOA
1782605P82-359
Editorial: Estrada da Outurela, 118, Parque Holanda - Edifício Holanda, 2790-114 CARNAXIDE
Tel: 214 169 210 **Fax:** 213 894 240
Email: metro@metroportugal.com **Web site:** http://www.readmetro.com
Date Established: 2004; **Freq:** Daily; **Cover Price:** Free; **Circ:** 92,500
Profile: Focused on the latest national and international news and current affairs.
Language(s): Portuguese
Readership: Distributed in the public transports of Lisboa, Évora, Faro and Leiria.
ADVERTISING RATES:
Full Page Mono .... EUR 6468
Full Page Colour .... EUR 6468
Mechanical Data: Type Area: 247 x 335 mm, Trim Size: 280 x 400 mm
Part of Series, see entry for: Metro Portugal
CONSUMER: CURRENT AFFAIRS & POLITICS

METRO PORTUGAL
1782607P82-413
Editorial: Estrada da Outurela, 118, Parque Holanda - Edifício Holanda, 2790-114 CARNAXIDE
Tel: 214 169 210 **Fax:** 213 894 240
Email: metro@metroportugal.com **Web site:** http://www.readmetro.com
Date Established: 2004; **Freq:** Daily; **Cover Price:** Free; **Circ:** 130,000
Usual Pagination: 24
Managing Director: Diogo Torgal Ferreira
Profile: Free newspaper concerning national and international news and current affairs.
Language(s): Portuguese
Readership: Aimed for Aveiro, Braga, Coimbra, Évora, Faro, Leiria, Lisboa and Porto regions.
ADVERTISING RATES:
Full Page Mono .... EUR 9240
Full Page Colour .... EUR 9240
Mechanical Data: Type Area: 247 x 335 mm, Trim Size: 280 x 400 mm
Series owner and contact point for the following titles, see individual entries:
Metro Casa
Metro Lisboa
CONSUMER: CURRENT AFFAIRS & POLITICS

MID / DIMENSÃO
19297P4-123
Editorial: Av. da Igreja, 37 - E, 1700-233 LISBOA
Tel: 217 939 775 **Fax:** 217 972 574
Email: mid@mid-net.com **Web site:** http://www.lamartine.pt
Date Established: 1982; **Freq:** Quarterly; **Cover Price:** EUR 4,4; **Circ:** 10,000
Usual Pagination: 84
Managing Director: Helena Ladeiro
Profile: Magazine about developments in architectural design.
Language(s): Portuguese
Readership: National.
ADVERTISING RATES:
Full Page Colour .... EUR 3250
Mechanical Data: Trim Size: 230 x 297 mm

MIRADOURO
1642877P72-89
Editorial: Casa Azenha, Boassas, Apartado 71, 4690-405 CINFÃES **Tel:** 255 561 337
Fax: 255 561 337
Email: jornalmiradouro@sapo.pt
Date Established: 1962; **Freq:** 26 issues yearly; **Cover Price:** EUR 1; **Circ:** 2,000
Usual Pagination: 8
Profile: Weekly newspaper with information about Castelo de Paiva, Cinfães and Resende regions. Politics, current affairs, society, sport, entertainment and events.
Language(s): Portuguese
Readership: Aimed for Castelo de Paiva, Cinfães and Resende locals.
ADVERTISING RATES:
Full Page Mono .... EUR 400
Full Page Colour .... EUR 500
Mechanical Data: Trim Size: 244 x 423 mm
LOCAL NEWSPAPERS

MOBILIÁRIO EM NOTÍCIA
1820766P23-2
Editorial: R. Passadouro, 84 - Lavra, Apartado 2153, 4451-901 MATOSINHOS **Tel:** 229 999 314
Fax: 229 999 319
Email: mobiliarioemnoticia@mail.telepac.pt **Web site:** http://www.mobiliarioemnoticia.pt
Date Established: 1997; **Freq:** 6 issues yearly; **Cover Price:** Free; **Circ:** 5,000
Usual Pagination: 100
Editor: Emídio C. Brandão; **Managing Director:** Júlio Pinto da Costa; **Advertising Manager:** Mário A. Costa
Profile: Magazine dedicated to the furniture market. National and international related news, events' agenda, thematical, furniture and decoration stores research across Portugal. Also published in Spanish. Published with: Público.
Language(s): Portuguese
Readership: National.
ADVERTISING RATES:
Full Page Colour .... EUR 1750
Mechanical Data: Type Area: 230 x 300 mm, Trim Size: 230 x 300 mm

MODA
1782638P74B-110
Editorial: R. Filipe Folque, N° 40 - 4° Andar, 1069-124 LISBOA **Tel:** 213 164 200 **Fax:** 213 164 205
Email: redaccao@rbarevistas.pt
Freq: Seasonal; **Cover Price:** Free; **Circ:** 73,682
Profile: The latest fashion trends: Spring/Summer and Autumn/Winter collection.
Language(s): Portuguese
Readership: Mainland.
Mechanical Data: Type Area: 176 x 246 mm, Trim Size: 228 x 297 mm
CONSUMER: WOMEN'S INTEREST CONSUMER MAGAZINES: Women's Interest - Fashion

MODA & MODA
19701P74B-55
Editorial: R. Braamcamp, 12 - R/C Esq., 1250-050 LISBOA **Tel:** 213 862 019 **Fax:** 213 862 426
Email: modaemoda@gmail.com
ISSN: 0874-5544
Date Established: 1984; **Freq:** Quarterly; **Cover Price:** EUR 5; **Circ:** 15,000
Usual Pagination: 148
Managing Director: Marionela de Gusmão
Profile: Fashion magazine.
Language(s): Portuguese
Readership: National.
ADVERTISING RATES:
Full Page Mono .... EUR 2500
Full Page Colour .... EUR 3100
Mechanical Data: Trim Size: 225 x 305 mm
CONSUMER: WOMEN'S INTEREST CONSUMER MAGAZINES: Women's Interest - Fashion

MODALIDADES
1896083P65A-20_108
Editorial: Travessa da Queimada, 23 - R/C, 1° e 2°, 1249-113 LISBOA **Tel:** 213 463 981 **Fax:** 213 464 503
Web site: http://www.abola.pt
Date Established: 2009; **Freq:** Occasional; **Cover Price:** Free; **Circ:** 120,000
Usual Pagination: 8
Profile: Provides special information about sports in general.
Language(s): Portuguese
Mechanical Data: Type Area: 259 x 348 mm, Trim Size: 281 x 400 mm
Section of: A Bola
NATIONAL DAILY & SUNDAY NEWSPAPERS: Unabhängiges konservatives MdEP

MODTISSIMO
1822729P47-112
Editorial: R. Fernando Mesquita, Edifício do Citeve, N° 2785 - Antas, Apartado 265, 4760-034 VILA NOVA DE FAMALICÃO **Tel:** 252 302 020
Email: jornaltextil@portugaltextil.com **Web site:** http://www.portugaltextil.com
Date Established: 2007; **Freq:** Occasional; **Cover Price:** Free; **Circ:** 4,000
Usual Pagination: 4
Profile: Special edition about Modtissimo, a famous exhibition regarding the textile and clothing industry of Portugal.
Language(s): Portuguese
Readership: Read in Braga region.
Mechanical Data: Type Area: 245 x 355 mm, Trim Size: 275 x 385 mm
Part of Series, see entry for: Jornal Têxtil

MOTO GUIA
1782660P77B-54
Editorial: Edifício Vale do Ave, Bloco A - 1° Esq, Portela, Apartado 1052, 4765-110 DELÃES
Tel: 252 905 511 **Fax:** 252 905 696
Email: administracao@motoguia.net **Web site:** http://www.motoguia.pt
Freq: Monthly; **Cover Price:** EUR 2,5; **Circ:** 25,500
Managing Director: José Luís Menezes
Profile: Publication dedicated to motocycles and motorized sports.
Language(s): Portuguese
Readership: National. Aimed at motorcycle enthusiasts.
ADVERTISING RATES:
Full Page Colour .... EUR 1100
Mechanical Data: Trim Size: 147 x 210 mm, Type Area: 135 x 197 mm

MOTO JORNAL
19371P31B-100
Editorial: R. Prof. Alfredo de Sousa, 1 - Loja, 1600-188 LISBOA **Tel:** 217 543 190 **Fax:** 217 543 199
Email: geral@motojornal.pt **Web site:** http://www.motojornal.pt
Date Established: 1984; **Freq:** Weekly; **Cover Price:** EUR 2,2; **Circ:** 25,000
Usual Pagination: 84
Editor-in-Chief: Fernando Neto; **Managing Director:** Mário Figueiras; **Advertising Manager:** Celina Dinis
Profile: Magazine covering the motorcycle trade. Includes national and international news, details on scooters and jet-skiing, tests and advice on customs.
Language(s): Portuguese
Readership: Mainland.
ADVERTISING RATES:
Full Page Colour .... EUR 1960
Mechanical Data: Trim Size: 205 x 290 mm, Type Area: 178 x 255 mm
BUSINESS: MOTOR TRADE: Motorcycle Trade

MOTO JORNAL - CATÁLOGO
1782662P77A-386
Editorial: R. Prof. Alfredo Sousa, 1 - Loja, 1600-188 LISBOA **Tel:** 217 543 140 **Fax:** 217 543 209
Email: geral@motojornal.pt **Web site:** http://www.motojornal.pt
Freq: Annual; **Cover Price:** EUR 4,5; **Circ:** 25,000
Usual Pagination: 140
Editor-in-Chief: Fernando Neto; **Managing Director:** Mário Figueiras
Profile: Magazine covering the motorcycle trade. Includes national and international news, details on scooters and jet-skiing, tests and advice on customs.
Language(s): Portuguese
Readership: Mainland.
Mechanical Data: Trim Size: 205 x 290 mm, Type Area: 180 x 260 mm

MOTOCICLISMO
19744P77B-50
Editorial: R. Policarpo Anjos, 4, 1495-742 CRUZ QUEBRADA/DAFUNDO **Tel:** 214 154 500
Fax: 214 154 501
Email: motociclismo@motorpress.pt **Web site:** http://www.motociclismo.pt
Date Established: 1991; **Freq:** Monthly; **Cover Price:** EUR 3,3; **Circ:** 18,000
Usual Pagination: 116
Managing Director: Luís Carlos Sousa
Profile: Magazine covering all aspects of motorcycling.
Language(s): Portuguese
Readership: Mainland. Aimed at motorcycle enthusiasts.
ADVERTISING RATES:
Full Page Colour .... EUR 2700
Mechanical Data: Trim Size: 215 x 280 mm, Type Area: 185 x 255 mm
CONSUMER: MOTORING & CYCLING: Motorcycling

MULHER MODERNA NA COZINHA
19713P74P-221
Editorial: R. da Impala, 33 A - Abrunheira, S. Pedro de Penaferrim, 2710-070 SINTRA **Tel:** 219 238 033
Fax: 219 238 044
Email: mmc@impala.pt **Web site:** http://www.impala.pt
Date Established: 1983; **Freq:** Monthly; **Cover Price:** EUR 1,75; **Circ:** 37,000
Editor-in-Chief: Ana Sofia Borges; **Managing Director:** Graça Morais; **Advertising Manager:** João Santos
Profile: Magazine focusing on cookery. Includes information on new products, recipes and expert advice.
Language(s): Portuguese
Readership: National. Aimed at women.
ADVERTISING RATES:
Full Page Colour .... EUR 3160
Mechanical Data: Type Area: 180 x 237 mm, Trim Size: 210 x 273 mm
Series owner and contact point for the following titles, see individual entries:
Diabetes
Estações
Receitas Práticas
CONSUMER: WOMEN'S INTEREST CONSUMER MAGAZINES: Food & Cookery

MULHER PORTUGUESA.COM
1642924P74A-112
Editorial: R. Campolide, 31 - 1° Dto., 1070-026 LISBOA **Tel:** 213 841 460 **Fax:** 213 841 461
Web site: http://www.mulherportuguesa.com
Freq: Daily; **Cover Price:** Free
Profile: Web site dedicated to women's interests. Nutrition, health, fashion and beauty, shopping, new therapies, celebrities and historical figures, new talents, communities, family section, photo gallery, chronicles, travelling and writing reviews, characterize this site.
Language(s): Portuguese
Readership: Women in general.
CONSUMER: WOMEN'S INTEREST CONSUMER MAGAZINES: Women's Interest

MUNDO DA PESCA
1642927P91R-8
Editorial: Av. Infante D. Henrique, 306, 1900-717 LISBOA **Tel:** 218 310 920 **Fax:** 219 310 939
Web site: http://www.grupov.com
Freq: Monthly; **Cover Price:** EUR 3,6; **Circ:** 12,700
Managing Director: Nuno Gomes
Language(s): Portuguese
Readership: National. 10 - 65. A, B, C1, C2.
ADVERTISING RATES:
Full Page Colour .... EUR 1550
Mechanical Data: Trim Size: 210 x 285 mm
CONSUMER: RECREATION & LEISURE: Recreation & Leisure Related

MUNDO DO DVD ROM
1642928P5C-61
Editorial: Av. das Robíneas, 10, Rinchoa, 2635-545 RIO DE MOURO **Tel:** 219 198 210 **Fax:** 219 171 053
Web site: http://www.beprofit.pt
Date Established: 1996; **Freq:** Monthly; **Cover Price:** EUR 3,9; **Circ:** 15,000
Usual Pagination: 48
Editor: Carlos Jorge Sequeira; **Managing Director:** Pedro Melo; **Advertising Manager:** Fátima Matos
Language(s): Portuguese
Readership: Mainland.
ADVERTISING RATES:
Full Page Colour .... EUR 800

Mechanical Data: Trim Size: 200 x 270 mm, Type Area: 170 x 252 mm
BUSINESS: COMPUTERS & AUTOMATION: Professional Personal Computers

O MUNDO EM... 1822759P1A-393
Editorial: R. Gonçalo Cristóvão, 111 - 6°, 4049-037 PORTO **Tel:** 223 399 404 **Fax:** 222 058 098
Email: redaccao@vidaeconomica.pt **Web site:** http://www.vidaeconomica.pt
ISSN: 0871-4320
Freq: Annual; **Cover Price:** Free; **Circ:** 45,000
Usual Pagination: 124
Profile: Published with: Vida Económica; Público.
Language(s): Portuguese
Readership: National.
ADVERTISING RATES:
Full Page Colour .... EUR 4500
Mechanical Data: Type Area: 178 x 250 mm, Trim Size: 203 x 267 mm

MUNDO MÉDICO 1642930P56A-162
Editorial: Edifício Lisboa Oriente Office, Av. Infante D.Henrique, 333 H - 5°, 1800-282 LISBOA
Tel: 218 504 000 **Fax:** 218 504 009
Email: mundomedico@jasfarma.com **Web site:** http://www.jasfarma.com
Date Established: 1998; **Freq:** 6 issues yearly; **Cover Price:** EUR 3; **Circ:** 20,000
Managing Director: José Alberto Soares
Language(s): Portuguese
Readership: National.
ADVERTISING RATES:
Full Page Colour .... EUR 3050
Mechanical Data: Trim Size: 220 x 280 mm
BUSINESS: HEALTH & MEDICAL

NATAL 1831661P65A-50_137
Editorial: Av. João Crisóstomo, 72, 1069-043 LISBOA **Tel:** 213 185 462 **Fax:** 213 540 695
Email: geral@correiomanha.pt **Web site:** http://www.cmjornal.pt
Date Established: 2007; **Freq:** Annual; **Cover Price:** Free; **Circ:** 159,800
Usual Pagination: 108
Profile: Christmas edition.
Language(s): Portuguese
Readership: National.
ADVERTISING RATES:
Full Page Mono .... EUR 2020
Full Page Colour .... EUR 3030
Mechanical Data: Type Area: 180 x 253 mm, Trim Size: 205 x 275 mm
Section of: Correio da Manhã
NATIONAL DAILY & SUNDAY NEWSPAPERS: Unabhängiges konservatives MdEP

NATIONAL GEOGRAPHIC 1606376P73-301
Editorial: R. Filipe Folque, 40 - 4°, 1069-124 LISBOA
Tel: 213 164 200 **Fax:** 213 164 201
Email: rbaportugal@rbarevistas.pt **Web site:** http://www.nationalgeographic.pt
Date Established: 2001; **Freq:** Monthly; **Cover Price:** EUR 3,5; **Circ:** 52,820
Managing Director: Gonçalo Pereira; **Advertising Manager:** Rui Tito Lopes
Profile: Magazine covering geographical subjects, natural history, environment, people and the way they live, plus other world interests.
Language(s): Portuguese
Readership: National.
ADVERTISING RATES:
Full Page Colour .... EUR 5750
Mechanical Data: Trim Size: 175 x 254 mm
CONSUMER: NATIONAL & INTERNATIONAL PERIODICALS

NAUTICAMPO 1822809P91-181
Editorial: Edifício S. Francisco de Sales, R. Calvet de Magalhães, 242, 2770-022 PAÇO DE ARCOS
Tel: 214 544 000 **Fax:** 214 435 310
Email: ipublishing@impresa.pt **Web site:** http://www.nauticampo.fil.pt
Date Established: 2007; **Freq:** Annual; **Cover Price:** Free; **Circ:** 150,675
Language(s): Portuguese
Readership: National.
ADVERTISING RATES:
Full Page Colour .... EUR 3600
Mechanical Data: Type Area: 237 x 307 mm, Trim Size: 260 x 330 mm
Part of Series, see entry for: Expresso
CONSUMER: RECREATION & LEISURE

NAVEGAR 19792P91A-100
Editorial: R. Policarpo Anjos, N° 4, 1495-742 CRUZ QUEBRADA/DAFUNDO **Tel:** 214 154 500
Fax: 214 154 501
Email: navegar@motorpress.pt **Web site:** http://www.mpl.com
Date Established: 1998; **Freq:** Monthly; **Cover Price:** EUR 5; **Circ:** 15,000
Managing Director: Vasco Macide; **Advertising Manager:** Fernando Pereira
Profile: Magazine about boating and sailing in Portugal.
Language(s): Portuguese
Readership: Mainland. Aimed at sailing enthusiasts.
ADVERTISING RATES:
Full Page Colour .... EUR 3100
Mechanical Data: Trim Size: 215 x 290 mm, Type Area: 181 x 249 mm
CONSUMER: RECREATION & LEISURE: Boating & Yachting

NEGÓCIOS & FRANCHISING 622951P14A-80
Editorial: R. Basílio Teles, 35 - 1° D, 1070-020 LISBOA **Tel:** 210 033 880 **Fax:** 210 033 888
Email: nf@ife.pt **Web site:** http://www.infofranchising.pt
ISSN: 0874-4564
Date Established: 1999; **Freq:** 6 issues yearly; **Cover Price:** EUR 3; **Circ:** 15,000
Usual Pagination: 100
Managing Director: Isa Amaral
Profile: Magazine covering all areas of franchising. Provides details of business opportunities, new ventures and products.
Language(s): Portuguese
Readership: Mainland. Aimed at members of the business community and prospective franchises.
ADVERTISING RATES:
Full Page Colour .... EUR 2185
Mechanical Data: Type Area: 200 x 275 mm, Trim Size: 210 x 285 mm
BUSINESS: COMMERCE, INDUSTRY & MANAGEMENT

NEW GOLF 1643356P75D-3
Editorial: Av. Columbano Bordalo Pinheiro, 87 - 5° Andar, 1070-042 LISBOA **Tel:** 213 303 330
Fax: 213 303 339
Email: geral@fgt.pt
ISSN: 1645-4456
Date Established: 2001; **Freq:** 6 issues yearly; **Cover Price:** EUR 2,2; **Circ:** 25,000
Usual Pagination: 68
Managing Director: Tiago Galvão-Teles
Language(s): English; Portuguese
Readership: Mainland.
ADVERTISING RATES:
Full Page Colour .... EUR 3850
Mechanical Data: Trim Size: 200 x 280 mm
CONSUMER: SPORT: Golf

NORTE 1822852P65A-50_125
Editorial: R. Manuel Pinto de Azevedo, 80 - 1, 4100-320 PORTO **Tel:** 225 322 300 **Fax:** 226 183 879
Email: geral@correiomanha.pt **Web site:** http://www.cmjornal.pt
Date Established: 2007; **Freq:** Daily; **Circ:** 158,796
Usual Pagination: 52
Language(s): Portuguese
ADVERTISING RATES:
Full Page Mono .... EUR 2020
Full Page Colour .... EUR 3030
Mechanical Data: Type Area: 257 x 338 mm, Trim Size: 273 x 370 mm
Section of: Correio da Manhã
NATIONAL DAILY & SUNDAY NEWSPAPERS: National Daily Newspapers

NOTÍCIAS DA COVILHÃ 1642943P72I-50
Editorial: R. Jornal Notícias da Covilhã, 65 R/C, 6201-015 COVILHÃ **Tel:** 275 330 700
Fax: 275 330 709
Email: geral@noticiasdacovilha.pt **Web site:** http://www.noticiasdacovilha.pt
Date Established: 1913; **Freq:** Weekly; **Cover Price:** EUR 0,65; **Circ:** 20,000
Usual Pagination: 24
Editor-in-Chief: Fernando Brito
Profile: Weekly regional newspaper with information about Covilhã region. Politics, current affairs, society, religion, sport, entertainment and events.
Language(s): Portuguese
Readership: Aimed for Covilhã region.
ADVERTISING RATES:
Full Page Mono .... EUR 600
Full Page Colour .... EUR 1320
Mechanical Data: Trim Size: 300 x 421 mm, Type Area: 266 x 379 mm
LOCAL NEWSPAPERS: Regional Weekly Newspapers

NOTÍCIAS DE CHAVES 1642947P72-114
Editorial: R. Santo António, 41 - 1° Andar, Apartado 66, 5400-909 CHAVES **Tel:** 276 334 447
Fax: 276 334 447
Email: noticiasdechaves@gmail.com **Web site:** http://www.noticiasdechaves.com
Date Established: 1950; **Freq:** Weekly; **Cover Price:** EUR 0,6; **Circ:** 3,800
Usual Pagination: 12
Profile: Weekly regional newspaper with information about Chaves. Politics, current affairs, society, religion, sport, entertainment and events.
Language(s): Portuguese
Readership: Read in Vila Real region.
ADVERTISING RATES:
Full Page Mono .... EUR 375
Full Page Colour .... EUR 600
Mechanical Data: Trim Size: 290 x 410 mm, Type Area: 260 x 347 mm
LOCAL NEWSPAPERS

NOTÍCIAS DE GOUVEIA 1642949P72-116
Editorial: R. Dr. António Mendes, 6290-311 GOUVEIA **Tel:** 238 491 626 **Fax:** 238 491 616
Email: ngred@abpg.pt
Date Established: 1913; **Freq:** Weekly; **Cover Price:** EUR 0,8; **Circ:** 3,000
Usual Pagination: 36
Editor-in-Chief: Paulo Prata; **Advertising Manager:** Armando Sousa
Profile: Weekly regional newspaper with information about Gouveia. Politics, current affairs, society, sport, entertainment and events.
Language(s): Portuguese
Readership: Read mainly by Gouveia locals.
ADVERTISING RATES:
Full Page Mono .... EUR 340
Full Page Colour .... EUR 400
Mechanical Data: Trim Size: 290 x 410 mm, Type Area: 260 x 350 mm
LOCAL NEWSPAPERS

NOTÍCIAS DE GUIMARÃES 1642950P72-117
Editorial: R. de Santo António, 125 A - 1°, Apartado 43, 4800-162 GUIMARÃES **Tel:** 253 512 674
Fax: 253 517 909
Email: not.guimaraes@mail.telepac.pt **Web site:** http://www.noticiasdeguimaraes.com
Date Established: 1932; **Freq:** Weekly; **Cover Price:** EUR 0,75; **Circ:** 5,000
Editor-in-Chief: Teresa Ferreira; **Managing Director:** Maria do Carmo Dias de Castro
Profile: Weekly regional newspaper with information about Guimarães. Politics, current affairs, society, religion, sport, entertainment and events.
Language(s): Portuguese
Readership: Read by Guimarães locals.
ADVERTISING RATES:
Full Page Mono .... EUR 495
Full Page Colour .... EUR 770
Mechanical Data: Trim Size: 285 x 415 mm, Type Area: 260 x 370 mm
LOCAL NEWSPAPERS

NOTÍCIAS DE MANTEIGAS 1642952P72-119
Editorial: R. General Póvoas, N° 7, 6260-173 MANTEIGAS **Tel:** 275 982 476 **Fax:** 275 982 481
Email: nmanteigas@gmail.com **Web site:** http://www.noticiasdemanteigas.blogspot.com
Freq: Monthly; **Cover Price:** EUR 0,95; **Circ:** 1,500
Usual Pagination: 12
Profile: Monthly regional newspaper with information about Manteigas. Politics, current affairs, society, sport, entertainment and events.
Language(s): Portuguese
Readership: Aimed for the population of Manteigas.
ADVERTISING RATES:
Full Page Mono .... EUR 415.38
Mechanical Data: Trim Size: 300 x 425 mm, Type Area: 260 x 370 mm
LOCAL NEWSPAPERS

NOTÍCIAS DE VISEU 1642956P72-123
Editorial: Complexo Conventurispress, Av. do Convento, N° 1, 3511-907 VISEU **Tel:** 232 410 410
Fax: 232 410 418
Email: geral@noticiasdeviseu.com **Web site:** http://www.noticiasdeviseu.com
Date Established: 1975; **Freq:** Weekly; **Cover Price:** EUR 0,6; **Circ:** 7,500
Usual Pagination: 36
Managing Director: Hélder Sequeira
Profile: Tabloid-sized regional newspaper that contains information and entertainment articles regarding Viseu. Politics, current affairs, society, religion, sport, entertainment and events.
Language(s): Portuguese
Readership: Read in Viseu region.
ADVERTISING RATES:
Full Page Mono .... EUR 400
Mechanical Data: Trim Size: 282 x 392 mm, Type Area: 250 x 330 mm
LOCAL NEWSPAPERS

NOTÍCIAS DE VIZELA 1642957P72-124
Editorial: R. Dr. Abílio Torres, 520, 4815-552 VIZELA
Tel: 253 584 010 **Fax:** 253 587 653
Email: noticiasdevizela@mail.telepac.pt
Date Established: 1947; **Freq:** Weekly; **Cover Price:** EUR 0,65; **Circ:** 2,500
Usual Pagination: 24
Editor: M. Sérgio Vinagre; **Managing Director:** Susana Ribeiro
Profile: Weekly regional newspaper with information about Braga. Politics, current affairs, society, sport, entertainment and events.
Language(s): Portuguese
Readership: Aimed for Braga region, mainly for Vizela population.
ADVERTISING RATES:
Full Page Mono .... EUR 200
Full Page Colour .... EUR 240
Mechanical Data: Trim Size: 290 x 400 mm, Type Area: 260 x 370 mm
LOCAL NEWSPAPERS

NOTÍCIAS DE VOUZELA 1642958P72I-11
Editorial: Praça da República, 17, 3670-245 VOUZELA **Tel:** 232 772 026 **Fax:** 232 772 074
Email: jnoticiasdevouzela@sapo.pt **Web site:** http://www.noticiasdevouzela.com
Date Established: 1935; **Freq:** Weekly; **Cover Price:** EUR 0,5; **Circ:** 5,220
Usual Pagination: 20
Managing Director: Lino Augusto Vinhal
Profile: Weekly regional newspaper with information about Viseu. Politics, current affairs, society, religion, sport, entertainment and events.
Language(s): Portuguese
Readership: Aimed for Viseu region, mainly for Vouzela population.
ADVERTISING RATES:
Full Page Mono .... EUR 385
Full Page Colour .... EUR 577.5
Mechanical Data: Trim Size: 290 x 410 mm, Type Area: 260 x 349 mm
LOCAL NEWSPAPERS: Regional Weekly Newspapers

NOTÍCIAS DO BOMBARRAL 1642960P72-127
Editorial: R. da Fonte Velha, 11 - B, 2540-909 BOMBARRAL **Tel:** 262 603 054 **Fax:** 262 603 054
Email: geral.nb@sapo.pt **Web site:** http://www.noticiasbombarral.netai.net
Date Established: 1985; **Freq:** 6 issues yearly; **Cover Price:** EUR 0,6; **Circ:** 2,600
Usual Pagination: 32
Profile: Fortnightly regional newspaper with information about Bombarral. Politics, current affairs, society, religion, sport, entertainment and events.
Language(s): Portuguese
Readership: Aimed for Bombarral locals.
ADVERTISING RATES:
Full Page Mono .... EUR 230
Full Page Colour .... EUR 350
Mechanical Data: Trim Size: 315 x 400 mm, Type Area: 275 x 340 mm
LOCAL NEWSPAPERS

NOTÍCIAS DO MAR 19397P45A-60
Editorial: Estrada Nacional 249/4, Lote 7 - 1° Andar, 2785-599 SÃO DOMINGOS DE RANA
Tel: 214 452 899 **Fax:** 214 673 061
Email: noticias.mar@gmail.com **Web site:** http://www.mar.com.pt
Date Established: 1985; **Freq:** Monthly; **Cover Price:** EUR 1,75; **Circ:** 9,600
Usual Pagination: 32
Managing Director: Antero dos Santos
Profile: Magazine concerning the aspects of the maritime industry.
Language(s): Portuguese
Readership: National.
ADVERTISING RATES:
Full Page Colour .... EUR 1575
Mechanical Data: Trim Size: 276 x 416 mm, Type Area: 254 x 380 mm
BUSINESS: MARINE & SHIPPING

NOTÍCIAS DOS ARCOS 1642962P72I-34
Editorial: Largo da Misericórdia, 65, 4974-009 ARCOS DE VALDEVEZ **Tel:** 258 514 440
Fax: 258 514 441
Email: noticias.arcos@portugalmail.pt **Web site:** http://www.noticiasdosarcos.com
ISSN: 1646-1673
Date Established: 1931; **Freq:** Weekly; **Cover Price:** EUR 0,6; **Circ:** 4,000
Profile: Weekly regional newspaper with information about Viana do Castelo. Politics, current affairs, society, religion, sport, entertainment and events.
Language(s): Portuguese
Readership: Read in Viana do Castelo region.
ADVERTISING RATES:
Full Page Mono .... EUR 400
Full Page Colour .... EUR 500
Mechanical Data: Trim Size: 285 x 407 mm, Type Area: 260 x 360 mm
LOCAL NEWSPAPERS: Regional Weekly Newspapers

NOTÍCIAS MAGAZINE 1782896P73-327
Editorial: Edifício Diário de Notícias, Av. da Liberdade, 266, 4°, 1250-149 LISBOA
Tel: 213 187 500 **Fax:** 213 187 506
Email: secretariado@noticiasmagazine.com.pt **Web site:** http://dn.sapo.pt/revistas/nm
Freq: Weekly; **Circ:** 300,000
Executive Editor: Sofia Barrocas
Profile: Published with: Jornal de Notícias; Diário de Notícias; DN Madeira.
Language(s): Portuguese
Readership: National.
ADVERTISING RATES:
Full Page Colour .... EUR 8100
Mechanical Data: Trim Size: 215 x 290 mm, Type Area: 205 x 280 mm
Series owner and contact point for the following titles, see individual entries:
Terra do Nunca
CONSUMER: NATIONAL & INTERNATIONAL PERIODICALS

Portugal

NOTÍCIAS MÉDICAS 1642854P56R-5
Editorial: R. Tristão Vaz, 15 - 2° Dto., 1449-023 LISBOA **Tel:** 213 011 989 **Fax:** 213 015 539
Email: noticiasmedicas@mail.telepac.pt
ISSN: 0870-2055
Freq: Weekly; **Cover Price:** EUR 0,01; **Circ:** 15,000
Language(s): Portuguese
Readership: National.
ADVERTISING RATES:
Full Page Colour .... EUR 1990
Mechanical Data: Trim Size: 280 x 390 mm, Type Area: 250 x 360 mm
BUSINESS: HEALTH & MEDICAL: Health Medical Related

NOTÍCIAS SÁBADO 1782899P82-235
Editorial: R. João da Silva, 20, 1900-271 LISBOA **Tel:** 218 440 700 **Fax:** 218 440 753
Email: ns@globalnoticias.pt **Web site:** http://dn.sapo.pt/revistas/ns
Freq: Weekly; **Cover Price:** Free; **Circ:** 180,249
Usual Pagination: 84
Editor: Albano Matos; **Executive Editor:** João Ferreira
Profile: Published with: Diário de Notícias; Jornal de Notícias.
Language(s): Portuguese
Readership: National.
ADVERTISING RATES:
Full Page Colour .... EUR 6260
Mechanical Data: Trim Size: 215 x 290 mm, Type Area: 190 x 260 mm
CONSUMER: CURRENT AFFAIRS & POLITICS

NOVA GENTE 19697P74A-99
Editorial: Edifício Impala, Ranholas, 2710-460 SINTRA **Tel:** 219 238 218 **Fax:** 219 238 197
Email: novagente@impala.pt **Web site:** http://www.impala.pt
Date Established: 1976; **Freq:** Weekly; **Cover Price:** EUR 1,25; **Circ:** 162,000
Editor: Diana Wong Cascalho; **Editor-in-Chief:** Magda Penas; **Managing Director:** Paulo Sérgio dos Santos
Profile: Magazine containing interviews with international stars, celebrities, gossip, royalty features, a society column and tv guide.
Language(s): Portuguese
Readership: Mainland.
ADVERTISING RATES:
Full Page Colour .... EUR 5920
Mechanical Data: Trim Size: 227 x 297 mm
CONSUMER: WOMEN'S INTEREST CONSUMER MAGAZINES: Women's Interest

NOVA GENTE DECORAÇÃO 1642742P74C-92
Editorial: Edifício Impala, Ranholas, 2710-460 SINTRA **Tel:** 219 238 400 **Fax:** 219 238 197
Email: novagente@impala.pt **Web site:** http://www.impala.pt
Date Established: 1997; **Freq:** Monthly; **Cover Price:** EUR 3,95; **Circ:** 15,500
Usual Pagination: 144
Profile: Magazine with house and garden decoration tips and latest news.
Language(s): Portuguese
Readership: National.
ADVERTISING RATES:
Full Page Colour .... EUR 3180
Mechanical Data: Type Area: 225 x 298 mm, Trim Size: 225 x 298 mm
CONSUMER: WOMEN'S INTEREST CONSUMER MAGAZINES: Home & Family

NOVA GUARDA 1642967P72I-29
Editorial: R. António Sérgio, Edifício Liberal, Loja Q, 6300-665 GUARDA **Tel:** 271 210 105
Fax: 271 210 106
Email: geral@novaguarda.pt **Web site:** http://www.novaguarda.pt
ISSN: 0873-996X
Date Established: 1996; **Freq:** Weekly; **Cover Price:** EUR 0,7; **Circ:** 5,100
Usual Pagination: 32
Managing Director: António Pereira de Andrade Pissarra; **Advertising Manager:** Paulo Pereira
Profile: Weekly newspaper with information about Guarda region. Politics, current affairs, society, religion, sport, entertainment and events.
Language(s): Portuguese
Readership: Read in Guarda region.
ADVERTISING RATES:
Full Page Colour .... EUR 350
Mechanical Data: Type Area: 258 x 365 mm, Trim Size: 300 x 400 mm
LOCAL NEWSPAPERS: Regional Weekly Newspapers

NOVA VERDADE 1642879P72-91
Editorial: R. Renato Leitão Lourenço, 11, 2580-335 ALENQUER **Tel:** 263 711 130
Email: presepioportugal@gmail.com **Web site:** http://www.novaverdade.com
Date Established: 1974; **Freq:** 26 issues yearly; **Cover Price:** EUR 0,85; **Circ:** 4,000
Usual Pagination: 30
Editor-in-Chief: A. Marques da Silva; **Managing Director:** Nuno Castilho de Matos
Profile: Fortnightly newspaper with information about Lisboa region. Politics, current affairs, society, sport, entertainment and events.
Language(s): Portuguese
Readership: Read in Lisboa region.
ADVERTISING RATES:
Full Page Mono .... EUR 210
Full Page Colour .... EUR 315
Mechanical Data: Trim Size: 280 x 410 mm, Type Area: 260 x 379 mm
LOCAL NEWSPAPERS

NURSING 19441P56B-100
Editorial: R. Padre Luis Aparicio, 11 - 3° A, 1150-248 LISBOA **Tel:** 213 584 301 **Fax:** 213 584 309
Email: geral@nursingportuguesa.com **Web site:** http://www.nursingportuguesa.com
ISSN: 0871-6196
Date Established: 1989; **Freq:** Monthly; **Cover Price:** EUR 6; **Circ:** 7,000
Usual Pagination: 52
Managing Director: Pedro Serra Pinto; **Advertising Manager:** Fátima Lima
Profile: Journal providing information about health and medicine with special focus on nursing.
Language(s): Portuguese
Readership: National. Aimed for professional nurses.
ADVERTISING RATES:
Full Page Colour .... EUR 1200
Mechanical Data: Trim Size: 205 x 270 mm
BUSINESS: HEALTH & MEDICAL: Nursing

OCASIÃO 1643034P2A-139
Editorial: R. Capitão Leitão, 66 N, 2800-133 ALMADA **Tel:** 707 260 260 **Fax:** 707 270 270
Email: feedback@ocasiao.pt **Web site:** http://www.ocasiao.pt
Date Established: 1990; **Freq:** Weekly; **Circ:** 30,295
Usual Pagination: 136
Profile: Weekly newspaper with classified advertisement. The two major headings are Real Estate, and Automotive, although there are many additional categories (e.g., Pets, Personals and Lost and Found).
Language(s): Portuguese
Readership: National.
ADVERTISING RATES:
Full Page Colour .... EUR 1878
Mechanical Data: Type Area: 262 x 369 mm, Trim Size: 285 x 400 mm
BUSINESS: COMMUNICATIONS, ADVERTISING & MARKETING

OPINIÃO PÚBLICA 1643039P72-132
Editorial: Editave Multimédia, Lda., R. 8 de Dezembro, Antas S. Tiago, 214, Apartado 410, 4760-016 VILA NOVA DE FAMALICÃO **Tel:** 252 308 145
Fax: 252 308 149
Email: informacao@opiniaopublica.pt **Web site:** http://www.opiniaopublica.pt
Date Established: 1991; **Freq:** Weekly; **Cover Price:** Free; **Circ:** 20,000
Usual Pagination: 20
Editor: Magda Ferreira; **Editor-in-Chief:** Cristina Azevedo
Profile: Newspaper with information about Vila Nova de Famalicão. Politics, current affairs, society, sport, entertainment and events.
Language(s): Portuguese
Readership: Aimed for Vila Nova de Famalicão locals.
ADVERTISING RATES:
Full Page Mono .... EUR 300
Full Page Colour .... EUR 450
Mechanical Data: Type Area: 253 x 364 mm, Trim Size: 283 x 397 mm
LOCAL NEWSPAPERS

PAIS & FILHOS 19780P88A-40
Editorial: R. Policarpo Anjos, 4, 1495-742 CRUZ QUEBRADA/DAFUNDO **Tel:** 214 154 500
Fax: 214 154 504
Email: paisefilhos@motorpress.pt **Web site:** http://www.paisefilhos.pt
Date Established: 1991; **Freq:** Monthly; **Cover Price:** EUR 3,2; **Circ:** 33,000
Usual Pagination: 116
Managing Director: Maria Jorge Costa
Profile: Magazine about education and teaching, including articles on health, beauty, children's fashion and motherhood.
Language(s): Portuguese
Readership: Mainland.
ADVERTISING RATES:
Full Page Colour .... EUR 5550
Mechanical Data: Trim Size: 207 x 280 mm, Type Area: 181 x 250 mm
CONSUMER: EDUCATION

PARQUES E VIDA SELVAGEM 1783044P57-143
Editorial: R. da Cunha, 4430-681 AVINTES
Tel: 227 878 120 **Fax:** 227 833 583
Email: revista@parquebiologico.pt **Web site:** http://www.parquebiologico.pt
ISSN: 1645-2607
Date Established: 2001; **Freq:** Monthly; **Cover Price:** Free; **Circ:** 120,000
Usual Pagination: 68
Editor-in-Chief: Jorge Gomes; **Managing Director:** Nuno Gomes Oliveira
Profile: Published with: Jornal de Notícias.
Language(s): Portuguese
Readership: National.
ADVERTISING RATES:
Full Page Colour .... EUR 3400
Mechanical Data: Trim Size: 215 x 290 mm, Type Area: 185 x 250 mm

PC GUIA 19303P5C-53
Editorial: R. Marcelino Mesquita, 15 - Loja 1, 2795-134 LINDA-A-VELHA **Tel:** 214 209 400
Email: ccosta@pcguia.fidemo.pt
Freq: Monthly; **Cover Price:** EUR 3,3; **Circ:** 30,000
Usual Pagination: 114
Editor: João Pedro Faria; **Managing Director:** Pedro Tróia; **Advertising Manager:** Cristina Fonseca
Profile: Magazine about the latest developments in the world of PCs.
Language(s): Portuguese
Readership: National.
ADVERTISING RATES:
Full Page Colour .... EUR 3400
Mechanical Data: Trim Size: 220 x 290 mm, Type Area: 193 x 267 mm
BUSINESS: COMPUTERS & AUTOMATION: Professional Personal Computers

PERFORMANCE 1643055P74G-79
Editorial: R. dos Bem Lembrados, 141, Manique, 2645-471 ALCABIDECHE **Tel:** 214 457 630
Fax: 214 449 691
Email: info@performance.pt **Web site:** http://www.performance.pt
ISSN: 1645-1406
Date Established: 1999; **Freq:** 6 issues yearly; **Cover Price:** EUR 1,5; **Circ:** 30,000
Usual Pagination: 68
Editor: Paula Cristovão Santos; **Managing Director:** João Guerra
Language(s): Portuguese
Readership: National.
ADVERTISING RATES:
Full Page Colour .... EUR 3200
Mechanical Data: Trim Size: 210 x 297 mm, Type Area: 155 x 258 mm
CONSUMER: WOMEN'S INTEREST CONSUMER MAGAZINES: Slimming & Health

PESSOAL 19335P14F-150
Editorial: Av. António Augusto de Aguiar, 106 - 7°, 1050-019 LISBOA **Tel:** 213 502 532 **Fax:** 213 522 713
Email: c.barosa@moonmedia.info **Web site:** http://www.rhonline.pt
ISSN: 0870-3027
Date Established: 2001; **Freq:** Monthly; **Cover Price:** EUR 3,5; **Circ:** 15,000
Usual Pagination: 82
Managing Director: Catarina Guerra Barosa; **Advertising Manager:** Miguel Sousa
Profile: Magazine focusing on personnel management and training. Includes interviews, reports, business advice, case studies and legal information.
Language(s): Portuguese
Readership: Mainland. Read by members of APG - the Portuguese Association of Human Resource Managers.
ADVERTISING RATES:
Full Page Colour .... EUR 2600
Mechanical Data: Trim Size: 230 x 280 mm, Type Area: 200 x 266 mm
BUSINESS: COMMERCE, INDUSTRY & MANAGEMENT: Training & Recruitment

PESSOAL - GREAT PLACE TO WORK (JN + S) 2094125P14A-296
Freq: Occasional; **Cover Price:** Free; **Circ:** 120,621
Usual Pagination: 60
Profile: Special edition with the best places to work.
Language(s): Portuguese
Readership: National.
Mechanical Data: Trim Size: 230 x 280 mm

PESSOAS & NEGÓCIOS 2094126P14A-297
Editorial: R. Augusto Lessa, 251 - 12, 4200-100 PORTO **Tel:** 225 091 181
Email: vertice.escolhido.geral@gmail.com **Web site:** http://www.verticeescolhido.pt
Freq: Monthly; **Cover Price:** EUR 4; **Circ:** 43,943
Usual Pagination: 52
Profile: People and business.
Language(s): Portuguese
Readership: National.
Mechanical Data: Trim Size: 210 x 300 mm

PLANO DE ACTIVIDADES 1823029P50-160
Editorial: Edifício Lisboa Oriente, Av. Infante D. Henrique, 333 H - Escritório 49, 1800-282 LISBOA
Tel: 218 508 110 **Fax:** 218 530 426
Email: lmpcom@lpmcom.pt **Web site:** http://www.visitlisboa.com
Date Established: 2006; **Freq:** Annual; **Cover Price:** Free; **Circ:** 2,500
Usual Pagination: 32
Profile: Magazine revealing the plan of activities, budget and tourist promotion for the city of Lisboa.
Language(s): Portuguese
Readership: National.
Mechanical Data: Type Area: 186 x 267 mm, Trim Size: 210 x 297 mm
Part of Series, see entry for: Turismo de Lisboa

PME LÍDER 1872784P14A-254
Editorial: R. Vieira da Silva, 45, 1350-342 LISBOA
Tel: 213 236 800 **Fax:** 213 236 801
Email: deconomico@economico.pt **Web site:** http://economico.pt
Date Established: 2009; **Freq:** Occasional; **Cover Price:** Free; **Circ:** 20,179
Profile: Supplement on the influence of the Small and Medium Enterprises in national economy and the internationalization of some Portuguese companies.
Language(s): Portuguese
Readership: National.
Mechanical Data: Type Area: 194 x 260 mm, Trim Size: 202 x 268 mm

PONTOS DE VISTA.COM.PT 1783143P1A-583
Editorial: R. Rei Ramiro, 870 - 6° B, 4400-281 VILA NOVA DE GAIA **Tel:** 220 993 250 **Fax:** 220 993 250
Email: geral@pontosdevista.com.pt **Web site:** http://www.pontosdevista.com.pt
Date Established: 2006; **Freq:** Monthly; **Cover Price:** Free; **Circ:** 50,121
Usual Pagination: 84
Editor: Ricardo Silva; **Managing Director:** Jorge Antunes
Profile: Published with: Público.
Language(s): Portuguese
Readership: National.
ADVERTISING RATES:
Full Page Colour .... EUR 2800
Mechanical Data: Type Area: 215 x 285 mm, Trim Size: 230 x 300 mm

PORTA DA ESTRELA 1643068P80-231
Editorial: Av. Luís Vaz de Camões, Edifício Jardim III, 6270-484 SEIA **Tel:** 238 315 240 **Fax:** 238 314 501
Email: geral@portadaestrela.com **Web site:** http://www.portadaestrela.com
Date Established: 1976; **Freq:** 104 issues yearly; **Cover Price:** EUR 0,6; **Circ:** 6,000
Usual Pagination: 20
Editor-in-Chief: Alcides Soares Henriques
Profile: Newspaper with information about Seia region. Politics, current affairs, society, sport, entertainment and events.
Language(s): Portuguese
Readership: Read by Guarda locals.
ADVERTISING RATES:
Full Page Mono .... EUR 300
Full Page Colour .... EUR 350
Mechanical Data: Trim Size: 290 x 411 mm, Type Area: 260 x 370 mm
CONSUMER: RURAL & REGIONAL INTEREST

PORTO 1823101P65A-181_124
Editorial: R. de Gonçalo Cristóvão, 195 - 219, 4049-011 PORTO **Tel:** 222 096 100 **Fax:** 222 096 140
Email: dpe@jn.pt **Web site:** http://www.jn.pt
ISSN: 0874-1352
Freq: Daily; **Circ:** 106,688
Usual Pagination: 72
Language(s): Portuguese
Readership: Distributed in Oporto.
ADVERTISING RATES:
Full Page Mono .... EUR 2340
Full Page Colour .... EUR 3276
Mechanical Data: Type Area: 253 x 370 mm, Trim Size: 290 x 400 mm
Section of: Jornal de Notícias
NATIONAL DAILY & SUNDAY NEWSPAPERS: National Daily Newspapers

PORTUGAL BRASIL 718428P50-180
Editorial: R. Joaquim António de Aguiar, 45 - 5° Esq., 1099-058 LISBOA **Fax:** 213 862 746
Email: geral@lucidus.pt **Web site:** http://portugalbrasil.sapo.pt
Freq: 6 issues yearly; **Circ:** 7,000
Profile: Magazine focusing on the relationship between Portugal and Brazil. Includes information on politics, culture and all the latest relevant news and issues.
Language(s): Portuguese
Readership: National.
Mechanical Data: Trim Size: 192 x 278 mm

PORTUGAL INOVADOR 1977288P1A-553
Editorial: R. Augusto Lessa, 251 Esc. - 13, 4200-100 PORTO **Tel:** 225 023 907 **Fax:** 225 023 908
Email: pagina.exclusiva.geral@gmail.com **Web site:** http://www.paginaexclusiva.pt
Date Established: 2010; **Freq:** Monthly; **Cover Price:** EUR 4; **Circ:** 10,000
Usual Pagination: 100
Profile: Published with: Público.
Language(s): Portuguese
Readership: National.
ADVERTISING RATES:
Full Page Colour .... EUR 1700
Mechanical Data: Type Area: 170 x 260 mm, Trim Size: 210 x 295 mm

PÓS GRADUAÇÕES, MESTRADOS, MBA 1823124P88A-111
Editorial: Edifício São Francisco de Sales, R. Calvet de Magalhães, 242, 2770-022 PAÇO DE ARCOS
Tel: 214 544 000 **Fax:** 214 698 547
Email: visao@edimpresa.pt **Web site:** http://www.visao.pt
ISSN: 0872-3540
Date Established: 2007; **Freq:** Occasional; **Cover Price:** Free; **Circ:** 125,100
Usual Pagination: 44
Language(s): Portuguese
Readership: National.
ADVERTISING RATES:
Full Page Colour .... EUR 6550
Mechanical Data: Type Area: 185 x 221 mm, Trim Size: 210 x 260 mm
CONSUMER: EDUCATION

POSTAL DO ALGARVE 19784P89A-120
Editorial: R. Dr. Silvestre Falcão, 13 C, 8800-412 TAVIRA **Tel:** 281 320 900 **Fax:** 281 320 915
Email: postal@mail.telepac.pt **Web site:** http://www.postaldoalgarve.com
Date Established: 1987; **Freq:** Weekly; **Cover Price:** EUR 1; **Circ:** 9,195
Usual Pagination: 40
Editor: Ricardo Claro; **Managing Director:** Henrique Dias Freire
Profile: Regional newspaper regarding Algarve.
Language(s): Portuguese
Readership: Read in Algarve region.
ADVERTISING RATES:
Full Page Mono .... EUR 960
Full Page Colour .... EUR 1200
Mechanical Data: Type Area: 260 x 370 mm, Trim Size: 290 x 410 mm
CONSUMER: HOLIDAYS & TRAVEL: Travel

POSTGRADUATE MEDICINE
1869318P56A-286
Editorial: Alameda António Sérgio, 22 - 4° B, Edifício Amadeo de Souza-Cardoso, Miraflores, 1495-132 ALGÉS **Tel:** 214 121 144 **Fax:** 214 121 145
Email: euromedice@mail.telepac.pt
ISSN: 0872-6590
Freq: Monthly; **Cover Price:** EUR 7,52; **Circ:** 9,000
Usual Pagination: 90
Managing Director: André Tomé
Profile: Magazine with practical issues for the year's daily medicine.
Language(s): Portuguese
Readership: National.
ADVERTISING RATES:
Full Page Colour .... EUR 1870
Mechanical Data: Trim Size: 207 x 280 mm

O POVO DE CORTEGAÇA
1643014P72-135
Editorial: Praceta Centro d'Villa, 15, Apartado 29, 3886-908 CORTEGAÇA **Tel:** 256 754 413
Fax: 256 752 437
Email: povocortegaca@portugalmail.pt
Freq: Monthly; **Cover Price:** EUR 1; **Circ:** 1,500
Usual Pagination: 16
Language(s): Portuguese
Readership: Read in Aveiro region.
ADVERTISING RATES:
Full Page Mono .... EUR 187
Mechanical Data: Type Area: 260 x 375 mm, Trim Size: 290 x 410 mm
LOCAL NEWSPAPERS

O POVO DE GUIMARÃES
1643015P72-136
Editorial: R. Gil Vicente, 123 - 1°, Apartado 157, 4801-910 GUIMARÃES **Tel:** 253 412 767
Fax: 253 412 767
Email: povoguimaraes@mail.telepac.pt **Web site:** http://www.povodeguimaraes.com
Date Established: 1978; **Freq:** Weekly; **Cover Price:** EUR 0,6; **Circ:** 3,000
Usual Pagination: 24
Managing Director: Jorge Castelar
Profile: Weekly newspaper with information about Guimarães region. Politics, current affairs, society, religion, sport, entertainment and events.
Language(s): Portuguese
Readership: Read by Guimarães region.
ADVERTISING RATES:
Full Page Mono .... EUR 350
Full Page Colour .... EUR 420
Mechanical Data: Trim Size: 250 x 350 mm, Type Area: 224 x 315 mm
LOCAL NEWSPAPERS

O POVO DO CARTAXO
1643016P72-137
Editorial: Largo do Valverde, 27, 2070-040 CARTAXO **Tel:** 243 702 154 **Fax:** 243 779 000
Email: opovodocartaxo@portugalmail.pt
Freq: 26 issues yearly; **Cover Price:** EUR 0,6; **Circ:** 5,000
Profile: Newspaper with information about Cartaxo. Politics, current affairs, society, sport, entertainment and events.
Language(s): Portuguese
Readership: Read by Cartaxo locals.
ADVERTISING RATES:
Full Page Mono .... EUR 700
Full Page Colour .... EUR 950
Mechanical Data: Trim Size: 315 x 405 mm, Type Area: 260 x 330 mm
LOCAL NEWSPAPERS

O POVO FAMALICENSE
1643017P72-138
Editorial: R. Camilo Castelo Branco, 45, Apartado 474, 4760-127 VILA NOVA DE FAMALICÃO
Tel: 252 378 165 **Fax:** 252 378 167
Email: povofamalicense@sapo.pt **Web site:** http://www.opovofamalicense.com
Date Established: 1999; **Freq:** Weekly; **Cover Price:** Free; **Circ:** 15,000
Editor-in-Chief: Filomena Lamego; **Managing Director:** Sandra Ribeiro Gonçalves
Profile: Free weekly newspaper with information about Vila Nova de Famalicão. Politics, current affairs, society, religion, sport, entertainment and events.
Language(s): Portuguese
Readership: Read by Vila Nova de Famalicão locals.
ADVERTISING RATES:
Full Page Mono .... EUR 600
Full Page Colour .... EUR 900
Mechanical Data: Trim Size: 290 x 415 mm, Type Area: 255 x 355 mm
LOCAL NEWSPAPERS

PÓVOA SEMANÁRIO 1643077P72I-46
Editorial: Praça do Almada, 10 - 1°, 4490-438 PÓVOA DE VARZIM **Tel:** 252 615 198
Fax: 252 627 636
Email: povoasemanario@povoasemanario.pt **Web site:** http://www.povoasemanario.pt
ISSN: 1646-2904
Freq: Weekly; **Cover Price:** EUR 0,75; **Circ:** 3,000
Usual Pagination: 32
Profile: Weekly newspaper with information about Póvoa de Varzim. Politics, current affairs, society, sport, entertainment and events.
Language(s): Portuguese
Readership: Read by Póvoa do Varzim locals.
ADVERTISING RATES:
Full Page Mono .... EUR 350
Full Page Colour .... EUR 450
Mechanical Data: Trim Size: 291 x 398 mm, Type Area: 258 x 348 mm
Series owner and contact point for the following titles, see individual entries:
Construção e Imobiliária
LOCAL NEWSPAPERS: Regional Weekly Newspapers

PRIMEIRA ESCOLHA
1783222P94X-588
Editorial: Av. João Crisóstomo, 72, Galeria, 1069-043 LISBOA **Tel:** 213 185 321 **Fax:** 213 540 392
Email: publicidade@sabado.cofina.pt **Web site:** http://www.sabado.pt
Freq: Weekly; **Cover Price:** Free; **Circ:** 108,500
Usual Pagination: 16
Profile: General interest magazine covering celebrities, arts and tourism.
Language(s): Portuguese
Readership: National.
ADVERTISING RATES:
Full Page Colour .... EUR 3475
Mechanical Data: Trim Size: 205 x 265 mm
Part of Series, see entry for: Sábado
CONSUMER: OTHER CLASSIFICATIONS: Miscellaneous

PRIMEIRA MÃO 1643080P72-141
Editorial: Av. Visconde Barreiros, 89 - 5° Andar, 4470-151 MAIA **Tel:** 229 439 380 **Fax:** 229 439 381
Email: geral@primeiramao.pt **Web site:** http://www.primeiramao.pt
Date Established: 2000; **Freq:** 26 issues yearly; **Cover Price:** EUR 0,5; **Circ:** 3,000
Usual Pagination: 24
Managing Director: José Freitas
Profile: Newspaper with information about Maia locals. Politics, current affairs, society, religion, sport, entertainment and events.
Language(s): Portuguese
Readership: Read in Porto region.
ADVERTISING RATES:
Full Page Colour .... EUR 400
Mechanical Data: Trim Size: 292 x 419 mm, Type Area: 260 x 375 mm
LOCAL NEWSPAPERS

O PRIMEIRO DE JANEIRO
1642883P72-93
Editorial: R. das Oliveirinhas, 36 - 1°, 4000-000 PORTO **Tel:** 220 967 847
Email: geral.cloverpress@oprimeirodejaneiro.pt **Web site:** http://www.oprimeirodejaneiro.pt
ISSN: 0873-168X
Date Established: 1868; **Freq:** Daily; **Cover Price:** EUR 0,6; **Circ:** 20,000
Usual Pagination: 40
Editor: Joaquim Sousa; **Managing Director:** Rui Alas Pereira
Language(s): Portuguese
Readership: National.
ADVERTISING RATES:
Full Page Mono .... EUR 600
Full Page Colour .... EUR 1000
Mechanical Data: Trim Size: 290 x 370 mm, Type Area: 260 x 320 mm
LOCAL NEWSPAPERS

PRIMEIRO EMPREGO
1823148P65A-50_127
Editorial: Av. João Crisóstomo, 72, 1069-043 LISBOA **Tel:** 213 185 462 **Fax:** 213 540 695
Email: geral@correiomanha.pt **Web site:** http://www.cmjornal.pt
Date Established: 2007; **Freq:** Weekly; **Cover Price:** Free; **Circ:** 160,521
Usual Pagination: 16
Language(s): Portuguese
Readership: National.
ADVERTISING RATES:
Full Page Colour .... EUR 3240
Mechanical Data: Type Area: 257 x 338 mm, Trim Size: 280 x 370 mm
Section of: Correio da Manhã
NATIONAL DAILY & SUNDAY NEWSPAPERS: National Daily Newspapers

PRO TESTE 1643083P74A-115
Editorial: Av. Eng. Arantes e Oliveira, 13 - 1° B, 1900-221 LISBOA **Tel:** 218 410 800 **Fax:** 218 410 802
Email: info@deco.proteste.pt **Web site:** http://www.deco.proteste.pt
ISSN: 0873-8785
Date Established: 1979; **Freq:** Monthly; **Cover Price:** EUR 7,68; **Circ:** 430,000
Usual Pagination: 56
Editor: Pedro Moreira
Language(s): Portuguese
Readership: National.
Mechanical Data: Trim Size: 210 x 285 mm, Type Area: 183 x 227 mm
CONSUMER: WOMEN'S INTEREST CONSUMER MAGAZINES: Women's Interest

PRODUÇÃO ÁUDIO 1643084P78B-2
Editorial: Edifício Central Park, R. Alexandre Herculano, 3 - 3° B, 2795-240 LINDA-A-VELHA
Tel: 214 131 600 **Fax:** 214 131 601
Email: proaudio@editorialbolina.com **Web site:** http://www.paudio.com.pt
Freq: Monthly; **Cover Price:** EUR 4,6; **Circ:** 10,000
Usual Pagination: 64
Managing Director: João Martins
Profile: Technical magazine about audio production and related information.
Language(s): Portuguese
Readership: Mainland.
ADVERTISING RATES:
Full Page Colour .... EUR 1500
Mechanical Data: Trim Size: 255 x 300 mm
CONSUMER: CONSUMER ELECTRONICS: Video & DVD

PRODUÇÃO PROFISSIONAL
19391P43B-60
Editorial: Edifício Central Park, R. Alexandre Herculano, 3 - 3° B, 2795-240 LINDA-A-VELHA
Tel: 214 131 600 **Fax:** 214 131 601
Email: redaccaopp@editorialbolina.com **Web site:** http://www.pp.com.pt
Freq: Monthly; **Cover Price:** EUR 4,6; **Circ:** 6,000
Usual Pagination: 56
Editor-in-Chief: Ana Rita Soares Dinis; **Managing Director:** João Martins
Profile: Magazine concerning radio, TV and video production. Provides analysis of markets and trends within the industry.
Language(s): Portuguese
Readership: Mainland. Aimed at TV, video and radio professionals.
ADVERTISING RATES:
Full Page Colour .... EUR 1850
Mechanical Data: Trim Size: 225 x 300 mm
BUSINESS: ELECTRICAL RETAIL TRADE: Radio & Hi-Fi

PRODUTO DO ANO 1983051P2A-195
Editorial: Av. da Liberdade, 266, 1250-149 LISBOA
Tel: 213 187 476 **Fax:** 213 187 425
Email: geral@globalnoticias.pt
Date Established: 2010; **Freq:** Occasional; **Cover Price:** Free; **Circ:** 158,420
Profile: Published with: Diário de Notícias; Global Notícias.
Language(s): Portuguese
Readership: National.
Mechanical Data: Type Area: 260 x 318 mm, Trim Size: 288 x 370 mm

PROFISSIONAIS DE TURISMO
1983204P50-276
Editorial: R. do Janes, 15 - 1°, 4700-318 BRAGA
Tel: 253 693 733 **Fax:** 253 693 733
Email: info@profissionaisdeturismo.pt **Web site:** http://www.profissionaisdeturismo.pt
Date Established: 2010; **Freq:** Quarterly; **Cover Price:** Free; **Circ:** 500
Managing Director: Miguel Mendes
Profile: Magazine about tourism.
Language(s): Portuguese
Readership: National.

O PROGRESSO DE PAREDES
1643085P72-143
Editorial: Praça Capitão Torres Meireles, 30 - 2°, sala H, 4580-211 PAREDES **Tel:** 255 781 520
Fax: 255 777 030
Email: jornalprogresso@gmail.com **Web site:** http://www.progressodeparedes.com.pt
Freq: 26 issues yearly; **Cover Price:** EUR 0,5; **Circ:** 4,750
Managing Director: Manuel Ferreira Coelho
Profile: Newspaper with information about Paredes. Politics, current affairs, society, sport, entertainment and events.
Language(s): Portuguese
Readership: Read by Paredes locals.
ADVERTISING RATES:
Full Page Mono .... EUR 225
Full Page Colour .... EUR 325
Mechanical Data: Trim Size: 290 x 400 mm, Type Area: 260 x 350 mm
LOCAL NEWSPAPERS

PÚBLICO 19476P65A-170
Editorial: R. Viriato, 13, 1069-315 LISBOA
Tel: 210 111 000 **Fax:** 210 111 006
Email: publico@publico.pt **Web site:** http://www.publico.pt
Date Established: 1990; **Freq:** Daily; **Cover Price:** EUR 1; **Circ:** 51,029
Usual Pagination: 48
Editor: Sérgio Aníbal; **Executive Editor:** Lurdes Ferreira; **Advertising Manager:** Luísa Agante
Profile: Tabloid-sized quality newspaper providing regional, national and international news, political coverage and in-depth information concerning finance, economics and new technologies. Also covers society, culture, media, sport and television. Contains comic strips, game puzzles and fait-divers.
Language(s): Portuguese
Readership: National. Aimed at decision-makers, managers and executives within the business community, IT professionals, university students and graduates.
ADVERTISING RATES:
Full Page Mono .... EUR 5332.05
Full Page Colour .... EUR 6273
Mechanical Data: Type Area: 257 x 339 mm, Trim Size: 280 x 400 mm
NATIONAL DAILY & SUNDAY NEWSPAPERS: National Daily Newspapers

PUBLITURIS 19410P50-60
Editorial: R. General Firmino Miguel, 3 - Torre 2, 3° Piso, 1600-100 LISBOA **Tel:** 210 410 300
Fax: 210 410 307
Email: geral@publituris.workmedia.pt **Web site:** http://www.publituris.pt
ISSN: 0870-2152
Date Established: 1968; **Freq:** Weekly; **Cover Price:** EUR 5; **Circ:** 4,500
Usual Pagination: 40
Editor: Fátima Valente
Profile: Publication covering all aspects of the travel and tourism trade in Portugal.
Language(s): Portuguese
Readership: National. Aimed at individuals or professsionals of the tourism market.
ADVERTISING RATES:
Full Page Colour .... EUR 1520
Mechanical Data: Trim Size: 240 x 335 mm, Type Area: 224 x 296 mm
BUSINESS: TRAVEL & TOURISM

RALLY DE PORTUGAL - REIS DA CONDUÇÃO 1820882P77D-186
Editorial: Av. Conde Valbom, 30 - 4°/5°, 1050-068 LISBOA **Tel:** 210 124 900 **Fax:** 213 151 315
Freq: Occasional; **Cover Price:** Free; **Circ:** 276,095
Usual Pagination: 48
Profile: Published with: Correio da Manhã; Record.
Language(s): Portuguese
Readership: National.
Mechanical Data: Type Area: 98 x 175 mm, Trim Size: 113 x 190 mm
CONSUMER: MOTORING & CYCLING: Motor Sports

RECEITAS PRÁTICAS
1823240P8-1035
Editorial: R. da Impala, N° 33 A - Abrunheira, S. Pedro de Penaferrim, 2710-070 SINTRA
Tel: 219 238 033 **Fax:** 219 238 044
Email: mmc@impala.pt **Web site:** http://www.impala.pt
Date Established: 2007; **Freq:** Occasional; **Cover Price:** Free; **Circ:** 43,000
Usual Pagination: 38
Language(s): Portuguese
Readership: National. Aimed at women.
ADVERTISING RATES:
Full Page Colour .... EUR 3080
Mechanical Data: Type Area: 970 x 140 mm, Trim Size: 110 x 165 mm
Part of Series, see entry for: Mulher Moderna na Cozinha
BUSINESS: BAKING & CONFECTIONERY

RECORD 19718P75A-120
Editorial: Av. Conde de Valbom, 30 - 4°/5°, 1050-068 LISBOA **Tel:** 210 124 900 **Fax:** 213 151 315

Portugal

Email: antoniomagalhaes@record.pt **Web site:** http://www.record.xl.pt
Date Established: 1949; **Freq:** Daily; **Cover Price:** EUR 0,85; **Circ:** 101,429
Usual Pagination: 48
Editor: João Seixas; **Executive Editor:** Luís Óscar; **Managing Director:** Alexandre Pais; **Advertising Manager:** C. Tavares
Profile: Sports newspaper.
Language(s): Portuguese
Readership: Mainland.
ADVERTISING RATES:
Full Page Mono .... EUR 5535
Full Page Colour .... EUR 8280
Mechanical Data: Type Area: 257 x 336 mm, Trim Size: 280 x 370 mm
Series owner and contact point for the following titles, see individual entries:
Agenda
Guia de Futebol
Jornal do Ténis
Um Ano em Revista
CONSUMER: SPORT

RECORDAR
1823243P74-294
Editorial: Av. João Crisóstomo, 72 - 4°, 1069-043 LISBOA **Tel:** 213 185 287 **Fax:** 213 540 380
Email: correio@flash.cofina.pt
ISSN: 0871-7362
Date Established: 2007; **Freq:** Occasional; **Cover Price:** Free; **Circ:** 100,000
Usual Pagination: 16
Language(s): Portuguese
Readership: National.
ADVERTISING RATES:
Full Page Colour .... EUR 4100
Mechanical Data: Trim Size: 230 x 297 mm, Type Area: 190 x 257 mm
CONSUMER: WOMEN'S INTEREST CONSUMER MAGAZINES

RECURSOS HUMANOS MAGAZINE
1643221P14F-151
Editorial: R. do Mercado, N°7, 1800-271 LISBOA
Tel: 218 551 203 **Fax:** 218 551 204
Email: geral@rhmagazine.publ.pt **Web site:** http://www.rhmagazine.publ.pt
Freq: 6 issues yearly; **Cover Price:** EUR 3; **Circ:** 15,000
Usual Pagination: 80
Managing Director: Ana Rijo da Silva
Language(s): Portuguese
Readership: Mainland.
ADVERTISING RATES:
Full Page Colour .... EUR 1000
Mechanical Data: Type Area: 185 x 273 mm, Trim Size: 210 x 297 mm
BUSINESS: COMMERCE, INDUSTRY & MANAGEMENT: Training & Recruitment

REFLEXOS MODA
1783353P74B-123
Editorial: Av. da Boavista, 3521 - 3°, Sala 303, 4100-139 PORTO **Tel:** 226 164 363 **Fax:** 223 321 576
Email: p.azevedo@reflexosmoda.com **Web site:** http://www.reflexosmoda.com
Freq: 3 issues yearly; **Cover Price:** EUR 5; **Circ:** 5,000
Usual Pagination: 72
Profile: Hairstyle magazine.
Language(s): Portuguese
Readership: National. Dedicated to hairstyle specialists.
ADVERTISING RATES:
Full Page Colour .... EUR 1200
Mechanical Data: Type Area: 190 x 265 mm, Trim Size: 210 x 310 mm

REFLEXOS MODA
1783353P74B-177
Editorial: Av. da Boavista, 3521 - 3°, Sala 303, 4100-139 PORTO **Tel:** 226 164 363 **Fax:** 223 321 576
Email: p.azevedo@reflexosmoda.com **Web site:** http://www.reflexosmoda.com
Freq: 3 issues yearly; **Cover Price:** EUR 5; **Circ:** 5,000
Usual Pagination: 72
Profile: Hairstyle magazine.
Language(s): Portuguese
Readership: National. Dedicated to hairstyle specialists.
ADVERTISING RATES:
Full Page Colour .... EUR 1200
Mechanical Data: Type Area: 190 x 265 mm, Trim Size: 210 x 310 mm

REGIÕES (DN + JN)
1988424P50-283
Editorial: Edifício Diário de Notícias, Av. da Liberdade, 266, 1250-149 LISBOA **Tel:** 213 187 500
Fax: 213 187 516
Email: dnot@dn.pt **Web site:** http://dn.sapo.pt
Date Established: 2010; **Freq:** Occasional; **Cover Price:** Free; **Circ:** 172,688
Usual Pagination: 16
Profile: Special edition about regional tourism. Published with: Diário de Notícias; Jornal de Notícias.
Language(s): Portuguese
Readership: National.
Mechanical Data: Trim Size: 210 x 290 mm

O REGIONAL
1643021P72I-2
Editorial: R. 11 de Outubro, 178, Apartado 135, 3700-210 SÃO JOÃO DA MADEIRA **Tel:** 256 822 783
Fax: 256 822 654
Email: jornal@oregional.pt **Web site:** http://www.oregional.pt
Freq: Weekly; **Cover Price:** EUR 0,5; **Circ:** 7,200
Profile: Weekly regional newspaper with information about São João da Madeira region. Politics, current affairs, society, sport, entertainment and events.
Language(s): Portuguese
Readership: Read in São João da Madeira region.
ADVERTISING RATES:
Full Page Mono .... EUR 400
Full Page Colour .... EUR 650
Mechanical Data: Trim Size: 290 x 410 mm, Type Area: 260 x 360 mm
LOCAL NEWSPAPERS: Regional Weekly Newspapers

RELÓGIOS & JÓIAS
19414P52B-150
Editorial: R. Policarpo Anjos, 4, 1495-742 CRUZ QUEBRADA/DAFUNDO **Tel:** 214 154 500
Fax: 214 154 504
Email: relogiosejoias@motorpress.pt **Web site:** http://www.mpl.pt
Date Established: 1994; **Freq:** 6 issues yearly; **Cover Price:** EUR 6; **Circ:** 15,000
Managing Director: Marina Oliveira; **Advertising Manager:** Carla Pinheiro
Profile: Magazine about clocks, watches and jewellery.
Language(s): Portuguese
Readership: Mainland. Read by jewellers, clockmakers and consumers in general.
ADVERTISING RATES:
Full Page Colour .... EUR 3775
Mechanical Data: Trim Size: 225 x 295 mm, Type Area: 185 x 255 mm
BUSINESS: GIFT TRADE: Clocks & Watches

RENASCIMENTO
1643227P80-233
Editorial: Av. General Humberto Delgado, 37 - R/C Esq., 3534-005 MANGUALDE **Tel:** 232 623 232
Fax: 232 622 295
Email: jrenascimento@sapo.pt
Date Established: 1927; **Freq:** 6 issues yearly; **Cover Price:** EUR 0,6; **Circ:** 4,262
Managing Director: Nelson Veiga
Profile: Fortnightly newspaper with information about Mangualde region. Politics, current affairs, society, religion, sport, entertainment and events.
Language(s): Portuguese
Readership: Aimed for Mangualde locals.
ADVERTISING RATES:
Full Page Mono .... EUR 366.62
Mechanical Data: Trim Size: 265 x 360 mm
CONSUMER: RURAL & REGIONAL INTEREST

RENOVÁVEIS MAGAZINE
1966802P58-22
Editorial: Praça da Corujeira, 38, Apartado 3825, 4300-144 PORTO **Tel:** 225 899 626 **Fax:** 225 899 629
Email: geral@publindustria.pt **Web site:** http://www.renovaveismagazine.pt
Date Established: 2010; **Freq:** Quarterly; **Cover Price:** EUR 9; **Circ:** 5,000
Usual Pagination: 130
Editor-in-Chief: Helena Paulino; **Managing Director:** Cláudio Monteiro; **Advertising Manager:** Júlio Almeida
Profile: Technical-professional magazine that provides information on renewable energies, new equipments, materials and technological processes and technical events.
Language(s): Portuguese
Readership: National.
ADVERTISING RATES:
Full Page Colour .... EUR 1146
Mechanical Data: Trim Size: 210 x 297 mm

REPÓRTER DO MARÃO
1643228P72-145
Editorial: R. Dr. Francisco Sá Carneiro, 230, Apartado 200, 4630-279 MARCO DE CANAVESES
Tel: 255 521 307 **Fax:** 255 437 000
Email: tamegapress@gmail.com **Web site:** http://www.reporterdomarao.com
Date Established: 1984; **Freq:** Monthly; **Cover Price:** EUR 1; **Circ:** 30,000
Usual Pagination: 48
Managing Director: Jorge Sousa
Profile: Magazine with information about Marão region. Politics, current affairs, society, religion, sport, entertainment and events.
Language(s): Portuguese
Readership: Read by Gondomar, Marão and Amarante locals.
ADVERTISING RATES:
Full Page Mono .... EUR 400
Full Page Colour .... EUR 575
Mechanical Data: Trim Size: 210 x 297 mm
LOCAL NEWSPAPERS

REVISTA ACP
19742P77A-200
Editorial: R. Rosa Araújo, 24 - 26, 1250-195 LISBOA
Tel: 213 180 184 **Fax:** 213 159 121
Email: revista@acp.pt **Web site:** http://www.acp.pt
ISSN: 0870-273X
Date Established: 1929; **Freq:** Monthly; **Cover Price:** EUR 1,5; **Circ:** 180,000
Usual Pagination: 92
Editor: Ricardo Lopes; **Advertising Manager:** Tomaz Alpoim
Profile: Official magazine of the Automobile Club of Portugal. Magazine includes tests on new models, traffic problems, travel and tourism.
Language(s): Portuguese
Readership: National.
ADVERTISING RATES:
Full Page Colour .... EUR 5300
Mechanical Data: Trim Size: 200 x 270 mm, Type Area: 180 x 244 mm
CONSUMER: MOTORING & CYCLING: Motoring

REVISTA DA QUEIMA DAS FITAS
1783415P65A-181_100
Editorial: R. Gonçalo Cristóvão, 195, 4049-011 PORTO **Tel:** 222 096 100 **Fax:** 222 006 330
Email: dpe@jn.pt **Web site:** http://www.jn.pt
ISSN: 0874-1352
Freq: Annual; **Cover Price:** Free; **Circ:** 105,942
Usual Pagination: 24
Profile: Magazine about students events in Porto University.
Language(s): Portuguese
Readership: National. University students (from the Porto region).
Mechanical Data: Trim Size: 195 x 270 mm
Section of: Jornal de Notícias
NATIONAL DAILY & SUNDAY NEWSPAPERS: Unabhängiges konservatives MdEP

REVISTA DE VINHOS
1643234P22A-17
Editorial: R. Mário Castelhano, 40, Queluz de Baixo, 2734-502 BARCARENA **Tel:** 214 369 450
Fax: 214 369 481
Email: llopes@mce.iol.pt **Web site:** http://www.revistadevinhos.iol.pt
Date Established: 1989; **Freq:** Monthly; **Cover Price:** EUR 4; **Circ:** 25,000
Usual Pagination: 226
Managing Director: Luís Ramos Lopes
Language(s): Portuguese
Readership: Mainland. Aimed at men aged 35 to 55. A, B, C1.
ADVERTISING RATES:
Full Page Colour .... EUR 2310
Mechanical Data: Trim Size: 230 x 297 mm, Type Area: 200 x 263 mm
BUSINESS: FOOD

REVISTA SEGURANÇA
1643249P54-1
Editorial: R. Sousa Viterbo, 48 - C, 1900-427 LISBOA
Tel: 218 131 944 **Fax:** 218 131 816
Email: geral@revistaseguranca.com **Web site:** http://www.revistaseguranca.com
Date Established: 1965; **Freq:** 6 issues yearly; **Circ:** 10,000
Managing Director: Maria Isabel Santos
Profile: Magazine covering the safety and firefighting industry, trade fairs and conferences.
Language(s): Portuguese
Readership: National.
ADVERTISING RATES:
Full Page Colour .... EUR 1226
Mechanical Data: Trim Size: 210 x 297 mm

REVISTA UNIBANCO
1643250P94H-4
Editorial: Edifício S. Francisco de Sales, R. Calvet de Magalhães, 242, 2770-022 PAÇO DE ARCOS
Tel: 214 544 000 **Fax:** 214 435 310
Email: mjdias@impresa.pt **Web site:** http://www.impresapublishing.pt/publicacoes/unibanco/unibanco_apresentacao.html
Freq: Quarterly; **Circ:** 101,940
Language(s): Portuguese
Readership: National.
ADVERTISING RATES:
Full Page Colour .... EUR 4815
Mechanical Data: Type Area: 175 x 230 mm, Trim Size: 205 x 260 mm
CONSUMER: OTHER CLASSIFICATIONS: Customer Magazines

REVISTA ÚNICA
1783961P94X-696
Editorial: Edifício S. Francisco de Sales, R. Calvet de Magalhães, 242, 2770-022 PAÇO DE ARCOS
Tel: 214 544 000 **Fax:** 214 435 310
Email: unica@expresso.impresa.pt **Web site:** http://www.expresso.pt
Date Established: 2000; **Freq:** Weekly; **Cover Price:** Free; **Circ:** 126,575
Usual Pagination: 132
Editor: José Cardoso
Language(s): Portuguese
Readership: National.
ADVERTISING RATES:
Full Page Colour .... EUR 5810
Mechanical Data: Type Area: 199 x 270 mm, Trim Size: 225 x 297 mm
Part of Series, see entry for: Expresso
CONSUMER: OTHER CLASSIFICATIONS: Miscellaneous

O RIBATEJO
19764P72I-31
Editorial: Centro Nacional de Exposições - Quinta das Cegonhas, Apartado 355, 2000-471 SANTARÉM
Tel: 243 309 600 **Fax:** 243 333 766
Email: info@oribatejo.pt **Web site:** http://www.oribatejo.pt
Date Established: 1985; **Freq:** Weekly; **Cover Price:** EUR 0,8; **Circ:** 15,000
Usual Pagination: 48
Editor-in-Chief: João Baptista; **Managing Director:** Joaquim Duarte
Profile: Newspaper featuring economic, business and general news about the Ribatejo region.
Language(s): Portuguese
Readership: Read in Santarém region.
ADVERTISING RATES:
Full Page Mono .... EUR 1100
Full Page Colour .... EUR 1200
Mechanical Data: Trim Size: 280 x 405 mm, Type Area: 255 x 340 mm
LOCAL NEWSPAPERS: Regional Weekly Newspapers

ROMA & ALVALADE
1823315P89C-26
Editorial: R. do Loreto, 16 - 2° Dto., 1200-242 LISBOA **Tel:** 213 408 090 **Fax:** 213 256 809
Email: email@convida.pt **Web site:** http://www.convida.pt
Date Established: 2003; **Freq:** Annual; **Cover Price:** Free; **Circ:** 60,000
Usual Pagination: 60
Language(s): English
ADVERTISING RATES:
Full Page Colour .... EUR 1950
Mechanical Data: Trim Size: 148 x 210 mm
Part of Series, see entry for: Convida
CONSUMER: HOLIDAYS & TRAVEL: Entertainment Guides

ROTAS & DESTINOS
19411P50-70
Editorial: Av. João Crisóstomo, 72, Galeria, 1069-043 LISBOA **Tel:** 213 185 428 **Fax:** 213 540 695
Email: ruifaria@revistas.cofina.pt **Web site:** http://rotas.xl.pt
Freq: Monthly; **Cover Price:** EUR 3,8; **Circ:** 24,000
Usual Pagination: 132
Editor: Teresa Frederico; **Managing Director:** Catarina Palma Armindo
Profile: Magazine for the travel trade. Covers forthcoming events, features on holiday destinations and articles with a historical and cultural background.
Language(s): Portuguese
Readership: National.
ADVERTISING RATES:
Full Page Colour .... EUR 4100
Mechanical Data: Trim Size: 205 x 275 mm, Type Area: 180 x 253 mm
BUSINESS: TRAVEL & TOURISM

ROTEIRO
1822265P50-157
Editorial: Edifício São Francisco de Sales, R. Calvet de Magalhães, 242, 2770-022 PAÇO DE ARCOS
Tel: 214 544 000 **Fax:** 214 698 547
Email: visao@edimpresa.pt **Web site:** http://www.visao.pt
ISSN: 0872-3540
Date Established: 2007; **Freq:** Occasional; **Cover Price:** Free; **Circ:** 120,175
Language(s): Portuguese
Readership: National.
ADVERTISING RATES:
Full Page Colour .... EUR 6550
Mechanical Data: Trim Size: 234 x 214 mm
BUSINESS: TRAVEL & TOURISM

ROTEIROS GASTRONÓMICOS
1823330P65A-181_125
Editorial: R. de Gonçalo Cristóvão 195-219, 4049-011 PORTO **Tel:** 222 096 100 **Fax:** 222 096 140
Email: dpe@jn.pt **Web site:** http://www.jn.pt
ISSN: 0874-1352
Date Established: 2007; **Freq:** Occasional; **Cover Price:** Free; **Circ:** 109,545
Usual Pagination: 48
Language(s): Portuguese
Readership: National.
ADVERTISING RATES:
Full Page Colour .... EUR 1500
Mechanical Data: Type Area: 135 x 188 mm, Trim Size: 150 x 210 mm
Section of: Jornal de Notícias
NATIONAL DAILY & SUNDAY NEWSPAPERS: National Daily Newspapers

RSM - SUPER MARKET
1643256P2A-106
Editorial: R. Luís de Camões, 10 - 12° Dto., 2685-219 PORTELA LRS **Tel:** 218 522 130
Fax: 218 522 130
Email: info@websmnews.com **Web site:** http://www.webrsm.com
Date Established: 1994; **Freq:** Monthly; **Cover Price:** EUR 10; **Circ:** 5,000
Usual Pagination: 52
Managing Director: João Paulo Gama; **Advertising Manager:** Ana Parente
Language(s): Portuguese
Readership: National.
ADVERTISING RATES:
Full Page Colour .... EUR 2500
Mechanical Data: Type Area: 180 x 260 mm, Trim Size: 210 x 290 mm
BUSINESS: COMMUNICATIONS, ADVERTISING & MARKETING

SÁBADO
1783491P82-264
Editorial: Av. João Crisóstomo, 72, Galeria, 1069-043 LISBOA **Tel:** 213 185 321 **Fax:** 213 540 392
Email: catarina@sabado.cofina.pt **Web site:** http://www.sabado.pt
Date Established: 2004; **Freq:** Weekly; **Cover Price:** EUR 2,8; **Circ:** 110,900
Usual Pagination: 172
Editor: Luís Silvestre; **Executive Editor:** João Carlos Silva; **Managing Director:** Miguel Pinheiro
Profile: Generalist magazine focused on the latest national and internacional news and current affairs, as well as a vast range of thematics of general interest such as economics, entertainment, politics or leisure.
Language(s): Portuguese
Readership: National.
ADVERTISING RATES:
Full Page Colour .... EUR 6660
Mechanical Data: Type Area: 180 x 253 mm, Trim Size: 205 x 275 mm
Series owner and contact point for the following titles, see individual entries:
Ensino Superior
Primeira Escolha
CONSUMER: CURRENT AFFAIRS & POLITICS

SANTARÉM
1823376P65A-50_128
Editorial: Av. João Crisóstomo, 72, 1069-043 LISBOA **Tel:** 213 185 462 **Fax:** 213 540 695
Email: geral@correiomanha.pt **Web site:** http://www.cmjornal.pt
Date Established: 2007; **Freq:** Occasional; **Cover Price:** Free; **Circ:** 155,915
Usual Pagination: 8
Language(s): Portuguese
Readership: National.
ADVERTISING RATES:
Full Page Mono .... EUR 2020
Full Page Colour .... EUR 3030
Mechanical Data: Type Area: 257 x 338 mm, Trim Size: 273 x 370 mm
Section of: Correio da Manhã
NATIONAL DAILY & SUNDAY NEWSPAPERS: National Daily Newspapers

SANTOS
1823378P89C-27
Editorial: R. do Loreto, 16 - 2° Dto., 1200-242 LISBOA **Tel:** 213 408 090 **Fax:** 213 256 809
Email: email@convida.pt **Web site:** http://www.convida.pt
Date Established: 2003; **Freq:** Annual; **Cover Price:** Free; **Circ:** 60,000
Usual Pagination: 60
Language(s): English
ADVERTISING RATES:
Full Page Colour .... EUR 1950
Mechanical Data: Trim Size: 148 x 210 mm
Part of Series, see entry for: Convida
CONSUMER: HOLIDAYS & TRAVEL: Entertainment Guides

SAÚDE
1823385P56A-230
Editorial: R. Arronches Junqueiro, 82, Apartado 182, 2902-000 SETÚBAL **Tel:** 265 528 132
Fax: 265 528 131
Email: director@osetubalense.pt **Web site:** http://www.osetubalense.pt
Date Established: 2007; **Freq:** Occasional; **Cover Price:** Free; **Circ:** 6,300
Usual Pagination: 8
Profile: Suplemento com especial destaque para o Dia Mundial da Saúde. Contém artigos sobre políticas de saúde, novas tecnologias, dados estatísticos relativos à medicina e dicas sobre como viver mais e melhor.
Language(s): Portuguese
Readership: Read in Setúbal region.
Mechanical Data: Type Area: 261 x 364 mm, Trim Size: 286 x 395 mm
Part of Series, see entry for: O Setubalense

SAÚDE
1860593P56A-281
Editorial: Av. João Crisóstomo, 72 - 1°, 1069-043 LISBOA **Tel:** 213 180 900 **Fax:** 213 540 361
Email: info@negocios.pt **Web site:** http://www.jornaldenegocios.pt
ISSN: 0874-1360
Date Established: 2008; **Freq:** Occasional; **Cover Price:** Free; **Circ:** 21,141
Profile: Edition about the national health legislation, investments and insurences.
Language(s): Portuguese
Readership: National.
Mechanical Data: Type Area: 257 x 336 mm, Trim Size: 280 x 370 mm
Part of Series, see entry for: Jornal de Negócios

SAÚDE
1823385P56A-298
Editorial: R. Arronches Junqueiro, 82, Apartado 182, 2902-000 SETÚBAL **Tel:** 265 528 132
Fax: 265 528 131
Email: director@osetubalense.pt **Web site:** http://www.osetubalense.pt
Date Established: 2007; **Freq:** Occasional; **Cover Price:** Free; **Circ:** 6,300
Usual Pagination: 8
Profile: Suplemento com especial destaque para o Dia Mundial da Saúde. Contém artigos sobre políticas de saúde, novas tecnologias, dados estatísticos relativos à medicina e dicas sobre como viver mais e melhor.
Language(s): Portuguese
Readership: Read in Setúbal region.
Mechanical Data: Type Area: 261 x 364 mm, Trim Size: 286 x 395 mm
Part of Series, see entry for: O Setubalense

SAÚDE (DN + JN)
1783490P56A-211
Editorial: Edifício Diário de Notícias, Av. da Liberdade, 266, 1250-149 LISBOA **Tel:** 213 187 500
Fax: 213 187 516
Email: dnot@dn.pt **Web site:** http://www.dn.pt
Date Established: 2006; **Freq:** Occasional; **Cover Price:** Free; **Circ:** 167,146
Usual Pagination: 16
Profile: Special edition about health. Published with: Diário de Notícias; Jornal de Notícias.
Language(s): Portuguese
Readership: National.
ADVERTISING RATES:
Full Page Colour .... EUR 5000
Mechanical Data: Trim Size: 210 x 280 mm, Type Area: 174 x 227 mm

SAÚDE (DN + JN)
1783490P56A-290
Editorial: Edifício Diário de Notícias, Av. da Liberdade, 266, 1250-149 LISBOA **Tel:** 213 187 500
Fax: 213 187 516
Email: dnot@dn.pt **Web site:** http://www.dn.pt
Date Established: 2006; **Freq:** Occasional; **Cover Price:** Free; **Circ:** 167,146
Usual Pagination: 16
Profile: Special edition about health. Published with: Diário de Notícias; Jornal de Notícias.
Language(s): Portuguese
Readership: National.
ADVERTISING RATES:
Full Page Colour .... EUR 5000
Mechanical Data: Trim Size: 210 x 280 mm, Type Area: 174 x 227 mm

SAÚDE & BELEZA
1783520P74B-126
Editorial: Edifício S. Francisco de Sales, R. Calvet de Magalhães, 242, 2770-022 PAÇO DE ARCOS
Tel: 214 544 000 **Fax:** 214 435 310
Email: bbettencourt@activa.impresa.pt **Web site:** http://aeiou.activa.pt
ISSN: 0874-0453
Freq: Occasional; **Cover Price:** Free; **Circ:** 88,400
Profile: Supplement containing recent studies and tips on Health and Beauty.
Language(s): Portuguese
Readership: Mainland.
ADVERTISING RATES:
Full Page Colour .... EUR 5950
Mechanical Data: Trim Size: 230 x 297 mm, Type Area: 194 x 260 mm
Part of Series, see entry for: Activa
CONSUMER: WOMEN'S INTEREST CONSUMER MAGAZINES: Women's Interest - Fashion

SAÚDE E BEM ESTAR
1930086P56A-314
Editorial: R. Gonçalo Cristóvão, 111 - 6°, 4049-037 PORTO **Tel:** 223 399 404 **Fax:** 222 058 098
Email: redaccao@vidaeconomica.pt **Web site:** http://www.vidaeconomica.pt
ISSN: 0871-4320
Date Established: 2009; **Freq:** Occasional; **Cover Price:** Free; **Circ:** 20,300
Profile: Health tourism.
Language(s): Portuguese
Readership: National. Aimed at managers and directors in business, finance and industry and politicians.
ADVERTISING RATES:
Full Page Mono .... EUR 1800
Full Page Colour .... EUR 2335
Mechanical Data: Type Area: 257 x 390 mm, Trim Size: 290 x 418 mm
Part of Series, see entry for: Vida Económica

SAÚDE E BEM ESTAR
1643266P74G-81
Editorial: R. Prof. Alfredo de Sousa, 1, Loja, 1600-188 LISBOA **Tel:** 217 543 140 **Fax:** 217 543 188
Email: saude@represse.pt **Web site:** http://saudebemestar.com.pt
Date Established: 1993; **Freq:** Monthly; **Cover Price:** EUR 2,8; **Circ:** 30,000
Usual Pagination: 100
Language(s): Portuguese
Readership: Mainland.
ADVERTISING RATES:
Full Page Colour .... EUR 2885
Mechanical Data: Type Area: 180 x 250 mm, Trim Size: 205 x 280 mm
CONSUMER: WOMEN'S INTEREST CONSUMER MAGAZINES: Slimming & Health

SAÚDE NOTÍCIAS
1995736P56A-337
Editorial: Largo Alberto Sampaio 3-A, 2795-007 LINDA-A-VELHA **Tel:** 214 146 217 **Fax:** 214 146 218
Email: agaspar@saudenoticias.pt **Web site:** http://www.saudenoticias.pt
Date Established: 2010; **Freq:** Monthly; **Cover Price:** Free; **Circ:** 20,000
Usual Pagination: 26
Advertising Manager: Ana Luz
Profile: Published with: Destak.
Language(s): Portuguese
ADVERTISING RATES:
Full Page Colour .... EUR 1350
Mechanical Data: Type Area: 260 x 313 mm, Trim Size: 285 x 345 mm

SAÚDE PÚBLICA
1783530P94X-629
Editorial: Edifício Lisboa Oriente Office, Av. Infante D. Henrique, 333 H - 5°, 1800-282 LISBOA
Tel: 218 504 000 **Fax:** 218 508 019
Email: saudepublica@saudepublica.pt **Web site:** http://www.jasfarma.com
Freq: Monthly; **Cover Price:** Free; **Circ:** 133,425
Usual Pagination: 8
Language(s): Portuguese
Readership: National.
ADVERTISING RATES:
Full Page Mono .... EUR 11000
Full Page Colour .... EUR 13000
Mechanical Data: Type Area: 178 x 227 mm, Trim Size: 260 x 340 mm
Part of Series, see entry for: Expresso
CONSUMER: OTHER CLASSIFICATIONS: Miscellaneous

SEGREDOS DE COZINHA
1643267P74P-223
Editorial: Edifício Impala, Ranholas, 2710-460 SINTRA **Tel:** 219 238 033 **Fax:** 219 238 044
Email: segredoscozinha@impala.pt **Web site:** http://www.impala.pt
Date Established: 1983; **Freq:** Weekly; **Cover Price:** EUR 0,8; **Circ:** 22,000
Usual Pagination: 44
Managing Director: Graça Morais
Profile: Weekly magazine containing various recipes.
Language(s): Portuguese
Readership: Mainland.
ADVERTISING RATES:
Full Page Colour .... EUR 1800
Mechanical Data: Type Area: 119 x 193 mm, Trim Size: 150 x 218 mm
Series owner and contact point for the following titles, see individual entries:
Sopas
Sushi
CONSUMER: WOMEN'S INTEREST CONSUMER MAGAZINES: Food & Cookery

SEGURANÇA INFANTIL (DN + JN)
1936052P54-13
Editorial: Av. da Liberdade, 266 - 4°, 1250-149 LISBOA **Tel:** 213 187 500 **Fax:** 213 187 506
Email: agenda@jn.pt **Web site:** http://www.jn.pt
Date Established: 2009; **Freq:** Occasional; **Cover Price:** Free; **Circ:** 156,833
Usual Pagination: 4
Profile: Special edition about child safety. Published with: Diário de Notícias; Jornal de Notícias.
Language(s): Portuguese
Readership: National.
ADVERTISING RATES:
Full Page Mono .... EUR 2700
Full Page Colour .... EUR 3780
Mechanical Data: Type Area: 252 x 366 mm, Trim Size: 288 x 398 mm

SELECÇÕES DO READERS DIGEST
19686P73-200
Editorial: Lagoas Park, Edifício 11, 1°, 2740-270 PORTO SALVO **Tel:** 213 810 000 **Fax:** 213 859 203
Email: clientes.portugal@seleccoes.pt **Web site:** http://www.seleccoes.pt
Freq: Monthly; **Cover Price:** EUR 3,85; **Circ:** 110,000
Managing Director: José Mendonça da Cruz; **Advertising Manager:** João Maria Pedrosa
Profile: Publication containing specially commissioned articles or reprinted from international publications.
Language(s): Portuguese
Readership: National.
ADVERTISING RATES:
Full Page Colour .... EUR 4900
Mechanical Data: Type Area: 129 x 179 mm, Trim Size: 134 x 184 mm
CONSUMER: NATIONAL & INTERNATIONAL PERIODICALS

SEMANA INFORMÁTICA
19308P5E-130
Editorial: Av. João Crisóstomo, 72, 1069-043 LISBOA **Tel:** 213 307 700 **Fax:** 213 307 799
Email: semanainformatica@xl.pt **Web site:** http://www.semanainformatica.xl.pt
Freq: Weekly; **Cover Price:** EUR 1,85; **Circ:** 7,500
Usual Pagination: 22
Editor-in-Chief: Cláudia Sargento; **Managing Director:** Carlos Marçalo; **Advertising Manager:** Cristina Fonseca
Profile: Magazine about information technology, data-communications, emerging technologies and telecommunications. National and international latest news on technology, related market and business companies, concerning articles, online store and thematical sections.
Language(s): Portuguese
Readership: Mainland.
ADVERTISING RATES:
Full Page Colour .... EUR 3000
Mechanical Data: Trim Size: 243 x 330 mm, Type Area: 217 x 290 mm
BUSINESS: COMPUTERS & AUTOMATION: Data Transmission

SEMANA MÉDICA
1643269P56A-169
Editorial: R. Padre Luís Aparício, 11 - 3° A, 1150-248 LISBOA **Tel:** 213 584 300 **Fax:** 213 584 309
Email: geral@semanamedica.com **Web site:** http://www.semanamedica.com
Freq: 26 issues yearly; **Cover Price:** EUR 1,99; **Circ:** 15,000
Usual Pagination: 66
Managing Director: Pedro Serra Pinto; **Advertising Manager:** Fátima Lima
Language(s): Portuguese
Readership: National.
ADVERTISING RATES:
Full Page Colour .... EUR 1800
Mechanical Data: Trim Size: 205 x 270 mm, Type Area: 178 x 229 mm
BUSINESS: HEALTH & MEDICAL

SEMANÁRIO TRANSMONTANO
1643270P82-65
Editorial: Praça Camões, 12 A - 2°, Apartado 91, 5400-150 CHAVES **Tel:** 276 333 333
Fax: 276 333 034
Email: transmontano@net.novis.pt **Web site:** http://www.semanariotransmontano.com
Freq: Weekly; **Cover Price:** EUR 0,5; **Circ:** 8,000
Usual Pagination: 20
Managing Director: Margarida Luzio
Profile: Weekly newspaper with information about Trás-os-Montes. Politics, current affairs, society, religion, sport, entertainment and events.
Language(s): Portuguese
Readership: Read in Vila Real region.
ADVERTISING RATES:
Full Page Mono .... EUR 350
Full Page Colour .... EUR 450
Mechanical Data: Trim Size: 286 x 410 mm, Type Area: 250 x 365 mm
CONSUMER: CURRENT AFFAIRS & POLITICS

O SETUBALENSE
1643025P80-236
Editorial: R. Arronches Junqueiro, 82, Apartado 182, 2902-000 SETÚBAL **Tel:** 265 528 130
Fax: 265 528 131
Email: director@osetubalense.pt **Web site:** http://www.osetubalense.pt
Date Established: 1855; **Freq:** 104 issues yearly; **Cover Price:** EUR 0,6; **Circ:** 6,300
Usual Pagination: 12
Managing Director: Rafael Fidalgo
Language(s): Portuguese
Readership: Read in Setúbal region.
ADVERTISING RATES:
Full Page Mono .... EUR 990
Full Page Colour .... EUR 1910
Mechanical Data: Trim Size: 286 x 395 mm, Type Area: 260 x 366 mm
Series owner and contact point for the following titles, see individual entries:
Saúde
Saúde
CONSUMER: RURAL & REGIONAL INTEREST

SISTEMAS DE INFORMAÇÃO GEOGRÁFICA
2094773P1A-622
Editorial: R. Vieira da Silva, 45, 1350-342 LISBOA
Tel: 213 236 800 **Fax:** 213 236 801
Email: deconomico@economico.pt **Web site:** http://economico.pt
Date Established: 2011; **Freq:** Occasional; **Cover Price:** Free; **Circ:** 20,179
Profile: Special edition on geography technological advances.
Language(s): Portuguese
Readership: National.
Mechanical Data: Type Area: 250 x 360 mm, Trim Size: 280 x 394 mm

SOBERANIA DO POVO
1643281P72I-10
Editorial: Av. Dr. Eugénio Ribeiro, 89, 3°, Apartado 145, 3754-909 ÁGUEDA **Tel:** 234 622 626
Fax: 234 601 836
Email: geral@soberaniadopovo.pt **Web site:** http://www.soberaniadopovo.pt
Date Established: 1879; **Freq:** Weekly; **Cover Price:** EUR 0,6; **Circ:** 11,000
Usual Pagination: 40
Profile: Weekly newspaper with information about Águeda region. Politics, current affairs, society, sport, entertainment and events.
Language(s): Portuguese
Readership: Aimed for Águeda locals.
ADVERTISING RATES:
Full Page Mono .... EUR 538
Mechanical Data: Trim Size: 287 x 410 mm, Type Area: 255 x 360 mm
LOCAL NEWSPAPERS: Regional Weekly Newspapers

SOPAS
1823503P74P-296
Editorial: Edifício Impala, Ranholas, 2710-460 SINTRA **Tel:** 219 238 033 **Fax:** 219 238 044

Email: segredoscozinha@impala.pt **Web site:** http://www.impala.pt
Date Established: 2007; **Freq:** Occasional; **Cover Price:** Free; **Circ:** 36,000
Usual Pagination: 8
Profile: Soup recipes.
Language(s): Portuguese
Readership: Mainland.
ADVERTISING RATES:
Full Page Colour .... EUR 1750
Mechanical Data: Type Area: 119 x 193 mm, Trim Size: 150 x 218 mm
Part of Series, see entry for: Segredos de Cozinha

SPORT
1823507P65A-50_131
Editorial: Av. João Crisóstomo, 72, 1069-043 LISBOA **Tel:** 213 185 462 **Fax:** 213 540 695
Email: geral@correiomanha.pt **Web site:** http://www.cmjornal.pt
Date Established: 2006; **Freq:** Weekly; **Cover Price:** Free; **Circ:** 160,521
Language(s): Portuguese
Readership: National.
ADVERTISING RATES:
Full Page Colour .... EUR 5400
Mechanical Data: Type Area: 257 x 338 mm, Trim Size: 280 x 370 mm
Section of: Correio da Manhã
NATIONAL DAILY & SUNDAY NEWSPAPERS: National Daily Newspapers

SPORT LIFE
1643284P75A-211
Editorial: R. Policarpo Anjos, 4, 1495-742 CRUZ QUEBRADA/DAFUNDO **Tel:** 214 154 500
Fax: 214 154 504
Email: sportlife@motorpress.pt **Web site:** http://www.sportlife.com.pt
Date Established: 2002; **Freq:** Monthly; **Cover Price:** EUR 295; **Circ:** 25,000
Managing Director: Isabel Pinto da Costa; **Advertising Manager:** Sandra Amaral
Language(s): Portuguese
Readership: National.
ADVERTISING RATES:
Full Page Colour .... EUR 4450
Mechanical Data: Trim Size: 207 x 280 mm, Type Area: 172 x 240 mm
CONSUMER: SPORT

SUPER BEBÉS
1643292P91D-150
Editorial: R. Prof. Alfredo de Sousa, N° 1, Loja, 1600-188 LISBOA **Tel:** 217 543 140 **Fax:** 217 543 188
Email: superbebes@represse.pt **Web site:** http://superbebes.com.pt
Freq: Monthly; **Cover Price:** EUR 2,5; **Circ:** 26,000
Usual Pagination: 84
Managing Director: Ana Madureira
Profile: Magazine focused on pregnancy, parenting and child care.
Language(s): Portuguese
Readership: National.
ADVERTISING RATES:
Full Page Colour .... EUR 2100
Mechanical Data: Trim Size: 205 x 280 mm, Type Area: 180 x 250 mm
CONSUMER: RECREATION & LEISURE: Children & Youth

SUPER CICLISMO
1643293P75A-214
Editorial: R. dos Carvalhais, 17, Vila Verde, 2705-879 TERRUGEM SNT **Tel:** 219 613 205 **Fax:** 219 613 206
Email: revista@superciclismo.pt **Web site:** http://www.superciclismo.pt
ISSN: 0874-7644
Date Established: 2000; **Freq:** Monthly; **Cover Price:** EUR 3; **Circ:** 20,000
Language(s): Portuguese
Readership: National.
Mechanical Data: Trim Size: 180 x 260 mm
CONSUMER: SPORT

SUPER FOTO DIGITAL
1643295P91R-9
Editorial: Av. Infante D. Henrique, 306, 1900-717 LISBOA **Tel:** 218 310 920 **Fax:** 218 310 939
Email: redaccao.foto@grupov.com **Web site:** http://www.editorialgrupov.com
Freq: Monthly; **Cover Price:** EUR 3,95; **Circ:** 8,500
Usual Pagination: 100
Editor-in-Chief: Ana Raquel Matos; **Managing Director:** Nuno Gomes
Language(s): Portuguese
Readership: Mainland. 18-55. A, B, C1.
ADVERTISING RATES:
Full Page Colour .... EUR 2110
Mechanical Data: Trim Size: 230 x 300 mm
CONSUMER: RECREATION & LEISURE: Recreation & Leisure Related

SUPER INTERESSANTE
623582P94J-170
Editorial: R. Policarpo Anjos, 4, 1495-702 CRUZ QUEBRADA/DAFUNDO **Tel:** 214 154 500
Fax: 214 154 504
Email: ilopes@motorpress.pt **Web site:** http://www.mpl.pt
Date Established: 1998; **Freq:** Monthly; **Cover Price:** EUR 2,95; **Circ:** 53,600
Usual Pagination: 104
Advertising Manager: Paulo Santos
Profile: Popular science magazine.
Language(s): Portuguese
Readership: Mainland. Read mainly by men and women between the ages of 18 and 44 years.
ADVERTISING RATES:
Full Page Colour .... EUR 5610
Mechanical Data: Trim Size: 207 x 280 mm, Type Area: 183 x 256 mm
CONSUMER: OTHER CLASSIFICATIONS: Popular Science

SURF PORTUGAL
1643301P75A-217
Editorial: Edifício S. Francisco de Sales, R. Calvet de Magalhães, 242, 2770-022 PAÇO DE ARCOS
Tel: 214 544 000 **Fax:** 214 435 310
Email: geral@surfportugal.pt **Web site:** http://surfportugal.pt
Freq: Monthly; **Cover Price:** EUR 2,95; **Circ:** 10,000
Editor: Gonçalo Cadilhe; **Managing Director:** João Valente; **Advertising Manager:** Paula Vieira
Language(s): Portuguese
Readership: Mainland.
ADVERTISING RATES:
Full Page Colour .... EUR 1290
Mechanical Data: Trim Size: 220 x 297 mm
CONSUMER: SPORT

SUSHI
1823527P74P-299
Editorial: Edifício Impala, Ranholas, 2710-460 SINTRA **Tel:** 219 238 033 **Fax:** 219 238 044
Email: segredoscozinha@impala.pt **Web site:** http://www.impala.pt
Date Established: 2007; **Freq:** Occasional; **Cover Price:** EUR 0,95; **Circ:** 25,000
Usual Pagination: 34
Profile: Supplement dedicated to sushi recipes.
Language(s): Portuguese
Readership: Mainland.
ADVERTISING RATES:
Full Page Colour .... EUR 1750
Mechanical Data: Type Area: 140 x 194 mm, Trim Size: 149 x 218 mm
Part of Series, see entry for: Segredos de Cozinha

T3
1643302P5C-63
Editorial: Av. Infante D. Henrique, 306 - Lote 6, R/C, 1950-421 LISBOA **Tel:** 218 621 530 **Fax:** 218 621 540
Email: geral.t3@goody.pt **Web site:** http://www.t3.com.pt
Date Established: 2002; **Freq:** Monthly; **Cover Price:** EUR 2,95; **Circ:** 15,000
Managing Director: Fernando Mendes; **Advertising Manager:** Lygia Perrolas
Language(s): Portuguese
Readership: National.
ADVERTISING RATES:
Full Page Colour .... EUR 5900
Mechanical Data: Trim Size: 230 x 300 mm
BUSINESS: COMPUTERS & AUTOMATION: Professional Personal Computers

TECNOHOSPITAL
622805P56A-331
Editorial: Praça da Corujeira, 38, Apartado 3825, 4300-144 PORTO **Tel:** 225 899 620 **Fax:** 225 899 625
Email: geral@publindustria.pt **Web site:** http://www.tecnohospital.pt
Date Established: 1998; **Freq:** 6 issues yearly; **Cover Price:** EUR 30; **Circ:** 4,000
Usual Pagination: 64
Profile: Magazine containing information about health projects, buildings, equipment maintenance, organisation, security and waste. Also includes interviews and details of national and international events.
Language(s): Portuguese
Readership: National. Aimed at technical engineers, architects, hospital managers, doctors and nurses.
ADVERTISING RATES:
Full Page Colour .... EUR 1030
Mechanical Data: Trim Size: 210 x 297 mm

TELE CABO
1783809P76C-197
Editorial: R. de Lisboa, 1 C, 2765-240 ESTORIL
Tel: 214 649 780 **Fax:** 214 670 374
Email: redaccao@telecabo.com **Web site:** http://www.telecabo.com
Date Established: 2002; **Freq:** Monthly; **Cover Price:** EUR 3; **Circ:** 79,700
Usual Pagination: 180
Managing Director: José H. Lancastre
Language(s): Portuguese
Readership: National.
ADVERTISING RATES:
Full Page Colour .... EUR 3000
Mechanical Data: Trim Size: 210 x 290 mm, Type Area: 185 x 270 mm
CONSUMER: MUSIC & PERFORMING ARTS: TV & Radio

TELE NOVELAS
1783814P76C-199
Editorial: Edifício S. Francisco de Sales, R. Calvet de Magalhães, 242, 2770-022 PAÇO DE ARCOS
Tel: 214 698 112 **Fax:** 214 698 546
Email: cmalves@impresa.pt **Web site:** http://www.edimpresa.pt
Freq: Weekly; **Cover Price:** EUR 0,65; **Circ:** 114,325
Editor: Ana Cristina Freitas; **Managing Director:** Teresa Pais
Profile: Magazine focusing on soap operas news and events.
Language(s): Portuguese
Readership: National.
ADVERTISING RATES:
Full Page Colour .... EUR 1650
Mechanical Data: Trim Size: 148 x 195 mm, Type Area: 130 x 173 mm
CONSUMER: MUSIC & PERFORMING ARTS: TV & Radio

TELE SATÉLITE
19731P2D-150
Editorial: R. Bernardo Lima, 35 - 3° A, 1150-075 LISBOA **Tel:** 213 570 418 **Fax:** 213 142 764
Email: telesatelite@telesatelite.net **Web site:** http://www.telesatelite.net
Freq: Monthly; **Cover Price:** EUR 4; **Circ:** 25,000
Usual Pagination: 100
Managing Director: Francisco Paulo de Oliveira Vieira
Profile: Guide to satellite television programmes containing more than 5.000 channels.
Language(s): Portuguese
Readership: Distributed in Portugal, Brazil and PALOP.
ADVERTISING RATES:
Full Page Colour .... EUR 2000
Mechanical Data: Trim Size: 210 x 297 mm, Type Area: 185 x 260 mm
BUSINESS: COMMUNICATIONS, ADVERTISING & MARKETING: Broadcasting

TELECULINÁRIA
1643309P74P-224
Editorial: Av. Duque de Ávila, 69 - R/C Esq., 1000-139 LISBOA **Tel:** 213 568 250 **Fax:** 213 524 050
Email: teleculinaria@edicoesplural.com **Web site:** http://www.teleculinaria.pt
Date Established: 1976; **Freq:** Weekly; **Cover Price:** EUR 1,1; **Circ:** 40,000
Usual Pagination: 32
Managing Director: Miguel Henriques; **Advertising Manager:** Carla Gomes
Language(s): Portuguese
Readership: Mainland.
ADVERTISING RATES:
Full Page Colour .... EUR 1430
Mechanical Data: Type Area: 190 x 255 mm, Trim Size: 210 x 275 mm
CONSUMER: WOMEN'S INTEREST CONSUMER MAGAZINES: Food & Cookery

O TEMPLÁRIO
1643028P72-153
Editorial: R. José Raimundo Ribeiro, 28, Apartado 152, 2304-909 TOMAR **Tel:** 249 322 733
Fax: 249 322 734
Email: geral@otemplario.pt **Web site:** http://www.otemplario.pt
ISSN: 1646-8260
Date Established: 1925; **Freq:** Weekly; **Cover Price:** EUR 0,8; **Circ:** 5,000
Usual Pagination: 44
Language(s): Portuguese
Readership: Read in Santarém region.
ADVERTISING RATES:
Full Page Mono .... EUR 500
Full Page Colour .... EUR 625
Mechanical Data: Trim Size: 286 x 410 mm, Type Area: 260 x 355 mm
LOCAL NEWSPAPERS

TEMPO LIVRE
19988P89A-123
Editorial: Calçada de Sant' Ana, 180, 1169-062 LISBOA **Tel:** 210 027 000 **Fax:** 210 027 061
Email: inatel@inatel.pt **Web site:** http://www.inatel.pt/topimagecontent.aspx?menuid=169
Freq: Monthly; **Cover Price:** EUR 2; **Circ:** 126,867
Usual Pagination: 84
Editor: Eugénio Alves
Profile: Official magazine of Inatel (organization dedicated to social services) focusing on travel, leisure and free time.
Language(s): Portuguese
Readership: National.
ADVERTISING RATES:
Full Page Colour .... EUR 3750
Mechanical Data: Trim Size: 200 x 270 mm, Type Area: 180 x 250 mm
Series owner and contact point for the following titles, see individual entries:
Turismo Social
CONSUMER: HOLIDAYS & TRAVEL: Travel

TEMPO MEDICINA
19438P56A-245
Editorial: R. Abranches Ferrão, N° 23, 3° Andar, 1600-296 LISBOA **Tel:** 214 788 620 **Fax:** 214 788 621
Email: tempomedicina@tempomedicina.com **Web site:** http://www.tempomedicina.com
Freq: Weekly; **Cover Price:** EUR 0,05; **Circ:** 15,000
Editor: João Paulo de Oliveira; **Managing Director:** José M. Antunes
Profile: Publication about medicine.
Language(s): Portuguese
Readership: National. Aimed at people in the medical profession.
ADVERTISING RATES:
Full Page Colour .... EUR 1947
Mechanical Data: Trim Size: 287 x 370 mm, Type Area: 252 x 326 mm

TERRA DO NUNCA
1783840P94X-675
Editorial: Edifício Diário de Notícias, Av. da Liberdade, 266, 4°, 1250-149 LISBOA
Tel: 213 187 500 **Fax:** 213 187 506
Email: secretariado@noticiasmagazine.com.pt **Web site:** http://dn.sapo.pt/revistas/nm
Freq: Weekly; **Cover Price:** Free; **Circ:** 300,000
Profile: Supplement with games, puzzles and hobbies for children.
Language(s): Portuguese
Readership: National. Aimed for children.
Mechanical Data: Type Area: 205 x 280 mm, Trim Size: 215 x 290 mm
Part of Series, see entry for: Notícias Magazine
CONSUMER: OTHER CLASSIFICATIONS: Miscellaneous

TERRA NOSTRA
1643313P74A-119
Editorial: Rua Praia dos Santos, 10, 9500-706 PONTA DELGADA **Tel:** 296 630 080
Fax: 296 630 089
Email: terranostra@publicor.pt **Web site:** http://publicor.pt/site/terranostra/index.php?area=30
Date Established: 1996; **Freq:** Weekly; **Cover Price:** EUR 0,75; **Circ:** 3,000
Usual Pagination: 12
Profile: Fortnightly newspaper with information about Ponta Delgada region. Politics, current affairs, society, religion, sport, entertainment and events.
Language(s): Portuguese
Readership: Read in Açores region.
ADVERTISING RATES:
Full Page Mono .... EUR 320
Mechanical Data: Trim Size: 305 x 395 mm, Type Area: 275 x 359 mm
CONSUMER: WOMEN'S INTEREST CONSUMER MAGAZINES: Women's Interest

TERRAS DA BEIRA
1643315P67B-6015
Editorial: R. Soeiro Viegas, 2 B, Apartado 201, 6300-758 GUARDA **Tel:** 271 223 110 **Fax:** 271 223 112
Email: tb@terrasdabeira.com **Web site:** http://www.terrasdabeira.com
Freq: Weekly; **Cover Price:** EUR 0,7; **Circ:** 5,000
Usual Pagination: 28
Editor: Gustavo Brás
Profile: Weekly newspaper with information about Guarda. Politics, current affairs, society, religion, sport, entertainment and events.
Language(s): Portuguese
Readership: Read in Guarda region.
ADVERTISING RATES:
Full Page Mono .... EUR 425
Full Page Colour .... EUR 552.5
Mechanical Data: Trim Size: 290 x 413 mm, Type Area: 260 x 355 mm
REGIONAL DAILY & SUNDAY NEWSPAPERS: Regional Daily Newspapers

TESTE SAÚDE
1643319P74G-84
Editorial: R. de Artilharia 1, 79 - 4°, 1269-160 LISBOA **Tel:** 218 410 800 **Fax:** 218 410 802
Email: sga@edideco.pt **Web site:** http://www.deco.proteste.pt
ISSN: 0873-8807
Freq: 6 issues yearly; **Cover Price:** EUR 6,85; **Circ:** 178,000
Managing Director: Pedro Moreira
Language(s): Portuguese
Readership: National.
Mechanical Data: Trim Size: 210 x 285 mm
CONSUMER: WOMEN'S INTEREST CONSUMER MAGAZINES: Slimming & Health

TIME OUT ALGARVE
1850273P74Q-133
Editorial: Av. da Liberdade 13, 1250-139 LISBOA
Tel: 213 593 100 **Fax:** 213 593 131
Email: geral@timeout.pt **Web site:** http://www.timeout.pt
Date Established: 2008; **Freq:** Weekly; **Cover Price:** Free; **Circ:** 11,520
Usual Pagination: 32
Profile: Suplemento com sugestões para o que fazer no Algarve durante o Verão: agenda de eventos, festas, bares, discotecas, restaurantes, exposições e espectáculos.
Language(s): Portuguese
Mechanical Data: Type Area: 137 x 202 mm, Trim Size: 145 x 210 mm
Part of Series, see entry for: Time Out

TIME OUT ALGARVE
1850273P74Q-142
Editorial: Av. da Liberdade 13, 1250-139 LISBOA
Tel: 213 593 100 **Fax:** 213 593 131
Email: geral@timeout.pt **Web site:** http://www.timeout.pt
Date Established: 2008; **Freq:** Weekly; **Cover Price:** Free; **Circ:** 11,520
Usual Pagination: 32
Profile: Suplemento com sugestões para o que fazer no Algarve durante o Verão: agenda de eventos, festas, bares, discotecas, restaurantes, exposições e espectáculos.
Language(s): Portuguese
Mechanical Data: Type Area: 137 x 202 mm, Trim Size: 145 x 210 mm
Part of Series, see entry for: Time Out

TIME OUT ALGARVE 1850273P74Q-157

Editorial: Av. da Liberdade 13, 1250-139 LISBOA **Tel:** 213 593 100 **Fax:** 213 593 131
Email: geral@timeout.pt **Web site:** http://www.timeout.pt
Date Established: 2008; **Freq:** Weekly; **Cover Price:** Free; **Circ:** 11,520
Usual Pagination: 32
Profile: Suplemento com sugestões para o que fazer no Algarve durante o Verão: agenda de eventos, festas, bares, discotecas, restaurantes, exposições e espectáculos.
Language(s): Portuguese
Mechanical Data: Type Area: 137 x 202 mm, Trim Size: 145 x 210 mm
Part of Series, see entry for: Time Out

TODO TERRENO 1643323P77A-272

Editorial: R. Bartolomeu Dias, 170 - 1° A, 1400-031 LISBOA **Tel:** 213 021 148 **Fax:** 213 020 431
Email: pubtt@netcabo.pt
Date Established: 1994; **Freq:** Monthly; **Cover Price:** EUR 3,9; **Circ:** 20,000
Usual Pagination: 84
Managing Director: Alexandre Correia
Language(s): Portuguese
Readership: National.
ADVERTISING RATES:
Full Page Colour .... EUR 3400
Mechanical Data: Trim Size: 225 x 297 mm, Type Area: 195 x 257 mm
CONSUMER: MOTORING & CYCLING: Motoring

TOM SOBRE TOM 1643324P15R-5

Editorial: R. Sampaio Pina, 58 - 2° Dto., 1070-250 LISBOA **Tel:** 213 825 610 **Fax:** 213 825 619
Email: marketing@companhiadascores.com **Web site:** http://www.companhiadascores.com
Freq: Quarterly; **Cover Price:** EUR 20; **Circ:** 6,500
Usual Pagination: 50
Managing Director: Francisco Sá da Bandeira
Profile: Magazine for professional hairdressers.
Language(s): Portuguese
Readership: National.
ADVERTISING RATES:
Full Page Colour .... EUR 1600
Mechanical Data: Trim Size: 205 x 285 mm
BUSINESS: COSMETICS & HAIRDRESSING: Cosmetics & Hairdressing Related

TRANSPORTES EM REVISTA

1643330P49A-6

Editorial: Av. Fontes Pereira de Melo, 35 - 14° D, 1050-118 LISBOA **Tel:** 213 559 015 **Fax:** 213 559 020
Email: info@transportesemrevista.com **Web site:** http://www.transportesemrevista.com
Date Established: 1999; **Freq:** Monthly; **Cover Price:** EUR 8,49; **Circ:** 9,000
Usual Pagination: 80
Managing Director: José Monteiro Limão; **Advertising Manager:** Margarida Nascimento
Profile: Business magazine about cargo, freight, passenger transport and urban mobility in its various modes of transport (road, rail, air, river and sea). In one month the issue highlights the sector of freight and goods, and in the next, the topics are the passengers and urban mobility. The editions are available on the website for free.
Language(s): Portuguese
Readership: National.
ADVERTISING RATES:
Full Page Colour .... EUR 1800
Mechanical Data: Trim Size: 208 x 270 mm, Type Area: 183 x 240 mm
BUSINESS: TRANSPORT

TREVIM 1643334P72I-20

Editorial: Praça Cândido dos Reis, 15, 3200-901 LOUSÃ **Tel:** 239 992 266 **Fax:** 239 991 117
Email: jornal.trevim@sapo.pt **Web site:** http://www.trevim.pt
ISSN: 0871-9217
Date Established: 1967; **Freq:** 26 times a year; **Cover Price:** Paid
Cover Price: EUR 0,5; **Circ:** 3,200 Unique Users
Usual Pagination: 20
Managing Director: Carlos Sêco
Profile: Fortnightly newspaper with information about Lousã. Politics, current affairs, society, sport, entertainment and events.
Language(s): Portuguese
Readership: Read by Lousã locals.
ADVERTISING RATES:
Full Page Mono .... EUR 462
Full Page Colour .... EUR 600
Mechanical Data: Trim Size: 290 x 370 mm, Type Area: 260 x 326 mm
LOCAL NEWSPAPERS: Regional Weekly Newspapers

TRIBUNA PACENSE 1642888P72-98

Editorial: Av. dos Templários, 318, 4590-509 PAÇOS DE FERREIRA **Tel:** 255 863 987 **Fax:** 255 862 456
Email: geral@tribuna.com.pt **Web site:** http://www.portugal-linha.pt/tribuna
Date Established: 1985; **Freq:** Weekly; **Cover Price:** EUR 0,5; **Circ:** 3,100
Usual Pagination: 24
Managing Director: António José G. Ribeiro
Language(s): Portuguese
Readership: Read in Paços de Ferreira region.
ADVERTISING RATES:
Full Page Mono .... EUR 400
Full Page Colour .... EUR 600
Mechanical Data: Trim Size: 305 x 430 mm, Type Area: 265 x 385 mm
LOCAL NEWSPAPERS

TURBO 19748P77D-150

Editorial: Av. Tomás Ribeiro, 129, Edifício Quinta do Jamor, Sala 11, 2790-466 QUEIJAS **Tel:** 211 918 875
Fax: 211 919 874
Email: turbo@turbo.pt **Web site:** http://www.turbo.pt
ISSN: 0874-0534
Date Established: 1987; **Freq:** Monthly; **Cover Price:** EUR 2,5; **Circ:** 27,500
Editor: Marco António; **Managing Director:** Júlio Santos
Profile: Magazine about automobiles.
Language(s): Portuguese
Readership: Mainland.
ADVERTISING RATES:
Full Page Colour .... EUR 4750
Mechanical Data: Type Area: 190 x 275 mm, Trim Size: 210 x 297 mm
CONSUMER: MOTORING & CYCLING: Motor Sports

TURISMO DE LISBOA 1783913P50-117

Editorial: Edifício Lisboa Oriente, Av. Infante D. Henrique, 333 H - Escritório 49, 1800-282 LISBOA
Tel: 218 508 110 **Fax:** 218 530 426
Email: lmpcom@lpmcom.pt **Web site:** http://www.visitlisboa.com
Date Established: 2004; **Freq:** Monthly; **Cover Price:** EUR 24; **Circ:** 2,000
Usual Pagination: 52
Managing Director: Mário Machado
Profile: Official magazine of the Turismo de Lisboa's association. Contains articles about business, arts, events and information regarding Lisboa region.
Language(s): Portuguese
Readership: National. Aimed for Turismo de Lisboa associates, business people, decision makers and students of turism industry.
ADVERTISING RATES:
Full Page Colour .... EUR 1500
Mechanical Data: Trim Size: 210 x 297 mm, Type Area: 186 x 267 mm
Series owner and contact point for the following titles, see individual entries:
Plano de Actividades

TURISMO SOCIAL 1783915P50-118

Editorial: Calçada de Sant' Ana, 180, 1169-062 LISBOA **Tel:** 210 027 000 **Fax:** 210 027 061
Email: tl@inatel.pt
Freq: Seasonal; **Cover Price:** Free; **Circ:** 175,522
Profile: Magazine about tourism.
Language(s): Portuguese
Readership: National.
ADVERTISING RATES:
Full Page Colour .... EUR 3000
Mechanical Data: Trim Size: 200 x 270 mm, Type Area: 180 x 250 mm
Part of Series, see entry for: Tempo Livre
BUSINESS: TRAVEL & TOURISM

TURISVER 19413P50-80

Editorial: R. da Cova da Moura, 2 - 2° Esq., 1350-177 LISBOA **Tel:** 213 929 640 **Fax:** 213 929 650
Email: turisver@netcabo.pt **Web site:** http://www.turisver.com
Date Established: 1985; **Freq:** 26 issues yearly; **Cover Price:** EUR 3; **Circ:** 6,500
Usual Pagination: 44
Managing Director: José Luís Elias
Profile: Magazine covering all aspects of travel, tourism and hotels in Portugal.
Language(s): Portuguese
Readership: National. Aimed at turism professionals.
ADVERTISING RATES:
Full Page Colour .... EUR 1550
Mechanical Data: Type Area: 200 x 277 mm, Trim Size: 226 x 303 mm
BUSINESS: TRAVEL & TOURISM

TV 1783920P65A-50_109

Editorial: Av. João Crisóstomo, 72, 1069-043 LISBOA **Tel:** 213 185 462 **Fax:** 213 540 695
Email: geral@correiomanha.pt **Web site:** http://www.cmjornal.pt
Freq: Weekly; **Cover Price:** Free; **Circ:** 160,521
Profile: Magazine about television, television celebrities and events. Contains the time schedules of national television stations.
Language(s): Portuguese
Readership: National.
ADVERTISING RATES:
Full Page Colour .... EUR 2880
Mechanical Data: Type Area: 135 x 186 mm, Trim Size: 145 x 200 mm
Section of: Correio da Manhã
NATIONAL DAILY & SUNDAY NEWSPAPERS: National Daily Newspapers

TV 7 DIAS 19728P76C-165

Editorial: Edifício Impala, Ranholas, 2710-460 SINTRA **Tel:** 219 238 120 **Fax:** 219 238 195
Email: tv7dias@impala.pt **Web site:** http://www.impala.pt
Date Established: 1987; **Freq:** Weekly; **Cover Price:** EUR 1,25; **Circ:** 181,600
Editor: Marta Plácido; **Editor-in-Chief:** Rui Pedro Pereira; **Managing Director:** José Paulo Canelas
Profile: Magazine providing listings of television programmes, along with technical information, as well as information about new releases in cinemas. Also contains the latest news regarding television celebrities.
Language(s): Portuguese
Readership: National. Aimed at teenagers and adults interested in TV and movie releases.
ADVERTISING RATES:
Full Page Colour .... EUR 4480
Mechanical Data: Type Area: 172 x 242 mm, Trim Size: 205 x 275 mm
Series owner and contact point for the following titles, see individual entries:
Cinema
CONSUMER: MUSIC & PERFORMING ARTS: TV & Radio

TV GUIA 19729P76C-180

Editorial: Av. João Crisóstomo, N° 72, Galeria, 1069-043 LISBOA **Tel:** 213 309 404 **Fax:** 213 540 695
Email: mjcoelho@tvguia.cofina.pt
ISSN: 0871-7362
Date Established: 1978; **Freq:** Weekly; **Cover Price:** EUR 1,25; **Circ:** 118,000
Usual Pagination: 132
Editor: Sandro Arruda; **Editor-in-Chief:** Paulo Abreu; **Managing Director:** Luisa Jeremias
Profile: Magazine providing listings of television programmes, along with technical information, as well as information about new releases in cinemas. Also contains the latest news regarding celebrities.
Language(s): Portuguese
Readership: Mainland.
ADVERTISING RATES:
Full Page Colour .... EUR 3960
Mechanical Data: Type Area: 190 x 257 mm, Trim Size: 230 x 297 mm
Series owner and contact point for the following titles, see individual entries:
Cozinha Portuguesa
CONSUMER: MUSIC & PERFORMING ARTS: TV & Radio

TV MAIS 19945P76C-190

Editorial: Edifício S. Francisco de Sales, R. Calvet de Magalhães, 242, 2770-022 PAÇO DE ARCOS
Tel: 214 544 000 **Fax:** 214 698 542
Email: tvmais@edimpresa.pt **Web site:** http://www.edimpresa.pt
ISSN: 0872-3559
Date Established: 1992; **Freq:** Weekly; **Cover Price:** EUR 1,25; **Circ:** 82,904
Usual Pagination: 150
Editor: Sandra Cerqueira
Profile: Magazine containing articles and information about forthcoming TV programs, including celebrity features.
Language(s): Portuguese
Readership: National. Aimed at people of all ages interested in TV.
ADVERTISING RATES:
Full Page Colour .... EUR 2750
Mechanical Data: Type Area: 182 x 267 mm, Trim Size: 205 x 295 mm
Series owner and contact point for the following titles, see individual entries:
Culinária
CONSUMER: MUSIC & PERFORMING ARTS: TV & Radio

UM ANO EM REVISTA

1823691P75A-406

Editorial: Av. Conde de Valbom, 30 - 4°/5°, 1050-068 LISBOA **Tel:** 210 124 900 **Fax:** 213 151 315
Email: antoniomagalhaes@record.pt **Web site:** http://www.record.xl.pt
Date Established: 2007; **Freq:** Annual; **Cover Price:** Free; **Circ:** 115,296
Usual Pagination: 16
Profile: Newspaper about the main sport events.
Language(s): Portuguese
Readership: Mainland.
ADVERTISING RATES:
Full Page Mono .... EUR 4980
Full Page Colour .... EUR 7470
SCC .... EUR 0.09
Mechanical Data: Type Area: 257 x 338 mm, Trim Size: 280 x 370 mm
Part of Series, see entry for: Record
CONSUMER: SPORT

A UNIÃO 1642816P67B-6027

Editorial: R. da Rosa, 19, 9700-171 ANGRA HEROÍSMO **Tel:** 295 214 275 **Fax:** 295 214 030
Email: auniao@auniao.com **Web site:** http://www.auniao.com
Date Established: 1893; **Freq:** Daily; **Cover Price:** EUR 0,5; **Circ:** 1,600
Profile: Daily newspaper with information about Angra do Heroísmo. Politics, current affairs, society, sport, entertainment and events.
Language(s): Portuguese
Readership: Read by Açores residents.
ADVERTISING RATES:
Full Page Mono .... EUR 270
Full Page Colour .... EUR 467
Mechanical Data: Trim Size: 283 x 428 mm, Type Area: 254 x 360 mm
REGIONAL DAILY & SUNDAY NEWSPAPERS: Regional Daily Newspapers

URBAN MAN 1933932P86C-30

Editorial: Av. Columbano Bordalo Pinheiro, 87 - 5°, 1070-062 LISBOA **Tel:** 213 303 330 **Fax:** 213 303 339
Email: rmilagres@matchscore.pt
Date Established: 2009; **Freq:** Monthly; **Cover Price:** EUR 1; **Circ:** 50,000
Usual Pagination: 92
Managing Director: Tiago Galvão-Teles
Profile: Men's magazine with topics such as sex, sports, culture, economics, among others.
Language(s): Portuguese
Readership: National. Aimed for men.
ADVERTISING RATES:
Full Page Colour .... EUR 3850
Mechanical Data: Trim Size: 210 x 297 mm

URBAN MAN 1933932P86C-30

Editorial: Av. Columbano Bordalo Pinheiro, 87 - 5°, 1070-062 LISBOA **Tel:** 213 303 330 **Fax:** 213 303 339
Email: rmilagres@matchscore.pt
Date Established: 2009; **Freq:** Monthly; **Cover Price:** EUR 1; **Circ:** 50,000
Usual Pagination: 92
Managing Director: Tiago Galvão-Teles
Profile: Men's magazine with topics such as sex, sports, culture, economics, among others.
Language(s): Portuguese
Readership: National. Aimed for men.
ADVERTISING RATES:
Full Page Colour .... EUR 3850
Mechanical Data: Trim Size: 210 x 297 mm

URBANISMO & CONSTRUÇÃO

19389P42A-100

Editorial: Av. Manuel Alpedrinha, 16 - D, 2720-354 AMADORA **Tel:** 214 998 600 **Fax:** 214 998 609
Email: redaccao.uec@net.vodafone.pt
Freq: Monthly; **Cover Price:** EUR 2,5; **Circ:** 60,000
Managing Director: Mário Pedro
Profile: Journal about construction and urbanisation.
Language(s): Portuguese
Readership: National. Aimed at builders and architects.
ADVERTISING RATES:
Full Page Colour .... EUR 930
Mechanical Data: Type Area: 265 x 355 mm, Trim Size: 290 x 385 mm
BUSINESS: CONSTRUCTION

VEÍCULOS COMERCIAIS

1643350P77A-273

Editorial: R. Policarpo Anjos, 4, 1495-742 CRUZ QUEBRADA/DAFUNDO **Tel:** 214 154 563
Fax: 214 154 504
Email: fandrade@motorpress.pt **Web site:** http://www.guiadoautomovel.pt
Date Established: 1991; **Freq:** 6 issues yearly; **Cover Price:** EUR 4; **Circ:** 20,000
Managing Director: Alexandre Rodrigues
Language(s): Portuguese
Readership: Mainland.
ADVERTISING RATES:
Full Page Colour .... EUR 3980
Mechanical Data: Type Area: 183 x 248 mm, Trim Size: 210 x 284 mm
CONSUMER: MOTORING & CYCLING: Motoring

VIAJAR 1643355P89A-130

Editorial: R. Prof. Alfredo Sousa, N° 1, Loja, 1600-188 LISBOA **Tel:** 217 543 140 **Fax:** 217 543 188
Email: viajar@represse.pt **Web site:** http://viajarmagazine.com.pt
Date Established: 1981; **Freq:** Monthly; **Cover Price:** EUR 2; **Circ:** 7,000
Usual Pagination: 48
Editor-in-Chief: Carolina Morgado; **Advertising Manager:** Guilherme Teixeira
Language(s): Portuguese
Readership: National.
ADVERTISING RATES:
Full Page Colour .... EUR 1100
Mechanical Data: Type Area: 205 x 310 mm, Trim Size: 240 x 340 mm
CONSUMER: HOLIDAYS & TRAVEL: Travel

VIDA ECONÓMICA 19281P1A-150

Editorial: R. Gonçalo Cristóvão, 111 - 6°, 4049-037 PORTO **Tel:** 223 399 404 **Fax:** 222 058 098
Email: redaccao@vidaeconomica.pt **Web site:** http://www.vidaeconomica.pt
ISSN: 0871-4320
Freq: Weekly; **Cover Price:** EUR 2,2; **Circ:** 20,200
Usual Pagination: 42
Editor: Fátima Ferrão; **Editor-in-Chief:** Virgílio Ferreira
Profile: Newspaper containing financial and economic information. Includes national and international news on stock exchange, business, foreign trade and the European Union market.
Language(s): Portuguese
Readership: National. Aimed at managers and directors in business, finance and industry and politicians.
ADVERTISING RATES:
Full Page Mono .... EUR 3034
Full Page Colour .... EUR 4074
Mechanical Data: Trim Size: 290 x 418 mm, Type Area: 257 x 390 mm
Series owner and contact point for the following titles, see individual entries:
Bolsa de Turismo de Lisboa

Indústria Farmacêutica
Indústria Farmacêutica
Inovação
Inovação
Saúde e Bem Estar
BUSINESS: FINANCE & ECONOMICS

VIDA IMOBILIÁRIA
1643358P74K-4
Editorial: R. Gonçalo Cristóvão, 111 - 6°, 4049-037 PORTO **Tel:** 223 399 400 **Fax:** 222 058 098
Email: gestao@vidaimobiliaria.com **Web site:** http://www.vidaimobiliaria.com
Freq: Monthly; **Cover Price:** EUR 10; **Circ:** 3,000
Editor: Susana Ribeiro; **Managing Director:** António Gil Machado
Language(s): Portuguese
Readership: National.
ADVERTISING RATES:
Full Page Colour .... EUR 1750
Mechanical Data: Trim Size: 225 x 287 mm
CONSUMER: WOMEN'S INTEREST CONSUMER MAGAZINES: Home Purchase

VIDA RIBATEJANA
1642890P72I-24
Editorial: R. dos Bombeiros, 44, 2600-116 VILA FRANCA DE XIRA **Tel:** 263 200 550 **Fax:** 263 200 560
Web site: http://www.vidaribatejana.pt
Date Established: 1917; **Freq:** Weekly; **Cover Price:** EUR 0,5; **Circ:** 10,000
Usual Pagination: 20
Editor: Sérgio Catoja
Language(s): Portuguese
Readership: Aimed at Lisboa region.
ADVERTISING RATES:
Full Page Mono .... EUR 665
Full Page Colour .... EUR 850
Mechanical Data: Type Area: 260 x 350 mm, Trim Size: 290 x 406 mm
LOCAL NEWSPAPERS: Regional Weekly Newspapers

VIDA RURAL
1643361P21A-75
Editorial: R. Basílio Teles, 35 - 1° Dto., 1070-020 LISBOA **Tel:** 210 033 800 **Fax:** 210 033 888
Email: imartins@ife.pt **Web site:** http://www.ife.pt
Date Established: 1953; **Freq:** Monthly; **Cover Price:** EUR 3,6; **Circ:** 11,000
Usual Pagination: 48
Managing Director: Isabel Martins
Language(s): Portuguese
Readership: National.
ADVERTISING RATES:
Full Page Colour .... EUR 2480
Mechanical Data: Trim Size: 230 x 297 mm, Type Area: 200 x 275 mm
BUSINESS: AGRICULTURE & FARMING

VIDA SAUDÁVEL (DN + JN)
1932403P56A-318
Editorial: Edifício Diário de Notícias, Av. da Liberdade, 266, 1250-149 LISBOA **Tel:** 213 187 500 **Fax:** 213 187 516
Email: dnot@dn.pt **Web site:** http://dn.sapo.pt
Date Established: 2009; **Freq:** Occasional; **Cover Price:** Free; **Circ:** 149,901
Usual Pagination: 4
Profile: Published with: Jornal de Notícias; Diário de Notícias.
Language(s): Portuguese
Readership: National.
Mechanical Data: Type Area: 257 x 370 mm, Trim Size: 290 x 400 mm

VILLAS & GOLFE
1643363P75D-4
Editorial: Centro Empresarial Lionesa, R. da Lionesa, 446 - Fracção G19, 4465-671 LEÇA DO BALIO **Tel:** 229 069 530 **Fax:** 229 069 539
Email: villasegolfe@villasegolfe.com **Web site:** http://www.villasegolfe.com/VillaseGolfe
ISSN: 1645-2798
Freq: 6 issues yearly; **Cover Price:** EUR 10; **Circ:** 50,000
Managing Director: Maria Amélia Pires
Language(s): Portuguese
Readership: National.
ADVERTISING RATES:
Full Page Colour .... EUR 5000
Mechanical Data: Trim Size: 240 x 340 mm, Type Area: 210 x 310 mm
CONSUMER: SPORT: Golf

VIP
1643364P74A-120
Editorial: R. da Impala, 33 - A, Abrunheira, S. Pedro de Penaferrim, 2710-070 SINTRA **Tel:** 219 238 100 **Fax:** 219 238 465
Email: vip@impala.pt **Web site:** http://www.impala.pt/site/vip
Date Established: 1997; **Freq:** Weekly; **Cover Price:** EUR 1,25; **Circ:** 53,600
Editor: José Lúcio Duarte
Language(s): Portuguese
Readership: National.
ADVERTISING RATES:
Full Page Colour .... EUR 3930
Mechanical Data: Trim Size: 230 x 296 mm
CONSUMER: WOMEN'S INTEREST CONSUMER MAGAZINES: Women's Interest

VIP SAÚDE E BELEZA
1784040P74B-129
Editorial: R. da Impala, 33 - A, Abrunheira, S. Pedro de Penaferrim, 2710-070 SINTRA **Tel:** 219 238 100 **Fax:** 219 238 465
Email: vip@impala.pt **Web site:** http://www.impala.pt
Freq: Annual; **Cover Price:** EUR 3,5; **Circ:** 75,400
Language(s): Portuguese
Readership: National.
ADVERTISING RATES:
Full Page Colour .... EUR 3730
Mechanical Data: Trim Size: 230 x 296 mm
CONSUMER: WOMEN'S INTEREST CONSUMER MAGAZINES: Women's Interest - Fashion

VISÃO
19688P73-300
Editorial: Edifício São Francisco de Sales, R. Calvet de Magalhães, 242, 2770-022 PAÇO DE ARCOS **Tel:** 214 544 000 **Fax:** 214 698 547
Email: visao@edimpresa.pt **Web site:** http://www.visao.pt
ISSN: 0872-3540
Date Established: 1993; **Freq:** Weekly; **Cover Price:** EUR 2,75; **Circ:** 107,000
Usual Pagination: 150
Editor: Pedro Dias de Almeida; **Executive Editor:** Filipe Luís; **Managing Director:** Pedro Camacho
Profile: Magazine containing articles about current events, weekly news, featuring economy, politics, culture.
Language(s): Portuguese
Readership: National.
ADVERTISING RATES:
Full Page Colour .... EUR 6550
Mechanical Data: Type Area: 176 x 236 mm, Trim Size: 210 x 280 mm
CONSUMER: NATIONAL & INTERNATIONAL PERIODICALS

VISÃO 7 GUIA
1823751P32H-258
Editorial: Edifício São Francisco de Sales, R. Calvet de Magalhães, 242, 2770-022 PAÇO DE ARCOS **Tel:** 214 544 000 **Fax:** 214 698 547
Email: visao@edimpresa.pt **Web site:** http://www.visao.pt
ISSN: 0872-3540
Date Established: 2007; **Freq:** Occasional; **Cover Price:** Free; **Circ:** 110,700
Usual Pagination: 150
Language(s): Portuguese
Readership: National.
ADVERTISING RATES:
Full Page Colour .... EUR 5200
Mechanical Data: Type Area: 185 x 221 mm, Trim Size: 210 x 260 mm
BUSINESS: LOCAL GOVERNMENT, LEISURE & RECREATION: Leisure, Recreation & Entertainment

VISÃO 7 LISBOA E SUL
1784057P94X-711
Editorial: Edifício São Francisco de Sales, R. Calvet de Magalhães, 242, 2770-022 PAÇO DE ARCOS **Tel:** 214 544 000 **Fax:** 214 698 547
Email: visao@edimpresa.pt **Web site:** http://www.visao.pt
ISSN: 0872-3540
Freq: Weekly; **Cover Price:** Free; **Circ:** 107,000
Usual Pagination: 150
Profile: Publication dedicated to entertainment and leisure activities.
Language(s): Portuguese
Readership: National. General population.
ADVERTISING RATES:
Full Page Colour .... EUR 3120
Mechanical Data: Type Area: 185 x 221 mm, Trim Size: 210 x 260 mm
CONSUMER: OTHER CLASSIFICATIONS: Miscellaneous

VISÃO 7 PORTO E NORTE
1784058P94X-712
Editorial: R. Monte dos Burgos, 1080, Laveiras, 4250-314 PORTO **Tel:** 228 347 525 **Fax:** 228 347 557
Email: visao@edimpresa.pt **Web site:** http://www.visao.pt
ISSN: 0872-3540
Freq: Weekly; **Cover Price:** Free; **Circ:** 107,000
Usual Pagination: 150
Profile: Publication dedicated to leisure and entertainment. Characterized by sections such as cinema, expositions, music, theatre, dance, restaurants and night life, as well as articles targeted at children.
Language(s): Portuguese
Readership: National. General population.
ADVERTISING RATES:
Full Page Colour .... EUR 2080
Mechanical Data: Type Area: 185 x 221 mm, Trim Size: 210 x 260 mm
CONSUMER: OTHER CLASSIFICATIONS: Miscellaneous

VISÃO GOURMET
1784061P74P-336
Editorial: Edifício S. Francisco de Sales, R. Calvet de Magalhães, 242, 2770-022 PAÇO DE ARCOS
Tel: 214 698 045 **Fax:** 214 435 310
Email: visao@edimpresa.pt **Web site:** http://www.visaoonline.pt
Freq: Half-yearly; **Cover Price:** EUR 1,5; **Circ:** 105,425
Usual Pagination: 72
Managing Director: Cláudia Lobo
Profile: Published with: Visão.
Language(s): Portuguese
Readership: National.
ADVERTISING RATES:
Full Page Colour .... EUR 4200
Mechanical Data: Trim Size: 220 x 280 mm, Type Area: 188 x 252 mm

VOGUE
1643369P74A-105
Editorial: Av. João Crisóstomo, 72, Galeria, 1069-043 LISBOA **Tel:** 213 185 428 **Fax:** 213 540 695
Email: fatimaferreira@vogue.cofina.pt **Web site:** http://www.vogue.xl.pt
Freq: Monthly; **Cover Price:** EUR 3,5; **Circ:** 50,000
Editor: Susana Chaves; **Editor-in-Chief:** Patrícia Barnabé; **Managing Director:** Paula Mateus;
Advertising Manager: Fernanda Cal
Language(s): Portuguese
Readership: National.
ADVERTISING RATES:
Full Page Colour .... EUR 6700
Mechanical Data: Trim Size: 220 x 285 mm
CONSUMER: WOMEN'S INTEREST CONSUMER MAGAZINES: Women's Interest

VOLTA AO MUNDO
19790P89E-250
Editorial: Edifício Diário de Notícias, Av. da Liberdade, 266, 1°, 1250-149 LISBOA
Tel: 213 187 779 **Fax:** 213 187 344
Email: daniel.j.barata@globalnoticias.pt
Date Established: 1994; **Freq:** Monthly; **Cover Price:** EUR 3,8; **Circ:** 28,230
Editor: Paulo Rolão; **Executive Editor:** Paulo Farinha; **Managing Director:** José Jaime Costa
Profile: Magazine containing articles and reports covering travel and tourism, culture, geography, money matters relating to travel and radical sports.
Language(s): Portuguese
Readership: National.
ADVERTISING RATES:
Full Page Colour .... EUR 5080
Mechanical Data: Trim Size: 230 x 295 mm, Type Area: 220 x 285 mm
CONSUMER: HOLIDAYS & TRAVEL: Holidays

VOZ DA FÁTIMA
1784104P80-735
Editorial: Santuário de Fátima - Apartado 31, 2496-908 FÁTIMA **Tel:** 249 539 600 **Fax:** 249 539 605
Email: ccs@santuario-fatima.pt **Web site:** http://www.fatima.pt
Date Established: 1921; **Freq:** Monthly; **Cover Price:** EUR 5
Free to qualifying individuals ; **Circ:** 118,000
Usual Pagination: 8
Language(s): Portuguese
Readership: Read in Fátima region.
Mechanical Data: Type Area: 265 x 378 mm, Trim Size: 304 x 430 mm
CONSUMER: RURAL & REGIONAL INTEREST

A VOZ DA FIGUEIRA
1642481P72-163
Editorial: R. do Paço, 8, Apartado 2224, 3081-903 FIGUEIRA DA FOZ **Tel:** 233 422 272
Email: vozdafigueira@iol.pt **Web site:** http://www.avozdafigueira.pt
Date Established: 1953; **Freq:** Weekly; **Cover Price:** EUR 0,85; **Circ:** 16,100
Usual Pagination: 16
Managing Director: Isabel Carvalho
Profile: Weekly newspaper with information about Figueira da Foz. Politics, current affairs, society, religion, sport, entertainment and events.
Language(s): Portuguese
Readership: Read by Figueira da Foz locals.
ADVERTISING RATES:
Full Page Mono .... EUR 370
Full Page Colour .... EUR 460
Mechanical Data: Trim Size: 300 x 423 mm, Type Area: 261 x 355 mm
LOCAL NEWSPAPERS

A VOZ DA PÓVOA
1642482P72-164
Editorial: Av. Vasco da Gama - Galerias Recife, N° 523 - Loja 13, 4490-410 PÓVOA DE VARZIM
Tel: 252 614 038 **Fax:** 252 614 038
Email: geral@vozdapovoa.com **Web site:** http://www.vozdapovoa.com
Date Established: 1938; **Freq:** Weekly; **Cover Price:** EUR 0,8; **Circ:** 5,000
Usual Pagination: 16
Managing Director: Tomás Postiga
Profile: Weekly newspaper with information about Póvoa do Varzim. Politics, current affairs, society, religion, sport, entertainment and events.
Language(s): Portuguese
Readership: Read by Póvoa do Varzim locals.
ADVERTISING RATES:
Full Page Colour .... EUR 400
Mechanical Data: Trim Size: 242 x 336 mm, Type Area: 220 x 300 mm
LOCAL NEWSPAPERS

A VOZ DE LOULÉ
1642818P80-222
Editorial: R. Major Olival, Centro Comercial Charlot, Loja 12, 8100-000 LOULÉ **Tel:** 289 410 640
Fax: 289 410 649
Email: voz.loule@net.novis.pt
Date Established: 1952; **Freq:** 6 issues yearly;
Cover Price: EUR 1; **Circ:** 4,000
Usual Pagination: 24
Editor: Luís Guerreiro
Profile: Newspaper with information about Loulé. Politics, current affairs, society, religion, sport, entertainment and events.
Language(s): Portuguese
Readership: Read by Loulé locals.
ADVERTISING RATES:
Full Page Mono .... EUR 448.9
Full Page Colour .... EUR 648.4
Mechanical Data: Type Area: 260 x 360 mm, Trim Size: 288 x 410 mm
CONSUMER: RURAL & REGIONAL INTEREST

A VOZ DE TRÁS-OS-MONTES
1642490P72-16
Editorial: R. D. António Valente da Fonseca, 22, Apartado 212, 5001-911 VILA REAL **Tel:** 259 340 290
Fax: 259 340 299
Email: geral@avozdetrasosmontes.com **Web site:** http://www.avozdetrasosmontes.com
Date Established: 1947; **Freq:** Weekly; **Cover Price:** EUR 0,7; **Circ:** 6,500
Usual Pagination: 48
Profile: Weekly newspaper with information about Trás-os-Montes region. Politics, current affairs, society, sport, entertainment and events.
Language(s): Portuguese
Readership: Read in Trás-os-Montes region.
ADVERTISING RATES:
Full Page Mono .... EUR 403
Full Page Colour .... EUR 564.2
Mechanical Data: Type Area: 260 x 365 mm, Trim Size: 290 x 411 mm
LOCAL NEWSPAPERS

VOZ DO DÃO
1643374P80-246
Editorial: R. António da Costa, 3, Apartado 39, 3441-999 SANTA COMBA DÃO **Tel:** 232 888 358
Fax: 232 881 135
Email: geral@vozdodao.net **Web site:** http://www.vozdodao.net
Date Established: 1985; **Freq:** 26 issues yearly;
Cover Price: EUR 0,5; **Circ:** 2,000
Usual Pagination: 20
Managing Director: António Manuel de Sousa Guedes
Profile: Fortnightly newspaper with information about Viseu. Politics, current affairs, society, religion, sport, entertainment and events.
Language(s): Portuguese
Readership: Read in Viseu region.
ADVERTISING RATES:
Full Page Mono .... EUR 975
Full Page Colour .... EUR 1462.5
Mechanical Data: Trim Size: 278 x 392 mm, Type Area: 258 x 372 mm
CONSUMER: RURAL & REGIONAL INTEREST

WEEKEND
1784124P74Q-124
Editorial: Av. João Crisóstomo, 72 - 1°, 1069-043 LISBOA **Tel:** 213 180 900 **Fax:** 213 540 361
Email: info@negocios.pt **Web site:** http://www.jornaldenegocios.pt
ISSN: 0874-1360
Freq: Weekly; **Cover Price:** Free; **Circ:** 18,381
Usual Pagination: 32
Profile: Lifestyle magazine covering art, literature, politics, wine, gastronomy and tourism.
Language(s): Portuguese
Readership: National. Aimed at businessmen and investors.
Mechanical Data: Type Area: 257 x 336 mm, Trim Size: 280 x 370 mm
Part of Series, see entry for: Jornal de Negócios

ZOOM I.T.
623747P78R-50
Editorial: R. Policarpo Anjos, 4, 1495-742 CRUZ QUEBRADA/DAFUNDO **Tel:** 214 154 500
Fax: 214 154 504
Email: connect@motorpress.pt **Web site:** http://www.zoomit.pt
Date Established: 1998; **Freq:** Monthly; **Cover Price:** EUR 3,5; **Circ:** 12,500
Usual Pagination: 100
Managing Director: Valter Leandro
Profile: Magazine focusing on mobile telephones, contains product reports and model comparisons.
Language(s): Portuguese
Readership: Mailand. Read by people wishing to purchase a mobile phone. Aimed at young people (18-34) living in urban centers. Men 93%. Class A and B 43%, C1 and C2 50%.
ADVERTISING RATES:
Full Page Colour .... EUR 3650
Mechanical Data: Type Area: 179 x 251 mm, Trim Size: 207 x 280 mm
CONSUMER: CONSUMER ELECTRONICS: Consumer Electronics Related

ZOOT MAGAZINE
1784142P74B-141
Editorial: R. Rodrigues Faria, 103, Edifício 1, Espaço 1.15, 1300-501 LISBOA **Tel:** 213 142 800
Fax: 213 142 800
Email: andrea@zootmagazine.com **Web site:** http://www.zootmag.com
ISSN: 1646-4869
Freq: Seasonal; **Cover Price:** EUR 5; **Circ:** 10,000
Usual Pagination: 256
Editor: Ann Shenton; **Advertising Manager:** Andrea Probosch

Profile: Fashion and music are the main themes of this magazine that is produced in Portugal but written in English.
Language(s): English; Portuguese
Readership: International.
ADVERTISING RATES:
Full Page Colour .... EUR 2187
Mechanical Data: Trim Size: 230 x 300 mm, Type Area: 205 x 275 mm

Romania

Time Difference: GMT + 2 hrs (EET - Eastern European Time)
National Telephone Code: +40
Continent: Europe
Capital: Bucharest
Principal Language: Romanian, German, Hungarian
Population: 22329977
Monetary Unit: Leu (RON)

EMBASSY HIGH COMMISSION: Embassy of Romania: Arundel House, 4 Palace Green, London, W8 4QD
Tel: 020 7937 9666/8
Fax: 020 7937 8069
Email: roemb@roemb.co.uk, press@roemb.co.uk
Website: http://www.roemb.co.uk

ADEVARUL 1500098RO65A-5
Editorial: Şos. Fabrica de Glucoză, nr 21, Sector 2, BUCURESTI **Tel:** 21 40 77 609 **Fax:** 21 40 77 602
Email: redactia@adevarulonline.ro **Web site:** http://www.adevarul.ro
Date Established: 1989; **Freq:** Daily - Monday to Saturday; **Annual Sub.:** RON 230.00; **Circ:** 100,000
Usual Pagination: 24
Editor-in-Chief: Grigore Cartianu
Profile: Independent newspaper containing news and background information; covers national and international politics, economics, finance, society information, culture and sports.
Language(s): Romanian
Readership: Read by a broad spectrum of the population.
ADVERTISING RATES:
Full Page Mono .... RON 17000.00
Full Page Colour .... RON 26000.00
Mechanical Data: Type Area: 295 x 500mm, Col Widths (Display): 45mm, No. of Columns (Display): 6
Copy instructions: *Copy Date:* 7 days prior to publishing
Average ad content per issue: 30%
NATIONAL DAILY & SUNDAY NEWSPAPERS: National Daily Newspapers

AZI 1500152RO65A-10
Editorial: Calea Victoriei 39 A, O.P. 49, C.P. 45, Sector 1, 70101 BUCURESTI **Tel:** 21 31 41 998
Fax: 21 31 20 128
Email: redactie@azi.ro **Web site:** http://www.azi.ro
Freq: Daily - Published Monday to Saturday; **Annual Sub.:** RON 60.00; **Circ:** 20,000
Editor: Ana Mod; **Editor-in-Chief:** Ruxandra Negrea; **Advertising Manager:** Cristina Baden
Profile: Newspaper covering news, economics, politics, sports and culture.
Language(s): Romanian
Readership: Read by a broad spectrum of the public.
ADVERTISING RATES:
Full Page Colour .... EUR 1700.00
NATIONAL DAILY & SUNDAY NEWSPAPERS: National Daily Newspapers

BIZ 762769RO14A-3
Editorial: Str. Alexandru Moruzzi Voievod nr. 9C, Sector 4, BUCURESTI **Tel:** 31 060 12 17
Fax: 31 060 12 22
Email: biz@revistabiz.ro **Web site:** http://www.revistabiz.ro
ISSN: 1454-8380
Date Established: 2000; **Freq:** 24 issues yearly; **Annual Sub.:** RON 100.00; **Circ:** 23,000
Usual Pagination: 80
Advertising Manager: Giuseppina Burlui
Profile: Magazine about business, economics and finance.
Language(s): English; Romanian
Readership: Read by managers, aged 25 to 45 years.
ADVERTISING RATES:
Full Page Colour .... EUR 3700.00
BUSINESS: COMMERCE, INDUSTRY & MANAGEMENT

BUCATARIA DE AZI 1934529RO74P-1
Editorial: str. Buzesti nr. 85, et. 4-8, sector 1, 011013 BUCURESTI **Tel:** 31 225 87 00 **Fax:** 31 225 87 15
Email: office@sanomahearst.ro **Web site:** http://www.sanomahearst.ro/bucataria_de_azi.htm
Freq: Monthly; **Circ:** 80,000
Editor-in-Chief: Irina Stanescu; **Publisher:** Lucian Ionita
Profile: Bucataria de azi is a practical guide for recipes and information useful in any kitchen.
Language(s): Romanian
ADVERTISING RATES:
Full Page Colour .... EUR 2400.00
CONSUMER: WOMEN'S INTEREST CONSUMER MAGAZINES: Food & Cookery

BURSA 762629RO65A-12
Editorial: Popa Tatu Str. Nr. 71, Sector 1, 010804 BUCURESTI **Tel:** 21 31 54 356 **Fax:** 21 31 24 556
Email: office@bursa.ro **Web site:** http://www.bursa.ro
Freq: Daily - Published Monday - Friday; **Circ:** 23,000
Editor: Anca Stanciu; **Advertising Director:** Geanina Voda
Profile: Newspaper providing extensive financial, economical and business cover.
Language(s): English; Romanian
Readership: Read by people working in business, finance or politics.
ADVERTISING RATES:
Full Page Mono .... EUR 3450.00
Agency Commission: 15%
Mechanical Data: Col Length: 520 mm, Col Widths (Display): 44 mm, No. of Columns (Display): 8
Copy instructions: *Copy Date:* Ads may be delivered until 5 pm, three days prior to publication
NATIONAL DAILY & SUNDAY NEWSPAPERS: National Daily Newspapers

CAPITAL 1600598RO14A-5
Editorial: B-dul Dimitrie Pomeiu, Nr 6, Sector 2, 020337 BUCURESTI **Tel:** 21 20 30 802
Fax: 21 20 30 902
Email: secretariat@capital.ro **Web site:** http://www.capital.ro
Date Established: 1992; **Freq:** Weekly - Published on Thursday; **Annual Sub.:** RON 110.00; **Circ:** 48,000
Usual Pagination: 68
Editor-in-Chief: Iulian Bortos; **Advertising Director:** Mirela Muraru
Profile: Publication featuring Romanian and international business and economics.
Language(s): Romanian
Readership: Aimed at managers, entrepreneurs, economists and students.
ADVERTISING RATES:
Full Page Mono .... RON 18000.00
Full Page Colour .... RON 24000.00
Agency Commission: 36%
Mechanical Data: Type Area: 265 x 380mm, Trim Size: 314 x 420mm, Screen: 48, Col Length: 390mm, Page Width: 380mm
Average ad content per issue: 35%
Supplement(s): Capital Cluj - 52xY, Capital Constructii - 52xY, Capital Dosar Energie - 52xY, Capital Investitii Straine - 52xY, Gadget - 52xY
BUSINESS: COMMERCE, INDUSTRY & MANAGEMENT

CHIP COMPUTER & COMMUNICATIONS 714132RO5C-30
Formerly: CHIP Computer Magazine
Editorial: Str. N.D. Cocea, Nr. 12, 500010 BRASOV
Tel: 268 41 51 58 **Fax:** 268 41 87 28
Email: redactie@3dmc.ro **Web site:** http://www.chip.ro
ISSN: 1453-7079
Date Established: 1992; **Freq:** Monthly; **Cover Price:** EUR 2.10; **Circ:** 27,000
Usual Pagination: 30
Editor: Ionuţ Bălan
Profile: Magazine containing information on computing covering hardware, software, multimedia, Internet, computer security and programming.
Language(s): Romanian
Readership: Aimed at IT decision makers in companies and organisations, also read by people interested in computers.
ADVERTISING RATES:
Full Page Colour .... EUR 2800.00
Mechanical Data: Type Area: 210 x 297mm
BUSINESS: COMPUTERS & AUTOMATION: Professional Personal Computers

COTIDIANUL 1500160RO65A-13
Editorial: Casa Presei Libere corp A3, etaj 4, Sector 1, BUCURESTI **Tel:** 21 31 03 128 **Fax:** 21 31 03 129
Email: redactia@cotidianul.ro **Web site:** http://www.cotidianul.ro
ISSN: 1220-692X
Freq: Daily; **Annual Sub.:** RON 259.00; **Circ:** 12,000
Features Editor: Alexandra Badicioiu; **Editor-in-Chief:** Oana Stanciulescu
Profile: Newspaper featuring politics, economics, finance, social issues and culture.
Language(s): Romanian
Readership: Read mainly by graduates.
Mechanical Data: Type Area: 530 x 390mm
NATIONAL DAILY & SUNDAY NEWSPAPERS: National Daily Newspapers

CURIERUL NATIONAL 1500166RO65A-20
Editorial: Str. Cristian Popisteanu 2-4, Sector 1, 10024 BUCURESTI **Tel:** 21 59 95 500
Fax: 21 31 21 300
Email: office@curierulnational.ro **Web site:** http://www.curierulnational.ro
Freq: Daily - Published Monday to Saturday; **Circ:** 35,000
News Editor: Valentin Bolocan; **Executive Editor:** Dan Manea; **Editor-in-Chief:** Stefan Radeanu
Profile: Newspaper covering news and background information on politics, economics, finance, sports and culture.
Language(s): Romanian
Supplement(s): Ghid TV - 52xY
NATIONAL DAILY & SUNDAY NEWSPAPERS: National Daily Newspapers

DIVA 1936746RO74A-73
Editorial: Bd. Dimitrie Pompeiu nr. 6, sector 2, BUCURESTI **Tel:** 21 203 0953 **Fax:** 21 203 5631
Email: contact@divaonline.ro **Web site:** http://www.divaonline.ro
Date Established: 2008; **Freq:** Weekly; **Circ:** 70,000
Editor-in-Chief: Cristiana Constantinescu
Profile: DIVA is The first weekly glossy magazine, positioned on the people segment. DIVA's target group includes urban young women aged between 18 and 35 years old. From the editorial point of view, DIVA offers to its readers news about Romanian and international celebrities, stories about them and their life-style. DIVA combines in a dynamic, original and harmonious way news about show-biz stars, fashion trends, cosmetics and beauty up-to-dates.
Language(s): Romanian
CONSUMER: WOMEN'S INTEREST CONSUMER MAGAZINES: Women's Interest

FEMEIA DE AZI 1934520RO74A-61
Editorial: Str. Buzesti, nr. 85, et. 4-8, sector 1, 011013 BUCURESTI **Tel:** 31 225 87 00
Fax: 31 225 87 15
Email: office@sanomahearst.ro **Web site:** http://www.sanomahearst.ro/femeia_de_azi.htm
Freq: Weekly; **Circ:** 250,000
Usual Pagination: 40
Editor-in-Chief: Irina Stanescu; **Publisher:** Lucian Ionita
Profile: Magazine focusing on health and health food, beauty, fashion, diet and fitness.
Language(s): Romanian
ADVERTISING RATES:
Full Page Colour .... EUR 4200.00
CONSUMER: WOMEN'S INTEREST CONSUMER MAGAZINES: Women's Interest

GANDUL 1839727RO65A-38
Editorial: Piata Presei Libere nr.1, Corp A3-A4, Sector 1, BUCURESTI **Tel:** 21 20 53 125
Fax: 21 20 53 188
Email: redactia@gandul.info **Web site:** http://www.gandul.info
Date Established: 2005; **Freq:** Daily - Published Monday to Friday; **Cover Price:** RON 1.20
Annual Sub.: RON 216.00; **Circ:** 16,000
Usual Pagination: 32
Editor-in-Chief: Claudiu Pândaru
Profile: National newspaper targeting educated and serious people that have high expectations and desires and are interested in what happens daily around them.
Language(s): Romanian
ADVERTISING RATES:
Full Page Colour .... EUR 5500.00
Mechanical Data: Type Area: 315 x 480mm
Copy instructions: *Copy Date:* 3 days prior to publication
NATIONAL DAILY & SUNDAY NEWSPAPERS: National Daily Newspapers

LIBERTATEA 1202247RO65A-36
Editorial: Bulevardul Dimitrie Pompeiu nr. 6, Sector 2, 020337 BUCURESTI **Tel:** 21 20 35 646
Fax: 21 20 30 830
Email: redactie@libertatea.ro **Web site:** http://www.libertatea.ro
Freq: Daily - Published Monday to Saturday; **Cover Price:** RON 0.50; **Circ:** 320,000
Editor: Irinel Antoniu; **Editor-in-Chief:** Ana Nita; **Advertising Manager:** Diana Sarbu
Profile: Tabloid newspaper covering news, politics, sports, society and culture.
Language(s): Romanian
ADVERTISING RATES:
Full Page Mono .... RON 21000.00
Full Page Colour .... RON 30100.00
Average ad content per issue: 35%
Supplement(s): Libertatea Weekend 52xY.
NATIONAL DAILY & SUNDAY NEWSPAPERS: National Daily Newspapers

MAGAZINUL PROGRESIV 1928696RO53-1
Editorial: Bd. Iuliu Maniu nr.7, corp A, et.2, Sector 6, BUCURESTI **Tel:** 21 31 59 031 **Fax:** 21 31 59 029
Email: office@cmgromania.ro **Web site:** http://www.magazinulprogresiv.ro
Freq: Monthly; **Circ:** 26,000
Editor: Roxana Baciu
Profile: Magazine focusing on the retail and fast moving consumer goods sector in Romania.
Language(s): Romanian
Readership: Aimed at the top decision makers in retail and the distribution of food and non-food goods.
BUSINESS: RETAILING & WHOLESALING

PROTV MAGAZIN 1935135RO76C-3
Editorial: Strada Baratiei, nr. 31, Sector 3, BUCURESTI **Tel:** 31 82 56 282 **Fax:** 31 82 56 285
Email: protv_guide@mpg.ro **Web site:** http://www.protvmagazin.ro
Freq: Weekly - Published on Monday; **Cover Price:** Free; **Circ:** 180,000
Editor-in-Chief: Anca Alexandroaie
Profile: PROTV MAGAZIN is a Romanian TV guide with the highest number of pages, the widest public, the highest number of TV programs, the best recommendations and the most interesting contests with prizes for the readers.
Language(s): Romanian
ADVERTISING RATES:
Full Page Colour .... EUR 5000.00
CONSUMER: MUSIC & PERFORMING ARTS: TV & Radio

ROMANIA LIBERA 1500192RO65A-30
Editorial: Str. Nerva Traian nr. 3, bl. M 101, etaj 4, Sector 3, CP 031041, BUCURESTI **Tel:** 21 202 81 55
Fax: 21 202 81 68
Email: redactia@romanialibera.ro **Web site:** http://www.romanialibera.com
Date Established: 1877; **Freq:** Daily - Published Monday to Saturday; **Circ:** 47,000
Usual Pagination: 28
Editor: Iosif Klein Medesan; **Editor-in-Chief:** Dan Cristian Turturica
Profile: Newspaper covering news, politics, economics, sports and culture.
Language(s): Romanian
Readership: Aimed at readers aged between 30 and 50 years with medium to high income.
ADVERTISING RATES:
Full Page Mono .... EUR 2500.00
Full Page Colour .... EUR 4500.00
Supplement(s): Ghidul Auto - 52xY, Ghidul Financiar - 52xY, Timpul liber - 52xY
NATIONAL DAILY & SUNDAY NEWSPAPERS: National Daily Newspapers

TV MANIA 1936748RO76C-5
Editorial: Novo Parc - 6, Dimitrie Pompeiu Blvd., District 2, 020337 BUCURESTI **Tel:** 21 20 30 953
Fax: 21 20 35 624
Email: office@tvmania.ro **Web site:** http://www.tvmania.ro
Freq: Weekly; **Cover Price:** RON 1.79; **Circ:** 90,100
Editor-in-Chief: Ruxandra Dinca; **Advertising Manager:** Gabriel Geru
Profile: TV Mania is the weekly TV guide, funny and intelligent, dedicated to the young and active people. TV Mania readers get valuable guidance within the TV programs of a great number of channels; they won't miss any of the broadcasts they have an interest in as the magazine offers complete information in a well structured and easy to read way.
Language(s): Romanian
ADVERTISING RATES:
Full Page Colour .... RON 15500.00
CONSUMER: MUSIC & PERFORMING ARTS: TV & Radio

XTREMPC MAGAZINE 1615479RO5D-101
Editorial: Splaiul Unirii 74, Sector 4, BUCURESTI
Tel: 21 33 11 133 **Fax:** 21 33 01 055
Email: redactia@xtrempc.ro **Web site:** http://www.xtrempc.ro
Date Established: 1999; **Freq:** Monthly; **Annual Sub.:** RON 116.00; **Circ:** 25,000
Usual Pagination: 124
Editor-in-Chief: Dorian Prodan; **Advertising Manager:** Cristina Savu
Profile: Magazine focusing on multimedia, games, hardware, software and the Internet.
Language(s): Romanian
Readership: Aimed at PC enthusiasts of all levels.
Mechanical Data: Type Area: 280 x 287mm, Bleed Size: 283 x 290mm
BUSINESS: COMPUTERS & AUTOMATION: Personal Computers

ZIARUL FINANCIAR 762718RO65A-33
Editorial: Strada Baratiei, nr. 31, Sector 3, BUCURESTI **Tel:** 318 256 282 **Fax:** 318 256 285
Email: zf@zf.ro **Web site:** http://www.zf.ro
Freq: Daily - Published Monday to Friday; **Circ:** 17,000
Editor-in-Chief: Sorin Pislaru; **Advertising Manager:** Nicoleta Nedea
Profile: Newspaper covering news and background information on economics, finance, business and politics.
Language(s): English; Romanian
Readership: Aimed at people working in finance and business.

Romania

ADVERTISING RATES:
Full Page Mono .... EUR 4350.00
Full Page Colour .... EUR 6500.00
NATIONAL DAILY & SUNDAY NEWSPAPERS: National Daily Newspapers

ZIUA
1500249RO65A-35
Formerly: The Daily Ziua Newspaper
Editorial: Strada C-tin Mille numarul 17, Sector 1, BUCURESTI **Tel:** 21 31 59 111 **Fax:** 21 31 59 160
Email: ziua@ziua.ro **Web site:** http://www.ziua.net
Date Established: 1930; **Freq:** Daily - Published Monday to Saturday; **Cover Price:** EUR 0.12; **Circ:** 12,000
Editor: Eduard Ivascu; **Editor-in-Chief:** Roland Catalin Pena; **Publisher:** Mihai Palsu
Profile: Newspaper covering national and international news, politics, economics, sports and culture.
Language(s): Romanian
Readership: Read by a broad spectrum of the public.
NATIONAL DAILY & SUNDAY NEWSPAPERS: National Daily Newspapers

Russian Federation

Time Difference: GMT + 2 hrs West, + 12 hrs East
National Telephone Code: +7
Continent: Europe
Capital: Moscow
Principal Language: Russian
Population: 144526000
Monetary Unit: Rouble (RUR)

EMBASSY HIGH

COMMISSION: Embassy of the Russian Federation: 6/7 Kensington Palace Gardens, London, W8 4QS
Tel: 020 72 29 36 28
Fax: 020 72 78 625
Website: http://www.rusemblon.org
Email: office@rusemblon.org/
Head of Mission HE Sternik Alekandr

4ROOM:
1774161RU4A-11
Editorial: ul. Sadovaya 122, SANKT PETERBURG
Tel: 12 438 15 38 **Fax:** 12 346 06 65
Email: ru@finestreet.ru **Web site:** http://www.finestreet.ru
Freq: 10 issues yearly; **Circ:** 25,000
Usual Pagination: 50
Executive Editor: Nikolai Bavrin; **Editor-in-Chief:** Ksenia Bandorina
Profile: Consists of 4 components: architecture, interior, design and fashion.
Language(s): Russian
Readership: Professional business to business publication aimed at architects and interior designers.
Mechanical Data: Type Area: A3
BUSINESS: ARCHITECTURE & BUILDING: Architecture

4X4 CLUB
1774049RU77A-63
Editorial: ul. Krylatskaya 12, 121552 MOSKVA
Tel: 495 737 44 44 **Fax:** 495 959 78 28
Email: club4x4@club4x4.ru **Web site:** http://media.club4x4.ru
Freq: Monthly; **Circ:** 5,000
Usual Pagination: 498
Editor: Ivan Evdokimov; **Executive Editor:** Varvara Fesenko; **Advertising Manager:** Mikhail Shkolnikov; **Publisher:** Vladislav Artemov
Profile: Monthly magazine about 4 wheel drive cars, jeeps and their accessories.
Language(s): Russian
ADVERTISING RATES:
Full Page Colour .... RUR 164000.00
Mechanical Data: Type Area: A4
CONSUMER: MOTORING & CYCLING: Motoring

625-NET
624234RU5B-10
Editorial: Malaya Nikiskaya 4, P.O. Box 143, MOSKVA, 121069 **Tel:** 495 291 77 24
Fax: 495 202 95 88
Email: magazine@625-net.ru **Web site:** http://www.625-net.ru
Date Established: 1999; **Freq:** 10 issues yearly; **Circ:** 14,000
Editor: Michail Zhitomirskiy; **Publisher:** Alexey Shapurov
Profile: Magazine 625 is a periodical dedicated to TV professionals of broadcasting and post-production.
Language(s): Russian
Readership: Aimed at IT professionals.
BUSINESS: COMPUTERS & AUTOMATION: Data Processing

ABOK JOURNAL (VENTILATION, HEATING, AIR-CONDITIONING)
1616117RU3B-1
Editorial: ul. Rozhdestvenskaya 11, 103754 MOSKVA
Tel: 495 921 69 46 **Fax:** 495 921 69 46
Email: abok@abok.ru **Web site:** http://www.abok.ru
Date Established: 1990; **Freq:** 8 issues yearly; **Circ:** 12,000
Usual Pagination: 136
Editor: Maria Eroshko; **Editor-in-Chief:** Yuriy Tabunschikov; **Advertising Manager:** Oksana Svatinya
Profile: Journal focusing on development of energy efficient construction technologies in Russia and abroad. Covers engineering, regulatory and social problems in energy conservation, new equipment and materials.
Language(s): English; Russian
Readership: Aimed at professionals and officials of federal ministries and agencies.
Mechanical Data: Type Area: 205 x 290mm
BUSINESS: HEATING & VENTILATION: Industrial Heating & Ventilation

AD/ARCHITECTURAL DIGEST
1773990RU4B-2
Editorial: Bolshaya Dmitrovka 11, str. 7, 125009 MOSKVA **Tel:** 495 745 55 67 **Fax:** 495 777 00 25
Email: editorial@admagazine.ru **Web site:** http://www.admagazine.ru
Date Established: 2002; **Freq:** Monthly; **Annual Sub.:** RUR 1440.00; **Circ:** 60,000
Usual Pagination: 200
Advertising Director: Brigitte Klein; **Publisher:** Anna Phelkina
Profile: Russian edition of American Architectural Digest about interior design, modern architecture and trade events. Facebook: http://www.facebook.com/pages/AD-Russia/210150678657.
Language(s): Russian
ADVERTISING RATES:
Full Page Colour .... RUR 320000.00
Mechanical Data: Type Area: 213x277mm
Copy instructions: *Copy Date:* 30 days prior publication date
BUSINESS: ARCHITECTURE & BUILDING: Interior Design & Flooring

ADRESA PETERBURGA
1774522RU7-514
Editorial: P.O. Box 12, 192007 SANKT PETERBURG
Tel: 12 962 42 41 **Fax:** 12 962 42 47
Email: info@adresaspb.ru **Web site:** http://www.adresaspb.ru
Date Established: 2003; **Freq:** 6 issues yearly; **Circ:** 20,000
Usual Pagination: 112
Editor: Sergey Yaroshetsky
Profile: Provides information about arts, culture, history and interesting places to see in St. Petersburg.
Language(s): Russian
ADVERTISING RATES:
Full Page Colour .... RUR 79800.00
Mechanical Data: Type Area: 230 x 300mm
BUSINESS: ANTIQUES

AEROFLOT
1774419RU89D-6
Editorial: ul. Valovaya 28, 115054 MOSKVA
Tel: 495 690 82 55
Web site: http://www.aeroflot.ru/templates/polet/magazine_9_2009_p.html
Freq: Monthly; **Cover Price:** Free; **Circ:** 100,000
Usual Pagination: 240
Advertising Director: Vera Kosyakova
Profile: Full-colour glossy magazine carrying news and entertainment articles typical for a high quality lifestyle edition intended for well-off consumers.
Language(s): English; Russian
ADVERTISING RATES:
Full Page Colour .... RUR 370000.00
Mechanical Data: Type Area: 212 x 276mm
CONSUMER: HOLIDAYS & TRAVEL: In-Flight Magazines

AEROFLOT PREMIUM
1600055RU89D-5
Editorial: ul. Valovaya 28, 115054 MOSKVA
Tel: 495 690 82 55
Web site: http://www.timeout.ru/aeroflot
Date Established: 2007; **Freq:** Monthly; **Cover Price:** Free; **Circ:** 20,000
Usual Pagination: 132
Editor-in-Chief: Yury Khnychkin; **Advertising Director:** Vera Kosyakova; **Publisher:** Pavel Zhezhel
Profile: Official in-flight magazine for business-class passengers flying with Aeroflot-Russian Airline.
Language(s): English; Russian
ADVERTISING RATES:
Full Page Colour .... RUR 380000.00
Agency Commission: 15%
Mechanical Data: Print Process: Offset, Trim Size: 264 x 210mm, Type Area: 212 x 276mm
Copy instructions: *Copy Date:* 4 weeks prior to publication date
Average ad content per issue: 40%
CONSUMER: HOLIDAYS & TRAVEL: In-Flight Magazines

AEROJETSTYLE
1774495RU6R-3
Editorial: ul. Kosmonavtov 18, korp. 2, 4 floor, office 4, 129301 MOSKVA **Tel:** 495 686 44 03
Fax: 495 686 57 30
Email: info@aerojetstyle.ru **Web site:** http://www.aerojetstyle.ru
Freq: Monthly; **Circ:** 20,000
Usual Pagination: 20
Editor: Sergey Lelekov; **Editor-in-Chief:** Alexander Omelchenko; **Advertising Manager:** Elizaveta Vlasova
Profile: Informative-analytical publication on business aviation, types of planes and their characteristics.
Language(s): Russian
ADVERTISING RATES:
Full Page Colour $2100.00
Mechanical Data: Type Area: 297 x 413mm
BUSINESS: AVIATION & AERONAUTICS: Aviation Related

AFISHA MIR
1896312RU89A-4
Editorial: Bolshoi Gnezdnikovski per. 7/28, str. 1, 125009 MOSKVA **Tel:** 495 785 17 00
Fax: 495 785 17 00
Email: travel@afisha.ru **Web site:** http://www.afisha.ru/magazine/afisha_mir
Freq: Monthly; **Circ:** 95,000
Managing Editor: Dmitri Beglyarov; **Advertising Director:** Inna Ovcharova
Profile: Monthly travel and lifestyle magazine with travel information and hundreds of vacation ideas, expert advice, opinions and facts.
Language(s): Russian
ADVERTISING RATES:
Full Page Colour .... RUR 510000.00
Mechanical Data: Type Area: 230x290mm
CONSUMER: HOLIDAYS & TRAVEL: Travel

AGRONOVOSTI
1774543RU21A-1
Editorial: ul. Chernyshevskogo 153, office 307, 410028 SARATOV **Tel:** 452 23 43 82
Fax: 452 23 83 14
Email: agronovosti@agro-bursa.ru **Web site:** http://www.agro-bursa.ru
Date Established: 2003; **Freq:** Weekly - Published on Mondays; **Annual Sub.:** RUR 863.76; **Circ:** 1,000
Usual Pagination: 6
Editor: Elena Vishnevskaya; **Advertising Manager:** Anastasiya Gorbyleva
Profile: Publication focused on agricultural issues.
Language(s): Russian
Readership: Aimed at farmers, agricultural managers and directors.
ADVERTISING RATES:
Full Page Mono .... RUR 35647.80
Mechanical Data: Type Area: 265 x 380mm
BUSINESS: AGRICULTURE & FARMING

AGROPROFI
1774644RU21A-5
Editorial: 2 Zvenigorodskaya ul. 2/1, 123100 MOSKVA **Tel:** 495 748 01 03 **Fax:** 495 748 01 03
Email: gleb@prph.ru **Web site:** http://agro-profi.ru
Freq: 6 issues yearly; **Annual Sub.:** RUR 4039.00; **Circ:** 6,000
Usual Pagination: 64
Editor-in-Chief: Elena Tkachenko; **Advertising Manager:** Olesya Proshenko
Profile: Professional magazine on newest technologies in plants' growing, cattle and livestock, agricultural management.
Language(s): Russian
Readership: Targets agricultural managers, agronomists, agro technicians, farm directors.
ADVERTISING RATES:
Full Page Colour .... EUR 1900.00
Mechanical Data: Type Area: 215x275mm
BUSINESS: AGRICULTURE & FARMING

AIF MOSKVA
763181RU82-10
Editorial: For all contact details see main record, Argumenty i Fakty **Tel:** 495 221 74 20
Fax: 495 925 61 82
Email: moskva@aif.ru **Web site:** http://www.aif.ru
Freq: Weekly - Published on Wednesday; **Circ:** 680,000
Editor: Roza Sargazieva; **Editor-in-Chief:** Nikolay Zyatkov; **Advertising Manager:** Aleksandr Avruh
Profile: Magazine featuring in-depth analysis of the latest events in Russian politics, economics and culture. Includes interviews with leading Russian politicians, businessmen, economists and artists.
Language(s): Russian
Readership: Aimed at those interested in current affairs.
ADVERTISING RATES:
Full Page Mono .... RUR 690000.00
Mechanical Data: Type Area: 265 x 367mm
Supplement to: Argumenty i Fakty
CONSUMER: CURRENT AFFAIRS & POLITICS

AIRUNION MAGAZINE
1774406RU89D-7
Editorial: Novodanilovskaya nab. 4a, 117105 MOSKVA **Tel:** 495 510 22 11 **Fax:** 495 510 49 69
Email: air@spn.ru **Web site:** http://www.spn.ru/publishing/journals/airunion
Date Established: 2006; **Freq:** Monthly; **Cover Price:** Free; **Circ:** 80,000
Editor-in-Chief: Irina Tiusonina; **Advertising Director:** Aleksey Ivanov
Profile: A glossy news and entertaining edition distributed free of charge on all AiRUnion flights.
Language(s): English; Russian
ADVERTISING RATES:
Full Page Colour .... RUR 255000.00
Mechanical Data: Type Area: 212 x 276mm
CONSUMER: HOLIDAYS & TRAVEL: In-Flight Magazines

AMBITSII
1774709RU14A-20
Editorial: P.O. Box 3, 129626 MOSKVA
Tel: 495 786 43 41 **Fax:** 495 789 37 80
Email: info@ambicii.com **Web site:** http://www.ambicii.com
Date Established: 1991; **Freq:** 10 issues yearly; **Circ:** 17,000
Usual Pagination: 76
Editor-in-Chief: Igor Tsykunov; **Advertising Director:** Nataliya Shagiakhmetova
Profile: Professional magazine about usage of psychological technologies in business and politics, PR and marketing campaigns.
Language(s): Russian
Mechanical Data: Type Area: 180 x 245mm
BUSINESS: COMMERCE, INDUSTRY & MANAGEMENT

AMCHAM NEWS
752651RU14A-2
Editorial: ul. Dolgorukovskaya 7, 14 Etage, Sadovaya Plaza, 127006 MOSKVA **Tel:** 495 961 21 41
Fax: 495 961 21 42
Email: info@amcham.ru **Web site:** http://www.amcham.ru
Freq: 6 issues yearly; **Circ:** 15,000
Profile: Provides authoritative analysis by member companies on the Russian economy and investment environment, outlines the Chamber's opinions on issues affecting its members and highlights salient information from conferences, forums and speaker events organized by the Chamber.
Language(s): English
Readership: Read by managers and executives of American companies in Russia.
ADVERTISING RATES:
Full Page Mono $1700.00
Full Page Colour $1900.00
Mechanical Data: Type Area: 270mm x 205mm
BUSINESS: COMMERCE, INDUSTRY & MANAGEMENT

APK-INFORM RUSSIA
1821870RU21A-3
Editorial: 1/60 Lev Tolstoi str., 305004 KURSK
Tel: 495 78 94 419 **Fax:** 495 78 94 419
Email: info@apk-inform.ru **Web site:** http://www.apk-inform.com
Freq: Monthly; **Annual Sub.:** $972.00; **Circ:** 2,000
Profile: Informative-analytical magazine on the market of grains, oilseeds and by-products in Russia, the CIS countries and world.
Language(s): Russian
Readership: Producers of grains and oilseeds, processors, traders, investment companies, banks, consulting agencies of Russia the CIS countries, world.
ADVERTISING RATES:
Full Page Mono $135.00
Full Page Colour $396.00
BUSINESS: AGRICULTURE & FARMING

APTEKAR'
1774627RU37-1
Editorial: ul. Profsoyuznaya 57, 117420 MOSKVA
Tel: 495 786 25 41 **Fax:** 495 334 22 55
Email: info@aptekarjournal.com **Web site:** http://www.aptekarjournal.com
Date Established: 2006; **Freq:** Monthly; **Circ:** 36,000
Usual Pagination: 72
Profile: Professional magazine about news in pharmacy and applied medicine.
Language(s): Russian
ADVERTISING RATES:
Full Page Colour $3950.00
Mechanical Data: Type Area: 168 x 240mm
BUSINESS: PHARMACEUTICAL & CHEMISTS

ARCHIDOM
1938325RU4A-12
Editorial: ul. Davydkovskaya 12, str. 3, 115184 MOSKVA **Tel:** 495 445 10 65 **Fax:** 495 445 10 83
Email: info@archidom.ru **Web site:** http://www.archidom.ru
Freq: 8 issues yearly; Free to qualifying individuals ; **Circ:** 40,000
Profile: Magazine on architecture and design, covering residential and public places interiors, events in the world of architecture and design, furniture, materials, accessories, new interiors of cafe, restaurants, cinemas and shops in Moscow and Saint Petersburg.
Language(s): Russian
Readership: Targets architects and designers, representatives of Russian Art, influential businessmen and politicians.
ADVERTISING RATES:
Full Page Colour .... EUR 6120.00
BUSINESS: ARCHITECTURE & BUILDING: Architecture

ARGUMENTI NEDELI
1774341RU65J-67
Editorial: pr. Aeroporta 11, 125167 MOSKVA
Tel: 495 981 68 36 **Fax:** 495 981 68 36
Email: argumenti@argumenti.ru **Web site:** http://www.argumenti.ru
Freq: Weekly - Published on Thursdays; **Annual Sub.:** RUR 851.00; **Circ:** 570,000
Usual Pagination: 48
Editor: Andrey Uglanov
Profile: Publication focused political analysis and social issues, business and economical developments.
Language(s): Russian
ADVERTISING RATES:
Full Page Mono .... RUR 240000.00
Mechanical Data: Type Area: 259 x 364mm
NATIONAL DAILY & SUNDAY NEWSPAPERS: National Weekly Newspapers

ARGUMENTY I FAKTY
763185RU65J-65
Editorial: ul.Elektrozavodskaya 42, str. 4, Business centre LeFort, 107996 MOSKVA **Tel:** 495 646 57 57
Fax: 495 646 47 03
Email: novosti@aif.ru **Web site:** http://www.aif.ru
Date Established: 1978; **Freq:** Weekly - Published on Wednesday; **Circ:** 2,700,000
Usual Pagination: 26
Editor: Roza Sargazieva; **Editor-in-Chief:** Nikolay Zyatkov
Profile: Weekly national newspaper featuring politics, economics, culture and arts.
Language(s): Russian
Readership: Aimed at those interested in current affairs.
ADVERTISING RATES:
Full Page Mono .... RUR 2450000.00
Mechanical Data: Type Area: 265 x 3767mm
Supplement(s): Aif Moskva - 52xY, AiF. Na Dache - 24xY
NATIONAL DAILY & SUNDAY NEWSPAPERS: National Weekly Newspapers

ART GOROD
1774515RU84A-3
Editorial: P.O. Box 531, 190000 SANKT PETERBURG **Tel:** 12 320 29 98 **Fax:** 12 702 77 35
Email: office@artcitiez.com **Web site:** http://www.artcitiez.com
Date Established: 2003; **Freq:** Quarterly; **Circ:** 3,000
Usual Pagination: 112
Profile: Publication focused on modern art, interviews with artists and designers, news of city art culture.
Language(s): Russian
Mechanical Data: Type Area: A4
CONSUMER: THE ARTS & LITERARY: Arts

AUDIT I NALOGOOBLOZHENIYE
1774287RU1M-1
Editorial: ul. Prechistenka 10, str. 1, office 49, 119034 MOSKVA **Tel:** 495 766 91 08
Fax: 499 766 92 21
Email: ain@complat.ru **Web site:** http://www.auditpress.ru
Date Established: 1993; **Freq:** Monthly; **Circ:** 5,500
Usual Pagination: 48
Editor: Anatoly Zaichenko
Profile: Publication focusing on taxation, accountancy and auditing.
Language(s): Russian
ADVERTISING RATES:
Full Page Mono .... RUR 10000.00
Mechanical Data: Type Area: 141 x 225mm
BUSINESS: FINANCE & ECONOMICS: Taxation

AUTOBUSINESS
1774668RU77A-62
Editorial: P. O. Box 79, 603022 NIZHNIY NOVGOROD **Tel:** 31 464 02 98 **Fax:** 31 434 53 94
Email: abiz@abiz.ru **Web site:** http://www.abiz.ru
Freq: 10 issues yearly; **Annual Sub.:** RUR 720.00; **Circ:** 20,000
Editor: Aleksandr L. Kozlov
Profile: Analytical publication on motoring business with economic statistics of countries and industries, on enterprises (Russian and foreign), on production volumes and legislation.
Language(s): Russian
Readership: Targets managerial and executive staff (directors, heads of strategic and operative marketing departments, finalists, etc) of automobile industry (and related industries) enterprises.
ADVERTISING RATES:
Full Page Colour .... EUR 5000.00
Mechanical Data: Type Area: 210x297mm
CONSUMER: MOTORING & CYCLING: Motoring

AVIAGLOBUS
1774284RU6A-2
Editorial: Sheremetevo, P.O. Box Aviaglobus, 141426 KHIMKI **Tel:** 495 518 63 81
Fax: 495 57 84 320
Email: pr@aviaglobus.ru **Web site:** http://www.aviaglobus.ru
Date Established: 1998; **Freq:** Monthly; **Cover Price:** RUR 140.00; **Circ:** 3,000
Usual Pagination: 40
Editor: Mikhail Puchenkin; **Advertising Manager:** Larisa Skripaleva
Profile: Informative-analytical publication focusing on problems in the aviation industry, aviation achievements and aviation carrier market.
Language(s): Russian
BUSINESS: AVIATION & AERONAUTICS

AVIATRANSPORTNOYE OBOZRENIYE
1774227RU6A-4
Editorial: P.O. Box 127, 119048 MOSKVA
Tel: 495 626 53 56 **Fax:** 495 933 02 97
Email: als@ato.ru **Web site:** http://www.ato.ru
Date Established: 1996; **Freq:** 10 issues yearly; **Annual Sub.:** RUR 2700.00; **Circ:** 5,000
Usual Pagination: 120
Editor-in-Chief: Aleksey Sinitsky; **Advertising Director:** Konstantin Rogov
Profile: Provides timely and objective business information on conditions and developments of civil aviation in Russia, CIS and rest of the world.
Language(s): Russian
Readership: Read by managers of Russian and CIS airlines, government authorities, industry suppliers and financial community, top executives of airlines, investment analysts and international consulting companies.
Mechanical Data: Type Area: A4
BUSINESS: AVIATION & AERONAUTICS

AVTOMIR
1600449RU77A-50
Editorial: Ulica Polkovaya, Dom 3, Stroenie 4, 127018 MOSKVA **Tel:** 495 797 98 53
Fax: 495 257 11 89
Email: automir@burda.ru **Web site:** http://www.burda.ru
Date Established: 1998; **Freq:** Weekly; **Annual Sub.:** $140.00; **Circ:** 140,000
Usual Pagination: 84
Editor-in-Chief: Viktor Fomin; **Advertising Manager:** Vyacheslav Breev Beniminovich; **Advertising Director:** Aleksandr Rudnev Vasilevich; **Publisher:** Denis Sedyakin
Profile: Car magazine, includes reviews of new models, test reports and general motoring information.
Language(s): Russian
Readership: Aimed at men aged 20 to 45 years.
ADVERTISING RATES:
Full Page Colour .... RUR 235000.00
Agency Commission: 15%
Mechanical Data: Screen: 60 lpc, Print Process: Offset, Type Area: 210 x 280mm
Copy instructions: *Copy Date:* 3 weeks prior to publication date
CONSUMER: MOTORING & CYCLING: Motoring

AVTOMOBILI
1774105RU77A-55
Editorial: MOSKVA **Tel:** 495 685 58 58
Fax: 495 685 58 58
Email: secretary@automobili.ru **Web site:** http://www.automobili.ru
Freq: Monthly; **Circ:** 150,000
Usual Pagination: 160
Editor: Andrey Dronin; **Advertising Manager:** Igor Kobenko
Profile: Magazine on cars, their comparison and testing, car accessories.
Language(s): Russian
ADVERTISING RATES:
Full Page Colour .... RUR 20000.00
Mechanical Data: Type Area: 220 x 297mm
CONSUMER: MOTORING & CYCLING: Motoring

AVTOMOBILI I TSENY
1774155RU77A-61
Editorial: Khoeroshevskoye shosse 32a, 123003 MOSKVA **Tel:** 495 940 18 97
Email: car@d-mir.ru **Web site:** http://auto.dmir.ru
Freq: Weekly; **Circ:** 110,000
Usual Pagination: 700
Editor: Oleg Ilyin
Profile: Each issue contains information on Moscow market car offers, other vehicles, spare parts, joint products and services.
Language(s): Russian
Readership: Targets private individuals living in Moscow and Russian regions interested in purchasing cars, spare parts and joint services in Moscow.
ADVERTISING RATES:
Full Page Colour .... RUR 78700.00
Mechanical Data: Type Area: A4, Trim Size: 210x265mm
CONSUMER: MOTORING & CYCLING: Motoring

AVTOPARK
1774404RU77A-58
Editorial: Novodanilovskaya nab. 4a, 117105 MOSKVA **Tel:** 495 510 22 11 **Fax:** 495 510 49 69
Email: niva@omskprint.ru **Web site:** http://www.park5.ru
Freq: 9 issues yearly; **Circ:** 20,000
Usual Pagination: 128
Executive Editor: Andrey Mashnin; **Editor-in-Chief:** Sergey Zhukov; **Advertising Director:** Anna Larina
Profile: Professional publication on commercial auto transport, car truck logistics, segments of the market and its developments.
Language(s): Russian
ADVERTISING RATES:
Full Page Colour .... RUR 178500.00
Mechanical Data: Type Area: 225x300mm
CONSUMER: MOTORING & CYCLING: Motoring

AVTOPILOT
1611068RU77A-51
Editorial: ul. Vrubelya dom 4, str. 1, 125080 MOSKVA
Tel: 495 943 97 50 **Fax:** 495 797 69 85
Email: autopilot@kommersant.ru **Web site:** http://autopilot.kommersant.ru
Freq: Monthly; **Circ:** 65,000
Editor: Nikolay Fomenko; **Executive Editor:** Igor Maltsev; **Advertising Manager:** Galina Kutepova; **Advertising Director:** Tatyana Pchelina
Profile: Magazine focusing on motoring includes car tests and car comparisons, expert advice and price guides.
Language(s): Russian
Readership: Aimed at motoring enthusiasts.
ADVERTISING RATES:
Full Page Mono .... RUR 207000.00
Agency Commission: 15%
Mechanical Data: Type Area: 206 x 125mm
CONSUMER: MOTORING & CYCLING: Motoring

BANKOVSKIYE TEKHNOLOGII
1774534RU1C-1
Editorial: ul. Klary Tsetkin 33, korpus 24, 125130 MOSKVA **Tel:** 495 601 92 08 **Fax:** 495 741 09 46
Email: info@finans-m.ru **Web site:** http://www.finans-m.ru
Date Established: 1994; **Freq:** Monthly; **Annual Sub.:** RUR 6000.00; **Circ:** 4,000
Usual Pagination: 80
Profile: Focused on implementation of new IT technologies in financial institutions, banking business and banking automation.
Language(s): Russian
Mechanical Data: Type Area: A3
BUSINESS: FINANCE & ECONOMICS: Banking

BANZAI
1774497RU86C-11
Editorial: ul. Uralskaya 3, office 8, YEKATERINBURG
Tel: 343 216 37 37 **Fax:** 343 216 37 38
Email: info@banzay.ru **Web site:** http://www.banzay.ru
Date Established: 2001; **Freq:** 11 issues yearly; **Circ:** 208,000
Usual Pagination: 152
Editor: Alexey Bogach; **Executive Editor:** Viktor Stepanov
Profile: Magazine for men providing information on politics, travel, cars, entertainment, girls.
Language(s): Russian
ADVERTISING RATES:
Full Page Colour .... RUR 48000.00
Mechanical Data: Type Area: A4
CONSUMER: ADULT & GAY MAGAZINES: Men's Lifestyle Magazines

BDI
1774006RU54B-1
Editorial: 16 Linia 7, office 86, 199034 SANKT PETERBURG **Tel:** 12 327 99 50 **Fax:** 12 327 99 20
Email: bdi@bdi.spb.ru **Web site:** http://www.bdi.spb.ru
Date Established: 1993; **Freq:** 6 issues yearly; Free to qualifying individuals ; **Circ:** 12,000
News Editor: Natalia Shkeneva; **Editor-in-Chief:** Valery Kislov
Profile: Magazine about work safety and security (data protection, physical security, security and safety devices, and fire protection).
Language(s): Russian
BUSINESS: SAFETY & SECURITY: Safety

BELYI BIZNES
1774181RU14A-25
Editorial: 11a Verhnyaya Krasnoselskaya str., Office 4, 107140 MOSKVA **Tel:** 495 666 32 62
Fax: 495 666 32 62
Email: info@bb-online.ru **Web site:** http://www.bb-online.ru
Freq: 10 issues yearly; **Cover Price:** RUR 352.00; **Circ:** 5,000
Usual Pagination: 80
Editor: Olga Redkina; **Executive Editor:** Evgeniya Osipova; **Editor-in-Chief:** Tatiana Ryutina
Profile: Magazine about business processes, business management and developments, newest technologies, analysis of the situation on Russian construction market, interaction between business and government.
Language(s): Russian
Readership: Aimed at specialists of Russian real estate and construction market and experts involved in decision-making related to project investment, advancement of crediting lines to developers and cooperation with development companies.
ADVERTISING RATES:
Full Page Mono .... RUR 117600.00
Mechanical Data: Type Area: 210 x 265mm
BUSINESS: COMMERCE, INDUSTRY & MANAGEMENT

BILLBOARD (RUSSIAN EDITION)
1774266RU76D-2
Editorial: ul. Nizhnyaya Krasnoselskaya 40/12, office 604, 105066 MOSKVA **Tel:** 495 620 49 58
Fax: 495 229 62 01
Email: info@billboard-magazine.ru **Web site:** http://www.billboard-magazine.ru
Freq: Monthly; **Annual Sub.:** RUR 1584.00; **Circ:** 25,000
Usual Pagination: 128
Editor: Ilya Buts; **Advertising Manager:** Evgeniy Fomichyov; **Advertising Director:** Oksana Deresh
Profile: Magazine about music industry and show business.
Language(s): Russian
ADVERTISING RATES:
Full Page Colour .... RUR 140000.00
Mechanical Data: Type Area: 280x342mm
CONSUMER: MUSIC & PERFORMING ARTS: Music

BIRZHA TRUDA
1774517RU88C-2
Editorial: ul. Aleksandra Nevskogo 12, 191167 SANKT PETERBURG **Tel:** 12 320 54 84
Fax: 12 271 02 86
Email: bt@ev.spb.ru **Web site:** http://www.birzha-truda.spb.ru
Date Established: 1992; **Freq:** 104 issues yearly - Published on Mondays and Thursdays; **Annual Sub.:** RUR 941.40; **Circ:** 25,000
Usual Pagination: 88
Editor: Nataliaya Tsvetkova; **Advertising Manager:** Svetlana Albova
Profile: Newspaper for jobseekers and recruiters.
Language(s): Russian
ADVERTISING RATES:
Full Page Mono .... RUR 5664.00
Mechanical Data: Type Area: 260 x 346mm
CONSUMER: EDUCATION: Careers

BIZNES OBOZRENIYE
1774547RU14A-23
Editorial: Novodanilovskaya nab. 4a, 117105 MOSKVA **Tel:** 495 411 86 08 **Fax:** 495 788 84 52
Email: bo@ex.ru **Web site:** http://www.bo.ex.ru
Date Established: 2002; **Freq:** Monthly; **Circ:** 30,000
Usual Pagination: 96
Editor-in-Chief: Aleksey Yashin
Profile: Provided up-to-date and detailed information on business issues, economics ratings and analytical materials.
Language(s): Russian
ADVERTISING RATES:
Full Page Mono .... RUR 110000.00
Mechanical Data: Type Area: A3
BUSINESS: COMMERCE, INDUSTRY & MANAGEMENT

BIZNES ZHURNAL
1774335RU1A-31
Editorial: 2 Roschinsky proyezd 8, 115419 MOSKVA
Tel: 495 633 14 24 **Fax:** 495 956 23 85
Email: info@b-mag.ru **Web site:** http://www.business-magazine.ru
Date Established: 2002; **Freq:** 24 issues yearly; **Circ:** 225,000
Usual Pagination: 120
Profile: Publication focused on financial and business issues, marketing and promoting of commercial activities in Russia.
Language(s): Russian
ADVERTISING RATES:
Full Page Colour .... RUR 473000.00
Mechanical Data: Type Area: 205x270mm
BUSINESS: FINANCE & ECONOMICS

BLIKI
1774059RU14A-19
Editorial: ul. Klary Tsetkin 33, korpus 24, 125130 MOSKVA **Tel:** 495 601 92 08 **Fax:** 495 601 92 09
Email: secretar@profi-press.ru **Web site:** http://www.blikimag.ru
Freq: Quarterly; **Circ:** 12,000
Usual Pagination: 112
Editor-in-Chief: Anastasiya Salomeeva
Profile: Aiming at businesswomen, successfully achieved top career positions, focuses on business ladies image, career, ideas and lifestyle.
Language(s): Russian
Mechanical Data: Type Area: 220 x 290mm
BUSINESS: COMMERCE, INDUSTRY & MANAGEMENT

BOLSHOY BUSINESS
1774392RU14A-24
Editorial: Zvezdny bulvar 21, str.3, office 406, 129085 MOSKVA **Tel:** 495 616 25 75
Email: zaitseva@astrel.ru **Web site:** http://www.bolshoybusiness.ru
Date Established: 2003; **Freq:** 10 issues yearly; **Circ:** 55,000
Usual Pagination: 160
Editor-in-Chief: Sergey Tsekhmistrenko; **Advertising Director:** Tamara Shafranova
Profile: Business monthly with analytical articles on world economics, its tendencies of development, experts' advice and overview of major business sectors of Russia.
Language(s): Russian
BUSINESS: COMMERCE, INDUSTRY & MANAGEMENT

BOSS
1774041RU14A-18
Editorial: Armyansky pereulok 9, korpus 1, str. 1, office 505, 101000 MOSKVA **Tel:** 495 789 32 93
Fax: 495 628 70 12
Email: nastyas@profi-press.ru **Web site:** http://www.bossmag.ru
Freq: Monthly; **Circ:** 10,000
Usual Pagination: 112
Editor-in-Chief: Alexander Polyansky; **Advertising Director:** Borislav Aidimirov
Profile: Publication featuring management issues, business and new technologies, new strategies and economics reviews.

Language(s): Russian
ADVERTISING RATES:
Full Page Colour $3500.00
Mechanical Data: Type Area: 190 x 253mm
BUSINESS: COMMERCE, INDUSTRY & MANAGEMENT

BRAND MANAGEMENT
1774001RU2A-11
Editorial: 2 Hutorskaya 38a, str.15, 127287 MOSKVA
Tel: 495 787 51 73 **Fax:** 495 787 51 74
Email: mail@grebennikov.ru **Web site:** http://www.grebennikov.ru
Date Established: 2001; **Freq:** 6 issues yearly;
Cover Price: RUR 1885.00
Annual Sub.: RUR 10200.00; **Circ:** 2,000
Usual Pagination: 64
Executive Editor: Tatiana Volkova; **Editor-in-Chief:** Vladimir Domnin
Profile: Magazine focusing on trade marks and brand management, companies' brand strategies and global branding.
Language(s): Russian
Mechanical Data: Type Area: A3
BUSINESS: COMMUNICATIONS, ADVERTISING & MARKETING

BRITISH STYLE
1774578RU74Q-6
Editorial: bld. 5/1, proezd Solomennoi, Storozhki, 125206 MOSKVA **Tel:** 495 772 20 44
Fax: 495 979 69 21
Email: info@british-style.ru **Web site:** http://www.british-style.ru
ISSN: 1742-2388
Date Established: 2004; **Freq:** Quarterly; **Cover Price:** RUR 200.00
Annual Sub.: RUR 800.00; **Circ:** 25,000
Usual Pagination: 112
Editor: Andrey Kharchenko
Profile: British Style magazine unites thousands of those who share a fascination with Britain, and strive to get a deeper understanding of its history and culture, get to know its traditions and tourism potential, explore benefits of quality British education, discover every facet of famed UK lifestyle, adopt experience, style and spirit of Britain's famous peoplethat achieved success and fame both in their home country and abroad.
Language(s): Russian
Readership: Targets directors of British Companies' representative offices in Russia, Russian Companies specializing in Finance and Investment, Banking and International Trade, members of international Business Associations and elite clubs, Art and Show-business Newsmakers, customers of elite British automobile brands, fashionable restaurants, golf-clubs, interior salons etc.; business-class passengers travelling from Sheremetyevo and Domodedovo, etc.
ADVERTISING RATES:
Full Page Colour £2500.00
Mechanical Data: Bleed Size: 240 x 290mm, Trim Size: 230 x 280mm
CONSUMER: WOMEN'S INTEREST CONSUMER MAGAZINES: Lifestyle

BROADCASTING
1814054RU2D-51
Editorial: 3-Magistralnaya ulitsa 30, P. O. Box 82, 123007 MOSKVA **Tel:** 495 60 93 231
Email: nikoforova@groteck.ru **Web site:** http://www.broadcasting.ru
Date Established: 1999; **Freq:** 8 issues yearly; **Circ:** 15,000
Usual Pagination: 96
Executive Editor: Anna Zavarzina; **Publisher:** Alexander Vlasov
Profile: Informs on new technologies and TV and radio broadcasting equipment, licensing and on major events and developments in this branch.
Language(s): Russian
Readership: Aimed at technical personnel and management of radio and TV stations.
ADVERTISING RATES:
Full Page Colour .... EUR 2499.00
BUSINESS: COMMUNICATIONS, ADVERTISING & MARKETING: Broadcasting

BTL-MAGAZINE
1774532RU2A-13
Editorial: ul. Kerchenskaya 26, 602086 NIZHNY NOVGOROD **Tel:** 312 417 88 32 **Fax:** 312 417 88 38
Email: btl@btl-magazine.ru **Web site:** www.btl-magazine.ru
Freq: 6 issues yearly; **Cover Price:** RUR 895.00
Annual Sub.: RUR 4964.00; **Circ:** 5,000
Usual Pagination: 120
Editor-in-Chief: Eugenia Vagina
Profile: Practical magazine about aim marketing and communications, branding and merchandising mobile marketing and PR campaigns.
Language(s): Russian
ADVERTISING RATES:
Full Page Colour .... RUR 23700.00
Mechanical Data: Bleed Size: 215 x 270mm
BUSINESS: COMMUNICATIONS, ADVERTISING & MARKETING

BUHGALTER I ZAKON
1774288RU1B-2
Editorial: P.O. Box, ul. Mashkova 3, str. 1, 111401 MOSKVA **Tel:** 495 621 69 49 **Fax:** 495 621 91 90
Email: post@financepress.ru **Web site:** http://www.financepress.ru
Date Established: 1999; **Freq:** Monthly; **Circ:** 5,500
Usual Pagination: 64
Editor: Vera Gorokhova
Profile: Focused on rights, duties and responsibilities, criminal liability of a bookkeeper with legal documentation and comments.
Language(s): Russian
ADVERTISING RATES:
Full Page Colour .... RUR 17346.00
Mechanical Data: Type Area: 170 x 240mm
BUSINESS: FINANCE & ECONOMICS: Accountancy

BUHGALTERSKY UCHET W BUDZHETNYKH I NEKOMMERCHESKIKH ORGANIZATSIYAKH
1774289RU1B-3
Editorial: P.O.Box 10, 111401 MOSKVA
Tel: 495 621 69 49 **Fax:** 495 621 91 90
Email: post@financepress.ru **Web site:** http://www.financepress.ru
Date Established: 1998; **Freq:** 24 issues yearly; **Circ:** 21,100
Usual Pagination: 64
Editor: Vera Gorokhova
Profile: Publication focusing on accounting, also covers non-commercial organizations. Offers practical advice and examples explained by experts.
Language(s): Russian
ADVERTISING RATES:
Full Page Colour .... RUR 30975.00
Mechanical Data: Type Area: 170 x 240mm
BUSINESS: FINANCE & ECONOMICS: Accountancy

BUHGALTERSKY UCHET W IZDATELSTVE I POLIGRAFII
1774290RU1B-4
Editorial: P.O. Box 10, 111401 MOSKVA
Tel: 495 621 69 49 **Fax:** 495 621 91 90
Email: post@financepress.ru **Web site:** http://www.financepress.ru
Date Established: 1999; **Freq:** Monthly; **Circ:** 5,950
Usual Pagination: 64
Editor: Vera Gorokhova
Profile: Publication featuring accountancy procedures in various organizations: in PR, publishing houses and media sector.
Language(s): Russian
ADVERTISING RATES:
Full Page Colour .... RUR 18585.00
Mechanical Data: Type Area: 170 x 240mm
BUSINESS: FINANCE & ECONOMICS: Accountancy

BULLETEN' NEDVIZHIMOSTI
1774632RU1E-2
Editorial: ul. Gagarina 1, office 633, 196105 SANKT PETERBURG **Tel:** 12 387 89 91
Email: editor@bnmail.ru **Web site:** http://www.bn.ru
Date Established: 1995; **Freq:** 104 issues yearly - Published on Mondays and Wednesdays; **Annual Sub.:** RUR 7200.00; **Circ:** 25,000
Usual Pagination: 300
Profile: Publication bringing property market, real estate, residential and commercial property news and events in St. Petersburg region.
Language(s): Russian
ADVERTISING RATES:
Full Page Mono .... RUR 11600.00
Mechanical Data: Type Area: 180 x 260mm
BUSINESS: FINANCE & ECONOMICS: Property

BULLETEN' STROYASHEYSYA NEDVIZHIMOSTI
1774062RU1E-6
Editorial: ul. Gagarina 1, office 633, 196105 SANKT PETERBURG **Tel:** 12 387 89 91 **Fax:** 12 346 57 98
Email: pr@bnmail.ru **Web site:** http://www.bn.ru
Date Established: 2003; **Freq:** Monthly; **Annual Sub.:** RUR 480.00; **Circ:** 8,000
Usual Pagination: 200
Profile: Informative-analytical monthly about property construction in St. Petersburg region.
Language(s): Russian
Readership: Aimed at professionals and people buying their first property.
Mechanical Data: Type Area: A 4
BUSINESS: FINANCE & ECONOMICS: Property

BURDA
624467RU74B-45
Editorial: Ulica Polkovaya, Dom 3, Stroenie 4, MOSKVA **Tel:** 495 787 33 68 **Fax:** 495 797 98 48
Email: burda@burda.ru **Web site:** http://www.burda.ru
Date Established: 1987; **Freq:** Monthly; **Circ:** 460,000
Usual Pagination: 164
Advertising Director: Nataliya Yakovets; **Publisher:** Alexander Moskovkin
Profile: Women's interest magazine focusing on fashion and lifestyle.
Language(s): Russian
Readership: Aimed at affluent women of all ages.
ADVERTISING RATES:
Full Page Colour .... RUR 370000.00
Mechanical Data: Col Length: 255mm, Trim Size: 213 x 275mm, Print Process: Offset, Bleed Size: 223 x 285mm
CONSUMER: WOMEN'S INTEREST CONSUMER MAGAZINES: Women's Interest - Fashion

BURENIYE I NEFT
1774085RU33-10
Editorial: Kashirsky proyezd 21, Office 32, 115201 MOSKVA **Tel:** 495 504 98 67 **Fax:** 499 613 93 17
Email: info@burneft.ru **Web site:** http://www.burneft.ru
Freq: 11 issues yearly; Free to qualifying individuals
Annual Sub.: RUR 5520.00; **Circ:** 7,000
Usual Pagination: 60
Executive Editor: Valeria Krylova; **Editor-in-Chief:** Ludmila Nechaikina
Profile: Magazine on new technologies in oil drilling, industry investments, branch scientific and economic developments.
Language(s): Russian
ADVERTISING RATES:
Full Page Mono .... RUR 45000.00
Full Page Colour .... RUR 60000.00
Mechanical Data: Type Area: A4
BUSINESS: OIL & PETROLEUM

BUSINESS & FINANCIAL MARKETS
1774320RU1A-36
Editorial: ul. 2-aya Khutorskaya 38A, str.23, 127994 MOSKVA **Tel:** 495 720 50 52 **Fax:** 495 720 50 53
Email: mail@businessfm.ru **Web site:** http://bfmgazeta.ru
Freq: Weekly; **Cover Price:** Paid
Executive Editor: Alexey Titkov; **Editor-in-Chief:** Grigoriy Beglaryan
Profile: Contains analytical in-depth materials about international and Russian financial markets and overview and research of their developments.
Language(s): Russian
Mechanical Data: Type Area: 259 x 314mm
BUSINESS: FINANCE & ECONOMICS

BUSINESS CLASS
1774101RU1A-44
Editorial: ul. Kommunisticheskaya 15a, 614000 PERM' **Tel:** 342 212 79 75 **Fax:** 342 210 58 05
Email: info@business-class.su **Web site:** http://business-class.su
Date Established: 1932; **Freq:** Weekly - Published on Mondays; **Annual Sub.:** RUR 950.00; **Circ:** 3,000
Usual Pagination: 36
Editor: Vadim Skovorodin; **Advertising Manager:** Anastasiya Iroshechkina
Profile: Business newspaper from Perm region covering regional business developments.
Language(s): Russian
ADVERTISING RATES:
SCC .... RUR 85.00
BUSINESS: FINANCE & ECONOMICS

BUSINESSWEEK ROSSIYA
1774293RU1A-18
Editorial: Bolshaya Andronevskaya 17, 109544 MOSKVA **Tel:** 495 745 84 01
Email: pr@idr.ru
Date Established: 2005; **Freq:** Monthly; **Annual Sub.:** RUR 1584.00; **Circ:** 75,000
Usual Pagination: 96
Advertising Manager: Tatiana Larina
Profile: Provides information on business and economics, analyses of business management, news on investment markets.
Language(s): Russian
ADVERTISING RATES:
Full Page Colour .... RUR 255000.00
Mechanical Data: Bleed Size: 208 x 275mm, Trim Size: 200 x 267mm
BUSINESS: FINANCE & ECONOMICS

BYTE
1613663RU5B-13
Editorial: ul. Marksistskaya 34, Korp. 10, office 338, 109147 MOSKVA **Tel:** 495 974 22 60
Fax: 495 974 22 63
Email: byte@bytemag.ru **Web site:** http://www.bytemag.ru
Date Established: 1998; **Freq:** Monthly; **Annual Sub.:** RUR 495.00; **Circ:** 20,000
Usual Pagination: 84
Editor: Andrey Borzenko; **Advertising Director:** Sergey Schabaev
Profile: Magazine focusing on IT systems, networking, operating platforms and solutions, software and communications.
Language(s): Russian
Readership: Aimed at IT professionals.
ADVERTISING RATES:
Full Page Colour .... RUR 188800.00
BUSINESS: COMPUTERS & AUTOMATION: Data Processing

CAPTAIN CLUB
1774488RU75M-1
Editorial: Petrovskaya kosa 7, 197110 SANKT PETERBURG **Tel:** 12 331 73 38 **Fax:** 12 320 06 93
Email: mail@captainclub.ru **Web site:** http://www.captainclub.ru
Date Established: 1997; **Freq:** 5 issues yearly; **Circ:** 15,000
Usual Pagination: 250
Editor: Zariy Chernyak; **Advertising Director:** Andrey Korneev
Profile: Magazine on motorboats, sailing yachts, PWC, inflatable and RIBs sailing racing power boating, seamanship, navigation communication safety at sea, equipment accessories, yacht charter cruising travelling, fishing diving water sports windsurfing.
Language(s): Russian
ADVERTISING RATES:
Full Page Colour $2450.00
Mechanical Data: Trim Size: 210 x 297mm, Type Area: 175 x 252mm
CONSUMER: SPORT: Water Sports

CHEFART
1774598RU11A-4
Editorial: ul. Dubininskaya 90, 115093 MOSKVA
Tel: 495 921 36 25 **Fax:** 495 921 36 25
Email: info@restoved.ru **Web site:** http://www.restoved.ru
Freq: Quarterly; **Circ:** 5,000
Usual Pagination: 120
Profile: Leading Russian publication on gastronomy, culinary technologies and cuisine fashion.
Language(s): Russian
Readership: Targets chefs, baking and confectionary professionals, restaurant managers.
ADVERTISING RATES:
Full Page Colour .... RUR 43500.00
Mechanical Data: Type Area: 210 x 297mm
BUSINESS: CATERING: Catering, Hotels & Restaurants

CHELOVEK I TRUD
1774420RU14F-2
Editorial: Yakovoapostolsky per. 6, str. 3, 105064 MOSKVA **Tel:** 495 917 76 36
Email: chelt@yandex.ru **Web site:** http://www.chelt.ru
Freq: Monthly; **Cover Price:** RUR 230.00; **Circ:** 5,000
Editor-in-Chief: M. Barinova
Profile: Magazine on social policies, employment market, payment and job motivation, HR and personnel.
Language(s): Russian
BUSINESS: COMMERCE, INDUSTRY & MANAGEMENT: Training & Recruitment

CHIP
714157RU5C-102
Editorial: ul. Polkovaya, Dom 3, Stroenie 4, 127018 MOSKVA **Tel:** 495 787 33 88 **Fax:** 495 787 94 31
Email: a.mokretsov@burda.ru **Web site:** http://www.ichip.ru
Date Established: 2001; **Freq:** Monthly; **Circ:** 100,500
Usual Pagination: 164
Advertising Director: Yaroslav Chernyakov; **Publisher:** Denis Sedyakin
Profile: Magazine focusing on the latest hardware, software and communication products for both private and business use.
Language(s): Russian
Readership: Aimed at IT professionals and home PC users.
ADVERTISING RATES:
Full Page Colour .... RUR 208000.00
Mechanical Data: Bleed Size: 225 x 295mm, Print Process: Offset, Trim Size: 215 x 285mm
BUSINESS: COMPUTERS & AUTOMATION: Professional Personal Computers

CIO
1613615RU5B-14
Editorial: 2 Roschinsky proyezd 8, 115419 MOSKVA
Tel: 495 232 22 63 **Fax:** 495 956 19 38
Email: inform@computerra.ru **Web site:** http://www.cio-world.ru
Date Established: 2002; **Freq:** Monthly; **Annual Sub.:** RUR 1979.00; **Circ:** 1,000
Usual Pagination: 144
Editor-in-Chief: Mikhail Rumyantev; **Publisher:** Dmitri Mendrelyuk
Profile: Magazine focusing on the influence of IT within the workplace.
Language(s): Russian
Readership: Aimed at chief information officers and other senior-level managers.
ADVERTISING RATES:
Full Page Colour $7900.00
Mechanical Data: Type Area: 210x290mm
BUSINESS: COMPUTERS & AUTOMATION: Data Processing

CK
1774651RU1A-35
Editorial: ul. Gorkogo 153, IZHEVSK
Tel: 3412 43 83 48 **Fax:** 3412 43 85 88
Email: ck@udm.ru **Web site:** http://www.soverkon.ru
Date Established: 2002; **Freq:** Weekly - Published on Thursdays; **Circ:** 30,000
Usual Pagination: 32
Editor: Valentina Kostina
Language(s): Russian
ADVERTISING RATES:
Full Page Mono .... RUR 40700.00
Mechanical Data: Type Area: A4
BUSINESS: FINANCE & ECONOMICS

COMMERCIAL REAL ESTATE
1774212RU1E-10
Editorial: 4 Roschinsky proyezd 20, str. 5, 115191 MOSKVA **Tel:** 495 540 73 40 **Fax:** 495 540 72 15
Email: info@cre.ru **Web site:** http://www.cre.ru
Freq: 24 issues yearly; Free to qualifying individuals
Annual Sub.: RUR 2800.00; **Circ:** 30,000
Usual Pagination: 136
News Editor: Rafael Khaibrakhmanov; **Editor-in-Chief:** Ekaterina Krylova; **Publisher:** Annette Wassenaar
Profile: Provides information on commercial property market of Russia: offices, retail and industrial real

estate, land, and hotels, quality objective analysis of problems and trends of market's development.
Language(s): English; Russian
Readership: Targets investors, developers, consultants, management companies, construction and engineering companies, architects and designers, lawyers, surveyors, service providers.
Mechanical Data: Type Area: 230 x 300mm
BUSINESS: FINANCE & ECONOMICS: Property

COMPUART
1613735RU41A-1
Editorial: Gorokhovskiy Per. 7, 105064 MOSKVA
Tel: 495 234 65 81 **Fax:** 495 234 65 81
Email: cart@compress.ru **Web site:** http://www.compuart.ru
Date Established: 1996; **Freq:** Monthly; **Circ:** 10,000
Editor: Boris Moltchanov; **Advertising Director:** Konstantin Babulin
Profile: Magazine focusing on printing, design, computer graphics and digital technologies. Features information on national and international exhibitions, articles on the latest hardware and software, expertise and testing on prepress and printing equipment.
Language(s): Russian
Readership: Aimed at users of modern editorial and printing equipment.
ADVERTISING RATES:
Full Page Colour $8000.00
Mechanical Data: Trim Size: 200 x 265mm, Bleed Size: 210 x 275mm
BUSINESS: PRINTING & STATIONERY: Printing

COMPUTER RESELLER NEWS RUSSIA
714174RU5C-103
Editorial: ul. Marksistkaya 34, Korp. 10, 109147 MOSKVA **Tel:** 495 974 22 60 **Fax:** 495 974 22 63
Email: crnre@crn.ru **Web site:** http://www.crn.ru
Date Established: 1996; **Freq:** 30 issues yearly; **Circ:** 10,200
Editor: Aleksandr Plitman; **Editor-in-Chief:** Elina Zolotova; **Advertising Manager:** Olga Marchenko
Profile: Magazine focusing on computer business, distribution, supply channels, service and support, hardware, software, networking systems and innovative technologies.
Language(s): Russian
Readership: Aimed at distributors, systems integrators, dealers and OEMs.
Agency Commission: 15%
Mechanical Data: Film: Positive, right reading. Emulsion side down, Trim Size: 336 x 247mm, Bleed Size: 346 x 257mm, Type Area: 319 x 224mm, Screen: 60lpc
BUSINESS: COMPUTERS & AUTOMATION: Professional Personal Computers

COMPUTERPRESS
763442RU5D-40
Editorial: Gorokhovskiy Per. 7, Korp. 1, 105064 MOSKVA **Tel:** 495 234 65 81 **Fax:** 495 234 65 82
Email: cpress@compress.ru **Web site:** http://www.compress.ru
Date Established: 1989; **Freq:** Monthly; **Circ:** 44,000
Usual Pagination: 192
Editor-in-Chief: Alexandr Sinev; **Advertising Director:** Konstantin Babulin; **Publisher:** Boris Moltchanov
Profile: Magazine highlighting problems in hardware, software, multimedia, networks, communications, new products, exhibitions and computer games.
Language(s): Russian
Readership: Aimed at those interested in computers.
ADVERTISING RATES:
Full Page Colour $10800.00
Mechanical Data: Type Area: A4, Bleed Size: 210 x 275mm, Trim Size: 200 x 265mm
BUSINESS: COMPUTERS & AUTOMATION: Personal Computers

COMPUTERRA
1774581RU5C-113
Editorial: 2 Roschinsky per. 8, 115419 MOSKVA
Tel: 495 232 22 63 **Fax:** 495 956 19 38
Email: inform@computerra.ru **Web site:** http://www.computerra.ru
Date Established: 1992; **Freq:** Weekly; **Circ:** 64,000
Usual Pagination: 96
Editor-in-Chief: Vladislav Biryukov; **Advertising Manager:** Elena Rybalko
Profile: Magazine on computing and IT technologies, their implementations and developments.
Language(s): Russian
ADVERTISING RATES:
Full Page Colour .... RUR 350000.00
Mechanical Data: Type Area: 210 x 297mm
BUSINESS: COMPUTERS & AUTOMATION: Professional Personal Computers

COMPUTERWORLD RUSSIA
714147RU5B-11
Editorial: Elektricheskiy Pereulok 8, Korp. 3, 123056 MOSKVA **Tel:** 495 253 92 06 **Fax:** 495 253 58 09
Email: cwr@osp.ru **Web site:** http://www.osp.ru
Date Established: 1995; **Freq:** Weekly - Published on Tuesday; **Circ:** 30,000
Usual Pagination: 56
Editor: Pavel Vyacheslavovich Khristov; **Advertising Manager:** Tatiana Filina; **Publisher:** Michael Borisov
Profile: Magazine providing news and analysis on personal computers, workstations, mid-range and central server hardware, software and networking products.
Language(s): Russian

Readership: Aimed at information systems executives, managers and professionals responsible for purchasing decisions of computers and networking technology.
ADVERTISING RATES:
Full Page Colour .... RUR 208860.00
Agency Commission: 15%
Mechanical Data: Screen: 54 lpc, Print Process: Offset, Trim Size: 342 x 260mm, Type Area: 316 x 240mm, Col Length: 316mm
Copy instructions: *Copy Date:* 2 weeks prior to publication date
BUSINESS: COMPUTERS & AUTOMATION: Data Processing

CONNECT! MIR SVYAZI
1774400RU18B-18
Editorial: ul. Selskokhozhyastvennaya 19, korpus 2, 129226 MOSKVA **Tel:** 495 925 11 18
Fax: 495 925 11 18
Email: editors@connect.ru **Web site:** http://www.connect.ru
Freq: Monthly; **Circ:** 10,000
Editor-in-Chief: Aleksandr Lomov
Profile: Professional publication on telecommunications and informative technologies.
Language(s): Russian
BUSINESS: ELECTRONICS: Telecommunications

CONTROL ENGINEERING RUSSIA
1774313RU5A-1
Editorial: ul Krasnoprudnaya 12/1, str. 1, office 17, 107140 MOSKVA **Tel:** 495 784 71 16
Fax: 495 784 71 16
Email: hc@trademedia.us **Web site:** http://www.controlengrussia.com
Freq: 10 issues yearly; **Circ:** 7,000
Executive Editor: Alexander Suranov; **Editor-in-Chief:** Inna Lukasik
Profile: Providing information on technology, products, news and trends inautomation, control and instrumentation, Russian automation market, control/instrumentation systems, components and equipment in manufacturing and non-manufacturing industries.
Language(s): Russian
Readership: Aimed at automation managers, production managers, automation and production engineers, experts and designers responsible for products and automation systems purchases for largest manufacturing plants in Russia.
ADVERTISING RATES:
Full Page Colour .... EUR 2284.00
Mechanical Data: Type Area: 200 x 267mm
BUSINESS: COMPUTERS & AUTOMATION: Automation & Instrumentation

COSMETICS IN RUSSIA
1865480RU15A-5
Editorial: 1 Volokolamsky proyezd 10, str. 1, Science & Technology Park, 123060 **Tel:** 495 981 94 91
Fax: 495 981 94 90
Email: info@cosmeticsinrussia.com **Web site:** http://www.cosmeticsinrussia.com
Freq: 3 issues yearly; Free to qualifying individuals ;
Circ: 3,000
Usual Pagination: 28
Editor: Svetlana Ryadchikova; **Advertising Manager:** Elena Karaseva
Profile: Publishes analytical reports on skin care, hair care, colour cosmetics, body care, bath care, oral care, male grooming, baby care, sun care, deodorants, perfumery, retail, distribution and manufacturing.
Language(s): English
Readership: Targets English-speaking audience, providing daily updated information on Russian and CIS countries perfumery and cosmetics markets.
ADVERTISING RATES:
Full Page Colour $900.00
Mechanical Data: Type Area: 220x307mm
BUSINESS: COSMETICS & HAIRDRESSING: Cosmetics

COSMOPOLITAN
763343RU74B-55
Editorial: ul. Polkovaya 3 zdaniye 1, 127018 MOSKVA **Tel:** 495 232 32 00 **Fax:** 495 232 17 61
Email: cosmopolitan@imedia.ru **Web site:** http://www.cosmo.ru
Date Established: 1994; **Freq:** Monthly; **Cover Price:** RUR 150.00
Annual Sub.: RUR 1370.00; **Circ:** 980,000
Advertising Director: Ludmila Gurey; **Publisher:** Ekaterina Kabakchi
Profile: Women's interest magazine covering fashion, beauty, family, careers and travel.
Language(s): Russian
Readership: Aimed at affluent women of all ages.
ADVERTISING RATES:
Full Page Colour .... RUR 1078000.00
CONSUMER: WOMEN'S INTEREST CONSUMER MAGAZINES: Women's Interest - Fashion

D'
1774577RU1R-2
Editorial: ul. Pravdy 24, office 623, 125866 MOSKVA
Tel: 495 609 64 98 **Fax:** 495 250 52 09
Email: d@expert.ru **Web site:** http://www.expert.ru
Date Established: 2005; **Freq:** 24 issues yearly; **Circ:** 50,500
Usual Pagination: 160
Editor: Evgenia Smolenskaya; **Advertising Manager:** Aleksandr Shukhmin; **Advertising Director:** Anastasiya Zhavoronkova
Profile: Dedicated to personal finance, investments, taxation and personal financial consulting.
Language(s): Russian
ADVERTISING RATES:
Full Page Colour .... RUR 203000.00
Mechanical Data: Type Area: 194 x 125mm
BUSINESS: FINANCE & ECONOMICS: Financial Related

DALNEVOSTOCHNY KAPITAL
1774460RU1R-1
Editorial: pr. Krasnogo Znameni 10, 690950 VLADIVOSTOK **Tel:** 4232 45 04 85
Fax: 4232 45 04 85
Email: zr@zrpress.ru **Web site:** http://www.zrpress.ru
Date Established: 2000; **Freq:** Monthly - First of every month; **Circ:** 5,500
Usual Pagination: 102
Editor: Larisa Zhironkina
Profile: Reviews about leading branches in Russian Far East, businessmen, the markets and infrastructure of business.
Language(s): Russian
ADVERTISING RATES:
Full Page Colour .... RUR 36000.00
Mechanical Data: Type Area: 217 x 296mm
BUSINESS: FINANCE & ECONOMICS: Financial Related

DELOVAYA MOSKVA
1774185RU14A-27
Editorial: Staromonetny prerulok 10, 3 floor, 119180 MOSKVA **Tel:** 495 950 83 12
Email: info@delpressa.ru **Web site:** http://delpressa.ru
Freq: Weekly - Published on Fridays; **Circ:** 55,000
Usual Pagination: 20
Advertising Director: Natalia Sukhanova
Profile: Contains information on business in Moscow region, tips for small business and management issues.
Language(s): Russian
ADVERTISING RATES:
Full Page Mono .... RUR 30000.00
Mechanical Data: Type Area: A3
BUSINESS: COMMERCE, INDUSTRY & MANAGEMENT

DELOVAYA NEDVIZHIMOST'
1774225RU1E-5
Editorial: ul. Gagarina 1, office 733, 196105 SANKT PETERBURG **Tel:** 12 387 88 39 **Fax:** 12 329 36 06
Email: dn@bnmail.ru **Web site:** http://www.bn.ru
Date Established: 2002; **Freq:** Monthly; **Circ:** 7,000
Usual Pagination: 120
Editor-in-Chief: Alexandr Zharkov
Profile: Informative-analytical professional publication on commercial property in Moscow. St. Petersburg and main regions of Russia.
Language(s): Russian
Readership: Aimed at developers, property managers and investors.
ADVERTISING RATES:
Full Page Mono .... RUR 18000.00
Mechanical Data: Type Area: 210 x 280mm
BUSINESS: FINANCE & ECONOMICS: Property

DELOVIE LYUDI
1201770RU1A-10
Formerly: Business in Russia
Editorial: ul. 1905 goda 7, MOSKVA 123995
Tel: 495 250 77 40 **Fax:** 495 250 77 46
Email: dl@mk.ru **Web site:** http://www.mk.ru
ISSN: 0868-9504
Date Established: 1990; **Freq:** Monthly; **Circ:** 50,000
Usual Pagination: 144
Editor: Ilya Ryabov
Profile: Magazine featuring business, commerce and politics.
Language(s): English; Russian
Readership: Aimed at business managers of the US and western companies and economists.
ADVERTISING RATES:
Full Page Mono $4600.00
Full Page Colour $6000.00
Mechanical Data: Bleed Size: 285mm x 220mm, Trim Size: 280mm x 215mm, Type Area: 275mm x 210mm, Col Length: 243mm, Col Widths (Display): 48mm, Screen: 150lpi
BUSINESS: FINANCE & ECONOMICS

DELOVOY KRESTIANIN
1774123RU21A-4
Editorial: ul. Goroda Volos 6, 8 floor, 344000 ROSTOV-NA-DONU **Tel:** 63 282 83 10
Email: director@krestianin.ru **Web site:** http://www.krestianin.ru
Freq: Monthly; **Cover Price:** Free; **Circ:** 20,000
Usual Pagination: 52
Advertising Director: Irina Danilova
Profile: Professional publication for managers of agricultural enterprises.
Language(s): Russian
ADVERTISING RATES:
Full Page Mono .... RUR 21251.00
Mechanical Data: Type Area: 210 x 240mm
BUSINESS: AGRICULTURE & FARMING

DELOVOY PETERBURG
1774520RU14A-8
Editorial: ul. Akademika Pavlova, River House, 5 floor, 197022 SANKT PETERBURG **Tel:** 12 326 97 00
Fax: 12 326 97 01
Email: Natalja.Mikhailova@dp.ru **Web site:** http://www.dpgazeta.ru
Date Established: 1993; **Freq:** 260 issues yearly;
Circ: 24,500
Usual Pagination: 56
News Editor: Maxim Vasyukov; **Executive Editor:** Dmitri Grozny; **Features Editor:** Alexey Kolomentsev;
Advertising Manager: Svetlana Titorenko;
Advertising Director: Marina Zabruskova
Profile: Newspaper about business and for business in St. Petersburg printed on pink paper.
Language(s): Russian
Mechanical Data: Type Area: A3
Supplement(s): Avtomobili, ElektroNeftegaz, Yachting - 52xY
BUSINESS: COMMERCE, INDUSTRY & MANAGEMENT

DELOVOY VTORNIK
1774268RU14A-38
Editorial: P.O. Box 34, 127137 MOSKVA
Tel: 495 257 38 45 **Fax:** 495 257 59 17
Email: vtornik@dvtornik.ru **Web site:** http://www.dvtornik.ru
Freq: Weekly; **Circ:** 1,800,000
Editor: Leonid Arikh
Profile: National weekly with financial, economic, business and political news.
Language(s): Russian
ADVERTISING RATES:
Full Page Mono $24000.00
Mechanical Data: Type Area: 378 x 515mm
BUSINESS: COMMERCE, INDUSTRY & MANAGEMENT

DENGI
763407RU1A-12
Editorial: ul. Vrubeliya 4/1, 125080 MOSKVA
Tel: 495 943 91 17 **Fax:** 495 943 97 28
Email: dengi@kommersant.ru **Web site:** http://www.kommersant.ru/money
Freq: Weekly; **Circ:** 85,000
Advertising Manager: Ekaterina Kuznetsova
Profile: Magazine featuring analysis and tendencies of financial markets, effective investments and practical information about new financial companies.
Language(s): Russian
Readership: Aimed at senior and middle level managers of state and private enterprises, politicians, managers of banks and financial institutions.
ADVERTISING RATES:
Full Page Mono .... RUR 425000.00
Full Page Colour .... RUR 425000.00
Agency Commission: 15%
Mechanical Data: Trim Size: 290 x 220mm, Type Area: 261x195mm, Col Length: 261mm, Screen: 70 lpc, Print Process: Offset
Copy instructions: *Copy Date:* 3 weeks prior to publication date
Supplement to: Kommersant
BUSINESS: FINANCE & ECONOMICS

DIGEST FINANSY
1774297RU1A-19
Editorial: P.O. Box 10, 111401 MOSKVA
Tel: 495 621 69 49 **Fax:** 495 621 91 90
Email: post@financepress.ru **Web site:** http://www.financepress.ru
Date Established: 1996; **Freq:** Monthly; **Circ:** 5,100
Usual Pagination: 76
Editor: Valentina Yedronova
Profile: Publication focused on finance, monetary circulation, credit, investments, and financial markets.
Language(s): Russian
ADVERTISING RATES:
Full Page Colour .... RUR 22656.00
Mechanical Data: Type Area: 170 x 240mm
BUSINESS: FINANCE & ECONOMICS

DIGITAL MAGAZINE
1774339RU18A-2
Editorial: 4a Novodanilovskaya nab, 117105 MOSKVA **Tel:** 495 510 22 11 **Fax:** 495 510 49 69
Email: i.bozhok@spn.ru **Web site:** http://www.spn.ru
Date Established: 2000; **Freq:** Monthly; **Circ:** 130,000
Editor: Mikhail Genin; **Advertisement Director:** Valery Mirochnik
Profile: Offers a comprehensible description and analysis of most interesting and most useful trends in the evolution of digital technologies: home theatres, top-class audio equipment, digital photo and video cameras, multimedia players, computers and notebooks, mobile devices and digital equipment.
Language(s): Russian
ADVERTISING RATES:
Full Page Colour .... RUR 208500.00
Mechanical Data: Type Area: 225 x 300mm
BUSINESS: ELECTRONICS

DIRECTORINFO
1613695RU14A-4
Editorial: Gorokhowskiy Per. 5, 113093 MOSKVA
Tel: 495 234 65 81 **Fax:** 495 234 65 81
Email: directorinfo@compress.ru **Web site:** http://www.directorinfo.ru
Date Established: 2001; **Freq:** Weekly; **Circ:** 30,000
Usual Pagination: 48
Advertising Director: Konstantin Babulin; **Publisher:** Boris Moltchanov
Profile: Magazine providing business executives with the relevant management tools, market analysis and

information on legal, financial and general business communications issues.
Language(s): Russian
Readership: Aimed at managers and executives.
ADVERTISING RATES:
Full Page Colour $7000.00
Mechanical Data: Trim Size: 200 x 265 mm
BUSINESS: COMMERCE, INDUSTRY & MANAGEMENT

DOMASHNII OCHAG 1600544RU74A-5
Editorial: ul. Polkovaya 3 zdaniye 1, 127018 MOSKVA **Tel:** 495 232 32 00 **Fax:** 495 23 21 761
Email: goodhouse@imedia.ru **Web site:** http://www.goodhouse.ru
Date Established: 1995; **Freq:** Monthly; **Circ:** 280,000
Usual Pagination: 330
Profile: Magazine covering lifestyle matters, includes fashion, home, family, cookery and health.
Language(s): Russian
Readership: Aimed at contemporary Russian women who strive to create a comfortable, creative and modern life for themselves and their families.
ADVERTISING RATES:
Full Page Colour .... RUR 508200.00
Agency Commission: 15%
Mechanical Data: Trim Size: 275 x 215mm
CONSUMER: WOMEN'S INTEREST CONSUMER MAGAZINES: Women's Interest

DOMODEDOVO 1938341RU89D-9
Editorial: ul. Marksistskaya, 34, bldg. 10, 109147 MOSKVA **Tel:** 495 974 22 60 **Fax:** 495 974 22 63
Email: vpred@vpolet.ru **Web site:** http://www.skpress.ru/in-flight/en/domodedovo
Date Established: 2001; **Freq:** 11 issues yearly - published on the 1st of every month; **Cover Price:** Free; **Circ:** 85,000
Usual Pagination: 100
Publisher: Anatoly Eides
Profile: Illustrated in-flight monthly for passengers of air companies flyingfrom Domodedovo Airport (Moscow). The first issue of the monthly Moscow Domodedovo International Airport was released in November 2001. Since then it has more than doubled in size, increased its circulation to 85,000 copies, and greatly extended the geography of flights.
Language(s): English; Russian
Readership: Audience of the monthly Domodedovo. Moscow Airport: members of the Russian regional business elite, managers of big and medium-size business, their family members and Muscovites, who maintain business contacts with regional partners.
ADVERTISING RATES:
Full Page Colour .... RUR 279000.00
Mechanical Data: Bleed Size: 210x264mm, Trim Size: 220x274mm
Copy instructions: *Copy Date:* a month prior the publication date
CONSUMER: HOLIDAYS & TRAVEL: In-Flight Magazines

DOROGOYE UDOVOLSTVIYE 1774094RU74Q-13
Editorial: Bolshaya Mariinskaya 9, str. 1, 3 floor, office 316, 129085 MOSKVA **Tel:** 495 616 99 66
Email: balburova@dorogoe.ru **Web site:** http://www.dorogoe.ru
Freq: Monthly; **Circ:** 54,000
Editor: Daria Filippova; **Editor-in-Chief:** Elena Balburova; **Advertising Manager:** Igor Ivanov
Profile: National glossy lifestyle magazine with fashion reviews, cosmetics news, celebrities, relationships, travel and entertainment.
Language(s): Russian
ADVERTISING RATES:
Full Page Colour .... RUR 60000.00
Mechanical Data: Type Area: A3
CONSUMER: WOMEN'S INTEREST CONSUMER MAGAZINES: Lifestyle

DVDXPERT 1774702RU78A-1
Editorial: ul. Timura Frunze 11, str. 44-45, 4 floor, 119992 MOSKVA **Tel:** 495 935 70 34
Fax: 495 780 88 24
Email: press@dvdexpert.ru **Web site:** http://www.dvdexpert.ru
Date Established: 2004; **Freq:** Monthly; **Circ:** 70,000
Usual Pagination: 160
Editor: Yaroslav Godyna; **Advertising Manager:** Oksana Akekhina; **Publisher:** Sergey Vereykin
Profile: Devoted to home cinema systems and audio and video technology with comprehensive reviews on latest gadgets from Hi-Fi/High End sectors.
Language(s): Russian
Readership: Targets passionate fans of home cinemas to help to find the way through numerous offerings on market.
Mechanical Data: Type Area: 210x297mm
CONSUMER: CONSUMER ELECTRONICS: Hi-Fi & Recording

EKONOMICHESKI ANALIZ: TEORIA I PRAKTIKA 1774333RU14A-7
Editorial: P.O. Box 10, 111401 MOSKVA
Tel: 495 621 69 49 **Fax:** 495 621 91 90
Email: post@financepress.ru **Web site:** http://www.financepress.ru
Date Established: 2002; **Freq:** 24 issues yearly; **Circ:** 11,670
Usual Pagination: 64
Editor: Nikolai Liubushin
Profile: Publication featuring economics analysis, investment news, financial and economic activities in the region.
Language(s): Russian
ADVERTISING RATES:
Full Page Colour .... RUR 38409.00
Mechanical Data: Type Area: 170 x 240mm
BUSINESS: COMMERCE, INDUSTRY & MANAGEMENT

EKONOMIKA I VREMYA 1774024RU1A-46
Editorial: ul. Aleksandra Nevskogo 12, 193167 SANKT PETERBURG **Tel:** 12 327 03 05
Email: info@ev.spb.ru **Web site:** http://ev.spb.ru
Date Established: 1994; **Freq:** Weekly; **Annual Sub.:** RUR 516.00; **Circ:** 13,500
Editor-in-Chief: Aleksandr Evseev; **Advertising Director:** Ludmila Veksler
Profile: Business newspaper with analytical and informative articles on economics in North-Western region of Russia, economic developments and business tendencies.
Language(s): Russian
ADVERTISING RATES:
Full Page Mono .... RUR 24000.00
Mechanical Data: Type Area: 266 x 360mm
BUSINESS: FINANCE & ECONOMICS

EKONOMIKA I ZHIZN 1611047RU1A-16
Editorial: Bumazhny Proezd 14, 2 floor, office 209, 127994 MOSKVA **Tel:** 495 152 51 38
Fax: 495 152 51 38
Email: LidiyaV@ekonomika.ru **Web site:** http://www.eg-online.ru
Date Established: 1994; **Freq:** Weekly; **Circ:** 52,000
Usual Pagination: 40
Editor: Ludmila Saveleva; **Editor-in-Chief:** Tatiana Ivanova; **Advertising Manager:** Lidia Vdovina
Profile: Magazine focusing on economics, business and finance.
Language(s): Russian
ADVERTISING RATES:
Full Page Mono $2000.00
Full Page Colour $3000.00
Agency Commission: 20%
Mechanical Data: Type Area: A3
Copy instructions: *Copy Date:* 14 days prior to publication date
BUSINESS: FINANCE & ECONOMICS

EKONOMIKO - PRAVOVOY BULLETEN 1774507RU1A-32
Editorial: ul. Chernyakhovskogo 16, 125319 MOSKVA **Tel:** 499 152 51 38 **Fax:** 499 152 68 65
Email: eg@ekonomika.ru **Web site:** http://www.akdi.ru
Date Established: 1996; **Freq:** Monthly; **Annual Sub.:** RUR 4560.00; **Circ:** 8,000
Editor: J. Samokhvalova; **Advertising Manager:** Elena Nizhelskaya
Profile: Gives practical advice on economics law, taxation and accountancy.
Language(s): Russian
ADVERTISING RATES:
Full Page Mono .... RUR 9000.00
Mechanical Data: Type Area: 142x200mm
BUSINESS: FINANCE & ECONOMICS

ELEKTROOBORUDOVANIYE: EKSPLUATATSIYA I REMONT 1862645RU17-3
Editorial: MOSKVA **Tel:** 495 945 32 28
Email: eakireeva@mail.ru **Web site:** http://oborud.promtransizdat.ru
Date Established: 2004; **Freq:** Monthly; **Annual Sub.:** RUR 6300.00; **Circ:** 5,300
Usual Pagination: 96
Profile: Production-technical magazine about exploitation of electrical energy equipment in industrial production.
Language(s): Russian
ADVERTISING RATES:
Full Page Colour .... RUR 12000.00
BUSINESS: ELECTRICAL

ELLE 749741RU74A-7
Editorial: ul. Shabolovka 31b, MOSKVA
Tel: 495 981 39 10 **Fax:** 495 981 39 11
Email: pr@elle.ru **Web site:** http://www.elle.ru
Date Established: 1996; **Freq:** Monthly; **Cover Price:** RUR 110.00; **Circ:** 220,000
Executive Editor: Tatiana Sycheva; **Advertising Director:** Elena Lakatosh
Profile: Magazine featuring fashion, beauty, health, fitness, astrology, shopping and articles on other women's issues.
Language(s): Russian
Readership: Aimed at women.
ADVERTISING RATES:
Full Page Colour .... RUR 587000.00
CONSUMER: WOMEN'S INTEREST CONSUMER MAGAZINES: Women's Interest

ELLE DECORATION 1774280RU74C-151
Formerly: ELLE Decor
Editorial: P.O. Box 64, 107045 MOSKVA
Tel: 495 981 39 10 **Fax:** 495 981 39 11
Email: elledecor@hfm.ru **Web site:** http://www.hfm.ru/elledecor
Date Established: 2001; **Freq:** Monthly; **Circ:** 75,000
Usual Pagination: 180
News Editor: Tatiana Parfenova; **Advertising Director:** Ludmila Stegniy
Profile: Magazine focusing on interior designs, decor and architecture.
Language(s): Russian
Readership: Aimed at wealthy and well-educated women in the age group 25-35.
ADVERTISING RATES:
Full Page Colour .... RUR 290000.00
Mechanical Data: Type Area: A4
CONSUMER: WOMEN'S INTEREST CONSUMER MAGAZINES: Home & Family

ENERGETIKA. PROMYSHLENNOST. REGIONY 1774091RU14B-2
Editorial: Shenkursky proyezd 3b, office 207, 127349 MOSKVA **Tel:** 495 406 48 65 **Fax:** 495 407 39 67
Email: amn@epr-journal.ru **Web site:** http://www.epr-journal.ru
Freq: Monthly; **Circ:** 5,000
Editor-in-Chief: Dmitry Kotelenets; **Advertising Director:** Vagan Martirosyan
Profile: Professional magazine on energy industry, engineering, metallurgy, oil and gas, and defence machinery industry.
Language(s): Russian
ADVERTISING RATES:
Full Page Colour .... RUR 120000.00
Mechanical Data: Type Area: 297 x 210mm
BUSINESS: COMMERCE, INDUSTRY & MANAGEMENT: Industry & Factories

ENERGORYNOK 1774007RU58-1
Editorial: ul. B. Pochtovaya 34, str. 8, 105066 MOSKVA **Tel:** 495 785 81 00 **Fax:** 495 785 81 00
Email: e-m@rcb.ru **Web site:** http://www.e-m.ru
Date Established: 2003; **Freq:** Monthly; **Annual Sub.:** RUR 7062.00; **Circ:** 6,000
Usual Pagination: 80
Editor: Elena Kolesnikova
Profile: Professional magazine about Russian market of energy, its developments and all aspects of functioning.
Language(s): Russian
ADVERTISING RATES:
Full Page Mono .... RUR 110000.00
Full Page Colour .... RUR 137000.00
Mechanical Data: Trim Size: 205 x 282mm
BUSINESS: ENERGY, FUEL & NUCLEAR

ENERGOSBEREZHENIYE 1616119RU3A-1
Editorial: ul. Rozhdestvenka 11, 107031 MOSKVA
Tel: 495 621 80 48 **Fax:** 495 621 64 29
Email: energo@abok.ru **Web site:** http://www.abok.ru
Date Established: 1999; **Freq:** 8 issues yearly; **Cover Price:** RUR 70.00
Annual Sub.: RUR 1132.80; **Circ:** 13,000
Usual Pagination: 104
Editor-in-Chief: Piotr Nikolaevich Aksionov; **Advertising Manager:** Aleksey Alexandrov
Profile: Journal focusing on new engineering, technological and legal development of energy and resource conservation in construction, housing & utility services and energy sector. Also covers analytical reviews, information on upcoming exhibitions and seminars.
Language(s): English; Russian
Readership: Read by engineering specialists, marketing and manufacturing companies and executives.
Mechanical Data: Type Area: A4
BUSINESS: HEATING & VENTILATION: Domestic Heating & Ventilation

EPIGRAPH 1774307RU1A-40
Editorial: ul.Derzhavina 28, office 604, 630091 NOVOSIBIRSK **Tel:** 3832 24 84 83
Email: inform@epig.ru **Web site:** http://www.epigraph.info
Freq: Weekly; **Annual Sub.:** RUR 1040.00; **Circ:** 13,000
Usual Pagination: 24
Editor-in-Chief: Ludmila Yankovenko; **Advertising Manager:** Anastasiya Chernikova
Profile: Regional weekly dedicated to problems of economics and economic developments in Novosibirsk, investments, regional commercial property and insurance.
Language(s): Russian
ADVERTISING RATES:
SCC .... RUR 330.00
Mechanical Data: Type Area: A 3
BUSINESS: FINANCE & ECONOMICS

THE EPOCH TIMES 1774236RU67B-199
Editorial: ul. Architektora Vlasova 21, korp. 3, 117335 MOSKVA **Tel:** 9265364789
Email: editor@epochtimes.ru **Web site:** http://www.epochtimes.ru
Freq: 24 issues yearly; **Circ:** 14,000
Usual Pagination: 16
Advertising Manager: Svetlana Kim
Profile: National newspaper about Russian-Chinese relations, political, cultural, economic news, health issues and tourism in Russian and Chinese languages.
Language(s): Chinese; Russian
ADVERTISING RATES:
Full Page Mono .... RUR 59280.00
Mechanical Data: Type Area: 250x360mm
REGIONAL DAILY & SUNDAY NEWSPAPERS: Regional Daily Newspapers

ESTETICHESKAYA MEDITSINA 1865454RU15A-3
Editorial: 1 Volokolamsky proyezd 10, str. 1, Science & Technology Park, 123060 MOSKVA
Tel: 495 981 94 93 **Fax:** 495 981 94 93
Email: aestued@cosmopress.ru **Web site:** http://cosmopress.ru
Freq: Quarterly; **Annual Sub.:** RUR 2000.00; **Circ:** 3,050
Usual Pagination: 100
Editor: Irina Taranova; **Executive Editor:** Violetta Dmitrieva
Profile: Publishes articles about latest scientific achievements and practical developments written by leading national and foreign specialists in aesthetic medicine.
Language(s): Russian
Readership: Scientific and practical magazine for plastic surgeons and dermatocosmetologists.
ADVERTISING RATES:
Full Page Colour .... RUR 71874.00
Mechanical Data: Type Area: 200x260mm
BUSINESS: COSMETICS & HAIRDRESSING: Cosmetics

EVRAZIA UFA 1774004RU2A-2
Editorial: ul. Oktyabrskoy Revolutsii 73, 450057 UFA
Tel: 3472 91 21 41 **Fax:** 3472 72 29 90
Email: eapress@ufanet.ru **Web site:** http://ewrasia.ru
Date Established: 1995; **Freq:** Weekly - Published on Thursdays; **Cover Price:** Free; **Circ:** 250,000
Usual Pagination: 40
Editor: Gulnara Fakhrova
Profile: Regional advertising-informative weekly.
Language(s): Russian
ADVERTISING RATES:
SCC .... RUR 50.00
Mechanical Data: Type Area: A3
BUSINESS: COMMUNICATIONS, ADVERTISING & MARKETING

EXPERT 1774298RU1A-27
Editorial: ul. Pravdy 24, 6 floor, 125866 MOSKVA
Tel: 495 789 44 65 **Fax:** 495 228 00 78
Email: vip@expert.ru **Web site:** http://www.expert.ru/printissues/expert
Date Established: 1995; **Freq:** Weekly; **Cover Price:** RUR 200.00; **Circ:** 85,000
Usual Pagination: 148
Editor: Valery Fadeev; **Advertising Director:** Anastasiya Zhavoronkova
Profile: Weekly business analytical magazine devoted to economical and financial issues in Russia.
Language(s): Russian
ADVERTISING RATES:
Full Page Colour .... RUR 460000.00
Mechanical Data: Trim Size: 210 x 280mm
Supplement(s): Expert Severo-Zapad - 52xY, Expert Volga - 52xY
BUSINESS: FINANCE & ECONOMICS

EXPERT SEVERO-ZAPAD 1774521RU1A-26
Editorial: ul. Razyazhaya 5, office 120, 191002 SANKT PETERBURG **Tel:** 12 324 80 25
Fax: 12 324 80 26
Email: info@expertnw.ru **Web site:** http://www.expert.ru/printissues/northwest
Date Established: 1999; **Freq:** Weekly; **Cover Price:** RUR 187.00; **Circ:** 10,000
Usual Pagination: 164
Editor: Dmitri Glumskov
Profile: Covers development of business, economics and companies in North-Western region of Russia and Baltic countries.
Language(s): Russian
ADVERTISING RATES:
Full Page Colour .... RUR 90000.00
Mechanical Data: Type Area: 210 x 280mm
Supplement to: Expert
BUSINESS: FINANCE & ECONOMICS

EXPERT VOLGA 1774367RU14A-21
Editorial: ul. Pravdy 24, 125866 MOSKVA
Tel: 495 789 44 65 **Fax:** 495 228 00 78
Email: ask@expert.ru **Web site:** http://www.expert.ru/printissues/volga
Date Established: 1999; **Freq:** Weekly; **Cover Price:** RUR 45.00; **Circ:** 10,200
Usual Pagination: 88
Editor-in-Chief: Vladimir Shtanov
Profile: Publication on economical growth and economical integrations, business developments in Volga region.
Language(s): Russian
ADVERTISING RATES:
Full Page Mono .... RUR 48415.00
Mechanical Data: Trim Size: 210 x 280mm + 5mm

Supplement to: Expert
BUSINESS: COMMERCE, INDUSTRY & MANAGEMENT

EZH-JURIST
1611051RU44-1
Editorial: ul. Chernyakhovskogo 16, 125319 MOSKVA **Tel:** 495 151 69 17 **Fax:** 495 152 02 90
Email: lawyer@ekonomika.ru **Web site:** http://www.gazeta-yurist.ru
Date Established: 1998; **Freq:** Weekly - Published on Friday; **Annual Sub.:** RUR 1938.00; **Circ:** 25,000
Usual Pagination: 16
Editor-in-Chief: Vasiliy Meshalkin; **Advertising Manager:** Lidia Vdovina
Profile: National newspaper focusing on legal news and issues.
Language(s): Russian
Readership: Read by lawyers and solicitors.
ADVERTISING RATES:
Full Page Mono .... RUR 34000.00
Agency Commission: 20%
Mechanical Data: Type Area: 264 x 380mm
Copy instructions: *Copy Date:* 10 days prior publication date
BUSINESS: LEGAL

F 13
1774037RU5C-112
Editorial: ul. Petukhova 16/1, office 706, 630088 NOVOSIBIRSK **Tel:** 383 342 15 98
Fax: 383 342 57 13
Email: news@f-13.ru **Web site:** http://www.f-13.ru
Freq: Monthly; **Circ:** 10,000
Usual Pagination: 64
Editor-in-Chief: Sergey Mist
Profile: Magazine dedicated to IT technologies, computing, software and hardware news.
Language(s): Russian
ADVERTISING RATES:
Full Page Colour .... RUR 18000.00
Mechanical Data: Type Area: 170x223mm
BUSINESS: COMPUTERS & AUTOMATION: Professional Personal Computers

FARMATSEVTICHESKOYE OBOZRENIYE
1774350RU37-2
Editorial: ul. Bolshaya Semenovskaya 42, 105094 MOSKVA **Tel:** 499 369 52 03 **Fax:** 499 369 48 01
Email: farmoboz@farmoboz.ru **Web site:** http://www.farmoboz.ru
Freq: Monthly; **Circ:** 15,000
Editor-in-Chief: Elena Sheveleva; **Advertising Manager:** Olga Danilova; **Publisher:** Elena Sheveleva
Profile: Provides practical solutions for pharmaceutical business.
Language(s): Russian
ADVERTISING RATES:
Full Page Colour .... EUR 800.00
Mechanical Data: Type Area: A3
BUSINESS: PHARMACEUTICAL & CHEMISTS

FARMATSEVTICHESKY VESTNIK
1615960RU37-5
Editorial: ul. Profsoyuznaya 57, office 249, 117420 MOSKVA **Tel:** 495 334 24 29 **Fax:** 495 334 29 82
Email: edition@pharmvestnik.ru **Web site:** http://www.pharmvestnik.ru
Date Established: 1994; **Freq:** 42 issues yearly; **Annual Sub.:** RUR 4347.00; **Circ:** 16,200
Usual Pagination: 32
Editor: S. Chervinsky
Profile: Informative-analytical weekly on pharmaceutical business in Russia, new medicine and technologies.
Language(s): Russian
ADVERTISING RATES:
Full Page Mono .... RUR 7900.00
Mechanical Data: Type Area: 274 x 385mm
BUSINESS: PHARMACEUTICAL & CHEMISTS

FASHION COLLECTION
1774468RU74B-223
Editorial: ul. Architektora Vlasova 3/1, 117218 MOSKVA **Tel:** 495 737 75 10 **Fax:** 495 737 75 11
Email: info@fcollection.ru **Web site:** http://fcollection.ru
Freq: Monthly; **Circ:** 117,500
Usual Pagination: 200
Editor-in-Chief: Marina Demchenko; **Advertising Manager:** Alexander Lareks
Profile: Russian fashion glossy magazine keeping track of latest fashion news, being a navigator in the world of fashion and style.
Language(s): Russian
ADVERTISING RATES:
Full Page Colour .... RUR 379000.00
Mechanical Data: Type Area: 230 x 297mm
CONSUMER: WOMEN'S INTEREST CONSUMER MAGAZINES: Women's Interest - Fashion

FHM
763148RU86C-2
Editorial: ul. Boshaya Andronevskaya 17, 109544 MOSKVA **Tel:** 495 745 84 12 **Fax:** 495 678 52 05
Email: fhm@fhm.ru **Web site:** http://www.fhm.ru
Date Established: 2001; **Freq:** Monthly; **Cover Price:** RUR 120.00; **Circ:** 110,000
Usual Pagination: 200
Editor: Maria Arzamasova
Profile: Men's lifestyle magazine for young men (25-35) with a good taste, fashion style and love for technical novelties.
Language(s): Russian
Readership: Aimed at men between 22 and 35 years.
ADVERTISING RATES:
Full Page Colour .... RUR 300000.00
Agency Commission: 15%
Mechanical Data: Type Area: 222 x 300mm, Col Length: 255mm, Trim Size: 275 x 215mm
Copy instructions: *Copy Date:* 6 weeks prior to publication date
CONSUMER: ADULT & GAY MAGAZINES: Men's Lifestyle Magazines

FINANS
1774685RU1A-50
Editorial: ul. Novodmitrovskaya 5a, str. 8, 127015 MOSKVA **Tel:** 495 660 17 27 **Fax:** 495 660 17 27
Email: inform@finansmag.ru **Web site:** http://www.finansmag.ru
Freq: Weekly; **Circ:** 48,700
Editor-in-Chief: Oleg Anisimov; **Advertising Director:** Marina Korsunova
Profile: Magazine on finance, credits, currencies, taxation, insurance, pensions, bank accounts, mortgage, pensions and property.
Language(s): Russian
ADVERTISING RATES:
Full Page Colour .... RUR 290000.00
Mechanical Data: Type Area: 210 x 275mm
BUSINESS: FINANCE & ECONOMICS

FINANSOVAYA GAZETA
1774331RU1A-20
Editorial: Staropimenovski pereulok 13, mail to P.O. box 598, Moskva 101000, 103006 MOSKVA
Tel: 499 166 04 12 **Fax:** 499 166 03 71
Email: fingazeta@fingazeta.ru **Web site:** http://www.fingazeta.ru
Date Established: 1991; **Freq:** Weekly - Published on Thurdays; **Circ:** 41,500
Usual Pagination: 16
Editor: Anna Malaya
Profile: Financial weekly covering all legal documentation of Ministry of Finance, taxation offices and Insurance Ministry.
Language(s): Russian
ADVERTISING RATES:
Full Page Mono .... RUR 100000.00
Mechanical Data: Type Area: 264 x 372mm
BUSINESS: FINANCE & ECONOMICS

FINANSOVY DIREKTOR
1774230RU1A-39
Editorial: M. Tolmachevski pereulok 1, 3 floor, 119017 MOSKVA **Tel:** 495 925 77 43
Fax: 495 933 54 46
Email: fd@fd.ru **Web site:** http://www.fd.ru
Date Established: 2002; **Freq:** 11 issues yearly; **Annual Sub.:** RUR 5412.00; **Circ:** 44,800
Usual Pagination: 96
Editor-in-Chief: Anna Chernetskaya; **Advertising Manager:** Lidia Bondareva
Profile: Presents financial news, information on macroeconomics events and financial markets reviews.
Language(s): Russian
ADVERTISING RATES:
Full Page Mono .... RUR 348000.00
Mechanical Data: Type Area: 170x 250mm
BUSINESS: FINANCE & ECONOMICS

FINANSY I KREDIT
1774332RU1A-21
Editorial: P.O. Box 10, 111401 MOSKVA
Tel: 495 621 69 49 **Fax:** 495 621 91 90
Email: post@financepress.ru **Web site:** http://www.financepress.ru
Date Established: 1995; **Freq:** Quarterly; **Circ:** 13,700
Usual Pagination: 100
Editor: Vera Gorokhova
Profile: Publication focused on finance, financial analysis, management and audit news.
Language(s): Russian
ADVERTISING RATES:
Full Page Mono .... RUR 38409.00
Mechanical Data: Type Area: 170 x 240mm
BUSINESS: FINANCE & ECONOMICS

FITNESS REPORT
1774005RU75P-1
Editorial: P. O. Box 25, 125167 MOSKVA
Tel: 495 925 51 56 **Fax:** 495 925 51 56
Email: elena@fitness-report.ru **Web site:** http://www.fitness-report.ru
Freq: Monthly; **Circ:** 10,000
Publisher: Alexander Popov
Profile: Professional magazine aiming at specialists of fitness industry.
Language(s): Russian
Mechanical Data: Type Area: 220x297mm
CONSUMER: SPORT: Fitness/Bodybuilding

FLOORING PROFESSIONAL MAGAZINE
1774110RU4B-5
Editorial: 4 Roschinsky proezd 20, str. 5, 115191 MOSKVA **Tel:** 495 540 73 40 **Fax:** 495 540 72 15
Email: info@flooringmagazine.ru **Web site:** http://www.flooringmagazine.ru
Freq: 6 issues yearly; **Cover Price:** RUR 180.00
Annual Sub.: RUR 1080.00; **Circ:** 5,000
News Editor: Nataliya Utkina; **Editor-in-Chief:** Roman Khaburgaev; **Publisher:** Annette Wassenaar
Profile: Keeps track of latest professional events, up-to-date marketing information about situation in national flooring market, about new trends, products, technologies, expert opinions and master classes, advice on organization of sales and ready-made design projects.
Language(s): Russian
Readership: Targets professionals of floor and flooring market: dealers, architects, interior designers, constructors, contractors and developers.
ADVERTISING RATES:
Full Page Colour .... EUR 2090.00
Mechanical Data: Type Area: A2
BUSINESS: ARCHITECTURE & BUILDING: Interior Design & Flooring

FOOD SERVICE
1774012RU11A-1
Editorial: 2 Zvenigorodskaya 2/1, 123100 MOSKVA
Tel: 495 228 19 66
Email: foodservice@moyo-delo.ru **Web site:** http://www.cafe-future.ru
Date Established: 2001; **Freq:** Monthly; **Cover Price:** RUR 200.00; **Circ:** 16,000
Usual Pagination: 68
Editor-in-Chief: Julia Matveeva; **Advertising Manager:** Marina Goluzinskaya; **Advertising Director:** Inga Lobjanidze
Profile: Russian edition of FoodService Europe & Middle East. Professional analytical magazine on eating out, catering and aiming at restaurants and cafes managers.
Language(s): Russian
ADVERTISING RATES:
Full Page Mono $2800.00
Full Page Colour $4000.00
Mechanical Data: Type Area: 230 x 300mm
BUSINESS: CATERING: Catering, Hotels & Restaurants

FOOTBALL
1774032RU75B-1
Editorial: ul. Timura Frunze 11, str. 44-45, 4 floor, 119992 MOSKVA **Tel:** 495 935 70 34
Fax: 495 780 88 24
Email: info@futbol-1960.ru **Web site:** http://futbol-1960.ru
Date Established: 1960; **Freq:** Weekly; **Cover Price:** RUR 20.00; **Circ:** 163,000
Usual Pagination: 52
Editor: Piyotr Kamenchenko; **Advertising Manager:** Marina Eremina; **Advertising Director:** Ruslan Kozlov
Profile: Popular weekly dedicated to football and all aspects related to this game.
Language(s): Russian
ADVERTISING RATES:
Full Page Colour .... RUR 200000.00
Mechanical Data: Type Area: 184x256mm
CONSUMER: SPORT: Football

FORBES
1774048RU14A-17
Editorial: 16 Dokukina str., building 1, floor 6, 129226 MOSKVA **Tel:** 495 98 05 252 **Fax:** 495 98 05 255
Email: info.forbes@axelspringer.ru **Web site:** http://www.forbesrussia.ru
Date Established: 2004; **Freq:** Monthly; **Annual Sub.:** RUR 1500.00; **Circ:** 140,000
Usual Pagination: 128
Editor-in-Chief: Maxim Kashulinsky; **Advertising Director:** Svetlana Laniyugova
Profile: Popular business magazine providing updated information opening fresh perspectives to its readers.
Language(s): Russian
ADVERTISING RATES:
Full Page Colour .... RUR 480000.00
Mechanical Data: Type Area: A4
BUSINESS: COMMERCE, INDUSTRY & MANAGEMENT

FOTODELO
1774599RU85A-1
Editorial: ul. Selskokhozhyastvennaya 19, korpus 2, 129226 MOSKVA **Tel:** 495 925 11 18
Fax: 495 925 11 18
Email: info@fotodelo.ru **Web site:** http://www.connect.ru
Date Established: 2002; **Freq:** Monthly; **Circ:** 50,000
Usual Pagination: 160
Profile: Popular magazine on photography in Russia and achievements of this art.
Language(s): Russian
Mechanical Data: Type Area: A3
CONSUMER: PHOTOGRAPHY & FILM MAKING: Photography

FREE TIME
1774514RU91R-2
Editorial: P.O. Box 137, 191002 SANKT PETERBURG **Tel:** 12 325 35 95 **Fax:** 12 575 63 86
Email: media@es.ru **Web site:** http://www.freetime-spb.ru
Date Established: 1998; **Freq:** Monthly; **Circ:** 40,000
Usual Pagination: 104
Editor: Andrey Andreev; **News Editor:** Olga Maksimova
Profile: Magazine offering ideas on how to spend your free time, provides information on fashion, holidays and entertainment.
Language(s): Russian
ADVERTISING RATES:
Full Page Colour .... RUR 160000.00
Mechanical Data: Type Area: 270 x 390mm
CONSUMER: RECREATION & LEISURE: Recreation & Leisure Related

GASTRONOMIYA. BAKALEYA
1774295RU22C-3
Editorial: Tverskoy bul. 22, 125009 MOSKVA
Tel: 495 629 05 35 **Fax:** 495 629 92 59
Email: gb@my-gb.ru **Web site:** http://www.my-gb.ru
Date Established: 1997; **Freq:** Weekly - Published on Tuesdays; **Cover Price:** Free; **Circ:** 9,340
Usual Pagination: 120
Editor: Dmitri Makhlin
Profile: Publication focused on food processing industry and gastronomy.
Language(s): Russian
Mechanical Data: Type Area: 200 x 275mm
BUSINESS: FOOD: Food Processing & Packaging

GAZETA
1774628RU65A-51
Editorial: ul. Zoologicheskaya 4, 123242 MOSKVA
Tel: 495 787 39 99 **Fax:** 495 787 39 99
Email: Kalugin@gzt.ru **Web site:** http://www.gzt.ru
Date Established: 2001; **Freq:** Daily; **Annual Sub.:** RUR 1500.00; **Circ:** 25,000
Usual Pagination: 40
Editor: Piotr Fadeev; **Advertising Director:** Aleksandr Shukhmin
Profile: National newspaper covering political news and facts, providing competent analysis and special reports.
Language(s): Russian
ADVERTISING RATES:
Full Page Mono .... RUR 219000.00
Mechanical Data: Type Area: 254x390mm
NATIONAL DAILY & SUNDAY NEWSPAPERS: National Daily Newspapers

GAZOVY BIZNES
1774352RU24-1
Editorial: Raskovoy Str. 22B, 125040 MOSKVA
Tel: 495 228 36 28 **Fax:** 495 228 36 26
Email: rgo@gazo.ru **Web site:** http://www.gazo.ru
Freq: 6 issues yearly; **Annual Sub.:** RUR 7700.00; **Circ:** 5,000
Usual Pagination: 80
Editor-in-Chief: Tatiana Yarkovaya
Profile: Professional magazine on natural gas prospecting, production, processing, transportation, contributing to establishing effective dialogs and build-up of intellectual potential of gas industry.
Language(s): Russian
Readership: Targets professionals of gas industry, CEOs of enterprises and gas companies, gas community.
ADVERTISING RATES:
Full Page Mono .... RUR 60000.00
Mechanical Data: Type Area: 210 x 297mm
BUSINESS: GAS

GDE DEN'GI
1774196RU1A-42
Editorial: ul. Sibirsky trakt 34, korpus 4, office 403-404, KAZAN' **Tel:** 432 511 49 67 **Fax:** 432 511 49 63
Email: post@g9e.ru **Web site:** http://www.g9e.ru
Freq: Weekly; **Circ:** 27,000
Editor: Anna Saushina; **Editor-in-Chief:** Sergey Kosheyev; **Publisher:** Alexander Andreyev
Profile: Major financial and business weekly in Tatarstan with reviews and analysis of banking sector, insurance, commerce, telecommunication and building.
Language(s): Russian
ADVERTISING RATES:
Full Page Mono .... RUR 49000.00
Mechanical Data: Type Area: 258 x 374mm
BUSINESS: FINANCE & ECONOMICS

GEO
1937463RU50-17
Editorial: Shmitovsky proyezd 3, str. 3, 123100 MOSKVA **Tel:** 495 937 60 90 **Fax:** 495 937 60 91
Email: geo@gjrussia.com **Web site:** http://www.geo.ru
Date Established: 1998; **Freq:** Monthly; **Cover Price:** RUR 85.00
Annual Sub.: RUR 660.00; **Circ:** 100,000
Usual Pagination: 250
Advertising Director: Elena Toporova
Profile: GEO is the reportage magazine about the world we live in, with an unmistakable optical design, comprehensive information and superb print quality, GEO gives its readers an expedition of the senses.
Language(s): Russian
Readership: GEO is a prime medium for reaching quality target groups in Russia. In the core target group aged 20-45 with higher education and higher household incomes, for years GEO has had a high and stable coverage of top target groups in Russia.
ADVERTISING RATES:
Full Page Colour .... RUR 430500.00
Mechanical Data: Type Area: 210x270mm, Trim Size: 213x270mm
BUSINESS: TRAVEL & TOURISM

GEOPROFI
1774274RU55-3
Editorial: Leninsky pr. 135, korp.2, 117513 MOSKVA
Tel: 495 223 32 78 **Fax:** 495 223 32 78
Email: info@geoprofi.ru **Web site:** http://www.geoprofi.ru
Freq: 6 issues yearly; **Circ:** 3,000
Usual Pagination: 72
Editor: M. Romanchikova; **Publisher:** V. Groshev

Profile: Professional magazine on geodesy, cartography and navigation.
Language(s): Russian
BUSINESS: APPLIED SCIENCE & LABORATORIES

GLAMOUR 1774448RU74B-222
Editorial: ul. Bolshaya Dmitrovka 11, 101999 MOSKVA **Tel:** 495 745 55 67 **Fax:** 495 777 00 25
Email: info@glamour.ru **Web site:** http://www.glamour.ru
Date Established: 2004; **Freq:** Monthly; **Annual Sub.:** RUR 900.00; **Circ:** 700,000
Executive Editor: Tatiana Kuznetsova; **Editor-in-Chief:** Alla Beliakova; **Advertising Manager:** Elena Rung; **Managing Editor:** Anna Verkholantseva; **Advertising Director:** Ekaterina Krylova; **Publisher:** Darya Pukhaeva
Profile: Glossy magazine covering beauty, fashion and celebrity features.
Language(s): Russian
ADVERTISING RATES:
Full Page Colour .... RUR 700000.00
Mechanical Data: Trim Size: 168 x 223mm
CONSUMER: WOMEN'S INTEREST CONSUMER MAGAZINES: Women's Interest - Fashion

GLASS PHYSICS AND CHEMISTRY 1600611RU12B-5
Editorial: Nab. Odoevskogo 24, Korpus 2, 199155 ST. PETERSBURG **Tel:** 12 328 85 84
Fax: 12 328 22 41
Email: gpcj@isc.ru **Web site:** http://www.maik.rssi.ru/journals/physglas.htm
ISSN: 1067-6596
Date Established: 1975; **Freq:** 6 issues yearly; **Circ:** 200
Editor-in-Chief: Vladimir Shevchenko
Profile: Publication of the Russian Academy of Sciences and the Institute of Silicate Chemistry focusing on manufacture of glass, theory and technologies.
Language(s): English; Russian
Readership: Aimed at scientists and manufacturers.
BUSINESS: CERAMICS, POTTERY & GLASS: Glass

GLAVBUKH 1774133RU1B-9
Editorial: P.O. Box 100, 127015 MOSKVA
Tel: 495 788 53 16 **Fax:** 495 788 53 17
Email: glavred@glavbukh.ru **Web site:** http://www.glavbukh.ru
Freq: 24 issues yearly; **Circ:** 181,850
Editor-in-Chief: Dmitri Voloshin
Profile: Professional magazine on accountancy, accountant issues and legal information.
Language(s): Russian
ADVERTISING RATES:
Full Page Colour .... RUR 245000.00
Mechanical Data: Trim Size: 173 x 255mm
BUSINESS: FINANCE & ECONOMICS: Accountancy

GLAVNY ENERGETIK 1862643RU58-19
Editorial: MOSKVA **Tel:** 495 945 32 28
Email: glavenergo@mail.ru **Web site:** http://glavenergo.promtransizdat.ru
Date Established: 2003; **Freq:** Monthly; **Annual Sub.:** RUR 6420.00; **Circ:** 3,000
Usual Pagination: 104
Publisher: A. Shkirmontov
Profile: Professional scientific-technical magazine on exploitation and optimisation of management of energy complex in industrial plants.
Language(s): Russian
Readership: Targets chief power engineering specialists.
BUSINESS: ENERGY, FUEL & NUCLEAR

GORNYI ZHURNAL 763722RU30-50
Editorial: Office G-563, Leninskii prospekt 6, 119991 MOSKVA **Tel:** 495 236 97 48 **Fax:** 495 236 97 18
Email: gornjournal@rudmet.ru **Web site:** http://www.rudmet.ru
Date Established: 1825; **Freq:** Monthly; **Annual Sub.:** RUR 13200.00; **Circ:** 3,000
Usual Pagination: 160
Advertising Manager: Natalia Kolykhalova; **Publisher:** Alexander Vorobiev
Profile: Magazine covering problems of mining and quarrying of mineral resources.
Language(s): Russian
Readership: Aimed at engineers and researchers.
ADVERTISING RATES:
Full Page Colour .... EUR 950.00
Mechanical Data: Type Area: 210 x 297mm
BUSINESS: MINING & QUARRYING

GORODOK+ 1774064RU2A-12
Editorial: ul. Zosimovskaya 9, 160035 VOLOGDA
Tel: 172 21 00 01
Email: mail@gazeta-gorodok.ru **Web site:** http://www.gazeta-gorodok.ru
Date Established: 1995; **Freq:** Weekly - Published on Fridays; **Cover Price:** Free; **Circ:** 142,800
Usual Pagination: 96
Advertising Manager: Svetlana Dubskaya
Profile: Weekly regional newspaper delivered free and containing advertising materials.
Language(s): Russian

ADVERTISING RATES:
Full Page Colour .... RUR 37700.00
Mechanical Data: Type Area: 420 x 291mm
BUSINESS: COMMUNICATIONS, ADVERTISING & MARKETING

GQ 1774047RU74Q-11
Editorial: Bolshaya Dmitrovka 11, 125009 MOSKVA
Tel: 495 745 55 65 **Fax:** 495 777 00 24
Email: editorial@gq.ru **Web site:** http://www.gq.ru
Date Established: 2007; **Freq:** Monthly; **Circ:** 100,000
Editor-in-Chief: Nikolay Uskov; **Advertising Director:** Irina Elizarova; **Publisher:** Dmitri Kreslavsky
Profile: Glossy lifestyle magazine for men, pictures by thebest photographers, photo shoots with the most beautiful women in the world, columns and essays by world renowned writers, and interviews with the most hard-to-get politicians, businessmen, stars of film and show business. Regularly features the latest news from leading designers, scientific developments, gastronomic discoveries and the best hotels in the world.
Language(s): Russian
ADVERTISING RATES:
Full Page Colour .... RUR 425000.00
Mechanical Data: Type Area: 230 x 300mm
CONSUMER: WOMEN'S INTEREST CONSUMER MAGAZINES: Lifestyle

GRAZIA 1774689RU74B-225
Editorial: ul. Polkovaya 3, str.1, 127018 MOSKVA
Tel: 495 232 03 200 **Fax:** 495 232 17 61
Email: k.kilibarda@imedia.ru **Web site:** http://www.graziamagazine.ru
Freq: Monthly; **Circ:** 120,000
Editor-in-Chief: Alena Peneva; **Advertising Director:** Yuliya Nemtsova; **Publisher:** Maria Zueva
Profile: Magazine on fashion, beauty and cosmetics, fashion events.
Language(s): Russian
ADVERTISING RATES:
Full Page Colour .... RUR 225000.00
Mechanical Data: Type Area: A3
CONSUMER: WOMEN'S INTEREST CONSUMER MAGAZINES: Women's Interest - Fashion

HARPER'S BAZAAR 1600531RU74A-10
Editorial: ul.Polkovaya 3, zdaniye 1, 127018 MOSKVA **Tel:** 495 23 23 200 **Fax:** 495 23 21 761
Email: s.evstigneeva@imedia.ru **Web site:** http://www.bazaar.ru
Date Established: 1996; **Freq:** Monthly; **Cover Price:** RUR 125.00; **Circ:** 135,000
Usual Pagination: 344
Advertising Director: Svetlana Penkina; **Publisher:** Ludmila Abramenko
Profile: Magazine with a mix of fashion, beauty, culture and high society features.
Language(s): Russian
Readership: Aimed at Russian women with a high disposable income.
ADVERTISING RATES:
Full Page Colour .... RUR 467500.00
Mechanical Data: Trim Size: 210 x 275 mm
CONSUMER: WOMEN'S INTEREST CONSUMER MAGAZINES: Women's Interest

HERMITAGE MAGAZINE 1873057RU84A-9
Editorial: Isaakievskaya pl. 4, 190000 SANKT PETERBURG **Tel:** 12 325 60 80 **Fax:** 12 314 21 20
Email: hermitage@sptimes.ru **Web site:** http://www.hermitagemagazine.com
Freq: Quarterly; **Annual Sub.:** RUR 400.00; **Circ:** 15,000
News Editor: Zoya Necheporenko; **Executive Editor:** Alexey Moskin; **Advertising Manager:** Oksana Bogomazova; **Advertising Director:** Yana Ermakova
Profile: Magazine about history, culture, museums, exhibitions, art galleries.
Language(s): English; Russian
ADVERTISING RATES:
Full Page Colour .... RUR 122500.00
Mechanical Data: Type Area: 224 x 280mm
CONSUMER: THE ARTS & LITERARY: Arts

HOMES & GARDENS 1826072RU4B-1
Editorial: ul. Lizy Chaykinoy 1, 6 floor, 125190 MOSKVA **Tel:** 495 93 30 720 **Fax:** 495 93 30 720
Email: reklama@arnold-prize.ru **Web site:** http://www.stylenews.ru
Date Established: 2006; **Freq:** Monthly; **Circ:** 100,000
Usual Pagination: 64
Advertising Manager: Vera Kolgushkina
Profile: Featuring information on interior design and gives advice on arranging homes.
Language(s): Russian
Readership: Aimed at successful young people in the age group from 25 to 35.
ADVERTISING RATES:
Full Page Colour .... RUR 222600.00
Mechanical Data: Trim Size: 450 x 289 mm
BUSINESS: ARCHITECTURE & BUILDING: Interior Design & Flooring

HOOLIGAN 1774044RU74Q-15
Editorial: ul. Timura Frunze 11, str. 44-45, 4 floor, 119992 MOSKVA **Tel:** 495 935 70 34
Fax: 495 780 88 24
Email: zinatulin@gameland.ru **Web site:** http://www.xyligan.ru
Freq: Monthly; **Circ:** 81,500
Usual Pagination: 112
Executive Editor: Anastasiya Fedorova; **Publisher:** Denis Kalinin
Profile: Provocative magazine on lifestyle and arts, urban tendencies in culture, music and design.
Language(s): Russian
ADVERTISING RATES:
Full Page Colour .... RUR 330000.00
Mechanical Data: Type Area: 230x270mm
CONSUMER: WOMEN'S INTEREST CONSUMER MAGAZINES: Lifestyle

HR-MANAGEMENT 1774229RU14F-1
Editorial: M. Tolmachevski pereulok 1, 3 floor, 119017 MOSKVA **Tel:** 495 933 55 19
Fax: 495 925 77 43
Email: reklama@b2bmedia.ru **Web site:** http://www.4hr.ru
Date Established: 2003; **Freq:** Monthly; **Annual Sub.:** RUR 3498.00; **Circ:** 16,000
Usual Pagination: 80
Editor-in-Chief: Kristina Ardelanu; **Advertising Manager:** Lidia Bondareva
Profile: Russian edition of British magazine Human Resources and writes about newest technologies in HR, companies' strategies, training and education.
Language(s): Russian
ADVERTISING RATES:
Full Page Mono .... RUR 145000.00
Mechanical Data: Type Area: 205 x 275mm
BUSINESS: COMMERCE, INDUSTRY & MANAGEMENT: Training & Recruitment

IDEI VASHEGO DOMA 1861976RU4B-9
Editorial: ul. Nagatinskaya 1, str. 29, 117105 MOSKVA **Tel:** 495 933 43 43 **Fax:** 495 937 52 15
Email: dsh@salonpress.ru **Web site:** http://www.ivd.ru
Date Established: 1997; **Freq:** 11 issues yearly; **Circ:** 280,000
Usual Pagination: 290
Advertising Manager: Daria Starodubova; **Advertising Director:** Dmitri Shakhnazarov
Profile: Provides advice on buying dwelling, interior style and design, re-planning and furnishing and all the construction and repair works, building materials and apartment planning, decoration methods and ideas.
Language(s): Russian
Readership: The magazine targets economically and socially active people aged 25-54, whose financial status can be attributed to the wealthy group of population. Over a half of the magazine's readers occupies prominent social positions of executives or high-paid professionals.
ADVERTISING RATES:
Full Page Colour .... RUR 265000.00
Mechanical Data: Type Area: 203x275mm
BUSINESS: ARCHITECTURE & BUILDING: Interior Design & Flooring

INFLIGHT REVIEW 1614094RU89D-8
Editorial: Novodanilovskaya nab.4a, 117105 MOSKVA **Tel:** 495 510 22 11 **Fax:** 495 510 49 69
Email: a.bashkeeva@spn.ru **Web site:** http://www.spn.ru/publishing/journals/inflight
Date Established: 1990; **Freq:** Monthly; **Cover Price:** Free; **Circ:** 70,000
Usual Pagination: 250
Editor: Alina Bashkeeva; **Editor-in-Chief:** Irina Tiusonina; **Advertising Manager:** Natalia Vasilieva; **Advertising Director:** Aleksey Ivanov
Profile: A full-colour glossy news & entertaining magazine in Russian and English distributed free of charge on all Russia State Transport Company flights.
Language(s): English; Russian
ADVERTISING RATES:
Full Page Colour .... RUR 285000.00
Mechanical Data: Type Area: 212 x 276mm
CONSUMER: HOLIDAYS & TRAVEL: In-Flight Magazines

INSTYLE 1805685RU74A-23
Editorial: Ul. Marksistskaya 34, build.10, MOSKVA, 109147 **Tel:** 495 974 22 60 **Fax:** 495 974 22 63
Email: instyle@instylemag.ru
Date Established: 2005; **Freq:** 10 issues yearly; **Cover Price:** RUR 90.00
Annual Sub.: RUR 1000.00; **Circ:** 120,000
Usual Pagination: 320
Advertising Manager: Denis Baserov; **Publisher:** Inga Ivanova
Profile: Everything about famous people, fabulous life and beautiful things.
Language(s): Russian
Readership: Aimed at women in the age group from 25 to 45 with over average income.
ADVERTISING RATES:
Full Page Colour .... RUR 386400.00
Mechanical Data: Type Area: 230 x 277mm
CONSUMER: WOMEN'S INTEREST CONSUMER MAGAZINES: Women's Interest

INTELLIGENT ENTERPRISE 1613662RU14A-3
Editorial: ul. Marksistkaya 34, Korp. 10, 109147 MOSKVA **Tel:** 495 974 22 60 **Fax:** 495 974 22 63
Email: partner@iemag.ru **Web site:** http://www.iemag.ru
Date Established: 1999; **Freq:** 30 issues yearly; **Circ:** 15,000
Editor: Konstantin Zimin; **Advertising Manager:** Nadezhda Aldoshkina; **Advertising Director:** Vladimir Boryshpolskiy
Profile: Magazine focusing on the economic aspects of implementing IT solutions in enterprises includes articles on management and technology issues. Also features interviews with leading IT managers from Russian and international companies.
Language(s): Russian
Readership: Aimed at IT managers and executives.
BUSINESS: COMMERCE, INDUSTRY & MANAGEMENT

INTERBIZNES 1774014RU14A-28
Editorial: ul. Mozhayskaya 15, 190013 SANKT PETERBURG **Tel:** 12 317 80 05 **Fax:** 12 317 80 02
Email: interbiz@poster-group.ru **Web site:** http://www.ibmagazine.ru
Date Established: 1993; **Freq:** 10 issues yearly; **Cover Price:** Free; **Circ:** 30,000
Usual Pagination: 180
Editor: Natalia Astakhova; **Editor-in-Chief:** Vera Dmitrieva; **Advertising Manager:** Ekaterina Markova; **Advertising Director:** Dmitiri Sorokin
Profile: Presents review of markets, interviews with outstanding businessmen, opinions of experts on economic issues, events and business developments in St. Petersburg region.
Language(s): Russian
ADVERTISING RATES:
Full Page Mono .... RUR 150000.00
Mechanical Data: Type Area: 230 x 295mm
BUSINESS: COMMERCE, INDUSTRY & MANAGEMENT

INTERFAX VREMYA 1615292RU65J-62
Editorial: ul. 1-ya Tverskaya-Yamskaya, d. 2, 127006 MOSKVA **Tel:** 495 251 67 82 **Fax:** 495 251 08 62
Email: adk27@adkbca.ru **Web site:** http://www.ifvremya.ru
Date Established: 1995; **Freq:** Weekly - Published on Monday; **Circ:** 1,140,000
Editor: Aleksey Valentinovich Chernyshev; **Advertising Director:** Maksim Zemyaninovich Yakovlev
Profile: Inter-regional newspaper covering national news, politics, economics, cultural and social issues.
Language(s): Russian
NATIONAL DAILY & SUNDAY NEWSPAPERS: National Weekly Newspapers

INTERIER + DIZAIN 1938305RU4B-12
Editorial: ul. Rochdelskaya 15, str. 10, 123022 MOSKVA **Tel:** 495 620 08 00 **Fax:** 495 620 08 01
Email: interior@forwarding.ru **Web site:** http://interior.ru
Date Established: 1996; **Freq:** 11 issues yearly; **Circ:** 95,000
Profile: Magazine about current trends in interior design, bringing the best of western and Russian interior culture.
Language(s): Russian
ADVERTISING RATES:
Full Page Colour .... RUR 290000.00
BUSINESS: ARCHITECTURE & BUILDING: Interior Design & Flooring

IT EXPERT 1774264RU5B-16
Editorial: Leningradskoye shosse 18, korp. 1, office 342, 125171 MOSKVA **Tel:** 495 775 16 76
Email: it.news@finestreet.ru **Web site:** http://www.finestreet.ru
Freq: Monthly; **Circ:** 5,000
Editor-in-Chief: Michael Grigoryev
Profile: Provides practical solutions for IT specialists.
Language(s): Russian
Mechanical Data: Type Area: A3
BUSINESS: COMPUTERS & AUTOMATION: Data Processing

IT MANAGER 1774136RU5B-17
Editorial: Leningradskoye shosse 18, korp. 1, office 342, 125171 MOSKVA **Tel:** 495 775 16 76
Email: it.news@finestreet.ru **Web site:** http://www.finestreet.ru
Freq: Monthly; **Circ:** 25,000
Editor: Andrey Vinogradov; **Executive Editor:** Elena Yakovenko
Profile: Professional publication on IT solutions aiming at companies' top managers.
Language(s): Russian
Mechanical Data: Type Area: A3
BUSINESS: COMPUTERS & AUTOMATION: Data Processing

IT NEWS 714149RU5C-100
Editorial: Leningradskoye shosse 18, korp. 1, office 342, 125171 MOSKVA **Tel:** 495 775 16 76
Fax: 12 346 06 65
Email: it.news@finestreet.ru **Web site:** http://www.finestreet.ru

Date Established: 1993; **Freq:** Monthly; **Circ:** 29,000
Editor: Andrey Vinogradov; **Executive Editor:** Elena Yakovenko; **Editor-in-Chief:** Gennady Belash; **Advertising Manager:** Veronika Pestova
Profile: Newspaper covering IT technologies, all aspects of computer systems design and applied software, computer networking and system integration.
Language(s): Russian
Readership: Aimed at IT and computer systems' specialists.
BUSINESS: COMPUTERS & AUTOMATION: Professional Personal Computers

---

ITIMES 1774435RU5B-18
Editorial: ul. Mamina-Sibiryaka 85, office 421, YEKATERINBURG **Tel:** 908 904 36 59
Email: pr@r2b.ru **Web site:** http://www.r2b.ru/itimes.php
Freq: Monthly; **Circ:** 3,000
Profile: Informative-analytical monthly publication on IT technologies in Ural region, their developments and tendencies.
Language(s): Russian
ADVERTISING RATES:
Full Page Mono .... RUR 30000.00
Mechanical Data: Type Area: A3
BUSINESS: COMPUTERS & AUTOMATION: Data Processing

ITOGI 763186RU82-50
Editorial: Leningradskoye Shosse 5 A, 125080 MOSKVA **Tel:** 495 753 80 58 **Fax:** 495 753 71 48
Email: itogi@7days.ru **Web site:** http://www.itogi.ru
Date Established: 1996; **Freq:** Weekly - Published on Monday; **Annual Sub.:** RUR 1603.20; **Circ:** 87,000
Usual Pagination: 84
Editor: Kirill Dibski; **Advertising Manager:** Svetlana Dolgih; **Advertising Director:** Nana Tsobekhia
Profile: Magazine featuring national and international news, also includes political cultural, social and business issues.
Language(s): Russian
Readership: Aimed at those interested in current affairs.
ADVERTISING RATES:
Full Page Mono .... RUR 210000.00
Full Page Colour .... RUR 330000.00
Agency Commission: 15%
Mechanical Data: Type Area: 250 x 192mm, Col Length: 250mm, Print Process: Offset
Copy instructions: *Copy Date:* B/W: 14 days prior to publication date. Colour: 20 days prior to publication date
CONSUMER: CURRENT AFFAIRS & POLITICS

IVAN 1774025RU86C-14
Editorial: ul. Malaya Pochtovaya 12, str., office 307, 105082 MOSKVA **Tel:** 495 229 62 00
Fax: 495 229 62 00
Web site: http://www.ivan-mag.ru
Freq: Monthly; **Cover Price:** RUR 90.00; **Circ:** 150,000
Usual Pagination: 160
Editor-in-Chief: Alexander Chechelev; **Advertising Director:** Marina Panteleeva
Profile: Men's magazine on men's fashion, women, lifestyle, cars, mobile phones and digital devices.
Language(s): Russian
ADVERTISING RATES:
Full Page Colour .... RUR 252000.00
Mechanical Data: Type Area: 200 x 277 mm
CONSUMER: ADULT & GAY MAGAZINES: Men's Lifestyle Magazines

IZVESTIA 1201772RU65A-5
Editorial: ul. Tverskaja 18, Korpus 1, 127994 MOSKVA **Tel:** 495 650 05 81 **Fax:** 495 20 93 620
Email: izv@izvestia.ru **Web site:** http://www.izvestia.ru
Date Established: 1917; **Freq:** Daily - Published Monday to Friday; **Circ:** 148,672
Usual Pagination: 16
Profile: National general interest quality daily paper covering all aspects of Russian politics and economy.
Language(s): Russian
ADVERTISING RATES:
Full Page Mono .... RUR 660000.00
Agency Commission: 15%
Mechanical Data: Type Area: 374 x 540mm
NATIONAL DAILY & SUNDAY NEWSPAPERS: National Daily Newspapers

---

JET 1774089RU6R-1
Editorial: Novy Arbat 15, str. 1, 13 floor, 119019 MOSKVA **Tel:** 495 730 57 28 **Fax:** 495 690 51 07
Email: info@jetmedia.ru **Web site:** http://www.jetmagazine.ru
Freq: Monthly; **Annual Sub.:** RUR 3000.00; **Circ:** 30,000
Usual Pagination: 160
Editor: Alexey Samolotov; **Advertising Manager:** Vadim Shivarihin
Profile: Provides competent analysis of business aviation, future and trends, usage of personal aircraft for business and leisure travel.
Language(s): English; Russian
ADVERTISING RATES:
Full Page Colour .... RUR 250000.00
Mechanical Data: Type Area: 215 x 285mm
BUSINESS: AVIATION & AERONAUTICS: Aviation Related

JOURNALIST 1774291RU2B-1
Editorial: ul. Chernyakhovskogo 16, 125319 MOSKVA **Tel:** 495 152 88 71 **Fax:** 495 152 88 71
Email: jour-nal@yandex.ru **Web site:** http://www.journalist-virt.ru
Date Established: 1914; **Freq:** Monthly; **Circ:** 8,352
Usual Pagination: 96
Editor: Gennady Maltsev
Profile: Professional magazine of Journalist association about media, journalism and with useful information for journalists.
Language(s): Russian
Mechanical Data: Type Area: A4
BUSINESS: COMMUNICATIONS, ADVERTISING & MARKETING: Press

KADROVOYE DELO 1774614RU14F-4
Editorial: ul. Novoslobodskaya 14/19, 127030 MOSKVA **Tel:** 495 775 77 65 **Fax:** 495 785 01 13
Email: kd@fr.ru **Web site:** http://www.kdelo.ru
Freq: Monthly; **Annual Sub.:** RUR 4212.00; **Circ:** 40,000
Usual Pagination: 128
Editor-in-Chief: Anna Vasenina
Profile: Journal for HR-managers, helps to solve problems of personnel office-work and HR-management. All personnel documentation, solutions of disputed situations, legal support for company, HR-experience of Russian and western companies.
Language(s): Russian
Mechanical Data: Type Area: A3
BUSINESS: COMMERCE, INDUSTRY & MANAGEMENT: Training & Recruitment

---

KALININGRADSKAYA PRAVDA 1774116RU67B-95
Editorial: ul. Karla Marksa 18, 236000 KALININGRAD
Tel: 4012 21 49 74 **Fax:** 4012 21 77 33
Email: info@kaliningradka.ru **Web site:** http://www.kaliningradka.ru
Date Established: 1946; **Freq:** 260 issues yearly; **Circ:** 22,000
Usual Pagination: 32
Editor: Damir Batyrshin
Profile: Daily regional with political, cultural, social news and entertainment.
Language(s): Russian
ADVERTISING RATES:
SCC .... RUR 50.00
Mechanical Data: Type Area: A3
REGIONAL DAILY & SUNDAY NEWSPAPERS: Regional Daily Newspapers

---

KAPITAL WEEKLY 1774452RU1A-47
Editorial: ul. Druzhby 34, 614990 PERM
Tel: 3422 48 03 60 **Fax:** 3422 48 03 60
Email: kapital@zvezda.nevod.ru **Web site:** http://www.kapital.perm.ru
Freq: Weekly - Published on Wednesdays; **Circ:** 15,000
Usual Pagination: 6
Editor: Nataliya Kopytova
Profile: Business weekly containing analytical information, regional stock exchange news, regional economics news.
Language(s): Russian
ADVERTISING RATES:
SCC .... RUR 45.00
Mechanical Data: Type Area: A2
BUSINESS: FINANCE & ECONOMICS

KARIERA 763180RU14A-13
Editorial: Ul. Bolshaya Andronevskaya 17, 109544 MOSKVA **Tel:** 495 745 84 01
Email: nklimenko@profilemedia.ru **Web site:** http://www.kariera.idr.ru
Date Established: 1998; **Freq:** 11 issues yearly; **Annual Sub.:** RUR 508.20; **Circ:** 80,000
Usual Pagination: 128
Editor: Mikhail Trubetskoy; **Editor-in-Chief:** Aleksander Zotikov; **Advertising Manager:** Sergey Vierbitsky; **Advertising Director:** Aleksander Rudnev
Profile: Magazine covering business issues, economics, investments and financial markets.
Language(s): Russian
Readership: Aimed at dynamic men between 22 and 35 years who want to make a business career.
ADVERTISING RATES:
Full Page Colour .... RUR 221000.00
Agency Commission: 15%
Mechanical Data: Trim Size: 220 x 280mm
Copy instructions: *Copy Date:* 1 month prior to publication date
BUSINESS: COMMERCE, INDUSTRY & MANAGEMENT

KARJALAN SANOMAT 718448RU72-500
Editorial: ul. Titova 3, 185610 PETROZAVODSK
Tel: 142 78 29 28 **Fax:** 142 78 29 15
Email: karjalansanomat@sampo.ru **Web site:** http://karjalansanomat.sampo.ru
Date Established: 1920; **Freq:** Weekly - Published on Wednesday; **Cover Price:** RUR 4.00
Annual Sub.: RUR 55.00; **Circ:** 1,100
Usual Pagination: 16
Editor-in-Chief: Robert Manner; **Managing Editor:** Mikko Nesvitski
Profile: Newspaper issued in Russian Carelia reporting on political, economic, cultural and other events.
Language(s): Finnish
Readership: Aimed at Finns and their descendants living in Russian Karelia, Finns in Finland interested in what is going on in former Finnish territories in Russian Carelia and those studying the Finnish language in Russia.
ADVERTISING RATES:
Full Page Mono .... EUR 543.00
LOCAL NEWSPAPERS

KAZANSKIYE VEDOMOSTI 1774612RU67B-410
Editorial: ul. Chistopolskaya 5, 420066 KAZAN
Tel: 43 542 98 16 **Fax:** 43 542 98 76
Email: gazeta@kazved.ru **Web site:** http://www.kazved.ru
Date Established: 1991; **Freq:** 260 issues yearly; **Annual Sub.:** RUR 996.00; **Circ:** 42,860
Usual Pagination: 24
Editor: Venera Yakupova; **Advertising Manager:** Marina Kubrina; **Advertising Director:** Liliya Kharisova
Profile: Regional daily with political, social and cultural news.
Language(s): Russian
ADVERTISING RATES:
Full Page Mono .... RUR 94300.00
Mechanical Data: Type Area: 250 x 370mm
REGIONAL DAILY & SUNDAY NEWSPAPERS: Regional Daily Newspapers

---

KHABAROVSKY KOMPYUTERNY RYNOK 1774097RU5C-114
Editorial: ul. Kim U Chena 65, KHABAROVSK
Tel: 4212 30 05 37 **Fax:** 4212 31 59 24
Email: hkr@hkr.ru
Freq: Weekly; **Circ:** 4,600
Usual Pagination: 92
Profile: Computer magazine with hardware and software news, mobile phones and computer games reviews.
Language(s): Russian
ADVERTISING RATES:
Full Page Mono .... RUR 1700.00
Full Page Colour .... RUR 6500.00
Mechanical Data: Type Area: 180x275mm
BUSINESS: COMPUTERS & AUTOMATION: Professional Personal Computers

---

KHLEBOPECHENIYE ROSSII 1611118RU8A-101
Editorial: Sadovaya-Spasskaya 18, komn. 601, 607, 107996 MOSCOW **Tel:** 495 607 17 70
Fax: 495 607 28 61
Email: foodprom@ropnet.ru **Web site:** http://www.foodprom.ru
Freq: 6 issues yearly; **Circ:** 3,000
Editor: Elena Kaouts; **Advertising Manager:** Ekaterina Varekha
Profile: Magazine providing information about bread baking processes.
Language(s): Russian
Readership: Aimed at bakers.
ADVERTISING RATES:
Full Page Mono .... RUR 1000.00
Full Page Colour .... RUR 1800.00
Mechanical Data: Type Area: 210 x 290mm, Trim Size: 210 x 290mm
BUSINESS: BAKING & CONFECTIONERY: Baking

KHLEBOPEKARNOYE PROIZVODSTVO 1862646RU8A-102
Editorial: MOSKVA **Tel:** 495 945 32 28
Email: topaz777@mtu-net.ru **Web site:** http://hleb.promtransizdat.ru
Date Established: 2004; **Freq:** Monthly; **Annual Sub.:** RUR 6670.00; **Circ:** 5,000
Usual Pagination: 80
Profile: Professional publication on new technologies, equipment, efficient methods of management in bread baking and confectionery.
Language(s): Russian
ADVERTISING RATES:
Full Page Colour .... RUR 12000.00
BUSINESS: BAKING & CONFECTIONERY: Baking

KHLEBOPRODUCTY 754472RU8A-100
Editorial: 1-y Shipkovsky Pereulok 20, 115093 MOSKVA **Tel:** 495 959 66 49 **Fax:** 495 959 66 74
Email: khlebprod@mtu-net.ru **Web site:** http://www.khlebprod.ru
ISSN: 0235-2508
Date Established: 1927; **Freq:** Monthly; **Annual Sub.:** RUR 4752.00; **Circ:** 3,000
Usual Pagination: 80
Advertising Manager: Yury Gargalyk
Profile: Magazine focusing on the baking industry. Includes information on flour products and pastas.
Language(s): Russian
Readership: Aimed at baking industry professionals.
ADVERTISING RATES:
Full Page Colour .... EUR 1020.00
Agency Commission: 15%
Mechanical Data: Type Area: 255 x 177mm, Trim Size: 290 x 210mm, Print Process: Offset, Col Length: 255mm
Copy instructions: *Copy Date:* 2 colours: 30 days prior to publication date. 4 colours: 45 days prior to publication date
Average ad content per issue: 40%
BUSINESS: BAKING & CONFECTIONERY: Baking

KHRANENIJE I PERERABOTKA SEL'KHOZSYRYA 1611170RU22C-1
Editorial: Sadovaya-Spasskaya 18, komn. 601, 607, 107996 MOSKVA **Tel:** 495 607 17 70
Fax: 495 607 28 61
Email: foodprom@ropnet.ru **Web site:** http://www.foodprom.ru
Freq: Monthly; **Cover Price:** RUR 330.00; **Circ:** 2,000
Editor: Olga Presnyakova
Profile: Scientific-theoretical magazine covering all the aspects of food processing industry.
Language(s): Russian
Readership: Read by food manufacturers and technologists.
ADVERTISING RATES:
Full Page Mono .... EUR 1000.00
Full Page Colour .... EUR 1800.00
BUSINESS: FOOD: Food Processing & Packaging

KHUDOZHESTVENNAYA SHKOLA 1774436RU84A-5
Editorial: ul. Urzhumskaya 4, str. 31, 3 floor, 129343 MOSKVA **Tel:** 495 504 09 37 **Fax:** 495 504 09 37
Email: redactor@art-publish.ru **Web site:** http://art-publish.ru
Date Established: 2003; **Freq:** 6 issues yearly; **Cover Price:** RUR 75.00; **Circ:** 6,000
Usual Pagination: 48
Editor: Nina Grom; **Advertising Director:** Olga Olevich
Profile: Informative magazine about arts: painting and drawing for teachers of arts schools.
Language(s): Russian
ADVERTISING RATES:
Full Page Colour .... RUR 30000.00
Mechanical Data: Trim Size: 210 x 287mm
CONSUMER: THE ARTS & LITERARY: Arts

KNIZHNYI BIZNES 1774305RU60A-3
Editorial: P.O. Box 417, 119017 MOSKVA
Tel: 495 951 81 86 **Fax:** 495 953 11 24
Email: info@kb-alvis.ru **Web site:** http://www.kb-alvis.ru
Date Established: 1993; **Freq:** 10 issues yearly; **Circ:** 4,000
Usual Pagination: 80
Editor: Vladimir Drabkin
Profile: Professional magazine for book business specialists.
Language(s): Russian
Readership: Aimed at publishers, book traders, librarians and specialists.
ADVERTISING RATES:
Full Page Colour .... RUR 32900.00
Mechanical Data: Type Area: 210 x 297mm
BUSINESS: PUBLISHING: Publishing & Book Trade

KOMMERCHESKAYA NEDVIZHIMOST ROSSII 1774149RU1E-18
Editorial: 4 Roschinsky proyezd 20, str. 5, 115191 MOSKVA **Tel:** 495 540 73 40 **Fax:** 495 540 72 15
Email: info@impressmedia.ru **Web site:** http://www.impressmedia.ru
Freq: Annual; **Circ:** 15,000
Usual Pagination: 160
Publisher: Annette Wassenaar
Profile: Presents comprehensive information on the state of commercial property market in Russia.
Language(s): English; Russian
Mechanical Data: Type Area: 168 x 240mm
BUSINESS: FINANCE & ECONOMICS: Property

KOMMERCHESKIY DIREKTOR 1774638RU2A-14
Editorial: M. Tolmachevski pereulok 1, 3 floor, 119017 MOSKVA **Tel:** 495 925 77 43
Fax: 495 933 54 46
Email: Andreeva@b2bmedia.ru **Web site:** http://www.kdonline.ru
Freq: Monthly; **Annual Sub.:** RUR 2508.00; **Circ:** 28,900
Usual Pagination: 80
Editor: Andrey Filatov; **Advertising Manager:** Lidia Bondareva
Profile: Russian edition of Sales & Marketing Management is a magazine with news and analysis of sales and marketing, commercial services and management.
Language(s): Russian
ADVERTISING RATES:
Full Page Colour .... RUR 200100.00
Mechanical Data: Type Area: 205 x 275mm
BUSINESS: COMMUNICATIONS, ADVERTISING & MARKETING

KOMMERCHESKIYE VESTI 1774384RU14A-36
Editorial: Krasny put 59, 644043 OMSK
Tel: 3812 24 04 67 **Fax:** 3812 24 28 02
Email: kv@kvnews.ru **Web site:** http://www.kvnews.ru
Freq: Weekly; **Circ:** 5,000
Usual Pagination: 32
Profile: Regional commercial weekly on economics, business, politics, energy sector, property, transport in Omsk region.
Language(s): Russian

ADVERTISING RATES:
Full Page Mono .... RUR 17300.00
Mechanical Data: Type Area: 271 x 375mm
BUSINESS: COMMERCE, INDUSTRY & MANAGEMENT

KOMMERSANT 763410RU1F-120
Editorial: ul. Vrubeliya 4/1, 125080 MOSKVA
Tel: 495 943 97 50 **Fax:** 495 943 97 28
Email: kommersant@kommersant.ru **Web site:** http://www.kommersant.ru
Freq: Daily - Published from Monday till Saturday; **Circ:** 110,000
Advertising Director: Valeria Lyubimova
Profile: Newspaper dedicated to the problems of economics and economic processes of Russian and international markets. Includes analyses of Russian micro- and macroeconomics, monetary and stock exchange markets and investments.
Language(s): Russian
Readership: Aimed at bank managers, stock exchange employees and decision makers within middle and high level state and private financial organisations and enterprises.
ADVERTISING RATES:
Full Page Mono .... RUR 1150000.00
Agency Commission: 15%
Mechanical Data: Type Area: 390 x 542mm, Col Length: 257mm, Print Process: Offset
Copy instructions: *Copy Date:* 2 weeks prior to publication date
Supplement(s): Dengi - 52xY, Vlast - 52xY, Weekend - 52xY
BUSINESS: FINANCE & ECONOMICS: Investment

KOMPANIYA 1615879RU14A-5
Editorial: ul.Bolshaya Andronevskaya 17, 109544 MOSKVA **Tel:** 495 745 84 10 **Fax:** 495 745 84 10
Email: ko@idr.ru **Web site:** http://www.ko.ru
Date Established: 1997; **Freq:** Weekly - Published on Monday; **Circ:** 78,000
Editor-in-Chief: Eugeniy Dodolev; **Advertising Director:** Elena Bezmenova
Profile: Magazine features news on general economic and management issues, analysis of basic economic developments, news about successful companies and people, description of new trends in company management and marketing, latest ideas to intensify your business.
Language(s): Russian
ADVERTISING RATES:
Full Page Mono .... RUR 270000.00
Mechanical Data: Type Area: 206 x 275mm
BUSINESS: COMMERCE, INDUSTRY & MANAGEMENT

KOMPONENTY I TEKHNOLOGII
1774188RU18A-3
Editorial: ul. Sadovaya 122, 190121 SANKT PETERBURG **Tel:** 12 438 15 38 **Fax:** 12 346 06 65
Email: power-e@finestreet.ru **Web site:** http://www.kit-e.ru
Freq: Monthly; **Circ:** 6,000
Usual Pagination: 160
Executive Editor: Ksenia Pritchina; **Editor-in-Chief:** Pavel Pravosudov; **Advertising Manager:** Olga Zaitseva
Profile: Professional magazine on electronic components and newest technologies in electronics.
Language(s): Russian
Readership: Targets managers of manufacturing companies, distributors, suppliers who have to know tendencies in power electronics market developments.
Mechanical Data: Type Area: 215 x 297mm
BUSINESS: ELECTRONICS

KOMSOMOLSKAYA PRAVDA
1615296RU65A-30
Editorial: Petrovsko-Razumovsky stary proyezd, 1/23, stroyeniye 1, 127287 MOSKVA **Tel:** 495 777 27 72
Email: kp@kp.ru **Web site:** http://www.kp.ru
Freq: Daily - Published from Monday to Saturday; **Circ:** 655,100
Usual Pagination: 48
Editor-in-Chief: Vladimir Nikolaevich Sungorkin; **Advertising Director:** Maxim Nikolaevich Bugachov
Profile: National newspaper covering politics, economics, social news and gossip, with latest news from Russia, the world, the CIS, photos and video.
Language(s): Russian
ADVERTISING RATES:
Full Page Mono .... RUR 1450000.00
Supplement(s): Gorodskaya Bankovskaya Gazeta - 12xY
NATIONAL DAILY & SUNDAY NEWSPAPERS: National Daily Newspapers

KOMSOMOLSKAYA PRAVDA V NOVOSIBIRSKE 1774380RU67B-270
Editorial: ul. Sovetskaya 64, 10 floor, 630091 NOVOSIBIRSK **Tel:** 3832 94 34 94
Email: kpnsk@apl.nsk.su **Web site:** http://www.nsk.kp.ru
Date Established: 1925; **Freq:** 260 issues yearly; **Circ:** 18,000
Usual Pagination: 24
Advertising Director: Ekaterina Mezintseva
Profile: Tabloid-sized regional issue of KP in Novosibirsk covering politics, gossip, entertainment.
Language(s): Russian

ADVERTISING RATES:
Full Page Mono .... RUR 57000.00
Mechanical Data: Type Area: 254x355mm
REGIONAL DAILY & SUNDAY NEWSPAPERS: Regional Daily Newspapers

KONDITERSKIYE IZDELIYA. CHAI, KOFE, KAKAO 1774308RU9B-1
Editorial: Tverskoy bul. 22, 125009 MOSKVA
Tel: 495 629 05 35 **Fax:** 495 629 92 59
Email: ki@my-ki.ru **Web site:** http://www.my-ki.ru
Date Established: 1997; **Freq:** Weekly - Published on Tuesdays; **Cover Price:** Free; **Circ:** 10,970
Usual Pagination: 180
Editor: Dmitri Makhlin
Profile: Professional magazine about non-alcoholic drinks: coffee, cacao and tea and confectionary.
Language(s): Russian
Mechanical Data: Type Area: 200 x 275mm
BUSINESS: DRINKS & LICENSED TRADE: Brewing

KONDITERSKOYE PROIZVODSTVO 1611177RU8B-1
Editorial: Sadovaya-Spasskaya 18, komn. 610, 107996 MOSKVA **Tel:** 495 607 17 70
Fax: 495 607 28 61
Email: foodprom@ropnet.ru **Web site:** http://www.foodprom.ru
Freq: 6 issues yearly; **Cover Price:** RUR 330.00; **Circ:** 2,500
Editor: Elena Kaouts; **Advertising Director:** Ekaterina Varekha
Profile: Magazine focusing on the technology, raw materials and equipment needed to manufacture various confectionery products in factories and shops, bakery plants and public catering institutions.
Language(s): Russian
Readership: Aimed at confectionery industry specialists.
ADVERTISING RATES:
Full Page Mono .... EUR 1000.00
Full Page Colour .... EUR 1800.00
Mechanical Data: Type Area: 220 x 300mm, Trim Size: 210 x 290mm
BUSINESS: BAKING & CONFECTIONERY: Confectionery Manufacturing

KONKURENTSIYA I RYNOK
1774036RU14A-26
Editorial: Nevsky prospekt 7/9, office 555, 191186 SANKT-PETERBURG **Tel:** 12 312 42 31
Email: info@konkir.ru **Web site:** http://www.konkir.ru
Date Established: 1998; **Freq:** Quarterly; **Cover Price:** RUR 500.00; **Circ:** 5,000
Usual Pagination: 160
Editor: Sergey Rozanov
Profile: Covers marketing and management, property and construction, advertising and public relations.
Language(s): Russian
ADVERTISING RATES:
Full Page Colour .... RUR 52038.00
Mechanical Data: Type Area: 210 x 297mm
BUSINESS: COMMERCE, INDUSTRY & MANAGEMENT

KONTEYNERNY BIZNES
1774382RU49R-1
Editorial: ul. Mikhailova 15/5, office 301, 195009 SANKT PETERBURG **Tel:** 12 702 16 43
Email: editor@transteka.ru **Web site:** http://www.containerbusiness.ru
Freq: 10 issues yearly; **Annual Sub.:** RUR 5000.00; **Circ:** 5,000
Editor: Svetlana Tsyrkunova; **Editor-in-Chief:** Nikolai Nilsky
Profile: Magazine about container business, ports and railway container terminals, logistics and container distribution.
Language(s): Russian
ADVERTISING RATES:
Full Page Mono .... RUR 41000.00
Mechanical Data: Type Area: A3
BUSINESS: TRANSPORT: Transport Related

KONTINENT SIBIR 1774373RU1A-48
Editorial: ul. Cheliuskintsev 50, 630132 NOVOSIBIRSK **Tel:** 3832 21 18 29
Fax: 3832 21 02 56
Email: post@sibpress.ru **Web site:** http://www.com.sibpress.ru
Freq: Weekly - Published on Fridays; **Circ:** 12,000
Usual Pagination: 32
Editor: Tatiana Nekhotina
Profile: Provides weekly analytical review of economic developments and business issues in Siberia region.
Language(s): Russian
ADVERTISING RATES:
Full Page Mono .... RUR 236000.00
Mechanical Data: Type Area: 390x 540mm
BUSINESS: FINANCE & ECONOMICS

KOSMETICHESKY RYNOK SEGODNYA 1865479RU15A-4
Editorial: 1 Volokolamsky proyezd 10, str. 1, Science & Technology Park, 123060 MOSKVA
Tel: 495 981 94 91 **Fax:** 495 981 94 90
Email: cosmarket@cosmopress.ru **Web site:** http://cosmopress.ru
Date Established: 1988; **Freq:** 20 issues yearly; Free to qualifying individuals ; **Circ:** 4,500
Usual Pagination: 36
Executive Editor: Violetta Dmitrieva; **Advertising Manager:** Viktor Bryginsky; **Advertising Director:** Irina Blinova
Profile: Covers perfumery and cosmetics news and provides analytical overviews of market segments, expert estimations, business-decisions, marketing communications and strategies.
Language(s): Russian
Readership: Targets cosmetics manufacturers of finished products, raw materials and packaging, distributors, exporters, importers, contract manufacturers and specialists in marketing.
ADVERTISING RATES:
Full Page Colour .... RUR 49000.00
Mechanical Data: Type Area: 210x297mm
BUSINESS: COSMETICS & HAIRDRESSING: Cosmetics

KOSTYOR 1774524RU84B-3
Editorial: ul. Mytinskaya 1/20, 191024 SANKT PETERBURG **Tel:** 12 274 15 72 **Fax:** 12 274 46 26
Email: root@kostyor.ru **Web site:** http://www.kostyor.ru
Date Established: 1936; **Freq:** Monthly; **Circ:** 5,000
Usual Pagination: 32
Editor: Nikolai Kharlampiev
Profile: Literary magazine for teenagers in the age group 10-14.
Language(s): Russian
ADVERTISING RATES:
Full Page Mono $250.00
Mechanical Data: Type Area: A4
CONSUMER: THE ARTS & LITERARY: Literary

KRASNAYA ZVEZDA 1774501RU40-6
Editorial: Khorosheyevskoye shosse 38, 123007 MOSKVA **Tel:** 495 941 21 58 **Fax:** 495 941 40 57
Email: mail@redstar.ru **Web site:** http://www.redstar.ru
Date Established: 1924; **Freq:** Daily; **Circ:** 80,000
Editor: Nikolai Efimov
Profile: Most reliable source of information about military issues and state of Russian Army.
Language(s): Russian
Mechanical Data: Type Area: A3
BUSINESS: DEFENCE

KRASNOYARSKAYA GAZETA
1774222RU65A-39
Editorial: ul. Respubliki 51, 660075 KRASNOYARSK
Tel: 3912 23 43 67 **Fax:** 3912 23 84 98
Email: kras_gazeta@mail.ru **Web site:** http://krsgz.narod.ru
Date Established: 1991; **Freq:** 104 issues yearly; **Annual Sub.:** RUR 1080.00; **Circ:** 8,000
Usual Pagination: 8
Editor: Oleg Paschenko
Profile: Regional socio-political and informative-entertaining newspaper.
Language(s): Russian
Mechanical Data: Type Area: A2
NATIONAL DAILY & SUNDAY NEWSPAPERS: National Daily Newspapers

KRASNOYARSKY RABOCHIY
1774218RU67B-190
Editorial: ul. Respubliki 51, 6 floor, 660075 KRASNOYARSK **Tel:** 3912 23 57 61
Fax: 3912 23 39 31
Email: krasrab@krsn.ru **Web site:** http://www.krasrab.com
Date Established: 1905; **Freq:** 208 issues yearly; **Circ:** 21,000
Usual Pagination: 32
Editor: Zoya Kasatkina; **Editor-in-Chief:** Vladimir Pavlovsky; **Advertising Manager:** Olga Zhilinskaya
Profile: Socio-political regional daily with regional economic and cultural news.
Language(s): Russian
ADVERTISING RATES:
Full Page Mono .... RUR 82600.00
Mechanical Data: Type Area: 395 x 510mm
REGIONAL DAILY & SUNDAY NEWSPAPERS: Regional Daily Newspapers

KRASNY SEVER 1774058RU67B-53
Editorial: ul. Cheliuskintsev 3, 160001 VOLOGDA
Tel: 172 72 00 33 **Fax:** 172 72 04 61
Email: ks@krassever.ru **Web site:** http://www.krassever.ru
Date Established: 1917; **Freq:** 156 issues yearly; **Circ:** 30,900
Usual Pagination: 40
Editor: Alexander Toropov; **Advertising Manager:** Nataliya Tsareva
Profile: Regional newspaper on political, economic issues, with society and culture, criminal news.
Language(s): Russian
ADVERTISING RATES:
Full Page Mono .... RUR 41651.00
SCC .... RUR 28.00
Mechanical Data: Type Area: A3
REGIONAL DAILY & SUNDAY NEWSPAPERS: Regional Daily Newspapers

KRASOTA I ZDOROVIYE
1774102RU74G-5
Editorial: Khoroshevskoye shosse 32, 123007 MOSKVA **Tel:** 495 940 18 97
Email: markina@d-mir.ru **Web site:** http://kiz.ru
Date Established: 2000; **Freq:** Monthly; **Circ:** 80,000
Usual Pagination: 200
Executive Editor: Ekaterina Semenova; **Advertising Director:** Alexander Shatokhin
Profile: Magazine on beauty and health, cosmetic surgeries, dieting and medical treatments.
Language(s): Russian
Readership: Targets those who care about their look and health.
ADVERTISING RATES:
Full Page Colour .... RUR 248000.00
Mechanical Data: Type Area: 215x285mm
CONSUMER: WOMEN'S INTEREST CONSUMER MAGAZINES: Slimming & Health

KUBAN' BUSINESS 1774173RU14A-6
Editorial: ul. Rashpilevskaya 106, office 2, 350000 KRASNODAR **Tel:** 61 255 35 56 **Fax:** 61 255 39 75
Email: redaktor@gazetavk.ru **Web site:** http://www.gazetavk.ru
Date Established: 1993; **Freq:** Weekly - Published on Fridays; **Annual Sub.:** RUR 374.00; **Circ:** 15,000
Usual Pagination: 8
Editor: Viktor Lameikin; **Advertising Director:** Tatiana Boyko
Profile: Provides information on business in Kuban region, about changes in business law and taxation.
Language(s): Russian
ADVERTISING RATES:
SCC .... RUR 25.00
Mechanical Data: Type Area: A3
Supplement to: Volnaya Kuban'
BUSINESS: COMMERCE, INDUSTRY & MANAGEMENT

KURIER PECHATI 1774340RU60A-2
Editorial: ul. Vyatskaya 49, str. 2, MOSKVA
Tel: 495 974 21 31
Email: jvolodina@kpechati.ru **Web site:** http://kpechati.ru
Date Established: 1998; **Freq:** 24 issues yearly; **Circ:** 2,500
Usual Pagination: 100
Editor: Evgenia Trushina; **Executive Editor:** Tatiana Chabykina
Profile: Professional publication about printed media market and distribution and aimed at media specialists and publishing houses.
Language(s): Russian
ADVERTISING RATES:
Full Page Mono .... RUR 8100.00
Full Page Colour .... RUR 13500.00
Mechanical Data: Trim Size: 189 x 277mm
BUSINESS: PUBLISHING: Publishing & Book Trade

KURSKAYA PRAVDA
1774257RU67B-218
Editorial: ul. Engelsa 109, 305007 KURSK
Tel: 4712 35 83 25
Email: bmk.90@mail.ru **Web site:** http://pravda.kursknet.ru
Date Established: 1917; **Freq:** 208 issues yearly; **Circ:** 25,000
Editor: Evgeniy Kotyaev; **Advertising Manager:** Boris Kiryaev
Profile: Socio-political newspaper covering regional issues.
Language(s): Russian
Mechanical Data: Type Area: A2
REGIONAL DAILY & SUNDAY NEWSPAPERS: Regional Daily Newspapers

KUZBASS 1774122RU67B-99
Editorial: pr. Oktyabrsky 28, 650630 KEMEROVO
Tel: 3842 52 32 74 **Fax:** 3842 52 12 10
Email: news@knews.polenet.ru **Web site:** http://www.mega.kemerovo.su/kuzbass
Date Established: 1922; **Freq:** 260 issues yearly; **Circ:** 28,000
Editor: Yuriy Kukhmar
Profile: Socio-political regional newspaper covering regional issues.
Language(s): Russian
Mechanical Data: Type Area: A2
REGIONAL DAILY & SUNDAY NEWSPAPERS: Regional Daily Newspapers

KVARTIRA, DACHA, OFIS
1774356RU1E-26
Editorial: Ogorodny proyezd 16, str. 17, 127254 MOSKVA **Tel:** 495 618 17 98
Email: news@kdo.ru **Web site:** http://kdo.ru
ISSN: 1561-8420
Freq: Weekly - Published on Tuesdays; **Circ:** 52,000
Usual Pagination: 32
News Editor: Sergey Nikolaev; **Editor-in-Chief:** Mikhail Morozov; **Advertising Manager:** Alexander Frolov; **Advertising Director:** Olga Mytnik
Profile: Informs about real estate market current news, tendencies in development and problems.
Language(s): Russian
ADVERTISING RATES:
Full Page Colour .... RUR 132000.00
Mechanical Data: Type Area: 262 x 390mm
BUSINESS: FINANCE & ECONOMICS: Property

KVARTIRNYI VOPROS - VSYO O NEDVIZHIMOSTI
1774649RU1E-7
Editorial: ul. Gagarina 1, office 651, 196105 SANKT PETERBURG **Tel:** 12 329 36 16
Email: info@tsn.spb.ru **Web site:** http://www.tsn.spb.ru
Date Established: 1999; **Freq:** Half-yearly; **Circ:** 10,000
Usual Pagination: 80
Profile: Informative directory about legal aspects of buying property and all property related issues.
Language(s): Russian
ADVERTISING RATES:
Full Page Mono .... RUR 15000.00
Mechanical Data: Type Area: 203 x 285mm
BUSINESS: FINANCE & ECONOMICS: Property

LAN
714158RU5B-12
Editorial: Elektricheskiy Pereulok 8, Korp. 3, 123056 MOSKVA **Tel:** 495 219 13 72 **Fax:** 495 253 92 04
Email: lan@lanmag.ru **Web site:** http://www.osp.ru/lan
Date Established: 1995; **Freq:** Monthly; **Circ:** 10,000
Usual Pagination: 160
Editor: Dimitriy Ganza; **Advertising Manager:** Elena Chekalina
Profile: Magazine focusing on networking solutions.
Language(s): Russian
Readership: Aimed at professionals in development of local and global networks, distributed information systems, IT managers and administrative staff of IT departments.
ADVERTISING RATES:
Full Page Mono $2800.00
Full Page Colour $4500.00
Mechanical Data: Type Area: 202 x 257mm
BUSINESS: COMPUTERS & AUTOMATION: Data Processing

LIPETSKAYA GAZETA
1774271RU67B-229
Editorial: ul. Moskovskaya 83, 398055 LIPETSK
Tel: 4742 31 40 75 **Fax:** 4742 31 40 89
Email: lg@pressa.lipetsk.ru **Web site:** http://www.lpgzt.ru
Freq: 256 issues yearly; **Circ:** 20,000
Usual Pagination: 16
Editor: Vladimir Miroshnik; **Advertising Manager:** Vyacheslav Kulikov
Profile: Socio-political regional newspaper covering regional politics, economics, entertainment and culture.
Language(s): Russian
ADVERTISING RATES:
SCC .... RUR 45.00
Mechanical Data: Type Area: A2
REGIONAL DAILY & SUNDAY NEWSPAPERS: Regional Daily Newspapers

LISA
624472RU74B-85
Editorial: ul. Polkovaya, Dom 3, Stroenie 4, 127018 MOSKVA **Tel:** 495 797 98 33 **Fax:** 495 787 94 46
Email: liza@burda.ru **Web site:** http://www.burda.ru
Date Established: 1995; **Freq:** Weekly; **Circ:** 750,000
Usual Pagination: 100
Editor: Kira Vladimirovna Burenina; **Advertising Manager:** Svetlana Kuzina; **Advertising Director:** Victoria Godunova
Profile: Weekly women's interest magazine about cosmetics, fashion, style and shopping.
Language(s): Russian
Readership: Aimed at women between 25 and 35 years.
ADVERTISING RATES:
Full Page Colour .... RUR 468700.00
Mechanical Data: Trim Size: 210 x 267mm, Bleed Size: 220 x 277mm
CONSUMER: WOMEN'S INTEREST CONSUMER MAGAZINES: Women's Interest - Fashion

LISA. MOY UYUTNY DOM
752650RU74C-150
Editorial: Ulica Polkovaya, Dom 3, Stroenie 4, MOSKVA **Tel:** 495 797 98 38 **Fax:** 495 787 94 45
Email: moydom@burda.ru **Web site:** http://www.burda.ru
Date Established: 1998; **Freq:** Monthly; **Circ:** 120,000
Usual Pagination: 68
Editor: Veronika Zubkova; **Advertising Manager:** Kristina Parkhomenko; **Advertising Director:** Andrey Rodionov
Profile: Lifestyle magazine including tips and ideas on how to furnish a home.
Language(s): Russian
Readership: Read by homeowners, mainly women.
ADVERTISING RATES:
Full Page Colour .... RUR 113400.00
Agency Commission: 15%
Mechanical Data: Type Area: 217 x 273mm, Col Length: 259mm, Screen: 60 lpc
Copy instructions: *Copy Date:* 1 month prior to publication date
CONSUMER: WOMEN'S INTEREST CONSUMER MAGAZINES: Home & Family

LISA. PRIYATNOGO APPETITA!
714148RU74P-200
Editorial: Ulica Polkovaya, Dom 3, Stroenie 4, MOSKVA **Tel:** 495 787 94 34 **Fax:** 495 787 94 45
Email: p.appetit@burda.ru **Web site:** http://www.burda.ru
Date Established: 1997; **Freq:** Monthly; **Circ:** 110,000
Usual Pagination: 52
Editor: Mikhail Lezhniev; **Editor-in-Chief:** Vera Pruzhinina; **Managing Director:** Aleksander Zork;
Advertising Manager: Olesya Mochalova;
Advertising Director: Ksenia Dmitrieva
Profile: Magazine providing information about cooking and baking.
Language(s): Russian
Readership: Aimed at women aged between 20 and 45 years of age.
ADVERTISING RATES:
Full Page Colour .... RUR 115000.00
Agency Commission: 15%
Mechanical Data: Type Area: 251 x 198mm, Col Length: 251mm, Screen: 60 lpc
Copy instructions: *Copy Date:* 1 month prior to publication date
CONSUMER: WOMEN'S INTEREST CONSUMER MAGAZINES: Food & Cookery

LOGISTIKA SEGODNYA
1774103RU49A-2
Editorial: 2 Khutornaya 38a, str. 15, 3 floor, 127287 MOSKVA **Tel:** 495 787 51 73 **Fax:** 495 787 5 174
Email: mail@grebennikov.ru **Web site:** http://www.grebennikov.ru
Freq: 6 issues yearly; **Cover Price:** RUR 1705.00
Annual Sub.: RUR 9200.00; **Circ:** 15,000
Usual Pagination: 64
Editor-in-Chief: V. Sergeyev
Profile: Professional magazine on optimization of business processes in a transport company, introduction of IT, newest management systems and logistics services.
Language(s): Russian
Mechanical Data: Type Area: A3
BUSINESS: TRANSPORT

LOYALTY.INFO
1774677RU2A-17
Editorial: ul. Deguninskaya 1, korp.3, 127486 MOSKVA **Tel:** 495 489 11 95 **Fax:** 495 488 23 15
Email: info@loyalty.info **Web site:** http://www.loyalty.info
Freq: 6 issues yearly; **Cover Price:** RUR 400.00; **Circ:** 5,000
Usual Pagination: 50
Advertising Manager: Nadezhda Hulapova
Profile: Professional magazine about loyalty programmes, marketing tools of keeping existing and gaining new customers, analysis of world experience and new technologies of stimulation of customer activity.
Language(s): Russian
Readership: Targets top managers, businessmen and marketing & sales managers of companies.
Mechanical Data: Type Area: A3
BUSINESS: COMMUNICATIONS, ADVERTISING & MARKETING

LUTSHIYE TSIFROVYE KAMERY
1774429RU78R-3
Editorial: ul. Timura Frunze 11, str. 44-45, 4 floor, 119992 MOSKVA **Tel:** 495 935 70 34
Fax: 495 780 88 24
Email: aldubaeva@gameland.ru **Web site:** http://www.kupikame.ru
Freq: Monthly; **Circ:** 50,000
Usual Pagination: 144
Editor: Maria Aldubaeva; **Executive Editor:** Anatoly Anikin; **Advertising Manager:** Oksana Alekhina;
Advertising Director: Igor Piskunov; **Publisher:** Alexander Sidorovsky
Profile: Buyers guide to digital cameras helping to choose a right digital camera and accessories with competent tests of new digital photo products.
Language(s): Russian
Readership: Targets digital camera buyers and photography lovers.
ADVERTISING RATES:
Full Page Colour .... RUR 280000.00
Mechanical Data: Type Area: 230x300mm
CONSUMER: CONSUMER ELECTRONICS: Consumer Electronics Related

MARIE CLAIRE
1600532RU74A-15
Editorial: ul. Myasnitskaya 35, 101000 MOSKVA
Tel: 495 981 39 10 **Fax:** 495 981 39 11
Email: marieclaire@hfm.ru **Web site:** http://marieclaire.ru
ISSN: 1562-5141
Date Established: 1997; **Freq:** Monthly; **Cover Price:** RUR 70.00
Annual Sub.: RUR 1080.00; **Circ:** 280,000
Usual Pagination: 210
Editor-in-Chief: Olga Zaretskaya; **Advertising Manager:** Antonina Romanova
Profile: Magazine covering lifestyle, addressing a wide range of issues.
Language(s): Russian
Readership: Aimed at professional women with higher education aged 20 to 35 years.
ADVERTISING RATES:
Full Page Colour .... RUR 255000.00
CONSUMER: WOMEN'S INTEREST CONSUMER MAGAZINES: Women's Interest

MARISKAYA PRAVDA
1774275RU67B-232
Editorial: ul. 70 letiya Vooruzhonnych sil 20, 424000 YOSHKAR-OLA **Tel:** 362 45 26 44 **Fax:** 362 45 18 18
Email: mp@mari-el.ru **Web site:** http://www.marpravda.ru
Date Established: 1921; **Freq:** Daily; **Annual Sub.:** RUR 320.00; **Circ:** 15,000
Usual Pagination: 16
Editor: Vasiliy Panchenko; **Advertising Director:** Marina Lastochkina
Profile: Regional daily covering regional economics, politics, culture and social issues.
Language(s): Russian
ADVERTISING RATES:
Full Page Mono .... RUR 15500.00
Mechanical Data: Type Area: 265 x 358mm
REGIONAL DAILY & SUNDAY NEWSPAPERS: Regional Daily Newspapers

MARKETING V ROSSII I ZA RUBEZHOM
1615965RU2A-19
Editorial: P.O. Box 530, 121096 MOSKVA
Tel: 495 148 95 62 **Fax:** 495 148 99 70
Email: red@dis.ru **Web site:** http://www.mavriz.ru
Date Established: 1997; **Freq:** 6 issues yearly;
Annual Sub.: RUR 7020.00; **Circ:** 6,500
Usual Pagination: 144
Editor: Evgeniy Golubkiov
Profile: Contains articles on methods and methodology of marketing, marketing research, marketing planning and its tools, organization of marketing process, competitiveness estimation, detailed description of products and price policies, advertising and PR.
Language(s): Russian
ADVERTISING RATES:
Full Page Colour .... RUR 30000.00
BUSINESS: COMMUNICATIONS, ADVERTISING & MARKETING

MASLOZHIROVAYA PROMYSHLENNOST
1611124RU22R-1
Editorial: Sadovaya-Spasskaya 18, komn. 601, 607, 107996 MOSKVA **Tel:** 495 607 17 70
Fax: 495 607 20 87
Email: foodprom@ropnet.ru **Web site:** http://www.foodprom.ru
Freq: 6 issues yearly; **Circ:** 1,500
Editor: Elena Kaouts; **Advertising Director:** Ekaterina Varekha
Profile: Magazine focusing on technology and equipment use in the manufacture of oils, margarine, mayonnaise and other food products.
Language(s): Russian
Readership: Aimed at specialists, manufacturers and university students.
ADVERTISING RATES:
Full Page Mono .... EUR 1000.00
Full Page Colour .... EUR 1800.00
Mechanical Data: Type Area: 210 x 290mm
BUSINESS: FOOD: Food Related

MATERIALY ELEKTRONNOI TEKHNIKI
1613582RU18A-1
Editorial: P. O. Box 49, 119049 MOSKVA
Tel: 495 236 03 04 **Fax:** 495 236 03 04
Email: osipov@misis.ru **Web site:** http://www.rudmet.ru
Date Established: 1998; **Freq:** Quarterly; **Annual Sub.:** RUR 3800.00; **Circ:** 500
Usual Pagination: 80
Editor: Yu. Parkhomenko; **Advertising Manager:** Natalia Kolykhalova
Profile: Journal devoted to the problems of production and application of semiconductors, dielectrics and magnetic materials.
Language(s): Russian
ADVERTISING RATES:
Full Page Mono .... EUR 400.00
Full Page Colour .... EUR 950.00
Mechanical Data: Type Area: A4
BUSINESS: ELECTRONICS

MAXI TUNING
1774500RU77A-60
Editorial: ul. Timura Frunze 11, str. 44-45, 4 floor, 119992 MOSKVA **Tel:** 495 935 70 34
Fax: 495 780 88 24
Email: zhutikov@gameland.ru **Web site:** http://www.maxi-tuning.ru
Date Established: 2006; **Freq:** Monthly; **Circ:** 90,000
Usual Pagination: 160
Editor: Aleksey Zhutikov; **Advertising Director:** Pavel Romanovski
Profile: Motoring magazine about cars, racing and techno-tuning.
Language(s): Russian
ADVERTISING RATES:
Full Page Colour .... RUR 280000.00
Mechanical Data: Type Area: 210x297mm
CONSUMER: MOTORING & CYCLING: Motoring

MAXIM
1774593RU86C-13
Editorial: MOSKVA **Tel:** 495 633 57 79
Email: maxim@maximonline.ru **Web site:** http://www.maximonline.ru
Freq: Monthly; **Circ:** 390,000
Editor: Igor Chersky; **Editor-in-Chief:** Alexander Malenkov; **Advertising Manager:** Kristina Tatarenkova; **Advertising Director:** Victoria Bukharkina
Profile: Men's magazine on lifestyle, fashion, women, music, curious facts and events.
Language(s): Russian
ADVERTISING RATES:
Full Page Colour .... RUR 46000.00
Mechanical Data: Type Area: A4
CONSUMER: ADULT & GAY MAGAZINES: Men's Lifestyle Magazines

MC (MOBILE COMPUTERS)
1774439RU5C-106
Editorial: ul. T. Frunze 11, str.44-45, 4 floor, 119992 MOSKVA **Tel:** 495 935 70 34
Email: letters@MConline.ru **Web site:** http://www.mconline.ru
Date Established: 2000; **Freq:** Monthly; **Cover Price:** RUR 140.00; **Circ:** 65,000
Usual Pagination: 128
Editor: Matvey Portnov; **Editor-in-Chief:** Denis Podolyak; **Advertising Manager:** Oksana Alekhina;
Advertising Director: Igor Piskunov
Profile: Magazine about smart phones, notebooks and all mobile devices.
Language(s): Russian
Readership: Aimed at young men aged 25-35, active users of mobile devices.
ADVERTISING RATES:
Full Page Colour .... RUR 271400.00
Mechanical Data: Type Area: 230 x 300mm
BUSINESS: COMPUTERS & AUTOMATION: Professional Personal Computers

MEDITSINSKI VESTNIK
1774310RU56A-1
Editorial: ul. Profsoyuznaya 57, MOSKVA
Tel: 495 332 63 80 **Fax:** 495 332 03 90
Email: edition@medvestnik.ru **Web site:** http://www.medvestnik.ru
Date Established: 1861; **Freq:** Weekly; **Annual Sub.:** RUR 2646.00; **Circ:** 30,000
Usual Pagination: 24
Editor: Elena Zorina
Profile: Professional publication with latest news of medical achievements and detailed medical information.
Language(s): Russian
Readership: Aimed at doctors, surgeries and pharmacists.
BUSINESS: HEALTH & MEDICAL

MEDVED
1877672RU86C-18
Editorial: Derbenevskaya nab. 7, str. 9, 113824 MOSKVA **Tel:** 495 620 08 07 **Fax:** 495 620 08 01
Email: s.yushkin@forwardmg.ru **Web site:** http://www.medved-magazine.ru
Date Established: 1995; **Freq:** Monthly; **Circ:** 85,000
Advertising Director: Ekaterina Sheremey
Profile: First men's magazine in Russia, a pioneer of Russia's luxury-style magazines, with the first issue was published in 1995.
Language(s): Russian
Readership: Target audience magazine are wealthy men aged 25 to 35 years old, self-confident, successfully implemented in business and other spheres of life.
ADVERTISING RATES:
Full Page Colour .... RUR 300000.00
Mechanical Data: Type Area: 210x280mm
CONSUMER: ADULT & GAY MAGAZINES: Men's Lifestyle Magazines

MEN'S HEALTH
1600535RU86C-5
Editorial: ul. Polkovaya 1 zdaniye 1, 127018 MOSKVA **Tel:** 495 232 32 00 **Fax:** 495 232 92 77
Email: mh@imedia.ru **Web site:** http://www.mhealth.ru
Date Established: 1997; **Freq:** Monthly; **Cover Price:** RUR 85.00
Annual Sub.: RUR 999.00; **Circ:** 270,000
Usual Pagination: 360
Advertising Director: Masha Kamenskaya;
Publisher: Margarita Tyrina
Profile: Magazine focusing on health and lifestyle issues.
Language(s): Russian
Readership: Aimed at professional men in their 20s and 30s.
ADVERTISING RATES:
Full Page Colour .... RUR 480000.00
Agency Commission: 15%
Average ad content per issue: 40%
CONSUMER: ADULT & GAY MAGAZINES: Men's Lifestyle Magazines

METALLY I TSENY
1774402RU27-2
Editorial: Ul. Marshalla Novikova 36, 197375 SANKT PETERBURG **Tel:** 12 322 52 59
Email: info@metal4u.ru **Web site:** http://metal4u.ru
Date Established: 2001; **Freq:** 24 issues yearly; **Cover Price:** RUR 60.00
Annual Sub.: RUR 660.00; **Circ:** 7,000
Usual Pagination: 100
Profile: Professional informative-advertising magazine about iron and steel industry, metal production and equipment, iron and steel suppliers and sellers, machinery and building sectors.
Language(s): Russian
ADVERTISING RATES:
Full Page Mono .... RUR 12950.00
Full Page Colour .... RUR 17790.00
Mechanical Data: Type Area: 185x260mm
BUSINESS: METAL, IRON & STEEL

Russian Federation

METRO MOSKVA 1895828RU65K-1
Editorial: ul. Krasnaya Presnya 1, 4 floor, 123242 MOSKVA **Tel:** 499 252 00 22 **Fax:** 499 252 63 44
Email: metro@gazetametro.ru **Web site:** http://www.gazetametro.ru
Freq: Mornings; **Cover Price:** Free; **Circ:** 500,000
Executive Editor: Viktoriya Melnikova; **Advertising Director:** Maksim Shehov
Profile: Entertainment newspaper with city news distributed for free in Moscow.
Language(s): Russian
ADVERTISING RATES:
Full Page Colour .... RUR 425000.00
Mechanical Data: Type Area: 261x377mm
NATIONAL DAILY & SUNDAY NEWSPAPERS: Metropolitan Daily Newspapers

METRO PETERBURG 1895832RU65K-2
Editorial: ul. Avtovskaya 2, 198096 SANKT PETERBURG **Tel:** 12 783 27 06 **Fax:** 12 783 44 45
Email: anna.ivanova@metro-russia.com **Web site:** http://www.gazetametro.ru
Freq: Mornings; **Cover Price:** Free; **Circ:** 500,000
Features Editor: Julia Nikoforova; **Advertising Director:** Olga Sakulina
Profile: City entertainment morning newspaper distributed for free in St. Petersburg.
Language(s): English
ADVERTISING RATES:
Full Page Colour .... RUR 314400.00
Mechanical Data: Type Area: 261x377mm
NATIONAL DAILY & SUNDAY NEWSPAPERS: Metropolitan Daily Newspapers

MEZHDUNARODNY BUHGALTERSKY UCHIOT 1774312RU1B-6
Editorial: P.O. Box 10, 111401 MOSKVA
Tel: 495 621 69 49 **Fax:** 495 621 91 90
Email: post@financepress.ru **Web site:** http://www.financepress.ru
Date Established: 1999; **Freq:** Monthly; **Circ:** 7,150
Usual Pagination: 72
Editor: Larisa Chaldayeva
Profile: Focused on international experience of accountancy systems, problems of switch of Russian accountancy to international standards.
Language(s): Russian
ADVERTISING RATES:
Full Page Colour .... RUR 22656.00
Mechanical Data: Type Area: 170 x 240mm
BUSINESS: FINANCE & ECONOMICS: Accountancy

MILITARY PARADE 1774281RU40-1
Editorial: 2-aya Entuziasov 5, korp. 36, 119330 MOSKVA **Tel:** 495 123 45 67 **Fax:** 495 123 45 69
Email: military@milparade.com **Web site:** http://www.milparade.com
Date Established: 1994; **Freq:** 6 issues yearly; **Circ:** 10,000
Usual Pagination: 120
Editor: Aleksandr Andrianov
Profile: Publication in English and Russian language featuring a unique source of information on activities of defence-industrial complex enterprises in Russia and other CIS countries. Offers information about new systems and military techniques, newest technology.
Language(s): English
ADVERTISING RATES:
Full Page Colour .... RUR 160000.00
Mechanical Data: Type Area: A4
BUSINESS: DEFENCE

MINI 1774140RU74B-224
Editorial: Polkovaya 3, str. 4, 127018 MOSKVA
Tel: 495 787 94 18
Email: mini@burda.ru **Web site:** http://www.minirussia.ru
Freq: Monthly; **Circ:** 250,000
Editor-in-Chief: Evgeniya Killikh; **Advertising Manager:** Ekaterina Klipova; **Advertising Director:** Nataliya Pecherskaya
Profile: Magazine for successful and active women about fashion, active lifestyle, fitness, beauty and cosmetics, job career, sex and relationships.
Language(s): Russian
ADVERTISING RATES:
Full Page Colour .... RUR 240900.00
Mechanical Data: Type Area: 167 x 223mm
CONSUMER: WOMEN'S INTEREST CONSUMER MAGAZINES: Women's Interest - Fashion

MIR ETIKETKI 1613701RU41A-2
Editorial: Gorokhowskiy Per. 7, str. 1, 105064 MOSKVA **Tel:** 495 234 65 81 **Fax:** 495 234 65 81
Email: labelworld@compress.ru **Web site:** http://www.labelworld.ru
Date Established: 2001; **Freq:** 6 issues yearly; **Circ:** 2,000
Usual Pagination: 32
Editor-in-Chief: Dimitriy Gudilin; **Advertising Director:** Konstantin Babulin; **Publisher:** Boris Moltchanov
Profile: Magazine focusing on label and packaging design and printing.
Language(s): Russian
Readership: Aimed at printing professionals and designers.
ADVERTISING RATES:
Full Page Mono $2000.00
Mechanical Data: Trim Size: 200 x 265mm
BUSINESS: PRINTING & STATIONERY: Printing

MIR NOVOSTEY 1774337RU65J-68
Editorial: ul. Schepkina 60/2, 129110 MOSKVA
Tel: 499 255 19 22 **Fax:** 495 681 28 12
Email: mirnov2000@mirnov.ru **Web site:** http://www.mirnov.ru
Date Established: 1993; **Freq:** Weekly - Published on Tuesdays; **Annual Sub.:** RUR 938.00; **Circ:** 850,000
Usual Pagination: 40
Editor: Nikolai Kruzhilin
Profile: Weekly newspaper providing political, economical and cultural information (with a TV guide).
Language(s): Russian
ADVERTISING RATES:
Full Page Mono .... RUR 295000.00
Full Page Colour .... RUR 295000.00
Mechanical Data: Type Area: 260 x 370mm
NATIONAL DAILY & SUNDAY NEWSPAPERS: National Weekly Newspapers

MIR PK 714172RU5C-101
Editorial: Elektricheskiy Pereulok 8, Korp. 3, 123O56 MOSKVA **Tel:** 495 253 92 27 **Fax:** 495 253 92 04
Email: pcworld@pcworld.ru **Web site:** http://www.osp.ru/pcworld
Date Established: 1988; **Freq:** Monthly; **Cover Price:** RUR 95.70
Annual Sub.: RUR 1148.40; **Circ:** 55,000
Editor: Alex Orlov; **Advertising Director:** Margarita Babayan; **Publisher:** Michael Borisov
Profile: Magazine focusing on domestic and global developments in the application and use of PCs and PC related products and services.
Language(s): Russian
Readership: Aimed at IT professionals and home PC users.
ADVERTISING RATES:
Full Page Mono $4800.00
Full Page Colour $6900.00
BUSINESS: COMPUTERS & AUTOMATION: Professional Personal Computers

MIROVAYA ENERGETIKA 1774190RU58-2
Editorial: Shenkursky proyezd 3b, office 207, 127349 MOSKVA **Tel:** 495 407 39 67 **Fax:** 495 406 48 65
Email: info@worldenergy.ru **Web site:** http://www.worldenergy.ru
Freq: Monthly; **Circ:** 11,000
Usual Pagination: 96
Editor: Vladimir Kiselev; **Editor-in-Chief:** Tatiana Khudyakova; **Advertising Director:** Vagan Martisrosyan
Profile: Professional publication about national interests of Russia on energy market, analysis of development tendencies of Russian and international energy industry.
Language(s): Russian
ADVERTISING RATES:
Full Page Mono .... RUR 150000.00
Mechanical Data: Trim Size: 297 x 210mm
BUSINESS: ENERGY, FUEL & NUCLEAR

MK MOSKOVSKY KOMSOMOLETS 1615821RU65A-29
Editorial: ul. 1905 goda, d. 7, D-22, 123995 MOSKVA
Tel: 495 250 72 72 **Fax:** 495 259 46 39
Email: mknews@mk.ru **Web site:** http://www.mk.ru
Freq: Daily; **Circ:** 750,000
Usual Pagination: 24
Editor: Pavel Nikolaevich Gusev; **Advertising Manager:** Ekaterina Karimova; **Advertising Director:** Sofia Hotchinskaya
Profile: Newspaper focusing on national and international affairs, events, meetings, scientific news, culture and arts.
Language(s): Russian
ADVERTISING RATES:
Full Page Mono .... RUR 903500.00
Mechanical Data: Type Area: 387 x 510mm
Supplement(s): MK-Bulvar - 52xY MK v voskreslenie - 52xY MK-Novosti - 52xY.
NATIONAL DAILY & SUNDAY NEWSPAPERS: National Daily Newspapers

MK SUBBOTA + VOSKRESENYE 1774504RU72I-13
Editorial: ul. 1905 goda 7, 123995 MOSKVA
Tel: 495 78 14 740 **Fax:** 495 781 47 36
Email: ok@mk.ru **Web site:** http://www.ok.mk.ru
Date Established: 2007; **Freq:** Weekly - Published on Saturdays; **Circ:** 600,000
Usual Pagination: 32
Advertising Manager: Ekaterina Karimova; **Advertising Director:** Sofia Hotchinskaya
Profile: Weekend entertaining Moscow newspaper with general and show biz news.
Language(s): Russian
ADVERTISING RATES:
Full Page Mono .... RUR 430000.00
Mechanical Data: Type Area: 245 x 352mm
LOCAL NEWSPAPERS: Regional Weekly Newspapers

MK V PITERE 1774525RU72I-38
Editorial: ul. Rubinsteina 23, 191002 SANKT PETERBURG **Tel:** 12 331 66 80 **Fax:** 12 331 66 80
Email: office@mk-piter.ru **Web site:** http://mk-piter.ru
Date Established: 1997; **Freq:** Weekly - Published on Wednesdays; **Annual Sub.:** RUR 830.00; **Circ:** 69,200
Usual Pagination: 40
Editor: Marina Povalyaeva
Profile: Regional weekly about social and cultural life in St. Petersburg.
Language(s): Russian
ADVERTISING RATES:
Full Page Mono .... RUR 71000.00
Mechanical Data: Type Area: 255 x 370mm
LOCAL NEWSPAPERS: Regional Weekly Newspapers

MK-BOULVAR 1774157RU76C-1
Editorial: ul. 1905 goda 7, 123995 MOSKVA
Tel: 495 253 20 94 **Fax:** 495 253 20 98
Email: blvd@mk.ru **Web site:** http://www.ok.mk.ru
ISSN: 1682-6930
Freq: Weekly - Published on Tuesdays; **Circ:** 305,000
Usual Pagination: 78
Advertising Manager: Polina Artemenko; **Advertising Director:** Irina Krasnikova
Profile: Entertaining magazine with news in show biz and fashion and a weekly TV programme.
Language(s): Russian
ADVERTISING RATES:
Full Page Mono .... RUR 213000.00
Mechanical Data: Trim Size: 200 x 256mm
CONSUMER: MUSIC & PERFORMING ARTS: TV & Radio

MOBI 1774438RU5D-154
Editorial: ul. Perovskaya 1, 111524 MOSKVA
Tel: 495 730 40 14 **Fax:** 495 730 40 14
Email: mail@mobimag.ru **Web site:** http://www.mobimag.ru
Freq: Monthly; **Cover Price:** RUR 120.00; **Circ:** 70,000
Usual Pagination: 180
Editor-in-Chief: Eujene Ter-Avyakan; **Advertising Manager:** Svetlana Popova; **Advertising Director:** Julia Odnakova
Profile: Magazine about mobile electronics and technologies, news in computing, digital hardware and software.
Language(s): Russian
Readership: Aimed at young men in the age group: 16-34.
ADVERTISING RATES:
Full Page Colour .... RUR 240000.00
Mechanical Data: Type Area: 210 x 297mm
BUSINESS: COMPUTERS & AUTOMATION: Personal Computers

MOBILE 1774519RU18B-15
Editorial: Novodanilovskaya Nab. 4a, 117105 MOSKVA **Tel:** 495 510 22 11 **Fax:** 495 510 49 69
Email: k.ostrikov@spn.ru **Web site:** http://www.rmob.ru
Date Established: 1998; **Freq:** Monthly; **Circ:** 250,000
Editor-in-Chief: Sergey Malenkovich; **Advertising Director:** Valery Mirochnik
Profile: Russia's most popular and most authoritative monthly devoted to mobile digital devices informing about cutting-edge mobile technologies and latest industry development trends.
Language(s): Russian
ADVERTISING RATES:
Full Page Colour .... RUR 262500.00
Mechanical Data: Bleed Size: 225 x 300mm
BUSINESS: ELECTRONICS: Telecommunications

MOBILNYE NOVOSTI 1774544RU18B-16
Editorial: ul. Mezdunarodnaya 28, korpus 1, office 123, 125009 MOSKVA **Tel:** 495 671 37 41
Fax: 12 325 75 18
Email: olga@pdg.ru **Web site:** http://mnovosti.ru
Freq: Monthly; **Circ:** 122,000
Usual Pagination: 144
Editor-in-Chief: Igor Volkov; **Advertising Manager:** Olga Vyunova; **Advertising Director:** Sergey Ivancha
Profile: Magazine on digital technologies, telecommunications and mobile networking.
Language(s): Russian
ADVERTISING RATES:
Full Page Colour .... RUR 480000.00
Mechanical Data: Type Area: A4
BUSINESS: ELECTRONICS: Telecommunications

MOBILNYE TELEKOMMUNIKATSII 1774343RU18B-1
Editorial: ul. Admirala Makarova 23, korpus 2, 125212 MOSKVA **Tel:** 495 502 92 62
Fax: 495 502 92 64
Email: mobile@profi-press.ru **Web site:** http://www.mobilecomm.ru
ISSN: 1562-4293
Date Established: 1999; **Freq:** 10 issues yearly; **Annual Sub.:** RUR 1870.00; **Circ:** 5,000
Usual Pagination: 80
Editor-in-Chief: Y. Gordeev
Profile: Provides information about telecommunication management, new technologies and standards.
Language(s): Russian
ADVERTISING RATES:
Full Page Mono $4720.00
Mechanical Data: Type Area: 205x295mm
BUSINESS: ELECTRONICS: Telecommunications

MOLODOY KOMMUNAR 1774075RU67B-56
Editorial: ul. Plekhanovskaya 53, 10 floor, 394026 VORONEZH **Tel:** 4732 59 31 73 **Fax:** 4732 46 53 88
Email: mkvrn@mail.ru **Web site:** http://mkommunar.ru
Date Established: 1918; **Freq:** 156 issues yearly; **Circ:** 10,000
Usual Pagination: 16
Editor: Alexander Saubanov; **Editor-in-Chief:** Alexander Pirogov
Profile: Regional daily covering industrial, trade, agricultural, economic, banking, social news, sports and entertainment.
Language(s): Russian
ADVERTISING RATES:
SCC .... RUR 100.00
Mechanical Data: Type Area: A3
REGIONAL DAILY & SUNDAY NEWSPAPERS: Regional Daily Newspapers

MONITOR+ 1773997RU5D-155
Editorial: office 307, pr. Sotsialisticheski 28, 3 floor, 656056 BARNAUL **Tel:** 3852 63 11 96
Fax: 3852 63 11 96
Email: monitor@barnaul.ru **Web site:** http://www.monitor.ab.ru
Date Established: 2002; **Freq:** 24 issues yearly; **Circ:** 4,500
Usual Pagination: 80
Editor-in-Chief: Dmitri Podaksenov
Profile: Magazine about computing issues, digital equipment and mobile computing.
Language(s): Russian
ADVERTISING RATES:
Full Page Mono .... RUR 5508.00
Full Page Colour .... RUR 10517.00
Mechanical Data: Type Area: 180 x 255mm
BUSINESS: COMPUTERS & AUTOMATION: Personal Computers

MORSKAYA BIRZHA 1774527RU45R-1
Editorial: ul. Blagodatnaya 6, lit. b, office 205, 196128 SAINT PETERSBURG **Tel:** 12 336 31 30
Fax: 12 336 31 32
Email: info@maritimemarket.ru **Web site:** http://www.maritimemarket.ru
Date Established: 2002; **Freq:** Quarterly; **Cover Price:** EUR 15.00
Annual Sub.: EUR 60.00; **Circ:** 3,000
Usual Pagination: 84
Editor-in-Chief: Viktor Efimov
Profile: Official publication of Management of sea and transport exhibitions of LENEXPO (St. Petersburg) and featured sections: Shipbuilding, Shipping, Ports, Ocean and Shelf Exploration.
Language(s): English; Russian
Readership: Targets at shipping companies managers, shipbuilding and research specialists, port officials, maritime equipment manufacturers, visitors to marine exhibitions as well as wide range of audience interested in marine issues.
ADVERTISING RATES:
Full Page Colour .... EUR 1800.00
Mechanical Data: Type Area: 250 x 330mm
BUSINESS: MARINE & SHIPPING: Marine Related

MOSCOW 1774491RU89C-11
Editorial: Pushkinskaya pl. 5, Office 410, 4 floor, 127994 MOSKVA **Tel:** 495 650 65 65
Fax: 495 694 34 39
Email: cityguide@mail.ru **Web site:** http://www.city-guide.msk.su
Freq: Quarterly; **Cover Price:** Free; **Circ:** 65,000
Editor: Svetlana Volkova
Profile: Colour illustrated bilingual Russian-English quarterly on entertainment events in Moscow: restaurants, shopping, galleries and museums.
Language(s): English; Russian
ADVERTISING RATES:
Full Page Colour .... EUR 1500.00
Mechanical Data: Trim Size: 146x210mm
CONSUMER: HOLIDAYS & TRAVEL: Entertainment Guides

THE MOSCOW NEWS 1936039RU65M-1
Editorial: 4, Zubovsky Boulevard, 119021 MOSCOW
Tel: 495 645 6565
Email: info@moscownews.ru **Web site:** http://www.mnweekly.ru
Freq: Weekly - Published weekly on Tuesdays (Twice-weekly on Tuesdays and Fridays starting from February 2010); **Circ:** 47,000
Usual Pagination: 24
Profile: Moscow newspaper containing articles on what happens in Russia and its capital each week, opinions of experts and analysis on various sectors of business, economics and finance.
Language(s): English
NATIONAL DAILY & SUNDAY NEWSPAPERS: Metropolitan Weekend Newspapers

THE MOSCOW TIMES
1500331RU67B-5
Editorial: ul. Polkovaya 3 zdaniye 1, stroyenie 4, 127018 MOSKVA **Tel:** 495 232 47 74
Fax: 495 232 65 28
Email: editors@themoscowtimes.com **Web site:** http://www.moscowtimes.ru
Date Established: 1992; **Freq:** 250 issues yearly; **Annual Sub.:** RUR 17490.00; **Circ:** 35,000
Editor: Andrew McChesney; **News Editor:** Nabi Abdullaev; **Managing Editor:** Scott Rose; **Advertising Director:** Elena Cheban; **Publisher:** Ekaterina Son
Profile: Newspaper covering national and international news and information.
Language(s): English
Readership: Aimed at the international business community in Moscow.
ADVERTISING RATES:
Full Page Colour .... EUR 12913.04
Agency Commission: 15%
Mechanical Data: Type Area: 372 x 265 mm, Col Length: 372mm, Col Widths (Display): 19mm, No. of Columns (Display): 5
Copy instructions: *Copy Date:* 3 days prior to publication date
Average ad content per issue: 40%
Supplement(s): Real Estate - 4xY
REGIONAL DAILY & SUNDAY NEWSPAPERS: Regional Daily Newspapers

MOSKOVSKAYA PRAVDA
1774314RU67B-484
Editorial: ul. 1905 goda, 7, 123846 MOSKVA
Tel: 495 259 82 33 **Fax:** 495 259 63 60
Email: newspaper@mospravda.ru **Web site:** http://www.mospravda.ru
Date Established: 1918; **Freq:** Daily - 7 days a week; **Annual Sub.:** RUR 1050.00; **Circ:** 400,000
Usual Pagination: 16
Editor-in-Chief: Shod Muladjadov
Profile: Regional newspaper covering national and international news, politics, economics, culture, social issues and current events in Moscow.
Language(s): Russian
ADVERTISING RATES:
Full Page Mono .... RUR 210000.00
Full Page Colour .... RUR 252000.00
Mechanical Data: Type Area: 310 x 534mm
REGIONAL DAILY & SUNDAY NEWSPAPERS: Regional Daily Newspapers

MOUNTAIN BIKE
1774199RU77C-1
Editorial: ul. Timura Frunze 11, str. 44-45, 4 floor, 119992 MOSKVA **Tel:** 495 935 70 34
Fax: 495 780 88 24
Email: goryachev@gameland.ru **Web site:** http://www.glc.ru
Freq: Monthly; **Circ:** 30,000
Usual Pagination: 112
Editor: Mikhail Goryachev; **Advertising Director:** Igor Piskunov
Profile: Mountain-biking magazine with tests and reviews of various equipment performed by most well-known riders, great pictures to enjoy, interviews and news from world of mountain-biking.
Language(s): Russian
Readership: Targets professional and amateur mountain-bikers.
ADVERTISING RATES:
Full Page Colour .... RUR 230000.00
Mechanical Data: Type Area: 230x300mm
CONSUMER: MOTORING & CYCLING: Cycling

MOY PREKRASNY SAD
752645RU93-200
Editorial: Ulica Polkovaya, Dom 3, Stroenie 4, MOSKVA **Tel:** 495 797 98 38 **Fax:** 495 787 94 45
Email: moysad@burda.ru **Web site:** http://www.burda.ru
Date Established: 1997; **Freq:** Monthly; **Circ:** 130,000
Usual Pagination: 84
Editor-in-Chief: Leonid Mazurik; **Advertising Manager:** Kristina Parkhomenko; **Advertising Director:** Andrey Rodionov
Profile: Gardening magazine, includes advice on garden layout and design, recommends plants and discusses problems.
Language(s): Russian
Readership: Aimed at those owning a garden or interested in gardening.
ADVERTISING RATES:
Full Page Colour .... RUR 172800.00
Mechanical Data: Type Area: 210 x 275mm
CONSUMER: GARDENING

MOY RAION - MOSKVA
1774169RU72I-41
Editorial: ul. Lobachika 11, 6 floor, 107113 MOSKVA
Tel: 495 925 55 25 **Fax:** 495 925 53 55
Email: info@mr-msk.ru **Web site:** http://www.mr-msk.ru
Freq: Weekly; **Cover Price:** Free; **Circ:** 400,000
Usual Pagination: 16
Executive Editor: Igor Romanenko; **Editor-in-Chief:** Dmitri Sumin; **Publisher:** Grigoriy Kunis
Profile: Entertainment weekly with information on holidays, shopping, city news.
Language(s): Russian
ADVERTISING RATES:
Full Page Colour .... RUR 588000.00
Mechanical Data: Type Area: 264 x 358mm
LOCAL NEWSPAPERS: Regional Weekly Newspapers

MOY RAION - SANKT PETERBURG
1774526RU72I-39
Editorial: ul. Odoevskogo 27, lit. A, 4 floor, 199155 SANKT PETERBURG **Tel:** 12 325 25 15
Fax: 12 325 55 15
Email: info@mr-spb.ru **Web site:** http://www.mr-spb.ru
Date Established: 2002; **Freq:** Weekly - Published on Fridays; **Cover Price:** Free; **Circ:** 350,000
Usual Pagination: 24
Executive Editor: Vera Verholantseva; **Editor-in-Chief:** Diana Kachalova; **Advertising Manager:** Julia Ismailova; **Advertising Director:** Dmitri Strelin
Profile: Entertainment newspaper with information on holidays, shopping, relaxation, local news and practical advice.
Language(s): Russian
ADVERTISING RATES:
Full Page Mono .... RUR 44462.00
Mechanical Data: Type Area: 262 x 355mm
LOCAL NEWSPAPERS: Regional Weekly Newspapers

MOYO DELO. MAGAZIN
1774418RU53-2
Editorial: 2 Zvenigorodskaya ul. 2/1, 123100 MOSKVA **Tel:** 495 748 01 03 **Fax:** 495 748 01 03
Email: prph@prph.ru **Web site:** http://www.moyo-delo.ru
Freq: Monthly; **Cover Price:** RUR 110.00; **Circ:** 60,000
Usual Pagination: 68
Executive Editor: Olga Dmitrieva; **Editor-in-Chief:** Andrey Cherkasov; **Advertising Manager:** Ludmila Belenkova; **Advertising Director:** Inga Lobdjanizde
Profile: Professional publication on retail trade in Russia.
Language(s): Russian
Readership: Aimed at retail managers, shop owners and wholesales distributors.
ADVERTISING RATES:
Full Page Mono $3850.00
Full Page Colour $5500.00
Mechanical Data: Type Area: 230 x 300mm
BUSINESS: RETAILING & WHOLESALING

MSFO
1774554RU1B-7
Editorial: M. Tolmachevski pereulok 1, 3 floor, 119017 MOSKVA **Tel:** 495 933 55 19
Fax: 495 933 54 46
Email: info@msfo-mag.ru **Web site:** http://www.msfo-magazine.ru
Date Established: 2004; **Freq:** 6 issues yearly; **Annual Sub.:** RUR 2310.00; **Circ:** 24,000
Usual Pagination: 104
Editor-in-Chief: Ekaterina Rubtsova; **Advertising Manager:** Lidia Bondareva
Profile: Informs about legal changes in Russian and international accountancy, existing standards, problems and perspectives of development of accountancy.
Language(s): Russian
ADVERTISING RATES:
Full Page Colour .... RUR 140000.00
Mechanical Data: Type Area: 170 x 250mm
BUSINESS: FINANCE & ECONOMICS: Accountancy

MUZHSKOY KLUB
1774114RU86C-12
Editorial: ul. Mira 25, 350000 KRASNODAR
Tel: 61 262 71 45 **Fax:** 61 262 71 45
Email: club@riaok.kuban.ru **Web site:** http://www.mans-club.ru
Freq: Monthly; **Cover Price:** Free; **Circ:** 12,000
Usual Pagination: 120
Editor: Anna Korneva; **Executive Editor:** Kseniya Donskaya; **Editor-in-Chief:** Gennadiy Shunin; **Advertising Manager:** Oksana Kondrahina
Profile: Regional glossy men's informative-entertaining magazine.
Language(s): Russian
ADVERTISING RATES:
Full Page Colour .... RUR 37500.00
Mechanical Data: Type Area: 220 x 280mm
CONSUMER: ADULT & GAY MAGAZINES: Men's Lifestyle Magazines

NA NEVSKOM
1774240RU74Q-12
Editorial: P.O. Box 137, 191002 SANKT PETERBURG **Tel:** 12 325 35 95 **Fax:** 12 575 63 86
Email: nn@es.ru **Web site:** http://www.nanevskom.ru
Freq: Monthly; **Circ:** 35,000
Usual Pagination: 132
Profile: Lifestyle magazine on fashion, news from cars world, interior design, cultural events.
Language(s): Russian
ADVERTISING RATES:
Full Page Colour .... RUR 160650.00
Mechanical Data: Type Area: 297x420mm
CONSUMER: WOMEN'S INTEREST CONSUMER MAGAZINES: Lifestyle

NARODNAYA GAZETA
1774654RU67B-433
Editorial: P.O. Box 54, 432063 ULYANOVSK
Tel: 422 30 17 10
Email: ng@mv.ru **Web site:** http://www.nargaz.ru
Date Established: 1991; **Freq:** 156 issues yearly; **Circ:** 14,000
Editor: Vera Matveeva
Profile: Socio-political newspaper covering regional news.
Language(s): Russian
ADVERTISING RATES:
Full Page Mono .... RUR 26180.00
Mechanical Data: Type Area: A3
REGIONAL DAILY & SUNDAY NEWSPAPERS: Regional Daily Newspapers

NASH SEVERNIY KRAI
1773995RU2A-1
Editorial: pl. Lenina 4, office 505, 163061 ARCHANGELSK **Tel:** 182 21 10 18 **Fax:** 182 26 85 45
Email: reklama@atk-media.ru
Date Established: 1993; **Freq:** Weekly - Published on Thursdays; **Cover Price:** Free; **Circ:** 76,000
Usual Pagination: 8
Editor: Zhanna Dimakova
Profile: Regional advertising-commercial weekly.
Language(s): Russian
ADVERTISING RATES:
Full Page Mono .... RUR 44000.00
Mechanical Data: Type Area: 250 x 360mm
BUSINESS: COMMUNICATIONS, ADVERTISING & MARKETING

NASHA VERSIA
1615283RU65J-71
Editorial: Smolenskaya pl. 13/21, 121099 MOSKVA
Tel: 495 544 30 20 **Fax:** 495 544 30 20
Email: versia@versia.ru **Web site:** http://versia.ru
Date Established: 1998; **Freq:** Weekly - Published on Monday; **Circ:** 170,000
Usual Pagination: 24
Editor: Oleg Bratishko
Profile: Newspaper covering national and international news, politics, economics and social issues.
Language(s): Russian
ADVERTISING RATES:
Full Page Mono .... RUR 150000.00
Mechanical Data: Type Area: 260 x 388mm
NATIONAL DAILY & SUNDAY NEWSPAPERS: National Weekly Newspapers

NASHA VLAST: DELA I LITSA
1774317RU82-163
Editorial: ul. Stanislavskogo 29, str. 1, 115054 MOSKVA **Tel:** 495 912 29 13 **Fax:** 495 912 29 13
Email: info@nashavlast.ru **Web site:** http://www.nashavlast.ru
Date Established: 2000; **Freq:** Monthly; **Cover Price:** RUR 290.00
Annual Sub.: RUR 3480.00; **Circ:** 10,000
Usual Pagination: 74
Editor: Alexander Novikov
Profile: National magazine on developments in politics and economics in Russia, banking and financial issues, society.
Language(s): Russian
ADVERTISING RATES:
Full Page Colour .... RUR 90000.00
Mechanical Data: Type Area: A4
CONSUMER: CURRENT AFFAIRS & POLITICS

NATIONAL BUSINESS
1774303RU14A-14
Editorial: ul. Uralskaya 3, office 8, YEKATERINBURG
Tel: 343 216 37 37 **Fax:** 343 216 37 35
Email: novikov@banzay.ru **Web site:** http://www.banzay.ru
Date Established: 2006; **Freq:** Monthly; **Circ:** 63,000
Usual Pagination: 192
Editor: Alexander Vasilevskiy
Profile: Monthly business magazine providing analysis, theory and practice of modern business management in non-capital cities of Russia.
Language(s): Russian
ADVERTISING RATES:
Full Page Colour .... RUR 36000.00
Mechanical Data: Type Area: 84x108 1/32
BUSINESS: COMMERCE, INDUSTRY & MANAGEMENT

NATIONAL GEOGRAPHIC RUSSIA
1937458RU50-16
Editorial: ul. Polkovaya 3, str. 1, 127018 MOSKVA
Tel: 495 232 32 00 **Fax:** 495 788 70 02
Email: ngm@imedia.ru **Web site:** http://www.national-geographic.ru/ngm/201001
Freq: Monthly; **Circ:** 140,000
Advertising Manager: Veronika Dery; **Publisher:** Tatiana Shalygina
Profile: A unique scientific and popular geographical magazine, official publication of the National Geographic Society (U.S.). National Geographic publishes an unprecedented photographs and exclusive materials about the history, archeology, science and culture.
Language(s): Russian
ADVERTISING RATES:
Full Page Colour .... RUR 382628.00
Mechanical Data: Trim Size: 141,8x218,4mm
BUSINESS: TRAVEL & TOURISM

NATIONAL GEOGRAPHIC TRAVELER
1937456RU89A-7
Editorial: ul. Polkovaya 3, str. 2, 127018 MOSKVA
Tel: 495 232 32 00 **Fax:** 495 710 76 40
Email: traveler@imedia.ru **Web site:** http://www.ngtraveler.ru
Date Established: 2007; **Freq:** 5 issues yearly; **Circ:** 100,000
Advertising Manager: Olga Shilova; **Publisher:** Tatiana Shalygina
Profile: Russian version of the legendary American edition, which for 20 years of its existence, gained the widest readership among magazines on travel. NG Traveler is a kind of manual for frequent travelers of people that can replace a travel guide. Stories about travel are accompanied here with all the necessary practical information, from the procedures for processing visa and air ticket reservation, features table booking in restaurants and nuances of the functioning of railways.
Language(s): Russian
ADVERTISING RATES:
Full Page Colour .... EUR 8100.00
CONSUMER: HOLIDAYS & TRAVEL: Travel

NATSIONALNYE INTERESY: PRIORITETY I BEZOPASTNOST'
1774316RU82-150
Editorial: P.O. Box 10, 111401 MOSKVA
Tel: 495 621 69 49 **Fax:** 495 621 91 90
Email: post@financepress.ru **Web site:** http://www.financepress.ru
Date Established: 2005; **Freq:** Monthly; **Circ:** 1,500
Usual Pagination: 88
Editor: Vera Gorokhova
Profile: Publication focused on actual problems of national interests and national priorities of Russia and security and protection in various spheres of economy, science and ecology.
Language(s): Russian
ADVERTISING RATES:
Full Page Mono .... RUR 18585.00
Full Page Colour .... RUR 43542.00
Mechanical Data: Type Area: 170 x 240mm
CONSUMER: CURRENT AFFAIRS & POLITICS

NATURAL
1774066RU74G-4
Editorial: ul. Gilyarovskogo 10, bld.1, 129090 MOSKVA **Tel:** 495 745 68 98 **Fax:** 495 745 68 99
Email: natural@veneto.ru **Web site:** http://www.veneto.ru
Date Established: 2001; **Freq:** Monthly; **Circ:** 100,000
Usual Pagination: 116
Editor: Rikka Ratina
Profile: Russian version of Natural health, magazine about healthy way of life and health, aimed at women in the middle age group.
Language(s): Russian
ADVERTISING RATES:
Full Page Colour .... RUR 170000.00
Mechanical Data: Type Area: A4
CONSUMER: WOMEN'S INTEREST CONSUMER MAGAZINES: Slimming & Health

NAUKA I ZHIZN
763441RU94J-100
Editorial: ul. Myasnitskaya 24, 101990 MOSKVA
Tel: 495 623 44 85 **Fax:** 495 625 05 90
Email: mail@nkj.ru **Web site:** http://www.nkj.ru
ISSN: 1683-9528
Date Established: 1890; **Freq:** Monthly; **Cover Price:** RUR 90.00; **Circ:** 42,000
Usual Pagination: 180
Editor: Igor Lagovsky
Profile: Magazine including information on general interest science, scientific advances, new technology, history, brain teasers and self-education.
Language(s): Russian
Readership: Aimed at corporate managers, businessmen, scientists, engineers, high school and college students.
ADVERTISING RATES:
Full Page Colour .... RUR 41600.00
Mechanical Data: Type Area: 216 x 131mm
CONSUMER: OTHER CLASSIFICATIONS: Popular Science

NAUKA V SIBIRI
1774369RU55-1
Editorial: Morskoy prospekt 2, 630090 NOVOSIBIRSK **Tel:** 3832 330 81 58
Fax: 3832 330 15 59
Email: presse@sbras.nsc.ru **Web site:** http://www.sbras.nsc.ru/HBC
Date Established: 1961; **Freq:** Weekly; **Circ:** 2,000
Usual Pagination: 16
Editor-in-Chief: Yuri Plotnikov
Profile: Covers life of Siberian scientific community: most significant results of theoretical and experimental research, expeditions, scientific conferences, international cooperation, professional training for science and information on scientific competitions.
Language(s): Russian
Readership: Aimed at scientific workers and experts working in the Academic or applied-research institutes, on professors and students, scientific and technical intellectuals.
ADVERTISING RATES:
SCC .... RUR 20.00

Mechanical Data: Type Area: A3
BUSINESS: APPLIED SCIENCE & LABORATORIES

NDT WORLD 1818143RU14B-1
Editorial: SVEN Ltd, P.O. Box 277, 195220 ST. PETERSBURG **Tel:** 12 448 18 84 **Fax:** 12 448 18 85
Email: editor@ndtworld.com **Web site:** http://www.ndtworld.com
Freq: Quarterly - Comes out in March, June, September and December; **Annual Sub.:** RUR 1160.00; **Circ:** 1,200
Profile: Publication covers testing problems in different areas of industry, transport and construction. Each issue of the journal includes articles on NDT in metallurgy, power generation industry, oil and gas supply industry, aerospace and shipbuilding industry, within the railway transport.
Language(s): English; Russian
Readership: Aimed at NDT laboratories and purchase departments of all big enterprises of Russia and other CIS countries and Baltic States. The journal is also read by the stuff of NDT trade and service companies.
ADVERTISING RATES:
Full Page Colour $1360.00
Mechanical Data: Type Area: A4 - 210 X 291 mm
BUSINESS: COMMERCE, INDUSTRY & MANAGEMENT: Industry & Factories

NEDELYA OBLASTI 1774542RU72I-44
Editorial: ul. Pugachevskaya 147/151, office 301, 410005 SARATOV **Tel:** 452 48 61 28
Fax: 452 48 62 26
Email: nedelia@renet.ru **Web site:** http://www.nedelia.ru
Date Established: 2002; **Freq:** Weekly - Published on Wednesdays; **Circ:** 8,000
Usual Pagination: 12
Editor: Irina Zhiganova
Profile: Socio-political regional covering regional legislation, regional news and social issues.
Language(s): Russian
ADVERTISING RATES:
SCC .... RUR 20.00
Mechanical Data: Type Area: A2
LOCAL NEWSPAPERS: Regional Weekly Newspapers

NEFT' I KAPITAL 1774692RU33-6
Editorial: ul. Profsouyznaya 57, 117420 MOSKVA
Tel: 495 933 66 93 **Fax:** 495 933 66 94
Email: nik@oilcapital.ru **Web site:** http://www.oilcapital.ru
Date Established: 1994; **Freq:** 11 issues yearly; **Annual Sub.:** RUR 9900.00; **Circ:** 14,000
Editor: Sergey Derevensky
Profile: Offers a qualitative analysis of events, trends and processes of fuel and energy complex of Russia and other former USSR countries.
Language(s): Russian
Readership: Aimed at top and middle management of companies of different oil and gas complex segments.
ADVERTISING RATES:
Full Page Mono .... RUR 150000.00
BUSINESS: OIL & PETROLEUM

NEFT' ROSSII 1774318RU33-2
Editorial: P.O. Box 230, 10100 MOSKVA
Tel: 495 627 16 90 **Fax:** 495 627 16 92
Email: nr@oilru.com **Web site:** http://www.oilru.com
Date Established: 1994; **Freq:** Monthly; **Circ:** 10,000
Usual Pagination: 120
Editor: Valery Andrianov
Profile: Publication focused on news of oil-and-gas industry.
Language(s): Russian
ADVERTISING RATES:
Full Page Colour .... RUR 94650.00
Mechanical Data: Type Area: A4
BUSINESS: OIL & PETROLEUM

NEFTEGAZ.RU 1842082RU33-9
Editorial: ul. Tverskaya 18, str. 1, office 806, 127006 MOSKVA **Tel:** 495 650 14 82 **Fax:** 495 694 39 24
Email: info@neftegaz.ru **Web site:** http:/neftegaz.ru
Freq: Monthly; **Annual Sub.:** RUR 1100.00; **Circ:** 40,000
Usual Pagination: 100
Editor-in-Chief: Denis Kozlov
Profile: Focuses on newest technologies in oil and gas industry, engineering and innovation projects, analytical reviews of energy sector and news of oil and gas companies.
Language(s): Russian
ADVERTISING RATES:
Full Page Colour .... RUR 210000.00
Mechanical Data: Type Area: 210 x 295mm
BUSINESS: OIL & PETROLEUM

NEFTESERVIS 1774131RU33-7
Editorial: ul. Profsouyznaya 57, 117420 MOSKVA
Tel: 495 933 66 93 **Fax:** 495 933 66 94
Email: info@indpg.ru **Web site:** http://www.oilcapital.ru
Date Established: 2001; **Freq:** Quarterly; **Circ:** 5,000
Editor: Sergey Savushkin
Profile: Magazine about service market and technologies for purposes of oil-gas complex industry.
Language(s): Russian
ADVERTISING RATES:
Full Page Mono .... RUR 170000.00
BUSINESS: OIL & PETROLEUM

NEFTYANAYA TORGOVLYA 1872710RU33-34
Editorial: ul. Profsoyuznaya 57, 117420 MOSKVA
Tel: 495 933 66 93 **Fax:** 495 933 66 94
Email: market@oilcapital.ru **Web site:** http://www.oilcapital.ru
Freq: Monthly; **Annual Sub.:** RUR 35640.00
Usual Pagination: 70
Profile: Includes a wide range of statistical information on performance of oil and gas complex enterprises and organizations of Russia and CIS countries.
Language(s): Russian
BUSINESS: OIL & PETROLEUM

NEFTYANYE VEDOMOSTI 1659570RU33-1
Editorial: ul. Bolshaya Ordynka 1, 115035 MOSKVA
Tel: 495 933 17 04 **Fax:** 495 933 18 00
Email: press@lukoil-overseas.ru **Web site:** http://eng.neftevedomosti.ru
Freq: 24 issues yearly; **Circ:** 1,700
Usual Pagination: 8
Editor-in-Chief: Grigory Volchek
Profile: Publication covering oil and gas industry, including the latest news, worldwide events and projects, business section and analysis.
Language(s): Russian
BUSINESS: OIL & PETROLEUM

NEON 1774401RU76D-3
Editorial: ul. Malaya Pochtovaya 12, korp. 1, 105082 MOSKVA **Tel:** 495 229 62 00 **Fax:** 495 229 62 01
Email: neon@neonmusic.ru **Web site:** http://www.neonmusic.ru
Freq: Monthly; **Circ:** 68,000
Usual Pagination: 134
Advertising Director: Marina Panteleeva; **Publisher:** Alena Dushko
Profile: Glossy magazine about styles and trends in pop-music, lifestyle.
Language(s): Russian
ADVERTISING RATES:
Full Page Colour .... RUR 90000.00
Mechanical Data: Type Area: 170x225mm
CONSUMER: MUSIC & PERFORMING ARTS: Music

NEPTUNE 21 CENTURY 1774503RU75M-2
Editorial: Butyrsky Val 20, str. 1, 125047 MOSKVA
Tel: 495 517 70 25 **Fax:** 495 720 67 39
Email: info@neptun21.ru **Web site:** http://www.neptun21.ru
Freq: 6 issues yearly; **Annual Sub.:** RUR 1200.00; **Circ:** 5,000
Profile: Magazine on underwater world (animals and plants) and underwater sports.
Language(s): Russian
ADVERTISING RATES:
Full Page Colour .... EUR 1600.00
Mechanical Data: Type Area: 210 x 290mm
CONSUMER: SPORT: Water Sports

THE NEW TIMES 1697684RU82-102
Editorial: Tverskoy bulvar 14, str. 1, 125009 MOSKVA **Tel:** 495 648 07 60 **Fax:** 495 980 87 20
Email: info@newtimes.ru **Web site:** http://www.newtimes.ru
Date Established: 1943; **Freq:** Weekly - Published on Mondays; **Circ:** 50,000
Usual Pagination: 68
Profile: Magazine covering politics, economics, social life and cultural events in Russia and abroad in English and Russian languages.
Language(s): Russian
Mechanical Data: Type Area: 230 x 270mm
CONSUMER: CURRENT AFFAIRS & POLITICS

NEZAVISIMAYA GAZETA 1615838RU65A-31
Editorial: ul. Myasnitskaya, d. 13, 101000 MOSKVA
Tel: 495 981 61 54 **Fax:** 495 925 55 43
Email: info@ng.ru **Web site:** http://www.ng.ru
Date Established: 1990; **Freq:** Daily - Double edition on Saturday issue; **Circ:** 56,000
Editor: Arkadiy Khancevich; **Advertising Manager:** Yulia Asmolova
Profile: Newspaper covering national and international news, politics, business and economy.
Language(s): Russian
ADVERTISING RATES:
Full Page Mono .... RUR 415000.00
Mechanical Data: Type Area: 310 x 476,25mm
NATIONAL DAILY & SUNDAY NEWSPAPERS: National Daily Newspapers

NICOTIANA ARISTOCRATICA 1774282RU51-1
Editorial: ul. Staraya Basmannaya 38/2, korp. 1, office 210, 105066 MOSKVA **Tel:** 495 933 85 62
Fax: 495 933 85 63
Email: nicotiana@rustabak.ru **Web site:** http://www.nicotiana.ru
ISSN: 1810-0570
Date Established: 2002; **Freq:** Quarterly; **Annual Sub.:** RUR 401.20; **Circ:** 23,000
Usual Pagination: 160
Editor: Maksim Korolev
Profile: Magazine for smokers presenting different topics, creating positive image of tobacco industry.
Language(s): Russian
BUSINESS: TOBACCO

NIZHNEGORODSKY RABOCHIY 1774362RU67B-257
Editorial: ul. Minina 35, 603155 NIZNIY NOVGOROD
Tel: 312 432 70 75 **Fax:** 312 432 70 28
Email: nworker@nr.nnov.ru **Web site:** http://nr.nnov.ru
Date Established: 1932; **Freq:** 260 issues yearly; **Annual Sub.:** RUR 1930.00; **Circ:** 5,500
Usual Pagination: 16
News Editor: Roman Filtsov; **Editor-in-Chief:** Tatiana Postnikova; **Advertising Manager:** Galina Bandina; **Advertising Director:** Denis Smirnov
Profile: Daily regional newspaper covering news and events from Nizhniy Novgorod.
Language(s): Russian
ADVERTISING RATES:
Full Page Mono .... RUR 15100.00
Full Page Colour .... RUR 18200.00
Mechanical Data: Type Area: 262x369mm
REGIONAL DAILY & SUNDAY NEWSPAPERS: Regional Daily Newspapers

NOGTEVOY SERVIS 1865366RU15A-2
Editorial: 1 Volokolamsky proyezd 10, str. 1, Science&Technology Park, 123060 MOSKVA
Tel: 495 981 94 91 **Fax:** 495 981 94 90
Email: lark@cosmopress.ru **Web site:** http://cosmopress.ru
Freq: 6 issues yearly; Free to qualifying individuals **Annual Sub.:** RUR 1080.00; **Circ:** 23,000
Usual Pagination: 166
Editor: Tatiana Grishina; **Executive Editor:** Aleksandra Merzlikina; **Advertising Manager:** Julia Venediktova; **Advertising Director:** Irina Blinova
Profile: Manual magazine for manicure and pedicure masters, specialists in nail drafting and modelling, administrators of beauty salons and nail studios.
Language(s): Russian
ADVERTISING RATES:
Full Page Colour .... RUR 68970.00
Mechanical Data: Type Area: 210 x 297 mm
BUSINESS: COSMETICS & HAIRDRESSING: Cosmetics

LES NOUVELLES ESTHETIQUES (RUSSIAN EDITION) 1864969RU15A-1
Editorial: 1 Volokolamsky proyezd 10, str. 1, Science &Technology Park, 123060 MOSKVA
Tel: 495 981 94 91 **Fax:** 495 981 94 90
Email: info@cosmopress.ru **Web site:** http://cosmopress.ru
Date Established: 1997; **Freq:** 6 issues yearly; **Annual Sub.:** RUR 2100.00; **Circ:** 13,300
Usual Pagination: 368
Executive Editor: Ekaterina Tchaikovskaya; **Advertising Manager:** Olga Lukina
Profile: Professional magazine on cosmetology and aesthetics, with theoretical knowledge and practical experience, reviews of new technologies, products, techniques.
Language(s): Russian
Readership: Targets professionals in field of cosmetology and applied aesthetics.
ADVERTISING RATES:
Full Page Colour .... RUR 127000.00
Mechanical Data: Type Area: 225 x 297mm
BUSINESS: COSMETICS & HAIRDRESSING: Cosmetics

NOVAYA TAMBOVSCHINA 1774582RU72I-65
Editorial: Morshanskoye shosse 14, 392602 TAMBOV **Tel:** 4752 53 51 34
Web site: http://www.newtambov.ru
Date Established: 2001; **Freq:** Weekly - Published on Wednesdays; **Circ:** 14,000
Usual Pagination: 16
Editor-in-Chief: Svetlana Serova
Profile: Regional social-political newspaper covering events in Tambov.
Language(s): Russian
ADVERTISING RATES:
Full Page Mono .... RUR 20000.00
Mechanical Data: Type Area: A3
LOCAL NEWSPAPERS: Regional Weekly Newspapers

NOVOSTI 1774474RU82-124
Editorial: ul. Kalinina 49A, 3 floor, post box 35-47, 690035 VLADIVOSTOK **Tel:** 4232 27 29 24
Fax: 4232 27 29 24
Email: news@novosti.vl.ru **Web site:** http://www.novosti.vl.ru
Date Established: 1993; **Freq:** 104 issues yearly; **Circ:** 22,000
Usual Pagination: 32
Editor-in-Chief: V. Sukhanov
Profile: Daily newspaper from Vladivostok providing political, economics, criminal, social and cultural news.
Language(s): Russian
ADVERTISING RATES:
SCC .... RUR 60.00
Mechanical Data: Type Area: A3
CONSUMER: CURRENT AFFAIRS & POLITICS

NOVOSTI YUGRY 1774645RU67B-426
Editorial: ul. Engelsa 14, 628011 KHANTY-MANSIISK
Tel: 34671 3 21 94 **Fax:** 34671 3 21 94
Web site: http://www.isurgut.ru/~company/newsofyugra
Date Established: 1931; **Freq:** 156 issues yearly; **Circ:** 52,000
Usual Pagination: 24
Editor: Alexey Dvizov
Profile: Socio-political newspaper focused on economic, cultural issues of the Siberian region.
Language(s): Russian
ADVERTISING RATES:
Full Page Mono .... RUR 55800.00
Full Page Colour .... RUR 66960.00
SCC .... RUR 80.00
Mechanical Data: Type Area: A3
REGIONAL DAILY & SUNDAY NEWSPAPERS: Regional Daily Newspapers

NOVY MIR 1774255RU67B-216
Editorial: ul. Gorkogo 84, 640000 KURGAN
Tel: 3522 46 17 22
Email: nm-reklama@yandex.ru **Web site:** http://newworldnews.ru
Date Established: 1917; **Freq:** 260 issues yearly - Published 5 days a week; **Annual Sub.:** RUR 3400.04; **Circ:** 12,000
Usual Pagination: 24
Editor-in-Chief: Galina Evseeva
Profile: Socio-political newspaper covering social, cultural and political issues and events in Kurgan region.
Language(s): Russian
ADVERTISING RATES:
SCC .... RUR 35.40
Mechanical Data: Type Area: A2
REGIONAL DAILY & SUNDAY NEWSPAPERS: Regional Daily Newspapers

NOVYE IZVESTIYA 1774539RU65A-50
Editorial: ul. Elektrozavodskaya 33, MOSKVA
Tel: 495 783 06 36 **Fax:** 495 783 06 37
Email: info@newnews.ru **Web site:** http://www.newizv.ru
Date Established: 2003; **Freq:** Daily; **Circ:** 108,200
Usual Pagination: 32
Editor: Valery Yakov; **Advertising Director:** Irina Varlamova
Profile: Fully colour daily newspaper covering political, social and economical news.
Language(s): Russian
ADVERTISING RATES:
Full Page Mono .... RUR 247500.00
Full Page Colour .... RUR 264000.00
Mechanical Data: Type Area: 383 x 503mm
NATIONAL DAILY & SUNDAY NEWSPAPERS: National Daily Newspapers

OBOGASHCHENIE RUD 763720RU30-150
Editorial: 22nd line 3, 199106 ST. PETERSBURG
Tel: 12 324 89 45 **Fax:** 12 324 89 45
Email: obrud@yandex.ru **Web site:** http://www.rudmet.ru
Date Established: 1956; **Freq:** 6 issues yearly; **Cover Price:** RUR 570.00; **Circ:** 1,000
Usual Pagination: 48
Editor: Viktor Fedotovich Baranov; **Advertising Manager:** Natalia Kolykhalova
Profile: Magazine covering the problems of mining processes and technological mineralogy.
Language(s): Russian
Readership: Aimed at engineers and researchers.
ADVERTISING RATES:
Full Page Mono .... EUR 400.00
Full Page Colour .... EUR 950.00
BUSINESS: MINING & QUARRYING

OBUSTROYSTVO 1774650RU4B-3
Editorial: ul. Mira 25, 350000 KRASNODAR
Tel: 61 262 71 45 **Fax:** 61 262 71 45
Email: market@riaok.kuban.ru **Web site:** http://www.obustrojstvo.ru
Freq: Monthly; **Circ:** 8,000
Usual Pagination: 100
Executive Editor: Kseniya Donskaya; **Editor-in-Chief:** Nataliya Milantyeva; **Advertising Manager:** Elena Dyshlyuk
Profile: Magazine for those who builds or renovates a house/flat with practical advice for house refurbishment.
Language(s): Russian

ADVERTISING RATES:
Full Page Colour .... RUR 20000.00
Mechanical Data: Type Area: 220 x 280mm
BUSINESS: ARCHITECTURE & BUILDING: Interior Design & Flooring

OFFISNIY INTERIER 1774205RU4B-4
Editorial: 4 Roschinsky proyezd, str. 5, 115191 MOSKVA **Tel:** 495 540 73 40 **Fax:** 495 540 72 15
Email: info@cre.ru **Web site:** http://www.interior.cre.ru
Freq: Quarterly; **Circ:** 20,000
Usual Pagination: 132
Editor-in-Chief: Tatiana Lomakina; **Publisher:** Annette Wassenaar
Profile: Professional magazine on office interior design and office furniture.
Language(s): Russian
BUSINESS: ARCHITECTURE & BUILDING: Interior Design & Flooring

OIL & GAS JOURNAL RUSSIA
1774562RU33-4
Editorial: ul. Rustaveli 12a, str. 2, MOSKVA
Tel: 495 253 90 20 **Fax:** 495 253 90 23
Email: ogj@ogj.ru **Web site:** http://www.ogj.ru
Date Established: 2006; **Freq:** Monthly; **Annual Sub.:** RUR 4473.00; **Circ:** 3,000
Usual Pagination: 80
Editor-in-Chief: Natalia Petrova
Profile: Provides information and news on oil and gas developments, new technologies and machinery.
Language(s): Russian
BUSINESS: OIL & PETROLEUM

OIL OF RUSSIA 1774269RU33-3
Editorial: 11 Sretensky Blvd., MOSKVA 101000
Tel: 495 627 16 90 **Fax:** 495 627 16 92
Email: editor@oilru.com **Web site:** http://www.oilru.com/or
Date Established: 1998; **Freq:** Quarterly; **Circ:** 10,000
Editor-in-Chief: Alexander Matveichuk; **Advertising Manager:** Andrei Soldatov; **Managing Editor:** Dmitry Gurtovoy
Profile: Provides coverage of oil and gas developments in Russia, the CIS and Eastern Europe.
Language(s): English
ADVERTISING RATES:
Full Page Colour .... RUR 94650.00
Mechanical Data: Type Area: A4
BUSINESS: OIL & PETROLEUM

OMSKAYA PRAVDA
1774389RU67B-275
Editorial: pr. K. Marksa 39, 644042 OMSK
Tel: 3812 31 22 05 **Fax:** 3812 30 57 54
Email: omskpravda@omskpravda.e4u.ru **Web site:** http://www.omskpravda.ru
Date Established: 1917; **Freq:** 104 issues yearly; **Circ:** 22,731
Usual Pagination: 32
Editor-in-Chief: Marina Vzdornova
Profile: Regional socio-political newspaper covering economics, culture and entertainment.
Language(s): Russian
ADVERTISING RATES:
Full Page Mono .... RUR 24480.00
Mechanical Data: Type Area: 250x320mm
REGIONAL DAILY & SUNDAY NEWSPAPERS: Regional Daily Newspapers

ONBOARD 1774417RU75G-2
Editorial: ul. Timura Frunze 11, str. 44-45, 4 floor, 119992 MOSKVA **Tel:** 495 935 70 34
Email: ryvkin@gameland.ru **Web site:** http://www.onboardmagazine.ru
Freq: Monthly; **Circ:** 20,000
Usual Pagination: 112
Editor: Dmitri Ryvkin; **Executive Editor:** Tatiana Romanova; **Advertising Manager:** Inna Ivanchenko; **Advertising Director:** Julia Mavlyanova
Profile: Publication about snowboarding with stylish photographs, mind-bogging tricks, interviews and profiles with famous riders, practical riding advice.
Language(s): Russian
Readership: Targets male inspired riders, from beginners to experts, in age group: 16-30.
ADVERTISING RATES:
Full Page Colour .... RUR 230000.00
Mechanical Data: Type Area: 230x300mm
CONSUMER: SPORT: Winter Sports

ORLOVSKAYA PRAVDA
1774443RU67B-310
Editorial: ul. Brestskaya 6, office 6, 302028 OREL
Tel: 622 43 51 72 **Fax:** 622 76 20 34
Email: orp@rekom.ru **Web site:** http://www.orp.orel.ru
Date Established: 1917; **Freq:** 260 issues yearly; **Circ:** 26,000
Usual Pagination: 16
Editor: Alexander Tikhonov
Profile: Regional socio-political newspaper aimed at all residents of the region.
Language(s): Russian
ADVERTISING RATES:
SCC .... RUR 40.00
Mechanical Data: Type Area: A 2, A3
REGIONAL DAILY & SUNDAY NEWSPAPERS: Regional Daily Newspapers

OTDEL PRODAZH 1774366RU11A-3
Editorial: ul. Dubininskaya 90, 115093 MOSKVA
Tel: 495 921 36 25 **Fax:** 495 921 36 25
Email: info@restoved.ru **Web site:** http://www.restoved.ru
Freq: Monthly; **Cover Price:** Free; **Circ:** 34,000
Advertising Director: Andrey Ivanov
Profile: Professional publication with information on goods for catering business and hotel accommodation business.
Language(s): Russian
ADVERTISING RATES:
Full Page Colour .... RUR 39000.00
Mechanical Data: Type Area: A4
BUSINESS: CATERING: Catering, Hotels & Restaurants

OTDOKHNI! 629835RU74Q-1
Editorial: Ulica Polkovaya, Dom 3, Stroenie 4, MOSKVA **Tel:** 495 797 98 68 **Fax:** 495 257 11 96
Email: otdochni@burda.ru **Web site:** http://www.burda.ru
Date Established: 1997; **Freq:** Weekly; **Circ:** 300,000
Usual Pagination: 84
Editor: Dmitriy Stanislavovich Zubanov; **Editor-in-Chief:** Inna Stepanova; **Advertising Director:** Nataliya Pushkina
Profile: Magazine featuring famous people and celebrities, horoscopes, career, health and culinary advice.
Language(s): Russian
Readership: Aimed at women aged between 30 and 45 years of age.
ADVERTISING RATES:
Full Page Mono .... RUR 300000.00
Mechanical Data: Type Area: 210 x 267mm
CONSUMER: WOMEN'S INTEREST CONSUMER MAGAZINES: Lifestyle

OTECHESTVENNYE ZAPISKI
1774321RU82-151
Editorial: ul. Pyatnitskaya 25, 115326 MOSKVA
Tel: 495 231 18 75 **Fax:** 495 974 39 47
Email: oz@vremya.ru **Web site:** http://www.strana-oz.ru
Date Established: 2001; **Freq:** 6 issues yearly; **Circ:** 2,000
Usual Pagination: 368
Editor: Tatiana Malkina
Profile: Analytical magazine providing in-depth research of state of Russian society, religion, culture and political issues.
Language(s): Russian
Mechanical Data: Type Area: 70x108/16
CONSUMER: CURRENT AFFAIRS & POLITICS

PACKAGING INTERNATIONAL/ PACKET 1894792RU35-11
Editorial: ul. Elektrozavodskaya 37/4, str. 7, 107140 MOSKVA **Tel:** 495 725 60 01 **Fax:** 495 725 60 01
Email: paket@kursiv.ru **Web site:** http://www.kursiv.ru
Date Established: 1999; **Freq:** 6 issues yearly; **Cover Price:** RUR 59.00; **Circ:** 5,000
Usual Pagination: 64
Managing Director: Nina Shapinova; **Advertising Manager:** Elena Maslova
Profile: Main topics of magazine: packaging technology, equipment and materials, labels and labelling, package and label design, recycling and environment, main industry exhibitions reviews and market researches.
Language(s): Russian
Readership: Targets consumer goods producers, packaging equipment & materials manufacturers and users.
ADVERTISING RATES:
Full Page Colour .... EUR 2000.00
Mechanical Data: Type Area: 215x297mm
BUSINESS: PACKAGING & BOTTLING

PARLAMENTSKAYA GAZETA
1774608RU32A-2
Editorial: 1 ul. Yamskogo Polya 28, 125993 MOSKVA
Tel: 499 257 50 90 **Fax:** 499 257 50 82
Email: pg@pnp.ru **Web site:** http://www.pnp.ru
ISSN: 1990-4924
Freq: Weekly; **Circ:** 35,000
Usual Pagination: 48
Editor: Andrey Fedotkin; **Advertising Director:** Maria Matveeva
Profile: Publishes official legislative documentation of Federal Parliament of Russia.
Language(s): Russian
ADVERTISING RATES:
Full Page Mono .... RUR 150000.00
Mechanical Data: Type Area: 256 x 356mm
BUSINESS: LOCAL GOVERNMENT, LEISURE & RECREATION: Local Government

PC+MOBILE 1774708RU18B-3
Editorial: ul. 4-aya Magistralnaya 11, MOSKVA
Tel: 495 510 15 25 **Fax:** 495 510 15 24
Email: samoylenko@mediasign.ru **Web site:** http://www.pc-mobile.ru
Date Established: 2006; **Freq:** Monthly; **Circ:** 36,000
Usual Pagination: 132
Editor: Maxim Samoylenko; **Editor-in-Chief:** Stanislav Kuprianov
Profile: Everything about PC gadgets: smart phones, notebooks, satellite navigation devices, palm tops, etc. and modern mobile technologies.
Language(s): Russian
BUSINESS: ELECTRONICS: Telecommunications

PC MAGAZINE 714167RU5D-150
Editorial: ul. Marksystskaya 34, Korp. 10, 109147 MOSKVA **Tel:** 495 974 22 60 **Fax:** 495 974 22 63
Email: red@pcmag.ru **Web site:** http://www.pcmag.ru
Date Established: 1991; **Freq:** Monthly; **Circ:** 40,000
Editor: Ruben Grigorevich Gerr; **Editor-in-Chief:** O. Lebedev; **Managing Director:** Leonid Teplitskiy; **Advertising Director:** Tatiana Sofronova; **Publisher:** Grigoriy Golman
Profile: Magazine concerning all aspects of personal computing.
Language(s): Russian
Readership: Aimed at IT professionals as well as individual computer users.
ADVERTISING RATES:
Full Page Mono .... RUR 162000.00
Full Page Colour .... RUR 200000.00
Mechanical Data: Trim Size: 275 x 205mm, Type Area: 250 x 180mm, Col Length: 250mm, Film: Positive, right reading, emulsion side down. Digital, Screen: 60 lpc
BUSINESS: COMPUTERS & AUTOMATION: Personal Computers

PC WEEK 714169RU5D-151
Editorial: ul. Marksitskaya 34, Korp. 10, 109147 MOSKVA **Tel:** 495 974 22 60 **Fax:** 495 974 22 63
Email: editorial@pcweek.ru **Web site:** http://www.pcweek.ru
Date Established: 1995; **Freq:** Weekly; **Circ:** 35,000
Editor: Eduard Predakov; **Editor-in-Chief:** Aleksey Maksimov; **Advertising Manager:** Olga Filatova; **Advertising Director:** Sofia Vaiserman
Profile: Magazine focusing on all aspects of PCs and the Internet.
Language(s): Russian
Readership: Aimed at home PC users.
ADVERTISING RATES:
Full Page Mono .... RUR 178200.00
Full Page Colour .... RUR 207900.00
Mechanical Data: Trim Size: 375 x 266mm, Type Area: 350 x 246mm, Col Length: 350mm, Film: Positive, right reading, emulsion side down, Screen: 60 lpc
BUSINESS: COMPUTERS & AUTOMATION: Personal Computers

PENZENSKAYA PRAVDA
1774446RU67B-312
Editorial: ul. Karla Marksa 16, 440026 PENZA
Tel: 412 56 00 85 **Fax:** 412 56 00 92
Email: true@penzenskaya-pravda.ru **Web site:** http://www.penzenskaya-pravda.ru
Date Established: 1917; **Freq:** 104 issues yearly; **Annual Sub.:** RUR 324.00; **Circ:** 20,000
Usual Pagination: 16
Editor: Larisa Reppe
Profile: Socio-political newspaper covering news and events from Penza region and Penza city.
Language(s): Russian
ADVERTISING RATES:
Full Page Mono .... RUR 30000.00
Full Page Colour .... RUR 36000.00
Mechanical Data: Type Area: A3
REGIONAL DAILY & SUNDAY NEWSPAPERS: Regional Daily Newspapers

PERSONA 1774322RU74Q-9
Editorial: ul. Novy Arbat 21, str. 1, 119019 MOSKVA
Tel: 495 291 20 05 **Fax:** 495 291 50 27
Email: persona-magazine@mail.ru **Web site:** htto://www.persona-magazine.ru
Date Established: 1997; **Freq:** 9 issues yearly; **Circ:** 10,000
Usual Pagination: 100
Editor: Larisa Shamikova
Profile: Publication presenting portraits of famous contemporary artists, politicians and writers, interviews and reviews.
Language(s): Russian
ADVERTISING RATES:
Full Page Colour .... RUR 25500.00
Mechanical Data: Type Area: 230 x 300mm
CONSUMER: WOMEN'S INTEREST CONSUMER MAGAZINES: Lifestyle

PETERBURGSKY DNEVNIK
1774523RU32A-1
Editorial: ul. Chapayeva 11/4, litera A, 197046 SANKT PETERBURG **Tel:** 12 331 06 88
Fax: 12 331 06 88
Email: editor@ipc.spb.ru **Web site:** http://www.spbdnevnik.ru
ISSN: 1992-8068
Date Established: 2003; **Freq:** Weekly - Published on Mondays; **Cover Price:** Free; **Circ:** 300,000
Usual Pagination: 20
Editor: Vladimir Malyshev
Profile: Official newspaper of St. Petersburg's local government and provides general city information and about decisions of local city administration.
Language(s): Russian
ADVERTISING RATES:
Full Page Mono .... RUR 150000.00
Full Page Colour .... RUR 195000.00
BUSINESS: LOCAL GOVERNMENT, LEISURE & RECREATION: Local Government

PISHCHEVAYA PROMYSHLENNOST 1611085RU22C-2
Editorial: Sadovaya-Spasskaya 18, komn. 610, 107996 MOSKVA **Tel:** 495 607 79 58
Fax: 495 607 20 87
Email: foodprom@ropnet.ru **Web site:** http://www.foodprom.ru
Date Established: 1930; **Freq:** Monthly; **Cover Price:** RUR 385.00; **Circ:** 8,000
Editor: Olga Presnyakova
Profile: Magazine focusing on the food industry containing information on technologies and equipment, exhibition calendars and overviews of events, company profiles, interviews with practitioners and managers, advertisement of machinery, raw materials and ingredients.
Language(s): Russian
Readership: Read by food industry managers and specialists.
ADVERTISING RATES:
Full Page Mono .... EUR 1000.00
Full Page Colour .... EUR 1800.00
Mechanical Data: Type Area: 210 x 290mm
BUSINESS: FOOD: Food Processing & Packaging

PISHCHEVYE INGREDIENTY: SYRIO I DOBAVKI 1611167RU22A-202
Editorial: Sadovaya-Spasskaya 18, komn. 610, 107996 MOSKVA **Tel:** 495 607 17 70
Fax: 495 607 28 61
Email: foodprom@ropnet.ru **Web site:** http://www.foodprom.ru
Freq: Half-yearly - Published in April and November; **Circ:** 3,000
Editor: Elena Kaouts; **Advertising Director:** Ekaterina Varekha
Profile: Magazine featuring manufacture and application of dyes, spices, thickeners, stabilizers, various food components, also covers reviews of thematic exhibitions and seminars.
Language(s): Russian
Readership: Read by manufacturers and suppliers of food components.
ADVERTISING RATES:
Full Page Mono .... EUR 1000.00
Full Page Colour .... EUR 1800.00
BUSINESS: FOOD

PIVO I NAPITKI 1611112RU9A-2
Editorial: Sadovaya-Spasskaya 18, komn. 604, 107996 MOSKVA **Tel:** 495 607 17 70
Fax: 495 607 28 61
Email: beerprom@ropnet.ru **Web site:** http://www.foodprom.ru
Freq: 6 issues yearly; **Cover Price:** RUR 407.00; **Circ:** 5,000
Editor: Olga Presnyakova
Profile: Magazine providing information on brewing, soft drink, liqueur and vodka industries, relating to ingredients, materials and machinery. Publishes reports from conferences and seminars.
Language(s): Russian
Readership: Aimed at specialists within the drinks industries.
ADVERTISING RATES:
Full Page Mono .... EUR 1000.00
Full Page Colour .... EUR 1800.00
BUSINESS: DRINKS & LICENSED TRADE: Drinks, Licensed Trade, Wines & Spirits

PLASTIKS: INDUSTRIYA PERERABOTKI PLASTMASS
1745918RU39-1
Formerly: Plastiks
Editorial: 1 Entuziastov 3, str. 1, 111024 MOSCOW
Tel: 495 231 21 15 **Fax:** 46 231 21 15
Email: pr@plastics.ru **Web site:** http://www.plastics.ru
Date Established: 2002; **Freq:** 10 issues yearly; **Circ:** 3,300
Usual Pagination: 88
Editor-in-Chief: Anna Vilens
Profile: Magazine focusing on plastics processing industry. Covers polymer technologies, raw materials, equipment and plastic products.
Language(s): Russian
Readership: Aimed at top management, technologists, specialists and plastic products manufacturing firms.
BUSINESS: PLASTICS & RUBBER

Russian Federation

PLAYBOY 1600534RU86C-10
Editorial: ul. Polkovaya, dom 3, str. 4, 127018 MOSKVA **Tel:** 495 797 45 60 **Fax:** 495 797 44 12
Email: playboy@burda.ru **Web site:** http://www.playboy.com.ru
Date Established: 1995; **Freq:** 11 issues yearly - July and August issues usually combined; **Cover Price:** RUR 100.00; **Circ:** 160,000
Usual Pagination: 180
Editor: Maksim Maslakov; **Editor-in-Chief:** Vladimir Lyaporov; **Advertising Manager:** Ekaterina Butova; **Advertising Director:** Oxana Zubova; **Publisher:** Olga Alekseenko
Profile: Magazine containing male interest photography, including features on food and wine, fashion and sport.
Language(s): Russian
Readership: Aimed at men aged 25 to 35 years.
ADVERTISING RATES:
Full Page Colour .... RUR 324400.00
Agency Commission: 10%
Mechanical Data: Trim Size: 275 x 215mm
Copy instructions: *Copy Date:* 2 months prior to publication date
CONSUMER: ADULT & GAY MAGAZINES: Men's Lifestyle Magazines

POD KLYLUCH 1774596RU4B-7
Editorial: ul. Razyezhaya 9, 191002 SANKT PETERBURG **Tel:** 12 325 35 95 **Fax:** 12 575 63 86
Email: key@es.ru **Web site:** http://www.podkluch-spb.ru
Freq: 11 issues yearly; **Circ:** 30,000
Usual Pagination: 104
Profile: Glossy magazine on architecture, interior design with photos from St. Petersburg's apartments.
Language(s): Russian
ADVERTISING RATES:
Full Page Colour .... RUR 126000.00
Mechanical Data: Type Area: 297x365mm
BUSINESS: ARCHITECTURE & BUILDING: Interior Design & Flooring

PODMOSKOVIYE 1774323RU67B-239
Editorial: ul. 1905 goda 7, 123022 MOSKVA
Tel: 495 707 27 68 **Fax:** 495 707 27 68
Email: enp@oblnews.ru **Web site:** http://enp.oblnews.ru
Date Established: 2001; **Freq:** 260 issues yearly; **Circ:** 65,000
Usual Pagination: 32
Editor: Piyotr Karapetyan
Profile: Provides informative analytical materials society, economics, social issues, culture and sports in Moscow region.
Language(s): Russian
Mechanical Data: Type Area: A2
REGIONAL DAILY & SUNDAY NEWSPAPERS: Regional Daily Newspapers

POISK 1697624RU55-5
Editorial: ul. Vavilova 30/6, 119991 MOSKVA
Tel: 499 135 35 67 **Fax:** 499 135 35 67
Email: editor@poisknews.ru **Web site:** http://www.poisknews.ru
Freq: Weekly; **Circ:** 10,000
Usual Pagination: 24
Advertising Manager: Marina Khruscheva
Profile: Provides news from research centres and universities, articles dedicated to actual problems of science & educational community, opinions of authorities in basic and applied science, reports by managers, stories about scientists and research teams.
Language(s): Russian
Readership: Targets professionals in field of science, teaching, IT and managers in the sphere of science and education.
ADVERTISING RATES:
Full Page Colour .... RUR 44000.00
Mechanical Data: Type Area: A3
BUSINESS: APPLIED SCIENCE & LABORATORIES

POPULARNYE FINANSY 1774531RU1A-37
Editorial: ul. 2-aya Khutorskaya 38A, str. 23, 127994 MOSKVA **Tel:** 495 660 88 75 **Fax:** 495 660 88 79
Email: info@popfin.com **Web site:** http://www.popfin.com
ISSN: 1817-034X
Date Established: 2000; **Freq:** Monthly; **Circ:** 60,400
Usual Pagination: 104
Editor-in-Chief: Dmitriy Lovyagin
Profile: Focuses on banking services, investments, insurance market, personal banking, luxury goods, holidays and lifestyle.
Language(s): Russian
Readership: Aimed at top managers, businessmen, finance, investment and insurance specialists.
ADVERTISING RATES:
Full Page Colour .... RUR 180000.00
Mechanical Data: Type Area: 200 x 255mm
BUSINESS: FINANCE & ECONOMICS

PRIKLADNAYA BIOKHIMIYA I MIKROBIOLOGIYA 1600608RU64F-5
Editorial: Profsoyuznaia 90, 117997 MOSKVA
Tel: 495 336 16 00 **Fax:** 495 336 06 66
Email: compmg@maik.ru **Web site:** http://www.maik.ru/journals/appbio.htm
ISSN: 0003-6838
Date Established: 1965; **Freq:** 6 issues yearly; **Circ:** 1,000
Executive Editor: Vladimir Shcherbukhin; **Editor-in-Chief:** Vladimir O. Popov
Profile: Publication covering the production and processing of biologically active substances, studies on the processing of raw materials and the microbiological synthesis of food and feed products.
Language(s): English
BUSINESS: OTHER CLASSIFICATIONS: Biology

PRO ALKOGOL 1774106RU9A-6
Editorial: Yegorevski proyezd 2, MOSKVA
Tel: 495 988 45 34
Email: info@alconews.ru **Web site:** http://www.alconews.ru
Freq: Monthly; Free to qualifying individuals ; **Circ:** 29,000
Editor: Tatiana Kasevich
Profile: Professional magazine about spirits production and alcohol trade in Russian Federation.
Language(s): Russian
ADVERTISING RATES:
Full Page Colour .... RUR 128700.00
Mechanical Data: Type Area: 220x295mm
BUSINESS: DRINKS & LICENSED TRADE: Drinks, Licensed Trade, Wines & Spirits

PRO DIGITAL 1774385RU5R-1
Editorial: pr. Pobedy 388, office 112, 454021 CHELYABINSK **Tel:** 343 216 37 37
Fax: 343 216 37 38
Email: pr@banzay.ru **Web site:** http://www.prodigital.su
Date Established: 2005; **Freq:** 11 issues yearly; **Circ:** 8,000
Usual Pagination: 44
Profile: Magazine about digital technologies, new scientific achievements and their implementation in technological production.
Language(s): Russian
ADVERTISING RATES:
Full Page Colour .... RUR 21000.00
Mechanical Data: Type Area: 215 x 280mm
BUSINESS: COMPUTERS & AUTOMATION: Computers Related

PROIZVODSTVO SPIRTA I LIKERO-VODOCHNYH IZDELIY 1611125RU9A-1
Editorial: Sadovaya-Spasskaya 18, komn. 601, 607, 107996 MOSKVA **Tel:** 495 607 17 70
Fax: 495 607 20 87
Email: beerprom@ropnet.ru **Web site:** http://www.foodprom.ru
Freq: Quarterly; **Cover Price:** RUR 275.00; **Circ:** 1,500
Editor: Olga Presnyakova; **Advertising Director:** Ekaterina Varekha
Profile: Magazine focusing on the spirit and alcoholic beverage industry, includes news about legislation, equipment and technologies.
Language(s): Russian
Readership: Read primarily by managers and practical specialists as well as suppliers of raw materials, machinery and accessories.
ADVERTISING RATES:
Full Page Mono .... EUR 1000.00
Full Page Colour .... EUR 1800.00
BUSINESS: DRINKS & LICENSED TRADE: Drinks, Licensed Trade, Wines & Spirits

PROMYSHLENNIK ROSSII 1774084RU14A-34
Editorial: Staraya ploschad 10/4, office 406, 103070 MOSKVA **Tel:** 495 748 41 46
Email: promros@mail.ru **Web site:** http://www.promros.ru
Freq: Monthly; **Circ:** 10,000
Usual Pagination: 80
Profile: Professional business magazine on economic developments in all regions of Russian and current state of Russian industry.
Language(s): Russian
ADVERTISING RATES:
Full Page Mono .... RUR 44000.00
Mechanical Data: Trim Size: 235 x 280mm
BUSINESS: COMMERCE, INDUSTRY & MANAGEMENT

PROMYSHLENNOST' POVOLZHYA 1774545RU14A-9
Editorial: PO box 217, 410005 SARATOV
Tel: 452 59 50 10 **Fax:** 452 45 96 49
Email: ivm@renet.ru **Web site:** http://www.i-v-m.ru
Date Established: 2000; **Freq:** 10 issues yearly; **Cover Price:** RUR 120.00; **Circ:** 10,000
Usual Pagination: 90
Editor: Sergey Grishin
Profile: Profile of industrial companies in Volga region and overview of region's economical developments.
Language(s): Russian
ADVERTISING RATES:
Full Page Colour .... RUR 30000.00
Mechanical Data: Type Area: 284 x 197mm
BUSINESS: COMMERCE, INDUSTRY & MANAGEMENT

PROMYSHLENNY MARKETING 1774178RU2A-15
Editorial: ul. Usacheva 11, office 529, 119992 MOSKVA **Tel:** 495 785 06 58 **Fax:** 495 514 83 05
Email: editor@ordeks.ru **Web site:** http://www.marketprom.ru
Freq: 6 issues yearly; **Annual Sub.:** RUR 5730.00; **Circ:** 5,000
Usual Pagination: 80
Editor: Yana Milovanova
Profile: Professional magazine on b2b, industry marketing, marketing services and marketing communication strategies.
Language(s): Russian
Readership: Aimed at marketing directors, marketing and advertising specialists, b2b departments of companies.
ADVERTISING RATES:
Full Page Mono .... RUR 84000.00
Mechanical Data: Type Area: A4
BUSINESS: COMMUNICATIONS, ADVERTISING & MARKETING

PROYEKT INTERNATIONAL 1616553RU4A-6
Editorial: Bolshoy Karetny per. 17, str. 2, 127051 MOSKVA **Tel:** 495 699 41 54 **Fax:** 495 699 41 54
Email: info@prorus.ru **Web site:** http://prorus.ru
Date Established: 1995; **Freq:** Quarterly; Free to qualifying individuals
Annual Sub.: RUR 2200.00; **Circ:** 6,000
Usual Pagination: 200
Editor-in-Chief: Bart Goldhoorn; **Advertising Director:** Olga Potapova
Profile: Magazine focusing on foreign architecture and design, includes information on latest projects, buildings and related issues.
Language(s): English; Russian
Readership: Aimed at architects and designers.
ADVERTISING RATES:
Full Page Colour .... EUR 3300.00
Mechanical Data: Trim Size: 225 x 280mm
BUSINESS: ARCHITECTURE & BUILDING: Architecture

PROYEKT KLASSIKA 1616555RU4A-7
Editorial: Bolshoy Karetny per. 17, str. 2, 127051 MOSKVA **Tel:** 495 699 41 54 **Fax:** 495 258 44 36
Email: editor@projectclassica.ru **Web site:** http://www.projectclassica.ru
Freq: Quarterly; **Annual Sub.:** RUR 660.00; **Circ:** 8,000
Usual Pagination: 160
Editor-in-Chief: Gregoriy Revzin; **Advertising Director:** Olga Potapova; **Publisher:** Sergey Pushkin
Profile: Magazine focusing on classical forms of design in architecture.
Language(s): Russian
Readership: Read by architects, interior designers and town planners.
BUSINESS: ARCHITECTURE & BUILDING: Architecture

PROYEKT ROSSIYA 1600715RU4A-5
Editorial: Bolshoy Karetny per. 17, str.2, 127051 MOSKVA **Tel:** 495 258 44 36 **Fax:** 495 258 44 36
Email: info@prorus.ru **Web site:** http://www.prorus.ru
Freq: Quarterly; **Annual Sub.:** RUR 1010.00; **Circ:** 10,000
Usual Pagination: 200
Editor: Bart Goldhoorn; **Editor-in-Chief:** Alexei Muratov; **Advertising Director:** Olga Potapova
Profile: Journal covering architecture, urbanism, design and construction in Russia.
Language(s): English; Russian
Readership: Aimed at architects, designers, architectural administrators and students of architecture.
ADVERTISING RATES:
Full Page Colour .... EUR 3300.00
Agency Commission: 15%
Mechanical Data: Print Process: Offset, Col Length: 280mm, No. of Columns (Display): 2, Type Area: 280 x 225mm, Trim Size: 225 x 280mm
Average ad content per issue: 20%
BUSINESS: ARCHITECTURE & BUILDING: Architecture

PSYKHOLOGICHESKAYA NAUKA I OBRAZOVANIYE 1774325RU55-2
Editorial: ul. Sretenka 29, 127051 MOSKVA
Tel: 495 632 99 59
Email: pno@inbox.ru **Web site:** http://www.psyedu.ru
Date Established: 1996; **Freq:** Quarterly; **Circ:** 2,100
Usual Pagination: 112
Editor-in-Chief: Anna Shvedkovskaya
Profile: Publication focused on psychology issues and education.
Language(s): Russian
Mechanical Data: Type Area: A4
BUSINESS: APPLIED SCIENCE & LABORATORIES

PYATIGORSKAYA PRAVDA 1774574RU67B-376
Editorial: pr. Lenina 2, office 601-610, 357500 PYATIGORSK **Tel:** 793 33 73 97 **Fax:** 793 34 26 43
Email: pravda@kmv.ru **Web site:** http://www.pravda-kmv.ru
Date Established: 1937; **Freq:** 156 issues yearly; **Circ:** 10,000
Editor: Sergey Drokin; **Advertising Director:** Olga Kostrova
Profile: Daily regional newspaper covering regional news from the Caucasus region, economics and politics.
Language(s): Russian
ADVERTISING RATES:
SCC .... RUR 27.50
Mechanical Data: Type Area: A2
REGIONAL DAILY & SUNDAY NEWSPAPERS: Regional Daily Newspapers

PYATOYE KOLESO 1774371RU77A-54
Editorial: Novodanilovskaya nab. 4a, 117105 MOSKVA **Tel:** 495 510 22 11 **Fax:** 495 510 49 69
Email: s.pavlov@spn.ru **Web site:** http://www.spn.ru
Date Established: 1993; **Freq:** Monthly; **Circ:** 152,000
Editor: Stanislav Pavlov; **News Editor:** Maxim Fedorov; **Editor-in-Chief:** Andrey Myazin; **Advertising Director:** Konstantin Ostrikov
Profile: Presents foreign and domestic auto news, latest news from official car dealers, interviews, automobile production novelties in Russia and abroad and new developments.
Language(s): Russian
Readership: Aimed at wide range of drivers, professional motorists and auto dealers.
ADVERTISING RATES:
Full Page Colour .... RUR 285000.00
CONSUMER: MOTORING & CYCLING: Motoring

RBC MAGAZINE 1937472RU1A-90
Editorial: ul. Profsoyuznaya 78, 117393 MOSKVA
Tel: 495 363 11 11 **Fax:** 495 363 11 25
Email: magazine@rbc.ru **Web site:** http://magazine.rbc.ru
Freq: Monthly; **Circ:** 100,000
Profile: The monthly magazine RBC keeps readers informed of major trends in economy and politics, offering a professional business process analysis, as well as info about the latest developments in various fields of knowledge and latest news in world culture. RBC is known for its calibrated and well-structured information, stylish design, easy navigation, the variety of journalistic genres, flawless Russian.
Language(s): Russian
Readership: The magazine is primarily aimed at owners and top managers of companies, but is also of interest to those who are used to keep abreast of the latest developments of Russia and the world of business.
ADVERTISING RATES:
Full Page Colour .... RUR 445000.00
Mechanical Data: Type Area: 215x285mm
BUSINESS: FINANCE & ECONOMICS

RBCC BULLETIN 1937454RU14C-1
Editorial: Business centre Galerelya Akter, office 402A, 16/2 Tverskaya St., 125009 MOSKVA
Tel: 495 961 21 60 **Fax:** 495 961 21 61
Email: infomoscow@rbcc.com **Web site:** http://rbcc.testcube.ru/media/bulleten
Date Established: 1918; **Freq:** 8 issues yearly; **Cover Price:** Free; **Circ:** 5,000
Usual Pagination: 48
Editor: Alexandra Kulikova
Profile: Publication of The Russo-British Chamber of Commerce, founded in 1916 as a private, non-profit making organisation, designed to facilitate businessbetween Britain and Russia.
Language(s): English; Russian
Readership: It has established itself as the leading Russo-British commercial digest for companies actively doing business between the two countries. It attracts a wide range of advertisers and articles covering all sectors of industry and ensures your products and services reach the leading business community in Moscow, St Petersburg and London.
ADVERTISING RATES:
Full Page Colour .... RUR 69000.00
Mechanical Data: Type Area: 180x250mm, Bleed Size: 215x285mm + 5mm
Copy instructions: *Copy Date:* 20th of the month prior to publication
BUSINESS: COMMERCE, INDUSTRY & MANAGEMENT: International Commerce

READER'S DIGEST (RUSSIA) 1201774RU73-5
Editorial: PO box 8, 117218 MOSKVA
Tel: 495 258 55 59 **Fax:** 495 258 55 59
Email: ed_ru@rd.com **Web site:** http://www.rdigest.ru
ISSN: 1018-3785
Date Established: 1991; **Freq:** 10 issues yearly; **Annual Sub.:** RUR 599.00; **Circ:** 411,000
Usual Pagination: 144
Editor: Eleonora Medvedeva; **Editor-in-Chief:** Eleonora Medvedeva; **Managing Director:** Yukha Pyukela
Profile: General interest magazine.
Language(s): Russian
Readership: Aimed at middle to high income earners all over Russia.

ADVERTISING RATES:
Full Page Colour .... RUR 184000.00
Agency Commission: 15%
Mechanical Data: Type Area: 170 x 110mm, Col Length: 170mm, Trim Size: 184 x 134mm, Bleed Size: 190 x 140mm, Screen: 54 lpc, Print Process: Offset
Copy instructions: *Copy Date:* 1st of month, 2 months prior to publication date
Average ad content per issue: 75%
CONSUMER: NATIONAL & INTERNATIONAL PERIODICALS

REALTOR
1774714RU1E-8
Editorial: ul. Usacheva 11, office 529, 119992 MOSKVA **Tel:** 495 785 06 58 **Fax:** 495 514 83 05
Email: editor@image-media.ru **Web site:** http://realtormag.ru
Freq: 6 issues yearly; **Annual Sub.:** RUR 5610.00; **Circ:** 5,000
Usual Pagination: 80
Editor-in-Chief: Timur Aslanov
Profile: Professional magazine about property market, investments and developments, mortgage and legal advice.
Language(s): Russian
Readership: Aimed at managers of property agencies, investors and developers.
ADVERTISING RATES:
Full Page Colour .... RUR 42000.00
Mechanical Data: Type Area: A4
BUSINESS: FINANCE & ECONOMICS: Property

REGIONALNAYA EKONOMIKA: TEORIYA I PRAKTIKA
1774326RU1A-38
Editorial: P.O. Box 10, 111401 MOSKVA
Tel: 495 621 69 49 **Fax:** 495 621 91 90
Email: post@financepress.ru **Web site:** http://www.financepress.ru
Date Established: 2003; **Freq:** 36 issues yearly; **Circ:** 6,250
Usual Pagination: 72
Editor: Larisa Chaldayeva
Profile: Publication featuring economic and political news of Russian regions. Covers culture, ecology, health system and demographics.
Language(s): Russian
ADVERTISING RATES:
Full Page Mono .... RUR 38409.00
Mechanical Data: Type Area: 170 x 240mm
BUSINESS: FINANCE & ECONOMICS

REKLAMA. OUTDOOR MEDIA
1774253RU2A-18
Editorial: ul. Ugreshskaya 2, str. 1, 4 floor, office 403, MOSKVA **Tel:** 495 627 59 39 **Fax:** 495 710 88 03
Email: info@outdoor.ru **Web site:** http://www.outdoormedia.ru
Freq: Monthly; **Annual Sub.:** RUR 2832.00
Editor-in-Chief: Maria Gromova
Profile: Professional magazine on outdoor advertising, in Out Of Home sector, perspectives of development, advertising and media companies in Russia and abroad, creative works.
Language(s): Russian
ADVERTISING RATES:
Full Page Colour .... RUR 51000.00
Mechanical Data: Type Area: 275 x 380mm
BUSINESS: COMMUNICATIONS, ADVERTISING & MARKETING

REMEDIUM
1774043RU37-4
Editorial: ul. Bakuninskaya 71, str. 10, 105082 MOSKVA **Tel:** 495 780 34 25 **Fax:** 495 780 34 26
Email: editor@remedium.ru **Web site:** http://www.remedium-journal.ru
Freq: Monthly; **Annual Sub.:** RUR 4646.00; **Circ:** 10,000
Usual Pagination: 96
Editor: Irina Shirokova; **News Editor:** Kira Apraksina; **Editor-in-Chief:** Aidar Ishmukhametov; **Advertising Manager:** Elena Sidorova; **Advertising Director:** Tatiana Zalihanova
Profile: Informative -analytical magazine on pharmaceutical market of Russia and medical equipment.
Language(s): Russian
Mechanical Data: Type Area: A4
BUSINESS: PHARMACEUTICAL & CHEMISTS

REMONT I STROITELSTVO
1774286RU4R-1
Editorial: ul. Gilyarovskogo 10, 129090 MOSKVA
Tel: 495 681 83 61 **Fax:** 495 681 73 59
Email: remont@veneto.ru **Web site:** http://www.remontinfo.ru
Date Established: 1996; **Freq:** Weekly - Published on Tuesdays; **Circ:** 115,000
Usual Pagination: 240
Profile: Magazine featuring articles on renovation of houses and price of building materials.
Language(s): Russian
ADVERTISING RATES:
Full Page Colour .... RUR 61000.00
Mechanical Data: Type Area: 180 x 240mm
BUSINESS: ARCHITECTURE & BUILDING: Building Related

RESTORANNYE VEDOMOSTI
1774315RU11A-2
Editorial: ul. Dubininskaya 90, 115093 MOSKVA
Tel: 495 921 36 25 **Fax:** 495 921 36 25
Email: info@restoved.ru **Web site:** http://www.restoved.ru
Freq: Monthly; **Cover Price:** RUR 250.00
Annual Sub.: RUR 3000.00; **Circ:** 18,700
Usual Pagination: 92
Editor-in-Chief: Alexander Pyankov; **Advertising Director:** Andrey Ivanov
Profile: Informative-analytical publication about catering business, restaurants and cafes in Russia.
Language(s): Russian
Readership: Targets catering professionals, chefs and restaurant managers.
ADVERTISING RATES:
Full Page Colour .... RUR 87000.00
Mechanical Data: Type Area: A4
BUSINESS: CATERING: Catering, Hotels & Restaurants

RISK MANAGEMENT
1774705RU14A-22
Editorial: M. Tolmachevski pereulok 1, 3 floor, 119017 MOSKVA **Tel:** 495 933 55 19
Fax: 495 925 77 43
Email: info@riskmanagement.ru **Web site:** http://www.riskmanagement.ru
Date Established: 2007; **Freq:** 6 issues yearly;
Annual Sub.: RUR 2112.00; **Circ:** 10,000
Usual Pagination: 120
Advertising Manager: Lidia Bondareva
Profile: Writes about business risk and insurance management in companies and public administration.
Language(s): Russian
ADVERTISING RATES:
Full Page Colour .... RUR 174000.00
Mechanical Data: Type Area: 205 x 275mm
BUSINESS: COMMERCE, INDUSTRY & MANAGEMENT

ROBB REPORT ROSSIYA
1773994RU74Q-10
Editorial: ul. Polkovaya 3, str. 1, 127018 MOSKVA
Tel: 495 232 32 00 **Fax:** 495 232 92 98
Email: robbreport@imedia.ru **Web site:** http://www.robbreport.ru
Date Established: 2004; **Freq:** 10 issues yearly;
Annual Sub.: RUR 4477.00; **Circ:** 25,000
Usual Pagination: 90
News Editor: Karen Gazaryan; **Editor-in-Chief:** Alexander Rymkevich; **Advertising Director:** Natalia Kharlamova; **Publisher:** Ludmila Abramenko
Profile: Russian edition of American luxury lifestyle magazine.
Language(s): Russian
ADVERTISING RATES:
Full Page Colour .... EUR 11000.00
Mechanical Data: Type Area: A4
CONSUMER: WOMEN'S INTEREST CONSUMER MAGAZINES: Lifestyle

ROLLING STONE
1774283RU76D-1
Editorial: Novodanilovskaya nab., 4a, 117105 MOSKVA **Tel:** 495 510 22 11 **Fax:** 495 510 49 69
Email: m.poroshina@spn.ru **Web site:** http://www.rollingstone.ru
Date Established: 2004; **Freq:** Monthly; **Circ:** 110,000
Usual Pagination: 100
Editor: Sergey Efremenko; **Advertising Manager:** Sergey Sakharov; **Advertising Director:** Valery Mirochnik
Profile: Russian-language version of the U.S. magazine. Full-colour glossy magazine about contemporary music and culture.
Language(s): Russian
ADVERTISING RATES:
Full Page Colour .... RUR 238500.00
Mechanical Data: Type Area: 230 x 300mm
CONSUMER: MUSIC & PERFORMING ARTS: Music

ROSSIISKAYA GAZETA
1615991RU65A-32
Editorial: ul. Pravdy 24, 125993 MOSKVA
Tel: 495 257 52 52 **Fax:** 495 257 58 92
Email: news@rg.ru **Web site:** http://www.rg.ru
Date Established: 1990; **Freq:** 312 issues yearly;
Annual Sub.: RUR 686.00; **Circ:** 218,905
Usual Pagination: 48
Editor: Varvara Dmitrieva; **Advertising Director:** Tatiana Pavlova
Profile: Newspaper covering national and international news, politics, economy, special reports and interview with government officials.
Language(s): Russian
Readership: Aimed at general public. According to TNS Gallup Media: 59% of the audience are the most active people aged 25 to 54 years. 56% of readers are women, 44% - men. 41% of readers with a high educational level. 45% of the audience are managers, professionals and employees.
ADVERTISING RATES:
Full Page Mono .... RUR 730000.00
Mechanical Data: Type Area: 383x518mm
Copy instructions: *Copy Date:* 4 days prior to publication
NATIONAL DAILY & SUNDAY NEWSPAPERS: National Daily Newspapers

ROSSIISKAYA TORGOVLYA
1774594RU53-5
Editorial: ul. Myasnitskaya 47, 107084 MOSKVA
Tel: 495 608 99 08 **Fax:** 495 607 76 96
Email: rtpress@mail.ru **Web site:** http://ros-torg.net
Freq: 104 issues yearly; **Annual Sub.:** RUR 1320.00; **Circ:** 50,000
Editor: Olga Vahontseva
Profile: Informative-analytical national newspaper about trade industry in Russia, promotion of Russian and good-quality foreign goods on Russian market.
Language(s): Russian
ADVERTISING RATES:
Full Page Mono .... RUR 50000.00
Mechanical Data: Type Area: 252 x 365mm
BUSINESS: RETAILING & WHOLESALING

ROSSIISKAYA FEDERATSIYA SEGODNYA
1774634RU82-164
Editorial: ul. Malaya Dmitrovka 3/10, 103800 MOSKVA **Tel:** 495 933 54 79 **Fax:** 495 933 54 74
Email: rfs@russia-today.ru **Web site:** http://russia-today.ru
Freq: 24 issues yearly; **Circ:** 50,000
Usual Pagination: 64
Editor: Y. Khrenov
Profile: Political magazine about the work of Russian Parliament, Russian government and state management of Russian regions, national authorities of federal and local jurisdiction.
Language(s): Russian
ADVERTISING RATES:
Full Page Colour .... RUR 160000.00
Mechanical Data: Type Area: 210x297mm
CONSUMER: CURRENT AFFAIRS & POLITICS

ROSSISKIYE APTEKI
1774092RU37-3
Editorial: ul. Bakuninskaya 72, str. 10, 105082 MOSKVA **Tel:** 495 780 34 25 **Fax:** 495 780 34 26
Email: gala@remedium.ru **Web site:** http://www.rosapteki.ru
Date Established: 1999; **Freq:** 24 issues yearly; Free to qualifying individuals
Annual Sub.: RUR 1800.00; **Circ:** 10,000
Usual Pagination: 36
Editor-in-Chief: Svetlana Abramova; **Advertising Manager:** Elena Sidorova; **Advertising Director:** Tatiana Zalihanova
Profile: Provides exclusive information including analytical reviews of range of pharmaceutical goods, articles on organisation and management of pharmaceutical institutions, new drugs, their characteristics and prospects of trade.
Language(s): Russian
Readership: Read by heads of pharmacies and health institutions, pharmacists, pharmaceutical chemists, members of distributor firms, health care workers, specialists in drugs provision.
Mechanical Data: Type Area: A4
BUSINESS: PHARMACEUTICAL & CHEMISTS

ROSSISKIYE NANOTEKHNOLOGII
1774587RU14A-55
Editorial: Leninskiye gory, str. 75G, korp. 6, office 626, 119991 MOSKVA **Tel:** 405 930 88 50
Fax: 495 930 87 07
Email: podpiska@nanorf.ru **Web site:** http://www.nanorf.ru
ISSN: 1992-7223
Freq: 6 issues yearly; **Cover Price:** RUR 1000.00; **Circ:** 700
Usual Pagination: 200
Editor: Sergey Ozerin; **Editor-in-Chief:** Mikhail Alfimov
Profile: Professional magazine on nanotechnologies in Russia, fundamental scientific research and practical approach.
Language(s): Russian
ADVERTISING RATES:
Full Page Colour .... RUR 23000.00
Mechanical Data: Type Area: 210x275mm
BUSINESS: COMMERCE, INDUSTRY & MANAGEMENT

ROSSIYA W GLOBALNOI POLITIKE
1773992RU82-156
Editorial: Nikitinsky pereulok 2, office 113, MOSKVA
Tel: 495 980 73 53 **Fax:** 495 937 76 11
Email: info@globalaffairs.ru **Web site:** http://www.globalaffairs.ru
Date Established: 2002; **Freq:** 6 issues yearly - Russia in Global Affairs (English language edition) is published quarterly; **Cover Price:** RUR 180.00; **Circ:** 25,000
Usual Pagination: 180
Executive Editor: Alexander Kuzyakov; **Editor-in-Chief:** Fyodor Lukyanov
Profile: Analytical magazine about international politics, international relations and role Russia plays on international arena.
Language(s): English; Russian
ADVERTISING RATES:
Full Page Mono $2000.00
Full Page Colour $3500.00
Mechanical Data: Type Area: 164 x 240mm
CONSUMER: CURRENT AFFAIRS & POLITICS

RUSSIA BEYOND THE HEADLINES
1774327RU65H-1
Editorial: ul. Pravdy 24, str. 4, floor 12, 125993 MOSKVA **Tel:** 495 775 31 14 **Fax:** 0870 9289823
Email: rbth@rg.ru **Web site:** http://rbth.rg.ru
Freq: Monthly
Usual Pagination: 8
Publisher: Eugene Abov
Profile: Covering Russian news, politics, economy, special reports and interviews with government officials.
Language(s): English
Mechanical Data: Type Area: 383 x 518mm
NATIONAL DAILY & SUNDAY NEWSPAPERS: National Colour Supplements

RUSSIA PROFILE
1842079RU82-162
Editorial: Zubovsky Blvd. 4, Office 3004, 119021 MOSKVA **Tel:** 495 645 64 86 **Fax:** 495 637 30 71
Email: info@russiaprofile.org **Web site:** http://www.russiaprofile.org
Freq: 10 issues yearly; **Cover Price:** $7.26
Annual Sub.: $51.70; **Circ:** 5,000
Editor: Andrei Zolotov
Profile: Provides an in-depth analysis on business, politics, current affairs and culture for Russia watchers around the world.
Language(s): English
ADVERTISING RATES:
Full Page Colour $2000.00
Mechanical Data: Type Area: 200 x 265mm
CONSUMER: CURRENT AFFAIRS & POLITICS

RUSSIA/CIS OBSERVER
1774329RU6A-3
Editorial: P.O. Box 127, 119048 MOSKVA
Tel: 495 626 53 56 **Fax:** 495 933 02 97
Email: maximp@ato.ru **Web site:** http://www.ato.ru
Date Established: 1918; **Freq:** Quarterly; **Annual Sub.:** $112.00; **Circ:** 2,500
Usual Pagination: 120
Editor-in-Chief: Maxim Pyadushkin; **Advertising Director:** Konstantin Rogov
Profile: Highly professional aerospace publication distributed at the world's largest air shows and by subscription, gives reliable, in-depth updates on latest trends in civil and defence aerospace industries, air transport sector and space business in Russia and post-Soviet marketplace.
Language(s): English
BUSINESS: AVIATION & AERONAUTICS

RUSSIAN JOURNAL OF HERPETOLOGY
1865575RU81A-1
Editorial: Zoological Institute of the Russian Academy of Sci, Universitetskaya nab., 1, 199034 SANKT PETERBURG
Email: azemiops@zin.ru **Web site:** http://rjh.folium.ru
ISSN: 1026-2296
Freq: Quarterly; **Annual Sub.:** $120.00
Profile: International multi-disciplinary journal devoted to herpetology, covering ecology, behaviour, conservation, systematics, evolutionary morphology, palaeontology, physiology, cytology and genetics of amphibians and reptiles.
Language(s): English
CONSUMER: ANIMALS & PETS: Animals & Pets Protection

RUSSKOYE ISKUSSTVO
1774665RU84A-6
Editorial: ul. Bakuninskaya 71, str. 10, 105082 MOSKVA **Tel:** 495 775 14 35
Email: russart@konliga.ru **Web site:** http://rusiskusstvo.ru
Date Established: 2004; **Freq:** 8 issues yearly;
Annual Sub.: RUR 1000.00; **Circ:** 3,000
Usual Pagination: 104
Editor: Olga Kostina; **Advertising Director:** Inna Pulikova
Profile: Features Russian art and culture, achievements and challenges of well-known and less well-known Russian artists and artisans, provides information about major exhibitions in Russia's great art museums and latest discoveries in Russian art.
Language(s): English; Russian
Mechanical Data: Type Area: 200x290mm
CONSUMER: THE ARTS & LITERARY: Arts

RUSSKY KURIER
1774518RU65J-66
Editorial: Luzhnetskaya nab.2.4, 119270 MOSKVA
Tel: 495 981 88 91
Email: ruscourier@ruscourier.ru **Web site:** http://www.ruscourier.ru
Date Established: 1990; **Freq:** Weekly; **Circ:** 102,700
Usual Pagination: 24
Editor: Oleg Vladykin; **Advertising Manager:** Nonna Gugeshashvili; **Advertising Director:** Tatiana Vereina
Profile: National newspaper bringing up political and economical issues of the country in the light of national interests.
Language(s): Russian
ADVERTISING RATES:
Full Page Mono .... RUR 51000.00
Mechanical Data: Type Area: 260 x 390mm
NATIONAL DAILY & SUNDAY NEWSPAPERS: National Weekly Newspapers

RUSSKY REPORTER
1774703RU82-146
Editorial: Bunazhny proyezd 14, str. 1, 125866 MOSKVA **Tel:** 495 609 66 74
Email: reporter@expert.ru **Web site:** http://www.expert.ru
Date Established: 2007; **Freq:** Weekly; **Circ:** 168,100
Editor: Vitaly Leibin; **Advertising Manager:** Tatiana Duniushkina; **Advertising Director:** Gleb Dunayevsky
Profile: Socio-political magazine, a Russian equivalent of The Time or Der Stern magazine.
Language(s): Russian
ADVERTISING RATES:
Full Page Colour .... RUR 295000.00
Mechanical Data: Type Area: A4
CONSUMER: CURRENT AFFAIRS & POLITICS

RYAZANSKIYE VEDOMOSTI
1774508RU67B-343
Editorial: ul. Mayakovskogo 9a, 390023 RYAZAN
Tel: 4912 21 08 13 **Fax:** 4912 21 08 11
Email: rv@rv.ryazan.ru **Web site:** http://rv.ryazan.ru
Date Established: 1997; **Freq:** 260 issues yearly; **Circ:** 16,500
Usual Pagination: 32
Editor: Galina Zaytseva
Profile: Socio-political newspaper covering news and events from Ryazan region.
Language(s): Russian
ADVERTISING RATES:
Full Page Mono .... RUR 40000.00
Mechanical Data: Type Area: 385x520mm
REGIONAL DAILY & SUNDAY NEWSPAPERS: Regional Daily Newspapers

RYNOK ELEKTORTEKHNIKI
1774000RU17-1
Editorial: ul. Usacheva 11, office 523, 119992 MOSKVA **Tel:** 495 921 20 65 **Fax:** 495 921 20 65
Email: mail@marketelectro.ru **Web site:** http://www.marketelectro.ru
Freq: Quarterly; **Annual Sub.:** RUR 2800.00; **Circ:** 15,000
Usual Pagination: 224
Editor: Eugeny Seryi; **Advertising Director:** Natalia Antipova
Profile: Provides news and tendencies of electro technical market, production and technologies, marketing and developments.
Language(s): Russian
ADVERTISING RATES:
Full Page Mono .... RUR 65760.00
Mechanical Data: Type Area: 180 x 263mm
BUSINESS: ELECTRICAL

SAKHARNAYA SVEKLA
754508RU22A-200
Editorial: Ulica 3 Projezd, Marinou Ruyshi, Dom 40, Korpus 1, Office 505, 127018 MOSKVA
Tel: 495 689 54 12 **Fax:** 495 689 54 12
Email: editor@sugarbeet.ru **Web site:** http://www.sugarbeet.ru
ISSN: 0036-3359
Date Established: 1956; **Freq:** 10 issues yearly; **Cover Price:** RUR 250.00
Annual Sub.: RUR 2500.00; **Circ:** 3,000
Usual Pagination: 32
Editor: Galina Balabanova; **Advertising Manager:** Irina Okhapkina
Profile: Magazine containing information on the cultivation of sugar beet and associated products.
Language(s): Russian
Readership: Read by manufacturers of sugar products and farmers.
BUSINESS: FOOD

SALON AUDIO VIDEO
1774242RU78B-1
Editorial: Oktyabrski per. 12, 127018 MOSKVA
Tel: 495 788 05 44 **Fax:** 495 788 05 50
Email: salonav@salonav.com **Web site:** http://www.salonav.com
Freq: Monthly; **Circ:** 50,000
Advertising Manager: Tatiana Rodimova
Profile: Magazine on home acoustic music systems, amplifiers and CD/DVD payers.
Language(s): Russian
ADVERTISING RATES:
Full Page Colour .... RUR 184000.00
Mechanical Data: Type Area: A4
CONSUMER: CONSUMER ELECTRONICS: Video & DVD

SALON INTERIOR
1976884RU4B-16
Editorial: ul. Nagatinskaya 1, str. 29, 117105 MOSKVA **Tel:** 495 933 43 43 **Fax:** 495 937 52 15
Email: okashenko@salonpress.ru **Web site:** http://www.salon.ru
Date Established: 1994; **Freq:** 11 issues yearly; **Annual Sub.:** RUR 2460.00; **Circ:** 55,000
Usual Pagination: 308
Executive Editor: Maria Petushkova; **Advertising Director:** Dmitri Shakhnazarov
Profile: SALON-interior is Russia's journal on architecture and design. All new, unique, exclusive designs created in the country, are reflected in the magazine, helping readers keep abreast of modern trends in Russia's architecture and design. It covers events, exhibitions in the world, reviews of accessories, historic buildings, landscape and floral solutions, all topics of the journal are intended to inform the reader on the world of architecture and design.
Language(s): Russian
Readership: Target audience of the magazine Salon-interior are wealthy people, representatives of political, artistic and business elite of Russia.
ADVERTISING RATES:
Full Page Colour .... RUR 378000.00
Mechanical Data: Type Area: 217x295mm
BUSINESS: ARCHITECTURE & BUILDING: Interior Design & Flooring

SALON NEDVIZHIMOSTI
1774684RU1E-28
Editorial: Devyatkin per. 2, MOSKVA
Tel: 495 621 80 71 **Fax:** 405 621 98 42
Email: info@salonn.ru **Web site:** http://www.salonn.ru
Date Established: 2001; **Freq:** Monthly; **Circ:** 30,000
Usual Pagination: 192
Editor: Marina Sytnikova; **Executive Editor:** Marina Sytnikova; **Editor-in-Chief:** Elena Ivanova; **Advertising Manager:** Elena Stroganova
Profile: Provides expert information on elite property in Moscow, in regions of Russia and abroad.
Language(s): Russian
ADVERTISING RATES:
Full Page Colour .... RUR 120000.00
Mechanical Data: Type Area: 225 x 295mm
BUSINESS: FINANCE & ECONOMICS: Property

SAMARSKAYA GAZETA
1774510RU67B-344
Editorial: ul. Galaktionovskaya 39, 443020 SAMARA
Tel: 46 979 75 80 **Fax:** 46 979 75 87
Email: samgazeta@samtel.ru **Web site:** http://www.sgpress.ru
Date Established: 1884; **Freq:** 260 issues yearly; **Circ:** 7,000
Usual Pagination: 48
Editor: Oksana Tikhomirova
Profile: Socio-political regional newspaper covering news and events in Samara region.
Language(s): Russian
ADVERTISING RATES:
Full Page Mono .... RUR 19254.00
Mechanical Data: Type Area: 250x320mm
REGIONAL DAILY & SUNDAY NEWSPAPERS: Regional Daily Newspapers

SANKT PETERBURGSKIYE VEDOMOSTI
1774535RU67B-350
Editorial: ul. Marata 25, 191025 SANKT PETERBURG **Tel:** 12 325 31 00 **Fax:** 12 764 48 40
Email: post@spbvedomosti.ru **Web site:** http://www.spbvedomosti.ru
Date Established: 1728; **Freq:** 260 issues yearly; **Circ:** 29,000
Usual Pagination: 16
Editor: Sergey Slobodskoy; **Advertising Manager:** Olga Gorodetskaya
Profile: Conservative socio-political daily covering politics, economics and culture in North-Western region of Russia.
Language(s): Russian
ADVERTISING RATES:
Full Page Mono .... RUR 150000.00
Mechanical Data: Type Area: 380x473mm
REGIONAL DAILY & SUNDAY NEWSPAPERS: Regional Daily Newspapers

SANTECHNIKA
1616120RU23C-1
Editorial: ul. Rozhdestvenkaya 11, 103754 MOSKVA
Tel: 495 621 80 76 **Fax:** 495 621 60 31
Email: st2006@abok.ru **Web site:** http://www.abok.ru
Date Established: 1999; **Freq:** 6 issues yearly; **Circ:** 10,000
Editor: Alexander Galusha; **Editor-in-Chief:** Yuriy Tabunschikov; **Advertising Manager:** Aleksey Lenkov
Profile: Journal covering range of sanitary equipment issues such as sanitary installation, baths, jacuzzis, water mixers, water treatment equipment, pumps, piping and valves. Also offers information on forthcoming exhibitions.
Language(s): Russian
Readership: Aimed at specialists and consumers.
BUSINESS: FURNISHINGS & FURNITURE: Furnishings & Furniture - Kitchens & Bathrooms

SAPR AND GRAFIKA
1613734RU5C-105
Editorial: Gorokhovskiy Per. 7, 105064 MOSKVA
Tel: 495 234 65 81 **Fax:** 495 234 65 81
Email: cad@compress.ru **Web site:** http://www.sapr.ru
Date Established: 1996; **Freq:** Monthly; **Circ:** 8,000
Usual Pagination: 102
Executive Editor: Konstantin Evchenko; **Editor-in-Chief:** Dmitriy Kraskovsky; **Advertising Manager:** D. Nasibullina; **Advertising Director:** Konstantin Babulin; **Publisher:** Boris Moltchanov
Profile: Magazine focusing on computer graphics, software and programming.
Language(s): Russian
Readership: Aimed at IT professionals and advanced home PC users.
ADVERTISING RATES:
Full Page Colour $8000.00
Mechanical Data: Trim Size: 200 x 265mm
BUSINESS: COMPUTERS & AUTOMATION: Professional Personal Computers

SARATROVSKI BUSINESS JOURNAL
1774546RU82-131
Editorial: ul. Tankistov 37, SARATOV
Tel: 452 43 61 40 **Fax:** 452 44 18 81
Email: saratov@b-mag.ru **Web site:** http://www.business-magazine.ru
Freq: 24 issues yearly; **Circ:** 7,000
Editor: Elena Lyanichenko
Profile: Regional business magazine on regional economic issues and developments.
Language(s): Russian
Mechanical Data: Type Area: A4
CONSUMER: CURRENT AFFAIRS & POLITICS

SCHASTLIVAYA SVADBA
1774354RU74L-1
Editorial: MOSKVA **Tel:** 495 256 91 72
Fax: 495 256 33 97
Email: happysvadba@mail.ru **Web site:** http://happysvadba.ru
Freq: Monthly; Free to qualifying individuals ; **Circ:** 10,000
Editor-in-Chief: Tatiana Glushkova
Profile: Magazine for grooms and brides-to-be with useful information and practical advice.
Language(s): Russian
Mechanical Data: Type Area: A4
CONSUMER: WOMEN'S INTEREST CONSUMER MAGAZINES: Brides

SCIENCE & TECHNOLOGY IN GAS INDUSTRY
1774119RU24-3
Editorial: ul. Obrucheva 27, korp. 2, 117630 MOSKVA **Tel:** 495 411 58 03 **Fax:** 495 719 64 76
Email: ed@hydrocarbons.ru **Web site:** http://hydrocarbons.ru
Date Established: 1999; **Freq:** Quarterly; **Cover Price:** RUR 700.00; **Circ:** 1,000
Usual Pagination: 120
Editor: Ekaterina Naschekina; **Editor-in-Chief:** Alexander Lipatov
Profile: Contains results of fundamental and applied science efforts, data on new high efficiency equipment, new technologies and advanced operational practice in natural gas industry.
Language(s): Russian
ADVERTISING RATES:
Full Page Mono .... RUR 50000.00
Mechanical Data: Type Area: 240 x 160mm
BUSINESS: GAS

SEVERNAYA OSETIYA
1774563RU67B-365
Editorial: pr. Kosta 11, 362015 VLADIKAVKAZ
Tel: 672 25 02 25 **Fax:** 672 75 50 31
Email: gazeta@osetia.ru **Web site:** http://gazeta.osetia.ru
Date Established: 1917; **Freq:** 260 issues yearly; **Circ:** 25,000
Editor: Olga Vyshlova
Profile: Regional daily covering social issues, cultural events and regional politics.
Language(s): Russian
Mechanical Data: Type Area: A2
REGIONAL DAILY & SUNDAY NEWSPAPERS: Regional Daily Newspapers

SEVERNY KRAI
1774711RU67B-480
Editorial: ul. Sobinova 1, 150000 YAROSLAVL'
Tel: 4852 32 90 53 **Fax:** 4852 32 90 53
Email: sevkray@yaroslavl.ru **Web site:** http://www.sevkray.ru
Date Established: 1898; **Freq:** 260 issues yearly; **Annual Sub.:** RUR 503.94; **Circ:** 12,000
Usual Pagination: 12
Editor: Andrey Grigoriev
Profile: Socio-political regional newspaper covering business, politics and culture.
Language(s): Russian
Mechanical Data: Type Area: A2
REGIONAL DAILY & SUNDAY NEWSPAPERS: Regional Daily Newspapers

SHAPE
1774306RU74G-3
Editorial: ul. Gilyarovskogo 10, bld. 1, 129090 MOSKVA **Tel:** 495 745 68 98 **Fax:** 495 681 73 59
Email: shape@veneto.ru **Web site:** http://www.shape.ru
Date Established: 2000; **Freq:** Monthly; **Circ:** 220,000
Usual Pagination: 164
Editor: Nataliya Orlova
Profile: Health, fitness and beauty magazine for young and active women.
Language(s): Russian
ADVERTISING RATES:
Full Page Colour .... RUR 439000.00
Mechanical Data: Type Area: A4
CONSUMER: WOMEN'S INTEREST CONSUMER MAGAZINES: Slimming & Health

SHEF
1774070RU1A-33
Editorial: ul. Srednemoskovskaya 7/192, 394030 VORONEZH **Tel:** 4732 39 25 30 **Fax:** 4732 39 25 33
Email: shef@rdw.vrn.ru **Web site:** http://www.idsocium.vrn.ru
Date Established: 2002; **Freq:** Monthly - Published on the 10th every month; **Circ:** 3,995
Usual Pagination: 36
Editor-in-Chief: Oleg Belenov
Profile: Monthly magazine for businessmen about small and medium business companies in Central Russia.
Language(s): Russian
ADVERTISING RATES:
Full Page Mono .... RUR 10620.00
Mechanical Data: Type Area: 190 x 210mm
BUSINESS: FINANCE & ECONOMICS

SHTAT
1774144RU14F-3
Editorial: Elektrichesky per. 3/10, office 314, 123557 MOSKVA **Tel:** 495 255 95 79
Email: hello@hrmedia.ru **Web site:** http://www.hrmedia.ru
Freq: 10 issues yearly; **Annual Sub.:** RUR 2600.00; **Circ:** 7,000
Usual Pagination: 90
Profile: Magazine on company's management, HR issues, job careers.
Language(s): Russian
ADVERTISING RATES:
Full Page Mono .... RUR 39000.00
Mechanical Data: Type Area: 200 x 260mm
BUSINESS: COMMERCE, INDUSTRY & MANAGEMENT: Training & Recruitment

SILOVAYA ELEKTRONIKA
1774499RU18A-4
Editorial: ul. Sadovaya 122, 190121 SANKT PETERBURG **Tel:** 12 438 15 38 **Fax:** 12 346 06 65
Email: power-e@finestreet.ru **Web site:** http://www.power-e.ru
Freq: Quarterly; **Circ:** 4,000
Usual Pagination: 100
Executive Editor: Ksenia Pritchina; **Editor-in-Chief:** Pavel Pravosudov
Profile: Informs on latest researches and developments in the field of power electronics, main trends, tendencies and future development of power electronics domestic and world market.
Language(s): Russian
Readership: Targets engineers and specialists in application of power electronics devices.
Mechanical Data: Type Area: 215x 297mm
BUSINESS: ELECTRONICS

SKIPASS
1774602RU75G-1
Editorial: ul. Timura Frunze 11, str. 44-45, floor 4, 119992 MOSKVA **Tel:** 495 935 70 34
Fax: 495 780 88 24
Email: potyagaeva@gameland.ru **Web site:** http://www.skipassmag.ru
Date Established: 2006; **Freq:** 8 issues yearly; **Circ:** 30,000
Usual Pagination: 112
Advertising Director: Julia Mavlyanova
Profile: Explores best ski resorts and latest skiing and aprs-ski fashion, events and opinions, interviews and photographs.
Language(s): Russian
Readership: Targets skiing enthusiasts, upper class men and women over 25 years of age.
ADVERTISING RATES:
Full Page Colour .... RUR 230000.00
Mechanical Data: Type Area: 230x300mm
CONSUMER: SPORT: Winter Sports

SLAVYANKA SEGODNYA
1774536RU67B-351
Editorial: ul. Karavaevskaya 30, 92177 SANKT PETERBURG **Tel:** 12 700 42 57 **Fax:** 12 700 42 57
Email: l.az@mail.ru **Web site:** http://www.nslav.spb.ru
Date Established: 1994; **Freq:** 40 issues yearly - Published on Fridays; **Cover Price:** Free; **Circ:** 100,000
Usual Pagination: 8
Editor: Aleksandr Seleznev; **Executive Editor:** M. Averchenkova
Profile: Provides general and city council news on life in St. Petersburg.
Language(s): Russian
Mechanical Data: Type Area: A3
REGIONAL DAILY & SUNDAY NEWSPAPERS: Regional Daily Newspapers

SLIYANIYA I POGLOSCHENIYA
1774206RU14A-32
Editorial: ul. Novopetrovskaya 1, str. 7, 125239 MOSKVA **Tel:** 495 234 43 24 **Fax:** 495 234 97 61
Email: info@ma-journal.ru **Web site:** http://www.ma-journal.ru
Date Established: 2003; **Freq:** Monthly; **Circ:** 7,000
Usual Pagination: 96
Editor-in-Chief: Anton Smirnov; **Advertising Manager:** Veronika Klubnikina
Profile: Professional analytical magazine on mergers and acquisitions and corporative control.
Language(s): Russian
Mechanical Data: Type Area: 210 x 297mm
BUSINESS: COMMERCE, INDUSTRY & MANAGEMENT

SMARTMONEY
1774629RU14A-16

Editorial: ul Polkovaya 3, str. 1, 127018 MOSKVA **Tel:** 495 232 32 00
Email: a.levinsky@vedomosti.ru **Web site:** http://www.smoney.ru
Date Established: 2006; **Freq:** Weekly - Published on Mondays; **Annual Sub.:** RUR 1478.40; **Circ:** 50,000
Usual Pagination: 64
Editor: Andrey Litvinov; **Editor-in-Chief:** Aleksander Malutin; **Advertising Director:** Olga Oreshnikova; **Publisher:** Ekaterina Son
Profile: Analytical business weekly magazine covering business issues and investments, markets analysis and business competition, economics and smart management.
Language(s): Russian
Readership: Aimed at top managers and businessmen in the age group 25-35, professionals with income level above average, predominantly male, who represent the most active part of the Russian business-community.
ADVERTISING RATES:
Full Page Colour .... RUR 320000.00
Mechanical Data: Type Area: 225 x 275mm
BUSINESS: COMMERCE, INDUSTRY & MANAGEMENT

SMOKE
1774015RU74Q-14

Editorial: ul. Timura Frunze 11, str. 44-45, 4 floor, 119992 MOSKVA **Tel:** 495 935 70 34
Fax: 495 780 88 24
Email: strekneva@gameland.ru **Web site:** http://www.glc.ru
Freq: 6 issues yearly; Free to qualifying individuals ; **Circ:** 30,000
Usual Pagination: 128
Editor: Oleg Chechilov; **Advertising Manager:** Svetlana Pinchuk
Profile: Lifestyle magazine and guide on smoking tobacco, cigars, entertainment and related issues.
Language(s): Russian
Mechanical Data: Type Area: 212x305mm
CONSUMER: WOMEN'S INTEREST CONSUMER MAGAZINES: Lifestyle

SMYSL
1774437RU82-153

Editorial: ul. Bolshaya Dmitrovka 5/6, str. 3, 125009 MOSKVA **Tel:** 495 692 04 65 **Fax:** 495 692 13 15
Email: office@smysl-project.ru **Web site:** http://www.smysl-project.ru
Date Established: 2006; **Freq:** 24 issues yearly; **Annual Sub.:** RUR 1360.00; **Circ:** 20,000
Usual Pagination: 160
Executive Editor: Andrey Pravov; **Editor-in-Chief:** Maxim Shevchenko
Profile: Analytical magazine about political, social and cultural issues in the world and contemporary Russia. Subtitle: World agenda in Russian language.
Language(s): Russian
ADVERTISING RATES:
Full Page Mono .... RUR 56000.00
Mechanical Data: Trim Size: 200 x 265mm
CONSUMER: CURRENT AFFAIRS & POLITICS

SOBESEDNIK
1774338RU82-117

Editorial: ul. Novoslobodskaya 73, str 1, 127055 MOSKVA **Tel:** 495 685 56 65 **Fax:** 495 973 20 54
Email: shapoval@sobesednik.ru **Web site:** http://www.sobesednik.ru
Date Established: 1984; **Freq:** Weekly - Published on Tuesdays; **Circ:** 260,560
Usual Pagination: 32
News Editor: Ekaterina Barova; **Editor-in-Chief:** Yury Pilipenko; **Advertising Manager:** Svetlana Bardonova
Profile: Weekly publication with political, economical, cultural news and social issues.
Language(s): Russian
ADVERTISING RATES:
Full Page Mono .... RUR 90000.00
Mechanical Data: Type Area: 247 x 358mm
CONSUMER: CURRENT AFFAIRS & POLITICS

LE SOMMELIER
1774095RU9C-1

Editorial: ul. 8 Marta 4, office 449, 620014 YEKATERINBURG **Tel:** 343 371 80 46
Fax: 343 378 07 42
Email: sommelier@analit.ur.ru **Web site:** http://www.le-sommelier.ru
Freq: 10 issues yearly; **Cover Price:** Free; **Circ:** 10,000
Editor: Konstantin Karasev
Profile: Glossy magazine about wine, wine consumption, wine produce and lifestyle.
Language(s): Russian
ADVERTISING RATES:
Full Page Colour .... RUR 49500.00
Mechanical Data: Type Area: A4
BUSINESS: DRINKS & LICENSED TRADE: Licensed Trade, Wines & Spirits

SOVETNIK
1774146RU2E-1

Editorial: ul. Miklukho-Maklaya 8, str.3, office 207, 117198 MOSKVA **Tel:** 495 781 20 71
Fax: 495 232 55 52
Email: info@sovetnik.ru **Web site:** http://www.sovetnik.ru
ISSN: 1608-0521
Date Established: 1996; **Freq:** Monthly; **Annual Sub.:** RUR 2640.00; **Circ:** 5,000
Editor: Vitaly Rasnitsin
Profile: Professional magazine about PR market in Russia and abroad.
Language(s): Russian
ADVERTISING RATES:
Full Page Mono .... RUR 28500.00
Full Page Colour .... RUR 36000.00
Mechanical Data: Type Area: A4
BUSINESS: COMMUNICATIONS, ADVERTISING & MARKETING: Public Relations

SOVETSKAYA SIBIR'
1774381RU82-121

Editorial: ul. Nemirovicha-Danchenko 104, 630048 NOVOSIBIRSK **Tel:** 3832 314 13 31
Email: sovsibir@sovsibir.ru **Web site:** http://sovsibir.ru
Date Established: 1919; **Freq:** 260 issues yearly; **Annual Sub.:** RUR 1070.00; **Circ:** 28,000
Usual Pagination: 32
Editor: Alexey Zharinov
Profile: Publication focused on education, history, culture, business and social problems of Novosibirsk region.
Language(s): Russian
Mechanical Data: Type Area: A2, A3
CONSUMER: CURRENT AFFAIRS & POLITICS

SOVETSKY SPORT
1774489RU75A-4

Editorial: Stary Petrovsko-Razumovsky proyezd 1/23, str. 1, 3 floor, 125993 MOSKVA
Tel: 495 637 64 33 **Fax:** 495 637 64 24
Email: info@sovietsport.ru **Web site:** http://www.sovsport.ru
Date Established: 1924; **Freq:** 300 issues yearly; **Cover Price:** RUR 11.00; **Circ:** 87,218
Usual Pagination: 32
Profile: Main sports publication of Russia presenting general news on all sports.
Language(s): Russian
Mechanical Data: Type Area: 283 x 391mm
CONSUMER: SPORT

SOVIETSKAYA ROSSIYA
1774370RU65A-55

Editorial: ul. Pravdy 24, 125993 MOSKVA
Tel: 499 257 53 00
Email: sovross@aha.ru **Web site:** http://www.sovross.ru
Date Established: 1956; **Freq:** Daily - Published 3 days a week: Tuesday, Thursday and Saturday; **Circ:** 300,000
Usual Pagination: 8
Editor-in-Chief: Valentin Chikin
Profile: Independent socialist political newspaper covering Russian issues.
Language(s): Russian
Mechanical Data: Type Area: A3
NATIONAL DAILY & SUNDAY NEWSPAPERS: National Daily Newspapers

SOVREMENNY SKLAD
1865660RU10-1

Editorial: ul. B. Semenovskaya 49, office 331, 107023 MOSKVA **Tel:** 499 369 79 20
Email: info@ssklad.ru **Web site:** http://www.ssklad.ru
Freq: 6 issues yearly; **Annual Sub.:** RUR 1463.40; **Circ:** 5,000
Usual Pagination: 64
Profile: Professional magazine about modern methods and logistics of warehousing.
Language(s): Russian
ADVERTISING RATES:
Full Page Colour .... RUR 55000.00
Mechanical Data: Type Area: 215x295mm
BUSINESS: MATERIALS HANDLING

SPIRTNIYE NAPITKI I PIVO
1774330RU9A-4

Editorial: Tverskoy bulvar 22, 125009 MOSKVA
Tel: 495 203 91 34
Email: sn@my-sn.ru **Web site:** http://www.my-sn.ru
Date Established: 1997; **Freq:** Weekly; **Cover Price:** Free; **Circ:** 12,720
Usual Pagination: 260
Profile: Publication focused on production of spirits, liquors and beer and their trade.
Language(s): Russian
Mechanical Data: Type Area: 200 x 275mm
BUSINESS: DRINKS & LICENSED TRADE: Drinks, Licensed Trade, Wines & Spirits

ST. PETERBURG
1774422RU89C-10

Editorial: ul. Aleksandra Nevskogo 22, 191167 SANKT PETERBURG **Tel:** 12 274 16 90
Fax: 12 327 82 41
Email: cg@ev.spb.ru **Web site:** http://www.city-guide.spb.ru
Freq: 6 issues yearly; **Cover Price:** Free; **Circ:** 45,000
Usual Pagination: 68
Editor: Svetlana Volkova
Profile: Aiming to provide most comprehensive information service for the city visitors, to attract more foreign tourists and business partners, as well as advertise St. Petersburg firms, goods, and services.
Language(s): English; Russian
ADVERTISING RATES:
Full Page Colour .... EUR 1500.00
Mechanical Data: Type Area: 146x210mm
CONSUMER: HOLIDAYS & TRAVEL: Entertainment Guides

THE ST. PETERSBURG TIMES
1774038RU67J-8

Editorial: 4 St. Isaac's Square, 190000 ST. PETERSBURG **Tel:** 12 325 60 80 **Fax:** 12 325 60 80
Email: letters@sptimes.ru **Web site:** http://www.sptimes.ru
Freq: 104 issues yearly - Published on Tuesdays and Fridays; **Annual Sub.:** RUR 2628.00; **Circ:** 12,000
Usual Pagination: 24
Editor: Tobin Auber
Profile: Premier English-language newspaper in St. Petersburg, providing readers with local, national and international news, as well as comprehensive coverage of arts, culture and entertainment.
Language(s): English
ADVERTISING RATES:
Full Page Mono .... RUR 126000.00
Full Page Colour .... RUR 136000.00
Mechanical Data: Type Area: 265 x 372mm
REGIONAL DAILY & SUNDAY NEWSPAPERS: Regional Newspapers (excl. dailies)

STAVROPOLSKAYA PRAVDA
1774566RU67B-368

Editorial: ul. Spartaka 8, 355035 STAVROPOL
Tel: 652 94 05 09 **Fax:** 652 94 17 08
Email: gazeta@stapravda.ru **Web site:** http://www.stapravda.ru
Date Established: 1917; **Freq:** 260 issues yearly; **Circ:** 20,000
Usual Pagination: 8
News Editor: Tatiana Sereda
Profile: Socio-political regional newspaper covering news and events in Stavropol region.
Language(s): Russian
ADVERTISING RATES:
Full Page Mono .... RUR 113144.00
SCC .... RUR 50.00
Mechanical Data: Type Area: 380x520mm
REGIONAL DAILY & SUNDAY NEWSPAPERS: Regional Daily Newspapers

STILNYIE PRICHESKY
1774134RU74H-1

Editorial: ul. Bakuninskaya 71, korp. 10, 105082 MOSKVA **Tel:** 495 775 14 35 **Fax:** 495 775 14 36
Email: v.schepin@konliga.ru **Web site:** http://www.prichesky.ru
Date Established: 2001; **Freq:** Monthly; **Cover Price:** RUR 70.00; **Circ:** 10,000
Usual Pagination: 92
Editor: Ya. Kononova; **Advertising Director:** Victor Schepin
Profile: Provides practical information on style and hairdressing for young women.
Language(s): Russian
ADVERTISING RATES:
Full Page Colour .... RUR 120000.00
Mechanical Data: Type Area: 166x240mm
CONSUMER: WOMEN'S INTEREST CONSUMER MAGAZINES: Hair & Beauty

STRATEGII USPEKHA
1774191RU14A-37

Editorial: ul. Cheliuskintsev 50, 630132 NOVOSIBIRSK **Tel:** 3832 21 18 29
Fax: 3832 21 49 71
Email: post@sibpress.ru **Web site:** http://www.com.sibpress.ru
Freq: Monthly; **Circ:** 15,500
Usual Pagination: 64
Profile: Informative-analytical regional magazine on regional business, companies and their success, marketing perspectives.
Language(s): Russian
ADVERTISING RATES:
Full Page Colour .... RUR 54752.00
Mechanical Data: Type Area: 220 x 290mm
Copy instructions: *Copy Date:* 18 days prior publication date
BUSINESS: COMMERCE, INDUSTRY & MANAGEMENT

STUFF
1774234RU5F-1

Editorial: ul. Rustaveli 12a, str. 2, 127254 MOSKVA
Tel: 495 253 92 28 **Fax:** 495 725 47 83
Email: prokirill@osp.ru **Web site:** http://stuff.osp.ru
Date Established: 2001; **Freq:** Monthly; **Circ:** 50,000
Usual Pagination: 128
Editor-in-Chief: Kirill Prokhodskiy; **Advertising Director:** Julia Shesheneva
Profile: Magazine about home computing, digital cameras, mobile devices and multimedia.
Language(s): Russian
ADVERTISING RATES:
Full Page Colour .... EUR 7000.00
BUSINESS: COMPUTERS & AUTOMATION: Multimedia

SUDOSTROYENIE
1774537RU45D-1

Editorial: 7 Promyshlennaya Street, 198095 ST PETERSBURG **Tel:** 12 786 05 30 **Fax:** 12 786 04 59
Email: cniits@telegraph.spb.ru **Web site:** http://www.crist.ru/issues/sudostroenie
Date Established: 1898; **Freq:** 6 issues yearly; **Circ:** 4,000
Usual Pagination: 80
Profile: Publication focused on shipbuilding, repairs, re-equipment, modernization and recycling of civil and military ships.
Language(s): English; Russian
ADVERTISING RATES:
Full Page Mono $1000.00
Full Page Colour $2000.00
Mechanical Data: Type Area: 210 x 297mm
BUSINESS: MARINE & SHIPPING: Marine Engineering Equipment

SURGUTSKAYA TRIBUNA
1774646RU67B-427

Editorial: ul. Mayakovskogo 12a, 628400 SURGUT
Tel: 3462 22 04 48 **Fax:** 3462 22 04 50
Email: tribuna@surgut.ru **Web site:** http://st.surgut.info
Date Established: 1934; **Freq:** 260 issues yearly; Free to qualifying individuals ; **Circ:** 22,100
Usual Pagination: 12
Editor: Alexander Schelkunov
Profile: Socio-political daily from Surgut region.
Language(s): Russian
ADVERTISING RATES:
SCC .... RUR 30.00
Mechanical Data: Type Area: A3
REGIONAL DAILY & SUNDAY NEWSPAPERS: Regional Daily Newspapers

SVOY BIZNES
1774250RU14A-30

Editorial: ul. Timura Frunze 11, str. 44-45, 4 floor, MOSKVA **Tel:** 495 935 70 34 **Fax:** 495 780 88 24
Email: letters@mybiz.ru **Web site:** http://www.mybiz.ru
Date Established: 2002; **Freq:** Monthly; **Cover Price:** RUR 90.00; **Circ:** 52,000
Usual Pagination: 96
Editor-in-Chief: Alexey Makurin; **Advertising Manager:** Marina Nesterova; **Publisher:** Tatiana Safronova
Profile: Presents practical business technologies and ideas, perspective markets and perfect marketing, how to gain investments and build up a team.
Language(s): Russian
Readership: Aimed at top managers and entrepreneurs.
ADVERTISING RATES:
Full Page Colour .... RUR 330000.00
Mechanical Data: Type Area: 210 x 273mm
BUSINESS: COMMERCE, INDUSTRY & MANAGEMENT

SYNC
1774013RU78R-5

Editorial: ul. Timura Frunze 11, atr. 44-45, 4 floor, 119992 MOSKVA **Tel:** 495 935 70 34
Fax: 495 780 88 24
Email: korsakov@gameland.ru **Web site:** http://www.glc.ru
Date Established: 2005; **Freq:** Monthly; **Circ:** 70,000
Usual Pagination: 112
Editor: Konstantin Korsakov; **Advertising Manager:** Evgeniya Goryacheva
Profile: Magazine about interesting innovations and trends in the world of gadgets and devices, their tests of quality and effectiveness.
Language(s): Russian
Readership: Targets those willing to purchase high-end technological solutions and gadgets.
ADVERTISING RATES:
Full Page Colour .... RUR 330000.00
Mechanical Data: Type Area: 204x276mm
CONSUMER: CONSUMER ELECTRONICS: Consumer Electronics Related

T3
1774395RU78R-2

Editorial: ul. Timura Frunze 11, str. 44-45, 4 floor, 119992 MOSKVA **Tel:** 495 935 70 34
Fax: 495 780 88 24
Email: info@t3.ru **Web site:** http://www.t3.ru
Date Established: 2002; **Freq:** Monthly; **Circ:** 42,100
Usual Pagination: 128
Editor-in-Chief: Stanislav Kuprianov; **Managing Editor:** Ludmila Ustinova; **Advertising Director:** Marina Komleva; **Publisher:** Kerim Tatevyan
Profile: Popular magazine on electronics, gadgets, mobile and digital technologies.
Language(s): Russian
ADVERTISING RATES:
Full Page Colour $11000.00
Mechanical Data: Type Area: 210x297mm
CONSUMER: CONSUMER ELECTRONICS: Consumer Electronics Related

TECHNO NEWS
1774414RU18A-6

Editorial: ul. Arhitektora Vlasova 3, 117335 MOSKVA
Tel: 495 746 59 39 **Fax:** 495 730 03 96
Email: pr@technonews.ru **Web site:** http://www.technonews.ru
Freq: 10 issues yearly; **Circ:** 70,000
Usual Pagination: 116
Editor-in-Chief: Andrey Sasinovsky; **Advertising Manager:** Marina Borisenko

Profile: Magazine on IT industry, new technologies, techno business, electronic and digital gadgets, mobile communication, Internet.
Language(s): Russian
ADVERTISING RATES:
Full Page Colour .... RUR 192500.00
Mechanical Data: Type Area: 220 x 297mm
BUSINESS: ELECTRONICS

TEKHNOLOGII I BIZNES NA RYNKE SYKHIKH STROITELNYKH SMESEY
1774344RU4E-2
Editorial: ul. Zheleznovodskaya 3, office 310, 199155 SANKT PETERBURG **Tel:** 12 350 54 11
Fax: 12 350 54 11
Email: info@spsss.ru **Web site:** http://www.spsss.ru
Freq: 7 issues yearly; **Cover Price:** Free; **Circ:** 1,500
Profile: Professional publication about market of dry building cements and mixes, new industry technologies and business.
Language(s): Russian
ADVERTISING RATES:
Full Page Mono .... RUR 41400.00
Mechanical Data: Type Area: A4
BUSINESS: ARCHITECTURE & BUILDING: Building

TELEKOM
1774440RU5R-3
Editorial: per. Dolomanovsky 12, 3 floor, 344002 ROSTOV NA DONU **Tel:** 63 255 98 57
Fax: 63 255 93 31
Email: telekom@aaanet.ru **Web site:** http://www.technograd.com/telekom.php
Freq: Weekly; **Circ:** 12,500
Usual Pagination: 192
Profile: Weekly publication on computers, telecommunications, office equipment, security systems.
Language(s): Russian
ADVERTISING RATES:
Full Page Mono .... RUR 7056.00
Mechanical Data: Type Area: 180 x 250mm
BUSINESS: COMPUTERS & AUTOMATION: Computers Related

TELE-SPUTNIK
714159RU2D-50
Editorial: PO Box 505, 190000 ST. PETERSBURG
Tel: 12 230 04 62 **Fax:** 12 230 93 51
Email: telesputnik@telesputnik.ru **Web site:** http://www.telesputnik.ru
Date Established: 1995; **Freq:** Monthly; **Annual Sub.:** RUR 726.00; **Circ:** 25,000
Usual Pagination: 100
News Editor: Vsevolod Kolyubakin; **Editor-in-Chief:** Nikolay Orlov; **Advertising Manager:** Alexey Novoselov
Profile: Magazine focusing on satellite and cable television and also digital terrestrial television.
Language(s): Russian
Readership: Aimed at telecommunications technicians.
ADVERTISING RATES:
Full Page Colour .... RUR 56000.00
Agency Commission: 10%
Mechanical Data: Bleed Size: 307mm x 220mm, Trim Size: 297mm x 210mm, Col Length: 259mm, Col Widths (Display): 90mm, Page Width: 185mm
Average ad content per issue: 20%
Supplement(s): CATV Handbook - 1xY, SATTV Handbook - 1xY
BUSINESS: COMMUNICATIONS, ADVERTISING & MARKETING: Broadcasting

TENNIS EXPERT
1774232RU75H-1
Editorial: ul. Zastavskaya 7, lit. A, office 205, SANKT PETERBURG **Tel:** 12 449 96 09
Email: org@tennis-expert.ru **Web site:** http://www.tennis-expert.ru
Date Established: 2002; **Freq:** 8 issues yearly; **Circ:** 10,000
Editor: Osipov
Profile: Magazine on professional and amateur tennis.
Language(s): Russian
Mechanical Data: Type Area: A4
CONSUMER: SPORT: Racquet Sports

TOMSK MAGAZINE
1774516RU82-143
Editorial: pr. Frunze 115, TOMSK **Tel:** 3822 26 41 66
Fax: 3822 26 41 66
Email: Miretzkaya@zr.tomsk.ru **Web site:** http://tm.zr.tomsk.ru
Date Established: 2004; **Freq:** 6 issues yearly; **Circ:** 5,000
Usual Pagination: 80
Editor: Ekaterina Miretzkaya; **Advertising Director:** Tatiana Rusanova
Profile: Glossy magazine featuring news about politics, economics, society and culture in the region.
Language(s): Russian
ADVERTISING RATES:
Full Page Colour .... RUR 20000.00
Mechanical Data: Type Area: A4
CONSUMER: CURRENT AFFAIRS & POLITICS

TOMSKY VESTNIK
1774637RU67B-419
Editorial: pr. Lenina 91, 634050 TOMSK
Tel: 3822 53 32 33 **Fax:** 3822 53 32 33
Email: vestnik@vestnik.tomsk.ru
Date Established: 1990; **Freq:** 260 issues yearly; **Circ:** 18,000
Usual Pagination: 24
Editor: Svetlana Sherstoboeva
Profile: Regional newspaper covering all aspects of life in Tomsk.
Language(s): Russian
ADVERTISING RATES:
SCC .... RUR 37.00
Mechanical Data: Type Area: A2
REGIONAL DAILY & SUNDAY NEWSPAPERS: Regional Daily Newspapers

TOPFLIGHT
1774396RU6R-2
Editorial: MOSKVA **Tel:** 495 787 03 95
Email: info@topflight.ru **Web site:** http://topflight.ru
Freq: Monthly; **Annual Sub.:** RUR 720.00; **Circ:** 2,500
Profile: Business aviation magazine for Russian readers containing up-to-date news, market research, statistics, contact information of leading market players.
Language(s): Russian
Readership: Targets private aviation buyers and flyers interested in private aircrafts.
Mechanical Data: Type Area:
BUSINESS: AVIATION & AERONAUTICS: Aviation Related

TOPLIVNY RYNOK
1774673RU58-5
Editorial: MOSKVA **Tel:** 495 649 92 84
Fax: 495 194 09 79
Email: info@top-r.ru **Web site:** http://www.top-r.ru
Freq: 6 issues yearly; **Annual Sub.:** RUR 3300.00; **Circ:** 20,000
Usual Pagination: 88
Advertising Director: Azarova
Profile: Professional informative-analytical magazine for those who trade with oil, petroleum, diesel and other kinds of fuel.
Language(s): Russian
Mechanical Data: Trim Size: 210 x 297mm
BUSINESS: ENERGY, FUEL & NUCLEAR

TORGOVAYA GAZETA
1774573RU53-3
Editorial: Varvarka 14, 109012 MOSKVA
Tel: 495 698 49 41 **Fax:** 495 698 48 48
Email: tg@centro.ru **Web site:** http://www.t-gazeta.ru
Freq: 104 issues yearly - Published on Wednesdays and Fridays; **Circ:** 76,000
Usual Pagination: 8
Editor: S. Shalyapina
Profile: Professional newspaper on consumer markets and services, goods and prices, sales networks and small business, safety and quality, legal aspects of trade.
Language(s): Russian
Mechanical Data: Type Area: A3
BUSINESS: RETAILING & WHOLESALING

TOTAL FOOTBALL
1774247RU75B-2
Editorial: ul. Timura Frunze 11, str. 44-45, 4 floor, 119992 MOSKVA **Tel:** 495 935 70 34
Fax: 495 780 88 24
Email: chernova@gameland.ru **Web site:** http://www.totalfootball.ru
Freq: Monthly; **Circ:** 300,000
Usual Pagination: 128
Editor: Nikolai Roganov; **Advertising Manager:** Julia Chernova
Profile: Entertaining and engaging magazine about football with unique photographs, exclusive interviews, football features.
Language(s): Russian
Readership: Targets readers with interest in the game and with its in-depth knowledge of subject.
ADVERTISING RATES:
Full Page Colour .... RUR 400000.00
Mechanical Data: Type Area: A3
CONSUMER: SPORT: Football

TOURBUSINESS
752627RU50-8
Editorial: PO Box 32, 107031 MOSKVA
Tel: 495 723 72 72 **Fax:** 495 723 72 72
Email: tb@tourbus.ru **Web site:** http://www.tourbus.ru
Date Established: 1998; **Freq:** 18 issues yearly; **Annual Sub.:** RUR 3398.40; **Circ:** 9,000
Advertising Director: Olga Maltseva
Profile: Magazine covering the travel business. Includes articles on hotels, insurance, tourist legislation, statistics and survey analyses.
Language(s): Russian
Readership: Aimed at travel agents, tour operators and hotel managers.
ADVERTISING RATES:
Full Page Mono $2500.00
Full Page Colour $3350.00
Mechanical Data: Type Area: 260 x 185mm, Col Length: 260mm, Bleed Size: 290 x 210mm, Trim Size: 280 x 205mm, Film: Positive, wrong reading, emulsion side down, Screen: 60 lpc
Copy instructions: *Copy Date:* 2 weeks prior to publication date
BUSINESS: TRAVEL & TOURISM

TOURINFO
1202223RU50-5
Formerly: Turinfo
Editorial: Aviatsionny Pereulok 4, P.O. Boc 54, 125319 MOSKVA **Tel:** 495 234 08 30
Fax: 499 155 70 56
Email: golubeva@tourinfo.ru **Web site:** http://www.tourinfo.ru
Date Established: 1993; **Freq:** Weekly; Free to qualifying individuals
Annual Sub.: $65.00; **Circ:** 5,000
Usual Pagination: 32
Editor: Ludmila Tupikova; **News Editor:** Ekaterina Sobol; **Executive Editor:** Ludmila Tupikova; **Advertising Director:** Andrey Pinchuk; **Publisher:** Vktor Remizov
Profile: Travel trade newspaper covering tourism business in Russia, events in Russian travel industry and abroad, providing tourism statistics, analytical surveys, tour operators' ratings, industry development projects, expert comments.
Language(s): Russian
Readership: Aimed at travel agents, Russian travel industry professionals.
ADVERTISING RATES:
Full Page Colour .... RUR 165000.00
Agency Commission: 10%
Mechanical Data: Type Area: 390 x 265mm, Col Length: 390mm
Average ad content per issue: 40%
BUSINESS: TRAVEL & TOURISM

TRANSPORT
1774238RU49A-1
Editorial: ul. Profsouyznaya 57, 117420 MOSKVA
Tel: 495 933 66 93 **Fax:** 495 933 66 94
Email: info@indpg.ru **Web site:** http://www.indpg.ru
Date Established: 2007; **Freq:** Monthly; **Annual Sub.:** RUR 7700.00; **Circ:** 10,000
Profile: Focused on different trends and projects that influence development of transport and logistics business in Russia and neighbouring countries. The publication's scope extends to all transport modes involved in freight traffic.
Language(s): Russian
Readership: Targets top managers of transport, forwarding, logistics and stevedore companies, management of banks, insurance and consulting companies connected with transport sector, transport machines manufacturing and large industrial enterprises divisions which are important consumers of transport business services.
ADVERTISING RATES:
Full Page Mono .... RUR 95000.00
BUSINESS: TRANSPORT

TRIBUNA
1774186RU65A-37
Editorial: Bumazhniy proyezd 14, str.1, 127015 MOSKVA **Tel:** 499 257 59 13 **Fax:** 499 257 07 04
Email: tribuna@tribuna.ru **Web site:** http://www.tribuna.ru
Date Established: 1969; **Freq:** Daily; **Circ:** 57,500
Usual Pagination: 48
Editor-in-Chief: Oleg Kuzin
Profile: National daily with analytical articles on politics, economics and social issues.
Language(s): Russian
ADVERTISING RATES:
Full Page Colour .... RUR 300000.00
Mechanical Data: Type Area: 317 x 500mm
NATIONAL DAILY & SUNDAY NEWSPAPERS: National Daily Newspapers

TRUD
1500339RU65A-20
Editorial: ul. Elektrozavodskaya 27, str. 4, Business Centre LeFort, MOSKVA **Tel:** 495 232 36 35
Email: pr@trud.ru **Web site:** http://www.trud.ru
Date Established: 1921; **Freq:** Daily - Published Tuesday - Saturday; **Circ:** 51,000
Editor-in-Chief: Vladimir Borodin
Profile: National newspaper covering national and international news.
Language(s): Russian
ADVERTISING RATES:
Full Page Mono .... RUR 415000.00
Mechanical Data: Screen: 65 lpc, Type Area: 378 x 520mm
NATIONAL DAILY & SUNDAY NEWSPAPERS: National Daily Newspapers

TVERSKAYA 13
763203RU32A-3
Editorial: ul. Novy Arbat 21, 119992 MOSKVA
Tel: 495 609 91 18 **Fax:** 495 605 91 27
Email: tverskaya-13@mtu-net.ru **Web site:** http://www.tver13.ru
Freq: 156 issues yearly; **Circ:** 100,000
Usual Pagination: 16
Editor-in-Chief: Mikhail Polyatykin
Profile: Newspaper of Moscow city council covering council services, transport, medicine services, trade and cultural events, and printing official administrative and legislative documentation.
Language(s): Russian
ADVERTISING RATES:
Full Page Mono .... RUR 160000.00
BUSINESS: LOCAL GOVERNMENT, LEISURE & RECREATION: Local Government

TVOYA IPOTEKA
1774239RU1G-1
Editorial: 4 Roschinsky proyezd 20, str. 5, 115191 MOSKVA **Tel:** 495 540 73 40 **Fax:** 495 540 72 15
Email: ipoteka@impressmedia.ru **Web site:** http://www.tvoya-ipoteka.ru
Freq: Monthly; Free to qualifying individuals
Annual Sub.: RUR 480.00; **Circ:** 60,000
Usual Pagination: 60
Profile: Magazine of financial services, obtaining a banking mortgage, newest banking tendencies and events.
Language(s): Russian
Mechanical Data: Type Area: 230x300mm
BUSINESS: FINANCE & ECONOMICS: Credit Trading

TYUMENSKAYA PRAVDA
1774641RU67B-422
Editorial: ul. Osipenko 81, 7 floor, office 711, 625002 TYUMEN' **Tel:** 3254 46 11 38 **Fax:** 3254 24 03 40
Email: redaktortp@yandex.ru **Web site:** http://pravda.port72.ru
Freq: 260 issues yearly; **Circ:** 16,000
Usual Pagination: 16
Editor: Larisa Vokhmina
Profile: Socio-political daily covering news from Tyumen' region.
Language(s): Russian
ADVERTISING RATES:
SCC .... RUR 47.20
Mechanical Data: Type Area: A2
REGIONAL DAILY & SUNDAY NEWSPAPERS: Regional Daily Newspapers

TYUMENSKIYE IZVESTIYA
1774643RU67B-424
Editorial: Dom Sovetov, ul. Respubliki 52, 625018 TYUMEN' **Tel:** 3452 46 54 07
Email: gazeta@t-i.ru **Web site:** http://www.t-i.ru
Date Established: 1990; **Freq:** 260 issues yearly; **Circ:** 16,000
Usual Pagination: 24
Editor: Vladimir Kuznetsov; **News Editor:** Dmitri Nevolin; **Advertising Director:** Anna Ostraya
Profile: Socio-political daily covering events and news from Tyumen region.
Language(s): Russian
Mechanical Data: Type Area: A2
REGIONAL DAILY & SUNDAY NEWSPAPERS: Regional Daily Newspapers

UCHET. NALOGI. PRAVO
1774579RU1M-2
Editorial: ul. B. Novodmitrovskaya 23, str.5, 127015 MOSKVA **Tel:** 495 788 53 14
Email: gl-red@gazeta-unp.ru **Web site:** http://gazeta-unp.ru
Freq: Weekly - Published on Tuesdays; **Circ:** 52,500
Editor-in-Chief: Alexey Starikov
Profile: Provides information on all changes in taxation and financial legal documentation.
Language(s): Russian
Readership: Aims at financial directors, accountants, companies' lawyers and audit inspectors.
ADVERTISING RATES:
Full Page Mono .... RUR 172500.00
Mechanical Data: Type Area: A4
BUSINESS: FINANCE & ECONOMICS: Taxation

UDMURTSKAYA PRAVDA
1774653RU67B-432
Editorial: ul. Pastukhova 13, 426057 IZHEVSK
Tel: 3412 51 46 63 **Fax:** 3412 68 38 89
Email: up@idz.ru **Web site:** http://www.udmpravda.ru
Date Established: 1917; **Freq:** 156 issues yearly; **Circ:** 14,000
Usual Pagination: 16
Editor: Svetlana Sentyakova; **Advertising Director:** Valentina Kozyreva
Profile: Socio-political newspaper covering news from Udmurtia region.
Language(s): Russian
ADVERTISING RATES:
Full Page Mono .... RUR 40320.00
Mechanical Data: Type Area: A2
REGIONAL DAILY & SUNDAY NEWSPAPERS: Regional Daily Newspapers

UGOL'
1774139RU30-152
Editorial: ul. Zemlyanoy val 64, str. 2, office 209, 109004 MOSKVA **Tel:** 495 915 56 80
Fax: 495 915 56 80
Email: ugol@spectrnet.ru **Web site:** http://www.ugolinfo.ru
Date Established: 1925; **Freq:** Monthly; **Annual Sub.:** RUR 3960.00; **Circ:** 3,800
Editor-in-Chief: Vladimir Schadov; **Advertising Manager:** Irina Tarazanova

Profile: Professional scientific-technical publication about developments in coal industry of energy sector of Russia and CIS, technical reviews, equipment and production issues.
Language(s): Russian
ADVERTISING RATES:
Full Page Colour .... RUR 28320.00
Mechanical Data: Type Area: 210 x 290mm
BUSINESS: MINING & QUARRYING

ULYANOVSKAYA PRAVDA
1774655RU67B-434
Editorial: Ul. Pushkinskaya 11, 1 floor, 432063 ULYANOVSK **Tel:** 422 30 15 89 **Fax:** 422 30 15 86
Email: ulpravda@mail.ru **Web site:** http://ulpravda.ru
Date Established: 1917; **Freq:** 156 issues yearly; **Circ:** 5,720
Usual Pagination: 24
Editor: Vladimir Luchnikov
Profile: Socio-political daily covering news and events in Ulyanovsk region.
Language(s): Russian
ADVERTISING RATES:
Full Page Mono .... RUR 25000.00
Mechanical Data: Type Area: A3
REGIONAL DAILY & SUNDAY NEWSPAPERS: Regional Daily Newspapers

---

UPGRADE
1613665RU5C-104
Editorial: ul. Timura Frunze 22, 119021 MOSKVA
Tel: 495 745 68 98 **Fax:** 495 681 73 59
Email: upgrade@upweek.ru **Web site:** http://www.upweek.ru
Date Established: 2000; **Freq:** Weekly - Published on Mondays; **Circ:** 92,000
News Editor: Nikolay Pankov; **Editor-in-Chief:** Danila Matveev; **Advertising Manager:** Pavel Vinogradov; **Advertising Director:** Vladimir Slivko
Profile: Magazine focusing on assembling and servicing PCs includes information on components, reconfiguring and all the latest computer technology.
Language(s): Russian
Readership: Read by IT professionals.
ADVERTISING RATES:
Full Page Colour .... RUR 232870.00
BUSINESS: COMPUTERS & AUTOMATION: Professional Personal Computers

---

UPGRADE SPECIAL
1774285RU5D-152
Editorial: ul. Pobedy 1, 119021 MOSKVA
Tel: 495 745 68 98 **Fax:** 495 681 73 59
Email: upspecial@veneto.ru **Web site:** http://www.upspecial.ru
Date Established: 2003; **Freq:** Monthly; **Circ:** 116,000
Usual Pagination: 148
Executive Editor: Gennadiy Boyko; **Editor-in-Chief:** Ruslan Shebukov; **Advertising Manager:** Pavel Vinogradov
Profile: Computer magazine offering solutions to usage problems, digital gadgets and mobile devices.
Language(s): Russian
ADVERTISING RATES:
Full Page Colour .... RUR 236060.00
Mechanical Data: Type Area: A4
BUSINESS: COMPUTERS & AUTOMATION: Personal Computers

UPRAVLENIYE NEDVIZHIMOSTYU
1774591RU1E-17
Editorial: 4 Roschinsky proyezd, str. 5, 115191 MOSKVA **Tel:** 495 540 73 40 **Fax:** 495 540 72 15
Email: pr@impressmedia.ru **Web site:** http://www.impressmedia.ru
Freq: Half-yearly; **Circ:** 25,000
Usual Pagination: 100
Publisher: Annette Wassenaar
Profile: Provides analytical and expert information on property management, property markets and companies on the market.
Language(s): English; Russian
Mechanical Data: Type Area: 168 x 240mm
BUSINESS: FINANCE & ECONOMICS: Property

URALSKI SADOVOD
1774450RU93-202
Editorial: P.O. Box 211, 620098 YEKATERINBURG
Tel: 343 372 74 22 **Fax:** 343 372 74 22
Email: alex@r66.ru **Web site:** http://uralsadovod.ru
Freq: Weekly; **Circ:** 25,000
Usual Pagination: 16
Editor: Alexander Chetverikov
Profile: Regional newspaper on gardening, with practical advice on growing of perspective plants, plant illnesses and fighting unwelcome insects.
Language(s): Russian
Readership: Targets amateur gardeners, farmers and private house owners.
ADVERTISING RATES:
SCC .... RUR 30.00
Mechanical Data: Type Area: A3
CONSUMER: GARDENING

VASH DOSUG
1937469RU89C-19
Editorial: Maly Drovyanoy per. 3, str.1, 109004 MOSKVA **Tel:** 495 956 76 26
Email: dosug@rdw.ru **Web site:** http://www.vashdosug.ru
Date Established: 1997; **Freq:** Weekly; **Circ:** 55,000
Usual Pagination: 220
Profile: 'Your Leisure' presents readers a broad overview of cultural events and opportunities for leisure in Moscow. All materials are accompanied by detailed background information. The basic content of the magazine are comments on current events and cultural life in the capital, interviews with stars, announcements of film premieres, repertoire for theaters, cinemas, concerts, classification of Moscow clubs, restaurants and other leisure activities, as well as reviews on tourism, beauty and health.
Language(s): Russian
Readership: A reader of 'Your Leisure' is a person with an active attitude to life, preferring to spend his/her money wisely and is ready to invest in a complete relaxation, fun and leisure.
ADVERTISING RATES:
Full Page Colour .... RUR 303730.00
CONSUMER: HOLIDAYS & TRAVEL: Entertainment Guides

VECHERNAYA MOSKVA
1615290RU65K-3
Editorial: ul. 1905 goda, d. 7, 123995 MOSKVA
Tel: 495 259 81 87 **Fax:** 495 259 81 87
Email: edit@vm.ru **Web site:** http://www.vm.ru
Date Established: 1923; **Freq:** Daily - Published Monday to Friday; **Circ:** 300,000
Usual Pagination: 40
Editor: Yury Riyazhsky; **Advertising Director:** Evgeniy Dimitrevich Shapochkin
Profile: Newspaper focusing on national and international news, politics, the economy, business and society.
Language(s): Russian
ADVERTISING RATES:
Full Page Mono .... RUR 220000.00
Mechanical Data: Type Area: 390 x 530mm
NATIONAL DAILY & SUNDAY NEWSPAPERS: Metropolitan Daily Newspapers

---

VECHERNY KRASNOYARSK
1774217RU67B-189
Editorial: ul. Respubliki 51, 11 floor, 660075 KRASNOYARSK **Tel:** 3912 23 29 26
Fax: 3912 23 29 82
Email: info@vecherka.ru **Web site:** http://www.vecherka.ru
Date Established: 1989; **Freq:** Weekly - Published on Wednesdays; **Circ:** 19,000
Usual Pagination: 32
Editor: Eugenia Leontyeva; **Advertising Manager:** Alla Grigorovich; **Advertising Director:** Irina Litvinova
Profile: Socio-political newspaper of Krasnoyarsk region.
Language(s): Russian
Mechanical Data: Type Area: A3
REGIONAL DAILY & SUNDAY NEWSPAPERS: Regional Daily Newspapers

---

VECHERNY NOVOSIBIRSK
1774379RU67B-269
Editorial: ul. Nemirovicha-Danchenko 104, 630048 NOVOSIBIRSK **Tel:** 3832 314 14 88
Fax: 3832 314 14 49
Email: vn@vn.ru **Web site:** http://www.vn.ru
Date Established: 1958; **Freq:** 260 issues yearly; **Circ:** 19,000
Usual Pagination: 16
Editor: Vladimir Kuzmenkin
Profile: Daily informative socio-political newspaper from Novosibirsk.
Language(s): Russian
ADVERTISING RATES:
SCC .... RUR 59.00
Mechanical Data: Type Area: A3
REGIONAL DAILY & SUNDAY NEWSPAPERS: Regional Daily Newspapers

---

VECHERNY OMSK - NEDELYA
1774055RU72I-17
Editorial: pr. K. Marksa 34a, OMSK
Tel: 3812 30 05 22 **Fax:** 3812 30 05 23
Email: vechorka55@mail.ru
Date Established: 1979; **Freq:** Weekly - Published on Wednesdays; **Annual Sub.:** RUR 450.00; **Circ:** 17,500
Usual Pagination: 32
Editor: Andrey Kotelevsky; **Advertising Manager:** Svetlana Yakovleva
Profile: Regional socio-political informative weekly.
Language(s): Russian
ADVERTISING RATES:
Full Page Mono .... RUR 28000.00
Mechanical Data: Type Area: 255 x 380mm
LOCAL NEWSPAPERS: Regional Weekly Newspapers

VECHERNY STAVROPOL'
1774567RU67B-369
Editorial: ul. Dovatortsov 28/30, 355000 STAVROPOL **Tel:** 652 37 34 19 **Fax:** 652 23 12 41
Email: info@vechorka.ru **Web site:** http://www.vechorka.ru
Date Established: 1989; **Freq:** 260 issues yearly; **Circ:** 25,473
Usual Pagination: 16
Editor: Mikhail Vasilenko; **Advertising Director:** Irina Lastovich
Profile: Regional socio-political newspaper with political, business and cultural news.
Language(s): Russian
ADVERTISING RATES:
SCC .... RUR 45.00
Mechanical Data: Type Area: A3
REGIONAL DAILY & SUNDAY NEWSPAPERS: Regional Daily Newspapers

---

VECHERNY TOMSK
1774621RU67B-415
Editorial: ul. Yelizarovykh 59, 634012 TOMSK
Tel: 3822 53 94 99 **Fax:** 3822 53 95 99
Email: wt@tspace.ru
Date Established: 1999; **Freq:** 260 issues yearly; **Circ:** 24,000
Usual Pagination: 8
Editor: Andrey Zaytsev
Profile: Regional socio-political informative newspaper.
Language(s): Russian
ADVERTISING RATES:
Full Page Mono .... RUR 30000.00
Mechanical Data: Type Area: A2
REGIONAL DAILY & SUNDAY NEWSPAPERS: Regional Daily Newspapers

---

VECHERNY VOLGOGRAD
1774051RU67J-9
Editorial: ul. Kommunisticheskaya 11, 400131 VOLGOGRAD **Tel:** 442 33 23 01 **Fax:** 442 33 21 95
Email: Vechorka@avtlg.ru **Web site:** http://www.volgograd.km.ru
Date Established: 1980; **Freq:** 156 issues yearly - Published on Tuesdays, Thursdays and Fridays; **Circ:** 15,000
Usual Pagination: 24
Editor: Grigori Naumov
Profile: Socio-political regional newspaper with political, business and cultural news.
Language(s): Russian
ADVERTISING RATES:
Full Page Mono .... RUR 30000.00
Mechanical Data: Type Area: A3
REGIONAL DAILY & SUNDAY NEWSPAPERS: Regional Newspapers (excl. dailies)

VECHERNY YEKATERINBURG
1774559RU67B-486
Editorial: ul. Malysheva 44, 620014 YEKATERINBURG **Tel:** 3432 377 66 00
Fax: 3432 377 66 69
Email: ve@urn.ru **Web site:** http://ur-ra.ru
Date Established: 1957; **Freq:** 312 issues yearly; **Circ:** 32,000
Usual Pagination: 6
Editor: Lev Koshcheyev
Profile: Socio-political and informative-analytical daily regional newspaper.
Language(s): Russian
ADVERTISING RATES:
Full Page Mono .... RUR 49700.00
Mechanical Data: Type Area: A2
REGIONAL DAILY & SUNDAY NEWSPAPERS: Regional Daily Newspapers

---

VECHERNYAYA KAZAN'
1774610RU67B-408
Editorial: ul. Dekabristov 2, 420066 KAZAN
Tel: 432 541 38 91 **Fax:** 432 541 38 42
Email: info@evening-kazan.ru **Web site:** http://www.evening-kazan.ru
Date Established: 1979; **Freq:** 208 issues yearly; **Annual Sub.:** RUR 720.00; **Circ:** 35,905
Editor: Khazbulat Shamsutdinov
Profile: Newspaper offering political, economic, cultural information and news about life in Tatarstan.
Language(s): Russian
ADVERTISING RATES:
SCC .... RUR 45.00
Mechanical Data: Type Area: A2
REGIONAL DAILY & SUNDAY NEWSPAPERS: Regional Daily Newspapers

---

VEDOMOSTI
1600793RU1A-24
Editorial: ul.Polkovaya 2 zdaniye 1, 2 Etage, 127018 MOSKVA **Tel:** 495 232 32 00 **Fax:** 495 956 07 16
Email: vedomosti@imedia.ru **Web site:** http://www.vedomosti.ru
Date Established: 1999; **Freq:** Daily - Published from Monday till Friday; **Circ:** 73,000
Usual Pagination: 12
Advertising Manager: Tatiana Sazhina
Profile: Newspaper covering business and finance issues, informs readers on a daily basis about most important economic, political, financial and corporate events, offering an in-depth analysis and forecasts.
Language(s): Russian
Readership: Aimed at top and middle management professionals.
ADVERTISING RATES:
Full Page Mono .... RUR 1200000.00
Agency Commission: 15%
Mechanical Data: Film: Positive, emulsion side down, Screen: 70 lpc, Type Area: 380 x 543mm
Copy instructions: *Copy Date:* 6 days prior to publication date
Supplement(s): Vedomosti - Kak potratit? - 14xY, Vedomosti - Nedvizhimost' - 10xY, Vedomosti. Pyatnitsa - 52xY
BUSINESS: FINANCE & ECONOMICS

VERTOLIOTNAYA INDUSTRIYA
1850113RU6A-6
Editorial: 3 Silikatny proyezd 4, korp. 1, 123308 MOSKVA **Tel:** 495 643 11 93
Email: info@helicopter.su **Web site:** http://www.helicopter.su
Date Established: 2006; **Freq:** Monthly; **Cover Price:** RUR 189.00
Free to qualifying individuals
Annual Sub.: RUR 2258.00; **Circ:** 2,500
Usual Pagination: 68
Profile: Provides competent analysis of Russian helicopter industry, news on both military and civil helicopters, aiming at senior managers and directors of companies in this industry sector.
Language(s): English; Russian
Mechanical Data: Type Area: 200 x 280mm
BUSINESS: AVIATION & AERONAUTICS

VINNAYA KARTA
1615242RU74P-201
Editorial: 2, Electrodnaya str., 111141 MOSKVA
Tel: 495 64 52 039 **Fax:** 495 64 52 039
Email: krasnogor@vitrina.com.ru **Web site:** http://www.vitrinapress.ru/en/contacts
Date Established: 1999; **Freq:** Monthly; **Cover Price:** RUR 90.00; **Circ:** 40,000
Editor-in-Chief: Olga Krasnogor; **Publisher:** Tatiana Zlodyreva
Profile: Newspaper providing a guide to wines, spirits and luxury dining.
Language(s): Russian
Readership: Aimed at wine connoisseurs.
ADVERTISING RATES:
Full Page Mono .... RUR 169000.00
Full Page Colour .... RUR 185000.00
Mechanical Data: Type Area: 297 x 420mm, Trim Size: 297x420mm
CONSUMER: WOMEN'S INTEREST CONSUMER MAGAZINES: Food & Cookery

---

VINODELIYE I VINOGRADARSTVO
1611172RU21H-1
Editorial: Sadovaya-Spasskaya 18, komn. 610, 107996 MOSCOW **Tel:** 495 607 17 70
Fax: 495 607 28 61
Email: beerprom@ropnet.ru **Web site:** http://www.foodprom.ru
Freq: 6 issues yearly; **Circ:** 1,500
Editor: Olga Presnyakova; **Advertising Director:** Ekaterina Varekha
Profile: Magazine covering all aspects of winemaking industry.
Language(s): Russian
Readership: Read by growers and producers.
ADVERTISING RATES:
Full Page Mono .... EUR 1000.00
Full Page Colour .... EUR 1800.00
BUSINESS: AGRICULTURE & FARMING: Vine Growing

VITRINA. MIR SUPERMARKETA
1824610RU53-1
Editorial: ul. Elektrodnaya 2, 111141 MOSKVA
Tel: 495 64 52 039 **Fax:** 495 64 52 039
Email: vitrina@vitrina.com.ru **Web site:** http://www.vitrinapress.ru/magazines/fm
Date Established: 1994; **Freq:** 11 issues yearly; **Circ:** 20,000
Usual Pagination: 40
Advertising Manager: Tania Grineva; **Publisher:** Tatiana Zlodyreva
Profile: Providing new business solutions, information about new products and tendencies, giving professional analysis of industry.
Language(s): Russian
Readership: Aimed at owners and managers of supermarkets and network shops.
ADVERTISING RATES:
Full Page Mono .... RUR 95000.00
Mechanical Data: Type Area: 230 x 297mm
BUSINESS: RETAILING & WHOLESALING

VLADIMIRSKIYE VEDOMOSTI
1774045RU67B-47
Editorial: ul. Pichugina 5, 60000 VLADIMIR
Tel: 4922 32 04 90 **Fax:** 4922 23 19 10
Email: vedom@vtsnet.ru **Web site:** http://www.vedom.ru
Date Established: 1998; **Freq:** 260 issues yearly - Published 5 days a week; **Circ:** 8,000
Usual Pagination: 32
Editor: Grigoriy Belov
Profile: Regional daily paper with business, political and cultural news.
Language(s): Russian
ADVERTISING RATES:
Full Page Mono .... RUR 35400.00

Full Page Colour .... RUR 42480.00
Mechanical Data: Type Area: A2
REGIONAL DAILY & SUNDAY NEWSPAPERS: Regional Daily Newspapers

VLADIVOSTOK 1774458RU67B-482
Editorial: Narodny pr. 13, 690600 VLADIVOSTOK **Fax:** 4232 41 56 60
Email: news@vladnews.ru **Web site:** http://www.vladnews.ru
Date Established: 1989; **Freq:** 208 issues yearly; **Circ:** 25,000
Usual Pagination: 40
Editor: Sergey Bulakh
Profile: Writes about socio-political life of the region, its education and culture.
Language(s): Russian
ADVERTISING RATES:
SCC .... RUR 60.00
Mechanical Data: Type Area: A3
REGIONAL DAILY & SUNDAY NEWSPAPERS: Regional Daily Newspapers

VLAST 1611066RU82-101
Editorial: ul. Vrubeliya 4, str. 1, 125080 MOSKVA **Tel:** 495 195 96 36 **Fax:** 499 943 97 28
Email: vlast@kommersant.ru **Web site:** http://www.kommersant.ru
Date Established: 1997; **Freq:** Weekly - Published on Mondays; **Circ:** 60,000
Features Editor: Vladislav Dorofeev; **Editor-in-Chief:** Maksim Kovalskiy; **Advertising Manager:** Tatyana Pchelina; **Advertising Director:** Valeria Lyubimova
Profile: Magazine covering politics, news and current affairs, economy, health and cultural issues.
Language(s): Russian
ADVERTISING RATES:
Full Page Mono .... RUR 315000.00
Full Page Colour .... RUR 315000.00
Mechanical Data: Type Area: 220 x 290mm
Supplement to: Kommersant
CONSUMER: CURRENT AFFAIRS & POLITICS

VOGUE 1799491RU74B-236
Editorial: ul. Bolshaya Dmitrovka 11, str. 7, 125009 MOSKVA **Tel:** 495 74 55 565 **Fax:** 495 29 23 657
Email: femeleeva@condenast.ru **Web site:** http://www.vogue.ru
Date Established: 1998; **Freq:** 11 issues yearly; **Circ:** 150,000
Usual Pagination: 500
Editor: Alena Doletskaya; **Advertising Director:** Irina Elizarova; **Publisher:** Kira Pokhiton
Profile: Magazine on fashion and lifestyle, with fashion and beauty news, photos from shows, topical trends in the new season.
Language(s): Russian
Readership: Read by professional women.
ADVERTISING RATES:
Full Page Colour .... RUR 580000.00
Mechanical Data: Type Area: A4
CONSUMER: WOMEN'S INTEREST CONSUMER MAGAZINES: Women's Interest - Fashion

VOKRUG SVETA 1774177RU89A-3
Editorial: ul. Meshcheryakova 5, korpus 1, 125362 MOSKVA **Tel:** 495 491 18 28 **Fax:** 495 490 56 55
Email: editor@vokrugsveta.ru **Web site:** http://www.vokrugsveta.ru
Date Established: 1861; **Freq:** Monthly; **Circ:** 250,000
Usual Pagination: 140
Editor: Elena Knyazeva
Profile: Geographic magazine with travel, latest discoveries in science and technology innovations, prominent people biographies and articles on animals.
Language(s): Russian
ADVERTISING RATES:
Full Page Colour .... RUR 520000.00
Mechanical Data: Trim Size: 210 x 290mm, Print Process: Offset
CONSUMER: HOLIDAYS & TRAVEL: Travel

VOLGOGRADSKAYA PRAVDA 1774050RU72-502
Editorial: ul. Kommunisticheskaya 11, 400131 VOLGOGRAD **Tel:** 442 33 21 76
Email: gazeta@vpravda.ru **Web site:** http://www.vpravda.ru
Date Established: 1917; **Freq:** 260 issues yearly; **Annual Sub.:** RUR 2665.00; **Circ:** 18,000
Usual Pagination: 8
Editor: Lev Kukanov
Profile: Regional socio-political paper with regional business and social news.
Language(s): Russian
ADVERTISING RATES:
Full Page Mono .... RUR 51000.00
Mechanical Data: Type Area: 381 x 525mm
LOCAL NEWSPAPERS

VOPROSY EKONOMIKI 1615872RU1A-17
Editorial: Pr. Nakhimovsky 32, 117218 MOSKVA **Tel:** 495 129 04 44 **Fax:** 495 124 52 28
Email: mail@vopreco.ru **Web site:** http://www.vopreco.ru
Date Established: 1929; **Freq:** Monthly; **Cover Price:** RUR 185.00
Annual Sub.: RUR 1680.00; **Circ:** 6,000
Usual Pagination: 160
Editor: Leonid Ivanovich Abalkin
Profile: Magazine of Economic Institute of Russian Academy of Science containing articles on business and economy, analyses and statistics on different market sectors and investments.
Language(s): Russian
Readership: Aimed at economists-researchers, lecturers and students, high-rank public officials, corporate and banking analysts.
ADVERTISING RATES:
Full Page Mono .... RUR 20000.00
Copy instructions: *Copy Date:* 15th of each month
BUSINESS: FINANCE & ECONOMICS

VORONEZH 1774065RU82-144
Editorial: ul. Plekhanovskaya 53, office 510, VORONEZH **Tel:** 4732 51 93 70 **Fax:** 4732 51 93 70
Email: vrn@vmail.ru **Web site:** http://ru.voronezh.ru
Date Established: 2002; **Freq:** Quarterly; **Circ:** 3,000
Usual Pagination: 68
Profile: Informative-analytical and cultural-entertaining magazine writes about life in Voronez, its political and economical news, culture, spots and ecology.
Language(s): Russian
ADVERTISING RATES:
Full Page Colour .... RUR 24000.00
Mechanical Data: Type Area: A4
CONSUMER: CURRENT AFFAIRS & POLITICS

VOSKRESNAYA GAZETA 1774003RU72I-18
Editorial: ul. Iaskaya 46, UFA **Tel:** 3742 50 13 92 **Fax:** 3742 50 13 92
Email: vg@vg-ufa.ru **Web site:** http://www.vg-ufa.ru
Date Established: 1991; **Freq:** Weekly; **Circ:** 25,000
Usual Pagination: 24
Editor: Dmitri Yefremov
Profile: Socio-political informative-entertaining regional weekly.
Language(s): Russian
Mechanical Data: Type Area: A3
LOCAL NEWSPAPERS: Regional Weekly Newspapers

VOSTOCHO-SIBIRSKAYA PRAVDA 1774111RU67B-91
Editorial: P.O. Box 111, 664011 IRKUTSK **Tel:** 3952 20 34 70 **Fax:** 3952 20 34 66
Email: wm@vsp.ru **Web site:** http://www.vsp.ru
Date Established: 1918; **Freq:** 260 issues yearly; **Circ:** 25,000
Usual Pagination: 32
Editor: Alexander Gimelstein
Profile: Socio-political and economic regional paper of Eastern Siberia.
Language(s): Russian
Mechanical Data: Type Area: A3
REGIONAL DAILY & SUNDAY NEWSPAPERS: Regional Daily Newspapers

VOTRE BEAUTÉ 1826071RU74B-221
Editorial: ul. Lizy Chaykinoy 1, 6 floor, 125190 MOSKVA **Tel:** 495 93 30 720 **Fax:** 495 93 30 720
Email: votre_beaute@arnold-prize.ru **Web site:** http://women.stylenews.ru/vb
Date Established: 2006; **Freq:** Monthly; **Cover Price:** RUR 75.00; **Circ:** 160,000
Usual Pagination: 160
Advertising Manager: Vera Kolgushkina
Profile: Covering news in cosmetics and perfumery, fashion and diet slimming.
Language(s): Russian
Readership: Aimed at modern women in the age group from 20 to 50.
ADVERTISING RATES:
Full Page Colour .... RUR 278400.00
Mechanical Data: Trim Size: 210 x 275 mm
CONSUMER: WOMEN'S INTEREST CONSUMER MAGAZINES: Women's Interest - Fashion

VOYENNO-PROMYSHLENNY KURIER 1774179RU40-3
Editorial: Leningradsky prospekt 80, 125190 MOSKVA **Tel:** 495 788 91 90 **Fax:** 495 158 25 01
Email: info@vpk-news.ru **Web site:** http://www.vpk-news.ru
ISSN: 1729-3928
Freq: Weekly; **Annual Sub.:** RUR 480.00; **Circ:** 50,240
Usual Pagination: 12
Editor: Igor Korotchenko
Profile: National newspaper with military and military industry news, new technologies in army and history.
Language(s): Russian
Mechanical Data: Type Area: A3
BUSINESS: DEFENCE

VOZDUSHNO-KOSMICHESKAYA OBORONA 1774035RU40-4
Editorial: Leningradsky prospekt 80, 125190 MOSLVA **Tel:** 495 788 91 90 **Fax:** 495 788 91 90
Email: info@vko.ru **Web site:** http://www.vko.ru
Freq: 6 issues yearly; **Annual Sub.:** RUR 2160.00; **Circ:** 5,400
Usual Pagination: 48
Editor: Milhail Khodarenok
Profile: Informative-analytical magazine about developments of military space defence, news on new missiles and radars, military cooperation.
Language(s): Russian
ADVERTISING RATES:
Full Page Mono .... RUR 56000.00
BUSINESS: DEFENCE

VOZDUSHNY TRANSPORT 1611062RU6A-1
Editorial: ul. Chernyakhovskogo 16, 125319 MOSKVA **Tel:** 499 152 15 92 **Fax:** 499 953 34 89
Email: airtransport@ekonomika.ru **Web site:** http://www.ideg.ru/izd/detail.php?ID=1061
Date Established: 1936; **Freq:** Weekly - Published on Tuesdays; **Circ:** 10,000
Usual Pagination: 20
Editor: Sergey Alexandrovich Gusyakov; **Advertising Manager:** Lidia Vdovina
Profile: Newspaper focusing on air transport issues and distributed at aerospace companies, airports, air carrier companied.
Language(s): Russian
Readership: Aimed at airline managers, manufacturers and other air transport professionals.
ADVERTISING RATES:
Full Page Mono .... RUR 42850.00
Mechanical Data: Type Area: 266x380mm
BUSINESS: AVIATION & AERONAUTICS

VREMYA I DEN'GI 1774477RU1A-41
Editorial: P.O. Box 308, 420111 KAZAN' **Tel:** 432 99 88 15 **Fax:** 432 99 88 13
Email: vid@e-vid.ru **Web site:** http://www.e-vid.ru
Date Established: 1992; **Freq:** 208 issues yearly; **Circ:** 10,000
Usual Pagination: 24
Profile: Provides business news, economic analysis and financial market news.
Language(s): Russian
ADVERTISING RATES:
Full Page Mono .... RUR 42000.00
Mechanical Data: Type Area: A3
BUSINESS: FINANCE & ECONOMICS

VREMYA NOVOSTEY 1774299RU65A-49
Editorial: ul. Pyatnitskaya 25, 115326 MOSKVA **Tel:** 495 231 18 77 **Fax:** 495 231 23 08
Email: info@vremya.ru **Web site:** http://www.vremya.ru
Date Established: 2000; **Freq:** Daily; **Circ:** 51,000
Usual Pagination: 12
Advertising Director: Natalia Volkova
Profile: Daily business, political and social newspaper.
Language(s): Russian
ADVERTISING RATES:
Full Page Mono .... RUR 255000.00
Mechanical Data: Type Area: 380 x 545mm
NATIONAL DAILY & SUNDAY NEWSPAPERS: National Daily Newspapers

VSYE DLYA BUHGALTERA 1774294RU1B-5
Editorial: P.O. Box 10, 111401 MOSKVA **Tel:** 495 621 69 49 **Fax:** 495 621 91 90
Email: post@financepress.ru **Web site:** http://www.financepress.ru
Date Established: 1996; **Freq:** Monthly; **Circ:** 13,700
Usual Pagination: 76
Editor: Vera Gorokhova
Profile: Publication focused on accountancy, covers official documentation, provides experts' comments and advice.
Language(s): Russian
ADVERTISING RATES:
Full Page Colour .... RUR 25842.00
Mechanical Data: Type Area: 170 x 240mm
BUSINESS: FINANCE & ECONOMICS: Accountancy

VTORAYA POLOVINA 1774334RU74A-24
Editorial: ul. Uralskaya 3, office 8, YEKATERINBURG **Tel:** 343 216 37 37 **Fax:** 343 216 37 36
Email: pr@banzay.ru **Web site:** http://www.banzay.ru
Date Established: 2004; **Freq:** 11 issues yearly; **Circ:** 15,000
Usual Pagination: 160
Editor: Oksana Ryzhkova
Profile: Magazine for women providing information about fashion, beauty and culture.
Language(s): Russian
ADVERTISING RATES:
Full Page Colour .... RUR 35000.00
Mechanical Data: Type Area: A5
Copy instructions: *Copy Date:* 20th of each month
CONSUMER: WOMEN'S INTEREST CONSUMER MAGAZINES: Women's Interest

VYATSKY KRAI 1774125RU67B-488
Editorial: ul. Stepana Khalturina 2A, 610000 KIROV **Tel:** 332 64 39 15 **Fax:** 332 64 15 64
Email: kray@kray.kirov.ru **Web site:** http://www.vk-smi.ru
Date Established: 1990; **Freq:** 260 issues yearly; **Circ:** 20,600
Usual Pagination: 24
Editor-in-Chief: Vasily Smirnov
Profile: Regional socio-political daily newspaper with political and cultural news.
Language(s): Russian
Mechanical Data: Type Area: A3
REGIONAL DAILY & SUNDAY NEWSPAPERS: Regional Daily Newspapers

VZLIOT 1774682RU6A-7
Editorial: P.O. Box 7, 125475 MOSKVA **Tel:** 495 644 17 33 **Fax:** 495 644 17 33
Email: info@take-off.ru **Web site:** http://www.take-off.ru
Freq: 10 issues yearly; **Annual Sub.:** RUR 900.00; **Circ:** 5,000
Usual Pagination: 96
Editor: Evgeniy Yerokhin; **Editor-in-Chief:** Andrey Fomin
Profile: National aerospace magazine with analytical-informative news, developments and maintenance aerospace industry, interviews and reviews.
Language(s): Russian
ADVERTISING RATES:
Full Page Colour .... RUR 56000.00
Mechanical Data: Type Area: 200 x 270mm
BUSINESS: AVIATION & AERONAUTICS

WHERE MOSCOW 1773993RU89C-9
Editorial: Novodanilovskaya nab. 4a, 117105 MOSKVA **Tel:** 495 510 22 11 **Fax:** 495 510 49 69
Email: a.semida@spn.ru **Web site:** http://www.wheremoscow.spn.ru
Date Established: 1996; **Freq:** Monthly; **Cover Price:** Free; **Circ:** 90,000
Usual Pagination: 140
Editor: Anna Semida; **Advertising Manager:** Natalia Vasilieva; **Advertising Director:** Tamara Tavrizyan; **Publisher:** Vladimir Tychinin
Profile: Full-colour glossy guide to culture and entertainment in Moscow (in Russian and English) with coverage of cultural events and entertainments of Moscow and provides information about shops, services and restaurants.
Language(s): English; Russian
ADVERTISING RATES:
Full Page Colour $4500.00
Mechanical Data: Type Area: 222 x 273mm
CONSUMER: HOLIDAYS & TRAVEL: Entertainment Guides

XXL 1971323RU86C-19
Editorial: ul. Bolshaya Andronevskaya 17, MOSKVA **Tel:** 495 745 84 43 **Fax:** 495 956 22 10
Email: xxl@idr.ru **Web site:** http://xxl-online.ru
Date Established: 1997; **Freq:** Monthly; **Circ:** 140,000
Usual Pagination: 128
Advertising Manager: Irina Scherbakova
Profile: Glossy magazine created for Russian men with practical and informative articles, entertainment.
Language(s): Russian
Readership: Targets young, actively interested in the country and the world, evolving and dynamic readers.
ADVERTISING RATES:
Full Page Colour .... RUR 325000.00
CONSUMER: ADULT & GAY MAGAZINES: Men's Lifestyle Magazines

YAKHTY. A BOAT INTERNATIONAL PUBLICATION 1842733RU91A-1
Editorial: Gruzinsky per. 3, korp. 1, office 219-220, 123056 MOSKVA **Tel:** 495 626 55 93 **Fax:** 495 635 86 61
Email: editorial@boatinternational.ru **Web site:** http://www.boatinternational.ru
Date Established: 2004; **Freq:** 8 issues yearly; **Annual Sub.:** RUR 4800.00; **Circ:** 15,000
Editor-in-Chief: Anastasiya Yushkova; **Advertising Director:** Alisa Lilchetskaya
Profile: Provides latest news from yacht builders and designers, exclusive interviews with yacht owners, charter & brokerage news and luxury lifestyle features.
Language(s): Russian
ADVERTISING RATES:
Full Page Colour .... RUR 104225.00
Mechanical Data: Type Area: 233 x 275mm
CONSUMER: RECREATION & LEISURE: Boating & Yachting

YAKUTSK VECHERNIY 1774553RU72I-30
Editorial: ul. Khabarova 50/1, 677000 YAKUTSK **Tel:** 4112 21 72 58 **Fax:** 4112 21 72 58
Email: vecher@ykt.ru **Web site:** http://www.vecherka.ykt.ru
Date Established: 1994; **Freq:** 260 issues yearly - Published on Fridays; **Circ:** 50,000
Usual Pagination: 60

Editor: Maria Ivanova; **News Editor:** Raisa Arzaeva; **Advertising Director:** Marina Osodoeva
Profile: Socio-political, informative-entertaining regional weekly newspaper.
Language(s): Russian
ADVERTISING RATES:
Full Page Mono .... RUR 38000.00
Full Page Colour .... RUR 76000.00
Mechanical Data: Type Area: 260 x 352mm
LOCAL NEWSPAPERS: Regional Weekly Newspapers

YURIST KOMPANII 1774476RU44-2

Editorial: ul. B. Novodmitrovskaya 23, str. 5, 127015 MOSKVA **Tel:** 495 788 53 14 **Fax:** 495 788 53 14
Email: inbox@lawyercom.ru **Web site:** http://www.lawyercom.ru
Freq: Monthly; **Circ:** 7,700
Usual Pagination: 96
Editor: Anna Aleksandrova
Profile: Professional magazine on business law targeting corporative lawyers.
Language(s): Russian
ADVERTISING RATES:
Full Page Colour .... RUR 50000.00
Mechanical Data: Type Area: 200 x 280mm
BUSINESS: LEGAL

ZA RULIOM - REGION

1774300RU77A-52
Editorial: Narshkinskaya alleya 5, str. 2, 127167 MOSKVA **Tel:** 499 978 03 89
Email: gazeta@zr.ru **Web site:** http://gzr.zr.ru
Date Established: 2001; **Freq:** 28 issues yearly - Published on Wednesdays; **Circ:** 250,000
Usual Pagination: 60
Editor: Leonid Klimanovich; **Advertising Manager:** Julia Sheveleva; **Advertising Director:** Semen Schadrin
Profile: National newspaper focusing on cars, motor racing and car repair service.
Language(s): Russian
Mechanical Data: Type Area: 290x317mm
CONSUMER: MOTORING & CYCLING: Motoring

ZAPOLYARNAYA PRAVDA

1774248RU67B-209
Editorial: ul. Borisa Khmelnitskogo 8, 663300 NORILSK **Tel:** 3912 34 26 00 **Fax:** 3912 34 26 00
Email: elena@gazetazp.ru **Web site:** http://www.gazetazp.ru
Date Established: 1953; **Freq:** 208 issues yearly; **Circ:** 7,100
Usual Pagination: 32
Editor: Tatiana Kramareva
Profile: Socio-political regional newspaper covering news and events in Norilsk.
Language(s): Russian
Mechanical Data: Type Area: A3
REGIONAL DAILY & SUNDAY NEWSPAPERS: Regional Daily Newspapers

ZAVTRA 1774301RU65J-69

Editorial: Frunzenskaya nab. 18-60, 119146 MOSKVA **Tel:** 495 726 54 83
Email: zavtra@zavtra.ru **Web site:** http://zavtra.ru
Date Established: 1993; **Freq:** Weekly - Published on Wednesdays; **Annual Sub.:** RUR 600.00; **Circ:** 100,000
Usual Pagination: 8
Editor: Alexander Prokhanov
Profile: Writes about political, economic and cultural events in Russia.
Language(s): Russian
ADVERTISING RATES:
Full Page Mono $3500.00
Mechanical Data: Type Area: A2
NATIONAL DAILY & SUNDAY NEWSPAPERS: National Weekly Newspapers

ZHILAYA SREDA 1774165RU4B-6

Editorial: Kamennoostrovsky per. 26-28, office 3, SANKT SETERBURG **Tel:** 12 438 15 38
Fax: 12 346 06 65
Email: real@finestreet.ru **Web site:** http://www.finestreet.ru
Freq: 10 issues yearly; **Circ:** 20,000
Usual Pagination: 152
Executive Editor: Nikolai Bavrin; **Editor-in-Chief:** Alexander Rechitsky; **Advertising Manager:** Vyacheslav Vorobyev
Profile: Publication on interior design, decor, furniture and home accessories.
Language(s): Russian
Mechanical Data: Type Area: A4
BUSINESS: ARCHITECTURE & BUILDING: Interior Design & Flooring

ZHIVOTNOVODSTVO ROSSII

763406RU21D-350
Editorial: Orlikov per., 3, build. 1, 107139 MOSKVA
Tel: 495 608 02 77 **Fax:** 495 975 19 94
Email: animal@east.ru **Web site:** http://www.zzr.ru
Date Established: 1987; **Freq:** 11 issues yearly; **Circ:** 2,000
Usual Pagination: 60
Editor: Natalia Sobol
Profile: Magazine featuring articles on livestock breeding.
Language(s): Russian
Readership: Aimed at cattle breeders and research staff.
ADVERTISING RATES:
Full Page Mono .... RUR 20000.00
BUSINESS: AGRICULTURE & FARMING: Livestock

ZOLOTOY ROG 1774456RU1A-25

Editorial: pr. Krasnogo Znameni 10, 690950 VLASIVOSTOK **Tel:** 4232 45 04 85
Fax: 4232 45 04 85
Email: zr@zrpress.ru **Web site:** http://www.zrpress.ru
Date Established: 1992; **Freq:** 104 issues yearly; **Circ:** 12,000
Usual Pagination: 32
Editor: Elena Barkova
Profile: Informs about business in the region, financial situation and companies in Russian Far East.
Language(s): Russian
ADVERTISING RATES:
Full Page Mono .... RUR 35000.00
Mechanical Data: Type Area: 262 x 368mm
BUSINESS: FINANCE & ECONOMICS

San Marino

Time Difference: GMT + 1 hr (CET - Central European Time)
National Telephone Code: +378
Continent: Europe
Capital: San Marino
Principal Language: Italian
Population: 29615
Monetary Unit: Euro (EUR)
EMBASSY HIGH
COMMISSION: Embassy of the Republic of San Marino: C/o Consulate of the Republic of San Marino, Flat 51, 162 Sloane Street, London, SW1X 9BS
Tel: 020 7823 4762
Fax: 020 7823 4768 Head of Mission: HE Contessa Marina Meneghetti de Camillo

ITINERARI GUSTOSI

1841407SM89A-251
Editorial: Strada Cardio, 10, GALAZZANO SM-47899
Tel: 339 2222095
Email: g.continolo@turit.it **Web site:** http://www.turit.it
Freq: 11 issues yearly; **Circ:** 5,000
Profile: Magazine containing information about the region, focusing on local products and gastronomy.
Language(s): Italian
CONSUMER: HOLIDAYS & TRAVEL: Travel

LA TRIBUNA SAMMARINESE

1841410SM65A-1
Editorial: Via Gino Giacomini, 86/A, SM-47890
Tel: 549 990420 **Fax:** 549 990398
Email: redazione@latribunasammarinese.net **Web site:** http://www.latribunasammarinese.net
Freq: Daily; **Cover Price:** EUR 1.00
Annual Sub.: EUR 120.00
Usual Pagination: 12
Editor: Riccardo Geminiani
Profile: National daily newspaper focussing on news, current affairs, politics, economics, culture and sport.
Language(s): Italian
NATIONAL DAILY & SUNDAY NEWSPAPERS: National Daily Newspapers

TURIT 763079SM89A-250

Formerly: Turismo all'aria aperta
Editorial: Strada Cardio, 10, GALAZZANO SM-47899
Tel: 549 94 13 78 **Fax:** 549 97 49 17
Email: s.benzi@turit.it **Web site:** http://www.turit.it
Date Established: 1994; **Freq:** 11 issues yearly;
Cover Price: EUR 4.00
Annual Sub.: EUR 35.00; **Circ:** 20,000
Usual Pagination: 164
Profile: Magazine containing information about the region, focusing on local products and tourist attractions.
Language(s): Italian
Readership: Read by visitors to San Marino.
CONSUMER: HOLIDAYS & TRAVEL: Travel

Serbia

Time Difference: GMT + 1 hr (CET - Central European Time)
National Telephone Code: +381
Continent: Europe
Capital: Beograd
Principal Language: Serbian, Albanian, Hungarian
Population: 7365507
Monetary Unit: Serbian Dinar (RSD)
EMBASSY HIGH
COMMISSION: Embassy of the Republic of Serbia: 28 Belgrave Square, London, SW1X 8QB
Tel: 020 7235 9049
Fax: 020 7235 7092
Website: http://www.serbianembassy.org.uk/ Head of Mission HE Dejan Popovic / temporarly- Mr Branimir Filipowic

BORBA 1808933YU65A-43

Editorial: Trg Nikole Pašića 7/II, BEOGRAD 11000
Tel: 11 339 81 37 **Fax:** 11 339 81 37
Email: redakcija@borba.rs **Web site:** http://www.borba.rs
Date Established: 1922; **Freq:** Daily; **Cover Price:** RSD 20.00; **Circ:** 15,000
Editor: Miona Kovačević; **Executive Editor:** Miloš Jevtović
Profile: Daily newspaper covering news, political comments, culture, economics and sport.
Language(s): Serbian
ADVERTISING RATES:
Full Page Colour .... RSD 109900.00
Mechanical Data: Type Area: 355 x 500mm
NATIONAL DAILY & SUNDAY NEWSPAPERS: National Daily Newspapers

DANAS 707864YU65A-40

Editorial: Alekse Nenadovica 19-23 / V, BEOGRAD 11000 **Tel:** 11 344 1186 **Fax:** 11 344 1186
Email: desk@danas.rs **Web site:** http://www.danas.rs
ISSN: 1450-538X
Date Established: 1997; **Freq:** Daily; **Cover Price:** RSD 30.00
Annual Sub.: RSD 78000.00; **Circ:** 30,000
Advertising Manager: Snežana Stojakov
Profile: Newspaper featuring domestic and international news, politics, economics, finance, culture and entertainment.
Language(s): Serbian
Readership: Aimed at well-educated members of the public.
ADVERTISING RATES:
Full Page Mono .... RSD 78000.00
Full Page Colour .... RSD 124800.00
Agency Commission: 15%
Mechanical Data: Trim Size: 360 x 269mm
NATIONAL DAILY & SUNDAY NEWSPAPERS: National Daily Newspapers

GLAS JAVNOSTI 1616500YU65A-42

Editorial: Vlajkovićeva 8, BEOGRAD 11000
Tel: 11 3249 125 **Fax:** 11 322 4780
Email: redakcija@glas-javnosti.rs **Web site:** http://www.glas-javnosti.rs
ISSN: 1450-7210
Date Established: 1874; **Freq:** Daily; **Cover Price:** RSD 20.00; **Circ:** 32,000
Editor-in-Chief: Ljiljana Staletović
Profile: Newspaper focusing on politics, economics, culture, sport and general news.
Language(s): Serbian
ADVERTISING RATES:
Full Page Mono .... RSD 51000.00
Full Page Colour .... RSD 95000.00
NATIONAL DAILY & SUNDAY NEWSPAPERS: National Daily Newspapers

POLITIKA 1836943YU65A-44

Editorial: Makedonska 29, 11000 BEOGRAD
Tel: 11 33 01 101 **Fax:** 11 33 73 163
Email: redakcija@politika.rs **Web site:** http://www.politika.rs
Date Established: 1904; **Freq:** Daily; **Cover Price:** RSD 30.00; **Circ:** 85,000
News Editor: Ozren Milanović; **Editor-in-Chief:** Dragan Bujosevic
Profile: Oldest daily on the Balkans covering politics, economics, social and cultural issues.
Language(s): Serbian
ADVERTISING RATES:
Full Page Mono .... RSD 185000.00
Full Page Colour .... RSD 270000.00
NATIONAL DAILY & SUNDAY NEWSPAPERS: National Daily Newspapers

VECERNJE NOVOSTI 766557YU65A-41

Editorial: Trg Nikole Pašića 7, BEOGRAD 11000
Tel: 11 30 28 000 **Fax:** 11 33 98 337
Email: redakcija@novosti.rs **Web site:** http://www.novosti.rs
Date Established: 1953; **Freq:** Daily; **Cover Price:** RSD 30.00; **Circ:** 200,000
Usual Pagination: 48
Editor-in-Chief: Manojlo Manjo Vukotić
Profile: Newspaper covering general news, politics, economics, culture and sport.
Language(s): Serbian
ADVERTISING RATES:
Full Page Mono .... RSD 189100.00
Full Page Colour .... RSD 293105.00
Mechanical Data: Type Area: 250 x 347mm
NATIONAL DAILY & SUNDAY NEWSPAPERS: National Daily Newspapers

Slovakia

Time Difference: GMT + 1 hr (CET - Central European Time)
National Telephone Code: +421
Continent: Europe
Capital: Bratislava
Principal Language: Slovak, Hungarian
Population: 5423567
Monetary Unit: Slovakian Koruna (SK)
EMBASSY HIGH
COMMISSION: Embassy of Slovakia: 25 Kensington Palace Gardens, London, W8 4QY
Tel: 020 73 13 64 70
Fax: 020 73 13 64 81
Email: emb.london@mzv.sk
Website: http://www.slovakembassy.co.uk/ Head of Mission HE Juraj Zervan

ALARM SECURITY 1775693SK54C-1

Editorial: Infodom s.r.o., Lubovnianska 5, 851 07 BRATISLAVA **Tel:** 2 63 53 31 41 **Fax:** 2 63 53 31 41
Email: info@infodom.sk **Web site:** http://www.infodom.sk
Freq: Quarterly; **Circ:** 8,000
Editor: Josef Gajdos
Profile: Magazine featuring news from security industry in Slovakia. Focuses on security systems, services, Legislation news, insurance, also offers practical advice.
Language(s): Slovak
Readership: Read by institutions involved in security industry.
BUSINESS: SAFETY & SECURITY: Security

EPI - EKONOMICKÝ A PRÁVNY PORADCA PODNIKATELA

765772SK14A-7
Formerly: EPP - Ekonomický a právny poradca podnikatela
Editorial: Martina Rázusa 23A, 010 01 ZILINA
Tel: 41 70 53 210 **Fax:** 41 70 53 214
Email: brouckova@absoluthotel.cz **Web site:** http://www.epi.sk
Freq: Monthly; **Annual Sub.:** SK 2040.00; **Circ:** 40,000
Editor: Juraj Málik; **Editor-in-Chief:** Daniela Hornikova
Profile: Magazine featuring legal advice, facts and regulations, information for businesses and acquisition of assets. Also covers employment law, civil law and insurance.
Language(s): English; French; Slovak
Readership: Aimed at business managers and business owners.
BUSINESS: COMMERCE, INDUSTRY & MANAGEMENT

HOSPODÁRSKE NOVINY

1600935SK65A-5
Editorial: Seberiniho 1, PO Box 35, 820 07 BRATISLAVA **Tel:** 2 48 23 81 02 **Fax:** 2 48 23 81 01

Slovakia

Email: redakcia@ecopress.sk **Web site:** http://hnonline.sk
ISSN: 1335-4701
Date Established: 1992; **Freq:** Daily - Published Monday to Friday; **Cover Price:** SK 12.00; **Circ:** 32,000
Editor-in-Chief: Peter Vavro; **Managing Director:** Milan Mokráň; **Advertising Director:** Juraj Lim
Profile: Broadsheet-sized newspaper featuring economics, politics, finances, national and international news, culture, sport and entertainment.
Language(s): English; German; Slovak
Readership: Aimed at business executives, government members and the general public.
ADVERTISING RATES:
Full Page Mono .... SK 99750.00
Mechanical Data: Trim Size: 285 x 420mm, No. of Columns (Display): 6, Col Widths (Display): 43mm
NATIONAL DAILY & SUNDAY NEWSPAPERS: National Daily Newspapers

KOSICKY DENNIK KORZAR
1775579SK67B-1
Editorial: Letna 47, 040 01 KOSICE **Tel:** 55 60 02 209 **Fax:** 55 60 02 230
Email: redakcia.ke@korzar.sk **Web site:** http://www.korzar.sk
ISSN: 1335-4566
Freq: Daily - Published Monday to Saturday; **Circ:** 22,153
Profile: Regional newspaper for Kosice.
Language(s): Slovak
ADVERTISING RATES:
Full Page Mono .... EUR 960.00
Full Page Colour .... EUR 1300.00
REGIONAL DAILY & SUNDAY NEWSPAPERS: Regional Daily Newspapers

MARKÍZA
765709SK76C-21
Editorial: Jasikova 2, 821 03 BRATISLAVA
Tel: 2 43 41 40 85 **Fax:** 2 43 41 40 87
Email: tvtip@tvtip.sk **Web site:** http://www.mojcasopis.sk
ISSN: 1335-2776
Date Established: 1998; **Freq:** Weekly - Published on Monday; **Annual Sub.:** SK 1196.00; **Circ:** 120,000
Usual Pagination: 100
Editor: Valéria Koszorouvá; **Editor-in-Chief:** Miriam Žiaková; **Advertising Director:** Pavol Sakál
Profile: Magazine focusing on celebrity lifestyle and television. Includes TV listings.
Language(s): Slovak
Readership: Read mainly by women aged 20 to 60 years.
ADVERTISING RATES:
Full Page Colour .... SK 150000.00
Mechanical Data: Trim Size: 208 x 280mm, No. of Columns (Display): 3
Copy instructions: *Copy Date:* 14 days prior to publication date
CONSUMER: MUSIC & PERFORMING ARTS: TV & Radio

MÓDA REVUE
1687631SK47A-1
Editorial: Jelsova 3, 831 01 BRATISLAVA
Tel: 2 54 79 20 44 **Fax:** 2 54 79 20 45
Email: info@modarevue.sk **Web site:** http://www.modarevue.sk
Freq: 6 issues yearly; **Annual Sub.:** SK 360.00; **Circ:** 8,000
Editor: Sylvia Laczova; **Editor-in-Chief:** Darina Vittekova; **Publisher:** Kamil Chmelár
Profile: Magazine focusing on new fashion trends, information about textile, footwear, leatherwear industry and trade.
Language(s): Slovak
Readership: Aimed at wholesalers and producers from textile, garment and leatherwear industry.
ADVERTISING RATES:
Full Page Colour .... SK 36800.00
Mechanical Data: Type Area: 210 x 297mm, Trim Size: 180 x 261mm
BUSINESS: CLOTHING & TEXTILES

NOVÝ CAS
765673SK65A-53
Editorial: Prievozka 14, 819 06 BRATISLAVA
Tel: 2 58 22 72 92 **Fax:** 2 58 22 73 50
Email: redakcia@novycas.sk **Web site:** http://www.cas.sk
Freq: Daily - Published Monday to Saturday; **Cover Price:** SK 9.00; **Circ:** 210,000
Usual Pagination: 32
Editor: Júlia Kováčová
Profile: Newspaper focusing on national and international news, politics, culture and sport.
Language(s): Slovak
Readership: Read by 20-49 years old with a household income over 15000 SK.
ADVERTISING RATES:
Full Page Mono .... EUR 7250.00
Full Page Colour .... EUR 8600.00
Mechanical Data: Type Area: 232 x 315mm, Trim Size: 206 x 268mm, Col Widths (Display): 38mm
NATIONAL DAILY & SUNDAY NEWSPAPERS: National Daily Newspapers

NOVY CAS VÍKEND
1668293SK65H-13
Editorial: Prievozská 14, PO Box 44, 820 04 BRATISLAVA **Tel:** 2 58 22 72 92 **Fax:** 2 58 22 73 50
Email: magazin@novycas.sk **Web site:** http://www.cas.sk
Freq: Weekly - Published on Saturday; **Circ:** 330,000
Editor: Júlia Kováčová; **Advertising Manager:** Olga Danihelová
Profile: Lifestyle magazine focusing on cinema, music, TV listings, showbiz features and events.
Language(s): Slovak
Readership: Read by women and men aged 20-29 with higher education and income of 20 000 SK.
ADVERTISING RATES:
Full Page Colour .... SK 170000.00
Mechanical Data: Type Area: 206 x 280mm, Trim Size: 188 x 252mm, Col Widths (Display): 44mm
NATIONAL DAILY & SUNDAY NEWSPAPERS: National Colour Supplements

PC REVUE
765746SK5C-1
Editorial: Kladnianska 60, 821 05 BRATISLAVA
Tel: 2 43 42 09 56 **Fax:** 2 43 42 09 58
Email: info@pcrevue.sk **Web site:** http://www.pcrevue.sk
Freq: Monthly; **Cover Price:** EUR 3.95; **Circ:** 22,000
Usual Pagination: 140
Editor: Michal Reiter; **Editor-in-Chief:** Ondrej Macko; **Advertising Manager:** Ludmila Gebauerova
Profile: Magazine focusing on new computer technology, programming, networking and mobile phones.
Language(s): Slovak
Readership: Aimed at IT professionals and computer enthusiasts.
ADVERTISING RATES:
Full Page Colour .... SK 59000.00
Mechanical Data: Type Area: 210 x 297mm
BUSINESS: COMPUTERS & AUTOMATION: Professional Personal Computers

PLUS 7 DNI
707617SK82-300
Editorial: Panónska cesta 9, 852 93 BRATISLAVA
Tel: 2 32 15 31 81 **Fax:** 2 32 15 31 82
Email: plus7dni@7plus.sk **Web site:** http://www.plus7dni.sk
Freq: Weekly - Published on Thursday; **Cover Price:** SK 28.00; **Circ:** 230,000
Usual Pagination: 100
Editor: Emil Polák; **News Editor:** Lenka Kapustová; **Editor-in-Chief:** Milos Luknár; **Advertising Director:** Mirjana Sikimič
Profile: Magazine covering news, culture and entertainment.
Language(s): Slovak
Readership: Read by 20 - 49 years old with household income above average.
ADVERTISING RATES:
Full Page Colour .... EUR 6605.59
Mechanical Data: Trim Size: 210 x 280mm
CONSUMER: CURRENT AFFAIRS & POLITICS

PRAVDA
707092SK65A-50
Editorial: Trnavská cesta 39/A, 831 04 BRATISLAVA 3 **Tel:** 2 49 59 69 99 **Fax:** 2 49 59 69 39
Email: pravda@pravda.sk **Web site:** http://www.pravda.sk
ISSN: 1335-4051
Freq: Daily - Published Monday to Saturday; **Circ:** 90,000
Editor-in-Chief: Petr Sabata; **Advertising Manager:** Erika Bokorova
Profile: Newspaper focusing on national and international news, finance, the economy, culture, entertainment and sport.
Language(s): English; Slovak
ADVERTISING RATES:
Full Page Mono .... EUR 4149.00
Full Page Colour .... EUR 5145.00
Agency Commission: 15%
Mechanical Data: Trim Size: 235 x 310mm, No. of Columns (Display): 5, Col Widths (Display): 39 mm, Type Area: 211x264 mm, Page Width: 211
Copy instructions: *Copy Date:* 5 working days prior publishing date
Supplement(s): Moment - 52xY.
NATIONAL DAILY & SUNDAY NEWSPAPERS: National Daily Newspapers

PRESOVKY DENNIK KORZAR
1775584SK67B-2
Editorial: Jarková 59, 080 01 PRESOV
Tel: 51 77 75 550 **Fax:** 51 77 75 154
Email: korzarpo@pobox.sk **Web site:** http://www.korzar.sk
ISSN: 1335-7611
Freq: Daily - Published Monday to Saturday; **Circ:** 12,200
Editor: Michal Frank; **Editor-in-Chief:** Peter Bercik
Profile: Newspaper aimed at Presov.
Language(s): Slovak
ADVERTISING RATES:
Full Page Mono .... EUR 960.00
Full Page Colour .... EUR 1300.00
REGIONAL DAILY & SUNDAY NEWSPAPERS: Regional Daily Newspapers

THE SLOVAK SPECTATOR
707111SK65J-1
Editorial: Lazaretska 12, 811 08 BRATISLAVA
Tel: 2 59 23 33 00 **Fax:** 2 59 23 33 19
Email: spectator@spectator.sk **Web site:** http://www.slovakspectator.sk
ISSN: 1335-9843
Date Established: 1995; **Freq:** Weekly - Published on Monday; **Cover Price:** SK 40.00; **Circ:** 8,500
Editor-in-Chief: Beata Balogova; **Advertising Manager:** Beata Fojtikova; **Publisher:** Jan Pallo
Profile: Newspaper focusing on general news, business issues, culture, opinion and features.
Language(s): English
Readership: Aimed at local business executives, expatriates and visitors to the country.
ADVERTISING RATES:
Full Page Mono .... EUR 2250.00
Full Page Colour .... EUR 2800.00
Agency Commission: 15%
Mechanical Data: Type Area: 280 x 380mm
NATIONAL DAILY & SUNDAY NEWSPAPERS: National Weekly Newspapers

SME
765565SK65A-51
Editorial: Lazaretská 12, 811 08 BRATISLAVA
Tel: 2 59 23 35 00 **Fax:** 2 59 23 36 69
Email: redakcia@sme.sk **Web site:** http://www.sme.sk
ISSN: 1335-4418
Freq: Daily - Published Monday to Saturday; **Annual Sub.:** SK 3478.00; **Circ:** 92,369
Usual Pagination: 40
Editor-in-Chief: Matus Kostolny
Profile: Newspaper focusing on national and international news, business, politics, culture and sport.
Language(s): English; Slovak
ADVERTISING RATES:
Full Page Mono .... EUR 3800.00
Full Page Colour .... EUR 5400.00
Mechanical Data: Col Widths (Display): 44mm, Trim Size: 380 x 280mm
Copy instructions: *Copy Date:* 13 days prior to publishing
Supplement(s): Auto Moto - 52xY, Bratislava - 52xY, Ekonomika - 365xY, Fórum - 52xY, Kariéra - 52xY, Pocitace - 52xY, Sport - 52xY, TV Oko - 52xY, Veda - 52xY, Víkend - 52xY, Zaujimavosti - 365xY, Zdravie - 52xY
NATIONAL DAILY & SUNDAY NEWSPAPERS: National Daily Newspapers

SPISSKY DENNIK KORZAR
1775586SK67B-3
Editorial: Zimná ulica 49, 052 01 SPISSKA NOVA VES **Tel:** 53 44 27 380
Email: redakcia.snv@korzar.sk **Web site:** http://www.korzar.sk
ISSN: 1335-759X
Freq: Daily - Published Monday to Saturday; **Circ:** 4,137
Editor: Monika Toporecova; **Editor-in-Chief:** Peter Bercik
Profile: Newspaper aimed at Spis.
Language(s): Slovak
ADVERTISING RATES:
Full Page Mono .... EUR 515.00
Full Page Colour .... EUR 690.00
REGIONAL DAILY & SUNDAY NEWSPAPERS: Regional Daily Newspapers

TATRANSKY DENNIK KORZAR
1775587SK67B-4
Editorial: Námestie Svätého Egídia 96/42, P.O.Box 77, 058 01 POPRAD **Tel:** 52 77 21 773
Email: richard.hudecek@korzar.sk **Web site:** http://www.korzar.sk
ISSN: 1335-7573
Freq: Daily - Published Monday to Saturday; **Circ:** 3,283
Editor: Richard Hudecek
Profile: Newspaper featuring reports from Transky region.
Language(s): Slovak
ADVERTISING RATES:
Full Page Mono .... EUR 370.00
Full Page Colour .... EUR 500.00
REGIONAL DAILY & SUNDAY NEWSPAPERS: Regional Daily Newspapers

TREND
707067SK1A-400
Editorial: Tomášikova 23, 821 01 BRATISLAVA 2
Tel: 2 20 82 22 22 **Fax:** 2 20 82 22 23
Email: redakcia@trend.sk **Web site:** http://www.etrend.sk
Date Established: 1990; **Freq:** Weekly; **Cover Price:** SK 30.60; **Circ:** 18,425
Usual Pagination: 36
Editor: Radoslav Bato; **Editor-in-Chief:** Jozef Andacky; **Advertising Manager:** Gabriela Horvathova
Profile: Magazine covering current affairs, economics, finance and telecommunications.
Language(s): Slovak
Readership: Read by professionals, businessmen and students.
ADVERTISING RATES:
Full Page Colour .... EUR 5010.00
Agency Commission: 15%
Mechanical Data: Trim Size: 183 x 254mm, Bleed Size: 210 x 280mm, Print Process: Offset
Average ad content per issue: 20%
BUSINESS: FINANCE & ECONOMICS

ÚJ SZÓ
1775577SK65A-54
Editorial: Lazaretská 12, 811 08 BRATISLAVA
Tel: 2 59 23 34 21 **Fax:** 2 59 23 34 69
Email: redakcia@ujszo.com **Web site:** http://www.ujszo.com
ISSN: 1335-7050
Date Established: 1948; **Freq:** Daily; **Cover Price:** EUR 0.37; **Circ:** 35,500
Profile: National newspaper for Hungarian speaking residents in Slovakia features: Home Affairs, Regions, International Affairs, Culture, Economics, Sports, Commentaries and Supplements.
Language(s): Hungarian
Readership: Aimed at Hungarians in Slovakia.
ADVERTISING RATES:
Full Page Mono .... EUR 2290.00
Full Page Colour .... EUR 2987.50
NATIONAL DAILY & SUNDAY NEWSPAPERS: National Daily Newspapers

ZEMPLINSKY DENNIK KORZAR
1775589SK67B-6
Editorial: Gorkého 1, 071 01 MICHALOVCE
Tel: 56 68 88 451
Email: redakcia.mi@korzar.sk **Web site:** http://www.korzar.sk
ISSN: 1335-7603
Freq: Daily - Published Monday to Saturday; **Circ:** 5,021
Editor: Lydia Verescakova; **Editor-in-Chief:** Peter Bercik
Profile: Newspaper focused on Zemplinsky region.
Language(s): Slovak
ADVERTISING RATES:
Full Page Mono .... EUR 515.00
Full Page Colour .... EUR 690.00
REGIONAL DAILY & SUNDAY NEWSPAPERS: Regional Daily Newspapers

ZIVOT
707174SK74A-201
Editorial: Prievozská 14, 820 09 BRATISLAVA
Tel: 2 58 22 78 21 **Fax:** 2 58 22 78 45
Email: zivot@ringier.sk **Web site:** http://lesk.cas.sk/se/10189/Zivot
Freq: Weekly - Published on Monday; **Annual Sub.:** SK 1190.00; **Circ:** 124,000
Usual Pagination: 76
Editor: Renáta Klacanská; **Advertising Manager:** Tibor Bondor
Profile: Magazine focused on family life, fashion, beauty, health, interior design, knitting, stitching and patchwork. Also includes celebrity gossip and features.
Language(s): Slovak
Readership: Aimed at women aged between 26 and 55.
ADVERTISING RATES:
Full Page Colour .... SK 160000.00
CONSUMER: WOMEN'S INTEREST CONSUMER MAGAZINES: Women's Interest

Slovenia

Time Difference: GMT + 1 hr (CET - Central European Time)
National Telephone Code: +386
Continent: Europe
Capital: Ljubljana
Principal Language: Slovene, Serbo-Croat, Italian
Population: 2011437
Monetary Unit: Tolar (SIT)

EMBASSY HIGH

COMMISSION: Embassy of the Republic of Slovenia: 10 Little College Street, London, SW1P 3SH
Tel: 020 7222 5700
Fax: 020 7222 5277
Email: vlo@gov.si
Website: http://london.embassy.si/ Head of Mision HE Mr Iztok Mirošič T: (+) 44 20 7222 5700
F: (+) 44 20 7222 5277
E: vlo(at)gov.si

ADUT
1699152SI2A-6
Editorial: Podjunska ulica 13, 1000 LJUBLJANA
Tel: 1 5838-400 **Fax:** 1 5838-409
Email: info@palegra.si **Web site:** http://www.adut.palegra.si
Freq: Monthly; **Circ:** 100,000
Editor-in-Chief: Aleksander Černe
Language(s): Slovenian
Mechanical Data: Trim Size: 275x415 mm
BUSINESS: COMMUNICATIONS, ADVERTISING & MARKETING

DELO
1202372SI65A-5
Editorial: Dunajska 5, 1509 LJUBLJANA **Tel:** 1 4737-400 **Fax:** 1 4737-420

Email: centralna@delo.si **Web site:** http://www.delo.si
Freq: Daily; **Circ:** 93,000
Editor: Darjan Košir
Profile: Newspaper focusing on national and international news, economics, finance, culture, entertainment and sport.
Language(s): Slovenian
ADVERTISING RATES:
Full Page Colour .... EUR 10500.00
Mechanical Data: Trim Size: 388 x 509mm, No. of Columns (Display): 8, Col Widths (Display): 45 mm, Bleed Size: 388 x 540mm
Supplement(s): DELO IN DOM - 52xY, DELO MATURANT&KA - 12xY, Delo Sobotna priloga - 52xY, MAG - 52xY, ONA - 52xY, POLET - 52xY, VIKEND - 52xY
NATIONAL DAILY & SUNDAY NEWSPAPERS: National Daily Newspapers

DELO IN DOM
1699172SI74C-2

Editorial: Dunajska 5, 1000 LJUBLJANA
Tel: 1 47 37 314 **Fax:** 1 473 73 25
Email: deloindom@delo.si **Web site:** http://www.delo.si/tiskano/html/zadnji/Delo+in+dom
Freq: Weekly; **Circ:** 202,600
Editor-in-Chief: Karina Cunder Reščič
Language(s): Slovenian
Mechanical Data: Trim Size: 202x270 mm
Supplement to: DELO
CONSUMER: WOMEN'S INTEREST CONSUMER MAGAZINES: Home & Family

DEMOKRACIJA
1699175SI65J-2

Editorial: Komenskega 11, p.p. 4315, 1000 LJUBLJANA **Tel:** 1 24 47 205 **Fax:** 1 24 47 204
Email: urednik@demokracija.si
ISSN: 1408-0494
Freq: Weekly; **Circ:** 11,000
Editor: Peter Avsenik; **Editor-in-Chief:** Metod Berlec
Profile: National weekly newspaper.
Language(s): Slovenian
Mechanical Data: Trim Size: 208x280 mm
NATIONAL DAILY & SUNDAY NEWSPAPERS: National Weekly Newspapers

DENAR & SVET NEPREMIČNIN
1699177SI1E-1

Editorial: Kopitarjeva 2 in 4, 1510 LJUBLJANA
Tel: 1 3082-100 **Fax:** 1 3082-369
Email: tomaz.bukovec@dnevnik.si **Web site:** http://www.dnevnik.si
Freq: 26 issues yearly; **Cover Price:** Free; **Circ:** 59,000
Editor-in-Chief: Miran Kump; **Advertising Manager:** Nives Roš
Language(s): Slovenian
Mechanical Data: Trim Size: 203x270 mm
Supplement to: DNEVNIK
BUSINESS: FINANCE & ECONOMICS: Property

DIREKT
1839882SI65A-11

Editorial: Kopitarjeva 2 in 4, 1510 LJUBLJANA
Tel: 1 30 82 282 **Fax:** 1 30 82 329
Email: bojan.pozar@direkt.si **Web site:** http://company.dnevnik.si/publications/direkt
Freq: Daily; **Circ:** 18,000
Editor: Bojan Požar
Profile: Tabloid size national daily.
Language(s): Slovenian
ADVERTISING RATES:
Full Page Colour .... EUR 3755.00
Mechanical Data: Type Area: 280 x 397mm, Col Widths (Display): 43 mm
NATIONAL DAILY & SUNDAY NEWSPAPERS: National Daily Newspapers

DNEVNIK
707708SI65A-7

Editorial: Kopitarjeva 2 in 4, 1510 LJUBLJANA
Tel: 1 3082-100 **Fax:** 1 3082-309
Email: info@dnevnik.si **Web site:** http://www.dnevnik.si
Freq: Daily; **Circ:** 59,000
Editor: Antiša Korljan; **Features Editor:** Toni Perić; **Editor-in-Chief:** Miran Lesjak; **Advertising Manager:** Nives Roš
Profile: Newspaper providing information on national and international politics, news, economics, finance, culture and entertainment.
Language(s): Slovenian
Readership: Aimed at the general public.
Mechanical Data: Trim Size: 280x397 mm
Supplement(s): ANTENA, DENAR & SVET NEPREMIČNIN, GAZELA, MOJ DOM, NIKA, PILOT
NATIONAL DAILY & SUNDAY NEWSPAPERS: National Daily Newspapers

DOBRO JUTRO
1699183SI67B-2

Editorial: Volkmerjev prehod, 2000 MARIBOR
Tel: 2 2346-630 **Fax:** 2 2346-637
Email: dobro.jutro@r-m.si **Web site:** http://www.dobrojutro.net
Freq: 26 issues yearly; **Circ:** 290,000
Editor-in-Chief: Saša Pukl
Language(s): Slovenian
Mechanical Data: Trim Size: 200x267 mm
REGIONAL DAILY & SUNDAY NEWSPAPERS: Regional Daily Newspapers

DRUŽINA
1616503SI65J-1

Editorial: Krekov trg 1, p.p. 95, 1000 LJUBLJANA
Tel: 1 3602-800 **Fax:** 1 3602-848
Email: druzina@siol.net **Web site:** http://www.druzina.si
Freq: Weekly; **Circ:** 53,000
Editor-in-Chief: Janez Gril
Profile: Newspaper covering all fields of life in the view of catholic social doctrine, features current affairs, cultural and other events.
Language(s): Slovenian
Readership: Aimed at Slovene families living in Slovenia and abroad.
Mechanical Data: Trim Size: 288x400 mm
NATIONAL DAILY & SUNDAY NEWSPAPERS: National Weekly Newspapers

DRUŽINSKI DELNIČAR
1699187SI1A-33

Editorial: Dunajska 5, 1509 LJUBLJANA **Tel:** 1 4737-481 **Fax:** 1 4737-483
Email: delnicar@delo.si **Web site:** http://www.delo.si
ISSN: 1561-4785
Freq: Monthly; **Cover Price:** Free; **Circ:** 133,000
Editor-in-Chief: Vasilij Krivec
Language(s): Slovenian
Mechanical Data: Trim Size: 180x250 mm
BUSINESS: FINANCE & ECONOMICS

GLAS GOSPODARSTVA
707670SI1A-30

Editorial: Dimičeva 13, 1000 LJUBLJANA
Tel: 1 58 98 000 **Fax:** 1 58 98 200
Email: info@gzs.si **Web site:** http://www.gzs.si
ISSN: 1318-3672
Freq: Monthly; **Circ:** 42,000
Editor-in-Chief: Robert Peklaj
Profile: Magazine providing in-depth coverage of Slovenian and international economics.
Language(s): Slovenian
Readership: Aimed at management executives.
Mechanical Data: Trim Size: 220x279mm
BUSINESS: FINANCE & ECONOMICS

IDEJA
1699206SI88R-1

Editorial: Lepi pot 6, 1000 LJUBLJANA **Tel:** 1 4790-232 **Fax:** 1 4790-230
Email: ideja@tzs.si **Web site:** http://www.tzs.si/ideja
Freq: Quarterly; **Circ:** 140,000
Editor-in-Chief: Maja Jug Hartman
Language(s): Slovenian
Mechanical Data: Trim Size: 210x297 mm
CONSUMER: EDUCATION: Education Related

MLADINA
1699237SI65A-10

Editorial: Trubarjeva 79, 1000 LJUBLJANA
Tel: 1 2306-500 **Fax:** 1 2306-510
Email: desk@mladina.si **Web site:** http://www.mladina.si
ISSN: 1580-5352
Freq: Weekly; **Circ:** 9,544
Editor-in-Chief: Jani Sever
Language(s): Slovenian
Mechanical Data: Trim Size: 220x280 mm
NATIONAL DAILY & SUNDAY NEWSPAPERS: National Daily Newspapers

MOBIL
1699238SI77B-1

Editorial: Dimičeva 16, 1000 LJUBLJANA
Tel: 1 4364-700 **Fax:** 1 4364-701
Email: adelita@email.si
Freq: Monthly; **Cover Price:** Free; **Circ:** 220,000
Editor: Matjaž Gregorič
Language(s): Slovenian
Mechanical Data: Trim Size: 220x265 mm
CONSUMER: MOTORING & CYCLING: Motorcycling

MOJ DOM
1699240SI74C-6

Editorial: Kopitarjeva 2 in 4, 1510 LJUBLJANA
Tel: 1 3082-100 **Fax:** 1 3082-369
Email: tomaz.bukovec@dnevnik.si **Web site:** http://www.dnevnik.si
Freq: 26 issues yearly; **Cover Price:** Free; **Circ:** 207,000
Editor-in-Chief: Tomaž Bukovec; **Advertising Manager:** Nives Roš
Language(s): Slovenian
Mechanical Data: Trim Size: 203x270 mm
Supplement to: DNEVNIK, NEDELJSKI DNEVNIK
CONSUMER: WOMEN'S INTEREST CONSUMER MAGAZINES: Home & Family

NEDELJSKI DNEVNIK
1648403SI65B-1

Editorial: Kopitarjeva 2 in 4, 1510 LJUBLJANA
Tel: 1 3082-100 **Fax:** 1 3082-369
Email: nedeljski@dnevnik.si **Web site:** http://www.dnevnik.si
ISSN: 1318-0339
Freq: Weekly; **Circ:** 148,000
Editor-in-Chief: Zlatko Šetinc; **Advertising Manager:** Nives Roš
Profile: Newspaper focusing on national and international news, politics, finance, culture and entertainment.
Language(s): Slovenian
Mechanical Data: Trim Size: 280x397 mm
Supplement to: DNEVNIK
NATIONAL DAILY & SUNDAY NEWSPAPERS: National Sunday Newspapers

NIKA
1699253SI73-4

Editorial: Kopitarjeva 2 in 4, 1510 LJUBLJANA
Tel: 1 3082-100 **Fax:** 1 3082-369
Email: nika@dnevnik.si **Web site:** http://www.dnevnik.si/nika
Freq: 26 issues yearly; **Cover Price:** Free; **Circ:** 207,000
Editor-in-Chief: Vesna Kalčič; **Advertising Manager:** Nives Roč
Language(s): Slovenian
Mechanical Data: Trim Size: 203x270 mm
Supplement to: DNEVNIK, NEDELJSKI DNEVNIK
CONSUMER: NATIONAL & INTERNATIONAL PERIODICALS

PREMOŽENJE
1699277SI1A-34

Editorial: Svetozarevska 14, 2000 MARIBOR
Tel: 2 2353-500 **Fax:** 2 2353-369
Email: desk@vecer.com **Web site:** http://www.vecer.com
Freq: Monthly; **Cover Price:** Free; **Circ:** 56,000
Editor-in-Chief: Darja Verbič
Language(s): Slovenian
Mechanical Data: Trim Size: 205x280 mm
Supplement to: VEČER
BUSINESS: FINANCE & ECONOMICS

REPORTER
1995153SI65J-3

Editorial: Prava smer d. o. o., Dunajska cesta 5, 1000 LJUBLJANA **Tel:** 1 620 9300 **Fax:** 1 620 9301
Email: info@revija-reporter.si **Web site:** http://www.revija-reporter.si
Freq: Weekly - Published on Monday; **Cover Price:** EUR 2.50; **Circ:** 15,000
Editor: Silvester Šurla
Language(s): Slovenian
NATIONAL DAILY & SUNDAY NEWSPAPERS: National Weekly Newspapers

SLOVENIA TIMES
1699295SI65G-1

Editorial: Šmartinska 106, 1000 LJUBLJANA
Tel: 1 5205-084
Email: info@sloveniatimes.com **Web site:** http://www.sloveniatimes.com
Freq: 26 issues yearly; **Circ:** 10,000
Editor: Rob Crawford; **Editor-in-Chief:** Jaka Terpinc
Language(s): English
Mechanical Data: Trim Size: 300x450 mm
NATIONAL DAILY & SUNDAY NEWSPAPERS: International Daily Newspapers

Spain

Time Difference: GMT + 1 hr (CET - Central European Time)
National Telephone Code: +34
Continent: Europe
Capital: Madrid
Principal Language: Spanish
Population: 41000000
Monetary Unit: Euro (EUR)

EMBASSY HIGH COMMISSION: Spanish Embassy: 39 Chesham Place, London, SW1X 8SB
Tel: 020 7235 5555
Fax: 020 7259 5392/ Head Of Mission : HE Carles Casajuana

EL 3 DE VUIT
763786X72-10

Editorial: Papiol 1, E-08720 VILAFRANCA DEL PENEDÈS (BARCELONA) **Tel:** 93 89 21 035
Fax: 93 81 80 236
Email: el3devuit@el3devuit.com **Web site:** http://www.troc.es
Freq: Weekly - Published on Friday; **Cover Price:** EUR 1.60; **Circ:** 7,000
Editor: Ricard Rafecas Ruiz
Language(s): Catalan; Spanish
LOCAL NEWSPAPERS

EL 9 NOU D'OSONA I DEL RIPOLLÈS
763788X67B-3730

Editorial: Pza. de la Catedral 2, E-08500 BARCELONA **Tel:** 93 88 94 949 **Fax:** 93 88 50 569
Email: noticies@vic.el9nou.com **Web site:** http://www.el9nou.com
Freq: 104 issues yearly - Published on Monday and Friday; **Cover Price:** EUR 1.90 (Friday); **Circ:** 10,985
Editor: Josep Cauma Juan
Profile: Regional daily newspaper focussing on news and current affairs.
Language(s): Catalan
ADVERTISING RATES:
Full Page Mono .... EUR 2800.00
Full Page Colour .... EUR 4100.00
REGIONAL DAILY & SUNDAY NEWSPAPERS: Regional Daily Newspapers

EL 9 NOU-VALLES ORIENTAL
763790X67B-3740

Editorial: Sant Jaime 16, 2º, 4, Edificio Vila Oberta, E-08400 GRANOLLERS **Tel:** 938 60 30 20
Fax: 938 70 70 55
Email: noticies@gra.el9nou.com **Web site:** http://www.el9nou.com
Freq: 102 issues yearly - Published on Monday and Friday; **Cover Price:** EUR 1.90 (Friday); **Circ:** 5,431
Editor: Juan Carlos Arredondo
Profile: Regional daily newspaper focussing on news and current affairs.
Language(s): Catalan
ADVERTISING RATES:
Full Page Mono .... EUR 2800.00
Full Page Colour .... EUR 4100.00
REGIONAL DAILY & SUNDAY NEWSPAPERS: Regional Daily Newspapers

ABC
52927X65A-10

Editorial: Juan Ignacio Luca de Tena 7, E-28027 MADRID **Tel:** 91 33 99 000 **Fax:** 91 32 03 620
Email: continuidad@abc.es **Web site:** http://www.abc.es
Freq: Daily; **Cover Price:** EUR 1.00
Annual Sub.: EUR 310.00; **Circ:** 359,842
Editor: Sergio Guijarro
Profile: Tabloid-sized quality newspaper containing national and international news and articles on the economy, finance, society, culture, opinion and sport.
Language(s): Spanish
Readership: Readership includes leaders in the business and financial sectors, civil servants and office personnel.
ADVERTISING RATES:
Full Page Mono .... EUR 19083.00
Full Page Colour .... EUR 27762.00
Supplement(s): ABC Cultural - 52xY ABC Inmobiliario - 52xY ABC Nuevo Trabajo - 52xY Guía del Motor - 52xY Qué de Qué - 52xY Blanco y Negro - 52xY Blanco y Negro Mujer - 52xY.
NATIONAL DAILY & SUNDAY NEWSPAPERS: National Daily Newspapers

ABOGACIA ESPAÑOLA
754313X44-1

Editorial: Paseo Recoletos 13, E-28004 MADRID
Tel: 91-52 32 593 **Fax:** 91-53 27 836
Email: prensa@cgae.es **Web site:** http://www.cgae.es
Freq: Quarterly; **Cover Price:** Free; **Circ:** 125,000
Editor: Laura Nuño
Profile: Magazine containing information on society and law.
Language(s): Spanish
Readership: Aimed at legal professionals.
BUSINESS: LEGAL

ACCIÓN COOPERATIVA
52268X21A-5

Editorial: Campo de Tajonar s/n, E-31192 TAJONAR (NAVARRA) **Tel:** 94 82 99 400 **Fax:** 94 82 99 420
Email: an@grupoan.com **Web site:** http://www.grupoan.com
Date Established: 1910; **Freq:** 11 issues yearly;
Annual Sub.: EUR 10.00; **Circ:** 140,000
Usual Pagination: 52
Editor: Fernando Beroíz
Profile: Journal about farming and livestock.
Language(s): Spanish
Readership: Aimed at farmers and students.
ADVERTISING RATES:
Full Page Colour .... EUR 750.00
BUSINESS: AGRICULTURE & FARMING

ACTUALIDAD ECONÓMICA
51898X1A-15

Editorial: Paseo de la Castellana 66, 4ª planta, E-28046 MADRID **Tel:** 91 33 73 220 **Fax:** 91 56 28 415
Email: aeconomica@recoletos.es **Web site:** http://www.actualidad-economica.com
Date Established: 1958; **Freq:** Weekly; **Cover Price:** EUR 3.00; **Circ:** 36,013
Features Editor: Tomás Lopéz; **Advertising Director:** Eliseo Soria
Profile: Magazine providing news and background information on national and international finance, economics and business.
Language(s): Spanish
Mechanical Data: Trim Size: 280 x 210mm, Type Area: 252 x 186mm, Col Length: 252mm, Film: Digital only
BUSINESS: FINANCE & ECONOMICS

Spain

AD ARCHITECTURAL DIGEST ESPAÑA
1930402X4A-103
Editorial: Paseo de la Castellana, 9-11, 28046 MADRID **Tel:** 91 700 41 70
Email: epastor@condenast.es **Web site:** www.revistaad.es
Freq: 11 issues yearly; **Annual Sub.:** EUR 24.75; **Circ:** 100,000
Editor: Enric Pastor; **Advertising Director:** Sofia Serrano
Profile: Monthly publication focussing architecture including decoration, interior design and art.
Language(s): Spanish
BUSINESS: ARCHITECTURE & BUILDING: Architecture

EL ADELANTADO DE SEGOVIA
53045X67B-3775
Editorial: Peñalara 3, Polígono Industrial el Cerro, E-40006 SEGOVIA **Tel:** 921 43 72 61 **Fax:** 921 44 24 32
Email: redaccion@eladelantado.com **Web site:** http://www.eladelantado.com
Date Established: 1901; **Freq:** Daily; **Cover Price:** EUR 1.00
Annual Sub.: EUR 300.00; **Circ:** 4,000
Editor: Jesús Martínez Calle; **Advertising Manager:** David Matarrá
Language(s): Spanish
ADVERTISING RATES:
Full Page Mono .... EUR 1585.00
Agency Commission: 10%
Average ad content per issue: 10%
REGIONAL DAILY & SUNDAY NEWSPAPERS: Regional Daily Newspapers

EL ADELANTO DE SALAMANCA
53038X67B-3800
Editorial: Gran Vía 56, E-37001 SALAMANCA
Tel: 902 879 767 **Fax:** 923 28 02 61
Email: eladelanto@elperiodico.com **Web site:** http://www.eladelanto.com
Date Established: 1883; **Freq:** Daily; **Cover Price:** EUR 1.00; **Circ:** 6,866
Editor: Alberto López; **Advertising Director:** Óscar Sánchez
Profile: Regional daily newspaper focussing news and current affairs.
Language(s): Spanish
ADVERTISING RATES:
Full Page Colour .... EUR 1296.00
Mechanical Data: Print Process: Offset rotation, Type Area: 390 x 290mm
REGIONAL DAILY & SUNDAY NEWSPAPERS: Regional Daily Newspapers

AGRONEGOCIOS
52271X21A-43_30
Editorial: Calle Claudio Coello 16, 1° dcha., E-28001 MADRID **Tel:** 91 42 64 430 **Fax:** 91 57 53 297
Email: redaccion@eumedia.es **Web site:** http://www.eumedia.es
Date Established: 1998; **Freq:** 42 issues yearly; **Annual Sub.:** EUR 58.00; **Circ:** 29,000
Usual Pagination: 16
Editor: Luis Mosquera; **Advertising Manager:** Vincente Santiago
Profile: Magazine containing business news for the agricultural sector. Provides information on EU policies, national and global developments, changes in legislation and details of relevant conferences and trade fairs.
Language(s): English; Spanish
Readership: Read by farmers, agricultural cooperatives, trade union members, government officials, manufacturers and distributors of agricultural products.
Agency Commission: 15%
Mechanical Data: Bleed Size: 355 x 256mm, Type Area: 282 x 207mm, Trim Size: 305 x 230mm, Col Length: 282mm, Page Width: 207mm
Copy instructions: *Copy Date:* 1 week prior to publication date
Average ad content per issue: 30%
BUSINESS: AGRICULTURE & FARMING

AIRELIBRE
53879X89A-10
Editorial: Paseo Marqués de Monistrol 7, 2° izda., E-28011 MADRID **Tel:** 91 52 68 080 **Fax:** 91 52 61 012
Email: grupoarthax@airelibre.com **Web site:** http://www.airelibre.com
Freq: Monthly; **Circ:** 900,000
Editor: Mercedes García; **Advertising Manager:** Pilar Fernández
Profile: Magazine about travel, culture and exploration, the environment, sport and outdoor pursuits, adventure travel and rural tourism.
Language(s): Spanish
Readership: Aimed at people who love the outdoor environment, travel and adventure.
CONSUMER: HOLIDAYS & TRAVEL: Travel

ALERTA-EL DIARIO DE CANTABRIA
53042X67B-3825
Formerly: Alerta - El Periódico de Cantábria
Editorial: Calle Primero de Mayo s/n, B° San Martín - Peñacastillo, E-39011 SANTANDER (CANTABRIA)
Tel: 942 32 00 33 **Fax:** 942 32 20 46
Email: administracion@eldiarioalerta.com **Web site:** http://www.eldiarioalerta.com/contacto.php
Freq: Daily; **Cover Price:** EUR 0.75; **Circ:** 26,610
Editor: Gonzalo Romero
Language(s): Spanish
ADVERTISING RATES:
Full Page Colour .... EUR 5300.00
REGIONAL DAILY & SUNDAY NEWSPAPERS: Regional Daily Newspapers

ALTA FIDELIDAD
52544X43B-8
Formerly: Alta Fidelidad en Audio y Vídeo
Editorial: Paseo San Gervasio 16-20, E-08022 BARCELONA **Tel:** 93 25 41 250 **Fax:** 93 25 41 263
Email: altafidelidad@mcediciones.es **Web site:** http://www.mcediciones.net
Date Established: 1990; **Freq:** Monthly; **Annual Sub.:** EUR 40.70; **Circ:** 25,000
Editor: Salvador Dangla
Profile: Magazine covering hi-fi and video. Includes technical and commercial news and information, interviews and product reviews. Also contains articles on electronics, music and accessories.
Language(s): Spanish
Readership: Aimed at retailers, engineers and manufacturers.
BUSINESS: ELECTRICAL RETAIL TRADE: Radio & Hi-Fi

AÑO CERO
53979X94E-10
Editorial: Calle Miguel Yuste 33 bis, E-28037 MADRID **Tel:** 91 32 77 950 **Fax:** 91 32 72 680
Email: ancero@eai.es **Web site:** http://www.eai.es
Freq: Monthly; **Circ:** 105,000
Editor: Paco González; **Advertising Manager:** Ana Barja de Quiroga
Profile: Magazine focusing on new frontiers in science, New Age matters and the paranormal.
Language(s): Spanish
ADVERTISING RATES:
Full Page Colour .... EUR 3500.00
Mechanical Data: Type Area: 285 x 210mm, Col Length: 285mm, Page Width: 210mm, Print Process: Offset
CONSUMER: OTHER CLASSIFICATIONS: Paranormal

ANPE
764843X62A-10
Editorial: Carretas 14, 5° A, E-28012 MADRID
Tel: 91 52 29 056 **Fax:** 91 52 21 237
Email: anpe@anpe.es **Web site:** http://www.anpe.es
Freq: Monthly; **Cover Price:** Free; **Circ:** 50,000
Usual Pagination: 64
Editor: Javier Carrascal
Profile: Educational, informative publication from the official Spanish teacher's union.
Language(s): Spanish
Readership: Aimed at teachers of children in primary and secondary schools.
Mechanical Data: Type Area: 265 x 185mm, Trim Size: 297 x 210mm
BUSINESS: CHURCH & SCHOOL EQUIPMENT & EDUCATION: Education

AR LA REVISTA DE ANA ROSA
754532X74A-5
Editorial: Avda. Cardenal Herrera Oria 3, E-28034 MADRID **Tel:** 91 72 87 000 **Fax:** 91 72 89 314
Email: ar@hachette.es **Web site:** http://www.ar-revista.wanadoo.es
Date Established: 2001; **Freq:** Monthly; **Cover Price:** EUR 2.50
Annual Sub.: EUR 19.20; **Circ:** 196,517
Editor: Cristina Planchuelo; **Advertising Director:** Amparo Bastiz; **Publisher:** Ana Rosa Quintana
Profile: Magazine focusing on fashion, health and lifestyle.
Language(s): Spanish
Readership: Aimed at women of all ages.
CONSUMER: WOMEN'S INTEREST CONSUMER MAGAZINES: Women's Interest

ARDATZA
52307X21J-15
Editorial: Pza. Simón Bolivar 14, 1°, E-01003 VITORIA **Tel:** 94 52 75 477 **Fax:** 94 52 75 731
Email: ehne@ehne.org **Web site:** http://www.ehne.org
Freq: 24 issues yearly; **Annual Sub.:** EUR 32.00; **Circ:** 23,350
Usual Pagination: 24
Editor: Xavier Elias; **Advertising Manager:** Josu Arregi
Profile: Guide to technology, management ideas, new crop varieties, innovations, new products and marketing information for the rural sector.
Language(s): Basque; Spanish
Agency Commission: 10%
Average ad content per issue: 25%
BUSINESS: AGRICULTURE & FARMING: Agriculture & Farming - Regional

ARMAS Y MUNICIONES
52485X40-20
Editorial: Los Nardos 2, San Lorenzo, E-28200 DEL EL ESCORIAL (MADRID) **Tel:** 91 89 02 290
Fax: 91 89 07 762
Email: valmayor@valmayor.net
Freq: Monthly; **Cover Price:** EUR 4.30; **Circ:** 24,000
Editor: Saúl Braceras
Profile: Magazine containing technical articles and information concerning weapons and ammunition. Provides analysis, reports and news, details of technological developments within the sector, interviews and features on military training.
Language(s): Spanish
Readership: Aimed at manufacturers and retailers of weapons and ammunition, members of military organisations and government officials.
BUSINESS: DEFENCE

ARQUITECTOS
51985X4A-10
Editorial: Paseo de la Castellana 12, E-28046 MADRID **Tel:** 91 43 52 200 **Fax:** 91 57 53 839
Email: revista@arquinex.es **Web site:** http://www.cscae.com
Date Established: 1975; **Freq:** Quarterly; **Cover Price:** Free; **Circ:** 42,880
Profile: Publication of the Spanish College of Architecture.
Language(s): Spanish
Agency Commission: 10%
Mechanical Data: Trim Size: 297 x 225mm
Average ad content per issue: 20%
BUSINESS: ARCHITECTURE & BUILDING: Architecture

ARROBA
52062X5E-5
Editorial: Avenida Meridiana 350, Planta 12 C, E-08027 BARCELONA **Tel:** 93 27 44 739
Fax: 95 23 64 101
Email: arroba2@megamultimedia.com **Web site:** http://www.megamultimedia.com/arroba
ISSN: 1138-1655
Freq: Monthly; **Annual Sub.:** EUR 4.95; **Circ:** 30,000
Editor: Gaby López
Profile: Internet and CD-ROM magazine.
Language(s): Spanish
Readership: Aimed at internet users.
Mechanical Data: Type Area: 297 x 210mm, Col Length: 297mm, Page Width: 210mm, Print Process: Offset. Rotative
BUSINESS: COMPUTERS & AUTOMATION: Data Transmission

AS
52928X65A-20
Editorial: Calle Albasanz 14, 4ª planta, E-28037 MADRID **Tel:** 91 37 52 500 **Fax:** 91 37 52 558
Email: diarioas@diarioas.es **Web site:** http://www.as.com
Date Established: 1967; **Freq:** Daily; **Cover Price:** EUR 0.90; **Circ:** 307,151
Editor: Tomás Roncero
Profile: Tabloid-sized newspaper concerning competitive sport, including results and interviews with sporting personalities.
Language(s): Spanish
Readership: Read by people with an interest in sport.
NATIONAL DAILY & SUNDAY NEWSPAPERS: National Daily Newspapers

ATLÁNTICO DIARIO
53059X67B-3875
Editorial: Avenida Camelias 102-104 bajo, E-36211 VIGO (PONTEVEDRA) **Tel:** 986 20 86 86
Fax: 986 20 12 69
Email: atlantico@atlantico.net **Web site:** http://www.atlantico.net
Freq: Daily; **Cover Price:** EUR 1.00
Annual Sub.: EUR 313.90; **Circ:** 5,359
Editor: José Luis Outeiriño Rodríguez
Profile: Regional daily newspaper focussing on news and current affairs.
Language(s): Spanish
ADVERTISING RATES:
Full Page Colour .... EUR 2895.50
REGIONAL DAILY & SUNDAY NEWSPAPERS: Regional Daily Newspapers

ATLETISMO ESPAÑOL
53546X75J-20
Editorial: Avenida de Valladolid 81, 1°, E-28008 MADRID **Tel:** 91 54 82 423 **Fax:** 91 54 76 113
Email: publicaciones@rfea.es **Web site:** http://www.sportec.es
Date Established: 1951; **Freq:** 11 issues yearly; **Cover Price:** EUR 4.40; **Circ:** 165,000
Usual Pagination: 64
Editor: Gerardo Cebrián
Profile: Publication of the Royal Spanish Federation of Athletics.
Language(s): Spanish
Readership: Aimed at all those interested in athletics.
ADVERTISING RATES:
Full Page Mono .... EUR 660.00
Full Page Colour .... EUR 1045.00
Agency Commission: 10%
Mechanical Data: No. of Columns (Display): 4, Screen: 70 lpc, Trim Size: 210x285mm
Copy instructions: *Copy Date:* 15th of month prior to publication date
Average ad content per issue: 20%
CONSUMER: SPORT: Athletics

AUSBANC
51934X1C-2
Editorial: Calle Alta Mirano 33, E-28008 MADRID
Tel: 91 54 16 161 **Fax:** 91 54 17 260
Email: ausbanc@ausbanc.com **Web site:** http://www.ausbanc.com
Freq: Monthly; **Cover Price:** EUR 2.50
Annual Sub.: EUR 75.00; **Circ:** 23,559
Editor: Juan José González; **Advertising Manager:** Isabel Medrano
Profile: Financial magazine of the Association of Users of Bank Services. Aiming to defend legitimate rights and interests of users of banking entities or any other type of financial services.
Language(s): Spanish
Readership: Aimed at businessmen and people in the financial sector.
ADVERTISING RATES:
Full Page Colour .... EUR 3500.00
BUSINESS: FINANCE & ECONOMICS: Banking

AUTO MAX
624874X77A-75
Editorial: Calle Duende 4, E-18214 NIVAR-GRANADA **Tel:** 902 10 36 63 **Fax:** 958 42 91 02
Email: info@auto-max.net **Web site:** http://www.auto-max.net
ISSN: 1139-2150
Date Established: 1996; **Freq:** Monthly; **Cover Price:** EUR 4.50
Annual Sub.: EUR 32.00; **Circ:** 150,000
Usual Pagination: 196
Editor: Celia Silva
Profile: Magazine covering all aspects of auto tuning, including road tests, new products and maintenance.
Language(s): Spanish
Readership: Aimed at motoring enthusiasts.
Agency Commission: 20%
Average ad content per issue: 40%
CONSUMER: MOTORING & CYCLING: Motoring

AUTO VÍA
52398X31A-48
Editorial: Calle Ancora 40, E-28045 MADRID
Tel: 91 34 70 100 **Fax:** 91 34 70 135
Email: autovia@mpib.es **Web site:** http://www.motorpress-iberica.com
Date Established: 2000; **Freq:** Monthly; **Cover Price:** EUR 1.00; **Circ:** 73,917
Editor: David Ayala
Profile: Magazine covering all aspects of the motor trade.
Language(s): Spanish
Readership: Aimed at car dealers, mechanics and manufacturers.
ADVERTISING RATES:
Full Page Colour .... EUR 5200.00
Mechanical Data: Bleed Size: 301 x 230mm
BUSINESS: MOTOR TRADE: Motor Trade Accessories

AUTOCEA
52399X31A-49
Editorial: Calle Almagro 31, E-28010 MADRID
Tel: 91 55 76 800 **Fax:** 91 55 76 835
Email: comunicacion@cea-online.es **Web site:** http://www.cea-online.es
Date Established: 1966; **Freq:** 11 issues yearly; **Cover Price:** Free; **Circ:** 80,000
Editor: Nuria Alonso Martínez-Losa
Profile: Magazine covering all aspects of the motor trade, including articles concerning tourism.
Language(s): Spanish
Readership: Distributed free to members of the CEA (the European Automobile Commission).
Agency Commission: 10%
Average ad content per issue: 25%
BUSINESS: MOTOR TRADE: Motor Trade Accessories

AUTOCLUB
53674X77E-20
Editorial: Calle Isaac Newton 4, E-28760 TRES CANTOS (MADRID) **Tel:** 91 59 47 400
Fax: 91 59 47 514
Email: prensa@race.es **Web site:** http://www.fia.com/tourisme/infoclub/race.htm
Freq: 6 issues yearly; **Circ:** 250,000
Editor: Diego de Azua
Profile: Magazine of the Royal Automobile Club of Spain.
Language(s): Spanish
Readership: Distributed free to all members.
Agency Commission: 10%
CONSUMER: MOTORING & CYCLING: Club Cars

LA AVENTURA DE LA HISTORIA
53996X94X-78
Editorial: Calle Javier Ferrero 9, E-28002 MADRID
Tel: 91 58 64 363 **Fax:** 91 58 64 314
Email: historia@ladh.com **Web site:** http://www.elmundo.es/ladh
Date Established: 1972; **Freq:** Monthly; **Cover Price:** EUR 3.60
Annual Sub.: EUR 34.56; **Circ:** 100,000
Editor: Asuncion Domenech; **Advertising Manager:** Pilar Torija; **Publisher:** Javier Villalba
Profile: Magazine containing articles and information concerning history throughout the world, but in particular focusing on Spain.
Language(s): Spanish
Readership: Aimed at those interested in history.
ADVERTISING RATES:
Full Page Mono .... EUR 6600.00
Full Page Colour .... EUR 7750.00
Mechanical Data: Print Process: Rotative, 4 colours
Copy instructions: *Copy Date:* Reservation until 20 days before publishing date; Advertisements accepted until 15 days before publishing date
CONSUMER: OTHER CLASSIFICATIONS: Miscellaneous

AVIÓN REVUE
52074X6A-15
Editorial: Calle Ancora 40, E-28045 MADRID
Tel: 91 34 70 100 **Fax:** 91 34 70 135

Email: avionrevue@mpib.es **Web site:** http://www.motorpress-iberica.es
Freq: Monthly; **Cover Price:** EUR 3.00; **Circ:** 27,750
Editor: Luis Calvo; **Publisher:** Esther Apesteguía
Profile: Journal about all aspects of professional aviation.
Language(s): Spanish
ADVERTISING RATES:
Full Page Colour .... EUR 3235.00
BUSINESS: AVIATION & AERONAUTICS

AVUI+ 52984X67B-3900
Formerly: Avui
Editorial: Enric Granados, 84, entresòl, E-08008 BARCELONA **Tel:** 93 31 63 900 **Fax:** 93 31 63 936
Email: avuicat@avui.cat **Web site:** http://www.avui.cat
Freq: Daily; **Cover Price:** EUR 1.00; **Circ:** 45,500
Editor: Albert Saez
Profile: Regional daily newspaper focussing on news and current affairs.
Language(s): Catalan
REGIONAL DAILY & SUNDAY NEWSPAPERS: Regional Daily Newspapers

BARCELONA DIVINA 53897X89C-15
Editorial: Calle Francisco Perez Cabrero 11 B, entresuelo 8°, E-08021 BARCELONA
Tel: 93 36 20 580 **Fax:** 93 36 20 581
Email: revistas@lugaresdivinos.com **Web site:** http://www.lugaresdivinos.com
Freq: Half-yearly - Published in May and November; **Cover Price:** EUR 3.00; **Circ:** 120,000
Editor: José Alarcón; **Advertising Manager:** Daniela Tonello
Profile: Guide to events and entertainment in Barcelona for Spring, Summer, Autumn and Winter.
Language(s): Spanish
Readership: Aimed at tourists and those living in Barcelona.
ADVERTISING RATES:
Full Page Colour .... EUR 3650.00
Agency Commission: 10%
Mechanical Data: Col Length: 300mm, Page Width: 230mm, Bleed Size: +3mm, Type Area: 300 x 230mm
Average ad content per issue: 60%
CONSUMER: HOLIDAYS & TRAVEL: Entertainment Guides

BRAVO 53456X74F-10
Editorial: Jacometrezo 15, 3ª planta, E-28013 MADRID **Tel:** 91 54 76 800 **Fax:** 91 55 90 818
Email: bravo@bauer.es **Web site:** http://www.bravoporti.com
ISSN: 1136-1239
Freq: 26 issues yearly; **Cover Price:** EUR 1.80; **Circ:** 230,590
Editor: Cristina Noe
Profile: Magazine containing general interest articles and features on music and films.
Language(s): Spanish
Readership: Aimed at teenagers.
CONSUMER: WOMEN'S INTEREST CONSUMER MAGAZINES: Teenage

BUTLLETI DE LA CAMBRA 52887X63-30
Editorial: Avda. Diagonal 452, E-08006 BARCELONA
Tel: 93 41 69 382 **Fax:** 93 41 69 396
Email: prensa@mail.cambrabcn.es **Web site:** http://www.cambrabcn.es
Freq: Quarterly; **Cover Price:** Free; **Circ:** 25,000
Usual Pagination: 16
Editor: Marta Rosés
Profile: Bulletin of the Chamber of Commerce, Industry and Navigation of Barcelona.
Language(s): Catalan; Spanish
Readership: Read by members of the local business community.
BUSINESS: REGIONAL BUSINESS

BYTE 754289X5A-15
Editorial: Avda. Generalisimo 14, 2° B, E-28660 BOADILLA DEL MONTE (MADRID) **Tel:** 91-63 23 827
Fax: 91-63 32 564
Email: byte@mkm-pi.com
Freq: Monthly; **Circ:** 25,000
Editor: Juan Manuel Sáez
Profile: Magazine focusing on IT and telecommunications.
Language(s): Spanish
Readership: Aimed at managers and professionals.
BUSINESS: COMPUTERS & AUTOMATION: Automation & Instrumentation

CALLE 20 1752944X91E-2
Editorial: Plaza Callao 4, 2ª planta, Palacio de la Prensa, E-28013 MADRID **Tel:** 91 70 15 600
Fax: 91 70 15 660
Email: redaccion@calle20.es **Web site:** http://calle20.20minutos.es
Freq: Monthly; **Cover Price:** Free; **Circ:** 150,000
Editor: Peio Hernández Riaño
Profile: Magazine focusing on culture, social and leisure information.
Language(s): Spanish
CONSUMER: RECREATION & LEISURE: Lifestyle

CAMP VALENCIA 52309X21J-20
Editorial: Calle Marques de 2 aguas, E-46002 VALENCIA **Tel:** 96 35 30 036 **Fax:** 96 35 30 018
Email: cparrado@launio.org
Date Established: 1977; **Freq:** Monthly; **Circ:** 30,000
Usual Pagination: 32
Editor: Llucia Labiós
Profile: Journal about farming and livestock.
Language(s): Spanish
Readership: Read by members of the farming community in Valencia.
Agency Commission: 10%
Copy instructions: *Copy Date:* 10th of the month prior to publication date
Average ad content per issue: 30%
BUSINESS: AGRICULTURE & FARMING: Agriculture & Farming - Regional

CANAL OCIO 712967X78B-131
Formerly: Ovidio
Editorial: José Abascal, 56, 7ª plta., E-28003 MADRID **Tel:** 91 45 64 711 **Fax:** 91 45 64 696
Email: tallerdeeditores@tallerdeeditores.com **Web site:** http://www.tallerdeeditores.com
Freq: Monthly; **Circ:** 120,000
Editor: Josè Maria Lacalle; **Advertising Director:** Alejandro Caballero
Profile: Magazine containing information about the latest in DVDs, videos and video games.
Language(s): Spanish
ADVERTISING RATES:
Full Page Colour .... EUR 1600.00
CONSUMER: CONSUMER ELECTRONICS: Video & DVD

CANARIAS 7 53072X67B-3975
Editorial: Urbanización El Sebadal, Calle Profesor Lozano 7, E-35008 LAS PALMAS DE GRAN CANARIA **Tel:** 928 30 13 00 **Fax:** 928 30 13 33
Email: redaccion@canarias7.es **Web site:** http://www.canarias7.es
Date Established: 1982; **Freq:** Daily; **Cover Price:** EUR 1.00
Annual Sub.: EUR 475.00; **Circ:** 30,152
Editor: Angeles Arencibia
Language(s): Spanish
ADVERTISING RATES:
Full Page Colour .... EUR 3352.00
REGIONAL DAILY & SUNDAY NEWSPAPERS: Regional Daily Newspapers

CAPITAL 764761X1A-46
Editorial: Calle Consuegra, 7 - 2da Planta, E-28036 MADRID **Tel:** 91 38 32 476 **Fax:** 91 38 32 571
Email: consuelo.calle@capital.es **Web site:** http://www.capitalrevista.es
Freq: 10 issues yearly; **Annual Sub.:** EUR 33.60; **Circ:** 88,151
Advertising Manager: Leticia Cebrián; **Advertising Director:** Elena Sánchez Fabrés
Profile: Financial magazine providing current economic analysis..
Language(s): Spanish
ADVERTISING RATES:
Full Page Colour .... EUR 6500.00
Mechanical Data: Type Area: 270 x 213mm, Print Process: Offset, Screen: 60 lpc
BUSINESS: FINANCE & ECONOMICS

CASA AL DIA 763957X74C-2_50
Editorial: López de Hoyos 141, E-28002 MADRID
Tel: 91 51 06 600 **Fax:** 91 51 94 813
Email: casa-al-dia@rba.es **Web site:** http://www.rba.es
Freq: 11 issues yearly; **Cover Price:** EUR 1.80; **Circ:** 166,267
Editor: Victoria Gómez; **Advertising Director:** Marta Blanco
Profile: Magazine focusing on home improvement and interior decoration.
Language(s): Spanish
Readership: Aimed at affluent people wishing to improve their living environment.
CONSUMER: WOMEN'S INTEREST CONSUMER MAGAZINES: Home & Family

CASA Y JARDÍN 53967X93-35
Formerly: Jardinería Casa Jardín
Editorial: Calle Ferraz 11, 1° izda., E-28008 MADRID
Tel: 91 54 01 880 **Fax:** 91 54 15 055
Email: grupocasa@edijardin.com **Web site:** http://www.edijardin.com
Date Established: 1977; **Freq:** 11 issues yearly; **Cover Price:** EUR 1.80
Annual Sub.: 29; **Circ:** 123,000
Usual Pagination: 260
Editor: Mariano Alonso Sánchez
Profile: Magazine concerning home decoration and gardening. Includes reports, advice and information on products, plant-care, garden design and methods.
Language(s): Spanish
Readership: Aimed at amateur gardeners and house owners.
CONSUMER: GARDENING

CASA DIEZ 53418X74C-4
Editorial: C/Santa Engracia, 23, 28010 MADRID
Tel: 91 7287000 **Fax:** 91 7289308
Email: therrero@hearst.es **Web site:** http://www.casadiez.elle.es
Date Established: 1997; **Freq:** Monthly; **Circ:** 126,834
Advertising Director: María Luisa Ruiz de Velasco
Profile: Magazine about interior design, home furnishings and decoration. Read mainly by women.
Language(s): Spanish
Readership: Read mainly by women.
ADVERTISING RATES:
Full Page Colour .... EUR 10350
Mechanical Data: Type Area: 268 x 200mm, Bleed Size: 297 x 228mm, Col Length: 280mm, Page Width: 200mm
CONSUMER: WOMEN'S INTEREST CONSUMER MAGAZINES: Home & Family

CASA MODA 52346X23A-4
Editorial: Calle Abtao 11, 2° C, E-28007 MADRID
Tel: 91 55 19 197 **Fax:** 91 50 12 388
Email: anfer@teleline.es
ISSN: 1133-6471
Freq: Half-yearly; **Circ:** 80,000
Editor: Ana García Herrera
Profile: Magazine containing information concerning the furniture trade in Spain.
Language(s): Spanish
Readership: Aimed at interior designers, manufacturers and DIY enthusiasts.
BUSINESS: FURNISHINGS & FURNITURE

CESVIMAP 52402X31A-65
Editorial: Ctra. Ávila a Valladolid, Km. 1, E-05004 ÁVILA **Tel:** 920 20 63 00 **Fax:** 920 20 63 19
Email: cesvimap@cesvimap.com **Web site:** http://www.revistacesvimap.com
ISSN: 1132-7103
Date Established: 1992; **Freq:** Quarterly; **Cover Price:** Free; **Circ:** 25,000
Usual Pagination: 66
Editor: Teresa Majeroni
Profile: Journal about the care and repair of vehicle bodywork and paint.
Language(s): Spanish
BUSINESS: MOTOR TRADE: Motor Trade Accessories

CINCO DÍAS 52929X65A-25
Editorial: Gran Vía 32, 2ª planta, E-28013 MADRID
Tel: 91 53 86 100 **Fax:** 91 52 31 128
Email: redaccion@cincodias.es **Web site:** http://www.cincodias.es
Freq: Daily; **Cover Price:** EUR 1.30; **Circ:** 46,252
Editor: Begona Barba
Profile: Tabloid-sized newspaper focusing on financial and business news and related issues.
Language(s): Spanish
Readership: Read by financial directors, senior executives and civil servants.
ADVERTISING RATES:
Full Page Mono .... EUR 6580.00
Full Page Colour .... EUR 8590.00
NATIONAL DAILY & SUNDAY NEWSPAPERS: National Daily Newspapers

CINEMANÍA 53582X76A-10
Editorial: Julián Camarillo, 29B - 1ª planta, E-28037 MADRID **Tel:** 91 53 86 104 **Fax:** 91 53 86 117
Email: cinemania@progresa.es **Web site:** http://www.progresa.es
Date Established: 1995; **Freq:** Monthly; **Cover Price:** EUR 2.70
Annual Sub.: EUR 30.00; **Circ:** 125,000
Editor: Javier Ocaña
Profile: Magazine focusing on films and the cinema. Features reviews of new releases, actor profiles and interviews and behind-the-scenes news.
Language(s): Spanish
Readership: Aimed at the general public.
ADVERTISING RATES:
Full Page Colour .... EUR 8700.00
Agency Commission: 10%
Mechanical Data: Type Area: 284 x 237mm, Col Length: 284mm, Page Width: 237mm
Copy instructions: *Copy Date:* 13th of the month prior to publication date
CONSUMER: MUSIC & PERFORMING ARTS: Cinema

CINERAMA 53585X76A-42
Editorial: Londres 38, E-28028 MADRID
Tel: 91 42 63 880 **Fax:** 91 72 57 735
Email: info@cinerama.es **Web site:** http://www.cinerama.es
Freq: Monthly; **Cover Price:** Free; **Circ:** 291,478
Editor: Alfonso Asúa
Profile: Magazine providing news and reviews of cinema releases in Spain.
Language(s): Spanish
Readership: Aimed at cinema enthusiasts of all ages.
ADVERTISING RATES:
Full Page Colour .... EUR 11000.00
Agency Commission: 10%
Mechanical Data: Bleed Size: +3mm, Trim Size: 297 x 210mm
Copy instructions: *Copy Date:* 15 days prior to publication date
Average ad content per issue: 18%
CONSUMER: MUSIC & PERFORMING ARTS: Cinema

CIUDAD DE ALCOY 52976X67B-4000
Editorial: Avenida Puente San Jorge 8 y 10, entreplanta, E-03803 ALCOY **Tel:** 966 52 15 48
Fax: 966 51 15 51
Email: ciudaddealcoy@elperiodico.com **Web site:** http://www.ciudaddealcoy.com
Freq: Daily - Published daily except Wednesday and Friday; **Cover Price:** EUR 1.00; **Circ:** 5,200
Language(s): Spanish
Readership: Regional daily newspaper focussing on news and current affairs.
ADVERTISING RATES:
Full Page Mono .... EUR 925.00
Full Page Colour .... EUR 1238.00
REGIONAL DAILY & SUNDAY NEWSPAPERS: Regional Daily Newspapers

CLARA 53393X74A-15
Editorial: Muntaner 40-42, E-08011 BARCELONA
Tel: 93 50 87 000 **Fax:** 93 45 48 071
Email: clara@hymsa.com **Web site:** http://www.hymsa.com
Date Established: 1992; **Freq:** Monthly; **Cover Price:** EUR 1.80
Annual Sub.: EUR 21.90; **Circ:** 285,133
Usual Pagination: 164
Editor: Aurora Gonzalo
Profile: Women's magazine covering fashion, beauty, cookery and family life.
Language(s): Spanish
Readership: Read mainly by women.
CONSUMER: WOMEN'S INTEREST CONSUMER MAGAZINES: Women's Interest

CLAXON GARRAF PENEDES 53901X72-804
Editorial: Rambla Samá 39, 2ª planta, local 8, E-08800 VILANOVA Y LA GELTRU (BARCELONA)
Tel: 93 81 41 017 **Fax:** 93 81 40 892
Email: publiclaxon@segundamano.es **Web site:** http://www.segundamano.es
Freq: Weekly; **Cover Price:** Free; **Circ:** 25,500
Usual Pagination: 32
Editor: Josep Ribas
Profile: Newspaper containing local news and information for the towns of Vilanova, Vilafranca, Cubelles, Sitges, Sant Pere de Ribas and Roquetes in Catalonia; includes entertainment, sport and culture.
Language(s): Catalan; Spanish
Mechanical Data: Type Area: 410 x 290mm, Col Length: 410mm, Page Width: 290mm
LOCAL NEWSPAPERS

CLAXON MANRESA 53903X72-805
Editorial: Casanova 4, 1° 2ª, E-08240 MANRESA
Tel: 93 87 24 410 **Fax:** 93 87 27 705
Email: encarnaavila@segundamano.es **Web site:** http://www.segundamano.es
Freq: 25 issues yearly; **Circ:** 40,000
Editor: Josep Ribas
Profile: Newspaper containing local news and information for the towns of Sant Joan de Vilatorrada, Sant Vicent de Castellet, Sant Fruitós del Bages and Sant Pedor i Navarcles in Catalonia; includes entertainment, sport and culture.
Language(s): Catalan
LOCAL NEWSPAPERS

CLAXON TARRAGONA 53904X72-803
Editorial: Comercio 5, E-43004 TARRAGONA
Tel: 977 23 85 11 **Fax:** 977 21 41 54
Email: tarragonaredaccio@segundamano.es **Web site:** http://www.segundamano.es
Date Established: 1969; **Freq:** Weekly - Published on Tuesday; **Circ:** 50,000
Editor: Alfonso Schwartz
Profile: Newspaper covering local news and information for Tarragona and surroundings; includes entertainment, sport and culture.
Language(s): Catalan; Spanish
LOCAL NEWSPAPERS

COCINA FÁCIL 53484X74P-60
Editorial: Muntaner 40-42, E-08011 BARCELONA
Tel: 93 50 87 000 **Fax:** 93 45 45 949
Email: cocina_facil@hymsa.com **Web site:** http://www.cocinafacil.com
Date Established: 1996; **Freq:** 11 issues yearly - Double issue in July/August; **Cover Price:** EUR 1.20
Annual Sub.: EUR 11.00; **Circ:** 142,589
Usual Pagination: 68
Editor: Julia Blázquez
Profile: Magazine covering all aspects of modern cookery, including recipes. Contains tips about easy and practical solutions.
Language(s): Spanish
Readership: Aimed at people who enjoy cooking.
CONSUMER: WOMEN'S INTEREST CONSUMER MAGAZINES: Food & Cookery

LA COMARCA D'OLOT 763793X72-30
Editorial: Plaça del Mig 2, local 406, E-17800 OLOT
Tel: 972 26 74 67 **Fax:** 972 26 36 05
Email: la-comarca@la-comarca.com **Web site:** http://www.la-comarca.net
Freq: Weekly - Published on Thursday; **Cover Price:** EUR 1.60
Annual Sub.: EUR 80.00; **Circ:** 3,800

Spain

Editor: Josep Murlá; **Advertising Director:** Cristina Valeri
Language(s): Catalan
ADVERTISING RATES:
Full Page Colour .... EUR 278.00
LOCAL NEWSPAPERS

COMER BIEN 53486X74P-180
Formerly: Comer Cada Día
Editorial: Muntaner 40-42, E-08011 BARCELONA
Tel: 93 50 87 000 **Fax:** 93 45 45 949
Email: comer_cada_dia@hymsa.com **Web site:** http://www.comerbien.com
Date Established: 1994; **Freq:** Monthly; **Cover Price:** EUR 2.05
Annual Sub.: EUR 20.60; **Circ:** 119,533
Usual Pagination: 132
Editor: Julia Blázquez
Profile: Cookery magazine containing recipes for the modern kitchen.
Language(s): Spanish
Readership: Aimed at people with an interest in cookery.
CONSUMER: WOMEN'S INTEREST CONSUMER MAGAZINES: Food & Cookery

EL COMERCIO 53008X67B-4025
Editorial: Calle del Diario El Comercio 1, E-33207 GIJÓN (ASTURIAS) **Tel:** 98 51 79 800
Fax: 98 53 40 955
Email: elcomercio@elcomercio-sa.es **Web site:** http://www.elcomerciodigital.com
Date Established: 1878; **Freq:** Daily; **Cover Price:** EUR 00.95; **Circ:** 40,000
Editor: Rubén Espiniella
Profile: Regional daily newspaper focussing on news and current affairs.
Language(s): Spanish
ADVERTISING RATES:
Full Page Colour .... EUR 2660.00
REGIONAL DAILY & SUNDAY NEWSPAPERS: Regional Daily Newspapers

COMPARTIR 52705X56A-275
Editorial: Avda. Josep Tarradellas 123-127, 4° planta, E-08029 BARCELONA **Tel:** 93 49 54 490
Fax: 93 49 54 492
Email: fundacionespriu@fundacionespriu.coop **Web site:** http://www.fundacionespriu.coop/aci/index.php?mq==
Date Established: 1991; **Freq:** Quarterly; **Cover Price:** Free; **Circ:** 35,000
Editor: Carles Torner Pifarré
Profile: International magazine about health co-operatives, the co-operative movement and medicine.
Language(s): Catalan; Spanish
Readership: Aimed at doctors.
Mechanical Data: Trim Size: 296 x 210mm, Screen: 60 lpc, Print Process: Offset
Copy instructions: *Copy Date:* 30 days prior to publication date
BUSINESS: HEALTH & MEDICAL

COMPRARCASA 754557X74K-100
Editorial: Retama 3, Edif. Ejesur, E-28045 MADRID
Tel: 90 24 04 151 **Fax:** 91 14 10 281
Email: publicaciones@comprarcasa.com **Web site:** http://www.comprarcasa.com
Date Established: 2000; **Freq:** Monthly; **Cover Price:** Free; **Circ:** 3,500,000
Usual Pagination: 24
Editor: Manuel Albiñana Rodríguez
Profile: Magazine focusing on moving house.
Language(s): Spanish
CONSUMER: WOMEN'S INTEREST CONSUMER MAGAZINES: Home Purchase

COMPUTER HOY 52048X78D-35_50
Formerly: Computer Hoy Juegos
Editorial: Los Vascos 17, E-28040 MADRID
Tel: 91 39 96 600 **Fax:** 91 39 96 930
Email: computerhoy@axelspringer.es **Web site:** http://www.axelspringer.es
Date Established: 1998; **Freq:** Monthly; **Annual Sub.:** EUR 39.50; **Circ:** 190,940
Editor: Andrés Purriños; **Advertising Director:** Elena Cabrera
Profile: Magazine providing news and information on computer and video games.
Language(s): Spanish
ADVERTISING RATES:
Full Page Colour .... EUR 7200.00
CONSUMER: CONSUMER ELECTRONICS: Games

COMPUTER MUSIC 761792X5D-25
Editorial: Calle Valportillo Primera No 11, E-28108 ALCOBENDAS (MADRID) **Tel:** 91 66 22 137
Fax: 91 66 14 754
Email: jaalvarez@grupov.es **Web site:** http://www.grupov.es
Freq: Monthly; **Cover Price:** EUR 5.95; **Circ:** 40,000
Advertising Manager: José María Seguido
Profile: Magazine covering all aspects of how to make music with a computer. Covers news, reviews and tutorials.
Language(s): Spanish
Readership: Aimed at people interested in making music using the latest technology.

ADVERTISING RATES:
Full Page Colour .... EUR 2115.00
Agency Commission: 10%
Mechanical Data: Print Process: Offset, Bleed Size: 279 x 230mm, Type Area: 259 x 210mm, Col Length: 259mm
Average ad content per issue: 20%
BUSINESS: COMPUTERS & AUTOMATION: Personal Computers

CONNECT 766489X18B-103
Editorial: Calle Ancora 40, E-28045 MADRID
Tel: 91 34 70 100 **Fax:** 91 347 02 36
Email: connect@mpib.es **Web site:** http://www.mpib.es
Freq: Monthly; **Cover Price:** EUR 3.00; **Circ:** 30,000
Editor: Miguel Ángel Muñoz
Profile: Magazine containing information about mobile communication includes telephones, palm-top computers and mobile technology software.
Language(s): Spanish
BUSINESS: ELECTRONICS: Telecommunications

CONSEJOS DE TU FARMACÉUTICO 53465X74G-8
Editorial: Beatriz de Suabia 57, E-41005 SEVILLA
Tel: 95 45 70 149 **Fax:** 95 49 80 185
Email: paula.rivero@consejos-e.com **Web site:** http://www.consejos-e.com
Freq: 11 issues yearly; **Circ:** 275,000
Editor: Paula Rivero
Profile: Magazine providing information and advice concerning health and medical issues. Distributed free in chemist shops throughout Spain.
Language(s): Spanish
Readership: Aimed at people interested in maintaining a healthy and balanced lifestyle.
Agency Commission: 10%
Average ad content per issue: 33%
CONSUMER: WOMEN'S INTEREST CONSUMER MAGAZINES: Slimming & Health

CONTIGO 712855X82-20
Editorial: Pujades 77-79, E-08005 BARCELONA
Tel: 93 30 01 101 **Fax:** 93 30 96 868
Email: medios@intervida.org **Web site:** http://www.intervida.org
Date Established: 1996; **Freq:** 3 issues yearly; **Cover Price:** Free; **Circ:** 275,000
Usual Pagination: 52
Editor: Marta Sol
Profile: Magazine focusing on social and economic development in third world countries.
Language(s): Spanish
CONSUMER: CURRENT AFFAIRS & POLITICS

CÓRDOBA 53004X67B-4050
Editorial: Ingeniero Juan de la Cierva 18, Polígono Industrial La Torrecilla, E-14013 CÓRDOBA
Tel: 957 42 03 02 **Fax:** 957 20 46 48
Email: cordoba2@elperiodico.es **Web site:** http://www.diariocordoba.com
Date Established: 1941; **Freq:** Daily; **Cover Price:** EUR 0.90; **Circ:** 17,294
Editor: José Murillo; **Advertising Manager:** María Jesús Querol
Profile: Regional daily newspaper focussing on news and current affairs.
Language(s): Spanish
ADVERTISING RATES:
Full Page Mono .... EUR 2860.00
Full Page Colour .... EUR 3718.00
Agency Commission: 10%
REGIONAL DAILY & SUNDAY NEWSPAPERS: Regional Daily Newspapers

EL CORREO 52988X67B-4100
Editorial: Pintor Losada 7, E-48004 BILBAO (VIZCAYA) **Tel:** 94 48 70 100 **Fax:** 94 48 70 111
Email: redaccion@diario-elcorreo.es **Web site:** http://www.diario-elcorreo.es
Date Established: 1910; **Freq:** Daily; **Cover Price:** EUR 0.95; **Circ:** 144,892
Features Editor: Javier Trigueros; **Advertising Manager:** Julio López
Language(s): Spanish
ADVERTISING RATES:
Full Page Mono .... EUR 4919.03
Full Page Colour .... EUR 7378.50
Mechanical Data: Type Area: 366 x 255mm, Col Length: 366mm, Page Width: 255mm
REGIONAL DAILY & SUNDAY NEWSPAPERS: Regional Daily Newspapers

EL CORREO DE ANDALUCÍA 53047X67B-4075
Editorial: Americo Vespucio 39, E-41092 ISLA DE LA CARTUCA (SEVILLA) **Tel:** 95 448 8500
Fax: 95 446 2881
Email: redaccion@correoandalucia.es **Web site:** http://www.correoandalucia.es
Freq: Daily; **Cover Price:** EUR 0.90; **Circ:** 20,774
Editor: Francisca Godoy
Profile: Regional daily newspaper focussing on news and current affairs.
Language(s): Spanish

ADVERTISING RATES:
Full Page Colour .... EUR 2650.00
REGIONAL DAILY & SUNDAY NEWSPAPERS: Regional Daily Newspapers

EL CORREO DE BURGOS 763505X67B-4085
Editorial: Plaza de Aragón, 5 bajo, E-09001 BURGOS
Tel: 947 10 10 00 **Fax:** 947 25 78 51
Email: info@ecb-elmundo.com **Web site:** http://www.elcorreodeburgos.com
Freq: Daily; **Cover Price:** EUR 1.00
Annual Sub.: EUR 290.81; **Circ:** 7,000
Editor: Ricardo Garcia Ureta; **Advertising Manager:** Yolanda Laglera
Profile: Regional daily newspaper focussing on news and current affairs.
Language(s): Spanish
ADVERTISING RATES:
Full Page Mono .... EUR 1202.00
Full Page Colour .... EUR 1562.60
REGIONAL DAILY & SUNDAY NEWSPAPERS: Regional Daily Newspapers

EL CORREO GALLEGO 53044X67B-4125
Editorial: Preguntoiro 29, E-15704 SANTIAGO DE COMPOSTELA (LA CORUÑA) **Tel:** 981 54 37 00
Fax: 981 56 23 96
Email: info@elcorreogallego.es **Web site:** http://www.elcorreogallego.es
ISSN: 1579-1572
Date Established: 1878; **Freq:** Daily; **Cover Price:** EUR 1.00; **Circ:** 20,000
Editor: Demetrio Peláez
Profile: Regional daily newspaper focussing on news and current affairs.
Language(s): Spanish
ADVERTISING RATES:
Full Page Colour .... EUR 2700.00
REGIONAL DAILY & SUNDAY NEWSPAPERS: Regional Daily Newspapers

CORRICOLARI 53547X75J-90
Editorial: Paseo Marqués de Monistrol 7, 2° izquierda., E-28011 MADRID **Tel:** 91 526 80 80
Fax: 91 52 61 021
Email: corricolari@corricolari.es **Web site:** http://www.corricolari.es
ISSN: 0157-1986
Date Established: 1986; **Freq:** Monthly; **Cover Price:** EUR 3.00
Annual Sub.: EUR 36.00; **Circ:** 210,000
Editor: Jesus Angel Omeñaca; **Advertising Manager:** Pilar Fernández
Profile: Magazine covering all aspects of athletics.
Language(s): Spanish
ADVERTISING RATES:
Full Page Colour .... EUR 4300.00
Mechanical Data: Trim Size: 205x275mm
CONSUMER: SPORT: Athletics

COSAS DE CASA 53423X74C-11
Editorial: Calle Lopéz de Hoyos 141, E-28002 MADRID **Tel:** 91 51 06 600 **Fax:** 91 51 94 813
Email: cosas-de-casa@rba.es **Web site:** http://www.rba.es
Freq: Monthly; **Cover Price:** EUR 1.20
Annual Sub.: EUR 9.95; **Circ:** 313,953
Editor: Nuria Sanfrutos; **Advertising Director:** Nuria Caballero
Profile: Magazine containing features on decorating, style, design, home products, gardens and cookery.
Language(s): Spanish
Readership: Aimed at home owners in Spain.
Supplement(s): Cosas de Casa Extras - 2xY.
CONSUMER: WOMEN'S INTEREST CONSUMER MAGAZINES: Home & Family

COSAS DE COCINA 53488X74P-210
Editorial: López de Hoyos 141, 5ª planta, E-28002 MADRID **Tel:** 91 51 06 600 **Fax:** 91 51 94 813
Email: mar-esteban@rba.es **Web site:** http://www.rba.es
Freq: Quarterly; **Circ:** 95,194
Editor: Mar Esteban; **Advertising Director:** Angelines Puentes
Profile: Magazine covering all aspects of cookery. Includes articles on kitchen decoration, utensils and equipment, recipes and reviews. Also provides information about nutrition and tips for planning menus.
Language(s): Spanish
Readership: Aimed at women who enjoy home cooking.
CONSUMER: WOMEN'S INTEREST CONSUMER MAGAZINES: Food & Cookery

COSMOPOLITAN 53394X74A-23
Editorial: Albasanz 15, Edificio A, E-28037 MADRID
Tel: 91 43 69 800 **Fax:** 91 43 58 701
Email: cosmopolitan@gyj.es **Web site:** http://www.cosmohispano.com
Freq: Monthly; **Annual Sub.:** EUR 31.20; **Circ:** 352,678
Editor: Angeles Aledo; **Advertising Manager:** Ángeles López; **Advertising Director:** Elena Sánchez Fabrés

Profile: Magazine covering fashion, health, beauty, travel and work.
Language(s): Spanish
Readership: Read mainly by women.
ADVERTISING RATES:
Full Page Colour .... EUR 14130.00
Agency Commission: 15%
Mechanical Data: Type Area: 277 x 213mm, Print Process: Offset, Screen: 60 lpc, Film: Positive, right reading, emulsion down, Bleed Size: + 3mm
CONSUMER: WOMEN'S INTEREST CONSUMER MAGAZINES: Women's Interest

LA CRÓNICA DE LEÓN 53017X67B-4150
Editorial: Calle Moises León 49, E-24006 LEÓN
Tel: 987 21 25 12 **Fax:** 987 20 09 01
Email: redaccion@la-cronica.net **Web site:** http://www.la-cronica.net
Freq: Daily; **Cover Price:** EUR 1.00; **Circ:** 7,874
Profile: Regional daily newspaper focussing on news and current affairs.
Language(s): Spanish
REGIONAL DAILY & SUNDAY NEWSPAPERS: Regional Daily Newspapers

CRÓNICA SANITARIA 625426X56B-20
Editorial: Edificio SATSE, Cuesta de Santo Domingo 6, E-28013 MADRID **Tel:** 91 54 24 805
Fax: 91 55 99 264
Email: cronica_sanitaria@satse.es **Web site:** http://www.satse.es
Freq: 11 issues yearly; **Circ:** 30,000
Editor: Marta Muñoz Fernández
Profile: Medical journal focusing on hygiene, safety and the hospital working environment.
Language(s): Spanish
Readership: Aimed at nurses.
BUSINESS: HEALTH & MEDICAL: Nursing

EL CROQUIS 51990X4A-30
Editorial: Avda. de los Reyes Católicos 9, E-28280 EL ESCORIAL (MADRID) **Tel:** 91 89 69 410
Fax: 91 89 69 411
Email: elcroquis@elcroquis.es **Web site:** http://www.elcroquis.es
Freq: 5 issues yearly - Published in February, April, June, September and November; **Annual Sub.:** EUR 190.00; **Circ:** 30,000
Editor: Paloma Poveda
Profile: Magazine focusing on architecture, industrial design and interiors.
Language(s): Spanish
Readership: Aimed at architects, surveyors, engineers, designers and professionals in the construction industry.
ADVERTISING RATES:
Full Page Colour .... EUR 3000.00
Agency Commission: 10%
Mechanical Data: Trim Size: 340 x 240mm, Print Process: Offset rotation
Average ad content per issue: 20%
BUSINESS: ARCHITECTURE & BUILDING: Architecture

CRUZ ROJA 52440X32G-50
Editorial: Rafael Villa s/n, E-28023 EL PLANTIO (MADRID) **Tel:** 91 33 54 444 **Fax:** 91 33 54 455
Web site: http://www.cruzroja.es
Freq: Quarterly; **Circ:** 700,000
Editor: Octavio Cabeza
Profile: Publication of the Spanish Red Cross Society.
Language(s): Spanish
Readership: Aimed at people in international aid agencies and those interested in Red Cross activities.
BUSINESS: LOCAL GOVERNMENT, LEISURE & RECREATION: Community Care & Social Services

DEIA 52989X67B-4175
Editorial: Camino de Capuchinos 6, 5°-C, E-48004 BILBAO **Tel:** 944 59 91 00 **Fax:** 944 59 91 20
Email: infodeia@deia.com **Web site:** http://www.deia.com
Date Established: 1977; **Freq:** Daily; **Cover Price:** EUR 1.00
Annual Sub.: EUR 341.97; **Circ:** 26,365
Editor: Iñaki González
Profile: Regional daily newspaper focussing on news and current affairs.
Language(s): Spanish
ADVERTISING RATES:
Full Page Colour .... EUR 3625.00
Agency Commission: 10%
Mechanical Data: Type Area: 172 x 125mm, Col Length: 172mm, Page Width: 125mm
REGIONAL DAILY & SUNDAY NEWSPAPERS: Regional Daily Newspapers

EL DÍA 763506X67B-4180
Editorial: Avenida Buenos Aires 71, E-38005 SANTA CRUZ DE TENERIFE **Tel:** 922 23 83 25
Fax: 922 21 38 34
Email: redaccioneldia@eldia.es **Web site:** http://www.eldia.es
Date Established: 1910; **Freq:** Daily; **Cover Price:** EUR 1.00; **Circ:** 28,018
Editor: José Luis Díaz Expósito
Profile: Regional daily newspaper focussing on news and current affairs.

Language(s): Spanish
ADVERTISING RATES:
Full Page Colour .... EUR 1515.15
Supplement(s): Jornada Deportiva - 52xY.
REGIONAL DAILY & SUNDAY NEWSPAPERS:
Regional Daily Newspapers

EL DÍA DE CORDOBA
763547X67B-4190
Editorial: Avda. Gran Capitán, 23, 2°, E-14008 CORDOBA **Tel:** 95 72 22 050 **Fax:** 95 72 22 072
Email: eldia@eldiadecordoba.com **Web site:** http://www.eldiadecordoba.com
Freq: Daily; **Cover Price:** EUR 0.75
Annual Sub.: EUR 251.34; **Circ:** 200,000
Editor: Luis Perez Bustamante
Profile: Regional daily newspaper focussing on news and current affairs.
Language(s): Spanish
REGIONAL DAILY & SUNDAY NEWSPAPERS:
Regional Daily Newspapers

EL DÍA DE CUENCA 53007X67B-4200
Editorial: Polígono La Carreja, Parcela 77-78, 16004 CUENCA **Tel:** 969 240 423 **Fax:** 969 225 361
Email: diadecuenca@citelan.es
Freq: Daily; **Cover Price:** EUR 1.00; **Circ:** 8,500
Editor: Esther Palenciano; **Advertising Manager:** Angel Hidalgo
Profile: Regional daily newspaper focussing on news and current affairs.
Language(s): Spanish
ADVERTISING RATES:
Full Page Mono .... EUR 1550.00
Full Page Colour .... EUR 2000.00
REGIONAL DAILY & SUNDAY NEWSPAPERS:
Regional Daily Newspapers

EL DÍA DE TOLEDO 53054X67B-4225
Editorial: Poligono La Carreja, Parcela 77-78, 16004 CUENCA **Tel:** 969 240 423 **Fax:** 969 225 351
Freq: Daily; **Cover Price:** EUR 1.00; **Circ:** 7,000
Editor: Esther de Andrés
Profile: Regional daily newspaper focussing on news and current affairs.
Language(s): Spanish
ADVERTISING RATES:
Full Page Mono .... EUR 1350.00
Full Page Colour .... EUR 1650.00
REGIONAL DAILY & SUNDAY NEWSPAPERS:
Regional Daily Newspapers

DIARI DE BALEARES 53065X67B-3925
Editorial: Palacio de la Prensa, Paseo Mallorca 9 A, E-07011 PALMA DE MALLORCA **Tel:** 971 78 83 22
Fax: 971 45 57 40
Email: master@diaridebalears.com **Web site:** http://www.diaridebalears.com
Freq: Daily; **Circ:** 15,325
Editor: Juan Rivera
Profile: Regional daily newspaper focussing on news and current affairs.
Language(s): Catalan
REGIONAL DAILY & SUNDAY NEWSPAPERS:
Regional Daily Newspapers

DIARI DE GIRONA 53009X67B-4300
Editorial: Paseo General Mendosa 2, E-17002 GIRONA **Tel:** 972 20 20 66 **Fax:** 972 20 20 05
Email: diaridegirona@epi.es **Web site:** http://www.diaridegirona.es
Date Established: 1889; **Freq:** Daily; **Cover Price:** EUR 1.00; **Circ:** 8,050
Editor: David Céspedes; **Advertising Manager:** Francisco Martí
Profile: Regional daily newspaper focussing on news and current affairs.
Language(s): Catalan; Spanish
ADVERTISING RATES:
Full Page Colour .... EUR 2250.00
Supplement(s): Dominical - 52xY, Motor - 52xY
REGIONAL DAILY & SUNDAY NEWSPAPERS:
Regional Daily Newspapers

DIARI DE SABADELL 53037X67B-4325
Editorial: Sant Quirze 37-41, E-08201 SABADELL (BARCELONA) **Tel:** 937 26 11 00 **Fax:** 937 27 08 65
Email: redaccio@diarisabadell.com **Web site:** http://www.diarisabadell.com
Date Established: 1976; **Freq:** Daily - Published Tuesday - Saturday; **Cover Price:** EUR 1.00; **Circ:** 6,309
Editor: Mathias Serracant
Profile: Regional daily newspaper focussing on news and current affairs.
Language(s): Catalan; Spanish
ADVERTISING RATES:
Full Page Mono .... EUR 840.00
Full Page Colour .... EUR 1092.00
REGIONAL DAILY & SUNDAY NEWSPAPERS:
Regional Daily Newspapers

DIARI DE TARRAGONA
53052X67B-4350
Editorial: Domènech Guansé 2, E-43005 TARRAGONA **Tel:** 977 29 97 00 **Fax:** 977 22 30 13
Email: tarragona@diaridetarragona.com **Web site:** http://www.diaridetarragona.com
Freq: Daily; **Cover Price:** EUR 1.00; **Circ:** 16,801
Editor: Francesc Joan; **Advertising Manager:** Pau Galí
Profile: Regional daily newspaper focussing on news and current affairs.
Language(s): Catalan; Spanish
Agency Commission: 10%
Mechanical Data: Type Area: 360 x 289mm, Col Widths (Display): 48mm, No. of Columns (Display): 5, Col Length: 360mm, Page Width: 289mm
Copy instructions: *Copy Date:* 48 hours prior to publication date
Average ad content per issue: 22%
REGIONAL DAILY & SUNDAY NEWSPAPERS:
Regional Daily Newspapers

DIARI DE TERRASSA 52985X67B-4750
Editorial: Vinyals 61, E-08221 TERRASSA (BARCELONA) **Tel:** 937 28 37 00 **Fax:** 937 28 37 18
Email: anuncios@diariterrassa.net **Web site:** http://www.diariterrassa.net
Date Established: 1977; **Freq:** Daily - Published Tuesday - Saturday; **Cover Price:** EUR 1.00; **Circ:** 6,488
Editor: Julián Sanz Soria; **Advertising Manager:** Julián Sanz Soria
Profile: Regional daily newspaper focussing on news and current affairs.
Language(s): Catalan; Spanish
ADVERTISING RATES:
Full Page Mono .... EUR 700.00
Full Page Colour .... EUR 900.00
Agency Commission: 15%
Mechanical Data: No. of Columns (Display): 6, Type Area: 402 x 280mm, Col Length: 402mm, Page Width: 280mm
Copy instructions: *Copy Date:* 2 days prior to publication date
REGIONAL DAILY & SUNDAY NEWSPAPERS:
Regional Daily Newspapers

DIARI DE VILANOVA 763785X72-50
Editorial: Carrer Jardí 37, Apartad de Correus 33, E-08800 VILANOVA I LA GELTRÚ (BARCELONA)
Tel: 93 81 49 191 **Fax:** 93 89 34 565
Email: diari@diaridevilanova.com **Web site:** http://www.diaridevilanova.com
Freq: Weekly - Published on Friday; **Cover Price:** EUR 1.60; **Circ:** 7,500
Editor: Rámon Francàs Martorrell; **Publisher:** Conxita Huguet Sesma
Language(s): Catalan; Spanish
LOCAL NEWSPAPERS

DIARIO DE ALCALÁ 53025X67B-4375
Editorial: Pza. de Navarra 3, 1° esc. izda 1° B, E-28804 ALCALÁ DE HENARES (MADRID)
Tel: 91 88 94 235 **Fax:** 91 88 95 115
Email: diarioalcala@tsai.es **Web site:** http://www.diarioalcala.es
Date Established: 1992; **Freq:** Daily - Published Monday - Saturday; **Cover Price:** EUR 1.00; **Circ:** 10,000
Editor: Sonia Romero; **Publisher:** Julio R. Naranjo
Profile: Regional daily newspaper focussing on news and current affairs.
Language(s): Spanish
ADVERTISING RATES:
Full Page Mono .... EUR 667.60
Full Page Colour .... EUR 902.50
Agency Commission: 10%
Copy instructions: *Copy Date:* 48 hours prior to publication date
REGIONAL DAILY & SUNDAY NEWSPAPERS:
Regional Daily Newspapers

DIARIO DE AVISOS 53073X67B-4450
Editorial: Calle Salamanca 5, E-38006 SANTA CRUZ DE TENERIFE **Tel:** 92 22 72 350 **Fax:** 92 22 41 039
Email: redaccion@diariodeavisos.com **Web site:** http://www.diariodeavisos.com
Date Established: 1890; **Freq:** Daily; **Cover Price:** EUR 1.00; **Circ:** 16,484
Editor: Candida Carballo
Profile: Regional daily newspaper focussing on news and current affairs.
Language(s): Spanish
ADVERTISING RATES:
Full Page Colour .... EUR 2440.00
REGIONAL DAILY & SUNDAY NEWSPAPERS:
Regional Daily Newspapers

DIARIO DE BURGOS 52991X67B-4475
Editorial: Avenida Castilla y Leon, 62 -64, E-09007 BURGOS **Tel:** 947 26 83 75 **Fax:** 947 26 80 03
Email: redaccion@diariodeburgos.es **Web site:** http://www.diariodeburgos.es
Date Established: 1891; **Freq:** Daily - Published Monday - Saturday; **Cover Price:** EUR 1.00; **Circ:** 14,078
Editor: Raul Briongos; **Publisher:** Antonio Méndez Pozo
Profile: Regional daily newspaper focussing on news and current affairs.
Language(s): Spanish
ADVERTISING RATES:
Full Page Mono .... EUR 1985.00
Full Page Colour .... EUR 2571.00
REGIONAL DAILY & SUNDAY NEWSPAPERS:
Regional Daily Newspapers

DIARIO DE CÁDIZ 52995X67B-4500
Editorial: Poligono el Trocadero Calle Francia s/n, E-11519 PUERTO REAL (CÁDIZ) **Tel:** 95 68 04 660
Fax: 95 68 36 717
Email: contactar@diariodecadiz.es **Web site:** http://www.diariodecadiz.es
Freq: Daily; **Cover Price:** EUR 0.90; **Circ:** 34,638
Editor: Ignacio de la Varga Pérez
Profile: Regional daily newspaper focussing on news and current affairs.
Language(s): Spanish
ADVERTISING RATES:
Full Page Colour .... EUR 3784.00
REGIONAL DAILY & SUNDAY NEWSPAPERS:
Regional Daily Newspapers

DIARIO DE IBIZA 53067X67B-4525
Editorial: Avda. de la Paz (esquina C/ Aubarca), E-07800 IBIZA **Tel:** 971 19 00 00 **Fax:** 971 19 03 21
Email: diariodeibiza@epi.es **Web site:** http://www.diariodeibiza.es
Freq: Daily; **Cover Price:** EUR 1.00; **Circ:** 9,151
Editor: Cristina Martin
Profile: Regional daily newspaper focussing on news and current affairs.
Language(s): Spanish
ADVERTISING RATES:
Full Page Mono .... EUR 1775.00
Full Page Colour .... EUR 2663.00
REGIONAL DAILY & SUNDAY NEWSPAPERS:
Regional Daily Newspapers

DIARIO DE JEREZ 52996X67B-4550
Editorial: Patricio Garvey s/n, 1°, E-11402 JEREZ DE LA FRONTERA (CADIZ) **Tel:** 95 63 21 411
Fax: 95 63 49 904
Email: redaccion@diariodejerez.com **Web site:** http://www.diariodejerez.com
Date Established: 1984; **Freq:** Daily; **Circ:** 13,000
Editor: Juan Pedro Simo
Profile: Regional daily newspaper focussing on news and current affairs.
Language(s): Spanish
ADVERTISING RATES:
Full Page Colour .... EUR 1710.00
REGIONAL DAILY & SUNDAY NEWSPAPERS:
Regional Daily Newspapers

DIARIO DE LEÓN 53018X67B-4600
Editorial: Carretera León-Astorga, Km. 4,5, E-24010 TROBAJO DEL CAMINO (LEÓN) **Tel:** 987 84 03 00
Fax: 987 84 03 14
Email: diariodeleon@diariodeleon.es **Web site:** http://www.diariodeleon.com
Date Established: 1906; **Freq:** Daily; **Cover Price:** EUR 1.00; **Circ:** 18,903
Editor: Vicente Pueyo; **Advertising Manager:** José Antonio Dominguez
Profile: Regional daily newspaper focussing on news and current affairs.
Language(s): Spanish
ADVERTISING RATES:
Full Page Colour .... EUR 2195.00
Agency Commission: 10%
REGIONAL DAILY & SUNDAY NEWSPAPERS:
Regional Daily Newspapers

DIARIO DE MALLORCA
53068X67B-4625
Editorial: Calle Puerto Rico 15, Poligono de Levante, E-07007 PALMA DE MALLORCA **Tel:** 971 17 03 00
Fax: 971 17 03 01
Email: cartas.diariodemallorca@epi.es **Web site:** http://www.diariodemallorca.es
Freq: Daily; **Circ:** 26,000
Profile: Regional daily newspaper focussing on news and current affairs.
Language(s): Spanish
ADVERTISING RATES:
Full Page Mono .... EUR 2455.00
Full Page Colour .... EUR 3685.00
REGIONAL DAILY & SUNDAY NEWSPAPERS:
Regional Daily Newspapers

DIARIO DE NAVARRA 53034X67B-4650
Editorial: Zapatería 49, Apdo. 5, E-31001 PAMPLONA **Tel:** 948 24 12 50 **Fax:** 948 15 04 84
Email: redaccion@diariodenavarra.es **Web site:** http://www.diariodenavarra.es
Freq: Daily; **Cover Price:** EUR 1.00; **Circ:** 67,524
Editor: José Miguel Iriberri
Profile: Regional daily newspaper focussing on news and current affairs.
Language(s): Spanish
ADVERTISING RATES:
Full Page Mono .... EUR 3225.00
Full Page Colour .... EUR 4837.00
REGIONAL DAILY & SUNDAY NEWSPAPERS:
Regional Daily Newspapers

DIARIO DE NOTICIAS DE NAVARRA 53012X67B-4675
Formerly: Diario de Noticias
Editorial: Altzutzate 8, Poligono Industrial Areta, E-31620 HUARTE (PAMPLONA) **Tel:** 948 33 25 33
Fax: 948 33 25 18
Email: redaccion@noticiasdenavarra.com **Web site:** http://www.noticiasdenavarra.com
Freq: Daily; **Cover Price:** EUR 1.00; **Circ:** 24,006
Profile: Regional daily newspaper focussing on news and current affairs.
Language(s): Spanish
ADVERTISING RATES:
Full Page Colour .... EUR 2300.00
REGIONAL DAILY & SUNDAY NEWSPAPERS:
Regional Daily Newspapers

DIARIO DE PONTEVEDRA
53035X67B-4700
Editorial: Calle Lepanto 5, E-36001 PONTEVEDRA
Tel: 986 01 11 00 **Fax:** 986 01 11 42
Email: diario@diariodepontevedra.com **Web site:** http://www.diariodepontevedra.com
Freq: Daily; **Cover Price:** EUR 1.00; **Circ:** 8,366
Profile: Regional daily newspaper focussing on news and current affairs.
Language(s): Spanish
ADVERTISING RATES:
Full Page Mono .... EUR 1335.00
Full Page Colour .... EUR 1730.00
REGIONAL DAILY & SUNDAY NEWSPAPERS:
Regional Daily Newspapers

DIARIO DE SEVILLA 763511X67B-4730
Editorial: Rioja 13, 1°, E- 41001 SEVILLA
Tel: 954 50 62 00 **Fax:** 954 50 62 22
Email: diariodesevilla@diariodesevilla.es **Web site:** http://www.diariodesevilla.es
Freq: Daily; **Cover Price:** EUR 1.00; **Circ:** 30,491
Editor: Adolfo Salvador; **Advertising Manager:** Angel Navarro
Profile: Regional daily newspaper focussing on news and current affairs.
Language(s): Spanish
REGIONAL DAILY & SUNDAY NEWSPAPERS:
Regional Daily Newspapers

DIARIO DE TERUEL 53053X67B-4775
Editorial: Avenida Sagunto 27, E-44002 TERUEL
Tel: 978 61 70 86 **Fax:** 978 60 47 02
Email: redaccion@diariodeteruel.net **Web site:** http://www.diariodeteruel.net
Date Established: 1936; **Freq:** Daily - Published Tuesday - Sunday; **Cover Price:** EUR 0.85; **Circ:** 4,000
Editor: Juan José Francisco Ballero; **Advertising Manager:** Isabel Ramirez Tena
Profile: Regional daily newspaper focussing on news and current affairs.
Language(s): Spanish
REGIONAL DAILY & SUNDAY NEWSPAPERS:
Regional Daily Newspapers

DIARIO DEL ALTO ARAGÓN
53014X67B-4800
Editorial: Ronda Estación 4, E-22005 HUESCA
Tel: 974 21 56 56 **Fax:** 974 21 56 57
Email: redaccion@diariodelaltoaragon.es **Web site:** http://www.diariodelaltoaragon.es
Date Established: 1985; **Freq:** Daily; **Cover Price:** EUR 1.00; **Circ:** 9,250
Editor: Jorge Naya; **News Editor:** Javier García Antón
Profile: Regional daily newspaper focussing on news and current affairs.
Language(s): Spanish
REGIONAL DAILY & SUNDAY NEWSPAPERS:
Regional Daily Newspapers

DIARIO MÁLAGA COSTA DEL SOL 53026X67B-4850
Editorial: Avenida García Morato 20, E-29004 MÁLAGA **Tel:** 952 24 43 53 **Fax:** 952 24 55 40
Email: redaccion@diariomalaga.com **Web site:** http://www.diariomalaga.com
Freq: Daily - Published Monday - Saturday; **Cover Price:** EUR 0.75; **Circ:** 17,000
Editor: Jesús Romano; **Advertising Manager:** Arantxa Crespo
Profile: Regional daily newspaper focussing on news and current affairs.
Language(s): Spanish
REGIONAL DAILY & SUNDAY NEWSPAPERS:
Regional Daily Newspapers

DIARIO MÉDICO 52711X56A-365
Editorial: Avenida de San Luis 25-27, E-28033 MADRID **Tel:** 91 443 50 00 **Fax:** 91 443 56 47
Email: eescala@unidadeditorial.es **Web site:** http://www.diariomedico.com
Date Established: 1992; **Freq:** 260 issues yearly - Published Monday - Friday; **Circ:** 49,211
Editor: Elena Escala; **Advertising Manager:** Rosario Serrano; **Advertising Director:** Daniel Julián
Profile: Newspaper discussing options and solutions to national and international health care issues, financing, health policy, health economics, managed care, medicare and medicaid, health philanthropy, and physician workforce issues.
Language(s): Spanish
BUSINESS: HEALTH & MEDICAL

EL DIARIO MONTAÑES
53043X67B-4875
Editorial: Calle la Prensa s/n, La Albericia, E-39012 SANTANDER **Tel:** 942 35 40 00 **Fax:** 942 34 18 06
Email: redaccion.dm@eldiariomontanes.es **Web site:** http://www.eldiariomontanes.es
Date Established: 1902; **Freq:** Daily; **Circ:** 38,078
Editor: Jesús Ferrera; **Advertising Director:** Juan Pelayo Valdeolivas
Profile: Regional daily newspaper focussing on news and current affairs.
Language(s): Spanish
ADVERTISING RATES:
Full Page Colour .... EUR 3300.00
REGIONAL DAILY & SUNDAY NEWSPAPERS: Regional Daily Newspapers

EL DIARIO PALENTINO
53033X67B-4900
Editorial: Mayor 52, E-34001 PALENCIA
Tel: 97 97 06 308 **Fax:** 97 97 06 651
Email: dp_local@diariopalentino.es **Web site:** http://www.diariopalentino.es
Date Established: 1881; **Freq:** Daily; **Cover Price:** EUR 1.00; **Circ:** 5,114
Editor: Jorge Cancho González; **Advertising Manager:** Antonia Sanz Casado; **Publisher:** Antonio Méndez Pozo
Profile: Regional daily newspaper focussing on news and current affairs.
Language(s): Spanish
REGIONAL DAILY & SUNDAY NEWSPAPERS: Regional Daily Newspapers

EL DIARIO VASCO
53041X67B-4925
Editorial: Camino de Portuetxe 2, E-20018 SAN SEBASTIÁN **Tel:** 943 41 07 00 **Fax:** 943 41 08 16
Email: redaccion@diariovasco.com **Web site:** http://www.diariovasco.com
Freq: Daily; **Cover Price:** EUR 0.95; **Circ:** 95,000
Editor: Javier Frias; **Features Editor:** Julio Diaz de Alda; **Advertising Director:** Iñigo Espinosa Vera
Profile: Regional daily newspaper focussing on news and current affairs.
Language(s): Spanish
REGIONAL DAILY & SUNDAY NEWSPAPERS: Regional Daily Newspapers

DIBUS
624891X91D-35
Editorial: Calle Fluviá 89, E-08019 BARCELONA
Tel: 93-30 34 038 **Fax:** 93-30 36 831
Email: exposito@norma-ed.es **Web site:** http://www.norma-ed.es
Freq: Monthly; **Circ:** 100,000
Editor: Maite Exposito; **Publisher:** Armand Zoroa
Profile: Cartoon magazine.
Language(s): Spanish
Readership: Read by children aged 7 to 14 years.
CONSUMER: RECREATION & LEISURE: Children & Youth

DIEZ MINUTOS
53396X74A-25
Editorial: Avda. Cardenal Herrera Oria 3, E-28034 MADRID **Tel:** 91 72 87 000 **Fax:** 91 72 89 279
Email: diezminutos@hachette.es **Web site:** http://www.diezminutos.wanadoo.es
Date Established: 1950; **Freq:** Weekly; **Cover Price:** EUR 1.80; **Circ:** 444,447
Editor: Rosa Ballarín; **Advertising Director:** María Luisa Ruiz de Velasco
Profile: Magazine containing lifestyle articles, competitions and puzzles.
Language(s): Spanish
Readership: Aimed at women.
Mechanical Data: Type Area: 268 x 200mm, Bleed Size: 297 x 228mm, Col Length: 268mm, Page Width: 200mm
CONSUMER: WOMEN'S INTEREST CONSUMER MAGAZINES: Women's Interest

DIGITAL PLUS
53597X76C-40
Formerly: Canal Satélite Digital
Editorial: Avda. de los Artesanos 6, E-28760 TRES CANTOS (MADRID) **Tel:** 91 736 70 00
Web site: http://www.plus.es
Freq: Monthly; **Cover Price:** Free; **Circ:** 1,882,555
Editor: Miriam Sarastizabal; **Advertising Manager:** Orestes Sánchez
Profile: Magazine covering satellite TV programmes.
Language(s): Spanish
Readership: Aimed at subscribers to satellite TV.
CONSUMER: MUSIC & PERFORMING ARTS: TV & Radio

DINERO
51904X1A-60
Editorial: Calle Pantoja 14, E-28002 MADRID
Tel: 91 43 27 600 **Fax:** 91 43 27 765
Email: pcaldez@negocios.com **Web site:** http://www.negocios.com
Freq: Monthly; **Annual Sub.:** EUR 30.05; **Circ:** 30,000
Editor: Miguel Ormaetxea; **Advertising Director:** Francisco Marín
Profile: Magazine focusing on business, economy and finance.
Language(s): Spanish
Readership: Aimed at those working in the finance industry.
BUSINESS: FINANCE & ECONOMICS

DINERO Y SALUD
52713X56A-372
Editorial: Calle Altamirano 33 bajo izquierda, E-28008 MADRID **Tel:** 91 54 72 662 **Fax:** 91 54 17 132
Email: dineroysalud@saludyocio.com
Freq: 10 issues yearly - Double issue, published in July/August and December/January; **Cover Price:** EUR 2.00
Annual Sub.: EUR 20.00; **Circ:** 30,000
Editor: Juan José González
Profile: Magazine providing news and opinion concerning the medical and pharmaceutical industries. Provides economic information relating to the health care sector.
Language(s): Spanish
Readership: Aimed at decision makers within the medical profession.
ADVERTISING RATES:
Full Page Colour .... EUR 3000.00
BUSINESS: HEALTH & MEDICAL

DIRIGENTES
52153X14A-25_50
Editorial: Calle Belmonte del Tajo 19, E-28019 MADRID **Tel:** 91 56 01 233 **Fax:** 91 56 51 569
Email: redaccion@dirigentes-negocios.com **Web site:** http://www.dirigentes-negocios.com
Freq: Monthly; **Circ:** 25,000
Editor: Borja Gómez; **Advertisement Director:** Andrea Martinotti
Profile: Review on business and finance.
Language(s): Spanish
Readership: Aimed at managers, directors and senior personnel.
Mechanical Data: Print Process: Offset
BUSINESS: COMMERCE, INDUSTRY & MANAGEMENT

DR DOBB'S ESPAÑA
765852X5B-251
Editorial: Avda. Generalisimo 14, 2° B, E-28660 BOADILLA DEL MONTE (MADRID) **Tel:** 91 63 23 827
Fax: 91 63 32 564
Email: mnavarro@mkm-pi.com **Web site:** http://www.mkm-pi.com
Freq: Monthly; **Cover Price:** EUR 5.00; **Circ:** 25,000
Editor: Manuel Navarro
Profile: Computing magazine covering system design, data security and operating systems.
Language(s): Spanish
Readership: Read by professional programmers, system designers and IT purchasers.
BUSINESS: COMPUTERS & AUTOMATION: Data Processing

DUPLEX PRESS
52656X52A-23
Editorial: Vía Layetana 71, pral., E-08003 BARCELONA **Tel:** 93 31 83 738 **Fax:** 93 31 85 984
Email: grupoduplex@grupoduplex.com **Web site:** http://www.grupoduplex.com
Date Established: 1993; **Freq:** 6 issues yearly;
Annual Sub.: EUR 15.00; **Circ:** 26,000
Usual Pagination: 60
Editor: Pedro Pérez Fernández; **Advertising Manager:** Pedro Pérez Fernández
Profile: Magazine containing news concerning the jewellery trade, including information on clocks and watches.
Language(s): Spanish
Readership: Aimed at jewellers, specialist retailers, gold- and silversmiths.
Agency Commission: 10%
Average ad content per issue: 40%
BUSINESS: GIFT TRADE: Jewellery

DVD ACTUALIDAD
754214X43D-20
Editorial: Carrer Roca i Batlle 5, entlo. 1ª, E-08023 BARCELONA **Tel:** 93-41 84 724 **Fax:** 93-41 84 312
Email: dvd@musicspain.com
Date Established: 1999; **Freq:** 11 issues yearly - Not published in August; **Cover Price:** EUR 2.85
Annual Sub.: EUR 28.50; **Circ:** 25,000
Usual Pagination: 96
Editor: Maribel Tomás
Profile: Magazine containing news concerning home theatre, new releases of films on DVD and hardware such as reproducers, loudspeakers and screens.
Language(s): Spanish
Readership: Aimed at people who would like to change their video for DVD equipment.
BUSINESS: ELECTRICAL RETAIL TRADE: Video

DXT
764780X75A-85
Editorial: Segovia 19, ES-28005 MADRID
Tel: 91 354 03 97 **Fax:** 91 354 03 14
Email: dxt@spain.com
Freq: Weekly; **Cover Price:** Free; **Circ:** 100,000
Editor: Juan Pérez Mateos; **Advertising Manager:** Francisco Linde
Profile: Magazine containing information about a variety of sports.
Language(s): Spanish
Mechanical Data: Print Process: Offset
CONSUMER: SPORT

LA ECONOMIA
765646X1A-209
Editorial: Calle De los Alejos 13, Apartado de correos 4233, E-30080 MURCIA **Tel:** 968 85 80 53
Fax: 968 30 51 78
Email: redaccion@laeconomia.com **Web site:** http://www.laeconomia.com
Freq: Monthly; **Circ:** 25,000
Editor: Francisco Poveda Navarro
Profile: Magazine containing information about Spanish economic issues and other general financial matters.
Language(s): Spanish
BUSINESS: FINANCE & ECONOMICS

EL ECONOMISTA
1743064X1A-229
Editorial: Condesa de Venadito 1 3ª planta, E-28027 MADRID **Tel:** 91 32 46 700 **Fax:** 91 32 46 727
Email: empresas@eleconomista.es **Web site:** http://www.eleconomista.es
Freq: Daily; **Cover Price:** EUR 1.00
Annual Sub.: EUR 206.00; **Circ:** 29,213
Editor: Joaquín Gomez; **Advertising Director:** Bernardo Carballido
Profile: Newspaper focusing on the stock market, financial and economics.
Language(s): Spanish
ADVERTISING RATES:
Full Page Mono .... EUR 7200.00
Full Page Colour .... EUR 9950.00
BUSINESS: FINANCE & ECONOMICS

EJECUTIVOS
51910X1A-93
Editorial: Calle Marquez Pico de Velazco 46 A, E-28027 MADRID **Tel:** 91 47 20 998
Email: info@redejecutivos.com **Web site:** http://www.redejecutivos.com
Date Established: 1988; **Freq:** 10 issues yearly;
Cover Price: EUR 4.00; **Circ:** 25,000
Usual Pagination: 116
Editor: Carlos Delgado; **Advertising Manager:** Ricardo López
Profile: Business and finance magazine that provides a news and information digest relating to all sectors of business and industry also included political information.
Language(s): Spanish
Readership: Aimed at managers and executives.
ADVERTISING RATES:
Full Page Colour .... EUR 4200
Agency Commission: 10%
Mechanical Data: Trim Size: 210 x 285mm, Type Area: 210 x 285mm, Col Length: 277mm, Bleed Size: + 3 mm
Copy instructions: *Copy Date:* On the 21st of the previous month
BUSINESS: FINANCE & ECONOMICS

ELLE
53397X74A-40
Editorial: Avda. Cardenal Herrea Oria 3, E-28034 MADRID **Tel:** 91 72 87 027 **Fax:** 91 35 85 473
Email: elle@hachette.es **Web site:** http://www.elle.wanadoo.es
Date Established: 1986; **Freq:** Monthly; **Cover Price:** EUR 3.00; **Circ:** 226,458
Editor: Benedetta Poletti; **Advertising Director:** Amparo Bastiz
Profile: Magazine focusing on lifestyle, beauty, fashion, food, home, relationships, sex, travel and leisure.
Language(s): Spanish
Readership: Aimed at modern women.
Mechanical Data: Type Area: 268 x 200mm, Bleed Size: 297 x 228mm, Col Length: 268mm, Page Width: 200mm
CONSUMER: WOMEN'S INTEREST CONSUMER MAGAZINES: Women's Interest

ELLE DECO
53424X74C-12
Formerly: Elle Decoración
Editorial: C/Santa Engracia, 23, 28010 MADRID
Tel: 91 7287000 **Fax:** 91 7289308
Email: therrero@hearst.es **Web site:** http://www.elle.es/elledeco
Date Established: 1989; **Freq:** Monthly; **Circ:** 184,154
Advertising Director: María Luisa Ruiz de Velasco
Profile: Magazine containing articles about home interiors and furnishings. Read mainly by women.
Language(s): Spanish
Readership: Read mainly by women.
ADVERTISING RATES:
Full Page Colour .... EUR 10450
Mechanical Data: Col Length: 297mm
CONSUMER: WOMEN'S INTEREST CONSUMER MAGAZINES: Home & Family

EMPRENDEDORES
52154X14A-32
Editorial: Santa Engracia 23, E-28010 MADRID
Tel: 91 72 87 000 **Fax:** 91 35 85 121
Email: emprende@hachette.es **Web site:** http://www.emprendedores.es
Date Established: 1997; **Freq:** Monthly; **Cover Price:** EUR 3.00; **Circ:** 188,000
Editor: Javier Inaraja; **Advertising Director:** Coral Garelly
Profile: Magazine covering business and industry.
Language(s): Spanish
ADVERTISING RATES:
Full Page Colour .... EUR 7200.00
Mechanical Data: Type Area: 268 x 200mm, Bleed Size: 297 x 228mm, Col Length: 268mm, Page Width: 200mm
BUSINESS: COMMERCE, INDUSTRY & MANAGEMENT

EN FRANQUICIA
52155X14A-36
Editorial: Alcala 128 1°, E-28009 MADRID
Tel: 91 30 96 513 **Fax:** 91 30 92 848
Email: comunicacion@bya.es **Web site:** http://www.quefranquicia.com
Freq: 11 issues yearly - Double issue in July/August;
Cover Price: EUR 3.00; **Circ:** 30,000
Editor: Antonio Sánchez Lorenzo; **Advertising Director:** Nieves Amavisca; **Publisher:** Santiago Barbadillo
Profile: Magazine focusing on the franchising business in Spain, includes articles on foreign markets.
Language(s): Spanish
Readership: Aimed at present and potential franchise operators and lenders.
BUSINESS: COMMERCE, INDUSTRY & MANAGEMENT

ENFERMERÍA FACULTATIVA
52781X56C-16_50
Formerly: Enfermería Actualidad
Editorial: Calle Fuente del Rey 2, E-28023 MADRID
Tel: 91 33 45 513 **Fax:** 91 33 45 523
Email: prensa@enfermundi.com **Web site:** http://www.enfermundi.com
Date Established: 1996; **Freq:** 10 issues yearly; **Circ:** 184,000
Usual Pagination: 44
Editor: Iñigo Lapetra
Profile: Newsletter focusing on nursing.
Language(s): Spanish
Readership: Aimed at nurses and students.
BUSINESS: HEALTH & MEDICAL: Hospitals

EQUIPO
53062X67B-4950
Editorial: Herman Cortés 37, E-50005 ZARAGOZA
Tel: 976 70 04 40 **Fax:** 976 70 04 49
Email: equipo@diarioequipo.com **Web site:** http://www.diarioequipo.com
Freq: Daily; **Cover Price:** EUR 0.90; **Circ:** 14,000
Editor: Nacho Martín
Profile: Newspaper providing coverage of sporting events in the Aragón region.
Language(s): Spanish
Readership: Read by people living in the region with an interest in sport.
REGIONAL DAILY & SUNDAY NEWSPAPERS: Regional Daily Newspapers

EQUIPOS PRODUCTOS INDUSTRIALES (EPI)
52171X14B-30_50
Editorial: Carrer Entença 28 entlo, E-08015 BARCELONA **Tel:** 93 29 24 638 **Fax:** 93 42 52 880
Email: epi@rbi.es **Web site:** http://www.rbi.es
Date Established: 1991; **Freq:** 11 issues yearly - Double issue published in July/August; **Circ:** 27,000
Editor: Manuel Masip
Profile: Journal concerning industrial products, including articles on management and safety.
Language(s): Spanish
Readership: Aimed at those in industry.
Agency Commission: 15%
Mechanical Data: Type Area: 280 x 400mm
BUSINESS: COMMERCE, INDUSTRY & MANAGEMENT: Industry & Factories

ESTADIO DEPORTIVO
53049X67B-4975
Editorial: Avda. San Francisco, Javier 2, Edif. Sevilla, Planta 11, Modelo 25, E-41018 SEVILLA
Tel: 95 49 33 940 **Fax:** 95 46 38 266
Email: redaccion@estadiodeportivo.com **Web site:** http://www.estadiodeportivo.com
Date Established: 1995; **Freq:** Daily; **Cover Price:** EUR 0.90; **Circ:** 11,774
Editor: José Manuel Diez Perales; **Advertising Director:** Manuel García
Profile: Newspaper providing coverage of sporting events in Seville, Spain and throughout the world.
Language(s): Spanish
ADVERTISING RATES:
Full Page Mono .... EUR 1458.00
Full Page Colour .... EUR 1884.00
REGIONAL DAILY & SUNDAY NEWSPAPERS: Regional Daily Newspapers

ESTRENOS DE VÍDEO
53586X76A-43
Editorial: José Abascal 55, entreplanta Izquierda, E-28003 MADRID **Tel:** 91 78 18 980 **Fax:** 91 57 79 109
Email: estrenos@estrenos21.com
Freq: 11 issues yearly - Double issue in July/August;
Circ: 320,000
Editor: Pablo Santiago
Profile: Magazine containing news and reviews of new video releases in Spain.
Language(s): Spanish
Readership: Aimed at those interested in new video releases.
ADVERTISING RATES:
Full Page Colour .... EUR 6900.00
Agency Commission: 10%
Mechanical Data: Trim Size: 297 x 210mm
Copy instructions: *Copy Date:* 15th of the month prior to publication date
Average ad content per issue: 10%
CONSUMER: MUSIC & PERFORMING ARTS: Cinema

EUROPA SUR
52997X67B-5000
Editorial: Calle Muro, 3, E-11201 ALGECIRAS (CÁDIZ) **Tel:** 95 67 62 022 **Fax:** 95 66 31 167

Email: redaccion@europasur.com **Web site:** http://www.europasur.com
Freq: Daily; **Circ:** 5,081
Editor: Federico Joly
Profile: Regional daily newspaper focussing on news, current affairs, economics, politics and sport.
Language(s): Spanish
ADVERTISING RATES:
Full Page Colour .... EUR 1490.00
REGIONAL DAILY & SUNDAY NEWSPAPERS: Regional Daily Newspapers

EXPANSIÓN
52932X65A-32
Editorial: Avenida de San Luis 25-27, E-28033 MADRID **Tel:** 91 443 61 62 **Fax:** 91 443 69 94
Email: vlozano@unidadeditorial.es **Web site:** http://www.expansion.com
Date Established: 1986; **Freq:** Daily - Published Monday - Saturday; **Cover Price:** EUR 1.50; **Circ:** 77,153
Editor: Darío Bravo Fuentes; **Advertising Director:** Pablo Sempere
Profile: Tabloid-sized newspaper focusing on the stock market, financial, economic and company news throughout Spain and Latin America.
Language(s): Spanish
Readership: Aimed at leaders in the financial and business sectors, senior executives, managers and civil servants.
ADVERTISING RATES:
Full Page Mono .... EUR 7140.00
Full Page Colour .... EUR 9967.00
Mechanical Data: Trim Size: 390 x 290mm, Type Area: 344 x 253mm, Col Length: 344mm, Film: Digital only
NATIONAL DAILY & SUNDAY NEWSPAPERS: National Daily Newspapers

FARMACÉUTICOS
52464X37-240
Editorial: Calle Villanueva 11, 7ª, E-28001 MADRID **Tel:** 91 43 12 560 **Fax:** 91 43 28 100
Email: congral@redfarma.org **Web site:** http://www.portalfarma.com
Date Established: 1959; **Freq:** 11 issues yearly; **Cover Price:** Free; **Circ:** 62,000
Usual Pagination: 68
Editor: Carlos Jardón
Profile: Magazine providing news and information concerning the pharmaceutical industry.
Language(s): Spanish
Readership: Aimed at pharmacists in Spain.
ADVERTISING RATES:
Full Page Colour .... EUR 1706.00
BUSINESS: PHARMACEUTICAL & CHEMISTS

EL FARO DE CEUTA
52998X67B-5050
Editorial: Sargento Mena 8, E-51001 CEUTA (CÁDIZ) **Tel:** 956 524 035 **Fax:** 956 524 147
Email: elfaro@retemail.es **Web site:** http://www.elfarodigita.es
Date Established: 1934; **Freq:** Daily; **Cover Price:** EUR 1.00; **Circ:** 3,500
Profile: Regional daily newspaper focussing on news, current affairs, economics, politics and sport.
Language(s): Spanish
ADVERTISING RATES:
Full Page Colour .... EUR 1750.00
REGIONAL DAILY & SUNDAY NEWSPAPERS: Regional Daily Newspapers

FARO DE VIGO
53060X67B-5075
Editorial: Avenida de Redondela Chapela s/n, E-36320 VIGO (PONTEVEDRA) **Tel:** 986 81 46 00
Fax: 986 81 46 14
Email: digital@farodevigo.es **Web site:** http://www.farodevigo.es
Date Established: 1853; **Freq:** Daily; **Cover Price:** EUR 1.00; **Circ:** 49,800
Editor: Juan Carlos Recondo; **Features Editor:** Salvador Rodríguez
Profile: Regional daily newspaper focussing on news, current affairs, economics, politics and sport.
Language(s): Galician; Spanish
ADVERTISING RATES:
Full Page Mono .... EUR 3510.00
Full Page Colour .... EUR 5270.00
REGIONAL DAILY & SUNDAY NEWSPAPERS: Regional Daily Newspapers

FINANCIAL FOOD
52330X22A-49
Editorial: Calle Santo Angel 21, E-28043 MADRID
Tel: 91 38 84 200 **Fax:** 91 30 00 610
Email: food@infonegocio.com
Freq: 11 issues yearly; **Circ:** 65,000
Editor: Maria Gil
Profile: Magazine focusing on all aspects of the food trade.
Language(s): Spanish
Readership: Aimed at food distributors and retailers.
Mechanical Data: Screen: Mono: 54 lpc; Colour: 60 lpc, Print Process: Offset
BUSINESS: FOOD

FLOTAS DE LEASE PLAN
52629X49D-40
Editorial: General Pardiñas 29, E-28001 MADRID
Tel: 91 43 11 725 **Fax:** 91 57 60 090
Email: ediauto@ediauto.es **Web site:** http://www.flotas.com
Freq: Quarterly; **Circ:** 30,000
Editor: Raúl Hoyo
Profile: Magazine about the leasing of fleets of vehicles.
Language(s): Spanish
Readership: Aimed at directors of car rental companies and fleet owners.
BUSINESS: TRANSPORT: Commercial Vehicles

FORMULA AUTOFACIL
764212X77A-195
Editorial: Cardenal Herrera Oria, 296, E-28035 MADRID **Tel:** 91 364 39 84 **Fax:** 91 354 01 55
Email: formulafacil@luike.com **Web site:** http://www.luike.com
Date Established: 2000; **Freq:** Monthly; **Cover Price:** EUR 2.00; **Circ:** 137,597
Usual Pagination: 244
Editor: Javier Garcia; **Advertising Manager:** Luis Espinosa de los Monteros
Profile: Magazine including tests, reviews and information on international automobile exhibitions also containing articles about all types of cars and prices.
Language(s): Spanish
Readership: Aimed at motoring enthusiasts.
ADVERTISING RATES:
Full Page Colour .... EUR 10550.00
Agency Commission: 10%
Mechanical Data: Type Area: 195 mm x 260 mm, Bleed Size: 173 mm x 243 mm, Trim Size: 195 mm x 260 mm, Page Width: 195 mm
Copy instructions: *Copy Date:* The 5th, one month prior to publication
Average ad content per issue: 35%
CONSUMER: MOTORING & CYCLING: Motoring

FOTO SISTEMA
53824X85A-50
Editorial: Calle Francia 15-25, Poligon Industrial Rosanes, E-08769 CASTELLVI DE ROSANES (BARCELONA) **Tel:** 93 77 68 800 **Fax:** 93 77 68 801
Email: jordisala@qss-fs.com **Web site:** http://www.cialit.com
Date Established: 1993; **Freq:** Quarterly; **Cover Price:** Free; **Circ:** 110,000
Usual Pagination: 54
Editor: Jordi Sala Thomas
Profile: Magazine providing advice and information about photography. Includes product reviews, technical advice and photography competitions. Also contains articles on travel and holidays.
Language(s): Spanish
Readership: Aimed at photography enthusiasts.
CONSUMER: PHOTOGRAPHY & FILM MAKING: Photography

FOTOGRAMAS & DVD
53587X76A-50
Formerly: Fotogramas & Video
Editorial: Gran Vía de les Corts, Catalanes 133, 2ª planta, E-08014 BARCELONA **Tel:** 93 22 30 353
Fax: 93 42 16 150
Email: fotogramas@hachette.es **Web site:** http://www.fotogramas.es
Date Established: 1946; **Freq:** Monthly; **Cover Price:** EUR 2.50
Annual Sub.: EUR 24.00; **Circ:** 158,301
Editor: Pere Vall; **Editor-in-Chief:** Paula Ponga
Profile: Magazine containing articles and reports about cinema and video releases.
Language(s): Spanish
ADVERTISING RATES:
Full Page Colour .... EUR 9000.00
Mechanical Data: Type Area: 272 x 200mm, Bleed Size: 300 x 228mm, Col Length: 272mm, Page Width: 200mm
CONSUMER: MUSIC & PERFORMING ARTS: Cinema

FRANQUICIAS Y NEGOCIOS
754614X14A-41_50
Editorial: Joaquin Molins 5, 5° 4ª, E-08028 BARCELONA **Tel:** 93-49 06 465 **Fax:** 93-49 01 962
Email: info@infofranquicias.com **Web site:** http://www.infofranquicias.com
Freq: 6 issues yearly; **Cover Price:** EUR 2.50
Annual Sub.: EUR 15.00; **Circ:** 27,000
Editor: Beatriz Rodriguez
Profile: Magazine focusing on franchising.
Language(s): Spanish
BUSINESS: COMMERCE, INDUSTRY & MANAGEMENT

FREESTYLE
707625X74G-30
Editorial: Plaza Marqués de Salamanca 9, 1° izq., E-28006 MADRID **Tel:** 91 42 63 880 **Fax:** 91 57 51 296
Email: promacentro@cinerama.es
Freq: Monthly; **Cover Price:** Free; **Circ:** 330,000
Editor: Juan Ignazio Chico
Profile: Magazine focusing on lifestyle, fitness, sport, fashion and leisure.
Language(s): Spanish
Readership: Read by health and fitness enthusiasts.
CONSUMER: WOMEN'S INTEREST CONSUMER MAGAZINES: Slimming & Health

LA GACETA DE LOS NEGOCIOS
52933X65A-35
Editorial: Calle Pantoja 14, E-28002 MADRID
Tel: 91 43 27 600 **Fax:** 91 43 27 656
Email: gaceta@negocios.com **Web site:** http://www.negocios.com/gaceta
Freq: Daily - Published Monday - Saturday; **Annual Sub.:** EUR 360.61; **Circ:** 31,000
Editor: Miguel Villarejo; **News Editor:** Hernando Calleja; **Advertising Director:** Victor M. Cifuentes
Profile: Tabloid-sized newspaper providing in-depth financial, economic and business news.
Language(s): Spanish
Readership: Readership includes company and financial directors, senior executives, managers, civil servants and economics students.
NATIONAL DAILY & SUNDAY NEWSPAPERS: National Daily Newspapers

GACETA DENTAL
52793X56D-72
Editorial: Calle Canillas 2, E-28002 MADRID
Tel: 91 56 34 907 **Fax:** 91 56 43 216
Email: pues@jet.es
ISSN: 1135-2949
Freq: Monthly; **Circ:** 24,000
Editor: Stefania Toscano
Profile: Journal providing news and information from the dental industry and dental profession.
Language(s): Spanish
Mechanical Data: Bleed Size: 280 x 210mm
BUSINESS: HEALTH & MEDICAL: Dental

GACETA INTERNACIONAL
53380X73-100
Editorial: Alonso Cano 66, 1° Local 6, E-28003 MADRID **Tel:** 91 55 47 354 **Fax:** 91 55 39 395
Email: info@aphis.org **Web site:** http://www.aphis.org
Date Established: 1989; **Freq:** Monthly; **Cover Price:** $3.00
Annual Sub.: $72.00; **Circ:** 150,000
Usual Pagination: 60
Editor: Yolanda Arratia; **Advertising Manager:** Armando Restrepo Bretón
Profile: General information magazine covering news, politics, Spanish and international economics, debate, science and culture.
Language(s): Spanish
Readership: Read by company executives and professionals.
ADVERTISING RATES:
Full Page Colour .... EUR 3300.00
Agency Commission: 10%
Mechanical Data: Type Area: 210 x 185mm, Col Length: 260mm, Page Width: 185mm, Trim Size: 280 x 210mm
Copy instructions: *Copy Date:* 20th of month prior to publication date
Average ad content per issue: 8%
CONSUMER: NATIONAL & INTERNATIONAL PERIODICALS

LA GACETA REGIONAL DE SALAMANCA
53039X67B-5125
Editorial: Avda. de los Cipreses 81, Apdo. 52, E-37004 SALAMANCA **Tel:** 923 12 52 52
Fax: 923 25 61 55
Email: local@lagacetadesalamanca.com **Web site:** http://www.lagacetadesalamanca.com
Date Established: 1920; **Freq:** Daily; **Cover Price:** EUR 1.00; **Circ:** 15,033
Usual Pagination: 64
Editor: Miguel Angel García; **Advertising Manager:** D. González Lucas
Profile: Regional daily newspaper focussing on news, current affairs, economics, politics and sport.
Language(s): Spanish
Agency Commission: 10%
Mechanical Data: Col Length: 386mm, Col Widths (Display): 47mm, Col Widths (Display): 5
REGIONAL DAILY & SUNDAY NEWSPAPERS: Regional Daily Newspapers

GACETA UNIVERSITARIA
53872X88B-80
Editorial: Paseo de la Castellana 66, E-28046 MADRID **Tel:** 91 33 70 011 **Fax:** 91 33 70 006
Email: gaceta@recoletos.es **Web site:** http://www.recoletos.es/gueb
Freq: Weekly - Published on Monday; **Cover Price:** Free; **Circ:** 155,000
Editor: Pilar Manzanares
Profile: Journal providing information about education at Spanish universities.
Language(s): Spanish
Readership: Read by students and staff.
CONSUMER: EDUCATION: Adult Education

GACETA UNIVERSITARIA DE BARCELONA
53869X88B-70
Editorial: Paseo de la Castellana 66, 4ª planta, E-08017 BARCELONA **Tel:** 93 22 76 700
Fax: 93 22 76 763
Email: gaceta@recoletos.es **Web site:** http://www.recoletos.es
Date Established: 1991; **Freq:** Weekly - Published on Monday; **Cover Price:** Free; **Circ:** 126,126
Editor: Pilar Manzanares; **Advertising Director:** Miguel García
Profile: Journal providing information about education at Barcelona University, including leisure.
Language(s): Spanish
Readership: Aimed at students and staff.
CONSUMER: EDUCATION: Adult Education

GENERACIÓN XXI
53761X83-60
Editorial: Carranza 13, 2° A, E-28004 MADRID
Tel: 91 44 63 845 **Fax:** 91 44 73 034
Email: redaccion@generacionxxi.com **Web site:** http://www.generacionxxi.com
ISSN: 1577-4465
Date Established: 1996; **Freq:** 24 issues yearly; **Cover Price:** Free; **Circ:** 200,000
Editor: Emilia Lanzas
Profile: Magazine focusing on culture and society. Provides opinion, interviews and book reviews, information on music, sport, IT and university matters.
Language(s): Spanish
Readership: Read by university students throughout Spain.
Agency Commission: 10%
Mechanical Data: Print Process: Offset, Trim Size: 297 x 210mm
CONSUMER: STUDENT PUBLICATIONS

GENTE EN BURGOS
712896X67B-6428
Editorial: Calle Victoria, 9, 1ª izquierda, E-09004 BURGOS **Tel:** 94 72 57 600 **Fax:** 94 72 57 453
Email: publicidad@genteenburgos.com **Web site:** http://www.genteenburgos.com
Freq: Weekly - Published on Fridays; **Cover Price:** Free; **Circ:** 50,000
Profile: Regional daily newspaper focussing on news, current affairs, economics, politics and sport.
Language(s): Spanish
Agency Commission: 10%
REGIONAL DAILY & SUNDAY NEWSPAPERS: Regional Daily Newspapers

EL GLOBAL
712871X56A-540
Editorial: Calle Hermanos Garcia Noblejas 37A, 2ª planta, E-28037 MADRID **Tel:** 91 38 34 324
Fax: 91 38 32 796
Email: jalvarez@contenidosdesalud.es **Web site:** http://www.elglobal.net
ISSN: 1576-0978
Freq: Weekly; **Annual Sub.:** EUR 50.00; **Circ:** 29,650
Editor: Gema Martínez
Profile: Magazine containing articles about the pharmaceutical industry, focusing on topics about distributions, management, legislation and drugs production.
Language(s): Spanish
BUSINESS: HEALTH & MEDICAL

LA GUÍA DEL EMBARAZO Y PARTO
53436X74D-27
Editorial: Parque de Negocios Mas Blau, Edificio Prima Muntadas Solsonés B-2, E-08820 EL PRAT DE LLOBREGAT (BARCELONA) **Tel:** 93 37 08 585
Fax: 93 37 05 060
Email: info@sfera.es **Web site:** http://www.aquimama.com
Freq: 7 issues yearly - Summer and Winter editions; **Circ:** 95,000
Editor: Edurne Romo
Profile: Magazine containing articles on the growth and health of unborn babies, nutrition, new products and advice on pregnancy.
Language(s): Spanish
Readership: Aimed at expectant mothers.
CONSUMER: WOMEN'S INTEREST CONSUMER MAGAZINES: Child Care

GUÍA DEL TRANSPORTE MARÍTIMO
52579X45C-15
Editorial: Santa Maria de la Cabeza, 11 Tpd., 2ª A., E-11007 CÁDIZ
Date Established: 1951; **Freq:** 26 issues yearly; **Circ:** 40,000
Editor: Manuel Camacho
Profile: Magazine providing trade news relating to the maritime industry.
Language(s): Spanish
Readership: Aimed at importers, exporters and industrial managers.
BUSINESS: MARINE & SHIPPING: Maritime Freight

HABITANIA
764768X74C-15
Editorial: Muntaner 40-42, E-08011 BARCELONA
Tel: 93 50 87 000 **Fax:** 93 45 45 051
Email: habitania@hymsa.com **Web site:** http://www.hymsa.com
Freq: 10 issues yearly; **Cover Price:** EUR 2.70
Annual Sub.: EUR 29.75; **Circ:** 95,183
Editor: Cinta Bosch
Profile: Magazine about home decoration, furnishing and style.
Language(s): Spanish
CONSUMER: WOMEN'S INTEREST CONSUMER MAGAZINES: Home & Family

HERALDO DE ARAGÓN
53063X67B-5175
Editorial: Paseo de la Independencia 29, Apdo. 175, E-50001 ZARAGOZA **Tel:** 976 76 50 00
Fax: 976 76 50 01
Email: heraldo@heraldo.es **Web site:** http://www.heraldo.es
Date Established: 1885; **Freq:** Daily; **Cover Price:** EUR 1.00
Annual Sub.: EUR 1.65; **Circ:** 100,000

Editor: Encarna Samitier
Profile: Regional daily newspaper focussing on news, current affairs, economics, politics and sport.
Language(s): Spanish
ADVERTISING RATES:
Full Page Mono .... EUR 3740.00
Full Page Colour .... EUR 5236.00
REGIONAL DAILY & SUNDAY NEWSPAPERS: Regional Daily Newspapers

---

HERALDO DE HUESCA
53015X67B-5200
Editorial: Coso Bajo 28, E-22001 HUESCA
Tel: 974 23 90 00 **Fax:** 974 23 90 05
Email: huesca@heraldo.es **Web site:** http://www.heraldo.es
Freq: Daily - Published Tuesday - Sunday; **Cover Price:** EUR 0.90; **Circ:** 5,819
Editor: Mariano Gallego
Profile: Regional daily newspaper focussing on news, current affairs, economics, politics and sport.
Language(s): Spanish
REGIONAL DAILY & SUNDAY NEWSPAPERS: Regional Daily Newspapers

---

HERALDO DE SORIA 7 DÍAS
53051X67B-5225
Editorial: El Collado 17, E-42002 SORIA
Tel: 975 23 36 07 **Fax:** 975 22 92 11
Email: soriaredaccion@heraldo.es **Web site:** http://www.heraldo.es
Freq: Daily; **Cover Price:** EUR 1.00; **Circ:** 4,199
Editor: Roberto Ortega
Language(s): Spanish
REGIONAL DAILY & SUNDAY NEWSPAPERS: Regional Daily Newspapers

---

HISTORIA NATIONAL GEOGRAPHIC
1696850X94X-151
Editorial: Pérez Galdós 36, E-08012 BARCELONA
Tel: 93 41 47 347 **Fax:** 93 21 77 374
Email: historia@rba.es **Web site:** http://www.rba.es
Freq: Monthly; **Cover Price:** EUR 2.95; **Circ:** 203,666
Editor: Josep María Casals; **Advertising Director:** Artur Alepuz
Profile: Information about history (Egypt, Greece, Romans, Middle Age,...), interviews, researching. Photography, maps.
Language(s): Spanish
Readership: People interested in history.
CONSUMER: OTHER CLASSIFICATIONS: Miscellaneous

HOGARES
53426X74C-35
Editorial: Pau Claris 99 -101, E-08009 BARCELONA
Tel: 93 31 80 101 **Fax:** 93 31 83 502
Email: hogares@curtediciones.com **Web site:** http://www.curtediciones.com
Freq: Monthly; **Circ:** 100,000
Editor: Martha Barbancho
Profile: Magazine containing articles on home decoration, furniture and furnishings, architecture and interior design.
Language(s): Spanish
Readership: Aimed at home owners.
ADVERTISING RATES:
Full Page Colour .... EUR 3726.00
CONSUMER: WOMEN'S INTEREST CONSUMER MAGAZINES: Home & Family

HOLA
53494X74Q-80
Editorial: Miguel Angel 1, 4ª planta, E-28010 MADRID **Tel:** 91 70 21 300 **Fax:** 91 31 96 444
Email: fotografias@hola.com **Web site:** http://www.hola.es
Freq: Weekly; **Annual Sub.:** EUR 93.60; **Circ:** 765,496
Editor: José Antonio Olivar; **Advertisement Director:** Elena Mendez
Profile: Celebrity and news magazine with interviews and photo sessions of famous people, world events and geographic features.
Language(s): Spanish
Readership: Aimed at the general public.
CONSUMER: WOMEN'S INTEREST CONSUMER MAGAZINES: Lifestyle

HORA NOVA
763792X72-150
Editorial: Méndez Nuñez 43-45, E-17600 FIGUERAS
Tel: 972 50 59 58 **Fax:** 972 67 85 37
Email: horanova@horanova.es **Web site:** http://www.horanova.es
Freq: Weekly - Published on Tuesday; **Cover Price:** EUR 1.50
Annual Sub.: EUR 77.54; **Circ:** 4,500
Editor: José María Benirl; **Advertising Manager:** José Puig
Language(s): Spanish
ADVERTISING RATES:
Full Page Mono .... EUR 325.00
Full Page Colour .... EUR 375.00
LOCAL NEWSPAPERS

HORAS PUNTA DEL MOTOR
52405X31A-80
Editorial: Avda. Transversal 16, urb. El Monte, E-28250 TORRELODONES (MADRID) **Tel:** 91 85 99 353
Fax: 91 85 99 361
Email: horaspunta@wanadoo.es
Date Established: 1993; **Freq:** Monthly; **Circ:** 25,000
Usual Pagination: 40
Editor: José María Bermejo
Profile: Newspaper containing news, product, equipment and accessories reviews, details of trade fairs, auctions and services within the motor industry. Includes information on the second-hand market.
Language(s): Spanish
Readership: Aimed at mechanics, sales managers, distributors and retailers of car spares and accessories.
Agency Commission: 10%
Mechanical Data: Type Area: 380 x 255mm, Col Length: 380mm, Page Width: 255mm
Copy instructions: *Copy Date:* 25th of the month prior to publication date
Average ad content per issue: 50%
BUSINESS: MOTOR TRADE: Motor Trade Accessories

HOY - DIARIO DE EXTREMADURA
52982X67B-5250
Editorial: Carretera Madrid-Lisboa 22, E-06008 BADAJOZ **Tel:** 924 21 43 00 **Fax:** 924 21 43 01
Email: redaccion.hoy@hoy.es **Web site:** http://www.hoy.es
Date Established: 1933; **Freq:** Daily; **Cover Price:** EUR 0.90
Annual Sub.: EUR 378.60; **Circ:** 25,892
Editor: José Orontos
Profile: Regional daily newspaper focussing on news, current affairs, economics, politics and sport.
Language(s): Spanish
ADVERTISING RATES:
Full Page Mono .... EUR 3158.00
Full Page Colour .... EUR 3790.00
REGIONAL DAILY & SUNDAY NEWSPAPERS: Regional Daily Newspapers

---

HUELVA INFORMACIÓN
53013X67B-5275
Editorial: Avenida Francisco Montenegro, 2° Transversal, s/n, E-21004 HUELVA **Tel:** 959 54 11 80
Fax: 959 25 94 67
Email: redaccion@huelvainformacion.es **Web site:** http://www.huelvainformacion.es
Date Established: 1983; **Freq:** Daily; **Cover Price:** EUR 0.90; **Circ:** 8,185
Editor: Antonio Peinazo Pleguezuelos; **Advertising Manager:** José Luis Camacho
Profile: Regional daily newspaper focussing on news, current affairs, economics, politics and sport.
Language(s): Spanish
ADVERTISING RATES:
Full Page Colour .... EUR 1660.00
Agency Commission: 10%
Mechanical Data: Film: Digital
REGIONAL DAILY & SUNDAY NEWSPAPERS: Regional Daily Newspapers

---

IDEAL
53011X67B-5300
Editorial: Poligono Asegra, Calle Huelva 2, E-18210 PELIGROS (GRANADA) **Tel:** 95 88 09 809
Fax: 95 84 05 072
Email: publicidad@ideal.es **Web site:** http://www.ideal.es
Freq: Daily; **Cover Price:** EUR 0.95; **Circ:** 37,765
Advertising Director: José Carlos Davo
Profile: Regional daily newspaper focussing on news, current affairs, economics, politics and sport.
Language(s): Spanish
ADVERTISING RATES:
Full Page Mono .... EUR 2450.00
Full Page Colour .... EUR 3675.00
REGIONAL DAILY & SUNDAY NEWSPAPERS: Regional Daily Newspapers

---

EL IDEAL GALLEGO
53005X67B-5325
Editorial: Poligono de Pocomaco, Parcela C 12, E-15190 MESOIRO LA CORUÑA **Tel:** 981 17 30 40
Fax: 981 29 93 27
Email: elidealgallego@elidealgallego.com **Web site:** http://www.elidealgallego.com
Date Established: 1917; **Freq:** Daily; **Cover Price:** EUR 0.90; **Circ:** 13,705
Editor: Ramón Barrena
Profile: Regional daily newspaper focussing on news, current affairs, economics, politics and sport.
Language(s): Spanish
REGIONAL DAILY & SUNDAY NEWSPAPERS: Regional Daily Newspapers

---

IMAGINATE
755523X74A-60
Editorial: Paseo Recoletos 16, E-28001 MADRID
Tel: 91 33 31 419 **Fax:** 91 43 14 215
Email: natalia.chientaroli@reporter.es
Date Established: 2001; **Freq:** Quarterly; **Cover Price:** EUR 1.00; **Circ:** 150,000
Editor: Natalia Chientaroli; **Advertising Manager:** Beatriz Santano
Profile: Magazine focusing on women's fashion, health and leisure.
Language(s): Spanish
Readership: Aimed at women of all ages.
ADVERTISING RATES:
Full Page Colour .... EUR 7000.00
CONSUMER: WOMEN'S INTEREST CONSUMER MAGAZINES: Women's Interest

---

INFORMACIÓN
52977X67B-5350
Editorial: Avenida del Doctor Rico, 17, Apdo. 214, E-03005 ALICANTE **Tel:** 965 98 91 00
Fax: 965 98 91 61
Email: informacion.redaccion@epi.es **Web site:** http://www.diarioinformacion.com
Date Established: 1984; **Freq:** Daily; **Cover Price:** EUR 1.00; **Circ:** 223,425
Editor: Mercedes Gallego; **Features Editor:** Paco Bernabe
Profile: Regional daily newspaper focussing on news, current affairs, economics, politics and sport, covering the Alicante province.
Language(s): Spanish
ADVERTISING RATES:
Full Page Mono .... EUR 3155.00
Full Page Colour .... EUR 4733.00
REGIONAL DAILY & SUNDAY NEWSPAPERS: Regional Daily Newspapers

---

INFORMATIU COMERÇ
52901X63-61
Editorial: Sardenya 544, 1°, 4 ª, E-08024 BARCELONA **Tel:** 93 28 48 911 **Fax:** 93 28 48 192
Email: informatiu@cambrescat.es
Freq: 11 issues yearly - Double issue in July/August; **Circ:** 24,500
Editor: Ana Vinyals; **Publisher:** Josep Francés Valls
Profile: Magazine of the Chamber of Commerce, Industry and Navigation of Catalonia. Features financial and security services, infrastructure, design, transport, equipment, IT and multimedia.
Language(s): Catalan; Spanish
Readership: Read by those in business and commerce.
BUSINESS: REGIONAL BUSINESS

INTERIORES, IDEAS Y TENDENCIAS
763961X74C-40
Editorial: Avda. Diagonal 477, 2ª planta, E-08036 BARCELONA **Tel:** 932 70 45 55 **Fax:** 932 70 45 82
Freq: Monthly; **Cover Price:** EUR 1.80; **Circ:** 240,162
Editor: Elena Matias
Profile: Magazine focusing on home improvement and interior decoration.
Language(s): Spanish
Readership: Aimed primarily at women interested in home decoration.
CONSUMER: WOMEN'S INTEREST CONSUMER MAGAZINES: Home & Family

INTERVIU
53382X73-150
Editorial: Calle O'Donnell 12, E-28009 MADRID
Tel: 91 58 63 300 **Fax:** 91 58 63 555
Email: interviu@grupozeta.es **Web site:** http://www.interviu.es
Date Established: 1976; **Freq:** Weekly; **Cover Price:** EUR 2.50; **Circ:** 215,500
Usual Pagination: 132
Editor: Juan José Fernández
Profile: Magazine containing articles and interviews covering lifestyle issues and related topics.
Language(s): Spanish
CONSUMER: NATIONAL & INTERNATIONAL PERIODICALS

INVERSIÓN Y CAPITAL
51949X1F-20
Editorial: Calle Jose Abascal 56, 7ª, E-28003 MADRID **Tel:** 91 45 63 320 **Fax:** 91 45 63 328
Email: r.rubio@inverca.com **Web site:** http://www.inversionycapital.com
Freq: Annual - Not published in August; **Cover Price:** EUR 2.70; **Circ:** 45,000
Usual Pagination: 100
Editor: Mariano Utrilla
Profile: Journal containing financial and investment news.
Language(s): Spanish
BUSINESS: FINANCE & ECONOMICS: Investment

JAÉN
53016X67B-5375
Editorial: Calle Torredonjimeno 1, Polígono los Olivares, Apdo. de Correos 81, E-23009 JAEN
Tel: 953 21 11 11 **Fax:** 953 21 11 25
Email: diariojaen@diariojaen.es **Web site:** http://www.diariojaen.es
Freq: Daily; **Cover Price:** EUR 1.00; **Circ:** 8,678
Editor: Juana González Cerezo; **Managing Director:** Tomás Raldan Cañas
Profile: Regional daily newspaper focussing on news, current affairs, economics, politics and sport.
Language(s): Spanish
ADVERTISING RATES:
Full Page Mono .... EUR 1176.00
Full Page Colour .... EUR 1647.00
REGIONAL DAILY & SUNDAY NEWSPAPERS: Regional Daily Newspapers

---

JANO MEDICINA Y HUMANIDADES
52726X56A-600
Editorial: Travesera de Gracia 17-21, E-08021 BARCELONA **Tel:** 93 20 00 711 **Fax:** 93 20 91 136
Email: jano@doyma.es **Web site:** http://www.doyma.es
ISSN: 0210-220X
Date Established: 1971; **Freq:** 44 issues yearly; **Circ:** 35,000
Editor: Aníbal Álvarez; **Publisher:** Javier López Iglesias
Profile: General medical journal.
Language(s): Spanish
Readership: Aimed at those in the medical profession.
BUSINESS: HEALTH & MEDICAL

JOYA MODA
52658X52A-34
Editorial: Calle Abtao 11, 2° C, E-28007 MADRID
Tel: 91 55 19 197 **Fax:** 91 50 12 388
Email: anfer@teleine.es
Freq: Half-yearly; **Circ:** 80,000
Editor: Ana García Herrera
Profile: Magazine about the international fashion jewellery trade.
Language(s): Spanish
BUSINESS: GIFT TRADE: Jewellery

EL JUEVES
53383X73-160
Editorial: Calle Viladomat 135, 3ª planta, E-08015 BARCELONA **Tel:** 93 29 22 217 **Fax:** 93 23 75 824
Email: redaccion@eljueves.es **Web site:** http://www.eljueves.es
Freq: Weekly; **Annual Sub.:** EUR 87.00; **Circ:** 134,347
Editor: Latorre; **Advertising Manager:** Maciej Zielaswick
Profile: Magazine containing political satire, gossip, jokes, cartoons and investigative journalism.
Language(s): Spanish
Readership: Read by members of the general public.
Mechanical Data: Bleed Size: 280 x 210mm, Trim Size: 255 x 182mm
CONSUMER: NATIONAL & INTERNATIONAL PERIODICALS

LABOREO
52298X21E-80
Editorial: Calle Gral. Moscardó 33, 1°E, E-280020 MADRID **Tel:** 91 53 61 129 **Fax:** 91 53 32 736
Email: laboreo@grupoyebenes.com **Web site:** http://www.grupoyebenes.com
Date Established: 1969; **Freq:** Monthly; **Circ:** 25,000
Editor: Julián Yébenes Guerrero
Profile: International magazine about agricultural mechanisation.
Language(s): Spanish
ADVERTISING RATES:
Full Page Colour .... EUR 1500.00
Mechanical Data: Trim Size: 297 x 210mm
BUSINESS: AGRICULTURE & FARMING: Agriculture - Machinery & Plant

---

LABORES DEL HOGAR
53449X74E-50
Editorial: Muntaner 40-42, E-08011 BARCELONA
Tel: 93 50 87 000 **Fax:** 93 45 40 551
Email: labores@hymsa.com **Web site:** http://www.labores.com
Freq: 11 issues yearly; **Cover Price:** EUR 3.30; **Circ:** 150,994
Editor: Eulalia Ubach; **Advertising Manager:** Margarita Massip
Profile: Magazine about embroidery, crochet, knitting, cross-stitch and other handicrafts.
Language(s): Spanish
Readership: Aimed at women interested in handicrafts.
CONSUMER: WOMEN'S INTEREST CONSUMER MAGAZINES: Crafts

LECTURAS
53458X74A-75
Editorial: Muntaner 40-42, E-08011 BARCELONA
Tel: 93 50 87 000 **Fax:** 93 45 41 322
Email: lecturas@hymsa.com **Web site:** http://www.lecturas.es
Freq: Weekly - Published on Thursday; **Cover Price:** EUR 1.50
Annual Sub.: EUR 93.60; **Circ:** 386,941
Editor: María José Díaz Plaja
Profile: Magazine containing short fictional stories and articles about celebrities.
Language(s): Spanish
Supplement(s): Lecturas Decoración - 10xY
CONSUMER: WOMEN'S INTEREST CONSUMER MAGAZINES: Women's Interest

---

LECTURAS ESPECIAL COCINA
764767X74P-236
Editorial: Muntaner 40-42, E-08011 BARCELONA
Tel: 93 50 87 000 **Fax:** 93 45 48 071
Email: lecturas_cocina@hymsa.com **Web site:** http://www.lecturascocina.com
Freq: 3 issues yearly - Published in May/June and November; **Cover Price:** EUR 3.16; **Circ:** 166,712
Editor: Julia Blázquez
Profile: Magazine about food and cookery, includes recipes, suggestions to healthy eating and a guide to seasonal produce.
Language(s): Spanish
Readership: Aimed at those who like cooking.
CONSUMER: WOMEN'S INTEREST CONSUMER MAGAZINES: Food & Cookery

LECTURAS MODA 764770X74B-45
Editorial: Muntaner 40-42, E-08011 BARCELONA
Tel: 93 50 87 000 **Fax:** 93 45 45 051
Email: lecturas_moda@hymsa.com **Web site:** http://www.lecturasmoda.com
Freq: 6 issues yearly; **Cover Price:** EUR 3.31; **Circ:** 149,291
Editor: Xandra Sarret
Profile: Magazine containing article about fashion.
Language(s): Spanish
CONSUMER: WOMEN'S INTEREST CONSUMER MAGAZINES: Women's Interest - Fashion

LEVANTE DE CASTELLÓN
52999X67B-5500
Editorial: Saragoza 11, E-12001 CASTELLON
Tel: 964 25 45 12 **Fax:** 964 25 08 89
Email: levantecs.rdc@epi.es **Web site:** http://www.levante-emv.com
Freq: Daily; **Circ:** 6,200
Editor: Joaquin Genis
Profile: Regional daily newspaper focussing on news, current affairs, economics, politics and sport.
Language(s): Spanish
REGIONAL DAILY & SUNDAY NEWSPAPERS: Regional Daily Newspapers

LEVANTE (EL MERCANTIL VALENCIANO) 53056X67B-5475
Editorial: Traginers 7, Edif. Levante, E-46014 VALENCIA **Tel:** 96 39 92 200 **Fax:** 96 39 92 308
Email: levante-emv@epi.es **Web site:** http://www.levante-emv.es
Date Established: 1872; **Freq:** Daily; **Cover Price:** EUR 1.00; **Circ:** 70,000
Editor: Miguel Angel Sánchez
Profile: Regional daily newspaper focussing on news, current affairs, economics, politics and sport.
Language(s): Spanish
Supplement(s): La Cartelera - 52xY.
REGIONAL DAILY & SUNDAY NEWSPAPERS: Regional Daily Newspapers

LIMPIEZA INFORM 52015X4F-90
Editorial: Calle Cadi 3, Polígon industrial Riu d'Or, E-08272 SANT FRUITÓS DE BAGES (BARCELONA)
Tel: 93 87 74 101 **Fax:** 93 87 74 078
Email: itel@itelspain.com **Web site:** http://www.itelspain.com
ISSN: 1135-0733
Date Established: 1980; **Freq:** 6 issues yearly; **Annual Sub.:** EUR 87.50; **Circ:** 22,500
Usual Pagination: 68
Editor: Valentín Casas
Profile: Magazine of the Spanish Technical Institute of Cleaning. Provides news and information about all aspects of industrial cleaning, including equipment reviews and details of training schemes.
Language(s): Spanish
Readership: Aimed at managers within the cleaning industry.
Agency Commission: 10%
BUSINESS: ARCHITECTURE & BUILDING: Cleaning & Maintenance

LINEAS DEL TREN 765686X49E-151
Editorial: Pº del Rey 30 - 1ª planta, E-28008 MADRID
Tel: 91 54 03 062 **Fax:** 91 54 03 091
Email: asuarez@renfe.es **Web site:** http://www.lineasdeltren.com/centro.htm
Freq: 26 issues yearly; **Circ:** 36,899
Editor: Ampara Suárez
Profile: Magazine published by the Spanish railway organisation includes details of the railway network.
Language(s): Spanish
BUSINESS: TRANSPORT: Railways

LLADRÓ PRIVILEGE 53710X79K-20
Formerly: Privilege
Editorial: Ctra. de Alboraya s/n, Pol. Lladró, Tavernes Blanques, E-46016 VALENCIA **Tel:** 96 31 87 000
Fax: 96 18 55 128
Email: gsastre@es.lladro.com **Web site:** http://www.lladro.es
Date Established: 2001; **Freq:** Half-yearly; **Cover Price:** Free; **Circ:** 100,000
Editor: Gemma Sastre; **Advertising Manager:** Silvia Garcia
Profile: Magazine of Lladró, a Spanish company manufacturing porcelain figurines. Contains society news and articles concerning art and culture.
Language(s): English; German; Italian; Japanese; Spanish
Readership: Read by members of the Privilege Society.
CONSUMER: HOBBIES & DIY: Collectors Magazines

LUGARES DIVINOS 53986X94G-155
Editorial: Calle Francisco Perez Cabrero 11 B, entresuelo 8ª, E-08021 BARCELONA
Tel: 93 36 20 580 **Fax:** 93 36 20 581
Email: vipclub@lugaresdivinos.com **Web site:** http://www.lugaresdivinos.com
Date Established: 1988; **Freq:** Annual - Published in January; **Cover Price:** EUR 24.00; **Circ:** 250,000
Usual Pagination: 400
Editor: Juan Robles; **Advertising Manager:** Daniela Tonello
Profile: Publication containing advice and information about quality restaurants and hotels in Spain, Andorra and Portugal.
Language(s): English; Spanish
Readership: Aimed at tourists, frequent and business travellers.
ADVERTISING RATES:
Full Page Colour .... EUR 3800.00
Agency Commission: 10%
Mechanical Data: Col Length: 290mm, Page Width: 230mm, Bleed Size: +3mm, Type Area: 290 x 230mm
Average ad content per issue: 20%
CONSUMER: OTHER CLASSIFICATIONS: Restaurant Guides

MAJORCA DAILY BULLETIN
53069X67B-5525
Editorial: Palacio de la Prensa, Paseo Mallorca 9A, E-07011 PALMA DE MALLORCA **Tel:** 971 78 84 00
Fax: 971 71 97 06
Email: editorial@majorcadailybulletin.es **Web site:** http://www.majorcadailybulletin.es
Date Established: 1962; **Freq:** Daily; **Cover Price:** EUR 0.90
Annual Sub.: EUR 180.30; **Circ:** 7,000
Editor: Humphrey Carter
Profile: Regional daily newspaper focussing on news, current affairs, economics, politics and sport.
Language(s): English
ADVERTISING RATES:
Full Page Mono .... EUR 916.00
Full Page Colour .... EUR 1374.00
Agency Commission: 10%
Mechanical Data: Col Length: 332mm, Type Area: 332 x 252mm, Print Process: Offset, Page Width: 252mm
REGIONAL DAILY & SUNDAY NEWSPAPERS: Regional Daily Newspapers

LA MAÑANA 763564X67B-5540
Editorial: Polígono industrial El Segre 118, Apdo. de Correus 11, E-25080 LLEIDA **Tel:** 973 20 46 00
Fax: 973 20 58 10
Email: manyana@lamanyana.es **Web site:** http://www.lamanyana.es
Freq: Daily; **Cover Price:** EUR 1.00
Annual Sub.: EUR 264.00; **Circ:** 7,358
Editor: Josep Ramón Ribé; **Advertising Manager:** Ramón Serrat Baiget
Profile: Regional daily newspaper focussing on news, current affairs, economics, politics and sport.
Language(s): Spanish
ADVERTISING RATES:
Full Page Mono .... EUR 1498.00
Full Page Colour .... EUR 1994.00
Supplement(s): Revista - 52xY, Tot motor - 52xY
REGIONAL DAILY & SUNDAY NEWSPAPERS: Regional Daily Newspapers

MARCA 52934X65A-45
Editorial: Avenida de San Luis, 25-27, E-28033 MADRID **Tel:** 90 299 61 11 **Fax:** 91 33 73 276
Email: cartasaldirector@recoletos.es **Web site:** http://www.marca.es
Date Established: 1938; **Freq:** Daily; **Cover Price:** EUR 1.00; **Circ:** 527,478
Editor: Gerardo Riquelme; **Advertising Director:** Carlos Linares
Profile: Tabloid-sized newspaper containing sport news from around the world.
Language(s): Spanish
Readership: Read by people of all ages interested in sports.
Mechanical Data: Trim Size: 390 x 290mm, Type Area: 340 x 250mm, Col Length: 340mm, Film: Digital only
NATIONAL DAILY & SUNDAY NEWSPAPERS: National Daily Newspapers

MARCA MOTOR 1774781X77D-301
Editorial: Paseo de la Castellana 66, E-28046 MADRID **Tel:** 91 33 73 202 **Fax:** 91 33 73 177
Email: marcamotorrevista@recoletos.es **Web site:** http://www.marca.com/marca_motor
Freq: Monthly; **Circ:** 123,261
Editor: Alberto Gómez
Language(s): Spanish
CONSUMER: MOTORING & CYCLING: Motor Sports

MARIE CLAIRE 53398X74A-80
Editorial: Albasanz 15, Edificio A, E-28037 MADRID
Tel: 91 43 69 800 **Fax:** 91 57 51 392
Email: mclaire@gyj.es **Web site:** http://www.marie-claire.es
Freq: Monthly; **Annual Sub.:** EUR 36.00; **Circ:** 168,588
Editor: Virginia Galvin; **Advertising Manager:** Rosa Alonso; **Advertising Director:** Elena Sánchez Fabrés
Profile: Magazine with articles on fashion, beauty, health, cookery and drink, interiors and worldwide sociopolitical issues.
Language(s): Spanish
Readership: Read mainly by women.
ADVERTISING RATES:
Full Page Colour .... EUR 10950.00
Agency Commission: 15%
Mechanical Data: Screen: 60 lpc, Film: Positive, right reading, emulsion down, Trim Size: 297 x 227mm
Supplement(s): La Casa Marie Claire - 12xY.
CONSUMER: WOMEN'S INTEREST CONSUMER MAGAZINES: Women's Interest

EL MEDICO 52737X56A-840
Editorial: Calle Capitán Haya 60, 1ª planta, E-28020 MADRID **Tel:** 91 74 99 508 **Fax:** 91 74 99 509
Email: elmedico@medynet.com **Web site:** http://www.elmedicointeractivo.com
ISSN: 0214-6363
Date Established: 1982; **Freq:** Weekly; **Cover Price:** EUR 4.00
Annual Sub.: EUR 130.00; **Circ:** 25,179
Editor: Leonor Rodriguez Guzman
Profile: Magazine providing articles and information concerning the medical profession. Dealing with all manners of medical issues from practical to insurance. Also includes legal debates and new discoveries.
Language(s): Spanish
Readership: Aimed at specialized doctors.
Mechanical Data: Type Area: 270 x 205mm, Col Length: 270mm, Page Width: 205mm
BUSINESS: HEALTH & MEDICAL

MENORCA DIARIO INSULAR
53070X67B-5600
Editorial: Cap de Cavallería 5, E-07714 MAHÓN
Tel: 97 13 51 600 **Fax:** 97 13 51 983
Email: redaccion@menorca.info
Freq: Daily; **Circ:** 7,000
Editor: Juan Carlos Ortego Elvira
Profile: Regional daily newspaper focussing on news, current affairs, economics, politics and sport.
Language(s): Spanish
REGIONAL DAILY & SUNDAY NEWSPAPERS: Regional Daily Newspapers

MEN'S HEALTH 764297X86C-165
Editorial: Calle Pedro i Pons 9-11, E-08034 BARCELONA **Tel:** 93 20 63 784 **Fax:** 93 20 48 829
Email: redaccionmh@mpib.es **Web site:** http://wwwmenshealth.es
Freq: Monthly; **Cover Price:** EUR 2.90
Annual Sub.: EUR 26.36; **Circ:** 118,273
Editor: Toni Orti
Profile: Magazine covering health, fitness and fashion issues.
Language(s): Spanish
Readership: Aimed at men.
ADVERTISING RATES:
Full Page Colour .... EUR 9115.00
CONSUMER: ADULT & GAY MAGAZINES: Men's Lifestyle Magazines

MERCADO DE DINERO
765648X1A-210
Editorial: Calle Altamirano 33, local izquierda, E-28008 MADRID **Tel:** 91 54 16 161 **Fax:** 91 54 17 260
Email: redaccionweb@mercado-dinero.es **Web site:** http://www.ausbanc.com
Freq: 26 issues yearly; **Cover Price:** EUR 1.00
Annual Sub.: EUR 22.00; **Circ:** 50,711
Editor: Juan José González; **Advertising Director:** Isabel Medrano
Profile: Newspaper focusing on financial and economic issues.
Language(s): Spanish
ADVERTISING RATES:
Full Page Colour .... EUR 4000.00
BUSINESS: FINANCE & ECONOMICS

MI BEBÉ Y YO 53438X74D-55
Editorial: Pol. Mas Blau, Ed. P. Muntadas, C. Solsonés B, E-08820 EL PRAT DE LLOBREGAT (BARCELONA) **Tel:** 93 37 08 585 **Fax:** 93 37 05 060
Email: info@sfera.es **Web site:** http://www.aquimama.com
Freq: Monthly; **Circ:** 170,000
Editor: Edurne Romo
Profile: Magazine containing information about child care, pregnancy, health, maternity wear, new products, education and development.
Language(s): Spanish
Readership: Aimed at expectant mothers and mothers with young babies.
Mechanical Data: Bleed Size: 270 x 205mm
Supplement(s): Guía Embarazo y Parto - 12xY Guía Primer Año - 12xY.
CONSUMER: WOMEN'S INTEREST CONSUMER MAGAZINES: Child Care

MI CARTERA DE INVERSIÓN
718878X1A-138
Formerly: Mi Cartera de Inversiones
Editorial: Juan Ignacio Luca de Tena 6, 3ª planta, E-28003 MADRID **Tel:** 91 342 14 65 **Fax:** 91 45 63 328
Email: redaccion@inverca.com **Web site:** http://www.hoyinversion.com
Date Established: 1999; **Freq:** Weekly - Published on Friday; **Annual Sub.:** EUR 100.00; **Circ:** 31,073
Editor: Antonio Miguel
Profile: Magazine focusing on business, economy and finance.
Language(s): Spanish
BUSINESS: FINANCE & ECONOMICS

MÍA 53399X74A-83
Editorial: Albasanz 15, Edificio A, E-28037 MADRID
Tel: 91 43 69 889 **Fax:** 91 57 58 880
Email: mia@gyj.es **Web site:** http://www.gyj.es
Date Established: 1986; **Freq:** Weekly; **Annual Sub.:** EUR 41.60; **Circ:** 293,659
Usual Pagination: 18
Editor: Beatriz Mañas; **Advertising Manager:** Cristina Torralba; **Advertising Director:** Elena Sánchez Fabrés
Profile: General interest magazine, includes lifestyle, health and beauty.
Language(s): Spanish
Readership: Read by women.
ADVERTISING RATES:
Full Page Colour .... EUR 9890.00
Agency Commission: 15%
Mechanical Data: Screen: 60 lpc, Film: Positive, right reading, emulsion down, Type Area: 285 x 224mm
Supplement(s): Especiales Mia Astrologia - 12xY Especiales Mia Belleza - 12xY Especiales Mia Cocina - 12xY Especiales Mia Decoracion - 12xY Especiales Mia Dietas - 12xY Especiales Mia Horoscopo - 12xY Especiales Mia Peinados - 12xY Especiales Mia Salud - 12xY Especiales Mia Trucos - 12xY Especiales Mia Trucos - 12xY Especiales Mia Derechos - 12xY.
CONSUMER: WOMEN'S INTEREST CONSUMER MAGAZINES: Women's Interest

MICASA 53429X74C-47
Editorial: Avenida Cardenal Herrera Oria 3, E-28034 MADRID **Tel:** 91 72 87 000 **Fax:** 91 72 89 371
Email: micasa@hachette.es **Web site:** http://www.hachette.es
Date Established: 1994; **Freq:** Monthly; **Cover Price:** EUR 1.95; **Circ:** 166,317
Editor: Cristina Sánchez; **Advertising Director:** María Luisa Ruiz de Velasco
Profile: Magazine containing information about home decoration and improvement. Provides design ideas and advice on refurbishments, furnishings and furniture.
Language(s): Spanish
Readership: Read by those interested in home improvements and DIY.
Agency Commission: 15%
Supplement(s): Extra Cocinas y Baños Micasa - 2xY Extra Reformas Micasa - 1xY Los Niños de Micasa - 1xY
CONSUMER: WOMEN'S INTEREST CONSUMER MAGAZINES: Home & Family

MON EMPRESARIAL 52902X63-63
Editorial: Carrer Jordi Girona 16, E-08034 BARCELONA **Tel:** 93 28 00 008 **Fax:** 93 28 00 002
Email: medigrup@medigrup.com **Web site:** http://www.medigrup.com
Freq: 11 issues yearly; **Circ:** 30,000
Editor: Montse Sitjà
Profile: Magazine focusing on business and industry in Catalonia. Places emphasis on professional training, as well as providing news on business developments within the region, economics and finance. Distributed free to companies in Catalonia.
Language(s): Catalan; Spanish
Readership: Aimed at company directors, senior management and those responsible for running company training schemes.
BUSINESS: REGIONAL BUSINESS

MONOGRAFICOS BYTE
754383X5R-75
Editorial: Avda. Generalisimo 14, 2° B, E-28660 BOADILLA DEL MONTE (MADRID) **Tel:** 91 63 23 827
Fax: 91 63 32 564
Email: byte@mkm-pi.com
Date Established: 2000; **Freq:** 11 issues yearly - Double issue in July/August; **Circ:** 25,000
Editor: Manuel Navarro
Profile: Magazine containing information on computing.
Language(s): Spanish
BUSINESS: COMPUTERS & AUTOMATION: Computers Related

EL MUEBLE 53430X74C-50
Editorial: Pérez Galdós 36 bis, E-08012 BARCELONA **Tel:** 934 157 374 **Fax:** 932 177378
Email: natalia-bosch@rba.es **Web site:** http://www.elmueble.com
Date Established: 1962; **Freq:** Monthly; **Cover Price:** EUR 2.50; **Circ:** 313,881
Advertising Director: Victoria Ibañez;
Advertisement Director: Ariadna Hernández
Profile: Magazine covering technical articles and features which include new and existing products, company profiles and furniture and machinery showcases. Aimed at people wishing to improve their home surroundings. Twitter Handle: http://twitter.com/ELMueble.
Language(s): Spanish
Readership: Aimed at people wishing to improve their home surroundings.
ADVERTISING RATES:
Full Page Colour .... EUR 22250
Mechanical Data: Col Length: 297mm
CONSUMER: WOMEN'S INTEREST CONSUMER MAGAZINES: Home & Family

MUFACE 52442X32K-200
Editorial: Paso de Juan XXIII, 26, E-28071 MADRID
Tel: 91 27 39 867 **Fax:** 91 27 39 876
Email: revista@muface.map.es **Web site:** http://www.map.es/muface
ISSN: 1234-5678

Date Established: 1978; **Freq:** Quarterly; **Cover Price:** Free; **Circ:** 760,000
Usual Pagination: 52
Editor: Alfonso Fernández Burgos
Profile: Journal of the General Mutual Society of Civil Servants. Covers public administration issues.
Language(s): Spanish
BUSINESS: LOCAL GOVERNMENT, LEISURE & RECREATION: Civil Service

MUJER HOY
753203X74A-95
Formerly: Mujer de Hoy
Editorial: Juan Ignacio Luca de Tena, 6, E-28027 MADRID **Tel:** 91 327 83 00 **Fax:** 91 327 83 01
Email: redaccion@hoymujer.com **Web site:** http://hoy.hoymujer.com
Date Established: 2001; **Freq:** Weekly - Published on Saturday; **Circ:** 1,189,533
Editor: María José Romero
Profile: Magazine covering fashion, beauty, business and technology.
Language(s): Spanish
Readership: Aimed at professional women.
ADVERTISING RATES:
Full Page Mono 17850.00
Full Page Colour .... EUR 22400.00
CONSUMER: WOMEN'S INTEREST CONSUMER MAGAZINES: Women's Interest

EL MUNDO CASTELLÓN AL DÍA
764907X67B-5615
Editorial: Calle Enmedio 81, E-12001 CASTELLÓN
Tel: 964 34 08 00 **Fax:** 964 21 75 06
Email: castellon.redaccion@el-mundo.es **Web site:** http://www.castellonaldia.es/hoy/index.html
Freq: Daily; **Cover Price:** EUR 1.00; **Circ:** 6,500
Editor: Victor Navarro
Profile: Regional daily newspaper focussing on news, current affairs, economics, politics and sport.
Language(s): Spanish
Mechanical Data: Type Area: 343 x 255
REGIONAL DAILY & SUNDAY NEWSPAPERS: Regional Daily Newspapers

EL MUNDO DE ALICANTE
764705X67B-5620
Editorial: García Morato 18, E-03004 ALICANTE
Tel: 96 59 82 244 **Fax:** 96 51 20 641
Email: alicante.redaccion@el-mundo.es **Web site:** http://www.elmundo.es
Freq: Daily; **Cover Price:** EUR 1.00; **Circ:** 14,302
Editor: Francisco Pascual; **Advertising Manager:** Miguel Ygueravide
Profile: Regional daily newspaper focussing on news, current affairs, economics, politics and sport.
Language(s): Spanish
REGIONAL DAILY & SUNDAY NEWSPAPERS: Regional Daily Newspapers

EL MUNDO DE ANDALUCIA
764706X67B-6426
Editorial: Avda. República Argentina 25 - 9ª planta, E-41011 SEVILLA **Tel:** 95 49 90 710
Fax: 95 49 90 712
Email: andalucia@elmundo.es **Web site:** http://www.elmundo.es
Freq: Daily - Published Monday to Saturday; **Cover Price:** EUR 1.00; **Circ:** 286,685
Editor: Javier Rubio; **Advertising Manager:** Rafael Marin
Profile: Regional daily newspaper focussing on news, current affairs, economics, politics and sport.
Language(s): Spanish
ADVERTISING RATES:
Full Page Mono .... EUR 2900.00
Full Page Colour .... EUR 3700.00
Mechanical Data: Type Area: 343 x 255mm
REGIONAL DAILY & SUNDAY NEWSPAPERS: Regional Daily Newspapers

EL MUNDO DE CASTILLA Y LEÓN
764707X67B-5623
Editorial: Avda. de Burgos 33, E-47009 VALLADOLID
Tel: 983 42 17 00 **Fax:** 983 42 17 15
Email: cartas.director@elmundo.es
Freq: Daily - Published Monday to Saturday; **Cover Price:** EUR 1.00; **Circ:** 26,461
Editor: Vidal Aranzo
Profile: Regional daily newspaper focussing on news, current affairs, economics, politics and sport.
Language(s): Spanish
Mechanical Data: Type Area: 343 x 255mm
REGIONAL DAILY & SUNDAY NEWSPAPERS: Regional Daily Newspapers

EL MUNDO DE CATALUNYA
52986X67B-5625
Editorial: Diputación 119, E-08015 BARCELONA
Tel: 93 49 62 415 **Fax:** 93 49 62 408
Email: catalunya@el-mundo.es **Web site:** http://www.el-mundo.es
Freq: Daily; **Cover Price:** EUR 1.00; **Circ:** 26,000
Editor: Félix Martínez; **Advertising Manager:** Josep Cantos
Language(s): Catalan; Spanish
Mechanical Data: Type Area: 343 x 255mm
REGIONAL DAILY & SUNDAY NEWSPAPERS: Regional Daily Newspapers

EL MUNDO DEL PAÍS VASCO
52990X67B-5675
Editorial: Camino Capucino de Vasurto 2, E-48013 BILBAO **Tel:** 94 47 39 110 **Fax:** 94 47 39 158
Email: sonia.andueza@el-mundo.es **Web site:** http://www.elmundo.es
Freq: Daily; **Cover Price:** EUR 1.00; **Circ:** 22,000
Editor: Mikel Moreno; **Features Editor:** Tito Poyo
Profile: Regional daily newspaper focussing on news, current affairs, economics, politics and sport.
Language(s): Spanish
Mechanical Data: Type Area: 353 x 262.5mm
REGIONAL DAILY & SUNDAY NEWSPAPERS: Regional Daily Newspapers

EL MUNDO DEL SIGLO VEINTIUNO
52936X65A-60
Editorial: Calle Pradillo 42, E-28002 MADRID
Tel: 91 58 64 800 **Fax:** 91 58 64 848
Email: nacional@elmundo.es **Web site:** http://www.elmundo.es
Date Established: 1989; **Freq:** Daily - Spain; **Circ:** 401,902
Editor: Rafael Moyano
Profile: Tabloid-sized quality newspaper covering regional, national and international news, politics, finance, culture, society and sport.
Language(s): Spanish
Readership: Readership includes executives, managers, university students and office personnel.
Mechanical Data: Trim Size: 399 x 291mm, Type Area: 343 x 255mm, Col Length: 343mm, Film: Digital only
Supplement(s): Ariadna - 52xY
NATIONAL DAILY & SUNDAY NEWSPAPERS: National Daily Newspapers

EL MUNDO DEPORTIVO
52935X65A-50
Editorial: Avda. Diagonal 477 - 5° planta, E-08036 BARCELONA **Tel:** 93 34 44 100 **Fax:** 93 34 44 250
Email: contacto@elmundodeportivo.es **Web site:** http://www.elmundodeportivo.es
Date Established: 1906; **Freq:** Daily; **Cover Price:** EUR 1.00; **Circ:** 100,737
Editor: Francesc Perarnau; **Managing Director:** Tomas Bly
Profile: Tabloid-sized newspaper focusing on all forms of competitive sport in Spain and throughout the world.
Language(s): Spanish
Readership: Read by a wide range of the population with an interest in sport.
ADVERTISING RATES:
Full Page Mono .... EUR 9330.00
Full Page Colour .... EUR 13120.00
Agency Commission: 10%
Mechanical Data: Type Area: 262,9x320,5 mm, Print Process: Offset, Screen: 85 lpc, Col Length: 49,2 mm, Col Length: 320,5, Col Widths (Display): 49,2, No. of Columns (Display): 5, Page Width: 262,9 mm
Copy instructions: *Copy Date:* 24h before published
NATIONAL DAILY & SUNDAY NEWSPAPERS: National Daily Newspapers

EL MUNDO DIARIO DE VALLADOLID
53057X67B-5650
Editorial: Avda. de Burgos 33, E-47009 VALLADOLID
Tel: 98 34 21 700 **Fax:** 98 34 21 715
Email: redaccion.valladolid@el-mundo.es **Web site:** http://www.elmundo.es/mapadelsitio
Freq: Daily; **Cover Price:** EUR 1.00; **Circ:** 9,368
Editor: Vidal Aranz; **News Editor:** Maria Romero Mayor
Profile: Regional daily newspaper focussing on news, current affairs, economics, politics and sport.
Language(s): Spanish
REGIONAL DAILY & SUNDAY NEWSPAPERS: Regional Daily Newspapers

EL MUNDO DIPLOMÁTICO
52187X14C-62_75
Editorial: Calle San Bernardo 107, E-28015 MADRID
Tel: 91 44 62 000 **Fax:** 91 44 74 666
Email: presidencia@elmundodiplomatico.com **Web site:** http://www.elmundodiplomatico.com
Freq: Monthly; **Cover Price:** Free; **Circ:** 43,000
Editor: Bachar Massaad; **Advertising Manager:** Juan López
Profile: Magazine focusing on politics, including news and information concerning business and international affairs.
Language(s): Spanish
Readership: Read by ambassadors, government officials and decision makers within the business community.
ADVERTISING RATES:
Full Page Colour .... EUR 13.000
BUSINESS: COMMERCE, INDUSTRY & MANAGEMENT: International Commerce

EL MUNDO / EL DIA DE BALEARES
764696X67B-5680
Editorial: Avda. 16 de Julio 75, (Polígono Son Castelló), E-07009 PALMA DE MALLORCA
Tel: 971 76 76 50 **Fax:** 971 76 76 33
Email: eldia.redaccion@el-mundo.es **Web site:** http://www.elmundo-eldia.com
Freq: Daily - Published Monday to Saturday; **Circ:** 19,894
Editor: Miguel Angel Font; **Advertising Manager:** José Maria Conrado
Profile: Regional daily newspaper focussing on news, current affairs, economics, politics and sport.
Language(s): Spanish
Mechanical Data: Type Area: 343 x 255mm
REGIONAL DAILY & SUNDAY NEWSPAPERS: Regional Daily Newspapers

MUNDO NEGRO
53856X87-150
Editorial: Calle Arturo Soria 101, E-28043 MADRID
Tel: 91 41 58 000 **Fax:** 91 51 92 550
Email: mundonegro@combonianos.com **Web site:** http://www.mundonegro.com
ISSN: 1134-7074
Date Established: 1960; **Freq:** 11 issues yearly; **Annual Sub.:** EUR 24.00; **Circ:** 100,000
Usual Pagination: 68
Editor: Gerardo González Calvo
Profile: Religious magazine about missionary work in Africa. Includes information about customs, social problems, politics and religion.
Language(s): Spanish
Average ad content per issue: 8%
CONSUMER: RELIGIOUS

MUNDO SANITARIO (PERIÓDICO DE ENFERMERÍA)
52783X56C-40
Editorial: Edificio SATSE, Cuesta de Santo Domingo 6, E-28013 MADRID **Tel:** 91 54 29 393
Fax: 91 55 99 264
Email: mundo_sanitario@satse.es **Web site:** http://www.satse.es
Freq: 20 issues yearly; **Circ:** 60,000
Editor: Monica Gonzalez
Profile: Magazine containing articles about health, hygiene and safety in hospital environments.
Language(s): Spanish
Readership: Aimed at nurses and hospital managers.
BUSINESS: HEALTH & MEDICAL: Hospitals

EL MUNDO VALENCIA
764709X67B-5685
Editorial: Eduardo Boscá 33 - 1° dcha, E-46023 VALENCIA **Tel:** 96 33 79 320 **Fax:** 96 33 71 650
Email: valencia@el-mundo.es
Freq: Daily; **Cover Price:** EUR 1.00; **Circ:** 15,409
Editor: Rafael Navarro; **Advertising Manager:** Miguel Ygueravide; **Advertising Director:** Manuel Huerta Miralles
Profile: Regional daily newspaper focussing on news, current affairs, economics, politics and sport.
Language(s): Spanish
ADVERTISING RATES:
Full Page Colour .... EUR 3280.00
Mechanical Data: Type Area: 343 x 255mm
REGIONAL DAILY & SUNDAY NEWSPAPERS: Regional Daily Newspapers

EL MUNDO Y LA GACETA DE CANARIAS
53075X67B-5100
Formerly: La Gaceta de Canarias
Editorial: Avda. el Paso, Edificio multiuso Los Majuelos, E-38108 LA LAGUNA (TENERIFE)
Tel: 922 82 15 55 **Fax:** 922 82 14 60
Email: publicidad@la-gaceta.net
Date Established: 1989; **Freq:** Daily; **Circ:** 17,000
Editor: Marco Rodriguez; **Advertising Manager:** Miguel Angel Ronda Casado
Profile: Regional daily newspaper focussing on news, current affairs, economics, politics and sport.
Language(s): Spanish
REGIONAL DAILY & SUNDAY NEWSPAPERS: Regional Daily Newspapers

MUY INTERESANTE
718235X94J-122
Editorial: Albasanz 15, Edificio A, E-28037 MADRID
Tel: 91 43 69 800 **Fax:** 91 57 51 280
Email: minteresante@gyj.es **Web site:** http://www.muyinteresante.es
Date Established: 1981; **Freq:** Monthly; **Annual Sub.:** EUR 24.00; **Circ:** 359,279
Usual Pagination: 160
Editor: Elena García de Guinea; **Advertising Manager:** Eduardo Alarcón; **Advertising Director:** Elena Sánchez Fabrés
Profile: Magazine containing articles about new scientific and technical developments and their influence on daily life. Includes culture, history, health, medicine, nutrition.
Language(s): Spanish
Readership: Aimed at members of the general public.
ADVERTISING RATES:
Full Page Colour .... EUR 14500.00
Mechanical Data: Film: Positive, right reading, emulsion down, Screen: 60 lpc, Type Area: 285 x 224mm, Print Process: Offset
CONSUMER: OTHER CLASSIFICATIONS: Popular Science

MUY SALUDABLE
764418X74G-50
Editorial: Perez 36, 2ª, E-08012 BARCELONA
Tel: 93 41 61 788 **Fax:** 93 23 70 659
Email: mamen-lorenzo@rba.es
Freq: Monthly; **Cover Price:** EUR 1.80; **Circ:** 237,407
Editor: Mamen Lorenzo
Profile: Magazine containing article about health, diet, fitness and nutrition.
Language(s): Spanish
Readership: Aimed at health-conscious people.
CONSUMER: WOMEN'S INTEREST CONSUMER MAGAZINES: Slimming & Health

NATIONAL GEOGRAPHIC MAGAZINE ESPAÑA
53385X73-207
Editorial: Pérez Galdós 36 bis, E-08012 BARCELONA **Tel:** 93 41 57 374 **Fax:** 93 21 77 378
Email: pep-cabello@rba.es **Web site:** http://www.rba.es
Date Established: 1997; **Freq:** Monthly; **Cover Price:** EUR 2.95; **Circ:** 250,340
Editor: Anna Lluch; **Advertising Director:** Pere Bou; **Advertisement Director:** Ariadna Hernández
Profile: Magazine providing geographic information, articles concerning natural history and society. Also includes news of general interest from around the world.
Language(s): Spanish
Readership: Read mainly by people aged 25 to 35 years.
CONSUMER: NATIONAL & INTERNATIONAL PERIODICALS

NEGOCIO & ESTILO DE VIDA
1790495X1A-214
Editorial: C/ Pedro de Valdivia, 16, Pozuelo de Alarcón, 28006 MADRID **Tel:** 915121760
Fax: 915121765
Email: redaccion@neg-ocio.com **Web site:** http://www.neg-ocio.com
Freq: Daily; **Circ:** 78,115
Editor: Mar Barrero
Profile: Business newspaper covering economics and finance, composed by a great team of professionals who work daily, with the aim of providing a newspaper with interesting, innovative, useful, accessible, independent and consistent business information.
Language(s): Spanish
ADVERTISING RATES:
Full Page Mono .... EUR 6897
Full Page Colour .... EUR 9627
BUSINESS: FINANCE & ECONOMICS

NEGOCIO INMOBILIARIO
51947X1E-50
Editorial: Plaza de España 18, 9 planta, E-28008 MADRID **Tel:** 91 54 81 808 **Fax:** 91 54 81 886
Email: redaccion@euroinmo.com **Web site:** http://www.euroinmo.com
Freq: Weekly; **Cover Price:** EUR 2.00; **Circ:** 25,000
Editor: Gema Fernández
Profile: Magazine covering property and the property construction industry.
Language(s): Spanish
BUSINESS: FINANCE & ECONOMICS: Property

EL NORTE DE CASTILLA
53058X67B-5700
Editorial: Vázquez de Menchaca 8-10, Polígono Industrial Argales, E-47008 VALLADOLID
Tel: 983 41 21 00 **Fax:** 983 41 21 11
Email: redaccion.nc@nortecastilla.es **Web site:** http://www.nortecastilla.es
Date Established: 1854; **Freq:** Daily; **Cover Price:** EUR 1.00; **Circ:** 40,000
Profile: Regional daily newspaper focussing on news, current affairs, economics, politics and sport.
Language(s): Spanish
REGIONAL DAILY & SUNDAY NEWSPAPERS: Regional Daily Newspapers

NOTICIAS MÉDICAS - EL SEMANARIO DE LA MEDICINA
52744X56A-1000
Formerly: Noticias Médicas - El Periódico de la Medicina
Editorial: Calle Alsasua 16, E-28023 MADRID
Tel: 91 38 60 033 **Fax:** 91 37 39 907
Email: comercial@edimsa.es
Freq: 42 issues yearly; **Circ:** 38,954
Editor: Antonio Chicharro Papiri; **Advertising Manager:** Raquel Moran
Profile: Newspaper covering all aspects of medicine. Includes news of the latest developments within the profession, articles on technology, new products and treatments.
Language(s): Spanish
Readership: Aimed at members of the medical profession.
Agency Commission: 15%
Mechanical Data: Bleed Size: 295 x 227mm
Average ad content per issue: 35%
BUSINESS: HEALTH & MEDICAL

NUESTROS NEGOCIOS
52165X14A-69_75
Formerly: Nuestros Negocios Hoy
Editorial: Calle Belmonte del Tajo 19, E-28019 MADRID **Tel:** 91 56 01 233 **Fax:** 91 56 51 569
Email: redaccion@dirigentes-negocios.com **Web site:** http://www.dirigentes-negocios.com

Date Established: 1993; **Freq:** 11 issues yearly - Combined issues July/August; **Cover Price:** EUR 3.00; **Circ:** 60,000
Editor: Borja Gómez; **Advertisement Director:** Andrea Martinotti
Profile: Magazine containing news and information about business.
Language(s): Spanish
Readership: Aimed at managers of small and medium-sized companies in Spain.
BUSINESS: COMMERCE, INDUSTRY & MANAGEMENT

NUEVA ALCARRIA
763766X67B-5745
Editorial: Francisco Aripio 76, E-19003 GUADALAJARA **Tel:** 949 24 74 72 **Fax:** 949 22 50 99
Email: redaccion@nuevaalcarria.com **Web site:** http://www.nuevaalcarria.com
Freq: 104 issues yearly - Published on Monday and Friday; **Cover Price:** EUR 1.00; **Circ:** 5,781
Profile: Regional daily newspaper focussing on news, current affairs, economics, politics and sport.
Language(s): Spanish
REGIONAL DAILY & SUNDAY NEWSPAPERS: Regional Daily Newspapers

LA NUEVA ESPAÑA
53032X67B-5750
Editorial: Calvo Sotelo 7, E-33007 OVIEDO
Tel: 98 52 79 700 **Fax:** 98 52 79 704
Email: pam@lne.es **Web site:** http://www.lanuevaespana.es
Freq: Daily; **Circ:** 60,000
Editor: Javier Cuervo; **News Editor:** Javier Neira
Profile: Regional daily newspaper focussing on news, current affairs, economics, politics and sport.
Language(s): Spanish
ADVERTISING RATES:
Full Page Colour .... EUR 3510.00
REGIONAL DAILY & SUNDAY NEWSPAPERS: Regional Daily Newspapers

NUEVO ESTILO
753207X74B-78
Editorial: Los Vascos 17, E-28040 MADRID
Tel: 91 51 40 600 **Fax:** 91 51 40 625
Email: nuevoestilo@axelspringer.es **Web site:** http://www.nuevo-estilo.es
Date Established: 1977; **Freq:** Monthly; **Circ:** 180,000
Editor: Pilar Barrio
Profile: Magazine containing articles on fashion and style.
Language(s): Spanish
Readership: Aimed at women.
Supplement(s): Nuevo Estilo Extra Diseño y Arquitectura - 3xY Nuevo Estilo Extra Cocina y Baño - 4xY Nuevo Estilo Extra Jardines y Terrazas - 1xY.
CONSUMER: WOMEN'S INTEREST CONSUMER MAGAZINES: Women's Interest - Fashion

EL NUEVO LUNES DE LA ECONOMÍA Y LA SOCIEDAD
51921X1A-145
Editorial: Plaza de España 18, Torre de Madrid 3-11, E-28008 MADRID **Tel:** 91 51 60 806
Fax: 91 51 60 824
Email: tpara@elnuevolunes.com **Web site:** http://www.elnuevolunes.com
Freq: 45 issues yearly - Published on Monday, not published in August; **Cover Price:** EUR 1.50; **Circ:** 50,000
Editor: José Luis Marco
Profile: Newspaper containing economic and financial news and information.
Language(s): Spanish
BUSINESS: FINANCE & ECONOMICS

NUEVO VALE
53459X74F-100
Editorial: Gran Vía Carlos III 124, 5° Planta, E-08034 BARCELONA **Tel:** 93 20 61 540 **Fax:** 93 28 05 555
Email: vale@publicacionesheres.com
Date Established: 1979; **Freq:** Weekly; **Cover Price:** EUR 1.00; **Circ:** 159,246
Editor: Ingrid Cervera; **Advertising Manager:** Rosa Martínez Román
Profile: Magazine containing articles about fashion, beauty, music, celebrities and sexuality.
Language(s): Spanish
Readership: Aimed at teenage girls.
Mechanical Data: Trim Size: 297 x 210mm
Copy instructions: *Copy Date:* 25 days prior to publication
Average ad content per issue: 30%
CONSUMER: WOMEN'S INTEREST CONSUMER MAGAZINES: Teenage

NURSING
52780X56B-70
Editorial: Travesera de Gracia 17-21, E-08021 BARCELONA **Tel:** 93 20 00 711 **Fax:** 93 20 91 136
Email: editorial@elsevier.com **Web site:** http://www.doyma.es
ISSN: 0212-5382
Freq: 10 issues yearly; **Circ:** 25,000
Editor: Margarita Peya Gascóns; **Advertising Manager:** Pat Wendelken; **Advertising Director:** Greg Pessagno
Profile: Journal containing articles concerning the education, training and practice of the nursing profession.
Language(s): Spanish
Readership: Aimed at nurses and training personnel.
BUSINESS: HEALTH & MEDICAL: Nursing

ODIEL INFORMACION
763744X67B-5760
Editorial: Pza. de las Monjas, 1, 5ª plantas, E-21001 HUELVA **Tel:** 959 54 08 32 **Fax:** 959 25 10 77
Email: odielinfor@odielpress.es **Web site:** http://www.odielinformacion.es
Date Established: 1999; **Freq:** Daily; **Cover Price:** EUR 1.00; **Circ:** 5,001
Editor: Javier Salas; **Managing Director:** Pedro Neble
Profile: Regional daily newspaper focussing on news, current affairs, economics, politics and sport.
Language(s): Spanish
ADVERTISING RATES:
Full Page Mono .... EUR 1376.00
Full Page Colour .... EUR 1789.00
REGIONAL DAILY & SUNDAY NEWSPAPERS: Regional Daily Newspapers

LA OPINIÓN A CORUÑA
763611X67B-5770
Editorial: Calle La Franja 40 - 42, E-15001 CORUNA
Tel: 981 21 74 00 **Fax:** 981 21 74 01
Email: opcoruna.local@epi.es **Web site:** http://www.laopinioncoruna.com
Freq: Daily; **Cover Price:** EUR 0.90; **Circ:** 8,924
Editor: Fernando Barela
Profile: Regional daily newspaper focussing on news, current affairs, economics, politics and sport.
Language(s): Spanish
REGIONAL DAILY & SUNDAY NEWSPAPERS: Regional Daily Newspapers

LA OPINIÓN DE MÁLAGA
763630X67B-5773
Editorial: Granada 42, E-29015 MÁLAGA
Tel: 95 21 26 200 **Fax:** 95 21 26 243
Email: laopiniondemalaga.rd2@epi.es **Web site:** http://www.laopiniondemalaga.es
Freq: Daily; **Cover Price:** EUR 0.80
Annual Sub.: EUR 270.46; **Circ:** 20,948
Editor: Juanjo Cabello
Profile: Regional daily newspaper focussing on news, current affairs, economics, politics and sport.
Language(s): Spanish
ADVERTISING RATES:
Full Page Colour .... EUR 1935.00
REGIONAL DAILY & SUNDAY NEWSPAPERS: Regional Daily Newspapers

LA OPINIÓN DE MURCIA
53029X67B-5775
Editorial: Pza. de Castilla 3, E-30009 MURCIA
Tel: 96 82 81 888 **Fax:** 96 82 81 861
Email: laopiniondemurcia.rdc@epi.es **Web site:** http://www.laopiniondemurcia.es
Date Established: 1988; **Freq:** Daily; **Circ:** 12,522
Profile: Regional daily newspaper focussing on news, current affairs, economics, politics and sport.
Language(s): Spanish
ADVERTISING RATES:
Full Page Colour .... EUR 1675.00
REGIONAL DAILY & SUNDAY NEWSPAPERS: Regional Daily Newspapers

LA OPINIÓN DE TENERIFE
763635X67B-5790
Editorial: Pza. de Santa Cruz de la Sierra, 2, planta baja, E-38003 SANTA CRUZ DE TENERIFE
Tel: 922 47 18 00 **Fax:** 922 47 18 01
Email: sugerencia@la-opinion.com **Web site:** http://www.la-opinion.com
Freq: Daily; **Cover Price:** EUR 1.00; **Circ:** 14,000
Editor: Luis Padilla
Language(s): Spanish
REGIONAL DAILY & SUNDAY NEWSPAPERS: Regional Daily Newspapers

LA OPINIÓN - EL CORREO DE ZAMORA
53061X67B-5800
Editorial: Rúa de los Francos 20, Apdo 468, E-49001 ZAMORA **Tel:** 980 53 47 59 **Fax:** 980 51 35 52
Email: laopinionzamora.rdc@epi.es **Web site:** http://www.laopiniondezamora.es
Freq: Daily; **Circ:** 7,325
Editor: Dalmiro Gavilan
Profile: Regional daily newspaper focussing on news, current affairs, economics, politics and sport.
Language(s): Spanish
REGIONAL DAILY & SUNDAY NEWSPAPERS: Regional Daily Newspapers

EL PAÍS
52937X65A-65
Editorial: Calle Miguel Yuste 40, E-28037 MADRID
Tel: 91 33 78 200 **Fax:** 91 30 48 766
Email: secretariaredaccion@elpais.es **Web site:** http://www.elpais.es
Date Established: 1976; **Freq:** Daily; **Cover Price:** EUR 1.00
Annual Sub.: EUR 335.00; **Circ:** 597,407
Editor: Berna González
Profile: Tabloid-sized newspaper providing extensive political coverage and in-depth articles concerning international affairs, finance, economics, society and culture.
Language(s): Spanish
Readership: Read by academics, opinion leaders, civil servants, senior executives and decision makers within the business community.
ADVERTISING RATES:
Full Page Mono .... EUR 18610.00
Full Page Colour .... EUR 26010.00
Mechanical Data: Col Length: 369mm, Print Process: Offset, Type Area: 369 x 249mm
Supplement(s): Babelia - 52xY, Ciber País - 52xY, Domingo - 52xY, EP3 - 52xY, Negocios - 52xY, El País Semanal - 52xY, Propiedades - 52xY, El Viajero - 52xY
NATIONAL DAILY & SUNDAY NEWSPAPERS: National Daily Newspapers

PATRONES
764766X74B-85
Editorial: Muntaner 40-42, E-08011 BARCELONA
Tel: 93 50 87 000 **Fax:** 93 45 48 071
Email: patrones@hymsa.com **Web site:** http://www.patrones.com
Date Established: 1982; **Freq:** 15 issues yearly - 15 per year: 12 (monthly) and 3 special editions; **Cover Price:** EUR 3.40
Annual Sub.: EUR 38; **Circ:** 96,142
Usual Pagination: 68
Editor: Carlota Palau
Profile: Magazine specializing in knitting, needlecraft, sewing and dressmaking.
Language(s): Spanish
Readership: Aimed at women.
CONSUMER: WOMEN'S INTEREST CONSUMER MAGAZINES: Women's Interest - Fashion

PC ACTUAL
52055X78E-8
Editorial: San Sotero 8, 4ª, E-23037 MADRID
Tel: 91 31 37 900 **Fax:** 91 32 73 704
Email: fernando-claver@rba.es **Web site:** http://www.pc-actual.com
ISSN: 1130-9954
Date Established: 1988; **Freq:** 11 issues yearly - Combined issue published in July/August; **Cover Price:** EUR 5.95
Annual Sub.: EUR 35.45; **Circ:** 115,455
Advertising Director: Miguel Onieva; **Publisher:** Fernando Claver
Profile: Magazine providing information about developments in personal computing and IT. Contains a product evaluation buyers' guide.
Language(s): Spanish
Readership: Aimed at IT professionals and PC users.
Agency Commission: 10%
Mechanical Data: Type Area: 246 x 186mm, Bleed Size: 280 x 210mm, Trim Size: 246 x 186mm, Col Length: 246mm, Page Width: 186mm, Film: Positive, right reading, emulsion side down, Screen: 60 lpc
Copy instructions: *Copy Date:* 15 days prior to publication date
CONSUMER: CONSUMER ELECTRONICS: Home Computing

PC PRO
761794X5B-87
Editorial: Calle Valportillo Primera No 11, E-28108 ALCOBENDAS (MADRID) **Tel:** 91 66 22 137
Fax: 91 66 14 754
Email: mjlozano@grupov.es **Web site:** http://www.grupov.es
Freq: 11 issues yearly - Not published in August; **Circ:** 65,000
Editor: María Jesús Lozano; **Advertising Director:** Carmina Ferrer
Profile: Magazine covering computer hardware, software and peripherals.
Language(s): Spanish
Readership: Aimed at professionals within the IT industry and advanced PC users.
ADVERTISING RATES:
Full Page Colour .... EUR 5300.00
Agency Commission: 10%
Mechanical Data: Print Process: Offset, Bleed Size: 297 x 210mm, Col Length: 297mm
Copy instructions: *Copy Date:* 15 days prior to publication date
Average ad content per issue: 20%
BUSINESS: COMPUTERS & AUTOMATION: Data Processing

PELUQUERIAS
52215X15B-10
Formerly: Peluquerías de Gran Selección
Editorial: Pza. de las Navas 11, E-08004 BARCELONA **Tel:** 93 29 25 840 **Fax:** 93 29 25 841
Email: info@hair-styles.com **Web site:** http://www.hair-styles.com
ISSN: 1134-5608
Date Established: 1969; **Freq:** 11 issues yearly; **Cover Price:** EUR 4.00; **Circ:** 25,000
Usual Pagination: 166
Editor: Luis Llongueras
Profile: Magazine containing news and information about hairdressing, fashion and beauty.
Language(s): English; French; Italian; Spanish
Readership: Aimed at hairdressers and beauticians.
Mechanical Data: Bleed Size: 285 x 215mm
BUSINESS: COSMETICS & HAIRDRESSING: Hairdressing

EL PERIÓDICO DE ARAGÓN
53064X67B-5850
Editorial: Calle Hernán Cortés 37, E-50005 ZARAGOZA **Tel:** 976 70 04 00 **Fax:** 976 70 04 62
Email: eparagon@elperiodico.es **Web site:** http://www.elperiodicodearagon.com
Freq: Daily; **Circ:** 18,656
Editor: Nicolas Espada
Language(s): Spanish
ADVERTISING RATES:
Full Page Mono .... EUR 2905.00
Full Page Colour .... EUR 3920.00
REGIONAL DAILY & SUNDAY NEWSPAPERS: Regional Daily Newspapers

EL PERIÓDICO DE CATALUNYA
52938X65A-70
Editorial: Consell de Cent 425-427, E-08009 BARCELONA **Tel:** 93 26 55 353 **Fax:** 93 48 46 512
Email: rnadal@elperiodico.com **Web site:** http://www.elperiodico.com
Freq: Daily; **Cover Price:** EUR 1.00; **Circ:** 236,000
Editor: Rafael Nadal; **Advertising Manager:** Sergio German
Profile: Tabloid-sized newspaper containing national, international and regional news focusing on Catalonia, events-listings and information on culture, society, the economy, politics, sport and television.
Language(s): Catalan; Spanish
Readership: Read by a broad spectrum of the population of Catalonia.
ADVERTISING RATES:
Full Page Mono .... EUR 14331.00
Full Page Colour .... EUR 21389.00
NATIONAL DAILY & SUNDAY NEWSPAPERS: National Daily Newspapers

EL PERIÓDICO DE EXTREMADURA
52992X67B-5875
Editorial: Dr. Marañón 2, local 7, E-10002 CÁCERES
Tel: 927 62 06 00 **Fax:** 927 62 06 26
Email: epextremadura@elperiodico.es **Web site:** http://www.elperiodicoextremadura.com
Freq: Daily; **Cover Price:** EUR 1.00; **Circ:** 9,047
Editor: José Guerra Iglesias
Language(s): Spanish
REGIONAL DAILY & SUNDAY NEWSPAPERS: Regional Daily Newspapers

PERIÓDICO ESTUDIANTES UNIVERSITARIOS
53764X83-100
Editorial: Timón 18 Pozuelo, Somosaguas Centro, E-28223 MADRID **Tel:** 91 35 22 800 **Fax:** 91 35 26 642
Email: periodicoeu@telefonica.net **Web site:** http://www.estudiantesuniversitarios.com
Date Established: 1989; **Freq:** 10 issues yearly - Not published in July and August; Free to qualifying individuals ; **Circ:** 130,000
Usual Pagination: 24
Editor: Cristina Roldán
Profile: General information newspaper for university students.
Language(s): Spanish
Readership: Aimed at university students and lecturers.
Agency Commission: 10%
Mechanical Data: Col Length: 365mm, Type Area: 365 x 255mm, Page Width: 255mm
Copy instructions: *Copy Date:* 17th of month prior to publication date
Average ad content per issue: 30%
CONSUMER: STUDENT PUBLICATIONS

EL PERIÓDICO LA VOZ DE ASTURIAS
53024X67B-5900
Editorial: C\ La Lila 6, E-33002 OVIEDO (ASTURIAS)
Tel: 985 10 15 00 **Fax:** 985 10 15 05
Email: vozredaccion@elperiodico.com **Web site:** http://www.redasturias.com
Freq: Daily; **Cover Price:** EUR 0.90; **Circ:** 27,953
Editor: José Carreño
Language(s): Spanish
REGIONAL DAILY & SUNDAY NEWSPAPERS: Regional Daily Newspapers

EL PERIODICO MEDITERRÁNEO
53000X67B-5575
Editorial: Carretera Almassora s/n, E-12005 CASTELLÓN DE LA PLANA **Tel:** 964 34 95 00
Fax: 964 34 95 05
Email: mediterraneo@elperiodico.com **Web site:** http://www.elperiodicomediterraneo.com
Freq: Daily; **Cover Price:** EUR 1.00; **Circ:** 18,500
Editor: Julio Sánchez
Language(s): Spanish
REGIONAL DAILY & SUNDAY NEWSPAPERS: Regional Daily Newspapers

PISCINAS
765120X32E-1
Editorial: Pau Claris 99-101, bajos, E-08009 BARCELONA **Tel:** 93 31 80 101 **Fax:** 93 31 83 505
Email: redaccionpiscinas@curtediciones.com **Web site:** http://www.curtediciones.com
Freq: Monthly; **Circ:** 40,000
Editor: Laura Curt

Profile: Magazine focusing on the construction, retail and maintenance of private or public swimming pools and aqua parks.
Language(s): Spanish
Readership: Aimed at manufacturers, retailers, installers and managers.
BUSINESS: LOCAL GOVERNMENT, LEISURE & RECREATION: Swimming Pools

PLAY2MANÍA
53694X78D-142
Formerly: Playmanía
Editorial: Los Vascos 17, E-28040 MADRID
Tel: 91 51 40 600 **Fax:** 91 39 96 932
Email: play2mania@axelspringer.es **Web site:** http://www.axelspringer.es
Date Established: 1999; **Freq:** Monthly; **Circ:** 135,460
Editor: Alberto Lloret; **Advertising Director:** Mónica Marín
Profile: Magazine providing features, news and reviews of computer games.
Language(s): Spanish
ADVERTISING RATES:
Full Page Colour .... EUR 5900.00
CONSUMER: CONSUMER ELECTRONICS: Games

PLAYBOY
53828X86A-180
Editorial: Avda. Diagonal 477, 2 ° planta, E-08036 BARCELONA **Tel:** 93 27 04 550 **Fax:** 93 27 04 582
Email: ecarnero@playboy.es **Web site:** http://www.playboy.com
Date Established: 1978; **Freq:** Monthly; **Cover Price:** EUR 3.46; **Circ:** 100,000
Editor: Eva Carnero
Profile: Magazine containing adult photography, along with articles on wine, nightlife, interviews, music and cinema.
Language(s): Spanish
Readership: Aimed at men.
CONSUMER: ADULT & GAY MAGAZINES: Adult Magazines

PLAYSTATION 2
764495X78D-144
Editorial: Calle O'Donnell 12, E-28009 MADRID
Tel: 91 58 63 300 **Fax:** 91 58 69 780
Email: ps2@grupozeta.es
Freq: Monthly; **Cover Price:** EUR 6.00; **Circ:** 140,000
Editor: Marcos García; **Advertising Manager:** Mar Lumbreras
Profile: Magazine focusing on the PlayStation 2 games console.
Language(s): Spanish
Readership: Aimed at PlayStation enthusiasts.
CONSUMER: CONSUMER ELECTRONICS: Games

PORCI
52916X64H-70
Editorial: Pasaje Virgen de la Alegría 14, E-28027 MADRID **Tel:** 91 40 51 595 **Fax:** 91 40 34 907
Email: aulaveterinaria@aulaveterinaria.com **Web site:** http://www.luzan5.es
ISSN: 1130-8451
Date Established: 1991; **Freq:** 6 issues yearly; **Circ:** 50,000
Usual Pagination: 96
Editor: Guillermo Garzón
Profile: Veterinary magazine focusing on the care of pigs.
Language(s): Spanish
Readership: Aimed at veterinary surgeons.
Agency Commission: 10%
Mechanical Data: Trim Size: 240 x 165mm
Copy instructions: *Copy Date:* 20th of the month prior to publication
Average ad content per issue: 16%
BUSINESS: OTHER CLASSIFICATIONS: Veterinary

PORTNEWSPAPER
52612X49A-47
Formerly: Spanish International Transport Newspaper
Editorial: Passeig de Colom 24 2° floor, E-08002 BARCELONA **Tel:** 93 30 15 516 **Fax:** 93 31 86 645
Email: men-car@men-car.com **Web site:** http://www.men-car.com
Freq: Monthly; **Circ:** 32,000
Editor: Juan Cardona Delclós; **Publisher:** Juan Cardona Delclós
Profile: Newspaper covering transport by road, rail, sea and air.
Language(s): Spanish
BUSINESS: TRANSPORT

PRIMERAS NOTICIAS DE COMUNICACIÓN Y PEDAGOGÍA
52883X62K-100
Editorial: Calle Aragon 466 E ntresuelo, E-08013 BARCELONA **Tel:** 93 20 75 052 **Fax:** 93 20 76 133
Web site: http://www.comunicacionypedagogia.com
Date Established: 1980; **Freq:** 8 issues yearly;
Annual Sub.: EUR 42.00; **Circ:** 30,000
Usual Pagination: 100
Editor: Raúl Mercadal
Profile: Magazine specialising in the educational applications within the communications field, with particular emphasis on new technology.
Language(s): Spanish
Readership: Aimed at teachers.
BUSINESS: CHURCH & SCHOOL EQUIPMENT & EDUCATION: Church & School Equipment

PRIMERAS NOTICIAS DE LITERATURA INFANTIL Y JUVENIL
52856X60A-100
Editorial: Calle Aragon 466 Entresuelo, E-08013 BARCELONA **Tel:** 93 20 75 052 **Fax:** 93 20 76 133
Email: info@comunicacionypedagogia.com **Web site:** http://www.comunicacionypedagogia.com
Date Established: 1980; **Freq:** 8 issues yearly;
Annual Sub.: EUR 42.00; **Circ:** 30,000
Usual Pagination: 100
Editor: José Domingo Aliaga Serrano
Profile: Magazine containing articles about children's literature.
Language(s): Spanish
Readership: Aimed at librarians, school teachers, students and professionals in related fields.
BUSINESS: PUBLISHING: Publishing & Book Trade

PRODUCTOS EQUIPOS CONSTRUCCIÓN PEC
52525X42A-71
Editorial: Zancoeta 9, 5ª planta, E-48013 BILBAO (VIZCAYA) **Tel:** 94 42 85 662 **Fax:** 94 42 85 624
Email: pec@rbi.es **Web site:** http://www.rbi.es
ISSN: 1576-446X
Date Established: 1997; **Freq:** 6 issues yearly;
Cover Price: Free; **Circ:** 23,000
Editor: Fernando Gómez Serranillos
Profile: Magazine providing information concerning new products and equipment for the construction industry.
Language(s): Spanish
Readership: Aimed at construction managers, engineers, architects, carpenters and retailers of construction materials and equipment.
Agency Commission: 10%
Mechanical Data: Type Area: 375 x 260mm, Col Length: 375mm, Page Width: 260mm, Print Process: Offset, Film: Positive
BUSINESS: CONSTRUCTION

EL PROGRESO
53023X67B-5925
Editorial: Calle Rivadeo 5, E-27002 LUGO
Tel: 982 29 81 00 **Fax:** 982 29 81 02
Email: correo@elprogreso.es **Web site:** http://www.elprogreso.es
Freq: Daily; **Cover Price:** EUR 1.00; **Circ:** 18,889
Editor: Tito Dieguez Sanchez
Language(s): Spanish
REGIONAL DAILY & SUNDAY NEWSPAPERS: Regional Daily Newspapers

PRONTO
53400X74A-120
Editorial: Gran Vía de Carlos III 124, 5ª planta, E-08034 BARCELONA **Tel:** 93 20 61 540
Fax: 93 28 05 555
Email: agencias@publicacionesheres.com
Date Established: 1972; **Freq:** Weekly - Published on Monday; **Cover Price:** EUR 1.00; **Circ:** 1,151,642
Editor: Montse Mayodomo
Profile: Magazine providing news, general information and articles on family life, health, beauty, cookery, relationships and society.
Language(s): Spanish
Readership: Aimed at women between 25 and 50 years of age.
Mechanical Data: Page Width: 210mm, Col Length: 297mm
CONSUMER: WOMEN'S INTEREST CONSUMER MAGAZINES: Women's Interest

LA PROVINCIA
53077X67B-5950
Editorial: Avda. Alcalde Ramírez Bethencourt, 8, E-35003 LAS PALMAS DE GRAN CANARIA
Tel: 928 47 94 00 **Fax:** 928 47 94 13
Email: laprovincia.publicidad@epi.es **Web site:** http://www.la-provincia.com
Date Established: 1911; **Freq:** Daily; **Circ:** 56,000
Features Editor: Diego Hernandez; **Advertising Manager:** José Alberto Jimenez
Language(s): Spanish
Mechanical Data: Print Process: Offset rotation
REGIONAL DAILY & SUNDAY NEWSPAPERS: Regional Daily Newspapers

LAS PROVINCIAS
718240X67B-6429
Editorial: C. Gremis 4, E-46014 VALENCIA
Tel: 96 35 02 211 **Fax:** 96 35 97 520
Email: editorial@federicodomenech.com **Web site:** http://www.lasprovincias.es
Date Established: 1886; **Freq:** Daily; **Cover Price:** EUR 1.00; **Circ:** 53,000
Editor: Pedro Ortiz
Profile: Broad size newspaper covering national and international news and current affairs, politics, economy, sport and culture.
Language(s): Spanish
Supplement(s): El Semanal - 52xY.
REGIONAL DAILY & SUNDAY NEWSPAPERS: Regional Daily Newspapers

PÚBLICO
1829672X65A-77
Editorial: Calle Caleruega 102, 1ª Planta, 28033 MADRID **Tel:** 91 838 77 74
Email: mlrosello@publico.es **Web site:** www.publico.es
Freq: Daily; **Circ:** 132,441

Profile: Newspaper covering regional, national and international news, politics, finance, culture, society and sport.
Language(s): Spanish
NATIONAL DAILY & SUNDAY NEWSPAPERS: National Daily Newspapers

EL PUNT
53010X67B-5975
Editorial: Carrer Santa Eugènia, 42, E-17005 GIRONA **Tel:** 972 18 64 00 **Fax:** 972 18 64 30
Email: direccio@elpunt.com **Web site:** http://www.elpunt.com
Freq: Daily; **Cover Price:** EUR 1.00; **Circ:** 24,500
Editor: Xevi Cyrgo
Language(s): Catalan
REGIONAL DAILY & SUNDAY NEWSPAPERS: Regional Daily Newspapers

EL PUNT (VALENCIA)
764727X72-802
Editorial: Historiador Diago 12 bis, 1° B, E-46007 VALENCIA **Tel:** 96 38 22 747 **Fax:** 96 38 51 581
Email: valencia@elpunt.com **Web site:** http://www.vilaweb.com/elpunt
Freq: Weekly; **Cover Price:** EUR 2.15; **Circ:** 8,000
Editor: Enric Orts
Language(s): Spanish
Mechanical Data: Trim Size: 375 x 290mm, Type Area: 326 x 250mm, Print Process: Offset
LOCAL NEWSPAPERS

PYMES
52197X14H-100
Editorial: Catra. Fuencarral-Alcobendas, Km. 14500, E-28108 ALCOBENDA (MADRID) **Tel:** 902 30 40 33
Fax: 902 38 78 95
Email: inma@tai.es **Web site:** http://www.tai.es
Date Established: 1993; **Freq:** 11 issues yearly;
Cover Price: EUR 2.50
Annual Sub.: EUR 26.00; **Circ:** 30,000
Usual Pagination: 100
Editor: Inmaculada Elizalde; **Advertising Manager:** Virginia Alcalde
Profile: Magazine providing information about business management, developments within the business community, information technology and the Internet. Also covers legislation, training, market analysis, economics and conventions.
Language(s): Spanish
Readership: Aimed at owners and directors of small and medium-sized businesses.
ADVERTISING RATES:
Full Page Colour .... EUR 3500.00
Agency Commission: 10%
Mechanical Data: Type Area: 280 x 210mm, Col Length: 280mm, Page Width: 210mm
Copy instructions: *Copy Date:* 10th of the month prior to publication date
Average ad content per issue: 30%
BUSINESS: COMMERCE, INDUSTRY & MANAGEMENT: Small Business

QUÉ ME DICES
53461X74F-140
Editorial: Avda. Cardenal Herrera Oria 3, E-28034 MADRID **Tel:** 91 72 87 000 **Fax:** 91 35 82 264
Email: qmd@hachette.es **Web site:** http://www.quemedices.wanadoo.es
Date Established: 1997; **Freq:** Weekly; **Cover Price:** EUR 1.20; **Circ:** 552,835
Editor: Raquel Vega; **Advertising Director:** María Luisa Ruiz de Velasco
Profile: Magazine containing articles and stories concerning romance and relationships.
Language(s): Spanish
Readership: Aimed at teenagers and women of all ages.
CONSUMER: WOMEN'S INTEREST CONSUMER MAGAZINES: Teenage

QUIÉN ES QUIÉN EN INFORMÁTICA Y TELECOMUNICACIONES
52072X5R-100
Editorial: Calle Marques de Lema 13, local bajo, E-28003 MADRID **Tel:** 91 45 62 660 **Fax:** 91 53 51 221
Email: kunker@kunker.com **Web site:** http://www.pvd.com
Freq: Annual - Published in December; **Circ:** 25,000
Usual Pagination: 450
Editor: Irene Cuevas
Profile: Magazine containing information concerning key personnel and companies throughout Spain within the fields of computing, IT and telecommunications.
Language(s): Spanish
BUSINESS: COMPUTERS & AUTOMATION: Computers Related

QUO
54000X94J-120
Editorial: Avda. Cardenal Herrera Oria 3, E-28034 MADRID **Tel:** 91 72 87 000 **Fax:** 91 72 91 48
Email: quo@hachette.es **Web site:** http://www.quo..es
Date Established: 1995; **Freq:** Monthly; **Circ:** 331,761
Editor: Lorena Sanchez Romero; **Advertising Director:** Pedro Mayenco
Profile: Magazine providing opinions on subjects relating to technology, society and modern living.
Language(s): Spanish
Readership: Aimed at the general public.
Mechanical Data: Type Area: 268 x 200mm, Bleed Size: 297 x 228mm, Col Length: 268mm, Page Width: 200mm
CONSUMER: OTHER CLASSIFICATIONS: Popular Science

RACC CLUB - REIAL AUTOMOBIL CLUB DE CATALUNYA
53677X77E-190
Editorial: Avenida Diagonal 687, E-08028 BARCELONA **Tel:** 93 49 55 029 **Fax:** 93 44 82 490
Email: premsa@racc.es **Web site:** http://www.racc.es
Date Established: 1963; **Freq:** Monthly - Not published in August; **Cover Price:** Free; **Circ:** 750,000
Usual Pagination: 84
Editor: Luis Falcon; **Advertising Manager:** Astriz Codina
Profile: Journal of the Royal Automobile Club of Catalonia, including tests of new cars, competition news, information and travel.
Language(s): Catalan; Spanish
Readership: Read by members.
ADVERTISING RATES:
Full Page Colour .... EUR 11500.00
Agency Commission: 10%
Copy instructions: *Copy Date:* 15 days prior to publication date
Average ad content per issue: 30%
CONSUMER: MOTORING & CYCLING: Club Cars

RAGAZZA
53462X74F-150
Editorial: Avda. Cardenal Herrera Oria 3, E-28034 MADRID **Tel:** 91 72 87 000 **Fax:** 91 72 89 149
Email: oggarcia@hachette.es **Web site:** http://www.ragazza.wanadoo.es
Date Established: 1989; **Freq:** Monthly; **Cover Price:** EUR 2.10; **Circ:** 150,753
Editor: Olga Gonzalo; **Advertising Director:** Amparo Bastiz
Profile: Magazine containing celebrity interviews and general information.
Language(s): Portuguese; Spanish
Readership: Aimed at teenagers in Spain.
Mechanical Data: Type Area: 260 x 193mm, Bleed Size: 297 x 228mm, Col Length: 260mm, Page Width: 193mm
CONSUMER: WOMEN'S INTEREST CONSUMER MAGAZINES: Teenage

LA RAZÓN
52939X65A-72
Editorial: Calle Josefa Valcarcel 42, E-28027 MADRID **Tel:** 91 32 47 000 **Fax:** 91 32 49 451
Email: internacional@larazon.es **Web site:** http://www.larazon.es
Freq: Daily; **Cover Price:** EUR 1.00; **Circ:** 207,631
Advertising Director: Juan Carlos Diaz
Profile: Tabloid-sized newspaper focusing on culture, society and opinion. Includes information on the economy, sport and events.
Language(s): Spanish
Readership: Read predominantly by public sector employees.
ADVERTISING RATES:
Full Page Mono .... EUR 10183.42
Full Page Colour .... EUR 19896.61
Supplement(s): El Dominical - 52xY El Cultural - 52xY.
NATIONAL DAILY & SUNDAY NEWSPAPERS: National Daily Newspapers

READER'S DIGEST SELECCIONES
763768X73-350
Editorial: Azalea 1 (mini parc) Edif. B 1ª Planta, El soto de la moraleja, E-28109 ALCOBENDAS (MADRID) **Tel:** 91 76 88 611 **Fax:** 91 30 20 223
Email: selecciones@rdselecciones.es **Web site:** http://www.selecciones.es
Freq: Monthly; **Cover Price:** EUR 3.50; **Circ:** 162,529
Editor: Natalia Alonso
Profile: General interest magazine.
Language(s): Spanish
CONSUMER: NATIONAL & INTERNATIONAL PERIODICALS

REGIÓ 7
52987X67B-6025
Editorial: Sant Antoni Mª Claret 32, E-08240 MANRESA (BARCELONA) **Tel:** 938 77 22 33
Fax: 938 74 03 52
Email: regio7@regio7.com **Web site:** http://www.regio7.com
Date Established: 1978; **Freq:** Daily - Published Monday, Tuesday, Thursday, Saturday and Sunday;
Cover Price: EUR 1.00
Annual Sub.: EUR 349.00; **Circ:** 9,778
Editor: Enric Badía
Language(s): Catalan; Spanish
ADVERTISING RATES:
Full Page Mono .... EUR 1398.00
Full Page Colour .... EUR 2097.00
REGIONAL DAILY & SUNDAY NEWSPAPERS: Regional Daily Newspapers

LA REGIÓN
53031X67B-6050
Editorial: Polígono San Ciprián de Viñas, Calle Cuatro 19, E-32901 OURENSE **Tel:** 988 38 38 38
Fax: 988 24 44 49

Email: redaccion@laregion.net **Web site:** http://www.laregion.es
Freq: Daily; **Cover Price:** EUR 1.00; **Circ:** 13,929
Editor: Angel Martinez; **Publisher:** José Luis Outeiriño Rodriguez
Language(s): Spanish
REGIONAL DAILY & SUNDAY NEWSPAPERS: Regional Daily Newspapers

REVISTA ADA
53652X77A-340
Editorial: Avenida de América 37, Edif. Torres Blancas, planta 22, E-28002 MADRID
Tel: 91 41 31 044 **Fax:** 91 41 33 330
Email: publicidad@ada.es **Web site:** http://www.ada.es
Freq: Quarterly - Published in January, April, July, December; **Cover Price:** EUR 2.50; **Circ:** 95,000
Usual Pagination: 52
Editor: Virgilio Hernández Rivadulla
Profile: Magazine containing motoring news, but also articles on tourism, gastronomy and lifestyle.
Language(s): Spanish
CONSUMER: MOTORING & CYCLING: Motoring

REVISTA TELEPROGRAMA
53601X76C-280
Editorial: Cardenal Herrera Oria 3, E-28034 MADRID
Tel: 91 72 87 000 **Fax:** 91 72 89 141
Email: tp@hachette.es **Web site:** http://www.teleprograma.tv
Date Established: 1966; **Freq:** Weekly; **Cover Price:** EUR 0.90; **Circ:** 156,280
Editor: Ana Martínez; **Advertising Director:** María Luisa Ruiz de Velasco
Profile: Magazine containing television listings and information about new cinema releases.
Language(s): Spanish
ADVERTISING RATES:
Full Page Colour .... EUR 6024.00
Mechanical Data: Type Area: 137 x 207mm
CONSUMER: MUSIC & PERFORMING ARTS: TV & Radio

REVISTA TOPE
52177X14B-49
Editorial: Puente de Deusto 7, 6°, E-48014 BILBAO
Tel: 94 475 38 13 **Fax:** 94 476 27 90
Email: mt@revistatope.com **Web site:** http://www.revistatope.com
ISSN: 1139-9767
Freq: 10 issues yearly; **Annual Sub.:** EUR 96.16; **Circ:** 25,000
Editor: Antonio Castro; **Advertising Manager:** Juan José González
Profile: Magazine focusing on production and industrial equipment, includes technical articles and reports written by qualified professionals.
Language(s): Spanish
BUSINESS: COMMERCE, INDUSTRY & MANAGEMENT: Industry & Factories

REVITEC
52387X28-60
Editorial: C. Cadi, 3, Polígono industrial Riu d'Or, E-08272 SANT FRUITÓS DE BAGES (BARCELONA)
Tel: 93 87 74 101 **Fax:** 93 87 74 078
Email: itel@itelspain.com **Web site:** http://www.itelspain.com
ISSN: 0214-7394
Date Established: 1966; **Freq:** 6 issues yearly; **Annual Sub.:** EUR 49.55; **Circ:** 24,500
Usual Pagination: 68
Editor: Valentín Casas
Profile: Magazine of the Spanish Technical Institute of Cleaning. Covers all aspects of dry- cleaning and dyeing, including equipment reviews and details of training schemes.
Language(s): Spanish
Readership: Aimed at managers of laundry and dry-cleaning facilities.
BUSINESS: LAUNDRY & DRY CLEANING

LA RIOJA
53022X67B-6075
Editorial: Vara del Rey 74, E-26002 LOGROÑO
Tel: 941 27 91 10 **Fax:** 941 27 91 06
Email: director@larioja.com **Web site:** http://www.larioja.com
Date Established: 1889; **Freq:** Daily; **Cover Price:** EUR 1.00; **Circ:** 17,000
Editor: J. del Río Sacristan; **News Editor:** Casimiro Somalo Somalo; **Features Editor:** Benjamín Blano
Language(s): Spanish
REGIONAL DAILY & SUNDAY NEWSPAPERS: Regional Daily Newspapers

RONDA IBÉRIA
53923X89D-150
Editorial: Calle O'Donnell 12, E-28009 MADRID
Tel: 91 58 63 300 **Fax:** 91 58 69 760
Email: rondaiberia@grupozeta.es **Web site:** http://www.grupozeta.es
Freq: Monthly; **Cover Price:** Free; **Circ:** 198,582
Editor: Manuel de Jesús; **Advertising Manager:** Carmen Yaguas
Profile: In-flight magazine for those flying with Iberian Airways, containing articles about travel and culture.
Language(s): Spanish
Readership: Aimed at Iberian Airways customers.
Mechanical Data: Print Process: Offset, Trim Size: 280 x 210mm
CONSUMER: HOLIDAYS & TRAVEL: In-Flight Magazines

SEGRE
53020X67B-6100
Editorial: Calle del Río 6, Apdo. 543, E-25007 LÉRIDA **Tel:** 973 24 80 00 **Fax:** 973 24 60 31
Email: comunicacio@segre.com **Web site:** http://www.segre.com
Freq: Daily; **Cover Price:** EUR 1.00; **Circ:** 19,394
Editor: Santiago Costa Miranda; **News Editor:** Josep Sanuya; **Features Editor:** Antonio Balleste
Language(s): Catalan; Spanish
ADVERTISING RATES:
Full Page Mono .... EUR 2380.00
Full Page Colour .... EUR 3090.00
Mechanical Data: Col Length: 357mm, No. of Columns (Display): 5, Type Area: 357 x 248mm
REGIONAL DAILY & SUNDAY NEWSPAPERS: Regional Daily Newspapers

SEGURITECNÍA
52674X54B-80
Editorial: Don Ramón de la Cruz 68, 6° derecha, E-28001 MADRID **Tel:** 91 40 29 607 **Fax:** 91 40 18 874
Email: seguritecnia@borrmart.es **Web site:** http://www.borrmart.es
Freq: 11 issues yearly; **Annual Sub.:** EUR 60.10; **Circ:** 25,000
Editor: Alberto Bueno; **Advertising Manager:** Javier Borredá
Profile: Journal covering all aspects of the safety and security industries. Member of Press Club CCTV.
Language(s): Spanish
Readership: Aimed at people in the security sector.
ADVERTISING RATES:
Full Page Colour .... EUR 1700.00
BUSINESS: SAFETY & SECURITY: Safety

SELECCIONES TO P.E.
754528X14B-100
Formerly: TO P.E. Piedra
Editorial: Puente de Deusto 7, 6°, E-48014 BILBAO
Tel: 94 47 53 813 **Fax:** 94 47 62 790
Email: mt@revistatope.com **Web site:** http://www.revistatope.com
Date Established: 1990; **Freq:** 3 issues yearly - Published in January, May and October; **Cover Price:** Free; **Circ:** 24,000
Editor: Antonio Castro; **Advertising Manager:** Ivan Gonzalez
Profile: Magazine focusing on steel production and industrial equipment for the stone industry.
Language(s): Spanish
Agency Commission: 10%
Mechanical Data: Trim Size: 297 x 210mm
BUSINESS: COMMERCE, INDUSTRY & MANAGEMENT: Industry & Factories

SEMANA
53496X74Q-200
Editorial: Cuesta San Vicente 28, 3°, E-28008 MADRID **Tel:** 91 20 40 687 **Fax:** 91 20 43 550
Email: directora@semana.es **Web site:** http://www.semana.es
Freq: Weekly; **Annual Sub.:** EUR 84.00; **Circ:** 352,379
Editor: Nacho Fresno
Profile: Magazine containing news and gossip about celebrities and society figures.
Language(s): Spanish
Readership: Aimed at women.
CONSUMER: WOMEN'S INTEREST CONSUMER MAGAZINES: Lifestyle

EL SEMANAL
1605141X91E-1
Editorial: José Abascal 56, 1°, E-28003 MADRID
Tel: 91 45 64 600 **Fax:** 91 45 64 703
Email: elsemanal@tallerdeeditores.com **Web site:** http://www.elsemanaldigital.com
Freq: Weekly - Published on Sunday; **Circ:** 1,664,014
Editor: Mercedes Baztan
Profile: Lifestyle magazine including articles on general news, fashion, food, health and leisure.
Language(s): Spanish
ADVERTISING RATES:
Full Page Colour .... EUR 33650.00
CONSUMER: RECREATION & LEISURE: Lifestyle

SETMANARI DE L'ALT EMPORDA
763802X72-600
Editorial: Ronda Barcelona 22, Apdo 21, E-17600 FIGUERES **Tel:** 972 51 07 15 **Fax:** 972 67 36 61
Email: redaccio@emporda.net **Web site:** http://www.emporda.net
Freq: Weekly - Published on Tuesday; **Cover Price:** EUR 1.50; **Circ:** 5,300
Editor: Jesús Navarro i Tavera; **Advertising Manager:** Susanna Pérez Lopez
Language(s): Catalan
ADVERTISING RATES:
Full Page Mono .... EUR 420
Full Page Colour .... EUR 552
Agency Commission: 10%
Mechanical Data: Col Length: 47 mm x 36 mm
LOCAL NEWSPAPERS

SIETE DÍAS MÉDICOS
52771X56A-1550
Editorial: Aribau 185-187, 2ª planta, E-08021 BARCELONA **Tel:** 93 20 90 255 **Fax:** 93 20 20 643
Email: edmayo@edicionesmayo.es **Web site:** http://www.edicionesmayo.es
ISSN: 0214-3011
Freq: 40 issues yearly; **Annual Sub.:** EUR 80.00; **Circ:** 25,000
Usual Pagination: 100
Editor: Antonio Vasconcellos
Profile: Magazine containing specialised medical features.
Language(s): Spanish
Readership: Aimed at general practitioners and other medical professionals.
Agency Commission: 10%
Mechanical Data: Print Process: Offset, Trim Size: 270 x 205mm, Bleed Size: +5mm
Copy instructions: *Copy Date:* 1 month prior to publication date
Average ad content per issue: 35%
BUSINESS: HEALTH & MEDICAL

EL SOCIALISTA
53757X82-150
Editorial: Gobelas 31, E-28023 MADRID
Tel: 91 58 20 044 **Fax:** 91 58 20 045
Email: elsocialista@elsocialista.es **Web site:** http://www.elsocialista.es
Freq: 6 issues yearly; **Circ:** 154,000
Editor: Ana Checa
Profile: Magazine containing articles on Socialism.
Language(s): Spanish
Readership: Aimed at socialists.
CONSUMER: CURRENT AFFAIRS & POLITICS

SÓLO CAMIÓN
52632X49D-80
Editorial: Gran Vía 8-10. 7ª, E-08902 L'HOSPITALET DE LLOBREGAT (BARCELONA) **Tel:** 93 43 15 533
Fax: 93 42 20 693
Email: solocamion@alesport.com **Web site:** http://www.alesport.com
Freq: Monthly; **Circ:** 60,000
Editor: Juan Montenegro
Profile: Journal about lorries and trucks.
Language(s): Spanish
Readership: Aimed at manufacturers, dealers and operators of lorry fleets.
Agency Commission: 10%
Mechanical Data: Trim Size: 285 x 220mm, Film: Positive, Page Width: 196mm, Type Area: 254 x 196mm, Col Length: 257mm, Bleed Size: + 3mm
Copy instructions: *Copy Date:* 15 days prior to publication date
Average ad content per issue: 26%
BUSINESS: TRANSPORT: Commercial Vehicles

SÓLO MOTO ACTUAL
52421X31B-70
Editorial: Gran Vía 8-10, 7ª, E-08908 HOSPITALET DE LLOBREGAT (BARCELONA) **Tel:** 93 43 15 533
Fax: 93 42 20 693
Email: solomoto@alesport.com **Web site:** http://www.solomoto.es
Freq: Weekly; **Cover Price:** EUR 2.50; **Circ:** 60,000
Editor: Pep Segalés
Profile: Magazine containing news and information about the motorcycling industry.
Language(s): Spanish
Readership: Aimed at motorcycle retailers.
Agency Commission: 10%
Mechanical Data: Type Area: 252 x 180mm, Col Length: 265mm, Page Width: 180mm, Print Process: Rotation offset, Screen: 60 lpc, Screen: Positive, Trim Size: 285 x 210mm, Bleed Size: + 3mm
Copy instructions: *Copy Date:* 5 days prior to publication date
Average ad content per issue: 45%
BUSINESS: MOTOR TRADE: Motorcycle Trade

EL SOMMELIER
52093X9C-85
Formerly: El Sommelier Español
Editorial: Rosellón 186, 4° 1ª, E-08008 BARCELONA
Tel: 93 32 31 491 **Fax:** 93 45 48 565
Email: edissa@telefonica.net **Web site:** http://www.revistasumiller.com
Date Established: 1988; **Freq:** 11 issues yearly; **Cover Price:** EUR 3.00
Annual Sub.: EUR 40.00; **Circ:** 30,000
Editor: Ricardo Fernández
Profile: Magazine focusing on the production of wines, spirits, liqueurs, beers and other general beverages.
Language(s): Spanish
Readership: Aimed at people involved in the spirit industries in Spain.
ADVERTISING RATES:
Full Page Colour .... EUR 1322.00
BUSINESS: DRINKS & LICENSED TRADE: Licensed Trade, Wines & Spirits

SPAIN GOURMETOUR
52129X50-202
Editorial: P° de la Castellana 14, E-28046 MADRID
Tel: 91 34 96 100 **Fax:** 91 43 58 876
Email: spaingourmetour@icex.es **Web site:** http://www.spaingourmetour.com
ISSN: 1135-8033
Date Established: 1986; **Freq:** 3 issues yearly; **Cover Price:** Free; **Circ:** 44,000
Usual Pagination: 140
Editor: Cathy Boirac
Profile: Magazine focusing on the Spanish tourism and gourmet industry.
Language(s): English; French; German; Spanish
Readership: Aimed at the catering trade, producers and the catering press.
BUSINESS: TRAVEL & TOURISM

SPORT
755529X65A-73
Editorial: Valencia 49-51bajos, E-08015 BARCELONA **Tel:** 93 22 79 400 **Fax:** 93 22 79 410
Email: redaccion@diariosport.com **Web site:** http://www.diariosport.com
Freq: Daily; **Cover Price:** EUR 1.00; **Circ:** 182,258
Editor: Lluís Mascaró; **Publisher:** José Maria Casanovas
Profile: Tabloid-sized covering sports show updating the latest scores, news and events.
Language(s): Spanish
Readership: Aimed at sport enthusiasts.
NATIONAL DAILY & SUNDAY NEWSPAPERS: National Daily Newspapers

SU PRIMER AÑO
53440X74D-110
Editorial: Parque de Negocios Mas Blau, Edificio Prima Muntadas Solsonés B-2, E-08820 EL PRAT DE LLOBREGAT (BARCELONA) **Tel:** 93 37 08 585
Fax: 93 37 05 060
Email: informacionweb@sfera.es **Web site:** http://www.aquimama.com
Freq: Half-yearly; **Circ:** 159,625
Editor: Edurne Romo
Profile: Magazine providing information about the development of babies throughout the first year of their life.
Language(s): Spanish
Readership: Aimed at pregnant women and the mothers of small children.
CONSUMER: WOMEN'S INTEREST CONSUMER MAGAZINES: Child Care

SUPER POP
53632X76E-400
Editorial: Gran Vía de Carlos III 124, 5ª planta, E-08034 BARCELONA **Tel:** 93 25 21 452
Fax: 93 25 21 450
Email: info@superpop.es
Date Established: 1977; **Freq:** 26 issues yearly; **Cover Price:** EUR 1.80; **Circ:** 218,867
Editor: Silvia Alemán; **Advertising Manager:** Rosa Martínez
Profile: Magazine focusing on popular music and covering cinema and television.
Language(s): Spanish
Readership: Aimed at young people.
ADVERTISING RATES:
Full Page Colour .... EUR 8500.00
Mechanical Data: Trim Size: 297 x 210mm, Col Widths (Display): 73mm
Copy instructions: *Copy Date:* 10 days prior to publication date
Average ad content per issue: 30%
CONSUMER: MUSIC & PERFORMING ARTS: Pop Music

SUPERTELE
53600X76C-295
Formerly: Revista Supertele
Editorial: Cardenal Herrera Oria 3, E-28034 MADRID
Tel: 91 72 87 000 **Fax:** 91 72 89 129
Email: supertele@hachette.es **Web site:** http://www.supertele.es
Date Established: 1992; **Freq:** Weekly; **Cover Price:** EUR 1.10; **Circ:** 111,276
Editor: Belen Alonso; **Advertising Director:** María Luisa Ruiz de Velasco
Profile: TV magazine with information about films, actors and reviews.
Language(s): Spanish
ADVERTISING RATES:
Full Page Colour .... EUR 6025.00
Mechanical Data: Trim Size: 228x297mm
CONSUMER: MUSIC & PERFORMING ARTS: TV & Radio

SUR
53027X67B-6125
Editorial: Avda. Dr Marañón 48, Apdo. 98, E-29009 MÁLAGA **Tel:** 95 26 49 600 **Fax:** 95 22 79 508
Email: redaccion@diariosur.es **Web site:** http://www.diariosur.es
Date Established: 1937; **Freq:** Daily; **Cover Price:** EUR 0.85; **Circ:** 43,634
Editor: José Vicente Astorga; **Advertisement Director:** Carlos Blanco
Language(s): Spanish
ADVERTISING RATES:
Full Page Mono .... EUR 4512.00
Full Page Colour .... EUR 6770.00
REGIONAL DAILY & SUNDAY NEWSPAPERS: Regional Daily Newspapers

TÉCNICA INDUSTRIAL
52258X19A-125
Editorial: Avenida Pablo Iglesias 2, 2°, E-28003 MADRID **Tel:** 91 55 41 806 **Fax:** 91 55 37 566
Email: ingetin@ingetin.es **Web site:** http://www.tecnicaindustrial.es
Freq: Quarterly; **Circ:** 62,000
Editor: Gonzálo Casino
Profile: Official publication of the Technical Industrial Foundation.
Language(s): Spanish
Readership: Read by members, engineers and technical workers.
BUSINESS: ENGINEERING & MACHINERY

TELENOVELA
53605X76C-330
Editorial: Cardenal Herrera Oria 3, E-28034 MADRID
Tel: 91 72 87 000 **Fax:** 91 35 81 348

Email: telenovela@hachette.es **Web site:** http://www.telenovela.es
Date Established: 1993; **Freq:** Weekly; **Cover Price:** EUR 1.00; **Circ:** 106,442
Editor: Maite Torrente; **Advertising Director:** María Luisa Ruiz de Velasco
Profile: TV magazine focusing on drama series and soap operas.
Language(s): Spanish
Readership: Aimed at the general public.
ADVERTISING RATES:
Full Page Colour .... EUR 6025.00
Mechanical Data: Type Area: 268 x 200mm, Bleed Size: 297 x 228mm, Col Length: 268mm, Page Width: 200mm
CONSUMER: MUSIC & PERFORMING ARTS: TV & Radio

TELVA
53401X74A-140
Editorial: Paseo de la Castellana 66 1ª planta, E-28046 MADRID **Tel:** 91 33 73 220 **Fax:** 91 33 73 143
Email: telva@recoletos.es **Web site:** http://www.recoletos.es/telva
Date Established: 1963; **Freq:** Monthly; **Circ:** 210,918
Editor: Isabela Muñoz; **Advertising Director:** Arancha González
Profile: Magazine containing articles on beauty, fashion, cooking, home decoration, fitness, travel and gifts.
Language(s): Spanish
Readership: Aimed at women.
CONSUMER: WOMEN'S INTEREST CONSUMER MAGAZINES: Women's Interest

TIEMPO DE HOY
53390X73-400
Formerly: Tiempo
Editorial: Calle O'Donnell 12, E-28009 MADRID **Tel:** 91 58 63 300 **Fax:** 91 58 63 346
Email: tiempo@grupozeta.es **Web site:** http://www.tiempodehoy.com
Freq: Weekly - Published on Monday; **Cover Price:** EUR 3.00; **Circ:** 98,863
Editor: José María Vals; **Advertising Manager:** Carlos Cerro
Profile: Magazine containing general information. Includes articles and reports about politics, technology, health, culture and society.
Language(s): Spanish
Readership: Read by people of all ages.
ADVERTISING RATES:
Full Page Colour .... EUR 11400.00
Mechanical Data: Trim Size: 290 x 205mm, Type Area: 271 x 182mm, Print Process: Offset
CONSUMER: NATIONAL & INTERNATIONAL PERIODICALS

LA TIERRA
52846X57-155
Editorial: Agustín de Betancourt, 17, 3°, E-28003 MADRID **Tel:** 91 533 83 55
Email: osanchez.publicidad@upa.es **Web site:** www.upa.es
Freq: 9 issues yearly; **Circ:** 72,000
Profile: Magazine focusing on nature and environmental concerns.
Language(s): Spanish
Readership: Aimed at the general public and managers of environmental agencies.
BUSINESS: ENVIRONMENT & POLLUTION

LA TIERRA DEL AGRICULTOR Y EL GANADERO
52284X21A-142
Editorial: Agustín de Bethancourt 17, E-28003 MADRID **Tel:** 91 55 41 621 **Fax:** 91 55 42 621
Email: latierra@upa.es **Web site:** http://www.upa.es
Date Established: 1984; **Freq:** 6 issues yearly; **Cover Price:** Free; **Circ:** 40,000
Editor: Esteban López
Profile: Farming and stockbreeding magazine published by the Union of Small-Scale Farmers. Contains information for ranchers and cattle breeders.
Language(s): Spanish
Readership: Aimed at farmers.
Supplement(s): Informe Sobre Agricultura Familiare - 1xY.
BUSINESS: AGRICULTURE & FARMING

TOCADO
52216X15B-40
Editorial: Muntaner, 401, Entlo 1ª, E-08021 BARCELONA **Tel:** 93 241 46 90 **Fax:** 93 200 15 44
Email: tocado@cosmobelleza.com **Web site:** http://www.editocado.com
Date Established: 1956; **Freq:** 11 issues yearly - Combined issue: July/August; **Cover Price:** EUR 7.00
Annual Sub.: EUR 45.00; **Circ:** 30,000
Usual Pagination: 150
Editor: Marga Sánchez; **Advertising Manager:** José Codina Perez
Profile: Magazine containing news and product information for the hairdressing trade, includes fashion and beauty.
Language(s): Spanish
Readership: Aimed at hairdressers and beauticians in Spain.
Agency Commission: 10%
Copy instructions: *Copy Date:* 1 month prior to publication date
Average ad content per issue: 15%
Supplement(s): Tecni-Moda - 11xY.
BUSINESS: COSMETICS & HAIRDRESSING: Hairdressing

TRABAJADORES DE LA ENSEÑANZA
52882X62J-200
Editorial: Pza. Cristino Martos, 4ª planta, E-28015 MADRID **Tel:** 91 54 09 203 **Fax:** 91 54 80 320
Email: fe@fe.ccoo.es **Web site:** http://www.fe.ccoo.es
ISSN: 1131-9615
Freq: 10 issues yearly; **Circ:** 80,000
Editor: José Benito Nieto
Profile: Teachers' union magazine.
Language(s): Spanish
BUSINESS: CHURCH & SCHOOL EQUIPMENT & EDUCATION: Teachers & Education Management

TRANSPORTE MUNDIAL
52617X49A-70
Editorial: Calle Ancora 40, E-28045 MADRID
Tel: 91 34 70 100 **Fax:** 91 34 70 236
Email: tm@mpib.es **Web site:** http://www.motorpress-iberica.es
Date Established: 1986; **Freq:** Monthly; **Cover Price:** EUR 2.50
Annual Sub.: EUR 23.08; **Circ:** 28,000
Usual Pagination: 118
Editor: Iñaqui Nuñez
Profile: Magazine covering news in topics related to transportation, with professional issues, technical tests and comparisons and market orientation.
Language(s): Spanish
Readership: Aimed at people in the transport industry.
BUSINESS: TRANSPORT

TRANSPORTE PROFESIONAL
52618X49A-85
Editorial: Calle López de Hoyos 141-4 planta Izda, E-28002 MADRID **Tel:** 91-74 40 395 **Fax:** 91-51 94 992
Email: tteprof@bgo.es **Web site:** http://www.cetm.es
Date Established: 1982; **Freq:** Monthly; **Annual Sub.:** EUR 73.00; **Circ:** 44,000
Usual Pagination: 98
Editor: Serafín Jiménez
Profile: Magazine covering freight road transport.
Language(s): Spanish
Agency Commission: 15%
Mechanical Data: Film: Positive, Print Process: Offset, Screen: 60 lpc, Type Area: 283 x 210mm, Col Length: 283mm, Page Width: 210mm
Copy instructions: *Copy Date:* 15-20th of the month prior to publication date
Average ad content per issue: 30%
Supplement(s): Foto V.O. -12xY- Catalogo de carroceros e industria auxiliar -1xY-.
BUSINESS: TRANSPORT

LA TRIBUNA DE ALBACETE
52974X67B-6150
Editorial: Paseo de la Cuba 14, E-02005 ALBACETE
Tel: 967 19 10 00 **Fax:** 967 21 12 75
Email: redaccion@latribunadealbacete.es **Web site:** http://www.latribunadealbacete.es
Freq: Daily; **Cover Price:** EUR 1.00; **Circ:** 6,000
Editor: Adolfo Giménez; **Advertising Manager:** Maribel López Vera
Language(s): Spanish
REGIONAL DAILY & SUNDAY NEWSPAPERS: Regional Daily Newspapers

LA TRIBUNA DE CIUDAD REAL
53003X67B-6175
Editorial: Calle Juan II 7, 1ª planta, E-13001 CIUDAD REAL **Tel:** 926 21 53 01 **Fax:** 926 21 53 06
Email: redaccion@diariolatribuna.com
Freq: Daily; **Circ:** 5,000
Editor: Gustavo Prieto
Language(s): Spanish
REGIONAL DAILY & SUNDAY NEWSPAPERS: Regional Daily Newspapers

LA TRIBUNA DE LA COSTA DEL SOL
53028X67B-6200
Formerly: La Tribuna de Hoy
Editorial: Ctra de Cádiz km 177.8, E-29600 MARBELLA (MÁLAGA) **Tel:** 95 28 67 484
Fax: 95 28 67 775
Email: publicidad@latribunamarbella.com
Date Established: 1988; **Freq:** Daily; **Cover Price:** Free; **Circ:** 15,000
Editor: Jorgelina Torres
Language(s): Spanish
REGIONAL DAILY & SUNDAY NEWSPAPERS: Regional Daily Newspapers

LA TRIBUNA DE SALAMANCA
53040X67B-6225
Editorial: Cañón de Río-Lobos, Parcela 14, Polígono el Montalvo 2, E-37008 SALAMANCA
Tel: 923 19 11 11 **Fax:** 923 19 11 52
Email: cartas.director@tribuna.net **Web site:** http://www.tribuna.net
Freq: Daily; **Cover Price:** EUR 1.00; **Circ:** 10,000
Editor: Luis Palomero
Language(s): Spanish
REGIONAL DAILY & SUNDAY NEWSPAPERS: Regional Daily Newspapers

TRIBUNA SANITARIA
52788X56C-80
Editorial: Avenida Menéndez Pelayo 93, E-28007 MADRID **Tel:** 91 55 26 604 **Fax:** 91 50 14 039
Email: oficina@codem.es **Web site:** http://www.cge.enfermundi.com
Freq: Monthly; **Cover Price:** Free; **Circ:** 38,000
Editor: Navarro Bartolomi
Profile: Journal containing articles about health and sanitation in Spanish hospitals.
Language(s): Spanish
Readership: Aimed at members of medical colleges.
BUSINESS: HEALTH & MEDICAL: Hospitals

ULTIMA HORA
53071X67B-6250
Editorial: Palacio de la Prensa, Paseo Mallorca 9 A, E-07011 PALMA DE MALLORCA **Tel:** 971 78 83 33
Fax: 971 45 41 90
Email: master@ultimahora.es **Web site:** http://www.ultimahora.es
Freq: Daily; **Circ:** 25,955
Editor: Lourdes Terrasa; **News Editor:** Pau Amer; **Features Editor:** Lola Olmo
Language(s): Spanish
REGIONAL DAILY & SUNDAY NEWSPAPERS: Regional Daily Newspapers

VALDECILLA NOTICIAS
52789X56C-100
Editorial: Avda. de los Castros 36, 1° A, E-39005 SANTANDER **Tel:** 942-29 12 00 **Fax:** 942-29 12 02
Email: valdecilla@mundivia.es
Freq: 6 issues yearly; **Cover Price:** Free; **Circ:** 35,000
Editor: Africa Fernández; **Advertisement Director:** Jesús Ibañez
Profile: Newsletter containing information concerning the Valdecilla Hospital in Santander.
Language(s): Spanish
Readership: Distributed free to staff.
BUSINESS: HEALTH & MEDICAL: Hospitals

LA VANGUARDIA
52940X65A-75
Editorial: Diagonal 477, 7°, E-08036 BARCELONA
Tel: 93 481 2200 **Fax:** 93 318 5587
Email: redaccion@lavanguardia.es **Web site:** http://www.lavanguardia.es
Freq: Daily; **Annual Sub.:** EUR 230.00; **Circ:** 240,978
Profile: Tabloid-sized newspaper providing in-depth international news, political information and articles on the environment, culture and current affairs. Also contains events-listings and arts reviews.
Language(s): Spanish
Readership: Read by university students, senior executives, managers and office staff, mainly read in Catalonia.
Supplement(s): Vivir en Barcelona - 360xY Deportes - 360xY Magazine - 52xY Qué Fem? - 52xY La Vanguardia Inmobiliaria - 24xY.
NATIONAL DAILY & SUNDAY NEWSPAPERS: National Daily Newspapers

LA VERDAD
53030X67B-6275
Editorial: Camino Viejo de Monteagudo s/n, Edif. La Verdad, E-30160 MURCIA **Tel:** 968 36 91 00
Fax: 968 36 91 47
Email: garciacruz@laverdad.es **Web site:** http://www.laverdad.es
Date Established: 1903; **Freq:** Daily; **Cover Price:** EUR 0.95; **Circ:** 48,506
Editor: Joaquín García Cruz; **Advertising Manager:** Damian Martínez
Language(s): Spanish
REGIONAL DAILY & SUNDAY NEWSPAPERS: Regional Daily Newspapers

LA VERDAD (ALBACETE)
52975X67B-6325
Editorial: Pza. de la Catedral 6, E-02001 ALBACETE
Tel: 967 21 93 11 **Fax:** 967 21 07 81
Email: albacete.lv@laverdad.es **Web site:** http://www.laverdad.es
Date Established: 1973; **Freq:** Daily; **Cover Price:** EUR 1.00; **Circ:** 3,662
Editor: José Fidel López
Language(s): Spanish
REGIONAL DAILY & SUNDAY NEWSPAPERS: Regional Daily Newspapers

LA VERDAD (ALICANTE)
52978X67B-6300
Editorial: Avda Oscar Esplá 4, E-03003 ALICANTE
Tel: 965 92 19 50 **Fax:** 965 92 22 48
Email: alicante.lv@laverdad.es **Web site:** http://www.laverdad.es
Freq: Daily; **Cover Price:** EUR 0.95
Annual Sub.: EUR 340.00; **Circ:** 17,000
Editor: Teresa Cobo; **Features Editor:** Pepe Antón
Language(s): Spanish
REGIONAL DAILY & SUNDAY NEWSPAPERS: Regional Daily Newspapers

LA VEU DE L'ANOIA
763800X72-800
Editorial: Retir 40, E-08700 IGUALADA
Tel: 93 80 42 451 **Fax:** 93 80 54 171
Email: laveu@veuanoia.com **Web site:** http://www.veuanoia.com
Freq: Weekly - Published on Friday; **Cover Price:** EUR 1.20; **Circ:** 6,000
Editor: Jaume Singla Sangra; **Advertising Manager:** Sina Plaza
Language(s): Catalan
LOCAL NEWSPAPERS

VIDA RURAL
52376X26C-110
Editorial: Calle Claudio Coello 16, 1° derecha., E-28001 MADRID **Tel:** 91 42 64 430 **Fax:** 91 57 53 297
Email: redaccion@eumedia.es **Web site:** http://www.eumedia.es
Freq: 21 issues yearly; **Circ:** 27,000
Editor: Estrella Martin; **Advertising Manager:** Julia Dominguez
Profile: Review focusing on the fruit and vegetable growing sector, including details of machinery and new products.
Language(s): Spanish
Readership: Aimed at those interested in national and EU-wide issues and news relating to horticulture.
Agency Commission: 15%
Mechanical Data: Bleed Size: 305 x 230mm, Trim Size: 282 x 207mm
Average ad content per issue: 30%
BUSINESS: GARDEN TRADE

VINO Y GASTRONOMÍA
52095X9C-90
Editorial: Calle Amador y Fernando 6, E-28040 MADRID **Tel:** 91 31 10 500 **Fax:** 91 45 95 700
Email: redaccion@vinoygastronomia.net
Freq: 6 issues yearly - Double issues in July/August and January/February; **Cover Price:** EUR 4.50
Annual Sub.: EUR 50.00; **Circ:** 30,000
Usual Pagination: 104
Editor: Beatriz Sánchez
Profile: Magazine focusing on wine and gastronomy. Provides articles on vine cultivation, quality and distribution.
Language(s): Spanish
Agency Commission: 10%
Mechanical Data: Bleed Size: 305 x 220mm, Trim Size: 265 x 180mm, Print Process: Offset
Copy instructions: *Copy Date:* 1st of the month prior to publication date
BUSINESS: DRINKS & LICENSED TRADE: Licensed Trade, Wines & Spirits

VINOS DE ESPAÑA
52304X21H-105
Editorial: Islas Marquesas 28 B, E-28035 MADRID
Tel: 91 38 65 152 **Fax:** 91 38 60 265
Email: vinos@mundonatura.es
Freq: 6 issues yearly; **Cover Price:** EUR 4.20; **Circ:** 30,000
Editor: Alberto Huerta; **Advertising Manager:** Antonio Perez
Profile: Magazine about Spanish wine, topics of interest to the wine and grape industry, with emphasis on grape growing, winemaking and marketing at various levels. Includes features on distribution and transportation, export and import issues, enology, viticulture, equipment and supplies, as well as industry leaders.
Language(s): Spanish
Readership: Aimed at viticulturists.
Agency Commission: 10%
Mechanical Data: Page Width: 210mm
Copy instructions: *Copy Date:* 15 days prior to publication date
Average ad content per issue: 25%
BUSINESS: AGRICULTURE & FARMING: Vine Growing

VIVE
54379X74A-130
Formerly: Saber Vivir
Editorial: Calle Covarrubias 1, 1ª Planta, E-28010 MADRID **Tel:** 91 44 71 202 **Fax:** 91 44 71 043
Email: vive@globuscom.es **Web site:** http://www.globuscom.es
Freq: Monthly; **Annual Sub.:** EUR 14.25; **Circ:** 145,667
Editor: Rosanna Rezusta; **Advertising Manager:** Natalia Onieva
Profile: Magazine covering health, nutrition, fashion, travel, beauty and gastronomy.
Language(s): Spanish
Readership: Aimed at women.
ADVERTISING RATES:
Full Page Colour .... EUR 6860.00
CONSUMER: WOMEN'S INTEREST CONSUMER MAGAZINES: Women's Interest

VOGUE BELLEZA
764947X74H-250
Editorial: Pº de la Castellana, 9-11, 2ª Plata, E-28046 MADRID **Tel:** 91 70 04 170 **Fax:** 91 31 99 325
Email: vogue@condenast.es **Web site:** http://www.vogue.es
Freq: 3 issues yearly; **Circ:** 100,000
Editor: Pepa Barrusell; **Advertising Manager:** María Jesús Navas
Profile: Magazine with news and tips about cosmetics, health and beauty.
Language(s): Spanish
Readership: Aimed at women.
Agency Commission: 10%
Mechanical Data: Trim Size: 285 x 220mm
Supplement to: Vogue España
CONSUMER: WOMEN'S INTEREST CONSUMER MAGAZINES: Hair & Beauty

VOGUE COLECCIONES
764948X74B-98
Editorial: P° de la Castellana, 9-11, 2ª Planta, E-28046 MADRID **Tel:** 91 70 04 170 **Fax:** 91 31 99 325
Email: vogue@condenast.es **Web site:** http://www.vogue.es
Freq: Half-yearly; **Circ:** 100,000
Editor: Pepa Barrusell; **Advertising Manager:** María Jesús Navas
Profile: Magazine featuring news about the latest fashion collections.
Language(s): Spanish
Readership: Aimed at women and men.
Mechanical Data: Trim Size: 285 x 220mm
Supplement to: Vogue España
CONSUMER: WOMEN'S INTEREST CONSUMER MAGAZINES: Women's Interest - Fashion

VOGUE ESPAÑA
53412X74B-100
Editorial: Paseo de la Castellana 9 y 11, 2ª planta, E-28046 MADRID **Tel:** 91 70 04 170 **Fax:** 91 31 99 325
Email: vogue@condenast.es **Web site:** http://www.vogue.es
Freq: Monthly; **Cover Price:** EUR 3.01; **Circ:** 150,411
Editor: Maria Contredas; **Advertising Director:** María Jesús Navas
Profile: Magazine containing articles about haute couture and beauty.
Language(s): Spanish
Readership: Read mainly by women.
ADVERTISING RATES:
Full Page Colour .... EUR 16400.00
Agency Commission: 10%
Mechanical Data: Trim Size: 285 x 220mm
Supplement(s): Vogue Belleza - 3xY, Vogue Colecciones - 2xY, Vogue Niños - 6xY, Vogue Novias - 2xY
CONSUMER: WOMEN'S INTEREST CONSUMER MAGAZINES: Women's Interest - Fashion

LA VOZ DE ALMERÍA
52979X67B-6350
Editorial: Avda. del Mediterraneo 159°, Edif. Laura 1° Planta, E-04007 ALMERÍA **Tel:** 950 28 00 36
Fax: 950 25 64 58
Email: edicion@lavozdealmeria.com **Web site:** http://www.lavozdealmeria.com
Freq: Daily; **Circ:** 9,500
Editor: Antonio Lao; **News Editor:** Antonio Lao; **Features Editor:** Jacinto Castillo; **Managing Director:** Francisco Iglesias
Language(s): Spanish
REGIONAL DAILY & SUNDAY NEWSPAPERS: Regional Daily Newspapers

LA VOZ DE AVILÉS - EL COMERCIO
52981X67B-6375
Editorial: Cámara 47, entlo., E-33400 AVILÉS (ASTURIAS) **Tel:** 985 52 00 56 **Fax:** 985 56 98 99
Email: lavozdeaviles@elcomerciodigital.com **Web site:** http://www.elcomerciodigital.com/diario/aviles.htm
Freq: Daily; **Circ:** 7,500
Editor: José María Urbano García; **News Editor:** Yolanda Luis
Language(s): Spanish
REGIONAL DAILY & SUNDAY NEWSPAPERS: Regional Daily Newspapers

LA VOZ DE GALICIA
53006X67B-6400
Editorial: Avda. de la Prensa 84-85, Polígono de Sabón, E-15142 ARTEIXO LA CORUÑA
Tel: 981 18 01 80 **Fax:** 981 18 04 10
Email: redac@lavoz.es **Web site:** http://www.lavozdegalicia.es
Freq: Daily; **Annual Sub.:** EUR 317.00; **Circ:** 123,639
Editor: Sofía Vázquez
Language(s): Galician; Spanish
ADVERTISING RATES:
Full Page Mono .... EUR 8589.00
Full Page Colour .... EUR 10886.00
Supplement(s): Guia de Galicia - 1xY.
REGIONAL DAILY & SUNDAY NEWSPAPERS: Regional Daily Newspapers

WOMAN
53403X74A-170
Editorial: Bailén 84, E-08009 BARCELONA
Tel: 93 48 46 600 **Fax:** 93 23 24 592
Email: woman@grupozeta.es **Web site:** http://www.grupozeta.es
Date Established: 1992; **Freq:** Monthly; **Cover Price:** EUR 3.00; **Circ:** 200,000
Editor: Silvia Martin
Profile: Magazine covering society, international politics, travel, work, fashion, beauty, sexuality and psychology. Includes opinion, interviews and consumer tests.
Language(s): Spanish
Mechanical Data: Print Process: Offset, Trim Size: 297 x 225mm, Type Area: 255 x 184mm
CONSUMER: WOMEN'S INTEREST CONSUMER MAGAZINES: Women's Interest

XORNAL DE GALICIA
1902474X67B-6431
Editorial: Rúa Galileo Galilei, Polígono Industrial A Grela, A CORUÑA 15008 **Tel:** 981 100 650
Email: redaccion@xornaldegalicia.com **Web site:** http://www.xornal.com
Freq: Daily; **Circ:** 15,000
Advertising Manager: Jacobo Sandino
Profile: Daily newspaper focused on pluralism and independence interests of Galicia.
Language(s): Galician
ADVERTISING RATES:
Full Page Mono .... EUR 2000.00
Full Page Colour .... EUR 3042.00
REGIONAL DAILY & SUNDAY NEWSPAPERS: Regional Daily Newspapers

Sweden

Time Difference: GMT + 1 hr (CET - Central European Time)
National Telephone Code: +46
Continent: Europe
Capital: Stockholm
Principal Language: Swedish
Population: 8975670
Monetary Unit: Swedish Krona (SEK)

EMBASSY HIGH COMMISSION: Swedish Embassy: 11 Montagu Place, London W1H 2AL
Tel: 020 7917 6400
Fax: 020 7724 4174
Email: ambassaden.london@foreign.ministry.se
Website: http://www.swedenabroad.com/london Head of Mission: H E (ms) Nicola Clase

101 NYA IDÉER
2003288W88D-2
Editorial: BONNIER TIDSKRIFTER, Sveavägen 53, 105 44 STOCKHOLM **Tel:** 8 736 53 00
Email: red@101ideer.se **Web site:** http://www.101ideer.se
Freq: 3 ggr/år; **Circ:** 55,000
Advertising Manager: Roger Nilsson
Language(s): Swedish
ADVERTISING RATES:
Full Page Colour .... SEK 29500
CONSUMER: EDUCATION: Crafts

1,6 MILJONERKLUBBEN
1835832W74G-218
Editorial: Grev Turegatan 27, 114 38 STOCKHOLM
Tel: 8 20 51 59
Email: info@1.6miljonerklubben.com **Web site:** http://www.1.6miljonerklubben.com
Circ: 28,000
Publisher: Ingemo Bonnier
Language(s): Swedish
ADVERTISING RATES:
Full Page Colour .... SEK 50000
SCC .... SEK 416.67
CONSUMER: WOMEN'S INTEREST CONSUMER MAGAZINES: Slimming & Health

2000-TALETS VETENSKAP
50656W56R-5
Editorial: Gångbrogatan 2, 372 37 RONNEBY
Tel: 457 267 49
Email: ingemar@2000taletsvetenskap.nu **Web site:** http://www.2000taletsvetenskap.nu
Date Established: 1996; **Freq:** Quarterly; **Circ:** 2,500
Editor: Bo Zackrisson; **Publisher:** Bengt Larsson
Profile: Journal about alternative medicine.
Language(s): Swedish
BUSINESS: HEALTH & MEDICAL: Health Medical Related

4 WHEEL DRIVE
51103W77A-20
Editorial: Box 529, 371 23 KARLSKRONA
Tel: 455 33 53 75 **Fax:** 455311715
Email: 4wd@fabas.se **Web site:** http://www.fabas.se
Date Established: 1983; **Freq:** Monthly; **Circ:** 16,300
Advertising Manager: Susanne Zec; **Publisher:** Stig L Sjöberg
Profile: Magazine containing motoring news, especially about 4 wheel drive vehicles, jeeps, vans and pick-ups.
Language(s): Swedish
ADVERTISING RATES:
Full Page Colour .... SEK 19200
SCC .... SEK 160
Copy instructions: *Copy Date:* 30 days prior to publication date
CONSUMER: MOTORING & CYCLING: Motoring

8 SIDOR
624506W67B-2950
Editorial: Box 9145, 102 72 STOCKHOLM
Tel: 8 640 70 90 **Fax:** 8 642 76 00
Email: 8sidor@8sidor.se **Web site:** http://www.8sidor.se
Date Established: 1984; **Freq:** Weekly; **Circ:** 14,000
Editor-in-Chief: Mats Ahlsén; **Publisher:** Mats Ahlsén
Language(s): Swedish
ADVERTISING RATES:
Full Page Colour .... SEK 16000
SCC .... SEK 80
REGIONAL DAILY & SUNDAY NEWSPAPERS: Regional Daily Newspapers

8 SIDOR; 8SIDOR.SE
1843137W65A-972
Editorial: Box 9145, 102 72 STOCKHOLM
Tel: 8 640 70 90 **Fax:** 8 642 76 00
Email: 8sidor@8sidor.se **Web site:** http://www.8sidor.se
Freq: Daily; **Cover Price:** Free; **Circ:** 20,000 Unique Users
Editor-in-Chief: Mats Ahlsén; **Publisher:** Mats Ahlsén
Language(s): Swedish
ADVERTISING RATES:
SCC .... SEK 16
NATIONAL DAILY & SUNDAY NEWSPAPERS: National Daily Newspapers

ACCENT
51165W82-20
Editorial: Box 12825, 112 97 STOCKHOLM
Tel: 8 672 60 50 **Fax:** 8 672 60 01
Email: accent@iogt.se **Web site:** http://www.accentmagasin.se
Date Established: 1970; **Freq:** Monthly; **Circ:** 43,000
Editor-in-Chief: Pierre Andersson; **Advertising Manager:** Roger Nydahl; **Publisher:** Pierre Andersson
Profile: Political and current affairs journal. Includes information on culture and international developments, as well as social policies.
Language(s): Swedish
ADVERTISING RATES:
Full Page Colour .... SEK 10500
SCC .... SEK 87
CONSUMER: CURRENT AFFAIRS & POLITICS

ACCENT; WEBB
1843130W62A-517
Editorial: Box 12825, 112 97 STOCKHOLM
Tel: 8 672 60 50 **Fax:** 8 672 60 01
Email: accent@iogt.se **Web site:** http://www.accentmagasin.se
Freq: Daily; **Cover Price:** Free; **Circ:** 17,200 Unique Users
Editor-in-Chief: Pierre Andersson; **Publisher:** Pierre Andersson
Language(s): Swedish
ADVERTISING RATES:
SCC .... SEK 18
BUSINESS: CHURCH & SCHOOL EQUIPMENT & EDUCATION: Education

ACTA DERMATO-VENEROLOGICA
634361W56A-2
Editorial: Trädgårdsgatan 14, 753 09 UPPSALA
Tel: 18 580 50 91 **Fax:** 18557332
Email: adv@medicaljournals.se **Web site:** http://www.medicaljournals.se/adv
Date Established: 1920; **Freq:** 6 issues yearly; **Circ:** 2,300
Profile: Journal containing scientific articles about skin infections.
Language(s): Swedish
Readership: Read by dermato-venereologists.
BUSINESS: HEALTH & MEDICAL

ACTA OTO-LARYNGOLOGICA
634367W56A-4_5
Editorial: Box 3255, 103 65 STOCKHOLM
Tel: 8 440 80 40 **Fax:** 8 440 80 50
Email: actaoto@informa.com **Web site:** http://informahealthcare.com/oto
Freq: Monthly; **Circ:** 1,900
Editor: Christer Lundberg; **Editor-in-Chief:** Matti Anniko
Profile: Journal featuring original articles of basic research interest regarding clinical questions at hand, s well as clinical studies in the field of otolaryngology, neck surgery and related subdisciplines.
Language(s): Swedish
Readership: Read by otorhinolaryngologists, audiologists, logopedics, head and neck surgeons.
BUSINESS: HEALTH & MEDICAL

ADVANCES IN PHYSIOTHERAPY
634372W56R-8
Editorial: c/o Informa Healthcare, Box 3255, 103 65 STOCKHOLM **Tel:** 8 440 80 40 **Fax:** 8 440 80 50
Email: advances@informa.com **Web site:** http://www.informahealthcare.com
Date Established: 1999; **Freq:** Quarterly; **Circ:** 4,500
Editor: Barbara Richardson; **Editor-in-Chief:** Gunnevi Sundelin
Profile: European journal covering all aspects of physiotherapy, aiming to place the physiotherapist at the core of a scientific debate.
Language(s): Swedish
Readership: Aimed at physiotherapists.
BUSINESS: HEALTH & MEDICAL: Health Medical Related

ADVOKATEN
50499W44-5
Editorial: Box 27321, 102 54 STOCKHOLM
Tel: 8 459 03 25 **Fax:** 8 662 30 19
Email: advokaten@advokatsamfundet.se **Web site:** http://www.advokatsamfundet.se/advokaten
Freq: 6 issues yearly; **Circ:** 7,100
Editor-in-Chief: Tom Knutson; **Publisher:** Ann Ramberg
Profile: Official publication of the Association of Swedish Lawyers.
Language(s): Swedish
ADVERTISING RATES:
Full Page Colour .... SEK 18000
SCC .... SEK 150
BUSINESS: LEGAL

ADVOKATEN; WEBB
1843144W44-66
Editorial: Box 27321, 102 54 STOCKHOLM
Tel: 8 459 03 25 **Fax:** 8 662 30 19
Email: tom.knutson@advokatsamfundet.se **Web site:** http://www.advokatsamfundet.se/advokaten
Freq: Daily; **Cover Price:** Free; **Circ:** 2,840 Unique Users
Editor-in-Chief: Tom Knutson; **Advertising Manager:** Lars Falk
Language(s): Swedish
ADVERTISING RATES:
SCC .... SEK 30
BUSINESS: LEGAL

AERO-MAGAZINET
634373W77A-255
Editorial: Volvo Aero Corporation, avd. 1500, 461 81 TROLLHÄTTAN **Tel:** 520 944 01 **Fax:** 520 985 00
Email: fredrik.fryklund@volvo.com **Web site:** http://www.volvoaero.com
Freq: Half-yearly; **Circ:** 13,000
Editor: Fredrik Fryklund; **Publisher:** Fredrik Fryklund
Profile: Magazine featuring news and information on Volvo cars.
Language(s): Swedish
CONSUMER: MOTORING & CYCLING: Motoring

AFASI-NYTT
50626W56L-5
Editorial: Kampementgatan 14, 115 38 STOCKHOLM **Tel:** 8 545 663 60 **Fax:** 854566379
Email: info@afasi.se **Web site:** http://www.afasi.se
Freq: Quarterly; **Circ:** 5,300
Editor-in-Chief: Marianne Åkerlund; **Advertising Manager:** Berith Bergman; **Publisher:** Lars Berge-Kleber
Profile: Journal containing information, articles and news about aphasia.
Language(s): Swedish
Readership: Read by members of the Swedish Aphasia Society and people working with the disease.
BUSINESS: HEALTH & MEDICAL: Disability & Rehabilitation

AFFÄRS- & KAPITALNYTT
50277W14A-10
Editorial: Båtbyggaregatan 198, 216 42 LIMHAMN
Tel: 40 15 30 50 **Fax:** 40153070
Email: info@affkapnytt.se **Web site:** http://www.affkapnytt.se
Date Established: 1994; **Freq:** 6 issues yearly; **Circ:** 20,500
Advertising Manager: Kerstin Grevelius Kjellvander
Profile: Magazine containing business and commercial news, focusing on the Oresund Region.
Language(s): Swedish
Readership: Business executives.
ADVERTISING RATES:
Full Page Colour .... SEK 41000
BUSINESS: COMMERCE, INDUSTRY & MANAGEMENT

AFFÄRS- & KAPITALNYTT; AFFKAPNYTT.SE
1843127W4E-159
Editorial: Båtbyggaregatan 198, 216 42 LIMHAMN
Tel: 40 15 30 50 **Fax:** 40 15 30 70
Email: info@affkapnytt.se **Web site:** http://www.affkapnytt.se
Freq: Daily; **Cover Price:** Free; **Circ:** 4,100 Unique Users
Editor: Ylva le Normand; **Editor-in-Chief:** Kerstin Grevelius Kjellvander; **Managing Director:** Kerstin Grevelius Kjellvander; **Advertising Manager:** Kerstin Grevelius Kjellvander; **Publisher:** Kerstin Grevelius Kjellvander
Language(s): Swedish
BUSINESS: ARCHITECTURE & BUILDING: Building

AFFÄRSLIV
1642074W2A-393
Editorial: Box 624, 114 56 STOCKHOLM
Tel: 733 16 00 37
Email: redaktionen@mfp.se **Web site:** http://www.mfp.se
Freq: Half-yearly; **Circ:** 87,300
Language(s): Swedish

ADVERTISING RATES:
Full Page Colour .... SEK 27000
BUSINESS: COMMUNICATIONS, ADVERTISING & MARKETING

AFFÄRSRESEMAGASINET
1835867W89C-257
Editorial: Travel Media Scandinavia, Grev Magnigatan 6, 114 55 STOCKHOLM
Tel: 8 545 660 00
Email: info@travelmedia.se **Web site:** http://www.inrikesmagasin.se
Freq: Monthly; **Cover Price:** Free; **Circ:** 39,900
Editor: Aleksander Kovacevic; **Advertising Manager:** Johanna Markbäck Zeilon; **Publisher:** Kjell Santesson
Language(s): Swedish
ADVERTISING RATES:
Full Page Colour .... SEK 38100
SCC .... SEK 317.5
CONSUMER: HOLIDAYS & TRAVEL: Entertainment Guides

AFFÄRSRESENÄREN
751104W10-85
Editorial: Box 145, 125 23 ÄLVSJÖ **Tel:** 8 568 790 30
Fax: 856879031
Email: redaktion@laprensa.se **Web site:** http://www.affarsresenaren.se
Freq: 6 issues yearly - (8 nr/år); **Circ:** 9,500
Editor-in-Chief: Antonio Inestal
Language(s): Swedish
ADVERTISING RATES:
Full Page Colour .... SEK 25000
SCC .... SEK 208.33
BUSINESS: MATERIALS HANDLING

AFFÄRSTIDNINGEN NÄRINGSLIV
51523W14A-115
Editorial: Box 2079, 433 02 SÄVEDALEN
Tel: 31 340 98 00 **Fax:** 313409801
Email: info@naringsliv.se **Web site:** http://www.naringsliv.se
Date Established: 1982; **Freq:** 6 issues yearly; **Circ:** 35,000
Publisher: Peter Fridén
Profile: Magazine focusing on Swedish business, industry and trade.
Language(s): Swedish
ADVERTISING RATES:
Full Page Colour .... SEK 36750
SCC .... SEK 183.75
Copy instructions: *Copy Date:* 15 days prior to publication date
BUSINESS: COMMERCE, INDUSTRY & MANAGEMENT

AFFÄRSTIDNINGEN NÄRINGSLIV; NARINGSLIV.SE
1843133W14A-325
Editorial: Box 2079, 433 02 SÄVEDALEN
Tel: 31 340 98 00 **Fax:** 31 340 98 01
Email: info@naringsliv.se **Web site:** http://www.naringsliv.se
Freq: Daily; **Cover Price:** Free; **Circ:** 7,000 Unique Users
Editor: Christer Andersson; **Editor-in-Chief:** Christer Andersson; **Publisher:** Peter Fridén
Language(s): Swedish
ADVERTISING RATES:
SCC .... SEK 37
BUSINESS: COMMERCE, INDUSTRY & MANAGEMENT

AFFÄRSVÄRLDEN
50147W1A-10
Editorial: Mäster Samuelsgatan 56, 106 12 STOCKHOLM **Tel:** 8 796 65 00
Email: redaktionen@affarsvarlden.se **Web site:** http://www.affarsvarlden.se
Date Established: 1901; **Freq:** Weekly; **Circ:** 17,300
Editor: Calle Froste
Profile: Magazine containing in-depth coverage, analysis and commentary on important developments and trends in Swedish companies and the international economy.
Language(s): Swedish
ADVERTISING RATES:
Full Page Colour .... SEK 35800
SCC .... SEK 329.16
Copy instructions: *Copy Date:* 12 days prior to publication date
BUSINESS: FINANCE & ECONOMICS

AFFÄRSVÄRLDEN; AFFÄRSVÄRLDEN24
1624538W14A-281
Editorial: 106 12 STOCKHOLM **Tel:** 8 796 65 00
Fax: 8 23 09 80
Email: redaktionen@affarsvarlden.se **Web site:** http://www.affarsvarlden.se
Circ: 22,363 Unique Users
Editor: Calle Froste; **Advertising Manager:** Michael Fällstrom; **Publisher:** Jon Åsberg
Language(s): Swedish
BUSINESS: COMMERCE, INDUSTRY & MANAGEMENT

AFGHANISTAN-NYTT
51402W90-5
Editorial: Trekantsvägen 1, 6tr., 117 43 STOCKHOLM **Tel:** 8 545 818 40 **Fax:** 8 545 818 55
Email: info@sak.se **Web site:** http://www.sak.se
Date Established: 1980; **Freq:** Quarterly; **Circ:** 10,000
Editor: Markus Håkansson
Profile: Magazine containing articles and information about Afghanistan and the work of the Swedish Afghanistan Committee.
Language(s): Swedish
CONSUMER: ETHNIC

AFTONBLADET
50754W65A-10
Editorial: Besöksadress: Västra Järnvägsgatan 21, 105 18 STOCKHOLM **Tel:** 8 725 20 00
Fax: 8 600 01 77
Email: 71000@aftonbladet.se **Web site:** http://www.aftonbladet.se
Date Established: 1830; **Freq:** Daily; **Circ:** 320,200
Profile: Tabloid-sized evening newspaper covering a broad range of national and international news, events and features.
Language(s): Swedish
Readership: Read by a broad range of the population, most of whom live in and around Stockholm.
ADVERTISING RATES:
Full Page Colour .... SEK 206927
NATIONAL DAILY & SUNDAY NEWSPAPERS: National Daily Newspapers

AFTONBLADET; AFTONBLADET.SE
751395W65A-92
Editorial: Budadress: Blekholmsgatan 18, 111 64 Stockholm, 105 18 STOCKHOLM **Tel:** 8 725 2000
Fax: 8 562 528 27
Email: webbnyheter@aftonbladet.se **Web site:** http://www.aftonbladet.se
Freq: Daily; **Circ:** 1,371,093 Unique Users
Editor: Björn Röhme
Language(s): Swedish
NATIONAL DAILY & SUNDAY NEWSPAPERS: National Daily Newspapers

AFTONBLADET; RÄTTSREDAKTIONEN
1697015W44-63
Editorial: Budadress: Blekholmsgatan 18, 111 64 Stockholm, 105 18 STOCKHOLM **Tel:** 8 725 20 00
Fax: 8 562 528 18
Email: krim@aftonbladet.se **Web site:** http://www.aftonbladet.se
Freq: Daily; **Circ:** 377,500
Language(s): Swedish
BUSINESS: LEGAL

AFTONBLADET; SPORTMAGASINET
1623579W75J-262
Editorial: Budadress: Blekholmsgatan 18, 111 64 Stockholm, 105 18 STOCKHOLM **Tel:** 8 725 20 00
Fax: 8 562 528 13
Email: sport@aftonbladet.se **Web site:** http://www.aftonbladet.se/sportmagasinet
Freq: Monthly; **Circ:** 25,000
Editor: Jonathan Jeppsson
Language(s): Swedish
CONSUMER: SPORT: Athletics

AGI
51803W41A-10
Editorial: Jörgen Kocksgatan 9, 211 20 MALMÖ
Tel: 40 12 78 40 **Fax:** 40 12 58 20
Email: news@agi.se **Web site:** http://www.agi.se
Freq: Monthly; **Circ:** 4,200
Editor: Johan Jönsson; **Editor-in-Chief:** Peter Ollén; **Managing Director:** Peter Ollén; **Advertising Manager:** Johan Haskå; **Publisher:** Peter Ollén
Language(s): Swedish
Readership: Read by the production managers of graphic arts companies in Europe who have more than 100 employees.
ADVERTISING RATES:
Full Page Colour .... SEK 26900
SCC .... SEK 224.17
BUSINESS: PRINTING & STATIONERY: Printing

AJOURODONT
634477W56D-10
Editorial: Järneksvägen 10, 131 40 NACKA
Tel: 8 718 51 30 **Fax:** 87164330
Email: info@ajourodont.com **Web site:** http://www.ajourodont.com
Freq: Quarterly; **Circ:** 2,000
Advertising Manager: Marie Ryd
Profile: Newsletter featuring up to date news on dental research.
Language(s): Swedish
BUSINESS: HEALTH & MEDICAL: Dental

ÅKA SKIDOR
51595W75G-10
Editorial: Box 164, 830 13 ÅRE **Tel:** 647 514 40
Fax: 64751444
Email: redaktionen@akaskidor.se **Web site:** http://www.akaskidor.se
Date Established: 1975; **Freq:** 6 issues yearly - (8 nr/år); **Circ:** 14,000
Editor: Mårten Pettersson; **Advertising Manager:** Anders Olofsson; **Publisher:** Patrik Leje
Profile: Magazine covering skiing, snowboarding and adventure sports.
Language(s): Swedish
Readership: Aimed at sports enthusiasts.
ADVERTISING RATES:
Full Page Colour .... SEK 33000
SCC .... SEK 275
Copy instructions: *Copy Date:* 25 days prior to publication date
CONSUMER: SPORT: Winter Sports

ÅKERI & ENTREPRENAD
1664276W10-93
Editorial: Tingsgatan 2, 827 32 LJUSDAL
Tel: 651 150 50 **Fax:** 651 133 33
Email: post@svenskamedia.se **Web site:** http://www.akerioentreprenad.se
Freq: 6 issues yearly; **Circ:** 24,000
Advertising Manager: Ylwa Stake
Language(s): Swedish
BUSINESS: MATERIALS HANDLING

ÅKERI & TRANSPORT; WEBB
1846520W49C-3
Editorial: 598 80 VIMMERBY **Tel:** 492 160 00
Fax: 492 101 02
Email: wesik@swepress.se **Web site:** http://www.akeritransport.se
Freq: Daily; **Cover Price:** Free; **Circ:** 9,120 Unique Users
Editor-in-Chief: Alf Wesik; **Advertising Manager:** Bert-Ove Svensson
Language(s): Swedish
ADVERTISING RATES:
SCC .... SEK 42
BUSINESS: TRANSPORT: Freight

AKT - TEATERFÖRBUNDETS TIDSKRIFT
50318W14L-5
Editorial: Teaterförbundet, Box 12710, 112 94 STOCKHOLM **Tel:** 8 28 01 48 **Fax:** 8280148
Email: magdalena.akt@tele2.se **Web site:** http://www.teaterforbundet.se
Freq: 6 issues yearly; **Circ:** 9,100
Publisher: Jaan Kolk
Profile: Official publication of the Swedish Theatre Trade Union. Contains news and feature material on theatre, film and dance.
Language(s): Swedish
ADVERTISING RATES:
Full Page Colour .... SEK 11000
SCC .... SEK 91.67
BUSINESS: COMMERCE, INDUSTRY & MANAGEMENT: Trade Unions

AKTIESPARAREN
50171W1F-10
Editorial: 113 89 STOCKHOLM **Tel:** 8 506 515 00
Fax: 8 32 61 22
Email: aktiespararen@aktiespararna.se **Web site:** http://www.aktiespararen.se
Date Established: 1967; **Freq:** Monthly; **Circ:** 65,700
Editor: Reza Rouzbehani; **Advertising Manager:** Bjarne Kristiansen; **Publisher:** Gunnar Johansson
Profile: Magazine about private finance. Contains advice, news and information about shares and bonds.
Language(s): Swedish
Readership: Aimed at active shareholders and investors.
ADVERTISING RATES:
Full Page Colour .... SEK 48000
SCC .... SEK 400
BUSINESS: FINANCE & ECONOMICS: Investment

AKTIESPARAREN; AKTIESPARARNA.SE
1843263W14A-326
Editorial: 113 89 STOCKHOLM **Tel:** 8 506 515 00
Fax: 8326122
Email: webbred@aktiespararna.se **Web site:** http://www.aktiespararna.se
Freq: Daily; **Cover Price:** Free; **Circ:** 23,000 Unique Users
Advertising Manager: Bjarne Kristiansen
Language(s): Swedish
BUSINESS: COMMERCE, INDUSTRY & MANAGEMENT

AKTIVA
51303W88R-10
Editorial: Box 655, 135 26 TYRESÖ
Tel: 8 410 053 40 **Fax:** 8 643 60 50
Email: info@familjemagasinet.se **Web site:** http://www.familjemagasinet.se
Freq: 6 issues yearly; **Circ:** 42,400
Editor-in-Chief: Petra Sundqvist; **Advertising Manager:** Joacim Nielsen
Profile: Magazine containing articles, information and news for parents who involve themselves in their children's education.
Language(s): Swedish
CONSUMER: EDUCATION: Education Related

AKTIVT SKOGSBRUK
1803921W46-127
Editorial: Box 626, 551 18 JÖNKÖPING
Tel: 36 30 17 50 **Fax:** 36308840
Email: information@sydved.se **Web site:** http://www.sydved.se
Freq: Quarterly; **Circ:** 31,000
Language(s): Swedish
BUSINESS: TIMBER, WOOD & FORESTRY

AKTUELL FORSKNING & UTVECKLING
1693283W55-53
Editorial: Storgatan 45, 171 52 SOLNA
Tel: 8 670 95 00
Email: joakim@nextworld.se **Web site:** http://www.teknolog.net
Freq: Half-yearly; **Circ:** 17,000
Editor: Joakim Hayenhjelm; **Advertising Manager:** Jan Nilsson; **Publisher:** Peter Lejdestad
Language(s): Swedish
ADVERTISING RATES:
Full Page Colour .... SEK 23000
BUSINESS: APPLIED SCIENCE & LABORATORIES

AKTUELL PRODUKTION
50486W42A-5
Editorial: Paviljongvägen 5, 132 40 SALTSJÖ-BOO
Tel: 8 642 68 05
Email: info@aktuellproduktion.com **Web site:** http://www.aktuell-produktion.com
Circ: 20,000
Editor-in-Chief: Christian Malmgren; **Advertising Manager:** Peter Malmgren; **Publisher:** Christian Malmgren
Profile: Magazine covering all aspects of the construction industry.
Language(s): Swedish
ADVERTISING RATES:
Full Page Colour .... SEK 11700
SCC .... SEK 97.5
BUSINESS: CONSTRUCTION

AKTUELL SÄKERHET
50575W54B-10
Editorial: Skeppargatan 27, 114 52 STOCKHOLM
Tel: 8 442 86 30 **Fax:** 86621180
Email: info@spearproduction.se **Web site:** http://www.aktuellsakerhet.se
Freq: 6 issues yearly; **Circ:** 16,400
Advertising Manager: Linda Larsson-Levin; **Publisher:** Anders Forsström
Profile: Magazine covering all aspects of the safety business.
Language(s): Swedish
ADVERTISING RATES:
Full Page Colour .... SEK 29200
SCC .... SEK 243.33
Copy instructions: *Copy Date:* 30 days prior to publication date
BUSINESS: SAFETY & SECURITY: Safety

AKTUELL SÄKERHET; AKTUELLSAKERHET.SE
1843649W54C-61
Editorial: 114 52 STOCKHOLM **Tel:** 8 442 86 30
Fax: 8 662 11 80
Email: info@spearproduction.se **Web site:** http://www.aktuellsakerhet.se
Freq: Daily; **Cover Price:** Free; **Circ:** 8,000 Unique Users
Editor-in-Chief: Lotta Eriksson; **Advertising Manager:** Linda Larsson-Levin
Language(s): Swedish
ADVERTISING RATES:
SCC .... SEK 48
BUSINESS: SAFETY & SECURITY: Security

AKTUELLA BYGGEN
50211W4E-5
Editorial: Box 24053, 104 50 STOCKHOLM
Tel: 8 506 244 00
Email: elin.bennewitz@conventusmedia.se **Web site:** http://www.branschnyheter.se
Date Established: 1988; **Freq:** 6 issues yearly; **Circ:** 4,900
Profile: Building and property development magazine.
Language(s): Swedish
ADVERTISING RATES:
Full Page Colour .... SEK 27850
SCC .... SEK 232.08
Copy instructions: *Copy Date:* 14 days prior to publication date
BUSINESS: ARCHITECTURE & BUILDING: Building

AKTUELLT I POLITIKEN
51166W67B-2955
Editorial: 105 60 STOCKHOLM **Tel:** 8 700 26 00
Fax: 8 411 65 42
Email: aip@sap.se **Web site:** http://www.aip.nu
Date Established: 1954
Circ: 7,100 Unique Users
Editor: Bo Bernhardsson; **Editor-in-Chief:** Fredrik Kornebäck; **Managing Director:** Jan Söderström; **Advertising Manager:** Jörgen Rosengren; **Publisher:** Eric Sundström
Profile: Newspaper of the Swedish Social Democratic Party.

Language(s): Swedish
REGIONAL DAILY & SUNDAY NEWSPAPERS: Regional Daily Newspapers

AKTUELLT I POLITIKEN; AIP.NU
1843245W14L-194
Editorial: 105 60 STOCKHOLM **Tel:** 8 700 26 00
Fax: 84116542
Email: aip@sap.se **Web site:** http://www.aip.nu
Freq: Daily; **Cover Price:** Free; **Circ:** 467 Unique Users
Editor-in-Chief: Eric Sundström
Language(s): Swedish
BUSINESS: COMMERCE, INDUSTRY & MANAGEMENT: Trade Unions

AKTUELLT OM VETENSKAP & HÄLSA
1824316W55-57
Editorial: Medicinska fakulteten, Lunds universitet, Box 117, 221 00 LUND **Tel:** 46 222 00 00
Email: ingela.bjorck@rektor.lu.se **Web site:** http://www.med.lu.se/forskning/aktuell_forskning/aktuellt_om_vetenskap_och_haelsa
Freq: Half-yearly; **Circ:** 7,000
Editor: Ingela Björck
Language(s): Swedish
BUSINESS: APPLIED SCIENCE & LABORATORIES

ALBA
634863W73-10
Editorial: Andra Långgatan 20, 413 28 GOTEBORG
Tel: 31 12 76 40 **Fax:** 31 14 37 77
Email: red@alba.nu **Web site:** http://www.alba.nu
Date Established: 1997; **Freq:** 6 times a year; **Circ:** 120,000 Unique Users
Publisher: Christer Wigerfelt
Profile: E-zine covering news and information on culture, science and the Swedish community.
Language(s): Swedish
CONSUMER: NATIONAL & INTERNATIONAL PERIODICALS

ÄLDREOMSORG
51564W74N-15
Editorial: Fortbildning AB Box 34, 171 11 SOLNA
Tel: 8 545 453 30 **Fax:** 8 545 453 49
Email: aldreomsorg@fortbild.se **Web site:** http://www.fortbild.se
Freq: 6 issues yearly; **Circ:** 8,680
Editor: Åsa Sundström; **Editor-in-Chief:** Elisabet Spjuth; **Managing Director:** Niklas Ekmark;
Advertising Manager: Ulf Jacobsson
Profile: Journal dealing with issues concerning the care of the elderly.
Language(s): Swedish
CONSUMER: WOMEN'S INTEREST CONSUMER MAGAZINES: Retirement

ALEKURIREN
633943W72-13
Editorial: Göteborgsvägen 94, 446 33 ÄLVÄNGEN
Tel: 303 74 99 40 **Fax:** 303 74 99 45
Email: info@alekuriren.se **Web site:** http://www.alekuriren.se
Date Established: 1996; **Freq:** Weekly; **Circ:** 15,100
Editor: Jonas Andersson; **Editor-in-Chief:** Per-Anders Klöversjö; **Managing Director:** Kent Hylander; **Publisher:** Per-Anders Klöversjö
Language(s): Swedish
ADVERTISING RATES:
Full Page Colour .... SEK 13500
SCC .... SEK 67.5
LOCAL NEWSPAPERS

ALEKURIREN; ALEKURIREN.SE
1843676W65A-1013
Editorial: Göteborgsvägen 94, 446 33 ÄLVÄNGEN
Tel: 303 74 99 40 **Fax:** 303 74 99 45
Email: info@alekuriren.se **Web site:** http://www.alekuriren.se
Freq: Daily; **Cover Price:** Free; **Circ:** 2,940 Unique Users
Editor: Jonas Andersson; **Editor-in-Chief:** Per-Anders Klöversjö; **Publisher:** Per-Anders Klöversjö
Language(s): Swedish
ADVERTISING RATES:
SCC .... SEK 14
NATIONAL DAILY & SUNDAY NEWSPAPERS: National Daily Newspapers

ALINGSÅS KURIREN
634867W72-17
Editorial: Box 627, 441 17 ALINGSÅS
Tel: 322 66 83 00 **Fax:** 322 66 83 01
Email: red@alingsaskuriren.se **Web site:** http://www.alingsaskuriren.se
Freq: Weekly. storutdelning 1ggr/m 47000; **Circ:** 25,300 Unique Users
Advertising Manager: Anders Granqvist; **Publisher:** Anna-Karin Jansson
Profile: E-zine featuring local news for Alingsås.
Language(s): Swedish
LOCAL NEWSPAPERS

ALINGSÅS TIDNING
633900W67B-3000
Editorial: Södra Ringgatan 14, 441 85 ALINGSÅS
Tel: 322 67 00 00 **Fax:** 322 67 00 66
Email: red@alingtid.se **Web site:** http://www.alingsastidning.se
Date Established: 1865
Circ: 13,000
Editor: Anders Thorn; **Publisher:** Bengt Michelsen
Language(s): Swedish
ADVERTISING RATES:
Full Page Colour .... SEK 31700
SCC .... SEK 158.50
REGIONAL DAILY & SUNDAY NEWSPAPERS: Regional Daily Newspapers

ALINGSÅS TIDNING; ALINGSASTIDNING.SE
1843675W65A-1012
Editorial: Södra Ringgatan 14, 441 85 ALINGSÅS
Tel: 322 67 00 00 **Fax:** 322670066
Email: red@alingtid.se **Web site:** http://www.alingsastidning.se
Freq: Daily; **Cover Price:** Free; **Circ:** 2,559 Unique Users
Language(s): Swedish
NATIONAL DAILY & SUNDAY NEWSPAPERS: National Daily Newspapers

ALKOHOL & NARKOTIKA
50628W56L-8
Editorial: Box 70412, 107 25 STOCKHOLM
Tel: 8 412 46 00 **Fax:** 8 10 46 41
Email: staffan.hasselgren@can.se **Web site:** http://www.can.se
Date Established: 1907; **Freq:** 6 issues yearly; **Circ:** 5,000
Editor-in-Chief: Staffan Hasselgren; **Advertising Manager:** Staffan Hasselgren; **Publisher:** Björn Hibell
Profile: Magazine covering trends, research and news in the field of drug and alcohol abuse.
Language(s): Swedish
Readership: Aimed at organisations working in the field of drugpolicy, drug and alcohol abuse. Including, researchers, medical professionals, teachers, socialworkers, and policymakers.
ADVERTISING RATES:
Full Page Colour .... SEK 1700
SCC .... SEK 14.17
BUSINESS: HEALTH & MEDICAL: Disability & Rehabilitation

ALLAS VECKOTIDNING
50950W74C-10
Editorial: 205 35 MALMO **Tel:** 40 38 59 00
Fax: 40 38 59 64
Email: mikael.frohm@allas.aller.se **Web site:** http://allas.se
Date Established: 1931; **Freq:** Weekly; **Circ:** 117,900
Profile: Magazine containing articles, advice and interviews. Covers issues of interest to the whole family such as recipes, DIY, short stories and gardening.
Language(s): Swedish
ADVERTISING RATES:
Full Page Colour .... SEK 41000
SCC .... SEK 342
CONSUMER: WOMEN'S INTEREST CONSUMER MAGAZINES: Home & Family

ALLERGI I PRAXIS
1668175W56A-342
Editorial: Box 17069, 104 62 STOCKHOLM
Tel: 8 506 282 16 **Fax:** 850628249
Email: lena.granstrom@astmaoallergiforbundet.se **Web site:** http://astmaoallergiforbundet.se
Freq: Quarterly; **Circ:** 18,000
Editor: Lena Granström
Language(s): Swedish
BUSINESS: HEALTH & MEDICAL

ALLERGIA
50583W56A-5
Editorial: Box 17069, 104 62 STOCKHOLM
Tel: 8 506 282 15 **Fax:** 8 506 282 49
Email: allergia@astmaoallergiforbundet.se **Web site:** http://www.astmaoallergiforbundet.se
Date Established: 1956; **Freq:** 6 issues yearly; **Circ:** 15,100
Advertising Manager: Anneli Stenberg; **Publisher:** Ingalill Björn
Profile: Medical journal containing articles about asthma and allergies.
Language(s): Swedish
Readership: Read by members of the Swedish Asthma & Allergy Association.
ADVERTISING RATES:
Full Page Colour .... SEK 17300
SCC .... SEK 144
BUSINESS: HEALTH & MEDICAL

ALLERS
50951W74C-20
Editorial: Allers Förlag, 251 85 HELSINGBORG
Tel: 42 17 35 00 **Fax:** 42 17 35 68
Email: redaktionen@allers.aller.se **Web site:** http://www.allersforlag.se
Freq: Weekly; **Circ:** 209,900
Editor: Lilian Ottosson
Profile: Magazine covering home and family matters, cookery and health tips.
Language(s): Swedish
ADVERTISING RATES:
Full Page Colour .... SEK 45000
SCC .... SEK 375
CONSUMER: WOMEN'S INTEREST CONSUMER MAGAZINES: Home & Family

ALLERS JULMAGASIN
1841534W74Q-172
Editorial: 251 85 HELSINGBORG **Tel:** 42 17 35 00
Fax: 42 17 35 68
Email: redaktionen@allers.se **Web site:** http://www.allersforlag.se
Freq: Annual; **Circ:** 50,000
Language(s): Swedish
ADVERTISING RATES:
Full Page Colour .... SEK 40000
SCC .... SEK 333,33
CONSUMER: WOMEN'S INTEREST CONSUMER MAGAZINES: Lifestyle

ALLERS TRÄDGÅRD
634375W74C-25
Editorial: 251 85 HELSINGBORG **Tel:** 42 17 35 00
Fax: 42 17 35 68
Email: at@aller.se **Web site:** http://www.allersforlag.se
Freq: 6 issues yearly; **Circ:** 46,400
Publisher: Eva Malmström
Profile: Magazine covering all aspects on how to design a garden.
Language(s): Swedish
Readership: Aimed at garden enthusiasts and professionals.
ADVERTISING RATES:
Full Page Colour .... SEK 19000
SCC .... SEK 158.33
Copy instructions: *Copy Date:* 30 days prior to publication date
CONSUMER: WOMEN'S INTEREST CONSUMER MAGAZINES: Home & Family

ALLMÄN MEDICIN
634377W56A-260
Editorial: SFAMs kansli, Box 503, 114 11 STOCKHOLM **Tel:** 8 23 24 05 **Fax:** 8200335
Email: chefredaktor@sfam.a.se **Web site:** http://www.sfam.se
Freq: 6 issues yearly - 6 nummer per år; **Circ:** 3,600
Editor: Stig Andersson; **Publisher:** Ingvar Krakau
Profile: Magazine covering scientific research, medical education for the improvement and training of general practitioners of the future.
Language(s): Swedish
Readership: Aimed at general practitioners and professionals in the medical field.
ADVERTISING RATES:
Full Page Colour .... SEK 17000
SCC .... SEK 141.67
Copy instructions: *Copy Date:* 30 days prior to publication date
BUSINESS: HEALTH & MEDICAL

ALLT I HEMMET
751096W74C-175
Editorial: Bonnier Tidskrifter AB, 105 44 STOCKHOLM **Tel:** 8 736 53 00 **Fax:** 8 736 54 41
Email: red@aih.bonnier.se **Web site:** http://www.alltihemmet.se
Freq: Monthly; **Circ:** 71,000
Advertising Manager: Johanna Källström
Language(s): Swedish
ADVERTISING RATES:
Full Page Colour .... SEK 42000
SCC .... SEK 350
Copy instructions: *Copy Date:* 28 days prior to publication date
CONSUMER: WOMEN'S INTEREST CONSUMER MAGAZINES: Home & Family

ALLT OM BRÖLLOP
1741133W74L-2
Editorial: Box 6320, 102 35 STOCKHOLM
Tel: 8 555 911 55 **Fax:** 855591130
Email: info@alltombrollop.com **Web site:** http://www.alltombrollop.com
Freq: Quarterly; **Circ:** 25,000
Advertising Manager: Natalie Goldbach; **Publisher:** Jens Christiansen
Language(s): Swedish
ADVERTISING RATES:
Full Page Colour .... SEK 28900
SCC .... SEK 240.83
CONSUMER: WOMEN'S INTEREST CONSUMER MAGAZINES: Brides

ALLT OM EGET FÖRETAG I SVERIGE
1667488W14R-65
Editorial: c/o Jobs and Society NyföretagarCentrum, 111 30 STOCKHOLM **Tel:** 8 14 44 00 **Fax:** 8 21 14 54
Email: mats.evergren@jobs-society.se **Web site:** http://www.egetforetag.se
Freq: Half-yearly; **Circ:** 40,000
Editor-in-Chief: Anders Modig; **Advertising Manager:** Nils-Erik Wickman; **Publisher:** Harry Goldman
Language(s): Swedish
BUSINESS: COMMERCE, INDUSTRY & MANAGEMENT: Commerce Related

ALLT OM FLUGFISKE
1665940W92-21
Editorial: Bergendorffsgatan 5 B, 652 24 KARLSTAD
Tel: 8 588 366 00
Email: redaktion.aof@lrfmedia.lrf.se **Web site:** http://www.lrfmedia.se
Freq: 6 issues yearly; **Circ:** 30,000
Editor-in-Chief: Nicolas Jändel; **Advertising Manager:** Ulla Jonsson; **Publisher:** Mats Gyllsand
Language(s): Swedish
CONSUMER: ANGLING & FISHING

ALLT OM FRITIDSHUS
1625131W74C-444
Editorial: 105 44 STOCKHOLM **Tel:** 8 736 53 00
Email: red@aof.bonnier.se **Web site:** http://www.palandet.nu
Freq: Monthly; **Circ:** 37,200
Editor-in-Chief: Bella Linde; **Advertising Manager:** Roger Nilsson
Language(s): Swedish
ADVERTISING RATES:
Full Page Colour .... SEK 23900
SCC .... SEK 199.16
CONSUMER: WOMEN'S INTEREST CONSUMER MAGAZINES: Home & Family

ALLT OM HISTORIA
1697475W94J-29
Editorial: Box 1206, 221 05 LUND **Tel:** 4 633 34 60
Email: red@alltomhistoria.se **Web site:** http://www.alltomhistoria.se
Freq: Monthly; **Circ:** 22,000
Editor: Åke Persson; **Advertising Manager:** Sara Jansson; **Publisher:** Erik Osvalds
Language(s): Swedish
Copy instructions: *Copy Date:* 37 days prior to publication date
CONSUMER: OTHER CLASSIFICATIONS: Popular Science

ALLT OM HJÄLPMEDEL
50629W56L-9
Editorial: Box 510, 162 15 VÄLLINGBY
Tel: 8 620 17 00 **Fax:** 87392152
Email: lena.udd@hi.se **Web site:** http://www.hi.se/aoh
Freq: 6 issues yearly; **Circ:** 2,500
Editor: Christina Sandqvist; **Editor-in-Chief:** Lena Udd; **Advertising Manager:** Lars-Göran Fransson
Profile: Magazine containing articles and information about aid for the disabled. Covers product news, research and debate.
Language(s): Swedish
Readership: Aimed at professionals working with disabled people.
ADVERTISING RATES:
Full Page Colour .... SEK 18100
SCC .... SEK 150.83
BUSINESS: HEALTH & MEDICAL: Disability & Rehabilitation

ALLT OM HJÄLPMEDEL; WEBB
1843651W55-64
Editorial: Box 510, 162 15 VÄLLINGBY
Tel: 8 620 17 00 **Fax:** 87392152
Email: aoh@hi.se **Web site:** http://www.hi.se/aoh
Freq: Daily; **Cover Price:** Free; **Circ:** 1,533 Unique Users
Editor-in-Chief: Lena Udd
Language(s): Swedish
BUSINESS: APPLIED SCIENCE & LABORATORIES

ALLT OM HOBBY
51143W79B-50
Editorial: Box 90133, 120 21 STOCKHOLM
Tel: 8 99 93 33 **Fax:** 8 99 88 66
Email: redaktion@hobby.se **Web site:** http://www.hobby.se
Date Established: 1966; **Freq:** 6 issues yearly; **Circ:** 18,300
Profile: Magazine covering model-making and technical and mechanical hobbies.
Language(s): Swedish
ADVERTISING RATES:
Full Page Colour .... SEK 12565
CONSUMER: HOBBIES & DIY: Models & Modelling

ALLT OM HOTELL & RESOR
1693451W50-113
Editorial: Storgatan 45, 171 52 SOLNA
Tel: 8670 95 00
Email: info@nextworld.se **Web site:** http://www.resorochhotell.se
Freq: Half-yearly; **Circ:** 15,000
Advertising Manager: Susanne Härlin; **Publisher:** Peter Lejdestad
Language(s): Swedish
ADVERTISING RATES:
Full Page Colour .... SEK 28000
SCC .... SEK 233.33
BUSINESS: TRAVEL & TOURISM

ALLT OM HUSVAGN & CAMPING
51339W91B-50
Editorial: Pyramidvägen 7, 16956 STOCKHOLM
Tel: 8 692 01 29 **Fax:** 8 692 01 55
Email: redaktionen@husvagnochcamping.se **Web site:** http://www.husvagnochcamping.se
Date Established: 1976; **Freq:** Monthly; **Circ:** 24,000

Editor: Jenny Flodén; **Advertising Manager:** Lennart Hammer; **Publisher:** Ulla Carle
Profile: Caravan and camping magazine.
Language(s): Swedish
ADVERTISING RATES:
Full Page Colour .... SEK 14800
SCC .... SEK 123.33
CONSUMER: RECREATION & LEISURE: Camping & Caravanning

ALLT OM JAKT & VAPEN
51024W75F-10
Editorial: Björkudden Lits Prästbord 126, 836 92 LIT
Tel: 63 13 45 65 **Fax:** 63 13 45 71
Email: jaktovapen@wallin-wiklund.se **Web site:** http://www.jaktovapen.com
Freq: Monthly; **Circ:** 25,000
Editor-in-Chief: Eric Wallin; **Advertising Manager:** Hans Engblom; **Publisher:** Eric Wallin
Profile: Magazine about hunting and weapons.
Language(s): Swedish
CONSUMER: SPORT: Shooting

ALLT OM KLOCKOR OCH SMYCKEN
1844675W74A-179
Editorial: Skalholtsgatan 2, 164 40 KISTA
Tel: 8 663 15 00
Email: kina@nextworld.se **Web site:** http://www.nextworld.se
Freq: Half-yearly; **Circ:** 40,000
Publisher: Peter Lejdestad
Language(s): Swedish
ADVERTISING RATES:
Full Page Colour .... SEK 39000
SCC .... SEK 325
CONSUMER: WOMEN'S INTEREST CONSUMER MAGAZINES: Women's Interest

ALLT OM KÖK OCH BAD
634379W74C-27
Editorial: Box 26206, 113 92 STOCKHOLM
Tel: 8 588 366 00 **Fax:** 8 506 678 09
Email: forogh.kargar@lrfmedia.lrf.se **Web site:** http://www.lrfmedia.se
Freq: 6 issues yearly; **Circ:** 80,000
Editor: Forogh Kargar; **Publisher:** Marie Flodin
Profile: Magazine containing information on designs for kitchens and bathrooms.
Language(s): Swedish
Readership: Aimed at householders and retailers.
ADVERTISING RATES:
Full Page Colour .... SEK 39800
SCC .... SEK 331.66
Copy instructions: *Copy Date:* 34 days prior to publication date
CONSUMER: WOMEN'S INTEREST CONSUMER MAGAZINES: Home & Family

ALLT OM MAT
1859404W74P-233
Editorial: Budadress: Rådmansgatan 49, 105 44 STOCKHOLM **Tel:** 8 736 53 00 **Fax:** 8 34 00 88
Email: red@aom.bonnier.se **Web site:** http://www.alltommat.se
Freq: 26 issues yearly; **Circ:** 99,600
Editor: Gunilla von Heland; **Advertising Manager:** Anna Björling
Language(s): Swedish
ADVERTISING RATES:
Full Page Colour .... SEK 55000
SCC .... SEK 458.33
Copy instructions: *Copy Date:* 28 days prior to publication date
CONSUMER: WOMEN'S INTEREST CONSUMER MAGAZINES: Food & Cookery

ALLT OM MAT; ALLTOMMAT.SE
1843646W74P-222
Editorial: Expressen, 105 15 STOCKHOLM
Tel: 8 738 30 00
Email: redaktion@alltommat.se **Web site:** http://www.alltommat.se
Freq: Daily; **Cover Price:** Free; **Circ:** 67,307 Unique Users
Editor: Josefine Lind; **Publisher:** Susanne B. Olsson
Language(s): Swedish
CONSUMER: WOMEN'S INTEREST CONSUMER MAGAZINES: Food & Cookery

ALLT OM MC
51111W77B-50
Editorial: Box 529, 371 23 KARLSKRONA
Tel: 455 33 53 30 **Fax:** 455 31 17 15
Email: alltommc@fabas.se **Web site:** http://www.alltommc.se
Date Established: 1965; **Freq:** Monthly; **Circ:** 23,400
Editor: Björn Magnusson; **Editor-in-Chief:** Göran Svensson; **Advertising Manager:** Therese Lindell Antonsson; **Publisher:** Stig Sjöberg
Profile: Motorcycling magazine containing product and equipment reviews, tests, tips and competition news.
Language(s): Swedish
Readership: Aimed at people interested in motorcycling.
ADVERTISING RATES:
Full Page Colour .... SEK 18400
SCC .... SEK 153.33
CONSUMER: MOTORING & CYCLING: Motorcycling

ALLT OM MÖBLER
1837002W74C-518
Editorial: Skalholtsgatan 2, 164 40 KISTA
Tel: 8 663 15 00
Email: info@nextworld.se **Web site:** http://www.alltommobler.se
Freq: Quarterly; **Circ:** 50,000
Advertising Manager: Birgit Björkhäll; **Publisher:** Peter Lejdestad
Language(s): Swedish
ADVERTISING RATES:
Full Page Colour .... SEK 28000
SCC .... SEK 233.33
CONSUMER: WOMEN'S INTEREST CONSUMER MAGAZINES: Home & Family

ALLT OM PC & TEKNIK
1625673W5D-51
Editorial: Box 3187, 350 43 VÄXJÖ **Tel:** 470 76 24 00
Fax: 470 76 24 25
Email: aopc@firstpublishing.se **Web site:** http://www.alltompc.se
Freq: Monthly; **Circ:** 12,000
Editor-in-Chief: Peter Alqvist
Language(s): Swedish
ADVERTISING RATES:
Full Page Colour .... SEK 19000
SCC .... SEK 158.33
BUSINESS: COMPUTERS & AUTOMATION: Personal Computers

ALLT OM RESOR
51619W89E-5
Editorial: Bonnier Tidskrifter, Sveavägen 53, 105 44 STOCKHOLM **Tel:** 8 736 53 00 **Fax:** 8 736 54 01
Email: red@aor.bonnier.se **Web site:** http://www.alltomresor.se
Date Established: 1998; **Freq:** Monthly; **Circ:** 32,600
Editor: Nina Hampusson; **Editor-in-Chief:** Frida Boisen; **Advertising Manager:** Mats Larson
Profile: Magazine focusing on travel. Contains articles, advice, information about specific destinations and interviews.
Language(s): Swedish
Readership: Aimed at people who enjoy travelling.
ADVERTISING RATES:
Full Page Colour .... SEK 34900
SCC .... SEK 290.83
CONSUMER: HOLIDAYS & TRAVEL: Holidays

ALLT OM STOCKHOLM
1804082W74Q-165
Editorial: c/o Aftonbladet, 105 18 STOCKHOLM
Tel: 872526 00
Email: red.aos@aftonbladet.se **Web site:** http://www.alltomstockholm.se
Circ: 180,000 Unique Users
Editor: Ida Lithell
Language(s): Swedish
CONSUMER: WOMEN'S INTEREST CONSUMER MAGAZINES: Lifestyle

ALLT OM TRÄDGÅRD
50991W93-10
Editorial: Bonnier Tidskrifter AB, 105 44 STOCKHOLM **Tel:** 8 736 53 00 **Fax:** 8 736 37 94
Email: redaktion@alltomtradgard.se **Web site:** http://www.alltomtradgard.se
Date Established: 1993; **Freq:** Monthly; **Circ:** 82,700
Editor: Ulrika Palmcrantz; **Advertising Manager:** Karolina Hülphers
Profile: Magazine containing articles and information about all aspects of gardens and gardening, covering product news and practical advice.
Language(s): Swedish
Readership: Aimed at owners of houses and holiday homes.
ADVERTISING RATES:
Full Page Colour .... SEK 31900
SCC .... SEK 265.83
Copy instructions: *Copy Date:* 30 days prior to publication date
CONSUMER: GARDENING

ALLT OM VETENSKAP
1643859W55-51
Editorial: Industrigatan 2A, 112 85 STOCKHOLM
Tel: 8 758 52 60
Email: red@alltomvetenskap.se **Web site:** http://www.alltomvetenskap.se
Freq: Monthly; **Circ:** 30,000
Editor-in-Chief: Lasse Zernell; **Publisher:** Michael Journath
Language(s): Swedish
ADVERTISING RATES:
Full Page Colour .... SEK 26000
SCC .... SEK 216.66
BUSINESS: APPLIED SCIENCE & LABORATORIES

ALLT OM VILLOR & HUS
1741130W1E-203
Editorial: Storgatan 45, 171 52 SOLNA
Tel: 8 670 95 00
Email: nilfjord@nextworld.se **Web site:** http://www.nextworld.se
Freq: Quarterly; **Circ:** 60,000
Editor: Ulrika Lindgren; **Publisher:** Mikael Karlsson
Language(s): Swedish
ADVERTISING RATES:
Full Page Colour .... SEK 50000
SCC .... SEK 416.66
BUSINESS: FINANCE & ECONOMICS: Property

ALLT OM VIN
750567W22A-100
Editorial: Allt om Vin, Box 1198, 181 23 LIDINGÖ
Email: info@alltomvin.se **Web site:** http://www.alltomvin.se
Freq: Monthly; **Circ:** 95,000
Advertising Manager: Stina Lundgren
Language(s): Swedish
ADVERTISING RATES:
Full Page Colour .... SEK 25900
SCC .... SEK 215.83
Copy instructions: *Copy Date:* 28 days prior to publication date
BUSINESS: FOOD

ALLT OM WHISKY
1835866W74P-219
Editorial: Nyvägen 55, 138 34 ÄLTA **Tel:** 8 39 27 72
Fax: 8396444
Email: info@alltomwhisky.nu **Web site:** http://www.alltomwhisky.se
Circ: 5,000
Publisher: Åke Jacobsson
Language(s): Swedish
ADVERTISING RATES:
Full Page Colour .... SEK 24900
SCC .... SEK 207.50
CONSUMER: WOMEN'S INTEREST CONSUMER MAGAZINES: Food & Cookery

ALLTOMBOSTAD.SE
1843666W1E-207
Editorial: Docu i Sverige AB, Tingsgatan 2 A, 827 32 LJUSDAL **Tel:** 651 760 420 **Fax:** 651760490
Email: info@alltombostad.se **Web site:** http://www.alltombostad.se
Freq: Daily; **Cover Price:** Free; **Circ:** 16,017 Unique Users
Editor: Susanne Mattsson; **Advertising Manager:** Jessica Larsson; **Publisher:** Mikael Sagström
Language(s): Swedish
BUSINESS: FINANCE & ECONOMICS: Property

ALMEGATIDNINGEN
634380W14L-10
Editorial: Box 55545, 102 04 STOCKHOLM
Tel: 8 762 69 00 **Fax:** 87626957
Email: lotta.oom@almega.se **Web site:** http://www.almega.se
Freq: Quarterly; **Circ:** 13,000
Publisher: Jonas Milton
Language(s): Swedish
ADVERTISING RATES:
Full Page Colour .... SEK 26000
SCC .... SEK 216.67
BUSINESS: COMMERCE, INDUSTRY & MANAGEMENT: Trade Unions

ALMEGATIDNINGEN; ALMEGA.SE
1843650W14A-330
Editorial: Box 55545, 102 04 STOCKHOLM
Tel: 8 762 69 00 **Fax:** 8 762 69 48
Email: lotta.oom@almega.se **Web site:** http://www.almega.se
Freq: Daily; **Cover Price:** Free; **Circ:** 4,333 Unique Users
Editor: Lotta Oom
Language(s): Swedish
ADVERTISING RATES:
SCC .... SEK 43.33
BUSINESS: COMMERCE, INDUSTRY & MANAGEMENT

ALUMA
1625413W14F-94
Editorial: Göran Olsgatan 1, 211 22 MALMO
Tel: 40 611 11 10
Email: red@aluma.nu **Web site:** http://www.aluma.nu
Freq: Monthly; **Circ:** 20,000
Editor: Maria Dåhmen; **Advertising Manager:** Anna Kind; **Publisher:** Jennie Järvå
Language(s): Swedish
Copy instructions: *Copy Date:* 11 days prior to publication date
BUSINESS: COMMERCE, INDUSTRY & MANAGEMENT: Training & Recruitment

ALUMINIUM SCANDINAVIA
50398W27-10
Editorial: Romfartuna, Nortuna, 725 94 VÄSTERÅS
Tel: 21 270 40 **Fax:** 21 270 45
Email: aluminium@nortuna.se **Web site:** http://www.aluminium.nu
Date Established: 1984; **Freq:** 6 issues yearly; **Circ:** 3,100
Editor: Staffan Mattson; **Editor-in-Chief:** Torbjörn Larsson; **Publisher:** Torbjörn Larsson
Profile: Magazine covering all aspects of the aluminium trade.
Language(s): Swedish
Readership: Read by constructors, product developers, executives, teachers and other professionals within the field.
BUSINESS: METAL, IRON & STEEL

ALZHEIMERTIDNINGEN
1803925W55-56
Editorial: Box 197, 221 00 LUND **Tel:** 46 14 73 66
Fax: 46188976
Email: gunnar@alzheimerforeningen.se **Web site:** http://www.alzheimerforeningen.se
Freq: Quarterly; **Circ:** 4,000
Editor: Gunnar Ekberg; **Publisher:** Krister Westerlund
Language(s): Swedish
BUSINESS: APPLIED SCIENCE & LABORATORIES

AMAZONABLADET
1821352W56A-355
Editorial: BCF (bröstcancerföreningen) amazona i Stockholms län, 113 26 STOCKHOLM **Tel:** 8 32 55 90
Email: info@amazona.se **Web site:** http://www.amazona.se
Freq: Quarterly; **Circ:** 2,500
Editor: Lisbeth Jonsson; **Publisher:** Maria Wiklund-Karlsson
Language(s): Swedish
ADVERTISING RATES:
Full Page Colour .... SEK 7900
BUSINESS: HEALTH & MEDICAL

AMBIO - A JOURNAL OF THE HUMAN ENVIRONMENT
50662W57-2
Editorial: Ambio, Kungl. Vetenskapsakademien, Box 50005, 104 05 STOCKHOLM **Tel:** 8 673 95 51
Fax: 8166251
Email: elisabet@ambio.kva.se **Web site:** http://ambio.allenpress.com/perlserv/?request=index-html&ct=1
Date Established: 1972; **Freq:** 6 issues yearly; **Circ:** 2,500
Profile: Journal providing information and debate articles about earth sciences, ecology, environmental economics, geology, geophysics, geochemistry, paleontology, hydrology, water resources, oceanography, meteorology and physical geography.
Language(s): Swedish
BUSINESS: ENVIRONMENT & POLLUTION

AMELIA
50942W74A-10
Editorial: Budadress: Malmskillnadsgatan 39, 105 44 STOCKHOLM **Tel:** 8 736 52 00 **Fax:** 8 24 02 13
Email: red@amelia.se **Web site:** http://www.amelia.se
Date Established: 1995; **Freq:** 26 issues yearly; **Circ:** 100,100
Editor: Alexandra Nyman; **Advertising Manager:** Martin Lundmark
Profile: Magazine for the modern woman aged between 25 and 44 years.
Language(s): Swedish
ADVERTISING RATES:
Full Page Colour .... SEK 77500
SCC .... SEK 620.83
Copy instructions: *Copy Date:* 28 days prior to publication date
CONSUMER: WOMEN'S INTEREST CONSUMER MAGAZINES: Women's Interest

AMELIA - BABY
1626242W86A-111
Editorial: 105 44 STOCKHOLM **Tel:** 8 736 52 00
Fax: 8 24 02 13
Email: red@amelia.se **Web site:** http://www.amelia.se
Freq: Annual; **Circ:** 50,000
Editor: Alexandra Nyman
Language(s): Swedish
ADVERTISING RATES:
Full Page Colour .... SEK 42900
SCC .... SEK 357.50
CONSUMER: ADULT & GAY MAGAZINES: Adult Magazines

AMELIA - BRUD & BRÖLLOP
1625695W74B-66
Editorial: 105 44 STOCKHOLM **Tel:** 8 736 52 00
Fax: 8 24 02 13
Email: red@amelia.se **Web site:** http://www.amelia.se
Freq: Annual; **Circ:** 50,000
Language(s): Swedish
ADVERTISING RATES:
Full Page Colour .... SEK 42900
SCC .... SEK 357.50
CONSUMER: WOMEN'S INTEREST CONSUMER MAGAZINES: Women's Interest - Fashion

AMELIA - HÅR & SKÖNHET
1625689W74B-65
Editorial: 105 44 STOCKHOLM **Tel:** 8 736 52 00
Fax: 8 24 02 13
Email: red@amelia.se **Web site:** http://www.amelia.se
Freq: Annual; **Circ:** 50,000
Language(s): Swedish
ADVERTISING RATES:
Full Page Colour .... SEK 42900
SCC .... SEK 357.50
CONSUMER: WOMEN'S INTEREST CONSUMER MAGAZINES: Women's Interest - Fashion

AMELIA - JUL
1625454W74E-206
Editorial: 105 44 STOCKHOLM **Tel:** 8 736 52 00
Fax: 8 24 02 13
Email: red@amelia.se **Web site:** http://www.amelia.se
Freq: Annual; **Circ:** 50,000
Editor: Susanne Uddman
Language(s): Swedish
ADVERTISING RATES:
Full Page Colour .... SEK 42900
SCC .... SEK 357.5
CONSUMER: WOMEN'S INTEREST CONSUMER MAGAZINES: Crafts

AMELIA - KROPP & SKÖNHET
1625688W74G-199
Editorial: 105 44 STOCKHOLM **Tel:** 8 736 52 00
Fax: 8 24 02 13
Email: red@amelia.se **Web site:** http://www.amelia.se
Freq: Annual; **Circ:** 50,000
Language(s): Swedish
ADVERTISING RATES:
Full Page Colour .... SEK 42900
SCC .... SEK 357.50
CONSUMER: WOMEN'S INTEREST CONSUMER MAGAZINES: Slimming & Health

AMELIA - SOMMAR
1659631W74A-147
Editorial: 105 44 STOCKHOLM **Tel:** 8 736 52 00
Fax: 8 24 02 13
Email: red@amelia.se **Web site:** http://www.amelia.se
Freq: Annual; **Circ:** 50,000
Editor: Alexandra Nyman
Language(s): Swedish
ADVERTISING RATES:
Full Page Colour .... SEK 42900
SCC .... SEK 357.5
CONSUMER: WOMEN'S INTEREST CONSUMER MAGAZINES: Women's Interest

AMELIA - VÄNTA BARN
1625711W74D-97
Editorial: 105 44 STOCKHOLM **Tel:** 8 736 52 00
Fax: 8 24 02 13
Email: red@amelia.se **Web site:** http://www.amelia.se
Freq: Annual; **Circ:** 50,000
Editor: Terri Herrera
Language(s): Swedish
ADVERTISING RATES:
Full Page Colour .... SEK 42900
SCC .... SEK 357.50
CONSUMER: WOMEN'S INTEREST CONSUMER MAGAZINES: Child Care

AMELIA - VIKT & HÄLSA
1625742W22A-143
Editorial: 105 44 STOCKHOLM **Tel:** 8 736 52 00
Fax: 8 24 02 13
Email: red@amelia.se **Web site:** http://www.amelia.se
Freq: Annual; **Circ:** 50,000
Language(s): Swedish
ADVERTISING RATES:
Full Page Colour .... SEK 42900
SCC .... SEK 357.50
BUSINESS: FOOD

AMNESTY PRESS
51167W82-53
Editorial: Box 4719, 116 92 STOCKHOLM
Tel: 8 729 02 00 **Fax:** 8 729 02 01
Email: ap@amnesty.se **Web site:** http://www2.amnesty.se/ap.nsf
Freq: Quarterly; **Circ:** 60,000
Publisher: Ulf B. Andersson
Profile: Magazine for supporters of the aims of the Amnesty International organisation.
Language(s): Swedish
CONSUMER: CURRENT AFFAIRS & POLITICS

AMNINGSNYTT
1667816W74D-100
Editorial: Ludvigslätt, 231 99 KLAGSTORP
Tel: 410 294 42
Email: kontoret@amningshjalpen.se **Web site:** http://www.amningshjalpen.se
Freq: Quarterly; **Circ:** 1,600
Editor: Eva-Lotta Funkquist
Language(s): Swedish
CONSUMER: WOMEN'S INTEREST CONSUMER MAGAZINES: Child Care

AMOS
1641075W87-204
Editorial: Box 22 543, 112 21 STOCKHOLM
Tel: 8 462 28 00 **Fax:** 8 644 76 86
Email: kristina.lindh@amosmagasin.se **Web site:** http://www.amosmagasin.com
Freq: 6 issues yearly; **Circ:** 567,700
Editor: Brita Häll; **Publisher:** Anders Ahlberg
Language(s): Swedish
CONSUMER: RELIGIOUS

ANBUDSJOURNALEN
50500W44-6
Editorial: Box 406, 791 28 FALUN **Tel:** 23 70 57 00
Fax: 23 70 57 05
Email: redaktion@allego.se **Web site:** http://www.allego.se
Date Established: 1994; **Freq:** Weekly; **Circ:** 3,400
Editor: Stefan Elg; **Editor-in-Chief:** Bo Höglander;
Managing Director: Claes Alduren; **Publisher:** Bo Höglander
Profile: Publication covering all aspects of official tendering. Features judicial issues and official tender advertisments.
Language(s): Swedish
ADVERTISING RATES:
Full Page Colour .... SEK 18000
SCC .... SEK 112.5
BUSINESS: LEGAL

ANBUDSJOURNALEN; ALLEGO.SE
1843673W14A-329
Editorial: Box 406, 791 28 FALUN **Tel:** 23 70 57 00
Fax: 23 70 57 05
Email: redaktion@allego.se **Web site:** http://www.allego.se
Freq: Daily; **Cover Price:** Free; **Circ:** 2,000 Unique Users
Editor-in-Chief: Bo Höglander; **Publisher:** Bo Höglander
Language(s): Swedish
ADVERTISING RATES:
SCC .... SEK 23
BUSINESS: COMMERCE, INDUSTRY & MANAGEMENT

ANHÖRIG, FMN
750841W56R-105
Editorial: Friluftsvägen 29, 172 40 SUNDBYBERG
Tel: 8 642 06 50 **Fax:** 8 640 00 65
Email: fmn.riks@fmn.org.se **Web site:** http://www.fmn.org.se
Circ: 10,000
Editor: Åke Johansson; **Publisher:** Gunilla Persson
Language(s): Swedish
BUSINESS: HEALTH & MEDICAL: Health Medical Related

ANNONSBLADET I SANDVIKEN
633978W72-25
Editorial: Box 176, 811 23 SANDVIKEN
Tel: 26 24 84 84 **Fax:** 26 24 84 85
Email: annons@annonsbladet.se **Web site:** http://www.annonsbladet.se
Date Established: 1980; **Freq:** Weekly; **Circ:** 25,000
Advertising Manager: Stefan Kleen; **Publisher:** Stefan Kleen
Language(s): Swedish
ADVERTISING RATES:
Full Page Colour .... SEK 24500
SCC .... SEK 153
LOCAL NEWSPAPERS

ANNONS-MARKNA'N
751203W80-475
Editorial: Kulla 11, 517 91 BOLLEBYGD
Tel: 33 28 41 20 **Fax:** 33 28 52 52
Email: annons@annonsmarknan.se **Web site:** http://www.annonsmarknan.se
Freq: 26 issues yearly; **Circ:** 13,200
Advertising Manager: Hans Björklund
Language(s): Swedish
CONSUMER: RURAL & REGIONAL INTEREST

ANNONSÖREN
1667884W2A-396
Editorial: Box 1327, 111 83 STOCKHOLM
Tel: 8 545 252 30 **Fax:** 8235510
Email: elisabeth.thornsten@annons.se **Web site:** http://www.annons.se
Freq: Quarterly; **Circ:** 4,000
Publisher: Anders Ericson
Language(s): Swedish
BUSINESS: COMMUNICATIONS, ADVERTISING & MARKETING

ANTIK & AUKTION
51230W79K-50
Editorial: 251 85 HELSINGBORG **Tel:** 42 17 35 00
Fax: 42 17 36 00
Email: carin.stentorp@aller.se **Web site:** http://www.antikochauktion.se
Date Established: 1975; **Freq:** Monthly; **Circ:** 45,000
Editor-in-Chief: Carin Stentorp; **Advertising Manager:** Christer Andersson
Profile: Magazine for those interested in antiques, art, auctions, history and interior decoration.
Language(s): Swedish
ADVERTISING RATES:
Full Page Colour .... SEK 22500
SCC .... SEK 187.50
CONSUMER: HOBBIES & DIY: Collectors Magazines

ANTIKVÄRLDEN
50256W7-100
Editorial: Lilla Nygatan 20, 111 28 STOCKHOLM
Tel: 8 545 470 40 **Fax:** 86948510
Email: antikred@antikvarlden.se **Web site:** http://www.antikvarlden.se
Freq: Monthly; **Circ:** 26,700
Editor: Eva Gustavsson; **Publisher:** Winston Håkanson
Profile: Magazine about antiques and fine art. Includes articles about antiques fairs, auctions and museums.
Language(s): Swedish
Readership: Read by auctioneers and collectors.
ADVERTISING RATES:
Full Page Colour .... SEK 14000
SCC .... SEK 116.67
Copy instructions: *Copy Date:* 30 days prior to publication date
BUSINESS: ANTIQUES

ANTIKVÄRLDEN; ANTIKVARLDEN.SE
1843670W7-843
Editorial: Lilla Nygatan 20, 111 28 STOCKHOLM
Tel: 8 545 470 40 **Fax:** 86948510
Email: antikred@antikvarlden.se **Web site:** http://www.antikvarlden.se
Freq: Daily; **Cover Price:** Free; **Circ:** 17,800 Unique Users
Publisher: Winston Håkanson
Language(s): Swedish
BUSINESS: ANTIQUES

APÉRITIF
50260W9A-10
Editorial: Skeppargatan 27, 114 52 STOCKHOLM
Tel: 8 442 86 30 **Fax:** 86621180
Email: editorvinochbar@spearproductions.se **Web site:** http://www.aperitifmag.se
Freq: 6 issues yearly; **Circ:** 14,500
Editor-in-Chief: Ewa Beit; **Publisher:** Anders Forsström
Profile: Magazine covering all aspects of the licensed trade.
Language(s): Swedish
ADVERTISING RATES:
Full Page Colour .... SEK 22200
SCC .... SEK 185
Copy instructions: *Copy Date:* 14 days prior to publication date
BUSINESS: DRINKS & LICENSED TRADE: Drinks, Licensed Trade, Wines & Spirits

APÉRITIF; APERITIFMAG.SE
1843674W74P-223
Editorial: Skeppargatan 27, 114 52 STOCKHOLM
Tel: 8 442 86 30 **Fax:** 86621180
Email: christer.w@spearproduction.se **Web site:** http://www.aperitifmag.se
Freq: Daily; **Cover Price:** Free; **Circ:** 5,800 Unique Users
Publisher: Anders Forsström
Language(s): Swedish
CONSUMER: WOMEN'S INTEREST CONSUMER MAGAZINES: Food & Cookery

APOTEKET - TIDNING FÖR APOTEKETS KUNDER
50448W37-35
Editorial: Apoteket AB, 118 81 STOCKHOLM
Tel: 10447 50 00 **Fax:** 8 466 15 90
Email: tidningen.apoteket@apoteket.se **Web site:** http://www.apoteket.se
Date Established: 1980; **Freq:** Quarterly; **Circ:** 250,000
Editor-in-Chief: Fredrik Hed
Profile: Publication of the Swedish Pharmaceutical Association. Includes information on new products and conditions.
Language(s): Swedish
ADVERTISING RATES:
Full Page Colour .... SEK 150000
SCC .... SEK 1250
BUSINESS: PHARMACEUTICAL & CHEMISTS

APROPÅ
51405W54C-10
Editorial: Box 1386, 111 93 STOCKHOLM
Tel: 8 401 87 00 **Fax:** 84119075
Email: info@bra.se **Web site:** http://www.bra.se
Freq: Quarterly; **Circ:** 6,500
Editor: Lisa Thorsén
Profile: Magazine published by the National Council for Crime Prevention. Covers evaluation, research, development and information activities within the field of criminal policy.
Language(s): Swedish
BUSINESS: SAFETY & SECURITY: Security

AQUA
51053W75M-170
Editorial: Svenska Simförbundet, 171 41 SOLNA
Tel: 8 627 46 43 **Fax:** 87246861
Email: ml.bergh@simforbundet.se **Web site:** http://www.simforbundet.se
Freq: Quarterly
Editor: Juan Martinez; **Advertising Manager:** Patrik Asp; **Publisher:** Marie Louise Bergh
Profile: Magazine for swimmers, swimming teachers and lifesavers. Published by the Swedish Swimming Association.
Language(s): Swedish
CONSUMER: SPORT: Water Sports

ARBETARBLADET
50781W67B-3050
Editorial: Box 287, 801 04 GÄVLE **Tel:** 26 15 93 00
Fax: 26 18 52 70
Email: redaktionen@arbetarbladet.se **Web site:** http://www.arbetarbladet.se
Date Established: 1902
Circ: 23,900
Editor: Anne Sjödin; **Publisher:** Sven Johansson
Language(s): Swedish
ADVERTISING RATES:
Full Page Colour .... SEK 30000
SCC .... SEK 150
REGIONAL DAILY & SUNDAY NEWSPAPERS: Regional Daily Newspapers

ARBETARBLADET; ARBETARBLADET.SE
751426W67B-8010
Editorial: Box 287, 801 04 GÄVLE **Tel:** 26 15 93 08
Fax: 26185270
Email: web@arbetarbladet.se **Web site:** http://www.arbetarbladet.se
Freq: Daily; **Cover Price:** Free; **Circ:** 27,000 Unique Users
Publisher: Sven Johansson
Language(s): Swedish
REGIONAL DAILY & SUNDAY NEWSPAPERS: Regional Daily Newspapers

ARBETAREN
50319W67B-3055
Editorial: Box 6507, 113 83 STOCKHOLM
Tel: 8 16 08 90
Email: redaktionen@arbetaren.se **Web site:** http://www.arbetaren.se
Date Established: 1922
Circ: 3,800
Publisher: Cecilia Irefalk
Profile: Trade union newspaper with features on politics, economics, satire and culture.
Language(s): Swedish
Readership: Read by members of the union.
ADVERTISING RATES:
Full Page Colour .... SEK 8900
REGIONAL DAILY & SUNDAY NEWSPAPERS: Regional Daily Newspapers

ARBETAREN; ARBETAREN.SE
1843661W65A-1008
Editorial: 113 83 STOCKHOLM **Tel:** 8 16 08 90
Email: redaktionen@arbetaren.se **Web site:** http://www.arbetaren.se
Freq: Daily; **Cover Price:** Free; **Circ:** 3,000 Unique Users
Editor-in-Chief: Mattias Pettersson
Language(s): Swedish
NATIONAL DAILY & SUNDAY NEWSPAPERS: National Daily Newspapers

ARBETARSKYDD
50576W54B-15
Editorial: 106 12 STOCKHOLM **Tel:** 8 796 64 50
Fax: 8 613 30 39
Email: redaktionen@arbetarskydd.se **Web site:** http://www.arbetarskydd.se
Date Established: 1975; **Freq:** Monthly; **Circ:** 16,200
Publisher: Johanna Kronlid
Profile: Magazine containing information and articles about safety at work.
Language(s): Swedish
ADVERTISING RATES:
Full Page Colour .... SEK 28500
SCC .... SEK 142.50
BUSINESS: SAFETY & SECURITY: Safety

ARBETSLIV
1625682W14L-188
Editorial: Box 20133, 104 60 STOCKHOLM
Tel: 8 402 02 00 **Fax:** 8 402 02 50
Email: info@prevent.se **Web site:** http://www.prevent.se/arbetsliv
Freq: Quarterly; **Circ:** 143,900
Editor-in-Chief: Marie Antman; **Advertising Manager:** Susanne Forswall; **Publisher:** Henrik Lindahl
Profile: Arbetsliv is Sweden's biggest trade magazine dealing with work environment and health and safety in the workplace. The magazine is Published by Prevent, a non-profit organization specialising in work environment, four times a year. The magazine gives a good overview of issues in the work place. Physical and psychological health and safety risks, research, and gender and diversity issues are some of the topics covered. The magazine's aim is to help readers improve their own working environment through practical advice and tips. Each issues has a theme which is explored in depth. The magazine's primary readers are health and safety offices, human resource managers, training managers, production and engineering managers, and environmental health officers. The magazine has a circulation of 143 000.
Language(s): Swedish
ADVERTISING RATES:
Full Page Colour .... SEK 36800
SCC .... SEK 306.66
Copy instructions: *Copy Date:* 30 days prior to publication date
BUSINESS: COMMERCE, INDUSTRY & MANAGEMENT: Trade Unions

ARBETSLIV; WEBB
1843656W14E-61
Editorial: Box 20133, 104 60 STOCKHOLM
Tel: 8 402 02 00 **Fax:** 84020250
Email: info@prevent.se **Web site:** http://www.prevent.se/arbetsliv
Freq: Daily; **Cover Price:** Free; **Circ:** 33,460 Unique Users

Editor: Marianne Zetterblom
Language(s): Swedish
BUSINESS: COMMERCE, INDUSTRY & MANAGEMENT: Work Study

ARBETSMARKNADEN 50307W14F-10
Editorial: Arbetsförmedlingen, 113 99 STOCKHOLM
Tel: 8508 801 00 **Fax:** 8 508 801 78
Email: arbetsmarknaden@arbetsformedlingen.se
Web site: http://www.arbetsmarknaden.se
Freq: 6 issues yearly; **Circ:** 14,000
Editor: Fredrik Wolffelt
Profile: Journal about the current job market in Sweden, looking at careers, career development and training.
Language(s): Swedish
ADVERTISING RATES:
Full Page Colour .... SEK 23500
SCC .... SEK 195.83
BUSINESS: COMMERCE, INDUSTRY & MANAGEMENT: Training & Recruitment

ARBETSMARKNADEN; ARBETSMARKNADEN.SE
1843658W62A-518
Editorial: Arbetsmarknadsstyrelsen, 113 99 STOCKHOLM **Tel:** 8 586 060 00 **Fax:** 858606485
Email: ewa.g.persson@arbetsformedlingen.se **Web site:** http://www.arbetsmarknaden.se
Freq: Daily; **Cover Price:** Free; **Circ:** 2,800 Unique Users
Language(s): Swedish
BUSINESS: CHURCH & SCHOOL EQUIPMENT & EDUCATION: Education

ARBETSTERAPEUTEN
50631W56L-10
Editorial: Box 760, 131 24 NACKA **Tel:** 8 466 24 40
Fax: 8 466 24 24
Email: arbetsterapeuten@akademikerhuset.se **Web site:** http://www.fsa.akademikerhuset.se
Circ: 9,900
Editor-in-Chief: Catharina B Tunestad; **Advertising Manager:** Tina Danielsson; **Publisher:** Inga-Britt Lindström
Profile: Magazine published by the Swedish Association of Occupational Therapists. Includes reports on the development and achievements within the field and provides information about social political issues.
Language(s): Swedish
ADVERTISING RATES:
Full Page Colour .... SEK 17800
SCC .... SEK 148.33
BUSINESS: HEALTH & MEDICAL: Disability & Rehabilitation

ARBOGA TIDNING 634876W67B-3100
Editorial: Storgatan 28 B, 732 46 ARBOGA
Tel: 589 857 00
Email: redaktionen.bblat@ingress.se **Web site:** http://bblat.se
Circ: 3,800
Editor-in-Chief: Anders Edström
Language(s): Swedish
REGIONAL DAILY & SUNDAY NEWSPAPERS: Regional Daily Newspapers

ARENA 51168W82-55
Editorial: Drottninggatan 83, 111 60 STOCKHOLM
Tel: 8 789 11 62 **Fax:** 8 411 42 42
Web site: http://www.arenagruppen.se
Freq: 6 issues yearly; **Circ:** 3,700
Editor: Håkan A Bengtsson; **Editor-in-Chief:** Per Wirtén; **Managing Director:** Håkan A Bengtsson; **Advertising Manager:** Per Wirtén; **Publisher:** Per Wirtén
Profile: Magazine about politics, culture and ideologies.
Language(s): Swedish
ADVERTISING RATES:
Full Page Colour .... SEK 15000
SCC .... SEK 125
CONSUMER: CURRENT AFFAIRS & POLITICS

ARENA; WEBB 1844959W82-485
Editorial: Drottninggatan 83, 111 60 STOCKHOLM
Tel: 8 789 11 62 **Fax:** 84114242
Email: devrim.mavi@arenagruppen.se **Web site:** http://www.tidskriftenarena.se
Freq: Daily; **Cover Price:** Free; **Circ:** 2,467 Unique Users
Editor-in-Chief: Devrim Mavi; **Publisher:** Per Wirtén
Language(s): Swedish
CONSUMER: CURRENT AFFAIRS & POLITICS

ÅRET RUNT 50978W74C-441
Editorial: Budadress: Humlegårdsgatan 6, Box 27715 115 91 Stockholm, 114 46 STOCKHOLM
Tel: 8 679 46 00 **Fax:** 8 661 36 15
Email: aretrunt@aller.se **Web site:** http://www.allersforlag.se
Freq: Weekly; **Circ:** 155,600
Editor: Per G Eriksson; **Editor-in-Chief:** Eva-Stina Sandstedt; **Advertising Manager:** Lotta Cederborn
Profile: Magazine about knitting, sewing, flower arranging and other handicrafts.
Language(s): Swedish
ADVERTISING RATES:
Full Page Colour .... SEK 39500
SCC .... SEK 329.16
CONSUMER: WOMEN'S INTEREST CONSUMER MAGAZINES: Home & Family

ARKITEKTEN 50198W4A-5
Editorial: Box 5027, 102 41 STOCKHOLM
Tel: 8 505 577 00 **Fax:** 8 505 577 05
Email: arkitekten@arkitekt.se **Web site:** http://www.arkitekt.se/arkitekten
Date Established: 1975; **Freq:** Monthly; **Circ:** 10,700
Editor-in-Chief: Per Lander; **Advertising Manager:** Margareta Karlsson; **Publisher:** Per Lander
Profile: Official journal of the Swedish Association of Graduates in Architecture, Landscape Architecture, Interior Architecture and Spatial Planning.
Language(s): Swedish
ADVERTISING RATES:
Full Page Colour .... SEK 26500
SCC .... SEK 215
BUSINESS: ARCHITECTURE & BUILDING: Architecture

ARKITEKTUR 50200W4A-20
Editorial: Box 4296, 102 66 STOCKHOLM
Tel: 8 702 78 50 **Fax:** 8 611 52 70
Email: redaktionen@arkitektur.se **Web site:** http://www.arkitektur.se
Circ: 7,000
Advertising Manager: Isa Ekstedt; **Publisher:** Olof Hultin
Profile: Architectural journal containing features on recreational buildings, new schools, housing, hospitals, factories and office buildings.
Language(s): Swedish
ADVERTISING RATES:
Full Page Colour .... SEK 15800
SCC .... SEK 224.16
Copy instructions: *Copy Date:* 30 days prior to publication date
BUSINESS: ARCHITECTURE & BUILDING: Architecture

ARVIKA NYHETER 50765W67B-3200
Editorial: Box 925, 671 29 ARVIKA **Tel:** 570 71 44 00
Fax: 570 149 30
Email: redaktion@arvikanyheter.se **Web site:** http://www.arvikanyheter.se
Date Established: 1895
Circ: 12,500
Advertising Manager: Lars Fredriksson; **Publisher:** Jan Nordenberg
Language(s): Swedish
ADVERTISING RATES:
Full Page Colour .... SEK 19872
SCC .... SEK 99.36
Copy instructions: *Copy Date:* 14 days prior to publication date
REGIONAL DAILY & SUNDAY NEWSPAPERS: Regional Daily Newspapers

ARVIKA NYHETER; ARVIKANYHETER.SE
1843654W65A-1006
Editorial: Box 925, 671 31 ARVIKA **Tel:** 570 71 44 00
Fax: 570176 00
Email: arvika@nwt.se **Web site:** http://www.arvikanyheter.se
Cover Price: Paid; **Circ:** 8,667 Unique Users
Editor-in-Chief: Jan Nordenberg; **Publisher:** Jan Nordenberg
Language(s): Swedish
ADVERTISING RATES:
SCC .... SEK 20
NATIONAL DAILY & SUNDAY NEWSPAPERS: National Daily Newspapers

ASPECT 50206W4C-50
Editorial: Sveriges Lantmätareförening, Box 3437, 103 68 STOCKHOLM **Tel:** 8 667 95 90
Fax: 8 24 54 64
Email: info@aspect.se **Web site:** http://www.aspect.se
Freq: Monthly; **Circ:** 2,000
Editor: Barbro Larson; **Publisher:** Thomas Nylund
Profile: Journal about land surveying.
Language(s): Swedish
BUSINESS: ARCHITECTURE & BUILDING: Surveying

ASSISTANS 1804031W56L-57
Editorial: Box 310 19, 400 32 GOTEBORG
Tel: 31 775 03 90
Email: redaktion@justmedia.se **Web site:** http://www.justmedia.se
Freq: 6 issues yearly; **Circ:** 9,000
Language(s): Swedish
BUSINESS: HEALTH & MEDICAL: Disability & Rehabilitation

ATL LANTBRUKETS AFFÄRSTIDNING 50361W21A-5
Editorial: Box 6044, 200 11 MALMO
Tel: 40 601 64 01 **Fax:** 40 601 64 99
Email: atl@lrfmedia.lrf.se **Web site:** http://www.atl.nu
Freq: 104 issues yearly; **Circ:** 51,700
Advertising Manager: Christer Karlsson; **Publisher:** Olle Sjökvist
Profile: Journal covering all aspects of farming and agriculture. Contains financial news and business information for people working within the agricultural field.
Language(s): Swedish
ADVERTISING RATES:
Full Page Colour .... SEK 26200
SCC .... SEK 131
Copy instructions: *Copy Date:* 8 days prior to publication date
BUSINESS: AGRICULTURE & FARMING

ATL LANTBRUKETS AFFÄRSTIDNING; ATL.NU
1843274W21A-83
Editorial: Box 6044, 200 11 MALMO
Tel: 40 601 64 60 **Fax:** 406016499
Email: info.atl@lrfmedia.lrf.se **Web site:** http://www.atl.nu
Freq: Daily; **Cover Price:** Free; **Circ:** 25,714 Unique Users
Editor-in-Chief: Helena Wennström
Language(s): Swedish
BUSINESS: AGRICULTURE & FARMING

ATT ADOPTERA 50971W74D-5
Editorial: Adoptionscentrum, Box 30073, 104 25 STOCKHOLM **Tel:** 8 587 499 00 **Fax:** 858749999
Email: anne.adre@telia.com **Web site:** http://www.adoptionscentrum.se
Freq: 6 issues yearly; **Circ:** 10,000
Editor: Anne Adre-Isaksson; **Advertising Manager:** Gertrud Appelqvist
Profile: Publication of the Swedish Adoption Centre. Covers all aspects of adoption.
Language(s): Swedish
CONSUMER: WOMEN'S INTEREST CONSUMER MAGAZINES: Child Care

ATT UNDERVISA 750933W94F-205
Editorial: Jakobsbergsgatan 29, 271 39 YSTAD
Tel: 411 122 43 **Fax:** 41112243
Email: ingrid.rudelius@telia.com **Web site:** http://www.sfsp.se
Freq: Quarterly; **Circ:** 5,000
Editor: Ingrid Rudelius; **Advertising Manager:** Sture Andersson; **Publisher:** Pia Blixt-Grahn
Language(s): Swedish
Copy instructions: *Copy Date:* 45 days prior to publication date
CONSUMER: OTHER CLASSIFICATIONS: Disability

AUDI MAGASIN 51597W77E-100
Editorial: Volkswagen Group Sverige AB/Audi, 151 88 SÖDERTÄLJE **Tel:** 8 553 865 00
Fax: 8 550 881 33
Email: audimagasin@audi.se **Web site:** http://www.audi.se
Date Established: 1995; **Freq:** Quarterly; **Circ:** 80,000
Editor: Lena Loheim; **Editor-in-Chief:** Eva-Maria Elstner; **Publisher:** Jens Wetterfors
Profile: Publication containing news, information and articles about Audi cars.
Language(s): Swedish
Readership: Aimed at owners and drivers of Audi cars.
CONSUMER: MOTORING & CYCLING: Club Cars

AUDIONYTT 634384W56G-20
Editorial: LIC Audio AB, Box 603, 194 26 UPPLANDS VÄSBY **Tel:** 8 590 00 450 **Fax:** 8 590 00 490
Email: borje@audionytt.se **Web site:** http://www.licaudio.se
Freq: Half-yearly; **Circ:** 3,500
Editor: Börje Olsson
Profile: Magazine featuring information on hearing aids.
Language(s): Swedish
Readership: Aimed at medical and hearing aid technicians.
BUSINESS: HEALTH & MEDICAL: Medical Equipment

AURIS 50632W56L-15
Editorial: Box 6605, 113 84 STOCKHOLM
Tel: 8 457 55 00 **Fax:** 84575503
Email: auris@hrf.se **Web site:** http://www.auris.nu
Freq: 6 issues yearly; **Circ:** 35,000
Advertising Manager: Mike Kolacz; **Publisher:** Stefan Andersson
Profile: Publication of the Association of the Hard of Hearing.
Language(s): Swedish
ADVERTISING RATES:
Full Page Colour .... SEK 19750
SCC .... SEK 164.58
Copy instructions: *Copy Date:* 9 days prior to publication date
BUSINESS: HEALTH & MEDICAL: Disability & Rehabilitation

AURORA 51598W84A-57
Editorial: c/o Katarina Wallin, Katarina Skolgata 38 A, 118 53 STOCKHOLM **Tel:** 8 592 505 27
Email: katarinawallin@home.se **Web site:** http://romantiskaforbundet.blogg.se
Freq: Quarterly; **Circ:** 300
Profile: Publication featuring articles about art, poetry and culture.
Language(s): Swedish
Readership: Aimed at people interested in all aspects of art and culture.
CONSUMER: THE ARTS & LITERARY: Arts

AUTO MOTOR & SPORT
51121W77D-15
Editorial: Gårdsvägen 4, 169 70 SOLNA
Tel: 8 470 92 60 **Fax:** 8 470 92 61
Email: info@automotorsport.se **Web site:** http://www.automotorsport.se
Date Established: 1994; **Freq:** 26 issues yearly; **Circ:** 21,800
Advertising Manager: Robert Svartling; **Publisher:** Gunnar Dackevall
Profile: General motoring magazine covering news, industry updates, test reports, consumer information and motor sports features.
Language(s): Swedish
Readership: Aimed at motoring enthusiasts.
ADVERTISING RATES:
Full Page Colour .... SEK 34000
SCC .... SEK 283.33
CONSUMER: MOTORING & CYCLING: Motor Sports

AUTO MOTOR & SPORT; AUTOMOTORSPORT.SE
1843664W77A-266
Editorial: Gårdsvägen 4, 169 70 SOLNA
Tel: 8 470 92 60 **Fax:** 8 470 92 61
Email: info@automotorsport.se **Web site:** http://www.automotorsport.se
Freq: Daily; **Cover Price:** Free; **Circ:** 19,128 Unique Users
Language(s): Swedish
CONSUMER: MOTORING & CYCLING: Motoring

AUTOMATION 50360W19J-15
Editorial: Box 2082, 169 02 SOLNA
Tel: 8 514 934 10 **Fax:** 851493419
Email: automation@vtf.se **Web site:** http://www.automation.se
Date Established: 1973; **Freq:** Monthly; **Circ:** 8,000
Advertising Manager: Anna Nilsson; **Publisher:** Staffan Lingmark
Profile: Journal covering automation in technical production, manufacturing, hydraulics, instrument-making, pneumatics and measurement.
Language(s): Swedish
ADVERTISING RATES:
Full Page Colour .... SEK 26955
SCC .... SEK 224.63
BUSINESS: ENGINEERING & MACHINERY: CAD & CIM (Computer Integrated Manufacture)

AUTOMOBIL 50408W31A-5
Editorial: Box 23800, 104 35 STOCKHOLM
Tel: 8 736 12 42 **Fax:** 8 736 12 49
Email: red@automobil.se **Web site:** http://www.automobil.se
Date Established: 1982; **Freq:** Monthly; **Circ:** 11,200
Advertising Manager: Claus Widell
Profile: Magazine covering every aspect of the motor trade in Sweden. Also contains information about motor sports.
Language(s): Swedish
ADVERTISING RATES:
Full Page Colour .... SEK 15000
SCC .... SEK 125
BUSINESS: MOTOR TRADE: Motor Trade Accessories

AUTOMOBIL; AUTOMOBIL.SE
1843662W77A-265
Editorial: Box 23800, 104 35 STOCKHOLM
Tel: 8 736 12 00 **Fax:** 87361249
Email: red@automobil.se **Web site:** http://www.automobil.se
Freq: Daily; **Cover Price:** Free; **Circ:** 10,400 Unique Users
Language(s): Swedish
CONSUMER: MOTORING & CYCLING: Motoring

AVESTA TIDNING 50766W67B-3250
Editorial: Box 163, 774 24 AVESTA **Tel:** 226 864 00
Fax: 226 864 19
Email: redaktionen.at@ingress.se **Web site:** http://www.avestatidning.com
Date Established: 1882
Circ: 7,000
Language(s): Swedish

ADVERTISING RATES:
Full Page Colour .... SEK 29460
SCC .... SEK 147.30
REGIONAL DAILY & SUNDAY NEWSPAPERS: Regional Daily Newspapers

AVFALL OCH MILJÖ 50227W4F-55
Editorial: Prostgatan 2, 211 25 MALMO
Tel: 40 35 66 00 **Fax:** 40 35 66 26
Email: office@avfallsverige.se **Web site:** http://www.avfallsverige.se
Date Established: 1986; **Freq:** Quarterly; **Circ:** 1,700
Advertising Manager: Chatarina Rutegård Media & information Ab; **Publisher:** Weine Wiqvist
Profile: Publication about waste management within the public and the private sector. Covers technical, environmental and political issues.
Language(s): Swedish
Readership: Aimed at decision-makers, officials, politicians and consultants.
ADVERTISING RATES:
Full Page Colour .... SEK 15000
BUSINESS: ARCHITECTURE & BUILDING: Cleaning & Maintenance

AVTRYCK 51193W82-180
Editorial: Grön Ungdom, Pustegränd 1-3, 118 20 STOCKHOLM **Tel:** 46 16 22 55
Email: avtryck@mp.se **Web site:** http://www.gronungdom.se
Freq: Quarterly; **Circ:** 2,000
Profile: Magazine covering politics, culture and philosophy.
Language(s): Swedish
CONSUMER: CURRENT AFFAIRS & POLITICS

AXESS MAGASIN 1625605W55-50
Editorial: Jakobsbergsgatan 2, 6tr., 111 44 STOCKHOLM **Tel:** 8 788 50 50
Email: redaktionen@axess.se **Web site:** http://www.axess.se
Freq: 6 issues yearly -, 9 nr per år; **Circ:** 7,000
Editor: Erik Wallrup; **Editor-in-Chief:** Johan Lundberg; **Advertising Manager:** Henrik Olsson
Language(s): Swedish
BUSINESS: APPLIED SCIENCE & LABORATORIES

BAD&KÖKGUIDEN 1804036W74C-514
Editorial: Skalholtsgatan 2, 164 40 KISTA
Tel: 8 670 95 00
Email: info@nextworld.se **Web site:** http://www.badochkokguiden.se
Freq: Quarterly; **Circ:** 50,000
Editor: Ulrika Lindgren; **Advertising Manager:** Mattias Högberg; **Publisher:** Peter Lejdestad
Language(s): Swedish
ADVERTISING RATES:
Full Page Colour .... SEK 50000
SCC .... SEK 416
CONSUMER: WOMEN'S INTEREST CONSUMER MAGAZINES: Home & Family

BALANS 50159W1B-20
Editorial: Box 6417, 113 82 STOCKHOLM
Tel: 8 506 112 40 **Fax:** 8 506 112 44
Email: red@tidskriftenbalans.se **Web site:** http://www.tidskriftenbalans.se
Date Established: 1975; **Freq:** Monthly; **Circ:** 15,700
Editor: Pernilla Halling; **Editor-in-Chief:** Åsa Ehlin; **Advertising Manager:** Bo Lindberg; **Publisher:** Åsa Ehlin
Profile: Magazine about accountancy, auditing and related topics.
Language(s): Swedish
ADVERTISING RATES:
Full Page Colour .... SEK 25400
SCC .... SEK 211.67
BUSINESS: FINANCE & ECONOMICS: Accountancy

BALANS; TIDSKRIFTENBALANS.SE 1843655W14A-328
Editorial: Box 6417, 113 82 STOCKHOLM
Tel: 8 506 112 40 **Fax:** 8 506 112 44
Email: red@tidskriftenbalans.se **Web site:** http://www.tidskriftenbalans.se
Freq: Daily; **Cover Price:** Free; **Circ:** 6,280 Unique Users
Editor: Anna Elgerot; **Editor-in-Chief:** Åsa Ehlin (ej aktiv); **Publisher:** Åsa Ehlin (ej aktiv)
Language(s): Swedish
ADVERTISING RATES:
SCC .... SEK 42
BUSINESS: COMMERCE, INDUSTRY & MANAGEMENT

BÅLSTA-UPPLANDS-BRO-BLADET 634027W72-28
Editorial: Box 8, 746 21 BÅLSTA **Tel:** 171 46 81 50
Fax: 171 46 70 17
Email: enab@enab-reklam.se **Web site:** http://www.enab-reklam.se
Date Established: 1970; **Freq:** Weekly; **Circ:** 24,000
Managing Director: Gustav Af Jocknick; **Advertising Manager:** Ben Isaksson
Profile: Newspaper covering local news in Häbo, Upplands-Bro, Grillby and Örsundsbro.
Language(s): Swedish
LOCAL NEWSPAPERS

BANG 51170W82-56
Editorial: Bang, Bergsundsgatan 25, 117 37 STOCKHOLM **Tel:** 8 15 71 75 **Fax:** 8 15 94 72
Email: lawen.mohtadi@bang.se **Web site:** http://www.bang.se
Date Established: 1991; **Freq:** Quarterly; **Circ:** 4,700
Profile: Feminist magazine covering cultural and political issues.
Language(s): Swedish
CONSUMER: CURRENT AFFAIRS & POLITICS

BÄRGSLAGSBLADET / ARBOGA TIDNING 50776W67B-3300
Editorial: Box 120, 731 23 KÖPING **Tel:** 221 365 00
Fax: 221 365 80
Email: redaktionen.bbl@ingress.se **Web site:** http://bblat.ingress.se
Date Established: 1890
Circ: 8,500
Editor-in-Chief: Anders Edström; **Advertising Manager:** Gert Söderström
Language(s): Swedish
ADVERTISING RATES:
Full Page Colour .... SEK 32485
SCC .... SEK 162.42
REGIONAL DAILY & SUNDAY NEWSPAPERS: Regional Daily Newspapers

BARN 50657W82-56_50
Editorial: Rädda Barnen, 107 88 STOCKHOLM
Tel: 8 698 90 00 **Fax:** 8 698 90 14
Email: barn@rb.se **Web site:** http://www.rb.se/tidningenbarn/Pages/default.aspx
Date Established: 1960; **Freq:** Quarterly; **Circ:** 128,900
Editor-in-Chief: Sophie Arnö
Profile: Official magazine of Save the Children. Covers children's rights and their situation in Sweden and internationally.
Language(s): Swedish
ADVERTISING RATES:
Full Page Colour .... SEK 28500
SCC .... SEK 237.50
CONSUMER: CURRENT AFFAIRS & POLITICS

BARN I STAN 1804026W89C-255
Editorial: Gröndalsvägen 38, 117 66 STOCKHOLM
Tel: 8 558 012 50
Email: tips@barnistan.se **Web site:** http://www.barnistan.se
Freq: Monthly; **Circ:** 30,000
Editor: Emilia Emtell Olofsgård; **Publisher:** Ulf Norrby
Language(s): Swedish
CONSUMER: HOLIDAYS & TRAVEL: Entertainment Guides

BARN & CANCER 50585W56A-10
Editorial: Box 5408, 114 84 STOCKHOLM
Tel: 8 584 209 00 **Fax:** 8 584 109 00
Email: redaktionen@barncancerfonden.se **Web site:** http://barnocancer.barncancerfonden.se
Freq: 6 issues yearly; **Circ:** 40,000
Editor: Ylva Andersson; **Publisher:** Olle Björk
Profile: Journal containing information, articles and the latest research on cancer in children. Official journal of the Children's Cancer Foundation.
Language(s): Swedish
BUSINESS: HEALTH & MEDICAL

BARN; TIDNINGENBARN.SE 1844546W74D-105
Editorial: Rädda Barnen, 107 88 STOCKHOLM
Tel: 8 698 90 00 **Fax:** 86989014
Email: barn@rb.se **Web site:** http://www.tidningenbarn.se
Freq: Daily; **Cover Price:** Free; **Circ:** 25,780 Unique Users
Editor: Nadja Debove; **Editor-in-Chief:** Sophie Arnö
Language(s): Swedish
CONSUMER: WOMEN'S INTEREST CONSUMER MAGAZINES: Child Care

BARNBLADET 1925367W56B-191
Editorial: Stensjöberg 15, 431 36 MÖLNDAL
Tel: 31 27 39 27
Email: redaktion@barnbladet.org **Web site:** http://www.barnbladet.org
Freq: 6 issues yearly; **Circ:** 3,500
Publisher: Berit Finnström
Language(s): Swedish
ADVERTISING RATES:
Full Page Colour .... SEK 16900
SCC .... SEK 330
Copy instructions: *Copy Date:* 20 days prior to publication date
BUSINESS: HEALTH & MEDICAL: Nursing

BARNBOKEN - TIDSKRIFT FÖR BARNLITTERATURFORSKNING 50691W60A-5
Editorial: Odengatan 61, 113 22 STOCKHOLM
Tel: 8 545 420 50 **Fax:** 8 545 420 54
Email: info@sbi.kb.se **Web site:** http://www.sbi.kb.se
Date Established: 1977; **Freq:** Half-yearly; **Circ:** 1,000
Editor: Lillemor Torstensson; **Publisher:** Jan Hansson
Profile: Magazine focusing on children's literature.
Language(s): Swedish
Readership: Aimed at researchers, students, tutors, teachers and librarians of universities and colleges.
ADVERTISING RATES:
Full Page Colour .... SEK 5000
SCC .... SEK 41.67
BUSINESS: PUBLISHING: Publishing & Book Trade

BARNBYAR 51171W32G-273
Editorial: Box 24165, 104 51 STOCKHOLM
Tel: 8 545 832 00 **Fax:** 8 545 832 22
Email: info@sos-barnbyar.se **Web site:** http://www.sos-barnbyar.se
Freq: Quarterly; **Circ:** 75,000
Editor: Carola Rydstedt; **Publisher:** Elisabet Andersson
Profile: Magazine about care facilities for children in third world countries.
Language(s): Swedish
Readership: Read mainly by members of the organisation SOS-Barnbyar Sverige.
BUSINESS: LOCAL GOVERNMENT, LEISURE & RECREATION: Community Care & Social Services

BARNENS FRAMTID 634386W1P-30
Editorial: Plan Sverige, Box 92150, 120 08 STOCKHOLM **Tel:** 8 587 755 00 **Fax:** 8 587 755 10
Email: annika.widholm@plansverige.org **Web site:** http://www.plansverige.org
Freq: Quarterly; **Circ:** 80,000
Editor: Annika Widholm; **Publisher:** Anna Hägg-Sjöquist
Profile: Magazine focusing on the PLAN organisation. Includes development projects and international issues that PLAN International is involved in all over the world.
Language(s): Swedish
Readership: Read by foster parents, donors, fundraisers and people interested in helping children in the third world.
BUSINESS: FINANCE & ECONOMICS: Fundraising

BAROMETERN - OT 50792W67B-3350
Editorial: 391 88 KALMAR **Tel:** 480 591 00
Fax: 480 864 06
Email: nyhetschefen@barometern.se **Web site:** http://www.barometern.se
Date Established: 1841
Circ: 43,000
Editor: Peter Ahlén; **Advertising Manager:** Eva Ekström; **Publisher:** Gunilla Sax
Language(s): Swedish
ADVERTISING RATES:
Full Page Colour .... SEK 40513
SCC .... SEK 202.56
REGIONAL DAILY & SUNDAY NEWSPAPERS: Regional Daily Newspapers

BAROMETERN-OT; BAROMETERN.SE 1843261W65A-977
Editorial: 391 88 KALMAR **Tel:** 480591 00
Email: nyhetschefen@barometern.se **Web site:** http://www.barometern.se
Freq: Daily; **Cover Price:** Free; **Circ:** 18,878 Unique Users
Publisher: Gunilla Sax
Language(s): Swedish
NATIONAL DAILY & SUNDAY NEWSPAPERS: National Daily Newspapers

BÅTBRANSCHEN 50521W45E-5
Editorial: Ö. Vittusgatan 36, 371 33 KARLSKRONA
Tel: 455 297 80 **Fax:** 455 36 97 99
Email: lars-ake.redeen@batliv.se **Web site:** http://www.sweboat.org
Freq: 6 issues yearly; **Circ:** 2,500
Editor: Lasse Bengtsson; **Editor-in-Chief:** Lars-Åke Redeén; **Managing Director:** Mats Eriksson; **Advertising Manager:** Michael Stenquist; **Publisher:** Mats Eriksson
Profile: Journal covering all aspects of the boat trade.
Language(s): Swedish
ADVERTISING RATES:
Full Page Colour .... SEK 9900
SCC .... SEK 82.5
BUSINESS: MARINE & SHIPPING: Boat Trade

BÅTLIV 51331W91A-20
Editorial: Ö. Vittusgatan 36, 371 38 KARLSKRONA
Tel: 455 297 80 **Fax:** 455 36 97 99
Email: info@batliv.se **Web site:** http://www.batliv.se
Date Established: 1983; **Freq:** 6 issues yearly; **Circ:** 147,100
Advertising Manager: Kristoffer Sturesson
Profile: Magazine covering sailing, including dinghies, yachts and motor-boats, equipment and boatbuilding exhibitions.
Language(s): Swedish
ADVERTISING RATES:
Full Page Colour .... SEK 34000
SCC .... SEK 275
CONSUMER: RECREATION & LEISURE: Boating & Yachting

BÅTLIV; BATLIV.SE 1846638W91A-304
Editorial: Ö. Vittusgatan 36, 371 33 KARLSKRONA
Tel: 455 297 80 **Fax:** 455 36 97 99
Email: info@batliv.se **Web site:** http://www.batliv.se
Freq: Daily; **Cover Price:** Free; **Circ:** 27,840 Unique Users
Editor: Lasse Bengtsson; **Editor-in-Chief:** Lars-Åke Redéen; **Publisher:** Lars-Åke Redéen
Language(s): Swedish
ADVERTISING RATES:
SCC .... SEK 55
CONSUMER: RECREATION & LEISURE: Boating & Yachting

BÅTNYTT 51332W91A-30
Editorial: Box 26206, 113 92 STOCKHOLM
Tel: 8 588 366 10 **Fax:** 8 588 369 39
Email: elias.johansson@lrfmedia.lrf.se **Web site:** http://www.batnytt.se
Date Established: 1961; **Freq:** Monthly; **Circ:** 35,000
Editor: Mats Göthlin; **Publisher:** Elias Johansson
Profile: Magazine containing boating and yachting news, including reviews of yachts, power cruisers and sailing dinghies.
Language(s): Swedish
Readership: Aimed at people who enjoy sailing as a leisure activity.
ADVERTISING RATES:
Full Page Colour .... SEK 28000
SCC .... SEK 233
Copy instructions: *Copy Date:* 34 days prior to publication date
CONSUMER: RECREATION & LEISURE: Boating & Yachting

BÄTTRE PRODUKTIVITET 1809872W14A-314
Editorial: Högbyvägen 155, 175 54 JÄRFÄLLA
Tel: 8 58 01 68 02 **Fax:** 8 58 08 24 24
Email: janbrink.media@telia.com **Web site:** http://www.battreproduktivitet.se
Freq: 6 issues yearly; **Circ:** 6,000
Editor-in-Chief: Sven Janbrink
Language(s): Swedish
ADVERTISING RATES:
Full Page Colour .... SEK 19500
SCC .... SEK 162.5
BUSINESS: COMMERCE, INDUSTRY & MANAGEMENT

BEBYGGELSEHISTORISK TIDSKRIFT 51373W94B-15
Editorial: Konstvetenskapliga institutionen, Stockholms Univ., 106 91 STOCKHOLM
Tel: 8 16 33 88 **Fax:** 8 16 14 07
Email: info@ssp.nu **Web site:** http://www.ssp.nu/bht.htm
Freq: Half-yearly; **Circ:** 1,000
Editor: Åsa Ahrland
Profile: Journal providing information about all aspects of history in relation to houses, buildings and monuments.
Language(s): Swedish
CONSUMER: OTHER CLASSIFICATIONS: Historic Buildings

BENSIN & BUTIK 50684W58-5
Editorial: Box 1763, 111 87 STOCKHOLM
Tel: 8 700 63 36 **Fax:** 87006349
Email: rolf.karlsson@svenskbensinhandel.se **Web site:** http://www.bensinochbutik.se
Freq: 6 issues yearly; **Circ:** 7,000
Editor-in-Chief: Rolf Karlsson; **Advertising Manager:** Nils-Erik Wickman; **Publisher:** Robert Dimmlich
Profile: Journal about petrol and the fuel industry. Distributed free to petrol stations, garages, manufacturers, suppliers and other professionals within the fuel and motor industries.
Language(s): Swedish
ADVERTISING RATES:
Full Page Colour .... SEK 27200
SCC .... SEK 170
BUSINESS: ENERGY, FUEL & NUCLEAR

BERBANG 51408W94D-15
Editorial: Box 5013, 131 05 NACKA **Tel:** 8 644 66 22
Fax: 8 650 21 20
Email: fkks@berbang.org **Web site:** http://www.berbang.org
Date Established: 1981; **Freq:** 6 issues yearly; **Circ:** 7,000
Editor: Qasim Qehremanî; **Editor-in-Chief:** Kovan Amedi; **Publisher:** Şermîn Bozarslan
Profile: Magazine covering articles and information of interest to the Kurd population in Sweden.
Language(s): Swedish
CONSUMER: OTHER CLASSIFICATIONS: Expatriates

BERGSMANNEN MED JERNKONTORETS ANNALER

50399W27-15

Editorial: Skeppargatan 27, 114 52 STOCKHOLM
Tel: 8 442 86 30 **Fax:** 86622950
Email: red@bergsmannen.se **Web site:** http://www.bergsmannen.se
Date Established: 1817; **Freq:** 6 issues yearly; **Circ:** 5,000
Editor-in-Chief: Marie Halldestam; **Advertising Manager:** Peter Edvall; **Publisher:** Anders Forsström
Profile: Journal about steel production and mining in Scandinavia.
Language(s): Swedish
Readership: Aimed at management, executives and engineers in steel. Also, mining and metal industries in the Nordic Countries.
ADVERTISING RATES:
SCC .... SEK 191.67
Copy instructions: *Copy Date:* 16 days prior to publication date
BUSINESS: METAL, IRON & STEEL

BERGSMANNEN MED JERNKONTORETS ANNALER; BERGSMANNEN.SE

1846286W10-97

Editorial: Skeppargatan 27, 114 52 STOCKHOLM
Tel: 8 442 86 30 **Fax:** 8 662 29 50
Email: info@spearheadproduction.se **Web site:** http://www.bergsmannen.se
Freq: Daily; **Cover Price:** Free; **Circ:** 3,467 Unique Users
Editor-in-Chief: Marie Halldestam; **Advertising Manager:** Rasmus Ohlin; **Publisher:** Anders Forsström
Language(s): Swedish
ADVERTISING RATES:
SCC .... SEK 38
BUSINESS: MATERIALS HANDLING

BERGSPORT

51032W75G-20

Editorial: Lagerlöfsgatan 8, 112 60 STOCKHOLM
Tel: 8 618 82 70
Email: bergsport@brant.se **Web site:** http://www.klatterforbundet.se
Date Established: 1972; **Freq:** Quarterly; **Circ:** 4,500
Editor: John Liungman; **Advertising Manager:** Tom Vikström
Profile: Magazine about climbing and other mountain sports.
Language(s): Swedish
CONSUMER: SPORT: Winter Sports

BIBLIOTEKET I FOKUS

51409W60B-8

Editorial: Mässans Gata 10, 412 51 GÖTEBORG
Tel: 31 708 66 86
Email: info@biblioteketifokus.se **Web site:** http://www.biblioteketifokus.se
Date Established: 1996; **Freq:** Quarterly; **Circ:** 73,800
Editor-in-Chief: Håkan Linger; **Advertising Manager:** Lotta Carlsson; **Publisher:** Mats Neuendorf
Profile: Magazine containing articles and information about libraries.
Language(s): Swedish
Readership: Aimed at librarians and people involved in the book trade.
BUSINESS: PUBLISHING: Libraries

BIBLIOTEKSBLADET, BBL

50696W60B-10

Editorial: Box 70380, 107 24 STOCKHOLM
Tel: 8 545 132 40 **Fax:** 8 545 132 31
Email: hz@bbl.biblioteksforeningen.org **Web site:** http://www.biblioteksforeningen.org
Date Established: 1915; **Freq:** Monthly; **Circ:** 4,700
Editor-in-Chief: Henriette Zorn; **Advertising Manager:** Bo Eriksson; **Publisher:** Henriette Zorn
Profile: Official journal of the Swedish Library Association. Publication carries informative articles, debates and book reviews concerning library and information issues.
Language(s): Swedish
ADVERTISING RATES:
Full Page Colour .... SEK 10200
SCC .... SEK 85
BUSINESS: PUBLISHING: Libraries

BIGTWIN

1803989W77A-261

Editorial: 106 78 STOCKHOLM **Tel:** 8 453 61 00
Email: red@bigtwin.se **Web site:** http://bigtwin.idg.se
Freq: Monthly; **Circ:** 12,000
Publisher: Björn Glansk
Language(s): Swedish
CONSUMER: MOTORING & CYCLING: Motoring

BIKE

51112W77B-52

Editorial: Box 23800, 104 35 SOLNA
Tel: 8 736 12 00 **Fax:** 8 736 12 49
Email: info@bike.se **Web site:** http://www.bike.se
Date Established: 1979; **Freq:** Monthly; **Circ:** 25,000
Editor: Oscar Algott; **Editor-in-Chief:** Magnus Johansson; **Publisher:** Magnus Johansson
Profile: Magazine providing motorcycling news and information. Includes articles on rallies, touring, new models and equipment. Also contains reviews, tests and competition advice.
Language(s): Swedish
Readership: Aimed at motorcycling enthusiasts.
ADVERTISING RATES:
Full Page Colour .... SEK 17200
SCC .... SEK 143.33
CONSUMER: MOTORING & CYCLING: Motorcycling

BIKE; BIKE.SE

1846265W77A-269

Editorial: Box 23800, 104 35 SOLNA
Tel: 8 736 12 00 **Fax:** 8 736 12 49
Email: info@bike.se **Web site:** http://www.bike.se
Freq: Daily; **Cover Price:** Free; **Circ:** 5,000 Unique Users
Editor: Oscar Algott; **Editor-in-Chief:** Magnus Johansson; **Publisher:** Magnus Johansson
Language(s): Swedish
ADVERTISING RATES:
SCC .... SEK 29
CONSUMER: MOTORING & CYCLING: Motoring

BILD I SKOLAN

50712W62B-15

Editorial: Box 12 239, 102 26 STOCKHOLM
Tel: 8 540 866 41
Email: annika.dzedina@lararforbundet.se **Web site:** http://www.bildiskolan.net
Freq: Quarterly; **Circ:** 3,200
Editor-in-Chief: Annika Dzedina; **Publisher:** Annika Dzedina
Profile: Magazine containing articles and information about the importance of creativity in education.
Language(s): Swedish
Readership: Aimed at art teachers.
BUSINESS: CHURCH & SCHOOL EQUIPMENT & EDUCATION: Education Teachers

BILD & LJUD HEMMA

1663292W78A-27

Editorial: Box 5240, 102 45 STOCKHOLM
Tel: 8 13 78 60
Email: info@bildochljud.se **Web site:** http://www.bildochljud.se
Freq: Monthly; **Circ:** 20,000
Editor: Geir Nordby; **Editor-in-Chief:** Lasse Svendsen; **Advertising Manager:** Lars Jonsson; **Publisher:** Lars Jonsson
Language(s): Swedish
ADVERTISING RATES:
Full Page Colour .... SEK 32900
SCC .... SEK 274.17
CONSUMER: CONSUMER ELECTRONICS: Hi-Fi & Recording

BILDKONSTNÄREN

51233W84A-60

Editorial: Karl Johans gata 2, 414 59 GÖTEBORG
Tel: 31 42 47 31 **Fax:** 31 14 36 55
Email: naemi@bure.info **Web site:** http://www.sv-konstnarsforb.se
Freq: Quarterly; **Circ:** 1,000
Editor: Naemi Bure; **Publisher:** Anders Österlin
Profile: Magazine for artists and art enthusiasts in Sweden.
Language(s): Swedish
CONSUMER: THE ARTS & LITERARY: Arts

BILKÅRISTEN

50462W40-15

Editorial: Box 5435, 114 84 STOCKHOLM
Tel: 8 579 388 90 **Fax:** 8 579 388 95
Email: bilkaristen@bilkaren.se **Web site:** http://www.skbr.se
Date Established: 1942; **Freq:** Quarterly; **Circ:** 7,000
Editor: Sören Lund; **Publisher:** Reidun Eklöw
Profile: Official journal of the Swedish Federation of Women's Motor Corps, providing news and information.
Language(s): Swedish
Readership: Read by members of the Federation.
BUSINESS: DEFENCE

BILSPORT

51122W77D-50

Editorial: Box 529, 371 23 KARLSKRONA
Tel: 455 33 53 25 **Fax:** 455 291 75
Email: bilsport@bilsport.se **Web site:** http://www.bilsport.se
Date Established: 1962; **Freq:** 26 issues yearly; **Circ:** 40,100
Editor: Jerker Johansson; **Editor-in-Chief:** Fredrik Sjöqvist; **Advertising Manager:** Per Östman; **Publisher:** Stig L Sjöberg
Profile: Magazine focusing on motor-sports.
Language(s): Swedish
ADVERTISING RATES:
Full Page Colour .... SEK 31600
SCC .... SEK 263.33
CONSUMER: MOTORING & CYCLING: Motor Sports

BILSPORT; BILSPORT.SE

1846646W75A-218

Editorial: Box 529, 371 23 KARLSKRONA
Tel: 455 33 53 25 **Fax:** 455 291 75
Email: bilsport@bilsport.se **Web site:** http://www.bilsport.se
Freq: Daily; **Cover Price:** Free; **Circ:** 22,400 Unique Users
Language(s): Swedish
ADVERTISING RATES:
SCC .... SEK 53
CONSUMER: SPORT

BILSPORT BÖRSEN

1841362W77A-264

Editorial: Box 529, 371 23 KARLSKRONA
Tel: 455 36 12 01 **Fax:** 455311715
Email: bilsport-borsen@fabas.se **Web site:** http://www.bilsportborsen.se
Freq: Monthly; **Circ:** 10,100
Advertising Manager: Simon Johansson
Language(s): Swedish
ADVERTISING RATES:
Full Page Colour .... SEK 10900
SCC .... SEK 90.83
CONSUMER: MOTORING & CYCLING: Motoring

BILSPORT CLASSIC

1624334W31A-87

Editorial: Box 529, 371 23 KARLSKRONA
Tel: 455 33 53 25 **Fax:** 455 31 17 15
Email: fabas@fabas.se **Web site:** http://www.fabas.se
Freq: Monthly; **Circ:** 29,700
Editor-in-Chief: Magnus Karlsson; **Advertising Manager:** Therese Lindell Antonsson; **Publisher:** Stig L. Sjöberg
Language(s): Swedish
ADVERTISING RATES:
Full Page Colour .... SEK 13700
SCC .... SEK 114.17
BUSINESS: MOTOR TRADE: Motor Trade Accessories

BILSPORT GATBILAR.SE

1803874W77A-258

Editorial: Box 529, 371 23 KARLSKRONA
Tel: 455 33 53 25 **Fax:** 455 186 60
Email: gatbilar@bilsport.se **Web site:** http://www.gatbilar.se
Freq: 6 issues yearly; **Circ:** 12,200
Editor: Daniel Lindstedt; **Advertising Manager:** Per Östman
Language(s): Swedish
ADVERTISING RATES:
Full Page Colour .... SEK 11400
SCC .... SEK 95
CONSUMER: MOTORING & CYCLING: Motoring

BILSPORT JUNIOR

1664777W77D-101

Editorial: Box 529, 371 23 KARLSKRONA
Tel: 455 33 53 25 **Fax:** 455 31 17 15
Email: bilsportjunior@fabas.se **Web site:** http://www.fabas.se
Freq: Monthly; **Circ:** 15,500
Editor: Erika Philipson; **Advertising Manager:** Simon Johansson
Language(s): Swedish
ADVERTISING RATES:
Full Page Colour .... SEK 12000
SCC .... SEK 100
CONSUMER: MOTORING & CYCLING: Motor Sports

BINDU

51374W74G-9

Editorial: Västmannagatan 62, 113 25 STOCKHOLM
Tel: 8 32 12 18 **Fax:** 8 31 44 06
Email: stockholm@yoga.se **Web site:** http://www.yoga.se
Date Established: 1971; **Freq:** Quarterly; **Circ:** 60,000
Editor: Marianne Larsson; **Publisher:** Marianne Larsson
Profile: International magazine for the Scandinavian School of Yoga.
Language(s): Swedish
CONSUMER: WOMEN'S INTEREST CONSUMER MAGAZINES: Slimming & Health

BIODIVERSE

634390W64F-20

Editorial: CBM, Box 7007, 750 07 UPPSALA
Tel: 18 67 13 94 **Fax:** 18 67 34 80
Email: biodiverse@cbm.slu.se **Web site:** http://www.cbm.slu.se
Freq: Quarterly; **Circ:** 4,500
Editor: Anna Maria Wremp; **Editor-in-Chief:** Oloph Demker; **Publisher:** Torbjörn Ebenhard
Profile: Journal containing information and research on Biology.
Language(s): Swedish
Readership: Aimed at people interested in biological studies.
BUSINESS: OTHER CLASSIFICATIONS: Biology

BIODYNAMISK ODLING

749964W21R-25

Editorial: Biodynamiska Föreningen, Box 97, 161 26 BROMMA **Tel:** 70 216 33 90 **Fax:** 8 730 13 46
Email: biodynamisk@btk.st **Web site:** http://www.biodynamisk.se/bf_sidor/bf_tidskrift.htm
Freq: 6 issues yearly; **Circ:** 2,500
Editor: Lasse Hellander; **Advertising Manager:** Lasse Hellander
Language(s): Swedish
BUSINESS: AGRICULTURE & FARMING: Agriculture & Farming Related

BIOENERGI

50685W58-6

Editorial: Torsgatan 12, 111 23 STOCKHOLM
Tel: 8 441 70 95 **Fax:** 8 441 70 89
Email: info@bioenergitidningen.se **Web site:** http://www.bioenergitidningen.se
Date Established: 1981; **Freq:** 6 issues yearly; **Circ:** 3,000
Advertising Manager: Nina Soliva
Profile: Official journal of the Swedish Association of Bioenergy.
Language(s): Swedish
Readership: Read by suppliers, buyers and others within the industry.
ADVERTISING RATES:
Full Page Colour .... SEK 13557
SCC .... SEK 112.97
Copy instructions: *Copy Date:* 20 days prior to publication date
BUSINESS: ENERGY, FUEL & NUCLEAR

BIOGUIDEN.SE

51073W76A-100

Editorial: Dorian Mabb AB, Box 20115, 104 60 STOCKHOLM **Tel:** 8 578 665 00 **Fax:** 8 578 665 19
Email: info@bioguiden.se **Web site:** http://www.bioguiden.se
Date Established: 1976
Circ: 365,000
Editor-in-Chief: Kent Brewitz
Profile: Magazine containing news and information about films.
Language(s): Swedish
Readership: Read by the cinema audience and people interested in the film industry.
CONSUMER: MUSIC & PERFORMING ARTS: Cinema

BIOTECH SWEDEN

1625555W37-36

Editorial: Karlbergsvägen 77, 106 78 STOCKHOLM
Tel: 8 453 60 00
Email: biotech@idg.se **Web site:** http://www.biotechscandinavia.com
Freq: Monthly; **Circ:** 11,000
Editor: Camilla Wernersson; **Advertising Manager:** Robert Petranyi; **Publisher:** Jörgen Lindqvist
Language(s): Swedish
ADVERTISING RATES:
Full Page Colour .... SEK 38600
SCC .... SEK 193
Copy instructions: *Copy Date:* 15 days prior to publication date
BUSINESS: PHARMACEUTICAL & CHEMISTS

BIOTECH SWEDEN; HTTP://BIOTECH.IDG.SE

1844774W13-106

Editorial: Karlbergsvägen 77, 106 78 STOCKHOLM
Tel: 8 453 60 00
Email: biotech@idg.se **Web site:** http://biotech.idg.se
Freq: Daily; **Cover Price:** Free; **Circ:** 762 Unique Users
Editor-in-Chief: Camilla Wernersson
Language(s): Swedish
ADVERTISING RATES:
SCC .... SEK 39
BUSINESS: CHEMICALS

BIS

51256W60B-20

Editorial: Rosenbadsgatan 9, 652 26 KARLSTAD
Tel: 54 10 18 13
Email: lennart.wettmark@gmail.com **Web site:** http://www.foreningenbis.org
Date Established: 1969; **Freq:** Quarterly; **Circ:** 550
Publisher: Lennart Wettmark
Profile: Magazine focusing on Swedish and International librarianship, including Swedish literature.
Language(s): Swedish
Readership: Read by librarians and people interested in library issues.
BUSINESS: PUBLISHING: Libraries

BLÅ BANDET

50633W56L-20

Editorial: Box 1233, 701 12 OREBRO
Tel: 19 13 05 75 **Fax:** 19121136
Email: redaktionen@blabandet.se **Web site:** http://www.blabandet.se
Date Established: 1883; **Freq:** 6 issues yearly; **Circ:** 4,800
Advertising Manager: Per-Olof Svensson; **Publisher:** Owe Ranebäck
Profile: Magazine about alcohol and drug dependency.
Language(s): Swedish
BUSINESS: HEALTH & MEDICAL: Disability & Rehabilitation

BLÅ STJÄRNAN

51411W40-18

Editorial: Box 2034, 169 02 SOLNA **Tel:** 8 629 63 60 **Fax:** 86296383
Email: sbs@svenskablastjarnan.se **Web site:** http://www.svenskablastjarnan.se
Freq: Quarterly; **Circ:** 8,000
Publisher: Christina Lind

rofile: Magazine providing information and news bout animal care within the military. Contains ticles about agriculture, farming and wildlife and ow to protect it in the event of war.
anguage(s): Swedish
eadership: Aimed at members of the military efence force.
USINESS: DEFENCE

LADET 750761W56B-75
ditorial: Landstinget Kronoberg, 351 88 VÄXJO
el: 470 58 85 61 Fax: 470 58 87 70
/eb site: http://www.ltkronoberg.se
req: 6 issues yearly; Circ: 7,500
ditor: Katharina Lundquist; Advertising Manager: ga-Lis Nilsson; Publisher: Ingrid Persson
anguage(s): Swedish
DVERTISING RATES:
ull Page Colour .... SEK 7000
CC .... SEK 35
USINESS: HEALTH & MEDICAL: Nursing

LÅTT 51172W82-58
ditorial: Box 2080, 103 12 STOCKHOLM
el: 8 676 81 52 Fax: 8 20 34 49
mail: markus.jonsson@moderat.se Web site: http://www.muf.se
req: Quarterly; Circ: 11,000
ditor: Markus Jonsson
rofile: Magazine focusing on politics.
anguage(s): Swedish
eadership: Read by young people in Moderata ungdomsförbundet.
ONSUMER: CURRENT AFFAIRS & POLITICS

BLEKINGE LÄNS TIDNING 50795W67B-3450
Editorial: 371 89 KARLSKRONA Tel: 455 770 00
ax: 455 821 70
Email: nyhetschef@blt.se Web site: http://www.blt.se
Date Established: 1869
Circ: 26,400
Editor: Klaus-Göran Ohlsson; Publisher: Kerstin Johansson
Language(s): Swedish
ADVERTISING RATES:
Full Page Colour .... SEK 31000
SCC .... SEK 155
REGIONAL DAILY & SUNDAY NEWSPAPERS: Regional Daily Newspapers

BLEKINGE LÄNS TIDNING; BLT.SE 752292W67B-8160
Editorial: 371 89 KARLSKRONA Tel: 455 770 00
Email: webred@blt.se Web site: http://www.blt.se
Freq: Daily; Cover Price: Free; Circ: 36,400 Unique Users
Publisher: Kerstin Johansson
Language(s): Swedish
REGIONAL DAILY & SUNDAY NEWSPAPERS: Regional Daily Newspapers

BLICKPUNKT: BYGG & FASTIGHET 51410W4E-22
Editorial: Sandvägen 2, 352 45 VÄXJÖ
Tel: 470 702 770 Fax: 470 702 771
Email: red@byggfast.com Web site: http://www.byggfast.com
Freq: Monthly -, 10 nr per år; Circ: 10,900
Editor: Tina Jukas
Profile: Magazine covering articles and news on the building industry.
Language(s): Swedish
Readership: Aimed at professionals in the building trade.
ADVERTISING RATES:
Full Page Colour .... SEK 25980
SCC .... SEK 216.50
Copy instructions: *Copy Date:* 30 days prior to publication date
BUSINESS: ARCHITECTURE & BUILDING: Building

BLOMSTER-BRANSCHEN 50392W26C-10
Editorial: Box 808, 161 24 BROMMA Tel: 8 25 97 31
Fax: 8 26 96 06
Email: blomster@blomster.se Web site: http://www.interflora.se/content.asp?PageID=88
Date Established: 1925; Freq: 6 issues yearly; Circ: 2,600
Editor-in-Chief: Catharina Rissel; Advertising Manager: Mia Lagerbäck; Publisher: John Lilja
Profile: Journal about floristry.
Language(s): Swedish
Readership: Aimed at florists.
ADVERTISING RATES:
Full Page Colour .... SEK 13800
SCC .... SEK 115
BUSINESS: GARDEN TRADE

BLOOD PRESSURE 634394W56A-13_5
Editorial: PO Box 418, 405 30 STOCKHOLM
Tel: 3 134 229 74 Fax: 31419368
Email: bloodpressure@pharm.gu.se Web site: http://www.tandf.no
Freq: 6 issues yearly; Circ: 1,000
Editor: Krzystof Narkiewicz
Profile: Medical magazine covering essential information on healthcare and scientific research on blood pressure.
Language(s): Swedish
Readership: Aimed at physicians, biochemists, endocrinologists and pharmacologists.
BUSINESS: HEALTH & MEDICAL

BMW MAGASIN 1624882W50-106
Editorial: c/o Chiffer AB, 118 20 STOCKHOLM
Tel: 8 410 321 00 Fax: 8 611 60 21
Email: margita.ingwall@chiffer.se Web site: http://www.chiffer.se
Freq: Quarterly; Circ: 45,000
Editor: Per Klemming; Editor-in-Chief: Margita Ingwall; Advertising Manager: Charlotte Blomfeldt; Publisher: Margita Ingwall
Language(s): Swedish
BUSINESS: TRAVEL & TOURISM

BO BÄTTRE 50213W4E-10
Editorial: Swedenborgsgatan 7, 118 48 STOCKHOLM Tel: 8 556 963 10 Fax: 8 641 95 44
Email: red@bobattre.se Web site: http://www.bobattre.se
Date Established: 1987; Freq: Quarterly; Circ: 19,700
Editor: Göran Olsson; Editor-in-Chief: Erik Hörnkvist; Advertising Manager: Mikael Andersson
Profile: Magazine covering all aspects of the building trade.
Language(s): Swedish
ADVERTISING RATES:
Full Page Colour .... SEK 27900
Copy instructions: *Copy Date:* 30 days prior to publication date
BUSINESS: ARCHITECTURE & BUILDING: Building

BODY MAGAZINE; BODY.SE 1844547W74G-220
Editorial: Hjemmet Mortensen AB, BODY Magazine, 113 78 STOCKHOLM Tel: 8 692 01 90
Fax: 86509705
Email: redax@body.se Web site: http://www.body.se
Freq: Daily; Cover Price: Free; Circ: 7,719 Unique Users
Language(s): Swedish
CONSUMER: WOMEN'S INTEREST CONSUMER MAGAZINES: Slimming & Health

BOFAST 50166W1E-10
Editorial: Box 474, 101 29 STOCKHOLM
Tel: 8 441 53 73
Email: info@bofast.net Web site: http://www.bofast.net
Freq: Monthly; Circ: 6,600
Advertising Manager: Göran Cavallin; Publisher: Christian Lacotte
Profile: Magazine covering real estate issues such as housing politics, architecture, financial aspects and technical and practical maintenance.
Language(s): Swedish
Readership: Aimed at all professionals within the housing trade.
ADVERTISING RATES:
Full Page Colour .... SEK 24800
SCC .... SEK 206.66
BUSINESS: FINANCE & ECONOMICS: Property

BOGGI 1803970W19E-101
Editorial: ATL/Boggi, Box 6044, 200 11 MALMÖ
Tel: 40 601 64 78 Fax: 40 601 64 99
Email: per.osterman@lrfmedia.lrf.se Web site: http://www.boggi.nu
Freq: Monthly; Circ: 10,000
Editor: Per Österman
Language(s): Swedish
BUSINESS: ENGINEERING & MACHINERY: Machinery, Machine Tools & Metalworking

BOHUSLÄNINGEN 50841W67B-3500
Editorial: 451 83 UDDEVALLA Tel: 522 990 00
Email: redaktionen@bohuslaningen.se Web site: http://www.bohuslaningen.se
Date Established: 1878
Circ: 31,600
Editor: Karin C Gistedt; Publisher: Ingalill Sundhage
Language(s): Swedish
ADVERTISING RATES:
Full Page Colour .... SEK 45600
SCC .... SEK 228
REGIONAL DAILY & SUNDAY NEWSPAPERS: Regional Daily Newspapers

BOHUSLÄNINGEN; BOHUSLANINGEN.SE 1843250W65A-974
Editorial: 451 83 UDDEVALLA Tel: 522 990 00
Email: webbmaster@bohuslaningen.se Web site: http://www.bohuslaningen.se
Freq: Daily. 34000 unika vecko besökare; Cover Price: Free; Circ: 34,000 Unique Users
Language(s): Swedish
NATIONAL DAILY & SUNDAY NEWSPAPERS: National Daily Newspapers

BOHUSLÄNINGEN ~ TANUMSHEDE 750339W74C-185
Editorial: Affärsvägen 1, 457 30 TANUMSHEDE
Tel: 525 292 40 Fax: 52520871
Email: tanum@bohuslaningen.se Web site: http://www.bohuslaningen.se
Circ: 32,600
Editor: Ann-Katrin Eklund
Language(s): Swedish
CONSUMER: WOMEN'S INTEREST CONSUMER MAGAZINES: Home & Family

BOKBODEN 634399W84B-20
Editorial: Nedre Tjärna 2, 780 41 GAGNEF
Tel: 241 618 09
Email: bokboden@telia.com Web site: http://web.telia.com/~u26706893
Date Established: 1987; Freq: Half-yearly; Circ: 100
Publisher: Erik Yvell
Profile: Magazine focusing on a wide range of literature.
Language(s): Swedish
CONSUMER: THE ARTS & LITERARY: Literary

BOLAGET 51618W9D-200
Editorial: Systembolaget AB, 103 84 STOCKHOLM
Tel: 8 503 300 00
Email: bolaget@systembolaget.se Web site: http://www.systembolaget.se
Freq: Quarterly; Cover Price: Free; Circ: 490,000
Publisher: Per Bergkrantz
Profile: Magazine covering news and information about off-licence stores in Sweden.
Language(s): Swedish
Readership: Aimed at retailers and customers.
ADVERTISING RATES:
Full Page Colour .... SEK 50000
SCC .... SEK 416
BUSINESS: DRINKS & LICENSED TRADE: Off-Licence

BOLLNÄSNYTT 634017W72-29
Editorial: Box 1059, Stationsgatan 8, 821 12 BOLLNÄS Tel: 278275 50 Fax: 278 132 18
Email: redaktion@bollnasnytt.se Web site: http://www.helahalsingland.se
Date Established: 1980; Freq: Weekly; Cover Price: Free; Circ: 14,200
Editor: Kristian Westin; Advertising Manager: Sara Sigvardsson; Publisher: Mats Omwall
Language(s): Swedish
ADVERTISING RATES:
Full Page Colour .... SEK 22320
SCC .... SEK 111.60
LOCAL NEWSPAPERS

BON MAGAZINE 1625598W74B-63
Editorial: Repslagargatan 17 B, 118 46 STOCKHOLM Tel: 8 449 46 90
Email: contact@bonmagazine.com Web site: http://www.bonmagazine.com
Freq: 6 issues yearly; Circ: 14,700
Editor: Anders Rydell; Publisher: Michael Elmenbeck
Language(s): Swedish
ADVERTISING RATES:
Full Page Colour .... SEK 26900
SCC .... SEK 224.16
CONSUMER: WOMEN'S INTEREST CONSUMER MAGAZINES: Women's Interest - Fashion

BORÅS TIDNING 50768W67B-3550
Editorial: Allégatan 67, 501 85 BORÅS
Tel: 33 700 07 00 Fax: 33 10 14 36
Email: nyhetschefen@bt.se Web site: http://www.bt.se
Date Established: 1826
Circ: 49,200
Advertising Manager: Tore Åkesson
Language(s): Swedish
ADVERTISING RATES:
Full Page Colour .... SEK 50880
SCC .... SEK 254
REGIONAL DAILY & SUNDAY NEWSPAPERS: Regional Daily Newspapers

BORÅS TIDNING; BT.SE 1844525W65A-1014
Editorial: Allégatan 67, 501 85 BORÅS
Tel: 33 700 07 00 Fax: 33101436
Email: bt.se@bt.se Web site: http://www.bt.se
Freq: Daily; Cover Price: Free; Circ: 16,578 Unique Users
Publisher: Jan Öjmertz
Language(s): Swedish
NATIONAL DAILY & SUNDAY NEWSPAPERS: National Daily Newspapers

BORÅS.BIZ 634021W89C-20
Editorial: Björkhemsgatan 38, 506 46 BORÅS
Tel: 33 10 10 03 Fax: 33 10 32 13
Email: info@borasarn.se Web site: http://www.boras.biz
Date Established: 1992; Freq: Daily; Cover Price: Paid; Circ: 40,000 Unique Users
Publisher: Benny Cederstrand
Profile: Magazine featuring news and information on entertainment, films, TV and restaurants.
Language(s): Swedish
CONSUMER: HOLIDAYS & TRAVEL: Entertainment Guides

BORÄTT, BOSTADSRÄTTS-FÖRENINGSTIDNINGEN 50992W74K-30
Editorial: Box 1236, 181 24 LIDINGÖ
Tel: 8 767 88 31 Fax: 8 765 71 74
Email: boratt@br-forlaget.se Web site: http://www.tidningenboratt.se
Date Established: 1985; Freq: Quarterly; Circ: 30,100
Editor-in-Chief: Lars-Göran Hedin; Advertising Manager: Lars Alfredsson; Publisher: Mats Gällman
Profile: Magazine for private property owners and tenants. Contains articles about home purchase and related issues.
Language(s): Swedish
ADVERTISING RATES:
Full Page Colour .... SEK 29900
SCC .... SEK 249
CONSUMER: WOMEN'S INTEREST CONSUMER MAGAZINES: Home Purchase

BORLÄNGE TIDNING 50770W67B-3600
Editorial: Box 29, 781 21 BORLÄNGE
Tel: 243 644 08 Fax: 243 644 61
Email: bt.red@dt.se Web site: http://www.dt.se
Date Established: 1885
Circ: 15,000
Editor: Sven-Erik Olsson; Publisher: Pär Fagerström
Language(s): Swedish
ADVERTISING RATES:
Full Page Colour .... SEK 23300
SCC .... SEK 116.50
REGIONAL DAILY & SUNDAY NEWSPAPERS: Regional Daily Newspapers

BÖRSVECKAN 50149W1A-20
Editorial: Box 1399, 111 93 STOCKHOLM
Tel: 8 10 33 50 Fax: 8 20 14 00
Email: redaktionen@borsveckan.se Web site: http://www.borsveckan.se
Freq: Weekly; Circ: 3,200
Editor: Daniel Svensson; Advertising Manager: Christian Danielsson; Publisher: Lars Frick
Profile: Magazine covering the world of finance and economics. Contains articles, stock-market news and up-to-date financial information.
Language(s): Swedish
ADVERTISING RATES:
Full Page Colour .... SEK 14900
SCC .... SEK 107.50
BUSINESS: FINANCE & ECONOMICS

BRAND NEWS 1626240W14F-95
Editorial: Box 3457, 103 69 STOCKHOLM
Tel: 8 406 09 00 Fax: 8 20 38 10
Email: mail@brandeye.se Web site: http://www.brandeye.se
Freq: Monthly; Circ: 2,000
Editor-in-Chief: Christer Löfgren; Publisher: Per Sahlqvist
Language(s): Swedish
ADVERTISING RATES:
Full Page Colour .... SEK 5000
SCC .... SEK 41.67
BUSINESS: COMMERCE, INDUSTRY & MANAGEMENT: Training & Recruitment

BRANDPOSTEN 1692630W54A-6
Editorial: Box 857, 501 15 BORÅS Tel: 10 516 50 00
Fax: 33417759
Email: ulf.wickstrom@sp.se Web site: http://www.sp.se
Freq: Half-yearly; Circ: 6,000
Editor: Magnus Arvidson; Advertising Manager: Fredrik Rosén; Publisher: Ulf Wickström
Language(s): Swedish
BUSINESS: SAFETY & SECURITY: Fire Fighting

BRANDSÄKERT 1692632W54A-7
Editorial: Luntmakargatan 90, 113 51 STOCKHOLM
Tel: 8 23 43 10
Email: info@brandsakert.se Web site: http://www.brandsakert.se
Freq: 6 issues yearly - (7 nr/år); Circ: 12,700
Editor: Karin Wandrell; Publisher: Göran Schnell
Language(s): Swedish
ADVERTISING RATES:
Full Page Colour .... SEK 24000
SCC .... SEK 200
Copy instructions: *Copy Date:* 30 days prior to publication date
BUSINESS: SAFETY & SECURITY: Fire Fighting

Sweden

BRANSCHNYHETER.SE
1846652W14A-353
Editorial: Box 24053, 10450 STOCKHOLM
Tel: 8 506 244 00 **Fax:** 8 506 244 99
Email: tommy.ekholm@conventusmedia.se **Web site:** http://www.branschnyheter.se
Freq: Daily; **Cover Price:** Free; **Circ:** 5,000 Unique Users
Editor-in-Chief: Tommy Ekholm
Language(s): Swedish
BUSINESS: COMMERCE, INDUSTRY & MANAGEMENT

BRANSCHTIDNINGEN FAST FOOD
1625061W11A-36
Editorial: Budadress: Tryffelslingan 10, Box 72001, 181 72 LIDINGÖ **Tel:** 8 6704158
Email: lotta.eriksson@mentoronline.se **Web site:** http://www.foodnet.se
Freq: 6 issues yearly; **Circ:** 7,500
Editor-in-Chief: Lotta Eriksson; **Advertising Manager:** Magnus Svenlert
Language(s): Swedish
ADVERTISING RATES:
SCC .... SEK 293
BUSINESS: CATERING: Catering, Hotels & Restaurants

BRANT
1639304W75L-191
Editorial: Amalia Jönssons gata 16, 421 31 VÄSTRA FRÖLUNDA **Tel:** 31 743 21 75 **Fax:** 31 743 20 90
Email: thomas@brant.se **Web site:** http://www.brant.se
Freq: 6 issues yearly; **Circ:** 20,000
Editor: Hanna Lindahl; **Editor-in-Chief:** Thomas Molin; **Advertising Manager:** Robert Nicklasson
Language(s): Swedish
ADVERTISING RATES:
Full Page Colour .... SEK 3600
SCC .... SEK 30
CONSUMER: SPORT: Outdoor

BREAD & CAKES
50257W8A-5
Editorial: Box 21105, 100 31 STOCKHOLM
Tel: 8 34 76 90 **Fax:** 8 31 86 70
Email: bread.cakes@comhem.se **Web site:** http://www.breadandcakes.se
Freq: Monthly; **Circ:** 4,200
Advertising Manager: Per Hansson
Profile: Magazine covering all aspects of the baking industry..
Language(s): Swedish
ADVERTISING RATES:
Full Page Colour .... SEK 15000
SCC .... SEK 125
BUSINESS: BAKING & CONFECTIONERY: Baking

BREEZE MAGAZINE
751001W62A-455
Editorial: Halmstads Studentkår, Box 847, 301 18 HALMSTAD **Tel:** 35 16 92 61
Email: breeze@karen.hh.se **Web site:** http://www.breezemagazine.se
Freq: Quarterly; **Circ:** 6,000
Editor: Mari-Louis Andersson; **Editor-in-Chief:** Kajsa Juslin
Language(s): Swedish
BUSINESS: CHURCH & SCHOOL EQUIPMENT & EDUCATION: Education

BRIS-TIDNINGEN BARN OCH UNGDOM
50973W74D-22
Editorial: Box 3415, Sveavägen 38, 103 68 STOCKHOLM **Tel:** 8 598 888 00 **Fax:** 859888801
Email: info@bris.se **Web site:** http://www.bris.se
Freq: Quarterly; **Circ:** 3,000
Editor-in-Chief: Cecilia Nauclér
Profile: Publication of the organisation Children's Rights in Society. Deals with everyday problems that children face and covers new research within the medical, psychological and educational fields.
Language(s): Swedish
Readership: Aimed at professionals working with children, members of BRIS, politicians and parents.
CONSUMER: WOMEN'S INTEREST CONSUMER MAGAZINES: Child Care

BRÖD
50258W8A-10
Editorial: Budadress: Storgatan 19, Box 556 80, 102 15 STOCKHOLM **Tel:** 8 762 60 00 **Fax:** 8 678 66 64
Email: kansli@bageri.se **Web site:** http://www.bageri.se
Freq: Monthly; **Circ:** 3,100
Advertising Manager: Birgitta Persdotter
Profile: Magazine covering all aspects of the baking trade.
Language(s): Swedish
ADVERTISING RATES:
Full Page Colour .... SEK 15500
SCC .... SEK 129
BUSINESS: BAKING & CONFECTIONERY: Baking

BRÖLLOPSGUIDEN
1804041W74A-166
Editorial: BröllopsGuiden Norden AB, Högbergsgatan 99, 118 54 STOCKHOLM
Tel: 8 545 245 55 **Fax:** 8 442 39 70
Email: info@brollopsguiden.se **Web site:** http://www.brollopsguiden.se
Freq: Half-yearly; **Circ:** 26,000
Publisher: Anna Lundgren
Language(s): Swedish
CONSUMER: WOMEN'S INTEREST CONSUMER MAGAZINES: Women's Interest

BRÖLLOPSMAGASINET
1639338W74L-1
Editorial: Björkbäcksvägen 9, 451 55 UDDEVALLA
Tel: 522 68 11 90 **Fax:** 522681199
Email: press@brollopsmagasinet.se **Web site:** http://www.brollopsmagasinet.se
Freq: Half-yearly; **Circ:** 25,000
Publisher: Anders Wallgren
Language(s): Swedish
CONSUMER: WOMEN'S INTEREST CONSUMER MAGAZINES: Brides

BRUKSHUNDEN
51156W81B-20
Editorial: Nordenskiöldsg 13, 211 19 MALMO
Tel: 4 061 190 11
Email: redaktion@brukshunden.se **Web site:** http://www.brukshunden.se
Freq: 6 issues yearly; **Circ:** 55,800
Editor-in-Chief: Fredrik Malmgren; **Advertising Manager:** Jeanette Forssman
Profile: Magazine of the Swedish Working Dogs Club.
Language(s): Swedish
Copy instructions: *Copy Date:* 30 days prior to publication date
CONSUMER: ANIMALS & PETS: Dogs

BUDBÄRAREN - EFS MISSIONSTIDNING
51281W87-10
Editorial: 751 70 UPPSALA **Tel:** 18 16 98 28
Fax: 18 16 98 02
Email: efs@efs.svenskakyrkan.se **Web site:** http://www.efs.nu/budbararen
Date Established: 1856; **Freq:** Monthly; **Circ:** 5,500
Editor-in-Chief: Erika Cyrillus; **Advertising Manager:** Elisabet Lundin
Profile: Magazine containing information, articles and news about religion and religious activities.
Language(s): Swedish
ADVERTISING RATES:
Full Page Colour .... SEK 21240
SCC .... SEK 132
CONSUMER: RELIGIOUS

BUFFÉ
51571W22A-2
Editorial: Budadress: Hälsingegatan 49, 113 31, Box 6630, 113 84 STOCKHOLM **Tel:** 8 728 23 00
Email: red.buffe@otw.se **Web site:** http://www.ica.se
Date Established: 1996; **Freq:** Monthly; **Circ:** 2,019,500
Editor: Lina Wallentinson
Profile: Magazine containing information on the food industry and related products.
Language(s): Swedish
Readership: Aimed at retailers.
ADVERTISING RATES:
Full Page Colour .... SEK 225000
SCC .... SEK 1583
Copy instructions: *Copy Date:* 40 days prior to publication date
BUSINESS: FOOD

BULLETINEN
634405W56A-14
Editorial: Västra Vägen 5B, 171 23 SOLNA
Tel: 8 730 05 72 **Fax:** 87300502
Email: bulletinen@celiaki.se **Web site:** http://www.celiaki.se
Freq: Quarterly; **Circ:** 18,000
Advertising Manager: Ulrika Brännman-Müller
Profile: Official magazine of the Swedish Coeliac Society.
Language(s): Swedish
Readership: Read by members.
BUSINESS: HEALTH & MEDICAL

BUMSEN
1625842W31A-88
Editorial: c/o Hagen Hopp, Grindtorpsvägen 35, 183 49 TÄBY **Tel:** 8 758 64 66
Email: hagen.hopp@bredband.net **Web site:** http://www.bmw-mc-klubben.se
Freq: Quarterly; **Circ:** 6,000
Editor-in-Chief: Hagen Hopp; **Publisher:** Hagen Hopp
Language(s): Swedish
BUSINESS: MOTOR TRADE: Motor Trade Accessories

BUSINESS
1841183W1A-214
Editorial: Box 111 19, 404 23 GOTEBORG
Tel: 31 61 24 02 **Fax:** 31612401
Email: redaktionen@businessregion.se **Web site:** http://www.businessregion.se
Cover Price: Free; **Circ:** 5,000
Language(s): Swedish
ADVERTISING RATES:
Full Page Mono .... SEK 5000
Full Page Colour .... SEK 5000
BUSINESS: FINANCE & ECONOMICS

BUSSBRANSCHEN
50540W49A-2_25
Editorial: Daldocksvägen 11, 34395 VINGÅKER
Tel: 221 175 00 **Fax:** 221 175 08
Email: ulo@busstidningen.se **Web site:** http://www.busstidningen.se
Freq: Monthly; **Circ:** 2,800
Editor: Thomas Johansson; **Advertising Manager:** Lena Nilsdotter; **Publisher:** Bjarne Wilmarsgård
Profile: Magazine containing news and information about bus transport.
Language(s): Swedish
Readership: Read by bus travellers and people involved in the bus trade.
ADVERTISING RATES:
Full Page Colour .... SEK 10900
SCC .... SEK 90.80
BUSINESS: TRANSPORT

BYAHORNET
51148W80-10
Editorial: Hägnaden 923, 247 96 SK. FAGERHULT
Tel: 433 500 80 **Fax:** 43350086
Email: info@byahornet.se **Web site:** http://www.byahornet.se
Freq: Quarterly; **Circ:** 2,000
Publisher: Cecilia Biarner
Profile: Magazine containing articles and information for people living in the southern parts of Sweden.
Language(s): Swedish
CONSUMER: RURAL & REGIONAL INTEREST

BYGD OCH NATUR
51375W94X-10
Editorial: Box 6167, 102 33 STOCKHOLM
Tel: 8 441 54 83 **Fax:** 8 34 74 74
Email: bygd.natur@hembygd.se **Web site:** http://www.hembygd.se
Freq: Quarterly; **Circ:** 12,000
Editor: Peter Johansson; **Editor-in-Chief:** Gunilla Lindberg; **Publisher:** Henrik Axiö
Profile: Magazine containing articles about nature and the countryside.
Language(s): Swedish
CONSUMER: OTHER CLASSIFICATIONS: Miscellaneous

BYGDEGÅRDEN
1837004W89C-258
Editorial: Bygdegårdarnas Riksförbund, Box 26017, 100 41 STOCKHOLM **Tel:** 8 440 51 90
Fax: 86115590
Email: info@bygdegardarna.se **Web site:** http://www.bygdegardarna.se
Freq: Quarterly; **Circ:** 7,000
Publisher: Monica Eriksson
Language(s): Swedish
ADVERTISING RATES:
Full Page Colour .... SEK 14000
SCC .... SEK 116
CONSUMER: HOLIDAYS & TRAVEL: Entertainment Guides

BYGG & TEKNIK
50201W4A-30
Editorial: Box 19099, 104 32 STOCKHOLM
Tel: 8 612 17 50 **Fax:** 8 612 54 81
Email: stig@byggteknikforlaget.se **Web site:** http://www.byggteknikforlaget.se
Date Established: 1909; **Freq:** 6 issues yearly; **Circ:** 6,700
Editor-in-Chief: Stig Dahlin; **Advertising Manager:** Roland Dahlin; **Publisher:** Stig Dahlin
Profile: Magazine for architects, building owners, engineers and building authorities.
Language(s): Swedish
ADVERTISING RATES:
Full Page Colour .... SEK 15800
SCC .... SEK 131
BUSINESS: ARCHITECTURE & BUILDING: Architecture

BYGGAREN
1833094W4E-157
Editorial: Box 2082, 169 02 SOLNA
Tel: 8 514 934 20 **Fax:** 8 514 934 29
Email: info@byggaren.se **Web site:** http://www.byggaren.se
Freq: 6 issues yearly; **Circ:** 11,300
Editor: Peter Norrbohm; **Editor-in-Chief:** Lars Cyrus; **Advertising Manager:** Thomas af Kleen
Language(s): Swedish
BUSINESS: ARCHITECTURE & BUILDING: Building

BYGGCHEFEN
634408W4E-25
Editorial: Burson Marsteller, Box 5266, 102 46 STOCKHOLM **Tel:** 8 440 12 20
Email: annica.holmberg@bm.com **Web site:** http://www.byggcheferna.se
Freq: Quarterly; **Circ:** 18,000
Editor: Annica Holmberg; **Advertising Manager:** Christian Danielsson; **Publisher:** Lars Bergqvist
Profile: Magazine containing information about the building industry.
Language(s): Swedish
Readership: Aimed at building contractors.
ADVERTISING RATES:
Full Page Colour .... SEK 19900
SCC .... SEK 165
BUSINESS: ARCHITECTURE & BUILDING: Building

BYGGETTAN
1837118W14E-6
Editorial: Box 1288, 171 25 SOLNA **Tel:** 8 734 65 00
Fax: 87346660
Email: byggettan@byggnads.se **Web site:** http://www.byggnads.se/byggettan
Circ: 18,000
Editor: Inger Fagerberg; **Publisher:** Johan Lindholm
Language(s): Swedish
ADVERTISING RATES:
Full Page Colour .... SEK 3600
SCC .... SEK 30
BUSINESS: COMMERCE, INDUSTRY & MANAGEMENT: Work Study

BYGGFAKTA PROJEKTNYTT
50215W4E-2
Editorial: Reed Business Information Sweden AB / Byggfakta, 827 81 LJUSDAL **Tel:** 651 55 25 00
Fax: 6 515 525 85
Email: catharina.olsson-lindh@byggfakta.se **Web site:** http://www.byggfakta.se
Date Established: 1989; **Freq:** 6 issues yearly; **Circ:** 14,100
Editor-in-Chief: Mikael Sagström; **Advertising Manager:** Hans Engblom; **Publisher:** Hans Strand
Profile: Journal containing news and articles about the building industry. Also contains information about forthcoming construction projects.
Language(s): Swedish
ADVERTISING RATES:
Full Page Colour .... SEK 26500
SCC .... SEK 220
Copy instructions: *Copy Date:* 15 days prior to publication date
BUSINESS: ARCHITECTURE & BUILDING: Building

BYGGINDUSTRIN
50217W4E-30
Editorial: Box 55 669, 102 15 STOCKHOLM
Tel: 8 665 36 50 **Fax:** 8 667 72 78
Email: red@byggindustrin.com **Web site:** http://www.byggindustrin.com
Date Established: 1931; **Freq:** 26 issues yearly; **Circ:** 10,400
Advertising Manager: Mike Kolacz; **Publisher:** Staffan Åkerlund
Profile: Magazine for contractors, building proprietors, designers and architects.
Language(s): Swedish
ADVERTISING RATES:
Full Page Colour .... SEK 33400
SCC .... SEK 271.66
Copy instructions: *Copy Date:* 9 days prior to publication date
BUSINESS: ARCHITECTURE & BUILDING: Building

BYGGINDUSTRIN; BYGGINDUSTRIN.COM
1844956W4E-160
Editorial: Box 55 669, 102 15 STOCKHOLM
Tel: 8 665 36 50 **Fax:** 8 667 72 78
Email: red@byggindustrin.com **Web site:** http://www.byggindustrin.com
Freq: Daily; **Cover Price:** Free; **Circ:** 4,000 Unique Users
Editor-in-Chief: Staffan Åkerlund; **Publisher:** Staffan Åkerlund
Language(s): Swedish
ADVERTISING RATES:
SCC .... SEK 54.2
BUSINESS: ARCHITECTURE & BUILDING: Building

BYGGKONTAKT
51005W4E-31
Editorial: Box 4152, 131 04 NACKA **Tel:** 8 448 25 50
Fax: 84482577
Email: byggkontakt@prodgr.se **Web site:** http://www.byggkontakt.nu
Freq: Quarterly; **Circ:** 16,000
Advertising Manager: Mats Eriksson
Language(s): Swedish
ADVERTISING RATES:
Full Page Colour .... SEK 15000
SCC .... SEK 125
BUSINESS: ARCHITECTURE & BUILDING: Building

BYGGNADSARBETAREN
50218W4E-32_50
Editorial: 106 32 STOCKHOLM **Tel:** 8 728 48 00
Fax: 8 728 49 80
Email: redaktionen@byggnadsarbetaren.se **Web site:** http://www.byggnadsarbetaren.se
Date Established: 1949; **Freq:** Monthly; **Circ:** 114,900
Editor: Margite Fransson; **Advertising Manager:** Lotta Vikström
Profile: Magazine covering all aspects of the building and construction trade.
Language(s): Swedish
Readership: Aimed at managers and employees in the building trade.
ADVERTISING RATES:
Full Page Colour .... SEK 42100
SCC .... SEK 334.16
BUSINESS: ARCHITECTURE & BUILDING: Building

BYGGNADSARBETAREN; BYGGNADSARBETAREN.SE
1846396W14F-113
ditorial: 106 32 STOCKHOLM **Tel:** 8 728 49 00
ax: 87284980
mail: redaktionen@byggnadsarbetaren.se **Web ite:** http://www.byggnadsarbetaren.se
req: Daily; **Cover Price:** Free; **Circ:** 26,200 Unique sers
ublisher: Kenneth Petterson
anguage(s): Swedish
BUSINESS: COMMERCE, INDUSTRY & MANAGEMENT: Training & Recruitment

BYGGNADSKULTUR
50219W4E-33
ditorial: Svenska byggnadsvårdsföreningen, Box 442, 113 82 STOCKHOLM **Tel:** 23 278 78
ax: 23 278 77
mail: kansli@byggnadsvard.se **Web site:** http://www.byggnadsvard.se
req: Quarterly; **Circ:** 7,000
ditor: Eva Kvarnström; **Advertising Manager:** Gunilla Lundgren; **Publisher:** Lotta Bylander
rofile: Magazine covering all aspects of the building rade.
anguage(s): Swedish
BUSINESS: ARCHITECTURE & BUILDING: Building

BYGGVÄRLDEN
1829380W42A-102
Editorial: 106 12 STOCKHOLM **Tel:** 8 796 66 50
Fax: 8 21 65 13
Email: redaktionen@byggvarlden.se **Web site:** http://www.byggvarlden.se
Freq: 26 issues yearly; **Circ:** 20,000
Advertising Manager: Marie Pettersson
Language(s): Swedish
ADVERTISING RATES:
Full Page Colour .... SEK 39500
SCC .... SEK 197.50
BUSINESS: CONSTRUCTION

BYTBIL.COM
2003291W53-91
Tel: 8 732 2800 **Fax:** 87322829
Email: info@bytbil.com **Web site:** http://bytbil.com
Freq: Daily; **Cover Price:** Free; **Circ:** 700,000 Unique Users
Language(s): Swedish
BUSINESS: RETAILING & WHOLESALING

C, IDÉTIDSKRIFT OM CEREALIER
634409W56A-268
Editorial: Box 30192, 104 25 STOCKHOLM
Tel: 8 657 42 20
Email: maud.lindbla@lantmannen.com **Web site:** http://www.lantmannen.com/sv/Lantmannen-COM/Om-koncernen/Publikationer/Idetidskriften-C
Freq: Quarterly; **Circ:** 30,000
Editor-in-Chief: Maud Lindblå
Language(s): Swedish
BUSINESS: HEALTH & MEDICAL

CAD & RITNYTT
634722W14J-20
Editorial: Bagersgatan 2, 211 25 MALMÖ
Tel: 40 23 22 37 **Fax:** 40 23 70 87
Email: info@ritnytt.com **Web site:** http://www.ritnytt.com
Date Established: 1982; **Freq:** Quarterly; **Circ:** 14,000
Editor: Irena Lauterbach; **Advertising Manager:** Irena Lauterbach; **Publisher:** Irena Lauterbach
Profile: Magazine focusing on design, drawing, materials and other aspects of technical and building design.
Language(s): Swedish
Readership: Aimed at engineers, architects and designers.
ADVERTISING RATES:
Full Page Colour .... SEK 20800
SCC .... SEK 173
BUSINESS: COMMERCE, INDUSTRY & MANAGEMENT: Commercial Design

CAFÉ
51279W86C-50
Editorial: BOX 27708, 115 91 Stockholm, 114 46 STOCKHOLM **Tel:** 8 57 80 10 00 **Fax:** 8 457 80 80
Email: cafe.red@cafe.se **Web site:** http://www.cafe.se
Date Established: 1990; **Freq:** Monthly; **Circ:** 28,700
Profile: Lifestyle magazine containing features on fashion, sport and current affairs.
Language(s): Swedish
Readership: Aimed at men aged between 20 and 35 years.
ADVERTISING RATES:
Full Page Colour .... SEK 55800
SCC .... SEK 465
CONSUMER: ADULT & GAY MAGAZINES: Men's Lifestyle Magazines

CAFÉ; CAFE.SE
751242W91R-205
Editorial: S:t Eriksplan 2, 113 93 STOCKHOLM
Tel: 8 457 80 00 **Fax:** 8 457 80 80
Email: victoria.nelson@cafe.se **Web site:** http://www.cafe.se
Freq: Daily; **Circ:** 8,233 Unique Users
Editor-in-Chief: Daniel Kjellson; **Advertising Manager:** Adam Stevens; **Publisher:** Fredrik Helmertz
Language(s): Swedish
CONSUMER: RECREATION & LEISURE: Recreation & Leisure Related

CAFÉ COLLECTIONS
1809893W86C-155
Editorial: S:t Eriksplan 2, 113 93 STOCKHOLM
Tel: 8 457 80 00 **Fax:** 8 457 80 80
Email: victoria.nelson@cafe.se **Web site:** http://www.cafe.se/collections
Freq: Half-yearly; **Circ:** 33,300
Publisher: Fredrik Helmertz
Language(s): Swedish
ADVERTISING RATES:
Full Page Colour .... SEK 55800
SCC .... SEK 465
CONSUMER: ADULT & GAY MAGAZINES: Men's Lifestyle Magazines

CAMINO
1809884W74Q-168
Editorial: House of Win-Win, Tredje Långgatan 13B, 413 03 GOTEBORG **Tel:** 31242426
Email: info@caminomagasin.se **Web site:** http://www.caminomagasin.se
Freq: Quarterly; **Circ:** 12,000
Advertising Manager: Caroline Petersson
Language(s): Swedish
CONSUMER: WOMEN'S INTEREST CONSUMER MAGAZINES: Lifestyle

CAMPUS EKONOMI
50150W1A-30
Editorial: Box 7053, 103 86 STOCKHOLM
Tel: 8 562 027 00 **Fax:** 8 562 930 50
Email: redaktionen@campus.se **Web site:** http://www.campus.se
Freq: Quarterly; **Circ:** 20,000
Editor: Malin Sund; **Advertising Manager:** Karin Almcrantz
Profile: Magazine for students of economics and business administration.
Language(s): Swedish
ADVERTISING RATES:
Full Page Colour .... SEK 39800
SCC .... SEK 331.60
BUSINESS: FINANCE & ECONOMICS

CAMPUS JURIST
1687080W44-62
Editorial: Box 7053, 103 86 STOCKHOLM
Tel: 8 56 20 27 00 **Fax:** 8 56 29 30 50
Email: redaktionen@campus.se **Web site:** http://www.campus.se
Freq: Quarterly; **Circ:** 5,000
Editor: Maija Mårtensgård; **Editor-in-Chief:** Sara Tuncel; **Advertising Manager:** Karin Almcrantz
Language(s): Swedish
ADVERTISING RATES:
Full Page Colour .... SEK 25000
SCC .... SEK 208
BUSINESS: LEGAL

CAMPUS TEKNIK
50344W19A-30
Editorial: Box 7053, 103 86 STOCKHOLM
Tel: 8 562 027 00 **Fax:** 856293050
Email: redaktionen@campus.se **Web site:** http://www.campus.se
Freq: Quarterly; **Circ:** 30,000
Advertising Manager: Karin Almcrantz
Profile: Magazine covering articles, news, and information about engineering technology.
Language(s): Swedish
Readership: Read mainly by Swedish engineering students.
ADVERTISING RATES:
Full Page Colour .... SEK 39800
SCC .... SEK 331
BUSINESS: ENGINEERING & MACHINERY

CAMPUS.SE
1846780W14F-124
Editorial: Box 7053, 103 86 STOCKHOLM
Tel: 8 56 20 27 00 **Fax:** 8 56 29 30 50
Email: redaktionen@campus.se **Web site:** http://www.campus.se
Freq: Daily; **Cover Price:** Free; **Circ:** 6,000 Unique Users
Language(s): Swedish
ADVERTISING RATES:
SCC .... SEK 66
BUSINESS: COMMERCE, INDUSTRY & MANAGEMENT: Training & Recruitment

CANCERVÅRDEN
1804044W56A-350
Editorial: c/o Diana lindén, Imatragatan 122, 164 78 KISTA **Tel:** 8 517 745 15
Email: diana.linden@karolinska.se **Web site:** http://www.cancervard.se
Freq: 6 issues yearly; **Circ:** 1,000
Publisher: Diana Lindén
Language(s): Swedish
BUSINESS: HEALTH & MEDICAL

CAP & DESIGN
50693W60A-10
Editorial: Karlbergsvägen 77-81, 106 78 STOCKHOLM **Tel:** 8 453 61 38
Email: pressmeddelande@capdesign.se **Web site:** http://www.capdesign.se
Freq: 6 issues yearly; **Circ:** 11,000
Editor: Jonas Mattsson; **Advertising Manager:** Magnus Mu Ray; **Publisher:** Andreas Leijon
Profile: Magazine about computer assisted publishing, graphic design and typography.
Language(s): Swedish
Readership: Read by publishers, designers and graphical producers.
ADVERTISING RATES:
Full Page Colour .... SEK 56800
SCC .... SEK 473.33
BUSINESS: PUBLISHING: Publishing & Book Trade

CAP & DESIGN; CAPDESIGN.SE
1844783W5E-117
Editorial: Karlbergsvägen 77-81, 106 78 STOCKHOLM **Tel:** 8 453 60 00
Email: pressmeddelande@capdesign.se **Web site:** http://capdesign.idg.se
Freq: Daily; **Cover Price:** Free; **Circ:** 3,012 Unique Users
Publisher: Andreas Leijon
Language(s): Swedish
BUSINESS: COMPUTERS & AUTOMATION: Data Transmission

CARAVANBLADET
51340W91B-80
Editorial: Kyrkvägen 25, 703 75 OREBRO
Tel: 19 23 46 10 **Fax:** 19 23 44 25
Email: redaktionen@caravanclub.se **Web site:** http://www.caravanclub.se
Date Established: 1959; **Freq:** 6 issues yearly; **Circ:** 21,400
Editor: Håkan Johansson; **Publisher:** Bill-Arne Andersson
Profile: Magazine of the Caravan Club of Sweden.
Language(s): Swedish
ADVERTISING RATES:
Full Page Colour .... SEK 15900
SCC .... SEK 132.50
CONSUMER: RECREATION & LEISURE: Camping & Caravanning

CENTERNYTT
1809865W14A-309
Editorial: Nordic Council of Shopping Centers, Slöjdgatan 9, 111 57 STOCKHOLM **Tel:** 8 611 11 42
Fax: 86111299
Email: agneta.uhrstedt@ncsc.se **Web site:** http://www.ncsc.se
Freq: Quarterly; **Circ:** 1,100
Publisher: Agneta Uhrstedt
Language(s): Swedish
BUSINESS: COMMERCE, INDUSTRY & MANAGEMENT

CF-BLADET
634413W56A-14_5
Editorial: Kålsängsgränd 10 D, 753 19 UPPSALA
Tel: 18 15 16 22 **Fax:** 18127074
Email: cf-bladet@rfcf.se **Web site:** http://www.rfcf.se
Date Established: 1970; **Freq:** Quarterly; **Circ:** 2,100
Advertising Manager: Kristina Radwan; **Publisher:** Lars U Granberg
Profile: Magazine focusing on research about cystic fibrosis and activities within the organisation.
Language(s): Swedish
Readership: Read by members of Riksförbundet Cystisk Fibros.
BUSINESS: HEALTH & MEDICAL

CHALMERS MAGASIN
750753W14R-40
Editorial: Informationsavdelningen, 412 96 GÖTEBORG **Tel:** 31 772 25 10 **Fax:** 31 772 25 61
Email: chalmersmagasin@chalmers.se **Web site:** http://www.chalmers.se/sections/aktuellt/chalmers-magasin
Freq: Quarterly; **Circ:** 41,000
Editor-in-Chief: Kerstin Törsäter; **Publisher:** Petra Ljung
Language(s): Swedish
ADVERTISING RATES:
Full Page Colour .... SEK 50000
SCC .... SEK 416.6
BUSINESS: COMMERCE, INDUSTRY & MANAGEMENT: Commerce Related

CHECK-IN
51415W89D-30
Editorial: 181 44 LIDINGÖ **Tel:** 660 37 09 79
Fax: 660 37 09 31
Email: g.mineur@check-in.se **Web site:** http://www.check-in.se
Date Established: 1989; **Freq:** Quarterly; **Circ:** 35,000
Editor-in-Chief: Gösta Mineur; **Advertising Manager:** Jan Åhlin; **Publisher:** Gösta Mineur
Profile: Magazine containing travel news and information.
Language(s): Swedish
Readership: Read by passengers and visitors at airports .
ADVERTISING RATES:
Full Page Colour .... SEK 34000
SCC .... SEK 283
CONSUMER: HOLIDAYS & TRAVEL: In-Flight Magazines

CHEF & LEDARSKAP
1741150W62A-509
Editorial: Box 12239, 102 26 STOCKHOLM
Tel: 8 737 65 40 **Fax:** 86190088
Email: chefochledarskap@lararforbundet.se **Web site:** http://www.chefochledarskap.se
Freq: 6 issues yearly; **Circ:** 6,300
Editor: Christina Thors; **Advertising Manager:** Evert Norberg; **Publisher:** Jonas Almquist
Language(s): Swedish
ADVERTISING RATES:
Full Page Colour .... SEK 14800
SCC .... SEK 123
BUSINESS: CHURCH & SCHOOL EQUIPMENT & EDUCATION: Education

CHEF & LEDARSKAP; CHEFOCHLEDARSKAP.SE
1846302W62A-521
Editorial: Box 12239, 102 26 STOCKHOLM
Tel: 8 737 65 00 **Fax:** 8 619 00 88
Email: chefochledarskap@lararforbundet.se **Web site:** http://www.chefochledarskap.se
Freq: Daily; **Cover Price:** Free; **Circ:** 7,000 Unique Users
Editor: Christina Thors; **Editor-in-Chief:** Jonas Almquist; **Publisher:** Jonas Almquist
Language(s): Swedish
ADVERTISING RATES:
SCC .... SEK 24.6
BUSINESS: CHURCH & SCHOOL EQUIPMENT & EDUCATION: Education

CHEFEN I FOKUS
1741158W14L-192
Editorial: Box 7825, 103 97 STOCKHOLM
Tel: 8 789 64 61 **Fax:** 8 789 64 79
Email: red@chefenifokus.se **Web site:** http://www.chefenifokus.se
Freq: 6 issues yearly; **Circ:** 15,800
Publisher: Kent Källqvist
Language(s): Swedish
ADVERTISING RATES:
Full Page Colour .... SEK 17000
SCC .... SEK 141.66
BUSINESS: COMMERCE, INDUSTRY & MANAGEMENT: Trade Unions

CHEFSTIDNINGEN, HR- OCH LEDARSKAPSMAGASIN FÖR AKADEMIKER
1895217W14F-126
Editorial: Drottninggatan 83, 111 60 STOCKHOLM
Tel: 8 789 11 70 **Fax:** 84114242
Email: redaktion@chefstidningen.se **Web site:** http://www.chefstidningen.se
Freq: 6 issues yearly -, 8 ggr/år; **Circ:** 15,000
Editor-in-Chief: Eva Brandsma
Language(s): Swedish
BUSINESS: COMMERCE, INDUSTRY & MANAGEMENT: Training & Recruitment

CINEMA
1659350W76A-189
Editorial: Birger Jarlsgatan 20, 114 34 STOCKHOLM
Tel: 8 667 92 10 **Fax:** 8 667 92 11
Email: cinema@cinemanews.se **Web site:** http://www.cinema.se
Freq: Monthly; **Circ:** 17,000
Editor: Stefan Nylén; **Editor-in-Chief:** Elin Larsson; **Advertising Manager:** Malou Hansson
Language(s): Swedish
ADVERTISING RATES:
Full Page Colour .... SEK 34500
SCC .... SEK 287.5
CONSUMER: MUSIC & PERFORMING ARTS: Cinema

CINEMA; CINEMA.SE
1843665W78B-24
Editorial: Birger Jarlsgatan 20, 114 34 STOCKHOLM
Tel: 8 667 92 10 **Fax:** 8 667 92 11
Email: alltomfilm@itsmedia.se **Web site:** http://www.alltomfilm.se
Freq: Daily; **Cover Price:** Free; **Circ:** 3,400 Unique Users
Editor-in-Chief: Lotten Sundgren
Language(s): Swedish
ADVERTISING RATES:
SCC .... SEK 58
CONSUMER: CONSUMER ELECTRONICS: Video & DVD

CIO SWEDEN
51606W14A-60
Editorial: IDG AB, Karlbergsvägen 77, 106 78 STOCKHOLM **Tel:** 8 453 64 00
Email: cio@idg.se **Web site:** http://www.cio.idg.se
Date Established: 2000; **Freq:** Monthly; **Circ:** 5,600
Editor: Jon Röhne; **Editor-in-Chief:** Alexandra Heymowska
Profile: Magazine containing information about the experiences of companies who have developed successful web strategies, trends in business

technology on the Internet and overviews of companies and suppliers.
Language(s): Swedish
Readership: Read by business leaders in the Swedish industry.
ADVERTISING RATES:
Full Page Colour .... SEK 45800
SCC .... SEK 381.67
BUSINESS: COMMERCE, INDUSTRY & MANAGEMENT

CIO SWEDEN; WEBB 1844673W5E-115

Editorial: IDG AB, Karlbergsvägen 77, 106 78 STOCKHOLM **Tel:** 8 453 60 00
Email: cio@idg.se **Web site:** http://www.cio.idg.se
Freq: Daily; **Cover Price:** Free; **Circ:** 4,586 Unique Users
Editor: Jon Röhne; **Editor-in-Chief:** Alexandra Heymowska
Language(s): Swedish
ADVERTISING RATES:
SCC .... SEK 76
BUSINESS: COMPUTERS & AUTOMATION: Data Transmission

CIRKELN 51226W83-97

Editorial: Studiefrämjandet Riksförbundet, Box 49013, 100 28 STOCKHOLM **Tel:** 8 545 707 00 **Fax:** 8 545 707 39
Email: info@studieframjandet.se **Web site:** http://www.cirkeln.nu
Freq: 6 issues yearly; **Circ:** 20,000
Editor-in-Chief: Hetty Rooth; **Advertising Manager:** Jan Dylicki; **Publisher:** Tjia Torpe
Profile: Student magazine containing educational, cultural and environmental news.
Language(s): Swedish
CONSUMER: STUDENT PUBLICATIONS

CIRKULATION, VA-TIDSKRIFTEN 50494W42C-35

Editorial: Box 508, 701 50 OREBRO **Tel:** 19 10 80 50 **Fax:** 19108055
Email: info@cirkulation.com **Web site:** http://www.cirkulation.com
Date Established: 1992; **Freq:** 6 issues yearly; **Circ:** 2,900
Advertising Manager: Peter Henricson
Profile: Magazine about water and wastewater.
Language(s): Swedish
Readership: Aimed at personnel within the waste and water industry.
ADVERTISING RATES:
Full Page Colour .... SEK 16900
SCC .... SEK 140.80
BUSINESS: CONSTRUCTION: Water Engineering

CIVIL 50433W40-20

Editorial: Box 2034, 169 02 SOLNA **Tel:** 8 629 63 72 **Fax:** 8 629 63 83
Email: red@civil.se **Web site:** http://www.civil.se
Date Established: 1937; **Freq:** Quarterly; **Circ:** 18,600
Publisher: Anders M Johansson
Profile: Journal containing articles and information about civil defence, survival and voluntary service.
Language(s): Swedish
ADVERTISING RATES:
Full Page Colour .... SEK 37200
SCC .... SEK 310
BUSINESS: DEFENCE

CIVILEKONOMEN 50151W88C-40

Editorial: Box 4720, 116 92 STOCKHOLM
Tel: 8 783 27 50 **Fax:** 8 783 27 52
Email: inkorgen@civilekonomen.se **Web site:** http://www.civilekonomen.se
Freq: Monthly -, 10 nr per år; **Circ:** 32,500
Editor-in-Chief: Torbjörn Askman; **Advertising Manager:** Berenika Westerlund
Profile: Magazine containing information about careers and articles concerning the economy.
Language(s): Swedish
Readership: Read by graduates and students at Swedish schools.
ADVERTISING RATES:
Full Page Colour .... SEK 35000
SCC .... SEK 170.83
CONSUMER: EDUCATION: Careers

CIVILEKONOMEN; CIVILEKONOMEN.SE

1846513W62A-522
Editorial: Box 4720, 116 92 STOCKHOLM
Tel: 8 783 27 50 **Fax:** 87832752
Email: civilekonomen@civilekonomerna.se **Web site:** http://www.civilekonomen.se
Freq: Daily; **Cover Price:** Free; **Circ:** 9,600 Unique Users
Publisher: Torbjörn Askman
Language(s): Swedish
BUSINESS: CHURCH & SCHOOL EQUIPMENT & EDUCATION: Education

CLASSIC BIKE 1663912W77B-68

Editorial: R&D Media AB, Gårdsvägen 4, 169 70 SOLNA **Tel:** 8 470 92 60
Email: info@classicbike.se **Web site:** http://www.classicbike.se
Freq: 6 issues yearly; **Circ:** 10,000
Editor: Henrik Nyberg; **Editor-in-Chief:** Robert Lavér; **Advertising Manager:** Björn Renvall
Language(s): Swedish
CONSUMER: MOTORING & CYCLING: Motorcycling

CLASSIC MOTOR 51134W77F-50

Editorial: Gävlegatan 22, 113 78 STOCKHOLM
Tel: 8 692 01 50 **Fax:** 8 692 01 55
Email: classic@classicmotor.se **Web site:** http://www.classicmotor.se
Freq: Monthly; **Circ:** 43,100
Editor: Björn Meyer; **Editor-in-Chief:** Thomas Sjölund; **Advertising Manager:** Marcus Friberg; **Publisher:** Thomas Sjölund
Profile: Magazine about classic cars.
Language(s): Swedish
ADVERTISING RATES:
Full Page Colour .... SEK 17000
SCC .... SEK 141.7
CONSUMER: MOTORING & CYCLING: Veteran Cars

CLASSIC MOTOR; CLASSICMOTOR.SE

1844809W77A-267
Editorial: Gävlegatan 22, 113 78 STOCKHOLM
Tel: 8 692 01 50 **Fax:** 8 692 01 55
Email: classic@classicmotor.se **Web site:** http://www.classicmotor.se
Freq: Daily; **Cover Price:** Free; **Circ:** 1,565 Unique Users
Editor: Björn Meyer; **Editor-in-Chief:** Thomas Sjölund; **Publisher:** Thomas Sjölund
Language(s): Swedish
ADVERTISING RATES:
SCC .... SEK 28
CONSUMER: MOTORING & CYCLING: Motoring

CLOSE-UP MAGAZINE

51095W76E-20
Editorial: Box 4411, 102 69 STOCKHOLM
Tel: 8 462 02 14 **Fax:** 8 462 02 15
Email: mail@closeupmagazine.net **Web site:** http://www.closeupmagazine.net
Date Established: 1991; **Freq:** 6 issues yearly; **Circ:** 16,500
Editor-in-Chief: Robban Becirovic; **Advertising Manager:** Robban Becirovic; **Publisher:** Robban Becirovic
Profile: Magazine about music.
Language(s): Swedish
Readership: Aimed at listeners of the latest rock music.
ADVERTISING RATES:
Full Page Colour .... SEK 14995
SCC .... SEK 124.9
CONSUMER: MUSIC & PERFORMING ARTS: Pop Music

COMMERSEN 750917W80-500

Editorial: Lotsgatan 5, 374 35 KARLSHAMN
Tel: 454 341 30 **Fax:** 454 341 39
Email: info@commersen.se **Web site:** http://www.commersen.se
Freq: Daily; **Cover Price:** Free; **Circ:** 80,000
Editor: Tinna Hiller Andreasson; **Publisher:** Peter Enckell
Language(s): Swedish
ADVERTISING RATES:
Full Page Colour .... SEK 26368
SCC .... SEK 105.10
CONSUMER: RURAL & REGIONAL INTEREST

COMPUTER SWEDEN 50231W5B-10

Editorial: IDG AB, Karlbergsvägen 77, 106 78 STOCKHOLM **Tel:** 8 453 60 00
Email: cs@idg.se **Web site:** http://www.computersweden.se
Date Established: 1983; **Freq:** 104 issues yearly; **Circ:** 52,000
Editor-in-Chief: Jörgen Lindqvist
Profile: Newspaper containing reports of national and international developments in information technology.
Language(s): Swedish
Readership: Aimed at IT managers, technicians and consultants.
ADVERTISING RATES:
Full Page Colour .... SEK 83900
SCC .... SEK 419.50
BUSINESS: COMPUTERS & AUTOMATION: Data Processing

COMPUTER SWEDEN; COMPUTERSWEDEN.SE

1843272W5E-111
Editorial: 106 78 STOCKHOLM **Tel:** 8 453 60 00
Email: cs@idg.se **Web site:** http://www.computersweden.se
Freq: Daily; **Cover Price:** Free; **Circ:** 34,250 Unique Users
Editor-in-Chief: Johan Hallsenius
Language(s): Swedish
BUSINESS: COMPUTERS & AUTOMATION: Data Transmission

COMPUTER SWEDEN; CS HEMMA 1643541W5R-128

Editorial: Karlbergsvägen 77, 106 78 STOCKHOLM
Tel: 8 453 60 00
Email: mats.glaad@idg.se **Web site:** http://www.computersweden.se
Freq: Monthly; **Circ:** 60,000
Language(s): Swedish
BUSINESS: COMPUTERS & AUTOMATION: Computers Related

CONNOISSEUR 634418W74Q-21

Editorial: Smedjegatan 8, 131 54 NACKA
Tel: 8 718 29 00 **Fax:** 8 716 23 00
Email: info@connoisseurint.se **Web site:** http://www.connoisseurint.se
Date Established: 1998; **Freq:** Quarterly; **Circ:** 40,300
Editor-in-Chief: Peter Lilliehök; **Advertising Manager:** Marcus Sääsk; **Publisher:** Susanne Ytterskog
Profile: Lifestyle magazine containing reports and information on travelling, culture, boats, fashion, fine arts and culture.
Language(s): Swedish
Readership: Aimed at people with a high disposable income.
CONSUMER: WOMEN'S INTEREST CONSUMER MAGAZINES: Lifestyle

CONTRA 51174W82-61

Editorial: Box 8052, 104 20 STOCKHOLM
Tel: 8 720 01 45
Email: redax@contra.nu **Web site:** http://www.contra.nu
Date Established: 1975; **Freq:** 6 issues yearly; **Circ:** 2,000
Editor: C G Holm; **Publisher:** Geza Molnar
Profile: Magazine dedicated to the promotion of political ideas in general and liberal ideas in particular. Covers national and international politics in theory and practice.
Language(s): Swedish
Readership: Read mainly by graduates.
CONSUMER: CURRENT AFFAIRS & POLITICS

CORA, EN TIDNING MED HJÄRTA 1663909W84B-292

Editorial: Bengt Ekehjelmsgatan 2B, 118 54 STOCKHOLM **Tel:** 8 668 74 92
Email: info@cora.se **Web site:** http://www.cora.se
Freq: Quarterly; **Circ:** 1,000
Editor-in-Chief: Yvonne Ihmels; **Publisher:** Yvonne Ihmels
Language(s): Swedish
CONSUMER: THE ARTS & LITERARY: Literary

CORPORATE INTELLIGENCE

1639383W14A-290
Editorial: Box 19063, 104 32 STOCKHOLM
Tel: 8 506 286 00 **Fax:** 850628720
Email: ingrid.larsson@intellecta.se **Web site:** http://www.intellecta.se
Freq: Half-yearly; **Circ:** 4,000
Publisher: Anders Borg
Language(s): Swedish
BUSINESS: COMMERCE, INDUSTRY & MANAGEMENT

COSMOPOLITAN 752111W74A-110

Editorial: 113 92 STOCKHOLM **Tel:** 8 588 366 00 **Fax:** 8 588 369 59
Email: maja.persson@cosmopolitan.se **Web site:** http://www.cosmopolitan.se
Date Established: 2001; **Freq:** Monthly; **Circ:** 53,000
Publisher: Maja Persson
Language(s): Swedish
ADVERTISING RATES:
Full Page Colour .... SEK 52900
SCC .... SEK 440.83
CONSUMER: WOMEN'S INTEREST CONSUMER MAGAZINES: Women's Interest

CRUISE & FERRY INFO

1641223W45A-106
Editorial: ShipPax Information, Box 7067, 300 07 HALMSTAD **Tel:** 35 21 83 70 **Fax:** 35130129
Email: editor@shippax.se **Web site:** http://www.shippax.se
Freq: Monthly; **Circ:** 3,300
Editor: Andreas Lundgren; **Editor-in-Chief:** Klas Brogren
Language(s): Swedish
Copy instructions: *Copy Date:* 30 days prior to publication date
BUSINESS: MARINE & SHIPPING

CSJOBB 1844681W88C-4

Editorial: 106 78 STOCKHOLM **Tel:** 8 453 63 00
Email: csjobb@idg.se **Web site:** http://www.csjobb.idg.se
Freq: Daily; **Cover Price:** Free; **Circ:** 6,736 Unique Users
Language(s): Swedish
CONSUMER: EDUCATION: Careers

CSO CHIEF SECURITY OFFICER

1835763W5E-10
Editorial: Karlbergsvägen 77, 106 78 STOCKHOLM
Tel: 8 453 60 00
Email: cio@idg.se **Web site:** http://www.cio.se
Circ: 8,000 Unique Users
Publisher: Alexandra Heymowska
Language(s): Swedish
BUSINESS: COMPUTERS & AUTOMATION: Data Transmission

CYKELTIDNINGEN KADENS

1809874W77C-92
Editorial: Box 22559, 112 21 STOCKHOLM
Tel: 8 545 535 38 **Fax:** 8 545 535 49
Email: redaktion@kadens.se **Web site:** http://www.kadens.se
Freq: 6 issues yearly; **Circ:** 14,000
Editor: Andreas Danielsson; **Editor-in-Chief:** Stefan Larsén; **Advertising Manager:** Lasse Strand; **Publisher:** Hans Lodin
Language(s): Swedish
ADVERTISING RATES:
Full Page Colour .... SEK 19950
SCC .... SEK 166.25
CONSUMER: MOTORING & CYCLING: Cycling

CYKLA 634424W77C-15

Editorial: Box 48, 591 21 MOTALA **Tel:** 141 22 32 90 **Fax:** 141 21 12 88
Email: info@vatternrundan.se **Web site:** http://www.cykla.com
Date Established: 1997; **Freq:** Quarterly; **Circ:** 30,000
Editor: Kjell-Erik Kristiansen; **Advertising Manager:** Björn Bettner; **Publisher:** Eva-Lena Frick
Profile: Magazine for cyclists.
Language(s): Swedish
CONSUMER: MOTORING & CYCLING: Cycling

CYKLING 1804078W77C-91

Editorial: Box 47, 250 53 HELSINGBORG
Tel: 8 545 910 30
Email: cykling@cykelframjandet.se **Web site:** http://www.cykelframjandet.se
Freq: Quarterly; **Circ:** 7,000
Publisher: Christian Juul
Language(s): Swedish
CONSUMER: MOTORING & CYCLING: Cycling

DÄCK DEBATT 1985643W14A-364

Editorial: c/o Stormen kommunikation, 432 44 VARBERG **Tel:** 340 67 3000
Email: pontus@stormen.nu **Web site:** http://www.ddebatt.se
Freq: Quarterly; **Circ:** 5,000
Editor: Björn Sundfeldt; **Advertising Manager:** Sven-Erik Bjarnesson
Language(s): Swedish
ADVERTISING RATES:
Full Page Colour .... SEK 17900
BUSINESS: COMMERCE, INDUSTRY & MANAGEMENT

DÄCK NYTT 1985644W14A-365

Editorial: ÖSTERBYBRUK **Tel:** 295 205 60
Email: press.reklam@swipnet.se **Web site:** http://www.dacknytt.se
Freq: Fem gånger om året; **Circ:** 6,600
Editor-in-Chief: Sven-Erik Johansson; **Advertising Manager:** Svante Svensson
Language(s): Swedish
BUSINESS: COMMERCE, INDUSTRY & MANAGEMENT

DÄCK-DEBATT 634446W31A-15

Editorial: Vasavägen 33, 352 61 VÄXJÖ
Tel: 470 637 63 **Fax:** 470 620 08
Email: press.reklam@swipnet.se **Web site:** http://www.pm-pressmedia.se
Freq: Quarterly; **Circ:** 5,000
Editor: Sven-Erik Johansson; **Advertising Manager:** Svante Svensson; **Publisher:** Anders Karpesjö
Profile: Magazine covering automobile tyres.
Language(s): Swedish
Readership: Aimed at manufacturers, retailers and suppliers.
BUSINESS: MOTOR TRADE: Motor Trade Accessories

DAGBLADET, NYA SAMHÄLLET; DAGBLADET.SE
1843247W65A-973
Editorial: Box 466, 851 06 SUNDSVALL
Tel: 60 66 35 82 **Fax:** 60 61 11 50
Email: webredaktion@dagbladet.se **Web site:** http://www.dagbladet.se
Freq: Daily; **Cover Price:** Free; **Circ:** 5,800 Unique Users
Publisher: Åke Hardfeldt
Language(s): Swedish
NATIONAL DAILY & SUNDAY NEWSPAPERS: National Daily Newspapers

DAGBLADET, NYA SAMHÄLLET; HUVUDREDAKTION
50836W67B-3700
Editorial: Box 466, 851 06 SUNDSVALL
Tel: 60 66 35 00 **Fax:** 60 61 11 50
Email: nyhetschef@dagbladet.se **Web site:** http://www.dagbladet.se
Date Established: 1900
Circ: 12,000
Editor: Els-Mari Bolin; **Publisher:** Åke Härdfeldt
Language(s): Swedish
ADVERTISING RATES:
Full Page Colour .... SEK 19440
SCC .... SEK 97
REGIONAL DAILY & SUNDAY NEWSPAPERS: Regional Daily Newspapers

DAGEN; DAGEN.SE
1844689W65A-1022
Editorial: 105 36 STOCKHOLM **Tel:** 8 619 24 00
Fax: 86566051
Email: redaktionen@dagen.se **Web site:** http://www.dagen.se
Freq: Daily; **Cover Price:** Free; **Circ:** 7,577 Unique Users
Publisher: Elisabeth Sandlund
Language(s): Swedish
NATIONAL DAILY & SUNDAY NEWSPAPERS: National Daily Newspapers

DAGENS ARBETE
50296W14B-40
Editorial: Dagens Arbete, 105 52 Stockholm, 105 52 STOCKHOLM **Tel:** 8 786 03 00 **Fax:** 8 796 81 59
Email: red@dagensarbete.se **Web site:** http://www.dagensarbete.se
Freq: Monthly; **Circ:** 442,600
Advertising Manager: Agneta Kempe Erneberg
Profile: Journal containing news, information and articles about trade and technology. Covers and analyses the development within industry and politics.
Language(s): Swedish
Readership: Aimed at professionals within trade and industry.
ADVERTISING RATES:
Full Page Colour .... SEK 49500
SCC .... SEK 374.16
BUSINESS: COMMERCE, INDUSTRY & MANAGEMENT: Industry & Factories

DAGENS ARBETE; DAGENSARBETE.SE
1844779W14L-196
Editorial: 105 52 STOCKHOLM **Tel:** 8 786 03 00
Fax: 8 796 81 59
Email: red@da.se **Web site:** http://www.dagensarbete.se
Freq: Daily; **Cover Price:** Free; **Circ:** 2,697 Unique Users
Editor-in-Chief: Hans Larsson; **Managing Director:** Hans Larsson; **Publisher:** Hans Larsson
Language(s): Swedish
ADVERTISING RATES:
SCC .... SEK 75
BUSINESS: COMMERCE, INDUSTRY & MANAGEMENT: Trade Unions

DAGENS ARENA
1846794W14F-121
Editorial: Drottninggatan 83, 111 60 STOCKHOLM
Tel: 8 789 11 60
Web site: http://www.dagensarena.se
Freq: Daily; **Cover Price:** Free; **Circ:** 5,000 Unique Users
Editor-in-Chief: Eric Sundström
Language(s): Swedish
BUSINESS: COMMERCE, INDUSTRY & MANAGEMENT: Training & Recruitment

DAGENS ETC
1664778W82-460
Editorial: Box 4403, 102 68 STOCKHOLM
Tel: 8 410 357 00 **Fax:** 8 410 357 01
Email: tidningen@etc.se **Web site:** http://www.etc.se
Freq: Weekly; **Circ:** 3,900
Advertising Manager: Andreas Gustavsson; **Publisher:** Johan Ehrenberg
Language(s): Swedish
ADVERTISING RATES:
Full Page Colour .... SEK 2000
SCC .... SEK 10
CONSUMER: CURRENT AFFAIRS & POLITICS

DAGENS HANDEL
50571W53-24
Editorial: Budadress: Tryffelsingan 10, Box 72001, 181 72 LIDINGÖ **Tel:** 8 670 41 00
Email: red@dagenshandel.se **Web site:** http://www.dagenshandel.se
Freq: Weekly; **Circ:** 23,400
Advertising Manager: Håkan Sandström; **Publisher:** Thomas Karlsson
Profile: Journal containing articles, information and news from the retailing trade.
Language(s): Swedish
ADVERTISING RATES:
Full Page Colour .... SEK 38000
SCC .... SEK 190
BUSINESS: RETAILING & WHOLESALING

DAGENS HANDEL; DAGENS HANDEL.SE
1639368W14A-289
Editorial: Box 72001, 181 72 LIDINGÖ
Tel: 8 670 41 00
Email: red@dagenshandel.se **Web site:** http://www.dagenshandel.se
Freq: Daily; **Cover Price:** Paid; **Circ:** 2,588 Unique Users
Editor: Sofia Callius; **Editor-in-Chief:** Thomas Karlsson; **Publisher:** Thomas Karlsson
Language(s): Swedish
ADVERTISING RATES:
SCC .... SEK 38
BUSINESS: COMMERCE, INDUSTRY & MANAGEMENT

DAGENS INDUSTRI
50755W65A-18
Editorial: Torsgatan 21, 113 90 STOCKHOLM
Tel: 8 573 650 00 **Fax:** 8 57365031
Email: red@di.se **Web site:** http://www.di.se
Date Established: 1976; **Freq:** Daily -, 6 ggr/vecka;
Circ: 101,700
Editor: Mats Brohagen; **Advertising Manager:** Erik Lennmark
Profile: Newspaper specialising in business matters. Provides financial, economic and political news and information.
Language(s): Swedish
Readership: Read predominantly by the business community, academics, civil servants and politicians.
ADVERTISING RATES:
Full Page Colour .... SEK 136900
SCC .... SEK 640
NATIONAL DAILY & SUNDAY NEWSPAPERS: National Daily Newspapers

DAGENS INDUSTRI; DI.SE
751473W65A-167
Editorial: Torsgatan 21, 113 90 STOCKHOLM
Tel: 8 573 650 50
Email: dise@di.se **Web site:** http://www.di.se
Freq: Daily; **Circ:** 278,861 Unique Users
Editor: Carl Björk
Language(s): Swedish
NATIONAL DAILY & SUNDAY NEWSPAPERS: National Daily Newspapers

DAGENS JURIDIK
1810384W44-65
Editorial: Nybrogatan 57 A, 114 40 STOCKHOLM
Tel: 8 579 366 00 **Fax:** 8 667 97 60
Email: fredrik.olsson@dagensjuridik.se **Web site:** http://www.dagensjuridik.se
Cover Price: Paid; **Circ:** 5,000 Unique Users
Editor-in-Chief: Fredrik Olsson; **Publisher:** Linda Frivik
Language(s): Swedish
BUSINESS: LEGAL

DAGENS MEDIA
634427W2E-40
Editorial: Postadress: Dagens Media, 106 12 STOCKHOLM **Tel:** 8 545 222 00
Email: red@dagensmedia.se **Web site:** http://www.dagensmedia.se
Freq: 26 issues yearly -,22 nr per år; **Circ:** 7,600
Profile: Dagens Media är en publikation som bevakat medie- och reklambranschen. Det finns även en webbversion. Tidningen lanserades i oktober 1998 med ett syfte att skapa ett nyhetsmedium till för medieköpare och marknadskommunikatörer, så att de lätt kan följa med i branschens utveckling. Läsare: Marknads-, reklam-, produkt, och informationschefer, medierådgivare, projektledare, reklamkreatörer, mediefolk samt personer inom PR- och eventbranschen. Startår: 1998 Ägare: Talentum Sweden AB Chefredaktör och Ansvarig utgivare: Fredrik Svedjetun Dagens Media is a publication writing about the media and advertising industries. There is also a web version. The newspaper was launched in October 1998 with a purpose to create a news forum for media buyers and marketing communicators so that they could easier follow the developments within the industry.
Language(s): Swedish
Readership: Aimed at professionals working in the media.
ADVERTISING RATES:
Full Page Colour .... SEK 42570
SCC .... SEK 266.06
BUSINESS: COMMUNICATIONS, ADVERTISING & MARKETING: Public Relations

DAGENS MEDIA; WEBB
1844953W2A-404
Editorial: Kungsgatan 56, 111 22 STOCKHOLM
Tel: 8 545 222 00
Email: red@dagensmedia.se **Web site:** http://www.dagensmedia.se
Freq: Daily; **Cover Price:** Free; **Circ:** 6,667 Unique Users
Editor-in-Chief: Fredrik Svedjetun; **Publisher:** Fredrik Svedjetun
Language(s): Swedish
ADVERTISING RATES:
SCC .... SEK 53
BUSINESS: COMMUNICATIONS, ADVERTISING & MARKETING

DAGENS MEDICIN
50587W56A-15
Editorial: Box 4612, 116 91 STOCKHOLM
Tel: 8 545 123 00 **Fax:** 8 411 01 02
Email: redaktionen@dagensmedicin.se **Web site:** http://www.dagensmedicin.se
Date Established: 1994; **Freq:** Weekly; **Circ:** 18,800
Advertising Manager: Stefan Hjärpe
Profile: Journal containing information, news and articles about the medical profession.
Language(s): Swedish
Readership: Aimed at people working in health care and within the medical profession.
ADVERTISING RATES:
Full Page Colour .... SEK 43100
SCC .... SEK 215.50
BUSINESS: HEALTH & MEDICAL

DAGENS MEDICIN; DAGENSMEDICIN.SE
1843267W56A-357
Editorial: Box 4612, 116 91 STOCKHOLM
Tel: 8 545 123 00 **Fax:** 84110102
Email: redaktionen@dagensmedicin.se **Web site:** http://www.dagensmedicin.se
Freq: Daily; **Cover Price:** Free; **Circ:** 25,800 Unique Users
Publisher: Per Gunnar Holmgren
Language(s): Swedish
BUSINESS: HEALTH & MEDICAL

DAGENS MÖJLIGHETER
1741135W14F-102
Editorial: Box 70368, 107 24 STOCKHOLM
Tel: 20 170 70 70 **Fax:** 855341915
Email: redaktionen@dagensmojligheter.se **Web site:** http://www.proffice.se
Freq: 6 issues yearly; **Cover Price:** Free; **Circ:** 5,000
Editor-in-Chief: Ola Söderlund; **Publisher:** Thomas Magnuson
Language(s): Swedish
ADVERTISING RATES:
Full Page Colour .... SEK 5000
SCC .... SEK 31.25
BUSINESS: COMMERCE, INDUSTRY & MANAGEMENT: Training & Recruitment

DAGENS NYHETER
50756W65A-20
Editorial: Gjörwellsgatan 30, 105 15 STOCKHOLM
Tel: 8 738 10 00 **Fax:** 8 738 21 90
Email: centralred@dn.se **Web site:** http://www.dn.se
Date Established: 1864; **Freq:** Daily; **Circ:** 298,200
Advertising Manager: Henrik Stangel
Profile: Broadsheet-sized quality newspaper providing in-depth coverage of national and international news, politics, economics, finance, business, culture, sports and events.
Language(s): Swedish
Readership: Read by academics, university students, civil servants, managers and executives.
ADVERTISING RATES:
Full Page Colour .... SEK 188000
SCC .... SEK 940
Sections:
Dagens Nyheter; Familjeredaktionen
NATIONAL DAILY & SUNDAY NEWSPAPERS: National Daily Newspapers

DAGENS NYHETER; DN.SE
750941W65A-232
Editorial: Gjörwellsgatan 30, 105 15 STOCKHOLM
Tel: 8 738 10 00 **Fax:** 8 738 18 80
Email: centralred@dn.se **Web site:** http://www.dn.se
Freq: Daily; **Circ:** 344,554 Unique Users
Language(s): Swedish
NATIONAL DAILY & SUNDAY NEWSPAPERS: National Daily Newspapers

DAGENS NYHETER; FAMILJEREDAKTIONEN
749969W65A-20_100
Editorial: Gjörwellsgatan 30, 105 15 STOCKHOLM
Tel: 8 738 10 00 **Fax:** 8 738 21 90
Email: familj@dn.se **Web site:** http://www.dn.se
Freq: Daily; **Circ:** 298,200
Editor: Karin Forsberg
Profile: Family section of Dagens Nyheter.
Language(s): Swedish
Section of: Dagens Nyheter
NATIONAL DAILY & SUNDAY NEWSPAPERS: Unabhängiges konservatives MdEP

DAGENS PS
1639393W14A-291
Editorial: Nybrogatan 18, 114 39 STOCKHOLM
Tel: 8 5280 08 99
Email: redaktion@dagensps.com **Web site:** http://www.dagensps.se
Freq: Daily; **Circ:** 170,000 Unique Users
Editor: Tommy Harnesk; **Editor-in-Chief:** Jesper Carlson; **Advertising Manager:** Rebecka Fant; **Publisher:** Bengt Uggla
Language(s): Swedish
BUSINESS: COMMERCE, INDUSTRY & MANAGEMENT

DAGENS SAMHÄLLE
1648534W32G-262
Editorial: 118 82 STOCKHOLM **Tel:** 8 452 73 00
Fax: 86423013
Email: centralanyheter@dagenssamhalle.se **Web site:** http://www.dagenssamhalle.se
Freq: Weekly; **Circ:** 31,200
Editor: Cecilia Granestrand; **Editor-in-Chief:** Mats Edman
Language(s): Swedish
ADVERTISING RATES:
Full Page Colour .... SEK 57500
SCC .... SEK 360
Copy instructions: *Copy Date:* 16 days prior to publication date
BUSINESS: LOCAL GOVERNMENT, LEISURE & RECREATION: Community Care & Social Services

DAGENS SAMHÄLLE; DAGENSSAMHALLE.SE
1844778W82-482
Editorial: 118 82 STOCKHOLM **Tel:** 8 452 73 00
Fax: 8 642 30 13
Email: pressmedd@dagenssamhalle.se **Web site:** http://www.dagenssamhalle.se
Freq: Daily; **Cover Price:** Free; **Circ:** 875 Unique Users
Editor-in-Chief: Lena Hörngren; **Publisher:** Lena Hörngren
Language(s): Swedish
ADVERTISING RATES:
SCC .... SEK 72
CONSUMER: CURRENT AFFAIRS & POLITICS

DAGENS SEKRETERARE
50990W74J-30
Editorial: Skeppargatan 27, 114 52 STOCKHOLM
Tel: 8 442 86 30 **Fax:** 8 662 11 80
Email: info@spearproduction.se **Web site:** http://www.ds.nu
Date Established: 1980; **Freq:** 6 issues yearly; **Circ:** 3,300
Editor-in-Chief: Susann Engqvist; **Managing Director:** Anders Forsström; **Advertising Manager:** Måns Åkesson; **Publisher:** Anders Forsström
Profile: Magazine for Swedish executive secretaries.
Language(s): Swedish
ADVERTISING RATES:
Full Page Colour .... SEK 20700
SCC .... SEK 172.5
CONSUMER: WOMEN'S INTEREST CONSUMER MAGAZINES: Secretary & PA

DALABYGDEN; DALABYGDEN.SE
1846301W65A-1075
Editorial: Box 280, 781 23 BORLÄNGE
Tel: 243 21 30 80 **Fax:** 243213085
Email: dalabygden@sveagruppen.se **Web site:** http://www.dalabygden.se
Freq: Daily; **Cover Price:** Free; **Circ:** 7,000 Unique Users
Editor-in-Chief: Bo Pettersson; **Advertising Manager:** Peter Svensson; **Publisher:** Olle Wärmlöf
Language(s): Swedish
NATIONAL DAILY & SUNDAY NEWSPAPERS: National Daily Newspapers

DALA-DEMOKRATEN
50779W67B-3750
Editorial: Box 825, 791 29 FALUN **Tel:** 23 475 00
Email: red@daladem.se **Web site:** http://www.dalademokraten.com
Date Established: 1917
Circ: 17,000
Editor: Mats Larsson; **Editor-in-Chief:** Göran Greider; **Advertising Manager:** Björn Eriksson; **Publisher:** Lennart Håkansson
Language(s): Swedish
ADVERTISING RATES:
Full Page Colour .... SEK 40176
SCC .... SEK 200.88
REGIONAL DAILY & SUNDAY NEWSPAPERS: Regional Daily Newspapers

DALA-DEMOKRATEN; DALADEMOKRATEN.SE
751497W67B-8330
Editorial: Box 825, 791 29 FALUN **Tel:** 23 475 00
Email: webmaster@daladem.se **Web site:** http://www.dalademokraten.se
Freq: Daily; **Cover Price:** Free; **Circ:** 21,600 Unique Users

Editor-in-Chief: Göran Greider; **Publisher:** Mats Larsson
Language(s): Swedish
REGIONAL DAILY & SUNDAY NEWSPAPERS: Regional Daily Newspapers

DALARNAS TIDNINGAR
751534W67B-8455
Editorial: Box 265, 791 26 FALUN **Tel:** 23 936 00
Fax: 2393610
Email: info@dt.se **Web site:** http://www.dt.se
Freq: Daily; **Circ:** 28,000 Unique Users
Editor: Tony Klintasp; **Publisher:** Pär Fagerström
Language(s): Swedish
REGIONAL DAILY & SUNDAY NEWSPAPERS: Regional Daily Newspapers

DALSLANDSKURIREN
634050W72-53
Editorial: Storgatan 20, 460 65 BRÅLANDA
Tel: 521 310 75 **Fax:** 521 310 75
Email: kurirenreklam@telia.com
Date Established: 1985; **Freq:** 26 issues yearly; **Circ:** 4,500
Editor-in-Chief: Folke Johansson; **Publisher:** Folke Johansson
Profile: Newspaper containing local news for Dalsland.
Language(s): Swedish
LOCAL NEWSPAPERS

DALSLÄNNINGEN / BENGTSFORS-TIDNINGEN
624323W67B-3770
Editorial: Box 53, 666 22 BENGTSFORS
Tel: 531 52 21 00
Email: redaktion@dalslanningen.se **Web site:** http://www.dalslanningen.se
Date Established: 1925
Circ: 7,400
Advertising Manager: Agneta Wallin; **Publisher:** Thomas Wallin
Language(s): Swedish
ADVERTISING RATES:
Full Page Colour .... SEK 25200
SCC .... SEK 126
REGIONAL DAILY & SUNDAY NEWSPAPERS: Regional Daily Newspapers

DAMERNAS VÄRLD
50944W74A-30
Editorial: Bonnier Tidskrifter, Budadress: Rådmansgatan 49, 105 44 STOCKHOLM
Tel: 8 736 53 00 **Fax:** 8 24 46 46
Email: red@dv.bonnier.se **Web site:** http://www.damernasvarld.se/damernas
Date Established: 1940; **Freq:** Monthly; **Circ:** 87,300
Editor-in-Chief: Martina Bonnier; **Advertising Manager:** Karolina Hulpers
Profile: Magazine covering fashion, beauty, health issues, interior decoration, cookery, gardening and relationships.
Language(s): Swedish
ADVERTISING RATES:
Full Page Colour .... SEK 67000
SCC .... SEK 540.80
Copy instructions: *Copy Date:* 30 days prior to publication date
CONSUMER: WOMEN'S INTEREST CONSUMER MAGAZINES: Women's Interest

DAMERNAS VÄRLD; DAMERNAS.SE
1844770W84B-298
Editorial: Bud: Rådmansgatan 49, 105 44 STOCKHOLM **Tel:** 8 736 53 00 **Fax:** 8 24 46 46
Email: red@dv.bonnier.se **Web site:** http://www.damernasvarld.se/damernas
Freq: Daily; **Cover Price:** Free; **Circ:** 2,497 Unique Users
Language(s): Swedish
CONSUMER: THE ARTS & LITERARY: Literary

DAMERNAS VÄRLD - DV MODE
1655341W74B-69
Editorial: 105 44 STOCKHOLM **Tel:** 8 736 53 00
Fax: 8 24 46 46
Email: red@dv.bonnier.se **Web site:** http://www.damernas.com
Freq: Half-yearly; **Circ:** 86,000
Language(s): Swedish
ADVERTISING RATES:
Full Page Colour .... SEK 49500
SCC .... SEK 412.50
CONSUMER: WOMEN'S INTEREST CONSUMER MAGAZINES: Women's Interest - Fashion

DANSTIDNINGEN
1643810W76G-1
Editorial: Box 2133, 103 14 STOCKHOLM
Tel: 703 34 69 98
Email: ann-marie@danstidningen.se **Web site:** http://www.danstidningen.se
Freq: 6 issues yearly; **Circ:** 3,000
Editor: Ann-Marie Wrange; **Advertising Manager:** Ann-Marie Wrange; **Publisher:** Ann-Marie Wrange
Language(s): Swedish
ADVERTISING RATES:
Full Page Colour .... SEK 8000
SCC .... SEK 66.67
CONSUMER: MUSIC & PERFORMING ARTS: Dance

DANSTIDNINGEN; DANSTIDNINGEN.SE
1844789W76G-2
Editorial: Box 2133, 103 14 STOCKHOLM
Tel: 703 34 69 98
Email: ann-marie@danstidningen.se **Web site:** http://www.danstidningen.se
Freq: Daily; **Cover Price:** Free; **Circ:** 1,000 Unique Users
Editor: Ann-Marie Wrange; **Advertising Manager:** Ann-Marie Wrange; **Publisher:** Ann-Marie Wrange
Language(s): Swedish
ADVERTISING RATES:
SCC .... SEK 13
CONSUMER: MUSIC & PERFORMING ARTS: Dance

DATORMAGAZIN
639457W5C-20
Editorial: Hjemmet Mortensen, 113 78 STOCKHOLM
Tel: 8 692 66 00
Email: mats.larsson@datormagazin.se **Web site:** http://www.datormagazin.se
Date Established: 2000; **Freq:** Monthly; **Circ:** 23,700
Editor: Thomas Forsberg; **Editor-in-Chief:** Mats Larsson; **Advertising Manager:** Benny Almqvist
Profile: Magazine covering PC products and solutions for advanced users.
Language(s): Swedish
Readership: Aimed at professional PC users.
ADVERTISING RATES:
Full Page Colour .... SEK 52000
SCC .... SEK 433
BUSINESS: COMPUTERS & AUTOMATION: Professional Personal Computers

DATORMAGAZIN; DATORMAGAZIN.SE
1844695W5E-116
Editorial: Hjemmet Mortensen, 113 78 STOCKHOLM
Tel: 8 692 66 00 **Fax:** 86509705
Email: mats.larsson@datormagazin.se **Web site:** http://www.datormagazin.se
Freq: Daily; **Cover Price:** Free; **Circ:** 15,000 Unique Users
Editor-in-Chief: Mats Larsson
Language(s): Swedish
BUSINESS: COMPUTERS & AUTOMATION: Data Transmission

DATORN I UTBILDNINGEN
634430W62B-25
Editorial: c/o Peter Becker, Förridargränd 16, 165 57 HÄSSELBY **Tel:** 8 32 57 76 **Fax:** 8 32 57 76
Email: peter.becker@diu.se **Web site:** http://www.diu.se
Date Established: 1987; **Freq:** 6 issues yearly; **Circ:** 3,000
Editor: Bo Andersson; **Editor-in-Chief:** Peter Becker; **Advertising Manager:** Petter Svärd; **Publisher:** Peter Becker
Profile: Magazine featuring computer training for teachers.
Language(s): Swedish
BUSINESS: CHURCH & SCHOOL EQUIPMENT & EDUCATION: Education Teachers

DEKÅR
750994W62A-390
Editorial: Studentkåren i Östersund, Mittuniversitetet, 831 25 ÖSTERSUND **Tel:** 63 16 54 80
Web site: http://www.sko.miun.se
Freq: Quarterly; **Cover Price:** Paid; **Circ:** 1,500 Unique Users
Language(s): Swedish
BUSINESS: CHURCH & SCHOOL EQUIPMENT & EDUCATION: Education

DELA MED
750949W14C-48
Editorial: 172 99 SUNDBYBERG **Tel:** 8 453 69 00
Fax: 8 453 69 29
Email: diakonia@diakonia.se **Web site:** http://www.diakonia.se
Date Established: 1980; **Freq:** Quarterly; **Circ:** 25,000
Editor: Viktoria Myren; **Publisher:** Bo Forsberg
Language(s): Swedish
BUSINESS: COMMERCE, INDUSTRY & MANAGEMENT: International Commerce

DEMENSFORUM
50646W56N-15
Editorial: Lundagatan 42A, 5tr., 117 27 STOCKHOLM **Tel:** 8 658 99 20 **Fax:** 86586068
Email: rdr@demensforbundet.se **Web site:** http://www.demensforbundet.se
Date Established: 1987; **Freq:** Quarterly; **Circ:** 16,000
Editor: Yvonne Jansson; **Publisher:** Stina-Clara Hjulström
Profile: Publication dealing with issues concerning people suffering from dementia.
Language(s): Swedish
BUSINESS: HEALTH & MEDICAL: Mental Health

DESTINATION HELSINGBORG
751035W2C-65
Editorial: Pålsjögatan 21 f, 252 40 HELSINGBORG
Tel: 42 12 43 00
Email: charlotte@destinationhelsingborg.se **Web site:** http://www.destinationhelsingborg.se
Freq: Monthly; **Circ:** 12,000
Publisher: Charlotte Blomfeldt
Language(s): Swedish
BUSINESS: COMMUNICATIONS, ADVERTISING & MARKETING: Conferences & Exhibitions

DETEKTOR SCANDINAVIA
50578W54C-25
Editorial: Västberga Allé 32, 126 30 HAGERSTEN
Tel: 8 556 306 80
Email: info@armedia.se **Web site:** http://www.detektor.com
Date Established: 1989; **Freq:** 6 issues yearly; **Circ:** 10,650
Advertising Manager: Deniz Baykal; **Publisher:** Lennart Alexandrie
Profile: Journal containing news and information about the security business. Covers the technical aspects and new products, market surveys, articles and international news and events.
Language(s): Swedish
Readership: Aimed at security officers, insurance companies, members of the emergency services, product distributions, electricians and installers of alarms and safety locks.
ADVERTISING RATES:
Full Page Colour .... SEK 22100
SCC .... SEK 184.16
BUSINESS: SAFETY & SECURITY: Security

DHB-DIALOG
50634W56L-25
Editorial: Kungsgatan 19, 703 61 OREBRO
Tel: 19 17 08 30
Web site: http://www.dhb.se
Freq: Quarterly; **Circ:** 2,500
Editor: Jörgen Hansen; **Publisher:** David Thölix
Profile: Magazine containing articles and information about people who are deaf, hard-of-hearing or language-impaired.
Language(s): Swedish
BUSINESS: HEALTH & MEDICAL: Disability & Rehabilitation

DIABETES
50588W56A-20
Editorial: Box 1107, 172 22 SUNDBYBERG
Tel: 8 564 821 00 **Fax:** 8 564 821 39
Web site: http://www.diabetes.se
Freq: 6 issues yearly; **Circ:** 32,000
Editor: Staffan Ohlson; **Editor-in-Chief:** Ann-Sofi Lindberg; **Advertising Manager:** Karin Hallin
Profile: Publication of the Swedish Diabetes Association.
Language(s): Swedish
ADVERTISING RATES:
Full Page Colour .... SEK 50000
SCC .... SEK 416.66
BUSINESS: HEALTH & MEDICAL

DIABETESVÅRD
1804056W56A-352
Editorial: c/o Britt-Marie Carlsson, Ljungås, 519 91 ISTORP **Tel:** 320 77 90 16
Email: britt-marie.sfsd@telia.com **Web site:** http://www.diabetesnurse.se
Freq: Quarterly; **Circ:** 1,800
Advertising Manager: Britt-Marie Carlsson
Language(s): Swedish
BUSINESS: HEALTH & MEDICAL

DIABETOLOGNYTT
634436W56R-25
Editorial: SU Sahlgrenska, 413 45 GOTEBORG
Tel: 31 342 10 00 **Fax:** 31270087
Email: stig.attvall@medicine.gu.se **Web site:** http://www.diabetolognytt.com
Freq: Quarterly; **Circ:** 3,000
Editor: Thomas Fritz; **Publisher:** Björn Eliasson
Language(s): Swedish
BUSINESS: HEALTH & MEDICAL: Health Medical Related

DIALÄSEN
752068W56B-85
Editorial: Getabocksvägen 4, 187 54 TABY
Tel: 8 510 515 00
Email: info@dialasen.com **Web site:** http://www.dialasen.com
Date Established: 1992; **Freq:** 6 issues yearly; **Circ:** 3,300
Advertising Manager: Pia Lundström
Language(s): Swedish
BUSINESS: HEALTH & MEDICAL: Nursing

DIALOGER
751106W76B-95
Editorial: c/o Santerus Förlag, Sturbrunnsgatan 56, 6 tr, 113 49 STOCKHOLM **Tel:** 8 30 34 62
Email: info@dialoger.se **Web site:** http://www.dialoger.se
Freq: Quarterly; **Circ:** 1,000
Editor: Maria Hammarén; **Publisher:** Bo Göranzon
Language(s): Swedish
CONSUMER: MUSIC & PERFORMING ARTS: Theatre

DIASPORA / DIJASPORA
752107W84B-241
Editorial: Åsbovägen 68, 152 52 SÖDERTÄLJE
Tel: 8 550 628 73
Email: dijaspora@bredband.net **Web site:** http://www.dijaspora.nu
Date Established: 1998; **Freq:** 6 issues yearly; **Circ:** 2,000
Publisher: Aco Dragicevic
Language(s): Swedish
CONSUMER: THE ARTS & LITERARY: Literary

DIETISTAKTUELLT
50589W56A-23
Editorial: Box 23, 261 07 ASMUNDTORP
Tel: 418 43 28 00 **Fax:** 418 43 28 00
Email: redaktionen@dietistaktuellt.com **Web site:** http://www.dietistaktuellt.com
Date Established: 1991; **Freq:** 6 issues yearly; **Circ:** 3,800
Editor-in-Chief: Magnus Forslin; **Advertising Manager:** Linda Larsson Levin; **Publisher:** Elisabeth Rothenberg
Profile: Journal covering food and nutrition and medical issues relating to dieticians.
Language(s): Swedish
Readership: Read by dieticians, nutritional therapists, doctors and nutrition nurses.
ADVERTISING RATES:
Full Page Colour .... SEK 18150
SCC .... SEK 151
BUSINESS: HEALTH & MEDICAL

DIGITAL FOTO
1624125W85A-1
Editorial: Box 3187, 350 43 VÄXJO **Tel:** 470 76 24 00
Fax: 470 76 24 25
Email: dfo@firstpublishing.se **Web site:** http://digitalfoto.fpgroup.se
Freq: Monthly; **Circ:** 54,000
Editor: Peter Hedenfalk; **Editor-in-Chief:** Dietmar Heinrich; **Advertising Manager:** Anders Löfgren
Language(s): Swedish
ADVERTISING RATES:
Full Page Colour .... SEK 39000
SCC .... SEK 325
CONSUMER: PHOTOGRAPHY & FILM MAKING: Photography

DIGITAL FOTO; WEBB
1846641W60A-74
Editorial: Box 3187, 350 43 VÄXJO **Tel:** 470 76 24 00
Fax: 470762425
Email: dfo@firstpublishing.se **Web site:** http://digitalfoto.fpgroup.se
Freq: Daily; **Cover Price:** Free; **Circ:** 11,400 Unique Users
Editor-in-Chief: Dietmar Heinrich; **Advertising Manager:** Anders Löfgren
Language(s): Swedish
BUSINESS: PUBLISHING: Publishing & Book Trade

DIGITAL LIFE
1697312W5F-3
Editorial: Videum Science Park, 351 96 VÄXJO
Tel: 470 72 47 17
Email: red@digitallife.se **Web site:** http://www.digitallife.se
Freq: 6 issues yearly; **Circ:** 15,000
Editor: Jonas Saha; **Advertising Manager:** Dragan Pavlovic
Language(s): Swedish
ADVERTISING RATES:
Full Page Colour .... SEK 17900
SCC .... SEK 149.17
BUSINESS: COMPUTERS & AUTOMATION: Multimedia

DIGITAL LIFE; DIGITALLIFE.SE
1846666W82-489
Editorial: Videum Science Park, 351 96 VÄXJO
Tel: 470 72 47 17
Email: red@digitallife.se **Web site:** http://www.digitallife.se
Freq: Daily; **Cover Price:** Free; **Circ:** 3,000 Unique Users
Advertising Manager: Dragan Pavlovic
Language(s): Swedish
CONSUMER: CURRENT AFFAIRS & POLITICS

DIGITALFOTO FÖR ALLA
1625789W85A-2
Editorial: Krusegränd 42 C, 212 25 MALMÖ
Tel: 40 601 88 00
Email: redaktionen@digitalfotoforalla.se **Web site:** http://www.digitalfotoforalla.se
Circ: 22,400
Editor: Rasmus Carlsson
Language(s): Swedish
ADVERTISING RATES:
Full Page Colour .... SEK 26000
SCC .... SEK 216.67
CONSUMER: PHOTOGRAPHY & FILM MAKING: Photography

DIGITALFOTO FÖR ALLA; DIGITALFOTOFORALLA.SE
1846490W60A-73
Editorial: Krusegränd 42 C, 212 25 MALMÖ
Tel: 40 601 88 00
Email: redaktionen@digitalfotoforalla.se **Web site:** http://www.digitalfotoforalla.se
Freq: Daily; **Cover Price:** Free; **Circ:** 20,000 Unique Users
Language(s): Swedish
ADVERTISING RATES:
SCC .... SEK 43.2
BUSINESS: PUBLISHING: Publishing & Book Trade

DIK-FORUM
51419W62R-35
Editorial: Box 760, 131 24 NACKA **Tel:** 8 466 24 00
Email: kansli@dik.se **Web site:** http://www.dik.se
Freq: Monthly; **Circ:** 20,800
Editor: Bo Westas; **Editor-in-Chief:** Elisabet Blomberg; **Advertising Manager:** Caroline Kejnemar; **Publisher:** Karin Åhström Iko
Profile: Journal containing academic and educational articles together with information of interest to people working with documentation and cultural issues.
Language(s): Swedish
Readership: Aimed at members of the SACO society.
ADVERTISING RATES:
Full Page Colour .... SEK 15500
SCC .... SEK 129
BUSINESS: CHURCH & SCHOOL EQUIPMENT & EDUCATION: Education Related

DINA BARNS UTVECKLING
1804022W62A-513
Editorial: International Business Media AB, Stora Åvägen 21, 436 34 ASKIM **Tel:** 431 156 12
Fax: 317238499
Email: kent@dinabarn.se **Web site:** http://www.dinabarn.se
Freq: Quarterly; **Circ:** 47,000
Advertising Manager: Lars-Erik Zetterberg
Language(s): Swedish
BUSINESS: CHURCH & SCHOOL EQUIPMENT & EDUCATION: Education

DINA VINER
50263W9C-35
Editorial: Box 26162, 100 41 STOCKHOLM
Tel: 8 662 90 50
Email: dinaviner@telia.com **Web site:** http://www.dinaviner.com
Date Established: 1989; **Freq:** Monthly; **Circ:** 2,500
Advertising Manager: Carl Silander
Profile: Newsletter containing news and information about wine.
Language(s): Swedish
ADVERTISING RATES:
Full Page Colour .... SEK 8500
SCC .... SEK 70.80
BUSINESS: DRINKS & LICENSED TRADE: Licensed Trade, Wines & Spirits

DIREKTKONTAKT - ENTREPENAD
1625584W19A-122
Editorial: Box 82, 533 04 HÄLLEKIS **Tel:** 510 862 00
Fax: 51086220
Email: roland@direktkontakt.se **Web site:** http://www.direktkontakt.se
Freq: Monthly -,10 nr per år; **Circ:** 13,000
Editor: Jeanette Persson; **Advertising Manager:** Ove Johansson
Language(s): Swedish
ADVERTISING RATES:
Full Page Colour .... SEK 24300
SCC .... SEK 121.50
Copy instructions: *Copy Date:* 10 days prior to publication date
BUSINESS: ENGINEERING & MACHINERY

DIREKTKONTAKT - SKOG
1623797W46-121
Editorial: Box 82, 533 04 HÄLLEKIS **Tel:** 510 862 00
Fax: 51086220
Email: roland@direktkontakt.se **Web site:** http://www.direktkontakt.se
Freq: Monthly -,10 nr per år; **Circ:** 10,000
Editor: Jeanette Persson; **Advertising Manager:** Ove Johansson
Language(s): Swedish
ADVERTISING RATES:
Full Page Colour .... SEK 24300
SCC .... SEK 121.50
Copy instructions: *Copy Date:* 10 days prior to publication date
BUSINESS: TIMBER, WOOD & FORESTRY

DIREKTKONTAKT - TRANSPORT
1625583W49C-1
Editorial: Box 82, 533 04 HÄLLEKIS **Tel:** 510 862 00
Email: roland@direktkontakt.se **Web site:** http://www.direktkontakt.se
Freq: Monthly -, 10 nr per år; **Circ:** 13,000
Editor: Jeanette Persson; **Advertising Manager:** Ove Johansson; **Publisher:** Roland Götblad
Language(s): Swedish
ADVERTISING RATES:
Full Page Colour .... SEK 24300
SCC .... SEK 121.50
Copy instructions: *Copy Date:* 10 days prior to publication date
BUSINESS: TRANSPORT: Freight

DISA
750679W14L-145
Editorial: 105 25 STOCKHOLM **Tel:** 8 698 50 00
Fax: 8 698 5606
Email: internalnews@sida.se **Web site:** http://www.sida.se
Freq: 6 issues yearly; **Circ:** 1,400
Language(s): Swedish
BUSINESS: COMMERCE, INDUSTRY & MANAGEMENT: Trade Unions

DISTRIKTSLÄKAREN
50591W56A-28
Editorial: Svenska Distriktsläkarföreningen, Box 5610, 114 86 STOCKHOLM **Tel:** 8 790 33 91
Fax: 8 790 33 95
Email: dl@mediahuset.se **Web site:** http://www.svdlf.se
Freq: 6 issues yearly; **Circ:** 7,000
Editor: Rune Kaalhus; **Editor-in-Chief:** Ulf Wahllöf; **Advertising Manager:** Tommy Samuelsson; **Publisher:** Rune Kaalhus
Profile: Magazine focusing on general medicine.
Language(s): Swedish
Readership: Aimed at district doctors.
BUSINESS: HEALTH & MEDICAL

DITT & DATT
50936W73-25
Editorial: Box 6903, 102 39 STOCKHOLM
Tel: 8 31 00 07
Email: alexander.scarlat@comhem.se
Freq: 6 issues yearly; **Circ:** 700
Editor-in-Chief: Alexander Scarlat; **Advertising Manager:** Marc Scarlat; **Publisher:** Alexander Scarlat
Profile: Magazine covering wide areas of interest such as culture, food and drink, entertainment and travel.
Language(s): Swedish
Readership: Aimed at executives and people with a high disposable income.
CONSUMER: NATIONAL & INTERNATIONAL PERIODICALS

DITT VAL
1976419W74D-112
Tel: 40 30 60 50
Email: info@reklamrutan.se **Web site:** http://www.reklamrutan.se
Freq: Quarterly; **Cover Price:** Free; **Circ:** 25,000
Language(s): Swedish
ADVERTISING RATES:
Full Page Colour .... SEK 19100
CONSUMER: WOMEN'S INTEREST CONSUMER MAGAZINES: Child Care

DIVAN-TIDSKRIFT FÖR PSYKOANALYS OCH KULTUR
50647W56N-20
Editorial: Psykoanalytiskt Forum, 141 38 HUDDINGE
Tel: 8 462 01 10
Email: redaktionen@divan.nu **Web site:** http://divan.nu
Freq: Half-yearly; **Circ:** 800
Editor: Carin Franzen; **Publisher:** Bengt Warren
Profile: Publication covering all aspects of psychoanalysis.
Language(s): Swedish
BUSINESS: HEALTH & MEDICAL: Mental Health

DJURENS RÄTT!
51153W81A-30
Editorial: Box 2005, 125 02 ÄLVSJÖ
Tel: 8 555 914 00 **Fax:** 8 555 914 50
Email: djr@djurensratt.se **Web site:** http://www.djurensratt.se
Date Established: 1975; **Freq:** 6 issues yearly; **Circ:** 40,000
Editor: Toivo Jokkala; **Editor-in-Chief:** Jonas Nilsson; **Publisher:** Jonas Nilsson
Profile: Magazine of the Swedish Society for Animal Rights. Covers political issues, consumer campaigns and changes in legislation. Also includes features on the treatment of farm animals, the fur trade and animal experiments.
Language(s): Swedish
Readership: Aimed at members and people with an active interest in the prevention of cruelty to animals.
CONSUMER: ANIMALS & PETS: Animals & Pets Protection

DJURSKYDDET
51154W81A-40
Editorial: Rökerigatan 19, 12162 JOHANNESHOV
Tel: 8 673 35 11 **Fax:** 8 673 36 66
Email: redaktionen@djurskyddet.se **Web site:** http://www.djurskyddet.se
Freq: Quarterly; **Circ:** 13,500
Editor: Elsa Frizell; **Advertising Manager:** Binh Tan; **Publisher:** Elsa Frizell
Profile: Magazine of the Society for the Prevention of Cruelty to Animals.
Language(s): Swedish
CONSUMER: ANIMALS & PETS: Animals & Pets Protection

DJURTIDNINGEN PETS
1625824W79K-56
Editorial: Box 702 72, 107 22 STOCKHOLM
Tel: 8 519 384 00 **Fax:** 8 519 384 40
Email: mirijam.pets@gmail.com
Freq: 6 issues yearly; **Circ:** 30,000
Editor: Marie Olsson
Language(s): Swedish
CONSUMER: HOBBIES & DIY: Collectors Magazines

DMH, DEN MODERNA HANTVERKAREN
1925368W88D-1
Editorial: Smidesvägen 10-12, 171 41 SOLNA
Tel: 8 510 608 90
Email: dmh@projektmedia.se **Web site:** http://www.denmodernahantverkaren.se
Freq: Monthly; **Circ:** 40,000
Editor-in-Chief: Rickard Carlsson; **Managing Director:** Rickard Carlsson; **Advertising Manager:** Roger Carlsson
Language(s): Swedish
ADVERTISING RATES:
Full Page Colour .... SEK 42500
CONSUMER: EDUCATION: Crafts

DOKTORN
1623708W74G-196
Editorial: c/o Erlandsson & Bloom, 113 27 STOCKHOLM **Tel:** 8 648 49 00
Web site: http://www.doktorn.com
Freq: Quarterly; **Circ:** 100,000
Editor: Pernilla Bloom; **Advertising Manager:** Johan Bloom
Language(s): Swedish
ADVERTISING RATES:
Full Page Colour .... SEK 40800
SCC .... SEK 323.70
CONSUMER: WOMEN'S INTEREST CONSUMER MAGAZINES: Slimming & Health

DORIAN MAGAZINE
1862728W86B-124
Editorial: Box 75 92, 103 93 STOCKHOLM
Tel: 8 715 06 80
Email: info@dorianmagazine.com **Web site:** http://www.dorianmagazine.com
Circ: 10,000
Editor: Jake Rydqvist; **Editor-in-Chief:** Benjamin Falk; **Managing Director:** Alexander Rafting; **Advertising Manager:** Göran Stråning; **Publisher:** Benjamin Falk
Language(s): Swedish
CONSUMER: ADULT & GAY MAGAZINES: Gay & Lesbian Magazines

DÖVAS TIDNING
51420W94F-20
Editorial: SDR, Förmansv. 2, plan 6, 117 43 STOCKHOLM **Tel:** 70 342 60 68 **Fax:** 86499046
Email: dovas.tidning@sdrf.se **Web site:** http://www.sdrf.se/sdr
Freq: 6 issues yearly - (8nr/år); **Circ:** 5,800
Editor: Lennart Tjärnström; **Editor-in-Chief:** Åsa Möller; **Advertising Manager:** Björn Holmberg; **Publisher:** Helena Fremnell Ståhl
Profile: Magazine containing articles and information of interest to people who are deaf or hard-of-hearing and their families.
Language(s): Swedish
CONSUMER: OTHER CLASSIFICATIONS: Disability

DRAGSPELSNYTT
634445W76D-57
Editorial: c/o R. Häggqvist, Lasarettsgatan 23, 891 32 ÖRNSKÖLDSVIK **Tel:** 660 21 16 43
Fax: 660 21 16 43
Email: info@dragspelsforbundet.se **Web site:** http://www.dragspelsforbundet.com
Freq: Quarterly; **Circ:** 3,000
Editor: Jessica Andersson; **Advertising Manager:** Agneta Nydahl; **Publisher:** Åke Hellman
Profile: Magazine containing special articles on the piano accordian featuring news, letters to the editor, and up to date reports .
Language(s): Swedish
Readership: Read by people interested in learning to play the piano accordian .
CONSUMER: MUSIC & PERFORMING ARTS: Music

DRIVA EGET
1836248W1A-213
Editorial: Poppelvägen 55, 135 52 TYRESÖ
Tel: 8 798 81 26
Email: red@driva-eget.se **Web site:** http://www.driva-eget.se
Freq: Quarterly; **Circ:** 25,000
Editor-in-Chief: Anders Andersson; **Advertising Manager:** Rasmus Thomsen
Language(s): Swedish
Copy instructions: *Copy Date:* 45 days prior to publication date
BUSINESS: FINANCE & ECONOMICS

DRÖMHEM & TRÄDGÅRD
1664975W74C-450
Editorial: 113 92 STOCKHOLM **Tel:** 8 588 365 90
Email: dromhem@lrfmedia.lrf.se **Web site:** http://lrfmedia.se/?Dromhemtradgard
Freq: Monthly; **Circ:** 61,500
Editor: Kerstin Holmberg
Language(s): Swedish
ADVERTISING RATES:
Full Page Colour .... SEK 36000
SCC .... SEK 300
Copy instructions: *Copy Date:* 34 days prior to publication date
CONSUMER: WOMEN'S INTEREST CONSUMER MAGAZINES: Home & Family

DRÖMHEM & TRÄDGÅRD - BYGGA NYTT & RENOVERA
1841520W4A-36
Editorial: LRF Media, 113 92 STOCKHOLM
Tel: 8 588 365 80
Email: dromhem@lrfmedia.lrf.se **Web site:** http://www.dromhem.se
Freq: Annual; **Circ:** 83,200
Language(s): Swedish
ADVERTISING RATES:
Full Page Colour .... SEK 36000
BUSINESS: ARCHITECTURE & BUILDING: Architecture

DRÖMHEM & TRÄDGÅRD - TRÄDGÅRD & BLOMMOR
1837056W26D-94
Editorial: LRF Media AB, 113 92 STOCKHOLM
Tel: 8 588 365 90
Email: dromhem@lrfmedia.lrf.se **Web site:** http://www.dromhem.se
Freq: Half-yearly; **Circ:** 50,000
Editor: Kerstin Holmberg; **Advertising Manager:** Petra Jängnemyr; **Publisher:** Ebba Svanholm
Language(s): Swedish
ADVERTISING RATES:
Full Page Colour .... SEK 17000
SCC .... SEK 141.66
BUSINESS: GARDEN TRADE: Garden Trade Horticulture

DSM
750614W2B-165
Editorial: Box 99, 563 22 GRÄNNA **Tel:** 390 107 50
Fax: 39010750
Email: redaktion@dsm.nu **Web site:** http://www.dsm.nu
Freq: 6 issues yearly; **Circ:** 1,600
Publisher: Jan Gillberg
Language(s): Swedish
BUSINESS: COMMUNICATIONS, ADVERTISING & MARKETING: Press

DU & CO
50311W14H-10
Editorial: Spoon Publishing, Kungstensg. 21 B, 113 57 STOCKHOLM **Tel:** 8 442 96 20 **Fax:** 8 442 96 39
Email: du.co@spoon.se **Web site:** http://www.posten.se/m/duco
Date Established: 1995; **Freq:** Quarterly; **Circ:** 92,800 Unique Users
Advertising Manager: Sebastian Tibbling
Profile: Magazine containing information, news and articles of interest to small businesses.
Language(s): Swedish
BUSINESS: COMMERCE, INDUSTRY & MANAGEMENT: Small Business

DU & JOBBET
50577W54B-20
Editorial: Box 17550, 118 91 STOCKHOLM
Tel: 8 442 46 00 **Fax:** 84424607
Email: redaktionen@duochjobbet.se **Web site:** http://www.duochjobbet.se
Date Established: 1913; **Freq:** Monthly; **Circ:** 20,200
Managing Director: Carina Lindvall; **Advertising Manager:** Corinne Nordell
Profile: Magazine containing information, news and articles about occupational health and safety.
Language(s): Swedish
ADVERTISING RATES:
Full Page Colour .... SEK 36900
SCC .... SEK 307.50
Copy instructions: *Copy Date:* 15 days prior to publication date
BUSINESS: SAFETY & SECURITY: Safety

DU & JOBBET; DUOCHJOBBET.SE
1846385W14E-63
Editorial: Box 17550, 118 91 STOCKHOLM
Tel: 8 442 46 00 **Fax:** 84424607
Email: redaktionen@duochjobbet.se **Web site:** http://www.duochjobbet.se
Freq: Daily; **Cover Price:** Free; **Circ:** 17,200 Unique Users
Managing Director: Carina Lindvall
Language(s): Swedish
BUSINESS: COMMERCE, INDUSTRY & MANAGEMENT: Work Study

DVDFORUM.NU
1846796W85A-5
Email: info@dvdforum.nu **Web site:** http://www.dvdforum.nu
Freq: Daily; **Cover Price:** Free; **Circ:** 8,214 Unique Users
Editor-in-Chief: Christian Magdu

Language(s): Swedish
CONSUMER: PHOTOGRAPHY & FILM MAKING: Photography

E24
1741126W82-466
Editorial: Västra Järnvägsgatan 21, 105 17 STOCKHOLM Tel: 8 725 98 00
Email: redaktionen@e24.se Web site: http://www.e24.se
Circ: 231,621 Unique Users
Editor: Anna-Karin Storwall
Language(s): Swedish
CONSUMER: CURRENT AFFAIRS & POLITICS

EDGE MAGAZINE
1803883W75L-193
Editorial: Nygatan 11, 722 14 VÄSTERÅS
Tel: 8 410 417 00
Email: leon@edgemagazine.se Web site: http://www.edgemagazine.se
Freq: 6 issues yearly; Circ: 20,000
Advertising Manager: Leon Grimaldi
Language(s): Swedish
ADVERTISING RATES:
Full Page Colour .... SEK 31000
SCC .... SEK 258.33
CONSUMER: SPORT: Outdoor

EFS.NU
1668496W87-205
Editorial: EFS, Kyrkans hus, 751 70 UPPSALA
Tel: 18 16 98 00 Fax: 18 16 98 01
Email: tidning@efs.nu Web site: http://www.efs.nu
Freq: Quarterly; Cover Price: Free; Circ: 16,000
Editor: Lotta Ring
Language(s): Swedish
CONSUMER: RELIGIOUS

EKOLOGISKT LANTBRUK
50664W57-75
Editorial: Sågargatan 10A, 753 18 UPPSALA
Tel: 18 10 10 06 Fax: 18101066
Email: tidningsred@ekolantbruk.se Web site: http://www.ekolantbruk.se
Date Established: 1985; Freq: Monthly; Circ: 5,000
Editor: Lena Karlsson; Advertising Manager: Kew Nordqvist; Publisher: Inger Källander
Profile: Magazine covering ecological issues.
Language(s): Swedish
BUSINESS: ENVIRONMENT & POLLUTION

EKON
751016W62A-395
Editorial: Box 680, 405 30 GÖTEBORG
Tel: 31 711 13 83
Email: ekon@hhgs.se Web site: http://www.hhgs.se
Freq: Quarterly; Circ: 4,900
Editor-in-Chief: Rasmus Wilhelmsson
Language(s): Swedish
BUSINESS: CHURCH & SCHOOL EQUIPMENT & EDUCATION: Education

EKONOMISK DEBATT
50152W1A-50
Editorial: Lunds universitet, Box 7082, 200 07 LUND
Tel: 4 622 286 76
Email: fredrik.andersson@nek.lu.se Web site: http://www.ekonomiskdebatt.se
Date Established: 1973; Freq: 6 issues yearly; Circ: 1,900
Advertising Manager: Elisabeth Gustafsson; Publisher: Assar Lindbeck
Profile: Journal containing debate articles about finance and economics.
Language(s): Swedish
ADVERTISING RATES:
Full Page Colour .... SEK 5300
SCC .... SEK 44.20
BUSINESS: FINANCE & ECONOMICS

EKONOMISK DEBATT; EKONOMISKDEBATT.SE
1844786W1A-219
Editorial: c/o Institutet för Näringslivsforskning, Box 55665, 102 15 STOCKHOLM Tel: 8 665 45 03
Email: elisabeth.gustafsson@ifn.se Web site: http://www.ekonomiskdebatt.se
Freq: Daily; Cover Price: Free; Circ: 1,267 Unique Users
Editor-in-Chief: Fredrik Andersson; Advertising Manager: Elisabeth Gustafsson
Language(s): Swedish
BUSINESS: FINANCE & ECONOMICS

ELBRANSCHEN
50334W17-10
Editorial: Box 6040, 200 11 MALMÖ
Tel: 40 611 06 90 Fax: 40 797 37
Email: elbranschen@bjinv.se Web site: http://www.elbranschen.nu
Date Established: 1928; Freq: 6 issues yearly; Circ: 6,000
Editor: Rolf Oward; Advertising Manager: Jörgen Dahlquist; Publisher: Jörgen Dahlquist
Profile: Journal for the electrical and electro-technical industry. Includes articles about power-generation, distribution, installation and lighting.
Language(s): Swedish
ADVERTISING RATES:
Full Page Colour .... SEK 18000
SCC .... SEK 150
BUSINESS: ELECTRICAL

ELECTRONIC ENVIRONMENT
1812937W18A-53
Editorial: Box 310 19, 400 32 GÖTEBORG
Tel: 31 775 03 90
Email: redaktion@justmedia.se Web site: http://www.justmedia.se
Freq: Quarterly; Circ: 9,000
Publisher: Dan Wallander
Language(s): Swedish
BUSINESS: ELECTRONICS

ELEKTOR
50337W18A-10
Editorial: Box 178, 444 22 STENUNGSUND
Tel: 303 77 04 90
Email: red@alltomelektronik.se Web site: http://www.alltomelektronik.se
Date Established: 1982; Freq: 6 issues yearly; Circ: 7,700
Editor-in-Chief: Bill Cedrum; Publisher: Bill Cedrum
Profile: Magazine containing information, articles, product news and practical advice about electronics.
Language(s): Swedish
Readership: Aimed at electricians and engineers.
BUSINESS: ELECTRONICS

ELEKTRIKERN
50320W14L-70
Editorial: Modern Teknik i Stockholm AB, Box 216, 162 13 VÄLLINGBY Tel: 70 590 09 02
Email: info@elektrikern.nu Web site: http://www.elektrikern.nu
Date Established: 1907; Freq: 6 issues yearly; Circ: 31,200
Editor-in-Chief: Pentti Lehto; Publisher: Pentti Lehto
Profile: Magazine published by the Swedish Electricians' Trade Union, SEF.
Language(s): Swedish
Readership: Read by electricians, technicians and engineers.
ADVERTISING RATES:
Full Page Colour .... SEK 30000
SCC .... SEK 250
BUSINESS: COMMERCE, INDUSTRY & MANAGEMENT: Trade Unions

ELEKTRIKERN; ELEKTRIKERN.NU
1844985W18A-56
Editorial: Modern Teknik i Stockholm AB, Box 216, 162 13 VÄLLINGBY Tel: 70 590 09 02
Email: info@elektrikern.nu Web site: http://www.elektrikern.nu
Freq: Daily; Cover Price: Free; Circ: 3,400 Unique Users
Editor-in-Chief: Pentti Lehto; Publisher: Pentti Lehto
Language(s): Swedish
ADVERTISING RATES:
SCC .... SEK 50
BUSINESS: ELECTRONICS

ELEKTRONIK I NORDEN
50338W18A-35
Editorial: Box 91, 182 11 DANDERYD
Tel: 8 445 20 70 Fax: 8 445 20 77
Email: redaktionen@elinor.se Web site: http://www.elektronikinorden.com
Date Established: 1992; Freq: 26 issues yearly; Circ: 25,600
Advertising Manager: Tommy Jägermo; Publisher: Gunnar Lilliesköld
Profile: Magazine about the electronics trade in Scandinavia.
Language(s): Swedish
ADVERTISING RATES:
Full Page Colour .... SEK 27700
SCC .... SEK 138.50
BUSINESS: ELECTRONICS

ELEKTRONIK I NORDEN; ELEKTRONIKINORDEN.COM
1846487W18A-60
Editorial: Box 91, 182 11 DANDERYD
Tel: 8 445 20 70 Fax: 8 445 20 77
Email: redaktionen@elinor.se Web site: http://www.elinor.se
Freq: Daily; Cover Price: Free; Circ: 10,240 Unique Users
Editor: Gunnar Lilliesköld; Editor-in-Chief: Göte Fagerfjäll; Advertising Manager: Tommy Jägermo; Publisher: Gunnar Lilliesköld
Language(s): Swedish
ADVERTISING RATES:
SCC .... SEK 28
BUSINESS: ELECTRONICS

ELEKTRONIKBRANSCHEN
50497W43A-10
Editorial: Box 22307, 104 22 STOCKHOLM
Tel: 8 508 938 57 Fax: 8 508 938 01
Email: jan@elektronikbranschen.se Web site: http://www.elektronikbranschen.se
Date Established: 1955; Freq: Monthly; Circ: 7,000
Editor: Ola Larsson; Editor-in-Chief: Jan Bjerkesjö; Advertising Manager: Daniel Skoglund; Publisher: Jan Bjerkesjö
Profile: Magazine about electrical and household appliances including radio, TV, hi-fi, photographic equipment, cable and satellite TV.
Language(s): Swedish
ADVERTISING RATES:
Full Page Colour .... SEK 29900
SCC .... SEK 235.41
BUSINESS: ELECTRICAL RETAIL TRADE

ELEKTRONIKBRANSCHEN.SE
1844771W78R-285
Editorial: Box 22307, 104 22 STOCKHOLM
Tel: 8 508 938 00 Fax: 8 508 938 01
Email: jan@elektronikbranschen.se Web site: http://www.elektronikbranschen.se
Freq: Daily; Cover Price: Free; Circ: 1,000 Unique Users
Editor-in-Chief: Jan Bjerkesjö
Language(s): Swedish
CONSUMER: CONSUMER ELECTRONICS: Consumer Electronics Related

ELEKTRONIKTIDNINGEN
50339W18A-45
Editorial: Katarinavägen 19, 1tr, 116 45 STOCKHOLM Tel: 8 644 51 20 Fax: 8 644 51 21
Email: redaktionen@elektroniktidningen.se Web site: http://www.elektroniktidningen.se
Date Established: 1992; Freq: 6 issues yearly; Circ: 13,900
Editor: Jan Tångring; Editor-in-Chief: Adam Edström; Advertising Manager: Fredrik Söderberg; Publisher: Adam Edström
Profile: Magazine covering all aspects of the electronics industry and electronic design.
Language(s): Swedish
Readership: Aimed at electronics engineers.
ADVERTISING RATES:
Full Page Colour .... SEK 30000
SCC .... SEK 250
BUSINESS: ELECTRONICS

ELEKTRONIKTIDNINGEN; ETN.SE
1846291W5E-121
Editorial: Katarinavägen 19, 116 45 STOCKHOLM
Tel: 8 644 51 20 Fax: 8 644 51 21
Email: redaktionen@etn.se Web site: http://www.etn.se
Freq: Daily; Cover Price: Free; Circ: 5,560 Unique Users
Editor: Adam Edström; Editor-in-Chief: Adam Edström; Advertising Manager: Fredrik Söderberg; Publisher: Adam Edström
Language(s): Swedish
ADVERTISING RATES:
SCC .... SEK 50
BUSINESS: COMPUTERS & AUTOMATION: Data Transmission

ELINSTALLATÖREN
50335W17-20
Editorial: Box 17537, 118 91 STOCKHOLM
Tel: 8 762 75 00 Fax: 86684014
Email: redaktionen@elinstallatoren.se Web site: http://www.elinstallatoren.se
Date Established: 1934; Freq: Monthly; Circ: 12,000
Editor: Lars-Göran Hedin; Editor-in-Chief: Henrik Nygård; Advertising Manager: Robert Weström
Profile: Magazine containing information about electrical installation.
Language(s): Swedish
Readership: Read by electricians, wholesalers, supply managers, automation specialists, security alarm installers, telecommunications workers, computer network installers and electric heating specialists.
ADVERTISING RATES:
Full Page Colour .... SEK 24900
SCC .... SEK 207.50
Copy instructions: *Copy Date:* 28 days prior to publication date
BUSINESS: ELECTRICAL

ELINSTALLATÖREN; ELINSTALLATOREN.SE
1846262W18A-57
Editorial: Box 17537, 118 91 STOCKHOLM
Tel: 8 762 75 00 Fax: 8 668 40 14
Email: redaktionen@elinstallatoren.se Web site: http://www.elinstallatoren.se
Freq: Daily; Cover Price: Free; Circ: 5,000 Unique Users
Editor: Lars-Göran Hedin; Editor-in-Chief: Henrik Nygård; Advertising Manager: Robert Weström; Publisher: Henrik Nygård
Language(s): Swedish
ADVERTISING RATES:
SCC .... SEK 41
BUSINESS: ELECTRONICS

ELLE
50945W74A-40
Editorial: Humlegårdsgatan 6, 114 46 STOCKHOLM
Tel: 8 57 80 10 00 Fax: 8 57801882
Email: ellered@elle.se Web site: http://www.elle.se
Freq: Monthly; Circ: 75,300
Editor: Josephine Aune
Profile: Elle is a French fashion magazine, one of the biggest fashion titles in the world. The Swedish edition was published in 1988 for the first time. Today Elle exist in over 40 countries.
Language(s): Swedish
ADVERTISING RATES:
Full Page Colour .... SEK 73100
SCC .... SEK 609
Copy instructions: *Copy Date:* 36 days prior to publication date
CONSUMER: WOMEN'S INTEREST CONSUMER MAGAZINES: Women's Interest

ELLE; ELLE.SE
1844687W74Q-173
Editorial: Postadress: Box 27 700, 115 91, 114 46 STOCKHOLM Tel: 8 457 80 00
Email: ellered@elle.se Web site: http://www.elle.se
Freq: Daily; Cover Price: Free; Circ: 5,979 Unique Users
Editor-in-Chief: Hermine Coyet Ohlén; Publisher: Hermine Coyet Ohlén
Language(s): Swedish
ADVERTISING RATES:
SCC .... SEK 122
CONSUMER: WOMEN'S INTEREST CONSUMER MAGAZINES: Lifestyle

ELLE INTERIÖR
50953W74C-32
Editorial: Postadress: Box 27 706, 115 91 STOCKHOLM Tel: 8 457 80 00 Fax: 8 457 80 80
Email: interior.red@elleinterior.se Web site: http://www.elleinterior.se
Freq: 6 issues yearly; Circ: 55,600
Editor: Anders Bergmark
Profile: Magazine about quality home furnishings and decor.
Language(s): Swedish
ADVERTISING RATES:
Full Page Colour .... SEK 59800
SCC .... SEK 498.33
CONSUMER: WOMEN'S INTEREST CONSUMER MAGAZINES: Home & Family

ELLE MAT & VIN
51001W74P-100
Editorial: Postadress: Box 27 700, 115 91, 114 46 STOCKHOLM Tel: 8 457 80 00 Fax: 84578080
Email: matochvin.red@elle.se Web site: http://www.ellematochvin.se
Freq: Quarterly; Circ: 32,700
Advertising Manager: Shatilla Holm; Publisher: Hermine Coyet Ohlén
Profile: Magazine about good food and eating out in Sweden.
Language(s): Swedish
ADVERTISING RATES:
Full Page Colour .... SEK 39800
SCC .... SEK 331.70
CONSUMER: WOMEN'S INTEREST CONSUMER MAGAZINES: Food & Cookery

EMMABODA TIDNING
634058W80-30
Editorial: 392 33 KALMAR Tel: 471 339 84
Email: tidningen@kalmarposten.se Web site: http://www.emmabodatidning.se
Date Established: 1967; Freq: Monthly; Cover Price: Free; Circ: 10,100
Publisher: Per-Olof Persson
Profile: Newspaper covering local news in Emmaboda.
Language(s): Swedish
Readership: Read by local residents.
ADVERTISING RATES:
Full Page Colour .... SEK 15330
SCC .... SEK 76.65
CONSUMER: RURAL & REGIONAL INTEREST

ENERGI & MILJÖ
50195W3B-50
Editorial: Vasagatan 52, 3 tr, 111 20 STOCKHOLM
Tel: 8 791 66 80 Fax: 8 660 39 44
Email: lindholm@emtf.se Web site: http://www.energi-miljo.se
Freq: Monthly; Circ: 11,200
Advertising Manager: Patrik Tjälldén; Publisher: Signhild Gehlin
Profile: Journal covering heating, ventilation, sanitation and refrigeration.
Language(s): Swedish
ADVERTISING RATES:
Full Page Colour .... SEK 25000
SCC .... SEK 208.33
BUSINESS: HEATING & VENTILATION: Industrial Heating & Ventilation

ENERGI & MILJÖ; SIKI.SE
1846258W58-105
Editorial: Vasagatan 52, 3 tr, 111 20 STOCKHOLM
Tel: 8 791 66 80 Fax: 86603944
Email: gehlin@emtf.se Web site: http://www.energi-miljo.se
Freq: Daily; Cover Price: Free; Circ: 4,000 Unique Users
Publisher: Bengt-Göran Jarefors
Language(s): Swedish
BUSINESS: ENERGY, FUEL & NUCLEAR

ENERGIGAS
50389W24-40
Editorial: Box 49134, 100 29 STOCKHOLM
Tel: 8 692 18 47 **Fax:** 86544615
Email: energigas@mediabaren.se **Web site:** http://www.gasforeningen.se
Date Established: 1969; **Freq:** Quarterly; **Circ:** 5,800
Advertising Manager: Karin Granqvist; **Publisher:** Anders Mathiasson
Profile: Journal containing information, news and articles about the gas industry.
Language(s): Swedish
ADVERTISING RATES:
Full Page Colour .... SEK 19000
SCC .... SEK 158.33
BUSINESS: GAS

ENERGIMAGASINET
50686W58-10
Editorial: Box 104, 301 04 HALMSTAD
Tel: 35 10 41 50 **Fax:** 35 18 65 09
Email: info@teknikfor.se **Web site:** http://www.energimagasinet.com
Date Established: 1979; **Freq:** 6 issues yearly; **Circ:** 7,500
Advertising Manager: Michael Karlsson; **Publisher:** Staffan Bengtsson
Profile: Magazine containing news and information about the use and production of energy.
Language(s): Swedish
ADVERTISING RATES:
Full Page Colour .... SEK 15400
SCC .... SEK 100
Copy instructions: *Copy Date:* 17 days prior to publication date
BUSINESS: ENERGY, FUEL & NUCLEAR

ENERGIMAGASINET; ENERGIMAGASINET.COM
1844800W18A-55
Editorial: Box 104, 301 04 HALMSTAD
Tel: 35 10 41 50 **Fax:** 35186509
Email: info@teknikfor.se **Web site:** http://www.energimagasinet.com
Freq: Daily; **Cover Price:** Free; **Circ:** 2,067 Unique Users
Advertising Manager: Michael Hultén; **Publisher:** Staffan Bengtsson
Language(s): Swedish
BUSINESS: ELECTRONICS

ENERGITEKNIK
51424W58-20
Editorial: Storgatan 45, 171 52 SOLNA
Tel: 8 670 95 00
Email: evy@nextworld.se **Web site:** http://www.energiguiden.com
Freq: Half-yearly; **Circ:** 25,000
Advertising Manager: Sten Söderberg
Profile: Magazine containing articles and information on energy, technology and environmental issues.
Language(s): Swedish
Readership: Aimed at professionals in the energy sector.
ADVERTISING RATES:
Full Page Colour .... SEK 24000
SCC .... SEK 200
BUSINESS: ENERGY, FUEL & NUCLEAR

ENERGIVÄRLDEN
1626256W18A-51
Editorial: Energimyndigheten, Box 310, 631 04 ESKILSTUNA **Tel:** 16 544 20 00 **Fax:** 165442099
Email: registrator@energimyndigheten.se **Web site:** http://www.energimyndigheten.se
Freq: Quarterly; **Circ:** 9,000
Editor: Gunilla Strömberg
Language(s): Swedish
BUSINESS: ELECTRONICS

ENIM
634586W87-30
Editorial: Fyrisborgsgatan 4, 754 50 UPPSALA
Tel: 18 12 71 09 **Fax:** 18 12 55 34
Web site: http://www.jatillivet.se
Freq: Quarterly; **Circ:** 10,500
Editor: Petra Oscarsson; **Publisher:** Johan Lundell
Language(s): Swedish
CONSUMER: RELIGIOUS

ENKÖPINGS-POSTEN
50772W67B-3800
Editorial: Box 918, 745 25 ENKÖPING
Tel: 171 41 46 55 **Fax:** 171 44 04 01
Email: redaktionen@eposten.se **Web site:** http://www.eposten.se
Date Established: 1880
Circ: 10,300
Editor: Gunilla Ejnersten; **Advertising Manager:** Lennart Carlsson Llull; **Publisher:** Thomaz Andersson
Language(s): Swedish
ADVERTISING RATES:
Full Page Colour .... SEK 26880
SCC .... SEK 134
REGIONAL DAILY & SUNDAY NEWSPAPERS: Regional Daily Newspapers

ENKÖPINGS-POSTEN; EPOSTEN.SE
1843271W65A-981
Editorial: Box 918, 745 25 ENKÖPING
Tel: 171 41 46 00 **Fax:** 171 440401
Email: redaktionen@eposten.se **Web site:** http://www.eposten.se
Freq: Daily; **Cover Price:** Free; **Circ:** 10,333 Unique Users
Editor-in-Chief: Thomaz Andersson; **Publisher:** Thomaz Andersson
Language(s): Swedish
ADVERTISING RATES:
SCC .... SEK 27
NATIONAL DAILY & SUNDAY NEWSPAPERS: National Daily Newspapers

ENTRÉ - FORSKNING OM ENTREPRENÖRSKAP OCH SMÅFÖRETAG
1673902W82-462
Editorial: ESBRI, Saltmätargatan 9, 113 59 STOCKHOLM **Tel:** 8 458 78 00
Email: entre@esbri.se **Web site:** http://www.esbri.se/tidning
Freq: Quarterly; **Circ:** 15,000
Editor: Jonas Gustafsson
Language(s): Swedish
CONSUMER: CURRENT AFFAIRS & POLITICS

ENTRÉ HALMSTAD
634064W73-30
Editorial: Fiskaregatan 21, 302 38 HALMSTAD
Tel: 730 29 81 48
Web site: http://www.hallandsposten.se
Date Established: 1996; **Freq:** 6 issues yearly; **Circ:** 45,000
Editor: Lina Keiloo; **Advertising Manager:** Thomas Ylander
Profile: News and general interest magazine for Halmstad.
Language(s): Swedish
CONSUMER: NATIONAL & INTERNATIONAL PERIODICALS

ENTREPRENADAKTUELLT
1859382W19E-102
Tel: 19 166 130 **Fax:** 19166145
Email: info@entreprenadaktuellt.se **Web site:** http://www.entreprenadaktuellt.se
Freq: Monthly; **Cover Price:** Free; **Circ:** 32,000
Editor: Micaela Nordberg
Language(s): Swedish
BUSINESS: ENGINEERING & MACHINERY: Machinery, Machine Tools & Metalworking

ENTREPRENÖR
50294W14A-25
Editorial: 114 82 STOCKHOLM **Tel:** 8 762 61 90
Email: redaktionen@entreprenor.se **Web site:** http://www.entreprenor.se
Date Established: 2001; **Freq:** Monthly; **Circ:** 69,500
Advertising Manager: Nicklas Jakobsson; **Publisher:** Nicklas Mattsson
Profile: Magazine of the Swedish Employers' Confederation. Covers personnel issues, wages, economics and legislation relating to employment.
Language(s): Swedish
Readership: Read by company owners and directors of mainly small and medium-sized businesses.
ADVERTISING RATES:
Full Page Colour .... SEK 43500
SCC .... SEK 380.41
BUSINESS: COMMERCE, INDUSTRY & MANAGEMENT

EQUIPAGE
1696272W81D-130
Editorial: Månskara Förlag, Skoghem, 179 96 SVARTSJÖ **Tel:** 8 545 510 61 **Fax:** 8 653 31 20
Email: red@equipage.se **Web site:** http://www.equipage.se
Freq: Monthly; **Circ:** 20,000
Editor: Sonja Di Gleria; **Editor-in-Chief:** Camilla R McCarthy; **Advertising Manager:** Björn Danell
Language(s): Swedish
ADVERTISING RATES:
Full Page Colour .... SEK 14500
CONSUMER: ANIMALS & PETS: Horses & Ponies

ERA
749809W18A-50
Editorial: 101 53 STOCKHOLM **Tel:** 8 677 26 20
Email: era@era.se **Web site:** http://www.era.se
Freq: Monthly; **Circ:** 12,500
Advertising Manager: Karin Granqvist
Language(s): Swedish
ADVERTISING RATES:
Full Page Colour .... SEK 26700
SCC .... SEK 222
BUSINESS: ELECTRONICS

ERA; ERA.SE
1846296W18A-59
Editorial: 101 53 STOCKHOLM **Tel:** 8 677 26 20
Fax: 8677 28 43
Email: webmaster@era.se **Web site:** http://www.era.se
Freq: Daily; **Cover Price:** Free; **Circ:** 5,000 Unique Users
Editor-in-Chief: Bengt Magnusson; **Advertising Manager:** Jan Nyman; **Publisher:** Bengt Magnusson
Language(s): Swedish
ADVERTISING RATES:
SCC .... SEK 44
BUSINESS: ELECTRONICS

ERGO
51217W83-20
Editorial: Övre Slottsgatan 7, 753 10 UPPSALA
Tel: 18 480 31 30 **Fax:** 18 480 31 29
Email: red@ergo.us.uu.se **Web site:** http://www.ergo.nu
Date Established: 1924; **Freq:** Monthly; **Circ:** 34,000
Editor: Gusten Holm; **Advertising Manager:** Mattias Arenius
Profile: Cultural magazine containing news of interest to students in Uppsala.
Language(s): Swedish
ADVERTISING RATES:
Full Page Colour .... SEK 16000
SCC .... SEK 100
CONSUMER: STUDENT PUBLICATIONS

ERGO; ERGO.NU
1846259W76B-110
Editorial: Övre Slottsgatan 7, 753 10 UPPSALA
Tel: 18 480 31 30 **Fax:** 18 480 31 29
Email: red@ergo.us.uu.se **Web site:** http://www.ergo.nu
Freq: Daily; **Cover Price:** Free; **Circ:** 6,800 Unique Users
Editor: Hanna Strandberg; **Editor-in-Chief:** Hanna Lundquist; **Publisher:** Hanna Lundquist
Language(s): Swedish
ADVERTISING RATES:
SCC .... SEK 20
CONSUMER: MUSIC & PERFORMING ARTS: Theatre

ESCAPE 360°
1668176W89A-65
Editorial: Box 6320, 102 35 STOCKHOLM
Tel: 8 555 911 55 **Fax:** 855591150
Email: press@escape360.com **Web site:** http://www.escape360.com
Freq: Monthly; **Circ:** 30,000
Advertising Manager: Linda Birgersson; **Publisher:** Jens Christiansen
Language(s): Swedish
ADVERTISING RATES:
Full Page Colour .... SEK 36900
SCC .... SEK 307.50
Copy instructions: *Copy Date:* 30 days prior to publication date
CONSUMER: HOLIDAYS & TRAVEL: Travel

ESKILSTUNA-KURIREN / STRENGNÄS TIDNING
50773W67B-3850
Editorial: Box 120, 631 02 ESKILSTUNA
Tel: 16 15 60 00
Email: redaktion@ekuriren.se **Web site:** http://www.ekuriren.se
Date Established: 1890
Circ: 30,700
Editor: Ewa Håkansson; **Managing Director:** Hans Rinkeborn; **Publisher:** Peo Wärring
Language(s): Swedish
ADVERTISING RATES:
Full Page Colour .... SEK 45500
SCC .... SEK 227.50
REGIONAL DAILY & SUNDAY NEWSPAPERS: Regional Daily Newspapers

ESKILSTUNA-KURIREN / STRENGNÄS TIDNING; WEBB
1843255W65A-976
Editorial: Box 120, 631 02 ESKILSTUNA
Tel: 1615 61 03
Email: webbredaktor@ekuriren.se **Web site:** http://www.ekuriren.se
Freq: Daily; **Cover Price:** Free; **Circ:** 29,472 Unique Users
Editor-in-Chief: Peo Wärring; **Publisher:** Peo Wärring
Language(s): Swedish
ADVERTISING RATES:
SCC .... SEK 45
NATIONAL DAILY & SUNDAY NEWSPAPERS: National Daily Newspapers

ETC.NU
51176W82-63
Editorial: Box 4403, 102 68 STOCKHOLM
Tel: 8 410 357 00 **Fax:** 841035701
Email: tidningen@etc.se **Web site:** http://www.etc.se
Circ: 6,000
Editor: Andreas Gustavsson; **Advertising Manager:** Gahangir Sarvari; **Publisher:** Johan Ehrenberg
Profile: Magazine covering society, economics, culture and related issues from a critical perspective.
Language(s): Swedish
ADVERTISING RATES:
Full Page Colour .... SEK 1000
SCC .... SEK 50
CONSUMER: CURRENT AFFAIRS & POLITICS

ETC.SE
1844944W14F-108
Editorial: Box 4403, 102 68 STOCKHOLM
Tel: 8 410 357 00 **Fax:** 841035701
Email: tidningen@etc.se **Web site:** http://www.etc.se
Freq: Daily; **Cover Price:** Free; **Circ:** 2,000 Unique Users
Publisher: Johan Ehrenberg
Language(s): Swedish
BUSINESS: COMMERCE, INDUSTRY & MANAGEMENT: Training & Recruitment

ETT23
1664974W83-154
Editorial: Box 31019, 400 32 GÖTEBORG
Tel: 31 775 03 83
Email: redaktion@justmedia.se **Web site:** http://www.justmedia.se
Freq: Quarterly; **Circ:** 22,500
Editor: Fredrik Good; **Publisher:** Dan Wallander
Language(s): Swedish
CONSUMER: STUDENT PUBLICATIONS

EVENT & EXPO
1623600W2E-232
Editorial: Box 6910, 102 39 STOCKHOLM
Tel: 8 459 24 00 **Fax:** 8 660 75 22
Email: press@eventexpo.se **Web site:** http://www.eventexpo.se
Freq: Quarterly; **Circ:** 8,800
Editor-in-Chief: Livia Jakobsson; **Advertising Manager:** Ulf Thörnholm
Language(s): Swedish
ADVERTISING RATES:
Full Page Colour .... SEK 14900
SCC .... SEK 124.17
BUSINESS: COMMUNICATIONS, ADVERTISING & MARKETING: Public Relations

EVOLUTION
50400W27-17
Editorial: AB SKF, 415 50 GOTEBORG
Tel: 31 337 10 00 **Fax:** 31 337 17 22
Email: evolution@skf.com **Web site:** http://evolution.skf.com
Freq: Quarterly; **Circ:** 115,000
Profile: International business and technology magazine from SKF.
Language(s): Swedish
Readership: Aimed at application engineers, technical teachers and students, decision makers, production managers, design engineers, manufacturing purchasing managers, managing directors and SKF employees.
BUSINESS: METAL, IRON & STEEL

EXECUTIVE REPORT
750009W14A-175
Editorial: 106 78 STOCKHOLM **Tel:** 8 453 60 00
Email: exr@idg.se **Web site:** http://www.exr.idg.se
Freq: Monthly; **Circ:** 1,500
Editor: Oskar Enerlund; **Editor-in-Chief:** Victor Falkteg; **Publisher:** Victor Falkteg
Language(s): Swedish
BUSINESS: COMMERCE, INDUSTRY & MANAGEMENT

EXPEDITION JORDEN RUNT
639355W50-17
Email: res@jordenrunt.nu **Web site:** http://www.jordenrunt.nu
Circ: 1,600 Unique Users
Publisher: Robert Karlsson
Language(s): Swedish
BUSINESS: TRAVEL & TOURISM

EXPO
1624069W86B-121
Editorial: Box 8165, 104 20 STOCKHOLM
Tel: 8 652 60 04 **Fax:** 86526204
Email: info@expo.se **Web site:** http://www.expo.se
Freq: Quarterly; **Circ:** 2,000
Editor: Anders Dalsbro; **Editor-in-Chief:** Daniel Poohl
Language(s): Swedish
CONSUMER: ADULT & GAY MAGAZINES: Gay & Lesbian Magazines

EXPRESSEN
50757W65A-30
Editorial: Gjörwellsgatan 30, 105 16 STOCKHOLM
Tel: 8 738 30 00 **Fax:** 8 619 04 50
Email: redaktionen@expressen.se **Web site:** http://www.expressen.se
Date Established: 1944; **Freq:** Daily; **Circ:** 286,500
Editor: Jan-Erik Berggren; **Advertising Manager:** Mikael Solberg
Profile: Tabloid-sized evening newspaper covering a broad range of national and international news, events and features. Read by a broad range of the population, most of whom live in and around Stockholm. AB Kvällstidningen Expressen publish three liberal evening tabloids. Expressen, GT and Kvällsposten.
Language(s): Swedish
Readership: Read by a broad range of the population, most of whom live in and around Stockholm.
ADVERTISING RATES:
Full Page Colour .... SEK 169900
SCC .... SEK 406.25
NATIONAL DAILY & SUNDAY NEWSPAPERS: National Daily Newspapers

EXPRESSEN; EXPRESSEN.SE
624277W65A-32
Editorial: Gjörwellsgatan 30, 105 16 STOCKHOLM
Tel: 8738 34 10 **Fax:** 8738 34 11
Email: expressen@expressen.se **Web site:** http://www.expressen.se
Freq: Daily
Profile: Internet version of the tabloid-sized evening newspaper, covering a broad range of national and international news, events and features.
Language(s): Swedish
Readership: Read by a broad range of the population, most of whom live in and around Stockholm.
NATIONAL DAILY & SUNDAY NEWSPAPERS: National Daily Newspapers

EXPRESSEN; GI&HÄLSA
1902908W74Q-180
Editorial: Gjörwellsgatan 30, 105 16 STOCKHOLM
Tel: 8 738 30 00
Email: gihalsa@expressen.se **Web site:** http://www.expressen.se
Freq: 6 issues yearly; **Circ:** 200,000
Editor: Elisabeth Montgomery; **Editor-in-Chief:** Thomas Mattsson
Language(s): Swedish
CONSUMER: WOMEN'S INTEREST CONSUMER MAGAZINES: Lifestyle

FACILITIES
1850047W1E-211
Editorial: Box 2076, 403 12 GOTEBORG
Tel: 31 704 45 80 **Fax:** 31136618
Email: red@facilities.se **Web site:** http://www.facilities.se
Freq: Quarterly; **Circ:** 6,000 Unique Users
Language(s): Swedish
BUSINESS: FINANCE & ECONOMICS: Property

FÅGLAR I NORRBOTTEN
1804033W81F-102
Editorial: c/o Stefan Holmberg Piteåvägen 19, 930 82 ARVIDSJAUR **Tel:** 960 50085
Email: stefan@abborrtrask.se **Web site:** http://www.nof.nu
Freq: Quarterly; **Circ:** 500
Editor: Andreas Livbom; **Publisher:** Andreas Livbom
Language(s): Swedish
CONSUMER: ANIMALS & PETS: Birds

FÅGLAR I UPPLAND
750645W57-80
Editorial: Upplands Ornitologiska Förening, Box 59, 751 03 UPPSALA **Tel:** 730 48 34 49
Email: redaktionen@uof.nu **Web site:** http://www.uof.nu
Freq: Quarterly; **Circ:** 1,500
Editor: Annika Rastén
Language(s): Swedish
BUSINESS: ENVIRONMENT & POLLUTION

FAKTUM
1625395W14F-93
Editorial: Stampgatan 50, 411 01 GOTEBORG
Tel: 31 63 22 90 **Fax:** 31159545
Email: red@faktum.nu **Web site:** http://www.faktum.nu
Freq: Monthly; **Circ:** 15,000
Editor: Martin Karlsson; **Managing Director:** Max Markusson; **Advertising Manager:** Amanda Holmbacka; **Publisher:** Malin Kling
Language(s): Swedish
BUSINESS: COMMERCE, INDUSTRY & MANAGEMENT: Training & Recruitment

FALKÖPINGS TIDNING
50778W67B-3950
Editorial: 521 42 FALKÖPING **Tel:** 515 67 04 00
Email: red.ft@vgt.se **Web site:** http://www.falkopingstidning.se
Date Established: 1857
Circ: 9,200
Editor: Marita Wass; **Advertising Manager:** Niclas Svensson; **Publisher:** Ronny Karlsson
Language(s): Swedish
ADVERTISING RATES:
Full Page Colour .... SEK 73440
SCC .... SEK 190.75
REGIONAL DAILY & SUNDAY NEWSPAPERS: Regional Daily Newspapers

FÄLTBIOLOGEN
50743W64F-50
Editorial: Brunnsg. 62, 802 52 Gävle, 802 52 GÄVLE
Tel: 26 61 06 70 **Fax:** 26 22 22 073
Web site: http://www.faltbiologerna.se
Freq: Quarterly; **Circ:** 5,000
Editor: Lisa Behrenfeldt; **Editor-in-Chief:** Erik Abel; **Publisher:** Erik Abel
Profile: Publication about nature conservation and field biology.
Language(s): Swedish
BUSINESS: OTHER CLASSIFICATIONS: Biology

FALU KURIREN
50780W67B-4000
Editorial: Box 265, 791 26 FALUN **Tel:** 23 935 00
Email: fk.red@dt.se **Web site:** http://www.dt.se
Date Established: 1894
Circ: 27,900
Editor: Lars Erik Måg; **Managing Director:** Pär Fagerström; **Publisher:** Ewa Wirén
Language(s): Swedish
ADVERTISING RATES:
Full Page Colour .... SEK 36288
SCC .... SEK 181.44
REGIONAL DAILY & SUNDAY NEWSPAPERS: Regional Daily Newspapers

FAMILJELIV
1864680W74D-107
Editorial: Familjeliv Media AB, Valhallavägen 117, 115 31 STOCKHOLM **Tel:** 8 473 33 60
Email: info@familjeliv.se **Web site:** http://www.familjeliv.se
Freq: Monthly - 10 nr/år; **Cover Price:** Free; **Circ:** 58,000
Editor: Kristin Gunnarsson; **Editor-in-Chief:** Anna Holmquist; **Advertising Manager:** Jenny Glantz
Language(s): Swedish
ADVERTISING RATES:
SCC .... SEK 234
CONSUMER: WOMEN'S INTEREST CONSUMER MAGAZINES: Child Care

FAMILY LIVING
1804002W62A-512
Editorial: Kungsgatan 34, 113 60 STOCKHOLM
Tel: 8 736 53 00
Email: ann@familyliving.se **Web site:** http://www.familyliving.se
Freq: 6 issues yearly; **Circ:** 31,400
Editor: Niklas Sessler; **Editor-in-Chief:** Anna Zethraeus; **Advertising Manager:** Hanna Gissberg
Language(s): Swedish
ADVERTISING RATES:
Full Page Colour .... SEK 44500
SCC .... SEK 370.83
BUSINESS: CHURCH & SCHOOL EQUIPMENT & EDUCATION: Education

FÅR JAG LOV
51096W76E-146
Editorial: Egmont Tidskrifter AB, 205 07 MALMO
Tel: 40 38 52 00
Email: diana.thylin@egmont.se **Web site:** http://www.fjl.se
Freq: 6 issues yearly; **Circ:** 8,900
Advertising Manager: Klas Persson
Profile: Magazine about pop music.
Language(s): Swedish
ADVERTISING RATES:
Full Page Colour .... SEK 16600
SCC .... SEK 138.30
CONSUMER: MUSIC & PERFORMING ARTS: Pop Music

FÄRGFABRIKEN MAGAZINE
1804058W7-841
Editorial: Färgfabriken, Lövholmsbrinken 1, 117 43 STOCKHOLM **Tel:** 8 645 07 07 **Fax:** 86455030
Email: pernilla@fargfabriken.se **Web site:** http://www.fargfabriken.se
Freq: Half-yearly; **Circ:** 10,000
Editor-in-Chief: Pernilla Lesse
Language(s): Swedish
BUSINESS: ANTIQUES

FARMACIFACKET
50451W37-25
Editorial: Västmannagatan 66, 113 25 STOCKHOLM
Tel: 8 31 64 10 **Fax:** 8340808
Email: farmacifacket@farmaciforbundet.se **Web site:** http://www.farmacifacket.se
Freq: Monthly; **Circ:** 8,400
Editor-in-Chief: Ewa-Maria Kriegholm
Profile: Publication for pharmaceutical chemists and their assistants.
Language(s): Swedish
ADVERTISING RATES:
Full Page Colour .... SEK 18700
SCC .... SEK 155.80
BUSINESS: PHARMACEUTICAL & CHEMISTS

FÅRSKÖTSEL
50371W21D-15
Editorial: Lillegården Brismene, 521 93 FALKÖPING
Tel: 515 530 45
Email: tidningen@faravelsforbundet.com **Web site:** http://www.faravelsforbundet.com
Date Established: 1917; **Freq:** 6 issues yearly; **Circ:** 3,500
Publisher: Einar de Wit
Profile: Magazine containing practical advice, information and articles about sheep farming.
Language(s): Swedish
Readership: Aimed at veterinary surgeons and sheep breeders.
BUSINESS: AGRICULTURE & FARMING: Livestock

FASTIGHETSFOLKET
50225W4F-20
Editorial: Box 70446, 107 25 STOCKHOLM
Tel: 8 696 11 50 **Fax:** 8 20 59 89
Email: fastighetsfolket@fastighets.se **Web site:** http://www.fastighetsfolket.se
Date Established: 1932; **Freq:** Monthly; **Circ:** 38,000
Advertising Manager: Johan Turian
Profile: Publication about property management, maintenance, cleaning and window-cleaning.
Language(s): Swedish
ADVERTISING RATES:
Full Page Colour .... SEK 21900
SCC .... SEK 182.50
BUSINESS: ARCHITECTURE & BUILDING: Cleaning & Maintenance

FASTIGHETSFOLKET; FASTIGHETSFOLKET.SE
1846254W14L-199
Editorial: Box 70446, 107 25 STOCKHOLM
Tel: 8 696 11 50 **Fax:** 8205989
Email: fastighetsfolket@fastighets.se **Web site:** http://www.fastighetsfolket.se
Freq: Daily; **Cover Price:** Free; **Circ:** 7,600 Unique Users
Language(s): Swedish
BUSINESS: COMMERCE, INDUSTRY & MANAGEMENT: Trade Unions

FASTIGHETSFÖRVALTAREN
50168W1E-20
Editorial: Drakenbergsgatan 2, 117 41 STOCKHOLM
Tel: 31 775 15 80
Email: redaktion@hexanova.se **Web site:** http://www.fastighetsforvaltaren.se
Date Established: 1989; **Freq:** 6 issues yearly; **Circ:** 22,300
Editor: Arne Öster; **Managing Director:** Urban Nilsson; **Advertising Manager:** Tinna Knape; **Publisher:** Urban Nilsson
Profile: Magazine covering the financial aspects of the building and property trade.
Language(s): Swedish
Readership: Aimed at estate agents, managers of banks and insurance companies and administrators.
ADVERTISING RATES:
Full Page Colour .... SEK 31500
SCC .... SEK 196.9
BUSINESS: FINANCE & ECONOMICS: Property

FASTIGHETSMÄKLAREN
50169W1E-30
Editorial: Box 1487, 171 28 SOLNA
Tel: 8 555 00 900 **Fax:** 8 555 00 999
Email: service@maklarsamfundet.se **Web site:** http://www.maklarsamfundet.se
Freq: 6 issues yearly; **Circ:** 8,000
Managing Director: Jeanette Gustafsdotter
Profile: Magazine containing news and information regarding the property trade.
Language(s): Swedish
Readership: Read by estate agents.
BUSINESS: FINANCE & ECONOMICS: Property

FASTIGHETSMARKNADEN
634077W74K-60
Editorial: Ilanda Gård 120, 653 50 KARLSTAD
Tel: 54 18 77 18 **Fax:** 54 53 45 80
Email: info@svenskmediakonsult.se **Web site:** http://www.svenskmediakonsult.se
Date Established: 1993; **Freq:** 6 issues yearly; **Circ:** 55,000
Managing Director: Joachim Svärdh; **Advertising Manager:** Joachim Svärdh; **Publisher:** Joachim Svärdh
Profile: Local newspaper covering the property market for Karlstad, Hammarö, Forshaga and Kil, includes articles about market trends.
Language(s): Swedish
CONSUMER: WOMEN'S INTEREST CONSUMER MAGAZINES: Home Purchase

FASTIGHETSNYTT
634799W1E-40
Editorial: Wallingatan 37, 111 24 STOCKHOLM
Tel: 8 652 89 80 **Fax:** 8 652 89 81
Email: info@fastighetsnytt.se **Web site:** http://www.fastighetsnytt.se
Date Established: 1994; **Freq:** 6 issues yearly; **Circ:** 7,800
Editor: Daniel Bergstrand; **Editor-in-Chief:** Daniel Bergstrand; **Advertising Manager:** Jonas Hedqvist; **Publisher:** Johan Zetterstedt
Profile: Magazine focusing on property administration including development and research.
Language(s): Swedish
Readership: Read by owners, architects, designers and builders.
ADVERTISING RATES:
Full Page Colour .... SEK 24900
SCC .... SEK 207.5
BUSINESS: FINANCE & ECONOMICS: Property

FASTIGHETSTIDNINGEN
50207W4D-5
Editorial: Intellecta Corporate, Box 19063, 104 32 STOCKHOLM **Tel:** 8 506 286 00 **Fax:** 8 506 287 00
Email: fastighetstidningen@intellecta.se **Web site:** http://www.fastighetstidningen.se
Freq: Monthly - (10 nr/år); **Circ:** 20,500
Editor-in-Chief: Per-Yngve Bengtsson; **Advertising Manager:** Simon Knudsen
Profile: Magazine about real estate management, finance, legislation, housing questions and matters relating to new buildings, restoration and rebuilding.
Language(s): Swedish
ADVERTISING RATES:
Full Page Colour .... SEK 29900
SCC .... SEK 249.20
BUSINESS: ARCHITECTURE & BUILDING: Planning & Housing

FASTIGHETSTIDNINGEN; FASTIGHETSTIDNINGEN.SE
1846274W4E-161
Editorial: /Intellecta Corporate, Box 19063, 104 32 STOCKHOLM **Tel:** 8 506 286 00 **Fax:** 8 506 287 00
Email: fastighetstidningen@intellecta.se **Web site:** http://www.fastighetstidningen.se
Freq: Daily; **Cover Price:** Free; **Circ:** 4,600 Unique Users
Language(s): Swedish
BUSINESS: ARCHITECTURE & BUILDING: Building

FASTIGHETSVÄRLDEN
749875W14A-180
Editorial: Box 3087, 103 61 STOCKHOLM
Tel: 8 631 90 20 **Fax:** 86119515
Email: red@fastighetsvarlden.se **Web site:** http://www.fastighetsvarlden.se
Freq: Monthly; **Circ:** 5,000
Publisher: Björn Rundquist
Language(s): Swedish
ADVERTISING RATES:
Full Page Colour .... SEK 21200
SCC .... SEK 176.70
BUSINESS: COMMERCE, INDUSTRY & MANAGEMENT

FASTIGHETSVÄRLDEN; FASTIGHETSVARLDEN.SE
1843276W14A-327
Editorial: Box 3087, 103 61 STOCKHOLM
Tel: 8 631 90 20 **Fax:** 8 611 95 15
Email: red@fastighetsvarlden.se **Web site:** http://www.fastighetsvarlden.se
Freq: Daily; **Cover Price:** Free; **Circ:** 1,667 Unique Users
Editor: Fredrik Engström; **Editor-in-Chief:** Willy Wredenmark; **Publisher:** Willy Wredenmark
Language(s): Swedish
ADVERTISING RATES:
SCC .... SEK 35
BUSINESS: COMMERCE, INDUSTRY & MANAGEMENT

FASTIGO
751111W4F-75
Editorial: Box 70397, 107 24 STOCKHOLM
Tel: 8 676 69 00 **Fax:** 8207575
Email: info@fastigo.se **Web site:** http://www.fastigo.se
Date Established: 1994; **Freq:** 6 issues yearly; **Circ:** 3,300
Editor: Anette Nordenfelt; **Advertising Manager:** Marie Harder; **Publisher:** Anders Skarin
Language(s): Swedish
ADVERTISING RATES:
Full Page Colour .... SEK 14400
SCC .... SEK 120
BUSINESS: ARCHITECTURE & BUILDING: Cleaning & Maintenance

FAUNA OCH FLORA
751112W64H-15
Editorial: Box 7007, 750 07 UPPSALA
Tel: 18 67 25 77
Email: faunaochflora@artdata.slu.se **Web site:** http://www.artdata.slu.se
Freq: Quarterly; **Circ:** 2,500
Editor: Ragnar Hall; **Editor-in-Chief:** Tomas Carlberg; **Publisher:** Tomas Carlberg
Language(s): Swedish
BUSINESS: OTHER CLASSIFICATIONS: Veterinary

FEMINA
50979W74A-42
Editorial: Landskronavägen 23, 251 85 HELSINGBORG **Tel:** 42 17 35 00 **Fax:** 42 17 36 82
Email: femina@aller.se **Web site:** http://femina.se
Freq: Monthly; **Circ:** 110,100 Unique Users
Editor: Clara Lindstrii
Profile: Magazine covering fashion, beauty, food and interior design.
Language(s): Swedish
Readership: Aimed at women aged between 25 and 49 years old with a high disposable income.
CONSUMER: WOMEN'S INTEREST CONSUMER MAGAZINES: Women's Interest

FIGHTER MAGAZINE
634482W75Q-80
Editorial: Karl Gustavsgatan 49, 411 31 GOTEBORG
Tel: 31 711 86 00
Email: marko.gyllenland@fightermag.com **Web site:** http://www.fightermag.com
Date Established: 1988; **Freq:** Monthly; **Circ:** 17,000
Editor: Anders Eriksson; **Advertising Manager:** Marko Gyllenland
Profile: Magazine featuring martial arts.
Language(s): Swedish
CONSUMER: SPORT: Combat Sports

FILIPSTADS TIDNING
633910W67B-4025
Editorial: Box 318, 682 27 FILIPSTAD
Tel: 590 79 15 50 **Fax:** 59015056
Email: redaktion@filipstadstid.se **Web site:** http://www.filipstadstid.se
Date Established: 1850
Circ: 4,000
Publisher: Lena Richardson
Language(s): Swedish
ADVERTISING RATES:
Full Page Colour .... SEK 16464
SCC .... SEK 82.32
Copy instructions: *Copy Date:* 14 days prior to publication date
REGIONAL DAILY & SUNDAY NEWSPAPERS: Regional Daily Newspapers

FILIPSTADS TIDNING; WEBB
1843270W65A-980
Editorial: Box 318, 682 27 FILIPSTAD
Tel: 59079 15 50 **Fax:** 590 150 56
Email: redaktion@filipstadstid.se **Web site:** http://www.filipstadstid.se
Freq: Daily; **Cover Price:** Free; **Circ:** 3,000 Unique Users
Editor-in-Chief: Lena Richardson; **Publisher:** Lena Richardson
Language(s): Swedish
ADVERTISING RATES:
SCC .... SEK 16
NATIONAL DAILY & SUNDAY NEWSPAPERS: National Daily Newspapers

FILM INTERNATIONAL
51070W76A-55
Editorial: Sunnanväg 6N, 222 26 LUND
Tel: 211 99 82
Email: daniel.lindvall@filmint.nu **Web site:** http://www.filmint.nu
Date Established: 1973; **Freq:** 6 issues yearly; **Circ:** 1,500
Editor-in-Chief: Daniel Lindvall; **Publisher:** Pär Linnertz
Profile: Magazine containing essays and interviews on film by distinguished scholars and journalists from all over the world. Includes a review section on books and new releases in the cinema and on DVD.The magazine is frequently used in schools and universities.
Language(s): Swedish
Readership: Read mainly by academics and students.
CONSUMER: MUSIC & PERFORMING ARTS: Cinema

FILM & TV
51078W76C-40
Editorial: Box 2068, Stora Nygatan 21, Gamla Stan, 103 12 STOCKHOLM **Tel:** 8 545 275 22
Fax: 8 545 275 09
Email: lahger@swipnet.se **Web site:** http://www.filmcentrum.se/Film_och_tv
Freq: Quarterly; **Circ:** 3,000
Editor: Håkan Lahger; **Advertising Manager:** Katrina Mathsson; **Publisher:** Stefan Jarl
Profile: Magazine providing information and listings of films and television programmes.
Language(s): Swedish
CONSUMER: MUSIC & PERFORMING ARTS: TV & Radio

FILMKONST
51071W76A-60
Editorial: Olof Palmes plats, 413 04 GÖTEBORG
Tel: 31 339 30 14 **Fax:** 31 41 00 63
Email: filmkonst@filmfestival.org **Web site:** http://www.filmfestival.org
Freq: 6 issues yearly; **Circ:** 5,000
Editor: Camilla Larsson
Profile: Magazine about the Gothenburg Film Festival.
Language(s): Swedish
Readership: Aimed at anyone with an interest in new releases.
CONSUMER: MUSIC & PERFORMING ARTS: Cinema

FILMKRETS
51136W78B-20
Editorial: Gröna Gatan 14 A, kv, 151 32 SÖDERTÄLJE **Tel:** 705 62 94 10
Email: red@filmkrets.se **Web site:** http://www.filmkrets.se
Freq: Half-yearly; **Circ:** 1,100
Editor: Johannes Runeborg
Profile: Magazine published by the Swedish Film and Video Society.
Language(s): Swedish
Readership: Read by amateur film makers producing documentaries and short films.
CONSUMER: CONSUMER ELECTRONICS: Video & DVD

FILMRUTAN
51072W76A-70
Editorial: Box 27126, 102 52 STOCKHOLM
Tel: 8 665 11 00
Web site: http://www.filmrutan.se
Date Established: 1958; **Freq:** Quarterly; **Circ:** 2,000
Editor: Marika Junström; **Advertising Manager:** Henry Lundström; **Publisher:** Mats Sladö
Profile: Magazine published by Swedish United Film Studios.
Language(s): Swedish
CONSUMER: MUSIC & PERFORMING ARTS: Cinema

FILOSOFEN
750519W62A-445
Editorial: StuFF, Trappan, Universitetet, 601 81 NORRKÖPING **Tel:** 13 28 28 87
Email: filosofen@stuff.liu.se **Web site:** http://www.stuff.liu.se
Freq: 6 issues yearly; **Circ:** 3,500
Editor-in-Chief: Carl Löfstrand; **Publisher:** Elin Larsson
Language(s): Swedish
BUSINESS: CHURCH & SCHOOL EQUIPMENT & EDUCATION: Education

FILTER
1835831W84B-297
Editorial: Östra Hamngatan 45, 411 10 GÖTEBORG
Tel: 31 711 98 82 **Fax:** 31 774 22 10
Email: info@magasinetfilter.se **Web site:** http://www.magasinetfilter.se
Freq: 6 issues yearly; **Circ:** 30,000
Editor: Ika Johannesson; **Editor-in-Chief:** Mattias Göransson; **Advertising Manager:** Richard Kruuse
Language(s): Swedish
CONSUMER: THE ARTS & LITERARY: Literary

FINANSVÄRLDEN
50162W1C-30
Editorial: Box 720, 101 34 STOCKHOLM
Tel: 8 614 03 00 **Fax:** 8 614 03 98
Email: finansvarlden@finansforbundet.se **Web site:** http://www.finansforbundet.se/finansvarlden
Freq: Monthly; **Circ:** 39,700
Editor: BrittMari Lantto; **Editor-in-Chief:** Stefan Ahlqvist; **Publisher:** Stefan Ahlqvist
Profile: Magazine published by the Swedish Bank Employees' Association. Contains articles, news and information about the world of finance.
Language(s): Swedish
ADVERTISING RATES:
Full Page Colour .... SEK 23900
SCC .... SEK 182.5
BUSINESS: FINANCE & ECONOMICS: Banking

FINANSVÄRLDEN; WEBB
1846482W14L-203
Editorial: Box 720, 101 34 STOCKHOLM
Tel: 8 614 03 00 **Fax:** 86140398
Email: finansvarlden@finansforbundet.se **Web site:** http://www.finansforbundet.se/finansvarlden
Freq: Daily; **Cover Price:** Free; **Circ:** 10,800 Unique Users
Editor: Åsa Berner; **Publisher:** Stefan Ahlqvist
Language(s): Swedish
BUSINESS: COMMERCE, INDUSTRY & MANAGEMENT: Trade Unions

FINNVEDEN NU; WEBB
1843269W65A-979
Editorial: Box 111, 331 32 VÄRNAMO
Tel: 370 69 16 40 **Fax:** 370 129 86
Email: redaktion@finnveden.nu **Web site:** http://www.finnveden.nu
Freq: Daily; **Cover Price:** Free; **Circ:** 15,667 Unique Users
Editor: Lena Gärdemalm; **Publisher:** Stefan Fels
Language(s): Swedish
ADVERTISING RATES:
SCC .... SEK 20
NATIONAL DAILY & SUNDAY NEWSPAPERS: National Daily Newspapers

FIRST POKER
1692629W78D-418
Editorial: Box 3187, 350 43 VÄXJO **Tel:** 470 76 24 00
Fax: 470762425
Email: poker@firstpublishing.se **Web site:** http://www.firstpoker.se
Freq: Monthly; **Circ:** 15,000
Editor: Olof Jisborg; **Editor-in-Chief:** Jonas Berg; **Advertising Manager:** Andreas Björck; **Publisher:** Patrick Ekelius
Language(s): Swedish
ADVERTISING RATES:
Full Page Colour .... SEK 36000
SCC .... SEK 300
CONSUMER: CONSUMER ELECTRONICS: Games

FISKE FÖR ALLA
51351W92-15
Editorial: Bergendorffsgatan 5B, 652 24 KARLSTAD
Tel: 54 775 25 20 **Fax:** 54 775 77 99
Email: info.jof@jof.se **Web site:** http://www.fiskeforalla.com
Freq: 6 issues yearly; **Circ:** 29,200
Editor: Mikael Engström; **Editor-in-Chief:** Mats Gyllsand; **Advertising Manager:** Jan Hagman; **Publisher:** Mats Gyllsand
Profile: Magazine about all aspects of angling and sports fishing.
Language(s): Swedish
CONSUMER: ANGLING & FISHING

FISKE-FEBER
1665941W92-22
Editorial: Box 22100, 250 23 HELSINGBORG
Tel: 42 211 22 **Fax:** 42 211 37
Email: info@fiske-feber.se **Web site:** http://www.fiske-feber.se
Freq: 6 issues yearly; **Circ:** 15,000
Editor: John Zafaradi; **Editor-in-Chief:** Jörgen Larsson; **Publisher:** Thorbjörn Östman
Language(s): Swedish
CONSUMER: ANGLING & FISHING

FISKEJOURNALEN
51352W92-17
Editorial: Box 104, 443 22 LERUM **Tel:** 302 244 40
Fax: 30224275
Email: redaktion@fiskejournalen.se **Web site:** http://www.fiskejournalen.se
Date Established: 1974; **Freq:** 6 issues yearly; **Circ:** 25,300
Advertising Manager: Håkan Otterberg; **Publisher:** Martin Falklind
Profile: Magazine about sport fishing in fresh and salt water.
Language(s): Swedish
CONSUMER: ANGLING & FISHING

FITNESS MAGAZINE
51057W75P-60
Editorial: c/o Forma Publishing Group AB, Box 6151, 102 33 STOCKHOLM **Tel:** 8 30 10 70 **Fax:** 8 30 16 70
Email: redaktion@fitness-magazine.com **Web site:** http://www.fitness-magazine.com
Date Established: 1995; **Freq:** Monthly; **Circ:** 45,000
Advertising Manager: Adam Stevens
Profile: Magazine containing news and information about sports, aerobics and fitness training. Also includes facts about food, nutrition and health.
Language(s): Swedish
Readership: Aimed at women aged between 18 and 42 years old who are concerned about their health and want to stay fit.
ADVERTISING RATES:
Full Page Colour .... SEK 31500
SCC .... SEK 262.50
CONSUMER: SPORT: Fitness/Bodybuilding

FITNESS MAGAZINE; WEBB
1846452W55-66
Editorial: Box 6151, 102 33 STOCKHOLM
Tel: 8 30 10 70 **Fax:** 8 30 16 70
Email: redaktion@fitness-magazine.com **Web site:** http://www.fitness-magazine.com
Freq: Daily; **Cover Price:** Free; **Circ:** 22,200 Unique Users
Editor-in-Chief: Marie Kjellnäs; **Advertising Manager:** Adam Stevens
Language(s): Swedish
ADVERTISING RATES:
SCC .... SEK 52
BUSINESS: APPLIED SCIENCE & LABORATORIES

FIXA SJÄLV
2010019W14A-372
Editorial: Bonnier Tidskrifter AB, 105 44 STOCKHOLM **Tel:** 8442 96 20
Email: info@spoon.se **Web site:** http://www.fixasjalv.se
Freq: 6 issues yearly; **Circ:** 30,000
Editor: Jonathan Leijonberg; **Editor-in-Chief:** Moa Suominen; **Advertising Manager:** Nina Rehnmark
Language(s): Swedish
BUSINESS: COMMERCE, INDUSTRY & MANAGEMENT

FJÄDERFÄ
50376W21F-10
Editorial: Näset, 741 91 KNIVSTA **Tel:** 18 34 62 52
Fax: 18346253
Email: journalistgruppen@secher.pp.se **Web site:** http://www.fjaderfa.se
Freq: Monthly; **Circ:** 2,000
Publisher: Sven Secher
Profile: Publication covering all aspects of poultry farming.
Language(s): Swedish
BUSINESS: AGRICULTURE & FARMING: Poultry

FJÄRDE VÄRLDEN
51315W90-25
Editorial: Box 16320, 103 26 STOCKHOLM
Tel: 8 84 49 15 **Fax:** 8201252
Email: post@f4world.org **Web site:** http://www.f4world.org
Freq: Quarterly; **Circ:** 1,500
Editor-in-Chief: Marita Tunbjer; **Publisher:** Birgitta Pihl
Profile: Magazine about indigenous people and ethnic minorities, focusing on politics and human rights around the world. Includes multi-cultural features on religion and fighting racism.
Language(s): Swedish
CONSUMER: ETHNIC

FJÄRRVÄRMETIDNINGEN
50196W3B-55
Editorial: Mitt ordval, Miraallén 21, 417 58 GÖTEBORG **Tel:** 31 22 78 11
Email: ann-sofie@mittordval.se **Web site:** http://www.svenskfjarrvarme.se
Date Established: 1981
Circ: 2,500
Advertising Manager: Thomas Palm; **Publisher:** Lena Sommestad
Profile: Journal providing information about district heating, power heating and district cooling.
Language(s): Swedish
BUSINESS: HEATING & VENTILATION: Industrial Heating & Ventilation

FLAMMAN; FLAMMAN.SE
1844781W65A-1028
Editorial: Kungsgatan 84, 112 27 STOCKHOLM
Tel: 8 650 80 10 **Fax:** 8 650 83 15
Email: nyhet@flamman.se **Web site:** http://www.flamman.se
Cover Price: Free; **Circ:** 1,800 Unique Users
Editor-in-Chief: Aron Etzler; **Publisher:** Aron Etzler
Language(s): Swedish
ADVERTISING RATES:
SCC .... SEK 7
NATIONAL DAILY & SUNDAY NEWSPAPERS: National Daily Newspapers

FLM
1833379W76B-107
Editorial: Tomtebogatan 3, 1 tr, 113 39 STOCKHOLM **Tel:** 705 26 53 45
Email: jacob@flm.nu **Web site:** http://www.flm.nu
Freq: Quarterly; **Circ:** 3,000
Editor: Jacob Lundström
Language(s): Swedish
CONSUMER: MUSIC & PERFORMING ARTS: Theatre

FLOTTANS MÄN
1698245W22A-148
Editorial: Teatergatan 3 1tr, 111 48 STOCKHOLM
Tel: 8 678 09 08 **Fax:** 8 678 09 08
Email: webmaster@flottansman.se **Web site:** http://www.flottansman.se
Freq: Quarterly; **Circ:** 4,500
Editor: Olle Melin; **Publisher:** Olle Melin
Language(s): Swedish
BUSINESS: FOOD

FLUGFISKE I NORDEN
51353W92-20
Editorial: Box 22032, Thommy Gustavsson / Flugfiske i Norden, 702 02 OREBRO **Tel:** 19 22 33 03
Email: flugfiskeinorden@telia.com **Web site:** http://www.flugfiskeinorden.se
Date Established: 1979; **Freq:** 6 issues yearly; **Circ:** 10,000
Editor: Thommy Gustavsson; **Advertising Manager:** Jan Sekander; **Publisher:** Erik Erlandson Hammargren
Profile: Magazine about fly fishing. Contains articles on techniques, competitions, equipment and holidays destinations.
Language(s): Swedish
Readership: Aimed at angling enthusiasts.
CONSUMER: ANGLING & FISHING

FLYGREVYN
50253W6A-20
Editorial: Övre Välsta gård, 137 92 TUNGELSTA
Tel: 8 500 379 00 **Fax:** 8 500 379 01
Email: redaktionen@flygrevyn.se **Web site:** http://www.flygtorget.se/flygfakta/flygrevyn
Freq: 6 issues yearly; **Circ:** 14,000
Editor-in-Chief: Christina Lindberg; **Advertising Manager:** Christina Lindberg; **Publisher:** Christina Lindberg
Profile: Magazine containing articles and information about aviation.
Language(s): Swedish
ADVERTISING RATES:
Full Page Colour .... SEK 21600
SCC .... SEK 180
BUSINESS: AVIATION & AERONAUTICS

FLYGTORGET AIRMAIL
1658778W6A-211
Editorial: Box 3389, 103 68 STOCKHOLM
Tel: 8 791 94 94 **Fax:** 8 791 97 99
Email: info@flygtorget.se **Web site:** http://www.flygtorget.se/nyheter/airmail/nyhetsbrev.asp
Freq: 104 issues yearly; **Circ:** 10,600
Editor: Albert Siösteen; **Publisher:** Peeter Puusepp
Language(s): Swedish
BUSINESS: AVIATION & AERONAUTICS

FOGNINGSTEKNIK
1894851W10-98
Tel: 8 564 886 44
Email: peter.bergqvist@verkstaderna.se **Web site:** http://www.verkstaderna.se
Freq: 6 issues yearly; **Circ:** 13,800
Publisher: Peter Bergqvist
Language(s): Swedish
BUSINESS: MATERIALS HANDLING

FOKUS
1741142W82-464
Editorial: FPG Media AB, Wallingatan 12, 111 60 STOCKHOLM **Tel:** 8 456 34 60 **Fax:** 8 456 34 72
Email: redaktion@fokus.se **Web site:** http://www.fokus.se
Freq: Weekly; **Circ:** 24,100
Editor: Thord Eriksson; **Publisher:** Martin Ahlquist
Language(s): Swedish

ADVERTISING RATES:
Full Page Colour .... SEK 29000
SCC .... SEK 241.66
CONSUMER: CURRENT AFFAIRS & POLITICS

FOKUS; FOKUS.SE 1846297W65A-1073
Editorial: EPG Media AB, Wallingatan 12, 111 60 STOCKHOLM **Tel:** 8456 34 60 **Fax:** 84563472
Email: redaktion@fokus.se **Web site:** http://www.fokus.se
Freq: Daily; **Cover Price:** Free; **Circ:** 7,600 Unique Users
Editor-in-Chief: Karin Pettersson; **Publisher:** Martin Ahlquist
Language(s): Swedish
NATIONAL DAILY & SUNDAY NEWSPAPERS: National Daily Newspapers

FOLKBLADET 50816W67B-4050
Editorial: Folkbladet, 601 84 NORRKÖPING
Tel: 11 20 04 00 **Fax:** 11 20 04 65
Email: redaktion@folkbladet.se **Web site:** http://www.folkbladet.se
Date Established: 1905
Circ: 9,500
Advertising Manager: Pär Lindegren; **Publisher:** Arne Lindh
Language(s): Swedish
ADVERTISING RATES:
Full Page Colour .... SEK 43920
SCC .... SEK 198
REGIONAL DAILY & SUNDAY NEWSPAPERS: Regional Daily Newspapers

FOLKBLADET; FOLKBLADET.SE 1843268W65A-978
Editorial: 601 84 NORRKÖPING **Tel:** 11 20 04 00
Fax: 11200465
Email: redaktion@folkbladet.se **Web site:** http://www.folkbladet.se
Freq: Daily; **Cover Price:** Free; **Circ:** 13,348 Unique Users
Publisher: Christer Sandberg
Language(s): Swedish
NATIONAL DAILY & SUNDAY NEWSPAPERS: National Daily Newspapers

FOLKET 50774W67B-4100
Editorial: Box 368, Besöksadress: J.A Selanders gata 1, 632 20 ESKILSTUNA **Tel:** 161775 50
Fax: 16 17 75 55
Email: redaktionen@folket.se **Web site:** http://www.folket.se
Date Established: 1905
Circ: 4,800
Editor-in-Chief: Marie Hillblom; **Managing Director:** Anders Boberg
Language(s): Swedish
ADVERTISING RATES:
Full Page Colour .... SEK 29045
SCC .... SEK 145.23
REGIONAL DAILY & SUNDAY NEWSPAPERS: Regional Daily Newspapers

FOLKET; FOLKET.SE 1843275W65A-982
Editorial: Box 368, 632 20 ESKILSTUNA
Tel: 16 177 571 **Fax:** 16 17 75 55
Email: webmaster@folket.se **Web site:** http://www.folket.se
Freq: Daily; **Cover Price:** Free; **Circ:** 7,014 Unique Users
Managing Director: Anders Boberg
Language(s): Swedish
NATIONAL DAILY & SUNDAY NEWSPAPERS: National Daily Newspapers

FOLKET I BILD / KULTURFRONT 51180W82-72
Editorial: Bondegatan 69, 116 34 STOCKHOLM
Tel: 8 644 50 32 **Fax:** 855695035
Email: red@fib.se **Web site:** http://www.fib.se
Date Established: 1972; **Freq:** Monthly; **Circ:** 2,000
Editor: Martin Shibbye
Profile: Magazine dealing with cultural matters and politics.
Language(s): Swedish
ADVERTISING RATES:
Full Page Colour .... SEK 4000
SCC .... SEK 33.33
CONSUMER: CURRENT AFFAIRS & POLITICS

FOLKET I BILD / KULTURFRONT; FIB.SE 1844794W76B-109
Editorial: Bondegatan 69, 116 34 STOCKHOLM
Tel: 8 644 50 32 **Fax:** 8 556 950 35
Email: webmaster@fib.se **Web site:** http://www.fib.se
Freq: Daily; **Cover Price:** Free; **Circ:** 667 Unique Users
Publisher: Kenneth Lundgren
Language(s): Swedish

ADVERTISING RATES:
SCC .... SEK 7
CONSUMER: MUSIC & PERFORMING ARTS: Theatre

FOLKHÖGSKOLAN 50732W62J-70
Editorial: SFHL, Box 1057, 172 22 SUNDBYBERG
Tel: 8 564 835 35
Email: staffanm@telia.com **Web site:** http://www.sfhl.se
Freq: 6 issues yearly; **Circ:** 3,300
Editor: Birgitta Tingdal; **Editor-in-Chief:** Staffan Myrbäck; **Publisher:** Staffan Myrbäck
Profile: Journal for teachers at Swedish high schools. Includes news, essays and features about education, learning and trade union matters.
Language(s): Swedish
BUSINESS: CHURCH & SCHOOL EQUIPMENT & EDUCATION: Teachers & Education Management

FÖNSTRET 50309W14F-35
Editorial: Box 522, 101 30 STOCKHOLM
Tel: 8 613 50 00 **Fax:** 8 24 69 56
Web site: http://www.fonstret.se
Date Established: 1954; **Freq:** Monthly; **Circ:** 35,000
Editor: Maria Ullsten; **Advertising Manager:** Birgitta Olsson; **Publisher:** Jonas Helling
Profile: Official journal of the Swedish Workers' Education Society.
Language(s): Swedish
ADVERTISING RATES:
Full Page Colour .... SEK 15300
SCC .... SEK 127.50
BUSINESS: COMMERCE, INDUSTRY & MANAGEMENT: Training & Recruitment

FOODWIRE.SE 1696581W22C-164
Editorial: Box 1011, 444 26 STENUNGSUND
Tel: 303 678 20 **Fax:** 708 10 44 31
Email: alla@foodwire.com **Web site:** http://www.foodwire.com
Freq: Daily; **Cover Price:** Paid; **Circ:** 1,500 Unique Users
Editor: Jonathan Newton; **Editor-in-Chief:** Stellan Löfving; **Publisher:** Stellan Löfving
Language(s): Swedish
ADVERTISING RATES:
Full Page Colour .... SEK 5000
BUSINESS: FOOD: Food Processing & Packaging

FÖR 51282W87-25
Editorial: Box 4312, 102 67 STOCKHOLM
Tel: 8 737 70 00 **Fax:** 8 737 71 45
Email: forsamlingsforbundet@svenskakyrkan.se **Web site:** http://www.forsamlingsforbundet.se
Date Established: 1947; **Freq:** 6 issues yearly; **Circ:** 5,800
Editor-in-Chief: Lars Lidström; **Publisher:** Torbjörn Zygmunt
Profile: Magazine for church communities about all aspects of church life.
Language(s): Swedish
CONSUMER: RELIGIOUS

FÖRÄLDRAKONTAKTEN 1625704W94F-212
Editorial: SRF, 122 88 ENSKEDE **Tel:** 8 39 92 98
Fax: 8 39 93 22
Email: jan.wiklund@srfriks.org **Web site:** http://www.srfriks.org
Freq: Quarterly; **Circ:** 1,500
Editor: Jan Wiklund; **Publisher:** Eva Björk
Language(s): Swedish
CONSUMER: OTHER CLASSIFICATIONS: Disability

FÖRÄLDRAKRAFT 1809930W56L-58
Editorial: Backebogatan 3, 129 40 HAGERSTEN
Tel: 8 410 056 36
Email: info@faktapress.se **Web site:** http://www.foraldrakraft.se
Freq: 6 issues yearly; **Circ:** 20,000
Editor-in-Chief: Sara Bengtsson; **Advertising Manager:** Frida-Louise Vikman; **Publisher:** Valter Bengtsson
Language(s): Swedish
Copy instructions: *Copy Date:* 40 days prior to publication date
BUSINESS: HEALTH & MEDICAL: Disability & Rehabilitation

FÖRÄLDRAR & BARN 50974W74D-40
Editorial: Budadress: Gävlegatan 22, 7tr, 113 92 STOCKHOLM **Tel:** 8588 366 00
Email: fob@lrfmedia.lrf.se **Web site:** http://www.foraldrarochbarn.se
Freq: Monthly; **Circ:** 45,000
Editor-in-Chief: Petra Aschberg; **Advertising Manager:** Jens Christiansen
Profile: Magazine about parents and children.
Language(s): Swedish
ADVERTISING RATES:
Full Page Colour .... SEK 33900
SCC .... SEK 282.50
CONSUMER: WOMEN'S INTEREST CONSUMER MAGAZINES: Child Care

FÖRÄLDRAR & BARN ATT VARA GRAVID 1673904W74D-101
Editorial: Box 4403, 102 68 STOCKHOLM
Tel: 8 588 33 848 **Fax:** 8 428 90 13
Email: fob@lrfmedia.lrf.se **Web site:** http://www.foraldrarochbarn.se
Freq: 6 issues yearly; **Circ:** 50,000
Editor: Yasemin Bayramoglou; **Editor-in-Chief:** Petra Achberg
Language(s): Swedish
ADVERTISING RATES:
Full Page Colour .... SEK 33900
SCC .... SEK 282.50
CONSUMER: WOMEN'S INTEREST CONSUMER MAGAZINES: Child Care

FÖRÄLDRAR & BARN JUNIOR 1834588W62A-515
Editorial: Box 4403, 113 92 STOCKHOLM
Tel: 8 588 366 00 **Fax:** 8 428 90 13
Email: fob@lrfmedia.lrf.se **Web site:** http://www.foraldrarochbarn.se
Freq: 6 issues yearly; **Circ:** 50,000
Editor: Yasemin Bayramoglu; **Editor-in-Chief:** Petra Aschberg; **Advertising Manager:** Daniel Johansson
Language(s): Swedish
ADVERTISING RATES:
Full Page Colour .... SEK 33900
SCC .... SEK 282.50
BUSINESS: CHURCH & SCHOOL EQUIPMENT & EDUCATION: Education

FÖRETAGAREN 1625668W14R-63
Editorial: Spoon Publishing AB, Kungstensgatan 21 B, 113 57 STOCKHOLM **Tel:** 8 406 17 00
Fax: 8 442 96 39
Email: foretagaren@foretagarna.se **Web site:** http://www.foretagarna.se
Freq: Monthly; **Circ:** 51,000
Editor: Stina Gerhardt; **Editor-in-Chief:** Peter Wiklund; **Advertising Manager:** Rasmus Thomsen
Language(s): Swedish
ADVERTISING RATES:
Full Page Colour .... SEK 43900
SCC .... SEK 274.37
BUSINESS: COMMERCE, INDUSTRY & MANAGEMENT: Commerce Related

FÖRETAGAREN; FORETAGARNA.SE 1846493W14A-342
Editorial: Spoon Publishing AB, Kungstensgatan 21 B, 113 57 STOCKHOLM **Tel:** 8 442 96 20
Fax: 8 442 96 39
Email: foretagaren@foretagarna.se **Web site:** http://www.foretagarna.se
Freq: Daily; **Cover Price:** Free; **Circ:** 10,200 Unique Users
Editor-in-Chief: Peter Wiklund
Language(s): Swedish
ADVERTISING RATES:
SCC .... SEK 55
BUSINESS: COMMERCE, INDUSTRY & MANAGEMENT

FÖRETAGSSKÖTERSKAN 1639397W32G-268
Editorial: Att: Kristina Andersson, Alviva AB, 374 38 KARLSHAMN **Tel:** 454 75 16 81
Email: britt-marie.silversund@comhem.se **Web site:** http://www.foretagsskoterskor.org
Freq: Quarterly; **Circ:** 1,500
Editor: Karin Björkman; **Advertising Manager:** Kristina Andersson; **Publisher:** Annika Claesson
Language(s): Swedish
BUSINESS: LOCAL GOVERNMENT, LEISURE & RECREATION: Community Care & Social Services

FÖRETAGSVÄRLDEN 1837057W14H-11
Editorial: Holländargatan 23, 111 60 STOCKHOLM
Tel: 8 791 96 75 **Fax:** 8 406 04 44
Email: produktion@ultimedia.se **Web site:** http://www.ultimedia.se
Freq: 6 issues yearly; **Circ:** 5,000
Managing Director: Donald Larsson; **Publisher:** Donald Larsson
Language(s): Swedish
ADVERTISING RATES:
SCC .... SEK 83.33
BUSINESS: COMMERCE, INDUSTRY & MANAGEMENT: Small Business

FÖRFATTAREN 51259W84B-50
Editorial: C/O Sveriges Författarförbund, Box 3157, 103 63 STOCKHOLM **Tel:** 8 545 132 00
Fax: 8 545 132 10
Email: forfattaren@sff.info **Web site:** http://www.forfattarforbundet.se
Date Established: 1969; **Freq:** 6 issues yearly; **Circ:** 3,000
Editor: Henrik C Enbohm; **Advertising Manager:** Marianne Lingserius
Profile: Journal of the Swedish Writers' Union.
Language(s): Swedish
ADVERTISING RATES:
Full Page Colour .... SEK 6000

SCC .... SEK 50
CONSUMER: THE ARTS & LITERARY: Literary

FORM 749949W23A-35
Editorial: Arvinius Förlag AB, Box 6040, 102 31 STOCKHOLM **Tel:** 8 32 00 15 **Fax:** 8320095
Email: info@arvinius.se **Web site:** http://www.tidskriftenform.se
Freq: Monthly -, 10 nr per år; **Circ:** 5,600
Language(s): Swedish
ADVERTISING RATES:
Full Page Colour .... SEK 26200
SCC .... SEK 218
BUSINESS: FURNISHINGS & FURNITURE

FORNVÄNNEN 1667549W94J-26
Editorial: Box 5622 Vitterhetsakademien, 114 86 STOCKHOLM **Tel:** 8 440 42 80 **Fax:** 8 440 42 90
Email: mr@vitterhetsakad.se **Web site:** http://www.vitterhetsakad.se
Freq: Quarterly; **Circ:** 1,800
Editor: Elisabet Regner; **Editor-in-Chief:** Lars Larsson; **Publisher:** Gustav Trotzig
Language(s): Swedish
CONSUMER: OTHER CLASSIFICATIONS: Popular Science

FORSKA 1625822W55-48
Editorial: Vetenskapsrådet, 103 78 STOCKHOLM
Tel: 8 546 440 00 **Fax:** 8 546 441 80
Email: forska@vr.se **Web site:** http://www.vr.se/forska
Freq: Quarterly; **Cover Price:** Free; **Circ:** 6,500
Editor: Ragnhild Romanus; **Publisher:** Tomas Nilsson
Language(s): Swedish
ADVERTISING RATES:
Full Page Colour .... SEK 3000
BUSINESS: APPLIED SCIENCE & LABORATORIES

FORSKNING 50347W19A-92
Editorial: Drottninggatan 9, 411 14 GOTEBORG
Tel: 31 701 07 30 **Fax:** 31 701 07 74
Email: lars@forskning.com **Web site:** http://www.forskning.com
Date Established: 1989; **Freq:** Quarterly; **Circ:** 12,100
Advertising Manager: Patrik Tjälldén; **Publisher:** Lars Alvegård
Profile: Magazine covering engineering, technology and science.
Language(s): Swedish
Readership: Aimed at researchers and engineers.
ADVERTISING RATES:
Full Page Colour .... SEK 18150
SCC .... SEK 151.25
Copy instructions: *Copy Date:* 45 days prior to publication date
BUSINESS: ENGINEERING & MACHINERY

FORSKNING FÖR HÄLSA 50593W56A-32
Editorial: Hjärt-Lungfonden, Box 5413, 114 84 STOCKHOLM **Tel:** 8 566 242 00 **Fax:** 8 566 242 29
Email: info@hjart-lungfonden.se **Web site:** http://www.hjart-lungfonden.se
Freq: Quarterly; **Circ:** 20,000
Editor: Karin Myhrström; **Publisher:** Karin Myrström
Profile: Journal containing information and articles about heart and lung related diseases.
Language(s): Swedish
BUSINESS: HEALTH & MEDICAL

FORSKNING & FRAMSTEG 51379W94X-37
Editorial: Gamla Brogatan 23B, 111 91 STOCKHOLM **Tel:** 555 198 00
Web site: http://www.fof.se
Date Established: 1966
Circ: 45,000
Editor: Lotta Fredholm; **Editor-in-Chief:** Patric Hadenius
Profile: Magazine containing scientific articles about development and research within the fields of energy, medicine, technology, psychology, physics, astronomy, ecology, history, civics and archaeology.
Language(s): Swedish
Readership: Aimed at people with a general interest in scientific matters and technology.
ADVERTISING RATES:
Full Page Colour .... SEK 50000
SCC .... SEK 416.66
CONSUMER: OTHER CLASSIFICATIONS: Miscellaneous

FORSKNING OCH FRAMSTEG; FOF.SE 1843273W55-63
Web site: http://www.fof.se
Circ: 17,640 Unique Users
Editor: Lotta Fredholm
Language(s): Swedish
BUSINESS: APPLIED SCIENCE & LABORATORIES

FORSKNING & MEDICIN
1625812W56A-332
Editorial: Vetenskapsrådet, 103 78 STOCKHOLM
Tel: 8 54 64 40 00
Email: pt@vr.se **Web site:** http://forskningmedicin.vr.se
Freq: Quarterly; **Circ:** 12,000
Editor: Peter Tillhammar; **Publisher:** Håkan Billig
Language(s): Swedish
ADVERTISING RATES:
Full Page Colour .... SEK 6500
SCC .... SEK 54.20
BUSINESS: HEALTH & MEDICAL

FÖRSKOLAN
50720W62C-60
Editorial: Box 12239, 102 26 STOCKHOLM
Tel: 8 737 65 51 **Fax:** 8 619 00 88
Email: forskolan@lararforbundet.se **Web site:** http://lararnasnyheter.se/forskolan
Freq: Monthly; **Circ:** 66,300
Editor-in-Chief: Helena Ingvarsdotter; **Advertising Manager:** Ann Spaak
Profile: Magazine about nursery school education.
Language(s): Swedish
ADVERTISING RATES:
Full Page Colour .... SEK 28700
SCC .... SEK 220.83
BUSINESS: CHURCH & SCHOOL EQUIPMENT & EDUCATION: Junior Education

FÖRSKOLETIDNINGEN
50721W62C-80
Editorial: Box 34, 171 11 SOLNA **Tel:** 8 545 453 30
Email: forskoletidningen@fortbild.se **Web site:** http://www.fortbild.se
Date Established: 1918; **Freq:** 6 issues yearly; **Circ:** 9,500
Editor: Harriet Jancke; **Editor-in-Chief:** Eva Wiklund-Dahl; **Advertising Manager:** Ulf Jacobsson
Profile: Journal about elementary education.
Language(s): Swedish
BUSINESS: CHURCH & SCHOOL EQUIPMENT & EDUCATION: Junior Education

FÖRSVARSUTBILDAREN
50461W40-10
Editorial: Box 5034, 102 41 STOCKHOLM
Tel: 8 587 742 00 **Fax:** 8 587 742 90
Email: forsvarsutbildaren@forsvarsutbildarna.se **Web site:** http://www.forsvarsutbildarna.se
Date Established: 1918; **Freq:** Quarterly; **Circ:** 35,000
Editor-in-Chief: Per Klingvall; **Advertising Manager:** Per Klingvall; **Publisher:** Leif Tyrén
Profile: Journal of the Central Federation for Voluntary Military Training.
Language(s): Swedish
Readership: Aimed at officers.
BUSINESS: DEFENCE

FORUM AID
1623597W23A-42
Editorial: Strandvägen 19, 114 56 STOCKHOLM
Tel: 8 555 400 00 **Fax:** 855540074
Email: forumaid@forumaid.com **Web site:** http://www.forumaid.com
Freq: Quarterly; **Circ:** 3,000
Advertising Manager: Christina Lund; **Publisher:** Daniel Golling
Language(s): Swedish
ADVERTISING RATES:
Full Page Colour .... SEK 23400
SCC .... SEK 195
BUSINESS: FURNISHINGS & FURNITURE

FOTBOLLSKANALEN.SE
1847159W75A-222
Editorial: TV4 AB, Tegeluddsvägen 3-5, 115 79 STOCKHOLM **Tel:** 8 459 40 00
Email: fotbollskanalen.se@tv4.se **Web site:** http://www.fotbollskanalen.se
Freq: Daily; **Cover Price:** Free; **Circ:** 45,300 Unique Users
Editor: Olof Lundh
Language(s): Swedish
CONSUMER: SPORT

FOTNOTEN
50713W62B-60
Editorial: Box 12239, 102 26 STOCKHOLM
Tel: 8 737 65 40 **Fax:** 8 619 00 88
Email: fotnoten@lararforbundet.se **Web site:** http://www.fotnoten.se
Freq: 6 issues yearly; **Circ:** 6,400
Editor-in-Chief: Annika Dzedina; **Advertising Manager:** Marie Lingensjö; **Publisher:** Annika Dzedina
Profile: Magazine for teachers of music, dance and drama.
Language(s): Swedish
BUSINESS: CHURCH & SCHOOL EQUIPMENT & EDUCATION: Education Teachers

FOTO
50455W38-10
Editorial: 251 85 HELSINGBORG **Tel:** 42 17 35 00
Fax: 42 17 37 90
Email: foto@aller.se **Web site:** http://www.tidningenfoto.se
Freq: Monthly; **Circ:** 22,900
Editor: Susanna Gordon; **Advertising Manager:** Martin Brolin; **Publisher:** Jan Almlöf
Profile: Magazine containing articles, news and information about photography. Contains product news, practical advice, information about coming events and exhibitions and interviews.
Language(s): Swedish
Readership: Read by amateur and professional photographers.
ADVERTISING RATES:
Full Page Colour .... SEK 29600
SCC .... SEK 246.70
BUSINESS: PHOTOGRAPHIC TRADE

FOTOGRAFISK TIDSKRIFT
50456W38-15
Editorial: Årstaängsvägen 5 B, S-117 43 STOCKHOLM **Tel:** 8 702 03 71 **Fax:** 8 641 22 10
Email: redaktion@sfoto.se **Web site:** http://www.sfoto.se
Freq: 6 issues yearly; **Circ:** 4,000
Editor: Stefan Ohlsson; **Editor-in-Chief:** Gösta Flemming; **Advertising Manager:** Hans Flygare; **Publisher:** Gösta Flemming
Profile: Review of photography, from the initial idea to the finished picture. Also covers printing and developing techniques, interviews and equipment reports.
Language(s): Swedish
ADVERTISING RATES:
Full Page Colour .... SEK 8000
SCC .... SEK 66.7
BUSINESS: PHOTOGRAPHIC TRADE

FOTOGRAFISK TIDSKRIFT; WEBB
1844782W85A-3
Editorial: Årstaängsvägen 5 B, 111 23 STOCKHOLM
Tel: 8 702 03 71 **Fax:** 8 641 22 10
Email: redaktion@sfoto.se **Web site:** http://www.sfoto.se
Freq: Daily; **Cover Price:** Free; **Circ:** 1,333 Unique Users
Editor: Stefan Ohlsson; **Editor-in-Chief:** Gösta Flemming; **Publisher:** Gösta Flemming
Language(s): Swedish
ADVERTISING RATES:
SCC .... SEK 13
CONSUMER: PHOTOGRAPHY & FILM MAKING: Photography

FRAMTIDER
1694689W94J-28
Editorial: Box 591, 101 31 STOCKHOLM
Tel: 8 402 12 00 **Fax:** 8245014
Email: info@framtidsstudier.se **Web site:** http://www.framtidsstudier.se
Freq: Quarterly; **Circ:** 6,000
Managing Director: Joakim Palme
Language(s): Swedish
CONSUMER: OTHER CLASSIFICATIONS: Popular Science

FRED OCH FRIHET
750728W74A-125
Editorial: Norrtullsgatan 45, 1 tr, 113 46 STOCKHOLM **Tel:** 8 702 98 10
Email: info@ikff.se **Web site:** http://www.ikff.se
Freq: Quarterly; **Circ:** 2,003
Editor: Josefine Karlsson; **Publisher:** Kirsti Kolthoff
Language(s): Swedish
CONSUMER: WOMEN'S INTEREST CONSUMER MAGAZINES: Women's Interest

FREDSTIDNINGEN PAX
51432W82-77
Editorial: Box 4134, 102 63 STOCKHOLM
Tel: 8 55 80 31 84 **Fax:** 8 702 18 46
Email: pax@svenskafreds.se **Web site:** http://www.svenskafreds.se/pax
Date Established: 1972; **Freq:** 6 issues yearly; **Circ:** 5,000
Editor: Eva Kellström Froste; **Publisher:** Eva Kellström Froste
Profile: Magazine concerning human rights, disarmament, security policies, foreign affairs and politics.
Language(s): Swedish
CONSUMER: CURRENT AFFAIRS & POLITICS

FREE
51576W74G-30
Editorial: Turistvägen 504, 794 93 ORSA
Tel: 250 55 20 05 **Fax:** 250 431 91
Email: info@free.com **Web site:** http://www.free.se
Date Established: 1982; **Freq:** 6 issues yearly; **Circ:** 26,900
Editor: Monica Katarina Frisk; **Advertising Manager:** Mats Östholm; **Publisher:** Monica Katarina Frisk
Profile: Magazine focusing on holistic medicine and spiritual development.
Language(s): Swedish
CONSUMER: WOMEN'S INTEREST CONSUMER MAGAZINES: Slimming & Health

FREEDOM
751115W73-95
Editorial: Månskärsvägen 10 A, 141 75 KUNGENS KURVA **Tel:** 8 615 21 81 **Fax:** 8 615 21 81
Email: editor@freedommag.org **Web site:** http://www.freedommag.org/swedish/index.htm
Freq: Half-yearly; **Circ:** 5,000
Editor-in-Chief: Gullevi Almgren; **Publisher:** Gullevi Almgren
Language(s): Swedish
CONSUMER: NATIONAL & INTERNATIONAL PERIODICALS

FREEDROM TRAVEL
2010028W50-142
Tel: 70947 96 53
Email: kontakt@freedomtravel.se **Web site:** http://www.freedomtravel.se
Circ: 1,000 Unique Users
Language(s): Swedish
BUSINESS: TRAVEL & TOURISM

FRI KÖPENSKAP
50379W22A-10
Editorial: Box 72001, 181 72 LIDINGÖ
Tel: 8 545 513 33 **Fax:** 86502491
Email: redaktionen@fri-kopenskap.se **Web site:** http://www.fri-kopenskap.se
Date Established: 1943; **Freq:** Weekly -, 40 nr per år; **Circ:** 30,700
Editor-in-Chief: Åke Rosengren; **Advertising Manager:** Mi Andrén
Profile: Journal about distribution and retailing within the food industry.
Language(s): Swedish
ADVERTISING RATES:
Full Page Colour .... SEK 78200
SCC .... SEK 391
BUSINESS: FOOD

FRI KÖPENSKAP; WEBB
1843265W22C-165
Editorial: Box 72001, 181 72 LIDINGÖ
Tel: 8 545 513 33 **Fax:** 86502491
Email: redaktionen@fri-kopenskap.se **Web site:** http://www.fri-kopenskap.se
Freq: Daily; **Cover Price:** Free; **Circ:** 1,320 Unique Users
Publisher: Åke Rosengren
Language(s): Swedish
BUSINESS: FOOD: Food Processing & Packaging

FRI SIKT
1803859W32G-269
Editorial: Jämtlands Läns Landsting, Landstingshuset, Box 654, 831 27 ÖSTERSUND
Tel: 63 14 76 29
Email: redaktionen@jll.se **Web site:** http://www.jll.se
Freq: Half-yearly; **Circ:** 5,200
Editor: Malin Gunnarsson; **Publisher:** Gun Råberg-Kjellerstrand
Language(s): Swedish
BUSINESS: LOCAL GOVERNMENT, LEISURE & RECREATION: Community Care & Social Services

FRIA FÖRETAGARE
1803998W14A-305
Editorial: Gamla Vägen 3, 262 43 ÄNGELHOLM
Tel: 20 760 761 **Fax:** 43183185
Email: info@ff.se **Web site:** http://www.ff.se
Freq: Quarterly; **Circ:** 47,500
Publisher: Per Lidström
Language(s): Swedish
ADVERTISING RATES:
Full Page Colour .... SEK 25000
BUSINESS: COMMERCE, INDUSTRY & MANAGEMENT

FRIDA
50982W74F-35
Editorial: Frida Förlag AB, Hammarby Kajväg 18, 120 30 STOCKHOLM **Tel:** 8 587 481 00
Email: frida@fridaforlag.se **Web site:** http://www.frida.se
Date Established: 1981; **Freq:** 26 issues yearly; **Circ:** 50,000
Editor-in-Chief: Beatrice Birkeldh; **Advertising Manager:** Nicolas Fuentes
Profile: Magazine covering fashion and cosmetics.
Language(s): Swedish
Readership: Aimed at teenagers and young women aged between 15 and 24 years.
ADVERTISING RATES:
Full Page Colour .... SEK 50000
SCC .... SEK 416.66
Copy instructions: *Copy Date:* 28 days prior to publication date
CONSUMER: WOMEN'S INTEREST CONSUMER MAGAZINES: Teenage

FRIDA SPECIAL
1841526W76D-290
Editorial: Frida Förlag AB, Hammarby Kajväg 18, 120 30 STOCKHOLM **Tel:** 8 587 481 00
Email: frida@fridaforlag.se **Web site:** http://www.frida.se
Freq: Half-yearly; **Circ:** 50,000
Language(s): Swedish
ADVERTISING RATES:
Full Page Colour .... SEK 50000
SCC .... SEK 416.67
CONSUMER: MUSIC & PERFORMING ARTS: Music

FRIDA; WEBB
1846467W76D-294
Editorial: Frida Förlag AB, Hammarby Kajväg 18, 120 30 STOCKHOLM **Tel:** 8 587 481 00
Email: frida@fridaforlag.se **Web site:** http://www.frida.se
Freq: Daily; **Cover Price:** Free; **Circ:** 15,800 Unique Users
Language(s): Swedish
CONSUMER: MUSIC & PERFORMING ARTS: Music

FRIHET
51182W82-80
Editorial: Box 115 44, 100 61 STOCKHOLM
Tel: 8 714 48 00 **Fax:** 8 714 95 08
Email: info@frihet.se **Web site:** http://www.frihet.se
Date Established: 1918; **Freq:** 6 issues yearly; **Circ:** 10,800
Editor: Becky Bergdahl; **Editor-in-Chief:** Mikael Feldbaum
Profile: Magazine for young people in the Swedish Social Democratic Party.
Language(s): Swedish
ADVERTISING RATES:
Full Page Colour .... SEK 20800
SCC .... SEK 173.33
CONSUMER: CURRENT AFFAIRS & POLITICS

FRILANSJOURNALISTEN
50184W2B-40
Editorial: c/o Garbo Reportage, Katarina Bangata 48, 116 39 STOCKHOLM
Email: red@frilansjournalisten.nu **Web site:** http://www.frilansjournalisten.nu
Freq: Quarterly; **Circ:** 2,300
Profile: Magazine for freelance journalists.
Language(s): Swedish
BUSINESS: COMMUNICATIONS, ADVERTISING & MARKETING: Press

FRILUFTSLIV - I ALLA VÄDER
50421W32D-50
Editorial: Instrumentsvägen 14, 126 53 HÄGERSTEN
Tel: 8 447 44 40 **Fax:** 8 447 44 44
Email: info@friluftsframjandet.se **Web site:** http://www.frilufts.se
Freq: Quarterly; **Circ:** 33,600
Editor-in-Chief: Per Göthlin; **Advertising Manager:** Nils-Erik Wickman; **Publisher:** Per Göthlin
Profile: Magazine about open-air sports facilities.
Language(s): Swedish
ADVERTISING RATES:
Full Page Colour .... SEK 31000
SCC .... SEK 258
BUSINESS: LOCAL GOVERNMENT, LEISURE & RECREATION: Parks

FRISKARE LIV, VISIR-AKTUELLT
51831W56A-278
Editorial: Hälsans Hus, Fjällgatan 23 A, 116 28 STOCKHOLM **Tel:** 8 591 282 11 **Fax:** 8 556 988 88
Email: visir@telia.com **Web site:** http://www.visir.a.se
Date Established: 1980; **Freq:** Quarterly; **Circ:** 3,000
Editor: Dick Jansson; **Publisher:** Arne Stråby
Profile: Magazine providing advice and articles concerning healthy living.
Language(s): Swedish
BUSINESS: HEALTH & MEDICAL

FRISKISPRESSEN
50985W74G-40
Editorial: Kungsholms Strand 127, 112 33 STOCKHOLM **Tel:** 8 20 19 25 **Fax:** 8 20 16 35
Email: info@friskispressen.se **Web site:** http://www.friskispressen.se
Freq: Quarterly; **Circ:** 193,000
Advertising Manager: Tina Reuterswärd; **Publisher:** Peter Rogeman
Profile: Magazine about health and fitness, diet and exercise.
Language(s): Swedish
ADVERTISING RATES:
Full Page Colour .... SEK 45000
SCC .... SEK 308.33
CONSUMER: WOMEN'S INTEREST CONSUMER MAGAZINES: Slimming & Health

FRISKSPORT
51349W91R-55
Editorial: Brahegatan 32A, 553 34 JÖNKÖPING
Tel: 36 71 17 46
Email: tidningen@frisksport.se **Web site:** http://www.frisksport.se
Date Established: 1935; **Freq:** 6 issues yearly; **Circ:** 6,000
Advertising Manager: Leif Dylicki; **Publisher:** Göran Bengtsson
Profile: Publication of the Swedish Association of Physical Culture.
Language(s): Swedish
Readership: Aimed at people interested in a healthy lifestyle.
CONSUMER: RECREATION & LEISURE: Recreation & Leisure Related

FRITID OCH PARK I SVERIGE
1625776W50-107
Editorial: OGSAW Förlags AB, Wallingatan 25, 784 34 BORLÄNGE **Tel:** 243 832 80
Email: info@fritidpark.se **Web site:** http://www.fritidpark.se
Freq: Quarterly; **Circ:** 6,000
Editor: Sven-Arne Wikén; **Editor-in-Chief:** Olof Schääf; **Advertising Manager:** Per Idborg; **Publisher:** Olof Schääf
Language(s): Swedish
ADVERTISING RATES:
Full Page Colour .... SEK 10700
SCC .... SEK 89
BUSINESS: TRAVEL & TOURISM

FRITIDSPEDAGOGEN
50722W62C-100
Editorial: Lärarförbundet, Box 12239, 102 26 STOCKHOLM **Tel:** 8 737 65 00 **Fax:** 8 619 00 88
Email: fritidspedagogen@lararforbundet.se **Web site:** http://www.fritidspedagogen.net
Date Established: 1980; **Freq:** 6 issues yearly; **Circ:** 14,800
Editor-in-Chief: Helena Gårdsäter; **Publisher:** Helena Gårdsäter
Profile: Magazine containing articles about the education of young children.
Language(s): Swedish
Readership: Read by teachers.
BUSINESS: CHURCH & SCHOOL EQUIPMENT & EDUCATION: Junior Education

FRONTFACE MAGAZINE
1666652W74A-152
Editorial: c/o Intellibra, Ortvik, Garvargatan 5, 112 21 STOCKHOLM **Tel:** 8 652 95 95
Email: info@frontface.se **Web site:** http://www.frontface.se
Freq: 6 times a year; **Cover Price:** Paid; **Circ:** 50,000 Unique Users
Editor-in-Chief: Peter Ortvik
Language(s): Swedish
CONSUMER: WOMEN'S INTEREST CONSUMER MAGAZINES: Women's Interest

FRONYTT
634502W40-28_75
Editorial: Box 19, 182 05 DJURSHOLM
Tel: 8 753 00 21
Email: fronytt@fro.se **Web site:** http://www.fro.se
Freq: Quarterly; **Circ:** 6,000
Editor: Lillemor Bohlin; **Editor-in-Chief:** Eva Neveling; **Advertising Manager:** Krister Ljungqvist; **Publisher:** Eva Neveling
Language(s): Swedish
BUSINESS: DEFENCE

FRYKSDALS-BYGDEN
50838W67B-4150
Editorial: Storgatan 22, 686 30 SUNNE
Tel: 565 68 82 00 **Fax:** 565 151 40
Email: redaktion@fryksdalsbygden.se **Web site:** http://www.fbygden.se
Date Established: 1941
Circ: 3,100
Advertising Manager: Eva Persson; **Publisher:** Britta Nyberg
Language(s): Swedish
ADVERTISING RATES:
Full Page Colour .... SEK 13104
SCC .... SEK 65.52
REGIONAL DAILY & SUNDAY NEWSPAPERS: Regional Daily Newspapers

FRYKSDALS-BYGDEN; FBYGDEN.SE
1844973W65A-1050
Editorial: Storgatan 22, 686 30 SUNNE
Tel: 565 68 82 00 **Fax:** 565 68 82 16
Email: redaktion@fbygden.se **Web site:** http://www.fbygden.se
Freq: Daily; **Cover Price:** Free; **Circ:** 4,000 Unique Users
Editor-in-Chief: Britta Nyberg; **Advertising Manager:** Lars Fredriksson; **Publisher:** Britta Nyberg
Language(s): Swedish
ADVERTISING RATES:
SCC .... SEK 13
NATIONAL DAILY & SUNDAY NEWSPAPERS: National Daily Newspapers

FUZZ
750985W76D-220
Editorial: 414 63 GÖTEBORG **Tel:** 31 711 68 06
Fax: 31 711 68 07
Email: info@fuzz.se **Web site:** http://www.fuzz.se
Freq: Monthly; **Circ:** 15,000
Editor: Per Boysen; **Editor-in-Chief:** Ulf Zackrisson; **Advertising Manager:** Ulf Zackrisson; **Publisher:** Ulf Zackrisson
Language(s): Swedish
CONSUMER: MUSIC & PERFORMING ARTS: Music

FYSIOTERAPI
50644W56L-55
Editorial: LSR/Fysioterapi, Box 3196, 103 63 STOCKHOLM **Tel:** 8 567 061 00
Email: fysioterapi@lsr.se **Web site:** http://www.sjukgymnastforbundet.se
Freq: 6 issues yearly; **Circ:** 12,100
Editor: Hilda Zollitsch Grill; **Advertising Manager:** Magnus Johansson; **Publisher:** Lois Steen Vivanco
Profile: Journal concerning research and treatment in the fields of physiotherapy and industrial physiotherapy.
Language(s): Swedish
ADVERTISING RATES:
Full Page Colour .... SEK 21850
SCC .... SEK 182.08
Copy instructions: *Copy Date:* 30 days prior to publication date
BUSINESS: HEALTH & MEDICAL: Disability & Rehabilitation

FYSIOTERAPI; WEBB
1846275W74G-221
Editorial: LSR/Fysioterapi, Box 3196, 103 63 STOCKHOLM **Tel:** 8 567 061 00 **Fax:** 8567 06 199
Email: fysioterapi@lsr.se **Web site:** http://www.sjukgymnastforbundet.se
Freq: Daily; **Cover Price:** Free; **Circ:** 4,840 Unique Users
Editor: Hilda Zollitsch Grill; **Editor-in-Chief:** Lois Steen Vivanco; **Publisher:** Lois Steen Vivanco
Language(s): Swedish
ADVERTISING RATES:
SCC .... SEK 36
CONSUMER: WOMEN'S INTEREST CONSUMER MAGAZINES: Slimming & Health

GAGNEFSBLADET
752364W80-520
Editorial: Gagnefsbyn 20, 780 41 GAGNEF
Tel: 241 616 00 **Fax:** 241 79 40 90
Email: elisabeth.lofkvist@gagnefsbladet.se **Web site:** http://www.gagnefsbladet.se
Freq: Weekly; **Circ:** 5,000
Publisher: Elisabeth Löfkvist
Language(s): Swedish
CONSUMER: RURAL & REGIONAL INTEREST

GALAGO
50937W73-35
Editorial: Box 17506, 118 91 STOCKHOLM
Tel: 8 462 44 00 **Fax:** 8 462 44 90
Email: galago@ordfront.se **Web site:** http://www.galago.se
Freq: Half-yearly; **Circ:** 5,000
Editor: Erik Uppenberg; **Publisher:** Getrud Åström
Profile: Cultural magazine containing articles about alternative comics. Contains interviews, causeries and satire.
Language(s): Swedish
CONSUMER: NATIONAL & INTERNATIONAL PERIODICALS

GALOPPMAGASINET
1813996W81D-134
Editorial: Örnaberga Gård, 272 94 SIMRISHAMN
Tel: 414 235 80 **Fax:** 41423125
Email: info@galoppmagasinet.se **Web site:** http://www.galoppmagasinet.se
Freq: Quarterly; **Circ:** 5,000
Editor: Sofia Nordin; **Editor-in-Chief:** Mats Genberg; **Publisher:** Mats Genberg
Language(s): Swedish
CONSUMER: ANIMALS & PETS: Horses & Ponies

GAMEREACTOR MAGAZINE
1625793W78D-411
Editorial: Hamngatan 10, 831 31 ÖSTERSUND
Tel: 63 10 11 23
Email: info@gamereactor.se **Web site:** http://www.gamereactor.se
Freq: Monthly; **Cover Price:** Free; **Circ:** 60,000
Editor: Jonas Mäki; **Editor-in-Chief:** Petter Hegevall; **Advertising Manager:** Morten Reichel; **Publisher:** Petter Hegevall
Language(s): Swedish
ADVERTISING RATES:
Full Page Colour .... SEK 10800
SCC .... SEK 90
CONSUMER: CONSUMER ELECTRONICS: Games

GAMEREACTOR MAGAZINE; WEBB
1844533W78D-420
Editorial: Hamngatan 10, 831 31 ÖSTERSUND
Tel: 63 10 11 23
Email: info@gamereactor.se **Web site:** http://www.gamereactor.se
Freq: Daily; **Cover Price:** Free; **Circ:** 24,466 Unique Users
Editor: Jonas Mäki; **Editor-in-Chief:** Petter Hegevall; **Publisher:** Petter Hegevall
Language(s): Swedish
ADVERTISING RATES:
SCC .... SEK 16
CONSUMER: CONSUMER ELECTRONICS: Games

GÅRD & TORP
1645381W57-114
Editorial: Lilla Nygatan 20, 111 28 STOCKHOLM
Tel: 8 702 13 40 **Fax:** 86948510
Email: red@gardochtorp.se **Web site:** http://www.gardochtorp.se
Freq: 6 issues yearly - 8 nr/år; **Circ:** 20,000
Editor-in-Chief: Gunilla von Platen; **Advertising Manager:** Anders Ericsson
Language(s): Swedish
ADVERTISING RATES:
Full Page Colour .... SEK 19100
SCC .... SEK 159.20
Copy instructions: *Copy Date:* 30 days prior to publication date
BUSINESS: ENVIRONMENT & POLLUTION

GASOLINE MAGAZINE
1803862W77A-257
Editorial: Box 65, 736 22 KUNGSÖR **Tel:** 227 121 40
Email: redaktion@gasolinemagazine.se **Web site:** http://www.gasolinemagazine.se
Freq: 6 issues yearly; **Circ:** 15,000
Editor: Peter Larsson; **Editor-in-Chief:** Mattias Hammarstedt; **Advertising Manager:** Dan Larsson
Language(s): Swedish
CONSUMER: MOTORING & CYCLING: Motoring

GÄSTRIKLANDS TIDNING; WEBB
1846269W65A-1062
Editorial: 806 45 GÄVLE **Tel:** 26 54 30 30
Fax: 26 54 30 35
Email: gastriklandstidning@sveagruppen.se **Web site:** http://www.gastriklandstidning.se
Freq: Daily; **Cover Price:** Free; **Circ:** 9,000 Unique Users
Editor-in-Chief: Bo Pettersson; **Advertising Manager:** Peter Svensson; **Publisher:** Olle Wärmlöf
Language(s): Swedish
NATIONAL DAILY & SUNDAY NEWSPAPERS: National Daily Newspapers

GASTROKURIREN
1804045W56A-351
Editorial: Mediahuset i Göteborg AB, Marieholmsgatan 10, 415 02 GOTEBORG
Tel: 31 707 19 30 **Fax:** 31848682
Email: leif.torkvist@ki.se **Web site:** http://www.svenskgastroenterologi.se
Freq: Quarterly; **Circ:** 2,800
Editor: Leif Törkvist
Language(s): Swedish
BUSINESS: HEALTH & MEDICAL

GATE REPORT
1809895W14A-312
Editorial: Mediafabriken, 111 27 STOCKHOLM
Tel: 8 508 807 78 **Fax:** 8 587 075 01
Email: tomas@gatereport.se **Web site:** http://www.mediafabriken.se
Freq: 6 issues yearly; **Circ:** 75,000
Editor: Tomas Borgå
Language(s): Swedish
BUSINESS: COMMERCE, INDUSTRY & MANAGEMENT

GAUDEAMUS
749789W62A-405
Editorial: Box 500 06, 104 05 STOCKHOLM
Tel: 8 674 62 49 **Fax:** 8 16 71 68
Email: gaudeamus@sus.su.se **Web site:** http://www.gaudeamus.se
Freq: 6 issues yearly; **Circ:** 23,800
Editor-in-Chief: Amalthea Frantz; **Advertising Manager:** Efva Bengtsson; **Publisher:** Amalthea Frantz
Language(s): Swedish
ADVERTISING RATES:
Full Page Colour .... SEK 25900
SCC .... SEK 161.88
BUSINESS: CHURCH & SCHOOL EQUIPMENT & EDUCATION: Education

GEFLA HÖGTRYCK
751004W62A-410
Editorial: Box 6018, 800 06 GÄVLE **Tel:** 26 64 86 23
Fax: 26 60 96 51
Email: gh@geflestudentkar.se **Web site:** http://www.midgardhig.se
Freq: 6 issues yearly; **Circ:** 2,500
Editor-in-Chief: Rossar Vestin; **Publisher:** Sandra Eklund
Language(s): Swedish
BUSINESS: CHURCH & SCHOOL EQUIPMENT & EDUCATION: Education

GEFLE DAGBLAD
50782W67B-4200
Editorial: Box 367, 801 05 GÄVLE **Tel:** 26 15 96 00
Email: gefle.dagblad@gd.se **Web site:** http://www.gd.se
Date Established: 1895
Circ: 26,500
Advertising Manager: Björn Ohlsson; **Publisher:** Christina Delby Vad-Schütt
Language(s): Swedish
ADVERTISING RATES:
Full Page Colour .... SEK 33360
SCC .... SEK 166.80
REGIONAL DAILY & SUNDAY NEWSPAPERS: Regional Daily Newspapers

GEFLE DAGBLAD; GD.SE
751243W74C-200
Editorial: Box 367, 801 05 GÄVLE **Tel:** 26 15 96 00
Email: gefle.dagblad@gd.se **Web site:** http://www.gd.se
Freq: Daily; **Cover Price:** Free; **Circ:** 14,181 Unique Users
Language(s): Swedish
CONSUMER: WOMEN'S INTEREST CONSUMER MAGAZINES: Home & Family

GENSVAR
51438W56A-280
Editorial: Box 1386, Sturegatan 4, 5 tr., 172 27 SUNDBYBERG **Tel:** 8 546 405 10 **Fax:** 8 546 405 14
Web site: http://www.fbis.se
Freq: Quarterly; **Circ:** 4,500
Advertising Manager: Eva Sarman
Profile: Magazine containing information, articles and news of interest to people suffering from haemophilia.
Language(s): Swedish
BUSINESS: HEALTH & MEDICAL

GENUS
752088W55-25
Editorial: Box 200, Nationella sekretariatet för genusforskning, 405 30 GOTEBORG
Tel: 31 786 56 02 **Fax:** 317865604
Email: siri.reuterstrand@genus.se **Web site:** http://www.genus.se
Freq: Quarterly; **Circ:** 14,000
Editor: Inga-Bodil Hermansson
Language(s): Swedish
BUSINESS: APPLIED SCIENCE & LABORATORIES

GEOLOGISKT FORUM
1842193W55-62
Editorial: c/o Qi-Media AB, Gjuterigatan 9, 553 18 JÖNKÖPING **Tel:** 708 20 50 10
Email: info@geologiskaforeningen.nu **Web site:** http://www.geologiskaforeningen.nu
Freq: Quarterly; **Circ:** 1,700
Language(s): Swedish
BUSINESS: APPLIED SCIENCE & LABORATORIES

GINSTEN
749818W56B-90
Editorial: Box 517, Landstinget Halland, 301 80 HALMSTAD **Tel:** 35 13 48 00
Email: ginsten@lthalland.se **Web site:** http://www.lthalland.se
Freq: 6 issues yearly; **Circ:** 9,000
Editor: Charlotte Johnsson; **Publisher:** Ann Fröström
Language(s): Swedish
BUSINESS: HEALTH & MEDICAL: Nursing

GITARR OCH LUTA
51081W76D-65
Editorial: c/o Mårten Falk, Järnvägsgatan 9, 640 34 SPARREHOLM **Tel:** 702 08 60 60
Email: redaktionen@sgls.nu **Web site:** http://www.sgls.nu
Freq: Quarterly; **Circ:** 1,100
Editor-in-Chief: Bengt Magnusson; **Advertising Manager:** Margareta Rörby
Profile: Magazine about the guitar and the flute.
Language(s): Swedish
CONSUMER: MUSIC & PERFORMING ARTS: Music

GJUTERIET
51439W14B-60
Editorial: Box 2033, 550 02 JÖNKÖPING
Tel: 36 301 217 **Fax:** 36 16 68 66
Email: gjuteriet@gjuteriforeningen.se **Web site:** http://www.gjuteriforeningen.se/gjuteriet
Date Established: 1911; **Freq:** Monthly; **Circ:** 1,800
Advertising Manager: Marie Gustafsson; **Publisher:** Dennis Karlsson
Profile: Magazine containing articles and information about casting and foundries.
Language(s): Swedish
ADVERTISING RATES:
Full Page Colour .... SEK 12000
SCC .... SEK 100
Copy instructions: *Copy Date:* 28 days prior to publication date
BUSINESS: COMMERCE, INDUSTRY & MANAGEMENT: Industry & Factories

GLAS
749805W4E-125
Editorial: Box 16286, 103 25 STOCKHOLM
Tel: 8 453 90 70 **Fax:** 84539071
Email: info@gbf.se **Web site:** http://www.gbf.se
Date Established: 1934; **Freq:** 6 issues yearly; **Circ:** 5,000
Advertising Manager: Hélène Ulvander; **Publisher:** Per Sjöhult
Language(s): Swedish
ADVERTISING RATES:
Full Page Colour .... SEK 16900
SCC .... SEK 140.83
BUSINESS: ARCHITECTURE & BUILDING: Building

GLAS OCH PORSLIN
50274W12B-75
Editorial: Haneson Förlag, Stationsvägen 2, 430 30 FRILLESÅS **Tel:** 340 65 77 20 **Fax:** 340 65 77 45

Web site: http://www.glasochporslin.se
Freq: Quarterly; **Circ:** 2,500
Editor: Titti Thorsell; **Managing Director:** Göran Eklund; **Publisher:** Göran Eklund
Profile: Magazine about the glass and porcelain trade.
Language(s): Swedish
Readership: Aimed at gift shop owners, designers and craftsmen.
ADVERTISING RATES:
Full Page Colour .... SEK 13000
SCC .... SEK 108.33
BUSINESS: CERAMICS, POTTERY & GLASS: Glass

GLAZE
1664365W74A-151
Editorial: Hammarby Kajväg 18, 120 30 STOCKHOLM **Tel:** 8 587 481 00
Email: glaze@fridaforlag.se **Web site:** http://www.fridaforlag.se
Freq: Monthly; **Circ:** 39,000
Advertising Manager: Nadja Nabelsi; **Publisher:** Ove Jerselius
Language(s): Swedish
ADVERTISING RATES:
Full Page Colour .... SEK 27900
SCC .... SEK 232.50
CONSUMER: WOMEN'S INTEREST CONSUMER MAGAZINES: Women's Interest

GLID MAGAZINE
1663915W75G-113
Editorial: Box 22 559, 104 22 STOCKHOLM
Tel: 7 704 571 16 **Fax:** 86520300
Email: info@glidmagazine.se **Web site:** http://www.glidmagazine.se
Freq: Annual; **Circ:** 10,000
Advertising Manager: Christopher Rimér; **Publisher:** Karin Bångman
Language(s): Swedish
CONSUMER: SPORT: Winter Sports

GLID- SVENSK LÄNGDÅKNING
1641224W75G-111
Editorial: Råstavägen 14, SE-169 54 STOCKHOLM
Tel: 8 545 535 30
Email: roberto.vacchi@glidmagazine.se **Web site:** http://www.glidmagazine.se
Freq: 6 issues yearly; **Circ:** 10,000
Language(s): Swedish
ADVERTISING RATES:
Full Page Colour .... SEK 26000
SCC .... SEK 216.67
CONSUMER: SPORT: Winter Sports

GLITTER
1804007W74Q-159
Editorial: Frida Förlag, Hammarby kajväg 18, 120 30 STOCKHOLM **Tel:** 8 587 481 00
Email: glitter@fridaforlag.se
Freq: Monthly; **Circ:** 35,000
Editor-in-Chief: Julia Svensson; **Publisher:** Ove Jerselius
Language(s): Swedish
ADVERTISING RATES:
Full Page Colour .... SEK 22900
SCC .... SEK 190.83
CONSUMER: WOMEN'S INTEREST CONSUMER MAGAZINES: Lifestyle

GLOBAL MAGAZINE
750979W14L-155
Editorial: AB Volvo VHK, 405 08 GÖTEBORG
Tel: 31 66 11 77
Email: global@volvo.com
Freq: 6 issues yearly; **Circ:** 30,000
Editor-in-Chief: Susanne Hanssen; **Publisher:** Susanne Hanssen
Language(s): Swedish
ADVERTISING RATES:
Full Page Colour .... SEK 39900
SCC .... SEK 249.38
BUSINESS: COMMERCE, INDUSTRY & MANAGEMENT: Trade Unions

GNAGAREN
1639401W75B-51
Editorial: Box 21166, 100 31 STOCKHOLM
Tel: 737 24 01 86
Email: gnagaren@blackarmy.se **Web site:** http://www.blackarmy.se
Freq: Quarterly; **Circ:** 2,500
Editor: Joakim Hall
Language(s): Swedish
CONSUMER: SPORT: Football

GO GIRL
1691668W74A-154
Editorial: Egmont Kärnan, 205 08 MALMO
Tel: 40 693 94 00
Email: gogirl@egmont.se
Freq: 6 issues yearly; **Circ:** 30,000
Editor: Marie Olsson
Language(s): Swedish
ADVERTISING RATES:
Full Page Colour .... SEK 12800
SCC .... SEK 106.66
CONSUMER: WOMEN'S INTEREST CONSUMER MAGAZINES: Women's Interest

GOAL
750754W75J-40
Editorial: 205 08 MALMO **Tel:** 40 693 94 00
Fax: 406939549
Email: goal@egmont.se **Web site:** http://www.egmonttidskrifter.se
Date Established: 1994; **Freq:** Monthly; **Circ:** 22,800
Language(s): Swedish
Copy instructions: *Copy Date:* 30 days prior to publication date
CONSUMER: SPORT: Athletics

GODA GRANNAR
1674295W74C-454
Editorial: Box 95, 162 12 VÄLLINGBY
Tel: 8 508 370 33 **Fax:** 8 508 611 68
Email: lars.bergstrom@svebo.se **Web site:** http://www.svebo.se
Freq: Quarterly - (4nr/år); **Circ:** 28,000
Editor: Kenneth Claesson
Language(s): Swedish
ADVERTISING RATES:
SCC .... SEK 208.33
CONSUMER: WOMEN'S INTEREST CONSUMER MAGAZINES: Home & Family

GODOME
1996693W4A-39
Editorial: Box: 3640, 103 59 STOCKHOLM
Email: redaktionen@godome.se **Web site:** http://www.godome.se
Freq: Monthly; **Cover Price:** Free; **Circ:** 190,000
Publisher: Peter Rydås
Language(s): Swedish
ADVERTISING RATES:
Full Page Colour .... SEK 60000
BUSINESS: ARCHITECTURE & BUILDING: Architecture

GODS & GÅRDAR
51440W80A-80
Editorial: Gävlegatan 22, 113 92 STOCKHOLM
Tel: 8 588 365 60 **Fax:** 858836989
Email: godsogard@lrfmedia.lrf.se **Web site:** http://www.godsochgardar.se
Date Established: 1996; **Freq:** Monthly; **Circ:** 28,900
Editor: Nenne Wåhlander; **Advertising Manager:** Marita Kokkonen; **Publisher:** Eva Källström
Profile: Magazine containing articles and information about all aspects of country living.
Language(s): Swedish
ADVERTISING RATES:
Full Page Colour .... SEK 31000
SCC .... SEK 258.33
Copy instructions: *Copy Date:* 34 days prior to publication date
CONSUMER: RURAL & REGIONAL INTEREST: Rural Interest

GOLF DIGEST
51579W75D-75
Editorial: Egmont tidskrifter, Pyramidvägen 7, 169 91 SOLNA **Tel:** 8 506 678 31 **Fax:** 8 506 678 09
Email: redaktionen@golfdigest.se **Web site:** http://www.golfdigest.se
Date Established: 1986; **Freq:** 6 issues yearly; **Circ:** 29,400
Advertising Manager: Magnus Åhlund; **Publisher:** Tommy Jeppsson
Profile: Magazine featuring news and information on golf.
Language(s): Swedish
Readership: Aimed at golf players and enthusiasts.
ADVERTISING RATES:
Full Page Colour .... SEK 25900
SCC .... SEK 215.80
Copy instructions: *Copy Date:* 45 days prior to publication date
CONSUMER: SPORT: Golf

GOLFBLADET
1803942W75A-210
Editorial: Skonertgränd 9, 260 93 TOREKOV
Tel: 431 152 50
Email: info@golfbladet.se **Web site:** http://www.golfbladet.se
Freq: Quarterly; **Circ:** 50,000
Advertising Manager: Pierre Åkerström; **Publisher:** Fredrik Richter
Language(s): Swedish
ADVERTISING RATES:
Full Page Colour .... SEK 29000
CONSUMER: SPORT

GOLFRESAN
1623573W75J-261
Editorial: Alströmergatan 20 A, 112 47 STOCKHOLM
Tel: 8 410 191 90 **Fax:** 86543819
Email: info@golfresan.se **Web site:** http://www.golfresan.se
Freq: 6 issues yearly; **Circ:** 32,700
Editor: Johan Dahlqvist; **Advertising Manager:** Johan Pagels; **Publisher:** Mikael Andersson
Language(s): Swedish
ADVERTISING RATES:
Full Page Colour .... SEK 39500
SCC .... SEK 329.16
CONSUMER: SPORT: Athletics

GOLF.SE
1844536W75A-213
Editorial: Box 84, 182 11 DANDERYD
Tel: 8 622 15 00 **Fax:** 8 755 84 39
Email: info@sgf.golf.se **Web site:** http://www.golf.se
Freq: Daily; **Cover Price:** Free; **Circ:** 86,711 Unique Users
Publisher: Tobias Bergman
Language(s): Swedish
CONSUMER: SPORT

GOLV TILL TAK
50205W4B-30
Editorial: Box 12250, 102 26 STOCKHOLM
Tel: 8 651 56 20
Email: redaktion@gtt.se **Web site:** http://www.golvtilltak.nu
Freq: 6 issues yearly; **Circ:** 2,500
Editor-in-Chief: Elisabeth Sedig
Profile: Journal about the flooring and wallcovering trades.
Language(s): Swedish
ADVERTISING RATES:
Full Page Colour .... SEK 17400
SCC .... SEK 145
BUSINESS: ARCHITECTURE & BUILDING: Interior Design & Flooring

GÖR DET SJÄLV
51142W79A-100
Editorial: Gör Det Själv, 205 50 MALMO
Tel: 8 555 454 02 **Fax:** 8 555 454 50
Email: redaktionen@gds.se **Web site:** http://www.gds.se
Freq: Monthly; **Circ:** 49,100
Profile: Magazine containing articles, news and information about DIY.
Language(s): Swedish
Readership: Read by DIY enthusiasts.
ADVERTISING RATES:
Full Page Colour .... SEK 33800
SCC .... SEK 281.70
CONSUMER: HOBBIES & DIY

GÖTEBORGS FRIA TIDNING; WEBB
1844772W65A-1024
Editorial: Såggatan 46, 414 67 GÖTEBORG
Tel: 31 704 80 80 **Fax:** 31 704 80 89
Email: tips@fria.nu **Web site:** http://www.goteborgsfria.nu
Freq: Daily; **Cover Price:** Free; **Circ:** 1,267 Unique Users
Editor: Madelene Axelsson
Language(s): Swedish
ADVERTISING RATES:
SCC .... SEK 17
NATIONAL DAILY & SUNDAY NEWSPAPERS: National Daily Newspapers

GÖTEBORGS-POSTEN
50783W67B-4250
Editorial: Polhemsplatsen 5, 405 02 GOTEBORG
Tel: 31 62 40 00 **Fax:** 31 80 27 69
Email: nyheter@gp.se **Web site:** http://www.gp.se
Freq: Daily; **Circ:** 228,200
Language(s): Swedish
ADVERTISING RATES:
Full Page Colour .... SEK 144000
SCC .... SEK 636.96
REGIONAL DAILY & SUNDAY NEWSPAPERS: Regional Daily Newspapers

GÖTEBORGS-POSTEN; GP.SE
752300W65A-605
Editorial: Polhemsplatsen 5, 405 02 GOTEBORG
Tel: 31 62 40 00
Email: webbred@gp.se **Web site:** http://www.gp.se
Freq: Daily; **Circ:** 125,492 Unique Users
Language(s): Swedish
NATIONAL DAILY & SUNDAY NEWSPAPERS: National Daily Newspapers

GÖTHEBORGSKE SPIONEN
51442W83-50
Editorial: Studenternas Hus, Götabergsgatan 17, 411 34 GÖTEBORG **Tel:** 31 773 53 70 **Fax:** 31 773 53 71
Email: redaktion@spionen.se **Web site:** http://www.spionen.se
Date Established: 1936; **Freq:** 6 issues yearly; **Circ:** 25,000
Editor-in-Chief: Lina Söderström; **Publisher:** Lina Söderström
Profile: Magazine covering all activities of the University of Gothenburg.
Language(s): Swedish
Readership: Aimed at students and employees.
ADVERTISING RATES:
Full Page Colour .... SEK 50000
SCC .... SEK 312.5
CONSUMER: STUDENT PUBLICATIONS

GOTLANDS ALLEHANDA
50851W67B-4300
Editorial: Box 1284, 621 23 VISBY **Tel:** 498 20 25 50
Fax: 498 20 25 97
Email: redaktion@gotlandsallehanda.se **Web site:** http://www.helagotland.se
Date Established: 1872
Circ: 10,100
Editor: Ingvar Andersson; **Publisher:** Ulrica Fransson Ingelmark
Language(s): Swedish
ADVERTISING RATES:
Full Page Colour .... SEK 31136
SCC .... SEK 155.68
REGIONAL DAILY & SUNDAY NEWSPAPERS: Regional Daily Newspapers

GOTLANDS ALLEHANDA; HELAGOTLAND.SE
1843254W65A-975
Editorial: Box 1284, 621 23 VISBY **Tel:** 49820 25 50
Fax: 49820 25 97
Email: redaktion@gotlandsallehanda.se **Web site:** http://www.helagotland.se
Freq: Daily; **Cover Price:** Free; **Circ:** 45,000 Unique Users
Publisher: Patrik Annerud
Language(s): Swedish
ADVERTISING RATES:
SCC .... SEK 31
NATIONAL DAILY & SUNDAY NEWSPAPERS: National Daily Newspapers

GOTLANDS TIDNINGAR
50852W67B-4350
Editorial: Box 1223, 621 23 VISBY **Tel:** 498 20 24 00
Fax: 498 20 24 30
Email: redaktion.gt@gotlandstidningar.se **Web site:** http://www.helagotland.se
Date Established: 1983
Circ: 21,800
Editor: Dage Ericsson; **Advertising Manager:** Göran Hellström; **Publisher:** Ulf Hammarlund
Language(s): Swedish
ADVERTISING RATES:
Full Page Colour .... SEK 31136
SCC .... SEK 155.68
REGIONAL DAILY & SUNDAY NEWSPAPERS: Regional Daily Newspapers

GOTLANDSGUIDEN
51604W89C-50
Editorial: Norra Hansegatan 18, 621 41 VISBY
Tel: 498 21 00 00 **Fax:** 498 27 15 48
Email: nyheter@gotlandsguiden.se **Web site:** http://www.gotlandsguiden.se
Freq: Annual; **Cover Price:** Free; **Circ:** 200,000
Editor: Nicka Hellenberg; **Managing Director:** Gunnar Danielsson; **Advertising Manager:** Gunnar Danielsson; **Publisher:** Gunnar Danielsson
Profile: Magazine covering activities, events, attractions and accommodation in Gotland.
Language(s): Swedish
Readership: Aimed at tourists visiting the town of Gotland.
CONSUMER: HOLIDAYS & TRAVEL: Entertainment Guides

GOTLÄNDSKA.SE
751043W80-530
Editorial: Box 1087, 621 21 VISBY **Tel:** 49827 13 00
Fax: 498 21 17 46
Email: redaktion@gotland.net **Web site:** http://www.gotland.net/sv
Freq: Daily; **Cover Price:** Paid; **Circ:** 18,917 Unique Users
Advertising Manager: Ralph Kellquist; **Publisher:** Bo Eriksson
Language(s): Swedish
CONSUMER: RURAL & REGIONAL INTEREST

GOURMET
51002W74P-150
Editorial: Box 302 10, 104 25 STOCKHOLM
Tel: 8 505 301 00 **Fax:** 8 505 301 01
Email: info@gourmet.se **Web site:** http://www.gourmet.se
Freq: Monthly -, 10 gånger per år; **Circ:** 30,000
Editor: Fredrik Lagerqvist; **Advertising Manager:** Chatarina Rutegård; **Publisher:** Lars Peder Hedberg
Profile: Food and wine magazine.
Language(s): Swedish
ADVERTISING RATES:
Full Page Colour .... SEK 35200
SCC .... SEK 293.30
CONSUMER: WOMEN'S INTEREST CONSUMER MAGAZINES: Food & Cookery

GRAFIKNYTT
50479W41A-15
Editorial: Hornsgatan 6, 118 20 STOCKHOLM
Tel: 33 41 98 60 **Fax:** 33 13 27 58
Email: grafiknytt@grafiskasallskapet.se **Web site:** http://www.grafiskasallskapet.se
Date Established: 1958; **Freq:** Quarterly; **Circ:** 2,200
Editor-in-Chief: Björn Bredström; **Advertising Manager:** Björn Bredström; **Publisher:** Björn Bredström
Profile: Magazine containing news and information about the graphics industry.
Language(s): Swedish
BUSINESS: PRINTING & STATIONERY: Printing

GRAFISKT FORUM
50480W41A-30
Editorial: Box 601, 251 06 HELSINGBORG
Tel: 42 490 19 00 **Fax:** 42 490 19 99
Email: grafisktforum@mentoronline.se **Web site:** http://www.graphicnet.se
Date Established: 1895; **Freq:** Monthly; **Circ:** 3,700
Editor: Veronica Rönnlund; **Editor-in-Chief:** Marcus Pettersson; **Advertising Manager:** Max Milan

Profile: Magazine covering all aspects of the graphics and printing industries. Also covers IT and media.
Language(s): Swedish
ADVERTISING RATES:
Full Page Colour .... SEK 22900
SCC .... SEK 190.8
BUSINESS: PRINTING & STATIONERY: Printing

GRAFISKT FORUM; WEBB
1844792W41A-96
Tel: 42 490 19 00 **Fax:** 42 490 19 99
Email: grafisktforum@mentoronline.se **Web site:** http://www.graphicnet.se
Freq: Daily; **Cover Price:** Free; **Circ:** 2,467 Unique Users
Editor: Veronica Rönnlund; **Editor-in-Chief:** Uffe Berggren; **Publisher:** Uffe Berggren
Language(s): Swedish
ADVERTISING RATES:
SCC .... SEK 38
BUSINESS: PRINTING & STATIONERY: Printing

GRANA
634513W56A-281
Editorial: Taylor & Francis AB, Box 3255, 103 65 STOCKHOLM **Tel:** 8 440 80 40 **Fax:** 8 440 80 50
Email: else.marie.friis@nrm.se **Web site:** http://www.tandf.no
Freq: Quarterly; **Circ:** 500
Editor: D. Cantrill
Language(s): Swedish
BUSINESS: HEALTH & MEDICAL

GRAND
1803920W74Q-167
Editorial: Grand Publishing AB, 115 56 STOCKHOLM
Tel: 8 535 280 50 **Fax:** 86639349
Email: info@grandpublishing.se **Web site:** http://www.grandpublishing.se
Freq: Quarterly; **Circ:** 31,700
Publisher: Britta Rossander
Language(s): Swedish
CONSUMER: WOMEN'S INTEREST CONSUMER MAGAZINES: Lifestyle

GREKER I NORDEN
751145W76A-155
Editorial: c/o Grekiska Riksförbundet, Box 1900, 104 32 STOCKHOLM **Tel:** 8 627 00 27 **Fax:** 8 627 00 26
Email: info@grekiskariksforbundet.se **Web site:** http://www.grekiskariksforbundet.se
Date Established: 1976; **Freq:** Quarterly; **Circ:** 3,200
Editor: Eleni Aloutzanidou; **Publisher:** Komninos Chaideftos
Language(s): Swedish
CONSUMER: MUSIC & PERFORMING ARTS: Cinema

GRIP MAGASIN (MALMÖ AVIATION'S MAGAZINE)
1697228W50-114
Editorial: Repslagargatan 17 B, 11846 STOCKHOLM
Tel: 8 545 064 00 **Fax:** 8 6795710
Email: nils.norberg@res.se
Freq: 6 issues yearly; **Circ:** 20,000
Publisher: Nils Norberg
Language(s): Swedish
BUSINESS: TRAVEL & TOURISM

GRIS
1625816W64H-16
Editorial: Berga, Stenåsen 311, 692 93 KUMLA
Tel: 19 57 60 90 **Fax:** 19 58 00 50
Email: gris@agrar.se **Web site:** http://grisportalen.se
Freq: Monthly; **Circ:** 3,700
Editor-in-Chief: Lars-Gunnar Lannhard; **Publisher:** Lars-Gunnar Lannhard
Language(s): Swedish
BUSINESS: OTHER CLASSIFICATIONS: Veterinary

GROBLAD
752005W84B-246
Editorial: c/o Johansson, Trastvägen 8, 374 50 ASARUM **Tel:** 454 874 75
Email: sonja.louise@telia.com **Web site:** http://www.nbv.se/skrivarklubben
Freq: Quarterly; **Circ:** 200
Editor: Gustav Karlsson; **Publisher:** Gustav Karlsson
Language(s): Swedish
CONSUMER: THE ARTS & LITERARY: Literary

GRÖNKÖPINGS VECKOBLAD
50938W73-43
Editorial: Box 2036, 103 11 STOCKHOLM
Tel: 8 643 38 46 **Fax:** 86433898
Email: gronkoping@lindco.se **Web site:** http://www.gronkoping.se
Date Established: 1902; **Freq:** Monthly; **Circ:** 13,500
Editor: Gunnar Ljusterdal; **Editor-in-Chief:** Ulf Schöldström; **Advertising Manager:** Fredrik Rydbeck
Profile: Magazine containing satire and humorous articles.
Language(s): Swedish
CONSUMER: NATIONAL & INTERNATIONAL PERIODICALS

GRÖNT
51185W82-87
Editorial: Pustegränd 1-3, 281 37 STOCKHOLM
Email: gront@mp.se **Web site:** http://www.mp.se/gront
Date Established: 1988; **Freq:** Quarterly; **Circ:** 8,500
Editor: Sofi Klang
Profile: Magazine containing articles, information and political news from the Swedish Green Party.
Language(s): Swedish
ADVERTISING RATES:
Full Page Colour .... SEK 17000
SCC .... SEK 141.66
CONSUMER: CURRENT AFFAIRS & POLITICS

GRÖNYTELEVERANTÖRERNA
50422W32D-60
Editorial: Vasagatan 20, 682 30 FILIPSTAD
Tel: 590 102 60 **Fax:** 590 102 60
Email: redaktion@gronyte.com **Web site:** http://www.gronyte.com
Date Established: 1995; **Freq:** Quarterly; **Circ:** 6,200
Editor: Jan Arvidson; **Editor-in-Chief:** Jan Arvidson; **Advertising Manager:** Jan Arvidson; **Publisher:** Jan Arvidson
Profile: Magazine for employers and employees working on the upkeep and maintenance of parks, gardens, golf courses, football fields and churchyards. Contains technical information as well as articles about entertainment and leisure.
Language(s): Swedish
ADVERTISING RATES:
Full Page Colour .... SEK 13900
BUSINESS: LOCAL GOVERNMENT, LEISURE & RECREATION: Parks

GRUFVAN
752006W76A-160
Editorial: Norra Parkv. 18, 730 91 RIDDARHYTTAN
Tel: 222 132 13
Email: info@larsanderssonforlag.se **Web site:** http://www.larsanderssonforlag.se
Freq: Half-yearly; **Circ:** 300
Publisher: Lars Andersson
Language(s): Swedish
CONSUMER: MUSIC & PERFORMING ARTS: Cinema

GRUNDSKOLETIDNINGEN
50725W62C-210
Editorial: Box 34, 171 11 SOLNA **Tel:** 8 545 453 30
Email: skolbarn@fortbild.se **Web site:** http://www.fortbild.se
Freq: 6 issues yearly; **Circ:** 7,800
Editor: Steve Wretman; **Editor-in-Chief:** Helene Moreau; **Advertising Manager:** Ulf Jacobsson
Profile: Magazine about changes and developments in primary and secondary schools.
Language(s): Swedish
Readership: Read by headmasters, teachers and people working in kindergartens and preschools.
BUSINESS: CHURCH & SCHOOL EQUIPMENT & EDUCATION: Junior Education

GRUNDVATTEN
50667W57-22
Editorial: SGU, Box 670, 751 28 UPPSALA
Tel: 18 17 90 00 **Fax:** 18 17 92 10
Email: kerstin.finn@sgu.se **Web site:** http://www.sgu.se
Freq: Half-yearly; **Circ:** 2,500
Editor-in-Chief: Birger Fogdestam; **Publisher:** Birger Fogdestam
Profile: Journal of the Swedish Geological Institute.
Language(s): Swedish
BUSINESS: ENVIRONMENT & POLLUTION

GT
633896W67B-4375
Editorial: Kungstorget 2, 401 26 GOTEBORG
Tel: 31 725 90 00
Email: redaktionen@gt.se **Web site:** http://www.gt.se
Date Established: 1902
Circ: 57,700
Editor: Kicki Lindbergh; **Editor-in-Chief:** Lars Näslund; **Publisher:** Thomas Mattson
Profile: Newspaper covering the western parts of Sweden.
Language(s): Swedish
ADVERTISING RATES:
Full Page Colour .... SEK 36900
SCC .... SEK 184.50
Copy instructions: *Copy Date:* 4 days prior to publication date
REGIONAL DAILY & SUNDAY NEWSPAPERS: Regional Daily Newspapers

GT; GT.SE
1843552W65A-1000
Editorial: Box 417, 401 26 GOTEBORG
Tel: 31 725 90 00
Email: redaktionen@gt.se **Web site:** http://www.gt.se
Freq: Daily; **Cover Price:** Free; **Circ:** 350,000 Unique Users
Publisher: Per-Anders Broberg
Language(s): Swedish
NATIONAL DAILY & SUNDAY NEWSPAPERS: National Daily Newspapers

GU-JOURNALEN
634514W62J-85
Editorial: Göteborgs universitet, Box 100, 405 30 GÖTEBORG **Tel:** 31 786 10 21 **Fax:** 31 786 43 54
Email: gu-journalen@gu.se **Web site:** http://www.gu-journalen.gu.se
Date Established: 1997; **Freq:** 6 issues yearly; **Circ:** 6,400
Editor: Eva Lundgren; **Editor-in-Chief:** Allan Eriksson; **Advertising Manager:** Anders Eurén; **Publisher:** Allan Eriksson
Profile: Magazine containing information about education and research at Gothenburg University.
Language(s): Swedish
Readership: Read by teachers, lecturers, professors and administrative personnel.
BUSINESS: CHURCH & SCHOOL EQUIPMENT & EDUCATION: Teachers & Education Management

GYMNASIEGUIDEN
634516W62D-100
Editorial: Box 1207, 131 52 NACKA STRAND
Tel: 8 545 424 50 **Fax:** 8 729 00 75
Email: info@framtid.se **Web site:** http://www.gymnasieguiden.se
Date Established: 1993; **Freq:** Quarterly; **Circ:** 125,000
Publisher: Kristoffer Jarefeldt
Profile: Magazine covering all aspects of secondary school education.
Language(s): Swedish
Readership: Aimed at students.
BUSINESS: CHURCH & SCHOOL EQUIPMENT & EDUCATION: Secondary Education

HABIT SKO & MODE
50533W47A-25
Editorial: Box 72001, 181 72 STOCKHOLM
Tel: 8 670 41 00 **Fax:** 8 661 64 55
Email: habitred@mentoronline.se **Web site:** http://www.habit.se
Freq: Monthly; **Circ:** 6,400
Advertising Manager: Carolina Ramsten; **Publisher:** Thomas Karlsson
Profile: Professional magazine for the fashion trade covering retail, manufacture, textiles and fashion fairs in Sweden and abroad. Clothing for men, women and children is featured including leisure and sports wear, leather, underwear and swimwear.
Language(s): Swedish
ADVERTISING RATES:
Full Page Colour .... SEK 28795
SCC .... SEK 239.95
Copy instructions: *Copy Date:* 24 days prior to publication date
BUSINESS: CLOTHING & TEXTILES

HÆMA
1828707W55-59
Tel: 703 47 47 63 **Fax:** 8 546 405 49
Email: haema@blodcancerforbundet.se **Web site:** http://www.blodcancerforbundet.se
Freq: Quarterly; **Circ:** 3,800
Editor: Hasse Sandberg
Language(s): Swedish
Copy instructions: *Copy Date:* 45 days prior to publication date
BUSINESS: APPLIED SCIENCE & LABORATORIES

HÄFTEN FÖR KRITISKA STUDIER
752008W84B-251
Editorial: c/o Fredriksson, Tulegatan 25 2 tr ög, 113 53 STOCKHOLM **Tel:** 8 673 22 07 **Fax:** 8 673 22 07
Email: red@haften.org **Web site:** http://www.haften.org
Freq: Quarterly; **Circ:** 1,300
Editor: Annika Åkerblom; **Advertising Manager:** Göran Fredriksson
Language(s): Swedish
CONSUMER: THE ARTS & LITERARY: Literary

HALLANDS AFFÄRER
51149W80-50
Editorial: Box 617, 301 16 HALMSTAD
Tel: 35 18 19 80
Email: haff@textmedia.se **Web site:** http://www.textmedia.se
Date Established: 1984; **Freq:** Monthly; **Circ:** 35,000
Editor: Torsten Nilsson; **Publisher:** Sverker Emanuelsson
Profile: Newspaper for the Halmstad region.
Language(s): Swedish
CONSUMER: RURAL & REGIONAL INTEREST

HALLANDS NYHETER
50777W67B-4400
Editorial: 311 81 FALKENBERG **Tel:** 346 290 00
Fax: 346 291 20
Email: redaktionen@hn.se **Web site:** http://www.hn.se
Date Established: 1905
Circ: 31,200
Editor: Anders Lindström; **Advertising Manager:** Lars Berander; **Publisher:** Anders Svensson
Language(s): Swedish
ADVERTISING RATES:
Full Page Colour .... SEK 38880
SCC .... SEK 194.40
REGIONAL DAILY & SUNDAY NEWSPAPERS: Regional Daily Newspapers

HALLANDS NYHETER; WWW.HN.SE
1843545W65A-994
Editorial: 311 81 FALKENBERG **Tel:** 346 290 00
Fax: 346 291 20
Email: redaktionen@hn.se **Web site:** http://www.hn.se
Freq: Daily; **Cover Price:** Free; **Circ:** 9,559 Unique Users
Publisher: Anders Svensson
Language(s): Swedish
NATIONAL DAILY & SUNDAY NEWSPAPERS: National Daily Newspapers

HALLANDSPOSTEN
50784W67B-4450
Editorial: 301 81 HALMSTAD **Tel:** 10471 51 00
Fax: 35 21 37 14
Email: redaktionen@hallandsposten.se **Web site:** http://www.hallandsposten.se
Circ: 32,900
Editor: Ulrika Ahlberg; **Publisher:** Viveka Hedbjörk
Language(s): Swedish
ADVERTISING RATES:
Full Page Colour .... SEK 50500
SCC .... SEK 252.50
REGIONAL DAILY & SUNDAY NEWSPAPERS: Regional Daily Newspapers

HALLANDSPOSTEN; WEBB
1843540W65A-989
Editorial: 301 81 HALMSTAD **Tel:** 35 14 75 00
Fax: 35213714
Email: redaktionen@hallandsposten.se **Web site:** http://www.hallandsposten.se
Freq: Daily; **Cover Price:** Free; **Circ:** 13,814 Unique Users
Publisher: Sverker Emanuelsson
Language(s): Swedish
NATIONAL DAILY & SUNDAY NEWSPAPERS: National Daily Newspapers

HÄLLEKIS-KURIREN; WEBB
1847164W65A-1086
Editorial: Duhagsvägen 1E, 53374 HÄLLEKIS
Tel: 510 540 022 **Fax:** 510 540 022
Email: info@hallekis.com **Web site:** http://www.hallekis.com
Freq: Daily; **Cover Price:** Free; **Circ:** 3,000 Unique Users
Editor-in-Chief: Stefan Sjöö; **Publisher:** Stefan Sjöö
Language(s): Swedish
NATIONAL DAILY & SUNDAY NEWSPAPERS: National Daily Newspapers

HÄLSA - FÖR KROPP OCH SJÄL I BALANS
50986W74G-50
Editorial: Budadress: Hälsingegatan 49, Forma Publishing Group, Box 6630, 113 82 STOCKHOLM
Tel: 8 728 24 66 **Fax:** 8 545 703 49
Email: info@halsa.se **Web site:** http://www.halsa.se
Date Established: 1940; **Freq:** Monthly; **Circ:** 56,900
Advertising Manager: Tomas Karlsson
Profile: Magazine for those interested in health food, exercise and the health food industry.
Language(s): Swedish
ADVERTISING RATES:
Full Page Colour .... SEK 32500
SCC .... SEK 270.83
Copy instructions: *Copy Date:* 27 days prior to publication date
CONSUMER: WOMEN'S INTEREST CONSUMER MAGAZINES: Slimming & Health

HÄLSA & VETENSKAP
1998219W74G-236
Tel: 8 790 33 00
Email: redaktionen@halsavetenskap.se **Web site:** http://www.halsavetenskap.se
Freq: Quarterly; **Circ:** 33,000
Advertising Manager: Britt-Marie Aronsson; **Publisher:** Jonas Hultkvist
Language(s): Swedish
Copy instructions: *Copy Date:* 38 days prior to publication date
CONSUMER: WOMEN'S INTEREST CONSUMER MAGAZINES: Slimming & Health

HÄLSAN I CENTRUM
752050W56B-95
Editorial: Mediahuset i Göteborg, 415 02 GÖTEBORG **Tel:** 31 707 19 30
Email: leila.haapaniemi@sll.se **Web site:** http://www.distriktssköterska.com
Freq: Quarterly; **Circ:** 7,500
Editor: Leila Haapaniemi; **Publisher:** Kristina Hesslund
Language(s): Swedish
BUSINESS: HEALTH & MEDICAL: Nursing

HÄLSOTECKEN
1803858W56A-346
Editorial: Landstinget i Östergötland, 581 91 LINKÖPING **Tel:** 13 22 20 00
Email: halsotecken@lio.se **Web site:** http://www.lio.se
Freq: Half-yearly; **Circ:** 220,000
Editor: Susanne Fridberg
Language(s): Swedish

ADVERTISING RATES:
Full Page Colour .... SEK 50000
SCC .... SEK 416.70
BUSINESS: HEALTH & MEDICAL

HANDBOLLSMAGASINET
51064W75X-205
Editorial: c/o Media Spjuth AB, Box 3288, 550 03 JÖNKÖPING **Tel:** 36 30 36 30 **Fax:** 36 19 02 60
Email: info@handbollsmagasinet.se **Web site:** http://www.handbollsmagasinet.se
Freq: Quarterly; **Circ:** 11,800
Advertising Manager: Bengt Spjuth
Profile: Magazine of the Swedish Handball Association.
Language(s): Swedish
ADVERTISING RATES:
Full Page Colour .... SEK 10395
CONSUMER: SPORT: Other Sport

HANDELSKAMMARTIDNINGEN
50738W63-125
Editorial: Box 16050, 103 21 STOCKHOLM
Tel: 8 555 100 00 **Fax:** 856631600
Email: info@chamber.se **Web site:** http://www.chamber.se
Freq: 6 issues yearly; **Circ:** 9,800
Advertising Manager: Sebastian Tibbling; **Publisher:** Marianne Andrée
Profile: Magazine covering news from the Chamber of Commerce in Stockholm.
Language(s): Swedish
ADVERTISING RATES:
Full Page Colour .... SEK 21500
SCC .... SEK 179.17
BUSINESS: REGIONAL BUSINESS

HANDELSNYTT
50572W53-30
Editorial: Box 1146, 111 81 STOCKHOLM
Tel: 8 412 68 00 **Fax:** 8 21 43 33
Email: handelsnytt@handels.se **Web site:** http://www.handelsnytt.se
Freq: Monthly; **Circ:** 149,000
Editor-in-Chief: Anna Filipsson; **Publisher:** Anna Filipsson
Profile: Magazine covering all aspects of the retail trade.
Language(s): Swedish
ADVERTISING RATES:
Full Page Colour .... SEK 24900
SCC .... SEK 207.5
BUSINESS: RETAILING & WHOLESALING

HANDELSNYTT; WEBB
1847181W14A-345
Editorial: Box 1146, 111 81 STOCKHOLM
Tel: 8 412 68 00 **Fax:** 8 21 43 33
Email: handelsnytt@handels.se **Web site:** http://www.handelsnytt.se
Freq: Daily; **Cover Price:** Free; **Circ:** 23,043 Unique Users
Editor-in-Chief: Anna Filipsson; **Advertising Manager:** Agneta Erneberg; **Publisher:** Anna Filipsson
Language(s): Swedish
ADVERTISING RATES:
SCC .... SEK 41
BUSINESS: COMMERCE, INDUSTRY & MANAGEMENT

HANDIKAPPIDROTT
51362W94F-50
Editorial: Sigma, Havregatan 7, 118 59 STOCKHOLM **Tel:** 8 640 90 21 **Fax:** 8 640 29 69
Email: handikappidrott@bostream.nu **Web site:** http://www.shif.se
Freq: 6 issues yearly; **Circ:** 4,000
Editor: Anita Gullberg; **Publisher:** Stig Carlsson
Profile: Magazine about sports for the disabled.
Language(s): Swedish
CONSUMER: OTHER CLASSIFICATIONS: Disability

HÄNT BILD
1639392W74Q-152
Editorial: Box 27870, 115 93 STOCKHOLM
Tel: 8 679 46 00 **Fax:** 86794677
Email: bengt.gustavsson@aller.se **Web site:** http://www.hantbild.se
Freq: 26 issues yearly; **Circ:** 54,400
Publisher: Bengt Gustavsson
Language(s): Swedish
ADVERTISING RATES:
Full Page Colour .... SEK 24000
SCC .... SEK 200
CONSUMER: WOMEN'S INTEREST CONSUMER MAGAZINES: Lifestyle

HÄNT EXTRA
50946W74A-42_5
Editorial: Budadress: Tysta Gatan 12, Box 27870, 115 93 STOCKHOLM **Tel:** 8 679 46 00
Fax: 8 679 46 77
Email: jan.bard@aller.se
Freq: Weekly; **Circ:** 128,800
Editor-in-Chief: Bo Liljeberg; **Publisher:** Bengt Gustavsson
Profile: Magazine containing features on beauty, fashion and health.
Language(s): Swedish
ADVERTISING RATES:
Full Page Colour .... SEK 34000
SCC .... SEK 283
CONSUMER: WOMEN'S INTEREST CONSUMER MAGAZINES: Women's Interest

HAPARANDABLADET/ HAAPARANNANLEHTI
624337W67B-4525
Editorial: Box 144, 953 23 HAPARANDA
Tel: 922 280 00 **Fax:** 922 280 10
Email: redaktionen@haparandabladet.se **Web site:** http://www.haparandabladet.se
Date Established: 1882
Circ: 4,200
Advertising Manager: Anne-Mari Lahti; **Publisher:** Örjan Pekka
Language(s): Swedish
ADVERTISING RATES:
Full Page Colour .... SEK 25715
SCC .... SEK 128.57
REGIONAL DAILY & SUNDAY NEWSPAPERS: Regional Daily Newspapers

HÄR&NU KOMMUNALPENSIONÄREN
1803906W74Q-158
Editorial: Box 310 19, 413 21 GOTEBORG
Tel: 31 775 03 90
Email: redaktion@justmedia.se **Web site:** http://www.justmedia.se
Freq: 6 issues yearly; **Circ:** 147,700
Language(s): Swedish
ADVERTISING RATES:
Full Page Colour .... SEK 31600
CONSUMER: WOMEN'S INTEREST CONSUMER MAGAZINES: Lifestyle

HÄRLIGA HUND
1687286W81B-52
Editorial: 113 92 STOCKHOLM **Tel:** 8 588 366 00
Fax: 8 588 369 89
Email: harligahund@lrfmedia.lrf.se **Web site:** http://lrfmedia.se/?HarligaHund
Freq: Monthly; **Circ:** 33,800
Editor: Helena Nilsson; **Editor-in-Chief:** Helena Nimbratt; **Advertising Manager:** Ulla Jonsson
Language(s): Swedish
ADVERTISING RATES:
Full Page Colour .... SEK 21900
SCC .... SEK 182.5
CONSUMER: ANIMALS & PETS: Dogs

HÄST & RYTTARE
1741161W81D-132
Editorial: Ridsportens Hus, 734 94 STRÖMSHOLM
Tel: 220 456 00
Email: info@hastryttare.se **Web site:** http://www.ridsport.se
Freq: Monthly; **Circ:** 87,800
Editor: Helena Stenman; **Editor-in-Chief:** Anna af Sillén; **Advertising Manager:** Lotta Vikström
Language(s): Swedish
ADVERTISING RATES:
Full Page Colour .... SEK 23000
CONSUMER: ANIMALS & PETS: Horses & Ponies

HÄSTEN
51161W81D-50
Editorial: Hästens förlag, Kampavall, 540 17 LERDALA **Tel:** 511 822 30
Email: tidningenhasten@telia.com **Web site:** http://www.hästen.nu
Date Established: 1920; **Freq:** 6 issues yearly; **Circ:** 10,000
Editor-in-Chief: Maria Cidh; **Publisher:** Maria Cidh
Profile: Magazine about horse-breeding, sport and leisure.
Language(s): Swedish
Readership: Aimed at owners and breeders of horses.
CONSUMER: ANIMALS & PETS: Horses & Ponies

HÄSTFOCUS
1696239W81D-129
Editorial: Box 7, 342 06 MOHEDA **Tel:** 472 705 25
Fax: 472 716 00
Email: ulf@hastfocus.se **Web site:** http://www.hastfocus.se
Freq: Monthly; **Circ:** 29,000
Editor: Ulf Norén; **Editor-in-Chief:** Emma Norén; **Advertising Manager:** Monika Söderlund; **Publisher:** Ulf Norén
Language(s): Swedish
CONSUMER: ANIMALS & PETS: Horses & Ponies

HÄSTMAGAZINET
752070W81D-115
Editorial: Skommarvägen 3, 783 50 GUSTAFS
Tel: 8 588 366 20 **Fax:** 243 24 00 28
Email: info@hastmagazinet.com **Web site:** http://www.hastmagazinet.com
Freq: Monthly; **Circ:** 59,000
Editor: AnnaKarin Spjuth-Elvin; **Editor-in-Chief:** Robert Solin; **Publisher:** Robert Solin
Language(s): Swedish
ADVERTISING RATES:
Full Page Colour .... SEK 16300
SCC .... SEK 135.8
CONSUMER: ANIMALS & PETS: Horses & Ponies

HÄSTSPORT
51020W75E-30
Editorial: PL 6171, 722 94 SALA **Tel:** 224 242 43
Fax: 224 242 00
Email: hastsport@hastsportguiden.com **Web site:** http://web.hastsport.com
Freq: Quarterly; **Circ:** 16,000
Editor: Nils-Otto Bernerup; **Editor-in-Chief:** Willy Nilsson; **Advertising Manager:** Nils-Otto Bernerup; **Publisher:** Stefan Mannfalk
Profile: Magazine about equestrian sport.
Language(s): Swedish
CONSUMER: SPORT: Horse Racing

HELSINGBORGS DAGBLAD
50789W67B-4550
Editorial: 251 83 HELSINGBORG **Tel:** 42 489 90 00
Fax: 42 489 90 01
Email: redaktionen@hd.se **Web site:** http://www.hd.se
Date Established: 1867
Circ: 76,100
Editor: Lotta Hördin; **Publisher:** Lars Johansson
Language(s): Swedish
ADVERTISING RATES:
Full Page Colour .... SEK 116256
SCC .... SEK 335
REGIONAL DAILY & SUNDAY NEWSPAPERS: Regional Daily Newspapers

HELSINGBORGS DAGBLAD; HD.SE
1843538W65A-988
Editorial: 251 83 HELSINGBORG **Tel:** 42 489 90 00
Fax: 42 489 90 01
Email: redaktionen@hd.se **Web site:** http://www.hd.se
Freq: Daily; **Cover Price:** Free; **Circ:** 53,141 Unique Users
Publisher: Sören Karlsson
Language(s): Swedish
NATIONAL DAILY & SUNDAY NEWSPAPERS: National Daily Newspapers

HEM LJUVA HEM
752069W26D-85
Editorial: Box 30210, 104 25 STOCKHOLM
Tel: 8 501 188 50
Email: redaktionen@hemljuvahem.info **Web site:** http://www.hemljuvahem.info
Date Established: 1926; **Freq:** Monthly; **Circ:** 61,700
Publisher: Marie Heidenfors
Language(s): Swedish
ADVERTISING RATES:
Full Page Colour .... SEK 32500
SCC .... SEK 270.80
Copy instructions: *Copy Date:* 45 days prior to publication date
BUSINESS: GARDEN TRADE: Garden Trade Horticulture

HEM LJUVA HEM TRÄDGÅRD
1667257W26D-91
Editorial: Box 30210, 104 25 STOCKHOLM
Tel: 8 501 188 50 **Fax:** 850118851
Email: kerstin@hemljuvahem.info
Freq: Monthly - /6 nr feb-juli); **Circ:** 38,500
Language(s): Swedish
ADVERTISING RATES:
Full Page Colour .... SEK 29500
SCC .... SEK 245.80
BUSINESS: GARDEN TRADE: Garden Trade Horticulture

HEM & ANTIK
1655798W74C-448
Editorial: 105 44 STOCKHOLM **Tel:** 8 736 53 00
Fax: 87365441
Email: red@hem-antik.bonnier.se **Web site:** http://www.hemochantik.se
Freq: 6 issues yearly; **Circ:** 32,500
Language(s): Swedish
ADVERTISING RATES:
Full Page Colour .... SEK 29000
SCC .... SEK 241.70
Copy instructions: *Copy Date:* 33 days prior to publication date
CONSUMER: WOMEN'S INTEREST CONSUMER MAGAZINES: Home & Family

HEM & HYRA
1804019W1E-204
Editorial: Postadress: Box 7514, 103 92 STOCKHOLM **Tel:** 8 519 103 00 **Fax:** 8 519 103 10
Email: redaktionen@hemhyra.se **Web site:** http://www.hemhyra.se
Circ: 537,400
Editor: Elin Jönsson; **Advertising Manager:** Mie Karlsson
Language(s): Swedish
ADVERTISING RATES:
Full Page Colour .... SEK 45320
SCC .... SEK 366.70
BUSINESS: FINANCE & ECONOMICS: Property

HEM OCH SAMHÄLLE
50954W74C-34
Editorial: C/O BiCo PR, Strandvägen 50, 193 30 SIGTUNA **Tel:** 8 592 565 90
Email: bico.pr@zeta.telenordia.se **Web site:** http://www.hemochsamhalle.se
Date Established: 1926; **Freq:** Quarterly; **Circ:** 10,000
Editor: Birgitta Collenius; **Publisher:** Siw Warholm
Profile: Magazine containing information about home decoration and improvement, lifestyle and society.
Language(s): Swedish
CONSUMER: WOMEN'S INTEREST CONSUMER MAGAZINES: Home & Family

HEMBYGDEN
51150W80-60
Editorial: Box 34056, 100 26 STOCKHOLM
Tel: 8 695 00 15 **Fax:** 86950022
Email: rikskansliet@folkdansringen.se **Web site:** http://www.folkdansringen.se
Freq: Quarterly; **Circ:** 17,000
Editor: Stig Hellemarck; **Publisher:** Åke Melin
Profile: Magazine containing regional and cultural information about Sweden.
Language(s): Swedish
Readership: Read by residents and visitors.
CONSUMER: RURAL & REGIONAL INTEREST

HEMMA I HSB
1809912W82-473
Editorial: Box 8310, 104 20 STOCKHOLM
Tel: 8 785 30 00
Email: hemmaihsb@hsb.se **Web site:** http://www.hsb.se/omhsb/vara-tidningar/hemma
Freq: 6 issues yearly - (8 nr/år); **Circ:** 434,800
Advertising Manager: Pierre Hultman
Language(s): Swedish
ADVERTISING RATES:
Full Page Colour .... SEK 54000
SCC .... SEK 450
Copy instructions: *Copy Date:* 23 days prior to publication date
CONSUMER: CURRENT AFFAIRS & POLITICS

HEMMABIO
752061W76A-165
Editorial: Box 230 84, 104 35 STOCKHOLM
Tel: 8 34 29 70 **Fax:** 8 34 29 71
Email: hemmabio@hifi-musik.se **Web site:** http://www.hemmabiotidningen.se
Freq: Monthly; **Circ:** 26,500
Editor: Magnus Fredholm; **Editor-in-Chief:** Jonas Olsson; **Advertising Manager:** Ulf Gustavsson
Language(s): Swedish
ADVERTISING RATES:
Full Page Colour .... SEK 18770
SCC .... SEK 156.42
CONSUMER: MUSIC & PERFORMING ARTS: Cinema

HEMMETS JOURNAL
50955W74C-35
Editorial: 205 07 MALMO **Tel:** 40 38 52 00
Fax: 40 38 53 93
Email: red.hj@egmont.se **Web site:** http://www.hemmetsjournal.se
Date Established: 1921; **Freq:** Weekly; **Circ:** 202,100
Editor: Helén Sambrant Winnberg; **Advertising Manager:** Martin Thornholm
Profile: Home and family journal including features on antiques, flower-arranging, handicrafts, family health and medicine, cookery, gardening, nature and beauty.
Language(s): Swedish
ADVERTISING RATES:
Full Page Colour .... SEK 46800
SCC .... SEK 390
CONSUMER: WOMEN'S INTEREST CONSUMER MAGAZINES: Home & Family

HEMMETS JOURNAL; WWW.HEMMETSJOURNAL.SE
1846659W74Q-176
Editorial: 205 07 MALMO **Tel:** 4038 52 00
Fax: 40 38 53 93
Email: red.hj@egmont.se **Web site:** http://www.hemmetsjournal.se
Freq: Daily; **Cover Price:** Free; **Circ:** 52,400 Unique Users
Editor: Celia Stahl; **Publisher:** Håkan Ström
Language(s): Swedish
CONSUMER: WOMEN'S INTEREST CONSUMER MAGAZINES: Lifestyle

HEMMETS VÄN
51186W82-90
Editorial: Box 220 10, 702 02 OREBRO
Tel: 19 16 54 20 **Fax:** 19124160
Email: redaktion@hemmetsvan.se **Web site:** http://www.hemmetsvan.se
Freq: Weekly - Arvika; **Circ:** 13,700
Editor: Per Danielsson
Profile: Political magazine with a Christian viewpoint.
Language(s): Swedish
ADVERTISING RATES:
Full Page Colour .... SEK 25200
SCC .... SEK 126
CONSUMER: CURRENT AFFAIRS & POLITICS

HEMMETS VECKOTIDNING
50956W74C-40
Editorial: Allers Förlag, 205 35 MALMO
Tel: 40 38 59 00 **Fax:** 40 38 59 14
Email: hemmets@aller.se
Date Established: 1929; **Freq:** Weekly; **Circ:** 197,600
Advertising Manager: Barbro Voss
Profile: Home and family magazine.
Language(s): Swedish
ADVERTISING RATES:
Full Page Colour .... SEK 39000
SCC .... SEK 325
CONSUMER: WOMEN'S INTEREST CONSUMER MAGAZINES: Home & Family

HEMSLÖJDEN
50980W74E-67
Editorial: Celia B. Dackenberg, Västra Kyrkogatan 3, 903 29 UMEÅ **Tel:** 90 71 83 02 **Fax:** 90 71 83 05
Email: redaktionen@hemslojden.org **Web site:** http://www.hemslojden.org
Date Established: 1933; **Freq:** 6 issues yearly; **Circ:** 13,400
Editor: Frida Engström; **Editor-in-Chief:** Celia B. Dackenberg; **Advertising Manager:** Liz Larsson
Profile: Magazine about Swedish and international traditional handicrafts.
Language(s): Swedish
Readership: Aimed at people interested in arts and crafts.
ADVERTISING RATES:
Full Page Colour .... SEK 14800
SCC .... SEK 123.33
CONSUMER: WOMEN'S INTEREST CONSUMER MAGAZINES: Crafts

HEMTRÄDGÅRDEN
51354W93-23
Editorial: Högåsvägen 6, 741 41 KNIVSTA
Tel: 18 34 29 72 **Fax:** 18341107
Email: hemtradgarden@tradgard.org **Web site:** http://www.tradgard.org
Date Established: 1945; **Freq:** 6 issues yearly; **Circ:** 29,400
Editor-in-Chief: Christina Säll; **Advertising Manager:** Hélène Ulvander
Profile: Magazine containing information, articles and practical advice for people interested in gardening.
Language(s): Swedish
ADVERTISING RATES:
Full Page Colour .... SEK 14000
SCC .... SEK 116.67
CONSUMER: GARDENING

HENRY - RÖDA KORSETS TIDNING
1836249W82-476
Editorial: Box 17563, 118 91 STOCKHOLM
Tel: 8 452 46 00 **Fax:** 8 452 48 01
Email: erik.olsson@redcross.se **Web site:** http://www.redcross.se
Freq: Quarterly; **Circ:** 258,600
Editor: Erik Olsson; **Editor-in-Chief:** Erik Halkjaer,; **Publisher:** Johan af Donner
Language(s): Swedish
ADVERTISING RATES:
Full Page Colour .... SEK 50000
SCC .... SEK 416.66
CONSUMER: CURRENT AFFAIRS & POLITICS

HIB-INFO
1695169W4E-153
Editorial: Box 5054, 102 42 STOCKHOLM
Tel: 8 698 58 73 **Fax:** 8 698 59 00
Email: lars.sandstrom@bygg.org **Web site:** http://www.haltagningsentreprenorerna.se
Freq: Quarterly; **Circ:** 1,500
Editor: Patrik Sjögren; **Publisher:** Lars Sandström
Language(s): Swedish
BUSINESS: ARCHITECTURE & BUILDING: Building

HIFI & MUSIK
50699W61-10
Editorial: Box 230 84, 104 35 STOCKHOLM
Tel: 8 34 29 70 **Fax:** 8 34 29 71
Email: info@hifi-musik.se **Web site:** http://www.hifi-musik.se
Freq: Monthly; **Circ:** 22,500
Editor: Jonas Bryngelsson; **Editor-in-Chief:** Jonas Bryngelsson; **Advertising Manager:** Erkki Salin
Profile: Magazine concerning the music industry. Includes information about hi-fis and recording studios.
Language(s): Swedish
ADVERTISING RATES:
Full Page Colour .... SEK 16870
SCC .... SEK 140.6
BUSINESS: MUSIC TRADE

HIT & DIT, TURISM & RESOR
50563W50-20
Editorial: Prästgården Kårstaby, 186 96 VALLENTUNA **Tel:** 8 512 36 20
Email: info@ladan.se **Web site:** http://www.hitodit.com
Date Established: 1991; **Freq:** 6 issues yearly; **Circ:** 5,000
Editor: Bengt Meder; **Advertising Manager:** Ove Persson
Profile: Magazine covering all aspects of the tourism trade.
Language(s): Swedish
ADVERTISING RATES:
Full Page Colour .... SEK 13200
SCC .... SEK 110
BUSINESS: TRAVEL & TOURISM

HJÄRNKRAFT
634564W56L-43
Editorial: Nybohovsgränd 12, 117 63 STOCKHOLM
Tel: 8 447 45 30 **Fax:** 8 447 45 39
Email: info@hjarnkraft.nu **Web site:** http://www.hjarnkraft.nu
Date Established: 1995; **Freq:** Quarterly; **Circ:** 4,500
Editor: Ann Turlock
Language(s): Swedish
BUSINESS: HEALTH & MEDICAL: Disability & Rehabilitation

HJÄRTEBARNET
1803969W56B-190
Editorial: Box 9087, 102 72 STOCKHOLM
Tel: 8 442 46 50 **Fax:** 8 442 46 59
Email: kansliet@hjartebarn.org **Web site:** http://www.hjartebarn.org
Freq: Quarterly; **Circ:** 3,500
Publisher: Johan Hallberg
Language(s): Swedish
BUSINESS: HEALTH & MEDICAL: Nursing

HONDA VISION
51128W77E-200
Editorial: Rubrik AB; Vallgatan 27, 411 16 GÖTEBORG **Tel:** 31 719 06 00 **Fax:** 31 15 34 46
Email: joe@rubrik.se **Web site:** http://www.rubrik.se
Date Established: 1990; **Freq:** Half-yearly; **Circ:** 70,000
Editor: Jan-Olof Ekelund; **Advertising Manager:** Karin Hedman; **Publisher:** Jan-Olof Ekelund
Profile: Magazine for Honda owners.
Language(s): Swedish
CONSUMER: MOTORING & CYCLING: Club Cars

HOOM
1687718W74C-456
Editorial: Gyllenstiernsgatan 10, 115 26 STOCKHOLM **Tel:** 8 717 06 00
Email: info@hoom.se **Web site:** http://www.hoom.se
Freq: 6 issues yearly; **Circ:** 40,000
Advertising Manager: Mikael Olsson
Language(s): Swedish
ADVERTISING RATES:
Full Page Colour .... SEK 34000
SCC .... SEK 283.33
CONSUMER: WOMEN'S INTEREST CONSUMER MAGAZINES: Home & Family

HOOM; WEBB
1846660W1E-210
Editorial: Gyllenstiernsgatan 10, 115 26 STOCKHOLM **Tel:** 8 442 85 00 **Fax:** 84428510
Email: info@hoom.se **Web site:** http://www.hoom.se
Freq: Daily; **Cover Price:** Free; **Circ:** 22,857 Unique Users
Language(s): Swedish
BUSINESS: FINANCE & ECONOMICS: Property

HORISONT
751121W84B-60
Editorial: Österskogsvägen 23, 590 12 BOXHOLM
Tel: 14 31 28 32
Email: peter.bjorkman@horisont.fi **Web site:** http://www.horisont.fi
Date Established: 1954; **Freq:** Quarterly; **Circ:** 1,000
Editor: Peter Björkman
Language(s): Swedish
CONSUMER: THE ARTS & LITERARY: Literary

HOTELL & RESTAURANG
1664275W11A-37
Editorial: Svenska Media Docu AB, Tingsgatan 2, 827 32 LJUSDAL **Tel:** 651 150 50 **Fax:** 65113333
Email: post@svenskamedia.se **Web site:** http://www.svenskamedia.se
Freq: Half-yearly; **Circ:** 16,500
Advertising Manager: AnnaKarin Larsson
Language(s): Swedish
Copy instructions: *Copy Date:* 15 days prior to publication date
BUSINESS: CATERING: Catering, Hotels & Restaurants

HOTELLREVYN
50273W11A-35
Editorial: Box 1143, 111 81 STOCKHOLM
Tel: 771 57 58 59 **Fax:** 8 20 47 28
Email: redaktionen@hotellrevyn.se **Web site:** http://www.hotellrevyn.se
Date Established: 1918; **Freq:** Monthly; **Circ:** 47,200
Advertising Manager: Jörgen Rosengren; **Publisher:** Susanna Lundell
Profile: Newsletter providing news and information on the Swedish Hotel & Restaurant Workers' Union (Hotel och Restaurang facket).
Language(s): Swedish
Readership: Read by members.
ADVERTISING RATES:
Full Page Colour .... SEK 24000
SCC .... SEK 200
BUSINESS: CATERING: Catering, Hotels & Restaurants

HOTELLREVYN; WEBB
1846460W14L-202
Editorial: Box 1143, 111 81 STOCKHOLM
Tel: 771 57 58 59 **Fax:** 8204728
Email: redaktionen@hotellrevyn.nu **Web site:** http://www.hotellrevyn.nu
Freq: Daily; **Cover Price:** Free; **Circ:** 19,067 Unique Users
Publisher: Susanna Lundell
Language(s): Swedish
BUSINESS: COMMERCE, INDUSTRY & MANAGEMENT: Trade Unions

HR-TIDNINGEN PERSONALCHEFEN
1625826W14F-92
Editorial: World Trade Center D8, 111 64 STOCKHOLM **Tel:** 8 20 21 10 **Fax:** 8 20 78 10
Email: info@personalchefen.nu **Web site:** http://www.personalchefen.nu
Freq: Quarterly; **Circ:** 20,000
Editor-in-Chief: Anders Åkerman; **Advertising Manager:** Sickan Palm; **Publisher:** Anders Åkerman
Language(s): Swedish
BUSINESS: COMMERCE, INDUSTRY & MANAGEMENT: Training & Recruitment

HSB UPPDRAGET
1625687W74C-446
Editorial: Box 8310, 104 20 STOCKHOLM
Tel: 8 785 32 81 **Fax:** 87853325
Email: uppdraget@hsb.se **Web site:** http://www.hsb.se
Freq: Quarterly; **Circ:** 25,500
Editor-in-Chief: Jenny Mattsson; **Advertising Manager:** Rober Wallner
Language(s): Swedish
ADVERTISING RATES:
Full Page Colour .... SEK 27900
SCC .... SEK 232.50
CONSUMER: WOMEN'S INTEREST CONSUMER MAGAZINES: Home & Family

HUDIKSVALLS TIDNING
50790W67B-4600
Editorial: Box 1201, 824 15 HUDIKSVALL
Tel: 650 355 00 **Fax:** 65035560
Email: redaktion@ht.se **Web site:** http://www.helahalsingland.se
Date Established: 1909
Circ: 15,700
Editor: Håkan Persson; **Managing Director:** Ruben Jacobsson; **Advertising Manager:** Michael Roos; **Publisher:** Mats Åmvall
Language(s): Swedish
ADVERTISING RATES:
Full Page Colour .... SEK 18720
SCC .... SEK 93.60
Copy instructions: *Copy Date:* 14 days prior to publication date
REGIONAL DAILY & SUNDAY NEWSPAPERS: Regional Daily Newspapers

HUDIKSVALLS TIDNING; HT.SE
1843537W65A-987
Editorial: 824 15 HUDIKSVALL **Tel:** 650 355 00 **Fax:** 650 355 60
Email: webmaster@ht.se **Web site:** http://helahalsingland.se/hudiksvall
Cover Price: Free; **Circ:** 3,055 Unique Users
Editor: Sandy Bergström; **Editor-in-Chief:** Mats Åmvall; **Publisher:** Mats Åmvall
Language(s): Swedish
ADVERTISING RATES:
SCC .... SEK 19
NATIONAL DAILY & SUNDAY NEWSPAPERS: National Daily Newspapers

HUJÅDÅ
51318W90-52
Editorial: Assyriska riksförbundet, Box 6019, 151 06 SÖDERTÄLJE **Tel:** 8 550 166 83 **Fax:** 36140661
Email: redaktionen@hujada.com **Web site:** http://www.hujada.com
Date Established: 1978; **Freq:** Monthly; **Circ:** 1,000
Editor: Moris Esa; **Publisher:** Rachel Hadodo
Profile: Journal containing news and information from the Assyrian Federation in Sweden.
Language(s): Swedish
CONSUMER: ETHNIC

HUMANETTEN
639398W62A-413
Editorial: Institutionen för humaniora, Växjö universitet, 351 95 VÄXJO **Tel:** 470 70 86 61
Fax: 470751888
Email: gunilla.byrman@vxu.se **Web site:** http://www.hum.vxu.se/publ/humanetten
Freq: Half-yearly; **Circ:** 4,153 Unique Users
Editor: Börje Björkman; **Publisher:** Anders Åberg
Language(s): Swedish
BUSINESS: CHURCH & SCHOOL EQUIPMENT & EDUCATION: Education

HUNDLIV
51157W81B-45
Editorial: Kampavall, 540 17 LERDALA
Tel: 511 822 30 **Fax:** 511 822 38
Email: info@hundliv.nu **Web site:** http://www.hundliv.nu
Date Established: 1995; **Freq:** 6 issues yearly; **Circ:** 15,000
Editor-in-Chief: Sandra Lundgren; **Publisher:** Maria Cidh
Profile: Magazine providing articles about dogs, including features on breeding, care, nutrition and training.
Language(s): Swedish
Readership: Aimed at dog owners and breeders.
ADVERTISING RATES:
Full Page Colour .... SEK 6000
CONSUMER: ANIMALS & PETS: Dogs

HUNDSPORT
51158W81B-50
Editorial: Box 20136, 161 02 BROMMA
Tel: 8 80 85 65 **Fax:** 8 80 85 95
Email: hundsport.online@swipnet.se **Web site:** http://www.hundsport.se
Freq: Monthly; **Circ:** 106,900
Editor-in-Chief: Torsten Widholm; **Advertising Manager:** Lars-Göran Fransson; **Publisher:** Ulf Uddman
Profile: Magazine of the Swedish Kennel Club. Contains news of events, shows and meetings and includes information on dog training and breeding.
Language(s): Swedish
Readership: Aimed at members, dog breeders and show organisers.
ADVERTISING RATES:
Full Page Colour .... SEK 37800
SCC .... SEK 315
CONSUMER: ANIMALS & PETS: Dogs

HUNDSPORT SPECIAL
1841361W64H-17
Editorial: Sv. Kennelklubben, Rinkebysvängen 70, 163 85 SPÅNGA **Tel:** 8 795 30 00
Email: hss@skk.se **Web site:** http://www.skk.se
Freq: Quarterly; **Circ:** 105,700
Editor: Inger Boström; **Editor-in-Chief:** Peter Fryksäter
Language(s): Swedish
ADVERTISING RATES:
Full Page Colour .... SEK 37800
SCC .... SEK 315
BUSINESS: OTHER CLASSIFICATIONS: Veterinary

HUNDSPORT; WEBB
1846654W64H-18
Editorial: Box 20136, 161 02 BROMMA
Tel: 8 80 85 65 **Fax:** 8 80 85 95
Email: hundsport@swipnet.se **Web site:** http://www.hundsport.se
Freq: Daily; **Cover Price:** Free; **Circ:** 20,200 Unique Users
Editor-in-Chief: Torsten Widholm; **Publisher:** Ulf Uddman
Language(s): Swedish
ADVERTISING RATES:
SCC .... SEK 63
BUSINESS: OTHER CLASSIFICATIONS: Veterinary

HUS & HEM
50957W74C-65
Editorial: Box 6630, 113 84 STOCKHOLM
Tel: 8 728 23 00
Email: red.husohem@formapg.se **Web site:** http://www.husohem.se
Freq: Monthly; **Circ:** 86,500
Editor: Iréne Hellström; **Advertising Manager:** Lars Zdilar
Profile: Magazine covering home decoration, improvement and furnishing.
Language(s): Swedish
Readership: Aimed at home owners in Sweden.
ADVERTISING RATES:
Full Page Colour .... SEK 58900
SCC .... SEK 490.80
CONSUMER: WOMEN'S INTEREST CONSUMER MAGAZINES: Home & Family

HUSBILEN TEST
1852603W77A-273
Editorial: 142 43 SKOGÅS **Tel:** 8 771 56 00
Fax: 8 771 56 00
Email: stefan.janeld@husbilentest.se **Web site:** http://www.husbilentest.se
Freq: Monthly; **Circ:** 10,000
Editor: Björn Genberg; **Editor-in-Chief:** Stefan Janeld; **Advertising Manager:** William Blanck; **Publisher:** Stefan Janeld
Language(s): Swedish
CONSUMER: MOTORING & CYCLING: Motoring

HUSBYGGAREN
50222W4E-40
Editorial: Box 4415, 102 69 STOCKHOLM
Tel: 8 462 17 90
Email: redaktion@husbyggaren.se **Web site:** http://www.husbyggaren.se
Date Established: 1958; **Freq:** 6 issues yearly; **Circ:** 10,500
Editor: Margot Granvik; **Advertising Manager:** Lena Rösund
Profile: Journal of the Swedish Building Engineers' Association, covering all aspects of the building trade.
Language(s): Swedish
ADVERTISING RATES:
Full Page Colour .... SEK 23500
SCC .... SEK 195.8
BUSINESS: ARCHITECTURE & BUILDING: Building

HUSDJUR 50373W21D-20
Editorial: Svensk Mjölk, Box 1146, 631 80 ESKILSTUNA **Tel:** 16 16 35 56 **Fax:** 1621125
Email: husdjur@svenskmjolk.se **Web site:** http://www.husdjur.se
Date Established: 1947; **Freq:** Monthly; **Circ:** 15,400
Editor: Ann Christin Olsson; **Editor-in-Chief:** Erik Pettersson; **Advertising Manager:** Marie Louise Ankarsten; **Publisher:** Lennart Andersson
Profile: Journal of the Swedish Dairy Association.
Language(s): Swedish
Readership: Read by livestock breeders, vets and agriculturists.
Copy instructions: *Copy Date:* 20 days prior to publication date
BUSINESS: AGRICULTURE & FARMING: Livestock

HUSHÅLLSVETAREN 50714W62B-80
Editorial: Box 12239, 102 26 STOCKHOLM
Tel: 8 737 65 43 **Fax:** 8 619 00 88
Email: hushallsvetaren@lararforbundet.se **Web site:** http://www.hushallsvetaren.se
Date Established: 1916; **Freq:** Quarterly; **Circ:** 2,300
Editor-in-Chief: Helena Gårdsäter; **Advertising Manager:** Marie Lingensjö; **Publisher:** Helena Gårdsäter
Profile: Magazine for home economics teachers. Contains articles regarding education in nutrition and hygiene, home environment and housekeeping.
Language(s): Swedish
ADVERTISING RATES:
Full Page Colour .... SEK 7500
SCC .... SEK 62.5
BUSINESS: CHURCH & SCHOOL EQUIPMENT & EDUCATION: Education Teachers

HYRESGÄSTFÖRENINGEN AKTUELLT 1625729W74C-447
Editorial: Box 7514, 103 92 STOCKHOLM
Tel: 8 791 02 00 **Fax:** 8 20 56 97
Email: peter.forsman@hyresgastforeningen.se **Web site:** http://www.hyresgastforeningen.se
Freq: 6 issues yearly; **Circ:** 5,000
Editor: Pär Svanberg
Language(s): Swedish
CONSUMER: WOMEN'S INTEREST CONSUMER MAGAZINES: Home & Family

I FOKUS - EN TIDNING FRÅN SAMHALL 750659W14L-150
Editorial: Box 27705, 115 91 STOCKHOLM
Tel: 8 553 411 20 **Fax:** 855341101
Email: lars.loow@samhall.se **Web site:** http://webnews.textalk.com/se/view.phtml?id=290
Freq: Quarterly; **Circ:** 33,000
Editor: Stefan Hladisch; **Editor-in-Chief:** Anneli Kamlin; **Publisher:** Lars Lööw
Language(s): Swedish
BUSINESS: COMMERCE, INDUSTRY & MANAGEMENT: Trade Unions

I FORM 749851W74G-207
Editorial: Pipersgatan 7, 112 24 STOCKHOLM
Tel: 8 441 07 90
Email: iform.redaktionen@telia.com **Web site:** http://www.iform.se
Freq: Monthly; **Circ:** 39,100
Language(s): Swedish
ADVERTISING RATES:
Full Page Colour .... SEK 36600
SCC .... SEK 305
CONSUMER: WOMEN'S INTEREST CONSUMER MAGAZINES: Slimming & Health

I&M, INVANDRARE & MINORITETER 51319W90-55
Editorial: Fittja gård, Värdshusvägen 46, 145 50 NORSBORG **Tel:** 8 531 757 60 **Fax:** 8 531 734 30
Email: info@iochm.com **Web site:** http://www.iochm.com
Date Established: 1973; **Freq:** 6 issues yearly; **Circ:** 2,000
Editor-in-Chief: Nora Weintraub; **Advertising Manager:** Lotta Bolin; **Publisher:** Nora Weintraub
Profile: Magazine about how migration and different cultures influence the Swedish society. Focuses on multicultural relations in modern society.
Language(s): Swedish
Readership: Read by professionals working on how to build a multicultural society. Also teachers, students and scientists.
CONSUMER: ETHNIC

I VÅRDEN 751166W56B-135
Editorial: Informa Healthcare, Box 3255, 103 65 STOCKHOLM **Tel:** 8 440 80 43 **Fax:** 8 440 80 50
Email: red@primarvard.se **Web site:** http://www.primarvard.se
Date Established: 1990; **Freq:** Monthly; **Circ:** 5,400
Advertising Manager: Per Sonnerfeldt
Language(s): Swedish
ADVERTISING RATES:
Full Page Colour .... SEK 19900
SCC .... SEK 165.83
BUSINESS: HEALTH & MEDICAL: Nursing

I VÅRDEN 634652W74N-45
Editorial: Taylor & Francis, Box 3255, 103 65 STOCKHOLM **Tel:** 8 440 80 51 **Fax:** 84408050
Email: redaktion@ivarden.se **Web site:** http://www.nordiskgeriatrik.se
Date Established: 1997; **Freq:** 6 issues yearly; **Circ:** 5,500
Advertising Manager: Per Sonnerfeldt; **Publisher:** Håkan Pårup
Profile: Magazine containing articles about finance, leisure and medical issues.
Language(s): Swedish
Readership: Read by pensioners.
CONSUMER: WOMEN'S INTEREST CONSUMER MAGAZINES: Retirement

I VÄREND OCH SUNNERBO 750625W73-100
Editorial: c/o Johansson, Hantverkaregatan 3, 341 36 LJUNGBY **Tel:** 372 624 61
Email: goran.hogstedt@ipbolaget.com **Web site:** http://www.hembygd.se/kronoberg
Freq: Quarterly; **Circ:** 1,700
Editor: Elisabet Johansson
Language(s): Swedish
CONSUMER: NATIONAL & INTERNATIONAL PERIODICALS

ICA-KURIREN 50958W74C-80
Editorial: Box 6630, 113 84 STOCKHOLM
Tel: 8 728 23 00
Email: red.kuriren@formapg.se **Web site:** http://www.icakuriren.se
Date Established: 1941; **Freq:** Weekly; **Circ:** 158,100
Editor: Kersti Byström; **Advertising Manager:** Tomas B Karlsson
Profile: Magazine focusing on all aspects of home and family life.
Language(s): Swedish
ADVERTISING RATES:
Full Page Colour .... SEK 71500
SCC .... SEK 620.83
CONSUMER: WOMEN'S INTEREST CONSUMER MAGAZINES: Home & Family

ICA-KURIREN; ICAKURIREN.SE 1843532W82-478
Editorial: Box 6630, 113 84 STOCKHOLM
Tel: 8 728 23 00 **Fax:** 87282350
Email: red.kuriren@formapg.se **Web site:** http://www.icakuriren.se
Freq: Daily; **Cover Price:** Free; **Circ:** 28,844 Unique Users
Language(s): Swedish
CONSUMER: CURRENT AFFAIRS & POLITICS

ICANYHETER 50384W22A-25
Editorial: Forma Publishing Group, 721 85 VÄSTERÅS **Tel:** 8 475 75 00 **Fax:** 21 475 75 93
Email: icanyheter@formapg.se **Web site:** http://www.icanyheter.se
Freq: Weekly; **Circ:** 18,200
Editor: Jim Cordts; **Advertising Manager:** Håkan Broberg
Profile: Magazine covering the food retail trade.
Language(s): Swedish
ADVERTISING RATES:
Full Page Colour .... SEK 74800
SCC .... SEK 374
Copy instructions: *Copy Date:* 7 days prior to publication date
BUSINESS: FOOD

IDG.SE 1844531W78R-283
Editorial: Karlbergsv. 77, 106 78 STOCKHOLM
Tel: 8 453 60 00
Email: webad@idg.se **Web site:** http://idg.se
Freq: Daily; **Cover Price:** Free; **Circ:** 61,876 Unique Users
Language(s): Swedish
CONSUMER: CONSUMER ELECTRONICS: Consumer Electronics Related

IDROTT & KUNSKAP 1665943W94J-25
Editorial: Roslagstullsbacken 11, Albanova Universitetscentrum, 106 91 STOCKHOLM
Tel: 8 30 99 05 **Fax:** 8 30 99 12
Email: christian.carlsson@idrottochkunskap.se **Web site:** http://www.idrottochkunskap.se
Freq: 6 issues yearly; **Circ:** 4,000
Language(s): Swedish
CONSUMER: OTHER CLASSIFICATIONS: Popular Science

IDROTTSLÄRAREN 51446W62A-415
Editorial: Box 12239, 102 26 STOCKHOLM
Tel: 8 737 67 30 **Fax:** 8 657 97 48
Email: idrottslararen@lararforbundet.se **Web site:** http://www.idrottslararen.net
Freq: Quarterly; **Circ:** 2,200
Editor: Björn Andersson; **Editor-in-Chief:** Björn Andersson; **Advertising Manager:** Gun Thil; **Publisher:** Björn Andersson
Profile: Magazine containing articles, news and information about physical education.
Language(s): Swedish
Readership: Aimed at teachers and coaches.
BUSINESS: CHURCH & SCHOOL EQUIPMENT & EDUCATION: Education

IKEA FAMILY LIVE 752043W74C-245
Editorial: Box 200, 260 35 ÖDÅKRA **Tel:** 42 25 26 35
Fax: 42 25 26 27
Web site: http://www.ikea.com
Freq: Quarterly; **Circ:** 736,800
Publisher: Jeanette Söderberg
Language(s): Swedish
CONSUMER: WOMEN'S INTEREST CONSUMER MAGAZINES: Home & Family

IKON1931 1809879W87-206
Editorial: 105 36 STOCKHOLM, 105 36 STOCKHOLM **Tel:** 8 619 24 38 **Fax:** 8 656 60 51
Email: rickard@ikon1931.se **Web site:** http://www.Ikon1931.se
Freq: 6 issues yearly; **Circ:** 5,100
Editor: Rickard Alvarsson
Language(s): Swedish
ADVERTISING RATES:
Full Page Colour .... SEK 8500
SCC .... SEK 70.83
CONSUMER: RELIGIOUS

ILCO-BLADET 749945W56B-100
Editorial: ILCO-förbundet, Box 1386, 172 27 SUNDBYBERG **Tel:** 8 546 405 20 **Fax:** 8 546 405 26
Email: info@ilco.nu **Web site:** http://www.ilco.nu
Date Established: 1966; **Freq:** Quarterly; **Circ:** 8,500
Editor: Eva Kindvall Vinkvist; **Advertising Manager:** Tomas Svensson; **Publisher:** Marie Stéen
Language(s): Swedish
Copy instructions: *Copy Date:* 45 days prior to publication date
BUSINESS: HEALTH & MEDICAL: Nursing

ILLUSTRERAD VETENSKAP; WEBB 1846630W55-68
Editorial: 205 50 MALMO **Tel:** 8 555 454 05
Web site: http://www.illustreradvetenskap.com
Freq: Daily; **Cover Price:** Free; **Circ:** 73,900 Unique Users
Publisher: Anna Rading Ploman
Language(s): Swedish
BUSINESS: APPLIED SCIENCE & LABORATORIES

IMPULS 51188W82-95
Editorial: Box 1109, 111 81 STOCKHOLM
Tel: 8 587 686 00 **Fax:** 8 587 686 03
Email: impuls@sv.se **Web site:** http://www.impuls.nu
Date Established: 1967
Circ: 28,200
Editor-in-Chief: Per Gustafsson; **Advertising Manager:** Ann-Marie Franzén; **Publisher:** Per Gustafsson
Profile: Political and current affairs magazine. Also covers culture, environmental concerns, the arts, the media, education and literature.
Language(s): Swedish
ADVERTISING RATES:
Full Page Colour .... SEK 15300
SCC .... SEK 127.5
CONSUMER: CURRENT AFFAIRS & POLITICS

IN TOUCH 1840875W74Q-171
Editorial: Box 3187, 350 43 VÄXJÖ **Tel:** 470 76 24 00
Fax: 470 76 24 25
Email: it@firstpublishing.se **Web site:** http://www.svenskaintouch.se
Freq: 26 issues yearly; **Circ:** 25,000
Editor: Henrietta Thollén; **Editor-in-Chief:** Sara Valfridsson
Language(s): Swedish
ADVERTISING RATES:
Full Page Colour .... SEK 27500
SCC .... SEK 229,17
CONSUMER: WOMEN'S INTEREST CONSUMER MAGAZINES: Lifestyle

INBLICK 749819W56B-105
Editorial: Box 712, 791 29 FALUN **Tel:** 23 49 04 92
Fax: 23490169
Email: michael.marklund@ltdalarna.se **Web site:** http://www.ltdalarna.se
Freq: Quarterly; **Circ:** 10,000
Editor: Michael Marklund; **Editor-in-Chief:** Catarina Nykvist-Lilliehöök; **Publisher:** Lena Sterner
Language(s): Swedish
BUSINESS: HEALTH & MEDICAL: Nursing

INBLICK ABB 1841359W58-104
Editorial: Communication Center, 721 83 VÄSTERÅS
Tel: 21 32 45 01
Email: annica.jansson@se.abb.com **Web site:** http://www.abb.se
Freq: Monthly; **Circ:** 10,000
Editor-in-Chief: Annica Jansson
Language(s): Swedish
ADVERTISING RATES:
Full Page Colour .... SEK 20000
SCC .... SEK 125,00
BUSINESS: ENERGY, FUEL & NUCLEAR

INCITAMENT 51566W56A-32_25
Editorial: Box 4173, 102 64 STOCKHOLM
Tel: 8 556 933 70 **Fax:** 8910907
Email: red@incitament.com **Web site:** http://www.incitament.com
Date Established: 1991; **Freq:** 6 issues yearly; **Circ:** 14,000
Advertising Manager: Annika Bergkvist; **Publisher:** Ove Ernström
Profile: Journal analysing the medical field, covering all aspects from issues concerning clinical laboratories to rehabilitation and therapy.
Language(s): Swedish
Readership: Aimed at doctors, nurses and people working with public health issues.
ADVERTISING RATES:
Full Page Colour .... SEK 25000
SCC .... SEK 208.33
Copy instructions: *Copy Date:* 14 days prior to publication date
BUSINESS: HEALTH & MEDICAL

INDIKAT 634428W2A-55
Editorial: Box 510, 192 05 SOLLENTUNA
Tel: 8 594 950 75
Email: indikat@indikat.se **Web site:** http://www.indikat.se
Freq: 104 issues yearly; **Circ:** 2,000
Publisher: Göran Swahn
Profile: Newsletter providing information on marketing, media and advertising.
Language(s): Swedish
BUSINESS: COMMUNICATIONS, ADVERTISING & MARKETING

INFLUENS 2010029W4A-40
Editorial: Svenska Teknik&Designföretagen, Box 555 45, 102 04 STOCKHOLM **Tel:** 8 762 67 00
Fax: 8 762 67 10
Email: mathias.lindow@std.se **Web site:** http://www.std.se
Freq: 3 gånger/år; **Circ:** 5,000
Editor: Åsa Rydén Antonsson
Language(s): Swedish
BUSINESS: ARCHITECTURE & BUILDING: Architecture

INFOTORG JURIDIKS 1642076W44-61
Editorial: InfoTorg AB, 105 99 STOCKHOLM
Tel: 8 738 48 00 **Fax:** 8 738 48 01
Web site: http://www.infotorgjuridik.se
Freq: Monthly - (8 ggr/år); **Circ:** 5,900
Language(s): Swedish
ADVERTISING RATES:
Full Page Colour .... SEK 21900
SCC .... SEK 182.50
BUSINESS: LEGAL

INFOTREND - NORDISK TIDSKRIFT FÖR INFORMATIONSSPEC. 1667550W14R-66
Editorial: Osquars Backe 25, c/o KTH, 100 44 STOCKHOLM **Tel:** 8 678 23 20
Email: kansliet@sfis.nu **Web site:** http://www.sfis.nu
Freq: Quarterly; **Circ:** 450
Editor: Peter Almerud
Language(s): Swedish
BUSINESS: COMMERCE, INDUSTRY & MANAGEMENT: Commerce Related

INGENJÖREN 50487W42A-15
Editorial: Box 1419, 111 84 STOCKHOLM
Tel: 8 613 80 00
Email: ingenjoren@sverigesingenjorer.se **Web site:** http://www.ingenjoren.se
Freq: Monthly; **Circ:** 124,800
Advertising Manager: Nicklas Larenholtz; **Publisher:** Jenny Grensman
Profile: Magazine containing articles and information about civil engineering and the construction industry.
Language(s): Swedish
ADVERTISING RATES:
Full Page Colour .... SEK 41700
SCC .... SEK 347.50
Copy instructions: *Copy Date:* 32 days prior to publication date
BUSINESS: CONSTRUCTION

INGENJÖREN; INGENJOREN.SE 1846518W14A-343
Editorial: Box 1419, 111 84 STOCKHOLM
Tel: 8 613 80 00
Email: ingenjoren@sverigesingenjorer.se **Web site:** http://www.ingenjoren.se
Freq: Daily; **Cover Price:** Free; **Circ:** 19,000 Unique Users
Advertising Manager: Berenika Westerlund; **Publisher:** Jenny Grensman
Language(s): Swedish
BUSINESS: COMMERCE, INDUSTRY & MANAGEMENT

Sweden

INKÖP+LOGISTIK 51567W10-90
Editorial: Box 1278, 164 29 KISTA **Tel:** 8 752 16 90 **Fax:** 8 750 64 10
Email: silfonline@silf.se **Web site:** http://www.inkop-logistik.org
Date Established: 1994; **Freq:** 6 issues yearly; **Circ:** 7,100
Editor-in-Chief: Anders Lindholm; **Managing Director:** Anders Lindholm; **Advertising Manager:** Magnus Johansson; **Publisher:** Anders Lindholm
Profile: Journal dealing with public purchase, logistics, materials handling, transport, raw materials, distribution and environmental issues.
Language(s): Swedish
Readership: Aimed at decision-makers and managers working with IT, production, logistics, buying and selling and transport.
ADVERTISING RATES:
Full Page Colour .... SEK 25000
SCC .... SEK 208.33
BUSINESS: MATERIALS HANDLING

INKÖPSJOURNALEN 50154W1A-70
Editorial: Rubanksgatan 6, 741 71 KNIVSTA
Tel: 18 34 90 85
Email: info@inkopsforum.se **Web site:** http://www.inkopsforum.se
Freq: 6 issues yearly; **Circ:** 9,000
Editor: Stefan Lind; **Editor-in-Chief:** Catharina Lind; **Advertising Manager:** Anders Bergström; **Publisher:** Catharina Lind
Profile: Journal dealing with issues concerning company purchase.
Language(s): Swedish
Readership: Read by purchase administrators and managers.
ADVERTISING RATES:
Full Page Colour .... SEK 18000
SCC .... SEK 90
BUSINESS: FINANCE & ECONOMICS

INNEBANDYMAGAZINET 751029W75J-80
Editorial: Karlagatan 21, 416 61 GOTEBORG
Tel: 31 40 52 33
Email: redaktion@innebandymagazinet.se **Web site:** http://www.innebandymagazinet.se
Freq: 6 issues yearly; **Circ:** 19,800
Editor: Robert Rappel; **Advertising Manager:** Martin Zetterstedt
Language(s): Swedish
CONSUMER: SPORT: Athletics

INSIKT OM HIV, SEX & SÅNT 750618W86A-105
Editorial: Box 175 33, 118 91 STOCKHOLM
Tel: 8 737 35 46
Email: martina.junstrom@sll.se **Web site:** http://www.lafa.nu
Freq: Quarterly; **Circ:** 12,000
Editor: Hanna Ådin; **Editor-in-Chief:** Martina Junström
Language(s): Swedish
CONSUMER: ADULT & GAY MAGAZINES: Adult Magazines

INSPIRERA BY INTERFLORA 1833151W74C-517
Editorial: Box 808, 161 24 BROMMA
Tel: 8 634 44 00 **Fax:** 8 26 96 06
Email: miriam.oucama@interflora.se **Web site:** http://www.interflora.se
Freq: 208 issues yearly; **Cover Price:** Free; **Circ:** 50,000
Editor-in-Chief: Miriam Oucama
Language(s): Swedish
CONSUMER: WOMEN'S INTEREST CONSUMER MAGAZINES: Home & Family

INTEGRITET I FOKUS 1841179W5E-109
Editorial: Box 8114, 104 20 STOCKHOLM
Tel: 8 657 61 00 **Fax:** 8 652 86 52
Email: redaktionen@datainspektionen.se **Web site:** http://www.datainspektionen.se
Freq: Quarterly; **Cover Price:** Free; **Circ:** 5,000
Editor: Göran Gräslund; **Publisher:** Göran Gräslund
Language(s): Swedish
ADVERTISING RATES:
Full Page Colour .... SEK 5000
SCC .... SEK 41,67
BUSINESS: COMPUTERS & AUTOMATION: Data Transmission

INTELLIGENT LOGISTIK 1809892W10-96
Editorial: Bastugatan 6, 118 20 STOCKHOLM
Tel: 8 641 54 08 **Fax:** 8 641 54 08
Email: gh@intelligentlogistik.se **Web site:** http://www.intelligentlogistik.se
Freq: 6 issues yearly; **Circ:** 11,000
Editor-in-Chief: Gösta Hultén
Language(s): Swedish
ADVERTISING RATES:
Full Page Colour .... SEK 25000
SCC .... SEK 208
BUSINESS: MATERIALS HANDLING

INTERNATIONAL FORUM OF PSYCHOANALYSIS 751123W56B-110
Editorial: Taylor & Francis AB, Box 3255, 103 65 STOCKHOLM **Tel:** 8 440 80 40 **Fax:** 8 440 80 50
Email: ifp@se.tandf.no **Web site:** http://www.tandf.no
Freq: Quarterly; **Circ:** 700
Editor-in-Chief: Christer Sjödin
Language(s): Swedish
BUSINESS: HEALTH & MEDICAL: Nursing

INTERNATIONALEN 51178W82-68
Editorial: Box 5073, 121 16 JOHANNESHOV
Tel: 8 31 70 70
Email: intis@internationalen.se **Web site:** http://www.internationalen.se
Date Established: 1974
Circ: 1,800
Editor: Linn Hjort; **Publisher:** Jörgen Hassler
Profile: Newspaper of the Swedish Socialist Party.
Language(s): Swedish
ADVERTISING RATES:
Full Page Colour .... SEK 5000
SCC .... SEK 31.25
CONSUMER: CURRENT AFFAIRS & POLITICS

INTERNATIONALEN; WEBB 1844773W65A-1025
Editorial: Box 5073, 121 16 JOHANNESHOV
Tel: 8 31 70 70
Email: intis@internationalen.se **Web site:** http://www.internationalen.se
Freq: Daily; **Cover Price:** Free; **Circ:** 1,200 Unique Users
Editor-in-Chief: Gunvor Kalrström; **Publisher:** Jörgen Hassler
Language(s): Swedish
NATIONAL DAILY & SUNDAY NEWSPAPERS: National Daily Newspapers

INTERNATIONELLA STUDIER 50302W14C-35
Editorial: Box 27035, 102 51 STOCKHOLM
Tel: 8 511 768 00 **Fax:** 851176899
Email: andreas.norman@ui.se **Web site:** http://www.ui.se
Freq: Quarterly; **Circ:** 1,500
Editor: Kerstin Furubrant
Profile: Magazine covering international economics and politics.
Language(s): Swedish
Readership: Aimed at researchers, students, teachers, academics and politicians.
BUSINESS: COMMERCE, INDUSTRY & MANAGEMENT: International Commerce

INTERNETWORLD 50249W5E-50
Editorial: IDG, Karlbergsvägen 77, 106 78 STOCKHOLM **Tel:** 8 453 61 70
Email: internetworld@idg.se **Web site:** http://www.internetworld.idg.se
Freq: Monthly; **Circ:** 8,000
Editor: Johan Larsson; **Publisher:** Magnus Höij
Profile: Magazine covering IT and the Internet. Contains product tests, articles, interviews, reviews, news and information. Also features suggested websites and information about Internet banking and shopping.
Language(s): Swedish
Readership: Aimed at PC and Mac users both in a professional capacity and at home.
ADVERTISING RATES:
Full Page Colour .... SEK 53500
SCC .... SEK 445.83
BUSINESS: COMPUTERS & AUTOMATION: Data Transmission

INTERNETWORLD; WEBB 1844686W5R-129
Editorial: Karlbergsv. 77, 106 78 STOCKHOLM
Tel: 8453 61 70
Email: webad@idg.se **Web site:** http://www.internetworld.idg.se
Freq: Daily; **Cover Price:** Free; **Circ:** 5,752 Unique Users
Editor-in-Chief: Magnus Höij
Language(s): Swedish
ADVERTISING RATES:
SCC .... SEK 89
BUSINESS: COMPUTERS & AUTOMATION: Computers Related

INTRUM MAGAZINE 1660582W14A-295
Editorial: c/o Intrum Justitia AB, 105 24 STOCKHOLM **Tel:** 8 546 102 00 **Fax:** 8 546 102 11
Email: info@intrum.com **Web site:** http://www.intrum.com
Freq: Quarterly; **Circ:** 8,000
Editor-in-Chief: Anders Antonsson; **Publisher:** Anders Antonsson
Language(s): Swedish
BUSINESS: COMMERCE, INDUSTRY & MANAGEMENT

INVANDRARKVINNAN 751124W14F-60
Editorial: Norrtullsgatan 45, 113 45 STOCKHOLM
Tel: 8 30 21 89 **Fax:** 8 33 53 23
Email: s.riffi@telia.com **Web site:** http://www.immi.se/tidskrifter/invandrarkvinnan.htm
Freq: Quarterly; **Circ:** 2,500
Editor: Mirja Huusko; **Publisher:** Meri Helena Forsberg
Language(s): Swedish
BUSINESS: COMMERCE, INDUSTRY & MANAGEMENT: Training & Recruitment

ISLAM & POLITIK 2010034W82-572
Email: abdulkader.habib@gmail.com **Web site:** http://broderskap.se
Circ: 40,000
Editor-in-Chief: Abdulkader Habib; **Advertising Manager:** Abdikani Muhammed
Language(s): Swedish
CONSUMER: CURRENT AFFAIRS & POLITICS

IT24 1803915W5E-103
Editorial: Karlbergsvägen 77, 106 78 STOCKHOLM
Tel: 8 453 60 00
Email: it24@idg.se **Web site:** http://www.it24.se
Circ: 12,618 Unique Users
Editor: Carl Grape; **Editor-in-Chief:** Daniel Goldberg; **Advertising Manager:** Britta Liljegren
Language(s): Swedish
BUSINESS: COMPUTERS & AUTOMATION: Data Transmission

IT I VÅRDEN 1809905W56A-354
Editorial: Computer Sweden, 106 78 STOCKHOLM
Tel: 8 453 60 50 **Fax:** 8 453 60 55
Email: red@itivarden.se **Web site:** http://itivarden.idg.se
Freq: Quarterly; **Circ:** 80,000
Editor: Maja Florin
Language(s): Swedish
ADVERTISING RATES:
Full Page Colour .... SEK 95000
BUSINESS: HEALTH & MEDICAL

IT I VÅRDEN; WEBB 1846448W14A-340
Editorial: Computer Sweden, 106 78 STOCKHOLM
Tel: 8 453 60 50 **Fax:** 8 453 60 55
Email: red@itivarden.se **Web site:** http://itivarden.idg.se
Freq: Daily; **Cover Price:** Free; **Circ:** 16,000 Unique Users
Editor: Maja Florin
Language(s): Swedish
BUSINESS: COMMERCE, INDUSTRY & MANAGEMENT

IT.BRANSCHEN 50234W5B-50
Editorial: IDG, Karlbergsvägen 77, 106 78 STOCKHOLM **Tel:** 8 453 60 00
Email: itbranschen@idg.se **Web site:** http://www.itbranschen.se
Date Established: 1996; **Freq:** Monthly; **Circ:** 14,000
Editor: Joakim Arstad Djurberg; **Editor-in-Chief:** Therese Järnankar; **Publisher:** Therese Järnankar
Profile: Magazine focusing on the IT industry in Sweden.
Language(s): Swedish
Readership: Aimed at manufacturers, distributors and retailers within the industry.
ADVERTISING RATES:
Full Page Colour .... SEK 47900
SCC .... SEK 400
BUSINESS: COMPUTERS & AUTOMATION: Data Processing

IT.BRANSCHEN; WEBB 1844976W5E-119
Editorial: IDG, Karlbergsvägen 77, 106 78 STOCKHOLM **Tel:** 8 453 60 00
Email: itbranschen@idg.se **Web site:** http://www.itbranschen.se
Freq: Daily; **Cover Price:** Free; **Circ:** 3,400 Unique Users
Editor-in-Chief: Therese Järnankar; **Publisher:** Therese Järnankar
Language(s): Swedish
ADVERTISING RATES:
SCC .... SEK 80
BUSINESS: COMPUTERS & AUTOMATION: Data Transmission

IT-CHEFEN 1666586W5F-1
Editorial: World Trade center D8, 111 64 STOCKHOLM **Tel:** 8 20 21 10
Email: info@it-chefen.se **Web site:** http://www.itchefen.com
Freq: Quarterly; **Circ:** 5,000
Advertising Manager: Anders Åkerman
Language(s): Swedish
ADVERTISING RATES:
Full Page Colour .... SEK 39500
SCC .... SEK 329
BUSINESS: COMPUTERS & AUTOMATION: Multimedia

IT-CHEFEN; WEBB 1844803W5E-118
Editorial: World Trade center D8, 111 64 STOCKHOLM **Tel:** 8 20 21 10 **Fax:** 820 78 10
Email: info@it-chefen.se **Web site:** http://www.itchefen.com
Freq: Daily; **Cover Price:** Free; **Circ:** 1,667 Unique Users
Publisher: Anders Åkerman
Language(s): Swedish
BUSINESS: COMPUTERS & AUTOMATION: Data Transmission

IT-NYTT.NU 1625768W18B-82
Editorial: VILL EJ HA PRESSMEDD. VIA BREV
Tel: 480 42 18 40
Email: press@fl-net.se **Web site:** http://www.it-nytt.nu
Freq: Weekly; **Circ:** 75,000 Unique Users
Editor: Michael Ländin
Language(s): Swedish
BUSINESS: ELECTRONICS: Telecommunications

IVA-AKTUELLT 50345W19A-60
Editorial: Box 5073, 102 42 STOCKHOLM
Tel: 8 791 29 79 **Fax:** 8 791 30 18
Email: par.ronnberg@iva.se **Web site:** http://www.iva.se
Freq: 6 issues yearly - (9 nr/år); **Circ:** 6,000
Editor-in-Chief: Pär Rönnberg
Profile: Journal containing information and news from the Royal Swedish Academy of Engineering Sciences.
Language(s): Swedish
ADVERTISING RATES:
Full Page Colour .... SEK 8700
SCC .... SEK 72.50
BUSINESS: ENGINEERING & MACHINERY

JABBOK 751125W87-155
Editorial: Skarpnäcks Allé 58, 128 33 SKARPNÄCK
Tel: 8 604 25 89
Email: benbenson@swipnet.se **Web site:** http://www.jabbok.se
Date Established: 1985; **Freq:** Quarterly; **Circ:** 2,000
Editor: Ben Benson; **Editor-in-Chief:** Ben Benson; **Advertising Manager:** Ben Benson
Language(s): Swedish
CONSUMER: RELIGIOUS

JAGAREN 1803922W56L-56
Editorial: Box 16145, 103 23 STOCKHOLM
Tel: 8 789 30 00 **Fax:** 8202085
Email: foreningen@jag.se **Web site:** http://www.jag.se
Freq: Quarterly; **Circ:** 3,000
Editor: Kerstin Sellin
Language(s): Swedish
BUSINESS: HEALTH & MEDICAL: Disability & Rehabilitation

JAKT & JÄGARE 51025W75F-40
Editorial: Slottsgatan 21, 722 11 VÄSTERÅS
Tel: 21 14 78 50 **Fax:** 21 14 73 50
Email: jakt.jagare@jrf-lj.org **Web site:** http://www.jaktojagare.se
Freq: Monthly; **Circ:** 24,700
Editor: Johan Boström; **Editor-in-Chief:** Anders Ljung; **Advertising Manager:** Ewa Westman; **Publisher:** Anders Ljung
Profile: Magazine about hunting, shooting, fishing and wildlife.
Language(s): Swedish
ADVERTISING RATES:
Full Page Colour .... SEK 12350
SCC .... SEK 102.91
CONSUMER: SPORT: Shooting

JAKTDEBATT - TIDSKRIFTEN SOM VÄRNAR OM DE VILDA DJUREN 1667817W75F-211
Editorial: Jägaregatan 106, 226 53 LUND
Tel: 46 30 72 12
Email: arne.e.ohlsson@telia.com **Web site:** http://www.jaktkritikerna.se/jaktdebatt
Freq: Quarterly; **Circ:** 550
Editor: Arne Ohlsson; **Publisher:** Arne Ohlsson
Language(s): Swedish
CONSUMER: SPORT: Shooting

JAKTJOURNALEN 51026W75F-50
Editorial: Box 100 13, 434 37 KUNGSBACKA
Tel: 300 306 20 **Fax:** 300 734 99
Email: holger.nilsson@jaktjournalen.se **Web site:** http://www.jaktjournalen.se
Freq: Monthly; **Circ:** 30,100
Editor: Ulf Lindroth; **Advertising Manager:** Maria Edlund; **Publisher:** Holger Nilsson
Profile: Magazine about hunting, gun-dogs, weaponry and rifle shooting.
Language(s): Swedish
CONSUMER: SPORT: Shooting

JAKTMARKER & FISKEVATTEN
51027W75F-70
Editorial: Bergendorffsgatan 5 B, 652 24 KARLSTAD
Tel: 54 775 25 10 **Fax:** 54 775 25 99
Email: info.jof@jof.se **Web site:** http://www.jof.se
Date Established: 1913; **Freq:** Monthly; **Circ:** 40,000
Editor-in-Chief: Mats Gyllsand; **Managing Director:** Mats Gyllsand; **Advertising Manager:** Ulla Jonsson; **Publisher:** Mats Gyllsand
Profile: Magazine about hunting and fishing.
Language(s): Swedish
Readership: Read by anglers and hunters.
ADVERTISING RATES:
Full Page Colour .... SEK 28900
SCC .... SEK 240.83
CONSUMER: SPORT: Shooting

JÄRN-BYGG-FÄRG, TIDSKRIFT FÖR FACKHANDELN
1639388W4E-152
Editorial: Box 2082, 169 02 SOLNA
Tel: 8 514 934 20 **Fax:** 8 514 934 29
Email: jaff@vtf.se **Web site:** http://www.jarnbyggfarg.se
Freq: Monthly; **Circ:** 7,800
Editor: Peter Norrbohm; **Advertising Manager:** Thomas af Kleen; **Publisher:** Lars Cyrus
Language(s): Swedish
ADVERTISING RATES:
Full Page Colour .... SEK 21800
SCC .... SEK 181.70
BUSINESS: ARCHITECTURE & BUILDING: Building

JNYTT.SE
1803853W72-835
Editorial: Gjuterigatan 9, 553 18 JÖNKÖPING
Tel: 36 340 300
Email: press@jnytt.se **Web site:** http://www.jnytt.se
Freq: Daily; **Cover Price:** Paid; **Circ:** 7,250 Unique Users
Editor-in-Chief: Gunilla Bunnvik; **Managing Director:** Krister Leimola; **Publisher:** Krister Leimola
Language(s): Swedish
LOCAL NEWSPAPERS

JÖNKÖPING NU; WEBB
1846509W65A-1081
Editorial: Box 264, 551 14 JÖNKÖPING
Tel: 36 30 94 90 **Fax:** 36 16 04 90
Email: redaktion@jonkoping.nu **Web site:** http://www.jonkoping.nu
Freq: Daily; **Cover Price:** Free; **Circ:** 22,667 Unique Users
Publisher: Stefan Fels
Language(s): Swedish
ADVERTISING RATES:
SCC .... SEK 29
NATIONAL DAILY & SUNDAY NEWSPAPERS: National Daily Newspapers

JÖNKÖPINGS-POSTEN
50791W67B-4700
Editorial: 551 80 JÖNKÖPING **Tel:** 36 30 40 50
Fax: 36 12 27 15
Email: red@jonkopingsposten.se **Web site:** http://www.jonkopingsposten.se
Date Established: 1865
Circ: 37,100
Editor: Janne Johansson; **Advertising Manager:** Gunnel Carlsson; **Publisher:** Mats Ottosson
Language(s): Swedish
ADVERTISING RATES:
Full Page Colour .... SEK 66350
SCC .... SEK 172.34
Editions:
Jönköpings-Posten; Kulturredaktionen
REGIONAL DAILY & SUNDAY NEWSPAPERS: Regional Daily Newspapers

JORD & SKOG
1837053W21A-81
Editorial: Fabriksgatan 21, 342 32 ALVESTA
Tel: 472 440 31 **Fax:** 47230091
Email: thomas.edgren@lokaltidningen.se **Web site:** http://www.lokaltidningen.se
Freq: 6 issues yearly; **Cover Price:** Free; **Circ:** 26,000
Advertising Manager: Stefan Johansson; **Publisher:** Cecilia Petersson
Language(s): Swedish
ADVERTISING RATES:
Full Page Colour .... SEK 22995
SCC .... SEK 114.90
BUSINESS: AGRICULTURE & FARMING

JORDEMODERN
50616W56B-30
Editorial: Baldersgatan 1, 114 27 STOCKHOLM
Tel: 8 10 70 88 **Fax:** 8244946
Email: margareta.rehn@barnmorskeforbundet.se
Web site: http://www.barnmorskeforbundet.se
Date Established: 1886; **Freq:** Monthly; **Circ:** 7,000
Advertising Manager: Maria Sahlin; **Publisher:** Ingela Wiklund
Profile: Publication of the Swedish Midwives Association.
Language(s): Swedish
Readership: Aimed at those working in the fields of antenatal, natal and post-natal care and gynaecology.
BUSINESS: HEALTH & MEDICAL: Nursing

JOURNAL
752059W76B-100
Editorial: c/o Sveriges Dramatikerförbund, Drottningg 85, 1 tr., 111 60 STOCKHOLM
Tel: 8 21 33 10 **Fax:** 8 613 39 79
Email: sdf@dramatiker.se **Web site:** http://www.dramatiker.se
Freq: Half-yearly; **Circ:** 1,100
Editor-in-Chief: Magnus Lind; **Publisher:** Rolf Börjlind
Language(s): Swedish
CONSUMER: MUSIC & PERFORMING ARTS: Theatre

JOURNAL CHOCOLAT
1803864W74P-211
Editorial: Box 204, 541 25 SKÖVDE
Tel: 500 43 55 10 **Fax:** 500 43 55 01
Email: leo.olsson@koncis.se **Web site:** http://www.journal-chocolat.se
Freq: Quarterly; **Circ:** 12,500
Editor: Leo Olsson; **Advertising Manager:** Karina von Brömsen
Language(s): Swedish
CONSUMER: WOMEN'S INTEREST CONSUMER MAGAZINES: Food & Cookery

JOURNALISTEN
50185W2B-60
Editorial: Box 1116, 111 81 STOCKHOLM
Tel: 8 613 75 00
Email: redaktionen@journalisten.se **Web site:** http://www.journalisten.se
Date Established: 1904; **Freq:** 26 issues yearly; **Circ:** 18,800
Advertising Manager: Eva Agrell Lundh; **Publisher:** Helena Giertta
Profile: Official magazine of the Swedish Union of Journalists. Covers press ethics, freedom of speech, copyright and working conditions in the EU.
Language(s): Swedish
ADVERTISING RATES:
Full Page Colour .... SEK 32000
SCC .... SEK 200
BUSINESS: COMMUNICATIONS, ADVERTISING & MARKETING: Press

JOURNALISTEN; JOURNALISTEN.SE
1846469W14F-117
Editorial: Box 1116, 111 81 STOCKHOLM
Tel: 8 613 75 00
Email: redaktionen@journalisten.se **Web site:** http://www.journalisten.se
Freq: Daily; **Cover Price:** Free; **Circ:** 8,200 Unique Users
Editor-in-Chief: Helena Giertta; **Advertising Manager:** Eva Agrell; **Publisher:** Helena Giertta
Language(s): Swedish
ADVERTISING RATES:
SCC .... SEK 40
BUSINESS: COMMERCE, INDUSTRY & MANAGEMENT: Training & Recruitment

JUDISK KRÖNIKA
51284W87-32
Editorial: Box 5053, 102 42 STOCKHOLM
Tel: 8 660 70 62 **Fax:** 8 660 38 72
Email: judisk.kronika@swipnet.se **Web site:** http://www.judiskkronika.se
Date Established: 1932; **Freq:** 6 issues yearly; **Circ:** 6,200
Editor: Jackie Jakubowski; **Editor-in-Chief:** Jackie Jakubowski; **Advertising Manager:** Lillemor Davin; **Publisher:** Jackie Jakubowski
Profile: Magazine about Jewish culture, politics and religion.
Language(s): Swedish
CONSUMER: RELIGIOUS

JULIA
752079W75J-100
Editorial: 205 08 MALMO **Tel:** 40 693 94 00
Fax: 406939544
Email: julia@egmont.se **Web site:** http://www.julia.egmont.se
Date Established: 2000; **Freq:** 26 issues yearly; **Circ:** 33,300
Advertising Manager: Jenny Frank
Language(s): Swedish
ADVERTISING RATES:
Full Page Colour .... SEK 20400
SCC .... SEK 170
CONSUMER: SPORT: Athletics

JULIA SPECIAL
1841524W74F-182
Editorial: 205 08 MALMÖ **Tel:** 40 693 94 00
Fax: 40 693 95 44
Email: julia@egmont.se **Web site:** http://www.julia.egmont.se
Freq: Quarterly; **Circ:** 27,700
Language(s): Swedish
ADVERTISING RATES:
Full Page Colour .... SEK 20400
SCC .... SEK 170
CONSUMER: WOMEN'S INTEREST CONSUMER MAGAZINES: Teenage

JUNIA
1664002W74A-149
Editorial: Rallarvägen 37, 184 40 ÅKERSBERGA
Tel: 8 540 203 28 **Fax:** 854020328
Email: info@junia.nu **Web site:** http://www.junia.se
Freq: 6 issues yearly; **Circ:** 9,000
Publisher: Marie Arnfjell
Language(s): Swedish
ADVERTISING RATES:
Full Page Colour .... SEK 14250
SCC .... SEK 118.75
CONSUMER: WOMEN'S INTEREST CONSUMER MAGAZINES: Women's Interest

JURIDISK TIDSKRIFT
50501W44-8
Editorial: Artillerigatan 67, 114 45 STOCKHOLM
Tel: 8 662 00 80 **Fax:** 8 662 00 86
Email: helena.forselius@jure.se **Web site:** http://www.jt.se
Date Established: 1988; **Freq:** Quarterly; **Circ:** 2,300
Editor: Kent Källström; **Publisher:** Kent Källström
Profile: Journal about law. Contains articles, debate and reviews.
Language(s): Swedish
BUSINESS: LEGAL

JUSEKTIDNINGEN
50502W44-10
Editorial: Box 5167, 102 44 STOCKHOLM
Tel: 8 665 29 20 **Fax:** 8 662 79 23
Email: info@jusektidningen.se **Web site:** http://www.jusektidningen.se
Date Established: 1951; **Freq:** Monthly; **Circ:** 80,300
Editor: Ulf Storm; **Advertising Manager:** Magnus Johansson; **Publisher:** Ann Marie Bergström
Profile: Magazine covering issues mainly concerning wages and career opportunities.
Language(s): Swedish
Readership: Aimed at law, business and economics graduates and system engineers.
ADVERTISING RATES:
Full Page Colour .... SEK 35700
SCC .... SEK 296.66
Copy instructions: *Copy Date:* 30 days prior to publication date
BUSINESS: LEGAL

JUSEKTIDNINGEN; WEBB
1843549W14L-195
Editorial: Box 5167, 102 44 STOCKHOLM
Tel: 8 665 29 20
Email: info@jusektidningen.se **Web site:** http://www.jusektidningen.se
Freq: Daily; **Cover Price:** Free; **Circ:** 15,200 Unique Users
Editor: Ulf Storm; **Editor-in-Chief:** Ann Marie Bergström; **Advertising Manager:** Magnus Johansson; **Publisher:** Ann Marie Bergström
Language(s): Swedish
ADVERTISING RATES:
SCC .... SEK 59
BUSINESS: COMMERCE, INDUSTRY & MANAGEMENT: Trade Unions

KALMAR LÄNS TIDNING / NYBRO TIDNING; WEBB
1846298W65A-1074
Editorial: Box 23, 386 21 FÄRJESTADEN
Tel: 485 307 19
Email: webben@kalmarlanstidning.se **Web site:** http://www.klt.nu
Freq: Daily; **Cover Price:** Free; **Circ:** 3,333 Unique Users
Publisher: Lina Watanen
Language(s): Swedish
ADVERTISING RATES:
SCC .... SEK 16
NATIONAL DAILY & SUNDAY NEWSPAPERS: National Daily Newspapers

KALMARPOSTEN
634159W80-75
Editorial: Jenny Nyströms gränd 2, 392 33 KALMAR
Tel: 480 72 02 00 **Fax:** 48 072 02 00
Email: tidningen@kalmarposten.se **Web site:** http://www.kalmarposten.se
Date Established: 1988; **Freq:** Weekly; **Cover Price:** Free; **Circ:** 74,900
Advertising Manager: Monika Ragnarsson; **Publisher:** Per-Olof Persson
Profile: Newspaper for Kalmar and surrounding areas.
Language(s): Swedish
Readership: Read by local residents.
ADVERTISING RATES:
Full Page Colour .... SEK 32412
SCC .... SEK 158.77
CONSUMER: RURAL & REGIONAL INTEREST

KAMERA OCH BILD
1697068W38-16
Editorial: Mediaprovider Scandinavia AB, Box 1054, 101 39 STOCKHOLM **Tel:** 8 503 057 04
Email: kamerabild@mediaprovider.se **Web site:** http://kamerabild.mkf.se
Freq: Monthly; **Circ:** 25,000
Editor-in-Chief: Magnus Fröderberg
Language(s): Swedish
ADVERTISING RATES:
Full Page Colour .... SEK 34000
SCC .... SEK 283.33
BUSINESS: PHOTOGRAPHIC TRADE

KAMERA OCH BILD; WEBB
1846450W60A-72
Editorial: Mediaprovider Scandinavia AB, Box 1054, 101 39 STOCKHOLM **Tel:** 8799 63 65
Email: kameraochbild@mediaprovider.se **Web site:** http://www.kamerabild.se
Freq: Daily; **Cover Price:** Free; **Circ:** 8,600 Unique Users
Editor-in-Chief: Magnus Fröderberg
Language(s): Swedish
ADVERTISING RATES:
SCC .... SEK 57
BUSINESS: PUBLISHING: Publishing & Book Trade

KAMRATPOSTEN
51343W91D-60
Editorial: 105 44 STOCKHOLM **Tel:** 8 736 53 00
Fax: 8 34 69 08
Web site: http://www.kpwebben.se
Date Established: 1892; **Freq:** Monthly; **Circ:** 60,000
Profile: Magazine containing information about current affairs.
Language(s): Swedish
Readership: Aimed at children aged between 8 and 15 years.
ADVERTISING RATES:
Full Page Colour .... SEK 50000
SCC .... SEK 416.66
CONSUMER: RECREATION & LEISURE: Children & Youth

KAMRATPOSTEN; KPWEBBEN.SE
1846427W74F-183
Editorial: 105 44 STOCKHOLM **Tel:** 8 736 53 00
Fax: 8346908
Email: kamratposten@kamratposten.nu **Web site:** http://www.kpwebben.se
Freq: Daily; **Cover Price:** Free; **Circ:** 12,000 Unique Users
Editor-in-Chief: Ola Lindholm
Language(s): Swedish
CONSUMER: WOMEN'S INTEREST CONSUMER MAGAZINES: Teenage

KANAL 12
752515W80-575
Editorial: Tage Erlanderg. 4, 652 20 KARLSTAD
Tel: 54 17 59 00
Email: kabeltv@kanal12.se **Web site:** http://www.kanal12.se
Freq: Daily; **Circ:** 32,000
Managing Director: Torsten Möller; **Publisher:** Torsten Möller
Language(s): Swedish
CONSUMER: RURAL & REGIONAL INTEREST

KÅRANEN
751010W62A-425
Editorial: Mälardalens studentkår, Smedjegatan 32 B, 632 20 ESKILSTUNA **Tel:** 16 15 37 11
Fax: 16 15 36 19
Email: chred.karanen@mds.mdh.se **Web site:** http://www.karanen.se
Freq: Quarterly; **Cover Price:** Free; **Circ:** 10,000
Editor-in-Chief: Veronica Larsen; **Advertising Manager:** Malin Swanström; **Publisher:** Malin Swanström
Language(s): Swedish
BUSINESS: CHURCH & SCHOOL EQUIPMENT & EDUCATION: Education

KARAVAN - LITTERÄR TIDSKRIFT PÅ RESA MELLAN KULTURER
51260W84B-80
Editorial: Box 17131, 104 62 STOCKHOLM
Tel: 8 442 02 13
Email: info@karavan.se **Web site:** http://www.karavan.se
Date Established: 1992; **Freq:** Quarterly; **Circ:** 2,000
Editor: Birgitta Wallin; **Advertising Manager:** Birgitta Wallin; **Publisher:** Birgitta Wallin
Profile: Publication containing news, information and articles about literature from Africa, Asia and Latin America. Also contains translations of fiction and poetry.
Language(s): Swedish
CONSUMER: THE ARTS & LITERARY: Literary

KÅRIREN
750999W76A-170
Editorial: Stridsvagnsvägen 8A, 291 39 KRISTIANSTAD **Tel:** 44 20 75 74 **Fax:** 44 12 58 25
Email: info@ksk.nu **Web site:** http://www.ksk.nu/kariren.asp
Freq: Quarterly; **Circ:** 6,500
Editor-in-Chief: Lasse Hörnäs; **Publisher:** Lasse Hörnäs
Language(s): Swedish
CONSUMER: MUSIC & PERFORMING ARTS: Cinema

KÅRKATT
750995W62A-430
Editorial: Studentkåren i Skövde, Södra Trängallén 4, 541 46 SKÖVDE **Tel:** 500 44 87 79
Email: redaktion@karkatt.se **Web site:** http://www.karkatt.se
Freq: Quarterly; **Circ:** 1,500
Editor-in-Chief: Viktor Rydbeck

Language(s): Swedish
ADVERTISING RATES:
Full Page Colour .... SEK 4000
BUSINESS: CHURCH & SCHOOL EQUIPMENT & EDUCATION: Education

KARLSKOGA TIDNING
50794W67B-4750
Editorial: Box 105, 691 22 KARLSKOGA
Tel: 586 72 13 00 **Fax:** 586 580 50
Email: redaktion@karlskogatidning.se **Web site:** http://nwt.se/karlskoga
Date Established: 1883
Circ: 7,500
Advertising Manager: Erik Wahlström; **Publisher:** Jonas Klint
Language(s): Swedish
ADVERTISING RATES:
Full Page Colour .... SEK 19680
SCC .... SEK 98.40
REGIONAL DAILY & SUNDAY NEWSPAPERS: Regional Daily Newspapers

KARLSKOGA-KURIREN
633911W67B-4725
Editorial: Kungsvägen 34, 691 24 KARLSKOGA
Tel: 586 784 300 **Fax:** 586 357 57
Email: redaktionen@karlskoga-kuriren.se **Web site:** http://www.karlskoga-kuriren.se
Date Established: 1902
Circ: 5,200
Editor: Annelie Gustavsson; **Advertising Manager:** Tommy Elovsson; **Publisher:** Göran Karlsson
Language(s): Swedish
ADVERTISING RATES:
Full Page Colour .... SEK 15900
SCC .... SEK 79.50
REGIONAL DAILY & SUNDAY NEWSPAPERS: Regional Daily Newspapers

KARLSKOGA-KURIREN; INSÄNDARAVDELNINGEN
751894W74C-265
Editorial: Box 211, 691 24 KARLSKOGA
Tel: 586 363 91 **Fax:** 58635757
Email: folketsrost@karlskoga-kuriren.se **Web site:** http://www.karlskoga-kuriren.se
Circ: 5,200
Editor: Annelie Gustavsson
Language(s): Swedish
CONSUMER: WOMEN'S INTEREST CONSUMER MAGAZINES: Home & Family

KARLSKOGA-KURIREN; WEBB
1843541W65A-990
Editorial: Kungsvägen 34, 691 24 KARLSKOGA
Tel: 586 363 90 **Fax:** 586 357 57
Email: redaktionen@karlskoga-kuriren.se **Web site:** http://www.karlskoga-kuriren.se
Freq: Daily; **Cover Price:** Free; **Circ:** 2,160 Unique Users
Editor-in-Chief: Göran Karlsson; **Publisher:** Göran Karlsson
Language(s): Swedish
ADVERTISING RATES:
SCC .... SEK 16
NATIONAL DAILY & SUNDAY NEWSPAPERS: National Daily Newspapers

KARLSTADS STUDENTTIDNING
1663936W83-153
Editorial: Karlstads Universitet, 651 88 KARLSTAD
Tel: 54 700 14 93
Email: press@karlstadstudentkar.se **Web site:** http://www.karlstadsstudenttidning.se
Freq: 6 issues yearly; **Circ:** 5,000
Editor-in-Chief: Anton Dyberg; **Advertising Manager:** Anna Stålhammar
Language(s): Swedish
CONSUMER: STUDENT PUBLICATIONS

KÄRNFULLT
1824317W82-475
Editorial: Box 210, 101 24 STOCKHOLM
Tel: 771 19 19 00 **Fax:** 8 20 87 90
Email: anna.ovesdotter@svenskmjolk.se **Web site:** http://www.svenskmjolk.se/Kärnfullt
Freq: 26 issues yearly; **Circ:** 9,000
Editor: Anna Ovesdotter
Language(s): Swedish
ADVERTISING RATES:
SCC .... SEK 150
CONSUMER: CURRENT AFFAIRS & POLITICS

KÅRSORDET
751067W74A-135
Editorial: Jönköpings Studentkår, Gjuterigatan 3 C, 553 18 JÖNKÖPING **Tel:** 36 15 75 86
Fax: 36 16 62 61
Email: karsordet@karen.hj.se **Web site:** http://www.karsordet.com
Date Established: 1984; **Freq:** 6 issues yearly; **Circ:** 8,500
Editor: Linus Norberg; **Advertising Manager:** Stina Hallman; **Publisher:** Emelie Danielsson
Language(s): Swedish
CONSUMER: WOMEN'S INTEREST CONSUMER MAGAZINES: Women's Interest

KATOLSKT MAGASIN
51285W87-35
Editorial: Box 2038, 750 02 UPPSALA
Tel: 18 13 61 40 **Fax:** 18136145
Email: redaktionen@katolsktmagasin.se **Web site:** http://www.katolsktmagasin.se
Freq: Monthly; **Circ:** 2,500
Editor-in-Chief: Margareta Murray-Nyman; **Advertising Manager:** Sofia Wahlstedt; **Publisher:** Kjell Blückert
Profile: Magazine about the Catholic church.
Language(s): Swedish
ADVERTISING RATES:
Full Page Colour .... SEK 5000
SCC .... SEK 41.67
CONSUMER: RELIGIOUS

KATOLSKT MAGASIN; WEBB
1844790W65A-1031
Editorial: Box 2038, 750 02 UPPSALA
Tel: 18 13 61 40 **Fax:** 18 13 61 45
Email: redaktionen@katolsktmagasin.se **Web site:** http://www.katolsktmagasin.se
Freq: Daily; **Cover Price:** Free; **Circ:** 833 Unique Users
Editor: Birgit Ahlberg-Hyse; **Editor-in-Chief:** Margareta Murray-Nyman; **Advertising Manager:** Sofia Wahlstedt
Language(s): Swedish
ADVERTISING RATES:
SCC .... SEK 8.2
NATIONAL DAILY & SUNDAY NEWSPAPERS: National Daily Newspapers

KATRINEHOLMS-KURIREN
50799W67B-4800
Editorial: Box 111, 641 22 KATRINEHOLM
Tel: 150 728 00 **Fax:** 150 539 00
Email: redaktion@kkuriren.se **Web site:** http://www.kkuriren.se
Circ: 12,400
Editor: Kristina Rönnqvist; **Managing Director:** Stefan Toll; **Advertising Manager:** Stefan Fredriksson
Language(s): Swedish
ADVERTISING RATES:
Full Page Colour .... SEK 31000
SCC .... SEK 155
REGIONAL DAILY & SUNDAY NEWSPAPERS: Regional Daily Newspapers

KATRINEHOLMS-KURIREN; WEBB
751594W67B-8935
Editorial: Box 111, 641 22 KATRINEHOLM
Tel: 150 728 00 **Fax:** 15053900
Email: redaktionen@kkuriren.se **Web site:** http://www.kkuriren.se
Freq: Daily; **Cover Price:** Free; **Circ:** 12,900 Unique Users
Language(s): Swedish
REGIONAL DAILY & SUNDAY NEWSPAPERS: Regional Daily Newspapers

KATTLIV
51607W81C-35
Editorial: Borgås gårdsväg 1, 434 39 KUNGSBACKA
Tel: 300 334 44 **Fax:** 30033749
Email: info@kattliv.com **Web site:** http://www.kattliv.com
Date Established: 1996; **Freq:** Daily; **Circ:** 16,000
Editor-in-Chief: Björn Segerblad; **Advertising Manager:** Christina Kristensen; **Publisher:** Åke Steinwall
Profile: Magazine containing articles and information about cats. Provides advice on feeding, illnesses and general care. Also contains interviews, details of different breeds and product reviews.
Language(s): Swedish
Readership: Aimed at cat owners of all ages.
CONSUMER: ANIMALS & PETS: Cats

KELEN
1836247W62A-516
Editorial: Åsögatan 37, 791 71 FALUN
Tel: 23 77 71 60 **Fax:** 23 77 71 67
Email: tidning@dalastudent.se **Web site:** http://tidning.dalastudent.se
Freq: Quarterly; **Cover Price:** Free; **Circ:** 2,000
Publisher: Joacim Svensson
Language(s): Swedish
BUSINESS: CHURCH & SCHOOL EQUIPMENT & EDUCATION: Education

KEMIVÄRLDEN BIOTECH MED KEMISK TIDSKRIFT
50276W13-105
Editorial: Box 72001, 181 72 LIDINGÖ
Tel: 8 670 41 00
Email: boel.j@mentoronline.se **Web site:** http://www.chemicalnet.se
Date Established: 1991; **Freq:** Monthly; **Circ:** 8,200
Editor-in-Chief: Boel Jönsson; **Advertising Manager:** Stephan Martins; **Publisher:** Boel Jönsson
Profile: Official magazine of the Swedish Chemical Society and the Swedish Association of Chemical Engineers. Reports important developments in chemistry and chemical engineering, relating to research and development.
Language(s): Swedish
ADVERTISING RATES:
Full Page Colour .... SEK 29700
SCC .... SEK 247.5
BUSINESS: CHEMICALS

KH AKTUELLT
750921W80-585
Editorial: Ilanda Gård 120, 653 50 KARLSTAD
Tel: 54 18 77 18 **Fax:** 54 18 76 77
Email: redaktionen@svenskmediakonsult.se **Web site:** http://www.svenskmediakonsult.se
Freq: Monthly; **Circ:** 65,000
Advertising Manager: Joachim Svärdh
Language(s): Swedish
CONSUMER: RURAL & REGIONAL INTEREST

KICK
51365W94F-130
Editorial: Vanadisvägen 21, 113 46 STOCKHOLM
Tel: 8 545 472 00 **Fax:** 8 545 472 10
Web site: http://www.rekryteringsgruppen.se
Freq: Quarterly; **Circ:** 3,500
Editor: Peter Andersson-Pope; **Advertising Manager:** Lena Persson; **Publisher:** Lena Sandström
Profile: Magazine focusing on rehabilitation. Includes information on sporting activities, athletics, leisure and recreation.
Language(s): Swedish
Readership: Aimed at disabled people.
CONSUMER: OTHER CLASSIFICATIONS: Disability

KICK OFF
1804061W2C-105
Editorial: Box 145, 125 23 ÄLVSJÖ **Tel:** 8 568 790 30
Fax: 8 568 790 31
Email: redaktion@laprensa.se **Web site:** http://www.kick-off.se
Freq: Monthly; **Cover Price:** Free; **Circ:** 16,700
Editor-in-Chief: Fredrik Gustafsson; **Advertising Manager:** Malin Thalén
Language(s): Swedish
ADVERTISING RATES:
Full Page Colour .... SEK 28950
SCC .... SEK 241.25
BUSINESS: COMMUNICATIONS, ADVERTISING & MARKETING: Conferences & Exhibitions

KING MAGAZINE
1666054W86C-151
Editorial: Pyramidvägen 7, 169 91 SOLNA
Tel: 8 617 36 40 **Fax:** 8 652 76 30
Email: king@egmont.se **Web site:** http://www.kingmagazine.se
Freq: Monthly; **Circ:** 30,500
Language(s): Swedish
ADVERTISING RATES:
Full Page Colour .... SEK 55400
SCC .... SEK 461
CONSUMER: ADULT & GAY MAGAZINES: Men's Lifestyle Magazines

KINGSIZE MAGAZINE
1803909W76D-276
Editorial: King Publishing AB, Erik Dahlbergsgatan 30, 115 32 STOCKHOLM **Tel:** 8 528 000 55
Fax: 8 528 000 51
Email: info@kingsizemagazine.se **Web site:** http://www.kingsizemagazine.se
Freq: 6 issues yearly; **Circ:** 19,000
Editor: Henry Stenberg; **Publisher:** Camilla Berg
Language(s): Swedish
CONSUMER: MUSIC & PERFORMING ARTS: Music

KINNARPS MAGAZINE
1803885W14A-300
Editorial: Kinnarps Marketing & Sales AB, 521 88 KINNARP **Tel:** 515 380 00 **Fax:** 515 337 01
Email: ida.gustafsson@kinnarps.se **Web site:** http://www.kinnarps.com
Freq: Half-yearly; **Circ:** 90,000
Publisher: Per-Ola Wennefors
Language(s): Swedish
BUSINESS: COMMERCE, INDUSTRY & MANAGEMENT

KIRUNA TIDNINGEN
51151W80-90
Editorial: Adolfs Hedinsvägen 58, 981 33 KIRUNA
Tel: 980 805 81 **Fax:** 98080191
Email: kiruna.tidningen@kiruna.nu **Web site:** http://www.kirunatidningen.se
Freq: Monthly; **Circ:** 3,300
Publisher: Kjell Törmä
Profile: Newspaper containing infomation about Kiruna.
Language(s): Swedish
ADVERTISING RATES:
Full Page Colour .... SEK 6000
CONSUMER: RURAL & REGIONAL INTEREST

KLASSIKER
1663514W77F-101
Editorial: Box 23800, 10435 STOCKHOLM
Tel: 8 736 12 00 **Fax:** 8 736 12 49
Email: red@klassiker.nu **Web site:** http://www.klassiker.nu
Freq: 6 issues yearly; **Circ:** 21,900
Editor-in-Chief: Carl Legelius; **Advertising Manager:** Maziar Zarrin; **Publisher:** Nils-Eric Frendin
Language(s): Swedish
ADVERTISING RATES:
Full Page Colour .... SEK 15000
SCC .... SEK 125
CONSUMER: MOTORING & CYCLING: Veteran Cars

KLIMATMAGASINET EFFEKT
1923947W57-122
Editorial: Box 17506, 118 91 STOCKHOLM
Tel: 708 88 17 23
Email: redaktionen@effektmagasin.se **Web site:** http://www.effektmagasin.se
Freq: 6 issues yearly; **Circ:** 2,000
Publisher: Sara Jeswani
Language(s): Swedish
BUSINESS: ENVIRONMENT & POLLUTION

KLOKA HEM
1837054W58-103
Editorial: Box 4403, 102 68 STOCKHOLM
Tel: 8 410 357 00 **Fax:** 8 410 357 01
Email: klokahem@etc.se
Freq: Quarterly; **Circ:** 40,000
Editor-in-Chief: Karin Holmberg; **Publisher:** Johan Ehrenberg
Language(s): Swedish
BUSINESS: ENERGY, FUEL & NUCLEAR

KOLLEGA
1833049W62A-514
Editorial: Attention Kollega, Olof Palmes Gata 17, 105 32 STOCKHOLM **Tel:** 8 504 150 00
Fax: 8 618 67 22
Email: brev@kollega.se **Web site:** http://www.kollega.se
Freq: Monthly; **Circ:** 484,000
Editor: Dag Bremberg
Language(s): Swedish
ADVERTISING RATES:
Full Page Colour .... SEK 54900
SCC .... SEK 457.50
BUSINESS: CHURCH & SCHOOL EQUIPMENT & EDUCATION: Education

KOLONITRÄDGÅRDEN
51355W93-50
Editorial: Åsögatan 149, 116 32 STOCKHOLM
Tel: 8 556 930 82 **Fax:** 8 640 38 98
Email: kolonitradgarden@koloni.org **Web site:** http://www.koloni.org
Date Established: 1918; **Freq:** Quarterly; **Circ:** 25,400
Editor: Ulrika Hallin; **Advertising Manager:** Marianne Lingserius; **Publisher:** Lars Oscarson
Profile: Magazine of interest to amateur gardeners. Contains general gardening information as well as news about research, literature, housing, environmental issues and reports.
Language(s): Swedish
Readership: Aimed at people of all ages interested in gardening.
ADVERTISING RATES:
Full Page Colour .... SEK 16000
SCC .... SEK 133.33
CONSUMER: GARDENING

KOM
750834W62A-440
Editorial: c/o Akademikerservice Box 3215, 103 64 STOCKHOLM **Tel:** 8 567 060 00 **Fax:** 8 567 060 99
Email: bo-goran.dahlberg@molndal.se **Web site:** http://www.visnet.se
Freq: Quarterly; **Circ:** 6,000
Editor-in-Chief: Bo-Göran Dahlberg; **Advertising Manager:** Bo-Göran Dahlberg; **Publisher:** Ronny Spångberg
Language(s): Swedish
BUSINESS: CHURCH & SCHOOL EQUIPMENT & EDUCATION: Education

KOM UT
51277W86B-50
Editorial: Box 350, 101 26 STOCKHOLM
Tel: 8 501 629 13 **Fax:** 850162999
Email: komut@rfsl.se **Web site:** http://www.rfsl.se/?p=357
Date Established: 1979; **Freq:** Monthly; **Circ:** 30,000
Editor: Lars Jonsson
Profile: Magazine for gay men, lesbians and bi-sexuals throughout Sweden.
Language(s): Swedish
ADVERTISING RATES:
Full Page Colour .... SEK 20000
SCC .... SEK 125
CONSUMER: ADULT & GAY MAGAZINES: Gay & Lesbian Magazines

KOMMUNAL EKONOMI
50415W32A-110
Editorial: Odinsgatan 20 A, 411 03 GOTEBORG
Tel: 31 13 02 56
Email: acta.skrivkultur@telia.com **Web site:** http://www.kommunalekonomi.se
Freq: 6 issues yearly; **Circ:** 3,900

Editor: Thomas Pettersson; **Advertising Manager:** Tommy Flink
Profile: Publication about local government finances.
Language(s): Swedish
BUSINESS: LOCAL GOVERNMENT, LEISURE & RECREATION: Local Government

KOMMUNALARBETAREN
50416W32A-115
Editorial: Box 19034, 104 32 STOCKHOLM
Tel: 10442 73 00 **Fax:** 8 30 61 42
Email: kommunalarbetaren@ka.se **Web site:** http://www.ka.se
Date Established: 1910; **Freq:** 26 issues yearly; **Circ:** 535,500
Advertising Manager: Jörgen Rosengren; **Publisher:** Liv Beckström
Profile: Magazine for municipal workers.
Language(s): Swedish
ADVERTISING RATES:
Full Page Colour .... SEK 47500
SCC .... SEK 390
BUSINESS: LOCAL GOVERNMENT, LEISURE & RECREATION: Local Government

KOMMUNALARBETAREN; WEBB
1846661W14F-120
Editorial: Box 190 34, 104 32 STOCKHOLM
Tel: 8 728 28 00 **Fax:** 8306142
Email: webbred@ka.se **Web site:** http://www.ka.se
Freq: Daily; **Cover Price:** Free; **Circ:** 46,100 Unique Users
Publisher: Liv Beckström
Language(s): Swedish
BUSINESS: COMMERCE, INDUSTRY & MANAGEMENT: Training & Recruitment

KONFERENSVÄRLDEN
50192W2C-20
Editorial: Box 6910, 102 39 STOCKHOLM
Tel: 8 459 24 00 **Fax:** 8 459 24 10
Email: info@konferensvarlden.se **Web site:** http://www.konferensvarlden.se
Date Established: 1989; **Freq:** 6 issues yearly; **Circ:** 14,600
Editor: Christina Rehn; **Advertising Manager:** Britt Edberg; **Publisher:** Erik Bergdorf
Profile: Magazine containing articles on how to plan business trips, conferences, congresses and conventions. Contains trends, ideas and information.
Language(s): Swedish
ADVERTISING RATES:
Full Page Colour .... SEK 19700
SCC .... SEK 224.16
BUSINESS: COMMUNICATIONS, ADVERTISING & MARKETING: Conferences & Exhibitions

KONSTHISTORISK TIDSKRIFT
51238W84A-90
Editorial: Taylor & Francis AB, Box 3255, 103 65 STOCKHOLM **Tel:** 8 440 80 40 **Fax:** 8 440 80 50
Email: kht@se.tandf.no **Web site:** http://www.tandf.no
Freq: Quarterly; **Circ:** 700
Editor: Görel Cavalli-Björkman
Profile: International journal containing articles about the history of art.
Language(s): Swedish
Readership: Read by art historians and those with a general cultural interest in European art.
CONSUMER: THE ARTS & LITERARY: Arts

KONSTNÄREN
51239W84A-100
Editorial: Norrtullsgatan 45, 117 43 STOCKHOLM
Tel: 8 545 420 83 **Fax:** 8 545 420 89
Email: red@tidningenkonstnaren.se **Web site:** http://www.kro.se
Freq: Quarterly; **Circ:** 6,600
Editor-in-Chief: Anders Rydell; **Advertising Manager:** Anders Rydell
Profile: Magazine covering all aspects of art.
Language(s): Swedish
Readership: Aimed at artists and people with a keen interest in art.
CONSUMER: THE ARTS & LITERARY: Arts

KONSTPERSPEKTIV
51240W84A-110
Editorial: Box 600 65, 216 10 MALMO
Tel: 40 36 26 60 **Fax:** 40162607
Email: info@konstperspektiv.nu **Web site:** http://www.konstperspektiv.nu
Freq: Quarterly; **Circ:** 16,000
Advertising Manager: Hilde Flaten
Profile: Magazine of the Swedish National Federation of Art Associations.
Language(s): Swedish
CONSUMER: THE ARTS & LITERARY: Arts

KONSTTIDNINGEN
51241W84A-115
Editorial: Ehrensvärdsgatan 3, nb, 112 35 STOCKHOLM **Tel:** 736 91 48 07
Date Established: 1990; **Freq:** Quarterly; **Circ:** 3,500
Editor: Lars Kollberg; **Publisher:** Lars Kollberg
Profile: Magazine focusing on art.
Language(s): Swedish
ADVERTISING RATES:
Full Page Colour .... SEK 7000
SCC .... SEK 35
CONSUMER: THE ARTS & LITERARY: Arts

KONSTVÄRLDEN & DISAJN
51242W84A-116
Editorial: IPG-sweden, Box 6320, 102 35 STOCKHOLM **Tel:** 8 555 911 00 **Fax:** 8 555 911 50
Email: info@ipg-sweden.com **Web site:** http://www.disajn.com
Freq: 6 issues yearly; **Circ:** 25,000
Editor-in-Chief: Göran Hellström; **Advertising Manager:** Nils Mörner; **Publisher:** Göran Hellström
Profile: Magazine covering all aspects of the art world from classical art to modern design.
Language(s): Swedish
ADVERTISING RATES:
Full Page Colour .... SEK 28900
SCC .... SEK 240.83
CONSUMER: THE ARTS & LITERARY: Arts

KONSULTEN
50161W1B-150
Editorial: Box 143, 791 23 FALUN **Tel:** 23 79 49 50
Fax: 23 637 88
Email: info@srfkonsult.se **Web site:** http://www.srfkonsult.se
Date Established: 1990; **Freq:** 6 issues yearly - (8 nr/år); **Circ:** 9,500
Editor: Lena Iredahl
Profile: Magazine covering all aspects of accountancy.
Language(s): Swedish
ADVERTISING RATES:
Full Page Colour .... SEK 18200
SCC .... SEK 138.33
BUSINESS: FINANCE & ECONOMICS: Accountancy

KONTAKTEN/CONTACT
750569W18B-75
Editorial: Box 1042, 164 21 KISTA **Tel:** 8 610 20 00
Email: jenz.nilsson@jgcommunication.se
Circ: 80,000
Editor: Jenz Nilsson; **Editor-in-Chief:** Jenz Nilsson
Language(s): Swedish
BUSINESS: ELECTRONICS: Telecommunications

KOREA-INFORMATION
1624428W14C-49
Email: christer@svenskkoreanska.se **Web site:** http://www.svenskkoreanska.se
Freq: Quarterly; **Circ:** 300
Language(s): Swedish
BUSINESS: COMMERCE, INDUSTRY & MANAGEMENT: International Commerce

KOSMETIK
50325W15A-100
Editorial: Mentor Communications AB, 181 72 STOCKHOLM **Tel:** 8 670 41 00
Web site: http://www.tidningenkosmetik.se
Date Established: 1996; **Freq:** Quarterly; **Circ:** 1,400
Managing Director: Mikael Heinig
Profile: Magazine covering the cosmetics industry.
Language(s): Swedish
Readership: Aimed at sales personnel at department stores and perfumeries.
ADVERTISING RATES:
Full Page Colour .... SEK 16800
SCC .... SEK 140
BUSINESS: COSMETICS & HAIRDRESSING: Cosmetics

KÖTTBRANSCHEN
50385W22D-10
Editorial: Box 55680, 102 15 STOCKHOLM
Tel: 8 762 65 25
Email: bo.lindmark@meatmag.se **Web site:** http://www.kcf.se
Freq: Monthly; **Circ:** 3,300
Editor-in-Chief: Bo Lindmark; **Advertising Manager:** Göran Månsson; **Publisher:** Åke Rutegård
Profile: Magazine covering all aspects of the butchers' trade including slaughtering, de-boning and processing.
Language(s): Swedish
ADVERTISING RATES:
Full Page Colour .... SEK 14500
SCC .... SEK 120.83
BUSINESS: FOOD: Meat Trade

KOUNTRY KORRAL MAGAZINE
51086W76D-77
Editorial: Box 6031, 791 06 FALUN **Tel:** 243 22 86 30
Fax: 243 673 23
Email: kountry@mailbox.as **Web site:** http://www.countrysweden.com/kk/kk.html
Date Established: 1968; **Freq:** Quarterly; **Circ:** 1,700
Editor: Lars Kjellberg; **Advertising Manager:** Sören Mattsson; **Publisher:** Lars Kjellberg
Profile: Magazine about country music.
Language(s): Swedish
CONSUMER: MUSIC & PERFORMING ARTS: Music

KRISTDEMOKRATEN
51189W82-100
Editorial: Box 2356, 103 18 STOCKHOLM
Tel: 8 723 25 81 **Fax:** 86127953
Email: red@kristdemokraten.com **Web site:** http://www.kristdemokraten.com
Date Established: 1979
Circ: 5,000
Editor: Anneli Ström Leijel; **Publisher:** Maria Wilhelmson
Profile: Journal of the Christian Democrats, covering political and social matters.
Language(s): Swedish
ADVERTISING RATES:
Full Page Colour .... SEK 22000
SCC .... SEK 110
Copy instructions: *Copy Date:* 7 days prior to publication date
CONSUMER: CURRENT AFFAIRS & POLITICS

KRISTDEMOKRATEN; WEBB
1844958W65A-1046
Editorial: Box 2356, 103 18 STOCKHOLM
Tel: 8 587 104 00 **Fax:** 8 612 79 53
Email: red@kristdemokraten.com **Web site:** http://www.kristdemokraten.com
Freq: Daily; **Cover Price:** Free; **Circ:** 2,867 Unique Users
Editor-in-Chief: Maria Wilhelmson; **Advertising Manager:** Sickan Palm; **Publisher:** Maria Wilhelmson
Language(s): Swedish
ADVERTISING RATES:
SCC .... SEK 22
NATIONAL DAILY & SUNDAY NEWSPAPERS: National Daily Newspapers

KRISTEN FOSTRAN
751132W87-160
Editorial: Gullbergsvägen 42, 511 59 KINNA
Tel: 320 134 49 **Fax:** 320 134 49
Email: rkf@crossnet.se **Web site:** http://www.kristenfostran.org
Date Established: 1884; **Freq:** 6 issues yearly; **Circ:** 3,500
Advertising Manager: Sven-Olof Olsson
Language(s): Swedish
CONSUMER: RELIGIOUS

KRISTIANSTADSBLADET; WEBB
752303W67B-9010
Editorial: 291 84 KRISTIANSTAD **Tel:** 44 18 55 00
Fax: 44 12 62 76
Email: webbredaktionen@skanemedia.se **Web site:** http://www.kristianstadsbladet.se
Freq: Daily; **Cover Price:** Free; **Circ:** 13,209 Unique Users
Language(s): Swedish
REGIONAL DAILY & SUNDAY NEWSPAPERS: Regional Daily Newspapers

KRISTINEHAMN-STORFORS AKTUELLT
634166W80-93
Editorial: Box 158, 681 23 KRISTINEHAMN
Tel: 550 199 00 **Fax:** 550 199 01
Email: redaktion@kristinehamnsaktuellt.se **Web site:** http://www.kristinehamnsaktuellt.se
Date Established: 1978; **Freq:** Monthly; **Cover Price:** Free; **Circ:** 18,000
Advertising Manager: Lina Jadolf; **Publisher:** Roland Thomas
Profile: Newspaper featuring local news for Kristinehamn and Storfors.
Language(s): Swedish
CONSUMER: RURAL & REGIONAL INTEREST

KRITISKA EU-FAKTA
634599W82-413
Editorial: c/o Torstensson, Rondovägen 312, 142 41 SKOGÅS **Tel:** 8 771 43 79
Email: kef@nejtilleu.se **Web site:** http://www.nejtilleu.se
Freq: Quarterly; **Circ:** 4,000
Editor: Gösta Torsensson; **Advertising Manager:** Gösta Torsensson; **Publisher:** Eva-Britt Svensson
Language(s): Swedish
CONSUMER: CURRENT AFFAIRS & POLITICS

KROPP & SJÄL
1809898W74G-217
Editorial: Årstaängsvägen 1A, 10 tr, 117 43 STOCKHOLM **Tel:** 8 555 930 00 **Fax:** 855593030
Email: poul.heie@villaaktuellt.se **Web site:** http://www.kroppochsjal.se
Freq: Quarterly; **Circ:** 2,400,000
Advertising Manager: Helene Ulvander; **Publisher:** Poul Heie
Language(s): Swedish
CONSUMER: WOMEN'S INTEREST CONSUMER MAGAZINES: Slimming & Health

KRUT - KRITISK UTBILDNINGSTIDSKRIFT
50706W62A-90
Editorial: Andra Långgatan 20, 413 28 GÖTEBORG
Tel: 31 12 76 40 **Fax:** 31 14 37 77
Email: tidskriften.krut@telia.com **Web site:** http://www.krut.a.se
Date Established: 1977; **Freq:** Quarterly; **Circ:** 1,000
Editor: Göran Folin; **Publisher:** Göran Folin
Profile: Magazine concerning issues in the world of teaching and education.
Language(s): Swedish
BUSINESS: CHURCH & SCHOOL EQUIPMENT & EDUCATION: Education

KTH &CO
1836388W55-60
Editorial: KTH Informationsenheten, 100 44 STOCKHOLM **Tel:** 8 790 78 09
Email: soold@kth.se **Web site:** http://www.kth.se
Circ: 8,000
Editor: Håkan Soold
Language(s): Swedish
ADVERTISING RATES:
Full Page Colour .... SEK 16000
SCC .... SEK 133.33
BUSINESS: APPLIED SCIENCE & LABORATORIES

KULTRYCKET
749813W31A-75
Editorial: c/o Hellgren, Kilby Vasängen 319, 748 91 ÖSTERBYBRUK **Tel:** 174 361 75
Email: hellgren.ulf@telia.com **Web site:** http://www.mhf.se/campingclub
Freq: 6 issues yearly; **Circ:** 3,000
Editor-in-Chief: Ulf Hellgren; **Advertising Manager:** Kjell Lidberg
Language(s): Swedish
BUSINESS: MOTOR TRADE: Motor Trade Accessories

KULTURENS VÄRLD
51243W84A-120
Editorial: S:t Paulsgatan 31, 118 48 STOCKHOLM
Tel: 8 640 15 01 **Fax:** 86401110
Email: redaktionen@kulturens-varld.se **Web site:** http://www.kulturens-varld.se
Date Established: 1985; **Freq:** Quarterly; **Circ:** 11,000
Advertising Manager: Marianne Lingserius; **Publisher:** Göran Hassler
Profile: Magazine about art, culture and history.
Language(s): Swedish
ADVERTISING RATES:
Full Page Colour .... SEK 12800
SCC .... SEK 106.66
CONSUMER: THE ARTS & LITERARY: Arts

KULTURTIDSKRIFTEN HJÄRNSTORM
51236W84A-75
Editorial: Box 4172, 102 64 STOCKHOLM
Tel: 18 782 94 58 **Fax:** 84474539
Email: hjarnstorm@gmail.com **Web site:** http://www.hjarnstorm.com
Freq: Quarterly; **Circ:** 1,500
Advertising Manager: Bo Pettersson; **Publisher:** Staffan Kling
Profile: Journal covering cultural critique and philosophical debate, mainly focusing on art and literature but with a broad interest in all areas of arts and ideology.
Language(s): Swedish
CONSUMER: THE ARTS & LITERARY: Arts

KULTURVÄRDEN
1694688W4A-33
Editorial: Box 2263, 103 16 STOCKHOLM
Tel: 8 696 70 00 **Fax:** 8 696 70 01
Email: kulturvarden@sfv.se **Web site:** http://www.sfv.se
Freq: Quarterly; **Circ:** 10,000
Editor-in-Chief: Hans Landberg
Language(s): Swedish
BUSINESS: ARCHITECTURE & BUILDING: Architecture

KUNGÄLVS-POSTEN
624367W72-130
Editorial: Box 523, 442 15 KUNGÄLV
Tel: 303 20 68 00 **Fax:** 303 155 41
Email: redaktion@kungalvsposten.se **Web site:** http://www.kungalvsposten.se
Date Established: 1956
Circ: 10,800
Editor-in-Chief: Ingrid Fredriksson; **Advertising Manager:** Karin Jacobsson; **Publisher:** Roger Boström
Language(s): Swedish
ADVERTISING RATES:
Full Page Colour .... SEK 17400
SCC .... SEK 87
LOCAL NEWSPAPERS

KUNGL KRIGSVETENSKAPS-AKADEMIENS HANDLINGAR OCH TIDSKRIFT
634601W40-40
Editorial: Teatergatan 3, 5 tr, 111 48 STOCKHOLM
Tel: 8 611 14 00 **Fax:** 8 667 22 53
Email: info@kkrva.se **Web site:** http://www.kkrva.se
Date Established: 1797; **Freq:** 6 issues yearly; **Circ:** 1,150
Publisher: Bo Hugemark
Profile: Magazine covering scientific analyses of military issues.
Language(s): Swedish
BUSINESS: DEFENCE

Sweden

KUPÉ 750750W74A-140
Editorial: Nordiska Tidningsbolaget, 111 40 STOCKHOLM **Tel:** 8 20 39 40
Email: kupe@tidningsbolaget.se **Web site:** http://www.tidningsbolaget.se
Freq: Monthly; **Circ:** 120,000
Advertising Manager: Robert Jonsson; **Publisher:** Claes Salomonsson
Language(s): Swedish
ADVERTISING RATES:
Full Page Colour .... SEK 39000
SCC .... SEK 325
CONSUMER: WOMEN'S INTEREST CONSUMER MAGAZINES: Women's Interest

KUSTBON 51320W90-55_50
Editorial: Roslagsgatan 57, 113 54 STOCKHOLM
Tel: 8 612 75 99 **Fax:** 8 612 77 85
Email: info@estlandssvenskarna.org **Web site:** http://www.estlandssvenskarna.org
Date Established: 1918; **Freq:** Quarterly; **Circ:** 1,300
Editor: Ingegerd Lindström; **Advertising Manager:** Ulla-Stina Rundgren; **Publisher:** Lars Rönnberg
Profile: Magazine providing information for Swedes with Estonian origin.
Language(s): Swedish
CONSUMER: ETHNIC

KVÄKARTIDSKRIFT 634603W87-43
Editorial: Box 9166, 102 72 STOCKHOLM
Tel: 175 604 25 **Fax:** 175 604 25
Email: kt@kvakare.se **Web site:** http://www.kvakare.se/kt
Date Established: 1948; **Freq:** Quarterly; **Circ:** 500
Editor-in-Chief: Tofte Frykman; **Publisher:** Tofte Frykman
Profile: Magazine focusing on the Quaker religion.
Language(s): Swedish
CONSUMER: RELIGIOUS

KVALITETSMAGASINET 50317W14K-50
Editorial: Box 104, 901 03 UMEÅ **Tel:** 90 70 09 00
Email: info@kvalitetsmagasinet.com **Web site:** http://www.kvalitetsmagasinet.com
Date Established: 1990; **Freq:** 6 issues yearly; **Circ:** 7,000
Advertising Manager: Antti Silventoinen; **Publisher:** Anna Nyström
Profile: Magazine about quality assurance within industry and the public sector.
Language(s): Swedish
ADVERTISING RATES:
Full Page Colour .... SEK 20900
SCC .... SEK 174.16
Copy instructions: *Copy Date:* 35 days prior to publication date
BUSINESS: COMMERCE, INDUSTRY & MANAGEMENT: Quality Assurance

KVALITETSMAGASINET; WEBB 1844802W14A-335
Editorial: Box 104, 901 03 UMEÅ **Tel:** 90 70 09 00
Fax: 9014 23 20
Email: info@kvalitetsmagasinet.com **Web site:** http://www.kvalitetsmagasinet.com
Freq: Daily; **Cover Price:** Free; **Circ:** 2,333 Unique Users
Managing Director: Anders Pauser; **Publisher:** Anna Nyström
Language(s): Swedish
BUSINESS: COMMERCE, INDUSTRY & MANAGEMENT

KVÄLLSPOSTEN; KVP.SE 1844539W65A-1016
Editorial: AB kvällstidningen Expressen Kvällsposten, 205 26 MALMÖ **Tel:** 40 602 01 00 **Fax:** 40 93 92 24
Email: redaktionen@kvp.se **Web site:** http://www.kvp.se
Freq: Daily; **Cover Price:** Free; **Circ:** 350,000 Unique Users
Editor-in-Chief: Thomas Mattsson; **Publisher:** Thomas Mattsson
Language(s): Swedish
ADVERTISING RATES:
SCC .... SEK 40
NATIONAL DAILY & SUNDAY NEWSPAPERS: National Daily Newspapers

KVÄLLSSTUNDEN 50959W74C-90
Editorial: Box 1080, 721 27 VÄSTERÅS
Tel: 21 19 04 15 **Fax:** 21 13 62 62
Email: bo.pettersson@tidningshuset.com **Web site:** http://www.kvallsstunden.se
Date Established: 1938; **Freq:** Weekly; **Circ:** 45,800
Editor-in-Chief: Bo Pettersson; **Managing Director:** Olle Wärmlöf; **Advertising Manager:** Berit Eklund
Profile: Leisure and recreational magazine for all the family.
Language(s): Swedish
ADVERTISING RATES:
Full Page Colour .... SEK 30450
SCC .... SEK 135
CONSUMER: WOMEN'S INTEREST CONSUMER MAGAZINES: Home & Family

KVINNOR MOT FUNDAMENTALISM 51321W90-55_55
Editorial: Box 7069, 402 32 GOTEBORG
Tel: 707 22 80 83
Email: avaiezan@gmail.com **Web site:** http://tvs.se/kf
Date Established: 1991; **Freq:** Half-yearly; **Circ:** 1,000
Publisher: Sholeh Irani
Profile: Journal focusing on women and religious fundamentalism. Contains news, articles and interviews.
Language(s): Swedish
Readership: Read by Iranian expatriates.
CONSUMER: ETHNIC

KVINNOTRYCK 1663910W74R-2
Editorial: Hornsgatan 66, 1 tr, 118 21 STOCKHOLM
Tel: 8 442 99 30 **Fax:** 86127325
Email: redaktion@kvinnotryck.se **Web site:** http://www.roks.se
Freq: 6 issues yearly; **Circ:** 3,000
Editor: Johanna Carlson
Language(s): Swedish
CONSUMER: WOMEN'S INTEREST CONSUMER MAGAZINES: Women's Interest Related

KYLA+VÄRMEPUMPAR 50441W3C-1
Editorial: Box 47122, 100 74 STOCKHOLM
Tel: 8 762 75 00 **Fax:** 8 669 78 37
Email: info@kyl.se **Web site:** http://www.kylavarme.se
Date Established: 1988; **Freq:** 6 issues yearly; **Circ:** 6,500
Editor: Johan Tegnelius; **Editor-in-Chief:** Johan Tegnelius; **Advertising Manager:** Cecilia Branting; **Publisher:** Johan Tegnelius
Profile: Magazine containing news and information about the cold storage and commercial refrigeration industry, including heatpumps and air-conditioning. Also provides articles on new products and materials.
Language(s): Swedish
Readership: Read by entrepreneurs, wholesalers, consultants and instructors.
ADVERTISING RATES:
Full Page Colour .... SEK 28600
SCC .... SEK 238.33
BUSINESS: HEATING & VENTILATION: Refrigeration & Ventilation

KYRKA OCH FOLK 1625820W87-201
Editorial: Träringen 52 ½, 416 79 GOTEBORG
Tel: 31 707 42 94 **Fax:** 317074295
Email: redaktion@kyrkaochfolk.se **Web site:** http://www.kyrkaochfolk.se
Freq: Weekly; **Circ:** 2,500
Publisher: Fredrik Sidenvall
Language(s): Swedish
CONSUMER: RELIGIOUS

KYRKANS TIDNING 634604W87-165
Editorial: Box 22543, 104 22 STOCKHOLM
Tel: 8 462 28 00 **Fax:** 8 644 76 86
Email: redaktionen@kyrkanstidning.se **Web site:** http://www.kyrkanstidning.se
Freq: Weekly; **Circ:** 40,800
Editor: Barbro Matzols; **Editor-in-Chief:** Anders Ahlberg; **Advertising Manager:** Jessy Fastevik; **Publisher:** Anders Ahlberg
Language(s): Swedish
ADVERTISING RATES:
Full Page Colour .... SEK 45520
SCC .... SEK 227.6
CONSUMER: RELIGIOUS

KYRKANS TIDNING; WEBB 1846500W87-214
Editorial: Box 22543, 104 22 STOCKHOLM
Tel: 8 462 28 00 **Fax:** 8 644 76 86
Email: redaktionen@kyrkanstidning.se **Web site:** http://www.kyrkanstidning.se
Freq: Daily; **Cover Price:** Free; **Circ:** 21,400 Unique Users
Editor-in-Chief: Anders Ahlberg; **Advertising Manager:** Ola Tallbom; **Publisher:** Anders Ahlberg
Language(s): Swedish
ADVERTISING RATES:
SCC .... SEK 45
CONSUMER: RELIGIOUS

KYRKFACK 50321W14L-123
Editorial: Box 300 78, 104 25 STOCKHOLM
Tel: 8 441 85 60 **Fax:** 8 441 85 77
Email: ann.thornblad@kyrka.se **Web site:** http://www.kyrka.se
Freq: 6 issues yearly; **Circ:** 5,500
Publisher: Bror Holm
Profile: Official journal of the Church Academics' Union.
Language(s): Swedish
BUSINESS: COMMERCE, INDUSTRY & MANAGEMENT: Trade Unions

KYRKOGÅRDEN 50750W64L-3
Editorial: Box 19071, 104 32 STOCKHOLM
Tel: 8 643 10 35 **Fax:** 8 612 80 36
Email: kansli@skkf.se **Web site:** http://www.skkf.se
Date Established: 1928; **Freq:** 6 issues yearly; **Circ:** 3,000
Editor-in-Chief: Bo Silfverberg; **Advertising Manager:** Martin Yde; **Publisher:** Ulf Lagerström
Profile: Official journal of the Swedish Society of Cemeteries and Crematoria.
Language(s): Swedish
BUSINESS: OTHER CLASSIFICATIONS: Funeral Directors, Cemeteries & Crematoria

KYRKOMUSIKERNAS TIDNING 51087W76D-80
Editorial: c/o Henrik Tobin, Giggvägen 6, 443 42 GRÅBO **Tel:** 302 412 37 **Fax:** 302 412 37
Email: kmt@kmr.se **Web site:** http://www.kmr.se
Date Established: 1934; **Freq:** Monthly; **Circ:** 4,200
Editor: Henrik Tobin; **Publisher:** Ingela Sjögren
Profile: Magazine about church music.
Language(s): Swedish
ADVERTISING RATES:
Full Page Colour .... SEK 9100
CONSUMER: MUSIC & PERFORMING ARTS: Music

LÅDAN 1667941W49R-1
Editorial: c/o Hans Fredriksson, Gullvivebacken 12, 554 56 JÖNKÖPING **Tel:** 36 17 67 15
Email: hans.fredriksson@home.se **Web site:** http://www.jsbs.se
Freq: Quarterly; **Circ:** 300
Publisher: Hans Fredriksson
Language(s): Swedish
BUSINESS: TRANSPORT: Transport Related

LAG & AVTAL 1844978W14R-68
Tel: 8 796 64 50
Circ: 4,800
Language(s): Swedish
ADVERTISING RATES:
Full Page Colour .... SEK 25500
SCC .... SEK 212.5
BUSINESS: COMMERCE, INDUSTRY & MANAGEMENT: Commerce Related

LÄKARTIDNINGEN 50595W56A-33
Editorial: Box 5603, 114 86 STOCKHOLM
Tel: 8 790 33 00 **Fax:** 8 20 76 19
Email: redaktionen@lakartidningen.se **Web site:** http://www.lakartidningen.se
Date Established: 1903; **Freq:** Weekly; **Circ:** 40,400
Editor: Jan Lind; **Publisher:** Jonas Hultkvist
Profile: Journal of the Swedish Doctors' Association.
Language(s): Swedish
ADVERTISING RATES:
Full Page Colour .... SEK 44000
SCC .... SEK 366.66
BUSINESS: HEALTH & MEDICAL

LÄKARTIDNINGEN; WWW.LAKARTIDNINGEN.SE 1846435W55-65
Editorial: Box 5603, 114 86 STOCKHOLM
Tel: 8 790 33 00 **Fax:** 8207619
Email: redaktionen@lakartidningen.se **Web site:** http://www.lakartidningen.se
Freq: Daily; **Cover Price:** Free; **Circ:** 23,200 Unique Users
Publisher: Jonas Hultkvist
Language(s): Swedish
BUSINESS: APPLIED SCIENCE & LABORATORIES

LÄKEMEDELSVÄRLDEN 50452W37-30
Editorial: Box 1136, 111 81 STOCKHOLM
Tel: 8 723 50 00 **Fax:** 8149580
Email: tips@lakemedelsvarlden.se **Web site:** http://www.lakemedelsvarlden.se
Date Established: 1896; **Freq:** Monthly - (8 nr/år); **Circ:** 11,400
Advertising Manager: Lars Sundberg; **Publisher:** Ingrid Stenberg
Profile: Magazine containing information, news and articles about health, pharmacy, medicine and nursing.
Language(s): Swedish
Readership: Aimed at doctors, nurses, pharmacists, politicians, scientists and students.
ADVERTISING RATES:
Full Page Colour .... SEK 22500
SCC .... SEK 187.50
Copy instructions: *Copy Date:* 21 days prior to publication date
BUSINESS: PHARMACEUTICAL & CHEMISTS

LÄKEMEDELSVÄRLDEN; LAKEMEDELSVARLDEN.SE 1844960W56A-359
Editorial: Box 1136, 111 81 STOCKHOLM
Tel: 8 723 50 00 **Fax:** 8149580
Email: tips@lakemedelsvarlden.se **Web site:** http://www.lakemedelsvarlden.se
Freq: Daily; **Cover Price:** Free
Publisher: Ingrid Stenberg
Language(s): Swedish
BUSINESS: HEALTH & MEDICAL

LAMBDA NORDICA 752199W55-35
Editorial: c/o Göran Söderström, 115 21 STOCKHOLM **Tel:** 704 63 17 40
Email: info@lambdanordica.se **Web site:** http://www.lambdanordica.se
Freq: Quarterly; **Circ:** 600
Editor: Dirk Gindt; **Editor-in-Chief:** Göran Söderström; **Publisher:** Göran Söderström
Language(s): Swedish
BUSINESS: APPLIED SCIENCE & LABORATORIES

LAND LANTBRUK; WEBB 1846671W82-490
Editorial: 113 92 STOCKHOLM **Tel:** 8 588 365 20
Fax: 858836949
Email: internetredaktionen@lrfmedia.lrf.se **Web site:** http://www.lantbruk.com
Freq: Daily; **Cover Price:** Free; **Circ:** 21,500 Unique Users
Publisher: Olle Eriksson
Language(s): Swedish
CONSUMER: CURRENT AFFAIRS & POLITICS

LAND SKOGSLAND 1837117W46-131
Editorial: Gävlegatan 22, 113 92 STOCKHOLM
Tel: 8 588 365 20 **Fax:** 858836949
Email: skogsland@lrfmedia.lrf.se **Web site:** http://www.skogsland.com
Freq: Weekly; **Circ:** 120,600
Editor: Rolf Segerstedt
Language(s): Swedish
ADVERTISING RATES:
Full Page Colour .... SEK 36000
SCC .... SEK 225
Copy instructions: *Copy Date:* 8 days prior to publication date
BUSINESS: TIMBER, WOOD & FORESTRY

LAND SKOGSLAND; WEBB 1846670W46-132
Editorial: Gävlegatan 22, 113 92 STOCKHOLM
Tel: 8 588 365 20 **Fax:** 858836949
Email: internetredaktionen@lrfmedia.lrf.se **Web site:** http://www.skogsland.com
Freq: Daily; **Cover Price:** Free; **Circ:** 21,500 Unique Users
Editor: Rolf Segerstedt; **Advertising Manager:** Christer Karlsson; **Publisher:** Olle Eriksson
Language(s): Swedish
BUSINESS: TIMBER, WOOD & FORESTRY

LANDSBYGD I NORR 1841180W21A-82
Editorial: Köpmangatan 2, 972 38 LULEÅ
Email: alec.lundstrom@hush.se **Web site:** http://www.hush.se/nord
Freq: Quarterly; **Circ:** 5,000
Editor: Alec Lundström
Language(s): Swedish
ADVERTISING RATES:
Full Page Colour .... SEK 5000
BUSINESS: AGRICULTURE & FARMING

LANDSKRONADIREKT.SE 1844682W65A-1021
Editorial: c/o Zebra Media, Säbygatan 16, 261 33 LANDSKRONA **Tel:** 418 227 60 **Fax:** 418 45 76 05
Email: info@landskronadirekt.com **Web site:** http://www.landskronadirekt.com
Freq: Daily; **Cover Price:** Free; **Circ:** 6,667 Unique Users
Advertising Manager: Kary Persson; **Publisher:** Håkan Karlsson
Language(s): Swedish
NATIONAL DAILY & SUNDAY NEWSPAPERS: National Daily Newspapers

LANDSTINGSNYTT 1625796W74G-198
Editorial: Box 1024, Informationsavdelningen, Landstingets kansli, 551 11 JÖNKÖPING
Tel: 36 32 40 45
Email: olle.hall@lj.se **Web site:** http://www.lj.se
Freq: Quarterly; **Circ:** 160,000
Editor: Olle Hall
Language(s): Swedish
CONSUMER: WOMEN'S INTEREST CONSUMER MAGAZINES: Slimming & Health

LANDSTINGSTIDNINGEN 749829W56B-120
Editorial: Norrbottens läns landsting, 971 89 LULEÅ
Tel: 920 28 43 64
Email: ulrika.englund@nll.se **Web site:** http://www.nll.se
Freq: 6 issues yearly; **Circ:** 12,900
Editor: Ulrika Englund
Language(s): Swedish
ADVERTISING RATES:
Full Page Colour .... SEK 25800
BUSINESS: HEALTH & MEDICAL: Nursing

LÄNS-POSTEN; LANSPOSTEN.SE 1843546W65A-995
Editorial: Box 22084, 702 03 OREBRO
Tel: 19 19 50 50 **Fax:** 19195055
Email: lansposten@sveagruppen.se **Web site:** http://www.lansposten.se
Freq: Daily; **Cover Price:** Free; **Circ:** 6,333 Unique Users
Editor-in-Chief: Bo Pettersson; **Advertising Manager:** Peter Svensson
Language(s): Swedish
NATIONAL DAILY & SUNDAY NEWSPAPERS: National Daily Newspapers

LÄNSTIDNINGEN NORR/ VIMMERBY TIDNING 50850W67B-7850
Editorial: 598 80 VIMMERBY **Tel:** 492 160 00
Fax: 492 141 02
Email: redaktion@vimmerbytidning.se **Web site:** http://www.vimmerbytidning.se
Circ: 9,000
Editor: Katarina Petersson; **Publisher:** Bengt Ingemarsson
Language(s): Swedish
ADVERTISING RATES:
Full Page Colour .... SEK 37560
SCC .... SEK 187.80
REGIONAL DAILY & SUNDAY NEWSPAPERS: Regional Daily Newspapers

LÄNSTIDNINGEN ÖSTERSUND 633915W67B-4975
Editorial: Kyrkgatan 52, 831 89 ÖSTERSUND
Tel: 63 15 55 00
Email: redaktionen@ltz.se **Web site:** http://www.ltz.se
Date Established: 1924
Circ: 14,300
Editor: Solbrith Eidenby; **Publisher:** Lennart Mattsson
Profile: Newspaper covering local news for Jämtland and Härjedalen.
Language(s): Swedish
ADVERTISING RATES:
Full Page Colour .... SEK 25056
SCC .... SEK 125.28
REGIONAL DAILY & SUNDAY NEWSPAPERS: Regional Daily Newspapers

LÄNSTIDNINGEN ÖSTERSUND; WEBB 751647W67B-9085
Editorial: Kyrkgatan 52, 831 89 ÖSTERSUND
Tel: 63 15 55 00
Email: redaktionen@ltz.se **Web site:** http://www.ltz.se
Freq: Daily; **Cover Price:** Free; **Circ:** 8,668 Unique Users
Editor-in-Chief: Lennart Mattsson; **Publisher:** Lennart Mattsson
Language(s): Swedish
ADVERTISING RATES:
SCC .... SEK 25
REGIONAL DAILY & SUNDAY NEWSPAPERS: Regional Daily Newspapers

LÄNSTIDNINGEN SÖDERTÄLJE; LT.SE 1843544W65A-993
Editorial: 151 82 SÖDERTÄLJE **Tel:** 8 550 921 00
Fax: 8 550 877 72
Email: redaktion@lt.se **Web site:** http://www.lt.se
Freq: Daily; **Cover Price:** Free; **Circ:** 8,756 Unique Users
Publisher: Thelma Kimsjö
Language(s): Swedish
NATIONAL DAILY & SUNDAY NEWSPAPERS: National Daily Newspapers

LANTBRUKETS AFFÄRER 751136W75F-205
Editorial: Tejarps Gård, 230 41 KLÅGERUP
Tel: 40 40 86 80
Email: info@lantbruketsaffarer.se **Web site:** http://www.lantbruketsaffarer.se
Date Established: 1994; **Freq:** Monthly; **Circ:** 4,500
Advertising Manager: Göran Månsson; **Publisher:** Agneta Lilliehöök
Language(s): Swedish
CONSUMER: SPORT: Shooting

LANTBRUKSMAGASINET 50366W21A-52
Editorial: Svenska Media Docu AB, Tingsgatan 2, 827 32 LJUSDAL **Tel:** 651 150 50 **Fax:** 651 133 33
Email: post@svenskamedia.se **Web site:** http://www.svenskamedia.se
Date Established: 1995; **Freq:** 6 issues yearly; **Circ:** 24,500
Advertising Manager: Tommy Flodberg
Profile: Magazine covering all aspects of life in the country. Contains reviews of new farming products.
Language(s): Swedish
ADVERTISING RATES:
Full Page Colour .... SEK 22900
SCC .... SEK 190.83
Copy instructions: *Copy Date:* 15 days prior to publication date
BUSINESS: AGRICULTURE & FARMING

LANTLIV 51009W74C-92
Editorial: Gävlegatan 22, 113 92 STOCKHOLM
Tel: 8 588 365 70 **Fax:** 8 588 369 89
Email: lantliv@lrfmedia.lrf.se **Web site:** http://www.tidningenlantliv.se
Date Established: 1999; **Freq:** Monthly; **Circ:** 45,000
Editor: Marie Flodin; **Advertising Manager:** Petra Jängnemyr
Profile: Magazine covering all aspects of country life. Contains articles about home decoration and purchase, along with items on gardening.
Language(s): Swedish
ADVERTISING RATES:
Full Page Colour .... SEK 29000
SCC .... SEK 241.66
Copy instructions: *Copy Date:* 34 days prior to publication date
CONSUMER: WOMEN'S INTEREST CONSUMER MAGAZINES: Home & Family

LANTMANNEN 50367W21A-55
Editorial: 113 92 STOCKHOLM **Tel:** 8 588 365 40
Fax: 8 588 369 49
Email: lantmannen@lrfmedia.lrf.se **Web site:** http://www.lantmannen.com
Date Established: 1879; **Freq:** Monthly; **Circ:** 8,400
Editor-in-Chief: Marcus Frennemark; **Advertising Manager:** Birgit Emilsson
Profile: Magazine containing articles, news and information about farming.
Language(s): Swedish
ADVERTISING RATES:
Full Page Colour .... SEK 14700
SCC .... SEK 122.50
Copy instructions: *Copy Date:* 30 days prior to publication date
BUSINESS: AGRICULTURE & FARMING

LANTMÄSTAREN 50368W21A-65
Editorial: Tejarps gård, 230 41 KLÅGERUP
Tel: 40 40 86 80
Email: info@lime.nu **Web site:** http://www.lime.nu
Date Established: 1937; **Freq:** 6 issues yearly; **Circ:** 4,500
Editor: Agneta Lilliehöök; **Advertising Manager:** Göran Månsson
Profile: Journal containing information and articles concerning farming and management of agriculture.
Language(s): Swedish
BUSINESS: AGRICULTURE & FARMING

LÄRARNAS TIDNING 50733W62J-120
Editorial: Box 12239, Segelbåtsvägen 15, Stora Essingen., 102 26 STOCKHOLM **Tel:** 8 737 65 00
Fax: 8 6579748
Email: lararnas.tidning@lararforbundet.se **Web site:** http://lararnasnyheter.se/lararnas-tidning
Freq: 26 issues yearly; **Circ:** 228,700
Profile: Journal covering professional and trade union issues concerning teachers at all levels from pre-school to secondary.
Language(s): Swedish
ADVERTISING RATES:
Full Page Colour .... SEK 65000
SCC .... SEK 374.37
BUSINESS: CHURCH & SCHOOL EQUIPMENT & EDUCATION: Teachers & Education Management

LÄRARNAS TIDNING; LARARNASTIDNING.NET 1846643W14L-204
Editorial: Box 12239, 102 26 STOCKHOLM
Tel: 8 737 65 00 **Fax:** 8 657 97 48
Email: lararnas.tidning@lararforbundet.se **Web site:** http://www.lararnastidning.net
Freq: Daily; **Cover Price:** Free; **Circ:** 24,400 Unique Users
Editor-in-Chief: Annica Grimlund; **Publisher:** Annica Grimlund
Language(s): Swedish
ADVERTISING RATES:
SCC .... SEK 75
BUSINESS: COMMERCE, INDUSTRY & MANAGEMENT: Trade Unions

LÄS OCH SKRIV 634620W56R-55
Editorial: c/o FMLS, Solnavägen 100, 169 51 SOLNA
Tel: 8 665 17 00 **Fax:** 86607977
Email: redaktion@dyslexiforbundet.se **Web site:** http://www.fmls.nu
Freq: 6 issues yearly; **Circ:** 17,000
Editor: Eva Hedberg; **Advertising Manager:** Carina Carlsson; **Publisher:** Sven Eklöf
Language(s): Swedish
BUSINESS: HEALTH & MEDICAL: Health Medical Related

LÅSMÄSTAREN 50579W54C-37
Editorial: Transportvägen 9, 117 43 STOCKHOLM
Tel: 8 721 40 55 **Fax:** 87214056
Email: kansli@slr.se **Web site:** http://www.slr.se
Date Established: 1977; **Freq:** Quarterly; **Circ:** 12,000
Editor: Erik Fahlander; **Publisher:** Mats Moberg
Profile: Official publication of the Swedish Locksmiths' Association.
Language(s): Swedish
BUSINESS: SAFETY & SECURITY: Security

LÄTTA LASTBILAR 50554W49D-15
Editorial: Box 82, 533 04 HÄLLEKIS **Tel:** 510 862 00
Fax: 51086220
Email: info@lattalastbilar.se **Web site:** http://www.lattalastbilar.se
Date Established: 1990; **Freq:** 6 issues yearly; **Circ:** 13,000
Advertising Manager: Ove Johansson
Profile: Magazine about light haulage.
Language(s): Swedish
ADVERTISING RATES:
Full Page Colour .... SEK 24300
SCC .... SEK 121.50
BUSINESS: TRANSPORT: Commercial Vehicles

LÄTTSMÄLT 749961W14A-215
Editorial: Box 116, 671 23 ARVIKA **Tel:** 570 100 90
Fax: 570 151 50
Email: sjmf@telia.com
Freq: Quarterly; **Circ:** 600
Editor: Per-Åke Fredricksson; **Publisher:** Per-Åke Fredricksson
Language(s): Swedish
BUSINESS: COMMERCE, INDUSTRY & MANAGEMENT

LEGALLY YOURS 1625849W44-56
Editorial: Banérgatan 16, 115 23 STOCKHOLM
Tel: 8 579 366 00 **Fax:** 8 667 97 60
Email: legally-yours@blendow.se **Web site:** http://www.legally-yours.se
Freq: 6 issues yearly; **Circ:** 17,000
Editor-in-Chief: Peter Johansson; **Advertising Manager:** Caroline Carlsson; **Publisher:** Peter Johansson
Language(s): Swedish
ADVERTISING RATES:
Full Page Colour .... SEK 34900
SCC .... SEK 290.83
BUSINESS: LEGAL

LEKMAN I KYRKAN 51287W87-45
Tel: 63 12 30 30
Email: madsensis@gmail.com **Web site:** http://www.lekmanikyrkan.se
Freq: Quarterly; **Circ:** 9,000
Editor: Britt-Louise Madsen; **Publisher:** Anders Nordberg
Profile: Magazine for lay-members of the Church of Sweden.
Language(s): Swedish
CONSUMER: RELIGIOUS

LERUMS TIDNING 634476W72-142
Editorial: Göteborgsvägen 3, 443 30 LERUM
Tel: 302 510 50 **Fax:** 302 510 51
Email: redaktion@lerumstidning.com **Web site:** http://www.lerumstidning.com
Date Established: 1969; **Freq:** Weekly; **Circ:** 18,600
Editor-in-Chief: Bengt Michelsen; **Advertising Manager:** Bengt Edvardsson; **Publisher:** Bengt Michelsen
Profile: Newspaper covering Lerum.
Language(s): Swedish
ADVERTISING RATES:
Full Page Colour .... SEK 17300
SCC .... SEK 86.5
LOCAL NEWSPAPERS

LERUMS TIDNING; LERUMSTIDNING.COM 1844808W65A-1037
Editorial: Göteborgsvägen 3, 443 30 LERUM
Tel: 302 510 50
Email: redaktion@lerumstidning.com **Web site:** http://www.lerumstidning.com
Freq: Daily; **Cover Price:** Free; **Circ:** 1,561 Unique Users
Advertising Manager: Maiwi Larsson
Language(s): Swedish
NATIONAL DAILY & SUNDAY NEWSPAPERS: National Daily Newspapers

LEVA MED DIABETES 1639370W74G-202
Editorial: Torsgatan 8, 111 23 STOCKHOLM
Tel: 8 654 00 40 **Fax:** 8 654 80 20
Email: red@ssdf.nu **Web site:** http://www.ssdf.nu
Freq: 6 issues yearly; **Circ:** 8,000
Editor: Susanna Pagels; **Publisher:** Inge-Britt Lundin
Language(s): Swedish
CONSUMER: WOMEN'S INTEREST CONSUMER MAGAZINES: Slimming & Health

LEVA MED SMÄRTA 1803923W74G-213
Editorial: Smärtföreningens kansli, Sabbatsbergs sjukhus, 113 24 STOCKHOLM **Tel:** 8 690 60 64
Email: info@levautansmarta.se **Web site:** http://www.levautansmarta.se
Freq: 6 issues yearly; **Circ:** 18,000
Advertising Manager: Anders Skogholm; **Publisher:** Rolf Malm
Language(s): Swedish
CONSUMER: WOMEN'S INTEREST CONSUMER MAGAZINES: Slimming & Health

LEVANDE STENAR - ELÄVÄT KIVET 751137W87-170
Editorial: Box 2281, 103 17 STOCKHOLM
Tel: 8 440 82 03 **Fax:** 8 440 82 01
Email: inkeri.toiviainen@svenskakyrkan.se **Web site:** http://www.svenskakyrkan.se/finskaforsamlingen/sv/forsamlingen/levande.asp?link=
Date Established: 1967; **Freq:** Quarterly; **Circ:** 9,000
Editor-in-Chief: Hakon Långström; **Advertising Manager:** Inkeri Toiviainen
Language(s): Swedish
CONSUMER: RELIGIOUS

LEVEL 1803884W78D-419
Editorial: Reset Media AB, Kungsgatan 55, 111 22 STOCKHOLM **Tel:** 8 24 41 14 **Fax:** 8 24 41 20
Email: level@resetmedia.se **Web site:** http://www.loading.se
Freq: Monthly; **Circ:** 9,600
Editor: Kacper Antonius; **Editor-in-Chief:** Tobias Bjarneby; **Advertising Manager:** Daniel Grigorov; **Publisher:** Tobias Bjarneby
Language(s): Swedish
ADVERTISING RATES:
Full Page Colour .... SEK 31900
SCC .... SEK 265.83
CONSUMER: CONSUMER ELECTRONICS: Games

LEVERANSTIDNINGEN ENTREPRENAD 50490W42B-30
Editorial: Box 72001, 181 72 LIDINGÖ
Tel: 8 670 41 00 **Fax:** 8 661 64 55
Email: tidningen@entreprenad.com **Web site:** http://www.entreprenad.com
Freq: 26 issues yearly; **Circ:** 11,100
Advertising Manager: John Sjögren
Profile: Magazine about road building and earth-moving machinery.
Language(s): Swedish
ADVERTISING RATES:
Full Page Colour .... SEK 26000
SCC .... SEK 130
Copy instructions: *Copy Date:* 21 days prior to publication date
BUSINESS: CONSTRUCTION: Roads

LEXAFFÄR 50156W1A-85
Editorial: Nota Bene AB, Prästgården Lönashult, 340 30 VISLANDA **Tel:** 470 72 66 30 **Fax:** 470726635
Web site: http://www.notabene.se
Freq: Weekly
Publisher: Kenny Fredlund
Profile: Newsletter containing business information. Distributed to subscribers via fax.
Language(s): Swedish
BUSINESS: FINANCE & ECONOMICS

LEXSKATT 50174W1M-25
Editorial: Nota Bene AB, Prästgården Lönashult, 340 30 VISLANDA **Tel:** 470 72 66 30 **Fax:** 470726635
Web site: http://www.lex.notabene.se
Date Established: 1995; **Freq:** 104 times a year
Publisher: Kenny Fredlund
Profile: Newspaper covering issues concerning the Swedish tax system. Distributed to subscribers via fax.
Language(s): Swedish
BUSINESS: FINANCE & ECONOMICS: Taxation

LIBERTAS 51222W83-75
Editorial: Box 11544, 100 61 STOCKHOLM
Tel: 8 714 48 00
Email: libertas@s-studenter.se **Web site:** http://www.s-studenter.se
Freq: 6 issues yearly; **Circ:** 2,000
Editor: Hanna-Linnéa Hellström
Profile: Magazine of the Swedish Social Democratic Students' Society.
Language(s): Swedish
CONSUMER: STUDENT PUBLICATIONS

LIDINGÖ TIDNING 624384W67B-4930
Editorial: Box 1274, 181 24 LIDINGÖ
Tel: 8 55055210 **Fax:** 8 731 90 80
Email: redaktion@lt.nu **Web site:** http://www.lt.nu
Date Established: 1910
Circ: 6,000
Editor: Martin Zettersten; **Managing Director:** Mikael Ericsson; **Advertising Manager:** Ghia Odéen; **Publisher:** Susann Thorngren
Language(s): Swedish
ADVERTISING RATES:
Full Page Colour .... SEK 26000
SCC .... SEK 130
REGIONAL DAILY & SUNDAY NEWSPAPERS: Regional Daily Newspapers

LIDINGÖ TIDNING; LT.NU
1846272W65A-1064
Editorial: Box 1274, 181 24 LIDINGÖ
Tel: 8 544 817 30 **Fax:** 85871 2315
Email: redaktion@lt.nu **Web site:** http://www.lt.nu
Freq: Daily; **Cover Price:** Free; **Circ:** 7,333 Unique Users
Language(s): Swedish
ADVERTISING RATES:
SCC .... SEK 26
NATIONAL DAILY & SUNDAY NEWSPAPERS: National Daily Newspapers

LIDKÖPINGSNYTT.NU
1663804W80-848
Editorial: Lidköpingsnytt.nu, Särnarksgatan 24, 531 31 LIDKÖPING **Tel:** 510 212 90 **Fax:** 31 313 13 03
Email: redaktion@lidkopingsnytt.nu **Web site:** http://www.lidkopingsnytt.nu
Freq: Daily; **Cover Price:** Paid; **Circ:** 50,000 Unique Users
Editor-in-Chief: Björn Smitterberg; **Advertising Manager:** Joakim Stegelmeyer; **Publisher:** Björn Smitterberg
Language(s): Swedish
CONSUMER: RURAL & REGIONAL INTEREST

LIEBLING
51191W82-120
Editorial: Box 6508, 113 83 STOCKHOLM
Tel: 8 410 242 00
Email: liebling@liberal.se **Web site:** http://www.liebling.nu
Date Established: 1961; **Freq:** Quarterly; **Circ:** 15,000
Editor-in-Chief: Aaron Israelson; **Publisher:** Mats Persson
Profile: Magazine of the Young Liberals in Sweden.
Language(s): Swedish
CONSUMER: CURRENT AFFAIRS & POLITICS

LIFESTYLE MAGAZINE
751139W74B-20
Editorial: Next World, Skalholtsgatan 2, 164 40 KISTA **Tel:** 8 670 95 00
Email: peter@nextworld.se **Web site:** http://www.lifestylemagazine.se
Freq: Quarterly; **Circ:** 46,000
Advertising Manager: Nicholas Psaros; **Publisher:** Peter Lejdestad
Language(s): Swedish
ADVERTISING RATES:
Full Page Colour .... SEK 49000
SCC .... SEK 408.33
CONSUMER: WOMEN'S INTEREST CONSUMER MAGAZINES: Women's Interest - Fashion

LIMHAMNS-TIDNINGEN
634174W80-96
Editorial: Järnvägsgatan 74, 216 16 LIMHAMN
Tel: 40 15 74 77 **Fax:** 40158680
Email: malmotidningen@telia.com
Date Established: 1955; **Freq:** Quarterly; **Circ:** 15,000
Publisher: Karl-Heinz Forsberg
Profile: Newspaper covering local news for Limhamn.
Language(s): Swedish
Readership: Read by local residents.
CONSUMER: RURAL & REGIONAL INTEREST

LINK MAGAZINE
1827072W1A-212
Editorial: Pipersgatan 1, 112 24 STOCKHOLM
Tel: 702 66 28 15
Email: info@linkmagazine.se **Web site:** http://www.linkmagazine.se
Freq: Quarterly; **Circ:** 8,000
Editor-in-Chief: Karin Palm; **Publisher:** Stefan Axelsson
Language(s): Swedish
BUSINESS: FINANCE & ECONOMICS

LINKÖPINGS-POSTEN
751223W80-595
Editorial: Badhusgatan 8, 582 22 LINKÖPING
Tel: 13 25 32 00 **Fax:** 13 12 24 92
Email: redaktion@linkopingsposten.se **Web site:** http://www.linkopingsposten.se
Circ: 78,400
Language(s): Swedish
ADVERTISING RATES:
Full Page Colour .... SEK 24200
SCC .... SEK 121
CONSUMER: RURAL & REGIONAL INTEREST

LIQUID INSPIRATION
1625784W22A-141
Editorial: Box 5314, 102 47 STOCKHOLM
Tel: 8 440 83 00 **Fax:** 8208780
Email: info.sweden@maxxium.com **Web site:** http://www.liquidinspiration.com
Freq: Half-yearly; **Circ:** 54,000
Publisher: Richard Viitanen
Language(s): Swedish
BUSINESS: FOOD

LIRA MUSIKMAGASIN
51088W76D-90
Editorial: Box 31036, 400 32 GOTEBORG
Tel: 31 13 44 10
Email: lira@lira.se **Web site:** http://www.lira.se
Date Established: 1994; **Freq:** Quarterly; **Circ:** 3,400
Advertising Manager: Elisabeth Tingdal; **Publisher:** Jonas Bergroth
Profile: Magazine about folk and world music.
Language(s): Swedish
ADVERTISING RATES:
Full Page Colour .... SEK 25000
SCC .... SEK 208.33
CONSUMER: MUSIC & PERFORMING ARTS: Music

LIS-AKTUELLT
752205W76D-230
Editorial: Landbogatan 4, 521 42 FALKÖPING
Tel: 21 30 38 55 **Fax:** 21 30 38 56
Email: info@elgkraft.se **Web site:** http://www.lis.nu
Freq: Quarterly; **Circ:** 700
Editor: Stina Elg; **Publisher:** Stig Josfalk
Language(s): Swedish
CONSUMER: MUSIC & PERFORMING ARTS: Music

LISETTEN
50715W62B-100
Editorial: c/o Annika Bergström, Virvelvindsgatan 12 A, 417 14 GÖTEBORG
Email: birgitta.anstrin@gmail.com **Web site:** http://www.lisa-riks.se
Freq: Quarterly; **Circ:** 1,100
Editor: Annika Bergström; **Advertising Manager:** Maria Pettersson; **Publisher:** Birgitta Anstrin-Åstedt
Profile: Magazine containing articles and information for language teachers.
Language(s): Swedish
BUSINESS: CHURCH & SCHOOL EQUIPMENT & EDUCATION: Education Teachers

LITHANIAN
751008W62A-450
Editorial: LinTek, Tekniska högskolan, 581 83 LINKÖPING **Tel:** 13 25 45 81
Email: chefred@lintek.liu.se **Web site:** http://www.lintek.liu.se
Freq: 6 issues yearly; **Circ:** 9,000
Editor-in-Chief: Anna Torstensson
Language(s): Swedish
BUSINESS: CHURCH & SCHOOL EQUIPMENT & EDUCATION: Education

LIU MAGASIN
1656398W83-152
Editorial: Externa relationer, Linköpings universitet, 581 83 LINKÖPING **Tel:** 13 28 16 93 **Fax:** 13 28 25 50
Email: alumni@liu.se **Web site:** http://www.liu.se/alumni/liu-magasin?l=sv
Freq: Quarterly; **Circ:** 20,000
Editor: Eva Bergstedt; **Editor-in-Chief:** Lennart Falklöf; **Advertising Manager:** Gunilla Bergstrand; **Publisher:** Lars Holberg
Language(s): Swedish
ADVERTISING RATES:
Full Page Colour .... SEK 32900
SCC .... SEK 274.16
CONSUMER: STUDENT PUBLICATIONS

LIV
51366W94F-160
Editorial: Box 2031, 169 02 SOLNA **Tel:** 8 629 27 80
Fax: 8 28 15 60
Web site: http://www.rtp.se
Freq: Quarterly; **Circ:** 16,000
Editor: Justina Öster; **Publisher:** Pelle Kölhed
Profile: Magazine for people who are disabled as a result of polio or traffic accidents.
Language(s): Swedish
ADVERTISING RATES:
Full Page Colour .... SEK 23000
SCC .... SEK 191.66
CONSUMER: OTHER CLASSIFICATIONS: Disability

LIVETS GODA
1625804W76D-267
Editorial: Box 4152, 131 04 NACKA **Tel:** 8 448 25 50
Fax: 84482577
Email: info@livetsgoda.se **Web site:** http://www.livetsgoda.se
Freq: 6 issues yearly; **Circ:** 17,000
Advertising Manager: Mats Eriksson
Language(s): Swedish
ADVERTISING RATES:
Full Page Colour .... SEK 15000
SCC .... SEK 125
Copy instructions: *Copy Date:* 30 days prior to publication date
CONSUMER: MUSIC & PERFORMING ARTS: Music

LIVETS GODA; LIVETSGODA.SE
1846505W74P-226
Editorial: Box 4152, 131 04 NACKA **Tel:** 8 448 25 50
Fax: 84482577
Email: info@livetsgoda.se **Web site:** http://www.livetsgoda.se
Freq: Daily; **Cover Price:** Free; **Circ:** 10,000 Unique Users
Advertising Manager: Mats Eriksson
Language(s): Swedish
CONSUMER: WOMEN'S INTEREST CONSUMER MAGAZINES: Food & Cookery

LIVSHÄLSAN
751141W22A-120
Editorial: Box 3010, 630 03 ESKILSTUNA
Tel: 16 13 58 03
Email: bo.niklasson@eskilstunamagasinet.se **Web site:** http://www.eskilstunamagasinet.se
Freq: Half-yearly; **Circ:** 130,000
Editor: Gösta Lööf; **Editor-in-Chief:** Fred Larsson; **Publisher:** Bo Niklasson
Language(s): Swedish
BUSINESS: FOOD

LIVSMEDEL I FOKUS
1639970W22C-163
Editorial: Tavastgatan 22, 118 24 STOCKHOLM
Tel: 8 714 50 46 **Fax:** 8 640 80 45
Email: asa.leife@livsmedelifokus.se **Web site:** http://www.livsmedelifokus.se
Freq: Monthly; **Circ:** 3,100
Advertising Manager: Thomas Palm; **Publisher:** Åsa Leife
Language(s): Swedish
ADVERTISING RATES:
Full Page Colour .... SEK 17500
SCC .... SEK 145.83
Copy instructions: *Copy Date:* 19 days prior to publication date
BUSINESS: FOOD: Food Processing & Packaging

LIVSMEDEL I FOKUS; LIVSMEDELIFOKUS.SE
1844814W22C-166
Editorial: Tavastgatan 22, 118 24 STOCKHOLM
Tel: 8 714 50 46 **Fax:** 8 640 80 45
Email: asa.leife@livsmedelifokus.se **Web site:** http://www.livsmedelifokus.se
Freq: Daily; **Cover Price:** Free; **Circ:** 2,067 Unique Users
Editor-in-Chief: Åsa Leife; **Advertising Manager:** Thomas Palm; **Publisher:** Åsa Leife
Language(s): Swedish
ADVERTISING RATES:
SCC .... SEK 29
BUSINESS: FOOD: Food Processing & Packaging

LJUD & BILD/ ELEKTRONIKVÄRLDEN
51141W78R-280
Editorial: Box 529, 371 23 KARLSKRONA
Tel: 455 30 80 40
Web site: http://www.ev.se
Date Established: 1929; **Freq:** Monthly; **Circ:** 14,000
Editor: Bertil Hellsten; **Advertising Manager:** Markus Dahl; **Publisher:** Anders Albinsson
Profile: Magazine focusing on all areas of consumer electronics, providing news and information.
Language(s): Swedish
ADVERTISING RATES:
Full Page Colour .... SEK 18100
SCC .... SEK 150.83
CONSUMER: CONSUMER ELECTRONICS: Consumer Electronics Related

LJUD & BILD/ ELEKTRONIKVÄRLDEN; EV.SE
1846531W5E-124
Editorial: Box 529, 371 23 KARLSKRONA
Tel: 455 30 80 40
Freq: Daily; **Cover Price:** Free; **Circ:** 18,400 Unique Users
Editor: Anders Albinsson; **Editor-in-Chief:** Anders Albinsson; **Publisher:** Anders Albinsson
Language(s): Swedish
ADVERTISING RATES:
SCC .... SEK 30
BUSINESS: COMPUTERS & AUTOMATION: Data Transmission

LJUSDALS-POSTEN
50805W67B-5000
Editorial: Box 707, 827 25 LJUSDAL
Tel: 651 58 50 00 **Fax:** 651 58 50 60
Email: redaktion@ljp.se **Web site:** http://helahalsingland.se/kontakt/ljusdalsposten
Date Established: 1914
Circ: 7,000
Editor: Maria Lindberg; **Publisher:** Mats Åmvall
Language(s): Swedish
ADVERTISING RATES:
Full Page Colour .... SEK 15240
SCC .... SEK 76.20
REGIONAL DAILY & SUNDAY NEWSPAPERS: Regional Daily Newspapers

LJUSDALS-POSTEN; LJP.SE
1843550W65A-998
Editorial: Box 707, 827 25 LJUSDAL
Tel: 651 58 50 00 **Fax:** 651 58 50 60
Email: redaktion@ljp.se **Web site:** http://www.helahalsingland.se
Freq: Daily; **Cover Price:** Free; **Circ:** 1,723 Unique Users
Editor-in-Chief: Mats Åmvall; **Publisher:** Mats Åmvall
Language(s): Swedish
ADVERTISING RATES:
SCC .... SEK 15
NATIONAL DAILY & SUNDAY NEWSPAPERS: National Daily Newspapers

LJUSKULTUR
50336W17-40
Editorial: Box 12653, 112 93 STOCKHOLM
Tel: 8 566 367 00
Email: info@ljuskultur.se **Web site:** http://www.ljuskultur.se
Freq: 6 issues yearly; **Circ:** 2,900
Editor-in-Chief: Magnus Frantzell; **Advertising Manager:** Mervi Rokka; **Publisher:** Magnus Frantzell
Profile: Journal about the electric lamp and lighting industry.
Language(s): Swedish
ADVERTISING RATES:
Full Page Colour .... SEK 18700
SCC .... SEK 155.83
BUSINESS: ELECTRICAL

LJUSNAN
50767W67B-5050
Editorial: Box 1059, 821 12 BOLLNÄS
Tel: 278 275 00 **Fax:** 27827517
Email: nyhetschefen@ljusnan.se **Web site:** http://www.helahalsingland.se
Date Established: 1912
Circ: 13,000
Editor: Siv Hedebrink; **Advertising Manager:** Stefan Jonsson; **Publisher:** Mats Åmvall
Language(s): Swedish
ADVERTISING RATES:
Full Page Colour .... SEK 20160
SCC .... SEK 100.80
Copy instructions: *Copy Date:* 14 days prior to publication date
REGIONAL DAILY & SUNDAY NEWSPAPERS: Regional Daily Newspapers

LJUSNAN; LJUSNAN.SE
1843547W65A-996
Editorial: Box 1059, 821 12 BOLLNÄS
Tel: 278 275 00 **Fax:** 278 275 17
Email: nyhetschefen@ljusnan.se **Web site:** http://www.ljusnan.se
Freq: Daily; **Cover Price:** Free; **Circ:** 3,087 Unique Users
Editor: Anders Eklund; **Editor-in-Chief:** Mats Åmvall; **Publisher:** Mats Åmvall
Language(s): Swedish
ADVERTISING RATES:
SCC .... SEK 20
NATIONAL DAILY & SUNDAY NEWSPAPERS: National Daily Newspapers

LJUVA LIVET
1804059W74Q-163
Editorial: Karlavägen 21, 172 76 SUNDBYBERG
Tel: 70 833 40 32
Email: redaktionen@ljuvalivet.se **Web site:** http://www.ljuvalivet.se
Freq: 6 issues yearly; **Circ:** 50,000
Editor: Emma Mollberg; **Advertising Manager:** Mohna Carlson
Language(s): Swedish
ADVERTISING RATES:
Full Page Colour .... SEK 42500
SCC .... SEK 354.16
CONSUMER: WOMEN'S INTEREST CONSUMER MAGAZINES: Lifestyle

THE LOCAL
1873499W89C-260
Editorial: Gjörwellsgatan 28, 112 60 STOCKHOLM
Tel: 8 656 65 13
Email: news@thelocal.se **Web site:** http://www.thelocal.se
Freq: Daily; **Cover Price:** Free; **Circ:** 48,916 Unique Users
Editor: Paul O'Mahony; **Managing Director:** Paul Rapacioli; **Advertising Manager:** Pelle Westerberg
Language(s): Swedish
CONSUMER: HOLIDAYS & TRAVEL: Entertainment Guides

LOCUS - TIDSKRIFT FÖR FORSKNING OM BARN OCH UNGDOMAR
50428W32G-100
Editorial: Stockholms universitet, 106 91 STOCKHOLM **Tel:** 8 737 55 85
Email: locus@buv.su.se **Web site:** http://www.buv.su.se/locus
Date Established: 1989; **Freq:** Quarterly; **Circ:** 800
Editor-in-Chief: Lucas Forsberg; **Publisher:** Peg Lindstrand
Profile: Magazine about child and youth research.
Language(s): Swedish
BUSINESS: LOCAL GOVERNMENT, LEISURE & RECREATION: Community Care & Social Services

LOFTBOOKAZINE
1858551W7-844
Editorial: Box 6067, 102 31 STOCKHOLM
Tel: 8 500 091 00 **Fax:** 850009119
Email: carina@loftcard.se **Web site:** http://www.loftbookazine.com

Freq: Monthly - 4 nummer per år; **Circ:** 40,000
Publisher: Mikael Becker
Language(s): Swedish
BUSINESS: ANTIQUES

LOGOPEDNYTT 50658W56R-60
Editorial: Box 760, 131 24 NACKA **Tel:** 8 466 24 00
Fax: 84662413
Web site: http://www.dik.se/logoped
Freq: 6 issues yearly; **Circ:** 1,200
Editor: Malin Sixt-Börjesson; **Editor-in-Chief:** Marika Schütz; **Advertising Manager:** Caroline Kejnemar; **Publisher:** Ulrika Guldstrand
Profile: Journal containing news, information and articles for professionals working with voice and speech training.
Language(s): Swedish
Readership: Read mainly by speech therapists and voice coaches.
BUSINESS: HEALTH & MEDICAL: Health Medical Related

LOKALGUIDEN 1803992W2A-399
Editorial: Torsgatan 5, 411 04 GOTEBORG
Tel: 31 23 71 00 **Fax:** 31 23 71 15
Email: redaktionen@lokalguiden.se **Web site:** http://www.lokalguiden.se
Freq: 6 issues yearly; **Circ:** 20,000
Editor: Elin Sjöberg; **Advertising Manager:** Jonas Svantsröm; **Publisher:** Tom Vikström
Language(s): Swedish
BUSINESS: COMMUNICATIONS, ADVERTISING & MARKETING

LOKALNYTT 1836387W14A-323
Editorial: Lokalförlaget i Göteborg AB, Trädgårdsgatan 1, 411 08 GÖTEBORG
Tel: 31 68 39 20 **Fax:** 31 68 39 60
Email: info@lokalnytt.se **Web site:** http://www.lokalnytt.se
Freq: 6 times a year; **Cover Price:** Paid; **Circ:** 5,000 Unique Users
Editor: Sofia Carlsson; **Managing Director:** Rolf Andersson; **Publisher:** Rolf Andersson
Language(s): Swedish
ADVERTISING RATES:
Full Page Colour .... SEK 5000
SCC .... SEK 41.66
BUSINESS: COMMERCE, INDUSTRY & MANAGEMENT

LOKALTIDNINGEN ÄNGELHOLM; WEBB 1846247W65A-1052
Editorial: Storgatan 40, 262 43 ÄNGELHOLM
Tel: 431 881 22
Email: redaktion.angelholm@lokaltidningen.se **Web site:** http://angelholm.lokaltidningen.se
Freq: Daily; **Cover Price:** Free; **Circ:** 6,733 Unique Users
Editor: Diana Larsson
Language(s): Swedish
ADVERTISING RATES:
SCC .... SEK 21
NATIONAL DAILY & SUNDAY NEWSPAPERS: National Daily Newspapers

LOKALTIDNINGEN AVENYN; WEBB 1846295W65A-1072
Editorial: Frykholmsgatan 17, 281 31 HÄSSLEHOLM
Tel: 451 38 61 51 **Fax:** 451 38 61 55
Email: redaktion.avenyn@lokaltidningen.se **Web site:** http://www.lokaltidningen.se/tidningar/?p=hassleholm
Freq: Daily; **Cover Price:** Free; **Circ:** 8,533 Unique Users
Editor: Maria Holm; **Advertising Manager:** Pia Törnkvist
Language(s): Swedish
ADVERTISING RATES:
SCC .... SEK 21
NATIONAL DAILY & SUNDAY NEWSPAPERS: National Daily Newspapers

LOKALTIDNINGEN BÅSTAD; WEBB 1844815W65A-1039
Editorial: Storgatan 40, 262 43 ÄNGELHOLM
Tel: 431 881 22
Email: redaktion.angelholm@lokaltidningen.se **Web site:** http://www.lokaltidningen.se/nyheter/?p=bastad
Freq: Daily; **Cover Price:** Free; **Circ:** 2,667 Unique Users
Editor: Diana Larsson; **Editor-in-Chief:** Alex Nielsen; **Publisher:** Alex Nielsen
Language(s): Swedish
ADVERTISING RATES:
SCC .... SEK 13
NATIONAL DAILY & SUNDAY NEWSPAPERS: National Daily Newspapers

LOKALTIDNINGEN HELSINGBORG; WEBB 1846421W65A-1077
Editorial: Bruksgatan 18, 252 23 HELSINGBORG
Tel: 42 19 47 00 **Fax:** 42 19 47 99
Email: redaktion.hbg@lokaltidningen.se **Web site:** http://helsingborg.lokaltidningen.se
Freq: Daily; **Cover Price:** Free; **Circ:** 20,133 Unique Users
Editor: Martin Wingren; **Editor-in-Chief:** Bo Furevi; **Advertising Manager:** Jessica Kuusk; **Publisher:** Bo Furevi
Language(s): Swedish
ADVERTISING RATES:
SCC .... SEK 32
NATIONAL DAILY & SUNDAY NEWSPAPERS: National Daily Newspapers

LOKALTIDNINGEN HÖGANÄS; WEBB 1844970W65A-1049
Editorial: Bruksgatan 18, 252 23 HELSINGBORG
Tel: 4219 47 00
Email: redaktion.hoganas@lokaltidningen.se **Web site:** http://hoganas.lokaltidningen.se
Freq: Daily; **Cover Price:** Free; **Circ:** 4,367 Unique Users
Editor: Susanne Gyllenlöf; **Advertising Manager:** Sebila Vickelli; **Publisher:** Bo Furevi
Language(s): Swedish
ADVERTISING RATES:
SCC .... SEK 16
NATIONAL DAILY & SUNDAY NEWSPAPERS: National Daily Newspapers

LOKALTIDNINGEN KÄVLINGE NYA 634168W80-80
Editorial: Mårtensgatan 2, 244 30 KÄVLINGE
Tel: 46 73 66 60 **Fax:** 46736675
Email: sven.bodestedt@lokaltidningen.se **Web site:** http://www.lokaltidningen.se
Date Established: 1981; **Freq:** 26 issues yearly; **Circ:** 30,000
Editor: Ann Lagerwall; **Advertising Manager:** Sven Bodestedt
Profile: Newspaper featuring local news for Kävlinge and surrounding areas.
Language(s): Swedish
ADVERTISING RATES:
Full Page Colour .... SEK 20700
SCC .... SEK 103.50
CONSUMER: RURAL & REGIONAL INTEREST

LOKALTIDNINGEN KÄVLINGE NYA; WEBB 1846290W65A-1070
Editorial: Mårtensgatan 2, 244 30 KÄVLINGE
Tel: 46 73 66 60 **Fax:** 46 73 66 75
Email: sven.bodestedt@lokaltidningen.se **Web site:** http://kavlinge.lokaltidningen.se
Freq: Daily; **Cover Price:** Free; **Circ:** 10,000 Unique Users
Editor: Ann Lagerwall; **Advertising Manager:** Birgitta Olshed
Language(s): Swedish
ADVERTISING RATES:
SCC .... SEK 21
NATIONAL DAILY & SUNDAY NEWSPAPERS: National Daily Newspapers

LOKALTIDNINGEN KLIPPAN/ PERSTORP/BJUV/ÅSTORP/ ÖRKELLJUNGA: WEBB 1846250W65A-1055
Editorial: Storgatan 40, 262 43 ÄNGELHOLM
Tel: 431 881 22
Email: alex.nielsen@lokaltidningen.se **Web site:** http://bjuv.lokaltidningen.se
Freq: Daily; **Cover Price:** Free; **Circ:** 3,000 Unique Users
Language(s): Swedish
ADVERTISING RATES:
SCC .... SEK 22
NATIONAL DAILY & SUNDAY NEWSPAPERS: National Daily Newspapers

LOKALTIDNINGEN KRISTIANSTAD; WEBB 1846419W65A-1076
Editorial: Tredalagatan 3, 291 34 KRISTIANSTAD
Tel: 44 12 74 90 **Fax:** 44 12 64 90
Email: redaktion.kristianstad@lokaltidningen.se **Web site:** http://kristianstad.lokaltidningen.se
Freq: Daily; **Cover Price:** Free; **Circ:** 14,433 Unique Users
Editor: Paola Nordgren; **Advertising Manager:** Stefan Åström
Language(s): Swedish
ADVERTISING RATES:
SCC .... SEK 32
NATIONAL DAILY & SUNDAY NEWSPAPERS: National Daily Newspapers

LOKALTIDNINGEN LAHOLM; WEBB 1844943W65A-1042
Editorial: Storgatan 40, 262 43 ÄNGELHOLM
Tel: 431 881 22
Email: alex.nielsen@lokaltidningen.se **Web site:** http://bjuv.lokaltidningen.se
Freq: Daily; **Cover Price:** Free; **Circ:** 5,500 Unique Users
Advertising Manager: Stefan Suokas
Language(s): Swedish
ADVERTISING RATES:
SCC .... SEK 16
NATIONAL DAILY & SUNDAY NEWSPAPERS: National Daily Newspapers

LOKALTIDNINGEN LANDSKRONA; WEBB 1846282W65A-1065
Editorial: Lilla Strandgatan 5 B, 261 31 LANDSKRONA **Tel:** 41844 66 51 **Fax:** 418 223 56
Email: trolle@lokaltidningen.se **Web site:** http://landskrona.lokaltidningen.se
Freq: Daily; **Cover Price:** Free; **Circ:** 9,000 Unique Users
Language(s): Swedish
ADVERTISING RATES:
SCC .... SEK 21
NATIONAL DAILY & SUNDAY NEWSPAPERS: National Daily Newspapers

LOKALTIDNINGEN LOMMABLADET 634182W80-100
Editorial: 234 30 KÄVLINGE **Tel:** 46 73 66 60
Fax: 46736675
Email: sven.bodestedt@lokaltidningen.se **Web site:** http://lommabladet.lokaltidningen.se
Date Established: 1994; **Freq:** 26 issues yearly; **Circ:** 28,100
Editor: Lena Karlsson; **Advertising Manager:** Sven Bodestedt
Profile: Local newspaper for Lomma.
Language(s): Swedish
Readership: Read by local residents.
ADVERTISING RATES:
Full Page Colour .... SEK 20104
SCC .... SEK 100.52
CONSUMER: RURAL & REGIONAL INTEREST

LOKALTIDNINGEN LOMMABLADET; WEBB 1846270W65A-1063
Editorial: Box 124, 244 30 KÄVLINGE
Tel: 4673 66 60 **Fax:** 46 73 66 75
Email: sven.bodestedt@lokaltidningen.se **Web site:** http://lommabladet.lokaltidningen.se
Freq: Daily; **Cover Price:** Free; **Circ:** 8,733 Unique Users
Editor: Lena Karlsson; **Advertising Manager:** Annelie Ekelöw
Language(s): Swedish
ADVERTISING RATES:
SCC .... SEK 20
NATIONAL DAILY & SUNDAY NEWSPAPERS: National Daily Newspapers

LOKALTIDNINGEN LUND; WEBB 1846473W65A-1079
Editorial: Paradisgatan 1, 223 50 LUND
Tel: 46 32 57 55 **Fax:** 46152900
Email: redaktion.lund@lokaltidningen.se **Web site:** http://lund.lokaltidningen.se
Freq: Daily; **Cover Price:** Free; **Circ:** 18,700 Unique Users
Editor: Sara Frostberg Lowery; **Advertising Manager:** Mehmet Eski
Language(s): Swedish
NATIONAL DAILY & SUNDAY NEWSPAPERS: National Daily Newspapers

LOKALTIDNINGEN MALMÖ; WEBB 1846636W65A-1082
Editorial: Celsiusgatan 31, 212 14 MALMO
Tel: 40 25 44 50 **Fax:** 40254469
Email: redaktion.malmo@lokaltidningen.se **Web site:** http://malmo.lokaltidningen.se
Freq: Daily; **Cover Price:** Free; **Circ:** 20,900 Unique Users
Editor: Markus Celander
Language(s): Swedish
NATIONAL DAILY & SUNDAY NEWSPAPERS: National Daily Newspapers

LOKALTIDNINGEN MELLANSKÅNE; WEBB 1846285W65A-1068
Editorial: Stora torg 2, 241 30 ESLÖV
Tel: 413 663 31 **Fax:** 413 109 66
Email: redaktion.mellanskane@lokaltidningen.se **Web site:** http://mellanskane.lokaltidningen.se
Freq: Daily; **Cover Price:** Free; **Circ:** 9,700 Unique Users
Editor: Kåre Sjöholm
Language(s): Swedish
ADVERTISING RATES:
SCC .... SEK 21
NATIONAL DAILY & SUNDAY NEWSPAPERS: National Daily Newspapers

LOKALTIDNINGEN SKURUP; WEBB 1844795W65A-1032
Editorial: Stationsplan, 212 14 SKURUP
Tel: 4025 44 60 **Fax:** 402544 69
Email: redaktion.skurup@lokaltidningen.se **Web site:** http://skurup.lokaltidningen.se
Freq: Daily; **Cover Price:** Free; **Circ:** 2,433 Unique Users
Editor: Pauline Bengtsson; **Editor-in-Chief:** Michael Figge Falk; **Publisher:** Michael Figge Falk
Language(s): Swedish
ADVERTISING RATES:
SCC .... SEK 19
NATIONAL DAILY & SUNDAY NEWSPAPERS: National Daily Newspapers

LOKALTIDNINGEN SVALÖV; WEBB 1844787W65A-1029
Editorial: Lilla Strandgatan 5b, 261 31 LANDSKRONA **Tel:** 418 44 66 66 **Fax:** 418 44 66 51
Email: lotta.wahlqvist@lokaltidningen.se **Web site:** http://landskrona.lokaltidningen.se
Freq: Daily; **Cover Price:** Free; **Circ:** 2,167 Unique Users
Language(s): Swedish
ADVERTISING RATES:
SCC .... SEK 12
NATIONAL DAILY & SUNDAY NEWSPAPERS: National Daily Newspapers

LOKALTIDNINGEN SVEDALA; WEBB 1844940W65A-1040
Editorial: Stationsplan, 212 14 MALMÖ
Tel: 40 25 44 60 **Fax:** 40 25 44 69
Email: redaktion.svedala@lokaltidningen.se **Web site:** http://svedala.lokaltidningen.se
Freq: Daily; **Cover Price:** Free; **Circ:** 3,000 Unique Users
Editor: Britta Abotsi; **Advertising Manager:** Henric Lind
Language(s): Swedish
ADVERTISING RATES:
SCC .... SEK 19
NATIONAL DAILY & SUNDAY NEWSPAPERS: National Daily Newspapers

LOKALTIDNINGEN TRELLEBORG; WEBB 1846249W65A-1054
Editorial: Box 100, 212 14 MALMÖ **Tel:** 40 25 44 60
Fax: 40 25 44 69
Email: asa.meierkord@lokaltidningen.se **Web site:** http://trelleborg.lokaltidningen.se
Freq: Daily; **Cover Price:** Free; **Circ:** 11,533 Unique Users
Editor: Åsa Meierkord
Language(s): Swedish
ADVERTISING RATES:
SCC .... SEK 17
NATIONAL DAILY & SUNDAY NEWSPAPERS: National Daily Newspapers

LOKALTIDNINGEN VÄSTBO ANDAN 634340W72-600
Editorial: Box 263, 332 25 GISLAVED
Tel: 371 58 91 50 **Fax:** 371 58 91 69
Email: redaktion.gislaved@lokaltidningen.se **Web site:** http://www.vastboandan.se
Date Established: 1994; **Freq:** Weekly; **Circ:** 24,400
Editor: Yvonne Cedergren; **Editor-in-Chief:** Joakim Olsson; **Advertising Manager:** Micael Ragnar
Language(s): Swedish
ADVERTISING RATES:
Full Page Colour .... SEK 18720
SCC .... SEK 93.6
LOCAL NEWSPAPERS

LOKALTIDNINGEN VÄSTBO ANDAN; WEBB 1846257W65A-1058
Editorial: Box 263, 332 25 GISLAVED
Tel: 371 58 91 50 **Fax:** 371 58 91 69
Email: redaktion.gislaved@lokaltidningen.se **Web site:** http://vastboandan.lokaltidningen.se
Freq: Daily; **Cover Price:** Free; **Circ:** 8,133 Unique Users
Editor: Therése Marttila; **Advertising Manager:** Mats Hammarlund
Language(s): Swedish
ADVERTISING RATES:
SCC .... SEK 19
NATIONAL DAILY & SUNDAY NEWSPAPERS: National Daily Newspapers

LOKALTIDNINGEN VELLINGE - NÄSET; WEBB 1844945W65A-1043
Editorial: 212 14 MALMÖ **Tel:** 410 35 15 10
Fax: 410 35 15 19
Email: redaktion.vellinge@lokaltidningen.se **Web site:** http://vellinge.lokaltidningen.se
Freq: Daily; **Cover Price:** Free; **Circ:** 5,487 Unique Users
Editor-in-Chief: Michael Figge Falk; **Advertising Manager:** Agnetha Schön Westberg; **Publisher:** Michael Figge Falk
Language(s): Swedish
ADVERTISING RATES:
SCC .... SEK 14
NATIONAL DAILY & SUNDAY NEWSPAPERS: National Daily Newspapers

Sweden

LOOK AT SCANDINAVIA
634617W1R-100
Editorial: Fiskhamnsgatan 2, 414 58 GÖTEBORG
Tel: 31 719 05 00
Email: redaktion@hexanova.se **Web site:** http://www.hexanova.se
Freq: Quarterly; **Circ:** 20,000
Editor: Klas Bergqvist; **Publisher:** Urban Nilsson
Language(s): Swedish
BUSINESS: FINANCE & ECONOMICS: Financial Related

LÖSNUMMER
51224W83-90
Editorial: Fakultetsgatan 3, 702 18 ÖREBRO
Tel: 19 676 23 53
Email: losnummer@karen.oru.se **Web site:** http://www.losnummer.net
Date Established: 1966; **Freq:** 6 issues yearly; **Circ:** 12,000
Editor: Emma Axelsson; **Editor-in-Chief:** Ida Andersson; **Publisher:** Ida Andersson
Profile: Magazine covering student interests such as politics, education and culture.
Language(s): Swedish
ADVERTISING RATES:
Full Page Colour .... SEK 12100
SCC .... SEK 60.5
CONSUMER: STUDENT PUBLICATIONS

LO-TIDNINGEN
50322W14L-125
Editorial: Box 1372, 111 93 STOCKHOLM
Tel: 8 796 25 00 **Fax:** 8 411 52 08
Email: lo-tidningen@lo.se **Web site:** http://lotidningen.lo.se
Freq: Weekly; **Circ:** 60,500
Advertising Manager: Anders Molander; **Publisher:** Johanna Kronlid
Profile: Magazine about the labour market, economy, politics and culture.
Language(s): Swedish
Readership: Read mainly by members of the organisation LO. (People who are interested in and campaign for the rights of workers).
ADVERTISING RATES:
Full Page Colour .... SEK 42700
SCC .... SEK 213.50
BUSINESS: COMMERCE, INDUSTRY & MANAGEMENT: Trade Unions

LO-TIDNINGEN; WEBB
1846387W14F-112
Editorial: Box 1372, 111 93 STOCKHOLM
Tel: 8 796 25 00 **Fax:** 84115208
Email: lo-tidningen@lo.se **Web site:** http://lotidningen.lo.se
Freq: Daily; **Cover Price:** Free; **Circ:** 25,760 Unique Users
Publisher: Tommy Öberg
Language(s): Swedish
BUSINESS: COMMERCE, INDUSTRY & MANAGEMENT: Training & Recruitment

LOTTANYTT
51460W40-50
Editorial: Box 2240, 103 16 STOCKHOLM
Tel: 8 666 10 80 **Fax:** 8 666 10 99
Email: info@svenskalottakaren.se **Web site:** http://www.svenskalottakaren.se
Freq: Quarterly; **Circ:** 15,000
Editor-in-Chief: Helena Rådemar
Profile: Magazine containing articles and information about the Swedish Women's Voluntary Defence Service.
Language(s): Swedish
Readership: Aimed at members.
BUSINESS: DEFENCE

LSF-MAGAZINET
50594W56A-32_50
Editorial: 114 21 STOCKHOLM **Tel:** 8 411 31 00
Fax: 8 21 03 26
Email: ordforande@lsf.se **Web site:** http://www.lsf.se
Freq: Monthly; **Circ:** 5,000
Editor: Bernt Andersson; **Advertising Manager:** Helena Zander Ögren
Profile: Journal containing information and articles of interest to medical secretaries.
Language(s): Swedish
BUSINESS: HEALTH & MEDICAL

LUCKYRIDER MAGAZINE
1696273W81D-131
Editorial: Box 16, 686 20 SUNNE **Tel:** 565 108 02
Fax: 565 108 02
Email: redaktion@luckyrider.se **Web site:** http://www.luckyrider.se
Freq: 6 issues yearly; **Circ:** 20,000
Editor-in-Chief: Åsa Wikberg; **Advertising Manager:** Carina Kvist; **Publisher:** Åsa Wikberg
Language(s): Swedish
CONSUMER: ANIMALS & PETS: Horses & Ponies

LUM, LUNDS UNIVERSITETS MAGASIN
51221W83-73
Editorial: Inf.enheten, Lunds universitet, Box 117, 221 00 LUND **Tel:** 46 222 95 24
Email: lum@rektor.lu.se **Web site:** http://www.lu.se/lum
Date Established: 1968; **Freq:** Monthly; **Circ:** 14,000
Editor: Maria Lindh; **Publisher:** Maria Lindh
Profile: Magazine about science, academic education and working life. Contains news from Lund University and information for and about students and student life.
Language(s): Swedish
ADVERTISING RATES:
Full Page Colour .... SEK 19500
SCC .... SEK 233.33
CONSUMER: STUDENT PUBLICATIONS

LYFTET
1639309W42R-1
Editorial: Box 22307, 111 22 STOCKHOLM
Tel: 8 508 938 00 **Fax:** 8 508 938 01
Email: mobilkran@branschkansliet.se **Web site:** http://www.mobilkranforeningen.se
Freq: Annual; **Circ:** 5,000
Editor: Jenny Forssell; **Editor-in-Chief:** Leena Haabma Hintze; **Publisher:** Leena Haabma Hintze
Language(s): Swedish
BUSINESS: CONSTRUCTION: Construction Related

LYRIKVÄNNEN
51262W84B-100
Editorial: Fredsgatan 6, 222 20 LUND
Tel: 46 32 32 95
Email: info@lyrikvannen.se **Web site:** http://www.lyrikvannen.se
Freq: 6 issues yearly; **Circ:** 3,500
Editor: Erik Magntorn
Profile: Magazine containing articles about poetry and lyric poetry, also featuring interviews with authors.
Language(s): Swedish
Readership: Aimed at readers of poetry.
CONSUMER: THE ARTS & LITERARY: Literary

LYSEKILSPOSTEN
50809W67B-5100
Editorial: Box 93, 453 22 LYSEKIL **Tel:** 523 66 70 81
Fax: 523 66 70 98
Email: redaktion@lysekilsposten.se **Web site:** http://www.lysekilsposten.se
Date Established: 1905
Circ: 3,000
Publisher: Helge Gustafzon
Language(s): Swedish
ADVERTISING RATES:
Full Page Colour .... SEK 20000
SCC .... SEK 51.94
REGIONAL DAILY & SUNDAY NEWSPAPERS: Regional Daily Newspapers

M3 DIGITAL WORLD
752214W14A-220
Editorial: Karlbergsvägen 77, 106 78 STOCKHOLM
Tel: 8 453 60 00
Email: m3@idg.se **Web site:** http://m3.idg.se
Freq: Monthly; **Circ:** 26,800
Editor: Mikael Lindkvist; **Publisher:** Daniel Sjöholm
Language(s): Swedish
ADVERTISING RATES:
Full Page Colour .... SEK 49900
SCC .... SEK 415.83
BUSINESS: COMMERCE, INDUSTRY & MANAGEMENT

M3 HEMMABIO
1803914W78B-23
Editorial: 106 78 STOCKHOLM **Tel:** 8 453 62 70
Email: m3@idg.se **Web site:** http://www.m3.idg.se
Freq: 6 issues yearly; **Circ:** 27,800
Editor: Mikael Lindkvist; **Publisher:** Daniel Sjöholm
Language(s): Swedish
ADVERTISING RATES:
Full Page Colour .... SEK 24300
SCC .... SEK 202.5
CONSUMER: CONSUMER ELECTRONICS: Video & DVD

M3; WEBB
1844527W5E-112
Editorial: Karlbergsvägen 77-81, 106 78 STOCKHOLM **Tel:** 8 453 60 00
Email: m3@idg.se **Web site:** http://www.m3.idg.se
Freq: Daily; **Cover Price:** Free; **Circ:** 21,081 Unique Users
Editor: Pontus Gunnarsson; **Editor-in-Chief:** Robert Brännström; **Publisher:** Daniel Sjöholm
Language(s): Swedish
BUSINESS: COMPUTERS & AUTOMATION: Data Transmission

MÅ BRA
50988W74G-60
Editorial: Budadress: Tysta Gatan 12, Box 27870, 115 93 STOCKHOLM **Tel:** 8 679 46 00
Email: redaktionen@mabra.aller.se **Web site:** http://www.mabra.com
Date Established: 1978; **Freq:** Monthly; **Circ:** 95,500
Advertising Manager: Edita Becker
Profile: Magazine about mental health and physical well-being.
Language(s): Swedish
ADVERTISING RATES:
Full Page Colour .... SEK 51000
SCC .... SEK 425
CONSUMER: WOMEN'S INTEREST CONSUMER MAGAZINES: Slimming & Health

MÅ BRA; MABRA.COM
1846664W91R-246
Editorial: Box 27870, 115 93 STOCKHOLM
Tel: 8 679 46 00
Email: redaktionen@mabra.aller.se **Web site:** http://www.mabra.com
Freq: Daily; **Cover Price:** Free; **Circ:** 39,400 Unique Users
Advertising Manager: Edita Becker; **Publisher:** Liselotte Stålberg
Language(s): Swedish
CONSUMER: RECREATION & LEISURE: Recreation & Leisure Related

MACWORLD
50242W5C-50
Editorial: IDG, Karlbergsvägen 77, 106 78 STOCKHOLM **Tel:** 8 453 60 00
Email: macworld@idg.se **Web site:** http://macworld.idg.se
Freq: Monthly; **Circ:** 16,000 Unique Users
Publisher: Andreas Leijon
Profile: Magazine focusing on the use of Macintosh systems.
Language(s): Swedish
Readership: Aimed at professional Macintosh users and network managers.
BUSINESS: COMPUTERS & AUTOMATION: Professional Personal Computers

MACWORLD;MACWORLD.SE
1844529W5E-113
Editorial: IDG, Karlbergsvägen 77, 106 78 STOCKHOLM **Tel:** 8 453 60 00
Email: macworld@idg.se **Web site:** http://www.macworld.se
Freq: Daily; **Cover Price:** Free; **Circ:** 21,158 Unique Users
Publisher: Andreas Leijon
Language(s): Swedish
BUSINESS: COMPUTERS & AUTOMATION: Data Transmission

MAGASIN1
1696115W76A-192
Editorial: Box 2009, 103 11 STOCKHOLM
Tel: 8 411 47 70
Email: redaktion@kultur1.se **Web site:** http://www.magasinett.net
Freq: Monthly; **Cover Price:** Paid; **Circ:** 4,116 Unique Users
Editor-in-Chief: Hans Alexander Gerlanius; **Publisher:** Hans Alexander Gerlanius
Language(s): Swedish
CONSUMER: MUSIC & PERFORMING ARTS: Cinema

MAGASIN ZOONEN
1817560W79K-58
Tel: 35 21 28 30
Web site: http://www.zoonen.com
Freq: Half-yearly; **Cover Price:** Free; **Circ:** 25,000
Editor: Hans Norling
Language(s): Swedish
CONSUMER: HOBBIES & DIY: Collectors Magazines

MAGASINET FASTIGHETSSVERIGE
1697016W1E-202
Editorial: Trädgårdsgatan 1, 411 08 GÖTEBORG
Tel: 31 13 91 16 **Fax:** 31 68 39 60
Email: red@fastighetssverige.se **Web site:** http://www.fastighetssverige.se
Circ: 10,000
Editor: Joachim Aronsson; **Editor-in-Chief:** Eddie Ekberg; **Publisher:** Rolf Andersson
Language(s): Swedish
ADVERTISING RATES:
Full Page Colour .... SEK 31950
SCC .... SEK 266.25
BUSINESS: FINANCE & ECONOMICS: Property

MAGASINET FOTBOLL
1625608W75J-264
Editorial: Box 1216, 171 23 SOLNA **Tel:** 8 735 09 00
Email: svff@svenskfotboll.se **Web site:** http://www.svenskfotboll.se
Freq: Quarterly; **Circ:** 8,000
Language(s): Swedish
CONSUMER: SPORT: Athletics

MAGASINET SKÅNE
1642358W80-846
Editorial: Svinaberga, 277 35 KIVIK **Tel:** 414 714 73
Email: red@magasinetskane.se **Web site:** http://www.magasinetskane.se
Freq: 6 issues yearly; **Circ:** 13,000
Publisher: Mattias Hansson
Language(s): Swedish
ADVERTISING RATES:
Full Page Colour .... SEK 19200
SCC .... SEK 160
CONSUMER: RURAL & REGIONAL INTEREST

MAGASINSKÄRGÅRD
1741129W50-116
Editorial: JE Mediaproduktion, PL 2178, 760 15 GRÄDDÖ **Tel:** 176 181 90
Email: josefin@magasinskargard.se **Web site:** http://www.magasinskargard.se
Freq: Half-yearly; **Circ:** 50,000
Editor-in-Chief: Josefin Ekberg; **Advertising Manager:** Lena Östergren
Language(s): Swedish
BUSINESS: TRAVEL & TOURISM

MAGAZIN24.SE
1844676W82-480
Editorial: Stora gatan 12, 731 30 KÖPING
Tel: 221 209 10 **Fax:** 221 760 090
Email: redaktion@magazin24.se **Web site:** http://www.magazin24.se
Freq: Daily; **Cover Price:** Free; **Circ:** 19,000 Unique Users
Editor-in-Chief: Patrick Mörk; **Publisher:** Josefin Svenberg
Language(s): Swedish
CONSUMER: CURRENT AFFAIRS & POLITICS

MAKALÖSA FÖRÄLDRAR
752204W74D-90
Editorial: Götgatan 100, 118 62 STOCKHOLM
Tel: 8 720 14 13
Email: kansli@makalosa.org **Web site:** http://www.makalosa.org
Freq: Quarterly; **Circ:** 2,000
Editor: Maria Lohe
Language(s): Swedish
CONSUMER: WOMEN'S INTEREST CONSUMER MAGAZINES: Child Care

MÄKLARVÄRLDEN
1839957W1E-205
Editorial: Skeppargatan 27, 114 52 STOCKHOLM
Tel: 8 442 86 30 **Fax:** 86621180
Email: info@spearproduction.se **Web site:** http://www.maklarvarlden.se
Freq: Quarterly; **Cover Price:** Free; **Circ:** 5,000
Editor: Anders Thorén
Language(s): Swedish
ADVERTISING RATES:
Full Page Colour .... SEK 5000
Copy instructions: *Copy Date:* 20 days prior to publication date
BUSINESS: FINANCE & ECONOMICS: Property

MÅL & MEDEL
50380W22A-60
Editorial: Box 1156, 111 81 STOCKHOLM
Tel: 8 796 29 00 **Fax:** 8208490
Email: malmedel@livs.se **Web site:** http://www.malmedel.nu
Freq: Monthly; **Circ:** 49,500
Advertising Manager: DA-media Ab
Profile: Journal focusing on issues relevant to the food trade.
Language(s): Swedish
Readership: Read by those working in the sector.
ADVERTISING RATES:
Full Page Colour .... SEK 21950
SCC .... SEK 182.92
BUSINESS: FOOD

MÅL & MEDEL; MALMEDEL.NU
1846412W14F-114
Editorial: Box 1156, 111 81 STOCKHOLM
Tel: 8 796 29 00 **Fax:** 8 20 84 90
Email: malmedel@livs.se **Web site:** http://www.malmedel.nu
Freq: Daily; **Cover Price:** Free; **Circ:** 8,720 Unique Users
Language(s): Swedish
BUSINESS: COMMERCE, INDUSTRY & MANAGEMENT: Training & Recruitment

MÄLARDALEN - BERGSLAGENS AFFÄRER
50739W63-8_20
Editorial: Storgatan 53, 703 63 ÖREBRO
Tel: 19 17 07 60 **Fax:** 19 12 56 42
Web site: http://www.mba.se
Freq: Quarterly; **Circ:** 4,300
Editor-in-Chief: Lars Berndtsson; **Advertising Manager:** Elizabeth Selvert; **Publisher:** Ronny Stenbergh
Profile: Magazine about business and industry in the middle regions of Sweden.
Language(s): Swedish
ADVERTISING RATES:
Full Page Colour .... SEK 23800
SCC .... SEK 198.33
BUSINESS: REGIONAL BUSINESS

MÅLAR'N
1834360W14E-59
Editorial: Målarettan, Svenska Målareförbundet avd 1, Box 42045, 126 12 STOCKHOLM **Tel:** 8 449 20 60
Fax: 84492089
Email: redaktionen@malarettan.se
Freq: Quarterly; **Circ:** 23,500
Language(s): Swedish
ADVERTISING RATES:
Full Page Colour .... SEK 29000

SCC .... SEK 241.67
BUSINESS: COMMERCE, INDUSTRY & MANAGEMENT: Work Study

MÅLARNAS FACKTIDNING
50330W16A-55
Editorial: Box 1113, 111 81 STOCKHOLM
Tel: 8 587 274 00
Email: post@malareforbundet.se **Web site:** http://www.malareforbundet.se
Freq: 6 issues yearly; **Circ:** 22,000
Profile: Magazine for Swedish artists.
Language(s): Swedish
ADVERTISING RATES:
Full Page Colour .... SEK 18900
SCC .... SEK 157.50
BUSINESS: DECORATING & PAINT

MÄLARÖARNAS NYHETER
634239W80-125
Editorial: Box 100, 178 22 EKERÖ **Tel:** 8560 358 00
Fax: 8 560 358 00
Email: red@malaroarnasnyheter.se **Web site:** http://www.malaro.com
Date Established: 1949; **Freq:** 26 issues yearly; **Circ:** 11,700
Editor: Lo Bäcklinder; **Publisher:** Laila Westerberg
Profile: Local newspaper for Ekerö kommun.
Language(s): Swedish
Readership: Read by local residents.
ADVERTISING RATES:
Full Page Colour .... SEK 22800
SCC .... SEK 114
CONSUMER: RURAL & REGIONAL INTEREST

MALMÖTIDNINGEN
634192W80-135
Editorial: Järnvägsgatan 74, 216 16 LIMHAMN
Tel: 40 15 74 77 **Fax:** 40158680
Email: malmotidningen@telia.com
Date Established: 1962; **Freq:** 6 issues yearly; **Circ:** 40,000
Editor: Ingrid Andersson; **Publisher:** Karl-Heinz Forsberg
Profile: Newspaper featuring local news for Malmö.
Language(s): Swedish
CONSUMER: RURAL & REGIONAL INTEREST

MAMA MAGASIN
1625825W74A-142
Editorial: Budadress: Rådmansgatan 49, 105 44 STOCKHOLM **Tel:** 8 736 53 00 **Fax:** 8 24 02 13
Email: mama@mama.bonnier.se **Web site:** http://www.mama.nu
Freq: Monthly; **Circ:** 56,400
Editor: Elin Fundell; **Editor-in-Chief:** Anna Zethraeus; **Advertising Manager:** Magdalena Egelin
Language(s): Swedish
ADVERTISING RATES:
Full Page Colour .... SEK 49500
SCC .... SEK 412.50
CONSUMER: WOMEN'S INTEREST CONSUMER MAGAZINES: Women's Interest

MANA
1641076W82-456
Editorial: Box 4514, 203 20 MALMO **Tel:** 40 18 70 05
Fax: 40 689 13 68
Email: post@uppmana.nu **Web site:** http://www.uppmana.nu
Freq: 6 issues yearly; **Circ:** 3,000
Publisher: Rebecca Selberg
Language(s): Swedish
CONSUMER: CURRENT AFFAIRS & POLITICS

MANAGEMENT OF TECHNOLOGY
50284W14A-81
Editorial: Vera Sandbergs allé 8, 412 96 GOTEBORG
Tel: 31 772 12 29
Email: info@imit.se **Web site:** http://www.imit.se
Freq: Quarterly; **Circ:** 19,000
Editor: Jennie Björk; **Publisher:** Mats Magnusson
Profile: Magazine covering international innovations, new technology, businesses, development and current related research.
Language(s): Swedish
Readership: Aimed at managers, directors, entrepreneurs, scientists and researchers.
ADVERTISING RATES:
Full Page Colour .... SEK 32470
SCC .... SEK 270.58
BUSINESS: COMMERCE, INDUSTRY & MANAGEMENT

MARIESTADS-TIDNINGEN
50813W67B-5150
Editorial: Box 242, 542 23 MARIESTAD
Tel: 501 687 00 **Fax:** 501 167 00
Email: redaktion@mariestadstidningen.se **Web site:** http://www.mariestadstidningen.se
Date Established: 1817
Circ: 13,300
Managing Director: Mats Muregård; **Advertising Manager:** Thomas Femrin; **Publisher:** Karin Eriksson
Language(s): Swedish
ADVERTISING RATES:
Full Page Colour .... SEK 26100
SCC .... SEK 130.50
REGIONAL DAILY & SUNDAY NEWSPAPERS: Regional Daily Newspapers

MARKBLADET
634195W72-199
Editorial: Box 113, 511 21 KINNA **Tel:** 320 20 91 40
Fax: 320 20 91 57
Email: redaktion@markbladet.se **Web site:** http://www.markbladet.se
Date Established: 1967; **Freq:** Weekly; **Circ:** 23,000
Editor: Per Niklasson; **Advertising Manager:** Matz Hammarström; **Publisher:** Matz Hammarström
Profile: Newspaper featuring local news for Marks and Viskafors.
Language(s): Swedish
ADVERTISING RATES:
Full Page Colour .... SEK 21700
SCC .... SEK 135.62
LOCAL NEWSPAPERS

MARKET
1804052W53-83
Editorial: 721 85 VÄSTERÅS **Tel:** 8 728 23 00
Fax: 21194182
Email: redaktionen@market.se **Web site:** http://www.market.se
Freq: Weekly; **Circ:** 8,000
Editor-in-Chief: David Jansson; **Publisher:** Eva Andersson
Language(s): Swedish
ADVERTISING RATES:
Full Page Colour .... SEK 33900
SCC .... SEK 169
BUSINESS: RETAILING & WHOLESALING

MARKET PLUS
1844780W14A-333
Editorial: 721 85 VÄSTERÅS **Tel:** 8 728 23 00
Fax: 21 19 41 82
Email: redaktionen@market.se **Web site:** http://www.market.se
Freq: Daily; **Cover Price:** Free; **Circ:** 2,704 Unique Users
Advertising Manager: Tomas Karlsson; **Publisher:** Eva Andersson
Language(s): Swedish
BUSINESS: COMMERCE, INDUSTRY & MANAGEMENT

MASEN
752367W80-625
Editorial: Box 220, 792 24 MORA **Tel:** 250 713 85
Web site: http://www.masen.se
Freq: Weekly; **Circ:** 16,500
Advertising Manager: Lina Norin; **Publisher:** Hans Nyström
Language(s): Swedish
CONSUMER: RURAL & REGIONAL INTEREST

MASKINENTREPRENÖREN / ME-TIDNINGEN
50488W42A-50
Editorial: Box 1609, 114 79 STOCKHOLM
Tel: 8 762 70 65
Email: micael.appelgren@me.se **Web site:** http://www.maskinentreprenoren.nu
Freq: Monthly; **Circ:** 7,500
Advertising Manager: Tomas Nordmark
Profile: Magazine for contractors in the construction industry.
Language(s): Swedish
ADVERTISING RATES:
Full Page Colour .... SEK 20500
SCC .... SEK 170.83
BUSINESS: CONSTRUCTION

MASKINENTREPRENÖREN / ME-TIDNINGEN; WEBB
1844946W42A-103
Editorial: Box 1609, 114 79 STOCKHOLM
Tel: 8 762 70 65
Email: micael.appelgren@me.se **Web site:** http://www.maskinentreprenoren.nu
Freq: Daily; **Cover Price:** Free; **Circ:** 3,000 Unique Users
Advertising Manager: Tomas Nordmark
Language(s): Swedish
BUSINESS: CONSTRUCTION

MASSAGE & KROPPSVÅRD
1648846W56Q-1
Editorial: Villa Ekeberga, 614 97 SÖDERKÖPING
Tel: 121 411 33 **Fax:** 121 411 33
Email: redaktionen@mok.se **Web site:** http://www.mok.se
Freq: Quarterly; **Circ:** 12,000
Editor-in-Chief: Rolf Elmström; **Publisher:** Rolf Elmström
Language(s): Swedish
BUSINESS: HEALTH & MEDICAL: Chiropractic

MAT & VÄNNER
1639402W74P-207
Editorial: Box 22100, 250 23 HELSINGBORG
Tel: 42 21 11 22 **Fax:** 42 21 11 37
Email: malin@matochvanner.se **Web site:** http://www.matochvanner.se
Freq: 6 issues yearly; **Circ:** 30,000
Advertising Manager: Robert Wallner; **Publisher:** Thorbjörn Östman
Language(s): Swedish
ADVERTISING RATES:
Full Page Colour .... SEK 24900
SCC .... SEK 207.50
Copy instructions: *Copy Date:* 10 days prior to publication date
CONSUMER: WOMEN'S INTEREST CONSUMER MAGAZINES: Food & Cookery

MAT & VÄNNER; MATOCHVANNER.SE
1846423W74P-225
Editorial: Box 22100, 250 23 HELSINGBORG
Tel: 42 21 11 22 **Fax:** 42211137
Email: malin@matochvanner.se **Web site:** http://www.matochvanner.se
Freq: Daily; **Cover Price:** Free; **Circ:** 16,400 Unique Users
Advertising Manager: Robert Wallner
Language(s): Swedish
CONSUMER: WOMEN'S INTEREST CONSUMER MAGAZINES: Food & Cookery

MATCH
51016W75B-50
Editorial: Box 2161, 403 13 GOTEBORG
Tel: 31 711 02 10 **Fax:** 31 700 81 89
Email: redaktion@matchplus.se **Web site:** http://www.matchplus.se
Date Established: 1993; **Freq:** Monthly; **Circ:** 50,000
Editor: Ulf Jörnvik; **Advertising Manager:** Patrick Heed
Profile: Magazine covering football. Contains news, articles, interviews and information about national and international football.
Language(s): Swedish
Readership: Read by football enthusiasts.
Copy instructions: *Copy Date:* 21 days prior to publication date
CONSUMER: SPORT: Football

MATMAGASINET
51003W74P-200
Editorial: 251 85 HELSINGBORG **Tel:** 42 17 35 00
Fax: 42 17 37 56
Email: matmagasinet@aller.se **Web site:** http://matmagasinet.se
Date Established: 1998; **Freq:** Monthly; **Circ:** 58,100
Editor-in-Chief: Maud Onnermark; **Publisher:** Ulla Cocke
Profile: Magazine containing articles and news about food and drink.
Language(s): Swedish
Readership: Aimed at people who enjoy cooking.
ADVERTISING RATES:
Full Page Colour .... SEK 24000
SCC .... SEK 200
CONSUMER: WOMEN'S INTEREST CONSUMER MAGAZINES: Food & Cookery

MC-FOLKET
51113W77B-60
Editorial: Forskargatan 3, 781 70 BORLÄNGE
Tel: 243 822 80
Email: redax@mc-folket.se **Web site:** http://www.svmc.se
Freq: 6 issues yearly; **Circ:** 58,800
Editor: Petra Holmlund; **Editor-in-Chief:** Magnus Klys; **Advertising Manager:** Rolf Eliasson; **Publisher:** Magnus Klys
Profile: Magazine about biking. Contains motorcycle proficiency tests, questions regarding safety and traffic and reader reports from motorcycle clubs. Published by the Swedish Motorcyclists' Federation.
Language(s): Swedish
ADVERTISING RATES:
Full Page Colour .... SEK 14500
SCC .... SEK 120.83
CONSUMER: MOTORING & CYCLING: Motorcycling

MCM - MOTORCYKELMAGASINET
51114W77B-65
Editorial: Torsgatan 65, 113 37 STOCKHOLM
Tel: 8 34 04 07 **Fax:** 8 34 04 22
Email: inge@mcm.se **Web site:** http://www.mcm.se
Date Established: 1985; **Freq:** 6 issues yearly; **Circ:** 20,500
Editor-in-Chief: Inge Persson-Carleson; **Publisher:** Inge Persson-Carleson
Profile: Magazine covering motorcycles. Contains articles, information and practical advice on maintenance, racing and leisure.
Language(s): Swedish
ADVERTISING RATES:
Full Page Colour .... SEK 16000
SCC .... SEK 133.33
CONSUMER: MOTORING & CYCLING: Motorcycling

MC-NYTT
51115W77B-67
Editorial: Box 23800, 104 35 STOCKHOLM
Tel: 8 736 12 00 **Fax:** 87361249
Email: manfred.holz@mcnytt.se **Web site:** http://www.mcnytt.se
Date Established: 1959; **Freq:** Monthly; **Circ:** 27,500
Advertising Manager: Ulrika Carlström
Profile: Magazine containing news, information and articles about motorcycles.
Language(s): Swedish
ADVERTISING RATES:
Full Page Colour .... SEK 15900
SCC .... SEK 132.50
CONSUMER: MOTORING & CYCLING: Motorcycling

MEDBARN
50975W74D-50
Editorial: c/o Lindberg, Bastugatan 27 3 tr, 118 25 STOCKHOLM **Tel:** 705 72 97 17
Email: marianne@barnfamiljen.com **Web site:** http://www.barnfamiljen.com
Date Established: 1993; **Freq:** Quarterly; **Cover Price:** Free; **Circ:** 55,000
Advertising Manager: Ingela Nicolausson
Profile: Magazine covering pregnancy and childcare.
Language(s): Swedish
Readership: Read by pregnant women and new parents.
CONSUMER: WOMEN'S INTEREST CONSUMER MAGAZINES: Child Care

MEDBORGAREN
51466W82-419
Editorial: Box 2080, 103 12 STOCKHOLM
Tel: 8 676 80 00 **Fax:** 8204171
Email: medborgaren@moderat.se **Web site:** http://www.moderat.se/web/medborgaren.aspx
Freq: 6 issues yearly; **Circ:** 48,700
Advertising Manager: Linda Davidson
Language(s): Swedish
ADVERTISING RATES:
Full Page Colour .... SEK 24900
SCC .... SEK 155.63
CONSUMER: CURRENT AFFAIRS & POLITICS

MEDIATRENDER; MEDIAFAX
1839788W2A-401
Editorial: Allégatan 5 B, 777 31 SMEDJEBACKEN
Tel: 240 706 66 **Fax:** 240 755 09
Email: ake.bergman@mediatrender.se **Web site:** http://www.mediatrender.se
Freq: Daily; **Cover Price:** Paid; **Circ:** 5,000 Unique Users
Editor-in-Chief: Åke Bergman; **Publisher:** Åke Bergman
Language(s): Swedish
ADVERTISING RATES:
Full Page Colour .... SEK 25200
BUSINESS: COMMUNICATIONS, ADVERTISING & MARKETING

MEDICINSK ACCESS
1666650W56A-340
Editorial: Nybohallen, 820 40 JÄRVSÖ
Tel: 651 150 50
Email: hakan@medicinskaccess.se **Web site:** http://www.medicinskaccess.se
Freq: 6 issues yearly; **Circ:** 19,200
Editor: Zvi Wirschubsky; **Editor-in-Chief:** Håkan Hedin
Language(s): Swedish
ADVERTISING RATES:
Full Page Colour .... SEK 25200
SCC .... SEK 210
BUSINESS: HEALTH & MEDICAL

MEDICINSK VETENSKAP
50597W56A-38_50
Editorial: Karolinska Institutet, 171 77 STOCKHOLM
Tel: 8 524 800 00 **Fax:** 8 33 88 33
Email: medicinskvetenskap@ki.se **Web site:** http://www.ki.se
Date Established: 1994; **Freq:** Quarterly; **Circ:** 21,600
Advertising Manager: Jan Nilsson
Profile: Journal covering development and research within the medical profession.
Language(s): Swedish
Readership: Read by scientists.
ADVERTISING RATES:
Full Page Colour .... SEK 24000
SCC .... SEK 200
BUSINESS: HEALTH & MEDICAL

MEDICINSK VETENSKAP & PRAXIS
1852523W56A-362
Editorial: Box 5650, 11486 STOCKHOLM
Tel: 8 411 32 00 **Fax:** 8 411 32 60
Email: info@sbu.se **Web site:** http://www.sbu.se/sv/Vetenskap–Praxis
Freq: 6 issues yearly - 4 ggr/ år; **Circ:** 230,000
Editor: Ragnar Levi; **Publisher:** Måns Rosén
Language(s): Swedish
BUSINESS: HEALTH & MEDICAL

MEDICOR MAGASIN
634911W56A-267
Editorial: Medicinska Föreningen i Stockholm, Box 250, 171 77 STOCKHOLM **Tel:** 8 524 830 70
Email: chefred@mf.ki.se **Web site:** http://www.mf.ki.se
Freq: Quarterly; **Circ:** 8,000
Language(s): Swedish
BUSINESS: HEALTH & MEDICAL

MEDIEVÄRLDEN 50186W2B-130
Editorial: Box 22500, 104 22 STOCKHOLM
Tel: 8 692 46 00 **Fax:** 8 692 46 13
Email: redaktion@medievarlden.se **Web site:** http://www.medievarlden.se
Date Established: 1920; **Freq:** Monthly; **Circ:** 10,200
Editor: Lisa Bjurwald; **Advertising Manager:** Carl Thörne; **Publisher:** Anders Ahlberg
Profile: Magazine of the Swedish Newspaper Publishers' Association.
Language(s): Swedish
Readership: Aimed at journalists and those working in the media.
ADVERTISING RATES:
Full Page Colour .... SEK 39000
SCC .... SEK 243.75
BUSINESS: COMMUNICATIONS, ADVERTISING & MARKETING: Press

MEDIEVÄRLDEN; MEDIEVARLDEN.SE 1843539W2A-402
Editorial: Box 22500, 104 22 STOCKHOLM
Tel: 8 692 46 00 **Fax:** 8 692 46 13
Email: redaktion@medievarlden.se **Web site:** http://www.medievarlden.se
Freq: Daily; **Cover Price:** Free; **Circ:** 3,400 Unique Users
Editor-in-Chief: Axel Andén
Language(s): Swedish
ADVERTISING RATES:
SCC .... SEK 49
BUSINESS: COMMUNICATIONS, ADVERTISING & MARKETING

MEDMÄNSKLIGHET 51447W82-94
Editorial: Box 45, 221 00 LUND **Tel:** 46 32 99 30
Fax: 46158309
Email: red@manniskohjalp.se **Web site:** http://www.manniskohjalp.se
Date Established: 1950; **Freq:** 6 issues yearly; **Circ:** 47,000
Editor: Åsa Bengtsson; **Publisher:** Bo Paulsson
Profile: Journal containing articles and information about the work of the humanitarian organisation Individual Aid, that provides help and support in the form of education, employment and health care for people in need.
Language(s): Swedish
CONSUMER: CURRENT AFFAIRS & POLITICS

MEDSOLS 50687W58-70
Editorial: c/o Folkkampanjen mot Kärnkraft och Kärnvapen, Tegelviksgatan 40, 118 20 STOCKHOLM
Tel: 8 84 14 90 **Fax:** 8 84 51 81
Email: info@folkkampanjen.se **Web site:** http://www.folkkampanjen.se
Freq: Quarterly; **Circ:** 2,500
Editor: Inger Widell
Profile: Journal about environment, energy, nuclear energy and nuclear weapons. Published and owned by the Swedish Anti-Nuclear Movement.
Language(s): Swedish
Readership: Aimed at members of the organisation.
BUSINESS: ENERGY, FUEL & NUCLEAR

MEDTECH MAGAZINE 1664171W56R-107
Editorial: Box 2001, 191 02 SOLLENTUNA
Tel: 708 80 04 07 **Fax:** 8 35 80 25
Email: redaktionen@medtechmagazine.se **Web site:** http://www.medtechmagazine.se
Freq: Quarterly; **Circ:** 6,000
Advertising Manager: Frida Axiö-Gelfgren
Language(s): Swedish
BUSINESS: HEALTH & MEDICAL: Health Medical Related

MEETINGS INTERNATIONAL 1695642W2C-104
Editorial: Box 1223, 164 28 KISTA **Tel:** 8 612 42 20
Fax: 86124280
Email: info@meetingsinternational.se **Web site:** http://www.meetingsinternational.se
Freq: 6 issues yearly; **Circ:** 13,900
Editor-in-Chief: Atti Soenarso; **Advertising Manager:** Roger Kellerman
Language(s): Swedish
ADVERTISING RATES:
Full Page Colour .... SEK 21700
SCC .... SEK 180.83
Copy instructions: *Copy Date:* 7 days prior to publication date
BUSINESS: COMMUNICATIONS, ADVERTISING & MARKETING: Conferences & Exhibitions

---

MEETINGS INTERNATIONAL; WEBB 1844969W2C-106
Editorial: Box 224, 271 25 YSTAD **Tel:** 8 612 42 20
Fax: 8 612 42 80
Email: info@meetingsinternational.se **Web site:** http://www.meetingsinternational.se
Freq: Daily; **Cover Price:** Free; **Circ:** 2,000 Unique Users
Editor-in-Chief: Atti Soenarso; **Publisher:** Atti Soenarso
Language(s): Swedish
BUSINESS: COMMUNICATIONS, ADVERTISING & MARKETING: Conferences & Exhibitions

---

MEKANIK- INFORMATION MED INDUSTRINYTT 50357W19F-65
Editorial: Box 30057, 200 61 LIMHAMN
Tel: 40 16 25 22 **Fax:** 40 16 25 23
Email: mekanikinfo@telia.com
Freq: Quarterly; **Circ:** 15,000
Editor-in-Chief: Rolf Jönsson; **Publisher:** Rolf Jönsson
Profile: Magazine covering all aspects of mechanical engineering.
Language(s): Swedish
ADVERTISING RATES:
Full Page Colour .... SEK 30000
SCC .... SEK 150
BUSINESS: ENGINEERING & MACHINERY: Production & Mechanical Engineering

---

MEKANISTEN 50358W19F-70
Editorial: Box 2045, 135 02 TYRESÖ
Tel: 8 667 93 20 **Fax:** 8 712 43 56
Email: info@smr.nu **Web site:** http://www.smr.nu
Date Established: 1985; **Freq:** Quarterly; **Circ:** 1,900
Publisher: Johan Bratthäll
Profile: Official journal of the Swedish Association of Mechanical Engineers (SMR).
Language(s): Swedish
Readership: Read by members of the SMR.
ADVERTISING RATES:
Full Page Colour .... SEK 5000
BUSINESS: ENGINEERING & MACHINERY: Production & Mechanical Engineering

---

MELLANRUMMET TIDSKR. OM BARN & UNGDOMSPSYKO. 1804055W56N-214
Editorial: c/o May Nilsson, Högalidsgatan 48, 117 30 STOCKHOLM **Tel:** 8 716 07 44 **Fax:** 8 716 07 44
Email: mellanrummet@hotmail.com **Web site:** http://www.enigma.se/mellanrummet
Freq: Half-yearly; **Circ:** 800
Editor: May Nilsson; **Publisher:** Britta Blomberg
Language(s): Swedish
BUSINESS: HEALTH & MEDICAL: Mental Health

MEMENTO 634636W87-175
Editorial: SBF, Upplagsvägen 1, 117 43 STOCKHOLM **Tel:** 8 556 811 80 **Fax:** 855681188
Email: info@memento.se **Web site:** http://www.begravningar.org
Date Established: 1945; **Freq:** Quarterly; **Circ:** 9,000
Language(s): Swedish
CONSUMER: RELIGIOUS

MENORAH 51289W87-55
Editorial: Förenade Israelinsamlingen, Box 5053, 102 42 STOCKHOLM **Tel:** 8 667 67 70 **Fax:** 86637676
Email: redaktion@menorah-sweden.com **Web site:** http://www.menorah-sweden.com
Date Established: 1970; **Freq:** Quarterly; **Circ:** 18,000
Editor-in-Chief: Margarete Nudel; **Advertising Manager:** Leone Metzger; **Publisher:** Regina Rodau
Profile: Magazine containing articles about Israel, Jews living in Sweden and elsewhere, their traditions and way of life. Also covers politics, business, tourism, immigration, medical research, literature and local news.
Language(s): Swedish
Readership: Aimed at members of the Jewish community and people interested in the Jewish culture.
CONSUMER: RELIGIOUS

MENTORONLINE.SE 1844678W14A-331
Editorial: Box 601, 251 06 HELSINGBORG
Tel: 42 490 19 00
Email: peter.k@mentoronline.se **Web site:** http://www.mentoronline.se
Freq: Daily; **Cover Price:** Free; **Circ:** 5,016 Unique Users
Editor-in-Chief: Peter Krusell
Language(s): Swedish
BUSINESS: COMMERCE, INDUSTRY & MANAGEMENT

MERSMAK 51582W74C-105
Editorial: Budadress: Svetsarvägen 4B, 171 88 SOLNA **Tel:** 8 743 10 00
Email: pressmersmak@coop.se **Web site:** http://www.coop.se/mersmak
Freq: Monthly; **Circ:** 945,000
Editor: Ewa Lundström; **Publisher:** Ivar Fransson
Profile: Magazine for the Swedish Consumers' Association.
Language(s): Swedish
Readership: Read by members and the general public.
ADVERTISING RATES:
Full Page Colour .... SEK 139000
SCC .... SEK 1208.33
Copy instructions: *Copy Date:* 54 days prior to publication date
CONSUMER: WOMEN'S INTEREST CONSUMER MAGAZINES: Home & Family

MET-AVIISI-TIDSKR. FÖR TORNEDALEN/MALMFÄLTEN 51152W80-150
Editorial: Box 118, 980 63 KANGOS **Tel:** 978 304 50
Email: metaviisi@swipnet.se **Web site:** http://www.str-t.com
Date Established: 1983; **Freq:** Quarterly; **Circ:** 1,500
Publisher: Sven Kostenius
Profile: Publication of the National Federation of Swedes from Tornedalen and Malmfälten.
Language(s): Swedish
CONSUMER: RURAL & REGIONAL INTEREST

METRO GÖTEBORG 622986W67B-5250
Editorial: Drottninggatan 36, Box 11275, 404 26 GOTEBORG **Tel:** 31 743 81 00 **Fax:** 31 743 81 19
Email: redaktion.gbg@metro.se **Web site:** http://www.metro.se
Date Established: 1998
Cover Price: Free; **Circ:** 115,900
Language(s): Swedish
ADVERTISING RATES:
Full Page Colour .... SEK 90156
SCC .... SEK 306
REGIONAL DAILY & SUNDAY NEWSPAPERS: Regional Daily Newspapers

---

METRO SKÅNE 633918W67B-5275
Editorial: Bergsgatan 20, Box 125, 201 21 MALMO
Tel: 40 660 07 50 **Fax:** 40 660 07 59
Email: red.skane@metro.se **Web site:** http://www.metro.se
Date Established: 1999
Cover Price: Free; **Circ:** 121,100
Profile: Newspaper covering national and international news, events and features.
Language(s): Swedish
Readership: Read by people in Skåne.
ADVERTISING RATES:
Full Page Colour .... SEK 79434
SCC .... SEK 292.50
REGIONAL DAILY & SUNDAY NEWSPAPERS: Regional Daily Newspapers

---

METRO STOCKHOLM 622981W67B-5200
Editorial: Ringvägen 52, Box 45075, 104 30 STOCKHOLM **Tel:** 8 402 20 30 **Fax:** 8 24 98 37
Email: redaktionen@metro.se **Web site:** http://www.metro.se
Date Established: 1995
Cover Price: Free; **Circ:** 289,700
Publisher: Per Gunne
Language(s): Swedish
ADVERTISING RATES:
Full Page Colour .... SEK 193221
SCC .... SEK 711.50
REGIONAL DAILY & SUNDAY NEWSPAPERS: Regional Daily Newspapers

---

METRO.SE 1803968W65A-922
Editorial: Ringvägen 52, Box 45075, 104 30 STOCKHOM **Tel:** 8 402 20 30 **Fax:** 8 24 98 37
Email: webb@metro.se **Web site:** http://www.metro.se
Circ: 516,334 Unique Users
Publisher: Per Gunne
Language(s): Swedish
NATIONAL DAILY & SUNDAY NEWSPAPERS: National Daily Newspapers

---

MICROBIAL ECOLOGY IN HEALTH AND DISEASE 634640W56A-297
Editorial: Taylor & Francis AB, Box 3255, 103 65 STOCKHOLM **Tel:** 8 440 80 40 **Fax:** 8 440 80 50
Email: journals@se.tandf.no **Web site:** http://www.tandf.no
Freq: Quarterly; **Circ:** 600
Editor-in-Chief: Tore Midtvedt
Language(s): Swedish
BUSINESS: HEALTH & MEDICAL

MILJÖ & HÄLSA 50670W57-33
Editorial: c/o Cicci Wik, Lingonstigen 5, 667 31 FORSHAGA **Tel:** 54 87 07 54
Email: redaktion@ymh.se **Web site:** http://www.ymh.se
Freq: Monthly; **Circ:** 1,800
Editor-in-Chief: Cicci Wik; **Advertising Manager:** Petra Karlberg; **Publisher:** Jan-Eric Bäck
Profile: Publication about environment and health. Contains articles about environmental auditing and environmental impact assessment.
Language(s): Swedish
ADVERTISING RATES:
Full Page Colour .... SEK 10950
SCC .... SEK 91.25
BUSINESS: ENVIRONMENT & POLLUTION

MILJÖ & UTVECKLING 50671W57-35
Editorial: Box 104, 901 03 UMEÅ **Tel:** 90 70 09 00
Email: info@miljo-utveckling.com **Web site:** http://www.miljo-utveckling.com
Freq: 6 issues yearly; **Circ:** 16,000
Editor-in-Chief: Catrin Offerman; **Managing Director:** Anders Pauser; **Advertising Manager:** Antti Silventoinen
Profile: Magazine containing information, news and articles about research and development concerning environmental issues.
Language(s): Swedish
ADVERTISING RATES:
Full Page Colour .... SEK 15900
SCC .... SEK 132.5
BUSINESS: ENVIRONMENT & POLLUTION

MILJÖ & UTVECKLING; WEBB 1844966W57-119
Editorial: Box 104, 121 62 JOHANNESHOV
Tel: 8670 88 47 **Fax:** 9014 23 20
Email: info@miljo-utveckling.com **Web site:** http://www.miljo-utveckling.com
Freq: Daily; **Cover Price:** Free; **Circ:** 3,400 Unique Users
Editor-in-Chief: Catrin Offerman; **Managing Director:** Anders Pauser; **Advertising Manager:** Christian Sjöström
Language(s): Swedish
ADVERTISING RATES:
SCC .... SEK 26
BUSINESS: ENVIRONMENT & POLLUTION

MILJÖAKTUELLT 50672W57-38
Editorial: 106 78 STOCKHOLM **Tel:** 8 453 60 00
Email: miljoaktuellt@idg.se **Web site:** http://www.miljoaktuellt.se
Date Established: 1973; **Freq:** 6 issues yearly; **Circ:** 11,700
Editor-in-Chief: Mikael Salo; **Advertising Manager:** Isabelle Delorme
Profile: Magazine containing articles and information about the protection of the environment.
Language(s): Swedish
ADVERTISING RATES:
Full Page Colour .... SEK 38200
SCC .... SEK 318.33
BUSINESS: ENVIRONMENT & POLLUTION

MILJÖAKTUELLT; MILJOAKTUELLT.SE 1844811W81A-103
Editorial: 106 78 STOCKHOLM **Tel:** 8 453 60 00
Email: miljoaktuellt@idg.se **Web site:** http://www.miljoaktuellt.se
Freq: Daily; **Cover Price:** Free; **Circ:** 1,968 Unique Users
Language(s): Swedish
CONSUMER: ANIMALS & PETS: Animals & Pets Protection

MILJÖFORSKNING 50216W4E-29_50
Editorial: Box 1206, 111 82 STOCKHOLM
Tel: 8 775 40 11
Email: birgitta.bruselius@formas.se **Web site:** http://miljoforskning.formas.se
Date Established: 2001
Editor-in-Chief: Birgitta Bruzelius
Profile: Journal of the Swedish Council for Building Research.
Language(s): Swedish
BUSINESS: ARCHITECTURE & BUILDING: Building

MILJÖLEDAREN 1645382W57-113
Editorial: Box 5191, 200 75 MALMÖ **Tel:** 40 26 77 09
Email: presence@telia.com **Web site:** http://www.miljoledaren.com
Freq: Weekly; **Circ:** 5,000
Publisher: Ann Gustrin
Language(s): Swedish
ADVERTISING RATES:
Full Page Colour .... SEK 5000
SCC .... SEK 41.66
BUSINESS: ENVIRONMENT & POLLUTION

MILJÖMAGASINET 624402W74C-108
Editorial: Box 11203, 100 61 STOCKHOLM
Tel: 8 640 82 80
Web site: http://www.miljomagasinet.se
Date Established: 1981
Circ: 2,300
Publisher: Lars Kollberg
Profile: Newspaper providing consumer information about the protection of the environment.
Language(s): Swedish
Readership: Aimed at the general public with an interest in environmental issues.
ADVERTISING RATES:
Full Page Colour .... SEK 14000
SCC .... SEK 70
CONSUMER: WOMEN'S INTEREST CONSUMER MAGAZINES: Home & Family

MILJÖRAPPORTEN 50675W57-50
Editorial: Box 10177, 100 55 STOCKHOLM
Tel: 78 23 47 10
Email: redaktionen@miljorapporten.se **Web site:** http://www.miljorapporten.se
Date Established: 1989; **Freq:** Monthly; **Circ:** 2,000

Profile: Newsletter about business and the environment in Sweden and Scandinavia.
Language(s): Swedish
Readership: Read by environmental managers, auditors, consultants and other professionals in the field.
ADVERTISING RATES:
SCC .... SEK 170
BUSINESS: ENVIRONMENT & POLLUTION

MILJÖTIDNINGEN 50676W57-55
Editorial: Box 7048, 402 31 GOTEBORG
Tel: 31 12 18 08 **Fax:** 31 12 18 17
Email: info@mjv.se **Web site:** http://www.mjv.se
Freq: Quarterly; **Circ:** 3,000
Profile: Magazine providing international environmental news. Official publication of Friends of the Earth Sweden.
Language(s): Swedish
BUSINESS: ENVIRONMENT & POLLUTION

MINHEMBIO.SE 1844528W78R-282
Editorial: Prisjakt Sverige AB, Storgatan 51, 262 32 ÄNGELHOLM **Tel:** 431 65 00 01
Email: info@minhembio.com **Web site:** http://www.minhembio.com
Freq: Daily; **Cover Price:** Free; **Circ:** 41,234 Unique Users
Advertising Manager: Magnus Bengtsson
Language(s): Swedish
CONSUMER: CONSUMER ELECTRONICS: Consumer Electronics Related

MITSUBISHI MOTORS MAGAZINE 51130W77E-350
Editorial: Box 8144, 163 08 SPÅNGA
Tel: 8 474 54 00 **Fax:** 8 621 18 61
Email: magazine@mitsubishimotors.se **Web site:** http://www.mitsubishimotors.se
Date Established: 1989; **Freq:** Half-yearly; **Circ:** 90,000
Editor: Rigmor Rodebäck
Profile: Magazine covering information and articles about Mitsubishi cars and products.
Language(s): Swedish
CONSUMER: MOTORING & CYCLING: Club Cars

MITT I TRAFIKEN-EN KUNSKAPSTIDNING OM TRAFIKSÄKERHET 50413W31D-200
Editorial: Järvgatan 4, 261 44 LANDSKRONA
Tel: 418 40 10 00 **Fax:** 418 132 50
Email: gunlog.stjerna@str.se **Web site:** http://www.str.se
Freq: Quarterly; **Circ:** 2,000
Editor-in-Chief: Gunlög Stjerna; **Publisher:** Berit Johansson
Profile: Journal of the National Swedish Driving Schools Association.
Language(s): Swedish
BUSINESS: MOTOR TRADE: Driving Schools

MJÖLKSPEGELN 50370W21C-5
Editorial: Box 210, 101 24 STOCKHOLM
Tel: 8 790 58 44 **Fax:** 8 20 87 90
Email: mjolkspegeln@mjolkframjandet.se **Web site:** http://www.mjolkframjandet.se
Freq: Quarterly; **Circ:** 55,000
Editor-in-Chief: Kerstin Wikmar; **Publisher:** Kerstin Wikmar
Profile: Journal about the production of milk and other dairy products.
Language(s): Swedish
ADVERTISING RATES:
Full Page Colour .... SEK 50000
SCC .... SEK 416.66
BUSINESS: AGRICULTURE & FARMING: Dairy Farming

M-MAGASIN 1804032W74Q-160
Editorial: Budadress: Malmskillnadsgatan 39, Kungsgatan 34, 105 44 STOCKHOLM
Tel: 8 736 53 00 **Fax:** 8 24 02 13
Email: redaktion@m-magasin.se **Web site:** http://www.m-magasin.se
Freq: Monthly; **Circ:** 87,800
Editor-in-Chief: Catharina Enblad Nordlund; **Publisher:** Amelia Adamo
Language(s): Swedish
ADVERTISING RATES:
Full Page Colour .... SEK 52700
SCC .... SEK 439.16
CONSUMER: WOMEN'S INTEREST CONSUMER MAGAZINES: Lifestyle

MOBIL 50340W18B-4_5
Editorial: Mediaprovider, Box 1054, 101 39 STOCKHOLM **Tel:** 8 545 121 10
Email: redaktion@mobil.se **Web site:** http://www.mobil.se
Freq: Monthly; **Circ:** 26,000
Editor: Erik Mörner; **Editor-in-Chief:** Linus Brohult; **Advertising Manager:** Jonas Ekstrand; **Publisher:** Pontus Brohult
Profile: Magazine covering the telecommunications industry in general and mobile communications in particular.
Language(s): Swedish
ADVERTISING RATES:
Full Page Colour .... SEK 42900
SCC .... SEK 357.50
BUSINESS: ELECTRONICS: Telecommunications

MOBIL; MOBIL.SE 1846528W55-67
Editorial: Mediaprovider, Box 1054, 101 39 STOCKHOLM **Tel:** 8 545 121 10
Email: redaktion@mobil.se **Web site:** http://www.mobil.se
Freq: Daily; **Cover Price:** Free; **Circ:** 16,200 Unique Users
Editor-in-Chief: Linus Brohult; **Advertising Manager:** Johan van der Kwast
Language(s): Swedish
BUSINESS: APPLIED SCIENCE & LABORATORIES

MODERN INTERIÖR 751152W23A-40
Editorial: Conventus Media House, 104 46 STOCKHOLM **Tel:** 8 506 244 00 **Fax:** 8 506 244 99
Email: john.hardwick@conventusmedia.se **Web site:** http://www.branschnyheter.se
Freq: 6 issues yearly; **Circ:** 12,000
Editor-in-Chief: John Hardwick; **Publisher:** John Hardwick
Language(s): Swedish
ADVERTISING RATES:
Full Page Colour .... SEK 23700
SCC .... SEK 197.5
BUSINESS: FURNISHINGS & FURNITURE

MODERN PSYKOLOGI 2001277W55-85
Tel: 8 555 103 46
Email: info@modernpsykologi.se **Web site:** http://www.modernpsykologi.se
Freq: 6 issues yearly; **Circ:** 10,000
Editor: Jonas Mattsson; **Editor-in-Chief:** Patrik Hadenius
Language(s): Swedish
BUSINESS: APPLIED SCIENCE & LABORATORIES

MODERN TEKNIK 1804001W18A-52
Editorial: Box 216, 162 13 VÄLLINGBY
Tel: 705 90 09 02
Email: info@modernteknik.nu **Web site:** http://www.modernteknik.nu
Freq: 6 issues yearly; **Circ:** 31,400
Advertising Manager: Stefan Lehto; **Publisher:** Pentti Lehto
Language(s): Swedish
ADVERTISING RATES:
Full Page Colour .... SEK 20000
SCC .... SEK 166.67
BUSINESS: ELECTRONICS

MODERN TEKNIK; MODERNTEKNIK.NU 1846267W18A-58
Editorial: Box 216, 162 13 VÄLLINGBY
Tel: 705 90 09 02
Email: info@modernteknik.nu **Web site:** http://www.modernteknik.nu
Freq: Daily; **Cover Price:** Free; **Circ:** 6,280 Unique Users
Advertising Manager: Stefan Lehto; **Publisher:** Pentti Lehto
Language(s): Swedish
BUSINESS: ELECTRONICS

MODERNA LÄKARE 50598W56A-300
Editorial: Box 5610, 114 86 STOCKHOLM
Tel: 8 790 33 66 **Fax:** 8 21 18 68
Email: info@modernalakare.se **Web site:** http://www.modernalakare.se
Freq: Quarterly; **Circ:** 13,900
Editor: Martin Wohlin
Profile: Journal dealing with issues concerning wages and education for doctors. Also covers medical care in general.
Language(s): Swedish
Readership: Aimed at senior registrars, junior doctors and medical students.
ADVERTISING RATES:
Full Page Colour .... SEK 22100
SCC .... SEK 184.17
BUSINESS: HEALTH & MEDICAL

MODERNA SPRÅK 51263W84B-120
Editorial: VÄXJÖ UNIVERSITET, 351 95 VÄXJÖ
Tel: 470 70 82 69 **Fax:** 470 75 18 88
Email: emil.tyberg@vxu.se **Web site:** http://www.modernasprak.com
Freq: Half-yearly; **Circ:** 800
Editor: Emil Tyberg; **Advertising Manager:** Emil Tyberg
Profile: Journal covering the study of the French, German, English and Spanish languages and their literature.
Language(s): Swedish
CONSUMER: THE ARTS & LITERARY: Literary

MODETTE.SE 1809899W74A-170
Editorial: Box 20093, 114 35 STOCKHOLM
Tel: 8 678 77 00 **Fax:** 8 122 09 254
Email: ehsan.fadakar@modette.se **Web site:** http://www.modette.se
Freq: Daily; **Circ:** 6,990 Unique Users
Managing Director: Per Kjellander
Language(s): Swedish
CONSUMER: WOMEN'S INTEREST CONSUMER MAGAZINES: Women's Interest

MÖLNDALS-POSTEN; MOLNDALSPOSTEN.SE 1846283W65A-1066
Editorial: Box 153, 431 22 MÖLNDAL
Tel: 31 86 84 00 **Fax:** 31 86 84 01
Email: redaktion@molndalsposten.se **Web site:** http://www.molndalsposten.se
Freq: Daily; **Cover Price:** Free; **Circ:** 9,000 Unique Users
Editor-in-Chief: Kjellåke Dahlin; **Managing Director:** Roger Boström; **Publisher:** Roger Boström
Language(s): Swedish
ADVERTISING RATES:
SCC .... SEK 16.2
NATIONAL DAILY & SUNDAY NEWSPAPERS: National Daily Newspapers

MONITOR 50498W43B-50
Editorial: Prästgatan 2, 416 66 GOTEBORG
Tel: 31 775 65 50 **Fax:** 317756549
Email: per@hansenmedia.se **Web site:** http://www.tidningenmonitor.se
Freq: Monthly; **Circ:** 12,000
Editor-in-Chief: Per Lundblad; **Advertising Manager:** Camilla Hansen; **Publisher:** Björn Hansen
Profile: Magazine containing business news, interviews, equipment reviews, reports and articles about new products within the professional video, audio and lighting industry. Covers broadcasting and media technology.
Language(s): Swedish
Readership: Aimed at sound technicians, video operators and other professionals within the field.
ADVERTISING RATES:
Full Page Colour .... SEK 27700
SCC .... SEK 230.83
BUSINESS: ELECTRICAL RETAIL TRADE: Radio & Hi-Fi

MONTESSORITIDNINGEN 50724W62C-180
Editorial: c/o Box Information, Drottninggatan 31, 411 14 GOTEBORG **Tel:** 31 17 11 10 **Fax:** 317112144
Email: anders@boxinformation.com **Web site:** http://www.montessoriforbundet.se
Date Established: 1981; **Freq:** 6 issues yearly; **Circ:** 11,300
Editor-in-Chief: Anders Carlsson; **Advertising Manager:** Rosi Tholin; **Publisher:** Peter Jorméus
Profile: Magazine containing articles about the use of Montessori methods within child-care and education.
Language(s): Swedish
Readership: Read by members (parents, teachers, people with a general interest in Montessori) of the Swedish Montessori Association.
BUSINESS: CHURCH & SCHOOL EQUIPMENT & EDUCATION: Junior Education

MOORE MAGAZINE; MOORE.SE 1844672W18B-83
Editorial: Skeppargatan 55, 114 59 STOCKHOLM
Tel: 8 702 22 8
Email: redaktionen@moore.se **Web site:** http://www.moore.se
Freq: Daily; **Cover Price:** Free; **Circ:** 7,264 Unique Users
Editor: Lena Furberg; **Editor-in-Chief:** Petter Axell; **Publisher:** Bingo Rimér
Language(s): Swedish
BUSINESS: ELECTRONICS: Telecommunications

MORA TIDNING 50814W67B-5300
Editorial: Strandgatan 28, 792 30 MORA
Tel: 250 59 24 20 **Fax:** 250 59 24 45
Email: mt.red@dt.se **Web site:** http://www.dt.se
Date Established: 1893
Circ: 11,100
Publisher: Pär Fagerström
Language(s): Swedish
ADVERTISING RATES:
Full Page Colour .... SEK 36288
SCC .... SEK 181.44
Copy instructions: *Copy Date:* 14 days prior to publication date
REGIONAL DAILY & SUNDAY NEWSPAPERS: Regional Daily Newspapers

MORGONBRIS, S-KVINNORS TIDNING 50947W74A-60
Editorial: Box 70458, 107 26 STOCKHOLM
Tel: 8 700 26 00 **Fax:** 8 411 65 42
Web site: http://www.s-kvinnor.se
Circ: 10,600
Editor-in-Chief: Lena Näslund; **Advertising Manager:** Marja Koivisto
Profile: Cultural and political magazine for women.
Language(s): Swedish
ADVERTISING RATES:
Full Page Colour .... SEK 9200
SCC .... SEK 76.66
CONSUMER: WOMEN'S INTEREST CONSUMER MAGAZINES: Women's Interest

MORNINGSTAR 1847298W1A-222
Editorial: Birger Jarlsgatan 25, 111 45 STOCKHOLM
Tel: 8 562 72 950
Email: jonas.lindmark@morningstar.se **Web site:** http://www.morningstar.se
Freq: Daily; **Cover Price:** Free; **Circ:** 5,000 Unique Users
Managing Director: George Sallfeldt; **Publisher:** Jonas Lindmark
Language(s): Swedish
BUSINESS: FINANCE & ECONOMICS

MOTALA & VADSTENA TIDNING 50815W67B-5350
Editorial: Industrigatan 9, 591 35 MOTALA
Tel: 141 22 36 00 **Fax:** 141 588 68
Email: redaktion@mvt.se **Web site:** http://mvt.se
Date Established: 1868
Circ: 7,400
Editor: Ylva Nydahl; **Advertising Manager:** P O Nordin; **Publisher:** Stefan Pettersson
Language(s): Swedish
ADVERTISING RATES:
Full Page Colour .... SEK 16700
SCC .... SEK 83.50
REGIONAL DAILY & SUNDAY NEWSPAPERS: Regional Daily Newspapers

MOTALA & VADSTENA TIDNING; MOTALATIDNING.SE 1843548W65A-997
Editorial: Industrigatan 9, 591 35 MOTALA
Tel: 141 22 36 00 **Fax:** 141 588 68
Email: redaktion@mvt.se **Web site:** http://mvt.se
Freq: Daily; **Cover Price:** Free; **Circ:** 5,017 Unique Users
Editor-in-Chief: Stefan Pettersson; **Publisher:** Göran Karlsson
Language(s): Swedish
ADVERTISING RATES:
SCC .... SEK 17
NATIONAL DAILY & SUNDAY NEWSPAPERS: National Daily Newspapers

MOTDRAG 51345W91D-85
Editorial: Box 128 25, 112 97 STOCKHOLM
Tel: 8 672 60 60 **Fax:** 86726001
Email: motdrag@unf.se **Web site:** http://www.unf.se
Freq: 6 issues yearly; **Circ:** 8,900
Publisher: Felicia Hedström
Profile: Magazine about youth culture and topics concerning alcohol and drugs.
Language(s): Swedish
ADVERTISING RATES:
Full Page Colour .... SEK 7500
SCC .... SEK 62.50
CONSUMER: RECREATION & LEISURE: Children & Youth

MOTOR 51105W77A-150
Editorial: Box 3265, Kungsgatan 48, 103 65 STOCKHOLM **Tel:** 8 50 55 62 21
Email: motor@otw.se **Web site:** http://www.motormannen.se
Date Established: 1943; **Freq:** Monthly -, 10 nr per år; **Circ:** 117,300
Editor-in-Chief: Michael Jonsson
Profile: Magazine providing information about new and old cars. Contains road- and crash test results, articles about new technology, maintenance and market research.
Language(s): Swedish
ADVERTISING RATES:
Full Page Colour .... SEK 34900
SCC .... SEK 271.66
Copy instructions: *Copy Date:* 31 days prior to publication date
CONSUMER: MOTORING & CYCLING: Motoring

MOTORBRANSCHEN 50411W31A-30
Editorial: Box 5611, 114 86 STOCKHOLM
Tel: 8 701 63 19 **Fax:** 8 20 67 47
Email: hans.bister@mrf.se **Web site:** http://www.mrf.se
Freq: 6 issues yearly; **Circ:** 5,200
Editor-in-Chief: Hans Bister; **Advertising Manager:** Inger Zetterwall; **Publisher:** Hans Bister
Profile: Magazine containing technical, financial and general news for the Swedish motor trade.
Language(s): Swedish
ADVERTISING RATES:
Full Page Colour .... SEK 20700
SCC .... SEK 172.5
BUSINESS: MOTOR TRADE: Motor Trade Accessories

MOTORFÖRAREN 51106W77A-170
Editorial: Heliosgatan 11, 120 30 STOCKHOLM
Tel: 8 555 765 55

Email: motorforaren@mhf.se **Web site:** http://www.mhf.se/motorforaren
Freq: 6 issues yearly; **Circ:** 39,400
Advertising Manager: B-G Werner; **Publisher:** Tom Bjerver
Profile: Motoring magazine.
Language(s): Swedish
ADVERTISING RATES:
Full Page Colour .... SEK 19000
SCC .... SEK 158.33
Copy instructions: *Copy Date:* 25 days prior to publication date
CONSUMER: MOTORING & CYCLING: Motoring

MOTORFÖRAREN; WEBB
1846462W56R-109
Editorial: Heliosgatan 11, 120 30 STOCKHOLM
Tel: 8 555 765 55
Email: motorforaren@mhf.se **Web site:** http://www.mhf.se/motorforaren
Freq: Daily; **Cover Price:** Free; **Circ:** 15,760 Unique Users
Publisher: Tom Bjerver
Language(s): Swedish
BUSINESS: HEALTH & MEDICAL: Health Medical Related

MOTOR-MAGASINET
50410W31A-25
Editorial: Box 72001, 181 72 LIDINGÖ
Tel: 8 564 886 40 **Fax:** 8 661 64 55
Email: olle.holm@mentoronline.se **Web site:** http://www.motormagasinet.se
Freq: Weekly; **Circ:** 15,600
Editor: Staffan Johnsson; **Editor-in-Chief:** Olle Holm; **Advertising Manager:** Camilla Stridh; **Publisher:** Olle Holm
Profile: Independent journal containing information for the motor trade.
Language(s): Swedish
Readership: Distributed free to all motor repair shops, car dealers, vulcanizers, petrol stations, body shops, motor-breakers, manufacturers, wholesalers and importers, technical schools and associated authorities and organisations.
ADVERTISING RATES:
Full Page Colour .... SEK 38700
SCC .... SEK 193.5
BUSINESS: MOTOR TRADE: Motor Trade Accessories

MOTOR-MAGASINET; MOTORMAGASINET.NET
1846289W77D-104
Editorial: Box 72001, 181 72 LIDINGÖ
Tel: 8564 886 40 **Fax:** 8 661 64 55
Email: olle.holm@mentoronline.se **Web site:** http://www.motormagasinet.se
Freq: Daily; **Cover Price:** Free; **Circ:** 6,240 Unique Users
Editor-in-Chief: Olle Holm; **Advertising Manager:** Peter Söderquist; **Publisher:** Olle Holm
Language(s): Swedish
ADVERTISING RATES:
SCC .... SEK 39
CONSUMER: MOTORING & CYCLING: Motor Sports

M-PLUS
1837003W81A-102
Editorial: Karlbergsvägen 77, 106 78 STOCKHOLM
Tel: 8 453 61 00
Email: miljoaktuellt@idg.se **Web site:** http://miljoaktuellt.idg.se
Freq: Monthly - (16 nr/år); **Circ:** 7,000
Publisher: Mikael Salo
Language(s): Swedish
ADVERTISING RATES:
Full Page Colour .... SEK 5800
CONSUMER: ANIMALS & PETS: Animals & Pets Protection

MUNSKÄNKEN MED VINJOURNALEN
50262W9A-20
Editorial: Box 92184, 120 09 STOCKHOLM
Tel: 8 30 10 43 **Fax:** 8301152
Email: kansli@munskankarna.se **Web site:** http://www.munskankarna.se
Date Established: 1958; **Freq:** 6 issues yearly; **Circ:** 14,500
Advertising Manager: Karolina Ekholm; **Publisher:** Lennart Rammer
Profile: Magazine covering all aspects of the licensed trade. Contains articles and information about new wines, shopping advice and related topics such as gastronomy.
Language(s): Swedish
ADVERTISING RATES:
Full Page Colour .... SEK 24940
SCC .... SEK 207.83
BUSINESS: DRINKS & LICENSED TRADE: Drinks, Licensed Trade, Wines & Spirits

MUSIKANT
751146W76D-235
Editorial: Sveriges Orkesterförbund, Box 163 44, 103 26 STOCKHOLM **Tel:** 8 470 24 42 **Fax:** 8 470 24 24
Email: info@orkester.nu **Web site:** http://www.orkester.nu
Date Established: 1965; **Freq:** Quarterly; **Circ:** 12,000
Advertising Manager: Marie Olausson; **Publisher:** Magnus Eriksson
Language(s): Swedish
CONSUMER: MUSIC & PERFORMING ARTS: Music

MUSIKERMAGASINET - MM
50701W61-45
Editorial: Prästgatan 2, 416 66 GÖTEBORG
Tel: 31 775 65 50 **Fax:** 31 775 65 49
Email: bjorn@hansenmedia.se **Web site:** http://www.musikermagasinet.com
Freq: Monthly; **Circ:** 16,000
Editor: Mats Grundberg; **Editor-in-Chief:** Henrik Vogel; **Advertising Manager:** Peter Marchione; **Publisher:** Björn Hansen
Profile: Publication covering all aspects of the music trade.
Language(s): Swedish
BUSINESS: MUSIC TRADE

MUSIKERN
50702W61-50
Editorial: Box 49144, 100 29 STOCKHOLM
Tel: 8 587 060 00 **Fax:** 8 16 80 20
Email: redaktionen@musikerforbundet.se **Web site:** http://www.musikerforbundet.se
Date Established: 1907; **Freq:** 6 issues yearly; **Circ:** 5,500
Editor: Benny Söderberg; **Advertising Manager:** Rune Liedström; **Publisher:** Jan Granvik
Profile: Magazine containing articles, interviews, reviews, information and news from the music trade.
Language(s): Swedish
Readership: Read by professional singers and musicians.
ADVERTISING RATES:
Full Page Colour .... SEK 11000
SCC .... SEK 91.66
BUSINESS: MUSIC TRADE

MUSIKINDUSTRIN, MI
751057W76D-240
Editorial: Box 34 245, 100 26 STOCKHOLM
Email: info@musikindustrin.se **Web site:** http://www.musikindustrin.se
Freq: Daily; **Cover Price:** Paid; **Circ:** 4,100 Unique Users
Editor: Claes Olson; **Editor-in-Chief:** Lars Nylin; **Advertising Manager:** Stefan Aronsson; **Publisher:** Lars Nylin
Language(s): Swedish
CONSUMER: MUSIC & PERFORMING ARTS: Music

MUSIKTIDNINGEN MUSIKOMANEN
751147W76D-245
Editorial: Box 6903, 102 39 STOCKHOLM
Tel: 8 31 00 07
Email: alexander.scarlat@comhem.se
Date Established: 1984; **Freq:** Half-yearly; **Circ:** 2,000
Editor-in-Chief: Alexander Scarlat; **Advertising Manager:** Alexander Scarlat; **Publisher:** Alexander Scarlat
Language(s): Swedish
CONSUMER: MUSIC & PERFORMING ARTS: Music

MY TELLUS.POCKET
634462W89A-60
Editorial: CIU, Ludvigsbergsgatan 22, 118 23 STOCKHOLM **Tel:** 8 440 87 80 **Fax:** 8 20 35 30
Email: info@ciu.org **Web site:** http://www.mytellus.com
Freq: Annual; **Circ:** 30,000
Editor: Cecilia Boija
Profile: Magazine featuring articles and news on young people interested in travel.
Language(s): Swedish
Readership: Aimed at young people aged between 12 to 18 years.
CONSUMER: HOLIDAYS & TRAVEL: Travel

NA BERGSLAGSPOSTEN
50802W67B-3400
Editorial: 711 81 LINDESBERG **Tel:** 581 844 00
Fax: 581 844 41
Email: nyhet@na.se **Web site:** http://na.se
Date Established: 1892
Circ: 9,900
Language(s): Swedish
REGIONAL DAILY & SUNDAY NEWSPAPERS: Regional Daily Newspapers

NACKA VÄRMDÖ POSTEN
634240W72-210
Editorial: Box 735, 131 24 NACKA **Tel:** 8 555 266 20
Fax: 8 555 266 41
Email: red@nvp.se **Web site:** http://www.nvp.se
Date Established: 1989; **Freq:** Weekly; **Circ:** 72,300
Managing Director: Patrik Staflin; **Advertising Manager:** Åsa Brandt; **Publisher:** Evelina Stucki
Profile: Newspaper featuring local news for Nacka and Värmdö.
Language(s): Swedish
ADVERTISING RATES:
Full Page Colour .... SEK 29235
SCC .... SEK 137.75
LOCAL NEWSPAPERS

NACKA VÄRMDÖ POSTEN; NVP.SE
1844805W65A-1036
Editorial: Box 735, 131 24 NACKA **Tel:** 8 555 266 20
Fax: 8 555 266 41
Email: red@nvp.se **Web site:** http://www.nvp.se
Freq: Daily; **Cover Price:** Free; **Circ:** 1,314 Unique Users
Editor-in-Chief: Evelina Stucki; **Managing Director:** Patrik Staflin; **Publisher:** Evelina Stucki
Language(s): Swedish
ADVERTISING RATES:
SCC .... SEK 27
NATIONAL DAILY & SUNDAY NEWSPAPERS: National Daily Newspapers

NÄMNDEMANNEN
50507W44-30
Editorial: Helsingborgsvägen 44, 262 72 ÄNGELHOLM **Tel:** 431 168 00 **Fax:** 431162 32
Email: mb@bureko.se **Web site:** http://www.nrf.cc
Freq: Quarterly; **Circ:** 9,000
Editor: Staffan Ringskog; **Advertising Manager:** Staffan Ringskog
Profile: Official journal of the Swedish Association of Lay Assessors. Contains articles and information about the Swedish judicial system.
Language(s): Swedish
BUSINESS: LEGAL

NÄRINGSLIV AFFÄRSTIDNINGEN I DITT LÄN
749967W14A-225
Editorial: Sjögatan 23, 852 34 SUNDSVALL
Tel: 60 16 21 45 **Fax:** 60 17 54 36
Email: redaktion@naringsliv.to **Web site:** http://www.naringsliv.to
Freq: Monthly; **Circ:** 11,800
Publisher: Olof Axelsson
Language(s): Swedish
ADVERTISING RATES:
Full Page Colour .... SEK 28700
SCC .... SEK 395.83
BUSINESS: COMMERCE, INDUSTRY & MANAGEMENT

NÄRINGSLIV I NORR
1804020W14A-307
Editorial: Nystades Företagscentrum, Idrottsvägen 5, 952 61 KALIX **Tel:** 923 789 40 **Fax:** 92310018
Web site: http://www.naringslivinorr.se
Freq: 6 issues yearly; **Circ:** 18,000
Editor-in-Chief: Reinhold Andefors; **Publisher:** Magnus Sjöberg
Language(s): Swedish
Copy instructions: *Copy Date:* 30 days prior to publication date
BUSINESS: COMMERCE, INDUSTRY & MANAGEMENT

NÄRINGSMEDICINSK TIDSKRIFT
1661722W56R-106
Editorial: Andra Långgatan 53, 413 27 GÖTEBORG
Tel: 31 42 12 46
Email: info@naringsmedicinsktidskrift.se **Web site:** http://www.naringsmedicinsktidskrift.se
Freq: 6 issues yearly; **Circ:** 2,700
Editor: Helene Sandström; **Editor-in-Chief:** Ulla Robertsson
Language(s): Swedish
BUSINESS: HEALTH & MEDICAL: Health Medical Related

NÄRINGSVÄRT - OM KOST OCH NÄRING
50590W56A-25
Editorial: Kost och Näring, c/o Ledarna, Box 12069, 102 22 STOCKHOLM **Tel:** 8 598 990 00
Email: info@kostochnaring.se **Web site:** http://www.kostochnaring.se/tidningen
Date Established: 1959; **Freq:** 6 issues yearly; **Circ:** 1,500
Editor: Monica Lindman; **Publisher:** Karin Lidén
Profile: Magazine of the Swedish Association of Dieticians. Contains articles on food therapy, dietetics, food service management and research and development within the food industry.
Language(s): Swedish
ADVERTISING RATES:
Full Page Colour .... SEK 18000
SCC .... SEK 150
BUSINESS: HEALTH & MEDICAL

NARKOTIKAFRÅGAN
51472W56L-50
Editorial: Ragvaldsgatan 14, 118 46 STOCKHOLM
Tel: 8 643 04 67 **Fax:** 8 643 04 98
Email: nf@rns.se **Web site:** http://www.rns.se
Freq: 6 issues yearly; **Circ:** 10,000
Editor: Pernilla Rönnlid; **Editor-in-Chief:** Gazal Amini; **Advertising Manager:** Ulla Söderberg
Language(s): Swedish
BUSINESS: HEALTH & MEDICAL: Disability & Rehabilitation

NATIONAL GEOGRAPHIC
1667718W94J-27
Editorial: Kundtjänst, 205 50 MALMÖ
Tel: 8 555 454 53 **Fax:** 8 555 454 50
Email: natgeo@mailbox.pp.se **Web site:** http://www.nationalgeographic.se
Freq: Monthly; **Circ:** 37,200
Publisher: Anna Rading Ploman
Language(s): Swedish
ADVERTISING RATES:
Full Page Colour .... SEK 43000
SCC .... SEK 358.33
CONSUMER: OTHER CLASSIFICATIONS: Popular Science

NATIONELLT PISTOLSKYTTE
751149W75F-210
Editorial: Box 5435, 114 84 STOCKHOLM
Tel: 8 553 401 60 **Fax:** 8 553 401 69
Email: kansli@pistolskytteforbundet.se **Web site:** http://www.pistolskytteforbundet.se
Freq: Quarterly; **Circ:** 16,000
Editor-in-Chief: Ulf Hansson; **Advertising Manager:** Ulf Hansson; **Publisher:** Mats Stoltz
Language(s): Swedish
CONSUMER: SPORT: Shooting

NÄTSMART
1986060W14A-368
Editorial: Erstagatan 26, 116 36 STOCKHOLM
Tel: 8 410 097 50 **Fax:** 86475174
Email: redaktion@natsmart.se **Web site:** http://www.natsmart.se
Freq: Quarterly; **Cover Price:** Free; **Circ:** 11,000
Editor: Erika Stenlund; **Publisher:** Tim Svensson
Language(s): Swedish
BUSINESS: COMMERCE, INDUSTRY & MANAGEMENT

NATURLIGT OM HÄLSA
751050W74G-175
Editorial: c/o Scantype Förlag & Media AB, 114 75 STOCKHOLM **Tel:** 8 663 55 30 **Fax:** 8 663 55 32
Email: lena.elisabet@scantype.se **Web site:** http://www.naturligtomhalsa.se
Date Established: 1999; **Freq:** Quarterly; **Circ:** 10,000
Advertising Manager: Malou Thorell; **Publisher:** Lena Götrich
Language(s): Swedish
ADVERTISING RATES:
Full Page Colour .... SEK 27500
SCC .... SEK 229.16
CONSUMER: WOMEN'S INTEREST CONSUMER MAGAZINES: Slimming & Health

NATURVETARE
50362W21A-10
Editorial: Box 2062, 131 24 NACKA
Tel: 8 562 920 00 **Fax:** 8 20 20 81
Email: redaktion@naturvetarna.se **Web site:** http://www.naturvetarna.se
Freq: Monthly; **Circ:** 8,300
Editor: Ulf Bergius; **Editor-in-Chief:** Lars-Erik Liljebäck; **Advertising Manager:** Lars-Erik Liljebäck; **Publisher:** Lars-Erik Liljebäck
Profile: Journal covering agriculture, horticulture, forestry, food and nutrition.
Language(s): Swedish
BUSINESS: AGRICULTURE & FARMING

NAUTISK TIDSKRIFT
749831W45A-90
Editorial: Gamla Brogatan 19, 111 20 STOCKHOLM
Tel: 8 10 60 15 **Fax:** 8 10 67 72
Email: info@sfbf.se **Web site:** http://www.sfbf.se
Freq: 6 issues yearly; **Circ:** 5,500
Editor: Marie Halvdanson; **Editor-in-Chief:** Marie Halvdanson; **Advertising Manager:** Ankie Nilsson; **Publisher:** Marie Halvdanson
Language(s): Swedish
BUSINESS: MARINE & SHIPPING

NEO
1741154W74Q-157
Editorial: Box 13028, 103 01 STOCKHOLM
Tel: 8 587 898 60
Web site: http://www.magasinetneo.se
Freq: 6 issues yearly; **Circ:** 7,000
Editor: Mattias Svensson; **Editor-in-Chief:** Paulina Neuding
Language(s): Swedish
ADVERTISING RATES:
Full Page Colour .... SEK 27000
SCC .... SEK 225
CONSUMER: WOMEN'S INTEREST CONSUMER MAGAZINES: Lifestyle

NERIKES ALLEHANDA
50821W67B-5400
Editorial: 701 92 OREBRO **Tel:** 19 15 50 00
Fax: 19 10 52 90
Email: nyhet@na.se **Web site:** http://www.na.se
Date Established: 1843
Circ: 60,700
Editor: Christina Eriksson; **Publisher:** Ulf Johansson
Language(s): Swedish
ADVERTISING RATES:
Full Page Colour .... SEK 64560

SCC .... SEK 322.80
REGIONAL DAILY & SUNDAY NEWSPAPERS: Regional Daily Newspapers

NERIKES ALLEHANDA; NA.SE
1625629W67E-5074
Editorial: N Strandgatan 5, 701 92 OREBRO **Tel:** 19 15 51 68 **Fax:** 19105290
Email: webb@na.se **Web site:** http://www.na.se
Freq: Daily; **Circ:** 61,300 Unique Users
Language(s): Swedish
REGIONAL DAILY & SUNDAY NEWSPAPERS: Regional Offices

NERVEN
749821W56B-125
Editorial: Box 601, 391 26 KALMAR **Tel:** 480 841 77
Email: nerven@ltkalmar.se **Web site:** http://www.ltkalmar.se
Freq: 6 issues yearly; **Circ:** 11,000
Publisher: Cecilia Kilander
Language(s): Swedish
BUSINESS: HEALTH & MEDICAL: Nursing

NEW ROUTES
51194W82-185
Editorial: Sysslomansgatan 7, 753 11 UPPSALA
Tel: 18 16 95 00 **Fax:** 18 69 30 59
Email: info@life-peace.org **Web site:** http://www.life-peace.org
Date Established: 1996; **Freq:** Quarterly; **Circ:** 1,200
Editor: Kristin Lundqvist
Profile: International journal offering analysis and commentary on issues of peace, justice and development.
Language(s): Swedish
CONSUMER: CURRENT AFFAIRS & POLITICS

NEWZ
1664273W89C-252
Editorial: Tingvallagatan 5A, 652 24 KARLSTAD
Tel: 704304836
Email: red@newzpaper.se **Web site:** http://www.newzpaper.se
Freq: Monthly; **Circ:** 15,000
Advertising Manager: Pauline Eriksson; **Publisher:** Staffan Johansson
Language(s): Swedish
CONSUMER: HOLIDAYS & TRAVEL: Entertainment Guides

NJURFUNK
1803880W56A-348
Editorial: Njurförbundet, Box 1386, 172 27 SUNDBYBERG **Tel:** 8 546 405 00 **Fax:** 8 546 405 04
Email: anna-lisa.lampinen@njurforbundet.se **Web site:** http://www.njurforbundet.se
Freq: Quarterly; **Circ:** 5,300
Editor: Anna-Lisa Lampinen; **Publisher:** Lars Nordstedt
Language(s): Swedish
BUSINESS: HEALTH & MEDICAL

NK STIL
1804067W74Q-164
Editorial: NK 100, 111 77 STOCKHOLM
Tel: 8 762 90 00 **Fax:** 8 792 90 89
Email: redaktion@nk-stil.se **Web site:** http://www.nk.se
Freq: Half-yearly; **Circ:** 80,000
Language(s): Swedish
CONSUMER: WOMEN'S INTEREST CONSUMER MAGAZINES: Lifestyle

NÖJESGUIDEN; GÖTEBORG
1873033W76B-116
Editorial: Viktoriagatan 3, 411 25 GOTEBORG
Tel: 31 20 36 66
Email: red@nojesguiden.se **Web site:** http://www.nojesguiden.se
Freq: Monthly; **Cover Price:** Free; **Circ:** 22,800
Editor: Carl Reinholdtzon Belfrage
Language(s): Swedish
ADVERTISING RATES:
Full Page Colour .... SEK 70965
SCC .... SEK 591.37
CONSUMER: MUSIC & PERFORMING ARTS: Theatre

NÖJESGUIDEN; MALMÖ/LUND
1873032W76B-115
Editorial: Baltzarsgatan 2, 211 36 MALMO
Tel: 736 43 88 60
Email: red@nojesguiden.se **Web site:** http://www.nojesguiden.se/malmo
Circ: 22,700
Language(s): Swedish
ADVERTISING RATES:
Full Page Colour .... SEK 70965
SCC .... SEK 591.38
CONSUMER: MUSIC & PERFORMING ARTS: Theatre

NÖJESGUIDEN; NOJESGUIDEN.SE
1847406W76B-112
Editorial: Östermalmsgatan 87d, 114 59 STOCKHOLM **Tel:** 8 456 45 00 **Fax:** 8 456 45 99
Email: red@nojesguiden.se **Web site:** http://www.nojesguiden.se
Freq: Daily; **Cover Price:** Free; **Circ:** 12,440 Unique Users
Editor: Carl Reinholdtzon Belfrage; **Editor-in-Chief:** Margret Atladottir
Language(s): Swedish
ADVERTISING RATES:
SCC .... SEK 83
CONSUMER: MUSIC & PERFORMING ARTS: Theatre

NÖJESGUIDEN; STOCKHOLM
51306W89C-100
Editorial: Östermalmsgatan 87 D, 114 59 STOCKHOLM **Tel:** 8 456 45 00 **Fax:** 8 456 45 99
Email: red@nojesguiden.se **Web site:** http://www.nojesguiden.se
Date Established: 1982; **Freq:** Monthly; **Cover Price:** Free; **Circ:** 59,400
Editor: Niklas Eriksson; **Editor-in-Chief:** Margret Atladottir
Profile: Entertainment guide to Stockholm, Malmö and Gothenburg.
Language(s): Swedish
ADVERTISING RATES:
Full Page Colour .... SEK 49900
SCC .... SEK 415.83
Copy instructions: *Copy Date:* 11 days prior to publication date
CONSUMER: HOLIDAYS & TRAVEL: Entertainment Guides

NÖJESMAGASINET CITY; UMEÅ
1693449W74A-156
Editorial: Nöjesmagasinet City c/o VK, 901 10 UMEÅ
Tel: 90 15 10 30 **Fax:** 90 10 05 15
Email: info@nojesmagasinet.se **Web site:** http://www.nojesmagasinet.se
Freq: Monthly; **Cover Price:** Free; **Circ:** 15,000
Editor-in-Chief: Mikael Sundberg; **Advertising Manager:** Dan Wiklander; **Publisher:** Mikael Sundberg
Language(s): Swedish
CONSUMER: WOMEN'S INTEREST CONSUMER MAGAZINES: Women's Interest

NÖJESMIX
1803896W73-140
Editorial: Box 367, 801 05 GÄVLE **Tel:** 26 15 96 78
Fax: 26661443
Email: red@nojesmix.com **Web site:** http://www.nojesmix.com
Freq: Monthly; **Cover Price:** Free; **Circ:** 15,000
Editor: Anna Utterberg; **Advertising Manager:** Henrik Nilsson; **Publisher:** Lasse Flach
Language(s): Swedish
ADVERTISING RATES:
Full Page Colour .... SEK 16700
SCC .... SEK 104.38
CONSUMER: NATIONAL & INTERNATIONAL PERIODICALS

NÖJESNYTT; HELSINGBORG
634257W89C-103
Editorial: Prästgatan 12, 252 24 HELSINGBORG
Tel: 42 21 20 80 **Fax:** 42 21 51 54
Email: info@nojesnytt.se **Web site:** http://www.nojesnytt.se
Date Established: 1996; **Freq:** 6 issues yearly; **Cover Price:** Free; **Circ:** 25,000
Editor-in-Chief: Mats Danielsson; **Managing Director:** Mats Danielsson; **Publisher:** Martina Edenfalk
Profile: Newspaper providing local news and information on entertainment, restaurants and events in Helsingborg.
Language(s): Swedish
Readership: Read by local residents and tourists.
CONSUMER: HOLIDAYS & TRAVEL: Entertainment Guides

NÖJESNYTT; JÖNKÖPING
1803879W89C-254
Editorial: Kompanigatan 1-2, 553 05 JÖNKÖPING
Tel: 36 71 00 12 **Fax:** 36 35 44 34
Email: sture@nojesnytt.se **Web site:** http://www.nojesnytt.se
Freq: 6 issues yearly; **Cover Price:** Free; **Circ:** 20,000
Editor-in-Chief: Mats Danielsson; **Managing Director:** Mats Danielsson; **Publisher:** Martina Edenfalk
Language(s): Swedish
CONSUMER: HOLIDAYS & TRAVEL: Entertainment Guides

NÖJESNYTT; KALMAR
1803860W89C-253
Editorial: Fiskaregatan 12, 392 32 KALMAR
Email: info@nojesnytt.se **Web site:** http://www.nojesnytt.se
Freq: 6 issues yearly; **Cover Price:** Free; **Circ:** 15,000
Editor-in-Chief: Mats Danielsson; **Advertising Manager:** Helen Berglund
Language(s): Swedish
CONSUMER: HOLIDAYS & TRAVEL: Entertainment Guides

NÖJESNYTT; VÄXJÖ
634259W89C-108
Editorial: Box 77, 351 03 VÄXJÖ **Tel:** 470 395 15
Fax: 47016420
Email: info@nojesnytt.se **Web site:** http://www.nojesnytt.se
Date Established: 1990; **Freq:** 6 issues yearly; **Cover Price:** Free; **Circ:** 20,000
Advertising Manager: Martina Edenfalk
Profile: Newspaper covering local events and entertainment in Växjö.
Language(s): Swedish
Readership: Read by local residents and tourists.
CONSUMER: HOLIDAYS & TRAVEL: Entertainment Guides

NOLLELVA
634245W89C-110
Editorial: Drottninggatan 55, 602 32 NORRKÖPING
Tel: 11 10 21 01
Email: redaktionen@nollelva.nu **Web site:** http://www.nollelva.nu
Date Established: 1996; **Freq:** 6 issues yearly; **Cover Price:** Free; **Circ:** 20,000
Advertising Manager: Karolina Norrbom Ericson; **Publisher:** Benny Nilsson
Profile: Newspaper featuring local entertainment for Norrköping. Includes personal profiles, theatre, restaurants, sports and book reviews.
Language(s): Swedish
Readership: Aimed at active people aged between 20 and 40 years.
CONSUMER: HOLIDAYS & TRAVEL: Entertainment Guides

NOLLNITTON
634246W89C-115
Editorial: Box 395, 701 47 OREBRO **Tel:** 19 10 84 90
Fax: 19108430
Email: peter.steen@hkm.se **Web site:** http://www.hkm.se
Date Established: 1995; **Freq:** 6 issues yearly; **Cover Price:** Free; **Circ:** 16,000
Advertising Manager: Dennis Karlsson; **Publisher:** Stefan Hallenius
Profile: Magazine focusing on local entertainment for Örebro. Includes personal profiles, food, books, cinema, sports etc.
Language(s): Swedish
Readership: Aimed at men and women aged between 18 and 40 years.
CONSUMER: HOLIDAYS & TRAVEL: Entertainment Guides

NOLLTRETTON
1626263W74B-67
Editorial: Box 320, 581 02 LINKÖPING
Tel: 13 12 26 16 **Fax:** 13239251
Email: redaktionen@nolltretton.se **Web site:** http://www.nolltretton.nu
Freq: Monthly; **Cover Price:** Free; **Circ:** 20,000
Editor: Tobias Pettersson; **Publisher:** Benny Nilsson
Language(s): Swedish
Copy instructions: *Copy Date:* 30 days prior to publication date
CONSUMER: WOMEN'S INTEREST CONSUMER MAGAZINES: Women's Interest - Fashion

NOLLTVÅ
1813995W89C-256
Editorial: Kupolen 112, 781 70 BORLÄNGE
Tel: 243 160 80 **Fax:** 24316039
Email: redaktionen@nolltva.se **Web site:** http://www.nolltva.se
Freq: Monthly; **Cover Price:** Free; **Circ:** 20,000
Publisher: Peter Thelin
Language(s): Swedish
CONSUMER: HOLIDAYS & TRAVEL: Entertainment Guides

NORD-EMBALLAGE
749779W41A-90
Editorial: Box 944, 251 09 HELSINGBORG
Tel: 42 20 71 66 **Fax:** 42 20 71 96
Email: bo.wallteg@n-e.nu **Web site:** http://www.n-e.nu
Freq: 6 issues yearly; **Circ:** 3,300
Editor: Jerry Pettersson; **Editor-in-Chief:** Bo Wallteg; **Advertising Manager:** Pia Andersson; **Publisher:** Bo Wallteg
Language(s): Swedish
ADVERTISING RATES:
Full Page Colour .... SEK 23200
SCC .... SEK 193.33
BUSINESS: PRINTING & STATIONERY: Printing

NORDENS TIDNING
51246W84A-150
Editorial: Box 12707, 112 94 STOCKHOLM
Tel: 8 506 113 00 **Fax:** 850611320
Email: torsten@norden.se **Web site:** http://www.norden.se
Date Established: 1944; **Freq:** Quarterly; **Circ:** 30,000
Editor-in-Chief: Torsten Hallberg
Profile: Scandinavian cultural magazine.
Language(s): Swedish
ADVERTISING RATES:
Full Page Colour .... SEK 20000
SCC .... SEK 166.67
CONSUMER: THE ARTS & LITERARY: Arts

NORDIC PULP AND PAPER RESEARCH JOURNAL
1656871W36-62
Editorial: Box 5515, 114 85 STOCKHOLM
Tel: 8 783 84 00 **Fax:** 8 661 73 44
Email: info@npprj.se **Web site:** http://www.npprj.se
Freq: Quarterly; **Circ:** 3,000
Editor: Per Stenius; **Editor-in-Chief:** Elisabet Brännvall
Language(s): Swedish
BUSINESS: PAPER

NORDISK ENERGI
1837055W18A-54
Editorial: Convenus Industry, Box 240 53, 104 50 STOCKHOLM **Tel:** 8 506 244 95 **Fax:** 850624499
Email: tips@branschnyheter.se **Web site:** http://www.energinyheter.se
Freq: 6 issues yearly - (8 nr/år); **Circ:** 15,000
Editor-in-Chief: Hanna S Backman; **Publisher:** Otto Marand
Language(s): Swedish
ADVERTISING RATES:
Full Page Colour .... SEK 23700
SCC .... SEK 197.50
BUSINESS: ELECTRONICS

NORDISK FILATELI
51144W79C-30
Editorial: Box 90, 277 21 KIVIK **Tel:** 414 702 30
Email: nordisk@filateli.se **Web site:** http://www.filateli.se
Date Established: 1937; **Freq:** Monthly; **Circ:** 7,000
Editor-in-Chief: Morten Persson; **Publisher:** Morten Persson
Profile: Journal about philately.
Language(s): Swedish
Readership: Read by stamp collectors.
CONSUMER: HOBBIES & DIY: Philately

NORDISK INDUSTRI
1625683W46-122
Editorial: Conventus Media House, Humlegårdsgatan 20, 114 46 STOCKHOLM
Tel: 8 506 244 00 **Fax:** 8 506 244 59
Email: tips@branschnyheter.se **Web site:** http://www.branschnyheter.se
Freq: 6 issues yearly; **Circ:** 2,600
Language(s): Swedish
ADVERTISING RATES:
Full Page Colour .... SEK 23700
BUSINESS: TIMBER, WOOD & FORESTRY

NORDISK INFRASTRUKTUR
634653W14A-222
Editorial: Conventus Media House AB, 114 46 STOCKHOLM **Tel:** 8 506 244 00
Email: john.hardwick@conventusmedia.se **Web site:** http://www.branschnyheter.se
Date Established: 1995; **Freq:** 6 issues yearly; **Circ:** 2,900
Publisher: John Hardwick
Language(s): Swedish
ADVERTISING RATES:
Full Page Colour .... SEK 23700
SCC .... SEK 197.50
BUSINESS: COMMERCE, INDUSTRY & MANAGEMENT

NORDISK JÄRNBANETIDSKRIFT
1809878W49E-109
Editorial: c/o Prenler, Kittåkers väg 16, 784 55 BORLÄNGE **Tel:** 705 24 24 61
Email: njt@precon.se **Web site:** http://www.njsforum.com
Freq: 6 issues yearly - 5 nr/år; **Circ:** 3,000
Editor: Mikael Prenler
Language(s): Swedish
BUSINESS: TRANSPORT: Railways

NORDISK PAPPERSTIDNING/ NORDIC PAPER JOURNAL
1639362W36-61
Editorial: Box 72001, 181 72 LIDINGÖ
Tel: 8 670 41 00 **Fax:** 86616455
Email: allan.a@mentoronline.se **Web site:** http://www.papernet.se
Freq: Monthly; **Circ:** 6,200
Editor-in-Chief: Allan Almegård; **Advertising Manager:** Ing-Marie Matsson
Language(s): Swedish
ADVERTISING RATES:
Full Page Colour .... SEK 29700
SCC .... SEK 247.50
Copy instructions: *Copy Date:* 20 days prior to publication date
BUSINESS: PAPER

NORDISK TIDSKRIFT FÖR VETENSKAP, KONST, INDUSTRI
51247W84A-160
Editorial: Box 22333, 104 22 STOCKHOLM
Tel: 8 654 75 70 **Fax:** 8 654 75 72
Email: info@letterstedtska.org **Web site:** http://www.letterstedtska.org
Date Established: 1878; **Freq:** Quarterly; **Circ:** 2,200
Publisher: Claes Wiklund
Profile: Politically independent journal containing articles about art, science and industry in Scandinavia.
Language(s): Swedish
CONSUMER: THE ARTS & LITERARY: Arts

NORDISKA PROJEKT
1903060W27-32
Editorial: Box 2132, 103 14 STOCKHOLM
Tel: 812207402
Email: info@ljungaforsmedia.se **Web site:** http://www.nordiskaprojekt.se
Freq: 6 issues yearly; **Circ:** 10,500
Editor-in-Chief: Janne Åström; **Advertising Manager:** Niklas Ljunggren
Language(s): Swedish
BUSINESS: METAL, IRON & STEEL

NORDMARKSBYGDEN
634251W80-200
Editorial: Elovsbyn, Hage, 670 10 TÖCKSFORS
Tel: 573 260 28 **Fax:** 57326062
Email: monica.leandersson@spray.se **Web site:** http://www.nordmarksbygden.nu
Date Established: 1964; **Freq:** Monthly; **Circ:** 8,100
Advertising Manager: Monica Leandersson Åhs
Profile: Newspaper featuring local news for Årlängs, Järnskog, Skillingmark, Långserud Svanskog, Lenungshammar and Gustavsfors.
Language(s): Swedish
Readership: Read by local residents.
CONSUMER: RURAL & REGIONAL INTEREST

NORRA HALLAND
624417W72-263
Editorial: Box 10244, 434 24 KUNGSBACKA
Tel: 300 107 95 **Fax:** 300 167 44
Email: redaktionen@norrahalland.se **Web site:** http://www.norrahalland.se
Date Established: 1921
Circ: 12,000
Advertising Manager: Pia Grapenstrand; **Publisher:** Kristian Alm
Language(s): Swedish
ADVERTISING RATES:
Full Page Colour .... SEK 25000
SCC .... SEK 125
LOCAL NEWSPAPERS

NORRA SKÅNE
50787W67B-5500
Editorial: 281 81 HÄSSLEHOLM **Tel:** 451 74 50 00
Fax: 451 74 50 32
Email: nyhetschefen@nsk.se **Web site:** http://www.nsk.se
Date Established: 1899
Circ: 20,700
Editor: Marie Strömberg-Andersson; **Editor-in-Chief:** Johan Hammarqvist; **Publisher:** Mimmi Karlsson-Bernfalk
Language(s): Swedish
ADVERTISING RATES:
Full Page Colour .... SEK 32160
SCC .... SEK 160.80
Copy instructions: *Copy Date:* 7 days prior to publication date
REGIONAL DAILY & SUNDAY NEWSPAPERS: Regional Daily Newspapers

NORRA SKÅNE; NSK.SE
1843536W65A-986
Editorial: 281 81 HÄSSLEHOLM **Tel:** 451 74 50 00
Fax: 451 74 50 32
Email: nyhetschefen@nsk.se **Web site:** http://www.nsk.se
Freq: Daily; **Cover Price:** Free; **Circ:** 16,667 Unique Users
Editor-in-Chief: Johan Hammarqvist; **Publisher:** Mimmi Karlsson-Bernfalk
Language(s): Swedish
NATIONAL DAILY & SUNDAY NEWSPAPERS: National Daily Newspapers

NORRAN
50830W67B-5550
Editorial: Box 58, 931 21 SKELLEFTEÅ
Tel: 910 577 00 **Fax:** 910 578 75
Email: nv@norran.se **Web site:** http://www.norran.se
Date Established: 1910; **Freq:** Daily; **Circ:** 27,500
Editor: Lars Andersson; **Advertising Manager:** Robert Brännström; **Publisher:** Anette Novak
Language(s): Swedish
ADVERTISING RATES:
Full Page Colour .... SEK 39718
SCC .... SEK 198.59
REGIONAL DAILY & SUNDAY NEWSPAPERS: Regional Daily Newspapers

NORRBOTTENS-KURIREN
50807W67B-5600
Editorial: 971 81 LULEÅ **Tel:** 920 26 29 03
Fax: 920 26 29 53
Email: redaktionen@kuriren.com **Web site:** http://www.kuriren.nu
Date Established: 1861
Circ: 25,200
Editor: Janne Enbom; **Advertising Manager:** Peder Stockman; **Publisher:** Mats Ehnbom
Language(s): Swedish
ADVERTISING RATES:
Full Page Colour .... SEK 39672
SCC .... SEK 198.36
REGIONAL DAILY & SUNDAY NEWSPAPERS: Regional Daily Newspapers

NORRBOTTENS-KURIREN; WEBB
751690W67B-9555
Editorial: 971 81 LULEÅ **Fax:** 92037628
Email: webredaktionen@kuriren.com **Web site:** http://www.kuriren.nu
Freq: Daily; **Circ:** 27,700 Unique Users
Publisher: Mats Ehnbom
Language(s): Swedish
REGIONAL DAILY & SUNDAY NEWSPAPERS: Regional Daily Newspapers

NORRKÖPINGS TIDNINGAR
50817W67B-5650
Editorial: 601 83 NORRKÖPING **Tel:** 11 20 00 00
Fax: 11 20 01 40
Email: redaktionen@nt.se **Web site:** http://www.nt.se
Date Established: 1758
Circ: 46,500
Editor: Jan Rådegård; **Editor-in-Chief:** Petra Wetterström; **Advertising Manager:** Theo Blanco; **Publisher:** Anders Nilsson
Language(s): Swedish
ADVERTISING RATES:
Full Page Colour .... SEK 55555
SCC .... SEK 277.77
REGIONAL DAILY & SUNDAY NEWSPAPERS: Regional Daily Newspapers

NORRKÖPINGS TIDNINGAR; NT.SE
1843534W65A-984
Editorial: 601 83 NORRKÖPING **Tel:** 11 20 01 60
Fax: 11 20 01 40
Email: webmaster@nt.se **Web site:** http://www.nt.se
Freq: Daily; **Cover Price:** Free; **Circ:** 27,063 Unique Users
Editor-in-Chief: Anders Nilsson; **Publisher:** Anders Nilsson
Language(s): Swedish
ADVERTISING RATES:
SCC .... SEK 55
NATIONAL DAILY & SUNDAY NEWSPAPERS: National Daily Newspapers

NORRLÄNDSKA SOCIALDEMOKRATEN
50808W67B-5700
Editorial: 971 83 LULEÅ **Tel:** 920 263 000
Fax: 920 263 039
Email: redaktion@nsd.se **Web site:** http://www.nsd.se
Date Established: 1919
Circ: 34,100
Editor: Ulf Bengtsson; **Advertising Manager:** Roland Lindgren; **Publisher:** Lena Olofsson
Language(s): Swedish
ADVERTISING RATES:
Full Page Colour .... SEK 30937
SCC .... SEK 154.69
REGIONAL DAILY & SUNDAY NEWSPAPERS: Regional Daily Newspapers

NORRLÄNDSKA SOCIALDEMOKRATEN; NSD.SE
1844545W65A-1019
Editorial: 971 83 LULEÅ **Tel:** 920 360 00
Fax: 920 892 10
Email: redaktion@nsd.se **Web site:** http://www.nsd.se
Freq: Daily; **Cover Price:** Free; **Circ:** 28,798 Unique Users
Language(s): Swedish
ADVERTISING RATES:
SCC .... SEK 31
NATIONAL DAILY & SUNDAY NEWSPAPERS: National Daily Newspapers

NORRTELJE TIDNING
50818W67B-5750
Editorial: 761 84 NORRTÄLJE **Tel:** 176 795 00
Fax: 176 100 08
Email: redaktionen@norrteljetidning.se **Web site:** http://www.norrteljetidning.se
Circ: 14,500
Editor: Ann Sjöblom; **Publisher:** Robert Jonsson
Language(s): Swedish
ADVERTISING RATES:
Full Page Colour .... SEK 36400
SCC .... SEK 182
REGIONAL DAILY & SUNDAY NEWSPAPERS: Regional Daily Newspapers

NORRTELJE TIDNING; NORRTELJETIDNING.SE
752318W67B-9660
Editorial: 761 84 NORRTÄLJE **Tel:** 176 795 00
Email: redaktionen@norrteljetidning.se **Web site:** http://www.norrteljetidning.se
Freq: Daily; **Cover Price:** Free; **Circ:** 3,097 Unique Users
Publisher: Katarina Ekspong
Language(s): Swedish
REGIONAL DAILY & SUNDAY NEWSPAPERS: Regional Daily Newspapers

NOSTALGIA
51135W77F-100
Editorial: Box 529, 371 23 KARLSKRONA
Tel: 455 33 53 25 **Fax:** 455 31 17 15
Email: nostalgia@fabas.se **Web site:** http://www.nostalgiamagazine.se
Date Established: 1993; **Freq:** Monthly; **Circ:** 43,400
Editor: Göran Ambell; **Editor-in-Chief:** Göran Ambell; **Advertising Manager:** Tony Thestrup; **Publisher:** Stig L Sjöberg
Profile: Magazine focusing on classic cars, boats and planes.
Language(s): Swedish
Readership: Aimed at owners of classic cars, people seeking to purchase a model and motoring enthusiasts.
ADVERTISING RATES:
Full Page Colour .... SEK 17400
SCC .... SEK 87
CONSUMER: MOTORING & CYCLING: Veteran Cars

NÖTKÖTT
50374W21D-25
Editorial: Box 1146, 631 81 ESKILSTUNA
Tel: 16 16 34 42 **Fax:** 16212 16
Email: notkott@svenskmjolk.se **Web site:** http://www.svenskmjolk.se
Date Established: 1982; **Freq:** 6 issues yearly; **Circ:** 5,600
Advertising Manager: Marie Louise Ankarsten; **Publisher:** Lena Widebeck
Profile: Magazine about beef production containing facts, information and debate articles.
Language(s): Swedish
Readership: Aimed at beef producers and farmers, advisers, veterinary surgeons and teachers.
BUSINESS: AGRICULTURE & FARMING: Livestock

NTT SÅG & TRÄ, NORDISK TRÄTEKNIK
1639403W46-124
Editorial: Box 72001, 181 72 LIDINGÖ
Tel: 8 670 41 00 **Fax:** 8 679 54 40
Email: ulf.a@mentoronline.se **Web site:** http://www.woodnet.se
Freq: 26 issues yearly; **Circ:** 4,200
Editor-in-Chief: Ulf Aronsson; **Advertising Manager:** Lars Bille; **Publisher:** Ulf Aronsson
Language(s): Swedish
ADVERTISING RATES:
Full Page Colour .... SEK 25900
SCC .... SEK 161.87
BUSINESS: TIMBER, WOOD & FORESTRY

NU - DET LIBERALA NYHETSMAGASINET
624430W67B-5770
Editorial: Box 2045, 103 11 STOCKHOLM
Tel: 8 410 242 00
Email: red@tidningen.nu **Web site:** http://www.tidningen.nu
Date Established: 1983
Circ: 5,200
Advertising Manager: Eva Bosved
Language(s): Swedish
ADVERTISING RATES:
Full Page Colour .... SEK 19000
SCC .... SEK 158.33
REGIONAL DAILY & SUNDAY NEWSPAPERS: Regional Daily Newspapers

NU - DET LIBERALA NYHETSMAGASINET; WEBB
1844952W65A-1044
Editorial: Box 6508, 111 27 STOCKHOLM
Tel: 8 410 242 00 **Fax:** 8 509 116 83
Email: red@tidningen.nu **Web site:** http://www.tidningen.nu
Freq: Daily; **Cover Price:** Free; **Circ:** 3,467 Unique Users
Editor-in-Chief: Jan Fröman; **Advertising Manager:** Eva Bosved
Language(s): Swedish
ADVERTISING RATES:
SCC .... SEK 32
NATIONAL DAILY & SUNDAY NEWSPAPERS: National Daily Newspapers

NUET
751156W74C-300
Editorial: Tobaksspinnargatan 2, 117 36 STOCKHOLM **Tel:** 8 720 20 80
Email: info@tundellsalmson.se **Web site:** http://www.tundellsalmson.se
Freq: 104 issues yearly; **Circ:** 400
Editor: Anita Björkqvist
Language(s): Swedish
CONSUMER: WOMEN'S INTEREST CONSUMER MAGAZINES: Home & Family

NUORAT
51328W90-59
Editorial: Adolf Hedinsvägen 36, 981 33 KIRUNA
Tel: 980 821 47 **Fax:** 980 270 77
Email: info@nuorat.se **Web site:** http://www.nuorat.se
Date Established: 1975; **Freq:** Quarterly; **Circ:** 600
Editor-in-Chief: Pia Sjögren
Profile: Journal containing information, news and articles about issues concerning the Swedish Saamis (Laplanders) such as minority rights and related topics. Published by the Swedish Saami Youth Association.
Language(s): Swedish
CONSUMER: ETHNIC

NY FRAMTID
51197W82-205
Editorial: Box 2373, 103 18 STOCKHOLM
Tel: 8 723 25 30 **Fax:** 8 723 25 10
Email: ny.framtid@kdu.se **Web site:** http://www.kdu.se
Freq: Quarterly; **Circ:** 5,000
Profile: Journal of the Christian Democratic Youth Party.
Language(s): Swedish
CONSUMER: CURRENT AFFAIRS & POLITICS

NY TEKNIK
50297W14B-90
Editorial: Mäster Samuelsgatan 56, 106 12 STOCKHOLM **Tel:** 8 796 66 00
Email: redaktion@nyteknik.se **Web site:** http://www.nyteknik.se
Freq: Weekly; **Circ:** 155,500
Publisher: Jan Huss
Profile: Magazine providing information, news and articles about science and technology. Covers solutions and inventions for industry.
Language(s): Swedish
Readership: Read by scientists, technicians and other professionals within industry.
ADVERTISING RATES:
Full Page Colour .... SEK 88500
SCC .... SEK 396
Copy instructions: *Copy Date:* 12 days prior to publication date
BUSINESS: COMMERCE, INDUSTRY & MANAGEMENT: Industry & Factories

NY TEKNIK; NY TEKNIK.SE
1623609W19J-16
Editorial: Mäster Samuelsgatan 56, 106 12 STOCKHOLM **Tel:** 8 796 66 00
Email: redaktion@nyteknik.se **Web site:** http://www.nyteknik.se
Circ: 27,612 Unique Users
Publisher: Jan Huss
Language(s): Swedish
BUSINESS: ENGINEERING & MACHINERY: CAD & CIM (Computer Integrated Manufacture)

NY TID
1835764W14F-105
Editorial: Heurlins plats 9, 413 01 GOTEBORG
Tel: 31 339 63 36 **Fax:** 31 339 63 01
Email: nytid@sap.se **Web site:** http://www.nytid.se
Freq: Weekly; **Circ:** 2,200
Editor-in-Chief: Eric Sundström
Language(s): Swedish
ADVERTISING RATES:
Full Page Colour .... SEK 10100
SCC .... SEK 63.12
Copy instructions: *Copy Date:* 9 days prior to publication date
BUSINESS: COMMERCE, INDUSTRY & MANAGEMENT: Training & Recruitment

NYA CYKELTIDNINGEN
51118W77C-90
Editorial: Torneågatan 10, 164 79 KISTA
Tel: 8 751 62 04
Email: kansli@svenska-cykelsallskapet.se **Web site:** http://www.svenska-cykelsallskapet.se
Date Established: 1980; **Freq:** Quarterly; **Circ:** 3,500
Editor-in-Chief: Lasse Brynolf; **Publisher:** Erkki Kärkkäinen
Profile: Magazine containing information and advice on the pleasures and pitfalls of cycling, including traffic and environmental news, tourism relating to cycling and consumer tests.
Language(s): Swedish
CONSUMER: MOTORING & CYCLING: Cycling

NYA KRISTINEHAMNS-POSTEN
50801W67B-5800
Editorial: Box 55, 681 22 KRISTINEHAMN
Tel: 550 41 25 00 **Fax:** 550 810 80

Email: redaktion@nkp.se **Web site:** http://www.nkp.se
Date Established: 1884
Circ: 8,100
Advertising Manager: Lars-Göran Johansson; **Publisher:** Lars Blomkvist
Language(s): Swedish
ADVERTISING RATES:
Full Page Colour .... SEK 18000
SCC .... SEK 90
REGIONAL DAILY & SUNDAY NEWSPAPERS: Regional Daily Newspapers

NYA KRISTINEHAMNS-POSTEN; NKP.SE 1844954W65A-1045
Editorial: Box 55, 681 31 KRISTINEHAMN
Tel: 550 41 25 51 **Fax:** 550 810 80
Email: redaktion@nkp.se **Web site:** http://nwt.se/kristinehamn
Freq: Daily; **Cover Price:** Free; **Circ:** 6,333 Unique Users
Language(s): Swedish
ADVERTISING RATES:
SCC .... SEK 18
NATIONAL DAILY & SUNDAY NEWSPAPERS: National Daily Newspapers

NYA LIDKÖPINGS-TIDNINGEN; NLT.SE 1843542W65A-991
Editorial: 531 81 LIDKÖPING **Tel:** 510 897 00
Fax: 51089730
Email: redaktionen@nlt.se **Web site:** http://www.nlt.se
Freq: Daily; **Cover Price:** Free; **Circ:** 18,333 Unique Users
Managing Director: Lennart Hörling; **Advertising Manager:** Thommy Johansson; **Publisher:** Anders Hörling
Language(s): Swedish
NATIONAL DAILY & SUNDAY NEWSPAPERS: National Daily Newspapers

NYA LUDVIKA TIDNING 50806W67B-5850
Editorial: Carlavägen 21, 771 30 LUDVIKA
Tel: 240 882 00 **Fax:** 240 882 30
Email: nlt.red@dt.se **Web site:** http://www.dt.se
Date Established: 1993
Circ: 9,500
Editor: Bo Johannesson
Language(s): Swedish
ADVERTISING RATES:
Full Page Colour .... SEK 36288
SCC .... SEK 181.44
REGIONAL DAILY & SUNDAY NEWSPAPERS: Regional Daily Newspapers

NYA SYNVÄRLDEN 1623595W94F-211
Editorial: SRF, 122 88 ENSKEDE **Tel:** 8 39 92 98
Email: jan.wiklund@srfriks.org **Web site:** http://www.ffsa.se/synvarlden.php
Freq: Quarterly; **Circ:** 1,500
Editor: Jan Wiklund; **Publisher:** Lena Söderberg
Language(s): Swedish
CONSUMER: OTHER CLASSIFICATIONS: Disability

NYA WERMLANDS-TIDNINGEN 50797W67B-5900
Editorial: Box 28, 651 02 KARLSTAD
Tel: 54 19 90 00 **Fax:** 54 19 96 00
Email: redaktion@nwt.se **Web site:** http://www.nwt.se
Date Established: 1836
Circ: 52,800
Editor: Mats Dahlberg; **Publisher:** Staffan Ander
Language(s): Swedish
ADVERTISING RATES:
Full Page Colour .... SEK 49680
SCC .... SEK 220.80
REGIONAL DAILY & SUNDAY NEWSPAPERS: Regional Daily Newspapers

NYA WERMLANDS-TIDNINGEN; NWT.SE 1843553W65A-1001
Editorial: Box 28, 651 02 KARLSTAD
Tel: 54 19 90 00 **Fax:** 54199600
Email: redaktion@nwt.se **Web site:** http://www.nwt.se
Freq: Daily; **Cover Price:** Free; **Circ:** 24,307 Unique Users
Publisher: Staffan Ander
Language(s): Swedish
NATIONAL DAILY & SUNDAY NEWSPAPERS: National Daily Newspapers

NYBRO-EXTRA 751078W80-675
Editorial: Box 119, 382 22 NYBRO **Tel:** 481 161 11
Fax: 48118864
Email: info@nybroextra.se **Web site:** http://www.nybroextra.se
Circ: 12,000
Publisher: Loa Arvidsson
Language(s): Swedish
Copy instructions: *Copy Date:* 7 days prior to publication date
CONSUMER: RURAL & REGIONAL INTEREST

NYHETER FRÅN LIVSMEDELSVERKET 1625818W14A-285
Editorial: Box 622, 751 26 UPPSALA
Tel: 18 17 55 00 **Fax:** 18 17 53 50
Email: livsmedelsverket@slv.se **Web site:** http://www.slv.se
Freq: 104 times a year; **Circ:** 3,000 Unique Users
Publisher: Eva Corp
Language(s): Swedish
BUSINESS: COMMERCE, INDUSTRY & MANAGEMENT

NYHETER FRÅN NICARAGUA 752021W74C-310
Editorial: VFSN, Tegelviksgatan 40, 118 46 STOCKHOLM **Tel:** 8 642 08 81 **Fax:** 8 641 11 35
Email: info@vfsn.se **Web site:** http://www.vfsn.se
Freq: Quarterly; **Circ:** 500
Language(s): Swedish
CONSUMER: WOMEN'S INTEREST CONSUMER MAGAZINES: Home & Family

NYHETSBREV SLUSSEN BUILDING SERVICES 1911082W58-109
Editorial: Slussen Building Services, S:t Göransgatan 84, 112 38 STOCKHOLM **Tel:** 8 518 018 00
Fax: 851801811
Email: redaktion@slussen.biz **Web site:** http://www.slussen.biz
Freq: Weekly; **Cover Price:** Free; **Circ:** 15,500
Language(s): Swedish
BUSINESS: ENERGY, FUEL & NUCLEAR

NYHETSBREVET DAGENS FASTIGHETSAKTIE 1841532W1E-206
Editorial: Wallingatan 18, 111 24 STOCKHOLM
Tel: 8 10 81 81 **Fax:** 8104140
Email: sf@centum.se **Web site:** http://www.fastighetsaktien.se
Freq: Daily; **Circ:** 8,000 Unique Users
Language(s): Swedish
BUSINESS: FINANCE & ECONOMICS: Property

NYHETSBREVET FOND & BANK 1692318W1A-208
Editorial: Box 17518, 118 91 STOCKHOLM
Tel: 8 442 44 90 **Fax:** 87204491
Email: fond.bank@nyhetsbrev.se **Web site:** http://www.nyhetsbrev.se
Freq: Monthly; **Circ:** 5,000
Editor: Hans Schmidt; **Publisher:** Gunnar Loxdal
Language(s): Swedish
ADVERTISING RATES:
Full Page Colour .... SEK 5000
BUSINESS: FINANCE & ECONOMICS

NYHETSBREVET FOND & BANK ONLINE 1683764W14A-296
Editorial: Svenska Nyhetsbrev AB, 113 46 STOCKHOLM **Tel:** 8 54 600 509 **Fax:** 8 54 600 599
Email: fond.bank@nyhetsbrev.se **Web site:** http://www.nyhetsbrev.se
Freq: Daily; **Circ:** 5,000
Editor: Hans Schmidt
Language(s): Swedish
ADVERTISING RATES:
Full Page Colour .... SEK 5000
BUSINESS: COMMERCE, INDUSTRY & MANAGEMENT

NYHETSBREVET NOTERAT 50737W63-100
Editorial: Box 5253, 402 25 GÖTEBORG
Tel: 31 83 59 00
Email: info@handelskammaren.net **Web site:** http://www.handelskammaren.net
Date Established: 2000; **Freq:** Weekly; **Circ:** 15,000
Editor: Anna Werner; **Publisher:** Robert Odenjung
Profile: Journal containing trade news for Chamber of Commerce members.
Language(s): Swedish
BUSINESS: REGIONAL BUSINESS

NYHETSBREVET PENSIONER & FÖRMÅNER 50173W1H-300
Editorial: Svenska Nyhetsbrev AB, 113 46 STOCKHOLM **Tel:** 8 546 005 00 **Fax:** 8 546 005 99
Email: pensioner.formaner@nyhetsbrev.se **Web site:** http://www.nyhetsbrev.se
Date Established: 1990; **Freq:** Monthly; **Circ:** 5,000
Editor: Alf Ohlén; **Advertising Manager:** Chris Lindström; **Publisher:** Gunnar Loxdal
Profile: Newsletter covering pensions, benefits and insurance.
Language(s): Swedish
ADVERTISING RATES:
Full Page Colour .... SEK 5000
BUSINESS: FINANCE & ECONOMICS: Pensions

NYHETSBREVET PHARMA ONLINE 1639315W37-37
Editorial: Svenska Nyhetsbrev AB, 113 46 STOCKHOLM **Tel:** 8 54 600 500 **Fax:** 8 54 600 599
Email: pharmaonline@nyhetsbrev.se **Web site:** http://www.nyhetsbrev.se
Freq: Daily; **Circ:** 5,000
Editor: Jonny Sågänger; **Publisher:** Gunnar Loxdal
Language(s): Swedish
ADVERTISING RATES:
Full Page Colour .... SEK 5000
BUSINESS: PHARMACEUTICAL & CHEMISTS

NYHETSBREVET RISK & FÖRSÄKRING 50165W1D-180
Editorial: Box 17518, 118 91 STOCKHOLM
Tel: 8 546 005 00 **Fax:** 8 546 005 99
Email: risk.forsakring@nyhetsbrev.se **Web site:** http://www.nyhetsbrev.se
Date Established: 1990; **Freq:** 26 issues yearly; **Circ:** 5,000
Editor: Georg Ebert; **Advertising Manager:** Chris Lindström; **Publisher:** Gunnar Loxdal
Profile: Newsletter containing debate articles, product information and news about insurance.
Language(s): Swedish
Readership: Aimed at managers in the insurance industry, insurance brokers, consultants and decision-makers dealing with insurance.
ADVERTISING RATES:
Full Page Colour .... SEK 5000
BUSINESS: FINANCE & ECONOMICS: Insurance

NYHETSBREVET TELEKOM ONLINE 50341W18B-20
Editorial: Svenska Nyhetsbrev AB, 113 46 STOCKHOLM **Tel:** 8 54 600 500 **Fax:** 8 54 600 599
Email: telekom@nyhetsbrev.se **Web site:** http://www.nyhetsbrev.se
Date Established: 1997; **Freq:** Daily; **Circ:** 5,000
Editor: Marlène Sellebråten; **Publisher:** Gunnar Loxdal
Profile: Newsletter concerning the telecommunications industry.
Language(s): Swedish
ADVERTISING RATES:
Full Page Colour .... SEK 5000
BUSINESS: ELECTRONICS: Telecommunications

NYHETSBREVET TELEKOM ONLINE SPECIAL 1841522W5E-110
Editorial: Svenska Nyhetsbrev AB, 113 46 STOCKHOLM **Tel:** 8 54 600 500 **Fax:** 8 54 600 599
Email: telekom@nyhetsbrev.se **Web site:** http://www.nyhetsbrev.se
Cover Price: Paid; **Circ:** 5,000 Unique Users
Editor: Marlène Sellebråten
Language(s): Swedish
ADVERTISING RATES:
Full Page Colour .... SEK 5000
BUSINESS: COMPUTERS & AUTOMATION: Data Transmission

NYHETSBREVET TELEKOMNYHETERNA 1865608W18B-85
Editorial: Box 4034, 102 61 STOCKHOLM
Tel: 8 455 67 70
Email: info@telekomnyheterna.se **Web site:** http://www.telekomnyheterna.se
Freq: Daily; **Circ:** 5,000
Editor-in-Chief: Mats Sjödin
Language(s): Swedish
BUSINESS: ELECTRONICS: Telecommunications

NYHETSTIDNINGEN SESAM 51359W94D-80
Editorial: Fraktflygargatan 18, 128 30 SKARPNÄCK
Tel: 8 600 80 80
Email: kerstin@sesam.nu **Web site:** http://www.sesam.nu
Date Established: 1999
Circ: 1,900
Publisher: Malin Bergendahl
Profile: Newspaper covering Swedish life and society for immigrants.
Language(s): Swedish
ADVERTISING RATES:
Full Page Colour .... SEK 15200
CONSUMER: OTHER CLASSIFICATIONS: Expatriates

NYHETSTIDNINGEN SESAM; SESAM.NU 1844986W65A-1051
Editorial: Fraktflygargatan 18, 128 30 SKARPNÄCK
Tel: 8 600 80 89
Email: red@nyhetstidningen.nu **Web site:** http://www.sesam.nu
Freq: Daily; **Cover Price:** Free; **Circ:** 1,500 Unique Users
Editor: Malin Bergendahl; **Publisher:** Malin Bergendahl
Language(s): Swedish
NATIONAL DAILY & SUNDAY NEWSPAPERS: National Daily Newspapers

NYLIBERALEN 51481W82-433
Editorial: BreviaBox 620, 114 79 STOCKHOLM
Tel: 8 34 56 47
Email: nyliberalen@bahnhof.se **Web site:** http://www.nyliberalen.nu
Date Established: 1983; **Freq:** Quarterly; **Circ:** 1,500
Editor-in-Chief: Hans Egnell; **Publisher:** Henrik Bejke
Language(s): Swedish
CONSUMER: CURRENT AFFAIRS & POLITICS

NYNÄSHAMNS POSTEN 50820W67B-5950
Editorial: Box 24, 149 21 NYNÄSHAMN
Tel: 8 524 404 00 **Fax:** 852440437
Email: np.redaktion@nhp.se **Web site:** http://www.nhp.se
Date Established: 1925
Circ: 7,400
Editor: Carina Knutas; **Advertising Manager:** Niclas Axelson; **Publisher:** Niklas Milberg
Language(s): Swedish
ADVERTISING RATES:
Full Page Colour .... SEK 21900
SCC .... SEK 109.50
Copy instructions: *Copy Date:* 14 days prior to publication date
REGIONAL DAILY & SUNDAY NEWSPAPERS: Regional Daily Newspapers

NYNÄSHAMNS POSTEN; NHP.SE 1846292W65A-1071
Editorial: Box 24, 149 21 NYNÄSHAMN
Tel: 8587 122 00
Email: np.redaktion@nhp.se **Web site:** http://www.nhp.se
Freq: Daily; **Cover Price:** Free; **Circ:** 7,000 Unique Users
Editor-in-Chief: Niklas Milberg; **Advertising Manager:** Niclas Axelson; **Publisher:** Niklas Milberg
Language(s): Swedish
ADVERTISING RATES:
SCC .... SEK 22
NATIONAL DAILY & SUNDAY NEWSPAPERS: National Daily Newspapers

NYTT FRÅN REVISORN 50160W1B-130
Editorial: Box 6497, 113 82 STOCKHOLM
Tel: 8 506 112 60 **Fax:** 850611258
Email: lars.waldengren@farsrsforlag.se **Web site:** http://www.nyttfranrevisorn.se
Date Established: 1994; **Freq:** Monthly; **Circ:** 86,200
Editor-in-Chief: Lars Waldengren; **Advertising Manager:** Inger Weman Åberg; **Publisher:** Marie Wernerman
Profile: Magazine published by FAR (The Institute for the Accounting Profession in Sweden).
Language(s): Swedish
Readership: Read by Swedish accountants and their clients.
ADVERTISING RATES:
Full Page Colour .... SEK 44000
SCC .... SEK 354.17
BUSINESS: FINANCE & ECONOMICS: Accountancy

OBEROENDE 50639W56L-53_75
Editorial: c/o RFHL Lagerlöfsgatan 8, 112 60 STOCKHOLM **Tel:** 8 545 560 60 **Fax:** 8 33 58 66
Email: info@rfhl.se **Web site:** http://www.rfhl.se
Freq: Quarterly; **Circ:** 5,000
Editor: Per Sternbeck; **Publisher:** Sonja Wallbom
Profile: Journal covering drug-related issues and social politics.
Language(s): Swedish
Readership: Aimed at people working with the rehabilitation of drug-addicts.
BUSINESS: HEALTH & MEDICAL: Disability & Rehabilitation

OFFENSIV; WEBB 1844777W65A-1027
Editorial: Box 73, 123 22 FARSTA **Tel:** 8 605 94 03
Fax: 8 556 252 52
Email: offensiv@socialisterna.org **Web site:** http://offensiv.socialisterna.org
Freq: Daily; **Cover Price:** Free
Language(s): Swedish
NATIONAL DAILY & SUNDAY NEWSPAPERS: National Daily Newspapers

OFFENTLIGA AFFÄRER 1667967W57-115
Editorial: Fiskhamnsgatan 2, 414 58 GÖTEBORG
Tel: 31 775 15 80 **Fax:** 31 775 15 89
Email: redaktion@hexanova.se **Web site:** http://www.hexanova.se
Freq: 6 issues yearly; **Circ:** 11,000
Managing Director: Urban Nilsson; **Publisher:** Urban Nilsson

Language(s): Swedish
ADVERTISING RATES:
Full Page Colour .... SEK 33550
SCC .... SEK 279.58
BUSINESS: ENVIRONMENT & POLLUTION

OFFICERSTIDNINGEN 50470W40-65
Editorial: Förbundskansliet, Box 5338, 102 47 STOCKHOLM **Tel:** 8 440 83 30 **Fax:** 84408340
Email: sandra.lang@officersforbundet.se **Web site:** http://www.officersforbundet.se
Freq: 6 issues yearly; **Circ:** 22,500
Editor-in-Chief: Daniel Skoglund; **Publisher:** Björn Lundell
Profile: Publication for military officers in the Swedish defence forces - the army, navy and air force. Published by the Swedish Association of Military Officers.
Language(s): Swedish
ADVERTISING RATES:
Full Page Colour .... SEK 23900
SCC .... SEK 199.17
BUSINESS: DEFENCE

OFFSIDE FOTBOLLSMAGASINET
1624984W75J-263
Editorial: Östra Hamngatan 45, 411 10 GOTEBORG
Tel: 31 13 79 81 **Fax:** 317742210
Email: tobias.regnell@offside.org **Web site:** http://www.offside.org
Freq: 6 issues yearly; **Circ:** 19,200
Editor: Henrik Ystén
Language(s): Swedish
CONSUMER: SPORT: Athletics

OKEJ 51097W76E-145
Editorial: OKEJ, Egmont Kärnan AB, 205 08 MALMO
Tel: 40 693 94 00
Email: okej@egmont.se **Web site:** http://www.okej.se
Date Established: 1980; **Freq:** Monthly; **Circ:** 24,900
Advertising Manager: Jenny Frank
Profile: Magazine about pop music, films and TV.
Language(s): Swedish
Readership: Aimed at young people.
ADVERTISING RATES:
Full Page Colour .... SEK 27600
SCC .... SEK 230
CONSUMER: MUSIC & PERFORMING ARTS: Pop Music

ÖLANDSBLADET 50769W67B-6000
Editorial: Västra Kyrkogatan 18, 387 22 BORGHOLM
Tel: 485 56 09 00 **Fax:** 485 56 09 19
Email: redaktion@olandsbladet.se **Web site:** http://www.olandsbladet.se
Date Established: 1867
Circ: 8,900
Language(s): Swedish
ADVERTISING RATES:
Full Page Colour .... SEK 36360
SCC .... SEK 181.80
REGIONAL DAILY & SUNDAY NEWSPAPERS: Regional Daily Newspapers

ÖLANDSBLADET; WEBB
1846248W65A-1053
Editorial: Västra Kyrkogatan 18, 387 22 BORGHOLM
Tel: 485 56 09 10 **Fax:** 485 56 09 09
Email: webben@olandsbladet.se **Web site:** http://www.olandsbladet.se
Freq: Daily; **Cover Price:** Free; **Circ:** 7,667 Unique Users
Advertising Manager: Jörgen Petersson
Language(s): Swedish
ADVERTISING RATES:
SCC .... SEK 36
NATIONAL DAILY & SUNDAY NEWSPAPERS: National Daily Newspapers

OM FÖRSVARSFÖRBUNDET
50434W32K-140
Editorial: Box 5328, 102 47 STOCKHOLM
Tel: 8 402 40 00 **Fax:** 8 20 56 92
Email: redaktion@forsvarsforbundet.se **Web site:** http://www.forsvarsforbundet.se
Freq: 6 issues yearly; **Circ:** 9,000
Editor-in-Chief: Ulrica Jansson; **Advertising Manager:** Ywonne Bjärkenrud; **Publisher:** Ulrica Jansson
Profile: Journal of the Civil Servants' Association.
Language(s): Swedish
BUSINESS: LOCAL GOVERNMENT, LEISURE & RECREATION: Civil Service

OMVÅRDNADSMAGASINET
1644263W56A-338
Editorial: Baldersgatan 1, 114 27 STOCKHOLM
Tel: 8 412 24 00 **Fax:** 8 412 24 24
Web site: http://www.omvardnadsmagasinet.se
Freq: 6 issues yearly; **Circ:** 75,300
Advertising Manager: Efva Bengtsson
Language(s): Swedish
ADVERTISING RATES:
Full Page Colour .... SEK 36000
SCC .... SEK 300
BUSINESS: HEALTH & MEDICAL

OMVÄRLDEN 50303W14C-38
Editorial: Sida, 105 25 STOCKHOLM
Tel: 8 698 50 65 **Fax:** 8 698 56 15
Email: redaktionen@omvarlden.se **Web site:** http://www.omvarlden.nu
Freq: 6 issues yearly; **Circ:** 10,000
Editor-in-Chief: Jesper Bengtsson; **Advertising Manager:** Lisa Ljadas
Profile: Official magazine of SIDA, the Swedish International Development Corporation Agency.
Language(s): Swedish
ADVERTISING RATES:
Full Page Colour .... SEK 20000
SCC .... SEK 125
BUSINESS: COMMERCE, INDUSTRY & MANAGEMENT: International Commerce

ONKOLOGI I SVERIGE
1698530W56A-345
Editorial: Tyra Lundgrens Väg 6, 134 40 GUSTAVSBERG **Tel:** 8 570 105 20
Email: ois@pharma-industry.se **Web site:** http://www.onkologiisverige.se
Freq: 6 issues yearly; **Circ:** 7,500
Language(s): Swedish
BUSINESS: HEALTH & MEDICAL

OPSIS BARNKULTUR 51346W91D-100
Editorial: St. Paulsgatan 13, 118 46 STOCKHOLM
Tel: 8 641 66 68 **Fax:** 86411668
Email: info@opsisbarnkultur.se **Web site:** http://www.opsiskalopsis.se
Date Established: 1986; **Freq:** Quarterly; **Circ:** 2,600
Publisher: Birgitta Fransson
Profile: Journal about culture for children.
Language(s): Swedish
ADVERTISING RATES:
Full Page Colour .... SEK 8000
SCC .... SEK 66.67
CONSUMER: RECREATION & LEISURE: Children & Youth

OPTIK 50625W56E-20
Editorial: Karlbergsvägen 22, 113 27 STOCKHOLM
Tel: 8 612 89 60 **Fax:** 8 612 56 90
Email: optik@radicalpr.se **Web site:** http://www.optikbranschen.se
Date Established: 1978; **Freq:** Monthly; **Circ:** 3,500
Editor: Mats Almegård; **Advertising Manager:** Gunilla Dagerman
Profile: Official journal of the Swedish Optometric Association.
Language(s): Swedish
ADVERTISING RATES:
Full Page Colour .... SEK 19600
SCC .... SEK 163.33
Copy instructions: *Copy Date:* 15 days prior to publication date
BUSINESS: HEALTH & MEDICAL: Optics

OPUS 1804004W76D-282
Editorial: Betaniaplan 3 B, 211 55 MALMÖ
Tel: 40 12 55 90 **Fax:** 40 12 55 90
Email: redaktion@opuspress.se **Web site:** http://www.opuspress.se
Freq: 6 issues yearly; **Circ:** 10,000
Language(s): Swedish
CONSUMER: MUSIC & PERFORMING ARTS: Music

ORD & BILD 51248W84A-180
Editorial: Box 31120, 400 32 GÖTEBORG
Tel: 31 743 99 10 **Fax:** 31 743 99 06
Email: red@tidskriftenordobild.se **Web site:** http://www.tidskriftenordobild.se
Date Established: 1892; **Freq:** 6 issues yearly; **Circ:** 2,000
Editor-in-Chief: Martin Engberg
Profile: Magazine about both visual and literary arts.
Language(s): Swedish
CONSUMER: THE ARTS & LITERARY: Arts

ORDFRONT MAGASIN
51264W84B-150
Editorial: Box 17506, 118 91 STOCKHOLM
Tel: 8 462 44 00 **Fax:** 8 462 44 90
Email: info@ordfront.se **Web site:** http://www.ordfront.se
Freq: Monthly; **Circ:** 20,000
Editor: Annika Hallman; **Advertising Manager:** Elisabeht Tingedal; **Publisher:** Johan Berggren
Profile: Magazine covering international literature, political and cultural issues.
Language(s): Swedish
CONSUMER: THE ARTS & LITERARY: Literary

ÖREBRO MARKNAD
1841360W14A-324
Editorial: HKM Publishing AB, Box 385, 703 47 ÖREBRO **Tel:** 19 10 84 90 **Fax:** 19 10 84 30
Email: stefan.hallenius@hkm.se **Web site:** http://www.hkm.se
Freq: 6 issues yearly; **Circ:** 12,000
Editor-in-Chief: Stefan Hallenius; **Advertising Manager:** Stefan Hallenius; **Publisher:** Stefan Hallenius
Language(s): Swedish
ADVERTISING RATES:
Full Page Colour .... SEK 23500
SCC .... SEK 146,88
BUSINESS: COMMERCE, INDUSTRY & MANAGEMENT

ÖREBROAR'N 634348W72-262
Editorial: Östra Bangatan 26, 703 61 OREBRO
Tel: 19 17 07 80 **Fax:** 19 12 83 20
Email: redaktion@orebroarn.se **Web site:** http://www.orebroarn.se
Date Established: 1988
Circ: 65,300
Editor: Marie Pallhed
Language(s): Swedish
LOCAL NEWSPAPERS

ORGELFORUM 51091W76D-190
Editorial: Västra Storgatan 7B, 694 30 HALLSBERG
Tel: 582 158 16
Email: dag@orgelsallskapet.se **Web site:** http://www.orgelsallskapet.se
Freq: Quarterly; **Circ:** 1,000
Editor-in-Chief: Dag Edholm; **Advertising Manager:** Dag Edholm; **Publisher:** Dag Edholm
Profile: Journal of the Swedish Organ Society covering all aspects of organ music and organ building.
Language(s): Swedish
Readership: Read by professional and amateur organists, organ builders and musicologists.
CONSUMER: MUSIC & PERFORMING ARTS: Music

ÖRGRYTE-HÄRLANDA TIDNING
634353W80-275
Editorial: 421 31 VÄSTRA FRÖLUNDA
Tel: 317 205 516 **Fax:** 314 954 00
Email: redaktion@gbg.direktpress.se **Web site:** http://www.ohposten.se
Date Established: 1994; **Freq:** Monthly; **Circ:** 32,000
Managing Director: Jan Larsson; **Publisher:** Michael "figge" Falk
Profile: Newspaper covering local news for Örgryte and Härlanda.
Language(s): Swedish
Readership: Read by local residents.
CONSUMER: RURAL & REGIONAL INTEREST

ORIENTALISKA STUDIER
51325W90-64
Editorial: Orientaliska Studier, Stockholms Universitet, Kräftriket 4B, 106 91 STOCKHOLM
Tel: 8 16 17 75 **Fax:** 8 15 54 64
Email: redaktion@orientaliskastudier.se **Web site:** http://www.orientaliskastudier.se
Date Established: 1969; **Freq:** Quarterly; **Circ:** 500
Editor: Fredrik Fällman; **Publisher:** Torbjörn Lodén
Profile: Journal about Oriental studies.
Language(s): Swedish
CONSUMER: ETHNIC

ORKESTER JOURNALEN - OM JAZZ 51092W76D-250
Editorial: Box 16344, 103 26 STOCKHOLM
Tel: 8 407 17 45 **Fax:** 8 407 17 49
Email: oj@swedejazz.com **Web site:** http://www.oj-jazz.com
Freq: Monthly; **Circ:** 3,500
Editor: Lars Grip; **Editor-in-Chief:** Lars Grip; **Advertising Manager:** Ewert Duell Media Ab; **Publisher:** Lars Grip
Profile: Magazine for jazz fans.
Language(s): Swedish
ADVERTISING RATES:
Full Page Colour .... SEK 8100
SCC .... SEK 67.5
CONSUMER: MUSIC & PERFORMING ARTS: Music

ORNIS SVECICA 1663294W81F-101
Editorial: c/o Sören Svensson, Ekologiska inst., Ekologihuset, 223 62 LUND **Tel:** 46 222 38 21
Fax: 46 222 47 16
Email: soren.svensson@zooekol.lu.se **Web site:** http://www.sofnet.org
Freq: Half-yearly; **Circ:** 1,300
Editor: Dennis Hasselquist; **Editor-in-Chief:** Sören Svensson; **Publisher:** Sören Svensson
Language(s): Swedish
CONSUMER: ANIMALS & PETS: Birds

ÖRNSKÖLDSVIKS ALLEHANDA
50823W67B-6100
Editorial: Box 110, 891 23 ÖRNSKÖLDSVIK
Tel: 660 29 55 00 **Fax:** 660 145 85
Email: oaredaktion@allehanda.se **Web site:** http://www.allehanda.se
Date Established: 1894
Circ: 17,400
Publisher: Jimmie Näslund
Language(s): Swedish
ADVERTISING RATES:
Full Page Colour .... SEK 32160
SCC .... SEK 160.80
REGIONAL DAILY & SUNDAY NEWSPAPERS: Regional Daily Newspapers

ÖRNSKÖLDSVIKS ALLEHANDA; WEBBREDAKTIONEN
752335W67B-9830
Editorial: Box 110, 891 23 ÖRNSKÖLDSVIK
Tel: 660 29 55 00
Email: webbredaktionen@allehanda.se **Web site:** http://www.allehanda.se
Freq: Daily; **Circ:** 20,000 Unique Users
Language(s): Swedish
REGIONAL DAILY & SUNDAY NEWSPAPERS: Regional Daily Newspapers

ORTOPEDISKT MAGASIN
634661W56A-303
Editorial: Everöd 19, 273 93 TOMELILLA
Tel: 417 310 26 **Fax:** 41731261
Email: borje@ortopedisktmagasin.se **Web site:** http://www.ortopedisktmagasin.se
Freq: Quarterly; **Circ:** 2,000
Advertising Manager: Börje Olsson; **Publisher:** Olle Svensson
Language(s): Swedish
BUSINESS: HEALTH & MEDICAL

ORUSTBLADET 752354W74C-325
Editorial: Box 91, 471 22 SKÄRHAMN
Tel: 304 67 12 42 **Fax:** 304674277
Freq: Monthly; **Circ:** 6,500
Advertising Manager: Staffan Nyström
Language(s): Swedish
CONSUMER: WOMEN'S INTEREST CONSUMER MAGAZINES: Home & Family

OSQLEDAREN 51486W83-93
Editorial: THS, 100 44 STOCKHOLM
Tel: 8 790 98 70 **Fax:** 8 20 62 03
Email: osqledaren@ths.kth.se **Web site:** http://www.ths.kth.se/osqledaren
Date Established: 1944; **Freq:** 6 issues yearly; **Circ:** 20,000
Editor-in-Chief: Marina Rantanen; **Publisher:** Marina Rantanen
Profile: Official publication of the students' organisation at the Royal Technical College (KTH). Covers news, articles and information about KTH and its activities and provides a forum for general debate.
Language(s): Swedish
Readership: Read by students and university staff.
ADVERTISING RATES:
Full Page Colour .... SEK 20900
SCC .... SEK 333.33
CONSUMER: STUDENT PUBLICATIONS

OSTEOPOROSNYTT 1639961W56A-337
Editorial: Riksföreningen Osteoporotiker, 414 51 GÖTEBORG **Tel:** 31 25 35 98
Email: osteo@telia.com **Web site:** http://www.osteoporos.org
Freq: Quarterly; **Circ:** 6,000
Editor: Wiva Asplund
Language(s): Swedish
BUSINESS: HEALTH & MEDICAL

ÖSTERLENMAGASINET
634352W72-265
Editorial: Storgatan 36A, 272 31 SIMRISHAMN
Tel: 414 179 80 **Fax:** 41428999
Web site: http://www.osterlenmagasinet.se
Date Established: 1986; **Freq:** Weekly; **Circ:** 20,000
Advertising Manager: Patrik Uttelius; **Publisher:** Dan Andersson
Profile: Newspaper featuring local news in Simrishamn.
Language(s): Swedish
ADVERTISING RATES:
Full Page Colour .... SEK 40000
SCC .... SEK 250
Copy instructions: *Copy Date:* 15 days prior to publication date
LOCAL NEWSPAPERS

ÖSTERMALMSNYTT 634355W72-270
Editorial: Box 5290, 102 46 STOCKHOLM
Tel: 8 545 870 70 **Fax:** 8 545 870 89
Email: info@direktpress.se **Web site:** http://www.ostermalmsnytt.se
Date Established: 1968; **Freq:** Weekly; **Cover Price:** Free; **Circ:** 41,700

Managing Director: Peter Rydås; Advertising Manager: Helena Englund; Publisher: Johan Bratt
Profile: Newspaper featuring local news from Östermalm.
Language(s): Swedish
ADVERTISING RATES:
Full Page Colour .... SEK 17850
SCC .... SEK 89.25
LOCAL NEWSPAPERS

ÖSTERSUNDS-POSTEN
50826W67B-6250
Editorial: Box 720, 831 28 ÖSTERSUND
Tel: 63 16 16 00 Fax: 63 16 16 55
Email: redaktion@op.se Web site: http://www.op.se
Circ: 28,800
Editor: Conny Pettersson; Editor-in-Chief: Hans Lindeberg; Publisher: Per Åhlin
Language(s): Swedish
ADVERTISING RATES:
Full Page Colour .... SEK 41952
SCC .... SEK 209.76
Copy instructions: *Copy Date:* 7 days prior to publication date
REGIONAL DAILY & SUNDAY NEWSPAPERS: Regional Daily Newspapers

ÖSTERSUNDS-POSTEN; INTERNET/WEBREDAKTIONEN
751871W67B-9855
Editorial: Box 720, 831 28 ÖSTERSUND
Tel: 63 16 16 59 Fax: 63161655
Email: webmaster@op.se Web site: http://www.op.se
Freq: Daily; Circ: 30,300 Unique Users
Editor-in-Chief: Hans Lindeberg
Language(s): Swedish
REGIONAL DAILY & SUNDAY NEWSPAPERS: Regional Daily Newspapers

ÖSTGÖTA CORRESPONDENTEN
50803W67B-6300
Editorial: 581 89 LINKÖPING Tel: 13 28 00 00
Fax: 13 28 03 24
Email: nyhet@corren.se Web site: http://www.corren.se
Date Established: 1838
Circ: 53,300
Editor: Fredrik Kylberg; Publisher: Charlotta Friborg
Language(s): Swedish
ADVERTISING RATES:
Full Page Colour .... SEK 64360
SCC .... SEK 301.32
REGIONAL DAILY & SUNDAY NEWSPAPERS: Regional Daily Newspapers

ÖSTGÖTA CORRESPONDENTEN; INTERNET-/ WEBBREDAKTIONEN
752336W67B-9920
Editorial: 581 89 LINKÖPING Tel: 13 28 00 00
Fax: 13 28 04 24
Email: itred@corren.se Web site: http://www.corren.se
Freq: Daily; Circ: 36,291 Unique Users
Language(s): Swedish
REGIONAL DAILY & SUNDAY NEWSPAPERS: Regional Daily Newspapers

ÖSTRAN / NYHETERNA - OSKARSHAMN; NYHETERNA.NET
1843543W65A-992
Editorial: Box 4, 572 21 OSKARSHAMN
Tel: 491 772 22 Fax: 49184349
Email: hans.hedenmalm@ostran.se Web site: http://www.nyheterna.net
Circ: 9,655
Advertising Manager: Mats Larsson; Publisher: Lennart Holmerin
Language(s): Swedish
NATIONAL DAILY & SUNDAY NEWSPAPERS: National Daily Newspapers

ÖSTRAN / NYHETERNA; OSTRAN.SE
1843551W65A-999
Editorial: Box 612, 391 26 KALMAR Tel: 480 613 00
Fax: 48087545
Email: hans.hedenmalm@ostran.se Web site: http://www.ostran.se
Freq: Daily; Cover Price: Free; Circ: 32,000 Unique Users
Advertising Manager: Mats Larsson; Publisher: Lennart Holmerin
Language(s): Swedish
NATIONAL DAILY & SUNDAY NEWSPAPERS: National Daily Newspapers

OTC - PLACERAREN
751159W1A-205
Editorial: Box 7137, 103 87 STOCKHOLM
Tel: 8 31 90 85 Fax: 317760601
Email: otc@otcplacer.a.se

Date Established: 1997; Freq: Monthly; Circ: 11,111
Publisher: Johan Lindstedt
Language(s): Swedish
BUSINESS: FINANCE & ECONOMICS

OUTSIDE
1741170W75L-192
Editorial: Smålandsgatan 6, 352 35 VÄXJO
Tel: 470 264 30
Email: info@outsideonline.se Web site: http://www.outsideonline.se
Freq: Monthly; Circ: 17,000
Editor-in-Chief: Glenn Mattsing; Advertising Manager: Patrik Adaktusson; Publisher: Jonas Hollander
Language(s): Swedish
ADVERTISING RATES:
Full Page Colour .... SEK 22900
SCC .... SEK 190.83
Copy instructions: *Copy Date:* 30 days prior to publication date
CONSUMER: SPORT: Outdoor

OXIEBLADET
751076W80-710
Editorial: Box 99, 238 22 OXIE Tel: 40 54 61 04
Email: oxiebladet@swipnet.se
Freq: Monthly; Circ: 4,000
Publisher: Lars Persson
Language(s): Swedish
CONSUMER: RURAL & REGIONAL INTEREST

PÅ GRÄNSEN
750742W14L-170
Editorial: Box 1220, 111 82 STOCKHOLM
Tel: 8 405 05 40 Fax: 8247146
Email: johan.lindgren@tullkust.se Web site: http://www.tullkust.se
Freq: 6 issues yearly; Circ: 3,800
Editor: Björn Roos
Language(s): Swedish
BUSINESS: COMMERCE, INDUSTRY & MANAGEMENT: Trade Unions

PÅ KRYSS
51333W91A-100
Editorial: Box 1189, 131 27 NACKA STRAND
Tel: 8 448 28 80
Email: pakryss@sxk.se Web site: http://www.pakryss.se
Freq: 6 issues yearly; Circ: 27,600
Editor-in-Chief: Micke Westin; Publisher: Per Berkhuizen
Profile: Sailing magazine covering power cruisers, sailing yachts and long distance sailing. Includes information about coastal cruising and ocean racing. Published by the Swedish Cruising Association.
Language(s): Swedish
Readership: Read by boat owners.
ADVERTISING RATES:
Full Page Colour .... SEK 28350
SCC .... SEK 236.25
CONSUMER: RECREATION & LEISURE: Boating & Yachting

PÅ TAL OM STOCKHOLM
752031W80-715
Editorial: 122 88 ENSKEDE Tel: 8 39 91 40
Fax: 8 659 26 25
Email: talomstockholm@iris.se Web site: http://www.irisintermedia.se
Freq: Weekly; Circ: 900
Editor: Helena lagercrantz
Language(s): Swedish
CONSUMER: RURAL & REGIONAL INTEREST

PÅ VÄG
1803897W42B-121
Editorial: Svevia, Box 4018, 171 04 SOLNA
Tel: 8 404 10 00 Fax: 8 404 10 50
Email: redaktor.pavag@svevia.se Web site: http://www.svevia.se/Nyheter/Tidningen-Pa-Vag
Freq: 6 issues yearly; Circ: 16,000
Editor: Johanna Berggren; Publisher: Charlotte Sandström
Language(s): Swedish
BUSINESS: CONSTRUCTION: Roads

PÅ VÄG
51495W62A-457
Editorial: Box 120, 161 26 BROMMA
Tel: 8 653 20 16 Fax: 8 650 80 11
Email: pavag@waldorf.se Web site: http://www.waldorf.se
Date Established: 1960; Freq: Quarterly; Circ: 2,500
Editor: Göran Fant; Publisher: Göran Fant
Language(s): Swedish
BUSINESS: CHURCH & SCHOOL EQUIPMENT & EDUCATION: Education

PACKMARKNADEN
50443W35-20
Editorial: Box 601, 251 06 HELSINGBORG
Tel: 42 490 19 00 Fax: 42 490 19 99
Email: packnet@mentoronline.se Web site: http://www.packnet.se
Date Established: 1978; Freq: Monthly; Circ: 4,000
Editor: Peter Nygren; Editor-in-Chief: Marcus Petersson; Advertising Manager: Mats Byrlén
Profile: Magazine for the Scandinavian packaging trade.

Language(s): Swedish
ADVERTISING RATES:
Full Page Colour .... SEK 29400
SCC .... SEK 183.75
BUSINESS: PACKAGING & BOTTLING

PÅHUGGET
1698600W10-95
Editorial: Box 3414, 165 23 HASSELBY
Tel: 8 89 29 19
Email: dahllof@pahugget.se Web site: http://www.pahugget.se
Freq: Weekly; Circ: 5,000
Publisher: Gunnar Dahllöf
Language(s): Swedish
ADVERTISING RATES:
Full Page Colour .... SEK 5000
BUSINESS: MATERIALS HANDLING

PALETTEN
51249W84A-200
Editorial: Heurlins Plats 1, 413 01 GÖTEBORG
Tel: 31 743 99 15 Fax: 31 743 99 16
Email: info@paletten.net Web site: http://www.paletten.net
Date Established: 1940; Freq: Quarterly; Circ: 2,000
Editor-in-Chief: Sophie Allgård; Advertising Manager: Christian Chambert
Profile: Magazine containing contemporary art, video performance and painting. Includes photos and reviews.
Language(s): Swedish
Readership: Aimed at artists, arts students and gallery visitors.
CONSUMER: THE ARTS & LITERARY: Arts

PAPPER & KONTOR
50485W41B-40
Editorial: Blå Kontoret, Drottninggatan 83, 111 60 STOCKHOLM Tel: 8 32 38 92
Email: nina.enstrom@papperkontor.nu
Freq: 6 issues yearly; Circ: 1,100
Publisher: Nina Enström
Profile: Magazine about stationery and office accessories.
Language(s): Swedish
ADVERTISING RATES:
Full Page Colour .... SEK 13750
SCC .... SEK 241.66
BUSINESS: PRINTING & STATIONERY: Stationery

PARKINSONJOURNALEN
1803894W56A-349
Editorial: Box 1386, 172 27 SUNDBYBERG
Tel: 8 546 405 27 Fax: 854640439
Email: parkinsonforbundet.kansli@telia.com Web site: http://www.parkinsonforbundet.se
Freq: Quarterly; Circ: 8,000
Editor: Curt Lundberg; Publisher: Karl-Gunnar Skoog
Language(s): Swedish
BUSINESS: HEALTH & MEDICAL

PARNASS
51265W84B-165
Editorial: c/o Söderbergh, Lädersättravägen 15, 176 70 JÄRFÄLLA Tel: 8 584 904 32
Email: catharina.soderbergh@telia.com Web site: http://www.dels.nu
Freq: Quarterly; Circ: 1,800
Editor: Catharina Söderbergh; Publisher: Bo Malmsten
Profile: Literary journal containing author profiles and articles.
Language(s): Swedish
CONSUMER: THE ARTS & LITERARY: Literary

PASSION FOR BUSINESS
1841181W74A-176
Editorial: c/o Network 21, Stureplan 4A, 114 35 STOCKHOLM Tel: 735206600
Email: redaktionen@passionforbusiness.se Web site: http://www.passionforbusiness.se
Freq: Quarterly - 6-8 ggr; Circ: 20,200
Editor: Åsa Mattsson; Publisher: Anna Carrfors Bråkenhielm
Language(s): Swedish
CONSUMER: WOMEN'S INTEREST CONSUMER MAGAZINES: Women's Interest

PATENT EYE
1625823W14F-91
Editorial: Box 3457, 103 69 STOCKHOLM
Tel: 8 406 09 00 Fax: 8 20 38 10
Email: mail@brandeye.se Web site: http://www.brandeye.se
Freq: 6 issues yearly; Circ: 600
Editor-in-Chief: Christer Löfgren
Language(s): Swedish
ADVERTISING RATES:
Full Page Colour .... SEK 17000
SCC .... SEK 141.66
BUSINESS: COMMERCE, INDUSTRY & MANAGEMENT: Training & Recruitment

PC FÖR ALLA
50238W5B-160
Editorial: Karlbergsvägen 77, 106 78 STOCKHOLM
Tel: 8 453 60 00
Email: pfa@idg.se Web site: http://pcforalla.idg.se

Freq: Monthly; Circ: 57,500
Editor: Jan Sandbladh; Publisher: Fredrik Agrén
Profile: Computer magazine covering all aspects of information technology.
Language(s): Swedish
Readership: Aimed at small companies and home users.
ADVERTISING RATES:
Full Page Colour .... SEK 70900
SCC .... SEK 590.83
BUSINESS: COMPUTERS & AUTOMATION: Data Processing

PC FÖR ALLA; WWW.PCFORALLA.IDG.SE
1844544W5E-114
Editorial: Karlbergsvägen 77, 106 78 STOCKHOLM
Tel: 8 453 60 00
Email: pfa@idg.se Web site: http://www.pcforalla.idg.se
Freq: Daily; Cover Price: Free; Circ: 180,000 Unique Users
Publisher: Fredrik Agrén
Language(s): Swedish
BUSINESS: COMPUTERS & AUTOMATION: Data Transmission

PC GAMER
51138W78D-238
Editorial: Gävlegatan 22, 113 78 STOCKHOLM
Tel: 8 692 66 00
Email: joakim.bennet@pcgamer.se Web site: http://www.pcgamer.se
Freq: Monthly; Circ: 21,300
Editor-in-Chief: Joakim Bennet; Advertising Manager: Tony Gustavsson
Profile: Magazine about computer games.
Language(s): Swedish
Readership: Read by computer game enthusiasts.
ADVERTISING RATES:
Full Page Colour .... SEK 34900
SCC .... SEK 290.83
CONSUMER: CONSUMER ELECTRONICS: Games

PC GAMER; PCGAMER.SE
1846392W5E-123
Editorial: Gävlegatan 22, 113 78 STOCKHOLM
Tel: 8 692 66 00
Email: joakim.bennet@pcgamer.se Web site: http://www.pcgamer.se
Freq: Daily; Cover Price: Free; Circ: 1,660 Unique Users
Editor: Thomas Petersson; Editor-in-Chief: Joakim Bennet; Publisher: Joakim Bennet
Language(s): Swedish
BUSINESS: COMPUTERS & AUTOMATION: Data Transmission

PC-TIDNINGEN
1640399W5C-83
Editorial: Attundavägen 19A, 168 58 BROMMA
Tel: 8 462 99 33 Fax: 8 579 733 00
Email: redaktion@pctidningen.se Web site: http://www.pctidningen.se
Circ: 31,900
Editor: Markus Dahlberg; Editor-in-Chief: Leif Jonasson; Publisher: Anna Rading Ploman
Language(s): Swedish
ADVERTISING RATES:
Full Page Colour .... SEK 28800
SCC .... SEK 240
BUSINESS: COMPUTERS & AUTOMATION: Professional Personal Computers

PC-TIDNINGEN; PCTIDNINGEN.SE
1846386W5E-122
Editorial: Attundavägen 19A, 168 58 BROMMA
Tel: 8 462 99 33 Fax: 857973300
Email: redaktion@pctidningen.se Web site: http://www.pctidningen.se
Freq: Daily; Cover Price: Free; Circ: 23,400 Unique Users
Publisher: Anna Rading Ploman
Language(s): Swedish
BUSINESS: COMPUTERS & AUTOMATION: Data Transmission

PEABJOURNALEN
1841093W4E-158
Editorial: Peab, Information, 260 92 FÖRSLÖV
Tel: 431 890 00 Fax: 431 45 00 83
Email: gosta.sjostrom@peab.se Web site: http://www.peab.se
Freq: Quarterly; Cover Price: Free; Circ: 5,000
Editor: Gösta Sjöström; Publisher: Gösta Sjöström
Language(s): Swedish
ADVERTISING RATES:
Full Page Colour .... SEK 10000
SCC .... SEK 83,33
BUSINESS: ARCHITECTURE & BUILDING: Building

PEDAGOGISKA MAGASINET
51488W62B-215
Editorial: Box 12239, Segelbåtsvägen 15 Stora Essingen, 102 26 STOCKHOLM Tel: 8 737 65 00
Fax: 8 6190088

Email: pedagogiska.magasinet@lararforbundet.se **Web site:** http://www.pedagogiskamagasinet.net
Freq: Quarterly; **Circ:** 223,600
Editor: Christina Thors; **Advertising Manager:** Evert Norberg
Profile: Magazine covering all aspects of teaching.
Language(s): Swedish
ADVERTISING RATES:
Full Page Colour .... SEK 32000
SCC .... SEK 248.33
BUSINESS: CHURCH & SCHOOL EQUIPMENT & EDUCATION: Education Teachers

PEDAGOGISKA MAGASINET; WEBB
1846668W62A-524
Editorial: Box 12239, 102 26 STOCKHOLM
Tel: 8 737 65 00 **Fax:** 8 619 00 88
Email: pedagogiska.magasinet@lararforbundet.se
Web site: http://www.pedagogiskamagasinet.net
Freq: Daily; **Cover Price:** Free; **Circ:** 22,180 Unique Users
Editor: Christina Thors; **Editor-in-Chief:** Leif Mathiasson; **Advertising Manager:** Maria Hamqvist; **Publisher:** Leif Mathiasson
Language(s): Swedish
ADVERTISING RATES:
SCC .... SEK 50
BUSINESS: CHURCH & SCHOOL EQUIPMENT & EDUCATION: Education

PEJL PÅ BOTKYRKA
1664001W80-849
Editorial: Botkyrka kommun, Munkhättevägen 45, 147 85 TUMBA **Tel:** 8 530 618 05 **Fax:** 8 530 616 36
Email: pejl@botkyrka.se **Web site:** http://www.botkyrka.se/pejl
Freq: 6 issues yearly; **Circ:** 34,000
Editor: Marianne Lundgren; **Publisher:** Kicki Morsing
Language(s): Swedish
CONSUMER: RURAL & REGIONAL INTEREST

PEJLING FRÅN SVENSK MJÖLK
750913W22C-160
Editorial: Box 210, 101 24 STOCKHOLM
Tel: 771 19 19 00 **Fax:** 8 21 83 63
Email: pejling@svenskmjolk.se **Web site:** http://www.svenskmjolk.se/pejling
Freq: Quarterly; **Circ:** 3,500
Editor-in-Chief: Carin Larsson; **Advertising Manager:** Helen Rubnell-Engström; **Publisher:** Inger Myresten
Language(s): Swedish
BUSINESS: FOOD: Food Processing & Packaging

PERSONAL & LEDARSKAP
50288W14A-97
Editorial: Box 5575, 114 85 STOCKHOLM
Tel: 8 545 684 00 **Fax:** 86627350
Email: personal@epok.se **Web site:** http://www.personal-ledarskap.com
Date Established: 1970; **Freq:** Monthly; **Circ:** 14,600
Editor: Linda Badner; **Publisher:** Kent Seifors
Profile: Magazine for and about personnel managers. Covers education, training and development.
Language(s): Swedish
ADVERTISING RATES:
Full Page Colour .... SEK 26000
SCC .... SEK 216.67
Copy instructions: *Copy Date:* 34 days prior to publication date
BUSINESS: COMMERCE, INDUSTRY & MANAGEMENT

PERSONALAKTUELLT
1625602W14L-190
Editorial: Benefit Media, Nybrogatan 35, 114 39 STOCKHOLM **Tel:** 8 66159 99 **Fax:** 8 660 07 70
Email: katarina@personalaktuellt.se **Web site:** http://www.personalaktuellt.se
Freq: Quarterly; **Circ:** 3,000
Editor-in-Chief: Katarina Sand; **Advertising Manager:** Lennart Sundberg
Language(s): Swedish
Copy instructions: *Copy Date:* 21 days prior to publication date
BUSINESS: COMMERCE, INDUSTRY & MANAGEMENT: Trade Unions

PERSPEKTIV PÅ HIV
50601W56A-45
Editorial: Stiftelsen Noaks Ark-Röda korset, Eriksbergsgatan 46, 114 30 STOCKHOLM
Tel: 8 700 46 00 **Fax:** 8 700 46 10
Email: l.g.moberg@telia.com **Web site:** http://www.pphiv.org
Freq: Half-yearly; **Circ:** 7,000
Editor: Lars Moberg; **Publisher:** Lars Moberg
Profile: Magazine about HIV and AIDS, including both the mental and physical care for sufferers.
Language(s): Swedish
Readership: Aimed at people working with HIV and AIDS patients.
BUSINESS: HEALTH & MEDICAL

PETIT MAGAZINE
1804051W74A-167
Editorial: Box 191 74, 104 32 STOCKHOLM
Tel: 8 33 34 65
Email: info@petit-magazine.com **Web site:** http://www.petit-magazine.com
Freq: Quarterly; **Circ:** 20,000
Publisher: Nina Midbrink
Language(s): Swedish
ADVERTISING RATES:
Full Page Colour .... SEK 25000
SCC .... SEK 208.33
CONSUMER: WOMEN'S INTEREST CONSUMER MAGAZINES: Women's Interest

PHARMA INDUSTRY
751361W55-40
Editorial: Tyra Lundgrens väg 6, 134 40 GUSTAVSBERG **Tel:** 8 570 105 20
Email: redaktionen@pharma-industry.se **Web site:** http://www.pharma-industry.se
Freq: 6 issues yearly; **Circ:** 7,600
Publisher: Niclas Ahlberg
Language(s): Swedish
ADVERTISING RATES:
Full Page Colour .... SEK 28500
SCC .... SEK 237.50
BUSINESS: APPLIED SCIENCE & LABORATORIES

PHARMA REPORT
1835476W56A-356
Editorial: Box 17518, 118 91 STOCKHOLM
Tel: 8 546 005 00 **Fax:** 854600599
Email: pharmaonline@nyhetsbrev.se **Web site:** http://www.nyhetsbrev.se
Freq: Monthly - (11nr/år)
Editor: Jonny Sågänger; **Advertising Manager:** Chris Lindström; **Publisher:** Gunnar Loxdal
Language(s): Swedish
BUSINESS: HEALTH & MEDICAL

PHILIPSON SÖDERBERG MAGAZINE
1665964W22A-147
Editorial: Box 29163, 100 52 STOCKHOLM
Tel: 8 598 112 00 **Fax:** 859811241
Email: info@philipsonsoderberg.se **Web site:** http://www.philipsonsoderberg.se
Freq: Quarterly; **Circ:** 33,000
Publisher: Erik Hultberg
Language(s): Swedish
ADVERTISING RATES:
Full Page Colour .... SEK 15510
SCC .... SEK 129.25
BUSINESS: FOOD

PHLINGAN
751002W75J-120
Editorial: GIH:s studentkår, Box 5626, 114 86 STOCKHOLM **Tel:** 8 20 06 18 **Fax:** 8 20 96 80
Email: phlingan@karen.ihs.se **Web site:** http://www.ihstudent.com
Freq: 6 issues yearly; **Circ:** 300
Editor-in-Chief: Gustav Lorenz
Language(s): Swedish
CONSUMER: SPORT: Athletics

PHRENICUS
1697281W56N-213
Editorial: Hantverkarg. 3G, 112 21 STOCKHOLM
Tel: 8 545 559 80
Email: office@schizofreniforbundet.se **Web site:** http://www.schizofreniforbundet.se
Freq: Quarterly; **Circ:** 5,000
Editor: Annica Holmberg; **Publisher:** Rakel Lundgren
Language(s): Swedish
BUSINESS: HEALTH & MEDICAL: Mental Health

PILOTMAGAZINET.SE
1657365W75N-211
Editorial: Stensundsvägen 23 B, 619 30 TROSA
Tel: 8 559 216 75
Email: info@pilotmagazinet.se **Web site:** http://www.pilotmagazinet.se
Freq: 156 times a year; **Cover Price:** Paid; **Circ:** 1,100 Unique Users
Publisher: Tom Svensson
Language(s): Swedish
CONSUMER: SPORT: Flight

PINGIS
51065W75X-100
Editorial: Svenska Bordtennisförbundet, 171 41 SOLNA **Tel:** 8 627 46 54 **Fax:** 8932733
Email: orjan.westberg@bordtennis.rf.se **Web site:** http://www.svenskbordtennis.com
Freq: 6 issues yearly; **Circ:** 10,500
Advertising Manager: Solveig Engstrand; **Publisher:** Ingmar Nygren Bonnier
Profile: Official magazine of the Swedish Table-Tennis Association.
Language(s): Swedish
CONSUMER: SPORT: Other Sport

PIRAJA
1666089W83-155
Editorial: Studentmedia AB, Box 3101, 103 62 STOCKHOLM **Tel:** 8 587 075 00 **Fax:** 8 587 075 01
Email: petrus@studentmedia.se **Web site:** http://www.piraja.se
Freq: Quarterly; **Circ:** 71,400
Editor-in-Chief: Måns Berg; **Managing Director:** Svante Randlert; **Advertising Manager:** Petter Ingmansson; **Publisher:** Teddy Hallin
Language(s): Swedish
ADVERTISING RATES:
Full Page Colour .... SEK 37500
SCC .... SEK 312.50
CONSUMER: STUDENT PUBLICATIONS

PITEÅ-TIDNINGEN
50827W67B-6400
Editorial: Box 193, 941 24 PITEÅ **Tel:** 911 645 00
Email: redaktionen@pitea-tidningen.se **Web site:** http://www.pitea-tidningen.se
Date Established: 1915
Circ: 15,900
Advertising Manager: Eva Lindberg; **Publisher:** Matti Lilja
Language(s): Swedish
ADVERTISING RATES:
Full Page Colour .... SEK 32832
SCC .... SEK 164.16
REGIONAL DAILY & SUNDAY NEWSPAPERS: Regional Daily Newspapers

PITEÅ-TIDNINGEN; PITEA-TIDNINGEN.SE
1843643W65A-1004
Editorial: Box 193, 941 24 PITEÅ **Tel:** 911 645 00
Fax: 91164640
Email: redaktionen@pitea-tidningen.se **Web site:** http://www.pitea-tidningen.se
Freq: Daily; **Cover Price:** Free; **Circ:** 13,677 Unique Users
Advertising Manager: Eva Lindberg; **Publisher:** Matti Lilja
Language(s): Swedish
NATIONAL DAILY & SUNDAY NEWSPAPERS: National Daily Newspapers

PLACERA.NU
1844548W14F-107
Editorial: Box 1399, 111 93 STOCKHOLM
Tel: 8 22 49 15
Email: info@placera.nu **Web site:** http://www.placera.nu
Freq: Daily; **Cover Price:** Free; **Circ:** 25,156 Unique Users
Editor: Frida Andersson
Language(s): Swedish
BUSINESS: COMMERCE, INDUSTRY & MANAGEMENT: Training & Recruitment

PLANERA BYGGA BO
50489W42A-75
Editorial: Boverket, Box 534, 371 23 KARLSKRONA
Tel: 455 35 30 00 **Fax:** 455 35 32 15
Email: pbb@boverket.se **Web site:** http://www.boverket.se
Freq: 6 issues yearly; **Circ:** 2,000
Advertising Manager: Jan Lindén; **Publisher:** Birgitta Frejd
Profile: Official journal of the Swedish National Board of Housing, Planning and Building.
Language(s): Swedish
ADVERTISING RATES:
Full Page Colour .... SEK 17000
SCC .... SEK 141.66
BUSINESS: CONSTRUCTION

PLASTFORUM
50458W39-40
Editorial: Box 601, 251 06 HELSINGBORG
Tel: 42 490 19 00 **Fax:** 42 490 19 99
Email: malin.f@mentoronline.se **Web site:** http://www.plastnet.se
Date Established: 2000; **Freq:** Monthly; **Circ:** 4,600
Editor: Malin Folkesson; **Editor-in-Chief:** Peter Schulz; **Advertising Manager:** Beth Holmkvist; **Publisher:** Peter Schulz
Profile: Journal about the plastics industry.
Language(s): Swedish
ADVERTISING RATES:
Full Page Colour .... SEK 28900
SCC .... SEK 240.83
BUSINESS: PLASTICS & RUBBER

PLÅT & VENT MAGASINET
749804W14E-55
Editorial: Box 17536, 118 91 STOCKHOLM
Tel: 8 762 75 85 **Fax:** 86160072
Email: p&vmagasinet@plr.se **Web site:** http://www.plr.se
Freq: Monthly; **Circ:** 2,500
Advertising Manager: Lennart Gustafsson
Language(s): Swedish
ADVERTISING RATES:
Full Page Colour .... SEK 17500
SCC .... SEK 145.83
Copy instructions: *Copy Date:* 27 days prior to publication date
BUSINESS: COMMERCE, INDUSTRY & MANAGEMENT: Work Study

PLAZA INTERIÖR
51585W4B-50
Editorial: Box 302 10, 104 25 Stockholm, 112 51 STOCKHOLM **Tel:** 8 501 188 00
Email: tove@plazainterior.se **Web site:** http://www.plazainterior.se
Date Established: 1995; **Freq:** Monthly; **Circ:** 34,900
Advertising Manager: Ulla Bergman
Profile: Magazine concerning decorating and interior design.
Language(s): Swedish
Readership: Aimed at professionals and those generally interested in interior design.
ADVERTISING RATES:
Full Page Colour .... SEK 40500
SCC .... SEK 329.16
BUSINESS: ARCHITECTURE & BUILDING: Interior Design & Flooring

PLAZA KVINNA
51610W74A-63
Editorial: Box 30210, 104 25 Stockholm, 112 51 STOCKHOLM **Tel:** 8 501 188 00 **Fax:** 8 501 188 01
Email: redaktion@plazakvinna.com **Web site:** http://www.plazakvinna.com
Freq: Monthly; **Circ:** 38,700
Advertising Manager: Therese Fernberg; **Publisher:** Jennie Birgmark
Profile: Magazine containing articles on fashion, beauty, travel, cars and boats. Also contains interviews and profiles.
Language(s): Swedish
Readership: Aimed at modern, well-educated women with a high disposable income.
ADVERTISING RATES:
Full Page Colour .... SEK 38000
SCC .... SEK 316.66
Copy instructions: *Copy Date:* 35 days prior to publication date
CONSUMER: WOMEN'S INTEREST CONSUMER MAGAZINES: Women's Interest

PLAZA MAGAZINE
51611W86C-100
Editorial: Box 30210, 104 25 Stockholm, 112 51 STOCKHOLM **Tel:** 8 501 188 00 **Fax:** 8 501 188 01
Email: info@plazamagazine.com **Web site:** http://www.plazamagazine.se
Date Established: 1994; **Freq:** Monthly -,10 nr/år; **Circ:** 18,200
Editor: Anders Kährström; **Publisher:** Elin af Klintberg
Profile: Magazine containing articles on fashion, travel, cars and boats. Also contains interviews and profiles.
Language(s): Swedish
Readership: Aimed at modern, well-educated men with a high disposable income.
ADVERTISING RATES:
Full Page Colour .... SEK 45000
SCC .... SEK 375
Copy instructions: *Copy Date:* 32 days prior to publication date
CONSUMER: ADULT & GAY MAGAZINES: Men's Lifestyle Magazines

PLAZA STORA; HUS, KÖK & BADGUIDEN
1841182W74C-519
Editorial: Box 3210, 104 25 Stockholm, 112 51 STOCKHOLM **Tel:** 8 501 188 00 **Fax:** 8 457 80 80
Email: info@plazapublishing.se **Web site:** http://www.plazastora.se
Freq: Quarterly - (6 nr/år); **Circ:** 50,000
Advertising Manager: Michael Mirahmadi
Language(s): Swedish
ADVERTISING RATES:
Full Page Colour .... SEK 39500
SCC .... SEK 329.17
CONSUMER: WOMEN'S INTEREST CONSUMER MAGAZINES: Home & Family

PLAZA WATCH
1803855W52B-1
Editorial: Plaza Publishing Group, Box 30210, 104 25 Stockholm, 112 51 STOCKHOLM **Tel:** 8 501 188 00
Fax: 8 501 188 01
Email: info@plazawatch.com **Web site:** http://www.plazawatch.com
Freq: Half-yearly; **Circ:** 30,000
Editor: Paul Sundvik; **Editor-in-Chief:** Anders Modig; **Publisher:** Christopher Östlund
Language(s): Swedish
BUSINESS: GIFT TRADE: Clocks & Watches

POCKETTIDNINGEN R
51267W82-207
Editorial: Stora Nygatan 31, 111 27 STOCKHOLM
Tel: 703 58 56 37
Email: redaktion@pockettidningenr.se **Web site:** http://www.pockettidningenr.se
Date Established: 1970; **Freq:** Quarterly; **Circ:** 5,000
Publisher: Kurt Nurmi
Profile: Magazine focusing on Swedish social politics, contains debate articles about changes in society.
Language(s): Swedish
CONSUMER: CURRENT AFFAIRS & POLITICS

POKER MAGAZINE
1681917W79F-126
Editorial: Birger Jarlsgatan 20, 114 34 STOCKHOLM
Tel: 8 653 59 00 **Fax:** 8 440 40 77
Email: info@pokermagazine.se **Web site:** http://www.pokermagazine.se
Freq: 6 issues yearly; **Circ:** 30,000
Editor-in-Chief: Murat Sahan; **Managing Director:** Krister Bengtsson; **Advertising Manager:** Carl Rinman; **Publisher:** Krister Bengtsson
Language(s): Swedish
ADVERTISING RATES:
Full Page Colour .... SEK 45000
SCC .... SEK 375
CONSUMER: HOBBIES & DIY: Games & Puzzles

POLISTIDNINGEN 50424W32F-60
Editorial: Box 5583, 114 85 STOCKHOLM
Tel: 8 676 97 00 **Fax:** 8 23 24 10
Email: polistidningen@polisforbundet.se **Web site:** http://www.polistidningen.se
Freq: 6 issues yearly; **Circ:** 22,700
Advertising Manager: Nina Flink
Profile: Journal containing information, articles, news and interviews concerning the Swedish police force.
Language(s): Swedish
ADVERTISING RATES:
Full Page Colour .... SEK 19500
SCC .... SEK 162.50
BUSINESS: LOCAL GOVERNMENT, LEISURE & RECREATION: Police

POLYMERVÄRLDEN 634682W39-60
Editorial: Box 2136, 250 02 HELSINGBORG
Tel: 42 13 85 00 **Fax:** 42 12 20 75
Email: polyinfo@polymervarlden.com **Web site:** http://www.polymervarlden.com
Date Established: 1995; **Freq:** Monthly; **Circ:** 5,000
Editor-in-Chief: Arne Jacobson; **Advertising Manager:** Maria Andersson; **Publisher:** Arne Jacobson
Profile: Magazine containing information about plastic and rubber.
Language(s): Swedish
Readership: Read by decision makers in the engineering industry.
ADVERTISING RATES:
Full Page Colour .... SEK 22000
SCC .... SEK 183.33
BUSINESS: PLASTICS & RUBBER

PONTON 634684W84B-258
Editorial: Punkt Medis, Box 17 604, 118 92 STOCKHOLM **Tel:** 8 508 308 23
Email: skriv@ponton.nu **Web site:** http://www.ponton.nu
Date Established: 1998; **Freq:** Quarterly; **Circ:** 1,200
Editor: Martina Lowden; **Publisher:** Staffan Engstrand
Language(s): Swedish
CONSUMER: THE ARTS & LITERARY: Literary

POPULÄR HÄLSA 1842200W74G-219
Editorial: Box 7438, 103 91 STOCKHOLM
Tel: 8 500 084 90
Email: daniel.pasztor@adaptionmedia.se **Web site:** http://www.popularhalsa.se
Freq: Quarterly; **Cover Price:** Free; **Circ:** 125,000
Language(s): Swedish
CONSUMER: WOMEN'S INTEREST CONSUMER MAGAZINES: Slimming & Health

POPULÄR HISTORIA 51391W94X-85
Editorial: Box 1206, 221 05 LUND **Tel:** 46 33 34 60
Fax: 46 18 96 85
Email: red@popularhistoria.se **Web site:** http://www.popularhistoria.se
Date Established: 1991; **Freq:** Monthly; **Circ:** 34,600
Publisher: Magnus Bergsten
Profile: History magazine.
Language(s): Swedish
ADVERTISING RATES:
Full Page Colour .... SEK 37400
SCC .... SEK 311.66
CONSUMER: OTHER CLASSIFICATIONS: Miscellaneous

POWER MAGAZINE 634687W31A-83
Editorial: Box 83, 239 21 SKANÖR **Tel:** 40 47 29 39
Email: power.magazine@telia.com **Web site:** http://www.powermagazine.com
Date Established: 1975; **Freq:** 6 issues yearly; **Circ:** 26,300
Editor-in-Chief: Kjell Gustafson; **Advertising Manager:** Erik Stigsson; **Publisher:** Kjell Gustafson
Language(s): Swedish
BUSINESS: MOTOR TRADE: Motor Trade Accessories

PRAKTIKAN 51493W56B-132
Editorial: Praktikertjänst AB, 103 55 STOCKHOLM
Tel: 8 789 40 00
Web site: http://www.ptj.se
Freq: 6 issues yearly; **Circ:** 16,800
Editor-in-Chief: Malin Bergh; **Advertising Manager:** Lisa Claesson
Language(s): Swedish
BUSINESS: HEALTH & MEDICAL: Nursing

PRAKTISKT BÅTÄGANDE 1625783W91A-301
Editorial: Gävlegatan 22C, 113 78 STOCKHOLM
Tel: 8 692 01 60 **Fax:** 86509710
Email: red@praktisktbatagande.se **Web site:** http://www.praktisktbatagande.se
Freq: Monthly; **Circ:** 20,900
Editor: Johannes Nordemar; **Editor-in-Chief:** Samuel Karlsson; **Advertising Manager:** Patrik Rehn
Language(s): Swedish
ADVERTISING RATES:
Full Page Colour .... SEK 19800
SCC .... SEK 165
Copy instructions: *Copy Date:* 14 days prior to publication date
CONSUMER: RECREATION & LEISURE: Boating & Yachting

PRIMA 1643943W14L-191
Editorial: AB Previa, Box 4080, 171 04 SOLNA
Tel: 8 627 43 00 **Fax:** 8 627 43 99
Email: informationsavdelningen@previa.se **Web site:** http://www.previa.se
Freq: Quarterly; **Circ:** 30,000
Editor: Katrin Malm
Language(s): Swedish
BUSINESS: COMMERCE, INDUSTRY & MANAGEMENT: Trade Unions

PRIME TIME MAGAZINE 1809875W89A-69
Editorial: Identitet c/o Community, Gustav Adolfs Torg 10B, 211 39 MALMÖ **Tel:** 40 66 55 792
Fax: 40 66 55 799
Email: redaktion@primetimemagazine.se **Web site:** http://www.primetimemagazine.se
Freq: Half-yearly; **Circ:** 65,000
Editor-in-Chief: Pelle Estborn
Language(s): Swedish
CONSUMER: HOLIDAYS & TRAVEL: Travel

PRIVATA AFFÄRER 50172W1F-75
Editorial: Sveavägen 53, 105 44 STOCKHOLM
Tel: 8 736 53 00 **Fax:** 8312560
Email: red@privataaffarer.se **Web site:** http://www.privataaffarer.se
Date Established: 1978; **Freq:** Monthly; **Circ:** 59,500
Advertising Manager: Christopher Grenö; **Publisher:** Per Hammarlund
Profile: Financial publication specialising in private business.
Language(s): Swedish
ADVERTISING RATES:
Full Page Colour .... SEK 61400
SCC .... SEK 511.66
BUSINESS: FINANCE & ECONOMICS: Investment

PRIVATA AFFÄRER PLACERINGSGUIDEN 1625554W74M-171
Editorial: c/o Privata Affärer, 105 44 STOCKHOLM
Tel: 8 736 53 00
Email: placeringsguiden@privataaffarer.se **Web site:** http://www.privataaffarer.se
Freq: Monthly; **Circ:** 31,800
Editor: Jan Sterner; **Publisher:** Per Hammarlund
Language(s): Swedish
ADVERTISING RATES:
Full Page Colour .... SEK 29000
SCC .... SEK 241.67
CONSUMER: WOMEN'S INTEREST CONSUMER MAGAZINES: Personal Finance

PRIVATA AFFÄRER; PRIVATAAFFARER.SE 1843641W1A-216
Editorial: Bonnier Tidskrifter AB, 105 44 STOCKHOLM **Tel:** 8 736 53 00 **Fax:** 8312560
Email: red@privataaffarer.se **Web site:** http://www.privataaffarer.se
Freq: Daily; **Cover Price:** Free; **Circ:** 32,009 Unique Users
Language(s): Swedish
BUSINESS: FINANCE & ECONOMICS

PRO HOCKEY 634691W75A-80
Editorial: Egmont Kärnan AB, 205 08 MALMO
Tel: 40 693 94 00 **Fax:** 406939549
Email: prohockey@egmont.se **Web site:** http://www.prohockey.egmont.se
Date Established: 1992; **Freq:** Monthly; **Circ:** 11,400
Editor: Linus Hugosson
Profile: Magazine covering all aspects of hockey.
Language(s): Swedish
Readership: Read by players, club members and coaches.
CONSUMER: SPORT

PROCESS NORDIC 1639306W14A-288
Editorial: Box 72001, 181 72 LIDINGÖ
Tel: 8 670 41 00 **Fax:** 8 661 64 55
Email: processnordic@mentoronline.se **Web site:** http://www.processnet.se
Freq: Monthly; **Circ:** 19,000
Editor-in-Chief: Sverker Nyman; **Advertising Manager:** Stephan Martins; **Publisher:** Marie Granmar
Language(s): Swedish
ADVERTISING RATES:
Full Page Colour .... SEK 48600
SCC .... SEK 303.75
BUSINESS: COMMERCE, INDUSTRY & MANAGEMENT

PROCESS NORDIC; PROCESSNET.SE 1846480W14A-341
Editorial: Box 72001, 181 72 LIDINGÖ
Tel: 8 670 41 00 **Fax:** 8 661 64 55
Email: processnordic@mentoronline.se **Web site:** http://www.processnet.se
Freq: Daily; **Cover Price:** Free; **Circ:** 2,500 Unique Users
Editor-in-Chief: Sverker Nyman; **Publisher:** Sverker Nyman
Language(s): Swedish
BUSINESS: COMMERCE, INDUSTRY & MANAGEMENT

PRODUKTAKTUELLT 1623596W4E-151
Editorial: Box 6910, 102 39 STOCKHOLM
Tel: 8 459 24 00 **Fax:** 8 660 75 22
Email: press@produktaktuellt.se **Web site:** http://www.produktaktuellt.se
Freq: Quarterly; **Circ:** 14,900
Editor: Stefan Karlebo
Language(s): Swedish
ADVERTISING RATES:
Full Page Colour .... SEK 23800
SCC .... SEK 198.33
BUSINESS: ARCHITECTURE & BUILDING: Building

PROFESSIONELL DEMOLERING 1623613W19A-121
Editorial: Box 786, 191 27 SOLLENTUNA
Tel: 8 631 90 70 **Fax:** 8 585 700 47
Email: info@pdworld.com **Web site:** http://www.pdworld.com
Freq: Quarterly; **Circ:** 5,100
Publisher: Jan Hermansson
Language(s): Swedish
ADVERTISING RATES:
Full Page Colour .... SEK 16900
BUSINESS: ENGINEERING & MACHINERY

PROFORMIA HÄLSA 752082W75J-140
Editorial: Box 15128, 167 15 BROMMA
Tel: 8 517 008 72
Email: info@proformia.se **Web site:** http://www.proformia.se
Date Established: 1997; **Freq:** 6 issues yearly; **Circ:** 5,000
Editor: Susanne Colliander; **Publisher:** Erland Colliander
Profile: Magazine focusing on athletics.
Language(s): Swedish
CONSUMER: SPORT: Athletics

PROLETÄREN 624435W82-212
Editorial: Box 31187, 400 32 GOTEBORG
Tel: 31 24 45 44 **Fax:** 31244464
Email: red@proletaren.se **Web site:** http://www.proletaren.se
Date Established: 1970
Circ: 3,400
Editor: Lars Rothelius
Profile: Communist newspaper covering national and international news, current affairs and politics.
Language(s): Swedish
Readership: Read by party members.
ADVERTISING RATES:
Full Page Colour .... SEK 6000
SCC .... SEK 30
CONSUMER: CURRENT AFFAIRS & POLITICS

PROLETÄREN; PROLETAREN.SE 1844813W65A-1038
Editorial: Box 31187, 400 32 GOTEBORG
Tel: 31 24 45 44 **Fax:** 31 24 44 64
Email: red@proletaren.se **Web site:** http://www.proletaren.se
Freq: Daily; **Cover Price:** Free; **Circ:** 2,000 Unique Users
Editor: Johan Wiman; **Publisher:** Lars Rothelius
Language(s): Swedish
NATIONAL DAILY & SUNDAY NEWSPAPERS: National Daily Newspapers

PROPENSIONÄREN 50997W74N-105
Editorial: Box 3274, 103 65 STOCKHOLM
Tel: 8 701 67 00 **Fax:** 8 20 33 58
Email: bettan.andersson@pro.se **Web site:** http://pensionaren.pro.se
Date Established: 1948; **Freq:** Monthly - 9 ggr/år; **Circ:** 303,200
Advertising Manager: Jhonny Sandin; **Publisher:** Bettan Andersson
Profile: Magazine for Swedish pensioners.
Language(s): Swedish
ADVERTISING RATES:
Full Page Colour .... SEK 43900
SCC .... SEK 365.83
CONSUMER: WOMEN'S INTEREST CONSUMER MAGAZINES: Retirement

PROVINSTIDNINGEN DALSLAND 633925W67B-6480
Editorial: Box 29, 662 21 ÅMÅL **Tel:** 532 123 90
Fax: 532 165 15
Email: redaktion@provinstidningen.se **Web site:** http://www.provinstidningen.se
Date Established: 1911
Circ: 4,800
Advertising Manager: Holger Andersson; **Publisher:** Sune Tholin
Profile: Newspaper featuring local news in Åmål.
Language(s): Swedish
ADVERTISING RATES:
Full Page Colour .... SEK 21240
SCC .... SEK 106.20
Copy instructions: *Copy Date:* 14 days prior to publication date
REGIONAL DAILY & SUNDAY NEWSPAPERS: Regional Daily Newspapers

PRYLPORTALEN.SE 1681918W76A-191
Editorial: Box 1054, 101 39 STOCKHOLM
Tel: 8 545 121 10 **Fax:** 8 545 121 19
Email: prylportalen@mediaprovider.se **Web site:** http://www.prylportalen.se
Freq: Daily; **Cover Price:** Paid; **Circ:** 12,000 Unique Users
Editor-in-Chief: Andreas Liebert; **Publisher:** Pontus Brohult
Language(s): Swedish
CONSUMER: MUSIC & PERFORMING ARTS: Cinema

PSORIASISTIDNINGEN 50602W56A-50
Editorial: Box 5173, 121 18 JOHANNESHOV
Tel: 8 600 36 36 **Fax:** 855610919
Email: marie.darin@pso.se **Web site:** http://www.pso.se
Freq: 6 issues yearly; **Circ:** 19,100
Advertising Manager: Marie Darin; **Publisher:** Lars Ettarp
Profile: Magazine containing information about psoriasis. Published by the Swedish Psoriasis Association.
Language(s): Swedish
ADVERTISING RATES:
Full Page Colour .... SEK 17000
SCC .... SEK 141.67
BUSINESS: HEALTH & MEDICAL

PSYKISK HÄLSA 50652W56N-200
Editorial: Box 3445, 103 69 STOCKHOLM
Tel: 8 34 70 65
Email: psykisk.halsa@sfph.se **Web site:** http://www.sfph.se
Freq: Quarterly; **Circ:** 4,000
Editor: Tina Holmgren; **Publisher:** PA Rydelius
Profile: Journal about psychology and psychiatry.
Language(s): Swedish
BUSINESS: HEALTH & MEDICAL: Mental Health

PSYKOLOGTIDNINGEN 50653W56N-205
Editorial: Box 3287, 103 65 STOCKHOLM
Tel: 8 567 064 50 **Fax:** 8 567 064 90
Email: tidningen@psykologforbundet.se **Web site:** http://www.psykologforbundet.se
Freq: 26 issues yearly; **Circ:** 9,600
Editor: Carin Waldenström; **Editor-in-Chief:** Eva Brita Järnefors; **Publisher:** Eva Brita Järnefors
Profile: Official journal of the Swedish Association of Psychologists.
Language(s): Swedish
ADVERTISING RATES:
Full Page Colour .... SEK 35000
SCC .... SEK 291.66
BUSINESS: HEALTH & MEDICAL: Mental Health

PULSEN 749825W56B-115
Editorial: Box 1024, Landstinget i Jönköpings län, 551 11 JÖNKÖPING **Tel:** 36 32 40 38
Email: mikael.bergstrom@lj.se **Web site:** http://www.lj.se
Freq: 6 issues yearly; **Circ:** 5,000
Editor: Mikael Bergström
Language(s): Swedish
ADVERTISING RATES:
Full Page Colour .... SEK 5000
BUSINESS: HEALTH & MEDICAL: Nursing

QTC AMATÖRRADIO 634701W43B-70
Editorial: FSS, Box 45, 191 21 SOLLENTUNA
Tel: 8 585 702 73 **Fax:** 8 585 702 74
Email: qtc@ssa.se **Web site:** http://www.ssa.se
Date Established: 1927; **Freq:** Monthly; **Circ:** 7,000
Editor: Jonas Ytterman; **Advertising Manager:** Anders Berglund; **Publisher:** Tore Andersson
Language(s): Swedish
BUSINESS: ELECTRICAL RETAIL TRADE: Radio & Hi-Fi

QX 51278W86B-100
Editorial: Box 17218, 104 62 STOCKHOLM
Tel: 8 720 30 01
Email: redaktionen@qx.se **Web site:** http://www.qx.se
Date Established: 1995; **Freq:** Monthly; **Circ:** 31,800
Editor: Magda Gad; **Editor-in-Chief:** Anders Öhrman; **Advertising Manager:** Ulrika Lahne; **Publisher:** Jon Voss
Profile: Magazine for lesbians and gay men distributed free in Stockholm, Gothenburg, Malmö and Copenhagen.
Language(s): Swedish
ADVERTISING RATES:
Full Page Colour .... SEK 27600
Copy instructions: *Copy Date:* 9 days prior to publication date
CONSUMER: ADULT & GAY MAGAZINES: Gay & Lesbian Magazines

QX; QX.SE 1844524W86B-123
Editorial: Box 17218, 104 62 STOCKHOLM
Tel: 8 720 30 01
Email: webred@qx.se **Web site:** http://www.qx.se
Freq: Daily; **Cover Price:** Free; **Circ:** 29,675 Unique Users
Editor: Magda Gad; **Editor-in-Chief:** Anders Öhrman; **Advertising Manager:** Ulrika Lahne; **Publisher:** Jon Voss
Language(s): Swedish
CONSUMER: ADULT & GAY MAGAZINES: Gay & Lesbian Magazines

RACE MC-SPORT 1834359W77A-263
Editorial: Box 101, 575 21 EKSJÖ **Tel:** 381 130 81
Fax: 381 130 84
Email: tidningen@racemcsport.com **Web site:** http://www.racemcsport.com
Freq: Monthly; **Circ:** 50,000
Editor-in-Chief: Jonas Hagren; **Advertising Manager:** Leo Larenholtz
Language(s): Swedish
ADVERTISING RATES:
Full Page Colour .... SEK 12400
SCC .... SEK 103.33
CONSUMER: MOTORING & CYCLING: Motoring

RÅD & RÖN 50963W74C-120
Editorial: Box 38001, 100 64 STOCKHOLM
Tel: 8 674 43 10 **Fax:** 8 6744325
Email: radron@radron.se **Web site:** http://www.radron.se
Date Established: 1958; **Freq:** Monthly; **Circ:** 137,000
Profile: Magazine containing consumer information such as product tests and household economy.
Language(s): Swedish
ADVERTISING RATES:
Full Page Colour .... SEK 46580
SCC .... SEK 388.16
CONSUMER: WOMEN'S INTEREST CONSUMER MAGAZINES: Home & Family

RÅD & RÖN; RADRON.SE 1843677W82-479
Editorial: Box 6086, 102 32 STOCKHOLM
Tel: 8 674 43 10 **Fax:** 8 674 43 25
Email: radron@radron.se **Web site:** http://www.radron.se
Freq: Daily; **Cover Price:** Free
Language(s): Swedish
CONSUMER: CURRENT AFFAIRS & POLITICS

RÄDDA LIVET 50603W56A-52
Editorial: David Bagares Gata 5, 101 55 STOCKHOLM **Tel:** 8 677 10 00 **Fax:** 86771001
Email: marita.onneby@cancerfonden.se **Web site:** http://www.cancerfonden.se
Freq: Quarterly; **Circ:** 35,000
Editor: Marita Önneby Eliasson; **Publisher:** Ursula Tengelin
Profile: Magazine about cancer research and medical developments within the field.
Language(s): Swedish
ADVERTISING RATES:
Full Page Colour .... SEK 27650
SCC .... SEK 230.42
BUSINESS: HEALTH & MEDICAL

RALLAREN 1657962W49E-107
Editorial: Göran Fält, Banverket, 781 85 BORLÄNGE
Tel: 243 44 55 73 **Fax:** 243 44 55 56
Email: goran.falt@banverket.se
Freq: Monthly; **Circ:** 12,000
Editor: Monica Näslund; **Editor-in-Chief:** Göran Fält
Language(s): Swedish
BUSINESS: TRANSPORT: Railways

READER'S DIGEST 749951W74A-115
Editorial: 117 34 STOCKHOLM **Tel:** 8 587 108 87
Fax: 8 587 108 89
Email: red@readersdigest.se **Web site:** http://www.readersdigest.se
Date Established: 1943; **Freq:** Monthly; **Circ:** 52,000
Editor: Monica Walldén; **Advertising Manager:** Annica Parhorn
Language(s): Swedish
ADVERTISING RATES:
Full Page Colour .... SEK 19950
SCC .... SEK 166.25
Copy instructions: *Copy Date:* 14 days prior to publication date
CONSUMER: WOMEN'S INTEREST CONSUMER MAGAZINES: Women's Interest

REALTID.SE 1657137W14A-294
Editorial: Alternativ Media Stockholm AB, Löjtnantsgatan 17, 115 50 STOCKHOLM
Tel: 8 545 871 30 **Fax:** 8 664 63 30
Email: redaktionen@realtid.se **Web site:** http://www.realtid.se
Freq: Daily; **Circ:** 10,635 Unique Users
Editor: Martin Lindgren; **Editor-in-Chief:** Per Agerman; **Advertising Manager:** Annika Guldroth; **Publisher:** Jonas Wiwen-Nilsson
Language(s): Swedish
BUSINESS: COMMERCE, INDUSTRY & MANAGEMENT

REBELL 634703W82-435
Editorial: Box 31187, 400 32 GOTEBORG
Tel: 31 24 44 17 **Fax:** 31 24 51 72
Web site: http://www.rebell.se
Date Established: 1994; **Freq:** 6 issues yearly; **Circ:** 4,000
Profile: Magazine focusing on politics.
Language(s): Swedish
Readership: Aimed at young socialists.
ADVERTISING RATES:
Full Page Colour .... SEK 5800
SCC .... SEK 29
CONSUMER: CURRENT AFFAIRS & POLITICS

RECYCLING & MILJÖTEKNIK 50679W57-57
Editorial: Box 601, 251 06 HELSINGBORG
Tel: 42 490 19 31 **Fax:** 42 490 19 98
Email: martin.d@mentoronline.se **Web site:** http://www.recyclingnet.se
Date Established: 1995; **Freq:** Monthly; **Circ:** 4,900
Editor-in-Chief: Martin Dyberg; **Advertising Manager:** Jerker Evaldsson; **Publisher:** Martin Dyberg
Profile: Journal covering environmental issues, such as the technical and economical aspects of environmental protection. Contains product news, articles and information about the environmental aspects of building and construction, materials handling and water and sewage systems.
Language(s): Swedish
ADVERTISING RATES:
Full Page Colour .... SEK 27200
SCC .... SEK 226.66
BUSINESS: ENVIRONMENT & POLLUTION

RED TEE 1665942W75D-151
Editorial: Box 5361, 102 49 STOCKHOLM
Tel: 734 14 91 49
Email: red@redtee.se **Web site:** http://www.redtee.se
Freq: Monthly; **Circ:** 22,800
Editor: Mary Anne Beckman; **Editor-in-Chief:** Bonnie Geijer; **Advertising Manager:** Cecilia Westman; **Publisher:** Bonnie Geijer
Language(s): Swedish
ADVERTISING RATES:
Full Page Colour .... SEK 23900
SCC .... SEK 199.17
CONSUMER: SPORT: Golf

REDAKTÖREN 50187W2B-150
Editorial: Rim, Kniva 129, 791 96 FALUN
Tel: 31 40 56 98
Email: gunnel@atlestam.se **Web site:** http://www.rim.se
Freq: Quarterly; **Circ:** 750
Editor: Gunnel Atlestam
Profile: Magazine covering articles and information about in-house publishing.
Language(s): Swedish
Readership: Aimed at editors of internal media.
BUSINESS: COMMUNICATIONS, ADVERTISING & MARKETING: Press

REFLEX 1623691W32G-257
Editorial: Box 49084, 100 28 STOCKHOLM
Tel: 8 677 70 10 **Fax:** 8241315
Email: nhr@nhr.se **Web site:** http://www.nhr.se
Freq: 6 issues yearly; **Circ:** 15,000
Editor: Thomas Ejderhov; **Publisher:** Stefan Käll
Language(s): Swedish
BUSINESS: LOCAL GOVERNMENT, LEISURE & RECREATION: Community Care & Social Services

REGIONMAGASINET 1639327W82-453
Editorial: Regionens Hus, Residenset, 462 80 VÄNERSBORG **Tel:** 521 27 58 19
Email: regionmagasinet@vgregion.se **Web site:** http://www.vgregion.se/regionmagasinet
Freq: Quarterly; **Circ:** 740,000
Editor-in-Chief: Jeanette Karlström; **Publisher:** Kerstin Einarsson
Language(s): Swedish
CONSUMER: CURRENT AFFAIRS & POLITICS

REKO 1861274W82-500
Editorial: c/o Redaktörerna, Box 92170, 120 08 STOCKHOLM **Tel:** 8 56 20 86 90
Email: redaktionen@magasinreko.se **Web site:** http://www.magasinreko.se
Freq: Quarterly; **Circ:** 50,000
Advertising Manager: Zahra Iggberg; **Publisher:** Lars Nellmer
Language(s): Swedish
CONSUMER: CURRENT AFFAIRS & POLITICS

RELATION 1645558W14A-293
Editorial: Box 1201, 751 42 UPPSALA
Tel: 18 60 44 80 **Fax:** 18 10 70 40
Email: info@relation.se **Web site:** http://www.relation.se
Freq: 6 issues yearly; **Circ:** 14,000
Editor: Anders Melldén; **Editor-in-Chief:** Anders Melldén; **Publisher:** Magnus Axelid
Language(s): Swedish
ADVERTISING RATES:
SCC .... SEK 196
BUSINESS: COMMERCE, INDUSTRY & MANAGEMENT

RELIGION & LIVSFRÅGOR 634705W87-177
Editorial: C/o Christina Osbeck, Ängskogsvägen 35, 656 71 SKATTÄRR **Tel:** 5 486 41 76
Email: christina.osbeck@kau.se **Web site:** http://www.flr.se/rol.html
Freq: Quarterly; **Circ:** 1,500
Editor: Sven-Göran Ohlsson; **Advertising Manager:** Gunnar Iselau; **Publisher:** Olof Franck
Language(s): Swedish
CONSUMER: RELIGIOUS

RENHETSTEKNIK / NORDISK JOURNAL FÖR RENHETSTEKNIK 751153W4F-85
Editorial: Box 65, 240 13 GENARP **Tel:** 40 50 01 18
Fax: 40 50 01 48
Email: berit.reinmuller@byv.kth.se **Web site:** http://www.r3nordic.com
Date Established: 1976; **Freq:** Quarterly; **Circ:** 2,000
Editor: Berit Reinmüller
Language(s): Swedish
BUSINESS: ARCHITECTURE & BUILDING: Cleaning & Maintenance

RENT 50228W4F-50
Editorial: Box 72001, 181 72 LIDINGÖ
Tel: 8 670 41 00 **Fax:** 86616455
Email: bo.l@mentoronline.se **Web site:** http://www.cleannet.se
Freq: 6 issues yearly; **Circ:** 3,100
Editor-in-Chief: Bo Lennholm; **Advertising Manager:** Sofia Häljeryd
Profile: Magazine containing information about the cleaning industry.
Language(s): Swedish
ADVERTISING RATES:
Full Page Colour .... SEK 26800
SCC .... SEK 223.33
BUSINESS: ARCHITECTURE & BUILDING: Cleaning & Maintenance

RES 749871W91R-235
Editorial: Repslagargatan 17B, 1tr, 118 46 STOCKHOLM **Tel:** 8 545 06 400 **Fax:** 8 679 57 10
Email: redaktionen@res.se **Web site:** http://www.res.se
Freq: Monthly; **Circ:** 27,300
Advertising Manager: Christian Wahls; **Publisher:** Johan Lindskog
Language(s): Swedish
ADVERTISING RATES:
Full Page Colour .... SEK 37400
SCC .... SEK 311.66
Copy instructions: *Copy Date:* 20 days prior to publication date
CONSUMER: RECREATION & LEISURE: Recreation & Leisure Related

RES & TRAFIKFORUM; WEBB 1847418W50-126
Editorial: Box 72001, 181 72 LIDINGÖ
Tel: 8670 41 00 **Fax:** 8661 64 55
Email: anders.k@mentoronline.se **Web site:** http://www.rt-forum.com
Freq: Daily; **Cover Price:** Free; **Circ:** 1,600 Unique Users
Advertising Manager: Peter Hall; **Publisher:** Anders Karlsson
Language(s): Swedish
BUSINESS: TRAVEL & TOURISM

RESERVOFFICEREN 50471W40-120
Editorial: Box 5417, 114 84 STOCKHOLM
Tel: 8 661 86 42
Email: reservofficeren@sverof.org **Web site:** http://www.sverof.org
Freq: Quarterly; **Circ:** 4,000
Editor: Ulrika Sjöström; **Advertising Manager:** Sven Hugosson
Profile: Military journal for officers of the reserve.
Language(s): Swedish
BUSINESS: DEFENCE

RESFORUM 751027W50-85
Editorial: Mentor Communications, Box 72001, 181 72 LIDINGÖ **Tel:** 8 670 41 00 **Fax:** 8 661 64 55
Email: redaktionen@rt-forum.com **Web site:** http://www.rt-forum.com
Freq: Monthly; **Circ:** 2,400
Advertising Manager: Gunilla Hagberg; **Publisher:** Ulo Maasing
Language(s): Swedish
ADVERTISING RATES:
Full Page Colour .... SEK 23175
SCC .... SEK 193.12
Copy instructions: *Copy Date:* 23 days prior to publication date
BUSINESS: TRAVEL & TOURISM

RESIDENCE 751171W91R-225
Editorial: 113 92 STOCKHOLM **Tel:** 8 588 366 00
Email: marten.nilehn@lrfmedia.lrf.se **Web site:** http://www.residencemagazine.se
Date Established: 2000; **Freq:** Monthly; **Circ:** 44,900
Publisher: Mårten Niléhn
Language(s): Swedish
ADVERTISING RATES:
Full Page Colour .... SEK 39900
SCC .... SEK 332.50
Copy instructions: *Copy Date:* 34 days prior to publication date
CONSUMER: RECREATION & LEISURE: Recreation & Leisure Related

RESIDENCE HEM & TREND 1741137W74C-458
Editorial: Box 26206, 113 92 STOCKHOLM
Tel: 8 588 366 00
Email: marten.nilehn@lrfmedia.lrf.se **Web site:** http://www.residencemagazine.se
Freq: Annual; **Circ:** 44,900
Publisher: Mårten Niléhn
Language(s): Swedish
ADVERTISING RATES:
Full Page Colour .... SEK 39900
SCC .... SEK 332.50
CONSUMER: WOMEN'S INTEREST CONSUMER MAGAZINES: Home & Family

RESMÅL 51311W89E-75
Editorial: Gränsö Slott, 593 92 VÄSTERVIK
Tel: 490 824 20 **Fax:** 490 354 46
Email: info@klarkullen.se **Web site:** http://www.klarkullen.se
Date Established: 1992; **Freq:** Half-yearly; **Circ:** 14,500
Editor: Per Johansson; **Publisher:** Per Johansson
Profile: Magazine containing information about travel destinations in Scandinavia.
Language(s): Swedish
Readership: Aimed at tourists.
ADVERTISING RATES:
Full Page Colour .... SEK 22400
SCC .... SEK 186.67
CONSUMER: HOLIDAYS & TRAVEL: Holidays

RESONER.NU 1847417W2A-409
Email: red@smrn.se **Web site:** http://www.resoner.nu
Freq: Daily; **Cover Price:** Free; **Circ:** 3,000 Unique Users
Editor: Mikael Karlsson; **Advertising Manager:** Henrik Hall
Language(s): Swedish
BUSINESS: COMMUNICATIONS, ADVERTISING & MARKETING

RESPONS FÖRETAGSTIDNING 750784W74G-180
Editorial: ENS 2000, Box 9003, 700 09 ÖREBRO
Tel: 19 27 10 10 **Fax:** 19 27 05 12
Email: info@ens2000.se **Web site:** http://www.ens2000.nu
Freq: 6 issues yearly; **Circ:** 9,300
Advertising Manager: Niclas Magnusson; **Publisher:** Lars Nenander
Language(s): Swedish
CONSUMER: WOMEN'S INTEREST CONSUMER MAGAZINES: Slimming & Health

RESPONS UNGDOMSTIDNING 750816W91D-115
Editorial: ENS 2000, Box 9003, 700 09 ÖREBRO
Tel: 19 27 10 10 **Fax:** 19 27 05 12
Email: info@ens2000.se **Web site:** http://www.ens2000.nu
Freq: Half-yearly; **Circ:** 9,000
Advertising Manager: Niclas Magnusson; **Publisher:** Lars Nenander

Language(s): Swedish
CONSUMER: RECREATION & LEISURE: Children & Youth

RESTAURANGER & STORKÖK
50270W11A-24
Editorial: Box 72001, 181 72 LIDINGÖ
Tel: 8 670 41 76 **Fax:** 86616455
Email: lena.i@mentoronline.se **Web site:** http://www.foodnet.se
Date Established: 1967; **Freq:** 6 issues yearly; **Circ:** 6,400
Editor-in-Chief: Anders Örnevall; **Advertising Manager:** Magnus Svenlert
Profile: Magazine for the hotel and restaurant trade focusing on technical and financial developments in catering around the world. Contains information about suppliers and food producers, legal matters and product news.
Language(s): Swedish
Readership: Aimed at professionals within the trade.
ADVERTISING RATES:
Full Page Colour .... SEK 35200
SCC .... SEK 293.33
Copy instructions: *Copy Date:* 21 days prior to publication date
BUSINESS: CATERING: Catering, Hotels & Restaurants

RESTAURANGVÄRLDEN
50269W11A-23
Editorial: Port-Anders gata T3, 721 85 VÄSTERÅS
Tel: 8 728 23 00 **Fax:** 21 19 42 10
Email: red.restaurangvarlden@formapg.se **Web site:** http://www.formapg.se
Date Established: 1979; **Freq:** Monthly; **Circ:** 5,500
Advertising Manager: Håkan Broberg
Profile: Magazine containing information, news and articles of interest to restaurant and hotel owners. Covers issues like hygiene and maintenance related to catering and canteen kitchens and food storage areas.
Language(s): Swedish
ADVERTISING RATES:
Full Page Colour .... SEK 35200
SCC .... SEK 293.33
BUSINESS: CATERING: Catering, Hotels & Restaurants

RESTAURATÖREN
749800W50-90
Editorial: Box3546, 103 69 STOCKHOLM
Tel: 8 762 74 00 **Fax:** 8 411 38 16
Email: redaktionen@restauratoren.se **Web site:** http://www.restauratoren.se
Date Established: 1996; **Freq:** Weekly; **Circ:** 8,700
Publisher: Ninni Dickson
Language(s): Swedish
ADVERTISING RATES:
Full Page Colour .... SEK 23700
SCC .... SEK 197.50
BUSINESS: TRAVEL & TOURISM

RESUMÉ
50180W2A-120
Editorial: Birgerjarlsgatan 6B, 113 90 STOCKHOLM
Tel: 8 736 30 00 **Fax:** 8 736 05 25
Email: red@resume.se **Web site:** http://www.resume.se
Freq: Weekly; **Circ:** 6,200
Profile: Resumé is a newspaper focusing on news within the media and marketingcommunication industries. It is published by Bonnier Tidskrifter 42 times a year. Start year: 1940 Owner: Resumé Förlag AB, owned by Bonnier Tidskrifter Editor-In-Chief and Publisher; Viggo Cavling.
Language(s): Swedish
Readership: Aimed at all professionals within the field.
ADVERTISING RATES:
Full Page Colour .... SEK 46224
SCC .... SEK 288.90
BUSINESS: COMMUNICATIONS, ADVERTISING & MARKETING

RESUMÉ; RESUME.SE
1843638W2A-403
Editorial: 113 90 STOCKHOLM **Tel:** 8 736 30 00
Fax: 8 736 05 25
Email: red@resume.se **Web site:** http://www.resume.se
Freq: Daily; **Cover Price:** Free; **Circ:** 20,480 Unique Users
Publisher: Viggo Cavling
Language(s): Swedish
BUSINESS: COMMUNICATIONS, ADVERTISING & MARKETING

RETORIKMAGASINET
752203W73-115
Editorial: Retorikförlaget AB, Box 10, 254 03 ÖDÅKRA **Tel:** 42 679 59 **Fax:** 42 679 54
Email: rm@retorikforlaget.se **Web site:** http://www.retorikforlaget.se/rm
Freq: Quarterly; **Circ:** 1,000
Editor: Karin Karlsson
Language(s): Swedish
CONSUMER: NATIONAL & INTERNATIONAL PERIODICALS

REUMATIKERVÄRLDEN
1938689W74G-229
Editorial: Reumatikerförbundet, 116 33 STOCKHOLM **Tel:** 8 556 06 446
Email: redaktionen@reumatikervarlden.se **Web site:** http://www.reumatikervarlden.se
Freq: 6 issues yearly; **Circ:** 60,000
Advertising Manager: Gun Hammar; **Publisher:** Anne Carlsson
Language(s): Swedish
ADVERTISING RATES:
Full Page Colour .... SEK 24900
CONSUMER: WOMEN'S INTEREST CONSUMER MAGAZINES: Slimming & Health

REV BULLETINEN
1664344W42A-101
Editorial: Riddargatan 35-37, 114 57 STOCKHOLM
Tel: 8 20 27 50 **Fax:** 8 20 74 78
Email: kansliet@revriks.se **Web site:** http://www.revriks.se
Freq: Quarterly; **Circ:** 8,000
Editor: Mats Karlström
Language(s): Swedish
BUSINESS: CONSTRUCTION

REVANSCH!
50429W32G-180
Editorial: Instrumentvägen 10, 2tr, 126 53 HAGERSTEN **Tel:** 8 772 33 60 **Fax:** 8 772 33 61
Email: rsmh@rsmh.se **Web site:** http://www.rsmh.se
Freq: 6 issues yearly; **Circ:** 9,300
Publisher: Östen Hannmyhr
Profile: Magazine containing articles and information about social and mental health.
Language(s): Swedish
BUSINESS: LOCAL GOVERNMENT, LEISURE & RECREATION: Community Care & Social Services

RIDSPORT
51021W75E-50
Editorial: Box 14, 619 21 TROSA **Tel:** 156 132 40
Fax: 15634878
Email: redaktionen@tidningenridsport.se **Web site:** http://www.tidningenridsport.se
Date Established: 1972; **Freq:** 26 issues yearly; **Circ:** 35,000
Editor: Lena Särnholm; **Advertising Manager:** Jan Bohlin
Profile: Magazine about equestrian sport.
Language(s): Swedish
ADVERTISING RATES:
Full Page Colour .... SEK 16000
SCC .... SEK 80
CONSUMER: SPORT: Horse Racing

RIDSPORT SPECIAL
51022W75E-60
Editorial: Box 14, 619 21 TROSA **Tel:** 156 132 40
Fax: 156 348 78
Email: redaktionen@tidningenridsport.se **Web site:** http://www.tidningenridsport.se
Date Established: 1989; **Freq:** Half-yearly; **Circ:** 40,000
Editor: Jan Bohlin; **Editor-in-Chief:** Jan Bohlin; **Advertising Manager:** Jan Bohlin; **Publisher:** Jan Bohlin
Profile: Journal about equestrian sports, horse racing and horse breeding.
Language(s): Swedish
ADVERTISING RATES:
Full Page Colour .... SEK 16000
SCC .... SEK 80
CONSUMER: SPORT: Horse Racing

RIG, KULTURHISTORISK TIDSKRIFT
750719W73-120
Editorial: Finngatan 8, 223 62 LUND **Tel:** 46 29 13 14
Fax: 462229849
Email: lars-eric.jonsson@etn.lu.se **Web site:** http://www.etn.lu.se/rig
Date Established: 1918; **Freq:** Quarterly; **Circ:** 600
Editor: Margareta Tellenbach; **Publisher:** Mats Hellspong
Language(s): Swedish
CONSUMER: NATIONAL & INTERNATIONAL PERIODICALS

RIKSDAG & DEPARTEMENT
51181W82-75
Editorial: 100 12 STOCKHOLM **Tel:** 8 786 40 00
Fax: 8 786 61 95
Email: kristina.gauthier@riksdagen.se **Web site:** http://www.rod.se
Date Established: 1976; **Freq:** Weekly; **Circ:** 10,800
Publisher: Nils Funcke
Profile: Pan-European magazine covering parliamentary debate.
Language(s): Swedish
ADVERTISING RATES:
Full Page Colour .... SEK 27800
SCC .... SEK 231.66
CONSUMER: CURRENT AFFAIRS & POLITICS

RIKSDAG & DEPARTEMENT; ROD.SE
1846293W14F-110
Editorial: 100 12 STOCKHOLM **Tel:** 8 786 40 00
Fax: 8 786 61 95
Email: nils.funcke@riksdagen.se **Web site:** http://www.rod.se
Freq: Daily; **Cover Price:** Free; **Circ:** 5,200 Unique Users
Editor-in-Chief: Mattias Croneborg; **Advertising Manager:** Jonas Thörne; **Publisher:** Mattias Croneborg
Language(s): Swedish
ADVERTISING RATES:
SCC .... SEK 46
BUSINESS: COMMERCE, INDUSTRY & MANAGEMENT: Training & Recruitment

RIKSETTAN
1698550W57-117
Editorial: Box 23 800, 104 35 STOCKHOLM
Tel: 8 736 12 13 **Fax:** 8 736 12 49
Email: redaktionen@riksettan.net **Web site:** http://www.riksettan.net
Freq: Half-yearly; **Circ:** 40,000
Editor-in-Chief: Jörgen Persson; **Publisher:** Nils-Eric Frendin
Language(s): Swedish
ADVERTISING RATES:
Full Page Colour .... SEK 15000
SCC .... SEK 125
BUSINESS: ENVIRONMENT & POLLUTION

RIKSTÄCKET
51505W74E-200
Editorial: Box 27, 191 21 SOLLENTUNA
Tel: 8 32 49 30
Email: info@rikstacket.se **Web site:** http://www.rikstacket.se
Freq: Quarterly; **Circ:** 3,200
Editor: Lena Lindqvist; **Publisher:** Lillemor Bergström
Profile: Magazine for Kviltföreningen Rikstäcket (Association of Patchwork Quiltmakers).
Language(s): Swedish
Readership: Read by members.
CONSUMER: WOMEN'S INTEREST CONSUMER MAGAZINES: Crafts

RIKSUTSTÄLLNINGAR
50193W2C-60
Editorial: Box 1033, 621 21 VISBY **Tel:** 498 79 90 00
Fax: 498 27 21 20
Email: info@riksutstallningar.se **Web site:** http://www.riksutstallningar.se
Date Established: 1989; **Freq:** Monthly - utkommer ungefär en gång i månaden; **Circ:** 10,000
Publisher: Eva Lundqvist
Profile: Magazine about travelling exhibitions and the exhibition as a communicative medium.
Language(s): Swedish
BUSINESS: COMMUNICATIONS, ADVERTISING & MARKETING: Conferences & Exhibitions

RÖD PRESS
51200W82-215
Editorial: Box 12660, 112 93 STOCKHOLM
Tel: 8 654 31 00 **Fax:** 8 650 85 57
Email: red@rodpress.nu **Web site:** http://www.rodpress.nu
Date Established: 1908; **Freq:** Quarterly; **Circ:** 3,000
Editor-in-Chief: Miro Anter
Profile: Magazine of the Youth Organisation of the Swedish Left Party. Covers politics, society, culture and youth.
Language(s): Swedish
CONSUMER: CURRENT AFFAIRS & POLITICS

RÖDA RUMMET
51199W82-214
Editorial: Box 7043, 402 31 GOTEBORG
Tel: 31 24 15 13
Email: redaktion@rodarummet.org **Web site:** http://www.rodarummet.org
Date Established: 1997; **Freq:** Quarterly; **Circ:** 2,700
Editor-in-Chief: Peter Belfrage; **Publisher:** Björn Rönnblad
Profile: Journal of the Socialist Party covering culture and politics. Also contains articles about economy, environment and literature.
Language(s): Swedish
CONSUMER: CURRENT AFFAIRS & POLITICS

RODEO
1643715W76A-186
Editorial: 114 59 STOCKHOLM **Tel:** 8 555 880 50
Fax: 8 545 682 41
Email: admin@rodeo.net **Web site:** http://www.rodeo.net
Freq: Quarterly; **Cover Price:** Free; **Circ:** 38,200
Publisher: Daniel Björk
Language(s): Swedish
ADVERTISING RATES:
Full Page Colour .... SEK 32000
SCC .... SEK 200
CONSUMER: MUSIC & PERFORMING ARTS: Cinema

RODEO; RODEO.NET
1847399W76B-111
Editorial: 114 59 STOCKHOLM **Tel:** 8 555 880 50
Fax: 8 545 682 41
Email: admin@rodeo.net **Web site:** http://www.rodeo.net
Freq: Daily; **Cover Price:** Free; **Circ:** 5,000 Unique Users
Editor: Agnes Braunerhielm; **Editor-in-Chief:** Lisa Corneliusson
Language(s): Swedish
CONSUMER: MUSIC & PERFORMING ARTS: Theatre

RONDEN, PERSONALTIDNING FÖR AKADEMISKA SJUKHUSET
1804028W32G-271
Editorial: Akademiska sjukhuset, 751 85 UPPSALA
Tel: 18 611 96 11
Email: ronden@akademiska.se **Web site:** http://www.akademiska.se
Freq: 6 issues yearly; **Circ:** 9,000
Editor: Ylva Porsklev; **Publisher:** Christina Bostedt
Language(s): Swedish
BUSINESS: LOCAL GOVERNMENT, LEISURE & RECREATION: Community Care & Social Services

ROOMSERVICE PRO
1803877W4E-156
Editorial: Box 73 44, 103 90 STOCKHOLM
Tel: 8 406 54 00 **Fax:** 8 406 54 99
Email: red@roomservicepro.se **Web site:** http://www.roomservicepro.se
Freq: Monthly; **Circ:** 4,000
Editor-in-Chief: Sofia Lundberg; **Publisher:** Ann-Charlotte Borgö
Language(s): Swedish
ADVERTISING RATES:
Full Page Colour .... SEK 21800
SCC .... SEK 181.66
BUSINESS: ARCHITECTURE & BUILDING: Building

RÖRELSE
50640W56L-54_50
Editorial: Box 8026, 104 20 STOCKHOLM
Tel: 8 677 73 00 **Fax:** 8 677 73 09
Email: rorelse@riks.rbu.se **Web site:** http://www.rbu.se
Freq: 6 issues yearly; **Circ:** 6,000
Editor: Mathias Roth; **Advertising Manager:** Ulla Wibom; **Publisher:** Agnetha Mbuyamba
Profile: Magazine containing information concerning the Swedish Society for Disabled Children and Youth.
Language(s): Swedish
Readership: Aimed at people working with disabled children and young people.
BUSINESS: HEALTH & MEDICAL: Disability & Rehabilitation

RÖRET
634728W56J-150
Editorial: Frostgränd 48, 931 51 SKELLEFTEÅ
Tel: 910 193 63 **Fax:** 91019363
Email: red@roret.com **Web site:** http://www.swedrad.se
Freq: Quarterly; **Circ:** 1,700
Advertising Manager: Vanja Kågström
Profile: Journal for the National Association of Medical Radiology.
Language(s): Swedish
BUSINESS: HEALTH & MEDICAL: Radiography

RUM
1645559W4A-31
Editorial: Birger Jarlsgatan 20, 114 34 STOCKHOLM
Tel: 8 667 92 10 **Fax:** 8 667 92 11
Email: redaktion@tidskriftenrum.se **Web site:** http://www.tidskriftenrum.se
Freq: Monthly; **Circ:** 10,000
Editor: Louisa Nyström; **Editor-in-Chief:** Emma Rost; **Publisher:** Jacop Merlini
Language(s): Swedish
ADVERTISING RATES:
Full Page Colour .... SEK 27900
SCC .... SEK 232.5
BUSINESS: ARCHITECTURE & BUILDING: Architecture

RUNNERS WORLD
750680W75J-180
Editorial: Box 22559, 104 22 STOCKHOLM
Tel: 8 545 535 30 **Fax:** 8 545 535 39
Email: hans@runnersworld.se **Web site:** http://www.runnersworld.se
Freq: Monthly; **Circ:** 20,600
Advertising Manager: Gunnar Lundqvist; **Publisher:** Hans Lodin
Language(s): Swedish
ADVERTISING RATES:
Full Page Colour .... SEK 26000
SCC .... SEK 216.66
CONSUMER: SPORT: Athletics

RYGGTIDNINGEN
1804021W56A-353
Editorial: Svenska Ryggföreningen, Box 244, 17724 STOCKHOLM **Tel:** 8 621 07 35
Email: info@ryggforening.se **Web site:** http://www.ryfs.nu
Freq: Quarterly; **Circ:** 5,000
Publisher: Christer Nyberg
Language(s): Swedish
BUSINESS: HEALTH & MEDICAL

SAAB MAGAZINE
51129W77E-475
Editorial: Box 101, 371 22 KARLSKRONA
Tel: 455 36 25 18 **Fax:** 455 36 25 01
Email: asa.melin@lennandia.com **Web site:** http://www.lennandia.com

Freq: Half-yearly; **Circ:** 75,000
Editor-in-Chief: Jan Lennartsson; **Publisher:** Annicka Troedsson
Profile: Magazine for owners of Saab and Opel cars.
Language(s): Swedish
Readership: Read by owners of Saab and Opel cars.
CONSUMER: MOTORING & CYCLING: Club Cars

SÄFFLE-TIDNINGEN; SAFFLETIDNING.SE
1844962W65A-1047
Editorial: Box 33, 661 21 SÄFFLE **Tel:** 533 464 30 **Fax:** 533 138 87
Email: redaktion@saffletidningen.se **Web site:** http://www.saffletidning.se
Freq: Daily; **Cover Price:** Free; **Circ:** 5,000 Unique Users
Editor-in-Chief: Sven-Erik Dahlström; **Advertising Manager:** Lars Fredriksson
Language(s): Swedish
ADVERTISING RATES:
SCC .... SEK 17
NATIONAL DAILY & SUNDAY NEWSPAPERS: National Daily Newspapers

SALA ALLEHANDA
50828W67B-6600
Editorial: Box 303, 733 25 SALA **Tel:** 224 561 00 **Fax:** 224 561 35
Email: redaktionen.sa@ingress.se **Web site:** http://www.salaallehanda.com
Circ: 9,000
Editor-in-Chief: Anna Bengtsdotter
Language(s): Swedish
ADVERTISING RATES:
Full Page Colour .... SEK 29460
SCC .... SEK 147.30
REGIONAL DAILY & SUNDAY NEWSPAPERS: Regional Daily Newspapers

SÄLJAREN
50289W14A-102
Editorial: Box 12668, 112 93 STOCKHOLM **Tel:** 8 617 02 21 **Fax:** 86521515
Email: saljaren@saljarnas.com **Web site:** http://www.saljarnas.com
Freq: Monthly; **Circ:** 7,600
Editor-in-Chief: Anna-Karin Rabe; **Advertising Manager:** Bengtsson & Sundström Media
Profile: Magazine containing information, news and articles about business and industry. Focuses heavily on sales techniques.
Language(s): Swedish
Readership: Aimed at sales people, business proprietors and managers.
ADVERTISING RATES:
Full Page Colour .... SEK 17700
SCC .... SEK 147.50
BUSINESS: COMMERCE, INDUSTRY & MANAGEMENT

SALT & PEPPAR
751360W74C-355
Editorial: Spoon Publishing, Kungstensgatan 21 B, 113 57 STOCKHOLM **Tel:** 8 442 96 20
Email: red.saltpeppar@vi-butikerna.se **Web site:** http://www.sth.vi-butikerna.se
Date Established: 1998; **Freq:** Quarterly; **Circ:** 145,000
Editor: Maud Onnermark; **Publisher:** Patrik Hjert
Language(s): Swedish
ADVERTISING RATES:
Full Page Colour .... SEK 75000
SCC .... SEK 625
CONSUMER: WOMEN'S INTEREST CONSUMER MAGAZINES: Home & Family

SAMEFOLKET
51507W90-58
Editorial: Box 86, 933 22 ARVIDSJAUR **Tel:** 960 134 30
Email: katarina@samefolket.se **Web site:** http://www.samefolket.se
Freq: Monthly; **Circ:** 2,000
Advertising Manager: Leif Dylicki; **Publisher:** Katarina Hällgren
Profile: Publication for the Swedish Laplanders Association.
Language(s): Swedish
ADVERTISING RATES:
Full Page Colour .... SEK 5000
SCC .... SEK 41.67
CONSUMER: ETHNIC

SAMHÄLLSBYGGAREN
652160W42A-100
Editorial: Box 3437, 103 68 STOCKHOLM **Tel:** 70 630 22 17 **Fax:** 8 24 54 64
Email: redaktionen@vbyggaren.se **Web site:** http://www.vbyggaren.se
Freq: 6 issues yearly; **Circ:** 3,600
Editor-in-Chief: Lars Hamrebjörk; **Advertising Manager:** Migge Sarrión
Language(s): Swedish
ADVERTISING RATES:
Full Page Colour .... SEK 17500
SCC .... SEK 145.83
Copy instructions: *Copy Date:* 20 days prior to publication date
BUSINESS: CONSTRUCTION

SAMHÄLLSTIDNINGEN RE:PUBLIC SERVICE
1667232W73-131
Editorial: Zoo, Grindsg 33 (vill ej ha pressmedd. via brev), 118 57 STOCKHOLM
Web site: http://www.republicservice.se
Freq: Quarterly; **Circ:** 10,000
Advertising Manager: Anders Birgersson
Language(s): Swedish
ADVERTISING RATES:
Full Page Colour .... SEK 14000
SCC .... SEK 116.66
CONSUMER: NATIONAL & INTERNATIONAL PERIODICALS

SÄNDAREN
51616W87-77
Editorial: Box 22543, 104 22 STOCKHOLM **Tel:** 8 545 784 50 **Fax:** 8 673 45 67
Email: sandaren@sandaren.se **Web site:** http://www.sandaren.se
Date Established: 1992; **Freq:** 26 issues yearly; **Circ:** 11,200
Editor-in-Chief: Anders Mellbourn
Profile: Magazine of the Mission Covenant Church of Sweden and the Swedish Baptist Union. Contains news and articles concerning religion, ethics, culture, society and human rights.
Language(s): Swedish
ADVERTISING RATES:
Full Page Colour .... SEK 29900
SCC .... SEK 186.88
CONSUMER: RELIGIOUS

SÄNDAREN; SANDAREN.SE
1846261W65A-1059
Editorial: Box 22543, 104 22 STOCKHOLM **Tel:** 8 545 784 50 **Fax:** 8 673 65 57
Email: anders.mellbourn@sandaren.se **Web site:** http://www.sandaren.se
Freq: Daily; **Cover Price:** Free; **Circ:** 6,600 Unique Users
Editor-in-Chief: Anders Mellbourn
Language(s): Swedish
ADVERTISING RATES:
SCC .... SEK 37
NATIONAL DAILY & SUNDAY NEWSPAPERS: National Daily Newspapers

SATS MAGASIN
1623602W74A-141
Editorial: Spoon Publishing, Kungstensgatan 21B, 113 57 STOCKHOLM **Tel:** 8 442 96 20 **Fax:** 8 442 96 39
Email: sats@spoon.se **Web site:** http://www.spoon.se
Freq: Quarterly; **Circ:** 75,000
Language(s): Swedish
CONSUMER: WOMEN'S INTEREST CONSUMER MAGAZINES: Women's Interest

SCAND. ACTUARIAL JOURNAL
634732W1D-230
Editorial: Box 3255, 103 65 STOCKHOLM **Tel:** 8 440 80 40 **Fax:** 8 440 80 50
Email: journals@tandf.no **Web site:** http://www.tandf.no
Date Established: 1918; **Freq:** Quarterly; **Circ:** 1,400
Editor: Boualem Djehiche
Profile: International specialised journal covering all aspects of insurance calculation.
Language(s): Swedish
Readership: Aimed at insurance brokers, claims adjusters and recording clerks.
BUSINESS: FINANCE & ECONOMICS: Insurance

SCAND. CARDIOVASCULAR JOURNAL
634733W56A-54_50
Editorial: Box 3255, 103 65 STOCKHOLM **Tel:** 8 440 80 40 **Fax:** 8 440 80 50
Email: rolf.ekroth@se.tandf.no **Web site:** http://www.informaworld.com
Freq: 6 issues yearly; **Circ:** 4,200
Editor: Knut Gjesdal; **Editor-in-Chief:** Rolf Ekroth
Profile: International medical journal.
Language(s): Swedish
Readership: Aimed at specialists in heart surgery, cardiologists and physiologists.
BUSINESS: HEALTH & MEDICAL

SCAND. JOURNAL OF INFECTIOUS DISEASES
634740W56A-57
Editorial: Box 3255, 103 65 STOCKHOLM **Tel:** 8 440 80 40 **Fax:** 8 440 80 50
Email: infectious@informa.com **Web site:** http://www.informahealthcare.com
Freq: 6 issues yearly; **Circ:** 1,900
Editor-in-Chief: Ragnar Norrby
Profile: International journal focusing on scientific research on infectious diseases.
Language(s): Swedish
Readership: Aimed at epidemiologists and professionals in the medical profession.
BUSINESS: HEALTH & MEDICAL

SCAND. JOURNAL OF PLASTIC AND RECONSTR. SURG.
634741W56A-313
Editorial: Department of Plastic Surgery, Sahlgrenska University Hospital, 413 45 GÖTEBORG **Tel:** 31 342 41 33 **Fax:** 31 342 12 09
Email: christina.andersson@plast.gu.se **Web site:** http://www.tandf.no
Freq: 6 issues yearly; **Circ:** 6,000
Editor-in-Chief: Jan Lilja
Language(s): Swedish
BUSINESS: HEALTH & MEDICAL

SCAND. JOURNAL OF UROLOGY AND NEPHROLOGY
751177W56A-315
Editorial: WHO Center Z5:00, Karolinska University Hospital Solna, 171 76 STOCKHOLM **Tel:** 8 440 80 40 **Fax:** 8 440 80 50
Email: diana.eriksson@ki.se **Web site:** http://www.tandf.no
Freq: 6 issues yearly; **Circ:** 1,900
Editor-in-Chief: Jan Adolfsson
Language(s): Swedish
BUSINESS: HEALTH & MEDICAL

SCANORAMA
51309W89D-150
Editorial: DG Communications, 111 57 STOCKHOLM **Tel:** 8 797 03 00 **Fax:** 87975315
Email: per.olsson@dgcom.se **Web site:** http://www.scanorama.com
Date Established: 1972; **Freq:** Monthly; **Circ:** 90,000
Editor: Rikard Lind; **Publisher:** Magnus Lindvall
Profile: Pan-European in-flight magazine of SAS, available on all domestic and international flights.
Language(s): Swedish
Readership: Read mainly by Scandinavians employed in high income management positions.
ADVERTISING RATES:
Full Page Colour .... SEK 107100
SCC .... SEK 892.50
CONSUMER: HOLIDAYS & TRAVEL: In-Flight Magazines

SCEN OCH SALONG
51307W89C-160
Editorial: AiP Media, 105 60 STOCKHOLM **Tel:** 8 700 26 46 **Fax:** 8 411 65 42
Email: sonja.tedelund@fhp.nu
Freq: Quarterly; **Circ:** 2,900
Editor: Sonja Tedelund; **Publisher:** Sonja Tedelund
Profile: Magazine containing news and information about events, entertainment and culture in Sweden.
Language(s): Swedish
ADVERTISING RATES:
Full Page Colour .... SEK 11200
SCC .... SEK 93.33
CONSUMER: HOLIDAYS & TRAVEL: Entertainment Guides

SCOOP
50188W2B-155
Editorial: Grävande Journalister, c/o JMK, Box 27861, 115 93 STOCKHOLM **Tel:** 8 16 44 25 **Fax:** 8 31 44 25
Email: kansli@fgj.se **Web site:** http://www.fgj.se
Freq: Quarterly; **Circ:** 1,500
Editor: Ylva Johnson; **Advertising Manager:** Åsa Sommar
Profile: Magazine for investigative journalists.
Language(s): Swedish
ADVERTISING RATES:
Full Page Colour .... SEK 7000
BUSINESS: COMMUNICATIONS, ADVERTISING & MARKETING: Press

SCOUTEN
1663911W91D-123
Editorial: Svenska Scoutrådet, Box 12 280, 102 27 STOCKHOLM **Tel:** 8 672 66 04
Email: scouten@scout.se **Web site:** http://www.scout.se
Freq: 6 issues yearly; **Circ:** 41,700
Editor-in-Chief: Emma Casserlöv; **Advertising Manager:** Hans Simons
Language(s): Swedish
CONSUMER: RECREATION & LEISURE: Children & Youth

SCOUTING SPIRIT
750749W91R-230
Editorial: Box 12825, 112 97 STOCKHOLM **Tel:** 8 672 60 80 **Fax:** 8 672 60 01
Email: scoutingspirit@nsf.scout.se **Web site:** http://www.nsf.scout.se
Freq: 6 issues yearly; **Circ:** 6,000
Editor: Nina Norén; **Publisher:** Birgitta Persson
Language(s): Swedish
CONSUMER: RECREATION & LEISURE: Recreation & Leisure Related

SCREEN&MARKNADEN
50194W2R-50
Editorial: Box 119, 643 22 VINGÅKER **Tel:** 151 303 10 **Fax:** 151 303 10
Email: info@screen-marknaden.se **Web site:** http://www.screen-marknaden.se
Date Established: 1989; **Freq:** 6 issues yearly; **Circ:** 3,500
Editor-in-Chief: Lars Knapasjö; **Publisher:** Lars Knapasjö
Profile: Magazine for the signmaking, display and screen printing trades.
Language(s): Swedish
ADVERTISING RATES:
Full Page Colour .... SEK 10300
SCC .... SEK 68.33
BUSINESS: COMMUNICATIONS, ADVERTISING & MARKETING: Communications Related

SE & HÖR
50941W73-90
Editorial: Budadress: Humlegårdsgatan 6, Box 27704, 115 91 STOCKHOLM **Tel:** 8 679 46 00 **Fax:** 8 679 46 33
Email: rolf.qvale@soh.aller.se **Web site:** http://www.soh.se
Freq: Weekly; **Circ:** 112,800
Editor-in-Chief: Carina Löfkvist
Profile: General and family interest magazine including listings of television and radio programmes.
Language(s): Swedish
ADVERTISING RATES:
Full Page Colour .... SEK 34000
SCC .... SEK 283.33
CONSUMER: NATIONAL & INTERNATIONAL PERIODICALS

SEASONS
1686803W89A-67
Editorial: Sergels Torg 12, 111 57 STOCKHOLM **Tel:** 8 797 03 10 **Fax:** 8 21 31 71
Email: peder.edvinsson@dgcom.se **Web site:** http://www.seasons-magazine.se
Freq: Quarterly; **Circ:** 68,600
Advertising Manager: Kerstin Adell; **Publisher:** Per Olsson
Language(s): Swedish
ADVERTISING RATES:
Full Page Colour .... SEK 57100
SCC .... SEK 475.83
CONSUMER: HOLIDAYS & TRAVEL: Travel

SEGLARBLADET
51334W91A-180
Editorial: GKSS Box 5039, 426 05 VÄSTRA FRÖLUNDA **Tel:** 31 29 90 40
Email: chefredaktor@gkss.se **Web site:** http://www.gkss.se
Date Established: 1911; **Freq:** Quarterly; **Circ:** 5,000
Editor-in-Chief: Alf Tornberg
Profile: Magazine of the Royal Gothenburg Yacht Club.
Language(s): Swedish
CONSUMER: RECREATION & LEISURE: Boating & Yachting

SEGLING
51335W91A-182
Editorial: 113 92 STOCKHOLM **Tel:** 8 506 678 00 **Fax:** 8 506 678 09
Email: info@segling.biz **Web site:** http://www.segling.biz
Date Established: 1981; **Freq:** Monthly; **Circ:** 60,000
Editor-in-Chief: Joakim Hermansson
Profile: Magazine covering all aspects of sailing.
Language(s): Swedish
ADVERTISING RATES:
Full Page Colour .... SEK 22600
SCC .... SEK 188.33
Copy instructions: *Copy Date:* 21 days prior to publication date
CONSUMER: RECREATION & LEISURE: Boating & Yachting

SEKOTIDNINGEN
50436W32K-210
Editorial: Box 1102, 111 81 STOCKHOLM **Tel:** 8 791 41 00 **Fax:** 8 21 16 94
Email: redaktionen@sekotidningen.se **Web site:** http://www.sekotidningen.se
Freq: 6 issues yearly; **Circ:** 129,300
Advertising Manager: Agneta Erneberg
Profile: Magazine covering matters concerning civil service, the Ministry for Civil Service Affairs, public administration and related topics. Official publication of the Union of Service and Communication Employees.
Language(s): Swedish
ADVERTISING RATES:
Full Page Colour .... SEK 24000
SCC .... SEK 300
BUSINESS: LOCAL GOVERNMENT, LEISURE & RECREATION: Civil Service

SEKOTIDNINGEN; SEKOTIDNINGEN.SE
1846415W14F-115
Editorial: Box 1102, 111 81 STOCKHOLM **Tel:** 8 791 41 00 **Fax:** 8211694
Email: redaktionen@sekotidningen.se **Web site:** http://www.sekotidningen.se
Freq: Daily; **Cover Price:** Free
Advertising Manager: Agneta Erneberg; **Publisher:** Mats Andersson
Language(s): Swedish
BUSINESS: COMMERCE, INDUSTRY & MANAGEMENT: Training & Recruitment

SERVICEHANDLAREN 50272W11A-30
Editorial: Servicehandlarn i Sverige AB, 716 31 FJUGESTA **Tel:** 585 317 01
Email: gunilla.pihlblad@servicehandlaren.se **Web site:** http://www.servicehandlaren.se
Freq: 6 issues yearly -, 8 nr per år; **Circ:** 18,300
Advertising Manager: Ann Tidqvist; **Publisher:** Gunilla Pihlblad
Profile: Magazine containing articles and information concerning the fast food and confectionery trade.
Language(s): Swedish
Readership: Read by owners of kiosks, convenience stores and fast-food units.
ADVERTISING RATES:
Full Page Colour .... SEK 44800
SCC .... SEK 257.50
BUSINESS: CATERING: Catering, Hotels & Restaurants

SFF-FILATELISTEN/SVENSK FILATELISTISK TIDSKRIFT
51145W79C-50
Editorial: Box 15074, 750 15 UPPSALA
Tel: 18 50 20 21
Email: redaktion@sff.nu **Web site:** http://www.sff.nu
Date Established: 1899; **Freq:** 6 issues yearly; **Circ:** 5,500
Editor: Bo Grendal; **Publisher:** Bo Grendal
Profile: Magazine about stamp-collecting.
Language(s): Swedish
CONSUMER: HOBBIES & DIY: Philately

SHERIFFI 1924923W76B-118
Editorial: Snoilskygatan 2b, 416 57 GOTEBORG
Tel: 708 58 82 35
Email: redaktionen@sheriffi.se **Web site:** http://www.sheriffi.se
Freq: Quarterly; **Circ:** 2,000
Editor-in-Chief: Sanna Posti Sjöman
Language(s): Swedish
CONSUMER: MUSIC & PERFORMING ARTS: Theatre

SHORTCUT 751051W14F-75
Editorial: Box 7691, 103 95 STOCKHOLM
Tel: 8 562 930 90
Email: info@shortcut.nu **Web site:** http://www.shortcut.nu
Date Established: 1999; **Freq:** Quarterly; **Circ:** 25,000
Editor: Malin Sund; **Editor-in-Chief:** Henrik Harr; **Advertising Manager:** Niclas Richtnér; **Publisher:** Andreas Dahlin
Language(s): Swedish
ADVERTISING RATES:
Full Page Colour .... SEK 37200
SCC .... SEK 310
Copy instructions: *Copy Date:* 30 days prior to publication date
BUSINESS: COMMERCE, INDUSTRY & MANAGEMENT: Training & Recruitment

SHOWROOM 1640912W2A-391
Editorial: Strandvägen 19, 114 56 STOCKHOLM
Tel: 8 661 18 90
Email: anna@sweetwilliams.se **Web site:** http://www.theshowroom.se
Freq: Quarterly; **Circ:** 1,000
Advertising Manager: Mikael Bergström
Language(s): Swedish
BUSINESS: COMMUNICATIONS, ADVERTISING & MARKETING

SHR-JOURNALEN 50660W15A-150
Editorial: Dalagatan 76, 113 24 STOCKHOLM
Tel: 8 30 94 40
Web site: http://www.shr.nu
Date Established: 1963; **Freq:** Quarterly; **Circ:** 1,700
Editor: Staffan Thomée; **Advertising Manager:** Staffan Thomée
Profile: Journal of the Swedish Association of Beauty Therapists.
Language(s): Swedish
BUSINESS: COSMETICS & HAIRDRESSING: Cosmetics

SIGNALEN 1835474W32G-275
Editorial: Box 5776, 114 87 STOCKHOLM
Tel: 8 407 30 00 **Fax:** 8 611 63 36
Email: signalen@sosalarm.se **Web site:** http://www.sosalarm.se
Freq: Quarterly; **Cover Price:** Free; **Circ:** 12,000
Editor: Bert Anderbring; **Publisher:** Sven-Runo Bergqvist
Language(s): Swedish
ADVERTISING RATES:
Full Page Colour .... SEK 6360
SCC .... SEK 53
BUSINESS: LOCAL GOVERNMENT, LEISURE & RECREATION: Community Care & Social Services

SIGNUM 51293W87-80
Editorial: Slottsgränd 6, 753 09 UPPSALA
Tel: 1858007 10 **Fax:** 1858007 20
Email: adm@signum.se **Web site:** http://www.signum.se
Freq: 6 issues yearly - (9 nr/år); **Circ:** 2,400
Advertising Manager: Per Lindqvist; **Publisher:** Frans Holin
Profile: Tabloid-sized Catholic newspaper covering religion, society and culture.
Language(s): Swedish
Readership: Read by people with an active interest in religion.
ADVERTISING RATES:
Full Page Colour .... SEK 5000
SCC .... SEK 41.66
CONSUMER: RELIGIOUS

SIGNUM; SIGNUM.SE
1844791W87-211
Editorial: Slottsgränd 6, 753 12 UPPSALA
Tel: 18580 07 10 **Fax:** 18580 07 20
Email: adm@signum.se **Web site:** http://www.signum.se
Freq: Daily; **Cover Price:** Free; **Circ:** 800 Unique Users
Editor-in-Chief: Ulf Jonsson; **Publisher:** Frans-J. Holin
Language(s): Swedish
ADVERTISING RATES:
SCC .... SEK 8.2
CONSUMER: RELIGIOUS

SIGTUNABYGDEN MÄRSTA TIDNING 634273W72-450
Editorial: Nymärstagatan 2, 195 30 MÄRSTA
Tel: 8 594 405 70 **Fax:** 8 594 405 99
Email: redaktion@sigtunabygden.se **Web site:** http://www.sigtunabygden.se
Date Established: 1984; **Freq:** Weekly; **Circ:** 27,400
Editor: Aina Liljefors; **Editor-in-Chief:** Maj-Lis Koivisto; **Advertising Manager:** Magnus Wranning; **Publisher:** Maj-Lis Koivisto
Profile: Newspaper featuring local news for Sigtuna.
Language(s): Swedish
ADVERTISING RATES:
Full Page Colour .... SEK 20640
SCC .... SEK 129
LOCAL NEWSPAPERS

SIMFRÄMJAREN LIVRÄDDAREN 51510W32E-150
Editorial: SLS, Spångavägen 47, 168 75 BROMMA
Tel: 31 744 16 52
Email: anders@pir87.se **Web site:** http://www.sls.a.se
Freq: Quarterly; **Circ:** 10,000
Editor-in-Chief: Anders Wernesten
Profile: Magazine featuring swimming and lifesaving.
Language(s): Swedish
Readership: Read by leisure centre personnel, professional swimming instructors, pool attendants and lifeguards.
BUSINESS: LOCAL GOVERNMENT, LEISURE & RECREATION: Swimming Pools

SISTA BREFVET 634745W62A-160
Editorial: Box 5015, 350 05 VÄXJÖ **Tel:** 470 75 54 62
Fax: 470 75 54 50
Email: sista.brefvet@siv.vxu.se **Web site:** http://www.siv.vxu.se
Date Established: 1969; **Freq:** 6 issues yearly; **Circ:** 10,000
Editor: Petter Ericsson
Profile: University magazine featuring a wide range of programmes and independent courses.
Language(s): Swedish
Readership: Aimed at undergraduates, researchers, lecturers and administrators at the Växjo university.
BUSINESS: CHURCH & SCHOOL EQUIPMENT & EDUCATION: Education

SITUATION STHLM 51615W82-217
Editorial: Box 19026, 104 32 STOCKHOLM
Tel: 8 545 95 38 **Fax:** 8 16 73 30
Email: red@situationsthlm.se **Web site:** http://www.situationsthlm.se
Date Established: 1995; **Freq:** Monthly; **Circ:** 22,000
Editor: Cyril Hellman; **Editor-in-Chief:** Ulf Stolt; **Managing Director:** Pia Læstadius; **Advertising Manager:** Herman Sundgren; **Publisher:** Ulf Stolt
Profile: Magazine is sold by homeless and unemployed people. Features general interest news and every day life in Stockholm.
Language(s): Swedish
Readership: Aimed at people aged between 20 and 40 years.
ADVERTISING RATES:
Full Page Colour .... SEK 24500
SCC .... SEK 204.17
CONSUMER: CURRENT AFFAIRS & POLITICS

SJ NYTT 1835868W49E-110
Editorial: Centralplan 19, 105 50 STOCKHOLM
Tel: 10 751 51 85
Circ: 3,200
Language(s): Swedish
ADVERTISING RATES:
Full Page Colour .... SEK 6400
SCC .... SEK 40
BUSINESS: TRANSPORT: Railways

SJÖBEFÄL 50519W45A-30
Editorial: Box 12100, 102 23 STOCKHOLM
Tel: 8 598 991 21 **Fax:** 86510848
Email: sjobefal@ledarna.se **Web site:** http://www.sbf.org.se
Date Established: 1891; **Freq:** 6 issues yearly; **Circ:** 4,600
Editor-in-Chief: Benkt Lundgren; **Advertising Manager:** Ankie Nilsson
Profile: Magazine covering technical, maritime and trade union topics concerning shipping.
Language(s): Swedish
Readership: Aimed at merchant marine officers working within the merchant fleet, on ferries and offshore units.
ADVERTISING RATES:
Full Page Colour .... SEK 9820
SCC .... SEK 81.83
BUSINESS: MARINE & SHIPPING

SJÖMANNEN 50511W45A-40
Editorial: Box 31176, 413 27 GOTEBORG
Tel: 31 42 94 20 **Fax:** 31429501
Email: sjomannen@seko.se **Web site:** http://www.sjomannen.se
Freq: 6 issues yearly; **Circ:** 12,000
Editor: Lennart Johnsson
Profile: European magazine about seafaring.
Language(s): Swedish
ADVERTISING RATES:
Full Page Colour .... SEK 24000
SCC .... SEK 200
BUSINESS: MARINE & SHIPPING

SJÖRAPPORTEN 752207W45A-100
Editorial: Sjöfartsverket, Huvudkontoret, 601 78 NORRKÖPING **Tel:** 11 19 14 35
Email: info@sjofartsverket.se **Web site:** http://www.sjofartsverket.se
Date Established: 1997; **Freq:** Monthly; **Circ:** 4,200
Publisher: Tommy Gardebring
Profile: Magazine of The Swedish Maritime Administration (SMA) dedicated to the maritime transport sector. To keep the sea lanes open and safe.
Language(s): Swedish
ADVERTISING RATES:
Full Page Colour .... SEK 8400
SCC .... SEK 70
BUSINESS: MARINE & SHIPPING

SJUKHUSLÄKAREN
1623570W32G-256
Editorial: Box 5610, 114 86 STOCKHOLM
Tel: 8 790 33 00
Email: gunilla.burenius@slf.se **Web site:** http://www.sjukhuslakaren.se
Freq: 6 issues yearly; **Circ:** 20,000
Editor: Christer Bark; **Advertising Manager:** Juris Purens; **Publisher:** Thomas Zilling
Language(s): Swedish
ADVERTISING RATES:
Full Page Colour .... SEK 30000
SCC .... SEK 250
Copy instructions: *Copy Date:* 11 days prior to publication date
BUSINESS: LOCAL GOVERNMENT, LEISURE & RECREATION: Community Care & Social Services

SJUKHUSLÄKAREN; SJUKHUSLAKAREN.SE
1846256W14L-200
Editorial: Box 5610, 114 86 STOCKHOLM
Tel: 8 790 33 00 **Fax:** 8 411 56 67
Email: helene.thornblad@slf.se **Web site:** http://www.sjukhuslakaren.se
Freq: Daily; **Cover Price:** Free; **Circ:** 4,000 Unique Users
Publisher: Thomas Zilling
Language(s): Swedish
BUSINESS: COMMERCE, INDUSTRY & MANAGEMENT: Trade Unions

SKANDINAVISK GALOPP
1655730W81D-128
Editorial: 161 89 STOCKHOLM **Tel:** 8 627 20 00
Fax: 8 764 50 28
Email: info@galoppsport.se **Web site:** http://www.skandinaviskgalopp.com
Freq: 26 issues yearly; **Circ:** 2,000
Editor: Björn Zachrisson; **Publisher:** Björn Eklund
Language(s): Swedish
CONSUMER: ANIMALS & PETS: Horses & Ponies

SKÅNEVETERANEN 751036W74C-360
Editorial: SPFs Distrikskansli i Höör, 243 31 HÖÖR
Tel: 413 291 14 **Fax:** 413 291 17
Email: spf.skane@telia.com **Web site:** http://www.spfpension.se/skanedistriktet
Freq: Quarterly; **Circ:** 30,000
Editor: Ulla Wilhelmsson
Language(s): Swedish
CONSUMER: WOMEN'S INTEREST CONSUMER MAGAZINES: Home & Family

SKÅNSKA DAGBLADET
50811W67B-6650
Editorial: Box 165, 201 21 MALMO **Tel:** 40 660 55 00
Fax: 40 704 45
Email: redaktion@skd.se **Web site:** http://www.skd.se
Date Established: 1888
Circ: 37,400
Editor: Carina Gavelin; **Publisher:** Jan A Johansson
Language(s): Swedish
ADVERTISING RATES:
Full Page Colour .... SEK 55125
SCC .... SEK 275
REGIONAL DAILY & SUNDAY NEWSPAPERS: Regional Daily Newspapers

SKÅNSKA LANTBRUK
634758W74C-123
Editorial: Hushållningssällskapet Kristianstad, 291 09 KRISTIANSTAD **Tel:** 44 22 99 01 **Fax:** 44229310
Email: elisabet.svensson@hush.se **Web site:** http://www.hush.se/l
Freq: Quarterly; **Circ:** 6,500
Publisher: Sven Fajersson
Profile: Magazine featuring home, household and garden.
Language(s): Swedish
Readership: Read by members of Hushållningsskapet Malmöhus.
Copy instructions: *Copy Date:* 21 days prior to publication date
CONSUMER: WOMEN'S INTEREST CONSUMER MAGAZINES: Home & Family

SKARABORGS ALLEHANDA
50831W67B-6700
Editorial: Box 407, 541 28 SKÖVDE
Tel: 500 46 75 00 **Fax:** 500 48 05 82
Email: redaktion@sla.se **Web site:** http://www.sla.se
Date Established: 1884
Circ: 24,300
Editor-in-Chief: Niclas Lindstrand; **Publisher:** Måns Johnson
Language(s): Swedish
ADVERTISING RATES:
Full Page Colour .... SEK 29900
SCC .... SEK 149.50
REGIONAL DAILY & SUNDAY NEWSPAPERS: Regional Daily Newspapers

SKARABORGS LÄNS TIDNING
50829W67B-6750
Editorial: Box 214, 532 23 SKARA **Tel:** 511 77 01 00
Fax: 511 77 01 90
Email: red.sklt@vgt.se **Web site:** http://www.vgt.se
Date Established: 1884
Circ: 7,250
Advertising Manager: Thomas Thomsen; **Publisher:** Dan Gillblad
Language(s): Swedish
ADVERTISING RATES:
Full Page Colour .... SEK 15000
SCC .... SEK 38.96
REGIONAL DAILY & SUNDAY NEWSPAPERS: Regional Daily Newspapers

SKARABORGSBYGDEN
624458W72-457
Editorial: Box 204, 532 23 SKARA **Tel:** 511 302 50
Fax: 51112620
Email: redaktion@skaraborgsbygden.se **Web site:** http://www.skaraborgsbygden.se
Date Established: 1955; **Freq:** Weekly; **Circ:** 11,600
Editor-in-Chief: Tomaz Magnusson; **Advertising Manager:** Gunilla Druve-Jansson; **Publisher:** Sven Gärdekrans
Language(s): Swedish
ADVERTISING RATES:
Full Page Colour .... SEK 15695
SCC .... SEK 78.48
Copy instructions: *Copy Date:* 7 days prior to publication date
LOCAL NEWSPAPERS

SKARABORGSBYGDEN; SKARABORGSBYGDEN.SE
1846266W65A-1061
Editorial: Box 204, 532 23 SKARA **Tel:** 511 302 50
Fax: 511 126 20
Email: redaktion@skaraborgsbygden.se **Web site:** http://www.skaraborgsbygden.se
Freq: Daily; **Cover Price:** Free; **Circ:** 10,666 Unique Users
Editor: Sven Gärdekrans; **Editor-in-Chief:** Thomaz Magnusson; **Advertising Manager:** Gunilla Druve-Jansson; **Publisher:** Thomaz Magnusson
Language(s): Swedish
ADVERTISING RATES:
SCC .... SEK 15.6
NATIONAL DAILY & SUNDAY NEWSPAPERS: National Daily Newspapers

SKÄRGÅRDEN; SKARGARDEN.SE 1846284W65A-1067
Editorial: Virkesvägen 2 B, 4 tr, 120 30 STOCKHOLM
Tel: 854 54 27 00 **Fax:** 8 545 427 27

Email: redaktionen@skargarden.se **Web site:** http://www.skargarden.se
Freq: Daily; **Cover Price:** Free; **Circ:** 3,400 Unique Users
Editor-in-Chief: Lasse Söderman; **Advertising Manager:** Ulf Gustavsson; **Publisher:** Lasse Söderman
Language(s): Swedish
ADVERTISING RATES:
SCC .... SEK 14
NATIONAL DAILY & SUNDAY NEWSPAPERS: National Daily Newspapers

SKÄRGÅRDSBÅTEN 51336W91A-185
Editorial: Nybrogatan 76, 114 41 STOCKHOLM
Tel: 8 662 89 02
Email: info@skargardsbaten.se **Web site:** http://home.swipnet.se/skargardsbaten/tidning.htm
Freq: Quarterly; **Circ:** 4,000
Editor: Gunnar Friberg; **Publisher:** Gunnar Friberg
Profile: Magazine about sailing around the Stockholm archipelago.
Language(s): Swedish
CONSUMER: RECREATION & LEISURE: Boating & Yachting

SKÄRGÅRDSLIV 1834439W4A-35
Editorial: Kustförlaget, Box 92173, 120 09 STOCKHOLM **Tel:** 8 545 427 00 **Fax:** 8 545 427 27
Email: skargardsliv@skargarden.se **Web site:** http://www.skargardsliv.se
Freq: 6 issues yearly; **Circ:** 30,000
Editor-in-Chief: Martin Goodwin; **Publisher:** Martin Goodwin
Language(s): Swedish
ADVERTISING RATES:
Full Page Colour .... SEK 23814
SCC .... SEK 198.45
BUSINESS: ARCHITECTURE & BUILDING: Architecture

SKATTENYTT 50175W1M-50
Editorial: Box 1994, 751 49 UPPSALA
Tel: 18 65 03 30 **Fax:** 18 69 30 99
Email: sn@iustus.se **Web site:** http://www.skattenytt.se
Date Established: 1953; **Freq:** Monthly; **Circ:** 2,500
Editor: Roger Persson Österman; **Advertising Manager:** Marita Dehlin; **Publisher:** Roger Persson Österman
Profile: Journal covering all aspects of taxation.
Language(s): Swedish
BUSINESS: FINANCE & ECONOMICS: Taxation

SKI & BOARD MAGAZINE 1664782W75G-114
Editorial: Svenska Skidförbundet Riksskidstadion, 791 19 FALUN **Tel:** 23 874 40 **Fax:** 23 874 41
Email: info@skiboardmagazine.se **Web site:** http://www.skiboardmagazine.se
Freq: 6 issues yearly; **Circ:** 2,500
Advertising Manager: Agneta Nydahl
Language(s): Swedish
CONSUMER: SPORT: Winter Sports

SKIDLÄRAREN 1655941W75G-112
Editorial: Torreby 38, 455 93 MUNKEDAL
Tel: 524 213 00 **Fax:** 524 211 22
Email: micke@skidlararforeningen.se **Web site:** http://www.skidlararforeningen.se
Freq: Quarterly; **Circ:** 700
Editor: Michael Seemann
Language(s): Swedish
CONSUMER: SPORT: Winter Sports

SKODAWORLD 634748W77E-485
Editorial: Skoda Auto Sverige, 151 88 SÖDERTÄLJE
Tel: 8 553 865 17
Email: henrik.svensson@skoda.se **Web site:** http://www.skoda.se
Date Established: 1995; **Freq:** Half-yearly; **Circ:** 130,000
Editor: Björn Sundefeldt; **Advertising Manager:** Michael Fant
Profile: Magazine about Skoda cars.
Language(s): Swedish
Readership: Read by owners.
CONSUMER: MOTORING & CYCLING: Club Cars

SKOG & INDUSTRI 50530W46-69
Editorial: Box 55525, 102 04 STOCKHOLM
Tel: 8 762 72 02 **Fax:** 86117122
Email: lotta.larson@skogsindustrierna.org **Web site:** http://www.skogsindustrierna.org
Freq: Quarterly; **Cover Price:** Free; **Circ:** 16,000
Profile: Official journal of the Swedish Forest Industries Association.
Language(s): Swedish
ADVERTISING RATES:
Full Page Colour .... SEK 28000
SCC .... SEK 233.33
BUSINESS: TIMBER, WOOD & FORESTRY

SKOG & SÅG 50526W46-60
Editorial: Box 37, 551 12 JÖNKÖPING
Tel: 36 34 30 00 **Fax:** 36 12 86 10
Email: info@sagisyd.se **Web site:** http://www.sagisyd.se
Freq: Quarterly; **Cover Price:** Free; **Circ:** 73,800
Editor: Sven Magnusson; **Advertising Manager:** Eva Raihle; **Publisher:** Henrik Asplund
Profile: Publication containing information about the forest and wood industry.
Language(s): Swedish
Readership: Aimed at forest owners in the south of Sweden.
ADVERTISING RATES:
Full Page Colour .... SEK 19500
SCC .... SEK 162.50
Copy instructions: *Copy Date:* 28 days prior to publication date
BUSINESS: TIMBER, WOOD & FORESTRY

SKOGEN 50527W46-65
Editorial: Box 1159, 111 81 STOCKHOLM
Tel: 8 412 15 00 **Fax:** 8 412 15 10
Email: info@skogen.se **Web site:** http://www.skogen.se
Date Established: 1914; **Freq:** Monthly; **Circ:** 15,500
Editor-in-Chief: Bengt Ek; **Advertising Manager:** Eva Ström; **Publisher:** Bengt Ek
Profile: Magazine concerning forestry policies, technology, economy and ecology.
Language(s): Swedish
Readership: Read by forestry employees, contractors and owners of forests.
ADVERTISING RATES:
Full Page Colour .... SEK 22100
SCC .... SEK 184.17
BUSINESS: TIMBER, WOOD & FORESTRY

SKOGEN I SKOLAN 750647W46-110
Editorial: Kansliet för lärarutbildning, Umeå universitet, 901 87 UMEÅ **Tel:** 90 786 68 58
Email: skogeniskolan@adm.umu.se **Web site:** http://www.skogeniskolan.se
Freq: Quarterly; **Circ:** 21,000
Publisher: Birgitta Wilhelmsson
Language(s): Swedish
BUSINESS: TIMBER, WOOD & FORESTRY

SKOGSAKTUELLT 1858701W21A-86
Editorial: Boställsvägen 4, 702 27 ÖREBRO
Tel: 19 16 61 30 **Fax:** 19 16 61 45
Email: info@skogsaktuellt.se **Web site:** http://www.skogsaktuellt.se
Freq: Monthly; **Cover Price:** Free; **Circ:** 92,000
Editor: Teresia Borgman; **Publisher:** Stefan Ljungdahl
Language(s): Swedish
BUSINESS: AGRICULTURE & FARMING

SKOGSEKO 50529W46-68
Editorial: Skogsstyrelsen, 551 83 JÖNKÖPING
Tel: 36 35 39 00 **Fax:** 36166170
Email: skogseko@skogsstyrelsen.se **Web site:** http://www.skogsstyrelsen.se
Freq: Quarterly; **Circ:** 260,000
Publisher: Rikard Flyckt
Profile: Newsletter for private forest owners.
Language(s): Swedish
ADVERTISING RATES:
Full Page Colour .... SEK 122200
SCC .... SEK 1018.33
BUSINESS: TIMBER, WOOD & FORESTRY

SKOGSSPORT 51051W75L-190
Editorial: Box 22, 171 18 SOLNA **Tel:** 8 587 720 00
Fax: 858772088
Email: skogssport@orientering.se **Web site:** http://www.orientering.se
Date Established: 1947; **Freq:** Monthly; **Circ:** 8,800
Advertising Manager: Knut Nord; **Publisher:** Jan Eric Goth
Profile: Magazine of the Swedish Orienteering Association.
Language(s): Swedish
Readership: Read by orienteers and outdoor enthusiasts.
Copy instructions: *Copy Date:* 30 days prior to publication date
CONSUMER: SPORT: Outdoor

SKOGSVÄRDEN 1803973W46-128
Editorial: Skogssällskapet, Box 5083, 402 22 GÖTEBORG **Tel:** 771 22 00 44 **Fax:** 31 335 89 07
Email: hans-joran.hildingsson@skogssallskapet.se
Web site: http://www.skogssallskapet.se
Freq: Quarterly; **Circ:** 12,000
Language(s): Swedish
ADVERTISING RATES:
Full Page Colour .... SEK 15000
SCC .... SEK 125
BUSINESS: TIMBER, WOOD & FORESTRY

SKOLHÄLSAN 50618W56B-50
Editorial: c/o Ewa Rensfelt, Okvägen 33, 281 51 HÄSSLEHOLM **Tel:** 45110781
Email: ewa.rensfelt@telia.com **Web site:** http://www.skolskoterskor.se
Freq: Quarterly; **Circ:** 2,300
Editor: Ewa Rensfelt; **Advertising Manager:** Gunnar Nornemark; **Publisher:** Gunilla Fagerholt
Profile: Official journal of the Swedish Association of School Nurses.
Language(s): Swedish
BUSINESS: HEALTH & MEDICAL: Nursing

SKOLHÄLSOVÅRD 1639389W74D-98
Editorial: Box 22543, 104 22 STOCKHOLM
Tel: 8 462 26 70 **Fax:** 84620322
Email: emma.wistrand@gothiaforlag.se **Web site:** http://www.gothiaforlag.se
Freq: Quarterly; **Circ:** 1,200
Editor: Annika Strandell; **Publisher:** Ingela Skantze
Language(s): Swedish
CONSUMER: WOMEN'S INTEREST CONSUMER MAGAZINES: Child Care

SKOLLEDAREN 1861519W62A-528
Editorial: Sveriges Skolledarförbund, Box 3266, 103 65 STOCKHOLM **Tel:** 8 567 062 00
Email: kerstin.weyler@skolledarna.se **Web site:** http://www.skolledarna.se
Circ: 7,900
Editor: Kerstin Weyler
Language(s): Swedish
ADVERTISING RATES:
Full Page Colour .... SEK 22000
SCC .... SEK 183.33
BUSINESS: CHURCH & SCHOOL EQUIPMENT & EDUCATION: Education

SKOLMATENS VÄNNER 1625772W22A-139
Editorial: 105 33 STOCKHOLM **Tel:** 70 237 99 29
Email: info@skolmatensvanner.org **Web site:** http://www.skolmatensvanner.se
Freq: Half-yearly; **Circ:** 35,000
Language(s): Swedish
BUSINESS: FOOD

SKOLVÄRLDEN 50710W62A-210
Editorial: Box 3265, 103 65 STOCKHOLM
Tel: 8 50 55 62 00 **Fax:** 8 55 62 90
Email: redaktionen@skolvarlden.se **Web site:** http://www.skolvarlden.se
Date Established: 1901; **Freq:** 26 issues yearly; **Circ:** 87,700
Advertising Manager: Britt Marie Classon
Profile: Journal covering issues of interest to teachers at all levels. Contains articles about different methods of teaching, political news and general information.
Language(s): Swedish
Readership: Aimed at teachers and other people working with education.
ADVERTISING RATES:
Full Page Colour .... SEK 35500
SCC .... SEK 366.66
BUSINESS: CHURCH & SCHOOL EQUIPMENT & EDUCATION: Education

SKOMAGAZINET 752073W74B-40
Editorial: Bergvägen 12 A, 182 46 ENEBYBERG
Tel: 8 768 85 03 **Fax:** 87688523
Email: tidningen@skomagazinet.se **Web site:** http://www.skomagazinet.se
Date Established: 1997; **Freq:** 6 issues yearly; **Circ:** 2,000
Advertising Manager: Mikael Holmertz; **Publisher:** Mariette Baecklund
Language(s): Swedish
Copy instructions: *Copy Date:* 30 days prior to publication date
CONSUMER: WOMEN'S INTEREST CONSUMER MAGAZINES: Women's Interest - Fashion

SKÖNA HEM 50964W74C-126
Editorial: 105 44 STOCKHOLM **Tel:** 8 736 52 00
Fax: 8 33 74 11
Email: skonahem@skonahem.com **Web site:** http://www.skonahem.com
Date Established: 1979; **Freq:** Monthly; **Circ:** 93,400
Editor-in-Chief: Bella Linde; **Publisher:** Claes Blom
Profile: Magazine about home furnishing, decor and interior design.
Language(s): Swedish
ADVERTISING RATES:
Full Page Colour .... SEK 54500
SCC .... SEK 454.16
Copy instructions: *Copy Date:* 28 days prior to publication date
CONSUMER: WOMEN'S INTEREST CONSUMER MAGAZINES: Home & Family

SKÖNA HEM - SKAPA STILEN 1803995W74C-512
Editorial: Bonnier Tidskrifter AB, 105 44 STOCKHOLM **Tel:** 8 736 52 00 **Fax:** 8 34 11 38
Email: per.wennberg@skonahem.com **Web site:** http://www.skonahem.com
Freq: Annual; **Circ:** 50,000
Editor-in-Chief: Bella Linde
Language(s): Swedish
ADVERTISING RATES:
Full Page Colour .... SEK 46500
SCC .... SEK 387.50
CONSUMER: WOMEN'S INTEREST CONSUMER MAGAZINES: Home & Family

SKÖNA HEM; SKONAHEM.COM 1844698W74C-520
Editorial: 105 44 STOCKHOLM **Tel:** 8 736 52 00
Fax: 8 33 74 11
Email: webredaktion@skonahem.com **Web site:** http://www.skonahem.com
Freq: Daily; **Cover Price:** Free
Advertising Manager: Karolina Hülphers; **Publisher:** Claes Blom
Language(s): Swedish
CONSUMER: WOMEN'S INTEREST CONSUMER MAGAZINES: Home & Family

SKRÄDDERI 50534W47A-75
Editorial: Sv Skrädderiförbund, Box 10111, 100 55 STOCKHOLM **Tel:** 8 662 07 45
Email: peter_magnusson@comhem.se **Web site:** http://www.skradderiforbundet.se
Date Established: 1893; **Freq:** Quarterly; **Circ:** 270
Editor-in-Chief: Eva Lundholm; **Publisher:** Eva Lundholm
Profile: Magazine read by tailors and employees of clothing factories.
Language(s): Swedish
BUSINESS: CLOTHING & TEXTILES

SKTF-TIDNINGEN 50417W32A-200
Editorial: Box 7825, 103 97 STOCKHOLM
Tel: 8 789 63 00 **Fax:** 8 789 64 79
Email: sktftidningen@sktf.se **Web site:** http://www.sktftidningen.nu
Freq: 26 issues yearly; **Circ:** 159,200
Advertising Manager: Mikael Stefansson; **Publisher:** Kent Källqvist
Profile: Magazine containing articles and information about municipal work and local government. Contains news about politics, economics and workers' rights.
Language(s): Swedish
Readership: Read by local government employees.
ADVERTISING RATES:
Full Page Colour .... SEK 38200
SCC .... SEK 238.75
BUSINESS: LOCAL GOVERNMENT, LEISURE & RECREATION: Local Government

SLITZ 51100W86C-150
Editorial: MDM Media AB, 120 30 STOCKHOLM
Tel: 8 506 122 00 **Fax:** 850612201
Email: red@slitz.se **Web site:** http://www.slitz.se
Freq: Monthly; **Circ:** 42,000
Publisher: Mats Drougge
Profile: Magazine containing lifestyle articles and information on popular music, fashion and culture.
Language(s): Swedish
Readership: Aimed at men aged between 20 and 40 years.
ADVERTISING RATES:
Full Page Colour .... SEK 59500
SCC .... SEK 495.83
Copy instructions: *Copy Date:* 30 days prior to publication date
CONSUMER: ADULT & GAY MAGAZINES: Men's Lifestyle Magazines

SLITZ; SLITZ.SE 1846679W5E-126
Editorial: Box 2229, 103 15 STOCKHOLM
Tel: 8 506 122 00 **Fax:** 8 506 122 01
Email: red@slitz.se **Web site:** http://www.slitz.se
Freq: Daily; **Cover Price:** Free; **Circ:** 24,286 Unique Users
Editor-in-Chief: Mats Drougge; **Managing Director:** Mats Drougge; **Publisher:** Mats Drougge
Language(s): Swedish
ADVERTISING RATES:
SCC .... SEK 99
BUSINESS: COMPUTERS & AUTOMATION: Data Transmission

SLÖJDFORUM 50718W62B-210
Editorial: 713 94 NORA **Tel:** 587 600 15
Email: slojdforum@lararforbundet.se **Web site:** http://www.slojdforum.se
Freq: 6 issues yearly; **Circ:** 6,600
Editor: Hasse Hedström; **Advertising Manager:** Lisen Skeppstedt; **Publisher:** Hasse Hedström
Profile: Magazine covering handicrafts as part of the education for children under 15 years of age.
Language(s): Swedish
Readership: Aimed at teachers.
BUSINESS: CHURCH & SCHOOL EQUIPMENT & EDUCATION: Education Teachers

SMÅLANDS NÄRINGSLIV 634765W63-85
Editorial: Smålands näringsliv, Stångågatan 46, 598 80 VIMMERBY **Tel:** 492 160 00 **Fax:** 492 101 02
Email: anders.lagerman@vimmerbytidning.se **Web site:** http://www.smalandsnaringsliv.se
Freq: 6 issues yearly; **Circ:** 28,800

Editor: Anders Lagerman; **Editor-in-Chief:** Bengt Ingermarsson; **Advertising Manager:** Bert-Ove Svensson; **Publisher:** Bengt Ingermarsson
Profile: Magazine focusing on business in the Småland region.
Language(s): Swedish
BUSINESS: REGIONAL BUSINESS

SMÅLANDSPOSTEN 50848W67B-6900
Editorial: 351 70 VÄXJO **Tel:** 470 77 05 00
Fax: 470 484 25
Email: nyhet.red@smp.se **Web site:** http://www.smp.se
Date Established: 1866
Circ: 38,600
Editor: Berne Persson; **Advertising Manager:** Ann Kjellberg; **Publisher:** Magnus Karlsson
Language(s): Swedish
ADVERTISING RATES:
Full Page Colour .... SEK 45744
SCC .... SEK 228.72
REGIONAL DAILY & SUNDAY NEWSPAPERS: Regional Daily Newspapers

SMÅLANDSPOSTEN; SMP.SE 1623572W67E-5041
Editorial: 351 70 VÄXJO **Tel:** 470 77 05 00
Fax: 47048425
Email: webbred@smp.se **Web site:** http://www.smp.se
Freq: Daily; **Cover Price:** Free; **Circ:** 40,200 Unique Users
Advertising Manager: Maria Thuresson; **Publisher:** Magnus Karlsson
Language(s): Swedish
REGIONAL DAILY & SUNDAY NEWSPAPERS: Regional Offices

SMÅLÄNNINGEN 50804W67B-6950
Editorial: Box 304, 341 26 LJUNGBY **Tel:** 372 692 00
Fax: 372 800 22
Email: redax@smalanningen.se **Web site:** http://www.smalanningen.se
Circ: 12,900
Editor: Gunnar Edwardsson; **Advertising Manager:** Sonny Knutsson
Language(s): Swedish
ADVERTISING RATES:
Full Page Colour .... SEK 25995
SCC .... SEK 129.97
REGIONAL DAILY & SUNDAY NEWSPAPERS: Regional Daily Newspapers

SMARTSON.SE 1844532W78R-284
Editorial: Industrigatan 4A, 112 46 STOCKHOLM
Tel: 8 545 201 60
Email: pressrelease@smartson.se **Web site:** http://www.smartson.se
Freq: Daily; **Cover Price:** Free; **Circ:** 22,556 Unique Users
Advertising Manager: Per Guinchard
Language(s): Swedish
CONSUMER: CONSUMER ELECTRONICS: Consumer Electronics Related

SMÉJOURNALEN 634277W72-470
Editorial: Tunprint AB, Box 457, 633 42 ESKILSTUNA
Tel: 16 200 30 20 **Fax:** 510 087
Email: redaktion@smejournalen.se **Web site:** http://www.smejournalen.se
Date Established: 1997; **Freq:** Weekly; **Cover Price:** Free; **Circ:** 46,120
Editor: Annika Dahlgren; **Managing Director:** Anders Boberg; **Advertising Manager:** Anders Bjuvsjö; **Publisher:** Staffan Lönner
Profile: Newspaper featuring local news for Kungsörs, Eskilstuna and Strängnäs.
Language(s): Swedish
ADVERTISING RATES:
Full Page Colour .... SEK 19000
SCC .... SEK 95
LOCAL NEWSPAPERS

SMITTSKYDD 1626238W56A-333
Editorial: Nobels väg 18, 171 82 SOLNA
Tel: 8 457 23 00
Web site: http://www.smittskyddsinstitutet.se
Freq: 6 issues yearly; **Circ:** 4,000
Editor-in-Chief: Marco Morner; **Publisher:** Ragnar Norrby
Language(s): Swedish
BUSINESS: HEALTH & MEDICAL

SNOW RIDER 634767W75G-97
Editorial: Sågbacksvägen 8, 792 91 MORA
Tel: 250 228 85 **Fax:** 250 228 83
Email: bjorn@snowrider.se **Web site:** http://www.snowrider.se
Date Established: 1997; **Freq:** 6 issues yearly; **Circ:** 8,300
Editor: Affe Sundström; **Editor-in-Chief:** Björn Friström; **Advertising Manager:** Björn Friström; **Publisher:** Björn Friström
Profile: Magazine featuring snowmobiles.
Language(s): Swedish
CONSUMER: SPORT: Winter Sports

SNOWMOBILE 51039W75G-95
Editorial: Klutmark 136, 931 97 SKELLEFTEÅ
Tel: 910 72 66 70 **Fax:** 910 72 66 80
Email: redaktionen@snowmobile.se **Web site:** http://www.snowmobile.se
Date Established: 1986; **Freq:** 6 issues yearly; **Circ:** 11,100
Editor-in-Chief: Patrik Edström; **Advertising Manager:** Stefan Jonsson
Profile: Magazine covering snowmobiling in Scandinavia and the USA. Largest snowmobile magazine outside North America.
Language(s): Swedish
Readership: Snowmobilers, mainly men aged 25-55. Outdoor life-style, high computer and mobile phone ownership.
CONSUMER: SPORT: Winter Sports

SOCIAL OMSORG 749792W32G-245
Tel: 410 73 32 53
Email: siv.bringetun@fso.nu **Web site:** http://www.fso.nu
Freq: 6 issues yearly; **Circ:** 3,000
Publisher: Siv Bringetun
Language(s): Swedish
BUSINESS: LOCAL GOVERNMENT, LEISURE & RECREATION: Community Care & Social Services

SOCIALMEDICINSK TIDSKRIFT 50607W56A-60
Editorial: Box 7245, 402 35 GÖTEBORG
Tel: 31 16 09 80
Web site: http://www.socialmedicinsktidskrift.se
Date Established: 1924; **Freq:** 6 issues yearly; **Circ:** 2,500
Editor: Bo J.A. Haglund
Profile: Journal covering health and social issues. Contains news and articles about the Swedish health service.
Language(s): Swedish
ADVERTISING RATES:
Full Page Colour .... SEK 3000
SCC .... SEK 25
BUSINESS: HEALTH & MEDICAL

SOCIALPOLITIK 601519W82-221
Editorial: Eriksberg 137, 451 96 UDDEVALLA
Tel: 31 14 48 08
Email: socialpolitik@socialpolitik.com **Web site:** http://www.socialpolitik.com
Date Established: 1994; **Freq:** Quarterly; **Circ:** 12,000
Advertising Manager: Efva Bengtsson; **Publisher:** Maria Wallin
Profile: International journal featuring articles on gender and social policy, citizenship, and the role of states in constructing and organising relations in the family, workplace and society.
Language(s): Swedish
Readership: Aimed at scholars, students and professional involved in gender studies, also those in the fields of history, sociology, political science, economics, philosophy and law.
ADVERTISING RATES:
Full Page Colour .... SEK 13900
SCC .... SEK 115.83
CONSUMER: CURRENT AFFAIRS & POLITICS

SOCIALVETENSKAPLIG TIDSKRIFT 751182W56N-210
Editorial: Institutionen för socialt arbete, Box 720, 405 30 GOTEBORG **Tel:** 31 773 1614
Email: margareta.back-wiklund@socwork.gu.se **Web site:** http://www.socwork2.gu.se//svt/svt.htm
Freq: Quarterly; **Circ:** 1,400
Publisher: Margareta Bäck-Wiklund
Language(s): Swedish
BUSINESS: HEALTH & MEDICAL: Mental Health

SOCIONOMEN 50432W32G-210
Editorial: Box 12800, 112 96 STOCKHOLM
Tel: 8 617 44 37 **Fax:** 8 617 44 40
Email: socionomen@akademssr.se **Web site:** http://www.socionomen.nu
Date Established: 1987; **Freq:** 6 issues yearly; **Circ:** 9,900
Editor-in-Chief: Lena Engelmark; **Publisher:** Lena Engelmark
Profile: Journal for qualified social workers.
Language(s): Swedish
ADVERTISING RATES:
Full Page Colour .... SEK 18900
SCC .... SEK 157.5
BUSINESS: LOCAL GOVERNMENT, LEISURE & RECREATION: Community Care & Social Services

SODA - SÖDERTÖRNS HÖGSKOLAS KÅRTIDNING 751030W62A-465
Editorial: SöderS, Södertörns Högskola, 141 89 HUDDINGE **Tel:** 8 608 40 35 **Fax:** 8 608 40 81
Email: sodared@soders.nu **Web site:** http://www.sodamag.se
Freq: 6 issues yearly; **Circ:** 2,000
Editor-in-Chief: Maria Gullstam; **Publisher:** Malin Karlsson
Language(s): Swedish
BUSINESS: CHURCH & SCHOOL EQUIPMENT & EDUCATION: Education

SÖDERHAMNS KURIREN 50833W67B-4500
Editorial: Box 514, 826 27 SÖDERHAMN
Tel: 270 740 00 **Fax:** 270 740 70
Email: redaktion@soderhamnskuriren.se **Web site:** http://www.helahalsingland.se
Date Established: 1895
Circ: 7,800
Editor: Maya Halldén; **Publisher:** Mats Åmvall
Language(s): Swedish
ADVERTISING RATES:
Full Page Colour .... SEK 30960
SCC .... SEK 154.80
REGIONAL DAILY & SUNDAY NEWSPAPERS: Regional Daily Newspapers

SÖDERHAMNS KURIREN; SODERHAMNSKURIREN.SE 1843669W65A-1010
Editorial: Box 514, 826 27 SÖDERHAMN
Tel: 270 740 00 **Fax:** 27074070
Email: webmaster@soderhamnskuriren.se **Web site:** http://www.helahalsingland.se
Freq: Daily; **Cover Price:** Free; **Circ:** 1,491 Unique Users
Publisher: Mats Åmvall
Language(s): Swedish
NATIONAL DAILY & SUNDAY NEWSPAPERS: National Daily Newspapers

SÖDERHAMNSNYTT 634294W72-475
Editorial: Box 514, 826 27 SÖDERHAMN
Tel: 270 26 53 50 **Fax:** 270 26 53 79
Email: redaktion@soderhamnsnytt.se **Web site:** http://www.soderhamnsnytt.se
Freq: Weekly; **Cover Price:** Free; **Circ:** 14,500
Editor: Sara Oscarsson
Language(s): Swedish
ADVERTISING RATES:
Full Page Colour .... SEK 22320
SCC .... SEK 111.6
LOCAL NEWSPAPERS

SÖDERMANLANDS NYHETER 50819W67B-7000
Editorial: 611 79 NYKÖPING **Tel:** 155 767 00
Email: redaktionen@sn.se **Web site:** http://www.sn.se
Cover Price: Free; **Circ:** 25,500
Editor: Pernilla Yderbo; **Managing Director:** Robert Jonsson; **Advertising Manager:** Åke Hökby; **Publisher:** Göran Carstorp
Language(s): Swedish
ADVERTISING RATES:
Full Page Colour .... SEK 41450
SCC .... SEK 207.25
REGIONAL DAILY & SUNDAY NEWSPAPERS: Regional Daily Newspapers

SÖDERMANLANDS NYHETER; SN.SE 1843660W65A-1007
Editorial: 611 79 NYKÖPING **Tel:** 155 767 00
Fax: 155 268 682
Email: redaktionen@sn.se **Web site:** http://www.sn.se
Freq: Daily; **Cover Price:** Free; **Circ:** 9,081 Unique Users
Editor-in-Chief: Göran Carstorp; **Advertising Manager:** Åke Hökby; **Publisher:** Göran Carstorp
Language(s): Swedish
ADVERTISING RATES:
SCC .... SEK 41
NATIONAL DAILY & SUNDAY NEWSPAPERS: National Daily Newspapers

SÖDERTÄLJE POSTEN 634298W72-480
Editorial: Bellevuegatan 6, 151 73 SÖDERTÄLJE
Tel: 8 550 641 14
Email: redaktion@sodertaljeposten.se **Web site:** http://www.sodertaljeposten.se
Date Established: 1993; **Freq:** 104 issues yearly; **Circ:** 47,800
Editor: Marie Pallhed; **Advertising Manager:** Nancy Lukic
Profile: Newspaper featuring news for Gnesta, Nykvarn and surrounding areas.
Language(s): Swedish
ADVERTISING RATES:
Full Page Colour .... SEK 33984
SCC .... SEK 130
LOCAL NEWSPAPERS

SÖDRA DALARNES TIDNING 50788W67B-7050
Editorial: Åsögatan 62, 776 31 HEDEMORA
Tel: 23 935 00 **Fax:** 225 59 54 40
Email: sdt.red@dt.se **Web site:** http://www.dt.se
Date Established: 1881
Circ: 6,100
Advertising Manager: Olov Norberg; **Publisher:** Pär Fagerström
Language(s): Swedish
ADVERTISING RATES:
Full Page Colour .... SEK 13000
SCC .... SEK 65
REGIONAL DAILY & SUNDAY NEWSPAPERS: Regional Daily Newspapers

SÖDRA KONTAKT 1836250W46-130
Editorial: 351 89 VÄXJÖ **Tel:** 470 890 00
Fax: 470 894 70
Email: sven-eric.petersson@sodra.com **Web site:** http://www.sodra.com
Freq: 6 times a year; **Cover Price:** Paid; **Circ:** 5,000 Unique Users
Editor: Sven-Eric Petersson; **Publisher:** Magnus Berg
Language(s): Swedish
ADVERTISING RATES:
Full Page Colour .... SEK 25000
SCC .... SEK 31.25
BUSINESS: TIMBER, WOOD & FORESTRY

SOLDAT & TEKNIK 2003292W40-119
Editorial: Förlags AB Albinsson & Sjöberg, Box 529, 371 29 KARLSKRONA
Email: info@fabas.se **Web site:** http://www.fabas.se
Circ: 6,000
Editor: Kjell Engström; **Editor-in-Chief:** Erika Philipson
Language(s): Swedish
BUSINESS: DEFENCE

SOLLENTUNAJOURNALEN 1804053W32G-272
Editorial: Sollentuna kommun, 191 86 SOLLENTUNA
Tel: 8 579 211 61
Email: peter.holstad@sollentuna.se **Web site:** http://www.sollentunajournalen.se
Freq: 6 issues yearly; **Circ:** 34,000
Editor: Peter Holstad; **Advertising Manager:** Eva Sandesjö; **Publisher:** Maria Sterner
Language(s): Swedish
BUSINESS: LOCAL GOVERNMENT, LEISURE & RECREATION: Community Care & Social Services

SOLO 634770W74A-75
Editorial: Hammarby Kajväg 18, 120 30 STOCKHOLM **Tel:** 8 587 481 00
Email: solo@fridaforlag.se **Web site:** http://www.solomag.se
Date Established: 1997; **Freq:** Monthly; **Circ:** 50,400
Editor: Jessica Laneborg
Profile: Magazine covering lifestyle, fashion, beauty and interior design.
Language(s): Swedish
Readership: Aimed at women of all ages.
ADVERTISING RATES:
Full Page Colour .... SEK 34600
SCC .... SEK 288.33
Copy instructions: *Copy Date:* 35 days prior to publication date
CONSUMER: WOMEN'S INTEREST CONSUMER MAGAZINES: Women's Interest

SONIC 1642075W76D-271
Editorial: Box 9142, 102 72 STOCKHOLM
Tel: 8 702 15 50
Email: redaktionen@sonicmagazine.com **Web site:** http://www.sonicmagazine.com
Freq: 6 issues yearly; **Circ:** 20,000
Editor: Håkan Steen; **Editor-in-Chief:** Pierre Hellqvist; **Advertising Manager:** Mårten Sterner
Language(s): Swedish
ADVERTISING RATES:
Full Page Colour .... SEK 18995
SCC .... SEK 158.29
CONSUMER: MUSIC & PERFORMING ARTS: Music

SOURZE 1657328W82-458
Editorial: Nättidningen Sourze AB, Box 3314, 113 59 STOCKHOLM **Tel:** 8 633 63 63
Email: info@sourze.se **Web site:** http://www.sourze.se
Freq: Daily; **Circ:** 8,000 Unique Users
Editor-in-Chief: Carl Olof Schlyter
Language(s): Swedish
CONSUMER: CURRENT AFFAIRS & POLITICS

SPCI/SVENSK PAPPERSTIDNING 50446W36-60
Editorial: SPCI, Box 5515, 114 85 STOCKHOLM
Tel: 8 783 84 00 **Fax:** 86617344
Email: info@svenskpapperstidning.se **Web site:** http://www.svenskpapperstidning.se
Date Established: 1887; **Freq:** Monthly; **Circ:** 10,000
Editor: Mikael Hedlund; **Editor-in-Chief:** Ewa Arve; **Advertising Manager:** Camilla Sinivaara; **Publisher:** Marina Asp
Profile: Journal covering the pulp and paper industry.
Language(s): Swedish
ADVERTISING RATES:
Full Page Colour .... SEK 29900
SCC .... SEK 249.17

Copy instructions: *Copy Date:* 21 days prior to publication date
BUSINESS: PAPER

SPECIALPEDAGOGIK
50731W62G-200
Editorial: 713 94 NORA **Tel:** 587 600 15
Email: specialpedagogik@lararforbundet.se **Web site:** http://www.specialpedagogik.se
Freq: 6 issues yearly; **Circ:** 14,500
Editor: Hasse Hedström; **Editor-in-Chief:** Hasse Hedström; **Advertising Manager:** Lisen Skeppstedt; **Publisher:** Hasse Hedström
Profile: Magazine for teachers of children with special needs.
Language(s): Swedish
BUSINESS: CHURCH & SCHOOL EQUIPMENT & EDUCATION: Special Needs Education

SPEGELN SVEDALABLADET
751075W80-765
Editorial: Box 830, 245 18 STAFFANSTORP
Tel: 46 25 02 02
Email: info@spegeln.se **Web site:** http://www.spegeln.se
Freq: Monthly; **Circ:** 17,000
Publisher: Stefan Svensson
Language(s): Swedish
CONSUMER: RURAL & REGIONAL INTEREST

SPELA BADMINTON
51043W75H-40
Editorial: Blekingegatan 8, 118 56 STOCKHOLM
Tel: 70 574 82 34
Email: eva.edbom@telia.com **Web site:** http://www.badminton.nu
Freq: Quarterly; **Circ:** 7,000
Editor: Eva Edbom; **Publisher:** Eva Edbom
Profile: Publication of the Swedish Badminton Association.
Language(s): Swedish
CONSUMER: SPORT: Racquet Sports

SPELMANNEN
51093W76D-210
Editorial: c/o Ahlbom, Bultvägen 5, 126 38 HÄGERSTEN **Tel:** 8 18 34 11 **Fax:** 8 407 16 50
Email: peter.ahlbom@rikskonserter.se **Web site:** http://www.spelmansforbund.org
Freq: Quarterly; **Circ:** 7,000
Editor: Peter Ahlbom; **Publisher:** Margaretha Mattsson
Profile: Folk music magazine.
Language(s): Swedish
CONSUMER: MUSIC & PERFORMING ARTS: Music

SPORTBILEN
752074W31A-85
Editorial: Gårdsvägen 4, 169 70 SOLNA
Tel: 8 470 92 60
Email: sportbilen@automotorsport.se **Web site:** http://www.sportbilen.nu
Date Established: 1999; **Freq:** Half-yearly; **Circ:** 12,000
Publisher: Gunnar Dackevall
Language(s): Swedish
BUSINESS: MOTOR TRADE: Motor Trade Accessories

SPORTDYKAREN
51587W75M-185
Editorial: Idrottshuset, 123 43 FARSTA
Tel: 8 605 88 05 **Fax:** 8 605 88 32
Email: sportdykaren@ssdf.se **Web site:** http://www.ssdf.se
Freq: Quarterly; **Circ:** 9,000
Editor-in-Chief: Johanna Strömgren; **Advertising Manager:** Lena Holmbring; **Publisher:** Lars Gustafsson
Profile: Sports magazine focusing on diving.
Language(s): Swedish
CONSUMER: SPORT: Water Sports

SPORTFACK
50538W48B-100
Editorial: Gävlegatan 22C, 113 78 STOCKHOLM
Tel: 8 692 66 70 **Fax:** 8 650 97 05
Email: info@sportfack.se **Web site:** http://www.sportfack.se
Date Established: 1993; **Freq:** Monthly; **Circ:** 2,200
Editor: Christer Flythström; **Editor-in-Chief:** Martin Willners; **Advertising Manager:** Thomas Sedin; **Publisher:** Martin Willners
Profile: Trade magazine for the Swedish sporting goods industry. Contains information about new companies, trends, financial reports and retailer education.
Language(s): Swedish
ADVERTISING RATES:
Full Page Colour .... SEK 19500
SCC .... SEK 162.5
BUSINESS: TOY TRADE & SPORTS GOODS: Sports Goods

SPORTFACK; SPORTFACK.SE
1844812W14A-332
Editorial: Gävlegatan 22C, 113 78 STOCKHOLM
Tel: 8 692 66 70 **Fax:** 8 650 97 05
Email: info@sportfack.se **Web site:** http://www.sportfack.se
Freq: Daily; **Cover Price:** Free; **Circ:** 656 Unique Users
Advertising Manager: Thomas Sedin; **Publisher:** Martin Willners
Language(s): Swedish
BUSINESS: COMMERCE, INDUSTRY & MANAGEMENT

SPORTGUIDEN
51588W75A-226
Editorial: Box 22541, 104 22 STOCKHOLM
Tel: 8 650 88 80
Email: info@mediapuls.com **Web site:** http://www.mediapuls.com
Date Established: 1990; **Freq:** 6 issues yearly; **Cover Price:** Free; **Circ:** 108,200
Publisher: Peder Stenson
Profile: Magazine covering sportswear, equipment, product tests, interviews and news.
Language(s): Swedish
Readership: Aimed at people interested in sports and general fitness.
ADVERTISING RATES:
Full Page Colour .... SEK 48000
SCC .... SEK 240
CONSUMER: SPORT

SPRÅKTIDNINGEN
1824318W55-58
Editorial: Folkungagatan 122, 116 30 302 43 HALMSTAD STOCKHOLM **Tel:** 8 551 109 50
Email: redaktionen@spraktidningen.se **Web site:** http://www.spraktidningen.se
Freq: 6 issues yearly; **Circ:** 15,000
Editor: Maria Arnstad; **Editor-in-Chief:** Patrik Hadenius; **Publisher:** Patrik Hadenius
Language(s): Swedish
BUSINESS: APPLIED SCIENCE & LABORATORIES

SPRF-TIDNINGEN
50998W74N-70
Editorial: Bjurholmsgatan 16, 116 38 STOCKHOLM
Tel: 8 702 28 80 **Fax:** 87022640
Email: redaktionen@sprf.se **Web site:** http://www.sprf.se
Freq: 6 issues yearly; **Circ:** 50,000
Publisher: Benny Hellis
Profile: Magazine for Swedish pensioners.
Language(s): Swedish
CONSUMER: WOMEN'S INTEREST CONSUMER MAGAZINES: Retirement

SR P4; EFTER TOLV
1863526W2D-14
Editorial: Verkstadsgatan 20, 651 03 KARLSTAD
Tel: 54 22 11 00 **Fax:** 54 18 26 21
Email: eftertolv@sr.se **Web site:** http://www.sverigesradio.se
Freq: Weekly - söndagar; **Circ:** 716,000
Language(s): Swedish
BUSINESS: COMMUNICATIONS, ADVERTISING & MARKETING: Broadcasting

SR P4 STOCKHOLM; NYHETSREDAKTIONEN
1863522W2D-12
Editorial: 105 10 STOCKHOLM **Tel:** 784 95 00
Fax: 8 651 61 66
Email: news.sth@sr.se **Web site:** http://www.sverigesradio.se/stockholm
Freq: Daily; **Circ:** 42,000
Language(s): Swedish
BUSINESS: COMMUNICATIONS, ADVERTISING & MARKETING: Broadcasting

SRF-PERSPEKTIV
50641W56L-54_60
Editorial: Sandsborgsvägen 52, 122 88 ENSKEDE
Tel: 8 39 90 00 **Fax:** 8399322
Email: srfperspektiv@srf.nu **Web site:** http://www.srfriks.org/Vara-tidningar/SRF-Perspektiv
Freq: 6 issues yearly; **Circ:** 15,000
Advertising Manager: Mattias Hannu; **Publisher:** Tiina Nummi-Södergren
Profile: Official journal of the Swedish Association for the Visually Handicapped. Contains news, articles and information.
Language(s): Swedish
Readership: Read by members of the organisation and people working with the visually handicapped.
BUSINESS: HEALTH & MEDICAL: Disability & Rehabilitation

SR.SE
1858731W14A-355
Editorial: 105 10 STOCKHOLM **Tel:** 8 784 50 00
Web site: http://www.sr.se
Freq: Daily; **Cover Price:** Paid; **Circ:** 212,000 Unique Users
Language(s): Swedish
BUSINESS: COMMERCE, INDUSTRY & MANAGEMENT

ST PRESS
1639964W32G-264
Editorial: Box 5044, 102 41 STOCKHOLM
Tel: 8 790 51 00 **Fax:** 8 790 52 86
Email: tidningen@st.org **Web site:** http://www.stpress.se
Circ: 87,500
Publisher: Alexander Armiento
Language(s): Swedish
ADVERTISING RATES:
Full Page Colour .... SEK 29000
SCC .... SEK 181.25
BUSINESS: LOCAL GOVERNMENT, LEISURE & RECREATION: Community Care & Social Services

ST PRESS; STPRESS.SE
1846433W14L-201
Editorial: Box 5044, 102 41 STOCKHOLM
Tel: 8 790 51 00 **Fax:** 87905286
Email: tidningen@st.org **Web site:** http://www.stpress.se
Freq: Daily; **Cover Price:** Free; **Circ:** 18,680 Unique Users
Publisher: Alexander Armiento
Language(s): Swedish
BUSINESS: COMMERCE, INDUSTRY & MANAGEMENT: Trade Unions

ST TIDNINGEN
641302W72-683
Editorial: Östra Köpmansgatan 18, 444 30 STENUNGSUND **Tel:** 303 72 82 30 **Fax:** 303 72 82 40
Email: redaktionen@sttidningen.se **Web site:** http://www.sttidningen.se
Freq: Weekly; **Circ:** 28,500 Unique Users
Editor: Kurt Nilsson; **Editor-in-Chief:** Thomas Clausson; **Advertising Manager:** Magnus Andreasson
Language(s): Swedish
LOCAL NEWSPAPERS

ST TIDNINGEN; STTIDNINGEN.SE
1847788W65A-1089
Editorial: Östra Köpmansgatan 18, 444 30 STENUNGSUND **Tel:** 303 72 82 30 **Fax:** 303 72 82 40
Email: redaktionen@sttidningen.se **Web site:** http://www.sttidningen.se
Freq: Daily; **Cover Price:** Free; **Circ:** 8,667 Unique Users
Editor-in-Chief: Thomas Clausson; **Advertising Manager:** Jimmy Stark; **Publisher:** Roger Boström
Language(s): Swedish
ADVERTISING RATES:
SCC .... SEK 21
NATIONAL DAILY & SUNDAY NEWSPAPERS: National Daily Newspapers

STADSBYGGNAD
50418W32A-206
Editorial: Hamngatan 6 B, 652 24 KARLSTAD
Tel: 54 15 32 92 **Fax:** 54153414
Email: stadsbyggnad@skt.se **Web site:** http://www.skt.se
Date Established: 1935; **Freq:** 6 issues yearly; **Circ:** 2,000
Publisher: Martin Edman
Profile: Official journal of the Swedish Municipal and Technical Union. Contains road and traffic information, articles about urban planning, maintenance, environment and architecture.
Language(s): Swedish
ADVERTISING RATES:
Full Page Colour .... SEK 18300
SCC .... SEK 152.50
Copy instructions: *Copy Date:* 14 days prior to publication date
BUSINESS: LOCAL GOVERNMENT, LEISURE & RECREATION: Local Government

STAND BY - SCANDINAVIAN TRAVEL TRADE JOURNAL
634773W50-95_50
Editorial: Eriksbergsgatan 46 4 tr, 114 30 STOCKHOLM **Tel:** 8 694 70 55 **Fax:** 86947075
Email: standby@telia.com **Web site:** http://www.standbynews.com
Freq: Monthly; **Circ:** 21,000
Advertising Manager: Christan Jahn
Profile: Magazine featuring the trade in travel.
Language(s): Swedish
Readership: Aimed at professionals in the travel industry.
ADVERTISING RATES:
Full Page Colour .... SEK 30200
SCC .... SEK 251.67
BUSINESS: TRAVEL & TOURISM

STANDARD MAGAZINE
1741160W14R-67
Editorial: 118 80 STOCKHOLM **Tel:** 8 555 520 00
Fax: 8 555 521 09
Email: standardmagazine@sis.se **Web site:** http://www.sis.se
Freq: Quarterly; **Circ:** 8,500
Editor: Lovisa Krebs; **Publisher:** Olle Axenborg
Language(s): Swedish
BUSINESS: COMMERCE, INDUSTRY & MANAGEMENT: Commerce Related

STÅNGMÄRKET
1644010W80-850
Editorial: Skärgårdsstiftelsen, Box 7669, 103 94 STOCKHOLM **Tel:** 8 440 56 00 **Fax:** 84405619
Email: kansliet@skargardsstiftelsen.se **Web site:** http://www.skargardsstiftelsen.se
Freq: 6 issues yearly; **Circ:** 26,000
Advertising Manager: Sten Hummelgren
Language(s): Swedish
CONSUMER: RURAL & REGIONAL INTEREST

STATUS
50609W56A-70
Editorial: Box 9090, 102 72 STOCKHOLM
Tel: 8 556 062 00 **Fax:** 86682385
Email: status@hjart-lung.se **Web site:** http://www.hjart-lung.se
Date Established: 1938; **Freq:** 6 issues yearly; **Circ:** 36,000
Editor: Ulrika Juto; **Advertising Manager:** Thomas Pettersson; **Publisher:** Berndt Nilsson
Profile: Magazine containing information, debate articles and medical reports relating to heart and lung diseases.
Language(s): Swedish
Readership: Aimed at cardiologists and other people working within the medical profession.
ADVERTISING RATES:
Full Page Colour .... SEK 18000
SCC .... SEK 150
BUSINESS: HEALTH & MEDICAL

STEN
50406W30-50
Editorial: Stenutveckling Nordiska AB, Värmdövägen 738-740, 132 35 SALTSJÖ-BOO **Tel:** 8 747 76 71
Fax: 87477641
Email: sten@stenutveckling.se **Web site:** http://www.sten.se
Date Established: 1939; **Freq:** Quarterly; **Circ:** 14,000
Advertising Manager: Robert Kjellén; **Publisher:** Kurt Johansson
Profile: Journal covering the use of stone as a building material.
Language(s): Swedish
Readership: Aimed at architects and building contractors.
ADVERTISING RATES:
Full Page Colour .... SEK 15850
SCC .... SEK 132.08
Copy instructions: *Copy Date:* 45 days prior to publication date
BUSINESS: MINING & QUARRYING

STILETTEN
750851W56B-140
Editorial: Arenavägen 63 7tr., 121 77 JOHANNESHOV **Tel:** 8 506 221 50 **Fax:** 850622170
Email: finn.hellman@stil.se **Web site:** http://www.stil.se
Freq: 6 issues yearly; **Circ:** 8,000
Editor: Sari Nykvist
Language(s): Swedish
BUSINESS: HEALTH & MEDICAL: Nursing

STIM-MAGASINET
50704W61-90
Editorial: Box 27327, 102 54 STOCKHOLM
Tel: 8 783 88 00 **Fax:** 8 783 95 95
Email: info@stim.se **Web site:** http://www.stim.se
Freq: Quarterly; **Circ:** 50,000
Editor: Margita Ljusberg; **Publisher:** Margita Ljusberg
Profile: Magazine covering all types of music.
Language(s): Swedish
Readership: Read by members of the Performing Arts Society.
BUSINESS: MUSIC TRADE

STOCKHOLMS FRIA TIDNING; STOCKHOLMSFRIA.NU
1844804W65A-1035
Editorial: Fraktflygargatan 18, 128 30 SKARPNÄCK
Tel: 8 600 80 90
Email: nyheter@fria.nu **Web site:** http://www.stockholmsfria.nu
Freq: Daily; **Cover Price:** Free; **Circ:** 1,600 Unique Users
Editor: Kristian Borg; **Advertising Manager:** Annika Lundmark
Language(s): Swedish
NATIONAL DAILY & SUNDAY NEWSPAPERS: National Daily Newspapers

STRIDSROPET
51294W87-90
Editorial: Box 5090, 102 42 STOCKHOLM
Tel: 8 562 282 00 **Fax:** 8 562 283 97
Email: stridsropet@fralsningsarmen.se **Web site:** http://www.fralsningsarmen.se
Date Established: 1883; **Freq:** 26 issues yearly; **Circ:** 11,000
Editor-in-Chief: Bert Åberg
Profile: Magazine of the Swedish Salvation Army.
Language(s): Swedish
ADVERTISING RATES:
Full Page Colour .... SEK 12000
SCC .... SEK 100
CONSUMER: RELIGIOUS

STRUTEN
634776W91D-120
Editorial: Box 12825, 112 97 STOCKHOLM
Tel: 8 672 60 52 **Fax:** 8 672 60 01

Email: struten@junis.org **Web site:** http://www.junis.org
Freq: 6 issues yearly; **Circ:** 25,000
Editor: Pontus Landström; **Publisher:** Pontus Landström
Profile: Magazine focusing on youthwork, includes articles on environmental issues, democracy, culture, adventure and activities for young people.
Language(s): Swedish
Readership: Read by members of IOGT-NTOs Juniorförbund.
CONSUMER: RECREATION & LEISURE: Children & Youth

STUDENTGUIDEN 51516W62A-250
Editorial: Vitsand, 152 95 SÖDERTÄLJE
Tel: 8 541 38 420
Email: info@studentguiden.com **Web site:** http://www.studentguiden.com
Freq: Quarterly; **Circ:** 80,000
Editor: Annika Wihlborg; **Advertising Manager:** Markku Käkelä
Profile: Magazine providing advice for secondary school students choosing a career.
Language(s): Swedish
Readership: Aimed at students, councillors and personnel managers.
ADVERTISING RATES:
Full Page Colour .... SEK 23000
SCC .... SEK 191.67
BUSINESS: CHURCH & SCHOOL EQUIPMENT & EDUCATION: Education

STUDENTLIV 51225W83-95
Editorial: TCO, 114 94 STOCKHOLM
Tel: 8 782 91 00 **Fax:** 8 662 36 79
Email: studentliv@tco.se **Web site:** http://www.studentliv.se
Freq: Quarterly; **Circ:** 214,400
Editor-in-Chief: Ylva Rehnberg; **Advertising Manager:** Gun Hammar; **Publisher:** Germán Bender-Pulido
Profile: Student magazine containing information about university life and higher education.
Language(s): Swedish
ADVERTISING RATES:
Full Page Colour .... SEK 49500
SCC .... SEK 386.66
CONSUMER: STUDENT PUBLICATIONS

STUDENTLIV; STUDENTLIV.SE
1846653W14F-118
Editorial: TCO, 114 94 STOCKHOLM
Tel: 8 782 91 00 **Fax:** 8 662 36 79
Email: studentliv@tco.se **Web site:** http://www.studentliv.se
Freq: Daily; **Cover Price:** Free; **Circ:** 21,330 Unique Users
Editor-in-Chief: Ylva Rehnberg; **Advertising Manager:** Gun Hammar
Language(s): Swedish
ADVERTISING RATES:
SCC .... SEK 38
BUSINESS: COMMERCE, INDUSTRY & MANAGEMENT: Training & Recruitment

STUDENTMAGASINET 51219W83-65
Editorial: Box 3101, 103 62 STOCKHOLM
Tel: 8 587 075 00 **Fax:** 8 587 075 01
Email: petrus@studentmedia.se **Web site:** http://www.studentmag.se
Freq: 6 issues yearly; **Circ:** 92,000
Advertising Manager: Michael Fridenborg; **Publisher:** Teddy Hallin
Profile: Student tabloid newspaper covering every aspect of student life.
Language(s): Swedish
CONSUMER: STUDENT PUBLICATIONS

STUDIA NEOPHILOLOGICA
752032W84B-271
Editorial: Taylor & Francis AB, Box 3255, 103 65 STOCKHOLM **Tel:** 8 440 80 40 **Fax:** 8 440 80 50
Web site: http://www.tandf.no
Freq: Half-yearly; **Circ:** 600
Editor-in-Chief: Gernot Müller
Language(s): Swedish
CONSUMER: THE ARTS & LITERARY: Literary

STUDIO 1625777W76D-266
Editorial: Att: Redaktionen, 106 78 STOCKHOLM
Tel: 8 453 64 70
Web site: http://www.studio.se
Freq: Monthly; **Circ:** 15,000
Editor-in-Chief: Björn E Olsberg; **Advertising Manager:** Andreas Hedberg; **Publisher:** Björn E Olsberg
Language(s): Swedish
ADVERTISING RATES:
Full Page Colour .... SEK 30800
SCC .... SEK 256.66
CONSUMER: MUSIC & PERFORMING ARTS: Music

STUDIO; STUDIO.SE
1844683W76D-292
Editorial: Karlbergsv. 77, 106 78 STOCKHOLM
Tel: 8 453 60 00
Web site: http://www.studio.se
Freq: Daily; **Cover Price:** Free; **Circ:** 3,000 Unique Users
Editor-in-Chief: Björn E Olsberg; **Publisher:** Björn E Olsberg
Language(s): Swedish
ADVERTISING RATES:
SCC .... SEK 51
CONSUMER: MUSIC & PERFORMING ARTS: Music

STUREPLAN.SE 1844957W74Q-174
Editorial: Webzine Stureplan AB, Box 55719, 114 83 STOCKHOLM **Tel:** 8 545 076 10
Email: redaktion@stureplan.se **Web site:** http://www.stureplan.se
Freq: Daily; **Cover Price:** Free; **Circ:** 33,000 Unique Users
Publisher: Carl M Sundevall
Language(s): Swedish
CONSUMER: WOMEN'S INTEREST CONSUMER MAGAZINES: Lifestyle

SUNDSVALLS TIDNING
50837W67B-7150
Editorial: 851 72 SUNDSVALL **Tel:** 60 19 70 00
Email: nyhetschef@st.nu **Web site:** http://www.st.nu
Date Established: 1841
Circ: 30,800
Editor: Sofia Mirjamsdotter; **Publisher:** Kjell Carnbro
Language(s): Swedish
ADVERTISING RATES:
Full Page Colour .... SEK 55238
SCC .... SEK 276.19
REGIONAL DAILY & SUNDAY NEWSPAPERS: Regional Daily Newspapers

SUNDSVALLS TIDNING; WWW.STONLINE.SE
752321W67B-10305
Editorial: 851 72 SUNDSVALL **Tel:** 60 19 70 00
Fax: 60 61 97 94
Email: tommy.klaar@st.nu **Web site:** http://www.stonline.se
Freq: Daily; **Cover Price:** Paid; **Circ:** 24,270 Unique Users
Editor: Tommy Klaar; **Editor-in-Chief:** Kjell Carnbro; **Publisher:** Kjell Carnbro
Language(s): Swedish
ADVERTISING RATES:
SCC .... SEK 55
REGIONAL DAILY & SUNDAY NEWSPAPERS: Regional Daily Newspapers

SUNT FÖRNUFT 50995W74M-150
Editorial: Box 3319, 103 66 STOCKHOLM
Tel: 8 613 17 00 **Fax:** 86131760
Email: ake.jungdalen@skattebetalarna.se **Web site:** http://www.skattebetalarna.se
Date Established: 1921; **Freq:** 6 issues yearly; **Circ:** 65,200
Editor: Åke Jungdalen; **Publisher:** Robert Gidehag
Profile: Magazine providing news from the Taxpayers' Association. Includes interviews, advice and articles concerning taxes, pensions, government schemes and EU developments.
Language(s): Swedish
ADVERTISING RATES:
Full Page Colour .... SEK 22900
SCC .... SEK 291.66
CONSUMER: WOMEN'S INTEREST CONSUMER MAGAZINES: Personal Finance

SVEA 1852604W50-133
Editorial: SCR, Box 5079, 402 22 GOTEBORG
Tel: 31 355 60 00 **Fax:** 313556003
Email: svea@scr.se **Web site:** http://www.scr.se
Freq: Quarterly; **Circ:** 3,000
Editor: Martin Juhos; **Advertising Manager:** Staffan Lundgren
Language(s): Swedish
BUSINESS: TRAVEL & TOURISM

SVENLJUNGA & TRANEMO TIDNING 634289W72-495
Editorial: Box 33, 514 23 TRANEMO **Tel:** 325 400 00
Fax: 325 406 58
Email: info@stthuset.com **Web site:** http://www.stthuset.com
Date Established: 1992; **Freq:** Weekly; **Cover Price:** Free; **Circ:** 25,050
Editor-in-Chief: Sune Strand; **Advertising Manager:** Sune Strand; **Publisher:** Sune Strand
Language(s): Swedish
ADVERTISING RATES:
Full Page Colour .... SEK 15860
SCC .... SEK 79.3
LOCAL NEWSPAPERS

SVENLJUNGA & TRANEMO TIDNING; WEBB 1846287W65A-1069
Editorial: Box 33, 514 23 TRANEMO **Tel:** 325 400 00
Fax: 325 406 58
Email: info@stthuset.com **Web site:** http://www.stthuset.com
Freq: Daily; **Cover Price:** Free; **Circ:** 7,000 Unique Users
Editor-in-Chief: Sune Strand; **Advertising Manager:** Sune Strand; **Publisher:** Sune Strand
Language(s): Swedish
ADVERTISING RATES:
SCC .... SEK 16
NATIONAL DAILY & SUNDAY NEWSPAPERS: National Daily Newspapers

SVENSK ÅKERITIDNING
50556W49D-75
Editorial: Box 508, 182 15 DANDERYD
Tel: 8 753 54 40 **Fax:** 8 755 88 95
Email: akeritidning@akeri.se **Web site:** http://www.akeritidning.com
Date Established: 1918; **Freq:** Monthly; **Circ:** 14,300
Editor: Frans Johansson; **Advertising Manager:** Inger Kalin; **Publisher:** Anders Josephsson
Profile: Magazine for truck owners and drivers, with emphasis on road haulage.
Language(s): Swedish
ADVERTISING RATES:
Full Page Colour .... SEK 32500
SCC .... SEK 270.83
BUSINESS: TRANSPORT: Commercial Vehicles

SVENSK ÅKERITIDNING; AKERITIDNING.COM
1846252W2A-405
Editorial: Box 508, 182 15 DANDERYD
Tel: 8753 54 00 **Fax:** 87556001
Email: akeritidning@akeri.se **Web site:** http://www.akeritidning.com
Freq: Daily; **Cover Price:** Free; **Circ:** 9,533 Unique Users
Advertising Manager: Inger Kalin; **Publisher:** Anders Josephsson
Language(s): Swedish
BUSINESS: COMMUNICATIONS, ADVERTISING & MARKETING

SVENSK BERGS- OCH BRUKSTIDNING 50407W30-80
Editorial: Box 6040, 200 11 MALMO
Tel: 40 611 06 90 **Fax:** 4079737
Email: svenskbergs-bruks@bjinv.se **Web site:** http://www.bergsbruks.nu
Date Established: 1922; **Freq:** Quarterly; **Circ:** 3,500
Publisher: Jörgen Dahlquist
Profile: Journal for the mining, ballast, crushing and steel industries.
Language(s): Swedish
ADVERTISING RATES:
Full Page Colour .... SEK 7000
SCC .... SEK 58.33
BUSINESS: MINING & QUARRYING

SVENSK BOKHANDEL 50695W60A-70
Editorial: Box 6888, 113 86 STOCKHOLM
Tel: 8 545 417 70 **Fax:** 8 545 417 75
Email: redaktion@svb.se **Web site:** http://www.svb.se
Freq: 26 issues yearly; **Circ:** 4,100
Advertising Manager: Karin Alexandersson; **Publisher:** Lasse Winkler
Profile: Book trade magazine.
Language(s): Swedish
Readership: Read by publishers, booksellers, librarians and the media.
ADVERTISING RATES:
Full Page Colour .... SEK 8100
SCC .... SEK 67.50
Copy instructions: *Copy Date:* 9 days prior to publication date
BUSINESS: PUBLISHING: Publishing & Book Trade

SVENSK BOKHANDEL; SVB.SE
1844980W14L-198
Editorial: Box 6888, 113 86 STOCKHOLM
Tel: 8 545 417 70 **Fax:** 854541775
Email: redaktion@svb.se **Web site:** http://www.svb.se
Freq: Daily; **Cover Price:** Free; **Circ:** 2,733 Unique Users
Advertising Manager: Annika Lundstedt; **Publisher:** Lasse Winkler
Language(s): Swedish
BUSINESS: COMMERCE, INDUSTRY & MANAGEMENT: Trade Unions

SVENSK BOTANISK TIDSKRIFT
50680W57-57_75
Editorial: c/o Växtekologiska avd. Villavägen 14, 752 36 UPPSALA **Tel:** 18 471 28 91 **Fax:** 18 55 34 19
Email: sbt@sbf.c.se **Web site:** http://www.sbf.c.se
Date Established: 1907; **Freq:** Quarterly; **Circ:** 2,500
Editor: Bengt Carlsson
Profile: Official journal of the Swedish Society of Botany. Covers ecology, flora and plant geography.
Language(s): Swedish
BUSINESS: ENVIRONMENT & POLLUTION

SVENSK CARDIOLOGI
1803878W56A-347
Editorial: Sveavägen 17, 8 tr, 111 57 STOCKHOLM
Tel: 8 546 910 00 **Fax:** 854691001
Email: christer.hoglund@gmail.com **Web site:** http://www.cardio.se
Freq: Quarterly; **Circ:** 3,000
Advertising Manager: Åsa Larsbo
Language(s): Swedish
BUSINESS: HEALTH & MEDICAL

SVENSK CURLING 51066W75X-170
Editorial: Idrottshuset, 123 43 FARSTA
Tel: 8 683 30 16 **Fax:** 8 604 70 78
Email: hakan.sundstrom@curling.se **Web site:** http://www.curling.se
Freq: Quarterly; **Circ:** 5,000
Publisher: Håkan Sundström
Profile: Magazine about the sport of curling in Sweden.
Language(s): Swedish
Readership: Read mainly by members of the SCF (the Swedish Curling Association).
CONSUMER: SPORT: Other Sport

SVENSK DAMTIDNING
50949W74A-80
Editorial: Budadress: Humlegårdsgatan 6, Box 27710, 115 91 STOCKHOLM **Tel:** 8 679 46 00
Web site: http://www.svenskdam.se
Freq: Weekly; **Circ:** 149,600
Publisher: Karin Lennmor
Profile: Magazine featuring celebrity interviews, cookery, fashion, beauty and short stories.
Language(s): Swedish
ADVERTISING RATES:
Full Page Colour .... SEK 34000
SCC .... SEK 283.33
CONSUMER: WOMEN'S INTEREST CONSUMER MAGAZINES: Women's Interest

SVENSK EXPORT 1803907W20-101
Editorial: Exportrådet, Box 240, 101 24 STOCKHOLM **Tel:** 8 588 660 00 **Fax:** 8 588 661 90
Email: svenskexport@swedishtrade.se **Web site:** http://www.swedishtrade.se/svenskexport
Freq: 6 issues yearly; **Circ:** 12,000
Editor: Camilla Garland
Language(s): Swedish
BUSINESS: IMPORT & EXPORT

SVENSK FALLSKÄRMSSPORT
51055W75N-210
Editorial: Himmelsdyk, Box 110, 438 23 LANDVETTER **Tel:** 31 91 88 01
Email: himmelsdyk@sff.se **Web site:** http://www.sff.se
Freq: 6 issues yearly; **Circ:** 3,500
Editor: Anna Oscarsson
Profile: Official magazine of the Swedish Parachute Association.
Language(s): Swedish
CONSUMER: SPORT: Flight

SVENSK FARMACI 50450W37-20
Editorial: Box 3215, 103 64 STOCKHOLM
Tel: 8 507 999 14 **Fax:** 8 507 999 99
Email: nils.bergea-nygrens@farmacevtforbundet.se
Web site: http://www.farmacevtforbundet.se
Freq: 6 issues yearly; **Circ:** 8,100
Editor-in-Chief: Nils Bergeá Nygren; **Advertising Manager:** Patrik Tjälldén
Profile: Journal about the pharmaceutical trade.
Language(s): Swedish
ADVERTISING RATES:
Full Page Colour .... SEK 22900
SCC .... SEK 190.83
BUSINESS: PHARMACEUTICAL & CHEMISTS

SVENSK FISKHANDEL 50515W45B-30
Editorial: Pirhus 1 Fiskhamnspiren, 414 58 GÖTEBORG **Tel:** 31 14 40 12 **Fax:** 31 14 40 12
Email: svensk.fiskhandel@telia.com **Web site:** http://www.fiskhandlarna.se
Date Established: 1946; **Freq:** Quarterly; **Circ:** 400
Publisher: Svante Wedin
Profile: Newsletter providing information about the Swedish fishing trade.
Language(s): Swedish
BUSINESS: MARINE & SHIPPING: Commercial Fishing

SVENSK FRÖTIDNING 50369W21A-79
Editorial: Box 96, 230 53 ALNARP **Tel:** 40 46 20 80
Fax: 40 46 20 85
Email: info@svenskraps.se **Web site:** http://www.svenskraps.se
Date Established: 1932; **Freq:** 6 issues yearly; **Circ:** 8,000

Editor: Jens Blomquist; **Advertising Manager:** Göran Månsson; **Publisher:** Johan Biärsjö
Profile: Publication of the Swedish Association of Seed and Oil Plant Cultivators.
Language(s): Swedish
Readership: Read by farmers and advisers.
BUSINESS: AGRICULTURE & FARMING

SVENSK GOLF
51019W75D-150
Editorial: Box 84, 182 11 DANDERYD
Tel: 8 622 15 00 **Fax:** 8 622 69 30
Email: info@golf.se **Web site:** http://www.golf.se
Date Established: 1946; **Freq:** Monthly; **Circ:** 315,000
Editor: Karin Klarström; **Advertising Manager:** Johan Laur
Profile: Magazine of the Swedish Golf Federation.
Language(s): Swedish
ADVERTISING RATES:
Full Page Colour .... SEK 59000
SCC .... SEK 575
Copy instructions: *Copy Date:* 30 days prior to publication date
CONSUMER: SPORT: Golf

SVENSK GRIS MED KNORR
749794W21D-45
Editorial: Näset, 741 91 KNIVSTA **Tel:** 18 34 62 52
Fax: 18346253
Email: journalistgruppen@secher.pp.se **Web site:** http://www.svenskgris.se
Freq: Monthly -,11 nr/år; **Circ:** 3,000
Publisher: Sven Secher
Language(s): Swedish
BUSINESS: AGRICULTURE & FARMING: Livestock

SVENSK HAMNTIDNING
50512W45A-50
Editorial: Box 5384, 102 49 STOCKHOLM
Tel: 8 762 71 51 **Fax:** 86111218
Email: ports@transportgruppen.se **Web site:** http://www.sverigeshamnar.se
Freq: Quarterly; **Circ:** 6,000
Publisher: Mikael Castanius
Profile: Journal containing articles and information about the port related trade in Sweden and throughout Europe.
Language(s): Swedish
Readership: Read by stevedores, dock workers, politicians, employers and other professionals within the field.
Copy instructions: *Copy Date:* 30 days prior to publication date
BUSINESS: MARINE & SHIPPING

SVENSK HANDELSTIDNING JUSTITIA
50290W14A-110
Editorial: 105 99 STOCKHOLM **Tel:** 8 519 012 00
Fax: 8169932
Email: info@shj.se **Web site:** http://www.shj.se
Freq: Weekly; **Circ:** 11,000
Publisher: Pontus Könberg
Profile: Magazine covering different aspects of national trade, business and commerce.
Language(s): Swedish
Readership: Read by financial directors, executives and other professionals within trade and finance.
BUSINESS: COMMERCE, INDUSTRY & MANAGEMENT

SVENSK HANDIKAPPTIDSKRIFT, SHT
51367W94F-200
Editorial: Box 47305, 100 74 STOCKHOLM
Tel: 8 685 80 70 **Fax:** 86456541
Email: redaktion@svenskhandikapptidskrift.se **Web site:** http://www.svenskhandikapptidskrift.se
Freq: Monthly; **Circ:** 19,900
Advertising Manager: Mie Karlsson; **Publisher:** Elisabet Geite
Profile: Magazine for and about people with disabilities.
Language(s): Swedish
ADVERTISING RATES:
Full Page Colour .... SEK 18700
SCC .... SEK 155.83
CONSUMER: OTHER CLASSIFICATIONS: Disability

SVENSK IDROTT
51014W75A-205
Editorial: Idrottens hus, 114 73 STOCKHOLM
Tel: 8 699 61 04 **Fax:** 8 94 81 84
Email: svidrott@rf.se **Web site:** http://www.svenskidrott.se/tidningen
Date Established: 1929; **Freq:** Monthly; **Circ:** 32,000
Editor: Pär Ånell; **Editor-in-Chief:** Pär Ånell; **Advertising Manager:** Patrik Swenzén
Profile: Official magazine of the Swedish Federation of Sports. Contains articles, interviews and information about competitions and other events.
Language(s): Swedish
Readership: Read by members of the organisation and other people interested in sport.
ADVERTISING RATES:
Full Page Colour .... SEK 19900
SCC .... SEK 165.83
CONSUMER: SPORT

SVENSK IDROTT; WEBB
1846515W75A-217
Editorial: Idrottens hus, 114 73 STOCKHOLM
Tel: 8 699 61 04 **Fax:** 8 94 81 84
Email: svidrott@rf.se **Web site:** http://www.svenskidrott.se/tidningen
Freq: Daily; **Cover Price:** Free; **Circ:** 12,800 Unique Users
Editor: Pär Ånell; **Editor-in-Chief:** Pär Ånell; **Advertising Manager:** Fredrik Johnsson
Language(s): Swedish
CONSUMER: SPORT

SVENSK IDROTTSMEDICIN
50611W56A-75
Editorial: Tuna Industriväg 4, 153 30 JÄRNA
Tel: 8 550 102 00 **Fax:** 855010409
Email: kansli@svenskidrottsmedicin.se **Web site:** http://www.svenskidrottsmedicin.se
Freq: Quarterly; **Circ:** 2,000
Editor: Tõnu Saartok; **Publisher:** Karin Henriksson-Larsén
Profile: Journal focusing on sports medicine issues in Sweden, including news and reviews.
Language(s): Swedish
Copy instructions: *Copy Date:* 30 days prior to publication date
BUSINESS: HEALTH & MEDICAL

SVENSK JAKT
51029W75F-150
Editorial: Öster Malma, 611 91 NYKÖPING
Tel: 155 24 62 90 **Fax:** 155 24 62 95
Email: svenskjakt@telia.com **Web site:** http://www.jagareforbundet.se
Date Established: 1862; **Freq:** Monthly; **Circ:** 141,900
Editor: Bertil Lundvik; **Advertising Manager:** Lennart Åström; **Publisher:** Jan Henricson
Profile: Magazine covering hunting, wildlife, shooting and hunting dogs.
Language(s): Swedish
ADVERTISING RATES:
Full Page Colour .... SEK 38850
CONSUMER: SPORT: Shooting

SVENSK JAKT NYHETER
1625810W14R-62
Editorial: Öster Malma, 611 91 NYKÖPING
Tel: 155 24 62 90 **Fax:** 155 24 62 95
Email: svenskjakt.nyheter@telia.com **Web site:** http://www.jagareforbundet.se/svenskjakt
Freq: Monthly - 11 ggr/år; **Circ:** 139,300
Editor: Magnus Rydholm; **Advertising Manager:** Fredrik Demotoni
Language(s): Swedish
ADVERTISING RATES:
Full Page Colour .... SEK 38000
BUSINESS: COMMERCE, INDUSTRY & MANAGEMENT: Commerce Related

SVENSK JURISTTIDNING
50508W44-50
Editorial: Box 1994, 751 49 UPPSALA
Tel: 18 65 03 30 **Fax:** 18 69 30 99
Email: svjt@iustus.se **Web site:** http://www.svjt.org
Date Established: 1916; **Freq:** Monthly; **Circ:** 3,500
Advertising Manager: Marita Dehlin; **Publisher:** Stefan Strömberg
Profile: Journal covering all aspects of Swedish law and the legal system.
Language(s): Swedish
BUSINESS: LEGAL

SVENSK KIRURGI
51770W56A-330
Editorial: Box 503, 114 46 STOCKHOLM
Tel: 8 440 02 30
Web site: http://www.tandf.no
Freq: 6 issues yearly; **Circ:** 1,600
Editor: Martin Björk
Profile: Official journal of the Swedish Surgical Society.
Language(s): Swedish
BUSINESS: HEALTH & MEDICAL

SVENSK KYRKOTIDNING
51297W87-95_5
Editorial: c/o Göran Lundstedth, Tryffelvägen 72, 756 46 UPPSALA **Tel:** 18 32 44 20
Email: svensk.kyrkotidning@telia.com **Web site:** http://www.svenskkyrkotidning.se
Freq: 26 issues yearly; **Circ:** 2,000
Editor: Göran Lundstedt; **Publisher:** Boel Hössjer Sundman
Profile: Christian magazine containing articles about religion, Swedish culture and related topics.
Language(s): Swedish
CONSUMER: RELIGIOUS

SVENSK LEVERANTÖRSTIDNING
50300W14B-120
Editorial: Fiskhamnsgatan 2, 41458 GÖTEBORG
Tel: 31 775 15 80 **Fax:** 31 775 15 89
Email: redaktion@hexanova.se **Web site:** http://webnews.textalk.com/se/view.php?id=9444
Date Established: 1984; **Freq:** 6 issues yearly; **Circ:** 20,000
Editor-in-Chief: Klas Bergqvist; **Publisher:** Urban Nilsson
Profile: Magazine containing articles and information about all aspects of trade and industry in Sweden.
Language(s): Swedish
Readership: Aimed at suppliers, buyers and sales people within the field.
ADVERTISING RATES:
Full Page Colour .... SEK 29100
SCC .... SEK 181.88
BUSINESS: COMMERCE, INDUSTRY & MANAGEMENT: Industry & Factories

SVENSK LINJE
51227W83-100
Editorial: c/o FMSF, Box 2294, 103 17 STOCKHOLM
Tel: 8 791 50 05
Email: student@moderat.se **Web site:** http://svenskLinje.se
Freq: 6 issues yearly; **Circ:** 4,000
Editor: Danjell Elgebrandt
Profile: Magazine of the Independent Conservative Students Organisation.
Language(s): Swedish
CONSUMER: STUDENT PUBLICATIONS

SVENSK MÅNGKAMP
634761W40-76
Editorial: SMKF, Östhammarsgatan 70, 115 28 STOCKHOLM **Tel:** 8 51439972 **Fax:** 851439970
Web site: http://www.mangkampsforbundet.org
Date Established: 1992; **Freq:** Quarterly; **Circ:** 1,000
Editor-in-Chief: Stig Reinodt; **Publisher:** Alf Sandqvist
Profile: Official journal for the Swedish Armed Forces.
Language(s): Swedish
BUSINESS: DEFENCE

SVENSK MISSIONSTIDSKRIFT
751189W87-185
Editorial: Box 1526, 751 45 UPPSALA
Tel: 18 13 00 60 **Fax:** 18 13 00 60
Email: sim@teol.uu.se
Date Established: 1913; **Freq:** Quarterly; **Circ:** 1,200
Editor: Magnus Lundberg; **Editor-in-Chief:** Robert Odén; **Advertising Manager:** Ove Gustafsson; **Publisher:** Aasulv Lande
Language(s): Swedish
CONSUMER: RELIGIOUS

SVENSK PASTORALTIDSKRIFT
1626234W87-202
Editorial: Box 2085, 750 02 UPPSALA
Tel: 18 51 09 86 **Fax:** 18 55 09 86
Email: pastoraltidskrift@telia.com **Web site:** http://www.pastoraltidskrift.nu
Freq: 26 issues yearly; **Circ:** 1,800
Editor: Erik Petrén; **Advertising Manager:** Bo Carlsson
Language(s): Swedish
CONSUMER: RELIGIOUS

SVENSK POLIS
50425W32F-70
Editorial: Box 12256, 102 26 STOCKHOLM
Tel: 8 401 90 00 **Fax:** 8 401 90 65
Email: webbredaktionen@rps.police.se **Web site:** http://www.svenskpolis.polisen.se
Date Established: 1962; **Freq:** Monthly; **Circ:** 31,800
Editor: Elin Törnqvist; **Editor-in-Chief:** Kerstin Magnusson; **Publisher:** Anders Hagquist
Profile: Magazine containing articles, information and news of interest to the Swedish police force.
Language(s): Swedish
Readership: Aimed at employees of the Swedish police force and governmental offices.
ADVERTISING RATES:
Full Page Colour .... SEK 25900
SCC .... SEK 215.83
BUSINESS: LOCAL GOVERNMENT, LEISURE & RECREATION: Police

SVENSK POLIS; WEBB
1846502W56R-110
Editorial: Box 12256, 102 26 STOCKHOLM
Tel: 8 401 90 00 **Fax:** 8 401 90 65
Email: webbredaktionen@rps.police.se **Web site:** http://www.svenskpolis.se
Freq: Daily; **Cover Price:** Free; **Circ:** 10,000 Unique Users
Editor: Elin Törnqvist; **Editor-in-Chief:** Kerstin Magnusson
Language(s): Swedish
ADVERTISING RATES:
SCC .... SEK 43
BUSINESS: HEALTH & MEDICAL: Health Medical Related

SVENSK RENTAL TIDNING
1625600W10-91
Editorial: SCOP AB, Box 786, 191 27 SOLLENTUNA
Tel: 8 585 700 46 **Fax:** 8 585 700 47
Email: info@pdworld.com **Web site:** http://www.svenskrental.se
Freq: Quarterly; **Circ:** 11,000
Editor: Anita do Rocio Hermansson; **Publisher:** Jan Hermansson
Language(s): Swedish
ADVERTISING RATES:
Full Page Colour .... SEK 17200
SCC .... SEK 140
BUSINESS: MATERIALS HANDLING

SVENSK RODD
51054W75M-200
Editorial: Box 131, 275 23 SJÖBO **Tel:** 415 410 95
Fax: 415 410 95
Email: svensk.rodd@sjobo.nu **Web site:** http://www.roddsverige.nu
Date Established: 1975; **Freq:** Quarterly; **Circ:** 5,300
Editor-in-Chief: Per Ekström; **Advertising Manager:** Per Ekström; **Publisher:** Jan Cederholm
Profile: Sports magazine about rowing.
Language(s): Swedish
CONSUMER: SPORT: Water Sports

SVENSK SJÖFARTS TIDNING
50518W45C-100
Editorial: Box 370, 401 25 GÖTEBORG
Tel: 31 62 95 70 **Fax:** 31 80 27 50
Email: redaktion@sjofart.se **Web site:** http://www.shipgaz.se
Date Established: 1905; **Freq:** Monthly; **Circ:** 14,500
Editor-in-Chief: Rolf P Nilsson; **Advertising Manager:** Agne Carlsson; **Publisher:** Rolf P Nilsson
Profile: International journal covering shipbuilding and the shipping trade.
Language(s): Swedish
BUSINESS: MARINE & SHIPPING: Maritime Freight

SVENSK SKOLIDROTT
50717W62B-220
Editorial: Idrottens hus, 114 73 STOCKHOLM
Tel: 8 699 60 00
Email: johan.sandler@skolidrott.se **Web site:** http://www.skolidrott.se
Date Established: 1949; **Freq:** 6 issues yearly; **Circ:** 8,000
Profile: Magazine covering physical education. Contains articles, interviews and information about school championships and other events.
Language(s): Swedish
BUSINESS: CHURCH & SCHOOL EQUIPMENT & EDUCATION: Education Teachers

SVENSK SKYTTESPORT
51028W75F-130
Editorial: Box 5435, 114 84 STOCKHOLM
Tel: 8 449 95 90 **Fax:** 8 449 95 99
Email: jessica.linnman@skyttesport.se **Web site:** http://www.svensk-skyttesport.se
Date Established: 1959; **Freq:** 6 issues yearly; **Circ:** 9,000
Editor: Göran Nygren; **Advertising Manager:** Kerstin Bodin; **Publisher:** Göran Nygren
Profile: Sports magazine about shooting.
Language(s): Swedish
Readership: Read by hunting enthusiasts.
CONSUMER: SPORT: Shooting

SVENSK SKYTTESPORT
750712W75J-200
Editorial: Harvens väg 11, 820 77 GNARP
Tel: 652 240 60 **Fax:** 652 240 60
Email: redaktionen@skyttesport.se **Web site:** http://svensk-skyttesport.se
Freq: Monthly; **Circ:** 5,500
Editor: Jessica Linnman; **Advertising Manager:** Leif Dyklicki; **Publisher:** Göran Nygren
Language(s): Swedish
CONSUMER: SPORT: Athletics

SVENSK TRAFIKTIDNING
50560W49E-90
Editorial: Box 2131, 103 14 STOCKHOLM
Tel: 8 14 29 65 **Fax:** 8108067
Email: kansli@tj.nu **Web site:** http://www.tj.nu
Freq: 6 issues yearly; **Circ:** 4,400
Editor: Ann Charlott Juliusson; **Publisher:** Jan Sandgren
Profile: Magazine containing articles and information for members of the Swedish Railway Employees' Federation.
Language(s): Swedish
BUSINESS: TRANSPORT: Railways

SVENSK VERKSTAD
1655493W19R-1
Editorial: Box 17244, c/o MVR Service AB, 104 62 STOCKHOLM **Tel:** 8 753 48 00 **Fax:** 8 545 161 69
Email: info@qimtek.se **Web site:** http://www.mvr.se
Freq: 6 issues yearly; **Circ:** 5,900
Advertising Manager: Johan Sköldberg; **Publisher:** Lars Svedje
Language(s): Swedish
ADVERTISING RATES:
Full Page Colour .... SEK 15500
SCC .... SEK 129.16
BUSINESS: ENGINEERING & MACHINERY: Engineering Related

SVENSK VETERINÄRTIDNING
50745W64H-10
Editorial: Box 12709, 112 94 STOCKHOLM
Tel: 8 545 558 30 **Fax:** 854555829
Email: johan.beck-friis@svf.se **Web site:** http://www.svf.se
Date Established: 1860; **Freq:** Monthly; **Circ:** 3,000
Advertising Manager: Birgitta Ahlkvist; **Publisher:** Johan Beck-Friis
Profile: Journal containing information, news, articles and practical advice for veterinary surgeons.
Language(s): Swedish
Readership: Aimed at veterinary surgeons in Sweden and Scandinavia.
ADVERTISING RATES:
Full Page Colour .... SEK 15500
SCC .... SEK 129.16
BUSINESS: OTHER CLASSIFICATIONS: Veterinary

SVENSKA BRANSCHMAGASINET
1696240W2A-397
Editorial: Voltavägen 2-4, 168 69 BROMMA
Tel: 8 704 22 30 **Fax:** 87042234
Email: info@branschmagasinet.se **Web site:** http://www.branschmagasinet.se
Freq: 6 issues yearly; **Circ:** 12,000
Publisher: Robert Wreder
Language(s): Swedish
Copy instructions: *Copy Date:* 33 days prior to publication date
BUSINESS: COMMUNICATIONS, ADVERTISING & MARKETING

SVENSKA DAGBLADET
50759W65A-40
Editorial: Besöksadress: Västra Järnvägsgatan 21, 105 17 STOCKHOLM **Tel:** 8 13 50 00 **Fax:** 8 13 50 01
Email: nyheter@svd.se **Web site:** http://www.svd.se
Date Established: 1884; **Freq:** Daily; **Circ:** 192,800
Editor-in-Chief: Lena Samuelsson
Profile: Svenska Dagbladet or "Svenskan" as it is sometimes referred to as, is one of Sweden's largest morningpapers. The paper is based in Stockholm and is owned by Norwegian Schibstedt Group. The newspaper is distributed via courier in most parts of the country. Its political stance is right wing independent. Readers: General Public, academics, university students, politicians, managers, decision-makers and civil servants. Start year: 1884 Editor-In-Chief and Publisher: Lena K Samuelsson PR Accepted in: Swedish.
Language(s): Swedish
Readership: Read by academics, university students, politicians, managers, decision-makers and civil servants.
ADVERTISING RATES:
Full Page Colour .... SEK 126500
SCC .... SEK 586
NATIONAL DAILY & SUNDAY NEWSPAPERS: National Daily Newspapers

SVENSKA DAGBLADET; K
1926344W84B-311
Editorial: Västra Järnvägsgatan 21, 105 17 STOCKHOLM **Tel:** 8 13 50 00
Email: kultur@svd.se **Web site:** http://www.svd.se
Freq: 104 issues yearly; **Circ:** 192,800
Editor: Magnus Gylje
Language(s): Swedish
CONSUMER: THE ARTS & LITERARY: Literary

SVENSKA DAGBLADET;SVD.SE
751770W65A-822
Editorial: Västra Järnvägsgatan 21, 105 17 STOCKHOLM **Tel:** 8 13 53 03 **Fax:** 8 13 54 40
Email: webbredaktion@svd.se **Web site:** http://www.svd.se
Freq: Daily; **Circ:** 195,962 Unique Users
Language(s): Swedish
NATIONAL DAILY & SUNDAY NEWSPAPERS: National Daily Newspapers

SVENSKA EPILEPSIA
50610W56A-73
Editorial: Box 1386, 172 27 SUNDBYBERG
Tel: 8 669 41 06 **Fax:** 8 669 15 88
Email: info@epilepsi.se **Web site:** http://www.epilepsi.se
Freq: Quarterly; **Circ:** 9,000
Editor: Susanne Lund; **Advertising Manager:** Irmeli Patricius; **Publisher:** Susanne Lund
Profile: Official journal of the Swedish Federation of Epilepsy.
Language(s): Swedish
Readership: Read by members of the organisation.
BUSINESS: HEALTH & MEDICAL

SVENSKA FRISÖRTIDNINGEN
50326W15B-10
Editorial: Box 626, Vasagatan 12, 101 32 STOCKHOLM **Tel:** 8 87 04 30 **Fax:** 8 445 88 00
Email: info@frisor.com **Web site:** http://www.frisorforetagarna.se
Date Established: 1902; **Freq:** 6 issues yearly; **Circ:** 7,000
Editor: Jens Kuhn; **Editor-in-Chief:** Jens Kuhn; **Managing Director:** Thomas Francke; **Advertising Manager:** Jens Kuhn; **Publisher:** Jens Kuhn
Profile: Journal containing articles about hairdressing. Covers new products, trends, interviews, information about coming events such as fairs and competitions and practical advice.
Language(s): Swedish
Readership: Aimed at professional hairdressers, students and apprentices.
BUSINESS: COSMETICS & HAIRDRESSING: Hairdressing

SVENSKA LIVSMEDEL
634778W22C-150
Editorial: Tejarps Gård, 230 41 KLÅGERUP
Tel: 40 40 86 90
Email: info@lime.nu **Web site:** http://www.cultimedia.se
Date Established: 1998; **Freq:** 6 issues yearly; **Circ:** 4,000
Profile: Magazine focusing on the food processing industry, includes articles on research, finance and production.
Language(s): Swedish
ADVERTISING RATES:
Full Page Colour .... SEK 13700
SCC .... SEK 114.16
BUSINESS: FOOD: Food Processing & Packaging

SVENSKA SÄNDEBUDET
51296W87-95
Editorial: Metodistkyrkan i Sverige, Danska Vägen 20, 412 66 GÖTEBORG **Tel:** 31 733 78 40
Fax: 31 733 78 49
Email: sandebudet@metodistkyrkan.se **Web site:** http://www.metodistkyrkan.se
Freq: Monthly; **Circ:** 1,200
Editor: Beatrice Alm; **Editor-in-Chief:** Tomas Boström; **Publisher:** Tomas Boström
Profile: Magazine of the Swedish Methodist Church.
Language(s): Swedish
CONSUMER: RELIGIOUS

SVENSKAFANS.COM
1844534W75A-215
Email: info@svenskafans.com **Web site:** http://www.svenskafans.com
Freq: Daily; **Cover Price:** Free; **Circ:** 81,085 Unique Users
Editor: Mickael Möller; **Editor-in-Chief:** Anders Nettelbladt; **Advertising Manager:** Mattias Ringmar
Language(s): Swedish
CONSUMER: SPORT

SVENSKAR I VÄRLDEN
634780W90-63
Editorial: Box 5501, 114 85 STOCKHOLM
Tel: 8 783 81 81 **Fax:** 86605264
Email: svenskar.i.varlden@sviv.se **Web site:** http://www.sviv.se
Date Established: 1938; **Freq:** Quarterly; **Circ:** 12,000
Editor: Axel Odelberg; **Publisher:** Örjan Berner
Profile: Magazine containing news, articles and information about Sweden.
Language(s): Swedish
Readership: Aimed at Swedish people living abroad.
CONSUMER: ETHNIC

SVERIGES NATUR
50681W57-58
Editorial: Box 4625, 116 91 STOCKHOLM
Tel: 8 702 65 00
Email: sveriges.natur@snf.se **Web site:** http://www.sverigesnatur.snf.se
Date Established: 1909; **Freq:** Quarterly - (5 nr/år); **Circ:** 116,100
Advertising Manager: Hans Simons; **Publisher:** Carl-Axel Fall
Profile: Journal containing information, articles and news about national and international environmental issues.
Language(s): Swedish
ADVERTISING RATES:
Full Page Colour .... SEK 29900
SCC .... SEK 249.16
Copy instructions: *Copy Date:* 30 days prior to publication date
BUSINESS: ENVIRONMENT & POLLUTION

SVETSEN
50356W19E-100
Editorial: Svetskommissionen, Box 5073, 102 42 STOCKHOLM **Tel:** 8 791 29 00 **Fax:** 8 679 94 04
Email: info@svets.se **Web site:** http://www.svets.se
Date Established: 1941; **Freq:** Quarterly; **Circ:** 2,300
Editor-in-Chief: Nina Niska; **Advertising Manager:** Patrik Swensén; **Publisher:** Lars Johansson
Profile: Journal about welding techniques.
Language(s): Swedish
ADVERTISING RATES:
Full Page Colour .... SEK 20700
SCC .... SEK 172.5
BUSINESS: ENGINEERING & MACHINERY: Machinery, Machine Tools & Metalworking

SVT NYHETER OCH SAMHÄLLE; AGENDA
1863323W2D-5
Editorial: Agenda, Sveriges Television, 105 10 STOCKHOLM **Tel:** 8 784 00 00
Email: agenda@svt.se **Web site:** http://www.svt.se/agenda
Circ: 840,000
Editor: Lars Eisjö
Language(s): Swedish
BUSINESS: COMMUNICATIONS, ADVERTISING & MARKETING: Broadcasting

SWEDEN ROCK MAGAZINE
1639360W76D-270
Editorial: Norjebokevägen 10, 294 76 SÖLVESBORG
Tel: 456 317 17 **Fax:** 456 310 50
Email: magazine@swedenrock.com **Web site:** http://www.swedenrockmagazine.com
Freq: Monthly; **Circ:** 14,000
Editor: Martin Forssman; **Editor-in-Chief:** Thomas Väänänen; **Managing Director:** Martin Forssman; **Advertising Manager:** Mark Frostenäs; **Publisher:** Martin Forssman
Language(s): Swedish
ADVERTISING RATES:
Full Page Colour .... SEK 18900
SCC .... SEK 157.5
CONSUMER: MUSIC & PERFORMING ARTS: Music

SWEDISH BOOK REVIEW
751187W84B-276
Editorial: Mossgatan 5, 413 21 GÖTEBORG
Tel: 31 16 62 20 **Fax:** 31 16 62 20
Web site: http://www.swedishbookreview.com
Freq: Half-yearly; **Circ:** 1,000
Editor: Linda Schenck; **Advertising Manager:** Sarah Death
Language(s): Swedish
CONSUMER: THE ARTS & LITERARY: Literary

SYDASIEN
51205W82-227
Editorial: Råbygatan 5 A, 223 61 LUND
Tel: 46 13 35 68
Email: sydasien@sydasien.se **Web site:** http://www.sydasien.se
Date Established: 1977; **Freq:** Quarterly; **Circ:** 1,400
Editor: John Senewiratne
Profile: Magazine covering politics, environment, religion and culture in South Asia.
Language(s): Swedish
CONSUMER: CURRENT AFFAIRS & POLITICS

SYDÖSTRAN
50796W67B-7200
Editorial: 371 88 KARLSKRONA **Tel:** 455 33 46 00
Fax: 455 124 03
Email: redaktion@sydostran.se **Web site:** http://www.sydostran.se
Circ: 13,800
Editor: Tina Pettersson; **Managing Director:** Håkan Johansson; **Advertising Manager:** Carina Andréasson; **Publisher:** Anders Hall
Language(s): Swedish
ADVERTISING RATES:
Full Page Colour .... SEK 31776
SCC .... SEK 158.88
REGIONAL DAILY & SUNDAY NEWSPAPERS: Regional Daily Newspapers

SYDÖSTRAN; SYDOSTRAN.SE
1843671W65A-1011
Editorial: 371 88 KARLSKRONA **Tel:** 455 33 46 00
Fax: 455 124 03
Email: redaktion@sydostran.se **Web site:** http://www.sydostran.se
Freq: Daily; **Cover Price:** Free; **Circ:** 35,000 Unique Users
Editor-in-Chief: Anders Hall; **Advertising Manager:** Carina Andreasson; **Publisher:** Anders Hall
Language(s): Swedish
ADVERTISING RATES:
SCC .... SEK 32
NATIONAL DAILY & SUNDAY NEWSPAPERS: National Daily Newspapers

SYDSVENSKAN
50812W67B-7250
Editorial: Krusegatan 19, 205 05 MALMO
Tel: 40 28 12 00
Email: nyhetsred@sydsvenskan.se **Web site:** http://www.sydsvenskan.se
Date Established: 1848
Circ: 116,600
Editor: Per Lindström; **Advertising Manager:** Peter Wallentin
Language(s): Swedish
ADVERTISING RATES:
Full Page Colour .... SEK 147216
SCC .... SEK 629
REGIONAL DAILY & SUNDAY NEWSPAPERS: Regional Daily Newspapers

SYDSVENSKAN; FEATUREREDAKTIONEN
1994732W84B-314
Editorial: 205 05 MALMO **Tel:** 40 28 11 71
Email: sondag@sydsvenskan.se **Web site:** http://www.sydsvenskan.se
Freq: Weekly; **Cover Price:** Free; **Circ:** 124,500
Language(s): Swedish
CONSUMER: THE ARTS & LITERARY: Literary

SYDSVENSKAN; SYDSVENSKAN.SE
1639413W67E-5090
Editorial: 205 05 MALMO **Tel:** 40 28 12 00
Email: internetred@sydsvenskan.se **Web site:** http://www.sydsvenskan.se
Freq: Daily; **Circ:** 123,200 Unique Users
Managing Director: Johan Ståhl; **Publisher:** Daniel Sandström
Language(s): Swedish
REGIONAL DAILY & SUNDAY NEWSPAPERS: Regional Offices

SYDSVENSKAN; TV
751775W76C-215
Editorial: Krusegatan 19, 205 05 MALMO
Tel: 40 28 12 44
Email: tvradio@sydsvenskan.se **Web site:** http://www.sydsvenskan.se
Freq: Daily; **Circ:** 124,500
Language(s): Swedish
CONSUMER: MUSIC & PERFORMING ARTS: TV & Radio

SYDSVENSKT NÄRINGSLIV
1646092W14A-297
Editorial: Sydsvenska Industri- och Handelskammaren, Skeppsbron 2, 211 20 MALMO
Tel: 40 690 24 00 **Fax:** 406902490
Email: kajsa.herner@handelskammaren.com **Web site:** http://www.handelskammaren.com
Freq: Quarterly; **Circ:** 5,000
Editor: Kajsa Larsson Herner
Language(s): Swedish
ADVERTISING RATES:
Full Page Colour .... SEK 10000
BUSINESS: COMMERCE, INDUSTRY & MANAGEMENT

SYMFONI
634782W76D-212
Editorial: Box 49144, 100 29 STOCKHOLM
Tel: 8 693 03 35 **Fax:** 84060555
Email: symfoni@symf.se **Web site:** http://www.symf.se
Freq: Quarterly; **Circ:** 2,400
Profile: Journal for Svenska Yrkesmusikersförbundet (Swedish Professional Musicians Association).
Language(s): Swedish
Readership: Read by members.
CONSUMER: MUSIC & PERFORMING ARTS: Music

SYNDIKALISTEN
750806W14F-85
Editorial: Box 6507, 113 83 STOCKHOLM
Tel: 8 673 35 59 **Fax:** 86733580
Email: syndikalisten@sac.se
Freq: 6 issues yearly; **Circ:** 7,900
Publisher: Anders Knutsson
Language(s): Swedish
BUSINESS: COMMERCE, INDUSTRY & MANAGEMENT: Training & Recruitment

TÅG
50561W49E-100
Editorial: Tingsvägen 17 4tr, 191 61 SOLLENTUNA
Tel: 8 84 04 01 **Fax:** 8 84 04 06
Email: tag@sjk.se **Web site:** http://www.sjk.se
Date Established: 1966; **Freq:** Monthly; **Circ:** 6,800
Advertising Manager: Lars-Olof Broberg; **Publisher:** Jan Lindahl
Profile: International magazine of the Swedish Railway Club.
Language(s): Swedish
Readership: Aimed at railway enthusiasts.
ADVERTISING RATES:
Full Page Colour .... SEK 13600
SCC .... SEK 113.33
BUSINESS: TRANSPORT: Railways

TANDHYGIENIST TIDNINGEN
50623W56D-57
Editorial: Box 1419, 111 84 STOCKHOLM
Tel: 8 442 44 60
Email: info@tandhygienistforening.se **Web site:** http://www.tandhygienistforening.se
Freq: 6 issues yearly; **Circ:** 3,700
Editor: Margaretha Malmquist; **Advertising Manager:** Lillemor Nordenhammar
Profile: Magazine containing articles, news and information about dental hygiene.
Language(s): Swedish
Readership: Aimed at dentists and dental technicians.
ADVERTISING RATES:
Full Page Colour .... SEK 7900
SCC .... SEK 65.83
BUSINESS: HEALTH & MEDICAL: Dental

TANDLÄKARTIDNINGEN
50624W56D-60
Editorial: Box 1217, 111 82 STOCKHOLM
Tel: 8 666 15 00 **Fax:** 8 666 15 95
Email: redaktionen@tandlakarforbundet.se **Web site:** http://www.tandlakartidningen.se
Date Established: 1909; **Freq:** Monthly; **Circ:** 9,900
Editor: Björn Klinge; **Advertising Manager:** Christer Johansson; **Publisher:** Christina Mörk
Profile: Official journal of the Swedish Dental Association.
Language(s): Swedish
ADVERTISING RATES:
Full Page Colour .... SEK 25650
SCC .... SEK 213.75
BUSINESS: HEALTH & MEDICAL: Dental

TANDLÄKARTIDNINGEN; TANDLAKARTIDNINGEN.SE
1844983W56A-360
Editorial: Box 1217, 111 82 STOCKHOLM
Tel: 8 666 15 00 **Fax:** 8 666 15 95
Email: redaktionen@tandlakarforbundet.se **Web site:** http://www.tandlakartidningen.se
Freq: Daily; **Cover Price:** Free; **Circ:** 3,960 Unique Users
Advertising Manager: Christer Johansson; **Publisher:** Christina Mörk
Language(s): Swedish
BUSINESS: HEALTH & MEDICAL

TANDSKÖTERSKETIDNINGEN
51527W56D-80
Editorial: Svenska tandsköterskeförbundet, Söder Mälarstrand 21, 118 20 STOCKHOLM
Tel: 8 411 19 12
Web site: http://www.svetf.se
Freq: Quarterly; **Circ:** 4,000
Publisher: Siv Widholm
Profile: Journal for the Swedish Dental Nurse Association.
Language(s): Swedish
BUSINESS: HEALTH & MEDICAL: Dental

TANDTEKNIKERN
634786W56D-95
Editorial: Skidvägen 10, 812 30 STORVIK
Tel: 707 60 22 28 **Fax:** 29012181
Email: tidningen.tandteknikern@hos.sandnet.se **Web site:** http://www.dentallab.se
Freq: 6 issues yearly; **Circ:** 2,000
Editor: Lena Nordkvist; **Advertising Manager:** Héléne Ulvander; **Publisher:** Bo Ekberg
Profile: Magazine focusing on the technical aspects of dental technology.
Language(s): Swedish
Readership: Aimed at dental technicians and laboratory assistants.
BUSINESS: HEALTH & MEDICAL: Dental

TARA
749250W74A-90
Editorial: Bonnier Tidskrifter, Bud: Malmskillnadsgatan 39, 105 44 STOCKHOLM
Tel: 8 736 52 00 **Fax:** 8 24 02 13
Email: red@tara.bonnier.se **Web site:** http://www.tara.se
Date Established: 2000; **Freq:** Monthly; **Circ:** 81,900
Advertising Manager: Camilla Hedin
Profile: Women's interest magazine focusing on health, fashion, beauty, interior design, medicine, travel and economy.
Language(s): Swedish
Readership: Aimed at women aged between 40 and 60 years.
ADVERTISING RATES:
Full Page Colour .... SEK 52500
SCC .... SEK 437.50
CONSUMER: WOMEN'S INTEREST CONSUMER MAGAZINES: Women's Interest

TASTELINE.COM
1810518W74P-217
Editorial: 105 18 STOCKHOLM **Tel:** 8 13 57 70
Fax: 8 13 54 35
Email: info@tasteline.com **Web site:** http://www.tasteline.com
Circ: 56,706 Unique Users
Editor-in-Chief: Magdalena Kvarning
Language(s): Swedish
CONSUMER: WOMEN'S INTEREST CONSUMER MAGAZINES: Food & Cookery

TAXI IDAG
50744W64G-200
Editorial: Skeppargatan 27, 114 52 STOCKHOLM
Tel: 708 88 96 07 **Fax:** 8 662 11 80
Email: maria.m@spearproduction.se **Web site:** http://www.taxiidag.com
Date Established: 1986; **Freq:** 6 issues yearly; **Circ:** 6,200
Editor-in-Chief: Maria Marteleur; **Publisher:** Anders Forsström
Profile: Magazine containing articles, information and news about the taxi trade.
Language(s): Swedish
Readership: Aimed at taxi drivers and chauffeurs.
ADVERTISING RATES:
Full Page Colour .... SEK 25300
SCC .... SEK 210.83
BUSINESS: OTHER CLASSIFICATIONS: Taxi Trade

TCO-TIDNINGEN
50438W14L-135
Editorial: 114 94 STOCKHOLM **Tel:** 8 782 91 00
Fax: 86624822
Email: tcotidningen@tco.se **Web site:** http://www.tcotidningen.se
Date Established: 1946; **Freq:** (5nr/år); **Circ:** 49,000
Publisher: Erling Forsman
Profile: Official publication of the Swedish Central Organisation of Civil Servants.
Language(s): Swedish
ADVERTISING RATES:
Full Page Colour .... SEK 43500
SCC .... SEK 217.50
BUSINESS: COMMERCE, INDUSTRY & MANAGEMENT: Trade Unions

TCO-TIDNINGEN; TCOTIDNINGEN.SE
1846455W14F-116
Editorial: 114 94 STOCKHOLM **Tel:** 8 782 91 00
Fax: 86624822
Email: tco.tidningen@tco.se **Web site:** http://www.tcotidningen.se
Freq: Daily; **Cover Price:** Free; **Circ:** 19,600 Unique Users
Publisher: Erling Forsman
Language(s): Swedish
BUSINESS: COMMERCE, INDUSTRY & MANAGEMENT: Training & Recruitment

TEATERFORUM
51076W76B-90
Editorial: Box 1194, 721 29 VÄSTERÅS
Tel: 21 470 41 64 **Fax:** 21 470 41 69
Email: teaterforum@atr.nu **Web site:** http://www.atr.nu
Date Established: 1967; **Freq:** 6 issues yearly; **Circ:** 6,000
Editor: Lena Lindstedt; **Editor-in-Chief:** Lena Lindstedt; **Advertising Manager:** Lena Lindstedt
Profile: Magazine for amateur dramatists.
Language(s): Swedish
CONSUMER: MUSIC & PERFORMING ARTS: Theatre

TEATERTIDNINGEN
50748W64K-82_50
Editorial: Box 4066, 102 62 STOCKHOLM
Tel: 8 84 92 87
Email: red@teatertidningen.se **Web site:** http://www.teatertidningen.se
Freq: Quarterly; **Circ:** 1,500
Editor-in-Chief: Birgitta Haglund; **Advertising Manager:** Rikard Hoogland
Profile: Magazine containing information, news and articles about all aspects concerning national and international theatre.
Language(s): Swedish
Readership: Aimed mainly at critics, actors, politicians, stage workers and other professionals within the field.
ADVERTISING RATES:
Full Page Colour .... SEK 4050
SCC .... SEK 33.75
BUSINESS: OTHER CLASSIFICATIONS: Cinema Entertainment

TEBLADET
750690W32G-250
Editorial: Box 1613, 701 16 OREBRO
Tel: 19 602 7358 **Fax:** 19107935
Email: tebladet@orebroll.se **Web site:** http://www.orebroll.se
Freq: Monthly; **Circ:** 13,000
Editor: Weine Ahlstrand; **Publisher:** Ann-Marie Wentzel
Language(s): Swedish
ADVERTISING RATES:
Full Page Colour .... SEK 26000
SCC .... SEK 130
BUSINESS: LOCAL GOVERNMENT, LEISURE & RECREATION: Community Care & Social Services

TECHWORLD
1809916W5E-104
Editorial: Karlbergsvägen 77, 106 78 STOCKHOLM
Tel: 8 453 62 22
Email: techworld@idg.se **Web site:** http://techworld.idg.se
Freq: Monthly; **Circ:** 13,400 Unique Users
Editor: Lars Dobos; **Editor-in-Chief:** Magnus Aschan; **Publisher:** Niclas Söderlund
Language(s): Swedish
BUSINESS: COMPUTERS & AUTOMATION: Data Transmission

TECHWORLD MIKRODATORN
1840042W5E-107
Editorial: IDG, Karlbergsvägen 77, 106 78 STOCKHOLM **Tel:** 8 453 62 20
Email: techworld@idg.se **Web site:** http://www.mikrodatorn.idg.se
Circ: 12,848 Unique Users
Editor: Jörgen Stadje; **Editor-in-Chief:** Öjvind Karlsson; **Advertising Manager:** Daniel Binett
Language(s): Swedish
BUSINESS: COMPUTERS & AUTOMATION: Data Transmission

TECHWORLD OPEN SOURCE
1846663W5E-135
Editorial: Karlbergsv. 77, 106 78 STOCKHOLM
Tel: 8 453 60 00
Email: magnus.andersson@idg.se **Web site:** http://opensource.idg.se
Freq: Daily; **Cover Price:** Free; **Circ:** 7,878 Unique Users
Editor: Lars Dobos; **Editor-in-Chief:** Magnus Aschan
Language(s): Swedish
ADVERTISING RATES:
SCC .... SEK 120
BUSINESS: COMPUTERS & AUTOMATION: Data Transmission

TECHWORLD; WEBB
1847796W5E-127
Editorial: Karlbergsv. 77, 106 78 STOCKHOLM
Tel: 8 453 60 00
Email: magnus.andersson@idg.se **Web site:** http://techworld.idg.se
Freq: Daily; **Cover Price:** Free; **Circ:** 27,609 Unique Users
Editor: Lars Dobos; **Editor-in-Chief:** Magnus Aschan
Language(s): Swedish
BUSINESS: COMPUTERS & AUTOMATION: Data Transmission

TECKNAREN
50324W14L-140
Editorial: Svenska Tecknare, Götgatan 48, 118 26 STOCKHOLM **Tel:** 8 556 029 18 **Fax:** 855602919
Email: tecknaren@svenskatecknare.se **Web site:** http://www.svenskatecknare.se
Freq: 6 issues yearly; **Circ:** 1,500
Profile: Journal covering issues concerning graphic design and illustrating.
Language(s): Swedish
Readership: Read mainly by trade union members.
ADVERTISING RATES:
Full Page Colour .... SEK 5000
SCC .... SEK 41.67
BUSINESS: COMMERCE, INDUSTRY & MANAGEMENT: Trade Unions

TEKNIKENS VÄRLD
51126W77D-100
Editorial: Sveavägen 53, 105 44 STOCKHOLM
Tel: 8 736 53 00 **Fax:** 8 736 00 11
Web site: http://www.teknikensvarld.com
Date Established: 1948; **Freq:** 26 times a year; **Circ:** 56,800 Unique Users
Publisher: Daniel Frodin
Profile: Magazine covering all aspects of motoring and motor-racing. Provides technical information, industry news, equipment reviews and information on racing venues.
Language(s): Swedish
Readership: Aimed at people who enjoy motor-racing.
Copy instructions: *Copy Date:* 21 days prior to publication date
CONSUMER: MOTORING & CYCLING: Motor Sports

TEKNIKENS VÄRLD; TEKNIKENSVARLD.COM
1843657W77D-103
Editorial: Sveavägen 53, 105 44 STOCKHOLM
Tel: 8 736 53 00 **Fax:** 87360011
Web site: http://www.teknikensvarld.se
Freq: Daily; **Cover Price:** Free; **Circ:** 22,822 Unique Users
Advertising Manager: Jens Jefferyd; **Publisher:** Daniel Frodin
Language(s): Swedish
CONSUMER: MOTORING & CYCLING: Motor Sports

TEKNIKFÖRETAGEN DIREKT
1657030W19R-2
Editorial: Box 5510, 114 85 STOCKHOLM
Tel: 8 782 08 00 **Fax:** 8 782 09 00
Email: jonas.cohen@teknikforetagen.se **Web site:** http://www.teknikforetagen.se
Freq: 6 issues yearly; **Circ:** 14,600
Publisher: Jonas Cohen
Language(s): Swedish
ADVERTISING RATES:
Full Page Colour .... SEK 29200
SCC .... SEK 182.50
BUSINESS: ENGINEERING & MACHINERY: Engineering Related

TELEKOM IDAG
50343W18B-50
Editorial: Box 104, 901 03 UMEÅ **Tel:** 90 70 09 00
Fax: 90 14 23 20
Email: info@telekomidag.com **Web site:** http://www.telekomidag.com
Date Established: 1994; **Freq:** Monthly; **Circ:** 18,000
Editor-in-Chief: Stefan Eriksson
Profile: Magazine covering development within the field of mobile computers and telecommunications.
Language(s): Swedish
Readership: Read by professional users and executives within the profession.
ADVERTISING RATES:
Full Page Colour .... SEK 28900
SCC .... SEK 240.83
BUSINESS: ELECTRONICS: Telecommunications

TELEKOM IDAG; TELEKOMIDAG.COM
1846280W5E-12
Editorial: Box 104, 901 03 UMEÅ **Tel:** 90 700 900
Fax: 90 14 23 20
Email: info@telekomidag.se **Web site:** http://www.telekomidag.com
Freq: Daily; **Cover Price:** Free; **Circ:** 10,000 Unique Users
Editor-in-Chief: Stefan Eriksson
Language(s): Swedish
ADVERTISING RATES:
SCC .... SEK 48
BUSINESS: COMPUTERS & AUTOMATION: Data Transmission

TELESCOPIUM
1656055W94J-22
Editorial: c/o D. Söderström, Götgatan 4, 753 15 UPPSALA **Tel:** 18 26 19 93
Email: telescopium@saaf.se **Web site:** http://www.saaf.se
Freq: Quarterly; **Circ:** 1,000
Editor: Daniel Söderström; **Publisher:** Daniel Söderström
Language(s): Swedish
CONSUMER: OTHER CLASSIFICATIONS: Popular Science

TENTAKEL
1803905W55-55
Editorial: Vetenskapsrådet, 103 78 STOCKHOLM
Tel: 8 546 440 00
Email: tentakel@vr.se **Web site:** http://www.tentakel.vr.se
Freq: Monthly; **Circ:** 6,000 Unique Users
Editor: Eva Barkeman; **Publisher:** Arne Johansson
Language(s): Swedish
BUSINESS: APPLIED SCIENCE & LABORATORIES

TF-BLADET
50622W56D-55
Editorial: Bergsunds Strand 9, 117 38 STOCKHOLM
Tel: 8 428 92 42 **Fax:** 8 641 90 81
Email: redaktionen@tf.nu **Web site:** http://www.tf.nu/tfbladet
Date Established: 1980; **Freq:** Quarterly; **Circ:** 10,000
Advertising Manager: Leif Löfkvist; **Publisher:** Mats Hanson
Profile: Journal providing information about the consequences of maltreatment within the dental profession.
Language(s): Swedish
Readership: Aimed at dental technicians, owners of dental practices, lawyers and patients.
BUSINESS: HEALTH & MEDICAL: Dental

TID & SMYCKEN
1641475W14J-60
Editorial: Gustaf Kjellbergsväg 2, 756 43 UPPSALA
Tel: 18 12 04 68 **Fax:** 417 312 61
Email: larsmagnus@tidochsmycken.se **Web site:** http://www.tidochsmycken.se
Freq: Quarterly; **Circ:** 5,000
Editor: Börje Ohlsson; **Publisher:** Lars Magnus Jansson
Language(s): Swedish
ADVERTISING RATES:
Full Page Colour .... SEK 10000
SCC .... SEK 83.33
BUSINESS: COMMERCE, INDUSTRY & MANAGEMENT: Commercial Design

TIDEN
750738W82-450
Editorial: 105 60 STOCKHOLM **Tel:** 8 700 26 00
Fax: 84116542
Email: bernhardsson.bo@telia.com **Web site:** http://www.arbetarrorelsenstankesmedja.se
Freq: 6 issues yearly; **Circ:** 5,000
Editor-in-Chief: Daniel Suhonen; **Publisher:** Bo Bernhardsson
Language(s): Swedish
ADVERTISING RATES:
Full Page Colour .... SEK 5000
SCC .... SEK 41.66
CONSUMER: CURRENT AFFAIRS & POLITICS

TIDEN; ARBETARRORELSEN-STANKESMEDJA.SE
1844776W82-481
Editorial: 111 23 STOCKHOLM **Tel:** 8 796 25 00
Fax: 84116542
Email: bernhardsson.bo@telia.com **Web site:** http://www.arbetarrorelsenstankesmedja.se
Freq: Daily; **Cover Price:** Free; **Circ:** 1,667 Unique Users
Publisher: Bo Bernhardsson
Language(s): Swedish
CONSUMER: CURRENT AFFAIRS & POLITICS

TIDIG MUSIK
51094W76D-215
Editorial: Box 16344, 103 26 STOCKHOLM
Tel: 8 407 17 23 **Fax:** 8 407 17 27
Email: red@tidigmusik.com **Web site:** http://www.tidigmusik.com
Date Established: 1979; **Freq:** Quarterly; **Circ:** 1,600
Editor: Hillevi Hogman; **Advertising Manager:** Per Axelsson; **Publisher:** Hillevi Hogman

Profile: Journal about music from the Middle Ages, the Renaissance and the Baroque.
Language(s): Swedish
CONSUMER: MUSIC & PERFORMING ARTS: Music

TIDNINGEN ÅNGERMANLAND

633929W67B-7275
Editorial: 871 81 HÄRNÖSAND **Tel:** 611 55 48 00
Fax: 611 156 60
Email: taredaktion@allehanda.se **Web site:** http://www.allehanda.se
Date Established: 2000
Circ: 20,400
Editor: Anneli Pettersson; **Publisher:** Jimmie Näslund
Language(s): Swedish
ADVERTISING RATES:
Full Page Colour .... SEK 40320
SCC .... SEK 201.60
REGIONAL DAILY & SUNDAY NEWSPAPERS: Regional Daily Newspapers

TIDNINGEN ÅTER

634852W57-59
Editorial: 521 94 GUDHEM **Tel:** 515 72 05 72
Email: ater@alternativ.nu **Web site:** http://www.alternativ.nu
Date Established: 1998; **Freq:** Quarterly; **Circ:** 5,100
Editor-in-Chief: Petter Bergström; **Publisher:** Petter Bergström
Profile: Magazine featuring all aspects of multimedia, including interactive entertainment.
Language(s): Swedish
Readership: Aimed at people mainly interested in music not available in the marketplace.
BUSINESS: ENVIRONMENT & POLLUTION

TIDNINGEN BROTTSOFFER

634404W32F-100
Editorial: Box 11014, 100 61 STOCKHOLM
Tel: 8 644 88 00 **Fax:** 8 644 88 28
Email: tidningenbrottsoffer@boj.se **Web site:** http://www.boj.se
Date Established: 1994; **Freq:** Quarterly; **Circ:** 15,000
Editor: Ninna Mörner; **Publisher:** Hans Klette
Profile: Magazine containing information about the criminal system in Sweden.
Language(s): Swedish
BUSINESS: LOCAL GOVERNMENT, LEISURE & RECREATION: Police

TIDNINGEN C.

1623694W82-452
Editorial: Centerpartiet, Box 2200, 103 15 STOCKHOLM **Tel:** 8 617 38 18 **Fax:** 8 617 38 10
Email: tidningenc@centerpartiet.se **Web site:** http://www.centerpartiet.se
Freq: Quarterly; **Circ:** 58,200
Editor: Elisabeth Jansson; **Editor-in-Chief:** Erik Bratthall; **Publisher:** Lena Forsman
Language(s): Swedish
ADVERTISING RATES:
Full Page Colour .... SEK 18000
CONSUMER: CURRENT AFFAIRS & POLITICS

TIDNINGEN CHEF

50308W14F-20
Editorial: Sveavägen 92, 113 50 STOCKHOLM
Tel: 8 555 245 00 **Fax:** 8 555 245 50
Email: red@chef.se **Web site:** http://www.chef.se
Date Established: 1995; **Freq:** Monthly; **Circ:** 110,800
Publisher: Vibeke Pålhaugen
Profile: Journal about human resource development and leadership, personnel administration and working life.
Language(s): Swedish
Readership: Aimed at managers at all levels.
ADVERTISING RATES:
Full Page Colour .... SEK 51900
SCC .... SEK 387.50
BUSINESS: COMMERCE, INDUSTRY & MANAGEMENT: Training & Recruitment

TIDNINGEN DYK

51052W75M-250
Editorial: Fjordvägen 4, 439 31 ONSALA
Tel: 300 600 77 **Fax:** 7026 9015
Email: redaktionen@dyk.net **Web site:** http://www.dyk.net
Freq: Monthly; **Circ:** 17,000
Editor-in-Chief: Martin Örnroth; **Advertising Manager:** Martin Baadsgaard; **Publisher:** Martin Örnroth
Profile: Magazine containing articles about the underwater world, scuba diving, adventure and travel.
Language(s): Swedish
Readership: Read by diving enthusiasts.
ADVERTISING RATES:
Full Page Colour .... SEK 17490
SCC .... SEK 145.75
CONSUMER: SPORT: Water Sports

TIDNINGEN DYK; DYK.NET

1844972W75M-251
Editorial: Fjordvägen 4, 439 31 ONSALA
Tel: 300 600 77
Email: redaktionen@dyk.net **Web site:** http://www.dykmag.net
Freq: Daily; **Cover Price:** Free; **Circ:** 3,400 Unique Users
Editor-in-Chief: Martin Örnroth; **Publisher:** Martin Örnroth
Language(s): Swedish
ADVERTISING RATES:
SCC .... SEK 29
CONSUMER: SPORT: Water Sports

TIDNINGEN FAMILJEDAGHEM

639356W32G-252
Editorial: Box 34, 171 11 SOLNA **Tel:** 8 545 453 30
Email: familjedaghem@fortbild.se **Web site:** http://www.fortbild.se
Freq: 6 times a year; **Cover Price:** Paid; **Circ:** 6,450 Unique Users
Editor-in-Chief: Eva Selin; **Advertising Manager:** Ulf Jakobsson
Language(s): Swedish
BUSINESS: LOCAL GOVERNMENT, LEISURE & RECREATION: Community Care & Social Services

TIDNINGEN FASTIGHETSAKTIEN

751069W14A-260
Editorial: Wallingatan 18, 111 24 STOCKHOLM
Tel: 8 10 81 81 **Fax:** 8104140
Email: sf@centum.se **Web site:** http://www.fastighetsaktien.se
Freq: 6 issues yearly; **Circ:** 7,000
Editor: Lars Eriksson; **Publisher:** Stefan Fröjdendahl
Language(s): Swedish
ADVERTISING RATES:
Full Page Colour .... SEK 27500
SCC .... SEK 229.17
BUSINESS: COMMERCE, INDUSTRY & MANAGEMENT

TIDNINGEN FASTIGHETSAKTIEN; WEBB

1844799W1E-209
Editorial: Wallingatan 18, 111 24 STOCKHOLM
Tel: 8 10 81 81 **Fax:** 8 10 41 40
Email: sf@centum.se **Web site:** http://www.fastighetsaktien.se
Freq: Daily; **Cover Price:** Free; **Circ:** 2,333 Unique Users
Editor: Lars Eriksson; **Editor-in-Chief:** Stefan Fröjdendahl; **Publisher:** Stefan Fröjdendahl
Language(s): Swedish
ADVERTISING RATES:
SCC .... SEK 46
BUSINESS: FINANCE & ECONOMICS: Property

TIDNINGEN HAMNARBETAREN

50509W45A-20
Editorial: c/o Ödesjö, Runmarö Söderby 610, 130 38 RUNMARÖ **Tel:** 70 527 09 19 **Fax:** 86678447
Email: micke@gbf.se **Web site:** http://www.hamn.nu
Freq: Quarterly; **Circ:** 3,000
Editor-in-Chief: Mikael Ödesjö; **Publisher:** Björn A Borg
Profile: Publication of the Swedish Dockworkers' Association.
Language(s): Swedish
BUSINESS: MARINE & SHIPPING

TIDNINGEN HEMVÄRNET

750721W40-110
Editorial: 107 85 STOCKHOLM **Tel:** 8 788 75 00
Fax: 8 664 57 90
Email: red@tidningenhemvarnet.se **Web site:** http://tidningenhemvarnet.se
Date Established: 1940; **Freq:** 6 issues yearly; **Circ:** 33,200
Editor-in-Chief: Therese Åkerstedt; **Publisher:** Lars Brink
Language(s): Swedish
BUSINESS: DEFENCE

TIDNINGEN HOCKEY

750729W75J-220
Editorial: Daus-huset, 893 80 BJÄSTA
Tel: 660 26 61 00 **Fax:** 660 26 61 11
Email: jan.dylicki@daus.se **Web site:** http://www.daus.se/hockey
Freq: Monthly; **Circ:** 8,000
Advertising Manager: Jan Dylicki
Language(s): Swedish
CONSUMER: SPORT: Athletics

TIDNINGEN KÖRSÅNG

750950W76D-255
Editorial: Box 163 44, 103 26 STOCKHOLM
Tel: 31 84 42 02
Email: red@sverigeskorforbund.se **Web site:** http://www.sverigeskorforbund.se
Freq: Quarterly; **Circ:** 16,000
Editor: Mia Malmstedt
Language(s): Swedish
CONSUMER: MUSIC & PERFORMING ARTS: Music

TIDNINGEN LUNDAGÅRD

51223W83-80
Editorial: Sandgatan 2, 223 50 LUND
Tel: 46 14 40 20
Email: lundagard@lundagard.se **Web site:** http://www.lundagard.se
Freq: Monthly; **Circ:** 25,900
Editor: Emma Svensson; **Advertising Manager:** Tobias Hansson; **Publisher:** Viktor Ström
Profile: Student newspaper with articles concerning higher education, culture and politics.
Language(s): Swedish
Readership: Read by students of Lund University.
ADVERTISING RATES:
Full Page Colour .... SEK 49400
SCC .... SEK 308.75
CONSUMER: STUDENT PUBLICATIONS

TIDNINGEN ÖPPET HUS

50224W4E-120
Editorial: Riksbyggen, 106 18 STOCKHOLM
Tel: 771 860 860 **Fax:** 8 698 41 10
Email: anna-maria.engqvist@riksbyggen.se **Web site:** http://www.riksbyggen.se
Freq: Quarterly; **Circ:** 182,000
Editor-in-Chief: Anna-Maria Engqvist; **Publisher:** Göran Krona
Profile: Journal containing information and news about the building trade. Also covers property purchase and maintenance.
Language(s): Swedish
Readership: Aimed at people working within the field.
ADVERTISING RATES:
Full Page Colour .... SEK 27000
BUSINESS: ARCHITECTURE & BUILDING: Building

TIDNINGEN PROFFS

50555W49D-50
Editorial: Kornhultsvägen 19, 310 21 HISHULT
Tel: 430 422 50 **Fax:** 43042232
Email: red@vagpress.se **Web site:** http://www.tidningenproffs.se
Date Established: 1990; **Freq:** Monthly; **Circ:** 14,700
Profile: Magazine about commercial vehicles and road transportation.
Language(s): Swedish
Readership: Aimed at truck operators, commercial drivers and transport administrators.
ADVERTISING RATES:
Full Page Colour .... SEK 31900
SCC .... SEK 159.50
BUSINESS: TRANSPORT: Commercial Vehicles

TIDNINGEN RUNTIKRIM

1983101W44-70
Tel: 11 496 37 90 **Fax:** 114963037
Email: runtikrim@kriminalvarden.se **Web site:** http://www.kriminalvarden.se/Publikationer/Tidningen-Runtikrim
Freq: Sex till sju nummer per år; **Cover Price:** Free; **Circ:** 17,500
Language(s): Swedish
BUSINESS: LEGAL

TIDNINGEN SKOGSTEKNIK

750725W14A-275
Editorial: Thulegatan 10A, 852 32 SUNDSVALL
Tel: 60 12 33 30 **Fax:** 60123339
Email: ove@midalva.se **Web site:** http://www.skogsteknik.com
Freq: Quarterly; **Circ:** 2,200
Advertising Manager: Tomas Nordmark; **Publisher:** Ove Jansson
Language(s): Swedish
BUSINESS: COMMERCE, INDUSTRY & MANAGEMENT

TIDNINGEN SNÖSKOTER

51038W75G-105
Editorial: Box 3163, 903 04 UMEÅ **Tel:** 90 14 93 70
Fax: 90 18 81 18
Email: info@skoter.se **Web site:** http://www.skoter.se
Freq: 6 issues yearly; **Circ:** 23,000
Editor: Carl Ivar Lidgren; **Editor-in-Chief:** Lars Wallmark; **Managing Director:** Carl Ivar Lidgren; **Advertising Manager:** Carl Ivar Lidgren; **Publisher:** Lars Wallmark
Profile: Magazine about transport by snow scooter in Scandinavia.
Language(s): Swedish
CONSUMER: SPORT: Winter Sports

TIDNINGEN SPIRA

1812361W87-208
Editorial: Box 521, 901 10 UMEÅ **Tel:** 90 200 25 00
Email: spira@svenskakyrkan.se **Web site:** http://www.tidningenspira.se
Freq: 6 issues yearly; **Circ:** 48,500
Editor: Ulrika Ljungblahd
Language(s): Swedish
CONSUMER: RELIGIOUS

TIDNINGEN STÅLBYGGNAD

1803846W4E-155
Editorial: Stålbyggnadsinstitutet, Box 27751, SE-115 92 STOCKHOLM **Tel:** 70 630 22 17 **Fax:** 84119226
Email: lars@sbi.se **Web site:** http://www.sbi.se
Freq: Quarterly; **Circ:** 5,000
Advertising Manager: Migge Sarrion; **Publisher:** Björn Uppfeldt
Language(s): Swedish
BUSINESS: ARCHITECTURE & BUILDING: Building

TIDNINGEN SVENSKT VATTEN

50495W42C-80
Editorial: Box 47607, 117 94 STOCKHOLM
Tel: 8 506 002 00 **Fax:** 850600210
Email: svensktvatten@svensktvatten.se **Web site:** http://www.svensktvatten.se
Freq: 6 issues yearly; **Circ:** 4,100
Editor: Catharina Olsson
Profile: Journal about water, waste water and drainage systems. Covers issues such as techniques, economy, information, education and environment.
Language(s): Swedish
ADVERTISING RATES:
Full Page Colour .... SEK 15300
SCC .... SEK 127.50
BUSINESS: CONSTRUCTION: Water Engineering

TIDNINGEN TRÄDGÅRDSLIV SVERIGE

1810820W26D-92
Editorial: Klubbacken 15, 129 39 HAGERSTEN
Tel: 707 53 33 83
Email: redaktion@tradgardsliv.net **Web site:** http://www.tradgardsliv.net
Freq: Quarterly; **Circ:** 10,000
Publisher: Klas Kihlberg
Language(s): Swedish
ADVERTISING RATES:
Full Page Colour .... SEK 18000
BUSINESS: GARDEN TRADE: Garden Trade Horticulture

TIDNINGEN TRAFIKMAGASINET

1641474W49A-402
Editorial: Trädgårdsgatan 35, 590 31 BORENSBERG
Tel: 42 23 64 48
Email: redaktionen@trafikmagasinet.nu **Web site:** http://www.trafikmagasinet.nu
Freq: Quarterly; **Circ:** 18,400
Editor: Stephan Fasth; **Advertising Manager:** Eva Nilsson; **Publisher:** Johan Rietz
Language(s): Swedish
ADVERTISING RATES:
Full Page Colour .... SEK 27000
SCC .... SEK 225
BUSINESS: TRANSPORT

TIDNINGEN ULLA

1625817W74B-62
Editorial: OTW Communication AB, Gekås Ullared, Box 34, 310 STOCKHOLM **Tel:** 346 37 500
Web site: http://www.gekas.se/Default.aspx?tabid=175
Freq: Quarterly; **Circ:** 122,000
Editor: Sofia Zetterman; **Managing Director:** Boris Lennerhov; **Publisher:** Boris Lennerhov
Language(s): Swedish
ADVERTISING RATES:
Full Page Colour .... SEK 36000
CONSUMER: WOMEN'S INTEREST CONSUMER MAGAZINES: Women's Interest - Fashion

TIDSKRIFT FÖR GENUSVETENSKAP

51008W74Q-59
Editorial: Linköpings Universitet, Linköpings Universitet, 581 83 LINKÖPING **Tel:** 1 328 2239
Email: tgv@mah.se **Web site:** http://www.tegeve.se
Date Established: 1980; **Freq:** Quarterly; **Circ:** 1,500
Editor: Anna Lundberg
Profile: Journal covering gender studies and the role of women within society and throughout history.
Language(s): Swedish
CONSUMER: WOMEN'S INTEREST CONSUMER MAGAZINES: Lifestyle

TIDSKRIFT FÖR LITTERATURVETENSKAP

51272W84B-231
Editorial: Box 200, 405 30 GÖTEBORG
Tel: 31 786 45 59 **Fax:** 31 786 44 60
Email: maria.jonsson@littvet.umu.se **Web site:** http://ojs.ub.gu.se/ojs/index.php/tfl
Date Established: 1971; **Freq:** Quarterly; **Circ:** 750
Editor: Maria Jonsson
Profile: Journal containing articles about the science and history of literature.
Language(s): Swedish
Readership: Read by scholars and students.
CONSUMER: THE ARTS & LITERARY: Literary

TIDSKRIFT FÖR SCHACK
51146W79F-120
Editorial: Slottsg 155, 602 20 NORRKÖPING
Tel: 11 10 74 20 **Fax:** 11 18 23 41
Email: kansliet@schack.se **Web site:** http://www.schack.se/tfs
Date Established: 1895; **Freq:** 6 issues yearly; **Circ:** 1,500
Editor: Niklas Sidmar
Profile: Journal of the Swedish Chess Association.
Language(s): Swedish
CONSUMER: HOBBIES & DIY: Games & Puzzles

TIDSKRIFT I SJÖVÄSENDET
50474W40-87
Editorial: VÄXJÖ **Tel:** 470 212 45
Web site: http://www.koms.se
Freq: Quarterly; **Circ:** 800
Editor: Thomas Engevall; **Advertising Manager:** Thomas Engevall; **Publisher:** Thomas Engevall
Profile: Publication of the Royal Swedish Society of Naval Sciences.
Language(s): Swedish
BUSINESS: DEFENCE

TIDSKRIFTEN 10TAL
750796W84B-281
Editorial: Box 19074, 104 32 STOCKHOLM
Tel: 8 612 10 49 **Fax:** 8 612 10 77
Email: redaktionen@10tal.se **Web site:** http://www.10tal.se
Freq: Quarterly; **Circ:** 4,000
Editor: Sara Stribe Pavell; **Editor-in-Chief:** Madeleine Grive; **Advertising Manager:** Madeleine Grive; **Publisher:** Madeleine Grive
Language(s): Swedish
ADVERTISING RATES:
Full Page Colour .... SEK 12000
SCC .... SEK 100
CONSUMER: THE ARTS & LITERARY: Literary

TIDSKRIFTEN ÄLDRE I CENTRUM
1803912W56B-189
Editorial: Gävlegatan 16, 113 30 STOCKHOLM
Tel: 8 690 58 00 **Fax:** 86906889
Email: inger.raune@aldreicentrum.se **Web site:** http://www.aldreicentrum.se
Freq: Quarterly; **Circ:** 4,000
Publisher: Inger Raune
Language(s): Swedish
BUSINESS: HEALTH & MEDICAL: Nursing

TIDSKRIFTEN BETONG
50214W4E-12
Editorial: Svenska Betongföreningen, 100 44 STOCKHOLM **Tel:** 8 564 102 14 **Fax:** 8 564 102 39
Email: redaktion@betong.se **Web site:** http://www.betong.se
Freq: 6 issues yearly; **Circ:** 3,500
Editor: Alexandra Cederquist; **Editor-in-Chief:** Roger Andersson; **Publisher:** Johan Silfwerbrand
Profile: Magazine covering all aspects of building and construction, especially concrete.
Language(s): Swedish
ADVERTISING RATES:
Full Page Colour .... SEK 19000
BUSINESS: ARCHITECTURE & BUILDING: Building

TIDSKRIFTEN FOLKUNIVERSITETET
50727W62F-70
Editorial: Folkuniversitetet, Box 26152, 100 41 STOCKHOLM **Tel:** 8 679 29 50 **Fax:** 8 678 15 44
Web site: http://www.folkuniversitetet.se
Freq: Quarterly; **Circ:** 5,000
Editor: Anette Riedel; **Advertising Manager:** Hans Flytström; **Publisher:** Michel Wlodarczyk
Profile: Magazine about all aspects of adult education and culture.
Language(s): Swedish
BUSINESS: CHURCH & SCHOOL EQUIPMENT & EDUCATION: Adult Education

TIDSKRIFTEN I IDROTT OCH HÄLSA
1663484W75A-206
Editorial: Tegelbruksgatan 17, 853 56 SUNDSVALL
Tel: 60 17 48 62
Email: idrottochhalsa@telia.com **Web site:** http://www.idrottslararna.se
Freq: 6 issues yearly; **Circ:** 2,700
Editor-in-Chief: Per Nylander; **Publisher:** Maria Mattsson
Language(s): Swedish
CONSUMER: SPORT

TIDSKRIFTEN KÄNGURU
634790W62A-330
Editorial: Box 50096, 104 05 STOCKHOLM
Tel: 8 16 76 63
Email: kanguru@tidskriftenkanguru.se **Web site:** http://www.tidskriftenkanguru.se
Date Established: 1995; **Freq:** Quarterly; **Circ:** 9,300
Editor-in-Chief: Petter Lindblad Ehnborg; **Publisher:** Petter Lindblad Ehnborg
Profile: Journal featuring articles on art and culture.
Language(s): Swedish
Readership: Aimed at students studying and interested in art and culture at Stockholm's University.
BUSINESS: CHURCH & SCHOOL EQUIPMENT & EDUCATION: Education

TIDSKRIFTEN KULT
1663396W84A-283
Editorial: Västergatan 11, 222 29 LUND
Tel: 46 39 99 40 **Fax:** 46399941
Email: info@svensktkulturarv.com **Web site:** http://www.svensktkulturarv.com
Freq: Quarterly; **Circ:** 1,000
Language(s): Swedish
CONSUMER: THE ARTS & LITERARY: Arts

TIDSKRIFTEN LABORATORIET
50582W55-10
Editorial: Röntgenv. 3, 141 52 HUDDINGE
Tel: 8 24 01 31
Email: laboratoriet@ibl-inst.se **Web site:** http://www.ibl-inst.se
Date Established: 1953; **Freq:** 6 issues yearly; **Circ:** 8,500
Advertising Manager: Bengt Tandberg
Profile: Publication for medical laboratory technologists within clinical chemistry, microbiology, cytology, clinical physiology, bio-chemistry, medical chemistry and blood group serology.
Language(s): Swedish
Readership: Aimed at Biomedical scientists.
BUSINESS: APPLIED SCIENCE & LABORATORIES

TIDSKRIFTEN OPERA
1625699W76D-269
Editorial: Väringatan 27, 113 33 STOCKHOLM
Tel: 8 643 95 44
Email: st@tidskriftenopera.nu **Web site:** http://www.tidskriftenopera.nu
Freq: Quarterly; **Circ:** 3,000
Editor: Sören Tranberg; **Editor-in-Chief:** Sören Tranberg; **Advertising Manager:** Magnus Zughaft, Ardeo Media Ab; **Publisher:** Sören Tranberg
Language(s): Swedish
CONSUMER: MUSIC & PERFORMING ARTS: Music

TIDSKRIFTEN OTTAR
1821343W86B-122
Editorial: RFSU, Box 4331, 102 67 STOCKHOLM
Tel: 8 692 07 28
Email: ottar@rfsu.se **Web site:** http://www.rfsu.se
Freq: Quarterly; **Circ:** 4,500
Editor-in-Chief: Carolina Hemlin; **Publisher:** Åsa Regnér
Language(s): Swedish
CONSUMER: ADULT & GAY MAGAZINES: Gay & Lesbian Magazines

TIDSKRIFTEN PLAN
750012W82-445
Editorial: Mats Johan Lundström, AQ Arkitekter, Box 235, 631 03 ESKILSTUNA **Fax:** 16 14 01 55
Email: plan@planering.org **Web site:** http://www.planering.org
Freq: Quarterly; **Circ:** 1,500
Editor-in-Chief: Mats Johan Lundström
Language(s): Swedish
CONSUMER: CURRENT AFFAIRS & POLITICS

TIDSKRIFTEN TRO & LIV
750643W87-190
Editorial: C/O Teologiska Högskolan Stockholm, Åkeshovsg 29, 168 39 BROMMA **Tel:** 8 564 357 16
Email: johnny.jonsson@ths.se **Web site:** http://www.ths.se/tro_liv.htm
Freq: 6 issues yearly; **Circ:** 1,600
Editor: Johnny Jonsson
Language(s): Swedish
CONSUMER: RELIGIOUS

TIDSKRIFTEN VÄSTERBOTTEN
750644W73-130
Editorial: Box 3183, 903 04 UMEÅ **Tel:** 90 17 18 02
Fax: 90779000
Email: ola.kellgren@vbm.se **Web site:** http://www.vasterbottensmuseum.se
Date Established: 1969; **Freq:** Quarterly; **Circ:** 3,500
Publisher: Ola Kellgren
Language(s): Swedish
CONSUMER: NATIONAL & INTERNATIONAL PERIODICALS

TOFSEN CHALMERS KÅRTIDNING
51530W62A-350
Editorial: Teknologgården 2, 412 58 GÖTEBORG
Tel: 31 772 39 23 **Fax:** 31 772 39 67
Email: tofsen@chs.chalmers.se **Web site:** http://www.tofsen.se
Freq: 6 issues yearly; **Circ:** 6,500
Editor-in-Chief: Isabella Flodström; **Advertising Manager:** Oscar Johansson
Profile: Student journal of Chalmers' University.
Language(s): Swedish
Readership: Read by teachers, students and postgraduates.
BUSINESS: CHURCH & SCHOOL EQUIPMENT & EDUCATION: Education

TOIVEKOTI & PUUTARHA
1861167W74C-539
Editorial: Gävlegatan 22, 113 92 STOCKHOLM
Email: toimitus@toivekoti.fi **Web site:** http://www.toivekoti.fi
ISSN: 2000-1096
Date Established: 2008; **Freq:** Monthly - Published 10/year; **Circ:** 50,000
Editor-in-Chief: Eeva Vähänäkki; **Managing Editor:** Henna Helne
Profile: Magazine about home and gardening.
Language(s): Finnish
ADVERTISING RATES:
Full Page Colour .... EUR 2990
SCC .... EUR 33.50
CONSUMER: WOMEN'S INTEREST CONSUMER MAGAZINES: Home & Family

TOPPHÄLSA
1655727W74G-205
Editorial: BUD: Rådmansgatan 49, 105 44 STOCKHOLM **Tel:** 8 736 52 00 **Fax:** 8 24 02 13
Email: red@topphalsa.se **Web site:** http://www.topphalsa.se
Freq: Monthly; **Circ:** 52,500
Language(s): Swedish
ADVERTISING RATES:
Full Page Colour .... SEK 39000
SCC .... SEK 325
CONSUMER: WOMEN'S INTEREST CONSUMER MAGAZINES: Slimming & Health

TORNEDALSBLADET
751209W80-770
Editorial: Ruokojärvivägen 28, 984 31 PAJALA
Tel: 978 102 15 **Fax:** 97810215
Email: jan-erik.lind@tornedalsbladet.se **Web site:** http://www.tornedalsbladet.se
Freq: 26 issues yearly; **Circ:** 4,300
Advertising Manager: Jan-Erik Lind
Language(s): Swedish
CONSUMER: RURAL & REGIONAL INTEREST

TORSLANDA TIDNINGEN
634304W72-525
Editorial: Flygmotorvägen 3, 423 37 TORSLANDA
Tel: 31 92 45 80 **Fax:** 31 92 25 87
Email: info@tidningen.se **Web site:** http://www.tidningen.se
Date Established: 1992; **Freq:** Weekly; **Circ:** 18,000
Editor-in-Chief: Bengt Wester; **Advertising Manager:** Lotta Nilsson; **Publisher:** Bengt Wester
Profile: Newspaper featuring news for Torslanda and surrounding areas.
Language(s): Swedish
LOCAL NEWSPAPERS

TOVE HEM & TRÄDGÅRD
1741134W74B-71
Editorial: Station 5 AB, Box 30210, 104 25 STOCKHOLM **Tel:** 8 501 188 50
Email: tove@tovemagazine.se **Web site:** http://www.tovemagazine.se
Freq: Monthly; **Circ:** 28,100
Advertising Manager: Ralf Lukovic; **Publisher:** Tove Oskarsson-Henckel
Language(s): Swedish
ADVERTISING RATES:
Full Page Colour .... SEK 38500
SCC .... SEK 416.66
CONSUMER: WOMEN'S INTEREST CONSUMER MAGAZINES: Women's Interest - Fashion

TRÄ & MÖBEL FORUM
1660643W46-125
Editorial: Box 55525, 102 04 STOCKHOLM
Tel: 8 762 72 50 **Fax:** 8 762 72 24
Email: info@tmf.se **Web site:** http://www.tmf.se
Freq: Quarterly; **Circ:** 6,000
Editor: Bengt Spjuth; **Managing Director:** Bengt Spjuth; **Publisher:** Susanne Rudenstam
Language(s): Swedish
BUSINESS: TIMBER, WOOD & FORESTRY

TRAFIK & MOTOR
50412W31A-60
Editorial: Box 6019, 175 06 Järfälla, 114 37 STOCKHOLM **Tel:** 8 761 82 82 **Fax:** 7 046 182 82
Email: fmk@fmk.se **Web site:** http://www.fmk.se
Freq: 6 issues yearly; **Circ:** 32,900
Editor-in-Chief: Staffan Swedenborg; **Publisher:** Bengt Wiktorsson
Profile: Magazine covering all aspects of the motor trade.
Language(s): Swedish
ADVERTISING RATES:
Full Page Colour .... SEK 23000
SCC .... SEK 191.67
BUSINESS: MOTOR TRADE: Motor Trade Accessories

TRAFIKFORUM
1625734W49A-401
Editorial: Box 72001, 181 72 LIDINGÖ
Tel: 8 670 41 00 **Fax:** 8 661 64 55
Email: info@rt-forum.com **Web site:** http://www.rt-forum.com
Freq: Monthly; **Circ:** 2,400
Editor-in-Chief: Anders Karlsson
Language(s): Swedish
ADVERTISING RATES:
Full Page Colour .... SEK 25975
SCC .... SEK 216.45
BUSINESS: TRANSPORT

TRAFIKVERKETS PERSONALTIDNING
1995111W49A-404
Editorial: 781 87 BORLÄNGE **Tel:** 771 921 921
Fax: 243 789 00
Email: itrafik@trafikverket.se **Web site:** http://www.trafikverket.se
Cover Price: Free; **Circ:** 9,000
Editor: Jennie Mörk
Language(s): Swedish
BUSINESS: TRANSPORT

TRAILER
50557W49D-100
Editorial: Box 529, 371 23 KARLSKRONA
Tel: 455 33 53 25 **Fax:** 455311528
Email: trailer@fabas.se **Web site:** http://www.trailer.se
Date Established: 1980; **Freq:** Monthly; **Circ:** 34,700
Advertising Manager: Martin Lindström; **Publisher:** Stig L Sjöberg
Profile: Magazine about lorries and other freight vehicles. Deals with political issues concerning transport.
Language(s): Swedish
Readership: Read by professionals involved in the transport trade throughout the Scandinavian countries.
ADVERTISING RATES:
Full Page Colour .... SEK 37900
SCC .... SEK 315.83
Copy instructions: *Copy Date:* 28 days prior to publication date
BUSINESS: TRANSPORT: Commercial Vehicles

TRAILER; TRAILER.SE
1846399W49A-403
Editorial: Box 529, 371 23 KARLSKRONA
Tel: 455 33 53 25 **Fax:** 455311528
Email: trailer@fabas.se **Web site:** http://www.trailer.se
Freq: Daily; **Cover Price:** Free; **Circ:** 16,400 Unique Users
Editor: Sture Bergendahl
Language(s): Swedish
BUSINESS: TRANSPORT

TRÄINFORMATION-EN TIDNING FRÅN SKOGSINDUSTRIERNA
1742366W4E-154
Editorial: Box 55525, 102 04 STOCKHOLM
Tel: 8 762 72 77 **Fax:** 87627990
Email: trainformation@skogsindustrierna.org **Web site:** http://www.skogsindustrierna.org/trainformation
Freq: Quarterly; **Circ:** 17,400
Advertising Manager: Hans Englund
Language(s): Swedish
ADVERTISING RATES:
Full Page Colour .... SEK 28000
SCC .... SEK 233.33
Copy instructions: *Copy Date:* 25 days prior to publication date
BUSINESS: ARCHITECTURE & BUILDING: Building

TRAKTOR POWER
1639381W21E-1
Editorial: 113 92 STOCKHOLM **Tel:** 8 588 365 51
Fax: 8 588 369 49
Email: kenneth.fransson@lrfmedia.lrf.se **Web site:** http://www.traktorpower.se
Freq: Monthly; **Circ:** 25,800
Editor: Kenneth Kauppi; **Editor-in-Chief:** Kenneth Fransson; **Advertising Manager:** Ulla Jonsson; **Publisher:** Kenneth Fransson
Language(s): Swedish
BUSINESS: AGRICULTURE & FARMING: Agriculture - Machinery & Plant

TRANÅS TIDNING
749754W74C-395
Editorial: Missionsgatan 2, 573 23 TRANAS
Tel: 140 674 40
Email: tranasred@smt.se **Web site:** http://www.tranastidning.se
Freq: Daily; **Circ:** 6,100
Publisher: Johan Hedberg
Language(s): Swedish
ADVERTISING RATES:
Full Page Colour .... SEK 13200
SCC .... SEK 34.28
CONSUMER: WOMEN'S INTEREST CONSUMER MAGAZINES: Home & Family

TRANÅS-POSTEN; TRANASPOSTEN.SE

1844964W65A-1048

Editorial: Box 1020, 573 28 TRANÅS
Tel: 140 38 55 70 **Fax:** 140 121 11
Email: red@tranasposten.se **Web site:** http://www.tranasposten.se
Freq: Daily; **Cover Price:** Free; **Circ:** 3,333 Unique Users
Editor: Ann-Christin Antonsson; **Editor-in-Chief:** Jan Justegård; **Advertising Manager:** Fredrik Söderholm; **Publisher:** Jan Justegård
Language(s): Swedish
ADVERTISING RATES:
SCC .... SEK 15
NATIONAL DAILY & SUNDAY NEWSPAPERS: National Daily Newspapers

TRANSITION

1625628W75X-206

Editorial: Swartling & Wranding Media AB, Sveavägen 62, 111 34 STOCKHOLM
Tel: 8 545 160 64 **Fax:** 8 545 160 69
Email: info@transition.se **Web site:** http://www.transition.se
Freq: 6 issues yearly; **Circ:** 15,000
Advertising Manager: Acke Stenquist; **Publisher:** Anders Neuman
Language(s): Swedish
CONSUMER: SPORT: Other Sport

TRANSPORT IDAG/ LOGISTIK IDAG

50549W49A-310

Editorial: Box 72001, 181 72 LIDINGÖ
Tel: 8 670 41 00 **Fax:** 86799050
Email: anders.k@mentoronline.se **Web site:** http://www.transportnet.se
Date Established: 1969; **Freq:** Monthly - (10 nr); **Circ:** 9,100
Advertising Manager: Jacob Albertsen; **Publisher:** Anders Karlsson
Profile: Magazine about transport, materials handling and logistics.
Language(s): Swedish
Readership: Aimed and decision-makers and managers.
ADVERTISING RATES:
Full Page Colour .... SEK 28200
SCC .... SEK 300
BUSINESS: TRANSPORT

TRANSPORT IDAG; TRANSPORTNET.SE

1848221W49C-4

Editorial: Box 72001, 181 72 LIDINGÖ
Tel: 8 670 41 00 **Fax:** 8 679 90 50
Email: kalle.l@mentoronline.se **Web site:** http://www.transportnet.se
Freq: Daily; **Cover Price:** Free; **Circ:** 5,000 Unique Users
Editor: Paul E Branke; **Editor-in-Chief:** Anders Karlsson; **Advertising Manager:** Jacob Albertsen; **Publisher:** Anders Karlsson
Language(s): Swedish
BUSINESS: TRANSPORT: Freight

TRANSPORTARBETAREN

50550W49A-340

Editorial: Box 714, Bud: Östra Järnvägsgatan 24 111 20 Stockholm, 101 33 STOCKHOLM
Tel: 10480 30 00 **Fax:** 8 723 00 76
Email: transport.fk@transport.se **Web site:** http://www.transport.se
Date Established: 1897; **Freq:** Monthly; **Circ:** 69,700
Editor: Pär Karlsson; **Publisher:** Jan Lindkvist
Profile: Magazine covering haulage, civil aviation, stevedoring and oil and newspaper distribution. Also contains articles about the bus, taxi and security trade.
Language(s): Swedish
Readership: Read by members of the Swedish Transport Workers' Union.
ADVERTISING RATES:
Full Page Colour .... SEK 24300
SCC .... SEK 202.50
BUSINESS: TRANSPORT

TRANSPORTNYTT

50548W49A-290

Editorial: Box 2082, 169 02 SOLNA
Tel: 8 514 934 70
Email: redaktion@transportnytt.se **Web site:** http://www.transportnytt.se
Date Established: 1958; **Freq:** Monthly; **Circ:** 7,000
Advertising Manager: Katarina Ungman; **Publisher:** Staffan Lingmark
Profile: Magazine about transport by air, land and sea. Also covers materials handling and packaging.
Language(s): Swedish
ADVERTISING RATES:
Full Page Colour .... SEK 22900
SCC .... SEK 190.83
Copy instructions: *Copy Date:* 10 days prior to publication date
BUSINESS: TRANSPORT

TRAVEL NEWS

50567W50-60

Editorial: Repslagargatan 17B, 1tr, 118 46 STOCKHOLM **Tel:** 8 545 064 20 **Fax:** 86795710
Email: redaktionen@travelnews.se **Web site:** http://www.travelnews.se
Date Established: 1985; **Freq:** Monthly; **Circ:** 11,500
Advertising Manager: Patrik Jerrestam; **Publisher:** Alexandra Kindblom
Profile: Magazine containing general travel trade news.
Language(s): Swedish
Readership: Read by professionals in the travel industry.
ADVERTISING RATES:
Full Page Colour .... SEK 37400
SCC .... SEK 311.67
BUSINESS: TRAVEL & TOURISM

TRAVEL NEWS; TRAVELNEWS.SE

1844984W50-123

Editorial: Box 20 123, 104 60 STOCKHOLM
Tel: 8 555 240 70 **Fax:** 8 679 57 10
Email: katarina.myrberg@travelnews.se **Web site:** http://www.travelnews.se
Freq: Daily; **Cover Price:** Free; **Circ:** 3,833 Unique Users
Editor-in-Chief: Katarina Myrberg; **Advertising Manager:** Patrik Jerrestam; **Publisher:** Katarina Myrberg
Language(s): Swedish
ADVERTISING RATES:
SCC .... SEK 62
BUSINESS: TRAVEL & TOURISM

TRAVHÄSTEN

752212W81D-125

Editorial: ASVT, 161 89 STOCKHOLM
Tel: 8 445 23 00 **Fax:** 8 445 23 09
Email: asvt@asvt.se **Web site:** http://www.asvt.se
Freq: 6 issues yearly; **Circ:** 4,500
Editor: Lotta Isacsson
Language(s): Swedish
CONSUMER: ANIMALS & PETS: Horses & Ponies

TRAVRONDEN

51023W75E-100

Editorial: Box 20046, 161 02 BROMMA
Tel: 8 564 820 00 **Fax:** 8283613
Email: redaktionen@travronden.se **Web site:** http://www.travronden.se
Freq: 104 issues yearly; **Circ:** 30,400
Advertising Manager: Thomas Johansson; **Publisher:** Anders Jonsson
Profile: Magazine focusing on horse racing.
Language(s): Swedish
CONSUMER: SPORT: Horse Racing

TRELLEBORGS ALLEHANDA

50840W67B-7300

Editorial: Box 73, 231 21 TRELLEBORG
Tel: 410 545 00
Email: red@trelleborgsallehanda.se **Web site:** http://www.trelleborgsallehanda.se
Circ: 9,200
Managing Director: Bo Wigernäs; **Advertising Manager:** Lena Söderlin; **Publisher:** Rickard Frank
Language(s): Swedish
ADVERTISING RATES:
Full Page Colour .... SEK 18720
SCC .... SEK 93.60
REGIONAL DAILY & SUNDAY NEWSPAPERS: Regional Daily Newspapers

TRELLEBORGS ALLEHANDA; WEBB

1625547W67E-5066

Editorial: Box 73, 231 21 TRELLEBORG
Tel: 410 545 25 **Fax:** 41017100
Email: webbredaktionen@skanemedia.se **Web site:** http://www.trelleborgsallehanda.se
Freq: Daily; **Cover Price:** Free; **Circ:** 10,400 Unique Users
Language(s): Swedish
REGIONAL DAILY & SUNDAY NEWSPAPERS: Regional Offices

TRUCKING SCANDINAVIA

1696631W10-94

Editorial: Box 529, 371 23 KARLSKRONA
Tel: 455 33 53 25 **Fax:** 455311715
Email: henrik.kindwall@fabas.se **Web site:** http://www.fabas.se
Freq: Monthly; **Circ:** 15,600
Language(s): Swedish
ADVERTISING RATES:
Full Page Colour .... SEK 13100
SCC .... SEK 109.17
BUSINESS: MATERIALS HANDLING

TS-TIDNINGEN

634807W2E-230

Editorial: 114 78 STOCKHOLM **Tel:** 8 507 424 00
Fax: 8 507 424 01
Email: info@ts.se **Web site:** http://www.ts.se
Freq: Quarterly; **Circ:** 5,000
Publisher: Magnus Paulsson
Profile: Official publication of Tidningsstatistik. Provides media statistics for Sweden, includes newspapers, television and radio.
Language(s): Swedish
ADVERTISING RATES:
Full Page Colour .... SEK 5000
BUSINESS: COMMUNICATIONS, ADVERTISING & MARKETING: Public Relations

TTELA

633906W67B-3775

Editorial: Box 111, 462 22 VÄNERSBORG
Tel: 521 26 46 00 **Fax:** 521 57 59 18
Email: redaktionen@ttela.se **Web site:** http://www.ttela.se
Date Established: 1885
Circ: 28,500
Editor: GunBritt Nord; **Editor-in-Chief:** Allan Johansson; **Publisher:** Bo Zetterlund
Profile: Newspaper covering local news in the Elfborg area.
Language(s): Swedish
ADVERTISING RATES:
Full Page Colour .... SEK 45600
SCC .... SEK 228
REGIONAL DAILY & SUNDAY NEWSPAPERS: Regional Daily Newspapers

TTELA ~ TROLLHÄTTAN

633932W67B-7325

Editorial: Box 54, 461 22 TROLLHÄTTAN
Tel: 520 49 42 00 **Fax:** 520 131 28
Email: redaktionen@ttela.se **Web site:** http://www.ttela.se
Date Established: 1906
Editor: Agnetha Andersson; **Advertising Manager:** Lennart Larsson
Profile: Newspaper covering local news in the Trollhättan.
Language(s): Swedish
REGIONAL DAILY & SUNDAY NEWSPAPERS: Regional Daily Newspapers

TTELA; TTELA.SE

1844696W65A-1023

Editorial: Box 111, 462 22 VÄNERSBORG
Tel: 521 26 46 00
Email: redaktionen@ttela.se **Web site:** http://www.ttela.se
Freq: Daily; **Cover Price:** Free; **Circ:** 7,309 Unique Users
Editor-in-Chief: Allan Johansson
Language(s): Swedish
NATIONAL DAILY & SUNDAY NEWSPAPERS: National Daily Newspapers

T-TIME

750591W14A-245

Editorial: Trelleborg AB, Box 153, 231 22 TRELLEBORG **Tel:** 410 670 00
Email: viktoria.bergman@trelleborg.com **Web site:** http://www.trelleborg.com/sv/Media/T-Time-
Freq: Quarterly; **Circ:** 40,000
Editor: Donna Guinivan; **Editor-in-Chief:** Rosman Jahja; **Publisher:** Viktoria Bergman
Language(s): Swedish
BUSINESS: COMMERCE, INDUSTRY & MANAGEMENT

TUIFLY MAGAZINE

1639325W89D-152

Editorial: Mediabolaget, Swedenborgsgatan 7, 118 48 STOCKHOLM **Tel:** 8 556 963 10 **Fax:** 8 641 95 44
Email: nils@mediabolaget.nu **Web site:** http://www.mediabolaget.nu
Freq: Half-yearly; **Circ:** 65,000
Editor: Nils Wennberg; **Editor-in-Chief:** Gunnar Wesslén; **Publisher:** Gunnar Wesslén
Language(s): Swedish
CONSUMER: HOLIDAYS & TRAVEL: In-Flight Magazines

TURIST

50568W50-70

Editorial: Box 17251, 104 62 STOCKHOLM
Tel: 8 463 21 00 **Fax:** 8 678 19 58
Email: turist@stfturist.se **Web site:** http://www.stfturist.se
Freq: Quarterly - 5 nr/år; **Circ:** 160,700
Advertising Manager: Patric Vedin; **Publisher:** Anders Tapper
Profile: Magazine covering all aspects of the tourism trade in Sweden.
Language(s): Swedish
ADVERTISING RATES:
Full Page Colour .... SEK 32900
SCC .... SEK 274.16
BUSINESS: TRAVEL & TOURISM

TURIST I VÄRMLAND

750531W50-100

Editorial: Gjutaregatan 2 E, 681 50 KRISTINEHAMN
Tel: 550 10988 **Fax:** 550 10988
Email: info@turistivarmland.se **Web site:** http://www.turistivarmland.se
Freq: Annual; **Circ:** 100,000
Editor-in-Chief: Kjell Ljung; **Managing Director:** Kjell Ljung; **Advertising Manager:** Kjell Ljung; **Publisher:** Kjell Ljung
Language(s): Swedish
BUSINESS: TRAVEL & TOURISM

TV3 ;TEXT-TV

1863424W2D-4

Editorial: Box 171 04, 104 62 STOCKHOLM
Tel: 8 562 023 00
Email: cecilia.bungss@mtgtv.se **Web site:** http://www.tv3.se
Freq: Daily; **Circ:** 397,000
Language(s): Swedish
BUSINESS: COMMUNICATIONS, ADVERTISING & MARKETING: Broadcasting

TV4; NYHETSKANALEN.SE

1852919W82-498

Editorial: 115 79 STOCKHOLM **Tel:** 8 459 40 00
Email: nyhetskanalen@tv4.se **Web site:** http://www.nyhetskanalen.se
Freq: Daily; **Cover Price:** Paid; **Circ:** 487,400 Unique Users
Editor: Ghita Huldén; **Publisher:** Kajsa Ericson
Profile: A site with local info covering general news and tourism.
Language(s): Swedish
CONSUMER: CURRENT AFFAIRS & POLITICS

TV4; TEXT-TV

1863420W2D-2

Editorial: Tegeluddsvägen 3-5, 115 79 STOCKHOLM
Tel: 8 459 40 00
Email: nyhetskanalen@tv4.se **Web site:** http://www.tv4.se
Freq: Daily; **Circ:** 1,120,000
Language(s): Swedish
BUSINESS: COMMUNICATIONS, ADVERTISING & MARKETING: Broadcasting

TVÄRDRAG

51208W82-245

Editorial: Box 11544, 100 61 STOCKHOLM
Tel: 8 714 48 06 **Fax:** 87149508
Email: daniel.suhonen@ssu.se **Web site:** http://www.tvardrag.se
Freq: Quarterly; **Circ:** 3,000
Profile: Political magazine of the Social Democratic Youth of Sweden.
Language(s): Swedish
ADVERTISING RATES:
Full Page Colour .... SEK 6000
SCC .... SEK 50
CONSUMER: CURRENT AFFAIRS & POLITICS

TYA-NYTT

50323W14L-185

Editorial: Box 1826, 171 26 SOLNA **Tel:** 8 734 52 00
Fax: 8 734 52 02
Email: info@tya.se **Web site:** http://www.tya.se
Freq: Quarterly; **Circ:** 13,400
Advertising Manager: Mikael Enbom
Profile: Journal providing news and information from the Transport Union.
Language(s): Swedish
BUSINESS: COMMERCE, INDUSTRY & MANAGEMENT: Trade Unions

TYNGDLYFTAREN

634815W75P-200

Editorial: Svenska Tyngdlyftningsförbundet, Box 15023, 700 15 ÖREBRO **Tel:** 19 17 55 80
Fax: 19 10 20 70
Email: office@tyngdlyftning.org **Web site:** http://www.tyngdlyftning.com
Freq: 6 issues yearly; **Circ:** 1,000
Editor-in-Chief: Håkan Johanson; **Advertising Manager:** Håkan Johanson; **Publisher:** Benny Johansson
Profile: Journal for the Swedish and Norwegian sports union.
Language(s): Swedish
Readership: Aimed at those interested in weightlifting and general sport enthusiasts.
CONSUMER: SPORT: Fitness/Bodybuilding

TYRESÖ NYHETER

634312W80-375

Editorial: Björkbacksvägen 37, 135 40 TYRESÖ
Tel: 8 798 91 01
Web site: http://www.tyresonyheter.nu
Date Established: 1972; **Freq:** 6 issues yearly; **Circ:** 16,000
Editor: Marita Bertilsson; **Advertising Manager:** Sune Linder; **Publisher:** Anders Linder
Profile: Newspaper covering local news for Tyresö.
Language(s): Swedish
CONSUMER: RURAL & REGIONAL INTEREST

UDDEVALLA-POSTEN; WEBB

1844941W65A-1041

Editorial: Junogatan 3, 451 41 UDDEVALLA
Tel: 522 350 50 **Fax:** 522 66 51 50
Email: redaktion@uddevallaposten.se **Web site:** http://www.uddevallaposten.se
Freq: Daily; **Cover Price:** Free; **Circ:** 4,000 Unique Users
Editor-in-Chief: Göran Nyberg; **Managing Director:** Göran Nyberg; **Advertising Manager:** Petra Jungner; **Publisher:** Göran Nyberg
Language(s): Swedish
ADVERTISING RATES:
SCC .... SEK 8
NATIONAL DAILY & SUNDAY NEWSPAPERS: National Daily Newspapers

UDDEVALLAREN

634315W72-565

Editorial: St. Hellevigsgatan 2, 451 55 UDDEVALLA
Tel: 522 384 80
Email: uddevallaren@telia.com **Web site:** http://www.uddevallaren.se
Freq: Monthly; **Circ:** 25,000
Advertising Manager: Sten Mattsson; **Publisher:** Sten Mattsson
Profile: Newspaper featuring local news for Uddevalla.

Language(s): Swedish
LOCAL NEWSPAPERS

UD-KURIREN 634819W32A-260

Editorial: 103 39 STOCKHOLM **Tel:** 8 405 59 35
Fax: 8 723 11 76
Email: information-ud@foreign.ministry.se **Web site:** http://www.regeringen.se
Freq: 6 issues yearly; **Circ:** 3,500
Editor: Taimi Köster
Profile: Newsletter for Utrikesdepartementet (Ministry for Foreign Affairs).
Language(s): Swedish
Readership: Read by local and national government officials.
BUSINESS: LOCAL GOVERNMENT, LEISURE & RECREATION: Local Government

UFO-AKTUELLT 51361W94E-20

Editorial: Box 175, 733 23 SALA **Tel:** 18 55 50 00
Email: info@ufo.se **Web site:** http://www.ufo.se
Freq: Quarterly; **Circ:** 2,000
Editor: Håkan Ekstrand; **Advertising Manager:** Håkan Ekstrand; **Publisher:** Clas Svahn
Profile: Magazine about unidentified flying objects.
Language(s): Swedish
CONSUMER: OTHER CLASSIFICATIONS: Paranormal

ULRICEHAMNS TIDNING 50842W67B-7350

Editorial: Box 310, 523 26 ULRICEHAMN
Tel: 321 262 00 **Fax:** 321 262 39
Email: red@ut.se **Web site:** http://www.ut.se
Date Established: 1869
Circ: 8,600
Publisher: Bo Högborn
Language(s): Swedish
ADVERTISING RATES:
Full Page Colour .... SEK 26688
SCC .... SEK 133.44
REGIONAL DAILY & SUNDAY NEWSPAPERS: Regional Daily Newspapers

ULRICEHAMNS TIDNING; UT.SE 1844788W65A-1030

Editorial: Box 310, 523 26 ULRICEHAMN
Tel: 321262 19
Email: ut.se@ut.se **Web site:** http://www.ut.se
Freq: Daily; **Cover Price:** Free; **Circ:** 1,130 Unique Users
Publisher: Gun Råberg-Kjellerstrand
Language(s): Swedish
NATIONAL DAILY & SUNDAY NEWSPAPERS: National Daily Newspapers

UNDERHÅLL OCH DRIFTSÄKERHET 50229W4F-65

Editorial: Box 601, 251 06 HELSINGBORG
Tel: 42 490 19 00 **Fax:** 42 490 19 99
Email: peter.o@mentoronline.se **Web site:** http://www.uochd.se
Freq: Monthly; **Circ:** 4,000
Editor-in-Chief: Peter Olofsson; **Publisher:** Peter Olofsson
Profile: Journal about maintenance and dependability within the field of construction, real estate and the shipping industry.
Language(s): Swedish
ADVERTISING RATES:
Full Page Colour .... SEK 35500
SCC .... SEK 216.25
BUSINESS: ARCHITECTURE & BUILDING: Cleaning & Maintenance

UNG CENTER 51198W82-210

Editorial: Box 2200, 103 15 STOCKHOLM
Tel: 8 617 38 54 **Fax:** 86173854
Email: andreas.langbergs@centerpartiet.se **Web site:** http://cuf.se
Freq: Quarterly; **Circ:** 5,000
Publisher: Andreas Långbergs
Profile: Magazine of the Centre Party in Sweden.
Language(s): Swedish
ADVERTISING RATES:
Full Page Colour .... SEK 5000
CONSUMER: CURRENT AFFAIRS & POLITICS

UNIK 1645724W94F-213

Editorial: Box 6436, 113 82 STOCKHOLM
Tel: 8 508 866 00 **Fax:** 850886666
Email: fub@fub.se **Web site:** http://www.fub.se/publikationer/tidningenunik
Freq: 6 issues yearly; **Circ:** 23,000
Language(s): Swedish
CONSUMER: OTHER CLASSIFICATIONS: Disability

UNIQUE GENERATION 1803984W86A-113

Editorial: Box 403, 401 26 GOTEBORG
Tel: 739 05 53 11
Email: redaktion@uniquegeneration.com **Web site:** http://www.uniquegeneration.com
Freq: 6 issues yearly; **Circ:** 15,000
Editor-in-Chief: Amanda Olsson
Language(s): Swedish
CONSUMER: ADULT & GAY MAGAZINES: Adult Magazines

UNIVERSEN 750553W62A-490

Editorial: Box 256, 751 05 UPPSALA
Tel: 18 471 19 86 **Fax:** 18 471 15 20
Email: universen@uadm.uu.se **Web site:** http://www.universen.uu.se
Freq: 6 issues yearly; **Circ:** 6,500
Editor: Annica Hulth; **Publisher:** Urban Lindberg
Language(s): Swedish
BUSINESS: CHURCH & SCHOOL EQUIPMENT & EDUCATION: Education

UNIVERSITETSLÄRAREN 50729W62F-240

Editorial: Box 1227, 111 82 STOCKHOLM
Tel: 8 505 836 00 **Fax:** 8208305
Email: universitetslararen@sulf.se **Web site:** http://www.sulf.se
Freq: 26 issues yearly; **Circ:** 20,400
Advertising Manager: Lena Löwenmark-André; **Publisher:** Eva Rådahl
Profile: Magazine containing articles, news and information about teaching at universities and colleges.
Language(s): Swedish
Readership: Aimed at university teachers.
ADVERTISING RATES:
Full Page Colour .... SEK 22500
SCC .... SEK 187.50
BUSINESS: CHURCH & SCHOOL EQUIPMENT & EDUCATION: Adult Education

UNIVERSITETSNYTT 750571W62A-475

Editorial: Stockholms universitet, 106 91 STOCKHOLM **Tel:** 8 16 44 64 **Fax:** 8 15 36 93
Email: per.larsson@kommunikation.su.se **Web site:** http://www.su.se/pub/jsp/polopoly.jsp?d=855&a=991
Freq: 6 issues yearly; **Circ:** 8,000
Editor: Per Larsson
Language(s): Swedish
BUSINESS: CHURCH & SCHOOL EQUIPMENT & EDUCATION: Education

UPP I NORR 750877W50-105

Editorial: Box 303, 901 07 UMEÅ **Tel:** 90 13 31 77
Fax: 90130986
Email: redaktion@mediakontakt.nu
Freq: Quarterly; **Circ:** 18,800
Editor: Emma Larsson; **Advertising Manager:** Lars Ekeberg; **Publisher:** Anders Kling
Language(s): Swedish
BUSINESS: TRAVEL & TOURISM

UPPDRAG MISSION 51283W87-28

Editorial: Västergatan 22, 211 21 MALMÖ
Tel: 40 17 11 64
Email: red@uppdragmission.se **Web site:** http://www.uppdragmission.se
Date Established: 1846; **Freq:** 6 issues yearly; **Circ:** 2,000
Editor: Marie Bosund Hedberg; **Advertising Manager:** Anneli Henriksson
Profile: Publication of the Church of Sweden and the Lund Missionary Society.
Language(s): Swedish
CONSUMER: RELIGIOUS

UPPFINNAREN/ KONSTRUKTÖREN 50348W19A-93

Editorial: Box 104, 301 04 HALMSTAD
Tel: 35 10 41 50 **Fax:** 35 18 65 09
Email: info@teknikfor.se **Web site:** http://www.teknikfor.se
Freq: 6 issues yearly; **Circ:** 5,300
Editor: Staffan Bengtsson; **Editor-in-Chief:** Per-Anders Bengtsson; **Managing Director:** Staffan Bengtsson; **Advertising Manager:** Michael Karlsson; **Publisher:** Per-Anders Bengtsson
Profile: Magazine dealing with product development, innovation and design.
Language(s): Swedish
ADVERTISING RATES:
Full Page Colour .... SEK 11700
SCC .... SEK 97.5
BUSINESS: ENGINEERING & MACHINERY

UPPFINNAREN/ KONSTRUKTÖREN; WEBB 1844942W14A-336

Editorial: Box 104, 301 04 HALMSTAD
Tel: 35 10 41 50 **Fax:** 35 18 65 09
Email: info@uppfinnaren.com **Web site:** http://www.uppfinnaren.com
Freq: Daily; **Cover Price:** Free; **Circ:** 2,120 Unique Users
Editor-in-Chief: Per-Anders Bengtsson; **Advertising Manager:** Jan-Erik Andersson; **Publisher:** Per-Anders Bengtsson
Language(s): Swedish
ADVERTISING RATES:
SCC .... SEK 19
BUSINESS: COMMERCE, INDUSTRY & MANAGEMENT

UPPHANDLING24 1803881W32G-270

Editorial: IDG, 106 78 STOCKHOLM **Tel:** 8 453 63 12
Email: bo.nordlin@idg.se **Web site:** http://upphandling24.idg.se
Freq: Monthly; **Circ:** 9,800
Editor: Malin Ulfvarson; **Editor-in-Chief:** Bo Nordlin
Language(s): Swedish
ADVERTISING RATES:
Full Page Mono .... SEK 43260
SCC .... SEK 360.50
BUSINESS: LOCAL GOVERNMENT, LEISURE & RECREATION: Community Care & Social Services

UPPLANDS NYHETER; WEBB 1846255W65A-1057

Editorial: Box 323, 751 05 UPPSALA **Tel:** 1818 30 50
Fax: 18183055
Email: upplandsnyheter@sveagruppen.se **Web site:** http://www.upplandsnyheter.se
Freq: Daily; **Cover Price:** Free; **Circ:** 11,333 Unique Users
Advertising Manager: Peter Svensson; **Publisher:** Bo Pettersson
Language(s): Swedish
NATIONAL DAILY & SUNDAY NEWSPAPERS: National Daily Newspapers

UPPSALADIREKT.SE 1844798W65A-1034

Email: info@uppsaladirekt.com **Web site:** http://www.uppsaladirekt.se
Freq: Daily; **Cover Price:** Free; **Circ:** 2,667 Unique Users
Language(s): Swedish
NATIONAL DAILY & SUNDAY NEWSPAPERS: National Daily Newspapers

UPPSNAPPAT 652157W5B-190

Editorial: Hjemmet Mortensen, 113 78 STOCKHOLM
Tel: 8 692 01 00
Email: uppsnappat@datormagazin.se **Web site:** http://www.datormagazin.se/uppsnappat
Freq: 104 times a year; **Circ:** 50,000 Unique Users
Editor: Thomas Forsberg
Language(s): Swedish
BUSINESS: COMPUTERS & AUTOMATION: Data Processing

UPPSPÅRAT 1657835W49E-106

Editorial: Banverket Produktion, 781 85 BORLÄNGE
Tel: 243 44 62 45 **Fax:** 243446250
Email: madelene.sandgren@infranord.se **Web site:** http://www.banverket.se/produktion
Freq: 6 issues yearly; **Circ:** 3,500
Editor: Stefan Bratt
Language(s): Swedish
BUSINESS: TRANSPORT: Railways

UPPTINGET 749816W56B-155

Editorial: Box 602, 751 25 UPPSALA
Tel: 18 611 60 94 **Fax:** 18 611 60 10
Email: upptinget@lul.se **Web site:** http://www.lul.se
Freq: 6 issues yearly; **Circ:** 16,000
Editor-in-Chief: Anna Yngvesson; **Publisher:** Noemi Katzenberg-Berger
Language(s): Swedish
BUSINESS: HEALTH & MEDICAL: Nursing

UPSALA NYA TIDNING 50845W67B-7400

Editorial: Box 36, 751 03 UPPSALA
Tel: 18 478 00 00
Email: nyhetsredaktionen@unt.se **Web site:** http://www.unt.se
Circ: 49,900
Publisher: Lars Nilsson
Language(s): Swedish
ADVERTISING RATES:
Full Page Colour .... SEK 63900
SCC .... SEK 313
REGIONAL DAILY & SUNDAY NEWSPAPERS: Regional Daily Newspapers

UPSALA NYA TIDNING; UNT.SE 751819W67B-10550

Editorial: Box 36, 751 03 UPPSALA
Tel: 18 478 00 00 **Fax:** 18129507
Email: carl-ake.eriksson@unt.se **Web site:** http://www.unt.se
Freq: Daily; **Cover Price:** Free; **Circ:** 60,900 Unique Users
Publisher: Carl-Åke Eriksson
Language(s): Swedish
REGIONAL DAILY & SUNDAY NEWSPAPERS: Regional Daily Newspapers

UTEMAGASINET 51350W91R-200

Editorial: Box 164, 830 13 ÅRE **Tel:** 647 514 40
Email: redaktionen@utemagasinet.se **Web site:** http://www.utemagasinet.se
Date Established: 1980; **Freq:** 6 issues yearly; **Circ:** 16,900
Editor: Kalle Grahn; **Editor-in-Chief:** Ingalill Forslund; **Advertising Manager:** Anders Olofsson; **Publisher:** Ingalill Forslund
Profile: Leisure magazine covering nature, walking, photography, skiing, cycling and canoeing.
Language(s): Swedish
ADVERTISING RATES:
Full Page Colour .... SEK 33000
SCC .... SEK 275
CONSUMER: RECREATION & LEISURE: Recreation & Leisure Related

UTEMAGASINET; WEBB 1844806W91R-244

Editorial: Box 164, 830 13 ÅRE **Tel:** 647 514 40
Email: redaktionen@utemagasinet.se **Web site:** http://www.utemagasinet.se
Freq: Daily; **Cover Price:** Free; **Circ:** 633 Unique Users
Editor: Erika Willners; **Editor-in-Chief:** Ingalill Forslund; **Advertising Manager:** Tommy Bjälkdahl; **Publisher:** Ingalill Forslund
Language(s): Swedish
ADVERTISING RATES:
SCC .... SEK 55
CONSUMER: RECREATION & LEISURE: Recreation & Leisure Related

UTEMILJÖ 50683W57-70

Editorial: Box 30, 432 03 TRÄSLÖVSLÄGE
Tel: 340 415 25 **Fax:** 340 417 95
Email: redaktion@utemiljo.com **Web site:** http://www.utemiljo.com
Date Established: 1967; **Freq:** 6 issues yearly; **Circ:** 2,900
Editor-in-Chief: Larseric Johanson; **Advertising Manager:** Birgitta Johansson; **Publisher:** Larseric Johanson
Profile: Magazine covering all aspects of the so called green sector which deals with environmental issues.
Language(s): Swedish
ADVERTISING RATES:
Full Page Colour .... SEK 8300
SCC .... SEK 69.17
BUSINESS: ENVIRONMENT & POLLUTION

V75-GUIDEN 1667630W75E-121

Editorial: 113 78 STOCKHOLM **Tel:** 8 692 66 80
Fax: 86920155
Email: guiden@guiden.se **Web site:** http://www.guiden.se
Freq: Weekly; **Circ:** 16,500
Editor: Håkan Danielsson; **Advertising Manager:** Ida Axelsson; **Publisher:** Hans Brolin
Language(s): Swedish
CONSUMER: SPORT: Horse Racing

VÄDER OCH VATTEN 50752W64N-100

Editorial: SMHI, Väder & Vatten, 601 76 NORRKÖPING **Tel:** 11 495 80 00 **Fax:** 11 495 80 01
Web site: http://www.smhi.se
Date Established: 1984; **Freq:** Monthly; **Circ:** 2,000
Editor: Carla Eggertsson-Karlström
Profile: Journal published by the Swedish Meteorological and Hydrological Institute containing articles about meteorology, hydrology and oceanography.
Language(s): Swedish
BUSINESS: OTHER CLASSIFICATIONS: Weather

VAGABOND 51313W89E-100

Editorial: Box 20123, 104 60 STOCKHOLM
Tel: 8 555 240 00 **Fax:** 855524001
Email: redaktionen@vagabond.se **Web site:** http://www.vagabond.se
Date Established: 1987; **Freq:** Monthly; **Circ:** 34,200
Editor: Barbro Janson; **Advertising Manager:** Jan Pettersson
Profile: Magazine containing information about travel and adventure.
Language(s): Swedish
Readership: Read by travel enthusiasts.
ADVERTISING RATES:
Full Page Colour .... SEK 39900
SCC .... SEK 332.50
Copy instructions: *Copy Date:* 30 days prior to publication date
CONSUMER: HOLIDAYS & TRAVEL: Holidays

VAGABOND; VAGABOND.SE 1846655W75L-194

Editorial: Box 20123, 104 60 STOCKHOLM
Tel: 8 555 240 00 **Fax:** 855524001
Email: redaktionen@vagabond.se **Web site:** http://www.vagabond.se
Freq: Daily; **Cover Price:** Free; **Circ:** 25,286 Unique Users
Editor: Fredrik Brändström; **Advertising Manager:** Jan Pettersson; **Publisher:** Tobias Larsson
Language(s): Swedish
CONSUMER: SPORT: Outdoor

VÄGBANAREN - TIDNINGEN SOM BANAR VÄG
634843W14A-137

Editorial: Fjärde Långgatan 48, 413 27 GOTEBORG
Tel: 31 42 94 30 **Fax:** 31429440
Email: vagbanaren@seko.se
Date Established: 1995; **Freq:** Quarterly; **Circ:** 25,000
Editor: Gunnar Larsson; **Publisher:** Per-Ove Andersson
Profile: Journal providing current information about Scandinavian industry, includes commerce, economics and culture.
Language(s): Swedish
Readership: Aimed at professionals from the Arabic speaking community.
BUSINESS: COMMERCE, INDUSTRY & MANAGEMENT

VÄGLEDAREN I UTBILDNING OCH ARBETSLIV
51545W62A-380

Editorial: c/o A.Söderlund, Västuguvägen 12, 862 41 NJURUNDA **Tel:** 60 310 89
Email: agneta.soderlund@skola.sundsvall.se **Web site:** http://www.vagledarforeningen.org
Freq: Quarterly; **Circ:** 1,100
Editor-in-Chief: Agneta Söderlund; **Advertising Manager:** Nina Flink; **Publisher:** Agneta Söderlund
Profile: Journal featuring information, discussions and opinions on education and careers.
Language(s): Swedish
BUSINESS: CHURCH & SCHOOL EQUIPMENT & EDUCATION: Education

VÄGMÄSTAREN
50492W42B-120

Editorial: Roxx Media Sverige, Box 164, 598 23 VIMMERBY **Tel:** 793 15 **Fax:** 793 49
Email: vagmastaren@fsv.se **Web site:** http://www.fsv.se
Freq: Quarterly; **Circ:** 2,300
Editor: Nils-Erik Pettersson; **Advertising Manager:** Anneli Lennartsson; **Publisher:** Stefan Wadbro
Profile: Journal containing articles and information of interest to road builders, contractors and engineers.
Language(s): Swedish
ADVERTISING RATES:
Full Page Colour .... SEK 5000
BUSINESS: CONSTRUCTION: Roads

VÄLFÄRD
51210W82-330

Editorial: Statistiska centralbyrån, Box 24300, 104 51 STOCKHOLM **Tel:** 8 506 940 00 **Fax:** 850694772
Email: tidskriften.valfard@scb.se **Web site:** http://www.scb.se/valfard
Freq: Quarterly; **Circ:** 2,500
Editor: Alexandra Kopf Axelman; **Editor-in-Chief:** Lena Johansson; **Publisher:** Berndt Öhman
Profile: Magazine covering current affairs and politics in Sweden and abroad. Contains general information about society and analyses facts about the welfare state and working life. Includes summaries of statistical reports describing the state's development.
Language(s): Swedish
Readership: Aimed at journalists, politicians, teachers and researchers interested in current affairs.
CONSUMER: CURRENT AFFAIRS & POLITICS

VALÖR, KONSTVETENSKAPLIGA STUDIER
51538W84A-240

Editorial: c/o Konstvetenskapliga institutionen, Box 630, 751 26 UPPSALA **Tel:** 18 471 58 35
Fax: 184712892
Email: valor@konstvet.uu.se **Web site:** http://www.konstvet.uu.se/valor
Date Established: 1986; **Freq:** Quarterly; **Circ:** 250
Publisher: Jessica Sjöholm Skrubbe
Profile: Magazine containing information on art history, research and literature reviews.
Language(s): Swedish
Readership: Read by scholars of Art History and others interested in the art scene.
CONSUMER: THE ARTS & LITERARY: Arts

VÅNING & VILLA
1664412W4F-87

Editorial: Mediehuset ST, 851 72 SUNDSVALL
Tel: 60 19 70 00 **Fax:** 60 12 22 12
Email: li.lestrade@st.nu **Web site:** http://www.vaningochvilla.nu
Freq: 26 issues yearly; **Circ:** 50,000
Advertising Manager: Eva Eriksson; **Publisher:** Camilla Boström
Language(s): Swedish
BUSINESS: ARCHITECTURE & BUILDING: Cleaning & Maintenance

VÄNSTERPRESS
51211W82-350

Editorial: Box 12660, 112 93 STOCKHOLM
Tel: 8 654 08 20 **Fax:** 86532385
Email: borje.graf@vansterpartiet.se **Web site:** http://www.vansterpartiet.se
Freq: Monthly; **Circ:** 14,000
Advertising Manager: Börje Graf
Profile: Left-wing political magazine.
Language(s): Swedish
ADVERTISING RATES:
Full Page Colour .... SEK 28000
SCC .... SEK 175
CONSUMER: CURRENT AFFAIRS & POLITICS

VAPENTIDNINGEN
51031W75F-200

Editorial: Box 23084, 104 35 STOCKHOLM
Tel: 8 34 29 70 **Fax:** 8342971
Email: redaktionen@vapentidningen.se **Web site:** http://www.vapentidningen.se
Freq: 6 issues yearly; **Circ:** 25,000
Editor-in-Chief: P-O Olsson; **Advertising Manager:** Ewa Westman
Profile: Magazine about guns, shooting and hunting.
Language(s): Swedish
CONSUMER: SPORT: Shooting

VÅR FÅGELVÄRLD
51163W81F-100

Editorial: Box 7006, 300 07 HALMSTAD
Tel: 35 374 53 **Fax:** 35 347 29
Email: anders.w@ornitologerna.se **Web site:** http://www.sofnet.org
Freq: 6 issues yearly; **Circ:** 10,000
Editor: Anders Wirdheim; **Advertising Manager:** Dirk Harmsen; **Publisher:** Anders Wirdheim
Profile: Journal of the Swedish Ornithology Society.
Language(s): Swedish
CONSUMER: ANIMALS & PETS: Birds

VÅR SKOLA SKOLÅR 1-3
749895W62A-495

Editorial: Skarpövägen 2, 185 91 VAXHOLM
Tel: 8 541 30160 **Fax:** 8 541 306 90
Email: gota@varskola.se **Web site:** http://www.varskola.se
Freq: 6 issues yearly; **Circ:** 1,500
Editor: Bodil Jönsson; **Editor-in-Chief:** Göta Englund; **Publisher:** Göta Englund
Language(s): Swedish
BUSINESS: CHURCH & SCHOOL EQUIPMENT & EDUCATION: Education

VÅR SKOLA SKOLÅR 4-7
749891W62A-500

Editorial: Skarpövägen 2, 185 91 VAXHOLM
Tel: 8 541 30160 **Fax:** 8 541 30690
Email: gota@varskola.se **Web site:** http://www.varskola.se
Freq: 6 issues yearly; **Circ:** 1,100
Editor: Christina Hansson; **Editor-in-Chief:** Göta Englund; **Publisher:** Göta Englund
Language(s): Swedish
BUSINESS: CHURCH & SCHOOL EQUIPMENT & EDUCATION: Education

VÅR SKOLA - SPECIALUNDERVISNING
749896W62A-505

Editorial: Skarpövägen 2, 185 91 VAXHOLM
Tel: 8 541 301 60 **Fax:** 8 541 306 90
Email: gota@varskola.se **Web site:** http://www.varskola.se
Freq: 6 issues yearly; **Circ:** 900
Editor: Eva Augustsson; **Editor-in-Chief:** Göta Englund; **Publisher:** Göta Englund
Language(s): Swedish
BUSINESS: CHURCH & SCHOOL EQUIPMENT & EDUCATION: Education

VÅR SYNPUNKT
1656508W94F-214

Editorial: Box 20074, 104 60 STOCKHOLM
Tel: 8 462 45 27 **Fax:** 84624502
Email: johan.rosengren@srfabi.org **Web site:** http://www.srfabi.org
Freq: 6 issues yearly; **Circ:** 4,000
Editor: Johan Rosengren
Language(s): Swedish
CONSUMER: OTHER CLASSIFICATIONS: Disability

VÅRA FISKEVATTEN
50514W45B-3

Editorial: 105 33 STOCKHOLM **Tel:** 8 787 50 00
Fax: 8 787 53 10
Email: andreas.martelius@swipnet.se **Web site:** http://www.fiskevatten.org
Freq: Quarterly; **Circ:** 5,000
Managing Director: Börje Waldebring
Profile: Journal containing articles and information about the management of Swedish fishing waters.
Language(s): Swedish
BUSINESS: MARINE & SHIPPING: Commercial Fishing

VÅRA KATTER
51160W81C-150

Editorial: Säby Nyckelbacken, 732 94 ARBOGA
Tel: 33 10 15 65 **Fax:** 33 10 08 99
Email: sverak@sverak.se **Web site:** http://www.sverak.se
Date Established: 1950; **Freq:** 6 issues yearly; **Circ:** 4,500
Editor: Ulf Lindström; **Advertising Manager:** Eva Porat
Profile: Magazine containing articles and information about cats.
Language(s): Swedish
Readership: Aimed at cat owners.
CONSUMER: ANIMALS & PETS: Cats

VÅRA ROVDJUR
1804023W81A-101

Editorial: Svenska rovdjursföreningen, Masthamnen, 116 30 STOCKHOLM **Tel:** 8 441 41 17
Email: redaktionen@rovdjur.se
Freq: Quarterly; **Circ:** 4,000
Editor: Tatjana Kontio; **Publisher:** Björn Ljunggren
Language(s): Swedish
CONSUMER: ANIMALS & PETS: Animals & Pets Protection

VARBERGS POSTEN
634327W72-583

Editorial: Box 93, 432 22 VARBERG **Tel:** 340 177 71
Fax: 340 144 70
Email: redaktion@varbergsposten.se **Web site:** http://www.varbergsposten.se
Date Established: 1996; **Freq:** Weekly; **Circ:** 28,800
Editor: Jessica Petersson; **Advertising Manager:** Ritva Niemi; **Publisher:** Roger Thilander
Language(s): Swedish
ADVERTISING RATES:
Full Page Colour .... SEK 28470
SCC .... SEK 142.35
LOCAL NEWSPAPERS

VARBERGS POSTEN; VARBERGSPOSTEN.SE
1846465W65A-1078

Tel: 340 177 71 **Fax:** 34014470
Email: redaktion@varbergsposten.se **Web site:** http://www.varbergsposten.se
Freq: Daily; **Cover Price:** Free; **Circ:** 14,000 Unique Users
Editor: Jessica Petersson; **Advertising Manager:** Martin Köllerström; **Publisher:** Roger Thilander
Language(s): Swedish
NATIONAL DAILY & SUNDAY NEWSPAPERS: National Daily Newspapers

VÅRDFOKUS
50619W56B-70

Editorial: Box 3207, 103 64 STOCKHOLM
Tel: 8 14 77 00 **Fax:** 8 14 77 00
Email: info.vardfokus@vardforbundet.se **Web site:** http://vardforbundet.se/vardfokus
Date Established: 1977; **Freq:** Monthly; **Circ:** 112,400
Editor: Annica Jonsson; **Advertising Manager:** Ewa Brandt
Profile: Magazine for nurses, midwives and laboratory assistants.
Language(s): Swedish
ADVERTISING RATES:
Full Page Colour .... SEK 38650
SCC .... SEK 278.75
BUSINESS: HEALTH & MEDICAL: Nursing

VÅRDGUIDEN
1623714W74G-197

Editorial: Hälso- och sjukvårdsnämndens förvaltning Box 690, Hantverkargatan 11 B, 102 39 STOCKHOLM **Tel:** 8123 132 70
Web site: http://www.vardguiden.se
Freq: Quarterly; **Circ:** 960,000
Editor: Anna Sjökvist; **Publisher:** Katarina Winell
Language(s): Swedish
CONSUMER: WOMEN'S INTEREST CONSUMER MAGAZINES: Slimming & Health

VÄRLDEN IDAG
1639406W87-203

Editorial: Box 6420, 751 36 UPPSALA
Tel: 18 430 40 00 **Fax:** 18 430 40 01
Email: redaktionen@varldenidag.se **Web site:** http://www.varldenidag.se
Freq: 104 issues yearly; **Circ:** 8,500
Editor: Mats Tunehag; **Editor-in-Chief:** Lukas Berggren; **Publisher:** Ulf Ekman
Language(s): Swedish
ADVERTISING RATES:
Full Page Colour .... SEK 17300
SCC .... SEK 108.12
Copy instructions: *Copy Date:* 7 days prior to publication date
CONSUMER: RELIGIOUS

VÄRLDEN IDAG; WEBB
1844982W87-213

Editorial: Box 6420, 751 36 UPPSALA
Tel: 18 430 40 00 **Fax:** 18 430 40 01
Email: webb@varldenidag.se **Web site:** http://www.varldenidag.se
Freq: Daily; **Cover Price:** Free; **Circ:** 3,400 Unique Users
Advertising Manager: Ingela Liljebäck; **Publisher:** Ruben Agnarsson
Language(s): Swedish
ADVERTISING RATES:
SCC .... SEK 22
CONSUMER: RELIGIOUS

VÄRLDENS TIDNING
1837364W87-209

Editorial: Svenska kyrkan, Informationsavdelningen, 751 70 UPPSALA **Tel:** 18 18 24 40 **Fax:** 18 16 99 31
Email: redaktionen@svenskakyrkan.se **Web site:** http://www.svenskakyrkan.se
Freq: Quarterly; **Cover Price:** Free; **Circ:** 180,000
Editor: Magdalena Wernefeldt
Language(s): Swedish
CONSUMER: RELIGIOUS

VÄRLDENS VINER
1804034W74P-214

Editorial: Nyvägen 55, 138 34 ÄLTA **Tel:** 8 39 27 72
Fax: 8396444
Email: info@tastynews.se
Freq: Quarterly; **Circ:** 10,000
Publisher: Åke Jacobsson
Language(s): Swedish
CONSUMER: WOMEN'S INTEREST CONSUMER MAGAZINES: Food & Cookery

VÄRLDSHORISONT
51212W82-353

Editorial: Box 15115, 104 65 STOCKHOLM
Tel: 8 462 25 58 **Fax:** 8 641 88 76
Email: varldshorisont@fn.se **Web site:** http://www.fn.se
Date Established: 1946; **Freq:** Quarterly; **Circ:** 9,000
Editor: AnnaLena Andrews
Profile: Magazine of the United Nations Association of Sweden.
Language(s): Swedish
CONSUMER: CURRENT AFFAIRS & POLITICS

VÄRLDSPOLITIKENS DAGSFRÅGOR
51213W82-355

Editorial: Box 27035, 102 51 STOCKHOLM
Tel: 8 511 768 00 **Fax:** 8 511 768 99
Email: lena.karlsson@ui.se **Web site:** http://www.ui.se
Date Established: 1938; **Freq:** Monthly; **Circ:** 4,500
Editor: Lena Karlsson
Profile: Journal about international politics.
Language(s): Swedish
Readership: Read by students, school pupils and interested general public.
CONSUMER: CURRENT AFFAIRS & POLITICS

VÄRMLANDS AFFÄRER
634845W63-110

Editorial: Säterivägen 7, 651 03 KARLSTAD
Tel: 5417 56 00 **Fax:** 54 20 35 15
Email: redaktion@varmlandsaffarer.se **Web site:** http://www.varmlandsaffarer.se
Date Established: 1992; **Freq:** 6 issues yearly; **Circ:** 40,000
Editor-in-Chief: Christina Wikström; **Publisher:** Christina Wikström
Profile: Magazine focusing on current business affairs in Värmland.
Language(s): Swedish
Readership: Aimed at professionals in the business sector.
ADVERTISING RATES:
Full Page Colour .... SEK 27540
BUSINESS: REGIONAL BUSINESS

VÄRMLANDS FOLKBLAD
50798W67B-7450

Editorial: Box 67, 651 03 KARLSTAD
Tel: 54 17 55 00 **Fax:** 54 17 55 99
Email: redaktion@vf.se **Web site:** http://www.vf.se
Circ: 19,500
Editor: Peter Franke
Language(s): Swedish
ADVERTISING RATES:
Full Page Colour .... SEK 21000
SCC .... SEK 105
REGIONAL DAILY & SUNDAY NEWSPAPERS: Regional Daily Newspapers

VÄRMLANDS FOLKBLAD; NÄRINGSLIV
51540W14A-160

Editorial: Box 67, 651 03 KARLSTAD
Tel: 54 17 55 00 **Fax:** 54175599
Email: redaktion@vf.se **Web site:** http://www.vf.se
Date Established: 1985
Circ: 24,700
Editor: Maria Eriksson
Profile: Journal focusing on business, trade and economy.
Language(s): Swedish
BUSINESS: COMMERCE, INDUSTRY & MANAGEMENT

VÄRMLANDS FOLKBLAD; VF.SE
751246W74C-435

Editorial: Box 67, 651 03 KARLSTAD
Tel: 54 17 55 00 **Fax:** 54175599
Email: redaktion@vf.se **Web site:** http://www.vf.se
Freq: Daily; **Cover Price:** Free; **Circ:** 24,700 Unique Users
Advertising Manager: Lars-Henrik Pamp; **Publisher:** Peter Franke
Language(s): Swedish
CONSUMER: WOMEN'S INTEREST CONSUMER MAGAZINES: Home & Family

VÄRMLÄNDSK KULTUR
1820772W76B-106
Editorial: Verkstadsgatan 1, 652 19 KARLSTAD
Tel: 54 10 06 19 **Fax:** 54100619
Email: kansliet@varmlandsk-kultur.com **Web site:** http://www.varmlandsk-kultur.com
Freq: Daily; **Circ:** 2,100 Unique Users
Publisher: Britt-Marie Insulander
Language(s): Swedish
Copy instructions: *Copy Date:* 45 days prior to publication date
CONSUMER: MUSIC & PERFORMING ARTS: Theatre

VÄRNAMO NYHETER
633939W67B-7475
Editorial: 331 84 VÄRNAMO **Tel:** 370 30 06 00
Fax: 37049090
Email: redaktion@varnamonyheter.se **Web site:** http://www.varnamonyheter.se
Date Established: 1930
Circ: 20,600
Editor: Lina Alkner; **Advertising Manager:** Mathias Duveskog; **Publisher:** Lars Alkner
Language(s): Swedish
ADVERTISING RATES:
Full Page Colour .... SEK 57966
SCC .... SEK 150.56
Copy instructions: *Copy Date:* 14 days prior to publication date
REGIONAL DAILY & SUNDAY NEWSPAPERS: Regional Daily Newspapers

VÅRT FÖRSVAR
50476W40-100
Editorial: Teatergatan 3, 111 48 STOCKHOLM
Tel: 8 678 15 10 **Fax:** 8 667 22 53
Email: aff@aff.a.se **Web site:** http://www.aff.a.se
Freq: Quarterly; **Circ:** 2,800
Editor: Tommy Jeppsson; **Publisher:** Maria Nyberg Ståhl
Profile: Journal containing information and articles about the Swedish total defence and security policies for Northern Europe.
Language(s): Swedish
BUSINESS: DEFENCE

VÅRT KUNGSHOLMEN
652175W72-800
Editorial: Box 5290, 102 46 STOCKHOLM
Tel: 8 545 870 70 **Fax:** 8 545 870 89
Email: vk@direktpress.se **Web site:** http://www.vartkungsholmen.se
Freq: Weekly; **Cover Price:** Free; **Circ:** 39,400 Unique Users
Managing Director: Peter Rydås; **Publisher:** Helene Claesson
Language(s): Swedish
ADVERTISING RATES:
Full Page Colour .... SEK 17085
SCC .... SEK 85.42
LOCAL NEWSPAPERS

VÅRT MALMÖ
634337W89C-210
Editorial: Malmö stad, Stadskontoret, 205 80 MALMO **Tel:** 40 34 10 00 **Fax:** 40 34 20 92
Email: info.malmo@givakt.se **Web site:** http://www.malmo.se/vartmalmo
Date Established: 1968; **Freq:** 6 issues yearly; **Circ:** 157,000
Editor: Åsa Lempert; **Advertising Manager:** Henrik Olsson; **Publisher:** Gunilla Konradsson
Profile: Newspaper featuring entertainment and news for Malmö.
Language(s): Swedish
ADVERTISING RATES:
Full Page Colour .... SEK 16900
SCC .... SEK 84.50
CONSUMER: HOLIDAYS & TRAVEL: Entertainment Guides

VÅRT NYA HEM
1863547W16A-58
Tel: 8 517 880 00 **Fax:** 851788001
Email: info@vartnyahem.se **Web site:** http://www.vartnyahem.se
Freq: Quarterly; **Circ:** 20,500
Editor-in-Chief: Lisa Kruse; **Advertising Manager:** Joséphine W Norgren
Language(s): Swedish
ADVERTISING RATES:
Full Page Colour .... SEK 50000
Copy instructions: *Copy Date:* 18 days prior to publication date
BUSINESS: DECORATING & PAINT

VÄSTERÅS TIDNING
634346W72-630
Editorial: Norra Källgatan 17, 722 11 VÄSTERÅS
Tel: 21 30 46 00 **Fax:** 21 30 46 09
Email: redaktion@vasterastidning.se **Web site:** http://www.vasterastidning.se
Date Established: 1992; **Freq:** Weekly; **Cover Price:** Free; **Circ:** 99,800
Editor-in-Chief: Britt Hallberg; **Publisher:** Lasse Blom
Language(s): Swedish
ADVERTISING RATES:
Full Page Colour .... SEK 47782
SCC .... SEK 208.84
LOCAL NEWSPAPERS

VÄSTERÅS TIDNING; WEBB
1846485W65A-1080
Editorial: Norra Källgatan 17, 722 11 VÄSTERÅS
Tel: 21 30 46 00 **Fax:** 21 30 46 09
Email: redaktion@vasterastidning.se **Web site:** http://www.vasterastidning.se
Freq: Daily; **Cover Price:** Free; **Circ:** 25,667 Unique Users
Editor-in-Chief: Britt Hallberg; **Managing Director:** Britt Hallberg; **Publisher:** Lasse Blom
Language(s): Swedish
ADVERTISING RATES:
SCC .... SEK 42
NATIONAL DAILY & SUNDAY NEWSPAPERS: National Daily Newspapers

VÄSTERBOTTEN MELLANBYGD
751226W74C-420
Editorial: Selet 138, 930 10 LÖVÅNGER
Tel: 913 240 00 **Fax:** 91310750
Email: annons@mellanbygden.nu **Web site:** http://www.mellanbygden.nu
Freq: 26 issues yearly; **Circ:** 9,000
Publisher: Gudmund Fahlén
Language(s): Swedish
CONSUMER: WOMEN'S INTEREST CONSUMER MAGAZINES: Home & Family

VÄSTERBOTTENS FOLKBLAD
50843W67B-7500
Editorial: Box 3164, 903 04 UMEÅ **Tel:** 90 17 00 00
Fax: 90 17 02 50
Email: redaktionen@folkbladet.nu **Web site:** http://www.folkbladet.nu
Circ: 13,000
Language(s): Swedish
ADVERTISING RATES:
Full Page Colour .... SEK 13600
SCC .... SEK 68
REGIONAL DAILY & SUNDAY NEWSPAPERS: Regional Daily Newspapers

VÄSTERBOTTENS FOLKBLAD; WEBB
1843652W65A-1005
Editorial: Box 3164, 903 04 UMEÅ **Tel:** 90 17 00 00
Fax: 90170250
Email: redaktionen@folkbladet.nu **Web site:** http://www.folkbladet.nu
Freq: Daily; **Cover Price:** Free; **Circ:** 14,876 Unique Users
Publisher: Roland Edlund
Language(s): Swedish
NATIONAL DAILY & SUNDAY NEWSPAPERS: National Daily Newspapers

VÄSTERBOTTENS-KURIREN
50844W67B-7550
Editorial: 901 70 UMEÅ **Tel:** 90 15 10 00
Fax: 90 77 46 47
Email: redaktion@vk.se **Web site:** http://www.vk.se
Circ: 35,800
Editor: Mats Olofsson; **Advertising Manager:** Peter Öystilä; **Publisher:** Sture Bergman
Language(s): Swedish
ADVERTISING RATES:
Full Page Colour .... SEK 37000
SCC .... SEK 185
REGIONAL DAILY & SUNDAY NEWSPAPERS: Regional Daily Newspapers

VÄSTERBOTTENS-KURIREN; VK.SE
752332W67B-10695
Editorial: 901 70 UMEÅ **Tel:** 9015 11 77
Fax: 90774647
Email: webred@vk.se **Web site:** http://www.vk.se
Freq: Daily; **Cover Price:** Free; **Circ:** 40,200 Unique Users
Advertising Manager: Peter Öystilä
Language(s): Swedish
REGIONAL DAILY & SUNDAY NEWSPAPERS: Regional Daily Newspapers

VÄSTERVIKS-TIDNINGEN
50847W67B-7650
Editorial: Stora Torget 2, 593 82 VÄSTERVIK
Tel: 490 666 00 **Fax:** 490 666 99
Email: vt.red@vt.se **Web site:** http://www.vt.se
Date Established: 1834
Circ: 11,800
Editor: Ilkka Ranta; **Advertising Manager:** Dag Lundblad; **Publisher:** Jennie Lorentsson
Language(s): Swedish
ADVERTISING RATES:
Full Page Colour .... SEK 25000
SCC .... SEK 125
REGIONAL DAILY & SUNDAY NEWSPAPERS: Regional Daily Newspapers

VÄSTERVIKS-TIDNINGEN; VT.SE
1844538W65A-1015
Editorial: Stora Torget 2, 593 82 VÄSTERVIK
Tel: 490 666 00 **Fax:** 49066699
Email: webmaster@vt.se **Web site:** http://www.vt.se
Freq: Daily; **Cover Price:** Free; **Circ:** 7,741 Unique Users
Language(s): Swedish
NATIONAL DAILY & SUNDAY NEWSPAPERS: National Daily Newspapers

VÄSTGÖTA-BLADET
50839W67B-7700
Editorial: Box 302, 522 30 TIDAHOLM
Tel: 502 77 03 00 **Fax:** 502 77 03 49
Email: red.vb@vgt.se **Web site:** http://www.vastgotabladet.se
Circ: 3,400
Advertising Manager: Niclas Svensson; **Publisher:** Dan Gillblad
Language(s): Swedish
ADVERTISING RATES:
Full Page Colour .... SEK 73440
SCC .... SEK 190.75
REGIONAL DAILY & SUNDAY NEWSPAPERS: Regional Daily Newspapers

VÄSTMANLANDS NYHETER; WEBB
1846264W65A-1060
Editorial: Box 1080, 721 27 VÄSTERÅS
Tel: 21 19 04 00 **Fax:** 21188434
Email: vastmanlandsnyheter@sveagruppen.se **Web site:** http://www.vastmanlandsnyheter.se
Freq: Daily; **Cover Price:** Free; **Circ:** 9,333 Unique Users
Editor-in-Chief: Bo Pettersson; **Advertising Manager:** Peter Svensson
Language(s): Swedish
NATIONAL DAILY & SUNDAY NEWSPAPERS: National Daily Newspapers

VÄSTMANNAKONTAKT
1623565W56B-186
Editorial: Landstingshuset, 721 51 VÄSTERÅS
Tel: 21 17 46 47 **Fax:** 21174509
Web site: http://www.ltvastmanland.se
Freq: 6 issues yearly; **Circ:** 7,500
Editor: Lars Thomasson
Language(s): Swedish
BUSINESS: HEALTH & MEDICAL: Nursing

VÄSTSAHARA
1640029W82-454
Editorial: c/o Afrikagrupperna, Linnégatan 21A, 413 04 GÖTEBORG **Tel:** 31 24 72 30
Email: vastsahara@brevet.nu **Web site:** http://www.vastsahara.net
Freq: Quarterly; **Circ:** 700
Editor: Lena Thunberg; **Publisher:** Jan Strömdahl
Language(s): Swedish
CONSUMER: CURRENT AFFAIRS & POLITICS

VÄXJÖBLADET/ KRONOBERGAREN; WEBB
1846253W65A-1056
Editorial: Västergatan 7, 352 31 VÄXJÖ
Tel: 470 71 99 50 **Fax:** 470 209 30
Email: redaktionen@vaxjobladet.se **Web site:** http://www.vaxjobladet.se
Freq: Daily; **Cover Price:** Free; **Circ:** 4,667 Unique Users
Language(s): Swedish
ADVERTISING RATES:
SCC .... SEK 32
NATIONAL DAILY & SUNDAY NEWSPAPERS: National Daily Newspapers

VECKANS AFFÄRER; VA.SE
1695641W74M-173
Editorial: 105 44 STOCKHOLM **Tel:** 8 736 53 00
Email: mikael.zackrisson@va.se **Web site:** http://www.va.se
Freq: Daily; **Circ:** 23,272 Unique Users
Editor-in-Chief: Pontus Schultz; **Advertising Manager:** Mikael Larsson
Language(s): Swedish
CONSUMER: WOMEN'S INTEREST CONSUMER MAGAZINES: Personal Finance

VECKANS NU
752110W74B-60
Editorial: Hammarby Kajväg 14, 120 30 STOCKHOLM **Tel:** 8 587 481 00 **Fax:** 8 587 48 107
Email: veckansnu@fridaforlag.se
Freq: 26 issues yearly; **Circ:** 70,000
Editor-in-Chief: Mira Palomäki
Language(s): Swedish
ADVERTISING RATES:
Full Page Colour .... SEK 29900
SCC .... SEK 249.16
CONSUMER: WOMEN'S INTEREST CONSUMER MAGAZINES: Women's Interest - Fashion

VECKO-REVYN
50984W74F-180
Editorial: Budadress: Malmskillnadsgatan 39, 111 38 Stockholm, 105 44 STOCKHOLM **Tel:** 8 736 52 00
Fax: 8 24 16 02
Email: red@veckorevyn.com **Web site:** http://www.veckorevyn.com
Freq: 26 issues yearly; **Circ:** 47,000
Publisher: Louise Bratt
Profile: Magazine covering fashion, beauty and topical issues.
Language(s): Swedish
Readership: Aimed at teenagers and young women.
ADVERTISING RATES:
Full Page Colour .... SEK 44500
SCC .... SEK 370.83
Copy instructions: *Copy Date:* 28 days prior to publication date
CONSUMER: WOMEN'S INTEREST CONSUMER MAGAZINES: Teenage

VECKO-REVYN; VECKOREVYN.COM
1842959W76D-291
Editorial: Sveavägen 53, 105 44 STOCKHOLM
Tel: 8 736 52 00 **Fax:** 8 24 16 02
Email: louise.bratt@veckorevyn.com **Web site:** http://www.veckorevyn.com
Freq: Daily; **Circ:** 20,865 Unique Users
Advertising Manager: Karolina Hülphers; **Publisher:** Louise Bratt
Language(s): Swedish
CONSUMER: MUSIC & PERFORMING ARTS: Music

VEGAN
51010W74Q-95
Editorial: Klövervägen 6, 647 30 MARIEFRED
Tel: 159 344 04
Email: info@vegan.se **Web site:** http://www.vegan.se
Freq: Quarterly; **Circ:** 2,000
Editor: Anette Svedberg; **Editor-in-Chief:** Ulla Troëng; **Advertising Manager:** Ulla Troëng
Profile: Magazine about the vegan lifestyle. Contains articles about diet and health, agriculture and animal protection.
Language(s): Swedish
Readership: Read by members of the organisation Veganföreningen (The Vegan Society).
CONSUMER: WOMEN'S INTEREST CONSUMER MAGAZINES: Lifestyle

VEGETAR
634658W74P-205
Editorial: Fjällgatan 23 B, 1 tr, 116 28 STOCKHOLM
Tel: 8 702 11 16
Email: svf@vegetarian.se **Web site:** http://www.vegetarian.se
Date Established: 1903; **Freq:** Quarterly; **Circ:** 4,000
Advertising Manager: Gert Jacobsson; **Publisher:** Kurt Svedros
Profile: Magazine focusing on vegetarianism and healthy cooking and eating.
Language(s): Swedish
Readership: Aimed at vegetarians.
CONSUMER: WOMEN'S INTEREST CONSUMER MAGAZINES: Food & Cookery

THE VEHICLE COMPONENT
1623605W49D-151
Editorial: Box 126, 793 23 LEKSAND **Tel:** 247 137 25
Email: tege.tornvall@telia.com **Web site:** http://www.fkg.se
Freq: 6 issues yearly; **Circ:** 3,900
Editor-in-Chief: Tege Tornvall; **Managing Director:** Svenåke Berglie; **Advertising Manager:** Daniel Skoglund; **Publisher:** Svenåke Berglie
Language(s): Swedish
ADVERTISING RATES:
Full Page Colour .... SEK 18700
SCC .... SEK 155.83
BUSINESS: TRANSPORT: Commercial Vehicles

VENTILEN
750522W56B-170
Editorial: c/o R. Nilsson, Gislövsvägen 2, 272 38 BRANTEVIK **Tel:** 414 224 47
Email: redaktionen@ventilen.se **Web site:** http://www.ventilen.se
Freq: Quarterly; **Circ:** 5,000
Editor: Isabell Fridh; **Editor-in-Chief:** Marianne Birke Englid; **Advertising Manager:** Gunnar Nornemark; **Publisher:** Marianne Birke Englid
Language(s): Swedish
BUSINESS: HEALTH & MEDICAL: Nursing

VERDANDISTEN
50711W82-367
Editorial: Slakthusgatan 9, 121 62 STOCKHOLM
Tel: 8 642 28 80 **Fax:** 86422820
Email: verdandisten@verdandi.se **Web site:** http://www.verdandi.se
Date Established: 1976; **Freq:** Quarterly; **Circ:** 11,000
Publisher: Helena Frisk
Profile: Magazine concerning social issues. Includes information on politics, education and drug problems.
Language(s): Swedish
CONSUMER: CURRENT AFFAIRS & POLITICS

VERKO
1665967W19R-3
Editorial: Datavägen 12 A, 436 32 ASKIM
Tel: 31 68 00 00 **Fax:** 31 68 00 09
Email: info@verko.se **Web site:** http://www.verko.se
Freq: Monthly; **Circ:** 5,300
Advertising Manager: Mattias Ek
Language(s): Swedish
BUSINESS: ENGINEERING & MACHINERY: Engineering Related

VERKSTÄDERNA 50350W19A-95
Editorial: 72001, Tryffelslingan 10, 181 72 LIDINGÖ
Tel: 8 52 22 53 35 **Fax:** 8 661 64 55
Email: info@verkstaderna.se **Web site:** http://www.verkstaderna.se
Date Established: 1905; **Freq:** Monthly; **Circ:** 13,800
Advertising Manager: Rose Marie Erikson;
Publisher: Peter Bergqvist
Profile: Journal covering the technology, machinery and the methods used within industrial workshops. Contains product news, articles, tests and general information.
Language(s): Swedish
ADVERTISING RATES:
Full Page Colour .... SEK 26900
SCC .... SEK 205
Copy instructions: *Copy Date:* 21 days prior to publication date
BUSINESS: ENGINEERING & MACHINERY

VERKSTÄDERNA; VERKSTADERNA.SE 1846294W27-30
Editorial: Box 72001, Tryffelslingan 10, 171 06 LIDINGÖ **Tel:** 8 52 22 53 35 **Fax:** 8 661 64 55
Email: info@verkstaderna.se **Web site:** http://www.verkstaderna.se
Freq: Daily; **Cover Price:** Free; **Circ:** 5,520 Unique Users
Advertising Manager: Rose-Marie Erikson;
Publisher: Peter Bergqvist
Language(s): Swedish
BUSINESS: METAL, IRON & STEEL

VERKSTADSFORUM 50301W14B-250
Editorial: Box 200 39, 104 60 STOCKHOLM
Tel: 8 30 79 90
Email: verdi.ogewell@verkstadsforum.se **Web site:** http://www.verkstadsforum.se
Date Established: 1992; **Freq:** 6 issues yearly -, 8 nr per år; **Circ:** 9,000
Editor: Bo Nyström; **Publisher:** Verdi Ogewell
Profile: Magazine covers the workshop industry. Focusing on Virtual Product Development and software in CAD-CAE-CAM, PDM, CPC, ERP, SCM CRM, visualisation, simulation and logistics.
Language(s): Swedish
Readership: Aimed at high and middle management, software users, and engineers in the IT industry.
ADVERTISING RATES:
Full Page Colour .... SEK 13500
SCC .... SEK 112.50
BUSINESS: COMMERCE, INDUSTRY & MANAGEMENT: Industry & Factories

VERKSTADSKONTAKT 50352W19A-120
Editorial: Box 82, 533 04 HÄLLEKIS **Tel:** 510 862 00
Fax: 51086220
Email: roland@verkstadskontakt.se **Web site:** http://www.verkstadskontakt.se
Date Established: 1990; **Freq:** 6 issues yearly; **Circ:** 13,000
Editor: Jeanette Persson; **Advertising Manager:** Anders Lidström
Profile: Magazine for people working in engineering workshops.
Language(s): Swedish
ADVERTISING RATES:
Full Page Colour .... SEK 11500
SCC .... SEK 57.50
Copy instructions: *Copy Date:* 10 days prior to publication date
BUSINESS: ENGINEERING & MACHINERY

VERKSTADSTIDNINGEN 50351W19A-100
Editorial: Box 2082, 169 02 SOLNA
Tel: 8 514 934 00
Web site: http://www.verkstadstidningen.se
Date Established: 1972; **Freq:** Monthly; **Circ:** 14,000
Editor: Per Sjögren; **Editor-in-Chief:** Ronald Andersson; **Advertising Manager:** Malin Jerre;
Publisher: Staffan Lingmark
Profile: Journal covering workshop practice.
Language(s): Swedish
Readership: Read by subcontractors and decision-makers in the manufacturing and engineering industry, machine tool shops and in the metal forming industry.
ADVERTISING RATES:
Full Page Colour .... SEK 21200
SCC .... SEK 176.66
BUSINESS: ENGINEERING & MACHINERY

VERTEX 51229W83-150
Editorial: Box 7652, 907 13 UMEÅ **Tel:** 90 786 90 20
Fax: 90 13 09 28
Email: red@vertex.nu **Web site:** http://www.vertex.nu
Date Established: 1960; **Freq:** Monthly; **Circ:** 18,000
Editor-in-Chief: Bertil Janson; **Advertising Manager:** Henrik Bjelkstål; **Publisher:** Bertil Janson
Profile: Magazine covering all aspects of student life.
Language(s): Swedish
Readership: Read by students at the University of Umeå.
ADVERTISING RATES:
Full Page Colour .... SEK 16400
SCC .... SEK 102.5
CONSUMER: STUDENT PUBLICATIONS

VERTEX; VERTEX.NU 1844974W62A-520
Editorial: Box 7652, 907 13 UMEÅ **Tel:** 90 786 90 20
Fax: 90 13 09 28
Email: red@vertex.nu **Web site:** http://www.vertex.nu
Freq: Daily; **Cover Price:** Free; **Circ:** 3,600 Unique Users
Editor-in-Chief: Bertil Janson; **Advertising Manager:** Henrik Bjelkstål; **Publisher:** Bertil Janson
Language(s): Swedish
ADVERTISING RATES:
SCC .... SEK 20
BUSINESS: CHURCH & SCHOOL EQUIPMENT & EDUCATION: Education

VESTMANLANDS LÄNS TIDNING 50846W67B-7750
Editorial: Box 3, 721 03 VÄSTERÅS **Tel:** 21 19 90 00
Fax: 21 19 90 60
Email: nyheter@vlt.se **Web site:** http://www.vlt.se
Circ: 42,200
Language(s): Swedish
ADVERTISING RATES:
Full Page Colour .... SEK 60165
SCC .... SEK 300.82
REGIONAL DAILY & SUNDAY NEWSPAPERS: Regional Daily Newspapers

VESTMANLANDS LÄNS TIDNING; VLT.SE 752326W67B-10815
Editorial: Box 3, 721 03 VÄSTERÅS **Tel:** 21 19 92 97
Fax: 21199060
Email: webben@vlt.se **Web site:** http://www.vlt.se
Freq: Daily; **Cover Price:** Free; **Circ:** 47,200 Unique Users
Language(s): Swedish
REGIONAL DAILY & SUNDAY NEWSPAPERS: Regional Daily Newspapers

VETERANEN 50999W74N-100
Editorial: Box 22574, 104 22 STOCKHOLM
Tel: 8 692 32 50 **Fax:** 8 651 15 53
Email: redaktionen@veteranen.se **Web site:** http://www.veteranen.se
Freq: Monthly - 9 nr/år; **Circ:** 204,300
Advertising Manager: Katarina Lindström;
Publisher: Ylva Bergman
Profile: Magazine of interest to active pensioners.
Language(s): Swedish
ADVERTISING RATES:
Full Page Colour .... SEK 41600
SCC .... SEK 311.66
CONSUMER: WOMEN'S INTEREST CONSUMER MAGAZINES: Retirement

VETLANDA-POSTEN 50849W67B-7800
Editorial: Box 63, 574 21 VETLANDA
Tel: 383 76 32 10 **Fax:** 383 152 94
Email: vetlandared@smt.se **Web site:** http://www.vetlandaposten.se
Circ: 8,800
Publisher: Johan Hedberg
Language(s): Swedish
ADVERTISING RATES:
Full Page Colour .... SEK 18200
SCC .... SEK 47.27
REGIONAL DAILY & SUNDAY NEWSPAPERS: Regional Daily Newspapers

VETLANDA-POSTEN ~ ÅSEDA 750489W74C-430
Editorial: Olovsgatan 17, 360 70 ÅSEDA
Tel: 474 712 68 **Fax:** 47412124
Email: asedared@smt.se **Web site:** http://www.vetlandaposten.se
Freq: Daily; **Circ:** 9,300
Editor: Eigert Petersson
Language(s): Swedish
CONSUMER: WOMEN'S INTEREST CONSUMER MAGAZINES: Home & Family

VI 50967W74C-140
Editorial: Box 2052, 103 12 STOCKHOLM
Tel: 8 769 86 00 **Fax:** 8 769 86 22
Email: redax@vi-tidningen.se **Web site:** http://www.vi-tidningen.se
Date Established: 1913; **Freq:** Monthly; **Circ:** 40,200
Editor: Anita Kratz; **Editor-in-Chief:** Sofia Wadensjö Karén
Profile: Family magazine containing articles, recipes and interviews. Also covers politics, aid projects and travel.
Language(s): Swedish
ADVERTISING RATES:
Full Page Colour .... SEK 33000
SCC .... SEK 275
CONSUMER: WOMEN'S INTEREST CONSUMER MAGAZINES: Home & Family

VI BÅTÄGARE 51338W91A-300
Editorial: 113 92 STOCKHOLM **Tel:** 8 588 366 70
Email: paul.bogatir@lrfmedia.lrf.se **Web site:** http://www.vibatagare.se
Freq: Monthly; **Circ:** 28,000
Editor: Anders Jelving; **Editor-in-Chief:** Paul Bogatir;
Publisher: Paul Bogatir
Profile: Magazine containing articles and information about motor boats. Covers new products, tests, maintenance and repair and related issues of interest to boat owners.
Language(s): Swedish
ADVERTISING RATES:
Full Page Colour .... SEK 23900
SCC .... SEK 199.17
CONSUMER: RECREATION & LEISURE: Boating & Yachting

VI BÅTÄGARE; WEBB 1846457W91R-245
Editorial: Box 26206, 113 92 STOCKHOLM
Tel: 8588 366 70 **Fax:** 850667809
Email: paul.bogatir@lrfmedia.lrf.se **Web site:** http://www.vibatagare.com
Freq: Daily; **Cover Price:** Free; **Circ:** 37,000 Unique Users
Advertising Manager: Thommy Andersson;
Publisher: Paul Bogatir
Language(s): Swedish
CONSUMER: RECREATION & LEISURE: Recreation & Leisure Related

VI BILÄGARE 1925961W82-544
Editorial: Box 23800, 104 35 STOCKHOLM
Tel: 8 736 12 00 **Fax:** 8 736 12 49
Email: redaktionen@vibilagare.se **Web site:** http://www.vibilagare.se
Freq: Monthly; **Circ:** 118,400
Editor-in-Chief: Niklas Carle
Language(s): Swedish
ADVERTISING RATES:
Full Page Colour .... SEK 47900
SCC .... SEK 457.50
CONSUMER: CURRENT AFFAIRS & POLITICS

VI BILÄGARE; WEBB 1846634W82-487
Editorial: Box 23800, 104 35 STOCKHOLM
Tel: 8 736 12 00 **Fax:** 8 736 12 49
Email: redaktionen@vibilagare.se **Web site:** http://www.vibilagare.se
Freq: Daily; **Cover Price:** Free; **Circ:** 40,400 Unique Users
Publisher: Nils-Eric Frendin
Language(s): Swedish
CONSUMER: CURRENT AFFAIRS & POLITICS

VI FÖRÄLDRAR 50977W74D-70
Editorial: Bonnier Tidskrifter, Budadress: Rådmansgatan 49, 105 44 STOCKHOLM
Tel: 8 736 53 00 **Fax:** 8 34 00 43
Email: red@vf.bonnier.se **Web site:** http://www.viforaldrar.se
Date Established: 1968; **Freq:** Monthly; **Circ:** 45,000
Editor-in-Chief: Åsa Rydgren; **Advertising Manager:** Hans Wånander
Profile: Magazine covering parenting issues and the upbringing and development of children.
Language(s): Swedish
Readership: Aimed at parents with newborn babies.
ADVERTISING RATES:
Full Page Colour .... SEK 48300
SCC .... SEK 402.50
CONSUMER: WOMEN'S INTEREST CONSUMER MAGAZINES: Child Care

VI FÖRÄLDRAR GRAVID 752072W74D-95
Editorial: Bonnier Tidskrifter AB, Budadress: Rådmansgatan 49, 105 44 STOCKHOLM
Tel: 8 736 53 00 **Fax:** 8 34 00 43
Email: red@vf.bonnier.se **Web site:** http://www.viforaldrar.se
Freq: 6 issues yearly; **Circ:** 17,700
Editor-in-Chief: Åsa Rydgren; **Advertising Manager:** Anna-Carin Enwall
Language(s): Swedish
ADVERTISING RATES:
Full Page Colour .... SEK 29250
SCC .... SEK 243.75
CONSUMER: WOMEN'S INTEREST CONSUMER MAGAZINES: Child Care

VI FÖRÄLDRAR; VIFORALDRAR.SE 1844691W62A-519
Editorial: Bonnier Tidskrifter, Budadress: Rådmansgatan 49, 105 44 STOCKHOLM
Tel: 8 736 53 00 **Fax:** 8 34 00 43
Email: red@vf.bonnier.se **Web site:** http://www.viforaldrar.se
Freq: Daily; **Cover Price:** Free; **Circ:** 4,726 Unique Users
Advertising Manager: Hans Wånander
Language(s): Swedish
BUSINESS: CHURCH & SCHOOL EQUIPMENT & EDUCATION: Education

VI I VASASTAN 634332W72-655
Editorial: Box 5290, 102 46 STOCKHOLM
Tel: 8 545 870 70 **Fax:** 8 545 870 89
Email: info@direktpress.se **Web site:** http://www.viivasastan.se
Date Established: 1979; **Freq:** Annual; **Cover Price:** Free; **Circ:** 38,500
Managing Director: Peter Rydås; **Publisher:** Helene Claesson
Language(s): Swedish
ADVERTISING RATES:
Full Page Colour .... SEK 17850
SCC .... SEK 89.25
LOCAL NEWSPAPERS

VI I VILLA 50969W74C-145
Editorial: Box 4040, 181 04 LIDINGÖ
Tel: 8 731 29 00 **Fax:** 8 731 00 22
Email: redaktionen@viivilla.se **Web site:** http://www.viivilla.se
Date Established: 1956
Cover Price: Free; **Circ:** 2,089,400
Publisher: Björn Vingård
Profile: Magazine containing information about furnishings, decoration and DIY.
Language(s): Swedish
Readership: Read by home owners.
ADVERTISING RATES:
Full Page Colour .... SEK 337000
SCC .... SEK 2650
CONSUMER: WOMEN'S INTEREST CONSUMER MAGAZINES: Home & Family

VI I VILLA; WEBB 1844549W1E-208
Editorial: Box 4040, 181 04 LIDINGÖ
Tel: 8 731 29 00 **Fax:** 8 731 00 22
Email: webbredaktionen@viivilla.se **Web site:** http://www.viivilla.se
Freq: Daily; **Cover Price:** Free
Publisher: Björn Vingård
Language(s): Swedish
BUSINESS: FINANCE & ECONOMICS: Property

VI LÄNKAR 51542W32G-230
Editorial: Box 9069, 126 09 HAGERSTEN
Tel: 8 18 96 88 **Fax:** 8182989
Email: rikslankarna@lankarna.nu **Web site:** http://www.lankarna.nu
Freq: 6 issues yearly; **Circ:** 2,300
Publisher: Ingemar Rosén
Profile: Magazine focusing on drug abuse and rehabilitation.
Language(s): Swedish
Readership: Read by social workers and reformed drug addicts.
BUSINESS: LOCAL GOVERNMENT, LEISURE & RECREATION: Community Care & Social Services

VI MÄNSKOR 51215W82-370
Editorial: Linnégatan 21 B, 1 tr, 413 04 GÖTEBORG
Tel: 31 14 40 28 **Fax:** 31 14 40 28
Email: vimanskor@gmail.com **Web site:** http://www.vimänskor.se
Freq: Quarterly; **Circ:** 1,500
Editor: Elsa Leth; **Publisher:** Evy Hagman
Profile: Political left-wing journal discussing social matters from a woman's perspective.
Language(s): Swedish
CONSUMER: CURRENT AFFAIRS & POLITICS

VI PÅ LANDET 1625611W74C-445
Editorial: Tidningsbyrån, Brunnsgatan 16, 553 16 JÖNKÖPING **Tel:** 36 340 600 **Fax:** 36340601
Email: info@tidningsbyran.se **Web site:** http://www.tidningsbyran.se
Freq: Quarterly; **Circ:** 25,000
Advertising Manager: Torbjörn Arvidsson;
Publisher: Olle Ekelund
Language(s): Swedish
CONSUMER: WOMEN'S INTEREST CONSUMER MAGAZINES: Home & Family

VI PÅ NÄSET 751387W80-845
Editorial: Järnvägsgatan 74, 216 16 MALMO
Tel: 40 15 74 77 **Fax:** 40158680
Email: malmotidningen@telia.com
Freq: 6 issues yearly; **Circ:** 18,000
Editor: Ingrid Andersson; **Publisher:** Karl-Heinz Forsberg
Language(s): Swedish
CONSUMER: RURAL & REGIONAL INTEREST

VI RESENÄRER 1804066W89A-68
Editorial: Box 70 387, 107 24 STOCKHOLM
Tel: 8 776 39 50
Email: press@vireser.se **Web site:** http://www.vireser.se
Freq: 6 issues yearly; **Circ:** 5,000
Editor: Ann-Christine Bosell
Language(s): Swedish
ADVERTISING RATES:
Full Page Colour .... SEK 5000
CONSUMER: HOLIDAYS & TRAVEL: Travel

VI SKOGSÄGARE 50532W46-100
Editorial: Stålbrandsgatan 5, 214 46 MALMO
Tel: 40 92 25 55
Email: par.fornling@lrfmedia.lrf.se **Web site:** http://www.atl.nu/skog

Freq: 6 issues yearly; **Circ:** 92,700
Advertising Manager: Birgit Emilsson; **Publisher:** Pär Fornling
Profile: Magazine about forestry.
Language(s): Swedish
Readership: Aimed at forest owners.
ADVERTISING RATES:
Full Page Colour .... SEK 24000
SCC .... SEK 200
Copy instructions: *Copy Date:* 31 days prior to publication date
BUSINESS: TIMBER, WOOD & FORESTRY

VIA STOCKHOLMS HAMNAR
1741155W50-119
Editorial: Box 27314, 102 54 STOCKHOLM
Tel: 8 670 26 00 **Fax:** 8 670 26 55
Email: red@stockholmshamnar.se **Web site:** http://www.stockholmshamnar.se
Freq: Quarterly; **Circ:** 4,000
Editor: Camilla Strümpel
Language(s): Swedish
BUSINESS: TRAVEL & TOURISM

VICE
1668289W91E-1
Editorial: Rosenlundsgatan 36 B, 118 53 STOCKHOLM **Tel:** 8 675 00 58 **Fax:** 8 692 62 74
Email: info@viceland.se **Web site:** http://www.viceland.com
Freq: Monthly; **Circ:** 45,000
Editor-in-Chief: Elin Unnes; **Publisher:** Elin Unnes
Language(s): Swedish
CONSUMER: RECREATION & LEISURE: Lifestyle

VILLA AKTUELLT
634335W74C-147
Editorial: Årstaängsvägen 1 A, 11tr, 117 43 STOCKHOLM **Tel:** 8 555 930 00 **Fax:** 8 555 930 30
Email: info@villaaktuellt.se **Web site:** http://www.villaaktuellt.se
Date Established: 1985; **Freq:** Monthly; **Circ:** 203,900
Editor: Per Löwendahl; **Advertising Manager:** Bengt Jervelius; **Publisher:** Poul Heie
Profile: Magazine featuring articles on house and garden.
Language(s): Swedish
ADVERTISING RATES:
Full Page Colour .... SEK 44000
SCC .... SEK 240
Copy instructions: *Copy Date:* 20 days prior to publication date
CONSUMER: WOMEN'S INTEREST CONSUMER MAGAZINES: Home & Family

VILLA & FRITID
50962W74C-110
Editorial: Box 344, 431 44 MÖLNDAL
Tel: 31 27 51 20 **Fax:** 31 27 68 61
Email: info@villafritid.se **Web site:** http://www.villafritid.se
Date Established: 1967; **Freq:** Monthly; **Circ:** 102,500
Advertising Manager: Elna Sirkka
Profile: Magazine about home and leisure time.
Language(s): Swedish
Readership: Aimed at tenants of properties owned by housing associations.
ADVERTISING RATES:
Full Page Colour .... SEK 29800
SCC .... SEK 231.66
CONSUMER: WOMEN'S INTEREST CONSUMER MAGAZINES: Home & Family

VILLAÄGAREN
749791W74C-440
Editorial: Box 27712, Aller Custom Publishing, 115 91 STOCKHOLM **Tel:** 8 578 010 14
Email: redaktion@villaagarna.se **Web site:** http://www.villaagarna.se
Freq: Quarterly - (5 nr/år); **Circ:** 321,300
Advertising Manager: Jens Lindahl; **Publisher:** Hans Lemker
Language(s): Swedish
ADVERTISING RATES:
Full Page Colour .... SEK 56900
SCC .... SEK 457.50
Copy instructions: *Copy Date:* 38 days prior to publication date
CONSUMER: WOMEN'S INTEREST CONSUMER MAGAZINES: Home & Family

VILLAAGARNA.SE
1846676W82-491
Editorial: Box 7118, 192 07 SOLLENTUNA
Tel: 10 750 01 00 **Fax:** 10750 02 50
Email: info@villaagarna.se **Web site:** http://www.villaagarna.se
Freq: Daily; **Cover Price:** Free; **Circ:** 95,200 Unique Users
Editor-in-Chief: Lotte Ivarsson
Language(s): Swedish
CONSUMER: CURRENT AFFAIRS & POLITICS

VILLAFAKTA
50970W74C-150
Editorial: Reed Business Sweden AB, 827 81 LJUSDAL **Tel:** 651 55 25 00 **Fax:** 651 55 25 90
Email: mikael.sagstrom@svenskamedia.se **Web site:** http://www.villafakta.se
Date Established: 1955; **Freq:** Half-yearly; **Circ:** 63,600
Editor-in-Chief: Mikael Sagström; **Advertising Manager:** Stefan Nilsson
Profile: Magazine about restoration of old houses.
Language(s): Swedish
Readership: Aimed at home-owners and people interested in DIY.
ADVERTISING RATES:
Full Page Colour .... SEK 53000
CONSUMER: WOMEN'S INTEREST CONSUMER MAGAZINES: Home & Family

VILLAFORUM
1674293W74C-453
Editorial: Box 100, 231 22 TRELLEBORG
Tel: 410 460 55 **Fax:** 410 460 45
Email: redaktionen@villaforum.se **Web site:** http://www.villaforum.se
Freq: Quarterly; **Circ:** 300,000
Editor: Rolf Flymen
Language(s): Swedish
CONSUMER: WOMEN'S INTEREST CONSUMER MAGAZINES: Home & Family

VILLALIV
1897061W74C-523
Editorial: Villaliv AB, Köpmansgatan 12, 302 42 HALMSTAD **Tel:** 35 27 11 90 **Fax:** 35 22 72 80
Email: red@villaliv.net **Web site:** http://www.villa-liv.se
Freq: 6 issues yearly; **Cover Price:** Free; **Circ:** 2,085,000
Editor: Mattias Kristensson; **Editor-in-Chief:** Ingrid Carlqvist; **Advertising Manager:** Eva Håkansson; **Publisher:** Fredrik Lindblahd
Language(s): Swedish
ADVERTISING RATES:
Full Page Colour .... SEK 335700
CONSUMER: WOMEN'S INTEREST CONSUMER MAGAZINES: Home & Family

VILLATIDNINGEN
1835765W14A-320
Editorial: Bergsbrunnagatan 18, 753 23 UPPSALA
Tel: 18 10 37 40 **Fax:** 18 10 37 80
Email: redaktionen@villatidningen.se **Web site:** http://www.villatidningen.se
Cover Price: Free; **Circ:** 800,100
Publisher: Dan Lindau
Language(s): Swedish
ADVERTISING RATES:
Full Page Colour .... SEK 238000
SCC .... SEK 1000
BUSINESS: COMMERCE, INDUSTRY & MANAGEMENT

VILLATIDNINGEN; WEBB
1846632W58-106
Editorial: Bergsbrunnagatan 22, 753 23 UPPSALA
Tel: 18 10 37 40 **Fax:** 18 10 37 80
Email: redaktionen@villatidningen.se **Web site:** http://www.villatidningen.se
Freq: Daily; **Cover Price:** Free; **Circ:** 15,000 Unique Users
Advertising Manager: Isak N-Johansson; **Publisher:** Dan Lindau
Language(s): Swedish
BUSINESS: ENERGY, FUEL & NUCLEAR

VIN&BARJOURNALEN
1685478W74P-210
Editorial: Skeppargatan 27, 114 52 STOCKHOLM
Tel: 8 442 86 30 **Fax:** 86621180
Email: vinochbar@pressdata.se **Web site:** http://www.vinochbar.se
Freq: 6 issues yearly; **Circ:** 16,600
Advertising Manager: Pia Lindberg; **Publisher:** Anders Forsström
Language(s): Swedish
ADVERTISING RATES:
Full Page Colour .... SEK 26900
SCC .... SEK 224.17
Copy instructions: *Copy Date:* 15 days prior to publication date
CONSUMER: WOMEN'S INTEREST CONSUMER MAGAZINES: Food & Cookery

VIN&BARJOURNALEN; VINOCHBAR.SE
1846390W74P-224
Editorial: Skeppargatan 27, 114 52 STOCKHOLM
Tel: 8 442 86 30 **Fax:** 86621180
Email: redaktion@vinochbar.se **Web site:** http://www.vinochbar.se
Freq: Daily; **Cover Price:** Free; **Circ:** 17,000 Unique Users
Advertising Manager: Anders Forsström
Language(s): Swedish
CONSUMER: WOMEN'S INTEREST CONSUMER MAGAZINES: Food & Cookery

VINNOVA-NYTT
1836386W14A-322
Editorial: 101 58 STOCKHOLM **Tel:** 8 473 30 00
Fax: 84733005
Email: vinnovanytt@vinnova.se **Web site:** http://www.VINNOVA.se
Freq: 6 issues yearly; **Cover Price:** Free; **Circ:** 5,000
Language(s): Swedish
ADVERTISING RATES:
Full Page Mono .... SEK 5000
SCC .... SEK 41.67
BUSINESS: COMMERCE, INDUSTRY & MANAGEMENT

VIOLA
50395W26C-70
Editorial: 105 33 STOCKHOLM **Tel:** 8 787 53 80
Fax: 8 787 53 81
Email: christina.sall@viola.se **Web site:** http://www.gro.se
Date Established: 1895; **Freq:** 26 issues yearly; **Circ:** 3,000
Editor: Anders Myrsten; **Editor-in-Chief:** Christina Säll; **Advertising Manager:** Urban Hedborg; **Publisher:** Christina Säll
Profile: Journal covering the vegetable, flower and gardening trade.
Language(s): Swedish
ADVERTISING RATES:
Full Page Colour .... SEK 14950
SCC .... SEK 124.58
BUSINESS: GARDEN TRADE

VIPÅTV
1695419W2B-179
Editorial: SVT, KH-BVO, 105 10 STOCKHOLM
Tel: 8 784 00 00 **Fax:** 8 663 8956
Email: vipatv@svt.se
Freq: 26 issues yearly; **Circ:** 5,500
Editor: Christer Mårtensson
Language(s): Swedish
BUSINESS: COMMUNICATIONS, ADVERTISING & MARKETING: Press

VOLKSWAGEN MAGASIN
750876W77E-500
Editorial: Volkswagen Personbilar, 151 88 SÖDERTÄLJE **Tel:** 8 553 865 00 **Fax:** 8 550 162 81
Email: marcus.thomasfolk@volkswagen.se **Web site:** http://personbilar.volkswagen.se
Date Established: 1956; **Freq:** Quarterly; **Circ:** 180,000
Editor: Bo Jönsson; **Publisher:** Marcus Thomasfolk
Language(s): Swedish
ADVERTISING RATES:
Full Page Colour .... SEK 44 900 kr
CONSUMER: MOTORING & CYCLING: Club Cars

VOLLEYBOLL
750762W75J-260
Editorial: Smidesvägen 5, 171 41 SOLNA
Tel: 8 627 40 85
Email: ake.sandberg@volleyboll.se **Web site:** http://www.volleyboll.se
Freq: Quarterly; **Circ:** 8,500
Language(s): Swedish
CONSUMER: SPORT: Athletics

VOLTIMUM
1626243W17-101
Editorial: Isafjordsgatan 22, 164 40 KISTA
Tel: 8 632 66 30 **Fax:** 8 632 66 39
Email: redaktionen@voltimum.se **Web site:** http://www.voltimum.se
Freq: Weekly; **Cover Price:** Free; **Circ:** 14,500 Unique Users
Editor-in-Chief: Björn Ahlgren; **Managing Director:** Lars Sandén
Language(s): Swedish
BUSINESS: ELECTRICAL

VOLVO LIFE
51131W77E-400
Editorial: VCI-2, 405 31 GÖTEBORG
Tel: 31 352 25 06 **Fax:** 31 325 27 70
Email: volvolif@volvocars.com **Web site:** http://www.volvocars.se
Date Established: 1930; **Freq:** Half-yearly; **Circ:** 320,000
Editor-in-Chief: Annika Bjerstaf; **Advertising Manager:** Per Mattsson; **Publisher:** Karin Larsson
Profile: Magazine containing information about Volvo cars, includes new models and accessories.
Language(s): Swedish
Readership: Read by owners.
ADVERTISING RATES:
Full Page Colour .... SEK 85000
CONSUMER: MOTORING & CYCLING: Club Cars

VOLVO PÅ VÄG
50558W49D-150
Editorial: Volvo Lastvagnar AB, LVA6, 405 08 GÖTEBORG **Tel:** 31 322 61 77 **Fax:** 31 330 20 42
Email: pavag@volvo.com **Web site:** http://www.volvopavag.com
Freq: Quarterly; **Circ:** 66,300
Editor: Stig-Arne Fredlund; **Editor-in-Chief:** Stig-Arne Fredlund; **Publisher:** Stig-Arne Fredlund
Profile: Magazine containing news and information about the transport business and Volvo vehicles. Covers road transportations, economy, trade and research.
Language(s): Swedish
Readership: Aimed at owners and drivers of heavy vehicles.
BUSINESS: TRANSPORT: Commercial Vehicles

VTI AKTUELLT
1834586W2A-400
Editorial: Olaus Magnus väg 35, 581 95 LINKÖPING
Tel: 13 20 40 00 **Fax:** 13 14 14 36
Email: vtiaktuellt@vti.se **Web site:** http://www.vti.se/tidningar
Freq: Quarterly; **Cover Price:** Free; **Circ:** 6,500
Editor: Magdalena Green
Language(s): Swedish
ADVERTISING RATES:
Full Page Mono .... SEK 13000
SCC .... SEK 108.33
BUSINESS: COMMUNICATIONS, ADVERTISING & MARKETING

VVS-FORUM
50197W3B-60
Editorial: Box 47014, 100 74 STOCKHOLM
Tel: 8 762 75 00 **Fax:** 8 669 12 04
Email: vvs.forum@vvsforum.se **Web site:** http://www.vvs-forum.se
Freq: Monthly; **Circ:** 17,900
Editor: Klas Sörbo; **Advertising Manager:** Anne-Marie Forsell; **Publisher:** Roine Kristianson
Profile: Journal about heating, plumbing, ventilation, cooling, energy and insulation.
Language(s): Swedish
ADVERTISING RATES:
Full Page Colour .... SEK 31000
SCC .... SEK 248.33
BUSINESS: HEATING & VENTILATION: Industrial Heating & Ventilation

VVS-FORUM; WEBB
1846271W14A-338
Editorial: Box 47014, 100 74 STOCKHOLM
Tel: 8 762 75 00 **Fax:** 8691204
Email: vvs.forum@vvsi.se **Web site:** http://www.vvs-forum.se
Freq: Daily; **Cover Price:** Free; **Circ:** 5,200 Unique Users
Advertising Manager: Lars Roselius
Language(s): Swedish
BUSINESS: COMMERCE, INDUSTRY & MANAGEMENT

WENDELAVISAN
634823W84A-280
Editorial: c/o Mattsson, Badhusgatan 8, 151 73 SÖDERTÄLJE **Tel:** 8 550 305 84
Email: info@wendelasvanner.se **Web site:** http://www.wendelasvanner.se
Freq: Quarterly; **Circ:** 1,000
Editor: Sven Eric Rönnby; **Publisher:** Per Eric Mattsson
Profile: Magazine covering culture, literature, music and journalism.
Language(s): Swedish
CONSUMER: THE ARTS & LITERARY: Arts

WHEELS MAGAZINE
51110W77A-250
Editorial: 113 78 STOCKHOLM **Tel:** 8 692 01 40
Fax: 8 692 01 55
Email: redaktionen@wheels-mag.se **Web site:** http://www.wheelsmagazine.se
Date Established: 1977; **Freq:** Monthly; **Circ:** 27,500
Profile: Magazine for car enthusiasts with an emphasis on American cars, car maintenance and drag racing.
Language(s): Swedish
CONSUMER: MOTORING & CYCLING: Motoring

WWF EKO
51155W81A-100
Editorial: Värdsnaturfonden WWF, Ulriksdals Slott, 170 81 SOLNA **Tel:** 8 624 74 00
Email: info@wwf.se **Web site:** http://www.wwf.se
Freq: Quarterly; **Circ:** 66,500
Profile: Official publication of the World Wildlife Fund.
Language(s): Swedish
Readership: Aimed at members of the organisation and people with an interest in wildlife protection.
CONSUMER: ANIMALS & PETS: Animals & Pets Protection

XPRESS, OMBORDMAGASIN PÅ ARLANDA EXPRESS
1697282W49E-108
Editorial: Grev Magnigatan 6 3tr, 114 55 STOCKHOLM **Tel:** 8 545 660 00 **Fax:** 8 545 660 01
Email: info@travelmedia.se **Web site:** http://www.travelmedia.se/tidningar/xpress
Freq: Monthly; **Circ:** 9,900
Advertising Manager: Susanne Lundh; **Publisher:** Kjell Santesson
Language(s): Swedish
ADVERTISING RATES:
Full Page Colour .... SEK 37800
SCC .... SEK 315
BUSINESS: TRANSPORT: Railways

YH-GUIDEN
1640298W88C-42
Editorial: Box 1207, 131 27 NACKA STRAND
Tel: 8 545 424 50 **Fax:** 8 729 00 75
Email: info@framtid.se **Web site:** http://www.kyguiden.se
Freq: Annual; **Circ:** 130,000
Editor: Maria Samuelsson; **Advertising Manager:** Magnus Rittnor; **Publisher:** Kristoffer Jarefeldt
Language(s): Swedish
CONSUMER: EDUCATION: Careers

YRKESFISKAREN 50517W45B-50
Editorial: Fiskets Hus, Fiskhamnsgatan 33, 414 58 GÖTEBORG **Tel:** 31 12 45 93 **Fax:** 31 24 86 35
Email: eva-britt.larsson@yrkesfiskarna.se **Web site:** http://www.yrkesfiskarna.se/yrkesfisk
Freq: Monthly; **Circ:** 4,000
Editor: Bernt Andersson; **Advertising Manager:** Maria Wernbom
Profile: Official journal of the Swedish National Association of Professional Fishermen.
Language(s): Swedish
ADVERTISING RATES:
Full Page Colour .... SEK 14350
SCC .... SEK 71.75
BUSINESS: MARINE & SHIPPING: Commercial Fishing

YRKESLANDSLAGET MAGASIN 1623793W88C-41
Editorial: c/o Appelberg, Box 7344, 103 90 STOCKHOLM **Tel:** 8 406 54 00 **Fax:** 8 406 54 99
Email: yrkeslandslaget@appelberg.com **Web site:** http://www.yrkeslandslaget.com
Freq: Half-yearly; **Circ:** 115,900
Language(s): Swedish
CONSUMER: EDUCATION: Careers

YRKESLÄRAREN 50735W62J-260
Editorial: c/o Britta Moberger, Byvägen 164, 187 45 TÄBY **Tel:** 8 34 99 66 **Fax:** 8 411 42 42
Email: yrke@lararforbundet.se **Web site:** http://www.yrkeslararen.se
Date Established: 1985; **Freq:** Quarterly; **Circ:** 5,000
Editor-in-Chief: Björn Andersson; **Advertising Manager:** Ann Spaak; **Publisher:** Björn Andersson
Profile: Magazine containing articles and information for people who teach at vocational training schools.
Language(s): Swedish
BUSINESS: CHURCH & SCHOOL EQUIPMENT & EDUCATION: Teachers & Education Management

YRKESLÄRAREN; WEBB 1848205W62A-526
Editorial: Box 12239, 102 26 STOCKHOLM
Tel: 8 737 67 30 **Fax:** 8 619 00 88
Email: yrkeslararen@lararforbundet.se **Web site:** http://www.yrkeslararen.se
Freq: Daily; **Cover Price:** Free; **Circ:** 5,000 Unique Users
Editor-in-Chief: Britta Moberger; **Advertising Manager:** Camilla Lundberg; **Publisher:** Britta Moberger
Language(s): Swedish
BUSINESS: CHURCH & SCHOOL EQUIPMENT & EDUCATION: Education

YSTADS ALLEHANDA 50853W67B-7900
Editorial: 271 81 YSTAD **Tel:** 411 55 78 00
Fax: 411 139 55
Email: red@ystadsallehanda.se **Web site:** http://www.ystadsallehanda.se
Circ: 24,000
Managing Director: Johan Ståhl; **Publisher:** Margaretha Engström
Language(s): Swedish
ADVERTISING RATES:
Full Page Colour .... SEK 17520
SCC .... SEK 87.60
REGIONAL DAILY & SUNDAY NEWSPAPERS: Regional Daily Newspapers

YSTADS ALLEHANDA; WEBB 752333W67B-10885
Editorial: 271 81 YSTAD **Tel:** 411 55 78 00
Fax: 41113955
Email: webbredaktionen@skanemedia.se **Web site:** http://www.ystadsallehanda.se
Freq: Daily; **Cover Price:** Free; **Circ:** 26,100 Unique Users
Editor: Carl Johan Engvall
Language(s): Swedish
REGIONAL DAILY & SUNDAY NEWSPAPERS: Regional Daily Newspapers

YTFORUM 50354W19C-100
Editorial: Box 462, 581 05 LINKÖPING
Tel: 13 31 41 75 **Fax:** 13143849
Email: ytforum@telia.com **Web site:** http://www.ytforum.com
Freq: 6 issues yearly; **Circ:** 2,000
Advertising Manager: Göran Ekström
Profile: Journal containing articles about different finishing methods and surface treatments for metal and wood.
Language(s): Swedish
ADVERTISING RATES:
Full Page Colour .... SEK 14500
SCC .... SEK 120.83
Copy instructions: *Copy Date:* 7 days prior to publication date
BUSINESS: ENGINEERING & MACHINERY: Finishing

YTFORUM; WEBB 1844793W27-29
Editorial: Box 462, 581 05 LINKÖPING
Tel: 13 31 41 75 **Fax:** 13143849
Email: ytforum@telia.com **Web site:** http://www.ytforum.com
Freq: Daily; **Cover Price:** Free; **Circ:** 667 Unique Users
Advertising Manager: Göran Ekström
Language(s): Swedish
BUSINESS: METAL, IRON & STEEL

ZERO MUSIC MAGAZINE 1685505W76D-274
Editorial: Box 2002, 403 11 GÖTEBORG
Tel: 706 88 63 11
Email: info@zeromagazine.nu **Web site:** http://www.zeromagazine.nu
Freq: Quarterly; **Circ:** 6,500
Editor: Jon Josefsson; **Editor-in-Chief:** Jon Josefsson; **Managing Director:** Jon Josefsson; **Advertising Manager:** Jon Josefsson; **Publisher:** Petter Jahnstedt
Language(s): Swedish
CONSUMER: MUSIC & PERFORMING ARTS: Music

Switzerland

Time Difference: GMT + 1 hr (CET - Central European Time)
National Telephone Code: +41
Continent: Europe
Capital: Berne
Principal Language: German, French, Italian, Romansch
Population: 7450867
Monetary Unit: Swiss Franc (CHF)

EMBASSY HIGH COMMISSION: Embassy of Switzerland: 16-18 Montagu Place, London W1H 2BQ
Tel: 020 7616 6000
Fax: 020 7724 7001
Website: http:// www.swissembassy.org.uk/ @ adress: swissembassy@lon .rep.admin.ch / Head of Mission HE Anton Thalmann

MANEGE 1656136S94X-669
Editorial: Eichhölzliweg 7, 3672 OBERDIESSBACH
Email: redaktion@circusfreunde.ch **Web site:** http://www.circusfreunde.ch
Freq: 6 issues yearly; Free to qualifying individuals
Annual Sub.: CHF 65,00; **Circ:** 800
Editor: Filip Vincenz
Profile: Magazine containing information about Swiss circuses.
Language(s): German
Copy instructions: *Copy Date:* 28 days prior to publication
CONSUMER: OTHER CLASSIFICATIONS: Miscellaneous

118 SWISSFIRE.CH 1640984S54A-43
Editorial: Morgenstr. 1, 3073 GÜMLIGEN
Tel: 31 9588118 **Fax:** 31 9588111
Email: sfz.redaktion@swissfire.ch **Web site:** http://www.swissfire.ch
Freq: Monthly; **Annual Sub.:** CHF 66,00; **Circ:** 16,647
Editor: Walter Pfammatter
Profile: Magazine for fire fighters about techniques, tactics, training, practice, assignment, security and fire protection.
Language(s): French; German; Italian
ADVERTISING RATES:
Full Page Mono .... CHF 3650
Full Page Colour .... CHF 3650
Mechanical Data: Type Area: 277 x 180 mm
Copy instructions: *Copy Date:* 38 days prior to publication
BUSINESS: SAFETY & SECURITY: Fire Fighting

20 MINUTEN 749069S72-60
Editorial: Brühlgasse 15, 9004 ST. GALLEN
Tel: 71 2268820 **Fax:** 71 2268821
Email: sascha.schmid@20minuten.ch **Web site:** http://www.20minuten.ch
Freq: 260 issues yearly; **Cover Price:** Free; **Circ:** 56,857
Editor: Sascha Schmid
Profile: Regional daily newspaper covering politics, economics, sport, travel, technology and the arts.
Language(s): German
ADVERTISING RATES:
SCC .... CHF 68,60
Mechanical Data: Type Area: 280 x 210 mm, No. of Columns (Display): 8, Col Widths (Display): 25 mm
Copy instructions: *Copy Date:* 2 days prior to publication
LOCAL NEWSPAPERS

50 PLUS - AUSG. BERN 1844603S74N-268
Editorial: Missionsstr. 36, 4012 BASEL
Tel: 61 2646450 **Fax:** 61 2646488
Email: verlag@reinhardt.ch **Web site:** http://www.50plus-magazin.ch
Freq: 6 issues yearly; **Cover Price:** Free; **Circ:** 22,595
Editor: Alfred Rüdisühli
Profile: Regional magazine for people older than 50 years of age about society, nature, health, travelling, fashion, finances, real estate and insurances.
Language(s): German
ADVERTISING RATES:
Full Page Mono .... CHF 5200
Full Page Colour .... CHF 5200
Mechanical Data: Type Area: 265 x 184 mm
Copy instructions: *Copy Date:* 20 days prior to publication

50 PLUS - AUSG. NORDWESTSCHWEIZ 1844604S74N-269
Editorial: Missionsstr. 36, 4012 BASEL
Tel: 61 2646450 **Fax:** 61 2646488
Email: verlag@reinhardt.ch **Web site:** http://www.50plus-magazin.ch
Freq: 6 issues yearly; **Cover Price:** Free; **Circ:** 23,450
Editor: Alfred Rüdisühli
Profile: Regional magazine.
Language(s): German
ADVERTISING RATES:
Full Page Mono .... CHF 5200
Full Page Colour .... CHF 5200
Mechanical Data: Type Area: 265 x 184 mm
Copy instructions: *Copy Date:* 20 days prior to publication

50 PLUS - AUSG. OSTSCHWEIZ 1844606S74N-271
Editorial: Missionsstr. 36, 4012 BASEL
Tel: 61 2646450 **Fax:** 61 2646488
Email: verlag@reinhardt.ch **Web site:** http://www.50plus-magazin.ch
Freq: 6 issues yearly; **Cover Price:** Free; **Circ:** 21,497
Editor: Alfred Rüdisühli
Profile: Regional magazine.
Language(s): German
ADVERTISING RATES:
Full Page Mono .... CHF 5200
Full Page Colour .... CHF 5200
Mechanical Data: Type Area: 265 x 184 mm
Copy instructions: *Copy Date:* 20 days prior to publication

50 PLUS - AUSG. ZÜRICH 1844605S74N-270
Editorial: Missionsstr. 36, 4012 BASEL
Tel: 61 2646450 **Fax:** 61 2646488
Email: verlag@reinhardt.ch **Web site:** http://www.50plus-magazin.ch
Freq: 6 issues yearly; **Cover Price:** Free; **Circ:** 25,120
Editor: Alfred Rüdisühli
Profile: Regional magazine.
Language(s): German
ADVERTISING RATES:
Full Page Mono .... CHF 5200
Full Page Colour .... CHF 5200
Mechanical Data: Type Area: 265 x 184 mm
Copy instructions: *Copy Date:* 20 days prior to publication

7SKY MAG 1623551S73-366
Editorial: 6, Mont-de-Faux, 1023 CRISSIER
Tel: 21 6374070 **Fax:** 21 6344110
Email: coco@7skymagazine.ch **Web site:** http://www.7skymagazine.ch
Freq: 10 issues yearly; **Circ:** 23,000
Editor: Corinne Tâche-Berther; **Advertising Manager:** Cira Riedel
Profile: Magazine about sport, music, cinema, fashion, society and events.
Language(s): German
ADVERTISING RATES:
Full Page Mono .... CHF 9950
Full Page Colour .... CHF 9950
Mechanical Data: Type Area: 283 x 203 mm
Copy instructions: *Copy Date:* 20 days prior to publication
CONSUMER: NATIONAL & INTERNATIONAL PERIODICALS

7SKY PEOPLE 1623552S73-367
Editorial: 6, Mont-de-Faux, 1023 CRISSIER
Tel: 21 6374070 **Fax:** 21 6344110
Email: admin@7skymagazine.ch **Web site:** http://www.7skymagazine.ch
Freq: 6 issues yearly; **Circ:** 150,000
Editor: Bernard Tâche
Profile: Magazine about sport, music, cinema, fashion, society and events.
Language(s): German
ADVERTISING RATES:
Full Page Mono .... CHF 12500
Full Page Colour .... CHF 12500
Mechanical Data: Type Area: 297 x 233 mm
Copy instructions: *Copy Date:* 27 days prior to publication

AARGAUER ZEITUNG AZ 719443S67B-40
Editorial: Neumattstr. 1, 5001 AARAU
Tel: 58 2005858 **Fax:** 58 2005354
Email: azredaktion@azag.ch **Web site:** http://www.aargauerzeitung.ch
Freq: 312 issues yearly; **Annual Sub.:** CHF 376,00; **Circ:** 104,697
Editor: Christian Dorer; **News Editor:** Christoph Bopp
Profile: Regional daily newspaper covering politics, economics, sport, travel, technology and the arts.
Language(s): German
ADVERTISING RATES:
SCC .... CHF 44,60
Mechanical Data: Type Area: 440 x 290 mm, No. of Columns (Display): 10, Col Widths (Display): 26 mm
Copy instructions: *Copy Date:* 2 days prior to publication
Supplement(s): AZ Live
REGIONAL DAILY & SUNDAY NEWSPAPERS: Regional Daily Newspapers

ABHÄNGIGKEITEN 719461S56L-15
Editorial: 14, av. Ruchonnet, 1001 LAUSANNE
Tel: 21 3212911 **Fax:** 21 3212940
Email: info@sucht-info.ch **Web site:** http://www.sucht-info.ch
Freq: 3 issues yearly; Free to qualifying individuals
Annual Sub.: CHF 53,00; **Circ:** 600
Editor: Regina Burri; **Advertising Manager:** Claude Saunier
Profile: Scientific journal focusing on people working against drug and alcohol abuse.
Language(s): German
Readership: Aimed at doctors, social workers, teachers and scientists.
Mechanical Data: Type Area: 205 x 110 mm
BUSINESS: HEALTH & MEDICAL: Disability & Rehabilitation

ACCEPT 1852294S14A-1275
Editorial: Hardturmstrasse 201, 8021 ZÜRICH
Tel: 44 8329162 **Fax:** 44 4463343
Email: info@six-multipay.com **Web site:** http://www.six-multipay.com
Freq: 3 issues yearly; **Circ:** 60,000
Editor: Ursula Seeberger
Profile: Customer magazine.
Language(s): French

ACCEPT 1852295S14A-1276
Editorial: Hardturmstrasse 201, 8021 ZÜRICH
Tel: 44 8329162 **Fax:** 44 4463343
Email: info@six-multipay.com **Web site:** http://www.six-multipay.com
Freq: 3 issues yearly; **Circ:** 60,000
Editor: Ursula Seeberger
Profile: Customer magazine.
Language(s): Italian

ACS AKTUELL 719510S77A-103
Editorial: Reckenbühlstr. 15, 6005 LUZERN
Tel: 41 3101985 **Fax:** 41 3101985
Email: acs-aktuell@gmx.net **Web site:** http://www.acs-luzern.ch
Freq: 6 issues yearly; **Circ:** 3,000
Editor: Jürg Kauffmann
Profile: Magazine of the Swiss Automobile Club ACS.
Language(s): German
ADVERTISING RATES:
Full Page Mono .... CHF 386
Mechanical Data: Type Area: 195 x 126 mm
Copy instructions: *Copy Date:* 14 days prior to publication

ACTA HÆMATOLOGICA 719516S56A-40
Editorial: Allschwiler Str. 10, 4055 BASEL
Tel: 61 3061344 **Fax:** 61 3061434
Email: aha@karger.ch **Web site:** http://www.karger.com/aha
Freq: 8 issues yearly; **Annual Sub.:** CHF 2659,20; **Circ:** 800
Editor: I. Ben-Bassat; **Advertising Manager:** Thomas Maurer
Profile: Magazine about haematology.
Language(s): English
ADVERTISING RATES:
Full Page Mono .... CHF 1780
Full Page Colour .... CHF 3340
Mechanical Data: Type Area: 224 x 180 mm

AERO REVUE 719624S6A-20
Editorial: Zurzacherstr. 64, 5200 BRUGG
Tel: 56 4429244 **Fax:** 56 4429243
Email: aerorevue@aeroclub.ch **Web site:** http://www.aero-revue.ch
Freq: 10 issues yearly; Free to qualifying individuals
Annual Sub.: CHF 60,00; **Circ:** 25,150
Editor: Jürg Wyss; **Advertising Manager:** Fabian Egger
Profile: Journal of the Aero Club of Switzerland.
Language(s): French; German
ADVERTISING RATES:
Full Page Mono .... CHF 3350
Full Page Colour .... CHF 4350
Mechanical Data: Type Area: 264 x 188 mm
Copy instructions: *Copy Date:* 21 days prior to publication
BUSINESS: AVIATION & AERONAUTICS

AERZTE/MEDICO JOURNAL 1847244S56A-2151
Editorial: Steinenbachgässlein 49, 4051 BASEL
Tel: 61 2817177 **Fax:** 61 2818118
Email: medipress@hin.ch
Freq: 6 issues yearly; **Annual Sub.:** CHF 78,50; **Circ:** 14,000
Editor: Wino E. Leuenberger; **Advertising Manager:** Anita Flückiger
Profile: Magazine with entertainment for physical doctors and pharmacists.
Language(s): French; German
ADVERTISING RATES:
Full Page Mono .... CHF 3280
Full Page Colour .... CHF 4870
Mechanical Data: Type Area: 216 x mm, No. of Columns (Display): 303
Copy instructions: *Copy Date:* 20 days prior to publication

AGOGIK 1852533S14A-1280
Editorial: Bühlermatte 12, 3018 BERN
Tel: 33 6550544
Email: redaktion@agogik.com **Web site:** http://www.agogik.com
Freq: Quarterly; **Annual Sub.:** CHF 56,00; **Circ:** 300
Editor: Peter Keimer
Profile: Magazine featuring subjects about social design.
Language(s): German
ADVERTISING RATES:
Full Page Mono .... CHF 250
Mechanical Data: Type Area: 165 x 110 mm
Copy instructions: *Copy Date:* 30 days prior to publication

AGORA 1855281S14A-1288
Editorial: Waldacker 1, 9000 ST. GALLEN
Tel: 71 2776067 **Fax:** 71 2776079
Email: info@agora-agenda.ch **Web site:** http://www.agora-agenda.ch
Freq: Monthly; **Annual Sub.:** CHF 47,00; **Circ:** 2,500
Editor: Alfons Wirth
Profile: Consumer magazine.
Language(s): German
Mechanical Data: Type Area: 300 x 200 mm, No. of Columns (Display): 3, Col Widths (Display): 64 mm
Copy instructions: *Copy Date:* 14 days prior to publication

AGRARFORSCHUNG 1640953S21A-585
Editorial: Tioleyre 4, 1725 POSIEUX **Tel:** 26 4077221
Fax: 26 4077300
Email: info@agrarforschungschweiz.ch **Web site:** http://www.agrarforschung.ch
Freq: 11 issues yearly; **Annual Sub.:** CHF 61,00; **Circ:** 2,000
Editor: Andrea Leuenberger-Minger
Profile: Magazine with results from agricultural research in Switzerland.
Language(s): German
ADVERTISING RATES:
Full Page Mono .... CHF 1500
Full Page Colour .... CHF 2300
Mechanical Data: Type Area: 260 x 184 mm, No. of Columns (Display): 3, Col Widths (Display): 62 mm
Copy instructions: *Copy Date:* 30 days prior to publication
Official Journal of: Organ d. Eidgenöss. Forschungsanstalten Agroscope Liebefeld-Posieux, Reckenholz-Tänikon, Changins-Wädenswil, d. ETH Zürich, Dep. Agrar- + Lebensmittelwissenschaft, d. Schweizer. Hochschule f. Landwirtschaft Zollikofen u. d. Bundesamtes f. Landwirtschaft

AGRI 764160S21A-568
Editorial: 1 av. de Jordils, 1000 LAUSANNE 6
Tel: 21 6130646 **Fax:** 21 6130640
Email: journal@agrihebdo.ch **Web site:** http://www.agrihebdo.ch
Freq: Weekly; **Annual Sub.:** CHF 125,00; **Circ:** 9,862
Editor: Christian Pidoux
Profile: Magazine about milk production.
Language(s): French
ADVERTISING RATES:
Full Page Mono .... CHF 5900
Full Page Colour .... CHF 5900
Mechanical Data: Type Area: 433 x 288 mm, No. of Columns (Display): 10, Col Widths (Display): 26 mm
Copy instructions: *Copy Date:* 2 days prior to publication
Official Journal of: Organ d. Union centrale des producteurs suisses de lait u. d. Chambres d'agriculture de suisse romande
BUSINESS: AGRICULTURE & FARMING

AKTIV 1855728S14A-1320
Editorial: Zieglerstr. 20, 3007 BERN **Tel:** 31 3906030
Fax: 31 3906020
Email: info@kvbern.ch **Web site:** http://www.kvbern.ch
Freq: 5 issues yearly; Free to qualifying individuals
Annual Sub.: CHF 10,00; **Circ:** 6,500
Editor: Kurt Amiet
Profile: Magazien form the Bernese Commercial Association about education and profession.
Language(s): German
ADVERTISING RATES:
Full Page Mono .... CHF 1590
Mechanical Data: Type Area: 281 x 197 mm

AKTUELLE NEUROLOGIE 719865G56A-180
Editorial: Bleulerstr. 60, 8008 ZÜRICH
Email: carmelina.renold@swissepi.ch **Web site:** http://www.thieme.de/aktneu
Freq: 10 issues yearly; **Annual Sub.:** CHF 324,60; **Circ:** 6,753
Editor: G. Krämer
Profile: All of the major neurological topics: guidelines of the DGN, scientifically recognized original research articles, sound overviews, CME-certified training, informative case studies, neuroscience quiz, forum of young neurologists, President Page: presentation of neurological societies.
Language(s): German
ADVERTISING RATES:
Full Page Mono .... EUR 2080
Full Page Colour .... EUR 3250
Mechanical Data: Type Area: 248 x 175 mm, No. of Columns (Display): 3, Col Widths (Display): 55 mm
Official Journal of: Organ d. Dt. Ges. f. Neurologie, d. Dt. Ges. f. Neurolog. Intensiv- u. Notfallmedizin, d. Berufsverb. Dt. Neurologen, d. Ges. f. Neuropädiatrie e.V., d. Ges. f. Neurotraumatologie u. klin. Neuropsychologie u. Dt. Interdisziplinäre Vereinigung f. Intensiv- u. Notfallmedizin
Supplement(s): Current congress
BUSINESS: HEALTH & MEDICAL

AKTUELLE TECHNIK 719876S18A-2
Editorial: Steinwiesenstr. 3, 8952 SCHLIEREN
Tel: 44 7333999 **Fax:** 44 7333989
Email: markus.back@blverlag.ch **Web site:** http://www.aktuelletechnik.ch
Freq: Monthly; **Annual Sub.:** CHF 54,00; **Circ:** 13,500
Editor: Markus Back
Profile: Magazine containing technical and computer news, focusing mainly on industrial electronics and automation.
Language(s): German
ADVERTISING RATES:
Full Page Mono .... CHF 4310
Full Page Colour .... CHF 4310
Mechanical Data: Type Area: 270 x 184 mm, No. of Columns (Display): 4, Col Widths (Display): 43 mm
Copy instructions: *Copy Date:* 20 days prior to publication
BUSINESS: ELECTRONICS

AL DENTE 1844567S74P-287
Editorial: Dufourstr. 23, 8008 ZÜRICH
Tel: 44 2596262 **Fax:** 44 2622976
Email: si@ringier.ch
Freq: Quarterly; **Circ:** 204,856
Advertising Manager: Brigitte Gemperle
Profile: Gourmet magazine.
Language(s): German
ADVERTISING RATES:
Full Page Mono .... CHF 26310
Full Page Colour .... CHF 26310
Mechanical Data: Type Area: 261 x 189 mm
Copy instructions: *Copy Date:* 17 days prior to publication
Supplement to: Schweizer Illustrierte

ALLGEMEINER ANZEIGER 1655952S72-9660
Editorial: Bahnhofstr. 99a, 9240 UZWIL
Tel: 58 3449551 **Fax:** 58 3449556
Email: redaktion@allgemeiner-anzeiger.ch **Web site:** http://www.allgemeiner-anzeiger.ch
Freq: Weekly; **Annual Sub.:** CHF 78,00; **Circ:** 2,904
Editor: Martin Wiesmann; **Advertising Manager:** Roland Rotach
Profile: Local official paper.
Language(s): German
ADVERTISING RATES:
SCC .... CHF 26,50
Mechanical Data: Type Area: 440 x 290 mm, No. of Columns (Display): 10, Col Widths (Display): 27 mm
Copy instructions: *Copy Date:* 1 day prior to publication
LOCAL NEWSPAPERS

ALLSCHWILER WOCHENBLATT 720019S72-320
Editorial: Missionsstr. 36, 4012 BASEL
Tel: 61 2646450 **Fax:** 61 2646488
Email: redaktion@allschwilerwochenblatt.ch **Web site:** http://www.reinhardt.ch
Freq: Weekly; **Annual Sub.:** CHF 75,00; **Circ:** 1,678
Profile: Regional weekly covering politics, economics, sport, travel, technology and the arts.
Language(s): German
ADVERTISING RATES:
SCC .... CHF 21,60
Mechanical Data: Type Area: 290 x 203 mm, No. of Columns (Display): 7, Col Widths (Display): 27 mm
Copy instructions: *Copy Date:* 4 days prior to publication
LOCAL NEWSPAPERS

DIE ALPEN 720032S75L-20
Editorial: Monbijoustr. 61, 3000 BERN 23
Tel: 31 3701885 **Fax:** 31 3701890
Email: alpen@sac-cas.ch **Web site:** http://www.sac-cas.ch
Freq: Monthly; Free to qualifying individuals
Annual Sub.: CHF 50,00; **Circ:** 75,000
Editor: Alexandra Rozkosny
Profile: Official journal of the Swiss Alpine Club.
Language(s): German
Readership: Read by club members.
ADVERTISING RATES:
Full Page Mono .... CHF 6160
Full Page Colour .... CHF 8560
Mechanical Data: Type Area: 275 x 181 mm, No. of Columns (Display): 2, Col Widths (Display): 88 mm
Copy instructions: *Copy Date:* 28 days prior to publication
CONSUMER: SPORT: Outdoor

ALPENROSEN 1655229S76D-597
Editorial: Bettlistr. 28, 8600 DÜBENDORF
Tel: 43 3559192 **Fax:** 43 3559193
Email: info@alpenrosen.ch **Web site:** http://www.alpenrosen.ch
Freq: 6 issues yearly; **Annual Sub.:** CHF 52,00; **Circ:** 10,600
Editor: Martin Sebastian
Profile: Magazine about traditional folk music.
Language(s): German
ADVERTISING RATES:
Full Page Mono .... CHF 1800
Full Page Colour .... CHF 1800
Mechanical Data: Type Area: 249 x 180 mm, No. of Columns (Display): 3, Col Widths (Display): 55 mm
Copy instructions: *Copy Date:* 40 days prior to publication
CONSUMER: MUSIC & PERFORMING ARTS: Music

ALTTOGGENBURGER 720097S67B-60
Editorial: Bahnhofstr. 10, 9602 KIRCHBERG
Tel: 71 9311012 **Fax:** 71 9313331
Email: redaktion@alttoggenburger.ch **Web site:** http://www.alttoggenburger.ch
Freq: 156 issues yearly; **Annual Sub.:** CHF 209,00; **Circ:** 4,661
Editor: Adi Lippuner; **Advertising Manager:** Matthias Pfändler
Profile: Regional daily newspaper covering politics, economics, sport, travel, technology and the arts.
Language(s): German
ADVERTISING RATES:
SCC .... CHF 29,60
Mechanical Data: Type Area: 440 x 287 mm, No. of Columns (Display): 10, Col Widths (Display): 26 mm
Copy instructions: *Copy Date:* 1 day prior to publication
REGIONAL DAILY & SUNDAY NEWSPAPERS: Regional Daily Newspapers

AM WÄGRAND 1843476S74N-267
Editorial: Natershusstr. 16, 3176 NEUENEGG
Tel: 31 7410117
Email: fred.aellen@kirchenbezirk-laupen.ch **Web site:** http://www.kirchenbezirk-laupen.ch/neuenegg
Freq: Half-yearly; **Cover Price:** Free; **Circ:** 700
Editor: Alfred Aellen
Profile: Magazine for the elderly on entertainment and information.
Language(s): German

AM WERKSTATTDATEN LEICHTE NUTZFAHRZEUGE BIS 3,5 T GESAMTGEWICHT 1656099S49D-1
Editorial: Wolleraustr. 11a, 8807 FREIENBACH
Tel: 848 333100 **Fax:** 55 4158200
Web site: http://www.eurotaxglass.ch
Freq: Annual; **Annual Sub.:** CHF 94,00; **Circ:** 3,300
Profile: Technical data about commercial vehicles up to 3,5 tons weight.
Language(s): French; German

AMTSBLATT 1656707S80-1537
Editorial: Obstmarkt 3, 9100 HERISAU
Tel: 71 3536111 **Fax:** 71 3521277
Freq: Weekly; **Annual Sub.:** CHF 32,00; **Circ:** 1,453
Profile: Regional official paper.
Language(s): German
Mechanical Data: Type Area: 167 x 108 mm
Copy instructions: *Copy Date:* 1 day prior to publication
CONSUMER: RURAL & REGIONAL INTEREST

AMTSBLATT DER STADT CHUR UND DER GEMEINDEN CHURWALDEN, FELSBERG, HALDENSTEIN, MALADERS, TRIMMIS, TSCHIERTSCHEN-PRADEN 1646194S72-9617
Editorial: Sonnenweg 1, 7000 CHUR
Tel: 81 2503431
Email: redaktion-stabla@suedostschweiz.ch
Freq: Weekly; **Annual Sub.:** CHF 20,00; **Circ:** 8,295
Editor: Walter Schmid
Profile: Local official paper.
Language(s): German
ADVERTISING RATES:
Full Page Mono .... CHF 1742
Full Page Colour .... CHF 2400
Mechanical Data: Type Area: 286 x 199 mm, No. of Columns (Display): 7, Col Widths (Display): 25 mm
Copy instructions: *Copy Date:* 3 days prior to publication
LOCAL NEWSPAPERS

AMTSBLATT DES KANTONS AARGAU 1656098S80-1534
Editorial: Henzmannstr. 20, 4800 ZOFINGEN
Tel: 62 7459355 **Fax:** 62 7459359
Email: amtsblatt@ztonline.ch **Web site:** http://www.amtsblatt-ag.ch
Freq: Weekly; **Annual Sub.:** CHF 95,00; **Circ:** 3,495
Profile: Regional official paper.
Language(s): German
Mechanical Data: Type Area: 255 x 174 mm, No. of Columns (Display): 2, Col Widths (Display): 85 mm
Copy instructions: *Copy Date:* 4 days prior to publication
CONSUMER: RURAL & REGIONAL INTEREST

AMTSBLATT DES KANTONS SOLOTHURN 1647423S80-1523
Editorial: Postfach, 4509 SOLOTHURN
Tel: 32 6272026 **Fax:** 32 6272994
Freq: Weekly; **Circ:** 4,792
Profile: Regional official paper.
Language(s): German
ADVERTISING RATES:
Full Page Mono .... CHF 425
Mechanical Data: Type Area: 165 x 109 mm
Copy instructions: *Copy Date:* 3 days prior to publication
CONSUMER: RURAL & REGIONAL INTEREST

AMTSBLATT DES KANTONS ST. GALLEN 764162S80-1480
Editorial: Regierungsgebäude, 9001 ST. GALLEN
Tel: 71 2293259 **Fax:** 71 2293955
Email: amtsblatt.sk@sg.ch **Web site:** http://www.amtsblatt-sg.ch
Freq: Weekly; **Annual Sub.:** CHF 65,00; **Circ:** 5,100
Profile: Regional official paper.
Language(s): German
Mechanical Data: Type Area: 180 x 117 mm, No. of Columns (Display): 1, Col Widths (Display): 117 mm
Copy instructions: *Copy Date:* 5 days prior to publication
CONSUMER: RURAL & REGIONAL INTEREST

AMTSBLATT DES KANTONS ZÜRICH 720512S80-1482
Editorial: Neumühlequai 10, 8090 ZÜRICH
Tel: 43 2592020 **Fax:** 43 2595939
Web site: http://www.amtsblatt.zh.ch
Freq: Weekly; **Annual Sub.:** CHF 61,40; **Circ:** 7,966
Profile: Regional official paper.
Language(s): German
Mechanical Data: Type Area: 440 x 286 mm, No. of Columns (Display): 4, Col Widths (Display): 68 mm
Copy instructions: *Copy Date:* 3 days prior to publication
CONSUMER: RURAL & REGIONAL INTEREST

ANDELFINGER ZEITUNG 720729S67B-280
Editorial: Landstr. 70, 8450 ANDELFINGEN
Tel: 52 3052909 **Fax:** 52 3171243
Email: redaktion@andelfinger.ch **Web site:** http://www.andelfinger.ch
Freq: 104 issues yearly; **Annual Sub.:** CHF 163,00; **Circ:** 5,988
Editor: Roland Spalinger
Profile: Regional daily newspaper covering politics, economics, sport, travel, technology and the arts.
Language(s): German
ADVERTISING RATES:
SCC .... CHF 30,90

Mechanical Data: Type Area: 430 x 285 mm, No. of Columns (Display): 10, Col Widths (Display): 25 mm
Copy instructions: *Copy Date:* 1 day prior to publication
REGIONAL DAILY & SUNDAY NEWSPAPERS: Regional Daily Newspapers

ANDERMATT GRUPPE JOURNAL
1843190S21A-611
Editorial: Stahlermatten 6, 6146 GROSSDIETWIL
Tel: 62 9175005 **Fax:** 62 9175006
Email: sales@biocontrol.ch **Web site:** http://www.biocontrol.ch
Freq: Annual; **Cover Price:** CHF 9,50; **Circ:** 1,300
Editor: Martin Andermatt
Profile: Company publication from the Andermatt Biocontrol AG about biological plant protection.
Language(s): French; German

ANIMAN
720760S94J-40
Editorial: Quai des Sirènes, 66, rte. de Lausanne, 1110 MORGES **Tel:** 21 6015255 **Fax:** 21 6015259
Email: thierry.peitrequin@animan.ch **Web site:** http://www.animan.ch
Freq: 6 issues yearly; **Annual Sub.:** CHF 82,00; **Circ:** 11,000
Editor: Thierry Peitrequin
Profile: Publication featuring prodigies of the world.
Language(s): German
ADVERTISING RATES:
Full Page Mono .... CHF 8250
Full Page Colour .... CHF 8250
Mechanical Data: Type Area: 245 x 195 mm, No. of Columns (Display): 3, Col Widths (Display): 65 mm
Copy instructions: *Copy Date:* 72 days prior to publication
CONSUMER: OTHER CLASSIFICATIONS: Popular Science

ANLAGETRENDS FONDS
1844822S1F-276
Editorial: Wengistr. 7, 8026 ZÜRICH **Tel:** 44 2654010
Fax: 44 2654011
Email: info@publicontext.com **Web site:** http://www.publicontext.com
Freq: Annual; **Cover Price:** Free; **Circ:** 37,700
Editor: Cécile Heusser-Bachmann
Profile: Finance magazine.
Language(s): German
ADVERTISING RATES:
Full Page Mono .... CHF 17100
Full Page Colour .... CHF 17100
Supplement to: Finanz und Wirtschaft

ANNABELLE
720781S74A-100
Editorial: Werdstr. 21, 8021 ZÜRICH **Tel:** 44 2486333
Fax: 44 2486328
Email: redaktion@annabelle.ch **Web site:** http://www.annabelle.ch
Freq: 22 issues yearly; **Annual Sub.:** CHF 110,00; **Circ:** 107,000
Editor: Lisa Feldmann
Profile: General women's interest magazine.
Language(s): German
ADVERTISING RATES:
Full Page Mono .... CHF 19510
Full Page Colour .... CHF 19510
Mechanical Data: Type Area: 249 x 193 mm, No. of Columns (Display): 4, Col Widths (Display): 46 mm
Copy instructions: *Copy Date:* 26 days prior to publication
CONSUMER: WOMEN'S INTEREST CONSUMER MAGAZINES: Women's Interest

ANNEMARIE WILDEISEN'S KOCHEN
1643466S74P-271
Editorial: Friedeckweg 2, 3007 BERN
Tel: 31 3002930 **Fax:** 31 3002931
Email: info@koch-magazin.ch **Web site:** http://www.wildeisen.ch
Freq: 10 issues yearly; **Annual Sub.:** CHF 58,00; **Circ:** 110,000
Editor: Annemarie Wildeisen; **Advertising Manager:** Dieter Maier
Profile: Cooking magazine.
Language(s): German
ADVERTISING RATES:
Full Page Mono .... CHF 13250
Full Page Colour .... CHF 13250
Mechanical Data: Type Area: 268 x 185 mm, No. of Columns (Display): 4, Col Widths (Display): 42 mm
Copy instructions: *Copy Date:* 23 days prior to publication

ANNUARIO IMPRESARI COSTRUTTORI TICINESI
1656100S4E-792
Editorial: via Cantonale, 34a, 6928 MANNO
Tel: 91 6002070 **Fax:** 91 6002074
Email: info@pubblicitasacchi.ch **Web site:** http://www.pubblicitasacchi.ch
Freq: Annual; **Cover Price:** Free; **Circ:** 3,500
Editor: Fabio Sacchi
Profile: Building business magazine.
Language(s): Italian
ADVERTISING RATES:
Full Page Mono .... CHF 1100
Full Page Colour .... CHF 1600
Mechanical Data: Type Area: 265 x 190 mm

ANTHOS
1844720S21A-613
Editorial: 1, av. Soguel, 2035 CORCELLES
Tel: 32 7303211 **Fax:** 32 7303211
Email: s.perrochet@tele2.ch **Web site:** http://www.anthos.ch
Freq: Quarterly; **Annual Sub.:** CHF 85,00; **Circ:** 2,800
Editor: Sabine Wolf
Profile: Magazine about landscape architecture.
Language(s): French; German
ADVERTISING RATES:
Full Page Mono .... CHF 2000
Full Page Colour .... CHF 2500
Mechanical Data: Type Area: 265 x 185 mm
Copy instructions: *Copy Date:* 21 days prior to publication
Official Journal of: Organ d. Vereinigung Schweizer Stadtgärtnereien u. Gartenbauämter u. d. Bund Schweizer Landschaftsarchitektinnen u. Landschaftsarchitekten

ANWALTS REVUE DE L'AVOCAT
1852536S1A-304
Editorial: Bollwerk 21, 3001 BERN **Tel:** 31 3283535
Fax: 31 3283540
Email: vonins@bollwerk21.ch **Web site:** http://www.swisslawyers.com
Freq: 10 issues yearly; Free to qualifying individuals
Annual Sub.: CHF 198,00; **Circ:** 8,543
Editor: Peter von Ins
Profile: Magazine of the Swiss Association of Lawyers.
Language(s): French; German
ADVERTISING RATES:
Full Page Mono .... CHF 2600
Full Page Colour .... CHF 3000
Mechanical Data: Type Area: 270 x 170 mm
Copy instructions: *Copy Date:* 28 days prior to publication
Official Journal of: Organ d. SAV/FSA

ANZEIGER
720880S72-540
Editorial: Eystr. 1, 3422 KIRCHBERG
Tel: 34 4452946 **Fax:** 34 4454537
Freq: Weekly; **Cover Price:** Free; **Circ:** 11,388
Editor: H. Kämpfer
Profile: Local official paper.
Language(s): German
ADVERTISING RATES:
Full Page Mono .... CHF 1858
Full Page Colour .... CHF 2158
Mechanical Data: Type Area: 432 x 287 mm, No. of Columns (Display): 10, Col Widths (Display): 26 mm
Copy instructions: *Copy Date:* 3 days prior to publication
LOCAL NEWSPAPERS

ANZEIGER AMT INTERLAKEN
1656711S72-9706
Editorial: Bahnhofstr. 15, 3800 INTERLAKEN
Tel: 33 8288080 **Fax:** 33 8288035
Email: anzeiger@schlaefli.ch **Web site:** http://www.anzeigerinterlaken.ch
Freq: Weekly; **Cover Price:** Free; **Circ:** 21,787
Profile: Local official paper.
Language(s): German
ADVERTISING RATES:
Full Page Mono .... CHF 3260
Full Page Colour .... CHF 3860
Mechanical Data: Type Area: 440 x 287 mm, No. of Columns (Display): 10, Col Widths (Display): 27 mm
Copy instructions: *Copy Date:* 3 days prior to publication
LOCAL NEWSPAPERS

ANZEIGER BÜREN UND UMGEBUNG
1648541S72-9633
Editorial: Rütifeldstr. 17, 3294 BÜREN
Tel: 32 3520430 **Fax:** 32 3520435
Email: anzeiger.bueren@aare-druck.ch
Freq: Weekly; **Cover Price:** Free; **Circ:** 10,887
Profile: Local official paper.
Language(s): German
ADVERTISING RATES:
Full Page Mono .... CHF 1980
Full Page Colour .... CHF 2280
Mechanical Data: Type Area: 440 x 286 mm, No. of Columns (Display): 10, Col Widths (Display): 26 mm
Copy instructions: *Copy Date:* 2 days prior to publication
LOCAL NEWSPAPERS

ANZEIGER DES AMTES WANGEN
720900S72-700
Editorial: Bahnhofstr. 39, 4900 LANGENTHAL
Tel: 62 9235555 **Fax:** 62 9235566
Email: inserate@aawangen.ch **Web site:** http://www.aawangen.ch
Freq: Weekly; **Cover Price:** Free; **Circ:** 15,935
Profile: Local official paper.
Language(s): German
ADVERTISING RATES:
Full Page Mono .... CHF 1804
Full Page Colour .... CHF 2254
Mechanical Data: Type Area: 440 x 291 mm, No. of Columns (Display): 10
Copy instructions: *Copy Date:* 3 days prior to publication
LOCAL NEWSPAPERS

ANZEIGER FÜR DAS MICHELSAMT
720911S72-820
Editorial: Aargauer Str. 12, 6215 BEROMÜNSTER
Tel: 41 9324050 **Fax:** 41 9324055
Email: redaktion@anzeigermichelsamt.ch **Web site:** http://www.anzeiger-michelsamt.ch
Freq: Weekly; **Annual Sub.:** CHF 119,00; **Circ:** 3,512
Editor: Werner Rinert
Profile: Regional weekly covering politics, economics, sport, travel, technology and the arts.
Language(s): German
ADVERTISING RATES:
SCC .... CHF 24,00
Mechanical Data: Type Area: 436 x 286 mm, No. of Columns (Display): 10, Col Widths (Display): 25 mm
Copy instructions: *Copy Date:* 2 days prior to publication
Supplement(s): Landwirtschaft aktuell
LOCAL NEWSPAPERS

ANZEIGER LANGENTHAL UND UMGEBUNG
1656708S72-9703
Editorial: Bahnhofstr. 39, 4900 LANGENTHAL
Tel: 62 9226555 **Fax:** 62 9229327
Email: duerrenmatt@anzeigerlangenthal.ch **Web site:** http://www.anzeigerlangenthal.ch/news.aspx
Freq: Weekly; **Cover Price:** Free; **Circ:** 22,469
Editor: Peter Dürrenmatt
Profile: Local official paper.
Language(s): German
ADVERTISING RATES:
Full Page Mono .... CHF 1892
Full Page Colour .... CHF 2192
Mechanical Data: Type Area: 440 x 291 mm, No. of Columns (Display): 10, Col Widths (Display): 26 mm
Copy instructions: *Copy Date:* 3 days prior to publication
LOCAL NEWSPAPERS

ANZEIGER LUZERN
720929S72-1040
Editorial: Reusseggstr. 9, 6002 LUZERN
Tel: 41 4919494 **Fax:** 41 4919495
Email: redaktion@anzeiger-luzern.ch **Web site:** http://www.anzeiger-luzern.ch
Freq: Weekly; **Cover Price:** Free; **Circ:** 123,800
Editor: Jörg Lüscher; **Advertising Manager:** Bruno Gluch
Profile: Advertising journal (house-to-house) concentrating on local stories.
Language(s): German
ADVERTISING RATES:
Full Page Mono .... CHF 7040
Full Page Colour .... CHF 8360
Mechanical Data: Type Area: 440 x 290 mm, No. of Columns (Display): 10, Col Widths (Display): 26 mm
Copy instructions: *Copy Date:* 2 days prior to publication
Supplement(s): Beauty
LOCAL NEWSPAPERS

ANZEIGER REGION BERN - REGIONALAUSG.
1655962S72-9666
Editorial: Postfach 5113, 3001 BERN
Tel: 32 3820000 **Fax:** 32 3821090
Web site: http://www.anzeigerbern.ch
Freq: 104 issues yearly; **Cover Price:** Free; **Circ:** 64,638
Profile: Advertising journal (house-to-house) concentrating on local stories.
Language(s): German
ADVERTISING RATES:
Full Page Mono .... CHF 4102
Full Page Colour .... CHF 5806
Mechanical Data: Type Area: 436 x 288 mm, No. of Columns (Display): 10, Col Widths (Display): 27 mm
Copy instructions: *Copy Date:* 2 days prior to publication
LOCAL NEWSPAPERS

ANZEIGER REGION BERN - STADTAUSG.
1655961S72-9665
Editorial: Postfach 5113, 3001 BERN
Tel: 32 3820000 **Fax:** 32 3821090
Web site: http://www.anzeigerbern.ch
Freq: 104 issues yearly; **Cover Price:** Free; **Circ:** 87,045
Profile: Advertising journal (house-to-house) concentrating on local stories.
Language(s): German
ADVERTISING RATES:
Full Page Mono .... CHF 4964
Full Page Colour .... CHF 6746
Mechanical Data: Type Area: 438 x 288 mm, No. of Columns (Display): 10, Col Widths (Display): 27 mm
Copy instructions: *Copy Date:* 2 days prior to publication
LOCAL NEWSPAPERS

ANZEIGER THAL GÄU OLTEN
1655959S72-9663
Editorial: Schanzenweg 45, 4612 WANGEN
Tel: 62 2139328 **Fax:** 62 2965127
Email: redaktion@gaeuanzeiger.ch **Web site:** http://www.gaeuanzeiger.ch
Freq: Weekly; **Annual Sub.:** CHF 83,00; **Circ:** 46,003
Editor: Thomas Knapp
Profile: Local official paper.
Language(s): German
Mechanical Data: No. of Columns (Display): 10, Type Area: 430 x 288 mm, Col Widths (Display): 27 mm
Copy instructions: *Copy Date:* 2 days prior to publication
Supplement(s): Beauty
LOCAL NEWSPAPERS

ANZEIGER TRACHSELWALD
1648540S72-9632
Editorial: Bahnhofstr. 9, 4950 HUTTWIL
Tel: 62 9598075 **Fax:** 62 9598074
Email: anzeiger@schuerch-druck.ch **Web site:** http://www.schuerch-druck.ch
Freq: Weekly; **Cover Price:** Free; **Circ:** 8,068
Editor: H. Thoenen
Profile: Local official paper.
Language(s): German
ADVERTISING RATES:
Full Page Mono .... CHF 1858
Full Page Colour .... CHF 2398
Mechanical Data: Type Area: 432 x 287 mm, No. of Columns (Display): 10, Col Widths (Display): 26 mm
Copy instructions: *Copy Date:* 3 days prior to publication
LOCAL NEWSPAPERS

ANZEIGER VON KERZERS
720933S72-1120
Editorial: Bahnhofstr. 1, 3210 KERZERS
Tel: 31 7560747 **Fax:** 31 7560750
Email: info@anzeigerkerzers.ch **Web site:** http://www.anzeigerkerzers.ch
Freq: Weekly; **Annual Sub.:** CHF 81,00; **Circ:** 1,426
Profile: Regional weekly covering politics, economics, sport, travel, technology and the arts.
Language(s): German
ADVERTISING RATES:
SCC .... CHF 11,90
Mechanical Data: Type Area: 440 x 285 mm, No. of Columns (Display): 8, Col Widths (Display): 33 mm
Copy instructions: *Copy Date:* 2 days prior to publication
LOCAL NEWSPAPERS

ANZEIGER VON SAANEN
720936S67B-360
Editorial: Kirchstr., 3780 GSTAAD **Tel:** 33 7488874
Fax: 33 7488884
Email: redaktion@anzeigervonsaanen.ch **Web site:** http://www.anzeigervonsaanen.ch
Freq: 104 issues yearly; **Annual Sub.:** CHF 106,00; **Circ:** 5,221
Editor: Anita Moser; **Advertising Manager:** Elsbeth Wyss
Profile: Regional daily newspaper covering politics, economics, sport, travel, technology and the arts.
Language(s): German
ADVERTISING RATES:
SCC .... CHF 20,80
Mechanical Data: Type Area: 440 x 288 mm, No. of Columns (Display): 10, Col Widths (Display): 27 mm
Copy instructions: *Copy Date:* 1 day prior to publication
REGIONAL DAILY & SUNDAY NEWSPAPERS: Regional Daily Newspapers

ANZEIGER VON WALLISELLEN
720939S72-1200
Editorial: Kirchstr. 2, 8304 WALLISELLEN
Tel: 44 8302309 **Fax:** 44 8310297
Email: info@avwa.ch **Web site:** http://www.avwa.ch
Freq: Monthly; **Cover Price:** Free; **Circ:** 7,640
Editor: M. Lorbe; **Advertising Manager:** Christian Albrecht
Profile: Advertising journal (house-to-house) concentrating on local stories.
Language(s): German
ADVERTISING RATES:
Full Page Mono .... CHF 3372
Full Page Colour .... CHF 3888
Mechanical Data: Type Area: 440 x 286 mm, No. of Columns (Display): 10, Col Widths (Display): 25 mm
Copy instructions: *Copy Date:* 2 days prior to publication
LOCAL NEWSPAPERS

ANZEIGER VON WALLISELLEN
720940S72-1220
Editorial: Kirchstr. 2, 8304 WALLISELLEN
Tel: 44 8302309 **Fax:** 44 8310297
Email: redaktion@avwa.ch **Web site:** http://www.avwa.ch
Freq: Weekly; **Annual Sub.:** CHF 78,00; **Circ:** 2,882
Editor: Markus Lorbe; **Advertising Manager:** Christian Albrecht
Profile: Regional weekly covering politics, economics, sport, travel, technology and the arts.
Language(s): German
ADVERTISING RATES:
SCC .... CHF 7,90

Mechanical Data: Type Area: 440 x 286 mm, No. of Columns (Display): 10, Col Widths (Display): 25 mm
Copy instructions: *Copy Date:* 2 days prior to publication
LOCAL NEWSPAPERS

APHASIE UND VERWANDTE GEBIETE/ET DOMAINES ASSOCIÉS
1858715S56A-2200
Editorial: Zähringerstr. 19, 6003 LUZERN
Tel: 41 2400583 **Fax:** 41 2400754
Email: info@aphasie.org **Web site:** http://www.aphasie.org
Freq: 3 issues yearly; Free to qualifying individuals
Annual Sub.: CHF 107,00; **Circ:** 500
Profile: Magazine on aphasy.
Language(s): French; German
Mechanical Data: Type Area: 174 x 115 mm, No. of Columns (Display): 2

APPENZELLER ZEITUNG
721011S67B-420
Editorial: Kasernenstr. 64, 9101 HERISAU
Tel: 71 3546474 **Fax:** 71 3546475
Email: redaktion@appon.ch **Web site:** http://www.appon.ch
Freq: 312 issues yearly; **Annual Sub.:** CHF 353,00; **Circ:** 14,045
Editor: Monika Egli
Profile: Daily newspaper with regional news and a local sports section.
Language(s): German
ADVERTISING RATES:
SCC .... CHF 41,20
Mechanical Data: Type Area: 438 x 291 mm, No. of Columns (Display): 10, Col Widths (Display): 27 mm
Copy instructions: *Copy Date:* 1 day prior to publication
Supplement(s): applaus; höckle ond gnüüsse
REGIONAL DAILY & SUNDAY NEWSPAPERS: Regional Daily Newspapers

ARCH
1789534S4E-807
Editorial: Postfach 203, 8024 ZÜRICH
Tel: 44 2413528 **Fax:** 44 2413528
Email: redaktion.arch@eternit.ch **Web site:** http://www.eternit.ch
Freq: 3 issues yearly; **Circ:** 16,500
Editor: Michael Hanak
Profile: Magazine for architects and the building business.
Language(s): German

ARCHI
1648668S4E-789
Editorial: via Cantonale, 15, 6900 LUGANO
Tel: 91 9214455
Email: caruso@rivista-archi.ch **Web site:** http://www.rivista-archi.ch
Freq: 6 issues yearly; **Annual Sub.:** CHF 120,00; **Circ:** 3,300
Editor: Alberto Caruso
Profile: Magazine on engineering and building.
Language(s): Italian
ADVERTISING RATES:
Full Page Mono .... CHF 1760
Full Page Colour .... CHF 2960
Mechanical Data: Type Area: 270 x 190 mm, No. of Columns (Display): 2, Col Widths (Display): 92 mm
Copy instructions: *Copy Date:* 21 days prior to publication
Official Journal of: Organ d. Ass. Ticinese di Economia delle Acque, Ordine Ticinese degli Ingegneri e degli Architetti u. Societá svizzera Ingegneri e Architetti, Sez. Ticino

ARCHITEKTUR TECHNIK
721129S4A-20
Editorial: Steinwiesenstr. 3, 8952 SCHLIEREN
Tel: 44 7333999 **Fax:** 44 7333991
Email: manuel.pestalozzi@bvverlag.ch **Web site:** http://www.architektur-technik.ch
Freq: Monthly; **Annual Sub.:** CHF 54,00; **Circ:** 8,000
Editor: Manuel Pestalozzi; **Advertising Manager:** Gabriela Hüppi
Profile: Magazine covering all aspects of architecture and modern building techniques and technology.
Language(s): German
Readership: Read by architects.
ADVERTISING RATES:
Full Page Mono .... CHF 5400
Full Page Colour .... CHF 5400
Mechanical Data: Type Area: 298 x 205 mm, No. of Columns (Display): 4, Col Widths (Display): 46 mm
Copy instructions: *Copy Date:* 20 days prior to publication
BUSINESS: ARCHITECTURE & BUILDING: Architecture

ARCHITHESE
721138S4A-1
Editorial: Holbeinstr. 31, 8008 ZÜRICH
Tel: 43 2434616 **Fax:** 43 2434611
Email: redaktion@archithese.ch **Web site:** http://www.archithese.ch
Freq: 6 issues yearly; Free to qualifying individuals
Annual Sub.: CHF 148,00; **Circ:** 8,500
Editor: J. Christoph Bürkle
Profile: Magazine covering all aspects of architecture.
Language(s): English; French; German
Readership: Read by architects and art historians.
ADVERTISING RATES:
Full Page Mono .... CHF 2770
Full Page Colour .... CHF 4155
Mechanical Data: Type Area: 267 x 200 mm, No. of Columns (Display): 4, Col Widths (Display): 45 mm
Official Journal of: Organ d. fédération suisse des architectes indépendent
BUSINESS: ARCHITECTURE & BUILDING: Architecture

AREA SICUREZZA
1855318S14A-1290
Editorial: Maulbeerstr. 14, 3011 BERN
Tel: 31 3055566
Email: areasicurezza@upi.ch **Web site:** http://www.bfu.ch
Freq: Quarterly; **Circ:** 1,100
Editor: Ursula Marti
Profile: Magazine about accident prevention.
Language(s): Italian

ARENA ALVA
721198S72-1280
Editorial: Chalet Central, 7018 FLIMS WALDHAUS
Tel: 81 9115559 **Fax:** 81 9113648
Email: arena-alva@suedostschweiz.ch **Web site:** http://www.suedostschweiz.ch
Freq: Weekly; **Annual Sub.:** CHF 91,00; **Circ:** 3,829
Editor: Sarah Nigg
Profile: Regional weekly covering politics, economics, sport, travel, technology and the arts.
Language(s): German
ADVERTISING RATES:
SCC .... CHF 16,50
Mechanical Data: Type Area: 286 x 199 mm, No. of Columns (Display): 7, Col Widths (Display): 25 mm
Copy instructions: *Copy Date:* 2 days prior to publication
LOCAL NEWSPAPERS

ARMEE-LOGISTIK
1859589S40-250
Editorial: Postfach 2840, 6002 LUZERN
Tel: 41 2403868 **Fax:** 41 2403869
Email: redaktion@armee-logistik.ch **Web site:** http://www.armee-logistik.ch
Freq: Monthly; Free to qualifying individuals
Annual Sub.: CHF 32,00; **Circ:** 6,340
Editor: Meinrad A. Schuler
Profile: Magazine of the Association of Swiss Sergeants.
Language(s): French; German; Italian
Copy instructions: *Copy Date:* 15 days prior to publication
Official Journal of: Organ d. Schweizer. Offiziersges. d. Logistik

AROSER ZEITUNG
721233S72-1320
Editorial: Haus Madrisa, 7050 AROSA
Tel: 79 4230043 **Fax:** 81 3772310
Email: aroser-zeitung@suedostschweiz.ch **Web site:** http://www.suedostschweiz.ch
Freq: Weekly; **Annual Sub.:** CHF 91,00; **Circ:** 3,370
Editor: Peter Lüscher
Profile: Weekly newspaper containing regional news and a local sports section.
Language(s): German
ADVERTISING RATES:
SCC .... CHF 16,50
Mechanical Data: Type Area: 286 x 199 mm, No. of Columns (Display): 7, Col Widths (Display): 25 mm
Copy instructions: *Copy Date:* 2 days prior to publication
LOCAL NEWSPAPERS

ARS MEDICI
721235S56A-100
Editorial: Schaffhauser Str. 13, 8212 NEUHAUSEN
Tel: 52 6755060 **Fax:** 52 6755061
Email: info@rosenfluh.ch **Web site:** http://www.rosenfluh.ch
Freq: 25 issues yearly; **Annual Sub.:** CHF 138,00; **Circ:** 8,000
Editor: Richard Altorfer
Profile: Official magazine of the Swiss Society for General Medicine.
Language(s): French; German
ADVERTISING RATES:
Full Page Mono .... CHF 3080
Full Page Colour .... CHF 4680
Mechanical Data: Type Area: 275 x 190 mm, No. of Columns (Display): 3
Copy instructions: *Copy Date:* 20 days prior to publication
Official Journal of: Organ Ärzte m. Patientenapotheke, Vereinigung d. selbstdispensierenden Ärzte d. Schweiz, Foederatio Medicorum Practicorum, Foederatio Medicarum Practicarum
Supplement(s): Ars Medici Dossier

ARS MEDICI
721235S56A-2163
Editorial: Schaffhauser Str. 13, 8212 NEUHAUSEN
Tel: 52 6755060 **Fax:** 52 6755061
Email: info@rosenfluh.ch **Web site:** http://www.rosenfluh.ch
Freq: 25 issues yearly; **Annual Sub.:** CHF 138,00; **Circ:** 8,000
Editor: Richard Altorfer
Profile: Official magazine of the Swiss Society for General Medicine.
Language(s): French; German
ADVERTISING RATES:
Full Page Mono .... CHF 3080
Full Page Colour .... CHF 4680
Mechanical Data: Type Area: 275 x 190 mm, No. of Columns (Display): 3
Copy instructions: *Copy Date:* 20 days prior to publication
Official Journal of: Organ Ärzte m. Patientenapotheke, Vereinigung d. selbstdispensierenden Ärzte d. Schweiz, Foederatio Medicorum Practicorum, Foederatio Medicarum Practicarum
Supplement(s): Ars Medici Dossier

ARS MEDICI DOSSIER
1786307S56A-2120
Editorial: Schaffhauser Str. 13, 8212 NEUHAUSEN
Tel: 52 6755060 **Fax:** 52 6755061
Email: info@rosenfluh.ch **Web site:** http://www.rosenfluh.ch
Freq: Monthly; **Circ:** 6,300
Editor: Richard Altorfer
Profile: Official magazine of the Swiss Society for General Medicine.
Language(s): French; German
ADVERTISING RATES:
Full Page Mono .... CHF 3060
Full Page Colour .... CHF 4680
Mechanical Data: Type Area: 275 x 190 mm
Supplement to: Ars Medici

ARS MEDICI DOSSIER
1786307S56A-2164
Editorial: Schaffhauser Str. 13, 8212 NEUHAUSEN
Tel: 52 6755060 **Fax:** 52 6755061
Email: info@rosenfluh.ch **Web site:** http://www.rosenfluh.ch
Freq: Monthly; **Circ:** 6,300
Editor: Richard Altorfer
Profile: Official magazine of the Swiss Society for General Medicine.
Language(s): French; German
ADVERTISING RATES:
Full Page Mono .... CHF 3060
Full Page Colour .... CHF 4680
Mechanical Data: Type Area: 275 x 190 mm
Supplement to: Ars Medici

ARS MEDICI THEMA PHYTOTHERAPIE
1643873S56A-2042
Editorial: Hirschmattsr. 46, 6003 LUZERN
Tel: 41 2103282 **Fax:** 41 2105282
Email: c.a.bachmann@bluewin.ch **Web site:** http://www.rosenfluh.ch
Freq: 6 issues yearly; **Annual Sub.:** CHF 42,00; **Circ:** 5,000
Editor: Christoph Bachmann
Profile: Magazine containing contributions and information about phytotherapy.
Language(s): German
ADVERTISING RATES:
Full Page Mono .... CHF 4880
Full Page Colour .... CHF 4880
Mechanical Data: Type Area: 297 x 210 mm
Copy instructions: *Copy Date:* 24 days prior to publication
Supplement to: Ars Medici

ARS MEDICI THEMA PHYTOTHERAPIE
1643873S56A-2173
Editorial: Hirschmattsr. 46, 6003 LUZERN
Tel: 41 2103282 **Fax:** 41 2105282
Email: c.a.bachmann@bluewin.ch **Web site:** http://www.rosenfluh.ch
Freq: 6 issues yearly; **Annual Sub.:** CHF 42,00; **Circ:** 5,000
Editor: Christoph Bachmann
Profile: Magazine containing contributions and information about phytotherapy.
Language(s): German
ADVERTISING RATES:
Full Page Mono .... CHF 4880
Full Page Colour .... CHF 4880
Mechanical Data: Type Area: 297 x 210 mm
Copy instructions: *Copy Date:* 24 days prior to publication
Supplement to: Ars Medici

ASMZ SICHERHEIT SCHWEIZ
763013S40-201
Editorial: Brunnenstr. 7, 8604 VOLKETSWIL
Tel: 44 9084560 **Fax:** 44 9084540
Email: redaktion@asmz.ch **Web site:** http://www.asmz.ch
Freq: 11 issues yearly; **Annual Sub.:** CHF 78,00; **Circ:** 19,500
Editor: Roland Beck; **Advertising Manager:** Patrick Kobelt
Profile: Magazine from the Swiss army.
Language(s): German
ADVERTISING RATES:
Full Page Mono .... CHF 3555
Full Page Colour .... CHF 6400
Mechanical Data: Type Area: 257 x 184 mm
Official Journal of: Organ d. Schweizer. Offiziersges.
Supplement(s): Military Power Revue
BUSINESS: DEFENCE

ASTROLOGIE HEUTE
1641781S94X-656
Editorial: Albisrieder Str. 232, 8047 ZÜRICH
Tel: 43 3433300 **Fax:** 43 3433301
Email: redaktion@astrologieheute.ch **Web site:** http://www.astrologieheute.ch
Freq: 6 issues yearly; **Annual Sub.:** CHF 68,00; **Circ:** 11,000
Editor: Armando Bertozzi; **Advertising Manager:** Trix Andrychowska
Profile: Magazine about astrology, psychology, esoterics and new subjects.
Language(s): German
ADVERTISING RATES:
Full Page Mono .... CHF 2080
Full Page Colour .... CHF 2480
Mechanical Data: Type Area: 257 x 184 mm, No. of Columns (Display): 3, Col Widths (Display): 58 mm
Copy instructions: *Copy Date:* 20 days prior to publication
CONSUMER: OTHER CLASSIFICATIONS: Miscellaneous

ATG BULLETIN TECHNIQUE DE L'ASSOCIATION DES ANCIENS ÉLÈVES DE L'ECOLE D'INGÉNIEURS DE GENÈVE
1646198S19E-185
Editorial: 31, ch.Pré-Marin, 1052 LE MONT-SUR-LAUSANNE **Tel:** 21 6530244
Freq: 3 issues yearly; Free to qualifying individuals
Annual Sub.: CHF 100,00; **Circ:** 1,200
Editor: L. Lakatos
Profile: Magazine with technical issues for former students of the Geneva School of Engineering.
Language(s): French
Mechanical Data: Type Area: 256 x 175 mm
Copy instructions: *Copy Date:* 30 days prior to publication

ATMOSPHÈRE
1852054S4E-829
Editorial: Postfach 1968, 8032 ZÜRICH
Tel: 43 4999930
Email: redaktion@richner.ch **Web site:** http://www.richner.ch/kundenmagazin
Freq: 3 issues yearly; **Cover Price:** Free; **Circ:** 25,000
Editor: Maja Fueter; **Advertising Manager:** Hansruedi Hofer
Profile: Company publication published by Richner, Gétaz, Rapin & Glasson.
Language(s): German
ADVERTISING RATES:
Full Page Mono .... CHF 6500
Full Page Colour .... CHF 6500
Mechanical Data: Type Area: 274 x 192 mm
Copy instructions: *Copy Date:* 74 days prior to publication

ATMOSPHÈRE
2009460S4E-857
Editorial: Postfach 1968, 8032 ZÜRICH
Tel: 43 4999930
Email: redaktion@richner.ch **Web site:** http://www.richner.ch/kundenmagazin
Freq: 3 issues yearly; **Cover Price:** Free; **Circ:** 12,000
Editor: Maja Fueter; **Advertising Manager:** Hansruedi Hofer
Profile: Company publication published by Richner, Gétaz, Rapin & Glasson.
Language(s): French
ADVERTISING RATES:
Full Page Mono .... CHF 6500
Full Page Colour .... CHF 6500
Mechanical Data: Type Area: 274 x 192 mm
Copy instructions: *Copy Date:* 74 days prior to publication

ATRIUM
721359S74C-80
Editorial: Rieterstr. 35, 8002 ZÜRICH
Tel: 44 2041851 **Fax:** 44 2041850
Email: hg.hildebrandt@archithema.com **Web site:** http://www.archithema.com
Freq: 6 issues yearly; **Annual Sub.:** CHF 37,80; **Circ:** 45,733
Editor: Hans Georg Hildebrandt; **Advertising Manager:** Emil M. Bisig
Profile: Magazine about interior and exterior house design.
Language(s): German
ADVERTISING RATES:
Full Page Mono .... CHF 7280
Full Page Colour .... CHF 10400
Mechanical Data: Type Area: 269 x 203 mm, No. of Columns (Display): 4, Col Widths (Display): 47 mm
Copy instructions: *Copy Date:* 42 days prior to publication
CONSUMER: WOMEN'S INTEREST CONSUMER MAGAZINES: Home & Family

AUSSENWIRTSCHAFT
721509S1R-200
Editorial: Bodanstr. 8, 9000 ST. GALLEN
Tel: 71 2242350 **Fax:** 71 2242298
Email: redaktion@journal-aussenwirtschaft.ch **Web site:** http://www.journal-aussenwirtschaft.ch
Freq: Quarterly; **Annual Sub.:** CHF 178,00; **Circ:** 1,000
Editor: Heinz Hauser

Profile: European review of international economic relations.
Language(s): English; German
ADVERTISING RATES:
Full Page Mono .... CHF 470
Mechanical Data: Type Area: 185 x 115 mm
Copy instructions: *Copy Date:* 30 days prior to publication
BUSINESS: FINANCE & ECONOMICS: Financial Related

AUTO ILLUSTRIERTE
1642001S77D-63
Editorial: Industriestr. 28, 8604 VOLKETSWIL
Tel: 44 8065588 **Fax:** 44 8065522
Email: ai@motorpresse.ch **Web site:** http://www.auto-illustrierte.ch
Freq: Monthly; **Annual Sub.:** CHF 78,00; **Circ:** 33,163
Editor: Ulrich Safferling; **Advertising Manager:** August Hug
Profile: Car magazine Facebook: http://de-de.facebook.com/autoillustrierte Twitter: http://twitter.com/#!/aischweiz This Outlet offers RSS (Really Simple Syndication).
Language(s): German
ADVERTISING RATES:
Full Page Mono .... CHF 7360
Full Page Colour .... CHF 8175
Mechanical Data: Type Area: 262 x 181 mm
Copy instructions: *Copy Date:* 14 days prior to publication
Official Journal of: Organ d. Schweizer. Autorennsport-Clubs
Supplement(s): auto illustrierte Formel 1 Guide; auto illustrierte Tuning Katalog
CONSUMER: MOTORING & CYCLING: Motor Sports

AUTO & ÉCONOMIE 1841035S14A-1244
Editorial: Riedstr. 10, 8953 DIETIKON
Tel: 43 4991860 **Fax:** 43 4991861
Email: redaktion@auto-wirtschaft.ch **Web site:** http://www.auto-wirtschaft.ch
Freq: 10 issues yearly; **Annual Sub.:** CHF 48,00; **Circ:** 1,500
Editor: Roland Christen; **Advertising Manager:** Giuseppe Cucchiara
Profile: Magazine for executives of the Swiss car sector.
Language(s): French
ADVERTISING RATES:
Full Page Mono .... CHF 515
Full Page Colour .... CHF 890
Mechanical Data: Type Area: 267 x 182 mm, No. of Columns (Display): 4, Col Widths (Display): 41 mm

AUTO & TECHNIK 1899853S14A-1355
Editorial: Riedstr. 10, 8953 DIETIKON
Tel: 43 4991860 **Fax:** 43 4991861
Email: redaktion@auto-wirtschaft.ch **Web site:** http://www.auto-wirtschaft.ch
Freq: 10 issues yearly; **Annual Sub.:** CHF 95,00; **Circ:** 6,500
Editor: Lukas Hasselberg; **Advertising Manager:** Giuseppe Cucchiara
Profile: Magazine for executives of the Swiss car sector.
Language(s): German
ADVERTISING RATES:
Full Page Mono .... CHF 965
Full Page Colour .... CHF 1650
Mechanical Data: Type Area: 267 x 182 mm, No. of Columns (Display): 4, Col Widths (Display): 41 mm

AUTO & WIRTSCHAFT
1656713S14A-1188
Editorial: Riedstr. 10, 8953 DIETIKON
Tel: 43 4991860 **Fax:** 43 4991861
Email: redaktion@auto-wirtschaft.ch **Web site:** http://www.auto-wirtschaft.ch
Freq: 10 issues yearly; **Annual Sub.:** CHF 95,00; **Circ:** 6,500
Editor: Lukas Hasselberg; **Advertising Manager:** Giuseppe Cucchiara
Profile: Magazine for executives of the Swiss car sector.
Language(s): French; German
ADVERTISING RATES:
Full Page Colour .... CHF 4225
Mechanical Data: Type Area: 267 x 182 mm, No. of Columns (Display): 4, Col Widths (Display): 41 mm
BUSINESS: COMMERCE, INDUSTRY & MANAGEMENT

AUTOMOBIL REVUE 762464S77A-81
Editorial: Dammweg 9, 3001 BERN **Tel:** 31 3303034
Fax: 31 3303032
Email: office@automobilrevue.ch **Web site:** http://www.automobilrevue.ch
Freq: Weekly; **Annual Sub.:** CHF 159,00; **Circ:** 33,494
Editor: Olaf Kuhlmann; **Advertising Manager:** Remo De Piano
Profile: Car magazine.
Language(s): German
ADVERTISING RATES:
Full Page Mono .... CHF 7952
Full Page Colour .... CHF 9404
Mechanical Data: Type Area: 380 x 263 mm
CONSUMER: MOTORING & CYCLING: Motoring

AZEIGER 720927S80-1484
Editorial: Fichtenweg, 4542 LUTERBACH
Tel: 32 6824074
Email: manfred.fluri@gmx.ch **Web site:** http://www.azeiger.ch
Freq: Weekly; **Cover Price:** Free; **Circ:** 78,340
Editor: Manfred Fluri
Profile: Advertising journal (house-to-house) concentrating on local stories.
Language(s): German
ADVERTISING RATES:
Full Page Mono .... CHF 1909
Full Page Colour .... CHF 2538
Mechanical Data: Type Area: 290 x 202 mm, No. of Columns (Display): 7, Col Widths (Display): 26 mm
Copy instructions: *Copy Date:* 2 days prior to publication
CONSUMER: RURAL & REGIONAL INTEREST

BASELLANDSCHAFTLICHE ZEITUNG BZ 721886S67B-440
Editorial: Rheinstr. 3, 4410 LIESTAL **Tel:** 61 9272600
Fax: 61 9212268
Email: info@bz-ag.ch **Web site:** http://www.bz-ag.ch
Freq: 208 issues yearly; **Annual Sub.:** CHF 368,00; **Circ:** 21,057
Editor: Thomas Dähler; **Advertising Manager:** Dieter Butz
Profile: Regional daily newspaper covering politics, economics, sport, travel, technology and the arts.
Language(s): German
ADVERTISING RATES:
SCC .... CHF 26,00
Mechanical Data: Type Area: 440 x 288 mm, No. of Columns (Display): 10, Col Widths (Display): 25 mm
Copy instructions: *Copy Date:* 2 days prior to publication
Supplement(s): TV täglich
REGIONAL DAILY & SUNDAY NEWSPAPERS: Regional Daily Newspapers

BASELLANDSCHAFTLICHE ZEITUNG BZ 721887S72-1440
Editorial: Rheinstr. 3, 4410 LIESTAL **Tel:** 61 9272600
Fax: 61 9212268
Email: info@bz-ag.ch **Web site:** http://www.bz-ag.ch
Freq: Weekly; **Cover Price:** Free; **Circ:** 83,861
Editor: Thomas Dähler
Profile: Advertising journal (house-to-house) concentrating on local stories.
Language(s): German
ADVERTISING RATES:
Full Page Mono .... CHF 7900
Full Page Colour .... CHF 9900
Mechanical Data: Type Area: 440 x 288 mm, No. of Columns (Display): 10, Col Widths (Display): 25 mm
Copy instructions: *Copy Date:* 2 days prior to publication
LOCAL NEWSPAPERS

BASLER ZEITUNG 1655505S67B-6630
Editorial: Aeschenplatz 7, 4002 BASEL
Tel: 61 6391111 **Fax:** 61 6391582
Email: redaktion@baz.ch **Web site:** http://www.baz.ch
Freq: 260 issues yearly; **Annual Sub.:** CHF 389,00; **Circ:** 88,187
Editor: Markus Somm; **News Editor:** Thomas Lüthi
Profile: Regional daily newspaper covering politics, economics, sport, travel, technology and the arts.
Language(s): German
ADVERTISING RATES:
SCC .... CHF 59,60
Mechanical Data: Type Area: 440 x 291 mm, No. of Columns (Display): 10, Col Widths (Display): 27 mm
Copy instructions: *Copy Date:* 2 days prior to publication
Supplement(s): Das Magazin; Neue Energie für die Schweiz; spatz; Vista
REGIONAL DAILY & SUNDAY NEWSPAPERS: Regional Daily Newspapers

BASLERSTAB 1655504S72-9652
Editorial: Hochbergerstr. 15, 4002 BASEL
Tel: 61 6391050 **Fax:** 61 6391102
Email: redaktion@baslerstab.ch **Web site:** http://www.baslerstab.ch
Cover Price: Free; **Circ:** 182,100
Editor: Marko Lehtinen; **Advertising Manager:** Isabella Pedrun
Profile: Advertising journal (house-to-house) concentrating on local stories.
Language(s): German
ADVERTISING RATES:
Full Page Mono .... CHF 10120
Full Page Colour .... CHF 13300
Mechanical Data: Type Area: 440 x 291 mm, No. of Columns (Display): 10, Col Widths (Display): 27 mm
Copy instructions: *Copy Date:* 2 days prior to publication
LOCAL NEWSPAPERS

BÂTITECH 721926S3B-3
Editorial: c.p., 1000 LAUSANNE 20 **Tel:** 21 6200124
Fax: 21 6200116
Email: batitech@diemand.ch **Web site:** http://www.batitech.ch
Freq: 11 issues yearly; Free to qualifying individuals
Annual Sub.: CHF 65,00; **Circ:** 4,250
Editor: Bernard Dätwyler; **Advertising Manager:** Rolf Niederberger
Profile: Magazine focusing on heating, ventilation, sanitation, plumbing and facilities management.
Language(s): French
Readership: Read by plumbing and heating engineers, architects, manufacturers, wholesalers and facilities managers.
ADVERTISING RATES:
Full Page Mono .... CHF 1775
Full Page Colour .... CHF 2975
Mechanical Data: Type Area: 264 x 184 mm
Copy instructions: *Copy Date:* 30 days prior to publication
BUSINESS: HEATING & VENTILATION: Industrial Heating & Ventilation

BAU FLASH 1642193S4E-781
Editorial: Postfach 940, 4142 MÜNCHENSTEIN 1
Tel: 61 3381638 **Fax:** 61 3381600
Email: bauflash@lupper.ch **Web site:** http://www.lupper.ch
Freq: 8 issues yearly; **Annual Sub.:** CHF 58,00; **Circ:** 6,100
Editor: Alfred Gysin
Profile: Building sector magazine.
Language(s): German
ADVERTISING RATES:
Full Page Mono .... CHF 2970
Full Page Colour .... CHF 3570
Mechanical Data: Type Area: 275 x 185 mm, No. of Columns (Display): 4, Col Widths (Display): 43 mm
Copy instructions: *Copy Date:* 25 days prior to publication

BAU INFO 1853314S4E-835
Editorial: Linsebühlstr. 89, 9004 ST. GALLEN
Tel: 71 2980006 **Fax:** 71 2985480
Email: dzverlag@bluewin.ch **Web site:** http://www.dz-verlag.ch
Freq: Monthly; **Annual Sub.:** CHF 85,00; **Circ:** 7,000
Editor: Clemens P. Zweifel; **Advertising Manager:** Clemens P. Zweifel
Profile: Building business magazine.
Language(s): German; Italian
ADVERTISING RATES:
Full Page Mono .... CHF 2520
Full Page Colour .... CHF 3020
Mechanical Data: Type Area: 270 x 184 mm, No. of Columns (Display): 2, Col Widths (Display): 90 mm

BAU LIFE 1842126S4E-814
Editorial: Leimgrubenweg 4, 4053 BASEL
Tel: 61 3382000 **Fax:** 61 3382022
Email: g.lutz@lifemedien.ch **Web site:** http://www.lifemedien.ch
Freq: Quarterly; **Annual Sub.:** CHF 45,00; **Circ:** 12,000
Editor: Georg Lutz
Profile: Building sector magazine.
Language(s): German
ADVERTISING RATES:
Full Page Mono .... CHF 3170
Full Page Colour .... CHF 3170
Mechanical Data: Type Area: 270 x 185 mm, No. of Columns (Display): 3, Col Widths (Display): 67 mm
Copy instructions: *Copy Date:* 28 days prior to publication

BAU & ARCHITEKTUR
1641406S4E-777
Editorial: Feldeggstr. 89, 8008 ZÜRICH
Tel: 43 4999901 **Fax:** 43 4999931
Email: sigrid.hanke@bluewin.ch
Freq: 5 issues yearly; **Circ:** 14,000
Editor: Sigrid Hanke; **Advertising Manager:** Ursula Kühne
Profile: Magazine on planning and building.
Language(s): German
ADVERTISING RATES:
Full Page Mono .... CHF 4350
Full Page Colour .... CHF 5700
Mechanical Data: Type Area: 270 x 185 mm

BAU- UND UMWELT-ZEITUNG
1776396S4E-804
Editorial: Rheinstr. 29, 4410 LIESTAL
Tel: 61 9255404 **Fax:** 61 9256948
Email: catia.allemann@bl.ch
Freq: Quarterly; **Circ:** 3,500
Editor: Adrian Baumgartner
Profile: Publication from the Basel cantonal administration.
Language(s): German

BAU- UND UMWELT-ZEITUNG
1776396S4E-824
Editorial: Rheinstr. 29, 4410 LIESTAL
Tel: 61 9255404 **Fax:** 61 9256948
Email: catia.allemann@bl.ch
Freq: Quarterly; **Circ:** 3,500
Editor: Adrian Baumgartner
Profile: Publication from the Basel cantonal administration.
Language(s): German

BAUEN HEUTE 721965S4E-200
Editorial: Werriker Str. 7, 8606 NÄNIKON
Tel: 44 9409953 **Fax:** 44 9420522
Email: info@bauenheute.ch **Web site:** http://www.bauenheute.ch
Freq: 10 issues yearly; **Annual Sub.:** CHF 62,00; **Circ:** 7,000
Editor: Ueli Buser; **Advertising Manager:** Ueli Buser
Profile: Magazine focusing on the building business and associated business.
Language(s): German
ADVERTISING RATES:
Full Page Mono .... CHF 2360
Full Page Colour .... CHF 3320
Mechanical Data: Type Area: 264 x 182 mm

BAUEN & RETTEN 745048S40-160
Editorial: Postfach, 5620 BREMGARTEN
Web site: http://www.bauenretten.ch
Freq: Quarterly; **Annual Sub.:** CHF 40,00; **Circ:** 1,500
Editor: Marion Romann
Profile: Magazine from the Society for Military Building Technology.
Language(s): French; German; Italian
ADVERTISING RATES:
Full Page Mono .... CHF 390
Full Page Colour .... CHF 390
Mechanical Data: Type Area: 266 x 180 mm
BUSINESS: DEFENCE

BAUERNZEITUNG 1749437S21A-602
Editorial: Thunstr. 78, 3000 BERN 15
Tel: 31 9583322 **Fax:** 31 9583323
Email: redaktion@bauernzeitung.ch **Web site:** http://www.bauernzeitung.ch
Freq: Weekly; **Annual Sub.:** CHF 86,00; **Circ:** 38,000
Editor: Ruedi Hagmann
Profile: Official newspaper of the Swiss Farmers' Association.
Language(s): German
ADVERTISING RATES:
Full Page Mono .... CHF 7095
Full Page Colour .... CHF 8145
Mechanical Data: Type Area: 430 x 290 mm, No. of Columns (Display): 10, Col Widths (Display): 26 mm
Copy instructions: *Copy Date:* 4 days prior to publication
Supplement(s): BauernZeitung Nordwestschweiz, Bern und Freiburg; BauernZeitung Zentralschweiz/Aargau

BAUERNZEITUNG NORDWESTSCHWEIZ, BERN UND FREIBURG 1842597S21A-609
Editorial: Thunstr. 78, 3000 BERN 15
Tel: 31 9583329 **Fax:** 31 9583339
Email: redaktion.be@bauernzeitung.ch **Web site:** http://www.bauernzeitung.ch
Freq: Weekly; **Circ:** 11,000
Editor: Alois Heinzer
Profile: Regional newspaper for Swiss farmers.
Language(s): German
ADVERTISING RATES:
Full Page Mono .... CHF 2000
Full Page Colour .... CHF 2600
Mechanical Data: Type Area: 290 x 209 mm, No. of Columns (Display): 7, Col Widths (Display): 26 mm
Copy instructions: *Copy Date:* 4 days prior to publication
Supplement to: BauernZeitung

BAUERNZEITUNG ZENTRALSCHWEIZ/AARGAU
1899581S21A-628
Editorial: Schellenrain 6, 6210 SURSEE
Tel: 41 9258029 **Fax:** 41 9217337
Email: bauernzeitung.sursee@luzernerbauern.ch
Web site: http://www.bauernzeitung.ch
Freq: Weekly; **Circ:** 13,750
Editor: Josef Scherer-Sigrist
Profile: Regional newspaper for Swiss farmers.
Language(s): German
Mechanical Data: Type Area: 430 x 290 mm, No. of Columns (Display): 10, Col Widths (Display): 26 mm
Copy instructions: *Copy Date:* 4 days prior to publication
Official Journal of: Organ d. Luzerner Bauernverb., d. Zentralschweizer Bauernbundes u. d. Aargau. Landwirtschaftl. Ges.
Supplement to: BauernZeitung

BAUHERREN MAGAZIN
2002272S4E-855
Editorial: Bahnhofstr. 24, 8803 RÜSCHLIKON
Tel: 44 7247777 **Fax:** 44 7247877
Email: redaktion@baublatt.ch **Web site:** http://www.bauherrenmagazin.ch
Freq: Quarterly; **Circ:** 8,500
Editor: Thomas Staenz; **Advertising Manager:** Martha Ammann
Profile: Magazine for house builders.
Language(s): French; German
ADVERTISING RATES:
Full Page Mono .... CHF 3670
Full Page Colour .... CHF 3670
Mechanical Data: Type Area: 265 x 185 mm
Copy instructions: *Copy Date:* 20 days prior to publication

BEOBACHTER 1859019S73-385
Editorial: Förrlibuckstr. 70, 8005 ZÜRICH
Tel: 43 4445200 **Fax:** 43 4445353
Email: redaktion@beobachter.ch **Web site:** http://www.beobachter.ch
Freq: 26 issues yearly; **Annual Sub.:** CHF 84,00; **Circ:** 308,527
Editor: Andres Büchi; **Advertising Manager:** Sandra Peiti
Profile: Journal containing articles about economics, politics and international news.
Language(s): German
ADVERTISING RATES:
Full Page Mono .... CHF 22698
Full Page Colour .... CHF 22698
Mechanical Data: Type Area: 237 x 182 mm, No. of Columns (Display): 3, Col Widths (Display): 58 mm
Copy instructions: *Copy Date:* 14 days prior to publication
Supplement(s): Beobachter Kompakt

BERGHILF-ZIITIG 1855357S21A-620
Editorial: Hauptplatz 5, 8640 RAPPERSWIL
Tel: 55 2208139 **Fax:** 55 2208177
Email: info@denon.ch **Web site:** http://www.berghilfe.ch
Freq: Quarterly; **Circ:** 160,000
Editor: Christoph Hämmig
Profile: Newspaper to support Swiss mountaidwellers in economic, natural and social issues.
Language(s): German

BERNE CAPITAL AREA
2002644S14A-1372
Editorial: Hauptplatz 5, 8640 RAPPERSWIL
Tel: 55 2208188
Email: julia.weber@denon.ch **Web site:** http://www.denon.ch
Freq: Annual; **Cover Price:** Free; **Circ:** 16,000
Editor: Julia Weber
Profile: Magazine on Business, Science and Living in the Canton of Berne, Switzerland.
Language(s): English

BERNE CAPITAL AREA
2002645S14A-1373
Editorial: Hauptplatz 5, 8640 RAPPERSWIL
Tel: 55 2208188
Email: julia.weber@denon.ch **Web site:** http://www.denon.ch
Freq: Annual; **Cover Price:** Free; **Circ:** 16,000
Editor: Julia Weber
Profile: Magazine on Business, Science and Living in the Canton of Berne, Switzerland.
Language(s): French

BERNER BÄR 722525S72-1500
Editorial: Dammweg 9, 3001 BERN **Tel:** 31 3303999
Fax: 31 3303990
Email: redaktion@bernerbaer.ch **Web site:** http://www.bernerbaer.ch
Freq: Weekly; **Cover Price:** Free; **Circ:** 139,172
Editor: Matthias Mast; **Advertising Manager:** Ruedi Lehmann
Profile: Advertising journal (house-to-house) concentrating on local stories.
Language(s): German
ADVERTISING RATES:
Full Page Mono .... CHF 7168
Full Page Colour .... CHF 8653
Mechanical Data: Type Area: 440 x 290 mm
Copy instructions: *Copy Date:* 1 day prior to publication
LOCAL NEWSPAPERS

BERNER KMU AKTUELL
765728S14A-1123
Editorial: Technikumstr. 14, 3401 BURGDORF
Tel: 34 4206565 **Fax:** 34 4230732
Email: info@bernerkmu.ch **Web site:** http://www.bernerkmu.ch
Freq: Monthly; **Circ:** 17,192
Editor: Hubert Will
Profile: Member magazine.
Language(s): German
ADVERTISING RATES:
Full Page Mono .... CHF 1950
Full Page Colour .... CHF 2550
Mechanical Data: Type Area: 260 x 177 mm
Copy instructions: *Copy Date:* 16 days prior to publication
BUSINESS: COMMERCE, INDUSTRY & MANAGEMENT

BERNER LANDBOTE
1656717S72-9709
Editorial: Schulhausgasse 16, 3110 MÜNSINGEN
Tel: 31 7206009 **Fax:** 31 7215333
Email: redaktion@berner-landbote.ch **Web site:** http://www.berner-landbote.ch
Freq: 26 issues yearly; **Cover Price:** Free; **Circ:** 79,475
Editor: Roland Docummon
Profile: Advertising journal (house-to-house) concentrating on local stories.
Language(s): German
ADVERTISING RATES:
Full Page Mono .... CHF 5289
Full Page Colour .... CHF 6149
Mechanical Data: Type Area: 430 x 290 mm, No. of Columns (Display): 10, Col Widths (Display): 25 mm
Copy instructions: *Copy Date:* 2 days prior to publication
LOCAL NEWSPAPERS

BERNER ZEITSCHRIFT FÜR GESCHICHTE 722536S94X-180_50
Editorial: Erlachstr. 9a, 3012 BERN **Tel:** 31 6318382
Email: martin.stuber@hist.unibe.ch **Web site:** http://www.bzgh.ch
Freq: Quarterly; Free to qualifying individuals
Annual Sub.: CHF 60,00; **Circ:** 1,500
Editor: Martin Stuber
Profile: Magazine focusing on local and national history and culture.
Language(s): German
ADVERTISING RATES:
Full Page Mono .... CHF 458
Mechanical Data: Type Area: 191 x 120 mm
Copy instructions: *Copy Date:* 28 days prior to publication
CONSUMER: OTHER CLASSIFICATIONS: Miscellaneous

BERNER ZEITUNG BZ
722537S67B-520
Editorial: Dammweg 9, 3013 BERN **Tel:** 31 3303111
Fax: 31 3327724
Email: redaktion@bernerzeitung.ch **Web site:** http://www.espace.ch
Freq: 312 issues yearly; **Annual Sub.:** CHF 348,00; **Circ:** 200,117
Editor: Michael Hug; **News Editor:** Adrian Zurbriggen; **Advertising Manager:** Michael Seiler
Profile: Regional daily newspaper covering politics, economics, sport, travel, technology and the arts.
Language(s): German
ADVERTISING RATES:
SCC .... CHF 243,60
Mechanical Data: Type Area: 440 x 292 mm, No. of Columns (Display): 10, Col Widths (Display): 27 mm
Copy instructions: *Copy Date:* 1 day prior to publication
Supplement(s): Neue Energie für die Schweiz; TV täglich; Vista
REGIONAL DAILY & SUNDAY NEWSPAPERS: Regional Daily Newspapers

BESCHAFFUNGS-MANAGEMENT 766531S10-44
Editorial: Bruechstr. 164, 8706 MEILEN
Tel: 44 7011441 **Fax:** 44 7011524
Email: redaktion@svme.ch **Web site:** http://www.svme.ch
Freq: 10 issues yearly; Free to qualifying individuals
Annual Sub.: CHF 65,00; **Circ:** 3,000
Editor: J. Luzius Ruppert
Profile: Member magazine.
Language(s): French; German
ADVERTISING RATES:
Full Page Mono .... CHF 1890
Full Page Colour .... CHF 2940
Mechanical Data: Type Area: 277 x 185 mm

BESCHAFFUNGS-MANAGEMENT 766531S10-54
Editorial: Bruechstr. 164, 8706 MEILEN
Tel: 44 7011441 **Fax:** 44 7011524
Email: redaktion@svme.ch **Web site:** http://www.svme.ch
Freq: 10 issues yearly; Free to qualifying individuals
Annual Sub.: CHF 65,00; **Circ:** 3,000
Editor: J. Luzius Ruppert
Profile: Member magazine.
Language(s): French; German
ADVERTISING RATES:
Full Page Mono .... CHF 1890
Full Page Colour .... CHF 2940
Mechanical Data: Type Area: 277 x 185 mm

BEZIRKS-AMTSBLATT
722665S72-1600
Editorial: Schulstr. 19, 7302 LANDQUART
Tel: 81 3000360 **Fax:** 81 3000361
Email: info@bezirksamtsblatt.ch **Web site:** http://www.bezirksamtsblatt.ch
Freq: Weekly; **Annual Sub.:** CHF 45,00; **Circ:** 19,139
Profile: Local official paper.
Language(s): German
Mechanical Data: Type Area: 288 x 203 mm, No. of Columns (Display): 7, Col Widths (Display): 27 mm
Copy instructions: *Copy Date:* 2 days prior to publication
LOCAL NEWSPAPERS

BIBO BIRSIGTAL-BOTE
1656719S72-9711
Editorial: Missionsstr. 36, 4012 BASEL
Tel: 61 2646434 **Fax:** 61 2646433
Email: redaktion@bibo.ch **Web site:** http://www.bibo.ch
Freq: Weekly; **Cover Price:** Free; **Circ:** 22,034
Editor: Georges Küng
Profile: Advertising journal (house-to-house) concentrating on local stories.
Language(s): German
ADVERTISING RATES:
Full Page Mono .... CHF 3520
Full Page Colour .... CHF 4884
Mechanical Data: Type Area: 440 x 288 mm, No. of Columns (Display): 10, Col Widths (Display): 27 mm
Copy instructions: *Copy Date:* 2 days prior to publication
LOCAL NEWSPAPERS

BIEL BIENNE 722829S72-1700
Editorial: Neuenburgstr. 140, 2501 BIEL
Tel: 32 3270911 **Fax:** 32 3270912
Email: news@bielbienne.com **Web site:** http://www.bielbienne.com
Freq: Weekly; **Cover Price:** Free; **Circ:** 107,834
Editor: M. Cortesi
Profile: Advertising journal (house-to-house) concentrating on local stories.
Language(s): French; German
ADVERTISING RATES:
Full Page Mono .... CHF 8619
Full Page Colour .... CHF 11579
Mechanical Data: Type Area: 442 x 290 mm, No. of Columns (Display): 10, Col Widths (Display): 25 mm
Copy instructions: *Copy Date:* 1 day prior to publication
LOCAL NEWSPAPERS

BIELER TAGBLATT 722837S67B-540
Editorial: Robert-Walser-Platz 7, 2501 BIEL
Tel: 32 3219111 **Fax:** 32 3219119
Email: btredaktion@bielertagblatt.ch **Web site:** http://www.bielertagblatt.ch
Freq: 312 issues yearly; **Annual Sub.:** CHF 366,00; **Circ:** 25,907
Editor: Catherine Duttweiler; **News Editor:** Erich Goetschi
Profile: Regional daily newspaper covering politics, economics, sport, travel, technology and the arts.
Language(s): German
ADVERTISING RATES:
SCC .... CHF 60,80
Mechanical Data: Type Area: 440 x 290 mm, No. of Columns (Display): 10, Col Widths (Display): 26 mm
Copy instructions: *Copy Date:* 1 day prior to publication
REGIONAL DAILY & SUNDAY NEWSPAPERS: Regional Daily Newspapers

BILAN 766448S14A-1134
Editorial: 11, rue des Rois, 1204 GENF
Tel: 22 3223636 **Fax:** 22 3223450
Email: bilan@bilan.ch **Web site:** http://www.bilan.ch
Freq: 22 issues yearly; **Annual Sub.:** CHF 119,00; **Circ:** 25,000
Editor: Stéphane Benoit-Godet
Profile: Industry and commerce magazine for West Switzerland.
Language(s): French
ADVERTISING RATES:
Full Page Mono .... CHF 10250
Full Page Colour .... CHF 10250
Mechanical Data: Type Area: 253 x 187 mm, No. of Columns (Display): 3, Col Widths (Display): 72 mm
Copy instructions: *Copy Date:* 13 days prior to publication
BUSINESS: COMMERCE, INDUSTRY & MANAGEMENT

BILANZ 762604S14A-1083
Editorial: Förrlibuckstr. 70, 8021 ZÜRICH
Tel: 43 4445520 **Fax:** 43 4445521
Email: redaktion@bilanz.ch **Web site:** http://www.bilanz.ch
Freq: 23 issues yearly; **Annual Sub.:** CHF 178,00; **Circ:** 50,000
Editor: Dirk Schütz; **Advertising Manager:** Sandra Bruderer
Profile: Industry and commerce magazine for managers.
Language(s): German
ADVERTISING RATES:
Full Page Mono .... CHF 16400
Full Page Colour .... CHF 16400
Mechanical Data: Type Area: 240 x 179 mm, No. of Columns (Display): 4, Col Widths (Display): 42 mm
Copy instructions: *Copy Date:* 21 days prior to publication
Supplement(s): Bilanz Invest; First. by Bilanz; FirstClass; Home Electronic Extra; Vorsorge

BILANZ 762604S14A-1346
Editorial: Förrlibuckstr. 70, 8021 ZÜRICH
Tel: 43 4445520 **Fax:** 43 4445521
Email: redaktion@bilanz.ch **Web site:** http://www.bilanz.ch
Freq: 23 issues yearly; **Annual Sub.:** CHF 178,00; **Circ:** 50,000
Editor: Dirk Schütz; **Advertising Manager:** Sandra Bruderer
Profile: Industry and commerce magazine for managers.
Language(s): German
ADVERTISING RATES:
Full Page Mono .... CHF 16400
Full Page Colour .... CHF 16400
Mechanical Data: Type Area: 240 x 179 mm, No. of Columns (Display): 4, Col Widths (Display): 42 mm
Copy instructions: *Copy Date:* 21 days prior to publication
Supplement(s): Bilanz Invest; First. by Bilanz; FirstClass; Home Electronic Extra; Vorsorge

BINNINGER ANZEIGER
1656720S72-9712
Editorial: Kirchweg 10, 4102 BINNINGEN
Tel: 61 4212580 **Fax:** 61 4215636
Email: redaktion@binningeranzeiger.ch **Web site:** http://www.binningeranzeiger.ch
Freq: Weekly; **Cover Price:** Free; **Circ:** 8,092
Editor: Rudolf Schweighauser
Profile: Advertising journal (house-to-house) concentrating on local stories.
Language(s): German
Mechanical Data: Type Area: 440 x 290 mm, No. of Columns (Display): 10, Col Widths (Display): 27 mm
Copy instructions: *Copy Date:* 3 days prior to publication
LOCAL NEWSPAPERS

BIO ACTUALITÉS 1850650S21A-614
Editorial: Ackerstr., 5070 FRICK **Tel:** 62 8657272
Fax: 62 8657273
Email: bioactualites@fibl.org **Web site:** http://www.fibl.org
Freq: 10 issues yearly; **Annual Sub.:** CHF 49,00; **Circ:** 615
Profile: Magazine from the Swiss Research Institute for Biological Agriculture.
Language(s): French
ADVERTISING RATES:
Full Page Mono .... CHF 557
Full Page Colour .... CHF 1224
Mechanical Data: Type Area: 270 x 186 mm
Copy instructions: *Copy Date:* 30 days prior to publication

BIO AKTUELL 1850653S21A-615
Editorial: Margarethenstr. 87, 4053 BASEL
Tel: 61 3850910 **Fax:** 61 3850911
Email: stephan.jaun@bio-suisse.de **Web site:** http://www.bioaktuell.ch
Freq: 10 issues yearly; **Annual Sub.:** CHF 49,00; **Circ:** 7,058
Editor: Stephan Jaun
Profile: Magazine about biological cultivation and agricultural policy.
Language(s): German
ADVERTISING RATES:
Full Page Mono .... CHF 1781
Full Page Colour .... CHF 3148
Mechanical Data: Type Area: 270 x 186 mm
Copy instructions: *Copy Date:* 30 days prior to publication

BIRSFELDER ANZEIGER
722990S72-1740
Editorial: Missionsstr. 36, 4012 BASEL
Tel: 61 2646450 **Fax:** 61 2646488
Email: redaktion@birsfelderanzeiger.ch **Web site:** http://www.reinhardt.ch
Freq: 11 issues yearly; **Cover Price:** Free; **Circ:** 13,015
Editor: Hanspeter Wipfli
Profile: Advertising journal (house-to-house) concentrating on local stories.
Language(s): German
ADVERTISING RATES:
Full Page Mono .... CHF 1685
Full Page Colour .... CHF 2680
Mechanical Data: Type Area: 290 x 203 mm, No. of Columns (Display): 7, Col Widths (Display): 27 mm
Copy instructions: *Copy Date:* 3 days prior to publication
LOCAL NEWSPAPERS

BLÄTTER FÜR ZÜRCHERISCHE RECHTSPRECHUNG 1641026S1A-277
Editorial: Zwinglipplatz 2, 8022 ZÜRICH
Tel: 44 2002999 **Fax:** 44 2002908
Email: schulthess@schulthess.com **Web site:** http://www.schulthess.com
Freq: 10 issues yearly; **Annual Sub.:** CHF 155,00; **Circ:** 1,650
Editor: Johann Zürcher
Profile: Juristical magazine informs about Zurich jurisdiction, contains judgements, decisions and court orders.
Language(s): German
ADVERTISING RATES:
Full Page Mono .... CHF 740
Full Page Colour .... CHF 740
Mechanical Data: Type Area: 190 x 130 mm
Copy instructions: *Copy Date:* 20 days prior to publication
Official Journal of: Judikaturorgan d. Kantons Zürich
BUSINESS: FINANCE & ECONOMICS

BLICK 723117S67B-600
Editorial: Dufourstr. 23, 8008 ZÜRICH
Tel: 44 2596262 **Fax:** 44 2596665
Email: redaktion@blick.ch **Web site:** http://www.blick.ch
Freq: 312 issues yearly; **Annual Sub.:** CHF 323,00; **Circ:** 240,066
Editor: Marc Walder; **News Editor:** Andrea Bleicher
Profile: Tabloid-sized newspaper covering regional, national and international news and sport. Facebook:

http://www.facebook.com/blick.ch This Outlet offers RSS (Really Simple Syndication).
Language(s): German
Readership: Read by office staff and factory workers.
Mechanical Data: Type Area: 290 x 204 mm, No. of Columns (Display): 3, Col Widths (Display): 67 mm
Copy instructions: *Copy Date:* 2 days prior to publication
Supplement(s): Reise Blick
REGIONAL DAILY & SUNDAY NEWSPAPERS: Regional Daily Newspapers

BODENSEE NACHRICHTEN
723325S72-1820
Editorial: Am Marktplatz 4, 9400 RORSCHACH
Tel: 71 8442365 **Fax:** 71 8442351
Email: redaktion@bodensee-nachrichten.ch **Web site:** http://www.bodensee-nachrichten.ch
Freq: Weekly; **Cover Price:** Free; **Circ:** 21,798
Editor: Flavio Razzino
Profile: Advertising journal (house-to-house) concentrating on local stories.
Language(s): German
ADVERTISING RATES:
Full Page Mono .... CHF 3600
Full Page Colour .... CHF 4200
Mechanical Data: Type Area: 440 x 286 mm, No. of Columns (Display): 10, Col Widths (Display): 25 mm
Copy instructions: *Copy Date:* 1 day prior to publication
LOCAL NEWSPAPERS

BOLERO
723364S74A-140
Editorial: Giesshübelstr. 62i, 8045 ZÜRICH
Tel: 44 4548282 **Fax:** 44 4548272
Email: service@boleroweb.ch **Web site:** http://www.boleroweb.ch
Freq: 10 issues yearly; **Annual Sub.:** CHF 110,00; **Circ:** 20,119
Editor: Sithara Atasoy
Profile: Magazine specialising in fashion and lifestyle.
Language(s): German
Readership: Read by urban women aged 25 to 50 years with a high disposable income.
ADVERTISING RATES:
Full Page Mono .... CHF 10570
Full Page Colour .... CHF 10570
Mechanical Data: Type Area: 249 x 185 mm, No. of Columns (Display): 4, Col Widths (Display): 39 mm
Copy instructions: *Copy Date:* 26 days prior to publication
Supplement(s): Rocks & Stones
CONSUMER: WOMEN'S INTEREST CONSUMER MAGAZINES: Women's Interest

BON À SAVOIR
1640956S74C-534
Editorial: 2, av. de la Rasude, 1001 LAUSANNE
Tel: 21 3100136 **Fax:** 21 3100139
Email: christian.chevrolet@bonasavoir.ch **Web site:** http://www.bonasavoir.ch
Freq: 11 issues yearly; **Annual Sub.:** CHF 29,00; **Circ:** 96,145
Editor: Christian Chevrolet
Profile: Consumers' guide.
Language(s): French
ADVERTISING RATES:
Full Page Mono .... CHF 10600
Full Page Colour .... CHF 10600
Mechanical Data: Type Area: 255 x 187 mm
CONSUMER: WOMEN'S INTEREST CONSUMER MAGAZINES: Home & Family

LA BORSA DELLA SPESA
1648545S74M-268
Editorial: c.p. 165, 6932 BREGANZONA
Tel: 91 9229755 **Fax:** 91 9220471
Email: acsi@acsi.ch **Web site:** http://www.acsi.ch
Freq: 8 issues yearly; Free to qualifying individuals
Annual Sub.: CHF 40,00; **Circ:** 9,500
Editor: Laura Bottani-Villa
Profile: Shopping guide.
Language(s): Italian
CONSUMER: WOMEN'S INTEREST CONSUMER MAGAZINES: Personal Finance

BOTE DER URSCHWEIZ
723434S67B-640
Editorial: Schmiedgasse 7, 6431 SCHWYZ
Tel: 41 8190811 **Fax:** 41 8117037
Email: reda@bote.ch **Web site:** http://www.bote.ch
Freq: 312 issues yearly; **Annual Sub.:** CHF 282,00; **Circ:** 15,136
Editor: Josias Clavadetscher; **Advertising Manager:** Christof Steiner
Profile: Regional daily newspaper covering politics, economics, sport, travel, technology and the arts.
Language(s): German
ADVERTISING RATES:
SCC .... CHF 36,00
Mechanical Data: Type Area: 440 x 286 mm, No. of Columns (Display): 10, Col Widths (Display): 25 mm
Copy instructions: *Copy Date:* 1 day prior to publication
REGIONAL DAILY & SUNDAY NEWSPAPERS: Regional Daily Newspapers

BOTE VOM UNTERSEE UND RHEIN
723442S67B-6624
Editorial: Seestr. 118, 8266 STECKBORN
Tel: 52 7620222 **Fax:** 52 7620223
Email: info@druckerei-steckborn.ch **Web site:** http://www.druckerei-steckborn.ch
Freq: 104 issues yearly; **Annual Sub.:** CHF 95,00; **Circ:** 5,000
Editor: Martin Keller
Profile: Regional daily newspaper covering politics, economics, sport, travel, technology and the arts.
Language(s): German
ADVERTISING RATES:
SCC .... CHF 26,60
Mechanical Data: Type Area: 435 x 280 mm, No. of Columns (Display): 6, Col Widths (Display): 42 mm
Copy instructions: *Copy Date:* 1 day prior to publication
REGIONAL DAILY & SUNDAY NEWSPAPERS: Regional Daily Newspapers

DIE BOTSCHAFT
723448S67B-680
Editorial: Hauptstr. 19, 5312 DÖTTINGEN
Tel: 56 2692525 **Fax:** 56 2692520
Email: redaktion@botschaft.ch **Web site:** http://www.botschaft.ch
Freq: 156 issues yearly; **Annual Sub.:** CHF 170,00; **Circ:** 9,416
Editor: Thomas Bürli
Profile: Regional daily newspaper covering politics, economics, sport, travel, technology and the arts.
Language(s): German
ADVERTISING RATES:
SCC .... CHF 16,50
Mechanical Data: Type Area: 442 x 289 mm, No. of Columns (Display): 10, Col Widths (Display): 27 mm
Copy instructions: *Copy Date:* 1 day prior to publication
REGIONAL DAILY & SUNDAY NEWSPAPERS: Regional Daily Newspapers

BRIGITTE
1848159S74A-501
Editorial: Zeltweg 15, 8032 ZÜRICH **Tel:** 44 2697070
Fax: 44 2697071
Email: guj.schweiz@guj.de **Web site:** http://www.guj.de
Freq: 26 issues yearly; **Cover Price:** CHF 4,70; **Circ:** 30,000
Editor: Monika Widler
Profile: Magazine for women. German edition inclusives four pages for switzerland, editorial staff in Germany Twitter: http://twitter.com/brigitteonline.
Language(s): German
ADVERTISING RATES:
Full Page Mono .... CHF 9600
Full Page Colour .... CHF 9600
Mechanical Data: Type Area: 231 x 185 mm, No. of Columns (Display): 4
Copy instructions: *Copy Date:* 23 days prior to publication

LA BROYE
1753834S72-9872
Editorial: 19, rue d'Yverdon, 1530 PAYERNE
Tel: 26 6624888 **Fax:** 26 6624899
Email: labroye@edipresse.ch **Web site:** http://www.labroye.ch
Freq: Weekly; **Annual Sub.:** CHF 68,00; **Circ:** 9,100
Editor: Danièle Pittet
Language(s): French
ADVERTISING RATES:
SCC .... CHF 19,60
Mechanical Data: Type Area: 440 x 290 mm, No. of Columns (Display): 10, Col Widths (Display): 26 mm
Copy instructions: *Copy Date:* 1 day prior to publication
LOCAL NEWSPAPERS

BÜLACHER INDUSTRIEN NACHRICHTEN
1843194S35-77
Editorial: Industriestrasse 3, 8610 USTER
Tel: 43 2660404 **Fax:** 43 2660405
Email: info@volltext.ch **Web site:** http://www.buelacher-industrien.ch
Freq: Quarterly; **Circ:** 20,000
Editor: Joachim Lienert
Profile: Information about the company cooperation Arbeitsgemeinschaft Bülacher Industrien.
Language(s): German

BULLETIN
1659062S58-192
Editorial: Luppmenstr. 1, 8320 FEHRALTORF
Tel: 44 9561111 **Fax:** 44 9561511
Email: bulletin@electrosuisse.ch **Web site:** http://www.electrosuisse.ch
Freq: 16 issues yearly; Free to qualifying individuals
Annual Sub.: CHF 205,00; **Circ:** 6,900
Editor: Christian Keller
Profile: Magazine of the Swiss Electro Technical Association.
Language(s): French; German
ADVERTISING RATES:
Full Page Mono .... CHF 3232
Full Page Colour .... CHF 4807
Mechanical Data: Type Area: 252 x 176 mm, No. of Columns (Display): 3, Col Widths (Display): 72 mm
Copy instructions: *Copy Date:* 14 days prior to publication
BUSINESS: ENERGY, FUEL & NUCLEAR

BULLETIN
1853317S74A-510
Editorial: Am Schanzengraben 29, 8002 ZÜRICH
Tel: 44 2063020 **Fax:** 44 2063021
Email: zh@frauenzentrale.ch **Web site:** http://www.frauenzentrale-zh.ch
Freq: Quarterly; Free to qualifying individuals
Annual Sub.: CHF 30,00; **Circ:** 3,500
Editor: Margaritha Felchlin
Profile: Membermagazine from the Zurich Cenrte for Women.
Language(s): German

BULLETIN ASSM
1852017S56A-2168
Editorial: Petersplatz 13, 4051 BASEL
Tel: 61 2699030 **Fax:** 61 2699039
Email: mail@samw.ch **Web site:** http://www.samw.ch
Freq: Quarterly; **Circ:** 800
Profile: Information from the Swiss Academy of Medical Sciences.
Language(s): French

BULLETIN BINATIONAL
1855385S74A-513
Editorial: Postfach 3063, 8021 ZÜRICH
Tel: 79 4166722
Email: bulletin@ig-binational.ch **Web site:** http://www.ig-binational.ch
Freq: Quarterly; Free to qualifying individuals
Annual Sub.: CHF 60,00; **Circ:** 400
Profile: Magazine about marriages between people of different nationalities.
Language(s): German

BULLETIN SAMW
1852016S56A-2167
Editorial: Petersplatz 13, 4051 BASEL
Tel: 61 2699030 **Fax:** 61 2699039
Email: mail@samw.ch **Web site:** http://www.samw.ch
Freq: Quarterly; **Circ:** 2,200
Profile: Information from the Swiss Academy of Medical Sciences.
Language(s): German

BULLETIN VSS/FDS
765730S47A-98
Editorial: Hohliebi, 3150 SCHWARZENBURG
Tel: 31 7310843 **Fax:** 31 7310360
Email: madeleine.raetz@dplanet.ch
Freq: Quarterly; **Circ:** 1,100
Editor: Madeleine Rätz; **Advertising Manager:** Madeleine Rätz
Language(s): French; German
ADVERTISING RATES:
Full Page Mono .... CHF 500
Copy instructions: *Copy Date:* 45 days prior to publication
BUSINESS: CLOTHING & TEXTILES

DER BUND
723893S67B-780
Editorial: Dammweg 9, 3001 BERN **Tel:** 31 3851111
Fax: 31 3851112
Email: redaktion@derbund.ch **Web site:** http://www.ebund.ch
Freq: 312 issues yearly; **Annual Sub.:** CHF 398,00; **Circ:** 124,026
Editor: Artur K. Vogel; **Advertising Manager:** Michael Seiler
Profile: Regional daily newspaper covering politics, economics, sport, travel, technology and the arts.
Language(s): German
ADVERTISING RATES:
SCC .... CHF 158,00
Mechanical Data: Type Area: 440 x 290 mm, No. of Columns (Display): 10, Col Widths (Display): 27 mm
Copy instructions: *Copy Date:* 1 day prior to publication
Supplement(s): Das Magazin; TV täglich
REGIONAL DAILY & SUNDAY NEWSPAPERS: Regional Daily Newspapers

BÜNDNER GEWERBE
723789S14A-240
Editorial: Hinterm Bach 40, 7002 CHUR
Tel: 81 2570323 **Fax:** 81 2570324
Email: info@kgv-gr.ch **Web site:** http://www.kgv-gr.ch
Freq: Quarterly; **Circ:** 6,300
Editor: Jürg Michel
Profile: Magazine from the Business Association in Graubuenden.
Language(s): German
ADVERTISING RATES:
Full Page Mono .... CHF 1500
Full Page Colour .... CHF 1500
Mechanical Data: Type Area: 265 x 180 mm
Copy instructions: *Copy Date:* 42 days prior to publication

DIE BÜNDNER KULTURBAHN
1665310S89A-348
Editorial: Postfach 662, 7002 CHUR **Tel:** 79 6098858
Email: fredy.pfister@club1889.ch **Web site:** http://www.historic-rhb.ch
Freq: Annual; **Cover Price:** Free; **Circ:** 30,000
Editor: Fredy Pfister; **Advertising Manager:** Fredy Pfister
Profile: Railway Society magazine.
Language(s): German
ADVERTISING RATES:
Full Page Mono .... CHF 2200
Full Page Colour .... CHF 2400
Mechanical Data: Type Area: 260 x 180 mm
Copy instructions: *Copy Date:* 60 days prior to publication

BÜNDNER NACHRICHTEN
1656723S72-9715
Editorial: Ringstr. 90, 7004 CHUR **Tel:** 81 2535777
Fax: 81 2535781
Email: a.kue@bluewin.ch **Web site:** http://www.buendner-nachrichten.ch
Freq: Weekly; **Cover Price:** Free; **Circ:** 21,066
Editor: Alex Künzle
Profile: Advertising journal (house-to-house) concentrating on local stories.
Language(s): German
ADVERTISING RATES:
Full Page Mono .... CHF 6556
Full Page Colour .... CHF 6956
Mechanical Data: Type Area: 440 x 286 mm, No. of Columns (Display): 10, Col Widths (Display): 25 mm
Copy instructions: *Copy Date:* 2 days prior to publication
LOCAL NEWSPAPERS

BÜNDNER WALD
1855384S21A-621
Editorial: Unter der Linde 16, 7304 MAIENFELD
Tel: 81 3022581
Email: sandro.kraettli@afw.gr.ch **Web site:** http://www.graubuendenwald.ch
Freq: 6 issues yearly; Free to qualifying individuals
Annual Sub.: CHF 80,00; **Circ:** 1,500
Editor: Sandro Krättli
Profile: Magazine about the Graubuendener Wald.
Language(s): German
ADVERTISING RATES:
Full Page Mono .... CHF 510
Full Page Colour .... CHF 830
Mechanical Data: Type Area: 206 x 144 mm
Copy instructions: *Copy Date:* 28 days prior to publication

BUS TRANSNEWS
1855767S49A-430
Editorial: Europastr. 15, 8152 GLATTBRUGG
Tel: 58 3449002 **Fax:** 58 3449001
Email: henrik.petro@motormedia.ch **Web site:** http://www.bustransnews.ch
Freq: Quarterly; **Annual Sub.:** CHF 55,00; **Circ:** 6,000
Editor: Henrik Petro; **Advertising Manager:** Herta Kornetzky
Profile: Bus magazine.
Language(s): German
ADVERTISING RATES:
Full Page Colour .... CHF 3910
Mechanical Data: Type Area: 265 x 192 mm, No. of Columns (Display): 3, Col Widths (Display): 61 mm

BÜWO BÜNDNER WOCHE
723794S72-9587
Editorial: Comercialstr. 22, 7007 CHUR
Tel: 81 2555279 **Fax:** 81 2555101
Email: redaktion-buewo@suedostschweiz.ch
Freq: Weekly; **Cover Price:** Free; **Circ:** 42,000
Editor: Barbara Paz Soldan
Profile: Advertising journal (house-to-house) concentrating on local stories.
Language(s): German
ADVERTISING RATES:
Full Page Mono .... CHF 2182
Full Page Colour .... CHF 2840
Mechanical Data: Type Area: 286 x 199 mm, No. of Columns (Display): 7, Col Widths (Display): 25 mm
Copy instructions: *Copy Date:* 2 days prior to publication
Supplement(s): Stadt Theater Chur-Journal
LOCAL NEWSPAPERS

CAMPCAR
764259S91B-405
Editorial: Maulbeerstr. 10, 3001 BERN
Tel: 31 3805000 **Fax:** 31 3805006
Email: touring@tcs.ch
Freq: 8 issues yearly; **Circ:** 18,000
Editor: Peter Widmer
Profile: Magazine about camping and caravanning.
Language(s): French; German
ADVERTISING RATES:
Full Page Mono .... CHF 3500
Full Page Colour .... CHF 3500
Mechanical Data: No. of Columns (Display): 4, Type Area: 290 x 208 mm
Copy instructions: *Copy Date:* 20 days prior to publication
CONSUMER: RECREATION & LEISURE: Camping & Caravanning

CAMPING REVUE
1655964S91B-424
Editorial: Würhestr. 13, 5724 DÜRRENÄSCH
Tel: 62 7774008 **Fax:** 62 7774009
Email: info@camping-revue.ch **Web site:** http://www.sccv.ch
Freq: 9 issues yearly; Free to qualifying individuals
Annual Sub.: CHF 25,00; **Circ:** 5,000
Editor: Josef Willi
Profile: Magazine about camping.
Language(s): French; German; Italian

ADVERTISING RATES:
Full Page Mono .... CHF 1000
Full Page Colour .... CHF 2390
Mechanical Data: Type Area: 265 x 187 mm
Copy instructions: *Copy Date:* 35 days prior to publication
CONSUMER: RECREATION & LEISURE: Camping & Caravanning

CANTIERI & ABITARE

1752955S4E-800
Editorial: via Cantonale, 34a, 6928 MANNO
Tel: 91 6002070 **Fax:** 91 6002074
Email: info@pubblicitasacchi.ch **Web site:** http://www.pubblicitasacchi.ch
Freq: 6 issues yearly; **Annual Sub.:** CHF 65,00; **Circ:** 3,200
Editor: Fabio Sacchi
Profile: Italian language magazine for the building industry.
Language(s): Italian
ADVERTISING RATES:
Full Page Mono .... CHF 1850
Full Page Colour .... CHF 2600
Mechanical Data: Type Area: 275 x 185 mm

CARROSSIER

763016S6A-361
Editorial: via Mulinet, 10, 7138 SURCUOLM
Tel: 81 9331684
Email: carrossier@vsci.ch
Freq: 8 issues yearly; Free to qualifying individuals
Annual Sub.: CHF 60,00; **Circ:** 1,700
Editor: Heinz H. Schneider
Language(s): German
ADVERTISING RATES:
Full Page Mono .... CHF 1480
Full Page Colour .... CHF 2390
Mechanical Data: Type Area: 260 x 185 mm
Copy instructions: *Copy Date:* 24 days prior to publication
BUSINESS: AVIATION & AERONAUTICS

CCS CRUISING

1642195S89A-352
Editorial: Marktgasse 9, 3000 BERN 7
Tel: 31 3101100 **Fax:** 31 3101109
Email: info@cruisingclub.ch **Web site:** http://www.cruisingclub.ch
Freq: 10 issues yearly; **Circ:** 6,100
Editor: Horst Niedhammer
Profile: Sailing club magazine with internal information.
Language(s): French; German
ADVERTISING RATES:
Full Page Mono .... CHF 990
Full Page Colour .... CHF 990
Mechanical Data: Type Area: 258 x 184 mm
Copy instructions: *Copy Date:* 16 days prior to publication

CEO*

724195S14A-280
Editorial: Birchstr. 160, 8050 ZÜRICH
Tel: 58 7924400 **Fax:** 58 7924410
Email: alexander.fleischer@ch.pwc.com **Web site:** http://www.pwc.ch
Freq: 3 issues yearly; **Cover Price:** Free; **Circ:** 26,000
Editor: Alexander Fleischer
Profile: Company publication published by PricewaterhouseCoopers AG.
Language(s): German

CEO*

724195S14A-1272
Editorial: Birchstr. 160, 8050 ZÜRICH
Tel: 58 7924400 **Fax:** 58 7924410
Email: alexander.fleischer@ch.pwc.com **Web site:** http://www.pwc.ch
Freq: 3 issues yearly; **Cover Price:** Free; **Circ:** 26,000
Editor: Alexander Fleischer
Profile: Company publication published by PricewaterhouseCoopers AG.
Language(s): German

CFD ZEITUNG

724206S82-480
Editorial: Falkenhöheweg 8, 3001 BERN
Tel: 31 3005060 **Fax:** 31 3005069
Email: info@cfd-ch.org **Web site:** http://www.cfd-ch.org
Freq: Quarterly; **Cover Price:** Free; **Circ:** 13,000
Profile: Magazine of the Christian Peace Service.
Language(s): German
CONSUMER: CURRENT AFFAIRS & POLITICS

CH-D WIRTSCHAFT

724227S63-20
Editorial: Tödistr. 60, 8002 ZÜRICH **Tel:** 44 2836161
Fax: 44 2836100
Email: redaktion@handelskammer-d-ch.ch **Web site:** http://www.handelskammer-d-ch.ch
Freq: 11 issues yearly; **Circ:** 5,200
Editor: Ralf J. Bopp
Profile: Official journal of the German-Swiss Chamber of Commerce.
Language(s): German
Readership: Aimed at managers and decision makers.
ADVERTISING RATES:
Full Page Mono .... CHF 2100
Full Page Colour .... CHF 3450
Mechanical Data: Type Area: 262 x 180 mm, No. of Columns (Display): 3, Col Widths (Display): 57 mm
Copy instructions: *Copy Date:* 31 days prior to publication
BUSINESS: REGIONAL BUSINESS

CHIFFRES, DONNÉES, FAITS SRG SSR IDÉE SUISSE

1828624S2A-670
Editorial: Giacomettistr. 1, 3000 BERN 31
Tel: 31 3509111
Email: publishing@srg-ssr.ch **Web site:** http://www.srg-ssr.ch
Freq: Annual; **Cover Price:** Free; **Circ:** 2,500
Editor: Dominic Witschi
Profile: Publication of the SRG SSR company.
Language(s): French

CHIMIA

724277S13-40
Editorial: Freiestr. 3, 3000 BERN 9 **Tel:** 31 6314359
Fax: 31 6313426
Email: philippe.renaud@chimia.ch **Web site:** http://www.chimia.ch
Freq: 10 issues yearly; **Annual Sub.:** CHF 220,00; **Circ:** 3,500
Editor: Philippe Renaud
Profile: International journal focusing on chemistry, including scientific, industrial, technical, ecological, social, political and economic aspects.
Language(s): English; French; German
ADVERTISING RATES:
Full Page Mono .... CHF 2150
Full Page Colour .... CHF 3740
Mechanical Data: Type Area: 270 x 190 mm, No. of Columns (Display): 4, Col Widths (Display): 45 mm
Copy instructions: *Copy Date:* 24 days prior to publication
BUSINESS: CHEMICALS

CHOISIR

1753164S87-2934
Editorial: 18, rue Jacques-Dalphin, 1227 CAROUGE
Tel: 22 8274675 **Fax:** 22 8274670
Email: redaction@choisir.ch **Web site:** http://www.choisir.ch
Freq: 11 issues yearly; **Annual Sub.:** CHF 95,00; **Circ:** 2,000
Editor: Lucienne Bittar; **Advertising Manager:** Jacqueline Huppi
Profile: Cultural magazine.
Language(s): French
ADVERTISING RATES:
Full Page Mono .... CHF 500
Full Page Colour .... CHF 500
Mechanical Data: Type Area: 205 x 145 mm, No. of Columns (Display): 2, Col Widths (Display): 55 mm
Copy instructions: *Copy Date:* 30 days prior to publication
CONSUMER: RELIGIOUS

CHRISCHONA PANORAMA

724307S87-380
Editorial: Chrischonarain 200, 4126 BETTINGEN
Tel: 61 6464557 **Fax:** 61 6464277
Email: medienstelle@chrischona.ch **Web site:** http://www.panorama.chrischona.org
Freq: 8 issues yearly; **Annual Sub.:** CHF 20,00; **Circ:** 12,200
Editor: Michael Gross; **Advertising Manager:** Wolfgang Binninger
Profile: Magazine of the Pilgrim Mission of St. Chrischona.
Language(s): German
Mechanical Data: Type Area: 270 x 184 mm, No. of Columns (Display): 3, Col Widths (Display): 58 mm
CONSUMER: RELIGIOUS

CIGAR

1853598S74P-296
Editorial: Stampfenbachstr. 117, 8042 ZÜRICH
Tel: 44 3602087 **Fax:** 44 3602089
Email: info@cigar.ch **Web site:** http://www.cigar.ch
Freq: Quarterly; **Annual Sub.:** CHF 39,00; **Circ:** 9,890
Editor: Tobias Hüberli; **Advertising Manager:** Stefan Schramm
Profile: Magazine promoting the sale of tobacco products. Available in hotels, restaurants and tobacconists.
Language(s): German
ADVERTISING RATES:
Full Page Mono .... CHF 6900
Full Page Colour .... CHF 6900
Mechanical Data: Type Area: 266 x 177 mm, No. of Columns (Display): 3, Col Widths (Display): 55 mm
Copy instructions: *Copy Date:* 30 days prior to publication

THE CLIPPER

767538S14C-224
Editorial: Baselstr. 48, 4125 RIEHEN **Tel:** 61 3869090
Fax: 61 3869099
Email: edit@agropress.com **Web site:** http://www.agropress.com
Freq: Quarterly; **Annual Sub.:** CHF 140,00; **Circ:** 3,000
Editor: G. H. Breuer; **Advertising Manager:** G. H. Breuer
Profile: Journal for production and trade of dried fruit and nuts worldwide.
Language(s): English; French; German; Spanish
Mechanical Data: Type Area: 263 x 184 mm

THE CLIPPER

767538S14C-236
Editorial: Baselstr. 48, 4125 RIEHEN **Tel:** 61 3869090
Fax: 61 3869099
Email: edit@agropress.com **Web site:** http://www.agropress.com
Freq: Quarterly; **Annual Sub.:** CHF 140,00; **Circ:** 3,000
Editor: G. H. Breuer; **Advertising Manager:** G. H. Breuer
Profile: Journal for production and trade of dried fruit and nuts worldwide.
Language(s): English; French; German; Spanish
Mechanical Data: Type Area: 263 x 184 mm

CLUBNACHRICHTEN SAC SEKTION BERN

724454S75L-40
Editorial: Postfach, 3000 BERN 7 **Tel:** 31 3010728
Email: redaktion-cn@sac-bern.ch **Web site:** http://www.sac-bern.ch
Freq: 6 issues yearly; **Circ:** 4,500
Editor: Ueli Seemann
Profile: Magazine of the Swiss Alpine Club, section Bern.
Language(s): German
ADVERTISING RATES:
Full Page Mono .... CHF 430
Mechanical Data: Type Area: 178 x 125 mm
CONSUMER: SPORT: Outdoor

CLUBZEITUNG

1664558S77A-114
Editorial: Föhrenweg 2, 8605 VOLKETSWIL
Tel: 44 9453430 **Fax:** 44 9453422
Email: ulrich.buehlmann@axept.ch **Web site:** http://www.borgward-ig.ch
Freq: Half-yearly; Free to qualifying individuals
Annual Sub.: CHF 15,00; **Circ:** 130
Editor: Ulrich Bühlmann
Profile: Information from Swiss Borgward car fans.
Language(s): German

COCKPIT

724472S6A-40
Editorial: Flughafen Bern, 3123 BELP
Tel: 31 9602249 **Fax:** 31 9602229
Email: info@redaktion-cockpit.com **Web site:** http://www.cockpit.aero
Freq: Monthly; **Annual Sub.:** CHF 87,00; **Circ:** 4,491
Editor: Max Ungricht; **Advertising Manager:** Beat Moser
Profile: Magazine covering aviation and space technology, the history of civilian and military aviation and news about airports and airlines.
Language(s): German
ADVERTISING RATES:
Full Page Mono .... CHF 1660
Full Page Colour .... CHF 2480
Mechanical Data: Type Area: 264 x 184 mm, No. of Columns (Display): 2, Col Widths (Display): 90 mm
Copy instructions: *Copy Date:* 20 days prior to publication
Official Journal of: Organ d. Swiss Helicopter Association u. d. AOPA Schweiz
BUSINESS: AVIATION & AERONAUTICS

COLLAGE

2002649S4E-856
Editorial: Vadianstr. 37, 9001 ST. GALLEN
Tel: 71 2225252 **Fax:** 71 2222609
Email: redaktion-collage@f-s-u.ch **Web site:** http://www.f-s-u.ch
Freq: 6 issues yearly; Free to qualifying individuals
Annual Sub.: CHF 85,00; **Circ:** 1,250
Profile: Magazine on planning, environment and town planning.
Language(s): French; German
ADVERTISING RATES:
Full Page Mono .... CHF 1190
Full Page Colour .... CHF 1190
Mechanical Data: Type Area: 271 x 176 mm
Official Journal of: Organ d. Kantonsplanerkonferenz

COMPUTER SPECTRUM

724558S5B-10
Editorial: Aarestr. 83, 5222 UMIKEN **Tel:** 56 4410043
Fax: 56 4414854
Email: editor@dplanet.ch **Web site:** http://www.computerspectrum.ch
Freq: Quarterly
Editor: Oskar Baldinger; **Advertising Manager:** Silvia Baumann
Profile: Magazine providing information on computer hard- and software, electronics, robotics, telecommunications, automation and logistics, networks and the Internet. Also covers ERP, CAD, measurement and control, electronics, digital photography and multimedia.
Language(s): German
ADVERTISING RATES:
Full Page Colour .... CHF 2400
BUSINESS: COMPUTERS & AUTOMATION: Data Processing

COMPUTERWORLD

765191S5-165
Editorial: Witikoner Str. 15, 8032 ZÜRICH
Tel: 44 3874444 **Fax:** 44 3874580
Email: hansjoerg.honegger@idg.ch **Web site:** http://www.computerworld.ch
Freq: 22 issues yearly; **Annual Sub.:** CHF 135,00; **Circ:** 10,000
Editor: Hansjörg Honegger
Profile: Magazine about informatics.
Language(s): German
ADVERTISING RATES:
Full Page Mono .... CHF 12450
Full Page Colour .... CHF 12450
Mechanical Data: Type Area: 276 x 184 mm, No. of Columns (Display): 4, Col Widths (Display): 42 mm
Copy instructions: *Copy Date:* 8 days prior to publication
BUSINESS: COMPUTERS & AUTOMATION

COMTEXTE

1927536S18B-398
Editorial: Looslistr. 15, 3027 BERN **Tel:** 31 9395226
Fax: 31 9395262
Email: redcom@syndicom.ch **Web site:** http://www.gewerkschaftkom.ch
Freq: 20 issues yearly; Free to qualifying individuals
Annual Sub.: CHF 45,00; **Circ:** 12,015
Editor: Gabriele Brodrecht; **Advertising Manager:** Beat Stettler
Profile: Magazine on communication.
Language(s): French; Italian
ADVERTISING RATES:
Full Page Mono .... CHF 3200
Full Page Colour .... CHF 3200
Mechanical Data: Type Area: 440 x 290 mm, No. of Columns (Display): 5, Col Widths (Display): 55 mm

CONNECT

1646204S19E-186
Editorial: Brown-Boveri-Str. 6, 5400 BADEN
Web site: http://www.abb.ch
Cover Price: Free; **Circ:** 39,000
Editor: Felix Fischer
Profile: Company publication published by ABB Schweiz.
Language(s): German

CONNECT

1674135S19E-192
Editorial: Brown-Boveri-Str. 6, 5400 BADEN
Web site: http://www.abb.ch
Cover Price: Free; **Circ:** 44,250
Editor: Felix Fischer
Profile: Company publication published by ABB Schweiz.
Language(s): French

CONTEXT

1855392S14A-1294
Editorial: Hans-Huber-Str. 4, 8002 ZÜRICH
Tel: 44 28345433
Email: context@kvschweiz.ch **Web site:** http://www.kvschweiz.ch
Freq: 11 issues yearly; Free to qualifying individuals
Annual Sub.: CHF 48,00; **Circ:** 50,470
Profile: Magazine of the Swiss Association of Merchants.
Language(s): German
ADVERTISING RATES:
Full Page Mono .... CHF 5950
Full Page Colour .... CHF 5950
Mechanical Data: Type Area: 269 x 188 mm, No. of Columns (Display): 3, Col Widths (Display): 65 mm
Copy instructions: *Copy Date:* 14 days prior to publication

COOP COOPZEITUNG

724644S94H-200
Editorial: St.-Jakobs-Str. 175, 4053 BASEL
Tel: 848 400044 **Fax:** 61 3367072
Email: coopzeitung@coop.ch **Web site:** http://www.coopzeitung.ch
Freq: Weekly; **Cover Price:** Free; **Circ:** 1,806,370
Editor: Matthias Zehnder; **Advertising Manager:** Tatjana Minzlaff
Profile: Information magazine of the Swiss Co-operative Society, with reports, enquiries, co-op news, items of general interest and articles about tourism.
Language(s): German
ADVERTISING RATES:
Full Page Mono .... CHF 20576
Full Page Colour .... CHF 34876
Mechanical Data: Type Area: 290 x 205 mm, No. of Columns (Display): 4, Col Widths (Display): 48 mm
Copy instructions: *Copy Date:* 10 days prior to publication
CONSUMER: OTHER CLASSIFICATIONS: Customer Magazines

COTE MAGAZINE

2080173S74A-531
Editorial: 37, rue Eugène Marziano, 1227 GENF
Tel: 22 7365656 **Fax:** 22 7363738
Email: redaction@cote-magazine.ch **Web site:** http://www.cotemagazine.com
Freq: 8 issues yearly; **Annual Sub.:** CHF 52,00; **Circ:** 22,522
Editor: Olivier Cerdan
Profile: Lifestylemagazine.
Language(s): French
ADVERTISING RATES:
Full Page Mono .... CHF 6150
Full Page Colour .... CHF 6150
Mechanical Data: Type Area: 270 x 210 mm

COURRIER DU MÉDECIN VAUDOIS
1853184S56A-2182
Editorial: 1, ch.de Mornex, 1002 LAUSANNE
Tel: 21 6510505 **Fax:** 21 6510500
Email: info@svmed.ch **Web site:** http://www.svmed.ch
Freq: 8 issues yearly; Free to qualifying individuals
Annual Sub.: CHF 50,00; **Circ:** 4,000
Editor: Pierre-André Repond
Profile: Magazine on health care and health care politics.
Language(s): French
ADVERTISING RATES:
Full Page Mono .... CHF 2364
Full Page Colour .... CHF 3315
Mechanical Data: Type Area: 275 x 185 mm
Copy instructions: *Copy Date:* 21 days prior to publication
Supplement(s): Guide des soins palliatifs du médecin vaudois

CR CHEMISCHE RUNDSCHAU
1638101S13-146
Editorial: Neumattstr. 1, 5001 AARAU
Tel: 58 2005688 **Fax:** 58 2005661
Email: redaktion@chemische-rundschau.ch **Web site:** http://www.chemische-rundschau.ch
Freq: 10 issues yearly; **Annual Sub.:** CHF 98,00; **Circ:** 12,000
Editor: Ralf Mayer
Profile: Magazine about chemistry, food technology, pharmacy and biotechnology.
Language(s): German
ADVERTISING RATES:
Full Page Mono .... CHF 3046
Full Page Colour .... CHF 4264
Mechanical Data: Type Area: 260 x 183 mm, No. of Columns (Display): 3, Col Widths (Display): 58 mm
Copy instructions: *Copy Date:* 24 days prior to publication
BUSINESS: CHEMICALS

CRATSCHLA
1859738S57-730
Editorial: Chastè Planta-Wildenberg, 7530 ZERNEZ
Tel: 81 8514111 **Fax:** 81 8514112
Email: lozza@nationalpark.ch **Web site:** http://www.nationalpark.ch
Freq: Half-yearly; **Annual Sub.:** CHF 24,00; **Circ:** 5,000
Editor: Hans Lozza
Profile: Magazine of the Foundation Schweitzer Nationalpark.
Language(s): German

CRB BULLETIN.
1790187S4E-811
Editorial: Steinstr. 21, 8036 ZÜRICH **Tel:** 44 4564520
Fax: 44 4564566
Email: info@crb.ch **Web site:** http://www.crb.ch
Freq: Quarterly; **Circ:** 7,000
Editor: Daniela Enz
Profile: Magazine for the building industry.
Language(s): French; German
Mechanical Data: Type Area: 260 x 183 mm
Copy instructions: *Copy Date:* 42 days prior to publication

CRYPTO MAGAZINE
1844894S18B-377
Editorial: Postfach 460, 6301 ZUG **Tel:** 41 7497781
Fax: 41 7412272
Email: gabriela.hofmann@crypto.ch **Web site:** http://www.crypto.ch
Freq: 3 issues yearly; **Circ:** 6,000
Editor: Gabriela Hofmann
Profile: Customer magazine from the Crypto AG about the the development and production of information security systems for civilian and military authorities worldwide.
Language(s): German

CRYPTO MAGAZINE
1844895S18B-378
Editorial: Postfach 460, 6301 ZUG **Tel:** 41 7497781
Fax: 41 7412272
Email: gabriela.hofmann@crypto.ch **Web site:** http://www.crypto.ch
Freq: 3 issues yearly; **Circ:** 6,000
Editor: Gabriela Hofmann
Profile: Customer magazine from the Crypto AG about the the development and production of information security systems for civilian and military authorities worldwide.
Language(s): English

CRYPTO MAGAZINE
1844896S18B-379
Editorial: Postfach 460, 6301 ZUG **Tel:** 41 7497781
Fax: 41 7412272
Email: gabriela.hofmann@crypto.ch **Web site:** http://www.crypto.ch
Freq: 3 issues yearly; **Circ:** 6,000
Editor: Gabriela Hofmann
Profile: Customer magazine from the Crypto AG about the the development and production of information security systems for civilian and military authorities worldwide.
Language(s): French

CRYPTO MAGAZINE
1844897S18B-380
Editorial: Postfach 460, 6301 ZUG **Tel:** 41 7497781
Fax: 41 7412272
Email: gabriela.hofmann@crypto.ch **Web site:** http://www.crypto.ch
Freq: 3 issues yearly; **Circ:** 6,000
Editor: Gabriela Hofmann
Profile: Customer magazine from the Crypto AG about the the development and production of information security systems for civilian and military authorities worldwide.
Language(s): Spanish

CRYPTO MAGAZINE
1844898S18B-381
Editorial: Postfach 460, 6301 ZUG **Tel:** 41 7497781
Fax: 41 7412272
Email: gabriela.hofmann@crypto.ch **Web site:** http://www.crypto.ch
Freq: 3 issues yearly; **Circ:** 6,000
Editor: Gabriela Hofmann
Profile: Customer magazine from the Crypto AG about the the development and production of information security systems for civilian and military authorities worldwide.
Language(s): Arabic

CURAVIVA
1614239S56R-458
Editorial: Zieglerstr. 53, 3000 BERN 14
Tel: 31 3853370 **Fax:** 31 3853334
Email: b.leuenberger@curaviva.ch **Web site:** http://www.curaviva.ch
Freq: 11 issues yearly; **Annual Sub.:** CHF 125,00; **Circ:** 4,000
Editor: Beat Leuenberger
Profile: Magazine for employees in care professions.
Language(s): German
ADVERTISING RATES:
Full Page Mono .... CHF 2064
Full Page Colour .... CHF 3440
Mechanical Data: Type Area: 270 x 180 mm
Copy instructions: *Copy Date:* 20 days prior to publication
BUSINESS: HEALTH & MEDICAL: Health Medical Related

D IMPULS MAGAZIN
1703513S94H-1439
Editorial: Lagerplatz 10, 8400 WINTERTHUR
Tel: 52 2692770 **Fax:** 52 2692777
Email: werbung@impuls-service.ch **Web site:** http://www.impulsdrogerie.ch
Freq: 8 issues yearly; **Cover Price:** Free; **Circ:** 109,804
Editor: Peter Binggeli; **Advertising Manager:** Franziska Peter
Language(s): German
ADVERTISING RATES:
Full Page Mono .... CHF 8800
Full Page Colour .... CHF 8800
Mechanical Data: No. of Columns (Display): 2, Col Widths (Display): 66 mm, Type Area: 230 x 175 mm
Copy instructions: *Copy Date:* 56 days prior to publication
CONSUMER: OTHER CLASSIFICATIONS: Customer Magazines

DIAGONAL
723716S32A-80
Editorial: Postgasse 60, 3000 BERN 8
Tel: 31 3111166 **Fax:** 31 3111118
Email: sekretariat@bspv.ch **Web site:** http://www.bspv.ch
Freq: 6 issues yearly; **Circ:** 6,800
Editor: Matthias Burkhalter
Profile: Publication covering academic and official news items.
Language(s): French; German
Readership: Aimed at administrators in the canton of Bern.
ADVERTISING RATES:
Full Page Mono .... CHF 1760
Full Page Colour .... CHF 1760
Mechanical Data: Type Area: 264 x 187 mm
Copy instructions: *Copy Date:* 28 days prior to publication
BUSINESS: LOCAL GOVERNMENT, LEISURE & RECREATION: Local Government

DIALOGUE
766585S87-2754
Editorial: Laupenstr. 5, 3001 BERN **Tel:** 31 3880542
Fax: 31 3880596
Email: redaction@swi.salvationarmy.org **Web site:** http://www.armeedusalut.ch
Freq: Monthly; **Annual Sub.:** CHF 46,00; **Circ:** 2,000
Editor: Martin Künzi
Profile: Christian magazine.
Language(s): French
CONSUMER: RELIGIOUS

DIMENSIONS
724953S56D-41
Editorial: Kleinriehenstr. 66, 4058 BASEL
Tel: 61 6832796 **Fax:** 61 6832797
Email: verenakoch@bluewin.ch
Freq: 6 issues yearly; Free to qualifying individuals
Annual Sub.: CHF 85,00; **Circ:** 2,006
Editor: Verena Koch
Profile: Magazine about all aspects of dentistry and dental hygiene.
Language(s): French; German
ADVERTISING RATES:
Full Page Mono .... CHF 1050
Full Page Colour .... CHF 2490
Mechanical Data: Type Area: 260 x 174 mm, Col Widths (Display): 62 mm
BUSINESS: HEALTH & MEDICAL: Dental

DISSONANCE
1643551S76D-582
Editorial: Postfach 96, 4009 BASEL **Tel:** 61 3016138
Fax: 22 3619122
Email: info@dissonance.ch **Web site:** http://www.dissonance.ch
Freq: Quarterly; Free to qualifying individuals
Annual Sub.: CHF 50,00; **Circ:** 2,500
Editor: Michael Kunkel
Profile: Magazine of the Swiss Musicians' Association.
Language(s): French; German
Mechanical Data: Type Area: 210 x 192 mm
Copy instructions: *Copy Date:* 30 days prior to publication
CONSUMER: MUSIC & PERFORMING ARTS: Music

LA DISTINCTION
766661S84A-524
Editorial: c.p. 125, 1018 LAUSANNE 18
Email: redaction@distinction.ch **Web site:** http://www.distinction.ch
Freq: 5 issues yearly; **Annual Sub.:** CHF 25,00; **Circ:** 1,200
Profile: Cultural magazine.
Language(s): French
Mechanical Data: No. of Columns (Display): 6, Col Widths (Display): 45 mm
CONSUMER: THE ARTS & LITERARY: Arts

D-JOURNAL
1655576S56A-2065
Editorial: 79, ch. de la Rêche, 1630 BULLE
Tel: 26 9129577
Email: mic.gremaud@bluewin.ch
Freq: 5 issues yearly; Free to qualifying individuals
Annual Sub.: CHF 40,00; **Circ:** 9,000
Editor: Michel Gremaud; **Advertising Manager:** Brigitte Fankhauser
Profile: Information for people suffering from diabetes in French-speaking Switzerland.
Language(s): French
ADVERTISING RATES:
Full Page Mono .... CHF 1155
Full Page Colour .... CHF 2240
Mechanical Data: Type Area: 260 x 180 mm, No. of Columns (Display): 3, Col Widths (Display): 55 mm

D-JOURNAL
725409S94F-120
Editorial: Vadianstr. 31, 9000 ST. GALLEN
Tel: 71 2235279
Email: kschedegger@sunrise.ch **Web site:** http://www.diabetesgesellschaft.ch
Freq: 6 issues yearly; Free to qualifying individuals
Annual Sub.: CHF 40,00; **Circ:** 19,600
Editor: Karl Scheidegger; **Advertising Manager:** Brigitte Fankhauser
Profile: Journal about diabetes.
Language(s): German
ADVERTISING RATES:
Full Page Mono .... CHF 1700
Full Page Colour .... CHF 3460
Mechanical Data: No. of Columns (Display): 2, Col Widths (Display): 79 mm, Type Area: 260 x 191 mm
Copy instructions: *Copy Date:* 45 days prior to publication
CONSUMER: OTHER CLASSIFICATIONS: Disability

DROGISTENSTERN
725667S94H-1315
Editorial: Nidaugasse 15, 2502 BIEL **Tel:** 32 3285040
Fax: 32 3285041
Email: h.gasser@drogistenverband.ch **Web site:** http://www.drogistenverband.ch
Freq: 10 issues yearly; **Annual Sub.:** CHF 25,00; **Circ:** 310,455
Editor: Heinrich Gasser; **Advertising Manager:** Susanne Werder
Profile: Customer magazine published by the Swiss Chemists Association.
Language(s): German
ADVERTISING RATES:
Full Page Mono .... CHF 18900
Full Page Colour .... CHF 18900
Mechanical Data: Type Area: 297 x 210 mm
Copy instructions: *Copy Date:* 61 days prior to publication
CONSUMER: OTHER CLASSIFICATIONS: Customer Magazines

DU
1615882S84A-535
Editorial: Stadelhoferstr. 25, 8001 ZÜRICH
Tel: 44 2668555 **Fax:** 44 2668558
Email: redaktion@du-magazin.com **Web site:** http://www.du-magazin.com
Freq: 10 issues yearly; **Annual Sub.:** CHF 160,00; **Circ:** 15,000
Editor: Stefan Kaiser; **Advertising Manager:** Oliver Burger
Language(s): German
ADVERTISING RATES:
Full Page Mono .... CHF 8500
Full Page Colour .... CHF 8500
Mechanical Data: Type Area: 253 x 196 mm, No. of Columns (Display): 3, Col Widths (Display): 62 mm
Copy instructions: *Copy Date:* 28 days prior to publication
CONSUMER: THE ARTS & LITERARY: Arts

ECHO
1772549S14A-1211
Editorial: 69, rue Jardinière, 2300 LA-CHAUX-DE-FONDS **Tel:** 32 9109403 **Fax:** 32 9109401
Email: info@practicefirms.ch **Web site:** http://www.practicefirms.ch
Freq: 3 issues yearly; **Circ:** 4,500
Editor: Annick Weber Richard
Profile: Company publication from the Swiss Central Office of Practice Firms.
Language(s): French; German

ECHO
1844736S14A-1258
Editorial: 69, rue Jardinière, 2300 LA-CHAUX-DE-FONDS **Tel:** 32 9109403 **Fax:** 32 9109401
Email: info@practicefirms.ch **Web site:** http://www.practicefirms.ch
Freq: Half-yearly; **Circ:** 4,500
Editor: Annick Weber Richard
Profile: Company publication from the Swiss Central Office of Practice Firms.
Language(s): German

ECO LIFE
1852316S57-725
Editorial: Pfadacher 5, 8623 WETZIKON
Tel: 43 4881848 **Fax:** 43 4881843
Email: info@profilepublishing.ch **Web site:** http://www.eco-life.info
Freq: 6 issues yearly; **Annual Sub.:** CHF 30,00; **Circ:** 80,000
Editor: Reto Wüthrich
Profile: Magazine providing information about developments in environment, economy and society.
Language(s): German
ADVERTISING RATES:
Full Page Mono .... CHF 8500
Full Page Colour .... CHF 8500
Mechanical Data: Type Area: 253 x 187 mm
Copy instructions: *Copy Date:* 52 days prior to publication

ECOLE ROMANDE
725892S62A-120
Editorial: 40, Crét-Mouton, 1091 GRANDVAUX
Tel: 21 7992883 **Fax:** 21 7992875
Email: adml@bluewin.ch **Web site:** http://www.epch.ch
Freq: 6 issues yearly; **Annual Sub.:** CHF 79,00; **Circ:** 3,100
Editor: André-Daniel Meylan
Profile: Magazine about education in French-speaking Swiss schools.
Language(s): French
ADVERTISING RATES:
Full Page Mono .... CHF 786
Mechanical Data: Type Area: 253 x 180 mm
Copy instructions: *Copy Date:* 30 days prior to publication
BUSINESS: CHURCH & SCHOOL EQUIPMENT & EDUCATION: Education

EDELWEISS
725915S74A-200
Editorial: 1, rue Chantepoulet, 1201 GENF
Tel: 21 3317300 **Fax:** 21 3317301
Email: edelweiss@ringier.ch **Web site:** http://www.edelweissmag.ch
Freq: 11 issues yearly; **Annual Sub.:** CHF 55,00; **Circ:** 24,185
Editor: Laurence Desbordes; **Advertising Manager:** Patrick Zanello
Profile: Women's interest magazine, containing articles about health, fashion, beauty and lifestyle.
Language(s): French
ADVERTISING RATES:
Full Page Mono .... CHF 10370
Full Page Colour .... CHF 10370
Mechanical Data: Type Area: 248 x 189 mm, No. of Columns (Display): 3, Col Widths (Display): 58 mm
Copy instructions: *Copy Date:* 31 days prior to publication
Supplement(s): edel girls; edelweiss men; Rocks & Stones; Type
CONSUMER: WOMEN'S INTEREST CONSUMER MAGAZINES: Women's Interest

EDELWEISS MEN
2059536S86C-65
Editorial: 1, rue Chantepoulet, 1201 GENF
Tel: 21 3317300 **Fax:** 21 3317301
Email: edelweiss@ringier.ch **Web site:** http://www.edelweissmag.ch
Freq: Half-yearly; **Circ:** 80,000
Editor: Laurence Desbordes; **Advertising Manager:** Patrick Zanello
Profile: Magazine for men, containing articles about health, fashion, beauty and lifestyle.
Language(s): French
ADVERTISING RATES:
Full Page Mono .... CHF 12900
Full Page Colour .... CHF 12900
Mechanical Data: Type Area: 246 x 185 mm, No. of Columns (Display): 2, Col Widths (Display): 88 mm
Supplement to: edelweiss, L'Hebdo

EDITO + KLARTEXT 1899862S2A-696

Editorial: Rebgasse 1, 4058 BASEL **Tel:** 61 6817937
Email: redaktion@edito-online.ch **Web site:** http://www.edito-online.ch
Freq: 6 issues yearly; Free to qualifying individuals
Annual Sub.: CHF 60,00; **Circ:** 7,860
Editor: Philipp Cueni
Profile: The Media MagazineEdito + Klartext is for all who want to know more about the media world, providing critical background. It's about print, radio, TV, online. It's about trends in journalism, to the economic development of the media sector, to media companies and working conditions. It is also about media policy to look to the editors and behind the scenes of the media houses in the world of media production and in the Swiss media scene Filmbranche.Der first part explores the current issues in the media houses and journalists. The second part offers media trends, analysis, opinion, reflection, and discusses the current trends. The third part comprises MEDIA LAB workshop reports, reflection on practice, the issues of education and training and research, tips on book, DVD and audio, controversial discussions to a media ethics case, and a trip to the online world. The magazine offers in each issue, a photo report.
Language(s): German
ADVERTISING RATES:
Full Page Mono .... CHF 5000
Full Page Colour .... CHF 5000
Mechanical Data: Type Area: 257 x 191 mm, No. of Columns (Display): 4, Col Widths (Display): 46 mm
Copy instructions: *Copy Date:* 18 days prior to publication

EDITO + KLARTEXT 1899863S2A-697

Editorial: 25, rue du Petit-Chêne, 1003 LAUSANNE
Tel: 79 6706264 **Fax:** 21 3112290
Email: redaction@edito-online.ch **Web site:** http://www.edito-online.ch
Freq: 6 issues yearly; Free to qualifying individuals
Annual Sub.: CHF 60,00; **Circ:** 3,434
Editor: Christian Campiche
Profile: The Media MagazineEdito + Klartext is for all who want to know more about the media world, providing critical background. It's about print, radio, TV, online. It's about trends in journalism, to the economic development of the media sector, to media companies and working conditions. It is also about media policy to look to the editors and behind the scenes of the media houses in the world of media production and in the Swiss media scene Filmbranche.Der first part explores the current issues in the media houses and journalists. The second part offers media trends, analysis, opinion, reflection, and discusses the current trends. The third part comprises MEDIA LAB workshop reports, reflection on practice, the issues of education and training and research, tips on book, DVD and audio, controversial discussions to a media ethics case, and a trip to the online world. The magazine offers in each issue, a photo report.
Language(s): French
ADVERTISING RATES:
Full Page Mono .... CHF 5000
Full Page Colour .... CHF 5000
Mechanical Data: Type Area: 257 x 191 mm, No. of Columns (Display): 4, Col Widths (Display): 46 mm
Copy instructions: *Copy Date:* 18 days prior to publication

EINFAMILIENHÄUSER 726014S4A-2

Editorial: Rieterstr. 35, 8002 ZÜRICH
Tel: 44 2041881 **Fax:** 44 2041850
Email: britta.limper@archithema.ch **Web site:** http://www.archithema.ch
Freq: Annual; **Cover Price:** CHF 8,50; **Circ:** 19,000
Editor: Britta Limper; **Advertising Manager:** Emil M. Bisig
Profile: Magazine focusing on architecture and building techniques.
Language(s): German
Readership: Read by architects, builders and developers.
ADVERTISING RATES:
Full Page Colour .... CHF 5280
Mechanical Data: Type Area: 265 x 200 mm
Copy instructions: *Copy Date:* 29 days prior to publication
Supplement to: Ideales Heim
BUSINESS: ARCHITECTURE & BUILDING: Architecture

EINSIEDLER ANZEIGER 726040S67B-880

Editorial: Bahnhofplatz 8, 8840 EINSIEDELN
Tel: 55 4189555 **Fax:** 55 4189556
Email: einsiedleranzeiger@eadruck.ch **Web site:** http://www.einsiedleranzeiger.ch
Freq: 104 issues yearly; **Annual Sub.:** CHF 174,00; **Circ:** 5,963
Editor: Victor Kälin
Profile: Regional daily newspaper covering politics, economics, sport, travel, technology and the arts.
Language(s): German
ADVERTISING RATES:
SCC .... CHF 25,50
Mechanical Data: Type Area: 440 x 286 mm, No. of Columns (Display): 10, Col Widths (Display): 25 mm
Copy instructions: *Copy Date:* 1 day prior to publication
REGIONAL DAILY & SUNDAY NEWSPAPERS: Regional Daily Newspapers

EINSIEDLER ANZEIGER 1642003S72-9597

Editorial: Bahnhofplatz 8, 8840 EINSIEDELN
Tel: 55 4189555 **Fax:** 55 4189556
Email: einsiedleranzeiger@eadruck.ch **Web site:** http://www.einsiedleranzeiger.ch
Freq: 18 issues yearly; **Cover Price:** Free; **Circ:** 10,280
Editor: Victor Kälin
Profile: Advertising journal (house-to-house) concentrating on local stories.
Language(s): German
ADVERTISING RATES:
Full Page Mono .... CHF 3520
Full Page Colour .... CHF 3700
Mechanical Data: Type Area: 440 x 286 mm, No. of Columns (Display): 10, Col Widths (Display): 25 mm
Copy instructions: *Copy Date:* 1 day prior to publication
LOCAL NEWSPAPERS

EL FORUM 1841074S17-176

Editorial: Sihlbruggstr. 105a, 6341 BAAR
Tel: 41 7677907 **Fax:** 41 7677911
Email: markus.frutig@elforum.ch **Web site:** http://www.elforum.ch
Freq: Monthly; **Annual Sub.:** CHF 30,00; **Circ:** 9,118
Editor: Markus Frutig; **Advertising Manager:** Bernhard Wettstein
Profile: Magazine about electronics and electrotechnology.
Language(s): German
ADVERTISING RATES:
Full Page Mono .... CHF 3185
Full Page Colour .... CHF 3785
Mechanical Data: Type Area: 266 x 185 mm, No. of Columns (Display): 4, Col Widths (Display): 42 mm
Copy instructions: *Copy Date:* 21 days prior to publication

ELECTRO REVUE 763027S17-161

Editorial: Militärstr. 36, 8021 ZÜRICH
Tel: 44 2994178 **Fax:** 44 2994140
Email: electrorevue@infel.ch
Freq: 24 issues yearly; Free to qualifying individuals
Annual Sub.: CHF 101,00; **Circ:** 3,600
Editor: Alexander Jacobi; **Advertising Manager:** Romaine Schilling
Profile: Magazine for electricians.
Language(s): French; German
ADVERTISING RATES:
Full Page Mono .... CHF 1715
Full Page Colour .... CHF 2450
Mechanical Data: Type Area: 270 x 186 mm
Copy instructions: *Copy Date:* 10 days prior to publication
Official Journal of: Organ d. Schweizer. Elektro-Einkaufs-Vereinigung
BUSINESS: ELECTRICAL

ELLE 1844596S74A-491

Editorial: 35, rue des Bains, 1205 GENF
Tel: 22 8099416 **Fax:** 22 7811414
Freq: 24 issues yearly; **Cover Price:** CHF 4,50; **Circ:** 25,000
Editor: Odile Habel
Profile: Magazine for women.
Language(s): French
ADVERTISING RATES:
Full Page Mono .... CHF 6200
Full Page Colour .... CHF 6200
Mechanical Data: Type Area: 259 x 180 mm, No. of Columns (Display): 4, Col Widths (Display): 49 mm
Copy instructions: *Copy Date:* 31 days prior to publication

EML EINKAUF MATERIALWIRTSCHAFT LOGISTIK 1642199S10-46

Editorial: Postfach 520, 4142 MÜNCHENSTEIN 1
Tel: 61 3381621 **Fax:** 61 3381600
Email: einkauf@lapper.ch **Web site:** http://www.einkauf.ch
Freq: 10 issues yearly; **Annual Sub.:** CHF 74,00; **Circ:** 4,500
Editor: H.-Joachim Behrend
Profile: Magazine on material management.
Language(s): German
ADVERTISING RATES:
Full Page Mono .... CHF 2250
Full Page Colour .... CHF 2850
Mechanical Data: Type Area: 250 x 185 mm, No. of Columns (Display): 4, Col Widths (Display): 42 mm
Copy instructions: *Copy Date:* 20 days prior to publication

EMPFEHLUNGEN 1846350S89A-388

Editorial: Jurastr. 29, 4901 LANGENTHAL
Tel: 62 9227721 **Fax:** 62 9230658
Email: tourismus@oberaargau.ch **Web site:** http://www.oberaargau.ch
Freq: Annual; **Cover Price:** Free; **Circ:** 10,000
Editor: Therese Ischi
Profile: Guide for Oberaargau.
Language(s): German

ENERGIE & UMWELT 726290S58-100

Editorial: Sihlquai 67, 8005 ZÜRICH **Tel:** 44 2752121
Email: info@energiestiftung.ch **Web site:** http://www.energiestiftung.ch
Freq: Quarterly; Free to qualifying individuals
Annual Sub.: CHF 30,00
Editor: Rafael Brand
Profile: Journal of the Swiss Energy Foundation, about energy and the environment.
Language(s): German
BUSINESS: ENERGY, FUEL & NUCLEAR

ENERGIES RENOUVELABLES 1852545S58-212

Editorial: Aarbergergasse 21, 3011 BERN
Tel: 31 3718000 **Fax:** 31 3718000
Email: redaktion@sses.ch **Web site:** http://www.sses.ch
Freq: 6 issues yearly; Free to qualifying individuals
Annual Sub.: CHF 70,00; **Circ:** 1,500
Editor: Ingrid Hess
Profile: Magazine from the Swiss Society for Solar Energy.
Language(s): French
ADVERTISING RATES:
Full Page Mono .... CHF 3200
Full Page Colour .... CHF 3200
Mechanical Data: Type Area: 272 x 183 mm, No. of Columns (Display): 3, Col Widths (Display): 58 mm
Copy instructions: *Copy Date:* 36 days prior to publication

ENERGIE-SPIEGEL 2002764S58-214

Editorial: 5232 VILLIGEN **Tel:** 56 3102956
Fax: 56 3104411
Email: energiespiegel@psi.ch **Web site:** http://www.psi.ch
Freq: 3 issues yearly; **Circ:** 15,000
Editor: Christian Bauer
Profile: Company publication about comprehensive analysis of energy systems.
Language(s): German

ENGADINER POST 726299S67B-920

Editorial: via Surpunt, 54, 7500 ST. MORITZ
Tel: 81 8379081 **Fax:** 81 8379082
Email: redaktion@engadinerpost.ch **Web site:** http://www.engadinerpost.ch
Freq: 156 issues yearly; **Annual Sub.:** CHF 169,00; **Circ:** 8,871
Editor: Reto Stifel
Profile: Regional daily newspaper covering politics, economics, sport, travel, technology and the arts.
Language(s): German
ADVERTISING RATES:
SCC .... CHF 33,80
Mechanical Data: Type Area: 430 x 286 mm, No. of Columns (Display): 10, Col Widths (Display): 25 mm
Copy instructions: *Copy Date:* 1 day prior to publication
Supplement(s): Marathon Post
REGIONAL DAILY & SUNDAY NEWSPAPERS: Regional Daily Newspapers

ENTREPRISE ROMANDE 1855407S14A-1297

Editorial: 98, rue de Saint-Jean, 1211 GENF 11
Tel: 22 7153244 **Fax:** 22 7153214
Email: er@entrepriseromande.ch **Web site:** http://www.fer-ge.ch
Freq: 26 issues yearly; **Annual Sub.:** CHF 65,00; **Circ:** 19,661
Editor: Véronique Kämpfen
Profile: Journal of the Employers' Federation in French-speaking Switzerland. Contains regional, national and international economic, political and social information.
Language(s): French
ADVERTISING RATES:
Full Page Mono .... CHF 4630
Full Page Colour .... CHF 5180
Mechanical Data: Type Area: 396 x 278 mm, No. of Columns (Display): 6, Col Widths (Display): 44 mm
Copy instructions: *Copy Date:* 4 days prior to publication

EPILEPTOLOGIE 726372S56A-580

Editorial: Seefeldstr. 84, 8042 ZÜRICH
Tel: 43 4886777 **Fax:** 43 4886778
Email: becker@epi.ch **Web site:** http://www.epi.ch
Freq: Quarterly; Free to qualifying individuals
Annual Sub.: CHF 50,00; **Circ:** 2,000
Editor: Margret Becker
Profile: Magazine for physical doctors, psychologists, teachers and clergymen.
Language(s): English; French; German
ADVERTISING RATES:
Full Page Mono .... CHF 3500
Full Page Colour .... CHF 3500

ERNEUERBARE ENERGIEN 1852546S58-213

Editorial: Aarbergergasse 21, 3011 BERN
Tel: 31 3718000 **Fax:** 31 3718000
Email: redaktion@sses.ch **Web site:** http://www.sses.ch
Freq: 6 issues yearly; Free to qualifying individuals
Annual Sub.: CHF 70,00; **Circ:** 6,700
Editor: Ingrid Hess
Profile: Information from the Swiss Society for Solar Energy.
Language(s): German
ADVERTISING RATES:
Full Page Mono .... CHF 3200
Full Page Colour .... CHF 3200
Mechanical Data: Type Area: 272 x 183 mm, No. of Columns (Display): 3, Col Widths (Display): 58 mm
Copy instructions: *Copy Date:* 36 days prior to publication

ESPOIR 766581S87-2753

Editorial: Laupenstr. 5, 3001 BERN **Tel:** 31 3880542
Fax: 31 3880596
Email: redaction@swi.salvationarmy.org **Web site:** http://www.armeedusalut.ch
Annual Sub.: CHF 48,00
Editor: Gabrielle Keller
Profile: Evangelical magazine.
Language(s): French
CONSUMER: RELIGIOUS

ESSEN & SCHLAFEN 1846352S89A-389

Editorial: Jurastr. 29, 4901 LANGENTHAL
Tel: 62 9227721 **Fax:** 62 9230658
Email: tourismus@oberaargau.ch **Web site:** http://www.oberaargau.ch
Freq: Annual; **Cover Price:** Free; **Circ:** 20,000
Profile: Gastronomy and accommodation facility guide for Oberaargau.
Language(s): German

ET ELEKTROTECHNIK 726577S17-60

Editorial: Neumattstr. 1, 5001 AARAU
Tel: 58 2005660 **Fax:** 58 2005661
Email: redaktion@elektrotechnik.ch **Web site:** http://www.elektrotechnik.ch
Freq: 11 issues yearly; **Annual Sub.:** CHF 119,00; **Circ:** 7,100
Editor: Hansjörg Wigger; **Advertising Manager:** Thomas Stark
Profile: Magazine for electricians, planners and electro engineers.
Language(s): German
ADVERTISING RATES:
Full Page Mono .... CHF 2495
Full Page Colour .... CHF 3695
Mechanical Data: Type Area: 264 x 184 mm
Copy instructions: *Copy Date:* 30 days prior to publication
BUSINESS: ELECTRICAL

ETH GLOBE 723856S14R-20

Editorial: Rämistr. 101, 8092 ZÜRICH
Tel: 44 6324252 **Fax:** 44 6323525
Email: ethglobe@hk.ethz.ch **Web site:** http://www.ethz.ch/ethglobe
Freq: Quarterly; **Circ:** 34,000
Editor: Martina Märki
Profile: Magazine covering economics, society, energy, environment and science.
Language(s): German
Readership: Aimed at managers, technologists and engineers.
ADVERTISING RATES:
Full Page Mono .... CHF 6800
Full Page Colour .... CHF 6800
Mechanical Data: Type Area: 288 x 213 mm
Copy instructions: *Copy Date:* 34 days prior to publication
BUSINESS: COMMERCE, INDUSTRY & MANAGEMENT: Commerce Related

ETHOS 726585S87-780

Editorial: Hinterburgstr. 8, 9442 BERNECK
Tel: 71 7272121 **Fax:** 71 7272123
Email: redaktion@ethos.ch **Web site:** http://www.ethos-magazin.ch
Freq: Monthly; **Annual Sub.:** CHF 69,80; **Circ:** 23,500
Editor: Rolf Höneisen
Profile: Christian family magazine.
Language(s): German
Mechanical Data: No. of Columns (Display): 4, Col Widths (Display): 45 mm, Type Area: 239 x 190 mm
CONSUMER: RELIGIOUS

EUROTEC 1779830S19E-193

Editorial: 25, rte. des Acacias, 1211 GENF 26
Tel: 22 3077837 **Fax:** 22 3077853
Email: pykohler@eurotec-bi.com **Web site:** http://www.eurotec.ch
Freq: 6 issues yearly; **Annual Sub.:** CHF 80,00; **Circ:** 10,000
Editor: Pierre-Yves Kohler; **Advertising Manager:** Nathalie Glattfelder
Profile: European technical news magazine about machine tools, precision tools, precision technical parts and automation and electronics.
Language(s): English; French; German
ADVERTISING RATES:
Full Page Mono .... CHF 5140
Full Page Colour .... CHF 5140
Mechanical Data: Type Area: 265 x 185 mm, No. of Columns (Display): 3, Col Widths (Display): 58 mm

FACHHEFTE GRAFISCHE INDUSTRIE BULLETIN TECHNIQUE
767109S41A-170
Editorial: Fabrikstr. 7, 3012 BERN **Tel:** 31 3013835
Email: rburi@schnittstelle-prepress.ch
Freq: 6 issues yearly; **Annual Sub.:** CHF 48,00,; **Circ:** 2,300
Editor: René Buri
Profile: Magazine with articles about modern technologies from information editing, production and distribution.
Language(s): French; German
ADVERTISING RATES:
Full Page Mono .... CHF 2950
Full Page Colour .... CHF 2950
Mechanical Data: Type Area: 258 x 190 mm
BUSINESS: PRINTING & STATIONERY: Printing

FACTS AND FIGURES SRG SSR IDÉE SUISSE
1828634S2A-671
Editorial: Giacomettistr. 1, 3000 BERN 31
Tel: 31 3509111
Email: publishing@srg-ssr.ch **Web site:** http://www.srg-ssr.ch
Freq: Annual; **Cover Price:** Free; **Circ:** 300
Editor: Dominic Witschi
Profile: Publication of the SRG SSR company.
Language(s): English

FAKTOR
1659976S4A-5
Editorial: Gubelstr. 59, 8050 ZÜRICH
Tel: 44 3161060 **Fax:** 44 3161061
Email: info@faktor.ch **Web site:** http://www.faktor.ch
Freq: 3 issues yearly; **Annual Sub.:** CHF 48,00; **Circ:** 11,200
Editor: Othmar Humm
Profile: Publications about architecture, technology and energy.
Language(s): German
ADVERTISING RATES:
Full Page Mono .... CHF 6700
Full Page Colour .... CHF 6700
Mechanical Data: Type Area: 255 x 195 mm

FAMILY
1645060S74A-469
Editorial: Witzbergstr. 7, 8330 PFÄFFIKON
Tel: 43 2888013 **Fax:** 43 2888011
Email: reda@bvmedia.ch **Web site:** http://www.family.ch
Freq: 6 issues yearly; **Annual Sub.:** CHF 32,70; **Circ:** 65,000
Editor: Martin Gundlach; **Advertising Manager:** Niklaus Mosimann
Profile: Christian magazine focusing on communication within relationships, potential conflict between family and job, sexuality and educational problems.
Language(s): German
ADVERTISING RATES:
Full Page Mono .... CHF 4146
Full Page Colour .... CHF 5439
Mechanical Data: Type Area: 258 x 188 mm, No. of Columns (Display): 4, Col Widths (Display): 44 mm
Copy instructions: *Copy Date:* 40 days prior to publication

FASSADE
1641411S4E-778
Editorial: Feldeggstr. 89, 8008 ZÜRICH
Tel: 43 4999901 **Fax:** 43 4999931
Email: sigrid.hanke@bluewin.ch
Freq: Annual; **Circ:** 26,000
Editor: Sigrid Hanke
Profile: Magazine on energy and architecture.
Language(s): German
ADVERTISING RATES:
Full Page Mono .... CHF 4550
Full Page Colour .... CHF 6500
Mechanical Data: Type Area: 268 x 189 mm, No. of Columns (Display): 2, Col Widths (Display): 92 mm
Copy instructions: *Copy Date:* 40 days prior to publication
Supplement to: Schweizer Energiefachbuch

FASSADE FAÇADE
727105S4E-400
Editorial: Riedstr. 14, 8953 DIETIKON
Tel: 44 7422434 **Fax:** 44 7415553
Email: fassade@szff.ch **Web site:** http://www.fassade.ch
Freq: Quarterly; **Annual Sub.:** CHF 40,00; **Circ:** 7,000
Editor: Rudolf Locher; **Advertising Manager:** Ruth Wasser
Profile: Swiss magazine on window and cladding techniques.
Language(s): French; German
ADVERTISING RATES:
Full Page Mono .... CHF 2680
Full Page Colour .... CHF 4000
Mechanical Data: Type Area: 270 x 190 mm
Copy instructions: *Copy Date:* 34 days prior to publication

FASSADE FAÇADE
727105S4E-830
Editorial: Riedstr. 14, 8953 DIETIKON
Tel: 44 7422434 **Fax:** 44 7415553
Email: fassade@szff.ch **Web site:** http://www.fassade.ch
Freq: Quarterly; **Annual Sub.:** CHF 40,00; **Circ:** 7,000
Editor: Rudolf Locher; **Advertising Manager:** Ruth Wasser
Profile: Swiss magazine on window and cladding techniques.
Language(s): French; German
ADVERTISING RATES:
Full Page Mono .... CHF 2680
Full Page Colour .... CHF 4000
Mechanical Data: Type Area: 270 x 190 mm
Copy instructions: *Copy Date:* 34 days prior to publication

FATTI E CIFRE SRG SSR IDÉE SUISSE
1828636S2A-672
Editorial: Giacomettistr. 1, 3000 BERN 31
Tel: 31 3509111
Email: publishing@srg-ssr.ch **Web site:** http://www.srg-ssr.ch
Freq: Annual; **Cover Price:** Free; **Circ:** 1,000
Editor: Dominic Witschi
Profile: Publication of the SRG SSR company.
Language(s): Italian

FEMINFO
1855409S74A-514
Editorial: Blaumatt 3, 3250 LYSS **Tel:** 32 3853725
Email: info@femwiss.ch **Web site:** http://www.femwiss.ch
Freq: Quarterly; Free to qualifying individuals
Annual Sub.: CHF 45,00; **Circ:** 1,100
Editor: Ursula Lipecki
Profile: Magazine about women and gender research, development of the university policy in Switzerland.
Language(s): French; German
ADVERTISING RATES:
Full Page Mono .... CHF 250

FER INFORMATIONS
1855410S14A-1298
Editorial: 98, rue de Saint-Jean, 1211 GENF 11
Tel: 22 7153269 **Fax:** 22 7153214
Email: anne-marie.barras@fer-ge.ch **Web site:** http://www.fer-ge.ch
Freq: 11 issues yearly; **Annual Sub.:** CHF 102,00; **Circ:** 1,300
Editor: Anne-Marie Barras
Profile: Economics magazine.
Language(s): French

FERMENT
727205S87-920
Editorial: Ostenbergstr. 18, 4410 LIESTAL
Tel: 61 9031144 **Fax:** 61 9031145
Email: ferment@bluewin.ch **Web site:** http://www.ferment.ch
Freq: 6 issues yearly; **Annual Sub.:** CHF 52,00; **Circ:** 17,000
Editor: Andreas Baumeister
Profile: Religious magazine.
Language(s): German
CONSUMER: RELIGIOUS

FINANZ UND WIRTSCHAFT
764875S14A-1104
Editorial: Hallwylstr. 71, 8004 ZÜRICH
Tel: 44 2983535 **Fax:** 44 2983550
Email: redaktion@fuw.ch **Web site:** http://www.fuw.ch
Freq: 104 issues yearly; **Annual Sub.:** CHF 305,00; **Circ:** 33,347
Editor: Peter Schuppli; **Advertising Manager:** Ruedi Minger
Profile: Regional daily newspaper covering politics, economics, sport, travel, technology and the arts.
Language(s): German
ADVERTISING RATES:
SCC .... CHF 38,60
Mechanical Data: Type Area: 440 x 297 mm, No. of Columns (Display): 10
Copy instructions: *Copy Date:* 2 days prior to publication
Supplement(s): Anlagetrends Fonds; Luxe
BUSINESS: COMMERCE, INDUSTRY & MANAGEMENT

FIRSTCLASS
1844828S14A-1260
Editorial: Wengistr. 7, 8026 ZÜRICH **Tel:** 44 2654010
Fax: 44 2654011
Email: info@publicontext.com **Web site:** http://www.publicontext.com
Freq: Annual; **Cover Price:** Free; **Circ:** 60,000
Editor: Ralph Spillmann
Profile: Magazine about business trips, supplement to the Swiss management- and financemagazine Bilanz.
Language(s): German
Supplement to: Bilanz

FIT FOR LIFE
727419S75J-20
Editorial: Neumattstr. 1, 5001 AARAU
Tel: 58 2005647 **Fax:** 58 2005644
Email: andreas.gonseth@fitforlife.ch **Web site:** http://www.fitforlife.ch
Freq: 11 issues yearly; **Annual Sub.:** CHF 84,00; **Circ:** 20,000
Editor: Andreas Gonseth; **Advertising Manager:** Sonja Schnider
Profile: Magazine about running and endurance sports.
Language(s): German
ADVERTISING RATES:
Full Page Mono .... CHF 5450
Full Page Colour .... CHF 5450
Mechanical Data: Type Area: 268 x 188 mm, No. of Columns (Display): 3, Col Widths (Display): 59 mm
Copy instructions: *Copy Date:* 17 days prior to publication
Supplement(s): Marathon Post; Trainings Tagebuch
CONSUMER: SPORT: Athletics

FLASH
1858745S2A-688
Editorial: Konradstr. 14, 8021 ZÜRICH
Tel: 44 3186464 **Fax:** 44 3186462
Email: contact@schweizerpresse.ch **Web site:** http://www.schweizerpresse.ch
Freq: 10 issues yearly; **Cover Price:** Free; **Circ:** 2,000
Editor: Urs F. Meyer
Profile: Official journal of the Swiss Society of Newspaper and Magazine Publishers.
Language(s): German
ADVERTISING RATES:
Full Page Mono .... CHF 1500
Full Page Colour .... CHF 1500
Mechanical Data: Type Area: 230 x 150 mm
Copy instructions: *Copy Date:* 10 days prior to publication

FLEISCH UND FEINKOST VIANDE ET TRAITEURS CARNE E COMMESTIBILI
1749176S22D-41
Editorial: Steinwiesstr. 59, 8032 ZÜRICH
Tel: 44 2507060 **Fax:** 44 2507061
Email: info@carnasuisse.ch **Web site:** http://www.metzgerei.ch
Freq: 26 issues yearly; **Annual Sub.:** CHF 97,80; **Circ:** 5,000
Language(s): French; German; Italian
ADVERTISING RATES:
Full Page Mono .... CHF 2480
Full Page Colour .... CHF 2980
Mechanical Data: Type Area: 280 x 202 mm, No. of Columns (Display): 4, Col Widths (Display): 47 mm
Copy instructions: *Copy Date:* 2 days prior to publication
BUSINESS: FOOD: Meat Trade

FOOD AKTUELL
735400S22D-40
Editorial: Freyastr. 4, 8004 ZÜRICH **Tel:** 44 2428520
Web site: http://www.mpv.ch
Freq: 25 issues yearly; Free to qualifying individuals
Annual Sub.: CHF 60,00; **Circ:** 5,165
Editor: Guido Böhler; **Advertising Manager:** Peter Küng
Profile: Journal covering all aspects of the butchers' trade.
Language(s): French; German; Italian
ADVERTISING RATES:
Full Page Mono .... CHF 1995
Full Page Colour .... CHF 2594
Mechanical Data: Type Area: 262 x 190 mm, No. of Columns (Display): 6
Copy instructions: *Copy Date:* 7 days prior to publication
BUSINESS: FOOD: Meat Trade

LA FORET
727621S46-1
Editorial: Rosenweg 14, 4501 SOLOTHURN
Tel: 21 6011077 **Fax:** 21 6011075
Email: gilardi@wvs.ch **Web site:** http://www.wvs.ch
Freq: 11 issues yearly; **Annual Sub.:** CHF 79,00; **Circ:** 1,735
Editor: Fabio Gilardi
Profile: Magazine containing information concerning forestry, the lumber trade, the use and sale of wood, work safety, nature protection, congresses and exhibitions.
Language(s): French
Readership: Read by owners and managers of forests, foresters, woodcutters and carpenters.
ADVERTISING RATES:
Full Page Mono .... CHF 1040
Full Page Colour .... CHF 1800
Mechanical Data: Type Area: 260 x 185 mm
Copy instructions: *Copy Date:* 14 days prior to publication
BUSINESS: TIMBER, WOOD & FORESTRY

FORM
1643907G2A-5546
Editorial: Viaduktstr. 42, 4051 BASEL
Tel: 61 5689861 **Fax:** 61 2050799
Email: redaktion@form.de **Web site:** http://www.birkhauser.ch
Freq: 6 issues yearly; **Cover Price:** CHF 33,00; **Circ:** 7,442
Editor: Gerrit Terstiege
Profile: Magazine focused on design.
Language(s): English; German
ADVERTISING RATES:
Full Page Mono .... CHF 4695
Full Page Colour .... CHF 4695
Mechanical Data: Type Area: 248 x 200 mm
Copy instructions: *Copy Date:* 20 days prior to publication
BUSINESS: COMMUNICATIONS, ADVERTISING & MARKETING

FORUM
1648588S87-2802
Editorial: Hirschengraben 72, 8023 ZÜRICH
Tel: 44 2661272 **Fax:** 44 2661273
Email: forum@zh.kath.ch **Web site:** http://www.kath.ch/zh/forum
Freq: 26 issues yearly; **Annual Sub.:** CHF 35,00; **Circ:** 172,546
Editor: Thomas Binotto
Profile: Paper of the Catholic Church in the canton of Zurich.
Language(s): German
ADVERTISING RATES:
Full Page Mono .... CHF 3925
Full Page Colour .... CHF 4225
Mechanical Data: Type Area: 270 x 186 mm, No. of Columns (Display): 4, Col Widths (Display): 43 mm
CONSUMER: RELIGIOUS

FORUM LANDTECHNIK
2038198S27-166
Editorial: Rosenstr. 14, 2562 PORT **Tel:** 32 3851791
Fax: 32 3851792
Email: info@publiprint.ch
Freq: 6 issues yearly; **Circ:** 1,400
Profile: Journal of the Swiss Metal Union.
Language(s): French; German
ADVERTISING RATES:
Full Page Mono .... CHF 1950
Full Page Colour .... CHF 1950
Mechanical Data: Type Area: 275 x 190 mm, No. of Columns (Display): 2, Col Widths (Display): 93 mm
Copy instructions: *Copy Date:* 26 days prior to publication
Supplement to: metall

FORUM RAUMENTWICKLUNG DU DÉVELOPPEMENT TERRITORIAL SVILUPPO TERRITORIALE
1614885S19A-204
Editorial: Kochergasse 10, 3003 BERN
Tel: 31 3224060 **Fax:** 31 3224716
Email: rudolf.menzi@are.admin.ch **Web site:** http://www.are.ch
Freq: 3 issues yearly; **Annual Sub.:** CHF 30,70; **Circ:** 4,000
Editor: Rudolf M. Menzi
Profile: Information about spatial planning, traffic and effective developments.
Language(s): French; German; Italian

FRAU UND KULTUR
727874G74A-1160
Editorial: Schlösslihalde 19, 6006 LUZERN
Tel: 41 413704230
Email: i.hildebrandt@bluewin.ch
Freq: Quarterly; Free to qualifying individuals
Annual Sub.: CHF 11,00; **Circ:** 4,500
Editor: Irma Hildebrandt
Profile: Magazine of the German Association for Women and Culture.
Language(s): German

FRAUENLAND
1842636S21A-610
Editorial: Thunstr. 78, 3000 BERN 15
Tel: 31 9583325 **Fax:** 31 9583313
Email: redaktion@frauenland.ch **Web site:** http://www.frauenland.ch
Freq: 6 issues yearly; **Annual Sub.:** CHF 35,00; **Circ:** 29,000
Editor: Christoph Greuter
Profile: Magazine for Swiss women living in rural regions.
Language(s): German
ADVERTISING RATES:
Full Page Mono .... CHF 2800
Full Page Colour .... CHF 3250
Mechanical Data: Type Area: 262 x 185 mm
Copy instructions: *Copy Date:* 21 days prior to publication

FREIBURGER NACHRICHTEN
727898S67B-1060
Editorial: Pérollesstr. 42, 1701 FREIBURG
Tel: 26 4264747 **Fax:** 26 4264740
Email: fn.redaktion@freiburger-nachrichten.ch **Web site:** http://www.freiburger-nachrichten.ch
Freq: 312 issues yearly; **Cover Price:** CHF 2,00; **Circ:** 16,003
Editor: Christoph Nussbaumer; **Advertising Manager:** Gilbert A. Bühler
Profile: Regional daily newspaper covering politics, economics, sport, travel, technology and the arts.
Language(s): German
ADVERTISING RATES:
SCC .... CHF 32,40
Mechanical Data: Type Area: 433 x 288 mm, No. of Columns (Display): 10, Col Widths (Display): 25 mm
Copy instructions: *Copy Date:* 2 days prior to publication
REGIONAL DAILY & SUNDAY NEWSPAPERS: Regional Daily Newspapers

Switzerland

DER FREISCHÜTZ 727937S67B-1100
Editorial: Seetalstr. 7, 5630 MURI **Tel:** 56 6751050 **Fax:** 56 6751055
Email: redaktion@freischuetz.ch
Freq: Weekly; **Annual Sub.:** CHF 105,00; **Circ:** 3,749
Editor: Thomas Kron; **Advertising Manager:** Therese Kron-Marty
Profile: Regional daily newspaper covering politics, economics, sport, travel, technology and the arts.
Language(s): German
ADVERTISING RATES:
SCC .... CHF 12,90
Mechanical Data: Type Area: 451 x 291 mm, No. of Columns (Display): 10, Col Widths (Display): 26 mm
Copy instructions: *Copy Date:* 2 days prior to publication
REGIONAL DAILY & SUNDAY NEWSPAPERS: Regional Daily Newspapers

FREUNDIN 1853326S74A-511
Editorial: Am Falter 11, 8966 OBERWIL
Tel: 56 6317717 **Fax:** 56 6317624
Email: info@fjf-intermedia.ch **Web site:** http://www.fjf-intermedia.ch
Freq: 26 issues yearly; **Annual Sub.:** CHF 104,00; **Circ:** 52,000
Editor: Dörte Welti
Profile: Magazine for women. German edition inclusives four pages for switzerland, editorial staff in Germany.
Language(s): German
ADVERTISING RATES:
Full Page Mono .... CHF 7100
Full Page Colour .... CHF 10160
Mechanical Data: Type Area: 229 x 175 mm, No. of Columns (Display): 4, Col Widths (Display): 40 mm
Copy instructions: *Copy Date:* 42 days prior to publication

FRIZ 728076S82-960
Editorial: Gartenhofstr. 7, 8004 ZÜRICH
Tel: 44 2422293 **Fax:** 44 2412926
Email: friz@efriz.ch **Web site:** http://www.efriz.ch
Freq: Quarterly; **Annual Sub.:** CHF 50,00; **Circ:** 3,500
Editor: Detlev Bruggmann
Profile: Magazine about peace policy.
Language(s): German
ADVERTISING RATES:
Full Page Mono .... CHF 1000
Mechanical Data: Type Area: 269 x 181 mm
Copy instructions: *Copy Date:* 13 days prior to publication
CONSUMER: CURRENT AFFAIRS & POLITICS

FS FREIER SCHWEIZER 727920S67B-1080
Editorial: Bahnhofstr. 39, 6403 KÜSSNACHT
Tel: 41 8542523 **Fax:** 41 8542520
Email: redaktion@freierschweizer.ch **Web site:** http://www.freierschweizer.ch
Freq: 104 issues yearly; **Annual Sub.:** CHF 132,00; **Circ:** 4,300
Editor: Alex von Däniken
Profile: Regional daily newspaper covering politics, economics, sport, travel, technology and the arts.
Language(s): German
ADVERTISING RATES:
SCC .... CHF 27,40
Mechanical Data: Type Area: 435 x 286 mm, No. of Columns (Display): 10, Col Widths (Display): 27 mm
Copy instructions: *Copy Date:* 1 day prior to publication
REGIONAL DAILY & SUNDAY NEWSPAPERS: Regional Daily Newspapers

G2W 729467S87-1040
Editorial: Birmensdorferstr. 52, 8036 ZÜRICH
Tel: 43 3222244 **Fax:** 43 3222240
Email: redaktion.g2w@bluewin.ch **Web site:** http://www.g2w.eu
Freq: 11 issues yearly; **Annual Sub.:** CHF 75,00; **Circ:** 1,900
Editor: Stefan Kube; **Advertising Manager:** Elisabeth Müller
Profile: Publication providing an ecumenical forum for discussions about religion and society in East and West.
Language(s): German
Mechanical Data: Type Area: 260 x 176 mm, No. of Columns (Display): 3, Col Widths (Display): 56 mm
Copy instructions: *Copy Date:* 25 days prior to publication
CONSUMER: RELIGIOUS

GALATEA 728267S74A-300
Editorial: via Besso, 42, 6903 LUGANO
Tel: 91 9663810 **Fax:** 91 9661447
Email: adv@adv-publishing.ch **Web site:** http://www.galatea.ch
Freq: 10 issues yearly; **Circ:** 15,000
Editor: Piero Del Giudice
Profile: Magazine concerning fashion and culture. Includes information about art, the theatre and the cinema.
Language(s): Italian
Readership: Aimed at professional women.
ADVERTISING RATES:
Full Page Mono .... CHF 1989
Full Page Colour .... CHF 3372
Mechanical Data: Type Area: 234 x 165 mm
Copy instructions: *Copy Date:* 14 days prior to publication
CONSUMER: WOMEN'S INTEREST CONSUMER MAGAZINES: Women's Interest

DER GARTENBAU L'HORTICULTURE 1913536S21A-630
Editorial: Gärtnerstr. 12, 4501 SOLOTHURN
Tel: 32 6226622 **Fax:** 32 6228162
Email: red.sigg@gartenbau-verlag.ch **Web site:** http://www.gartenbau-online.ch
Freq: Weekly; **Annual Sub.:** CHF 138,00; **Circ:** 5,918
Editor: Claudia-Regina Sigg; **Advertising Manager:** Reto Maurer
Profile: Magazine covering landscaping, nurseries, flower production, cut flowers, trees, shrubs, perennials and vegetables.
Language(s): French; German
ADVERTISING RATES:
Full Page Mono .... CHF 1675
Full Page Colour .... CHF 2150
Mechanical Data: Type Area: 259 x 180 mm, No. of Columns (Display): 4, Col Widths (Display): 40 mm
Copy instructions: *Copy Date:* 8 days prior to publication
Official Journal of: Organ d. Schweizer. Fachvereinigung Gebäudebegrünung, d. Schweizer. Schnittblumenproduzenten, d. VSB Verb. Schweizer. Baumschulen, d. GBS Grüne Berufe Schweiz, d. VEOe Verein Ehemaliger d. kantonalen Gartenbauschule Oeschberg, d. Garten-Center Fachverb. Schweiz u. d. Bundes Schweizer Baumpflege BSB

DER GARTENFREUND LE JARDIN FAMILIAL 1641412S93-104
Editorial: Sturzeneggstr. 23, 9015 ST. GALLEN
Tel: 71 3112719 **Fax:** 71 2744078
Email: waschaffner@bluewin.ch **Web site:** http://www.familiengaertner.ch
Freq: Monthly; Free to qualifying individuals
Annual Sub.: CHF 24,00; **Circ:** 27,000
Editor: Walter Schaffner
Profile: Magazine for garden fans.
Language(s): French; German
ADVERTISING RATES:
Full Page Mono .... CHF 1865
Full Page Colour .... CHF 2660
Mechanical Data: Type Area: 252 x 188 mm
Copy instructions: *Copy Date:* 19 days prior to publication
CONSUMER: GARDENING

GASTRO JOURNAL 764174S11A-343
Editorial: Blumenfeldstr. 20, 8046 ZÜRICH
Tel: 44 3775305 **Fax:** 44 3775070
Email: redaktion@gastrojournal.ch **Web site:** http://www.gastrojournal.ch
Freq: Weekly; Free to qualifying individuals
Annual Sub.: CHF 135,00; **Circ:** 26,500
Editor: Matthias Nold; **Advertising Manager:** Claudia Antener
Profile: Magazine about hotels, restaurants and tourism.
Language(s): French; German
ADVERTISING RATES:
Full Page Mono .... CHF 7656
Full Page Colour .... CHF 7656
Mechanical Data: Type Area: 440 x 290 mm, No. of Columns (Display): 10, Col Widths (Display): 27 mm
Copy instructions: *Copy Date:* 4 days prior to publication
BUSINESS: CATERING: Catering, Hotels & Restaurants

GASTROFÜHRER 1859749S89A-399
Editorial: Spalenring 4, 4055 BASEL **Tel:** 61 2814672
Email: a.honegger@guide-bleu.ch **Web site:** http://www.guide-bleu.ch
Freq: Annual; **Cover Price:** CHF 48,00; **Circ:** 20,000
Editor: Anton Herbert Honegger; **Advertising Manager:** Samuel Abt
Profile: Gastronomy guide.
Language(s): German
ADVERTISING RATES:
Full Page Mono .... CHF 4000
Full Page Colour .... CHF 4000
Mechanical Data: Type Area: 154 x 85 mm

GAULT MILLAU GUIDE SCHWEIZ 728370S89A-80
Editorial: Dufourstr. 23, 8008 ZÜRICH
Tel: 44 2596900 **Fax:** 44 2620442
Email: gaultmillau@ringier.ch **Web site:** http://www.ringier.ch
Freq: Annual; **Cover Price:** CHF 49,90; **Circ:** 30,000
Editor: Urs Heller
Profile: Swiss gastronomy guide.
Language(s): German
ADVERTISING RATES:
Full Page Mono .... CHF 4650
Full Page Colour .... CHF 5950
Mechanical Data: Type Area: 184 x 113 mm
Copy instructions: *Copy Date:* 60 days prior to publication

GDI IMPULS 728391S14A-460
Editorial: Landhaldenstr. 21, 8803 RÜSCHLIKON
Tel: 44 7246111 **Fax:** 44 7246262
Email: impuls@gdi.ch **Web site:** http://www.gdi-impuls.ch
Freq: Quarterly; **Annual Sub.:** CHF 120,00; **Circ:** 3,022
Editor: Detlef Gürtler
Profile: Journal of the Gottlieb Duttweiler Institute for Economic and Social Studies.
Language(s): German
ADVERTISING RATES:
Full Page Mono .... CHF 2420
Full Page Colour .... CHF 2420
Mechanical Data: Type Area: 213 x 177 mm, No. of Columns (Display): 3, Col Widths (Display): 56 mm
Copy instructions: *Copy Date:* 37 days prior to publication
BUSINESS: COMMERCE, INDUSTRY & MANAGEMENT

GEBÄUDEHÜLLE SCHWEIZ 1852126S4E-831
Editorial: Lindenstr. 4, 9240 UZWIL **Tel:** 71 9557030 **Fax:** 71 9557040
Email: chantal.hueppi@gh-schweiz.ch **Web site:** http://www.gh-schweiz.ch
Freq: 11 issues yearly; **Annual Sub.:** CHF 95,00; **Circ:** 1,600
Editor: Chantal Hüppi
Profile: Building sector magazine.
Language(s): German
ADVERTISING RATES:
Full Page Mono .... CHF 920
Full Page Colour .... CHF 1970
Mechanical Data: Type Area: 265 x 185 mm

GEFIEDERTER FREUND 1648739S81X-290
Editorial: Gässlimattweg 8, 5703 SEON
Tel: 62 7774258 **Fax:** 62 7774259
Email: schriftleitung@exotis.ch **Web site:** http://www.exotis.ch
Freq: 8 issues yearly; Free to qualifying individuals
Annual Sub.: CHF 72,00; **Circ:** 1,500
Editor: Markus Lüscher; **Advertising Manager:** Markus Lüscher
Profile: Magazine about keeping, breeding and protecting exotic birds.
Language(s): German
ADVERTISING RATES:
Full Page Mono .... CHF 600
Full Page Colour .... CHF 600
Mechanical Data: No. of Columns (Display): 3, Col Widths (Display): 60 mm
Copy instructions: *Copy Date:* 35 days prior to publication
CONSUMER: ANIMALS & PETS

GEGENWART 764265S82-2208
Editorial: Burgunderstr. 132, 3018 BERN
Tel: 31 9914823 **Fax:** 31 9914823
Freq: Quarterly; **Annual Sub.:** CHF 70,00; **Circ:** 1,500
Editor: Gerold Aregger
Profile: Magazine about social, soul and life questions.
Language(s): German
ADVERTISING RATES:
Full Page Mono .... CHF 350
Mechanical Data: Type Area: 183 x 133 mm
CONSUMER: CURRENT AFFAIRS & POLITICS

DER GEMÜSEBAU LE MARAÎCHER 728644S26C-30
Editorial: Kapellenstr. 5, 3001 BERN **Tel:** 31 3853620 **Fax:** 31 3853630
Email: info@vsgp-ums.ch **Web site:** http://www.swissveg.com
Freq: 6 issues yearly; **Annual Sub.:** CHF 56,00; **Circ:** 3,000
Editor: David Eppenberger
Profile: Journal of the Swiss Vegetable Producers' Union.
Language(s): French; German
Readership: Read by vegetable growers and vegetable research consultants.
ADVERTISING RATES:
Full Page Mono .... CHF 1200
Full Page Colour .... CHF 1575
Mechanical Data: Type Area: 272 x 192 mm, No. of Columns (Display): 2, Col Widths (Display): 94 mm
Copy instructions: *Copy Date:* 13 days prior to publication
BUSINESS: GARDEN TRADE

GENERAL-ANZEIGER GA 1656721S72-9713
Editorial: Storchengasse 15, 5201 BRUGG
Tel: 56 4607750 **Fax:** 56 4607780
Email: s.killias@general-anzeiger.ch **Web site:** http://www.effingerhof.ch
Freq: Weekly; **Cover Price:** Free; **Circ:** 23,595
Editor: Sonja Killias; **Advertising Manager:** Othmar Vogel
Profile: Advertising journal (house-to-house) concentrating on local stories.
Language(s): German
ADVERTISING RATES:
Full Page Mono .... CHF 3916
Full Page Colour .... CHF 4224
Mechanical Data: Type Area: 440 x 290 mm, No. of Columns (Display): 10, Col Widths (Display): 25 mm
Copy instructions: *Copy Date:* 2 days prior to publication
LOCAL NEWSPAPERS

GENETIC COUNSELING 1853328S56A-2192
Editorial: 46, ch. de la Mousse, 1225 CHÊNE-BOURG **Tel:** 22 7029311 **Fax:** 22 7029355
Email: administration@medhyg.ch **Web site:** http://www.medecinehygiene.ch
Freq: Quarterly; **Annual Sub.:** CHF 294,00; **Circ:** 400
Editor: J.P. Fryns
Profile: Publication about the medical, psychological and ethical aspects of genetic counselling.
Language(s): English

GESUNDHEITSPOLITISCHE INFORMATIONEN GPI POLITIQUE DE SANTÉ: INFORMATIONS PSI 1644490S56A-2050
Editorial: Postfach 686, 3000 BERN 8
Tel: 31 3138866 **Fax:** 31 3138899
Email: redaktion@sggp.ch **Web site:** http://www.sggp.ch
Freq: Quarterly; **Circ:** 1,384
Profile: Magazine providing health political information.
Language(s): English; French; German
BUSINESS: HEALTH & MEDICAL

GESUNDHEITSSCHUTZ UND UMWELTTECHNIK 2002173S57-737
Editorial: Postfach 2250, 8645 RAPPERSWIL-JONA
Tel: 55 2128404 **Fax:** 55 2129774
Email: peyer.presse@bluewin.ch
Freq: Quarterly; **Cover Price:** CHF 80,00
Free to qualifying individuals ; **Circ:** 1,100
Editor: W. Peyer; **Advertising Manager:** Susanne Bruderer
Profile: Journal covering health and environmental technology.
Language(s): German
ADVERTISING RATES:
Full Page Mono .... CHF 1400
Full Page Colour .... CHF 2360
Mechanical Data: Type Area: 265 x 178 mm
Copy instructions: *Copy Date:* 28 days prior to publication

DAS GESUNDHEITSWESEN IN DER SCHWEIZ LEISTUNGEN, KOSTEN, PREISE 728851S56A-740
Editorial: Petersgraben 35, 4003 BASEL
Tel: 61 2643434 **Fax:** 61 2643435
Email: info@interpharma.ch **Web site:** http://www.interpharma.ch
Freq: Annual; **Cover Price:** Free; **Circ:** 35,000
Profile: Magazine on the Swiss health care system.
Language(s): German

GEWERBE LUZERN 1855854S14A-1329
Editorial: Eichwaldstr. 15, 6002 LUZERN
Tel: 41 3180318 **Fax:** 41 3181319
Email: info@gewerbeverband-lu.ch **Web site:** http://www.gewerbeverband-lu.ch
Freq: 10 issues yearly; Free to qualifying individuals
Annual Sub.: CHF 35,00; **Circ:** 8,500
Editor: Ursula Schürmann-Häberli
Profile: Regional business magazine.
Language(s): German
Mechanical Data: Type Area: 270 x 185 mm
Copy instructions: *Copy Date:* 18 days prior to publication

GF GESCHÄFTSFÜHRER 1842139S14A-1246
Editorial: Leimgrubenweg 4, 4053 BASEL
Tel: 61 3382000 **Fax:** 61 3382002
Email: n.freundlieb@prestigemedia.ch **Web site:** http://www.der-geschaeftsfuehrer.ch
Freq: Quarterly; **Annual Sub.:** CHF 19,00; **Circ:** 15,000
Editor: Niggi Freundlieb
Profile: Regional Basle business magazine.
Language(s): German
ADVERTISING RATES:
Full Page Mono .... CHF 3600
Full Page Colour .... CHF 3600
Mechanical Data: Type Area: 270 x 180 mm, No. of Columns (Display): 3, Col Widths (Display): 60 mm
Copy instructions: *Copy Date:* 25 days prior to publication

GHI GENÈVE HOME INFORMATIONS 728920S72-3320
Editorial: 22, av. du Mail, 1211 GENF 4
Tel: 22 8072211 **Fax:** 22 8072233
Email: redaction@ghi.ch **Web site:** http://www.ghi.ch
Freq: Weekly; **Cover Price:** Free; **Circ:** 258,000
Editor: Charles-André Aymon; **Advertising Manager:** Christine Fudez

Profile: Advertising journal (house-to-house) concentrating on local stories.
Language(s): French
ADVERTISING RATES:
Full Page Mono .... CHF 9812
Full Page Colour .... CHF 15708
Mechanical Data: Type Area: 440 x 290 mm, No. of Columns (Display): 10, Col Widths (Display): 25 mm
Copy instructions: *Copy Date:* 5 days prior to publication
LOCAL NEWSPAPERS

GLARISSIMO BUSINESS
1843484S14A-1250
Editorial: Zwinglistr. 6, 8750 GLARUS
Tel: 55 6452828 **Fax:** 55 6406440
Web site: http://www.suedostschweiz.ch
Freq: Half-yearly; **Circ:** 9,000
Profile: Regional business information.
Language(s): German
ADVERTISING RATES:
Full Page Mono .... CHF 2150
Full Page Colour .... CHF 2150
Mechanical Data: Type Area: 252 x 190 mm
Copy instructions: *Copy Date:* 31 days prior to publication

GLÜCKS POST
1844609S74A-492
Editorial: Dufourstr. 49, 8008 ZÜRICH
Tel: 44 2596378 **Fax:** 44 4548272
Email: gluueckspost@ringier.ch **Web site:** http://www.glueckspost.ch
Freq: Weekly; **Annual Sub.:** CHF 159,00; **Circ:** 219,000
Editor: Beatrice Zollinger; **Advertising Manager:** Reinelde Wegmann
Profile: Women's magazine with information about the home and family, beauty, fashion and people. Also includes shopping features and competitions.
Language(s): German
ADVERTISING RATES:
Full Page Mono .... CHF 12885
Full Page Colour .... CHF 12885
Mechanical Data: Type Area: 261 x 189 mm, No. of Columns (Display): 4, Col Widths (Display): 45 mm
Copy instructions: *Copy Date:* 14 days prior to publication
Supplement(s): Glücks Post Super-Rätsel; TV täglich

DAS GOETHEANUM
729063S94X-300_50
Editorial: Postfach, 4143 DORNACH 1
Tel: 61 7064464 **Fax:** 61 7064465
Email: redaktion@dasgoetheanum.ch **Web site:** http://www.dasgoetheanum.ch
Freq: 45 issues yearly; **Annual Sub.:** CHF 160,00; **Circ:** 8,327
Editor: Sebastian Jüngel
Profile: International journal relating to the spiritual teachings of Rudolf Steiner.
Language(s): German
ADVERTISING RATES:
Full Page Mono .... CHF 2050
Mechanical Data: Type Area: 276 x 200 mm, No. of Columns (Display): 3, Col Widths (Display): 64 mm
Copy instructions: *Copy Date:* 9 days prior to publication
Supplement(s): Anthroposophie weltweit
CONSUMER: OTHER CLASSIFICATIONS: Miscellaneous

GOLD'OR
1641304S52A-42
Editorial: Postfach 1034, 6341 BAAR
Tel: 41 7660044 **Fax:** 41 7660055
Email: info@goldor.ch **Web site:** http://www.goldor.ch
Freq: 10 issues yearly; **Annual Sub.:** CHF 96,00; **Circ:** 3,300
Editor: Rahel Marschall; **Advertising Manager:** Tanja Fuhrer
Profile: Magazine containing information on the jewellery, clock and watch trade.
Language(s): French; German
ADVERTISING RATES:
Full Page Mono .... CHF 1900
Full Page Colour .... CHF 2990
Mechanical Data: Type Area: 280 x 205 mm
Copy instructions: *Copy Date:* 30 days prior to publication
BUSINESS: GIFT TRADE: Jewellery

G'PLUS
729162S26C-40
Editorial: Forchstr. 287, 8008 ZÜRICH
Tel: 44 3885354 **Fax:** 44 3885340
Email: redaktion@gplus.ch **Web site:** http://www.gplus.ch
Freq: 24 issues yearly; **Annual Sub.:** CHF 97,00; **Circ:** 4,000
Editor: Anita Kägi Vontobel; **Advertising Manager:** Urs Günther
Profile: Magazine of the Swiss Gardeners Association.
Language(s): German
ADVERTISING RATES:
Full Page Mono .... CHF 1500
Full Page Colour .... CHF 1950
Mechanical Data: Type Area: 269 x 182 mm
Copy instructions: *Copy Date:* 7 days prior to publication
BUSINESS: GARDEN TRADE

GRENCHNER TAGBLATT GT
729223S67B-1180
Editorial: Zuchwiler Str. 21, 4501 SOLOTHURN
Tel: 32 6247474 **Fax:** 32 6247788
Email: info@gtonline.ch **Web site:** http://www.gtonline.ch
Freq: 312 issues yearly; **Annual Sub.:** CHF 369,00; **Circ:** 4,470
Profile: Daily newspaper with regional news and a local sports section.
Language(s): German
Mechanical Data: Type Area: 430 x 290 mm, No. of Columns (Display): 10, Col Widths (Display): 26 mm
Copy instructions: *Copy Date:* 1 day prior to publication
REGIONAL DAILY & SUNDAY NEWSPAPERS: Regional Daily Newspapers

IL GRIGIONE ITALIANO
729241S72-3720
Editorial: strada S. Bartolomeo, 7742 POSCHIAVO
Tel: 81 8440163 **Fax:** 81 8441323
Freq: Weekly; **Annual Sub.:** CHF 80,00; **Circ:** 3,246
Editor: Remo Tosio
Profile: Regional weekly covering politics, economics, sport, travel, technology and the arts.
Language(s): Italian
ADVERTISING RATES:
SCC .... CHF 13,10
Mechanical Data: Type Area: 433 x 289 mm, No. of Columns (Display): 10, Col Widths (Display): 25 mm
Copy instructions: *Copy Date:* 2 days prior to publication
LOCAL NEWSPAPERS

DIE GRÜNE
729297S21A-220
Editorial: Thunstr. 78, 3000 BERN 15
Tel: 31 9583312 **Fax:** 31 9583313
Email: redaktion@diegruene.ch **Web site:** http://www.diegruene.ch
Freq: 26 issues yearly; **Annual Sub.:** CHF 92,00; **Circ:** 16,000
Editor: Stefan Kohler
Profile: Magazine about Swiss agriculture.
Language(s): German
ADVERTISING RATES:
Full Page Mono .... CHF 2800
Full Page Colour .... CHF 3250
Mechanical Data: Type Area: 262 x 185 mm, No. of Columns (Display): 3, Col Widths (Display): 57 mm
Copy instructions: *Copy Date:* 8 days prior to publication
BUSINESS: AGRICULTURE & FARMING

GUIDE CAMPING CAMPING FÜHRER GUIDA DEI CAMPEGGI
1852324S89A-393
Editorial: 4, chemin de Blandonnet, 1214 VERNIER
Tel: 22 4172030 **Fax:** 22 4172042
Email: cpg@tcs.ch **Web site:** http://www.campingtcs.ch
Freq: Annual; **Cover Price:** CHF 18,90; **Circ:** 13,000
Editor: Gloria Noualhat; **Advertising Manager:** Gloria Noualhat
Profile: Camping guide for Switzerland, Austria, Italy, France, Spain, Portugal and Croatia.
Language(s): English; French; German; Italian
Mechanical Data: Type Area: 200 x 105 mm

GUIDE PLAISIRS GASTRONOMIE MAGAZINE
1851146S89A-391
Editorial: 4, rue de l'Etang, 2013 COLOMBIER
Tel: 32 8417250 **Fax:** 32 8411521
Freq: Annual; **Cover Price:** CHF 35,00; **Circ:** 14,000
Editor: R. Gessler
Profile: Gastronomy magazie.
Language(s): French
ADVERTISING RATES:
Full Page Colour .... CHF 3850

GWA
2002840S58-216
Editorial: Grütlistr. 44, 8027 ZÜRICH **Tel:** 44 2883333
Fax: 44 2883326
Email: e.pintimalli@svgw.ch **Web site:** http://www.gwa.ch
Freq: Monthly; **Annual Sub.:** CHF 205,00; **Circ:** 3,000
Editor: Susanne Mettler
Profile: Magazine on gas, water, sewage about energy and environment.
Language(s): French; German
ADVERTISING RATES:
Full Page Mono .... CHF 1956
Full Page Colour .... CHF 3260
Mechanical Data: Type Area: 259 x 185 mm
Official Journal of: Organ d. Verb. Schweizer Abwasser- u. Gewässerschutzfachleute

GYM LIVE
1775811S75A-386
Editorial: Bahnhofstr. 38, 5001 AARAU
Tel: 62 8378200 **Fax:** 62 8231011
Email: peter.friedli@stv-fsg.ch **Web site:** http://www.stv-fsg.ch
Freq: 6 issues yearly; **Annual Sub.:** CHF 20,00; **Circ:** 110,199
Editor: Peter Friedli
Language(s): German
ADVERTISING RATES:
Full Page Mono .... CHF 7900
Full Page Colour .... CHF 7900
Mechanical Data: Type Area: 268 x 188 mm
Supplement(s): GYM tech
CONSUMER: SPORT

GYM LIVE
1775812S75A-387
Editorial: c.p. 1344, 1870 MONTHEY
Tel: 79 2722571
Email: corinne.gabioud@stv-fsg.ch **Web site:** http://www.stv-fsg.ch
Freq: 6 issues yearly; **Annual Sub.:** CHF 20,00; **Circ:** 17,417
Editor: Corinne Gabioud
Language(s): French
ADVERTISING RATES:
Full Page Mono .... CHF 7900
Full Page Colour .... CHF 7900
Mechanical Data: Type Area: 268 x 188 mm
Copy instructions: *Copy Date:* 28 days prior to publication
Supplement(s): GYM tech
CONSUMER: SPORT

GYM LIVE
1775813S75A-388
Editorial: vicollo alla Monda, 17, 6517 ARBEDO
Tel: 91 8358135 **Fax:** 91 8358136
Email: red-arbedo@stv-fsg.ch **Web site:** http://www.stv-fsg.ch
Freq: 6 issues yearly; **Annual Sub.:** CHF 20,00; **Circ:** 3,140
Editor: Emiliano Camponova
Language(s): Italian
ADVERTISING RATES:
Full Page Mono .... CHF 1000
Full Page Colour .... CHF 2330
Mechanical Data: Type Area: 268 x 188 mm
Copy instructions: *Copy Date:* 28 days prior to publication
CONSUMER: SPORT

GYNÄKOLOGIE
729456S56A-760
Editorial: Schaffhauser Str. 13, 8212 NEUHAUSEN
Tel: 52 6755182 **Fax:** 52 6755061
Email: hirrle@rosenfluh.ch **Web site:** http://www.rosenfluh.ch
Freq: 6 issues yearly; **Annual Sub.:** CHF 46,00; **Circ:** 5,000
Editor: Bärbel Hirrle
Profile: Journal about medicine and gynaecology.
Language(s): German
ADVERTISING RATES:
Full Page Mono .... CHF 3280
Full Page Colour .... CHF 4880
Mechanical Data: Type Area: 281 x 175 mm
Copy instructions: *Copy Date:* 25 days prior to publication

GYNÄKOLOGIE
729456S56A-2170
Editorial: Schaffhauser Str. 13, 8212 NEUHAUSEN
Tel: 52 6755182 **Fax:** 52 6755061
Email: hirrle@rosenfluh.ch **Web site:** http://www.rosenfluh.ch
Freq: 6 issues yearly; **Annual Sub.:** CHF 46,00; **Circ:** 5,000
Editor: Bärbel Hirrle
Profile: Journal about medicine and gynaecology.
Language(s): German
ADVERTISING RATES:
Full Page Mono .... CHF 3280
Full Page Colour .... CHF 4880
Mechanical Data: Type Area: 281 x 175 mm
Copy instructions: *Copy Date:* 25 days prior to publication

GYNÄKOLOGISCH-GEBURTSHILFLICHE RUNDSCHAU
729460S56A-780
Editorial: Allschwiler Str. 10, 4055 BASEL
Tel: 61 3061111 **Fax:** 61 3061234
Email: karger@karger.ch **Web site:** http://www.karger.com/ggr
Freq: Quarterly; **Annual Sub.:** CHF 1150,60; **Circ:** 1,950
Editor: D. Fink; **Advertising Manager:** Thomas Maurer
Profile: Magazine about gynaecology and obstetrics.
Language(s): English; French; German
ADVERTISING RATES:
Full Page Mono .... CHF 1760
Full Page Colour .... CHF 3200
Mechanical Data: Type Area: 242 x 180 mm
Official Journal of: Organ d. Österr. Ges. f. Gynäkologie u. Geburtshilfe u. d. Schweizer. Ges. f. Gynäkologie u. Geburtshilfe

HAGEL KURIER
729493S1D-21
Editorial: Seilergraben 61, 8021 ZÜRICH
Tel: 44 2572211 **Fax:** 44 2572212
Email: info@hagel.ch **Web site:** http://www.hagel.ch
Freq: Half-yearly; **Circ:** 900
Profile: Magazine for employees of Schweizer Hagel.
Language(s): German

HANDEL HEUTE
1656748S14A-1189
Editorial: Industriestr. 37, 3178 BÖSINGEN
Tel: 31 7409730 **Fax:** 31 7409739
Email: info@handel-heute.ch **Web site:** http://www.handel-heute.ch
Freq: 6 issues yearly; **Annual Sub.:** CHF 48,00; **Circ:** 34,500
Editor: Reto Wüthrich; **Advertising Manager:** Hans-Peter Streit
Profile: Magazine from the Swiss retail trade industry.
Language(s): German
ADVERTISING RATES:
Full Page Mono .... CHF 5980
Full Page Colour .... CHF 7480
Mechanical Data: Type Area: 249 x 182 mm, No. of Columns (Display): 4, Col Widths (Display): 43 mm
Copy instructions: *Copy Date:* 18 days prior to publication

HANDEL + FREIZEIT
1656749S72-9723
Editorial: Klosterstr. 32, 9403 GOLDACH
Tel: 71 8416262 **Fax:** 71 8452606
Email: info@handelverlag.ch **Web site:** http://www.handelverlag.ch
Freq: 9 issues yearly; **Cover Price:** Free; **Circ:** 104,940
Editor: Kurt Höhener; **Advertising Manager:** Kurt Höhener
Profile: Advertising journal (house-to-house) concentrating on local stories.
Language(s): German
ADVERTISING RATES:
Full Page Mono .... CHF 2900
Full Page Colour .... CHF 2900
Mechanical Data: Type Area: 285 x 209 mm, No. of Columns (Display): 4, Col Widths (Display): 50 mm
Copy instructions: *Copy Date:* 8 days prior to publication
LOCAL NEWSPAPERS

HANDELN >>>>>>
1645466S87-2797
Editorial: Seminarstrasse 28, 8042 ZÜRICH
Tel: 44 3608800 **Fax:** 44 3608801
Email: info@heks.ch **Web site:** http://www.heks.ch
Freq: Quarterly; **Annual Sub.:** CHF 10,00; **Circ:** 52,000
Editor: Susanne Stahel
Profile: Magazine of the Swiss Evangelical churches.
Language(s): German
CONSUMER: RELIGIOUS

HANDELSZEITUNG & THE WALL STREET JOURNAL
729701S14A-500
Editorial: Förrlibuckstr. 70, 8021 ZÜRICH
Tel: 43 4445900 **Fax:** 43 4445930
Email: redaktion@handelszeitung.ch **Web site:** http://www.handelszeitung.ch
Freq: Weekly; **Annual Sub.:** CHF 218,00; **Circ:** 43,940
Editor: Beat Balzli; **News Editor:** Alice Chalupny
Profile: Regional weekly covering politics, economics, sport, travel, technology and the arts.
Language(s): German
ADVERTISING RATES:
SCC .... CHF 92,00
Mechanical Data: Type Area: 438 x 291 mm, No. of Columns (Display): 10, Col Widths (Display): 27 mm
Copy instructions: *Copy Date:* 2 days prior to publication
Supplement(s): First. by Handelszeitung; Home Electronic Extra; Leader spezial
BUSINESS: COMMERCE, INDUSTRY & MANAGEMENT

HANDICAPFORUM
1693434S94F-589
Editorial: Klybeckstr. 64, 4057 BASEL
Tel: 61 2052929 **Fax:** 61 2052928
Email: info@behindertenforum.ch **Web site:** http://www.behindertenforum.ch
Freq: Quarterly; **Circ:** 5,500
Editor: Barbara Imobersteg
Profile: Magazine from the handicapped self aid group in Basel.
Language(s): German
ADVERTISING RATES:
Full Page Mono .... CHF 1100
Full Page Colour .... CHF 1250
Mechanical Data: Type Area: 274 x 180 mm
CONSUMER: OTHER CLASSIFICATIONS: Disability

L' HEBDO
729898S73-120
Editorial: 3, pont Bessières, 1005 LAUSANNE
Tel: 21 3317600 **Fax:** 21 3317601
Email: hebdo@ringier.ch **Web site:** http://www.hebdo.ch
Freq: Weekly; **Annual Sub.:** CHF 215,00; **Circ:** 60,000
Editor: Alain Jeannet
Profile: French language magazine containing news and articles about politics, economy, society and culture.
Language(s): French
ADVERTISING RATES:
Full Page Mono .... CHF 12900
Full Page Colour .... CHF 12900
Mechanical Data: Type Area: 244 x 182 mm, No. of Columns (Display): 3, Col Widths (Display): 58 mm
Copy instructions: *Copy Date:* 7 days prior to publication

Supplement(s): Montres Passion; Type
CONSUMER: NATIONAL & INTERNATIONAL PERIODICALS

HEIMATBLATT FÜR DIE GEMEINDEN THAYNGEN (MIT ALTDORF, BARZHEIM, BIBERN, HOFEN UND OPFERTSHOFEN), BÜTTENHARDT, DÖRFLINGEN, LOHN UND STETTEN
1614897S72-9584
Editorial: Im Merzenbrunnen, 8240 THAYNGEN
Tel: 52 6454125 **Fax:** 52 6454199
Email: heimatblatt.redaktion@augustin.ch
Freq: Weekly; **Annual Sub.:** CHF 93,00; **Circ:** 1,849
Editor: Ulrich Flückiger; **Advertising Manager:** Janine Basler
Profile: Regional weekly covering politics, economics, sport, travel, technology and the arts.
Language(s): German
Mechanical Data: Type Area: 217 x 145 mm, No. of Columns (Display): 5, Col Widths (Display): 27 mm
Copy instructions: *Copy Date:* 2 days prior to publication
LOCAL NEWSPAPERS

HEIMATSCHUTZ PATRIMOINE
1847744S57-715
Editorial: Seefeldstr. 5a, 8008 ZÜRICH
Tel: 44 2545700 **Fax:** 44 2522870
Email: redaktion@heimatschutz.ch **Web site:** http://www.heimatschutz.ch
Freq: Quarterly; Free to qualifying individuals
Annual Sub.: CHF 30,00; **Circ:** 18,000
Editor: Peter Egli
Profile: Magazine focusing on environmental and architectural protection.
Language(s): French; German

HELVETICA CHIMICA ACTA
1853335S37-805
Editorial: Hofwiesenstr. 26, 8042 ZÜRICH
Tel: 44 3602434 **Fax:** 44 3602435
Email: vhca@vhca.ch
Freq: Monthly; **Annual Sub.:** CHF 2484,00; **Circ:** 1,500
Editor: M. Volkan Kisakürek
Profile: Magazine covering all aspects of chemistry.
Language(s): English
ADVERTISING RATES:
Full Page Mono .... CHF 1400
Full Page Colour .... CHF 2720
Mechanical Data: Type Area: 200 x 125 mm
Copy instructions: *Copy Date:* 21 days prior to publication

HK GEBÄUDETECHNIK
730337S3D-100
Editorial: Neumattstr. 1, 5001 AARAU
Tel: 58 2005611 **Fax:** 58 2005661
Email: peter.warthmann@hk-gebaeudetechnik.ch
Web site: http://www.hk-gebaeudetechnik.ch
Freq: Monthly; **Annual Sub.:** CHF 120,00; **Circ:** 8,500
Editor: Peter Warthmann; **Advertising Manager:** Rolf Niederberger
Profile: Magazine about air conditioning, air and environment technologies, use of energy.
Language(s): German
ADVERTISING RATES:
Full Page Mono .... CHF 2715
Full Page Colour .... CHF 3915
Mechanical Data: Type Area: 264 x 184 mm, No. of Columns (Display): 4
Copy instructions: *Copy Date:* 30 days prior to publication
BUSINESS: HEATING & VENTILATION: Heating & Plumbing

HOCHPARTERRE
730378S4A-3
Editorial: Ausstellungsstr. 25, 8005 ZÜRICH
Tel: 44 4442888 **Fax:** 44 4442889
Email: gantenbein@hochparterre.ch **Web site:** http://www.hochparterre.ch
Freq: 10 issues yearly; **Annual Sub.:** CHF 158,00; **Circ:** 8,000
Editor: Jakob Gantenbein; **Advertising Manager:** Susanne von Arx
Profile: Magazine focusing on design and architecture. Contains details of design tenders.
Language(s): German
Readership: Read by architects and designers.
ADVERTISING RATES:
Full Page Mono .... CHF 4500
Full Page Colour .... CHF 6920
Mechanical Data: Type Area: 306 x 225 mm, No. of Columns (Display): 4, Col Widths (Display): 53 mm
Copy instructions: *Copy Date:* 30 days prior to publication
BUSINESS: ARCHITECTURE & BUILDING: Architecture

HOCHPARTERRE. WETTBEWERBE
766484S4E-772
Editorial: Ausstellungsstr. 25, 8005 ZÜRICH
Tel: 44 4442888 **Fax:** 4144 4442889
Email: wettbewerbe@hochparterre.ch **Web site:** http://www.hochparterre.ch
Freq: 5 issues yearly; **Annual Sub.:** CHF 169,00; **Circ:** 2,000
Editor: Ivo Bösch; **Advertising Manager:** Agnes Schmid
Profile: Magazine on the documentation of architectural competitions in Switzerland.
Language(s): French; German; Italian
ADVERTISING RATES:
Full Page Mono .... CHF 1800
Full Page Colour .... CHF 2500
Mechanical Data: Type Area: 267 x 181 mm

HOCHZEITSFÜHRER
1641105S74L-1
Editorial: Maihofstr. 76, 6002 LUZERN
Tel: 41 4295252 **Fax:** 41 4295222
Email: info@lzfachverlag.ch **Web site:** http://www.hochzeitsfuehrer.ch
Freq: Annual; **Cover Price:** Free; **Circ:** 10,000
Editor: Carolina Hügi
Profile: Magazine containing wedding advice.
Language(s): German
ADVERTISING RATES:
Full Page Mono .... CHF 3400
Full Page Colour .... CHF 3400
Mechanical Data: Type Area: 265 x 188 mm

HÖFNER VOLKSBLATT
730407S67B-1220
Editorial: Verenastr. 2, 8832 WOLLERAU
Tel: 44 7870300 **Fax:** 44 7870301
Email: info@theilerdruck.ch **Web site:** http://www.theilerdruck.ch
Freq: 260 issues yearly; **Annual Sub.:** CHF 208,00; **Circ:** 11,588
Profile: Regional daily newspaper covering politics, economics, sport, travel, technology and the arts.
Language(s): German
ADVERTISING RATES:
SCC .... CHF 27,00
Mechanical Data: Type Area: 440 x 286 mm, No. of Columns (Display): 10, Col Widths (Display): 25 mm
Copy instructions: *Copy Date:* 1 day prior to publication
REGIONAL DAILY & SUNDAY NEWSPAPERS: Regional Daily Newspapers

HOME ELECTRONICS
730494S78R-1
Editorial: Zypressenstr. 60, 8040 ZÜRICH
Tel: 44 2454511 **Fax:** 44 2454500
Email: redaktion@home-electronics.ch **Web site:** http://www.home-electronics.ch
Freq: 11 issues yearly; **Annual Sub.:** CHF 78,00; **Circ:** 9,532
Editor: Rolf Frank; **Advertising Manager:** Dominik Achermann
Profile: Magazine about the sale and repair of video recorders.
Language(s): German
ADVERTISING RATES:
Full Page Mono .... CHF 6940
Full Page Colour .... CHF 6940
Mechanical Data: Type Area: 262 x 197 mm
Copy instructions: *Copy Date:* 28 days prior to publication
CONSUMER: CONSUMER ELECTRONICS: Consumer Electronics Related

HORIZONTE
719614S74N-20
Editorial: Baarerstr. 131, 6300 ZUG **Tel:** 41 7275050
Fax: 41 7275060
Email: christian.seeberger@zg.pro-senectute.ch **Web site:** http://www.zg.pro-senectute.ch
Freq: Half-yearly; **Cover Price:** Free; **Circ:** 12,000
Editor: Christian Seeberger; **Advertising Manager:** Milian Hunkeler
Profile: Event magazine for the elderly from the Swiss region of Zug.
Language(s): German
ADVERTISING RATES:
Full Page Colour .... CHF 3150
Mechanical Data: Type Area: 280 x 180 mm
Copy instructions: *Copy Date:* 50 days prior to publication

HUNDE
1641363S81B-1
Editorial: Belchenstr. 30, 5012 SCHÖNENWERD
Tel: 62 8270504 **Fax:** 62 8490377
Email: redaktion@skg.ch **Web site:** http://www.hundeweb.org
Freq: Monthly; **Annual Sub.:** CHF 75,00; **Circ:** 19,947
Editor: Ursula Känel Kocher
Profile: Magazine from the Swiss Kynologic Association.
Language(s): German
ADVERTISING RATES:
Full Page Mono .... CHF 2215
Full Page Colour .... CHF 4465
Mechanical Data: Type Arèa: 266 x 188 mm, No. of Columns (Display): 4, Col Widths (Display): 44 mm
Copy instructions: *Copy Date:* 10 days prior to publication
CONSUMER: ANIMALS & PETS: Dogs

ICT IN FINANCE
1852325S18B-385
Editorial: Postfach 228, 8907 WETTSWIL
Tel: 44 7778363 **Fax:** 44 7778366
Email: b.strebel@ict-magazine.ch **Web site:** http://www.ict-magazine.ch
Freq: Quarterly; **Annual Sub.:** CHF 37,00; **Circ:** 7,000
Editor: Brigitte Strebel; **Advertising Manager:** Marcel Bosshard
Profile: Magazine about information- and communications technologies for banking houses and insurances.
Language(s): German
ADVERTISING RATES:
Full Page Mono .... CHF 5640
Full Page Colour .... CHF 5640
Mechanical Data: Type Area: 243 x 178 mm
Copy instructions: *Copy Date:* 20 days prior to publication

ICT KOMMUNIKATION
733054S18B-342
Editorial: Hinterbergstr. 2, 8604 VOLKETSWIL
Tel: 44 9451333 **Fax:** 44 3813443
Email: karlheinz.pichler@ictk.ch **Web site:** http://www.ictk.ch
Freq: 10 issues yearly; **Annual Sub.:** CHF 44,00; **Circ:** 10,200
Editor: Karlheinz Pichler
Profile: Journal covering the whole communications field, including computing and telecommunications.
Language(s): German
ADVERTISING RATES:
Full Page Mono .... CHF 5600
Mechanical Data: Type Area: 270 x 184 mm, No. of Columns (Display): 4, Col Widths (Display): 43 mm
Copy instructions: *Copy Date:* 20 days prior to publication

IDEA
730759S4E-440
Editorial: Steinwiesenstr. 3, 8952 SCHLIEREN
Tel: 44 7333999 **Fax:** 44 7333989
Email: marianne.kuersteiner@blverlag.ch **Web site:** http://www.blverlag.ch
Freq: 6 issues yearly; **Annual Sub.:** CHF 34,00; **Circ:** 7,000
Editor: Marinne Kürsteiner; **Advertising Manager:** Gabriela Hüppi
Profile: Magazine for architects.
Language(s): French
ADVERTISING RATES:
Full Page Mono .... CHF 5100
Full Page Colour .... CHF 5100
Mechanical Data: Type Area: 270 x 184 mm, No. of Columns (Display): 4, Col Widths (Display): 43 mm
Copy instructions: *Copy Date:* 20 days prior to publication

IDEELLE
1641790S74A-466
Editorial: Haldenweg 9c, 4450 SISSACH
Tel: 61 2222380
Email: m.lienhard@bluewin.ch **Web site:** http://www.sgf.ch
Freq: 6 issues yearly; **Annual Sub.:** CHF 35,00; **Circ:** 3,300
Editor: Margrit Lienhard-Müller
Profile: Magazine for women.
Language(s): German
Mechanical Data: Type Area: 260 x 183 mm

IDPURE
1846743S19B-2
Editorial: 4a, chemin du Pré, 1110 MORGES 1
Tel: 848 437873
Email: redac@idpure.ch **Web site:** http://www.idpure.ch
Freq: Quarterly; **Annual Sub.:** CHF 42,00; **Circ:** 9,500
Editor: Thierry Hausermann
Profile: Magazine dedicated to professionals working in the graphic arts, images and design.
Language(s): English; French; German
ADVERTISING RATES:
Full Page Mono .... CHF 5800
Full Page Colour .... CHF 5800
Mechanical Data: Type Area: 280 x 220 mm
Copy instructions: *Copy Date:* 22 days prior to publication

ILLUSTRAZIONE TICINESE
1852554S73-383
Editorial: via Massagno, 10, 6908 LUGANO
Tel: 91 9732620 **Fax:** 91 9724565
Email: info@illustrazione.ch **Web site:** http://www.illustrazione.ch
Freq: Monthly; **Cover Price:** Free; **Circ:** 130,776
Editor: Matthias Werder
Profile: Family magazine.
Language(s): Italian
ADVERTISING RATES:
Full Page Mono .... CHF 7150
Full Page Colour .... CHF 10945
Mechanical Data: Type Area: 235 x 180 mm, No. of Columns (Display): 4, Col Widths (Display): 40 mm

L' ILLUSTRÉ
730866S73-140
Editorial: 3, pont Bessières, 1002 LAUSANNE
Tel: 21 3317500 **Fax:** 21 3317501
Email: illustre@ringier.ch **Web site:** http://www.illustre.ch
Freq: Weekly; **Annual Sub.:** CHF 179,00; **Circ:** 108,000
Editor: Michel Jeanneret; **Advertising Manager:** Patrick Zanello
Language(s): French
ADVERTISING RATES:
Full Page Mono .... CHF 18700
Full Page Colour .... CHF 18700
Mechanical Data: Type Area: 268 x 200 mm, No. of Columns (Display): 3, Col Widths (Display): 62 mm
Copy instructions: *Copy Date:* 9 days prior to publication
Supplement(s): al dente; Miss Suisse Magazine
CONSUMER: NATIONAL & INTERNATIONAL PERIODICALS

IMMOBILIEN BUSINESS
730916S1E-20
Editorial: Grubenstr. 56, 8045 ZÜRICH
Tel: 43 3333949 **Fax:** 43 3333950
Email: breiner@ibverlag.ch **Web site:** http://www.immobilienbusiness.ch
Freq: Monthly; **Annual Sub.:** CHF 120,00; **Circ:** 14,500
Editor: Rolf Breiner; **Advertising Manager:** Moritz Weibel
Profile: Magazine focusing on the business property trade.
Language(s): German
ADVERTISING RATES:
Full Page Mono .... CHF 6900
Full Page Colour .... CHF 6900
Mechanical Data: Type Area: 254 x 182 mm, No. of Columns (Display): 3, Col Widths (Display): 81 mm
Copy instructions: *Copy Date:* 14 days prior to publication
BUSINESS: FINANCE & ECONOMICS: Property

IMPACT
1858634S2A-685
Editorial: Giacomettistr. 15, 3000 BERN 31
Tel: 31 3583111 **Fax:** 31 3583100
Email: webteam@publisuisse.ch **Web site:** http://www.publisuisse.ch
Freq: 3 issues yearly; **Cover Price:** Free; **Circ:** 6,000
Editor: Markus Hollenstein
Profile: Magazine with information about recent issues from the media, concentrating on TV.
Language(s): German
Supplement(s): impact zoom

IMPULS
1648674S21A-594
Editorial: Schwarztorstr. 26, 3001 BERN
Tel: 31 3903336 **Fax:** 31 3903335
Email: info@alis.ch **Web site:** http://www.alis.ch
Freq: 11 issues yearly; **Annual Sub.:** CHF 60,00; **Circ:** 1,300
Editor: Michéle Joliat
Profile: Magazine from the Association of Agricultural Engineers.
Language(s): French; German
ADVERTISING RATES:
Full Page Mono .... CHF 1160
Full Page Colour .... CHF 1715
Mechanical Data: Type Area: 259 x 179 mm
Copy instructions: *Copy Date:* 20 days prior to publication

IMPULS
1648674S21A-618
Editorial: Schwarztorstr. 26, 3001 BERN
Tel: 31 3903336 **Fax:** 31 3903335
Email: info@alis.ch **Web site:** http://www.alis.ch
Freq: 11 issues yearly; **Annual Sub.:** CHF 60,00; **Circ:** 1,300
Editor: Michéle Joliat
Profile: Magazine from the Association of Agricultural Engineers.
Language(s): French; German
ADVERTISING RATES:
Full Page Mono .... CHF 1160
Full Page Colour .... CHF 1715
Mechanical Data: Type Area: 259 x 179 mm
Copy instructions: *Copy Date:* 20 days prior to publication

IN DUBIO
1752885S1A-290
Editorial: Malerweg 4, 3601 THUN **Tel:** 33 2222266
Fax: 33 2222267
Email: willener@rechtsanwaelte-thun.ch
Freq: 5 issues yearly; **Annual Sub.:** CHF 25,00; **Circ:** 1,600
Editor: Jürg Friedli
Profile: Magazine for lawyers.
Language(s): German
ADVERTISING RATES:
Full Page Mono .... CHF 620
Mechanical Data: Type Area: 171 x 125 mm

INDEX
1859761S14A-1349
Editorial: Felsenstr. 88, 9000 ST. GALLEN
Tel: 71 2284580 **Fax:** 71 2284540
Email: info@persens.ch **Web site:** http://www.indexonline.ch
Freq: Quarterly; **Annual Sub.:** CHF 92,00; **Circ:** 8,000
Editor: Otto Belz
Profile: Magazine about business economy.
Language(s): German
ADVERTISING RATES:
Full Page Mono .... CHF 4500
Full Page Colour .... CHF 4500
Mechanical Data: Type Area: 250 x 184 mm, No. of Columns (Display): 2, Col Widths (Display): 90 mm

INDUSTRIEARCHÄOLOGIE
731000S84A-529
Editorial: Aarestr. 83, 5222 UMIKEN **Tel:** 56 4410043 **Fax:** 56 4414854
Email: editor@dplanet.ch **Web site:** http://www.industriegeschichte.ch
Freq: Quarterly; **Annual Sub.:** CHF 89,00; **Circ:** 800
Editor: Oskar Baldinger; **Advertising Manager:** Silvia Baumann
Profile: European magazine covering industrial heritage, tourism and art.
Language(s): German
Readership: Read by architects, engineers, museum directors and government agencies for the protection of cultural heritage.
ADVERTISING RATES:
Full Page Colour .... CHF 2400
Mechanical Data: Type Area: 240 x 185 mm, No. of Columns (Display): 3, Col Widths (Display): 58 mm
Copy instructions: *Copy Date:* 30 days prior to publication
CONSUMER: THE ARTS & LITERARY: Arts

INFECTION
1794908S56A-2131
Editorial: Rämistr. 100, 8091 ZÜRICH
Tel: 44 2555731 **Fax:** 44 2554558
Email: christian.ruef@usz.ch
Freq: 6 issues yearly; **Annual Sub.:** CHF 234,50; **Circ:** 1,800
Editor: Christian Ruef; **Advertising Manager:** Sigrid Christ
Profile: The journal Infection is a peer-reviewed forum for the presentation and discussion of clinically relevant information on infectious diseases for readers and contributors from all over the world. Articles deal with etiology, pathogenesis, diagnosis and treatment of infectious diseases in outpatient and inpatient setting. Public health issues of local, regional and international importance related to infectious diseases are covered along with progress and problems in hospital epidemiology. The main contents include original articles describing results of research projects; brief reports on new observations that enhance the knowledge of clinicians; and state-of-the-art reviews on topics relevant to physicians diagnosing or treating infectious diseases. Case reports describing new infectious etiologies or clinical manifestations are also offered. Infection adheres to a high standard of quality of all published material.
Language(s): English
ADVERTISING RATES:
Full Page Mono .... EUR 1750
Full Page Colour .... EUR 2730
Mechanical Data: Type Area: 240 x 174 mm
Official Journal of: Organ d. Dt. Ges. f. Infektiologie, d. Paul-Ehrlich-Ges. f. Chemotherapie u. d. Dt. Sepsis-Ges.

INFO.
1656007S57-681
Editorial: Hardstr. 73, 5430 WETTINGEN
Tel: 56 4371228 **Fax:** 56 4371207
Email: heinz.sager@nagra.ch **Web site:** http://www.nagra.ch
Freq: 3 issues yearly; **Cover Price:** Free; **Circ:** 65,000
Editor: Heinz Sager
Profile: Magazine with news about nuclear waste disposal.
Language(s): French; German; Italian

INFO-BLATT
1849160S4E-821
Editorial: Hauptstr. 19, 3252 WORBEN
Tel: 32 3872050 **Fax:** 32 3872056
Email: info@worben.ch **Web site:** http://www.worben.ch
Freq: 3 issues yearly; **Circ:** 1,100
Profile: Customer newspaper about IT in the building industry.
Language(s): German

INFO-BLATT
1849160S4E-858
Editorial: Hauptstr. 19, 3252 WORBEN
Tel: 32 3872050 **Fax:** 32 3872056
Email: info@worben.ch **Web site:** http://www.worben.ch
Freq: 3 issues yearly; **Circ:** 1,100
Profile: Customer newspaper about IT in the building industry.
Language(s): German

INFOS, FÜR JUNGE KAUFLEUTE
1844835S14A-1261
Editorial: Zinggstr. 1, 3000 BERN 23 **Tel:** 31 3700111 **Fax:** 31 3700110
Email: patrick.naumann@maxomedia.ch **Web site:** http://www.maxomedia.ch
Freq: 11 issues yearly; **Annual Sub.:** CHF 98,80; **Circ:** 4,000
Editor: Patrick Naumann
Profile: Magazine containing information for trainee salespeople.
Language(s): German
ADVERTISING RATES:
Full Page Mono .... CHF 1660
Full Page Colour .... CHF 1660
Mechanical Data: Type Area: 254 x 195 mm
Copy instructions: *Copy Date:* 21 days prior to publication

INSPIRATION
2002179S2A-704
Editorial: Zürichstrasse 98, 8600 DÜBENDORF 1
Tel: 44 9103230 **Fax:** 44 9105260
Email: info@inspiration-press.com **Web site:** http://www.inspiration-press.com
Freq: 6 issues yearly; **Annual Sub.:** CHF 157,00; **Circ:** 10,000
Editor: Huguette Maier; **Advertising Manager:** Brigitte Tavernini
Profile: Magazine about shop windows and shop decorations, presentation of articles.
Language(s): English; German
ADVERTISING RATES:
Full Page Mono .... CHF 1800
Full Page Colour .... CHF 2766
Mechanical Data: Type Area: 207 x 211 mm, No. of Columns (Display): 2, Col Widths (Display): 103 mm
Copy instructions: *Copy Date:* 60 days prior to publication

INTENSIV-NEWS
1858764S56A-2201
Editorial: Baarer Str. 86a, 6300 ZUG **Tel:** 41 7123131 **Fax:** 41 7123130
Email: reto.stocker@usz.ch **Web site:** http://www.medicom.cc
Freq: 6 issues yearly; **Circ:** 5,000
Editor: Reto Stocker; **Advertising Manager:** Nina Kotar
Profile: Magazine for physical doctors.
Language(s): French; German
Copy instructions: *Copy Date:* 14 days prior to publication

INTERCLASSIC
1656126S49A-403
Editorial: Wolleraustr. 11a, 8807 FREIENBACH
Tel: 848 333100 **Fax:** 55 4158200
Web site: http://www.eurotaxglass.ch
Freq: Half-yearly; **Annual Sub.:** CHF 307,00; **Circ:** 1,120
Profile: Magazine with reports on the special car market.
Language(s): French; German; Italian
Mechanical Data: Type Area: 200 x 138 mm
Copy instructions: *Copy Date:* 30 days prior to publication

INTERIEUR
731345S23A-100
Editorial: Dorfplatz 3, 8126 ZUMIKON
Tel: 44 9181844 **Fax:** 44 9181884
Email: leipzigerpr@bluewin.ch **Web site:** http://www.interieur-suisse.ch
Freq: Monthly; Free to qualifying individuals
Annual Sub.: CHF 89,00; **Circ:** 4,000
Editor: Emil Schreyger; **Advertising Manager:** André Schöller
Profile: Journal of the Swiss Association of Furnishers, Furniture Manufacturers and Upholsterers.
Language(s): French; German
ADVERTISING RATES:
Full Page Mono .... CHF 2850
Full Page Colour .... CHF 3300
Mechanical Data: Type Area: 267 x 185 mm, No. of Columns (Display): 2, Col Widths (Display): 88 mm
Copy instructions: *Copy Date:* 20 days prior to publication
Official Journal of: Organ d. Schweizerischen Verb. d. Innendekorateure, d. Möbelfachhandels u. d. Sattler
BUSINESS: FURNISHINGS & FURNITURE

INTERNATIONAL JOURNAL OF PUBLIC HEALTH
1852814S56A-2181
Editorial: Niesenweg 6, 3012 BERN **Tel:** 31 6313519 **Fax:** 31 6313430
Email: ijph@ispm.unibe.ch **Web site:** http://www.birkhauser.ch/ijph
Freq: 6 issues yearly; **Annual Sub.:** CHF 498,00; **Circ:** 420
Editor: Thomas Abel
Profile: Magazine about social and preventive medicine.
Language(s): English; French; German
ADVERTISING RATES:
Full Page Mono .... CHF 950
Mechanical Data: Type Area: 240 x 170 mm
Official Journal of: Organ d. Swiss Society for Public Health

INTERNATIONAL REGISTER OF FORWARDING AND LOGISTICS COMPANIES
1843485S49A-425
Editorial: Grosspeterstr. 23, 4002 BASEL
Tel: 58 9589514 **Fax:** 58 9589590
Email: tim-oliver.frische@transportjournal.com **Web site:** http://www.transportjournal.com
Freq: 3 issues yearly; **Annual Sub.:** CHF 40,00; **Circ:** 10,000
Profile: Directory lists addresses of forwarding and logistics companies.
Language(s): English
ADVERTISING RATES:
Full Page Mono .... CHF 650
Full Page Colour .... CHF 2000
Mechanical Data: Type Area: 126 x 86 mm, No. of Columns (Display): 1, Col Widths (Display): 86 mm
Copy instructions: *Copy Date:* 56 days prior to publication

INTERNATIONAL TRADE FORUM
1853463S14C-240
Editorial: Palais des Nations, 1211 GENF 10
Tel: 22 7300111 **Fax:** 22 7337176
Email: itcreg@intracen.org **Web site:** http://www.intracen.org
Freq: Quarterly; **Annual Sub.:** $45,00; **Circ:** 17,000
Editor: Natalie Domeisen
Profile: Magazine aimed at developing and transition economies, it analyses export trends and opportunities and informs about ITC events and services.
Language(s): English

IO NEW MANAGEMENT
1640774S14A-1144
Editorial: Förrlibuckstr. 70, 8021 ZÜRICH
Tel: 43 4445888 **Fax:** 43 4445935
Email: ionewmanagement@axelspringer.ch **Web site:** http://www.ionewmanagement.ch
Freq: 8 issues yearly; Free to qualifying individuals
Annual Sub.: CHF 159,00; **Circ:** 12,000
Editor: Beatrice Brenner; **Advertising Manager:** Christine Lesnik
Profile: Scientific management magazine.
Language(s): German
ADVERTISING RATES:
Full Page Mono .... CHF 7460
Full Page Colour .... CHF 7460
Mechanical Data: Type Area: 231 x 175 mm, No. of Columns (Display): 3, Col Widths (Display): 50 mm
Copy instructions: *Copy Date:* 28 days prior to publication
Official Journal of: Organ d. ETH-Zentrum f. Unternehmenswissenschaften (BWI), ETH Alumni Engineering Management, Schweizer. Managementges.
Supplement(s): Leader spezial
BUSINESS: COMMERCE, INDUSTRY & MANAGEMENT

IT BUSINESS
764677S18B-322
Editorial: Postfach 29, 4124 SCHÖNENBUCH
Tel: 61 6838876 **Fax:** 61 6838877
Email: redaktion@itbusiness.ch **Web site:** http://www.itbusiness.ch
Freq: 5 issues yearly; **Annual Sub.:** CHF 49,00; **Circ:** 15,000
Editor: Petra De Meo; **Advertising Manager:** Leonardo De Meo
Profile: The Swiss magazine for ICT - provides analysis, trend reports, background stories, opinions and news from the ICT industry at home and abroad. Each issue provides several key issues to the fore in the market environment and practical and compact and focused reports on selected special areas will be. The magazine is an excellent communication platform in the area of ICT This dar. the human factor is of central importance.
Language(s): German
ADVERTISING RATES:
Full Page Mono .... CHF 4785
Full Page Colour .... CHF 6045
Mechanical Data: Type Area: 260 x 186 mm, No. of Columns (Display): 3, Col Widths (Display): 57 mm
Copy instructions: *Copy Date:* 21 days prior to publication

ITJ INTERNATIONAL TRANSPORT JOURNAL - (ENGL. AUSG.)
763585S49A-382
Editorial: Grosspeterstr. 23, 4002 BASEL
Tel: 58 9589514 **Fax:** 58 9589590
Email: tim-oliver.frische@transportjournal.com **Web site:** http://www.transportjournal.com
Freq: 22 issues yearly; **Annual Sub.:** CHF 220,00; **Circ:** 9,084
Editor: Tim-Oliver Frische; **Advertising Manager:** Patricia Hunziker
Profile: Magazine for the transport and logistics industry.
Language(s): English; German
ADVERTISING RATES:
Full Page Mono .... CHF 4300
Full Page Colour .... CHF 6450
Mechanical Data: Type Area: 268 x 185 mm, No. of Columns (Display): 3, Col Widths (Display): 58 mm
Copy instructions: *Copy Date:* 20 days prior to publication

JAHRBUCH MARKETING KOMMUNIKATION
1645662S2A-644
Editorial: Geltenwilenstr. 8a, 9001 ST. GALLEN
Tel: 71 2269292 **Fax:** 71 2269293
Email: info@kbmedien.ch **Web site:** http://www.kbmedien.ch
Freq: Annual; **Annual Sub.:** CHF 49,00; **Circ:** 8,000
Editor: Vera Hermes; **Advertising Manager:** Urs Dick
Profile: Annual about creative communications, management and marketing.
Language(s): German
ADVERTISING RATES:
Full Page Mono .... CHF 3700
Full Page Colour .... CHF 5050
Mechanical Data: Type Area: 270 x 180 mm
Copy instructions: *Copy Date:* 60 days prior to publication

JAHRESBERICHT
1855826S50-146
Editorial: Dufourstr. 40a, 9000 ST. GALLEN
Tel: 71 2242525 **Fax:** 71 2242536
Email: idthsg@unisg.ch **Web site:** http://www.idt.unisg.ch
Freq: Annual; **Cover Price:** Free; **Circ:** 400
Editor: Nicole Denk
Profile: Annual of the Swiss tourism business.
Language(s): German

JARDIN ROMAND
731907S93-20
Editorial: 190, rte. de Cossonay, 1020 RENENS
Tel: 21 7031306 **Fax:** 21 7031305
Email: magazine@jardin.ch **Web site:** http://www.jardin.ch
Freq: 9 issues yearly; **Annual Sub.:** CHF 64,00; **Circ:** 10,000
Editor: Marc-Henri Jan
Profile: Gardening magazine, includes advice on types of plants and garden design. Also features recipes using seasonal garden produce.
Language(s): French
ADVERTISING RATES:
Full Page Mono .... CHF 2435
Full Page Colour .... CHF 3930
Mechanical Data: Type Area: 270 x 184 mm
Copy instructions: *Copy Date:* 30 days prior to publication
CONSUMER: GARDENING

JAZZ TIME
763465S76D-563
Editorial: Täfernstr. 37, 5405 BADEN
Tel: 56 4833737 **Fax:** 56 4833739
Email: eduard.keller@jazztime.com **Web site:** http://www.jazztime.com
Freq: Monthly; **Annual Sub.:** CHF 46,00; **Circ:** 8,000
Editor: Eduard Keller
Profile: Programme of events.
Language(s): German
ADVERTISING RATES:
Full Page Mono .... CHF 1440
Mechanical Data: Type Area: 190 x 128 mm, No. of Columns (Display): 4, Col Widths (Display): 48 mm
Copy instructions: *Copy Date:* 8 days prior to publication
CONSUMER: MUSIC & PERFORMING ARTS: Music

JOURNAL DES ARTS ET MÉTIERS
732024S74E-1
Editorial: Schwarztorstr. 26, 3007 BERN
Tel: 31 3801426 **Fax:** 31 3801415
Email: redaktion@sgv-usam.ch **Web site:** http://www.sgv-usam.ch
Freq: Monthly; **Cover Price:** Free; **Circ:** 50,000
Editor: Sarah Steinweg
Profile: Journal of the Swiss Union of Arts and Crafts.
Language(s): French
ADVERTISING RATES:
Full Page Mono .... CHF 6600
Full Page Colour .... CHF 6600
Mechanical Data: Type Area: 440 x 288 mm, No. of Columns (Display): 10, Col Widths (Display): 27 mm
Copy instructions: *Copy Date:* 3 days prior to publication
CONSUMER: WOMEN'S INTEREST CONSUMER MAGAZINES: Crafts

LE JOURNAL DU JURA
1656415S67B-6639
Editorial: Robert-Walser-Platz 7, 2501 BIEL
Tel: 32 3219000 **Fax:** 32 3219009
Email: redactionjj@journaldujura.ch **Web site:** http://www.journaldujura.ch
Freq: 312 issues yearly; **Annual Sub.:** CHF 347,00; **Circ:** 10,978
Editor: Stéphane Devaux
Profile: Regional daily newspaper covering politics, economics, sport, travel, technology and the arts.
Language(s): French
ADVERTISING RATES:
SCC .... CHF 48,40
Mechanical Data: Type Area: 440 x 290 mm, No. of Columns (Display): 10, Col Widths (Display): 26 mm
Copy instructions: *Copy Date:* 2 days prior to publication
REGIONAL DAILY & SUNDAY NEWSPAPERS: Regional Daily Newspapers

JOURNAL FRANZ WEBER
732047S57-260
Editorial: case postale, 1820 MONTREUX 1
Tel: 21 9643737 **Fax:** 21 9645736
Email: ffw@ffw.ch **Web site:** http://www.ffw.ch
Freq: Quarterly; **Annual Sub.:** CHF 20,00; **Circ:** 120,000
Editor: Franz Weber
Profile: Magazine about nature, animal and environmental protection and events of the day.
Language(s): German

JOURNAL SWISSMEDIC
1655811S56A-2066
Editorial: Hallerstr. 7, 3000 BERN 9 **Tel:** 31 3220211 **Fax:** 31 3220212
Email: media@swissmedic.ch **Web site:** http://www.swissmedic.ch
Freq: Monthly; **Annual Sub.:** CHF 150,00; **Circ:** 2,850

Profile: Magazine on drugs for Switzerland.
Language(s): French; German

JOYCE 1645065S74A-470
Editorial: Witzbergstr. 7, 8330 PFÄFFIKON
Tel: 43 2888013 **Fax:** 43 2888011
Email: reda@bvmedia.ch **Web site:** http://www.joyce.ch
Freq: Quarterly; **Annual Sub.:** CHF 29,10; **Circ:** 18,500
Editor: Melanie Carstens; **Advertising Manager:** Niklaus Mosimann
Profile: Church magazine for women.
Language(s): German
ADVERTISING RATES:
Full Page Mono .... CHF 3557
Full Page Colour .... CHF 4682
Mechanical Data: Type Area: 258 x 188 mm, No. of Columns (Display): 4, Col Widths (Display): 44 mm
Copy instructions: *Copy Date:* 40 days prior to publication

JUMI 1656127S91D-899
Editorial: Hirschengraben 52, 6000 LUZERN 7
Tel: 41 3609377
Email: redaktion@jumi.ch **Web site:** http://www.jumi.ch
Freq: 8 issues yearly; **Annual Sub.:** CHF 20,00; **Circ:** 47,000
Editor: Christine Weber
Profile: Magazine for children aged between 7 to 12 years.
Language(s): German
CONSUMER: RECREATION & LEISURE: Children & Youth

K GELD 1655379S1F-258
Editorial: Wolfbachstr. 15, 8024 ZÜRICH
Tel: 44 2661707 **Fax:** 44 2661700
Email: redaktion@kgeld.ch **Web site:** http://www.konsuminfo.ch
Freq: 6 issues yearly; **Annual Sub.:** CHF 31,00; **Circ:** 48,216
Editor: Bernhard Bircher-Suits
Profile: Magazine about finances.
Language(s): German
ADVERTISING RATES:
Full Page Mono .... CHF 8000
Full Page Colour .... CHF 8000
Mechanical Data: Type Area: 276 x 209 mm
Copy instructions: *Copy Date:* 14 days prior to publication
BUSINESS: FINANCE & ECONOMICS: Investment

K TIPP 733362S74C-58
Editorial: Wolfbachstr. 15, 8024 ZÜRICH
Tel: 44 2661717 **Fax:** 44 2661700
Email: redaktion@ktipp.ch **Web site:** http://www.konsuminfo.ch
Freq: 20 issues yearly; **Annual Sub.:** CHF 31,50; **Circ:** 302,609
Editor: Ernst Meierhofer
Profile: Magazine providing information for general consumers.
Language(s): German
ADVERTISING RATES:
Full Page Mono .... CHF 22400
Full Page Colour .... CHF 22400
Mechanical Data: Type Area: 276 x 209 mm
CONSUMER: WOMEN'S INTEREST CONSUMER MAGAZINES: Home & Family

KANTON URI AMTSBLATT 732385S80-1495
Editorial: Rathausplatz 1, 6460 ALTDORF
Tel: 41 8752017 **Fax:** 41 8706651
Email: amtsblatt@ur.ch **Web site:** http://www.ur.ch
Freq: Weekly; **Annual Sub.:** CHF 84,00; **Circ:** 2,763
Profile: Regional official paper.
Language(s): German
ADVERTISING RATES:
Full Page Mono .... CHF 337
Mechanical Data: Type Area: 180 x 117 mm, No. of Columns (Display): 2, Col Widths (Display): 57 mm
Copy instructions: *Copy Date:* 2 days prior to publication
CONSUMER: RURAL & REGIONAL INTEREST

KARDIOVASKULÄRE MEDIZIN MÉDECINE CARDIOVASCULAIRE 762647S56A-1961
Editorial: Farnsburger Str. 8, 4132 MUTTENZ
Tel: 61 4678555 **Fax:** 61 4678556
Email: verlag@emh.ch **Web site:** http://www.cardiovascmed.ch
Freq: 11 issues yearly; **Annual Sub.:** CHF 125,00; **Circ:** 8,100
Editor: Thomas F. Lüscher; **Advertising Manager:** Silvia Fuchs
Profile: Magazine for cardiologists.
Language(s): French; German
ADVERTISING RATES:
Full Page Mono .... CHF 2400
Full Page Colour .... CHF 4350
Mechanical Data: Type Area: 268 x 186 mm
Official Journal of: Organ d. Schweizer. Ges. f. Kardiologie, d. Schweizer. Hypertonie-Ges. u. d. Schweizer. Ges. f. Pädiatr. Kardiologie

KARGER GAZETTE 732403S56A-2060
Editorial: Allschwiler Str. 10, 4055 BASEL
Tel: 61 3061111 **Fax:** 61 3061234
Email: gazette@karger.ch **Web site:** http://www.karger.com/gazette
Freq: Annual; **Cover Price:** Free; **Circ:** 20,000
Editor: Dagmar Horn
Profile: Company publication published by Karger.
Language(s): English

KATALOG DER AUTOMOBIL REVUE CATALOGUE DE LA REVUE AUTOMOBILE 1994482S77A-136
Editorial: Dammweg 9, 3001 BERN **Tel:** 31 3303034 **Fax:** 31 3303032
Email: office@automobilrevue.ch **Web site:** http://www.katalog.automobilrevue.ch
Freq: Annual; **Annual Sub.:** CHF 49,00; **Circ:** 42,000
Editor: Pierre-André Schmitt; **Advertising Manager:** Remo De Piano
Profile: Car magazine.
Language(s): French; German
Mechanical Data: Type Area: 271 x 203 mm
Copy instructions: *Copy Date:* 90 days prior to publication

KF INFO 1849104S74M-285
Editorial: Grossmannstr. 29, 8049 ZÜRICH
Tel: 44 3445060 **Fax:** 44 3445066
Email: forum@konsum.ch **Web site:** http://www.konsum.ch
Circ: 2,700
Profile: Member magazine from the Konsumerforum.
Language(s): German

KIDY SWISS FAMILY 1641445S74D-5
Editorial: Zürcher Str. 601, 9015 ST. GALLEN
Tel: 71 3140444 **Fax:** 70 3140445
Email: c.boesiger@kueba.ch **Web site:** http://www.swissfamily.ch
Freq: 6 issues yearly; **Annual Sub.:** CHF 48,00; **Circ:** 25,000
Editor: Christina Bösiger
Profile: Publication containing information about children from the first year of age up to enrolment in elementary school.
Language(s): German
ADVERTISING RATES:
Full Page Mono .... CHF 5100
Full Page Colour .... CHF 5100
Mechanical Data: Type Area: 270 x 195 mm, No. of Columns (Display): 3, Col Widths (Display): 65 mm
Copy instructions: *Copy Date:* 42 days prior to publication
Supplement(s): Unser Baby; Werdendes Leben
CONSUMER: WOMEN'S INTEREST CONSUMER MAGAZINES: Child Care

KIRCHE HEUTE 738851S87-2040
Editorial: Innere Margarethenstr. 26, 4051 BASEL
Tel: 61 3630170 **Fax:** 61 3630171
Email: redaktion@kirche-heute.ch **Web site:** http://www.kirche-heute.ch
Freq: 41 issues yearly; **Annual Sub.:** CHF 36,00; **Circ:** 69,000
Editor: Alois Schuler; **Advertising Manager:** Regula Schmidt
Profile: Read by Catholics in Switzerland.
Language(s): German
Readership: Read by catholics in Switzerland.
ADVERTISING RATES:
Full Page Mono .... CHF 1440
Full Page Colour .... CHF 1800
Copy instructions: *Copy Date:* 14 days prior to publication
CONSUMER: RELIGIOUS

KLEINBUSSE UND LIEFERWAGEN MINIBUS ET VÉHICULES DE LIVRAISON MINIBUS E FURGONI 1656131S49A-405
Editorial: Wolleraustr. 11a, 8807 FREIENBACH
Tel: 848 333100 **Fax:** 55 4158200
Web site: http://www.eurotaxglass.ch
Freq: Quarterly; **Annual Sub.:** CHF 210,00; **Circ:** 1,230
Profile: Magazine reporting on the market of mini buses and vans.
Language(s): French; German; Italian

KLOSTERSER ZEITUNG 732888S72-9627
Editorial: Gotschnastr. 14, 7250 KLOSTERS
Tel: 81 4221315 **Fax:** 81 4224948
Email: klosterserzeitung@budag.ch **Web site:** http://www.budag.ch
Freq: Weekly; **Annual Sub.:** CHF 79,00; **Circ:** 2,871
Editor: Johannes Haltiner
Profile: Regional weekly covering politics, economics, sport, travel, technology and the arts.
Language(s): German
ADVERTISING RATES:
SCC .... CHF 17,00
Mechanical Data: Type Area: 420 x 287 mm, No. of Columns (Display): 10, Col Widths (Display): 26 mm
Copy instructions: *Copy Date:* 2 days prior to publication
LOCAL NEWSPAPERS

KLOTENER ANZEIGER 720896S72-660
Editorial: Gerbegasse 2, 8302 KLOTEN
Tel: 44 8001111 **Fax:** 44 8001134
Email: redaktion@kloteneranzeiger.ch **Web site:** http://www.kloteneranzeiger.ch
Freq: Weekly; **Cover Price:** CHF 2,00; **Circ:** 3,425
Editor: Leo Niessner; **Advertising Manager:** Kathrin Spross
Profile: Regional weekly covering politics, economics, sport, travel, technology and the arts.
Language(s): German
ADVERTISING RATES:
SCC .... CHF 11,10
Mechanical Data: Type Area: 440 x 296 mm, No. of Columns (Display): 10, Col Widths (Display): 26 mm
Copy instructions: *Copy Date:* 2 days prior to publication
LOCAL NEWSPAPERS

KLOTENER ANZEIGER 1647285S72-9625
Editorial: Gerbegasse 2, 8302 KLOTEN
Tel: 44 8001111 **Fax:** 44 8001134
Email: redaktion@kloteneranzeiger.ch **Web site:** http://www.kloteneranzeiger.ch
Freq: Monthly; **Cover Price:** Free; **Circ:** 11,025
Editor: Leo Niessner; **Advertising Manager:** Kathrin Spross
Profile: Advertising journal (house-to-house) concentrating on regional coverage.
Language(s): German
ADVERTISING RATES:
Full Page Mono .... CHF 4136
Full Page Colour .... CHF 4340
Mechanical Data: Type Area: 440 x 286 mm, No. of Columns (Display): 10, Col Widths (Display): 25 mm
Copy instructions: *Copy Date:* 2 days prior to publication
LOCAL NEWSPAPERS

KMU-PRAXIS 732902S14A-620
Editorial: Hardturmstr. 120, 8005 ZÜRICH
Tel: 44 2784500 **Fax:** 44 2784505
Email: jacqueline.grob@obt.ch **Web site:** http://www.obt.ch
Freq: Annual; **Cover Price:** Free; **Circ:** 20,000
Editor: Jacqueline Grob; **Advertising Manager:** Jacqueline Grob
Profile: Magazine for small and medium sized businesses.
Language(s): German
ADVERTISING RATES:
Full Page Colour .... CHF 3900
Mechanical Data: Type Area: 262 x 180 mm, No. of Columns (Display): 4, Col Widths (Display): 42 mm

KÖ. 1641414S2A-639
Editorial: Geltenwilenstr. 8a, 9001 ST. GALLEN
Tel: 71 2269292 **Fax:** 71 2269293
Email: info@kbmedien.ch **Web site:** http://www.koe.ch
Freq: Annual; **Annual Sub.:** CHF 49,00; **Circ:** 10,000
Profile: Directory for the communications and production sectors.
Language(s): German
ADVERTISING RATES:
Full Page Mono .... CHF 3600
Full Page Colour .... CHF 4950
Mechanical Data: Type Area: 270 x 180 mm

KOORDINIERTER SANITÄTSDIENST SERVICE SANITAIRE COORDONNÉ SERVIZIO SANITARIO COORDINATO 1667400S40-221
Editorial: Worblentalstr. 36, 3063 ITTIGEN
Tel: 31 3242842 **Fax:** 31 3242744
Email: info-ksd@vtg.admin.ch **Web site:** http://www.ksd-ssc.ch
Freq: Quarterly; **Cover Price:** Free; **Circ:** 8,800
Editor: Esther Bärtschi
Profile: Information from the Swiss Sanitary Services.
Language(s): English; French; German

KRANKENPFLEGE SOINS INFIRMIERS CURE INFERMIERISTICHE 733252S56R-280
Editorial: Choisystr. 1, 3001 BERN **Tel:** 31 3883637 **Fax:** 31 3883635
Email: redaktion@sbk-asi.ch **Web site:** http://www.sbk-asi.ch
Freq: Monthly; Free to qualifying individuals
Annual Sub.: CHF 95,00; **Circ:** 30,000
Editor: Urs Lüthi
Profile: Magazine on nursing.
Language(s): French; German; Italian
ADVERTISING RATES:
Full Page Mono .... CHF 3530
Full Page Colour .... CHF 4730
Mechanical Data: Type Area: 260 x 185 mm
Copy instructions: *Copy Date:* 30 days prior to publication
BUSINESS: HEALTH & MEDICAL: Health Medical Related

KUNST BULLETIN 733529S84A-240
Editorial: Zeughausstr. 55, 8026 ZÜRICH
Tel: 44 2983030 **Fax:** 44 2983038
Email: info@kunstbulletin.ch **Web site:** http://www.kunstbulletin.ch
Freq: 10 issues yearly; **Annual Sub.:** CHF 68,00,; **Circ:** 13,500
Editor: Claudia Jolles
Profile: Official journal of the Swiss Art Association.
Language(s): French; German; Italian
ADVERTISING RATES:
Full Page Mono .... CHF 1620
Full Page Colour .... CHF 1880
Mechanical Data: Type Area: 190 x 131 mm, No. of Columns (Display): 2, Col Widths (Display): 63 mm
Copy instructions: *Copy Date:* 21 days prior to publication
CONSUMER: THE ARTS & LITERARY: Arts

KUNST + STEIN 1647565S4E-788
Editorial: Aarberger Gasse 16, 3011 BERN
Tel: 31 9700881 **Fax:** 31 9700882
Email: daniela.urfer@kamberpartner.ch **Web site:** http://www.vsbs.ch
Freq: 6 issues yearly; **Annual Sub.:** CHF 91,00,; **Circ:** 1,200
Editor: Daniela Urfer
Profile: Magazine on the arts, tomb history and restoration.
Language(s): German
ADVERTISING RATES:
Full Page Mono .... CHF 1100
Full Page Colour .... CHF 2470
Mechanical Data: Type Area: 248 x 171 mm, No. of Columns (Display): 3, Col Widths (Display): 54 mm
Copy instructions: *Copy Date:* 21 days prior to publication

KV. NACHRICHTEN 1855842S14A-1326
Editorial: Aeschengraben 13, 4002 BASEL
Tel: 61 2715470 **Fax:** 61 2722441
Email: stephan.schoettli@kvbasel.ch **Web site:** http://www.kvbasel.ch
Freq: 6 issues yearly; **Circ:** 7,500
Editor: Stephan Schöttli
Profile: Member magazine form the Basle Professional Association for Commercial Employees and Trainees.
Language(s): German

KV ZUG AKTUELL 1855847S14A-1328
Editorial: Postfach 235, 6312 STEINHAUSEN
Tel: 41 7114660 **Fax:** 41 7402778
Email: kv.verein.zug@datazug.ch **Web site:** http://www.kvschweiz.ch/zug
Freq: Quarterly; Free to qualifying individuals ; **Circ:** 750
Editor: Jeannine Hegglin
Profile: Member magazine from the Commercial Association of the Canton Zug.
Language(s): German

KVT AKTUELL 733668S19A-203
Editorial: Lagerstr. 8, 8953 DIETIKON
Tel: 44 7433333 **Fax:** 44 7406566
Email: info@kvt.ch **Web site:** http://www.kvt.ch
Freq: Half-yearly; **Cover Price:** Free; **Circ:** 14,000
Editor: Ralf Dorner
Profile: Magazine of the Koenig Verbindungstechnik company.
Language(s): German

LABMED SCHWEIZ SUISSE SVIZZERA 733686S55-18
Editorial: 3, rue Louis-de-Meuron, 2074 MARIN
Tel: 32 7543740 **Fax:** 32 7543741
Email: merlotti@labmed.ch **Web site:** http://www.labmed.ch
Freq: 11 issues yearly; Free to qualifying individuals
Annual Sub.: CHF 100,00; **Circ:** 2,600
Editor: Jacqueline Merlotti-Noyer
Profile: Magazine about medical laboratories.
Language(s): French; German; Italian
Readership: Read by medical laboratory scientists and biologists.
ADVERTISING RATES:
Full Page Mono .... CHF 2550
Full Page Colour .... CHF 2550
Mechanical Data: Type Area: 267 x 182 mm
BUSINESS: APPLIED SCIENCE & LABORATORIES

DER LANDANZEIGER 733752S72-4520
Editorial: Schönenwerderstr. 13, 5036 OBERENTFELDEN **Tel:** 62 7379000 **Fax:** 62 7379005
Email: redaktion@landanzeiger.ch **Web site:** http://www.landanzeiger.ch
Freq: Monthly; **Cover Price:** Free; **Circ:** 51,000
Editor: Markus Schenk; **Advertising Manager:** Claudia Hunziker
Profile: Advertising journal (house-to-house) concentrating on local stories.
Language(s): German

ADVERTISING RATES:
Full Page Mono .... CHF 3652
Full Page Colour .... CHF 4224
Mechanical Data: Type Area: 440 x 290 mm, No. of Columns (Display): 10, Col Widths (Display): 25 mm
Copy instructions: *Copy Date:* 2 days prior to publication
LOCAL NEWSPAPERS

DER LANDBOTE 733768S67B-1520
Editorial: Garnmarkt 10, 8401 WINTERTHUR
Tel: 52 2669900 **Fax:** 52 2669911
Email: redaktion@landbote.ch **Web site:** http://www.landbote.ch
Freq: 260 issues yearly; **Annual Sub.:** CHF 337,00; **Circ:** 33,896
Editor: Colette Gradwohl; **News Editor:** Luca de Carli
Profile: Daily newspaper for the Winterthur region.
Language(s): German
ADVERTISING RATES:
SCC .... CHF 36,80
Mechanical Data: Type Area: 437 x 290 mm, No. of Columns (Display): 10, Col Widths (Display): 26 mm
Copy instructions: *Copy Date:* 1 day prior to publication
REGIONAL DAILY & SUNDAY NEWSPAPERS: Regional Daily Newspapers

DER LANDBOTE 1777071S72-9898
Editorial: Garnmarkt 10, 8401 WINTERTHUR
Tel: 52 2669901 **Fax:** 52 2669911
Email: redaktion@landbote.ch **Web site:** http://www.landbote.ch
Freq: Weekly; **Cover Price:** Free; **Circ:** 91,281
Editor: Colette Gradwohl
Profile: Daily newspaper for the Winterthur region.
Language(s): German
ADVERTISING RATES:
Full Page Mono .... CHF 8700
Full Page Colour .... CHF 10900
Mechanical Data: Type Area: 437 x 290 mm, No. of Columns (Display): 10, Col Widths (Display): 26 mm
Copy instructions: *Copy Date:* 1 day prior to publication
LOCAL NEWSPAPERS

LASTWAGEN CAMIONS 1656135S49A-406
Editorial: Wolleraustr. 11a, 8807 FREIENBACH
Tel: 848 333100 **Fax:** 55 4158200
Web site: http://www.eurotaxglass.ch
Freq: Half-yearly; **Annual Sub.:** CHF 357,00; **Circ:** 700
Profile: Magazine reporting on the market of buying and selling trucks.
Language(s): French; German
Mechanical Data: Type Area: 138 x 95 mm
Copy instructions: *Copy Date:* 30 days prior to publication

LEADER 2078993S14A-1381
Editorial: Zürcher Str. 170, 9014 ST. GALLEN
Tel: 71 2728050 **Fax:** 71 2728051
Email: leader@metrocomm.ch **Web site:** http://www.leaderonline.ch
Freq: 14 issues yearly; **Annual Sub.:** CHF 60,00; **Circ:** 7,274
Editor: Michael Baumgartner; **Advertising Manager:** Martin Schwizer
Profile: The mix of regional economic relevance and economic Boulevard, reports, interviews with key business leaders and political "pull the stings" allows an intimate look into the entire micro-cosmic tension between the Eastern Swiss and Liechtenstein economic environment. These insights and guide service vessels encounter increasingly wide interest, both the readers and the advertisers. The strength of the Leader is also based on a peculiarity of a homogeneously dominated eastern Switzerland and Liechtenstein economy, reflected confidence in their own publication provides. Anhören Umschrift.
Language(s): German
ADVERTISING RATES:
Full Page Mono .... CHF 2900
Full Page Colour .... CHF 3300
Mechanical Data: Type Area: 265 x 178 mm, No. of Columns (Display): 3, Col Widths (Display): 57 mm

LEBEN & GLAUBEN 734001S74C-60_50
Editorial: Neuenhoferstr. 101, 5401 BADEN
Tel: 56 2032200 **Fax:** 56 2032299
Email: redaktion@lebenundglauben.ch **Web site:** http://www.lebenundglauben.ch
Freq: Weekly; **Annual Sub.:** CHF 205,75; **Circ:** 30,050
Editor: Regina Müller
Profile: General interest Protestant family magazine.
Language(s): German
ADVERTISING RATES:
Full Page Mono .... CHF 4000
Full Page Colour .... CHF 4000
Mechanical Data: Type Area: 265 x 190 mm, No. of Columns (Display): 4, Col Widths (Display): 45 mm
Copy instructions: *Copy Date:* 10 days prior to publication
Supplement(s): TV täglich
CONSUMER: WOMEN'S INTEREST CONSUMER MAGAZINES: Home & Family

LEBENSLAUF >> 1645064S74N-254
Editorial: Witzbergstr. 7, 8330 PFÄFFIKON
Tel: 43 2888013 **Fax:** 43 2888011
Email: reda@bvmedia.ch **Web site:** http://www.lebenslauf-magazin.ch
Freq: 6 issues yearly; **Annual Sub.:** CHF 37,20; **Circ:** 15,000
Editor: Agnes Wedell; **Advertising Manager:** Niklaus Mosimann
Profile: Christian magazine for the elderly.
Language(s): German
ADVERTISING RATES:
Full Page Mono .... CHF 2500
Full Page Colour .... CHF 3075
Mechanical Data: Type Area: 258 x 188 mm, No. of Columns (Display): 4, Col Widths (Display): 44 mm
Copy instructions: *Copy Date:* 40 days prior to publication

LENZBURGER BEZIRKS-ANZEIGER 1656758S72-9728
Editorial: Kronenplatz 12, 5600 LENZBURG
Tel: 58 2005802 **Fax:** 58 2005821
Email: hubert.keller@lenzburger-lba.ch.ch **Web site:** http://www.aargauerzeitung.ch
Freq: Weekly; **Cover Price:** Free; **Circ:** 29,492
Editor: Hubert Keller
Profile: Regional newspaper.
Language(s): German
ADVERTISING RATES:
Full Page Mono .... CHF 4048
Full Page Colour .... CHF 4312
Mechanical Data: Type Area: 440 x 290 mm, No. of Columns (Display): 10, Col Widths (Display): 25 mm
Copy instructions: *Copy Date:* 2 days prior to publication
LOCAL NEWSPAPERS

LOGISTIK & FÖRDERTECHNIK 1625981S10-45
Editorial: Grosspeterstr. 23, 4002 BASEL
Tel: 58 9589500 **Fax:** 58 9589590
Email: klaus.koch@logistik-online.ch **Web site:** http://www.logistik-online.ch
Freq: 11 issues yearly; **Annual Sub.:** CHF 105,00; **Circ:** 8,180
Editor: Klaus Koch; **Advertising Manager:** Annaröss Hürlimann
Profile: Magazine on logistics, flow of material, elevation technology, transport and storage technologies and cleaning technology as well as the automation and propulsion technologies within these sectors.
Language(s): French; German
ADVERTISING RATES:
Full Page Mono .... CHF 3100
Full Page Colour .... CHF 4750
Mechanical Data: Type Area: 265 x 181 mm, No. of Columns (Display): 3, Col Widths (Display): 57 mm
Copy instructions: *Copy Date:* 15 days prior to publication
Official Journal of: Organ d. Schweizer. Verb. f. d. Berufsbildung in d. Logistik (SVBL), d. Swiss Shippers' Council (SSC) u. d. Schweizer. Verb. f. Kühl- u. Tiefkühllogistik (SVKTL/ASLF)
BUSINESS: MATERIALS HANDLING

L-T LEBENSMITTEL-TECHNOLOGIE 733981S22A-180
Editorial: Basler Str. 15, 5080 LAUFENBURG
Tel: 62 8697930 **Fax:** 62 8697901
Email: edirlinger@lt-magazin.ch **Web site:** http://www.lt-magazin.ch
Freq: 10 issues yearly; Free to qualifying individuals
Annual Sub.: CHF 78,00; **Circ:** 4,150
Editor: Eva Dirlinger; **Advertising Manager:** Thomas Rehmann
Profile: Official publication of the Swiss Society for Food Science and Technology. Covers food and drinks technology. Includes discussions of the implications of GATT decisions and possible EU entry.
Language(s): German
Readership: Read by food scientists, senior executives and production managers.
ADVERTISING RATES:
Full Page Mono .... CHF 2750
Full Page Colour .... CHF 3800
Mechanical Data: Type Area: 260 x 190 mm, No. of Columns (Display): 3, Col Widths (Display): 61 mm
Copy instructions: *Copy Date:* 27 days prior to publication
Official Journal of: Organ d. Schweizer. Ges. f. Lebensmittel-Wissenschaft u. -Technologie
BUSINESS: FOOD

DAS MAGAZIN 734656S67B-6630_500
Editorial: Werdstr. 21, 8021 ZÜRICH **Tel:** 44 2484501
Fax: 44 2484487
Email: redaktion@dasmagazin.ch **Web site:** http://www.dasmagazin.ch
Freq: Weekly; **Circ:** 500,000
Editor: Finn Canonica; **Advertising Manager:** Michel Eggenberger
Profile: Weekend supplement to the Tages-Anzeiger.
Language(s): German
ADVERTISING RATES:
Full Page Mono .... CHF 25490
Full Page Colour .... CHF 25490
Mechanical Data: Type Area: 258 x 184 mm
Copy instructions: *Copy Date:* 10 days prior to publication
Supplement to: Basler Zeitung, Berner Zeitung BZ, Der Bund, Tages Anzeiger
REGIONAL DAILY & SUNDAY NEWSPAPERS: Regional Daily Newspapers

MANAGEMENT-ANDRAGOGIK UND ORGANISATIONSENT-WICKLUNG (MAO) 1855458S14A-1310
Editorial: Felsentr. 88, 9000 ST. GALLEN
Tel: 71 7800955 **Fax:** 71 7800956
Email: mao@stiefel-rolf-th.ch **Web site:** http://www.stiefel-rolf-th.ch
Freq: Quarterly; **Annual Sub.:** CHF 190,00; **Circ:** 800
Editor: Rolf Th. Stiefel
Profile: Manager magazine.
Language(s): German

MÄNNERIZEITUNG 1853474S86C-63
Editorial: Mühlegasse 14, 3400 BURGDORF
Tel: 34 4225008
Email: ivo.knill@maennerzeitung.ch **Web site:** http://www.maennerzeitung.ch
Freq: Quarterly; **Annual Sub.:** CHF 45,00; **Circ:** 4,000
Editor: Ivo Knill
Profile: Lifestyle magazine for men.
Language(s): German
ADVERTISING RATES:
Full Page Mono .... CHF 1000
Mechanical Data: Type Area: 260 x 168 mm
Copy instructions: *Copy Date:* 42 days prior to publication

MARCH-ANZEIGER 734780S67B-1860
Editorial: Alpenblickstr. 26, 8853 LACHEN
Tel: 55 4510888 **Fax:** 55 4510889
Email: redaktion@marchanzeiger.ch **Web site:** http://www.marchanzeiger.ch
Annual Sub.: CHF 221,00
Editor: Stefan Grüter
Profile: Regional daily newspaper covering politics, economics, sport, travel, technology and the arts.
Language(s): German
REGIONAL DAILY & SUNDAY NEWSPAPERS: Regional Daily Newspapers

MARIE CLAIRE 1844629S74A-493
Editorial: 1, Ch. du Bugnon, 1803 CHARDONNE
Tel: 21 9221690 **Fax:** 21 9221691
Email: info@marieclaire-suisse.ch **Web site:** http://www.marieclaire-suisse.ch
Freq: Monthly; **Circ:** 30,000
Editor: Hélène Béziat
Profile: Magazine for women.
Language(s): French
ADVERTISING RATES:
Full Page Mono .... CHF 8200
Full Page Colour .... CHF 8200
Mechanical Data: Type Area: 270 x 215 mm, No. of Columns (Display): 4, Col Widths (Display): 54 mm
Copy instructions: *Copy Date:* 49 days prior to publication

MARKET.CH 1643475S14A-1166
Editorial: 49, route des Jeunes, 1227 CAROUGE
Tel: 22 3017548 **Fax:** 22 3015914
Email: redaction@market.ch **Web site:** http://www.market.ch
Freq: 11 issues yearly; **Annual Sub.:** CHF 72,00; **Circ:** 40,500
Editor: Muriel Delucinge; **Advertising Manager:** John Hartung
Profile: Business magazine.
Language(s): French
ADVERTISING RATES:
Full Page Mono .... CHF 9000
Full Page Colour .... CHF 9000
Mechanical Data: Type Area: 280 x 213 mm, No. of Columns (Display): 3, Col Widths (Display): 72 mm

MARKET.CH 1985660S14A-1365
Editorial: 49, route des Jeunes, 1227 CAROUGE
Tel: 22 3017548 **Fax:** 22 3015914
Email: redaction@market.ch **Web site:** http://www.market.ch
Freq: 11 issues yearly; **Annual Sub.:** CHF 72,00; **Circ:** 21,500
Editor: Muriel Delucinge; **Advertising Manager:** John Hartung
Profile: Business magazine.
Language(s): German
ADVERTISING RATES:
Full Page Mono .... CHF 9000
Full Page Colour .... CHF 9000
Mechanical Data: Type Area: 280 x 213 mm, No. of Columns (Display): 3, Col Widths (Display): 72 mm

MARMITE 734928S74P-160
Editorial: Grubenstr.56, 8045 ZÜRICH
Tel: 43 3333952 **Fax:** 43 3333950
Email: a.willi@marmite.ch **Web site:** http://www.marmite.ch
Freq: 6 issues yearly; **Annual Sub.:** CHF 54,00; **Circ:** 13,053
Editor: Andrin C. Willi; **Advertising Manager:** Daniel Pauletto
Profile: Magazine for lovers of cooking and entertaining.
Language(s): German
ADVERTISING RATES:
Full Page Mono .... CHF 5900
Full Page Colour .... CHF 5900
Mechanical Data: Type Area: 260 x 190 mm

MARMITE 734928S74P-295
Editorial: Grubenstr.56, 8045 ZÜRICH
Tel: 43 3333952 **Fax:** 43 3333950
Email: a.willi@marmite.ch **Web site:** http://www.marmite.ch
Freq: 6 issues yearly; **Annual Sub.:** CHF 54,00; **Circ:** 13,053
Editor: Andrin C. Willi; **Advertising Manager:** Daniel Pauletto
Profile: Magazine for lovers of cooking and entertaining.
Language(s): German
ADVERTISING RATES:
Full Page Mono .... CHF 5900
Full Page Colour .... CHF 5900
Mechanical Data: Type Area: 260 x 190 mm

MASCHINENBAU 1656371S19E-188
Editorial: Carl-Böckli-Weg 1, 9410 HEIDEN
Tel: 71 8988010 **Fax:** 71 8988020
Email: maschinenbau@pph.ch **Web site:** http://www.maschinenbau-schweiz.ch
Freq: 13 issues yearly; **Annual Sub.:** CHF 55,00; **Circ:** 7,500
Editor: Christian Schlumpf
Profile: Magazine about engine construction.
Language(s): German
ADVERTISING RATES:
Full Page Mono .... CHF 2975
Full Page Colour .... CHF 4175
Mechanical Data: Type Area: 270 x 186 mm, No. of Columns (Display): 4, Col Widths (Display): 43 mm
Copy instructions: *Copy Date:* 25 days prior to publication

MASCHINENBAU 1656371S19E-198
Editorial: Carl-Böckli-Weg 1, 9410 HEIDEN
Tel: 71 8988010 **Fax:** 71 8988020
Email: maschinenbau@pph.ch **Web site:** http://www.maschinenbau-schweiz.ch
Freq: 13 issues yearly; **Annual Sub.:** CHF 55,00; **Circ:** 7,500
Editor: Christian Schlumpf
Profile: Magazine about engine construction.
Language(s): German
ADVERTISING RATES:
Full Page Mono .... CHF 2975
Full Page Colour .... CHF 4175
Mechanical Data: Type Area: 270 x 186 mm, No. of Columns (Display): 4, Col Widths (Display): 43 mm
Copy instructions: *Copy Date:* 25 days prior to publication

MEDIA LEX 1853018S2A-683
Editorial: Wölflistr. 1, 3001 BERN **Tel:** 31 3006666
Fax: 31 3006688
Email: redaktion@medialex.ch **Web site:** http://www.staempfliverlag.com
Freq: Quarterly; **Annual Sub.:** CHF 143,00; **Circ:** 750
Editor: Oliver Sidler
Profile: Publication about rights and the law relating to communications.
Language(s): French; German
ADVERTISING RATES:
Full Page Mono .... CHF 1025
Full Page Colour .... CHF 1025
Mechanical Data: Type Area: 260 x 185 mm

MEDIA TENOR 1865329S2A-694
Editorial: Rothstr. 54, 8057 ZÜRICH **Tel:** 43 2551920
Fax: 4143 2551929
Email: medien-tenor@innovatio.de **Web site:** http://www.medien-tenor.de
Freq: Quarterly; **Annual Sub.:** CHF 99,00; **Circ:** 2,000
Editor: Roland Schatz; **Advertising Manager:** Zuzana Beluska
Profile: Publication with media trends for journalists, company spokesmen, political parties, governments and trade unions.
Language(s): English
ADVERTISING RATES:
Full Page Mono .... CHF 980
Full Page Colour .... CHF 1980
Copy instructions: *Copy Date:* 10 days prior to publication

MEDIA TENOR 735143G2A-3160
Editorial: Rothstr. 54, 8057 ZÜRICH **Tel:** 43 2551926
Fax: 43 2551929
Email: r.schatz@mediatenor.com **Web site:** http://www.innovatio.de
Freq: Quarterly; **Annual Sub.:** CHF 94,00; **Circ:** 1,000
Editor: Roland Schatz
Profile: Publication covering media trends for journalists, company press officers, political parties, governments and trade unions.
Language(s): German
ADVERTISING RATES:
Full Page Mono .... CHF 980
Full Page Colour .... CHF 1980
Copy instructions: *Copy Date:* 10 days prior to publication

MEDIA TREND JOURNAL
735100S2A-260
Editorial: Neugasse 10, 8031 ZÜRICH
Tel: 44 2502830 **Fax:** 44 2502851
Email: pc.meier@werbewoche.ch **Web site:** http://www.mediatrend.ch
Freq: Quarterly; **Circ:** 4,000
Editor: Pierre C. Meier; **Advertising Manager:** Daniela Hämmerle
Profile: Magazine which looks behind the scenes of media. Includes analyses of future trends.
Language(s): German
Readership: Read by advertisers and media planners.
ADVERTISING RATES:
Full Page Mono .... CHF 5700
Full Page Colour .... CHF 5700
Mechanical Data: Type Area: 250 x 182 mm, No. of Columns (Display): 3, Col Widths (Display): 57 mm
Copy instructions: *Copy Date:* 12 days prior to publication
Official Journal of: Organ d. Interessengemeinschaft Media-Agenturen u. d. Vereinigung Schweizer Verlagsfachleute
Supplement to: WerbeWoche
BUSINESS: COMMUNICATIONS, ADVERTISING & MARKETING

MEDICAL TRIBUNE
735115S56A-1240
Editorial: Grosspeterstr. 23, 4002 BASEL
Tel: 58 9589603 **Fax:** 58 9589660
Email: redaktion@medical-tribune.ch **Web site:** http://www.medical-tribune.ch
Freq: Weekly; **Annual Sub.:** CHF 156,00; **Circ:** 10,400
Editor: Markus Meier; **Advertising Manager:** Patricia Hunziker
Profile: Publication containing national and international medical news.
Language(s): German
ADVERTISING RATES:
Full Page Mono .... CHF 7200
Full Page Colour .... CHF 7200
Mechanical Data: Type Area: 390 x 286 mm
Copy instructions: *Copy Date:* 28 days prior to publication
Supplement(s): Labor und Devices; Medical Tribune Kolloquium; Medical Tribune public; Psyche und Soma; Selecta
BUSINESS: HEALTH & MEDICAL

MEDICAL TRIBUNE KOLLOQUIUM
735117S56A-1260
Editorial: Grosspeterstr. 23, 4002 BASEL
Tel: 58 9589600 **Fax:** 58 9589660
Email: redaktion@medical-tribune.ch **Web site:** http://www.medical-tribune.ch
Freq: 15 issues yearly; **Circ:** 10,400
Editor: Petra Genetzky; **Advertising Manager:** Patricia Hunziker
Profile: Highlights of major conferences and review of current science in the main areas of family medicine. The newspaper format and the typical journalistic and creative presence of the parent booklet complements Medical Tribune Kolloqium to an environment that is in its presentation and editorial preparation of a more academic emphasis. The content is based largely on scientific meetings.
Language(s): German
ADVERTISING RATES:
Full Page Mono .... CHF 5732
Full Page Colour .... CHF 5732
Mechanical Data: Type Area: 242 x 184 mm
Copy instructions: *Copy Date:* 27 days prior to publication
Supplement to: Medical Tribune

[MEDICOS]
735121S56A-20
Editorial: Lättendörfli 3, 8114 DÄNIKON
Tel: 44 8451593 **Fax:** 44 8451613
Email: g.stauber@hispeed.ch
Freq: 5 issues yearly; **Annual Sub.:** CHF 42,00; **Circ:** 6,300
Editor: Gisela Stauber-Reichmuth
Profile: Magazine on dermatology, venerology, esthetic surgery, medical cosmetics and allergology.
Language(s): German
ADVERTISING RATES:
Full Page Mono .... CHF 3280
Full Page Colour .... CHF 4880
Mechanical Data: Type Area: 238 x 175 mm
Copy instructions: *Copy Date:* 24 days prior to publication

[MEDICOS]
735121S56A-2171
Editorial: Lättendörfli 3, 8114 DÄNIKON
Tel: 44 8451593 **Fax:** 44 8451613
Email: g.stauber@hispeed.ch
Freq: 5 issues yearly; **Annual Sub.:** CHF 42,00; **Circ:** 6,300
Editor: Gisela Stauber-Reichmuth
Profile: Magazine on dermatology, venerology, esthetic surgery, medical cosmetics and allergology.
Language(s): German
ADVERTISING RATES:
Full Page Mono .... CHF 3280
Full Page Colour .... CHF 4880
Mechanical Data: Type Area: 238 x 175 mm
Copy instructions: *Copy Date:* 24 days prior to publication

MEDKALENDER
735178S56A-1280
Editorial: Farnsburger Str. 8, 4132 MUTTENZ
Tel: 61 4678555 **Fax:** 61 4678556
Email: medkalender@emh.ch **Web site:** http://www.emh.ch
Freq: Annual; **Annual Sub.:** CHF 55,00; **Circ:** 3,000
Editor: Susanne Redler
Profile: Directory listing pharmaceutical products.
Language(s): German

MEGALINK
735189S5F-2
Editorial: Neumattstr. 1, 5001 AARAU
Tel: 58 2005659 **Fax:** 58 2005651
Email: patrick.mueller@megalink.ch **Web site:** http://www.megalink.ch
Freq: Monthly; **Annual Sub.:** CHF 85,00; **Circ:** 10,500
Editor: Patrick Müller; **Advertising Manager:** Thosten Krüger
Profile: Magazine focusing on research, electronics, telecommunications and multimedia.
Language(s): German
Readership: Aimed at senior management in the electronics, computer and communications industries. Also read by lecturers and students in technical colleges.
ADVERTISING RATES:
Full Page Mono .... CHF 3190
Full Page Colour .... CHF 4390
Mechanical Data: Type Area: 264 x 184 mm, No. of Columns (Display): 4, Col Widths (Display): 46 mm
Copy instructions: *Copy Date:* 26 days prior to publication
BUSINESS: COMPUTERS & AUTOMATION: Multimedia

LE MENU
1853621S74P-298
Editorial: Weststr. 10, 3000 BERN 6 **Tel:** 31 3595754
Fax: 31 3595855
Email: redaktion@lemenu.ch **Web site:** http://www.lemenu.ch
Freq: 10 issues yearly; **Annual Sub.:** CHF 49,00; **Circ:** 60,406
Editor: Barbara Paulsen Gysin
Profile: Magazine containing recipes, kitchen and cooking tips.
Language(s): German
ADVERTISING RATES:
Full Page Mono .... CHF 9500
Full Page Colour .... CHF 9500
Mechanical Data: Type Area: 239 x 177 mm
Copy instructions: *Copy Date:* 25 days prior to publication

MESSPUNKT
1846756S4E-817
Editorial: Pflanzschulstr. 17, 8411 WINTERTHUR
Tel: 52 2345050 **Fax:** 52 2345099
Email: info@hunzikerwater.ch **Web site:** http://www.hunzikerwater.ch
Freq: Annual; **Circ:** 2,000
Profile: Company publication.
Language(s): German

METALL
1999603S19E-200
Editorial: Seestr. 105, 8027 ZÜRICH **Tel:** 44 2857777
Fax: 44 2857778
Email: metall@smu.ch **Web site:** http://www.metallunion.ch
Freq: Monthly; Free to qualifying individuals
Annual Sub.: CHF 120,00; **Circ:** 6,027
Editor: René Pellaton
Profile: Journal of the Swiss Metal Union. Focuses on architecture in metal.
Language(s): French; German
ADVERTISING RATES:
Full Page Mono .... CHF 2150
Full Page Colour .... CHF 3650
Mechanical Data: Type Area: 270 x 190 mm, No. of Columns (Display): 2, Col Widths (Display): 93 mm
Copy instructions: *Copy Date:* 20 days prior to publication

MINERALIENFREUND
1776199S79K-279
Editorial: Sticki, 6468 ATTINGHAUSEN
Tel: 79 3535965
Email: info@mineralienfreund.ch **Web site:** http://www.mineralienfreund.ch
Freq: Quarterly; Free to qualifying individuals
Annual Sub.: CHF 48,00; **Circ:** 1,300
Editor: Bruno Müller
Language(s): German
ADVERTISING RATES:
Full Page Mono .... CHF 250
Full Page Colour .... CHF 400
Mechanical Data: Type Area: 177 x 117 mm
Copy instructions: *Copy Date:* 30 days prior to publication
CONSUMER: HOBBIES & DIY: Collectors Magazines

MITENAND
1827942S74N-265
Editorial: Heideweg 10, 6440 BRUNNEN
Tel: 41 8250825 **Fax:** 41 8250826
Email: alterswohnheim@brunnen.ch **Web site:** http://www.brunnen.ch/alterswohnheim
Freq: Quarterly; **Annual Sub.:** CHF 18,00; **Circ:** 1,600
Editor: Reinhold Roten
Profile: Magazine for the elderly.
Language(s): German

MITTELALTER MOYEN AGE MEDIOEVO TEMP MEDIEVAL
736237S94X-380
Editorial: Blochmonterstr. 22, 4054 BASEL
Tel: 61 3612444 **Fax:** 61 3639405
Email: info@burgenverein.ch **Web site:** http://www.burgenverein.ch
Freq: Quarterly; Free to qualifying individuals
Annual Sub.: CHF 45,00; **Circ:** 1,256
Editor: Thomas Bitterli-Waldvogel
Profile: Magazine from the Swiss Castel Association about archaeology and culture of mediaeval times, castle explorations and castle archaeology.
Language(s): French; German; Italian
CONSUMER: OTHER CLASSIFICATIONS: Miscellaneous

MK MARKETING & KOMMUNIKATION
736296S2A-340
Editorial: Zweierstr. 35, 8036 ZÜRICH
Tel: 44 2961040 **Fax:** 44 2961049
Email: redaktion@m-k.ch **Web site:** http://www.m-k.ch
Freq: Monthly; Free to qualifying individuals
Annual Sub.: CHF 198,00; **Circ:** 9,000
Editor: Anne-Friedericke Heinrich
Profile: Magazine about sales, marketing and communications.
Language(s): German
ADVERTISING RATES:
Full Page Mono .... CHF 4900
Full Page Colour .... CHF 5900
Mechanical Data: Type Area: 282 x 200 mm, No. of Columns (Display): 4, Col Widths (Display): 47 mm
Copy instructions: *Copy Date:* 21 days prior to publication
Official Journal of: Organ d. Schweizer Werbung SW, d. Schweizer. Public Relations Ges., d. Schweizer. Marketing Clubs, d. Verb. Schweizer Marketing- u. Sozialforscher, d. Schweizer. Direktmarketing Verb., d. Fachvereinigung f. Marketing-Kommunikation u. d. WEMAR
BUSINESS: COMMUNICATIONS, ADVERTISING & MARKETING

MOBILITÄT
767646S18B-333
Editorial: Obergasse 34, 8402 WINTERTHUR
Tel: 52 2132317 **Fax:** 52 2132319
Email: groborg@mobilitaet-verlag.ch **Web site:** http://www.mobilitaet-verlag.ch
Freq: Quarterly; **Annual Sub.:** CHF 70,00; **Circ:** 12,000
Editor: Rolf Grob; **Advertising Manager:** Rolf Grob
Profile: Magazine on traffic, energy, environment, security, logistics, infrastructure, development, research, industry and economy.
Language(s): German
ADVERTISING RATES:
Full Page Mono .... CHF 3780
Full Page Colour .... CHF 4760
Mechanical Data: Type Area: 273 x 185 mm, No. of Columns (Display): 3
Copy instructions: *Copy Date:* 30 days prior to publication

MODELL FLUGSPORT
763048S79B-102
Editorial: Postfach 175, 8335 HITTNAU
Email: editor@modellflugsport.ch **Web site:** http://www.modellflugsport.ch
Freq: 6 issues yearly; **Annual Sub.:** CHF 42,00; **Circ:** 8,100
Editor: E. C. Giezendanner
Profile: Magazine for model aviators.
Language(s): French; German; Italian
ADVERTISING RATES:
Full Page Mono .... CHF 1298
Full Page Colour .... CHF 1998
Mechanical Data: Type Area: 267 x 185 mm
Copy instructions: *Copy Date:* 30 days prior to publication
Official Journal of: Organ d. Schweizer. Modellflugverb. (FSAM)
CONSUMER: HOBBIES & DIY: Models & Modelling

MONTAGNA
1851543S21A-619
Editorial: Sellerstr. 4, 3001 BERN **Tel:** 31 3821010
Fax: 31 3821016
Email: vincent.gillioz@sab.ch **Web site:** http://www.sab.ch
Freq: 10 issues yearly; Free to qualifying individuals
Annual Sub.: CHF 80,00; **Circ:** 4,000
Editor: Vincent Gillioz
Profile: Monthly for mountainous regions of the Alps.
Language(s): French; German; Italian
ADVERTISING RATES:
Full Page Mono .... CHF 985
Full Page Colour .... CHF 985
Mechanical Data: Type Area: 252 x 192 mm
Official Journal of: Organ d. Schweizer. alpwirtschaftl. Verb. (SAV) u. d. Schweizer. ArGe f. d. Berggebiete (SAB)

MOTOCLASSIC
1656139S31B-1
Editorial: Wolleraustr. 11a, 8807 FREIENBACH
Tel: 848 333100 **Fax:** 55 4158200
Web site: http://www.eurotaxglass.ch
Freq: Annual; **Annual Sub.:** CHF 82,00; **Circ:** 650
Profile: Magazine reporting on the market of special motorbikes.
Language(s): French; German; Italian
Mechanical Data: Type Area: 200 x 138 mm
Copy instructions: *Copy Date:* 30 days prior to publication

MOTOR SPORT AKTUELL
1633970S77D-69
Editorial: Industriestr. 28, 8604 VOLKETSWIL
Tel: 44 8065566 **Fax:** 44 8065511
Email: msa@motorpresse.ch **Web site:** http://www.motorsport-aktuell.com
Freq: Weekly; **Annual Sub.:** CHF 149,00; **Circ:** 45,506
Editor: Leopold Wieland; **Advertising Manager:** August Hug
Profile: Close to the race track. After the races from the weekend, Europe's fastest motor sport newspaper the only one already on Tuesday after all, what makes the heart of motorsport interested later: cutting-edge and comprehensive race reports on the national and international automobile and motorcycle racing. What the TV and newspaper coverage can not deliver, namely depth analysis and commentary, get interested persons, Fans, Active and decision makers in Motor Sport aktuell. Professionally and competently the whole range of issues of racing will be covered: all formula classes, touring car and rally racing, popular sports, Moto Grand Prix scene, the World Superbike Championship and Motocross. In short: Who has a say in racing, says it currently in Motor Sport aktuell - the source of information about the motor sports. Week after week, all the news from the market- and opinion leaders. As part of the annual readers' choice "Racer of the Year" highly interesting market research data to the racing market are made, can be represented as a long-term trends. This includes not only awareness and sympathy points from manufacturers, teams, equipment manufacturers and sponsors also estimates the development of motor sport and the individual race series.
Language(s): German
ADVERTISING RATES:
Full Page Mono .... CHF 12720
Full Page Colour .... CHF 12720
Mechanical Data: Type Area: 289 x 206 mm
Copy instructions: *Copy Date:* 12 days prior to publication
CONSUMER: MOTORING & CYCLING: Motor Sports

MP MIETRECHTSPRAXIS
1648432S1A-287
Editorial: Hardstr. 319, 8005 ZÜRICH
Tel: 44 2782805
Email: redaktion@mietrecht.ch **Web site:** http://www.mietrecht.ch
Freq: Quarterly; **Annual Sub.:** CHF 86,00; **Circ:** 2,876
Editor: Claude Roy; **Advertising Manager:** Peter Macher
Profile: Magazine about tenancy law in Switzerland.
Language(s): German
ADVERTISING RATES:
Full Page Mono .... CHF 1900

MQ MANAGEMENT UND QUALITÄT
736559S14R-280
Editorial: Kasernenstr. 35, 3012 BERN
Tel: 31 3485019 **Fax:** 31 3485023
Email: henninghz@bluewin.ch
Freq: 10 issues yearly; **Annual Sub.:** CHF 125,00; **Circ:** 7,000
Editor: Hans-Henning Herzog
Profile: Magazine on integrated management systems.
Language(s): German
ADVERTISING RATES:
Full Page Mono .... CHF 2700
Full Page Colour .... CHF 3700
Mechanical Data: Type Area: 268 x 200 mm, No. of Columns (Display): 4, Col Widths (Display): 43 mm
Copy instructions: *Copy Date:* 15 days prior to publication
Official Journal of: Organ d. Swiss Association for Quality
BUSINESS: COMMERCE, INDUSTRY & MANAGEMENT: Commerce Related

MSM LE MENSUEL DE L'INDUSTRIE
1842247S19E-194
Editorial: 11, Chemin du Pâquier, 1688 VUISTERNENS-DEVANT-ROMONT **Tel:** 26 6550447
Fax: 26 6550448
Email: jrgonthier@msm.ch **Web site:** http://www.msm.ch
Freq: 11 issues yearly; **Circ:** 8,500
Editor: Jean-René Gonthier; **Advertising Manager:** Trudi Halama
Profile: Contents: Technical articles, case studies, current reports on all major trade fairs at home and abroad, latest product news, current industry news. Editorial expertise: All editors of the MSM have a sound technical and / or business training at a university or college. Along with a permanent training in journalism, they guarantee a technically correct and pleasing journalistic reporting.
Language(s): French
ADVERTISING RATES:
Full Page Mono .... CHF 3517
Full Page Colour .... CHF 5162
Mechanical Data: Type Area: 267 x 185 mm, No. of Columns (Display): 3, Col Widths (Display): 59 mm
Copy instructions: *Copy Date:* 20 days prior to publication

Official Journal of: Organ d. Swiss Welding Institute, d. Institut Suisse du Soudage, d. Swissmechanic u. d. GIM-CH Association pour les petites et moyennes entreprises de la branche mécanique et technique.

DER MURTENBIETER
736720S67B-1900
Editorial: Irisstr. 12, 3280 MURTEN **Tel:** 26 6723441 **Fax:** 26 6723449
Email: redaktion@murtenbieter.ch **Web site:** http://www.murtenbieter.ch
Freq: 104 issues yearly; **Annual Sub.:** CHF 101,00; **Circ:** 4,226
Editor: Christoph Nussbaumer
Profile: Regional daily newspaper covering politics, economics, sport, travel, technology and the arts.
Language(s): German
ADVERTISING RATES:
SCC .... CHF 14,90
Mechanical Data: Type Area: 440 x 286 mm, No. of Columns (Display): 8, Col Widths (Display): 33 mm
Copy instructions: *Copy Date:* 2 days prior to publication
REGIONAL DAILY & SUNDAY NEWSPAPERS: Regional Daily Newspapers

DER MURTENBIETER
736719S72-6080
Editorial: Irisweg 12, 3280 MURTEN **Tel:** 26 6703441 **Fax:** 26 6723449
Email: redaktion@murtenbieter.ch **Web site:** http://www.murtenbieter.ch
Freq: Monthly; **Cover Price:** Free; **Circ:** 18,398
Editor: Christoph Nussbaumer
Profile: Advertising journal (house-to-house) concentrating on local stories.
Language(s): German
ADVERTISING RATES:
Full Page Mono .... CHF 3168
Mechanical Data: Type Area: 440 x 286 mm, No. of Columns (Display): 8, Col Widths (Display): 33 mm
Copy instructions: *Copy Date:* 2 days prior to publication
LOCAL NEWSPAPERS

MUTTENZER ANZEIGER
1655532S72-9654
Editorial: Missionsstr. 36, 4012 BASEL
Tel: 61 2646450 **Fax:** 61 2646488
Email: redaktion@muttenzeranzeiger.ch **Web site:** http://www.reinhardt.ch
Freq: 2444 issues yearly; **Circ:** 3,339
Profile: Regional weekly covering politics, economics, sport, travel, technology and the arts.
Language(s): German
ADVERTISING RATES:
SCC .... CHF 23,40
Mechanical Data: Type Area: 290 x 203 mm, No. of Columns (Display): 7, Col Widths (Display): 27 mm
LOCAL NEWSPAPERS

NACHRICHTEN AERO-CLUB OSTSCHWEIZ
764301S75N-1
Editorial: Postfach 279, 9320 ARBON
Tel: 79 4467066
Email: redaktion@aeroclub-ostschweiz.ch **Web site:** http://www.aeroclub-ostschweiz.ch
Freq: 6 issues yearly; **Circ:** 2,000
Profile: Aero sport club magazine for East Switzerland.
Language(s): German
ADVERTISING RATES:
Full Page Mono .... CHF 1140
Full Page Colour .... CHF 2112
Mechanical Data: Type Area: 190 x 128 mm
CONSUMER: SPORT: Flight

NATUR UND MENSCH
736999S57-400
Editorial: Weinsteig 192, 8201 SCHAFFHAUSEN
Tel: 52 6252667 **Fax:** 52 6252651
Email: redaktion@rheinaubund.ch **Web site:** http://www.rheinaubund.ch
Freq: 6 issues yearly; Free to qualifying individuals
Annual Sub.: CHF 45,00; **Circ:** 3,000
Editor: Günther Frauenlob
Profile: Swiss paper about nature and homeland protection.
Language(s): German
Official Journal of: Organ d. Schweizer. Vereinigung gegen d. Hochrheinschiffahrt, d. ArGe z. Schutz d. Aare, d. Interessengemeinschaft Bielersee, d. Landschaftsschutzverb. Hallwilersee, d. Aqua Viva Nationale ArGe z. Schutz d. Flüsse u. Seen, d. Pro Rein Anteriur, d. Bodensee-Stiftung, d. Verb. z. Schutze d. Greifensees u. d. ArGe Pro Thur

NATÜRLICH LEBEN
736946S74G-240
Editorial: Neumattstr. 1, 5001 AARAU
Tel: 58 2005638 **Fax:** 58 2005644
Email: markus.kellenberger@natuerlich-leben.ch
Web site: http://www.natuerlich-leben.ch
Freq: Monthly; **Annual Sub.:** CHF 84,00; **Circ:** 48,000
Editor: Markus Kellenberger
Profile: Magazine about health and nature. Includes features on medicine, keeping fit, eating well and the natural world.
Language(s): German
Readership: Aimed at adults aged between 40 and 50 years old.
ADVERTISING RATES:
Full Page Colour .... CHF 6300
Mechanical Data: No. of Columns (Display): 3, Col Widths (Display): 59 mm, Type Area: 268 x 185 mm
Copy instructions: *Copy Date:* 24 days prior to publication
CONSUMER: WOMEN'S INTEREST CONSUMER MAGAZINES: Slimming & Health

NEBELSPALTER
737028S73-150
Editorial: Bahnhofstr. 17, 9326 HORN
Tel: 71 8468876 **Fax:** 71 8468879
Email: marco.ratschiller@nebelspalter.ch **Web site:** http://www.nebelspalter.ch
Freq: 10 issues yearly; **Annual Sub.:** CHF 98,00; **Circ:** 21,000
Editor: Marco Ratschiller; **Advertising Manager:** Roger Pfranger
Profile: Satirical publication.
Language(s): German
ADVERTISING RATES:
Full Page Mono .... CHF 5800
Full Page Colour .... CHF 5800
Mechanical Data: Type Area: 265 x 187 mm, No. of Columns (Display): 3, Col Widths (Display): 60 mm
CONSUMER: NATIONAL & INTERNATIONAL PERIODICALS

NEONATOLOGY
722964S56A-140
Editorial: Allschwiler Str. 10, 4055 BASEL
Tel: 61 3061360 **Fax:** 61 3061434
Email: neo@karger.ch **Web site:** http://www.karger.com/neo
Freq: 8 issues yearly; **Annual Sub.:** CHF 2627,20; **Circ:** 900
Editor: H. L. Halliday; **Advertising Manager:** Thomas Maurer
Profile: Journal is a source of information in the area of fetal and neonatal research.
Language(s): English
ADVERTISING RATES:
Full Page Mono .... CHF 1780
Full Page Colour .... CHF 3340
Mechanical Data: Type Area: 224 x 180 mm

NEPHRON
737049S56A-1340
Editorial: Allschwiler Str. 10, 4055 BASEL
Tel: 61 3061111 **Fax:** 61 3061234
Email: karger@karger.ch **Web site:** http://www.karger.com/nef
Freq: Monthly; **Annual Sub.:** CHF 4627,80; **Circ:** 2,800
Editor: L. G. Fine; **Advertising Manager:** Thomas Maurer
Profile: Magazine with recent information about nephrology.
Language(s): English
ADVERTISING RATES:
Full Page Mono .... CHF 1950
Full Page Colour .... CHF 3510
Mechanical Data: Type Area: 224 x 180 mm

NEPHRO-NEWS
1859133S56A-2203
Editorial: Baarer Str. 86a, 6300 ZUG **Tel:** 41 7123131 **Fax:** 41 7123130
Email: office@medicom.ch **Web site:** http://www.medicom.cc
Freq: 6 issues yearly; **Circ:** 3,000
Profile: Magazine containing information about nephrology und hypertensiology.
Language(s): German
Mechanical Data: Type Area: 260 x 180 mm
Copy instructions: *Copy Date:* 14 days prior to publication

NETCOM MAGAZIN
1656314S18B-343
Editorial: via del Tiglio, 24B, 6605 LOCARNO
Tel: 91 7600888 **Fax:** 91 7600889
Email: redaktion@eis.ch **Web site:** http://www.netcom-magazin.ch
Freq: Half-yearly; **Annual Sub.:** CHF 15,00; **Circ:** 15,000
Editor: Peter Fischer; **Advertising Manager:** Peter Fischer
Profile: Magazine about network and telecommunications.
Language(s): German
ADVERTISING RATES:
Full Page Mono .... CHF 3380
Full Page Colour .... CHF 4250
Mechanical Data: Type Area: 250 x 190 mm
Copy instructions: *Copy Date:* 30 days prior to publication

NETCOM MAGAZIN
1656314S18B-384
Editorial: via del Tiglio, 24B, 6605 LOCARNO
Tel: 91 7600888 **Fax:** 91 7600889
Email: redaktion@eis.ch **Web site:** http://www.netcom-magazin.ch
Freq: Half-yearly; **Annual Sub.:** CHF 15,00; **Circ:** 15,000
Editor: Peter Fischer; **Advertising Manager:** Peter Fischer
Profile: Magazine about network and telecommunications.
Language(s): German
ADVERTISING RATES:
Full Page Mono .... CHF 3380
Full Page Colour .... CHF 4250
Mechanical Data: Type Area: 250 x 190 mm
Copy instructions: *Copy Date:* 30 days prior to publication

NEUE FRICKTALER ZEITUNG
1655521S67B-6631
Editorial: Albrechtsplatz 3, 4310 RHEINFELDEN
Tel: 61 8350035 **Fax:** 61 8350099
Email: redaktion@nfz.ch **Web site:** http://www.nfz.ch
Freq: 104 issues yearly; **Annual Sub.:** CHF 178,00; **Circ:** 8,981
Editor: Walter Herzog
Profile: Regional daily newspaper covering politics, economics, sport, travel, technology and the arts.
Language(s): German
ADVERTISING RATES:
SCC .... CHF 29,80
Mechanical Data: Type Area: 440 x 291 mm, No. of Columns (Display): 10, Col Widths (Display): 25 mm
Copy instructions: *Copy Date:* 1 day prior to publication
REGIONAL DAILY & SUNDAY NEWSPAPERS: Regional Daily Newspapers

NEUE FRICKTALER ZEITUNG
1656449S72-9694
Editorial: Albrechtsplatz 3, 4310 RHEINFELDEN
Tel: 61 8350035 **Fax:** 61 8350099
Email: redaktion@nfz.ch **Web site:** http://www.nfz.ch
Freq: Weekly; **Cover Price:** Free; **Circ:** 36,391
Editor: Walter Herzog
Profile: Advertising journal (house-to-house) concentrating on local stories.
Language(s): German
ADVERTISING RATES:
Full Page Mono .... CHF 5280
Full Page Colour .... CHF 6600
Mechanical Data: Type Area: 440 x 291 mm, No. of Columns (Display): 10, Col Widths (Display): 25 mm
Copy instructions: *Copy Date:* 2 days prior to publication
LOCAL NEWSPAPERS

NEUE LUZERNER ZEITUNG
737149S67B-1920
Editorial: Maihofstr. 76, 6002 LUZERN
Tel: 41 4295151 **Fax:** 41 4295181
Email: redaktion@neue-lz.ch **Web site:** http://www.zisch.ch
Freq: 312 issues yearly; **Annual Sub.:** CHF 348,00; **Circ:** 133,304
Editor: Thomas Bornhauser; **News Editor:** Dominik Buholzer
Profile: Regional daily newspaper covering politics, economics, sport, travel, technology and the arts.
Language(s): German
ADVERTISING RATES:
SCC .... CHF 84,20
Mechanical Data: Type Area: 440 x 290 mm, No. of Columns (Display): 10, Col Widths (Display): 26 mm
Copy instructions: *Copy Date:* 2 days prior to publication
Supplement(s): Apéro; Montag; NZZ Folio; ZAP
REGIONAL DAILY & SUNDAY NEWSPAPERS: Regional Daily Newspapers

NEUE NIDWALDNER ZEITUNG
737163S67B-1940
Editorial: Maihofstr. 76, 6002 LUZERN
Tel: 41 4295151 **Fax:** 41 4295181
Email: redaktion@neue-lz.ch **Web site:** http://www.zisch.ch
Freq: 312 issues yearly; **Annual Sub.:** CHF 398,00; **Circ:** 15,417
Profile: Daily newspaper with regional news and a local sports section.
Language(s): German
ADVERTISING RATES:
SCC .... CHF 18,20
Mechanical Data: Type Area: 440 x 290 mm, No. of Columns (Display): 10, Col Widths (Display): 26 mm
Copy instructions: *Copy Date:* 2 days prior to publication
Supplement(s): Montag; ZAP
REGIONAL DAILY & SUNDAY NEWSPAPERS: Regional Daily Newspapers

NEUE OBWALDNER ZEITUNG
737169S67B-1960
Editorial: Maihofstr. 76, 6002 LUZERN
Tel: 41 4295141 **Fax:** 41 4295181
Email: redaktion@neue-oz.ch **Web site:** http://www.zisch.ch
Freq: 312 issues yearly; **Annual Sub.:** CHF 398,00; **Circ:** 15,417
Profile: Daily newspaper with regional news and a local sports section.
Language(s): German
ADVERTISING RATES:
SCC .... CHF 18,20
Mechanical Data: Type Area: 440 x 290 mm, No. of Columns (Display): 10, Col Widths (Display): 26 mm
Copy instructions: *Copy Date:* 2 days prior to publication
Supplement(s): Montag; ZAP
REGIONAL DAILY & SUNDAY NEWSPAPERS: Regional Daily Newspapers

NEUE OLTNER ZEITUNG NOZ
1641972S72-9595
Editorial: Ringstr. 41, 4603 OLTEN **Tel:** 62 2055445 **Fax:** 62 2055446
Email: redaktion@noz.ch **Web site:** http://www.noz.ch
Freq: Weekly; **Cover Price:** Free; **Circ:** 32,171
Editor: Fredi Köbeli; **Advertising Manager:** Roli Diglas
Profile: Advertising journal (house-to-house) concentrating on local stories.
Language(s): German
ADVERTISING RATES:
Full Page Mono .... CHF 5984
Full Page Colour .... CHF 6384
Mechanical Data: Type Area: 440 x 286 mm, No. of Columns (Display): 10, Col Widths (Display): 25 mm
Copy instructions: *Copy Date:* 1 day prior to publication
LOCAL NEWSPAPERS

NEUE PRODUKTE
1642212S14A-1165
Editorial: Postfach 940, 4142 MÜNCHENSTEIN 1
Tel: 61 3381638 **Fax:** 61 3381600
Email: neueprodukte@lauper.ch **Web site:** http://www.neueprodukte.ch
Freq: 10 issues yearly; **Annual Sub.:** CHF 51,00; **Circ:** 5,400
Editor: Luca Taiana
Profile: International market overview for industry, trade and service providers.
Language(s): German
ADVERTISING RATES:
Full Page Mono .... CHF 1550
Full Page Colour .... CHF 2350
Mechanical Data: Type Area: 275 x 185 mm, No. of Columns (Display): 4, Col Widths (Display): 45 mm
Copy instructions: *Copy Date:* 25 days prior to publication

DIE NEUE SCHULPRAXIS
764927S62A-528
Editorial: Bruggli 3, 8754 NETSTAL
Email: heinrich.marti@os-verwaltung-eschenbach.ch
Freq: 11 issues yearly; **Annual Sub.:** CHF 87,00; **Circ:** 10,200
Editor: Heinrich Marti; **Advertising Manager:** Markus Turani
Profile: Magazine for teachers.
Language(s): German
ADVERTISING RATES:
Full Page Mono .... CHF 1620
Full Page Colour .... CHF 2205
Mechanical Data: Type Area: 268 x 176 mm, No. of Columns (Display): 2, Col Widths (Display): 86 mm
Copy instructions: *Copy Date:* 25 days prior to publication
BUSINESS: CHURCH & SCHOOL EQUIPMENT & EDUCATION: Education

NEUE SCHWYZER ZEITUNG
737213S67B-1980
Editorial: Maihofstr. 76, 6002 LUZERN
Tel: 41 4295151 **Fax:** 41 4295181
Email: redaktion@neue-lz.ch **Web site:** http://www.zisch.ch
Freq: 312 issues yearly; **Annual Sub.:** CHF 398,00; **Circ:** 3,640
Profile: Daily newspaper with regional news and a local sports section.
Language(s): German
ADVERTISING RATES:
SCC .... CHF 13,40
Mechanical Data: Type Area: 440 x 290 mm, No. of Columns (Display): 10, Col Widths (Display): 26 mm
Copy instructions: *Copy Date:* 2 days prior to publication
Supplement(s): Montag; ZAP
REGIONAL DAILY & SUNDAY NEWSPAPERS: Regional Daily Newspapers

DIE NEUE STEUERPRAXIS
1647230S1A-286
Editorial: Münstergasse 3, 3011 BERN
Tel: 31 6334360
Freq: 6 issues yearly; **Annual Sub.:** CHF 75,00; **Circ:** 900
Profile: Magazine on taxes.
Language(s): French; German
ADVERTISING RATES:
Full Page Mono .... CHF 350
Mechanical Data: Type Area: 194 x 120 mm
Copy instructions: *Copy Date:* 28 days prior to publication

NEUE URNER ZEITUNG
737258S67B-2000
Editorial: Maihofstr. 76, 6002 LUZERN
Tel: 41 4295151 **Fax:** 41 4295181
Email: redaktion@neue-lz.ch **Web site:** http://www.zisch.ch
Freq: 312 issues yearly; **Annual Sub.:** CHF 398,00; **Circ:** 4,310
Profile: Daily newspaper with regional news and a local sports section.
Language(s): German
ADVERTISING RATES:
SCC .... CHF 12,20
Mechanical Data: Type Area: 440 x 290 mm, No. of Columns (Display): 10, Col Widths (Display): 26 mm

Copy instructions: *Copy Date:* 2 days prior to publication
Supplement(s): Montag; ZAP
REGIONAL DAILY & SUNDAY NEWSPAPERS: Regional Daily Newspapers

NEUE ZUGER ZEITUNG
737287S67B-2020
Editorial: Maihofstr. 76, 6002 LUZERN
Tel: 41 4295151 **Fax:** 41 4295181
Email: redaktion@neue-lz.ch **Web site:** http://www.zisch.ch
Freq: 312 issues yearly; **Annual Sub.:** CHF 398,00; **Circ:** 19,816
Editor: Christian P. Meier
Profile: Daily newspaper with regional news and a local sports section.
Language(s): German
ADVERTISING RATES:
SCC .... CHF 20,70
Mechanical Data: Type Area: 440 x 290 mm, No. of Columns (Display): 10, Col Widths (Display): 26 mm
Copy instructions: *Copy Date:* 2 days prior to publication
Supplement(s): Montag; NZZ Folio; ZAP
REGIONAL DAILY & SUNDAY NEWSPAPERS: Regional Daily Newspapers

NEUE ZÜRCHER ZEITUNG
737286S65A-20
Editorial: Falkenstr. 11, 8021 ZÜRICH
Tel: 44 2581111 **Fax:** 44 2521329
Email: redaktion@nzz.ch **Web site:** http://www.nzz.ch
Freq: 312 issues yearly; **Annual Sub.:** CHF 512,00; **Circ:** 139,732
Editor: Markus Spillmann; **News Editor:** Luzi Bernet; **Advertising Manager:** Walter Vontobel
Profile: Tabloid-sized quality newspaper covering regional, national and international news, politics, finance, economics, sport, culture and leisure.
Language(s): German
Readership: Aimed at company directors, business executives and students.
ADVERTISING RATES:
SCC .... CHF 254,40
Mechanical Data: Type Area: 440 x 291 mm, No. of Columns (Display): 10, Col Widths (Display): 25 mm
Copy instructions: *Copy Date:* 2 days prior to publication
Supplement(s): NZZ Campus; NZZ Folio; Z Die Schönen Seiten
NATIONAL DAILY & SUNDAY NEWSPAPERS: National Daily Newspapers

NEUES BÜLACHER TAGBLATT
1656009S67B-6632
Editorial: Bahnhofstr. 44, 8180 BÜLACH
Tel: 44 8641515 **Fax:** 44 8641550
Email: redaktion@nbt.ch **Web site:** http://www.nbt.ch
Freq: 260 issues yearly; **Annual Sub.:** CHF 298,00; **Circ:** 22,544
Editor: Rolf Haecky
Profile: Regional daily newspaper covering politics, economics, sport, travel, technology and the arts.
Language(s): German
ADVERTISING RATES:
SCC .... CHF 21,90
Mechanical Data: Type Area: 440 x 286 mm, No. of Columns (Display): 10, Col Widths (Display): 26 mm
Copy instructions: *Copy Date:* 1 day prior to publication
REGIONAL DAILY & SUNDAY NEWSPAPERS: Regional Daily Newspapers

NEUES BÜLACHER TAGBLATT
1656143S72-9673
Editorial: Bahnhofstr. 44, 8180 BÜLACH
Tel: 44 8641515 **Fax:** 44 8641550
Email: redaktion@nbt.ch **Web site:** http://www.nbt.ch
Freq: Weekly; **Cover Price:** Free; **Circ:** 80,239
Editor: Rolf Haecky
Profile: Advertising journal (house-to-house) concentrating on local stories.
Language(s): German
ADVERTISING RATES:
Full Page Mono .... CHF 7680
Full Page Colour .... CHF 11792
Mechanical Data: Type Area: 440 x 286 mm, No. of Columns (Display): 10, Col Widths (Display): 26 mm
Copy instructions: *Copy Date:* 2 days prior to publication
LOCAL NEWSPAPERS

NEURODEGENERATIVE DISEASES
1641966S56A-2040
Editorial: Allschwiler Str. 10, 4055 BASEL
Tel: 61 3061358 **Fax:** 61 3061434
Email: ndd@karger.ch **Web site:** http://www.karger.com/ndd
Freq: 6 issues yearly; **Annual Sub.:** CHF 1440,40; **Circ:** 800
Editor: R. M. Nitsch; **Advertising Manager:** Thomas Maurer
Profile: Magazine about neurodegenerative diseases.
Language(s): English
ADVERTISING RATES:
Full Page Mono .... CHF 1780
Full Page Colour .... CHF 3340
Mechanical Data: Type Area: 224 x 180 mm

NEUROIMMUNOMODULATION
1641141S56A-2030
Editorial: Allschwiler Str. 10, 4055 BASEL
Tel: 61 3061356 **Fax:** 61 3061434
Email: nim@karger.ch **Web site:** http://www.karger.com/nim
Freq: 6 issues yearly; **Annual Sub.:** CHF 1701,40; **Circ:** 800
Editor: W. Savino; **Advertising Manager:** Thomas Maurer
Profile: Research about the interaction between the nervous and the immune systems.
Language(s): English
ADVERTISING RATES:
Full Page Mono .... CHF 1950
Full Page Colour .... CHF 3510
Mechanical Data: Type Area: 224 x 180 mm
Official Journal of: Organ d. Internat. Society for Neuroimmunomodulation

NEUROPSYCHOBIOLOGY
737321S56A-1360
Editorial: Allschwiler Str. 10, 4055 BASEL
Tel: 61 3061111 **Fax:** 61 3061234
Email: karger@karger.ch **Web site:** http://www.karger.com/nps
Freq: 8 issues yearly; **Annual Sub.:** CHF 2387,00; **Circ:** 800
Editor: W. Strik; **Advertising Manager:** Thomas Maurer
Profile: Neurobiological aspects concerning behaviour and mental disorders.
Language(s): English
ADVERTISING RATES:
Full Page Mono .... CHF 1950
Full Page Colour .... CHF 3510
Mechanical Data: Type Area: 224 x 180 mm
Official Journal of: Organ d. Internat. Pharmaco-EEG Society

NEWS
1820131S18B-376
Editorial: Rotzbergstr. 15, 6362 STANSSTAD
Tel: 41 6180808 **Fax:** 41 6180818
Email: info@telcom-ag.ch **Web site:** http://www.telcom-ag.ch
Freq: Half-yearly; **Circ:** 3,500
Profile: Publication from the telecommunications provider Telcom.
Language(s): German

NEWSLETTER
1774434S14A-1215
Editorial: Münsterplatz 3, 3011 BERN
Tel: 31 6334120 **Fax:** 31 6334088
Email: info@berneinvest.com **Web site:** http://www.berneinvest.com
Freq: Half-yearly; **Cover Price:** Free; **Circ:** 20,000
Editor: Virve Resta
Profile: Information from the business development department of the Swiss Canton Bern.
Language(s): French; German

NEWSLETTER
1855470S14A-1312
Editorial: Herrenacker 15, 8200 SCHAFFHAUSEN
Tel: 52 6740615 **Fax:** 52 6740609
Email: petra.roost@generis.ch **Web site:** http://www.economy.sh
Freq: Quarterly; Free to qualifying individuals ; **Circ:** 3,300
Profile: Regional business magazine.
Language(s): German
ADVERTISING RATES:
Full Page Mono .... CHF 2400
Full Page Colour .... CHF 3600
Mechanical Data: Type Area: 271 x 190 mm, No. of Columns (Display): 3, Col Widths (Display): 60 mm

NEWSLETTER
2002658S14A-1374
Editorial: Münsterplatz 3, 3011 BERN
Tel: 31 6334120 **Fax:** 31 6334088
Email: info@berneinvest.com **Web site:** http://www.berneinvest.com
Freq: Half-yearly; **Cover Price:** Free; **Circ:** 20,000
Editor: Virve Resta
Profile: Information from the business development department of the Swiss Canton Bern.
Language(s): French

NEXT FLOOR
765524S4E-775
Editorial: Zuger Str. 13, 6030 EBIKON
Tel: 41 4454356 **Fax:** 41 4454435
Email: nextfloor@ch.schindler.com **Web site:** http://www.schindler.ch
Freq: Half-yearly; **Cover Price:** Free; **Circ:** 44,900
Editor: Beat Baumgartner
Profile: Magazine for customers of the Schindler Aufzüge company.
Language(s): German

NIDWALDNER BLITZ
737442S72-6260
Editorial: Dorfplatz 2, 6383 DALLENWIL
Tel: 41 6297979 **Fax:** 41 6297997
Email: guido.infanger@dod.ch **Web site:** http://www.nw-blitz.ch
Freq: Weekly; **Cover Price:** Free; **Circ:** 21,000
Editor: Guido Infanger; **Advertising Manager:** Adrian Näpflin
Profile: Advertising journal (house-to-house) concentrating on local stories.
Language(s): German
ADVERTISING RATES:
Full Page Mono .... CHF 386
Full Page Colour .... CHF 559
Mechanical Data: Type Area: 205 x 145 mm, No. of Columns (Display): 4, Col Widths (Display): 33 mm
Copy instructions: *Copy Date:* 2 days prior to publication
LOCAL NEWSPAPERS

NOCH ERFOLGREICHER!
1855476S14A-1317
Editorial: Augustin-Keller-Str. 31, 5600 LENZBURG
Tel: 62 8884054 **Fax:** 62 8884055
Email: chefredakteur@noch-erfolgreicher.com **Web site:** http://www.noch-erfolgreicher.com
Freq: Quarterly; **Annual Sub.:** CHF 59,90; **Circ:** 40,000
Profile: Magazine for managers.
Language(s): German
ADVERTISING RATES:
Full Page Mono .... CHF 7350
Full Page Colour .... CHF 7350
Mechanical Data: Type Area: 277 x 190 mm, No. of Columns (Display): 3, Col Widths (Display): 56 mm
Copy instructions: *Copy Date:* 51 days prior to publication

LE NOUVELLISTE
737688S67B-1700
Editorial: 13, rue de l'Industrie, 1950 SION
Tel: 27 3297511 **Fax:** 27 3297578
Email: redaction@nouvelliste.ch **Web site:** http://www.lenouvelliste.ch
Freq: 312 issues yearly; **Annual Sub.:** CHF 387,00; **Circ:** 42,671
Editor: Jean-François Fournier; **News Editor:** Michel Gratzl
Profile: Regional daily newspaper covering politics, economics, sport, travel, technology and the arts.
Language(s): French
ADVERTISING RATES:
SCC .... CHF 46,90
Mechanical Data: Type Area: 440 x 288 mm, No. of Columns (Display): 10, Col Widths (Display): 25 mm
Copy instructions: *Copy Date:* 2 days prior to publication
Supplement(s): Le Nouvelliste
REGIONAL DAILY & SUNDAY NEWSPAPERS: Regional Daily Newspapers

NOVITATS
737690S72-6380
Editorial: Voa Davos Lai 2, 7078 LENZERHEIDE
Tel: 81 3843440 **Fax:** 81 3846107
Email: novitats@suedostschweiz.ch **Web site:** http://www.suedostschweiz.ch
Freq: Weekly; **Annual Sub.:** CHF 91,00; **Circ:** 4,669
Editor: Monika Werder
Profile: Regional weekly covering politics, economics, sport, travel, technology and the arts.
Language(s): German
ADVERTISING RATES:
SCC .... CHF 17,30
Mechanical Data: Type Area: 286 x 199 mm, No. of Columns (Display): 7, Col Widths (Display): 25 mm
Copy instructions: *Copy Date:* 2 days prior to publication
LOCAL NEWSPAPERS

OBERSEE NACHRICHTEN
737839S72-6480
Editorial: Hauptplatz 5, 8640 RAPPERSWIL-JONA
Tel: 55 2208181 **Fax:** 55 2208191
Email: redaktion@obersee-nachrichten.ch **Web site:** http://www.obersee-nachrichten.ch
Freq: Weekly; **Cover Price:** Free; **Circ:** 63,136
Editor: Andreas Knobel; **Advertising Manager:** Hanspeter Haussener
Profile: Advertising journal (house-to-house) concentrating on local stories.
Language(s): German
ADVERTISING RATES:
Full Page Mono .... CHF 4928
Full Page Colour .... CHF 5852
Mechanical Data: Type Area: 440 x 286 mm, No. of Columns (Display): 10, Col Widths (Display): 25 mm
Copy instructions: *Copy Date:* 2 days prior to publication
LOCAL NEWSPAPERS

OBJECTIF SÉCURITÉ
1855491S14A-1319
Editorial: Maulbeerstr. 14, 3011 BERN
Tel: 31 3055566
Email: objectif@bpa.ch **Web site:** http://www.bfu.ch
Freq: Quarterly; **Circ:** 3,300
Editor: Ursula Marti
Profile: Magazine about accident prevention.
Language(s): French

OBZ OBERBASELBIETER ZEITUNG
1648560S72-9637
Editorial: Hauptstr. 22, 4437 WALDENBURG
Tel: 61 9659765 **Fax:** 61 9659769
Email: redaktion@dietschi.ch
Freq: Weekly; **Cover Price:** Free; **Circ:** 42,433
Editor: Marc Schaffner
Profile: Advertising journal (house-to-house) concentrating on local stories.
Language(s): German
ADVERTISING RATES:
Full Page Mono .... CHF 5260
Full Page Colour .... CHF 7912
Mechanical Data: Type Area: 442 x 288 mm, No. of Columns (Display): 10, Col Widths (Display): 25 mm
Copy instructions: *Copy Date:* 3 days prior to publication
LOCAL NEWSPAPERS

OEKOSKOP
1853233S56A-2185
Editorial: Hauptstr. 52, 4461 BÖCKTEN
Tel: 61 9813877 **Fax:** 61 9814127
Freq: Quarterly; Free to qualifying individuals
Annual Sub.: CHF 30,00; **Circ:** 2,500
Editor: Rita Moll
Profile: Magazine on environmental protection.
Language(s): German

ÖKK DOSSIER FÜR UNTERNEHMEN
1896518S1D-29
Editorial: Bahnhofstr. 9, 7302 LANDQUART
Tel: 58 4561115 **Fax:** 58 4561011
Email: dossier@oekk.ch **Web site:** http://www.oekk.ch
Freq: Half-yearly; **Circ:** 14,500
Editor: Peter Werder
Profile: Customer magazine from the ÖKK.
Language(s): German
Mechanical Data: Type Area: 297 x 210 mm
Copy instructions: *Copy Date:* 30 days prior to publication

ÖKK MAGAZIN
763660S74M-261
Editorial: Bahnhofstr. 9, 7302 LANDQUART
Tel: 58 4561115 **Fax:** 58 4561011
Email: magazin@oekk.ch **Web site:** http://www.oekk.ch
Freq: Quarterly; **Cover Price:** Free; **Circ:** 84,000
Editor: Peter Werder
Profile: Customer magazine from the ÖKK.
Language(s): French; German; Italian
ADVERTISING RATES:
Full Page Mono .... CHF 3000
Full Page Colour .... CHF 3000
Mechanical Data: Type Area: 297 x 210 mm
Copy instructions: *Copy Date:* 30 days prior to publication
CONSUMER: WOMEN'S INTEREST CONSUMER MAGAZINES: Personal Finance

ÖKK MAGAZINE
1847759S74M-284
Editorial: Bahnhofstr. 9, 7302 LANDQUART
Tel: 58 4561115 **Fax:** 58 4561011
Email: magazin@oekk.ch **Web site:** http://www.oekk.ch
Freq: Quarterly; **Cover Price:** Free; **Circ:** 4,000
Editor: Peter Werder
Profile: Customer magazine from the ÖKK.
Language(s): Italian
ADVERTISING RATES:
Full Page Mono .... CHF 3000
Full Page Colour .... CHF 3000
Mechanical Data: Type Area: 297 x 210 mm
Copy instructions: *Copy Date:* 30 days prior to publication

ÖKOLOGO
2002190S21A-637
Editorial: Schützengässchen 5, 3001 BERN
Tel: 31 3126400 **Fax:** 31 3126403
Email: vkmb@bluewin.ch **Web site:** http://www.kleinbauern.ch
Freq: Quarterly; Free to qualifying individuals
Annual Sub.: CHF 30,00; **Circ:** 22,000
Editor: Herbert Karch
Profile: Magazine about ecology.
Language(s): German

OLTNER TAGBLATT OT
738208S67B-2120
Editorial: Ziegelfeldstr. 60, 4601 OLTEN
Tel: 62 2057676 **Fax:** 62 2057600
Email: redaktion@oltnertagblatt.ch **Web site:** http://www.oltnertagblatt.ch
Freq: 312 issues yearly; **Cover Price:** CHF 2,50; **Circ:** 16,624
Editor: Beat Nützi
Profile: Regional daily newspaper covering politics, economics, sport, travel, technology and the arts.
Language(s): German
ADVERTISING RATES:
SCC .... CHF 43,10
Mechanical Data: Type Area: 440 x 290 mm, No. of Columns (Display): 10, Col Widths (Display): 26 mm
Copy instructions: *Copy Date:* 2 days prior to publication
REGIONAL DAILY & SUNDAY NEWSPAPERS: Regional Daily Newspapers

OPHTHALMOLOGICA
738263S56A-1420
Editorial: Allschwiler Str. 10, 4055 BASEL
Tel: 61 3061358 **Fax:** 61 3061434
Email: oph@karger.ch **Web site:** http://www.karger.com/oph
Freq: 6 issues yearly; **Annual Sub.:** CHF 1701,40; **Circ:** 1,000
Editor: J. Cunha-Vaz; **Advertising Manager:** Thomas Maurer
Profile: Magazine containing patient oriented scientific reports on all aspects of ophthalmology.
Language(s): English
ADVERTISING RATES:
Full Page Mono .... CHF 1780
Full Page Colour .... CHF 3340
Mechanical Data: Type Area: 224 x 180 mm
Official Journal of: Organ d. Netherlands Ophtalmological Society

ORGANISATOR
1641419S14A-1150
Editorial: Geltenwilenstr. 8a, 9000 ST. GALLEN
Tel: 71 2225661 **Fax:** 71 2225662
Email: redaktion@organisator.ch **Web site:** http://www.organisator.ch
Freq: 10 issues yearly; **Annual Sub.:** CHF 174,00; **Circ:** 13,200
Editor: Thomas Berner
Profile: Manager magazine.
Language(s): German
ADVERTISING RATES:
Full Page Mono .... CHF 4500
Full Page Colour .... CHF 5700
Mechanical Data: Type Area: 270 x 224 mm, No. of Columns (Display): 4, Col Widths (Display): 52 mm
Copy instructions: *Copy Date:* 22 days prior to publication
Official Journal of: Organ d. Controllervereins, d. SWG Schweiz, d. Ges. d. Wirtschaftsberater, d. Time/system-Clubs u. d. Verb. d. Personal- u. Ausbildungsfachleute
BUSINESS: COMMERCE, INDUSTRY & MANAGEMENT

ORL
738318S56A-1440
Editorial: Allschwiler Str. 10, 4055 BASEL
Tel: 61 3061358 **Fax:** 61 3061434
Email: orl@karger.ch **Web site:** http://www.karger.com/orl
Freq: 6 issues yearly; **Annual Sub.:** CHF 1461,40; **Circ:** 900
Editor: B. W. O'Malley, Jr.; **Advertising Manager:** Thomas Maurer
Profile: Reports on research and practice about oto-rhino-laryngology and its related specialities.
Language(s): English
ADVERTISING RATES:
Full Page Mono .... CHF 1780
Full Page Colour .... CHF 3340
Mechanical Data: Type Area: 224 x 180 mm

ORNATIP
1855948S14A-1335
Editorial: Ausstellungsstr. 25, 8005 ZÜRICH
Tel: 44 4442888 **Fax:** 44 4442889
Email: verlag@hochparterre.ch **Web site:** http://www.hochparterre.ch
Freq: Half-yearly; **Cover Price:** CHF 6,50; **Circ:** 30,000
Editor: Monika Widler
Profile: Magazine for the novelty- and trend-fair.
Language(s): French; German
ADVERTISING RATES:
Full Page Mono .... CHF 3100
Full Page Colour .... CHF 4100
Mechanical Data: Type Area: 269 x 188 mm

DER ORNITHOLOGISCHE BEOBACHTER
738321S81F-110
Editorial: 6204 SEMPACH **Tel:** 41 4629700
Fax: 41 4629710
Email: peter.knaus@vogelwarte.ch **Web site:** http://www.vogelwarte.ch
Freq: Quarterly; Free to qualifying individuals
Annual Sub.: CHF 65,00; **Circ:** 1,900
Editor: Peter Knaus
Profile: Journal of the Swiss Society for Ornithology and the Protection of Birds.
Language(s): German
ADVERTISING RATES:
Full Page Mono .... CHF 580
Mechanical Data: Type Area: 187 x 130 mm
Copy instructions: *Copy Date:* 40 days prior to publication
CONSUMER: ANIMALS & PETS: Birds

OTX WORLD
1851465S37-800
Editorial: Zürcher Str. 17, 8173 NEERACH
Tel: 44 8591000 **Fax:** 44 8591009
Email: contact@sanatrend.ch **Web site:** http://www.sanatrend.ch
Freq: 10 issues yearly; **Cover Price:** CHF 5,80; **Circ:** 12,092
Editor: Isabelle Mahrer; **Advertising Manager:** Daniel M. Späni
Profile: Magazine for specialised traders, industry and all interested.
Language(s): German
ADVERTISING RATES:
Full Page Mono .... CHF 7500
Full Page Colour .... CHF 7500
Mechanical Data: Type Area: 290 x 208 mm, No. of Columns (Display): 3, Col Widths (Display): 60 mm
Copy instructions: *Copy Date:* 24 days prior to publication

OTX WORLD
1851466S37-801
Editorial: Zürcher Str. 17, 8173 NEERACH
Tel: 44 8591000 **Fax:** 44 8591009
Email: contact@sanatrend.ch **Web site:** http://www.sanatrend.ch
Freq: 10 issues yearly; **Cover Price:** CHF 5,80; **Circ:** 2,200
Editor: Isabelle Mahrer; **Advertising Manager:** Daniel M. Späni
Profile: Magazine for specialised traders, industry and all interested.
Language(s): French
ADVERTISING RATES:
Full Page Mono .... CHF 3200
Full Page Colour .... CHF 3200
Mechanical Data: Type Area: 290 x 208 mm, No. of Columns (Display): 3, Col Widths (Display): 60 mm
Copy instructions: *Copy Date:* 24 days prior to publication

PÄ PÄDIATRIE
738485S56A-1500
Editorial: Schützenmattstr. 1, 4051 BASEL
Tel: 61 2632535 **Fax:** 61 2632536
Email: claudia.reinke@medsciences.ch **Web site:** http://www.rosenfluh.ch
Freq: 6 issues yearly; **Annual Sub.:** CHF 46,00; **Circ:** 5,000
Editor: Claudia M. Reinke
Profile: Medical journal focusing on paediatrics.
Language(s): German
Readership: Aimed at paediatricians and general practitioners.
ADVERTISING RATES:
Full Page Mono .... CHF 3280
Full Page Colour .... CHF 4880
Mechanical Data: Type Area: 238 x 175 mm, No. of Columns (Display): 3
Copy instructions: *Copy Date:* 23 days prior to publication

PÄ PÄDIATRIE
738485S56A-2172
Editorial: Schützenmattstr. 1, 4051 BASEL
Tel: 61 2632535 **Fax:** 61 2632536
Email: claudia.reinke@medsciences.ch **Web site:** http://www.rosenfluh.ch
Freq: 6 issues yearly; **Annual Sub.:** CHF 46,00; **Circ:** 5,000
Editor: Claudia M. Reinke
Profile: Medical journal focusing on paediatrics.
Language(s): German
Readership: Aimed at paediatricians and general practitioners.
ADVERTISING RATES:
Full Page Mono .... CHF 3280
Full Page Colour .... CHF 4880
Mechanical Data: Type Area: 238 x 175 mm, No. of Columns (Display): 3
Copy instructions: *Copy Date:* 23 days prior to publication

PACK AKTUELL
1641037S35-75
Editorial: Sihlbruggstr. 105a, 6341 BAAR
Tel: 41 7677914 **Fax:** 41 7677911
Email: joachim.kreuter@packaktuell.ch **Web site:** http://www.packaktuell.ch
Freq: 18 issues yearly; **Annual Sub.:** CHF 127,00; **Circ:** 5,300
Editor: Joachim Kreuter
Profile: Trade magazine for packaging and packaging design.
Language(s): German
ADVERTISING RATES:
Full Page Mono .... CHF 2520
Full Page Colour .... CHF 3720
Mechanical Data: Type Area: 270 x 190 mm
Copy instructions: *Copy Date:* 14 days prior to publication
BUSINESS: PACKAGING & BOTTLING

LA PAGINA DA SURMEIR
767620S67B-6620
Editorial: Stradung 23, 7460 SAVOGNIN
Tel: 81 6842838 **Fax:** 81 6843262
Email: pagina@bluewin.ch **Web site:** http://www.u-r-s.ch
Freq: Weekly; **Circ:** 1,700
Editor: Reto Capeder
Profile: Regional weekly newspaper covering politics, economics, sport, travel, technology and the arts.
Language(s): German
Mechanical Data: Type Area: 286 x 199 mm, No. of Columns (Display): 7, Col Widths (Display): 25 mm
Copy instructions: *Copy Date:* 2 days prior to publication
REGIONAL DAILY & SUNDAY NEWSPAPERS: Regional Daily Newspapers

PALLIATIVE-CH
1789503S56A-2123
Editorial: Seebahnstr. 231, 8004 ZÜRICH
Tel: 44 2401621 **Fax:** 44 2429535
Email: admin@palliative.ch
Freq: Quarterly; Free to qualifying individuals
Annual Sub.: CHF 55,00; **Circ:** 2,127
Editor: Claude Fuchs
Profile: Magazine about pallative medicine.
Language(s): French; German; Italian
ADVERTISING RATES:
Full Page Mono .... CHF 1680
Full Page Colour .... CHF 2370
Mechanical Data: Type Area: 297 x 210 mm

PALLIATIVE-CH
1789503S56A-2166
Editorial: Seebahnstr. 231, 8004 ZÜRICH
Tel: 44 2401621 **Fax:** 44 2429535
Email: admin@palliative.ch
Freq: Quarterly; Free to qualifying individuals
Annual Sub.: CHF 55,00; **Circ:** 2,127
Editor: Claude Fuchs
Profile: Magazine about pallative medicine.
Language(s): French; German; Italian
ADVERTISING RATES:
Full Page Mono .... CHF 1680
Full Page Colour .... CHF 2370
Mechanical Data: Type Area: 297 x 210 mm

PANCREATOLOGY
762742S56A-1967
Editorial: Allschwiler Str. 10, 4055 BASEL
Tel: 61 3061357 **Fax:** 61 3061434
Email: pan@karger.ch **Web site:** http://www.karger.com/pan
Freq: 6 issues yearly; **Annual Sub.:** CHF 2464,40; **Circ:** 1,600
Editor: R. Urrutia; **Advertising Manager:** Thomas Maurer
Profile: International forum for pancreatology.
Language(s): English
ADVERTISING RATES:
Full Page Mono .... CHF 1780
Full Page Colour .... CHF 3340
Mechanical Data: Type Area: 224 x 180 mm
Official Journal of: Organ d. Internat. Association of Pancreatology, d. European Pancreatic Club, d. Club Español de Enfermedades Biliopancreáticas u. d. Pancreatic Society of Great Britain and Ireland

PANTHER POST
1853486S74N-275
Editorial: Im Ettingerhof 2, 4055 BASEL
Tel: 61 3010667
Email: info@grauepanther.ch **Web site:** http://www.grauepanther.ch
Freq: Half-yearly; **Circ:** 2,500
Editor: Susanne Wenger; **Advertising Manager:** Susanne Wenger
Profile: Magazine for the elderly.
Language(s): German
Copy instructions: *Copy Date:* 31 days prior to publication

PAPIER & UMWELT
738549S34-80
Editorial: Kohlenberggasse 21, 4001 BASEL
Tel: 61 2708400 **Fax:** 61 2708401
Email: poldervaart@kohlenberg.ch **Web site:** http://www.kohlenberg.ch
Freq: Quarterly; Free to qualifying individuals
Annual Sub.: CHF 25,00; **Circ:** 1,800
Editor: Pieter Poldervaart; **Advertising Manager:** Barbara Würmli
Profile: Magazine promoting the use of recycled or environmentally-friendly supplies for offices.
Language(s): German
Mechanical Data: Type Area: 245 x 190 mm, No. of Columns (Display): 2, Col Widths (Display): 92 mm
Copy instructions: *Copy Date:* 21 days prior to publication
BUSINESS: OFFICE EQUIPMENT

PCTIPP
765523S5-168
Editorial: Witikoner Str. 15, 8032 ZÜRICH
Tel: 44 3874437 **Fax:** 44 3874582
Email: hansjoerg.honegger@idg.ch **Web site:** http://www.pctipp.ch
Freq: Monthly; **Annual Sub.:** CHF 49,00; **Circ:** 90,000
Editor: Hansjörg Honegger
Profile: Computer magazine.
Language(s): German
ADVERTISING RATES:
Full Page Mono .... CHF 11167
Full Page Colour .... CHF 11167
Mechanical Data: Type Area: 286 x 202 mm, No. of Columns (Display): 3, Col Widths (Display): 64 mm
Copy instructions: *Copy Date:* 11 days prior to publication
BUSINESS: COMPUTERS & AUTOMATION

PERSONENWAGEN VOITURES DE TOURISME AUTOVETTURE
1656148S49A-408
Editorial: Wolleraustr. 11a, 8807 FREIENBACH
Tel: 848 333100 **Fax:** 55 4158200
Web site: http://www.eurotaxglass.ch
Freq: 11 issues yearly; **Annual Sub.:** CHF 453,00; **Circ:** 1,800
Profile: Magazine reporting on the market of buying and bartering cars.
Language(s): French; German; Italian
Mechanical Data: Type Area: 138 x 95 mm
Copy instructions: *Copy Date:* 30 days prior to publication

PERSÖNLICH
1851468S2A-679
Editorial: Hauptplatz 5, 8640 RAPPERSWIL
Tel: 55 2208171 **Fax:** 55 2208177
Email: info@persoenlich.com **Web site:** http://www.persoenlich.com
Freq: 10 issues yearly; **Annual Sub.:** CHF 135,00; **Circ:** 6,922
Editor: Matthias Ackeret; **Advertising Manager:** Roman Frank
Profile: Magazine about marketing and management.
Language(s): German
ADVERTISING RATES:
Full Page Mono .... CHF 5850
Full Page Colour .... CHF 5850
Mechanical Data: Type Area: 275 x 210 mm, No. of Columns (Display): 3, Col Widths (Display): 66 mm

PERSORAMA
1642109S14F-5
Editorial: Industriestr. 176, 8957 SPREITENBACH
Tel: 56 4015191
Email: redaktion@persorama.ch **Web site:** http://www.persorama.ch
Freq: Quarterly; Free to qualifying individuals
Annual Sub.: CHF 75,00; **Circ:** 6,000
Editor: Manuel Fischer
Profile: Magazine from the Swiss Society für Human Ressources.
Language(s): French; German
ADVERTISING RATES:
Full Page Mono .... CHF 3040
Full Page Colour .... CHF 4140
Mechanical Data: Type Area: 260 x 184 mm, No. of Columns (Display): 3, Col Widths (Display): 58 mm
Copy instructions: *Copy Date:* 28 days prior to publication
BUSINESS: COMMERCE, INDUSTRY & MANAGEMENT: Training & Recruitment

PERSPECTIVE
1656315S27-152
Editorial: Neugutstr. 12, 8304 WALLISELLEN
Tel: 44 8787060 **Fax:** 44 8787055
Email: perspective@swissavant.ch **Web site:** http://www.swissavant.ch
Freq: 24 issues yearly; Free to qualifying individuals
Annual Sub.: CHF 104,00; **Circ:** 2,000
Editor: Christoph Rotermund; **Advertising Manager:** Kurt Scheuermeier
Profile: Magazine on hardware and tools.
Language(s): French; German
ADVERTISING RATES:
Full Page Mono .... CHF 1425
Full Page Colour .... CHF 2685
Mechanical Data: Type Area: 257 x 184 mm, No. of Columns (Display): 3, Col Widths (Display): 56 mm
Copy instructions: *Copy Date:* 15 days prior to publication

PHARMA-FLASH
1853352S56A-2194
Editorial: 46, ch. de la Mousse, 1225 CHÊNE-BOURG **Tel:** 22 7029311 **Fax:** 22 7029355
Email: administration@medhyg.ch **Web site:** http://www.medecinehygiene.ch
Freq: 6 issues yearly; **Annual Sub.:** CHF 52,00; **Circ:** 1,600
Editor: J. Desmeules
Profile: Magazine about pharmacy.
Language(s): French

PHARMAJOURNAL
1853243S37-803
Editorial: Stationsstr. 12, 3097 LIEBEFELD
Tel: 31 9785858 **Fax:** 31 9785859
Web site: http://www.pharma-journal.ch
Freq: 25 issues yearly; Free to qualifying individuals
Annual Sub.: CHF 260,00; **Circ:** 6,000
Editor: Christa Rüedi; **Advertising Manager:** H.R. Schindler
Profile: Magazine for pharmacists in Switzerland.
Language(s): French; German
ADVERTISING RATES:
Full Page Mono .... CHF 1530
Full Page Colour .... CHF 2900
Mechanical Data: Type Area: 268 x 176 mm
Copy instructions: *Copy Date:* 21 days prior to publication

PHARMA-KRITIK
1853353S56A-2195
Editorial: Bergliweg 17, 9500 WIL **Tel:** 71 9100866
Fax: 71 9100877
Email: infomed@infomed.ch **Web site:** http://www.infomed.org
Freq: 20 issues yearly; **Annual Sub.:** CHF 102,00; **Circ:** 5,200
Editor: Etzel Gysling
Profile: Magazine on pharmaceutical therapies.
Language(s): German

PHARMA-MARKT SCHWEIZ
738918S37-580
Editorial: Petersgraben 35, 4003 BASEL
Tel: 61 2643434 **Fax:** 61 2643435
Email: info@interpharma.ch **Web site:** http://www.interpharma.ch
Freq: Annual; **Cover Price:** Free; **Circ:** 23,000
Profile: Magazine with data of the Swiss pharmaceutical market.
Language(s): German

PIPETTE
1842657S56A-2145
Editorial: Farnsburger Str. 8, 4132 MUTTENZ
Tel: 61 4678555 **Fax:** 61 4678556

Email: redaktion@sulm.ch **Web site:** http://www.sulm.ch
Freq: 6 issues yearly; **Annual Sub.:** CHF 89,00; **Circ:** 16,000
Editor: Andreas R. Huber
Profile: Magazine about laboratory medicine in Switzerland.
Language(s): German
ADVERTISING RATES:
Full Page Mono .... CHF 3145
Full Page Colour .... CHF 5130
Mechanical Data: Type Area: 266 x 168 mm
Copy instructions: *Copy Date:* 30 days prior to publication
Official Journal of: Organ d. SULM Schweizer. Union f. Laboratoriumsmedizin

PITCH
1855957S14A-1336
Editorial: Grünaustr. 10, 3084 WABERN
Tel: 31 9615481 **Fax:** 31 9615130
Email: charly.federer@verkaufschweiz.ch **Web site:** http://www.verkaufschweiz.ch
Freq: 10 issues yearly; **Circ:** 8,500
Editor: Charly Federer
Profile: Magazine on sales and marketing in Switzerland.
Language(s): French; German; Italian
ADVERTISING RATES:
Full Page Mono .... CHF 1600
Full Page Colour .... CHF 2100
Mechanical Data: Type Area: 265 x 169 mm, No. of Columns (Display): 3, Col Widths (Display): 53 mm
Copy instructions: *Copy Date:* 29 days prior to publication

PME MAGAZINE
1835755S14A-1242
Editorial: 109, rue de Lyon, 1203 GENF
Tel: 22 9197900 **Fax:** 22 7400959
Email: infopme@pme.ch **Web site:** http://www.pme.ch
Freq: Monthly; **Annual Sub.:** CHF 115,00; **Circ:** 11,878
Editor: Olivier Toublan; **Advertising Manager:** Claudia Köpfli
Profile: Journal about management and administration, including sections on finance, trade, communications, marketing and computers.
Language(s): French
ADVERTISING RATES:
Full Page Mono .... CHF 8550
Full Page Colour .... CHF 8550
Mechanical Data: Type Area: 252 x 180 mm, No. of Columns (Display): 4, Col Widths (Display): 44 mm
Copy instructions: *Copy Date:* 28 days prior to publication
Supplement(s): First. by PME Magazine

POLICE
1648684S32F-27
Editorial: Murtenstr. 3, 3270 AARBERG
Tel: 79 3925213
Email: police.d@vspb.org **Web site:** http://www.vspb.org
Freq: Monthly; Free to qualifying individuals
Annual Sub.: CHF 50,00; **Circ:** 23,000
Editor: Markus Nobs
Profile: Member magazine from the Swiss Police Association.
Language(s): French; German; Italian
ADVERTISING RATES:
Full Page Mono .... CHF 1770
Full Page Colour .... CHF 2970
Mechanical Data: Type Area: 258 x 190 mm
BUSINESS: LOCAL GOVERNMENT, LEISURE & RECREATION: Police

POPOLO E LIBERTÀ
739223S82-2206
Editorial: via Ghiringhelli, 7, 6500 BELLINZONA
Tel: 91 8251245 **Fax:** 91 8258551
Email: redazione@popolo-liberta.ch **Web site:** http://www.ppd-ti.ch
Freq: Weekly; **Annual Sub.:** CHF 135,00; **Circ:** 6,000
Editor: Marco Romano; **Advertising Manager:** Michele Romagnoli
Profile: Newspaper of the People's Democratic Party of Ticino.
Language(s): Italian
ADVERTISING RATES:
SCC .... CHF 22,40
Mechanical Data: Type Area: 450 x 289 mm, No. of Columns (Display): 10, Col Widths (Display): 25 mm
CONSUMER: CURRENT AFFAIRS & POLITICS

PÖSCHTLI
739156S72-6660
Editorial: Neudorfstr. 17, 7430 THUSIS
Tel: 81 6500075 **Fax:** 81 6500079
Email: poeschtli@suedostschweiz.ch
Freq: Weekly; **Annual Sub.:** CHF 91,00; **Circ:** 8,432
Editor: Albert Pitschi
Profile: Local official paper.
Language(s): German
ADVERTISING RATES:
SCC .... CHF 17,80
Mechanical Data: Type Area: 286 x 199 mm, No. of Columns (Display): 7, Col Widths (Display): 25 mm
Copy instructions: *Copy Date:* 2 days prior to publication
LOCAL NEWSPAPERS

PRÄTTIGAUER UND HERRSCHÄFTLER
739295S67B-2160
Editorial: Bahnhofstr. 120, 7220 SCHIERS
Tel: 81 3281566 **Fax:** 81 3281955
Email: info@drucki.ch **Web site:** http://www.drucki.ch
Freq: 156 issues yearly; **Annual Sub.:** CHF 109,00; **Circ:** 3,510
Editor: Marco Schnell
Profile: Regional daily newspaper covering politics, economics, sport, travel, technology and the arts.
Language(s): German
ADVERTISING RATES:
SCC .... CHF 16,50
Mechanical Data: Type Area: 450 x 290 mm, No. of Columns (Display): 10, Col Widths (Display): 27 mm
Copy instructions: *Copy Date:* 1 day prior to publication
REGIONAL DAILY & SUNDAY NEWSPAPERS: Regional Daily Newspapers

PRATTLER ANZEIGER
739310S72-6720
Editorial: Missionsstr. 36, 4012 BASEL
Tel: 61 2646450 **Fax:** 61 2646488
Email: redaktion@prattleranzeiger.ch **Web site:** http://www.reinhardt.ch
Freq: 2444 issues yearly; **Annual Sub.:** CHF 74,00; **Circ:** 3,339
Editor: Verena Fiva
Profile: Regional weekly covering politics, economics, sport, travel, technology and the arts.
Language(s): German
ADVERTISING RATES:
SCC .... CHF 23,40
Mechanical Data: Type Area: 290 x 203 mm, No. of Columns (Display): 7, Col Widths (Display): 27 mm
LOCAL NEWSPAPERS

DIE PRAXIS
1852567S1A-305
Editorial: Elisabethenstr. 8, 4051 BASEL
Tel: 61 2289070 **Fax:** 61 2989071
Email: zeitschriften@helbing.ch **Web site:** http://www.helbing.ch
Freq: Monthly; **Annual Sub.:** CHF 298,00; **Circ:** 1,933
Editor: Sylvia Frei
Profile: Magazine focusing on important decisions regarding the law and social security.
Language(s): German
ADVERTISING RATES:
Full Page Mono .... CHF 1200
Full Page Colour .... CHF 1600
Mechanical Data: Type Area: 195 x 120 mm
Copy instructions: *Copy Date:* 21 days prior to publication

PRAXIS
1853247S56A-2187
Editorial: Länggassstr. 76, 3000 BERN 9
Tel: 31 3004576 **Fax:** 31 3004627
Email: redaktion@praxis.ch **Web site:** http://www.praxis.ch
Freq: 25 issues yearly; **Annual Sub.:** CHF 197,00; **Circ:** 2,700
Editor: E. Battegay; **Advertising Manager:** H.R. Schindler
Profile: Magazine on medicine from Switzerland.
Language(s): French; German
ADVERTISING RATES:
Full Page Mono .... CHF 1820
Full Page Colour .... CHF 3040
Mechanical Data: Type Area: 273 x 180 mm
Copy instructions: *Copy Date:* 20 days prior to publication

DIE PRAXIS DES FAMILIENRECHTS LA PRATIQUE DU DROIT DE LA FAMILLE LA PRASSI DEL DIRETTO DI FAMIGLIA FAMPRA.CH
1853025S1A-308
Editorial: Wölflistr. 1, 3001 BERN **Tel:** 31 3006666
Fax: 31 3006688
Email: verlag@staempfli.com **Web site:** http://www.staempfliverlag.com
Freq: Quarterly; **Annual Sub.:** CHF 366,00; **Circ:** 500
Editor: Ingeborg Schwenzer
Profile: Juristic magazine about Swiss family law.
Language(s): French; German; Italian
ADVERTISING RATES:
Full Page Mono .... CHF 1080
Full Page Colour .... CHF 1080
Mechanical Data: Type Area: 210 x 128 mm

PRIMARY CARE
762649S56A-1962
Editorial: Farnsburger Str. 8, 4132 MUTTENZ
Tel: 61 4678554 **Fax:** 61 4678556
Email: marty@primary-care.ch **Web site:** http://www.primary-care.ch
Freq: 20 issues yearly; Free to qualifying individuals
Annual Sub.: CHF 170,00; **Circ:** 12,300
Editor: Natalie Marty
Profile: Magazine for general practitioners.
Language(s): French; German
ADVERTISING RATES:
Full Page Mono .... CHF 2950
Full Page Colour .... CHF 5200
Mechanical Data: Type Area: 268 x 186 mm
Official Journal of: Organ d. Kollegiums f. Hausarztmedizin, d. Schweizer. Ges. f. Allgemeinmedizin, d. Schweizer. Ges. f. Innere Medizin, d. Schweizer. Ges. f. Pädiatrie, d. Schweizer. Akademie f. Psychosomat. u. Psychsoziale Medizin u. d. Berufsverb. d. Haus- u. Kinderärzte

PRINTMEDIEN SCHWEIZ ZEITSCHRIFTEN
1645663S2A-645
Editorial: Geltenwilenstr. 8a, 9001 ST. GALLEN
Tel: 71 2269292 **Fax:** 71 2269293
Email: info@kbmedien.ch **Web site:** http://www.kbmedien.ch
Freq: Annual; **Cover Price:** Free; **Circ:** 10,000
Advertising Manager: Urs Dick
Profile: Publication providing an overview of Swiss magazines.
Language(s): German
ADVERTISING RATES:
Full Page Mono .... CHF 2400
Full Page Colour .... CHF 2400
Mechanical Data: Type Area: 262 x 170 mm
Copy instructions: *Copy Date:* 55 days prior to publication

PRIVATE BANKING
1835757S1F-273
Editorial: 109, rue Lyon, 1203 GENF **Tel:** 22 9197900
Fax: 22 7400959
Web site: http://www.privatebankingmagazine.ch
Freq: 10 issues yearly; **Annual Sub.:** CHF 95,00; **Circ:** 10,000
Editor: Olivier Toublan; **Advertising Manager:** Christian Santa
Profile: Journal about management and administration, including sections on finance, trade, communications, marketing and computers.
Language(s): French
ADVERTISING RATES:
Full Page Mono .... CHF 7960
Full Page Colour .... CHF 7960
Mechanical Data: Type Area: 265 x 181 mm

PRO MENTE SANA AKTUELL
1648501S56A-2063
Editorial: Hardturmstr. 261, 8031 ZÜRICH
Tel: 44 5638600 **Fax:** 44 5638617
Email: kontakt@promentesana.ch **Web site:** http://www.promentesana.ch
Freq: Quarterly; **Annual Sub.:** CHF 40,00; **Circ:** 4,050
Editor: Anna Beyme; **Advertising Manager:** Dominique Schönenberger
Profile: Magazine on psychiatry.
Language(s): French; German
ADVERTISING RATES:
Full Page Mono .... CHF 990
Full Page Colour .... CHF 990
Mechanical Data: Type Area: 249 x 163 mm, No. of Columns (Display): 3, Col Widths (Display): 50 mm
BUSINESS: HEALTH & MEDICAL

PRO NATURA MAGAZIN
1844855S57-713
Editorial: Dornacherstr. 192, 4053 BASEL
Tel: 61 3179191 **Fax:** 61 3179266
Email: raphael.weber@pronatura.ch **Web site:** http://www.pronatura.ch
Freq: 5 issues yearly; **Circ:** 75,713
Editor: Raphael Weber
Profile: Magazine about nature protection.
Language(s): German
ADVERTISING RATES:
Full Page Mono .... CHF 6000
Full Page Colour .... CHF 6000
Mechanical Data: Type Area: 280 x 174 mm, No. of Columns (Display): 2, Col Widths (Display): 84 mm
Copy instructions: *Copy Date:* 46 days prior to publication

PROBLEM
1641038S79F-21
Editorial: Postfach 4066, 6002 LUZERN
Tel: 41 3102823
Freq: 25 issues yearly; **Annual Sub.:** CHF 59,00; **Circ:** 4,600
Editor: Markus Elminger
Profile: Puzzle magazine for German-speaking part of Switzerland.
Language(s): German
Mechanical Data: Type Area: 220 x 150 mm
Copy instructions: *Copy Date:* 14 days prior to publication
CONSUMER: HOBBIES & DIY: Games & Puzzles

PROFESSIONAL COMPUTING
739545S5E-200
Editorial: Frauenfelder Str. 49, 8370 SIRNACH
Tel: 71 5115054 **Fax:** 71 9661069
Email: redaction-pc@utk.ch **Web site:** http://www.utk.ch
Freq: 5 issues yearly; **Annual Sub.:** CHF 20,00; **Circ:** 10,000
Editor: Jörg Schelling; **Advertising Manager:** Pascal Tobler
Profile: Magazine focusing on network technology as well as binding techniques, products and services, practical assistance with the solution of problems, information about new products and detailed information about new technologies and their use.
Language(s): German
Readership: Read by decision makers involved with network technology and IT.
ADVERTISING RATES:
Full Page Mono .... CHF 3700
Full Page Colour .... CHF 3700
Mechanical Data: Type Area: 266 x 185 mm
Copy instructions: *Copy Date:* 20 days prior to publication
BUSINESS: COMPUTERS & AUTOMATION: Data Transmission

PROFIL
739563S74A-400
Editorial: 17, rue de Genève, 1002 LAUSANNE
Tel: 21 3314141 **Fax:** 21 3314110
Email: k.berger@agefi.com **Web site:** http://www.profilfemme.ch
Freq: 6 issues yearly; **Annual Sub.:** CHF 55,00; **Circ:** 24,500
Editor: Katia Berger
Profile: Women's interest magazine. Contains articles about fashion, beauty, travel and lifestyle.
Language(s): French
ADVERTISING RATES:
Full Page Mono .... CHF 8280
Full Page Colour .... CHF 8280
Mechanical Data: Type Area: 297 x 225 mm
Copy instructions: *Copy Date:* 21 days prior to publication
Supplement(s): Work
CONSUMER: WOMEN'S INTEREST CONSUMER MAGAZINES: Women's Interest

PROPRIÉTÉ
739651S1E-40
Editorial: 15, rue du Midi, 1003 LAUSANNE
Tel: 21 3414142 **Fax:** 21 3414146
Email: mail@fri.ch **Web site:** http://www.fri.ch
Freq: 8 issues yearly; **Annual Sub.:** CHF 50,00; **Circ:** 20,979
Editor: Philippe Leuba
Profile: Magazine about property and home ownership.
Language(s): French
Readership: Aimed at estate agents.
ADVERTISING RATES:
Full Page Mono .... CHF 3990
Full Page Colour .... CHF 3990
Mechanical Data: Type Area: 260 x 190 mm
BUSINESS: FINANCE & ECONOMICS: Property

PSYCHE UND SOMA
741856S56A-1720
Editorial: Grosspeterstr. 23, 4002 BASEL
Tel: 58 9589600 **Fax:** 58 9589660
Email: redaktion@medical-tribune.ch **Web site:** http://www.medical-tribune.ch
Freq: 6 issues yearly; **Circ:** 10,400
Editor: Winfried Powolik; **Advertising Manager:** Patricia Hunziker
Profile: Magazine for gynaecologists, urologists, dermatologists and general practitioners.
Language(s): German
ADVERTISING RATES:
Full Page Mono .... CHF 3692
Full Page Colour .... CHF 3692
Mechanical Data: Type Area: 265 x 180 mm
Supplement to: Medical Tribune
BUSINESS: HEALTH & MEDICAL

PSYCHOSCOPE
1647584S55-556
Editorial: Choisystr. 11, 3000 BERN 14
Tel: 31 3888827 **Fax:** 31 3888801
Email: redaktion@psychoscope.ch **Web site:** http://www.psychologie.ch
Freq: 10 issues yearly; Free to qualifying individuals
Annual Sub.: CHF 85,00; **Circ:** 6,900
Editor: Susanne Birrer; **Advertising Manager:** Christian Wyniger
Profile: Magazine from the Federation of Swiss Psychologists.
Language(s): French; German
ADVERTISING RATES:
Full Page Mono .... CHF 1980
Full Page Colour .... CHF 1980
Mechanical Data: Type Area: 276 x 190 mm, No. of Columns (Display): 3, Col Widths (Display): 60 mm
Copy instructions: *Copy Date:* 26 days prior to publication
BUSINESS: APPLIED SCIENCE & LABORATORIES

PSYCHOTHÉRAPIES
1853355S56A-2196
Editorial: 46, ch. de la Mousse, 1225 CHÊNE-BOURG **Tel:** 22 7029311 **Fax:** 22 7029355
Email: administration@medhyg.ch **Web site:** http://www.medecinehygiene.ch
Freq: Quarterly; **Annual Sub.:** CHF 125,00; **Circ:** 600
Profile: Magazine about psychotherapy.
Language(s): French

PUNKT
1842658S1F-274
Editorial: Pfingstweidstr. 6, 8005 ZÜRICH
Email: schicker@financialmedia.ch **Web site:** http://www.punktmagazin.com
Freq: 6 issues yearly; **Annual Sub.:** CHF 29,50; **Circ:** 10,000
Editor: Cyril schicker
Profile: Investment magazine.
Language(s): German
ADVERTISING RATES:
Full Page Mono .... CHF 4950
Full Page Colour .... CHF 4950
Mechanical Data: Type Area: 312 x 232 mm

RADIO MAGAZIN 1641452S76C-305
Editorial: Brunnenhofstr. 22, 8024 ZÜRICH
Tel: 43 3005200 **Fax:** 43 3005201
Email: redaktion@radiomagazin.ch **Web site:** http://www.radiomagazin.ch
Freq: Weekly; **Annual Sub.:** CHF 79,00; **Circ:** 41,335
Editor: Peter Salvisberg
Profile: Detailed information about music and the arts as well as radio programme listings.
Language(s): German
ADVERTISING RATES:
Full Page Mono .... CHF 4800
Full Page Colour .... CHF 4800
Mechanical Data: Type Area: 275 x 199 mm
CONSUMER: MUSIC & PERFORMING ARTS: TV & Radio

READER'S DIGEST SCHWEIZ 722587S80-1464
Editorial: Räffelstr. 11, 8045 ZÜRICH
Tel: 44 4557339 **Fax:** 44 4557119
Email: redaktion@readersdigest.ch **Web site:** http://www.readersdigest.ch
Freq: Monthly; **Annual Sub.:** CHF 71,90; **Circ:** 103,175
Editor: Michael Kallinger; **Advertising Manager:** Sabine Kölsch
Profile: Journal containing articles about people and their lives in the Zug region, short stories and advertising.
Language(s): German
Readership: Aimed at people in the Zug region of Switzerland.
ADVERTISING RATES:
Full Page Mono .... CHF 9980
Full Page Colour .... CHF 9980
Mechanical Data: Type Area: 176 x 124 mm, No. of Columns (Display): 2, Col Widths (Display): 60 mm
Copy instructions: *Copy Date:* 35 days prior to publication
CONSUMER: RURAL & REGIONAL INTEREST

READER'S DIGEST SUISSE 2010375S73-407
Editorial: Räffelstr. 11, 8045 ZÜRICH
Tel: 44 4557339 **Fax:** 44 4557119
Email: redaktion@readersdigest.ch **Web site:** http://www.readersdigest.ch
Freq: Monthly; **Annual Sub.:** CHF 71,90; **Circ:** 32,555
Editor: Michael Kallinger; **Advertising Manager:** Sabine Kölsch
Profile: Journal containing articles about people and their lives in the Zug region, short stories and advertising.
Language(s): French
ADVERTISING RATES:
Full Page Mono .... CHF 4750
Full Page Colour .... CHF 4750
Mechanical Data: Type Area: 176 x 124 mm, No. of Columns (Display): 2, Col Widths (Display): 60 mm
Copy instructions: *Copy Date:* 35 days prior to publication

RECHT 1853027S1A-309
Editorial: Falkenplatz 18, 3012 BERN
Tel: 31 6318981 **Fax:** 31 6313790
Email: redaktion@recht.ch
Freq: 6 issues yearly; **Annual Sub.:** CHF 165,00; **Circ:** 1,600
Editor: Marlis Koller-Tumler
Profile: Magazine about juristic training and practice.
Language(s): German
ADVERTISING RATES:
Full Page Mono .... CHF 1150
Full Page Colour .... CHF 1150
Mechanical Data: Type Area: 256 x 180 mm

RECHTSPRECHUNG IN STRAFSACHEN BULLETIN DE JURISPRUDENCE PÉNALE 1853029S1A-310
Editorial: 26, av. du Premier-Mars, 2000 NEUCHÂTEL
Freq: Quarterly; **Annual Sub.:** CHF 44,00; **Circ:** 2,600
Editor: Pierre-Henri Bolle
Profile: Magazine about criminal law.
Language(s): French; German

REFLEXIONEN 728766S14A-480
Editorial: Loorenstr. 14, 5443 NIEDERROHRDORF
Tel: 56 4963243
Email: rxredaktion@ivcg.org **Web site:** http://www.ivcg.org
Freq: 6 issues yearly; **Annual Sub.:** CHF 40,00; **Circ:** 15,000
Editor: Oscar Meier
Profile: Christian magazine.
Language(s): German
BUSINESS: COMMERCE, INDUSTRY & MANAGEMENT

REGION 740129S72-6900
Editorial: Maihofstr. 76, 6002 LUZERN
Tel: 41 2403165 **Fax:** 41 4295439
Email: pam@dieregion.ch **Web site:** http://www.dieregion.ch
Freq: Quarterly; **Cover Price:** Free; **Circ:** 31,000
Editor: Peter A. Meyer
Profile: Advertising journal (house-to-house) concentrating on local stories.
Language(s): German
ADVERTISING RATES:
Full Page Mono .... CHF 4400
Full Page Colour .... CHF 4800
Mechanical Data: Type Area: 437 x 290 mm, No. of Columns (Display): 10, Col Widths (Display): 26 mm
Copy instructions: *Copy Date:* 1 day prior to publication
LOCAL NEWSPAPERS

REGION 740130S72-6920
Editorial: Maihofstr. 76, 6002 LUZERN
Tel: 41 4295442 **Fax:** 41 4295439
Email: pam@dieregion.ch **Web site:** http://www.dieregion.ch
Freq: Weekly; **Annual Sub.:** CHF 125,00; **Circ:** 6,000
Editor: Peter A. Meyer
Profile: Regional weekly covering politics, economics, sport, travel, technology and the arts.
Language(s): German
ADVERTISING RATES:
SCC .... CHF 17,50
Mechanical Data: Type Area: 437 x 290 mm, No. of Columns (Display): 10, Col Widths (Display): 26 mm
Copy instructions: *Copy Date:* 2 days prior to publication
LOCAL NEWSPAPERS

LE REPUBLICAIN 740301S72-4980
Editorial: 116, av. de la Gare, 1470 ESTAVAYER-LE-LAC **Tel:** 26 6631267 **Fax:** 26 6632521
Email: journal@lerepublicain.ch **Web site:** http://www.lerepublicain.ch
Freq: Weekly; **Annual Sub.:** CHF 50,00; **Circ:** 3,611
Editor: Léon Borcard; **Advertising Manager:** Léon Borcard
Profile: Regional weekly covering politics, economics, sport, travel, technology and the arts.
Language(s): French
ADVERTISING RATES:
SCC .... CHF 12,70
Mechanical Data: Type Area: 420 x 290 mm, No. of Columns (Display): 10, Col Widths (Display): 25 mm
Copy instructions: *Copy Date:* 2 days prior to publication
LOCAL NEWSPAPERS

REVUE AUTOMOBILE 1643875S77A-104
Editorial: Dammweg 9, 3001 BERN **Tel:** 31 3303060 **Fax:** 31 3303032
Email: office@revueautomobile.ch **Web site:** http://www.revueautomobile.ch
Freq: 24 issues yearly; **Annual Sub.:** CHF 104,00; **Circ:** 17,312
Editor: Olaf Kuhlmann; **Advertising Manager:** Remo de Piano
Profile: Online car magazine.
Language(s): French
ADVERTISING RATES:
Full Page Mono .... CHF 4851
Full Page Colour .... CHF 6036
Mechanical Data: Type Area: 380 x 263 mm
Copy instructions: *Copy Date:* 1,56

REVUE JUIVE 766293S87-2746
Editorial: Tödistr. 42, 8027 ZÜRICH **Tel:** 44 2064200 **Fax:** 44 2064210
Email: redaktion@tachles.ch **Web site:** http://www.tachles.ch
Freq: 5 issues yearly; **Cover Price:** CHF 4,50; **Circ:** 4,000
Editor: Yves Kugelmann; **Advertising Manager:** Daniel Treuhaft
Profile: Jewish weekly magazine.
Language(s): French
ADVERTISING RATES:
Full Page Mono .... CHF 5310
Full Page Colour .... CHF 5310
Mechanical Data: Type Area: 272 x 203 mm, No. of Columns (Display): 4, Col Widths (Display): 47 mm
Copy instructions: *Copy Date:* 14 days prior to publication
CONSUMER: RELIGIOUS

REVUE MÉDICALE SUISSE 1655888S56A-2074
Editorial: 46, ch. de la Mousse, 1225 CHÊNE-BOURG **Tel:** 22 7029311 **Fax:** 22 7029366
Email: redac@revmed.ch **Web site:** http://www.revmed.ch
Freq: Weekly; Free to qualifying individuals
Annual Sub.: CHF 138,00; **Circ:** 6,500
Editor: Bertrand Kiefer
Profile: Medical magazine.
Language(s): French
ADVERTISING RATES:
Full Page Mono .... CHF 3700
Full Page Colour .... CHF 3700
Mechanical Data: Type Area: 297 x 210 mm, No. of Columns (Display): 3, Col Widths (Display): 72 mm
Copy instructions: *Copy Date:* 21 days prior to publication
Official Journal of: Organ d. Soc. Médicale de la Suisse Romande

REVUE MÉDICALE SUISSE 1655888S56A-2162
Editorial: 46, ch. de la Mousse, 1225 CHÊNE-BOURG **Tel:** 22 7029311 **Fax:** 22 7029366
Email: redac@revmed.ch **Web site:** http://www.revmed.ch
Freq: Weekly; Free to qualifying individuals
Annual Sub.: CHF 138,00; **Circ:** 6,500
Editor: Bertrand Kiefer
Profile: Medical magazine.
Language(s): French
ADVERTISING RATES:
Full Page Mono .... CHF 3700
Full Page Colour .... CHF 3700
Mechanical Data: Type Area: 297 x 210 mm, No. of Columns (Display): 3, Col Widths (Display): 72 mm
Copy instructions: *Copy Date:* 21 days prior to publication
Official Journal of: Organ d. Soc. Médicale de la Suisse Romande

REVUE MILITAIRE SUISSE 763540S40-203
Editorial: 3, av. de Florimont, 1006 LAUSANNE
Tel: 21 3114817 **Fax:** 21 3119709
Email: administration@revuemilitairesuisse.ch **Web site:** http://www.revuemilitairesuisse.ch
Freq: 8 issues yearly; **Annual Sub.:** CHF 60,00; **Circ:** 3,000
Editor: Alexandre Vautravers
Profile: Swiss army magazine.
Language(s): French
ADVERTISING RATES:
Full Page Mono .... CHF 1600
Full Page Colour .... CHF 2700
Mechanical Data: Type Area: 297 x 210 mm
Official Journal of: Organ d. Soc. suisse des officiers

DER RHEINTALER 740441S67B-2220
Editorial: Hafnerwisenstr. 1, 9442 BERNECK
Tel: 71 7472241 **Fax:** 71 7472220
Email: bruderer@rheintalverlag.ch **Web site:** http://www.rheintalverlag.ch
Freq: 260 issues yearly; **Annual Sub.:** CHF 355,00; **Circ:** 17,547
Advertising Manager: Heinz Duppenthaler
Profile: Daily newspaper with regional news and a local sports section.
Language(s): German
ADVERTISING RATES:
SCC .... CHF 42,00
Mechanical Data: Type Area: 438 x 291 mm, No. of Columns (Display): 10, Col Widths (Display): 27 mm
Copy instructions: *Copy Date:* 1 day prior to publication
REGIONAL DAILY & SUNDAY NEWSPAPERS: Regional Daily Newspapers

RHEINTALISCHE VOLKSZEITUNG 740443S67B-2240
Editorial: Hafnerwisenstr. 1, 9442 BERNECK
Tel: 71 7472241 **Fax:** 71 7472220
Email: redaktion@rheintalverlag.ch **Web site:** http://www.rheintalverlag.ch
Freq: 312 issues yearly; **Annual Sub.:** CHF 271,00; **Circ:** 6,081
Editor: Gert Bruderer
Profile: Regional daily newspaper covering politics, economics, sport, travel, technology and the arts.
Language(s): German
ADVERTISING RATES:
SCC .... CHF 30,50
Mechanical Data: Type Area: 435 x 287 mm, No. of Columns (Display): 10, Col Widths (Display): 26 mm
Copy instructions: *Copy Date:* 1 day prior to publication
REGIONAL DAILY & SUNDAY NEWSPAPERS: Regional Daily Newspapers

RHEINTALISCHE VOLKSZEITUNG 740444S72-7120
Editorial: Hafnerwisenstr. 1, 9442 BERNECK
Tel: 71 7472241 **Fax:** 71 7472220
Email: redaktion@rheintalverlag.ch **Web site:** http://www.rheintalverlag.ch
Freq: Weekly; **Cover Price:** Free; **Circ:** 28,466
Editor: Gert Bruderer
Profile: Advertising journal (house-to-house) concentrating on local stories.
Language(s): German
ADVERTISING RATES:
Full Page Mono .... CHF 4510
Full Page Colour .... CHF 5355
Mechanical Data: Type Area: 435 x 287 mm, No. of Columns (Display): 10, Col Widths (Display): 26 mm
Copy instructions: *Copy Date:* 1 day prior to publication
LOCAL NEWSPAPERS

RIEHENER ZEITUNG 740479S67B-2260
Editorial: Schopfgässchen 8, 4125 RIEHEN 1
Tel: 61 6451006 **Fax:** 61 6451010
Email: redaktion@riehener-zeitung.ch **Web site:** http://www.riehener-zeitung.ch
Freq: Weekly; **Annual Sub.:** CHF 78,00; **Circ:** 6,100
Editor: Dieter Wüthrich; **Advertising Manager:** V. Stoll
Profile: Regional weekly covering politics, economics, sport, travel, technology and the arts.
Language(s): German
ADVERTISING RATES:
SCC .... CHF 28,00
Mechanical Data: Type Area: 440 x 288 mm, No. of Columns (Display): 10, Col Widths (Display): 27 mm
Copy instructions: *Copy Date:* 3 days prior to publication
REGIONAL DAILY & SUNDAY NEWSPAPERS: Regional Daily Newspapers

RIGI ANZEIGER 740491S72-7180
Editorial: Luzernerstr. 2c, 6037 ROOT
Tel: 41 2289002 **Fax:** 41 2289009
Email: redaktion@rigianzeiger.ch **Web site:** http://www.rigianzeiger.ch
Freq: Weekly; **Cover Price:** Free; **Circ:** 31,905
Editor: Linda Kolly-Bisch; **Advertising Manager:** Urs Suter
Profile: Advertising journal (house-to-house) concentrating on local stories.
Language(s): German
ADVERTISING RATES:
Full Page Mono .... CHF 3465
Full Page Colour .... CHF 3825
Mechanical Data: Type Area: 440 x 290 mm, No. of Columns (Display): 10, Col Widths (Display): 26 mm
Copy instructions: *Copy Date:* 4 days prior to publication
Supplement(s): info Adligenswil
LOCAL NEWSPAPERS

RIGI-POST 740494S72-7240
Editorial: Gutenbergweg 3, 6410 ARTH
Tel: 41 8551241 **Fax:** 41 8551247
Email: rp@kaelindruck.ch **Web site:** http://www.rigipost.ch
Freq: Weekly; **Circ:** 3,290
Profile: Regional weekly covering politics, economics, sport, travel, technology and the arts.
Language(s): German
ADVERTISING RATES:
SCC .... CHF 19,60
Mechanical Data: Type Area: 440 x 286 mm, No. of Columns (Display): 10, Col Widths (Display): 25 mm
Copy instructions: *Copy Date:* 1 day prior to publication
LOCAL NEWSPAPERS

RIVISTA DI LUGANO 740528S72-4360
Editorial: via Canonica, 6, 6900 LUGANO
Tel: 91 9235631 **Fax:** 91 9213043
Email: rivistadilugano@ticino.com
Freq: 46 issues yearly; **Annual Sub.:** CHF 98,00; **Circ:** 6,256
Editor: Roberto Guidi; **Advertising Manager:** Christian Bernasconi
Profile: Family magazine.
Language(s): Italian
ADVERTISING RATES:
Full Page Mono .... CHF 1200
Full Page Colour .... CHF 1200
Mechanical Data: Type Area: 276 x 188 mm
Copy instructions: *Copy Date:* 8 days prior to publication
LOCAL NEWSPAPERS

ROSENBLATT 1859621S21A-625
Editorial: Kirchstr.12, 3427 UTZENSTORF
Tel: 32 6553575
Email: redaktion@rosenfreunde.ch **Web site:** http://www.rosenfreunde.ch
Freq: Monthly; **Circ:** 3,600
Editor: Anna Barbara Hofer
Profile: Magazine from the Swiss Rose Society.
Language(s): German; Italian
ADVERTISING RATES:
Full Page Mono .... CHF 650
Mechanical Data: Type Area: 190 x 130 mm, No. of Columns (Display): 3, Col Widths (Display): 39 mm
Copy instructions: *Copy Date:* 16 days prior to publication

RPW RECHT UND POLITIK DES WETTBEWERBS DPC DROIT ET POLITIQUE DE LA CONCURRENCE DPC DIRITTO E POLITICA DELLA CONCORRENZA 1855827S14A-1325
Editorial: Monbijoustr. 43, 3003 BERN
Tel: 31 3222040 **Fax:** 31 3222053
Email: weko@weko.admin.ch **Web site:** http://www.wettbewerbskommission.ch
Freq: Quarterly; **Annual Sub.:** CHF 120,00; **Circ:** 1,500
Profile: National official paper.
Language(s): French; German; Italian

RUNDBRIEF 1850868S74A-502
Editorial: Badener Str. 134, 8004 ZÜRICH
Tel: 44 2404422 **Fax:** 4144 2404423
Email: contact@fiz-info.ch **Web site:** http://www.fiz-info.ch
Freq: Half-yearly; **Circ:** 5,000
Editor: Doro Winkler
Profile: Magazine fights trafficking in women and other forms of exploitation of and violence against

migrant women from Africa, Asia, Latin America and Eastern Europe.
Language(s): German

RUNDSCHAU RS 1656779S72-9732
Editorial: Storchengasse 15, 5201 BRUGG
Tel: 56 4607798 **Fax:** 56 4607780
Email: f.saiger@effingerhof.ch **Web site:** http://www.effingerhof.ch
Freq: Weekly; **Cover Price:** Free; **Circ:** 18,700
Editor: Friderike Saiger; **Advertising Manager:** Roger Keller
Profile: Local official paper.
Language(s): German
ADVERTISING RATES:
Full Page Mono .... CHF 3564
Full Page Colour .... CHF 3828
Mechanical Data: Type Area: 440 x 290 mm, No. of Columns (Display): 10, Col Widths (Display): 25 mm
Copy instructions: *Copy Date:* 2 days prior to publication
LOCAL NEWSPAPERS

RZ RHONE ZEITUNG 1699346S72-9812
Editorial: Saltinaplatz 1, 3900 BRIG-GLIS
Tel: 27 9222911 **Fax:** 27 9222910
Email: escher@rz-online.ch **Web site:** http://www.rz-online.ch
Freq: Weekly; **Cover Price:** Free; **Circ:** 37,303
Editor: German Escher; **Advertising Manager:** Claudine Studer
Profile: Advertising journal (house-to-house) concentrating on local stories.
Language(s): German
ADVERTISING RATES:
Full Page Mono .... CHF 2814
Full Page Colour .... CHF 2814
Mechanical Data: Type Area: 290 x 212 mm
Copy instructions: *Copy Date:* 2 days prior to publication
LOCAL NEWSPAPERS

SAFETY-PLUS 740953S14A-880
Editorial: Tägernstr. 1, 8127 FORCH **Tel:** 43 3662024
Fax: 43 3662030
Email: info@mediasec.ch **Web site:** http://www.safety-plus.ch
Freq: Quarterly; **Annual Sub.:** CHF 78,00; **Circ:** 4,000
Editor: Stefan Kühnis; **Advertising Manager:** Markus Good
Language(s): German
ADVERTISING RATES:
Full Page Mono .... CHF 2630
Full Page Colour .... CHF 3770
Mechanical Data: No. of Columns (Display): 3, Col Widths (Display): 55 mm, Type Area: 266 x 186 mm
Copy instructions: *Copy Date:* 31 days prior to publication
BUSINESS: COMMERCE, INDUSTRY & MANAGEMENT

SAISON-KÜCHE 1647407S74P-275
Editorial: Limmatplatz 6, 8005 ZÜRICH
Tel: 44 4473606 **Fax:** 44 4473679
Email: redaktion@saison.ch **Web site:** http://www.saison.ch
Freq: Monthly; Free to qualifying individuals
Annual Sub.: CHF 39,00; **Circ:** 128,491
Editor: Christine Kunovits; **Advertising Manager:** Reto Feurer
Profile: Magazine about seasonal cooking.
Language(s): German
ADVERTISING RATES:
Full Page Mono .... CHF 17600
Full Page Colour .... CHF 17600
Mechanical Data: Type Area: 263 x 190 mm
CONSUMER: WOMEN'S INTEREST CONSUMER MAGAZINES: Food & Cookery

SALDO 1641453S74M-263
Editorial: Schifflände 22, 8001 ZÜRICH
Tel: 44 2543232 **Fax:** 44 2543230
Email: redaktion@saldo.ch **Web site:** http://www.saldo.ch
Freq: 20 issues yearly; **Annual Sub.:** CHF 34,50; **Circ:** 107,332
Editor: René Schumacher
Profile: Consumer magazine.
Language(s): German

SALDO 1641453S74M-286
Editorial: Schifflände 22, 8001 ZÜRICH
Tel: 44 2543232 **Fax:** 44 2543230
Email: redaktion@saldo.ch **Web site:** http://www.saldo.ch
Freq: 20 issues yearly; **Annual Sub.:** CHF 34,50; **Circ:** 107,332
Editor: René Schumacher
Profile: Consumer magazine.
Language(s): German

SARGANSERLÄNDER
741090S67B-2280
Editorial: Zeughausstr. 50, 8887 MELS
Tel: 81 7253232 **Fax:** 81 7253230
Email: redaktion@sarganserlaender.ch

Freq: 260 issues yearly; **Annual Sub.:** CHF 176,00; **Circ:** 10,263
Editor: Heinz Gmür
Profile: Regional daily newspaper covering politics, economics, sport, travel, technology and the arts.
Language(s): German
ADVERTISING RATES:
SCC .... CHF 24,60
Mechanical Data: Type Area: 440 x 286 mm, No. of Columns (Display): 10, Col Widths (Display): 25 mm
Copy instructions: *Copy Date:* 1 day prior to publication
REGIONAL DAILY & SUNDAY NEWSPAPERS: Regional Daily Newspapers

SAV SCHWEIZERISCHE AKTUARVEREINIGUNG ASA ASSOCIATIONSUISSE DES ACTUAIRES SAA SWISS ASSOCIATION OF ACTUARIES MITTEILUNGEN - BULLETIN
1853033S1D-28
Editorial: Wölflistr. 1, 3001 BERN **Tel:** 31 3006666
Fax: 31 3006688
Email: verlag@staempfli.com **Web site:** http://www.staempfli.com
Freq: Half-yearly; **Annual Sub.:** CHF 183,00; **Circ:** 1,230
Profile: Magazine on Swiss insurance.
Language(s): English; French; German

SÄZ SCHWEIZERISCHE ÄRZTEZEITUNG BMS BOLLETTINO DEI MEDICI SVIZZERI BULLETIN DES MÉDECINS SUISSES
1645541S56A-2052
Editorial: Farnsburger Str. 8, 4132 MUTTENZ
Tel: 61 4678555 **Fax:** 61 4678556
Email: redaktion.saez@emh.ch **Web site:** http://www.saez.ch
Freq: Weekly; **Annual Sub.:** CHF 365,00; **Circ:** 35,400
Editor: Bruno Kesseli
Profile: Magazine for Swiss physical doctors.
Language(s): French; German
ADVERTISING RATES:
Full Page Mono .... CHF 3650
Full Page Colour .... CHF 5900
Mechanical Data: Type Area: 268 x 186 mm
Copy instructions: *Copy Date:* 14 days prior to publication

SCHAFFHAUSER BOCK
741155S72-7460
Editorial: Wiesengasse 20, 8222 BERINGEN
Tel: 52 6323059 **Fax:** 52 6323090
Email: redaktion@bockonline.ch **Web site:** http://www.bockonline.ch
Freq: Weekly; **Cover Price:** Free; **Circ:** 50,325
Editor: Ursula Litmanowitsch; **Advertising Manager:** Francesco Berenati
Profile: Advertising journal (house-to-house) concentrating on local stories.
Language(s): German
ADVERTISING RATES:
Full Page Mono .... CHF 5852
Mechanical Data: Type Area: 440 x 290 mm, No. of Columns (Display): 10, Col Widths (Display): 29 mm
Copy instructions: *Copy Date:* 1 day prior to publication
LOCAL NEWSPAPERS

SCHAFFHAUSER NACHRICHTEN 741157S67B-2300
Editorial: Vordergasse 58, 8201 SCHAFFHAUSEN
Tel: 52 6333111 **Fax:** 52 6333401
Email: redaktion@shn.ch **Web site:** http://www.shn.ch
Freq: 260 issues yearly; **Annual Sub.:** CHF 339,00; **Circ:** 23,559
Editor: Norbert Neininger; **Advertising Manager:** Sacha Meier
Profile: Regional daily newspaper covering politics, economics, sport, travel, technology and the arts.
Language(s): German
ADVERTISING RATES:
SCC .... CHF 54,60
Mechanical Data: Type Area: 440 x 290 mm, No. of Columns (Display): 10, Col Widths (Display): 26 mm
Copy instructions: *Copy Date:* 1 day prior to publication
Supplement(s): express
REGIONAL DAILY & SUNDAY NEWSPAPERS: Regional Daily Newspapers

SCHAFFHAUSER NACHRICHTEN 763741S72-9524
Editorial: Vordergasse 58, 8201 SCHAFFHAUSEN
Tel: 52 6333111 **Fax:** 52 6333401
Email: redaktion@shn.ch **Web site:** http://www.shn.ch
Freq: Weekly; **Cover Price:** Free; **Circ:** 48,419
Editor: Norbert Neininger; **Advertising Manager:** Sacha Meier
Profile: Advertising journal (house-to-house) concentrating on local stories.

Language(s): German
ADVERTISING RATES:
Full Page Mono .... CHF 6700
Full Page Colour .... CHF 8490
Mechanical Data: Type Area: 440 x 290 mm, No. of Columns (Display): 10, Col Widths (Display): 26 mm
Copy instructions: *Copy Date:* 1 day prior to publication
LOCAL NEWSPAPERS

SCHAUSTELLER 1856002S14A-1337
Editorial: Zuger Str. 123, 8820 WÄDENSWIL
Tel: 44 2523378
Email: info@vsvs.ch **Web site:** http://www.vsvs.ch
Freq: 11 issues yearly; **Circ:** 1,000
Editor: Daniel Kägi; **Advertising Manager:** René Bourquin
Profile: Magazine from the Swiss Fairground Entertainer's Association.
Language(s): German

SCHULBLATT 741436S62A-360
Editorial: Entfelder Str. 61, 5001 AARAU
Tel: 62 8236619 **Fax:** 62 8240260
Email: schulblatt@alv-ag.ch **Web site:** http://www.alv-ag.ch
Freq: 24 issues yearly; **Annual Sub.:** CHF 56,00; **Circ:** 11,597
Editor: Irene Wegmann
Profile: Magazine for teachers.
Language(s): German
ADVERTISING RATES:
Full Page Mono .... CHF 1720
Full Page Colour .... CHF 2220
Mechanical Data: Type Area: 271 x 177 mm
Copy instructions: *Copy Date:* 16 days prior to publication
BUSINESS: CHURCH & SCHOOL EQUIPMENT & EDUCATION: Education

SCHULBLATT DES KANTONS ST. GALLEN 720243S80-1473
Editorial: Davidstr. 31, 9001 ST. GALLEN
Tel: 71 2294383 **Fax:** 71 2294479
Email: info.schulblatt@sg.ch **Web site:** http://www.schule.sg.ch
Freq: 11 issues yearly; **Annual Sub.:** CHF 40,00; **Circ:** 7,000
Editor: Ursula Meiler
Profile: Official school publication of the canton of St. Gallen.
Language(s): German
Readership: Aimed at teachers.
ADVERTISING RATES:
Full Page Mono .... CHF 490
Mechanical Data: Type Area: 175 x 116 mm, No. of Columns (Display): 2, Col Widths (Display): 58 mm
CONSUMER: RURAL & REGIONAL INTEREST

SCHULE KONKRET 741443S62A-400
Editorial: Schürlirain 40, 3172 NIEDERWANGEN
Tel: 31 9880033
Email: kurt.heller@swch.ch **Web site:** http://www.swch.ch
Freq: 8 issues yearly; **Annual Sub.:** CHF 89,00; **Circ:** 3,061
Editor: Kurt Heller-Lindt
Profile: Magazine for teachers.
Language(s): German
ADVERTISING RATES:
Full Page Mono .... CHF 1650
Full Page Colour .... CHF 2700
Mechanical Data: Type Area: 245 x 180 mm
Copy instructions: *Copy Date:* 39 days prior to publication
BUSINESS: CHURCH & SCHOOL EQUIPMENT & EDUCATION: Education

SCHWEIZ 741665S50-65
Editorial: Rathausgasse 20a, 4501 SOLOTHURN
Tel: 32 6231632 **Fax:** 32 6235036
Email: wandermagazin@rothus.ch **Web site:** http://www.rothus.ch
Freq: 10 issues yearly; **Annual Sub.:** CHF 98,00; **Circ:** 16,577
Editor: Toni Kaiser
Profile: International magazine covering all aspects of the Swiss travel business.
Language(s): French; German
ADVERTISING RATES:
Full Page Mono .... CHF 4200
Full Page Colour .... CHF 4200
Mechanical Data: Type Area: 270 x 188 mm, No. of Columns (Display): 4, Col Widths (Display): 44 mm
Copy instructions: *Copy Date:* 30 days prior to publication

SCHWEIZ 741665S50-142
Editorial: Rathausgasse 20a, 4501 SOLOTHURN
Tel: 32 6231632 **Fax:** 32 6235036
Email: wandermagazin@rothus.ch **Web site:** http://www.rothus.ch
Freq: 10 issues yearly; **Annual Sub.:** CHF 98,00; **Circ:** 16,577
Editor: Toni Kaiser
Profile: International magazine covering all aspects of the Swiss travel business.
Language(s): French; German
ADVERTISING RATES:
Full Page Mono .... CHF 4200

Full Page Colour .... CHF 4200
Mechanical Data: Type Area: 270 x 188 mm, No. of Columns (Display): 4, Col Widths (Display): 44 mm
Copy instructions: *Copy Date:* 30 days prior to publication

SCHWEIZER BANK 1847383S1C-48
Editorial: Förrlibuckstr. 70, 8021 ZÜRICH
Tel: 43 4445111 **Fax:** 43 4445091
Email: schweizerbank@handelszeitung.ch **Web site:** http://www.schweizerbank.ch
Freq: Monthly; **Annual Sub.:** CHF 116,00; **Circ:** 15,000
Editor: Claudia Gabriel-Schneider; **Advertising Manager:** Christian Santa
Profile: Magazine for executives of banks and finances in Switzerland.
Language(s): German
ADVERTISING RATES:
Full Page Mono .... CHF 8920
Full Page Colour .... CHF 8920
Mechanical Data: Type Area: 265 x 180 mm, No. of Columns (Display): 3, Col Widths (Display): 56 mm
Copy instructions: *Copy Date:* 31 days prior to publication
Supplement(s): Leader spezial

SCHWEIZER BAUER 765072S21A-572
Editorial: Dammweg 9, 3001 BERN **Tel:** 31 3303416
Fax: 31 3303395
Email: redaktion@schweizerbauer.ch **Web site:** http://www.schweizerbauer.ch
Freq: 104 issues yearly; **Annual Sub.:** CHF 179,00; **Circ:** 31,302
Editor: Rudolf Haudenschild
Profile: Magazine for Swiss farmers.
Language(s): German
ADVERTISING RATES:
Full Page Mono .... CHF 7260
Full Page Colour .... CHF 7620
Mechanical Data: Type Area: 440 x 292 mm, No. of Columns (Display): 10, Col Widths (Display): 27 mm
Copy instructions: *Copy Date:* 2 days prior to publication
Supplement(s): Schweizer Land + Leben
BUSINESS: AGRICULTURE & FARMING

SCHWEIZER BAUWIRTSCHAFT
1655331S42A-2
Editorial: Weinbergstr. 49, 8006 ZÜRICH
Tel: 44 2588333 **Fax:** 44 2610324
Email: mwalser@baumeister.ch **Web site:** http://www.schweizerbauwirtschaft.ch
Freq: 24 issues yearly; Free to qualifying individuals
Annual Sub.: CHF 115,00; **Circ:** 7,600
Editor: Martin A. Walser; **Advertising Manager:** Claudio von Känel
Profile: Building business magazine.
Language(s): French; German; Italian
ADVERTISING RATES:
Full Page Mono .... CHF 1800
Full Page Colour .... CHF 2750
Mechanical Data: Type Area: 263 x 185 mm, No. of Columns (Display): 2, Col Widths (Display): 90 mm
Copy instructions: *Copy Date:* 10 days prior to publication
Official Journal of: Organ d. Schweizer. Baumeisterverb. u. seiner Fachgruppen
BUSINESS: CONSTRUCTION

SCHWEIZER ENERGIEFACHBUCH 1641422S58-186
Editorial: Feldeggstr. 89, 8008 ZÜRICH
Tel: 43 4999901 **Fax:** 43 4999931
Email: sigrid.hanke@bluewin.ch
Freq: Annual; **Annual Sub.:** CHF 290,00; **Circ:** 8,000
Editor: Sigrid Hanke
Profile: Magazine on energy.
Language(s): German
ADVERTISING RATES:
Full Page Mono .... CHF 4150
Full Page Colour .... CHF 5200
Mechanical Data: Type Area: 268 x 189 mm, No. of Columns (Display): 2, Col Widths (Display): 92 mm
Copy instructions: *Copy Date:* 40 days prior to publication
Supplement(s): Fassade

SCHWEIZER FAMILIE
741595S74C-533
Editorial: Werdstr. 21, 8021 ZÜRICH **Tel:** 44 2486106
Fax: 44 2486096
Email: redaktion@schweizer-familie.ch **Web site:** http://www.schweizer-familie.ch
Freq: Weekly; **Annual Sub.:** CHF 194,00; **Circ:** 185,174
Editor: Daniel Dunkel; **Advertising Manager:** Goran Vukota
Profile: Home and family magazine.
Language(s): German
ADVERTISING RATES:
Full Page Mono .... CHF 18500
Full Page Colour .... CHF 18500
Mechanical Data: Type Area: 249 x 182 mm, No. of Columns (Display): 4, Col Widths (Display): 42 mm
Copy instructions: *Copy Date:* 16 days prior to publication
Supplement(s): TV täglich
CONSUMER: WOMEN'S INTEREST CONSUMER MAGAZINES: Home & Family

SCHWEIZER GARTEN

741597S26B-100

Editorial: Bahnhofplatz 1, 3110 MÜNSINGEN
Tel: 31 7205384 **Fax:** 31 7205377
Email: i.hofer@schweizergarten.ch **Web site:** http://www.schweizergarten.ch
Freq: Monthly; **Annual Sub.:** CHF 99,00; **Circ:** 20,000
Editor: Livia Hofer; **Advertising Manager:** Marco Fedalto
Profile: Magazine containing advice and information on gardening and outdoor and indoor plants.
Language(s): German
Readership: Read by managers and staff of garden centres.
ADVERTISING RATES:
Full Page Mono .... CHF 2468
Full Page Colour .... CHF 3734
Mechanical Data: Type Area: 253 x 185 mm
Copy instructions: *Copy Date:* 23 days prior to publication
BUSINESS: GARDEN TRADE: Garden Trade Supplies

SCHWEIZER GEMEINDE COMMUNE SUISSE COMUNE SVIZZERO VISCHNANCA SVIZRA

1646250S32A-468

Editorial: Solothurnstr. 22, 3322 URTENEN
Tel: 31 8583116 **Fax:** 31 8583115
Email: info@chgemeinden.ch **Web site:** http://www.chgemeinden.ch
Freq: 11 issues yearly; Free to qualifying individuals
Annual Sub.: CHF 90,00; **Circ:** 4,600
Editor: Steff Schneider
Profile: Magazine for authorities and administrations of the political communities, cities and federal states in Switzerland.
Language(s): French; German; Italian
ADVERTISING RATES:
Full Page Mono .... CHF 2100
Full Page Colour .... CHF 3870
Mechanical Data: Type Area: 256 x 185 mm, No. of Columns (Display): 3, Col Widths (Display): 59 mm
Copy instructions: *Copy Date:* 28 days prior to publication
Official Journal of: Organ d. Schweizer. Konferenz d. Stadt- u. Gemeindeschreiber
BUSINESS: LOCAL GOVERNMENT, LEISURE & RECREATION: Local Government

SCHWEIZER HOLZBAU

741600S46-75_50

Editorial: Weinbergstr. 49, 8006 ZÜRICH
Tel: 44 2588259 **Fax:** 44 2610324
Email: flipp@baumeister.ch **Web site:** http://www.schweizerholzbau.ch
Freq: Monthly; Free to qualifying individuals
Annual Sub.: CHF 90,00; **Circ:** 5,000
Editor: Franz Ferry Lipp; **Advertising Manager:** Guido Hüppi
Profile: Magazine about wood use in carpentry and construction.
Language(s): German
Readership: Read by carpenters, architects, engineers and those involved in wood-based trade.
ADVERTISING RATES:
Full Page Mono .... CHF 1700
Full Page Colour .... CHF 2650
Mechanical Data: No. of Columns (Display): 2, Col Widths (Display): 90 mm, Type Area: 263 x 185 mm
Copy instructions: *Copy Date:* 14 days prior to publication
Official Journal of: Organ d. Verb. holzbau schweiz
BUSINESS: TIMBER, WOOD & FORESTRY

SCHWEIZER ILLUSTRIERTE

741602S73-280

Editorial: Dufourstr. 23, 8008 ZÜRICH
Tel: 44 2596363 **Fax:** 44 2620442
Email: info@schweizer-illustrierte.ch **Web site:** http://www.schweizer-illustrierte.ch
Freq: Weekly; **Circ:** 255,000
Editor: Stephan Sutter; **News Editor:** Marcel Huwyler; **Advertising Manager:** Reinelde Wegmann
Profile: General interest illustrated magazine.
Language(s): German
ADVERTISING RATES:
Full Page Mono .... CHF 26310
Full Page Colour .... CHF 26310
Mechanical Data: Type Area: 261 x 189 mm, No. of Columns (Display): 4, Col Widths (Display): 45 mm
Copy instructions: *Copy Date:* 21 days prior to publication
Supplement(s): al dente; event.; Miss Schweiz Magazin; Mister Schweiz Magazin; Schweizer Illustrierte Auto; Schweizer Illustrierte Gruen; shopping; style; TV täglich; Uhren Welt
CONSUMER: NATIONAL & INTERNATIONAL PERIODICALS

SCHWEIZER LAND + LEBEN

766068S21A-576

Editorial: Dammweg 9, 3001 BERN **Tel:** 31 3303171
Fax: 31 3303395
Email: redaktion@landleben.ch **Web site:** http://www.schweizerbauer.ch
Freq: 6 issues yearly; **Circ:** 34,000
Editor: Max Welter
Profile: Supplement to the Schweizer Bauer magazine for Swiss farmers.
Language(s): German
ADVERTISING RATES:
Full Page Mono .... CHF 3390
Full Page Colour .... CHF 3700
Mechanical Data: Type Area: 275 x 185 mm, No. of Columns (Display): 6, Col Widths (Display): 27 mm
Copy instructions: *Copy Date:* 14 days prior to publication
Official Journal of: Organ d. Schweizer. Verbände d. Kath. Bauern, Bäuerinnen u. Landjugend
Supplement to: Schweizer Bauer

SCHWEIZER LANDLIEBE

2077904S74P-302

Editorial: Dufourstr. 49, 8008 ZÜRICH
Tel: 44 2596111 **Fax:** 44 2596844
Email: redaktion@landliebe-magazin.ch **Web site:** http://www.landliebe-magazin.ch
Freq: Quarterly; **Annual Sub.:** CHF 24,00; **Circ:** 200,000
Editor: Urs Heller; **Advertising Manager:** Stefan Reinli
Profile: With the new Swiss magazine Schweizer LandLiebe to take on the trend of a new sense of life, the wins in Switzerland is becoming increasingly important. Back to nature! We bring authentic stories about people who are rooted in their living room and there is doing amazing things. Our protagonists are people like the last blacksmith in a region and its trade. The farmer who has prescribed the conservation of rare breeds of farm animals, or the fisherman on the lake early in the morning interprets its nets. The woman with the green thumb that turns her garden into a paradise. All photographed in front of the magnificent panoramic scenery as the seasons change. Flora and fauna also play a crucial role, our stars are donkeys and bats, or the most beautiful mushrooms that there is to see the autumn. Rare English Rose varieties and how they flourish in your garden. Fine vegetables for planting and use in the kitchen. We are down-position and show our Switzerland from its traditional and rural side.
Language(s): German
ADVERTISING RATES:
Full Page Mono .... CHF 17500
Full Page Colour .... CHF 17500
Mechanical Data: Type Area: 261 x 189 mm, No. of Columns (Display): 3, Col Widths (Display): 61 mm

SCHWEIZER LANDTECHNIK

763311S27-143

Editorial: Ausserdorfstr. 31, 5223 RINIKEN
Tel: 56 4511859 **Fax:** 56 4416731
Email: red@agrartechnik.ch **Web site:** http://www.agrartechnik.ch
Freq: 11 issues yearly; Free to qualifying individuals
Annual Sub.: CHF 107,00; **Circ:** 20,000
Editor: Ueli Zweifel
Profile: Magazine informs about agricultural technology, renewable energies and the Swiss Association for Agricultural Technologies.
Language(s): German
ADVERTISING RATES:
Full Page Mono .... CHF 3100
Full Page Colour .... CHF 3460
Mechanical Data: Type Area: 261 x 183 mm, No. of Columns (Display): 4, Col Widths (Display): 42 mm

SCHWEIZER LOGISTIK KATALOG

763312S10-43

Editorial: Basler Str. 15, 5080 LAUFENBURG
Tel: 62 8697900 **Fax:** 62 8697901
Email: jules.kistler@swissonline.ch **Web site:** http://www.schweizerlogistikkatalog.ch
Freq: Annual; **Cover Price:** CHF 45,00; **Circ:** 4,500
Editor: Jules Kistler
Profile: Directory for the logistics industry.
Language(s): German
ADVERTISING RATES:
Full Page Mono .... CHF 3240
Full Page Colour .... CHF 3240
Mechanical Data: Type Area: 267 x 195 mm
Copy instructions: *Copy Date:* 70 days prior to publication

SCHWEIZER PERSONALVORSORGE PREVOYANCE PROFESSIONNELLE SUISSE

1648509S32G-454

Editorial: Taubenhausstr. 38, 6002 LUZERN
Tel: 41 3170707 **Fax:** 41 3170700
Email: vps@vps.ch **Web site:** http://www.vps.ch
Freq: Monthly; **Annual Sub.:** CHF 310,00; **Circ:** 4,000
Editor: Peter Schnider; **Advertising Manager:** Bruno E. Durrer
Profile: Magazine on occupational provisions and social insurance.
Language(s): French; German
ADVERTISING RATES:
Full Page Mono .... CHF 3400
Full Page Colour .... CHF 5500
Mechanical Data: Type Area: 257 x 175 mm, No. of Columns (Display): 3, Col Widths (Display): 55 mm
Copy instructions: *Copy Date:* 15 days prior to publication
BUSINESS: LOCAL GOVERNMENT, LEISURE & RECREATION: Community Care & Social Services

SCHWEIZER PR- & MEDIEN-VERZEICHNIS RÉPERTOIRE RP & MÉDIAS SUISSES

1859067S2A-689

Editorial: Hopfenstr. 10, 8045 ZÜRICH
Tel: 44 4514647 **Fax:** 44 4513638
Email: contact@renteria.ch **Web site:** http://www.renteria.ch
Freq: Annual; **Annual Sub.:** CHF 135,00; **Circ:** 2,000
Editor: Michelle Freund
Profile: Swiss directory about PR and the media.
Language(s): English; French; German
ADVERTISING RATES:
Full Page Mono .... CHF 2125
Full Page Colour .... CHF 2575
Mechanical Data: Type Area: 215 x 135 mm, No. of Columns (Display): 2, Col Widths (Display): 62 mm
Copy instructions: *Copy Date:* 75 days prior to publication

SCHWEIZER SOLDAT

763057S40-202

Editorial: Weinbergstr. 11, 8268 SALENSTEIN
Tel: 71 6632644
Email: redaktion@schweizer-soldat.ch **Web site:** http://www.schweizer-soldat.ch
Freq: 11 issues yearly; **Annual Sub.:** CHF 55,00; **Circ:** 6,300
Editor: Peter Forster
Profile: Swiss army magazine about defence and civil protection.
Language(s): German
ADVERTISING RATES:
Full Page Mono .... CHF 3860
Full Page Colour .... CHF 5800
Mechanical Data: Type Area: 266 x 184 mm
BUSINESS: DEFENCE

SCHWEIZER SPORT & MODE SPORT & MODE SUISSE

1656783S47A-100

Editorial: Oergelackerstr. 4, 8707 UETIKON
Tel: 44 9207940 **Fax:** 44 9207941
Email: info@sportbiz.ch **Web site:** http://www.sportbiz.ch
Freq: Quarterly; Free to qualifying individuals
Annual Sub.: CHF 98,00; **Circ:** 3,100
Editor: Beat Ladner
Profile: Magazine from the Swiss sport equipment industry.
Language(s): French; German
ADVERTISING RATES:
Full Page Mono .... CHF 1500
Full Page Colour .... CHF 1500
Mechanical Data: Type Area: 322 x 235 mm
Copy instructions: *Copy Date:* 7 days prior to publication
Official Journal of: Organ d. Verb. Schweizer Sportfachhandel ASMAS
BUSINESS: CLOTHING & TEXTILES

DER SCHWEIZER TREUHÄNDER L'EXPERT-COMPTABLE SUISSE

1656156S1A-288

Editorial: Limmatquai 120, 8023 ZÜRICH
Tel: 44 2677575 **Fax:** 44 2677555
Email: redaktionst@treuhand-kammer.ch **Web site:** http://www.treuhaender.ch
Freq: 10 issues yearly; Free to qualifying individuals
Annual Sub.: CHF 195,00; **Circ:** 12,000
Editor: Annelies Keller
Profile: Magazine about certified accountancy, business accountancy, company and tax accountancy.
Language(s): French; German
ADVERTISING RATES:
Full Page Mono .... CHF 2380
Full Page Colour .... CHF 4730
Mechanical Data: Type Area: 248 x 174 mm, No. of Columns (Display): 3, Col Widths (Display): 56 mm
BUSINESS: FINANCE & ECONOMICS

SCHWEIZER VERPACKUNGS KATALOG

763313S35-21

Editorial: Basler Str. 15, 5080 LAUFENBURG
Tel: 55 4622451 **Fax:** 62 8697901
Email: irene.jung@text-technik.ch **Web site:** http://www.schweizerverpackungskat.ch
Freq: Annual; **Cover Price:** CHF 48,00; **Circ:** 4,500
Editor: Irene Jung; **Advertising Manager:** Marianne Leimroth
Profile: Swiss annual about packaging.
Language(s): German
ADVERTISING RATES:
Full Page Mono .... CHF 3550
Full Page Colour .... CHF 3550
Mechanical Data: Type Area: 267 x 185 mm, No. of Columns (Display): 3, Col Widths (Display): 59 mm
Copy instructions: *Copy Date:* 70 days prior to publication

SCHWEIZER VERSICHERUNG

1647231S1D-25

Editorial: Förrlibuckstr. 70, 8021 ZÜRICH
Tel: 43 4445111 **Fax:** 43 4445091
Email: wrueedi@handelszeitung.ch **Web site:** http://www.schweizerversicherung.ch
Freq: Monthly; **Annual Sub.:** CHF 116,00; **Circ:** 8,733
Editor: Werner Rüedi; **Advertising Manager:** Christian Santa
Profile: Magazine on Swiss finances and insurance.
Language(s): French; German
ADVERTISING RATES:
Full Page Mono .... CHF 8410
Full Page Colour .... CHF 8410
Mechanical Data: Type Area: 254 x 187 mm, No. of Columns (Display): 3, Col Widths (Display): 59 mm
Copy instructions: *Copy Date:* 30 days prior to publication
Official Journal of: Organ d. Schweiz. Vereinigung d. diplomierten Versicherungsfachleute, d. Schweiz. Verb. d. Versicherungs-Generalagenten u. d. Schweizer. Verb. d. Versicherungs-Inspektoren u. -Agenten
Supplement(s): Leader spezial
BUSINESS: FINANCE & ECONOMICS: Insurance

SCHWEIZER ZEITSCHRIFT FÜR ERNÄHRUNGSMEDIZIN

1643877S56A-2044

Editorial: Schützenmattstr. 1, 4051 BASEL
Tel: 61 2632535 **Fax:** 61 2632536
Email: claudia.reinke@medsciences.ch
Freq: 5 issues yearly; **Annual Sub.:** CHF 42,00; **Circ:** 7,000
Editor: Claudia M. Reinke
Profile: Swiss magazine featuring contributions and information about nutrition medicine.
Language(s): German
ADVERTISING RATES:
Full Page Mono .... CHF 3280
Full Page Colour .... CHF 4880
Mechanical Data: Type Area: 238 x 175 mm
Copy instructions: *Copy Date:* 23 days prior to publication

SCHWEIZER ZEITSCHRIFT FÜR ERNÄHRUNGSMEDIZIN

1643877S56A-2175

Editorial: Schützenmattstr. 1, 4051 BASEL
Tel: 61 2632535 **Fax:** 61 2632536
Email: claudia.reinke@medsciences.ch
Freq: 5 issues yearly; **Annual Sub.:** CHF 42,00; **Circ:** 7,000
Editor: Claudia M. Reinke
Profile: Swiss magazine featuring contributions and information about nutrition medicine.
Language(s): German
ADVERTISING RATES:
Full Page Mono .... CHF 3280
Full Page Colour .... CHF 4880
Mechanical Data: Type Area: 238 x 175 mm
Copy instructions: *Copy Date:* 23 days prior to publication

SCHWEIZER ZEITSCHRIFT FÜR ONKOLOGIE

1643878S56A-2045

Editorial: Schaffhauser Str. 13, 8212 NEUHAUSEN
Tel: 52 6755182 **Fax:** 52 6755061
Email: hirrle@rosenfluh.ch **Web site:** http://www.rosenfluh.ch
Freq: 5 issues yearly; **Annual Sub.:** CHF 42,00; **Circ:** 4,200
Editor: Bärbel Hirrle
Profile: Magazine about further education in oncological diagnosis and therapy.
Language(s): German
ADVERTISING RATES:
Full Page Mono .... CHF 3730
Full Page Colour .... CHF 5330
Mechanical Data: Type Area: 280 x 175 mm
Copy instructions: *Copy Date:* 31 days prior to publication

SCHWEIZER ZEITSCHRIFT FÜR ONKOLOGIE

1643878S56A-2176

Editorial: Schaffhauser Str. 13, 8212 NEUHAUSEN
Tel: 52 6755182 **Fax:** 52 6755061
Email: hirrle@rosenfluh.ch **Web site:** http://www.rosenfluh.ch
Freq: 5 issues yearly; **Annual Sub.:** CHF 42,00; **Circ:** 4,200
Editor: Bärbel Hirrle
Profile: Magazine about further education in oncological diagnosis and therapy.
Language(s): German
ADVERTISING RATES:
Full Page Mono .... CHF 3730
Full Page Colour .... CHF 5330
Mechanical Data: Type Area: 280 x 175 mm
Copy instructions: *Copy Date:* 31 days prior to publication

DER SCHWEIZERISCHE HAUSEIGENTÜMER

741611S74K-40

Editorial: Seefeldstr. 60, 8032 ZÜRICH
Tel: 44 2549020 **Fax:** 44 2549021
Email: info@hev-schweiz.ch **Web site:** http://www.hev-schweiz.ch
Freq: 22 issues yearly; Free to qualifying individuals
Annual Sub.: CHF 34,50; **Circ:** 299,423
Editor: Ansgar Gmür
Profile: Journal of the Swiss Home-owners' Association.
Language(s): German
ADVERTISING RATES:
Full Page Mono .... CHF 16294
Full Page Colour .... CHF 19094
Mechanical Data: Type Area: 438 x 291 mm, No. of Columns (Display): 10

Copy instructions: *Copy Date:* 19 days prior to publication
Supplement(s): Sofa
CONSUMER: WOMEN'S INTEREST CONSUMER MAGAZINES: Home Purchase

SCHWEIZERISCHE WEINZEITUNG
1641424S9C-1
Editorial: Grubenstr. 11, 8045 ZÜRICH
Tel: 44 4504410
Email: wolfram.meister@schweizerische-weinzeitung.ch **Web site:** http://www.schweizerische-weinzeitung.ch
Freq: 10 issues yearly; **Annual Sub.:** CHF 111,00; **Circ:** 8,000
Editor: Wolfram Meister
Profile: Swiss magazine on wine.
Language(s): French; German; Italian
ADVERTISING RATES:
Full Page Mono .... CHF 3000
Full Page Colour .... CHF 3000
Mechanical Data: Type Area: 274 x 205 mm
Copy instructions: *Copy Date:* 14 days prior to publication
BUSINESS: DRINKS & LICENSED TRADE: Licensed Trade, Wines & Spirits

SCHWEIZERISCHE ZEITSCHRIFT FÜR FORSTWESEN
764121S46-8
Editorial: Mythenstr. 2, 8308 ILLNAU
Tel: 52 3472179 **Fax:** 52 3472176
Email: szf@forstverein.ch **Web site:** http://www.forstverein.ch/szf
Freq: Monthly; Free to qualifying individuals
Annual Sub.: CHF 175,00; **Circ:** 1,133
Editor: Barbara Allgaier Leuch
Profile: Swiss scientific and practical magazine about forestry.
Language(s): English; French; German; Italian
ADVERTISING RATES:
Full Page Mono .... CHF 1550
Full Page Colour .... CHF 1550
Mechanical Data: Type Area: 264 x 192 mm
Copy instructions: *Copy Date:* 18 days prior to publication
BUSINESS: TIMBER, WOOD & FORESTRY

SCHWEIZERISCHE ZEITSCHRIFT FÜR SPORTMEDIZIN UND SPORTTRAUMATOLOGIE REVUE SUISSE DE MÉDECINE ET DE TRAUMATOLOGIE DU SPORT RIVISTA SVIZZERA DI MEDICINA E TRAUMATOLOGIA DELLO SPORT
1643881S56A-2046
Editorial: Winterthurer Str. 190, 8057 ZÜRICH
Tel: 1 6357078 **Fax:** 1 6356863
Email: boutellier.urs@access.unizh.ch **Web site:** http://www.sgsm.ch
Freq: Quarterly; Free to qualifying individuals
Annual Sub.: CHF 60,00; **Circ:** 1,500
Editor: Urs Boutellier
Profile: Magazine on sports medicine.
Language(s): English; French; German
ADVERTISING RATES:
Full Page Mono .... CHF 1450
Full Page Colour .... CHF 2350
Mechanical Data: Type Area: 258 x 175 mm
Copy instructions: *Copy Date:* 28 days prior to publication
BUSINESS: HEALTH & MEDICAL

SCHWEIZERISCHER FORSTKALENDER
2002075S21A-634
Editorial: Zürcher Str. 180, 8501 FRAUENFELD
Tel: 52 7236050 **Fax:** 52 7236059
Email: info@verlaghuber.ch **Web site:** http://www.ofv.ch
Freq: Annual; **Cover Price:** CHF 32,00; **Circ:** 3,000
Editor: Stefan Schweizer
Profile: Calendar for forestry, wood business and hunting.
Language(s): German
Mechanical Data: Type Area: 144 x 94 mm
Copy instructions: *Copy Date:* 60 days prior to publication

SCHWEIZERISCHES ARCHIV FÜR VOLKSKUNDE
741617S94X-520
Editorial: Wiesenstr. 7, 8008 ZÜRICH
Tel: 44 6342433 **Fax:** 44 6344994
Email: ugyr@ipk.unizh.ch **Web site:** http://www.volkskunde.ch
Freq: Half-yearly; **Annual Sub.:** CHF 62,00; **Circ:** 800
Editor: Ueli Gyr
Profile: Magazine covering folklore containing articles on history and traditions.
Language(s): French; German; Italian
CONSUMER: OTHER CLASSIFICATIONS: Miscellaneous

SCHWEIZERISCHES MEDIZINISCHES JAHRBUCH ANNUAIRE MÉDICAL SUISSE
741620S56A-1700
Editorial: Farnsburger Str. 8, 4132 MUTTENZ
Tel: 61 4678555 **Fax:** 61 4678556
Email: smj@emh.ch **Web site:** http://www.smj.ch
Freq: Annual; **Cover Price:** CHF 150,00; **Circ:** 1,200
Editor: Natalie Marty; **Advertising Manager:** Silvia Fuchs
Profile: Directory listing addresses of the Swiss health care system.
Language(s): French; German
Mechanical Data: Type Area: 248 x 169 mm

SCHWEIZERISCHES ZENTRALBLATT FÜR STAATS- UND VERWALTUNGSRECHT
1641060S44-345
Editorial: Zwingliplatz 2, 8022 ZÜRICH
Tel: 44 2002999 **Fax:** 44 2002908
Email: schulthess@schulthess.com **Web site:** http://www.schulthess.com
Freq: Monthly; **Cover Price:** CHF 18,00; **Circ:** 1,430
Editor: August Mächler
Profile: Magazine with contributions about public law.
Language(s): German
ADVERTISING RATES:
Full Page Mono .... CHF 680
Full Page Colour .... CHF 680
Mechanical Data: Type Area: 190 x 135 mm
Copy instructions: *Copy Date:* 16 days prior to publication
BUSINESS: LEGAL

SCHWEIZISCHE ZEITSCHRIFT FÜR OBST- UND WEINBAU
763600S22A-221
Editorial: Schloss, 8820 WÄDENSWIL
Tel: 44 7836325 **Fax:** 44 7836379
Email: uta.gafner@acw.admin.ch **Web site:** http://www.szow.ch
Freq: 24 issues yearly; **Annual Sub.:** CHF 95,00; **Circ:** 2,981
Editor: Hans Peter Ruffner
Profile: Magazine about fruit and wine growing and selling.
Language(s): German
ADVERTISING RATES:
Full Page Mono .... CHF 1349
Full Page Colour .... CHF 1754
Mechanical Data: Type Area: 260 x 184 mm, No. of Columns (Display): 4, Col Widths (Display): 45 mm
Copy instructions: *Copy Date:* 15 days prior to publication
Official Journal of: Organ d. Forschungsanstalt Agroscope Changins-Wädenswil ACW, d. Schweizer. Obstverb., d. Branchenverb. Deutschschweizer Wein, d. Schweizer. Kellermeisterverb., d. Schweizer. Brennerverb., d. Zürcher Hochschule f. Angewandte Wissenschaften ZHAW, Netzwerk Wädenswil u. d. Berufsbildungszentrum Wädenswil
BUSINESS: FOOD

SCHWYZER GEWERBE
1752682S14A-1209
Editorial: Gribschrain 16, 6403 KÜSSNACHT
Tel: 79 4088340 **Fax:** 41 8504314
Email: redaktion@ksgv.ch **Web site:** http://www.ksgv.ch
Freq: 11 issues yearly; **Circ:** 2,400
Editor: Ernst Sidler
Profile: Business magazine.
Language(s): German
ADVERTISING RATES:
Full Page Mono .... CHF 690
Full Page Colour .... CHF 990
Mechanical Data: Type Area: 272 x 185 mm

SCHWYZER PANDA
741683S57-440
Editorial: Wilenstr. 133, 8832 WILEN **Tel:** 43 8444951
Fax: 43 8444952
Email: res.knobel@oekobuero.ch
Freq: Quarterly; Free to qualifying individuals
Annual Sub.: CHF 20,00; **Circ:** 9,000
Editor: Res Knobel
Profile: Magazine of the World Wide Fund for Nature.
Language(s): German
ADVERTISING RATES:
Full Page Mono .... CHF 1300
Full Page Colour .... CHF 1600
Mechanical Data: No. of Columns (Display): 3, Col Widths (Display): 60 mm, Type Area: 272 x 190 mm
Copy instructions: *Copy Date:* 40 days prior to publication
BUSINESS: ENVIRONMENT & POLLUTION

SEESPIEGEL
1687115S57-687
Editorial: Bahnhofsstr. 55, 8510 FRAUENFELD
Tel: 52 7242432 **Fax:** 52 7242848
Email: marco.sacchetti@tg.ch **Web site:** http://www.seespiegel.de
Freq: Half-yearly; **Cover Price:** Free; **Circ:** 13,000
Editor: Marco Sacchetti
Profile: Information on water quality of Lake Constance, and to the riparian zone and catchment area of the lake (natural environment, living and working space, residential and utility room, recovery room).
Language(s): German

SEETALER BOTE
741721S72-7520
Editorial: Hauptstr. 42, 6280 HOCHDORF
Tel: 41 9140950 **Fax:** 41 9140999
Email: redaktion@seetalerbote.ch **Web site:** http://www.seetalerbote.ch
Freq: Weekly; **Annual Sub.:** CHF 129,00; **Circ:** 5,204
Editor: Peter Gerber Plech
Profile: Regional weekly covering politics, economics, sport, travel, technology and the arts.
Language(s): German
ADVERTISING RATES:
SCC .... CHF 14,60
Mechanical Data: Type Area: 435 x 286 mm, No. of Columns (Display): 10, Col Widths (Display): 26 mm
Copy instructions: *Copy Date:* 2 days prior to publication
Supplement(s): Landwirtschaft aktuell
LOCAL NEWSPAPERS

DER SEETALER-DER LINDENBERG
1656784S72-9734
Editorial: Kronenplatz 12, 5600 LENZBURG
Tel: 58 2005802 **Fax:** 58 2005821
Email: hubert.keller@lenzburger-lba.ch **Web site:** http://www.aargauerzeitung.ch
Cover Price: Free
Editor: Hubert Keller
Profile: Advertising journal (house-to-house) concentrating on local stories.
Language(s): German
LOCAL NEWSPAPERS

SELECTA
1643916S56A-2047
Editorial: Grosspeterstr. 23, 4002 BASEL
Tel: 58 9589600 **Fax:** 58 9589660
Email: redaktion@medical-tribune.ch **Web site:** http://www.medical-tribune.ch
Freq: 6 issues yearly; **Circ:** 14,500
Editor: Winfried Powollik; **Advertising Manager:** Patricia Hunziker
Profile: Magazine for physical doctors.
Language(s): German
ADVERTISING RATES:
Full Page Mono .... CHF 4650
Full Page Colour .... CHF 4650
Mechanical Data: Type Area: 257 x 185 mm, No. of Columns (Display): 3, Col Widths (Display): 59 mm
Copy instructions: *Copy Date:* 28 days prior to publication
Supplement to: Medical Tribune

SELECTA
1843296S56A-2148
Editorial: Grosspeterstr. 23, 4002 BASEL
Tel: 58 9589600 **Fax:** 58 9589660
Email: redaktion@medical-tribune.ch **Web site:** http://www.medical-tribune.ch
Freq: 3 issues yearly; **Circ:** 4,800
Editor: Winfried Powollik; **Advertising Manager:** Patricia Hunziker
Profile: Magazine for physical doctors.
Language(s): French
ADVERTISING RATES:
Full Page Mono .... CHF 3345
Full Page Colour .... CHF 3345
Mechanical Data: Type Area: 257 x 185 mm, No. of Columns (Display): 3, Col Widths (Display): 59 mm
Copy instructions: *Copy Date:* 28 days prior to publication
Supplement to: Tribune Médicale

SÉLECTION
741769S73-320
Editorial: Räffelstr. 11, 8045 ZÜRICH
Tel: 44 4557339 **Fax:** 44 4557119
Email: edwin.surbeck@readersdigest.ch **Web site:** http://www.readersdigest.ch
Freq: Monthly; **Annual Sub.:** CHF 79,80; **Circ:** 40,932
Editor: Edwin Surbeck; **Advertising Manager:** Sabine Kölsch
Profile: Journal containing articles about people and their lives in the Zug region, short stories and advertising.
Language(s): French
ADVERTISING RATES:
Full Page Mono .... CHF 3275
Full Page Colour .... CHF 5380
Mechanical Data: Type Area: 176 x 124 mm, No. of Columns (Display): 2, Col Widths (Display): 66 mm
Copy instructions: *Copy Date:* 35 days prior to publication
CONSUMER: NATIONAL & INTERNATIONAL PERIODICALS

SEMPACHER WOCHE
741793S72-7600
Editorial: Sempachstr. 7, 6203 SEMPACH-STATION
Tel: 41 4673019 **Fax:** 41 4672355
Email: redaktion@sempacherwoche.ch **Web site:** http://www.sempacherwoche.ch
Freq: Weekly; **Annual Sub.:** CHF 133,00; **Circ:** 2,711
Editor: Marcel Schmid-Helfenstein
Profile: Regional weekly covering politics, economics, sport, travel, technology and the arts.
Language(s): German
ADVERTISING RATES:
SCC .... CHF 17,00
Mechanical Data: Type Area: 434 x 286 mm, No. of Columns (Display): 10, Col Widths (Display): 25 mm
Copy instructions: *Copy Date:* 2 days prior to publication
LOCAL NEWSPAPERS

SERVICE PUBLIC
1828660S2A-673
Editorial: Giacomettistr. 1, 3000 BERN 31
Tel: 31 3509111
Email: publishing@srg-ssr.ch **Web site:** http://www.srg-ssr.ch
Freq: Annual; **Cover Price:** Free; **Circ:** 3,000
Editor: Dominic Witschi
Profile: Publication of the SRG SSR company.
Language(s): German

LE SERVICE PUBLIC
1828661S2A-674
Editorial: Giacomettistr. 1, 3000 BERN 31
Tel: 31 3509111
Email: publishing@srg-ssr.ch **Web site:** http://www.srg-ssr.ch
Freq: Annual; **Cover Price:** Free; **Circ:** 1,500
Editor: Dominic Witschi
Profile: Publication of the SRG SSR company.
Language(s): French

SERVICE PUBLIC
2004672S2A-705
Editorial: Giacomettistr. 1, 3000 BERN 31
Tel: 31 3509111
Email: publishing@srg-ssr.ch **Web site:** http://www.srg-ssr.ch
Freq: Annual; **Cover Price:** Free; **Circ:** 1,000
Editor: Dominic Witschi
Profile: Publication of the SRG SSR company.
Language(s): German

SERVIZIO PUBBLICO
1828662S2A-675
Editorial: Giacomettistr. 1, 3000 BERN 31
Tel: 31 3509111
Email: publishing@srg-ssr.ch **Web site:** http://www.srg-ssr.ch
Freq: Annual; **Cover Price:** Free; **Circ:** 800
Editor: Dominic Witschi
Profile: Publication of the SRG SSR company.
Language(s): Italian

SFA/ISPA CONTACT
1648599S56B-640
Editorial: 14, av. Ruchonnet, 1001 LAUSANNE
Tel: 21 3212974 **Fax:** 21 3212940
Email: info@sfa-ispa.ch **Web site:** http://www.sfa-ispa.ch
Freq: Quarterly; **Annual Sub.:** CHF 12,00; **Circ:** 80,000
Editor: Monique Helfer
Language(s): French; German
ADVERTISING RATES:
Full Page Mono .... CHF 1500
BUSINESS: HEALTH & MEDICAL: Nursing

SHAB.CH SCHWEIZERISCHES HANDELSAMTSBLATT FOSC.CH FEUILLE OFFICIELLE SUISSE DU COMMERCE FUSC.CH FOGLIO UFFICIALE SVIZZERO DI COMMERCIO
1643919S14A-1168
Editorial: Effingerstr. 1, 3001 BERN **Tel:** 31 3240992
Fax: 31 3240961
Email: markus.tanner@seco.admin.ch **Web site:** http://www.shab.ch
Freq: 252 issues yearly; **Annual Sub.:** CHF 150,00; **Circ:** 8,000
Editor: Markus Tanner
Profile: National official paper.
Language(s): French; German; Italian
Mechanical Data: Type Area: 435 x 288 mm, No. of Columns (Display): 10, Col Widths (Display): 27 mm
Copy instructions: *Copy Date:* 2 days prior to publication
Official Journal of: Organ d. Eidgenossenschaft
BUSINESS: COMMERCE, INDUSTRY & MANAGEMENT

SHOP AKTUELL
1856013S14A-1338
Editorial: Suhrer Str. 57, 5036 OBERENTFELDEN
Tel: 62 7372525 **Fax:** 62 7372550
Email: usco@umdasch.com **Web site:** http://www.umdasch-shop-concept.com
Freq: 6 issues yearly; **Cover Price:** CHF 9,00
Free to qualifying individuals ; **Circ:** 10,000
Profile: Company publication.
Language(s): English; German

SHR SCHWEIZER HOLZ-REVUE
1642223S46-7
Editorial: Postfach 940, 4142 MÜNCHENSTEIN 1
Tel: 61 3381638 **Fax:** 61 3381600
Email: holzrevue@laupper.ch **Web site:** http://www.holzrevue.ch
Freq: 8 issues yearly; **Annual Sub.:** CHF 48,00; **Circ:** 6,850
Editor: Laura Luthiger

Profile: Magazine for the wood processing and associated business.
Language(s): German
ADVERTISING RATES:
Full Page Mono .... CHF 1925
Full Page Colour .... CHF 2525
Mechanical Data: Type Area: 275 x 185 mm, No. of Columns (Display): 4, Col Widths (Display): 44 mm
Copy instructions: *Copy Date:* 25 days prior to publication

SICHER LEBEN 1855872S14A-1333
Editorial: Maulbeerstr. 14, 3011 BERN
Tel: 31 3055566
Email: sicherleben@bfu.ch **Web site:** http://www.bfu.ch
Freq: Quarterly; **Circ:** 9,200
Editor: Ursula Marti
Profile: Magazine about accident prevention.
Language(s): German

SICHERHEIT SÉCURITÉ SICUREZZA 1640985S54B-5
Editorial: Nüschelerstr. 45, 8001 ZÜRICH
Tel: 44 2174327 **Fax:** 44 2117030
Email: safety@swissi.ch **Web site:** http://www.swissi.ch
Freq: Quarterly; **Annual Sub.:** CHF 95,00; **Circ:** 5,000
Editor: Christian Jaberg
Profile: Magazine with information about fire, explosions, environment, burglary and thievery protection, work security and health protection.
Language(s): French; German; Italian
ADVERTISING RATES:
Full Page Mono .... CHF 2700
Full Page Colour .... CHF 2700
Mechanical Data: Type Area: 253 x 177 mm
Copy instructions: *Copy Date:* 31 days prior to publication
BUSINESS: SAFETY & SECURITY: Safety

SICHERHEIT SFORUM 1648511S14A-1178
Editorial: Tägernstr. 1, 8127 FORCH **Tel:** 43 3662020
Fax: 43 3662030
Email: info@mediasec.ch **Web site:** http://www.sicherheitsforum.ch
Freq: 6 issues yearly; **Annual Sub.:** CHF 142,00; **Circ:** 4,000
Editor: Urs Häni; **Advertising Manager:** Cristian Sina
Profile: Magazine about security.
Language(s): German
ADVERTISING RATES:
Full Page Mono .... CHF 2700
Full Page Colour .... CHF 4140
Mechanical Data: Type Area: 266 x 187 mm, No. of Columns (Display): 3, Col Widths (Display): 55 mm
Copy instructions: *Copy Date:* 39 days prior to publication

SICHERHEITSPOLITIK 1855868S14A-1332
Editorial: Stüsslingerstr. 1, 4654 LOSTORF
Tel: 62 2980157 **Fax:** 62 2980156
Email: kamber@kambermedia.ch **Web site:** http://www.sicherheitspolitik.ch
Freq: 6 issues yearly; **Annual Sub.:** CHF 160,00; **Circ:** 4,000
Editor: Dominik I. Kamber
Profile: Information about safety policy in administrations, economy and population.
Language(s): German
ADVERTISING RATES:
Full Page Mono .... CHF 2100
Full Page Colour .... CHF 2900
Mechanical Data: Type Area: 275 x 185 mm, No. of Columns (Display): 2, Col Widths (Display): 90 mm
Copy instructions: *Copy Date:* 18 days prior to publication

SIGRISTEN-VERBAND AKTUELL 1655273S87-2807
Editorial: Trislerstr. 15, 8952 SCHLIEREN
Tel: 44 7344012 **Fax:** 44 7344007
Email: red.sigrist@hispeed.ch **Web site:** http://www.sigristen.ch
Freq: 6 issues yearly; Free to qualifying individuals
Annual Sub.: CHF 30,00; **Circ:** 1,300
Editor: Ursula Räbsamen; **Advertising Manager:** Bruno Lüscher
Profile: Christian magazine.
Language(s): German
ADVERTISING RATES:
Full Page Mono .... CHF 268
Full Page Colour .... CHF 600
Mechanical Data: Type Area: 170 x 115 mm
Copy instructions: *Copy Date:* 33 days prior to publication
CONSUMER: RELIGIOUS

SIR MEDICAL 765073S5-164
Editorial: Steinenvorstadt 33, 4001 BASEL
Tel: 61 5350911 **Fax:** 4161 5356820
Email: redaktion@med-ict.ch **Web site:** http://www.med-ict.ch
Freq: 6 issues yearly; **Annual Sub.:** CHF 40,00; **Circ:** 10,000
Editor: Thomas Wacker
Language(s): German
ADVERTISING RATES:
Full Page Mono .... CHF 5000
Full Page Colour .... CHF 5000
Mechanical Data: Type Area: 240 x 180 mm
BUSINESS: COMPUTERS & AUTOMATION

SJZ SCHWEIZERISCHE JURISTEN-ZEITUNG REVUE SUISSE DE JURISPRUDENCE 1641043S1A-278
Editorial: Zwingliplatz 2, 8022 ZÜRICH
Tel: 44 2002999 **Fax:** 44 2002908
Email: schulthess@schulthess.com **Web site:** http://www.schulthess.com
Freq: 24 issues yearly; **Annual Sub.:** CHF 189,00; **Circ:** 3,600
Editor: Gaudenz Zindel
Profile: Magazine about company, corporate, antitrust and financial law.
Language(s): French; German
ADVERTISING RATES:
Full Page Mono .... CHF 1330
Full Page Colour .... CHF 2960
Mechanical Data: Type Area: 230 x 167 mm, No. of Columns (Display): 2, Col Widths (Display): 81 mm
Copy instructions: *Copy Date:* 17 days prior to publication
BUSINESS: FINANCE & ECONOMICS

SKO ASC ASQ LEADER 1772707S14A-1212
Editorial: Schaffhauser Str. 2, 8006 ZÜRICH
Tel: 43 3005054 **Fax:** 43 3005051
Email: leader@sko.ch **Web site:** http://www.sko.ch/de/leader
Freq: 5 issues yearly; Free to qualifying individuals ; **Circ:** 13,000
Editor: Petra Kalchofner; **Advertising Manager:** Jeannette Häsler
Profile: Magazine for managers and experts.
Language(s): French; German
ADVERTISING RATES:
Full Page Mono .... CHF 2200
Full Page Colour .... CHF 3500
Mechanical Data: Type Area: 265 x 186 mm, No. of Columns (Display): 3, Col Widths (Display): 59 mm
BUSINESS: COMMERCE, INDUSTRY & MANAGEMENT

SKO ASC ASQ LEADER SPEZIAL 1985657S14A-1364
Editorial: Schaffhauser Str. 2, 8006 ZÜRICH
Tel: 43 3005054 **Fax:** 43 3005051
Email: leader@sko.ch **Web site:** http://www.sko.ch/de/leader
Freq: Annual; **Cover Price:** Free; **Circ:** 128,500
Editor: Petra Kalchofner; **Advertising Manager:** Jeannette Häsler
Profile: Magazine for managers and experts.
Language(s): French; German
ADVERTISING RATES:
Full Page Mono .... CHF 4000
Full Page Colour .... CHF 5500
Mechanical Data: Type Area: 258 x 186 mm, No. of Columns (Display): 3, Col Widths (Display): 58 mm
Supplement to: Handelszeitung & The Wall Street Journal, io new management, Schweizer Bank, Schweizer Versicherung, stocks

SKR DIE SCHWEIZERISCHE KOMMUNAL-REVUE 765879S32A-453
Editorial: Schützenmattstr. 39a, 4051 BASEL
Tel: 61 2050380 **Fax:** 61 2050381
Email: lmbu@fachpresse.com **Web site:** http://www.fachpresse.com
Freq: Quarterly; **Annual Sub.:** CHF 39,00; **Circ:** 12,000
Editor: Liévin M'Bu
Profile: Magazine for supply departments of public administrations.
Language(s): German
ADVERTISING RATES:
Full Page Mono .... CHF 5050
Full Page Colour .... CHF 5500
Mechanical Data: Type Area: 260 x 186 mm
BUSINESS: LOCAL GOVERNMENT, LEISURE & RECREATION: Local Government

SKYNEWS.CH 1663229S6A-377
Editorial: Oberteufenerstr. 58, 8428 TEUFEN
Tel: 44 8817261 **Fax:** 44 8817263
Email: info@skynews.ch **Web site:** http://www.skynews.ch
Freq: Monthly; **Annual Sub.:** CHF 79,00; **Circ:** 8,000
Editor: Hansjörg Bürgi
Language(s): German
ADVERTISING RATES:
Full Page Mono .... CHF 2700
Full Page Colour .... CHF 2700
Mechanical Data: Type Area: 261 x 187 mm
Copy instructions: *Copy Date:* 10 days prior to publication
BUSINESS: AVIATION & AERONAUTICS

SMF SCHWEIZERISCHES MEDIZIN-FORUM SWISS MEDICAL FORUM FMS FORUM MÉDICAL SUISSE 744108S56A-1780
Editorial: Farnsburger Str. 8, 4132 MUTTENZ
Tel: 61 4678551 **Fax:** 61 4678556
Email: verlag@emh.ch **Web site:** http://www.medicalforum.ch
Freq: Weekly; **Annual Sub.:** CHF 175,00; **Circ:** 35,400
Editor: Reto Krapf; **Advertising Manager:** Ariane Furrer
Profile: Magazine on further education of physical doctors in Switzerland.
Language(s): German
ADVERTISING RATES:
Full Page Mono .... CHF 3300
Full Page Colour .... CHF 5550
Mechanical Data: Type Area: 268 x 186 mm
Copy instructions: *Copy Date:* 14 days prior to publication

SMM GUIDE MSM GUIDE 1842255S19E-196
Editorial: Seestr. 95, 8800 THALWIL **Tel:** 44 7227791
Fax: 44 7227701
Email: matthias_boehm@vogel-media.ch **Web site:** http://www.ssmguide.ch
Freq: Annual; **Cover Price:** CHF 20,00; **Circ:** 8,000
Editor: Matthias Böhm; **Advertising Manager:** Trudi Halama
Profile: Technical magazine for the Swiss machine industry.
Language(s): French; German
ADVERTISING RATES:
Full Page Mono .... CHF 3517
Full Page Colour .... CHF 5162
Mechanical Data: Type Area: 267 x 185 mm, No. of Columns (Display): 3, Col Widths (Display): 59 mm
Copy instructions: *Copy Date:* 51 days prior to publication

SMM SCHWEIZER MASCHINENMARKT 1842254S19E-195
Editorial: Seestr. 95, 8800 THALWIL **Tel:** 44 7227791
Fax: 44 7201078
Email: matthias_boehm@vogel-media.ch **Web site:** http://www.smm.ch
Freq: 24 issues yearly; **Annual Sub.:** CHF 160,00; **Circ:** 14,400
Editor: Matthias Böhm; **Advertising Manager:** Trude Halama
Profile: Contents: Technical articles, case studies, current reports on all major trade fairs at home and abroad, latest product news, current industry news. Editorial expertise: All editors of the SMM have a sound technical and / or business training at a university or college. Along with a permanent training in journalism, they guarantee a technically correct and pleasing journalistic reporting.
Language(s): German
ADVERTISING RATES:
Full Page Mono .... CHF 3517
Full Page Colour .... CHF 5162
Mechanical Data: Type Area: 267 x 185 mm, No. of Columns (Display): 3, Col Widths (Display): 59 mm
Copy instructions: *Copy Date:* 14 days prior to publication

S'MOTO 1853649S77A-130
Editorial: Hauptstr. 28, 5113 HOLDERBANK
Fax: 62 5341008
Email: smoto@hispeed.ch **Web site:** http://www.fam-amv.ch
Freq: Quarterly; **Circ:** 3,000
Profile: Classic motorcycle club magazine with internal information.
Language(s): French; German; Italian

SOCIETY 1985669S73-401
Editorial: Seewenweg 5, 4153 REINACH
Tel: 61 6907777 **Fax:** 61 6907788
Email: info@swissbusiness-society.ch **Web site:** http://www.swissbusiness-society.ch
Freq: Quarterly; **Annual Sub.:** CHF 58,00; **Circ:** 10,000
Editor: Robert Gloor; **Advertising Manager:** Robert Gloor
Profile: Business & Lifestyle for Top Management.
Language(s): English
ADVERTISING RATES:
Full Page Mono .... CHF 6900
Full Page Colour .... CHF 6900
Mechanical Data: Type Area: 297 x 210 mm
Copy instructions: *Copy Date:* 14 days prior to publication

SOLOTHURNER ZEITUNG SZ 742132S67B-2360
Editorial: Zuchwiler Str. 21, 4501 SOLOTHURN
Tel: 32 6247474 **Fax:** 32 6247788
Email: info@szonline.ch **Web site:** http://www.szonline.ch
Freq: 312 issues yearly; **Annual Sub.:** CHF 369,00; **Circ:** 35,681
Editor: Theodor Eckert
Profile: Regional daily newspaper covering politics, economics, sport, travel, technology and the arts.
Language(s): German
ADVERTISING RATES:
SCC .... CHF 45,50
Mechanical Data: Type Area: 430 x 290 mm, No. of Columns (Display): 10, Col Widths (Display): 26 mm
Copy instructions: *Copy Date:* 1 day prior to publication
REGIONAL DAILY & SUNDAY NEWSPAPERS: Regional Daily Newspapers

SOLUTIONS 1855884S14A-1334
Editorial: Culmannstr. 37, 8006 ZÜRICH
Tel: 44 2458585 **Fax:** 44 2458595
Email: info@finesolutions.ch **Web site:** http://www.finesolutions.ch
Freq: Annual; **Circ:** 4,500
Profile: Customer magazine from the logistics service provider FineSolutions AG.
Language(s): German

SONNTAG 742155S87-2380
Editorial: Neuenhofer Str. 101, 5401 BADEN
Tel: 56 2032200 **Fax:** 56 2032299
Email: redaktion@dersonntag.ch **Web site:** http://www.dersonntag.ch
Freq: Weekly; **Annual Sub.:** CHF 205,75; **Circ:** 35,050
Editor: Thomas Schnelling
Profile: Catholic family magazine.
Language(s): German
ADVERTISING RATES:
Full Page Mono .... CHF 4600
Full Page Colour .... CHF 4600
Mechanical Data: Type Area: 265 x 190 mm, No. of Columns (Display): 4, Col Widths (Display): 45 mm
Copy instructions: *Copy Date:* 10 days prior to publication
Supplement(s): TV täglich
CONSUMER: RELIGIOUS

SONNTAGS BLICK 742190S72-7700
Editorial: Dufourstr. 23, 8008 ZÜRICH
Tel: 44 2596464 **Fax:** 44 2518006
Email: sobli@ringier.ch **Web site:** http://www.sonntagsblick.ch
Freq: Weekly; **Annual Sub.:** CHF 164,00; **Circ:** 247,449
Editor: Karsten Witzmann; **News Editor:** Silvana Guanziroli
Profile: National weekly covering politics, economics, sport, travel, technology and the arts.
Language(s): German
Mechanical Data: Type Area: 290 x 204 mm
Copy instructions: *Copy Date:* 9 days prior to publication
Supplement(s): Ferien Post
LOCAL NEWSPAPERS

SONNTAGS ZEITUNG 742224S72-7720
Editorial: Werdstr. 21, 8004 ZÜRICH **Tel:** 44 2484040
Fax: 44 2484748
Email: redaktion@sonntagszeitung.ch **Web site:** http://www.sonntagszeitung.ch
Freq: Weekly; **Annual Sub.:** CHF 169,00; **Circ:** 194,764
Editor: Martin Spieler; **News Editor:** Oliver Zihlmann;
Advertising Manager: Adriano Valeri
Profile: Regional weekly covering politics, economics, sport, travel, technology and the arts.
Language(s): German
Readership: Read by company directors, senior managers, office personnel, skilled workers and university students.
ADVERTISING RATES:
SCC .... CHF 271,30
Mechanical Data: Type Area: 440 x 296 mm, No. of Columns (Display): 10, Col Widths (Display): 26 mm
Copy instructions: *Copy Date:* 4 days prior to publication
Supplement(s): Alpha; more; Neue Energie für die Schweiz
LOCAL NEWSPAPERS

SPEKTRUM GEBÄUDETECHNIK 764413S17-162
Editorial: Bollackerweg 2, 5024 KÜTTIGEN
Tel: 62 8398075 **Fax:** 62 8274501
Email: rudolf.bolliger@robe-verlag.ch **Web site:** http://www.robe-verlag.ch
Freq: 6 issues yearly; **Annual Sub.:** CHF 75,00; **Circ:** 8,500
Editor: Rudolf Bolliger; **Advertising Manager:** Hans-Peter Christ
Profile: Magazine about building equipment, automation and maintenance.
Language(s): German
ADVERTISING RATES:
Full Page Mono .... CHF 2800
Full Page Colour .... CHF 4120
Mechanical Data: Type Area: 264 x 184 mm
Copy instructions: *Copy Date:* 30 days prior to publication

SPI SWISSPACK INTERNATIONAL 1656318S10-47
Editorial: Herrligstr. 35, 8048 ZÜRICH
Tel: 44 4316445 **Fax:** 44 4316497
Email: info@swisspack.ch **Web site:** http://www.swisspack.ch
Freq: 5 issues yearly; **Annual Sub.:** CHF 30,00; **Circ:** 4,390

Editor: Peter Senecky
Profile: Magazine about packaging, elevation technologies, storage technologies, logistics and trade.
Language(s): German
ADVERTISING RATES:
Full Page Mono .... CHF 2290
Full Page Colour .... CHF 3310
Mechanical Data: Type Area: 254 x 175 mm, No. of Columns (Display): 3, Col Widths (Display): 55 mm
Copy instructions: *Copy Date:* 14 days prior to publication

ST. GALLER BAUER 1656025S21A-596
Editorial: Magdenauer Str. 2, 9230 FLAWIL
Tel: 71 3946015 **Fax:** 71 3936019
Email: redaktion@sgbauer.ch **Web site:** http://www.bauern-sg.ch
Freq: Weekly; **Annual Sub.:** CHF 96,00; **Circ:** 11,317
Editor: Doris Ammann-Süess
Profile: Official publication of the St. Gallische Farmers' Association.
Language(s): German
ADVERTISING RATES:
Full Page Mono .... CHF 1400
Full Page Colour .... CHF 2016
Mechanical Data: Type Area: 200 x 133 mm, No. of Columns (Display): 4, Col Widths (Display): 32 mm
Copy instructions: *Copy Date:* 3 days prior to publication
BUSINESS: AGRICULTURE & FARMING

ST. GALLER TAGBLATT
741056S67B-2380
Editorial: Fürstenlandstr. 122, 9014 ST. GALLEN
Tel: 71 2727711 **Fax:** 71 2727476
Email: zentralredaktion@tagblatt.ch **Web site:** http://www.tagblatt.ch
Freq: 312 issues yearly; **Annual Sub.:** CHF 353,00; **Circ:** 125,500
Editor: Philipp Landmark; **News Editor:** Thomas Griesser
Profile: Regional daily newspaper covering politics, economics, sport, travel, technology and the arts.
Language(s): German
ADVERTISING RATES:
SCC .... CHF 131,00
Mechanical Data: Type Area: 438 x 291 mm, No. of Columns (Display): 10, Col Widths (Display): 27 mm
Copy instructions: *Copy Date:* 1 day prior to publication
Supplement(s): NZZ Folio
REGIONAL DAILY & SUNDAY NEWSPAPERS: Regional Daily Newspapers

ST SCHWEIZER TOURISTIK
1852576S50-144
Editorial: Forchstr. 60, 8032 ZÜRICH
Tel: 44 3889977 **Fax:** 44 3803170
Email: thomas.borowski@lzfachverlag.ch **Web site:** http://www.lzfachverlag.ch
Freq: 26 issues yearly; **Annual Sub.:** CHF 96,00; **Circ:** 7,000
Editor: Thomas Borowski; **Advertising Manager:** Nathalie Michelberger
Profile: Magazine for the travel market and the tourism business.
Language(s): German
ADVERTISING RATES:
Full Page Mono .... CHF 4840
Full Page Colour .... CHF 6590
Mechanical Data: Type Area: 260 x 201 mm, No. of Columns (Display): 3, Col Widths (Display): 64 mm
Copy instructions: *Copy Date:* 7 days prior to publication

STADTANZEIGER 1647592S72-9630
Editorial: Ziegelfeldstr. 60, 4601 OLTEN
Tel: 62 2057596 **Fax:** 62 2057586
Email: info@stadtanzeiger-olten.ch **Web site:** http://www.stadtanzeiger-olten.ch
Freq: Weekly; **Cover Price:** Free; **Circ:** 48,000
Profile: Advertising journal (house-to-house) concentrating on local stories.
Language(s): German
ADVERTISING RATES:
Full Page Mono .... CHF 4300
Full Page Colour .... CHF 6000
Mechanical Data: Type Area: 440 x 290 mm, No. of Columns (Display): 10, Col Widths (Display): 26 mm
Copy instructions: *Copy Date:* 1 day prior to publication
LOCAL NEWSPAPERS

STADT-ANZEIGER AARAU
1656473S72-9696
Editorial: Kronenplatz 12, 5600 LENZBURG
Tel: 58 2005802 **Fax:** 58 2005821
Email: hubert.keller@stadtanzeiger-aargau.ch **Web site:** http://www.azag.ch
Freq: Weekly; **Cover Price:** Free; **Circ:** 34,351
Editor: Hubert Keller
Profile: Advertising journal (house-to-house) concentrating on local stories.
Language(s): German
ADVERTISING RATES:
Full Page Mono .... CHF 4048
Full Page Colour .... CHF 4356
Mechanical Data: Type Area: 440 x 290 mm, No. of Columns (Display): 10, Col Widths (Display): 25 mm
Copy instructions: *Copy Date:* 3 days prior to publication
LOCAL NEWSPAPERS

STADT-ANZEIGER BADEN
1656479S72-9699
Editorial: Kronenplatz 12, 5600 LENZBURG
Tel: 58 2005802 **Fax:** 58 2005821
Email: hubert.keller@stadtanzeiger-aargau.ch **Web site:** http://www.azag.ch
Freq: Weekly; **Cover Price:** Free; **Circ:** 45,104
Editor: Hubert Keller
Profile: Advertising journal (house-to-house) concentrating on local stories.
Language(s): German
ADVERTISING RATES:
Full Page Mono .... CHF 4268
Full Page Colour .... CHF 4752
Mechanical Data: Type Area: 440 x 290 mm, No. of Columns (Display): 10, Col Widths (Display): 25 mm
Copy instructions: *Copy Date:* 3 days prior to publication
LOCAL NEWSPAPERS

STAFFLE-BLITZ 1853499S74N-277
Editorial: Staffelnhofstr. 60, 6015 REUSSBÜHL
Tel: 41 2593030 **Fax:** 41 2593039
Email: staffelnhof@littau.ch **Web site:** http://www.littau.ch
Freq: Quarterly; **Circ:** 500
Editor: Werner Steiger
Profile: Newspaper for the Center for the elderly Staffelnhofen.
Language(s): German

STANDPUNKT DER WIRTSCHAFT 1842942S14A-1249
Editorial: Altmarktstr. 96, 4410 LIESTAL
Tel: 61 9276464 **Fax:** 61 9276550
Email: standpunkt@kmu.org **Web site:** http://www.kmu.org
Freq: Monthly; **Circ:** 17,500
Editor: Edi Borer
Profile: Regional business chamber magazine.
Language(s): German

STAR PLUS 1842683S74A-487
Editorial: Bahnhofstr. 111, 9240 UZWIL
Tel: 71 9557711 **Fax:** 71 9557717
Email: christine.greuter@star-plus.ch **Web site:** http://www.star-plus.ch
Freq: Monthly; **Annual Sub.:** CHF 50,00; **Circ:** 50,000
Editor: Christine Greuter
Profile: Swiss event and artists magazine.
Language(s): German
ADVERTISING RATES:
Full Page Mono .... CHF 3490
Full Page Colour .... CHF 3490
Mechanical Data: Type Area: 297 x 210 mm

STEUER REVUE REVUE FISCALE 764061S1A-263
Editorial: Mariahalde 8, 8555 MÜLLHEIM
Tel: 52 7300538 **Fax:** 52 7300539
Freq: 11 issues yearly; **Annual Sub.:** CHF 254,00; **Circ:** 3,400
Editor: Wolfgang Maute; **Advertising Manager:** Petra Schmutz
Profile: Information about Swiss tax law.
Language(s): French; German
ADVERTISING RATES:
Full Page Mono .... CHF 920
Full Page Colour .... CHF 1400
Mechanical Data: Type Area: 170 x 110 mm
Copy instructions: *Copy Date:* 14 days prior to publication
BUSINESS: FINANCE & ECONOMICS

DER STEUERENTSCHEID STE
743349S1M-2
Editorial: Elisabethenstr. 8, 4051 BASEL
Tel: 61 2289070 **Fax:** 61 2989071
Email: zeitschriften@helbing.ch **Web site:** http://www.helbing.ch
Freq: 10 issues yearly; **Annual Sub.:** CHF 359,00; **Circ:** 1,163
Editor: M. Reich
Profile: Publication with information about tax laws.
Language(s): French; German
ADVERTISING RATES:
Full Page Mono .... CHF 1000
Full Page Colour .... CHF 1000
Mechanical Data: Type Area: 265 x 170 mm
Copy instructions: *Copy Date:* 14 days prior to publication
BUSINESS: FINANCE & ECONOMICS: Taxation

STOCKS 743534S1F-200
Editorial: Förrlibuckstr. 70, 8021 ZÜRICH
Tel: 43 4445901 **Fax:** 43 4445937
Email: redaktion@stocks.ch **Web site:** http://www.stocks.ch
Freq: 26 issues yearly; **Annual Sub.:** CHF 135,00; **Circ:** 22,014
Editor: Volker Strohm; **Advertising Manager:** Musti Asaf
Profile: Swiss financial investment magazine.
Language(s): German
ADVERTISING RATES:
Full Page Mono .... CHF 9850
Full Page Colour .... CHF 9850
Mechanical Data: Type Area: 249 x 187 mm, No. of Columns (Display): 4, Col Widths (Display): 43 mm
Copy instructions: *Copy Date:* 8 days prior to publication
Supplement(s): Leader spezial
BUSINESS: FINANCE & ECONOMICS: Investment

STRASSE UND VERKEHR ROUTE ET TRAFIC 1852143S49A-427
Editorial: Sihlquai 255, 8005 ZÜRICH
Tel: 44 2694020 **Fax:** 44 2523130
Email: m.etter@vss.ch **Web site:** http://www.vss.ch
Freq: 10 issues yearly; Free to qualifying individuals
Annual Sub.: CHF 112,65; **Circ:** 3,000
Editor: Martin Etter
Profile: Journal published by the Swiss Association of Road and Traffic Engineers.
Language(s): French; German
ADVERTISING RATES:
Full Page Mono .... CHF 1500
Full Page Colour .... CHF 3000
Mechanical Data: Type Area: 268 x 171 mm

STRASSEN TRANSPORT
764654S49A-384
Editorial: Weissenbühlweg 3, 3007 BERN
Tel: 31 3708542 **Fax:** 31 3708588
Email: e.kartnaller@astag.ch **Web site:** http://www.astag.ch
Freq: 10 issues yearly; **Annual Sub.:** CHF 99,00; **Circ:** 8,000
Editor: Erwin Kartnaller
Profile: Information from the Swiss Association for Commercial Vehicles.
Language(s): French; German; Italian
ADVERTISING RATES:
Full Page Mono .... CHF 3800
Full Page Colour .... CHF 4750
Mechanical Data: Type Area: 277 x 190 mm
Copy instructions: *Copy Date:* 10 days prior to publication

STRASSEN TRANSPORT
764654S49A-436
Editorial: Weissenbühlweg 3, 3007 BERN
Tel: 31 3708542 **Fax:** 31 3708588
Email: e.kartnaller@astag.ch **Web site:** http://www.astag.ch
Freq: 10 issues yearly; **Annual Sub.:** CHF 99,00; **Circ:** 8,000
Editor: Erwin Kartnaller
Profile: Information from the Swiss Association for Commercial Vehicles.
Language(s): French; German; Italian
ADVERTISING RATES:
Full Page Mono .... CHF 3800
Full Page Colour .... CHF 4750
Mechanical Data: Type Area: 277 x 190 mm
Copy instructions: *Copy Date:* 10 days prior to publication

DIE SÜDOSTSCHWEIZ
743938S67B-2400
Editorial: Comercialstr. 22, 7007 CHUR
Tel: 81 2555050 **Fax:** 81 2555102
Email: zentralredaktion@suedostschweiz.ch **Web site:** http://www.suedostschweiz.ch
Freq: 312 issues yearly; **Circ:** 126,697
Editor: David Sieber
Profile: Regional daily newspaper covering politics, economics, sport, travel, technology and the arts.
Language(s): German
ADVERTISING RATES:
SCC .... CHF 172,70
Mechanical Data: Type Area: 440 x 286 mm, No. of Columns (Display): 10, Col Widths (Display): 25 mm
Copy instructions: *Copy Date:* 2 days prior to publication
Supplement(s): aboplus
REGIONAL DAILY & SUNDAY NEWSPAPERS: Regional Daily Newspapers

SULZER TECHNICAL REVIEW
744365S19R-3
Editorial: Zürcher Str. 14, 8401 WINTERTHUR
Tel: 52 2626554 **Fax:** 52 2620025
Email: sulzertechnicalreview@sulzer.com **Web site:** http://www.sulzer.com/str
Freq: Quarterly; **Annual Sub.:** CHF 70,00; **Circ:** 16,000
Editor: Gabriel Barroso
Profile: Magazine for customers of the Sulzer company.
Language(s): German

SUNNIGI NACHRICHTE
1853508S74N-278
Editorial: Werdstr. 34, 8004 ZÜRICH **Tel:** 44 2418050 **Fax:** 44 2417585
Email: bruno-thomas@bluewin.ch **Web site:** http://www.evergreens.ch
Freq: Quarterly; **Annual Sub.:** CHF 20,00; **Circ:** 2,000
Editor: Bruno-Thomas Eltschinger
Profile: Cultural club magazine with internal information.
Language(s): German

SURSEER WOCHE 744036S72-7980
Editorial: Unterstadt 22, 6210 SURSEE
Tel: 41 9218521 **Fax:** 41 9217533
Email: redaktion@surseerwoche.ch **Web site:** http://www.surseerwoche.ch
Freq: Weekly; **Annual Sub.:** CHF 133,00; **Circ:** 8,528
Editor: Andrea Willimann Misticoni
Profile: Regional weekly covering politics, economics, sport, travel, technology and the arts.
Language(s): German
ADVERTISING RATES:
SCC .... CHF 23,00
Mechanical Data: Type Area: 434 x 286 mm, No. of Columns (Display): 10, Col Widths (Display): 25 mm
Copy instructions: *Copy Date:* 2 days prior to publication
LOCAL NEWSPAPERS

SVS AKTUELL 744062S45A-80
Editorial: Südquaistr. 14, 4019 BASEL
Tel: 61 6312727 **Fax:** 61 6311483
Email: svs@swissonline.ch **Web site:** http://www.svs-online.ch
Freq: 10 issues yearly; Free to qualifying individuals
Annual Sub.: CHF 90,00; **Circ:** 1,200
Editor: André Auderset; **Advertising Manager:** André Auderset
Profile: Magazine about seafaring and harbour and marine business.
Language(s): German
ADVERTISING RATES:
Full Page Mono .... CHF 1800
Full Page Colour .... CHF 1800
Mechanical Data: Type Area: 256 x 170 mm, No. of Columns (Display): 3, Col Widths (Display): 53 mm
Copy instructions: *Copy Date:* 10 days prior to publication
BUSINESS: MARINE & SHIPPING

SWISS AIDS NEWS 1774832S56A-2101
Editorial: Postfach 1118, 8031 ZÜRICH
Tel: 44 4471111 **Fax:** 44 4471112
Email: rainer.kamber@aids.ch **Web site:** http://www.aids.ch
Freq: 6 issues yearly; **Annual Sub.:** CHF 40,00; **Circ:** 5,000
Editor: Rainer Kamber
Profile: magazine provides medical and juristic information about HIV and Aids.
Language(s): French; German

SWISS BANKING YEARBOOK
1750003S1C-44
Editorial: 35, rue des Bains, 1205 GENF
Tel: 22 8099460 **Fax:** 22 7811414
Web site: http://www.promoedition.ch
Freq: Annual; **Cover Price:** CHF 25,00; **Circ:** 22,000
Editor: Véronique Buhlmann
Profile: Bank magazine.
Language(s): English
ADVERTISING RATES:
Full Page Mono .... CHF 8600
Full Page Colour .... CHF 8600
Mechanical Data: Type Area: 270 x 192 mm

SWISS BANKING YEARBOOK
1750003S1C-52
Editorial: 35, rue des Bains, 1205 GENF
Tel: 22 8099460 **Fax:** 22 7811414
Web site: http://www.promoedition.ch
Freq: Annual; **Cover Price:** CHF 25,00; **Circ:** 22,000
Editor: Véronique Buhlmann
Profile: Bank magazine.
Language(s): English
ADVERTISING RATES:
Full Page Mono .... CHF 8600
Full Page Colour .... CHF 8600
Mechanical Data: Type Area: 270 x 192 mm

SWISS CAMION 1859144S49A-432
Editorial: 26, rue de la Chocolatière, 1026 ECHANDENS **Tel:** 21 7062000 **Fax:** 21 7062009
Email: hpsteiner@routiers.ch **Web site:** http://www.routiers.ch
Freq: 11 issues yearly; **Annual Sub.:** CHF 75,00; **Circ:** 11,731
Editor: Hans-Peter Steiner; **Advertising Manager:** Elisabeth Koehli
Profile: Magazine for professional and private drivers and on transport in general.
Language(s): German
ADVERTISING RATES:
Full Page Mono .... CHF 3560
Full Page Colour .... CHF 3560
Mechanical Data: Type Area: 266 x 192 mm
Copy instructions: *Copy Date:* 22 days prior to publication

SWISS ENGINEERING RTS
1623554S14R-608
Editorial: 10, rte. de Châtillon, 2830 COURRENDLIN
Tel: 32 4351772 **Fax:** 32 4351773
Email: r.keller@kbmedien.ch

Freq: 10 issues yearly; **Annual Sub.:** CHF 75,00; **Circ:** 7,400
Editor: Roland Keller
Profile: Engineering magazine.
Language(s): French
ADVERTISING RATES:
Full Page Mono .... CHF 3450
Full Page Colour .... CHF 4500
Mechanical Data: Type Area: 270 x 185 mm
Official Journal of: Organ d. UTS Union Technique Suisse
BUSINESS: COMMERCE, INDUSTRY & MANAGEMENT: Commerce Related

SWISS ENGINEERING STZ
1623555S19A-206
Editorial: Technoparkstr. 1, 8005 ZÜRICH
Tel: 44 4451991 **Fax:** 44 4451992
Email: rosatzin@sprachwerk.ch
Freq: 10 issues yearly; **Annual Sub.:** CHF 85,00; **Circ:** 16,500
Editor: Christa Rosatzin; **Advertising Manager:** Roger Frischknecht
Profile: Magazine focused on technology used in polytechnic engineering.
Language(s): German
ADVERTISING RATES:
Full Page Mono .... CHF 3450
Full Page Colour .... CHF 4500
Mechanical Data: Type Area: 270 x 185 mm
Supplement(s): By Rail.Now!; Plastics.Now!
BUSINESS: ENGINEERING & MACHINERY

SWISS EQUITY MAGAZIN
1643872S1F-255
Editorial: Freigutstr. 26, 8002 ZÜRICH
Tel: 43 3005381 **Fax:** 43 3005388
Email: redaktion@se-medien.ch **Web site:** http://www.se-medien.ch
Freq: 11 issues yearly; **Annual Sub.:** CHF 154,00; **Circ:** 3,500
Editor: Björn Zern; **Advertising Manager:** Stefanie Keusen
Profile: Magazine for financial investors focusing on Swiss joint stock companies.
Language(s): German
ADVERTISING RATES:
Full Page Mono .... CHF 3150
Full Page Colour .... CHF 3150
Mechanical Data: Type Area: 236 x 180 mm, No. of Columns (Display): 3, Col Widths (Display): 57 mm
Copy instructions: *Copy Date:* 10 days prior to publication

SWISS EXPORT JOURNAL
1853510S14C-241
Editorial: Staffelstr. 8, 8045 ZÜRICH **Tel:** 44 2043484
Fax: 44 2043480
Email: redaktion@se-journal.com **Web site:** http://www.se-journal.com
Freq: Quarterly; **Annual Sub.:** CHF 40,00; **Circ:** 40,000
Editor: Claudia Moerker
Profile: Magazine of the Swiss Export Association.
Language(s): English; German
ADVERTISING RATES:
Full Page Mono .... CHF 2950
Full Page Colour .... CHF 3850
Mechanical Data: Type Area: 240 x 170 mm
Copy instructions: *Copy Date:* 15 days prior to publication

SWISS IT RESELLER
1663677S5C-2
Editorial: Seestr. 95, 8800 THALWIL **Tel:** 44 7227700
Fax: 44 7201078
Email: redaktion_it@vogel-media.ch **Web site:** http://www.swissitreseller.ch
Freq: Monthly; **Circ:** 4,500
Editor: Marcel Wüthrich; **Advertising Manager:** Benedikt Bitzi
Profile: Business magazine about PCs and the retail and re-sale of computers.
Language(s): German
ADVERTISING RATES:
Full Page Mono .... CHF 5500
Full Page Colour .... CHF 5500
Mechanical Data: Type Area: 260 x 190 mm, No. of Columns (Display): 4, Col Widths (Display): 44 mm
Copy instructions: *Copy Date:* 10 days prior to publication

SWISS IT RESELLER
1663677S43A-2
Editorial: Seestr. 95, 8800 THALWIL **Tel:** 44 7227700
Fax: 44 7201078
Email: redaktion_it@vogel-media.ch **Web site:** http://www.swissitreseller.ch
Freq: Monthly; **Circ:** 4,500
Editor: Marcel Wüthrich; **Advertising Manager:** Benedikt Bitzi
Profile: Business magazine about PCs and the retail and re-sale of computers.
Language(s): German
ADVERTISING RATES:
Full Page Mono .... CHF 5500
Full Page Colour .... CHF 5500
Mechanical Data: Type Area: 260 x 190 mm, No. of Columns (Display): 4, Col Widths (Display): 44 mm
Copy instructions: *Copy Date:* 10 days prior to publication

SWISS MEDICAL INFORMATICS
1849053S56A-2152
Editorial: Steinentorstr. 13, 4010 BASEL
Tel: 61 2789565 **Fax:** 61 2789566
Email: verlag@schwabe.ch **Web site:** http://www.schwabe.ch
Freq: 3 issues yearly; Free to qualifying individuals
Annual Sub.: CHF 55,00; **Circ:** 1,000
Editor: Hans Rudolf Straub; **Advertising Manager:** Lydia Zimmer
Profile: Magazine from the Swiss Association of Medical Informatics.
Language(s): English; French; German
ADVERTISING RATES:
Full Page Mono .... CHF 1700
Full Page Colour .... CHF 3200
Mechanical Data: Type Area: 262 x 180 mm
Official Journal of: Organ d. Schweizer. Ges. f. Medizininformatik

SWISS MEDICAL WEEKLY
744110S56A-1820
Editorial: Farnsburger Str. 8, 4132 MUTTENZ
Tel: 61 4678555 **Fax:** 61 4678556
Email: red@smw.ch **Web site:** http://www.smw.ch
Freq: 26 issues yearly; **Annual Sub.:** CHF 150,00; **Circ:** 1,350
Editor: Andreas Schaffner
Profile: General medical journal.
Language(s): English
Readership: Read by members of the medical profession and medical students.
ADVERTISING RATES:
Full Page Mono .... CHF 2000
Full Page Colour .... CHF 3950
Mechanical Data: Type Area: 268 x 186 mm
Copy instructions: *Copy Date:* 22 days prior to publication
Official Journal of: Organ d. Swiss Society of Internal Medicine, d. Swiss Respiratory Society u. d. Swiss Society of Infectious diseases
BUSINESS: HEALTH & MEDICAL

SWISSCLASSICS REVUE
1664151S77A-112
Editorial: Schlyffistr. 21, 8806 FREIENBACH
Tel: 43 8880005 **Fax:** 43 8880946
Email: info@swissclassics.com **Web site:** http://www.swissclassics.com
Freq: Quarterly; **Annual Sub.:** CHF 29,00; **Circ:** 14,000
Editor: Markus Rühle
Profile: Magazine about oldtimer cars.
Language(s): German
ADVERTISING RATES:
Full Page Mono .... CHF 1990
Full Page Colour .... CHF 1990
Mechanical Data: Type Area: 260 x 170 mm, No. of Columns (Display): 3, Col Widths (Display): 40 mm
Copy instructions: *Copy Date:* 30 days prior to publication

SWISSMECHANIC
1859361S17-185
Editorial: Felsenstr. 6, 8570 WEINFELDEN
Tel: 71 6262800 **Fax:** 71 6262809
Email: redaktion@swissmechanic.ch **Web site:** http://www.swissmechanic.ch
Freq: 10 issues yearly; **Annual Sub.:** CHF 80,00; **Circ:** 2,600
Profile: Magazine about mechanics and technology.
Language(s): French; German
ADVERTISING RATES:
Full Page Mono .... CHF 1600
Full Page Colour .... CHF 2100
Mechanical Data: Type Area: 266 x 185 mm
Copy instructions: *Copy Date:* 20 days prior to publication
Official Journal of: Organ d. Schweizer. Verb. mechan.-techn. Betriebe

SWISSPLASTICS
1642210S13-149
Editorial: Neumattstr. 1, 5001 AARAU
Tel: 55 4622451 **Fax:** 58 2005661
Email: irene.portmann@azmedien.ch **Web site:** http://www.swissplastics.ch
Freq: 10 issues yearly; **Annual Sub.:** CHF 96,00; **Circ:** 6,000
Editor: Irene Portmann
Profile: Magazine about producing, processing and applying synthetic materials and new materials.
Language(s): German
ADVERTISING RATES:
Full Page Mono .... CHF 2506
Full Page Colour .... CHF 3580
Mechanical Data: Type Area: 260 x 185 mm, No. of Columns (Display): 4, Col Widths (Display): 43 mm
Copy instructions: *Copy Date:* 21 days prior to publication
BUSINESS: CHEMICALS

SWISSQUOTE
1977071S1F-291
Editorial: 6, rue Abraham-Gevray, 1201 GENF
Tel: 22 9191919 **Fax:** 22 9191918
Email: info@largenetwork.com **Web site:** http://www.swissquote.ch/magazine/d
Freq: 6 issues yearly; **Annual Sub.:** CHF 40,00; **Circ:** 40,000
Editor: Gabriel Sigrist
Profile: Investor magazine of Swissquote Bank.
Language(s): German
ADVERTISING RATES:
Full Page Mono .... CHF 11500
Full Page Colour .... CHF 11500
Mechanical Data: Type Area: 220 x 160 mm
Copy instructions: *Copy Date:* 30 days prior to publication

SYNAPSE
762652S56A-1964
Editorial: Farnsburger Str. 8, 4132 MUTTENZ
Tel: 61 4678555 **Fax:** 61 4678556
Email: synapse@emh.ch **Web site:** http://www.aerzte-bl.ch
Freq: 8 issues yearly; **Annual Sub.:** CHF 50,00; **Circ:** 2,600
Profile: Magazine for physical doctors in the region of Baselland.
Language(s): German
ADVERTISING RATES:
Full Page Mono .... CHF 2550
Full Page Colour .... CHF 3450
Mechanical Data: Type Area: 268 x 186 mm
Official Journal of: Organ d. Ärzteges. Baselland u. d. Medizinische Ges. Ba.

SZIER SCHWEIZERISCHE ZEITSCHRIFT FÜR INTERNATIONALES UND EUROPÄISCHES RECHT RSDIE REVUE SUISSE DE DROIT INTERNATIONAL ET EUROPÉEN
1641041S44-344
Editorial: Zwinglиplatz 2, 8022 ZÜRICH
Tel: 44 2002999 **Fax:** 44 2002908
Email: schulthess@schulthess.com **Web site:** http://www.schulthess.com
Freq: 5 issues yearly; **Annual Sub.:** CHF 250,00; **Circ:** 800
Editor: Richard Schmidt
Profile: Juristical magazine about international and European law.
Language(s): French; German
ADVERTISING RATES:
Full Page Mono .... CHF 680
Mechanical Data: Type Area: 190 x 120 mm
Copy instructions: *Copy Date:* 14 days prior to publication
BUSINESS: LEGAL

TAGBLATT
723326S67B-620
Editorial: Fürstenlandstr. 122, 9014 ST. GALLEN
Tel: 71 2727711 **Fax:** 71 2727476
Email: zentralredaktion@tagblatt.ch **Web site:** http://www.tagblatt.ch
Freq: 312 issues yearly; **Annual Sub.:** CHF 353,00; **Circ:** 12,726
Profile: Daily newspaper with regional news and a local sports section.
Language(s): German
ADVERTISING RATES:
SCC .... CHF 45,40
Mechanical Data: Type Area: 438 x 291 mm, No. of Columns (Display): 10, Col Widths (Display): 27 mm
Copy instructions: *Copy Date:* 1 day prior to publication
REGIONAL DAILY & SUNDAY NEWSPAPERS: Regional Daily Newspapers

TAGES ANZEIGER
744220S67B-2420
Editorial: Werdstr. 21, 8021 ZÜRICH **Tel:** 44 2484411
Fax: 44 2484471
Email: redaktion@tages-anzeiger.ch **Web site:** http://www.tages-anzeiger.ch
Freq: 312 issues yearly; **Annual Sub.:** CHF 364,00; **Circ:** 209,297
Editor: Andreas Strehle; **News Editor:** Dominique Eigenmann; **Advertising Manager:** Andy Bürki
Profile: Tabloid-sized quality newspaper covering regional, national and international news, politics, economics, finance, culture, science and sport.
Language(s): German
Readership: Aimed at senior executives, managers, office personnel and students.
ADVERTISING RATES:
SCC .... CHF 174,60
Mechanical Data: Type Area: 440 x 296 mm, No. of Columns (Display): 10, Col Widths (Display): 26 mm
Copy instructions: *Copy Date:* 2 days prior to publication
Supplement(s): Alpha; BuchJournal Schweiz; Futura; Das Magazin; Neue Energie für die Schweiz; Stellen-Anzeiger; TV täglich; Vista; züritipp
REGIONAL DAILY & SUNDAY NEWSPAPERS: Regional Daily Newspapers

TEC 21
763253S4E-741
Editorial: Staffelstr. 12, 8045 ZÜRICH
Tel: 44 2889060 **Fax:** 44 2889070
Email: tec21@tec21.ch **Web site:** http://www.tec21.ch
Freq: 42 issues yearly; Free to qualifying individuals
Annual Sub.: CHF 280,00; **Circ:** 12,000
Editor: Judith Solt
Profile: Magazine on architecture, engineering and environment.
Language(s): German
ADVERTISING RATES:
Full Page Mono .... CHF 2980
Full Page Colour .... CHF 4180
Mechanical Data: No. of Columns (Display): 3, Col Widths (Display): 60 mm, Type Area: 260 x 188 mm
Copy instructions: *Copy Date:* 12 days prior to publication
Official Journal of: Organ d. Schweizer. Ingenieur- u. Architekten-Vereine, d. Netzwerk d. Absolventinnen u. Absolventen d. ETH Zürich, d. Schweizer. Vereinigung d. Beratender Ingenieure, d. Bund Schweizer Architekten u. d. Association amicale des anciens élèves de l'EPFL

TECHNICA
1626143S19R-2
Editorial: Neumattstr. 1, 5001 AARAU
Tel: 58 2005641 **Fax:** 58 2005661
Email: eugen.albisser@azmedien.ch **Web site:** http://www.technica-online.ch
Freq: Monthly; **Annual Sub.:** CHF 95,00; **Circ:** 10,500
Editor: Eugen Albisser; **Advertising Manager:** Peter Spycher
Profile: Magazine about industrial technology.
Language(s): German
ADVERTISING RATES:
Full Page Mono .... CHF 3190
Full Page Colour .... CHF 4390
Mechanical Data: Type Area: 264 x 184 mm, No. of Columns (Display): 4, Col Widths (Display): 43 mm
Copy instructions: *Copy Date:* 21 days prior to publication
Official Journal of: Organ d. Schweizer. Vereins f. Schweisstechnik
BUSINESS: ENGINEERING & MACHINERY: Engineering Related

TECHNIQUE AGRICOLE
764655S27-146
Editorial: Ausserdorfstr. 31, 5223 RINIKEN
Tel: 56 4511859 **Fax:** 56 4416731
Email: red@agrartechnik.ch **Web site:** http://www.agrartechnik.ch
Freq: 11 issues yearly; Free to qualifying individuals
Annual Sub.: CHF 107,00; **Circ:** 5,000
Editor: Ueli Zweifel
Profile: Magazine about agricultural technologies.
Language(s): French
ADVERTISING RATES:
Full Page Mono .... CHF 1550
Full Page Colour .... CHF 1790
Mechanical Data: Type Area: 261 x 183 mm, No. of Columns (Display): 4, Col Widths (Display): 42 mm
BUSINESS: METAL, IRON & STEEL

TECHNISCHE RUNDSCHAU
745424S14R-540
Editorial: Basler Str. 15, 5080 LAUFENBURG
Tel: 62 8697917 **Fax:** 62 8697901
Email: pmuehlemann@technische-rundschau.ch
Web site: http://www.technische-rundschau.ch
Freq: Monthly; **Annual Sub.:** CHF 148,00; **Circ:** 15,350
Editor: Peter R. Mühlemann; **Advertising Manager:** Udo Oppermann
Profile: Swiss industrial magazine.
Language(s): German
ADVERTISING RATES:
Full Page Mono .... CHF 3388
Full Page Colour .... CHF 4318
Mechanical Data: Type Area: 267 x 185 mm, No. of Columns (Display): 3, Col Widths (Display): 56 mm
Copy instructions: *Copy Date:* 10 days prior to publication
Official Journal of: Organ d. Engineering Workflow Association
BUSINESS: COMMERCE, INDUSTRY & MANAGEMENT: Commerce Related

TECHNO SCOPE
1667997S19A-208
Editorial: Seidengasse 16, 8001 ZÜRICH
Tel: 44 2265011 **Fax:** 44 2265020
Email: redaktion.technoscope@satw.ch **Web site:** http://www.satw.ch
Freq: 3 issues yearly; **Cover Price:** Free; **Circ:** 7,000
Editor: Béatrice Miller
Profile: Magazine about technology.
Language(s): German

TEENSMAG
744399S74F-350
Editorial: Witzbergstr. 7, 8330 PFÄFFIKON
Tel: 43 2888013 **Fax:** 43 2888011
Email: reda@bvmedia.ch **Web site:** http://www.teensmag.net
Freq: 6 issues yearly; **Annual Sub.:** CHF 31,30; **Circ:** 28,000
Editor: Janine Anliker; **Advertising Manager:** Niklaus Mosimann
Profile: Evangelical magazine for teenagers and young people.
Language(s): German
ADVERTISING RATES:
Full Page Mono .... CHF 1833
Full Page Colour .... CHF 2321
Mechanical Data: Type Area: 258 x 188 mm, No. of Columns (Display): 4, Col Widths (Display): 44 mm
Copy instructions: *Copy Date:* 40 days prior to publication
CONSUMER: WOMEN'S INTEREST CONSUMER MAGAZINES: Teenage

TELE
744409S76C-60
Editorial: Förrlibuckstr. 70, 8005 ZÜRICH
Tel: 43 4445540 **Fax:** 43 4445541
Email: gion.stecher@tvzeitschriften.ch **Web site:** http://www.tvzeitschriften.ch

Freq: Weekly; **Annual Sub.:** CHF 169,00; **Circ:** 144,369
Editor: Gion Stecher; **Advertising Manager:** Sandra Peiti
Profile: Magazine containing weekly programme listings, interviews and articles about celebrities, new cinema releases and multimedia issues.
Language(s): German
ADVERTISING RATES:
Full Page Mono .... CHF 15500
Full Page Colour .... CHF 15500
Mechanical Data: Type Area: 261 x 189 mm, No. of Columns (Display): 4, Col Widths (Display): 45 mm
Copy instructions: *Copy Date:* 14 days prior to publication
CONSUMER: MUSIC & PERFORMING ARTS: TV & Radio

LE TEMPS 744461S67B-1740
Editorial: 3, pl. de Cornavin, 1211 GENF 2
Tel: 22 7995858 **Fax:** 22 7995859
Email: info@letemps.ch **Web site:** http://www.letemps.ch
Freq: 312 issues yearly; **Annual Sub.:** CHF 480,00; **Circ:** 45,506
Editor: Pierre Veya
Profile: Tabloid-sized quality newspaper covering a broad range of news and current affairs.
Language(s): French
Readership: Read by company directors, managers, office personnel, civil servants and university students.
ADVERTISING RATES:
SCC .... CHF 108,50
Mechanical Data: Type Area: 440 x 290 mm, No. of Columns (Display): 10, Col Widths (Display): 26 mm
Copy instructions: *Copy Date:* 2 days prior to publication
Supplement(s): TV8
REGIONAL DAILY & SUNDAY NEWSPAPERS: Regional Daily Newspapers

TERTIANUM 1852496S74N-273
Editorial: Seestr. 78, 8267 BERLINGEN
Tel: 52 7625151 **Fax:** 52 7611206
Email: h.bachmaier@tertianum.ch **Web site:** http://www.tertianum.ch
Freq: Quarterly; **Circ:** 15,943
Editor: Helmut Bachmaier; **Advertising Manager:** Ramona Schmidt
Profile: German magazine of the generations.
Language(s): German

TESSINER ZEITUNG MIT AGENDA 744492S67B-2440
Editorial: via Luini, 19, 6601 LOCARNO
Tel: 91 7562460 **Fax:** 91 7562479
Email: tz@tessinerzeitung.ch **Web site:** http://www.tessinerzeitung.ch
Freq: Weekly; **Annual Sub.:** CHF 139,00; **Circ:** 7,852
Editor: Marianne Baltisberger
Profile: Magazine for holiday guests and holiday house owners in the Ticino canton.
Language(s): German
ADVERTISING RATES:
SCC .... CHF 29,80
Mechanical Data: Type Area: 440 x 289 mm, No. of Columns (Display): 10, Col Widths (Display): 25 mm
Copy instructions: *Copy Date:* 2 days prior to publication
Supplement(s): ticinosette; TV täglich
REGIONAL DAILY & SUNDAY NEWSPAPERS: Regional Daily Newspapers

THEMA UMWELT 744632S57-480
Editorial: Hottingerstr. 4, 8024 ZÜRICH
Tel: 44 2674411 **Fax:** 44 2674414
Email: mail@umweltschutz.ch **Web site:** http://www.umweltschutz.ch
Freq: Quarterly; Free to qualifying individuals
Annual Sub.: CHF 50,00; **Circ:** 2,300
Editor: Ion Karagounis
Profile: Magazine focusing on environmental problems, presents solutions to decision makers in public institutions.
Language(s): German
Readership: Aimed at directors in municipal government, local authority members, politicians and administration secretaries.
BUSINESS: ENVIRONMENT & POLLUTION

THERAPEUTISCHE UMSCHAU 1853280S56A-2188
Editorial: Länggassstr. 76, 3000 BERN 9
Tel: 31 3004569 **Fax:** 31 3004591
Email: verlag@hanshuber.com **Web site:** http://www.therapeutischeumschau.ch
Freq: Monthly; **Annual Sub.:** CHF 179,00; **Circ:** 2,400
Editor: W. Reinhart; **Advertising Manager:** H.R. Schindler
Profile: Magazine for physical doctors.
Language(s): German
ADVERTISING RATES:
Full Page Mono .... CHF 1820
Full Page Colour .... CHF 3080
Mechanical Data: Type Area: 262 x 160 mm

THERAPIE FAMILIALE 1853372S56A-2197
Editorial: 46, ch. de la Mousse, 1225 CHÊNE-BOURG **Tel:** 22 7029311 **Fax:** 22 7029355
Email: administration@medhyg.ch **Web site:** http://www.medecinehygiene.ch
Freq: Quarterly; **Annual Sub.:** CHF 92,00; **Circ:** 2,000
Editor: Brigitte Waternaux
Profile: Magazine about family therapy.
Language(s): French

THURGAUER BAUER 763315S21J-1
Editorial: Industriestr. 9, 8570 WEINFELDEN
Tel: 71 6262888 **Fax:** 71 6262889
Email: thurgauer.bauer@vtgl.ch **Web site:** http://www.vtgl.ch
Freq: Weekly; **Annual Sub.:** CHF 74,00; **Circ:** 4,100
Editor: Hermine Hascher; **Advertising Manager:** Hanni Hächler
Profile: Magazine for farmers in the Thurgau region.
Language(s): German
ADVERTISING RATES:
Full Page Mono .... CHF 736
Full Page Colour .... CHF 1440
Mechanical Data: Type Area: 200 x 126 mm
Copy instructions: *Copy Date:* 3 days prior to publication
BUSINESS: AGRICULTURE & FARMING: Agriculture & Farming - Regional

THURGAUER ZEITUNG 744711S67B-2540
Editorial: Promenadenstr. 16, 8500 FRAUENFELD
Tel: 52 7235757 **Fax:** 52 7235707
Email: redaktion@thurgauerzeitung.ch **Web site:** http://www.thurgauerzeitung.ch
Freq: 312 issues yearly; **Annual Sub.:** CHF 359,00; **Circ:** 44,000
Advertising Manager: Daniel Schneider
Profile: Regional daily newspaper covering politics, economics, sport, travel, technology and the arts.
Language(s): German
ADVERTISING RATES:
SCC .... CHF 54,60
Mechanical Data: Type Area: 438 x 291 mm, No. of Columns (Display): 10, Col Widths (Display): 27 mm
Copy instructions: *Copy Date:* 1 day prior to publication
Supplement(s): TV täglich; Vista
REGIONAL DAILY & SUNDAY NEWSPAPERS: Regional Daily Newspapers

TICINO BUSINESS 1655951S17-169
Editorial: Corso Elvezia, 16, 6900 LUGANO
Tel: 91 9115132 **Fax:** 91 9115112
Email: pantini@cci.ch **Web site:** http://www.cciati.ch
Freq: 10 issues yearly; **Annual Sub.:** CHF 50,00; **Circ:** 2,500
Editor: Lisa Pantini
Profile: Magazine about electro technology and installation.
Language(s): Italian
ADVERTISING RATES:
Full Page Mono .... CHF 1200
Full Page Colour .... CHF 1600
Mechanical Data: Type Area: 260 x 180 mm
Copy instructions: *Copy Date:* 14 days prior to publication

TICINO MANAGEMENT 1852501S14A-1279
Editorial: via Vergiò, 8, 6932 BREGANZONA
Tel: 91 6102929 **Fax:** 91 6102910
Email: redazione@ticinomanagement.ch **Web site:** http://www.ticinomanagement.ch
Freq: 11 issues yearly; **Annual Sub.:** CHF 100,00; **Circ:** 19,960
Editor: Alberto Pattono; **Advertising Manager:** Valerio De Giorgi
Profile: Economics magazine.
Language(s): Italian
ADVERTISING RATES:
Full Page Mono .... CHF 3430
Full Page Colour .... CHF 4915
Mechanical Data: Type Area: 252 x 178 mm, No. of Columns (Display): 3, Col Widths (Display): 54 mm
Copy instructions: *Copy Date:* 15 days prior to publication

TIR TRANSNEWS 763063S49A-381
Editorial: Europastr. 15, 8152 GLATTBRUGG
Tel: 58 3449002 **Fax:** 58 3449001
Email: henrik.petro@motormedia.ch **Web site:** http://www.tir.ch
Freq: 11 issues yearly; **Annual Sub.:** CHF 95,00; **Circ:** 7,000
Editor: Henrik Petro; **Advertising Manager:** Herta Kornetzky
Profile: Journal on commercial vehicles.
Language(s): German
ADVERTISING RATES:
Full Page Colour .... CHF 3910
Mechanical Data: Type Area: 265 x 192 mm, No. of Columns (Display): 3, Col Widths (Display): 61 mm
Copy instructions: *Copy Date:* 15 days prior to publication
Official Journal of: Organ d. Schweizer. Fahrzeugflottenbesitzer-Verb.
BUSINESS: TRANSPORT

TOGGENBURGER NACHRICHTEN UND "OBERTOGGENBURGER WOCHENBLATT" 745065S67B-2580
Editorial: Sonneggstr. 28, 9642 EBNAT-KAPPEL
Tel: 71 9926022 **Fax:** 71 9926021
Email: info@toggenburgernachrichten.ch **Web site:** http://www.toggenburgernachrichten.ch
Freq: 104 issues yearly; **Annual Sub.:** CHF 118,00; **Circ:** 4,400
Editor: Elisabeth Scherrer; **Advertising Manager:** Marcel Bornhauser
Profile: Regional daily newspaper covering politics, economics, sport, travel, technology and the arts.
Language(s): German
ADVERTISING RATES:
SCC .... CHF 29,00
Mechanical Data: Type Area: 438 x 291 mm, No. of Columns (Display): 10, Col Widths (Display): 27 mm
Copy instructions: *Copy Date:* 1 day prior to publication
REGIONAL DAILY & SUNDAY NEWSPAPERS: Regional Daily Newspapers

TOP 745201S14R-520
Editorial: Förrlibuckstr. 70, 8021 ZÜRICH
Tel: 43 4445900 **Fax:** 43 4445932
Email: redaktion@handelszeitung.ch **Web site:** http://www.handelszeitung.ch
Freq: Annual; **Cover Price:** CHF 69,00; **Circ:** 10,000
Editor: Martin Spieler
Profile: Mercantile and telephone directory.
Language(s): German
ADVERTISING RATES:
Full Page Colour .... CHF 5000
Mechanical Data: Type Area: 275 x 185 mm
Copy instructions: *Copy Date:* 60 days prior to publication
BUSINESS: COMMERCE, INDUSTRY & MANAGEMENT: Commerce Related

TOP INFORMATIONEN 1856055S14A-1339
Editorial: Postfach 2114, 5430 WETTINGEN
Tel: 56 4371916 **Fax:** 56 4371910
Email: info@kvagost.ch **Web site:** http://www.kvschweiz.ch/aargau-ost
Freq: Quarterly; Free to qualifying individuals ; **Circ:** 1,280
Editor: Silvia Vogt
Profile: Member magazine from the Commercial Association Aargau Ost.
Language(s): German

TOP KÖCHE GRAUBÜNDEN 1842945S74P-285
Editorial: Rancho, 7031 LAAX **Tel:** 79 6813181
Email: rchatelain@exclusiv.ch **Web site:** http://www.exclusiv.ch
Freq: Annual; **Cover Price:** CHF 12,00; **Circ:** 20,000
Editor: René Chatelain
Profile: Regional gastronomy magazine.
Language(s): German
ADVERTISING RATES:
Full Page Mono .... CHF 3080
Full Page Colour .... CHF 3080
Mechanical Data: Type Area: 266 x 192 mm, No. of Columns (Display): 2, Col Widths (Display): 93 mm
Copy instructions: *Copy Date:* 30 days prior to publication

DER TÖSSTHALER 745060S67B-2620
Editorial: Tösstalstr. 74, 8488 TURBENTHAL
Tel: 52 3852090 **Fax:** 52 3852901
Email: redaktion@toessthaler.ch **Web site:** http://www.toessthaler.ch
Freq: 156 issues yearly; **Annual Sub.:** CHF 118,00; **Circ:** 4,286
Editor: Hanspeter Blattmann; **Advertising Manager:** Luzia Diggelmann
Profile: Regional daily newspaper covering politics, economics, sport, travel, technology and the arts.
Language(s): German
ADVERTISING RATES:
SCC .... CHF 28,90
Mechanical Data: Type Area: 429 x 287 mm, No. of Columns (Display): 10, Col Widths (Display): 26 mm
Copy instructions: *Copy Date:* 2 days prior to publication
REGIONAL DAILY & SUNDAY NEWSPAPERS: Regional Daily Newspapers

TOUR 1859298S49A-435
Editorial: Dählhölzliweg 12, 3000 BERN 6
Tel: 31 3592323 **Fax:** 31 3592310
Email: info@voev.ch **Web site:** http://www.voev.ch
Freq: Annual; **Cover Price:** Free; **Circ:** 5,500
Advertising Manager: Urs Rölli
Profile: Magazine from the Swiss Association for Public Transport.
Language(s): French; German
ADVERTISING RATES:
Full Page Mono .... CHF 4950
Full Page Colour .... CHF 4950
Mechanical Data: Type Area: 248 x 176 mm, No. of Columns (Display): 2, Col Widths (Display): 90 mm
Copy instructions: *Copy Date:* 41 days prior to publication

TOURBILLON 2097101S74A-532
Editorial: Heinestr. 17, 9008 ST. GALLEN
Tel: 71 2456362 **Fax:** 71 2454127
Email: redaktion@tourbillon-magazin.ch **Web site:** http://www.tourbillon-magazin.ch
Freq: Quarterly; **Cover Price:** CHF 40,00; **Circ:** 40,000
Editor: Karl Heinz Nuber
Profile: Tourbillon - the "Swiss Made" watches magazine draws on the first and only German-speaking Swiss consumer magazine that amplifies visible interest in luxury Swiss watches, which is especially mechanical watches in the upper price segment: the tourbillon, the pinnacle of Swiss watchmaking, new releases and proven classics of recent years. An editorial portion guides the reader with brief information in the world of luxury watches, the rich and famous. What events took place where? Which watch maker has what, how and where to launch? Where do which watch brand, has opened a new shop? Who wears what at what time Clock? In fast forward, the reader information shortly and will be more aware of the upcoming topics in the magazine content. Corporate Information characterize the contents of chapter business. Connected with a cover story, which is the focus of this section and portätiert always a personality in the watch industry. The focus is always on the person - down - the makers of the Swiss watch industry. Another constant in this chapter is the statement by Jean-Daniel Pasche, president of the Swiss Watch Federation (FHS), and various economic, market and press worldwide. Product-related information, new developments in the watch industry, book tips, and other topics are in the foreground. This chapter is accompanied by a statement from each André Hirschi, president of the Association VSGU Swiss goldsmith and watch retailers. In the editorial section, "lifestyle" find the consumer world of the luxury goods industry continued. The clock as a central issue should not be considered in isolation, it is always a complementary part of the lifestyle. From the purely functional to the state's Accessories and conversation piece! Part of the lifestyle are also expensive cars, fascinating Oldtimers, noble desginer clothing, welted shoes, high-quality cosmetics, narrow boats, seductive travel destinations, exclusive hotels and resorts, selected and rare wines, champagne and spirits, well kept vintage cigars and much more whose content is always on the "high potential readers," who see their passion as a hobby and meticulously value system, are aligned.
Language(s): German
ADVERTISING RATES:
Full Page Mono .... CHF 15000
Full Page Colour .... CHF 15000
Mechanical Data: Type Area: 280 x 220 mm, No. of Columns (Display): 3, Col Widths (Display): 70 mm

TOUT L'IMMOBILIER 745236S74K-80
Editorial: 8, rue Jacques Grosselin, 1227 CAROUGE
Tel: 22 3070220 **Fax:** 22 3070222
Email: info@toutimmobilier.ch **Web site:** http://www.toutimmobilier.ch
Freq: 46 issues yearly; **Cover Price:** Free; **Circ:** 184,102
Editor: Thierry B. Oppikofer; **Advertising Manager:** Gregory Pavoni
Profile: Publication containing information about houses for sale or rent, includes information about finance and housing trends.
Language(s): French
Readership: Read by those wishing to move house.
ADVERTISING RATES:
Full Page Mono .... CHF 4500
Full Page Colour .... CHF 5400
Mechanical Data: Type Area: 289 x 204 mm
Copy instructions: *Copy Date:* 1 day prior to publication
CONSUMER: WOMEN'S INTEREST CONSUMER MAGAZINES: Home Purchase

TP LEADER 1852421S14A-1278
Editorial: Freigutstr. 8, 8027 ZÜRICH
Tel: 43 3050590 **Fax:** 43 3050599
Email: info@senarclens.com **Web site:** http://www.senarclens.com
Freq: Half-yearly; **Circ:** 15,000
Editor: Andrea Leu
Profile: Company publication.
Language(s): German
ADVERTISING RATES:
Full Page Mono .... CHF 3800
Full Page Colour .... CHF 3800
Mechanical Data: Type Area: 261 x 186 mm
Copy instructions: *Copy Date:* 28 days prior to publication

TRACÉS 763254S4E-742
Editorial: 4, rue de Bassenges, 1024 ECUBLENS
Tel: 21 6932098 **Fax:** 21 6932084
Email: fdc@revue-traces.ch **Web site:** http://www.revue-traces.ch
Freq: 22 issues yearly; **Annual Sub.:** CHF 170,00; **Circ:** 4,500
Editor: Francesco Della Casa
Profile: Magazine for architects and engineers.
Language(s): French
ADVERTISING RATES:
Full Page Mono .... CHF 2300
Full Page Colour .... CHF 3500
Mechanical Data: No. of Columns (Display): 2, Col Widths (Display): 90 mm, Type Area: 260 x 188 mm
Copy instructions: *Copy Date:* 14 days prior to publication
Official Journal of: Organ d. Soc. suisse des ingénieurs et des architectes, d. Union suisse des

ingénieures-conseils, d. Association des anciens élèves de l'EPFL u. d. Anciens élèves de l'EPFZ

TRANSPORT ROUTIER
1859364S49A-437
Editorial: Weissenbühlweg 3, 3007 BERN
Tel: 31 3708542 **Fax:** 31 3708588
Email: e.kartnaller@astag.ch **Web site:** http://www.astag.ch
Freq: 10 issues yearly; **Annual Sub.:** CHF 99,00; **Circ:** 2,000
Editor: Erwin Kartnaller
Profile: Magazine from the Swiss Association for Commercial Vehicles.
Language(s): French; Italian
ADVERTISING RATES:
Full Page Mono .... CHF 3800
Full Page Colour .... CHF 4750
Mechanical Data: Type Area: 277 x 190 mm
Copy instructions: *Copy Date:* 10 days prior to publication

TRAVEL INSIDE
745316S50-127
Editorial: Hammerstr. 81, 8032 ZÜRICH
Tel: 44 3875757 **Fax:** 44 3875707
Email: info@travelinside.ch **Web site:** http://www.travelinside.ch
Freq: Weekly; **Annual Sub.:** CHF 84,00; **Circ:** 8,750
Editor: Angelo Heuberger
Profile: Magazine on tourism.
Language(s): German
ADVERTISING RATES:
Full Page Mono .... CHF 4990
Full Page Colour .... CHF 6690
Mechanical Data: Type Area: 290 x 210 mm, No. of Columns (Display): 4, Col Widths (Display): 49 mm
Copy instructions: *Copy Date:* 7 days prior to publication
Supplement(s): MIC Meeting Industry Magazine

TRAVEL INSIDE
1642053S50-131
Editorial: 14, pl. Cornavin, 1211 GENF
Tel: 22 9086900 **Fax:** 22 9086909
Email: ti-gva@travelinside.ch **Web site:** http://www.travelinside.de
Freq: 26 issues yearly; **Annual Sub.:** CHF 59,00; **Circ:** 3,250
Editor: Dominique Sudan
Profile: Magazine on tourism.
Language(s): French
ADVERTISING RATES:
Full Page Mono .... CHF 3580
Full Page Colour .... CHF 4930
Mechanical Data: Type Area: 290 x 210 mm, No. of Columns (Display): 4, Col Widths (Display): 49 mm
Copy instructions: *Copy Date:* 7 days prior to publication

TRAVEL INSIDE
745316S50-139
Editorial: Hammerstr. 81, 8032 ZÜRICH
Tel: 44 3875757 **Fax:** 44 3875707
Email: info@travelinside.ch **Web site:** http://www.travelinside.ch
Freq: Weekly; **Annual Sub.:** CHF 84,00; **Circ:** 8,750
Editor: Angelo Heuberger
Profile: Magazine on tourism.
Language(s): German
ADVERTISING RATES:
Full Page Mono .... CHF 4990
Full Page Colour .... CHF 6690
Mechanical Data: Type Area: 290 x 210 mm, No. of Columns (Display): 4, Col Widths (Display): 49 mm
Copy instructions: *Copy Date:* 7 days prior to publication
Supplement(s): MIC Meeting Industry Magazine

TRAVEL INSIDE
1642053S50-140
Editorial: 14, pl. Cornavin, 1211 GENF
Tel: 22 9086900 **Fax:** 22 9086909
Email: ti-gva@travelinside.ch **Web site:** http://www.travelinside.de
Freq: 26 issues yearly; **Annual Sub.:** CHF 59,00; **Circ:** 3,250
Editor: Dominique Sudan
Profile: Magazine on tourism.
Language(s): French
ADVERTISING RATES:
Full Page Mono .... CHF 3580
Full Page Colour .... CHF 4930
Mechanical Data: Type Area: 290 x 210 mm, No. of Columns (Display): 4, Col Widths (Display): 49 mm
Copy instructions: *Copy Date:* 7 days prior to publication

TRAVELMANAGER
1642054S50-132
Editorial: Hammerstr. 81, 8032 ZÜRICH
Tel: 44 3875787 **Fax:** 44 3875707
Email: redaktion@travelmanager.ch **Web site:** http://www.travelmanager.ch
Freq: 10 issues yearly; **Annual Sub.:** CHF 95,00; **Circ:** 3,000
Editor: Beat Eichenberger
Profile: Swiss monthly on tourism.
Language(s): English; German
ADVERTISING RATES:
Full Page Mono .... CHF 3990
Full Page Colour .... CHF 5340
Mechanical Data: Type Area: 265 x 185 mm
Copy instructions: *Copy Date:* 14 days prior to publication

TRAVELMANAGER
1642054S50-141
Editorial: Hammerstr. 81, 8032 ZÜRICH
Tel: 44 3875787 **Fax:** 44 3875707
Email: redaktion@travelmanager.ch **Web site:** http://www.travelmanager.ch
Freq: 10 issues yearly; **Annual Sub.:** CHF 95,00; **Circ:** 3,000
Editor: Beat Eichenberger
Profile: Swiss monthly on tourism.
Language(s): English; German
ADVERTISING RATES:
Full Page Mono .... CHF 3990
Full Page Colour .... CHF 5340
Mechanical Data: Type Area: 265 x 185 mm
Copy instructions: *Copy Date:* 14 days prior to publication

TRAVELTIP
1642055S89A-346
Editorial: Hammerstr. 81, 8032 ZÜRICH
Tel: 44 3875757 **Fax:** 44 3875707
Email: info@traveltip.ch **Web site:** http://www.traveltip.ch
Freq: Quarterly; **Annual Sub.:** CHF 20,00; **Circ:** 121,000
Editor: Urs Hirt
Profile: Travel fair magazine.
Language(s): German
ADVERTISING RATES:
Full Page Mono .... CHF 5200
Full Page Colour .... CHF 6950
Mechanical Data: No. of Columns (Display): 3, Col Widths (Display): 58 mm, Type Area: 265 x 185 mm

LA TRIBUNE DE GENÈVE
745384S67B-2640
Editorial: 11, rue des Rois, 1204 GENF
Tel: 22 3224000 **Fax:** 22 7810107
Web site: http://www.tribune.ch
Freq: 312 issues yearly; **Annual Sub.:** CHF 359,00; **Circ:** 62,003
Editor: Pierre Ruetschi
Profile: Regional daily newspaper covering politics, economics, sport, travel, technology and the arts.
Language(s): French
Mechanical Data: Type Area: 440 x 290 mm, No. of Columns (Display): 10, Col Widths (Display): 26 mm
Copy instructions: *Copy Date:* 2 days prior to publication
Supplement(s): Cinéma tout écran; Guide Loisirs; Tribune des Arts; Tribune Rives-Lac
REGIONAL DAILY & SUNDAY NEWSPAPERS: Regional Daily Newspapers

TRUMPF-AS
745437S76D-577
Editorial: Unterdorfstr. 8, 7206 IGIS **Tel:** 81 3228174
Fax: 44 3228579
Email: info@trumpf-as.ch **Web site:** http://www.trumpf-as.ch
Freq: 6 issues yearly; **Annual Sub.:** CHF 35,00; **Circ:** 5,000
Editor: Fabian Cadonau; **Advertising Manager:** Rudolf Kupfer
Profile: Magazine with news and information about jass-games.
Language(s): German
Mechanical Data: No. of Columns (Display): 3, Col Widths (Display): 60 mm
Copy instructions: *Copy Date:* 14 days prior to publication
CONSUMER: MUSIC & PERFORMING ARTS: Music

TVSTAR
1746012S76C-307
Editorial: Förrlibuckstr. 70, 8005 ZÜRICH
Tel: 43 4445537 **Fax:** 43 4445541
Email: gion.stecher@tvzeitschriften.ch **Web site:** http://www.tvzeitschriften.ch
Freq: Weekly; **Annual Sub.:** CHF 139,00; **Circ:** 155,563
Editor: Gion Stecher; **Advertising Manager:** Sandra Peiti
Language(s): German
ADVERTISING RATES:
Full Page Mono .... CHF 8500
Full Page Colour .... CHF 8500
Mechanical Data: Type Area: 244 x 186 mm, No. of Columns (Display): 4, Col Widths (Display): 43 mm
Copy instructions: *Copy Date:* 14 days prior to publication
CONSUMER: MUSIC & PERFORMING ARTS: TV & Radio

UFA REVUE
1645581S21A-591
Editorial: Schaffhauser Str. 6, 8401 WINTERTHUR
Tel: 52 2642728 **Fax:** 52 2132161
Email: info@ufarevue.ch **Web site:** http://www.landi.ch
Freq: 11 issues yearly; **Circ:** 62,524
Editor: Roman Engeler; **Advertising Manager:** Martina Bernet
Profile: Magazine for farmers.
Language(s): French; German
ADVERTISING RATES:
Full Page Mono .... CHF 7015
Full Page Colour .... CHF 8515
Mechanical Data: Type Area: 256 x 192 mm, No. of Columns (Display): 4, Col Widths (Display): 45 mm
Copy instructions: *Copy Date:* 20 days prior to publication

UFA REVUE
1851176S21A-616
Editorial: Schaffhauser Str. 6, 8401 WINTERTHUR
Tel: 52 2642728 **Fax:** 52 2132161
Email: info@ufarevue.ch **Web site:** http://www.landi.ch
Freq: 11 issues yearly; **Circ:** 13,465
Editor: Cyril de Poret; **Advertising Manager:** Martina Bernet
Profile: Magazine for farmers.
Language(s): French
ADVERTISING RATES:
Full Page Mono .... CHF 2180
Full Page Colour .... CHF 3680
Mechanical Data: Type Area: 256 x 192 mm, No. of Columns (Display): 4, Col Widths (Display): 45 mm
Copy instructions: *Copy Date:* 20 days prior to publication

UMWELT
1648781S57-674
Editorial: Postfach, 3003 BERN **Tel:** 31 3229356
Fax: 31 3227054
Email: georg.ledergerber@bafu.admin.ch **Web site:** http://www.umwelt-schweiz.ch
Freq: Quarterly; **Cover Price:** Free; **Circ:** 38,000
Editor: Georg Ledergerber
Profile: Magazine about environmental protection.
Language(s): German

UMWELT
1824023S57-704
Editorial: Postfach 669, 3900 BRIG-GLIS
Tel: 27 9236162
Email: umweltsekretariat@rhone.ch **Web site:** http://www.umwelt-oberwallis.ch
Circ: 1,700
Editor: Brigitte Wolf
Profile: Regional information about environment protection.
Language(s): German

UMWELT
1824023S57-729
Editorial: Postfach 669, 3900 BRIG-GLIS
Tel: 27 9236162
Email: umweltsekretariat@rhone.ch **Web site:** http://www.umwelt-oberwallis.ch
Circ: 1,700
Editor: Brigitte Wolf
Profile: Regional information about environment protection.
Language(s): German

UMWELT PERSPEKTIVEN
1841087S57-710
Editorial: Kempttalstr. 56, 8308 ILLNAU
Tel: 52 3552111 **Fax:** 52 3552110
Email: info@umweltperspektiven.ch **Web site:** http://www.umweltperspektiven.ch
Freq: 6 issues yearly; **Annual Sub.:** CHF 125,00; **Circ:** 4,000
Editor: Roger Strässle; **Advertising Manager:** Urs Heutschi
Profile: Magazine focusing on the environment, including management, technology and investment aspects.
Language(s): German
ADVERTISING RATES:
Full Page Mono .... CHF 2690
Full Page Colour .... CHF 4130
Mechanical Data: Type Area: 266 x 186 mm, No. of Columns (Display): 3, Col Widths (Display): 55 mm
Copy instructions: *Copy Date:* 24 days prior to publication

UMWELTRECHT IN DER PRAXIS DROIT DE L'ENVIRONNEMENT DANS LA PRATIQUE
1859154S1A-313
Editorial: Postfach 2430, 8026 ZÜRICH
Tel: 44 2417691 **Fax:** 44 2417905
Email: info@vur-ade.ch **Web site:** http://www.vur-ade.ch
Freq: 9 issues yearly; Free to qualifying individuals
Annual Sub.: CHF 140,00; **Circ:** 1,000
Profile: Juristic magazine about environmental law.
Language(s): French; German

UMWELTTECHNIK SCHWEIZ
1642226S57-669
Editorial: Postfach 940, 4142 MÜNCHENSTEIN 1
Tel: 61 3381616 **Fax:** 61 3381600
Email: umwelttechnik@laupper.ch **Web site:** http://www.umwelt-technik.ch
Freq: 10 issues yearly; **Annual Sub.:** CHF 83,00; **Circ:** 4,850
Editor: Pieter Poldervaart
Profile: Magazine about environmental technologies.
Language(s): German
ADVERTISING RATES:
Full Page Mono .... CHF 2100
Full Page Colour .... CHF 2700
Mechanical Data: Type Area: 275 x 185 mm, No. of Columns (Display): 4, Col Widths (Display): 45 mm
Copy instructions: *Copy Date:* 20 days prior to publication

UNIJOURNAL
745778S83-340
Editorial: Rämistr. 42, 8001 ZÜRICH **Tel:** 44 6344433
Fax: 44 6342346
Email: unijournal@unicom.uzh.ch **Web site:** http://www.unizh.ch
Freq: 6 issues yearly; **Cover Price:** Free; **Circ:** 14,500
Editor: David Werner
Profile: Magazine of the University of Zurich.
Language(s): German
Readership: Read by students and university staff, editors in Kanton Zürich and selected editors in Switzerland, also other universities.
ADVERTISING RATES:
Full Page Mono .... CHF 2500
Full Page Colour .... CHF 4400
Mechanical Data: Type Area: 384 x 263 mm
CONSUMER: STUDENT PUBLICATIONS

UNTERNEHMER-ZEITUNG
765197S14A-1105
Editorial: Köschenrütistr. 109, 8052 ZÜRICH
Tel: 44 3064704 **Fax:** 44 3064711
Email: info@unternehmerzeitung.ch **Web site:** http://www.unternehmerzeitung.ch
Freq: 10 issues yearly; **Annual Sub.:** CHF 40,00; **Circ:** 82,000
Editor: Peter Blattner; **Advertising Manager:** Urs C. Keller
Profile: Magazine for owners and managers of small and medium sized companies.
Language(s): German
ADVERTISING RATES:
Full Page Mono .... CHF 7200
Full Page Colour .... CHF 9900
Mechanical Data: Type Area: 290 x 208 mm, No. of Columns (Display): 4, Col Widths (Display): 50 mm
Copy instructions: *Copy Date:* 14 days prior to publication
Supplement(s): Genesis; Zürcher Unternehmer
BUSINESS: COMMERCE, INDUSTRY & MANAGEMENT

DIE UNTERNEHMUNG
1856074S14A-1341
Editorial: 90, bd. de Pérolles, 1700 FREIBURG
Tel: 26 3008294 **Fax:** 26 3009659
Email: martin.wallmeier@unifr.ch **Web site:** http://www.dieunternehmung.ch
Freq: Quarterly; **Annual Sub.:** CHF 115,00; **Circ:** 1,000
Editor: Martin Wallmeier
Profile: Magazine focusing on business management.
Language(s): English; German
ADVERTISING RATES:
Full Page Mono .... CHF 750
Mechanical Data: Type Area: 195 x 138 mm
Official Journal of: Organ d. Schweizer. Ges. f. Betriebswirtschaft

URNER WOCHENBLATT
746033S67B-2680
Editorial: Gitschenstr. 9, 6460 ALTDORF
Tel: 41 8741677 **Fax:** 41 8741670
Email: mail@urnerwochenblatt.ch **Web site:** http://www.urnerwochenblatt.ch
Freq: 104 issues yearly; **Annual Sub.:** CHF 196,00; **Circ:** 10,129
Editor: Erich Herger
Profile: Regional daily newspaper covering politics, economics, sport, travel, technology and the arts.
Language(s): German
ADVERTISING RATES:
SCC .... CHF 28,10
Mechanical Data: Type Area: 440 x 283 mm, No. of Columns (Display): 10, Col Widths (Display): 26 mm
Copy instructions: *Copy Date:* 2 days prior to publication
REGIONAL DAILY & SUNDAY NEWSPAPERS: Regional Daily Newspapers

UROLOGIA INTERNATIONALIS
746037S56A-1920
Editorial: Allschwiler Str. 10, 4055 BASEL
Tel: 61 3061424 **Fax:** 61 3061434
Email: uin@karger.ch **Web site:** http://www.karger.com/uin
Freq: 8 issues yearly; **Annual Sub.:** CHF 3999,20; **Circ:** 800
Editor: M. Porena; **Advertising Manager:** Thomas Maurer
Profile: Magazine about research on urology.
Language(s): English
ADVERTISING RATES:
Full Page Mono .... CHF 1870
Full Page Colour .... CHF 3430
Mechanical Data: Type Area: 224 x 180 mm

ÜSI MEINIG
745649S57-580
Editorial: Postfach 1613, 8201 SCHAFFHAUSEN
Tel: 52 6722819
Email: hugo.mahler@bluewin.ch **Web site:** http://www.vcs-sh.ch
Freq: Quarterly; **Circ:** 2,900
Editor: Hugo Mahler
Profile: Magazine of the Traffic Club of Switzerland.
Language(s): German
ADVERTISING RATES:
Full Page Mono .... CHF 360
Full Page Colour .... CHF 360
Mechanical Data: Type Area: 208 x 145 mm, No. of Columns (Display): 2, Col Widths (Display): 72 mm

Copy instructions: *Copy Date:* 25 days prior to publication
Official Journal of: Organ d. WWF u. d. VCS, Sektionen Schaffhausen

USIC NEWS 1859627S4E-844
Editorial: Aarberger Gasse 16, 3011 BERN
Tel: 31 9700881 **Fax:** 31 9700882
Email: usic@usic.ch **Web site:** http://www.usic.ch
Freq: Half-yearly; **Circ:** 2,500
Profile: Magazine with information for the building business about law and politics.
Language(s): French; German

VELO 1846534S89A-390
Editorial: Jurastr. 29, 4901 LANGENTHAL
Tel: 62 9227721 **Fax:** 62 9230658
Email: tourismus@oberaargau.ch **Web site:** http://www.oberaargau.ch
Freq: Annual; **Cover Price:** Free; **Circ:** 6,000
Profile: Guide for Oberaargau.
Language(s): German

VELOJOURNAL 1641945S77C-260
Editorial: Cramerstr. 17, 8004 ZÜRICH
Tel: 44 2426035 **Fax:** 44 2416032
Email: info@velojournal.ch **Web site:** http://www.velojournal.ch
Freq: 6 issues yearly; **Annual Sub.:** CHF 30,00; **Circ:** 22,500
Editor: Pete Mijnssen-Hemmi
Profile: Magazine for leisure time bicyclists.
Language(s): German
ADVERTISING RATES:
Full Page Mono .... CHF 3400
Full Page Colour .... CHF 3400
Mechanical Data: Type Area: 270 x 176 mm
CONSUMER: MOTORING & CYCLING: Cycling

VERBANDS MANAGEMENT 1859695S14A-1347
Editorial: 90, bd. de Pérolles, 1701 FREIBURG
Tel: 26 3008400 **Fax:** 26 3009755
Email: info@vmi.ch **Web site:** http://www.vmi.ch
Freq: 3 issues yearly; Free to qualifying individuals ; **Circ:** 900
Profile: Information about management.
Language(s): English; French; German
ADVERTISING RATES:
Full Page Mono .... CHF 700
Full Page Colour .... CHF 1450
Mechanical Data: Type Area: 228 x 165 mm

VIA 746474S94H-1220
Editorial: Militärstr. 36, 8021 ZÜRICH
Tel: 44 2994122 **Fax:** 44 2994140
Email: redaktion@via.ch **Web site:** http://www.via.ch
Freq: 10 issues yearly; **Annual Sub.:** CHF 28,00; **Circ:** 186,000
Editor: Simon B. Bühler
Profile: Magazine for travellers on Swiss railways.
Language(s): German
ADVERTISING RATES:
Full Page Mono .... CHF 10372
Full Page Colour .... CHF 10372
Mechanical Data: No. of Columns (Display): 4, Col Widths (Display): 46 mm, Type Area: 261 x 202 mm
Copy instructions: *Copy Date:* 45 days prior to publication
Official Journal of: Organ d. Schweizer. Bundesbahnen SBB u.d. Verb. öffentl. Verkehr VöV
CONSUMER: OTHER CLASSIFICATIONS: Customer Magazines

VIERTELJAHRSSCHRIFT DER NATURFORSCHENDEN GESELLSCHAFT IN ZÜRICH 746511S64F-200
Editorial: Winterthurerstr. 190, 8057 ZÜRICH
Tel: 44 6355168 **Fax:** 44 6355906
Email: conradin.burga@geo.uzh.ch **Web site:** http://www.ngzh.ch
Freq: Quarterly; Free to qualifying individuals
Annual Sub.: CHF 90,00; **Circ:** 2,000
Editor: Conradin A. Burga
Profile: Research magazine focusing on natural science, medicine and biology.
Language(s): German
Readership: Read by academics and library staff.
ADVERTISING RATES:
Full Page Mono .... CHF 1000
Mechanical Data: Type Area: 216 x 174 mm, No. of Columns (Display): 2, Col Widths (Display): 84 mm
BUSINESS: OTHER CLASSIFICATIONS: Biology

VINUM 746540G9C-5
Editorial: Thurgauer Str. 66, 8050 ZÜRICH
Tel: 44 2685260 **Fax:** 44 2685265
Email: redaktion@vinum.de **Web site:** http://www.vinum.de
Freq: 10 issues yearly; **Annual Sub.:** CHF 62,00; **Circ:** 36,774
Editor: Britta Wiegelmann; **Advertising Manager:** Regine Axhami
Profile: Vinum has been published since 1980 and enjoys a high acceptance at the Grand, the interested audience and wine producers, in retail and upscale restaurants. Vinum - that is enjoying a high level. Stories about the heritage of wine from the wine regions of Switzerland, Germany, Austria, Italy, France and the world are constant themes. Extensive tastings, recommendations offer the reader a sound basis for orientation and wine purchases. Travel and Culture Features invite you to linger. Upscale Dining and stylish accessories complete the range of topics. Facebook: http://www.facebook.com/pages/Vinum-Europas-Weinmagazin/370970693167 This Outlet offers RSS (Really Simple Syndication).
Language(s): German
Readership: Aimed at wine connoisseurs and enthusiasts.
ADVERTISING RATES:
Full Page Mono .... EUR 3038
Full Page Colour .... EUR 5494
Mechanical Data: Type Area: 260 x 190 mm, No. of Columns (Display): 4, Col Widths (Display): 43 mm
Copy instructions: *Copy Date:* 35 days prior to publication
BUSINESS: DRINKS & LICENSED TRADE: Licensed Trade, Wines & Spirits

VINUM 746541S74P-240
Editorial: Thurgauer Str. 66, 8050 ZÜRICH
Tel: 44 2685260 **Fax:** 44 2685265
Email: redaktion@vinum.ch **Web site:** http://www.vinum.ch
Freq: 10 issues yearly; **Annual Sub.:** CHF 124,00; **Circ:** 21,000
Editor: Britta Wiegelmann; **Advertising Manager:** Patric Preite
Profile: European wine magazine..
Language(s): German
ADVERTISING RATES:
Full Page Mono .... CHF 4675
Full Page Colour .... CHF 7380
Mechanical Data: Type Area: 260 x 190 mm, No. of Columns (Display): 4, Col Widths (Display): 43 mm
Copy instructions: *Copy Date:* 42 days prior to publication
Supplement(s): extra Vinum
CONSUMER: WOMEN'S INTEREST CONSUMER MAGAZINES: Food & Cookery

LA VOCE DELLE VALLI/IL SAN BERNADINO 746605S72-4600
Editorial: 6535 ROVEREDO **Tel:** 91 8272631
Fax: 91 8274531
Email: marcotognola@bluewin.ch **Web site:** http://www.rezzonico.ch
Freq: Weekly; **Annual Sub.:** CHF 65,00; **Circ:** 1,026
Editor: Marco Tognola; **Advertising Manager:** Ivan Raineri
Profile: Regional weekly covering politics, economics, sport, travel, technology and the arts.
Language(s): Italian
ADVERTISING RATES:
SCC .... CHF 13,50
Mechanical Data: Type Area: 445 x 289 mm, No. of Columns (Display): 10, Col Widths (Display): 25 mm
Copy instructions: *Copy Date:* 4 days prior to publication
LOCAL NEWSPAPERS

VOGEL GRYFF 1655548S72-9658
Editorial: Riehentorstr. 15, 3005 BERN
Tel: 61 6910666 **Fax:** 61 6913635
Email: rolf.zenklusen@vogelgryff.ch **Web site:** http://www.vogelgryff.ch
Freq: 26 issues yearly; **Cover Price:** Free; **Circ:** 29,000
Editor: Rolf Zenklusen; **Advertising Manager:** Robert Schlosser
Profile: Advertising journal (house-to-house) concentrating on local stories.
Language(s): German
ADVERTISING RATES:
Full Page Mono .... CHF 2578
Full Page Colour .... CHF 3796
Mechanical Data: Type Area: 290 x 203 mm, No. of Columns (Display): 7, Col Widths (Display): 29 mm
Copy instructions: *Copy Date:* 2 days prior to publication
Official Journal of: Organ d. Interessengemeinschaft Kleinbasel
LOCAL NEWSPAPERS

VOLKSSTIMME 746671S67B-2700
Editorial: Hauptstr. 33, 4450 SISSACH
Tel: 61 9761030 **Fax:** 61 9761013
Email: redaktion@volksstimme.ch **Web site:** http://www.volksstimme.ch
Freq: 156 issues yearly; **Annual Sub.:** CHF 169,00; **Circ:** 7,626
Editor: Christian Horisberger
Profile: Regional daily newspaper covering politics, economics, sport, travel, technology and the arts.
Language(s): German
ADVERTISING RATES:
SCC .... CHF 23,00
Mechanical Data: Type Area: 440 x 291 mm, No. of Columns (Display): 10, Col Widths (Display): 25 mm
Copy instructions: *Copy Date:* 2 days prior to publication
REGIONAL DAILY & SUNDAY NEWSPAPERS: Regional Daily Newspapers

VOLKSSTIMME 1656036S72-9670
Editorial: Hauptstr. 33, 4450 SISSACH
Tel: 61 9761030 **Fax:** 61 9761013
Email: redaktion@volksstimme.ch **Web site:** http://www.volksstimme.ch
Freq: 18 issues yearly; **Cover Price:** Free; **Circ:** 20,060
Editor: Christian Horisberger
Profile: Advertising journal (house-to-house) concentrating on local stories.
Language(s): German
ADVERTISING RATES:
Full Page Mono .... CHF 4300
Full Page Colour .... CHF 5000
Mechanical Data: Type Area: 440 x 291 mm, No. of Columns (Display): 10, Col Widths (Display): 25 mm
Copy instructions: *Copy Date:* 2 days prior to publication
LOCAL NEWSPAPERS

DIE VOLKSWIRTSCHAFT 762917S1R-1862
Editorial: Effingerstr. 1, 3003 BERN **Tel:** 31 3222939
Fax: 31 3222740
Email: redaktion@dievolkswirtschaft.ch **Web site:** http://www.dievolkswirtschaft.ch
Freq: 10 issues yearly; **Annual Sub.:** CHF 149,00; **Circ:** 6,500
Editor: Geli Spescha
Profile: Information about recent economic trends and issues from economic policy.
Language(s): German
ADVERTISING RATES:
Full Page Mono .... CHF 3900
Full Page Colour .... CHF 3900
Mechanical Data: Type Area: 275 x 180 mm
Copy instructions: *Copy Date:* 31 days prior to publication
Supplement(s): Konjukturtendenzen
BUSINESS: FINANCE & ECONOMICS: Financial Related

VORSORGE 1844824S1F-278
Editorial: Wengistr. 7, 8026 ZÜRICH **Tel:** 44 2654010
Fax: 44 2654011
Email: info@publicontext.com **Web site:** http://www.publicontext.com
Freq: Annual; **Cover Price:** Free; **Circ:** 56,000
Editor: Ralph Spillmann
Profile: Finance magazine.
Language(s): German
ADVERTISING RATES:
Full Page Mono .... CHF 18500
Full Page Colour .... CHF 18500
Mechanical Data: Type Area: 270 x 195 mm
Copy instructions: *Copy Date:* 38 days prior to publication
Supplement to: Bilanz

[VORSORGE 1856061S14A-1340
Editorial: Paulstr. 9, 8401 WINTERTHUR
Tel: 52 2613677 **Fax:** 52 2613788
Email: redaktion.vorsorge@axa-winterthur.ch **Web site:** http://www.winterthur-leben.ch/vorsorge
Freq: 3 issues yearly; **Cover Price:** Free; **Circ:** 86,000
Editor: Eva-Maria Jonen
Profile: Company publication published by Winterthur Leben.
Language(s): German

VSAO JOURNAL 1853376S56A-2198
Editorial: Bahnhofplatz 10a, 3001 BERN
Tel: 31 3504488 **Fax:** 31 3504489
Email: journal@vsao.ch **Web site:** http://www.vsao.ch
Freq: 6 issues yearly; **Annual Sub.:** CHF 50,00; **Circ:** 18,000
Editor: Catherine Aeschbacher
Profile: Magazine for physical doctors.
Language(s): French; German; Italian
ADVERTISING RATES:
Full Page Mono .... CHF 4400
Full Page Colour .... CHF 4400
Mechanical Data: Type Area: 272 x 178 mm

WALD UND HOLZ 746854S46-3
Editorial: Rosenweg 14, 4501 SOLOTHURN
Tel: 32 6258800 **Fax:** 32 6258899
Email: tschannen@wvs.ch **Web site:** http://www.waldundholz.ch
Freq: Monthly; **Annual Sub.:** CHF 89,00; **Circ:** 7,184
Editor: Walter Tschannen
Profile: Journal focusing on forestry, forestry industry, forestry politics, wood trade and related political issues.
Language(s): German
Readership: Read by foresters, leaders of local authorities and politicians dealing with forestry issues.
ADVERTISING RATES:
Full Page Mono .... CHF 1540
Full Page Colour .... CHF 2215
Mechanical Data: Type Area: 260 x 185 mm
Copy instructions: *Copy Date:* 14 days prior to publication
BUSINESS: TIMBER, WOOD & FORESTRY

WALLISER BOTE 746866S67B-2740
Editorial: Furkastr. 21, 3900 BRIG-GLIS
Tel: 27 9229988 **Fax:** 27 9229989
Email: info@walliserbote.ch **Web site:** http://www.walliserbote.ch
Freq: 312 issues yearly; **Cover Price:** CHF 2,20; **Circ:** 25,261
Editor: Thomas Rieder; **Advertising Manager:** Nicolas Mengis
Profile: Regional daily newspaper covering politics, economics, sport, travel, technology and the arts.
Language(s): German
ADVERTISING RATES:
SCC .... CHF 42,40
Mechanical Data: Type Area: 440 x 282 mm, No. of Columns (Display): 10, Col Widths (Display): 25 mm
Copy instructions: *Copy Date:* 1 day prior to publication
Supplement(s): WB extra
REGIONAL DAILY & SUNDAY NEWSPAPERS: Regional Daily Newspapers

WANDERLAND 746887S75L-120
Editorial: Monbijoustr. 61, 3000 BERN 23
Tel: 31 3701030 **Fax:** 31 3701021
Email: wanderland@wandern.ch **Web site:** http://www.wandern.ch
Freq: 6 issues yearly; **Annual Sub.:** CHF 46,00; **Circ:** 23,000
Editor: Sam Junker
Profile: Hiking magazine.
Language(s): German
ADVERTISING RATES:
Full Page Mono .... CHF 4140
Full Page Colour .... CHF 4140
Mechanical Data: Type Area: 260 x 180 mm
Copy instructions: *Copy Date:* 18 days prior to publication
CONSUMER: SPORT: Outdoor

WEGE UND GESCHICHTE LES CHEMINS ET L'HISTOIRE STRADE E STORIA 764837S49A-385
Editorial: Kapellenstr. 5, 3011 BERN **Tel:** 31 3007050
Fax: 31 3007069
Email: info@viastoria.ch **Web site:** http://www.viastoria.ch
Freq: Half-yearly; Free to qualifying individuals
Annual Sub.: CHF 30,00; **Circ:** 5,000
Profile: Magazine from the Center of Transport History.
Language(s): French; German; Italian

WEINWISSER 1847349S74P-293
Editorial: Lavaterstr. 40, 8002 ZÜRICH
Tel: 55 2445244 **Fax:** 55 2445245
Email: stephan.reinhardt@weinwisser.com **Web site:** http://www.weinwisser.com
Freq: Monthly; **Annual Sub.:** CHF 175,00; **Circ:** 5,000
Editor: Stephan Reinhardt; **Advertising Manager:** Petra Binz-Lockenvitz
Profile: Magazine about wine.
Language(s): German
ADVERTISING RATES:
Full Page Mono .... CHF 1840
Mechanical Data: Type Area: 255 x 182 mm
Copy instructions: *Copy Date:* 21 days prior to publication

DIE WELTWOCHE 747149S65J-1
Editorial: Förrlibuckstr. 70, 8005 ZÜRICH
Tel: 43 4445700 **Fax:** 43 4445669
Email: redaktion@weltwoche.ch **Web site:** http://www.weltwoche.ch
Freq: Weekly; **Annual Sub.:** CHF 213,00; **Circ:** 110,000
Editor: Roger Köppel
Profile: Newspaper focusing on worldwide news, current affairs and general interest articles.
Language(s): German
Mechanical Data: Type Area: 269 x 208 mm
Copy instructions: *Copy Date:* 6 days prior to publication
Supplement(s): Home Electronic Extra
NATIONAL DAILY & SUNDAY NEWSPAPERS: National Weekly Newspapers

WERBEWOCHE 1859305S2A-693
Editorial: Neugasse 10, 8031 ZÜRICH
Tel: 44 2502830 **Fax:** 44 2502852
Email: info@werbewoche.ch **Web site:** http://www.werbewoche.ch
Freq: 22 issues yearly; **Annual Sub.:** CHF 298,00; **Circ:** 3,500
Editor: Pierre C. Meier; **Advertising Manager:** Thomas Stuchert
Profile: Magazine about advertising, media, marketing and communications business.
Language(s): German
ADVERTISING RATES:
Full Page Mono .... CHF 6500
Full Page Colour .... CHF 6500
Mechanical Data: Type Area: 330 x 254 mm, No. of Columns (Display): 5, Col Widths (Display): 49 mm
Copy instructions: *Copy Date:* 6 days prior to publication
Supplement(s): media Trend Journal

WERDENBERGER & OBERTOGGENBURGER 748387S67B-2720
Editorial: Bahnhofstr. 14, 9471 BUCHS
Tel: 81 7500200 **Fax:** 81 7562960

Email: info@wundo.ch **Web site:** http://www.w-und-o.ch
Freq: 312 issues yearly; **Annual Sub.:** CHF 288,00; **Circ:** 9,315
Editor: Thomas Schwizer
Profile: Regional daily newspaper covering politics, economics, sport, travel, technology and the arts.
Language(s): German
ADVERTISING RATES:
SCC .... CHF 27,60
Mechanical Data: Type Area: 440 x 286 mm, No. of Columns (Display): 10, Col Widths (Display): 25 mm
Copy instructions: *Copy Date:* 1 day prior to publication
Supplement(s): sofa
REGIONAL DAILY & SUNDAY NEWSPAPERS: Regional Daily Newspapers

WERDENBERGER & OBERTOGGENBURGER
748388S72-8660
Editorial: Bahnhofstr. 14, 9471 BUCHS
Tel: 81 7500200 **Fax:** 81 7502960
Email: info@wundo.ch
Freq: Weekly; **Cover Price:** Free; **Circ:** 19,896
Editor: Thomas Schwizer
Profile: Advertising journal (house-to-house) concentrating on local stories.
Language(s): German
ADVERTISING RATES:
Full Page Mono .... CHF 3815
Full Page Colour .... CHF 5535
Mechanical Data: Type Area: 440 x 286 mm, No. of Columns (Display): 10, Col Widths (Display): 25 mm
Copy instructions: *Copy Date:* 1 day prior to publication
LOCAL NEWSPAPERS

WERK, BAUEN + WOHNEN
1858821S4E-843
Editorial: Talstr. 29, 8001 ZÜRICH **Tel:** 44 2181430
Fax: 44 2181434
Email: redaktion@wbw.ch **Web site:** http://www.werkbauenundwohnen.ch
Freq: 10 issues yearly; Free to qualifying individuals
Annual Sub.: CHF 200,00; **Circ:** 8,000
Editor: Nott Caviezel
Profile: Magazine on architecture and town planning.
Language(s): English; French; German
ADVERTISING RATES:
Full Page Mono .... CHF 3380
Full Page Colour .... CHF 5300
Mechanical Data: Type Area: 275 x 205 mm
Copy instructions: *Copy Date:* 31 days prior to publication
Official Journal of: Organ d. Bund Schweizer Architekten, d. Vereinigung Schweizer Innenarchitekten u. d. Verb. Schweizer InnenarchitektInnen

WERKSPUREN
747195S62B-140
Editorial: Loretohöhe 46b, 6300 ZUG
Tel: 41 7101085 **Fax:** 41 7201088
Email: info@werkspuren.ch **Web site:** http://www.werkspuren.ch
Freq: Quarterly; Free to qualifying individuals
Annual Sub.: CHF 60,00; **Circ:** 1,500
Editor: Viktor Dittli-Zehnder; **Advertising Manager:** Viktor Dittli-Zehnder
Profile: Magazine about technical and design education.
Language(s): German
ADVERTISING RATES:
Full Page Mono .... CHF 750
Mechanical Data: Type Area: 266 x 185 mm, No. of Columns (Display): 2, Col Widths (Display): 90 mm
Copy instructions: *Copy Date:* 30 days prior to publication
BUSINESS: CHURCH & SCHOOL EQUIPMENT & EDUCATION: Education Teachers

WILLISAUER BOTE
747443S67B-2800
Editorial: Am Viehmarkt 1, 6130 WILLISAU
Tel: 41 9726030 **Fax:** 41 9726021
Email: redaktion@willisauerbote.ch **Web site:** http://www.willisauerbote.ch
Freq: 104 issues yearly; **Annual Sub.:** CHF 213,00; **Circ:** 9,267
Editor: Stefan Calivers
Profile: Regional daily newspaper covering politics, economics, sport, travel, technology and the arts.
Language(s): German
ADVERTISING RATES:
SCC .... CHF 10,60
Mechanical Data: Type Area: 240 x 290 mm, No. of Columns (Display): 26, Col Widths (Display): 10 mm
Copy instructions: *Copy Date:* 2 days prior to publication
REGIONAL DAILY & SUNDAY NEWSPAPERS: Regional Daily Newspapers

WINTERTHURER STADTANZEIGER
1643407S72-9600
Editorial: Garnmarkt 10, 8401 WINTERTHUR
Tel: 52 2669977 **Fax:** 52 2669913
Email: redaktion@stadi-online.ch **Web site:** http://www.stadi-online.ch
Freq: Weekly; **Cover Price:** Free; **Circ:** 66,312
Editor: Lucia M. Eppmann; **Advertising Manager:** Pablo Vecchi
Profile: Advertising journal (house-to-house) concentrating on local stories.
Language(s): German
ADVERTISING RATES:
Full Page Mono .... CHF 6337
Full Page Colour .... CHF 7735
Mechanical Data: Type Area: 437 x 290 mm, No. of Columns (Display): 10, Col Widths (Display): 26 mm
Copy instructions: *Copy Date:* 1 day prior to publication
LOCAL NEWSPAPERS

WIR ELTERN
1647604S74C-540
Editorial: Stadtturmstr. 19, 5401 BADEN
Tel: 58 2005666 **Fax:** 58 2005667
Email: redaktion@wireltern.ch **Web site:** http://www.wireltern.ch
Freq: 11 issues yearly; **Annual Sub.:** CHF 72,00; **Circ:** 58,000
Editor: Nicole Althaus; **Advertising Manager:** Jean-Orphée Reuter
Profile: Magazine for parents in Switzerland.
Language(s): German
ADVERTISING RATES:
Full Page Mono .... CHF 10100
Full Page Colour .... CHF 10100
Mechanical Data: Type Area: 268 x 185 mm, No. of Columns (Display): 4, Col Widths (Display): 42 mm
Copy instructions: *Copy Date:* 30 days prior to publication
CONSUMER: WOMEN'S INTEREST CONSUMER MAGAZINES: Home & Family

WIRBELWIND
1853378S74A-512
Editorial: Postfach 197, 8053 ZÜRICH
Tel: 81 9433300 **Fax:** 81 9433300
Email: redaktion@elternzeitschrift.org **Web site:** http://www.elternzeitschrift.org
Freq: 6 issues yearly; **Annual Sub.:** CHF 33,00; **Circ:** 52,000
Editor: Nicole Christina Ritsch
Profile: Parents' magazine.
Language(s): German
ADVERTISING RATES:
Full Page Mono .... CHF 1200
Mechanical Data: Type Area: 255 x 175 mm
Copy instructions: *Copy Date:* 62 days prior to publication

WIRTSCHAFTS FLASH
732901S14A-600
Editorial: Buchenstr. 101, 4500 SOLOTHURN
Tel: 32 6247685 **Fax:** 32 6247444
Email: dejo-press@bluewin.ch **Web site:** http://www.wirtschaftsflash.ch
Freq: 6 issues yearly; Free to qualifying individuals
Annual Sub.: CHF 25,00; **Circ:** 6,191
Editor: Joseph Weibel
Profile: Voice of business and commerce in the canton of Solothurn. The business related personalities come here to speak. Interesting companies with exemplary ideas are portrayed. Economic dedicated flash for a business-friendly policies. If necessary, in this magazine are also "hot iron" taken up and explained where subparticipants of the shoe pinches.
Language(s): German
ADVERTISING RATES:
Full Page Mono .... CHF 2300
Full Page Colour .... CHF 2760
Mechanical Data: Type Area: 252 x 176 mm, No. of Columns (Display): 3, Col Widths (Display): 56 mm
Copy instructions: *Copy Date:* 18 days prior to publication

WIRTSCHAFTSJOURNALIST
747728G2B-940
Editorial: Im Buechwald 12, 9242 OBERUZWIL
Tel: 71 3400966
Email: markus.wiegand@wirtschaftsjournalist-online.de **Web site:** http://www.wirtschaftsjournalist-online.de
Freq: 6 issues yearly; **Annual Sub.:** CHF 42,00; **Circ:** 6,030
Editor: Markus Wiegand; **Advertising Manager:** Martha Steinwender
Profile: Financial and business journalists to a large extent determine the success or failure of a company. How about a company on the Economic part is reported shapes the market price, the confidence of investors, customers and employees. The "Wirtschaftsjournalist" reaches every two months this exclusive target group.
Language(s): German
ADVERTISING RATES:
Full Page Mono .... EUR 3750
Full Page Colour .... EUR 3750
Mechanical Data: Type Area: 254 x 190 mm
Copy instructions: *Copy Date:* 21 days prior to publication
Supplement(s): Autojournalist; Food- und Agrarjournalist; Medizin & Wissenschaftsjournalist; Umweltjournalist
BUSINESS: COMMUNICATIONS, ADVERTISING & MARKETING: Press

WIRTSCHAFTSPSYCHOLOGIE
747757G14F-102
Editorial: Kreuzplatz 5, 8092 ZÜRICH
Tel: 44 6327088 **Fax:** 44 6321186
Email: twehner@ethz.ch **Web site:** http://www.wirtschafts-psychologie.net
Freq: Quarterly; **Annual Sub.:** CHF 45,00; **Circ:** 3,800
Editor: Theo Wehner; **Advertising Manager:** Wolfgang Pabst
Profile: Wirtschaftspsychologie publishes timely, practical contributions to the fields of labor, industrial and organizational psychology: a review, and detailed illustrations, interviews and briefings. For ABO-psychologists is as indispensable as the magazine for managers want to use psychological skills in their work (eg HR managers).
Language(s): German
Readership: Aimed at psychologists and consultants within institutions and organisations.
ADVERTISING RATES:
Full Page Mono .... EUR 971
Full Page Colour .... EUR 1294
Mechanical Data: Type Area: 240 x 177 mm, No. of Columns (Display): 2, Col Widths (Display): 68 mm
Copy instructions: *Copy Date:* 30 days prior to publication
BUSINESS: COMMERCE, INDUSTRY & MANAGEMENT: Training & Recruitment

WOCHEN-ZEITUNG
748202S72-8980
Editorial: Dorfplatz, 6354 VITZNAU **Tel:** 41 3970303
Fax: 41 3971747
Email: wochenzeitung@bucherdruck.ch **Web site:** http://www.bucherdruck.ch
Freq: Weekly; **Annual Sub.:** CHF 95,00; **Circ:** 2,600
Profile: Regional weekly covering politics, economics, sport, travel, technology and the arts.
Language(s): German
ADVERTISING RATES:
SCC .... CHF 17,50
Mechanical Data: Type Area: 284 x 203 mm, No. of Columns (Display): 7, Col Widths (Display): 55 mm
Copy instructions: *Copy Date:* 2 days prior to publication
LOCAL NEWSPAPERS

WOHNEN
1852427S4E-832
Editorial: Bucheggstr. 109, 8057 ZÜRICH
Tel: 44 3602652 **Fax:** 44 3626971
Email: richard.liechti@svw.ch **Web site:** http://www.svw.ch
Freq: 10 issues yearly; **Annual Sub.:** CHF 48,00; **Circ:** 10,311
Editor: Richard Liechti
Profile: Magazine with information about Swiss Building Societies.
Language(s): German
ADVERTISING RATES:
Full Page Mono .... CHF 3300
Full Page Colour .... CHF 4800
Mechanical Data: Type Area: 271 x 188 mm
Copy instructions: *Copy Date:* 36 days prior to publication
Official Journal of: Organ d. Logis Suisse, d. Hypothekar-Bürgschaftsgenossenschaft u. d. Allg. Baugenossenschaft Zü.

WOHNREVUE
748269S74C-520
Editorial: Stationsstr. 49, 8902 URDORF
Tel: 44 7358000 **Fax:** 44 7358001
Email: redaktion@wohnrevue.ch **Web site:** http://www.wohnrevue.ch
Freq: Monthly; **Annual Sub.:** CHF 84,00; **Circ:** 19,500
Editor: Nina Huber; **Advertising Manager:** Patrick Boll
Profile: Magazine containing information about furniture and furnishings.
Language(s): German
ADVERTISING RATES:
Full Page Mono .... CHF 5500
Full Page Colour .... CHF 6400
Mechanical Data: Type Area: 257 x 184 mm
Copy instructions: *Copy Date:* 30 days prior to publication
CONSUMER: WOMEN'S INTEREST CONSUMER MAGAZINES: Home & Family

WOHNWAGEN CARAVANES
1656172S49A-411
Editorial: Wolleraustr. 11a, 8807 FREIENBACH
Tel: 848 333100 **Fax:** 55 4158200
Web site: http://www.eurotaxglass.ch
Freq: Annual; **Annual Sub.:** CHF 297,00; **Circ:** 650
Profile: Information about the evaluation of caravans.
Language(s): French; German
Mechanical Data: Type Area: 138 x 95 mm

WOHNIWIRTSCHAFT
1753054S74K-111
Editorial: Stadtturmstr. 19, 5401 BADEN
Tel: 56 2005050 **Fax:** 56 2229018
Email: info@hev-aargau.ch **Web site:** http://www.hev-aargau.ch
Freq: 10 issues yearly; **Cover Price:** CHF 3,00
Free to qualifying individuals ; **Circ:** 33,681
Editor: Martin Meili
Profile: Magazine for house and land owners.
Language(s): German
ADVERTISING RATES:
Full Page Mono .... CHF 2900
Full Page Colour .... CHF 4355
Mechanical Data: Type Area: 264 x 186 mm, No. of Columns (Display): 3, Col Widths (Display): 58 mm
Copy instructions: *Copy Date:* 15 days prior to publication
CONSUMER: WOMEN'S INTEREST CONSUMER MAGAZINES: Home Purchase

WORK
2059545S74A-529
Editorial: 17, rue de Genève, 1002 LAUSANNE
Tel: 21 3314141 **Fax:** 21 3314110
Email: k.berger@agefi.com **Web site:** http://www.profilfemme.ch
Freq: Half-yearly; **Circ:** 31,500
Editor: Katia Berger; **Advertising Manager:** Marie Dautruche
Profile: Women's interest magazine. Contains articles about fashion, beauty, travel and lifestyle.
Language(s): French
ADVERTISING RATES:
Full Page Mono .... CHF 9800
Full Page Colour .... CHF 9800
Mechanical Data: Type Area: 245 x 147 mm
Copy instructions: *Copy Date:* 21 days prior to publication
Supplement to: L'Agefi, profil

WORK
2059546S74A-530
Editorial: 17, rue de Genève, 1002 LAUSANNE
Tel: 21 3314141 **Fax:** 21 3314110
Email: k.berger@agefi.com **Web site:** http://www.profilfemme.ch
Freq: Half-yearly; **Circ:** 10,500
Editor: Katia Berger
Profile: Women's interest magazine. Contains articles about fashion, beauty, travel and lifestyle.
Language(s): German
ADVERTISING RATES:
Full Page Mono .... CHF 9800
Full Page Colour .... CHF 9800
Mechanical Data: Type Area: 245 x 147 mm
Copy instructions: *Copy Date:* 21 days prior to publication
Supplement to: Women in Business

WORT+WÄRCH
748414S87-2660
Editorial: Postfach 101, 3048 WORBLAUFEN
Tel: 31 3304643 **Fax:** 31 3304640
Email: redaktion@egw.ch **Web site:** http://www.egw.ch
Freq: Monthly; Free to qualifying individuals
Annual Sub.: CHF 43,00; **Circ:** 3,000
Editor: Gertrud Trittibach; **Advertising Manager:** Gertrud Trittibach
Profile: Magazine about all aspects of religion.
Language(s): German
Readership: Read by members and friends of the Evangelisches Gemeinschaftswerk.
ADVERTISING RATES:
Full Page Mono .... CHF 599
Full Page Colour .... CHF 599
Mechanical Data: Type Area: 268 x 172 mm, No. of Columns (Display): 4, Col Widths (Display): 40 mm
Copy instructions: *Copy Date:* 30 days prior to publication
CONSUMER: RELIGIOUS

WOZ DIE WOCHENZEITUNG
748346S72-9140
Editorial: Hardturmstr. 66, 8031 ZÜRICH
Tel: 44 4481414 **Fax:** 44 4481415
Email: woz@woz.ch **Web site:** http://www.woz.ch
Freq: Weekly; **Annual Sub.:** CHF 265,00; **Circ:** 17,000
Editor: Susan Boos
Profile: Regional weekly covering politics, economics, sport, travel, technology and the arts.
Language(s): German
ADVERTISING RATES:
SCC .... CHF 38,00
Mechanical Data: Type Area: 430 x 291 mm, No. of Columns (Display): 5, Col Widths (Display): 55 mm
Copy instructions: *Copy Date:* 7 days prior to publication
Supplement(s): Le Monde diplomatique; WoZ Literatur
LOCAL NEWSPAPERS

WWF MAGAZIN
1859269S57-726
Editorial: Hohlstr. 110, 8004 ZÜRICH
Tel: 44 2972121 **Fax:** 44 2972100
Email: info@wwf.ch **Web site:** http://www.wwf.ch
Freq: Quarterly; **Circ:** 165,000
Profile: Magazine about environmental protection.
Language(s): German
ADVERTISING RATES:
Full Page Mono .... CHF 8300
Full Page Colour .... CHF 11100
Mechanical Data: Type Area: 251 x 175 mm

WWF RIVISTA
1859270S57-727
Editorial: P. Indipendenza, 6, 6501 BELLINZONA
Tel: 91 8206000 **Fax:** 91 8206008
Email: servizio@wwf.ch **Web site:** http://www.wwf.ch
Freq: Quarterly; **Circ:** 10,000
Profile: Magazine of the World Wide Fund for Nature.
Language(s): Italian
ADVERTISING RATES:
Full Page Mono .... CHF 1180
Full Page Colour .... CHF 2080
Mechanical Data: Type Area: 251 x 175 mm

YACHTING SWISS BOAT
1656323S75M-148
Editorial: Ekkehardstr. 16, 8006 ZÜRICH
Tel: 91 6046258 **Fax:** 32 3848634

Email: stefan.detjen@yachting.ch **Web site:** http://www.yachting.ch
Freq: 6 issues yearly; **Annual Sub.:** CHF 45,00; **Circ:** 8,500
Editor: tefan Detjen
Profile: Yacht magazine.
Language(s): German
ADVERTISING RATES:
Full Page Mono .... CHF 4300
Full Page Colour .... CHF 4300
Mechanical Data: Type Area: 260 x 195 mm, No. of Columns (Display): 4, Col Widths (Display): 43 mm
Copy instructions: *Copy Date:* 27 days prior to publication
Official Journal of: Organ d. Schweizer. Interessengemeinschaft Bootssport
CONSUMER: SPORT: Water Sports

Z DIE SCHÖNEN SEITEN
1846544G65A-263_108
Editorial: Falkenstr. 11, 8021 ZÜRICH
Tel: 44 2581111 **Fax:** 44 2581323
Email: nzzastil@nzz.ch **Web site:** http://www.magazin-z.ch
Freq: Quarterly; **Circ:** 322,000
Editor: Jeroen van Rooijen
Profile: «Z Die Schönen Seiten» is the magazine for the delightful and beautiful aspects of life. It is aimed at an intelligent and free-spending readers with the need for high-goods and services. The magazine "Z" was launched in early 2007, which offers a high range and is noticeable for the special format that is unique to Switzerland. "Z" is published eight times per year and by the Saturday edition of the enclosed "Neue Zürcher Zeitung" and the "NZZ am Sonntag ". The "Frankfurter Allgemeine Zeitung"and the "Neue Zürcher Zeitung" produce a big new edition of the lifestyle magazine supplement "Z Die Schönen Seiten". The magazine "Z" is thus produced four times a year in accordance with the high journalistic claims of the two editors of NZZ and FAZ.
Language(s): German
ADVERTISING RATES:
Full Page Mono .... EUR 29500
Full Page Colour .... EUR 29500
Mechanical Data: Type Area: 372 x 256 mm, No. of Columns (Display): 4, Col Widths (Display): 61 mm
Copy instructions: *Copy Date:* 29 days prior to publication
Supplement to: Frankfurter Allgemeine, Neue Zürcher Zeitung, NZZ am Sonntag
NATIONAL DAILY & SUNDAY NEWSPAPERS: Unabhängiges konservatives MdEP

ZAHLEN, DATEN, FAKTEN SRG SSR IDÉE SUISSE
1828704S2A-676
Editorial: Giacomettistr. 1, 3000 BERN 31
Tel: 31 3509111
Email: publishing@srg-ssr.ch **Web site:** http://www.srg-ssr.ch
Freq: Annual; **Cover Price:** Free; **Circ:** 5,000
Editor: Dominic Witschi
Profile: Publication of the SRG SSR company.
Language(s): German

ZBGR SCHWEIZERISCHE ZEITSCHRIFT FÜR BEURKUNDUNGS- UND GRUNDBUCHRECHT RNRF REVUE SUISSE DU NOTARIAT ET DU REGISTRE FONCIER
1841089S1A-298
Editorial: Sunnebüelstr. 34, 8604 VOLKETSWIL
Tel: 43 5344596
Email: juerg.schmid@zbgr.ch **Web site:** http://www.zbgr.ch
Freq: 6 issues yearly; **Annual Sub.:** CHF 69,00; **Circ:** 2,100
Editor: Jürg Schmid
Profile: Magazine from the Zurich Association of Notaries.
Language(s): French; German
ADVERTISING RATES:
Full Page Mono .... CHF 710
Mechanical Data: Type Area: 175 x 108 mm
Copy instructions: *Copy Date:* 30 days prior to publication
Official Journal of: Organ d. Verband Schweizer. Grundbuchverwalter

ZEITLUPE
1656044S74N-255
Editorial: Schulhausstr. 55, 8027 ZÜRICH
Tel: 44 2838913 **Fax:** 44 2838910
Email: marianne.noser@zeitlupe.ch **Web site:** http://www.zeitlupe.ch
Freq: 10 issues yearly; **Annual Sub.:** CHF 42,00; **Circ:** 70,612
Editor: Marianne Noser
Profile: Magazine for the elderly.
Language(s): German
ADVERTISING RATES:
Full Page Mono .... CHF 4840
Full Page Colour .... CHF 6460
Mechanical Data: Type Area: 256 x 183 mm, No. of Columns (Display): 4, Col Widths (Display): 43 mm
Copy instructions: *Copy Date:* 25 days prior to publication
CONSUMER: WOMEN'S INTEREST CONSUMER MAGAZINES: Retirement

ZEITPUNKT
1852627S73-384
Editorial: Werkhofstr. 19, 4500 SOLOTHURN
Tel: 32 6218111 **Fax:** 32 6218110
Email: mail@zeitpunkt.ch **Web site:** http://www.zeitpunkt.ch
Freq: 6 issues yearly; **Annual Sub.:** CHF 54,00; **Circ:** 8,000
Editor: Christoph Pfluger
Profile: Magazine about people living their dreams.
Language(s): German
ADVERTISING RATES:
Full Page Mono .... CHF 1600
Full Page Colour .... CHF 1750
Mechanical Data: Col Widths (Display): 55 mm, Type Area: 238 x 174 mm, No. of Columns (Display): 3
Copy instructions: *Copy Date:* 24 days prior to publication

ZEITSCHRIFT DES BERNISCHEN JURISTENVEREINS REVUE DE LA SOCIÉTÉ DES JURISTES BERNOIS ZBJV
1853051S1A-312
Editorial: Wölflistr. 1, 3001 BERN **Tel:** 31 3006666
Fax: 31 3006688
Email: verlag@staempfli.com **Web site:** http://www.staempfliverlag.com
Freq: 11 issues yearly; **Annual Sub.:** CHF 148,00; **Circ:** 3,700
Editor: Heinz Hausheer
Profile: Magazine from the Association of Jurists in Bern.
Language(s): French; German
ADVERTISING RATES:
Full Page Mono .... CHF 780
Full Page Colour .... CHF 780
Mechanical Data: Type Area: 175 x 104 mm
Copy instructions: *Copy Date:* 24 days prior to publication
Official Journal of: Organ f. schweizer. Rechtspflege u. Gesetzgebung

ZEITSCHRIFT FÜR KINDER- UND JUGENDPSYCHIATRIE UND PSYCHOTHERAPIE
1853298S56A-2189
Editorial: Länggassstr. 76, 3000 BERN 9
Tel: 31 3004500 **Fax:** 31 3004590
Email: zeitschriften@hanshuber.com **Web site:** http://www.verlag-hanshuber.com/zkjp
Freq: 6 issues yearly; Free to qualifying individuals
Annual Sub.: CHF 245,00; **Circ:** 1,600
Advertising Manager: H.R. Schindler
Profile: Magazine about psychiatry and psychotherapy used in the treatment of children and adolescents.
Language(s): German
ADVERTISING RATES:
Full Page Mono .... CHF 640
Full Page Colour .... CHF 1390
Mechanical Data: Type Area: 250 x 170 mm
Official Journal of: Organ d. Dt. Ges. f. Kinder- u. Jugendpsychiatrie, Psychosomatik u. Psychotherapie

ZEITSCHRIFT FÜR KINDES- UND ERWACHSENENSCHUTZ REVUE DELA PROTECTION DES MINEURS ET DES ADULTES RIVISTA DELLA PROTIZIONE DEL MINORI E DEGLI ADULTI
1641067S32A-461
Editorial: Werftstr. 1, 6002 LUZERN **Tel:** 41 3674857
Fax: 41 3674849
Web site: http://www.kokes.ch
Freq: 6 issues yearly; **Annual Sub.:** CHF 78,00
Editor: Kurt Affolter
Profile: Essays on recent family law topics and similar issues.
Language(s): French; German; Italian
BUSINESS: LOCAL GOVERNMENT, LEISURE & RECREATION: Local Government

ZEITSCHRIFT FÜR PÄDAGOGIK
748720G62B-3195
Editorial: Riehenstr. 154, 4058 BASEL
Tel: 61 4674972 **Fax:** 61 4674969
Email: berit.oetsch@unibas.ch
Freq: 6 issues yearly; **Annual Sub.:** CHF 110,30; **Circ:** 1,600
Editor: Roland Reichenbach; **Advertising Manager:** Claudia Klinger
Profile: The journal is the forum for discussion of educational science. It represents the current state of the epistemological and methodological disputes, establish and evaluate scientific issues of public interest in the fields of education and socialization, education and youth policy. The magazine informs about the results of empirical educational research, historical education and international developments.
Language(s): German
ADVERTISING RATES:
Full Page Mono .... EUR 780
Mechanical Data: Type Area: 198 x 130 mm
Copy instructions: *Copy Date:* 51 days prior to publication
BUSINESS: CHURCH & SCHOOL EQUIPMENT & EDUCATION: Education Teachers

ZOFINGER TAGBLATT ZT
748948S67B-2860
Editorial: Henzmannstr. 20, 4800 ZOFINGEN
Tel: 62 7459350 **Fax:** 62 7459419
Email: redaktion@zofingertagblatt.ch **Web site:** http://www.ztonline.ch
Freq: 312 issues yearly; **Annual Sub.:** CHF 385,55; **Circ:** 15,114
Editor: Beat Kirchhofer; **Advertising Manager:** Thomas Schwabe
Profile: Regional daily newspaper covering politics, economics, sport, travel, technology and the arts.
Language(s): German
ADVERTISING RATES:
SCC .... CHF 33,90
Mechanical Data: Type Area: 440 x 290 mm, No. of Columns (Display): 10, Col Widths (Display): 26 mm
Copy instructions: *Copy Date:* 2 days prior to publication
REGIONAL DAILY & SUNDAY NEWSPAPERS: Regional Daily Newspapers

ZOOM
1648565S14A-1179
Editorial: Buchenstr. 101, 4500 SOLOTHURN
Tel: 32 6247685 **Fax:** 32 6247444
Email: info@dejo-press.ch **Web site:** http://www.dejo-press.ch
Freq: 3 issues yearly; **Cover Price:** Free; **Circ:** 50,000
Editor: Joseph Weibel
Profile: Customer magazine about business consulting, trusts, taxes and law.
Language(s): German

ZUGER WOCHE
749024S72-9260
Editorial: Oberdorfstr. 11, 6342 BAAR
Tel: 41 7697040 **Fax:** 41 7697049
Email: redaktion@zugerwoche.ch **Web site:** http://www.zugerwoche.ch
Freq: Weekly; **Cover Price:** Free; **Circ:** 43,618
Editor: Dany Kammüller
Profile: Advertising journal (house-to-house) concentrating on local stories.
Language(s): German
ADVERTISING RATES:
Full Page Mono .... CHF 6952
Full Page Colour .... CHF 7352
Mechanical Data: Type Area: 440 x 286 mm, No. of Columns (Display): 10, Col Widths (Display): 25 mm
Copy instructions: *Copy Date:* 1 day prior to publication
LOCAL NEWSPAPERS

ZÜRCHER BAUER
1859159S21A-623
Editorial: Nüschelerstr. 35, 8001 ZÜRICH
Tel: 44 2177733 **Fax:** 44 2177732
Email: bauernverband@zbv.ch **Web site:** http://www.zbv.ch
Freq: Weekly; **Annual Sub.:** CHF 63,00; **Circ:** 10,538
Profile: Regional daily newspaper covering politics, economics, sport, travel, technology and the arts.
Language(s): German
ADVERTISING RATES:
SCC .... CHF 48,00
Mechanical Data: Type Area: 420 x 286 mm, No. of Columns (Display): 10, Col Widths (Display): 25 mm
Copy instructions: *Copy Date:* 2 days prior to publication
Official Journal of: Organ d. Zürcher Bauernverb., d. Zürcher Landfrauen-Vereinigung, d. Obstbauverein Kanton Zü., d. Verein Zürcher u. Schaffhauser Bio-Produzenten u. d. Zürcher IP-Bauern

DER ZÜRCHER HAUSEIGENTÜMER
1647607S74K-108
Editorial: Albisstr. 28, 8038 ZÜRICH **Tel:** 44 4871700
Fax: 44 4871777
Email: hev@hev-zuerich.ch **Web site:** http://www.hev-zuerich.ch
Freq: Monthly; Free to qualifying individuals
Annual Sub.: CHF 20,00; **Circ:** 57,726
Editor: Luca Roncoroni; **Advertising Manager:** Markus Turani
Profile: Magazine of the House Owners' Association in Zurich.
Language(s): German
ADVERTISING RATES:
Full Page Mono .... CHF 1230
Full Page Colour .... CHF 1690
Mechanical Data: Type Area: 180 x 130 mm
Copy instructions: *Copy Date:* 25 days prior to publication
CONSUMER: WOMEN'S INTEREST CONSUMER MAGAZINES: Home Purchase

ZÜRCHER UMWELT PRAXIS
748996S57-660
Editorial: Stampfenbachstr. 14, 8006 ZÜRICH
Tel: 43 2592417 **Fax:** 43 2595126
Email: isabel.flynn@bd.zh.ch **Web site:** http://www.umweltschutz.zh.ch
Freq: Quarterly; **Cover Price:** Free; **Circ:** 4,000
Editor: Isabel Flynn
Profile: Magazine about practical environmental protection in the canton of Zurich.
Language(s): German

ZÜRCHER UNTERLÄNDER
748998S67B-2920
Editorial: Seestr. 86, 8712 STÄFA **Tel:** 44 9285811
Fax: 44 9285810
Email: redaktion@zuonline.ch **Web site:** http://www.zuonline.ch
Freq: 260 issues yearly; **Annual Sub.:** CHF 298,00; **Circ:** 22,544
Editor: Michael Schönenberger
Profile: Regional daily newspaper covering politics, economics, sport, travel, technology and the arts.
Language(s): German
ADVERTISING RATES:
SCC .... CHF 21,90
Mechanical Data: Type Area: 440 x 286 mm, No. of Columns (Display): 10, Col Widths (Display): 26 mm
Copy instructions: *Copy Date:* 1 day prior to publication
Supplement(s): Fespo Magazin
REGIONAL DAILY & SUNDAY NEWSPAPERS: Regional Daily Newspapers

ZÜRCHER UNTERNEHMER
1847773S14A-1263
Editorial: Köschenrütistr. 109, 8052 ZÜRICH
Tel: 44 3064704 **Fax:** 44 3064711
Email: blattner@zuercherunternehmer.ch **Web site:** http://www.zuercherunternehmer.ch
Freq: 10 issues yearly; **Circ:** 29,000
Editor: Peter Blattner; **Advertising Manager:** Richard Leimbacher
Profile: Magazine for owners and managers of small and medium sized companies.
Language(s): German
ADVERTISING RATES:
Full Page Mono .... CHF 3600
Full Page Colour .... CHF 4800
Mechanical Data: Type Area: 290 x 208 mm, No. of Columns (Display): 4, Col Widths (Display): 50 mm
Copy instructions: *Copy Date:* 14 days prior to publication
Supplement to: Unternehmer-Zeitung

ZÜRCHER WIRTSCHAFT
766172S14A-1125
Editorial: Badener Str. 21, 8050 ZÜRICH
Tel: 43 2883368 **Fax:** 43 2883360
Email: zuercherwirtschaft@kgv.ch **Web site:** http://www.kgv.ch
Freq: 10 issues yearly; Free to qualifying individuals
Annual Sub.: CHF 50,00; **Circ:** 19,500
Editor: Thomas Pfyffer
Language(s): German
ADVERTISING RATES:
Full Page Mono .... CHF 3760
Full Page Colour .... CHF 3760
Mechanical Data: Type Area: 284 x 208 mm
Copy instructions: *Copy Date:* 30 days prior to publication
BUSINESS: COMMERCE, INDUSTRY & MANAGEMENT

ZÜRCHER WIRTSCHAFTS MAGAZIN
1852989S14A-1285
Editorial: Postfach, 8010 ZÜRICH **Tel:** 44 2922075
Fax: 44 2922068
Email: zwm@zkb.ch **Web site:** http://www.zkb.ch
Freq: Quarterly; **Cover Price:** Free; **Circ:** 25,000
Editor: Othmar Köchle
Profile: Company publication published by Zürcher Kantonalbank.
Language(s): German

ZÜRICHSEE-ZEITUNG
1655218S67B-6628
Editorial: Seestr. 86, 8712 STÄFA **Tel:** 44 9285811
Fax: 44 9285810
Email: redaktion.horgen@zsz.ch **Web site:** http://www.zsz.ch
Annual Sub.: CHF 328,00
Profile: Regional daily newspaper covering politics, economics, sport, travel, technology and the arts.
Language(s): German
Supplement(s): Fespo Magazin
REGIONAL DAILY & SUNDAY NEWSPAPERS: Regional Daily Newspapers

ZÜRICHSEE-ZEITUNG
1655219S67B-6629
Editorial: Seestr. 86, 8712 STÄFA **Tel:** 44 9285555
Fax: 44 9285550
Email: redaktion@zlzeitung.ch **Web site:** http://www.zsz.ch
Freq: 260 issues yearly; **Annual Sub.:** CHF 328,00; **Circ:** 41,957
Editor: Benjamin Geiger
Profile: Regional daily newspaper covering politics, economics, sport, travel, technology and the arts.
Language(s): German
Mechanical Data: Type Area: 440 x 286 mm, No. of Columns (Display): 10, Col Widths (Display): 25 mm
Supplement(s): Fespo Magazin
REGIONAL DAILY & SUNDAY NEWSPAPERS: Regional Daily Newspapers

ZÜRICHSEE-ZEITUNG
1655220S72-9648
Editorial: Burghaldenstr. 4, 8810 HORGEN
Tel: 44 7181020 **Fax:** 44 7181025
Email: redaktion.horgen@zsz.ch **Web site:** http://www.zsz.ch
Cover Price: Free
Editor: Lukas Matt
Profile: Advertising journal (house-to-house) concentrating on local stories.
Language(s): German
LOCAL NEWSPAPERS

ZÜRICHSEE-ZEITUNG
1655221S72-9649
Editorial: Seestr. 86, 8712 STÄFA **Tel:** 44 9285555
Fax: 44 9285550
Email: redaktion.staefa@zsz.ch **Web site:** http://www.zsz.ch
Freq: Weekly; **Cover Price:** Free; **Circ:** 75,884
Editor: Christian Dietz-Saluz
Profile: Advertising journal (house-to-house) concentrating on local stories.
Language(s): German
ADVERTISING RATES:
Full Page Mono .... CHF 7900
Full Page Colour .... CHF 9200
Mechanical Data: Type Area: 440 x 286 mm, No. of Columns (Display): 10, Col Widths (Display): 25 mm
LOCAL NEWSPAPERS

ZÜRISPORT
1656175S75A-376
Editorial: Postfach, 8702 ZOLLIKON **Tel:** 44 3962555
Fax: 44 3962552
Email: zuerisport@xess.ch **Web site:** http://www.zss.ch
Freq: Quarterly; **Circ:** 37,017
Editor: Erich Ogi
Profile: Magazine containing information for athletes.
Language(s): German
ADVERTISING RATES:
Full Page Mono .... CHF 3300
Full Page Colour .... CHF 4125
Mechanical Data: Type Area: 286 x 203 mm, No. of Columns (Display): 4, Col Widths (Display): 48 mm
Copy instructions: *Copy Date:* 15 days prior to publication
CONSUMER: SPORT

ZWEIRAD DEUX ROUES DUE RUOTE
1656177S31B-3
Editorial: Wolleraustr. 11a, 8807 FREIENBACH
Tel: 848 333100 **Fax:** 55 4158200
Web site: http://www.eurotaxglass.ch
Freq: Quarterly; **Annual Sub.:** CHF 228,00; **Circ:** 1,010
Profile: Fahrzeugbewertungen für Kleinmotorräder, Motorräder und Roller.
Language(s): French; German; Italian
Mechanical Data: Type Area: 138 x 93 mm
Copy instructions: *Copy Date:* 30 days prior to publication

Turkey

Time Difference: GMT + 2 hrs (EET - Eastern European Time)
National Telephone Code: +90
Continent: Europe
Capital: Ankara
Principal Language: Turkish, Kurdish
Population: 68893918
Monetary Unit: New Turkish Lira (YTL)

EMBASSY HIGH COMMISSION: Embassy of the Republic of Turkey: 43 Belgrave Sq, London SW1X 8PA
Tel: 020 7393 0202
Fax: 020 7393 0066
Email:turkemb.london@mfa.gov.tr /Website: http://london.emb.mfa.gov.tr/ Head of Mission: H E Ahmet Unal Cevikoz

AKŞAM
763123TR65A-222
Editorial: Davutpaşa C. No.34 34020, Zeytinburnu, İSTANBUL **Tel:** 212 4493000 **Fax:** 212 4819561
Email: haber@aksam.com.tr **Web site:** http://www.aksam.com.tr
Freq: Daily; **Cover Price:** YTL 0,25; **Circ:** 142,277
News Editor: Kader Balikci
Profile: Newspaper focusing on national and international news and current affairs.
Language(s): Turkish
ADVERTISING RATES:
SCC .... YTL 44.25
NATIONAL DAILY & SUNDAY NEWSPAPERS: National Daily Newspapers

AKSIYON
766200TR73-1
Editorial: Fevzi Çakmak Mah. A. Taner Kışlalı Cad. No:6 34194, Yenibosna, İSTANBUL **Tel:** 212 4541454
Fax: 212 4548625
Email: okur@aksiyon.com.tr **Web site:** http://www.aksiyon.com.tr
Freq: Weekly; **Cover Price:** YTL 2,00; **Circ:** 23,698
Editor: Kadir Dikbas
Profile: Magazine covering news and current affairs.
Language(s): Turkish
CONSUMER: NATIONAL & INTERNATIONAL PERIODICALS

AUTO SHOW
753045TR77A-50
Editorial: Hürriyet Medya Towers 34212, Güneşli, İSTANBUL **Tel:** 212 4103440 **Fax:** 212 4103442
Email: autoshow@doganburda.com
Freq: Weekly; **Cover Price:** YTL 2,50; **Circ:** 9,036
Profile: Magazine featuring cars and accessories.
Language(s): Turkish
Readership: Read predominantly by men aged between 18 and 24 years.
CONSUMER: MOTORING & CYCLING: Motoring

AYDIN TICARET ODASI DERGISI
1615417TR63-1
Editorial: Ürgen Paşa Cd. No:15, Merkez, AYDIN
Tel: 256 2132202 **Fax:** 256 2128254
Email: atob@atob.org.tr
Freq: 6 issues yearly; **Cover Price:** YTL Ücretsiz; **Circ:** 4,000
Profile: Official publication of the Chamber of Commerce of Aydin.
Language(s): Turkish
Readership: Read by members of the local business community.
BUSINESS: REGIONAL BUSINESS

BANYO MUTFAK
1615839TR23C-1
Editorial: Matbaacılar Sitesi 1.Cd. No:115 34554, Bağcılar, İSTANBUL **Tel:** 212 4133333
Fax: 212 6290575
Email: msezen@boyut.com.tr
Freq: 6 issues yearly; **Cover Price:** YTL 5,00; **Circ:** 16,000
Profile: Magazine focusing on improvements, technology, design and decoration in the kitchen and bathroom.
Language(s): Turkish
Readership: Read by interior designer, decorators and architects.
BUSINESS: FURNISHINGS & FURNITURE: Furnishings & Furniture - Kitchens & Bathrooms

BUSINESS TRAVEL IN TURKEY
1615667TR89D-6
Editorial: Nispetiye Cd. No:48/11 80630, Etiler, İSTANBUL **Tel:** 212 2870532 **Fax:** 212 2870531
Email: btt@isseyahatleri.com
Freq: Quarterly; **Cover Price:** YTL 2.000.000; **Circ:** 12,000
Profile: Magazine focusing on business and incentive travel and meetings.
Language(s): English; Turkish
Readership: Read by corporate travellers and decision makers.
CONSUMER: HOLIDAYS & TRAVEL: In-Flight Magazines

CAPITAL
762396TR1A-8
Formerly: Capital Magazine
Editorial: Hürriyet Medya Towers, 34212 GÜNESLI - ISTANBUL **Tel:** 212 41 03 228 **Fax:** 212 41 03 227
Email: sseckin@capital.com.tr **Web site:** http://www.capital.com.tr
Freq: Monthly; **Circ:** 15,395
Editor: Volkan Aki
Profile: Magazine focusing on finance and economics. Includes articles on business and politics.
Language(s): Turkish
BUSINESS: FINANCE & ECONOMICS

CD OYUN
1615323TR78D-2
Editorial: Şölen Sk. No:10/2 06550, Çankaya, ANKARA **Tel:** 312 2873152 **Fax:** 312 2846037
Email: gulsun@cdoyun.com
Freq: Monthly; **Cover Price:** YTL 6.000.000; **Circ:** 12,100
Profile: Magazine focusing on computer and console games. Includes computing news, new games and ratings.
Language(s): Turkish
CONSUMER: CONSUMER ELECTRONICS: Games

CHAT
1614093TR91E-1
Editorial: HSBC Bank A:Ş HSBC Plaza Ayazağa Mahallesi Ahi Evran Cad. Dereboyu Sok. 34398, Maslak, İSTANBUL **Tel:** 212 3663000
Fax: 212 3663411
Freq: 6 issues yearly; **Cover Price:** YTL Ücretsiz; **Circ:** 40,000
Profile: Magazine containing celebrity interviews, fashion, food and drink, travel and general issues. Each issue covers a themed topic.
Language(s): Turkish
Readership: Aimed at top spending account holders of HSBC Bank.
CONSUMER: RECREATION & LEISURE: Lifestyle

CHIP
764037TR5B-20
Editorial: Hürriyet Medya Towers, Güneşli, 34212 İSTANBUL **Tel:** 212 410 36 00 **Fax:** 212 410 33 57
Web site: http://www.chip.com.tr
Date Established: 1996; **Freq:** Monthly; **Cover Price:** YTL 5,90; **Circ:** 48,951
Editor: Cem Sinanoğlu
Profile: Magazine containing information on computer technology and applications. Includes specialist features, market overviews and hardware and software tests.
Language(s): Turkish
Readership: Aimed at decision makers in companies responsible for data processing and people who are interested in computers.
ADVERTISING RATES:
Full Page Colour .... YTL 28500.00
BUSINESS: COMPUTERS & AUTOMATION: Data Processing

CORNUCOPIA
766502TR84A-1
Editorial: CC 480 80303, Mecidiyeköy, İSTANBUL
Tel: 212 2483607 **Fax:** 212 2483607
Email: cornucopia@atlas.net.tr
Freq: 3 issues yearly; **Cover Price:** YTL 20000000; **Circ:** 28,500
Profile: Magazine focusing on Turkey, containing illustrated articles on people, places, food, travel, interior, history and current affairs.
Language(s): English
Readership: Read by those interested in history and culture.
CONSUMER: THE ARTS & LITERARY: Arts

COSMO GIRL!
1640326TR74F-1
Editorial: Barbaros Bulvan Cam Han No:125, Beşiktaş, İSTANBUL **Tel:** 212 4112000
Fax: 212 3544745
Email: abone@merkezdergi.com.tr **Web site:** http://www.cosmogirl.com.tr
Freq: Monthly; **Cover Price:** YTL 4,00; **Circ:** 18,410
Profile: Magazine focusing on beauty, fashion and make up. Each issue has insider beauty and fashion secrets from stars and their stylists.
Language(s): Turkish
Readership: Read by women aged 15 to 30 years old. Over 50% are teenagers aged 15 to 17 years.
CONSUMER: WOMEN'S INTEREST CONSUMER MAGAZINES: Teenage

CUMHURIYET
762382TR65A-2
Editorial: Türkocağı Cd. No:39/41 34334 (P.K.246 34435 Sirkeci-İst.), Cağaloğlu, İSTANBUL
Tel: 212 343 72 74 **Fax:** 212 291 49 76
Email: posta@cumhuriyet.com.tr **Web site:** http://www.cumhuriyet.com.tr
Freq: Daily; **Cover Price:** YTL 0,50; **Circ:** 62,583
Managing Director: İbrahim Yıldız
Profile: Newspaper containing national and international news, business, current affairs and sport.
Language(s): English; Turkish
NATIONAL DAILY & SUNDAY NEWSPAPERS: National Daily Newspapers

EGE LIFE
1640566TR89C-2
Editorial: Cumhuriyet bulvan No:231 Kat:7 Daire:13, Alsancak, İZMIR **Tel:** 232 4648588 **Fax:** 232 4648588
Email: info@egelife.com
Freq: Monthly; **Cover Price:** YTL 5,00; **Circ:** 7,500
Profile: Magazine featuring art, travel, city tours, cartoons, history, recipes, city guide, music, cinema, drama, entertainment places, shopping and cars. Special editions in the summer for tourists.
Language(s): Turkish
Readership: Read by people with a high disposable income, businessmen and tourists.
CONSUMER: HOLIDAYS & TRAVEL: Entertainment Guides

EKONOMIST
1201084TR1A-15
Editorial: Hürriyet Medya Towers 34212, Güneşli, İSTANBUL **Tel:** 212 4103256 **Fax:** 212 4103255
Email: ekonomist@doganburda.com **Web site:** http://www.ekonomist.com.tr
Freq: Weekly; **Cover Price:** YTL 3,00; **Circ:** 9,500
Profile: Magazine covering the economy.
Language(s): Turkish
BUSINESS: FINANCE & ECONOMICS

ELEGANS
766198TR82-1
Editorial: Valikonağı Cd. Yapı Kredi.V. Binası K:5 D.3 34363, Nişantaşı, İSTANBUL **Tel:** 212 2336506
Fax: 212 2312878
Email: elegans@elegans.com.tr
Freq: 6 issues yearly; **Cover Price:** YTL 5,00; **Circ:** 12,000
Profile: Magazine focusing on the economy, politics and non-governmental organisations.
Language(s): English; Turkish
Readership: Aimed at Turkish businessmen.
CONSUMER: CURRENT AFFAIRS & POLITICS

ELLE
749736TR74A-50
Editorial: Hürriyet Medya Towers, 34212 GÜNESLI - ISTANBUL **Tel:** 212 41 03 421 **Fax:** 212 41 03 528
Email: igormus@dmg.com.tr **Web site:** http://www.elle.com.tr
Date Established: 1999; **Freq:** Monthly; **Cover Price:** YTL 6.00
Annual Sub.: YTL 60.00; **Circ:** 22,402
Editor: Esra Aysan
Profile: Magazine featuring fashion, beauty, health, fitness, astrology, shopping and articles on women's issues.
Language(s): Turkish
ADVERTISING RATES:
Full Page Colour .... EUR 16000.00
Copy instructions: *Copy Date:* 4 weeks prior publication
CONSUMER: WOMEN'S INTEREST CONSUMER MAGAZINES: Women's Interest

FANATIK
762420TR75A-34
Editorial: Doğan Medya Center 34204, Bağcılar, İSTANBUL **Tel:** 212 5056542 **Fax:** 212 5056523
Freq: Daily; **Cover Price:** YTL 0,25; **Circ:** 190,595
Profile: Tabloid-sized newspaper focusing on sport with a special emphasize on football; includies previews, results, reports and interviews.
Language(s): Turkish
Readership: Aimed at sport enthusiasts.
CONSUMER: SPORT

FANATIK BASKET
762421TR75X-50
Editorial: Doğan Medya Center 34204, Bağcılar, İSTANBUL **Tel:** 212 5056524 **Fax:** 212 5056558
Freq: Weekly; **Cover Price:** YTL 0,40; **Circ:** 9,000
Profile: Newspaper featuring in-depth coverage of national and international professional and amateur basketball leagues.
Language(s): Turkish
Readership: Aimed at basketball enthusiasts.
CONSUMER: SPORT: Other Sport

GASTRONOMI
1615841TR22A-1
Editorial: Matbaacılar Sitesi 1.Cd. No:115 34554, Bağcılar, İSTANBUL **Tel:** 212 4133333
Fax: 212 4133334
Email: gastronomi@boyut.com.tr
Date Established: 1995; **Freq:** 6 issues yearly; **Cover Price:** YTL 7,00
Annual Sub.: YTL 36.00; **Circ:** 15,000
Profile: Magazine focusing on food and drinks from around the world.
Language(s): Turkish
Readership: Read by people who work in the tourism and food and drink sector.
BUSINESS: FOOD

THE GUIDE ANKARA
1615380TR89A-4
Editorial: Ali Kaya Sk. No:7 80720, Levent, İSTANBUL **Tel:** 212 283 20 61 **Fax:** 212 280 82 75
Email: guide@apa.com.tr
Freq: Annual; **Cover Price:** YTL 2.750.000; **Circ:** 25,000
Profile: Magazine focusing on Ankara and its surroundings. Includes arts and culture, business, hotels, cafés, shopping, restaurants, nightlife, sports and sightseeing.
Language(s): English; Turkish
Readership: Aimed at tourists planning to visit Ankara and expatriates.
CONSUMER: HOLIDAYS & TRAVEL: Travel

THE GUIDE ANTALYA
1615382TR89A-3
Editorial: Ali Kaya Sk. No:7 80720, Levent, İSTANBUL **Tel:** 212 2832061 **Fax:** 212 2808275
Email: guide@apa.com.tr
Freq: Annual; **Cover Price:** YTL 3.500.000; **Circ:** 40,000
Profile: Magazine focusing on Antalya and its surroundings. Includes arts and culture, business, hotels, cafés, shopping, restaurants, nightlife, sports and sightseeing.
Language(s): English; German; Turkish
Readership: Aimed at tourists planning to visit Antalya and expatriates.
CONSUMER: HOLIDAYS & TRAVEL: Travel

THE GUIDE BODRUM
1615385TR89A-2
Editorial: Ali Kaya Sk. No:7 80720, Levent, İSTANBUL **Tel:** 212 2802061 **Fax:** 212 2808275
Email: guide@apa.com.tr
Freq: Annual; **Cover Price:** YTL 2.750.000; **Circ:** 40,000

Profile: Magazine focusing on Bodrum and its surroundings. Includes arts and culture, business, hotels, cafés, shopping, restaurants, nightlife, sports and sightseeing.
Language(s): English; Turkish
Readership: Aimed at tourists planning to visit Bodrum and expatriates.
CONSUMER: HOLIDAYS & TRAVEL: Travel

THE GUIDE İSTANBUL
1615387TR89A-1
Editorial: Büyükdere Cad. No:191 34330, Levent, İSTANBUL **Tel:** 212 2832061 **Fax:** 212 2706370
Email: guide@apa.com.tr
Freq: 6 issues yearly; **Cover Price:** YTL 5.000.000; **Circ:** 25,000
Profile: Magazine focusing on Istanbul and its surroundings. Includes arts and culture, business, hotels, cafés, shopping, restaurants, nightlife, sports, sightseeing, museums, economy and politics, also features profiles of important people.
Language(s): English
Readership: Aimed at tourists planning to visit Istanbul and expatriates.
CONSUMER: HOLIDAYS & TRAVEL: Travel

GÜNEŞ 763001TR65A-224
Editorial: Merkezefendi Mh. Davutpaşa Cd. No:34, Zeytinburnu, İSTANBUL **Tel:** 212 4493010
Fax: 212 4819924
Web site: http://www.gunes.com
Freq: Daily; **Cover Price:** YTL 0,20; **Circ:** 124,911
Profile: Newspaper featuring national and international news, economy, sport and features.
Language(s): Turkish
NATIONAL DAILY & SUNDAY NEWSPAPERS: National Daily Newspapers

HUMAN RESOURCES 765886TR14F-1
Editorial: CemiBağdat Caddesi, Esen Apt. No.175 Daire:7, Kadıköy, İSTANBUL **Tel:** 216 3600111
Fax: 216 3600920
Email: info@hrdergi.com **Web site:** http://www.hrdergi.com/tr
Freq: Monthly; **Cover Price:** YTL 8,00
Annual Sub.: YTL 88.00; **Circ:** 5,500
Profile: Magazine focusing on recruitment, career planning, performance monitoring, e-learning and outsourcing of personnel. Includes company news and profiles. Provides a forum for discussion.
Language(s): Turkish
Readership: Read by HR professionals.
BUSINESS: COMMERCE, INDUSTRY & MANAGEMENT: Training & Recruitment

HÜRRIYET
1201093TR65A-5
Editorial: Hürriyet Medya Towers 34212, Güneşli, İSTANBUL **Tel:** 212 6770000 **Fax:** 212 6770327
Email: editor@hurriyet.com.tr **Web site:** http://www.hurriyet.com.tr
Freq: Daily; **Cover Price:** YTL 0,35; **Circ:** 467,478
Profile: Newspaper focusing on national and international news, politics, business and sport.
Language(s): Turkish
ADVERTISING RATES:
SCC .... YTL 119.98
NATIONAL DAILY & SUNDAY NEWSPAPERS: National Daily Newspapers

KAZETE 763266TR74R-1
Editorial: 1391 Sok. No 4/201, Alsancak, IZMIR
Tel: 232 46 36 300 **Fax:** 232 46 35 300
Email: kazete@kazete.com.tr **Web site:** http://www.kazete.com.tr
Freq: 6 issues yearly; **Annual Sub.:** YTL 18.75; **Circ:** 3,500
Editor: Berrin Delikçi
Profile: Women's magazine focusing on politics, society, law, education and women's issues.
Language(s): Turkish
ADVERTISING RATES:
Full Page Mono .... YTL 1100.00
Full Page Colour .... YTL 1500.00
CONSUMER: WOMEN'S INTEREST CONSUMER MAGAZINES: Women's Interest Related

LEVEL 766807TR78D-1
Editorial: Hürriyet Medya Towers, 34212 Güneşli, İSTANBUL **Tel:** 212 2179371 **Fax:** 212 2179532
Email: level@level.com.tr **Web site:** http://www.level.com.tr
Freq: Monthly; **Cover Price:** YTL 5,50; **Circ:** 13,542
Editor: Elif Akça
Profile: Magazine focusing on computer games, contains articles about new games and strategies.
Language(s): Turkish
Readership: Aimed at computer game players.
CONSUMER: CONSUMER ELECTRONICS: Games

MARKETING TÜRKIYE
1201266TR2A-5
Editorial: Prof.N.Mazhar Öksen Sk.No:1Rota Binasi34360, Şişli, İSTANBUL **Tel:** 212 2240144
Fax: 212 2337243
Email: rota@rotayayin.com.tr **Web site:** http://www.marketingturkiye.com/yeni
ISSN: 1303-457X
Freq: 24 issues yearly; **Cover Price:** YTL 6,00; **Circ:** 5,700
Editor: Elif Erman
Profile: Magazine covering marketing and advertising.
Language(s): Turkish
Readership: Aimed at people working in marketing and communication.
BUSINESS: COMMUNICATIONS, ADVERTISING & MARKETING

MATBAA TEKNIK 1200717TR41A-5
Editorial: İhlas Holding Merkez Binası Magazin Grubu 29 Ekim Cd. No:23 34520, Yenibosna, İSTANBUL
Tel: 212 4542520 **Fax:** 212 4542555
Email: img@img.com.tr
Freq: Monthly; **Cover Price:** YTL 10.000.000; **Circ:** 4,715
Profile: Magazine covering the printing and publishing industry; includes the latest technology, the economy, management, company news, market studies and reports.
Language(s): English; Turkish
BUSINESS: PRINTING & STATIONERY: Printing

MEDIKAL & TEKNIK 1200741TR56G-5
Editorial: 29 Ekim Mah., İhlas Holding Medya Blok Kat:1, 34530 YENIBOSNA - ISTANBUL
Tel: 212 45 42 503 **Fax:** 212 45 42 506
Email: info@ihlasfuar.com **Web site:** http://www.medikalteknik.com.tr
ISSN: 1301-0034
Date Established: 1987; **Freq:** Monthly; **Cover Price:** YTL 10.00; **Circ:** 10,200
Usual Pagination: 200
Editor: Dilek Doğan; **Advertising Director:** Ahmet Erarslan
Profile: Magazine covering medical equipment and suppliers, hospital management, market analysis and recent developments in the field.
Language(s): English; Turkish
ADVERTISING RATES:
Full Page Colour .... EUR 1500.00
Agency Commission: 15%
Mechanical Data: Bleed Size: 300 x 218 mm, Print Process: Offset
Copy instructions: *Copy Date:* 15th of month prior to publication date
BUSINESS: HEALTH & MEDICAL: Medical Equipment

MILLIYET
762407TR65A-8
Editorial: Doğan Medya Center 34204, Bağcılar, İSTANBUL **Tel:** 212 5056111 **Fax:** 212 5056233
Web site: http://www.milliyet.com.tr
Freq: Daily; **Cover Price:** YTL 0,25; **Circ:** 194,037
Editor: Sami Kohen
Profile: Newspaper focusing on national and international news, politics, business and sport.
Language(s): Turkish
ADVERTISING RATES:
SCC .... YTL 37.76
Supplement(s): Milliyet Arabam.com - 52xY, Milliyet Business - 52xY, Milliyet Business Bursa - 52xY, Milliyet Ek2, Milliyet İnsan Kaynaklan - 365xY, Milliyet Kariyerim - 52xY
NATIONAL DAILY & SUNDAY NEWSPAPERS: National Daily Newspapers

MOBILYA TEKSTIL 1615842TR4B-1
Editorial: Matbaacılar Sitesi 1.Cd. No:115 34204, Bağcılar, İSTANBUL **Tel:** 212 4133333
Fax: 212 4133334
Email: sektorel@boyut.com.tr
Freq: Quarterly; **Cover Price:** YTL 5,00; **Circ:** 15,000
Profile: Magazine focusing on home decoration.
Language(s): Turkish
BUSINESS: ARCHITECTURE & BUILDING: Interior Design & Flooring

OFIS İLETIŞIM 1615845TR34-1
Editorial: Matbaacılar Sitesi 1.Cd. No:115 34204, Bağcılar, İSTANBUL **Tel:** 212 4133333
Fax: 212 4133334
Email: sektorel@boyut.com.tr
Freq: Half-yearly; **Cover Price:** YTL 5,00; **Circ:** 12,500
Profile: Magazine focusing on office equipment, including flooring, lighting, air-conditioning. Offers suggestions for a stress-free working environment.
Language(s): Turkish
BUSINESS: OFFICE EQUIPMENT

PC NET 762523TR5D-200
Editorial: Hürriyet Medya Towers 34212, Güneşli, İSTANBUL **Tel:** 212 4103346 **Fax:** 212 4103357
Email: pcnet@pcnet.com.tr **Web site:** http://www.pcnet.com.tr
Date Established: 1997; **Freq:** Monthly; **Cover Price:** YTL 5,90; **Circ:** 60,807
Editor: Eylem Aksunger
Profile: Magazine featuring information about PC hardware, software and Internet technology.
Language(s): Turkish
Readership: Aimed at home PC owners and Internet enthusiasts.
BUSINESS: COMPUTERS & AUTOMATION: Personal Computers

POPÜLER BILIM 766024TR94J-1
Editorial: 5.Basın Sitesi Duyu Sk. B Bl. 45/28, Çankaya, ANKARA **Tel:** 312 4413345
Fax: 312 4426838
Email: populerbilim@populerbilim.com.tr
Freq: Monthly; **Cover Price:** YTL 3,50; **Circ:** 10,000
Profile: Science magazine, containing articles about food, neurology and psychology.
Language(s): Turkish
Readership: Read mainly by men aged 20 to 40 years.
CONSUMER: OTHER CLASSIFICATIONS: Popular Science

POSTA 762416TR65A-229
Editorial: Doğan Medya Center 34204, Bağcılar, İSTANBUL **Tel:** 212 5056111 **Fax:** 212 5056520
Email: info@posta-gazetesi.net **Web site:** http://www.posta-gazetesi.net
Freq: Daily; **Cover Price:** YTL 0,25; **Circ:** 498,240
Editor: M. Ali Birand
Profile: Newspaper focusing on national and international news, society, entertainment and sport.
Language(s): Turkish
ADVERTISING RATES:
SCC .... YTL 23.60
NATIONAL DAILY & SUNDAY NEWSPAPERS: National Daily Newspapers

RADIKAL 762413TR65A-9
Editorial: Doğan Medya Center 34204, Bağcılar, İSTANBUL **Tel:** 212 5056111 **Fax:** 212 505 65 80
Email: iletisim@radikal.com.tr **Web site:** http://www.radikal.com.tr
Freq: Daily; **Cover Price:** YTL 0,40; **Circ:** 38,201
Managing Editor: Erdal Güven
Profile: Newspaper focusing on national and international news, economics, business and politics, as well as culture and the arts.
Language(s): Turkish
Readership: Aimed at young, intellectual and educated urban readers.
NATIONAL DAILY & SUNDAY NEWSPAPERS: National Daily Newspapers

ROTARY 767362TR32G-1
Editorial: 1571 Sk. No:16 35110, Çınarlı, İZMIR
Tel: 232 4619642 **Fax:** 232 4619646
Freq: 6 issues yearly; **Cover Price:** YTL Ücretsiz; **Circ:** 7,600
Profile: Official magazine of Rotary in Turkey. Covers news of Rotary events, personalities, club and district activities.
Language(s): English; Turkish
Readership: Read by Rotarians who are directors, managers and key executives in commerce, trade, industry and professional organisations.
BUSINESS: LOCAL GOVERNMENT, LEISURE & RECREATION: Community Care & Social Services

SABAH 1200817TR65A-10
Editorial: Barbaros Bulvarı Cam Han No:125 K:5, Beşiktaş, İSTANBUL **Tel:** 212 3543000
Email: editor@sabah.com.tr **Web site:** http://sabah.com.tr
ISSN: 1301-5796
Date Established: 1985; **Freq:** Daily; **Cover Price:** YTL 0,35; **Circ:** 344,344
Profile: Newspaper focusing on national and international news, politics, business and sport.
Language(s): Turkish
ADVERTISING RATES:
SCC .... YTL 59.00
NATIONAL DAILY & SUNDAY NEWSPAPERS: National Daily Newspapers

STAR 762947TR65A-223
Editorial: Mehmet Akif Mh. İnönü Cd. Basın Ekspres Yolu Star Sk. No:2 34679, İkitelli, İSTANBUL
Tel: 212 4488000 **Fax:** 212 4488260
Email: editor@stargazete.com **Web site:** http://www.stargazete.com
Freq: Daily; **Cover Price:** YTL 0,25; **Circ:** 113,214
News Editor: Filiz Guler
Profile: Newspaper focusing on national and international news, economy, current affairs and sport.
Language(s): Turkish
ADVERTISING RATES:
SCC .... YTL 35.40
Supplement(s): Star Ve Gol - 365xY
NATIONAL DAILY & SUNDAY NEWSPAPERS: National Daily Newspapers

TEKSTIL TEKNIK 1200721TR47A-10
Editorial: İhlas Holding Merkez Binası Magazin Grubu 29 Ekim Cd. No:23 34520 Kat:1, Yenibosna, İSTANBUL **Tel:** 212 4542520 **Fax:** 212 4542555
Email: img@img.com.tr
Freq: Monthly; **Cover Price:** YTL 10.000.000; **Circ:** 11,531
Profile: Magazine containing information about textiles; includes information on fibre and yarn manufacture, woven fabric manufacture and household textiles.
Language(s): English; Turkish
BUSINESS: CLOTHING & TEXTILES

TELEPATI TELEKOM 766729TR18B-1
Editorial: Yıldız Caddesi Konak Apt. No: 43/2, Beşiktaş, İSTANBUL 34353 **Tel:** 212 3108181
Fax: 212 2278925
Email: telepati@telepati.com.tr **Web site:** http://www.telepati.com
Freq: Monthly; **Cover Price:** YTL 8,50; **Circ:** 10,000
News Editor: Cenk Yapici
Profile: Magazine containing information about mobile communications; includes information on telephones and mobile technology software.
Language(s): Turkish
Readership: Read by manufacturers, suppliers and retailers.
BUSINESS: ELECTRONICS: Telecommunications

TERMODINAMIK 766796TR3B-1
Editorial: Alinazım Sok. No:30 34718 Koşuyolu, Kadıköy, İSTANBUL **Tel:** 216 3278010
Fax: 216 3277925
Email: info@dogayayin.com
Freq: Monthly; **Cover Price:** YTL 4500000; **Circ:** 4,000
Profile: Magazine focusing on heating, air conditioning, water purifiers, natural gas, ventilation, refrigeration, (HVAC-R installation) and insulation.
Language(s): Turkish
Readership: Read by technical managers in the public and private sector, hospital managers, shopping centre managers and hotel managers.
BUSINESS: HEATING & VENTILATION: Industrial Heating & Ventilation

TESISAT MARKET 1611035TR3B-2
Editorial: Alinazım Sok.No:30 34718 Koşuyolu, Kadıköy, İSTANBUL **Tel:** 216 3278010
Fax: 216 327 79 25
Email: info@dogayayin.com
Freq: Monthly; **Cover Price:** YTL 4.000.000; **Circ:** 7,000
Profile: Magazine focusing on heating, air conditioning, ventilation, refrigeration (HVAC-R installation), water purifiers, natural gas, insulation and sanitary information.
Language(s): Turkish
Readership: Read by purchasing managers in the public and private sector, hospital managers, shopping centre managers, hotel managers and managers of sanitary firms.
BUSINESS: HEATING & VENTILATION: Industrial Heating & Ventilation

TICARET GAZETESI 1201105TR67B-5
Editorial: 1571 Sk. No:16 35110, Çınarlı, İZMIR
Tel: 232 461 96 42 **Fax:** 232 4619646
Email: ticinfo@unimedya.net.tr
Freq: 312 issues yearly; **Cover Price:** YTL 190.000; **Circ:** 4,970
Language(s): Turkish
Readership: Aimed at businessmen, bankers and people in the commodity markets.
REGIONAL DAILY & SUNDAY NEWSPAPERS: Regional Daily Newspapers

TODAY S ZAMAN 1803679TR65A-256
Editorial: Ahmet Taner Kislali Cad. No: 6, 34194 Yenibosna, İSTANBUL **Tel:** 212 4541444
Fax: 212 4541497
Email: editor@todayszaman.com **Web site:** http://www.todayszaman.com
Freq: Daily; **Cover Price:** YTL 0,35; **Circ:** 4,928
Usual Pagination: 20
Executive Editor: Abdullah Bozkurt; **Features Editor:** Pinar Vurucu; **Managing Editor:** Okan Udo Bassey
Profile: Today's Zaman is filled with national and international news in the fields of business, diplomacy, politics, culture, arts, sports and economics, in addition to commentaries, specials and features.
Language(s): English
NATIONAL DAILY & SUNDAY NEWSPAPERS: National Daily Newspapers

TURKISH DAILY NEWS
762409TR65A-14
Editorial: Hurriyet Medya Towers, Gunesli, İSTANBUL **Tel:** 212 2516580 **Fax:** 212 2454730
Email: tdn@tdn.com.tr **Web site:** http://www.turkishdailynews.com.tr
ISSN: 1300-0721
Date Established: 1961; **Freq:** Daily; **Cover Price:** YTL 1,50; **Circ:** 2,535
News Editor: Nejat Basar; **Executive Editor:** Eyup Can Saglik; **Editor-in-Chief:** David Judson;
Advertising Manager: Gunes H. Eren
Profile: Newspaper focusing on national and international news, politics, economics, society and culture.
Language(s): English
NATIONAL DAILY & SUNDAY NEWSPAPERS: National Daily Newspapers

TÜRKIYE 1201154TR65A-15
Editorial: İhlas Holding Medya Plaza 29 Ekim Cd. No:23 34197, Yenibosna, İSTANBUL
Tel: 212 4542000 **Fax:** 212 4543100
Email: info@tg.com.tr **Web site:** http://www.turkiyegazetesi.com
Freq: Daily; **Cover Price:** YTL 0,30; **Circ:** 140,927

News Editor: Kazim Celiker
Profile: Newspaper focusing on national and international news, politics, business, culture and sport.
Language(s): Turkish
ADVERTISING RATES:
SCC .... YTL 29.50
Supplement(s): Türkiye Ticari Araç
NATIONAL DAILY & SUNDAY NEWSPAPERS: National Daily Newspapers

VIP
762628TR86C-400
Editorial: Süleyman Seba Cd.Spor Apt.No:62 34357, Maçka, İSTANBUL **Tel:** 212 227 20 50
Fax: 212 2276134
Freq: 6 issues yearly; **Cover Price:** YTL 5,00; **Circ:** 10,250
Profile: Magazine containing articles on lifestyle issues, fashion, celebrity interviews, motoring and leisure.
Language(s): Turkish
CONSUMER: ADULT & GAY MAGAZINES: Men's Lifestyle Magazines

WINDOWS NET MAGAZINE
1615677TR5C-102
Editorial: Vefa Bayın Sok. Gayrettepe İş Merkezi B.Blok 34349, Gayrettepe, İSTANBUL
Tel: 212 217 93 71 **Fax:** 212 217 95 32
Freq: Monthly; **Cover Price:** YTL 6,00; **Circ:** 7,500
Profile: Magazine focusing on Windows systems and the Internet.
Language(s): Turkish
Readership: Read by professional users.
BUSINESS: COMPUTERS & AUTOMATION: Professional Personal Computers

YELKEN DÜNYASI
628706TR91A-225
Editorial: Cevdet Paşa Cd. Eczane Sk. Mürvet Apt. 336/1 80810, Bebek, İSTANBUL **Tel:** 212 2654527
Fax: 212 5586785
Email: yelken@yelkendunyasi.com
Freq: Monthly; **Cover Price:** YTL 3.500.000; **Circ:** 3,817
Profile: Magazine covering boats, luxury and sailing yachts, windsurfs, cruising and racing and navigation. Includes technical articles, interviews of boat-builders, designers, tests, electronics, international and local news, boat shows and fishing.
Language(s): Turkish
CONSUMER: RECREATION & LEISURE: Boating & Yachting

YENI ASIR
763080TR67B-8
Editorial: Gaziosmanpaşa Bulvarı No:5 35210, Çankaya, İZMIR **Tel:** 232 4415000 **Fax:** 232 4464222
Email: yasir@yeniasir.com.tr **Web site:** http://www.yeniasir.com.tr
Freq: Daily; **Cover Price:** YTL 0,50; **Circ:** 37,106
Profile: Newspaper containing national and international news, business and current affairs.
Language(s): Turkish
REGIONAL DAILY & SUNDAY NEWSPAPERS: Regional Daily Newspapers

YENI ŞAFAK
762881TR65A-150
Editorial: Yenidoğan Mah. Şenay Sok. No:2 Kat:1, Bayrampaşa, İSTANBUL **Tel:** 212 6122930
Fax: 212 6121903
Email: halkilaliskiler@yenisafak.com **Web site:** http://yenisafak.com.tr
Freq: Daily; **Cover Price:** YTL 0,35; **Circ:** 104,129
News Editor: Fatma DemIRcIOĞLu
Profile: Newspaper focusing on national and international news, economics, politics, culture, society and sport.
Language(s): Turkish
ADVERTISING RATES:
SCC .... YTL 23.60
Supplement(s): Yeni Şafak Kitap, Yeni Şafak Pazar - 52xY
NATIONAL DAILY & SUNDAY NEWSPAPERS: National Daily Newspapers

ZAMAN
762859TR65A-220
Editorial: Zaman Gazetesi, 34194 Yenibosna, İSTANBUL **Tel:** 212 454 14 54 **Fax:** 212 454 14 67
Email: zaman@zaman.com.tr **Web site:** http://www.zaman.com.tr
Freq: Daily; **Cover Price:** YTL 0,35; **Circ:** 873,954
Editor: Mehmet Yılmaz; **Advertising Director:** Hakan Dikmen
Profile: Daily newspaper covering political, business, financial, economic, cultural, social and sports news.
Language(s): Turkish
NATIONAL DAILY & SUNDAY NEWSPAPERS: National Daily Newspapers

Ukraine

Time Difference: GMT + 2 hrs (EET - Eastern European Time)
National Telephone Code: +380
Continent: Europe
Capital: Kiev (Kyiv)
Principal Language: Ukrainian, Russian, Romanian, Polish, Hungarian
Population: 52000000
Monetary Unit: Hryvnia (UAH)

EMBASSY HIGH

COMMISSION: Embassy of Ukraine: 60 Holland Park, London W11 3SJ
Tel: 020 7727 6312
Fax: 020 7792 1708/
Website: www.ukremb.org.uk/Email adress: emb_gb@mfa.gov.ua / Head Of Mission H.E. IHOR KHARCHENKO

AGROBIZNES SEGODNYA
1819381UA21A-3
Editorial: ul. Gheroyev Stalingrada 48A, P.O. Box 35, 04213 KIEV **Tel:** 44 23 92 216 **Fax:** 44 45 14 781
Email: agro@impress-media.kiev.ua
Freq: 24 issues yearly; **Cover Price:** UAH 5.00
Annual Sub.: UAH 112.00; **Circ:** 30,000
Usual Pagination: 48
Profile: Covers issues of economics and agriculture and gives professional information on agro business.
Language(s): Ukrainian
Readership: Aimed at agricultural specialists, scientists and entrepreneurs.
ADVERTISING RATES:
Full Page Mono .... UAH 1470.00
Full Page Colour .... UAH 2600.00
BUSINESS: AGRICULTURE & FARMING

AUTOCENTRE
1613746UA77A-1
Editorial: ul. Degtyarevskaya 52, 04112 KYIV
Tel: 44 20 65 601 **Fax:** 44 20 65 601
Email: editor@autocentre.ua **Web site:** http://www.autocentre.ua
ISSN: 1605-5330
Date Established: 1997; **Freq:** Weekly - Published on Monday; **Cover Price:** UAH 5.50; **Circ:** 200,000
Usual Pagination: 68
Editor: Sergiy Martysyak; **Advertising Manager:** Oksana Chabanenko
Profile: Magazine focusing on latest models in car world and second-hand cars. Features technical specifications, tests and comparisons.
Language(s): Russian
Readership: Aimed at motoring enthusiasts, car buyers and dealers.
ADVERTISING RATES:
Full Page Mono .... UAH 36000.00
Mechanical Data: Type Area: 230 x 300mm
Copy instructions: *Copy Date:* 10 days prior publication date
CONSUMER: MOTORING & CYCLING: Motoring

BURDA-UKRAINA
1611067UA74E-1
Editorial: ul. Vladimirskaya 101, Korpus 2, 4th Floor, 01033 KYIV **Tel:** 44 49 08 368 **Fax:** 44 49 08 360
Email: office@burda.ua **Web site:** http://www.burda.ua
Freq: Monthly; **Circ:** 80,000
Usual Pagination: 164
Advertising Manager: Svetlana Sovinskaya
Profile: Fashion magazine featuring step-by-step guides on how to make a garment, providing measurements and details on pattern sheets. Also features cross-stitching, beauty and health, make-up tips and recipes.
Language(s): Russian
Readership: Aimed at needle and handiwork enthusiasts.
ADVERTISING RATES:
Full Page Colour .... EUR 3100.00
Mechanical Data: Trim Size: 213 x 275 mm, Type Area: 223 x 285 mm, Print Process: Offset
CONSUMER: WOMEN'S INTEREST CONSUMER MAGAZINES: Crafts

CHIP
714237UA5B-1
Editorial: ul. Vladimirskaya 101, 01033 KIEV
Tel: 44 49 08 350 **Fax:** 44 49 08 364
Email: chip@burda.ua **Web site:** http://www.ichip.com.ua
Date Established: 1996; **Freq:** Monthly; **Cover Price:** UAH 12.95
Annual Sub.: UAH 191.52; **Circ:** 30,000
Usual Pagination: 148
Editor: Maksim Bartiuk
Profile: Magazine containing information on computer technology and applications.
Language(s): Russian
Readership: Aimed at IT enthusiasts, managers, professionals and decision makers.
ADVERTISING RATES:
Full Page Colour .... UAH 25000.00
Mechanical Data: Bleed Size: 220 x 285mm, Trim Size: 215 x 285mm, Print Process: Offset
Copy instructions: *Copy Date:* 4 weeks prior to publication
BUSINESS: COMPUTERS & AUTOMATION: Data Processing

DEN
749242UA65A-50
Editorial: Blvd. Marshala Tymoshenka 2L, 04212 KYIV **Tel:** 44 41 44 331 **Fax:** 44 41 46 760
Email: chedit@day.kiev.ua **Web site:** http://www.day.kiev.ua
Date Established: 1996; **Freq:** Daily; **Cover Price:** UAH 0.85
Annual Sub.: UAH 120.00; **Circ:** 62,500
Usual Pagination: 24
Editor-in-Chief: Larysa Ivshina; **Advertising Manager:** Elena Karandai; **Advertising Director:** Olena Burchevska
Profile: Newspaper in Ukrainian, Russian and English versions covering politics, current-affairs, economics and culture.
Language(s): English; Russian; Ukrainian
Readership: Aimed at politicians, public servants and university graduates.
ADVERTISING RATES:
Full Page Mono $5000.00
Supplement(s): Weekly Digest - 52xY.
NATIONAL DAILY & SUNDAY NEWSPAPERS: National Daily Newspapers

DOMASHNIY PC
766595UA5D-2
Editorial: pr. Krasnozvezdny 51, 03110 KYIV
Tel: 44 24 39 233 **Fax:** 44 27 03 891
Email: dpk@itc.ua **Web site:** http://www.dpk.com.ua
Date Established: 1998; **Freq:** Monthly; **Cover Price:** UAH 10.00; **Circ:** 41,000
Usual Pagination: 144
Profile: Magazine covering news and features latest developments in computing, information systems, IT innovations and technological developments.
Language(s): Russian
ADVERTISING RATES:
Full Page Colour $4500.00
Mechanical Data: Trim Size: 221 x 303 mm
Copy instructions: *Copy Date:* 25 days prior publication date
BUSINESS: COMPUTERS & AUTOMATION: Personal Computers

DONBASS
1611122UA65A-155
Editorial: Kievsky Avenue 48, 83118 DONETSK
Tel: 62 3116 610 **Fax:** 62 3112101
Email: che@donbass.dn.ua **Web site:** http://www.donbass.dn.ua
Date Established: 1917; **Freq:** Daily - Ukraine; **Circ:** 22,000
Usual Pagination: 16
Executive Editor: Sergey Chernykh; **Editor-in-Chief:** Alexander Brizh
Profile: Tabloid-sized newspaper featuring national news, politics, business, culture and sport.
Language(s): Russian
ADVERTISING RATES:
Full Page Mono .... UAH 6089
Full Page Colour .... UAH 7161
Mechanical Data: Type Area: A3
NATIONAL DAILY & SUNDAY NEWSPAPERS: National Daily Newspapers

FAKTY I KOMMENTARII
766566UA65A-159
Editorial: ul. Vandy Vasilevskoy 27/29, 04116 KYIV
Tel: 44 24 45 781 **Fax:** 44 24 68 550
Email: info@facts.kiev.ua **Web site:** http://www.facts.kiev.ua
Date Established: 1997; **Freq:** Daily - Published Monday to Saturday; **Cover Price:** UAH 0.75; **Circ:** 784,275
Advertising Manager: Viktor Ivanenko
Profile: Newspaper covering news, politics, the economy, culture, foreign affairs and sport.
Language(s): Russian
ADVERTISING RATES:
Full Page Mono .... UAH 40280.00
Full Page Colour .... UAH 37100.00
NATIONAL DAILY & SUNDAY NEWSPAPERS: National Daily Newspapers

KOMMERSANT UKRAINA
1839830UA14A-3
Editorial: ul. Rybalskaya 22, 01011 KIEV
Tel: 44 49 63 720 **Fax:** 44 49 63 724
Email: editor@kommersant.ua **Web site:** http://www.kommersant.ua
Date Established: 1991; **Freq:** Daily; **Annual Sub.:** UAH 540.00; **Circ:** 30,000
Editor-in-Chief: Andrey Gogolev; **Advertising Director:** Irina Naumenko
Profile: Daily business newspaper covering economics, finance and business in Ukraine and abroad.
Language(s): Russian
ADVERTISING RATES:
Full Page Mono $10000.00
Mechanical Data: Type Area: 310 x 510mm
BUSINESS: COMMERCE, INDUSTRY & MANAGEMENT

KYIV POST
719286UA65J-57
Editorial: Prosp. Bazhana 14-a, 7th Fl, 02140 KYIV
Tel: 44 49 64 563 **Fax:** 44 49 64 567
Email: stephan@kppublications.com **Web site:** http://www.kyivpost.com
Date Established: 2001; **Freq:** Weekly - Published on Thursdays; **Cover Price:** UAH 5.00
Annual Sub.: $95.00; **Circ:** 25,000
Editor: Katya Gorchinskaya; **Publisher:** Jed Sunden
Profile: Newspaper containing national and international news, business and current affairs.
Language(s): English
Readership: Aimed at the general public.
ADVERTISING RATES:
Full Page Colour .... UAH 30300.00
NATIONAL DAILY & SUNDAY NEWSPAPERS: National Weekly Newspapers

LEVIY BEREG
1936348UA65J-59
Editorial: ul. Chapaeva 4, office 18, 01030 KIEV
Tel: 44 235 98 69
Email: info@lb.com.ua **Web site:** http://lb.com.ua
Date Established: 2008; **Freq:** Weekly - Published on Fridays; **Circ:** 90,000
Profile: Weekly newspaper covering political and social events in Ukraine.
Language(s): Russian
NATIONAL DAILY & SUNDAY NEWSPAPERS: National Weekly Newspapers

MOBILITY
1824098UA18B-2
Editorial: pr. Krasnozvezdny 51, 03110 KYIV
Tel: 44 24 39 233 **Fax:** 44 27 03 891
Email: mobility@itc.ua **Web site:** http://www.itcpublishing.com/mobility
Date Established: 2004; **Freq:** Monthly; **Circ:** 34,000
Usual Pagination: 126
Advertising Manager: Irina Perlovskaya; **Advertising Director:** Larisa Akrytova
Profile: Covering news on mobile phones, pocket PCs and palmtops, laptops, services and accessories. Provides latest news, products reviews and analysis of services from operators.
Language(s): Russian
ADVERTISING RATES:
Full Page Mono $3400.00
Full Page Colour $4300.00
Mechanical Data: Type Area: 221 x 303 mm
Copy instructions: *Copy Date:* 15 days prior to publication
BUSINESS: ELECTRONICS: Telecommunications

MOTOR NEWS
1851284UA77A-5
Editorial: pr. Pobedy 50, 6 floor, office 642, KIEV
Tel: 44 20 65 662 **Fax:** 44 20 65 662
Email: group@motornews.ua **Web site:** http://www.motornews.ua
Date Established: 1994; **Freq:** Monthly; **Annual Sub.:** UAH 120.00; **Circ:** 55,000
Usual Pagination: 136
News Editor: Evgeniy Yegorov; **Editor-in-Chief:** Nikolai Zakharenkov
Profile: Monthly automobile magazine with car news, car reviews and information on accessories.
Language(s): Russian
ADVERTISING RATES:
Full Page Colour .... UAH 40163.00
Mechanical Data: Type Area: 222x300mm, Trim Size: 227x310mm, Print Process: Offset
CONSUMER: MOTORING & CYCLING: Motoring

SEGODNYA
1611069UA65A-154
Editorial: Ul. Borshagovskaya 152-B, 03056 KYIV 56
Tel: 44 45 72 399 **Fax:** 44 45 72 387
Email: info@segodnya.ua **Web site:** http://www.segodnya.ua
Date Established: 1997; **Freq:** Daily - published 6 days a week except Sunday; **Cover Price:** UAH 1.00; **Circ:** 135,000
Usual Pagination: 16
Editor-in-Chief: Igor Guzhva; **Advertising Manager:** Pavel Matiash
Profile: Newspaper covering national and international news, politics, sport and entertainment.
Language(s): Russian
ADVERTISING RATES:
Full Page Colour .... UAH 60000.00
Mechanical Data: Type Area: 349 x 250 mm
NATIONAL DAILY & SUNDAY NEWSPAPERS: National Daily Newspapers

SMS
1851484UA18B-11
Editorial: ul. Gaidara 27, office 10, KIEV
Tel: 44 200 45 45 **Fax:** 44 200 45 45
Email: reklama@ad-world.com.ua **Web site:** http://sms-ua.com.ua
Date Established: 2004; **Freq:** Monthly; **Circ:** 78,000
Editor-in-Chief: Evgeniy Golovko; **Advertising Manager:** Maxim Prokopenko

Ukraine

Profile: Magazine on mobile phones, mobile technologies, test and reviews, mobile phones' news.
Language(s): Russian
ADVERTISING RATES:
Full Page Colour $4000.00
Mechanical Data: Type Area: A4
BUSINESS: ELECTRONICS: Telecommunications

UKRAINA MOLODA 766571UA65A-152

Editorial: pr. Peremogi 50, 5 floor, 03047 KYIV
Tel: 44 45 48 392 **Fax:** 44 45 48 392
Email: post@umoloda.kiev.ua **Web site:** http://uamedia.visti.net/um
Freq: Daily - published 5 days a week except Sunday and Monday; **Cover Price:** UAH 0.50
Annual Sub.: UAH 120.00; **Circ:** 130,884
Usual Pagination: 16
Editor: Mihailo Doroshenko; **Advertising Manager:** Natasha Yankovskaya; **Advertising Director:** Jeliena Georgyevna Primak; **Publisher:** Mihailo Doroshenko
Profile: Informative -analytical newspaper covering news, politics and economic issues.
Language(s): Ukrainian
ADVERTISING RATES:
Full Page Mono .... UAH 18000.00
Mechanical Data: Type Area: 256 x 372mm
NATIONAL DAILY & SUNDAY NEWSPAPERS: National Daily Newspapers

VECHIRNIY KYIV 100 763011UA65J-58

Formerly: Vechirniy Kyiv
Editorial: ul. Marshala Grechka 13, 04136 KYIV
Tel: 44 43 46 109 **Fax:** 44 44 39 609
Email: office@vk-100.ua **Web site:** http://www.vechirnij.kiev.ua
Freq: Weekly; **Circ:** 20,000
Usual Pagination: 16
Advertising Manager: Oxana Mihaylovna
Profile: National newspaper, covering politics, business and current affairs.
Language(s): Ukrainian

ADVERTISING RATES:
Full Page Colour .... UAH 7000.00
NATIONAL DAILY & SUNDAY NEWSPAPERS: National Weekly Newspapers

XXL MAGAZINE 1611079UA86C-1

Editorial: ul. Melnikova 12A, Office 8, 04050 KYIV
Tel: 44 56 85 798 **Fax:** 44 56 85 896
Email: info@xxl.ua **Web site:** http://www.xxl.ua
Date Established: 2001; **Freq:** 11 issues yearly;
Cover Price: UAH 14.00; **Circ:** 65,000
Advertising Director: Tatiana Drobiazko
Profile: Magazine focusing on lifestyle, entertainment, sex, sport and fashion.
Language(s): Russian
Readership: Aimed at men aged 25 to 44 years.
ADVERTISING RATES:
Full Page Colour .... EUR 7200.00
Mechanical Data: Type Area: 213 x 295mm
CONSUMER: ADULT & GAY MAGAZINES: Men's Lifestyle Magazines

ZERKALO NEDELI 766559UA65J-51

Editorial: ul. Tverskaya 6, 03150 KYIV
Tel: 44 52 97 822 **Fax:** 44 52 97 452
Email: info@mirror.kiev.ua **Web site:** http://www.zerkalo-nedeli.com
Freq: Weekly - Published on Saturday; **Cover Price:** UAH 3.50
Annual Sub.: UAH 117.00; **Circ:** 57,515
Usual Pagination: 24
Editor-in-Chief: Vladimir Mostovyy; **Advertising Director:** Ludmila Rozhdestvenskaya
Profile: Newspaper covering national and international news with features on business and finance, politics, lifestyle, entertainment and sport.
Language(s): Russian; Ukrainian
ADVERTISING RATES:
Full Page Mono .... UAH 51200.00
Mechanical Data: Type Area: 530 x 385mm, Col Length: 530mm
NATIONAL DAILY & SUNDAY NEWSPAPERS: National Weekly Newspapers

Vatican City

Time Difference: GMT + 1 hr (CET - Central European Time)
National Telephone Code: +39
Continent: Europe
Capital: Vatican City
Principal Language: Italian
Population: 860
Monetary Unit: Euro (EUR)

EMBASSY HIGH COMMISSION: Apostolic Nunciature: 54 Parkside, London SW19 5NE
Tel: 02089 447189
Fax: 02089 472494 Head of Mission: His Excellency Archishop Faustino Sainz Muñoz
Email: nuntius@globalnet.co.uk

L' OSSERVATORE ROMANO 13972VR65A-1

Editorial: Via Del Pellegrino, 00120 CITTÀ DEL VATICANO **Tel:** 06 69 88 34 61 **Fax:** 06 69 88 36 75
Email: ornet@ossrom.va **Web site:** http://www.vatican.va/news_services/or/home_ita.html
Date Established: 1861; **Freq:** Daily - Published Tuesday - Sunday; **Cover Price:** EUR 1.00
Annual Sub.: EUR 199.00; **Circ:** 40,000
Usual Pagination: 14
Editor: Antonio Chilà
Profile: Broadsheet-sized newspaper containing political, social, cultural and religious news from a Catholic viewpoint.
Language(s): English; French; German; Italian; Polish; Portuguese; Spanish
Readership: Read by people interested in the opinions of the Catholic Church.
Mechanical Data: Film: Positive, Print Process: Rotation offset, Screen: Mono: 34 lpc. Colour: 80 lpc, Trim Size: 600 x 430mm, Col Length: 375mm
Copy instructions: *Copy Date:* 24 hours prior to publication
NATIONAL DAILY & SUNDAY NEWSPAPERS: National Daily Newspapers

VATICAN RADIO 1836209VR2D-1

Editorial: Palazzo Pio, Piazza Pia 3, 00120 CITTÀ DEL VATICANO **Tel:** 06 698 832 37
Fax: 06 698 832 37
Email: sedoc@vatiradio.va **Web site:** http://www.vaticanradio.org
Editor: Susie Hodges
Profile: Broadcasting station of the Holy See focussing on communication and evangelisation, serving the Pope's ministry.
Language(s): English; Italian
BUSINESS: COMMUNICATIONS, ADVERTISING & MARKETING: Broadcasting

Willings Volume 2
Section 5

Publishers' Index

A-Z Index to Publishers in Europe

The Index cross-refers to all the Publishers in the section which follows, Section 6. Each listing gives, in brackets, the country in which the Publisher is based.

Publishers' Index

A

Publishers' Index

B

Publishers' Index

C

D

Publishers' Index

E

Publishers' Index

F

Publishers' Index

G

H

Publishers' Index

I

Publishers' Index

J

K

Publishers' Index

L

M

Publishers' Index

Section 5 Publishers' Index

N

Publishers' Index

O

P

Publishers' Index

Q

R

Section 5 Publishers' Index

Publishers' Index

S

Publishers' Index

Publishers' Index

T

U

Publishers' Index

V

W

X

Publishers' Index

Y

Z

Willings Volume 2
Section 6

Publishers by Country

Publishers around Europe, with the titles they publish

This section is in alphabetical order by country, and then by publisher.

Albania

PANORAMA GROUP 1750355
Rr "Jordan Misja", behind Harry Fulltz School, Palace 1, Shk. 2/2, TIRANA **Tel:** 4 273 207
Fax: 4 273 206
Email: info@panorama.com.al
Web site: www.panorama.com.al

Titles:
PANORAMA

SHEKULLI MEDIA GROUP 699396
Rruga Aleksandër Moisiu, ish-Kinostudio, pranë A1 TV, TIRANE **Tel:** 4 23 35 72 **Fax:** 4 25 14 20
Email: kontakt@shekulli.com.al

Titles:
SHEKULLI
SPORTI SHQIPTAR

STANDARD SHPK 1772087
ad. rruga e Kavajes, nr.67, TIRANA **Tel:** 4 2260695
Fax: 4 2255646
Web site: info@standard.al

Titles:
STANDARD

Andorra

ANDORRANA DE PUBLICACIONES SA 21043
Parc de la Mola, 10 Torre Caldea, 7° Piso, LES ESCALDES - ENGORDANY **Tel:** 73 62 00
Fax: 73 62 10
Email: redaccio@andorra.elperiodico.com
Web site: www.elperiodico.com

Titles:
EL PERIODIC D'ANDORRA

JENLAI SL 21279
Verge del Pilar 5, 3° planta, dpcho 4, Aptdo. 1130, ANDORRA LA VELLA AD500 **Tel:** 86 78 88
Fax: 86 78 87
Email: jenlai@andorra.ad

Titles:
ANDORRA MAGAZINE

PREMSA ANDORRANA SA 20744
Avda. Riberaygua 39, 5° piso, AD 500, ANDORRA LA VELLA **Tel:** 87 74 77 **Fax:** 86 38 00
Email: diaridigital@diariandorra.ad
Web site: www.diariandorra.ad

Titles:
7 DIES
DIARI D'ANDORRA
INFORMACIONS

LA VEU DEL POBLE S.L. 1710855
Carre Maria Pla 28, 1ª planta, ANDORRA LA VELLA **Tel:** 80 88 88 **Fax:** 82 88 88

Titles:
BONDIA

Austria

A3 WIRTSCHAFTSVERLAG GMBH 677338
Wiener Str. 2/1/6, 2340 MÖDLING
Tel: 2236 42528 **Fax:** 2236 26311
Email: a3@a3verlag.com
Web site: http://www.a3verlag.com

Titles:
A3 BAU
A3 BOOM!
A3 ECO
A3 EURO

A & W VERLAG GMBH 1649409
Inkustr. 16, 3403 KLOSTERNEUBURG
Tel: 2243 368400 **Fax:** 2243 36840593
Email: redaktion@autoundwirtschaft.at
Web site: http://www.autoundwirtschaft.at

Titles:
AUTO & WIRTSCHAFT

AB WIRTSCHAFTSDIENST GMBH 678549
Herzog-Odilo-Str. 52, 5310 MONDSEE
Tel: 6232 21051 **Fax:** 6232 210515
Email: redaktion@boersenbrief.at
Web site: http://www.boersenbrief.at

Titles:
AUSTRIA BÖRSENBRIEF

ABLINGER & GARBER GMBH 682544
Medienturm Saline Hall, 6060 HALL
Tel: 5223 5130 **Fax:** 5223 51320
Email: verlag@ablinger-garber.at
Web site: http://www.ablinger-garber.at

Titles:
HALLER BLATT
R 19

ABSOLVENTENVERBAND DER BUNDESHANDELSAKADEMIE UND BUNDESHANDELSSCHULE I WELS 690452
Ringstr. 27, 4600 WELS **Tel:** 7242 43074
Fax: 732 2100228101
Email: walter-christa.dannecker@liwest.at

Titles:
WELSER MERKUR

ADVANTAGE ZEITSCHRIFTENVERLAG GMBH 1717966
Bahnhofstr. 10, 9300 ST. VEIT **Tel:** 4212 3323320
Fax: 4212 332336
Email: info@advantage.at
Web site: http://www.advantage.at

Titles:
ADVANTAGE

AEP 677363
Müllerstr. 26, 6020 INNSBRUCK **Tel:** 512 583698
Fax: 512 583698
Email: informationen@aep.at
Web site: http://www.aep.at

Titles:
AEP-INFORMATIONEN

AFCOM ALEXANDER FAULAND COMMUNICATION, VERLAG UND MEDIENPRODUKTIONEN GMBH 1644531
Lange Gasse 20, 1080 WIEN **Tel:** 1 4023555
Fax: 1 4060922
Email: office@afcom.at
Web site: http://www.afcom.at

Titles:
MEDMIX

AGRAR POST-VERLAG DR. BRUNO MÜLLER GMBH 677428
Schulstr. 64, 2103 LANGENZERSDORF
Tel: 2244 46470 **Fax:** 2244 464723
Email: muellers.buero@speed.at

Titles:
AGRAR POST

AGRO WERBUNG GMBH 1643809
Harrachstr. 12, 4010 LINZ **Tel:** 732 776641
Fax: 732 784067
Email: post@agrowerbung.at
Web site: http://www.agrowerbung.at

Titles:
LUST AUFS LAND

AHEAD MEDIABERATUNGS GMBH 677441
Engerthstr. 151, 1020 WIEN **Tel:** 1 2140601
Fax: 1 214060111
Email: kontakt@aheadmedia.com
Web site: http://www.aheadmedia.com

Titles:
H.O.M.E.

AKZENTE SALZBURG 689813
Glockengasse 4c, 5020 SALZBURG
Tel: 662 849291 **Fax:** 662 84929116
Email: ultimo@akzente.net
Web site: http://www.akzente.net

Titles:
ULTIMO

ALBATROS MEDIA GMBH 698166
Grüngasse 16, 1050 WIEN **Tel:** 1 4053610
Fax: 1 405361027
Email: office@albatros-media.at
Web site: http://www.albatros-media.at

Titles:
HANDBUCH WERBUNG
MEDIENMANAGER

ALMWIRTSCHAFT ÖSTERREICH 677682
Postfach 73, 6010 INNSBRUCK **Tel:** 680 1175560
Email: johann.jenewein@almwirtschaft.com
Web site: http://www.almwirtschaft.com

Titles:
DER ALM- UND BERGBAUER

ALPEN-ADRIA-UNIVERSITÄT KLAGENFURT 685852
Universitätsstr. 65, 9020 KLAGENFURT
Tel: 463 27009301 **Fax:** 463 27009399
Email: unisono@uni-klu.ac.at
Web site: http://www.uni-klu.ac.at/unisonoonline

Titles:
UNISONO PLUS

ALT-NEUSTADT, ABSOLVENTENVEREINIGUNG DER THERESIANISCHEN MILITÄRAKADEMIE 1600348
Schwarzenbergplatz 1, 1010 WIEN **Tel:** 1 7153759
Fax: 1 7121964
Email: office@alt-neustadt.at
Web site: http://www.alt-neustadt.at

Titles:
ALT-NEUSTADT MITTEILUNGSBLATT

ALUMINIUM-FENSTER-INSTITUT 677737
Johnstr. 4/8, 1150 WIEN **Tel:** 1 9834205
Fax: 1 9834206
Email: office@alufenster.at
Web site: http://www.alufenster.at

Titles:
ALU FENSTER NEWS

ANGESTELLTENBETRIEBSRAT VOESTALPINE STAHL DONAWITZ GMBH & CO KG 690234
Kerpelystr. 199, 8700 LEOBEN **Tel:** 50304253129
Fax: 50304653132
Email: alexander.lechner@voestalpine.com

Titles:
VOESTALPINE ANGESTELLTE

ARBEITERKAMMER KÄRNTEN 689473
Bahnhofplatz 3, 9021 KLAGENFURT **Tel:** 50477
Email: arbeiterkammer@akktn.at
Web site: http://kaernten.arbeiterkammer.at

Titles:
AK TIP

ARBEITSGEMEINSCHAFT ERNEUERBARE ENERGIE - DACHVERBAND 681401
Feldgasse 19, 8200 GLEISDORF **Tel:** 3112 5886
Email: office@aee.at
Web site: http://www.aee.at

Titles:
ERNEUERBARE ENERGIE

ARBEITSGEMEINSCHAFT NATURSCHUTZ 1641035
Gasometergasse 10, 9020 KLAGENFURT
Tel: 463 329666 **Fax:** 463 3296664
Email: office@arge-naturschutz.at
Web site: http://www.arge-naturschutz.at

Titles:
HABITAT

ARBEITSMARKTSERVICE OBERÖSTERREICH 677779
Europaplatz 9, 4021 LINZ **Tel:** 732 69630
Fax: 732 696320290
Email: ams.oberoesterreich@ams.at
Web site: http://www.ams.at/ooe

Titles:
AMS-DIREKT

ARBÖ, AUTO-, MOTOR- UND RADFAHRERBUND ÖSTERREICHS 682130
Mariahilfer Str. 180, 1150 WIEN **Tel:** 1 89121257
Fax: 1 89121227
Email: freiefahrt@arboe.at
Web site: http://www.freiefahrt.at

Titles:
FREIE FAHRT

ARWAG HOLDING-AG 678370
Würtzlerstr. 15, 1030 WIEN **Tel:** 1 79700700
Fax: 1 79700790
Email: info@arwag.at
Web site: http://www.arwag.at

Titles:
ARWAG NEWS

ARZT UND PRAXIS VERLAGSGES. MBH 1644484
Hasenauerstr. 23, 1180 WIEN **Tel:** 1 4790578
Fax: 1 479057830
Email: office@arztundpraxis.at
Web site: http://www.arztundpraxis.at

Titles:
ARZT & PRAXIS

ÄRZTE WOCHE SPRINGER VERLAG GMBH 699936
Sachsenplatz 4, 1201 WIEN **Tel:** 1 5131047
Fax: 1 5134783
Email: springermedizin@springer.at
Web site: http://www.springermedizin.at

Titles:
ÄRZTE WOCHE
HAUTNAH
RHEUMA PLUS
ZAHN ARZT

ÄRZTEKAMMER FÜR KÄRNTEN 684168
St.-Veiter Str. 34, 9020 KLAGENFURT
Tel: 463 585626 **Fax:** 463 585644
Email: presse@aekktn.at
Web site: http://www.aekktn.at

Titles:
KÄRNTNER ÄRZTEZEITUNG

ÄRZTEKAMMER FÜR OBERÖSTERREICH 683406
Dinghoferstr. 4, 4010 LINZ **Tel:** 732 7783710
Fax: 732 778371258
Email: aekooe@aekooe.or.at
Web site: http://www.gesundesooe.at

Titles:
OÖ ÄRZTE

ÄRZTEKAMMER FÜR STEIERMARK 688935
Kaiserfeldgasse 29, 8010 GRAZ **Tel:** 316 80440
Fax: 316 815671
Email: presse@aekstmk.or.at
Web site: http://www.aekstmk.or.at

Titles:
AERZTE STEIERMARK

ÄRZTEKAMMER FÜR TIROL 677385
Anichstr. 7/IV, 6021 INNSBRUCK **Tel:** 512 520580
Fax: 512 52058130
Email: kammer@aektirol.at
Web site: http://www.aektirol.at

Titles:
MITTEILUNGEN ÄRZTEKAMMER FÜR TIROL

ÄRZTEKAMMER FÜR WIEN, FACHGRUPPE DERMATOLOGIE 688185
Margaretenstr. 72, 1050 WIEN **Tel:** 1 5866161

Titles:
SCHRIFTTUM UND PRAXIS

ÄRZTEKAMMER FÜR WIEN, SERVICESTELLE FÜR ARBEITSLOSE JUNGMEDIZINERINNEN 684125
Weihburggasse 10, 1010 WIEN **Tel:** 1 515011276
Fax: 1 515011429
Email: stellenboerse@aekwien.at
Web site: http://www.aekwien.at

Titles:
JUNGE MEDIZINER

ÄRZTEKRONE VERLAGSGES. MBH 698395
Seidengasse 9/1/1, 1070 WIEN **Tel:** 1 40731110
Fax: 1 4073114
Email: aerztekrone@medmedia.at
Web site: http://www.medmedia.at

Titles:
APOTHEKER KRONE
ÄRZTE KRONE

ASSCOMPACT GMBH 1713673
Kollingerfeld 9, 4563 MICHELDORF
Tel: 7582 511120 **Fax:** 7582 5111219
Email: info@asscompact.at
Web site: http://www.asscompact.at

Titles:
ASSCOMPACT AUSTRIA

ATELIER OLSCHINSKY GRAFIK UND DESIGN GMBH 1791375
Gonzagagasse 12, 1010 WIEN **Tel:** 1 5356762
Email: office@olschinsky.at
Web site: http://www.olschinsky.at

Titles:
NEVERTHELESS

AUSTRIAN STANDARDS INSTITUTE 680343
Heinestr. 38, 1020 WIEN **Tel:** 1 21300317
Fax: 1 21300327
Email: connex@as-institute.at
Web site: http://www.as-institute.at

Titles:
CONNEX

AUSTRO CLASSIC VERLAGS GMBH 678560
Lenaugasse 10, 3412 KLOSTERNEUBURG
Tel: 2243 87476 **Fax:** 2243 87476
Email: office@austroclassic.com
Web site: http://www.austroclassic.at

Titles:
AUSTRO CLASSIC

AUSTROPAPIER ZEITSCHRIFTENVERLAGSGES. MBH 686917
Gumpendorfer Str. 6, 1061 WIEN **Tel:** 1 58886
Fax: 1 58886222
Email: papier.aus.oesterreich@austropapier.at
Web site: http://www.austropapier.at

Titles:
PAPIER AUS ÖSTERREICH

AV+ASTORIA DRUCKZENTRUM GMBH 1726531
Faradaygasse 6, 1030 WIEN **Tel:** 1 79785
Fax: 1 79785115
Email: office@av-astoria.at
Web site: http://www.av-astoria.at

Titles:
TRUPPENDIENST

BARBARA MUCHA MEDIA GMBH 678648
Mariahilfer Str. 89a, 1060 WIEN **Tel:** 1 58040
Fax: 1 5804070
Web site: http://www.diemucha.at

Titles:
SIGNORA

BERGMAYER & PARTNER PRODUCER OG 685456
Billrothstr. 55/8, 1190 WIEN **Tel:** 1 40335830
Email: mediabiz@mediabiz.at
Web site: http://www.mediabiz.at

Titles:
MEDIA BIZ
MEDIA BIZ BRANCHENFÜHRER

BERUFSVERBAND ÖSTERREICHISCHER CHIRURGEN 1715955
Hollandstr. 14, 1020 WIEN **Tel:** 1 5333542
Fax: 1 533354219
Email: chirurgie@aon.at
Web site: http://www.boec.at

Titles:
CHIRURGIE

BESSER WOHNEN VERLAGSGES. MBH 679195
Stelzhamergasse 4/9, 1030 WIEN **Tel:** 1 7125692
Fax: 1 712569250
Email: office@besser-wohnen.co.at
Web site: http://www.besser-wohnen.co.at

Titles:
BESSER WOHNEN

BEYARS GMBH 1690856
Hauptstr. 34/34a, 5202 NEUMARKT
Tel: 6216 20000
Email: office@beyars.com
Web site: http://www.beyars.com

Titles:
BEYARS.COM

BEZIRKSKAMMER FÜR LAND- UND FORSTWIRTSCHAFT MURAU 686061
St. Egidi 110, 8850 MURAU **Tel:** 3532 21680
Fax: 3532 21685251
Email: bk-murau@lk-stmk.at
Web site: http://www.agrarnet.info/murau

Titles:
BK-AKTUELL

BIK VERLAGSGES. MBH 684562
Karlsgasse 9, 1040 WIEN **Tel:** 1 505580752
Fax: 1 5053211
Email: office@arching.at
Web site: http://www.daskonstruktiv.at

Titles:
KONSTRUKTIV

BIO AUSTRIA 681404
Ellbognerstr. 60, 4020 LINZ **Tel:** 732 654884
Fax: 732 65488440
Email: office@bio-austria.at
Web site: http://www.bio-austria.at

Titles:
BIO AUSTRIA

BOHMANN DRUCK & VERLAG GMBH & CO. KG 678227
Leberstr. 122, 1110 WIEN **Tel:** 1 740950
Fax: 1 74095183
Web site: http://www.bohmann.at

Titles:
AQUA PRESS INTERNATIONAL
ARCHITEKTURJOURNAL WETTBEWERBE
ATG TANKSTELLEN- UND WERKSTÄTTENJOURNAL
AUSTRIA INNOVATIV
CITY
ISR INTERNATIONALE SEILBAHN-RUNDSCHAU
MONITOR
ONRAIL
DIE ÖSTERREICHISCHE FEUERWEHR
DER ÖSTERREICHISCHE INSTALLATEUR
SICHERE ARBEIT
UMWELTSCHUTZ
VERKEHR

BUNDESARBEITSKAMMER FÜR ARBEITER UND ANGESTELLTE 690678
Prinz-Eugen-Str. 20, 1040 WIEN **Tel:** 1 501650
Web site: http://www.arbeiterkammer.at

Titles:
WIRTSCHAFT & UMWELT
WIRTSCHAFTS- UND SOZIALSTATISTISCHES TASCHENBUCH

BUNDESGEMÜSEVERBAND ÖSTERREICH 682474
Linzer Str. 4, 4070 EFERDING **Tel:** 5069023530
Fax: 50690293530
Email: stefan.hamedinger@bgvoe.at
Web site: http://www.bgvoe.at

Titles:
GEMÜSEBAUPRAXIS

BUNDESMINISTERIUM FÜR LAND- UND FORSTWIRTSCHAFT, UMWELT UND WASSERWIRTSCHAFT 1643723
Stubenring 1, 1012 WIEN **Tel:** 1 711000
Fax: 1 711002140
Email: office@lebensministerium.at
Web site: http://www.lebensministerium.at

Titles:
GRÜNER BERICHT

BUNDESZENTRALE DER TIERVERSUCHSGEGNER ÖSTERREICHS 689596
Radetzkystr. 21, 1030 WIEN **Tel:** 1 7130823
Fax: 1 713082310
Email: transparent@chello.at
Web site: http://www.tierversuchsgegner.at

Titles:
TRANSPARENT

BURDA ÖSTERREICH 679943
Max-Schrems-Gasse 5/3/9, 2345 BRUNN
Tel: 2236 320068 **Fax:** 2236 320072
Email: office@weginger-media.at

Titles:
FREUNDIN

BURGENLÄNDISCHE GEBIETSKRANKENKASSE 1643891
Esterhazyplatz 3, 7000 EISENSTADT
Tel: 2682 6080 **Fax:** 2682 6081041
Email: wie.gehts@bgkk.at
Web site: http://www.bgkk.at

Titles:
WIE GEHT'S

BURGENLÄNDISCHE LANDWIRTSCHAFTSKAMMER 685429
Esterházystr. 15, 7000 EISENSTADT
Tel: 2682 7020 **Fax:** 2682 702190
Email: presse@lk-bgld.at
Web site: http://www.lk-bgld.at

Titles:
MBL

BURGENLÄNDISCHER SENIORENBUND 679956
Ing.-Julius-Raab-Str. 7, 7000 EISENSTADT
Tel: 2682 79944 **Fax:** 2682 79945
Email: office.osb@oevp-burgenland.at
Web site: http://www.bgld.seniorenbund.at

Titles:
BURGENLÄNDISCHER FEIERABEND

BUSINESS BESTSELLER VERLAGSGES. MBH 697926
Europahaus, 6020 INNSBRUCK **Tel:** 512 561740
Fax: 512 561741
Email: office@business-bestseller.com
Web site: http://www.business-bestseller.com

Titles:
BUSINESS BESTSELLER

CB-VERLAGS GMBH 678569
Haydngasse 6, 1060 WIEN **Tel:** 1 5974985
Fax: 1 597498515
Email: office@cbverlag.at
Web site: http://www.cbverlag.at

Titles:
AUTO AKTUELL
BUS & HOTEL REPORT INTERNATIONAL
REISE AKTUELL

CDA VERLAGS- UND HANDELSGES. MBH 680092
Tobra 9, 4320 PERG **Tel:** 7262 575570
Fax: 7262 5755744
Web site: http://www.cda-verlag.com

Titles:
CD AUSTRIA
PC NEWS

COMO GMBH 686794
Am Winterhafen 11, 4020 LINZ **Tel:** 732 77422217
Fax: 732 77422250
Email: birgit.mayrhofer@como.at
Web site: http://www.como.at

Titles:
AUGENOPTIK & HÖRAKUSTIK

CORPORATE MEDIA SERVICE GMBH 1763642
Arche-Noah-Gasse 8, 8020 GRAZ
Tel: 316 903310 **Fax:** 316 903312754
Email: office@cm-service.at
Web site: http://www.cm-service.at

Titles:
AKTIV & GESUND
VIA
VIA GASTROGUIDE
XUND

D + R VERLAGSGES. MBH NFG. KG 677596
Leberstr. 122, 1110 WIEN **Tel:** 1 740770
Fax: 1 74077888
Email: office@d-r.at
Web site: http://www.dundr.at

Titles:
A LA CARTE
SLOW

DAVID - JÜDISCHER KULTURVEREIN 680509
Hofgraben 1/1, 2490 EBENFURTH **Tel:** 1 8886945
Fax: 1 8886945
Email: david_kultur@gmx.at
Web site: http://www.davidkultur.at

Titles:
DAVID

DEUTSCHE HANDELSKAMMER IN ÖSTERREICH 680692
Schwarzenbergplatz 5/3/1, 1030 WIEN
Tel: 1 5451417 **Fax:** 1 5452259
Email: office@dhk.at
Web site: http://www.dhk.at

Titles:
DHK ASPEKTE

DIABLA MEDIA VERLAG 1769064
Karlsplatz 1/18, 1010 WIEN **Tel:** 1 8900881
Fax: 1 890088115
Web site: http://www.diabla.at

Titles:
SKYLINES

DIÖZESE EISENSTADT, PASTORALAMT 679957
St.-Rochus-Str. 21, 7001 EISENSTADT
Tel: 2682 777243 **Fax:** 2682 777431
Email: office@martinus.at
Web site: http://www.martinus.at

Titles:
MARTINUS

DIRNINGER & DIRNINGER, HANDELS-, VERLAGS- UND WERBEGES. MBH 678032
Emil-Kralik-Gasse 3/24, 1050 WIEN
Tel: 1 5452811 **Fax:** 1 54528115
Email: info@dirninger.com
Web site: http://www.dirninger.com

Titles:
WIEN EXCLUSIV MAGAZIN

DR. A. SCHENDL GMBH & CO. MEDIEN KG 678192
Geblergasse 95, 1170 WIEN **Tel:** 1 9068011
Fax: 1 9068091199
Email: info@schendl.at
Web site: http://www.schendl.at

Titles:
AUSTROPACK
UMWELT JOURNAL

ECHO IN SALZBURG GMBH 1690190
Carl-Zuckmayer-Str. 38, 5020 SALZBURG
Tel: 662 457090 **Fax:** 662 45709020
Email: info@echosalzburg.at
Web site: http://www.echoonline.at

Titles:
ECHO

ECHO ZEITSCHRIFTEN- UND VERLAGS GMBH 681048
Eduard-Bodem-Gasse 6, 6020 INNSBRUCK
Tel: 512 342170 **Fax:** 512 34217020
Email: info@echotirol.at
Web site: http://www.echoonline.at

Titles:
ECHO

ECHOMEDIA VERLAGSGES. MBH 691034
Schottenfeldgasse 24, 1070 WIEN **Tel:** 1 5247086
Fax: 1 5247086903
Web site: http://www.echo.at

Titles:
ZIVILSCHUTZ AKTUELL

ECO.NOVA VERLAGS GMBH 681088
Hunoldstr. 20, 6020 INNSBRUCK
Tel: 512 2900880 **Fax:** 512 29008870
Email: office@econova.at
Web site: http://www.econova.at

Titles:
ECO.NOVA

ELEKTRO & WIRTSCHAFT ZEITSCHRIFTENVERLAGSGES. MBH 681469
Wilhelminenstr. 91/IIc, 1160 WIEN
Tel: 1 48531490 **Fax:** 1 486903230
Email: verkauf@elektro.at
Web site: http://www.elektro.at

Titles:
E&W

ENGEL AUSTRIA GMBH 698320
Ludwig-Engel-Str. 1, 4311 SCHWERTBERG
Tel: 506200
Email: press@engel.at
Web site: http://www.engelglobal.com

Titles:
INJECTION

ERZDIÖZESE SALZBURG 1643374
Kaigasse 8, 5020 SALZBURG **Tel:** 662 872223
Fax: 662 87222313
Email: rupertusblatt@kommunikation.kirchen.net
Web site: http://www.kirchen.net/rupertusblatt

Titles:
RUPERTUSBLATT

EUGEN RUSS VORARLBERGER ZEITUNGSVERLAG UND DRUCKEREI GMBH 678343
Gutenbergstr. 1, 6858 SCHWARZACH
Tel: 5572 5010 **Fax:** 5572 501245
Web site: http://www.medienhaus.at

Titles:
VN VORARLBERGER NACHRICHTEN
WANN & WO AM SONNTAG

EUROTAXGLASS'S ÖSTERREICH GMBH 681521
Dresdner Str. 89/3/9, 1200 WIEN **Tel:** 1 3323000
Fax: 1 3323000100
Email: vienna@eurotax.com
Web site: http://www.eurotaxglass.at

Titles:
EUROTAX-AUTO-INFORMATION

EWF-VERLAGSGES. MBH 681556
Klostergasse 9/10, 1180 WIEN **Tel:** 1 4703850
Fax: 1 4703849
Email: eastwestforum@gmx.at
Web site: http://www.east-west-forum.com

Titles:
EWF EAST WEST FORUM

EXCLUSIV-VERLAGSGES. MBH & CO. KG 1649599
Schloss Lichtenegg 1, 4600 WELS
Tel: 7242 67823 **Fax:** 7242 29707
Email: office@mmga.at
Web site: http://www.mmga.at

Titles:
4WD FOUR WHEEL DRIVE

F & H GASTRO VERLAG GMBH 682349
Gersthofer Str. 87, 1180 WIEN **Tel:** 1 4798430
Fax: 1 479843016
Email: gastro@gastroverlag.at
Web site: http://www.gastroverlag.at

Titles:
GASTRO

FACHVERLAG + KOMMUNIKATION JOHANN ALMER 698110
Lenaugasse 15/11, 1080 WIEN **Tel:** 1 40719910
Fax: 1 407199175
Email: hans.almer@verlag-almer.at
Web site: http://www.baeckerzeitung.at

Titles:
DER NEUE KONDITOR
ÖSTERREICHISCHE BÄCKER ZEITUNG

FACHVERLAG WIEN DR. SEPP K. FISCHER 684875
DOK IV NW 21, 2301 GROSS-ENZERSDORF
Tel: 2249 4104 **Fax:** 2249 7481
Email: info@labor.at
Web site: http://www.labor.at

Titles:
ÖSTERREICHISCHE CHEMIE ZEITSCHRIFT
ÖSTERREICHISCHE KUNSTSTOFF ZEITSCHRIFT

FACULTAS VERLAGS- UND BUCHHANDELS AG 679550
Berggasse 5, 1090 WIEN **Tel:** 1 3105356
Fax: 1 3197050
Email: verlage@facultas.at
Web site: http://www.facultas.at

Titles:
GANZHEITSMEDIZIN
IMAGINATION
PSYCHOLOGISCHE MEDIZIN

FALSTAFF VERLAGS GMBH 681508
Heiligenstädter Str. 43, 1190 WIEN
Tel: 1 90421410 **Fax:** 1 9042141450
Email: redaktion@falstaff.at
Web site: http://www.falstaff.at

Titles:
FALSTAFF

FALTER VERLAGSGES. MBH 1775922
Marc-Aurel-Str. 9, 1011 WIEN **Tel:** 1 536600
Fax: 1 53660935
Email: service@falter.at
Web site: http://www.falter.at

Titles:
CREATION/PRODUCTION
FALTER BEST OF VIENNA
WIEN, WIE ES ISST ...

FALTER ZEITSCHRIFTEN GMBH 680417
Marc-Aurel-Str. 9, 1011 WIEN **Tel:** 1 536600
Fax: 1 53660935
Email: service@falter.at
Web site: http://www.falter.at

Titles:
FALTER - AUSG. WIEN

FINANZMEDIENVERLAG GMBH 1744847
Gentzgasse 43, 1180 WIEN **Tel:** 1 21322852
Fax: 1 21322800
Web site: http://www.boersen-kurier.at

Titles:
BÖRSEN-KURIER

FISHMEDIA WERBE- & VERLAGS GMBH 1745174
Rotenturmstr. 17, 1010 WIEN **Tel:** 1 533326080
Fax: 1 533326015
Email: office@fishmedia.at
Web site: http://www.fishmedia.at

Titles:
OIZ ÖSTERREICHISCHE IMMOBILIEN ZEITUNG

FONDS PROFESSIONELL MULTIMEDIA GMBH 1644619
Rechte Wienzeile 237/1, 1120 WIEN
Tel: 1 81554840 **Fax:** 1 815548418
Email: office@fondsprofessionell.com
Web site: http://www.fondsprofessionell.at

Titles:
FONDS PROFESSIONELL
IM INSTITUTIONAL MONEY

FONDSMAGAZIN VERLAGSGES. MBH 697505
Donaufelder Str. 247, 1220 WIEN **Tel:** 1 71370500
Fax: 1 713705040
Email: office@fondsverlag.com
Web site: http://www.fondsverlag.com

Titles:
FONDS EXKLUSIV - AUSG. DEUTSCHLAND
FONDS EXKLUSIV - AUSG. ÖSTERR.

FRIEDRICH VDV VEREINTE DRUCKEREIEN- UND VERLAGS-GMBH & CO KG 1643901
Zamenhofstr. 43, 4020 LINZ **Tel:** 732 6696270
Fax: 732 6696275
Email: office@friedrichvdv.com
Web site: http://www.friedrichvdv.com

Titles:
FORUM GAS WASSER WÄRME

FÜHRUNGSUNTERSTÜTZUNGSBATAILLON 2, KROBATINKASERNE 683221
Salzburgerstr. 3, 5600 ST. JOHANN
Tel: 502018231600 **Fax:** 502018217300
Email: fueub2.s5@bmlvs.gv.at

Titles:
DER KOMMUNIKATOR

DIE FURCHE ZEITSCHRIFTEN-BETRIEBSGES. MBH & CO. KG 682270
Lobkowitzplatz 1, 1010 WIEN **Tel:** 1 5125261
Fax: 1 5128215
Email: furche@furche.at
Web site: http://www.furche.at

Titles:
DIE FURCHE

DIE GANZE WOCHE GMBH 697930
Heiligenstädter Str. 121, 1190 WIEN **Tel:** 1 291600
Fax: 1 2916062
Email: office@dgw.at
Web site: http://www.ganzewoche.at

Titles:
DIE GANZE WOCHE
TV DABEI

GASSNER & HLUMA COMMUNICATIONS 1605978
Bischof-Faber-Platz 14/4, 1180 WIEN
Tel: 1 4798182 **Fax:** 1 479818283
Email: susanna.gassner@gh-pr.at
Web site: http://www.austria.info/bulletin

Titles:
BULLETIN

GASTROWERKSTATT GMBH 1640583
Ignanz-Köck-Str. 17, 1210 WIEN **Tel:** 1 29130425
Fax: 1 29130420
Email: willkommen@lustundleben.at
Web site: http://www.lustundleben.at

Titles:
LUST & LEBEN

GEBRÜDER WEISS GMBH 686853
Wiener Str. 26, 2326 MARIA-LANZENDORF
Tel: 1 797997922 **Fax:** 1 797997925
Email: ost-news@gw-world.com
Web site: http://www.gw-world.com

Titles:
OSTNEWS

GEFCO VERLAGSGES. MBH & CO. KG 677630
Beckgasse 24, 1130 WIEN **Tel:** 1 8779711
Fax: 1 87797114
Email: gefco-verlag@allesauto.at
Web site: http://www.allesauto.at

Titles:
ALLES AUTO

GEKO PUBLIC RELATIONS 682406
Raffelspergergasse 33, 1190 WIEN
Tel: 1 4799127 **Fax:** 1 479912711

Titles:
GEKO NEWS

GEMEINDE TREFFEN 689613
Marktplatz 2, 9521 TREFFEN **Tel:** 4248 2805
Fax: 434248 280525
Email: treffen@ktn.gde.at
Web site: http://www.treffen.at

Titles:
TREFFNER GEMEINDEZEITUNG

GEMEINDEVERBAND FÜR ABFALLWIRTSCHAFT IM RAUM SCHWECHAT 678637
Hauptplatz 5, 2432 SCHWADORF **Tel:** 2230 2418
Fax: 2230 24188
Email: info@avschwechat.at
Web site: http://www.abfallverband.at/schwechat

Titles:
AWS REPORT

GEMEINDEVERBAND FÜR ABFALLWIRTSCHAFT UND ABGABENEINHEBUNG IM VERWALTUNGSBEZIRK BADEN 682855
Schulweg 6, 2441 MITTERNDORF
Tel: 2234 74151 **Fax:** 2234 741554
Email: office@gvabaden.at
Web site: http://www.gvabaden.at

Titles:
ABFALL & UMWELT

GEMEINDEVERBAND FÜR UMWELTSCHUTZ IN DER REGION AMSTETTEN 1746166
Mostviertelplatz 1, 3362 ÖHLING
Tel: 7475 53340200
Email: info@gvuam.at
Web site: http://www.abfallverband.at/amstetten

Titles:
FORUM UMWELT

GESELLSCHAFTSPOLITISCHE VEREINIGUNG 690899
Dr.-Josef-Ender-Str. 21, 4400 STEYR
Tel: 7252 50065 **Fax:** 7252 50065
Email: z.zeitbuehne@aon.at
Web site: http://www.zeitbuehne.at

Titles:
ZEITBÜHNE

GESÜNDER LEBEN VERLAGSGES. MBH 1762637
Siebenbrunngasse 17, 1050 WIEN
Tel: 1 3100700310 **Fax:** 1 3100700600
Email: office@gesuender-leben.com
Web site: http://www.gesuender-leben.com

Titles:
GESÜNDER LEBEN

GLOBAL 2000 VERLAGSGES. MBH 682632
Neustiftgasse 36, 1070 WIEN **Tel:** 1 8125730
Fax: 1 8125728
Email: globalnews@global2000.at
Web site: http://www.global2000.at

Titles:
GLOBAL NEWS

GRAPHISCHER BILDUNGSVERBAND 682719
Alfred-Dallinger-Platz 1, 1030 WIEN
Tel: 1 30121495 **Fax:** 1 30171495
Web site: http://www.bildungsverband.at

Titles:
GRAPHISCHE REVUE ÖSTERREICHS

GRAZER WECHSELSEITIGE VERSICHERUNG AG 682727
Herrengasse 18, 8011 GRAZ **Tel:** 316 80370
Fax: 316 80376490
Email: service@grawe.at
Web site: http://www.grawe.at

Titles:
GRAWE AKTUELL

GRENZ-VERLAG MÜHLHAUSER & CO. KG 1649430
Floßgasse 6, 1020 WIEN **Tel:** 1 2141715
Fax: 1 214171530
Email: office@grenzverlag.at
Web site: http://www.grenzverlag.at

Titles:
FINANZ JOURNAL

GRUBER-SEEFRIED-ZEK VERLAGS OG 1737333
Lindaustr. 10, 4820 BAD ISCHL **Tel:** 6235 20541
Fax: 6235 20541
Email: office@zekmagazin.at
Web site: http://www.zek.at

Titles:
ZEK ZUKUNFTSENERGIE + KOMMUNALTECHNIK

GRÜNE BÄUERINNEN UND BAUERN ÖSTERREICH 1724084
Landgutstr. 17, 4040 LINZ **Tel:** 732 73940017
Fax: 732 73940099
Email: bauern@gruene.at
Web site: http://www.bauern.gruene.at

Titles:
GRÜNESLAND

GRÜNE FRAUEN WIEN 1644478
Lindengasse 40, 1070 WIEN **Tel:** 1 52125234
Fax: 1 5269119
Email: gruene.frauen.wien@gruene.at
Web site: http://wien.gruene.at/gruenefrauen

Titles:
BROT & ROSEN

GRUNER + JAHR VERLAGSGES. MBH 678839
Parkring 12, 1010 WIEN **Tel:** 1 51256470
Fax: 1 5125732

Titles:
BRIGITTE
SCHÖNER WOHNEN
SCHÖNER WOHNEN

GUTENBERG WERBERING GMBH 682022
Anastasius-Grün-Str. 6, 4020 LINZ **Tel:** 732 69620
Fax: 732 6962250
Email: office@gutenberg.at
Web site: http://www.gutenberg.at

Titles:
FORUM GESUNDHEIT - AUSG. OBERÖSTERREICH

HELGU-VERLAG 1713634
Geidorfgürtel 40, 8010 GRAZ **Tel:** 316 711540
Fax: 316 718611
Email: redaktion@helguverlag.at

Titles:
LANDWIRTSCHAFTLICHES TAGEBUCH

HEROLD DRUCK UND VERLAG AG 681495
Faradaygasse 6, 1030 WIEN **Tel:** 1 795940
Fax: 1 79594150
Email: herold@herold.cc
Web site: http://www.herold.cc

Titles:
EUROPÄISCHE RUNDSCHAU

HILDEGARD-BURJAN-INSTITUT 677689
Stubenbastei 12/14, 1010 WIEN **Tel:** 1 5134800
Fax: 1 513480023
Email: clubalpha@alphafrauen.org
Web site: http://www.alphafrauen.org

Titles:
ALPHA

"HOW TO SPEND IT" ZEITSCHRIFTEN VERLAG GMBH 678483
Geiselbergstr. 15, 1110 WIEN **Tel:** 1 60117311
Fax: 1 60117156
Web site: http://www.businesspeople.at

Titles:
BUSINESS PEOPLE

ICEP WIRTSCHAFT UND ENTWICKLUNG GMBH 1645357
Möllwaldplatz 5, 1040 WIEN **Tel:** 1 9690254
Fax: 1 96902545
Email: icep@icep.at
Web site: http://www.icep.at

Titles:
CORPORAID MAGAZIN

ICG INFORA CONSULTING GROUP GMBH 680936
Entenplatz 1a, 8020 GRAZ **Tel:** 316 7189400
Fax: 316 71894040
Email: office@icg.eu.com
Web site: http://www.icg.eu.com

Titles:
CHANGE MANAGEMENT

IDEE WERBEAGENTUR LTD. 690775
Werksgasse 71, 8786 ROTTENMANN
Tel: 3614 20330 **Fax:** 3614 20317
Email: office@idee-werbeagentur.at
Web site: http://www.idee-werbeagentur.at

Titles:
WOHNTRAUM LIFESTYLE - (AUSG. LIEZEN)

IMMOBILIEN MEDIEN VERLAG GMBH 683542
Millennium Tower, Handelskai 94, 1020 WIEN
Tel: 1 252540 **Fax:** 1 25254320
Email: office@imv-medien.at
Web site: http://www.immobilien-magazin.at

Titles:
IMMOBILIEN MAGAZIN

IMPACTMEDIA 1764448
Witthauergasse 6/2, 1180 WIEN **Tel:** 1 4788170
Fax: 1 478817010
Email: office@impactmedia.at
Web site: http://www.impactmedia.at

Titles:
KR KERAMISCHE RUNDSCHAU
ÖBM DER ÖSTERREICHISCHE BAUSTOFFMARKT

INDEX VERLAG 684075
Frimmelgasse 41, 1190 WIEN **Tel:** 1 3701577
Fax: 1 3704693
Email: redaktion@indexverlag.at
Web site: http://www.indexverlag.at

Titles:
JOURNALISTEN MEDIEN & PR-INDEX

INDUSTRIEMAGAZIN VERLAG GMBH 683529
Lindengasse 56, 1070 WIEN **Tel:** 1 58590000
Fax: 1 585900016
Web site: http://www.industriemagazin.at

Titles:
FACTORY
DAS ÖSTERREICHISCHE INDUSTRIE MAGAZIN
SOLID

INFO TECHNOLOGIE VERLAG GMBH 1643823
Halbgasse 3, 1070 WIEN **Tel:** 1 52305080
Fax: 1 523050833
Web site: http://www.computerwelt.at

Titles:
COMPUTERWELT

ING. HANS LANG GMBH 686319
Alte Landstr. 44, 6123 TERFENS **Tel:** 5242 69050
Fax: 5242 65418
Email: office@langbau.at
Web site: http://www.langbau.at

Titles:
NEUES VON LANG

INNTAL VERLAG GMBH 1723958
Eduard-Bodem-Gasse 6, 6020 INNSBRUCK
Tel: 512 345701 **Fax:** 512 345702
Web site: http://www.bezirksblaetter.com

Titles:
BEZIRKSBLÄTTER KUFSTEIN
BEZIRKSBLÄTTER SCHWAZ

ISRAELITISCHE KULTUSGEMEINDE 682423
Seitenstettengasse 4, 1010 WIEN **Tel:** 1 53104271
Fax: 1 53104279
Email: redaktion@ikg-wien.at
Web site: http://www.ikg-wien.at

Titles:
DIE GEMEINDE

IT MEDIA GMBH 683873
Scheibengasse 1, 1190 WIEN **Tel:** 1 36980670
Fax: 1 369806722
Email: office@itmedia.at
Web site: http://www.itmedia.at

Titles:
IT&T BUSINESS

JOHANN OBERAUER GMBH 686663
Fliederweg 4, 5301 EUGENDORF **Tel:** 6225 27000
Fax: 6225 270011
Email: vertrieb@oberauer.com
Web site: http://www.oberauer.com

Titles:
DER ÖSTERREICHISCHE JOURNALIST

JULIUS BLUM GMBH, BESCHLÄGEFABRIK 679529
Industriestr. 1, 6973 HÖCHST **Tel:** 5578 7050
Fax: 5578 70544
Email: info@blum.com
Web site: http://www.blum.com

Titles:
BLUM JOURNAL
BLUM NEWS
BLUM-BLÄTTLE

KAMMER DER ARBEITER UND ANGESTELLTEN IN DER LAND- UND FORSTWIRTSCHAFT FÜR OÖ. 684208
Scharitzerstr. 9, 4010 LINZ **Tel:** 732 65638126
Fax: 732 65638129
Email: office@lak-ooe.at
Web site: http://www.landarbeiterkammer.at/ooe

Titles:
KAMMER AKTUELL

KAMMER DER ARCHITEKTEN UND INGENIEURKONSULENTEN FÜR WIEN, NIEDERÖSTERREICH UND BURGENLAND 678320
Karlsgasse 9, 1040 WIEN **Tel:** 1 5051781
Fax: 1 5051005
Email: kammer@arching.at
Web site: http://wien.arching.at

Titles:
DERPLAN

KAMMER FÜR ARBEITER UND ANGESTELLTE FÜR TIROL 677520
Maximilianstr. 7/II, 6010 INNSBRUCK
Tel: 512 5340 **Fax:** 512 53401290
Email: ak@tirol.com
Web site: http://www.ak-tirol.com

Titles:
AK TIROL TIROLER ARBEITERZEITUNG

KAMMER FÜR ARBEITER UND ANGESTELLTE IN DER LAND- UND FORSTWIRTSCHAFT IN NIEDERÖSTERREICH 682793
Marco-d'Aviano-Gasse 1/1, 1015 WIEN
Tel: 1 512160110 **Fax:** 1 5139366
Email: doris.fischer@lak-noe.at
Web site: http://www.landarbeiterkammer.at/noe

Titles:
GRÜNE WELT

KAMMER FÜR LAND- UND FORSTWIRTSCHAFT IN KÄRNTEN 684169
Museumgasse 5, 9020 KLAGENFURT
Tel: 463 5850 **Fax:** 463 58501389
Email: presse@lk-kaernten.at
Web site: http://www.lk-kaernten.at

Titles:
KÄRNTNER BAUER

KÄRNTNER GEBIETSKRANKENKASSE 1641590
Kempfstr. 8, 9021 KLAGENFURT **Tel:** 5058552012
Fax: 50585582010
Email: direktion1@kgkk.at
Web site: http://www.forumgesundheit.at

Titles:
FORUM GESUNDHEIT

KÄRNTNER MONAT ZEITUNGSGES. MBH 684176
Eiskellerstr. 3/2, 9020 KLAGENFURT
Tel: 463 47858 **Fax:** 463 4785815
Email: kaerntner@monat.at
Web site: http://www.monat.at

Titles:
KÄRNTNER MONAT

KÄRNTNER SENIORENBUND 684178
Bahnhofstr. 20/2, 9020 KLAGENFURT
Tel: 463 586242 **Fax:** 463 586243
Email: presse@seniorenbund.org
Web site: http://www.seniorenbund.org

Titles:
KÄRNTNER SENIORENZEITUNG

KÄRNTNER WOCHE ZEITUNGS-GMBH & CO KG 1630536
Völkermarkter Ring 25/1, 9020 KLAGENFURT
Tel: 676 845501 **Fax:** 463 5800636
Email: office.kaernten@woche.at
Web site: http://www.woche.at

Titles:
WOCHE VÖLKERMARKT & JAUNTAL

KATASTROPHENHILFE ÖSTERREICHISCHER FRAUEN 684498
Krugerstr. 3, 1010 WIEN **Tel:** 1 5125800
Fax: 1 5128037
Email: wien@koef.at
Web site: http://www.koef.at

Titles:
KÖF-INFORMATIONSDIENST

KATHOLISCHE ARBEITNEHMER, BILDUNGS- UND HILFSWERK ÖSTERREICH 690963
Göllnergasse 8, 1030 WIEN

Titles:
ZEIT ZEICHEN

KATHOLISCHER FAMILIENVERBAND ÖSTERREICHS 679721
Spiegelgasse 3/3/9, 1010 WIEN **Tel:** 1 515523201
Fax: 1 515523699
Email: info@familie.at
Web site: http://www.familie.at

Titles:
EHE UND FAMILIEN

KERCSELICS & SCHULTZ VERLAG GMBH & CO. KG 682691
Karl-Meißl-Str. 7/7, 1203 WIEN **Tel:** 1 3326105
Fax: 1 332610533
Email: office@goodlife-magazin.com

Titles:
GOOD LIFE

KLAUS HÖNIGSBERGER 1757658
Spieljochweg 9, 6271 UDERNS **Tel:** 5337 62050
Fax: 5337 62060
Email: info@skiareatest.com
Web site: http://www.skigebietstest.at

Titles:
S&BT SEILBAHN BUS TOURISMUS

KLEINE ZEITUNG GMBH & CO. KG 684439
Schönaugasse 64, 8010 GRAZ **Tel:** 316 8750
Fax: 316 8753004
Web site: http://www.kleinezeitung.at

Titles:
KLEINE ZEITUNG

KLIMABÜNDNIS ÖSTERREICH 684452
Hütteldorfer Str. 63, 1150 WIEN **Tel:** 1 5815881
Fax: 1 5815880
Email: office@klimabuendnis.at
Web site: http://www.klimabuendnis.at

Titles:
KLIMABÜNDNIS

KLIPP ZEITSCHRIFTEN KG 686269
Friedhofgasse 20, 8020 GRAZ **Tel:** 316 4260800
Fax: 316 426080122
Email: office@klippmagazin.at
Web site: http://www.klippmagazin.at

Titles:
KL!PP

KOLPING ÖSTERREICH 686683
Paulanergasse 11, 1040 WIEN **Tel:** 1 58735420
Fax: 1 5879900
Email: office@kolping.at
Web site: http://www.kolping.at

Titles:
KOLPING ÖSTERREICH

KRAUSE & PACHERNEGG GMBH VERLAG FÜR MEDIZIN UND WIRTSCHAFT 684068
Mozartgasse 10, 3003 GABLITZ **Tel:** 2231 612580
Fax: 2231 6125810
Email: katharina.grabner@kup.at
Web site: http://www.kup.at
Titles:
JOURNAL FÜR GASTROENTEROLOGISCHE UND HEPATOLOGISCHE ERKRANKUNGEN
JOURNAL FÜR HYPERTONIE
JOURNAL FÜR KARDIOLOGIE
JOURNAL FÜR MINERALSTOFFWECHSEL
JOURNAL FÜR NEUROLOGIE, NEUROCHIRURGIE UND PSYCHIATRIE
JOURNAL FÜR REPRODUKTIONSMEDIZIN UND ENDOKRINOLOGIE
JOURNAL FÜR UROLOGIE UND UROGYNÄKOLOGIE

KREDITSCHUTZVERBAND VON 1870 682027
Wagenseilgasse 7, 1120 WIEN **Tel:** 501870
Fax: 501870991000
Email: ksv@ksv.at
Web site: http://www.ksv.at
Titles:
FORUM.KSV

KRENNZGENIAL WERBEAGENTUR + VERLAG GMBH 1654260
Brauhausstr. 8, 2320 SCHWECHAT
Tel: 1 70781910 **Fax:** 1 707819133
Email: office@krennzgenial.at
Web site: http://www.krennzgenial.at
Titles:
ALL4FAMILY

KRONE-VERLAG GMBH & CO. KG 684690
Muthgasse 2, 1190 WIEN **Tel:** 1 360110
Fax: 1 3698385
Web site: http://www.krone.at
Titles:
KRONEN ZEITUNG

KURIER ZEITUNGSVERLAG UND DRUCKEREI GMBH 682155
Lindengasse 52, 1070 WIEN **Tel:** 1 521000
Fax: 1 521112481
Web site: http://www.kurier.at
Titles:
KURIER

LAND SALZBURG, LANDESPRESSEBÜRO 684905
Chiemseehof, 5010 SALZBURG
Tel: 662 80422365 **Fax:** 662 80422161
Email: landespressebuero@salzburg.gv.at
Web site: http://www.salzburg.gv.at/pressebuero/lpb
Titles:
SLZ SALZBURGER LANDES-ZEITUNG

LAND & FORST BETRIEBE ÖSTERREICH 677558
Schauflergasse 6/5, 1010 WIEN **Tel:** 1 5330227
Fax: 1 5332104
Email: office@landforstbetriebe.at
Web site: http://www.landforstbetriebe.at
Titles:
AKTUELL

LANDESHAUPTSTADT, ABT. PRESSE UND INFORMATION 684413
Neuer Platz 1, 9010 KLAGENFURT
Tel: 463 5372271 **Fax:** 463 516990
Email: presse@klagenfurt.at
Web site: http://www.klagenfurt.at
Titles:
KLAGENFURT

LANDESSCHULRAT FÜR NIEDERÖSTERREICH 690111
Rennbahnstr. 29, 3109 ST. PÖLTEN **Tel:** 2742 280
Fax: 2742 2801111
Email: office@lsr-noe.gv.at
Web site: http://www.lsr-noe.gv.at
Titles:
VERORDNUNGSBLATT DES LANDESSCHULRATES FÜR NIEDERÖSTERREICH

LANDESUMWELTANWALTSCHAFT BURGENLAND 1736758
Ing.-Hans-Sylvester-Str. 7, 7000 EISENSTADT
Tel: 2682 6002192
Titles:
NATUR & UMWELT IM PANNONISCHEN RAUM

LANDESVERTEIDIGUNGS-AKADEMIE, INSTITUT FÜR FRIEDENSSICHERUNG UND KONFLIKTMANAGEMENT 1646168
Stiftgasse 2a, 1070 WIEN **Tel:** 502011028700
Fax: 502011017262
Email: lvak.ifk@bmlvs.gv.at
Web site: http://www.bundesheer.at/organisation/beitraege/lvak/ifk/ifk.shtml
Titles:
IFK AKTUELL

LANDESVERTEIDIGUNGS-AKADEMIE, ZENTRALDOKUMENTATION 683654
Stiftgasse 2a, 1070 WIEN **Tel:** 502011028630
Fax: 502011017109
Titles:
INFORMATION-DOKUMENTATION
INFORMATION-DOKUMENTATION

LANDWIRT AGRARMEDIEN GMBH 1642295
Hofgasse 5, 8010 GRAZ **Tel:** 316 821636
Fax: 316 835612
Web site: http://www.landwirt.com
Titles:
BIENEN AKTUELL
FLECKVIEH AUSTRIA
DER FORTSCHRITTLICHE LANDWIRT
LANDKALENDER
SCHAFE & ZIEGEN AKTUELL

LANDWIRTSCHAFTSKAMMER FÜR VORARLBERG 689917
Montfortstr. 9, 6900 BREGENZ **Tel:** 5574 400441
Fax: 5574 400600
Email: presse@lk-vbg.at
Web site: http://www.diekammer.info
Titles:
UNSER LÄNDLE

LANDWIRTSCHAFTSKAMMER OBERÖSTERREICH 678841
Auf der Gugl 3, 4021 LINZ **Tel:** 5069021364
Fax: 5069021707
Email: ref-presse@lk-ooe.at
Web site: http://www.lk-ooe.at
Titles:
DER BAUER

LANDWIRTSCHAFTSKAMMER ÖSTERREICH 1714895
Schauflergasse 6, 1014 WIEN **Tel:** 1 534418520
Email: office@lk-oe.at
Web site: http://www.lk-oe.at
Titles:
BAUERNJOURNAL

LANDWIRTSCHAFTSKAMMER TIROL 684915
Brixner Str. 1, 6021 INNSBRUCK **Tel:** 592921052
Fax: 592921059
Email: presse@lk-tirol.at
Web site: http://www.lk-tirol.info
Titles:
LANDWIRTSCHAFTLICHE BLÄTTER

LANDWIRTSCHAFTSKAMMER WIEN 698088
Gumpendorfer Str. 15, 1060 WIEN **Tel:** 1 5879528
Fax: 1 587952821
Email: direktion@lk-wien.at
Web site: http://www.lk-wien.at
Titles:
DIE INFORMATION

LANDWIRTSCHAFTSVERLAG GMBH 698927
Südstadtzentrum 1/14/1, 2344 MARIA ENZERSDORF **Tel:** 2236 287000
Fax: 2236 2870010
Email: verlag@lv-topagrar.at
Web site: http://www.landwirtschaftsverlag.com
Titles:
TOP AGRAR ÖSTERREICH

LASER VERLAG GMBH 678290
Hochstr. 103, 2380 PERCHTOLDSDORF
Tel: 1 8695829 **Fax:** 1 869582920
Titles:
ARCHITEKTUR

LEOPOLD STOCKER VERLAG 677685
Hofgasse 5, 8010 GRAZ **Tel:** 316 821636
Fax: 316 835612
Email: office@kochenundkueche.com
Web site: http://www.kochenundkueche.com
Titles:
KOCHEN UND KÜCHE

LEXISNEXIS VERLAG ARD ORAC GMBH & CO KG 678323
Marxergasse 25, 1030 WIEN **Tel:** 1 534520
Fax: 1 53452141
Email: verlag@lexisnexis.at
Web site: http://www.lexisnexis.at
Titles:
ARD
RDW ÖSTERREICHISCHES RECHT DER WIRTSCHAFT
RWZ RECHT & RECHNUNGSWESEN
ZIK INSOLVENZRECHT & KREDITSCHUTZ

LINDE VERLAG WIEN GMBH 678405
Scheydgasse 24, 1210 WIEN **Tel:** 1 246300
Fax: 1 2463053
Email: office@lindeverlag.at
Web site: http://www.lindeverlag.at
Titles:
ASOK ARBEITS- UND SOZIALRECHTSKARTEI
GESRZ DER GESELLSCHAFTER
SWI STEUER & WIRTSCHAFT INTERNATIONAL
SWK STEUER- UND WIRTSCHAFTSKARTEI

LISEY GMBH 681209
Walfischgasse 11/1/8, 1010 WIEN **Tel:** 1 5131395
Fax: 1 5127369
Email: verlag@lisey.at
Web site: http://www.lisey.at
Titles:
E.L.B.W. UMWELTTECHNIK
ÖSTERREICHISCHE BETRIEBS TECHNIK

LÜRZER GMBH 685220
Keinergasse 29/7, 1030 WIEN **Tel:** 1 7152424
Fax: 1 7152470
Email: office@luerzersarchive.com
Web site: http://www.luerzersarchive.com
Titles:
LÜRZER'S ARCHIV - (DT. AUSG.)

LW WERBE- UND VERLAGS GMBH 689583
Ringstr. 44/1, 3500 KREMS **Tel:** 2732 8200030
Fax: 2732 8200082
Email: office@lwmedia.at
Web site: http://www.lwmedia.at
Titles:
FERTIGHAUS TRÄUME
LAND DER BERGE
LAND DER BERGE SPECIAL
LAND DER BERGE SPECIAL
LAUFSPORT MARATHON
RADWELT
UNIVERSUM

MACK-CROSS-MEDIA 1641477
Zedlitzgasse 5/104, 1010 WIEN **Tel:** 2236 8123304
Fax: 2236 8123300
Email: office@mackcrossmedia.at
Web site: http://www.mackcrossmedia.at
Titles:
CC JOURNAL

MAGISTRAT 677895
Hauptplatz 1, 4041 LINZ **Tel:** 732 70701341
Fax: 732 70701313
Email: komm@mag.linz.at
Web site: http://www.linz.at
Titles:
AMTSBLATT DER LANDESHAUPTSTADT LINZ

MANSTEIN ZEITSCHRIFTENVERLAGSGES. MBH 697618
Brunner Feldstr. 45, 2380 PERCHTOLDSDORF
Tel: 1 866480 **Fax:** 1 86648100
Email: office@manstein.at
Web site: http://www.manstein.at
Titles:
BESTSELLER
C.A.S.H
HGV PRAXIS
HORIZONT
HOTEL & TOURISTIK
INTERN
ÖSTERREICHISCHE TEXTIL ZEITUNG
TRAVELLER
UHREN & JUWELEN
VM DER VERSICHERUNGSMAKLER

MANZ'SCHE VERLAGS- UND UNIVERSITÄTSBUCHHANDLUNG GMBH 681084
Johannesgasse 23, 1015 WIEN **Tel:** 1 531610
Fax: 1 53161181
Email: verlag@manz.at
Web site: http://www.manz.at
Titles:
IMMOLEX
ÖSTERREICHISCHE NOTARIATS ZEITUNG
PRESSEHANDBUCH
RECHT DER UMWELT RDU

MARGIT HAAS VERLAG 690541
Tenschertstr. 5, 1230 WIEN **Tel:** 664 3236000
Fax: 664 2286000
Email: office@lokalfuehrer.at
Web site: http://www.lokalfuehrer.at
Titles:
WIENER LOKALFÜHRER

MARKTGEMEINDE ARNOLDSTEIN 686136
Gemeindeplatz 4, 9601 ARNOLDSTEIN
Tel: 4255 22600 **Fax:** 4255 226033
Email: arnoldstein@ktn.gde.at
Web site: http://www.arnoldstein.gv.at
Titles:
NACHRICHTENBLATT MARKTGEMEINDE ARNOLDSTEIN

MBO MEDIA VERLAGS GMBH 1644390
Ameisgasse 49, 1140 WIEN **Tel:** 1 415390
Fax: 1 4153966
Email: office@mbo-media.at
Titles:
EHZ AUSTRIA

MEDIA SERVICE VERLAGS- UND DIENSTLEISTUNGS GMBH 677753
Dr.-Ammann-Str. 34, 8130 FROHNLEITEN
Titles:
AM DAS ÖSTERREICHISCHE AUTOMAGAZIN

MEDIAMED VERLAGS- UND HANDELSGES. MBH 687181
Pillergasse 13/34, 1150 WIEN **Tel:** 1 89748600
Fax: 1 897486022
Email: angermayr@mediamed.at
Web site: http://www.myguides.at
Titles:
40 PLUS GUIDE
TRAVEL GUIDE

MEDIAPRINT ZEITUNGS- UND ZEITSCHRIFTENVERLAG GMBH & CO. KG 698270
Muthgasse 2, 1190 WIEN **Tel:** 1 360003737
Email: office@kurieranzeigen.at
Web site: http://www.kurieranzeigen.at
Titles:
IMMO KURIER

MEDIAUNIT VERLAGS GMBH & CO. KG 1655088
Rainergasse 1/3, 1041 WIEN **Tel:** 1 50135283
Titles:
DINERS CLUB MAGAZIN

MEDICOM VERLAGS GMBH 1644608
Koloman-Wallisch-Platz 12, 8600 BRUCK
Tel: 3862 56400 **Fax:** 3862 5640016
Email: office@medicom.cc
Web site: http://www.medicom.cc
Titles:
INTENSIV-NEWS
NEPHRO-NEWS

MEDIEN & RECHT VERLAGS GMBH 682566
Danhauser Gasse 6, 1040 WIEN **Tel:** 1 5052766
Fax: 1 505276615
Email: verlag@medien-recht.com
Web site: http://www.medien-recht.com
Titles:
MEDIEN UND RECHT

MEDIENGRUPPE "ÖSTERREICH" GMBH 1721366
Friedrichstr. 10, 1010 WIEN **Tel:** 1 588110
Email: office@oe24.at
Web site: http://www.oe24.at
Titles:
ÖSTERREICH

MEDIZIN MEDIEN AUSTRIA GMBH 680239
Wiedner Hauptstr. 120, 1050 WIEN **Tel:** 1 54600
Fax: 1 54600710
Email: office@medizin-medien.at
Web site: http://www.medizin-medien.at
Titles:
ÄRZTE MAGAZIN
CLINICUM
DOKTOR IN WIEN
GERIATRIE PRAXIS ÖSTERREICH
KREBS:HILFE!
MEDICAL TRIBUNE - AUSG. ÖSTERREICH

MEDMEDIA VERLAG UND MEDIASERVICE GMBH 699517
Seidengasse 9/1/1, 1070 WIEN **Tel:** 1 40731110
Fax: 1 4073114
Email: office@medmedia.at
Web site: http://www.medmedia.at
Titles:
DIABETES FORUM
FAKTEN DER RHEUMATOLOGIE
GYN-AKTIV
NEPHROSCRIPT
UNIVERSUM INNERE MEDIZIN

MERKUR WARENHANDELS AG 1774391
IZ NÖ Süd, Str. 3/16, 2355 WIENER NEUDORF
Tel: 2236 6006730 **Fax:** 2236 6006770
Email: redaktion@maxima.co.at
Web site: http://www.maxima.at
Titles:
MAXIMA

MILDE VERLAG GMBH 682160
Ocwirkgasse 3, 1210 WIEN **Tel:** 1 27703
Fax: 1 2770326
Email: office@mildeverlag.at
Web site: http://www.mildeverlag.at
Titles:
FREIZEIT-JOURNAL

MODERN TIMES MEDIA VERLAGSGES. MBH 685922
Palais Spittelwiese 8, 4020 LINZ **Tel:** 732 795577
Fax: 732 795580
Email: linz@moderntimesmedia.at
Web site: http://www.moderntimesmedia.at
Titles:
MODERN TIMES

MOENY TREND VERLAG GMBH 1644630
Kutschkergasse 42, 1180 WIEN **Tel:** 1 476860
Fax: 1 4768621
Email: v.weege@webway.at
Web site: http://www.buergermeisterzeitung.at
Titles:
BÜRGERMEISTER ZEITUNG

MONOPOL MEDIEN GMBH 1644688
Favoritenstr. 4/10, 1040 WIEN **Tel:** 1 9076766
Fax: 1 907676699
Email: wien@monopol.at
Web site: http://www.monopol.at
Titles:
TBA - (AUSG. ÖSTERR.)

MOTOR FREIZEIT & TRENDS PRESSEGES. MBH 685980
Im Plattner 17, 6833 KLAUS **Tel:** 5523 51581
Fax: 5523 51134
Email: redaktion@motor-freizeit-trends.at
Web site: http://www.motor-freizeit-trends.at
Titles:
MOTOR FREIZEIT TRENDS

MPV MEDIZINISCH-PHARMAZEUTISCHER VERLAG GMBH 683013
Kutschkergasse 26, 1180 WIEN **Tel:** 1 5260501
Email: redaktionsbuero@mpv.co.at
Web site: http://www.hausarzt-online.at
Titles:
HAUSARZT

MUCHA VERLAG GMBH 681596
Zieglergasse 1, 1072 WIEN **Tel:** 1 521310
Fax: 1 5239217
Web site: http://www.mucha.at
Titles:
EXTRADIENST
FAKTUM. FM

M.V. MEDIENCONSULTING & VERLAGSGES. MBH 1645402
Reininghausstr. 13a, 8020 GRAZ
Tel: 316 5849460 **Fax:** 316 58494619
Titles:
GOURMETREISE

NATIONALPARKGESELL-SCHAFT NEUSIEDLER SEE-SEEWINKEL, INFORMATIONSZENTRUM 686165
Hauswiese, 7142 ILLMITZ **Tel:** 2175 34420
Fax: 2175 34424
Email: info@nationalpark-neusiedlersee-seewinkel.at
Web site: http://www.nationalpark-neusiedlersee-seewinkel.at
Titles:
NATIONALPARK GESCHNATTER

NATURFREUNDE ÖSTERREICHS 1710337
Viktoriagasse 6, 1150 WIEN **Tel:** 1 8923534
Fax: 1 892353448
Email: info@naturfreunde.at
Web site: http://www.naturfreunde.at
Titles:
NATURFREUND

NATURSCHUTZBUND OBERÖSTERREICH 683704
Promenade 37, 4020 LINZ **Tel:** 732 779279
Fax: 732 785602
Email: ooenb@gmx.net
Web site: http://www.naturschutzbund-ooe.at
Titles:
INFORMATIV

NATURSCHUTZBUND ÖSTERREICH 686202
Museumsplatz 2, 5020 SALZBURG
Tel: 662 64290913 **Fax:** 662 6437344
Email: natur-land@naturschutzbund.at
Web site: http://www.naturschutzbund.at
Titles:
NATUR UND LAND

NATURSCHUTZBUND STEIERMARK 686203
Herdergasse 3, 8010 GRAZ **Tel:** 316 322377
Fax: 316 3223774
Email: post@naturschutzbundsteiermark.at
Web site: http://www.naturschutzbundsteiermark.at
Titles:
NATUR UND LANDSCHAFTSSCHUTZ IN DER STEIERMARK

NEUES LAND MEDIEN GMBH 698518
Reitschulgasse 3, 8011 GRAZ **Tel:** 316 8263610
Fax: 316 82636116
Email: office@neuesland.at
Web site: http://www.neuesland.at
Titles:
NEUES LAND

NEW BUSINESS VERLAG GMBH 686363
Otto-Bauer-Gasse 6, 1060 WIEN **Tel:** 1 23513660
Fax: 1 2351366999
Email: kontakt@newbusiness.at
Web site: http://www.newbusiness.at
Titles:
EXPORTER'S
NEW BUSINESS

NIEDERÖSTERREICH-FONDS, AMT DER NÖ LANDESREGIERUNG, ABT. KULTUR UND WISSENSCHAFT 685963
Landhausplatz 1, 3109 ST. PÖLTEN
Tel: 2742 900513729
Email: office@morgen.at
Web site: http://www.morgen.at
Titles:
MORGEN

NIEDERÖSTERREICHISCHE GRATISMEDIEN GMBH 698175
Gutenbergstr. 12, 3100 ST. PÖLTEN
Tel: 2742 744635571 **Fax:** 2742 744635522
Email: office@kurz-und-buendig.at
Web site: http://www.kurz-und-buendig.at
Titles:
KURZ&BÜNDIG AMSTETTEN
KURZ&BÜNDIG KREMS
KURZ&BÜNDIG MELK-ERLAUFTAL
KURZ&BÜNDIG ST. PÖLTEN

NIEDERÖSTERREICHISCHE LANDESREGIERUNG 677802
Landhausplatz 1, 3109 ST. PÖLTEN
Tel: 2742 900512181 **Fax:** 2742 900513550
Email: presse@noel.gv.at
Web site: http://www.noel.gv.at
Titles:
AMTLICHE NACHRICHTEN NIEDERÖSTERREICH

NIEDERÖSTERREICHISCHER LANDESVERBAND FÜR PSYCHOTHERAPIE 686457
Hauptstr. 22, 2326 MARIA-LANZENDORF
Tel: 2235 42965 **Fax:** 2235 44039
Email: noelp@aon.at
Web site: http://www.psychotherapie.at/noelp
Titles:
NÖLP-NACHRICHTEN

NIEDERÖSTERREICH-WERBUNG GMBH 689561
Niederösterreichring 2, 3100 ST. PÖLTEN
Tel: 2742 900019800 **Fax:** 2742 900019804
Email: presse@noe.co.at
Web site: http://www.niederoesterreich.at
Titles:
TOURISMUS INTERN

NORBERT JAKOB SCHMID VERLAGSGES. MBH 684069
Leberstr. 122, 1110 WIEN **Tel:** 1 74032733
Fax: 1 74032740
Email: office@schmid-verlag.at
Web site: http://www.bohmann-verlag.at
Titles:
PERSPEKTIVEN
WIENER BALLKALENDER

ÖAMTC-VERLAG GMBH 678606
Tauchnergasse 5, 3400 KLOSTERNEUBURG
Tel: 2243 4042700 **Fax:** 2243 4042721
Email: autotouring.verlag@oeamtc.at
Web site: http://www.oeamtc.at
Titles:
AUTO TOURING
CAMPING REVUE

OBERLÄNDER VERLAGS-GMBH 1748423
Bahnhofstr. 24, 6410 TELFS **Tel:** 5262 67491
Fax: 5262 6749113
Email: office@oberlandverlag.at
Web site: http://www.oberlandverlag.at
Titles:
MEIN MONAT
RUNDSCHAU

OBERÖSTERREICH TOURISMUS 687499
Freistädter Str. 119, 4041 LINZ **Tel:** 732 7277100
Fax: 732 7277130
Email: tourismus@lto.at
Web site: http://www.oberoesterreich-tourismus.at
Titles:
RADTOUREN IN ÖSTERREICH.

OBERÖSTERREICHISCHE MEDIA DATA VERTRIEBS- UND VERLAGSGES. MBH 1644340
Hafenstr. 1, 4010 LINZ **Tel:** 732 76060
Fax: 732 7606707
Email: verlagsleitung@volksblatt.at
Web site: http://www.volksblatt.at
Titles:
NEUES VOLKSBLATT

OBERÖSTERREICHISCHER PRESSECLUB 686974
Landstr. 31, 4020 LINZ **Tel:** 732 775634
Fax: 732 772016205
Email: ooe@presseclub.at
Web site: http://www.presseclub.at
Titles:
CLUB-NEWS

OBERÖSTERREICHISCHER SENIORENBUND 690623
Obere Donaulände 7, 4010 LINZ **Tel:** 732 7753110
Fax: 732 775311729
Email: office@ooe-seniorenbund.at
Web site: http://www.ooe-seniorenbund.at
Titles:
TREFFPUNKT WIR SENIOREN

ÖKO-INVEST-VERLAGS-GMBH 686626
Schweizertalst. 8-10/5, 1130 WIEN **Tel:** 1 8760501
Fax: 1 405717129
Email: oeko-invest@teleweb.at
Web site: http://www.oeko-invest.de
Titles:
ÖKO INVEST

OÖ TECHNOLOGIE- UND MARKETINGGES. MBH 1710710
Hafenstr. 47, 4020 LINZ **Tel:** 732 798105013
Fax: 732 798105008
Email: info@tmg.at
Web site: http://www.tmg.at
Titles:
INNOVATIVES OBERÖSTERREICH

ORF-ENTERPRISE GMBH & CO. KG 686803
Würzburggasse 30, 1136 WIEN **Tel:** 1 8787813998
Fax: 1 8787813743
Email: nachlese@orf.at
Web site: http://enterprise.orf.at
Titles:
ORF NACHLESE

ÖSTERREICHISCHE BEAMTENVERSICHERUNG 686608
Grillparzerstr. 14, 1016 WIEN **Tel:** 1 401201120
Fax: 1 401201001
Email: publicrelations@oebv.com
Web site: http://www.oebv.com
Titles:
ÖBVAKTIV

ÖSTERREICHISCHE BUNDES-SPORTORGANISATION 686677
Prinz-Eugen-Str. 12, 1040 WIEN **Tel:** 1 5044455
Fax: 1 504445566
Email: office@bso.or.at
Web site: http://www.bso.or.at
Titles:
ÖSTERREICH SPORT

ÖSTERREICHISCHE FRAUENBEWEGUNG
1643373
Lichtenfelsgasse 7, 1010 WIEN **Tel:** 1 40126655
Fax: 1 4066245
Email: frauen@oevp.at
Web site: http://www.frauenoffensive.at

Titles:
DIE ÖSTERREICHISCHE FRAU

ÖSTERREICHISCHE GESELLSCHAFT FÜR ABSATZWIRTSCHAFT
685370
Augasse 2, 1090 WIEN **Tel:** 1 313364609
Fax: 1 31336732
Email: arne.floh@wu-wien.ac.at
Web site: http://www.dermarkt.or.at

Titles:
DER MARKT

ÖSTERREICHISCHE GESELLSCHAFT FÜR SCHWEISSTECHNIK
688262
Arsenal, Objekt 207, 1030 WIEN **Tel:** 1 7982168
Fax: 1 7982168
Email: schweiss-prueftechnik@aon.at
Web site: http://www.oegs.org

Titles:
SCHWEISS- & PRÜFTECHNIK

ÖSTERREICHISCHE LANDSMANNSCHAFT
681076
Fuhrmannsgasse 18a, 1080 WIEN **Tel:** 1 4082273
Fax: 1 4022882
Email: info@oelm.at
Web site: http://www.oelm.at

Titles:
DER ECKART

ÖSTERREICHISCHE OFFIZIERSGESELLSCHAFT
1642247
Schwarzenbergplatz 1, 1010 WIEN **Tel:** 1 7121510
Fax: 1 7129963
Email: info@oeog.at
Web site: http://www.oeog.at

Titles:
DER OFFIZIER

ÖSTERREICHISCHE WERBEWISSENSCHAFTLICHE GESELLSCHAFT
689589
Augasse 2, 1090 WIEN **Tel:** 1 313364617
Fax: 1 3176699
Email: wwg@wu-wien.ac.at
Web site: http://www.wwgonline.at

Titles:
TRANSFER

ÖSTERREICHISCHER AERO-CLUB, SEKTION MODELLFLUG
687387
Prinz-Eugen-Str. 12, 1040 WIEN **Tel:** 1 5051028
Fax: 1 5057923
Email: redaktion@prop.at
Web site: http://www.prop.at

Titles:
PROP

ÖSTERREICHISCHER AGRARVERLAG, DRUCK- UND VERLAGSGES. MBH NFG. KG
1742630
Sturzgasse 1a, 1140 WIEN **Tel:** 1 981770
Fax: 1 98177111
Email: office@agrarverlag.at
Web site: http://www.agrarverlag.at

Titles:
AGRARISCHE RUNDSCHAU
BAUERNBUND KALENDER
BESSERES OBST
CENTRALBLATT FÜR DAS GESAMTE FORSTWESEN
FORSTZEITUNG
GARTEN + HAUS
GÄRTNER + FLORIST
HOLZDESIGN
HOLZKURIER
ÖSTERREICHISCHE BAUERNZEITUNG
DIE PALETTE
DER PFLANZENARZT
RAIFFEISEN BLATT
DER WINZER

ÖSTERREICHISCHER ALPENVEREIN
677687
Olympiastr. 37, 6020 INNSBRUCK
Tel: 512 595470 **Fax:** 512 575528
Email: office@alpenverein.at
Web site: http://www.alpenverein.at

Titles:
BERGAUF

ÖSTERREICHISCHER APOTHEKER VERLAG GMBH
678199
Spitalgasse 31, 1090 WIEN **Tel:** 1 4023588
Fax: 1 4085355
Email: direktion@apoverlag.at
Web site: http://www.apoverlag.at

Titles:
DA DIE APOTHEKE
ÖAZ ÖSTERREICHISCHE APOTHEKER-ZEITUNG

ÖSTERREICHISCHER BIOMASSE-VERBAND
686625
Franz-Josefs-Kai 13, 1010 WIEN **Tel:** 1 53307970
Fax: 1 533079790
Email: office@biomasseverband.at
Web site: http://www.biomasseverband.at

Titles:
ÖKOENERGIE

ÖSTERREICHISCHER CARTELLVERBAND
677267
Lerchenfelder Str. 14, 1080 WIEN
Tel: 1 405162230 **Fax:** 1 495162244
Email: academia@oecv.at
Web site: http://www.oecv.at

Titles:
ACADEMIA

ÖSTERREICHISCHER FAMILIENBUND
681681
Schulgasse 3, 3100 ST. PÖLTEN **Tel:** 2742 77304
Fax: 2742 7730420
Email: gs@familienbund.at
Web site: http://www.familienbund.at

Titles:
FAMILIE & KINDERBETREUUNG

ÖSTERREICHISCHER FISCHEREIVERBAND
686693
Ing.- Etzel- Str. 63, 6020 INNSBRUCK
Tel: 512 582458 **Fax:** 512 582458
Email: office@fischerei-verband.at
Web site: http://www.fischerei-verband.at

Titles:
ÖSTERREICHS FISCHEREI

ÖSTERREICHISCHER GEWERBEVEREIN
1718326
Eschenbachgasse 11, 1010 WIEN **Tel:** 1 5873633
Fax: 1 5870192
Web site: http://www.gewerbeverein.at

Titles:
ÖSTERREICHS WIRTSCHAFT

ÖSTERREICHISCHER INGENIEUR- UND ARCHITEKTEN-VEREIN
686622
Eschenbachgasse 9, 1010 WIEN **Tel:** 1 5873536
Fax: 1 58735365
Email: office@oiav.at
Web site: http://www.oiav.at

Titles:
ÖIAZ ÖSTERREICHISCHE INGENIEUR- UND ARCHITEKTEN-ZEITSCHRIFT

ÖSTERREICHISCHER JAGD- UND FISCHEREI-VERLAG DER JFB GMBH
683893
Wickenburggasse 3, 1080 WIEN **Tel:** 1 405163639
Fax: 1 405163636
Email: verlag@jagd.at
Web site: http://www.jagd.at

Titles:
WEIDWERK

ÖSTERREICHISCHER KOMMUNAL-VERLAG GMBH
684538
Löwelstr. 6/2, 1010 WIEN **Tel:** 1 5322388
Fax: 1 532238822
Email: kommunalverlag@kommunal.at
Web site: http://www.kommunal.at

Titles:
KOMMUNAL
MACH MIT!
ÖSTERREICHISCHE SPARKASSENZEITUNG

ÖSTERREICHISCHER KRANKENPFLEGEVERBAND
686666
Wilhelminenstr. 91/2e, 1160 WIEN
Tel: 1 47827100 **Fax:** 1 47827109
Email: pflegezeitschrift@oegkv.at
Web site: http://www.oegkv.at

Titles:
ÖSTERREICHISCHE PFLEGEZEITSCHRIFT

ÖSTERREICHISCHER NATURSCHUTZBUND WIEN
690543
Museumsplatz 1, Stiege 13, 1070 WIEN
Tel: 1 5223597 **Fax:** 1 5223597
Email: wien@naturschutzbund.at
Web site: http://www.naturschutzbund.at

Titles:
WIENER NATURSCHUTZ-NACHRICHTEN

ÖSTERREICHISCHER RUDERVERBAND
687854
Blattgasse 6, 1030 WIEN **Tel:** 1 7120878
Fax: 1 712087815
Email: office@rudern.at
Web site: http://www.rudern.at

Titles:
RUDERREPORT

ÖSTERREICHISCHER VERBAND DER WIRTSCHAFTSINGENIEURE
1640615
Kopernikusgasse 24/3, 8010 GRAZ
Tel: 316 8737795 **Fax:** 316 8737797
Email: office@wing-online.at
Web site: http://www.wing-online.at

Titles:
WING BUSINESS

ÖSTERREICHISCHER WIRTSCHAFTSBUND
684038
Mozartgasse 4, 1041 WIEN **Tel:** 1 50547960
Fax: 1 505479640
Email: office@wirtschaftsbund.at
Web site: http://www.wirtschaftsbund.at

Titles:
WB WIRTSCHAFT IM BLICK

ÖSTERREICHISCHER WIRTSCHAFTSBUND WIEN
690551
Lothringerstr. 14, 1030 WIEN **Tel:** 1 5127631
Fax: 1 512763134
Email: office@wirtschaftsbund-wien.at
Web site: http://www.wirtschaftsbund-wien.at

Titles:
WIRTSCHAFTSREPORT

ÖSTERREICHISCHER WIRTSCHAFTSVERLAG GMBH
678294
Wiedner Hauptstr. 120, 1051 WIEN **Tel:** 1 546640
Fax: 1 54664528
Email: office@wirtschaftsverlag.at
Web site: http://www.wirtschaftsverlag.at

Titles:
BAUHANDBUCH
CONTRACT
DACH WAND
ELEKTRO JOURNAL
FORUM
GEBÄUDE INSTALLATION
KFZWIRTSCHAFT
LK DIE HANDELSZEITUNG
METALL
OESTERREICHS ENERGIE
ÖGZ CAFÉ JOURNAL
ÖGZ ÖSTERREICHISCHE GASTRONOMIE- & HOTEL-ZEITUNG
ÖPV ÖSTERREICHISCHER PERSONENVERKEHR
ÖSTERREICHISCHE BAU.ZEITUNG
ÖSTERREICHISCHE FLEISCHER ZEITUNG
ÖSTERREICHISCHE TRAFIKANTEN ZEITUNG
SCHWIMMBAD + THERME
SKIN
STERNE-APARTMENTS, GASTHÖFE, PENSIONEN IN ÖSTERREICH
STERNEHOTELS IN ÖSTERREICH
STRASSENGÜTERVERKEHR
TISCHLER JOURNAL
TRUCKER EXPRESS
WIENER WIRTSCHAFT
DIE WIRTSCHAFT

ÖSTERREICHISCHES INSTITUT FÜR BAUBIOLOGIE UND -ÖKOLOGIE
683441
Alserbachstr. 5/8, 1090 WIEN **Tel:** 1 3192005
Fax: 1 319200550
Email: ibo@ibo.at
Web site: http://www.ibo.at

Titles:
IBOMAGAZIN

ÖSTERREICHISCHES INSTITUT FÜR BAUTECHNIK
697838
Schenkenstr. 4, 1010 WIEN **Tel:** 1 5336550
Fax: 1 5336423
Email: mail@oib.or.at
Web site: http://www.oib.or.at

Titles:
OIB AKTUELL

ÖSTERREICHISCHES INSTITUT FÜR RAUMPLANUNG
687528
Franz-Josefs-Kai 27, 1010 WIEN **Tel:** 1 533874721
Fax: 1 533874766
Email: neulinger@oir.at
Web site: http://www.raum-on.at

Titles:
RAUM

OSTTIROLER BOTE MEDIENUNTERNEHMEN GMBH
686559
Schweizer Gasse 26, 9900 LIENZ
Tel: 4852 651510 **Fax:** 4852 65510
Email: info@osttirolerbote.at
Web site: http://www.osttirol-online.at

Titles:
OBERKÄRNTNER VOLLTREFFER
OSTTIROLER BOTE

OTTMAR F. STEIDL GMBH
688464
Kirchenstr. 25 A, 5301 EUGENDORF
Tel: 6225 7290 **Fax:** 6225 729014
Email: office@simagazin.at
Web site: http://www.simagazin.at

Titles:
SI SEILBAHNEN INTERNATIONAL

OTTO MÜLLER-VERLAG
685133
Ernest-Thun-Str. 11, 5020 SALZBURG
Tel: 662 8819740 **Fax:** 662 872387
Email: info@omvs.at
Web site: http://www.omvs.at

Titles:
LITERATUR UND KRITIK

ÖTZTAL TOURISMUS, ABT. WERBUNG
1748991
Gemeindestr. 4, 6450 SÖLDEN **Tel:** 57200
Fax: 57200201
Email: info@oetztal.com
Web site: http://www.oetztal.com

Titles:
ÖTZTAL NATUR FÜHLEN CAMPING . . .

PANZERGRENADIER-BATAILLON 13
680908
Kasernstr. 10, 4910 RIED **Tel:** 502014431604
Fax: 502014417310

Titles:
13ER-KURIER

PARNASS VERLAG GMBH
686938
Porzellangasse 43/19, 1090 WIEN **Tel:** 1 3195375
Fax: 1 31953755
Email: office@parnass.at
Web site: http://www.parnass.at

Titles:
PARNASS

PARTNER ZEITUNGSVERLAGSGES. MBH
686941
Leibnitzer Str. 76, 8403 LEBRING
Tel: 699 16004070 **Fax:** 3182 49406540
Email: info@partnerzeitung.at
Web site: http://www.partnerzeitung.at

Titles:
PARTNER

PENSIONISTENVERBAND ÖSTERREICHS 686676
Gentzgasse 129, 1180 WIEN **Tel:** 1 313720
Fax: 1 3137278
Email: redaktion@pvoe.at
Web site: http://www.pvoe.at

Titles:
ÖSTERREICHISCHER PENSIONISTEN-KALENDER
UG UNSERE GENERATION

PHARMA-TIME VERLAGS GMBH 687093
Teichgasse 20, 2325 HIMBERG **Tel:** 2235 879431
Fax: 2235 879434
Email: office@pharmatime.at
Web site: http://www.pharmatime.at

Titles:
PHARMA-TIME
PKA JOURNAL

PHARMIG VERBAND DER PHARMAZEUTISCHEN INDUSTRIE ÖSTERREICHS 687094
Garnisongasse 4/1/6, 1090 WIEN **Tel:** 1 4060290
Fax: 1 40602909
Email: kommunikation@pharmig.at
Web site: http://www.pharmig.at

Titles:
PHARMIG INFO

PHOIBOS VERLAG 1717748
Anzengrubergasse 16, 1050 WIEN
Tel: 1 54403191 **Fax:** 1 54403199
Email: office@phoibos.at
Web site: http://www.phoibos.at

Titles:
BIBLOS

PLANSEE SE 687130
6600 REUTTE **Tel:** 5672 6000
Email: pin@plansee.com
Web site: http://www.plansee-group.com

Titles:
PIN

POHL & PARTNER VERLAGS GMBH 699260
Rennweg 9, 6020 INNSBRUCK **Tel:** 512 571985
Fax: 512 57198519

Titles:
WIA WIRTSCHAFT IM ALPENRAUM

POLAK MEDIASERVICE 1774366
Kramergasse 11, 6460 IMST **Tel:** 5412 66712
Fax: 5412 90806
Email: info@polak-mediaservice.at
Web site: http://www.polak-mediaservice.at

Titles:
ÖTZTAL INTERN

DIE PRESSE VERLAGSGES. MBH & CO. KG 687281
Hainburger Str. 33, 1030 WIEN **Tel:** 1 514140
Fax: 1 51414334
Email: geschaeftsfuehrung@diepresse.com
Web site: http://www.diepresse.com

Titles:
DIE PRESSE

PRINT & PUBLISHING INTERNATIONAL VERLAG GMBH 687296
Rotenmühlgasse 11/10, 1120 WIEN
Tel: 1 9830640 **Fax:** 1 983064018
Email: office@printernet.at
Web site: http://www.printernet.at

Titles:
PACKAGING AUSTRIA
PRINT & PUBLISHING

PRINT ZEITUNGSVERLAG GMBH 679245
Münchner Bundesstr. 142/2, 5020 SALZBURG
Tel: 662 22330 **Fax:** 662 2233233
Email: salzburg@bezirksblaetter.com
Web site: http://www.bezirksblaetter.com

Titles:
BEZIRKSBLÄTTER PINZGAU
BEZIRKSBLÄTTER REUTTE
HALLO INNSBRUCK

PRIVATVERMIETER VERBAND TIROL 1791349
Brixnerstr. 3, 6020 INNSBRUCK **Tel:** 512 587748
Fax: 512 581144
Email: info@privatvermieter-tirol.at
Web site: http://www.privatvermieter-tirol.at

Titles:
MITGLIEDER MAGAZIN

PROMETUS VERLAG 1712650
Mühldorf 389, 8330 MÜHLDORF **Tel:** 3152 39582
Fax: 1 9623359582
Email: office@prometus.at
Web site: http://www.prometus.at

Titles:
ARZT+KIND
ARZT+PATIENT

PUBLICITY WERBEGES. MBH 684496
Lindengasse 26, 1070 WIEN **Tel:** 1 5261952
Fax: 1 526195246
Email: publicity@kochundback.at
Web site: http://www.kochundback.at

Titles:
KOCH & BACK JOURNAL
PRIMA

QUEHENBERGER LOGISTIKGRUPPE 1690946
Handelszentrum 3, 5101 BERGHEIM
Tel: 662 46800
Web site: http://www.quehenberger.com

Titles:
Q-SPIRIT

QUERVERKEHR, EINE DIVISION OF WEB ENGINEERING GMBH 1763881
Kaiserstr. 50/10, 1070 WIEN **Tel:** 1 9665848
Fax: 1 96658489
Email: retail@querverkehr.at
Web site: http://www.querverkehr.at

Titles:
RETAIL

RAIFFEISEN MEDIA GMBH 699072
Friedrich-Wilhelm-Raiffeisen-Platz 1, 1020 WIEN
Tel: 1 211362580 **Fax:** 1 211362551
Email: verlag@raiffeisenzeitung.at
Web site: http://www.raiffeisenzeitung.at

Titles:
RAIFFEISEN ZEITUNG

RAINER KRAFTFAHRZEUGHANDELS AG 687508
Wiedner Gürtel 3a, 1040 WIEN **Tel:** 1 601660
Fax: 1 60166105
Email: georg.berner@rainer.co.at
Web site: http://www.rainer.co.at

Titles:
RAINER

READER'S DIGEST ÖSTERREICH: VERLAG DAS BESTE GMBH 679199
Singerstr. 2, 1010 WIEN **Tel:** 1 5132554
Fax: 1 5139752
Web site: http://www.readersdigest.at

Titles:
READER'S DIGEST ÖSTERREICH

RED BULLETIN GMBH 1784215
Am Brunnen 1, 5330 FUSCHL
Email: office@seitenblicke.at
Web site: http://www.seitenblicke.at

Titles:
SEITENBLICKE
SERVUS IN STADT & LAND

REFORMVERBAND ÖSTERREICHISCHER HAUSBESITZER 686661
Bösendorfer Str. 2/4/13, 1010 WIEN
Tel: 1 5056177 **Fax:** 1 5056171
Email: rv-hausbesitzer@chello.at
Web site: http://www.rv-hausbesitzer.at

Titles:
DER ÖSTERREICHISCHE HAUSBESITZ

REGAL VERLAGS GMBH 687575
Floridsdorfer Hauptstr. 1, 1210 WIEN
Tel: 1 3686713 **Fax:** 1 368671318
Email: marketing@regal.at
Web site: http://www.regal.at

Titles:
REGAL

REGE VERLAGS- UND HANDELSGES. MBH 690845
Mühlgasse 13, 2500 BADEN **Tel:** 2252 88731
Email: yachtinfo@yachtinfo.at
Web site: http://www.yachtinfo.at

Titles:
YACHT INFO

DER REITWAGEN ZEITSCHRIFTENVERLAGSGES. MBH 687624
Obertriesting 49, 2572 KAUMBERG
Tel: 2765 88033 **Fax:** 2765 88045
Email: verlag@reitwagen.at
Web site: http://www.reitwagen.at

Titles:
DER REITWAGEN

REPORT VERLAG GMBH & CO. KG 689294
Nattergasse 4, 1170 WIEN **Tel:** 1 902990
Fax: 1 9029937
Email: office@report.at
Web site: http://www.report.at

Titles:
REPORT (+) PLUS
TELEKOM + IT REPORT

RUDOLF SCHERMANN GMBH 684369
Keplergasse 8, 1100 WIEN **Tel:** 1 6035626
Fax: 1 60664104
Email: office@kirche-in.at
Web site: http://www.kirche-in.at

Titles:
KIRCHE IN

RZ REGIONALZEITUNGS GMBH 681740
Rosengasse 5, 6800 FELDKIRCH **Tel:** 5522 72330
Fax: 5522 7233085
Email: info@rzg.at
Web site: http://www.rzg.at

Titles:
BLUDENZER ANZEIGER
WALGAUBLATT

SALZBURGER GEBIETSKRANKENKASSE 1752707
Engelbert-Weiß-Weg 10, 5021 SALZBURG
Tel: 662 88890 **Fax:** 662 88891058
Email: redaktion@sgkk.at
Web site: http://www.sgkk.at

Titles:
FORUM GESUNDHEIT - AUSG. SALZBURG

SALZBURGER KRIEGSOPFERVERBAND 687987
Haunspergstr. 39, 5020 SALZBURG
Tel: 662 872240 **Fax:** 662 87224015
Email: skov@hostprofis.at

Titles:
SALZBURGER KRIEGSOPFER

SALZBURGER NACHRICHTEN VERLAGSGES. MBH & CO. KG 687988
Karolingerstr. 40, 5021 SALZBURG
Tel: 662 83730 **Fax:** 662 8373105
Web site: http://www.salzburg.com

Titles:
SALZBURGER NACHRICHTEN

SCANIA ÖSTERREICH GMBH 1640569
Johann-Steinböck-Str. 4, 2345 BRUNN
Tel: 2236 39020 **Fax:** 2236 390286
Email: office@scania.at
Web site: http://www.scania.at

Titles:
SCANIA BEWEGT

SCHAFFLER VERLAG GMBH 1641059
Wickenburggasse 32, 8010 GRAZ
Tel: 316 8205650 **Fax:** 316 82056520
Email: office@schaffler-verlag.com
Web site: http://www.schaffler-verlag.com

Titles:
DAS ÖSTERREICHISCHE GESUNDHEITSWESEN ÖKZ
QUALITAS

SCHEUCH GMBH 1743016
Weierfing 68, 4971 AUROLZMÜNSTER
Tel: 7752 9050 **Fax:** 7752 905370
Email: office@scheuch.com
Web site: http://www.scheuch.com

Titles:
EMISSIONEN

SCHLÜSSELVERLAG J. S. MOSER GMBH 689493
Ing.-Etzel-Str. 30, 6021 INNSBRUCK **Tel:** 50403
Fax: 50403543
Email: service@tt.com
Web site: http://www.tt.com

Titles:
TIROLER TAGESZEITUNG

SCHMUTZER VERLAG GMBH 1775524
Bahnstr. 6, 2345 BRUNN **Tel:** 2236 31520
Fax: 2236 31529
Email: schmutzer@bauverlag.at
Web site: http://www.bauverlag.at

Titles:
ÖSTERREICHISCHES BAU- UND ENERGIESPAR HANDBUCH

SEELSORGEAMT DER DIÖZESE GURK 684174
Tarviser Str. 30, 9020 KLAGENFURT
Tel: 463 58772502
Email: sonntag@kath-kirche-kaernten.at
Web site: http://www.sonntag-kaernten.at

Titles:
SONNTAG KIRCHENZEITUNG KATHOLISCHE KIRCHE KÄRNTEN

SIMA-DRUCK, AIGNER UND WEISI GMBH 690513
Fabrikstr. 15, 8530 DEUTSCHLANDSBERG
Tel: 3462 25240 **Fax:** 3462 252423
Email: rundschau@simadruck.at
Web site: http://www.simadruck.at

Titles:
WESTSTEIRISCHE RUNDSCHAU

SOZIALDEMOKRATISCHE ÄRZTEVEREINIGUNG 678033
Landgerichtsstr. 16, 1010 WIEN **Tel:** 1 3108829
Fax: 1 319928227
Email: office@bsa.at
Web site: http://www.sozdemaerzte.at

Titles:
ANALYSE

SOZIALVERSICHERUNGS-ANSTALT DER GEWERBLICHEN WIRTSCHAFT 1776030
Wiedner Hauptstr. 84, 1050 WIEN **Tel:** 1 546540
Web site: http://esv-sva.sozvers.at

Titles:
SVA AKTUELL

SPEEDCOMPANY OEG 1791542
Schönkirchnerstr. 4, 2231 STRASSHOF
Tel: 676 5440235
Email: office@motorandmore.at

Titles:
MOTOR & MORE WIEN SÜD

SPORTVERLAG GMBH & CO KG 683137
Geiselbergstr. 15, 1110 WIEN **Tel:** 1 601170
Fax: 1 60117680
Web site: http://www.styria-multi-media.com

Titles:
SPORT MAGAZIN
SPORTWOCHE

SPORTZEITUNG VERLAGS-GMBH 686311
Linke Wienzeile 40/22, 1061 WIEN
Tel: 1 5855757401 **Fax:** 1 5855757411
Email: sportzeitung@lwmedia.at
Web site: http://www.sportzeitung.at

Titles:
SPORTZEITUNG

SPRINGER-VERLAG GMBH 677295
Sachsenplatz 4, 1201 WIEN **Tel:** 1 33024150
Fax: 1 3302426
Web site: http://www.springer.at

Titles:
ACTA MECHANICA
ACTA NEUROCHIRURGICA
AMINO ACIDS
ARCHITEKTUR.AKTUELL
ARCHIVES OF WOMEN'S MENTAL HEALTH
BANKARCHIV
BAURECHTLICHE BLÄTTER:BBL
BHM BERG- UND HÜTTENMÄNNISCHE MONATSHEFTE
E & I
EUROPEAN SURGERY
JOURNAL OF NEURAL TRANSMISSION
MICROCHIMICA ACTA
MONATSHEFTE FÜR CHEMIE CHEMICAL MONTHLY
ÖSTERREICHISCHE WASSER- UND ABFALLWIRTSCHAFT
PÄDIATRIE & PÄDOLOGIE
PSYCHOPRAXIS
SPEKTRUM DER AUGENHEILKUNDE
STOMATOLOGIE
WIENER KLINISCHE WOCHENSCHRIFT
WIENER KLINISCHES MAGAZIN
WMW WIENER MEDIZINISCHE WOCHENSCHRIFT

SPV PRINTMEDIEN GMBH 1643415
Margaretenstr. 22/2/9, 1040 WIEN **Tel:** 1 5812890
Fax: 1 581289023

Titles:
BLICK INS LAND

STADT ATTNANG-PUCHHEIM 686127
Rathausplatz 9, 4800 ATTNANG-PUCHHEIM
Tel: 7674 6150 **Fax:** 7674 61544
Email: stadtamt@attnang-puchheim.ooe.gv.at
Web site: http://www.attnang-puchheim.at

Titles:
UNSER ATTNANG-PUCHHEIM

STADT LEOBEN 688821
Erzherzog-Johann-Str. 2, 8700 LEOBEN
Tel: 3842 4062258 **Fax:** 3842 4062327
Email: presse@leoben.at
Web site: http://www.leoben.at

Titles:
LEOBEN STADTMAGAZIN

STADT, MAGISTRAT 686189
Hauptstr. 1, 4041 LINZ **Tel:** 732 70701862
Fax: 732 70701874
Email: nast@mag.linz.at
Web site: http://www.linz.at/umwelt

Titles:
BERICHTE FÜR ÖKOLOGIE UND NATURSCHUTZ DER STADT LINZ

STADT STEYR 688963
Stadtplatz 27, 4400 STEYR **Tel:** 7252 575354
Fax: 7252 48386
Email: amtsblatt@steyr.gv.at
Web site: http://www.steyr.at

Titles:
STEYR

STANDARD VERLAGSGES. MBH 688867
Herrengasse 19, 1010 WIEN **Tel:** 1 531700
Fax: 1 53170131
Email: marketing@derstandard.at
Web site: http://www.derstandarddigital.at

Titles:
DER STANDARD

STAPF TEXTIL GMBH 697894
Streleweg 20, 6460 IMST **Tel:** 5412 69990
Fax: 5412 699954
Email: stapftextilimst@aon.at
Web site: http://www.stapftextil.at

Titles:
DIRNDL REVUE

STARMÜHLER AGENTUR & VERLAG GMBH 680499
Schellinggasse 1/7/3, 1010 WIEN **Tel:** 1 9613888
Fax: 1 961388850
Email: office@starmuehler.at
Web site: http://www.starmuehler.at

Titles:
ADGAR
STARMÜHLER'S

STEIERMÄRKISCHE LANDARBEITERKAMMER 684933
Raubergasse 20, 8010 GRAZ **Tel:** 316 832507
Fax: 316 83250720
Email: office@lak-stmk.at
Web site: http://www.landarbeiterkammer.at/steiermark

Titles:
LAND- UND FORSTARBEIT HEUTE

STEIERMÄRKISCHER FORSTVEREIN 682790
Herrengasse 13/I, 8010 GRAZ **Tel:** 316 825325
Fax: 316 825325
Email: forstverein.steiermark@utanet.at
Web site: http://www.steirischerwald.at

Titles:
GRÜNER SPIEGEL

STYRIA MULTI MEDIA CORPORATE GMBH & CO KG 1758111
Geiselbergstr. 15, 1110 WIEN **Tel:** 1 601170
Fax: 1 60117190
Web site: http://www.styria-multi-media.com

Titles:
ACTIVE BEAUTY
PROGENIO

STYRIA MULTI MEDIA LADIES GMBH & CO KG 1710152
Geiselbergstr. 15, 1110 WIEN **Tel:** 1 60117966
Fax: 1 60117240
Email: diva@diva-online.at
Web site: http://www.diva-online.at

Titles:
DIVA
MISS
WIENERIN

SÜDWIND AGENTUR GMBH 686780
Laudongasse 40, 1080 WIEN **Tel:** 1 40555150
Fax: 1 4055519
Email: suedwind.magazin@suedwind.at
Web site: http://www.suedwind-magazin.at

Titles:
SÜDWIND

SZABO-SCHEIBL VERLAG + PR OG 1645433
Liebhartsgasse 36, 1160 WIEN **Tel:** 1 4934945
Fax: 1 4934946
Email: office@bankundboerse.at
Web site: http://www.bankundboerse.at

Titles:
BANK & BÖRSE

T.A.I. FACHZEITUNGSVERLAG GMBH 700054
Weyrgasse 8/9, 1030 WIEN **Tel:** 1 588810
Fax: 1 5888120
Email: verlag@tai.at
Web site: http://www.tai.at

Titles:
TAI TOURISMUSWIRTSCHAFT AUSTRIA & INTERNATIONAL

TEAM-I ZEITSCHRIFTENVERLAG GMBH 1644397
Stockerauer Str. 43a/5, 2100 KORNEUBURG
Tel: 32262 74650 **Fax:** 2262 7465030

Titles:
DAS INSTALLATIONS-MAGAZIN

TECHNIK & MEDIEN VERLAGSGES. MBH 1632826
Hietzinger Kai 175, 1130 WIEN **Tel:** 1 87683790
Fax: 1 876837915
Email: mm@technik-medien.at
Web site: http://www.maschinenmarkt.at

Titles:
MM MASCHINENMARKT

TELEKOM PRESSE DR. PETER F. MAYER KG 1654548
Getreidemarkt 10, 1010 WIEN **Tel:** 1 58120810
Fax: 1 581208199
Email: chefredaktion@pfm-magazin.at
Web site: http://www.peterfmayer.at

Titles:
PFM-MAGAZIN FÜR INFRASTRUKTUR UND TECHNOLOGIE

TELE-ZEITSCHRIFTENVERLAGSGES. MBH & CO. KG 689282
Lothringerstr. 14, 1030 WIEN **Tel:** 1 605900
Fax: 1 6059041
Email: office@tele.at
Web site: http://www.tele.at

Titles:
TELE

TIPS ZEITUNGS GMBH & CO KG 1644301
Promenade 23, 4010 LINZ **Tel:** 732 7895290
Fax: 732 785955
Web site: http://www.tips.at

Titles:
ENNS STADTMAGAZIN
TIPS FREISTADT
TIPS LINZ
TIPS VÖCKLABRUCK

TIROLER JÄGERVERBAND 683894
Adamgasse 7a/2, 6020 INNSBRUCK
Tel: 512 571093 **Fax:** 512 57109315
Email: info@tjv.at
Web site: http://www.tjv.at

Titles:
JAGD IN TIROL

TIROLER JUNGBAUERNSCHAFT/ LANDJUGEND 685174
Brixner Str. 1, 6020 INNSBRUCK
Tel: 512 5990020 **Fax:** 512 5990031
Email: tjblj@tiroler-bauernbund.at
Web site: http://www.tjblj.at

Titles:
LOGO

TIROLER LANDESREGIERUNG 679627
Neues Landhaus, 6020 INNSBRUCK
Tel: 512 5082184 **Fax:** 512 5082185
Web site: http://www.tirol.gv.at

Titles:
BOTE FÜR TIROL

TIROLERIN VERLAGSGES. MBH 689483
Industriezone C6, 6166 FULPMES
Tel: 5225 63921 **Fax:** 5225 64196
Email: office@tirolerin.at
Web site: http://www.tirolerin.at

Titles:
TIROLERIN

TOPTIMES MEDIEN GMBH 1724178
Belgiergasse 3, 8020 GRAZ **Tel:** 316 903312786
Fax: 316 903312764
Email: office@toptimes.at
Web site: http://www.sport10.at

Titles:
TOPTIMES

UCM-VERLAG B2B FACHVERLAG GMBH 689049
Salzweg 17, 5081 ANIF **Tel:** 6246 897999
Fax: 6246 897989
Email: office@ucm-verlag.at
Web site: http://www.ucm-verlag.at

Titles:
STYLE IN PROGRESS
STYLE IN PROGRESS

UCM-VERLAG B2C CORPORATE-PUBLISHING GMBH 1719942
Salzweg 17, 5081 ANIF **Tel:** 6246 897999
Fax: 6246 897989
Email: office@ucm-verlag.at
Web site: http://www.ucm-verlag.at

Titles:
WÜSTENROT MAGAZIN

UCOM-S GMBH 1789317
Nonntaler Hauptstr. 20, 5020 SALZBURG
Tel: 662 236624
Web site: http://www.designers-digest.de

Titles:
DESIGNERS DIGEST

UFO, DIE GRÜNEN PRESSBAUM 1714680
Kaiserbrunnstr. 73, 3021 PRESSBAUM
Tel: 2233 55070 **Fax:** 2233 55070
Email: peter.samec@gruene.at
Web site: http://www.ufo-pressbaum.at

Titles:
UMWELTFORUM PRESSBAUM

UMDASCH SHOP-CONCEPT GMBH 688412
Josef-Umdasch-Platz 1, 3300 AMSTETTEN
Tel: 7472 6050 **Fax:** 7472 63487
Email: shop.aktuell@umdasch.com
Web site: http://www.umdasch-shop-concept.com

Titles:
SHOP AKTUELL

UNIVERSIMED PUBLISHING GMBH 679501
Markgraf-Rüdiger-Str. 8, 1150 WIEN
Tel: 1 87679560 **Fax:** 1 876795620
Email: office@universimed.com
Web site: http://www.universimed.com

Titles:
JATROS DIABETES & STOFFWECHSEL
JATROS HÄMATOLOGIE & ONKOLOGIE
JATROS KARDIOLOGIE & GEFÄSSMEDIZIN
JATROS MEDIZIN FÜR DIE FRAU
JATROS NEUROLOGIE & PSYCHIATRIE
JATROS ORTHOPÄDIE
JATROS VACCINES
UROLOGIK

UPG VERLAGSGES. MBH 681907
Simmeringer Hauptstr. 152/19, 1110 WIEN
Tel: 664 8468645
Email: wcm@wcm.at
Web site: http://www.wcm.at

Titles:
ITSELLER
WCM

URANUS VERLAGSGES. M.B.H 1641652
Neustiftgasse 115a/20, 1070 WIEN
Tel: 1 4039111 **Fax:** 1 403911133
Email: verlag@uranus.at
Web site: http://www.uranus.at

Titles:
SONNENZEITUNG

VCÖ VERKEHRSCLUB ÖSTERREICH 690010
Bräuhausgasse 7, 1050 WIEN **Tel:** 1 8932697
Fax: 1 8932431
Email: vcoe@vcoe.at
Web site: http://www.vcoe.at

Titles:
MOBILITÄT MIT ZUKUNFT
VCÖ-MAGAZIN

VERBAND BIO AUSTRIA SALZBURG 687984
Schwarzstr. 19, 5020 SALZBURG
Tel: 662 870571314 **Fax:** 662 878074
Email: salzburg@bio-austria.at
Web site: http://www.bio-austria.at

Titles:
BIO AUSTRIA SALZBURG

VERBAND DER ÖSTERREICHISCHEN AUTOTAXIUNTERNEHMER 686699
Hetzgasse 34/1/7, 1030 WIEN **Tel:** 1 71549800
Fax: 1 715498012
Email: taxiverband@fachliste.at
Web site: http://www.fachliste.at

Titles:
ÖTZ ÖSTERREICHISCHE TAXIZEITUNG

VERBAND DER REGIONALMEDIEN ÖSTERREICHS 690310
Esterházygasse 4a/2/17, 1060 WIEN
Tel: 1 5857737 **Fax:** 1 585773737
Email: vrm@vrm.at
Web site: http://www.vrm.at

Titles:
VRM PRESSEHANDBUCH

VERBAND ÖSTERREICHISCHER INGENIEURE 690231
Eschenbachgasse 9, 1010 WIEN **Tel:** 1 5874198
Fax: 1 5868268
Email: voi@voi.at
Web site: http://www.voi.at

Titles:
DER INGENIEUR

VERBAND ÖSTERREICHISCHER WIRTSCHAFTSAKADEMIKER 1712970
Teinfaltstr. 1, 1010 WIEN **Tel:** 1 53368760
Fax: 1 533687633
Email: office@voewa.at
Web site: http://www.voewa.at

Titles:
VÖWA WIRTSCHAFTSKURIER

VERBAND ÖSTERREICHISCHER ZEITUNGEN 687284
Wipplingerstr. 15, 1010 WIEN **Tel:** 1 53379790
Fax: 1 5337979422
Email: office@voez.at
Web site: http://www.voez.at

Titles:
VÖZ AKTUELL

VEREIN AGROZUCKER 677434
Donau-City-Str. 9, 1220 WIEN **Tel:** 1 211370
Fax: 1 211372998
Email: info.ab@agrana.at
Web site: http://www.agrana.com

Titles:
AGRO ZUCKER STÄRKE

VEREIN FAHRGAST-DIE ÖSTERREICHISCHE FAHRGASTVERTRETUNG 681653
Magdalenenstr. 13/1/2, 1060 WIEN
Tel: 1 5871069 **Fax:** 1 5856269
Email: fahrgast@gmx.at
Web site: http://www.fahrgast.at

Titles:
FAHRGAST

VEREIN FRAUENFORSCHUNG UND WEIBLICHER LEBENSZUSAMMENHANG 688968
Diefenbachgasse 38/1, 1150 WIEN **Tel:** 1 8129886
Fax: 1 8129886
Email: office@stichwort.or.at
Web site: http://www.stichwort.or.at

Titles:
STICHWORT-NEWSLETTER

VEREIN FÜR KONSUMENTENINFORMATION 680992
Mariahilfer Str. 81, 1060 WIEN **Tel:** 1 588770
Fax: 1 5887773
Email: konsument@vki.at
Web site: http://www.konsument.at

Titles:
KONSUMENT

VEREIN MANUSKRIPTE 685339
Sackstr. 17, 8010 GRAZ **Tel:** 316 825608
Fax: 316 825605
Email: lz@manuskripte.at
Web site: http://www.manuskripte.at

Titles:
MANUSKRIPTE

VEREIN REGENWALD DER ÖSTERREICHER 1727474
Währinger Str. 182/24, 1180 WIEN **Tel:** 1 4701935
Fax: 1 470193520
Email: info@regenwald.at
Web site: http://www.regenwald.at

Titles:
REGENWALD-NACHRICHTEN

VEREIN SOL-MENSCHEN FÜR SOLIDARITÄT, OEKOLOGIE UND LEBENSSTIL 1644641
Penzingerstr. 18/2, 1140 WIEN **Tel:** 1 8767924
Fax: 1 878129283
Email: sol@nachhaltig.at
Web site: http://www.nachhaltig.at

Titles:
SOL

VEREIN UNSER LAGERHAUS 689918
Wienerbergstr. 3, 1100 WIEN **Tel:** 1 605155660
Fax: 1 605155679
Email: unserland@rwa.at
Web site: http://www.lagerhaus.at

Titles:
UNSER LAND

VEREINIGUNG ÖSTERREICHISCHER WIRTSCHAFTSTREUHÄNDER GMBH 690677
Kärntner Str. 8, 1010 WIEN **Tel:** 1 5122069
Fax: 1 512206920
Email: vwt@vwt.at
Web site: http://www.vwt.at

Titles:
WT DER WIRTSCHAFTSTREUHÄNDER

VERLAG DAS GRÜNE HAUS 682785
Tuttenhofstr. 63, 2103 LANGENZERSDORF
Tel: 2244 292370 **Fax:** 2244 2923733
Email: verlag@gruenehaus.at
Web site: http://www.gesundheitswelten.com

Titles:
DAS GRÜNE HAUS

VERLAG DER MEDIZINER GMBH 685488
Steirer Str. 24, 9375 HÜTTENBERG
Tel: 4263 20034 **Fax:** 4263 20074
Email: office@mediziner.at
Web site: http://www.mediziner.at

Titles:
DER MEDIZINER

VERLAG DER SPÖ GMBH 1781981
Löwelstr. 18, 1014 WIEN **Tel:** 1 53427399
Fax: 431 53427363
Email: manfred.lang@spoe.at
Web site: http://www.diezukunft.at

Titles:
ZUKUNFT

VERLAG DES ÖSTERREICHISCHEN GEWERKSCHAFTSBUNDES GMBH 677646
Johann-Böhm-Platz 1, 1020 WIEN
Tel: 1 66232960 **Fax:** 1 662329639793
Email: office@oegbverlag.at
Web site: http://www.oegbverlag.at

Titles:
ARBEIT & WIRTSCHAFT
BAU-HOLZ
FSG DIREKT
KOMPETENZ

VERLAG DIETER GÖSCHL GMBH 682955
Hernalser Hauptstr. 213, 1170 WIEN
Tel: 1 4864240 **Fax:** 1 4854902
Email: info@goeschl.co.at
Web site: http://www.medizinprodukte.at

Titles:
HANDBUCH FÜR DIE SANITÄTSBERUFE ÖSTERREICHS
ÖMP ÖSTERREICHISCHES MEDIZINPRODUKTE-HANDBUCH

VERLAG FRANZ STEINER 685434
Wolfeggstr. 19, 6900 BREGENZ **Tel:** 5574 46462
Fax: 5574 44033
Email: franz.steiner@vol.at
Web site: http://www.modellbahnwelt.at

Titles:
MBW MODELLBAHNWELT

VERLAG GESUNDHEIT GMBH 682546
Stoß im Himmel 1, 1010 WIEN **Tel:** 1 5322540
Fax: 1 532254020
Web site: http://www.gesundheit.co.at

Titles:
GESUNDHEIT

VERLAG HELENE GAMPER 679496
Schützenstr. 11, 6332 KUFSTEIN
Tel: 5372 623320 **Fax:** 5372 623324
Email: gamper-werbung@kufnet.at
Web site: http://www.blickpunkt-lkw-bus.com

Titles:
BLICKPUNKT LKW & BUS

VERLAG LEEB!ENSZEICHEN 687153
Knappensteig 12, 9500 VILLACH
Tel: 664 9762859
Email: planetalpen@gmx.at
Web site: http://www.alpen-adria-planet.org

Titles:
PLANET ALPEN

VERLAG MAG. KLAUS GARMS 682732
Plüddemanngasse 39, 8010 GRAZ
Tel: 316 475112 **Fax:** 316 466366
Email: redaktion@garms.co.at
Web site: http://www.garms.at

Titles:
MEINE TANKSTELLE

VERLAG ÖSTERREICH GMBH 677901
Bäckerstr. 1, 1010 WIEN **Tel:** 1 610770
Fax: 1 61077419
Email: office@verlagoesterreich.at
Web site: http://www.verlagoesterreich.at

Titles:
ZEITSCHRIFT DER UNABHÄNGIGEN VERWALTUNGSSENATE
ZEITSCHRIFT FÜR ABGABEN-, FINANZ- UND STEUERRECHT AFS
ZEITSCHRIFT FÜR GESELLSCHAFTSRECHT UND ANGRENZENDES STEUERRECHT
ZEITSCHRIFT FÜR VERGABERECHT RPA

VERLAG PETER GÜNZL 688391
Kirchenstr. 11, 9220 VELDEN **Tel:** 4274 3313
Fax: 4274 50710
Email: redaktion@veldnerzeitung.at
Web site: http://www.veldnerzeitung.at

Titles:
SERVUS AM WÖRTHERSEE

VERLAG PETER SCHOBER 686558
10.-Oktober-Str. 66, 9800 SPITTAL
Tel: 4762 4060 **Fax:** 4762 406014
Email: okn.schober@aon.at
Web site: http://www.okn.at

Titles:
OBERKÄRNTNER NACHRICHTEN

VERLAG STROHMAYER KG 1776295
Weitmosergasse 30, 1100 WIEN **Tel:** 1 6172635
Fax: 1 6172635
Email: office@verlag-strohmayer.at
Web site: http://www.verlag-strohmayer.at

Titles:
GIESSEREI RUNDSCHAU
WOHNKULTUR

VERLAG UND WERBEGRAFIK LABER GMBH 679321
Oberwaltersdorferstr. 36, 2512 TRIBUSWINKEL
Tel: 2252 259912 **Fax:** 2252 80204
Email: verlag@biker.at
Web site: http://www.biker.at

Titles:
BIKER IN ÖSTERREICH

VERLAG WACHTER-SIEG 1745171
Lambrechtstr. 16, 1040 WIEN **Tel:** 664 1342966
Fax: 1 9437900
Email: hannelore.wachter-sieg@dlv.de
Web site: http://www.motorist.at

Titles:
AGRAR TECHNIK ÖSTERREICH

VERLAG WEGE 690407
Rankar 12, 4692 NIEDERTHALHEIM
Tel: 7676 7017
Email: redaktion@wege.at
Web site: http://www.wege.at

Titles:
WEGE

VERLAG WIRL 689582
Tautenhayngasse 21/3, 1150 WIEN
Tel: 1 7863781 **Fax:** 1 786378119
Email: wirl@verlagwirl.at
Web site: http://www.verlagwirl.at

Titles:
KULTURMAGAZIN DER WIENER FREMDENFÜHRER
TRAINING

VERLAGSANSTALT TYROLIA GMBH 681754
Exlgasse 20, 6020 INNSBRUCK **Tel:** 512 2233202
Fax: 512 2233206
Email: buchverlag@tyrolia.at
Web site: http://www.tyrolia-verlag.at

Titles:
REIMMICHLS VOLKSKALENDER

VERLAGSGRUPPE NEWS GMBH 1643907
Taborstr. 1, 1020 WIEN **Tel:** 1 213120
Fax: 1 213126650
Web site: http://www.news.at

Titles:
AUTO REVUE
E-MEDIA
FORMAT
GOLF REVUE
GUSTO
NEWS
PROFIL
TREND
WOMAN

VERLAGSHAUS DER ÄRZTE GMBH 680156
Nibelungengasse 13, 1010 WIEN **Tel:** 1 5124486
Fax: 1 512448624
Email: office@aerzteverlagshaus.at
Web site: http://www.aerzteverlagshaus.at

Titles:
MEDIZIN POPULÄR
ÖSTERREICHISCHE ÄRZTEZEITUNG
PHARMAINFORMATION

VORARLBERGER GEBIETSKRANKENKASSE 682020
Jahngasse 4, 6850 DORNBIRN **Tel:** 5084551111
Fax: 50845581111
Email: forum.gesundheit@vgkk.at
Web site: http://www.vgkk.at

Titles:
FORUM GESUNDHEIT

VORARLBERGER LANDESREGIERUNG, ABTEILUNG RAUMPLANUNG UND BAURECHT 1643257
Landhaus, 6900 BREGENZ **Tel:** 5574 51127105
Email: raumplanung@vorarlberg.at
Web site: http://www.vorarlberg.at/gemeindeentwicklung

Titles:
VORUM

VWZ ZEITSCHRIFTENVERLAG GMBH 685613
Schottenfeldgasse 24, 1070 WIEN **Tel:** 1 5247086
Fax: 1 5247086903
Web site: http://www.wienerbezirksblatt.at

Titles:
WIENER BEZIRKS BLATT

WAILAND & WALDSTEIN GMBH 682571
Stiftgasse 31, 1071 WIEN **Tel:** 1 521240
Fax: 1 5212440
Email: gewinn@gewinn.com
Web site: http://www.gewinn.com

Austria

Titles:
GEWINN
TOP GEWINN

WALLIG ENNSTALER DRUCKEREI UND VERLAGSGES. MBH
681308
Mitterbergstr. 36, 8962 GRÖBMING
Tel: 3685 2212113 **Fax:** 3685 22321
Email: ennstaler@walligdruck.at
Web site: http://www.derennstaler.at

Titles:
DER ENNSTALER

WEBERMEDIA
691035
Zieglergasse 3/2/2, 1072 WIEN **Tel:** 1 52504
Fax: 1 5254020
Email: verlag@webermedia.at
Web site: http://www.webermedia.at

Titles:
ZUKUNFTSBRANCHEN

WEIZER ZEITUNG GMBH & CO KG
682627
Südtiroler Platz 2, 8160 WEIZ **Tel:** 3172 3790
Fax: 3172 379021
Web site: http://www.woche.at/weiz

Titles:
WOCHE WEIZ & BIRKFELD

WEKA VERLAG GMBH
678951
Dresdner Str. 45, 1200 WIEN **Tel:** 1 97000100
Fax: 1 970005100
Web site: http://www.weka.at

Titles:
AUTO SERVICE
BBB BAUMASCHINE BAUGERÄT BAUSTELLE
BM BAUMAGAZIN
DISPO
ELEKTRONIK REPORT
FIRMENWAGEN
HLK HEIZUNG LÜFTUNG KLIMATECHNIK
PUNKTUM
RENOVATION
SCHUH & LEDERWAREN REVUE
TECHNIK REPORT
TGA TECHNISCHE GEBÄUDEAUSRÜSTUNG
TOPGEBRAUCHTE.AT
TRAKTUELL

WELLNESS MAGAZIN ZEITSCHRIFTENVERLAGS GMBH
690451
Ölzeltgasse 3, 1030 WIEN **Tel:** 1 4191095
Fax: 1 419109510
Email: office@wellness-magazin.at
Web site: http://www.wellness-magazin.at

Titles:
WELLNESS MAGAZIN

WELT DER FRAU VERLAGS GMBH
690457
Lustenauer Str. 21, 4020 LINZ **Tel:** 732 77000112
Fax: 732 77000124
Email: office@welt-der-frau.at
Web site: http://www.welt-der-frau.at

Titles:
WELT DER FRAU

WERBEAGENTUR HARALD ECKERT
684548
Landstraßer Hauptstr. 141/3a/5, 1030 WIEN
Tel: 1 7122036 **Fax:** 1 7122070
Email: werbeagentur.harald.eckert@chello.at
Web site: http://www.kompack.info

Titles:
KOMPACK

WERBEAGENTUR KARIN MAYERHOFER
1725078
Stemolakgasse 29, 1220 WIEN **Tel:** 1 2856108
Fax: 1 285610813
Email: office@grafik-hauk.at

Titles:
KLEINGÄRTNER

WESTPOINT KURT HERRAN
690511
Holzhammerstr. 15/3/1, 6020 INNSBRUCK
Tel: 664 3165777
Email: kurt.herran@chello.at
Web site: http://www.westpoint.at

Titles:
WESTPOINT

WIENER ARBEITSKREIS FÜR METAPHYSIK E. V.
679238
Postfach 36, 1042 WIEN **Tel:** 1 4709850
Fax: 1 9207080
Email: office@bewusst-sein.net
Web site: http://www.bewusst-sein.net

Titles:
BEWUSST SEIN

WIENER SENIORENBUND
690545
Biberstr. 9, 1010 WIEN **Tel:** 1 51543600
Fax: 1 51543609
Email: wiener@seniorenbund.at
Web site: http://www.ab5zig.at

Titles:
AB5ZIG

WIENER STÄDTISCHE VERSICHERUNG AG
1640579
Schottenring 30, 1010 WIEN **Tel:** 1 5035021336
Fax: 1 503509921039
Email: presseabteilung@staedtische.co.at
Web site: http://www.wienerstaedtische.at

Titles:
IMPULS

WIENER VERLAGS GMBH & CO KG
697406
Geiselbergstr. 15, 1110 WIEN **Tel:** 1 601170
Fax: 1 60117350
Email: wiener@wiener-online.at
Web site: http://www.wienerpost.at

Titles:
WIENER

WIENER ZEITUNG GMBH
690552
Wiedner Gürtel 10, 1040 WIEN **Tel:** 1 206990
Fax: 1 20699100
Email: abo-center@wienerzeitung.at
Web site: http://www.wienerzeitung.at

Titles:
WIENER JOURNAL
WIENER ZEITUNG

WIMMER MEDIEN GMBH & CO. KG
679250
Promenade 23, 4010 LINZ **Tel:** 732 78050
Fax: 732 785955
Email: a.cuturi@nachrichten.at
Web site: http://www.nachrichten.at

Titles:
OÖ NACHRICHTEN

WIRTSCHAFTSBLATT VERLAG AG
690651
Geiselbergstr. 15, 1110 WIEN **Tel:** 1 601170
Fax: 1 6022858
Email: redaktion@wirtschaftsblatt.at
Web site: http://www.wirtschaftsblatt.at

Titles:
WIRTSCHAFTSBLATT
WIRTSCHAFTSBLATT DELUXE
WIRTSCHAFTSBLATT INVESTOR

WIRTSCHAFTSFORUM DER FÜHRUNGSKRÄFTE
690396
Lothringer Str. 12, 1030 WIEN **Tel:** 1 7126510
Fax: 1 711352912
Email: r.graf@wdf.at
Web site: http://www.wdf.at

Titles:
LEADERSHIP

WIRTSCHAFTSKAMMER BURGENLAND
679958
Robert-Graf-Platz 1, 7000 EISENSTADT
Tel: 5909074511 **Fax:** 5909074515
Email: redaktion@wkbgld.at
Web site: http://wko.at/bgld

Titles:
BURGENLÄNDISCHE WIRTSCHAFT

WIRTSCHAFTSKAMMER OBERÖSTERREICH
677534
Hessenplatz 3, 4020 LINZ **Tel:** 5909093314
Fax: 5909093311
Email: medien@wkooe.at
Web site: http://wko.at/ooe

Titles:
OÖ WIRTSCHAFT

WIRTSCHAFTSKAMMER ÖSTERREICH, ABT. FÜR STATISTIK
1643702
Wiedner Hauptstr. 63, 1045 WIEN
Tel: 5909004103 **Fax:** 590900246
Email: statistik@wko.at
Web site: http://www.wko.at/statistik

Titles:
ANALYSE DER VERBRAUCHERPREISE

WIRTSCHAFTSKAMMER SALZBURG
677439
Julius-Raab-Platz 1, 5027 SALZBURG
Tel: 662 8888345 **Fax:** 662 8888388
Email: salzburger-wirtschaft@wks.at
Web site: http://wko.at/sbg

Titles:
S.W. SALZBURGER WIRTSCHAFT

WIRTSCHAFTSKAMMER TIROL
689495
Meinhardstr. 14, 6020 INNSBRUCK
Tel: 5909051482 **Fax:** 5909051461
Email: presse@wktirol.at
Web site: http://www.tirolerwirtschaft.at

Titles:
TIROLER WIRTSCHAFT

WIRTSCHAFTSLISTE SALZBURG, FRAKTION IN DER WIRTSCHAFTSKAMMER SALZBURG
690631
Franz-Josef-Str. 12, 5020 SALZBURG
Tel: 662 878147 **Fax:** 662 876649
Email: office@wirtschaftsliste.at
Web site: http://www.wirtschaftsliste.at

Titles:
WIRTSCHAFT AKTIV

WIRTSCHAFTSNACHRICHTEN ZEITSCHRIFTEN VERLAGSGES. MBH
680008
Stempfergasse 3, 8010 GRAZ **Tel:** 316 834020
Fax: 316 83402010
Email: steiermark@euromedien.at
Web site: http://www.wn-online.at

Titles:
WIRTSCHAFTSNACHRICHTEN SÜD

WOCHENZEITUNGS GMBH STEIERMARK
686063
Murtaler Platz 1, 8750 JUDENBURG
Tel: 3572 8580024 **Fax:** 3572 8580026
Email: murtaler.zeitung@styria.com
Web site: http://www.murtalerzeitung.at

Titles:
MURTALER ZEITUNG
WOCHE OBERSTEIERMARK

WOCHENZEITUNGS GMBH STEIERMARK, WOCHE HARTBERG
683056
Am Ökopark 9, 8230 HARTBERG
Tel: 3332 623940 **Fax:** 3332 6239494
Email: hbz@woche.at
Web site: http://www.woche.at/hbz

Titles:
WOCHE HARTBERGER BEZIRKSZEITUNG

WORK FLOWS. AGENTUR & VERLAG
1741677
Roseggerweg 36, 2201 GERASDORF
Tel: 2246 21922 **Fax:** 2246 2192220
Email: office@workflows.at
Web site: http://www.workflows.at

Titles:
OUT-OF-HOME

WWF PANDA GMBH
686894
Ottakringer Str. 114, 1160 WIEN **Tel:** 1 48817237
Fax: 1 48817278
Web site: http://www.wwf.at

Titles:
PANDAMAGAZIN

ZEIT FÜR MICH ZEITSCHRIFTENVERLAGS GMBH
1762768
Altmannsdorfer Str. 104, 1120 WIEN
Tel: 1 2988888888 **Fax:** 1 2988883
Email: office@zeit-fuer-mich.cc
Web site: http://www.fuer-mich.at

Titles:
FRATZ&CO

ZEITUNGS- UND VERLAGSGES. MBH
686329
Gutenbergstr. 1, 6858 SCHWARZACH
Tel: 5572 501850 **Fax:** 5572 501860

Titles:
NEUE VORARLBERGER TAGESZEITUNG

ZENTRALVEREIN DER WIENER LEHRERINNEN
691048
Rauhensteingasse 5/4, 1010 WIEN **Tel:** 1 8130811
Fax: 1 8130815
Email: perspektive.zv@gmx.at
Web site: http://www.zv-wien.at

Titles:
PERSPEKTIVE

ZG ZEITSCHRIFTEN GMBH & CO KG
1751613
Geiselbergstr. 15, 1110 WIEN **Tel:** 1 60117
Fax: 1 60117680
Web site: http://www.styria-multi-media.com

Titles:
MOTORRAD MAGAZIN

ZIELGRUPPEN-ZEITUNGSVERLAGS GMBH
680132
Zamenhofstr. 9, 4020 LINZ **Tel:** 732 696440
Fax: 732 696441
Email: office@zzv.at
Web site: http://www.zzv.at

Titles:
CHEFINFO

Belarus

ADMINISTRATION OF THE PRESIDENT OF THE BELARUS REPUBLIC
699476
vul. Khmelnitskogo 10A, 220013 MINSK
Tel: 17 29 21 432 **Fax:** 17 29 21 432

Titles:
SOVIETSKAYA BELORUSSIA

BELARUSKOYE TELEGRAFNOYE AGENSTVO
1651168
ul. Kirova 26, 220030 MINSK **Tel:** 17 22 71 992
Fax: 17 22 71 346
Email: oper@belta.by
Web site: http://www.belta.by

Titles:
7 DNEY

BELGAZETA
699504
ul. Kalvariskaya 17 A, office 616A, MINSK 220004 **Tel:** 17 22 33 373 **Fax:** 17 22 04 050
Email: bg@bg.org.by
Web site: http://www.belgazeta.by

Titles:
BELGAZETA

KOMSIS
1732289
pr. Nezavisimosti 77, 220013 MINSK

Titles:
EXPRESS NOVOSTI

MINISTERIUM OF THE REPUBLIC OF BELARUS
697939
ul. Bogdana Khmyalnitskogo 10a, MINSK 220013 **Tel:** 17 26 82 615 **Fax:** 17 26 82 612

Titles:
RESPUBLIKA

NARODNAYA GAZETA
1200846
ul. Khmelnitskogo 10A, Etazh 7, 220013 MINSK
Tel: 17 26 82 870 **Fax:** 17 26 82 806

Titles:
NARODNAYA GAZETA

NESTOR PUBLISHERS
697888
PO Box 563, 220113 MINSK **Tel:** 17 28 93 713
Fax: 17 33 46 790
Email: mg@nestormedia.com
Web site: http://www.nestor.minsk.by/nestoren.htm

Titles:
KOMPUTERNAYA GAZETA
VIRTUAL JOYS

OOO IZDATELSKIY DOM VECHERNY MINSK 699590
Pr. Fr. Skoriny 44, 220005 MINSK
Tel: 17 28 82 532 **Fax:** 17 28 82 532
Titles:
VECHERNY MINSK

SPN REMATIS 1747474
per. Fedotova 14, MINSK **Tel:** 17 29 15 909
Titles:
MC MOBILNAYA SVYAZ'

UPRAVLYENYE PO DELOM MALADYOZHY MINISTERSTVA OBROZOVANYA RESPSPUBLIKI BELARUSI 1622035
ul. Khmelnitskogo 10 A, 220013 MINSK
Titles:
ZNAMYA YUNOSTI

ZAO ASA 1201270
ul. Kalinovskogo 55, 220103 MINSK
Tel: 17 26 54 739 **Fax:** 17 26 54 741
Email: abw@abw.by
Web site: http://www.ab-daily.by
Titles:
AUTOBUSINESS WEEKLY

Belgium

ACKROYD PUBLICATIONS 1784809
Chaussée de Waterloo, 1038 BRUXELLES
Tel: 2373 83 26 **Fax:** 23759822
Titles:
THE BULLETIN

ALTERNET 1690647
Quai d'Aa, 6, 1070 BRUXELLES **Tel:** 2526 93 25
Fax: 25245700
Titles:
MARIAGE.BE

ARPEGE MEDIA 1645470
Rue de la Terre Franche, 31, 5310 LONGCHAMPS **Tel:** 8143 24 80 **Fax:** 81432489
Titles:
AGENDA PLUS

ARS NV 1785805
Ambachtenlaan 13, 3294 MOLENSTEDE-DIEST
Tel: 13 78 07 90 **Fax:** 13 77 75 66
Titles:
IMAGO

ATON PUBLISHING 1784813
Aton Publishing, Rue Jules Lahaye 82, 1090 BRUXELLES **Tel:** 2772 40 47 **Fax:** 27719801
Titles:
LE JOURNAL DE L'ARCHITECTE - ARCHITECTENKRANT

BACK TO BASICS 1645660
Taxanderlei, 43, 2900 SCHOTEN **Tel:** 3658 09 68
Fax: 36583708
Titles:
LES JARDINS D'EDEN-TUINEN VAN EDEN

BEST OF PUBLISHING 1645657
Rodenbachstraat 70, 1190 BRUSSELS
Tel: 2 349 35 50 **Fax:** 2 349 35 97
Titles:
INSIDE
PC WORLD

BOERENBOND 1645506
Diestsevest 40, 3000 LEUVEN **Tel:** 1628 63 02
Fax: 16286309
Titles:
LANDBOUW & TECHNIEK

CMP MEDICA BELGIUM 1784783
Rue du Bourdon, 100, 1180 BRUXELLES
Tel: 2333 34 11 **Fax:** 23323958
Titles:
DIALOGUE & SANTE

CONCENTRA 1646059
Katwilgweg, 2 - Bus 3, 2050 ANVERS
Tel: 3210 30 50 **Fax:** 32103051
Titles:
AMBIANCE CULINAIRE
HET BELANG VAN LIMBURG
GAZET VAN ANTWERPEN

CONFEDERATIE BELGISCHE BIETENPLANTERS 1785881
Bd Anspach 111 - B 10, 1000 BRUXELLES
Tel: 2551 11 74 **Fax:** 25121988
Titles:
DE BIETPLANTER - LE BETTERAVIER

CORELIO (EX VUM NV) 1784691
Kouter 150, 9000 GENT **Tel:** 9 268 72 70
Fax: 9 268 72 71
Titles:
DE GENTENAAR - NIEUWSBLAD
HEY NIEUWSBLAD OP ZONDAG
NB MAGAZINE
PASSE-PARTOUT
DE STANDAARD

DAVIDSFONDS 1784872
Blijde Inkomststraat, 79-81, 3000 LEUVEN
Tel: 1631 06 00 **Fax:** 16310608
Titles:
OMTRENT

DE BOECK & LARCIER 1784794
Coupure Rechts 298, 9000 GENT **Tel:** 9269 97 96
Fax: 92699799
Titles:
DROIT BANCAIRE ET FINANCIER - BANK- EN FINANCIEEL RECHT

DE GROEVE 1785893
Postbus, 728, 8400 OOSTENDE **Tel:** 59702 8 14
Fax: 59702834
Titles:
ZWERFAUTO MAGAZINE

DE MORGEN 1784696
De Morgen, Arduinkaai 29, 1000 BRUSSELS
Tel: 2 556 68 11 **Fax:** 2 520 35 15
Titles:
DE MORGEN

DE PERSGROEP 1784690
Brusselsesteenweg 347, 1730 ASSE/ KOBBEGEM **Tel:** 2454 26 16 **Fax:** 24542615
Titles:
7SUR7.BE
DAG ALLEMAAL
DEMORGEN.BE
HLN - HET LAATSTE NIEUWS / DE NIUEWE GAZET

DECHAMPS - DIFFUSIONS SPRL 1785898
Clos des Lilas, 5, 1380 OHAIN **Tel:** 2660 69 40
Fax: 26600943
Titles:
VOTRE BEAUTE

DECOM 1645562
Stationstraat, 108, 2800 MALINES **Tel:** 2219 28 32
Fax: 25233962
Titles:
LE COURRIER DU BOIS/HOUTNIEUWS
GEZOND THUIS
SMILE

DUPEDI SA 1784953
Rue de Stalle 70-82, 1180 BRUXELLES
Tel: 2 333 07 00 **Fax:** 2 332 05 98
Titles:
L' ÉVÉNEMENT

EDER SA 1761595
Rue Golden Hope, 1, 1620 DROGENBOS
Tel: 2378 21 27 **Fax:** 2378 37 29
Titles:
VILLAS

EDICLAM 1761564
Rue de la Pavée, 6, 5101 ERPENT **Tel:** 8132 22 61
Fax: 8132 22 69
Titles:
UNION & ACTIONS

EDITECO 1645559
Marktplatz, 8, 4700 EUPEN **Tel:** 8759 13 22
Fax: 87553457
Titles:
GRENZ-ECHO
NETTO (SUPP. DE TIJD)

EDITING MEDIA GROUP 1793046
Gravendreef, 9 - B 8, 9120 BEVEREN
Tel: 3 750 90 20 **Fax:** 3 750 90 29
Titles:
STORECHECK

EDITIONS CHANGER D'R 1645517
Avenue Brugmann, 29, 1060 BRUXELLES
Tel: 2345 04 78 **Fax:** 2345 85 44
Titles:
BIOINFO

EDITIONS CINE TELE REVUE 1761573
Editions Ciné Revue, Av. Reine Marie-Henriette, 101, 1190 BRUXELLES **Tel:** 2290 04 80
Fax: 2343 12 72
Titles:
LOU MAGAZINE

EDITIONS DUPUIS 1784886
Rue de Stallestraat 70-82, 1180 BRUXELLES
Tel: 2 333 07 00 **Fax:** 2 332 05 98
Titles:
GENIETEN

EDITIONS VENTURES 1784686
Chaussée de Louvain 431d, 1380 LASNE
Tel: 2379 29 90 **Fax:** 23792999
Titles:
ELLE BELGIQUE DECORATION
ELLE WMEN

EMG 1785883
Edition Média Group, Gravendreef, 9 - Bus 8, 9120 BEVEREN **Tel:** 3750 90 20 **Fax:** 37509029
Titles:
ELECTRO-VENTE
ELEKTRO-VERKOOP

EMM BVBA 1785798
Redactiebureau INK, Stationstraat, 12, 8210 LOPPEM **Tel:** 5082 43 75 **Fax:** 50824380
Titles:
DECOSTYLE

EUROPEAN BUSINESS PRESS SA 1788958
144 Avenue E. Plasky, 1030 BRUXELLES
Tel: 2 740 00 50 **Fax:** 2 740 00 59
Titles:
EE TIMES EUROPE

EUROPEAN WIND ENERGY ASSOCIATION 1690997
Renewable Energy House, 66 Rue d'Arlon, BRUSSELS 1040 **Tel:** 2 546 1940 **Fax:** 2 546 1944
Email: ewea@ewea.org
Web site: http://www.ewea.org
Titles:
WIND DIRECTIONS

EVOLUTION MEDIA GROUP 1784723
Vlasstraat, 17, 8710 WIELSBEKE **Tel:** 5660 73 33
Fax: 56610583
Titles:
FOOD & MEAT DE SLAGER/LE BOUCHER
HORECA REVUE
HOTEL BUSINESS

FONDS NATIONAL DE LA RECHERCHE SCIENTIFIQUE 1645688
Rue d'Egmont, 5, 1000 BRUXELLES
Tel: 2504 92 11 **Fax:** 25049292
Titles:
LA LETTRE DU FNRS

G.V.C. 1784804
Leemveldstraat, 42, 3090 OVERIJSE
Tel: 2785 02 80 **Fax:** 27319798
Titles:
LAN NEWS / ELECTRONICS HIGH-TECH

HIMALAYA 1645923
Himalaya NV Kerkplein, 24, Bus 7, 1930 ZAVENTEM **Tel:** 2717 00 10 **Fax:** 27170011
Titles:
DECOUVREZ LA FRANCE

HI-MEDIA BELGIUM 1785901
Rue de l'Arbre Bénit, 93, 1050 BRUXELLES
Tel: 2646 71 30 **Fax:** 2502 40 24
Titles:
VITAT.BE

IPM - INFO. ET PRODUCTIONS MULTIMEDIA 1784802
Rue des Francs, 79, 1040 BRUXELLES
Tel: 2211 28 49 **Fax:** 2211 28 70
Titles:
LA DERNIÈRE HEURE / LES SPORTS
PARIS MATCH

ITI PUBLISHING 1784823
ITI Publishing, Avenue Coghen, 119, 1180 BRUXELLES **Tel:** 2340 77 51 **Fax:** 23448770
Titles:
KIOSQUE

KLUWER 1645465
Ragheno Business Park, Motstraat, 30, 2800 MECHELEN **Tel:** 1536 15 30 **Fax:** 15361899
Titles:
PUB MAGAZINE
VRAAG & AANBOD

KRISTELIJKE ARBEIDERS VROUWENBEWEGING 1785896
Urbain Britsierslaan 5, 1030 BRUSSELS
Tel: 2246 51 11 **Fax:** 22465110
Titles:
VROUW & WERELD

KVLV 1645583
Remylaan 4b, 3018 WIJGMAAL-LEUVEN
Tel: 1624 39 99 **Fax:** 16243909
Titles:
VROUWEN MET VAART

LIGUE DES FAMILLES 1645668
Avenue Émile de Beco 109, 1050 BRUXELLES
Tel: 2507 72 11 **Fax:** 2507 72 00
Titles:
LE LIGUEUR

MAGNET MAGAZINES 1645491
Brandekensweg 2, 2627 SCHELLE
Tel: 3880 84 50 **Fax:** 3844 61 52
Titles:
GOED GEVOEL
TV FAMILIE

MAINPRESS NV 1785808
Diamantstraat, 5, 2275 LILLE **Tel:** 3326 56 16
Fax: 33265636
Titles:
CONTROL & AUTOMATION MAGAZINE
MAINTENANCE MAGAZINE

MASS TRANSIT MEDIA 1645939
S.A. Mass Transit Media, Galerie Ravenstein 4, 1000 BRUSSELS **Tel:** 2227 93 43 **Fax:** 2227 93 41
Titles:
METRO

Belgium

MASSIN 1785807
Place des Carabiniers, 15, 1030 BRUXELLES
Tel: 2241 55 55 **Fax:** 22415533

Titles:
ART ET DECORATION CAHIER BELGIQUE

MEDIA ACCESS 1645535
Jan van Gentstraat 1, Bus 102, 2000 ANTWERP
Tel: 3 234 05 50

Titles:
BUSINESS LOGISTICS / SUPPLY CHAIN SOLUTIONS

MEDIA OFFICE 1645663
For all contact details see main record, KNACK, 1130 **Tel:** 2702 71 31 **Fax:** 27027132

Titles:
BATIR

MEDIAFIN 1784677
Havenlaan 86 C, 1000 BRUSSELS
Tel: 2 423 18 39 **Fax:** 2 423 18 15

Titles:
DE TIJD
L' ECHO

META MEDIA 1645705
Wettersestraat, 64, 9260 SCHELLEBELLE
Tel: 9369 31 73 **Fax:** 93693293

Titles:
MENZO SPORTS

MINOC BUSINESS PRESS 1645549
Parklaan, 22, Bus 10, 2300 TURNHOUT
Tel: 1446 23 00 **Fax:** 1446 23 66

Titles:
CLICKX MAGAZINE
PC MAGAZINE
SMART BUSINESS STRATEGIES

MMM BUSINESS MEDIA 1784943
Parc Artisanal 11-13, 4671 BARCHON
Tel: 2778 62 00 **Fax:** 27786222

Titles:
FEDERAUTO MAGAZINE
FLEET & BUSINESS

NEW EDITIONS NV 1785880
NinOffices, Graanmarkt, 42 A1, 9400 NINOVE
Tel: 5451 55 10 **Fax:** 54515515

Titles:
DECORS

OMICRON 1645550
Omicron NV, Hoornstraat, 16 B, 8730 BEERNEM
Tel: 50250 1 70 **Fax:** 50250171

Titles:
OMICRON NV VAKTIJDSCHRIFT: GARDEN STYLE

PM GROUP - PROFESSIONAL MEDIA GROUP 1784806
Torhoutsesteenweg, 226, Bus 2, 8210 ZEDELGEM **Tel:** 5024 04 04 **Fax:** 50240445

Titles:
DECODESIGN
DECORATIE
DELICATESSE
METALLERIE
MOTION CONTROL/SNACKBLAD
SANILEC
SHOES MAGAZINE

PRO VOEDING 1785891
Tweekerkenstraat 29, 1000 BRUSSELS
Tel: 2238 05 57 **Fax:** 22380596

Titles:
SUPER MAGAZINE

REKAD UITGEVERIJ 1784797
Geelseweg, 47 A, 2200 HERENTALS
Tel: 1428 60 80 **Fax:** 14214774

Titles:
ENTREPRISE AGRICOLE
JARDINS & LOISIRS/HOBBYTUIN

RMG - ROULARTA MEDIA GROUP 1784680
Raketstraat 50, 1130 BRUSSELS **Tel:** 2702 71 07
Fax: 2660 36 00

Titles:
DATA NEWS
DATANEWS CAREERS
FOCUS KNACK
GRAFISCH NIEUWS - NOUVELLES GRAPHIQUES
GRANDE
ITM - INDUSTRIE TECHNIQUE & MANAGEMENT - INDUSTRIE TECHNISCH & MANAGEMENT
KNACK
KRANT VAN WEST VLAANDEREN - SIEGE SOCIAL
PLUS MAGAZINE
SPORT VOETBAL MAGAZINE
TÉLÉPRO MAGAZINE
TRENDS - TENDENCES
DE ZONTAG

ROSSEL & CIE 1645582
Avenue Léon Grosjean 92, 1140 EVERE
Tel: 2 730 33 11 **Fax:** 2 730 35 80

Titles:
7DIMANCHE
LE SOIR
LE SOIR MAGAZINE
ZAP (SUPP. LE SOIR)

ROULARTA PUBLISHING 1645766
Z.I. Research Park, 20, 1731 ZELLIK
Tel: 2467 61 68 **Fax:** 24676162

Titles:
FLEET (EDITION NL)
LE LION - DE LEEUW
NEST
SENSA - GALERIA
SPORT FOOT MAGAZINE
UITMAGAZINE
LE VIF/L'EXPRESS

SA EDITIONS PME-KMO UITGEVERIJEN NV 1784848
Avenue du Pérou 77b, 1000 BRUXELLES
Tel: 1635 91 50 **Fax:** 16359158

Titles:
PME-KMO MAGAZINE

SAIPM 1784709
Rue des Francs, 79, 1040 BRUXELLES
Tel: 2 211 27 11 **Fax:** 2 21128 32

Titles:
LA LIBRE BELGIQUE - GAZETTE DE LIÈGE

SCIENCES TODAY 1645634
Rue de Rixensart, 18, Bâtiment 17, Boite 3, 1332 GENVAL **Tel:** 2653 21 58 **Fax:** 26532158

Titles:
HEALTH AND FOOD

SMB - SANOMA MAGAZINES BELGIUM 1784693
Pulsebaan, 50/1, 2242 PULDERBOS
Tel: 3466 00 66 **Fax:** 34660067

Titles:
ATTITUDE
FEELING
FEMMES D'AUJOURD'HUI
FLAIR
GAEL
GAEL MAISON / FEELING WONEN
GLAM-IT
HUMO
LES JARDINS DE FEMMES D'AUJOURD'HUI (SUPP. FEMMES D'AUJOURD'HUI)
LIBELLE
LIBELLE PROEVEN
LIBELLE.BE
LOVING YOU FEESTZALENGIDS
LOVING YOU - LE MAGAZINE DU MARIAGE
MARIE CLAIRE BELGIQUE
TÉLÉ MOUSTIQUE
TEVE BLAD
VITAYA MAGAZINE

SUD-PRESSE 1785797
Rue Royale, 120, 1000 BRUXELLES
Tel: 2225 56 00 **Fax:** 22255913

Titles:
LA CAPITALE - REDACTION CENTRALE - BRUXELLES
LA MEUSE SIEGE ADMINISTRATIF
NORD-ECLAIR - SIEGE ADMINISTRATIF
LA NOUVELLE GAZETTE SIEGE ADMINISTRATIF
LA PROVINCE SIEGE ADMINISTRATIF

THE ECONOMIST GROUP 1784858
International Press Centre, Résidence Palace, Rue de la Loi 155, Boite 6, 1040 BRUXELLES
Tel: 2540 90 90 **Fax:** 2540 90 71

Titles:
EUROPEAN VOICE

TOURING 1784792
Rue de la Loi 44, 1040 BRUXELLES
Tel: 2233 24 72 **Fax:** 22332469

Titles:
TOURING EXPLORER (FRENCH EDITION)

TRAVEL PRODUCTIONS NV 1785816
Hanswijkstraat 23, 2800 MECHELEN
Tel: 15 450 350 **Fax:** 15 450 360

Titles:
TRAVEL MAGAZINE

UITGEVERIJ CASCADE 1784803
Duboisstraat 50, 2060 ANTWERP **Tel:** 3680 24 90
Fax: 3680 25 64

Titles:
EOS MAGAZINE
MAMA

VINOPRES 1645751
Rue de Merode, 60, (Saint Gilles), 1060 BRUXELLES **Tel:** 2533 27 60 **Fax:** 25332761

Titles:
VINO MAGAZINE

Bosnia-Herzegovina

AROTO PRESS 672100
Tešanjska 24b, 71000 SARAJEVO **Tel:** 33 281 391
Fax: 33 281 441
Email: redakcija@avaz.ba
Web site: http://www.dnevniavaz.ba

Titles:
DNEVNI AVAZ
SPORT

AUTO MEDIA GROUP D.O.O. 1744856
Šibenska 3/5, 71000 SARAJEVO **Tel:** 33 26 26 00
Fax: 33 26 26 06
Email: auto@auto.ba
Web site: http://auto.ba

Titles:
AUTO

D.O.O. CIVITAS 699233
Skenderpašina 4, 71000 SARAJEVO
Tel: 33 22 04 62 **Fax:** 33 65 17 89
Web site: http://www.bhdani.com

Titles:
DANI

D.O.O. PRES-SING 699179
Čekaluša Čikma 6, 71000 SARAJEVO
Tel: 33 44 40 41 **Fax:** 33 44 48 95
Email: sl.bos@bih.net.ba
Web site: http://www.slobodna-bosna.ba

Titles:
SLOBODNA BOSNA

MAXI PRESS D.O.O 1744680
Maršala Tita 30/V, 71000 SARAJEVO
Tel: 33 21 35 72 **Fax:** 33 21 35 72
Email: redakcija@maxi.co.ba
Web site: http://www.maxi.co.ba

Titles:
MAXISTARS

N.I.G.D. DNEVNE NEZAVISNE NOVINE D.O.O. 699262
Braće Pišteljića 1, 78000 BANJA LUKA
Tel: 51 33 18 50 **Fax:** 51 33 18 51
Email: nnsekretar@nezavisne.com
Web site: http://www.nezavisne.com

Titles:
NEZAVISNE NEDJELJNE NOVINE
NEZAVISNE NOVINE

NIK DENAMEDA D.O.O 699171
M. Snajedera 5, 71000 SARAJEVO
Tel: 33 61 144 979 **Fax:** 33 204 060
Web site: http://www.startbih.info

Titles:
START BIH

OSLOBODJENJE D. D. 699230
Džemala Bijedića 185, 71000 SARAJEVO
Tel: 33 27 69 00 **Fax:** 33 46 80 90
Email: redaction@oslobodjenje.com.ba
Web site: http://www.oslobodjenje.com.ba

Titles:
OSLOBODJENJE

Bulgaria

7 DNI SPORT LTD. 1743952
6 Al. Jendov St., Glavproekt, 1113 SOFIA
Tel: 2 807 65 85 **Fax:** 2 807 65 61

Titles:
7 DNI SPORT

BOOMERANG-BG INC. 1743951
73 Yavorov District, ap.11, 1111 SOFIA
Tel: 2 971 11 72 **Fax:** 2 971 11 65

Titles:
ATAKA

CASH LTD. 1726661
5B Triaditsa St., 1000 SOFIA **Tel:** 2 988 00 00
Fax: 2 988 55 15

Titles:
BUSINESS WEEK BULGARIA

CBA GROUP LTD. 1726662
19-21 Drazki St., 9000 VARNA **Tel:** 52 616 725
Fax: 52 615 891

Titles:
REKLAMA

ECONOMEDIA 1726603
20 Ivan Vazov St., 1000 SOFIA **Tel:** 2 937 61 22
Fax: 2 937 64 40

Titles:
CAPITAL

EUROFOOTBALLPRINT 1743965
1 Koloman St, 1618 SOFIA **Tel:** 2 818 91 75
Fax: 2 818 91 69

Titles:
EUROFOOTBALL

KOMPAKT-MERIDIAN 1726611
113A Tsarigradsko Shose Blvd, 1784 SOFIA
Tel: 2 975 25 96 **Fax:** 2 975 25 95

Titles:
MERIDIAN MATCH

MEDIA HOLDING 1726601
47 Tsarigradsko Shose Blvd, 1504 SOFIA
Tel: 2 942 25 14 **Fax:** 2 942 28 19

Titles:
24 CHASSA
DNEVEN TRUD

NEWSPAPER GROUP BULGARIA 1726612
47 Tsarigradsko Shose Blvd, 1504 SOFIA
Tel: 2 942 27 32 **Fax:** 2 942 28 24

Titles:
168 CHASSA

PIKS LTD. 1726689
1 St. Georgi Sofiiski 1., 1431 SOFIA
Tel: 2 952 6303 **Fax:** 2 952 6314

Titles:
FORUM MEDIKUS

PRESS GROUP MONITOR 1726606
113A Tsarigradsko Shose Blvd, 1784 SOFIA
Tel: 2 960 22 12 **Fax:** 2 975 24 64

Titles:
TELEGRAF

ROAD RUNNER LTD 1726704
65 B Manastirski Livadi, entrance B, floor 6, 1404 SOFIA **Tel:** 2 700 10 400

Titles:
BG MENU

SANOMA BLIASAK 1726642
6 Alexander Jendov St., fl.6, 1113 SOFIA
Tel: 2 970 68 68 **Fax:** 2 970 68 31
Titles:
JOURNAL ZA JENATA

SANOMA BLIASAK BULGARIA 1726678
6 Alexander Zhendov Str., 1113 SOFIA
Tel: 2 970 6891 **Fax:** 2 970 6819
Titles:
NATIONAL GEOGRAPHIC BULGARIA

SANOMA BLYASUK BULGARIA 1726702
6 Alekdander Jendov, floor 6, 1113 SOFIA
Tel: 2 970 68 68 **Fax:** 2 970 68 31
Titles:
CULINARY JOURNAL FOR THE WOMAN

STANDART NEWS 1726602
49 Bulgaria Blvd, Vitosha Business Center, 1404 SOFIA **Tel:** 2 818 23 11 **Fax:** 2 818 23 55
Titles:
STANDART

Croatia

NOVI LIST D.D. 1691640
Zvonimirova 20a, 51 000 RIJEKA **Tel:** 51 650-011 **Fax:** 51 672-114
Titles:
NOVI LIST

SLOBODNA DALMACIJA D.D. 1691634
Hrvatske mornarice 4, 21 000 SPLIT
Titles:
SLOBODNA DALMACIJA

TISKARA ZAGREB D.O.O. 1691618
Radnička cesta 210, 10 000 ZAGREB
Titles:
24SATA

Cyprus

ACTION PUBLICATION 699976
PO Box 24676, 1302 LEFKOSIA **Tel:** 22 81 88 84 **Fax:** 22 87 36 63
Email: mediainfo@actionprgroup.com
Titles:
SUNJET
SUNJET RUSSIAN EDITION

ARKTINOS PUBLICATIONS LTD 1639593
8 Vassileiou Voulgaroktonou Str., NICOSIA 1524
Tel: 22 86 18 61 **Fax:** 22 86 18 71
Titles:
POLITIS

BEN PUBLISHING LTD 1761048
P.O.Box 41091, 6309 LARNAKA **Tel:** 24 648090 **Fax:** 24 648089
Email: benzar@spidernet.com.cy
Web site: http://www.popka-news.com
Titles:
POPKA

CYPRUS LABOUR FEDERATION 699983
PO Box 21185, 29 Archermos, 1045 NICOSIA
Tel: 22 86 64 00 **Fax:** 22 34 93 82
Email: peo@peo.org.cy
Web site: http://www.peo.org.cy
Titles:
ERGATIKO VIMA

CYPRUS MAIL CO LTD 1200730
24 Vassilios Voulgaroktonos Str., PO Box 21 44, 1502 Nicosia, NICOSIA 1010 **Tel:** 22 81 85 85 **Fax:** 22 67 63 85
Email: cyprus.mail@cytanet.com.cy
Web site: http://www.cynew.com
Titles:
CYPRUS MAIL

CYPRUS WORKERS' CONFEDERATION (SEK) 1639653
P.O. Box 25 018, NICOSIA 1306 **Tel:** 22 84 98 49 **Fax:** 22 84 98 50
Email: sek@sek.org.cy
Web site: http://www.sek.org.cy
Titles:
ERGATIKI PHONI

CYWEEKLY LIMITED 623148
PO Box 24977, NICOSIA 1306 **Tel:** 22 744400 **Fax:** 22 744440
Titles:
THE CYPRUS WEEKLY

DIAS PUBLISHING HOUSE LTD 1200734
Aigaleo 5, Second Floor, 2057 STROVOLOS
Tel: 22 58 05 80 **Fax:** 22 58 05 99
Email: surievi@dias.com.cy
Web site: http://www.dias.com.cy
Titles:
CITY FREE PRESS
I SIMERINI
O TILETHEATIS

DROSITIS EKDOTIKES LTD 1639657
24 Elia Papakyriakou, Dafne Building, 1st floor, Acropoli, P.O.Box 28685, 2081 NICOSIA
Tel: 22 49 14 00 **Fax:** 22 49 12 30
Titles:
ANTILOGOS

HALKIN SESI 1639668
172 Girne Caddesi, P.O. Box 339, Mersin 10, LEFKOSA **Tel:** 392 227 31 41 **Fax:** 392 227 26 12
Titles:
HALKIN SESI

KIBRISLI 1639658
Mecidiye Sok. No: 44, Mersin 10, LEFKOŞA
Tel: 392 22 76 146 **Fax:** 392 22 75 703
Titles:
KIBRISLI

NDD EIDIKES EKDOSEIS 1638856
7 E Nicou Kranidioti Str., 3th fl., Engomi, 2411 NICOSIA **Tel:** 22 47 24 72 **Fax:** 22 66 48 60
Email: must@must-magazine.com
Titles:
MUST DECO

N.G. CYPRUS ADVERTISER LTD 1735692
14b Byron Str., 1 Park Tower, LIMASSOL
Tel: 25 58 21 20 **Fax:** 25 58 49 20
Email: info@vestnikkipra.com
Web site: http://www.vewstnikkipra.com
Titles:
VESTNIK KIPRA

PASYDY 1200949
3 Demosthenis Severis Avenue, 1066 NICOSIA
Tel: 22 84 44 50 **Fax:** 22 66 51 99
Email: pasydy@spidernet.com.cy
Web site: http://www.pasydy.org
Titles:
DIMOSSIOS YPALLILOS

O PHILELEFTHEROS LTD 1200731
PO Box 21094, Commercial Centre, 1 Diogenous, 3rd floor, Engomi, NICOSIA 1501
Tel: 22 59 00 00 **Fax:** 22 59 01 22
Email: artemiou@phileleftheros.com
Titles:
O PHILELEFTHEROS
TV MANIA

P.J.P. CHRISES ANGELIES PUBLISHING LTD. 1761631
14 Spyrou Kyprianou Ave., Ag. Omologites, 2nd floor, P.O.Box 26560, 1075 NICOSIA
Titles:
CHRYSES EFKAIRIES

SANADELFI CO LTD 1761047
Tel: 25 581133 **Fax:** 25 582749
Titles:
EVROPA-KIPR

TRAVEL NEWS EUROPE LTD 1686968
8 Vitsi Street, 1 floor, 2373 NICOSIA
Tel: 22 45 93 59 **Fax:** 22 45 93 61
Email: news@travelnewseurope.com
Web site: http://www.travelnewseurope.com
Titles:
TRAVEL NEWS EUROPE

YENIDÜZEN LTD. 1639672
Yeni Sanayi Bölgesi, Mersin 10, LEFKOŞA-KIBRIS **Tel:** 392 22 56 658 **Fax:** 392 22 53 240
Titles:
YENIDÜZEN

Czech Republic

AC&C, PUBLIC RELATIONS 1687950
Čistovická 249/11, 16300 PRAHA 6
Titles:
VOLKSWAGEN MAGAZÍN

AENNE BURDA GMBH & CO. 1687627
Tel: 81843513 **Fax:** 81843513
Přemyslovská 2845/43, 13000 PRAHA 3
Tel: 222513525 **Fax:** 222522648
Titles:
HALENKY, SUKNĚ, KALHOTY (EDICE BURDA)
KŘÍŽKOVÁ VÝŠIVKA (VELKÁ EDICE BURDA)
MÓDA PRO DĚTI
MÓDA PRO DROBNÉ ŽENY
MÓDA PRO PLNOŠTÍHLÉ
ŠKOLA PLETENÍ (EDICE BURDA)
VERENA
VZORY PRO RUČNÍ PLETENÍ (EDICE BURDA)

AFFINITY MEDIA 1756579
Mikanova 3251/7, 10600 PRAHA 10
Titles:
BUDEME MÍT MIMINKO - BABY GUIDE
MIMINKO

AGROSPOJ 1687596
Těšnov 17, 11705 PRAHA 1
Titles:
AGROSPOJ

ALITRON CZ 1689153
Kotěrova 5543, 76001 ZLÍN
Titles:
RALLY

AMARO 1687621
Smetanova 973, 75501 VSETÍN
Titles:
AMATÉRSKÉ RADIO

AMINOSTAR 1688341
Ohrazenice 188, 51101 OHRAZENICE
Titles:
IRON MAN

AQUA VIVA 1688579
Pod Štěpem 9a/1231, 10200 PRAHA 10
Titles:
BAZÉN A SAUNA

ASTRON STUDIO CZ 1687656
Veselská 699, 19900 PRAHA 9 - LETŇANY
Titles:
PEUGEOT STYLE

ASTROSAT 1687833
Přátelství 986, 10424 PRAHA 10 - UHŘÍNĚVES
Titles:
CHEF GURMÁN
GLANC
ŠÍP PLUS
TV STAR

ATEMI 1687999
Velvarská 1626/45, 16000 PRAHA 6
Titles:
FOTOVIDEO

ATOZ MARKETING SERVICES 1687742
Holečkova 657/29, 15095 PRAHA 5
Titles:
ZBOŽÍ & PRODEJ

AXEL SPRINGER PRAHA 1687666
Dělnická 12, 17000 PRAHA 7
Titles:
AUTO TIP
SVĚT MOTORŮ
TOP DÍVKY
TRUCKSALON

AZZA PERFEKT 1774507
Suchardova 515, 27201 KLADNO
Titles:
PATRIOT

B1 1719866
Dopravákû 3, 18000 PRAHA 8
Titles:
G2010

BAUER MEDIA 1719731
Victora Huga 6, P.O.Box 125, 15000 PRAHA 5
Tel: 225008111 **Fax:** 257327103
Titles:
BRAVO GIRL!
BYDLENÍ
CLAUDIA
DÍVKA
NAPSÁNO ŽIVOTEM
PESTRÝ SVĚT
RYTMUS ŽIVOTA
ŠTĚSTÍ A NESNÁZE
TINA
TV PLUS
TV REVUE
TVŮJ SVĚT
VAŘÍME
ŽENA A ŽIVOT

BBPRESS 1689084
Zelný trh 12, 60200 BRNO
Titles:
PROBRNO

BIKES PUBLISHING 1687915
Starochuchelská 1/14, 15900 PRAHA 5
Titles:
ČESKÉ MOTOCYKLOVÉ NOVINY (ČMN)
MOTORKÁŘ

BODY 1740495
Mozartova 24, 77200 OLOMOUC
Titles:
BODY

BOHEMIA AUTO TUNING 1687680
Na Haldě 1837, 53003 PARDUBICE
Titles:
AUTOSPORT & TUNING

BOOMERANG PUBLISHING 1687635
Nad Kazankou 37/708, 17100 PRAHA 7 - TRÓJA
Titles:
DETAIL (BAŤA)

BOREMI INVEST 1761080
Dlouhá 705/16, 11000 PRAHA 1
Titles:
FITSTYL
PULS

BURDA PRAHA 1687672
Přemyslovská 2845/43, 13000 PRAHA 3
Tel: 221589311 **Fax:** 222515837
Titles:
AUTOHIT
BETYNKA
BURDA
CHIP
JOY
KATKA
KATKA NÁŠ ÚTULNÝ BYT
KATKA NEJLEPŠÍ RECEPTY
NAŠE KRÁSNÁ ZAHRADA
POČÍTAČ PRO KAŽDÉHO
POŠLI RECEPT
SVĚT ŽENY

Czech Republic

BUSINESS MEDIA CZ 1743017
Nádražní 762/32, 15000 PRAHA 5
Titles:
AUTOMOBIL REVUE
AUTOTEC & AUTOSALON REVUE
MODERNÍ BYT
MŮJ DŮM
OPEL MAGAZÍN
RODINNÝ DŮM
STAVBA
SVĚT KOUPELEN
SVĚT KUCHYNÍ
TRUCKER

CAR TIP BRNO 1687839
Rokycanova 80, 61500 BRNO
Titles:
CAR TIP

ČASOPISY 2005 1688124
Táborská 5/979, 14000 PRAHA 4
Titles:
FLORA NA ZAHRADĚ
ZDRAVÍ

ČASOPISY PRO VOLNÝ ČAS 1688022
Šaldova 7, 18000 PRAHA 8
Titles:
DOMOV

ČESKÁ LÉKAŘSKÁ SPOLEČNOST J.E.PURKYNĚ 1687625
Sokolská 31, 12026 PRAHA 2 Tel: 224266226
Fax: 224266265
Titles:
ČESKÁ A SLOVENSKÁ FARMACIE
ČESKÁ A SLOVENSKÁ OFTALMOLOGIE
ČESKO-SLOVENSKÁ PEDIATRIE
PRACOVNÍ LÉKAŘSTVÍ
REHABILITACE A FYZIKÁLNÍ LÉKAŘSTVÍ
REVUE ČESKÉ LÉKAŘSKÉ SPOLEČNOSTI J. E. PURKYNĚ
ROZHLEDY V CHIRURGII

ČESKÁ SPOLEČNOST CHEMICKÁ 1688271
Novotného lávka 200/5, 11668 PRAHA 1
Titles:
CHEMICKÉ LISTY

ČESKÉ A SLOVENSKÉ ODBORNÉ NAKLADATELSTVÍ 1688131
Rosmarin Business Center, Dělnická 213/12, Praha 7 - Holešovice, 17000 PRAGUE
Tel: 270003961 Fax: 270003977
Titles:
MODERNÍ OBCHOD
SVĚT BALENÍ

ČESKÝ HYDROMETEOROLOGICKÝ ÚSTAV 1687595
Na Šabatce 2050/17, 14306 PRAHA 4 - KOMOŘANY Tel: 244031111 Fax: 244032634
Titles:
METEOROLOGICKÉ ZPRÁVY

ČESKÝ SVAZ VČELAŘŮ 1688904
Křemencova 177/8, 11524 PRAHA 1
Titles:
VČELAŘSTVÍ

ČESKÝ SVAZ ZAMĚSTNAVATELŮ V ENERGETICE (ČSZE) 1688076
Partyzánská 7, 17005 PRAHA 7 - HOLEŠOVICE
Titles:
ENERGETIKA

ČESKÝ ZAHRÁDKÁŘSKÝ SVAZ 1689695
Kněžská 11, 37001 ČESKÉ BUDĚJOVICE
Tel: 386354203
Titles:
ZAHRÁDKÁŘ

ČNTL - ČESKÉ NAKLADATELSTVÍ TECHNICKÉ LITERATURY 1687938
Ježkova 1, 13000 PRAHA 3 Tel: 222721164-5
Fax: 222722380
Titles:
CHLAZENÍ A KLIMATIZACE

CONCEPT 2M 1689160
Václavská 316/12, 12000 PRAHA 2
Titles:
REAL-CITY (SEVERNÍ MORAVA A VALAŠSKO)

COOPER PRESS 1688513
Ohradní 61, 14000 PRAHA 4 - BRANÍK
Titles:
KONKURSNÍ NOVINY

COSMETIC KARL HADEK INTERNATIONAL 1687646
Přemyslovců 653/24, 40007 ÚSTÍ NAD LABEM
Titles:
AROMATERAPIE

C.O.T. MEDIA 1687600
Opletalova 55, P.O.Box 772-HP, 11184 PRAHA 1
Titles:
C.O.T. BUSINESS

CPRESS MEDIA 1763772
Holandská 8, Spielberk Office Centre, 63900 BRNO
Titles:
BIZ
COMPUTER
CONNECT!
DIGIFOTO
JAK NA POČÍTAČ
MOBILITY

CREST COMMUNICATIONS 1688132
Ostrovní 126/30, 11000 PRAHA 1
Titles:
FORD REVUE

CRUX 1719896
Havlíčkova 304, 53803 HEŘMANŮV MĚSTEC
Titles:
RODINNÉ DOMY SE SNÍŽENOU SPOTŘEBOU ENERGIÍ

CZECH PRESS GROUP 1688501
Klíšská 1432/18, 40001 ÚSTÍ NAD LABEM
Titles:
KOKTEJL
KOKTEJL EXTRA PRO ŽENY
KOKTEJL SPECIÁL

ČZT 1687594
Těšnov 17, 11705 PRAHA 1
Titles:
DOVOLENÁ PRO VÁS
STAVOSPOJ

DANA FULÍNOVÁ - ANTISA 1689620
Pražského povstání 1974, 25601 BENEŠOV
Titles:
VŠE PRO DŮM - BYT - ZAHRADU - HOBBY

DAVID RUBEK - DR. ABÉ 1763792
Družstevní 63, 27364 DOKSY
Titles:
LIFESTYLE PRO MOU RODINU

DIGIRAMA 1689519
Bolívarova 23, 16900 PRAHA 6
Titles:
TYPOGRAFIA

DM - DROGERIE MARKT 1719707
Jeronýmova 1485/19, 37001 ČESKÉ BUDĚJOVICE
Titles:
ACTIVE BEAUTY

DŮM TECHNIKY OSTRAVA 1688399
Mariánské náměstí 480/5, 70928 OSTRAVA - MARIÁNSKÉ HORY
Titles:
KVALITA PRO ŽIVOT

ECONOMIA 1687693
Dobrovského 25, 17055 PRAHA 7 Tel: 233071111
Fax: 233072003
Titles:
EKONOM
EXPORTÉR
HOSPODÁŘSKÉ NOVINY
HRM
PROČ NE?!

EDUKAFARM 1688100
V Lipkách 647, 15400 PRAHA 5 - SLIVENEC
Titles:
LÉKY A LÉKÁRNA

EGMONT ČR 1687694
Žirovnická 3124, 10600 PRAHA 10
Titles:
PRO FOOTBALL
PRO HOCKEY

EIFFEL OPTIC 1728445
Ječná 507/6, 12000 PRAHA 2
Titles:
OPTICA MODA

ENTRE 1687639
Chodovecké náměstí 8, 14100 PRAHA 4 - CHODOV
Titles:
O2 ARENA

EUROFIRMA 1688088
Husitská 90, 13000 PRAHA 3
Titles:
EUROFIRMA

EURONEWS 1688053
Holečkova 103, P.O.Box 23, 15000 PRAHA 5
Tel: 251026124 Fax: 257328774
Titles:
EURO

EVROPSKÉ VYDAVATELSTVÍ 1687822
Bratranců Veverkových 816, 53002 PARDUBICE, ZELENÉ PŘEDMĚSTÍ
Titles:
EVROPSKÉ NOVINY
KRAJSKÉ NOVINY

EVW 1688647
Nádražní 1301/24, 15000 PRAHA 5
Titles:
MADAME RENÉE

EXTRA PUBLISHING 1728414
Hrnčířská 23, 60200 BRNO
Titles:
EXTRA PC
SVĚT

FCC PUBLIC 1687673
Pod Vodárenskou věží 1143/4, 18208 PRAHA 8
Titles:
SVĚTLO

FINE TECH 1728411
Branická 140/514, 14700 PRAHA 4
Titles:
ESTETIKA

FIRE EDIT 1688186
Blanická 13, 12000 PRAHA 2
Titles:
ALARM REVUE HASIČŮ A ZÁCHRANÁŘŮ

FLOREN CAPITAL 1728453
Americká 17, 12000 PRAHA 2
Titles:
RODIČE

FRONTPAGE 1767469
Roháčova 77, 13000 PRAHA 3
Titles:
HATTRICK

FUTURA 1688182
Politických vězňů 9, P.O.Box 836, 11121 PRAHA 1 Tel: 222897335 Fax: 224224822
Titles:
HALÓ NOVINY

G SERVIS CZ 1774532
Tiskařská 10/257, 10800 PRAHA 10
Titles:
RODINNÉ DOMY - PROJEKTY A REALIZACE

GENERAL INVEST COMPANY 1688158
Václavské náměstí 64, 11000 PRAHA 1
Titles:
GENERAL REALITY

GRAND PRINC 1688171
Vinohradská 174, 13000 PRAHA 3
Titles:
GRAND AUTO
GRAND BIBLIO
GRAND DEVELOPER
GRAND REALITY (PRAHA A STŘEDOČESKÝ KRAJ)
HOUSER

GRANIT 1719849
Nad cementárnou 12/473, 14700 PRAHA 4
Titles:
VADEMECUM ZDRAVÍ

HACHETTE FILIPACCHI 2000 1687632
Na Zátorce 3, 16000 PRAHA 6 Tel: 233023100
Fax: 233023101
Titles:
APETIT
ELLE
MARIANNE
MARIANNE BYDLENÍ
MAXIM

HEARST-STRATOSFÉRA 1687873
Drtinova 8, 15000 PRAHA 5 Tel: 234109801
Fax: 234109199
Titles:
COSMOPOLITAN

HELMA 1687612
U Pekařky 234/7, 18000 PRAHA 8 - LIBEŇ
Tel: 283840140-2 Fax: 283842785
Titles:
ALBERT

HEXXA KOMUNIKAČNÍ AGENTURA 1719806
Pekárenská 42, 76001 ZLÍN - PŘÍLUKY
Tel: 577043111 Fax: 577011480
Titles:
OKNO DO KRAJE

HIGH SOCIETY 1688181
Malířská 16, 17000 PRAHA 7
Titles:
HAIR & BEAUTY

HLAVNÍ MĚSTO PRAHA 1688614
Mariánské náměstí 2, 11000 PRAHA 1
Tel: 224482127
Titles:
LISTY HLAVNÍHO MĚSTA PRAHY

HOMEDECO SMP 1748188
Lomnického 7/1705, 14079 PRAHA 4
Titles:
DŮM A ZAHRADA

HP PUBLISHING 1719729
8. listopadu 871/53, 16200 PRAHA 6
Titles:
BOARD

HYUNDAI MOTOR CZ 1688268
Bucharova 1186/16, 15500 PRAHA 5
Tel: 251025363 Fax: 251626965
Titles:
NA CESTĚ

IDG CZECH 1687825
Seydlerova 2451/11, 15500 PRAHA 5 - NOVÉ BUTOVICE
Titles:
CIO BUSINESS WORLD
COMPUTERWORLD
SECURITY WORLD

IDITARA 1719792
Záhřebská 157/24, 12000 PRAHA 2
Titles:
KURÝR PRAHA

I.M.P. - INTERNATIONAL MEDICAL PUBLICATIONS 1687845
Dlouhá 16, 11000 PRAHA 1
Titles:
DR. PALEČEK

ING. MILOSLAV ROTREKL 1688270
Boženy Němcové 2625, 53002 PARDUBICE
Tel: 466411800 Fax: 466414161
Titles:
CHEMAGAZÍN

ING. VÁCLAV DOSTÁL - TERRAPOLIS 1689435
U Botanické zahrady 4, 77900 OLOMOUC
Tel: 585411240 Fax: 585411118
Titles:
TERRA

IVAN RUDZINSKYJ 1688121
nábřeží Závodu míru 1888, 53002 PARDUBICE - ZELENÉ PŘEDMĚSTÍ
Titles:
FITNESS
SVĚT KULTURISTIKY

JAGA MEDIA 1687649
Pražská 1279/18, 10200 PRAHA 10
Titles:
ASB (ČR)

JAN KOVÁŘ - AGENTURA ESO 1689179
Kapitána Nálepky 18, 56802 SVITAVY - PŘEDMĚSTÍ
Titles:
REGIONÁLNÍ NOVINY ESO

JANA HAMERNÍKOVÁ - DLOUHÁ 1688432
Heranova 1550/1, P.O.Box 15, 15500 PRAHA 5 - STODŮLKY
Titles:
K REVUE

JAROSLAV BACHORA 1689392
nám. Svobody 728/1, 16000 PRAHA 6
Titles:
ŠESTKA

JIK - 05 1689504
Ostromečská 8/1227, 13000 PRAHA 3
Titles:
TV POHODA

JUDR. KAREL HAVLÍČEK 1763777
Ostrovní 2064/5, 11000 PRAHA 1
Titles:
SOUDCE

JULIUS MACHÁČEK - KABINET 1748171
Národní Obrany 574/38, 16000 PRAHA 6 - BUBENEČ
Titles:
ARCHITEKT

KATEŘINA SEKYRKOVÁ, ING. 1688442
Nuderova 622, 33901 KLATOVY II.
Titles:
KALIMERA

KONSTRUKCE MEDIA 1688515
Českobratrská 1663/6, 70200 OSTRAVA
Titles:
KONSTRUKCE

KOVOHUTĚ PŘÍBRAM NÁSTUPNICKÁ 1689633
Příbram VI. č.p. 530, 26181 PŘÍBRAM VI.
Tel: 318470111
Titles:
XANTYPA

LADISLAV SOBOLÍK - INFORM ART 1689626
Veverkova 1343, 50002 HRADEC KRÁLOVÉ 2
Titles:
VÝCHODOČESKÉ STAVEBNÍ NOVINY

LAKTAČNÍ LIGA 1688664
Vídeňská 800, 14000 PRAHA 12 - KUNRATICE
Titles:
MAMITA

LESNICKÁ PRÁCE, VYDAVATELSTVÍ A NAKLADATELSTVÍ 1688587
Zámek 1, P.O.Box 25, 28163 KOSTELEC NAD ČERNÝMI LESY Tel: 321679413-4
Fax: 321679413-4
Titles:
LESNICKÁ PRÁCE

LIBERECKÝ KRAJ 1688596
U jezu 642/2a, 46180 LIBEREC 2 Tel: 485226302
Fax: 485226330
Titles:
LIBERECKÝ KRAJ

LOBBY ČESKÁ REPUBLIKA 1688629
Amforová 1885, 15000 PRAHA 5
Titles:
LOBBY

LUXURY SHOPPING GUIDE 1750512
Na Maninách 14, 17000 PRAHA 7
Titles:
LUXURY GUIDE

M1N >>> V KONKURSU OD 11/2007 1767487
Františka Křížka 1, 17030 PRAHA 7
Titles:
RAZ DVA TŘI

MAFRA 1688651
Karla Engliše 519/11, 15000 PRAHA 5
Titles:
LIDOVÉ NOVINY
MAGAZÍN DNES + TV
MLADÁ FRONTA DNES
PÁTEK LIDOVÉ NOVINY

MARTA HANUSKOVÁ - SCHELLENBERG 1731848
Hradčany 86, 28906 HRADČANY
Titles:
TATRANSKÉ PUTOVÁNÍ

MAXIMA REALITY 1688674
Nerudova 234/45, 11000 PRAHA 1
Titles:
MAXIMA MAGAZÍN

MED COMPANY 1743877
Na Jamech 731, 25230 ŘEVNICE
Titles:
LOOK MAGAZINE

MEDIA LABORATORY 1728428
Vinohradská 138, 13000 PRAHA 3
Titles:
RECEPTY PRIMA NÁPADŮ

MEDIACOP 1688327
Panská 7/890, Kaunický palác, 11000 PRAHA 1
Titles:
INSTINKT
TÝDEN

MEDICA HEALTHWORLD 1728404
Václavské nám. 832/19, 11000 PRAHA 1
Titles:
VNITŘNÍ LÉKAŘSTVÍ

MEDICAL TRIBUNE CZ 1688176
Na Moráni 5, 12800 PRAHA 2
Titles:
MEDICAL TRIBUNE

MĚSTO ZLÍN 1688655
Náměstí Míru 12, 76140 ZLÍN, OKR. ZLÍN
Titles:
MAGAZÍN ZLÍN

METRO ČESKÁ REPUBLIKA 1688693
Na Florenci 19, 11000 PRAHA 1
Titles:
MEN ONLY / WOMAN ONLY
METRO

MGR. ZUZANA JANKŮ 1688144
Suchý vršek 2122, 15800 PRAHA 5
Tel: 723435033 Fax: 224491309
Titles:
FREUNDSCHAFT

MINISTERSTVO FINANCÍ ČR 1687848
Letenská 15, 11810 PRAHA 1
Titles:
FINANČNÍ ZPRAVODAJ

MLADÁ FRONTA 1687997
Mezi Vodami 1952/9, 14300 PRAHA 4 - MODŘANY
Titles:
BYDLENÍ STAVBY REALITY
DIETA
JUICY
MAMINKA
MOJE PSYCHOLOGIE
MOJE ZDRAVÍ
OBCHODNÍ TÝDENÍK
TRAVEL IN THE CZECH REPUBLIC
ZOOM

MOJE GENERACE 1750517
Drhovy 16, 23601 DOBŘÍŠ
Titles:
MOJE GENERACE 40+

MORAVA PLUS 1688747
Velehradská 507, 76701 KROMĚŘÍŽ
Titles:
MORAVSKÝ REGION

MORAVSKÝ VETERÁN 1688750
Nemilany - Heská čtvrť 28, 78302 OLOMOUC 19
Tel: 585414639
Titles:
MORAVSKÝ VETERÁN

MOTOR - PRESSE BOHEMIA 1687661
U Krčského nádraží 36, 14000 PRAHA 4 - KRČ
Tel: 241721151-4 Fax: 241721905
Titles:
AUTO 7
AUTO MOTOR A SPORT
AUTO PRŮVODCE
GEO
MOTOCYKL
MOTOCYKL PRŮVODCE

MOTORCOM 1687615
Žerotínova 43, 13000 PRAHA 3
Titles:
AUTO FORUM

MUDR. BOHUMIL ŽDICHYNEC CSC. - AESCULAPUS K-S 1689570
V Pátém 226, 19014 PRAHA 9 Tel: 281961204
Titles:
VÁŠ OSOBNÍ LÉKAŘ

MYSLIVOST 1688767
Seifertova 81, 13000 PRAHA 3
Titles:
MYSLIVOST

NAKLADATELSTVÍ MINERVA CZ 1745816
Říčanská 10/1923, 10100 PRAHA 10 - VINOHRADY
Titles:
SVĚT PSŮ

NAKLADATELSTVÍ MISE 1687669
Sluneční 43/7, 74720 VŘESINA
Titles:
PROGRAM (NAKLADATELSTVÍ MISE)

NEXUS GROUP 1688833
V Křovinách 1708/22, 14700 PRAHA 4
Titles:
BYTY, DOMY, ZAHRADY

NEXUS PUBLISHING 1734122
Pod Pekárnami 3, 18000 PRAH 8 Tel: 266312379
Fax: 266312379
Titles:
ČESKOPIS

ODBOROVÝ SVAZ PRACOVNÍKŮ DŘEVOZPRACUJÍCÍCH ODVĚTVÍ, LESNÍHO A VODNÍHO HOSPODÁŘST 1688042
náměstí W. Churchilla 2, 11359 PRAHA 3
Titles:
DŘEVO, LESY, VODA

OMEGA PUBLISHING GROUP 1688000
Nad koupadly 1b, 14200 PRAHA 4 - LHOTKA
Titles:
LA CUCINA ITALIANA

ORBIS IN 1719796
Jaurisova 1499/23, 14000 PRAHA 4
Titles:
MÁMA A JÁ

PANEL PLUS PRESS 1719809
Koněvova 2660/141, 13083 PRAHA 3
Titles:
PANEL PLUS

PETR ROŠTLAPIL 1688097
Kapitána Nálepky 59, 58602 SVITAVY
Titles:
FAKTA PRESS

Czech Republic

PETROLMEDIA 1688991
Josefa Suka 31, 67431 TŘEBÍČ
Titles:
PETROLMAGAZÍN

PETRSKÁ REKLAMNÍ A MEDIÁLNÍ 1688798
Jiráskova 84, 19600 PRAHA 9
Titles:
VŠE PRO DÍTĚ

PHARMA NEWS 1748227
Jakobiho 326, 10900 PRAHA 10
Titles:
SANTÉ

PHDR. IVAN RICHTER - ŽIVNOSTENSKÉ LISTY 1689027
Košťálkova 1105/1, 18200 PRAHA 8 - KOBYLISY
Titles:
PODNIKÁNÍ A OBCHOD

PHDR. OTAKAR ŠTAJF - OSMIUM VYDAVATELSTVÍ NAKLADATELSTVÍ 1688107
Mistřínská 394, 15521 PRAHA 5
Titles:
SETKÁNÍ (AUTOMOBILY A STK)

PLAYPRESS 1769122
Dominova 2463/15, 15800 PRAHA 5
Titles:
PLAYBOY

PLM REKLAMA 1687598
Žerotínova 483/1, 37004 ČESKÉ BUDĚJOVICE
Titles:
AHOJ BUDĚJOVICE

PONTIUM 1719902
Brněnská 700/25, 50006 HRADEC KRÁLOVÉ
Titles:
STAVEBNICTVÍ (PONTIUM)

PRAGUE INTERNATIONAL MARATHON 1688667
Záhořanského 3/1644, 12000 PRAHA 2
Tel: 224919209 Fax: 224923355
Titles:
MARATHON MAGAZINE

PRAŽSKÁ VYDAVATELSKÁ SPOLEČNOST 1687996
Na Poříčí 1048/28-30, 11000 PRAHA 1
Titles:
JEZDECTVÍ
MEDUŇKA
PES PŘÍTEL ČLOVĚKA
PRAKTIK
STŘELECKÁ REVUE

PREMISA 1689334
Hošťálkova 1949/29, 16900 PRAHA 6 - BŘEVNOV Tel: 251562535 Fax: 251562535
Titles:
SNPLUS

PRESS PUBLISHING GROUP 1689455
Neklanova 15/122, 12000 PRAHA 2
Titles:
KLADNO

PROFITNESS ČESKÁ REPUBLIKA 1689599
Na Pankráci 1618/30, 14000 PRAHA 4
Titles:
VITALAND

PROSAM 1731828
Nad Údolím 3, 14700 PRAHA 4
Titles:
HAPPY BABY

PROVIZI 1688872
Mírové náměstí 152/25, 41201 LITOMĚŘICE
Titles:
MĚSÍC V REGIONU

RADIOSERVIS 1689515
Olšanská 3/54, 13000 PRAHA 3
Titles:
TÝDENÍK ROZHLAS

RATTLESNAKE PUBLISHING 1687738
Jeseniova 780/101, 13000 PRAHA 3
Titles:
MOTOHOUSE KATALOG AUTOMOBILŮ

READER'S DIGEST VÝBĚR 1689159
V Celnici 1031/4, 11000 PRAHA 1
Titles:
RECEPTÁŘ PRO ZDRAVÍ
RECEPTY RECEPTÁŘE

REAL SPEKTRUM 1689161
Lidická 77/718, 60200 BRNO
Titles:
REAL SPEKTRUM

REGENERACE 1689170
Starostřešovická 79/15, 16200 PRAHA 6
Tel: 233313708 Fax: 233313708
Titles:
REGENERACE

RESPEKT PUBLISHING 1741960
Dobrovského 1278/25, 17055 PRAHA 7
Titles:
RESPEKT

RINGIER ČR 1687565
Komunardů 1584/42, 17000 PRAHA 7
Titles:
AHA! (DENÍK)
AHA! (NEDĚLNÍ)
AHA! TV MAGAZÍN
BLESK
BLESK PRO ŽENY
BLESK ZDRAVÍ
NEDĚLNÍ BLESK
NEDĚLNÍ SPORT
REFLEX
SPORT
SPORT MAGAZÍN

RNDR. PAVEL KLIMEŠ - VESELÝ VÝLET 1689584
Temný Důl 46, 54226 HORNÍ MARŠOV
Titles:
VESELÝ VÝLET

ROBERT BEZOUŠKA 1689498
Choceradská 3120/8, 10000 PRAHA 10
Titles:
TUNING MAGAZINE

ROBERT NĚMEC - PRAGMA 1689169
Uhelný Trh 413/8, 11000 PRAHA 1
Titles:
REGENA

ROBERT ZOREK 1688924
Domky 319, 74781 OTICE, OKR. OPAVA
Titles:
OPAVSKÉ REKLAMNÍ NOVINY

ROBERTS PUBLISHING MEDIA GROUP 1745774
Václavské náměstí 832/19, 11000 PRAHA 1
Titles:
CENTRAL & EASTERN EUROPEAN CIJ

ROCK MEDIA 1741937
Drtinova 8, 15000 PRAHA 5
Titles:
F1 - RACING

RYBÁŘ 1689231
Nad Olšinami 31, 10000 PRAHA 10
Titles:
RYBÁŘSTVÍ

SANOMA MAGAZINES PRAHA 1687691
Lomnického 7, 14000 PRAHA 4 Tel: 296162111
Fax: 296162420
Titles:
FAJN ŽIVOT
NATIONAL GEOGRAPHIC
PRAKTICKÁ ŽENA
STORY
TÝDENÍK KVĚTY
VLASTA
ŽENA & KUCHYNĚ

SEZNAM.CZ 1689321
Radlická 608/2, 15000 PRAHA 5 Tel: 257313181
Titles:
SREALITY

ŠKODA AUTO 1689395
Václava Klementa 869/II, 29360 MLADÁ BOLESLAV
Titles:
ŠKODA MAGAZÍN

SLAVONIA PRESS 1767461
Šafaříkova 371/22, 12000 PRAHA 2
Titles:
MEN'S SPORTS

STANFORD 1689093
Francouzská 284/94, 10100 PRAHA 10
Titles:
PROFIT

STATUTÁRNÍ MĚSTO OSTRAVA, ÚŘAD MĚSTSKÉHO OBVODU 1771366
Hlučínská 135, 72529 OSTRAVA - PETŘKOVICE
Titles:
PRIO - PORUBSKÁ RADNICE INFORMUJE OBČANY

STOPLUS CZ 1774429
Návazná 40/679, 16500 PRAHA 6
Titles:
100+1

STRATEGIC CONSULTING 1688456
Na Poříčí 8, 11000 PRAHA 1
Titles:
JIŽNÍ LISTY (OSTRAVA)
KRAJ VYSOČINA
KRAJSKÉ LISTY
MORAVSKOSLEZSKÝ KRAJ
PLZEŇSKÝ KRAJ
TUČŇÁK

STRATOSFÉRA 1687840
Drtinova 8, 15000 PRAHA 5
Titles:
AUTOCAR
ESQUIRE
FHM
HARPER'S BAZAAR
JACKIE
LOVE STAR
SPEED
SPY
STUFF
STYLE
TOP GEAR

SUCHÝ - VYDAVATELSTVÍ 1761059
náměstí Antonie Bejdové 1791/5, 70800 OSTRAVA - PORUBA
Titles:
LEVNÉ RECEPTY SPECIÁL

ŠUMAVSKÉ TISKÁRNY 1777027
Včelná pod Boubínem 5, 38421 BUK, OKR. PRACHATICE
Titles:
SUPER INFO

SVAZ PRŮMYSLU PAPÍRU A CELULÓZY 1688960
K Hrušovu 292/4, 10223 PRAHA 10
Tel: 271081125 Fax: 271081135
Titles:
PAPÍR A CELULÓZA

TEPLÁRENSKÉ SDRUŽENÍ ČR 1687567
Bělehradská 458, P.O.Box 17, 53009 PARDUBICE 9
Titles:
3T - TEPLO, TECHNIKA, TEPLÁRENSTVÍ

TESCOMA 1777031
U Tescomy 241, 76001 ZLÍN, OKR. ZLÍN
Titles:
TESCOMA MAGAZÍN

TIGIS 1687606
Havlovického 16, 14700 PRAHA 4
Titles:
VETERINÁRNÍ LÉKAŘ

TIPSPORT 1688881
Václavské náměstí 56/802, 11000 PRAHA 1
Titles:
O.K. TIP

TOMÁŠ ROLÍNEK - IPR 1719877
Ječná 516/28, 12000 PRAHA 2
Titles:
KAM V PRAZE

TRADE & LEISURE PUBLICATIONS 1688032
Pernerova 35a, 18600 PRAHA 8 - KARLÍN
Tel: 225386575 Fax: 225386555
Titles:
STEREO & VIDEO

UNILEVER ČR 1688770
Thámova 18, 18000 PRAHA 8 - KARLÍN
Titles:
NA DOMA

VÁCLAV JANDA - VYDAVATELSTVÍ VT MEDIA 1687866
Otakara Jaroše 1656, 27401 SLANÝ, OKR. KLADNO
Titles:
CO JSME NAKOUPILI, TO SI UVAŘÍME
PANELÁK DOMOV MŮJ

VERLAG DASHÖFER, NAKLADATELSTVÍ 1687967
Na Příkopě 18, P.O.Box 756, 11121 PRAHA 1
Titles:
PRAKTICKÝ PORADCE V DAŇOVÝCH OTÁZKÁCH

VICTORY MEDIA 1688238
Ve Stromkách 460/10, P.O.Box 114, 40021 ÚSTÍ NAD LABEM 2
Titles:
SPIRIT

VISUAL AGENCY 1689786
Lazebnická 60/12, 58601 JIHLAVA
Titles:
ŽIJEME NA PLNÝ PLYN

VLTAVA-LABE-PRESS 1687716
Náměstí Přemysla Otakara II. 8/5, 37021 ČESKÉ BUDĚJOVICE
Titles:
DENÍK ČECHY (SÍŤ)
DENÍK ČESKÁ REPUBLIKA (SÍŤ)
DENÍK JIŽNÍ ČECHY (SÍŤ)
DENÍK SEVERNÍ ČECHY (SÍŤ)
DENÍK STŘEDNÍ ČECHY + PRAŽSKÝ DENÍK (SÍŤ)
DENÍK VÝCHODNÍ ČECHY (SÍŤ)
KULTURA (PLZEŇ)
PRAŽSKÝ DENÍK

VLTAVA-LABE-PRESS - DIVIZE SEVER 1688689
Klíšská 1702/25, 40001 ÚSTÍ NAD LABEM
Titles:
MĚSTSKÉ NOVINY (ÚSTÍ NAD LABEM)

VOJENSKÁ ZDRAVOTNÍ POJIŠŤOVNA ČR - ÚSTŘEDÍ 1689764
Drahobejlova 1404/4, 19003 PRAHA 9
Tel: 284021307 Fax: 284021250
Titles:
ZPRAVODAJ VOJENSKÉ ZDRAVOTNÍ POJIŠŤOVNY ČESKÉ REPUBLIKY

VRATISLAV MLČOCH - VYDAVATELSTVÍ VRAM 1688791
Vychodilova 2531/13, 63500 BRNO - ŽABOVŘESKY
Titles:
NAŠE NOVINY (BRNO)

WALD PRESS 1734140
Španělská 1073/10, 12000 PRAHA 2
Titles:
SANQUIS

WE MAKE MEDIA 1739286
Jeseniova 55, 13000 PRAHA 3
Titles:
GRAND ZDRAVÍ A KRÁSA

WWW.SCIO.CZ 1759825
Pobřežní 34, 18600 PRAHA 8
Titles:
UČITELSKÝ ZPRAVODAJ

ZDENĚK KAMENČÁK - GRAFIK 1688557
Staňkova 18a, 70030 OSTRAVA 3 Tel: 596737053
Fax: 596737053
Titles:
LIDOVÉ RECEPTY SPECIÁL

Denmark

AARS AVIS A/S 1727227
Himmerlandsgade 150, 9600 AARS
Tel: 98 62 17 11 Fax: 98 62 27 99
Titles:
AARS AVIS
VORT LANDBOBLAD

ADRESSEAVISEN KALØ VIG A/S 1727930
Grenåvej 10A, 8410 RØNDE Tel: 86 37 10 28
Fax: 86 37 11 91
Titles:
ADRESSEAVISEN SYDDJURS

ÆLDRE SAGEN 1727135
Nørregade 49, 1165 KØBENHAVN K
Tel: 33 96 86 86 Fax: 33 96 86 87
Titles:
ÆLDRE SAGEN NU

ALLER BUSINESS A/S 1727618
Marielundvej 46D, Postbox 537, 2730 HERLEV
Tel: 70 15 02 22 Fax: 44 85 89 19
Titles:
LICITATIONEN
TRANSPORTMAGASINET

ALLER CLIENT PUBLISHING 1793719
Otto Mønsteds gade 3, 1571 COPENHAGEN
Tel: 72 34 12 00 Fax: 72 34 12 01
Titles:
WHERE2GO

ALLER INTERNATIONAL 1792467
Havneholmen 33, 1561 COPENHAGEN
Tel: 44 85 88 08
Titles:
STREET BOYS

ALLER INTERNATIONAL A/S 1727173
Otto Mønsteds Gade 3, 1571 KØBENHAVN K
Tel: 36 15 33 00 Fax: 36 15 33 02
Titles:
GOLFMAGASINET

ALLER MAGASINER A/S 1727613
Vigerslev Alle 18, 2500 VALBY Tel: 36 15 20 00
Fax: 36 15 27 91
Titles:
ANTIK & AUKTION

ALLER PRESS 1793790
Havneholmen 33, 1561 KØBENHAVN V
Tel: 72 34 20 00 Fax: 72 34 20 05
Titles:
SØNDAG

ALLER PRESS A/S 1756672
Havneholmen 33, 1561 COPENHAGEN
Tel: 72 34 20 00
Titles:
BAZAR
BILLED-BLADET
FAMILIE JOURNAL
FEMINA
KIG IND
LIVING DESIGN
MAD!
MAD OG BOLIG
SE OG HØR
UDE OG HJEMME
VI UNGE

ALLER PRESSE 1793756
Havneholmen 33, 1561 COPENHAGEN
Tel: 72 34 20 00
Titles:
PSYKOLOGI

ÅRHUS STIFTSTIDENDE A/S 1727095
Nørregade 7, 8900 RANDERS Tel: 87 12 20 00
Fax: 87 12 20 10
Titles:
RANDERS AMTSAVIS

ÅRHUS STIFTSTIDENDE K/S 1726951
Banegårdspladsen 11, 8000 ÅRHUS C
Tel: 87 40 10 10 Fax: 87 40 13 21
Titles:
ÅRHUS STIFTSTIDENDE

ARKITEKTENS FORLAG 1727893
Overgaden oven Vandet 10, 1, 1415 KØBENHAVN K Tel: 32 83 69 53
Titles:
ARKITEKTEN
ARKITEKTUR DK

ARKITEKTENS FORLAG/ FORENINGEN AF BYPLANLÆGGERE 1727764
Nørregade 36, 1165 KØBENHAVN K
Tel: 33 17 72 81
Titles:
BYPLAN NYT

ARTILLERI OFFICERS FORENINGEN 1727557
Hjertingvej 127, 6800 VARDE Tel: 76 95 50 00
Fax: 76 95 54 14
Titles:
DANSK ARTILLERI-TIDSSKRIFT

ASSURANDØR KREDSEN 1793132
APPLEBYS PLADS 5, DK-1411 COPENHAGEN
Tel: 32 66 1357
Titles:
ASSURANDØR KREDSEN

AUDIO MEDIA A/S 1726972
Sejrøgade 7-9, 2100 KØBENHAVN Ø
Tel: 33 74 71 33 Fax: 33 74 71 91
Titles:
ALT OM DATA
DATATID

BÅDMAGASINET APS 1793171
Rungsted Havn 1D, 2960 RUNGSTED KYST
Tel: 88 77 00 00
Titles:
BÅDMAGASINET

BENJAMIN MEDIA 1793211
Finsensvej 6D, 2000 FREDERIKSBERG
Tel: 39 10 30 22 Fax: 70 22 02 56
Titles:
COSTUME

BERLINGSKE LOKALAVISER 1727340
Aldersrogade 6A, 2100 KØBENHAVN Ø
Tel: 35 42 25 15 Fax: 35 42 81 51
Titles:
ØSTERBRO AVIS
SORØ AVIS
VALBY BLADET

BERLINGSKE LOKALAVISER A/S 1727451
Ramsherred 47, 6200 AABENRAA
Tel: 74 62 60 00 Fax: 74 63 25 34
Titles:
AABENRAA UGE-AVIS
CITY AVISEN
FREDERIKSBERG BLADET
FREDERIKSVÆRK UGEBLAD, HALSNÆS POSTEN
VESTEGNEN

BERLINGSKE LOKALAVISER, DANSKE DISTRIKTSBLADE 1727734
centrumgade 7, 2750 BALLERUP Tel: 44 60 03 30
Fax: 44 60 03 31
Titles:
BAGSVÆRD/SØBORG BLADET
BALLERUP BLADET

BERLINGSKE LOKALBLADE 1727751
Østergade 3, 1.sal, 6400 SØNDERBORG
Tel: 87 54 25 42 Fax: 87 54 25 43
Titles:
SØNDERBORG UGEAVIS

BERLINGSKE MEDIA 1750267
Pilestræde 34, 1147 KØBENHAVN K
Tel: 33 75 75 75 Fax: 33 75 20 20
Titles:
BERLINGSKE
BERLINGSKE NYHEDSMAGASIN
BERLINGSKE REJSELIV

BERLINGSKE TIDENDE A/S 1791616
Studiestræde 50, 1554 KØBENHAVN V
Tel: 33 76 20 00 Fax: 33 76 20 01
Titles:
BOLIGEN
VESTERBROBLADET

BILLEDKUNSTNERNES FORBUND / BKF 1727912
Vingårdstræde 21, 1070 KØBENHAVN K
Tel: 33 12 81 72
Titles:
BILLEDKUNSTNEREN

BILLUND BOGTRYKERI 1727733
Højmarksvej 5, 7190 BILLUND Tel: 75 33 12 18
Fax: 75 35 37 08
Titles:
BILLUND UGEAVIS

BIOENERGISEKTIONEN DANSK LANDBRUG, DANBIO OG FORENINGEN FOR DANSKE BIOGASANLÆG. 1739790
Sdr. Tingvej 10, 6630 RØDDING Tel: 73 84 85 45
Titles:
BIOENERGI

BJERRINGBRO AVIS S.M.B.A. 1727921
Banegårdspladsen 3, 8850 BJERRINGBRO
Tel: 86 68 17 55 Fax: 86 68 03 87
Titles:
BJERRINGBRO AVIS

BK MEDIA 1735461
Sdr. Strandvej 18, 3000 HELSINGØR
Tel: 70 20 98 38
Titles:
MONITOR

BLÅ AVIS A/S 1727534
Marselisborg, Havnevej 26 Box 180, 8100 ÅRHUS C Tel: 87 31 31 31 Fax: 87 31 31 91
Titles:
DEN BLÅ AVIS VEST

BLADGRUPPEN VEST 1727316
Sct. Knuds Alle 3, 6740 BRAMMING
Tel: 75 17 40 00 Fax: 75 17 37 87
Titles:
UGEAVISEN FOR BRAMMING OG OMEGN
UGEAVISEN FOR RIBE OG OMEGN

BOLIGSELSKABERNES LANDSFORENING 1727952
Studiestræde 50, 1554 KØBENHAVN V
Tel: 33 76 20 00 Fax: 33 96 20 01
Titles:
BEBOERBLADET

BONNIER PUBLICATION A/S 1726992
Strandboulevarden 130, 2100 COPENHAGEN
Tel: 39 17 20 00 Fax: 39172300
Titles:
ILLUSTRERET VIDENSKAB
NATIONAL GEOGRAPHIC DENMARK

BONNIER PUBLICATIONS 1762111
Finsensvej 6 D, 2000 FREDERIKSBERG
Tel: 70 22 02 55 Fax: 70 22 02 56
Titles:
ARENA
BILMAGASINET
BOLIG MAGASINET
FHM
M!
WOMAN

BONNIER PUBLICATIONS A/S 1726923
Strandboulevarden 122, 2100 KØBENHAVN Ø
Tel: 39 17 20 00
Titles:
HISTORIE
SPIS BEDRE

BONNIER PUBLICATIONS INTERNATIONAL AS 1727021
Strandboulevarden 130, 2100 COPENHAGEN
Tel: 39 17 20 00 Fax: 39 29 01 99
Titles:
BO BEDRE
DIGITAL FOTO
GØR DET SELV
I FORM
PENGE & PRIVATØKONOMI

BONNIER RESPONSMEDIER 1793595
Strandboulevarden 130, 2100 COPENHAGEN
Tel: 39 17 20 00
Titles:
IDÉNYT

BONNIER TIDSKRIFTER AB, STOCKHOLM 1726963
Bistrup Park 40, 3460 BIRKERØD Tel: 45 81 29 32
Fax: 70 27 11 56
Titles:
ALT OM HAVEN

Denmark

BONNIERS PUBLICATIONS INTERNATIONAL AS 1727985
Strandboulevarden 130, 2100 KØBENHAVN Ø
Tel: 39 17 20 00 **Fax:** 39 17 23 09
Titles:
KOMPUTER FOR ALLE

BORNHOLMS TIDENDE 1740718
Nørregade 11-19, 3700 RØNNE **Tel:** 56 90 30 00
Fax: 56 90 30 91
Titles:
RYTTERKNÆGTEN

A/S BORNHOLMS TIDENDE 1727847
Nørregade 11-19, 3700 RØNNE **Tel:** 56 90 30 00
Fax: 56 95 31 65
Titles:
BORNHOLMS TIDENDE

BRANDE BLADET A/S 1727732
Storegade 25, Posboks 169, 7330 BRANDE
Tel: 97 18 28 38 **Fax:** 97 18 00 93
Titles:
BRANDE BLADET

BRYLLUPSMAGASINET DANMARK AS 1793177
Enrum Slot, Strandvejen 341, 2940 VEDBÆK
Tel: 38 76 01 98 **Fax:** 70 21 42 14
Titles:
BRYLLUPSMAGASINET

B.T. A/S 1790980
Pilestræde 34, 1147 COPENHAGEN
Tel: 33 75 75 33 **Fax:** 33752033
Titles:
B.T.

BUDSTIKKEN A/S 1739930
Bredgade 33, 1. sal, 6000 KOLDING
Tel: 75 50 24 20 **Fax:** 75 50 55 20
Titles:
BUDSTIKKEN KOLDING

BUDSTIKKEN VOJENS A/S 1727170
Nørreport 5, 6200 ÅBENRÅ **Tel:** 74 62 12 75
Fax: 74 62 12 76
Titles:
BUDSTIKKEN AABENRAA
BUDSTIKKEN SØNDERBORG

BUND DEUTCHER NORDSCHLESWIGER 1727484
Skibbroen 4, 6200 AABENRAA **Tel:** 74 62 38 80
Fax: 74 62 94 30
Titles:
NORDSCHLESWIGER

B.U.P.L 1792596
Blegdamsvej 124, DK-2100 COPENHAGEN
Tel: 35 46 50 00 **Fax:** 35465039
Titles:
BØRN & UNGE

BUSINESS TRAVELLER DENMARK 1793181
Rymarksvej 46, 2900 HELLERUP **Tel:** 33 11 44 13
Fax: 33 114414
Titles:
BUSINESS TRAVELLER DENMARK

BYGGEPLADS DANMARK APS 1793398
Solvang 23, Postboks 146, 3450 ALLERØD
Tel: 48 17 0078
Titles:
BYGGEPLADS

C3 ORGANISATION 1735617
Søtorvet 5, Postboks 2043, 1012 KØBENHAVN K **Tel:** 36 91 91 11 **Fax:** 33 14 11 49
Titles:
C3 MAGASINET OM LEDELSE OG ØKONOMI

CENTRALFORENINGEN FOR STAMPERSONEL 1727680
Centralforeningen for Stampersonel, Trommesalen 3, 1614 KØBENHAVN V
Tel: 36 90 89 39 **Fax:** 33 31 10 33
Titles:
CS-BLADET

CENTRALTRYKKERIET VORDINGBORG A/S 1727753
Torvestræde 4, 4760 VORDINBORG
Tel: 55 37 00 09 **Fax:** 55 34 00 11
Titles:
SYDSJÆLLANDS TIDENDE

CHAUFFØRERNES FAGFØRENING 1727726
Svanevej 22, 2400 KØBENHAVN NV
Tel: 88 92 27 66 **Fax:** 38 14 06 09
Titles:
CHAUFFØREN

CHILI A/S 1793174
Otto Mønsteds Gade 3, 1571 COPENHAGEN
Tel: 72 341200 **Fax:** 72 341201
Titles:
CHILI MAGAZINE

CO-INDUSTRI 1791439
Vester Søgade 12, 2. sal, 1790 COPENHAGEN
Tel: 33 63 80 00 **Fax:** 33 63 80 90
Titles:
CO-INDUSTRI MAGASINET

DÆKBRANCHENS FÆLLESRÅD 1794295
Hans Edvard Teglers Vej 5, 2920 CHARLOTTENLUND **Tel:** 39 63 97 79
Fax: 39 63 92 79
Titles:
DÆK-MAGASINET

DAGBLADET BØRSEN A/S 1817
Møntergade 19, 1140 KØBENHAVN K
Tel: 33 32 01 02 **Fax:** 33 12 24 45
Titles:
BØRSEN
BØRSEN PLEASURE.DK
BØRSEN UDLAND
BØRSEN VÆKST DANMARK

DAGENS MEDICIN A/S 1727649
Christian IX's Gade 3, 1. sal; Postboks 194, 1006 KØBENHAVN K **Tel:** 33 32 44 00 **Fax:** 33 18 86 66
Titles:
DAGENS MEDICIN

DANISH TRANSPORT AND LOGISTICS 1793228
Grønningen 17, Postboks 2250, 1019 COPENHAGEN **Tel:** 70 15 95 00 **Fax:** 70159522
Titles:
DTL MAGASINET

DANMARKS APOTEKERFORENING 1727298
Bredgade 54, 1260 KØBENHAVN K
Tel: 33 76 76 00 **Fax:** 33 76 76 97
Titles:
FARMACI

DANMARKS BRIDGEFORBUND 1727389
Smedevej 1, 9340 ASAA **Tel:** 32 55 52 13
Fax: 48 47 62 13
Titles:
DANSK BRIDGE

DANMARKS EXPORTRÅD 1727258
Danmarks Exportråd, Asiatisk Plads 2, 1448 KØBENHAVN K **Tel:** 33 92 00 00 **Fax:** 32 54 19 18
Titles:
FOCUS DENMARK

DANMARKS JÆGERFORBUND 1728134
Højnæsvej 56, 2610 RØDOVRE **Tel:** 36 73 05 00
Fax: 36 72 09 11
Titles:
JÆGER

DANMARKS JURIST- OG ØKONOMFORBUND 1793873
Gothersgade 133, Postboks 2126, 1123 COPENHAGEN **Tel:** 33 95 97 00 **Fax:** 33959991
Titles:
DJØF BLADET

DANMARKS LÆRERFORENING 1727249
P.O. Box 2139, 1015 KØBENHAVN K
Tel: 33 69 63 00 **Fax:** 33 69 64 26
Titles:
FOLKESKOLEN
UNDERVISERE

DANMARKS NATURFREDNINGSFORENING 1727553
Masnedøgade 20, 2100 KØBENHAVN Ø
Tel: 39 17 40 00 **Fax:** 39 17 41 41
Titles:
NATUR OG MILJØ

DANMARKS RESTAURANTER & CAFEER 1793612
Islands Brygge 26, 2300 KØBENHAVN S
Tel: 33 25 1011 **Fax:** 33 25 3099
Titles:
DRC-BLADET / RESTAURANT & CAFÉ

DANMARKS SKOHANDLERFORENING 1794112
Langebrogade 5, 1411 COPENHAGEN
Tel: 33 91 46 07
Titles:
SKO, SHOES & MORE

DANMARKS SLØJDLÆRERFORENING 1726969
Møldrupvej 53 A, 9510 ARDEN **Tel:** 98 56 53 43
Titles:
SLØJD

DANMARKS SPORTSFISKERFORBUND 1728019
Worsåesgade 1, 7100 VEJLE **Tel:** 75 82 06 99
Fax: 75 82 02 09
Titles:
SPORTSFISKEREN

DANMARKS TEKNISKE UNIVERSITET 1794341
Anker Engelunds Vej 1, Bygning 101, 2800 LYNGBY **Tel:** 45 25 10 76 **Fax:** 45 88 80 40
Titles:
DTU AVISEN

DANMARKS TRANSPORT FORLAG A/S 1794324
Jernbanegade 18, 6330 PADBORG
Tel: 70 10 05 06 **Fax:** 74 67 40 47
Titles:
DANMARKS TRANSPORT-TIDENDE

DANSK AGRAR FORLAG A/S/ JORDBRUGERE 1728126
Birk Centerpark 36, 7400 HJØRRING
Tel: 96 26 52 87 **Fax:** 76 20 79 60
Titles:
AGROLOGISK

DANSK AKTIONÆRFORENING 1793859
Amagertorv 9, 3.sal, Postboks 1140, 1010 COPENHAGEN **Tel:** 45 82 15 91 **Fax:** 45 41 15 90
Titles:
AKTIONÆREN

DANSK AUTOMATIONSSELSKAB 1794304
Hannemanns Alle 25, 2300 COPENHAGEN
Tel: 39 90 39 55
Titles:
DAU BLADET

DANSK AVIS TRYK A/S 1727110
Klostermosevej 101, 3000 HELSINGØR
Tel: 49 22 21 10 **Fax:** 49 26 65 05
Titles:
HELSINGØR DAGBLAD

DANSK BYGGERI 1727780
Nr. Voldgade 106, Postboks 2125, 1055 KØBENHAVN K **Tel:** 72 16 00 00 **Fax:** 72 16 00 10
Titles:
BYGGERIET

DANSK CAMPING UNION 1728028
Korsdalsvej 134, 2605 BRØNDBY **Tel:** 33 21 06 00
Fax: 33 21 01 08
Titles:
CAMPING-FRITID

DANSK CYKLIST FORBUND 1727673
Rømersgade 7, 1362 KØBENHAVN K
Tel: 33 32 31 21 **Fax:** 33 32 76 83
Titles:
CYKLISTER

DANSK EJENDOMSMÆGLER-FORENING 1793308
Islands Brygge 43, 2300 COPENHAGEN
Tel: 70 25 09 99 **Fax:** 32 64 45 99
Titles:
EJENDOMSMÆGLEREN

DANSK EL-FORBUND 1727349
Vodroffsvej 26, 1900 FREDERIKSBERG C
Tel: 33 29 70 00 **Fax:** 33 29 70 70
Titles:
ELEKTRIKEREN

DANSK ERHVERVSFORLAG APS 1791830
Tinggårdsvej 4, 4130 VIBY **Tel:** 82 30 75 00
Titles:
LEVNEDSMIDDEL & FØDEVARE MAGASINET

DANSK FORENING FOR KVALITET 1727938
Jersie Solvænge 16, 2680 SOLRØD STRAND
Tel: 70 20 32 13 **Fax:** 70 20 32 23
Titles:
MAGASINET KVALITET

DANSK FORMANDS FORENING 1793862
Prags Boulevard 45, 2300 COPENHAGEN
Tel: 32 96 56 22 **Fax:** 32 96 58 22
Titles:
FORMANDSBLADET

DANSK FUNKTIONÆRFORBUND - SERVICEFORBUNDET 1727052
Upsalagade 20, 2100 KØBENHAVN Ø
Tel: 70 15 04 00 **Fax:** 70 15 04 05
Titles:
SERVICE

DANSK GAS FORENING 1727186
Dr. Neergaards Vej 5B, 2970 HØRSHOLM
Tel: 97 51 45 95 **Fax:** 97 51 33 95
Titles:
GASTEKNIK

DANSK GOLF UNION 1727596
Idrættens Hus Brøndby Stadion 20, 2605 BRØNDBY **Tel:** 43 26 27 00 **Fax:** 43 26 27 01
Titles:
DANSK GOLF

DANSK HANDELSBLAD A/S 1793230
Fenrisvej 11, 8230 ÅBYHØJ **Tel:** 86 15 80 11 **Fax:** 86 158252
Titles:
DANSK HANDELSBLAD

DANSK HANDICAP FORBUND 1727125
Hans Knudsens Plads 1A, 2100 KØBENHAVN Ø **Tel:** 39 29 35 55 **Fax:** 39 29 39 48
Titles:
HANDICAP-NYT

DANSK HUSFLIDSSELSKAB 1727045
Tyrebakken 11, 5300 KERTEMINDE **Tel:** 63 32 20 96 **Fax:** 63 32 20 97
Titles:
HUSFLID

DANSK IDRÆTS-FORBUND 1727005
Idrættens Hus, Brøndby Stadion 20, 2605 BRØNDBY **Tel:** 43 26 26 26 **Fax:** 43 26 26 30
Titles:
IDRÆTSLIV

DANSK INDUSTRI 1793241
Hannemanns Alle 25, 2300 COPENHAGEN **Tel:** 33 77 33 77 **Fax:** 33 773300
Titles:
DI BUSINESS

DANSK JOURNALISTFORBUND 1727949
Gl. Strand 46, 1202 KØBENHAVN K **Tel:** 33 42 80 00 **Fax:** 33 42 80 08
Titles:
JOURNALISTEN
MAGASIN K

DANSK KENNEL KLUB 1728016
Mediehuset Wiegården, Postboks 315, 9500 HOBRO **Tel:** 98 51 20 66 **Fax:** 98 51 20 06
Titles:
HUNDEN

DANSK KIROPRAKTOR FORENING 1728020
Vendersgade 6, 2.tv, 1011 KØBENHAVN K **Tel:** 33 93 04 00 **Fax:** 33 93 04 89
Titles:
KIROPRAKTOREN

DANSK LÆGESEKRETÆRFORENING/ HK 1727917
P.O. Box 1297, 7500 HOLSTEBRO **Tel:** 97 41 13 54 **Fax:** 97 40 43 54
Titles:
DL MAGASINET

DANSK LANDBRUGS GROVVARESELSKAB 1726983
Axelborg, Vesterbrogade 4A, 1503 KØBENHAVN V **Tel:** 33 68 30 00 **Fax:** 33 68 87 28
Titles:
DLG NYT

DANSK LANDBRUGS MEDIER 1726981
Vester Farimagsgade 6, 2. sal, 1606 KØBENHAVN V **Tel:** 33 39 47 00 **Fax:** 33 39 47 39
Titles:
LAND & LIV
LANDBRUGSAVISEN
LANDBRUGSAVISEN
LANDBRUGSAVISEN.DK
MAGASINET HEST
MARK

DANSK MAGISTERFORENING 1727541
Nimbusparken 16, 2000 FREDERIKSBERG **Tel:** 38 15 66 25 **Fax:** 38 15 66 65
Titles:
MAGISTERBLADET

DANSK METAL 1727677
Nyropsgade 38, Postboks 308, 1780 KØBENHAVN V **Tel:** 33 63 20 00 **Fax:** 33 63 21 51
Titles:
METALMAGASINET

DANSK SELSKAB FOR SYGEHUSLEDELSE 1727934
Niels Bohrs Vej 30, 9200 AALBORG **Tel:** 99 27 27 30
Titles:
TIDSSKRIFT FOR DANSK SUNDHEDSVÆSEN

DANSK SKOVFORENING 1726984
Amalievej 20, 1875 FREDERIKSBERG C **Tel:** 33 78 52 15 **Fax:** 33 24 02 42
Titles:
SKOVEN

DANSK SKYTTE UNION 1728058
Idrættens Hus, Brøndby Stadion 20, 2605 BRØNDBY **Tel:** 43 26 26 26 **Fax:** 43 26 23 55
Titles:
SKYTTEBLADET

DANSK SLÆGTSGÅRDSFORENING 1726982
Skælskør Landevej 83, Lundforlund, 4200 SLAGELSE **Tel:** 58 58 40 16
Titles:
SLÆGTSGAARDEN

DANSK SVEJSETEKNISK LANDSFORENING 1728048
c/o Dansk Svejseteknisk Landsforening, Park Allé 345, 2605 BRØNDBY **Tel:** 40 61 30 90 **Fax:** 43 26 70 11
Titles:
SVEJSNING

DANSK SYGEPLEJERÅD 1728023
Sankt Annæ Plads 30, postboks 1084, 1008 KØBENHAVN K **Tel:** 33 15 15 55 **Fax:** 33 15 18 41
Titles:
SYGEPLEJERSKEN

DANSK TRANSPORT FORLAG A/S 1727752
Jernbanegade 18, 6330 PADBORG **Tel:** 70 10 05 06 **Fax:** 74 67 40 47
Titles:
TRANS INFORM

DANSK UNIX-SYSTEM BRUGER GRUPPE 1727465
Fruebjergvej 3, 2100 KØBENHAVN Ø **Tel:** 39 17 99 44
Titles:
DKUUG-NYT

DANSK VANDRELAUG 1727156
Kultorvet 7, 1, 1175 KØBENHAVN K **Tel:** 33 12 11 65
Titles:
FRITIDSLIV

DANSKE FAGMEDIER A/S 1793981
Marielundsvej 46 E, 2730 HERLEV **Tel:** 70 11 59 57 **Fax:** 44 85 10 13
Titles:
MESTER TIDENDE

DANSKE FYSIOTERAPEUTER 1727192
Nørre Voldgade 90, 1358 KØBENHAVN K **Tel:** 33 41 46 29 **Fax:** 33 41 46 14
Titles:
FYSIOTERAPEUTEN

DANSKE MALERMESTRE 1727565
Islands Brygge 26, Postboks 1989, 2300 KØBENHAVN S **Tel:** 32 63 03 70 **Fax:** 32 63 03 99
Titles:
DE FARVER

DANSKE SÆLGERE 1793855
Nørre Farimagsgade 49, 1364 COPENHAGEN **Tel:** 33 74 02 00 **Fax:** 33 74 0290
Titles:
INBUSINESS

DANSKE SKOV- OG LANDSKABSINGENIØRER 1726985
Emdrupvej 28A, 2100 KØBENHAVN Ø **Tel:** 33 23 00 45 **Fax:** 38 71 03 23
Titles:
SKOV & LAND

DANSKE SKYTTEFORENINGER 1726980
Vingstedvej 27, 7182 BREDSTEN **Tel:** 75 86 42 22 **Fax:** 75 86 54 75
Titles:
SKYTTEN

DANSKE SPEJDERKORPS 1727769
Arsenalvej 10, 1436 KØBENHAVN K **Tel:** 32 64 00 50 **Fax:** 32 64 00 75
Titles:
BROEN

DANSKE SUKERROEDYRKERE 1727966
Axelborg, Axeltorv 3, 1., 1609 KØBENHAVN K **Tel:** 33 39 40 00 **Fax:** 33 39 41 51
Titles:
SUKKERROE NYT

DANSKE TORPARE 1727556
Landskronagade 82, 2100 KØBENHAVN Ø **Tel:** 39 29 52 82 **Fax:** 39 29 59 82
Titles:
TORPARE BLADET

DE BERGSKE BLADE 1727145
Bergs plads 5, 6900 SKJERN **Tel:** 96 81 53 13 **Fax:** 96 81 53 01
Titles:
UGEPOSTEN SKJERN
VIBORG NYT

DET DANSKE HAVESELSKAB 1727119
Clausholmvej 316, 8370 HADSTEN **Tel:** 86 49 17 33 **Fax:** 86 49 17 35
Titles:
HAVEN

DET KONSERVATIVE FOLKEPARTI 1727282
Nyhavn 4, 1051 KØBENHAVN K **Tel:** 33 13 41 40 **Fax:** 33 93 37 73
Titles:
POLITISK HORISONT

DG MEDIA 1727593
Region Midtjylland, Tingvej 15, 8800 VIBORG **Tel:** 87 28 58 12
Titles:
MAGASINET MIDT

DIABETESFORENINGEN - LANDSFORENINGEN FOR SUKKERSYGE 1727502
Rytterkasernen 1, 5000 ODENSE C **Tel:** 66 12 90 06 **Fax:** 65 91 49 08
Titles:
DIABETES

DIVER GROUP SCANDINAVIA APS 1727372
Rentemestervej 64, 2400 KØBENHAVN NV **Tel:** 70 26 30 15 **Fax:** 70 26 90 15
Titles:
DYK

DJURSLANDSPOSTEN A/S 1727522
Østerbrogade 45, 8500 GRENÅ **Tel:** 87 58 55 00 **Fax:** 87 58 55 16
Titles:
DJURSLANDSPOSTEN

DK-CAMP 1727736
DK-Camp, Industrivej 5 D, 7120 VEJLE Ø **Tel:** 75 71 29 60 **Fax:** 75 71 29 66
Titles:
CAMPISTEN

DMC 1727665
Haverslevvej 47, Ersted, 9520 SKØRPING **Tel:** 98 37 36 93 **Fax:** 98 37 28 81
Titles:
DMC BLADET

DR 1727194
DR Byen, Emil Holms Kanal 20, 0999 KØBENHAVN C **Tel:** 35 20 45 20 **Fax:** 35 20 46 46
Titles:
DR NYHEDER TV AVISEN 21.00
DR P4 BORNHOLM FORMIDDAG

DSB 1726975
Sølvgade 40, 1349 KØBENHAVN K **Tel:** 33 54 44 76 **Fax:** 33 54 42 40
Titles:
UD & SE

EGMONT MAGASINER 1793142
Hellerupvej 51, 2900 HELLERUP **Tel:** 39 45 75 51
Titles:
BOLIGLIV
GASTRO

EGMONT MAGASINER A/S 1726976
Hellerupvej 51, 2900 HELLERUP **Tel:** 39 45 75 00
Titles:
ALT FOR DAMERNE
GRAVID - ALT OM DIG
HENDES VERDEN
HER OG NU
HJEMMET
PC PLANET
SIRENE
VI FORÆLDRE

EGMONT SERIEFORLAGET A/S 1727230
Vognmagergade 11, 1148 KBH K **Tel:** 33 30 57 13 **Fax:** 33 30 57 60
Titles:
ANDERS AND & CO
GOAL
PLAYRIGHT PLAYRIGHT.DK
WENDY

EJENDOMSAVISEN/BILAVISEN A/S 1726943
Værkmestergade 11, 2. sal, 8000 ÅRHUS C **Tel:** 87 69 69 69 **Fax:** 86 12 73 90
Titles:
BILAVISEN
BYGGEAVISEN

EJENDOMSFORENINGEN DANMARK 1793877
Nørre Voldgade 2, 4. sal, 1358 COPENHAGEN **Tel:** 33 12 03 30 **Fax:** 33 12 62 75
Titles:
HUSET

ERHVERVSBLADET A/S 1792535
Pilestræde 34, 1147 COPENHAGEN **Tel:** 33 75 38 01 **Fax:** 33 75 36 96
Titles:
ERHVERVSBLADET

EUROINVESTOR.COM A/S 1748456
Øster Allé 42, 5., 2100 COPENHAGEN
Titles:
EUROINVESTOR.DK

EUROMAN PUBLICATIONS A/S 1793209
Hellerupvej 51, 2900 HELLERUP **Tel:** 39 45 75 00
Titles:
EUROMAN
EUROWOMAN

EXTRA POSTEN A/S 1727903
Nygade 30, 4900 NAKSKOV **Tel:** 54 92 48 00 **Fax:** 54 95 10 20
Titles:
EXTRA POSTEN

FAGBLADSFORLAGET TEKNIK & VIDEN APS 1727995
Glostrup Torv 6, Postbox 162, 2600 GLOSTRUP **Tel:** 43 46 67 00 **Fax:** 43 43 15 13
Titles:
AUTOMATIK

FAGBLADSGRUPPEN A/S 1727778
Birk Centerpark 36, 7400 HERNING **Tel:** 96 26 52 82 **Fax:** 96 26 52 96
Titles:
BYGGETEKNIK
MASKINBLADET

FAGLIG SAMMENSLUTN. AF SUNDHEDSPLEJERSKER 1724757
H.P. Hansensvej 17, DK-6100 HADERSLEV
Titles:
SUNDHEDSPLEJERSKEN

FDB 1727084
Ragnesminde, Vallensbæk Torvevej 9, 2620 ALBERTSLUND **Tel:** 39 47 00 31 **Fax:** 39 47 00 01
Titles:
SAMVIRKE

FINANSFORBUNDET 1793129
Applebys Plads 5, Postboks 1960, 1411 COPENHAGEN **Tel:** 32 96 46 00 **Fax:** 32 961225
Titles:
FINANS

FINANS/INVEST 1793329
Holmstrupgårdvej 140, 8210 ÅRHUS **Tel:** 86 24 29 90 **Fax:** 86 24 30 42
Titles:
FINANS/INVEST

FINANSRÅDET 1793962
Finansrådets Hus, Amaliegade 7, 1256 KØBENHAVN K **Tel:** 33 70 10 00
Titles:
FINANSRÅDETS NYHEDSBREV

FISK OG FRI K.S. 1727276
Christians Brygge 28, st. tv., 1559 KØBENHAVN V **Tel:** 33 11 14 88 **Fax:** 33 93 81 70
Titles:
FISK & FRI

FISKE AVISEN 1727273
Vestskellet 21, 3250 GILLELEJE **Tel:** 48 30 13 68 **Fax:** 48 35 44 54
Titles:
FISKE AVISEN

FOLKEBLADET FOR GLOSTRUP OG VESTEGNEN A/S 1727894
Glostrup Torv 6, 2600 GLOSTRUP **Tel:** 43 96 00 31 **Fax:** 43 63 28 41
Titles:
FOLKEBLADET FOR GLOSTRUP, BRØNDBY OG VALLENSBÆK

FOLKEKIRKENS NØDHJÆLP 1727353
Nørregade 13, 1165 KØBENHAVN K **Tel:** 33 15 28 00 **Fax:** 33 18 78 16
Titles:
MAGASINET

FONDEN FOR TIDSSKRIFT FOR PRAKTISK LÆGEGERNING 1727315
Stockholmsgade 55, 2100 KØBENHAVN Ø **Tel:** 35 26 67 85 **Fax:** 35 26 04 15
Titles:
MÅNEDSSKRIFT FOR PRAKTISK LÆGEGERNING

FORÆLDRE & BØRN A/S 1793634
Vigerslev Allé 18, 2500 VALBY **Tel:** 36 15 21 41 **Fax:** 36152698
Titles:
FORÆLDRE & BØRN

FORÆLDREORGANISATIONEN SKOLE OG SAMFUND 1726993
Gammel Kongevej 140 A, 1850 FREDERIKSBERG C **Tel:** 33 26 17 21 **Fax:** 33 26 17 22
Titles:
SKOLEBØRN

FORBRUGERRÅDET 1794064
Fiolstræde 17, Postbox 2188, 1017 KØBENHAVN K **Tel:** 77 41 77 41 **Fax:** 77 41 77 42
Titles:
TÆNK PENGE

FORBRUGSFORENINGEN 1793336
Knabrostræde 12, Postboks 1114, 1210 COPENHAGEN **Tel:** 33 18 86 00 **Fax:** 33 15 87 60
Titles:
F BLADET

FORBUNDET AF OFFENTLIGT ANSATTE FOA 1793356
Staunings Plads 1-3, 1790 COPENHAGEN **Tel:** 46 97 26 26
Titles:
FAGBLADET FOA

FORBUNDET TRÆ-INDUSTRI-BYG I DANMARK 1727311
Mimersgade 41, 2200 KÆ **Tel:** 88 18 70 00 **Fax:** 88 18 71 10
Titles:
FAGBLADET TIB

FORENEDE DANSKE ZONETERAPEUTER 1727449
Dyrehavevej 90, 5800 NYBORG **Tel:** 65 31 28 85 **Fax:** 70 27 99 50
Titles:
ZONETERAPEUTEN

FORENINGEN AF KLINISKE DIÆTISTER 1727499
Landmærket 10, 1012 KØBENHAVN K **Tel:** 33 32 00 39 **Fax:** 38 71 03 22
Titles:
DIÆTISTEN

FORENINGEN DANSK MUSIK TIDSKRIFT 1727525
Strandvejen 100 D, 3070 SNEKKERSTEN **Tel:** 33 24 42 48 **Fax:** 33 24 42 46
Titles:
DANSK MUSIK TIDSSKRIFT

FORENINGEN DANSKE REVISORER 1794305
Munkehatten 32, 5220 ODENSE **Tel:** 65 93 25 00 **Fax:** 65 93 25 08
Titles:
DANSKE REVISORER

FORENINGEN NORDEN 1727517
Malmøgade 3, 2100 KØBENHAVN Ø **Tel:** 35 42 63 25 **Fax:** 35 42 80 88
Titles:
NORDEN NU

FORENINGEN REGISTREREDE REVISORER FRR 1793988
Åmarksvej 1, 2650 HVIDOVRE **Tel:** 36 34 44 22 **Fax:** 36 344444
Titles:
REVISORBLADET

FORENINGEN SKOPET & AOF AALBORG 1727681
Kjellerupsgade 16-18, 9000 AALBORG **Tel:** 98 16 70 82 **Fax:** 98 16 70 52
Titles:
KULTURMAGASINET SKOPET

FORENINGEN TIL DYRENES BESKYTTELSE I DANMARK 1727369
Alhambravej 15, 1826 FREDERIKSBERG C **Tel:** 33 28 70 00 **Fax:** 33 25 14 60
Titles:
DYREVENNEN

FORLAGET AKTUEL SIKKERHED 1794221
Glostrup Torv 6 Box 162, 2600 GLOSTRUP **Tel:** 43 43 51 12 **Fax:** 43431513
Titles:
AKTUEL SIKKERHED

FORLAGET AMT OG KOMMUNEINFORMATION A/S 1727882
Glostrup Torv 6, 2600 GLOSTRUP **Tel:** 43 43 31 21 **Fax:** 43 43 15 13
Titles:
STAT & KOMMUNE INDKØB

FORLAGET CORONET A/S 1793330
Traverbanevej 10, 2920 CHARLOTTENLUND **Tel:** 35 25 34 00 **Fax:** 35 25 34 04
Titles:
ENTREPRENØREN

FORLAGET KSI A/S 1727667
Faendediget 1A, 2, 4600 KØGE **Tel:** 56 27 64 44 **Fax:** 56 27 65 29
Titles:
STUDY ABROAD
UDDANNELSESAVISEN

FORLAGET MAGNUS A/S SKATTEKARTOTEKET 1794150
Palægade 4, 1261 COPENHAGEN **Tel:** 70 20 33 14 **Fax:** 33 96 01 01
Titles:
TIDSSKRIFT FOR SKATTER OG AFGIFTER

FORLAGET MARKEDSFØRING A/S 1793094
Postboks 40, 2000 FREDERIKSBERG **Tel:** 38 11 87 87 **Fax:** 38118747
Titles:
MARKEDSFØRING

FORLAGET MEALS 1727801
Gl. Bregnerødvej 12, 3520 FARUM **Tel:** 44 99 90 01
Titles:
UGEBREVET MEALS

FORLAGET MOTOR 1792492
Firskovvej 32, 2800 KGS. LYNGBY **Tel:** 45 27 07 07 **Fax:** 45270989
Titles:
MOTOR

FORLAGET ODSGARD A/S 1727782
Stationsparken 25, 2600 GLOSTRUP **Tel:** 43 43 29 00 **Fax:** 43 43 13 28
Titles:
BYGGERI
PACKMARKEDET

FORLAGET OLE CAMÅE 1793895
Lerbjergstien 18, 3460 BIRKERØD **Tel:** 48 17 62 82 **Fax:** 48 177880
Titles:
DANISH OFFSHORE INDUSTRY

FORLAGET SMAG & BEHAG APS 1791831
Abildgårdsparken 5, 3460 BIRKERØD **Tel:** 33 97 43 43 **Fax:** 33 111762
Titles:
SMAG & BEHAG

FORLAGET THOMSON A/S 1793987
Nytorv 5, 1450 COPENHAGEN **Tel:** 33 74 07 00 **Fax:** 33 12 16 36
Titles:
REVISION & REGNSKABSVÆSEN
SR-SKAT

FYENS STIFTSTIDENDE A/S 1727036
Banegårdspladsen, 5100 ODENSE C **Tel:** 66 11 11 11 **Fax:** 65 45 52 88
Titles:
FYENS STIFTSTIDENDE

FYNSKE MEDIER P/S 1752508
Sankt Nicolai Gade 1A, 5700 SVENDBORG **Tel:** 62 21 73 21 **Fax:** 62 22 30 09
Titles:
UGEAVISEN SVENDBORG

GAFFA A/S 1793360
Enghavevej 40, 1674 COPENHAGEN **Tel:** 70 27 06 00 **Fax:** 86 189222
Titles:
GAFFA

GAMEZ PUBLISHING 1793366
Strandvejen 72, 2900 COPENHAGEN **Tel:** 45 88 76 00
Titles:
GAMEREACTOR

GARANTSELSKABET SKIVE FOLKEBLAD 1727004
Gemsevej 7-9, 7800 SKIVE **Tel:** 97 51 34 11 **Fax:** 97 51 28 35
Titles:
SKIVE FOLKEBLAD

GIGTFORENINGEN 1735644
Gentoftegade 118, 2820 GENTOFTE **Tel:** 39 77 80 14
Titles:
LEDSAGER

GIVE BOGTRYKKERI A/S 1727885
Vestergade 7 E, 7323 GIVE **Tel:** 75 73 22 00 **Fax:** 75 73 23 46
Titles:
GIVE AVIS

GLADSAXE BLADET APS 1752358
Søborg Hovedgade 119, 4 sal, 2860 SØBORG **Tel:** 39 56 12 75 **Fax:** 39 56 14 35
Titles:
GLADSAXE BLADET

GRENAA BLADET A/S 1727879
Storegade 37, 8500 GRENÅ **Tel:** 86 32 16 77 **Fax:** 86 32 46 11
Titles:
GRENAA BLADET

HAANDVÆRKERFORENINGEN I KJØBENHAVN 1727006
Dronningens Tværgade 2 A, 1302 KØBENHAVN K **Tel:** 48 48 17 88 **Fax:** 33 14 16 25
Titles:
HÅND & VÆRK

HÆRENS KONSTABEL- OG KORPORALFORENING HKKF 1727309
Kronprinsensgade 8, 1114 KØBENHAVN K **Tel:** 33 93 65 22 **Fax:** 33 93 65 23
Titles:
FAGLIGT FORSVAR

HELSINGØR DAGBLAD A/S 1727538
Frederikssundsvej 322 A, 2700 BRØNSHØJ **Tel:** 38 60 30 03 **Fax:** 38 60 01 47
Titles:
BRØNSHØJ-HUSUM AVIS

HERNING BLADET A/S 1727860
Bredgade 33, 2. sal, 7400 HERNING **Tel:** 97 12 15 00 **Fax:** 97 22 20 42
Titles:
HERNING BLADET

HERNING FOLKEBLAD A/S 1727031
Østergade 25, 7400 HERNING **Tel:** 96 26 37 00 **Fax:** 97 22 36 00
Titles:
HERNING FOLKEBLAD

HEST OG RYTTER 1727635
Hejreskovvej 20, 3490 KVISTGÅRD **Tel:** 49 13 92 00 **Fax:** 49 13 85 00
Titles:
HEST OG RYTTER

HESTESPORTENS TRYKCENTER A/S 1727071
Traverbanevej 10, 2920 CHARLOTTENLUND **Tel:** 39 96 20 20 **Fax:** 39 63 91 65
Titles:
VÆDDELØBSBLADET

HILLERØD MEDIECENTER I/S (POLITIKENS LOKALAVISER A/S) 1752048
M.D Madsensvej 13, 3450 ALLERØD **Tel:** 70 13 11 00 **Fax:** 45 90 82 23
Titles:
ALLERØD NYT

HJERTEFORENINGEN 1793172
Hausers Plads 10, 1127 COPENHAGEN **Tel:** 33 93 17 88
Titles:
HJERTENYT

HK/KOMMUNAL 1728071
Weidekampsgade 8, 0900 KØBENHAVN C **Tel:** 33 30 43 85 **Fax:** 33 30 44 49
Titles:
HK KOMMUNALBLADET

HK/STAT 1727077
Weidekampsgade 8, PostBoks 470, 0900 KØBENHAVN C **Tel:** 33 30 43 43 **Fax:** 33 30 42 22
Titles:
HK/STAT MAGASINET

HOBRO AVIS A/S 1727857
Adelgade 56, 9500 HOBRO **Tel:** 98 52 70 30 **Fax:** 98 51 18 88
Titles:
HOBRO AVIS

HOLBÆK AMTS VENSTREBLAD 1727729
Centervej 33, 4270 HØNG **Tel:** 88 88 42 90 **Fax:** 58 85 20 75
Titles:
UGEBLADET VESTSJÆLLAND

HOLSTEBRO ONSDAG 1726948
Hærens Kampskole, 6840 OKSBØL **Tel:** 76 54 12 00 **Fax:** 76 54 14 09
Titles:
KENTAUR

HORESTA 1727062
HORESTA, Vodroffsvej 32, 1900 FREDERIKSBERG C **Tel:** 35 24 80 80 **Fax:** 35 24 80 85
Titles:
VISITOR

HORISONT GRUPPEN A/S 1726934
Center Boulevard 5, 2300 KØBENHAVN S **Tel:** 32 47 32 30 **Fax:** 32 47 32 39
Titles:
CSR
SCM

HORSENS FOLKEBLAD A/S 1726973
Søndergade 47, 8700 HORSENS **Tel:** 76 27 20 00
Titles:
EJENDOMSAVISEN HORSENS POSTEN
HORSENS FOLKEBLAD

HOVEDORGANISATIONEN AF OFFICERER I DK (HOD) 1727560
Olof Palmes Gade 10, 2100 KØBENHAVN Ø **Tel:** 33 15 02 33 **Fax:** 33 14 46 26
Titles:
DANSKE OFFICERER

HOVEDORGANISATIONEN FOR PERSONEL AF RESERVEN I DK 1727166
Rigensgade 9, 1316 KØBENHAVN K **Tel:** 33 14 16 01
Titles:
RESERVEN

HUS & HAVE AVISEN APS 1793632
Traverbanevej 10, 2920 CHARLOTTENLUND **Tel:** 70 20 01 82 **Fax:** 36 70 50 63
Titles:
HUS & HAVE AVISEN

HVIDOVRE AVIS A/S 1727853
Hvidovrevej 301, 2650 HVIDOVRE **Tel:** 36 49 55 55 **Fax:** 36 77 25 55
Titles:
HVIDOVRE AVIS

HVIDOVRE MILJØFORUM OG HVIDOVRE KOMMUNE 1727650
Hvidovrevej 278, 2650 HVIDOVRE **Tel:** 36 39 35 00 **Fax:** 36 39 36 58
Titles:
MILJØAVISEN HVIDOVRE

IDG DANMARK A/S 1791457
Carl Jacobsens Vej 25, 2500 VALBY **Tel:** 77 30 03 00 **Fax:** 77300304
Titles:
PCWORLD.DK

INGENIØREN A/S 1793871
Skelbækgade 4, 1717 KØBENHAVN V **Tel:** 33 26 53 00 **Fax:** 33 26 53 01
Titles:
INGENIØREN

INSTITUTTET FOR FREMTIDSFORSKNING 1793923
Nørre Farimagsgade 65, 1364 COPENHAGEN **Tel:** 33 11 71 76
Titles:
SCENARIO

INTECH PUBLICATIONS 1748054
St. Kongensgade 14, 1., 2164 KØBENHAVN K **Tel:** 33 30 82 62
Titles:
JYLLANDS-POSTEN, MORGENAVISEN; GISMO

INTERNATIONAL SOLID WASTE ASSOCIATION 1728154
Vesterbrogade 74, 3rd floor, 1620 KØBENHAVN V **Tel:** 32 96 15 88 **Fax:** 32 96 15 84
Titles:
WASTE MANAGEMENT WORLD

ISABELLA SMITH A/S OG ALLER PRESS A/S 1793720
Hesede Hovedgård 3, 4690 HASLEV **Tel:** 70 70 14 14
Titles:
ISABELLAS

ISWA 1793283
Overgaden Oven Vandet 48 E, DK-1415 COPENHAGEN **Tel:** 32 96 15 88 **Fax:** 32 96 15 84
Titles:
WASTE MANAGEMENT & RESEARCH

JP/POLITIKENS HUS A/S 1789312
Bygmestervej 61, 2400 COPENHAGEN **Tel:** 77 30 57 57
Titles:
24TIMER FORBRUG
EKSTRA BLADET NYHEDER
JYLLANDS POSTEN
POLITIKEN

JSL PUBLICATIONS A/S 1793763
Dortheavej 59, 2400 COPENHAGEN **Tel:** 32 71 12 00
Titles:
MAD&VENNER

JUNGERSTED-VERMØ 1774020
Frederiksberg Runddel 1, 2000 FREDERIKSBERG **Tel:** 35 25 05 25 **Fax:** 35 26 87 60
Titles:
HELSE

JURIST- OG ØKONOMFORBUNDETS FORLAG A/S 1727090
Gothersgade 133, P.O. Box 2126, 1015 KØBENAVHN K **Tel:** 33 95 97 00 **Fax:** 33 95 99 99
Titles:
SAMFUNDSØKONOMEN

JYDSKE VESTKYSTEN A/S 1727515
Vestergade 2D, 6600 VEJEN **Tel:** 75 36 00 22 **Fax:** 75 36 03 90
Titles:
VEJEN AVIS

KABEL OG LINIEMESTERFORENINGEN 1727962
Ørbækvej 47, 7330 BRANDE **Tel:** 97 18 03 77 **Fax:** 97 18 13 53
Titles:
KABEL OG LINIEMESTEREN

KATOLSKE KIRKE I DANMARK 1728053
Gl. Kongevej 15, 1610 KØBENHAVN V **Tel:** 33 55 60 40 **Fax:** 33 24 49 75
Titles:
KATOLSK ORIENTERING

KFUM/KFUK 1793184
Valby Langgade 19, 2500 VALBY **Tel:** 36 16 60 33 **Fax:** 36 160818
Titles:
BRICKS

KL PUBLISHING 1793493
Trommesalen 5, 2. sal, DK-1614 COPENHAGEN **Tel:** 31 21 26 28
Titles:
BYGGE & ANLÆGSAVISEN

KØBENHAVNS UNIVERSITET 1727781
Københavns Universitet, Nørregade 10, 1005 KØBENHAVN K **Tel:** 35 32 28 98 **Fax:** 35 32 29 20
Titles:
UNIVERSITETSAVISEN

KØGE MEDIE CENTER A/S 1752409
Søndre Alle 1, 4600 KØGE **Tel:** 56 65 82 00 **Fax:** 56 65 93 09
Titles:
LØRDAGSAVISEN KØGE

KOLONIHAVEFORBUNDET FOR DANMARK 1727120
Frederikssundsvej 304 A, 2700 BRØNSHØJ **Tel:** 38 28 87 50 **Fax:** 38 28 83 50
Titles:
HAVEBLADET

A/S KRISTELIGT DAGBLAD 1791254
Rosengården 14, 1174 COPENHAGEN **Tel:** 33 48 05 00 **Fax:** 33480502
Titles:
KRISTELIGT DAGBLAD

KRYDSFELT 1739794
Anker Engelundsvej 1, DTU bygn. 101E, 2800 KGS. LYNGBY **Tel:** 77 42 44 17
Titles:
KRYDSFELT

LÆGEFORENINGENS FORLAG 1727271
Øster Farimagsgade 5, Postboks 2099, 1014 KØBENHAVN K **Tel:** 35 32 65 90 **Fax:** 35 32 65 91
Titles:
PRACTICUS

LÆGEFORENINGENS FORLAG, KØBENHAVN 1727496
Trondhjemsgade 9, 2100 KØBENHAVN Ø **Tel:** 35 44 85 00 **Fax:** 35 44 85 02
Titles:
UGESKRIFT FOR LÆGER

LANDBRUG FYN A/S 1727362
Odensevej 29, 5550 LANGESKOV **Tel:** 70 15 12 37 **Fax:** 70 15 12 47
Titles:
EFFEKTIVT LANDBRUG
LANDBRUG FYN

LANDBRUG NORD 1743930
Østre Allé, 9530 STØVRING **Tel:** 98 35 12 37 **Fax:** 98 33 12 37
Titles:
LANDBRUG NORD

LANDBRUG ØST 1743932
Huginsvej 11, 4100 RINGSTED **Tel:** 55 50 12 37 **Fax:** 55 50 12 31
Titles:
LANDBRUG ØST

LANDBRUG SYD APS 1727910
Skolegade 1A, 6650 BRØRUP **Tel:** 75 38 15 00 **Fax:** 75 38 15 16
Titles:
LANDBRUG SYD

LANDSFORENINGEN AF DANSKE MÆLKEPROD. & BØRS-MARK A/S 1727566
Vestergade 19, 7600 STRUER **Tel:** 97 84 13 80 **Fax:** 97 84 13 70
Titles:
DANSKE MÆLKEPRODUCENTER

LANDSFORENINGEN AF MENIGHEDSRÅDSMED-LEMMER 1727688
Vesterport 3, 1., 8000 ÅRHUS C **Tel:** 87 32 21 33 **Fax:** 86 19 80 40
Titles:
MENIGHEDSRÅDENES BLAD

LANDSFORENINGEN FOR BEDRE HØRELSE 1727022
Kløverprisvej 10 B, 2650 HVIDOVRE **Tel:** 61 38 54 94 **Fax:** 36 38 85 80
Titles:
HØRELSEN

LANDSFORENINGEN FOR BYGNINGS OG LANDSKABSKULT 1727767
Borgergade 111, 1022 KØBENHAVN K **Tel:** 70 22 12 99 **Fax:** 70 22 12 90
Titles:
BY OG LAND

LANDSFORENINGEN MC TOURING CLUB DANMARK 1727471
Markvangen 6, 8260 VIBY J **Tel:** 86 11 62 00 **Fax:** 86 11 62 59
Titles:
TOURING NYT

LANDSFORENINGEN PRAKTISK ØKOLOGI 1735735
Vestenskovvej 11, 4900 NAKSKOV **Tel:** 70 20 83 81
Titles:
HAVENYT.DK

Denmark

LASTBILMAGASINET APS 1727881
Kongensgade 72, 1. sal, 5000 ODENSE C
Fax: 66 16 01 47
Titles:
LASTBIL MAGASINET

LEDERNES HOVEDORGANISATION 1793925
Vermlandsgade 65, DK-2300 COPENHAGEN
Tel: 32 83 32 83 **Fax:** 32 833284
Titles:
LEDELSE I DAG LEDELSEIDAG.DK

LEDERNES HOVEDORGANISATION 1793926
Vermlandsgade 65, 2300 COPENHAGEN
Tel: 32 83 32 83 **Fax:** 32833284
Titles:
LEDERNE

LEJERNES LANDSORGANISATION I DANMARK 1727709
Reventlowsgade 14, 1651 KØBENHAVN V
Tel: 33 86 09 10 **Fax:** 33 86 09 20
Titles:
VI LEJERE

LEMVIG FOLKEBLAD A/S 1727042
Bredgade 20, 7620 LEMVIG **Tel:** 96 63 04 00
Fax: 96 63 04 18
Titles:
FOLKEBLADET LEMVIG

LOKALAVISEN DJURSLAND OG KALØ VIG A/S 1727839
Tingvej 36, 8543 HORNSLET **Tel:** 86 99 45 11
Fax: 86 99 55 49
Titles:
LOKALAVISEN KALØ VIG

LOLLAND-FALSTERS ERHVERVSFORLAG APS 1727800
Marrebæk Norvej 1, 4873 VÆGGERLØSE
Tel: 54 17 73 00 **Fax:** 54 17 73 43
Titles:
LANDBRUGS-NYT

LOLLANDS-POSTEN A/S 1727391
Banegårdspladsen 2, 4930 MARIBO
Tel: 54 76 04 88 **Fax:** 54 88 03 61
Titles:
LOLLANDS POSTEN

LUNGEFORENINGEN BOSERUP MINDE 1726899
Old Gyde 74, 5620 GLAMSBJERG
Tel: 64 72 13 57 **Fax:** 64 72 13 77
Titles:
LUNGEFORENINGEN BOSERUP MINDE

MAGASINET DIGITALT 1762112
Christiansborggade 1, 1558 KØBENHAVN V
Tel: 33 32 90 66
Titles:
MAGASINET DIGITALT

MALERFORBUNDET I DANMARK 1727359
Lersø Park Allé 109, 2100 KØBENHAVN Ø
Tel: 39 16 79 00 **Fax:** 39 16 79 10
Titles:
MALEREN
VOGNMALEREN

MASKIN- OG MATERIAL MAGASINET 1727724
Gustav Wieds Vej 53, 8600 SILKEBORG
Tel: 86 80 44 99 **Fax:** 86 80 44 49
Titles:
MASKIN & MATERIAL MAGASINET

MAX HAVELAAR DANMARK 1793341
Nørregade 15, 4. sal, 1165 COPENHAGEN
Tel: 70 23 13 45
Titles:
FAIR NOK

MAZAFAKA MEDIA APS 1727323
Stefansgade 7, Baghuset, st., 2200 KØBENHAVN N **Tel:** 33 91 30 32 **Fax:** 33 91 30 36
Titles:
PC PLAYER

MEDIACTIVE APS 1793343
Dronnings Tværgade 8 A, 1302 COPENHAGEN
Tel: 36 92 70 70
Titles:
FITNEWS MAGAZINE

MEDIAPROVIDER A/S 1736202
Hørkær 18, 2730 HERLEV **Tel:** 77 30 02 70
Titles:
CRN
MOBIL

MEDIECENTRET HERLEV BLADET 1727861
Herlev Bygade 39, 2730 HERLEV **Tel:** 44 94 10 10
Fax: 44 94 13 63
Titles:
HERLEV BLADET

MEDIEFORLAGET CHILI GROUP 1793359
Bispevej 4, 2.sal, 2400 COPENHAGEN
Tel: 33 38 63 33 **Fax:** 33386300
Titles:
FRIKVARTER
KULØR
LIME

MEDIEHUSET LUKSUS 1793718
Vesterbrogade 74, 4, 1620 KØBENHAVN N
Tel: 29 71 61 75
Titles:
LUKSUS

MEDIESELSKABET NORDVESTSJÆLLAND 1727072
Bladhuset i Holbæk, Ahlgade 1, 4300 HOLBÆK
Tel: 88 88 43 00 **Fax:** 59 44 50 34
Titles:
HOLBÆK AMTS VENSTREBLAD
JYDERUP POSTEN
ODSHERREDS KYSTEN

MEJERIFORENINGEN 1727169
Frederiks Allé 22, 8000 ÅRHUS **Tel:** 87 31 20 00
Fax: 87 31 20 01
Titles:
&MÆLK

MIDTJYLLANDS AVIS 1739947
Papirfabrikken 18, 8600 SILKEBORG
Tel: 86 82 13 00 **Fax:** 86 82 13 60
Titles:
EKSTRA-POSTEN

MIDTJYSK UGEBLAD A/S 1727806
Jernbanegade 25, 7200 GRINDSTED
Tel: 75 32 05 00 **Fax:** 75 32 31 95
Titles:
MIDTJYSK UGEAVIS

MIDTJYSKE MEDIER 1740935
Lægårdsvej 86, 7500 HOLSTEBRO
Tel: 99 12 84 10 **Fax:** 97 41 03 20
Titles:
DAGBLADET HOLSTEBRO/STRUER
VIBORG STIFTS FOLKEBLAD

MILJØSTYRELSEN MILJØ- OG ENERGIMINISTERIET 1727544
Højbro Plads 4, 1200 KØBENHAVN K
Tel: 33 92 76 00 **Fax:** 32 66 04 79
Titles:
MILJØDANMARK

MOMENT KOMMUNIKATION 1727871
Gothersgade 11, 1123 KØBENHAVN K
Tel: 70 20 18 35 **Fax:** 33 11 10 88
Titles:
MOMENT

MORSØ FOLKEBLAD A/S 1727624
Elsøvej 105, 7900 NYKØBING MORS
Tel: 97 72 10 00 **Fax:** 97 72 10 10
Titles:
MORSØ FOLKEBLAD
MORSØ FOLKEBLADS UGEAVIS

MURERFAGETS OPLYSNINGSRÅD 1727855
Lille Strandstræde 20C, 1254 KØBENHAVN K
Tel: 33 32 34 84 **Fax:** 33 32 22 97
Titles:
TEGL

MUSIKBRANCHENS REKLAMEBUREAU APS 1727228
Wilders Plads 15C, 1403 KØBENHAVN K
Tel: 32 96 06 12 **Fax:** 32 96 06 21
Titles:
MUSIKKALENDEREN

NÆRINGS- & NYDELSES-MIDDELSARBEJDER FORBUNDET 1727520
C.F. Richs vej 103, DK-2000 FREDERIKSBERG
Tel: 38 18 72 72 **Fax:** 38 18 72 30
Titles:
NNF-ARBEJDEREN

NÆSTVED-BLADET A/S 1726958
Ringstedgade 11, 4700 NÆSTVED
Tel: 55 73 50 00 **Fax:** 55 73 55 79
Titles:
NÆSTVED-BLADET

NETPOSTEN A/S 1794037
Kigkurren 8 D, 3t.h., 2300 COPENHAGEN
Tel: 83 30 00 00
Titles:
NPINVESTOR NPINVESTOR.DK

NORDJYSK MEDIECENTER 1727815
Langagervej 1, 9220 AALBORG Ø
Tel: 99 35 35 35 **Fax:** 99 35 35 34
Titles:
MIDT-VEST AVIS

NORDJYSKE MEDIER 1727104
Langagervej 1, DK-9220 AALBORG
Tel: 99 35 33 00
Titles:
FRIII
LOKALAVISEN FREDERIKSHAVN
NORDJYSKE STIFTSTIDENDE
NORDJYSKE STIFTSTIDENDE AALBORG
NORDJYSKE STIFTSTIDENDE FREDERIKSHAVN
NORDJYSKE STIFTSTIDENDE HIMMERLAND
NORDJYSKE STIFTSTIDENDE HJØRRING
NØRRESUNDBY AVIS
OPLANDSAVISEN
THISTED DAGBLAD
THISTED POSTEN
VEJGAARD AVIS
VENDELBO POSTEN

NORDSJÆLLANDS AVIS A/S 1740487
Klostermosevej 101, 3000 HELSINGØR
Tel: 49 22 21 10 **Fax:** 49 22 11 08
Titles:
LOKALAVISEN NORDSJÆLLAND

NYHEDSBUREAUET NEWSPAQ APS 1793921
St. Regnegade 12, 1.sal, 1100 COPENHAGEN
Tel: 70 27 90 70 **Fax:** 31 410191
Titles:
MEDIAWATCH MEDIAWATCH.DK

ODSGARD 1728141
Stationsparken 25, 2600 GLOSTRUP
Tel: 43 43 29 00 **Fax:** 43 43 13 28
Titles:
BYG TEK

ODSGARD A/S 1727175
Stationsparken 25, 2600 GLOSTRUP
Tel: 43 43 29 00 **Fax:** 43 43 13 28
Titles:
MESTER & SVEND
PUFF
TELEKOMMUNIKATION

ODSGARD REKLAME OG MARKETING A/S 1793305
Stationsparken 25, 2600 GLOSTRUP
Tel: 43 45 10 63 **Fax:** 43 43 13 28
Titles:
ELEKTRONIK & DATA

ØJENFORENINGEN VÆRN OM SYNET 1727615
Ny Kongensgade 20, 1557 KØBENHAVN K
Tel: 33 69 11 00 **Fax:** 33 69 11 01
Titles:
VÆRN OM SYNET

OMRÅDE AVISEN NORDFYN A/S 1727787
Østergade 14, 5400 BOGENSE **Tel:** 65 45 57 00
Fax: 64 86 11 45
Titles:
UGEAVISEN NORDFYN

ONSDAGS-AVISEN HORSENS A/S 1727792
Nørregade 22, 8700 HORSENS **Tel:** 75 61 28 77
Fax: 75 61 20 30
Titles:
ONSDAGSAVISEN HORSENS

ØRSKOV GRUPPEN 1726918
Gentoftegade 118, 2820 GENTOFTE
Tel: 39 77 80 14 **Fax:** 39 65 11 96
Titles:
LEDSAGER - ALT OM GIGT OG GODE VANER

OXYGEN A/S 1793834
Oxygen A/S, Thoravej 13, 3.sal, 2400 COPENHAGEN **Tel:** 39 16 26 16
Titles:
VORES BØRN

P E J GRUPPEN 1727691
Bitsovvej 2, 7400 HERNING **Tel:** 97 11 89 00
Fax: 97 11 85 11
Titles:
TID & TENDENSER

PARCELHUSEJERNES LANDSFORENING 1727685
Kjærstrupvej 36, 2500 VALBY **Tel:** 38 74 76 88
Fax: 38 74 76 12
Titles:
MIT HUS

PETER WINDING OG ELSEBETH LOHFERT 1793281
Postboks 75, Vandværksvej 11, 5690 TOMMERUP **Tel:** 64 75 22 84 **Fax:** 64 75 28 44
Titles:
VINBLADET

PHARMADANMARK 1735727
Rygårds Alle 1, 2900 HELLERUP **Tel:** 39 46 36 00
Fax: 39 46 36 39
Titles:
FAGBLADET FARMA

POLITIKENS FORLAG 1791060
Rådhuspladsen 37, 1785 COPENHAGEN
Tel: 33 47 25 65
Titles:
TURENGAARTIL.DK

POLITIKENS LOKALAVISER 1727244
Stationsporten 9, 2620 ALBERTSLUND
Tel: 45 90 82 26 **Fax:** 45 90 82 31
Titles:
ALBERTSLUND POSTEN
UGE-NYT FREDENSBORG

POLITIKENS LOKALAVISER A/S 1727093
Møllestræde 9, 3400 HILLERØD **Tel:** 70 13 11 00
Fax: 48 24 16 16
Titles:
HILLERØD POSTEN
LOKALAVISEN UGE NYT

PRO-F A.M.B.A 1793599
Vejrøvænget 85, 5500 MIDDELFART
Tel: 75 85 80 90
Titles:
KROP & FYSIK

PROSA 1727255
Ahlefeldtsgade 16, 1359 KØBENHAVN K
Tel: 33 36 41 41 **Fax:** 33 91 90 44
Titles:
PROSABLADET
PROSIT

RADIOTELEGRAFIST FORENINGEN AF 1917 1726990
Trommesalen 3, DK-1614 KØBENHAVN K
Titles:
RADIOTELEGRAFEN

REDERIFORENINGEN FOR MINDRE SKIBE 1727867
Rederiforeningen for Mindre Skibe, Amaliegade 33, 1256 KØBENHAVN K **Tel:** 33 11 40 88
Fax: 33 11 62 10
Titles:
SKIPPEREN

REJSEMAGASINET VAGABOND APS 1791048
Bregnerødvej 132, 3460 BIRKERØD
Tel: 70 22 44 36 **Fax:** 48131507
Titles:
VAGABOND REJS

REVIFORA 1726931
Revifora, Kronprinsessegade 8, 1306 KØBENHAVN K **Tel:** 33 15 15 19 **Fax:** 33 93 15 19
Titles:
INSPI

RMB DANSK REKLAME FILM A/S 1727290
Borgergade 14, 4. sal, 1300 KØBENHAVN K
Tel: 33 32 54 00 **Fax:** 33 15 71 70
Titles:
FILM GUIDE

ROSKILDE UNIVERSITETSCENTER 1735589
Postboks 260, 4000 ROSKILDE **Tel:** 46 74 20 13
Titles:
RUCNYT

SAMARBEJDENDE MERKONOMER 1794291
Ramsingsvej 28 A, stuen, 2500 VALBY
Tel: 31 22 25 77 **Fax:** 31 22 25 32
Titles:
MERKONOMBLADET

SAMFUNDS-KONTAKT A/S 1727669
Postboks 596, 2200 KØBENHAVN N
Tel: 21 48 19 27 **Fax:** 35 35 51 60
Titles:
CHAUFFØRNYT

SAMMENSLUTNINGEN AF FIRMA-FUNKTIONÆRER 1727279
Paghs Gård, Overstræde 2b, 5100 ODENSE C
Tel: 63 13 85 50 **Fax:** 63 13 85 55
Titles:
FRIE

SAMVIR ENERGI- & MILJØKONTORER, SEK OG OVE 1793282
Dannebrogsgade 8 A, 8000 ÅRHUS
Tel: 86 76 04 44 **Fax:** 86 76 05 44
Titles:
VEDVARENDE ENERGI & MILJØ

SCANPUBLISHER A/S 1765404
Emiliekildevej 35, 2930 KLAMPENBORG
Tel: 39 90 80 00 **Fax:** 39 90 82 80
Titles:
LÆGEMAGASINET

SILKEBORG AVIS A/S 1727026
Papirfabrikken 18, 8600 SILKEBORG
Tel: 86 82 13 00 **Fax:** 86 81 35 77
Titles:
MIDTJYLLANDS AVIS SILKEBORG

SJÆLLANDSKE MEDIER A/S 1743879
Søgade 4-12, 4100 RINGSTED **Tel:** 57 61 25 00
Fax: 57 61 06 22
Titles:
DAGBLADET RINGSTED
DAGBLADET ROSKILDE
FAXE BUGTEN
HASLEV POSTEN
KØGE ONSDAG
MIDTSJÆLLANDS FOLKBLAD
UGEBLADET FOR MØN
UGEBLADET NÆSTVED OG OMEGN
UGEBLADET SYDSJÆLLAND

SKANDINAVISK BLADFORLAG A/S 1790988
Vester Voldgade 83,3, 1553 KØBENHAVN V
Tel: 33 26 8400 **Fax:** 33 26 8401
Titles:
TAKE OFF TAKEOFF.DK

SKANDINAVISK MOTOR CO. A/S 1793128
Park Allé 355, 2605 BRØNDBY **Tel:** 43 28 82 00
Titles:
BILSNAK

SKATTEREVISORFORENINGEN 1727014
Alperosevej 11, 4600 KØGE **Tel:** 21 75 22 92
Titles:
SKATTEREVISOREN

SOCIALDEMOKRATIET 1726962
Danasvej 7, 1910 FREDERIKSBERG
Tel: 72 30 08 00 **Fax:** 33 93 67 70
Titles:
SOCIALDEMOKRATEN

SOCIALPÆDAGOGERNES LANDSFORBUND 1728049
Brolæggerstræde 9, 1211 KØBENHAVN K
Tel: 72 48 60 00 **Fax:** 72 48 60 01
Titles:
SOCIALPÆDAGOGEN

SØNDAGSAVISEN A/S 1727341
Gladsaxe Møllevej 28, 2860 SØBORG
Tel: 39 57 75 00 **Fax:** 39577600
Titles:
SØNDAGSAVISEN CENTRALREDAKTIONEN
UGE NYT SLAGELSE

SPASTIKERFORENINGEN 1726937
Spastikerforeningen, Flintholm Allé 8, 2000 FREDERIKSBERG **Tel:** 38 88 45 75
Fax: 38 88 45 76
Titles:
SPASTIKEREN

SPILDEVANDSTEKNISK FORENING 1726919
Bøgevej 12, 8660 SKANDERBORG
Tel: 86 52 41 08
Titles:
SPILDEVANDSTEKNISK TIDSSKRIFT

STAND BY PUBLISHING 1790987
Carl Jacobsens Vej 20, 1. sal, 2500 VALBY
Tel: 33 26 84 00 **Fax:** 33 26 84 01
Titles:
STAND BY

STANDBY PUBLISHING APS I SAMARBEJDE M. BILLUND LUFTHAVN 1741846
Vesterbrogade 19, 1620 KØBENHAVN V
Tel: 33 26 84 00 **Fax:** 33 26 84 01
Titles:
CHECK-IN BILLUND

STARK 1727687
Søren Frichs Vej 18, 8100 ÅRHUS
Tel: 89 34 34 34
Titles:
BYGGEMAGASINET

SUNDHEDSGUIDEN MEDIA APS 1748652
Hollandsvej 12, 2800 LYNGBY **Tel:** 39 13 10 10
Titles:
SUNDHEDSGUIDEN.DK

SUPER AVISEN APS 1793812
Grønholmsvej 12, 4340 TØLLØSE **Tel:** 59 18 54 30
Fax: 59 18 58 12
Titles:
SUPER AVISEN

A/S SVENDBORG AVIS 1727196
Sankt Nicolai Gade 3, BOX 40, 5700 SVENDBORG **Tel:** 62 21 46 21 **Fax:** 62 22 06 10
Titles:
FYNS AMTS AVIS

TÅRNBY BLADET A/S 1727642
Englandsvej 290, Postboks 34, 2770 KASTRUP
Tel: 32 50 92 90 **Fax:** 32 50 92 93
Titles:
TÅRNBY BLADET

TECHMEDIA A/S 1726928
Naverland 35, 2600 GLOSTRUP **Tel:** 43 24 26 28
Fax: 43 24 26 26
Titles:
ELTEKNIK
INSTALLATIONS NYT
MASKIN AKTUELT
RENS & VASK
SCANDINAVIAN FOOD & DRINK
TEKNISK NYT
TRÆ- & MØBELINDUSTRI

TECHMEDIA A/S SAMT PLASTINDUSTRIEN I DANMARK 1727312
Naverland 35, 2600 GLOSTRUP **Tel:** 43 24 26 01
Fax: 43 24 26 26
Titles:
PLAST PANORAMA

TEKNIQ INSTALLATØRERNES ORGANISATION 1727350
Paul Bergsøes Vej 6, 2600 GLOSTRUP
Tel: 77 42 42 23 **Fax:** 43 43 21 03
Titles:
ELECTRA

TEKNISK LANDSFORBUND 1727960
Nørre Voldgade 12, 1358 KØBENHAVN K
Tel: 33 43 65 00 **Fax:** 33 43 66 67
Titles:
TEKNIKEREN

TIPS-BLADET A/S 1727637
Kristen Bernikowsgade 4, 3. sal, 1105 KØBENHAVN K **Tel:** 49 70 89 00 **Fax:** 49 70 88 30
Titles:
TIPSBLADET

TV 2 / DANMARK 1727059
Teglholm Allé 16, DK-2450 KØBENHAVN SV
Titles:
TV 2 / DANMARK NYHEDERNE; 18.00
TV 2 FINANS FINANS.TV2.DK

UGEAVISEN ODENSE 1727913
Banegårdspladsen, 5100 ODENSE C
Tel: 66 14 14 10 **Fax:** 66 12 22 00
Titles:
DALUM-HJALLESE AVIS

UGEAVISEN ODENSE A/S 1727354
Vestergade 70-74, 5100 ODENSE C
Tel: 66 14 14 10 **Fax:** 66 12 22 00
Titles:
UGEAVISEN ODENSE

UGEAVISEN SVENSTRUP A/S 1727735
Godthåbsvej 7, 9230 SVENSTRUP
Tel: 98 38 14 77 **Fax:** 98 38 19 65
Titles:
UGEAVISEN SVENSTRUP

VEJLE AMTS FOLKEBLAD A/S 1726959
Bugattivej 8, 7100 VEJLE **Tel:** 75 83 10 00
Fax: 75 72 17 27
Titles:
UGEAVISEN VEJLE

VERMØ A/S 1793804
Øresundsvej 49, 4 t.v., 2300 COPENHAGEN
Tel: 60 7777 61
Titles:
TJECK MAGAZINE

VESTERGAARD REKLAMEBUREAU 1736229
Frederik Den VII's Gade 10, 4800 NYKØBING F
Tel: 54 85 11 85 **Fax:** 54 82 74 00
Titles:
ERHVERVSAVISEN FOR LOLLAND, FALSTER, SYDSJÆLLAND OG MØN

A/S VESTKYSTENS DISTRIKTSBLADE 1727460
Jernbanegade 18, 6700 ESBJERG
Tel: 75 15 52 00 **Fax:** 75 13 82 77
Titles:
MÅNEDSMAGASINET ERHVERV

VIDEBÆK BOGTRYKKERI 1727821
Falkevej 4, 6920 VIDEBÆK **Tel:** 97 17 11 22
Fax: 97 17 31 11
Titles:
LOKALPOSTEN LEM UGEAVIS

VIDENSCENTER FOR ARBEJDSMILJØ VED ARBEJDSMILJØINSTI. 1728064
Lersø Parkallé 105, 2100 KØBENHAVN Ø
Tel: 39 16 54 94 **Fax:** 39 16 52 01
Titles:
ARBEJDSMILJØ

VIDENSCENTRET FOR DØVBLINDEBLEVNE 1727367
Generatorvej 2A, 2730 HERLEV **Tel:** 44 85 60 30
Fax: 44 85 60 99
Titles:
NYT

VILLABYERNES MEDIECENTER 1727707
Ordrupvej 101 3. sal, 2920 CHARLOTTENLUND
Tel: 39 63 51 11 **Fax:** 39 63 81 36
Titles:
VILLABYERNE

Denmark

WILLIAMS REKLAMEBUREAU AS 1727124
Klostermosevej 140, 3000 HELSINGØR
Tel: 49 22 37 00 **Fax:** 49 22 37 46
Titles:
ROAD LIFE MAGAZINE

WINDPOWER MONTHLY A/S 1727535
P.O. Box 100, 8250 EGAA **Tel:** 86 36 54 65
Fax: 86 36 56 26
Titles:
WINDPOWER MONTHLY

WWF VERDENSNATURFONDEN 1727850
WWF Verdensnaturfonden, Ryesgade 3F, 2200 KØBENHAVN N **Tel:** 35 36 36 35 **Fax:** 35 24 78 68
Titles:
LEVENDE NATUR

Estonia

ÄRIPÄEVA KIRJASTUSE AS 1201335
Pärnu mnt. 105, TALLINN 19094 **Tel:** 66 70 222
Fax: 66 70 265
Titles:
ÄRIPÄEV

AS AJAKIRJADE KIRJASTUS 697823
Maakri 23 A, 10145 TALLINN **Tel:** 66 62 600
Fax: 63 11 460
Email: kirjastus@kirjastus.ee
Web site: http://www.kirjastus.ee
Titles:
KROONIKA
TALLINN THIS WEEK
TERVIS PLUSS

EESTI EKSPRESSI KIRJATUSE AS 1201369
Narva mnt. 11 E, 10151 TALLINN **Tel:** 66 98 080
Fax: 66 98 154
Email: ekspress@ekspress.ee
Web site: http://www.ekspress.ee
Titles:
EESTI EKSPRESS

EESTI MEEDIA 1757180
Maakri 23a, TALLINN 10145 **Tel:** 666 2350
Fax: 666 2351
Web site: http://www.eestimeedia.ee
Titles:
POSTIMEES
SL ÕHTULEHT

EESTI PÄEVALEHT AS 699016
Narva mnt. 13, 10151 TALLINN **Tel:** 6 80 44 00
Fax: 6 80 44 01
Email: mail@epl.ee
Web site: http://www.epl.ee
Titles:
EESTI PÄEVALEHT

GUIDE MARKETING OÜ 698940
L. Koidula 5, 10125 TALLINN **Tel:** 60 13 335
Fax: 60 13 324
Titles:
THE BALTIC GUIDE

MAALEHT AS 697638
Toompuiestee 16, 10137 TALLINN **Tel:** 66 13 718
Fax: 66 22 292
Titles:
MAALEHT

MOLES AS 698966
Tartu mnt. 53, 10115 TALLINN **Tel:** 6 14 34 00
Fax: 6 14 34 06
Titles:
MOLODJOZ ESTONIJ

NORD PRINT OÜ 1757183
Pärnu mnt 139f, 11317 TALLINN
Titles:
MK-ESTONIA

OÜ SKP MEDIA 1757186
Läänemere tee 70/1, office 30, TALLINN 13914
Titles:
KOMSOMOLSKAJA PRAVDA

POSTIMEES AS 697920
Maakri 23a, 5th floor, TALLINN **Tel:** 73 90 300
Fax: 73 90 369
Titles:
POSTIMEES (RUSSIAN EDITION)

ZEROMARK OÜ 1621883
Peterburgskoe shosse, 53, TALLINN 11415
Tel: 67 88 288 **Fax:** 67 88 290
Titles:
DEN ZA DNJOM

Finland

AAMUPOSTI-MEDIAT OY 1790012
PL 14/ Kauppakatu 12, 11101 RIIHIMAKI
Tel: 20 77 03 462
Titles:
AAMUPOSTI

AARNIO NEWS OY 1621249
PL 68/ Tiurinsaarenkatu 8, 49401 HAMINA
Tel: 50 40 75 212
Titles:
TRANSPORT NEWS

ABB KONSERNIPALVELUT VIESTINTÄPALVELU 1789303
PL 210, 00381 HELSINKI **Tel:** 10 22 11
Titles:
POWER

ACACOM MEDIA OY 1774276
Erottajankatu 15-17, 00130 HELSINKI
Tel: 20 74 39 900 **Fax:** 20 74 39 909
Titles:
IMPROBATUR

ACACOM PRINT OY 671412
Erottajankatu 15-17, 00130 HELSINKI
Tel: 20 74 39 900 **Fax:** 20 74 39 909
Titles:
CAMPUS.FI

ADATO ENERGIA OY 1790217
PL 1427/ Fredrikinkatu 51-53 B 5. krs, 00101 HELSINKI **Tel:** 9 53 05 27 00 **Fax:** 9 53 05 27 01
Titles:
ENERGIAUUTISET
SÄHKÖVIESTI

ADNI OY 1789876
Raisiontie 6 D, 00280 HELSINKI **Tel:** 9 62 22 500
Fax: 3 61 25 500
Titles:
IKKUNAPAIKKA

AHTAUS- JA HUOLINTA-ALAN TEKNISET AHT 671231
Lastenkodinkuja 1, 00180 HELSINKI
Tel: 9 69 48 132 **Fax:** 9 69 48 043
Titles:
AHT-TEKNISET

AIVOHALVAUS- JA DYSFASIALIITTO RY 671122
Suvilinnantie 2, 20900 TURKU **Tel:** 2 21 38 200
Fax: 2 21 38 210
Titles:
AVH
DYSFASIA

AJAN SANA OY 1790022
PL 205/Kuninkaanlahdenkatu 7, 28101 PORI
Tel: 44 73 00 200 **Fax:** 2 63 00 280
Titles:
UUSI AIKA

AKAAN SEUTU LEHTI OY 1790324
PL 60 /Alventie 4, 37801 TOIJALA
Tel: 3 54 09 600 **Fax:** 3 54 09 630
Titles:
AKAAN SEUTU

A-KATSASTUS OY 671600
PL 510/ Vetokuja 4, 01601 VANTAA
Tel: 75 32 32 000 **Fax:** 75 32 32 003
Titles:
KATSASTUSLEHTI

AKAVAN ERITYISALOJEN KESKUSLIITTO AEK RYHMÄ 1792285
Maistraatinportti 4 A, 6 krs, 00240 HELSINKI
Tel: 20 12 35 340 **Fax:** 9 14 72 42
Titles:
YHTEENVETO

ÅLANDS TIDNINGS TRYCKERI AB 1791038
PB 50/ Strandgatan 16, 22101 MARIEHAMN
Tel: 18 26 026 **Fax:** 18 15 755
Titles:
ÅLAND

ALAVIESKAN VIRI RY 1794013
PL 20 / Pääskyntie 1, 85201 ALAVIESKA
Tel: 8 43 01 59 **Fax:** 8 43 12 40
Titles:
ALAVIESKA

A-LEHDET OY 1789260
Risto Rytin tie 33, 00081 A-LEHDET **Tel:** 9 75 961
Fax: 9 75 98 31 01
Titles:
APU
AVOTAKKA
DEMI
EEVA
KAUNEUS & TERVEYS
MAKU
MEIDÄN MÖKKI
MEIDÄN TALO
OP-POHJOLA
TUULILASI
URHEILULEHTI
VIHERPIHA
VOI HYVIN

ALEKSANTERI-INSTITUUTTI 1793167
Aleksanteri-instituutti, PL 42/ Unioninkatu 33, 00014 HELSINGIN YLIOPISTO **Tel:** 9 19 12 41 75
Fax: 9 19 12 36 15
Titles:
IDÄNTUTKIMUS

ALKO OY 670661
PL 33/ Salmisaarenaukio 1, 00181 HELSINKI
Tel: 20 71 111 **Fax:** 20 71 15 263
Titles:
ETIKETTI

ALLER MEDIA OY 1789348
PL 124/ Pursimiehenkatu 29-31 A, 00151 HELSINKI **Tel:** 9 86 21 70 00 **Fax:** 9 86 21 71 77
Titles:
7 PÄIVÄÄ
FIT
KATSO!
KOTI JA KEITTIÖ
MISS MIX

ALLERGIA-JA ASTMALIITTO 7699
Paciuksenkatu 19, 00270 HELSINKI
Tel: 9 47 33 51 **Fax:** 9 47 33 53 90
Titles:
ALLERGIA & ASTMA

ALMA 360 ASIAKASMEDIA 1792346
Alma 360 Asiakasmedia, PL 502/ Munkkiniemen puistotie 25, 00101 HELSINKI **Tel:** 10 66 51 02
Titles:
X-LEHTI

ALMA 360 ASIAKASMEDIA OY 1792342
Alma 360 Asiakasmedia Oy, PL 502/ Munkkiniemen puistotie 25, 5. krs, 00101 HELSINKI **Tel:** 10 66 51 02 **Fax:** 10 66 52 533
Titles:
YHTEISHYVÄ

ALMA MEDIA 1791501
PL 1364/ Eteläesplanadi 20, 6. krs, 00101 HELSINKI **Tel:** 10 66 52 800 **Fax:** 10 66 52 423
Titles:
ALMA MEDIAN HELSINGIN TOIMITUS

AMMATTIVIESTIT OY 1789844
Itkonniemenkatu 13 A, 70500 KUOPIO
Tel: 17 36 86 000
Titles:
TEOLLISUUSSUOMI

ARBETARFÖRLAGET AB 1789853
PB 140/ Aspnäsgatan 7-9, 00531 HELSINGFORS **Tel:** 9 77 32 844 **Fax:** 9 70 18 845
Titles:
ARBETARBLADET

ASEMAN LAPSET RY 671599
Vuorikatu 8 A 14, 00100 HELSINKI **Tel:** 9 65 47 40
Fax: 9 68 42 05 10
Titles:
ASEMAN LAPSET

AUTO- JA KULJETUSALAN TYÖNTEKIJÄLIITTO AKT 1790960
PL 313/ John Stenbergin ranta 6, 00531 HELSINKI **Tel:** 9 61 31 12 38 **Fax:** 9 61 31 12 97
Titles:
AKT

AUTO-BON OY 1619214
PL 115, 01511 VANTAA
Titles:
VOILÀ CITROËN

B YHTIÖT OY 1789865
Nuijamiestentie 5 A, 00400 HELSINKI
Tel: 9 54 76 21 **Fax:** 9 54 76 22 46
Titles:
AJOLINJA
AUTO, TEKNIIKKA JA KULJETUS

BBM OY 1791941
PL3/ Laturinkuja 10, 02601 ESPOO
Tel: 9 54 21 01 00 **Fax:** 9 54 21 01 32
Titles:
KAUPAN MAAILMA

BIODYNAMINEN YHDISTYS RY 7625
Uudenmaankatu 25 A 4, 00120 HELSINKI
Tel: 9 64 41 60 **Fax:** 9 68 02 591
Titles:
DEMETER-LEHTI

BM MEDIA OY 1789854
Sinikalliontie 11, 02630 ESPOO **Tel:** 9 42 47 38 60
Fax: 9 45 22 206
Titles:
ASUNTOINFO.NET

BONNIER JULKAISUT OY 1774149
Siltasaarenkatu 18-20 A, 00530 HELSINKI
Tel: 20 76 08 500 **Fax:** 20 76 08 520
Titles:
DIVAANI

BONNIER PUBLICATIONS OY 1790303
Siltasaarenkatu 18-20 A, 00530 HELSINKI
Tel: 20 76 08 500 **Fax:** 20 76 08 520
Titles:
DIGIKUVA
KOTIMIKRO
KUNTO PLUS
NATIONAL GEOGRAPHIC
OLIVIA
TEE ITSE
TIETEEN KUVALEHTI

BRIDAL PUBLISHING GROUP 1782123
Vattuniemenranta 2, 00210 HELSINKI
Tel: 9 32 95 11 00 **Fax:** 9 32 95 11 09
Titles:
HÄÄT JA JUHLAT

C & E ROSENBERG OY 1789848
Purjeentekijänkuja 7 B 15, 00210 HELSINKI
Tel: 9 45 59 17 24 **Fax:** 9 45 59 17 23
Titles:
A. VOGELIN TERVEYSUUTISET

CADI OY 1789301
Ruosilankuja 3 A, 00390 HELSINKI
Tel: 9 54 22 65 00 **Fax:** 9 54 22 66 00
Titles:
CAD-Q NEWS

CITYPRESS OY/ JANTON 1789980
PL 80/ Hankasuontie 3, 00391 HELSINKI
Tel: 9 56 15 63 00 **Fax:** 9 56 15 63 21
Titles:
CITY-HELSINKI
CITY-JYVÄSKYLÄ

COUNTRY MEDIA OY 1793130
Liisankatu 11 C 69, 28100 PORI **Tel:** 2 63 24 310
Fax: 2 63 24 313
Titles:
FARMI

CRUISE MEDIA OY LTD. 1784118
Palokuja 6 A 17, 04250 KERAVA **Tel:** 50 51 49 085
Titles:
CRUISE BUSINESS REVIEW

CSC-TIETEELLINEN LASKENTA OY 1789846
PL 405/ Keilaranta 14, 02101 ESPOO
Tel: 9 45 72 001 **Fax:** 9 45 72 302
Titles:
@CSC-SIVUSTO

CSC-TIETEEN TIETOTEKNIIKAN KESKUS OY 1788324
PL 405/ Keilaranta 14, 02101 ESPOO
Tel: 9 45 72 001 **Fax:** 9 45 72 302
Titles:
CSC NEWS
TIETEEN TIETOTEKNIIKKA

DIALOGI OY 1728944
PL 410/ Risto Rytin tie 33, 00811 HELSINKI
Tel: 9 42 42 73 30 **Fax:** 9 42 42 73 33
Titles:
BIRKA
CLUB ONE
MAALI!
MAATILAN PIRKKA - ÅKER BIRKA
PIRKKA

DRAKA NK CABLES OY 671259
PL 419/ Kimmeltie 1, 00101 HELSINKI
Tel: 10 56 61 **Fax:** 10 56 63 394
Titles:
JOHDIN

DREAM CATCHER PRODUCTIONS 1622406
Vilhonvuorenkatu 11 B, 00500 HELSINKI
Tel: 9 68 96 74 20 **Fax:** 9 68 96 74 21
Titles:
SIX DEGREES

DRIFTSINGENJÖRSFÖR-BUNDET I FINLAND 674959
PB 75/ Banvaktsgatan 2, 00521 HELSINGFORS
Tel: 9 47 67 717 **Fax:** 9 47 67 73 47
Titles:
GULA BLADET

ECONOMIC SOCIETY OF FINLAND 1793166
ISES/ Åbo Akademi, Fänriksgatan 3 B, 20500
ÅBO **Tel:** 2 21 54 163
Titles:
EKONOMISKA SAMFUNDETS TIDSKRIFT

EDITUS OY 671240
Meritullinkatu 11 K, 00170 HELSINKI
Tel: 9 26 00 470 **Fax:** 9 26 00 471
Titles:
HÄÄT-LEHTI

EGMONT KUSTANNUS OY AB 1789369
PL 1269/ Vuorikatu 14 A, 00101 HELSINKI
Tel: 20 13 32 222 **Fax:** 20 13 32 360
Titles:
ELÄINMAAILMA KOIRAT
HEVOSHULLU
JÄÄKIEKKOLEHTI

EKENÄS TRYCKERI AB 1790158
PB 26/ Genvägen 4, 10601 EKENÄS
Tel: 19 22 28 22 **Fax:** 19 22 28 14
Titles:
VÄSTRA NYLAND
VÄSTRA NYLAND HANGÖ
VÄSTRA NYLAND KARIS
VÄSTRA NYLAND KYRKSLÄTT

EKOKEM OY AB 671329
PL 181/ Kuulojankatu 1, 11101 RIIHIMÄKI
Tel: 10 75 51 000 **Fax:** 10 75 51 300
Titles:
EKO-ASIAA

ELÄKELÄISET RY 670928
Mechelininkatu 20 A 1, 00100 HELSINKI
Tel: 20 74 33 610 **Fax:** 20 74 33 619
Titles:
ELÄKELÄINEN

ELÄKELIITTO RY 1791610
Kalevankatu 61, 00180 HELSINKI
Tel: 9 72 57 11 00 **Fax:** 9 72 57 11 98
Titles:
EL-SANOMAT

ELÄKETURVAKESKUS 671356
Kirjurinkatu 3, 00065 ELÄKETURVAKESKUS
Tel: 10 75 11 **Fax:** 10 75 12 205
Titles:
ARBETSPENSION
TYÖELÄKE
TYÖVOITTO

ELÄKKEENSAAJIEN KESKUSLIITTO EKL RY 1791953
PL 168/ Haapaniemenkatu 14, 2 krs, 00531
HELSINKI **Tel:** 9 61 26 840 **Fax:** 9 17 06 99
Titles:
ELÄKKEENSAAJA

ELIMÄEN SANOMAT OY 1790015
PL 10/Vanhamaantie 7, 47201 ELIMÄKI
Tel: 5 74 00 500 **Fax:** 57400510
Titles:
ELIMÄEN SANOMAT

ELONKEHÄ RY 671286
Aurinkotehdas, Kirkkotie 6-10, 20540 TURKU
Tel: 2 23 35 930 **Fax:** 2 23 71 670
Titles:
ELONKEHÄ

ENERGIANSÄÄSTÖN PALVELUKESKUS MOTIVA 671491
PL 489/ Urho Kekkosenkatu 4-6 A, 00101
HELSINKI **Tel:** 424 28 11 **Fax:** 424 28 12 99
Titles:
MOTIVA XPRESS

EQ PANKKI OY 1791297
Acacom Print Oy, Erottajankatu 15-17, 00130
HELSINKI **Tel:** 20 74 39 900
Titles:
MEKLARI

ERNST & YOUNG OY 1639948
Elielinaukio 5 B, 00100 HELSINKI
Tel: 20 72 80 190
Titles:
ERNIE

ESAB 1600518
Ruosilantie 18, 00390 HELSINKI **Tel:** 9 54 77 61
Fax: 9 54 77 771
Titles:
HITSAUSUUTISET

ESAN KIRJAPAINO OY 1790547
PL 80/ Ilmarisentie 7, 15101 LAHTI **Tel:** 3 75 751
Fax: 3 75 75 469
Titles:
ETELÄ-SUOMEN SANOMAT

ESAN PAIKALLISLEHDET OY 1790485
PL 10/Lampikatu 8, 18101 HEINOLA
Tel: 3 75 75 05 **Fax:** 3 75 75 765
Titles:
ITÄ-HÄME
UUSI LAHTI

ESV-JULKAISUT OY 1782884
Patteristonkatu 2 C, 50100 MIKKELI
Tel: 15 33 70 111
Titles:
ETEVÄ-SAVO

ETELÄ-SAVON PAIKALLISLEHDET OY 1789888
Joroisniementie 4, 79600 JOROINEN
Tel: 15 35 03 154 **Fax:** 15 35 03 151
Titles:
JOROISTEN LEHTI
JUVAN LEHTI
KANGASNIEMEN KUNNALLISLEHTI
PURUVESI

ETUOVI.COM 1789223
PL 368/ Aleksanterinkatu 9, 00101 HELSINKI
Tel: 10 66 51 05 **Fax:** 10 66 55 019
Titles:
ASUNTOMEDIA

EXPRESSBUS 1649516
Lauttasaarentie 8, 00200 HELSINKI
Tel: 9 68 27 01
Titles:
EXPRESSI

FAKTAPRO OY 1792964
PL 4/ Jänismäki 1 A, 02941 ESPOO
Tel: 9 54 79 74 10 **Fax:** 9 51 22 033
Titles:
TOSIMIES

FAKTAVISA AB 670606
Tampereentie 484, 33880 LEMPÄÄLÄ
Tel: 20 75 79 700 **Fax:** 20 75 79 701
Titles:
EUROMETALLI
EUROPÖRSSI

FAZER AMICA OY 1793393
PL 37/ Laulukuja 6, 00421 HELSINKI
Tel: 20 72 96 000 **Fax:** 20 72 96 012
Titles:
RAKKAUDESTA RUOKAAN

FENNIA-RYHMÄ 671517
Televisiokatu 1, 00017 FENNIA **Tel:** 10 50 31
Fax: 10 50 35 300
Email: info@fennia.fi
Web site: http://www.fennia.fi
Titles:
FENNIA

FIN-EL OY 1792122
Merikasarminkatu 7, 00160 HELSINKI
Tel: 9 66 89 850 **Fax:** 9 65 75 62
Titles:
SÄHKÖ & TELE

FINLANDS SVENSKA MARTHAFÖRBUND RF 671020
Lönnrotsgatan 3 A 7, 00120 HELSINGFORS
Tel: 9 69 62 250 **Fax:** 9 68 01 188
Titles:
MARTHA

FINNET FOCUS FINLAND OY 670726
PL 949/Sinebrychoffinkatu 11, 00101 HELSINKI
Tel: 9 31 53 15 **Fax:** 9 31 53 82 44
Titles:
FINNET KOTIASIAKASLEHTI
FINNET YRITYSASIAKASLEHTI

FINNISH BUSINESS & SOCIETY RY 1728923
Mikonkatu 17, 5 krs, 00100 HELSINKI
Titles:
VASTUULLINEN VAIKUTTAJA

FINNISH ECONOMIC ASSOCIATION 7556
Palkansaajien tutkimuslaitos, Pitkänsillanranta 3
A, 00530 HELSINKI **Tel:** 9 25 35 73 45
Titles:
KANSANTALOUDELLINEN AIKAKAUSKIRJA

FINNISH GOLF CONSULTING OY 1793175
Viestintä Tarmio Oy, Kivenlahdenkatu 1 B, 5 krs,
02320 ESPOO **Tel:** 9 80 16 849 **Fax:** 9 80 16 806
Titles:
SUOMEN GOLFLEHTI

FINNISH SOCIETY OF FOREST SCIENCE 7679
PL 18/ Jokiniemenkuja 1, 01301 VANTAA
Tel: 10 21 12 144 **Fax:** 10 21 12 102
Titles:
SILVA FENNICA

FINNMETKO OY 1791756
Sitratie 7, 00420 HELSINKI **Tel:** 40 90 09 410
Fax: 9 56 30 329
Titles:
KONEYRITTÄJÄ

FINN-NICHE LTD 675024
Aleksanterinkatu 17, 00100 HELSINKI
Tel: 9 24 14 511 **Fax:** 9 24 14 611
Titles:
FINN NICHE

FINPRO RY 1791726
Viestintätoimisto Sanakunta Oy, Kristiinankatu 3
B, 20100 TURKU **Tel:** 20 46 951
Titles:
FINPRO IN FRONT

FINSKA LÄKARSÄLLSKAPET 671540
PB 82/ Johannesbergsvägen 8, 00251
HELSINGFORS **Tel:** 9 47 76 80 90 **Fax:** 9 43 62 055
Titles:
FINSKA LÄKARESÄLLSKAPETS HANDLINGAR

FÖRLAGS AB FORUM FÖR EKONOMI OCH TEKNIK 1791724
Mannerheimvägen 20 A, 7 vån, 00100
HELSINGFORS **Tel:** 9 54 95 55 00
Fax: 9 54 95 55 77
Titles:
FORUM FÖR EKONOMI OCH TEKNIK

FÖRLAGS AB SYDVÄSTKUSTEN 1789817
PB 211/ Auragatan 1 B, 3 vån, 20101 ÅBO
Tel: 2 27 49 900 **Fax:** 2 23 11 394
Titles:
ÅBO UNDERRÄTTELSER
PARGAS KUNGÖRELSER - PARAISTEN KUULUTUKSET

FORMA MAGAZINES OY 1790297
Elimäenkatu 17-19, 6 krs., 00510 HELSINKI
Tel: 9 77 39 51 **Fax:** 9 77 39 53 21
Titles:
KOTIVINKKI

FORMA MESSUT OY 7638
Mannerheimintie 40 D 82, 00100 HELSINKI
Tel: 10 82 09 800 **Fax:** 10 82 09 806
Titles:
FORMA & FURNITURE

FORMA PUBLISHING GROUP OY 1789878
Elimäenkatu 17-19, 6 krs., 00510 HELSINKI
Tel: 9 77 39 51 **Fax:** 9 77 39 53 99
Titles:
TALO & KOTI
TRENDI

FÖRSAMLINGSFÖRBUNDETS FÖRLAGS AB 1789547
Mannerheimvägen 16 A 9, 00100 HELSINGFORS
Tel: 9 61 26 15 49 **Fax:** 9 27 84 138
Titles:
KYRKPRESSEN

FORSSAN KIRJAPAINO OY 622949
PL 38/ Esko Aaltosen katu 2, 30101 FORSSA
Tel: 3 41 551 **Fax:** 3 41 55 724
Titles:
FORSSAN LEHTI

FORUM-LEHDET OY 1638622
PL 226/ Nilatie 3, 50101 MIKKELI **Tel:** 15 36 63 91
Fax: 15 36 63 94
Titles:
AGRIFORUM

FOURPRESS OY 671091
PL 69/ Jäämerentie 4 A, 99601 SODANKYLÄ
Tel: 16 61 29 11 **Fax:** 16 61 30 00
Titles:
SOMPIO

FUJITSU SERVICES OY 670627
PL 100/ Valimotie 16, 00012 FUJITSU
Tel: 45 78 800
Titles:
NET

FUTURE CAD OY 674242
Sahaajankatu 26 A, 00880 HELSINKI
Tel: 9 47 85 400 **Fax:** 9 47 85 45 00
Titles:
FUTURE MAAILMA

GARANTIFÖRENINGEN FÖR FINLANDS FREDSFÖRBUND 671289
Fredsstationen, Loktorget 3, 00520
HELSINGFORS **Tel:** 9 14 29 15 **Fax:** 9 14 72 97
Titles:
FREDSPOSTEN

GRAFISKA INDUSTRI AB 1794168
Blåbergsvägen 5 B, 02630 ESBO **Tel:** 9 50 23 490
Fax: 95023486
Titles:
FRISK BRIS

HAAPAJÄRVI-SEURA RY 1790272
PL 74/ Puistokatu 37, 85801 HAAPAJÄRVI
Tel: 8 77 27 500 **Fax:** 87727555
Titles:
MAASELKÄ

HÄMEEN SANOMAT OY 1789931
PL 530/ Vanajatie 7, 13111 HÄMEENLINNA
Tel: 3 61 511 **Fax:** 3 61 51 492
Titles:
HÄMEEN SANOMAT
HÄMEEN SANOMAT RIIHIMÄKI

HÄMEEN VIESTINTÄ OY 1790066
Lamminraitti 25, 16900 LAMMI **Fax:** 3 63 32 382
Titles:
KESKI-HÄME

HÄMEENKYRÖN SANOMAT OY 1793934
PL 13 / Nuijamiestentie 1, 39101 HÄMEENKYRÖ
Tel: 3 31 43 31 00 **Fax:** 3 37 15 788
Titles:
HÄMEENKYRÖN SANOMAT

HELSINGIN ALUEEN INSINÖÖRIT HI RY 670642
Tietäjäntie 4, 02130 ESPOO **Tel:** 9 47 74 540
Fax: 9 47 74 54 42
Titles:
UUDENMAAN ALUEEN INSINÖÖRI

HELSINGIN CC KUSTANNUS OY 1792984
PL 313/ Linnanrakentajantie 4, 00811 HELSINKI
Tel: 50 57 67 062
Titles:
KUNTA JA INVESTOINNIT

HELSINGIN ENERGIA 671365
Kampinkuja 2, 00090 HELEN **Tel:** 9 61 71
Fax: 9 61 72 360
Titles:
HELEN
HELEN B.

HELSINGIN KAUPUNGINTEATTERI 1791042
Ensi Linja 2, 00530 HELSINKI **Tel:** 9 39 401
Fax: 9 39 40 404
Titles:
TEATTERIIN

HELSINGIN KAUPUNKI 1792022
PL 1/ Pohjoisesplanadi 11-13, 00099 HELSINGIN
KAUPUNKI **Tel:** 9 31 01 641 **Fax:** 9 31 03 65 85
Titles:
HELSINKI-INFO

HELSINGIN PUBLICATIO OY 674405
Lammaslammentie 13, 01710 VANTAA
Tel: 9 70 12 565
Titles:
TIETOTEKNIIKAN TUOTEUUTISET

HELSINGIN RESERVIUPSEERIPIIRI RY 1794183
Döbelninkatu 2, 00260 HELSINKI
Tel: 9 40 56 20 80 **Fax:** 9 44 86 59
Titles:
HELSINGIN RESERVIN SANOMAT

HELSINGIN TIETOJENKÄSITTELY-YHDISTYS RY (HETK 1782246
Lars Sonckin kaari 12, 02600 ESPOO
Tel: 400 83 26 98 **Fax:** 20 74 19 889
Titles:
HETKY

HELSINKI EXPERT OY 1776806
Pohjoinen Makasiinikatu 4, 00130 HELSINKI
Tel: 9 22 88 13 33 **Fax:** 9 22 88 13 99
Titles:
HELSINKI THIS WEEK

HENGITYSLIITTO HELI RY 1794077
PL 40/ Oltermannintie 8, 00621 HELSINKI
Tel: 20 75 75 000
Titles:
HENGITYS

HJK HELSINKI 676660
Finnair Stadium, Urheilukatu 5, 00250 HELSINKI
Tel: 9 74 21 66 00 **Fax:** 9 74 21 66 66
Titles:
KLUBI

HSO-SIHTEERIT RY 670589
Eerikinkatu 20 C 37, 00100 HELSINKI
Tel: 9 58 65 020 **Fax:** 9 58 65 021
Titles:
SULKAKYNÄ

HSS MEDIA AB 1748486
PB 22/Jakobsgatan 13, 68601 JAKOBSTAD
Tel: 6 78 48 800 **Fax:** 6 78 48 883
Titles:
ÖSTERBOTTENS TIDNING
ÖSTERBOTTENS TIDNING NYKARLEBY
PIETARSAAREN SANOMAT
VASABLADET
VASABLADET HELSINGFORS
VASABLADET JAKOBSTAD-NYKARLEBY
VASABLADET KARLEBY
VASABLADET MALAX KORSNÄS
VASABLADET NÄRPES
VASABLADET ORAVAIS-VÖRÅ-MAXMO

H-TOWN OY 700578
PL 1378/ Museokatu 44 C 115, 00101 HELSINKI
Tel: 9 43 69 37 57 **Fax:** 9 43 69 37 58
Titles:
PELAA!

HUFVUDSTADSBLADET AB 1789304
PB 217/ Mannerheimvägen 18, 00101
HELSINGFORS **Tel:** 9 12 531 **Fax:** 9 12 53 500
Titles:
TV RADIO BLADET

HUITTISTEN SANOMALEHTI OY 1793936
PL 36/Karpintie 13, 32701 HUITTINEN
Tel: 2 55 54 200 **Fax:** 2 55 54 220
Titles:
LAUTTAKYLÄ

IF SUURASIAKKAAT 1634303
Niittyportti 4 A, 00025 IF
Titles:
RISK CONSULTING

IITINLEHTI OY 1793938
PL 37/ Kauppakatu 6, 47401 KAUSALA
Tel: 5 32 60 355 **Fax:** 53260321
Titles:
IITINSEUTU

IKAALINEN OY 1790321
PL 24 / Keskisenkatu 1, 39501 IKAALINEN
Tel: 3 45 89 300 **Fax:** 3 45 87 736
Titles:
POHJOIS-SATAKUNTA

ILKKA OY 1789739
Kirjapainonkuja 2, 63300 ALAVUS
Tel: 6 24 77 576 **Fax:** 6 24 77 864
Titles:
ILKKA ALAVUS
ILKKA KAUHAJOKI
JURVAN SANOMAT

ILMAJOKI-LEHTI 1790179
PL 12 / Mikontie 3, 60801 ILMAJOKI
Tel: 6 42 44 800 **Fax:** 6 42 44 834
Titles:
ILMAJOKI-LEHTI

ILMANSUOJELUYHDISTYS RY 671074
PL 136, 00215 HELSINKI **Tel:** 9 27 12 076
Fax: 9 34 45 274
Titles:
ILMANSUOJELU

ILMATORJUNTAUPSEERIYHDISTYS RY 671337
PL 5, 04301 TUUSULA **Tel:** 9 18 16 21 11
Fax: 9 18 16 23 16
Titles:
ILMATORJUNTAUPSEERI

ILVES RY/ JALKAPALLOJAOSTO 1788343
Rieväkatu 2, 33540 TAMPERE **Tel:** 207 48 26 80
Fax: 3 26 12 614
Titles:
ILVES MURISEE

IMAGE KUSTANNUS OY 1790172
PL 212/ Risto Rytin tie 33, 00811 HELSINKI
Tel: 9 75 96 779 **Fax:** 9 75 98 38 04
Titles:
IMAGE
MONDO

I-MEDIAT OY 1790020
PL 60/Koulukatu 10, 60101 SEINÄJOKI
Tel: 6 24 77 865 **Fax:** 6 24 77 869
Titles:
ETELÄ-POHJANMAA
ILKKA
POHJALAINEN

INCHCAPE MOTORS FINLAND OY 1792336
Vetokuja 1, 01610 VANTAA **Tel:** 20 77 04 300
Titles:
MAZDA

INFO CENTER FINLAND ICF OY 1644550
Info Center Finland Oy, Kantolankatu 7, 13110
HÄMEENLINNA **Tel:** 3 65 700 **Fax:** 3 63 36 430
Titles:
INTERNET-UUTISET

INMIND PRODUCTION OY 1784536
Antbackantie 4 D 22, 02400 KIRKKONUMMI
Tel: 400 39 26 60
Titles:
MAINE

INNOVA MAGAZINES 1776828
Sahaajankatu 20-22 D, 00880 HELSINKI
Tel: 9 42 41 34 10
Titles:
KAUNIIT KODIT

INNOVA MAGAZINES OY 1652832
Takkatie 6, 00370 HELSINKI **Tel:** 9 42 41 34 10
Fax: 9 42 41 34 11
Titles:
SISUSTA.

INTRUM JUSTITIA OY 676835
PL 47/ Hitsaajankatu 20, 00811 HELSINKI
Tel: 9 22 91 11 **Fax:** 9 22 91 19 11
Titles:
INTRESSI

INVALIDILIITTO RY 1789263
Omnipress Oy, Hämeentie 13 B, 00530
HELSINKI **Tel:** 9 75 99 620 **Fax:** 9 75 99 62 30
Titles:
IT INVALIDITYÖ

ITÄ-SAVO OY 1791500
PL 101/ Olavinkatu 60, 57101 SAVONLINNA
Tel: 15 35 03 400 **Fax:** 15 35 03 444
Titles:
ITÄ-SAVO

ITELLA OYJ 670979
PL 1, 00011 ITELLA **Tel:** 20 45 11
Fax: 20 45 15 645
Titles:
POSTIA SINULLE

JAAMEDIA 1776821
PL 57, 33711 TAMPERE **Tel:** 50 56 91 969
Titles:
TANSSIVIIHDE

JALASJÄRVI OY 1789891
PL 53 / Torikuja 9, 61601 JALASJÄRVI
Tel: 6 45 65 100 **Fax:** 6 45 61 420
Titles:
JP KUNNALLISSANOMAT

JÄRVISEUTU-SEURA RY 1790180
PL 29/ Maneesintie 4, 62601 LAPPAJÄRVI
Tel: 20 79 40 510 **Fax:** 20 79 40 512
Titles:
JÄRVISEUDUN SANOMAT

JMS NORDIC OY 1774794
Jäspilänkatu 28 D, 04250 KERAVA
Tel: 9 85 61 93 00 **Fax:** 9 85 61 93 01
Titles:
MP MAAILMA

JOENSUUN KUSTANNUS OY YRITYSMAAILMA 671186
Teollisuuskatu 11, 80100 JOENSUU
Tel: 10 82 05 700 **Fax:** 10 82 05 750
Titles:
YRITYSMAAILMA

JOKILAAKSOJEN KUSTANNUS OY 1789979
Tähtelänkuja 2, 86600 HAAPAVESI
Tel: 20 75 04 640 **Fax:** 207504641
Titles:
HAAPAVESI-LEHTI
KALAJOKILAAKSO
LESTIJOKI
NIVALA-LEHTI
PERHONJOKILAAKSO

JOUTSAN SEUTU OY 1790176
PL 15/ Jousitie 31, 19651 JOUTSA
Tel: 20 18 76 100 **Fax:** 20 18 76 101
Titles:
JOUTSAN SEUTU
PAIKALLISUUTISET

JOUTSEN MEDIA OY 1775529
PL 52 / Lekatie 4, 90101 OULU **Tel:** 8 53 70 022
Fax: 8 53 70 327
Titles:
OULU-LEHTI

JULKAISU BOOKERS OY 1788357
Kumppania Oy, Pohjoisranta 11, 28100 PORI
Tel: 9 23 16 31 21
Titles:
TERVE POTILAS

JULKIS- JA YKSITYISALOJEN TOIMIHENKILÖLIITTO JYTY 670717
Asemamiehenkatu 4, 00520 HELSINKI
Tel: 20 78 93 799
Titles:
JYTY

JULKISTEN JA HYVINVOINTIALOJEN LIITTO JHL RY 1774138
PL 101/ Sörnäisten rantatie 23, 00531 HELSINKI
Tel: 10 77 031 **Fax:** 107703410
Titles:
MOTIIVI

JUUKA-SEURA RY 1793309
Juuantie 9 A, 83900 JUUKA **Tel:** 10 83 54 004
Fax: 132481310
Titles:
VAAROJEN SANOMAT

JYVÄSKYLÄN KAUPUNKISEURAKUNTA 1790215
Yliopistokatu 12 B, 40100 JYVÄSKYLÄ
Tel: 14 63 67 80 **Fax:** 14 63 67 85
Titles:
HENKI & ELÄMÄ

JYVÄSKYLÄN YLIOPISTON NYKYKULTTUURIN TUTKIMUSKESKUS 1793168
Nykykulttuurin tutkimuskeskus, PL 35, 40014 JYVÄSKYLÄN YLIOPISTO **Tel:** 14 26 01 317
Fax: 14 26 01 311
Titles:
KULTTUURINTUTKIMUS

KAARINAN LEHTI OY 1790174
PL 73/Pyhän Katariinantie 7, 20781 KAARINA
Tel: 2 58 88 600 **Fax:** 22743610
Titles:
KAARINA

KAATUNEITTEN OMAISTEN LIITTO RY 671179
PL 600/ Ratamestarinkatu 9 C, 00521 HELSINKI
Tel: 2 25 88 790 **Fax:** 2 25 88 792
Titles:
HUOLTOVIESTI

KADETTIKUNTA RY 670554
Eino Leinonkatu 12 E 64, 00250 HELSINKI
Tel: 9 49 09 32 **Fax:** 9 44 62 62
Titles:
KYLKIRAUTA

KALATALOUDEN KESKUSLIITTO 670836
Malmin kauppatie 26, 00700 HELSINKI
Tel: 9 68 44 590 **Fax:** 9 68 44 59 59
Titles:
SUOMEN KALASTUSLEHTI

KALEVA KUSTANNUS OY 1789954
Lekatie 6, 90510 OULU **Tel:** 20 75 45 700
Fax: 20 75 45 701
Titles:
FORUM 24
KALEVA
KALEVA KEMI-TORNIO
KALEVA KUUSAMO
KALEVA RAAHE
KALEVA VAALA
KALEVA YLIVIESKA

KÄLVIÄN SEUDUN SANOMAT OY 1790270
Kälviäntie 36, 68300 KÄLVIÄ **Tel:** 6 82 43 822
Fax: 68243848
Titles:
KÄLVIÄN SEUDUN SANOMAT

KAMERASEURA RY 1789754
Lastenkodinkatu 5, 00180 HELSINKI
Tel: 9 68 11 490 **Fax:** 9 69 40 166
Titles:
KAMERA-LEHTI

KANGASALAN SANOMALEHTI OY 1793935
PL 40/Myllystenpohjantie 2, 36201 KANGASALA
Tel: 3 37 76 900 **Fax:** 3 37 70 668
Titles:
KANGASALAN SANOMAT

KANSALLINEN SENIORILIITTO RY. 1789870
Kansakoulukatu 5 A 6, 00100 HELSINKI
Tel: 20 74 88 444 **Fax:** 9 75 30 931
Titles:
PATINA

KANSALLISKUSTANNUS OY 1794315
Runeberginkatu 5 B, 7. krs, 00100 HELSINKI
Tel: 20 74 88 488 **Fax:** 20 74 88 507
Titles:
NYKYPÄIVÄ

KANSAN UUTISET OY 1789327
Väinönkatu 28 B 14, 40100 JYVÄSKYLÄ
Tel: 9 75 96 02 51 **Fax:** 975960319
Titles:
KANSAN UUTISET JYVÄSKYLÄ
KANSAN UUTISET TAMPERE
KANSAN UUTISET TURKU
KANSAN UUTISET VERKKOLEHTI
KANSAN UUTISET VIIKKOLEHTI
SATAKUNNAN TYÖ

KANSANELÄKELAITOS 671249
PL 450/ Nordenskiöldinkatu 12, 00101 HELSINKI
Tel: 20 63 411 **Fax:** 20 63 45 058
Titles:
ELÄMÄSSÄ - MITT I ALLT

KARAS-SANA OY 1791942
Kaisaniemenkatu 8, 4. krs, 00100 HELSINKI
Tel: 20 76 81 700
Titles:
SANA

KARPRINT OY 1789788
Vanha Turuntie 371, 03150 HUHMARI
Tel: 9 41 39 73 00
Titles:
ENERGIA JA YMPÄRISTÖ
IKÄPLUS
KIINTEISTÖ JA ISÄNNÖINTI
SUOMI+
TALOMESTARI

KAUHAJOEN KUNNALLISLEHTI OY 1789405
PL 5 / Puistotie 25, 61801 KAUHAJOKI
Tel: 6 23 57 100 **Fax:** 6 23 12 210
Titles:
KAUHAJOKI-LEHTI

KAUPPALEHTI OY 1789981
PL 189 / Eteläesplanadi 20, 00101 HELSINKI
Tel: 10 66 51 01
Titles:
KAUPPALEHTI
KAUPPALEHTI OPTIO

KAUPPAPUUTARHALIITTO RY JA PUUTARHALIITTO 1791944
Larin Kyöstintie 6, 00650 HELSINKI
Tel: 9 72 88 210 **Fax:** 9 72 88 21 28
Titles:
PUUTARHA & KAUPPA

KAUPPATEKNIKKOLIITTO RY 670664
Uudenmaankatu 44, 00120 HELSINKI
Titles:
KAUPPATEKNIKKO

KAUPUNKILEHDET 1792396
PL 203/ Mannerheimintie 94, 00531 HELSINKI
Tel: 45 13 800 **Fax:** 9 43 65 00 13
Titles:
KAUPUNKISANOMAT

KAUPUNKILEHTI TAMPERELAINEN OY 1790486
PL 375/ Mustanlahdenkatu 3-7, 33101 TAMPERE **Tel:** 20 61 00 170 **Fax:** 20 77 03 040
Titles:
TAMPERELAINEN

KAUPUNKILEHTI TURKULAINEN OY 1789895
PL 396/ Läntinen Pitkäkatu 34, 4.krs, 20101 TURKU **Tel:** 20 61 00 160 **Fax:** 20 77 03 038
Titles:
TURKULAINEN

KD-MEDIAT OY 670918
Karjalankatu 2 C, 7 krs, 00520 HELSINKI
Tel: 9 34 88 22 30 **Fax:** 9 34 88 22 38
Titles:
KD

KEA-INVEST OY 670509
Itäportti 4 A, 02210 ESPOO **Tel:** 20 74 88 521
Fax: 9 85 50 586
Titles:
UUSI ESPOO

KESKI-KARJALAN KUSTANNUS OY 1789889
Parikkalantie 18, 59100 PARIKKALA
Tel: 10 23 08 900 **Fax:** 5 43 00 83
Titles:
PARIKKALAN-RAUTJÄRVEN SANOMAT

KESKI-KARJALAN PAIKALLISLEHTI OY 1790178
PL 34 / Pokentie 8, 82501 KITEE **Tel:** 13 68 48 411
Fax: 13 41 45 93
Titles:
KOTI-KARJALA

KESKINÄINEN ELÄKEVAKUUTUSKASSA ETERA 1792188
PL 20/Palkkatilanporttl 1, 00241 HELSINKI
Tel: 10 55 33 00 **Fax:** 10 55 33 477
Titles:
ETERA

KESKINÄINEN ELÄKEVAKUUTUSYHTIÖ ILMARINEN 1793207
Porkkalankatu 1, 00018 ILMARINEN
Tel: 10 28 411 **Fax:** 10 28 42 580
Titles:
ILMARINEN

KESKINÄINEN ELÄKEVAKUUTUSYHTIÖ VARMA 1792126
PL 1/ Salmisaarenranta 11, 00098 VARMA
Tel: 10 24 40 **Fax:** 10 24 45 037
Titles:
VARMA

KESKI-POHJANMAAN KIRJAPAINO OYJ 1781407
Kalajoentie 4, 85100 KALAJOKI **Tel:** 8 46 01 66
Fax: 8460543
Titles:
KALAJOEN SEUTU
KALAJOKI

KESKI-POHJANMAAN KUSTANNUS OY 1790159
PL 45/ Rantakatu 10, 67101 KOKKOLA
Tel: 20 75 04 400 **Fax:** 20 75 04 444
Titles:
KESKIPOHJANMAA
KESKIPOHJANMAA HAAPAJÄRVI
KESKIPOHJANMAA KALAJOKI
KESKIPOHJANMAA PIETARSAARI
KESKIPOHJANMAA VETELI
KESKIPOHJANMAA YLIVIESKA

KESKISUOMALAINEN OYJ 670324
PL 159/ Aholaidantie 3, 40101 JYVÄSKYLÄ
Tel: 14 62 20 00 **Fax:** 14 62 22 72
Titles:
KESKISUOMALAINEN
KESKISUOMALAINEN ÄÄNEKOSKI
KESKISUOMALAINEN JÄMSÄ
KESKISUOMALAINEN KEURUU
KESKISUOMALAINEN SAARIJÄRVI
SUNNUNTAISUOMALAINEN
SUUR-JYVÄSKYLÄN LEHTI
YRITYSMAAKUNTA

KESKI-SUOMEN VIIKKOLEHTI OY 1790173
PL 273/ Vasarakatu 1, 40101 JYVÄSKYLÄ
Tel: 10 42 34 900 **Fax:** 10 42 34 909
Titles:
KESKI-SUOMEN VIIKKO

KIINTEISTÖALAN KUSTANNUS OY 1783109
Annankatu 24, 2. krs., 00100 HELSINKI
Tel: 9 41 66 76 500 **Fax:** 9 64 87 45
Titles:
LOCUS

KIINTEISTÖALAN KUSTANNUS OY-REP LTD 1794102
Annankatu 24 A 4 krs, 00100 HELSINKI
Tel: 9 16 67 65 00 **Fax:** 9 64 87 45
Titles:
SUOMEN KIINTEISTÖLEHTI

KIURUVESI LEHTI OY 1781718
PL 69/ Hovinpelto 3, 74701 KIURUVESI
Tel: 17 77 07 700 **Fax:** 17 77 07 770
Titles:
KIURUVESI

KIVITEOLLISUUSLIITTO RY 674999
PL 381/ Unioninkatu 14, 00131 HELSINKI
Tel: 9 12 99 300 **Fax:** 9 12 99 414
Titles:
KIVI

Finland

K-KAUPPIASLIITTO RY 1790056
Kruunuvuorenkatu 5 A, 00160 HELSINKI
Tel: 10 53 010 Fax: 105336206
Titles:
KAUPPIAS
KEHITTYVÄ KAUPPA

KL KULJETUS&LOGISTIIKKA 1783032
Artturinkatu 2, 20200 TURKU Tel: 2 24 44 110
Fax: 2 23 22 382
Titles:
KULJETUS JA LOGISTIIKKA

KLIPPI DESIGN MANAGEMENT OY 671225
Hämeentie 153 B, 00560 HELSINKI
Tel: 9 66 15 11 Fax: 9 66 15 21
Titles:
PUUVENE

KL-KUSTANNUS OY 1789860
Toinen linja 14, 00530 HELSINKI Tel: 9 77 11
Titles:
KUNTALEHTI
KUNTATEKNIIKKA

KOILLISSANOMAT OY 1789407
Kitkantie 31-33, 93600 KUUSAMO
Tel: 8 86 00 620 Fax: 8 86 00 621
Titles:
KOILLISSANOMAT

KOKOOMUKSEN TAMPEREEN ALUEJÄRJESTÖ RY 1775528
Kuninkaankatu 13 B, 33210 TAMPERE
Tel: 50 56 45 054
Titles:
NYKY-TAMPERE

KOKOOMUKSEN VANTAAN KUNNALLISJÄRJESTÖ RY 1792936
Pakkalankuja 5, 01510 VANTAA Tel: 20 74 88 523
Titles:
UUSI VANTAA

KOLMIOKIRJA OY 7765
PL 246/Lekatie 6, 90101 OULU Tel: 8 53 70 033
Fax: 8 53 06 118
Titles:
REGINA
TOSI ELÄMÄÄ

KORPELAN VOIMA 697501
PL 13/ Junkalantie 15, 69101 KANNUS
Tel: 6 87 47 311 Fax: 6 87 04 08
Titles:
KORPELA PLUS

KORPILAHDEN PAIKALLISLEHTI OY 1792566
Kokkotie 11 C 17, 41800 KORPILAHTI
Tel: 40 19 77 400 Fax: 14822471
Titles:
KORPILAHTI

KOTIMAA OY 7811
PL 200/ Kirkkokatu 1, 02771 ESPOO
Tel: 20 75 42 000 Fax: 9 80 50 22 85
Titles:
ESSE
KIRKKO JA KOTI
RAUHAN TERVEHDYS
TAMPEREEN KIRKKOSANOMAT

KRAFT&KULTUR 1781679
Rauhankatu 16 A 26, 65100 VAASA
Tel: 6 35 77 750 Fax: 6 35 77 791
Titles:
HUILI

KSF MEDIA 1790328
PB 217/ Mannerheimvägen 18, 00101
HELSINGFORS Tel: 9 12 531 Fax: 9 64 29 30
Titles:
HUFVUDSTADSBLADET
PAPPER

KTA-YHTIÖT OY 1605428
Kutojantie 5, 02630 ESPOO Tel: 9 75 90 71
Fax: 9 78 55 54
Titles:
PISTE

KUHMOISTEN SANOMAT OY 1794009
PL 8 / Toritie 52, 17801 KUHMOINEN
Tel: 3 55 51 437 Fax: 3 55 56 538
Titles:
KUHMOISTEN SANOMAT

KUNTARAHOITUS OY 692686
PL 744/ Antinkatu 3 C, 5. krs, 00101 HELSINKI
Tel: 9 68 03 56 66 Fax: 9 68 03 56 69
Titles:
HUOMISTA TEHDÄÄN

KURIKKA-LEHTI OY 1791052
PL 50 / Laulajantie 4, 61301 KURIKKA
Tel: 6 45 15 500 Fax: 6 45 15 532
Titles:
KURIKKA-LEHTI

KURIRENS FÖRLAG AB 1794314
Skeppsgatan 3, 65101 VASA Tel: 6 31 81 900
Fax: 6 31 81 911
Titles:
KURIREN

KUSTANNUS OY AAMULEHTI 1789306
PL 327, 33101 TAMPERE Tel: 10 66 51 11
Fax: 10 66 53 140
Titles:
AAMULEHTI
AAMULEHTI MÄNTTÄ
AAMULEHTI MORO
AAMULEHTI ORIVESI
AAMULEHTI PARKANO
AAMULEHTI VALKEAKOSKI
AAMULEHTI VALO
AAMULEHTI VAMMALA

KUSTANNUS OY DEMARI 1790445
PL 338/ Haapaniemenkatu 7-9 B, 00531
HELSINKI Tel: 9 70 10 41 Fax: 9 70 10 567
Titles:
UUTISPÄIVÄ DEMARI
UUTISPÄIVÄ DEMARI TAMPERE
UUTISPÄIVÄ DEMARI TURKU
UUTISPÄIVÄ DEMARI VAASA
VIIKKO-HÄME

KUSTANNUS OY ILTALEHTI 1789350
PL 372/ Aleksanterinkatu 9, 00101 HELSINKI
Tel: 10 66 51 00 Fax: 9 17 73 13
Titles:
ILTALEHTI
ILTALEHTI ILONA
ILTALEHTI ONLINE
ILTALEHTI TURKU

KUSTANNUS OY JUOKSIJA 1789872
Olympiastadion, Eteläkaarre B 10, 00250
HELSINKI Tel: 9 43 42 040 Fax: 9 43 42 04 44
Titles:
JUOKSIJA

KUSTANNUS OY KANSAN TAHTO 1790441
PL 61/Mäkelininkatu 29, 90101 OULU
Tel: 8 53 71 724 Fax: 8 37 13 14
Titles:
KANSAN TAHTO

KUSTANNUS OY KOTIMAA 1789934
PL 279/ Hietalahdenranta 13, 00181 HELSINKI
Tel: 20 75 42 257
Titles:
ASKEL
KIRKKO & KAUPUNKI
KOTIMAA

KUSTANNUS OY MOBILISTI 7893
Niittyläntie 11, 00620 HELSINKI Tel: 9 27 27 100
Fax: 9 27 27 10 27
Titles:
MOBILISTI

KUSTANNUS OY PUOLANGAN DTP 1794016
PL 15 / Kajaanintie 5, 89201 PUOLANKA
Tel: 8 65 32 200 Fax: 86532229
Titles:
PUOLANKA-LEHTI

KUSTANNUS OY RAJATIETO 1792300
Salojärventie 36, 17950 KYLÄMÄ Tel: 3 55 58 101
Fax: 3 55 58 111
Titles:
ULTRA

KUSTANNUS OY RAKENNUSTEKNIIKKA 670653
Töölönkatu 4, 1.krs, 00100 HELSINKI
Tel: 20 71 20 600 Fax: 20 71 20 619
Titles:
RAKENNUSTEKNIIKKA

KUSTANNUS OY SUOMEN MIES 670563
Döbelninkatu 2, 00260 HELSINKI
Tel: 10 42 38 380 Fax: 10 42 38 389
Titles:
SUOMEN SOTILAS

KUSTANNUS OY TASE-BALANS 1789744
Fredrikinkatu 61 A 35, 00100 HELSINKI
Tel: 9 69 44 064 Fax: 9 69 49 215
Titles:
TILINTARKASTUS

KUSTANNUS OY VEROTUS 670727
PL 223/ Paasitie 12 A 1, 00101 HELSINKI
Tel: 9 66 20 06 Fax: 9 66 20 06
Titles:
VEROTUS

KUSTANNUS OY YHTEISSANOMAT 1789775
Peltoinlahdentie 24, 54800 SAVITAIPALE
Tel: 5 67 73 300 Fax: 5 47 72 211
Titles:
LÄNSI-SAIMAAN SANOMAT

KUSTANNUSHUONE OY 1654034
Finlaysoninkuja 22, 33210 TAMPERE
Tel: 3 22 38 688 Fax: 3 22 38 680
Titles:
KOTIAVAIN

KUSTANNUSOSAKEYHTIÖ KÄRKI 671312
Yliopistonkatu 12 a A 402, 20100 TURKU
Tel: 2 25 10 899
Titles:
SUE

KUSTANNUS-OSAKEYHTIÖ KOTIMAA OY 1791728
PL 922/ Eerikinkatu 3, 20101 TURKU
Tel: 2 26 17 111 Fax: 2 26 17 289
Titles:
KIRKKO JA ME, KYRKAN OCH VI

KUSTANNUSOSAKEYHTIÖ METSÄLEHTI 1789971
Soidinkuja 4, 00700 HELSINKI Tel: 20 77 29 120
Fax: 20 77 29 139
Titles:
METSÄLEHTI

KUSTANNUSOSAKEYHTIÖ PERHEMEDIAT OY 1782568
Purpuripolku 6, 00420 HELSINKI
Tel: 9 42 82 10 00 Fax: 9 42 82 10 30
Titles:
BUSINESS FINLAND

KYMEN SANOMALEHTI OY 7749
PL 27/Tornatorintie 3, 48101 KOTKA
Tel: 5 21 00 15 Fax: 5 21 00 52 06
Titles:
KYMEN SANOMAT
KYMEN SANOMAT HAMINA

KYMEN VIIKKOLEHTI OY 1789760
PL 140/ Kymenlaaksonkatu 10, 48101 KOTKA
Tel: 5 22 51 122 Fax: 5 21 81 157
Titles:
VIIKKO-ETEENPÄIN

KYMENVIESTINTÄ OY 1790160
PL 40/Lehtikaari 1, 45101 KOUVOLA
Tel: 5 28 00 14 Fax: 5 28 00 47 06
Titles:
KOUVOLAN SANOMAT
KOUVOLAN SANOMAT VALKEALA

KYMPPIMEDIAT OY 670666
Hämeenpuisto 44, 33200 TAMPERE
Tel: 3 22 34 035 Fax: 3 22 34 882
Titles:
KONEKURIIRI

KYMPPIVOIMA OY 1644314
PL 29/ Töölönkatu 4, 00101 HELSINKI
Tel: 10 21 02 10 Fax: 10 21 02 15
Titles:
KYMPPI

KYNÄMIES OY 629264
Kynämies Oy, Köydenpunojankatu 2 aD, 00180
HELSINKI Tel: 9 15 661 Fax: 915668600
Titles:
OMISTAJA & SIJOITTAJA

KYRÖNMAA-LAIHIA OY 1791051
PL 61/Ruutintie 2 C, 66401 LAIHIA
Tel: 6 47 76 116 Fax: 64776114
Titles:
KYRÖNMAA-LEHTI

LÄÄKEALAN TURVALLISUUS- JA KEHITTÄMISKESKUS FIMEA 1788312
PL 55, 00301 HELSINKI Tel: 9 47 33 41
Titles:
SIC!

LAHDEN SEURAKUNTYHTYMÄ 671550
PL 84/ Kirkkokatu 5, 15111 LAHTI Tel: 3 89 111
Fax: 3 78 30 891
Titles:
KIRKONSEUTU

LAHTI ENERGIA OY 693986
PL 93/ Kauppakatu 31, 15141 LAHTI Tel: 3 82 300
Fax: 3 82 34 567
Titles:
LAHTIWATTI

LALLI OY 1774656
Teljänkatu 8, 28130 PORI Tel: 2 63 44 563
Fax: 2 63 44 511
Titles:
SATAKUNNAN VIIKKO

LÄNSI-SAVO OY 1790982
PL 6/ Teollisuuskatu 2-6, 50101 MIKKELI
Tel: 15 35 01
Titles:
LÄNSI-SAVO
LÄNSI-SAVO PIEKSÄMÄKI

LÄNSI-SUOMI OY 1790258
PL 5/ Susivuorentie 2, 26101 RAUMA
Tel: 10 83 361 Fax: 10 83 36 659
Titles:
LÄNSI-SUOMI

LÄNSI-UUSIMAA OY 1789892
PL 60/ Suurlohjankatu 10, 08101 LOHJA
Tel: 20 61 00 130 **Fax:** 20 77 03 048
Titles:
LÄNSI-UUSIMAA

LAPUA SÄÄTIÖ 1793939
Sanomatie 1, 62100 LAPUA **Tel:** 6 43 87 352
Fax: 6 43 38 901
Titles:
LAPUAN SANOMAT

LASTEN PÄIVÄN SÄÄTIÖ 671452
PL 37/ Tivolikuja 1, 00101 HELSINKI
Tel: 9 77 39 91 **Fax:** 9 76 81 52
Titles:
LINNANMÄKI-UUTISET

LASTENSUOJELUN KESKUSLIITTO 1794319
Armfeltintie 1, 00150 HELSINKI **Tel:** 9 32 96 011
Fax: 9 32 96 02 99
Titles:
LAPSEN MAAILMA

LASTENTARHANOPETTA-JALIITTO 1783075
Rautatieläisenkatu 6, 00520 HELSINKI
Tel: 20 74 89 400 **Fax:** 9 14 27 20
Titles:
LASTENTARHA

LEGENDA OY 1789835
Nuijatie 11 B, 01650 VANTAA **Tel:** 3 85 53 260
Fax: 38532009
Titles:
PÄÄKAUPUNKISEUDUN AUTOUUTISET

LEGENDIUM OY 1789843
Melkonkatu 28 D, 00210 HELSINKI
Titles:
PAPERI JA PUU

LEHTIPISTE OY 1791752
PL 1/ Koivuvaarankuja 2, 01641 VANTAA
Tel: 9 85 281 **Fax:** 9 85 28 444
Titles:
LEHTIPISTEUUTISET

LEHTITAITO OY 1638547
Rihvelimäki 3 D 36, 02770 ESPOO
Tel: 9 85 93 001
Titles:
AUTO & KULJETUS

LEMPÄÄLÄN-VESILAHDEN SANOMAT OY 1790269
PL 38 / Tampereentie 17, 37501 LEMPÄÄLÄ
Tel: 3 34 29 000 **Fax:** 3 34 29 030
Titles:
LEMPÄÄLÄN-VESILAHDEN SANOMAT

LIEKSAN LEHTI OY 1789404
PL 22/ Siltakatu 1, 81701 LIEKSA
Tel: 10 23 08 650 **Fax:** 10 23 08 690
Titles:
LIEKSAN LEHTI

LIHAKESKUSLIITTO RY 1791755
Vuorikatu 8 A 19, 00100 HELSINKI
Tel: 9 41 88 76 32 **Fax:** 941887634
Titles:
LIHALEHTI

LIHASTAUTILIITTO 7702
Läntinen Pitkäkatu 35, 20100 TURKU
Tel: 2 27 39 700 **Fax:** 2 27 39 701
Titles:
PORRAS

LIIKETALOUDEN LIITTO RY 1783110
Asemamiehenkatu 2, 00520 HELSINKI
Tel: 9 22 94 71 71 **Fax:** 9 86 83 42 50
Titles:
LIIKETALOUS

LIIKETALOUSTIETEELLINEN YHDISTYS RY 670577
PL 1210/ Runeberginkatu 22-24, 00101
HELSINKI **Tel:** 9 43 13 84 69 **Fax:** 9 43 13 86 78
Titles:
LIIKETALOUDELLINEN AIKAKAUSKIRJA

LINJA-AUTOLIITTO RY 670676
Lauttasaarentie 8, 00200 HELSINKI
Tel: 9 68 27 01 **Fax:** 9 69 22 787
Titles:
BUSSIAMMATTILAINEN

LIPERIN KOTISEUTU-UUTISET KY 1790271
PL 14 / Keskustie 20, 83101 LIPERI
Tel: 10 66 66 081 **Fax:** 132525013
Titles:
KOTISEUTU-UUTISET

LOGISTIIKAN TOIMIHENKILÖT RY 697432
Asemamiehenkatu 4, 00520 HELSINKI
Tel: 20 11 30 200 **Fax:** 20 11 30 201
Titles:
LOG ON

LOVIISAN SANOMAIN OY 1790274
PL 42 / Sibeliuksenkatu 10, 07901 LOVIISA
Tel: 19 53 27 01 **Fax:** 19 53 27 06
Titles:
LOVIISAN SANOMAT

LRF MEDIA 1788356
Kehävuorenkuja 16, 01690 VANTAA
Tel: 50 32 34 794
Titles:
TRACTOR POWER

LUHTAWAY MEDIA & TEKNIIKKA OY 1791763
Luhtapolku 7, 99140 KÖNGÄS **Tel:** 16 65 31 55
Fax: 16 65 31 55
Titles:
LEVI. NYT!

LUMON OY 1605991
Kaitilankatu 11, 45130 KOUVOLA
Tel: 20 74 03 200
Titles:
NÄKÖALOJA

LUOMURA RY 677060
Keskitie 5, 36760 LUOPIOINEN **Tel:** 3 26 51 022
Titles:
TERVE TALO

LUONNONTIETEIDEN AKATEEMISTEN LIITTO - LAL 671150
Pohjoinen Makasiinikatu 6 A, 4. kerros, 00130
HELSINKI **Tel:** 9 25 11 16 60 **Fax:** 9 25 11 16 71
Titles:
LUONNONTIETEIDEN AKATEEMISET

LUONTAISTUNTIJAT OSUUSKUNTA 670940
Laivanvarustajankatu 9 A, 00140 HELSINKI
Tel: 9 80 94 481 **Fax:** 9 80 94 482
Titles:
LUONTAISTUNTIJA

LUONTO-LIITON UUDENMAAN PIIRI RY 671220
Mechelininkatu 36, 00260 HELSINKI
Tel: 9 44 63 13 **Fax:** 9 44 66 04
Titles:
LUPPI

LXRY FINLAND OY 1776837
PL 1421, 00101 HELSINKI **Tel:** 44 95 63 308
Titles:
LXRY MAGAZINE

MAA- JA KOTITALOUSNAISTEN KESKUS RY 1794309
PL 251/ Urheilutie 6, 01301 VANTAA
Tel: 20 74 72 400 **Fax:** 20 74 72 401
Titles:
KOTI

MAA- JA METSÄTALOUSMINISTERIÖ 671245
PL 30/ Hallituskatu 3 A, 00023
VALTIONEUVOSTO **Tel:** 9 16 02 299
Fax: 9 16 02 190
Titles:
60 DEGREES NORTH

MAA- JA METSÄTALOUSTUOTTAJAIN KESKUSLIITTO 1783395
PL 510/ Simonkatu 6, 00101 HELSINKI
Tel: 20 41 31 **Fax:** 20 41 32 425
Titles:
MTK-VIESTI

MAAILMANKAUPPOJEN LIITTO RY 676438
c/o Saloranta, Rengonraitti 22 as 1, 14300
RENKO **Tel:** 45 67 05 645
Titles:
MAAILMANKAUPPALEHTI

MAAKUNNAN SANOMAT OY 1640177
PL 12/Keskustie 32, 41521 HANKASALMI
Tel: 14 84 11 45 **Fax:** 14841961
Titles:
HANKASALMEN SANOMAT
HEINÄVEDEN LEHTI
KOILLIS-SAVO
LAUKAA-KONNEVESI
MATTI JA LIISA
MIILU
PIEKSÄMÄEN LEHTI
PIELAVESI - KEITELE
PITÄJÄLÄINEN
SAMPO-LEHTI
SISÄ-SAVO
SISÄ-SUOMEN LEHTI
SOISALON SEUTU
UUTIS-JOUSI
VIISPIIKKINEN
VIITASAAREN SEUTU

MAAN AUTO OY 671157
Tiilenpolttajankuja 5 A, 01720 VANTAA
Tel: 10 76 86 200 **Fax:** 10 76 86 330
Titles:
AJA HYVIN / PEUGEOT

MAANMITTAUSLAITOS 674452
PL 84/ Opastinsilta 12 C, 00521 HELSINKI
Tel: 20 54 15 441 **Fax:** 20 54 15 454
Titles:
POSITIO
TIETOA MAASTA

MAANOMISTAJAIN LIITTO RY 670818
Urheilutie 6 D, 01370 VANTAA **Tel:** 9 13 56 511
Fax: 9 13 57 100
Titles:
MAANOMISTAJA

MAANPUOLUSTUSYHTIÖ MPY OY 7664
Döbelninkatu 2, 00260 HELSINKI
Tel: 9 40 56 20 16 **Fax:** 9 40 56 20 96
Titles:
RESERVILÄINEN

MAATALOUSTUOTTAJAIN PALVELU OY 7743
PL 440/Simonkatu 6, 00101 HELSINKI
Tel: 9 13 11 51 **Fax:** 9 69 43 717
Titles:
KYLVÖSIEMEN

MAINOSTAJIEN LIITTO 1627167
Erottajankatu 19 B, 00130 HELSINKI
Tel: 9 68 60 840 **Fax:** 9 68 60 84 20
Titles:
MAINOSTAJA

MALISILLA OY 671455
Puolikuu 5 B-C, 02210 ESPOO **Tel:** 9 88 70 840
Fax: 9 88 70 84 66
Titles:
MENNÄÄN NAIMISIIN

MANNERHEIMIN LASTENSUOJELULIITTO RY 1794186
PL 141/Toinen Linja 17, 00531 HELSINKI
Tel: 75 32 451 **Fax:** 75 32 45 403
Titles:
LAPSEMME

MARTTALIITTO RY 1789974
Lapinlahdenkatu 3 A, 00180 HELSINKI
Tel: 10 83 85 500 **Fax:** 10 83 85 601
Titles:
MARTAT

MATKAILUN EDISTÄMISKESKUS 670729
PL 625/Töölönkatu 11, 00101 HELSINKI
Tel: 10 60 58 00 **Fax:** 10 60 58 333
Titles:
MATKAILUSILMÄ

MEDIA TORI 691091
Kölikatu 14, 20810 TURKU **Tel:** 2 23 96 616
Fax: 2 23 96 616
Titles:
KAUPPA JA TEOLLISUUS

MEDIAATTORI OY 1784415
Varraskuja 1, 15880 HOLLOLA **Tel:** 10 32 07 200
Titles:
PODIUM

MEDIAUNIONI MDU RY 1791725
Museokatu 13 A 4, 00100 HELSINKI
Tel: 9 45 42 18 40 **Fax:** 9496276
Titles:
FAKTORI

MEHILÄINEN OY 670935
Pohjoinen Hesperiankatu 17 C, 00260 HELSINKI
Tel: 10 41 43 036 **Fax:** 10 41 43 095
Titles:
MEHILÄINEN

MERIVOIMIEN ESIKUNTA 691160
PL 105, 00201 HELSINKI **Tel:** 9 18 12 42 96
Fax: 9 18 12 42 99
Titles:
RANNIKON PUOLUSTAJA

METALLITYÖVÄEN LIITTO 670841
PL 107/ Hakaniemenranta 1, 6 krs, 00531
HELSINKI **Tel:** 20 77 40 01 **Fax:** 20 77 41 240
Titles:
AHJO

METO - METSÄALAN ASIANTUNTIJAT RY 671222
Hietalahdenkatu 8 A, 00180 HELSINKI
Tel: 9 61 26 55 15 **Fax:** 9 61 26 55 30
Titles:
METSÄTALOUS-FORESTRY

METSÄ-BOTNIA AB 700100
PL 165, 26101 RAUMA **Tel:** 10 46 68 999
Fax: 10 46 68 372
Titles:
BOTNIA ECHO

METSÄHALLITUS 677021
PL 94/ Vernissakatu 4, 01301 VANTAA
Tel: 20 56 41 00 **Fax:** 20 56 45 050
Titles:
METSÄ.FI

METSÄNHOITOYHDISTYS 671458
Terveystie 2, 90900 KIIMINKI **Tel:** 8 81 61 036
Fax: 8 81 61 833
Titles:
METSÄVIESTI

Finland

METSÄNTUTKIMUSLAITOS METLA 671457
PL 18/ Jokiniemenkuja 1, 01301 VANTAA
Tel: 10 21 11 **Fax:** 10 21 12 101
Titles:
METSÄTIETEEN AIKAKAUSKIRJA

METSÄSTÄJÄIN KESKUSJÄRJESTÖ - JÄGARNAS CENTRALFÖRBUND 1774278
Fantsvägen 13-14, 00890 HELSINGFORS
Tel: 9 27 27 81 16 **Fax:** 9 27 27 81 30
Titles:
JÄGAREN
METSÄSTÄJÄ

METSÄTRANS -LEHTI OY 1783397
Myllärinkatu 21 A, 65100 VAASA **Tel:** 6 31 82 820
Fax: 6 31 82 821
Titles:
METSÄTRANS

MICROSOFT OY 1641012
Keilaranta 7, 02150 ESPOO
Titles:
CIRCLE

MIKKELIN TYÖVÄENLEHTI OY 1794003
PL 228/Porrassalmenkatu 2, 50101 MIKKELI
Tel: 15 32 13 70 **Fax:** 15 36 03 27
Titles:
VIIKKO VAPAUS

MINISTRY FOR FOREIGN AFFAIRS 7597
PL 176, 00161 HELSINKI **Tel:** 9 16 055
Fax: 9 16 05 63 75
Titles:
KAUPPAPOLITIIKKA
KEHITYS-UTVECKLING

MOOTTORIPYÖRÄKERHO 69 R.Y. 696905
Lepolantie 108, 35610 PIHLAISTO
Tel: 50 52 89 239
Titles:
MOTORISTI

MOTOPOINT OY 674595
Ahdenkallionkatu 46, 05820 HYVINKÄÄ
Tel: 10 61 72 410 **Fax:** 10 29 61 841
Titles:
MOTO-YKKÖNEN

MTKL VIREÄ MIELI AB 1789858
Malmin kauppatie 26, 00700 HELSINKI
Tel: 9 56 57 730 **Fax:** 956577334
Titles:
KÄSIKÄDESSÄ

OY MTKL VIREÄ MIELI AB 1794083
Ratakatu 9, 00120 HELSINKI **Tel:** 9 56 57 730
Fax: 9 56 57 73 34
Titles:
REVANSSI

MUOTIKAUPAN LIITTO RY 1789873
Mannerheimintie 76 B, 00250 HELSINKI
Tel: 9 68 44 73 21 **Fax:** 9 68 44 73 44
Titles:
MODIN

MUOTIMAAILMA OY 1789975
Mikkolantie 1 A, 00640 HELSINKI **Tel:** 9 75 21 469
Fax: 9 75 21 439
Titles:
MUOTIMAAILMA

MUOVIYHDISTYS RY 1791861
Pälkäneentie 18, 00510 HELSINKI
Tel: 9 86 89 910 **Fax:** 986899115
Titles:
MUOVI-PLAST

MUSIIKKILEHTI RONDO 1791952
Ilmalankuja 2 L, 00240 HELSINKI
Tel: 9 72 51 40 11
Titles:
RONDO-CLASSICA

MYYNNIN JA MARKKINOINNIN AMMATTILAISET SMKJ 1790000
PL 1100/ Töölönkatu 11 A, 5 krs, 00101
HELSINKI **Tel:** 9 47 80 77 00 **Fax:** 9 47 80 77 30
Titles:
MYYNTI & MARKKINOINTI

NANTUCKET OY 1789344
Taipaleentie 380, 31640 HUMPPILA
Tel: 10 42 26 590 **Fax:** 34378591
Titles:
PORTAALI

NATUR OCH MILJÖ RF 671288
Annegatan 26, 00100 HELSINGFORS
Tel: 9 61 22 290 **Fax:** 9 61 22 29 10
Titles:
FINLANDS NATUR

NESTE OIL OYJ 1677127
PL 95, 00095 NESTE **Tel:** 10 45 811
Fax: 10 45 84 442
Titles:
REFINE

NEUVOTTELEVAT SÄHKÖSUUNNITTELIJAT NSS RY 1792289
Alppikatu 13 B 15, 00530 HELSINKI
Tel: 9 70 14 611 **Fax:** 9 76 82 45
Titles:
PLAANI

NORDEA BANK PLC 1792338
Alma 360 Asiakasmedia, PL 502/ Munkkiniemen puistotie 35, 5 krs, 00101 HELSINKI
Tel: 10 66 51 02 **Fax:** 10 66 52 533
Titles:
AJASSA

NORDEA RAHOITUS SUOMI OY 1686019
Nihtisillantie 3 G, 00020 NORDEA
Titles:
TORI

NORDIC LAN & WAN COMMUNICATION OY 1641587
PL 128/ Sinikalliontie 16, 02631 ESPOO
Tel: 9 42 43 55 55
Titles:
BUSINESS NETWORKS

OY NOVOMEDIA LTD 1776798
Kaupintie 16 B 16, 00440 HELSINKI
Tel: 9 85 45 320 **Fax:** 9 85 45 32 50
Titles:
VENÄJÄN AIKA

NUORTEN LÄÄKÄRIEN YHDISTYS RY 1789488
PL 49/ Mäkelänkatu 2 A, 5 krs, 00501 HELSINKI
Tel: 9 39 30 873 **Fax:** 9 39 30 773
Titles:
NUORI LÄÄKÄRI - YNGRE LÄKARE

NURMEKSEN KIRJAPAINO OY 1789890
PL 5/Pappilansuora 15, 75501 NURMES
Tel: 10 23 08 600 **Fax:** 10 23 08 620
Titles:
YLÄ-KARJALA

NYA ÅLANDS TIDNING AB 1791039
PB 21/Uppgårdsvägen 6, 22101 MARIEHAMN
Tel: 18 23 444 **Fax:** 18 23 449
Titles:
NYA ÅLAND

NYLANDS BRIGAD 677121
Nylands Brigad, 10640 DRAGSVIK
Tel: 19 18 14 739 **Fax:** 19 18 14 741
Titles:
FANBÄRAREN

ODL TERVEYS OY 1776813
PL 365/ Uusikatu 50, 90101 OULU
Tel: 10 34 52 000
Titles:
OODI

ÖLJYALAN PALVELUKESKUS OY 671119
Eteläranta 8, 00130 HELSINKI **Tel:** 9 62 26 150
Fax: 9 62 22 042
Titles:
LÄMMÖLLÄ

OPETUSALAN AMMATTIJÄRJESTÖ OAJ RY 1794187
PL 94/ Rautatieläisenkatu 6, 00521 HELSINKI
Tel: 20 74 89 600 **Fax:** 20 74 89 760
Titles:
OPETTAJA

OP-KESKUS 1776799
PL 308/ Teollisuuskatu 1b, 00101 HELSINKI
Tel: 10 25 20 10
Titles:
KULTAJYVÄ

OP-POHJOLA-RYHMÄ 670813
PL 308, 00101 HELSINKI **Tel:** 10 25 20 11
Fax: 9 40 42 135
Titles:
CHYDENIUS
HIPPO
METSÄRAHA
O & P
OP-POHJOLA-NYTT

ORIVEDEN SANOMALEHTI OY 1789886
PL 33 / Lehmilaidantie 6, 35301 ORIVESI
Tel: 3 35 89 500 **Fax:** 3 35 89 535
Titles:
ORIVEDEN SANOMAT

OSAKESÄÄSTÄJIEN KESKUSLIITTO RY 1743541
PL 502, 00100 HELSINKI **Tel:** 10 66 51 02
Fax: 10 66 52 533
Titles:
VIISAS RAHA

ÖSTRA NYLANDS TIDNINGAR AB 1789208
PB 200 / Mannerheimgatan 9-11, 06101 BORGÅ
Tel: 20 75 69 622 **Fax:** 19 53 48 244
Titles:
BORGÅBLADET
ÖSTRA NYLAND

OSTROMEDIA OY 694295
PL 181, 00161 HELSINKI **Tel:** 9 62 29 640
Fax: 9 62 29 64 64
Titles:
NEW HORIZONS

OSUUSKUNTA METSÄLIITTO 670825
Revontulentie 6, 02100 ESPOO **Tel:** 10 46 01
Fax: 10 46 94 562
Titles:
METSÄLIITON VIESTI

OTAVAMEDIA OY 1789346
Esterinportti 1, 00015 OTAVAMEDIA **Tel:** 9 15 665
Fax: 9 15 66 62 06
Titles:
ALIBI
ANNA
DEKO
ERÄ
HYMY
KAKSPLUS
KANAVA
KÄYTÄNNÖN MAAMIES
KG
KIPPARI
KM VET
KOTILÄÄKÄRI
KOTILIESI
KOULULAINEN
LEMMIKKI
LEPPIS
MAALLA
METSÄSTYS JA KALASTUS
MODA
MOOTTORI
PARNASSO
SEURA
SUOMEN KUVALEHTI
SUOSIKKI
TEKNIIKAN MAAILMA
TM RAKENNUSMAAILMA
TV-MAAILMA
VAUHDIN MAAILMA
VENE
VILLIVARSA
VIVA

PÄÄLLYSTÖLIITTO RY.- BEFÄLSFÖRBUNDET RF. 670565
Ratamestarinkatu 11, 7 krs, 00520 HELSINKI
Tel: 50 35 57 289 **Fax:** 9 72 62 299
Titles:
PÄÄLLYSTÖLEHTI

PADASJOEN SANOMAT OY 1793234
PL 3/ Koivutie 8, 17501 PADASJOKI
Tel: 3 55 27 500 **Fax:** 3 55 27 525
Titles:
PADASJOEN SANOMAT

PAIKALLISLEHTI TEJUKA OY 1794015
PL 16 / Tiilitie 2, 64701 TEUVA **Tel:** 6 24 74 300
Fax: 62474321
Titles:
TEJUKA

PAIKALLISOSUUSPANKIT 676794
PL 1290/ Yliopistonkatu 7, 00101 HELSINKI
Tel: 9 68 11 700 **Fax:** 9 68 11 70 70
Titles:
KOIVUNLEHTI

PAINOMAAILMA OY 1793876
Markkinointiviestintä Dialogi Oy, PL 410, 00811
HELSINKI **Tel:** 9 42 42 73 30 **Fax:** 942427333
Titles:
PAINOMAAILMA

PALKANSAAJAJÄRJESTÖ PARDIA RY 1794193
Ratamestarinkatu 11, 00520 HELSINKI
Tel: 75 32 47 575 **Fax:** 75 32 47 576
Titles:
PARDIANYT

PALKANSAAJIEN TUTKIMUSLAITOS 677066
Pitkänsillanranta 3 A, 6 krs, 00530 HELSINKI
Tel: 9 25 35 73 30 **Fax:** 9 25 35 73 32
Titles:
TALOUS & YHTEISKUNTA

PALO- JA PELASTUSTIETO RY 1790224
Pasilankatu 8, 00240 HELSINKI **Tel:** 9 22 93 380
Fax: 9 22 93 38 33
Titles:
PELASTUSTIETO-RÄDDNING

PALTAMON KIRJAPAINO KY 670475
Sairaalatie 8, 88300 PALTAMO **Tel:** 8 87 17 41
Fax: 8 87 20 21
Titles:
VUOLIJOKI -LEHTI

PALVELUALOJEN AMMATTILIITTO PAM RY 1791857
PL 54/ Paasivuorenkatu 4-6 A, 2 krs, 00531
HELSINKI **Tel:** 20 77 40 02 **Fax:** 207742055
Titles:
PAM

PAPERILIITTO RY 7657
PL 326/ Paasivuorenkatu 4-6 A, 00531 HELSINKI
Tel: 9 70 891 **Fax:** 9 70 12 279
Titles:
PAPERILIITTO-LEHTI

PAPERINKERÄYS OY 1789655
PL 143/ Porkkalankatu 20 a, 3. krs, 00181 HELSINKI **Tel:** 9 22 81 91 **Fax:** 9 17 71 09
Titles:
KIERROSSA

PELIPEITTO OY 670585
PL 275/ Yliopistokatu 23 A, 20101 TURKU
Tel: 2 25 01 738 **Fax:** 2 25 16 970
Titles:
LOUNAISRANTA SYDVÄSTBLADET
RAKENNUSSANOMAT

PELLERVO-SEURA RY 1789999
PL 77/ Simonkatu 6, 00101 HELSINKI
Tel: 9 47 67 501 **Fax:** 9 69 48 845
Titles:
KODIN PELLERVO
LIHATALOUS
MAATILAN PELLERVO

PERFORMANCE MAGAZINES OY 692531
Olarinluoma 15, 02200 ESPOO **Tel:** 10 77 86 404
Fax: 9 88 15 21 01
Titles:
AUTOSOUND TECHNICAL MAGAZINE

PERNIÖNSEUDUN LEHTI OY 1794005
PL 35 / Salontie 2, 25501 PERNIÖ
Tel: 2 73 52 301 **Fax:** 27352284
Titles:
PERNIÖNSEUDUN LEHTI

PERUNANTUTKIMUSLAITOS 670838
Ruosuontie 156, 16900 LAMMI **Tel:** 3 65 63 00
Fax: 3 65 63 030
Titles:
TUOTTAVA PERUNA

PETÄJÄVEDEN PETÄJÄISET RY 1794008
Asematie 6, 41900 PETÄJÄVESI **Tel:** 14 85 42 40
Fax: 14854904
Titles:
PETÄJÄVESI

PHARMAPRESS OY 1789392
Pieni Roobertinkatu 14 C, 00120 HELSINKI
Tel: 9 22 87 11 **Fax:** 9 64 82 43
Titles:
APTEEKKARI
TERVEYDEKSI!

PIENTALORAKENTAMISEN KOULUTUSKESKUS OY PRK 671253
Vetotie 3 A, 01610 VANTAA **Tel:** 20 73 12 310
Fax: 20 73 12 319
Titles:
VIIHTYISÄ KOTI

PIHTIPUDAS-SEURA RY 1790177
Keskustie 8, 44800 PIHTIPUDAS
Tel: 20 79 31 620 **Fax:** 14 56 25 28
Titles:
KOTISEUDUN SANOMAT

PIRKANMAAN KIINTEISTÖYHDISTYS 670995
Hallituskatu 11 C, 33200 TAMPERE
Tel: 3 31 25 02 00 **Fax:** 3 31 25 02 22
Titles:
PIRKANMAAN KIINTEISTÖVIESTI

PIRKANMAAN YRITTÄJÄT OY 1789879
PL 7/ Kehräsaari B, 2. krs., 33201 TAMPERE
Tel: 3 25 16 500 **Fax:** 32516516
Titles:
PIRKANMAAN YRITTÄJÄ

PITÄJÄSANOMAT OY 1791049
PL 5 / Erkontie 17, 16301 ORIMATTILA
Tel: 3 87 66 78 **Fax:** 37774244
Titles:
ORIMATTILAN SANOMAT

PLARI OY 1789977
PL 8/Keskuskatu 2, 23801 LAITILA **Tel:** 2 85 006
Fax: 2 85 008
Titles:
LAITILAN SANOMAT

PLAZA PUBLISHING GROUP AB 1774764
Simonkatu 12 B 13, 00100 HELSINKI
Tel: 10 38 78 700 **Fax:** 10 38 78 788
Titles:
OMA KOTI KULLAN KALLIS
PLAZAKOTI

PLUS-LEHDET OY 671545
Iso Roobertinkatu 43 A, 00120 HELSINKI
Tel: 9 68 44 550 **Fax:** 9 60 70 42
Titles:
OLE HYVÄ!

POGOSTAN SANOMAT OY 1794012
PL 41/ Kauppatie 29, 82901 ILOMANTSI
Tel: 10 23 08 800 **Fax:** 10 23 08 802
Titles:
POGOSTAN SANOMAT

POHJAKYRÖN MEDIA OY 1789406
Pohjankyröntie 128, 61501 ISOKYRÖ
Tel: 6 47 15 214 **Fax:** 6 47 14 400
Titles:
POHJANKYRÖ-LEHTI

POHJANMAAN LÄHISANOMAT OY 1789978
PL 33 / Hoiskontie 4, 62901 ALAJÄRVI
Tel: 6 24 77 890 **Fax:** 6 24 77 899
Titles:
JÄRVISEUTU
SUUPOHJAN SANOMAT
VIISKUNTA

POHJOIS-KARJALAN PAIKALLISLEHDET OY 1774462
PL 7 / Koulukatu 2, 83501 OUTOKUMPU
Tel: 10 23 08 850 **Fax:** 10 23 08 860
Titles:
OUTOKUMMUN SEUTU
PIELISJOKISEUTU

POHJOIS-SUOMEN MEDIA OY 1789366
PL 150/ Kauppakatu 11, 87101 KAJAANI
Tel: 8 61 66 333 **Fax:** 8 62 34 00
Titles:
KAINUUN SANOMAT
KOILLIS-LAPPI
LAPIN KANSA
LAPIN KANSA INARI-UTSJOKI
LAPIN KANSA KEMIJÄRVI-SALLA-PELKOSENNIEMI
LAPIN KANSA KITTILÄ-MUONIO-ENONTEKIÖ
LAPIN KANSA SODANKYLÄ
POHJOLAN SANOMAT
POHJOLAN SANOMAT KOLARI
POHJOLAN SANOMAT PELLO
POHJOLAN SANOMAT TORNIO
POHJOLAN SANOMAT YLITORNIO

POHJOIS-SUOMEN PAIKALLISUUTISET OY 1789375
PL 24 / Puistotie 2, 93100 PUDASJÄRVI
Tel: 8 86 00 715 **Fax:** 8 86 00 731
Titles:
IIJOKISEUTU
RANTALAKEUS
SIIKAJOKILAAKSO

POHJOIS-SUOMEN SANOMALEHTI OY 1790314
PL 18, 90400 OULU **Tel:** 40 55 50 239
Fax: 8 31 15 540
Titles:
OULUN SANOMAT
POHJOLAN TYÖ

POHJOLAN LUOMU FINLAND OY 1759484
Kankurinkatu 4-6, 05800 HYVINKÄÄ
Tel: 40 30 11 230 **Fax:** 40 30 11 239
Titles:
POHJOLAN LUOMU

POLARLEHDET OY 7874
Katajaranta 24, 96400 ROVANIEMI
Tel: 16 31 16 11 **Fax:** 16 31 28 45
Titles:
TRAVEL ROVANIEMI

PORI ENERGIA OY 1653474
PL 9/ Radanvarsi 2, 28101 PORI **Tel:** 2 62 12 233
Titles:
WATTIVIESTI

PRETAX OY 1605464
Antinkatu 3 C, 3. krs, 00100 HELSINKI
Tel: 20 74 42 300 **Fax:** 20 74 42 001
Titles:
PRETAX

PRIIMUS MEDIA OY 1790268
PL 2/Kartanomäenkatu 4, 32201 LOIMAA
Tel: 2 58 88 000 **Fax:** 2 76 31 233
Titles:
LOIMAAN LEHTI

PRIIMUS MEDIA OY AURANMAAN VIIKKOLEHTI 1790014
PL 15 / Kehityksentie 3, 21801 KYRÖ
Tel: 2 48 64 950 **Fax:** 2 48 68 053
Titles:
AURANMAAN VIIKKOLEHTI

PRIVAT-MEDI OY 1621153
Virmantie 7, 90830 HAUKIPUDAS
Tel: 40 57 41 237
Titles:
HOIVAPALVELUT

PROAGRIA ETELÄ-POHJANMAA 670804
Huhtalantie 2, 60220 SEINÄJOKI **Tel:** 6 41 63 111
Fax: 6 41 63 448
Titles:
ITUA

PROAGRIA KESKI-POHJANMAA RY 670810
Ristirannankatu 1, 67100 KOKKOLA
Tel: 20 74 73 250 **Fax:** 20 74 73 299
Titles:
PROAGRIA KESKI-POHJANMAA

PROAGRIA OULUN MAASEUTUKESKUS 670822
PL 106/ Kauppurienkatu 23, 90101 OULU
Tel: 8 31 68 611 **Fax:** 8 37 30 75
Titles:
MAAVIESTI

PROAGRIA POHJOIS-KARJALA 1789850
PL 5/ Koskikatu 11 C, 80101 JOENSUU
Tel: 13 25 83 311 **Fax:** 132583399
Titles:
PROAGRIA ITÄ-SUOMI

PUBLICO OY 1789299
Pälkäneentie 19 A, 00510 HELSINKI
Tel: 9 68 66 250 **Fax:** 9 68 52 940
Titles:
NORDICUM
PROINTERIOR

PUNKALAITUMEN SANOMAT OY 1790322
PL 1 / Lauttakyläntie 4, 31901 PUNKALAIDUN
Tel: 2 76 74 256 **Fax:** 27674225
Titles:
PUNKALAITUMEN SANOMAT

PUOLUSTUSVOIMAT 671382
PL 25/ Korkeavuorenkatu 21, 00131 HELSINKI
Tel: 9 18 12 24 32 **Fax:** 9 18 12 24 40
Titles:
RUOTUVÄKI

PUU & TEKNIIKKA OY 1732118
Faktapro Oy, PL 4, 02941 ESPOO
Tel: 9 54 79 74 10 **Fax:** 9 51 22 033
Titles:
PUU & TEKNIIKKA

PUU- JA ERITYISALOJEN LIITTO-TRÄ- OCH SPECIALBRANCHERNAS FÖRBUND 1794065
PL 318/Haapaniemenkatu 7-9 B, 00531 HELSINKI **Tel:** 9 61 51 61 **Fax:** 97532506
Titles:
SÄRMÄ

PUUINFORMAATIO RY 1789224
Snellmaninkatu 13, 00170 HELSINKI
Tel: 9 68 65 450 **Fax:** 9 68 65 45 30
Titles:
PUU

PUUMALA-SEURA RY 1794011
PL 12 / Kenttätie 7, 52201 PUUMALA
Tel: 15 46 81 225 **Fax:** 154681833
Titles:
PUUMALA

PUUMIESTEN LIITTO RY 7678
Keskustie 20 D, 40100 JYVÄSKYLÄ
Tel: 14 21 56 36 **Fax:** 14 21 56 52
Titles:
PUUMIES

PUUTARHALIITTO-TRÄDGÅRDSFÖRBUNDET RY. 1792124
Viljatie 4 C, 00700 HELSINKI **Tel:** 9 58 41 66
Fax: 9 58 41 65 55
Titles:
KOTIPUUTARHA

PYHÄJÄRVEN SANOMAT OY 1790325
PL 41/ Asematie 2, 86801 PYHÄSALMI
Tel: 8 77 29 000 **Fax:** 8 77 29 040
Titles:
PYHÄJÄRVEN SANOMAT

PYHÄJÄRVISEUDUN PAIKALLISLEHTI OY 1793937
PL 19/ Eurantie 6, 27511 EURA **Tel:** 2 83 87 92 00
Fax: 2 86 51 961
Titles:
ALASATAKUNTA

RAHTARIT RY 1789875
Pitkäniemenkatu 11, 33330 TAMPERE
Tel: 3 34 33 710 **Fax:** 33433752
Titles:
RAHTARIT

RAJASEUTULIITTO RY 1790218
Tunturikatu 6 A 19, 00100 HELSINKI
Tel: 9 44 42 38 **Fax:** 9493701
Titles:
RAJASEUTU

RAJAVARTIOLAITOS 7663
PL 3/ Korkeavuorenkatu 21, 00131 HELSINKI
Tel: 71 87 21 333 **Fax:** 71 87 21 009
Titles:
RAJAMME VARTIJAT

Section 6 Publishers by Country

RAKENNUSINSINÖÖRIT JA ARKKITEHDIT RIA RY 1791938
PL 357/ Albertinkatu 23 A 13, 00121 HELSINKI
Tel: 9 61 22 770 **Fax:** 961227733
Titles:
RAKENNUSINSINÖÖRI JA -ARKKITEHTI RIA

RAKENNUSLIITTO 670853
PL 307/ Siltasaarenkatu 4, 00531 HELSINKI
Tel: 20 77 40 03 **Fax:** 20 77 43 061
Titles:
RAKENTAJA

RAKENNUSMESTARIEN KESKUSLIITTO RY 670652
PL 1004/ Runebergínkatu 5, 00101 HELSINKI
Tel: 9 54 95 570 **Fax:** 9 54 95 53 90
Titles:
MESTARI-INSINÖÖRI
RAKENNUSTAITO

RAKENNUSTARKASTUSYHDISTYS RTY RY 1789849
Rakennustieto Oy, PL 1004, 00101 HELSINKI
Tel: 20 74 76 400 **Fax:** 207476320
Titles:
RY RAKENNETTU YMPÄRISTÖ

RAKENNUSTIETO OY 1791747
PL 1370, 00101 HELSINKI **Tel:** 9 56 58 310
Fax: 9 27 87 364
Titles:
KOTITALO

RAKENTAJAN TIETOPALVELU RTI OY 1774275
Maailman-Matti 2 A 2, 02230 ESPOO
Tel: 9 54 07 310 **Fax:** 95031810
Titles:
OMAKOTISANOMAT

RANTAPOHJA OY 1794017
PL 15/Huvipolku 6, 90831 HAUKIPUDAS
Tel: 8 56 37 200 **Fax:** 8 54 72 433
Titles:
RANTAPOHJA

RANTASALMEN LEHTI OY 1789609
PL 4 / Kylätie 37, 58901 RANTASALMI
Tel: 15 44 07 51 **Fax:** 15440775
Titles:
RANTASALMEN LEHTI

OY REED BUSINESS INFORMATION FINLAND OY 1789256
Ruukinkuja 3, 02330 ESPOO **Tel:** 9 80 99 11
Fax: 980991400
Titles:
RAKENNA OIKEIN

REHURAISIO OY 671558
PL 101, 21201 RAISIO **Tel:** 2 44 32 111
Fax: 2 44 32 137
Titles:
REHUMAKASIINI

REISJÄRVI-LEHTI OY 1794004
PL 2/ Kirkkotie 3 H, 85901 REISJÄRVI
Tel: 8 77 70 20 **Fax:** 8777021
Titles:
REISJÄRVI

RPS-MARKKINOINTI OY 670552
PL 23/ Hietakummuntie 18, 00701 HELSINKI
Tel: 44 07 00 401 **Fax:** 9 22 45 148
Titles:
JULKAISIJA

RPT DOCU OY 1789254
Ruukinkuja 3, 02330 ESPOO **Tel:** 9 80 99 11
Fax: 9 80 99 14 00
Titles:
PROJEKTIUUTISET
TEOLLISUUS NYT

RUKA-KUUSAMO MATKAILUYHDISTYS RY 1712678
Torangintaival 2, 93600 KUUSAMO
Tel: 8 85 21 300 **Fax:** 8 85 21 305
Titles:
RUKA-KUUSAMO

RUOVEDEN SANOMALEHTI OY 1790323
PL 2/ Honkalantie 2, 2 krs, 34601 RUOVESI
Tel: 3 47 61 400 **Fax:** 3 47 61 424
Titles:
RUOVESI
TEISKO-AITOLAHTI

SAARIMEDIA KY 1621871
PL 56, 08101 LOHJA **Tel:** 44 30 01 070
Fax: 19 33 33 13
Titles:
HIRSITALO

SADANKOMITEA JA RAUHANLIITTO 671305
Rauhanasema, Veturitori 3, 00520 HELSINKI
Tel: 9 14 13 36 **Fax:** 9 14 72 97
Titles:
PAX

SAHAYRITTÄJÄT RY 670828
Kiljavantie 6 rak.12, 05200 RAJAMÄKI
Tel: 9 85 58 990 **Fax:** 9 85 58 991
Titles:
SAHAYRITTÄJÄ

SÄHKÖALOJEN AMMATTILIITTO RY 670859
PL 747/Aleksanterinkatu 15, 33101 TAMPERE
Tel: 3 25 20 111 **Fax:** 3 25 20 210
Titles:
VASAMA

SÄHKÖINFO OY 1793838
PL 55/ Harakantie 18, 02601 ESPOO
Tel: 9 54 76 10 **Fax:** 954761310
Titles:
SÄHKÖALA
SÄHKÖMAAILMA

SAK (SUOMEN AMMATTILIITTOJEN KESKUSJÄRJESTÖ RY.) 1792340
c/o Alma 360 Asiakasmedia, PL 502/ Munkkiniemen puistotie 25, 5 krs, 00101 HELSINKI **Tel:** 10 66 51 02 **Fax:** 10 66 52 533
Titles:
ARVO

SAKSALAIS-SUOMALAINEN KAUPPAKAMARI 671409
PL 83/ Mikonkatu 25, 00101 HELSINKI
Tel: 9 61 22 120 **Fax:** 9 64 28 59
Titles:
DEUTSCH-FINNISCHER HANDEL

SAL RY. 670773
Haapaniemenkatu 7-9 B, 10 krs, 00530 HELSINKI **Tel:** 10 23 99 080 **Fax:** 10 23 99 089
Titles:
HYVINVOINTI

SALON SEUDUN SANOMAT OY 1790175
PL 29/Vistantie 38, 21531 PAIMIO **Tel:** 2 47 76 66
Fax: 2 47 76 600
Titles:
KUNNALLISLEHTI PAIMIO-SAUVO-KAARINA
SALON SEUDUN SANOMAT
SOMERO
YKKÖSSANOMAT

SANOMA LEHTIMEDIA OY 1790019
PL 3/Lauritsalantie 1, 53501 LAPPEENRANTA
Tel: 5 53 88 13 **Fax:** 5 53 88 32 07
Titles:
ETELÄ-SAIMAA
ETELÄ-SAIMAA IMATRA

SANOMA MAGAZINES FINLAND OY 7582
PL 100/ Lapinmäentie 1, 00040 SANOMA MAGAZINES **Tel:** 9 12 01 **Fax:** 9 12 05 354
Titles:
AESCULAPIUS
APOTEEKKI
AUTO BILD SUOMI
AUTOT
BLUE WINGS
COSMOPOLITAN
ET-LEHTI
EXCLUSIVE
GEO
GLORIA
GLORIAN ANTIIKKI
GLORIAN KOTI
GLORIAN RUOKA & VIINI
GTI-MAGAZINE
HYVÄ TERVEYS
KODIN KUVALEHTI
MATKAOPAS
ME NAISET
MEIDÄN PERHE
MIKROBITTI
PELIT
PROSESSORI
RAKENNUSLEHTI
SARA. SPORT
SUURI KÄSITYÖLEHTI
TIEDE
TIETOKONE
V8-MAGAZINE
VAUVA

SANOMA MAGAZINES OY 1774147
PL 44/ Hämeentie 33, 00501 HELSINKI
Tel: 9 12 01 **Fax:** 20 74 18 622
Titles:
KODINRAKENTAJA

SANOMA NEWS OY 1789558
PL 85, 00089 SANOMA **Tel:** 9 12 21
Fax: 9 12 22 366
Titles:
HELSINGIN SANOMAT
HELSINGIN SANOMAT KAUPUNKITOIMITUS
HELSINGIN SANOMAT KOTIMAANTOIMITUS
HELSINGIN SANOMAT KUOPIO
HELSINGIN SANOMAT KUUKAUSILIITE
HELSINGIN SANOMAT LAPPEENRANTA
HELSINGIN SANOMAT MATKAILU
HELSINGIN SANOMAT NYT-VIIKKOLIITE
HELSINGIN SANOMAT OULU
HELSINGIN SANOMAT SUNNUNTAITOIMITUS
HELSINGIN SANOMAT TALOUSTOIMITUS
HELSINGIN SANOMAT TAMPERE VAASA
HELSINGIN SANOMAT TURKU
HELSINGIN SANOMAT VERKKOLIITE
ILTA-SANOMAT
JOUTSENO
KAAKONKULMA
KELTAINEN PÖRSSI
KESKILAAKSO
LUUMÄEN LEHTI
METRO
PITÄJÄNUUTISET
VEIKKAAJA

SANOMALEHTI KARJALAINEN OY 1789241
PL 99/ Kosti Aaltosen tie 9, 80141 JOENSUU
Tel: 10 23 08 080 **Fax:** 10 23 08 081
Titles:
KARJALAINEN
KARJALAINEN KESÄLAHTI
KARJALAINEN KITEE
KARJALAINEN LIEKSA
KARJALAINEN NURMES

SANOMALEHTI UUSI POHJOIS-KARJALA OY 1789885
PL 97/ Niskakatu 7, 80101 JOENSUU
Tel: 13 73 75 811 **Fax:** 13 74 33 07
Titles:
VIIKKO POHJOIS-KARJALA

SANOMALEHTIEN LIITTO 1792783
PL 415/Lönnrotinkatu 11, 00121 HELSINKI
Tel: 9 22 87 73 00 **Fax:** 9 60 79 89
Titles:
SUOMEN LEHDISTÖ - FINLANDS PRESS

SATAKUNNAN KIRJATEOLLISUUS OY 1789816
PL 58/ Pohjoisranta 11 E, 28101 PORI
Tel: 10 66 58 318 **Fax:** 10 66 58 330
Titles:
SATAKUNNAN KANSA
SATAKUNNAN KANSA EURA
SATAKUNNAN KANSA HUITTINEN
SATAKUNNAN KANSA KANKAANPÄÄ

SAVON MEDIAT OY 1789953
PL 11/Kilpivirrantie 7, 74101 IISALMI
Tel: 17 83 51 311 **Fax:** 17 83 51 401
Titles:
IISALMEN SANOMAT
SAVON SANOMAT
SAVON SANOMAT KESKI-SAVON ALUETOIMITUS
SAVON SANOMAT PIEKSÄMÄKI
SAVON SANOMAT YLÄ-SAVON ALUETOIMITUS

SAVONLINNAN OOPPERAJUHLIEN KANNATUSYHDISTYS 671114
Olavinkatu 27, 57130 SAVONLINNA
Tel: 15 47 67 50 **Fax:** 15 47 67 540
Titles:
OOPPERAUUTISET

OY SCAN-AUTO AB 1789129
PL 59/ Muonamiehentie 1, 00391 HELSINKI
Tel: 10 55 50 10 **Fax:** 10 55 55 317
Titles:
SCANIA MAAILMA

SFC-MARKKINOINTI OY 1791179
Viipurintie 58, 13210 HÄMEENLINNA
Tel: 3 61 53 140 **Fax:** 3 61 53 162
Titles:
CARAVAN

SIEVI-SEURA R.Y. 1794014
PL 23/Haikolantie 23, 85411 SIEVI **Tel:** 8 48 02 78
Fax: 8480278
Titles:
SIEVILÄINEN

SKAL KUSTANNUS OY 1791746
PL 38 /Nuijamiestentie 7, 00401 HELSINKI
Tel: 9 47 89 99 **Fax:** 9 58 78 520
Titles:
KULJETUSYRITTÄJÄ

SKOGSBRUKETS UTVECKLINGSCENTRAL TAPIO 1791949
Orrspelsgränden 4 A, 00700 HELSINGFORS
Tel: 20 77 29 000 **Fax:** 207729008
Titles:
SKOGSBRUKET

SL-MEDIAT OY 670680
Takojankatu 11, 33540 TAMPERE **Tel:** 3 38 07 700
Fax: 3 38 07 701
Titles:
AMMATTIAUTOT
AUTOPOKKARI
KONEPÖRSSI
URAKOINTI-UUTISET

SLO OY 1792290
PL 88/ Ritakuja 2, 01741 VANTAA **Tel:** 10 28 311
Fax: 102832010
Titles:
ESSELLOO EXPRÈS

SLY-KAUPUNKILEHDET OY 1774274
PL 350/ Rälssitie 7 A, 01511 VANTAA
Tel: 20 61 00 110 **Fax:** 20 77 03 016
Titles:
LÄNSIVÄYLÄ
VANTAAN SANOMAT

SLY-PAIKALLISLEHDET OY 1774398
PL 52/ Klaavolantie 5, 04301 TUUSULA
Tel: 20 77 03 101 **Fax:** 20 77 03 000
Titles:
KESKI-UUSIMAA
SIPOON SANOMAT

SOSIAALILÄÄKETIETEEN YHDISTYS RY 676333
Siirtolaisuusinstituutti, Eerikinkatu 34, 20100 TURKU **Tel:** 2 33 38 543
Titles:
SOSIAALILÄÄKETIETEELLINEN AIKAKAUSLEHTI

SOTILASAMMATTILIITTO SOAL RY 671129
Ratamestarinkatu 11, 7.krs, 00520 HELSINKI
Tel: 9 14 86 915 **Fax:** 9 27 87 854
Titles:
AMMATTISOTILAS

SOTILASKOTILIITTO - SOLDATHEMSFÖRBUNDET RY 671026
Simonkatu 12 A 9, 00100 HELSINKI
Tel: 9 56 57 20 22 **Fax:** 9 56 57 20 25
Titles:
SOTILASKOTI

SP-JULKAISUT OY 670752
PL 68/ Linnoitustie 9, 02601 ESPOO
Tel: 9 54 80 51
Titles:
SÄÄSTÖPANKKI

STELLATUM OY 7964
Purotie 1 B, 00380 HELSINKI **Tel:** 9 54 21 01 00
Web site: http://www.stellatum.fi
Titles:
ALARA
ASU JA RAKENNA
HALLINTO

STORA ENSO OYJ 671497
PL 309/ Kanavaranta 1, 00101 HELSINKI
Tel: 20 46 21 296 **Fax:** 20 46 21 267
Titles:
TERVE METSÄ

SUGAR BEET RESEARCH CENTRE 7626
Toivonlinnantie 518, 21500 PIIKKIÖ
Tel: 10 43 10 62 **Fax:** 2 73 76 409
Titles:
JUURIKASSARKA

SULKAVAN KOTISEUTULEHTI OY 670446
Uitonrinne 18, 58700 SULKAVA **Tel:** 15 47 15 44
Fax: 15 67 63 26
Titles:
SULKAVA-LEHTI

SUOMALAINEN LÄÄKÄRISEURA DUODECIM 7701
PL 713/ Kalevankatu 11 A, 00101 HELSINKI
Tel: 9 61 88 51 **Fax:** 9 61 88 52 00
Titles:
LÄÄKETIETEELLINEN AIKAKAUSKIRJA DUODECIM

SUOMEN 4H-LIITTO RY 1789869
Suomen 4H-liitto/4H-Pilke-lehti, Karjalankatu 2 A, 00520 HELSINKI **Tel:** 9 75 12 42 00
Fax: 9 75 12 42 55
Titles:
PILKE

SUOMEN AIKAKAUSLEHDENTOIMITTAJAIN LIITTO 1788313
Hietalahdenkatu 2 B 23, 00180 HELSINKI
Tel: 9 61 10 55
Titles:
LÖÖPPI

SUOMEN ANTROPOSOFINEN LIITTO R.Y. 671199
Uudenmaankatu 25 A 4, 00120 HELSINKI
Tel: 9 69 62 520 **Fax:** 9 68 02 591
Titles:
TAKOJA

SUOMEN ARKKITEHTILIITTO RY 1774977
Runeberginkatu 5 A, 00100 HELSINKI
Tel: 9 58 44 48 **Fax:** 958444222
Titles:
ARKKITEHTI

SUOMEN ARKKITEHTILIITTO-FINLANDS ARKITEKTFÖRBUND RY (SAFA) 1791168
Runeberginkatu 5 A, 00100 HELSINKI
Tel: 9 58 44 48 **Fax:** 958444222
Titles:
ARKKITEHTIUUTISET-ARKITEKTNYTT

SUOMEN ASIAKASTIETO OY 670580
PL 16/ Työpajankatu 10 A, 00581 HELSINKI
Tel: 9 14 88 61 **Fax:** 9 73 53 38
Titles:
LUOTTOLISTA

SUOMEN ATOMITEKNILLINEN SEURA RY 671537
Fennovoima, Salmisaarenaukio 1, 00180 HELSINKI **Tel:** 20 72 25 057 **Fax:** 20 72 25 000
Titles:
ATS YDINTEKNIIKKA

SUOMEN BENSIINIKAUPPIAITTEN LIITTO SBL RY 670660
Mannerheimintie 40 D 84, 00100 HELSINKI
Tel: 9 75 19 55 00 **Fax:** 9 75 19 55 25
Titles:
BENSIINIUUTISET

SUOMEN DIABETESLIITTO RY 1794078
Kirjoniementie 15, 33680 TAMPERE
Tel: 3 28 60 111 **Fax:** 3 28 60 422
Titles:
DIABETES

SUOMEN EKONOMILIITTO 1789997
Kynämies, Köydenpunojankatu 2 aD, 00180 HELSINKI **Tel:** 9 15 66 85 10 **Fax:** 9 15 66 86 00
Titles:
EKONOMI

SUOMEN EUROOPPALIIKE-EUROPARÖRELSEN I FINLAND 1776804
PL 332, 00121 HELSINKI **Tel:** 46 98 08 227
Titles:
EUROMETRI

SUOMEN EUROOPPALIIKE-EUROPARÖRELSEN I FINLAND RY. 671190
PL 332, 00121 HELSINKI **Tel:** 10 60 55 055
Fax: 10 60 55 904
Titles:
EUROOPAN TIEDE JA TEKNOLOGIA

SUOMEN FARMASIALIITTO RY 1791605
Iso Roobertinkatu 7 A, 00120 HELSINKI
Tel: 9 69 62 270 **Fax:** 9 60 51 12
Titles:
FARMASIA

SUOMEN HENKILÖKESKUSJÄRJESTÖ-STTK RY 671128
PL 421/ Mikonkatu 8 A, 6 krs, 00101 HELSINKI
Tel: 9 13 15 21 **Fax:** 9 65 23 67
Titles:
STTK-LEHTI

SUOMEN HEVOSURHEILULEHTI OY 1790603
Tulkinkuja 3, 02650 ESPOO **Tel:** 20 76 05 300
Fax: 20 76 05 390
Titles:
HEVOSURHEILU

SUOMEN HITSAUSTEKNILLINEN YHDISTYS RY 7643
Mäkelänkatu 36 A 2, 00510 HELSINKI
Tel: 9 77 32 199 **Fax:** 9 77 32 661
Titles:
HITSAUSTEKNIIKKA-SVETSTEKNIK

SUOMEN KALANKASVATTAJALIITTO RY 670835
Malmin kauppatie 26, 00700 HELSINKI
Tel: 50 52 48 582 **Fax:** 9 68 44 59 59
Titles:
SUOMEN KALANKASVATTAJA

SUOMEN KANSALLISOOPPERA 692702
PL 176/ Helsinginkatu 58, 00251 HELSINKI
Tel: 9 40 30 21 **Fax:** 9 40 30 22 95
Titles:
OOPPERASANOMAT

SUOMEN KÄTILÖLIITTO RY 1791757
PL 100/ Asemamiehenkatu 4, 00060 TEHY
Tel: 9 54 22 74 91 **Fax:** 961500268
Titles:
KÄTILÖLEHTI

SUOMEN KEKSIJÄIN KESKUSLIITTO RY 671441
Radiokatu 20, 2 krs, 00240 HELSINKI
Tel: 9 27 80 00 02 **Fax:** 9 27 22 037
Titles:
KEKSINTÖUUTISET

SUOMEN KENNELLIITTO-FINSKA KENNELKLUBBEN RY. 1794226
Torikatu 2 B 12, 14200 TURENKI **Tel:** 3 68 50 80
Fax: 3 68 50 816
Titles:
KOIRAMME - VÅRA HUNDAR

SUOMEN KIRURGIYHDISTYS RY- FINNISH SURGICAL SOCIETY 1784160
PL 49/ Mäkelänkatu 2 A, 00501 HELSINKI
Tel: 9 39 30 91 **Fax:** 9 39 30 794
Titles:
SCANDINAVIAN JOURNAL OF SURGERY
SJS

SUOMEN KONEPÄÄLLYSTÖLIITTO SKL 670692
Lastenkodinkuja 1, 00180 HELSINKI
Tel: 9 58 60 48 10 **Fax:** 9 69 48 798
Titles:
VOIMA JA KÄYTTÖ - KRAFT OCH DRIFT

SUOMEN LÄÄKÄRILIITTO RY-FINLANDS LÄKARFÖRBUND 1774140
PL 49/Mäkelänkatu 2 A, 00501 HELSINKI
Tel: 9 39 30 91 **Fax:** 9 39 30 795
Titles:
SUOMEN LÄÄKÄRILEHTI

SUOMEN LÄÄKÄRILIITTO RY-FINLANDS LÄKARFÖRBUND RF 1790001
Mäkikatu 3 B 50-51, 70110 KUOPIO
Tel: 17 36 20 389
Titles:
LÄÄKÄRISANOMAT

SUOMEN LAATUYHDISTYS RY. 671205
Keilaranta 12, 02150 ESPOO **Tel:** 20 77 91 470
Fax: 20 77 91 499
Titles:
LAATU

SUOMEN LÄHETYSSEURA - FINSKA MISSIONSSÄLLSKAPET 7816
PL 154/ Tähtitorninkatu 18, 00141 HELSINKI
Tel: 9 12 971 **Fax:** 9 12 97 294
Titles:
LÄHETYSSANOMAT
MISSION

SUOMEN LÄHI- JA PERUSHOITAJALIITTO SUPER 1794181
Ratamestarinkatu 12, 00520 HELSINKI
Tel: 9 27 27 910 **Fax:** 9 27 27 91 20
Titles:
SUPER

SUOMEN LÄHIKAUPPA OY 1789747
PL 1/ Sörnäistenkatu 2, 00581 HELSINKI
Tel: 20 70 03 00 **Fax:** 20 70 03 570
Titles:
LÄHIS
ME

SUOMEN LAKIMIESLIITTO RY 7877
Uudenmaankatu 4-6 B 10, 00120 HELSINKI
Tel: 9 85 61 03 00 **Fax:** 9 85 61 03 06
Titles:
LAKIMIESUUTISET-JURISTNYTT

SUOMEN LATU RY 1794231
Radiokatu 20, 00240 HELSINKI **Tel:** 44 72 26 300
Fax: 9663376
Titles:
LATU JA POLKU

SUOMEN LEHTIYHTYMÄ OY 1776796
Keskuskatu 4, 04601 MÄNTSÄLÄ
Tel: 20 61 00 152 **Fax:** 20 77 03 019
Titles:
MÄNTSÄLÄ

SUOMEN LEIPURILIITTO RY 7588
PL 115/ Pasilankatu 2, 00241 HELSINKI
Tel: 9 14 88 73 00 **Fax:** 9 14 88 73 01
Titles:
LEIPURI

SUOMEN LIONS-LIITTO RY 671095
Kirkonkyläntie 10, 00700 HELSINKI
Tel: 9 56 55 95 11 **Fax:** 9 56 55 95 55
Titles:
LION/LEIJONA

SUOMEN LUONNONSUOJELULIITTO 1791764
Kotkankatu 9, 00510 HELSINKI **Tel:** 9 22 80 81
Fax: 922808200
Titles:
LUONNONSUOJELIJA
SUOMEN LUONTO

SUOMEN MATKAKUSTANTAMO OY 675341
Kreetankuja 2, 21200 RAISIO **Tel:** 2 27 78 080
Fax: 2 27 78 099
Titles:
RAKENTAJAPOSTI
SUOMEN MATKAILULEHTI
TEOLLISUUSSANOMAT

SUOMEN MEDIA-KAMARI OY 670646
Pisteenkaari 4, 03100 NUMMELA **Tel:** 9 22 26 565
Fax: 9 22 26 515
Titles:
KIINTEISTÖPOSTI

SUOMEN METROTUOTANTO OY 1791863
Joukahaisenkatu 67, 53500 LAPPEENRANTA
Tel: 50 30 31 000
Titles:
METROPOLI

SUOMEN METSÄNHOITAJALIITTO RY 670826
Kruunuvuorenkatu 5 F 25, 00160 HELSINKI
Tel: 9 68 40 810 **Fax:** 9 68 40 81 22
Titles:
METSÄNHOITAJA

SUOMEN METSÄSTÄJÄLIITTO RY 1793133
PL 91/ Kinturinkuja 4, 11101 RIIHIMAKI
Tel: 10 84 10 050 **Fax:** 10 84 10 051
Titles:
JAHTI - JAKT

SUOMEN MIELENTERVEYSSEURA RY 1794179
Maistraatinportti 4 A, 00240 HELSINKI
Tel: 9 61 55 16 **Fax:** 961551770
Titles:
MIELENTERVEYS

SUOMEN MS-LIITTO RY 1794076
PL 15/ Seppäläntie 90, 21251 MASKU
Tel: 2 43 92 111 **Fax:** 2 43 92 133
Titles:
AVAIN

SUOMEN NAISTUTKIMUKSEN SEURA RY 671582
PL 111, 80101 JOENSUU **Tel:** 40 51 15 039
Titles:
NAISTUTKIMUS - KVINNOFORSKNING

SUOMEN NIVELYHDISTYS RY 1794113
c/o Jyrki Laakso, Pajutie 16, 07940 LOVIISA
Tel: 44 55 44 555
Titles:
NIVELTIETO

SUOMEN NLP-YHDISTYS RY 677162
Kaupinkuja 21, 01360 VANTAA **Tel:** 9 34 24 24 14
Titles:
NLP-MIELILEHTI

SUOMEN OMAKOTILIITTO RY. 1792339
Sompiontie 1, 00730 HELSINKI **Tel:** 9 68 03 710
Fax: 9 68 03 71 55
Titles:
SUOMEN OMAKOTILEHTI

SUOMEN OPASLIITTO RY 7687
Verkatehtaankatu 2, 33100 TAMPERE
Tel: 3 21 10 802 **Fax:** 3 21 10 802
Titles:
OPAS-GUIDE

SUOMEN OSTO- JA LOGISTIIKKAYHDISTYS LOGY RY 1776795
Särkiniementie 3, 00210 HELSINKI
Tel: 9 69 63 752 **Fax:** 9 63 16 72
Titles:
LOGISTIIKKA

SUOMEN OSUUSKAUPPOJEN KESKUSKUNTA (SOK) 1792960
PL 1/ Fleminginkatu 34, 00088 S-RYHMÄ
Tel: 10 76 80 11 **Fax:** 10 76 80 380
Titles:
ÄSSÄ

SUOMEN PAIKALLISLIIKENNELIITTO OY 1789605
Unioninkatu 22, 3. krs, 00130 HELSINKI
Tel: 9 22 89 95 10 **Fax:** 922899550
Titles:
PAIKALLISLIIKENNE

SUOMEN PAIKALLISSANOMAT OY 1789403
Lindemaninkatu 3, 42100 JÄMSÄ
Tel: 10 66 55 149 **Fax:** 10 66 55 152
Titles:
JÄMSÄN SEUTU
JANAKKALAN SANOMAT
KANKAANPÄÄN SEUTU
KMV-LEHTI
KUHMOLAINEN
LUOTEISVÄYLÄ
MERIKARVIALEHTI
NOKIAN UUTISET
PYHÄJOKISEUTU
RAAHEN SEUTU
RANNIKKOSEUTU
SOTKAMO-LEHTI
SUUR-KEURUU
SYDÄN-SATAKUNTA
TYRVÄÄN SANOMAT
VALKEAKOSKEN SANOMAT
YLÄ-KAINUU

SUOMEN PAKKAUSYHDISTYS RY 1789398
Ritarikatu 3 b A, 00170 HELSINKI **Tel:** 9 68 40 340
Fax: 968403410
Titles:
PAKKAUS

SUOMEN PANKKI 671358
PL 160, 00101 HELSINKI **Tel:** 10 83 11
Titles:
EURO & TALOUS

SUOMEN PARKINSON-LIITTO RY 1794080
PL 905/ Suvilinnantie 2, 20101 TURKU
Tel: 2 27 40 400 **Fax:** 2 27 40 444
Titles:
PARKINSON-POSTIA

SUOMEN PARTIOLAISET - FINLANDS SCOUTER RY 1789756
Töölönkatu 55, 00250 HELSINKI
Tel: 9 88 65 11 00 **Fax:** 988651199
Titles:
PARTIO

SUOMEN PROVIISORILIITTO 1791604
Iso Roobertinkatu 7 A, 00120 HELSINKI
Tel: 9 69 62 270 **Fax:** 9 60 51 12
Titles:
DOSIS

SUOMEN PROVIISORIYHDISTYS RY 671276
Kaisaniemenkatu 1 B a, 7 krs, 00100 HELSINKI
Tel: 9 17 77 71 **Fax:** 9 68 43 99 11
Titles:
PROVIISORI

SUOMEN PUNAINEN RISTI 7723
PL 168/Tehtaankatu 1 a, 00141 HELSINKI
Tel: 9 12 931 **Fax:** 9 12 93 226
Titles:
ABO
AVUN MAAILMA

SUOMEN RAUHANTURVAAJALIITTO RY 671030
Aittastentie 138, 27320 IHODE **Tel:** 44 51 23 944
Titles:
RAUHANTURVAAJA

SUOMEN REUMALIITTO RY 670946
Iso Roobertinkatu 20-22 A, 00120 HELSINKI
Tel: 9 47 61 55 **Fax:** 9 64 22 86
Titles:
REUMA

SUOMEN RK-RYHMÄ 1789836
Rydöntie 24, 20360 TURKU **Tel:** 2 23 84 223
Fax: 22383335
Titles:
RASKASSARJA

SUOMEN RÖNTGENHOITAJALIITTO RY 671614
PL 140/ Asemamiehenkatu 4, 00060 TEHY
Tel: 9 54 22 75 22 **Fax:** 9 61 50 02 67
Titles:
RADIOGRAFIA

SUOMEN RUSKALIITTO RY 670947
Fredrikinkatu 62 A 1, 00100 HELSINKI
Tel: 9 49 27 43 **Fax:** 9 40 66 67
Titles:
RUSKALEHTI

SUOMEN SAIRAANHOITAJALIITTO RY 1789859
Asemamiehenkatu 2, 00520 HELSINKI
Tel: 9 22 90 020 **Fax:** 922900240
Titles:
SAIRAANHOITAJA - SJUKSKÖTERSKAN

SUOMEN SOTAVETERAANILIITTO RY - FINLANDS KRIGSVETERANFÖRBUND RF 670950
Ratamestarinkatu 9 C, 00520 HELSINKI
Tel: 9 61 26 200 **Fax:** 9 61 26 20 20
Titles:
SOTAVETERAANI - KRIGSVETERANEN

SUOMEN SYDÄNLIITTO RY 1794079
PL 50/ Oltermannintie 8, 00621 HELSINKI
Tel: 9 75 27 521
Titles:
SYDÄN

SUOMEN TALOKESKUS OY 692590
Pihlajistonkuja 4, 00710 HELSINKI
Tel: 9 72 51 55 00 **Fax:** 9 72 51 55 99
Titles:
KIINTEISTÖSEKTORI

SUOMEN TEOLLISUUSLÄÄKETIETEEN YHDISTYS 670800
PL 713/ Kalevankatu 11 A, 00101 HELSINKI
Tel: 9 61 88 52 11 **Fax:** 9 61 88 52 60
Titles:
TYÖTERVEYSLÄÄKÄRI

SUOMEN TEOLLISUUSSIJOITUS OY 1715125
PL 685/ Kalevankatu 9 A, 00101 HELSINKI
Tel: 9 68 03 680
Titles:
TEOLLISUUSSIJOITUS

SUOMEN TIEYHDISTYS RY 1784117
PL 55/ Kaupintie 16 A, 00441 HELSINKI
Tel: 20 78 61 000 **Fax:** 20 78 61 009
Titles:
TIE JA LIIKENNE

SUOMEN UNIFEM 1621872
Töölöntorinkatu 2 B, 8 krs, 00260 HELSINKI
Titles:
UN WOMEN -UUTISET

SUOMEN VALOTEKNILLINEN SEURA RY 1788327
Särkiniementie 3, 00210 HELSINKI
Tel: 400 86 93 39
Titles:
VALO

SUOMEN VAPAA-AJANKALASTAJIEN KESKUSJÄRJESTÖ 670885
Vanha Talvitie 2-6 A 11, 00580 HELSINKI
Tel: 9 22 89 13 12 **Fax:** 9 68 49 904
Titles:
VAPAA-AJAN KALASTAJA

SUOMEN VARUSMIESLIITTO 1791980
PL 1303/ Asemapäällikönkatu 1, 00101 HELSINKI **Fax:** 9 77 41 833
Titles:
VARUSMIES

SUOMEN VENEILYLIITTO RY 1792344
Westendinkatu 7, 02160 ESPOO **Tel:** 20 79 64 200
Fax: 20 79 64 111
Titles:
NAUTIC

SUOMEN VIRO-YHDISTYSTEN LIITTO RY 698698
PL 464/ Mariankatu 8 b C 12, 00171 HELSINKI
Tel: 9 68 42 84 64 **Fax:** 9 68 42 84 65
Titles:
VIRO.NYT

SUOMEN YLEISLÄÄKÄRIT GPF RY 1792296
PL 49 / Mäkelänkatu 2, 00501 HELSINKI
Tel: 9 39 30 758 **Fax:** 9 39 30 773
Titles:
YLEISLÄÄKÄRI

SUOMEN YRITTÄJIEN SYPOINT OY 1791352
PL 999/ Mannerheimintie 76 A, 00101 HELSINKI
Tel: 9 22 92 21 **Fax:** 9 22 92 29 99
Titles:
SUOMEN YRITTÄJÄSANOMAT
YRITTÄJÄ

SUOMENMAAN KUSTANNUS OY 670352
PL 52/Lekatie 4, 90101 OULU **Tel:** 8 53 70 011
Fax: 8 53 70 229
Titles:
APOLLO
SUOMENMAA
SUOMENMAA OULUN TOIMITUS

SUOMI-KIINA-SEURA RY. 671443
Ludviginkatu 3-5 A 52, 00130 HELSINKI
Tel: 9 60 58 12 **Fax:** 9 60 53 15
Titles:
KIINA SANOIN JA KUVIN

SUOMI-SAKSA YHDISTYSTEN LIITTO RY 692585
Pohjoinen Makasiinikatu 7, 00130 HELSINKI
Tel: 9 62 27 02 00 **Fax:** 9 62 27 02 77
Titles:
SILTA-BRÜCKE

SUOMI-SEURA RY 671029
Mariankatu 8 B c 15, 00170 HELSINKI
Tel: 9 68 41 210 **Fax:** 9 68 41 21 40
Titles:
SUOMEN SILTA

SUOMI-UNKARI SEURA RY 677065
Kaisaniemenkatu 10, 00100 HELSINKI
Tel: 9 85 69 85 66
Titles:
SUOMI-UNKARI

SUOMI-VENÄJÄ-SEURA 671444
PL 194/ Haapaniemenkatu 7-9 B, 12. krs, 00531 HELSINKI **Tel:** 9 69 38 31 **Fax:** 9 61 23 787
Titles:
KONTAKT

SUORAMEDIA OY 1790166
Lapinrinne 3, 00100 HELSINKI **Tel:** 9 61 55 15
Fax: 9 61 55 18 00
Titles:
SUOMELA

SUPERMEDIA ADV OY 699375
Larin Kyöstin katu 16, 13130 HÄMEENLINNA
Tel: 20 74 12 240 **Fax:** 20 74 12 249
Titles:
KONE & KULJETUS

KONETYÖ
KULJETUS-VARASTO-LOGISTIIKKA

SUSAMURU OY 1789401
Henry Fordin katu 5 H 5 krs, 00150 HELSINKI
Tel: 9 61 16 80
Titles:
WELCOME TO FINLAND

SVENSKA FOLKPARTIET 670919
PB 430/ Simonsgatan 8 A, 00101 HELSINGFORS **Tel:** 9 69 30 70 **Fax:** 9 69 31 968
Titles:
MEDBORGARBLADET

SVENSKA LANTBRUKS-PRODUCENTERNAS CENTRALFÖRBUND 1783060
Fredriksgatan 61 A 34, 00100 HELSINGFORS
Tel: 9 58 60 460 **Fax:** 9 69 41 358
Titles:
LANDSBYGDENS FOLK

SVENSKA ÖSTERBOTTENS LITTERATURFÖRENING 7763
Hörnvägen 2 A 7, 64200 NÄRPES
Tel: 50 37 14 963
Titles:
HORISONT

SVENSKA PENSIONÄRSFÖRBUNDET RF 670932
PB 129/ Annegatan 25 A, 3 vån, 00101 HELSINGFORS **Tel:** 20 72 88 810
Fax: 9 72 88 82 15
Titles:
GOD TID

SYDÄN-HÄMEEN KUSTANNUS OY 1792479
PL 16 / Onkkaalantie 58, 36601 PÄLKÄNE
Tel: 3 53 99 800 **Fax:** 3 53 99 888
Titles:
SYDÄN-HÄMEEN LEHTI

SYD-ÖSTERBOTTENS TIDNINGS AB 1790021
PB 6/ Närpesvägen 4, 64201 NÄRPES
Tel: 6 78 48 700 **Fax:** 6 78 48 887
Titles:
SYD-ÖSTERBOTTEN

SYÖPÄJÄRJESTÖT 1790575
Pieni Roobertinkatu 9, 00130 HELSINKI
Tel: 9 13 53 31 **Fax:** 9 13 51 093
Titles:
SYÖPÄ-CANCER

TALENTUM MEDIA OY 1789257
PL 920/ Annankatu 34-36 B, 00101 HELSINKI
Tel: 20 44 240 **Fax:** 20 44 24 677
Titles:
ARVOPAPERI
FAKTA
MARKKINOINTI & MAINONTA
MEDIUUTISET
MIKROPC
TALOUSELÄMÄ
TALOUSELÄMÄ PLATINUM
TEKNIIKKA & TALOUS
TIETOVIIKKO
URATIE

TALOTEKNIIKKA-JULKAISUT OY 1794096
Lönnrotinkatu 4 B, 00120 HELSINKI
Tel: 20 74 35 760 **Fax:** 20 74 35 761
Titles:
TALOTEKNIIKKA

TALOUSHALLINTOLIITON JULKAISUT OY 1792118
MCI Press Oy, Mikonkatu 18 B, 00100 HELSINKI
Tel: 9 68 50 57 55 **Fax:** 9 69 49 596
Titles:
TILISANOMAT

TALOUSSANOMAT OY 1774744
PL 45/ Töölönlahdenkatu 2, 00089 SANOMA
Tel: 9 12 21 **Fax:** 9 12 24 179
Titles:
ITVIIKKO
TALOUSSANOMAT

TALSO OY 676316
Annankatu 25 5. krs, 00100 HELSINKI
Tel: 9 41 30 06 00 **Fax:** 9 41 30 06 01
Titles:
VAPAAT TOIMITILAT

TAPATURMAVAKUUTUS-KESKUS TVK 696906
PL 275/ Bulevardi 28, 00121 HELSINKI
Tel: 9 68 04 01
Titles:
TAPATURMAVAKUUTUS

TAPIOLA-YHTIÖT 671056
Revontulentie 7, 02010 TAPIOLA **Tel:** 9 45 31
Fax: 9 45 33 166
Web site: http://www.tapiola.fi
Titles:
TAPIOLA OMA TALOUS

TEAM TEOLLISUUSALOJEN AMMATTILIITTO RY 1774042
PL 324 / Siltasaarenkatu 2, 00531 HELSINKI
Tel: 9 77 39 71 **Fax:** 9 75 38 511
Titles:
INTIIM

TEKNIIKAN AKATEEMISTEN LIITTO TEK RY 1790013
Ratavartijankatu 2, 00520 HELSINKI
Tel: 9 22 91 21 **Fax:** 9 22 91 29 11
Titles:
TEK

TEKNIIKAN HISTORIAN SEURA THS RY 670635
Tieteiden Talo, Kirkkokatu 6, 00170 HELSINKI
Tel: 9 46 82 126
Titles:
TEKNIIKAN WAIHEITA

TEKNIKUM-YHTIÖT 677127
PL 13/ Nokiankatu 1, 38211 SASTAMALA
Tel: 3 51 911 **Fax:** 3 51 91 33 30
Titles:
KUMIVIESTI

TEKNOLOGIATEOLLISUUS RY 670617
PL 10/Eteläranta 10, 00131 HELSINKI
Tel: 9 45 12 706 **Fax:** 9 62 44 62
Titles:
METALLITEKNIIKKA
OHUTLEVY

TEKSTIVIESTIT OY 1790216
Köydenpunojankatu 4 a D, 00180 HELSINKI
Tel: 9 60 25 44 **Fax:** 9 61 16 70
Titles:
TEKSTIVIESTIT OY

TEOLLISUUDEN VOIMA OY 1680548
Olkiluoto, 27160 EURAJOKI **Tel:** 2 83 811
Fax: 2 83 81 52 09
Titles:
YTIMEKÄS

TERÄSRAKENNEYHDISTYS R.Y. 1792298
PL 381/ Unioninkatu 14, 4. kerros, 00131 HELSINKI **Tel:** 9 12 99 514 **Fax:** 9 12 99 214
Titles:
TERÄSRAKENNE

TERVAREITTI OY 1792882
PL 63/ Aaronkuja 5, 91501 MUHOS
Tel: 8 53 13 700 **Fax:** 8 53 32 179
Titles:
TERVAREITTI

TERVEYDEN- JA SOSIAALIHUOLTOALAN AMMATTIJÄRJ. 1774141
PL 10/Asemamiehenkatu 4, 00060 TEHY
Tel: 9 54 22 70 00 **Fax:** 9 61 50 02 73
Titles:
TEHY-LEHTI

TIETOMEDIAT OY 1792299
Hämeenpuisto 44, 33200 TAMPERE
Tel: 3 22 34 380 **Fax:** 3 22 34 381
Titles:
HANKINTAVINKIT

TIETOYHTEISKUNNAN KEHITTÄMISKESKUS TIEKE RY 671077
Salomonkatu 17 A, 10 krs., 00100 HELSINKI
Tel: 9 47 63 04 00 **Fax:** 9 47 63 03 99
Titles:
TIEDOSTA

TILAUSAJOKULJETTAJAT RY. 671403
Pruukintuvantie 7 A 20, 60200 SEINÄJOKI
Tel: 45 67 65 865 **Fax:** 6 41 22 456
Titles:
CHARTER CLUB

TILMA MEDIAT OY 671426
PL 164, 20101 TURKU **Tel:** 20 71 21 254
Fax: 20 71 21 251
Titles:
KULTTUURIHAITARI
SAARISTOUUTISET

TK-MEDIATALO OY 1641517
Hämeenkatu 14, 3 krs, 11100 RIIHIMÄKI
Tel: 10 42 15 000
Titles:
TERVEYSUUTISET

TLH MEDIA OY 1794149
Sulankuja 3, 04300 TUUSULA **Tel:** 10 42 04 120
Fax: 9 27 31 301
Titles:
BIKE

TOHMAJÄRVI-VÄRTSILÄ LEHTI OY 1790233
PL 6 / Asemantie 2, 82601 TOHMAJÄRVI
Tel: 10 42 24 000 **Fax:** 104224005
Titles:
UUTIS ALASIN

TOURING FINLANDIA MK RY 699686
Karstulantie 4, 00550 HELSINKI **Tel:** 9 77 34 573
Titles:
MOOTTORITURISTI

TOYOTA-YHTIÖT 671227
PL 12/ Korpivaarantie 1, 01451 VANTAA
Tel: 9 85 181 **Fax:** 9 85 18 22 21
Titles:
TOYOTA PLUS

OY TRADING WEAL LTD 1782985
Koulukatu 10 A, 53100 LAPPEENRANTA
Tel: 5 54 12 245 **Fax:** 5 54 12 246
Titles:
KONEIKKUNA

TT-TUULET AVOIN YHTIÖ 1788314
Huvilakatu 8, 06100 PORVOO
Titles:
TUULET

TULLIHALLITUS 671482
PL 512/ Erottajankatu 2, 00101 HELSINKI
Tel: 9 61 41 **Fax:** 20 49 22 852
Titles:
TULLIVIESTI

TURUN OMAKOTILEHTI OY 671566
PL 943/ Itäinen Rantakatu 68 C 48, 20101 TURKU **Tel:** 2 23 66 790 **Fax:** 2 23 66 790
Titles:
TURUN OMAKOTILEHTI

TURUN SANOMAT OY 1789552
PL 95/ Kauppiaskatu 5, 20101 TURKU
Tel: 2 26 93 311
Titles:
TS. TURUN SANOMAT
TURUN SANOMAT HUITTINEN
TURUN SANOMAT LOHJA
TURUN SANOMAT LOIMAA
TURUN SANOMAT RAUMA
TURUN SANOMAT SÄKYLÄ
TURUN SANOMAT SALO
TURUN SANOMAT UUSIKAUPUNKI

TURUN SEUDUN VAPAIDEN SEURAKUNTIEN VIESTINTÄYHDISTYS A&O RY 1776808
Kalastajankatu 1 B, 20100 TURKU
Tel: 2 25 15 385 **Fax:** 2 25 15 384
Titles:
A & O

TURUN SEUTU OY 1794006
Elotie 26, 21360 LIETO AS. **Tel:** 2 48 92 00
Fax: 2 48 92 099
Titles:
TURUN TIENOO

TURUN TIETOTARJONTA OY 1790016
PL 600/ Yliopistonkatu 14, 20101 TURKU
Tel: 2 26 93 900 **Fax:** 2 26 94 51
Titles:
AAMUSET

TURVALLISUUDEN JA RISKIENHALLINNAN (T&RH) TIETOPALVELU OY 1792294
Kumitehtaankatu 5, 04260 KERAVA
Tel: 40 58 40 212 **Fax:** 10 42 19 601
Titles:
TURVALLISUUS & RISKIENHALLINTA

TYÖSUOJELURAHASTO TSR JA TYÖTURVALLISUUSKESKUS TTK 1792119
Lönnrotinkatu 4 B, 00120 HELSINKI
Tel: 9 61 62 61 **Fax:** 9 61 21 287
Titles:
TELMA

TYÖTEHOSEURA RY 1794307
PL 5/ Kiljavantie 6, 05201 RAJAMÄKI
Tel: 9 29 04 12 00 **Fax:** 9 51 29 07 20
Titles:
TEHO

TYÖTERVEYSLAITOS 1792297
Topeliuksenkatu 41 a A, 00250 HELSINKI
Tel: 30 47 41 **Fax:** 30 47 42 478
Titles:
TYÖ TERVEYS TURVALLISUUS

ULKOPOLIITTINEN INSTITUUTTI 1790516
PL 400/ Kruunuvuorenkatu 4, 00161 HELSINKI
Tel: 9 43 27 700
Titles:
ULKOPOLITIIKKA

ULVILAN SEUTU OY 1794010
PL 11/ Friitalantie 13, 28401 ULVILA
Tel: 2 53 11 721 **Fax:** 25311710
Titles:
ULVILAN SEUTU

UNIONIMEDIA 670857
PL 36/ Kaupintie 16 A, 3 krs, 00441 HELSINKI
Tel: 9 41 33 44 10 **Fax:** 9 41 33 44 33
Titles:
PRO TOIMIHENKILÖUNIONI

UPC MEDIA OY 699808
Gerbyntie 18, 65230 VAASA **Tel:** 6 32 18 000
Fax: 6 32 18 001
Titles:
ASUNTOLEHTI - BOSTADSBLADET

UPM-KYMMENE OYJ 674488
PL 380/ Eteläesplanadi 2, 00101 HELSINKI
Tel: 20 41 51 11 **Fax:** 20 41 50 512
Titles:
GRIFFIN

UPSEERILIITTO RY 671198
Laivastokatu 1 B, 00160 HELSINKI
Tel: 9 66 89 40 16 **Fax:** 9 66 89 40 20
Titles:
SOTILASAIKAKAUSLEHTI

URHEILUHALLIT OY 676134
Helsinginkatu 25, 00510 HELSINKI
Tel: 9 34 88 600
Titles:
OMA LIIKUNTA

URJALAN SANOMAT OY 1794007
PL 61/ Urjalantie 26, 31761 URJALA
Tel: 40 18 13 020 **Fax:** 3 54 66 660
Titles:
URJALAN SANOMAT

UTGIVARFÖRENINGEN FÖR TIDSKRIFTEN ASTRA NOVA 7766
Tallbergsgatan 1/71, 00180 HELSINGFORS
Tel: 9 61 24 80 80 **Fax:** 9 44 29 26
Titles:
ASTRA NOVA

UUDENKAUPUNGIN SANOMAT OY 1791658
PL 68/ Alinenkatu 29, 23501 UUSIKAUPUNKI
Tel: 2 58 88 302 **Fax:** 2 84 24 940
Titles:
UUDENKAUPUNGIN SANOMAT

UUDENMAAN, HÄMEEN, PIRKANMAAN, SATAKUNNAN JA 1775008
Vanajantie 10 B, 13110 HÄMEENLINNA
Tel: 20 74 73 000
Titles:
PROAGRIA SATOA

UUSI INSINÖÖRILIITTO IL RY. 1789855
Ratavartijankatu 2 A, 8krs, 00520 HELSINKI
Tel: 20 18 01 801 **Fax:** 20 18 01 880
Titles:
UUSI INSINÖÖRI

UUSIMAA OY 1790214
PL 15/Teollisuustie 19, 06151 PORVOO
Tel: 20 61 00 140 **Fax:** 20 77 03 021
Titles:
UUSIMAA

VAASA OY 7848
Raatihuoneenkatu 7, 68600 PIETARSAARI
Tel: 6 24 77 581 **Fax:** 6 24 77 957
Titles:
POHJALAINEN PIETARSAARI
POHJALAINEN SEINÄJOKI
POHJALAINEN SUUPOHJA

VAILLA VAKINAISTA ASUNTOA RY 1791130
Kinaporinkatu 2, 00500 HELSINKI
Tel: 10 54 81 900 **Fax:** 10 54 81 999
Titles:
ASUKKI

VAKKA-SUOMEN SANOMAIN KUNTAYHTYMÄ 1790484
PL 84/ Rauhankatu 8 A, 23501 UUSIKAUPUNKI
Tel: 2 84 26 300 **Fax:** 2 84 16 142
Titles:
VAKKA-SUOMEN SANOMAT

VAKUUTUSVÄEN LIITTO VVL 670763
Asemamiehenkatu 2, 00520 HELSINKI
Tel: 9 85 67 24 00 **Fax:** 9 85 67 24 01
Titles:
VAKUUTUSVÄKI - FÖRSÄKRINGSMANNABLADET

VALITUT PALAT - READERS DIGEST AB 1774148
PL 106/ Pitäjänmäentie 14, 00381 HELSINKI
Tel: 9 50 34 41 **Fax:** 9 50 34 499
Titles:
MEIDÄN SUOMI

VALITUT PALAT-READER'S DIGEST OY AB 1793870
PL 106/ Pitäjämäentie 14, 00381 HELSINKI
Tel: 9 50 34 41 **Fax:** 9 50 34 499
Titles:
VALITUT PALAT

VAMMAISTEN KOULUTUKSEN JA TYÖLLISTYMISEN TUKI VKTT RY 1792291
Pasilanraitio 5, 00240 HELSINKI **Tel:** 9 41 55 15 00
Titles:
TUKILINJA

VANHUS- JA LÄHIMMÄISPALVELUN LIITTO RY. 671432
Hämeentie 58-60 A 52, 00500 HELSINKI
Tel: 9 77 45 900 **Fax:** 9 70 15 474
Titles:
UUDET TUULET

VANHUSTYÖN KESKUSLIITTO 671541
Malmin kauppatie 26, 00700 HELSINKI
Tel: 9 35 08 600 **Fax:** 9 35 08 60 10
Titles:
VANHUSTYÖ - SENIORARBETE

VANTAAN ENERGIA OY 698715
PL 95/ Peltolantie 27, 01301 VANTAA
Tel: 9 82 901 **Fax:** 9 82 65 17
Titles:
ENERGIAVIRTAA

VANTAAN EVANKELIS-LUTERILAISET SEURAKUNNAT 1792286
PL 56/ Unikkotie 5 B, 01301 VANTAA
Tel: 9 83 06 274 **Fax:** 9 82 30 136
Titles:
VANTAAN LAURI

VANTAAN SOSIALIDEMOKRAATTINEN KUNNALLISJÄRJESTÖ 1792881
Lehdokkitie 2, 2 krs, 01300 VANTAA
Tel: 9 82 30 595 **Fax:** 9 82 30 596
Titles:
VANTAALAINEN

VAPAA-AJATTELIJOIDEN LIITTO RY. 1790221
Neljäs linja 1, 00530 HELSINKI **Tel:** 44 71 56 01
Fax: 9 71 56 02
Titles:
VAPAA AJATTELIJA

VEGAANILIITTO RY 676855
Hämeentie 48, 00500 HELSINKI **Tel:** 9 29 63 025
Fax: 9 22 15 696
Titles:
VEGAIA

VEHO GROUP OY AB 1689826
Salomonkatu 17 B, 00100 HELSINKI
Tel: 10 56 92 202
Titles:
MERCEDES

VERONMAKSAJAIN KESKUSLIITTO RY 670571
Kalevankatu 4, 5 krs, 00100 HELSINKI
Tel: 9 61 88 71 **Fax:** 9 60 80 87
Titles:
TALOUSTAITO
TALOUSTAITO YRITYS
VEROUUTISET

VEROVIRKAILIJAIN LIITTO 671136
Ratamestarinkatu 11, 00520 HELSINKI
Tel: 9 22 93 36 34 **Fax:** 9 22 93 36 36
Titles:
VEROVÄKI

VESAISTEN KESKUSLIITTO RY 676319
Asemapäällikönkatu 1, 00520 HELSINKI
Tel: 20 75 52 696 **Fax:** 20 75 52 627
Titles:
VIISARI

VIA GROUP 1735322
Westendinkatu 7, 02160 ESPOO **Tel:** 20 74 02 800
Fax: 20 74 02 830
Titles:
VIA LEADERSHIP

VIESTILEHDET OY 1789389
PL 440/Simonkatu 6, 00101 HELSINKI
Tel: 20 41 32 155 **Fax:** 20 41 62 233
Titles:
AARRE
KONEVIESTI
MAASEUDUN TULEVAISUUS
SUOMALAINEN MAASEUTU

VIESTINTÄYHDISTYS A&O RY 691093
Kalastajankatu 1 B, 20100 TURKU
Tel: 2 25 15 385 **Fax:** 2 25 15 384
Titles:
AJAN FAKTA

VIHREÄ LANKA OY 1790222
Fredrikinkatu 33, 3 krs, 00120 HELSINKI
Tel: 9 58 60 41 23 **Fax:** 9 58 60 41 24
Titles:
VIHREÄ LANKA

VIKINGROAD 1640018
Vironkatu 9, 00170 HELSINKI **Tel:** 9 69 80 442
Fax: 9 68 13 07 11
Titles:
METSÄALAN AMMATTILEHTI

VOIMA KUSTANNUS OY 1792292
Hämeentie 48, 00500 HELSINKI **Tel:** 9 77 44 31 20
Fax: 9 77 32 328
Titles:
VOIMA

VOLVO AUTO OY AB 1792337
c/o Alma 360 Asiakasmedia, PL 502, 00101 HELSINKI **Tel:** 10 66 52 01
Titles:
VOLVO VIESTI

VOLVO FINLAND AB 1788331
PL 50/ Vetokuja 1 E, 01611 VANTAA
Tel: 10 65 500 **Fax:** 10 65 55 895
Titles:
VOLVO VISIITTI

VR OSAKEYHTIÖ 1789755
Alma 360 Asiakasmedia, PL 502/ Munkkiniemen puistotie 25, 5.krs, 00101 HELSINKI
Tel: 10 66 51 02 **Fax:** 10 66 52 533
Titles:
MATKAAN

VUORIMIESYHDISTYS - BERGSMANNAFÖRENINGEN R.Y. 671534
Kaskilaaksontie 3 D 108, 02360 ESPOO
Tel: 9 81 34 758 **Fax:** 9 81 34 758
Titles:
MATERIA

VV-AUTO OY 671238
Hitsaajankatu 7 B, 00810 HELSINKI **Tel:** 9 75 831
Fax: 9 75 94 20 11
Titles:
ETUMATKAA

VVO-YHTYMÄ OY 670915
PL 40/ Mannerheimintie 168, 00301 HELSINKI
Tel: 20 50 83 10 **Fax:** 20 50 83 790
Titles:
ASUKAS

WÄDE PRODUCTION OY 671543
PL 35/ Kivivuorentie 4, 01621 VANTAA
Tel: 9 29 03 250 **Fax:** 9 29 03 255
Titles:
HYVÄ KAUPPA

WARKAUDEN LEHTI OY 1790442
Pirnankatu 4, 78200 VARKAUS **Tel:** 17 77 83 631
Fax: 17 55 22 375
Titles:
WARKAUDEN LEHTI

WHEELMEDIA 1726818
PL 235, 01301 VANTAA
Titles:
KAASUJALKA

WINDJAMMER MEDIA OY 1788339
Haraldsby, 22410 GODBY **Tel:** 18 41 869
Titles:
SCANDINAVIAN MAGAZINE

WOODPUBLISHER OY LTD 1792295
PL 211/ Puistokatu 9 A, 15101 LAHTI
Tel: 3 73 31 501 **Fax:** 37331511
Titles:
WOODWORKING PUUNTYÖSTÖ

WWF VERDENSNATURFONDEN 1783760
Lintulahdenkatu 10, 00500 HELSINKI
Tel: 9 77 40 100 **Fax:** 9 77 40 21 39
Titles:
PANDAN POLKU

YARA SUOMI 671085
PL 900/ Mechelininkatu 1 A, 00181 HELSINKI
Tel: 10 86 15 11 **Fax:** 10 86 21 619
Titles:
LEIPÄ LEVEÄMMÄKSI

YHDYSKUNTASUUNNITTELUN SEURA RY (YSS) 675960
Tieteiden Talo, Kirkkokatu 6, 00170 HELSINKI
Tel: 9 22 86 92 70
Titles:
YHDYSKUNTASUUNNITTELU

YLÄ-SATAKUNNAN SANOMALEHTI OY 1790963
PL 6 / Parkanontie 63, 39701 PARKANO
Tel: 3 44 381 **Fax:** 3 44 38 44
Titles:
YLÄ-SATAKUNTA

YLIOPISTON APTEEKKI 1616846
Valimotie 7, 00380 HELSINKI **Tel:** 9 54 20 46
Titles:
APTEEKIN HYLLYLTÄ

YLIOPISTON FARMASIAKUNTA RY 7659
PL 56/ Viikinkaari 5, 00014 HELSINGIN YLIOPISTO **Tel:** 9 37 45 273 **Fax:** 9 37 45 273
Titles:
MDS

YLÖJÄRVEN SANOMAT OY 1792879
PL 26/ Mikkolantie 7, 33471 YLÖJÄRVI
Tel: 3 34 77 200 **Fax:** 3 34 77 221
Titles:
YLÖJÄRVEN UUTISET

YMPÄRISTÖASIANTUNTIJOIDEN KESKUSLIITTO YKL RY
1784103
Vuorikatu 22 A 15, 00100 HELSINKI
Tel: 9 62 26 850 **Fax:** 9 62 26 85 50

Titles:
YMPÄRISTÖASIANTUNTIJA

YMPÄRISTÖMINISTERIÖ JA SUOMEN YMPÄRISTÖKESKUS
671230
PL 140/ Mechelininkatu 34 A, 00251 HELSINKI
Tel: 20 49 02 762 **Fax:** 20 49 02 790

Titles:
YMPÄRISTÖ

ZAO MEDIA PRESS
692530
Koulukatu 10 B, 53100 LAPPEENRANTA
Tel: 5 41 85 101 **Fax:** 5 41 85 102

Titles:
STOP IN FINLAND

ZONETRADE SERVICES
1782056
Pengerkatu 2, 67100 KOKKOLA **Tel:** 46 57 48 571

Titles:
MADE IN EU

France

1,2,3... DETENTE
1785099
163 quai du Docteur-Dervaux, 92601, CEDEX ASNIERES **Tel:** 1 41 32 73 15 **Fax:** 141327305

Titles:
1,2,3... DETENTE

20 MINUTES FRANCE SAS
1640592
50-52 boulevard Haussmann, CS 10300, 75427 CEDEX 09 PARIS **Tel:** 1 53 26 65 65
Fax: 1 53 26 65 68

Titles:
20 MINUTES PARIS

A PARIS VILLE DE PARIS
1625483
4 rue de Lobau, 75196, CEDEX 4 PARIS
Tel: 1 42 76 79 82 **Fax:** 142767995

Titles:
A PARIS VILLE DE PARIS

ABC
1622711
84 boulevard de Sébastopol, 75003 PARIS
Tel: 1 42 74 28 00 **Fax:** 1 42 74 29 36

Titles:
AGRA PRESSE HEBDO
FLD - FRUITS ET LEGUMES
LES MARCHES
VSB - VINS SPIRITUEUX BOISSONS

ADOUR PRESSE INFORMATION
1622621
Antenne à Paris, 3 rue Séguier, 75006 PARIS
Tel: 5 59 52 55 33 **Fax:** 5 59 52 84 01

Titles:
LA GAZETTE OFFICIELLE DU TOURISME

AGENCE IPANEMA
1622849
Agence Ipanema, 10 rue Pergolèse, 75016 PARIS **Tel:** 1 44 17 34 34 **Fax:** 1 44 17 34 39

Titles:
CARREFOUR SAVOIRS

AISNE CONSEIL GENERAL DE L'AISNE
1784735
Hôtel-du-Département, Rue Paul-Doumer, 02013 CEDEX LAON **Tel:** 3 23 24 62 80 **Fax:** 323246284

Titles:
L' AISNE CONSEIL GENERAL DE L'AISNE

AMAURY
1626955
25 avenue Michelet, 93408 SAINT-OUEN
Tel: 1 40 10 30 30 **Fax:** 1 40 10 35 17

Titles:
AUJOURD'HUI EN FRANCE
LE PARISIEN - AUJOURD'HUI EN FRANCE ECONOMIE SUPPLEMENT DU QUOTIDIEN LE PARISIEN
LE PARISIEN - PARIS

ANGELINE'S MAG
1625253
83 avenue de Clichy, 75017 PARIS

Titles:
ANGELINE'S MAG

AQUITAINE CONSEIL REGIONAL D'AQUITAINE
1624620
14 rue François-de-Sourdis, 33077 BORDEAUX CEDEX **Tel:** 5 57 57 02 80 **Fax:** 5 57 57 02 47

Titles:
L' AQUITAINE CONSEIL REGIONAL D'AQUITAINE

ARTCLAIR EDITIONS
1622998
8 rue Borromée, 75015 PARIS **Tel:** 1 48 42 90 00
Fax: 1 48 42 90 01

Titles:
LE JOURNAL DES ARTS
L' OEIL

ASF
1790764
68 rue Marjolin, CEDEX, 92309 LEVALLOIS PERRET **Tel:** 1 45 19 58 00 **Fax:** 1 45 19 58 16

Titles:
TELE MAGAZINE

ATC
1790699
ATC, 23 rue Dupont des Loges, BP 90 146 CEDEX 1, 57004 METZ **Tel:** 3 87 69 18 18
Fax: 3 87 69 18 14

Titles:
AFRIQUE AGRICULTURE
L' ARBORICULTURE FRUITIERE
CIRCUITS CULTURE
CULTURE LEGUMIERE
VITI

AXIS SANTE
1790745
AXIS SANTE, 15 rue des Sablons, 75116 PARIS
Tel: 1 47 55 31 41 **Fax:** 1 47 55 31 32

Titles:
CARDIOLOGIE PRATIQUE

AYACHE
1790714
53 avenue Victor Hugo, 75116 PARIS
Tel: 1 56 88 98 00 **Fax:** 1 56 88 98 32

Titles:
NUMERO
QUESTIONS DE FEMMES
REPONSE A TOUT

B & B MEDIA
1784841
40 rue de Paradis, 75010 PARIS
Tel: 1 53 34 98 00 **Fax:** 1 53 34 98 05

Titles:
MAXIMOTO

BAUER
1623129
30/32 rue de Chabrol, 75010 PARIS
Tel: 1 40 22 75 00 **Fax:** 1 48 24 08 40

Titles:
MAXI
MAXI CUISINE

BAYARD
1626958
18 rue Barbès, 92128 CEDEX MONTROUGE
Tel: 1 74 31 60 60 **Fax:** 1 74 31 60 01

Titles:
LES PARENTS & ENFANTS SUPPLEMENT HEBDOMADAIRE DU JOURNAL LA CROIX
PRIONS EN EGLISE

BAYARD PRESSE
1790627
18 rue Barbès, CEDEX, 92128 MONTROUGE
Tel: 1 74 31 60 60 **Fax:** 1 74 31 60 01

Titles:
LA CROIX
ENFANT MAGAZINE
JE BOUQUINE
NOTRE TEMPS MAGAZINE
OKAPI
PELERIN

BLEUCOM
1790759
BLEUCOM, 10-12 villa Thoreton, 75015 PARIS
Tel: 1 45 71 75 00

Titles:
MAMAN !
NEUF MOIS MAGAZINE

BOOST EDITIONS
1785800
BP 337, CEDEX, 80103 ABBEVILLE
Tel: 3 22 20 15 63 **Fax:** 3 22 24 90 27

Titles:
BOOST TUNING

BOTANIC
1786665
Botanic IBP Archamps, BP 64106, 74161 CEDEX SAINT-JULIEN-EN-GENEVOIS **Tel:** 4 50 31 27 00
Fax: 450312701

Titles:
BOTANIC

BSC
1790685
45 rue de l'Est, 92100 BOULOGNE BILLANCOURT **Tel:** 1 48 25 11 33
Fax: 1 48 25 47 42

Titles:
MULTIMEDIA A LA UNE

BTP RETRAITE
1790844
BP 300, CEDEX, 6800 CAGNES-SUR-MER
Tel: 4 92 13 78 74

Titles:
LE FIL DES ANS

BURDA - DIPA
1790792
26 avenue de l'Europe, BP 60052, CEDEX, 67013 STRASBOURG **Tel:** 3 88 19 25 25
Fax: 3 88 19 40 76

Titles:
BURDA

CENTRE FRANCE
1784689
45 rue du Clos-Four, BP 83, 63056 CEDEX 2 CLERMONT-FERRAND **Tel:** 4 73 17 17 17
Fax: 4 73 17 18 19

Titles:
LA MONTAGNE CLERMONT-FERRAND
LE POPULAIRE DU CENTRE: EDITION HAUTE-VIENNE

CENTRE FRANCE LA MONTAGNE
1623298
Rue de la Halte, BP 93035, 45403 CEDEX FLEURY-LES-AUBRAIS **Tel:** 2 38 78 79 80
Fax: 2 38 78 79 79

Titles:
LA RÉPUBLIQUE DU CENTRE - EDITION DU LOIRET

CFDT
1790677
4 Boulevard de la Villette, CEDEX 19, 75955 PARIS **Tel:** 1 42 03 82 00 **Fax:** 1 53 72 85 68

Titles:
CFDT MAGAZINE

CMPMEDICA
1790694
21 rue Camille Desmoulins, CEDEX 9, 92789 ISSY LES MOULINEAUX **Tel:** 1 73 28 14 70
Fax: 1 73 28 14 71

Titles:
LE GENERALISTE
LE QUOTIDIEN DU MEDECIN
LE QUOTIDIEN DU PHARMACIEN

COM-PRESSE
1790819
COM-PRESSE, 6 rue Tarnac, 47220 ASTAFFORT **Tel:** 5 53 48 17 60 **Fax:** 5 53 66 71 64

Titles:
VIE PRATIQUE FEMININ
VIE PRATIQUE GOURMAND

CPPD
1790776
6 bis rue Campagne Première, 75014 PARIS
Tel: 1 56 80 20 80 **Fax:** 1 56 80 20 85

Titles:
TETU

DGT ASSOCIÉS
1790650
DGT Associés, 46 rue du Général Chanzy, 94130 NOGENT-SUR-MARNE **Tel:** 1 48 77 37 06
Fax: 1 48 77 37 36

Titles:
L' ESSENTIEL DE LA MAROQUINERIE

DI GROUP
1622965
16 rue du Quatre-Septembre, CEDEX 2, 75112 PARIS **Tel:** 1 44 88 55 00 **Fax:** 1 44 88 51 88

Titles:
CONNAISSANCE DES ARTS
INVESTIR

DISNEY HACHETTE PRESSE
1622696
10 rue Thierry Le Luron, CEDEX, 92592 LEVALLOIS PERRET **Tel:** 1 41 34 85 00
Fax: 1 41 34 88 61

Titles:
LE JOURNAL DE MICKEY
KID'S MAG
PICSOU MAGAZINE
SUPER PICSOU GEANT

DNA
1623281
17-21 rue de la Nuée-Bleue, BP 406, 67077 CEDEX STRASBOURG **Tel:** 3 88 21 55 00
Fax: 3 88 21 55 15

Titles:
DNA - DERNIERES NOUVELLES D'ALSACE STRASBOURG

DPE EDITIONS
1790766
SAP, 9 rue de l'Arbre Sec, 69001 LYON
Tel: 4 72 98 26 60 **Fax:** 4 72 98 26 80

Titles:
ENVIRONNEMENT ET TECHNIQUE

EBRA
1784678
40 quai des Bons-Enfants, BP 273, 88026 CEDEX EPINAL **Tel:** 29 82 98 00 **Fax:** 3 29 82 99 29

Titles:
VOSGES MATIN EPINAL

EDIFA
1790722
EDIFA, 15/27 rue Moussorgski, CEDEX 18, 75895 PARIS **Tel:** 1 53 26 35 00 **Fax:** 1 53 26 35 05

Titles:
FAMILLE CHRETIENNE

EDIMETIERS
1644578
EDIMETIERS, 137 quai de Valmy, 75010 PARIS
Tel: 1 40 05 23 23 **Fax:** 1 40 05 23 24

Titles:
LE MONDE DES ARTISANS

EDIT OUEST
1786501
108 rue Victor Boissel, BP 529, CEDEX, 53005 LAVAL **Tel:** 2 43 59 10 40 **Fax:** 2 43 49 03 91

Titles:
LE COURRIER DE LA MAYENNE

EDITIALIS
1790637
13 rue Louis Pasteur, CEDEX, 92513 BOULOGNE BILLANCOURT **Tel:** 1 46 99 93 93
Fax: 1 46 99 81 40 97 71

Titles:
ACTION COMMERCIALE
DECISION ACHATS
MARKETING DIRECT
MARKETING MAGAZINE
RELATION CLIENT

EDITIONS DE LA R.H.F
1790767
9 rue Labie, CEDEX 17, 75838 PARIS
Tel: 1 45 74 21 62 **Fax:** 1 45 74 01 03

Titles:
L' INDUSTRIE HOTELIERE

EDITIONS DE L'ECLUSE
1790742
36 boulevard de la Bastille, 75012 PARIS
Tel: 1 40 19 90 00 **Fax:** 1 40 19 09 72

Titles:
FLUVIAL

EDITIONS DE L'ETOILE
1790640
65 rue Montmartre, 75002 PARIS
Tel: 1 53 44 75 75 **Fax:** 1 43 43 95 04

Titles:
LES CAHIERS DU CINEMA

EDITIONS DE L'UNION
1623283
55 rue La Boétie, 75384 CEDEX 08 PARIS
Tel: 1 40 74 08 00 **Fax:** 140740780

Titles:
LE MAGAZINE DU MOUVEMENT POPULAIRE

France

EDITIONS DE VERNEUIL 1623115
35 rue de Liège, 75008 PARIS **Tel:** 1 44 70 66 66
Fax: 1 44 70 66 69

Titles:
GESTION DE FORTUNE

EDITIONS D.P.E. 1622960
9 rue de l'Arbre-Sec, 69281 CEDEX 01 LYON
Tel: 4 72 98 26 60 **Fax:** 4 72 98 26 80

Titles:
VERTITUDE MAGAZINE

EDITIONS DU BOISBAUDRY 1789970
13 square du Chêne Germain, CS 77711, CEDEX, 35577 CESSON-SEVIGNE
Tel: 2 99 32 21 21 **Fax:** 2 99 32 14 17

Titles:
LINEAIRES
PROCESS ALIMENTAIRE
RAYON BOISSONS

EDITIONS HUBERT BURDA MEDIA 1790711
67 rue de Dunkerque, 75009 PARIS
Tel: 1 53 63 10 27 **Fax:** 1 53 63 82 38

Titles:
MAISON BRICOLAGE ET DECORATION
SAVEURS

EDITIONS JALOU 1784785
10 rue du Plâtre, 75004 PARIS **Tel:** 1-53-01-10-30
Fax: 1-53-01-11-93

Titles:
JALOU GALLERY
L' OFFICIEL
L' OPTIMUM
LA REVUE DES MONTRES

EDITIONS LARIVIERE 1784869
Immeuble Sirius, 9 allée Jean Prouvé, CEDEX, 92387 CLICHY **Tel:** 1 41 40 33 33
Fax: 1 47 40 31 00

Titles:
ECRAN TOTAL
FASHION DAILY NEWS
MICRO PRATIQUE
LE MONDE DU CAMPING CAR
LE MONDE DU PIN AIR
MOTO REVUE
LE QUOTIDIEN DU TOURISME
ROCK & FOLK

EDITIONS NIVEALES 1790719
6 rue Irvoy, CEDEX 1, 38027 GRENOBLE
Tel: 4 76 70 92 60 **Fax:** 4 76 70 54 12

Titles:
GRANDS REPORTAGES

EDITIONS SEBAN 1790800
5 bis rue Faÿs, 94160 SAINT-MANDE
Tel: 1 41 74 10 00 **Fax:** 1 41 74 11 21

Titles:
MARIONS NOUS !

EDITIONS SEDEC 1790680
11 rue de Milan, CEDEX 09, 75440 PARIS
Tel: 1 53 80 74 00

Titles:
LE MONITEUR DU COMMERCE INTERNATIONAL

ELIAZ EDITIONS 1623367
4 avenue de Corbéra, 75012 PARIS
Tel: 1 53 02 06 60 **Fax:** 1 43 44 07 08

Titles:
LA TERRASSE

ELSEVIER-MASSON 1790691
62 rue Camille Desmoulins, CEDEX, 92442 ISSY LES MOULINEAUX **Tel:** 1 71 16 55 00
Fax: 1 71 16 51 99

Titles:
LE PHARMACIEN HOSPITALIER

ELTA - MBC 1790667
16 rue Saint Fiacre, 75002 PARIS
Tel: 1 42 36 51 02 **Fax:** 1 42 36 04 62

Titles:
LA REVUE DES COMPTOIRS
LA REVUE DES TABACS

EMI 1784682
6 rue Faidherbe, 94160 SAINT-MANDE
Tel: 1 48 12 35 31 **Fax:** 1 48 12 35 52

Titles:
COTE SANTE

EST REPUBLICAIN 1623321
7 boulevard du Chanoine Kir, BP 21 550, CEDEX, 21015 DIJON **Tel:** 3 80 42 42 42
Fax: 3 80 42 42 10

Titles:
LE BIEN PUBLIC - S DEPECHES
LE JOURNAL DE SAONE ET LOIRE

ESTYLE 1790666
5 rue Boudreau, 75009 PARIS **Tel:** 1 42 60 25 61
Fax: 1 42 60 24 40

Titles:
ESTETICA FRANCE

ETAI 1622525
Parc Antony II, 10 place du Général de Gaulle, 92160 ANTONY **Tel:** 1 77 92 92 92
Fax: 1 77 92 98 20

Titles:
FRANCE GRAPHIQUE
INFO CHIMIE MAGAZINE

FAIRCHILD PUBLICATIONS INC 1646179
9 rue Royale, 75008 PARIS **Tel:** 1 44 51 13 00
Fax: 1 42 68 16 41

Titles:
WWD

FRANCE AGRICOLE 1790686
8 Cité Paradis, CEDEX 10, 75493 PARIS
Tel: 1 40 22 79 00 **Fax:** 1 40 22 70 80

Titles:
LA FRANCE AGRICOLE
RIA - REVUE DE L'INDUSTRIE
LA VIGNE

FRANCE EDITION 1686129
27 rue Pétion de Villeneuve, 75011 PARIS
Tel: 1 43 79 07 37 **Fax:** 1 43 79 76 88

Titles:
AGRANDIR ET PROTEGER SA MAISON
CHEMINEES MAGAZINE

FRANCE EST MEDIAS 1623289
L'Est Républicain, Rue Théophraste-Renaudot, 54185 CEDEX HEILLECOURT **Tel:** 3 83 59 09 15
Fax: 383598013

Titles:
L' EST MAGAZINE

FREQUENCES 1785813
9 rue Charlot, 75003 PARIS **Tel:** 1 44 78 04 78
Fax: 1 42 78 70 36

Titles:
SATELLIFAX (NEWSLETTER)

GENTLEMEN DRIVERS MAGAZINE 1773115
PBR, 18 rue de Pontoise, 95160 MONTMORENCY **Tel:** 8 72 70 79 89
Email: pboidron@yahoo.fr
Web site: http://www.gentlemendrivers-mag.net

Titles:
P4 RADIO; MICHAEL DIREKTE

GHM - GROUPE HERSANT MEDIA 1623291
214 route de Grenoble, 06290 CEDEX 3 NICE
Tel: 4 93 18 28 38 **Fax:** 4 93 18 29 51

Titles:
NICE-MATIN NICE - SIEGE SOCIAL
PARIS NORMANDIE ROUEN
L' UNION REIMS
VAR-MATIN NICE-MATIN TOULON SIEGE SOCIAL

GLOBAL MEDIA SANTE 1784864
114 avenue Charles de Gaulle, CEDEX, 92522 NEUILLY SUR SEINE **Tel:** 1 55 62 68 00
Fax: 1 55 62 68 29

Titles:
PANORAMA DU MEDECIN

GRAND TOULOUSE INFOS COMMUNAUTE D'AGGLOMERATION DU GRAND TOULOUSE 1646250
1 place de la Légion-d'Honneur, BP 5821, 31505 CEDEX 5 TOULOUSE **Tel:** 5 34 41 59 00
Fax: 534415901

Titles:
GRAND TOULOUSE INFOS COMMUNAUTE D'AGGLOMERATION DU GRAND TOULOUSE

GROUPE 01 1622938
12 rue d'Oradour S/Glane, CEDEX 15, 75504 PARIS **Tel:** 1 71 18 54 00 **Fax:** 1 71 18 52 50

Titles:
ELECTRONIQUES
ELECTRONIQUES.BIZ

GROUPE AMAURY 1790628
21 rue Vincent Chevard, BP 50189, 28004 CHARTRES **Tel:** 2 37 88 88 88

Titles:
L' ECHO REPUBLICAIN
L' EQUIPE
L' EQUIPE MAGAZINE
FRANCE FOOTBALL

GROUPE ARTEMIS 1790869
74 avenue du Maine, 75014 PARIS
Tel: 1 44 10 10 10 **Fax:** 1 44 10 54 47

Titles:
L' HISTOIRE

GROUPE BOLLORE 1784889
31-32 quai de Dion Bouton, 92800 PUTEAUX
Tel: 1 46 96 31 00 **Fax:** 1 46 96 40 94

Titles:
DIRECT MATIN PLUS
DIRECT SOIR

GROUPE CENTRE FRANCE - LA MONTAGNE 1790634
1 rue du Général Ferrié, CEDEX, 18023 BOURGES **Tel:** 2 48 27 63 63 **Fax:** 2 48 27 63 65

Titles:
LE BERRY REPUBLICAIN
LE JOURNAL DU CENTRE

GROUPE DAUPHINE LIBERE 1790625
Les Iles Cordées, CEDEX, 38913 VEUREY
Tel: 4 76 88 71 00 **Fax:** 4 76 85 80 20

Titles:
LE DAUPHINE LIBERE

GROUPE DEPECHE DU MIDI 1790632
A Paris, 5 rue du Hanovre, 75002 PARIS
Tel: 5 62 11 33 00 **Fax:** 5 62 11 34 59

Titles:
LA DEPECHE DU MIDI
LA NOUVELLE REPUBLIQUE DES PYRENEES
LE PETIT BU DU LOT ET GARONNE

GROUPE EXPRESS EXPANSION - ROULARTA 1790723
29 rue de Châteaudun, CEDEX 09, 75308 PARIS
Tel: 1 75 55 10 00

Titles:
MAISON FRANCAISE
MAISON MAGAZINE
MAISONS COTE EST
MAISONS COTE OUEST
MAISONS COTE SUD

GROUPE EXPRESS ROULARTA 1790675
29 rue de Châteaudun, CEDEX 09, 75308 PARIS
Tel: 1 75 55 10 00 43 13 **Fax:** 1 75 55 41 20

Titles:
L' ENTREPRISE

GROUPE EXPRESS-EXPANSION 1790669
29 rue de Châteaudun, CEDEX 09, 75308 PARIS
Tel: 1 75 55 10 00

Titles:
L' EXPANSION
L' EXPRESS
LIRE

GROUPE HERSANT MEDIA 1790623
2 rue Sergent Casalonga, 20000 AJACCIO
Tel: 4 95 51 74 00 **Fax:** 4 95 51 74 01

Titles:
CORSE MATIN
L' EST ECLAIR
LIBERATION CHAMPAGNE
LIBERTE DIMANCHE
LES NOUVEL DE TAHITI
LA PROVENCE

GROUPE ICF 1790678
6 bis rue Gambetta, CEDEX, 92022 NANTERRE
Tel: 1 46 69 11 33 **Fax:** 1 46 69 11 98

Titles:
FRANCHISE MAGAZINE

GROUPE IMPACT MEDECINE 1790693
152 avenue de Malakoff, 75116 PARIS
Tel: 1 53 93 36 00 **Fax:** 1 53 93 37 75

Titles:
IMPACT MEDECINE
INFO SANTE

GROUPE INDUSTRIE SERVICES INFO 1784755
Antony Parc 2, 10 place du Général de Gaulle, 92160 ANTONY **Tel:** 1 77 92 92 92
Fax: 1 77 92 98 19

Titles:
L' ARGUS DE ASSURANCE
L' ECHO TOURISTIQUE
EMBALLAGES MAGAZINE
IT, INDUSTRIE ET TECHNOLOGIES
LSA
NEO RESTAURATION MAGAZINE
L' USINE NOUVELLE

GROUPE J 1622914
11 route de la Butte du Moulin, 78125 POIGNY LA FORET **Tel:** 1 34 84 70 60 **Fax:** 1 34 84 70 55

Titles:
JARDINERIES

GROUPE LA VOIX DU NORD 1790713
PGLM, 29 rue Esquermoise, 59000 LILLE
Tel: 3 20 44 80 00 **Fax:** 3 20 44 33 55

Titles:
LILLEPLUS

GROUPE LE POINT 1790716
74 avenue du Maine, CEDEX 14, 75682 PARIS
Tel: 1 44 10 10 10 **Fax:** 1 43 21 43 24

Titles:
LE POINT

GROUPE LE REVENU 1784842
1 bis avenue de la République, 75011 PARIS
Tel: 1 49 29 30 00 **Fax:** 1 49 29 30 98

Titles:
LE REVENU LE MENSUEL CONSEIL POUR VOS PLACEMENTS
LE REVENU L'HEBDO CONSEIL DE LA BOURSE

GROUPE LES ECHOS 1622528
16 rue du 4 septembre, CEDEX 02, 75112 PARIS
Tel: 1 49 53 64 40 **Fax:** 1 49 53 68 62

Titles:
CAPITAL FINANCE
LES ECHOS
ENJEUX - LES ECHOS
INVESTIR MAGAZINE

GROUPE LYON POCHE PRESSE 1790643
3 rue de la Claire, 69009 LYON **Tel:** 4 78 64 84 64
Fax: 4 78 43 49 51

Titles:
LYON POCHE

GROUPE MARIE CLAIRE 1790710
10 boulevard des Frères Voisin, CEDEX 9, 92792 ISSY LES MOULINEAUX **Tel:** 1 41 46 89 03 88 88
Fax: 1 41 46 87 77

Titles:
LES AVANTAGES
COSMOPOLITAN
CUISINE ET VINS DE FRANCE
FAMILI
MARIE CLAIRE

MARIE CLAIRE IDEES
MARIE CLAIRE MAISON
MARIE FRANCE
LA REVUE DU VIN DE FRANCE
VOTRE BEAUTE

GROUPE MONITEUR 1622676
17 rue d'Uzès, CEDEX 02, 75108 PARIS
Tel: 1 40 13 30 30 **Fax:** 1 40 13 32 02
Titles:
AMC - LE MONITEUR ARCHITECTURE
LE COURRIER DES MAIRES
LA GAZETTE DES COMMUNES
LE MONITEUR DES TRAVAUX PUBLICS
NEGOCE

GROUPE OUEST FRANCE - INFOMER 1790708
ZI Rennes Chantepie, 13 rue du Breil, CS 46305 CEDEX, 35063 RENNES **Tel:** 2 99 32 58 80
Fax: 2 99 32 58 88
Titles:
CULTURES MARINES
PRODUITS DE LA MER

GROUPE PROGRES 1790809
4 rue Montrochet, 69002 LYON **Tel:** 4 78 14 77 91
Titles:
LYONPLUS

GROUPE PUBLIHEBDOS 1790802
3 boulevard Victor Hugo, BP 22, CEDEX, 77001 MELUN **Tel:** 1 64 87 50 00 **Fax:** 1 64 52 14 92
Titles:
LA REPUBLIQUE DE SEINE ET MARNE

GROUPE REVENU MULTIMEDIA 1790659
1 bis avenue de la République, 75011 PARIS
Tel: 1 49 29 32 00 **Fax:** 1 49 29 32 01
Titles:
AIR ET COSMOS

GROUPE ROULARTA 1790715
23 rue de Châteaudun, CEDEX 09, 75308 PARIS
Tel: 1 75 55 17 00 **Fax:** 1 75 55 10 22
Titles:
LE POINT DE VUE

GROUPE SOPHIA PUBLICATIONS 1790670
74 avenue du Maine, 75014 PARIS
Tel: 1 44 10 10 10
Titles:
LA RECHERCHE

GROUPE SUD OUEST 1790781
ZI n° 3, CEDEX 9, 16903 ANGOULEME
Tel: 5 45 94 16 00 **Fax:** 5 45 94 17 19 16 19
Titles:
LA CHARENTE LIBRE

GROUPE TESTS 1790683
12 rue d'Oradour S/Glane, 75015 PARIS
Tel: 1 71 18 54 00 **Fax:** 1 71 18 52 50
Titles:
01 INFORMATIQUE
MESURES
MICRO HEBDO
L' ORDINATEUR INDIVIDUEL

GROUPE TOUATI 1622878
1 rue des Entrepreneurs, 93400 SAINT OUEN
Tel: 1 40 11 44 44 **Fax:** 1 40 11 55 50
Titles:
COURRIER CADRES

HACHETTE FILIPACCHI ASSOCIES 1790631
124 rue Danton, 92300 LEVALLOIS PERRET
Tel: 1 41 34 60 00 **Fax:** 1 41 34 95 59
Titles:
CAMPAGNE DECORATION
ELLE
ELLE A TABLE
ELLE DECORATION
ICI PARIS
LE JOURNAL DE LA MAISON
LE JOURNAL DU DIMANCHE
MON JARDIN ET MA MAISON
PARENTS
PARIS MATCH
PARISCOPE

HACHETTE FILIPACCHI MEDIAS 1790630
149 rue Anatole France, 92300 LEVALLOIS PERRET **Tel:** 1 41 34 60 00 **Fax:** 1 41 34 95 26
Titles:
AUTO MOTO
FRANCE DIMANCHE
PHOTO
PUBLIC
TELE 7 JOURS

HARMONIE COMMUNAUTE D'AGGLOMERATION DE MONTPELLIER 1646211
50 place Zeus - CS 39556, BP 9531, 34961 MONTPELLIER CEDEX 2 **Tel:** 4 67 13 60 00
Fax: 4 67 13 64 00
Titles:
HARMONIE COMMUNAUTE D'AGGLOMERATION DE MONTPELLIER

HAUTE-VIENNE LE MAGAZINE CONSEIL GENERAL DE LA HAUTE- VIENNE 1785771
Hôtel-du-Département, 43 avenue de la Libération, 87031 CEDEX LIMOGES
Tel: 5 55 45 12 54 **Fax:** 555795781
Titles:
HAUTE-VIENNE LE MAGAZINE CONSEIL GENERAL DE LA HAUTE- VIENNE

HAUT-RHIN MAGAZINE CONSEIL GENERAL DU HAUT-RHIN 1784739
Hôtel-du-Département, 100 avenue d'Alsace, BP 20351, 68006 CEDEX COLMAR **Tel:** 3 89 30 60 70
Fax: 389217285
Titles:
HAUT-RHIN MAGAZINE CONSEIL GENERAL DU HAUT-RHIN

HEBE 1713611
60 rue de Miromesnil, 75008 PARIS
Tel: 1 56 43 35 30 **Fax:** 1 56 43 35 29
Titles:
MOVING MAGAZINE

HOMMELL - SETC 1790763
48/50 Boulevard Sénard, 92210 SAINT CLOUD
Tel: 1 47 11 20 00 **Fax:** 1 46 02 31 51
Titles:
TELECABLE SAT HEBDO

HOMMELL - SFEP 1790652
SFEP, 48/50 Boulevard Sénard, 92210 SAINT CLOUD **Tel:** 1 47 11 20 43 **Fax:** 1 46 02 09 10
Titles:
AUTO-HEBDO
NITRO

INFO MAGAZINE CLERMONT-FERRAND 1626060
7 place de Jaude, 63038, CEDEX 1 CLERMONT-FERRAND **Tel:** 4 73 43 50 50 **Fax:** 473342997
Titles:
INFO MAGAZINE CLERMONT-FERRAND

INFOPRO COMMUNICATION 1790656
Immeuble Parc II, 10 place du Général de Gaulle, 92160 ANTONY **Tel:** 1 77 92 92 92
Fax: 1 77 92 98 26
Titles:
L' AUTOMOBILE & ENTREPRISE

INRS 1790734
30 rue Olivier Noyer, CEDEX 14, 75680 PARIS
Tel: 1 40 44 31 54 **Fax:** 1 40 44 30 41
Titles:
TRAVAIL ET SECURITE

IT NEWS INFO 1784919
40 boulevard Henri-Sellier, 92150 SURESNES
Tel: 1 41 97 02 02 **Fax:** 1 41 97 02 01
Titles:
DISTRIBUTIQUE.COM

JIBENA 1790704
BP 100, CEDEX, 86101 CHATELLERAULT
Tel: 5 49 85 49 85 **Fax:** 5 49 85 49 99
Titles:
CHASSEUR D'IMAGES

JOURNAL DE LA VENDEE CONSEIL GENERAL DE LA VENDEE 1785076
40 rue Maréchal-Foch, 85923 CEDEX 9 LA ROCHE-SUR-YON **Tel:** 2 51 44 79 10
Fax: 251447911
Titles:
LE JOURNAL DE LA VENDEE CONSEIL GENERAL DE LA VENDEE

JOURNAL DU CALVADOS CONSEIL GENERAL DU CALVADOS 1785772
Conseil Général du Calvados, 9 rue Saint-Laurent, BP 20520, 14035 CEDEX 1 CAEN
Tel: 2 31 57 11 07 **Fax:** 231571139
Titles:
LE JOURNAL DU CALVADOS CONSEIL GENERAL DU CALVADOS

LES JOURNAUX DU MIDI 1630410
ADT Communication, 450 route de Nîmes, 34920 LE CRES **Tel:** 4 67 87 05 60 **Fax:** 4 67 87 02 36
Titles:
DANS L'AIR DU TEMPS

LA DEPECHE DU MIDI 1784703
20 place Carnot, 11000 CARCASSONNE
Tel: 4 68 11 90 11 **Fax:** 4 68 11 90 12
Titles:
LA DEPECHE DU MIDI EDITION DE L'AUDE
LA DEPECHE DU MIDI EDITION DE L'AVEYRON
LA DEPECHE DU MIDI EDITION DU LOT-ET-GARONNE
LA DEPECHE DU MIDI EDITION DU TARN SUD
LA DEPECHE DU MIDI EDITION DU TARN-ET-GARONNE
MPS - MIDI PRESSE SERVICE TOULOUSE

LA MARSEILLAISE 1784829
10 rue Berny, (entrée rue Parmentier), 83500 LA SEYNE-SUR-MER **Tel:** 4 94 94 76 67
Fax: 4 94 94 82 63
Titles:
LA MARSEILLAISE EDITION DU VAR

LA NOUVELLE REPUBLIQUE DU CENTRE OUEST 1784975
232 avenue de Grammont, 37048 CEDEX 1 TOURS **Tel:** 2 47 31 70 00 **Fax:** 2 47 31 70 70
Titles:
LA NOUVELLE REPUBLIQUE DU CENTRE-OUEST EDITION D'INDRE-ET-LOIRE TOURS ET LA BANLIEUE

LA VIE - LE MONDE 1784688
8 rue Jean-Antoine-de-Baïf, 75212 CEDEX 13 PARIS **Tel:** 1 55 30 55 62 **Fax:** 1 45 22 08 45
Titles:
SORTIR TELERAMA SUPPLEMENT DE TELERAMA

LA VOIX DU NORD 1784760
8 place du Général-de-Gaulle, BP 549, 59023 CEDEX LILLE **Tel:** 3 20 78 40 40 **Fax:** 3 20 78 42 44
Titles:
LA VOIX DU NORD EDITION DU NORD LILLE

L'AGENCE INNOVAPRESSE SARL 1784837
1 place Boieldieu, 75002 PARIS **Tel:** 1 48 24 08 97
Fax: 1 42 47 00 76
Titles:
D'A (D'ARCHITECTURES)

L'AME SASU 1790795
18 rue de Thann, CEDEX 9, 68945 MULHOUSE
Titles:
EN ALSACE
PAYS COMTOIS

LE DAUPHINE LIBERE 1784830
19 avenue du Grand-Tissage, BP 223, 38305 BOURGOIN-JALLIEU **Tel:** 4 74 28 03 00
Fax: 4 74 28 89 95
Titles:
LE DAUPHINE LIBERE EDITION ISERE NORD BOURGOIN - VILLE NOUVELLE

LE MONDE 1790629
LE MONDE INTERACTIF, 80 boulevard Auguste Blanqui, 75013 PARIS **Tel:** 1 53 38 42 60
Fax: 1 53 38 42 96
Titles:
LEMONDE.FR
LE MONDE
LE MONDE DIPLOMATIQUE

LE MONDE SA 1784715
80 boulevard Auguste-Blanqui, 75707 CEDEX 13 PARIS **Tel:** 1 57 28 20 00 **Fax:** 1 57 28 21 05
Titles:
LE MONDE DES LIVRES SUPPLEMENT DU QUOTIDIEN LE MONDE
LE MONDE ECONOMIE SUPPLEMENT DU QUOTIDIEN LE MONDE
LE MONDE EDUCATION SUPPLEMENT DU QUOTIDIEN LE MONDE

LE NOUVEL OBSERVATEUR 1790718
10/12 place de la Bourse, CEDEX 02, 75081 PARIS **Tel:** 1 44 88 34 34
Titles:
LE NOUVEL OBSERVATEUR

LE PROGRES 1784779
4 rue Paul-Montrochet, 69002 LYON
Tel: 4 72 22 23 23 **Fax:** 4 78 14 77 10
Titles:
LE PROGRES EDITION LYON-VILLEURBANNE-CALUIRE
LA TRIBUNE LE PROGRES SAINT-ETIENNE

LE REPUBLICAIN LORRAIN 1785011
24 rue Serpenoise, 57000 METZ
Tel: 3 87 38 58 00 **Fax:** 3 87 38 58 01
Titles:
LE REPUBLICAIN LORRAIN METZ

LE TELEGRAMME DE BREST ET DE L'OUEST 1784786
7 voie d'Accès-au-Port, BP 67243, 29672 CEDEX MORLAIX **Tel:** 2 98 62 11 33
Fax: 2 98 63 20 99
Titles:
LE TELEGRAMME DE BREST ET DE L'OUEST MORLAIX
LE TELEGRAMME DIMANCHE
LE TELEGRAMME DU FINISTERE NORD EDITIONS DE BREST OUEST BREST EST ET BREST

LEN MEDICAL 1623047
LEN MEDICAL, 15 rue des Sablons, 75116 PARIS **Tel:** 1 47 55 31 31 **Fax:** 1 47 55 32 32
Titles:
DERMATOLOGIE PRATIQUE

LES JOURNAUX DU MIDI 1784758
80 boulevard Auguste-Blanqui, 75683 CEDEX 14 PARIS **Tel:** 1 44 71 80 44 **Fax:** 144718046
Titles:
L' INDEPENDANT BUREAU PARISIEN
L' INDEPENDANT RIVESALTES
MIDI LIBRE BUREAU PARISIEN

L'EST REPUBLICAIN 1784942
Rue Théophraste-Renaudot, Houdemont, 54185 CEDEX HEILLECOURT **Tel:** 3 83 59 88 01
Titles:
L' EST REPUBLICAIN HOUDEMONT

LETTRE DE LA REGION CONSEIL REGIONAL PROVENCE-ALPES-COTE D'AZUR
1788543
Hôtel-de-Région, 27 place Jules-Guesde, 13481 CEDEX 20 MARSEILLE **Tel:** 4 91 57 50 57 **Fax:** 491575205

Titles:
LA LETTRE DE LA REGION CONSEIL REGIONAL PROVENCE-ALPES-COTE D'AZUR

L'ETUDIANT
1784733
23 rue de Châteaudun, CEDEX 09, 75308 PARIS **Tel:** 1 75 55 40 40

Titles:
L' ETUDIANT
LYCEE MAG

LIEN HORTICOLE SA
1790705
Rédaction - Parc Club du Millénaire - Bât 9, 1025 rue Henri Becquerel, 34000 MONTPELLIER **Tel:** 4 67 50 42 60 **Fax:** 4 67 50 19 02

Titles:
LIEN HORTICOLE

LORRAINE ET VOUS CONSEIL REGIONAL DE LORRAINE
1712671
1 place Gabriel-Hocquard, BP 81004, 57036 METZ CEDEX 1 **Tel:** 3 87 33 60 00 **Fax:** 3 87 33 61 57

Titles:
LORRAINE ET VOUS CONSEIL REGIONAL DE LORRAINE

LUXMEDIA GROUP
1784863
4 rue Reyer, CEDEX, 6414 CANNES **Tel:** 4 97 06 95 95 **Fax:** 4 97 06 95 96

Titles:
EDGAR

MA REGION HAUTE-NORMANDIE CONSEIL REGIONAL
1624628
5 rue Robert Schuman, BP 1129, 76174 ROUEN CEDEX 1 **Tel:** 2 35 52 56 82 **Fax:** 2 35 52 57 97

Titles:
MA REGION HAUTE-NORMANDIE CONSEIL REGIONAL

MAGAZINE DU CONSEIL GENERAL DE LA GIRONDE
1784736
Hôtel-du-Département, Esplanade Charles-de-Gaulle, 33074 CEDEX BORDEAUX **Tel:** 5 56 99 33 10 **Fax:** 556993399

Titles:
LE MAGAZINE DU CONSEIL GENERAL DE LA GIRONDE

MAINE-ET-LOIRE LE MAGAZINE DU CONSEIL GENERAL DE MAINE-ET-LOIRE
1624592
Hôtel-du-Département, Place Michel-Debré, BP 94104, 49941 ANGERS CEDEX 09 **Tel:** 2 41 81 43 86 **Fax:** 2 41 81 49 94

Titles:
MAINE-ET-LOIRE LE MAGAZINE DU CONSEIL GENERAL DE MAINE-ET-LOIRE

MALESHERBES PUBLICATIONS
1623447
80 boulevard Auguste Blanqui, CEDEX 13, 75707 PARIS **Tel:** 1 48 88 46 00 **Fax:** 1 48 88 46 01

Titles:
LA VIE

MANCHE MAG' CONSEIL GÉNÉRAL DE LA MANCHE
1785777
98 route de Candol, 50008 CEDEX SAINT-LO **Tel:** 2 33 05 95 00 **Fax:** 233059565

Titles:
MANCHE MAG' CONSEIL GÉNÉRAL DE LA MANCHE

MARNE LE MAG CONSEIL GENERAL DE LA MARNE
1787064
Hôtel-du-Département, 40 rue Carnot, 51038 CEDEX CHALONS-EN-CHAMPAGNE **Tel:** 3 26 69 51 51 **Fax:** 326214981

Titles:
LA MARNE LE MAG CONSEIL GENERAL DE LA MARNE

MIDI LIBRE
1784831
rue du Mas-de-Grille, 34438 CEDEX SAINT-JEAN-DE-VEDAS **Tel:** 4 67 07 67 07 **Fax:** 4 67 07 68 57

Titles:
MIDI LIBRE MONTPELLIER

MILAN PRESSE
1622620
Savoie Technolac, 12 allée du Lac de Garde, BP 308 CEDEX, 73377 LE BOURGET DU LAC **Tel:** 4 79 26 28 26 **Fax:** 4 79 26 27 89

Titles:
ALPES MAGAZINE
BRETAGNE MAGAZINE
JULIE
PAYS BASQUE MAGAZINE

MONDADORI FRANCE
1785986
Immeuble Trait d'Union, 8 rue François Ory, 92120 MONTROUGE **Tel:** 1 46 48 48 06 **Fax:** 1 46 48 48 60

Titles:
L' AMI DES JARDINS ET DE LA MAISON
AUTO PLUS
BIBA
LE CHASSEUR FRANCAIS
CLOSER
DIAPASON
LE FILM FRANCAIS
MODES ET TRAVAUX
NOUS DEUX
LA PLEINE VIE
REPONSES PHOTO
LA SCIENCE & VIE
SCIENCE & VIE JUNIOR
TELE POCHE
TELE STAR
TOP SANTE

MONDADORI MAGAZINES FRANCE
1790654
Immeuble Trait d'Union, 8 rue François Ory, 92120 MONTROUGE **Tel:** 1 41 33 50 00 **Fax:** 1 41 33 57 04

Titles:
L' AUTO JOURNAL

LA MONTAGNE
1623027
CCI de Clermont-Ferrand-Issoire, 148 boulevard Lavoisier, 63037 CLERMONT-FERRAND CEDEX 1 **Tel:** 4 73 43 43 43 **Fax:** 4 73 43 43 42

Titles:
LA VOIX DES ENTREPRISES CLERMONT-FERRAND

MONTAIGNE PUBLICATIONS
1784725
72 boulevard Berthier, 75017 PARIS **Tel:** 1 47 63 90 95 48 00 **Fax:** 1 47 63 49 08

Titles:
DREAMS
MONSIEUR MAGAZINE

MOTOR PRESSE FRANCE
1784838
12 rue Rouget de Lisle, CEDEX, 92442 ISSY LES MOULINEAUX **Tel:** 1 41 33 37 37 **Fax:** 1 41 33 37 99

Titles:
L' AUTOMOBILE MAGAZINE
CAMPING CAR MAGAZINE
CAMPING ET CARAVANING - LE CARAVANIER
L' HOTELIER DE PLEIN AIR
JOGGING INTERNATIONAL
MOTO JOURNAL
L' OFFICIEL DES TERRAINS DE CAMPINGS

NANTES METROPOLE COMMUNAUTE D'AGGLOMERATION DE NANTES
1732889
2 cours du Champ-de-Mars, 44923 CEDEX 9 NANTES **Tel:** 2 40 99 48 27 **Fax:** 240994800

Titles:
NANTES METROPOLE COMMUNAUTE D'AGGLOMERATION DE NANTES

NEMM & CIE
1790757
15 rue Duphot, 75001 PARIS **Tel:** 1 56 88 17 73 **Fax:** 1 49 53 08 31

Titles:
JAZZ MAGAZINE

NOUVEL OBSERVATEUR
1622993
10-12 place de la Bourse, 75081 CEDEX 02 PARIS **Tel:** 1 44 88 35 70 **Fax:** 1 44 88 35 15

Titles:
TELEOBS PARIS - TELE CINE OBS

NSP
1622675
8 quai de Bir Hakeim, CEDEX, 94417 SAINT MAURICE **Tel:** 1 43 97 95 23 **Fax:** 1 43 97 20 07

Titles:
CONFORTIQUE MAGAZINE - LE MAGAZINE

NUIT ET JOUR
1790717
26 rue Vercingétorix, CEDEX 14, 75685 PARIS **Tel:** 1 40 64 31 31 **Fax:** 1 40 64 31 30

Titles:
LE NOUVEAU DETECTIVE

OFF-ROADS
1790653
61 avenue Gambetta, 94100 SAINT MAUR DES FOSSES **Tel:** 1 77 01 83 00 **Fax:** 1 77 01 83 19

Titles:
LAND

OPTION FINANCE
1790662
91 bis rue Cherche-Midi, 75006 PARIS **Tel:** 1 53 63 55 55 **Fax:** 1 53 63 55 50

Titles:
L' OPTION FINANCE

ORACOM
1622942
168-170 rue Raymond Losserand, 75014 PARIS **Tel:** 1 44 78 93 00 **Fax:** 1 44 78 97 67 98 34

Titles:
MOBILES MAGAZINE

OUEST FRANCE
1622559
10 rue du Breil, ZI Sud Est, 35051 CEDEX 9 RENNES **Tel:** 2 99 32 67 26 **Fax:** 2 99 32 62 63

Titles:
DIMANCHE OUEST FRANCE
LE MAINE LIBRE - EDITION LE MANS
OUEST FRANCE RENNES
PRESSE OCEAN NANTES

PGV MAISON
1790725
15 à 27 rue Moussorgski, 75018 PARIS **Tel:** 1 53 26 30 06 **Fax:** 1 53 26 33 03

Titles:
SYSTEME D

PLAY BAC PRESSE
1622888
Play Bac Presse, 14 bis rue des Minimes, CEDEX 03, 75140 PARIS **Tel:** 1 53 01 23 60 **Fax:** 1 53 01 23 99

Titles:
MON QUOTIDIEN

PR EDITIONS
1790695
91 rue Jean Jaurès, CEDEX, 92807 PUTEAUX **Tel:** 1 43 34 73 00 **Fax:** 1 43 34 73 24

Titles:
LES PHARMACEUTIQUES

PRESSE SPORT INVESTISSEMENT
1790833
4 cours de l'Ile Seguin, BP 10302, 92102 BOULOGNE BILLANCOURT **Tel:** 1 40 93 20 20 **Fax:** 1 40 93 27 78

Titles:
SPORT ET STYLE

PRISMA CORPORATE MEDIA
1784684
6 rue Daru, 75379 CEDEX 08 PARIS **Tel:** 1 44 15 30 00

Titles:
LES AEROPORTS DE PARIS MAGAZINE
CANALSAT - LE MAGAZINE DES ABONNES
PLUS LE MAGAZINE DES ABONNES DE CANAL+

PRISMA PRESSE
1624701
13 rue Henri Barbusse, 92624 GENNEVILLIERS **Tel:** 1 73 05 60 24

Titles:
CA M'INTERESSE
CAPITAL
LA CUISINE ACTUELLE
CUISINE GOURMANDE
LA FEMME ACTUELLE
GALA
GEO
MANAGEMENT
NATIONAL GEOGRAPHIC FRANCE
PRIMA
TELE 2 SEMAINES
TELE LOISIRS
TELE LOISIRS GUIDE CUISINE
TV GRANDES CHAINES
VOICI
VSD

PUBLI NEWS
1784724
47 rue Aristide-Briand, 92300 LEVALLOIS-PERRET **Tel:** 1 41 49 93 60 **Fax:** 1 47 57 37 25

Titles:
SECURITE INFORMATIQUE

PUBLICATIONS CONDE NAST SA
1790724
26 rue Cambacérès, 75008 PARIS **Tel:** 1 53 43 61 72 60 00 **Fax:** 1 53 43 61 70

Titles:
AD - ARCHITECTURAL DIGEST
AIR FRANCE MADAME
GLAMOUR
VOGUE

PUBLICATIONS G. VENTILLARD
1790755
2/12 rue de Bellevue, CEDEX 19, 75940 PARIS **Tel:** 1 44 84 84 84 **Fax:** 1 44 84 84 67

Titles:
SONO MAGAZINE

PUBLICATIONS METRO FRANCE
1784976
35, rue Greneta, 75002 PARIS **Tel:** 1 55 34 45 00 **Fax:** 1 55 34 45 03

Titles:
METRO FRANCE (PARIS & LOCAL EDITIONS)

PYC EDITION
1622576
16/18 place de la Chapelle, 75018 PARIS **Tel:** 1 53 26 48 00 **Fax:** 1 53 26 48 01

Titles:
TRAITEMENTS & MATERIAUX

PYRENEES PRESSE
1790626
6-8 rue Despourrins, 64000 PAU **Tel:** 5 59 82 29 29 **Fax:** 5 59 27 79 31

Titles:
L' ECLAIR PYRENEES
LA REPUBLIQUE DES PYRENEES

REED BUSINESS INFORMATION
1623111
Forum 55, 52 rue Camille Desmoulins, 92448 ISSY LES MOULINEAUX **Tel:** 1 46 29 46 29

Titles:
COSMETIQUE MAGAZINE
ELECTRONIC PRODUCT NEWS
LES VIES DE FAMILLE

REFLETS DU LOIRET CONSEIL GENERAL DU LOIRET
1624601
Hôtel-du-Département, 15 rue Eugène-Vignat, BP 2019, 45010 CEDEX 1 ORLEANS **Tel:** 2 38 25 43 25 **Fax:** 238254347

Titles:
REFLETS DU LOIRET CONSEIL GENERAL DU LOIRET

REUSSIR
1790688
2 avenue du Pays de Caen, Colombelles, CEDEX 9, 14902 CAEN **Tel:** 2 31 35 77 00 **Fax:** 2 31 82 29 63

Titles:
REUSSIR - GRANDES CULTURES
REUSSIR - LAIT
REUSSIR - VIGNE

REUSSIR SA 1622548
2 avenue du Pays-de-Caen, Colombelles, 14902 CEDEX 9 CAEN **Tel:** 2 31 35 77 00 **Fax:** 2 31 35 77 18
Titles:
DIRECT AFFAIRES

RHONE-ALPES CONSEIL REGIONAL RHONE-ALPES 1723996
78 route de Paris, BP 19, 69751 CHARBONNIERES-LES-BAINS CEDEX **Tel:** 4 72 59 40 00 **Fax:** 4 72 59 42 18
Titles:
RHONE-ALPES CONSEIL REGIONAL RHONE-ALPES

ROBERT LAFONT PRESSE 1790679
CAHETEL, 70 avenue de Strasbourg, 94300 VINCENNES **Tel:** 1 49 57 99 46 **Fax:** 1 70 79 06 23
Titles:
ENTREPRENDRE
L' ESSENTIEL DE AUTO

ROSSEL 1785125
42 rue du Général-Sarrail, 59100 ROUBAIX **Tel:** 3 20 25 62 37 **Fax:** 3 20 25 62 98
Titles:
NORD ÉCLAIR - ROUBAIX

ROULARTA 1623126
23 rue de Châteaudun, CEDEX 09, 75308 PARIS **Tel:** 1 75 55 10 00 **Fax:** 1 75 55 12 61
Titles:
A NOUS PARIS

RUSTICA SA 1790706
15-27 rue Moussorgski, CEDEX 18, 75895 PARIS **Tel:** 1 53 26 33 00 **Fax:** 1 53 26 33 01
Titles:
RUSTICA
VOTRE MAISON - VOTRE JARDIN

SAONE & LOIRE INFO CONSEIL GENERAL DE SAONE-ET-LOIRE 1624603
Hôtel-du-Département, Rue de Lingendes, 71026 CEDEX 9 MACON **Tel:** 3 85 39 66 90 **Fax:** 385396666
Titles:
SAONE & LOIRE INFO CONSEIL GENERAL DE SAONE-ET- LOIRE

SAP L'ALSACE 1790624
18 rue de Thann, CEDEX 9, 68945 MULHOUSE **Tel:** 3 89 32 70 00 **Fax:** 3 89 32 11 26
Titles:
L' ALSACE

SARTHE CONSEIL GENERAL DE LA SARTHE 1624577
Hôtel-du-Département, Place Aristide-Briand, 72072 CEDEX 9 LE MANS **Tel:** 2 43 54 70 26 **Fax:** 2 43 54 70 31
Titles:
LA SARTHE CONSEIL GENERAL DE LA SARTHE

SEINE-MARITIME LE MAGAZINE CONSEIL GENERAL DE SEINE-MARITIME 1788542
Hôtel-du-Département, Quai Jean-Moulin, 76101 CEDEX 1 ROUEN **Tel:** 2 35 03 54 17 **Fax:** 235036774
Titles:
SEINE-MARITIME LE MAGAZINE CONSEIL GENERAL DE SEINE-MARITIME

SELECTION DU READER'S DIGEST 1786134
1-7 avenue Louis-Pasteur, 92220 CEDEX BAGNEUX **Tel:** 1 77 75 29 01 **Fax:** 1 46 74 85 75
Titles:
READER'S DIGEST SELECTION

SEM (SOCIETE EDITRICE DU MONDE) 1785806
1 avenue Stéphen-Pichon, 75013 PARIS **Tel:** 1 53 94 96 01 **Fax:** 153969626
Titles:
MANIERE DE VOIR

SER 1781829
14 rue d'Assas, 75006 PARIS **Tel:** 1 44 39 48 48 **Fax:** 1 44 39 48 17
Titles:
ETUDES

SERNAS 1623269
21 rue du Faubourg Saint Antoine, CEDEX 11, 75550 PARIS **Tel:** 1 44 87 87 87 **Fax:** 1 44 87 87 79
Titles:
VOILES ET VOILIERS

SFR MINIMAG 1624541
SFR - Tour Séquoia, 1 place Carpeaux, 92915 PARIS-LA-DEFENSE **Tel:** 1 71 08 32 96 **Fax:** 1 71 08 90 34
Titles:
SFR MINIMAG

SIAC 1784844
84 boulevard de Sébastopol, 75003 PARIS **Tel:** 1 43 96 16 16 **Fax:** 1 43 96 16 16
Titles:
LA REVUE VINICOLE INTERNATIONALE

SIPA 1790633
Boulevard Albert Blanchoin, BP 10728, CEDEX 01, 49007 ANGERS **Tel:** 2 41 68 86 88 **Fax:** 2 41 44 31 43
Titles:
LE COURRIER DE L'OUEST

SOCIETE ALSACIENNE DE PUBLICATIONS 1622887
85-87 rue de la République, BP 84, 68502 GUEBWILLER **Tel:** 3 89 76 81 05 **Fax:** 389748242
Titles:
L' ALSACE EDITION DE GUEBWILLER

SOCIETE D'EDITION DU TV MAGAZINE 1790762
14 boulevard Haussmann, CEDEX 09, 75438 PARIS **Tel:** 1 57 08 72 00 **Fax:** 1 57 08 72 22
Titles:
TV MAGAZINE

SOCIETE GENERALE DE PRESSE 1623038
13 avenue de l'Opéra, CEDEX 01, 75039 PARIS **Tel:** 1 40 15 17 89 **Fax:** 1 40 15 17 15
Titles:
BILANS HEBDOMADAIRES
LA CORRESPONDANCE ECONOMIQUE

SOCPRESSE 1784694
14 boulevard Haussmann, 75009 PARIS **Tel:** 1 57 08 50 00
Titles:
LE FIGARO
LE FIGARO MAGAZINE
LE FIGAROSCOPE
MADAME FIGARO
LE PARTICULIER

SOFETEC 1623180
Editions SOFETEC, 66 rue Escudier, 92100 BOULOGNE BILLANCOURT **Tel:** 1 48 25 50 30 **Fax:** 1 48 25 90 54
Titles:
MACHINES PRODUCTION

SOPREDA 2 1784888
7 route de Nanfray, 74960 CRAN-GEVRIER **Tel:** 4 50 33 35 35 **Fax:** 4 50 52 11 06
Titles:
ACTIVES, LES PAYS DE SAVOIE
ECO DES PAYS DE SAVOIE

STRATEGIES 1623043
Forum 55, 52 rue Camille Desmoulins, BP 62, 92448 ISSY LES MOULINEAUX **Tel:** 1 46 29 46 29 **Fax:** 1 46 29 46 09
Titles:
STRATEGIES

SUD COMMUNICATION 1790635
9 place Michelet, BP 24, CEDEX, 43001 LE PUY-EN-VELAY **Tel:** 4 71 09 32 14 **Fax:** 4 71 02 94 08
Titles:
L' EVEIL DE LA HAUTE LOIRE

SUD OUEST 1623227
23 quai de Queyries, 33094 BORDEAUX **Tel:** 5 35 31 31 31
Titles:
SUD OUEST BORDEAUX
SUD OUEST DIMANCHE

TELERAMA 1622865
6/8 rue Jean Antoine de Baïf, CEDEX 13, 75212 PARIS **Tel:** 1 55 30 55 30
Titles:
TELERAMA

TEXTUEL 1790797
TEXTUEL, 146 rue du Faubourg Poissonnière, 75010 PARIS **Tel:** 1 53 21 21 00 **Fax:** 1 53 21 22 49
Titles:
DU COTE DE CHEZ VOUS
LE TGV MAGAZINE

THOMAS INDUSTRIAL MEDIA 1785884
15/17 rue de Vanves, 92100 BOULOGNE BILLANCOURT **Tel:** 1 41 31 74 50 **Fax:** 1 57 67 12 41
Titles:
PEI - PRODUITS EQUIPEMENTS INDUSTRIELS

TOPIX MEDIAS 1623031
5 rue François-Ponsard, 75116 PARIS **Tel:** 1 55 74 62 00 **Fax:** 155746210
Titles:
MITI NEWS

TOUT LE BAS RHIN CONSEIL GENERAL DU BAS-RHIN 1624609
Hôtel-du-Département, Place du Quartier-Blanc, 67964 CEDEX 9 STRASBOURG **Tel:** 3 88 76 67 67 **Fax:** 388766917
Titles:
TOUT LE BAS RHIN CONSEIL GENERAL DU BAS-RHIN

TRANSFAC/ GR L'ETUDIANT 1790775
23 rue de Châteaudun, CEDEX 09, 75308 PARIS **Tel:** 1 75 55 40 40
Titles:
TRANSFAC - L'EXPRESS

TRANSOCEANIC 1786074
TRANSOCEANIC, 3 boulevard Ney, 75018 PARIS **Tel:** 1 44 65 80 80 **Fax:** 1 44 65 80 90
Titles:
HI FI VIDEO HOME CINEMA
SONOVISION VIDEO BROADCAST

TSP 1790727
4 rue des Beaumonts, 94120 FONTENAY-SOUS-BOIS **Tel:** 1 71 33 15 88
Titles:
CINEMA CHEZ SOI

TUTELAIRE 1785768
45 rue Eugène-Oudiné, 75013 PARIS **Tel:** 1 44 06 89 42 **Fax:** 144239567
Titles:
LA TUTELAIRE

UFC - QUE CHOISIR 1625227
233 boulevard Voltaire, CEDEX 11, 75555 PARIS **Tel:** 1 43 48 55 48 **Fax:** 1 43 48 44 35
Titles:
QUE CHOISIR

UNI EDITION 1790709
22 rue Letellier, cedex 15, 75739 PARIS **Tel:** 1 43 23 45 72 **Fax:** 1 43 23 04 95
Titles:
L' AMATEUR DE BORDEAUX

UNI EDITIONS 1622952
22 rue Letellier, CEDEX 15, 75739 PARIS **Tel:** 1 43 23 45 72 **Fax:** 1 43 23 04 95
Titles:
DETENTE JARDIN
DETOURS EN FRANCE
LE DOSSIER FAMILIAL
LA MAISON CREATIVE
REGAL
SANTE MAGAZINE

VALMONDE ET CIE 1790720
3/5 rue Saint Georges, 75009 PARIS **Tel:** 1 40 54 11 00 **Fax:** 1 40 54 12 85
Titles:
VALEURS ACTUELLES

VAUCLUSE CONSEIL GENERAL DE VAUCLUSE 1624611
Hôtel-du-Département, Rue Viala, 84909 CEDEX 9 AVIGNON **Tel:** 4 90 16 11 12 **Fax:** 490161117
Titles:
VAUCLUSE CONSEIL GENERAL DE VAUCLUSE

VEILLE 1625147
134 avenue Henri-Ginoux, 92120 MONTROUGE **Tel:** 1 46 65 55 37 **Fax:** 1 78 76 51 20
Titles:
VEILLE

VICTOIRES EDITIONS 1785073
38 rue Croix des Petits Champs, 75001 PARIS **Tel:** 1 53 45 89 00 **Fax:** 1 53 45 89 11
Titles:
ENVIRONNEMENT MAGAZINE
RECYCLAGE RECUPERATION MAGAZINE

VIP INTERNATIONAL 1622927
111 avenue Victor-Hugo, 75016 PARIS **Tel:** 1 47 55 63 63 **Fax:** 1 47 55 63 53
Titles:
LES MAISONS DE CAMPAGNE
MAISONS NORMANDES
RESTAURER SA MAISON
TOUTE LA MAISON

VIVRE EN SOMME CONSEIL GENERAL DE LA SOMME 1714683
53, rue de la république, BP 32615, 80026 AMIENS CEDEX 1 **Tel:** 3 22 71 97 16 **Fax:** 3 22 71 83 50
Titles:
VIVRE EN SOMME CONSEIL GENERAL DE LA SOMME

VOCATIS 1622894
34/38 rue Camille Pelletan, CEDEX, 92309 LEVALLOIS PERRET **Tel:** 1 41 06 59 00 **Fax:** 1 41 06 59 09
Titles:
STUDYRAMAG

WOLTERS KLUWER - GROUPE LIAISONS 1790649
1 rue Eugène et Armand Peugeot, Case Postale 706, CEDEX, 92856 RUEIL MALMAISON **Tel:** 1 76 73 33 01 **Fax:** 1 76 73 48 85
Titles:
ENTREPRISE ET CARRIERES
LE MONITEUR DES PHARMACIES
TOUR HEBDO

YELLOW MEDIA 1784849
101/109 rue Jean Jaurès, 92300 LEVALLOIS PERRET **Tel:** 1 41 27 38 38 **Fax:** 1 41 27 38 39
Titles:
COMPUTER ARTS
CONSOLES +
JEUX VIDEO MAGAZINE
MICRO ACTUEL
NINTENDO - LE MAGAZINE OFFICIEL
PC ACHAT
PC JEUX
PSM3
WINDOWS NEWS

YONNE REPUBLICAINE 1785127
8-12 avenue Jean-Moulin, 89025 CEDEX AUXERRE **Tel:** 3 86 49 52 15 **Fax:** 3 86 46 99 90
Titles:
L' YONNE RÉPUBLICAINE AUXERRE
L' YONNE RÉPUBLICAINE: EDITION SUD

Germany

"DER KLEINE" VERLAG 1769155
Hegwiesen 10, 72764 REUTLINGEN
Tel: 7121 240459 **Fax:** 7121 210542
Email: info@heyd-pr.de
Web site: http://www.die-kleine-zeitschrift.de

Titles:
DIE KLEINE

"DIE STIFTUNG" MEDIA GMBH 1763436
Hofmannstr. 7a, 81379 MÜNCHEN
Tel: 89 20003390 **Fax:** 89 200033939
Email: info@die-stiftung.de
Web site: http://www.die-stiftung.de

Titles:
DIE STIFTUNG

11 FREUNDE VERLAG GMBH & CO. KG 1706788
Palisadenstr. 48, 10243 BERLIN **Tel:** 30 4039360
Fax: 30 403936122
Email: info@11freunde.de
Web site: http://www.11freunde.de

Titles:
11 FREUNDE

4IMEDIA AGENTURGRUPPE FÜR JOURNALISTISCHE KOMMUNIKATION 1728291
Friedrich-List-Platz 2, 04103 LEIPZIG
Tel: 341 8709840 **Fax:** 341 87098414
Email: laekb@4imedia.com
Web site: http://www.4imedia.com

Titles:
BRANDENBURGISCHES ÄRZTEBLATT

A. BEIG DRUCKEREI UND VERLAG GMBH & CO. KG 678786
Damm 9, 25421 PINNEBERG **Tel:** 4101 5350
Fax: 4101 5356006
Email: info@a-beig.de
Web site: http://www.a-beig.de

Titles:
BARMSTEDTER ZEITUNG
PINNEBERGER TAGEBLATT
QUICKBORNER TAGEBLATT
SCHENEFELDER TAGEBLATT
TIP AM SONNTAG
TIP AM SONNTAG
WEDEL-SCHULAUER TAGEBLATT

A. BERNECKER VERLAG GMBH 677935
Unter dem Schöneberg 1, 34212 MELSUNGEN
Tel: 5661 7310 **Fax:** 5661 731400
Email: info@bernecker.de
Web site: http://www.bernecker.de

Titles:
BUND+BERUF
XCENTRIC

A. MILLER, ZEITUNGSVERLAG KG 689605
Marienstr. 12, 83278 TRAUNSTEIN
Tel: 861 98770 **Fax:** 861 9877119
Web site: http://www.traunsteiner-tagblatt.de

Titles:
TRAUNSTEINER TAGBLATT

A & C DRUCK UND VERLAG GMBH 677697
Waterloohain 6, 22769 HAMBURG
Tel: 40 4325890 **Fax:** 40 43258950
Email: kontakt@auc-hamburg.de
Web site: http://www.auc-hamburg.de

Titles:
TELEMONAT

ABBOTT GMBH DIAGNOSTIKA 677228
Max-Planck-Ring 2, 65205 WIESBADEN
Tel: 6122 580 **Fax:** 6122 581277
Web site: http://www.abbottdiagnostik.de

Titles:
ABBOTT TIMES

A.B.C. ALBERT BITTER CONSULTING VERLAG & MARKETING GMBH 689541
Corneliusstr. 85, 40215 DÜSSELDORF
Tel: 211 865120 **Fax:** 211 8651232
Email: duesseldorf@top-magazin.de
Web site: http://www.top-magazin-duesseldorf.de

Titles:
TOP MAGAZIN DÜSSELDORF

ABCVERLAG GMBH 1649537
Waldhofer Str. 19, 69123 HEIDELBERG
Tel: 6221 757040 **Fax:** 6221 75704109
Email: info@abcverlag.de
Web site: http://www.abcverlag.de

Titles:
BASKET
EAT MAGAZINE
GIS.BUSINESS
GIS.TRENDS+MARKETS

DER ABITURIENT VERLAG 1621033
Taubfeld 6, 66121 SAARBRÜCKEN
Tel: 681 3946760 **Fax:** 681 39467610
Email: info@derabiturient.de
Web site: http://www.derabiturient.de

Titles:
DER ABITURIENT

ABL BAUERNBLATT VERLAG GMBH 689836
Bahnhofstr. 31, 59065 HAMM **Tel:** 2381 492288
Fax: 2381 492221
Email: verlag@bauernstimme.de
Web site: http://www.bauernstimme.de

Titles:
UNABHÄNGIGE BAUERNSTIMME

ABSOLUT RESEARCH GMBH 1685575
Große Elbstr. 277a, 22767 HAMBURG
Tel: 40 3037790 **Fax:** 40 30377915
Email: info@absolut-report.de
Web site: http://www.absolut-report.de

Titles:
ABSOLUTIREPORT

AC/CONSENS AGENTUR FÜR COMMUNICATION GMBH 683039
Ruhrallee 185, 45136 ESSEN **Tel:** 201 8945270
Fax: 201 894545
Email: consens@cityweb.de

Titles:
HAUS & MARKT - AUSG. DÜSSELDORF

ACE-VERLAG GMBH 677272
Schmidener Str. 227, 70374 STUTTGART
Tel: 711 53030 **Fax:** 711 5303168
Email: ace@ace-online.de
Web site: http://www.ace-online.de

Titles:
ACE LENKRAD

ACOUSTIC MUSIC GMBH & CO. KG 1626611
Jahnstr. 1a, 49080 OSNABRÜCK **Tel:** 541 710020
Fax: 541 708667
Email: order@acoustic-music.de
Web site: http://www.acoustic-music.de

Titles:
AKUSTIK GITARRE

ACV VERLAGS- UND WIRTSCHAFTSDIENST GMBH 677312
Goldgasse 2, 50668 KÖLN **Tel:** 221 9126910
Fax: 221 91269126
Email: acv@acv.de
Web site: http://www.acv.de

Titles:
ACV PROFIL

ADAC VERLAG GMBH 677314
Am Westpark 8, 81373 MÜNCHEN **Tel:** 89 76760
Fax: 89 76764770
Email: verlag@adac.de
Web site: http://www.adac.de

Titles:
ADAC BUNGALOW MOBILHEIM FÜHRER
ADAC CAMPING CARAVANING FÜHRER
ADAC CAMPING CARAVANING FÜHRER
ADAC MOTORWELT
ADAC REISEMAGAZIN
ADAC REISEMAGAZIN SKI
ADAC SKIGUIDE
ADAC SPECIAL GEBRAUCHTWAGEN
ADAC STELLPLATZ FÜHRER

ADAMAS MEDIA & MORE GMBH 1741908
Am Gentenberg 117, 40489 DÜSSELDORF
Tel: 211 4371350 **Fax:** 211 4371351
Email: ruhnke@adamas-media.de
Web site: http://www.adamas-media.de

Titles:
MBZ METALLBAUZEITUNG

ADIEU TRISTESSE VERLAG 1729649
Immanuelkirchstr. 38, 10405 BERLIN
Tel: 30 44351940 **Fax:** 30 443519420
Email: info@at-reisemagazin.de
Web site: http://www.at-reisemagazin.de

Titles:
ADIEU TRISTESSE

AD-MEDIA GMBH 680001
Industriestr. 180, 50999 KÖLN **Tel:** 2236 962390
Fax: 2236 962396
Email: info@ad-media.de
Web site: http://www.ad-media.de

Titles:
BTI BETON TEKNIK INTERNATIONAL
BWI BETONWERK INTERNATIONAL
C&PI CALCESTRUZZO & PREFABBRICAZIONE INTERNATIONAL
CPI CONCRETE PLANT INTERNATIONAL
CPI CONCRETE PLANT INTERNATIONAL
FCI FABRICA DE CONCRETO INTERNACIONAL
PBI PRÉFA BÉTON INTERNATIONAL
PHI PLANTA DE HORMIGÓN INTERNACIONAL
STEINE+ERDEN
ZBI ZAKLADY BETONOWE INTERNATIONAL

ADOLF DEIL GMBH & CO. KG 1741028
Schachenstr. 1, 66954 PIRMASENS
Tel: 6331 80050 **Fax:** 6331 800529
Email: verlag@pirmasenser-zeitung.de
Web site: http://www.pirmasenser-zeitung.de

Titles:
PZ PIRMASENSER ZEITUNG

ADOLF ENKE GMBH & CO. KG 677628
Steinweg 73, 38518 GIFHORN **Tel:** 5371 8080
Fax: 5371 808117
Web site: http://www.aller-zeitung.de

Titles:
ALLER-ZEITUNG
ALLER-ZEITUNG.DE
WOLFSBURGER ALLGEMEINE

ADOLF REMPPIS VERLAG GMBH + CO. KG 685340
König-Wilhelm-Platz 2, 71672 MARBACH
Tel: 7144 85000 **Fax:** 7144 5000
Email: verlag@marbacher-zeitung.zgs.de

Titles:
MARBACH & BOTTWARTAL
MARBACHER ZEITUNG

ADOLF-GRIMME-INSTITUT GES. FÜR MEDIEN, BILDUNG UND KULTUR MBH 683934
Eduard-Weitsch-Weg 25, 45768 MARL
Tel: 2365 91890 **Fax:** 2365 918989
Email: info@grimme-institut.de
Web site: http://www.grimme-institut.de

Titles:
JAHRBUCH FERNSEHEN

A.E.C. GERONIMO VERLAG GMBH 687536
Hospeltstr. 32, 50825 KÖLN **Tel:** 221 5708120
Fax: 221 570812121
Email: info@raveline.de
Web site: http://www.raveline.de

Titles:
RAVELINE

AEDIFICATIO VERLAG GMBH 700415
Schlierbergstr. 80, 79100 FREIBURG
Tel: 761 8818650 **Fax:** 761 8818651
Email: office@aedificat.de
Web site: http://www.aedificat.de

Titles:
RESTORATION OF BUILDINGS AND MONUMENTS

AFRICA POSITIVE E.V. 1627023
Rheinische Str. 147, 44147 DORTMUND
Tel: 231 7978590 **Fax:** 231 72592735
Email: info@africa-positive.de
Web site: http://www.africa-positive.de

Titles:
AFRICA POSITIVE

AG DER DILLINGER HÜTTENWERKE 689970
Werkstr. 1, 66763 DILLINGEN **Tel:** 6831 473126
Fax: 6831 473078
Email: nicole.munninger@dillinger.biz
Web site: http://www.dillinger.de

Titles:
USHÜTT

AGASAAT GMBH & CO. KG-MAISHANDELSGES. 1784258
Pascalstr. 11, 47506 NEUKIRCHEN-VLUYN
Tel: 2845 9369724 **Fax:** 2845 936979
Email: info@agasaat-mais.de
Web site: http://www.agasaat-mais.de

Titles:
MAISREPORT

AGENTUR DREIKLANG DEUTSCHLAND GBR 1600374
Johannesstr. 15b, 17034 NEUBRANDENBURG
Tel: 395 5824020 **Fax:** 395 5825635
Email: info@piste-neubrandenburg.de
Web site: http://www.piste.de

Titles:
PISTE

AGENTUR JANKE GMBH 1653010
Stammheimer Str. 47a, 50735 KÖLN
Tel: 221 7680270 **Fax:** 221 76802713
Email: info@agentur-janke.de
Web site: http://www.agentur-janke.de

Titles:
FEIERN IM BERGISCHEN LAND
HERA HOCHZEIT - REG.-AUSG. F. NORDRHEIN-WESTFALEN/RHEINLAND-PFALZ/HESSEN

AGRIMEDIA GMBH & CO. KG 690920
Klein Sachau 4, 29459 CLENZE
Tel: 5844 9711880 **Fax:** 5844 9711889
Email: mail@agrimedia.com
Web site: http://www.agrimedia.com

Titles:
FRISCHELOGISTIK
ZEITSCHRIFT FÜR ARZNEI- & GEWÜRZPFLANZEN

AGT VERLAG THUM GMBH 677435
Teinacher Str. 34, 71634 LUDWIGSBURG
Tel: 7141 22310 **Fax:** 7141 223131
Email: info@agt-verlag.de
Web site: http://www.agt-verlag.de

Titles:
DHF INTRALOGISTIK
DIMA
HOB DIE HOLZBEARBEITUNG
[ME] MECHATRONIK & ENGINEERING

AHEAD MEDIA GMBH 683339
Schlesische Str. 29, 10997 BERLIN
Tel: 30 6113080 **Fax:** 30 6113088
Email: ahead.berlin@aheadmedia.com
Web site: http://www.aheadmedia.com

Titles:
H.O.M.E.

AID INFODIENST ERNÄHRUNG, LANDWIRTSCHAFT, VERBRAUCHERSCHUTZ E.V. 677456
Heilsbachstr. 16, 53123 BONN **Tel:** 228 84990
Fax: 228 8499177
Email: aid@aid.de
Web site: http://www.aid.de

Titles:
B&B AGRAR

AIDS-HILFE DÜSSELDORF E.V. 683600
Johannes-Weyer-Str. 1, 40227 DÜSSELDORF
Tel: 211 7709541 **Fax:** 211 7709545
Email: info@duesseldorf.aidshilfe.de
Web site: http://www.duesseldorf.aidshilfe.de

Titles:
:INFO

AKADEMIE FÜR SEXUALMEDIZIN E.V. 1785697
Amsterdamer Weg 78, 44269 DORTMUND
Tel: 231 56763181 **Fax:** 231 9062451
Email: geschaeftsstelle@sexualmedizin-akademie.de
Web site: http://www.sexualmedizin-akademie.de

Titles:
SEXUOLOGIE

AKADEMIE VERLAG GMBH 677727
Markgrafenstr. 12, 10969 BERLIN
Tel: 30 42200640 **Fax:** 30 42200657
Email: info@akademie-verlag.de
Web site: http://www.akademie-verlag.de

Titles:
ARCHÄOLOGISCHES NACHRICHTENBLATT

AKRIBIE ARBEITSKREIS FÜR INFORMATION BIELEFELD/ OSTWESTFALEN-LIPPE E.V.- EIN REGIONALVERBAND DER DGI 688155
Vennhofallee 79, 33689 BIELEFELD
Tel: 5205 20888 **Fax:** 5205 20888
Email: ewald.bittner@t-online.de
Web site: http://www.akribie.de

Titles:
SCHNITT-STELLE

AKTIV DRUCK & VERLAG GMBH 1713093
An der Lohwiese 36, 97500 EBELSBACH
Tel: 9522 943570 **Fax:** 9522 943577
Email: ai@aktiv-druck.de
Web site: http://www.aktiv-druck.de

Titles:
A&I ANÄSTHESIOLOGIE & INTENSIVMEDIZIN

AKTIV VERLAG UND MEDIENSERVICE GMBH 1653435
Pirminstr. 145, 78479 REICHENAU
Tel: 7534 999950 **Fax:** 7534 999951
Email: kontakt@aktiv-verlag.com
Web site: http://www.aktiv-verlag.com

Titles:
VIDEOAKTIV DIGITAL

AKTIVMEDIA GMBH 679402
Hopfenfeld 5, 31311 UETZE **Tel:** 5173 98270
Fax: 5173 982739
Email: info@aktivmedia-online.de
Web site: http://www.aktivmedia-online.de

Titles:
BLACHREPORT
BLACHREPORT AUTOMOBIL EVENTS
BLACHREPORT MESSE + MARKETING
BLACHREPORT MUSEUM
STAGEREPORT

AKTUELL-VERLAG MODROW GMBH 683033
Martinistr. 5, 45701 HERTEN **Tel:** 209 16218555
Fax: 209 16218557
Email: info@av-westerholt.de
Web site: http://www.av-westerholt.de

Titles:
HAUS UND GRUND JOURNAL - AUSG. STADT U. REGION AACHEN

AKZENT VERLAGS-GMBH 677584
Moltkestr. 2, 78467 KONSTANZ
Tel: 7531 9914800 **Fax:** 7531 9914870
Email: info@akzent-magazin.com
Web site: http://www.akzent-magazin.com

Titles:
AKZENT

ALBA FACHVERLAG GMBH & CO. KG 679994
Willstätterstr. 9, 40549 DÜSSELDORF
Tel: 211 520130 **Fax:** 211 5201358
Email: vertrieb@alba-verlag.de
Web site: http://www.alba-verlag.de

Titles:
GÜTERBAHNEN
DER NAHVERKEHR

ALBA PUBLIKATION ALF TELOEKEN GMBH & CO. KG 681185
Am Meerkamp 20, 40667 MEERBUSCH
Tel: 2132 913950 **Fax:** 2132 9139558
Email: vertrieb@alba-verlag.de
Web site: http://www.alba-verlag.de

Titles:
EISENBAHN MODELLBAHN MAGAZIN
MODELL MAGAZIN
N BAHN MAGAZIN

ALFONS W. GENTNER VERLAG GMBH & CO. KG 677353
Forststr. 131, 70193 STUTTGART **Tel:** 711 636720
Fax: 711 63672747
Email: gentner@gentner.de
Web site: http://www.gentner.de

Titles:
ARBEITSMEDIZIN SOZIALMEDIZIN UMWELTMEDIZIN
ÄRZTEBLATT BADEN-WÜRTTEMBERG
ASUPROTECT
F+K FAHRZEUG + KAROSSERIE
GEBÄUDE ENERGIEBERATER
GLASWELT
DIE KÄLTE- UND KLIMATECHNIK
DER MEDIZINISCHE SACHVERSTÄNDIGE
PHOTOVOLTAIK
SBZ MONTEUR
SBZ SANITÄR.HEIZUNG.KLIMA
TGA FACHPLANER

ALFRED TOEPFER AKADEMIE FÜR NATURSCHUTZ 685710
Hof Möhr, 29640 SCHNEVERDINGEN
Tel: 5199 9890 **Fax:** 5199 98946
Email: nna@nna.niedersachsen.de
Web site: http://www.nna.de

Titles:
MITTEILUNGEN AUS DER NNA
NNA BERICHTE

ALLER-WESER VERLAGSGES. MBH 1619203
Werkstr. 2, 28857 SYKE **Tel:** 4242 58273
Fax: 4242 58276
Email: verlag@aller-weser-verlag.de
Web site: http://www.aller-weser-verlag.de

Titles:
BARNSTORFER WOCHENBLATT
DIEPHOLZER WOCHENBLATT
SCHWARMSTEDTER RUNDSCHAU
WALSRODER MARKT
WOCHEN-TIPP FÜR SYKE, STUHR, WEYHE UND BRUCHHAUSEN-VILSEN

ALLES GUTE VERLAG LTD. 1785756
Bärheide 1, 38442 WOLFSBURG
Tel: 5362 949733
Web site: http://www.allesguteverlag.de

Titles:
FREIZEIT VERGNÜGEN
VON FRAU ZU FRAU

ALLGÄUER ZEITUNGSVERLAG GMBH 1781411
Heisinger Str. 14, 87437 KEMPTEN **Tel:** 831 2060
Fax: 831 206379
Email: anzeigen@azv.de
Web site: http://www.all-in.de

Titles:
ALLGÄUER ZEITUNG
BUCHLOER ZEITUNG
MEMMINGER ZEITUNG

ALLGEMEINER ANZEIGER WERBE- UND VERTRIEBSGES. MBH 677207
Gottstedter Landstr. 6, 99092 ERFURT
Tel: 361 2275033 **Fax:** 361 2275034
Email: geschaeftsfuehrung@allgemeiner-anzeiger.de
Web site: http://www.allgemeiner-anzeiger.de

Titles:
ALLGEMEINER ANZEIGER
ALLGEMEINER ANZEIGER EICHSFELD
ALLGEMEINER ANZEIGER EISENACH
ALLGEMEINER ANZEIGER ERFURT
ALLGEMEINER ANZEIGER GERA/ SCHMÖLLN
ALLGEMEINER ANZEIGER GOTHA
ALLGEMEINER ANZEIGER HOLZLANDBOTE
ALLGEMEINER ANZEIGER JENA
ALLGEMEINER ANZEIGER MÜHLHAUSEN/ BAD LANGENSALZA
ALLGEMEINER ANZEIGER NORDHAUSEN/ SONDERSHAUSEN
ALLGEMEINER ANZEIGER SAALFELD/ RUDOLSTADT/PÖSSNECK
ALLGEMEINER ANZEIGER SÖMMERDA/ ARTERN
ALLGEMEINER ANZEIGER THÜRINGER VOGTLAND
ALLGEMEINER ANZEIGER WEIMAR/APOLDA

ALLGEMEINER DEUTSCHER FAHRRAD-CLUB BERLIN E.V. 687502
Brunnenstr. 28, 10119 BERLIN **Tel:** 30 4484724
Fax: 30 44340520
Email: kontakt@adfc-berlin.de
Web site: http://www.adfc-berlin.de

Titles:
RADZEIT

ALLIANZ DEUTSCHER DESIGNER AGD 677407
Steinstr. 3, 38100 BRAUNSCHWEIG
Tel: 531 16757 **Fax:** 531 16989
Email: info@agd.de
Web site: http://www.agd.de

Titles:
AGD VIERTEL

ALLIANZ DEUTSCHLAND AG 677669
Königinstr. 28, 80802 MÜNCHEN **Tel:** 89 38000
Fax: 89 380082712
Web site: http://www.allianz.de

Titles:
ALLIANZ FIRMEN INFO

ALOIS ERDL KG 677702
Gabelsbergerstr. 4, 83308 TROSTBERG
Tel: 8621 8080 **Fax:** 8621 80810
Email: info@erdl-verlag.de
Web site: http://www.chiemgau-online.de

Titles:
ALTBAYERISCHE HEIMATPOST
TRAUNREUTER ANZEIGER
TROSTBERGER TAGBLATT

ALPHA INFORMATIONS GMBH 697897
Finkenstr. 10, 68623 LAMPERTHEIM
Tel: 6206 9390 **Fax:** 6206 939232
Email: info@alphapublic.de
Web site: http://www.alphapublic.de

Titles:
ZUKUNFTSMOTOR METROPOLREGION RHEIN-NECKAR

ALSTERSPREE VERLAG GMBH 1768184
Schumannstr. 17, 10117 BERLIN
Tel: 30 21960830 **Fax:** 30 21960832
Email: info@procontra-online.de
Web site: http://www.procontra-online.de

Titles:
PROCONTRA

ALTMEPPEN VERLAG GMBH & CO. KG 686054
Bahnhofstr. 8, 48431 RHEINE **Tel:** 5971 4040
Fax: 5971 404199
Email: anzeigen@mv-online.de
Web site: http://www.mv-online.de

Titles:
MÜNSTERLÄNDISCHE VOLKSZEITUNG

ALTOP VERLAGS- UND VERTRIEBSGES. FÜR UMWELTFREUNDLICHE PRODUKTE MBH 1763441
Gotzingerstr. 48, 81371 MÜNCHEN
Tel: 89 7466110 **Fax:** 89 74661160
Email: info@eco-world.de
Web site: http://www.eco-world.de

Titles:
ECO WORLD
FORUM NACHHALTIG WIRTSCHAFTEN

ALTÖTTINGER LIEBFRAUENBOTE VERLAGSGES. MBH 677725
Neuöttinger Str. 5, 84503 ALTÖTTING
Tel: 8671 92730 **Fax:** 8671 927329
Email: kieswimmer@liebfrauenbote.de
Web site: http://www.liebfrauenbote.de

Titles:
ALTÖTTINGER LIEBFRAUENBOTE

ALU MEDIA GMBH 677739
Am Bonneshof 5, 40474 DÜSSELDORF
Tel: 211 4796422 **Fax:** 211 4796424
Email: info@alu-media.de
Web site: http://www.alu-media.de

Titles:
ALUMINIUM LIEFERVERZEICHNIS

AMEDIA INFORMATIONS GMBH 688552
Bei den Kornschrannen 18, 86720 NÖRDLINGEN
Tel: 9092 96830 **Fax:** 9092 9683990
Email: info@wochenzeitung.de

Titles:
SONNTAGS-ZEITUNG AKTUELL - AUSG. NÖRDLINGEN
WOCHEN ZEITUNG WZ AKTUELL - AUSG. ANSBACH
WOCHEN ZEITUNG WZ AKTUELL - AUSG. DINKELSBÜHL
WOCHEN ZEITUNG WZ AKTUELL - AUSG. HEIDENHEIM

AMG OWNERS CLUB E.V. 1741767
Mariental 12, 99817 EISENACH **Tel:** 3691 296336
Fax: 3691 296363
Email: info@amg-owners-club.org
Web site: http://www.amg-owners-club.org

Titles:
AMG OWNERS CLUB

ANALYTICA VERLAGSGES. MBH 690874
Leuvenstr. 25, 58515 LÜDENSCHEID
Tel: 2351 458890 **Fax:** 2351 458895
Email: info@analytica-verlag.de
Web site: http://www.zau-net.de

Titles:
ZAU ZEITSCHRIFT FÜR ANGEWANDTE UMWELTFORSCHUNG

ÄND ÄRZTENACHRICHTENDIENST VERLAGSGESELLSCHAFT MBH 1690731
Kattjahren 4, 22359 HAMBURG **Tel:** 40 6091540
Fax: 40 60915444
Web site: http://www.aend.de

Titles:
FACHARZT.DE

ANDERS UND SEIM NEUE MEDIEN AG 1651527
Raiffeisenstr. 10, 63225 LANGEN **Tel:** 6103 59730
Fax: 6103 597318
Email: office@andersundseim.de
Web site: http://www.bildschirmschoner.de

Titles:
BILDSCHIRMSCHONER.DE

ANDRÉ CITROËN CLUB 678053
Rheingauer Str. 8, 55122 MAINZ **Tel:** 6131 41818
Fax: 6131 41817
Email: citroen-club@t-online.de
Web site: http://www.andre-citroen-club.de

Titles:
ANDRÉ CITROËN-CLUB RUNDBRIEF

ANDREAE-NORIS ZAHN AG 678133
Solmsstr. 25, 60486 FRANKFURT **Tel:** 69 792030
Fax: 69 79203299
Email: kontakt@anzag.de
Web site: http://www.anzag.de

Titles:
APOTHEKENMANAGER

ANNA SCHWEIZAR VERLAG 683047
Eberle-Kögl-Str. 6, 87616 MARKTOBERDORF
Tel: 8342 96420 **Fax:** 8342 964220
Email: service@zielpunkte.de
Web site: http://www.zielpunkte.de

Titles:
ZIELPUNKTE REISEN

ANTIM-VERLAG GMBH 694637
Wächterstr. 2, 90489 NÜRNBERG **Tel:** 911 22814
Fax: 911 22815
Email: antim@bjv-report.de

Titles:
BJV REPORT
PUBLIC RELATIONS FORUM FÜR WISSENSCHAFT UND PRAXIS

ANTON SCHLECKER 1652455
Talstr. 14, 89579 EHINGEN **Tel:** 7391 5841222
Fax: 7391 5841855
Email: service@schlecker.net
Web site: http://www.schlecker.com

Titles:
SCHLECKER

Germany

ANZEIGEN VERTRIEB & MARKETING VERLAG 1622352
Ochsenfurter Str. 56, 97286 SOMMERHAUSEN
Tel: 9333 904990 **Fax:** 9333 9049915
Email: info@world-of-bike.de
Web site: http://www.world-of-bike.de
Titles:
WORLD OF BIKE

ANZEIGENBLATT EICHSFELD GMBH & CO. KG 682903
Breitenbacher Str. 18, 37327 LEINEFELDE-WORBIS **Tel:** 3605 519974 **Fax:** 3605 519976
Email: hallo-eichsfeld@madsack.de
Web site: http://www.hallo-eichsfeld.de
Titles:
HALLO SONNTAG IM EICHSFELD

ANZEIGENBLATT-VERLAG LAHN-DILL GMBH 684888
Elsa-Brandström-Str. 18, 35578 WETZLAR
Tel: 6441 959277 **Fax:** 6441 75166
Email: anzeigen.lda@mittelhessen.de
Web site: http://www.lahn-dill-anzeiger.de
Titles:
LDA - AUSG. WETZLAR

ANZEIGER VERLAG GMBH 686844
Bahnhofstr. 58, 27711 OSTERHOLZ-SCHARMBECK **Tel:** 4791 96650 **Fax:** 4791 966555
Email: ohz@anzeiger-verlag.de
Web site: http://www.anzeiger-verlag.de
Titles:
BREMERVÖRDER ANZEIGER
OSTERHOLZER ANZEIGER

AOL DEUTSCHLAND MEDIEN GMBH 1651414
Zirkusweg 1, 20359 HAMBURG **Tel:** 40 361590
Fax: 40 361597060
Web site: http://www.aol.de
Titles:
AOL.DE

AP VERLAG GMBH 1650440
Flossmannstr. 4, 85560 EBERSBERG
Tel: 8092 247020 **Fax:** 8092 2470229
Email: info@ap-verlag.de
Web site: http://www.ap-verlag.de
Titles:
MANAGE IT

APART VERLAG GMBH 1782375
Hildegardstr. 9, 80539 MÜNCHEN
Tel: 89 24207505 **Fax:** 89 24207504
Email: contact@alps-magazine.com
Web site: http://www.alps-magazine.com
Titles:
ALPS ALPINE LEBENSART

APOTHEKERKAMMER NORDRHEIN 694860
Poststr. 4, 40213 DÜSSELDORF **Tel:** 211 83880
Fax: 211 8388222
Email: info@aknr.de
Web site: http://www.aknr.de
Titles:
KAMMER IM GESPRÄCH

AQUENSIS VERLAG PRESSEBÜRO BADEN-BADEN GMBH 1773073
Pariser Ring 37, 76532 BADEN-BADEN
Tel: 7221 971450 **Fax:** 7221 9714510
Email: buero@presse-baden.de
Web site: http://www.aquensis-verlag.de
Titles:
BADEN BADEN INTERNATIONALES OLDTIMER-MEETING
ROSENBOGEN

ARAL AG 1630531
Wittener Str. 45, 44789 BOCHUM
Tel: 234 3153625
Web site: http://www.aral.de
Titles:
24/7
BUSINESS NEWS

ARBEITER-SAMARITER-BUND DEUTSCHLAND E.V. 678387
Sülzburgstr. 140, 50937 KÖLN **Tel:** 221 47605324
Fax: 221 47605297
Email: magazin@asb.de
Web site: http://www.asb.de
Titles:
ASB MAGAZIN

ARBEITGEBERVERBAND DER VERSICHERUNGSUNTER-NEHMEN IN DEUTSCHLAND 684397
Arabellastr. 29, 81925 MÜNCHEN
Tel: 89 9220010 **Fax:** 89 92200151
Email: agvvers@agv-vers.de
Web site: http://www.agv-vers.de
Titles:
KI SOZIALPOLITISCHE KURZINFORMATIONEN

ARBEITSGEMEINSCHAFT PARTNERSCHAFT IN DER WIRTSCHAFT E.V. 677416
Wilhelmshöher Allee 283a, 34131 KASSEL
Tel: 561 9324250 **Fax:** 561 9324252
Email: info@agpev.de
Web site: http://www.agpev.de
Titles:
AGP-MITTEILUNGEN

ARBEITSGEMEINSCHAFT REGENWALD UND ARTENSCHUTZ E.V. 1654186
August-Bebel-Str. 16, 33602 BIELEFELD
Tel: 521 65943 **Fax:** 521 64975
Email: ara@araonline.de
Web site: http://www.araonline.de
Titles:
ARA MAGAZIN

ARBEITSKAMMER DES SAARLANDES 678244
Fritz-Dobisch-Str. 6, 66111 SAARBRÜCKEN
Tel: 681 4005406 **Fax:** 681 4005401
Email: presse@arbeitskammer.de
Web site: http://www.arbeitskammer.de
Titles:
ARBEITNEHMER

ARBEITSKREIS BERLINER NAHVERKEHR E.V. 679139
Friedrichshaller Str. 31, 14199 BERLIN
Tel: 30 8223245 **Fax:** 30 3424855
Email: post@verkehrsblaetter.de
Web site: http://www.verkehrsblaetter.de
Titles:
BERLINER VERKEHRSBLÄTTER

ARBEITSKREIS CHRISTLICHER PUBLIZISTEN E.V. 677284
Schöne Aussicht 8, 34305 NIEDENSTEIN
Tel: 5624 5259 **Fax:** 5624 6921
Email: info@acp-international.de
Web site: http://www.acp-international.de
Titles:
ACP ARBEITSKREIS CHRISTLICHER PUBLIZISTEN

ARBEITSKREIS VERKEHR UND UMWELT UMKEHR E.V. 683698
Exerzierstr. 20, 13357 BERLIN **Tel:** 30 4927473
Fax: 30 4927972
Email: bestellung@mobilogisch.de
Web site: http://www.mobilogisch.de
Titles:
MOBILOGISCH!

ARCELORMITTAL EISENHÜTTENSTADT GMBH 681197
Werkstr. 1, 15890 EISENHÜTTENSTADT
Tel: 3364 372460 **Fax:** 3364 37652460
Web site: http://www.arcelormittal.com/eisenhuettenstadt
Titles:
EKO AKTUELL

ARCH+ VERLAG GMBH 678319
Kurbrunnenstr. 22, 52066 AACHEN
Tel: 241 508303 **Fax:** 241 54831
Email: verlag@archplus.net
Web site: http://www.archplus.net
Titles:
ARCH+

ARCOR AG & CO.KG 678322
Alfred-Herrhausen-Allee 1, 65760 ESCHBORN
Tel: 69 21693024 **Fax:** 69 21693027
Email: magazin.mail@arcor.net
Web site: http://www.arcor.de
Titles:
ARCOR MAGAZIN

ARCUS VERLAG NÜRNBERG-PRAG-WIEN GDBR 1654384
Lanzenweg 2a, 90455 NÜRNBERG
Tel: 911 880087 **Fax:** 911 880087
Email: peter.verbata@fek-ev.de
Web site: http://www.eurojournal.info
Titles:
EURO JOURNAL PRO MANAGEMENT

ARDEY-VERLAG GMBH 680566
An den Speichern 6, 48157 MÜNSTER
Tel: 251 4132213 **Fax:** 251 413220
Email: service@westfalenspiegel.de
Web site: http://www.westfalenspiegel.de
Titles:
WESTFALENSPIEGEL

ARD-WERBUNG SALES & SERVICES GMBH 685463
Bertramstr. 8/D-Bau, 60320 FRANKFURT
Tel: 69 154240 **Fax:** 69 15424199
Web site: http://www.media-perspektiven.de
Titles:
MEDIA PERSPEKTIVEN
MEDIA PERSPEKTIVEN BASISDATEN
MEDIA PERSPEKTIVEN DOKUMENTATION

ARGUMENT VERLAG 678332
Glashüttenstr. 28, 20357 HAMBURG
Tel: 40 4018000 **Fax:** 40 40180020
Email: verlag@argument.de
Web site: http://www.argument.de
Titles:
JAHRBUCH FÜR KRITISCHE MEDIZIN UND GESUNDHEITSWISSENSCHAFTEN

ARIVA.DE AG 1651434
Walkerdamm 17, 24103 KIEL **Tel:** 431 971080
Fax: 431 9710829
Email: info@ariva.de
Web site: http://www.ariva.de
Titles:
ARIVA.DE

ARS PUBLICA MARKETING GMBH 1676028
Markt 10, 18528 BERGEN **Tel:** 3838 809970
Fax: 3838 809977
Email: info@apmarketing.de
Web site: http://www.apmarketing.de
Titles:
À LA CARTE

ART GENERATION GMBH 1758298
Neuer Zollhof 2, 40221 DÜSSELDORF
Tel: 211 22950500 **Fax:** 211 229505013
Titles:
DEUTSCH
LINIE INTERNATIONAL

ÄRZTE ZEITUNG VERLAGSGES. MBH 677376
Am Forsthaus Gravenbruch 5, 63263 NEU-ISENBURG **Tel:** 6102 5060 **Fax:** 6102 506123
Email: info@aerztezeitung.de
Web site: http://www.aerztezeitung.de
Titles:
ÄRZTE ZEITUNG
ÄRZTE ZEITUNG ONLINE
WIRTSCHAFTSTIPP DERMATOLOGEN/ALLERGOLOGEN
WIRTSCHAFTSTIPP GYNÄKOLOGEN
WIRTSCHAFTSTIPP ORTHOPÄDEN/RHEUMATOLOGEN
WIRTSCHAFTSTIPP PÄDIATER
WIRTSCHAFTSTIPP UROLOGEN

ÄRZTEKAMMER SACHSEN-ANHALT 677371
Doctor-Eisenbart-Ring 2, 39120 MAGDEBURG
Tel: 391 60546 **Fax:** 391 60547000
Email: info@aeska.de
Web site: http://www.aeksa.de
Titles:
ÄRZTEBLATT SACHSEN-ANHALT

ASANGER VERLAG GMBH 1644655
Bödldorf 3, 84178 KRÖNING **Tel:** 8744 7262
Fax: 8744 967755
Email: verlag@asanger.de
Web site: http://www.asanger.de
Titles:
ZEITSCHRIFT FÜR PSYCHOTRAUMATOLOGIE PSYCHOTHERAPIEWISSENSCHAFT PSYCHOLOGISCHE MEDIZIN ZPPM

ASCHENDORFF MEDIA & SALES 1785737
An der Hansalinie 1, 48163 MÜNSTER
Tel: 251 6900 **Fax:** 251 6904570
Email: zeitschriften@aschendorff.de
Web site: http://www.aschendorff.de
Titles:
WIRTSCHAFTS SPIEGEL

ASCHENDORFF MEDIEN GMBH & CO. KG 695184
An der Hansalinie 1, 48163 MÜNSTER
Tel: 251 6900 **Fax:** 251 690105
Web site: http://www.aschendorff.de
Titles:
AHLENER ZEITUNG
STEINFURTER KREISBLATT
WESTFÄLISCHE NACHRICHTEN

ASCHENDORFF VERLAG GMBH & CO. KG 677839
Soester Str. 13, 48155 MÜNSTER **Tel:** 251 6900
Fax: 251 690143
Email: buchverlag@aschendorff.de
Web site: http://www.aschendorff-buchverlag.de
Titles:
CATHOLICA
IHK PLUS

ASCHENDORFF VERLAG GMBH & CO.KG MEDIA & SALES 1744326
Bredeneyer Str. 2b, 45133 ESSEN
Tel: 201 5237464 **Fax:** 201 5237463
Email: zeitschriften@aschendorff.de
Web site: http://www.aschendorff.de
Titles:
MEO

ASGARD-VERLAG DR. WERNER HIPPE GMBH 687636
Einsteinstr. 10, 53757 ST. AUGUSTIN
Tel: 2241 31640 **Fax:** 2241 316436
Email: info@asgard.de
Web site: http://www.asgard.de
Titles:
DIE RENTENVERSICHERUNG RV

ASIA VISION VERLAG MARTIN BRÜCKNER 683579
Rudolfstr. 22, 60327 FRANKFURT
Tel: 69 6656320 **Fax:** 69 66563222
Email: info@asiavision.de
Titles:
IN ASIEN!

ASSEKURANZ AKTUELL-VERLAG SIGNE HORN 678412
Schubertstr. 8, 65232 TAUNUSSTEIN
Tel: 6128 85604 **Fax:** 6128 84795
Titles:
ASSEKURANZ AKTUELL

ASTORIA REISEBÜRO GMBH 1762638
Dielingerstr. 1, 49074 OSNABRÜCK
Tel: 541 330930 **Fax:** 541 26842
Email: info@kreuzfahrt-zeitung.de
Web site: http://www.kreuzfahrt-zeitung.de
Titles:
KREUZFAHRT-ZEITUNG

ASTRO ZEITSCHRIFTENVERLAGS GMBH & CO. MEDIEN KG 678422
Karlsruher Str. 31, 76437 RASTATT
Tel: 7222 13402 **Fax:** 7222 13333
Email: info@vpm.de
Titles:
ASTRO WOCHE
ASTRO WOCHE

ATEC BUSINESS INFORMATION GMBH 1603067
Hackerbrücke 6, 80335 MÜNCHEN
Tel: 89 898170 **Fax:** 89 89817300
Email: info@atec-bi.de
Web site: http://www.atec-bi.de
Titles:
DIGITAL PRODUCTION
RECYCLING MAGAZIN

ATELIER VERLAG URSULA FRITZSCHE KG 678430
Hospeltstr. 47, 50825 KÖLN **Tel:** 221 9545858
Fax: 221 9545860
Email: info@atelier-verlag.de
Web site: http://www.atelier-verlag.de
Titles:
ATELIER

AT-FACHVERLAG GMBH 681218
Saarlandstr. 28, 70734 FELLBACH
Tel: 711 9529510 **Fax:** 711 95295199
Email: at@at-fachverlag.de
Web site: http://www.at-fachverlag.de
Titles:
EL INFO ELEKTRONIK INFORMATIONEN
HOTEL & TECHNIK
PHOTONIK
SI INFORMATIONEN

ATLAS COPCO TOOLS CENTRAL EUROPE GMBH 1653598
Langemarckstr. 35, 45141 ESSEN **Tel:** 201 21770
Fax: 201 2177100
Email: dk-info@de.atlascopco.com
Web site: http://www.atlascopco.com
Titles:
DRUCKLUFT KOMMENTARE

ATLAS SPEZIAL GMBH 682683
Brienner Str. 41, 80333 MÜNCHEN
Tel: 89 552410 **Fax:** 89 55241100
Email: info@atlas-verlag.de
Web site: http://www.atlas-verlag.de
Titles:
GOLF JOURNAL

ATLAS VERLAG GMBH 1769595
Brienner Str. 41, 80333 MÜNCHEN
Tel: 89 552410 **Fax:** 89 55241100
Email: info@atlas-verlag.de
Web site: http://www.atlas-verlag.de
Titles:
KANU MAGAZIN
KANU MAGAZIN

ATON VERLAG GMBH & CO. KG 688351
Max-Planck-Str. 25, 59423 UNNA
Tel: 2303 86745 **Fax:** 2303 81333
Email: info@aton-verlag.de
Web site: http://www.aton-verlag.de
Titles:
DER SELBSTÄNDIGE DSMAGAZIN

AUDI AG, ABT. I/VM-43 678456
Auto-Union-Str., 85057 INGOLSTADT
Tel: 841 8936017 **Fax:** 841 8939919
Email: anja.weinhofer@audi.de
Web site: http://www.audimagazin.de
Titles:
AUDI MAGAZIN

AUDIMAX MEDIEN GMBH 678457
Hauptmarkt 6, 90403 NÜRNBERG
Tel: 911 237790 **Fax:** 911 204939
Email: info@audimax.de
Web site: http://www.audimax.de
Titles:
AUDIMAX DIE HOCHSCHULZEITSCHRIFT
AUDIMAX ONLINE

AUDIN VERLAG GMBH 681948
Westenriederstr. 49, 80331 MÜNCHEN
Tel: 89 2422830 **Fax:** 89 24228319
Email: fml@audin.de
Web site: http://www.audin.de
Titles:
FML DER FAHRZEUG- UND METALL-LACKIERER/DAS LACKIERHANDWERK

AULA-VERLAG GMBH 681675
Industriepark 3, 56291 WIEBELSHEIM
Tel: 6766 903141 **Fax:** 6766 903320
Email: vertrieb@aula-verlag.de
Web site: http://www.verlagsgemeinschaft.com
Titles:
DER FALKE
DIE VOGELWELT

AUMA AUSSTELLUNGS- UND MESSE-AUSSCHUSS DER DEUTSCHEN WIRTSCHAFT E.V. 678503
Littenstr. 9, 10179 BERLIN **Tel:** 30 240000
Fax: 30 24000330
Email: info@auma.de
Web site: http://www.auma.de
Titles:
AUMA_MESSEGUIDE DEUTSCHLAND
AUSLANDSMESSEPROGRAMM DER BUNDESREPUBLIK DEUTSCHLAND UND DER BUNDESLÄNDER
DIE MESSEWIRTSCHAFTIBILANZ
REVIEW GERMAN TRADE FAIR INDUSTRY

AUTENTIC.INFO GMBH 1788153
Lange Gasse 19, 88239 WANGEN
Tel: 7522 931073 **Fax:** 7522 7079832
Web site: http://www.autentic.info
Titles:
CONCEPT OPHTHALMOLOGIE

AUTO & REISE GMBH VERLAG UND WIRTSCHAFTSDIENST 678609
Oberntiefer Str. 20, 91438 BAD WINDSHEIM
Tel: 9841 4090 **Fax:** 9841 409190
Web site: http://www.arcd.de
Titles:
AUTO & REISE

AUTODROM PUBLIKATIONEN, WOLFRAM NICKEL VERLAG 678578
Mehlemer Weg 25e, 53340 MECKENHEIM
Tel: 2225 945773 **Fax:** 2225 945774
Email: info@autodrom-online.de
Web site: http://www.autodrom-online.de
Titles:
AUTOSALON AUTOPARADE

AUTOMAXX VERLAG 680926
Rosenstr. 4, 84171 BAIERBACH **Tel:** 8705 1503
Fax: 8705 9511
Email: automaxx-verlag@t-online.de
Web site: http://www.automaxx.de
Titles:
AUTOMAXX

AVA AGRAR-VERLAG ALLGÄU GMBH 677639
Porschestr. 2, 87437 KEMPTEN **Tel:** 831 571420
Fax: 831 79008
Email: info@ava-verlag.de
Web site: http://www.ava-verlag.de
Titles:
ALLGÄUER BAUERNBLATT
MILCH PUR
DAS SCHÖNE ALLGÄU

AVIATIC VERLAG GMBH 685230
Kolpingring 16, 82041 OBERHACHING
Tel: 89 6138900 **Fax:** 89 61389010
Email: aviatic@aviatic.de
Web site: http://www.aviatic.de
Titles:
LUFT- UND RAUMFAHRT

AV-NEWS GMBH 1709631
Arabellastr. 4, 81925 MÜNCHEN
Tel: 89 92223173 **Fax:** 89 92223171
Email: information@av-finance.com
Web site: http://www.av-finance.com
Titles:
BANKEN & SPARKASSEN
EVIKO BANKENEINKAUFSFÜHRER
IT BANKEN & VERSICHERUNGEN

AVR AGENTUR FÜR WERBUNG UND PRODUKTION GMBH 683292
Weltenburger Str. 4, 81677 MÜNCHEN
Tel: 89 4196940 **Fax:** 89 4705364
Email: info@avr-werbeagentur.de
Web site: http://www.avr-werbeagentur.de
Titles:
HOCHZEITSPLANER
MAVIDA
SOUS

AWO BUNDESVERBAND E.V. 678631
Blücherstr. 62, 10961 BERLIN **Tel:** 30 263090
Fax: 30 2630932599
Email: info@awo.org
Web site: http://www.awo.org
Titles:
ANSICHT

AXEL SPRINGER AG 690455
Axel-Springer-Str. 65, 10969 BERLIN
Tel: 30 25910
Web site: http://www.welt.de
Titles:
AUTO BILD
AUTO BILD KLASSIK
BERLINER WIRTSCHAFT
BILD
BILD AM SONNTAG
BILD BERLIN-BRANDENBURG
BILD BREMEN
BILD CHEMNITZ
BILD DER FRAU
BILD DER FRAU GUT KOCHEN & BACKEN
BILD DRESDEN
BILD DÜSSELDORF
BILD HALLE
BILD HAMBURG
BILD HANNOVER
BILD KÖLN
BILD LEIPZIG
BILD MAGDEBURG
BILD MAINZ-WIESBADEN
BILD MECKLENBURG-VORPOMMERN
BILD MÜNCHEN
BILD NÜRNBERG
BILD RHEIN-NECKAR
BILD SAARLAND
BILD STUTTGART
BILD THÜRINGEN
BILDWOCHE
COMPUTER BILD
FEINE WELT
FEINE WELT
FEINE WELT
FEINE WELT
FRAU VON HEUTE
FUNK UHR
HÖRZU
HÖRZU WISSEN
ICON
TV NEU
DIE WELT
WELT AKTUELL
WELT AM SONNTAG

AXEL SPRINGER AG, TV DIGITAL 1743060
Axel-Springer-Platz 1, 20355 HAMBURG
Tel: 40 34700 **Fax:** 40 34721701
Titles:
TV DIGITAL

AXEL SPRINGER AUTO VERLAG GMBH 678574
Hansastr. 4a, 91126 SCHWABACH
Tel: 9122 985220 **Fax:** 9122 985222
Web site: http://www.axelspringer.de
Titles:
AUTO BILD ALLRAD
AUTO BILD MOTORSPORT
AUTO BILD SPORTSCARS
AUTO TEST
AUTO TEST 4X4 EXTRA
AUTO TEST CABRIO
AUTO TEST VAN-EXTRA

AXEL SPRINGER MEDIAHOUSE BERLIN GMBH 682996
Mehringdamm 33, 10961 BERLIN
Tel: 30 30881880 **Fax:** 30 3088188223
Email: info@axel-springer-mediahouse-berlin.de
Web site: http://www.axel-springer-mediahouse-berlin.de
Titles:
METAL HAMMER
MUSIKEXPRESS. ROLLING STONE

AXEL SPRINGER VERLAG AG 1649510
Axel-Springer-Str. 65, 10969 BERLIN
Tel: 30 25910 **Fax:** 30 25911608
Titles:
HAMBURGER ABENDBLATT
WELT ONLINE

AZ ALFELDER ZEITUNG DOBLER GMBH & CO. KG 677611
Ravenstr. 45, 31061 ALFELD **Tel:** 5181 80020
Fax: 5181 800247
Email: alfelder-zeitung@alfelder-zeitung.de
Web site: http://www.alfelder-zeitung.de
Titles:
ALFELDER ZEITUNG

B. BEHR'S VERLAG GMBH & CO. KG 690491
Averhoffstr. 10, 22085 HAMBURG
Tel: 40 2270080 **Fax:** 40 2201091
Email: info@behrs.de
Web site: http://www.behrs.de
Titles:
>>DLR DEUTSCHE LEBENSMITTEL-RUNDSCHAU

B. BOLL VERLAG DES SOLINGER TAGEBLATTES GMBH & CO. KG 686748
Mummstr. 9, 42651 SOLINGEN **Tel:** 212 2990
Fax: 212 299118
Email: b.boll@solinger-tageblatt.de
Web site: http://www.solinger-tageblatt.de
Titles:
DAS SOLINGER AM MITTWOCH
SOLINGER-TAGEBLATT.DE
ST SOLINGER TAGEBLATT

B+B MEDIA COMPANY GMBH 689509
Hildebrandtstr. 24, 40215 DÜSSELDORF
Tel: 211 83030 **Fax:** 211 324862
Email: info@bb-mediacompany.com
Web site: http://www.bb-mediacompany.com
Titles:
TM

B & B PUBLISHING GMBH 680103
Schmiedberg 2a, 86415 MERING **Tel:** 8233 4117
Fax: 8233 30206
Email: verlag@ce-markt.de
Web site: http://www.ce-markt.de
Titles:
CE MARKT

B&L MEDIENGMBH & CO. KG 678711
Max-Volmer-Str. 28, 40724 HILDEN
Tel: 2103 2040 **Fax:** 2103 204204
Email: info@blmedien.de
Web site: http://www.blmedien.de
Titles:
BÄCKER BLUME
BLICK FF DELIKAT
FIRST CLASS
FT FLEISCHEREI TECHNIK MEAT TECHNOLOGY
GENIESSEN & MEHR
GVMANAGER
JOURNAL FÜR PERFEKTES HAUSHALTEN
LUKULLUS

BACK JOURNAL VERLAGSGES. MBH 1758887
Luisenstr. 1a, 49074 OSNABRÜCK
Tel: 541 58054451 **Fax:** 541 58054499
Email: info@backjournal.de
Web site: http://www.backjournal.de
Titles:
BACK JOURNAL

BÄCKER-INNUNG NÜRNBERG 678715
Ostendstr. 149, 90482 NÜRNBERG
Tel: 911 541949 **Fax:** 911 542828
Titles:
BÄCKER-WERK

BACKMEDIA VERLAGSGES. MBH 680521
Vierhausstr. 112, 44807 BOCHUM
Tel: 234 901990 **Fax:** 234 9019919
Email: info@backmedia.info
Web site: http://www.backmedia.info
Titles:
BÄCKER ZEITUNG
D.B.Z MAGAZIN
D.B.Z WECKRUF

BACKTECHNIK VERLAGSGES. MBH
1742580
Friedrichstr. 9, 49076 OSNABRÜCK
Tel: 541 58054451 **Fax:** 541 58054499
Email: waclawek@backtechnik-online.de
Web site: http://www.backtechnik-online.de

Titles:
GETREIDETECHNOLOGIE [CEREAL TECHNOLOGY]

BADENIA VERLAG UND DRUCKEREI GMBH
684557
Rudolf-Freytag-Str. 6, 76189 KARLSRUHE
Tel: 721 95450 **Fax:** 721 9545125
Email: vertrieb@konradsblatt.de
Web site: http://www.konradsblatt-online.de

Titles:
KONRADSBLATT

BADEN-MEDIEN REDAKTION + VERTRIEB
685144
Aschmattstr. 8, 76532 BADEN-BADEN
Tel: 7221 502340 **Fax:** 7221 502344
Email: kontakt@baden-medien.de
Web site: http://www.baden-medien.de

Titles:
LIVE MAGAZIN

BADEN-WÜRTTEMBERGISCHER GENOSSENSCHAFTSVERBAND E.V.
1759881
Lauterbergstr. 1, 76137 KARLSRUHE
Tel: 721 3520 **Fax:** 721 3521482
Email: aktuelles@bgvnet.de
Web site: http://www.bwgv-info.de

Titles:
GENOGRAPH

BADISCHE ANZEIGEN-VERLAGS-GMBH
678678
Herzogstr. 10, 68723 SCHWETZINGEN
Tel: 6202 9400 **Fax:** 6202 940133
Email: verlag@baz-medien.de
Web site: http://www.baz-medien.de

Titles:
BAZ BADISCHE ANZEIGEN-ZEITUNG - AUSG. 2
BAZ BADISCHE ANZEIGEN-ZEITUNG ZUM SONNTAG - AUSG. A
BAZ BERGSTRÄSSER ANZEIGEN-ZEITUNG - AUSG. 21

BADISCHE NEUESTE NACHRICHTEN BADENDRUCK GMBH
677275
Linkenheimer Landstr. 133, 76149 KARLSRUHE
Tel: 721 7890 **Fax:** 721 789155
Email: vertrieb@bnn.de
Web site: http://www.bnn.de

Titles:
ACHER- UND BÜHLER BOTE
BADISCHE NEUESTE NACHRICHTEN
BRETTENER NACHRICHTEN
BRUCHSALER RUNDSCHAU
PFORZHEIMER KURIER

BADISCHE ZEITSCHRIFTEN GMBH
684544
Unterwerkstr. 5, 79115 FREIBURG
Tel: 761 45153400 **Fax:** 761 45153401
Email: info@badische-zeitschriften.de
Web site: http://www.badische-zeitschriften.de

Titles:
BADEN INTERN
BADISCHES WEIN MAGAZIN

BADISCHER LANDWIRTSCHAFTS-VERLAG GMBH
678684
Friedrichstr. 43, 79098 FREIBURG
Tel: 761 271330 **Fax:** 761 2713357
Email: verlag@blv-freiburg.de

Titles:
DER BADISCHE WINZER
BBZ BADISCHE BAUERN ZEITUNG

BADISCHER TURNER-BUND E.V.
678683
Am Fächerbad 5, 76131 KARLSRUHE
Tel: 721 18150 **Fax:** 721 26176
Email: kurt.klumpp@badischer-turner-bund.de
Web site: http://www.badischer-turner-bund.de

Titles:
BADISCHE TURNZEITUNG

BADISCHER VERLAG GMBH & CO. KG
678685
Basler Str. 88, 79115 FREIBURG **Tel:** 761 4960
Fax: 761 4961099
Email: info@badische-zeitung.de
Web site: http://www.badische-zeitung.de

Titles:
BADISCHE ZEITUNG
BADISCHE ZEITUNG.DE

BADISCHES TAGBLATT GMBH
678682
Stephanienstr. 1, 76530 BADEN-BADEN
Tel: 7221 2150 **Fax:** 7221 2151490
Email: info@badisches-tagblatt.de
Web site: http://www.badisches-tagblatt.de

Titles:
BADISCHES TAGBLATT
WOCHENJOURNAL WO

BAHN FACHVERLAG GMBH
678736
Linienstr. 214, 10119 BERLIN **Tel:** 30 20095220
Fax: 30 200952229
Email: info@bahn-fachverlag.de
Web site: http://www.bahn-fachverlag.de

Titles:
DEINE BAHN

BANGER VERLAG GMBH
690099
Guldenbachstr. 1, 50935 KÖLN **Tel:** 221 460140
Fax: 221 4601425
Email: banger@banger.de
Web site: http://www.banger.de

Titles:
ZEITSCHRIFTEN

BANK-VERLAG MEDIEN GMBH
678764
Wendelinstr. 1, 50933 KÖLN **Tel:** 221 54900
Fax: 221 5490315
Email: info@bank-verlag-medien.de
Web site: http://www.bank-verlag-medien.de

Titles:
DIE BANK
RISIKO MANAGER

BÄRENREITER-VERLAG GMBH & CO. KG
1720378
Heinrich-Schütz-Allee 35, 34131 KASSEL
Tel: 561 31050 **Fax:** 561 3105240
Email: info@baerenreiter.com
Web site: http://www.baerenreiter.com

Titles:
MUSIK & KIRCHE
DIE MUSIKFORSCHUNG

BARMER GEK
678784
Lichtscheider Str. 89, 42285 WUPPERTAL
Tel: 18 500990 **Fax:** 18 500991459
Email: redaktion@barmer-gek.de
Web site: http://www.barmer-gek.de

Titles:
GESUNDHEIT KONKRET

BARMER GEK, ABT. UNTERNEHMENSPOLITIK UND KOMMUNIKATION
1745521
42271 WUPPERTAL **Tel:** 18500 991836
Fax: 18500 991389
Email: nahdran@barmer-gek.de
Web site: http://www.barmer-gek.de

Titles:
NAHDRAN

BAU- UND LIEGENSCHAFTSBETRIEB NRW, ÖFFENTLICHKEITSARBEIT UND KOMMUNIKATION
1728899
Mercedesstr. 12, 40470 DÜSSELDORF
Tel: 211 61700180 **Fax:** 211 61700182
Email: info@blb.nrw.de
Web site: http://www.blb.nrw.de

Titles:
BLB.NRW

BAUER DIGITAL KG
1748106
Burchardstr. 11, 20095 HAMBURG **Tel:** 40 30190
Fax: 40 30191991
Email: info@bauerdigital.de

Titles:
BRAVO.DE
SELBST.DE

BAUER MEDIA GROUP
678843
Burchardstr. 11, 20095 HAMBURG
Tel: 40 30191037 **Fax:** 40 30191043
Email: kommunikation@bauermedia.com
Web site: http://www.bauermedia.com

Titles:
INTERN
INTOUCH

BAUER MEDIA GROUP, YVONNE BAUER REDAKTIONS KG
1763000
Burchardstr. 11, 20095 HAMBURG **Tel:** 40 30190
Fax: 40 30191043
Email: kommunikation@bauermedia.com
Web site: http://www.bauermediagroup.de

Titles:
TV PUR

BAUER MEDIA KG
1783354
Burchardstr. 11, 20095 HAMBURG **Tel:** 40 30190
Fax: 40 30191043
Email: kommunikation@bauermedia.com
Web site: http://www.bauermedia.com

Titles:
TINA KOCH & BACK-IDEEN

BAUER PROGRAMM GMBH
681769
Burchardstr. 11, 20095 HAMBURG **Tel:** 40 30190
Fax: 40 30191043
Email: kommunikation@bauermedia.com
Web site: http://www.bauermedia.com

Titles:
AUF EINEN BLICK
TV HÖREN UND SEHEN
TV MOVIE
TV MOVIE.DE

BAUER WOMEN GMBH
1685859
Burchardstr. 11, 20095 HAMBURG **Tel:** 40 30190
Fax: 40 30195449
Email: mail@maxi.de
Web site: http://www.hbv.de

Titles:
MAXI

BAUERNBLATT GMBH
678844
Am Kamp 19, 24768 RENDSBURG
Tel: 4331 12770 **Fax:** 4331 127762
Email: verlag@bauernblatt.com
Web site: http://www.bauernblatt.com

Titles:
BAUERNBLATT

BAUERNVERBAND SCHLESWIG-HOLSTEIN E.V., KREISBAUERNVERBAND DITHMARSCHEN
680789
Waldschlößchenstr. 39, 25746 HEIDE
Tel: 481 850420 **Fax:** 481 8504220
Email: kbv@bauernverbandsh.de
Web site: http://www.bauernverbandsh.de

Titles:
DITHMARSCHER BAUERNBRIEF

BAUERNVERBAND SCHLESWIG-HOLSTEIN E.V., KREISBAUERNVERBAND RENDSBURG-ECKERNFÖRDE
686149
Am Kamp 19, 24768 RENDSBURG
Tel: 4331 127761 **Fax:** 4331 127718
Email: kbv.rd-eck@bauernverbandsh.de
Web site: http://www.bauernverbandsh.de

Titles:
NACHRICHTEN FÜR DIE LANDWIRTSCHAFT

BAUERNVERBAND SCHLESWIG-HOLSTEIN E.V., KREISBAUERNVERBAND SCHLESWIG
1793299
Lise-Meitner Str. 2, 24837 SCHLESWIG
Tel: 4621 3057010 **Fax:** 4621 3057015
Email: kbv.schleswig@bauernverbandsh.de

Titles:
INFORMATIONEN DES KREISBAUERNVERBANDES SCHLESWIG

BAUGEWERBE-VERBAND NIEDERSACHSEN
678882
Baumschulenallee 12, 30625 HANNOVER
Tel: 511 957570 **Fax:** 511 9575740
Email: kontakt@bvn.de
Web site: http://www.bvn.de

Titles:
DIE BAUSTELLE

BAUGEWERBEVERBAND RHEINLAND-PFALZ E.V.
678864
Max-Hufschmidt-Str. 11, 55130 MAINZ
Tel: 6131 983490 **Fax:** 6131 9834949
Email: bgv@bgvmz.de
Web site: http://www.bgv-rheinland-pfalz.de

Titles:
BAU-JOURNAL

BAUGEWERBEVERBAND SCHLESWIG-HOLSTEIN
1600367
Hopfenstr. 2e, 24114 KIEL **Tel:** 431 535470
Fax: 431 5354777
Email: info@bau-sh.de
Web site: http://www.bau-sh.de

Titles:
BAU AKTUELL

BAUMEISTER VERLAG
689042
Uhlandstr. 104, 73614 SCHORNDORF
Tel: 7181 253231 **Fax:** 7181 258878
Email: info@baumeister-verlag.de
Web site: http://www.baumeister-verlag.de

Titles:
AKTIV IM LEBEN
GENERATION 55PLUS
GENERATION 55PLUS
GENERATION 55PLUS
GENERATION 55PLUS
GENERATION 55PLUS

BAUVERBÄNDE WESTFALEN
678850
Westfalendamm 229, 44141 DORTMUND
Tel: 231 9411580 **Fax:** 231 94115840
Email: info@bauverbaende.de
Web site: http://www.bauverbaende.de

Titles:
BAUDIREKT
BAUDIREKT FORT- UND WEITERBILDUNG IN DER BAUWIRTSCHAFT

BAUVERLAG BV GMBH
678852
Avenwedder Str. 55, 33335 GÜTERSLOH
Tel: 5241 8090884 **Fax:** 5241 80690880
Email: leserservice@bauverlag.de
Web site: http://www.bauverlag.de

Titles:
AT INTERNATIONAL MINERAL PROCESSING
BAUHANDWERK
BAUMARKT BAUWIRTSCHAFT
BAUVERLAG EINKAUFSFÜHRER BAU
BAUWELT
BETON BAUTEILE
BFT INTERNATIONAL
BRANDSCHUTZ IN ÖFFENTLICHEN UND PRIVATWIRTSCHAFTLICHEN GEBÄUDEN
BUNDESBAUBLATT
COMPUTER SPEZIAL
DACH + HOLZBAU
DBZ DEUTSCHE BAUZEITSCHRIFT
DBZ LICHT+RAUM
FACILITY MANAGEMENT
KKA KÄLTE KLIMA AKTUELL
LICHT + RAUM
METALLBAU
SHK PROFI
STADT BAUWELT
TAB
TIS GALA BAU
TIS TIEFBAU INGENIEURBAU STRASSENBAU
TUNNEL
WHO IS WHO FACILITY MANAGEMENT
ZI ZIEGELINDUSTRIE INTERNATIONAL
ZI-JAHRBUCH
ZKG INTERNATIONAL

BAYARD MEDIA GMBH & CO. KG
1643762
Böheimstr. 8, 86153 AUGSBURG
Tel: 821 4554810 **Fax:** 821 45548110
Web site: http://www.bayard-media.de

Titles:
FRAU IM LEBEN
LEBEN & ERZIEHEN
PLUS MAGAZIN
RENTE & CO

BAYARTZ CONSULTING 678896
Bennostr. 6, 52134 HERZOGENRATH
Tel: 2406 669006
Email: info@bayartz.de
Web site: http://www.bayartz.de

Titles:
BAYARTZ NEWS & FACTS

BAYER AG, KONZERNKOMMUNIKATION, BAYERWERK, GEBÄUDE W 11 678897
51368 LEVERKUSEN **Tel:** 214 301
Fax: 214 3071985
Web site: http://www.bayer.com

Titles:
BAYER REPORT

BAYER CROPSCIENCE AG 677433
Alfred-Nobel-Str. 50, 40789 MONHEIM
Tel: 2173 383540 **Fax:** 2173 383454
Email: bernhard.grupp@bayercropscience.com
Web site: http://www.bayercropscience.com

Titles:
CORREO
CURIERUL
HIRADÓ
KURIER OCHRONY ROSLIN

BAYERISCHE LANDESANSTALT FÜR WALD UND FORSTWIRTSCHAFT 1728311
Hans-Carl-von-Carlowitz-Platz 1, 85354 FREISING **Tel:** 8161 714881 **Fax:** 8161 714971
Email: redaktion@lwf.bayern.de
Web site: http://www.lwf.bayern.de

Titles:
LWF AKTUELL

BAYERISCHE LANDESÄRZTEKAMMER 678918
Mühlbaurstr. 16, 81677 MÜNCHEN
Tel: 89 4147274 **Fax:** 89 4147202
Email: aerzteblatt@blaek.de
Web site: http://www.blaek.de

Titles:
BAYERISCHES ÄRZTEBLATT

BAYERISCHE LANDESBANK 1621158
Brienner Str. 18, 80333 MÜNCHEN
Tel: 89 217101 **Fax:** 89 217123578

Titles:
PUNKT

BAYERISCHE RUNDSCHAU VERLAG & MEDIEN GMBH & CO. KG 678917
E.-C.-Baumann-Str. 5, 95326 KULMBACH
Tel: 9221 9490 **Fax:** 9221 949378
Email: verlagsleitung@bayerische-rundschau.de
Web site: http://www.infranken.de

Titles:
BAYERISCHE RUNDSCHAU

BAYERISCHER LANDES-SPORTVERBAND E.V. 678939
Georg-Brauchle-Ring 93, 80992 MÜNCHEN
Tel: 89 157020 **Fax:** 89 15702444
Email: info@blsv.de
Web site: http://www.blsv.de

Titles:
BAYERNSPORT

BAYERISCHER LEHRER- UND LEHRERINNENVERBAND E.V. 678921
Bavariaring 37, 80336 MÜNCHEN
Tel: 89 7210010 **Fax:** 89 7250324
Email: bllv@bllv.de
Web site: http://www.bllv.de

Titles:
BAYERISCHE SCHULE

BAYERISCHER TURNVERBAND E.V. 678942
Georg-Brauchle-Ring 93, 80992 MÜNCHEN
Tel: 89 15702318 **Fax:** 89 15702317
Email: bayernturner@turnverband-bayern.de
Web site: http://www.turnverband-bayern.de

Titles:
BAYERN TURNER

BAYERISCHER WALDBESITZERVERBAND E.V. 678929
Max-Joseph-Str. 9, 80333 MÜNCHEN
Tel: 89 5803080 **Fax:** 89 5807015
Email: bayer.waldbesitzerverband@t-online.de
Web site: http://www.bayer-waldbesitzerverband.de

Titles:
DER BAYERISCHE WALDBESITZER

BAYERISCHES SONNTAGSBLATT VERLAGSGES. MBH 678925
Lange Str. 335, 59067 HAMM **Tel:** 2381 940400
Fax: 2381 9404040
Email: verlag@liborius.de
Web site: http://www.bayerisches-sonntagsblatt.de

Titles:
BAYERISCHES SONNTAGSBLATT

BBE-MEDIA GMBH & CO. KG 677308
Am Hammergraben 14, 56567 NEUWIED
Tel: 2631 879400 **Fax:** 2631 879403
Email: info@bbe-media.de
Web site: http://www.bbe-media.de

Titles:
BBE CHEF-TELEGRAMM
BBE CHEF-TELEGRAMM APOTHEKEN SPEZIAL
BBE STEUERPRAXIS

BBG BETRIEBSBERATUNGS GMBH 693231
Bindlacher Str. 4, 95448 BAYREUTH
Tel: 921 757580 **Fax:** 921 7575820
Email: info@asscompact.de
Web site: http://www.asscompact.de

Titles:
ASSCOMPACT

BBSG VERLAG 1759177
Schillerstr. 18, 69226 NUSSLOCH

Titles:
MAMMA MIA!

BBV BILDUNG + BUSINESS = VERANTWORTUNG 683612
Helmlinger Str. 1, 77839 LICHTENAU
Tel: 7227 505010 **Fax:** 7227 505050
Email: info@b-b-v.de
Web site: http://www.b-b-v.de

Titles:
INFO-ATLAS
PS PÄDAGOGEN SERVICE

BCA AG 693299
Siemensstr. 27, 61352 BAD HOMBURG
Tel: 6172 495510 **Fax:** 6172 495550
Email: willkommen@bca.de
Web site: http://www.bca.de

Titles:
TOPNEWS

BCD TRAVEL GERMANY GMBH 1640645
Otto-Lilienthal-Str. 1, 28199 BREMEN
Tel: 421 3500861 **Fax:** 421 3500638
Email: imke.reichert@bcdtravel.de
Web site: http://www.bcdtravel.de

Titles:
MOVE

BDM VERLAGS GMBH 1738274
Steintor 2a, 19243 WITTENBURG
Tel: 38852 90630 **Fax:** 38852 906322
Web site: http://www.bdm-verband.de

Titles:
BDM AKTUELL

BDST STEUERZAHLER SERVICE GMBH 1627233
Adolfsallee 22, 65185 WIESBADEN
Tel: 611 3410750 **Fax:** 611 34107599
Email: info@steuerzahler-service.de
Web site: http://www.steuerzahler-service.de

Titles:
NORD-KURIER
DIE NRW NACHRICHTEN
DER STEUERZAHLER

BDZ-DEUTSCHE ZOLL- UND FINANZGEWERKSCHAFT 678978
Friedrichstr. 169, 10117 BERLIN **Tel:** 30 40816600
Fax: 30 40816633
Email: post@bdz.eu
Web site: http://www.bdz.dbb.de

Titles:
BDZ MAGAZIN

BEAM-ELEKTRONIK VERLAGS- UND VERTRIEBS GMBH 677778
Krummbogen 14, 35039 MARBURG
Tel: 6421 96140 **Fax:** 6421 961423
Email: info@beam-verlag.de
Web site: http://www.beam-verlag.de

Titles:
H & E HAUS & ELEKTRONIK
HF-PRAXIS

BECHTLE, GRAPH. BETRIEBE UND VERLAGSGES. (BECHTLE VERLAG UND ESSLINGER ZEITUNG) GMBH & CO. KG 681445
Zeppelinstr. 116, 73730 ESSLINGEN
Tel: 711 93100 **Fax:** 711 9310440
Email: info@ez-online.de
Web site: http://www.esslinger-zeitung.de

Titles:
ESSLINGER ZEITUNG
NECKAR JOURNAL

BECKMANN VERLAG GMBH & CO. KG 680883
Heidecker Weg 112, 31275 LEHRTE
Tel: 5132 85910 **Fax:** 5132 859125
Email: info@beckmann-verlag.de
Web site: http://www.beckmann-verlag.de

Titles:
DPS
KOMMUNALTECHNIK
LOHNUNTERNEHMEN

BELGIEN TOURISMUS WALLONIE-BRÜSSEL 1725040
Cäcilienstr. 46, 50667 KÖLN **Tel:** 221 277590
Fax: 221 27759100
Email: info@belgien-tourismus.de
Web site: http://www.belgien-tourismus.de

Titles:
SAVOIR VIVRE

BELLEVUE AND MORE GMBH 679042
Dorotheenstr. 64, 22301 HAMBURG
Tel: 40 6965950 **Fax:** 40 696595199
Email: info@bellevue.de
Web site: http://www.bellevue.de

Titles:
BELLEVUE
BELLEVUE
HOUSE AND MORE

BEM MEDIA GMBH & CO. KG 1752532
Koblenzer Str. 97, 32584 LÖHNE
Tel: 5731 981040 **Fax:** 5731 6641009
Email: post@bem-media.de
Web site: http://www.bem-media.de

Titles:
GROSSHANDELSMARKT
PREDPRINIMATEL

BENEDIKTINERINNEN-ABTEI FULDA 695187
Nonnengasse 16, 36037 FULDA **Tel:** 661 9024531
Fax: 661 9024545
Email: garten@abtei-fulda.de
Web site: http://www.abtei-fulda.de

Titles:
WINKE FÜR DEN BIOGÄRTNER

BERCHTESGADENER ANZEIGER KG 679055
Griesstätter Str. 1, 83471 BERCHTESGADEN
Tel: 8652 95840 **Fax:** 8652 958419
Email: anzeigen@berchtesgadener-anzeiger.de
Web site: http://www.berchtesgadener-anzeiger.de

Titles:
BERCHTESGADENER ANZEIGER

BERGEDORFER BUCHDRUCKEREI VON ED. WAGNER (GMBH & CO.) 679061
Curslacker Neuer Deich 50, 21029 HAMBURG
Tel: 40 725660 **Fax:** 40 72566209
Web site: http://www.bergedorfer-zeitung.de

Titles:
BERGEDORFER ZEITUNG
BILLE WOCHENBLATT
LAUENBURGISCHE LANDESZEITUNG

BERGISCHE VERLAGSGES. MENZEL GMBH & CO. KG 679078
Neumarktstr. 10, 42103 WUPPERTAL
Tel: 202 451654 **Fax:** 202 450086
Email: info@bvg-menzel.de
Web site: http://www.bvg-menzel.de

Titles:
BERGISCHE WIRTSCHAFT

BERGISCHER NATURSCHUTZVEREIN E.V. 1606079
Schmitzbüchel 2, 51491 OVERATH
Tel: 2204 7977 **Fax:** 2204 74258
Email: rbnoverath@t-online.de
Web site: http://www.bergischer-naturschutzverein.de

Titles:
RBN RUNDBRIEF DES BERGISCHEN NATURSCHUTZVEREIN

BERGISCHES HANDELSBLATT GMBH & CO. KG 679077
Hauptstr. 97, 51465 BERGISCH GLADBACH
Tel: 2202 20080 **Fax:** 2202 2008499
Email: joachim.hesse@mds.de
Web site: http://www.rheinische-anzeigenblaetter.de

Titles:
BERGISCHES HANDELSBLATT

BERLIN FACES VERLAGSGES. 1728157
Bamberger Str. 18, 10779 BERLIN
Tel: 30 21458410 **Fax:** 30 21458479
Email: info@elsweyer-hoffmann.de
Web site: http://www.elsweyer-hoffmann.de

Titles:
DER MITTELSTAND.

BERLIN TOURISMUS MARKETING GMBH 679148
Am Karlsbad 11, 10785 BERLIN **Tel:** 30 2647480
Fax: 30 264748968
Email: elatacz@btm.de
Web site: http://www.visitberlin.de

Titles:
BERLIN STADTPLAN
BERLIN TO GO
BUSSTOP
CITY GUIDE
HOTEL GUIDE BERLIN
MEETING GUIDE
SALES MANUAL

BERLINER ÄRZTE-VERLAG GMBH 1653948
Flemingstr. 12, 10557 BERLIN **Tel:** 30 8336066
Fax: 30 84309677
Web site: http://www.berliner-aerzteblatt.de

Titles:
BERLINER ÄRZTEBLATT

BERLINER REISE VERLAG 690194
Haeselerstr. 22c, 14050 BERLIN **Tel:** 30 3028145
Email: dirk.jacobs@vip-reisemagazin.de
Web site: http://www.vip-reisemagazin.de

Titles:
V.I.P. REISE MAGAZIN

BERLINER VERLAG GMBH 1767281
Karl-Liebknecht-Str. 29, 10178 BERLIN
Tel: 30 23279 **Fax:** 30 23276171
Web site: http://www.berlinonline.de

Titles:
BERLINER ZEITUNG

BERLINER VERLAG GMBH & CO. 679123
Karl-Liebknecht-Str. 29, 10178 BERLIN
Tel: 30 23279 **Fax:** 30 23275254
Web site: http://www.berlinonline.de

Titles:
BERLINER KURIER
BERLINER KURIER AM SONNTAG

Germany

BERLINER VORWÄRTS VERLAGSGES. MBH 679131
Stresemannstr. 30, 10963 BERLIN
Tel: 30 25594100 **Fax:** 30 25594192
Email: verlag@vorwaerts.de
Web site: http://www.vorwaerts.de
Titles:
DEMO
VORWÄRTS

BERLINER WISSENSCHAFTS-VERLAG GMBH 682192
Markgrafenstr. 12, 10969 BERLIN **Tel:** 30 8417700
Fax: 30 84177021
Email: bwv@bwv-verlag.de
Web site: http://www.bwv-verlag.de
Titles:
OSTEUROPA
OSTEUROPA WIRTSCHAFT
ZEUS

BERLINER WOCHENBLATT VERLAG GMBH 679142
Wilhelmstr. 139, 10963 BERLIN **Tel:** 30 259178400
Fax: 30 259138448
Email: verlagsleitung@berliner-woche.de
Web site: http://www.berliner-woche.de
Titles:
SPANDAUER VOLKSBLATT - SPANDAUER ZTG.-HAVELLÄND. ZTG.-SPANDAUER ANZEIGER, LOKALZTG. F. D. HAVELSTADT AUSG. NORD F. D. ORTSTEILE SPANDAU, FALKENHAGENER FELD, HAKENFELDE, HASELHORST U. SIEMENSSTADT

BERLINONLINE STADTPORTAL GMBH & CO. KG 1626625
Karl-Liebknecht-Str. 29, 10178 BERLIN
Tel: 1805 807737 **Fax:** 1805 002897
Email: info@berlin.de
Web site: http://www.berlin.de
Titles:
BERLIN.DE

BERNHARD GÖTZ VERLAG 685985
Ahornweg 4, 74255 ROIGHEIM **Tel:** 6298 928884
Fax: 6298 928981
Email: info@motorrad-gespanne.de
Web site: http://www.motorrad-gespanne.de
Titles:
MOTORRAD GESPANNE

BERUFSGENOSSENSCHAFT DER BAUWIRTSCHAFT 678824
Hildegardstr. 29, 10715 BERLIN **Tel:** 30 857810
Fax: 30 85781500
Email: info@bgbau.de
Web site: http://www.bgbau.de
Titles:
BG BAU AKTUELL
TIPPS

BERUFSGENOSSENSCHAFT ENERGIE TEXTIL ELEKTRO MEDIENERZEUGNISSE 679775
Gustav-Heinemann-Ufer 130, 50968 KÖLN
Tel: 221 37780 **Fax:** 221 37781199
Email: info@bgetem.de
Web site: http://www.bgetem.de
Titles:
BRÜCKE - INFORMATIONEN F. ARBEITSSICHERHEIT U. GESUNDHEITSSCHUTZ, AUSG. ELEKTRO FEINMECHANIK
IMPULS
INFORMATIONEN FÜR DEN BETRIEBSARZT
INFORMATIONEN FÜR DEN SICHERHEITSBEAUFTRAGTEN
INFORMATIONEN FÜR DIE SICHERHEITSFACHKRAFT

BERUFSGENOSSENSCHAFT FÜR GESUNDHEITSDIENST UND WOHLFAHRTSPFLEGE 690854
Pappelallee 35, 22089 HAMBURG **Tel:** 40 202070
Fax: 40 20207525
Titles:
YOUNG LOOK

BERUFSGENOSSENSCHAFT HOLZ UND METALL 686474
Seligmannallee 4, 30173 HANNOVER
Tel: 511 8118366 **Fax:** 511 8118200
Email: klaus.taubitz@bghm.de
Web site: http://www.bghm.de
Titles:
BGHM-AKTUELL

BERUFSGENOSSENSCHAFT ROHSTOFFE UND CHEMISCHE INDUSTRIE 1783009
Kurfürsten-Anlage 62, 69115 HEIDELBERG
Tel: 6221 5230 **Fax:** 6221 523323
Email: info@bgrci.de
Web site: http://www.bgrci.de
Titles:
BGRCI.MAGAZIN

BERUFSVERBAND DER HEILPRAKTIKER E.V. NORDRHEIN-WESTFALEN 690936
Kasernenstr. 26, 42651 SOLINGEN
Tel: 212 47285 **Fax:** 212 42711
Email: redaktion@verlag-zfn.de
Web site: http://www.verlag-zfn.de
Titles:
ZEITSCHRIFT FÜR NATURHEILKUNDE

BERUFSVERBAND DEUTSCHER INTERNISTEN E.V. 700408
Schöne Aussicht 5, 65193 WIESBADEN
Tel: 611 181330 **Fax:** 611 1813350
Email: info@bdi.de
Web site: http://www.bdi.de
Titles:
BDI AKTUELL

BETA VERLAG & MARKETINGGES. MBH 684021
Celsiusstr. 43, 53125 BONN **Tel:** 228 919370
Fax: 228 9193723
Email: info@beta-publishing.com
Web site: http://www.beta-publishing.com
Titles:
MEDICAL CORPS INTERNATIONAL FORUM
WEHRMEDIZIN UND WEHRPHARMAZIE
WEHRMEDIZINISCHE MONATSSCHRIFT

BEURONER KUNSTVERLAG 1725037
Abteistr. 2, 88631 BEURON **Tel:** 7466 17228
Fax: 7466 17209
Email: info@beuroner-kunstverlag.de
Web site: http://www.beuroner-kunstverlag.de
Titles:
ERBE UND AUFTRAG

BEUTH VERLAG GMBH 680755
Burggrafenstr. 6, 10787 BERLIN **Tel:** 30 26010
Fax: 30 260142750
Web site: http://www.beuth.de
Titles:
DIN MITTEILUNGEN

BEZIRKSREDAKTION ARZ GMBH 677273
Am Marktplatz 4, 77704 OBERKIRCH
Tel: 7802 80424 **Fax:** 7802 80441
Email: lokales.oberkirch@reiff.de
Titles:
ACHER-RENCH-ZEITUNG

BFB BESTMEDIA4BERLIN GMBH 1763357
Bundesallee 23, 10717 BERLIN **Tel:** 30 863030
Fax: 30 86303200
Email: info@bfb.de
Web site: http://www.bfb.de
Titles:
CHARLOTTENBURG KOMPAKT
MITTE KOMPAKT
PRENZLAUER BERG KOMPAKT
REINICKENDORF KOMPAKT
STEGLITZ KOMPAKT
TEMPELHOF KOMPAKT
TREPTOW KOMPAKT
WEISSENSEE KOMPAKT
ZEHLENDORF KOMPAKT

BFS. VERLAG 1747679
Gürtelstr. 25, 10247 BERLIN **Tel:** 30 32534730
Fax: 30 32534731
Email: info@sleazemag.de
Web site: http://www.sleazemag.de
Titles:
SLEAZE

BGA BERATUNGSSTELLE FÜR GUSSASPHALTANWENDUNG E.V. 682840
Dottendorfer Str. 86, 53129 BONN
Tel: 228 239899 **Fax:** 228 239399
Email: info@gussasphalt.de
Web site: http://www.gussasphalt.de
Titles:
GUSS I ASPHALT MAGAZIN

BGL-MEDIEN UND DRUCK GMBH & CO. KG 679264
Schachtstr. 4, 83435 BAD REICHENHALL
Tel: 8651 9810 **Fax:** 8651 981160
Email: info@bgl-medien.de
Web site: http://www.bgl-medien.de
Titles:
FREILASSINGER ANZEIGER
REICHENHALLER TAGBLATT

BI MEDIEN GMBH 679268
Faluner Weg 33, 24109 KIEL **Tel:** 431 535920
Fax: 431 5359225
Email: info@bi-medien.de
Web site: http://www.bi-medien.de
Titles:
AUSSCHREIBUNGSBLATT BI
BI BAUFAHRZEUGE
BI BAUMAGAZIN
BI GALABAU
BI UMWELTBAU

BIBLIOMED MEDIZINISCHE VERLAGSGES. MBH 682261
Stadtwaldpark 10, 34212 MELSUNGEN
Tel: 5661 73440 **Fax:** 5661 8360
Email: info@bibliomed.de
Web site: http://www.bibliomed.de
Titles:
ARZT UND KRANKENHAUS
F & W FÜHREN UND WIRTSCHAFTEN IM KRANKENHAUS
PFLEGE- & KRANKENHAUSRECHT-PKR
DIE SCHWESTER DER PFLEGER

BIERMANN VERLAG GMBH 694687
Otto-Hahn-Str. 7, 50997 KÖLN **Tel:** 2236 3760
Fax: 2236 376999
Email: info@biermann.net
Web site: http://www.biermann.net
Titles:
ARTHROSE NACHRICHTEN
ÄRZTLICHE PRAXIS GYNÄKOLOGIE
ÄRZTLICHE PRAXIS NEUROLOGIE PSYCHIATRIE
ÄRZTLICHE PRAXIS ONKOLOGIE
KOMPAKT GASTROENTEROLOGIE
KOMPAKT PNEUMOLOGIE
OPHTHALMOLOGISCHE NACHRICHTEN
ORTHOPÄDISCHE NACHRICHTEN
UROLOGISCHE NACHRICHTEN

BILD DIGITAL GMBH & CO. KG 1627260
Axel-Springer-Str. 65, 10888 BERLIN
Tel: 30 25910
Email: info@bild.de
Web site: http://www.bild.de
Titles:
BILD.DE

BILDUNGSHAUS SCHULBUCHVERLAGE WESTERMANN SCHROEDEL DIESTERWEG SCHÖNINGH WINKLERS GMBH 682498
Georg-Westermann-Allee 66, 38104 BRAUNSCHWEIG **Tel:** 531 7080 **Fax:** 531 7088340
Email: schulservice@westermann.de
Web site: http://www.westermann.de
Titles:
BÜROWIRTSCHAFT
GRUNDSCHULE
L.A. MULTIMEDIA
PRAXIS GEOGRAPHIE
PRAXIS GESCHICHTE
PRAXIS GRUNDSCHULE
PRAXIS SCHULE 5-10
WINKLERS ILLUSTRIERTE

BILFINGER BERGER AG 1637139
Carl-Reiß-Platz 1, 68165 MANNHEIM
Tel: 621 4590 **Fax:** 621 4592366
Titles:
BILFINGER BERGER MAGAZIN

BIO RITTER GMBH VERLAG UND VERSAND 679356
Monatshauser Str. 8, 82327 TUTZING
Tel: 8158 8022 **Fax:** 8158 7142
Email: bioritter@aol.com
Web site: http://www.ritter24.de
Titles:
BIO

BIO VERLAG GMBH 686187
Magnolienweg 23, 63741 ASCHAFFENBURG
Tel: 6021 44890 **Fax:** 6021 4489499
Email: info@bioverlag.de
Web site: http://www.bioverlag.de
Titles:
NATURKOST.DE
SCHROT & KORN

BIOGRAPH VERLAG PETER LIESE 679358
Citadellstr. 14, 40213 DÜSSELDORF
Tel: 211 8668212 **Fax:** 211 8668222
Email: info@biograph-online.de
Web site: http://www.biograph-online.de
Titles:
BIOGRAPH

BIOKREIS E.V., VERBAND FÜR ÖKOLOGISCHEN LANDBAU UND GESUNDE ERNÄHRUNG 679368
Stelzlhof 1, 94034 PASSAU **Tel:** 851 7565016
Fax: 851 7565025
Email: info@biokreis.de
Web site: http://www.biokreis.de
Titles:
BIONACHRICHTEN

BIOLAND VERLAGS GMBH 679361
Kaiserstr. 18, 55116 MAINZ **Tel:** 6131 1408693
Fax: 6131 1408697
Email: redaktion@bioland.de
Web site: http://www.bioland-verlag.de
Titles:
BIOLAND

BIOMEDPARK MEDIEN GMBH 1643750
Sofienstr. 5, 69115 HEIDELBERG
Tel: 6221 137470 **Fax:** 6221 1374777
Email: info@biomedpark.de
Web site: http://www.biomedpark.de
Titles:
PÄDIATRIX

BIOPRESS VERLAG MARIA SENTZ E.K. 679370
Schulstr. 10, 74927 ESCHELBRONN
Tel: 6226 4351 **Fax:** 6226 40047
Email: presse@biopress.de
Web site: http://www.biopress.de
Titles:
BIOPRESS

BIOWELT VERLAGSGES. MBH 1687329
Luisenstr. 1a, 49074 OSNABRÜCK
Tel: 541 58054443 **Fax:** 541 58054499
Email: info@biowelt-online.de
Web site: http://www.biowelt-online.de
Titles:
BIOWELT

BIT-VERLAG WEINBRENNER GMBH & CO. KG 679386
Fasanenweg 18, 70771 LEINFELDEN-ECHTERDINGEN **Tel:** 711 75910 **Fax:** 711 7591348
Email: info@bitverlag.de
Web site: http://www.bitverlag.de
Titles:
BIT
BOSS
DI DIGITAL IMAGING
HOBBYART
KULT AM PULT
PBS AKTUELL

BIZ VERLAG GMBH 679392
Ehrig-Hahn-Str. 4, 16356 AHRENSFELDE
Tel: 30 437380 **Fax:** 30 43738111
Email: info@biz-verlag.de
Web site: http://www.zuhause3.de

Titles:
MEIN SCHÖNES ZU HAUSE[3]

BKK BUNDESVERBAND 1685818
Kronprinzenstr. 6, 45128 ESSEN **Tel:** 201 17901
Fax: 201 1791010
Email: info@bkk-bv.de
Web site: http://www.bkk.de

Titles:
BKK GESUNDHEITSREPORT

BKK BUNDESVERBAND GBR 679400
Kronprinzenstr. 6, 45128 ESSEN **Tel:** 201 17901
Fax: 201 1791000
Email: diebkk@bkk-bv.de
Web site: http://www.bkk.de

Titles:
DIE BKK

BKK IHV 1736751
Äppelallee 27, 65203 WIESBADEN
Tel: 611 186860 **Fax:** 611 1868610
Email: info@bkk-ihv.de
Web site: http://www.bkk-ihv.de

Titles:
DER GESUNDHEITSPARTNER

BLACKWELL VERLAG GMBH 678030
Rotherstr. 21, 10245 BERLIN **Tel:** 30 47031400
Fax: 30 47031410
Web site: http://www.blackwell.de

Titles:
ANDROLOGIA
IMAGING DECISIONS MRI
JDDG JOURNAL DER DEUTSCHEN DERMATOLOGISCHEN GESELLSCHAFT JOURNAL OF THE GERMAN SOCIETY OF DERMATOLOGY
MEDREPORT
MEDREVIEW
MYCOSES
REPRODUCTION IN DOMESTIC ANIMALS

BLÄTTER VERLAGSGES. MBH 679415
Torstr. 178, 10115 BERLIN **Tel:** 30 30883644
Fax: 30 30883645
Email: info@blaetter.de
Web site: http://www.blaetter.de

Titles:
BLÄTTER FÜR DEUTSCHE UND INTERNATIONALE POLITIK

BLIX-VERLAG GMBH & CO. KG 1675686
Hauptstr. 93/1, 88326 AULENDORF
Tel: 7525 92120 **Fax:** 7525 921222
Email: info@blix.info
Web site: http://www.blix.info

Titles:
BLIX

BLUE OCEAN ENTERTAINMENT AG 1717936
Breitscheidstr. 10, 70174 STUTTGART
Tel: 711 2202990 **Fax:** 711 22029919
Email: reale@blue-ocean-ag.de
Web site: http://www.blue-ocean-ag.de

Titles:
FRAG DOCH MAL DIE MAUS

BM MEDIEN VERLAG 694698
Industriestr. 131c, 50996 KÖLN **Tel:** 221 6501166
Fax: 221 65011688
Email: info@bm-medien-verlag.de
Web site: http://www.bm-medien-verlag.de

Titles:
VIP INTERNATIONAL HONEYMOONER
VIP INTERNATIONAL TRAVELLER
VIP INTERNATIONAL TRAVELLER GOLD EDITION

BMV BISTUMSZEITUNG MÜNSTER VERLAGSGES. MBH 684382
Auf dem Graben 2, 45657 RECKLINGHAUSEN
Tel: 2361 582880 **Fax:** 2361 5828855
Email: info@bmv-verlag.de
Web site: http://www.kircheundleben.de

Titles:
KIRCHE + LEBEN

BMW VETERANEN-CLUB DEUTSCHLAND E.V. 694672
Bahnhofstr. 17, 35745 HERBORN **Tel:** 2772 41665
Fax: 2772 41666
Email: info@bmw-veteranenclub.de
Web site: http://www.bmw-veteranenclub.de

Titles:
CN BMW VETERANEN-CLUB NACHRICHTEN

BOCK + HERCHEN VERLAG 679289
Reichenberger Str. 11e, 53604 BAD HONNEF
Tel: 2224 5775 **Fax:** 2224 78310
Email: buh@bock-net.de
Web site: http://www.b-u-b.de

Titles:
BUB FORUM BIBLIOTHEK UND INFORMATION

BODO'S POWER SYSTEMS 1716501
Katzbek 17a, 24235 LABOE **Tel:** 4343 421790
Fax: 4343 421789
Email: editor@bodospower.com
Web site: http://www.bodospower.com

Titles:
BODO'S POWER SYSTEMS

BÖHLAU VERLAG GMBH & CIE. 678299
Ursulaplatz 1, 50668 KÖLN **Tel:** 221 913900
Fax: 221 9139011
Email: vertrieb@boehlau.de
Web site: http://www.boehlau.de

Titles:
L' HOMME

BONIFATIUS GMBH, DRUCK-BUCH-VERLAG 1687301
Karl-Schurz-Str. 26, 33100 PADERBORN
Tel: 5251 1530 **Fax:** 5251 153104
Email: karl.wegener@bonifatius.de
Web site: http://www.derdom.de

Titles:
DER DOM

BONNER ZEITUNGSDRUCKEREI UND VERLAGSANSTALT H. NEUSSER GMBH 682477
Justus-von-Liebig-Str. 15, 53121 BONN
Tel: 228 66880 **Fax:** 228 6688170
Email: verlag@ga-bonn.de
Web site: http://www.general-anzeiger-bonn.de

Titles:
GENERAL-ANZEIGER
GENERAL-ANZEIGER ONLINE

BORBECKER NACHRICHTEN WILHELM WIMMER GMBH & CO. KG 679604
Vinckestr. 2, 45355 ESSEN **Tel:** 201 867000
Fax: 201 678360

Titles:
BORBECKER NACHRICHTEN

BORN VERLAG - J. H. BORN GMBH 679862
Am Walde 23, 42119 WUPPERTAL
Tel: 202 243080 **Fax:** 202 2430819
Email: born@born-verlag.de
Web site: http://www.born-verlag.de

Titles:
HAUS UND GRUND-MAGAZIN WUPPERTAL

BÖRSE AKTUELL VERLAG AG 679567
Fritz-Elsas-Str. 49, 70174 STUTTGART
Tel: 711 61414111 **Fax:** 711 61414333
Email: kundenservice@boerse-aktuell.de
Web site: http://www.boerse-aktuell.de

Titles:
BÖRSE-AKTUELL

BÖRSENMEDIEN AG 677516
Am Eulenhof 14, 95326 KULMBACH
Tel: 9221 90510 **Fax:** 9221 90514000
Email: info@boersenmedien.de
Web site: http://www.boersenmedien.de

Titles:
DER AKTIONÄR
DER AKTIONÄR

BOSCH REXROTH AG, UNTERNEHMENSKOMMUNIKATION 687742
Maria-Theresien-Str. 23, 97816 LOHR
Tel: 9352 181091 **Fax:** 9352 181190
Email: drive-control@boschrexroth.de
Web site: http://www.boschrexroth.com

Titles:
DRIVE & CONTROL

B.O.S.S DRUCK UND MEDIEN GMBH 681364
von-Monschaw-Str. 5, 47574 GOCH
Tel: 2823 929980 **Fax:** 2823 9299899
Email: info@boss-druck.de
Web site: http://www.boss-druck.de

Titles:
NIEDERRHEIN

BOULEVARD ILLUSTRIERTEN VERLAG GMBH 682209
Weberstr. 17, 55130 MAINZ **Tel:** 6131 965110
Fax: 6131 9651190
Email: info@frizzgehtaus.de
Web site: http://www.frizz-mainz.de

Titles:
FRIZZ

BOX MEDIEN GMBH 679641
Christianstr. 52, 50825 KÖLN **Tel:** 221 95433335
Fax: 221 3553387259
Email: box@box-medien.de
Web site: http://www.box-online.de

Titles:
BOX

BOYENS MEDIEN GMBH & CO. KG 1681421
Wulf-Isebrand-Platz 1, 25746 HEIDE
Tel: 481 68860 **Fax:** 481 688690199
Email: boyens@boyens-medien.de
Web site: http://www.boyens-medien.de

Titles:
BRUNSBÜTTELER ZEITUNG
DITHMARSCHER LANDESZEITUNG
MARNER ZEITUNG

B-QUADRAT VERLAGS GMBH & CO. KG 681494
Kolpingstr. 46, 86916 KAUFERING
Tel: 8191 96410 **Fax:** 8191 964141
Email: info@b-quadrat.de
Web site: http://www.b-quadrat.de

Titles:
EUROPÄISCHER LASER MARKT
LASER
MPA MESSEN PRÜFEN AUTOMATISIEREN
MPA MESSEN PRÜFEN AUTOMATISIEREN

BRAND EINS VERLAG GMBH & CO. OHG 679657
Speersort 1, 20095 HAMBURG **Tel:** 40 32331670
Fax: 40 32331680
Email: verlag@brandeins.de
Web site: http://www.brandeins.de

Titles:
BRAND EINS
BRAND EINS NEULAND

BRANDEIS VERLAG UND MEDIEN GMBH & CO. KG 685927
Schulstr. 53, 65795 HATTERSHEIM
Tel: 6190 800900 **Fax:** 6190 800910
Email: info@brandeisweb.de
Web site: http://www.brandeisweb.de

Titles:
DER MÖBELSPEDITEUR

BRANDENBURGER LANDFRAUENVERBAND E.V. 1767671
Dorfstr. 1, 14513 TELTOW **Tel:** 3328 319300
Fax: 3328 319305
Email: blv_ev@t-online.de
Web site: http://www.brandenburger-landfrauen.de

Titles:
LAND FRAUEN JOURNAL

BRANDENBURGISCHE ANZEIGENZEITUNG GMBH 687252
Neustädtischer Markt 7, 14776 BRANDENBURG
Tel: 3381 52570 **Fax:** 3381 525739

Titles:
DER POTSDAMER

BRANDENBURGISCHE UNIVERSITÄTSDRUCKEREI 679659
Karl-Liebknecht-Str. 24, 14476 POTSDAM
Tel: 331 56890 **Fax:** 331 568916
Web site: http://www.bud-potsdam.de

Titles:
N UND L NATURSCHUTZ UND LANDSCHAFTSPFLEGE IN BRANDENBURG

BRANDES & APSEL VERLAG GMBH 677396
Scheidswaldstr. 22, 60385 FRANKFURT
Tel: 69 272995170 **Fax:** 69 2729951710
Email: info@brandes-apsel-verlag.de
Web site: http://www.brandes-apsel-verlag.de

Titles:
ANALYTISCHE KINDER- UND JUGENDLICHEN-PSYCHOTHERAPIE

BRAUNSCHWEIG REPORT MEDIENGES. MBH & CO. KG 679677
Kreuztor 8, 38126 BRAUNSCHWEIG
Tel: 531 3800014 **Fax:** 531 3800020
Email: info@braunschweigreport.de

Titles:
BRAUNSCHWEIG REPORT
WOCHENBLATT ZUM SONNTAG

BRAUNSCHWEIGER ZEITUNGSVERLAG GMBH & CO. KG 679672
Hamburger Str. 277, 38114 BRAUNSCHWEIG
Tel: 531 39000 **Fax:** 531 3900610
Email: vertrieb@bzv.de
Web site: http://www.newsclick.de

Titles:
BRAUNSCHWEIGER ZEITUNG
NEWSCLICK.DE
SALZGITTER-ZEITUNG
WOLFSBURGER NACHRICHTEN

BRAUTMEDIA GMBH 679680
Hörsterplatz 2b, 48147 MÜNSTER
Tel: 251 539020 **Fax:** 251 5390230
Web site: http://das.braut.net

Titles:
BRAUT & BRÄUTIGAM

BREMENPORTS GMBH & CO. KG 690492
Hafenstr. 49, 28217 BREMEN **Tel:** 421 30901615
Fax: 421 309019615
Email: claudia.stuhrmann@bremenports.de
Web site: http://www.bremenports.de

Titles:
WESER LOTSE LOGISTICS PILOT

BREMER ANZEIGER GMBH 679702
Martinistr. 33, 28195 BREMEN
Tel: 421 518045600 **Fax:** 421 518045601
Email: anzeigen@bremer-anzeiger.de
Web site: http://www.bremer-anzeiger.de

Titles:
BREMER ANZEIGER - AUSG. WEST

BREMER BLATT VERLAGS GMBH 679315
Altenwall 9, 28195 BREMEN **Tel:** 421 790070
Fax: 421 7900777
Email: info@bremer.de
Web site: http://www.bremer.de

Titles:
BREMER
BREMER SPECIAL
BREMER SPECIAL

BREMER TAGESZEITUNGEN AG 679705
Martinistr. 43, 28195 BREMEN **Tel:** 421 36710
Fax: 421 328327
Email: vertrieb@btag.info

Titles:
BREMEN 4U
BREMER NACHRICHTEN
KURIER AM SONNTAG

REGIONALE RUNDSCHAU
VERDENER NACHRICHTEN
WESER-KURIER
WESER-KURIER ONLINE

BREMISCHE EVANGELISCHE KIRCHE 1729562
Franziuseck 2, 28199 BREMEN **Tel:** 421 5597221
Fax: 421 5597207
Email: redaktion@kirche-bremen.de
Web site: http://www.kirche-bremen.de

Titles:
BREMER KIRCHENZEITUNG

BREU & SCHNEIDER GMBH 686050
Donnersbergerstr. 22, 80634 MÜNCHEN
Tel: 89 8090920 **Fax:** 89 80909212
Email: info@muenchenanzeiger.de
Web site: http://www.muenchenanzeiger.de

Titles:
NEUHAUSER NYMPHENBURGER ANZEIGER

BRINKMANN HENRICH MEDIEN GMBH 693431
Heerstr. 5, 58540 MEINERZHAGEN
Tel: 2354 77990 **Fax:** 2354 779977
Email: info@bhmg.de
Web site: http://www.bhmg.de

Titles:
NORDIC SPORTS MAGAZIN
SKIMAGAZIN

BRINKSCHULTE MEDIEN GMBH & CO. KG 1630455
Möhnestr. 55, 59755 ARNSBERG **Tel:** 2932 97750
Fax: 2932 977525
Email: arnsberg@brinkschulte.com
Web site: http://www.brinkschulte.com

Titles:
REVIER MANAGER
SÜDWESTFALEN MANAGER

BRONNERMEDIA VERLAG 1767140
An der Frauenkirche 12, 01067 DRESDEN
Tel: 351 82129880
Email: akb@bronnermedia.de
Web site: http://www.bronnermedia.com

Titles:
AUDIOPHIL

BROT UND SPIELE GMBH 1732886
Bahnhofstr. 18b, 61250 USINGEN
Tel: 6081 5828733 **Fax:** 6081 5828734
Email: info@spieletipps.de
Web site: http://www.spieletipps.de

Titles:
SPIELETIPPS.DE

BRUCKMANN VERLAG GMBH 679083
Infanteriestr. 11a, 80797 MÜNCHEN
Tel: 89 1306990 **Fax:** 89 130699100
Email: info@bruckmann.de
Web site: http://www.bruckmann.de

Titles:
BERGSTEIGER

BRUDERVERLAG ALBERT BRUDER GMBH & CO. KG 678837
Stolberger Str. 84, 50993 KÖLN **Tel:** 221 54970
Fax: 221 5497326
Email: info@bruderverlag.de
Web site: http://www.rudolf-mueller.de

Titles:
BAUEN MIT HOLZ
DER ZIMMERMANN

BRUKER BIOSPIN GMBH 1606297
Silberstreifen 4, 76287 RHEINSTETTEN
Tel: 721 51610 **Fax:** 721 517101
Email: marcom@bruker-biospin.de
Web site: http://www.bruker-biospin.de

Titles:
ALMANAC

BRUNE-METTCKER DRUCK- UND VERLAGSGES. MBH 1681103
Am Markt 18, 26409 WITTMUND **Tel:** 4462 9890
Fax: 4462 989119
Email: verlag@harlinger.de
Web site: http://www.harlinger.de

Titles:
ANZEIGER FÜR HARLINGERLAND

BRUNE-METTCKER DRUCK- UND VERLAGS-GMBH 1782990
Wangerstr. 14, 26441 JEVER **Tel:** 4461 9440
Fax: 4461 944219
Email: info@jeversches-wochenblatt.de
Web site: http://www.jeversches-wochenblatt.de

Titles:
JEVERSCHES WOCHENBLATT
WILHELMSHAVENER ZEITUNG

BSH-VERLAG 679804
Gartenweg 5, 26203 WARDENBURG
Tel: 4407 5111 **Fax:** 4407 6760
Email: info@bsh-natur.de
Web site: http://www.bsh-natur.de

Titles:
BSH NVN NATUR SPECIAL REPORT

BSMO GMBH 1686192
Schwedter Str. 263, 10119 BERLIN
Tel: 30 88429390 **Fax:** 30 884293941
Email: info@bsmo.de
Web site: http://www.bsmo.de

Titles:
LIFELINE
SPRINGERMEDIZIN

BT VERLAG GMBH 1640229
Rosenheimer Str. 145i, 81671 MÜNCHEN
Tel: 89 4570960 **Fax:** 89 45709610
Email: info@bt.de
Web site: http://www.bt.de

Titles:
HAUS&WELLNESS

BTA VERLAGS- UND MEDIENSERVICE 1766961
Geranienweg 1, 85598 BALDHAM
Tel: 8106 379480 **Fax:** 8106 306804
Email: info@eventlocations.info
Web site: http://www.eventlocations.info

Titles:
EVENTLOCATIONS

BÜCHEREI DES DEUTSCHEN GARTENBAUES E.V. 690870
Potsdamer Str. 187, 14469 POTSDAM
Tel: 331 502471
Web site: http://www.gartenbaubuecherei.de

Titles:
ZANDERA

BUCHHALTUNGSSERVICEGES. DER VER.DI MBH 1744089
Köpenicker Str. 31, 10179 BERLIN
Tel: 30 30877340 **Fax:** 30 30877325
Email: daniela.schueler@verdi-bsg.de
Web site: http://www.verdi-publik.de

Titles:
VER.DI PUBLIK

BUCHMARKT VERLAG K. WERNER GMBH 1626642
Sperberweg 4a, 40668 MEERBUSCH
Tel: 2150 91910 **Fax:** 2150 919191
Email: redaktion@buchmarkt.de
Web site: http://www.buchmarkt.de

Titles:
BUCHMARKT

BÜCHSENMACHER-VERLAG GMBH 679842
Pastorenberg 4, 31167 BOCKENEM
Tel: 5067 247150 **Fax:** 5067 247153
Email: redaktion@buechsenmacherverlag.de
Web site: http://www.buechsenmacherverlag.de

Titles:
BÜCHSENMACHER MESSER & SCHERE

BÜCKER-FACHVERLAG GMBH & CO. KG 684180
Rheintalstr. 6, 53498 BAD BREISIG
Tel: 2633 45400 **Fax:** 2633 97415
Email: info@milch-marketing.de
Web site: http://www.moproweb.de

Titles:
KÄSE-THEKE
MILCH-MARKETING

BÜHNENSCHRIFTEN-VERTRIEBSGES. MBH 679850
Feldbrunnenstr. 74, 20148 HAMBURG
Tel: 40 445185 **Fax:** 40 456002
Email: buehnenschriften@buehnengenossenschaft.de
Web site: http://www.buehnengenossenschaft.de

Titles:
BÜHNENGENOSSENSCHAFT

BUND DER DEUTSCHEN LANDJUGEND 678975
Claire-Waldoff-Str. 7, 10117 BERLIN
Tel: 30 31904253 **Fax:** 30 31904206
Email: info@landjugend.de
Web site: http://www.landjugend.de

Titles:
BDL
BDL SPEZIAL

BUND DER ENERGIEVERBRAUCHER E.V. 1626699
Frankfurter Str. 1, 53572 UNKEL
Tel: 2224 9603436 **Fax:** 2224 10321
Email: info@energieverbraucher.de
Web site: http://www.energieverbraucher.de

Titles:
ENERGIEDEPESCHE

BUND DEUTSCHER FORSTLEUTE 1783687
Friedrichstr. 169/170, 10117 BERLIN
Tel: 30 40816700 **Fax:** 30 40816710
Email: info@bdf-online.de
Web site: http://www.bdf-online.de

Titles:
BDF AKTUELL

BUND DEUTSCHER KRIMINALBEAMTER 1783718
Poststr. 4, 10178 BERLIN **Tel:** 30 24630450
Fax: 30 246304529
Email: bdk.bgs@bdk.de
Web site: http://www.bdk.de

Titles:
DER KRIMINALIST

BUND FREISCHAFFENDER FOTO-DESIGNER E.V. 679258
Tuttlinger Str. 95, 70619 STUTTGART
Tel: 711 473422 **Fax:** 711 475280
Email: info@bff.de
Web site: http://www.bff.de

Titles:
BFF JAHRBUCH

BUND FÜR UMWELT UND NATURSCHUTZ DEUTSCHLAND, LANDESVERBAND BERLIN E.V. 1709755
Crellestr. 35, 10827 BERLIN **Tel:** 30 7879000
Fax: 30 78790018
Email: redaktion@bundzeit.de
Web site: http://www.bundzeit.de

Titles:
BUNDZEIT

BUND FÜR UMWELT UND NATURSCHUTZ DEUTSCHLAND LANDESVERBAND NORDRHEIN-WESTFALEN E.V. 1724173
Merowingerstr. 88, 40225 DÜSSELDORF
Tel: 211 3020050 **Fax:** 211 30200526
Email: bund.nrw@bund.net
Web site: http://www.bund-nrw.de

Titles:
NRW-INFO

BUND FÜR UMWELT UND NATURSCHUTZ DEUTSCHLAND, LANDESVERBAND SAARLAND E.V. 1755663
Evangelisch-Kirch-Str. 8, 66111 SAARBRÜCKEN
Tel: 681 813700 **Fax:** 681 813720
Email: info@bund-saar.de
Web site: http://www.bund-saar.de

Titles:
UMWELTMAGAZIN SAAR

BUND KATHOLISCHER UNTERNEHMER E.V. 693253
Georgstr. 18, 50676 KÖLN **Tel:** 221 272370
Fax: 221 2723727
Email: unterberg@bku.de
Web site: http://www.bku.de

Titles:
BKU JOURNAL

BUND NATURSCHUTZ IN BAYERN E.V. 1692079
Dr.-Johann-Maier-Str. 4, 93049 REGENSBURG
Tel: 941 2972022 **Fax:** 941 2972030
Email: info@bund-naturschutz.de
Web site: http://www.bund-naturschutz.de

Titles:
NATUR + UMWELT

BUND NATURSCHUTZ IN BAYERN E.V., KREISGRUPPE AUGSBURG 1687144
Heilig-Kreuz-Str. 6, 86152 AUGSBURG
Tel: 821 37695 **Fax:** 821 514787
Email: bn_kg_augsburg@augustakom.net
Web site: http://www.bund-naturschutz-augsburg.de

Titles:
DIE ARCHE

BUND NATURSCHUTZ IN BAYERN E.V. KREISGRUPPE BAYREUTH 1650968
Alexanderstr. 9, 95444 BAYREUTH
Tel: 921 27230 **Fax:** 921 851497
Email: bayreuth@bund-naturschutz.de
Web site: http://www.bayreuth.bund-naturschutz.de

Titles:
BUND NATURSCHUTZ IN BAYERN E.V. KREISGRUPPE BAYREUTH-RUNDBRIEF

BUND NATURSCHUTZ IN BAYERN E.V., KREISGRUPPE WÜRZBURG 686233
Luitpoldstr. 7a, 97082 WÜRZBURG
Tel: 931 43972 **Fax:** 931 42553
Email: info@bn-wuerzburg.de
Web site: http://www.wuerzburg.bund-naturschutz.de

Titles:
NETZ

BUND NATURSCHUTZ OBERSCHWABEN E.V. 694655
Rosengarten 1, 88410 BAD WURZACH
Tel: 7564 93120 **Fax:** 7564 931222
Email: vorstand@bno-ev.de
Web site: http://www.bno-ev.de

Titles:
OBERSCHWABEN NATURNAH

BUNDESAMT FÜR SEESCHIFFFAHRT UND HYDROGRAPHIE 681179
Bernhard-Nocht-Str. 78, 20359 HAMBURG
Tel: 40 31900 **Fax:** 40 31905000
Email: posteingang@bsh.de
Web site: http://www.bsh.de

Titles:
SEEKARTEN UND BÜCHER KATALOG
WINTERBETONNUNG DER DEUTSCHEN KÜSTENGEWÄSSER

BUNDESANZEIGER VERLAGSGES. MBH. 678635
Amsterdamer Str. 192, 50735 KÖLN
Tel: 221 976680 **Fax:** 221 97668278
Email: vertrieb@bundesanzeiger.de
Web site: http://www.bundesanzeiger-verlag.de

Titles:
AW-PRAX
DER BAUSACHVERSTÄNDIGE

BUNDESARBEITSGEMEINSCHAFT DER SENIOREN-ORGANISATIONEN E.V. 678729
Bonngasse 10, 53111 BONN **Tel:** 228 2499930
Fax: 228 24999320
Email: kontakt@bagso.de
Web site: http://www.bagso.de

Titles:
DIE BAGSO NACHRICHTEN

BUNDESARBEITSGEMEINSCHAFT FÜR SICHERHEIT UND GESUNDHEIT BEI DER ARBEIT (BASI) E.V. 1627232
Alte Heerstr. 111, 53757 ST. AUGUSTIN
Tel: 2241 2316000 **Fax:** 2241 2316111
Email: basi@hvbg.de
Web site: http://www.basi.de

Titles:
INFOPRINT

BUNDESAUSSCHUSS OBST UND GEMÜSE, FACHGRUPPE OBSTBAU 1685497
Godesberger Allee 142, 53175 BONN
Tel: 228 8100224 **Fax:** 228 8100264
Email: info@obstbau.org
Web site: http://www.obstbau.org

Titles:
OBSTBAU

BUNDESINSTITUT FÜR BAU-, STADT- UND RAUMFORSCHUNG IM BUNDESAMT FÜR BAUWESEN UND RAUMORDNUNG 683662
Deichmanns Aue 31, 53179 BONN
Tel: 22899 4012209 **Fax:** 22899 4011270
Email: selbstverlag@bbr.bund.de
Web site: http://www.bbsr.bund.de

Titles:
INFORMATIONEN AUS DER FORSCHUNG DES BBSR
INFORMATIONEN ZUR RAUMENTWICKLUNG
WERKSTATT: PRAXIS

BUNDESKONTAKTSTELLE GESTEINSABBAU DER GRÜNEN LIGA 688921
Prof.-Virchow-Str. 8, 08280 AUE **Tel:** 371 8321272
Email: gesteinsabbau@grueneliga.de
Web site: http://www.grueneliga.de/gesteinsabbau

Titles:
STEINBEISSER

BUNDESMINISTERIUM DER VERTEIDIGUNG, JUGENDMARKETING 1630456
Postfach 1328, 53003 BONN **Tel:** 228 1200
Fax: 228 125357
Email: infopost@nw-w.de

Titles:
INFOPOST

BUNDESMINISTERIUM DER VERTEIDIGUNG, LEITER DES PRESSE- UND INFORMATIONSSTABES 1651197
Stauffenbergstr. 18, 10785 BERLIN
Tel: 1888 248232 **Fax:** 1888 248240

Titles:
IF

BUNDESMINISTERIUM DER VERTEIDIGUNG, PRESSE- UND INFORMATIONSSTAB 3 1687212
Stauffenbergstr. 18, 10785 BERLIN
Tel: 30 200429030 **Fax:** 30 200429036
Email: aktuell@bundeswehr.de
Web site: http://www.aktuell.bundeswehr.de

Titles:
AKTUELL

BUNDESMINISTERIUM FÜR UMWELT, NATURSCHUTZ UND REAKTORSICHERHEIT, REF. ÖFFENTLICHKEITSARBEIT 689823
11055 BERLIN **Tel:** 30 183050 **Fax:** 30 183052044
Email: bmu@broschuerenversand.de
Web site: http://www.bmu.de

Titles:
UMWELT

BUNDESMINISTERIUM FÜR WIRTSCHAFT UND TECHNOLOGIE 1638691
Scharnhorststr. 34, 10115 BERLIN
Fax: 30 186157010
Email: oeffentlichkeitsarbeit@bmwi.bund.de
Web site: http://www.bmwi.de

Titles:
GRÜNDERZEITEN
JAHRESWIRTSCHAFTSBERICHT

BUNDESVERBAND BETONBAUTEILE DEUTSCHLAND E.V. 1767862
Kochstr. 6, 10969 BERLIN **Tel:** 30 259229210
Fax: 30 259229219
Email: gf@betoninfo.de
Web site: http://www.betoninfo.de

Titles:
SPECTRUM

BUNDESVERBAND DER ARZNEIMITTEL-HERSTELLER E.V. 1621607
Ubierstr. 71, 53173 BONN **Tel:** 228 9574547
Fax: 228 9574590
Email: bah@bah-bonn.de
Web site: http://www.bah-bonn.de

Titles:
DAS FREIE MEDIKAMENT

BUNDESVERBAND DER DEUTSCHEN GIESSEREI-INDUSTRIE 684560
Sohnstr. 70, 40237 DÜSSELDORF
Tel: 211 6871223 **Fax:** 211 6871365
Email: info@bdguss.de
Web site: http://www.bdguss.de

Titles:
KONSTRUIEREN + GIESSEN

BUNDESVERBAND DER PRESSEBILD-AGENTUREN UND BILDARCHIVE E.V. 679328
Sächsische Str. 63, 10707 BERLIN
Tel: 30 3249917 **Fax:** 30 3247001
Email: info@bvpa.org
Web site: http://www.bvpa.org

Titles:
DER BILDERMARKT
BILDHONORARE

BUNDESVERBAND DER VERTRAGSPSYCHOTHERAPEUTEN E.V. 1783757
Schwimmbadstr. 22, 79100 FREIBURG
Tel: 761 7910245 **Fax:** 761 7910243
Email: bvvp@bvvp.de
Web site: http://www.bvvp@bvvp.de

Titles:
PROJEKT PSYCHOTHERAPIE

BUNDESVERBAND DES DEUTSCHEN BRIEFMARKENHANDELS 679936
Universitätsstr. 5, 50937 KÖLN **Tel:** 221 407900
Fax: 221 409597
Email: bundesverband@aphv.de
Web site: http://www.aphv.de

Titles:
APHVMAGAZIN

BUNDESVERBAND DES SCHORNSTEINFEGERHANDWERKS 688175
Westerwaldstr. 6, 53757 ST. AUGUSTIN
Tel: 2241 34070 **Fax:** 2241 340710
Email: ziv@schornsteinfeger.de
Web site: http://www.schornsteinfeger.de

Titles:
SCHORNSTEINFEGERHANDWERK

BUNDESVERBAND DEUTSCHER STAHLHANDEL AG 688864
Max-Planck-Str. 1, 40237 DÜSSELDORF
Tel: 211 864970 **Fax:** 211 8649722
Email: info-bds@stahlhandel.com
Web site: http://www.stahlhandel.com

Titles:
STAHLREPORT

BUNDESVERBAND DEUTSCHER VERSICHERUNGSKAUFLEUTE E.V. 690117
Kekuléstr. 12, 53115 BONN **Tel:** 228 228050
Fax: 228 2280550
Email: versverm@bvk.de
Web site: http://www.bvk.de

Titles:
VERSICHERUNGSVERMITTLUNG

BUNDESVERBAND DEUTSCHER VOLKS- UND BETRIEBSWIRTE E.V. 1603086
Florastr. 29, 40217 DÜSSELDORF
Tel: 211 371022 **Fax:** 211 379468
Email: info@bdvb.de
Web site: http://www.bdvb.de

Titles:
BDVB AKTUELL

BUNDESVERBAND DIREKTVERTRIEB DEUTSCHLAND E.V. 679906
Bundesallee 221, 10719 BERLIN **Tel:** 30 23635680
Fax: 30 23635688
Email: info@bundesverband-direktvertrieb.de
Web site: http://www.bundesverband-direktvertrieb.de

Titles:
DIREKT!

BUNDESVERBAND FÜR KÖRPER- UND MEHRFACHBEHINDERTE E.V. 678761
Brehmstr. 5, 40239 DÜSSELDORF
Tel: 211 640040 **Fax:** 211 6400420
Email: info@bvkm.de
Web site: http://www.bvkm.de

Titles:
DAS BAND

BUNDESVERBAND GROSSHANDEL, AUSSENHANDEL, DIENSTLEISTUNGEN E.V. 680764
Am Weidendamm 1a, 10117 BERLIN
Tel: 30 59009950 **Fax:** 30 590099519
Email: info@bga.de
Web site: http://www.bga.de

Titles:
DIREKT AUS BERLIN

BUNDESVERBAND GÜTERKRAFTVERKEHR LOGISTIK UND ENTSORGUNG E.V. 679263
Breitenbachstr. 1, 60487 FRANKFURT
Tel: 69 79190 **Fax:** 69 7919227
Email: bgl@bgl-ev.de
Web site: http://www.bgl-ev.de

Titles:
BGL-INFODIENST

BUNDESVERBAND HÖHERER BERUFE DER TECHNIK, WIRTSCHAFT UND GESTALTUNG E.V. 689308
Baumschulweg 6, 53639 KÖNIGSWINTER
Tel: 2244 92427 **Fax:** 2244 924299
Email: bvt-online@online.de
Web site: http://www.bvt-online.de

Titles:
TEMA

BUNDESVERBAND MEDIATION E.V. 1745667
Kirchweg 80, 34119 KASSEL **Tel:** 561 7396413
Fax: 561 7396412
Email: info@bmev.de
Web site: http://www.bmev.de

Titles:
SPEKTRUM DER MEDIATION

BUNDESVERBAND ROLLLADEN + SONNENSCHUTZ E.V. 687917
Hopmannstr. 2, 53177 BONN **Tel:** 228 952100
Fax: 228 9521010
Email: info@rs-fachverband.de
Web site: http://www.rs-fachverband.de

Titles:
R + S ROLLLADEN + SONNENSCHUTZ

BUNDESVERBAND SELBSTHILFE KÖRPERBEHINDERTER E.V. 679806
Altkrautheimer Str. 20, 74238 KRAUTHEIM
Tel: 6294 42810 **Fax:** 6294 428179
Email: info@bsk-ev.org
Web site: http://www.bsk-ev.org

Titles:
LEBEN&WEG

BUNDESVERBAND SENIORENTANZ E.V. 688380
Hemmstr. 202, 28215 BREMEN **Tel:** 421 441180
Fax: 421 4986217
Email: verband@seniorentanz.de
Web site: http://www.seniorentanz.de

Titles:
ST SENIOREN TANZEN

BUNDESVERBAND TANKSTELLEN UND GEWERBLICHE AUTOWÄSCHE DEUTSCHLAND E.V. 678610
Stiftstr. 35, 32427 MINDEN **Tel:** 571 886080
Fax: 571 8860820
Email: info@btg-minden.de
Web site: http://www.btg-minden.de

Titles:
DIE AUTOWÄSCHE

BUNDESVERBAND WINDENERGIE E.V. 1626842
Marienstr. 19, 10117 BERLIN **Tel:** 30 28482130
Fax: 30 28482139
Email: info@neueenergie.net
Web site: http://www.neueenergie.net

Titles:
NEUE ENERGIE
NEW ENERGY

BUNDESVEREINIGUNG LEBENSHILFE FÜR MENSCHEN MIT GEISTIGER BEHINDERUNG E.V. 681627
Raiffeisenstr. 18, 35043 MARBURG
Tel: 6421 4910 **Fax:** 6421 491167
Email: presse@lebenshilfe.de
Web site: http://www.lebenshilfe.de

Titles:
LEBENSHILFE ZEITUNG

BUNDES-VERLAG GMBH 678464
Bodenborn 43, 58452 WITTEN **Tel:** 2302 930930
Fax: 2302 93093689
Email: info@bundes-verlag.de
Web site: http://www.bundes-verlag.de

Titles:
AUF ATMEN
CHRISTSEIN HEUTE
DRAN
FAMILY
JESUS.DE
JOYCE
KLÄX
LEBENSLAUF >>
TEENSMAG

BUND-VERLAG GMBH 678263
Heddernheimer Landstr. 144, 60439 FRANKFURT **Tel:** 69 79501082 **Fax:** 69 133077666
Email: kontakt@bund-verlag.de
Web site: http://www.bund-verlag.de

Titles:
AIB ARBEITSRECHT IM BETRIEB
AUR ARBEIT UND RECHT
COMPUTER UND ARBEIT
GUTE ARBEIT. DER PERSONALRAT
SOZIALE SICHERHEIT

BUNKVERLAG GMBH 680224
Friedensallee 7, 22765 HAMBURG
Tel: 40 3992950 **Fax:** 40 39929529
Email: info@bunkverlag.de
Web site: http://www.bunkverlag.de

Titles:
KULTURNEWS

BUNTE ENTERTAINMENT VERLAG GMBH 1791434
Arabellastrasse 23, 81925 MÜNCHEN
Tel: 88 5567205

Titles:
BUNTE
BUNTE ONLINE
INSTYLE
PRELUDIUM

BURDA SENATOR VERLAG GMBH 1782114
Hubert-Burda-Platz 1, 77652 OFFENBURG
Tel: 781 8401 **Fax:** 781 842299

Titles:
ARD BUFFET
FRAU IM TREND
FREIZEIT REVUE
FREIZEIT SPASS
GARTEN SPASS
GLÜCKS REVUE
MEIN SCHÖNER GARTEN
MEIN SCHÖNER GARTEN ONLINE

BÜRGER- UND VERKEHRSVEREIN TÜBINGEN 1723645
An der Neckarbrücke 1, 72072 TÜBINGEN
Tel: 7071 91360
Email: mail@tuebingen-info.de
Web site: http://www.tuebingen-info.de

Titles:
ESSEN UND TRINKEN IN TÜBINGEN

BÜRGERINITIATIVE UMWELTSCHUTZ E.V. 689825
Stephanusstr. 25, 30449 HANNOVER
Tel: 511 443303
Email: umweltdepesche@biu-hannover.de
Web site: http://www.biu-hannover.de

Titles:
UMWELT DEPESCHE

BÜRO FÜR MEDIEN OLIVER LEHNERT E.K. 1718489
Westheimer Str. 18, 86356 NEUSÄSS
Tel: 821 48685290 **Fax:** 821 48685293
Email: verlag@wissensmanagement.net
Web site: http://www.wissensmanagement.net

Titles:
WISSENS MANAGEMENT

BUSCHE VERLAGSGES. MBH 680494
Schleefstr. 1, 44287 DORTMUND **Tel:** 231 444770
Fax: 231 4447777
Email: info@busche.de
Web site: http://www.busche.de

Titles:
ARAL AUTO-ATLAS
ARAL DEUTSCHLAND-ATLAS
ARAL STRASSEN-ATLAS
BUSCHE HOTELS & RESTAURANTS
BUSCHE WINZER & WEINGÜTER
GUT & PREISWERT BED & BREAKFAST FRANKREICH
GUT & PREISWERT BETT MIT BAD BIS 50 EURO
GUT & PREISWERT MIT DEM BIKE ÜBERNACHTEN
GUT & PREISWERT MIT KINDERN ÜBERNACHTEN
GUT & PREISWERT MIT TIEREN ÜBERNACHTEN
SCHLUMMER ATLAS
TAGUNGSHOTELS

BUSINESS CLUB AACHEN MAASTRICHT 1743940
Grüner Weg 13, 52070 AACHEN **Tel:** 241 9183011
Fax: 241 9183050
Email: info@businessclub-aachen.com
Web site: http://www.businessclub-aachen.com

Titles:
BUSINESS LIVE

BÜTTNER MEDIEN GMBH 687449
Sigmund-Freud-Str. 77a, 60435 FRANKFURT
Tel: 69 7561900 **Fax:** 69 75619041
Email: jbuettner@buemed.de
Web site: http://www.buemed.de

Titles:
VATER - MUTTER - KIND
WO BEKOMME ICH MEIN BABY?

BVA BIELEFELDER VERLAG GMBH & CO. KG 677532
Niederwall 53, 33602 BIELEFELD **Tel:** 521 5950
Fax: 521 595518
Email: kontakt@bva-bielefeld.de
Web site: http://www.bva-bielefeld.de

Titles:
AUTORÄDERREIFEN - GUMMIBEREIFUNG
RADMARKT
SONNE WIND & WÄRME
SUN & WIND ENERGY

BVA BIKEMEDIA GMBH 1789249
Fraunhoferstr. 9, 85737 ISMANING
Tel: 89 41615400 **Fax:** 89 416154019
Email: kontakt@bva-bikemedia.de

Titles:
AKTIV RADFAHREN

BVM BERUFSVERBAND DEUTSCHER MARKT- UND SOZIALFORSCHER E.V. 679997
Friedrichstr. 187, 10117 BERLIN **Tel:** 30 49907420
Fax: 30 49907421
Email: info@bvm.org
Web site: http://www.bvm.org

Titles:
BVM INBRIEF
MARKTFORSCHUNG ...

BVW VERLAG GMBH 688796
Georgstr. 14, 49074 OSNABRÜCK
Tel: 541 357870 **Fax:** 541 24602
Email: office@stadtblatt-osnabrueck.de
Web site: http://www.stadtblatt-osnabrueck.de

Titles:
STADTBLATT LIVE
STADTBLATT OSNABRÜCK

BVZ ANZEIGENZEITUNGEN GMBH 679109
Karl-Liebknecht-Str. 29, 10178 BERLIN
Tel: 30 2938888 **Fax:** 30 29388877
Email: anzeigen@abendblatt-berlin.de
Web site: http://www.abendblatt-berlin.de

Titles:
BERLINER ABENDBLATT
BERLINER ABENDBLATT
EASTGATE
LICHTENBERGER RATHAUSNACHRICHTEN
MÄRKISCHES ZENTRUM NEWS
MITTE JOURNAL
WARNOW KURIER AM MITTWOCH

BW BRANDMANN & WEPPLER VERLAGS OHG 1792257
Bargkoppelweg 72, 22145 HAMBURG
Tel: 40 79699771 **Fax:** 40 79699773
Email: office@pos-kompakt.net
Web site: http://www.pos-kompakt.net

Titles:
P.O.S.KOMPAKT

BWE-SERVICE 1639883
Marienstr. 19, 10117 BERLIN **Tel:** 30 28482106
Fax: 30 28482107
Email: service@wind-energie.de
Web site: http://www.wind-energie.de

Titles:
WIND ENERGY MARKET
WIND ENERGY MARKET

B.Z. ULLSTEIN GMBH 1733301
Kurfürstendamm 21, 10719 BERLIN
Tel: 30 259173607 **Fax:** 30 259171193

Titles:
B.Z. B.Z. AM SONNTAG

C. BECKERS BUCHDRUCKEREI GMBH & CO. KG 677667
Gr. Liederner Str. 45, 29525 UELZEN
Tel: 581 80891100 **Fax:** 581 80891191
Email: redaktion@cbeckers.de
Web site: http://www.az-online.de

Titles:
ALLGEMEINE ZEITUNG DER LÜNEBURGER HEIDE
ALTMARK ZEITUNG
ISENHAGENER KREISBLATT

C. BÖSENDAHL GMBH & CO. KG 688093
Klosterstr. 32, 31737 RINTELN **Tel:** 5751 40000
Fax: 5751 4000544
Email: sz@schaumburger-zeitung.de
Web site: http://www.schaumburger-zeitung.de

Titles:
SCHAUMBURGER ZEITUNG

C. F. MÜLLER VERLAGSGRUPPE HÜTHIG JEHLE REHM GMBH 1650243
Im Weiher 10, 69121 HEIDELBERG
Tel: 6221 4890 **Fax:** 6221 489529
Email: info@hjr-verlag.de
Web site: http://www.hjr-verlag.de

Titles:
WISTRA

C. H. WÄSER KG GMBH & CO. 683123
Hamburger Str. 26, 23795 BAD SEGEBERG
Tel: 4551 9040 **Fax:** 4551 90464
Email: info@segeberger-zeitung.de
Web site: http://www.segeberger-zeitung.de

Titles:
SZ SEGEBERGER ZEITUNG

C. KOHLMANN, DRUCK & VERLAG GMBH 684829
Hauptstr. 36, 37431 BAD LAUTERBERG
Tel: 5524 85000 **Fax:** 5524 850039
Email: info@kohlmann-druck.de
Web site: http://www.kohlmann-druck.de

Titles:
DISTANZ AKTUELL
MASTERRIND

C. MAURER DRUCK UND VERLAG GMBH & CO. KG 678507
Schubartstr. 21, 73312 GEISLINGEN
Tel: 7331 9300 **Fax:** 7331 930191
Email: c.maurer@maurer-online.de
Web site: http://www.maurer-online.de

Titles:
AUSBAU + FASSADE
DER FUSS
ORTHOPÄDIE SCHUHTECHNIK

CALA-VERLAG GMBH & CO. KG 1763623
Juri-Gagarin-Ring 68, 99084 ERFURT
Tel: 361 6633632 **Fax:** 361 6028502
Email: info@cala-verlag.de
Web site: http://www.cala-verlag.de

Titles:
60PLUSMINUS - AUSG. DRESDEN
60PLUSMINUS - AUSG. THÜRINGEN

CAMPING-ERHOLUNGSVEREIN BAYERN E.V. 1616849
Leipartstr. 22, 81369 MÜNCHEN **Tel:** 89 7242573
Fax: 89 72400595
Email: campingerholungsverein@arcor.de

Titles:
CEB AKTUELL

CAMPUS-TRADING HANDELSGES. MBH 1720592
Brucknerstr. 4, 01309 DRESDEN
Tel: 351 21330011 **Fax:** 351 21330022
Email: zentrale@port01.com
Web site: http://www.port01.com

Titles:
PORT01.CITY-FLASH BREMEN
PORT01.CITY-FLASH CHEMNITZ
PORT01.CITY-FLASH DRESDEN
PORT01.CITY-FLASH JENA WEIMAR
PORT01.CITY-FLASH LEIPZIG
PORT01.CITY-FLASH PLAUEN ZWICKAU
PORT01.CITY-FLASH STUTTGART LUDWIGSBURG
PORT01.CITY-FLASH WÜRZBURG

CARL ED. SCHÜNEMANN KG ZEITSCHRIFTENVERLAG 678836
Zweite Schlachtpforte 7, 28195 BREMEN
Tel: 421 3690372 **Fax:** 421 3690334
Email: zeitschriften@schuenemann-verlag.de
Web site: http://www.schuenemann-verlag.de

Titles:
BAUEN IN UND UM BREMEN
SCHACH MAGAZIN 64
WIRTSCHAFT IN BREMEN

CARL HANSER VERLAG GMBH & CO. KG 679451
Kolbergerstr. 22, 81679 MÜNCHEN
Tel: 89 998300 **Fax:** 89 99830623
Email: info@hanser.de
Web site: http://www.hanser.de

Titles:
FORM+WERKZEUG
HANSER AUTOMOTIVE
HTM JOURNAL OF HEAT TREATMENT AND MATERIALS
INTERNATIONAL JOURNAL OF MATERIALS RESEARCH
KERNTECHNIK
KUNSTSTOFFE
LASER+PHOTONIK
LASER+PRODUKTION
MP MATERIALPRÜFUNG MATERIALS TESTING
PRAKTISCHE METALLOGRAPHIE PRACTICAL METALLOGRAPHY
QM-INFOCENTER.DE
QZ QUALITÄT UND ZUVERLÄSSIGKEIT
RAPIDX

SCHWEIZER PRÄZISIONS-FERTIGUNGSTECHNIK
SWISS QUALITY PRODUCTION
TENSIDE SURFACTANTS DETERGENTS
WB WERKSTATT+BETRIEB
ZULIEFERMARKT FÜR KONSTRUKTEURE UND TECHNISCHE EINKÄUFER
ZWF ZEITSCHRIFT FÜR WIRTSCHAFTLICHEN FABRIKBETRIEB

CARL HEYMANNS VERLAG GMBH/WOLTERS KLUWER DEUTSCHLAND 679429
Luxemburger Str. 449, 50939 KÖLN
Tel: 221 943730 **Fax:** 221 94373901
Web site: http://www.wolterskluwer.de

Titles:
DEUTSCHE RICHTERZEITUNG
DEUTSCHES VERWALTUNGSBLATT DVBL MIT VERWALTUNGSARCHIV
DER KONZERN
MARKENR
MONATSSCHRIFT FÜR KRIMINOLOGIE UND STRAFRECHTSREFORM
DER ÖFFENTLICHE DIENST
DIE POLIZEI
RDE - RECHT DER ENERGIEWIRTSCHAFT
ZFA ZEITSCHRIFT FÜR ARBEITSRECHT
ZFW ZEITSCHRIFT FÜR WASSERRECHT
ZZP ZEITSCHRIFT FÜR ZIVILPROZESS

CARL LINK -WOLTERS KLUWER DEUTSCHLAND GMBH 1635458
Adolf-Kolping-Str. 10, 96317 KRONACH
Tel: 9261 9690 **Fax:** 9261 96939
Email: info@wolterskluwer.de
Web site: http://www.wolterskluwer.de

Titles:
SCHULVERWALTUNG BW
SCHULVERWALTUNG BY
SCHULVERWALTUNG NRW

CARTELL AGENTUR FÜR CITYMEDIEN 680907
Walter-Oertel-Str. 50, 09112 CHEMNITZ
Tel: 371 355030 **Fax:** 371 3550314
Email: info@371stadtmagazin.de
Web site: http://www.371stadtmagazin.de

Titles:
FRUNCH

CARTELLVERBAND DER KATHOLISCHEN DEUTSCHEN STUDENTENVERBINDUNGEN 677266
Linzer Str. 82, 53604 BAD HONNEF
Tel: 2224 960020 **Fax:** 2224 9600220
Email: sekretariat@cartellverband.de
Web site: http://www.cartellverband.de

Titles:
ACADEMIA

CASH.PRINT GMBH 680072
Stresemannstr. 163, 22769 HAMBURG
Tel: 40 514440 **Fax:** 40 51444120
Email: info@cash-online.de
Web site: http://www.cash-online.de

Titles:
CASH.

C.A.T.-VERLAG BLÖMER GMBH 682765
Freiligrathring 18, 40878 RATINGEN
Tel: 2102 20270 **Fax:** 2102 202790
Web site: http://www.cat-verlag.de

Titles:
IMAGING + FOTO CONTACT
INTERNATIONAL CONTACT
POS-MAIL
PREPRESS WORLD OF PRINT

CBS INTERACTIVE GMBH 1626932
Willy-Brandt-Allee 2, 81829 MÜNCHEN
Tel: 89 25555700 **Fax:** 89 25555750
Email: petra.gottschalk@cbs.com
Web site: http://www.zdnet.de

Titles:
ZDNET.DE

CB-VERLAG CARL BOLDT 679110
Baseler Str. 80, 12205 BERLIN **Tel:** 30 8337087
Fax: 30 8339125
Email: cb-verlag@t-online.de
Web site: http://www.cb-verlag.de

Titles:
BERLINER ANWALTSBLATT
BK BAUKAMMER BERLIN
VERBANDSNACHRICHTEN

CCA AGENTUR FÜR KOMMUNIKATION GMBH 1751474
Adam-Klein-Str. 156, 90431 NÜRNBERG
Tel: 911 47790730 **Fax:** 911 47790777
Email: redaktion@spiritmagazin.de
Web site: http://www.spiritmagazin.de

Titles:
SPIRIT

C/C/C CLEF CREATIVE COMMUNICATIONS GMBH 1762264
Steinstr. 44, 81667 MÜNCHEN **Tel:** 89 99548460
Fax: 89 99548466
Email: golf@clef.de
Web site: http://www.golf-genuss.de

Titles:
GOLF GENUSS

CCUNIRENT SYSTEM GMBH 1741330
Allersberger Str. 185/F, 90461 NÜRNBERG
Tel: 911 4804990 **Fax:** 911 48049929
Email: info@ccunirent.com
Web site: http://www.ccunirent.com

Titles:
KRAFTSTOFF

CELLESCHE ZEITUNG SCHWEIGER & PICK VERLAG PFINGSTEN GMBH & CO. KG 680101
Bahnhofstr. 1, 29221 CELLE **Tel:** 5141 9900
Fax: 5141 990290
Email: verlag@cellesche-zeitung.de
Web site: http://www.cellesche-zeitung.de

Titles:
CELLER MARKT
CELLESCHE ZEITUNG

CETO-VERLAG GMBH 679725
Industriestr. 85, 04229 LEIPZIG **Tel:** 341 4924010
Fax: 341 4924012
Email: info@brennstoffspiegel.de
Web site: http://www.brennstoffspiegel.de

Titles:
BRENNSTOFFSPIEGEL UND MINERALÖLRUNDSCHAU

CHARLES COLEMAN VERLAG GMBH & CO. KG 681707
Stolberger Str. 84, 50933 KÖLN **Tel:** 221 54970
Fax: 221 5497326
Email: info@coleman-verlag.de
Web site: http://www.mt-metallhandwerk.de

Titles:
M & T METALLHANDWERK
M & T ONLINE

CHEFBÜRO MEDIA VERLAG STEFAN BEUCHEL 680131
Oberer Eisbergweg 7, 73734 ESSLINGEN
Tel: 711 3482070 **Fax:** 711 3482071
Email: chefbuero@chefbuero.de
Web site: http://www.chefbuero.de

Titles:
CHEFBÜRO

CHEFMEDIA VERLAG 1643745
Bechsteinstr. 27, 99423 WEIMAR **Tel:** 3643 41580
Fax: 3643 415819
Email: info@chefmedia.de
Web site: http://www.chefmedia.de

Titles:
BUONGIORNO ITALIA

CHEMNITZER VERLAG UND DRUCK GMBH & CO. KG 682132
Brückenstr. 15, 09111 CHEMNITZ **Tel:** 371 6560
Fax: 371 643042
Email: die.tageszeitung@freiepresse.de
Web site: http://www.freiepresse.de

Titles:
FREIE PRESSE
FREIEPRESSE.DE

CHIP COMMUNICATIONS GMBH 680154
Poccistr. 11, 80336 MÜNCHEN **Tel:** 89 746420
Fax: 89 7460560
Email: info@chip.de
Web site: http://www.chip.de/media

Titles:
CHIP
CHIP FOTO-VIDEO
CHIP TEST & KAUF

CHIP XONIO ONLINE GMBH 1626654
Poccistr. 11, 80336 MÜNCHEN **Tel:** 89 74642500
Fax: 89 74642261
Email: info@chipxonio.com
Web site: http://www.chip-xonio.de

Titles:
CHIP ONLINE.DE

CHOICES VERLAG JOACHIM BERNDT 1626655
Maastrichter Str. 6, 50672 KÖLN
Tel: 221 2725260 **Fax:** 221 2725288
Email: info@choices.de
Web site: http://www.choices.de

Titles:
CHOICES

CHRISTEN IN DER WIRTSCHAFT E.V. 680186
Morianstr. 10, 42103 WUPPERTAL
Tel: 202 24419121 **Fax:** 202 24419122
Email: info@ciw.de
Web site: http://www.ciw.de

Titles:
FAKTOR C

CHRISTIAN HARTMANN VERLAG GMBH 698264
Agnes-Bernauer-Str. 129, 80687 MÜNCHEN
Tel: 89 6936560 **Fax:** 89 69365656

Titles:
I. PROGRAMM FÜR MÜNCHEN & BAYERN

CHRISTIAN VERLAG GMBH 1655393
Infanteriestr. 11a, 80797 MÜNCHEN
Tel: 89 1306990 **Fax:** 89 13069911
Email: info@christian-verlag.de
Web site: http://www.christian-verlag.de

Titles:
GAULT MILLAU DEUTSCHLAND
GAULT MILLAU WEINGUIDE DEUTSCHLAND

CHRISTLICHE POST- UND TELEKOMVEREINIGUNG 1744488
Im Dorf 9a, 27404 HEESLINGEN
Email: geschaeftsstelle@cptv-online.de
Web site: http://www.cptv-online.de

Titles:
DIE CHRISTUS-POST

CHRISTLICHER MEDIENVERBUND KEP E.V. 687315
Steinbühlstr. 3, 35578 WETZLAR
Tel: 6441 915151 **Fax:** 6441 915157
Email: info@kep.de
Web site: http://www.kep.de

Titles:
PRO

CINEMA VERLAG GMBH 680199
Christoph-Probst-Weg 1, 20251 HAMBURG
Tel: 40 41310 **Fax:** 40 41312024
Email: info@milchstrasse.de
Web site: http://www.milchstrasse.de

Titles:
CINEMA

CITY ANZEIGENBLATT GMBH 680965
Karl-Geusen-Str. 185, 40231 DÜSSELDORF
Tel: 211 903060 **Fax:** 211 9030619
Email: kontakt@duesseldorfer-anzeiger.de
Web site: http://www.duesseldorfer-anzeiger.de

Titles:
DÜSSELDORFER ANZEIGER

CITY WERBEVERLAGS GMBH 680137
Lindenthaler Hauptstr. 98, 04158 LEIPZIG
Tel: 341 4618213 **Fax:** 341 4618214
Email: info@blitz-world.de
Web site: http://www.blitz-world.de

Titles:
BLITZ! - AUSG. CHEMNITZ
BLITZ! - AUSG. DRESDEN
BLITZ! - AUSG. HALLE
BLITZ! - AUSG. LEIPZIG
BLITZ! - AUSG. THÜRINGEN

CITYOFFERS.DE L & G OHG 1709756
Am Brixener Hof 12, 93047 REGENSBURG
Tel: 941 5956080 **Fax:** 941 59560810
Email: info@cityoffers.de
Web site: http://www.cityoffers.de

Titles:
FILTER

CITY-POST ZEITSCHRIFTENVERLAGS GMBH 680832
Schwanthalerstr. 10, 80336 MÜNCHEN
Tel: 89 5990810 **Fax:** 89 59908133
Email: redaktion@cpz.de
Web site: http://www.cpz.de

Titles:
DACH, WAND & BODEN
DAS EINFAMILIEN HAUS
FENSTER, TÜREN & GARAGENTORE
HEIZUNG & ENERGIESPAREN
UMBAUEN & MODERNISIEREN
UNSER HAUS FÜR DIE GANZE FAMILIE

CL. ATTENKOFER'SCHE BUCH- UND KUNSTDRUCKEREI 677655
Ludwigsplatz 30, 94315 STRAUBING
Tel: 9421 9400
Web site: http://www.idowa.de

Titles:
ALLGEMEINE LABER-ZEITUNG - HEIMATAUSG. D. STRAUBINGER TAGBLATTS
BOGENER ZEITUNG - HEIMATAUSG. D. STRAUBINGER TAGBLATTS
CHAMER ZEITUNG
CHAMLAND AKTUELL
DEGGENDORF AKTUELL
DONAU-POST
GÄUBODEN AKTUELL
ISAR AKTUELL
KÖTZTINGER ZEITUNG
LANDAUER ZEITUNG
PLATTLINGER ANZEIGER
STRAUBINGER TAGBLATT

CLASSIC BRITISH BIKE CLUB E.V. 1741825
Im Winkel 8, 56653 WEHR **Tel:** 160 96907210
Email: klaus.lonnendonker@web.de
Web site: http://www.cbbc.de

Titles:
CBBC-INFO

CLASSIC DRIVER GMBH 700384
Mittelweg 158b, 20148 HAMBURG
Tel: 40 2800830 **Fax:** 40 28008350
Email: empfang@classicdriver.de
Web site: http://www.classicdriver.de

Titles:
CLASSIC DRIVER

CLIPS VERLAGS GMBH 694670
Wilhelm-Backhaus-Str. 2, 50931 KÖLN
Tel: 221 9440670 **Fax:** 221 94406710
Email: verlag@clips-verlag.de
Web site: http://www.clips-verlag.de

Titles:
CLIPS

CMAC GMBH & CO. VERLAGS KG 682893
August-Röbling-Str. 28, 99091 ERFURT
Tel: 361 740550 **Fax:** 361 7405560
Email: info@diehallos.de
Web site: http://www.diehallos.de

Titles:
WWW.DIEHALLOS.DE IN THÜRINGEN ZUM SONNTAG - AUSG. BAD SALZUNGEN
WWW.DIEHALLOS.DE IN THÜRINGEN ZUM SONNTAG - AUSG. WEIMAR U. APOLDA

CMC PUBLISHING GMBH 697791
Kaiserstr. 72, 60329 FRANKFURT **Tel:** 69 2740420
Fax: 69 27404222
Email: christian.beese@cmc-publishing.de
Web site: http://www.inqueery.de

Titles:
GAB

CMP-WEKA VERLAG GMBH & CO. KG 1685865
Gruber Str. 46a, 85586 POING **Tel:** 8121 951301
Fax: 8121 951396
Email: info@cmp-weka.de
Web site: http://www.cmp-weka.de

Titles:
COMPUTER RESELLER NEWS

COBRA IG DEUTSCHLAND 1788389
Fahrweg 20, 53773 HENNEF
Web site: http://www.cobra-ig.de

Titles:
COBRA NEWS

COBURGER TAGEBLATT VERLAG & MEDIEN GMBH & CO. KG 699940
Hindenburgstr. 3a, 96450 COBURG
Tel: 9561 888100 **Fax:** 9561 888102
Email: info@infranken.de
Web site: http://www.infranken.de

Titles:
COBURGER TAGEBLATT

CO.IN. MEDIEN VERLAGSGES. MBH 1684574
Otto-von-Guericke-Ring 3a, 65205 WIESBADEN
Tel: 6122 705450 **Fax:** 6122 705470
Email: hamm@coin-online.de
Web site: http://www.coin-online.de

Titles:
BANKEN + PARTNER

COMDIRECT BANK AG 1651619
Pascalkehre 15, 25451 QUICKBORN
Tel: 4106 7040 **Fax:** 4106 7042508
Web site: http://www.comdirect.de

Titles:
.COMDIRECT

CO'MED VERLAGSGES. MBH 680291
Rüdesheimer Str. 40, 65239 HOCHHEIM
Tel: 6146 90740 **Fax:** 6146 907444
Email: verlag@comedverlag.de
Web site: http://www.comedverlag.de

Titles:
CO'MED

COMMUNICATION NETWORK MEDIA 1774105
Ridlerstr. 35a, 80339 MÜNCHEN
Tel: 89 72959915 **Fax:** 89 72959918
Email: info@commnet-media.de
Web site: http://www.commnet-media.de

Titles:
MARKE41
MEDIA41

COMPACT PUBLISHING GMBH 678853
Hackerbrücke 6, 80335 MÜNCHEN
Tel: 89 89817212 **Fax:** 89 89817102
Email: info@compactpublishing.de
Web site: http://www.compactpublishing.de

Titles:
DER BAUHERR

COMPANIONS GMBH 1605981
Rödingsmarkt 9, 20459 HAMBURG
Tel: 40 30604600 **Fax:** 40 30604690
Email: info@companions.de
Web site: http://www.companions.de

Titles:
KIND IM RHEIN-MAIN-GEBIET
KIND IM RUHRGEBIET
KIND IN BERLIN MIT POTSDAM UND BERLINER UMLAND
KIND IN DÜSSELDORF
KIND IN HAMBURG
KIND IN KÖLN/BONN
KIND IN MÜNCHEN
KIND IN STUTTGART

COMPUTEC MEDIA AG 682311
Dr.-Mack-Str. 83, 90762 FÜRTH **Tel:** 911 2872100
Fax: 911 2872200
Email: info@computec.de
Web site: http://www.computec.de

Titles:
GAMES AKTUELL
KIDS ZONE
N-ZONE
PC ACTION
PC GAMES
PC GAMES
PC GAMES HARDWARE
SFT
WIDESCREEN

CONBRIO VERLAGSGES. MBH
684001
Brunnstr. 23, 93053 REGENSBURG
Tel: 941 945930 **Fax:** 941 9459350
Email: info@conbrio.de
Web site: http://www.conbrio.de

Titles:
NMZ NEUE MUSIKZEITUNG

CONCARDIS GMBH
1630438
Solmsstr. 4, 60486 FRANKFURT **Tel:** 69 79220
Fax: 69 79224500
Web site: http://www.concardis.com

Titles:
DIREKT

CONDÉ NAST VERLAG GMBH
677313
Karlstr. 23, 80333 MÜNCHEN **Tel:** 89 381040
Fax: 89 38104230
Web site: http://www.condenast.de

Titles:
AD ARCHITECTURAL DIGEST
GLAMOUR
GQ
GQ CARE
GQ STYLE
GQ UHREN
MYSELF
VOGUE

CONFRUCTA MEDIEN GMBH
681924
Raiffeisenstr. 27, 56587 STRASSENHAUS
Tel: 2634 92350 **Fax:** 2634 923535
Email: info@confructa-medien.com
Web site: http://www.confructa-medien.com

Titles:
FLÜSSIGES OBST
FRUIT PROCESSING

CONGRESS COMPACT VERLAG
1739793
Bleibtreustr. 12a, 10623 BERLIN **Tel:** 30 32708233
Fax: 30 32708234
Email: info@congress-compact.de
Web site: http://www.congress-compact.de

Titles:
ZEITSCHRIFT FÜR WUNDHEILUNG

CONOCOPHILLIPS GERMANY GMBH
1685238
Überseering 27, 22297 HAMBURG **Tel:** 40 638010
Fax: 40 63801454

Titles:
JET KONTAKT

CONPART VERLAG GMBH & CO. ZEITSCHRIFTEN KG
679685
Bäckerstr. 14, 25709 MARNE **Tel:** 4851 964766
Fax: 4851 964767
Email: contact@conpart-verlag.de
Web site: http://www.conpart-verlag.de

Titles:
DAS BESTE AUS MEIN BEKENNTNIS
DAS BESTE FÜR DIE FRAU
DAS BESTE FÜR DIE FRAU REZEPTE & MEHR!
FRAU IM BLICK
FREIZEIT EXTRA
FREIZEIT ILLUSTRIERTE
DAS MACHT SPASS!
MEIN BEKENNTNIS
MEIN GEHEIMNIS
MEINE SCHICKSALS STORY
SCHICKSALS-ERLEBNISSE
SCHÖNE FREIZEIT!
SCHÖNE FREIZEIT! EINFACH BACKEN

CONSENS-MEDIEN-VERLAG WOLFGANG-MICHAEL DUSCHL
1788156
An der Oberpforte 1, 55128 MAINZ
Tel: 6131 364579 **Fax:** 6131 369740
Email: info@consens-seniorenmagazin.de
Web site: http://www.consens-seniorenmagazin.de

Titles:
CONSENS MAINZ
CONSENS WIESBADEN

CONTINENTALE KRANKENVERSICHERUNG A.G.
690595
Ruhrallee 92, 44139 DORTMUND
Tel: 231 9192255 **Fax:** 231 9193094
Email: presse@continentale.de
Web site: http://www.continentale.de

Titles:
WIR AKTUELL

CONTITECH AG
1622098
Vahrenwalder Str. 9, 30165 HANNOVER
Tel: 511 93801 **Fax:** 511 93881770
Email: service@contitech.de
Web site: http://www.contitech.de

Titles:
CONTITECH INITIATIV
CONTITECH INITIATIV

CONTRASTE E.V.
680361
Postfach 104520, 69035 HEIDELBERG
Tel: 6221 162467
Email: contraste@online.de
Web site: http://www.contraste.org

Titles:
CONTRASTE

CORPS. CORPORATE PUBLISHING SERVICES GMBH
700410
Kasernenstr. 69, 40213 DÜSSELDORF
Tel: 211 54227700 **Fax:** 211 54227722
Email: info@corps-verlag.de
Web site: http://www.corps-verlag.de

Titles:
CHANCEN
DEUTSCHES ARCHITEKTENBLATT
INITIATIVBANKING

COTTBUSER GENERAL-ANZEIGER VERLAG GMBH
685273
Wernerstr. 21, 03046 COTTBUS **Tel:** 355 381310
Fax: 355 3813120
Email: post@cga-verlag.de
Web site: http://www.maerkischerbote.de

Titles:
DER MÄRKISCHE BOTE

CRAIN COMMUNICATIONS GMBH
696985
Argelsrieder Feld 13, 82234 WESSLING
Tel: 8153 907400 **Fax:** 8153 907426
Email: automobilwoche@craincom.de
Web site: http://www.automobilwoche.de

Titles:
AUTOMOBILWOCHE

CREDITREFORM DÜSSELDORF FROMMANN KG
680419
Heesenstr. 65, 40549 DÜSSELDORF
Tel: 211 16710 **Fax:** 211 1671108

Titles:
WIRTSCHAFTSSPIEGEL

CRM CENTRUM FÜR REISEMEDIZIN GMBH
1685491
Hansaallee 321, 40549 DÜSSELDORF
Tel: 211 904290 **Fax:** 211 9042999
Email: info@crm.de
Web site: http://www.crm.de

Titles:
CRM-HANDBUCH REISEMEDIZIN
CRM-HANDBUCH REISEN MIT VORERKRANKUNGEN

CUBUS MEDIEN VERLAG GMBH
1627025
Knauerstr. 1, 20249 HAMBURG **Tel:** 40 28096750
Fax: 40 28096752
Email: cubus@fassadentechnik.de
Web site: http://www.fassadentechnik.de

Titles:
FASSADENTECHNIK

CUXHAVEN-NIEDERELBE VERLAGSGES. MBH & CO. KG
680439
Kaemmererplatz 2, 27472 CUXHAVEN
Tel: 4721 5850 **Fax:** 4721 585336
Email: cn@cuxonline.de
Web site: http://www.cn-online.de

Titles:
CUXHAVENER NACHRICHTEN
NIEDERELBE-ZEITUNG

CV COMPUTERN-VERLAGS GMBH
680319
Beethovenplatz 2, 80336 MÜNCHEN
Tel: 89 5446560 **Fax:** 89 531327
Email: info@cv-verlag.de
Web site: http://www.handwerke.de

Titles:
COMPUTERN IM H@NDWERK

CYBERMEDIA VERLAGSGES. MBH
678460
Wallbergstr. 10, 86415 MERING **Tel:** 8233 74010
Fax: 8233 740117
Email: info@cybermediaverlag.de
Web site: http://www.cybermediaverlag.de

Titles:
MIGAMES
SAT + KABEL

DA CAPO VERLAG & AGENTUR
680456
Ebertallee 45a, 38104 BRAUNSCHWEIG
Tel: 531 798347 **Fax:** 531 798343
Email: da-capo@t-online.de

Titles:
DA CAPO

DAA DEUTSCHEANWALTAKADEMIE GMBH
680596
Littenstr. 11, 10179 BERLIN **Tel:** 30 7261530
Fax: 30 726153111
Email: daa@anwaltakademie.de
Web site: http://www.anwaltakademie.de

Titles:
DEUTSCHEANWALTAKADEMIE SEMINARVERZEICHNIS

DACHVERBAND DEUTSCHE LEUKÄMIE-FORSCHUNGSHILFE - AKTION FÜR KREBSKRANKE KINDER E.V.
690581
Adenauerallee 134, 53113 BONN **Tel:** 228 688460
Fax: 228 6884644
Email: dlfhbonn@kinderkrebsstiftung.de
Web site: http://www.kinderkrebsstiftung.de

Titles:
WIR

DÄHNE VERLAG GMBH
678229
Am Erlengraben 8, 76275 ETTLINGEN
Tel: 7243 5750 **Fax:** 7243 575100
Email: info@daehne.de
Web site: http://www.daehne.de

Titles:
AQUARISTIK VEREINT MIT AQUARIUM LIVE
DIY
DIY INTERNATIONAL
GARTENTEICH
HOLZ FORUM MIT FENSTER- UND TÜRENMARKT
PET

DAIMLER AG, COMMUNICATIONS, E 402
693377
Mercedesstr. 132, 70567 STUTTGART
Tel: 711 1759298 **Fax:** 711 1779095134
Email: mirjam.bendak@daimler.com
Web site: http://www.mercedes-benz.de

Titles:
MERCEDESMAGAZIN

DAIMLER AG, DAIMLER TRUCK GROUP, MARKETING-KOMMUNIKATION
698861
Postfach Z602, 70546 STUTTGART
Tel: 711 1790468 **Fax:** 711 1790944
Web site: http://www.mercedes-benz.de

Titles:
MERCEDES-BENZ ROUTE
MERCEDES-BENZ ROUTE
MERCEDES-BENZ TRANSPORT

DARC VERLAG GMBH
680411
Lindenallee 6, 34225 BAUNATAL
Tel: 561 9498873 **Fax:** 561 9498855
Email: verlag@darcverlag.de
Web site: http://www.darcverlag.de

Titles:
CQ DL

DATA BECKER GMBH & CO. KG
683817
Merowingerstr. 30, 40223 DÜSSELDORF
Tel: 211 933470 **Fax:** 211 9334710
Web site: http://www.databecker.de

Titles:
GRILL MAGAZIN
INTERNET INTERN
PC PR@XIS

DATAKONTEXT, VERLAGSGRUPPE HÜTHIG JEHLE REHM GMBH
677613
Augustinusstr. 9d, 50226 FRECHEN
Tel: 2234 966100 **Fax:** 2234 966109
Email: fachverlag@datakontext.com
Web site: http://www.datakontext.com

Titles:
HR PERFORMANCE
HR SERVICES
IT-SICHERHEIT
LOHN+GEHALT
LOHNSTEUER-MITTEILUNGEN
RDV RECHT DER DATENVERARBEITUNG

DATES MEDIEN VERLAG GMBH
680504
Zum Handelshof 7, 39108 MAGDEBURG
Tel: 391 7325230 **Fax:** 391 7325231
Email: kontakt@dates-online.de
Web site: http://www.bewegungsmelder.de/dates

Titles:
DATES
DATES
STUDIEREN IN MAGDEBURG

DATEV EG
1605946
Paumgartnerstr. 6, 90429 NÜRNBERG
Tel: 911 3190 **Fax:** 911 3193196
Email: info@datev.de
Web site: http://www.datev.de

Titles:
DATEV MAGAZIN

DAV DEUTSCHE AKTUARVEREINIGUNG E.V.
1765931
Hohenstaufenring 47, 50674 KÖLN
Tel: 221 9125540 **Fax:** 221 91255444
Email: info@aktuar.de
Web site: http://www.aktuar.de

Titles:
AKTUAR AKTUELL

DAYLIGHT VERLAG
687143
Am Brink 4, 18057 ROSTOCK **Tel:** 381 7698633
Fax: 381 7698645
Email: rostock@piste.de
Web site: http://www.piste-rostock.de

Titles:
PISTE

DAZ VERLAG VERLAGSGRUPPE GMBH & CO. KG
678598
An der Strusbek 23, 22926 AHRENSBURG
Tel: 4102 47870 **Fax:** 4102 478795
Email: info@daz-verlag.de
Web site: http://www.daz24.de

Titles:
AUTO-MOBILES TRÄUME WAGEN
BAUMA MOBILES INTERNATIONAL
DAZ AUTO TOTAL
DAZ CARS!
DAZ TRANSPORTER
TRUCK MOBILES INTERNATIONAL

DBB VERLAG GMBH
694684
Friedrichstr. 165, 10117 BERLIN **Tel:** 30 72619170
Fax: 30 726191740
Email: kontakt@dbbverlag.de
Web site: http://www.dbbverlag.de

Titles:
AKTIV IM RUHESTAND
DIE BERUFSBILDENDE SCHULE
BTB MAGAZIN
DBB MAGAZIN
DURCHBLICK
POLIZEISPIEGEL
ZFPR ZEITSCHRIFT FÜR PERSONALVERTRETUNGSRECHT

DCC-WIRTSCHAFTSDIENST UND VERLAG GMBH
680029
Mandlstr. 28, 80802 MÜNCHEN **Tel:** 89 3801420
Fax: 89 38014242
Email: info@camping-club.de
Web site: http://www.camping-club.de

Titles:
CAMPING
DCC-CAMPINGFÜHRER EUROPA

DEERE & COMPANY 1767532
John-Deere-Str. 70, 68163 MANNHEIM
Tel: 621 8298418 **Fax:** 621 8298300
Web site: http://www.johndeere.de

Titles:
DE VOOR
FÅRA
FÅRAN
FLUR UND FURCHE
FUREN
THE FURROW
LE SILLON
IL SOLCO
SULCO
VAKO

DEHNE DIENSTLEISTUNGS-GMBH 1771901
Azaleenstr. 87, 26639 WIESMOOR
Tel: 4944 920486 **Fax:** 4944 919416
Email: info@dehne.de
Web site: http://www.dehne-internet.de

Titles:
HORTIVISION

DEISTER- UND WESERZEITUNG VERLAGSGES. MBH & CO. KG 680548
Osterstr. 15, 31785 HAMELN **Tel:** 5151 2000
Fax: 5151 200305
Email: mail@dewezet.de
Web site: http://www.dewezet.de

Titles:
ANZEIGER FÜR BODENWERDER
DEWEZET
PYRMONTER NACHRICHTEN

DELIUS KLASING VERLAG GMBH 678803
Siekerwall 21, 33602 BIELEFELD **Tel:** 521 5590
Fax: 521 559116
Email: info@delius-klasing.de
Web site: http://www.delius-klasing.de

Titles:
BIKE
BOOTE
BOOTE EXCLUSIV
GUTE FAHRT
KÄFER REVUE
MODELL FAHRZEUG
SURF
TOUR SPEZIAL RENNRAD MARKT
TUNING
VW CLASSIC
VW SPEED
YACHT

DELTA MEDIEN GMBH 685507
Melchiorstr. 1, 68167 MANNHEIM
Tel: 621 338800 **Fax:** 621 333367
Email: info@meier-online.de
Web site: http://www.meier-online.de

Titles:
MEIER
MEIER SUMMERTIME

DEMETER BADEN-WÜRTTEMBERG 680556
Hauptstr. 82, 70771 LEINFELDEN-ECHTERDINGEN **Tel:** 711 902540
Fax: 711 9025454
Email: info@demeter-bw.de
Web site: http://www.demeter-bw.de

Titles:
DEMETER GARTENRUNDBRIEF

DENTAL TRIBUNE INTERNATIONAL GMBH 1690017
Holbeinstr. 29, 04229 LEIPZIG **Tel:** 341 48474302
Fax: 341 48474173
Email: j.boegershausen@dental-tribune.com
Web site: http://www.dental-tribune.com

Titles:
DENTAL TRIBUNE

DESCH ANTRIEBSTECHNIK GMBH & CO. KG 680579
Kleinbahnstr. 21, 59759 ARNSBERG
Tel: 2932 3000 **Fax:** 2932 300899
Email: birgitt.cordes@desch.de
Web site: http://www.desch.de

Titles:
DESCH AKTUELL

DESIGNWERK VERLAG 697756
Uhlenbroicher Weg 30a, 47269 DUISBURG
Tel: 203 729207 **Fax:** 203 719378
Email: info@design-werk.net

Titles:
DER DUISBURGER
DER OBERHAUSENER

DESOTRON VERLAGSGES. DR. GÜNTER HARTMANN & PARTNER GBR 1621959
Juri-Gagarin-Ring 152, 99084 ERFURT
Tel: 361 5621865 **Fax:** 361 5621865
Email: verlag@desotron.de
Web site: http://www.verlag.desotron.de

Titles:
INGENIEUR-NACHRICHTEN

DETEMEDIEN GMBH 1690865
Wiesenhüttenstr. 18, 60329 FRANKFURT
Tel: 69 26820 **Fax:** 69 26827890
Email: info@detemedien.de
Web site: http://www.detemedien.de

Titles:
GELBESEITEN

DEUBNER VERLAG GMBH & CO. KG 695569
Oststr. 11, 50996 KÖLN **Tel:** 221 9370180
Fax: 221 93701890
Email: kundenservice@deubner-verlag.de
Web site: http://www.deubner-verlag.de

Titles:
STEUER-TELEX

DEUTSCHE ARBEITSGEMEINSCHAFT FÜR EVANGELISCHE GEHÖRLOSENSEELSORGE E.V. 695148
Ständeplatz 18, 34117 KASSEL **Tel:** 561 7394051
Fax: 561 7394052
Email: info@dafeg.de
Web site: http://www.dafeg.de

Titles:
UNSERE GEMEINDE

DEUTSCHE BANK PRIVAT- UND GESCHÄFTSKUNDEN AG 1643272
Theodor-Heuss-Allee 72, 60486 FRANKFURT
Web site: http://www.deutsche-bank.de/start

Titles:
MÄRKTE & TRENDS

DEUTSCHE BUNDESSTIFTUNG UMWELT 1764601
An der Bornau 2, 49090 OSNABRÜCK
Tel: 541 96330 **Fax:** 541 9633990
Email: zuk-info@dbu.de
Web site: http://www.dbu.de

Titles:
DBU AKTUELL

DEUTSCHE BUNSEN-GESELLSCHAFT FÜR PHYSIKALISCHE CHEMIE E.V. 1728900
Theodor-Heuss-Allee 25, 60486 FRANKFURT
Tel: 69 7564620 **Fax:** 69 7564622
Email: woehler@bunsen.de
Web site: http://www.bunsen.de

Titles:
BUNSENMAGAZIN

DEUTSCHE GEFÄSSLIGA E.V. 1728834
Postfach 4038, 69254 MALSCH **Tel:** 7253 26228
Fax: 7253 278160
Email: info@deutsche-gefaessliga.de
Web site: http://www.deutsche-gefaessliga.de

Titles:
GEFÄSSREPORT AKTUELL

DEUTSCHE GESELLSCHAFT FÜR BIOMEDIZINISCHE TECHNIK E.V. IM VDE 680684
Stresemannallee 15, 60596 FRANKFURT
Tel: 69 6308208 **Fax:** 69 96315219
Email: dgbmt@vde.com
Web site: http://www.dgbmt.de

Titles:
HEALTH TECHNOLOGIES

DEUTSCHE GESELLSCHAFT FÜR DAS BADEWESEN E.V. 1606102
Alfredstr. 73, 45130 ESSEN **Tel:** 201 879690
Fax: 201 8796920
Email: info@baederportal.com
Web site: http://www.baederportal.com

Titles:
AB ARCHIV DES BADEWESENS

DEUTSCHE GESELLSCHAFT FÜR FLÖTE E.V. 681911
Strubbergstr. 80, 60489 FRANKFURT
Tel: 69 5962443
Email: floete@floete.net
Web site: http://www.floete.net

Titles:
FLÖTE AKTUELL

DEUTSCHE GESELLSCHAFT FÜR INTERNATIONALE ZUSAMMENARBEIT 1723955
Dag-Hammarskjöld-Weg 1, 65760 ESCHBORN
Tel: 6196 790 **Fax:** 6196 791115
Email: info@giz.de
Web site: http://www.giz.de

Titles:
AKZENTE

DEUTSCHE GESELLSCHAFT FÜR MUSKELKRANKE E.V. 686094
Im Moos 4, 79112 FREIBURG **Tel:** 7665 94470
Fax: 7665 944720
Email: info@dgm.org
Web site: http://www.dgm.org

Titles:
MUSKELREPORT

DEUTSCHE GESELLSCHAFT FÜR PERSONALFÜHRUNG E.V. 687014
Niederkasseler Lohweg 16, 40547 DÜSSELDORF **Tel:** 211 59780 **Fax:** 211 5978199
Email: info@dgfp.de
Web site: http://www.dgfp.de

Titles:
PERSONALFÜHRUNG

DEUTSCHE GESELLSCHAFT FÜR SONNENENERGIE E.V. 1743605
Emmy-Noether-Str. 2, 80992 MÜNCHEN
Tel: 89 524071 **Fax:** 89 521668
Email: info@dgs.de
Web site: http://www.dgs.de

Titles:
SONNENENERGIE

DEUTSCHE GESELLSCHAFT FÜR ZELLBIOLOGIE E.V. 1739525
Im Neuenheimer Feld 280, 69120 HEIDELBERG
Tel: 6221 423451 **Fax:** 6221 423452
Email: dgz@dkfz.de
Web site: http://www.zellbiologie.de

Titles:
CELL NEWS

DEUTSCHE GESELLSCHAFT FÜR ZERSTÖRUNGSFREIE PRÜFUNG 690976
Max-Planck-Str. 6, 12489 BERLIN **Tel:** 30 678070
Fax: 30 67807109
Email: mail@dgzfp.de
Web site: http://www.dgzfp.de

Titles:
ZFP-ZEITUNG

DEUTSCHE HERZSTIFTUNG E.V. 683188
Vogtstr. 50, 60322 FRANKFURT **Tel:** 69 9551280
Fax: 69 955128313
Email: info@herzstiftung.de
Web site: http://www.herzstiftung.de

Titles:
HERZ HEUTE
HERZBLATT

DEUTSCHE LEUKÄMIE- UND LYMPHOM-HILFE E.V. 680812
Thomas-Mann-Str. 40, 53111 BONN
Tel: 228 33889200 **Fax:** 228 33889222
Email: info@leukaemie-hilfe.de
Web site: http://www.leukaemie-hilfe.de

Titles:
DLH INFO

DEUTSCHE STEUER-GEWERKSCHAFT, LANDESVERBAND BERLIN 1746291
Motzstr. 32, 10777 BERLIN **Tel:** 30 21473040
Fax: 30 21473041
Email: info@dstg-berlin.de
Web site: http://www.dstg-berlin.de

Titles:
DAS STEUER- UND GROLLBLATT BERLIN

DEUTSCHE ZENTRALBÜCHEREI FÜR BLINDE ZU LEIPZIG 679649
Gustav-Adolf-Str. 7, 04105 LEIPZIG
Tel: 341 71130 **Fax:** 341 7113125
Email: info@dzb.de
Web site: http://www.dzb.de

Titles:
RATGEBER-AKTUELL

DEUTSCHE ZENTRALE FÜR GLOBETROTTER E.V. 689662
Rußhütter Str. 26, 66287 QUIERSCHIED
Tel: 700 45623876
Email: vorstand@globetrotter.org
Web site: http://www.globetrotter.org

Titles:
DER TROTTER

DEUTSCHER AGRARVERLAG 680598
Claire-Waldoff-Str. 7, 10117 BERLIN
Tel: 30 31904242 **Fax:** 30 31904431
Email: presse@bauernverband.net
Web site: http://www.bauernverband.de

Titles:
DBK DEUTSCHE BAUERN KORRESPONDENZ

DEUTSCHER ALLERGIE- UND ASTHMABUND E.V. 677624
Fliethstr. 114, 41061 MÖNCHENGLADBACH
Tel: 2161 814940 **Fax:** 2161 8149430
Email: info@daab.de
Web site: http://www.daab.de

Titles:
ALLERGIE KONKRET

DEUTSCHER ALPENVEREIN E.V. 679057
Von-Kahr-Str. 2, 80997 MÜNCHEN
Tel: 89 140030 **Fax:** 89 14000398
Email: dav-panorama@alpenverein.de
Web site: http://www.alpenverein.de

Titles:
DAV PANORAMA

DEUTSCHER ANWALTVERLAG GMBH 677350
Wachsbleiche 7, 53111 BONN **Tel:** 228 919117
Fax: 228 9191123
Email: kontakt@anwaltverlag.de
Web site: http://www.anwaltverlag.de

Titles:
AE ARBEITSRECHTLICHE ENTSCHEIDUNGEN
ANWALTSBLATT
ASR ANWALT/ANWÄLTIN IM SOZIALRECHT
FORUM FAMILIENRECHT
FOVO FORDERUNG & VOLLSTRECKUNG
MITGLIEDERBRIEF BAYERISCHER ANWALTVERBAND
DER VERKEHRSANWALT

DEUTSCHER APOTHEKER VERLAG 678202
Birkenwaldstr. 44, 70191 STUTTGART
Tel: 711 25820 **Fax:** 711 2582290
Email: service@deutscher-apotheker-verlag.de
Web site: http://www.deutscher-apotheker-verlag.de

Titles:
AP APOTHEKEN PRAXIS
AWA - AKTUELLER WIRTSCHAFTSDIENST FÜR APOTHEKER
AZ APOTHEKER ZEITUNG
DAZ DEUTSCHE APOTHEKERZEITUNG
GESCHICHTE DER PHARMAZIE

KRANKENHAUSPHARMAZIE
MMP MEDIZINISCHE MONATSSCHRIFT FÜR PHARMAZEUTEN
NEUE ARZNEIMITTEL
PKA AKTIV
PTA HEUTE
STUDENT UND PRAKTIKANT

DEUTSCHER ÄRZTE-VERLAG GMBH 680629

Dieselstr. 2, 50859 KÖLN **Tel:** 2234 70110
Fax: 2234 7011515
Web site: http://www.aerzteverlag.de

Titles:
DENTAL MAGAZIN
DEUTSCHES ÄRZTEBLATT
DIVI
HNO INFORMATIONEN
HNO MITTEILUNGEN
ORALPROPHYLAXE & KINDERZAHNHEILKUNDE
PRAXIS
REISEMAGAZIN
SPECTATOR-DENTISTRY
ZFA ZEITSCHRIFT FÜR ALLGEMEINMEDIZIN
ZM ZAHNÄRZTLICHE MITTEILUNGEN
ZZI ZEITSCHRIFT FÜR ZAHNÄRZTLICHE IMPLANTOLOGIE

DEUTSCHER ÄRZTINNENBUND E.V. 1766965

Herbert-Lewin-Platz 1, 10623 BERLIN
Tel: 30 400456540 **Fax:** 30 400456541
Email: gsdaeb@aerztinnenbund.de
Web site: http://www.aerztinnenbund.de

Titles:
ÄRZTIN

DEUTSCHER BANKANGESTELLTEN-VERBAND 693235

Oststr. 10, 40211 DÜSSELDORF
Tel: 211 3694558 **Fax:** 211 369679
Email: info@dbv-gewerkschaft.de
Web site: http://www.dbv-gewerkschaft.de

Titles:
DER FINANZDIENSTLEISTER

DEUTSCHER BAUERNVERLAG GMBH 678236

Wilhelmsaue 37, 10713 BERLIN **Tel:** 30 464060
Fax: 30 46406205
Email: info@bauernverlag.de
Web site: http://www.bauernverlag.de

Titles:
BAUERN ZEITUNG
DEUTSCHES BIENEN JOURNAL
GARTEN ZEITUNG
DER HUND
VDL-JOURNAL

DEUTSCHER BETRIEBSWIRTE-VERLAG GMBH 679222

Bleichstr. 20, 76593 GERNSBACH
Tel: 7224 93970 **Fax:** 7224 9397905
Email: info@betriebswirte-verlag.de
Web site: http://www.betriebswirte-verlag.de

Titles:
DER BETRIEBSWIRT

DEUTSCHER BUNDESWEHRVERBAND E.V. 679937

Südstr. 123, 53175 BONN **Tel:** 228 38230
Fax: 228 3823219
Email: presse@dbwv.de
Web site: http://www.dbwv.de

Titles:
DIE BUNDESWEHR

DEUTSCHER CARITASVERBAND E.V. 680053

Karlstr. 40, 79104 FREIBURG **Tel:** 761 2000
Fax: 761 200509
Email: info@caritas.de
Web site: http://www.caritas.de

Titles:
NEUE CARITAS

DEUTSCHER DRUCKER VERLAGSGES. MBH & CO. KG 1784355

Riedstr. 25, 73760 OSTFILDERN **Tel:** 711 448170
Fax: 711 442099
Email: info@print.de
Web site: http://www.print.de

Titles:
DEUTSCHER DRUCKER
GRAFISCHE PALETTE - AUSG. BADEN-WÜRTTEMBERG
GRAFISCHE PALETTE - AUSG. BAYERN
GRAFISCHE PALETTE - AUSG. NORD
GRAFISCHE PALETTE - AUSG. NORDRHEIN-WESTFALEN
GRAFISCHE PALETTE - AUSG. OST
GRAFISCHE PALETTE - AUSG. SÜDWEST
PRINT.DE

DEUTSCHER FACHVERLAG GMBH 677405

Mainzer Landstr. 251, 60326 FRANKFURT
Tel: 69 759501 **Fax:** 69 75952999
Email: info@dfv.de
Web site: http://www.dfv.de

Titles:
AFZ ALLGEMEINE FLEISCHER ZEITUNG
AGRARZEITUNG
DIALOG
ENTSORGA
FEEDMAGAZINE KRAFTFUTTER
FLEISCHWIRTSCHAFT
FLEISCHWIRTSCHAFT INTERNATIONAL
FLEISCHWIRTSCHAFT.DE
FOOD SERVICE
GV-PRAXIS
DER HANDEL. HORIZONT
HORIZONT.NET
JAHRBUCH LÄDEN
LEBENSMITTEL ZEITUNG
LEBENSMITTEL ZEITUNG
LEBENSMITTEL ZEITUNG DIREKT
LEBENSMITTEL ZEITUNG SPEZIAL
MELLIAND TEXTILBERICHTE
PACKMITTEL
PACKREPORT
PLANUNG & ANALYSE
TEXTILWIRTSCHAFT
TEXTILWIRTSCHAFT ONLINE
TW THE GLOBAL MAGAZINE FOR MEETING, INCENTIVE AND EVENT PROFESSIONALS
WOCHENBLATT FÜR PAPIERFABRIKATION
WRP
ZEITSCHRIFT FÜR UMWELTPOLITIK & UMWELTRECHT
ZLR

DEUTSCHER FACHVERLAG GMBH, M+A INTERNATIONALE MESSEMEDIEN 683815

Mainzer Landstr. 251, 60326 FRANKFURT
Tel: 69 759502 **Fax:** 69 75951280
Email: mua@dfv.de
Web site: http://www.m-averlag.com

Titles:
M+A MESSEPLANER
M+A REPORT
TW TAGUNGSREGIONEN

DEUTSCHER FAMILIENVERBAND 680682

Luisenstr. 48, 10117 BERLIN **Tel:** 30 30882960
Fax: 30 30882961
Email: post@deutscher-familienverband.de
Web site: http://www.deutscher-familienverband.de

Titles:
DFV-FAMILIE

DEUTSCHER FRAUENRAT E.V. 1616866

Axel-Springer-Str. 54a, 10117 BERLIN
Tel: 30 2045690 **Fax:** 30 20456944
Email: kontakt@frauenrat.de
Web site: http://www.frauenrat.de

Titles:
FRAUENRAT

DEUTSCHER GENOSSENSCHAFTS-VERLAG EG 677421

Leipziger Str. 35, 65191 WIESBADEN
Tel: 611 50660 **Fax:** 611 50661500
Email: direct@dgverlag.de
Web site: http://www.dgverlag.de

Titles:
BI BANKINFORMATION
BONUS
PERSPEKTIVEPRAXIS.DE
VR FUTURE
VR PRIMAX

DEUTSCHER HEBAMMENVERBAND E.V. 1639647

Gartenstr. 26, 76133 KARLSRUHE
Tel: 721 981890 **Fax:** 721 9818920
Email: info@hebammenverband.de
Web site: http://www.hebammenverband.de

Titles:
HEBAMMEN FORUM

DEUTSCHER HOCHSCHULVERBAND 681987

Rheinallee 18, 53173 BONN **Tel:** 228 9026615
Fax: 228 9026690
Email: dhv@hochschulverband.de
Web site: http://www.hochschulverband.de

Titles:
FORSCHUNG & LEHRE

DEUTSCHER JUGENDBUND FÜR NATURBEOBACHTUNG 1736239

Geiststr. 2, 37073 GÖTTINGEN
Email: djn@naturbeobachtung.de
Web site: http://www.naturbeobachtung.de

Titles:
NATURKUNDLICHE BEITRÄGE DES DJN

DEUTSCHER KINDERSCHUTZBUND E.V. 684694

Schöneberger Str. 15, 10963 BERLIN
Tel: 30 2148090 **Fax:** 30 21480999
Email: info@dksb.de
Web site: http://www.kinderschutzbund.de

Titles:
KSA KINDERSCHUTZ AKTUELL

DEUTSCHER LAND ROVER CLUB E.V. 1732457

Damaschkestr. 11, 52066 AACHEN
Tel: 241 9214900 **Fax:** 241 9214901
Email: info@dlrc.org
Web site: http://www.dlrc.org

Titles:
ROVER-BLATT

DEUTSCHER LANDSCHRIFTENVERLAG GMBH 681756

Maarstr. 96, 53227 BONN **Tel:** 228 963020
Fax: 228 9630233
Email: info@bauernhofurlaub.com
Web site: http://www.bauernhofurlaub.com

Titles:
HOF DIREKT
LUST AUFS LAND
RAUF AUF DIE BERGE
RAUS AUFS LAND

DEUTSCHER LANDWIRTSCHAFTSVERLAG GMBH 1709825

Mars-la-Tour-Str. 4, 26121 OLDENBURG
Tel: 441 801221 **Fax:** 441 801249
Email: dlv.oldenburg@dlv.de
Web site: http://www.dlv.de

Titles:
AFZ DER WALD ZUSAMMEN MIT FORST UND HOLZ
AGRAR TECHNIK
DER ALMBAUER
BAYERISCHES LANDWIRTSCHAFTLICHES WOCHENBLATT
BAYERNS PFERDE ZUCHT + SPORT
DIE BIENE
DEUTSCHER WALDBESITZER
DLZ AGRARMAGAZIN
FORST & TECHNIK
GEMÜSE
IMKERFREUND
DER JAGDGEBRAUCHSHUND
JOULE
KRAUT&RÜBEN
LAND & FORST
NIEDERSÄCHSISCHER JÄGER
NL NEUE LANDWIRTSCHAFT
PFERDEFORUM
PIRSCH
PRIMUS RIND
PRIMUS SCHWEIN
RINDERZUCHT BRAUNVIEH
RINDERZUCHT FLECKVIEH
SÄNGER & MUSIKANTEN
UNSERE JAGD

DEUTSCHER MARINEBUND E.V. 685012

Strandstr. 92, 24235 LABOE **Tel:** 4343 427062
Fax: 4343 427067
Email: vz@deutscher-marinebund.de
Web site: http://www.deutscher-marinebund.de

Titles:
LEINEN LOS!

DEUTSCHER ORDEN 684595

Kurparkstr. 15, 63619 BAD ORB **Tel:** 6052 800250
Fax: 6052 800259
Email: konturen@do-suchthilfe.de
Web site: http://www.konturen.de

Titles:
KONTUREN

DEUTSCHER PSORIASIS BUND E.V. 1640125

Seewartenstr. 10, 20459 HAMBURG
Tel: 40 2233990 **Fax:** 40 22339922
Email: info@psoriasis-bund.de
Web site: http://www.psoriasis-bund.de

Titles:
PSO MAGAZIN

DEUTSCHER PSYCHOLOGEN VERLAG GMBH 687270

Am Köllnischen Park 2, 10179 BERLIN
Tel: 30 209166410 **Fax:** 30 209166413
Email: verlag@psychologenverlag.de
Web site: http://www.psychologenverlag.de

Titles:
RP REPORT PSYCHOLOGIE
WIRTSCHAFTSPSYCHOLOGIE AKTUELL

DEUTSCHER RAIFFEISENVERBAND E.V. 687504

Adenauerallee 127, 53113 BONN **Tel:** 228 1060
Fax: 228 106266
Email: presse@drv.raiffeisen.de
Web site: http://www.raiffeisen.de

Titles:
RAIFFEISEN MAGAZIN

DEUTSCHER RÄTSELVERLAG GMBH & CO. KG 1721073

Münchener Str. 101/Geb. 09, 85737 ISMANING
Tel: 89 272707811 **Fax:** 89 272707890
Email: info@raetsel.de
Web site: http://www.raetsel.de

Titles:
A DIE AKTUELLE LIEBE & SCHICKSAL
A DIE AKTUELLE PREIS RÄTSEL MAGAZIN
BASTEI EXTRA RÄTSEL

DEUTSCHER RICHTERBUND, LANDESVERBAND NORDRHEIN-WESTFALEN 1783722

Martin-Luther-Str. 11, 59065 HAMM
Tel: 2381 29814 **Fax:** 2381 22568
Email: info@drb-nrw.de
Web site: http://www.drb-nrw.de

Titles:
RICHTER UND STAATSANWALT IN NRW

DEUTSCHER SPARKASSEN VERLAG GMBH 677418

Am Wallgraben 115, 70565 STUTTGART
Tel: 711 7820 **Fax:** 711 7821635
Web site: http://www.sparkassenverlag.de

Titles:
AUSSENWIRTSCHAFT
BETRIEBSWIRTSCHAFTLICHE BLÄTTER
DEUTSCHER SPARKASSENKALENDER
FONDS MAGAZIN
GELDPROFI
PROFITS
SPARKASSE
SPARKASSEN MARKT
DIE SPARKASSEN ZEITUNG
TR€FFPUNKT

DEUTSCHER TECKELKLUB 1888 E.V. 680465

Prinzenstr. 38, 47058 DUISBURG **Tel:** 203 330005
Fax: 203 330007
Email: dachshund@dtk1888.de
Web site: http://www.dtk1888.de

Titles:
DER DACHSHUND

DEUTSCHER VERBAND FRAU UND KULTUR E.V. 682109

Bösenseller Str. 152, 48161 MÜNSTER
Tel: 2536 201 **Fax:** 2536 201
Web site: http://www.verband-frau-und-kultur.de

Titles:
FRAU UND KULTUR

DEUTSCHER VERBAND FÜR FREIKÖRPERKULTUR (DFK) E.V., VERBAND FÜR FAMILIEN-, BREITENSPORT UND NATURISMUS E.V. 681879
Ferdinand-Wilhelm-Fricke Weg 10, 30169 HANNOVER **Tel:** 511 12685500 **Fax:** 511 12685515
Email: dfk@dfk.org
Web site: http://www.dfk.org

Titles:
FREI KÖRPER KULTUR

DEUTSCHER VEREIN FÜR VERMESSUNGSWESEN - BAYERN E.V. 685807
Alexandrastr. 4, 80538 MÜNCHEN
Tel: 89 21291527 **Fax:** 89 212921527
Email: dvw-bayern@lvg.bayern.de
Web site: http://www.dvw-bayern.de

Titles:
DVW BAYERN E.V.

DEUTSCHER VERKEHRSSICHERHEITSRAT E.V. 681003
Auguststr. 29, 53229 BONN **Tel:** 228 400010
Fax: 228 4000167
Email: info@dvr.de
Web site: http://www.dvr.de

Titles:
DVR REPORT

DEUTSCHER WETTERDIENST WEIHENSTEPHAN 694525
Alte Akademie 16, Weihenstephaner Berg, 85354 FREISING **Tel:** 8161 537690 **Fax:** 8161 5376950
Email: lw.weihenstephan@dwd.de
Web site: http://www.dwd.de

Titles:
AGRARMETEOROLOGISCHER MONATSBERICHT FÜR BAYERN

DEUTSCHER ZENTRALVEREIN HOMÖOPATHISCHER ÄRZTE E.V. 1744030
Am Hofgarten 5, 53113 BONN **Tel:** 228 2425330
Fax: 228 2425331
Email: sekretariat@dzvhae.de
Web site: http://www.welt-der-homoeopathie.de

Titles:
HOMÖOPATHIE

DEUTSCHES AKTIENINSTITUT E.V. 681848
Niedenau 13, 60325 FRANKFURT **Tel:** 69 929150
Fax: 69 9291512
Email: dai@dai.de
Web site: http://www.dai.de

Titles:
FINANZPLATZ

DEUTSCHES AUSSCHREIBUNGSBLATT GMBH 679925
Höherweg 278, 40231 DÜSSELDORF
Tel: 211 370848 **Fax:** 211 381607
Email: service@deutsches-ausschreibungsblatt.de
Web site: http://www.deutsches-ausschreibungsblatt.de

Titles:
DEUTSCHES AUSSCHREIBUNGSBLATT

DEUTSCHES INSTITUT FÜR URBANISTIK GGMBH 679091
Zimmerstr. 13, 10969 BERLIN **Tel:** 30 390010
Fax: 30 39001130
Email: presse@difu.de
Web site: http://www.difu.de

Titles:
BERICHTE
KOMMUNALWISSENSCHAFTLICHE DISSERTATIONEN

DEUTSCHES VERKEHRSFORUM E.V. 683632
Klingelhöferstr. 7, 10785 BERLIN
Tel: 30 26395430 **Fax:** 30 26395422
Email: info@verkehrsforum.de
Web site: http://www.verkehrsforum.de

Titles:
FORUM VERKEHR NEWSLETTER

DEUTSCHES ZENTRALINSTITUT FÜR SOZIALE FRAGEN 688566
Bernadottestr. 94, 14195 BERLIN **Tel:** 30 8390010
Fax: 30 8314750
Email: verlag@dzi.de
Web site: http://www.dzi.de

Titles:
SOZIALE ARBEIT

DEUTSCHLAND-LAND DER IDEEN MARKETING FÜR DEUTSCHLAND GMBH 1741775
Unter den Linden 74, 10117 BERLIN
Tel: 30 2064590 **Fax:** 30 20645937
Email: info@land-der-ideen.de
Web site: http://www.land-der-ideen.de

Titles:
NEUES AUS DEM LAND DER IDEEN

DEVIL INC. PRESSEVERLAG 684999
Lessingstr. 28, 66121 SAARBRÜCKEN
Tel: 681 3907660 **Fax:** 681 3907661
Email: patric@legacy.de

Titles:
LEGACY

DEWI GMBH DEUTSCHES WINDENERGIE-INSTITUT 680677
Ebertstr. 96, 26382 WILHELMSHAVEN
Tel: 4421 48080 **Fax:** 4421 4808843
Email: dewi@dewi.de
Web site: http://www.dewi.de

Titles:
DEWI MAGAZIN

DFM MEDIA GMBH 1709753
Piechlerstr. 18, 86356 NEUSÄSS
Tel: 821 44471300 **Fax:** 821 44471390
Email: info@dfm.de
Web site: http://www.dfm.eu

Titles:
DFM

DFS GMBH DER FACHVERLAG FÜR SICHERHEIT 1600385
Barbarossastr. 21, 63517 RODENBACH
Tel: 6184 95080 **Fax:** 6184 54524
Email: info@security-service.com
Web site: http://www.security-service.com

Titles:
CD SICHERHEITS-MANAGEMENT
SECURITY POINT

DGFK-DPRG GES. FÜR KOMMUNIKATIONSSERVICE MBH 1630577
Marienstr. 24, 10117 BERLIN **Tel:** 30 80409733
Fax: 30 80409734
Email: info@dprg.de
Web site: http://www.dprg.de

Titles:
DER DPRG-INDEX PR-BERATER

DGW-VERLAG - MONIKA BUSCH & REINER SCHMIDT GBR 680606
Nansenstr. 11, 58300 WETTER **Tel:** 2335 739801
Fax: 2335 739802
Email: verlag@deutschegetraenkewirtschaft.de
Web site: http://www.deutschegetraenkewirtschaft.de

Titles:
DEUTSCHE GETRÄNKE WIRTSCHAFT

DHBV GMBH 1600352
Hans-Willy-Mertens-Str. 2, 50858 KÖLN
Tel: 2234 48455 **Fax:** 2234 49314
Email: info@dhbv.de
Web site: http://www.dhbv.de

Titles:
SCHÜTZEN & ERHALTEN

DHV-DIENSTLEISTUNGS GMBH 680594
Droopweg 31, 20537 HAMBURG **Tel:** 40 6328020
Fax: 40 63280218
Email: gmbh@dhv-cgb.de
Web site: http://www.dhv-cgb.de

Titles:
DEUTSCHE ANGESTELLTEN ZEITUNG DHV

DIABOLO VERLAGS GMBH 680698
Wallstr. 11, 26122 OLDENBURG **Tel:** 441 218350
Fax: 441 2183520
Email: info@diabolo-mox.de
Web site: http://www.diabolo-mox.de

Titles:
DIABOLO

DIAKONIESTATION KREUZTAL 684673
Martin-Luther-Str. 2, 57223 KREUZTAL
Tel: 2732 582470 **Fax:** 2732 582472
Email: seniorenberatung@diakoniestation-kreuztal.de
Web site: http://www.diakoniestation-kreuztal.de

Titles:
MEINE KREUZTALER SENIORENPOST

DIATRA-VERLAG GMBH 680725
Kiedricher Str. 25, 65343 ELTVILLE
Tel: 6123 73478 **Fax:** 6123 73287
Email: dj@diatra-verlag.de
Web site: http://www.diatra-verlag.de

Titles:
DIATRA JOURNAL

DIEBURGER ANZEIGER GMBH & CO. KG 680733
Schlossergasse 4, 64807 DIEBURG
Tel: 6071 25005 **Fax:** 6071 81358
Email: service@op-online.de
Web site: http://www.op-online.de

Titles:
DIEBURGER ANZEIGER
GROSS-ZIMMERNER LOKAL-ANZEIGER

DIERICHS GMBH & CO. KG 683281
Frankfurter Str. 168, 34121 KASSEL
Tel: 561 20300 **Fax:** 561 2032116
Email: info@hna.de
Web site: http://www.hna.de

Titles:
FRANKENBERGER ALLGEMEINE
FRITZLAR-HOMBERGER ALLGEMEINE
HESSISCHE ALLGEMEINE HNA
HNA HESSISCHE/NIEDERSÄCHSISCHE ALLGEMEINE
HNA.DE
HOFGEISMARER ALLGEMEINE
MELSUNGER ALLGEMEINE
MÜNDENER ALLGEMEINE
NORTHEIMER NEUESTE NACHRICHTEN
ROTENBURG-BEBRAER ALLGEMEINE
SCHWÄLMER ALLGEMEINE
SOLLINGER ALLGEMEINE
WALDECKISCHE ALLGEMEINE
WITZENHÄUSER ALLGEMEINE
WOLFHAGER ALLGEMEINE

DIESBACHMEDIEN GMBH 683166
Friedrichstr. 24, 69469 WEINHEIM
Tel: 6201 81100 **Fax:** 6201 81179
Email: mail@diesbachmedien.de

Titles:
ODENWÄLDER ZEITUNG
WEINHEIMER NACHRICHTEN

DIETRICH'S AG 1715153
Hauptstr 37, 85579 NEUBIBERG **Tel:** 89 6144210
Fax: 89 61442144
Email: info@dietrichs.com
Web site: http://www.dietrichs.com

Titles:
NEUES! FÜR DIE HOLZBAUBRANCHE IN DEUTSCHLAND-ÖSTERREICH-SCHWEIZ

DIÖZESAN-CARITAS-VERBÄNDE IN NORDRHEIN-WESTFALEN 680057
Lindenstr. 178, 40233 DÜSSELDORF
Tel: 211 51606620 **Fax:** 211 51606625
Email: redaktion@caritas-nrw.de
Web site: http://www.caritas-nrw.de

Titles:
CARITAS IN NRW

DIRECTA BULDT FACHVERLAG 678880
Lübecker Str. 8, 23611 BAD SCHWARTAU
Tel: 451 499990 **Fax:** 451 4999940
Email: info@directa-verlag.de
Web site: http://www.directa-verlag.de

Titles:
GASTRONOMIE-PRAXIS
MODERNE METALLTECHNIK M

DISPLAY VERLAGS GMBH 680781
Am Neumarkt 30, 22041 HAMBURG
Tel: 40 30060560 **Fax:** 40 300605622
Email: info@display.de
Web site: http://www.display.de

Titles:
DISPLAY

DJH SERVICE GMBH 681606
Bismarckstr. 8, 32756 DETMOLD **Tel:** 5231 74010
Fax: 5231 7401811
Email: service@djh.de
Web site: http://www.djh-service.de

Titles:
EXTRATOUR

DKV-WIRTSCHAFTS- UND VERLAGS GMBH 684225
Bertaallee 8, 47055 DUISBURG **Tel:** 203 997590
Fax: 203 9975961
Email: verlag@kanu.de
Web site: http://www.kanu-verlag.de

Titles:
KANU SPORT

DLG AGROFOOD MEDIEN GMBH 1769901
Clemens-August-Str. 12, 53115 BONN
Tel: 228 9694260 **Fax:** 228 630311
Email: info@dlg-agrofoodmedien.de
Web site: http://www.dlg-agrofoodmedien.de

Titles:
GETREIDE MAGAZIN
KARTOFFELBAU
MAIS
MILCHPRAXIS
RAPS
ZUCKERRÜBE

DLG-VERLAG GMBH 681334
Eschborner Landstr. 122, 60489 FRANKFURT
Tel: 69 247880 **Fax:** 69 24788480
Email: dlg-verlag@dlg.org
Web site: http://www.dlg-verlag.de

Titles:
DLG TEST LANDWIRTSCHAFT
MASCHINENRING AKTUELL
QUARTERLY JOURNAL OF INTERNATIONAL AGRICULTURE
RURAL 21
ZEITSCHRIFT FÜR BEWÄSSERUNGSWIRTSCHAFT

DMB-MIETERVEREIN BOCHUM, HATTINGEN UND UMGEGEND E.V. 685545
Brückstr. 58, 44787 BOCHUM **Tel:** 234 961140
Fax: 234 9611411
Email: info@mvbo.de
Web site: http://www.mvbo.de

Titles:
MIETERFORUM

DMB-VERLAG VERLAGS- UND VERWALTUNGSGES. DES DEUTSCHEN MIETERBUNDES MBH 685619
Littenstr. 10, 10179 BERLIN **Tel:** 30 223230
Fax: 30 22323100
Email: info@mieterbund.de
Web site: http://www.mieterbund.de

Titles:
MIETERZEITUNG

DÖBELNER VERLAGSGES. MBH 680829
Rosa-Luxemburg-Str. 5, 04720 DÖBELN
Tel: 3431 71940 **Fax:** 3431 719499
Email: da.verlag@dd-v.de
Web site: http://www.doebelneranzeiger.de

Titles:
DÖBELNER ANZEIGER

DOCMATISCHE GESELLSCHAFT VERLAGS GMBH 1783689
Wallstr. 28, 21335 LÜNEBURG **Tel:** 4131 2661195
Email: redaktion@docma.info
Web site: http://www.docma.info

Titles:
DOCMA

DOGAN MEDIA INTERNATIONAL GMBH 1632823
An der Brücke 20, 64546 MÖRFELDEN-WALLDORF **Tel:** 6105 327130 **Fax:** 6105 327999
Email: verlag@dogan-media.com
Web site: http://www.doganmedia.de

Titles:
HÜRRIYET - DEUTSCHLANDAUSG. D. TÜRK. TAGESZTG.

DOLDEMEDIEN VERLAG GMBH 680030
Postwiesenstr. 5a, 70327 STUTTGART
Tel: 711 134660 **Fax:** 711 1346668
Email: info@doldemedien.de
Web site: http://www.doldemedien.de

Titles:
CAMPING CARS & CARAVANS
CAMPINGIMPULSE
REISEMOBIL INTERNATIONAL
REISEMOBIL INTERNATIONAL BORDATLAS

DOMOWINA-VERLAG GMBH 1650341
Tuchmacherstr. 27, 02625 BAUTZEN
Tel: 3591 5770 **Fax:** 3591 577243
Email: geschaeftsfuehrung@domowina-verlag.de
Web site: http://www.domowina-verlag.de

Titles:
SERBSKE NOWINY

DONAUKURIER VERLAGSGES. MBH & CO. KG 677453
Stauffenbergstr. 2a, 85051 INGOLSTADT
Tel: 841 96660 **Fax:** 841 9666255
Email: redaktion@donaukurier.de
Web site: http://www.donaukurier.de

Titles:
DONAUKURIER
DONAUKURIER.DE
EICHSTÄTTER KURIER
HILPOLTSTEINER KURIER
PFAFFENHOFENER KURIER
SCHROBENHAUSENER ZEITUNG

DOPPEL D WERBESERVICE 1650187
Alt Fermersleben 77, 39122 MAGDEBURG
Tel: 391 4011000 **Fax:** 391 5419805
Email: mdkurier@aol.com

Titles:
MAGDEBURGER KURIER

DORSTENER UND HALTERNER ZEITUNGSVERLAGSGES. MBH & CO. KG 1638606
Südwall 27, 46282 DORSTEN **Tel:** 2362 92770
Fax: 2362 927729

Titles:
DORSTENER ZEITUNG
HALTERNER ZEITUNG

DOW JONES NEWS GMBH, BEREICH BUSINESS NEWSLETTERS 679982
Wilhelm-Leuschner-Str. 78, 60329 FRANKFURT
Tel: 69 29725163 **Fax:** 69 29725160
Web site: http://www.djnewsletters.de

Titles:
DOW JONES ENERGY WEEKLY

DOZ-VERLAG OPTISCHE FACHVERÖFFENTLICHUNG GMBH 680879
Luisenstr. 14, 69115 HEIDELBERG
Tel: 6221 905170 **Fax:** 6221 905171
Email: doz@doz-verlag.de
Web site: http://www.doz-verlag.de

Titles:
DOZ OPTOMETRIE & FASHION

DPW VERLAGSGES. MBH 678624
Borsigstr. 1, 63150 HEUSENSTAMM
Tel: 6104 6060 **Fax:** 6104 606317

Titles:
AVR ALLGEMEINER VLIESSTOFF-REPORT

DR. BREITSOHL VERLAGSGES. MBH 678423
Löffelstr. 1, 70597 STUTTGART **Tel:** 711 7696370
Fax: 711 76963729
Email: info@breitsohl.de
Web site: http://www.breitsohl.de

Titles:
DIE NEWS

DR. CURT HAEFNER-VERLAG GMBH 677460
Dischingerstr. 8, 69123 HEIDELBERG
Tel: 6221 644660 **Fax:** 6221 644640
Email: info@haefner-verlag.de
Web site: http://www.haefner-verlag.de

Titles:
DGUV FAKTOR ARBEITSSCHUTZ
ERGO-MED
FERRUM
MENSCH & BÜRO
PAPIER + TECHNIK
PHARMAREPORT
SICHERHEITSBEAUFTRAGTER
SICHERHEITSINGENIEUR
ZENTRALBLATT FÜR ARBEITSMEDIZIN, ARBEITSSCHUTZ UND ERGONOMIE

DR. GUPTA VERLAG 682297
Am Stadion 3b, 40878 RATINGEN
Tel: 2102 93450 **Fax:** 2102 934520
Email: info@gupta-verlag.de
Web site: http://www.gupta-verlag.de

Titles:
GAK GUMMI-FASERN-KUNSTSTOFFE

DR. HARNISCH VERLAGSGES. MBH 680516
Blumenstr. 15, 90402 NÜRNBERG **Tel:** 911 20180
Fax: 911 2018100
Email: service@harnisch.com
Web site: http://www.harnisch.com

Titles:
DEDICA
DRINK TECHNOLOGY & MARKETING
ELEMENT + BAU
FNG-MAGAZIN
FOOD TECHNOLOGIE
GETRÄNKE!
HYGIENE REPORT
PUK PROZESSTECHNIK UND KOMPONENTEN
WIN WOODWORKING INTERNATIONAL

DR. ING. H.C. F. PORSCHE AG 680184
Porscheplatz 1, 70435 STUTTGART
Tel: 711 91125278 **Fax:** 711 91125208
Email: cpm@porsche.de
Web site: http://www.porsche.com/christophorus

Titles:
CHRISTOPHORUS

DR. JOSEF RAABE VERLAGS-GMBH 689828
Kaiser-Friedrich-Str. 90, 10585 BERLIN
Tel: 30 2129870 **Fax:** 30 21298730
Email: umweltbriefe@raabe.de
Web site: http://www.umweltbriefe.de

Titles:
UMWELTBRIEFE

DR. KLAUS-PETER KALWITZKI 690098
Eduardstr. 4, 45468 MÜLHEIM **Tel:** 208 33031
Fax: 208 3881588
Email: redaktion@verkehrszeichen-online.de
Web site: http://www.verkehrszeichen-online.de

Titles:
VERKEHRSZEICHEN

DR. MARTIN STEFFAN MEDIA 1773869
Markgrafenstr. 3, 33602 BIELEFELD
Tel: 521 5251310 **Fax:** 521 5251311
Email: redaktion@autogas-journal.de
Web site: http://www.autogas-journal.de

Titles:
DAS AUTOGAS JOURNAL

DR. NEINHAUS VERLAG AG 677420
Wollgrasweg 31, 70599 STUTTGART
Tel: 711 451275 **Fax:** 711 456603
Email: info@neinhaus-verlag.de
Web site: http://www.neinhaus-verlag.de

Titles:
AGRARGEWERBLICHE WIRTSCHAFT
GARTENBAU IN BADEN-WÜRTTEMBERG
DER JÄGER IN BADEN-WÜRTTEMBERG
LANDPOST
DER WALDWIRT

DR. R. KADEN VERLAG GMBH & CO. KG 678487
Maaßstr. 32/1, 69123 HEIDELBERG
Tel: 6221 1377610 **Fax:** 6221 29910
Email: info@kaden-verlag.de
Web site: http://www.kaden-verlag.de

Titles:
DER AUGENARZT
CHIRURGISCHE ALLGEMEINE
HNO KOMPAKT
OPHTHALMOCHIRURGIE
PLASTISCHE CHIRURGIE
ZPA

DR. ROLF M. WOLF MEDIA GMBH 682219
Lindemannstr. 12, 40237 DÜSSELDORF
Tel: 211 991040 **Fax:** 211 663162
Email: info@fruchthandel.de
Web site: http://www.fruchthandel.de

Titles:
FRUCHTHANDEL MAGAZIN

DR. VOLLMER GMBH 1732274
Siegfriedstr. 5, 63785 OBERNBURG
Tel: 6022 61980 **Fax:** 6022 619823
Email: redaktion@tk-report.de
Web site: http://www.tk-report.de

Titles:
TKREPORT

DR. WIMMERSHOF GMBH + CO. 689991
Marktplatz 15, 71665 VAIHINGEN **Tel:** 7042 9190
Fax: 7042 91955
Email: info@vkz.de
Web site: http://www.vkz.de

Titles:
VAIHINGER KREISZEITUNG
WOCHENBLATT + SACHSENHEIM POST

DREI BRUNNEN VERLAG GMBH & CO. KG 681491
Heusee 19, 73655 PLÜDERHAUSEN
Tel: 7181 86020 **Fax:** 7181 860229
Email: mail@drei-brunnen-verlag.de
Web site: http://www.drei-brunnen-verlag.de

Titles:
ECC EUROPA CAMPING + CARAVANING
FERIEN-BUNGALOW-FÜHRER

DRESDNER DRUCK- UND VERLAGSHAUS GMBH & CO. KG 680140
Ostra-Allee 20, 01067 DRESDEN **Tel:** 351 48640
Fax: 351 48642800
Email: sz.geschaeftsfuehrung@dd-v.de
Web site: http://www.sz-online.de

Titles:
CHEMNITZER MORGENPOST
DRESDNER MORGENPOST
MORGENPOST AM SONNTAG
SZ-ONLINE.DE

DRESDNER MAGAZIN VERLAG GMBH 678497
Ostra-Allee 18, 01067 DRESDEN
Tel: 351 48642408 **Fax:** 351 48642679
Email: info@maz-online.de

Titles:
AUGUSTO
MAZ MOTOR AUTO ZEITUNG - AUSG. CHEMNITZ

DRUCK- UND PRESSEHAUS NAUMANN GMBH & CO. KG 679843
Gutenbergstr. 1, 63571 GELNHAUSEN
Tel: 6051 833201 **Fax:** 6051 833230
Email: redaktion@gnz.de
Web site: http://www.gnz.de

Titles:
GELNHÄUSER NEUE ZEITUNG

DRUCK & SERVICE GARHAMMER GMBH 1638605
Straßfeld 5, 94209 REGEN **Tel:** 9921 904093
Fax: 9921 904094
Email: info@garhammer-druck.de

Titles:
DA WAIDLER

DRUCK + VERLAG ERNST VÖGEL GMBH 678906
Kalvarienbergstr. 22, 93491 STAMSRIED
Tel: 9466 94000 **Fax:** 9466 1276
Email: voegel@voegel.com
Web site: http://www.verlag-voegel.de

Titles:
DAS BAYERISCHE KAMINKEHRERHANDWERK
BR BAURECHTS-REPORT
PLANERRECHTS-REPORT
VERGABERECHTS-REPORT

DRUCK UND VERLAG KONRAD KIRCH GMBH 689193
Bahnhofstr. 18, 48607 OCHTRUP **Tel:** 2553 93940
Fax: 2553 3000
Email: info@tageblatt-online.de
Web site: http://www.tageblatt-online.de

Titles:
TAGEBLATT FÜR DEN KREIS STEINFURT

DRUCK + VERLAG O. HUNDT GMBH & CO. KG 689069
An der Lohmühle 7, 58840 PLETTENBERG
Tel: 2391 90930 **Fax:** 2391 10904
Email: st@mzv.net
Web site: http://www.suederlaender-tageblatt.de

Titles:
SÜDERLÄNDER TAGEBLATT

DRUCK- UND VERLAGSANSTALT NEUE PRESSE GMBH 1752022
Steinweg 51, 96450 COBURG **Tel:** 9561 8500
Fax: 9561 850110
Email: verlag@np-coburg.de
Web site: http://www.np-coburg.de

Titles:
NEUE PRESSE

DRUCK- UND VERLAGSGES. BIETIGHEIM MBH 679314
Kronenbergstr. 10, 74321 BIETIGHEIM-BISSINGEN **Tel:** 7142 4030 **Fax:** 7142 403125
Email: info@bietigheimerzeitung.de
Web site: http://www.bietigheimerzeitung.de

Titles:
BIETIGHEIMER ZEITUNG
BÖNNIGHEIMER ZEITUNG
SACHSENHEIMER ZEITUNG

DRUCK- UND VERLAGSGES. KÖHRING GMBH & CO. KG 681204
Wallstr. 22, 29439 LÜCHOW **Tel:** 5841 1270
Fax: 5841 127350
Email: ejz@ejz.de
Web site: http://www.ejz.de

Titles:
ELBE-JEETZEL-ZEITUNG

DRUCK + VERLAGSGES. SÜDWEST MBH 678630
Ostring 6, 76131 KARLSRUHE **Tel:** 721 62830
Fax: 721 628310
Email: info@druck-verlag-sw.de
Web site: http://www.druck-verlag-sw.de

Titles:
EISENBAHN-LANDWIRT
HAUS UND GARTEN
HESSISCHER KLEINGÄRTNER
SENIORENBLICKPUNKT

DRUCK- UND VERLAGSHAUS E. WEIDENBACH GMBH & CO. KG 680751
Rathausstr. 1, 35683 DILLENBURG
Tel: 2771 8740 **Fax:** 2771 874220
Email: anzeigen@dill.de
Web site: http://www.dill.de

Titles:
DILL-ZEITUNG
DILL-ZEITUNG AM SONNTAG
HAIGERER KURIER
HAIGERER KURIER AM SONNTAG
HERBORNER ECHO
HERBORNER ECHO AM SONNTAG

DRUCK- UND VERLAGSHAUS FRANKFURT AM MAIN GMBH 1717723
Karl-Gerold-Platz 1, 60594 FRANKFURT
Tel: 69 21991 **Fax:** 69 21993421
Email: chefredaktion@fr-online.de
Web site: http://www.fr-online.de

Titles:
FRANKFURTER RUNDSCHAU
FRANKFURTER RUNDSCHAU AM FREITAG MITTAG
HEIMSPIEL

DRUCK + VERLAGSHAUS HERMANN DANIEL GMBH + CO. KG 682767
Grünewaldstr. 15, 72336 BALINGEN
Tel: 7433 2660 **Fax:** 7433 266201
Email: zak@zak.de
Web site: http://www.zak.de

Titles:
IBN
ZOLLERN-ALB KURIER

DRUCK- UND VERLAGSHAUS HÜPKE & SOHN WESERLAND-VERLAG GMBH 688085
Zeppelinstr. 10, 37603 HOLZMINDEN
Tel: 5531 93040 **Fax:** 5531 930441
Email: info@tah.de
Web site: http://www.tah.de

Titles:
SCHAUFENSTER
TÄGLICHER ANZEIGER

DRUCK- UND VERLAGSHAUS J. C. ERHARDT GMBH 677571
Bahnhofstr. 18, 31832 SPRINGE **Tel:** 5041 7890
Fax: 5041 78989
Web site: http://www.ndz.de

Titles:
NEUE DEISTER-ZEITUNG

DRUCK- UND VERLAGSHAUS ZARBOCK GMBH & CO. KG 1650984
Sontraer Str. 6, 60386 FRANKFURT
Tel: 69 42090372 **Fax:** 69 42090370
Email: verlag@zarbock.de
Web site: http://www.zarbock.de

Titles:
OFFENBACHER WIRTSCHAFT

DRUCKEREI RICHARD MACK GMBH & CO. KG 687719
Friedenstr. 9, 97638 MELLRICHSTADT
Tel: 9776 81210 **Fax:** 9776 812133
Email: tr@mack-druck.de
Web site: http://www.mack-druck.de

Titles:
RHÖN- UND STREUBOTE

DRUCKEREI STARK GMBH 682424
Benzstr. 24, 76316 MALSCH **Tel:** 7246 922828
Fax: 7246 922879
Email: anzeiger@druckerei-stark.de
Web site: http://www.druckerei-stark.de

Titles:
GEMEINDE ANZEIGER

DRUCKEREI UND VERLAG ENNO SÖKER 697830
Marienkamper Str. 1, 26427 ESENS
Tel: 4971 91050 **Fax:** 4971 910550
Email: info@soeker-druck.de
Web site: http://www.soeker-druck.de

Titles:
DE UTKIEKER

DRUCKHAUS GRATZFELD GMBH & CO. KG 679996
Langgasse 16, 35510 BUTZBACH
Tel: 6033 96060 **Fax:** 6033 960649
Email: mail@butzbacher-zeitung.de
Web site: http://www.butzbacher-zeitung.de

Titles:
BUTZBACHER ZEITUNG

DRUCKHAUS WAIBLINGEN REMSTAL-BOTE GMBH 1621276
Albrecht-Villinger-Str. 10, 71332 WAIBLINGEN
Tel: 7151 5660 **Fax:** 7151 566323
Web site: http://www.dhw.de

Titles:
IHK MAGAZIN WIRTSCHAFT

DRUCKSPIEGEL VERLAGSGES. MBH & CO. KG 680943
Borsigstr. 1, 63150 HEUSENSTAMM
Tel: 6104 6060 **Fax:** 6104 606444
Email: ds@kepplermediengruppe.de
Web site: http://www.druckspiegel.de

Titles:
DER DRUCKSPIEGEL

DRW-VERLAG WEINBRENNER GMBH & CO. KG 679189
Fasanenweg 18, 70771 LEINFELDEN-ECHTERDINGEN **Tel:** 711 75910 **Fax:** 711 7591217
Email: info@drw-verlag.de
Web site: http://www.drw-verlag.de

Titles:
DESIGN + BESCHLAG MAGAZIN
EXAKT
FURNIER MAGAZIN
HK HOLZ- UND KUNSTSTOFFVERARBEITUNG
HOLZBAU MAGAZIN
HOLZ-ZENTRALBLATT
LAMINAT MAGAZIN
MDF MAGAZIN

DSV DEUTSCHER SPORTVERLAG GMBH 677604
Im Mediapark 8, 50670 KÖLN **Tel:** 221 25870
Fax: 221 2587200
Email: kontakt@sportverlag.de
Web site: http://www.sportverlag.de

Titles:
BOX SPORT
SPORT-WELT
VOLLBLUT

DUH UMWELTSCHUTZ-SERVICE GMBH 1753291
Fritz-Reichle-Ring 4, 78315 RADOLFZELL
Tel: 7732 99950 **Fax:** 7732 999577

Titles:
ZEO2

DUKE COMMUNICATIONS GMBH 686397
Zugspitzstr. 7, 86932 PÜRGEN **Tel:** 8196 7084
Fax: 8196 1239
Email: iabenthum@newsolutions.de
Web site: http://www.newsolutions.de

Titles:
NEWSOLUTIONS

DÜKER GMBH & CO. KGAA 680960
Hauptstr. 39, 63846 LAUFACH **Tel:** 6093 870
Fax: 6093 87246
Email: info@dueker.de
Web site: http://www.dueker.de

Titles:
DÜKER NACHRICHTEN

DUMMY VERLAG GMBH 1731688
Torstr. 109, 10119 BERLIN **Tel:** 30 300230233
Fax: 30 300230231
Email: redaktion@dummy-magazin.de
Web site: http://www.dummy-magazin.de

Titles:
DUMMY

DUMONT REISEVERLAG GMBH & CO. KG 683055
Marco-Polo-Str. 1, 73760 OSTFILDERN
Tel: 711 45020 **Fax:** 711 4502135
Email: info@dumontreise.de
Web site: http://www.dumontreise.de

Titles:
DUMONT BILDATLAS

DUNCKER & HUMBLOT GMBH 678079
Carl-Heinrich-Becker-Weg 9, 12165 BERLIN
Tel: 30 7900060 **Fax:** 30 79000631
Email: info@duncker-humblot.de
Web site: http://www.duncker-humblot.de

Titles:
APPLIED ECONOMICS QUARTERLY
KREDIT UND KAPITAL
SOZIALER FORTSCHRITT
DIE VERWALTUNG
ZEITSCHRIFT FÜR HISTORISCHE FORSCHUNG

DURCHBLICK-SIEGEN INFORMATION UND MEDIEN E.V. 1775470
Marienborner Str. 151, 57074 SIEGEN
Tel: 271 61647
Email: redaktion@durchblick-siegen.de
Web site: http://www.durchblick-siegen.de

Titles:
DURCHBLICK

DÜSI COMPUTER SOFTWARE 1652598
Römerturmstr. 25, 73547 LORCH
Tel: 7172 926060 **Fax:** 7172 9260699
Email: info@duesicomputersoftware.de
Web site: http://www.duesicomputersoftware.de

Titles:
WWW.ONLINESPIELE.DE

DIE DÜSSELDORFER BRANCHEN VERLAGS GMBH 1641055
Wielandstr. 24, 40699 ERKRATH
Tel: 211 5203091 **Fax:** 211 5203092
Email: info@branchen-duesseldorf.de
Web site: http://www.branchen-duesseldorf.de

Titles:
DÜSSELDORFER BRANCHEN

DÜSSELDORF-EXPRESS GMBH & CO. KG 680968
Königsallee 27, 40212 DÜSSELDORF
Tel: 211 13930 **Fax:** 211 324835
Email: duesseldorf@express.de
Web site: http://www.express.de

Titles:
DÜSSELDORF EXPRESS

DUSTRI-VERLAG DR. KARL FEISTLE GMBH & CO. KG 678433
Bajuwarenring 4, 82041 OBERHACHING
Tel: 89 6138610 **Fax:** 89 6135412
Email: info@dustri.de
Web site: http://www.dustri.de

Titles:
ALLERGOLOGIE
ATEMWEGS- UND LUNGENKRANKHEITEN
CLINICAL NEUROPATHOLOGY
DERMATOLOGIE IN BERUF UND UMWELT
INTENSIV- UND NOTFALLBEHANDLUNG
INTERNATIONAL JOURNAL OF CLINICAL PHARMACOLOGY AND THERAPEUTICS
NEUROPSYCHIATRIE
NIEREN- UND HOCHDRUCKKRANKHEITEN
PRÄVENTION UND REHABILITATION
TRACE ELEMENTS AND ELECTROLYTES
VERDAUUNGSKRANKHEITEN

DVS MEDIA GMBH 683962
Aachener Str. 172, 40223 DÜSSELDORF
Tel: 211 15910 **Fax:** 211 1591150
Email: media@dvs-hg.de
Web site: http://www.dvs-media.info

Titles:
JAHRBUCH SCHWEISSTECHNIK
DER PRAKTIKER
SCHWEISSEN UND SCHNEIDEN
WELDING AND CUTTING

DVS-WIRTSCHAFTSGES. MBH 690115
Breite Str. 98, 53111 BONN **Tel:** 228 982230
Fax: 228 631651
Email: wirtschaftsgesellschaft@dvs-schutzverband.de
Web site: http://www.dvs-schutzverband.de

Titles:
DIE VERSICHERUNGSPRAXIS

DVV MEDIA GROUP GMBH 677469
Nordkanalstr. 36, 20097 HAMBURG
Tel: 40 2371401 **Fax:** 40 23714244
Email: info@dvvmedia.com
Web site: http://www.dvvmedia.com

Titles:
DVZ BRIEF
DVZ DEUTSCHE LOGISTIK-ZEITUNG
EI DER EISENBAHNINGENIEUR
EIK EISENBAHN INGENIEUR KALENDER
INTERNATIONALES VERKEHRSWESEN
LOG. KOMPASS
OFFIZIELLES SPEDITEUR-ADRESSBUCH
QUER DURCH HAMBURG/SCHLESWIG-HOLSTEIN SCHIFFFAHRT UND TRANSPORT
RTR EUROPEAN RAIL TECHNOLOGY REVIEW
SCHIFF & HAFEN
SIGNAL + DRAHT

DVW HESSEN E.V. GESELLSCHAFT FÜR GEODÄSIE, GEOINFORMATON UND LANDMANAGEMENT 681007
Schaperstr. 16, 65195 WIESBADEN
Tel: 611 5355345 **Fax:** 611 5355490
Email: bernhard.heckmann@hvbg.hessen.de
Web site: http://www.dvwhessen.de

Titles:
DVW MITTEILUNGEN HESSEN-THÜRINGEN

DVZ-VERLAGS-GMBH 1784743
Daniel-Vorländer-Str. 6, 06120 HALLE
Tel: 345 6932554 **Fax:** 345 6932555
Email: verlag@dvz-halle.de
Web site: http://www.ausschreibungsanzeiger.com

Titles:
AUSSCHREIBUNGSANZEIGER SACHSEN-ANHALT

DWA DEUTSCHE VEREINIGUNG FÜR WASSERWIRTSCHAFT, ABWASSER UND ABFALL E.V. 1686029
Theodor-Heuss-Allee 17, 53773 HENNEF
Tel: 2242 8720 **Fax:** 2242 872135
Web site: http://www.dwa.de

Titles:
GEWÄSSER-INFO

DWJ VERLAGS-GMBH 1677343
Rudolf-Diesel-Str. 46, 74572 BLAUFELDEN
Tel: 7953 97870 **Fax:** 7953 9787880
Email: info@dwj-verlag.de
Web site: http://www.dwj.de

Titles:
DWJ DEUTSCHES WAFFEN-JOURNAL

EAT SMARTER GMBH & CO. KG 1770671
Schulterblatt 58, 20357 HAMBURG
Email: info@eatsmarter.de
Web site: http://www.eatsmarter.de

Titles:
EATSMARTER!

EBERHARD A. BREINLINGER VERLAG 689179
Rheinallee 71, 53173 BONN **Tel:** 228 363433
Fax: 228 363401
Email: e.breinlinger@szeneonline.de
Web site: http://www.szeneonline.de

Titles:
SZENE KÖLN / BONN

EBERL MEDIEN GMBH & CO. KG 1605942
Kirchplatz 6, 87509 IMMENSTADT **Tel:** 8323 8020
Fax: 8323 802112
Email: info@eberl.de
Web site: http://www.eberl.de

Titles:
ALLGÄUER ANZEIGEBLATT

EBNER VERLAG GMBH & CO KG 677918
Karlstr. 41, 89073 ULM **Tel:** 731 152002
Fax: 731 1520175
Email: info@ebnerverlag.de
Web site: http://www.ebnerverlag.de

Titles:
CHRONOS
EYEBIZZ
FEUERWEHR MAGAZIN
KLASSIK UHREN
NATURSTEIN
RETTUNGS MAGAZIN
UHREN MAGAZIN
VFDB ZEITSCHRIFT

EC-GMBH, INCENTIVE-, MARKETING- & CONSULTING GES. 1600483
Keltenring 22, 85658 EGMATING **Tel:** 8095 87260
Fax: 8095 872629
Email: ec@icj-mm.de
Web site: http://www.icj-mm.de

Titles:
ICJ MICE MAGAZINE

ECHO ANZEIGENBLATT GMBH & CO. KG 681444
Zeppelinstr. 116, 73730 ESSLINGEN
Tel: 711 7587000 **Fax:** 711 758700148
Email: esslingen@ihr-wochenblatt-echo.de
Web site: http://www.ihr-wochenblatt-echo.de

Titles:
ESSLINGER ECHO
NÜRTINGER ECHO

ECHO KREATIVPLANUNG GMBH 680817
Holzhofallee 25, 64295 DARMSTADT
Tel: 6151 387223 **Fax:** 6151 387525
Email: verlag@echo-kp.de
Web site: http://www.echo-kreativplanung.de

Titles:
D.M.K DIE MODERNE KÜCHE

ECHO ZEITUNGEN GMBH 680488
Holzhofallee 25, 64295 DARMSTADT
Tel: 6151 3871 **Fax:** 6151 387383
Web site: http://www.echo-online.de

Titles:
DARMSTÄDTER ECHO

GROSS-GERAUER ECHO
ODENWÄLDER ECHO
RÜSSELSHEIMER ECHO
STARKENBURGER ECHO
WIRTSCHAFTSECHO

ECOMED MEDIZIN, VERLAGSGRUPPE HÜTHIG JEHLE REHM GMBH 681336
Justus-von-Liebig-Str. 1, 86899 LANDSBERG
Tel: 8191 1250 **Fax:** 8191 125492
Email: info@ecomed.de
Web site: http://www.ecomed-medizin.de

Titles:
IMPFDIALOG
SUCHTMEDIZIN IN FORSCHUNG UND PRAXIS
UMWELTMEDIZIN IN FORSCHUNG UND PRAXIS

ECOMED SICHERHEIT VERLAGSGRUPPE HÜTHIG JEHLE REHM GMBH 682387
Justus-von-Liebig-Str. 1, 86899 LANDSBERG
Tel: 8191 125295 **Fax:** 8191 125151
Email: info@ecomed.de
Web site: http://www.ecomed-sicherheit.de

Titles:
GEFAHRGUT AKTUELL

ECON VERLAG 1758061
Friedrichstr. 126, 10117 BERLIN **Tel:** 30 23456300
Fax: 30 23456303
Web site: http://www.econ.de

Titles:
JAHRBUCH DER WERBUNG

ECONA INTERNET AG 1762136
Chausseestr. 8, 10115 BERLIN **Tel:** 30 9210640
Fax: 30 92106431
Email: info@econa.com
Web site: http://www.econa.com

Titles:
GIGA.DE
WINLOAD.DE

ECONOMY.ONE GMBH 1741773
Kasernenstr. 67, 40213 DÜSSELDORF
Tel: 211 8870 **Fax:** 211 8872980
Web site: http://www.vhb.de

Titles:
KARRIERE.DE
WIWO.DE

ECOREPORTER.DE AG 1651718
Weidenbohrerweg 15, 44269 DORTMUND
Tel: 231 47735960 **Fax:** 231 47735961
Email: info@ecoreporter.de
Web site: http://www.ecoreporter.de

Titles:
ECOREPORTER

ECV-EDITIO CANTOR VERLAG FÜR MEDIZIN UND NATURWISSENSCHAFTEN GMBH 678372
Baendelstockweg 20, 88326 AULENDORF
Tel: 7525 9400 **Fax:** 7525 940180
Email: info@ecv.de
Web site: http://www.ecv.de

Titles:
ARZNEIMFORSCH DRUGRES
ARZNEIMITTEL FORSCHUNG DRUG RESEARCH
PHARMIND DIE PHARMAZEUTISCHE INDUSTRIE

EDEKA VERLAGSGES. MBH 682963
New-York-Ring 6, 22297 HAMBURG
Tel: 40 63772469 **Fax:** 40 63772570
Email: verlag@edeka.de
Web site: http://www.edeka-handelsrundschau.de

Titles:
HANDELSRUNDSCHAU

EDITION LIT. EUROPE MEYER/ MÜLLER GBR 679430
Monumentenstr. 26, 10965 BERLIN
Tel: 30 7868547 **Fax:** 30 7866215
Email: blattgold.berlin@snafu.de
Web site: http://www.blattgold-berlin.de

Titles:
BLATTGOLD

EDITION PROFESSIONELL 678886
Im Ried 4, 79429 MALSBURG **Tel:** 7626 977410
Fax: 7626 977419
Email: info@ed-pro.de
Web site: http://www.ed-pro.de

Titles:
EDITION PROFESSIONELL - AUSG. BAU

EDITION SIGMA 689269
Leuschnerdamm 13, 10999 BERLIN
Tel: 30 6232363 **Fax:** 30 6239393
Email: verlag@edition-sigma.de
Web site: http://www.edition-sigma.de

Titles:
TECHNIKGESCHICHTE

EDITION STIFTERVERBAND - VERWALTUNGSGES. FÜR WISSENSCHAFTSPFLEGE MBH 690680
Barkhovenallee 1, 45239 ESSEN **Tel:** 201 8401181
Fax: 201 8401459
Email: wuw@stifterverband.de
Web site: http://www.stifterverband.de

Titles:
WIRTSCHAFT & WISSENSCHAFT

EDITION TEXT + KRITIK IM RICHARD BOORBERG VERLAG GMBH & CO KG 678780
Levelingstr. 6a, 81673 MÜNCHEN
Tel: 89 43600012 **Fax:** 89 43600019
Email: info@etk-muenchen.de
Web site: http://www.etk-muenchen.de

Titles:
MUSIK-KONZEPTE

EFFILEE GMBH 1757868
Rothenbaumchaussee 73, 20148 HAMBURG
Tel: 40 809053580 **Fax:** 40 809053822
Email: info@effilee.de
Web site: http://www.effilee.de

Titles:
EFFILEE

EFFIZIENZ-AGENTUR NRW 681111
Mülheimer Str. 100, 47057 DUISBURG
Tel: 203 3787930 **Fax:** 203 3787944
Email: efa@efanrw.de
Web site: http://www.efanrw.de

Titles:
EFA FORUM

EGMONT EHAPA VERLAG GMBH 679050
Wallstr. 59, 10179 BERLIN **Tel:** 30 240080
Fax: 30 24008599
Email: info@ehapa-service.de
Web site: http://www.ehapa.de

Titles:
BARBIE
BENJAMIN BLÜMCHEN
BIBI BLOCKSBERG
BIBI & TINA
DISNEY EINFACH TIERISCH
DISNEY PRINZESSIN
DISNEY WINNIE PUUH
GO GIRL
LÖWENZAHN
SPONGEBOB
WALT DISNEY MICKY MAUS MAGAZIN
WENDY
WITCH

EHEMALIGENVERBAND SCHÖNBRUNN-WEIHENSTEPHAN E.V. 1621202
Am Lurzenhof 3, 84036 LANDSHUT
Tel: 871 9521100 **Fax:** 871 9521102
Email: ehemaligenverb.scheller@freenet.de
Web site: http://www.ehemaligenverband.de

Titles:
EHEMALIGENVERBAND SCHÖNBRUNN-WEIHENSTEPHAN MITTEILUNGEN

EHI RETAIL INSTITUTE GMBH 687660
Spichernstr. 55, 50672 KÖLN **Tel:** 221 5799364
Fax: 221 5799345
Email: vertrieb@ehi.org
Web site: http://www.ehi.org

Titles:
RT RETAIL TECHNOLOGY
STORES + SHOPS

EIERS INC & CO. KG 1791543
Saarlouiser Str. 18, 80997 MÜNCHEN
Tel: 89 381697750 **Fax:** 89 381697759
Email: info@senioren-und-pflegemagazin.de
Web site: http://www.senioren-und-pflegemagazin.de

Titles:
SENIOREN- UND PFLEGEMAGAZIN

EIGENVERLAG THOMAS BULLMANN 1758521
Waldstr. 226, 63071 OFFENBACH
Tel: 69 80106782 **Fax:** 69 80106784
Email: info@frizz-offenbach.de
Web site: http://www.frizz-offenbach.de

Titles:
FRIZZ

EILBOTE BOOMGAARDEN VERLAG GMBH 681134
Winsener Landstr. 7, 21423 WINSEN
Tel: 4171 78350 **Fax:** 4171 783535
Email: verlag@eilbote-online.de
Web site: http://www.eilbote-online.de

Titles:
EILBOTE

EINHORN-PRESSE VERLAG GMBH 697353
Neuer Wall 80, 20354 HAMBURG **Tel:** 40 3615750
Fax: 40 36157516
Email: info@einhorn-presse-verlag.de
Web site: http://www.einhorn-presse-verlag.de

Titles:
HCP JOURNAL
JOURNAL DER DEUTSCHEN GESELLSCHAFT FÜR PLASTISCHE UND WIEDERHERSTELLUNGSCHIRURGIE E.V.

EINKAUFSBÜRO DEUTSCHER EISENHÄNDLER GMBH 687446
EDE-Platz 1, 42389 WUPPERTAL
Tel: 202 6096865 **Fax:** 202 609670739
Email: wolfgang.pott@ede.de
Web site: http://www.ede.de

Titles:
PVH MAGAZIN

EISENBAHN- UND VERKEHRSGEWERKSCHAFT 689592
Chausseestr. 84, 10115 BERLIN **Tel:** 30 42439075
Fax: 30 42439071
Email: redaktion@evg-online.org
Web site: http://www.evg-online.org

Titles:
EVG IMTAKT

EISENWAREN-ZEITUNG GMBH 681190
Eichendorffstr. 3, 40474 DÜSSELDORF
Tel: 211 4705066 **Fax:** 211 4705064
Email: ez.hz@gmx.de
Web site: http://www.ez-hz.de

Titles:
EZ TOOLS & TRADE EISENWAREN-ZEITUNG
HZ HAUSRAT-ZEITUNG HAUSHALT & ELEKTRO

EISSPORTCLUB PEITING 693286
Alfons-Peter-Str. 4, 86971 PEITING
Tel: 8861 68232 **Fax:** 8861 68231
Email: info@ecpeiting.de
Web site: http://www.ecpeiting.de

Titles:
OVERTIME

EK-VERLAG GMBH 681184
Lörracher Str. 16, 79115 FREIBURG
Tel: 761 703100 **Fax:** 761 7031050
Email: service@eisenbahn-kurier.de
Web site: http://www.eisenbahn-kurier.de

Titles:
EISENBAHN KURIER
STADTVERKEHR

ELBE-WOCHENBLATT VERLAGSGES. MBH & CO. KG 677726
Harburger Rathausstr. 40, 21073 HAMBURG
Tel: 40 7660000 **Fax:** 40 76600024
Email: info@elbe-wochenblatt-verlag.de
Web site: http://www.elbe-wochenblatt.de

Titles:
ALTONAER WOCHENBLATT
EIDELSTEDTER WOCHENBLATT
ELBVORORTE WOCHENBLATT
HARBURGER WOCHENBLATT
LURUPER WOCHENBLATT
SÜDERELBE WOCHENBLATT
WILHELMSBURGER WOCHENBLATT

ELEKTOR-VERLAG GMBH 681212
Süsterfeldstr. 25, 52072 AACHEN **Tel:** 241 889090
Fax: 241 8890977
Email: info@elektor.de
Web site: http://www.elektor.de

Titles:
ELEKTOR

ELEMENT VERLAG GMBH & CO BETRIEBS KG 682257
Ernst-Heinkel-Str. 4/2, 70734 FELLBACH
Tel: 711 5057165 **Fax:** 711 5057166
Email: element-verlag@t-online.de
Web site: http://www.elementverlag.de

Titles:
F+I-BAU BAUEN MIT SYSTEMEN

ELITE MAGAZINVERLAGS GMBH 1761241
Boslerstr. 29, 71088 HOLZGERLINGEN
Tel: 7031 7440 **Fax:** 7031 744195
Email: verlag@wissen-karriere.com
Web site: http://www.wissen-karriere.com

Titles:
MONEYMAKER
WISSEN+KARRIERE

ELLA VERLAG ELKE LATUPERISA E.K. 697978
Emil-Hoffmann-Str. 55, 50999 KÖLN
Tel: 2236 84880 **Fax:** 2236 380233
Email: info@ella-verlag.de
Web site: http://www.ella-verlag.de

Titles:
CITY FASZINATIONEN
CITY FASZINATIONEN WEIHNACHTSMARKT
GOURMET KOMPASS
PACKAGING JOURNAL
REISEN EXCLUSIV

ELLE VERLAG GMBH 681232
Arabellastr. 23, 81925 MÜNCHEN **Tel:** 89 92500
Fax: 89 92502315
Web site: http://www.elle.de

Titles:
ELLE
ELLE DECORATION

ELSEVIER GMBH 677293
Hackerbrücke 6, 80335 MÜNCHEN **Tel:** 89 53830
Fax: 89 5383939
Email: info@elsevier.de
Web site: http://www.elsevier.de

Titles:
AEÜ INTERNATIONAL JOURNAL OF ELECTRONICS AND COMMUNICATION
CHEMIE DER ERDE GEOCHEMISTRY
DEUTSCHE ZEITSCHRIFT FÜR AKUPUNKTUR
EUROPEAN JOURNAL OF CELL BIOLOGY
FLORA
FUSS & SPRUNGGELENK
KRANKENHAUS-HYGIENE + INFEKTIONSVERHÜTUNG
LIMNOLOGICA
L.O.G.O.S. INTERDISZIPLINÄR
MIKROKOSMOS
OPTIK
OSTEOPATHISCHE MEDIZIN
PEDOBIOLOGIA
SPORT ORTHOPÄDIE TRAUMATOLOGIE
ZEITSCHRIFT FÜR EVIDENZ, FORTBILDUNG UND QUALITÄT IM GESUNDHEITSWESEN
ZEITSCHRIFT FÜR MEDIZINISCHE PHYSIK
DER ZOOLOGISCHE GARTEN
ZOOLOGISCHER ANZEIGER

ELWIN STAUDE VERLAG GMBH 680607
Fuchsrain 18a, 30657 HANNOVER
Tel: 511 651003 **Fax:** 511 651788
Email: info@staudeverlag.de
Web site: http://www.staudeverlag.de

Titles:
DEUTSCHE HEBAMMEN ZEITSCHRIFT

EMDER ZEITUNG GMBH & CO. KG 681255
Ringstr. 17a, 26721 EMDEN **Tel:** 4921 89000
Fax: 4921 8900489
Web site: http://www.emderzeitung.de

Titles:
EMDER ZEITUNG

EMMA FRAUENVERLAGS GMBH 681258
Bayenturm, 50678 KÖLN **Tel:** 221 6060600
Fax: 221 60606029
Email: info@emma.de
Web site: http://www.emma.de

Titles:
EMMA

EMMINGER & PARTNER GMBH 680631
Oraniendamm 68, 13469 BERLIN
Tel: 30 40304330 **Fax:** 30 40304340
Email: info@emminger-net.de
Web site: http://www.emminger-net.de

Titles:
LOP LANDWIRTSCHAFT OHNE PFLUG

ENDURO-VERLAGSGES. MBH 681273
Adlerstr. 6, 73540 HEUBACH **Tel:** 7173 714500
Fax: 7173 7145020
Email: redaktion@enduro-press.de
Web site: http://www.enduro-press.de

Titles:
ENDURO

ENERGIE INFORMATIONSDIENST GMBH 681365
Neue Burg 2, 20457 HAMBURG **Tel:** 40 3037350
Fax: 40 30373535
Email: info@eid.de
Web site: http://www.eid-aktuell.de

Titles:
EID ENERGIE INFORMATIONSDIENST

ENERGIE & MANAGEMENT VERLAGSGES. MBH 681290
Schloß Mühlfeld 20, 82211 HERRSCHING
Tel: 8152 93110 **Fax:** 8152 931122
Email: info@energiemarkt-medien.de
Web site: http://www.energiemarkt-medien.de

Titles:
ENERGIE & MANAGEMENT

ENERGIE & MEDIEN VERLAG GMBH 681362
Gustav-Siegle-Str. 16, 70193 STUTTGART
Tel: 711 2535900 **Fax:** 711 25359028
Email: post@energie-medien-verlag.de
Web site: http://www.energie-medien-verlag.de

Titles:
UNSERE REGION

ENERGIS GMBH 1690435
Heinrich-Böcking-Str. 10, 66121 SAARBRÜCKEN **Tel:** 681 90690 **Fax:** 681 90691575
Email: service@energis.de
Web site: http://www.energis.de

Titles:
SCHLAUER STROMER

ENGELS VERLAG JOACHIM BERNDT 680198
Maastrichter Str. 6, 50672 KÖLN
Tel: 221 2725260 **Fax:** 221 2725288
Email: info@engels-kinokultur.de
Web site: http://www.engels-kinokultur.de

Titles:
ENGELS

EPK MEDIA GMBH & CO.KG 1732474
Altstadt 296, 84028 LANDSHUT **Tel:** 871 4306330
Fax: 871 43063311
Email: info@beteiligungsreport.de
Web site: http://www.beteiligungsreport.de

Titles:
BETEILIGUNGSIREPORT
PELIKANS BETEILIGUNGS-KOMPASS

EPPINGER-VERLAG OHG 678525
Stauffenbergstr. 18, 74523 SCHWÄBISCH HALL
Tel: 791 950610 **Fax:** 791 9506141
Email: info@eppinger-verlag.de

Titles:
DER GEMEINDERAT

ERF ONLINE 1627172
Berliner Ring 62, 35576 WETZLAR
Tel: 6441 9572000 **Fax:** 6441 9572001
Email: online@erf.de
Web site: http://www.erf.de

Titles:
BIBELSERVER.COM
JOEMAX.DE

ERGONOMIA GMBH & CO. KG 690919
Julius-Hölder-Str. 29a, 70597 STUTTGART
Tel: 711 7280473 **Fax:** 711 7280492
Email: info@ergonomia.de
Web site: http://www.ergonomia.de

Titles:
ZEITSCHRIFT FÜR ARBEITSWISSENSCHAFT

ERICH SCHMIDT VERLAG GMBH & CO. 689438
Paosostr. 7, 81243 MÜNCHEN **Tel:** 89 8299600
Fax: 89 82996010
Email: esv.muenchen@esvmedien.de
Web site: http://www.esv.info

Titles:
BAUPORTAL

ERICH SCHMIDT VERLAG GMBH & CO. KG 677720
Genthiner Str. 30g, 10785 BERLIN
Tel: 30 2500850 **Fax:** 30 250085305
Email: esv@esvmedien.de
Web site: http://www.esv.info

Titles:
ALTLASTEN SPEKTRUM
BODENSCHUTZ
IDEENMANAGEMENT
IMMISSIONSSCHUTZ
KRV DIE KRANKENVERSICHERUNG
MÜLL UND ABFALL
PERSV DIE PERSONALVERTRETUNG
SICHER IST SICHER ARBEITSSCHUTZ AKTUELL
SRTOUR STEUER- UND RECHTSBRIEF TOURISTIK
STBP DIE STEUERLICHE BETRIEBSPRÜFUNG
V + T BETRIEBSPRAXIS UND RATIONALISIERUNG
V + T VERKEHR UND TECHNIK
WZS WEGE ZUR SOZIALVERSICHERUNG
ZIR ZEITSCHRIFT INTERNE REVISION

ERNST REINHARDT VERLAG 682222
Kemnatenstr. 46, 80639 MÜNCHEN
Tel: 89 1780160 **Fax:** 89 17801630
Email: info@reinhardt-verlag.de
Web site: http://www.reinhardt-verlag.de

Titles:
FRÜHFÖRDERUNG INTERDISZIPLINÄR
PSYCHOLOGIE IN ERZIEHUNG UND UNTERRICHT
UNSERE JUGEND

ERNST & SOHN VERLAG FÜR ARCHITEKTUR UND TECHNISCHE WISSENSCHAFTEN GMBH & CO. KG 678872
Rotherstr. 21, 10245 BERLIN **Tel:** 30 47031200
Fax: 30 47031270
Email: info@ernst-und-sohn.de
Web site: http://www.ernst-und-sohn.de

Titles:
BAUPHYSIK
BAUTECHNIK
BETON- UND STAHLBETONBAU
BETONKALENDER
DIBT MITTEILUNGEN
GEOMECHANIK UND TUNNELBAU
MAUERWERK
MAUERWERK-KALENDER
STAHLBAU
STEEL CONSTRUCTION
UNTERNEHMERBRIEF BAUWIRTSCHAFT

ERZ.ART GMBH 1782991
Markt 9, 09456 ANNABERG-BUCHHOLZ
Tel: 3733 5002933 **Fax:** 3733 5002934
Email: info@erz-art.de
Web site: http://www.erz-art.de

Titles:
SUPER TRABI

ESPRIT MEDIA GBR WERBEAGENTUR UND VERLAG 685199
Schwemannstr. 8, 31134 HILDESHEIM
Tel: 5121 37073 **Fax:** 5121 132458
Email: info@esprit-media.de
Web site: http://www.esprit-media.de

Titles:
PUBLIC

DIE ESSENER BRANCHEN VERLAGS-GMBH 1626988
Dahlhauser Str. 106, 45279 ESSEN
Tel: 201 2799646 **Fax:** 201 2799452
Email: info@dieessener.com
Web site: http://www.essener-branchenbuch.de

Titles:
DIE ESSENER

ESSENER KIRCHENZEITUNG VERLAGSGES. MBH 687870
Alfredistr. 31, 45127 ESSEN **Tel:** 201 810900
Fax: 201 8109010
Email: verlag@ruhrwort.de
Web site: http://www.ruhrwort.de

Titles:
RUHRWORT

ETV GMBH 681297
Montebruchstr. 2, 45219 ESSEN **Tel:** 2054 95320
Fax: 2054 953260
Email: energie-und-technik-verlag@etvessen.de

Titles:
ENERGIEWIRTSCHAFTLICHE TAGESFRAGEN ET

EUBUCO EURO BUSINESS COMMUNICATION VERLAG GMBH 689565
Geheimrat-Hummel-Platz 4, 65239 HOCHHEIM
Tel: 6146 6050 **Fax:** 6146 605201
Web site: http://www.touristik-aktuell.de

Titles:
TOURISTIK AKTUELL

EUBUCO VERLAG GMBH 687148
Geheimrat-Hummel-Platz 4, 65239 HOCHHEIM
Tel: 6146 6050 **Fax:** 6146 605204
Email: verlag@eubuco.de
Web site: http://www.eubuco.de

Titles:
MOUNTAIN MANAGER
PLAKATIV
PRINT & PRODUKTION
PROFESSIONAL PRODUCTION

EUGEN G. LEUZE VERLAG KG 682309
Karlstr. 4, 88348 BAD SAULGAU **Tel:** 7581 48010
Fax: 7581 480110
Email: info@leuze-verlag.de
Web site: http://www.leuze-verlag.de

Titles:
GALVANOTECHNIK
JAHRBUCH OBERFLÄCHENTECHNIK
PLUS PRODUKTION VON LEITERPLATTEN UND SYSTEMEN

EUGEN HEINZ DRUCK- UND VERLAGSGES. MBH 679636
Bessemerstr. 7, 70435 STUTTGART
Tel: 711 820000 **Fax:** 711 8200030
Email: verlagheinz@eheinz.de
Web site: http://www.eheinz.de

Titles:
FEUERBACHER WOCHE
WEILIMDORFER ANZEIGER MIT GIEBEL-NACHRICHTEN. ZUFFENHÄUSER WOCHE

EUGEN ULMER KG 678845
Wollgrasweg 41, 70599 STUTTGART
Tel: 711 45070 **Fax:** 711 4507120
Email: info@ulmer.de
Web site: http://www.ulmer.de

Titles:
ACKERPLUS
BAUERNKALENDER
BW AGRAR LANDWIRTSCHAFTLICHES WOCHENBLATT
CAMPOS
DEGA GALABAU
DEGA GRÜNER MARKT
DEGA PRODUKTION & HANDEL
DGS
EUROPEAN JOURNAL OF HORTICULTURAL SCIENCE
FLORIEREN!
GARTENPRAXIS
GEFIEDERTE WELT
JOURNAL OF PLANT DISEASES AND PROTECTION
KLEINBRENNEREI
NATURSCHUTZ UND LANDSCHAFTSPLANUNG
OBST & GARTEN
REBE & WEIN
SCHAFZUCHT
WOCHENBLATT MAGAZIN

EULENSPIEGEL GMBH 681468
Gubener Str. 47, 10243 BERLIN **Tel:** 30 29346311
Fax: 30 29346321
Email: verlag@eulenspiegel-zeitschrift.de
Web site: http://www.eulenspiegel-zeitschrift.de

Titles:
EULENSPIEGEL

EURO SECURITY FACHVERLAGE 681518
Peckhauser Str. 29, 40822 METTMANN
Tel: 2104 958972 **Fax:** 2104 5728
Web site: http://www.euro-security.de

Titles:
EURO SECURITY

EUROKUNST A. R. PURTAUF 681486
Am Salzpfad 26, 35633 LAHNAU
Tel: 6441 5673787
Email: eurokunst@web.de
Web site: http://www.eurokunst.com

Titles:
EUROKUNST

EURO-SCHULEN NORDRHEIN-WESTFALEN GMBH 1650220
Hamburger Allee 26, 30161 HANNOVER
Tel: 511 336179330 **Fax:** 511 336179355
Email: info@asc-hannover.de

Titles:
ASC-KURIER

EUROSHELL DEUTSCHLAND GMBH 1771687
Suhrenkamp 71, 22335 HAMBURG
Tel: 40 694090 **Fax:** 40 51319090
Email: card-kundenservice@shell.com

Titles:
CARD

EUROSOLAR E.V. 1621593
Kaiser-Friedrich-Str. 11, 53113 BONN
Tel: 228 362373 **Fax:** 228 361279
Email: info@eurosolar.org
Web site: http://www.eurosolar.org

Titles:
SOLARZEITALTER

EUROTAXSCHWACKE GMBH 688230
Wilhelm-Röntgen-Str. 7, 63477 MAINTAL
Tel: 6181 4050 **Fax:** 6181 405111
Email: info@eurotaxschwacke.de
Web site: http://www.schwacke.de

Titles:
SCHWACKELISTE LANDMASCHINEN
SCHWACKELISTE NUTZFAHRZEUGE
SCHWACKELISTE PKW
SCHWACKELISTE SUPERSCHWACKE
SCHWACKELISTE ZWEIRAD

EUROTRANSPORTMEDIA VERLAGS- UND VERANSTALTUNGS-GMBH 678589
Handwerkstr. 15, 70565 STUTTGART
Tel: 711 784980 **Fax:** 711 7849824
Email: info@etm-verlag.de
Web site: http://www.etm-verlag.de

Titles:
AUTOHOF GUIDE LKW
AUTOHOF GUIDE PKW
FERNFAHRER
FIRMENAUTO
KEP AKTUELL
LASTAUTO OMNIBUS
LASTAUTO OMNIBUS KATALOG
SCANIA BEWEGT
TRANS AKTUELL
TRANS AKTUELL SPEZIAL
WHO IS WHO IM FLOTTENMARKT

EUWID EUROPÄISCHER WIRTSCHAFTSDIENST GMBH 681526
Bleichstr. 20, 76593 GERNSBACH
Tel: 7224 93970 **Fax:** 7224 9397900
Email: info@euwid.de
Web site: http://www.euwid.de

Titles:
EUWID EUROPÄISCHER WIRTSCHAFTSDIENST KUNSTSTOFF
EUWID EUROPÄISCHER WIRTSCHAFTSDIENST LAUBHOLZ
EUWID EUROPÄISCHER WIRTSCHAFTSDIENST MÖBEL
EUWID EUROPÄISCHER WIRTSCHAFTSDIENST NEUE ENERGIEN

EUWID EUROPÄISCHER WIRTSCHAFTSDIENST PAPIER UND ZELLSTOFF
EUWID EUROPÄISCHER WIRTSCHAFTSDIENST RECYCLING UND ENTSORGUNG
EUWID EUROPÄISCHER WIRTSCHAFTSDIENST VERPACKUNG
EUWID WASSER SPECIAL
EUWID WASSER UND ABWASSER

EVANGELISCHE GEMEINDEPRESSE GMBH 693290
Augustenstr. 124, 70197 STUTTGART
Tel: 711 601000 **Fax:** 711 6010076
Email: verlag@evanggemeindeblatt.de
Web site: http://www.evangelisches-gemeindeblatt.de

Titles:
BENJAMIN
EVANGELISCHES GEMEINDEBLATT FÜR WÜRTTEMBERG UND STUTTGARTER EVANGELISCHES SONNTAGSBLATT

EVANGELISCHE LANDJUGENDAKADEMIE 684367
Dieperzbergweg 13, 57610 ALTENKIRCHEN
Tel: 2681 95160 **Fax:** 2681 70206
Email: info@lja.de
Web site: http://www.lja.de

Titles:
ÜBER LAND

EVANGELISCHER PRESSEVERBAND FÜR BAYERN E.V. 681113
Birkerstr. 22, 80636 MÜNCHEN **Tel:** 89 121720
Fax: 89 12172138
Email: info@epv.de
Web site: http://www.epv.de

Titles:
SONNTAGSBLATT

EVANGELISCHER PRESSEVERBAND FÜR WESTFALEN UND LIPPE E.V. 680740
Cansteinstr. 1, 33647 BIELEFELD **Tel:** 521 94400
Fax: 521 9440136
Email: info@medienhaus-bielefeld.de
Web site: http://www.medienhaus-bielefeld.de

Titles:
UK UNSERE KIRCHE

EVANGELISCHER PRESSEVERLAG NORD GMBH 686476
Gartenstr. 20, 24103 KIEL **Tel:** 431 55779200
Fax: 431 55779292

Titles:
EVANGELISCHE ZEITUNG FÜR HAMBURG & SCHLESWIG-HOLSTEIN

EVANGELISCHES MEDIENHAUS GMBH 1783085
Blumenstr. 76, 04155 LEIPZIG **Tel:** 341 711410
Fax: 341 7114150
Email: info@eva-leipzig.de
Web site: http://www.eva-leipzig.de

Titles:
DER SONNTAG

EVANGELIUMS-RUNDFUNK DEUTSCHLAND E.V. 1764665
Berliner Ring 62, 35576 WETZLAR
Tel: 6441 9572000 **Fax:** 6441 9572001
Email: online@erf.de
Web site: http://www.erf.de

Titles:
ERF.DE

EVOBUS GMBH, SETRA OMNIBUSSE 688393
Carl-Zeiss-Str. 2, 89231 NEU-ULM
Tel: 731 1812396 **Fax:** 731 1812418
Web site: http://www.setra.de

Titles:
SETRA FAMILIE
SETRA FAMILIE

EVOLUZIONE MEDIA AG 683234
Dillwächterstr. 4, 80686 MÜNCHEN
Tel: 89 7690030 **Fax:** 89 76900339
Email: info@evoluzione.de
Web site: http://www.evoluzione.de

Titles:
HIGH POTENTIAL
UNICOMPACT

EVONIK RÖHM GMBH 687173
Kirschenallee, 64293 DARMSTADT
Tel: 6151 1801 **Fax:** 6151 1802
Email: info@designinacrylics.de
Web site: http://www.plexiglas.net

Titles:
DESIGN IN ACRYLICS

EW MEDIEN UND KONGRESSE GMBH 681482
Kleyerstr. 88, 60326 FRANKFURT
Tel: 69 7104687447 **Fax:** 69 7104687451
Email: manfred.goebel@ew-online.de
Web site: http://www.ew-online.de

Titles:
EUROHEAT & POWER
EUROHEAT & POWER
EW - DAS MAGAZIN FÜR DIE ENERGIE WIRTSCHAFT
NETZPRAXIS
STROM PRAXIS

EXCLUSIVE & LIVING DIGITAL GMBH 685147
Am Baumwall 11, 20459 HAMBURG
Tel: 40 37034214 **Fax:** 40 37034212

Titles:
LIVING AT HOME
LIVING AT HOME.DE

EXIT MEDIEN GMBH 1621772
Sternstr. 49, 40479 DÜSSELDORF
Tel: 211 41667440 **Fax:** 211 41667441
Email: info@exit-magazin.de
Web site: http://www.exit-magazin.de

Titles:
EXIT

EXPERT FACHMEDIEN GMBH 1783108
Aachener Str. 172, 40223 DÜSSELDORF
Tel: 211 1591210 **Fax:** 211 1591150
Email: keramik@dvs-hg.de
Web site: http://www.expert-fachmedien.de

Titles:
INTERCERAM
KERAMISCHE ZEITSCHRIFT

EXPERTEN-NETZWERK GMBH 1763359
Pelkovenstr. 81b, 80992 MÜNCHEN
Tel: 89 21961220 **Fax:** 89 219612220
Email: info@experten.de
Web site: http://www.experten.de

Titles:
E EXPERTEN REPORT

EXPULS-VERLAG 681580
Hochstr. 8, 92637 WEIDEN **Tel:** 961 390820
Fax: 961 3908226
Email: redaktion@expuls.de
Web site: http://www.expuls.de

Titles:
EXPULS

EXTRA TIP WERBEGES. MBH 681602
Kölnische Str. 16, 34117 KASSEL **Tel:** 561 707007
Fax: 561 7070224
Email: info@ks.extratip.de
Web site: http://www.extratip.de

Titles:
EXTRA TIP

EXTRA TIP WERBUNGS- UND VERTRIEBSGES. MBH 681601
Prinzenstr. 10, 37073 GÖTTINGEN
Tel: 551 383860 **Fax:** 551 3838630
Email: info@extratip-goettingen.de
Web site: http://www.extratip-goettingen.de

Titles:
EXTRA TIP

EXTRAKTE-TEAM-VERLAG GMBH 681600
Wolfgang-Döring-Str. 2, 40595 DÜSSELDORF
Tel: 211 701011 **Fax:** 211 701013

Titles:
EXTRAKTE

F2M FOOD MULTIMEDIA GMBH 679761
Behnstr. 61, 22767 HAMBURG **Tel:** 40 39901227
Fax: 40 39901229
Email: info@foodmultimedia.de
Web site: http://www.foodmultimedia.de

Titles:
BROT + BACKWAREN

F. H. KLEFFMANN VERLAG GMBH 680463
Herner Str. 299, 44809 BOCHUM **Tel:** 234 953910
Fax: 234 9539130
Email: info@kleffmann-verlag.de
Web site: http://www.kleffmann-verlag.de

Titles:
FASSADE
RTS MAGAZIN

DER FABRIK VERLAG GMBH 683169
Friedrich-Ebert-Str. 36, 03044 COTTBUS
Tel: 355 431240 **Fax:** 355 4312424
Email: fabrikverlag@lausitz.net
Web site: http://www.hermannimnetz.de

Titles:
HERMANN

FACHPRESSE-VERLAG MICHAEL STEINERT 693300
An der Alster 21, 20099 HAMBURG
Tel: 40 2484540 **Fax:** 40 2803788
Email: service@snfachpresse.de
Web site: http://www.snfachpresse.de

Titles:
EUROFISH MAGAZINE
FISCHMAGAZIN
FLEISCH MAGAZIN

FACHSCHRIFTEN-VERLAG GMBH & CO. KG 677717
Höhenstr. 17, 70736 FELLBACH **Tel:** 711 52061
Fax: 711 5206300
Email: info@fachschriften.de
Web site: http://www.fachschriften.de

Titles:
ALTHAUS MODERNISIEREN
BAUEN!
BAUEN & RENOVIEREN
FERTIGHÄUSER
HAUS TEST
HAUSBAU
HÄUSER BAUEN & SPAREN
KAMINE & KACHELÖFEN
MEIN HOLZHAUS
DIE NEUEN BÄDER
PRO FERTIG HAUS
SCHWIMMBAD & SAUNA

FACHVERBAND DEUTSCHER HEILPRAKTIKER, LV BERLIN-BRANDENBURG 699720
Mommsenstr. 45, 10629 BERLIN **Tel:** 30 3233050
Fax: 30 3249761
Email: buero@heilpraktiker-berlin.org
Web site: http://www.heilpraktiker-berlin.org

Titles:
BERLINER HEILPRAKTIKER NACHRICHTEN

FACHVERBAND STEINZEUGINDUSTRIE E.V. 688930
Alfred-Nobel-Str. 17, 50226 FRECHEN
Tel: 2234 507271 **Fax:** 2234 507204
Email: fachverband@steinzeug.com
Web site: http://www.fachverband-steinzeug.de

Titles:
STEINZEUG-INFORMATION

FACHVERLAG DER VERLAGSGRUPPE HANDELSBLATT GMBH 677259
Grafenberger Allee 293, 40237 DÜSSELDORF
Tel: 211 8870 **Fax:** 211 8871410
Email: info@fachverlag.de
Web site: http://www.fachverlag.de

Titles:
ABSATZWIRTSCHAFT
DER AUFSICHTSRAT
DER BETRIEB
BILANZEN IM MITTELSTAND
CORPORATE FINANCE BIZ
CORPORATE FINANCE LAW
CREDITREFORM
DATENSCHUTZ-BERATER
KOR
KURS
ORGANISATIONSENTWICKLUNG
PHARMA MARKETING JOURNAL
SBR
WUW WIRTSCHAFT UND WETTBEWERB
ZFBF

FACHVERLAG DR. FRAUND GMBH 695562
Weberstr. 9, 55130 MAINZ **Tel:** 6131 62050
Fax: 6131 620541
Email: verlag@fraund.de
Web site: http://www.fraund.de

Titles:
DAS DEUTSCHE WEINMAGAZIN
LW HESSEN.RHEINLAND-PFALZ LANDWIRTSCHAFTLICHES WOCHENBLATT
PFERDESPORT JOURNAL
WEIN+MARKT

FACHVERLAG DR. H. ARNOLD GMBH 681222
Siegburgstr. 5, 44359 DORTMUND
Tel: 231 33690 **Fax:** 231 336920

Titles:
ELEKTRO WIRTSCHAFT
NAHVERKEHRS...PRAXIS

FACHVERLAG HANS CARL GMBH 679311
Andernacher Str. 33a, 90411 NÜRNBERG
Tel: 911 952850 **Fax:** 911 952858120
Email: info@hanscarl.com
Web site: http://www.hanscarl.com

Titles:
BRAUWELT
BRAUWELT INTERNATIONAL
KUNSTCHRONIK
MITTEILUNGSBLATT DEUTSCHER BRAUMEISTER- UND MALZMEISTER-BUND

FACHVERLAG MÖLLER E.K. 680897
Neustr. 163, 42553 VELBERT **Tel:** 2053 981250
Fax: 2053 981256
Email: info@fachverlag-moeller.de
Web site: http://www.fachverlag-moeller.de

Titles:
DREHTEIL + DREHMASCHINE
FRÄSEN + BOHREN
SCHLEIFEN + POLIEREN
DER SCHNITT- & STANZWERKZEUGBAU
DER STAHLFORMENBAUER

FACHVERLAG PETER SABO 687262
Am Sonnenberg 17, 55270 SCHWABENHEIM
Tel: 6130 7760 **Fax:** 6130 7971
Email: peter.sabo@t-online.de
Web site: http://www.sabo-buch.de

Titles:
PRÄVENTION

FACHVERLAG SAGKOB 1728907
Von-Ketteler-Str. 16, 84416 TAUFKIRCHEN
Tel: 8084 4133660 **Fax:** 8084 4133661
Email: info@fs-on.de

Titles:
MOBILE NEWS

FACHVERLAG SCHIELE & SCHÖN GMBH 679367
Markgrafenstr. 11, 10969 BERLIN **Tel:** 30 2537520
Fax: 30 25375299
Email: service@schiele-schoen.de
Web site: http://www.schiele-schoen.de

Titles:
DEUTSCHES INGENIEURBLATT
FKT
GIESSEREI-PRAXIS
GREENBUILDING
VIDEOFILMEN

FACHZEITSCHRIFTEN-PORTAL VERLAG 1651777
Südstr. 18, 58644 ISERLOHN **Tel:** 2371 77270
Fax: 2371 772720
Email: info@fachzeitschriften-portal.de
Web site: http://www.fachzeitschriften-portal.de

Titles:
FACHZEITSCHRIFTEN-PORTAL

FACTORY MEDIA GMBH 1783691
Gabelsbergerstr. 36, 80333 MÜNCHEN
Tel: 89 5427200 **Fax:** 89 54272080

Titles:
FREEDOMBMX
SKATEBOARD

SNOWBOARDER
SURFERS

FACTORY PUBLISHING GBR
1689810
Heinrich-Heine-Str. 9, 35039 MARBURG
Tel: 6421 15233 **Fax:** 6421 166815
Email: info@factory-magazin.de
Web site: http://www.factory-magazin.de

Titles:
FACTORY

FACTS VERLAG GMBH
681641
Theodor-Althoff-Str. 45, 45133 ESSEN
Tel: 201 87126800 **Fax:** 201 87126810
Email: redaktion@factsverlag.de
Web site: http://www.factsverlag.de

Titles:
FACTS

FACTUM-GES. FÜR STATISTIK, WISSENSCHAFTLICHE INFORMATION UND KOMMUNIKATION MBH
1668758
Kaiserstr. 51, 63065 OFFENBACH
Tel: 69 8297140 **Fax:** 69 8004924
Email: info@bestmedlink.de
Web site: http://www.factum.com

Titles:
BEST-MED-LINK

FAIRKEHR VERLAGSGES. MBH
681671
Niebuhrstr. 16b, 53113 BONN **Tel:** 228 9858545
Fax: 228 9858550
Email: redaktion@fairkehr.de
Web site: http://www.fairkehr.de

Titles:
FAIRKEHR
VERTRÄGLICH REISEN

FALK FOUNDATION E.V.
1760521
Leinenweberstr. 5, 79108 FREIBURG
Tel: 761 15140 **Fax:** 761 1514321
Email: literaturservice@falkfoundation.de
Web site: http://www.falkfoundation.de

Titles:
FALK GASTRO REVIEW JOURNAL

FALKEMEDIA KOCHMEDIEN GMBH
1788323
An der Halle 400 1, 24143 KIEL **Tel:** 431 20076600
Fax: 431 20076650
Email: info@falkemedia.de
Web site: http://www.falkemedia.de

Titles:
LANDGENUSS
SO ISST ITALIEN

FAMILIENHEIM UND GARTEN VERLAGSGES. MBH
681687
Oberer Lindweg 2, 53129 BONN **Tel:** 228 604680
Fax: 228 6046830
Email: verlag@fug-verlag.de
Web site: http://www.fug-verlag.de

Titles:
FAMILIENHEIM UND GARTEN

FAMILIEN-WIRTSCHAFTSRING E.V.
687180
Neubrückenstr. 60, 48143 MÜNSTER
Tel: 251 490180 **Fax:** 251 4901828
Email: info@fwr-muenster.de
Web site: http://www.fwr-muenster.de

Titles:
PLUSPUNKTE

FAMILY HOME VERLAG GMBH
1605998
Mörikestr. 67, 70199 STUTTGART
Tel: 711 96666999 **Fax:** 711 96666980
Web site: http://www.hurra-wir-bauen.de

Titles:
FAMILY HOME

FAMILY MEDIA GMBH & CO. KG
1642277
Schnewlinstr. 6, 79098 FREIBURG
Tel: 761 705780 **Fax:** 761 70578653
Email: online@familymedia.de
Web site: http://www.familymedia.de

Titles:
FAMILIE & CO
FAMILIE.DE

KINDERZEIT
SPIELEN UND LERNEN
TREFF

FASCINATION VERLAGSGES. MBH
680330
Baumschulenweg 12a, 48159 MÜNSTER
Tel: 251 2652744 **Fax:** 251 2652745
Email: info@computervideo.de
Web site: http://www.computervideo.de

Titles:
COMPUTER VIDEO

F.A.Z.-INSTITUT FÜR MANAGEMENT-, MARKT- UND MEDIENINFORMATIONEN GMBH
684885
Mainzer Landstr. 199, 60326 FRANKFURT
Tel: 69 75910 **Fax:** 69 75911966
Email: info@faz-institut.de
Web site: http://www.faz-institut.de

Titles:
AUSSENWIRTSCHAFT

FBG-FÖRDERGES. DES BAYERISCHEN GARTENBAUES
682329
Hirschgartenallee 19, 80639 MÜNCHEN
Tel: 89 178670 **Fax:** 89 1786799
Email: service@bgv-muenchen.de
Web site: http://www.bgv-muenchen.de

Titles:
GARTENBAU AKTUELL

FBR DIALOG GMBH
1744025
Havelstr. 7a, 64295 DARMSTADT
Tel: 6151 339257 **Fax:** 6151 339258
Email: info@fbr.de
Web site: http://www.fbr.de

Titles:
FBR-WASSERSPIEGEL

FEGERS DRUCK- UND VERLAG GMBH
682749
Rosental 51, 41334 NETTETAL **Tel:** 2153 91680
Fax: 2153 916829
Email: info@grenzlandnachrichten.de
Web site: http://www.grenzlandnachrichten.de

Titles:
MAHLZEIT

FEMINISTISCHES FRAUEN GESUNDHEITS ZENTRUM E.V.
680240
Bamberger Str. 51, 10777 BERLIN
Tel: 30 2139597 **Fax:** 30 2141927
Email: ffgzberlin@snafu.de
Web site: http://www.ffgz.de

Titles:
CLIO

FERDINAND HOLZMANN VERLAG GMBH
678273
Weidestr. 120a, 22083 HAMBURG
Tel: 40 6320180 **Fax:** 40 6307510
Email: holzmann@holzmann.de
Web site: http://www.holzmann.de

Titles:
ARCADE
DER KÜCHENPROFI
MÖBEL FERTIGUNG
MÖBEL KULTUR
SPOT MARKT

FERNSPRECHBUCH-VERLAG SCHWANN KG
680969
Markenstr. 21, 40227 DÜSSELDORF
Tel: 211 7773131 **Fax:** 211 7883325
Email: info@duesseldorf-guide.de
Web site: http://www.duesseldorf-guide.de

Titles:
DÜSSELDORF GUIDE>

FEUERTRUTZ GMBH VERLAG FÜR BRANDSCHUTZPUBLIKA-TIONEN
1748169
Stolberger Str. 84, 50933 KÖLN **Tel:** 221 5497500
Fax: 221 5497140
Email: redaktion@feuertrutz.de
Web site: http://www.feuertrutz.de

Titles:
FEUERTRUTZ

FGG FÖRDERUNGSGES. GARTENBAU MBH
691047
Godesberger Allee 142, 53175 BONN
Tel: 228 810020 **Fax:** 228 8100248
Email: zvg-report@g-net.de
Web site: http://www.g-net.de

Titles:
ZVG GARTENBAU REPORT

F.G.H. MEDIAWERK GMBH
1735978
Greflingerstr. 3, 93055 REGENSBURG
Tel: 941 796070 **Fax:** 941 7960710
Email: activewoman@fgh-mediawerk.de
Web site: http://www.activewoman.de

Titles:
ACTIVE WOMAN

FID-VERLAG GMBH FACHVERLAG FÜR INFORMATIONSDIENSTE
690113
Koblenzer Str. 99, 53177 BONN **Tel:** 228 9550600
Fax: 228 354472
Web site: http://www.fid-verlag.de

Titles:
DER VERSANDHAUSBERATER
DER VERSANDHAUSBERATER SPEZIAL
VERZEICHNIS DES VERSANDHANDELS

FILM & MEDIENBÜRO NIEDERSACHSEN E.V.
681835
Lohstr. 45a, 49074 OSNABRÜCK **Tel:** 541 28426
Fax: 541 29507
Email: info@filmbuero-nds.de
Web site: http://www.filmbuero-nds.de

Titles:
RUNDBRIEF FILM & MEDIENBÜRO NIEDERSACHSEN

FINANCIAL GATES GMBH
698653
Mainzer Landstr. 199, 60326 FRANKFURT
Tel: 69 75912494 **Fax:** 69 75912495
Email: info@finance-magazin.de
Web site: http://www.finance-magazin.de

Titles:
FINANCE
FINANCE
MARKT UND MITTELSTAND

FINANCIAL TIMES BUSINESS LTD.
1709886
Nibelungenplatz 3, 60318 FRANKFURT
Tel: 69 15685115 **Fax:** 69 5975528
Email: dpn@ft.com
Web site: http://www.dpn-online.com

Titles:
DPN

FINANZ COLLOQUIUM HEIDELBERG GMBH
1768512
Plöck 32a, 69117 HEIDELBERG **Tel:** 6221 998980
Fax: 6221 9989899
Email: info@fc-heidelberg.de
Web site: http://www.fc-heidelberg.de

Titles:
BANKPRAKTIKER

FINANZEN VERLAG GMBH
694730
Bayerstr. 71, 80335 MÜNCHEN **Tel:** 89 272640
Fax: 89 27264189
Email: verlag@finanzen.net
Web site: http://www.finanzen.net

Titles:
€URO
€URO AM SONNTAG
€URO BEST-BUY
€URO EXTRA

FINANZEN.NET GMBH
1626715
Hirschstr. 2, 76133 KARLSRUHE
Tel: 721 1617660
Web site: http://www.finanzen.net

Titles:
FINANZEN.NET

FINE ART MEDIA GMBH
1691585
Dr.-Gessler-Str. 16a, 93051 REGENSBURG
Tel: 941 465270260 **Fax:** 941 465270299
Email: kontakt@fine-art-media.de
Web site: http://www.finestfinance.com

Titles:
FINEST.FINANCE!

FIRE&FOOD VERLAG GMBH
1684995
Waldseer Str. 3, 88250 WEINGARTEN
Tel: 751 56177518 **Fax:** 751 56177559
Email: post@fire-food.com
Web site: http://www.fire-food.com

Titles:
FIRE&FOOD

FISCHER'S ARCHIV MEDIEN GMBH
1626717
Bei den Mühren 91, 20457 HAMBURG
Tel: 40 3698320 **Fax:** 40 36983236
Email: info@fischers-archiv.de
Web site: http://www.fischers-archiv.de

Titles:
DIALOGMARKETING-TRENDS
FISCHER'S ARCHIV

FIT FOR FUN VERLAG GMBH
681872
Christoph-Probst-Weg 1, 20251 HAMBURG
Tel: 40 41313401 **Fax:** 40 41312040
Email: service@fitforfun.de
Web site: http://www.fitforfun.de

Titles:
FIT FOR FUN

FIWA VERLAG GMBH
1744294
Elisabeth-Breuer-Str. 9, 51065 KÖLN
Tel: 221 940820 **Fax:** 221 9408211
Email: info@orthopress.de
Web site: http://www.orthopress.de

Titles:
ORTHO PRESS

F.K.W. FACHVERLAG FÜR KOMMUNIKATION UND WERBUNG
678701
Nelmannwall 4, 59494 SOEST **Tel:** 2921 36090
Fax: 2921 360929
Email: info@fkwverlag.com
Web site: http://www.fkwverlag.com

Titles:
SOESTMAGAZIN
WARSTEINER

FLORIAN HEISE
1690956
Landsberger Str. 18, 86932 PÜRGEN
Tel: 8196 998167 **Fax:** 8196 998169
Email: info@druckerchannel.de
Web site: http://www.druckerchannel.de

Titles:
DRUCKERCHANNEL

FLOTTENMANAGEMENT VERLAG GMBH
1643727
Rudolf-Diesel-Str. 14, 53859 NIEDERKASSEL
Tel: 228 4595470 **Fax:** 228 4595479
Email: post@flotte.de
Web site: http://www.flotte.de

Titles:
FLOTTEN MANAGEMENT

FOCUS MAGAZIN VERLAG GMBH
679525
Arabellastr. 23, 81925 MÜNCHEN **Tel:** 89 92500
Fax: 89 92502026
Email: anzeigen@focus.de
Web site: http://www.medialine.de

Titles:
FOCUS
FOCUS MONEY
FOCUS SCHULE

FOERSTER & THELEN MARKTFORSCHUNG-FELDSERVICE GMBH
681743
Stühmeyerstr. 16, 44787 BOCHUM
Tel: 234 50740 **Fax:** 234 5074199
Email: info@ftmafo.de
Web site: http://www.ftmafo.de

Titles:
FELDSALAT

FONDS PROFESSIONELL MULTIMEDIA GMBH
1737503
Neuenhöfer Allee 153, 50935 KÖLN
Tel: 221 4759797 **Fax:** 221 4759798
Email: office@fondsprofessionell.com
Web site: http://www.fondsprofessionell.de

Titles:
FONDS PROFESSIONELL
IM INSTITUTIONAL MONEY

FONDS & FRIENDS VERLAGSGES. MBH 681965
Goldbekplatz 3, 22303 HAMBURG
Tel: 40 40199950 **Fax:** 40 40199960
Email: info@dasinvestment.com
Web site: http://www.dasinvestment.com

Titles:
DAS INVESTMENT
DAS INVESTMENT.COM

FOOD PROMOTION GMBH 1728288
Baumstr. 4, 80469 MÜNCHEN **Tel:** 89 2002713
Fax: 89 20027150
Email: apero@fp-food.de
Web site: http://www.fp-food.de

Titles:
APÉRO

FÖRDERUNGSVEREIN DEUTSCHER SOLDATENVERBÄNDE E.V. 686255
Rheinallee 55, 53173 BONN **Tel:** 228 361007
Fax: 228 361008
Email: vds.bund.bonn@t-online.de

Titles:
SOLDAT IM VOLK

FORM+ZWECK VERLAG GBR 1621361
Dorotheenstr. 4, 12557 BERLIN **Tel:** 30 6555722
Fax: 30 65880653
Email: info@formundzweck.com
Web site: http://www.formundzweck.com

Titles:
FORM+ZWECK

FORSTFACHVERLAG GMBH & CO. KG 1627053
Moorhofweg 11, 27383 SCHEESSEL
Tel: 4263 93950 **Fax:** 4263 939521
Email: info@forstfachverlag.de
Web site: http://www.forstfachverlag.de

Titles:
ENERGIE PFLANZEN
FORSTMASCHINEN PROFI

FORUM JUNGE ANWALTSCHAFT IM DEUTSCHER ANWALTVEREIN E.V. 1771305
Littenstr. 11, 10179 BERLIN **Tel:** 30 7261520
Fax: 30 26152195
Email: info@davforum.de
Web site: http://www.davforum.de

Titles:
ADVOICE

FORUM MEDIZIN VERLAGSGES. MBH 682026
Peterstr. 11, 26382 WILHELMSHAVEN
Tel: 4421 7556615 **Fax:** 4421 7556610
Email: sekretariat@forum-medizin.de
Web site: http://www.forum-medizin.de

Titles:
DIE NATURHEILKUNDE

FORUM ZEITSCHRIFTEN UND SPEZIALMEDIEN GMBH 680080
Mandichostr. 18, 86504 MERCHING
Tel: 8233 381361 **Fax:** 8233 381212
Email: service@forum-zeitschriften.de
Web site: http://www.forum-zeitschriften.de

Titles:
CATERING MANAGEMENT
DER FACILITY MANAGER
INDUSTRIEBAU
DIE REITERIN

FORUMSPROJEKT GMBH 1764773
Prinzessinenstr. 19, 10969 BERLIN
Tel: 30 609824950 **Fax:** 30 609824959
Email: sandra.broschat@aufstiegundfall.com

Titles:
AUFSTIEG UND FALL

FOTOFORUM-VERLAG 680723
Ludwig-Wolker-Str. 37, 48157 MÜNSTER
Tel: 251 143930 **Fax:** 251 143939
Email: info@fotoforum.de
Web site: http://www.fotoforum.de

Titles:
FOTOFORUM

FRANKENPOST VERLAG GMBH 681810
Poststr. 9, 95028 HOF **Tel:** 9281 8160
Fax: 9281 816440
Email: verlag@frankenpost.de
Web site: http://www.frankenpost.de

Titles:
FRANKENPOST
FRANKENPOST SECHSÄMTER NEUESTE NACHRICHTEN
FRANKENPOST SECHSÄMTERBOTE
HOFER ANZEIGER
MARKTREDWITZER TAGBLATT FRANKENPOST
MÜNCHBERG-HELMBRECHTSER TAGESZEITUNG
REHAUER TAGBLATT FRANKENPOST

FRANKEN-REPORT VERLAGS-GMBH 682075
Winklerstr. 15, 90403 NÜRNBERG **Tel:** 911 23310
Fax: 911 2331292
Email: info@frankenreport.info
Web site: http://www.frankenreport.info

Titles:
FRANKEN REPORT

FRANKFURTER ALLGEMEINE ZEITUNG GMBH 679840
Hellerhofstr. 2, 60327 FRANKFURT **Tel:** 69 75910
Fax: 69 75912172
Web site: http://www.faz.net

Titles:
FAZ.NET
FRANKFURTER ALLGEMEINE
FRANKFURTER ALLGEMEINE HOCHSCHULANZEIGER
FRANKFURTER ALLGEMEINE HOCHSCHULANZEIGER.DE
FRANKFURTER ALLGEMEINE SONNTAGSZEITUNG
Z DIE SCHÖNEN SEITEN

FRANKFURTER SOCIETÄTS-DRUCKEREI GMBH 680484
Frankenallee 71, 60327 FRANKFURT
Tel: 69 75010 **Fax:** 69 75014877
Email: fsd@fsd.de
Web site: http://www.fsd.de

Titles:
FRANKFURTER NEUE PRESSE
HÖCHSTER KREISBLATT
HPR HESSISCHE POLIZEIRUNDSCHAU
LOYAL
MAIN FEELING
NASSAUISCHE NEUE PRESSE
DAS PARLAMENT
TAUNUS ZEITUNG
UK PT KONTAKT

FRÄNKISCHE LANDESZEITUNG GMBH 682057
Nürnberger Str. 9, 91522 ANSBACH
Tel: 981 95000 **Fax:** 981 9500122
Web site: http://www.flz.de

Titles:
FRÄNKISCHE LANDESZEITUNG

FRÄNKISCHE NACHRICHTEN VERLAGS-GMBH 682058
Schmiederstr. 19, 97941 TAUBERBISCHOFSHEIM **Tel:** 9341 830
Fax: 9341 83161
Web site: http://www.fnweb.de

Titles:
(FN WEB
FRÄNKISCHE NACHRICHTEN
FRÄNKISCHE WOCHENPOST - AUSG. A TAUBERBISCHOFSHEIM

FRANZ STEINER VERLAG GMBH 677486
Birkenwaldstr. 44, 70191 STUTTGART
Tel: 711 25820 **Fax:** 711 2582390
Email: service@steiner-verlag.de
Web site: http://www.steiner-verlag.de

Titles:
GELD UND KAPITAL
GEOGRAPHISCHE ZEITSCHRIFT
HISTORIA
HMRG HISTORISCHE MITTEILUNGEN
MEDIZIN, GESELLSCHAFT UND GESCHICHTE
MEDIZIN HISTORISCHES JOURNAL
SUDHOFFS ARCHIV
ZBW ZEITSCHRIFT FÜR BERUFS- UND WIRTSCHAFTSPÄDAGOGIK

FRANZMEDIEN GMBH 680572
Im Ikaruspark/Lilienthalstr. 3, 82178 PUCHHEIM
Tel: 89 8299470 **Fax:** 89 82994716
Email: info@franzmedien.com
Web site: http://www.franzmedien.com

Titles:
DENTAL:SPIEGEL

FRAUENVERBAND COURAGE E.V. 680396
Holsteiner Str. 28, 42107 WUPPERTAL
Tel: 202 4969749
Email: frauenverband-courage@t-online.de
Web site: http://www.fvcourage.de

Titles:
COURAGE

FRAUNHOFER INSTITUT FÜR PRODUKTIONSTECHNIK UND AUTOMATISIERUNG IPA 1675714
Nobelstr. 12, 70569 STUTTGART
Tel: 711 9701667 **Fax:** 711 9701400
Email: presse@ipa.fraunhofer.de
Web site: http://www.ipa.fraunhofer.de

Titles:
INTERAKTIV

FRAUNHOFER-INSTITUT FÜR FABRIKBETRIEB UND -AUTOMATISIERUNG IFF 1746321
Sandtorstr. 22, 39106 MAGDEBURG
Tel: 391 40900 **Fax:** 391 4090596
Email: presse@iff.fraunhofer.de
Web site: http://www.iff.fraunhofer.de

Titles:
IFFOCUS

FRAUNHOFER-INSTITUT FÜR PRODUKTIONSANLAGEN UND KONSTRUKTIONSTECHNIK 682281
Pascalstr. 8, 10587 BERLIN **Tel:** 30 39006140
Fax: 30 39006392
Email: info@ipk.fraunhofer.de
Web site: http://www.ipk.fraunhofer.de

Titles:
FUTUR

FREIBURGER STADTKURIER VERLAGSGES. MBH 688817
Bismarckallee 8, 79098 FREIBURG
Tel: 761 207190 **Fax:** 761 2071919
Email: verlag@stadtkurier.de
Web site: http://www.stadtkurier.de

Titles:
STADTKURIER

FREIBURGER WOCHENBERICHT VERLAGS GMBH 682124
Basler Str. 88, 79115 FREIBURG
Tel: 761 45153500 **Fax:** 761 45153501
Email: anzeigen@freiburger-wochenbericht.de
Web site: http://www.freiburger-wochenbericht.de

Titles:
FREIBURGER WOCHENBERICHT

DER FREIE BERATER VERLAGS GMBH & CO. KG 1627026
Steinheimer Str. 117, 63500 SELIGENSTADT
Tel: 6182 9938400 **Fax:** 6182 9938444
Email: info@derfreieberater.de
Web site: http://www.derfreieberater.de

Titles:
DER FREIE BERATER

DER FREIE BERUF DIENSTLEISTUNGS- UND VERLAGS GMBH 682128
Reinhardtstr. 34, 10117 BERLIN **Tel:** 30 28444438
Fax: 30 28444479
Email: redaktion@der-freie-beruf.de
Web site: http://www.der-freie-beruf.de

Titles:
DER FREIE BERUF

DER FREITAG MEDIENGES. MBH & CO. KG 1681084
Hegelplatz 1, 10117 BERLIN **Tel:** 30 2500870
Fax: 30 25008799
Email: info@freitag.de
Web site: http://www.freitag.de

Titles:
DER FREITAG

FREIWILLIGE SELBSTKONTROLLE FERNSEHEN E.V. 1789105
Heidestr. 3, 10557 BERLIN **Tel:** 30 2308360
Fax: 30 23083670
Email: tvdiskurs@fsf.de
Web site: http://www.fsf.de

Titles:
TV DISKURS

FREIZEIT & KULTUR VERLAG 682258
Dorfstr. 28, 79249 MERZHAUSEN
Tel: 761 1307703 **Fax:** 761 405341
Email: anzeigen@fipps-freiburg.de
Web site: http://www.fipps-freiburg.de

Titles:
FIPPS

FREIZEIT + WASSERSPORT VERLAG GMBH 688478
Am Windfeld 15, 83714 MIESBACH
Tel: 8025 294243 **Fax:** 8025 294271
Email: skipper@skipperonline.de
Web site: http://www.skippermagazin.de

Titles:
SKIPPER

FREIZEIT-VERLAG LANDSBERG GMBH 678517
Celsiusstr. 7, 86899 LANDSBERG
Tel: 8191 947160 **Fax:** 8191 9471666
Email: verlag@tophotel.de
Web site: http://www.freizeit-verlag.de

Titles:
AUSGEWÄHLTE TAGUNGSHOTELS ZUM WOHLFÜHLEN
AUSGEWÄHLTE WELLNESSHOTELS ZUM WOHLFÜHLEN
TOP HOTEL

FREIZEITWOCHE VERLAG GMBH & CO. KG 1643344
Karlsruher Str. 31, 76437 RASTATT **Tel:** 7222 130
Fax: 7222 13218

Titles:
FREIZEIT WOCHE
SUPER FREIZEIT

FRESH! MEDIA GMBH 1640327
Rupertistr. 32, 83278 TRAUNSTEIN
Tel: 861 166290 **Fax:** 861 1662929
Web site: http://www.ludwig-magazin.de

Titles:
LUDWIG - SÜDOSTBAYERNS TRENDMAGAZIN, AUSG. RO-TS-BGL-AÖ-MÜ-PAN

FRESHMILK CREATIVE MEDIA GMBH 1784339
Stralauer Allee 2a, 10245 BERLIN
Tel: 30 364440950 **Fax:** 30 364440999
Email: postamt@freshmilk.de
Web site: http://www.freshmilk.de/creativemedia

Titles:
CONDOR

FREUDENSTADT TOURISMUS 694822
Marktplatz 64, 72250 FREUDENSTADT
Tel: 7441 864730 **Fax:** 7441 864777
Email: touristinfo@freudenstadt.de
Web site: http://www.freudenstadt-tourismus.de

Titles:
URLAUBSWELTEN

FREUNDE DES GESPRÄCHS E.V. 682538
Dorfstr. 10, 23883 KLEIN ZECHER
Email: gueges@t-online.de
Web site: http://www.gadf.de

Titles:
DAS GESPRÄCH AUS DER FERNE

FREUNDIN VERLAG GMBH 682175
Arabellastr. 23, 81925 MÜNCHEN **Tel:** 89 92500
Fax: 89 92503991
Email: freundin@burda.com
Web site: http://www.freundin.de

Titles:
FREUNDIN
FREUNDIN DONNA
FREUNDIN KALENDER
FREUNDIN WELLFIT

FRIEDRICH BERLIN VERLAGSGES. MBH 678746
Knesebeckstr. 59, 10719 BERLIN **Tel:** 30 2544950
Fax: 30 25449512
Email: verlag@friedrichberlin.de
Web site: http://www.friedrichberlin.de

Titles:
DIE DEUTSCHE BÜHNE
LITERATUREN
OPERNWELT
THEATER HEUTE

FRIEDRICH VERLAG GMBH 677728
Im Brande 17, 30926 SEELZE **Tel:** 511 400040
Fax: 511 40004119
Email: info@friedrich-verlag.de
Web site: http://www.friedrich-verlag.de

Titles:
COMPUTER + UNTERRICHT
GRUNDSCHULE MUSIK
DIE GRUNDSCHULZEITSCHRIFT
KUNST + UNTERRICHT
LERN CHANCEN
LERNENDE SCHULE
PRAXIS DEUTSCH
UNTERRICHT BIOLOGIE

FRIEDRICH ZUFALL GMBH & CO. KG INTERNATIONALE SPEDITION 1716008
Robert-Bosch-Breite 11, 37079 GÖTTINGEN
Tel: 551 607271 **Fax:** 551 607244
Email: carolin.heinrichs@zufall.de
Web site: http://www.zufall.de

Titles:
ZUFALL REPORT

FRIENDS MEDIEN LEMANCZYK & PARTNER 680289
Max-Eyth-Str. 22, 71686 REMSECK
Tel: 7146 286330 **Fax:** 7146 286332
Email: info@friends-medien.com
Web site: http://www.friends-medien.com

Titles:
FRIENDS THE GAYMAP - AUSG. ALICANTE
FRIENDS THE GAYMAP - AUSG. AMSTERDAM
FRIENDS THE GAYMAP - AUSG. ANTWERPEN
FRIENDS THE GAYMAP - AUSG. BARCELONA
FRIENDS THE GAYMAP - AUSG. BENIDORM
FRIENDS THE GAYMAP - AUSG. BERLIN
FRIENDS THE GAYMAP - AUSG. BRÜSSEL
FRIENDS THE GAYMAP - AUSG. BUDAPEST
FRIENDS THE GAYMAP - AUSG. CITTÀ DEL VATICANO
FRIENDS THE GAYMAP - AUSG. COLOGNE
FRIENDS THE GAYMAP - AUSG. COPENHAGEN
FRIENDS THE GAYMAP - AUSG. DÜSSELDORF
FRIENDS THE GAYMAP - AUSG. FORT LAUDERDALE
FRIENDS THE GAYMAP - AUSG. FRANKFURT/MAIN
FRIENDS THE GAYMAP - AUSG. HAMBURG
FRIENDS THE GAYMAP - AUSG. HANNOVER
FRIENDS THE GAYMAP - AUSG. IBIZA EIVISSA
FRIENDS THE GAYMAP - AUSG. KEY WEST
FRIENDS THE GAYMAP - AUSG. LISSABON
FRIENDS THE GAYMAP - AUSG. LONDON
FRIENDS THE GAYMAP - AUSG. MADRID
FRIENDS THE GAYMAP - AUSG. MANNHEIM
FRIENDS THE GAYMAP - AUSG. MIAMI
FRIENDS THE GAYMAP - AUSG. MONTRÉAL
FRIENDS THE GAYMAP - AUSG. MÜNCHEN-MUNICH
FRIENDS THE GAYMAP - AUSG. NEW YORK CITY
FRIENDS THE GAYMAP - AUSG. NÜRNBERG
FRIENDS THE GAYMAP - AUSG. ORLANDO
FRIENDS THE GAYMAP - AUSG. PARIS
FRIENDS THE GAYMAP - AUSG. PLAYA DEL INGLES
FRIENDS THE GAYMAP - AUSG. PRAG
FRIENDS THE GAYMAP - AUSG. ROMA
FRIENDS THE GAYMAP - AUSG. ROTTERDAM
FRIENDS THE GAYMAP - AUSG. RUHR
FRIENDS THE GAYMAP - AUSG. SITGES
FRIENDS THE GAYMAP - AUSG. STUTTGART
FRIENDS THE GAYMAP - AUSG. TEL AVIV
FRIENDS THE GAYMAP - AUSG. VIAREGGIO & TORRE DEL LAGO
FRIENDS THE GAYMAP - AUSG. WIEN
FRIENDS THE GAYMAP - AUSG. ZÜRICH
SPA-GUIDE

FRIZZ MEDIA & MARKETING DARMSTADT 682211
Wilhelminenstr. 7A, 64283 DARMSTADT
Tel: 6151 915810 **Fax:** 6151 915858
Email: magazin@frizz-darmstadt.de
Web site: http://www.frizz-darmstadt.de

Titles:
FRIZZ

DIE FÜHRUNGSKRÄFTE E.V. 1640391
Mohrenstr. 11, 50670 KÖLN **Tel:** 221 9218290
Fax: 221 9218296
Email: koeln@die-fuehrungskraefte.de
Web site: http://www.die-fuehrungskraefte.de

Titles:
PERSPEKTIVEN

FÜRSTLICH CASTELL'SCHE KANZLEI 680075
Rathausplatz 1, 97355 CASTELL **Tel:** 9325 60136
Fax: 9325 60126
Email: pr@castell-bank.de
Web site: http://www.castell-bank.de

Titles:
CASTELLER NACHRICHTEN

FÜSSEN TOURISMUS UND MARKETING 682249
Kaiser-Maximilian-Platz 1, 87629 FÜSSEN
Tel: 8362 93850 **Fax:** 8362 938520
Email: tourismus@fuessen.de
Web site: http://www.tourismus-fuessen.de

Titles:
FÜSSEN IM ALLGÄU
FÜSSEN IM ALLGÄU
FÜSSEN IM ALLGÄU
FÜSSEN IN THE KING'S NOOK
FÜSSEN NELLA TERRA DEL RE

FVG FACHVERLAG TECHNISCHE GEBÄUDEAUSRÜSTUNG 683766
Arnikaweg 8, 85521 OTTOBRUNN **Tel:** 89 604075
Fax: 89 6016135
Email: redaktion@instandhaltungsjournal.de
Web site: http://www.instandhaltungsjournal.de

Titles:
INSTANDHALTUNGSJOURNAL & GEBÄUDEMANAGEMENT

FW-VERLAG GMBH 1622255
Söhnleinstr. 17, 65201 WIESBADEN
Tel: 611 267660 **Fax:** 611 2676618
Email: info@finanzwelt.de
Web site: http://www.finanzwelt.de

Titles:
FINANZWELT

G. BRAUN VERLEGER-SERVICES GMBH 1639663
Lichtentaler Str. 35, 76530 BADEN-BADEN
Tel: 7221 211924 **Fax:** 7221 211930
Email: medienmarketing@pruefer.com
Web site: http://www.pruefer.com

Titles:
IHK WIRTSCHAFT IN DER TECHNOLOGIEREGION KARLSRUHE

G + J AG & CO. KG 681242
Weihenstephaner Str. 7, 81673 MÜNCHEN
Tel: 89 415200 **Fax:** 89 4152627
Web site: http://www.gujmedia.de

Titles:
ELTERN
ELTERN FAMILY
ELTERN RATGEBER ARZT UND SCHWANGERSCHAFT
ELTERN RATGEBER DAS GESUNDE KIND
ELTERN RATGEBER KLINIKFÜHRER GEBURT
ELTERN RATGEBER - (PRAXIS-RATGEBER) AUSG. KINDERARZT
FIFTY

G + J CORPORATE EDITORS GMBH 1770693
Stubbenhuk 10, 20459 HAMBURG **Tel:** 40 37030
Fax: 40 37035010
Email: info@corporate-editors.com
Web site: http://www.corporate-editors.com

Titles:
>COMPASS
LUFTHANSA EXCLUSIVE MAGAZIN
MOBIL
VOLKSWAGEN MAGAZIN
WOMAN'S WORLD

G + J ELECTRONIC MEDIA SALES GMBH 682835
Stubbenhuk 5, 20459 HAMBURG
Tel: 40 37037373 **Fax:** 40 37035734
Email: marketing@ems.guj.de
Web site: http://www.ems.guj.de

Titles:
G+J EMS NEWSLETTER

G+J ENTERTAINMENT MEDIA GMBH & CO. KG 679492
Weihenstephaner Str. 7, 81673 MÜNCHEN
Tel: 89 451140 **Fax:** 89 45114444
Email: emv@e-media.de
Web site: http://www.e-media.de

Titles:
GAMESHOP
KINO.DE
TREFFPUNKT KINO
VIDEOTIPP

G + J WIRTSCHAFTSMEDIEN GMBH & CO KG 1763096
Am Baumwall 11, 20459 HAMBURG
Tel: 40 37030 **Fax:** 40 37038310

Titles:
BÖRSE ONLINE
BÖRSE ONLINE
BUSINESS PUNK
CAPITAL
CAPITAL.DE
FINANCIAL TIMES DEUTSCHLAND
GRÜNDERZEIT
IMPULSE
IMPULSE ONLINE

G + J WOMEN NEW MEDIA GMBH 1764603
Weihenstephaner Str. 7, 81673 MÜNCHEN
Tel: 89 415200 **Fax:** 89 4152651

Titles:
BRIGITTE.DE
ELTERN.DE

G + J/RBA GMBH & CO. KG 686164
Am Baumwall 11, 20459 HAMBURG
Tel: 40 37035521 **Fax:** 40 37035599
Web site: http://www.nationalgeographic.de

Titles:
NATIONAL GEOGRAPHIC DEUTSCHLAND

G & K TECHMEDIA GMBH 681901
Am Stollen 6/1, 79261 GUTACH **Tel:** 7685 918110
Fax: 7685 909011
Email: info@flexo.de
Web site: http://www.flexo.de

Titles:
FLEXO&GRAVURE INTERNATIONAL
FLEXO+TIEF-DRUCK

GABLER VERLAG/SPRINGER FACHMEDIEN WIESBADEN GMBH 1627123
Abraham-Lincoln-Str. 46, 65189 WIESBADEN
Tel: 611 78780 **Fax:** 611 7878400
Email: springerfachmedien-wiesbaden@springer.com
Web site: http://www.gabler.de

Titles:
BANKFACHKLASSE
BANKMAGAZIN
CALLCENTER PROFI
CONTROLLING & MANAGEMENT
ENGLISH@OFFICE
INNOVATIVE VERWALTUNG
MIR MANAGEMENT INTERNATIONAL REVIEW
SALES BUSINESS
VERSICHERUNGS MAGAZIN
WI WIRTSCHAFTSINFORMATIK
WORKING@OFFICE
ZFB ZEITSCHRIFT FÜR BETRIEBSWIRTSCHAFT

GABRIEL.LLOYD MARTENS.GMBH 1653874
Römerstr. 3, 94032 PASSAU **Tel:** 851 9290865
Fax: 851 9290866
Email: redaktion@pastaonline.de
Web site: http://www.pastaonline.de

Titles:
PASTA!

GAMIGO AG 1626738
Behringstr. 16b, 22765 HAMBURG
Tel: 40 226305260 **Fax:** 40 226305255
Email: support@gamigo.de
Web site: http://www.gamigo.de

Titles:
GAMIGO

GANDERSHEIMER KREISBLATT GMBH & CO. KG 682313
Alte Gasse 19, 37581 BAD GANDERSHEIM
Tel: 5382 98110 **Fax:** 5382 6356
Email: kreisblatt@t-online.de
Web site: http://www.gandersheimer-kreisblatt.de

Titles:
GANDERSHEIMER KREISBLATT

GASTEIG MÜNCHEN GMBH 682340
Rosenheimer Str. 5, 81667 MÜNCHEN
Tel: 89 480980 **Fax:** 89 480981000
Email: zentral@gasteig.de
Web site: http://www.gasteig.de

Titles:
GASTEIG KULTUR FÜR MÜNCHEN

GASTGEWERBE INFORMATIONS-, MEDIEN- UND VERLAGSGES. MBH 1654152
Hammer Landstr. 45, 41460 NEUSS
Tel: 2131 7518200 **Fax:** 2131 7518201
Email: verlag@gastgewerbe.us
Web site: http://www.gastgewerbe-magazin.de

Titles:
GASTGEWERBE

GASTRONOMIE REPORT VERLAGS GMBH 682353
Weißenburger Str. 19, 81667 MÜNCHEN
Tel: 89 4480409 **Fax:** 89 4807514
Email: faber@gastronomie-report.de
Web site: http://www.gastronomie-report.de

Titles:
GASTRONOMIE REPORT

GAUKE GMBH-VERLAG FÜR SOZIALÖKONOMIE 690944
Hofholzallee 67, 24109 KIEL **Tel:** 431 6793650
Fax: 431 6793651
Email: mail@gauke.net
Web site: http://www.gauke.net

Titles:
ZFSÖ ZEITSCHRIFT FÜR SOZIALÖKONOMIE

GAZETTE VERBRAUCHERMAGAZIN GMBH 682368
Badensche Str. 44, 10715 BERLIN
Tel: 30 8449330 **Fax:** 30 84493313
Email: info@gazette-berlin.de
Web site: http://www.gazette-berlin.de

Titles:
GAZETTE - AUSG. CHARLOTTENBURG

DIE GAZETTE VERLAGS GMBH 1643286
Kunigundenstr. 42, 80805 MÜNCHEN
Tel: 89 36039666 **Fax:** 89 36039667
Email: glunk@gazette.de
Web site: http://www.gazette.de

Titles:
DIE GAZETTE

GBI-GENIOS DEUTSCHE WIRTSCHAFTSDATENBANK GMBH 1690864
Freischützstr. 96, 81927 MÜNCHEN
Tel: 89 9928790 **Fax:** 89 99287999
Email: info@genios.de
Web site: http://www.genios.de

Titles:
GENIOS GERMAN BUSINESS INFORMATION

GD GOTHA DRUCK UND VERPACKUNG GMBH & CO. KG 1653910
Gutenbergstr. 3, 99869 GÜNTHERSLEBEN-WECHMAR **Tel:** 36256 280 **Fax:** 36256 280132
Email: info@gothadruck.de
Web site: http://www.gothadruck.de

Titles:
APOTHEKEN KURIER

GDL-VERMÖGENSTRÄGERGES. MBH 682376
Baumweg 45, 60316 FRANKFURT
Tel: 69 4057090 **Fax:** 69 405709129
Email: info@gdl.de
Web site: http://www.gdl.de

Titles:
GDL MAGAZIN VORAUS

GDMB INFORMATIONSGES. MBH 681424
Paul-Ernst-Str. 10, 38678 CLAUSTHAL-ZELLERFELD **Tel:** 5323 93720 **Fax:** 5323 937237
Email: gdmb@gdmb.de
Web site: http://www.gdmb.de

Titles:
MARKSCHEIDEWESEN
WORLD OF METALLURGY - ERZMETALL
WORLD OF MINING - SURFACE UNDERGROUND

G.D.T. GMBH DIVISION MEDIA PRODUCTION 1709754
Heinrich-Kemp-Weg 10, 52499 BAESWEILER
Tel: 2401 8010813 **Fax:** 2401 8010814
Web site: http://www.dynamit-magazin.de

Titles:
DYNAMIT

GEA WESTFALIA SEPARATOR GMBH 1650992
Werner-Habig-Str. 1, 59302 OELDE **Tel:** 2522 770
Fax: 2522 772488
Email: ws.info@geagroup.com
Web site: http://www.westfalia-separator.com

Titles:
SEPARATOR'S DIGEST

GEBR. GERSTENBERG GMBH & CO. KG 683242
Rathausstr. 18, 31134 HILDESHEIM
Tel: 5121 1060 **Fax:** 5121 106217
Email: info@hildesheimer-allgemeine.de
Web site: http://www.hildesheimer-allgemeine.de

Titles:
HILDESHEIMER ALLGEMEINE ZEITUNG

GEBR. MÄRKLIN & CIE. GMBH, VERLAGSBEREICH MÄRKLIN MAGAZIN 685278
Stuttgarter Str. 55, 73033 GÖPPINGEN
Tel: 7161 79491 **Fax:** 7161 79439
Web site: http://www.maerklin.de

Titles:
MÄRKLIN MAGAZIN

GEBR. STORCK GMBH & CO. VERLAGS-OHG 678207
Duisburger Str. 375/C-Geb., 46049 OBERHAUSEN **Tel:** 208 8480224 **Fax:** 208 8480242
Email: birgit.voelkel@storckverlag.de
Web site: http://www.storckverlag.de

Titles:
APOTHEKEN MAGAZIN
APOTHEKEN RÄTSEL MAGAZIN 50+
RATGEBER AUS IHRER APOTHEKE

GEE MEDIA & MARKETING GMBH 1758454
Hongkongstr. 7, 20457 HAMBURG
Tel: 40 226335962 **Fax:** 40 226335989
Email: hansch@geemag.de
Web site: http://www.geemag.de

Titles:
GEE

GEFFKEN & KÖLLNER DRUCK- UND VERLAGSGES. MBH 679536
Sedanstr. 87, 28201 BREMEN **Tel:** 421 557080
Fax: 421 5570822
Email: service@geffkenkoellner.de
Web site: http://www.geffkenkoellner.de

Titles:
BLZ

GEHE PHARMA HANDEL GMBH, NEUE MEDIEN 1690726
Neckarstr. 131, 70376 STUTTGART
Tel: 711 577190 **Fax:** 711 57719790
Email: info@apotheke.com
Web site: http://www.apotheke.com

Titles:
APOTHEKE.COM

GEIER-DRUCK-VERLAG KG 688109
Bahnhofstr. 70, 67105 SCHIFFERSTADT
Tel: 6235 92690 **Fax:** 6235 926933
Email: info@geier-druck-verlag.de
Web site: http://www.schifferstadter-tagblatt.de

Titles:
SCHIFFERSTADTER TAGBLATT

GEISLINGER ZEITUNG VERLAGSGES. MBH & CO. KG 682401
Hauptstr. 38, 73312 GEISLINGEN **Tel:** 7331 2020
Fax: 7331 20240
Email: geislinger-zeitung.vertrieb@swp.de
Web site: http://www.geislinger-zeitung.de

Titles:
GEISLINGER ZEITUNG

GELD UND VERBRAUCHER VERLAGS-GMBH & CO. 687974
Neckargartacher Str. 90, 74080 HEILBRONN
Tel: 7131 913320 **Fax:** 7131 91332114
Email: info@geldundverbraucher.de
Web site: http://www.geldundverbraucher.de

Titles:
SALDO

GELNHÄUSER TAGEBLATT VERLAGSGES. MBH & CO. KG 1767106
Barbarossastr. 5, 63571 GELNHAUSEN
Tel: 6051 8240 **Fax:** 6051 824333
Email: info@gelnhaeuser-tageblatt.de
Web site: http://www.gelnhaeuser-tageblatt.de

Titles:
GELNHÄUSER TAGEBLATT

GEMEINDE BOBENHEIM-ROXHEIM, SENIORENBEIRAT 1622291
Rathausplatz, 67240 BOBENHEIM-ROXHEIM
Tel: 6239 9391304
Web site: http://www.bobenheim-roxheim.de/gemeinde/senioren/index.htm

Titles:
SENIOREN JOURNAL GOLDENER HERBST

GEMEINDETAG BADEN-WÜRTTEMBERG 682422
Panoramastr. 33, 70174 STUTTGART
Tel: 711 225720 **Fax:** 711 2257247
Email: zentrale@gemeindetag-bw.de
Web site: http://www.gemeindetag-bw.de

Titles:
DIE GEMEINDE

GEMEINNÜTZIGE MEDIENHAUS GMBH 681534
Rechneigrabenstr. 10, 60311 FRANKFURT
Tel: 69 92107401 **Fax:** 69 92107422
Email: medienhaus@ekhn.de
Web site: http://www.ev-medienhaus.de

Titles:
EVANGELISCHE SONNTAGS-ZEITUNG

GEMEINSCHAFT DER FLIEGER DEUTSCHER STREITKRÄFTE E.V. 1768908
Südstr. 66a, 53797 LOHMAR **Tel:** 2246 3037375
Fax: 2246 3037375
Email: gdf.gf@gmx.de
Web site: http://www.fliegergemeinschaft.de

Titles:
FLIEGERBLATT

GEMEINSCHAFTSWERK DER EVANGELISCHEN PUBLIZISTIK GGMBH 679049
Emil-von-Behring-Str. 3, 60439 FRANKFURT
Tel: 69 580980 **Fax:** 69 58098100
Email: info@gep.de
Web site: http://www.gep.de

Titles:
EPD FILM
EPD MEDIEN
EPD SOZIAL
GEMEINDEBRIEF
JS MAGAZIN

GENERAL FLUGSICHERHEIT IN DER BUNDESWEHR 1767086
Postfach 906110, 51127 KÖLN **Tel:** 2203 9083124
Fax: 2203 9084092

Titles:
FLUGSICHERHEIT

GENERAL LOGISTICS SYSTEMS GERMANY GMBH & CO. OHG 693339
GLS-Germany-Str. 1, 36286 NEUENSTEIN
Tel: 6677 170 **Fax:** 6677 17111
Email: info@gls-germany.com
Web site: http://www.gls-group.eu

Titles:
INSIGHT

GENERALI VERSICHERUNGEN 682481
Adenauerring 7, 81737 MÜNCHEN
Tel: 89 51212864 **Fax:** 89 51211045
Email: presse@generali.de
Web site: http://www.generali.de

Titles:
LÖWENKURIER

GENOSSENSCHAFTSVERBAND BAYERN E.V. 682492
Türkenstr. 22, 80333 MÜNCHEN **Tel:** 89 28683400
Fax: 89 28683405
Email: profil@gv-bayern.de
Web site: http://www.gv-bayern.de

Titles:
PROFIL

GENOSSENSCHAFTSVERBAND E.V. 1741907
Wilhelm-Haas-Platz 2, 63263 NEU-ISENBURG
Tel: 69 69780 **Fax:** 69 6978124
Email: marketing.intern@genossenschaftsverband.de
Web site: http://www.genossenschaftsverband.de

Titles:
MARKETING INTERN
NETZWERK

GENOSSENSCHAFTSVERBAND WESER-EMS E.V. 682491
Raiffeisenstr. 26, 26122 OLDENBURG
Tel: 441 210030 **Fax:** 441 21003529

Titles:
GENOSSENSCHAFTS-MAGAZIN WESER-EMS

GEORG GRAF VON BAUDISSIN VERLAG NORDFRIESLAND PALETTE KG 696934
Norderstr. 22, 25813 HUSUM **Tel:** 4841 83560
Fax: 4841 835660
Email: ktv-verlag@moinmoin.de
Web site: http://www.nf-palette.de

Titles:
NORDFRIESLAND PALETTE

GEORG HAUSER GMBH + CO. ZEITUNGSVERLAG KG 1718315
Hindenburgstr. 6, 72555 METZINGEN
Tel: 7123 9450 **Fax:** 7123 945160

Titles:
REUTLINGER NACHRICHTEN
SÜDWEST PRESSE

GEORG THIEME VERLAG KG 677464
Rüdigerstr. 14, 70469 STUTTGART
Tel: 711 89310 **Fax:** 711 8931298
Email: kundenservice@thieme.de
Web site: http://www.thieme.de

Titles:
AINS ANÄSTHESIOLOGIE INTENSIVMEDIZIN NOTFALLMEDIZIN SCHMERZTHERAPIE
AKTUELLE DERMATOLOGIE
AKTUELLE ERNÄHRUNGSMEDIZIN
AKTUELLE NEUROLOGIE
AKTUELLE RHEUMATOLOGIE
AKTUELLE UROLOGIE
ALLGEMEIN- UND VISZERALCHIRURGIE UP2DATE
BALINT-JOURNAL
BVGD INFO
CENTRAL EUROPEAN NEUROSURGERY
DEUTSCHE GESELLSCHAFT FÜR CHIRURGIE MITTEILUNGEN
DEUTSCHE GESELLSCHAFT FÜR UNFALLCHIRURGIE E.V. MITTEILUNGEN UND NACHRICHTEN
DIABETES AKTUELL FÜR DIE HAUSARZTPRAXIS
DIABETESIDE KONKRET
DIABETOLOGIE UND STOFFWECHSEL
DIALYSE AKTUELL
DMW DEUTSCHE MEDIZINISCHE WOCHENSCHRIFT
ENDO-PRAXIS
ENDOSCOPY
ENDOSKOPIE HEUTE
EUROPEAN JOURNAL OF PEDIATRIC SURGERY
FLUGMEDIZIN TROPENMEDIZIN REISEMEDIZIN
FORTSCHRITTE DER NEUROLOGIE - PSYCHIATRIE
FRAUENHEILKUNDE UP2DATE
GASTROENTEROLOGIE UP2DATE
GEBURTSHILFE UND FRAUENHEILKUNDE
GESUNDHEITSÖKONOMIE & QUALITÄTSMANAGEMENT
DAS GESUNDHEITSWESEN
HANDCHIRURGIE MIKROCHIRURGIE PLASTISCHE CHIRURGIE
HORMONE AND METABOLIC RESEARCH
INTENSIV
INTERNATIONAL JOURNAL OF SPORTS MEDICINE
KARDIOLOGIE UP2DATE
KLINISCHE MONATSBLÄTTER FÜR AUGENHEILKUNDE
KLINISCHE NEUROPHYSIOLOGIE
KLINISCHE PÄDIATRIE
KRANKENHAUSHYGIENE UP2DATE
LARYNGO- RHINO- OTOLOGIE
MINIMALLY INVASIVE NEUROSURGERY
NEUROREHA
DER NOTARZT
NOTFALLMEDIZIN UP2DATE
OP-JOURNAL
ORTHOPÄDIE MITTEILUNGEN
ORTHOPÄDIE UND UNFALLCHIRUGIE UP2DATE
PÄDIATRIE UP2DATE
PHARMACOPSYCHIATRY
PHYSIKALISCHE MEDIZIN REHABILITATIONSMEDIZIN KURORTMEDIZIN
PID PSYCHOTHERAPIE IM DIALOG
PNEUMOLOGIE
PPMP PSYCHOTHERAPIE PSYCHOSOMATIK MEDIZINISCHE PSYCHOLOGIE
PSYCH. PFLEGE HEUTE
PSYCHIATRIE UND PSYCHOTHERAPIE UP2DATE
PSYCHIATRISCHE PRAXIS
RADIOLOGIE UP2DATE
RADIOPRAXIS
DIE REHABILITATION
RÖFO FORTSCHRITTE AUF DEM GEBIET DER RÖNTGENSTRAHLEN UND DER BILDGEBENDEN VERFAHREN
SENOLOGIE
SPORTVERLETZUNG SPORTSCHADEN
SPRACHE - STIMME - GEHÖR
SUCHTTHERAPIE
SYNFACTS
SYNLETT
SYNTHESIS
THE THORACIC AND CARDIOVASCULAR SURGEON
TUMORDIAGNOSTIK & THERAPIE
ULTRASCHALL IN DER MEDIZIN EUROPEAN JOURNAL OF ULTRASOUND
ZEITSCHRIFT FÜR GASTROENTEROLOGIE
ZEITSCHRIFT FÜR ORTHOPÄDIE UND UNFALLCHIRURGIE
ZEITSCHRIFT FÜR PALLIATIVMEDIZIN
ZEITSCHRIFT FÜR SEXUALFORSCHUNG
ZENTRALBLATT FÜR CHIRURGIE
ZGN ZEITSCHRIFT FÜR GEBURTSHILFE & NEONATOLOGIE

GERAMOND VERLAG GMBH 1707111
Infanteriestr. 11a, 80797 MÜNCHEN
Tel: 89 1306990 **Fax:** 89 130699100
Email: info@geramond.de
Web site: http://www.geramond.de

Titles:
AUTO CLASSIC
FLUGZEUG CLASSIC
MODELLFAN
TRAKTOR CLASSIC

GERD ACHILLES VERLAG 681647
Dorotheenstr. 64, 22301 HAMBURG
Tel: 40 46856587 **Fax:** 40 46863297
Email: info@schiffsreisenportal.de
Web site: http://www.schiffsreisenportal.de

Titles:
SCHIFFSREISEN INTERN.

GERHARD VERLAG GMBH 1773181
Gutenbergstr. 1, 26632 IHLOW **Tel:** 4928 910066
Fax: 4928 911012
Email: christhard.wendt@gerhard-verlag.de
Web site: http://www.gerhard-verlag.de

Titles:
HANDELSFORUM

GERLINDE KLÄRNER 1724659
Heimstr. 70, 27749 DELMENHORST
Tel: 4221 155350 **Fax:** 4221 155352
Email: info@reifezeit.net
Web site: http://www.reifezeit.net
Titles:
REIFEZEIT

GERT WOHLFARTH GMBH 678822
Stresemannstr. 20, 47051 DUISBURG
Tel: 203 305270 **Fax:** 203 30527820
Email: info@wohlfarth.de
Web site: http://www.wohlfarth.de
Titles:
BAUBESCHLAG TASCHENBUCH
BAUELEMENT + TECHNIK
BAUSTOFF MARKT
BAUSTOFFPRAXIS
LEBENSRÄUME
LEBENSRÄUME-SPEZIAL
SCHLOSS + BESCHLAG MARKT
SICHERHEITS MAGAZIN

GESAMTVERBAND DER DEUTSCHEN VERSICHERUNGSWIRTSCHAFT E.V. 1641876
Wilhelmstr. 43/43G, 10117 BERLIN
Tel: 30 20205118 **Fax:** 30 20206604
Email: positionen@gdv.de
Web site: http://www.gdv.de
Titles:
POSITIONEN ZU POLITIK, WIRTSCHAFT UND GESELLSCHAFT

GESELLSCHAFT ANTHROPOSOPHISCHER ÄRZTE IN DEUTSCHLAND 685573
Roggenstr. 82, 70794 FILDERSTADT
Tel: 711 7799711 **Fax:** 711 7799712
Email: info@gaed.de
Web site: http://www.gaed.de
Titles:
DER MERKURSTAB

GESELLSCHAFT DEUTSCHER CHEMIKER 686116
Varrentrappstr. 40, 60486 FRANKFURT
Tel: 69 7917462 **Fax:** 69 7917463
Email: nachrichten@gdch.de
Web site: http://www.gdch.de
Titles:
NACHRICHTEN AUS DER CHEMIE

GESELLSCHAFT DEUTSCHER ROSENFREUNDE E.V. 687791
Waldseestr. 14, 76530 BADEN-BADEN
Tel: 7221 31302 **Fax:** 7221 38337
Email: info@rosenfreunde.de
Web site: http://www.rosenfreunde.de
Titles:
ROSEN-JAHRBUCH

GESELLSCHAFT FÜR BIOLOGISCHE KREBSABWEHR E.V. 1743186
Voßstr. 3, 69115 HEIDELBERG **Tel:** 6221 138020
Fax: 6221 1380220
Email: information@biokrebs.de
Web site: http://www.biokrebs.de
Titles:
IMPULSE

GESELLSCHAFT FÜR FREIE PUBLIZISTIK E.V. 682131
Postfach 1216, 72641 OBERBOIHINGEN
Tel: 7022 39941
Web site: http://www.gfp-netz.de
Titles:
DAS FREIE FORUM

GESELLSCHAFT FÜR GESCHICHTE DES WEINES E.V. 688183
Schloßbergstr. 17, 55452 RÜMMELSHEIM
Tel: 6721 43489
Email: gerhard.stumm@gmx.de
Web site: http://www.geschichte-des-weines.de
Titles:
VERZEICHNIS DER SCHRIFTEN ZUR WEINGESCHICHTE

GESELLSCHAFT FÜR KIRCHLICHE PUBLIZISTIK MAINZ MBH 679587
Liebfrauenplatz 10, 55116 MAINZ
Tel: 6131 287550 **Fax:** 6131 2875522
Email: info@kirchenzeitung.de
Web site: http://www.kirchenzeitung.de
Titles:
BONIFATIUSBOTE
GLAUBE UND LEBEN
DER SONNTAG

GESELLSCHAFT FÜR KOMMUNIKATION UND WIRTSCHAFTSINFORMATION MBH 681487
Landersumer Weg 40, 48431 RHEINE
Tel: 5971 921630 **Fax:** 5971 921163896
Email: info@europa-kurier.com
Web site: http://www.europa-kurier.com
Titles:
EUROPAKURIER

GESELLSCHAFT FÜR MEDIENENTWICKLUNG GBR 1772320
Isestr. 26, 20149 HAMBURG
Titles:
MESSAGE

GESELLSCHAFT FÜR WISSENSCHAFTLICHE GESPRÄCHS-PSYCHOTHERAPIE E.V. 698118
Melatengürtel 125a, 50825 KÖLN
Tel: 221 9259080 **Fax:** 221 92590819
Email: gwg@gwg-ev.org
Web site: http://www.gwg-ev.org
Titles:
GESPRÄCHSPSYCHOTHERAPIE UND PERSONZENTRIERTE BERATUNG

GESELLSCHAFT ZUR FÖRDERUNG DES LEHRSTUHLS FÜR WASSERGÜTE- UND ABFALLWIRTSCHAFT DER TECHNISCHEN UNIVERSITÄT MÜNCHEN 1668820
Am Coulombwall, 85748 GARCHING
Tel: 89 28913700 **Fax:** 89 28913718
Email: foerderverein@bv.tum.de
Web site: http://www.wga.bv.tum.de
Titles:
FORUM

GESTALT-INSTITUT KÖLN GMBH/GIK BILDUNGSWERKSTATT KÖLN 1622462
Rurstr. 9, 50937 KÖLN **Tel:** 221 416163
Fax: 221 447652
Email: gik-gestalttherapie@gmx.de
Web site: http://www.gestalt.de
Titles:
GESTALT KRITIK

GEVA GASTRONOMIEDIENSTE GMBH 1713105
Albert-Einstein-Str. 18, 50226 FRECHEN
Tel: 2234 1834171 **Fax:** 2234 1834179
Email: haake@geva.com
Web site: http://www.geva.com
Titles:
GAST FREUNDSCHAFT

GEWANDHAUS ZU LEIPZIG 682563
Augustusplatz 8, 04109 LEIPZIG **Tel:** 341 12700
Fax: 341 1270200
Email: publicrelations@gewandhaus.de
Web site: http://www.gewandhaus.de
Titles:
VORSCHAU

GEWERBE-REPORT, VERLAGSGEMEINSCHAFT GBR 682565
Hüttenbergstr. 38, 66538 NEUNKIRCHEN
Tel: 6821 306251 **Fax:** 6821 306241
Email: info@esd-ev.de
Web site: http://www.esd-ev.de
Titles:
GEWERBE REPORT

GEWERKSCHAFT ERZIEHUNG UND WISSENSCHAFT, LANDESVERBAND HAMBURG 1744274
Rothenbaumchaussee 15, 20148 HAMBURG
Tel: 40 4146330 **Fax:** 40 440877
Email: hlz@gew-hamburg.de
Web site: http://www.gew-hamburg.de
Titles:
HLZ

GEWERKSCHAFT NAHRUNG-GENUSS-GASTSTÄTTEN 681160
Haubachstr. 76, 22765 HAMBURG **Tel:** 40 380130
Fax: 40 38013220
Email: hv.redaktion@ngg.net
Web site: http://www.ngg.net
Titles:
EINIGKEIT

GFA-GESELLSCHAFT ZUR FÖRDERUNG DER ABWASSERTECHNIK E.V. 678451
Theodor-Heuss-Allee 17, 53773 HENNEF
Tel: 2242 8720 **Fax:** 2242 872151
Email: bringewski@dwa.de
Web site: http://www.dwa.de
Titles:
KA KORRESPONDENZ ABWASSER ABFALL
KA-BETRIEBS-INFO
KW KORRESPONDENZ WASSERWIRTSCHAFT

GFE GES. ZUR FÖRDERUNG DER ELEKTROHANDWERKE NIEDERSACHSEN/BREMEN MBH 1600543
Baumschulenallee 12, 30625 HANNOVER
Tel: 511 9575744 **Fax:** 511 9575799
Email: liv@eh-nb.de
Web site: http://www.eh-nb.de
Titles:
DAS NEUE SPRACHROHR ELEKTROHANDWERK NORD

GFI. GES. FÜR MEDIZINISCHE INFORMATION MBH 678203
Paul-Wassermann-Str. 15, 81829 MÜNCHEN
Tel: 89 4366300 **Fax:** 89 436630210
Email: info@gfi-online.de
Web site: http://www.gfi-medien.de
Titles:
APOTHEKEN-DEPESCHE
GYN-DEPESCHE
NEURO-DEPESCHE
PRAXIS-DEPESCHE

GFK GRUPPE 695583
Nordwestring 101, 90419 NÜRNBERG
Tel: 911 3954440 **Fax:** 911 3954041
Email: public.relations@gfk.com
Web site: http://www.gfk.com
Titles:
GFK INSITE

GFM GES. FÜR MASCHINENDIAGNOSE MBH 1622230
Köpenicker Str. 325/40, 12555 BERLIN
Tel: 30 65762565 **Fax:** 30 65762564
Email: mailbox@maschinendiagnose.de
Web site: http://www.maschinendiagnose.de
Titles:
MASCHINENDIAGNOSE-NEWS

GFMK KG VERLAGSGES. 1675682
Gezelinallee 37, 51375 LEVERKUSEN
Tel: 214 310570 **Fax:** 214 3105719
Email: info@gfmk.com
Web site: http://www.gfmk.com
Titles:
ALLERGIKUS
BEFUND KREBS
LEBEN? LEBEN!

GFW PHOTO PUBLISHING GMBH 681214
Holzstr. 2, 40221 DÜSSELDORF **Tel:** 211 390090
Fax: 211 3900955
Email: info@gfw.de
Web site: http://www.gfw.de
Titles:
FOTO HITS EINKAUFSFÜHRER
INPHO IMAGING & BUSINESS
PICTORIAL
PROFIFOTO

GIESEL VERLAG GMBH 677736
Hans-Böckler-Allee 9, 30173 HANNOVER
Tel: 511 73040 **Fax:** 511 7304157
Email: info@giesel.de
Web site: http://www.giesel-verlag.de
Titles:
ALUMINIUM
ALUMINIUM PRAXIS
ASPHALT
K KUNSTSTOFF-BERATER
K ZEITUNG
METALL
DIE SCHWEIZER BAUSTOFF-INDUSTRIE DSB
STRASSEN- UND TIEFBAU ST

GIESSENER ANZEIGER VERLAGS GMBH & CO. KG 1682195
Am Urnenfeld 12, 35396 GIESSEN
Tel: 641 95043505 **Fax:** 641 95043511
Email: redaktion@giessener-anzeiger.de
Web site: http://www.giessener-anzeiger.de
Titles:
GIESSENER ANZEIGER

GIESSEREI-VERLAG GMBH 680409
Sohnstr. 65, 40237 DÜSSELDORF **Tel:** 211 67070
Fax: 211 6707517
Email: giesserei@stahleisen.de
Web site: http://www.giesserei-verlag.de
Titles:
CP + T CASTING PLANT AND TECHNOLOGY INTERNATIONAL
GIESSEREI
GIESSEREI-ERFAHRUNGSAUSTAUSCH
GIESSEREIFORSCHUNG INTERNATIONAL FOUNDRY RESEARCH

GIG VERLAGS GMBH 682598
Sauerländer Weg 2a, 48145 MÜNSTER
Tel: 251 987230 **Fax:** 251 9872350
Email: office@gig-online.de
Web site: http://www.gig-online.de
Titles:
GIG
UNI-GIG

GIT VERLAG GMBH & CO. KG 677473
Rößlerstr. 90, 64293 DARMSTADT
Tel: 6151 80900 **Fax:** 6151 8090146
Email: info@gitverlag.com
Web site: http://www.gitverlag.com
Titles:
BIOFORUM
CHEMANAGER
CIT PLUS
G.I.T. LABORATORY JOURNAL EUROPE
GIT LABOR-FACHZEITSCHRIFT
GIT SICHERHEIT + MANAGEMENT
INSPECT
MANAGEMENT & KRANKENHAUS
MESSTEC DRIVES AUTOMATION
ORTHOPÄDIE IM PROFIL
PRO-4-PRO

GITO MBH-VERLAG FÜR INDUSTRIELLE INFORMATIONSTECHNIK UND ORGANISATION 683592
Detmolder Str. 62, 10715 BERLIN
Tel: 30 41938364 **Fax:** 30 41938367
Email: service@gito.de
Web site: http://www.gito.de
Titles:
INDUSTRIE MANAGEMENT
PRODUCTIVITY MANAGEMENT

GK MITTELSTANDSMAGAZIN VERLAG GMBH 1760013
Gärtnerkoppel 3, 24259 WESTENSEE
Tel: 4305 992995 **Fax:** 4305 992993
Email: info@mitmagazin.com
Web site: http://www.mitmagazin.com
Titles:
MITTELSTANDSMAGAZIN

GKM-ZENTRALREDAKTION GMBH 1655249
Boslerstr. 29, 71088 HOLZGERLINGEN
Tel: 7031 744201 **Fax:** 7031 744199
Email: verlag@network-karriere.com
Web site: http://www.network-karriere.com
Titles:
NETWORK-KARRIERE

Germany

GLOBUS MEDIEN GMBH 1706789
Erich-Weinert-Str. 22, 10439 BERLIN
Tel: 30 50178145 **Fax:** 30 920372065
Email: info@frankreicherleben.de
Web site: http://www.globus-medien.de

Titles:
FRANKREICH ERLEBEN

GO! PRESSEBÜRO & VERLAG GMBH 1710446
Harvestehuder Weg 94, 20149 HAMBURG
Tel: 40 45038410 **Fax:** 40 45038411
Email: verlag@go-presse.de
Web site: http://www.go-presse.de

Titles:
SAVOIR-VIVRE

GO VERLAG GMBH & CO. KG 1681463
Alleenstr. 158, 73230 KIRCHHEIM
Tel: 7021 97500 **Fax:** 7021 975033
Email: info@teckbote.de
Web site: http://www.teckbote.de

Titles:
DER TECKBOTE

GOING PUBLIC MEDIA AG 682662
Hofmannstr. 7a, 81379 MÜNCHEN
Tel: 89 20003390 **Fax:** 89 200033939
Email: info@goingpublic.de
Web site: http://www.goingpublic.de

Titles:
GOINGPUBLIC
HV MAGAZIN
UNTERNEHMER EDITION
VENTURECAPITAL

GOLDAMMER VERLAG GMBH & CO. KG 679727
Langes Gräthlein 45, 97078 WÜRZBURG
Tel: 931 24006 **Fax:** 931 29201
Email: info@goldammer.com
Web site: http://www.goldammer.com

Titles:
WOHLAU-STEINAUER HEIMATBLATT

GOLF TIME VERLAG GMBH 682686
Oskar-von-Miller-Str. 11, 82008 UNTERHACHING **Tel:** 89 42718181
Fax: 89 42718171
Email: redaktion@golftime.de
Web site: http://www.golftime.de

Titles:
GOLF TIME

GOLF-MASTERS 1793383
Forststr. 34, 12163 BERLIN **Tel:** 30 8236502
Fax: 30 8234098
Email: golf-masters@t-online.de
Web site: http://www.golf-masters.de

Titles:
GOLF IN BERLIN UND BRANDENBURG

GÖLLER VERLAG GMBH 680012
Aschmattstr. 8, 76532 BADEN-BADEN
Tel: 7221 502200 **Fax:** 7221 502222
Email: info@goeller-verlag.de
Web site: http://www.goeller-verlag.de

Titles:
CFI CERAMIC FORUM INTERNATIONAL
ECONOMIC ENGINEERING
FLIEGE. INGENIEURBLATT FÜR BADEN-WÜRTTEMBERG
OFFICE & PAPER
TOYS

GONG VERLAG GMBH & CO. KG 677329
Münchener Str. 101, 85737 ISMANING
Tel: 89 272700 **Fax:** 89 272707990
Email: kontakt@gongverlag.de
Web site: http://www.gong-verlag.de

Titles:
2 DIE ZWEI
A DIE AKTUELLE
BILD + FUNK
DU UND DAS TIER
EIN HERZ FÜR TIERE
GELIEBTE KATZE
NURTV
OTC TOOLS
PARTNER HUND
TV 4X7
TV DIREKT
TV KOCHEN
TV PICCOLINO

GÖRRES DRUCKEREI UND VERLAG GMBH 1653049
Carl-Spaeter-Str. 1, 56070 KOBLENZ
Tel: 261 884190 **Fax:** 261 8841980
Email: info@goerres-druckerei.de
Web site: http://www.goerres-verlag.de

Titles:
IHK JOURNAL KOBLENZ

GOSLARSCHE ZEITUNG KARL KRAUSE GMBH & CO. KG 1767295
Bäckerstr. 31, 38640 GOSLAR **Tel:** 5321 3330
Fax: 5321 333399
Email: verlag@goslarsche-zeitung.de
Web site: http://www.goslarsche.de

Titles:
GOSLARSCHE ZEITUNG

GÖTTINGER TAGEBLATT GMBH & CO. KG 694782
Dransfelder Str. 1, 37079 GÖTTINGEN
Tel: 551 901200 **Fax:** 551 901278
Email: info@goettinger-tageblatt.de
Web site: http://www.goettinger-tageblatt.de

Titles:
BLICK
GÖTTINGER TAGEBLATT

GOVI-VERLAG, PHARMAZEUTISCHER VERLAG GMBH 686240
Carl-Mannich-Str. 26, 65760 ESCHBORN
Tel: 6196 9280 **Fax:** 6196 928203
Email: service@govi.de
Web site: http://www.govi.de

Titles:
NEUE APOTHEKEN ILLUSTRIERTE
NEUE APOTHEKEN ILLUSTRIERTE EXTRA
DIE PHARMAZIE
PTA FORUM
PZ PHARMAZEUTISCHE ZEITUNG
PZ PHARMAZEUTISCHE ZEITUNG ONLINE
PZ PRISMA

GRAEWIS VERLAG GMBH 681141
Wallstr. 60, 10179 BERLIN **Tel:** 30 3088240
Fax: 30 30882420
Email: verlag@graewis.de
Web site: http://www.einblick.dgb.de

Titles:
EINBLICK

GRÄFE UND UNZER VERLAG GMBH 1640636
Grillparzerstr. 12, 81675 MÜNCHEN
Tel: 89 419810 **Fax:** 89 41981113
Web site: http://www.graefe-und-unzer.de

Titles:
GAMBERO ROSSO VINI D'ITALIA
DER KLEINE JOHNSON
OSTERIE D'ITALIA

GRAFSCHAFTER NACHRICHTEN GMBH & CO. KG 682648
Coesfelder Hof 2, 48527 NORDHORN
Tel: 5921 7070 **Fax:** 5921 707470
Email: gn@gn-online.de
Web site: http://www.gn-online.de

Titles:
GN GRAFSCHAFTER NACHRICHTEN

GRAFSCHAFTER WOCHENBLATT VERLAGS- UND WERBE-GMBH 682711
Max-Planck-Str. 4, 48529 NORDHORN
Tel: 5921 5055 **Fax:** 5921 77297
Web site: http://www.grafschafter-wochenblatt.de

Titles:
GRAFSCHAFTER WOCHENBLATT AM MITTWOCH

GRAPHISCHE BETRIEBE F. W. RUBENS KG 683157
Ostring 2, 59423 UNNA **Tel:** 2303 2020
Fax: 2303 202163
Email: verlag@hellwegeranzeiger.de
Web site: http://www.hellwegeranzeiger.de

Titles:
HELLWEGER ANZEIGER
HELLWEGER ANZEIGER

GREENPEACE MEDIA GMBH 694791
Große Elbstr. 145d, 22767 HAMBURG
Tel: 40 808128080 **Fax:** 40 808128099
Email: gpm@greenpeace-magazin.de
Web site: http://www.greenpeace-magazin.de

Titles:
GREENPEACE
GREENPEACE MAGAZIN.

GRIMMESCHE HOFBUCHDRUCKEREI, ZWEIGNIEDERLASSUNG DER C. BÖSENDAHL GMBH & CO. KG 688094
Lange Str. 20, 31675 BÜCKEBURG
Tel: 5722 96870 **Fax:** 5722 9687566
Email: lz@landes-zeitung.de
Web site: http://www.landes-zeitung.de

Titles:
SCHAUMBURG-LIPPISCHE LANDES-ZEITUNG

GRIN VERLAG GMBH 1651685
Marienstr. 17, 80331 MÜNCHEN **Tel:** 89 5505590
Fax: 89 55055910
Email: info@grin.com
Web site: http://www.grin.com

Titles:
HAUSARBEITEN.DE

GRONE VERLAG 685388
Sickingmühler Str. 99, 45772 MARL
Tel: 2365 65055 **Fax:** 2365 65400
Email: verlag@vest-aktuell.de
Web site: http://www.vest-aktuell.de

Titles:
MARL AKTUELL SONNTAGSBLATT

GROSSE VERLAG 684627
Brandenburgische Str. 18, 10707 BERLIN
Tel: 30 8867490 **Fax:** 30 88674999
Email: info@grosse-verlag.de
Web site: http://www.grosse-verlag.de

Titles:
KOCH-METSCHNIKOW JOURNAL
KOSMETISCHE MEDIZIN

GRUNDEIGENTUM-VERLAG GMBH 682804
Potsdamer Str. 143, 10783 BERLIN
Tel: 30 4147690 **Fax:** 30 4113025
Email: vertrieb@grundeigentum-verlag.de
Web site: http://www.grundeigentum-verlag.de

Titles:
DAS GRUNDEIGENTUM
DAS HAUSEIGENTUM

GRÜNE LIGA BERLIN E.V. 679115
Prenzlauer Allee 8, 10405 BERLIN
Tel: 30 4433910 **Fax:** 30 44339133
Email: berlin@grueneliga.de
Web site: http://www.grueneliga-berlin.de

Titles:
DER RABE RALF

GRÜNE LIGA E.V. 677670
Greifswalder Str. 4, 10405 BERLIN
Tel: 30 2044745 **Fax:** 30 2044468
Email: alligator@grueneliga.de
Web site: http://www.grueneliga.de

Titles:
ALLIGATOR

DER GRÜNE PUNKT-DUALES SYSTEM DEUTSCHLAND GMBH 687440
Frankfurter Str. 720, 51145 KÖLN
Tel: 2203 937507 **Fax:** 2203 937191
Email: pressestelle@gruener-punkt.de
Web site: http://www.gruener-punkt.de

Titles:
PUNKT

GRUNER + JAHR AG & CO. KG 687182
Weihenstephaner Str. 7, 81673 MÜNCHEN
Tel: 89 415200 **Fax:** 89 4152565
Web site: http://www.guj.de

Titles:
ART
BRIGITTE
BRIGITTE BALANCE
BRIGITTE KALENDER
BRIGITTE WOMAN
ESSEN & TRINKEN
ESSEN & TRINKEN FÜR JEDEN TAG
FLORA GARTEN
GEO
GEO EPOCHE
GEO SAISON
GEO SPECIAL
GEO.DE
GEOLINO
HÄUSER
JAMIE
P.M. HISTORY
P.M. LOGIK-TRAINER
P.M. MAGAZIN
SCHÖNER WOHNEN
STERN
STERN GESUND LEBEN

GS1 GERMANY GMBH 680371
Maarweg 133, 50825 KÖLN **Tel:** 221 947140
Fax: 221 94714990
Email: info@gs1-germany.de
Web site: http://www.gs1-germany.de

Titles:
STANDARDS

GSFP MBH 1686489
Dudel 1, 17207 BOLLEWICK **Tel:** 39931 54726
Fax: 39931 54727
Web site: http://www.berlinerdebatte.de

Titles:
BERLINER DEBATTE INITIAL

GTV - BUNDESVERBAND GEOTHERMIE E.V. 682503
Stralauer Platz 34, 10243 BERLIN
Tel: 30 726102841 **Fax:** 30 72610280
Email: info@geothermie.de
Web site: http://www.geothermie.de

Titles:
GEOTHERMISCHE ENERGIE

GUIDES & MORE MEDIENAGENTUR UND VERLAGSGMBH 1685873
Knesebeckstr. 11, 10623 BERLIN
Tel: 30 30641410 **Fax:** 30 30641411
Email: office@guidesandmore.com
Web site: http://www.guidesandmore.com

Titles:
HUBERTUS VON HOHENLOHES 500 VERY SPECIAL HOTELS

GUIDO BRÖER & ANDREAS WITT GBR 688512
Bültestr. 70b, 32584 LÖHNE **Tel:** 5731 83460
Fax: 5731 83469
Email: redaktion@solarthemen.de
Web site: http://www.solarthemen.de

Titles:
SOLARTHEMEN
SOLARTHEMEN:KOM

GÜNTER KOHL PR + MARKETING 695106
Gärtnerkoppel 3, 24259 WESTENSEE
Tel: 4305 992992 **Fax:** 4305 992993
Email: gkprkiel@t-online.de

Titles:
DIE INSEL
SYLT MAGAZIN

GÜTERSLOHER VERLAGSHAUS GMBH 678312
Carl-Miele-Str. 214, 33335 GÜTERSLOH
Tel: 5241 74050 **Fax:** 5241 740548
Email: info@gtvh.de
Web site: http://www.gtvh.de

Titles:
GESTERN HEUTE + MORGEN

GW-VERLAG, GES. FÜR GASTGEWERBLICHE FACHPUBLIKATIONEN MBH 682348
Theodor-Althoff-Str. 39, 45133 ESSEN
Tel: 201 87126948 **Fax:** 201 87126941
Web site: http://www.gwverlag.de

Titles:
GASTROHOTEL

GZSZ GMBH 1626754
Picassoplatz 1, 50679 KÖLN **Tel:** 221 45660
Fax: 221 45669999
Email: gzsz-support@rtl.de
Web site: http://gzsz.rtl.de

Titles:
GUTE ZEITEN SCHLECHTE ZEITEN

H. HOFMANN GMBH + CO. KG
1741057
Lautenthaler Str. 3, 38723 SEESEN
Tel: 5381 93650 **Fax:** 5381 936526
Email: anzeigen@seesener-beobachter.de
Web site: http://www.seesener-beobachter.de

Titles:
BEOBACHTER

H. RISIUS KG DRUCKEREI UND VERLAG
687684
Risiusstr. 6, 26826 WEENER **Tel:** 4951 9300
Fax: 4951 930150
Email: info@rheiderland.de
Web site: http://www.rheiderland.de

Titles:
RHEIDERLAND

H & P VERLAG HOYER GMBH
685143
Mainzer Str. 23, 66111 SAARBRÜCKEN
Tel: 681 9601034 **Fax:** 681 9601035
Email: info@live-magazin.de
Web site: http://www.live-magazin.de

Titles:
LIVE

HAHNSCHE BUCHHANDLUNG
682984
Leinstr. 32, 30159 HANNOVER **Tel:** 511 80718040
Fax: 511 363698
Email: verlag@hahnsche-buchhandlung.de
Web site: http://www.hahnsche-buchhandlung.de

Titles:
SCHULVERWALTUNGSBLATT FÜR NIEDERSACHSEN

HALLER KREISBLATT VERLAGS GMBH
682043
Gutenbergstr. 2, 33790 HALLE **Tel:** 5201 1501
Fax: 5201 15166
Email: anzeigen@haller-kreisblatt.de
Web site: http://www.haller-kreisblatt.de

Titles:
HALLER KREISBLATT

HALLO-VERLAG GMBH & CO. KG
682895
Hans-Pinsel-Str. 9a, 85540 HAAR **Tel:** 89 4623355
Fax: 89 462335299
Email: info@hallo-verlag.de
Web site: http://www.hallo-verlag.de

Titles:
HALLO BERG AM LAIM
HALLO HAAR/VATERSTETTEN
HALLO MÜNCHNER NORDOSTEN

HAMBURG FÜHRER VERLAG GMBH
682916
Alter Wall 65, 20457 HAMBURG **Tel:** 40 448185
Fax: 40 452368
Email: info@hamburg-fuehrer.de
Web site: http://www.hamburg-fuehrer.de

Titles:
HAMBURG FÜHRER
HAMBURG GUIDE

HAMBURG TOURISMUS GMBH
689562
Steinstr. 7, 20095 HAMBURG **Tel:** 40 30051103
Fax: 40 30051210
Email: feigl-harms@hamburg-tourismus.de
Web site: http://www.hamburg-tourismus.de

Titles:
TOURISMUS REPORT HAMBURG

HAMBURGER ÄRZTE VERLAG GMBH & CO KG
682918
Humboldtstr. 56, 22083 HAMBURG
Tel: 40 202299205 **Fax:** 40 202299400
Email: verlag@aekhh.de

Titles:
HAMBURGER ÄRZTEBLATT

HAMBURGER BUCH- UND ZEITSCHRIFTENVERLAG GMBH
1742916
Doormannsweg 22, 20259 HAMBURG
Tel: 40 414333830 **Fax:** 40 414333818
Email: info@hbzv.com
Web site: http://www.hbzv.com

Titles:
HAMBURGER UNTERNEHMENSPORTRAITS

HAMBURGER STADTILLUSTRIERTEN VERLAGSGES. MBH
689180
Behringstr. 14, 22765 HAMBURG **Tel:** 40 4328420
Fax: 40 43284230
Email: info@hsi-verlag.de
Web site: http://www.szene-hamburg.de

Titles:
HAMBURG:PUR
SZENE HAMBURG ESSEN + TRINKEN
SZENE HAMBURG KAUFT EIN!

HAMBURGISCHER ANWALTVEREIN E.V.
1715921
Sievekingplatz 1, 20355 HAMBURG
Tel: 40 6116350 **Fax:** 40 354231
Email: info@hav.de
Web site: http://www.hav.de

Titles:
HAV INFO

HANAUER ANZEIGER GMBH + CO. DRUCK- UND VERLAGSHAUS
682943
Donaustr. 5, 63452 HANAU **Tel:** 6181 29030
Fax: 6181 2903500
Email: verlag@hanauer.de
Web site: http://www.hanauer.de

Titles:
HANAUER ANZEIGER
HANAUER WOCHENPOST
LANGENSELBOLDER ZEITUNG

HANDBALLWOCHE GMBH
1752745
Gänsemarkt 1, 24534 NEUMÜNSTER
Tel: 4321 9465400 **Fax:** 4321 9465419
Web site: http://www.handballwoche.de

Titles:
HANDBALL WOCHE

HANDELSAUSKUNFT HEINRICH TÜFFERS GMBH + CO. KG
682960
Grafenberger Allee 39, 40237 DÜSSELDORF
Tel: 211 686766 **Fax:** 211 6798605
Email: info@handelsauskunft.de
Web site: http://www.handelsauskunft.de

Titles:
HANDELSAUSKUNFT

HANDELSBLATT GMBH
1681126
Kasernenstr. 67, 40213 DÜSSELDORF
Tel: 211 8870 **Fax:** 211 8872980
Email: handelsblatt@vhb.de
Web site: http://www.handelsblatt.com

Titles:
HANDELSBLATT
WIRTSCHAFTSWOCHE

HANF VERLAG DARMSTADT GMBH
1634280
Liebenauer Str. 19a, 34396 LIEBENAU
Tel: 5676 920920 **Fax:** 5676 920920
Email: info@grow.de
Web site: http://www.grow.de

Titles:
GROW!

HANNOVER MARKETING UND TOURISMUS GMBH
687632
Bahnhofstr. 6, 30159 HANNOVER
Tel: 511 12345111 **Fax:** 511 12345112
Email: info@hannover-tourismus.de
Web site: http://www.hannover-tourismus.de

Titles:
HANNOVER HOTELS
HANNOVER ... SCHÖNSTE SEITEN!

HANNOVERANER VERBAND E.V.
682979
Lindhooper Str. 92, 27283 VERDEN
Tel: 4231 6730 **Fax:** 4231 67312
Email: redaktion@hannoveraner.com
Web site: http://www.hannoveraner.com

Titles:
DER HANNOVERANER

HANNOVERSCHE ÄRZTE-VERLAGS-UNION GMBH
686429
Berliner Allee 20, 30175 HANNOVER
Tel: 511 3802282 **Fax:** 511 3802281
Email: info@haeverlag.de
Web site: http://www.haeverlag.de

Titles:
NIEDERSÄCHSISCHES ÄRZTEBLATT

HANS MARSEILLE VERLAG GMBH
678373
Bürkleinstr. 12, 80538 MÜNCHEN **Tel:** 89 227988
Fax: 89 2904643
Email: office@marseille-verlag.com
Web site: http://www.marseille-verlag.com

Titles:
PÄDIATRISCHE PRAXIS

HANS SOLDAN GMBH
1622064
Bocholder Str. 259, 45356 ESSEN
Tel: 201 8612123 **Fax:** 201 8612222
Email: info@soldan.de
Web site: http://www.soldan.de

Titles:
JURMEDIA

HANS-BREDOW-INSTITUT
678324
Heimhuder Str. 21, 20148 HAMBURG
Tel: 40 4502170 **Fax:** 40 45021777
Email: info@hans-bredow-institut.de
Web site: http://www.hans-bredow-institut.de

Titles:
ARD JAHRBUCH

HANSEATISCHES WERBEKONTOR HEUSER & CO. KG
682952
Schützenwall 9, 22844 NORDERSTEDT
Tel: 40 5252051 **Fax:** 40 5251088
Email: hwk.heuser@web.de

Titles:
HANDBUCH FÜR DAS GESUNDHEITSWESEN IN HAMBURG

HANSISCHES DRUCK- UND VERLAGSHAUS GMBH
680169
Emil-von-Behring-Str. 3, 60439 FRANKFURT
Tel: 69 580980 **Fax:** 69 58098254
Email: hdv@chrismon.de
Web site: http://www.chrismon.de

Titles:
CHRISMON PLUS
DIAKONIE MAGAZIN

HANSISCHES VERLAGSKONTOR GMBH
678380
Mengstr. 16, 23552 LÜBECK **Tel:** 451 703101
Fax: 451 7031253
Email: info@hansisches-verlagskontor.de
Web site: http://www.hansisches-verlagskontor.de

Titles:
KINDER- UND JUGENDARZT

HAPPY READ PUBLISHING LTD.
1685538
Promenadeplatz 12, 80333 MÜNCHEN
Tel: 89 244488810 **Fax:** 89 244488829
Email: info@harepu.eu
Web site: http://www.deal-magazin.com

Titles:
DEAL MAGAZIN

HARDWARELUXX MEDIA GMBH
1709758
Zum Wiehegraben 5, 30519 HANNOVER
Tel: 511 4756963 **Fax:** 511 4756491
Email: dbode@hardwareluxx.com
Web site: http://www.hardwareluxx.de

Titles:
HARDWARE LUXX

HARENBERG KOMMUNIKATION VERLAGS- UND MEDIEN GMBH & CO. KG
677542
Königswall 21, 44137 DORTMUND **Tel:** 231 90560
Fax: 231 9056110
Email: info@buchreport.de
Web site: http://www.buchreport.de

Titles:
BUCHREPORT EXPRESS
BUCHREPORT MAGAZIN

HARZ KURIER VERLAGSGES. MBH & CO. KG
1751985
Gipsmühlenweg 2, 37520 OSTERODE
Tel: 5522 31700 **Fax:** 5522 3170480
Email: anzeigen@harzkurier.de
Web site: http://www.harzkurier.de

Titles:
ECHO ZUM SONNTAG
HARZ KURIER
HARZER WOCHENSPIEGEL

HARZER HIGHLIGHTS E.V.
1766056
Goetheweg 1, 06502 THALE
Email: info@harzer-highlights.de
Web site: http://www.harzer-highlights.de

Titles:
HARZER HIGHLIGHTS

HASSFURTER TAGBLATT VERLAG GMBH
683009
Augsfelder Str. 19, 97437 HASSFURT
Tel: 9521 6990 **Fax:** 9521 69911
Email: anzeigen@hassfurter-tagblatt.de
Web site: http://www.hassfurter-tagblatt.de

Titles:
HASSFURTER TAGBLATT

HATJE CANTZ VERLAG
679044
Zeppelinstr. 32, 73760 OSTFILDERN
Tel: 711 44050 **Fax:** 711 4405220
Email: contact@hatjecantz.de
Web site: http://www.hatjecantz.de

Titles:
KQ KUNSTQUARTAL

HAUFE PUBLISHING
694631
Fraunhoferstr. 5, 82152 PLANEGG **Tel:** 89 895170
Fax: 89 89517250
Email: online@haufe.de
Web site: http://www.haufe.de

Titles:
DER TIPP DES TAGES

HAUFE-LEXWARE GMBH & CO. KG
689225
Tangstedter Landstr. 83, 22415 HAMBURG
Tel: 40 5201030 **Fax:** 40 52010330
Email: info@hammonia.de
Web site: http://www.hammonia.de

Titles:
ACQUISA
BAV SPEZIAL
BILANZ + BUCHHALTUNG
DIREKT MARKETING
DW DIE WOHNUNGSWIRTSCHAFT
IMMOBILIENWIRTSCHAFT
PERSONAL
PERSONALMAGAZIN
PROFIRMA
STEUERCONSULTANT
WI WOHNUNGSPOLITISCHE INFORMATIONEN
WIRTSCHAFT+WEITERBILDUNG

HAUPTMANN GMBH
688247
August-Bebel-Str. 22, 95126 SCHWARZENBACH **Tel:** 9284 349
Fax: 9284 800460
Email: hauptmann-verlag@t-online.de

Titles:
SCHWARZENBACHER AMTS-BLATT

HAUPTVERBAND DER DEUTSCHEN BAUINDUSTRIE E.V.
678857
Kurfürstenstr. 129, 10785 BERLIN **Tel:** 30 212860
Fax: 30 21286240
Email: bauind@bauindustrie.de
Web site: http://www.bauindustrie.de

Titles:
BAUINDUSTRIE AKTUELL

HAUS & GRUND BAYERN VERLAG UND SERVICE GMBH
678903
Sonnenstr. 11, 80331 MÜNCHEN
Tel: 89 540413322 **Fax:** 89 540413355
Email: info@bayerische-hausbesitzer-zeitung.de
Web site: http://www.bayerische-hausbesitzer-zeitung.de

Titles:
BAYERISCHE HAUSBESITZER-ZEITUNG

HAUS & GRUND KIEL - VERLAG & SERVICE GMBH
686473
Stresemannplatz 4, 24103 KIEL **Tel:** 431 6636123
Fax: 431 6636180
Email: info@haus-und-grund-kiel.de
Web site: http://www.haus-und-grund-kiel.de

Titles:
DIE NORDDEUTSCHE HAUSBESITZER ZEITUNG

HAUSÄRZTEVERBAND WESTFALEN-LIPPE E.V. 683014
Wilhelm-Brand-Str. 1a, 44141 DORTMUND
Tel: 231 821175 **Fax:** 231 825364
Email: bda-westfalen-lippe@t-online.de
Web site: http://www.hausaerzteverband-wl.de

Titles:
DER HAUSARZT IN WESTFALEN

HAYMARKET MEDIA GMBH 1757622
Wieblinger Weg 17, 69123 HEIDELBERG
Tel: 6221 33100 **Fax:** 6221 3310222
Email: office@kress.de
Web site: http://www.kress.de

Titles:
DOCUMENTS
DRUCK & MEDIEN
KRESS KÖPFE
KRESS REPORT
KRESS.DE
KRESSTHEMA LUXUS
PR REPORT
PR REPORT COMPENDIUM

HAYMARKET MEDIA GMBH & CO. KG 682328
Frankfurter Str. 3d, 38122 BRAUNSCHWEIG
Tel: 531 380040 **Fax:** 531 3800425
Email: info@haymarket.de
Web site: http://www.haymarket.de

Titles:
DEUTSCHE BAUMSCHULE
FLORIST
FRIEDHOFSKULTUR
G & V GESTALTEN UND VERKAUFEN
GB GÄRTNERBÖRSE
JAHRBUCH DER BAUMPFLEGE
JAHRBUCH GARTENBAU
TASPO
TASPO BAUMZEITUNG
TASPO DAS MAGAZIN
TASPO GARTEN DESIGN

HEALTH AND BEAUTY BUSINESS MEDIA GMBH 678983
Karl-Friedrich-Str. 14, 76133 KARLSRUHE
Tel: 721 1650 **Fax:** 721 165150
Email: info@health-and-beauty.com
Web site: http://www.health-and-beauty.com

Titles:
BEAUTY FORUM
BODY LIFE
COSSMA
KARLSRUHER WIRTSCHAFTSSPIEGEL
TRAINER

HEBU MUSIKVERLAG GMBH 679425
Gottlieb-Daimler-Str. 22, 76703 KRAICHTAL
Tel: 7250 92280 **Fax:** 7250 922829
Email: info@hebu-music.de
Web site: http://www.hebu-music.de

Titles:
DIE BLASMUSIK

HECKNER DRUCK- UND VERLAGSGES. MBH & CO. KG 679175
Harzstr. 23, 38300 WOLFENBÜTTEL
Tel: 5331 800840 **Fax:** 5331 800820
Email: hecknerdruck@t-online.de

Titles:
WIRTSCHAFT UND ERZIEHUNG

HEEL VERLAG GMBH 678346
Gut Pottscheidt, 53639 KÖNIGSWINTER
Tel: 2223 92300 **Fax:** 2223 923013
Email: service@heel-verlag.de
Web site: http://www.heel-verlag.de

Titles:
Ä APICIUS
ARMBAND UHREN
FERRARI WORLD
OLDTIMER KATALOG
PORSCHE FAHRER
SPACEVIEW
TRAKTOR OLDTIMER KATALOG

DAS HEFT ZEITSCHRIFTENVERLAG 683063
Haarener Str. 32, 33178 BORCHEN
Tel: 5251 62624 **Fax:** 5251 62628
Email: mail@heft.de
Web site: http://www.heft.de

Titles:
DAS HEFT

HEIDE & KLAUS GBR 1752257
Salisweg 30d, 63454 HANAU **Tel:** 6181 966570
Fax: 6181 966571
Email: info@security-insight.com
Web site: http://www.security-insight.com

Titles:
SECURITY INSIGHT

HEIDELBERGER LESE-ZEITEN VERLAG 1788412
Happelstr. 12, 69120 HEIDELBERG
Tel: 6221 804827
Email: universitas@heidelberger-lese-zeiten-verlag.de
Web site: http://www.heidelberger-lese-zeiten-verlag.de

Titles:
UNIVERSITAS

HEIDENHEIMER NEUE PRESSE GMBH 683068
Marienstr. 9, 89518 HEIDENHEIM
Tel: 7321 347201 **Fax:** 7321 347200

Titles:
HEIDENHEIMER NEUE PRESSE

HEIDENHEIMER ZEITUNG GMBH & CO. KG 679726
Olgastr. 15, 89518 HEIDENHEIM **Tel:** 7321 3470
Fax: 7321 347100
Email: pressehaus@hz-online.de
Web site: http://www.hz-online.de

Titles:
BRENZTAL-BOTE
HEIDENHEIMER ZEITUNG

HEILBRONNER STIMME GMBH & CO. KG 682896
Allee 2, 74072 HEILBRONN **Tel:** 7131 6150
Fax: 7131 615200
Email: servicecenter@stimme.de
Web site: http://www.stimme.de

Titles:
HEILBRONNER STIMME
HOHENLOHER ZEITUNG
KRAICHGAU STIMME

HEIMATANZEIGER ANZEIGENBLATT GMBH 683084
Konrad-Adenauer-Str. 2, 42853 REMSCHEID
Tel: 2191 9090 **Fax:** 2191 909180
Email: heimatanzeiger@rga-online.de

Titles:
HEIMATANZEIGER FÜR RADEVORMWALD MIT WUPPERORTSCHAFTEN

HEIMATBOTE-VERLAG P. OSTHEIMER 683095
Laudenbacher Str. 4, 63825 SCHÖLLKRIPPEN
Tel: 6024 67210 **Fax:** 6024 7763
Email: peter.ostheimerheimatbote@t-online.de

Titles:
DER HEIMATBOTE

HEIMATBUND LÜTTRINGHAUSEN E.V. 685221
Gertenbachstr. 20, 42899 REMSCHEID
Tel: 2191 50663 **Fax:** 2191 54598
Email: luettringhauser-anzeiger@t-online.de
Web site: http://www.luettringhauser-anzeiger.de

Titles:
LÜTTRINGHAUSER ANZEIGER

HEINRICH BAUER SMARAGD KG 679688
Charles-de-Gaulle-Str. 8, 81737 MÜNCHEN
Tel: 89 67860 **Fax:** 89 67867588
Web site: http://www.bauerverlag.de

Titles:
BRAVO

HEINRICH BAUER VERLAG KG 1788385
Burchardstr. 11, 20095 HAMBURG **Tel:** 40 30190
Fax: 40 30191043
Web site: http://www.bauermedia.com

Titles:
ADEL EXKLUSIV

HEINRICH BAUER ZEITSCHRIFTEN VERLAG KG 678471
Burchardstr. 11, 20095 HAMBURG **Tel:** 40 30190
Fax: 40 30191043
Email: kommunikation@bauermedia.com
Web site: http://www.bauermedia.com

Titles:
ALLES FÜR DIE FRAU
AUTO ZEITUNG
BELLA
BRAVO GIRL!
HAPPINEZ
KOCHEN & GENIESSEN
LAURA
LAURA WOHNEN KREATIV
LECKER
LIFE&STYLE
DAS NEUE
DAS NEUE BLATT
NEUE POST
REZEPTE PUR
SELBST IST DER MANN
TINA
TINA WOMAN
TV14
TV KLAR
WOHNIDEE

HEINRICH RÜTTGERODT GMBH & CO. KG 681138
Marktplatz 12, 37574 EINBECK **Tel:** 5561 4002
Fax: 5561 73383
Email: info@einbecker-morgenpost.de
Web site: http://www.einbecker-morgenpost.de

Titles:
EINBECKER MORGENPOST

HEINRICHS-VERLAG GMBH 677999
Heinrichsdamm 32, 96047 BAMBERG
Tel: 951 51920 **Fax:** 951 519215
Email: ramer@heinrichs-verlag.de
Web site: http://www.heinrichs-verlag.de

Titles:
HEINRICHSBLATT

HEINRICH-THÖNE VOLKSHOCHSCHULE, SENIORENREDAKTION 1622284
Bergstr. 1, 45479 MÜLHEIM
Email: redaktion@alt-na-und.de
Web site: http://www.alt-na-und.de

Titles:
ALT? NA UND!

HEINZ MAGAZIN VERLAG 683141
Tannenbergstr. 35, 42103 WUPPERTAL
Tel: 202 371700 **Fax:** 202 3717023
Email: info@heinz-magazin.de
Web site: http://www.heinz-magazin.de

Titles:
HEINZ
HEINZ
HEINZ

HEINZ MAGAZIN VERLAGS GMBH 1654465
Brassertstr. 6, 45130 ESSEN **Tel:** 201 7988663
Fax: 201 7988664
Email: redaktion@heinz-magazin.de
Web site: http://www.heinz-magazin.de

Titles:
HEINZ
HEINZ

HEINZE GMBH 1759939
Bremer Weg 184, 29223 CELLE **Tel:** 5141 500
Fax: 5141 50104
Email: kundenservice@heinze.de
Web site: http://www.heinze.de

Titles:
JOURNAL

HEISE ZEITSCHRIFTEN VERLAG GMBH & CO. KG 1626939
Karl-Wiechert-Allee 10, 30625 HANNOVER
Tel: 511 53520 **Fax:** 511 5352129
Email: kontakt@heise.de
Web site: http://www.heise.de

Titles:
C'T MAGAZIN FÜR COMPUTERTECHNIK
HEISE ONLINE
IX
TECHNOLOGY REVIEW

DER HEISSE DRAHT VERLAGSGES. MBH & CO. KG 678584
Drostestr. 14, 30161 HANNOVER **Tel:** 511 390910
Fax: 511 39091252
Email: zentrale@dhd.de
Web site: http://www.dhd24.com

Titles:
DHD24 FRIENDS
OLDTIMER ANZEIGER
OLDTIMER INSERAT
PFERDE ANZEIGER

HEIZUNGS-JOURNAL VERLAGS-GMBH 683143
Eibenweg 20, 71364 WINNENDEN
Tel: 7195 928401 **Fax:** 7195 928411
Email: media@heizungsjournal.de
Web site: http://www.heizungsjournal.de

Titles:
HEIZUNGSJOURNAL
SANITÄRJOURNAL

HEKATRON VERTRIEBS GMBH 1768229
Brühlmatten 9, 79295 SULZBURG **Tel:** 7634 5000
Fax: 7634 6419
Email: info@hekatron.de
Web site: http://www.hekatron.de

Titles:
HEKATRON TREND

HELFRECHT VERLAG UND DRUCK 1600642
Markgrafenstr. 32, 95680 BAD ALEXANDERSBAD **Tel:** 9232 6010
Fax: 9232 601282
Email: redaktion@helfrecht.de
Web site: http://www.helfrecht.de

Titles:
HELFRECHT METHODIK

HELIOS MEDIA GMBH 1681177
Werderscher Markt 13, 10117 BERLIN
Tel: 30 848590 **Fax:** 30 84859200
Email: info@helios-media.com
Web site: http://www.helios-media.com

Titles:
PRESSESPRECHER

HELMHOLTZ-ZENTRUM FÜR UMWELTFORSCHUNG GMBH-UFZ 1728911
Permoserstr. 15, 04318 LEIPZIG **Tel:** 341 2351269
Fax: 341 2352649
Email: info@ufz.de
Web site: http://www.ufz.de

Titles:
UFZ-NEWSLETTER

HELMUT W. QUAST 1638520
Rabenkopfweg 32, 65931 FRANKFURT
Tel: 69 363560 **Fax:** 69 362654
Email: verlag@hehandelszeitung.com
Web site: http://www.hehandelszeitung.com

Titles:
H & E

HENKEL AG & CO. KGAA, BAUTECHNIK DEUTSCHLAND 687330
40191 DÜSSELDORF **Tel:** 211 73790
Fax: 211 7379319
Email: thomsit.bautechnik@henkel.de
Web site: http://www.thomsit.de

Titles:
PROFI

HENRICH PUBLIKATIONEN GMBH 1686809
Talhofstr. 24b, 82205 GILCHING **Tel:** 8105 38530
Fax: 8105 385311
Email: info@verlag-henrich.de
Web site: http://www.verlag-henrich.de

Titles:
:K
> E ENERGIESPEKTRUM
A AUTOMATION
BBR
BZM BRENNSTOFFZELLEN MAGAZIN
G+H GEBÄUDETECHNIK UND HANDWERK
LOGISTIK JOURNAL
MASCHINE + WERKZEUG

HERAUSGEBERGEMEINSCHAFT AMBULANTER PFLEGERISCHER DIENSTE DER DIAKONIE IN HAMBURG UND UMGEBUNG 1767653
Forsmannstr. 19, 22303 HAMBURG
Tel: 40 517845 **Fax:** 40 27806540
Titles:
URBANES

HERAUSGEBERGEMEINSCHAFT WERTPAPIER-MITTEILUNGEN, KEPPLER, LEHMANN GMBH & CO. KG 679572
Düsseldorfer Str. 16, 60329 FRANKFURT
Tel: 69 27320 **Fax:** 69 234186
Web site: http://www.wmrecht.com
Titles:
BÖRSEN-ZEITUNG
RENDITE

HERBERT WICHMANN VERLAG IM VDE VERLAG GMBH 678622
Merianstr. 29, 63069 OFFENBACH
Tel: 69 8400061121 **Fax:** 69 8400069121
Email: olbrich@vde-verlag.de
Web site: http://www.wichmann-verlag.de
Titles:
AVN ALLGEMEINE VERMESSUNGS-NACHRICHTEN

HERFORDER KREISBLATT BUSSE GMBH & CO. KG 679853
Brüderstr. 30, 32052 HERFORD **Tel:** 5221 59080
Fax: 5221 590837
Titles:
HERFORDER KREISBLATT
LÖHNER ZEITUNG

HERMANN IMSIECKE DRUCK UND VERLAG GMBH 700076
Lange Str. 9, 49661 CLOPPENBURG
Tel: 4471 1780 **Fax:** 4471 17830
Email: info@mt-news.de
Web site: http://www.mt-news.de
Titles:
MÜNSTERLÄNDISCHE TAGESZEITUNG

HERMANN KUHN GMBH & CO. KG 1718316
Bert-Brecht-Str. 15, 78054 VILLINGEN-SCHWENNINGEN **Tel:** 7720 3940
Fax: 7720 394294
Email: info@kuhnverlag.de
Web site: http://www.nq-online.de
Titles:
SÜDWEST PRESSE DIE NECKARQUELLE

HESS VERLAG 1712744
Trappentreustr. 31, 80339 MÜNCHEN
Tel: 89 51997020
Email: hess@photo-international.de
Web site: http://www.photo-international.de
Titles:
PHOTO INTERNATIONAL

HESSISCHER TENNIS-VERBAND E.V. 689548
Auf der Rosenhöhe 68, 63069 OFFENBACH
Tel: 69 9840320 **Fax:** 69 98403220
Email: monika.vestweber@htv-tennis.de
Web site: http://www.htv-tennis.de
Titles:
TOP SPIN

HESSISCHES SOZIALMINISTERIUM 694815
Dostojewskistr. 4, 65187 WIESBADEN
Tel: 611 8170 **Fax:** 611 8173566
Email: herbert.ujma@hsm.hessen.de
Web site: http://www.hsm.hessen.de
Titles:
HESSISCHE SENIOREN BLÄTTER

HEWES GMBH 1622120
Weg zur Platte 15a, 45133 ESSEN
Tel: 201 413482 **Fax:** 201 411272
Email: hewesgmbh45133@aol.com
Web site: http://www.treff-punkt.info
Titles:
TREFFPUNKT DÜSSELDORF
TREFFPUNKT ESSEN

HEY + HOFFMANN VERLAG GMBH & CO. KG 1729609
Gertrudenkirchhof 10, 20095 HAMBURG
Tel: 40 37423600 **Fax:** 40 374236020
Email: info@hey-hoffmann.de
Web site: http://www.hey-hoffmann.de
Titles:
UNISCENE

HIGHLIGHT VERLAGSGES. MBH 683230
Braugasse 2, 59602 RÜTHEN **Tel:** 2952 9759200
Fax: 2952 9759201
Email: info@highlight-verlag.de
Web site: http://www.highlight-web.de
Titles:
HIGHLIGHT
LIGHT-EVENT + ARCHITECTURE

HIGHTEXT VERLAG OHG 683445
Wilhelm-Riehl-Str. 13, 80687 MÜNCHEN
Tel: 89 5783870 **Fax:** 89 57838799
Email: info@ibusiness.de
Web site: http://www.ibusiness.de
Titles:
IBUSINESS EXECUTIVE SUMMARY

HILLE MEDIEN 679235
Karlstr. 8, 79104 FREIBURG **Tel:** 761 29280240
Fax: 761 29380348
Email: hille@bewusster-leben.de
Web site: http://www.bewusster-leben.de
Titles:
BEWUSSTER LEBEN

HINNERK VERLAG 683257
Steindamm 11, 20099 HAMBURG
Tel: 40 2841150 **Fax:** 40 28411580
Email: redaktion@hinnerk.de
Web site: http://www.hinnerk.de
Titles:
HINNERK

HINZ & KUNZT VERLAGS- UND VERTRIEBS GGMBH 683261
Altstädter Twiete 1, 20095 HAMBURG
Tel: 40 32108311 **Fax:** 40 30399638
Email: info@hinzundkunzt.de
Web site: http://www.hinzundkunzt.de
Titles:
HINZ&KUNZT

HIPPOCAMPUS VERLAG KG 686353
Bismarckstr. 8, 53604 BAD HONNEF
Tel: 2224 919480 **Fax:** 2224 919482
Email: verlag@hippocampus.de
Web site: http://www.hippocampus.de
Titles:
NEUROLOGIE & REHABILITATION

HIPPOKRATES VERLAG IN MVS MEDIZINVERLAGE STUTTGART GMBH & CO. KG 677578
Oswald-Hesse-Str. 50, 70469 STUTTGART
Tel: 711 89310 **Fax:** 711 8931706
Web site: http://www.medizinverlage.de
Titles:
DIE HEBAMME
OM ZEITSCHRIFT FÜR ORTHOMOLEKULARE MEDIZIN

HITZEROTH DRUCK + MEDIEN GMBH & CO. KG 678160
Franz-Tuczek-Weg 1, 35039 MARBURG
Tel: 6421 4090 **Fax:** 6421 409117
Email: info@op-marburg.de
Web site: http://www.op-marburg.de
Titles:
ANZEIGER EXTRA
OBERHESSISCHE PRESSE

HK HOBBY- UND KLEINTIERZÜCHTER VERLAGSGES. MBH & CO. KG 1638648
Wilhelmsaue 37, 10713 BERLIN
Tel: 30 897454300 **Fax:** 30 897454555
Web site: http://www.hk-verlag.de
Titles:
GEFLÜGEL ZEITUNG
KANINCHEN ZEITUNG

HLBS VERLAG GMBH 679541
Kölnstr. 202, 53757 ST. AUGUSTIN
Tel: 2241 8661750 **Fax:** 2241 8661759
Email: verlag@hlbs.de
Web site: http://www.hlbs.de
Titles:
BN BETRIEBSWIRTSCHAFTLICHE NACHRICHTEN FÜR DIE LANDWIRTSCHAFT
HLBS REPORT
STEUER- UND WIRTSCHAFTS-NACHRICHTEN DER LANDWIRTSCHAFTLICHEN BUCHSTELLEN IM HLBS

HMC HAMBURG MEDIA COMPANY GMBH 1728890
Beim Strohhause 27, 20097 HAMBURG
Tel: 40 4136390 **Fax:** 40 41363911
Email: info@hmc.de
Web site: http://www.hmc.de
Titles:
WOHNEN

HOEHL-DRUCK GMBH + CO. HERSFELDER ZEITUNG KG 683429
Gutenbergstr. 1, 36251 BAD HERSFELD
Tel: 6621 1610 **Fax:** 6621 161148
Email: anzeigen@hersfelder-zeitung.de
Web site: http://www.hersfelder-zeitung.de
Titles:
HZ HERSFELDER ZEITUNG

HOENER'S BUREAU - VERLAG & AGENTUR 1758455
Aegidii-Markt 7, 48143 MÜNSTER
Tel: 251 7036430 **Fax:** 251 7036435
Email: info@indiansummer-magazin.de
Web site: http://www.indiansummer-magazin.de
Titles:
INDIANSUMMER MAGAZIN

HOFFMANN UND CAMPE VERLAG GMBH CORPORATE PUBLISHING 677410
Harvestehuder Weg 42, 20149 HAMBURG
Tel: 40 44188251 **Fax:** 40 44188210
Email: cp@hoca.de
Web site: http://cp.hoca.de
Titles:
BMW MAGAZIN - AUSG. DEUTSCHLAND
CONCEPTS BY HOCHTIEF
FOLIO
RESULTS
RWE KOMPAKT
STEINKOHLE

HOFMANN DRUCK NÜRNBERG GMBH & CO. KG 690642
Emmericher Str. 10, 90411 NÜRNBERG
Tel: 911 52030 **Fax:** 911 5203148
Email: media@hofmann-infocom.de
Web site: http://www.hofmann-infocom.de
Titles:
JOHANNITER
WIM WIRTSCHAFT IN MITTELFRANKEN

HOFMANN-VERLAG GMBH & CO. KG 682584
Steinwasenstr. 6, 73614 SCHORNDORF
Tel: 7181 4020 **Fax:** 7181 402111
Email: info@hofmann-verlag.de
Web site: http://www.hofmann-verlag.de
Titles:
INTERNATIONAL JOURNAL OF PHYSICAL EDUCATION
MOTORIK

HOGREFE VERLAG GMBH & CO. KG 698813
Rohnsweg 25, 37085 GÖTTINGEN
Tel: 551 496090 **Fax:** 551 4960988
Email: verlag@hogrefe.de
Web site: http://www.hogrefe.de
Titles:
DIAGNOSTICA
KINDHEIT UND ENTWICKLUNG
ZEITSCHRIFT FÜR GESUNDHEITSPSYCHOLOGIE
ZEITSCHRIFT FÜR KLINISCHE PSYCHOLOGIE UND PSYCHOTHERAPIE

HOHENLOHE+SCHWÄBISCH HALL TOURISMUS E.V. 1731743
Münzstr. 1, 74523 SCHWÄBISCH HALL
Tel: 791 7557444 **Fax:** 791 7557447
Email: info@hs-tourismus.de
Web site: http://www.hs-tourismus.de
Titles:
GASTGEBERVERZEICHNIS HOHENLOHE+SCHWÄBISCH HALL

HOHENLOHER DRUCK- UND VERLAGSHAUS VERLAG HOHENLOHER TAGBLATT RICHTER UND GEBR. WANKMÜLLER GMBH & CO. KG 1751987
Ludwigstr. 6, 74564 CRAILSHEIM **Tel:** 7951 4090
Fax: 7951 409119
Email: t.scherf-clavel@swp.de
Web site: http://www.hohenloher-tagblatt.de
Titles:
HOHENLOHER TAGBLATT

HOHENTWIEL VERLAG & INTERNET GMBH 1651315
Dr.-Andler-Str. 28, 78224 SINGEN
Tel: 7731 912310 **Fax:** 7731 9123130
Email: info@hohentwielverlag.de
Web site: http://www.hohentwielverlag.de
Titles:
WELLNESS BODY & SPIRIT
WIRTSCHAFTSSPIEGEL

HOHENZOLLERISCHE ZEITUNG GMBH + CO KG 683320
Obertorplatz 19, 72379 HECHINGEN
Tel: 7471 93150 **Fax:** 7471 2045
Email: hoz.anzeigen@swp.de
Web site: http://www.suedwest-aktiv.de
Titles:
HOHENZOLLERISCHE ZEITUNG

HOLIMED VERLAGSGES. MBH 1739519
Uhlemeyerstr. 16, 30175 HANNOVER
Tel: 511 3882639 **Fax:** 511 9904430
Email: info@holimed-verlag.de
Web site: http://www.estheticpure.de
Titles:
ESTHETIC PURE

HOLZER DRUCK UND MEDIEN GMBH + CO. KG 690497
Fridolin-Holzer-Str. 22, 88171 WEILER-SIMMERBERG **Tel:** 8387 3990 **Fax:** 8387 39955
Email: info@westallgaeuer-zeitung.de
Web site: http://www.westallgaeuer-zeitung.de
Titles:
DER WESTALLGÄUER

HOLZMANN MEDIEN GMBH & CO. KG 679555
Gewerbestr. 2, 86825 BAD WÖRISHOFEN
Tel: 8247 35401 **Fax:** 8247 354170
Email: info@holzmann-medien.de
Web site: http://www.holzmann-medien.de
Titles:
BODEN WAND DECKE
DEUTSCHE HANDWERKS ZEITUNG
ESTRICHTECHNIK & FUSSBODENBAU
DIE FLEISCHEREI
GFF
GI GELDINSTITUTE
HANDWERK MAGAZIN
RATIONELL REINIGEN
RW TEXTILSERVICE
SICHT + SONNENSCHUTZ
VB VERSICHERUNGSBETRIEBE

HÖMA-VERLAG GMBH & CO. KG 1650273
Im Schlangengarten 56, 76877 OFFENBACH
Tel: 6348 959391 **Fax:** 6348 959392
Email: info@hoema-verlag.de
Web site: http://www.hoemaverlag.de
Titles:
URLAUBS- UND GÄSTEZEITUNG ROMANTISCHER RHEIN

HOMÖOPATHIE FORUM E.V. 683343
Grubmühlerfeldstr. 14a, 82131 GAUTING
Tel: 89 89999617 **Fax:** 89 89999610
Email: info@homoeopathie-forum.de
Web site: http://www.homoeopathie-forum.de
Titles:
HOMÖOPATHIE ZEITSCHRIFT

HOPPENSTEDT PUBLISHING GMBH 678766
Havelstr. 9, 64295 DARMSTADT **Tel:** 6151 380130
Fax: 6151 380131
Email: service@hoppenstedt.de
Web site: http://www.hoppenstedt-zeitschriften.de

Titles:
CAD-CAM REPORT
EDM REPORT
HANDLING
KUNSTSTOFF MAGAZIN
LABO
MTA DIALOG
SCOPE

HOSPITALITY ALLIANCE AG DEUTSCHLAND 1783759
Braunser Weg 12, 34454 BAD AROLSEN
Tel: 5691 878207 **Fax:** 5691 878407
Web site: http://www.ramada.de

Titles:
SCHÖNE ZEITEN

HÖTZEL, RFS & PARTNER GMBH 690633
Boschstr. 1, 48703 STADTLOHN
Tel: 2563 929200 **Fax:** 2563 929900
Email: info@wirtschaft-aktuell.de
Web site: http://www.wirtschaft-aktuell.de

Titles:
WIRTSCHAFT AKTUELL
WIRTSCHAFT AKTUELL
WIRTSCHAFT AKTUELL
WIRTSCHAFT AKTUELL - AUSG. EMSLAND
WIRTSCHAFT AKTUELL - AUSG. OSNABRÜCK
WIRTSCHAFT AKTUELL - AUSG. STEINFURT
WIRTSCHAFT AKTUELL - AUSG. WARENDORF

HPB WELTHANDEL VERLAG GMBH 690460
Postfach 650909, 22369 HAMBURG
Tel: 40 6004670 **Fax:** 40 6013114
Email: info@hpb-w.de

Titles:
WELTHANDEL

HUBER VERLAG GMBH & CO. KG 679322
Markircher Str. 9a, 68229 MANNHEIM
Tel: 621 483610 **Fax:** 621 4836111
Email: info@huber-verlag.de
Web site: http://www.huber-verlag.de

Titles:
BIKERS NEWS
CUSTOMBIKE
DREAM-MACHINES
MOTOR MANIACS
REISE MOTORRAD RIDE ON!
TÄTOWIER MAGAZIN

HUDDLE VERLAGS GMBH 683393
Laubacher Str. 10, 14197 BERLIN
Tel: 30 82009331 **Fax:** 30 82009353
Email: huddle@huddle-verlag.de
Web site: http://www.huddle-verlag.de

Titles:
HUDDLE

HUSS-MEDIEN GMBH 678266
Am Friedrichshain 22, 10407 BERLIN
Tel: 30 421510 **Fax:** 30 42151273
Email: huss.medien@hussberlin.de
Web site: http://www.huss.de/huss-medien.htm

Titles:
ARBEIT UND ARBEITSRECHT
EP ELEKTROPRAKTIKER
EP ELEKTROPRAKTIKER PHOTOVOLTAIK
FEUERWEHR
GASTRONOMIE & HOTELLERIE
GV KOMPAKT
HEBEZEUGE FÖRDERMITTEL
IMMOBILIEN VERMIETEN & VERWALTEN
MODERNE GEBÄUDETECHNIK
RFE ELEKTRO HÄNDLER EH
WWT WASSERWIRTSCHAFT WASSERTECHNIK

HUSS-VERLAG GMBH 679989
Joseph-Dollinger-Bogen 5, 80807 MÜNCHEN
Tel: 89 323910 **Fax:** 89 32391416
Email: management@huss-verlag.de
Web site: http://www.huss-verlag.de

Titles:
BUSPLANER INTERNATIONAL
FAHRER-JAHRBUCH
LOGISTIK HEUTE
LOGISTRA FUHRPARK
LOGISTRA LAGERLOGISTIK
DIE PROFI WERKSTATT
RECYCLING TECHNOLOGY
TAXI HEUTE
TRANSPORT

HÜTHIG ELEKTRONIK JOURNAL GMBH 1757663
Justus-von-Liebig-Str. 1, 86899 LANDSBERG
Tel: 8191 1250
Email: info@elektronikjournal.de
Web site: http://www.elektronikjournal.com

Titles:
ELEKTRONIK JOURNAL - DEUTSCHLAND-AUSG.

HÜTHIG GMBH 678608
Im Weiher 10, 69121 HEIDELBERG
Tel: 6221 4890 **Fax:** 6221 489481
Email: info@huethig.de
Web site: http://www.huethig.de

Titles:
AUTOMOBIL-ELEKTRONIK
CHEMIE TECHNIK
ELEKTRONIK INDUSTRIE
IEE
KGK KAUTSCHUK GUMMI KUNSTSTOFFE
KI KÄLTE LUFT KLIMATECHNIK
NEUE VERPACKUNG
PHARMA+FOOD
PHOTOVOLTAIC PRODUCTION
PLASTVERARBEITER
PRODUCTRONIC

HÜTHIG & PFLAUM VERLAG GMBH & CO. FACHLITERATUR KG 680537
Lazarettstr. 4, 80636 MÜNCHEN **Tel:** 89 12607299
Fax: 89 12607310
Web site: http://www.de-online.info

Titles:
DE DER ELEKTRO- UND GEBÄUDETECHNIKER
DER ELEKTRO FACHMANN
ELEKTROMASCHINEN UND ANTRIEBE
ELEKTROTECHNIK FÜR HANDWERK UND INDUSTRIE
EMA ELEKTRISCHE MASCHINEN
E.PUNKT NRW
GEBÄUDETECHNIK

HV HANSEATIC-VERLAGSGES. MBH 700017
Waidmannstr. 35, 22769 HAMBURG
Tel: 40 8500607 **Fax:** 40 8512808
Email: info@hanse-art.net
Web site: http://www.hanse-art.net

Titles:
HANSE-ART

H.W.G. VERLAG & WERBUNG 680366
Wiedbachstr. 50, 56567 NEUWIED
Tel: 2631 96460 **Fax:** 2631 964640
Email: info@hwg-media.de
Web site: http://www.hwg-media.de

Titles:
CONVENTION INTERNATIONAL
PICTURE
QUEENS

HW-VERLAG 683331
Sonnenblumenring 35, 86415 MERING
Tel: 8233 32761 **Fax:** 8233 32762

Titles:
WERKSTOFFE IN DER FERTIGUNG

HYDRA E.V. 694736
Köpenicker Str. 187, 10997 BERLIN
Tel: 30 6110023 **Fax:** 30 6110021
Email: kontakt@hydra-ev.org
Web site: http://www.hydra-ev.org

Titles:
EXPRESSCHEN ANGEBOTSKALENDER

HYDROGEIT VERLAG 1724976
Gartenweg 5, 16727 OBERKRÄMER
Tel: 33055 21322 **Fax:** 33055 21320
Email: kontakt@hydrogeit.de
Web site: http://www.hydrogeit-verlag.de

Titles:
HZWEI

H² MEDIA FACTORY GMBH 1690875
Osdorfer Landstr. 20, 22607 HAMBURG
Tel: 40 81992737 **Fax:** 40 81992739
Email: redaktion@netzwelt.de
Web site: http://www.netzwelt.de

Titles:
NETZWELT

I. WEBER VERLAG 681836
Ohmstr. 15, 80802 MÜNCHEN **Tel:** 89 38308680
Fax: 89 38308683
Email: redaktion@kameramann.de
Web site: http://www.kameramann.de

Titles:
FILM & TV KAMERAMANN

IAS INSTITUT FÜR ARBEITS- UND SOZIALHYGIENE STIFTUNG 683434
Steinhäuserstr. 19, 76135 KARLSRUHE
Tel: 721 82040 **Fax:** 721 8204400
Email: service@ias-stiftung.de
Web site: http://www.ias-stiftung.de

Titles:
IAS IMPULSE

IBP INTERNATIONAL BUSINESS PRESS PUBLISHERS GMBH 680133
Mainzer Landstr. 251, 60326 FRANKFURT
Tel: 69 759501 **Fax:** 69 75952999
Email: info@dfv.de
Web site: http://www.dfv.de

Titles:
CHEMICAL FIBERS INTERNATIONAL

ICT INNOVATIVE COMMUNICATION TECHNOLOGIES AG 687118
Erscheckweg 1, 72664 KOHLBERG
Tel: 7025 1020 **Fax:** 7025 7111
Email: info@ict.de
Web site: http://www.ict.de

Titles:
PICTURE

IDC CORPORATE PUBLISHING GMBH 1654065
Hammerbrookstr. 93, 20097 HAMBURG
Tel: 40 226211280 **Fax:** 40 226211270
Email: info@lfi-online.de
Web site: http://www.lfi-online.de

Titles:
LFI LEICA FOTOGRAFIE INTERNATIONAL
LFI LEICA FOTOGRAFIE INTERNATIONAL

IDEA E.V. EVANGELISCHE NACHRICHTENAGENTUR 683456
Steinbühlstr. 3, 35578 WETZLAR **Tel:** 6441 9150
Fax: 6441 915118
Email: idea@idea.de
Web site: http://www.idea.de

Titles:
IDEA ONLINE
IDEA SPEKTRUM

IDEAL WERBEAGENTUR GMBH 686789
Junkerstr. 21, 53177 BONN **Tel:** 228 559020
Fax: 228 5590222
Email: info@idealbonn.de

Titles:
SENIOREN AKTIV TERMINE

IDG BUSINESS MEDIA GMBH 680320
Lyonel-Feininger-Str. 26, 80807 MÜNCHEN
Tel: 89 360860 **Fax:** 89 36086118
Web site: http://www.idg.de

Titles:
CHANNELPARTNER
CHANNELPARTNER
CIO
CIO
COMPUTERWOCHE
COMPUTERWOCHE.DE
TECCHANNEL

IDG ENTERTAINMENT MEDIA GMBH 1737327
Lyonel-Feininger-Str. 26, 80807 MÜNCHEN
Tel: 89 360860 **Fax:** 89 36086118
Web site: http://www.idgmedia.de

Titles:
GAMEPRO
GAMEPRO.DE
GAMESTAR
GAMESTAR.DE

IDG MAGAZINE MEDIA GMBH 685264
Lyonel-Feininger-Str. 26, 80807 MÜNCHEN
Tel: 89 360860 **Fax:** 89 36086118
Web site: http://www.idgcom.de

Titles:
DIGITAL.WORLD
MACWELT
MACWELT
PC WELT
PC WELT

IDW-VERLAG GMBH 690670
Tersteegenstr. 14, 40474 DÜSSELDORF
Tel: 211 4561222 **Fax:** 211 4561206
Email: post@idw-verlag.de
Web site: http://www.idw-verlag.de

Titles:
DIE WIRTSCHAFTSPRÜFUNG WPG

IFB EIGENSCHENK GMBH 1715853
Mettener Str. 33, 94469 DEGGENDORF
Tel: 991 370150 **Fax:** 991 33918
Email: mail@eigenschenk.de
Web site: http://www.eigenschenk.de

Titles:
AUFGESCHLOSSEN

IG METALL 683484
Wilhelm-Leuschner-Str. 79, 60329 FRANKFURT
Tel: 69 66932672 **Fax:** 69 66932870
Email: pressestelle@igmetall.de
Web site: http://www.igmetall.de

Titles:
IGM DIREKT
METALLZEITUNG

I.G.T. INFORMATIONSGES. TECHNIK MBH 683769
Oskar-Maria-Graf-Ring 23, 81737 MÜNCHEN
Tel: 89 6736970 **Fax:** 89 67369719
Email: info@igt-verlag.de
Web site: http://www.igt-verlag.de

Titles:
MECHATRONIK
METALLOBERFLÄCHE MO
MO MAGAZIN FÜR OBERFLÄCHENTECHNIK
PROTECTOR
W&S

IHLAS MEDIA + TRADE CENTER GMBH 689700
Starkenburgstr. 7, 64546 MÖRFELDEN-WALLDORF **Tel:** 6105 98130 **Fax:** 6105 9813171
Email: info@ihlas.de
Web site: http://www.ihlas.de

Titles:
TÜRKIYE

IKEA DEUTSCHLAND GMBH & CO. KG 1686188
Am Wandersmann 2, 65719 HOFHEIM
Email: redaktion@ikeafamilylive.de
Web site: http://www.ikeafamilylive.de

Titles:
IKEA FAMILY LIVE

IMAGE VERLAGS GMBH 683519
Alois-Harbeck-Platz 3, 82178 PUCHHEIM
Tel: 89 894184510 **Fax:** 89 894184512

Titles:
IMAGE HIFI

IMC AG 1626787
Altenkesseler Str. 17, 66115 SAARBRÜCKEN
Tel: 681 94760 **Fax:** 681 9476530
Email: info@im-c.de
Web site: http://www.im-c.de

Titles:
IM INFORMATION MANAGEMENT & CONSULTING

IMMERGRÜN MEDIEN GMBH 1788391
Südliche Hauptstr. 21, 83700 ROTTACH-EGERN
Tel: 89 80928050 **Fax:** 89 27264333
Email: info@immergruen-medien.de
Web site: http://www.immergruen-medien.de

Titles:
FONDS & CO.

IMMOBILIEN MANAGER VERLAG IMV GMBH & CO. KG
683544
Stolberger Str. 84, 50933 KÖLN **Tel:** 221 5497131
Fax: 221 5496131
Email: imv@immobilienmanager.de
Web site: http://www.immobilienmanager.de

Titles:
IMMOBILIEN MANAGER

IN FRANKEN ELEKTRONISCHE MEDIEN GMBH & CO. KG 1763996
Gutenbergstr. 1, 96050 BAMBERG **Tel:** 951 1880
Fax: 951 188335
Email: info@infranken.de
Web site: http://www.infranken.de

Titles:
INFRANKEN.DE

IN VERLAG GMBH & CO. KG
1766312
Rosenthaler Str. 40, 10178 BERLIN
Tel: 30 319914100 **Fax:** 30 319914400
Email: in@in-verlag.de
Web site: http://www.in-starmagazin.de

Titles:
IN DAS STAR & STYLE MAGAZIN

INDUSTRIE- UND HANDELSKAMMER FULDA 690650
Heinrichstr. 8, 36037 FULDA **Tel:** 661 2840
Fax: 661 28444
Email: info@fulda.ihk.de
Web site: http://www.ihk-fulda.de

Titles:
WIRTSCHAFT REGION FULDA

INDUSTRIE- UND HANDELSKAMMER FÜR MÜNCHEN UND OBERBAYERN
690629
Max-Joseph-Str. 2, 80333 MÜNCHEN
Tel: 89 51160 **Fax:** 89 5116306
Email: ihkmail@muenchen.ihk.de
Web site: http://www.muenchen.ihk.de

Titles:
WIRTSCHAFT

INDUSTRIE - UND HANDELSKAMMER HANNOVER
1627100
Schiffgraben 49, 30175 HANNOVER
Tel: 511 3107269 **Fax:** 511 3107450
Email: kommunikation@hannover.ihk.de
Web site: http://www.hannover.ihk.de

Titles:
NIEDERSÄCHSISCHE WIRTSCHAFT

INDUSTRIE- UND HANDELSKAMMER REUTLINGEN
1627160
Hindenburgstr. 54, 72762 REUTLINGEN
Tel: 7121 2010 **Fax:** 7121 2014120
Email: ihk@reutlingen.ihk.de
Web site: http://www.reutlingen.ihk.de

Titles:
WIRTSCHAFT NECKAR-ALB

INDUSTRIE- UND HANDELSKAMMER ZU DORTMUND
683486
Märkische Str. 120, 44141 DORTMUND
Tel: 231 54170 **Fax:** 231 5417109
Email: info@dortmund.ihk.de
Web site: http://www.dortmund.ihk24.de

Titles:
RUHR WIRTSCHAFT

INDUSTRIE- UND HANDELSKAMMER ZU SCHWERIN
690662
Graf-Schack-Allee 12, 19053 SCHWERIN
Tel: 385 51030 **Fax:** 385 5103999
Email: info@schwerin.ihk.de
Web site: http://www.ihkzuschwerin.de

Titles:
WIKO WIRTSCHAFTSKOMPASS

INDUSTRIEGEWERKSCHAFT BAUEN-AGRAR-UMWELT 682254
Olof-Palme-Str. 19, 60439 FRANKFURT
Tel: 69 957370 **Fax:** 69 95737139
Web site: http://www.igbau.de

Titles:
DER GRUNDSTEIN

INDUSTRIEGEWERKSCHAFT BERGBAU, CHEMIE, ENERGIE
685285
Königsworther Platz 6, 30167 HANNOVER
Tel: 511 7631329 **Fax:** 511 7000891
Email: presse@igbce.de
Web site: http://www.igbce.de

Titles:
IG BCE KOMPAKT

INFO WOCHENZEITUNG OHG
683611
Rudolf-Roth-Str. 18, 88299 LEUTKIRCH
Tel: 7561 800244 **Fax:** 7561 8009733
Email: info@info-wochenzeitung.de
Web site: http://www.info-wochenzeitung.de

Titles:
INFO EHINGEN

INFO-MARKT GMBH 1654213
Fischerstr. 49, 40477 DÜSSELDORF
Tel: 211 6878550 **Fax:** 211 68785525
Email: kontakt@infomarkt.de
Web site: http://www.infomarkt.de

Titles:
INFOMARKT
INFOMARKT

INFORMA VERLAG GMBH 682091
Johann-Wilhelm-Lindlar-Str. 9, 51465 BERGISCH GLADBACH **Tel:** 2202 9369010
Fax: 2202 9369022
Web site: http://www.franzz.de

Titles:
FRANZZ

INFORMATIONS- UND BILDUNGSZENTRUM EMAIL E.V. 685753
An dem Heerwege 10, 58093 HAGEN
Tel: 2331 788651 **Fax:** 2331 22662
Email: ibe@emailverband.de
Web site: http://www.emailverband.de

Titles:
EMAIL

INFORMATIONSKREIS FÜR RAUMPLANUNG E.V. 687531
Hansastr. 26, 44137 DORTMUND **Tel:** 231 759570
Fax: 231 759597
Email: redaktion@ifr-ev.de
Web site: http://www.ifr-ev.de

Titles:
RAUMPLANUNG

INFOSTELLE INDUSTRIEVERBAND MASSIVUMFORMUNG E.V. 688149
Goldene Pforte 1, 58093 HAGEN
Tel: 2331 958828 **Fax:** 2331 958728
Email: orders@metalform.de
Web site: http://www.metalform.de

Titles:
SCHMIEDE JOURNAL

INFOTERM-VERLAG GMBH 682162
Plochinger Str. 102, 73730 ESSLINGEN
Tel: 711 9318350 **Fax:** 711 93183535
Email: freizeitspiegel@fzsinfo.de
Web site: http://www.freizeitspiegel-home.de

Titles:
FREIZEIT SPIEGEL

INGE SEELIG 690403
Werkhof Kukate, 29496 WADDEWEITZ
Tel: 5849 468 **Fax:** 5849 1202
Email: info@werkhof-kukate.de
Web site: http://www.webenplus.de

Titles:
WEBEN+

INGENIEUR VERLAG NAGEL
680555
Uhlandstr. 1, 72631 AICHTAL **Tel:** 7127 56609
Fax: 7127 56649
Email: info@pumps-directory.com
Web site: http://www.pumps-directory.com

Titles:
DELTA P

INMAGAZIN VERLAGS GMBH
683727
Hohenstaufenstr. 1, 80801 MÜNCHEN
Tel: 89 3899710 **Fax:** 89 390351
Email: info@in-muenchen.de
Web site: http://www.in-muenchen.de

Titles:
IN MÜNCHEN

INMEDIA VERLAGS- UND REDAKTIONSBÜRO GMBH 687786
Lucile-Grahn-Str. 37, 81675 MÜNCHEN
Tel: 89 4572610 **Fax:** 89 45726150
Email: post@rondomagazin.de
Web site: http://www.rondomagazin.de

Titles:
RONDO

INNOVATIVES NIEDERSACHSEN GMBH 1767068
Kurt-Schumacher-Str. 24, 30159 HANNOVER
Tel: 511 7607260 **Fax:** 511 76072619
Email: info@nds.de
Web site: http://www.innovatives.niedersachsen.de

Titles:
PLIETSCH*

INNSIDE VERLAG UND WERBEAGENTUR
683741
Wiener Str. 37, 94032 PASSAU **Tel:** 851 32001
Fax: 851 32004
Email: innside@t-online.de
Web site: http://www.innside-passau.de

Titles:
INNSIDE

INPUNKTO MEDIA GMBH 678216
Agnes-Bernauer-Str. 129, 80687 MÜNCHEN
Tel: 89 6936560 **Fax:** 89 69365656
Email: info@inpunkto-media.de
Web site: http://www.inpunkto-media.de

Titles:
KONZERTNEWS

DAS INSERAT VERLAG GMBH
683541
Frankfurter Str. 39, 63303 DREIEICH
Tel: 6103 48400 **Fax:** 6103 4840440
Email: info@das-inserat.de
Web site: http://www.das-inserat.de

Titles:
KFZ-INSERAT

INSIDE GETRÄNKE VERLAGS-GMBH
683748
St.-Jakobs-Platz 12, 80331 MÜNCHEN
Tel: 89 23249060 **Fax:** 89 232490610
Email: info@inside-getraenke.de
Web site: http://www.inside-getraenke.de

Titles:
INSIDE

INSIDE WOHNEN VERLAGS-GMBH
683749
Destouchesstr. 6, 80803 MÜNCHEN
Tel: 89 3835670 **Fax:** 89 342124
Email: info@inside-wohnen.de
Web site: http://www.inside-wohnen.de

Titles:
INSIDE

INSIDE-INTERMEDIA ONLINEVERLAG GMBH & CO. KG
1690738
Bahnhofstr. 11, 50321 BRÜHL **Tel:** 2232 5044600
Fax: 2232 5044609
Web site: http://www.inside-intermedia.de

Titles:
INSIDE-DIGITAL.DE
INSIDE-HANDY.DE

INSTANT CORPORATE CULTURE GMBH
1630458
Leerbachstr. 57, 60322 FRANKFURT
Tel: 69 79588780 **Fax:** 69 795887818
Email: office@e-instant.de
Web site: http://www.e-instant.de

Titles:
INSTANT
INSTANT DDC

INSTITUT DER DEUTSCHEN WIRTSCHAFT KÖLN MEDIEN GMBH
677522
Konrad-Adenauer-Ufer 21, 50668 KÖLN
Tel: 221 49810 **Fax:** 221 4981445
Email: iwmedien@iwkoeln.de
Web site: http://www.iwmedien.de

Titles:
BLICKPUNKT WIRTSCHAFT
WIR UND DIE WIRTSCHAFT

INSTITUT DER WIRTSCHAFTSPRÜFER IN DEUTSCHLAND E.V.
683467
Tersteegenstr. 14, 40474 DÜSSELDORF
Tel: 211 45610 **Fax:** 211 4561204
Email: info@idw.de
Web site: http://www.idw.de

Titles:
IDW FACHNACHRICHTEN

INSTITUT DES DEUTSCHEN TEXTILEINZELHANDELS GMBH
679812
An Lyskirchen 14, 50676 KÖLN **Tel:** 221 92150955
Fax: 221 92150910
Email: marketingberater@bte.de
Web site: http://www.bte.de

Titles:
MB MARKETING BERATER

INSTITUT FEUERVERZINKEN GMBH
694749
Sohnstr. 66, 40237 DÜSSELDORF
Tel: 211 6907650 **Fax:** 211 689599
Email: holger.glinde@feuerverzinken.com
Web site: http://www.feuerverzinken.com

Titles:
FEUERVERZINKEN

INSTITUT FÜR ARBEITSMARKT- UND BERUFSFORSCHUNG DER BUNDESAGENTUR FÜR ARBEIT
681983
Regensburger Str. 104, 90478 NÜRNBERG
Tel: 911 1790 **Fax:** 911 1798418
Email: iab.wmk@iab.de
Web site: http://www.iab.de

Titles:
IAB FORUM

INSTITUT FÜR BAUBIOLOGIE + OEKOLOGIE GMBH, ABT. VERLAG
690778
Holzham 25, 83115 NEUBEUERN **Tel:** 8035 2039
Fax: 8035 8164
Email: institut@baubiologie.de
Web site: http://www.baubiologie.de

Titles:
WOHNUNG + GESUNDHEIT

INSTITUT FÜR DEMOSKOPIE ALLENSBACH
677622
Radolfzeller Str. 8, 78476 ALLENSBACH
Tel: 7533 8050 **Fax:** 7533 3048
Email: presse@ifd-allensbach.de
Web site: http://www.ifd-allensbach.de

Titles:
AWA ALLENSBACHER MARKT- UND WERBETRÄGERANALYSE AWA

INSTITUT FÜR INTERNATIONALE ARCHITEKTUR-DOKUMENTATION GMBH & CO. KG
680589
Hackerbrücke 6, 80335 MÜNCHEN
Tel: 89 3816200 **Fax:** 89 398670
Email: mail@detail.de
Web site: http://www.detail.de

Titles:
DETAIL
DETAIL

DETAIL GREEN
DETAIL.DE

INSTITUT FÜR TEXTILTECHNIK DER RHEINISCH-WESTFÄLISCHEN TECHNISCHEN HOCHSCHULE 694937
Otto-Blumenthal-Str. 1, 52074 AACHEN
Tel: 241 8023490 **Fax:** 241 8022422
Email: ita@ita.rwth-aachen.de
Web site: http://www.ita.rwth-aachen.de
Titles:
MITTEILUNGEN DES INSTITUTES FÜR TEXTILTECHNIK DER RHEINISCH-WESTFÄLISCHEN TECHNISCHEN HOCHSCHULE AACHEN

INSTITUT FÜR ZWEIRADSICHERHEIT E.V. 695639
Gladbecker Str. 425, 45329 ESSEN
Tel: 201 835390 **Fax:** 201 8353999
Email: info@ifz.de
Web site: http://www.ifz.de
Titles:
MOTORRADTRAINING TERMINE

INSTITUT SCHWEIZER FINANZ-DIENSTLEISTUNGEN GMBH 1653094
Eysseneckstr. 31, 60322 FRANKFURT
Tel: 69 15300611 **Fax:** 69 15300610
Email: info@isf-schweiz.ch
Web site: http://www.isf-schweiz.ch
Titles:
MANDANTEN-KURIER

INTEGRATA AG 688368
Zettachring 4, 70567 STUTTGART
Tel: 711 72846269 **Fax:** 711 72846108
Email: elmar.probst@integrata.de
Web site: http://www.integrata.de
Titles:
INFORMATIONSTECHNOLOGIE

INTER PUBLISH GMBH 1639930
Karlsruher Str. 31, 76437 RASTATT **Tel:** 7222 130
Titles:
BLITZ ILLU.DE
COUPÉ

INTERDISZIPLINÄRES ÖKOLOGISCHES ZENTRUM DER TECHNISCHEN UNIVERSITÄT BERGAKADEMIE FREIBERG 1724180
Brennhausgasse 14, 09599 FREIBERG
Tel: 3731 392297 **Fax:** 3731 394060
Web site: http://www.ioez.tu-freiberg.de
Titles:
UMFELD UMWELT

INTER-EURO MEDIEN GMBH 1605468
Eisenacher Str. 10, 80804 MÜNCHEN
Tel: 89 36037427 **Fax:** 89 32667553
Email: info@eurocosmetics-magazine.com
Web site: http://www.eurocosmetics-magazine.com
Titles:
EURO COSMETICS

INTERGERMA MARKETING GMBH & CO. KG 683779
Alfred-Fischer-Weg 12, 59073 HAMM
Tel: 2381 307090 **Fax:** 2381 3070919
Email: info@intergerma.de
Web site: http://www.intergerma.de
Titles:
INTERGERMA HOTELS UND TAGUNGSSTÄTTEN

INTERIEUR-VERLAG CLAUS BIRKNER GMBH 684704
Rotländerweg 13, 59846 SUNDERN
Tel: 2933 5071 **Fax:** 2933 7400
Email: info@interieur-verlag.de
Web site: http://www.interieur-verlag.de
Titles:
KÜCHEN HANDEL
KÜCHEN NEWS

INTERMEDIA WERBE- & VERLAGSGES. MBH 688732
Tömperweg 1, 47669 WACHTENDONK
Tel: 2836 972950 **Fax:** 2836 9729565
Email: info@intermedia-verlag.de
Web site: http://www.intermedia-verlag.de
Titles:
SPORT REVUE

INTERNATIONAL BUSINESS VERLAG GMBH 679985
Landersumer Weg 40, 48431 RHEINE
Tel: 5971 92160 **Fax:** 5971 92161854
Email: ibv@international-business.de
Web site: http://www.european-business-journal.com
Titles:
EUROPEAN BUSINESS JOURNAL

INTERNATIONAL HERALD TRIBUNE 4315
Friedrichstrasse 52, 60323 FRANKFURT
Tel: 1 41 43 93 00 **Fax:** 1 41 43 93 38
Titles:
INTERNATIONAL HERALD TRIBUNE - FRANKFURT

INTERNATIONALE GEWÄSSER-SCHUTZKOMMISSION FÜR DEN BODENSEE 1677019
Kernerplatz 9, 70182 STUTTGART
Tel: 711 1261533 **Fax:** 711 1261509
Email: bruno.blattner@um.bwl.de
Web site: http://www.igkb.org
Titles:
SEESPIEGEL

INTERNATIONALE WIRTSCHAFTSNACHRICHTEN VERLAGSGES. MBH 681087
Timmerhellstr. 39, 45478 MÜLHEIM
Tel: 208 377080 **Fax:** 208 380077
Email: info@iwn-verlag.de
Web site: http://www.iwn-verlag.de
Titles:
ECONOMY TRIBUNE
REGIONALEUROPÄISCHER WIRTSCHAFTS-SPIEGEL

INTERNET MAGAZIN VERLAG GMBH 683011
Arabellastr. 23, 81925 MÜNCHEN **Tel:** 89 92500
Fax: 89 92503055
Web site: http://www.haus.de
Titles:
DAS HAUS
DAS HAUS

INTERPRESS MEDIA COMMUNICATIONS 1774463
Friedländer Weg 45, 37085 GÖTTINGEN
Tel: 551 41121 **Fax:** 551 42270
Email: achim.stahn@interpress-ipr.de
Titles:
NEW METROPOLIS

INTERVINUM AG 690188
Otto-Raggenbass-Str. 11, 78462 KONSTANZ
Tel: 7531 132823 **Fax:** 7531 132813
Email: info@vinum.de
Web site: http://www.vinum.de
Titles:
VINUM

INTRAKUSTIK GMBH & CO. KG 694844
Thomasstr. 27, 12053 BERLIN **Tel:** 30 6889080
Fax: 30 68890832
Email: info@intrakustik.de
Web site: http://www.intrakustik.de
Titles:
INTRAS

INTRO GMBH & CO. KG 683824
Venloer Str. 241, 50823 KÖLN **Tel:** 221 949930
Fax: 221 9499399
Email: verlag@intro.de
Web site: http://www.intro.de
Titles:
INTRO

I.P.A. VERLAG GMBH 685511
Max-Planck-Str. 13, 28857 SYKE **Tel:** 4242 9610
Fax: 4242 961110
Email: info@ipaverlag.de
Web site: http://www.ipaverlag.de
Titles:
RUNDSCHREIBEN FÜR IHRE KUNDENZEITUNG

IPM MAGAZIN-VERLAG GMBH 680068
Rosenkavalierplatz 14, 81925 MÜNCHEN
Tel: 89 9100930 **Fax:** 89 91009353
Web site: http://www.ipm-verlag.de
Titles:
20 PRIVATE WOHNTRÄUME
CASA DECO
COUNTRY HOMES
HAIR UND BEAUTY
HAIRSTYLE!
HOMES & GARDENS

IPW MEDIEN GMBH & CO. KG 1774770
Rüsterstr. 11, 60325 FRANKFURT
Tel: 69 20737620 **Fax:** 69 20737584
Email: edit@ipwonline.de
Web site: http://www.ipwonline.de
Titles:
IPW

ISGATEC GMBH 1731726
Am Exerzierplatz 1a, 68167 MANNHEIM
Tel: 621 71768880 **Fax:** 621 71768888
Email: info@isagatec.com
Web site: http://www.isgatec.com
Titles:
DICHT!

ISI MEDIEN GMBH 698026
Albert-Schweitzer-Str. 66, 81735 MÜNCHEN
Tel: 89 9048620 **Fax:** 89 90486255
Email: info@isreport.de
Web site: http://www.isreport.de
Titles:
IS REPORT

I.S.O.-INSTITUT GMBH 684551
Schubartstr. 24, 73529 SCHWÄBISCH GMÜND
Tel: 7171 4959473 **Fax:** 7171 4959474
Email: info@kompetent.de
Web site: http://www.kompetent.de
Titles:
KOMPETENT FÜR KOMMUNIKATION - AUSG. KARLSRUHE/NORDSCHWARZWALD/RHEIN-NECKAR/PFALZ/SAAR
KOMPETENT FÜR KOMMUNIKATION - AUSG. SÜDBADEN/BODENSEE
KOMPETENT FÜR KOMMUNIKATION - AUSG. WÜRTTEMBERG

IT VERLAG FÜR INFORMATIONSTECHNIK GMBH 680447
Rudolf-Diesel-Ring 32, 82054 SAUERLACH
Tel: 8104 64940 **Fax:** 8104 649422
Web site: http://www.it-verlag.de
Titles:
IT MANAGEMENT
IT SECURITY

ITH-VERLAG MICHAEL KLÜCKMANN 685468
Badestr. 7, 31020 SALZHEMMENDORF
Tel: 5153 1898 **Fax:** 5153 964814
Email: ith-verlag@medical-special.de
Web site: http://www.medical-special.de
Titles:
MEDICAL SPECIAL

ITM VERLAGS GMBH & CO. KG 688679
Debert 32, 91320 EBERMANNSTADT
Tel: 9194 73780 **Fax:** 9194 737820
Email: spielzeug@spielzeuginternational.de
Web site: http://www.spielzeuginternational.de
Titles:
SPIELZEUG INTERNATIONAL

ITP VERLAG GMBH 680237
Kolpingstr. 26, 86916 KAUFERING
Tel: 8191 96490 **Fax:** 8191 70661
Email: service@midrange.de
Web site: http://www.midrange.de
Titles:
LANLINE
MIDRANGE MAGAZIN

IVD GMBH & CO.KG 1758220
Wilhelmstr. 240, 49479 IBBENBÜREN
Tel: 5451 9330 **Fax:** 5451 933195
Email: verlag@ivd.de
Web site: http://www.ivd.de/verlag
Titles:
WESTFÄLISCHES ÄRZTEBLATT

IVZ.MEDIEN GMBH & CO. KG 683437
Wilhelmstr. 240, 49475 IBBENBÜREN
Tel: 5451 9330 **Fax:** 5451 933192
Email: info@ivz-online.de
Web site: http://www.ivz-online.de
Titles:
IBBENBÜRENER VOLKSZEITUNG

IWW INSTITUT FÜR WIRTSCHAFTSPUBLIZISTIK VERLAG STEUERN RECHT WIRTSCHAFT GMBH & CO. KG 1741736
Aspastr. 24, 59394 NORDKIRCHEN
Tel: 2596 9220 **Fax:** 2596 92299
Email: info@iww.de
Web site: http://www.iww.de
Titles:
WIRTSCHAFTSDIENST VERSICHERUNGSMAKLER

IZ IMMOBILIEN ZEITUNG VERLAGSGES. MBH 683552
Luisenstr. 24, 65185 WIESBADEN
Tel: 611 973260 **Fax:** 611 9732631
Email: info@iz.de
Web site: http://www.immobilien-zeitung.de
Titles:
IMMOBILIEN ZEITUNG

J. A. BARTH VERLAG IM GEORG THIEME VERLAG KG 681272
Rüdigerstr. 14, 70469 STUTTGART
Tel: 711 89310 **Fax:** 711 8931298
Email: kundenservice@thieme.de
Web site: http://www.thieme.de
Titles:
ENDOKRINOLOGIE INFORMATIONEN
EXPERIMENTAL AND CLINICAL ENDOCRINOLOGY & DIABETES

J. C. C. BRUNS BETRIEBS-GMBH 685633
Obermarktstr. 26, 32423 MINDEN **Tel:** 571 8820
Fax: 571 882240
Email: info@jccbruns.de
Web site: http://www.jccbruns.de
Titles:
MINDENER TAGEBLATT
VLOTHOER ANZEIGER

J. ESSLINGER GMBH + CO. KG 686442
Poststr. 5, 75172 PFORZHEIM **Tel:** 7231 9330
Fax: 7231 93332393
Email: webmaster@pz-news.de
Web site: http://www.pz-news.de
Titles:
PFORZHEIMER ZEITUNG

J. F. BOFINGER KG 682708
Jägerhofstr. 4, 78532 TUTTLINGEN
Tel: 7461 70150 **Fax:** 7461 701537
Titles:
GRÄNZBOTE
HEUBERGER BOTE
TROSSINGER ZEITUNG

J. F. ZELLER GMBH & CO. 688360
Gartenstr. 4, 27404 ZEVEN **Tel:** 4281 9450
Fax: 4281 945949
Email: t.ditzen-blanke@t-online.de
Titles:
ZEVENER ZEITUNG

J. F. ZIEGLER KG, DRUCKEREI UND VERLAG 679075
Konrad-Adenauer-Str. 2, 42853 REMSCHEID
Tel: 2191 9090 **Fax:** 2191 909182
Email: verlag@rga-online.de
Web site: http://www.rga-online.de

Titles:
BERGISCHER ANZEIGER
REMSCHEIDER GENERAL-ANZEIGER
RGA-ONLINE

J. FINK VERLAG GMBH & CO. KG 1653424
Zeppelinstr. 10, 73760 OSTFILDERN
Tel: 711 28040600 Fax: 711 280406070
Email: kontakt@jfink-verlag.de
Web site: http://www.jfink-verlag.de

Titles:
MEIN EIGENHEIM

J. GRONEMANN KG, VERLAG WALSRODER ZEITUNG 690347
Lange Str. 14, 29664 WALSRODE
Tel: 5161 60050 Fax: 5161 600528
Email: walsroderzeitung@wz-net.de
Web site: http://www.wz-net.de

Titles:
WALSRODER ZEITUNG
WOCHEN SPIEGEL AM SONNTAG

J. HOFFMANN GMBH & CO. KG 1767089
An der Stadtgrenze 2, 31582 NIENBURG
Tel: 5021 9660 Fax: 5021 966113
Email: info@dieharke.de
Web site: http://www.dieharke.de

Titles:
DIE HARKE

J. LATKA VERLAG GMBH 677754
Heilsbachstr. 17, 53123 BONN Tel: 228 919320
Fax: 228 9193217
Email: info@latka.de
Web site: http://www.latka.de

Titles:
AMERICA JOURNAL
ASIA & MIDDLE EAST FOOD TRADE
SÜD-AFRIKA

J. MERGELSBERG GMBH & CO. KG 679610
Bahnhofstr. 6, 46325 BORKEN Tel: 2861 9440
Fax: 2861 944109
Email: verlag@borkenerzeitung.de
Web site: http://www.borkenerzeitung.de

Titles:
BORKENER ZEITUNG

J. P. BACHEM MEDIEN GMBH 677934
Ursulaplatz 1, 50668 KÖLN Tel: 221 16190
Fax: 221 1619205
Email: verlag@bachem.de
Web site: http://www.bachem.de/verlag

Titles:
KIRCHENZEITUNG FÜR DAS ERZBISTUM KÖLN

J&S DIALOG-MEDIEN GMBH 686779
Bei den Mühren 91, 20457 HAMBURG
Tel: 40 3698320 Fax: 40 36983236
Email: info@jsdialog.de
Web site: http://www.onetoone.de

Titles:
ONE TO ONE
ONE TO ONE BOOK

J. WECK GMBH UND CO. KG-VERLAG 687832
Wehratalstr. 3, 79664 WEHR Tel: 7761 9350
Fax: 7761 57691
Email: ratgeber@weck.de
Web site: http://www.weck.de

Titles:
R RATGEBER FRAU UND FAMILIE
R RATGEBER FRAU UND FAMILIE SPEZIAL WEIHNACHTEN

JACKWERTH VERLAG GMBH & CO. KG 688446
Tempelhofer Ufer 11, 10963 BERLIN
Tel: 30 2355390 Fax: 30 23553919
Email: verlag@jackwerth.de

Titles:
SIEGESSÄULE

JAGDSPANIEL-KLUB E.V. 683895
Adelbyerstr. 41, 24943 FLENSBURG
Tel: 461 48089990 Fax: 461 48089991
Email: geschaeftsstelle@jagdspaniel-klub.de
Web site: http://www.jagdspaniel-klub.de

Titles:
DER JAGDSPANIEL

JAGUAR ASSOCIATION GERMANY E.V. 1639706
Lönsstr. 18, 40880 RATINGEN Tel: 177 6043600
Fax: 2102 445948
Email: geschaeftsstelle@jaguar-association.de
Web site: http://www.jaguar-association.de

Titles:
JAG MAG

JAHR TOP SPECIAL VERLAG GMBH & CO. KG 678057
Troplowitzstr. 5, 22529 HAMBURG
Tel: 40 389060 Fax: 40 38906300
Web site: http://www.jahr-tsv.de

Titles:
AERO INTERNATIONAL
BLINKER
ESOX
FLIEGENFISCHEN
FLIEGER MAGAZIN
FOTO MAGAZIN
FOTO WIRTSCHAFT
GOLFMAGAZIN
JÄGER
OUTDOOR.MARKT
ROTORBLATT
SEGELN
ST. GEORG
TAUCHEN
TENNIS MAGAZIN

JAHRESZEITEN VERLAG GMBH 678506
Poßmoorweg 2, 22301 HAMBURG Tel: 40 27170
Fax: 40 27172056
Email: jahreszeitenverlag@jalag.de
Web site: http://www.jalag.de

Titles:
A & W ARCHITEKTUR & WOHNEN
COUNTRY
DER FEINSCHMECKER
DER FEINSCHMECKER BOOKAZINE
DER FEINSCHMECKER GOURMET-SHOP
FÜR SIE
MERIAN
PETRA
PRINZ
SELBER MACHEN
VITAL
ZUHAUSE WOHNEN
ZUHAUSE WOHNEN EXTRA

JAMVERLAG GMBH 1621084
Lausitzer Str. 9, 63075 OFFENBACH
Tel: 69 86711404 Fax: 69 86711406
Email: info@jamverlag.de
Web site: http://www.jamverlag.de

Titles:
VERPFLEGUNGS-MANAGEMENT

JEDERMANN-VERLAG GMBH 1616896
Mittelgewannweg 15, 69123 HEIDELBERG
Tel: 6221 14510 Fax: 6221 145119
Email: hem-baden@jedermann.de
Web site: http://www.jedermann.de

Titles:
HAUS & GRUND

JEHLE, VERLAGSGRUPPE HÜTHIG JEHLE REHM GMBH 1690186
Hultschiner Str. 8, 81677 MÜNCHEN
Tel: 89 21837222 Fax: 89 21837620
Email: info@hjr-verlag.de
Web site: http://www.huethig-jehle-rehm.de

Titles:
DER BAYERISCHE BÜRGERMEISTER

JO KLATT DESIGN+DESIGN VERLAG 680584
Körnerstr. 5, 22301 HAMBURG Tel: 40 2792223
Fax: 40 2798132
Email: joklatt@design-und-design.de
Web site: http://www.design-und-design.de

Titles:
DESIGN+DESIGN

JOH. HEIDER VERLAG GMBH 677568
Paffrather Str. 102, 51465 BERGISCH GLADBACH Tel: 2202 95400 Fax: 2202 21531
Email: heider@heider-verlag.de
Web site: http://www.heider-verlag.de

Titles:
DHB MAGAZIN

JOH. HEINR. MEYER GMBH DRUCKEREI + VERLAG 679674
Ernst-Böhme-Str. 20, 38112 BRAUNSCHWEIG
Tel: 531 3108523 Fax: 531 3108521
Email: verlag@braunschweig-medien.de
Web site: http://www.meyer-medien.de

Titles:
DER MARKT IN MITTELDEUTSCHLAND

JOHANN MICHAEL SAILER VERLAG GMBH & CO. KG 679051
Lina-Ammon-Str. 30, 90471 NÜRNBERG
Tel: 911 6600100 Fax: 911 6600110
Email: sailer@sailer-verlag.de
Web site: http://www.sailer-verlag.de

Titles:
BENNI
STAFETTE

JOHANN OBERAUER GMBH 680438
Postfach 1152, 83381 FREILASSING
Tel: 6225 27000 Fax: 6225 270011
Email: vertrieb@oberauer.com
Web site: http://www.oberauer.com

Titles:
MEDIUM
WIRTSCHAFTSJOURNALIST

JOHANN WILHELM NAUMANN VERLAG GMBH 677662
Dominikanerplatz 8, 97070 WÜRZBURG
Tel: 931 308630 Fax: 931 3086333
Email: info@die-tagespost.de
Web site: http://www.die-tagespost.de

Titles:
ASZ DIE ALLGEMEINE SONNTAGSZEITUNG
DIE TAGESPOST

JOHANNES MARTIN SÖHNE VIERNHEIMER DRUCK- UND VERLAGSHAUS 690171
Rathausstr. 43, 68519 VIERNHEIM
Tel: 6204 96660 Fax: 6204 966666
Email: verlag@viernheimertageblatt.de

Titles:
VIERNHEIMER TAGEBLATT

JÖRG LOOSE CONSULTING E.K. 1709604
Eutiner Ring 2, 23611 BAD SCHWARTAU
Tel: 451 7021167 Fax: 451 7021189
Email: info@joerg-loose-consulting.de
Web site: http://www.joerg-loose-consulting.de

Titles:
PISTE

JOSEF KELLER GMBH & CO. VERLAGS-KG 682469
Seebreite 9, 82335 BERG Tel: 8151 7710
Fax: 8151 771190
Email: info@keller-verlag.de
Web site: http://www.keller-verlag.de

Titles:
T>AKT

JOSEF THOMANN'SCHE BUCHDRUCKEREI VERLAG 682889
Altstadt 89, 84028 LANDSHUT Tel: 871 8500
Fax: 871 850132
Email: service@idowa.de
Web site: http://www.idowa.de

Titles:
HALLERTAUER ZEITUNG
LANDSHUT AKTUELL
LANDSHUTER ZEITUNG
MOOSBURGER ZEITUNG
VILSBIBURGER ZEITUNG

JOURNAL INTERNATIONAL VERLAGS- UND WERBEGES. MBH 681615
Hanns-Seidel-Platz 5, 81737 MÜNCHEN
Tel: 89 6427970 Fax: 89 64279777
Email: info@journal-international.de
Web site: http://www.journal-international.de

Titles:
GLOSS

JS-FILMPRODUKTION GMBH 691012
Postfach 5324, 79020 FREIBURG
Tel: 761 6966043 Fax: 761 66310
Web site: http://www.riogrande.de

Titles:
ZÜGE

JS-WERBEBERATUNG 1737061
Max-Samson-Str. 24, 33165 LICHTENAU
Tel: 5292 930640 Fax: 5292 930641
Email: info@werbeberatung.org
Web site: http://www.werbeberatung.org

Titles:
HALLO TOURIST!

JUGENDHAUS DÜSSELDORF E.V. 678971
Carl-Mosterts-Platz 1, 40477 DÜSSELDORF
Tel: 211 46930 Fax: 211 4693120
Email: jhd@jugendhaus-duesseldorf.de
Web site: http://www.jugendhaus-duesseldorf.de

Titles:
JUGEND & BUNDESWEHR

JULIUS BELTZ GMBH + CO. KG 686878
Werderstr. 10, 69469 WEINHEIM Tel: 6201 60070
Fax: 6201 6007310
Email: info@beltz.de
Web site: http://www.beltz.de

Titles:
PÄDAGOGIK
PSYCHOLOGIE HEUTE
ZEITSCHRIFT FÜR PÄDAGOGIK

JUNGE PRESSE NORDRHEIN-WESTFALEN E.V. 1679953
Hammacherstr. 33, 45127 ESSEN
Tel: 201 2480358 Fax: 201 2480348
Email: info@junge-presse.de
Web site: http://www.junge-presse.de

Titles:
VERANSTALTUNGSKALENDER

JUNGLE WORLD VERLAGS GMBH 1654085
Bergmannstr. 68, 10961 BERLIN Tel: 30 61282732
Fax: 30 6182055
Email: verlag@jungle-world.com
Web site: http://www.jungle-world.com

Titles:
JUNGLE WORLD

JUNIOR-VERLAG GMBH & CO. KG 684119
Raboisen 30, 20095 HAMBURG Tel: 40 344434
Fax: 40 352540
Email: info@junior-verlag.de
Web site: http://www.wireltern.de

Titles:
JUNGE FAMILIE
KINDER

JÜRGEN HARTMANN VERLAG GMBH 678362
Seefeld 18, 91093 HESSDORF Tel: 9135 71230
Fax: 9135 712340
Email: kontakt@hartmann-verlag.de
Web site: http://www.hartmann-verlag.de

Titles:
HERZ MEDIZIN

JUSTUS-LIEBIG-UNIVERSITÄT 689853
Ludwigstr. 23, 35390 GIESSEN Tel: 641 9912040
Fax: 641 9912049
Email: christel.lauterbach@admin.uni-giessen.de
Web site: http://www.uni-giessen.de

Titles:
SPIEGEL DER FORSCHUNG

JUVE VERLAG FÜR JURISTISCHE INFORMATION GMBH 678641
Sachsenring 6, 50677 KÖLN **Tel:** 221 9138800
Fax: 221 91388018
Email: info@juve.de
Web site: http://www.juve.de

Titles:
JUVE HANDBUCH WIRTSCHAFTSKANZLEIEN
JUVE RECHTSMARKT

JUVENTA VERLAG GMBH 679013
Ehretstr. 3, 69469 WEINHEIM **Tel:** 6201 90200
Fax: 6201 902013
Email: juventa@juventa.de
Web site: http://www.juventa.de

Titles:
DEUTSCHE JUGEND ZEITSCHRIFT FÜR DIE JUGENDARBEIT
GEMEINSAM LEBEN
SOZIALMAGAZIN

K. G. SAUR VERLAG. EIN IMPRINT DER WALTER DE GRUYTER GMBH & CO. KG 679279
Mies-van-der-Rohe-Str. 1, 80807 MÜNCHEN
Tel: 89 769020 **Fax:** 89 76902150
Email: info@degruyter.com
Web site: http://www.saur.de

Titles:
BIBLIOTHEK FORSCHUNG UND PRAXIS

K&H VERLAGS-GMBH 1684903
Wilhelm-Giese-Str. 26, 27616 BEVERSTEDT
Tel: 4747 87410 **Fax:** 4747 8741222
Email: info@kran-und-hebetechnik.de
Web site: http://www.kran-und-hebetechnik.de

Titles:
KRAN & HEBETECHNIK

K&K VERLAG GMBH 681821
Mörkenstr. 12, 22767 HAMBURG
Tel: 40 589657970 **Fax:** 40 589657977
Email: info@filemaker-magazin.de
Web site: http://www.filemaker-magazin.de

Titles:
FILEMAKER MAGAZIN

K+S AG 684795
Bertha-von-Suttner-Str. 7, 34131 KASSEL
Tel: 561 93011043 **Fax:** 561 93011666
Email: uwe.handke@k-plus-s.com
Web site: http://www.k-plus-s.com

Titles:
K+S INFORMATION

KAPITALFORUM AG 684227
Hopfenrain 1, 35114 HAINA **Tel:** 6456 81200
Fax: 6456 81205
Email: culex@t-online.de
Web site: http://www.kapitalforum.info

Titles:
KAPITALFORUM

KARL DEMETER VERLAG IM GEORG THIEME VERLAG KG 677330
Rüdigerstr. 14, 70469 STUTTGART
Tel: 711 89310 **Fax:** 711 8931298
Web site: http://www.thieme.de

Titles:
KLINIKARZT

KARL ELSER GMBH BUCH- UND ZEITUNGSVERLAG 686019
Kißlingweg 35, 75417 MÜHLACKER
Tel: 7041 8050 **Fax:** 7041 80570
Email: info@muehlacker-tagblatt.de
Web site: http://www.muehlacker-tagblatt.de

Titles:
MÜHLACKER TAGBLATT

KARL F. HAUG VERLAG IN MVS MEDIZINVERLAGE STUTTGART GMBH & CO. KG 677651
Oswald-Hesse-Str. 50, 70469 STUTTGART
Tel: 711 89310 **Fax:** 711 8931706
Web site: http://www.medizinverlage.de

Titles:
ALLGEMEINE HOMÖOPATHISCHE ZEITUNG
DEUTSCHE ZEITSCHRIFT FÜR ONKOLOGIE
DO DEUTSCHE ZEITSCHRIFT FÜR OSTEOPATHIE
ERFAHRUNGSHEILKUNDE
ZEITSCHRIFT FÜR KLASSISCHE HOMÖOPATHIE
ZEITSCHRIFT FÜR PHYTOTHERAPIE

KARL MÜLLER VORM. FR. FEUERLEIN GMBH 690390
Allee 2, 91154 ROTH **Tel:** 9171 970311
Fax: 9171 970326
Email: wochenanzeiger.roth-schwabach@pressenetz.de
Web site: http://www.wa-wochenanzeiger.de

Titles:
WA WOCHEN ANZEIGER

KASSELER SONNTAGSBLATT VERLAGSGES. MBH 680621
Werner-Heisenberg-Str. 7, 34123 KASSEL
Tel: 561 9592521 **Fax:** 561 9592514
Email: vertrieb@kasseler-sonntagsblatt.de
Web site: http://www.kasseler-sonntagsblatt.de

Titles:
KASSELER SONNTAGSBLATT

KASSENÄRZTLICHE VEREINIGUNG BADEN-WÜRTTEMBERG 1726871
Albstadtweg 11, 70567 STUTTGART
Tel: 711 78750 **Fax:** 711 78753274
Email: info@kvbawue.de
Web site: http://www.kvbawue.de

Titles:
ERGO

KASSENÄRZTLICHE VEREINIGUNG BERLIN 684866
Masurenallee 6a, 14057 BERLIN **Tel:** 30 31003223
Fax: 30 31003210
Email: kvblatt-berlin@kvberlin.de
Web site: http://www.kvberlin.de

Titles:
KV BLATT BERLIN

KASSENÄRZTLICHE VEREINIGUNG MECKLENBURG-VORPOMMERN 1716504
Postfach 160145, 19091 SCHWERIN
Tel: 385 7431213 **Fax:** 385 7431386
Email: presse@kvmv.de
Web site: http://www.kvmv.de

Titles:
JOURNAL

KASSENÄRZTLICHE VEREINIGUNG NIEDERSACHSEN 1739879
Berliner Allee 22, 30175 HANNOVER
Tel: 511 3803133 **Fax:** 511 3803491
Email: detlef.haffke@kvn.de
Web site: http://www.kvn.de

Titles:
KVN-PRO

KASSENÄRZTLICHE VEREINIGUNG RHEINLAND-PFALZ 1739164
Isaac-Fulda-Allee 14, 55124 MAINZ
Tel: 6131 326326 **Fax:** 6131 326327
Email: kvpraxis@kv-rlp.de
Web site: http://www.kv-rlp.de

Titles:
KV RHEINLAND-PFALZ PRAXIS

KASTNER AG - DAS MEDIENHAUS 678937
Schloßhof 2, 85283 WOLNZACH **Tel:** 8442 92530
Fax: 8442 2289
Email: verlag@kastner.de
Web site: http://www.kastner.de

Titles:
BRANDWACHT
EURO MOTORHOME
HOLZBAU DIE NEUE QUADRIGA
JAGD IN BAYERN
MEDINTERN

KATHOLISCHE FRAUENGEMEINSCHAFT DEUTSCHLANDS, BUNDESVERBAND E.V. 682110
Prinz-Georg-Str. 44, 40477 DÜSSELDORF
Tel: 211 4499240 **Fax:** 211 4499275
Email: sekretariat@kfdfum.de
Web site: http://www.fraundmutter.de

Titles:
FRAU + MUTTER

KATHOLISCHE UNIVERSITÄT EICHSTÄTT-INGOLSTADT, RECHENZENTRUM 683724
Ostenstr. 24, 85072 EICHSTÄTT **Tel:** 8421 931214
Fax: 8421 932745
Email: urz-direktion@ku-eichstaett.de
Web site: http://www.ku-eichstaett.de/Rechenzentrum/dienstleist/schriften/inkuerze

Titles:
IN KUERZE

KATHOLISCHE VERLAGSGES. MBH ST. ANSGAR 686268
Schmilinskystr. 80, 20099 HAMBURG
Tel: 40 24877111 **Fax:** 40 24877119
Email: info@ansgar-verlag.de
Web site: http://www.neue-kirchenzeitung.de

Titles:
NEUE KIRCHENZEITUNG

KATHOLISCHES MILITÄRBISCHOFSAMT 685628
Am Weidendamm 2, 10117 BERLIN
Tel: 30 206170 **Fax:** 30 20617199
Web site: http://www.katholische-militaerseelsorge.de

Titles:
VERORDNUNGSBLATT DES KATHOLISCHEN MILITÄRBISCHOFS FÜR DIE DEUTSCHE BUNDESWEHR

KATJA GEHRING 1748637
Hellweg 1, 15234 FRANKFURT **Tel:** 335 2288794
Fax: 335 2288794
Email: red@frankfurterfamilienseiten.de
Web site: http://www.frankfurterfamilienseiten.de

Titles:
DIE FRANKFURTER FAMILIENSEITEN

KAUPERT MEDIA GMBH 1757240
Spandauer Damm 89, 14059 BERLIN
Tel: 30 30301401 **Fax:** 30 30301482
Email: team@kaupertmedia.de
Web site: http://www.kaupertmedia.de

Titles:
KAUPERTS STRASSENFÜHRER DURCH BERLIN MIT GEMEINDEVERZEICHNIS LAND BRANDENBURG

KELKHEIMER ZEITUNG 1757621
Theresenstr. 2, 61462 KÖNIGSTEIN
Tel: 6174 93850 **Fax:** 6174 938550
Email: kw@hochtaunus.de
Web site: http://www.hochtaunus.de/kw

Titles:
KELKHEIMER ZEITUNG

KERN & KERN MEDIA VERLAG OHG 682687
Körnerstr. 28, 53175 BONN **Tel:** 228 9354800
Fax: 228 93548020
Email: info@kernkern.de
Web site: http://www.golfwelt.net

Titles:
LADYSLOUNGE

KERN VERLAG, INH. ANNETTE DWORAK 695084
Tiroler Weg 1b, 79285 EBRINGEN
Tel: 7664 611511 **Fax:** 7664 611512
Email: info@kern-verlag.de
Web site: http://www.kern-verlag.de

Titles:
ZWEIRAD ADRESSBUCH

KETTELER VERLAG GMBH 684159
Bernhard-Letterhaus-Str. 26, 50670 KÖLN
Tel: 221 7722134 **Fax:** 221 7722135
Email: kontakt@ketteler-verlag.de
Web site: http://www.ketteler-verlag.de

Titles:
KAB IMPULS

KG WOCHENKURIER VERLAGSGES. MBH & CO. BRANDENBURG 678692
Geierswalder Str. 14, 02979 ELSTERHEIDE
Tel: 3571 4670 **Fax:** 3571 406891
Email: wochenkurier@cwk-verlag.de
Web site: http://www.wochenkurier.info

Titles:
COTTBUSER WOCHENKURIER
ELBE-ELSTER WOCHENKURIER - AUSG. BAD LIEBENWERDA
ELBE-ELSTER WOCHENKURIER - AUSG. FINSTERWALDE
ELBE-ELSTER WOCHENKURIER - AUSG. HERZBERG
HOYERSWERDAER WOCHENKURIER
KAMENZER WOCHENKURIER
SENFTENBERGER WOCHENKURIER
SPREE-NEISSE WOCHENKURIER - AUSG. FORST
SPREE-NEISSE WOCHENKURIER - AUSG. GUBEN
SPREE-NEISSE WOCHENKURIER - AUSG. SPREMBERG
SPREEWÄLDER WOCHENKURIER - AUSG. CALAU
SPREEWÄLDER WOCHENKURIER - AUSG. LÜBBEN
SPREEWÄLDER WOCHENKURIER - AUSG. LUCKAU

KG WOCHENKURIER VERLAGSGES. MBH & CO. DRESDEN 678888
Wettiner Platz 10, 01067 DRESDEN
Tel: 351 491760 **Fax:** 351 4917674
Email: wochenkurier-dresden@dwk-verlag.de
Web site: http://www.wochenkurier.info

Titles:
BAUTZNER WOCHENKURIER
BISCHOFSWERDAER WOCHENKURIER
DIPPOLDISWALDER WOCHENKURIER
FREITALER WOCHENKURIER
GÖRLITZER WOCHENKURIER
GROSSENHAINER WOCHENKURIER
LÖBAUER WOCHENKURIER
MEISSNER WOCHENKURIER
NIESKYER WOCHENKURIER
PIRNAER WOCHENKURIER
RIESAER WOCHENKURIER
SEBNITZER WOCHENKURIER
WEISSWASSERANER WOCHENKURIER
ZITTAUER WOCHENKURIER

KHS GMBH 684298
Juchostr. 20, 44143 DORTMUND
Tel: 231 5691339 **Fax:** 231 5691226
Email: info@khs.com
Web site: http://www.khs.com

Titles:
KHS COMPETENCE

KIBRA VERLAG & MEDIENSERVICE DALICHAU & SCHREIBER GBR 1684759
Fuhrberger Weg 10, 30900 WEDEMARK
Tel: 5130 928190 **Fax:** 5130 9281929
Web site: http://www.kibra.de

Titles:
KINDER BRANCHENBUCH

KIDSGO VERLAG GMBH 1641639
Carl-Giesecke-Str. 4, 37079 GÖTTINGEN
Tel: 551 997250 **Fax:** 551 99725299
Email: willkommen@kidsgo.de
Web site: http://www.kidsgo.de

Titles:
MEIN BABY MEIN KIDSGO
MEIN BABY MEIN KIDSGO
MEIN BABY MEIN KIDSGO - AUSG. BERLIN
MEIN BABY MEIN KIDSGO - AUSG. DÜSSELDORFER RAUM
MEIN BABY MEIN KIDSGO - AUSG. KÖLN
MEIN BABY MEIN KIDSGO - AUSG. MÜNCHEN

KIEBACK&PETER GMBH & CO. KG 1742940
Tempelhofer Weg 50, 12347 BERLIN
Tel: 30 60095135 **Fax:** 30 60095163
Email: symanczik@kieback-peter.de
Web site: http://www.kieback-peter.de

Titles:
TECHNOLOGISCH

KIEL - MARKETING E.V. 684317
Andreas-Gayk-Str. 31, 24103 KIEL
Tel: 431 6791028 **Fax:** 431 6791099
Email: info@kurskiel.de
Web site: http://www.kurskiel.de

Titles:
KURS KIEL

KIEL - MARKETING E.V. CITY- & STADTMANAGEMENT 1771318
Andreas-Gayk-Str. 31, 24103 KIEL
Tel: 431 6791050 **Fax:** 431 6791099
Email: j.schmidt@kiel-marketing.de
Web site: http://www.stadtmarketing-kiel.de

Titles:
SHOP'N JOY

KIELER ZEITUNG VERLAGS- UND DRUCKEREI KG-GMBH & CO. 684311
Fleethörn 1, 24103 KIEL **Tel:** 431 9030
Fax: 431 9032935
Email: ph.gf@kieler-nachrichten.de
Web site: http://www.kn-online.de

Titles:
ECKERNFÖRDER RUNDSCHAU
KIELER EXPRESS AM WOCHENENDE - AUSG. OST
KIELER EXPRESS - AUSG. NORD
KIELER NACHRICHTEN

K.I.-MEDIENGES. MBH 684505
Vorgebirgstr. 59, 50677 KÖLN **Tel:** 221 35558711
Fax: 221 35558741 1
Email: verwaltung@koelner.de
Web site: http://www.koelner.de

Titles:
KÖLNER GASTRO-SPECIAL
KÖLNER ILLUSTRIERTE
LIVE!

KIRCHE HEUTE VERLAGS-GGMBH 684365
Postfach 1406, 84498 ALTÖTTING
Tel: 8671 880430 **Fax:** 8671 880431
Email: info@kirche-heute.de
Web site: http://www.kirche-heute.de

Titles:
KIRCHE HEUTE

KIRCHENBOTE DES BISTUMS OSNABRÜCK 684372
Kleine Domsfreiheit 23, 49074 OSNABRÜCK
Tel: 541 318500 **Fax:** 541 318530
Email: verlag@kirchenbote.de
Web site: http://www.kirchenbote.de

Titles:
KIRCHENBOTE

KIRCHERBURKHARDT GMBH 1686514
Heiligegeistkirchplatz 1, 10178 BERLIN
Tel: 30 440320 **Fax:** 30 4403220
Email: info@kircher-burkhardt.com
Web site: http://www.kircher-burkhardt.com

Titles:
Y

KIRRROYAL GENIESSERVERLAG E.KFR. 1753043
Hafnerstr. 13, 83043 BAD AIBLING
Tel: 8061 392788 **Fax:** 8061 392790
Email: office@kirroyal.eu
Web site: http://www.kirroyal-geniesserjournal.de

Titles:
KIR ROYAL

KIRSCHBAUM VERLAG GMBH 679988
Siegfriedstr. 28, 53179 BONN **Tel:** 228 954530
Fax: 228 9545327
Email: info@kirschbaum.de
Web site: http://www.kirschbaum.de

Titles:
BUS MAGAZIN
GÜTERVERKEHR
STRASSE UND AUTOBAHN
STRASSENVERKEHRSTECHNIK

KITZINGER VERLAG UND MEDIEN GMBH & CO. KG 1793384
Herrnstr. 10, 97318 KITZINGEN **Tel:** 9321 70090
Fax: 9321 700944
Email: anzeigen.kitzingen@infranken.de
Web site: http://www.infranken.de/diekitzinger

Titles:
DIE KITZINGER

KKH-ALLIANZ 684408
Karl-Wiechert-Allee 61, 30625 HANNOVER
Tel: 511 28020 **Fax:** 511 28029999
Email: service@kkh-allianz.de
Web site: http://www.kkh-allianz.de

Titles:
NACHRICHTEN

KKV HANSA MÜNSTER E.V. 684411
Klosterstr. 28, 48143 MÜNSTER **Tel:** 251 214690
Web site: http://www.kkv-muenster.de

Titles:
KKV INFORMATION

KLAMBT-STYLE-VERLAG GMBH & CO. KG 1771313
Gänsemarkt 21, 20354 HAMBURG
Tel: 40 4118825301 **Fax:** 40 4118825302
Email: info@grazia-magazin.de
Web site: http://www.grazia-magazin.de

Titles:
GRAZIA

KLAMBT-VERLAG GMBH & CIE 1681427
Rotweg 8, 76532 BADEN-BADEN **Tel:** 7221 35010
Fax: 7221 3501204
Email: kontakt@klambt.de
Web site: http://www.klambt.de

Titles:
7 TAGE
DIE 80 BESTEN GRATINS WOCHE DER FRAU
DIE 80 BESTEN GRILL-REZEPTE WOCHE DER FRAU
DIE 80 BESTEN PASTA-REZEPTE WOCHE DER FRAU
DIE 80 BESTEN SCHNITZEL-REZEPTE WOCHE DER FRAU
ADEL AKTUELL
DIE BESTEN OBSTKUCHEN
HEIM UND WELT
LANDKÜCHE WOCHE DER FRAU
DIE NEUE FRAU
DIE NEUE FRAU DIE BESTEN FRÜHLINGSTORTEN UND KUCHEN
DIE NEUE FRAU DIE BESTEN LANDFRAUEN-KUCHEN
WOCHE DER FRAU
WOCHE DER FRAU DIE 90 BESTEN WEIHNACHTSPLÄTZCHEN
WOCHE DER FRAU EXTRA UNSERE 111 LIEBLINGSREZEPTE

KLATSCHMOHN VERLAG, DRUCK + WERBUNG GMBH 1643239
Am Campus 25, 18182 BENTWISCH
Tel: 381 2066811 **Fax:** 381 2066812
Email: info@klatschmohn.de
Web site: http://www.klatschmohn.de

Titles:
ESSEN UND TRINKEN IN MECKLENBURG-VORPOMMERN

KLAUS MERSE-VERLAG GMBH 683329
Schulstr. 20, 25335 ELMSHORN **Tel:** 4121 26730
Fax: 4121 267334
Email: anzeigen@holsteiner-allgemeine.de
Web site: http://www.holsteiner-allgemeine.de

Titles:
HOLSTEINER ALLGEMEINE

KLAUS RESCH VERLAG KG 679186
Moorbeker Str. 31, 26197 GROSSENKNETEN
Tel: 4435 96120 **Fax:** 4435 961296
Email: info@berufsstart.de
Web site: http://www.berufsstart.de

Titles:
UNTERNEHMEN STELLEN SICH VOR

KLAUS SCHULZ VERLAGS GMBH 686875
Böckmannstr. 15, 20099 HAMBURG
Tel: 40 248777 **Fax:** 40 249448
Email: info@oxmoxhh.de
Web site: http://www.oxmoxhh.de

Titles:
OXMOX
UPDATE

KLEINER GMBH 1714914
Göppinger Str. 2, 75179 PFORZHEIM
Tel: 7231 60720 **Fax:** 7231 60701039
Email: marketing@kleiner-gmbh.de
Web site: http://www.kleiner-gmbh.de

Titles:
KLEINER INTERN

KLERUSBLATT-VERLAG 684447
Stephansplatz 3, 80337 MÜNCHEN
Tel: 89 265464 **Fax:** 89 266671
Email: klerusverband@t-online.de

Titles:
KLERUSBLATT

KLETT MINT GMBH 1770569
Rotebühlstr. 77, 70178 STUTTGART
Tel: 711 66720 **Fax:** 711 66722004
Web site: http://www.klett-mint.de

Titles:
LIFE + SCIENCE

KLETT-COTTA J. G. COTTA'SCHE BUCHHANDLUNG NACHF. 680389
Rotebühlstr. 77, 70178 STUTTGART
Tel: 711 66721648 **Fax:** 711 66722032
Email: th.kleffner@klett-cotta.de
Web site: http://www.klett-cotta.de

Titles:
KINDERANALYSE
MUSIK & ÄSTHETIK

KLIMASCHUTZAGENTUR REGION HANNOVER GMBH 1723469
Prinzenstr. 12, 30159 HANNOVER
Tel: 511 61623109 **Fax:** 511 61623975
Email: info@klimaschutzagentur.de
Web site: http://www.klimaschutz-hannover.de

Titles:
KLIMAINFOS

KLINIKUM INGOLSTADT GMBH 1728596
Krumenauerstr. 25, 85049 INGOLSTADT
Tel: 841 8801060 **Fax:** 841 880661060
Email: presse@klinikum-ingolstadt.de
Web site: http://www.klinikum-ingolstadt.de

Titles:
KLINIKUMMEDICUS

KLOCKE VERLAG GMBH 677595
Höfeweg 40, 33619 BIELEFELD **Tel:** 521 911110
Fax: 521 9111112
Email: info@klocke-verlag.de
Web site: http://www.klocke-verlag.de

Titles:
À LA CARTE
COUNTRY STYLE
HIDEAWAYS
HIGH LIFE

KM VERLAGS GMBH 1616907
Eichendorffstr. 47, 64347 GRIESHEIM
Tel: 6155 823030 **Fax:** 6155 823032
Email: hellmich@kmverlag.de
Web site: http://www.kmverlag.de

Titles:
BÜHNEN MAGAZIN
SCHWERTRANSPORT MAGAZIN

KMA MEDIEN IN GEORG THIEME VERLAG KG 684456
Rüdigerstr. 14, 70469 STUTTGART
Tel: 711 89310 **Fax:** 711 8931298
Web site: http://www.kma-online.de

Titles:
KMA DAS GESUNDHEITSWIRTSCHAFTSMAGAZIN

KMS KAFITZ MEDIENSERVICE GMBH 698284
Max-Planck-Str. 38, 50858 KÖLN **Tel:** 2234 99080
Fax: 2234 9908130
Email: info@kms.eu
Web site: http://www.kms.eu

Titles:
MULTIMEDIA MAGAZIN

KNAAK VERLAG 695189
Kaiserstr. 8, 13589 BERLIN **Tel:** 30 3751515
Fax: 30 3754424
Email: peterknaak@aol.com

Titles:
BAU

KNEIPP-VERLAG GMBH 684479
Adolf-Scholz-Allee 6, 86825 BAD WÖRISHOFEN
Tel: 8247 3002160 **Fax:** 8247 3002199
Email: kneippverlag@t-online.de
Web site: http://www.kneippverlag.de

Titles:
KNEIPP JOURNAL

KNITTLER MEDIEN GMBH 687611
Mittlerer Hubweg 5, 72227 EGENHAUSEN
Tel: 7453 9385787 **Fax:** 7453 9385797
Email: info@knittler.de
Web site: http://www.knittler.de

Titles:
REINIGUNGS MARKT

KNÜPFER VERLAG GMBH 1743545
Prager Str. 2b, 01069 DRESDEN **Tel:** 351 800700
Fax: 351 8007070
Email: post@maxity.de
Web site: http://www.knve.de

Titles:
CITY GUIDE DRESDEN
FEIERN & TAGEN DRESDEN
KAUFMACHER DRESDEN
MAXITY DRESDNER ELBLAND
MUSEUMS IN DRESDEN
SOMMEROASEN CHEMNITZ
SOMMEROASEN DRESDEN

KÖLLEN DRUCK+VERLAG GMBH 679597
Ernst-Robert-Curtius-Str. 14, 53117 BONN
Tel: 228 9898280 **Fax:** 228 9898299
Email: verlag@koellen.de
Web site: http://www.koellen.de

Titles:
GOLF MANAGER
GREENKEEPERS JOURNAL
HARTMANNBUND MAGAZIN

KÖLNER ANZEIGENBLATT GMBH & CO. KG 681122
Stolberger Str. 114a, 50933 KÖLN
Tel: 221 9544140 **Fax:** 221 954414499
Email: joachim.hesse@mds.de
Web site: http://www.rheinische-anzeigenblaetter.de

Titles:
KÖLN 8 AKTUELL
KÖLNER WOCHENSPIEGEL - AUSG. STADTBEZIRK EHRENFELD
PORZ AKTUELL

KÖLNISCHE RÜCKVERSICHERUNGS-GESELLSCHAFT AG 1724695
Theodor-Heuss-Ring 11, 50668 KÖLN
Tel: 221 77521001 **Fax:** 221 77521007
Web site: http://www.genre.com

Titles:
BUZAKTUELL
RPAKTUELL

KÖLNTOURISMUS GMBH 684240
Kardinal-Höffner-Platz 1, 50667 KÖLN
Tel: 221 22130400 **Fax:** 221 22130410
Email: info@koelntourismus.de
Web site: http://www.koelntourismus.de

Titles:
HOTELS UND PENSIONEN
KÖLN. DIE STADT
DER STADTPLAN
DIE WEIHNACHTSMÄRKTE

KOLPING VERLAG GMBH 683461
Kolpingplatz 5, 50667 KÖLN **Tel:** 221 207010
Fax: 221 2070138
Email: joachim.flieher@kolping.de
Web site: http://www.kolping.de

Titles:
KOLPING MAGAZIN

KOMBA GEWERKSCHAFT RHEINLAND-PFALZ 1783716
Josef-Görres-Platz 17, 56068 KOBLENZ
Tel: 261 35766 **Fax:** 261 38257
Email: rp@komba.de
Web site: http://www.komba.de

Titles:
KOMMUNALES ECHO

KOMET DRUCK- UND VERLAGSHAUS GMBH 684527
Molkenbrunner Str. 10, 66954 PIRMASENS
Tel: 6331 51320 **Fax:** 6331 31480
Email: info@komet-pirmasens.de
Web site: http://www.komet-pirmasens.de

Titles:
DER KOMET

KOMMUNAL-VERLAG GMBH 1767092
Klingelhöferstr. 8, 10785 BERLIN
Tel: 30 22070477 **Fax:** 30 2207478
Email: info@kommunal-verlag.com
Web site: http://www.kommunal-verlag.com

Titles:
KOPO KOMMUNALPOLITISCHE BLÄTTER

KOMMUNIKATION & WIRTSCHAFT GMBH 686756
Baumschulenweg 28, 26127 OLDENBURG
Tel: 441 93530 **Fax:** 441 9353300
Email: info@kuw.de
Web site: http://www.kuw.de

Titles:
OLDENBURGISCHE WIRTSCHAFT
WIRTSCHAFT OSTFRIESLAND & PAPENBURG

KOMMUNIKATIONSVERBAND, CLUB STUTTGART 690038
Alte Steige 17, 73732 ESSLINGEN
Tel: 711 9378930 **Fax:** 711 9378939
Email: info@werbeagentur-beck.de
Web site: http://www.werbeagentur-beck.de

Titles:
VERANSTALTUNGSPROGRAMM

KOMPART VERLAGSGES. MBH & CO. KG 1770707
Rosenthaler Str. 31, 10178 BERLIN
Tel: 30 220110 **Fax:** 30 22011105
Email: info@kompart.de
Web site: http://www.kompart.de

Titles:
G+G GESUNDHEIT UND GESELLSCHAFT

KÖNIGSTEINER WOCHE 684518
Theresenstr. 2, 61462 KÖNIGSTEIN
Tel: 6174 93850 **Fax:** 6174 938550
Email: kw@hochtaunus.de
Web site: http://www.hochtaunus.de/kw

Titles:
KÖNIGSTEINER WOCHE

KONRAD THEISS VERLAG GMBH 677732
Mönchhaldenstr. 28, 70191 STUTTGART
Tel: 711 255270 **Fax:** 711 2552717
Email: service@theiss.de
Web site: http://www.theiss.de

Titles:
ARCHÄOLOGIE IN DEUTSCHLAND

KONRADIN MEDIEN GMBH 678817
Ernst-Mey-Str. 8, 70771 LEINFELDEN-ECHTERDINGEN **Tel:** 711 75940 **Fax:** 711 7594390
Email: info@konradin.de
Web site: http://www.konradin.de

Titles:
BBA BAU BERATUNG ARCHITEKTUR
BILD DER WISSENSCHAFT
BILD DER WISSENSCHAFT
BPZ BAUPRAXIS ZEITUNG
DAMALS
DB DEUTSCHE BAUZEITUNG
DDS
DESIGN REPORT
GLAS
LACKIERERBLATT
MALERBLATT
NATUR+KOSMOS

KONRADIN RELATIONS GMBH 1709807
Ernst-Mey-Str. 8, 70771 LEINFELDEN-ECHTERDINGEN **Tel:** 711 7594340
Fax: 711 75945897
Email: relations@konradin.de
Web site: http://www.konradin-relations.de

Titles:
ARCGUIDE.DE

KONRADIN SELECTION GMBH 1758048
Ernst-Mey-Str. 8, 70771 LEINFELDEN-ECHTERDINGEN **Tel:** 711 75940
Web site: http://www.konradin.de

Titles:
DIGEST
DTZ DIE TABAK ZEITUNG
SELECTION
SMOKERS CLUB
TJI TOBACCO JOURNAL INTERNATIONAL

KONRADIN VERLAG ROBERT KOHLHAMMER GMBH 678493
Ernst-Mey-Str. 8, 70771 LEINFELDEN-ECHTERDINGEN **Tel:** 711 75940 **Fax:** 711 7594390
Email: info@konradin.de
Web site: http://www.konradin.de

Titles:
DER AUGENOPTIKER
BESCHAFFUNG AKTUELL
BM
CAV CHEMIE-ANLAGEN + VERFAHREN
DEI DIE ERNÄHRUNGSINDUSTRIE
ELEKTRO AUTOMATION
EPP ELEKTRONIK PRODUKTION & PRÜFTECHNIK
EPP EUROPE
INDUSTRIE ANZEIGER
KEM
DIE KONTAKTLINSE
MAV KOMPETENZ IN DER SPANENDEN FERTIGUNG
MD INTERNATIONAL DESIGNSCOUT FOR FURNITURE, INTERIOR AND DESIGN
QUALITY ENGINEERING
SUPPLY

KONSUM DRESDEN EG 1781603
Tharandter Str. 69, 01187 DRESDEN
Tel: 351 41360 **Fax:** 351 4136291
Email: info@konsum-dresden.de
Web site: http://www.konsum.de

Titles:
FRIDA

KONTAKT IN KRISEN E.V. 679771
Magdeburger Allee 116, 99086 ERFURT
Tel: 361 74981134 **Fax:** 361 74981139
Email: strassenzeitung@kontaktinkrisen.de
Web site: http://www.kontaktinkrisen.de

Titles:
BRÜCKE

KONTAKT VERLAGS- UND WERBE GMBH 679986
Landsberger Str. 77, 82205 GILCHING
Tel: 8105 376390 **Fax:** 8105 376392
Email: info@top-kontakt.de
Web site: http://www.top-kontakt.de

Titles:
BUSINESS PER TOPKONTAKT
TOPKONTAKT MARKETING & WERBUNG

KONTOR FÜR MEDIENDIENSTE GMBH 1737324
Aulergasse 9, 55496 ARGENTHAL
Tel: 6761 947620

Titles:
DIRK JASPER FILMLEXIKON

KONZEPT VERLAGSGES. MBH 694679
Ludwigstr. 33, 60327 FRANKFURT **Tel:** 69 974600
Fax: 69 97460699
Email: info@konzept-verlagsgesellschaft.de
Web site: http://www.konzept-verlagsgesellschaft.de

Titles:
IHK WIRTSCHAFTSFORUM

KOPP & THOMAS VERLAG GMBH 685934
Am Friedenshügel 2, 24941 FLENSBURG
Tel: 461 5880 **Fax:** 461 58858
Email: ktv-verlag@moinmoin.de
Web site: http://www.moinmoin.de

Titles:
MOIN MOIN FLENSBURG
MOIN MOIN KAPPELN/ANGELN
MOIN MOIN SCHLESWIG
MOIN MOIN SÜDTONDERN

KÖSEL-VERLAG, VERLAGSGRUPPE RANDOM HOUSE GMBH 684256
Flüggenstr. 2, 80639 MÜNCHEN **Tel:** 89 178010
Fax: 89 17801111
Email: info@koesel.de
Web site: http://www.koesel.de

Titles:
KATECHETISCHE BLÄTTER
WELT DES KINDES

KOSMETIK INTERNATIONAL VERLAG GMBH 682945
Medienplatz 1, 76571 GAGGENAU **Tel:** 7225 9160
Fax: 7225 916109
Email: service@ki-verlag.de
Web site: http://www.ki-online.de

Titles:
KOSMETIK INTERNATIONAL

KPS VERLAGSGES. MBH 677249
Contrescarpe 75a, 28195 BREMEN
Tel: 421 3666167 **Fax:** 421 3666192
Email: info@weserreport.de
Web site: http://www.weserreport.de

Titles:
EVENT.

KRAD-VERLAG JÜRGEN GREIF 1752020
Grundweg 8, 89250 SENDEN **Tel:** 7307 961026
Fax: 7307 961027
Email: krad-verlag@t-online.de
Web site: http://www.motorrad-kurier.de

Titles:
MOTORRAD KURIER

KRAFTHAND VERLAG WALTER SCHULZ GMBH 678599
Walter-Schulz-Str. 1, 86825 BAD WÖRISHOFEN
Tel: 8247 30070 **Fax:** 8247 300770
Email: info@krafthand.de
Web site: http://www.krafthand.de

Titles:
AUTOMOBIL WIRTSCHAFT
BD BAUMASCHINENDIENST
KRAFTHAND

KRAMMER VERLAG DÜSSELDORF AG 680359
Goethestr. 75, 40237 DÜSSELDORF
Tel: 211 91493 **Fax:** 211 9149450
Email: krammer@krammerag.de
Web site: http://www.krammerag.de

Titles:
BERATENDE INGENIEURE
RAS INTERNATIONAL
SANITÄR + HEIZUNGSTECHNIK
SHK REPORT
SPORT BÄDER FREIZEIT BAUTEN
STÄDTE UND GEMEINDERAT
WOHNBADEN

KREATIV KONZEPT GBR - VERLAG ENGEL 686355
Kleine Heide 2, 28844 WEYHE **Tel:** 4203 8045490
Fax: 4203 8045499
Email: verlag@vdbum.de
Web site: http://www.vdbum.de

Titles:
VDBUM INFORMATION

KREIS-ANZEIGER VERLAGS GMBH + CO. KG 684648
Gabelsbergerstr. 1, 89407 DILLINGEN
Tel: 9071 79360 **Fax:** 9071 793650
Email: verlag@kreisanzeiger.de
Web site: http://www.kreisanzeiger.de

Titles:
KREIS-ANZEIGER

KREISBOTEN-VERLAG MÜHLFELLNER KG 684654
Am Weidenbach 8, 82362 WEILHEIM
Tel: 881 6860 **Fax:** 881 68653
Web site: http://www.kreisbote.de

Titles:
KREISBOTE WEILHEIM-SCHONGAU
WOCHENENDE KREISBOTE WEILHEIM UND MURNAU

KREISZEITUNG BÖBLINGER BOTE WILHELM SCHLECHT GMBH & CO. KG 1605473
Bahnhofstr. 27, 71034 BÖBLINGEN
Tel: 7031 62000 **Fax:** 7031 227443
Email: info@bb-live.de
Web site: http://www.bb-live.de

Titles:
KREISZEITUNG

KREISZEITUNG VERLAGSGES. MBH & CO. KG 677277
Am Ristedter Weg 17, 28857 SYKE **Tel:** 4242 580
Fax: 4242 58238
Email: anzeigen@kreiszeitung.de
Web site: http://www.kreiszeitung.de

Titles:
ACHIMER KREISBLATT
DIEPHOLZER KREISBLATT
KREISZEITUNG
SULINGER KREISZEITUNG
THEDINGHÄUSER ZEITUNG
VERDENER ALLER-ZEITUNG

KRESSE & DISCHER MEDIENVERLAG GMBH 1634344
Marlener Str. 2, 77656 OFFENBURG
Tel: 781 95500 **Fax:** 781 955050
Email: kontakt@kd-medienverlag.de
Web site: http://www.kd-medienverlag.de

Titles:
SUPER TROOPER

KRESSE & DISCHER WIRTSCHAFTSVERLAG GMBH 1649466
Marlener Str. 2, 77656 OFFENBURG
Tel: 781 955061 **Fax:** 781 955063
Email: verlag@econo.de
Web site: http://www.econo.de

Titles:
HIDDEN-CHAMPIONS

KREUZER MEDIEN GMBH 700637
Brühl 54, 04109 LEIPZIG **Tel:** 341 2698080
Fax: 341 2698088
Email: info@kreuzer-leipzig.de
Web site: http://www.kreuzer-leipzig.de

Titles:
CHIQUE
KREUZER
LEIPZIG TAG & NACHT
LEIPZIG TAG & NACHT

KRIMINALISTIK VERLAG, VERLAGSGRUPPE HÜTHIG JEHLE REHM GMBH 684681
Im Weiher 10, 69121 HEIDELBERG
Tel: 6221 489416 **Fax:** 6221 489624
Email: judith.hamm@hjr-verlag.de
Web site: http://www.hjr-verlag.de

Titles:
KRIMINALISTIK

KSM VERLAG 1675987
Schaffnerstr. 5, 89073 ULM **Tel:** 731 3783293
Fax: 731 3783299
Email: info@ksm-verlag.de
Web site: http://www.ksm-verlag.de

Titles:
SPAZZ

KUHN FACHVERLAG GMBH & CO. KG 1736789
Bert-Brecht-Str. 15, 78054 VILLINGEN-SCHWENNINGEN **Tel:** 7720 3940
Fax: 7720 394175
Email: kataloge@kuhnverlag.de
Web site: http://www.kuhn-kataloge.de

Titles:
BOGENSPORT MAGAZIN
GETRÄNKEHERSTELLUNG DEUTSCHLAND
HOLZ- UND MÖBELINDUSTRIE DEUTSCHLAND
KOMMUNALE FAHRZEUGE
KUNSTSTOFFVERARBEITUNG DEUTSCHLAND
MASCHINENBAU UND METALLBEARBEITUNG DEUTSCHLAND
REGIOTRANS

KULTURWERK DES BBK E.V. 684756
Weberstr. 61, 53113 BONN **Tel:** 228 216107
Fax: 228 96699690
Email: info@bbk-bundesverband.de
Web site: http://www.bbk-bundesverband.de

Titles:
KULTUR POLITIK

KUNSTVOLL VERLAG GBR, PETRA JENDRYSSEK & SUSANNA KHOURY 699698
Pleicher Kirchplatz 11, 97070 WÜRZBURG
Tel: 931 329160 **Fax:** 931 3291666
Email: kvv@kunstvoll-verlag.de
Web site: http://www.kunstvoll-verlag.de

Titles:
LEPORELLO

KUR- UND FREIZEIT GMBH SCHMALLENBERGER SAUERLAND 1644651
Poststr. 7, 57392 SCHMALLENBERG
Tel: 2972 97400 **Fax:** 2792 974026
Email: info@schmallenberger-sauerland.de
Web site: http://www.schmallenberger-sauerland.de

Titles:
DAS WANDERWELTMAGAZIN

KUR UND TOURISMUS SERVICE 679875
Südstrand 11, 25761 BÜSUM **Tel:** 4834 9090
Fax: 4834 909166
Email: info@buesum.de
Web site: http://www.buesum.de

Titles:
NORDSEE-HEILBAD BÜSUM URLAUBSMAGAZIN

KURATORIUM DEUTSCHE ALTERSHILFE 687316
An der Pauluskirche 3, 50677 KÖLN
Tel: 221 93184710 **Fax:** 221 9318476
Email: proalter@kda.de
Web site: http://www.proalter.de

Titles:
PRO ALTER

KURATORIUM FÜR LANDTECHNIK UND BAUWESEN IN DER LANDWIRTSCHAFT E.V. 1744192
Bartningstr. 49, 64289 DARMSTADT
Tel: 6151 70010 **Fax:** 6151 7001123
Email: ktbl@ktbl.de

Titles:
LANDTECHNIK

KURIER VERLAG GMBH 685532
Glendalestr. 8, 87700 MEMMINGEN
Tel: 8331 85610 **Fax:** 8331 856161
Email: anzeigen@kurierverlag.de
Web site: http://www.kurierverlag.de

Titles:
MEMMINGER KURIER

KURIER VERLAG LENNESTADT GMBH 688055
Kölner Str. 18, 57368 LENNESTADT
Tel: 2721 1360 **Fax:** 2721 136177
Email: info@sauerlandkurier.de
Web site: http://www.sauerlandkurier.de

Titles:
SAUERLANDKURIER FÜR OLPE, DROLSHAGEN, WENDEN UND UMGEBUNG
SAUERLANDKURIER FÜR SCHMALLENBERG, AUE-W., ESLOHE UND UMGEBUNG

KURIERVERLAGS GMBH & CO. KG 1649324
Friedrich-Engels-Ring 29, 17033 NEUBRANDENBURG **Tel:** 395 45750
Fax: 395 4575104
Email: gf@nordkurier.de
Web site: http://www.nordkurier.de

Titles:
NORDKURIER
UCKERMARK KURIER
USEDOM KURIER

KURSANA RESIDENZEN GMBH 1641527
Mauerstr. 85, 10117 BERLIN **Tel:** 30 20252525
Fax: 30 20252540
Email: mehls@dussmann.de
Web site: http://www.kursana.de

Titles:
KURSANA MAGAZIN

KURT VIEBRANZ VERLAG (GMBH & CO. KG) 677554
Schefestr. 11, 21493 SCHWARZENBEK
Tel: 4151 88900 **Fax:** 4151 889033
Email: info@viebranz.de
Web site: http://www.viebranz.de

Titles:
BÜCHENER ANZEIGER
GEESTHACHTER ANZEIGER
LAUENBURGER RUFER
SCHWARZENBEKER ANZEIGER
WOCHENEND ANZEIGER

KVDA-VERLAG 678379
Langer Weg 18, 60489 FRANKFURT
Tel: 69 97843251 **Fax:** 69 97843253
Email: kvda.de@t-online.de
Web site: http://www.kvda-online.de

Titles:
ARZT + AUTO

KVG KISSINGER VERLAGSGES. MBH & CO. KG 678686
Theresienstr. 19, 97688 BAD KISSINGEN
Tel: 971 80400 **Fax:** 971 8040209
Web site: http://www.infranken.de

Titles:
SAALE-ZEITUNG

KVV KONKRET VERTRIEBSGES. FÜR DRUCK UND ANDERE MEDIEN GMBH & CO. KG 684555
Ehrenbergstr. 59, 22767 HAMBURG
Tel: 40 8512531 **Fax:** 40 8512514
Email: verlag@konkret-magazin.de
Web site: http://www.konkret-verlage.de

Titles:
KONKRET

L. A. CH. SCHULZ GMBH 680245
Mattentwiete 5, 20457 HAMBURG
Tel: 40 3698040 **Fax:** 40 36980444
Email: info@lachschulz.de
Web site: http://www.lachschulz.de

Titles:
GOLF IN HAMBURG

L. N. SCHAFFRATH NEUEMEDIEN GMBH & CO. KG 688075
Marktweg 42, 47608 GELDERN **Tel:** 2831 3960
Fax: 2831 396110
Email: kontakt@schaffrath.de
Web site: http://www.schaffrath.de

Titles:
TW THEMA WIRTSCHAFT

LABHARD MEDIEN GMBH 1737897
Saalhausener Str. 51b, 01159 DRESDEN
Tel: 351 7958830 **Fax:** 351 79588315
Email: sachsen@labhard.de
Web site: http://www.labhard.de

Titles:
BODENSEE MAGAZIN
BODENSEE MAGAZIN AKTUELL
GARTENTOUR
OBERSCHWABEN MAGAZIN
SACHSEN MAGAZIN
WIRTSCHAFTSMAGAZIN BODENSEE

LAFARGE ZEMENT GMBH 694891
Frankfurter Landstr. 2, 61440 OBERURSEL
Tel: 6171 614320 **Fax:** 6171 614689
Web site: http://www.lafarge.de

Titles:
FORUM

LAHRER ZEITUNG GMBH 1719252
Kreuzstr. 9, 77933 LAHR **Tel:** 7821 27830
Fax: 7821 2783150
Email: info@lahrer-zeitung.de

Titles:
LAHRER ZEITUNG

LAIBLE VERLAGSPROJEKTE 1739243
Prof.-Schmieder-Str. 8c, 78476 ALLENSBACH
Tel: 7533 98300 **Fax:** 7533 98301
Email: laible@phk-verlag.de
Web site: http://www.phk-verlag.de

Titles:
PASSIVHAUS KOMPENDIUM

LAMBDA VERLAG GMBH 683859
Hauptstr. 6, 83536 GARS **Tel:** 8073 2550
Fax: 8073 2535
Email: info@isolier-technik.de
Web site: http://www.isolier-technik.de

Titles:
ISOLIER TECHNIK

LAND & MEER VERLAGS GMBH 684934
Neumühlen 46, 22763 HAMBURG
Tel: 40 3907681 **Fax:** 40 3907682
Email: mail@landundmeer.de
Web site: http://www.landundmeer.de

Titles:
LAND & MEER
LAND & MEER FAHRRAD WANDERN-WALKING

LANDESAMT FÜR NATUR, UMWELT UND VERBRAUCHERSCHUTZ NORDRHEIN-WESTFALEN 685164
Leibnizstr. 10, 45659 RECKLINGHAUSEN
Tel: 2361 3050 **Fax:** 2361 305215
Email: poststelle@nua.nrw.de
Web site: http://www.lanuv.nrw.de

Titles:
NATUR IN NRW

LANDESAPOTHEKERKAMMER HESSEN 684893
Am Leonhardsbrunn 5, 60487 FRANKFURT
Tel: 69 97950911 **Fax:** 69 97950922
Email: info@apothekenkammer.de
Web site: http://www.apothekenkammer.de

Titles:
LAK KONKRET

LANDESBETRIEB FORST BRANDENBURG, STABSSTELLE PRESSE- UND ÖFFENTLICHKEITSARBEIT 1790185
Karl-Marx-Str. 73, 14612 FALKENSEE
Tel: 3322 243749 **Fax:** 3322 243750
Web site: http://www.mil.brandenburg.de

Titles:
BRANDENBURGISCHE FORSTNACHRICHTEN

LANDESHAUPTSTADT DÜSSELDORF, AMT FÜR KOMMUNIKATION 680964
Marktplatz 2, 40213 DÜSSELDORF
Tel: 211 8993131 **Fax:** 211 894179
Email: presse@duesseldorf.de
Web site: http://www.duesseldorf.de

Titles:
DÜSSELDORFER AMTSBLATT

LANDESJUGENDRING MECKLENBURG-VORPOMMERN E.V. 1676527
Goethestr. 73, 19053 SCHWERIN **Tel:** 385 760760
Fax: 385 7607620
Email: ljr@inmv.de
Web site: http://www.jugend.inmv.de

Titles:
FERIENKALENDER

LANDESNOTARKAMMER BAYERN 1638778
Ottostr. 10, 80333 MÜNCHEN **Tel:** 89 55166660
Fax: 89 55166234
Email: mittbaynot@notarkasse.de
Web site: http://www.notare.bayern.de

Titles:
MITTBAYNOT MITTEILUNGEN DES BAYERISCHEN NOTARVEREINS, DER NOTARKASSE UND DER LANDESNOTARKAMMER BAYERN

LANDESSENIORENVERTRETUNG NORDRHEIN-WESTFALEN E.V. 1622290
Friesenring 32, 48147 MÜNSTER **Tel:** 251 212050
Fax: 251 2006613
Email: info@lsv-nrw.de
Web site: http://www.lsv-nrw.de

Titles:
NUN REDEN WIR

LANDESSPORTBUND BERLIN E.V. 688711
Jesse-Owens-Allee 2, 14053 BERLIN
Tel: 30 30002109 **Fax:** 30 30002119
Email: sib@lsb-berlin.de
Web site: http://www.lsb-berlin.de

Titles:
SPORT IN BERLIN

LANDESSPORTBUND NORDRHEIN-WESTFALEN E.V. 687455
Friedrich-Alfred-Str. 25, 47055 DUISBURG
Tel: 203 73810 **Fax:** 203 7381615
Email: info@lsb-nrw.de
Web site: http://www.wir-im-sport.de

Titles:
WIR IM SPORT

LANDESVERBAND DER STEUERBERATENDEN UND WIRTSCHAFTSPRÜFENDEN BERUFE IN BAYERN E.V. 690046
Implerstr. 11, 81371 MÜNCHEN **Tel:** 89 2732140
Fax: 89 2730656
Email: info@lswb.de
Web site: http://www.lswb.de

Titles:
LSWB INFO

LANDESVERBAND FÜR DAS PERSONENVERKEHRS-GEWERBE HAMBURG E.V. 689244
Alsterdorfer Str. 276, 22297 HAMBURG
Tel: 40 448643 **Fax:** 40 453551
Email: info@taxiverband-hamburg.de
Web site: http://www.taxiverband-hamburg.de

Titles:
TAXI RUNDSCHAU

LANDESVERBAND FÜR PRÄVENTION UND REHABILITATION VON HERZ-KREISLAUFERKRANKUNGEN RHEINLAND-PFALZ E.V. 683189
Friedrich-Ebert-Ring 38, 56068 KOBLENZ
Tel: 261 309233 **Fax:** 261 309232
Email: info@rheinland-pfalz.dgpr.de
Web site: http://www.rheinland-pfalz.dgpr.de

Titles:
HERZ-ECHO

LANDESZEITUNG FÜR DIE LÜNEBURGER HEIDE GMBH 681605
Am Sande 18, 21335 LÜNEBURG **Tel:** 4131 7400
Fax: 4131 740255
Email: lz-anzeigen@landeszeitung.de
Web site: http://www.landeszeitung.de

Titles:
LANDESZEITUNG FÜR DIE LÜNEBURGER HEIDE
LANDESZEITUNG FÜR DIE LÜNEBURGER HEIDE ONLINE

LANDEVERBAND DER BAYERISCHEN JUSTIZVOLLZUGSBEDIENSTETEN E.V. 684154
Königreichweg 24, 94315 STRAUBING
Tel: 9421 923401 **Fax:** 9421 923402
Web site: http://www.jvb-bayern.de

Titles:
JVB-PRESSE

LANDFRAUENVERBAND HESSEN E.V. 1713684
Taunusstr. 151, 61381 FRIEDRICHSDORF
Tel: 6172 77073 **Fax:** 6172 77075
Email: mail@lfv-hessen.de
Web site: http://www.lfv-hessen.de

Titles:
RUNDBRIEF

LANDKREIS LINDAU (BODENSEE) 1646166
Stiftsplatz 4, 88131 LINDAU **Tel:** 8382 270155
Fax: 8382 27077155
Email: tourismus@landkreis-lindau.de
Web site: http://www.landkreis-lindau.de

Titles:
FREIZEITBERATER

LANDKREIS SAARLOUIS, LEITSTELLE ÄLTERWERDEN 1643225
Kaiser-Wilhelm-Str. 4, 66740 SAARLOUIS
Tel: 6831 444226 **Fax:** 6831 444620
Email: amt59@kreis-saarlouis.de
Web site: http://www.kreis-saarlouis.de
Titles:
ÄLTER WERDEN IM LANDKREIS SAARLOUIS

LANDRATSAMT 677848
Marktplatz 8, 97753 KARLSTADT
Tel: 9353 793113 **Fax:** 9353 793252
Email: poststelle@lramsp.de
Web site: http://www.mainspessart.de
Titles:
AMTSBLATT

LANDRATSAMT ASCHAFFENBURG 1770271
Bayernstr. 18, 63739 ASCHAFFENBURG
Tel: 6021 3940 **Fax:** 6021 394998
Web site: http://www.landkreis-aschaffenburg.de
Titles:
LEBENSBOGEN

LANDRATSAMT CHAM, SENIORENKONTAKTSTELLE 1622408
Rachelstr. 6, 93413 CHAM **Tel:** 9971 78291
Fax: 9971 845291
Email: senioren@lra.landkreis-cham.de
Web site: http://www2.landkreis-cham.de
Titles:
ABSEITS-DENKSTE

LANDRATSAMT ROTH 1725025
Weinbergweg 1, 91154 ROTH **Tel:** 9171 81251
Fax: 9171 817251
Email: rothkehlchen@landratsamt-roth.de
Web site: http://www.landratsamt-roth.de
Titles:
ROTHKEHLCHEN

LANDRATSAMT ROTH, KULTUR UND TOURISMUS 682158
Weinbergweg 1, 91154 ROTH **Tel:** 9171 81329
Fax: 9171 81399
Email: tourismus@landratsamt-roth.de
Web site: http://www.urlaub-roth.de
Titles:
GASTGEBERVERZEICHNIS

LANDSCHAFTSVERBAND RHEINLAND, ZENTRUM FÜR MEDIEN UND BILDUNG 679327
Bertha-von-Suttner-Platz 1, 40227 DÜSSELDORF **Tel:** 211 274043189
Fax: 211 82842910
Email: manfred.kremers@lvr.de
Web site: http://www.medien-und-bildung.lvr.de
Titles:
MEDIENBRIEF

LANDVOLK-VERLAG GMBH 681014
Karl-Tesche-Str. 3, 56073 KOBLENZ
Tel: 261 304220 **Fax:** 261 304221000
Email: vertrieb@rheinische-bauernzeitung.de
Web site: http://www.lv-net.de
Titles:
DWZ DIE WINZER-ZEITSCHRIFT
RHEINISCHE BAUERNZEITUNG

LANDWIRTSCHAFTSKAMMER NRW 687700
Siebengebirgsstr. 200, 53229 BONN
Tel: 228 7030 **Fax:** 228 7038498
Email: info@lwk.nrw.de
Web site: http://www.landwirtschaftskammer.de
Titles:
UNTERNEHMENSERGEBNISSE BUCHFÜHRENDER BETRIEBE IN NRW

LANDWIRTSCHAFTSVERLAG GMBH 677429
Hülsebrockstr. 2, 48165 MÜNSTER
Tel: 2501 8010 **Fax:** 2501 801204
Email: zentrale@lv.de
Web site: http://www.lv.de
Titles:
AGRAR- UND UMWELTRECHT
ELITE
FLEISCHRINDER JOURNAL
IM GARTEN
LANDFRAUEN AKTUELL
LANDLUST
LANDWIRTSCHAFTLICHES WOCHENBLATT WESTFALEN-LIPPE
MILCHRIND
PFERDEMARKT
PROFI
REITER & PFERDE IN WESTFALEN
RHEINISCH-WESTFÄLISCHER JÄGER
SUS SCHWEINEZUCHT UND SCHWEINEMAST
TOP AGRAR
TOP AGRAR ONLINE
DIE WALDBAUERN IN NRW

LANDWIRTSCHAFTSVERLAG HESSEN GMBH 683195
Taunusstr. 151, 61381 FRIEDRICHSDORF
Tel: 6172 71060 **Fax:** 6172 710610
Email: info@lv-hessen.de
Titles:
HESSENJÄGER
LEBENSRAUM
LW HESSEN.RHEINLAND-PFALZ LANDWIRTSCHAFTLICHES WOCHENBLATT

LATTKE UND LATTKE GMBH 1626944
Schloß Reichenberg, 97234 REICHENBERG
Tel: 931 660660 **Fax:** 931 6606690
Email: post@lattkeundlattke.de
Web site: http://www.lattkeundlattke.de
Titles:
FLEET MAGAZINE

LAUPENMÜHLEN DRUCK GMBH & CO. KG 1740568
Hüttenstr. 3, 44795 BOCHUM **Tel:** 234 94410
Fax: 234 9441124
Email: info@l-d.de
Web site: http://www.l-d.de
Titles:
KOMPASS VOR ORT

LAUT AG 1652141
Seilerstr. 7, 78467 KONSTANZ **Tel:** 7531 6923800
Fax: 7531 6923811
Email: redaktion@laut.de
Web site: http://www.laut.de
Titles:
LAUT.DE

LECTURA GMBH VERLAG & MARKETING SERVICE 678868
Ritter-von-Schuh-Platz 3, 90459 NÜRNBERG
Tel: 911 4308990 **Fax:** 911 43089920
Email: info@lectura.de
Web site: http://www.lectura.de
Titles:
BAUMASCHINEN

LEIPZIG TOURISMUS UND MARKETING GMBH 1655323
Augustusplatz 9, 04109 LEIPZIG **Tel:** 341 7104265
Fax: 341 7104276
Email: presse@ltm-leipzig.de
Web site: http://www.ltm-leipzig.de
Titles:
NÄHER > DRAN

LEIPZIGER ANZEIGENBLATT VERLAG GMBH & CO. KG 679613
Floßplatz 6, 04107 LEIPZIG **Tel:** 341 21812900
Fax: 341 21812695
Email: th.jochemko@leipziger-anzeigenblatt-verlag.de
Web site: http://www.leipziger-rundschau.de
Titles:
LEIPZIGER RUNDSCHAU

LEIPZIGER VERLAGS- UND DRUCKEREIGES. MBH & CO. KG 1626806
Peterssteinweg 19, 04107 LEIPZIG
Tel: 341 21811260 **Fax:** 341 21811794
Email: post@lvz-online.de
Web site: http://www.lvz-online.de
Titles:
DÖBELNER ALLGEMEINE ZEITUNG
LEIPZIGER VOLKSZEITUNG
LVZ ONLINE
OSCHATZER ALLGEMEINE
OSTERLÄNDER VOLKSZEITUNG

LEIPZIGER VERLAGSANSTALT GMBH 677370
Paul-Gruner-Str. 62, 04107 LEIPZIG
Tel: 341 71003990 **Fax:** 341 71003999
Email: info@l-va.de
Web site: http://www.l-va.de
Titles:
ÄRZTEBLATT MECKLENBURG-VORPOMMERN
ÄRZTEBLATT RHEINLAND-PFALZ
ÄRZTEBLATT SACHSEN
ÄRZTEBLATT THÜRINGEN
BERLINER ÄRZTE
HESSISCHES ÄRZTEBLATT
SAARLÄNDISCHES ÄRZTEBLATT

LEIPZIGER WOCHENKURIER VERLAGSGES. MBH & CO. KG 679614
Gerberstr. 15, 04105 LEIPZIG **Tel:** 341 9881440
Fax: 341 9881547
Email: info@lwk-verlag.de
Web site: http://www.wochenkurier.info
Titles:
DÖBELNER WOCHENKURIER
HALLO! LEIPZIG
LEIPZIG IM FOKUS
LEIPZIGER LAND WOCHENKURIER - AUSG. BORNA
LEIPZIGER LAND WOCHENKURIER - AUSG. GEITHAIN
LEIPZIGER LAND WOCHENKURIER - AUSG. WURZEN
NORDSÄCHSISCHER WOCHENKURIER - AUSG. EILENBURG
NORDSÄCHSISCHER WOCHENKURIER - AUSG. OSCHATZ
NORDSÄCHSISCHER WOCHENKURIER - AUSG. TORGAU

LEMMENS MEDIEN GMBH 680679
Matthias-Grünewald-Str. 1, 53175 BONN
Tel: 228 421370 **Fax:** 228 4213729
Email: info@lemmens.de
Web site: http://www.lemmens.de
Titles:
WISSENSCHAFTSMANAGEMENT
WISSENSCHAFTSMANAGEMENT SPECIAL

LESBENRING E.V. 685033
Postfach 110214, 69071 HEIDELBERG
Tel: 441 2097137 **Fax:** 441 2097137
Email: buero@lesbenring.de
Web site: http://www.lesbenring.de
Titles:
LESBENRING-INFO

LEUKÄMIEHILFE RHEIN-MAIN E.V. 683607
Falltorweg 6, 65428 RÜSSELSHEIM
Tel: 6142 32240 **Fax:** 6142 175642
Email: buero@lhrm.de
Web site: http://www.lhrm.de
Titles:
INFO

LEXISNEXIS DEUTSCHLAND GMBH 1728868
Feldstiege 100, 48161 MÜNSTER **Tel:** 2533 93000
Fax: 2533 930055380
Web site: http://www.lexisnexis.de
Titles:
ANWALT24.DE

LEXISNEXIS DEUTSCHLAND GMBH - DEUTSCHER RENO VERLAG 1769634
Feldstiege 100, 48161 MÜNSTER **Tel:** 2533 93000
Fax: 2533 930050
Web site: http://www.lexisnexis.de
Titles:
RENOPRAXIS

LEXISNEXIS DEUTSCHLAND GMBH - ZAP VERLAG 679648
Feldstiege 100, 48161 MÜNSTER **Tel:** 2533 93000
Fax: 2533 930050
Email: service@lexisnexis.de
Web site: http://www.lexisnexis.de
Titles:
INSBÜRO
ZAP ZEITSCHRIFT FÜR DIE ANWALTSPRAXIS
ZFE ZEITSCHRIFT FÜR FAMILIEN- UND ERBRECHT
ZGS ZEITSCHRIFT FÜR VERTRAGSGESTALTUNG, SCHULD- UND HAFTUNGSRECHT
ZINSO ZEITSCHRIFT FÜR DAS GESAMTE INSOLVENZRECHT
ZNOTP ZEITSCHRIFT FÜR DIE NOTARPRAXIS

LEXXION VERLAGSGES. MBH 1606025
Güntzelstr. 63, 10717 BERLIN **Tel:** 30 8145060
Fax: 30 81450622
Email: mail@lexxion.de
Web site: http://www.lexxion.de
Titles:
ABFALLR ZEITSCHRIFT FÜR DAS RECHT DER ABFALLWIRTSCHAFT
CCLR CARBON & CLIMATE LAW REVIEW
DER DEUTSCHE WIRTSCHAFTSANWALT
EFFL EUROPEAN FOOD AND FEED LAW REVIEW
EPPPL EUROPEAN PUBLIC PRIVATE PARTNERSHIP LAW REVIEW
EUROPEAN STATE AID LAW QUARTERLY
JUSTAMENT
ZEITSCHRIFT FÜR STOFFRECHT STOFFR

LIBELLE VERLAGS- UND VERTRIEBS GMBH 678391
Weichertstr. 20, 63741 ASCHAFFENBURG
Tel: 6021 396140 **Fax:** 6021 396150
Email: verlag@aschaffenburger-stadtmagazin.de
Web site: http://www.aschaffenburger-stadtmagazin.de
Titles:
ASCHAFFENBURGER STADT MAGAZIN

LIBERAL-VERLAG, UNIVERSUM KOMMUNIKATION UND MEDIEN AG 685063
Reinhardtstr. 16, 10117 BERLIN **Tel:** 30 27572875
Fax: 30 27572880
Email: renate.metzenthin@liberalverlag.de
Web site: http://www.liberalverlag.de
Titles:
LIBERAL

LICHT.DE - FÖRDERGEMEINSCHAFT GUTES LICHT 685078
Lyoner Str. 9, 60528 FRANKFURT
Tel: 69 6302353 **Fax:** 69 6302400
Email: licht.de@zvei.org
Web site: http://www.licht.de
Titles:
LICHT.FORUM

LIFE! MAGAZIN GMBH 1739880
Gasstr. 14, 22761 HAMBURG **Tel:** 40 3890400
Fax: 40 38904020
Web site: http://www.foodandtravel.de
Titles:
FOOD AND TRAVEL

LIMBACH DRUCK- UND VERLAG GMBH 682802
Ernst-Böhme-Str. 20, 38112 BRAUNSCHWEIG
Tel: 531 3108543 **Fax:** 531 3108521
Email: verlag@braunschweig-medien.de
Web site: http://www.limbach-medien.de
Titles:
IHK WIRTSCHAFT

LIMPERT VERLAG GMBH 687856
Industriepark 3, 56291 WIEBELSHEIM
Tel: 6766 903160 **Fax:** 6766 903360
Email: vertrieb@limpert.de
Web site: http://www.limpert.de
Titles:
SPORT PRAXIS

LINDENHAUS VERLAGSGES. MBH & CO. KG 680418
Wilmersdorfer Str. 6, 16278 ANGERMÜNDE
Tel: 33334 85200 **Fax:** 33334 852029
Email: redaktion@lindenhaus-verlag.de
Web site: http://verlag.lindenhaus-verlag.info
Titles:
CREATIV VERPACKEN

LINGUAMED VERLAGS-GMBH 678335
Friedensallee 30, 63263 NEU-ISENBURG
Tel: 6102 71570 **Fax:** 6102 715771
Email: info@linguamed.de
Web site: http://www.linguamed.de
Titles:
ARGUMENTE + FAKTEN DER MEDIZIN

LINUX NEW MEDIA AG 1603400
Putzbrunner Str. 71, 81739 MÜNCHEN
Tel: 89 9934110 **Fax:** 89 99341199
Email: info@linuxnewmedia.de
Web site: http://www.linuxnewmedia.de
Titles:
EASYLINUX!
LINUX MAGAZIN

LIPPISCHER ZEITUNGSVERLAG GIESDORF GMBH & CO. KG 685117
Ohmstr. 7, 32758 DETMOLD **Tel:** 5231 9110
Fax: 5231 911100
Email: lz@lz-online.de
Titles:
LIPPISCHE LANDES-ZEITUNG

LIQUIDIAGENTUR FÜR GESTALTUNG 1746032
Kohlergasse 20, 86152 AUGSBURG
Tel: 821 34999090 **Fax:** 821 34999093
Web site: http://www.tatendrang.info
Titles:
TATENDRANG

L.I.S. VERLAG GMBH 688090
Theresienstr. 9, 94032 PASSAU **Tel:** 851 932000
Fax: 851 9320049
Email: info@style-guide.biz
Web site: http://www.style-guide.biz
Titles:
STYLE GUIDE

LISKOW DRUCK UND VERLAG GMBH 678209
Oldenburger Allee 23, 30659 HANNOVER
Tel: 511 5635853 **Fax:** 511 56358555
Email: info@liskow.de
Web site: http://www.liskow.de
Titles:
APOTHEKERKAMMER NACHRICHTEN

LIVING & MORE VERLAG GMBH 697101
Böheimstr. 8, 86153 AUGSBURG **Tel:** 781 924490
Web site: http://www.livingandmore.de
Titles:
GÄRTNERN LEICHT GEMACHT
GRÜN

LIVING-CROSSMEDIA GMBH & CO. KG 1789151
Zweibrückenstr. 1, 80331 MÜNCHEN
Tel: 89 80038063
Email: info@goliving.de
Web site: http://www.goliving.de
Titles:
GOLIVING.DE IN BERLIN
GOLIVING.DE IN HAMBURG
GOLIVING.DE IN KÖLN/BONN
GOLIVING.DE IN MÜNCHEN

LMC MEDIACONSULT GMBH 1769156
Braschoßer Str. 55, 53721 SIEGBURG
Tel: 2241 234260 **Fax:** 2241 2342626
Email: lmc_mediaconsult@t-online.de
Web site: http://www.koeln-bonn-manager.de
Titles:
KÖLN-BONN MANAGER

LOBBE HOLDING GMBH & CO KG 695109
Bernhard-Hülsmann-Weg 2, 58644 ISERLOHN
Tel: 2371 8880 **Fax:** 2371 888108
Web site: http://www.lobbe.de
Titles:
TATSACHEN

LOCAL GLOBAL GMBH 1626809
Marienstr. 5, 70178 STUTTGART
Tel: 711 2255880 **Fax:** 711 22558811
Email: info@localglobal.de
Web site: http://www.localglobal.de
Titles:
SOURCING_ASIA

LOKA MEDIA GMBH 689182
Langenfelde 11, 23611 BAD SCHWARTAU
Tel: 451 21047 **Fax:** 451 26039
Email: lokamedia@arcor.de
Web site: http://www.szeneluebeck.de
Titles:
SZENE LÜBECK

LOKAL-ANZEIGER VERLAG MAX BISCHOFF 685188
Kattunbleiche 37, 22041 HAMBURG
Tel: 40 681988 **Fax:** 4552 9933081
Email: hb@lokalanzeiger.info
Web site: http://www.lokal-anzeiger-hamburg.de
Titles:
LOKAL-ANZEIGER - AUSG. BARMBEK/ WINTERHUDE

LOKALBOTE VERLAGS-GMBH 685194
Maikäferweg 10, 29640 SCHNEVERDINGEN
Tel: 40 7546118 **Fax:** 40 7546861
Email: info@lokalbote-hamburg.de
Web site: http://www.lokalbote-hamburg.de
Titles:
LOKAL BOTE

LOUIS MOTORRADVERTRIEB 1638851
Rungedamm 35, 21035 HAMBURG
Email: info@louis.de
Web site: http://www.louis.de
Titles:
LOUIS

LÖWE & SCHÜTZE VERLAG UND MEDIENAGENTUR 1732133
Weidenstr. 15, 46499 HAMMINKELN
Tel: 2852 968631 **Fax:** 2852 968632
Email: info@gesundheitheute.com
Web site: http://www.gesundheitheute.com
Titles:
GESUNDHEIT HEUTE

LPV LEBENSMITTEL PRAXIS VERLAG NEUWIED GMBH 680079
Am Hammergraben 14, 56567 NEUWIED
Tel: 2631 8790 **Fax:** 2631 879123
Web site: http://www.lebensmittelpraxis.de
Titles:
CATERING INSIDE
CONVENIENCE SHOP
HANDELSJOURNAL
KÜCHE
LEBENSMITTEL PRAXIS

LR MEDIENVERLAG UND DRUCKEREI GMBH 681202
Str. der Jugend 54, 03050 COTTBUS
Tel: 355 4810 **Fax:** 355 481245
Email: lr@lr-online.de
Titles:
LAUSITZER RUNDSCHAU

LT FOOD MEDIEN-VERLAG GMBH 684991
Bugdahnstr. 5, 22767 HAMBURG
Tel: 40 38609301 **Fax:** 40 38609385
Email: service@lebensmitteltechnik-online.de
Web site: http://www.lebensmitteltechnik-online.de
Titles:
LEBENSMITTEL TECHNIK

LÜBECKER NACHRICHTEN GMBH 683064
Herrenholz 10, 23556 LÜBECK **Tel:** 451 1440
Fax: 451 1441029
Email: ln@ln-luebeck.de
Web site: http://www.ln-online.de
Titles:
LÜBECKER NACHRICHTEN

LÜBECKER NACHRICHTEN ONLINE GMBH 1630215
Herrenholz 10, 23556 LÜBECK **Tel:** 451 1442263
Email: info@ln-online.de
Web site: http://www.ln-online.de
Titles:
LÜBECKER NACHRICHTEN

LUCIUS & LUCIUS VERLAGSGES. MBH 678035
Gerokstr. 51, 70184 STUTTGART **Tel:** 711 242060
Fax: 711 242088
Email: lucius@luciusverlag.com
Web site: http://www.luciusverlag.com
Titles:
ARBEIT
TW ZEITSCHRIFT FÜR TOURISMUSWISSENSCHAFT
ZEITSCHRIFT FÜR WIRTSCHAFTSPOLITIK
ZFGG ZEITSCHRIFT FÜR DAS GESAMTE GENOSSENSCHAFTSWESEN

LUDWIGSBURGER WOCHENBLATT GMBH + CO. KG 685216
Lindenstr. 15, 71634 LUDWIGSBURG
Tel: 7141 96200 **Fax:** 7141 9620533
Email: gerald.probst@luwo.de
Web site: http://www.ludwigsburger-wochenblatt.de
Titles:
LUDWIGSBURGER WOCHENBLATT

LÜHMANNDRUCK HARBURGER ZEITUNGSGES. MBH & CO. KG 1781416
Harburger Rathausstr. 40, 21073 HAMBURG
Tel: 40 77177177 **Fax:** 40 77177360
Email: vertrieb@han-online.de
Web site: http://www.han-online.de
Titles:
HARBURGER ANZEIGEN UND NACHRICHTEN
HARBURGER ANZEIGEN UND NACHRICHTEN

LUTHERISCHES VERLAGSHAUS GMBH 680713
Knochenhauerstr. 38, 30159 HANNOVER
Tel: 511 1241720 **Fax:** 511 3681098
Email: info@lvh.de
Web site: http://www.lvh.de
Titles:
EZ EVANGELISCHE ZEITUNG - CHRISTL. WOCHENZTG. F. NIEDERSACHSEN, AUSG. LANDESKIRCHE BRAUNSCHWEIG

LUTZISCHULZ MARKETING & KOMMUNIKATION GMBH 1771104
Lindersrain 2, 35708 HAIGER **Tel:** 2773 74370
Fax: 2773 743729
Email: mail@werdewelt.info
Web site: http://www.werdewelt.info
Titles:
LAHNDILL WIRTSCHAFT

LUTZ-VERLAG 1745947
Postfach 1420, 65764 KELKHEIM
Tel: 172 6712118 **Fax:** 6195 65118
Email: presse-lutz@gmx.net
Titles:
AKTUALITÄTSLEXIKON UMWELTSCHUTZ
LUTZ'SCHES KURZ-INFO

LYDIA-VERLAG GERTH MEDIEN GMBH 685252
Dillerberg 1, 35614 ASSLAR **Tel:** 6443 6839
Fax: 6443 686839
Email: info@lydia.net
Web site: http://www.lydia.net
Titles:
LYDIA

M. DUMONT SCHAUBERG GMBH & CO. KG 684509
Amsterdamer Str. 192, 50735 KÖLN
Tel: 221 2240 **Fax:** 221 2242142
Web site: http://www.dumont.de
Titles:
KÖLNER STADT-ANZEIGER
KSTA.DE KÖLNER STADT-ANZEIGER
LEVERKUSENER ANZEIGER
OBERBERGISCHER ANZEIGER
RHEIN-SIEG-ANZEIGER

M. DUMONT SCHAUBERG-EXPEDITION DER KÖLNISCHEN ZEITUNG GMBH & CO. KG 679073
Amsterdamer Str. 192, 50735 KÖLN
Tel: 221 2240 **Fax:** 221 2242142
Web site: http://www.dumont.de
Titles:
BERGISCHE LANDESZEITUNG
BONN EXPRESS
BONNER RUNDSCHAU
EXPRESS
EXPRESS.DE
KÖLNISCHE RUNDSCHAU
OBERBERGISCHE VOLKSZEITUNG
RHEIN-SIEG RUNDSCHAU
SONNTAG EXPRESS

M. & H. SCHAPER GMBH 1729096
Bischofsholer Damm 24, 30173 HANNOVER
Tel: 511 8503050 **Fax:** 511 85030510
Email: info@schaper-verlag.de
Web site: http://www.schaper-verlag.de
Titles:
KLEINTIERPRAXIS

M+M VERLAG GMBH 1621641
Zur Tannenburg 43, 66280 SULZBACH
Tel: 6897 983886 **Fax:** 6897 983686
Email: renate.graf@m-m-verlag.de
Web site: http://www.m-m-verlag.de
Titles:
DER FREIE ARZT
HP NATUR-HEILKUNDE

M+T RITTHAMMER PUBLISHING GMBH 694952
Andernacher Str. 5a, 90411 NÜRNBERG
Tel: 911 955780 **Fax:** 911 9557878
Email: info@material-technik.de
Web site: http://www.material-technik.de
Titles:
MATERIAL+TECHNIK MÖBEL

MABUSE-VERLAG GMBH 680834
Kasseler Str. 1a, 60486 FRANKFURT
Tel: 69 70799615 **Fax:** 69 704152
Email: info@mabuse-verlag.de
Web site: http://www.mabuse-verlag.de
Titles:
DR. MED. MABUSE

MADAME VERLAG GMBH 1782093
Leonrodstr. 52, 80636 MÜNCHEN **Tel:** 89 551350
Fax: 89 55135299
Email: mailbox@madame.de
Web site: http://www.madame.de
Titles:
MADAME
L' OFFICIEL HOMMES

MADE MARKETING DEVELOPMENT GMBH 697752
Rudolf-Diesel-Str. 5, 86470 THANNHAUSEN
Tel: 8281 799660 **Fax:** 8281 7996650
Email: golonglife@made.de
Web site: http://www.golonglife.de
Titles:
GO LONGLIFE!
GO LONGLIFE!

MAENKEN KOMMUNIKATION GMBH 1653034
Von-der-Wettern-Str. 25, 51149 KÖLN
Tel: 2203 35840 **Fax:** 2203 3584185
Email: info@maenken.com
Web site: http://www.maenken.com
Titles:
KÖLN MAGAZIN
KÖLNERLEBEN
PERSPEKTIVEN
RATGEBER BAUEN
WIRTSCHAFT IM DIALOG
ZVO REPORT

MAG04 PUBLISHING GMBH 1652893
Haußmannstr. 240, 70188 STUTTGART
Tel: 711 99797264 **Fax:** 711 99797393
Web site: http://www.stuff-mag.de
Titles:
STUFF

MAGAZIN VERLAG HAMBURG HMV GMBH 677698
Barkhausenweg 11, 22339 HAMBURG
Tel: 40 5389300 **Fax:** 40 53893011
Email: anzeigen@alster-net.de
Web site: http://www.alster-net.de
Titles:
ALSTERTAL MAGAZIN

MAGAZIN VERLAGSGES. SÜDDEUTSCHE ZEITUNG MBH 689068
Hultschiner Str. 8, 81677 MÜNCHEN
Tel: 89 21839540 **Fax:** 89 21839570

Titles:
SÜDDEUTSCHE ZEITUNG GOLF SPIELEN
SÜDDEUTSCHE ZEITUNG MAGAZIN
SÜDDEUTSCHE ZEITUNG WOHLFÜHLEN

MAGDEBURGER VERLAGS- UND DRUCKHAUS GMBH 677721
Bahnhofstr. 17, 39104 MAGDEBURG
Tel: 391 59990 **Fax:** 391 5999400

Titles:
BÖRDE VOLKSSTIMME
GENERAL-ANZEIGER BURG
GENERAL-ANZEIGER GENTHIN
GENERAL-ANZEIGER HALBERSTADT
GENERAL-ANZEIGER HALDENSLEBEN/ WOLMIRSTEDT
GENERAL-ANZEIGER LÜCHOW-DANNENBERG
GENERAL-ANZEIGER MAGDEBURG
GENERAL-ANZEIGER SCHÖNEBECK
GENERAL-ANZEIGER UELZEN
GENERAL-ANZEIGER WERNIGERODE
GENERAL-ANZEIGER ZERBST
HALBERSTÄDTER VOLKSSTIMME
HALDENSLEBER VOLKSSTIMME
HARZER VOLKSSTIMME
MAGDEBURGER VOLKSSTIMME
OSTERBURGER VOLKSSTIMME
SALZWEDELER VOLKSSTIMME
SCHÖNEBECKER VOLKSSTIMME
STASSFURTER VOLKSSTIMME
STENDALER VOLKSSTIMME
ZERBSTER VOLKSSTIMME

MAGSEVEN GMBH 1641575
Alte Hattinger Str. 29, 44789 BOCHUM
Tel: 234 6239789
Email: office@magseven.biz
Web site: http://www.magseven.biz

Titles:
STREETWEAR TODAY

MAIN-POST GMBH & CO. KG 678687
Berner Str. 2, 97084 WÜRZBURG
Tel: 931 6001239 **Fax:** 931 6001233
Email: markt-anzeigen@mainpost.de
Web site: http://www.markt.mainpost.de

Titles:
MAINPOST.DE
MARKT AM MITTWOCH - AUSG. BAD KISSINGEN
MARKT AM MITTWOCH - AUSG. KITZINGEN/ GEROLZHOFEN/MAINSCHLEIFE
MARKT AM MITTWOCH - AUSG. RHÖN-GRABFELD
MARKT AM MITTWOCH - AUSG. SCHWEINFURT
MARKT WOCHENMITTE - AUSG. LOHR/ MARKTHEIDENFELD

MAINTAL TAGESANZEIGER VERLAGS-GMBH 679062
Kennedystr. 44, 63477 MAINTAL **Tel:** 6181 40900
Fax: 6181 409040
Email: redaktion@maintaltagesanzeiger.de
Web site: http://www.maintaltagesanzeiger.de

Titles:
FECHENHEIMER ANZEIGER

MAIRS GEOGRAPHISCHER VERLAG KURT MAIR GMBH & CO. 1759389
Marco-Polo-Str. 1, 73760 OSTFILDERN
Tel: 711 45020 **Fax:** 711 4502340
Email: info@mairdumont.com
Web site: http://www.mairdumont.com

Titles:
DER VARTA-FÜHRER

MAKOSSA DRUCK UND MEDIEN GMBH 698854
Pommernstr. 17, 45889 GELSENKIRCHEN
Tel: 209 980850 **Fax:** 209 9808585
Email: druck.medien@makossa.de
Web site: http://www.makossa.de

Titles:
BERGBAU

MANAGEMENT + KARRIERE VERLAG 677342
Brandenburgstr. 3, 40629 DÜSSELDORF
Tel: 211 6914535 **Fax:** 211 6914537
Web site: http://www.management-karriere.de

Titles:
PERSONALBERATER
TRAINER + SEMINARANBIETER

MANAGER MAGAZIN VERLAGSGES. MBH 681840
Dovenfleet 5, 20457 HAMBURG **Tel:** 40 30072551
Fax: 40 30072247
Email: mm_redaktion@manager-magazin.de
Web site: http://www.manager-magazin.de

Titles:
HARVARD BUSINESS MANAGER
MANAGER MAGAZIN

MANAGERSEMINARE VERLAGS GMBH 685328
Endenicher Str. 41, 53115 BONN **Tel:** 228 977910
Fax: 228 616164
Email: info@managerseminare.de
Web site: http://www.managerseminare.de

Titles:
MANAGE_HR
MANAGERSEMINARE
TRAINING AKTUELL

MANNHEIMER MORGEN GROSSDRUCKEREI UND VERLAG GMBH 685333
Dudenstr. 12, 68167 MANNHEIM **Tel:** 621 39201
Fax: 621 3921252
Email: verlag@mamo.de
Web site: http://www.morgenweb.de

Titles:
MANNHEIMER MORGEN
SÜDHESSEN MORGEN

MANNHEIMER WOCHENBLATT VERLAGSGES. MBH + CO. KG 690727
Melchiorstr. 1, 68167 MANNHEIM
Tel: 621 127920 **Fax:** 621 1279220
Email: egon.timm@wobla.de
Web site: http://www.wobla.de

Titles:
WOCHENBLATT MIT AMTSBLATT STADT MANNHEIM

MARBUCH VERLAG GMBH 682592
Ernst-Giller-Str. 20a, 35039 MARBURG
Tel: 6421 68440 **Fax:** 6421 684444
Email: feedback@marbuch-verlag.de
Web site: http://www.marbuch-verlag.de

Titles:
GIESSENER MAGAZIN EXPRESS
MARBURGER MAGAZIN EXPRESS

MARCELLINO'S AG 695621
Kaistr. 12, 40221 DÜSSELDORF **Tel:** 211 3006690
Fax: 211 30066930
Email: mail@marcellinos.de
Web site: http://www.marcellinos.de

Titles:
MARCELLINO'S DEUTSCHLAND HOTEL REPORT
MARCELLINO'S DEUTSCHLAND RESTAURANT REPORT
MARCELLINO'S RESTAURANT REPORT - AUSG. BERLIN U. UMGEBUNG
MARCELLINO'S RESTAURANT REPORT - AUSG. DÜSSELDORF KREFELD WUPPERTAL NEUSS MÖNCHENGLADBACH
MARCELLINO'S RESTAURANT REPORT - AUSG. FRANKFURT U. UMGEBUNG
MARCELLINO'S RESTAURANT REPORT - AUSG. HAMBURG U. UMGEBUNG
MARCELLINO'S RESTAURANT REPORT - AUSG. KÖLN BONN BAD NEUENAHR BERGISCH GLADBACH
MARCELLINO'S RESTAURANT REPORT - AUSG. MALLORCA
MARCELLINO'S RESTAURANT REPORT - AUSG. MÜNCHEN U. UMGEBUNG
MARCELLINO'S RESTAURANT REPORT - AUSG. RUHRGEBIET
MARCELLINO'S RESTAURANT REPORT - AUSG. STUTTGART HEILBRONN TÜBINGEN ESSLINGEN BÖBLINGEN
MARCELLINO'S RESTAURANT REPORT - AUSG. SYLT, AMRUM U. FÖHR

MAREVERLAG GMBH & CO. OHG 685346
Pickhuben 2, 20457 HAMBURG **Tel:** 40 3698590
Fax: 40 36985990
Email: mare@mare.de
Web site: http://www.mare.de

Titles:
MARE

MARIANNE BREUER VERLAG 681024
Wandersmannstr. 15, 65205 WIESBADEN
Tel: 611 976160 **Fax:** 611 712429
Email: info@breuerpresse.de
Web site: http://www.breuerpresse.de

Titles:
WIESBADENER ERBENHEIMER ANZEIGER

MARITIM HOTELGES. MBH 685360
Herforder Str. 2, 32105 BAD SALZUFLEN
Tel: 5222 9530
Email: info.vkd@maritim.de
Web site: http://www.maritim.de

Titles:
MARITIM JOURNAL

MARKEN VERLAG GMBH 678652
Hansaring 97, 50670 KÖLN **Tel:** 221 9574270
Fax: 221 95742777
Email: marken-info@markenverlag.de
Web site: http://www.markenverlag.de

Titles:
AKTIV LAUFEN
BABY POST
FIT + 50
JA ZUM BABY
KREATIV MAGAZIN
LEICHTATHLETIK SPECIAL
PROFILE
TREND FRISUREN
VEGETARISCH FIT!
WEIGHT WATCHERS

MARKETING CLUB BERLIN E.V. 1724752
Schumannstr. 5, 10117 BERLIN **Tel:** 30 27594500
Fax: 30 27594513
Email: info@marketingclubberlin.de
Web site: http://www.marketingclubberlin.de

Titles:
USP MENSCHEN IM MARKETING

MÄRKISCHE VERLAGS- UND DRUCK-GESELLSCHAFT MBH POTSDAM 685271
Friedrich-Engels-Str. 24, 14473 POTSDAM
Tel: 331 28400 **Fax:** 331 2840310

Titles:
MAERKISCHEALLGEMEINE.DE

MÄRKISCHE VERLAGS- UND DRUCK-GMBH POTSDAM 1683605
Friedrich-Engels-Str. 24, 14473 POTSDAM
Tel: 331 28400 **Fax:** 331 99123
Email: vertriebsleitung@mazonline.de
Web site: http://www.maerkischeallgemeine.de

Titles:
MÄRKISCHE ALLGEMEINE

MÄRKISCHER ZEITUNGSVERLAG GMBH & CO. KG 1719920
Schillerstr. 20, 58511 LÜDENSCHEID
Tel: 2351 1580 **Fax:** 2351 158281
Email: ln@come-on.de
Web site: http://www.come-on.de

Titles:
ALLGEMEINER ANZEIGER
ALTENAER KREISBLATT
LÜDENSCHEIDER NACHRICHTEN
MEINERZHAGENER ZEITUNG
SÜDERLÄNDER VOLKSFREUND

MÄRKISCHER ZEITUNGSVERLAG ZWEIGNIEDERLASSUNG DER WESTFÄLISCHER ANZEIGER VERLAGSGES. MBH & CO. KG 682717
Lehnitzstr. 13, 16515 ORANIENBURG
Tel: 3301 59630 **Fax:** 3301 596333
Email: info@oranienburger-generalanzeiger.de
Web site: http://www.die-mark-online.de

Titles:
GRANSEE-ZEITUNG
ORANIENBURGER GENERALANZEIGER
RUPPINER ANZEIGER

MÄRKISCHES VERLAGS- UND DRUCKHAUS GMBH & CO. KG 685274
Kellenspring 6, 15230 FRANKFURT
Tel: 335 55300 **Fax:** 335 5530320
Email: verlagsleitung@moz.de
Web site: http://www.moz.de

Titles:
MÄRKISCHE ODERZEITUNG
MÄRKISCHER MARKT - AUSG. BAD FREIENWALDE

MARKT 1 VERLAGSGES. MBH 1774135
Markt 1, 45127 ESSEN **Tel:** 201 1095195
Fax: 201 1095141
Email: info@markt1-verlag.de
Web site: http://www.cp-verlagsgesellschaft.de

Titles:
REISEWELT

MARKT CONTROL MULTIMEDIA VERLAG GMBH & CO. KG 681904
Am Büschchen 2a, 47179 DUISBURG
Tel: 203 554248 **Fax:** 203 547970
Email: info@marktcontrol.de
Web site: http://www.marktcontrol.de

Titles:
CLEVER REISEN!

MARKT INTERN VERLAG GMBH 678772
Grafenberger Allee 30, 40237 DÜSSELDORF
Tel: 211 66980 **Fax:** 211 6698222
Email: info@markt-intern.de
Web site: http://www.markt-intern.de

Titles:
KAPITAL-MARKT INTERN
MARKT INTERN APOTHEKE PHARMAZIE
MARKT INTERN INSTALLATION SANITÄR/ HEIZUNG
MARKT INTERN MITTELSTAND

MARKTSPIEGEL VERLAG GMBH 679968
Marktstr. 16, 31303 BURGDORF **Tel:** 5136 89940
Fax: 5136 899430
Email: gf.hoffmann@marktspiegel-verlag.de
Web site: http://www.marktspiegel-verlag.de

Titles:
BURGWEDELER NACHRICHTEN
MARKTSPIEGEL

MARKTVERLAG JOACHIM MÜHLER 685372
Am Teichfeld 24, 06567 BAD FRANKENHAUSEN
Tel: 34671 63087 **Fax:** 34671 77539
Email: marktanzeigerost@t-online.de
Web site: http://www.marktanzeiger-ost.de

Titles:
MARKT ANZEIGER OST

MARTIN KELTER VERLAG GMBH & CO. KG 677765
Mühlenstieg 16, 22041 HAMBURG
Tel: 40 6828950 **Fax:** 40 68289550
Email: info@kelter.de
Web site: http://www.kelter.de

Titles:
MEINE WAHRHEIT

MARVI VERLAG 1789950
Nordfelder Reihe 20, 30159 HANNOVER
Tel: 511 2625399 **Fax:** 511 2625399
Email: marvi@marvi-verlag.de

Titles:
BIO LIFE

MATECO AG 1747296
Bottroper Str. 16, 70376 STUTTGART
Tel: 711 955560 **Fax:** 711 9555699
Email: info@mateco.de
Web site: http://www.mateco.de

Titles:
MATECO NEWS

MATHILDE E.V. 685407
Postfach 130269, 64242 DARMSTADT
Tel: 6151 537937
Email: redaktion@mathilde-frauenzeitung.de
Web site: http://www.mathilde-frauenzeitung.de

Titles:
MATHILDE

MATTEI MEDIEN GMBH 687733
Norbertstr. 2, 50670 KÖLN **Tel:** 221 390660
Fax: 221 3906622
Email: verlag@mattei-medien.de
Web site: http://www.mattei-medien.de

Titles:
RIK

MATTHAES MEDIEN GMBH & CO. KG 1650241
Motorstr. 38, 70499 STUTTGART
Tel: 711 8060820 **Fax:** 711 80608250

Titles:
REITERJOURNAL

MATTHAES VERLAG GMBH, EIN UNTERNEHMEN DER VERLAGSGRUPPE DEUTSCHER FACHVERLAG 1676997
Silberburgstr. 122, 70176 STUTTGART
Tel: 711 21330 **Fax:** 711 2133290
Email: kontaktm@matthaes.de
Web site: http://www.matthaes-verlag.de

Titles:
ABZ ALLGEMEINE BÄCKERZEITUNG
ALLGEMEINE HOTEL- UND GASTRONOMIE-ZEITUNG
DEHOGA MAGAZIN
DEUTSCHER HOTELFÜHRER
KONDITOREI & CAFÉ

MATTHIAS KYNAST WINDKRAFTBETEILIGUNGS-PROJEKTE 1745770
Am Wördehoff 2, 59597 ERWITTE
Tel: 2945 963212 **Fax:** 2945 963213
Email: mk@windinvestor.de
Web site: http://www.windinvestor.de

Titles:
WINDBRIEF SÜDWESTFALEN

MATTHIAS-GRÜNEWALD-VERLAG DER SCHWABENVERLAG AG 680307
Senefelderstr. 12, 73760 OSTFILDERN
Tel: 711 4406140 **Fax:** 711 4406138
Email: petra.haertel@schwabenverlag.de
Web site: http://www.gruenewaldverlag.de

Titles:
COMMUNICATIO SOCIALIS

MAV-VERLAGSGES. MBH 1621620
Gögginger Str. 2, 72505 KRAUCHENWIES
Tel: 7576 961850 **Fax:** 7576 9618599

Titles:
0-100 STREET PERFORMANCE
PS DAS AUTOMAGAZIN

MAX-EYTH-VERLAG MBH 680811
Eschborner Landstr. 122, 60489 FRANKFURT
Tel: 69 247880 **Fax:** 69 24788481
Email: dlg-mitteilungen@dlg.org
Web site: http://www.dlg-mitteilungen.de

Titles:
DLG MITTEILUNGEN

MAXSELL WERBEAGENTUR & PARTNER GMBH 690635
Großen Str. 37, 27356 ROTENBURG
Tel: 4261 819990 **Fax:** 4261 8199999
Email: kontakt@maxsell.de
Web site: http://www.maxsell.de

Titles:
INTERMEZZO

MAYER + SÖHNE DRUCK- UND MEDIENGRUPPE GMBH + CO. KG 677451
Oberbernbacher Weg 7, 86551 AICHACH
Tel: 8251 880100 **Fax:** 8251 880109
Email: mrabl@aichacher-zeitung.de
Web site: http://www.aichacher-zeitung.de

Titles:
AICHACHER ZEITUNG

MAZ VERLAG GMBH 685880
Katharinengasse 12, 35390 GIESSEN
Tel: 641 79460 **Fax:** 641 794617
Email: info@maz-verlag.de
Web site: http://www.maz-verlag.de

Titles:
MAZ MITTELHESSISCHE ANZEIGEN ZEITUNG - AUSG. ALSFELD
MAZ MITTELHESSISCHE ANZEIGEN ZEITUNG - AUSG. HINTERLAND

MBM MARTIN BRÜCKNER MEDIEN GMBH 1762439
Rudolfstr. 22, 60327 FRANKFURT
Tel: 69 66563225 **Fax:** 69 66563222
Email: service@mbmmedien.de
Web site: http://www.maerkte-weltweit.de

Titles:
ASIA BRIDGE
NACHRICHTEN FÜR AUSSENHANDEL

MDV MÖNCHHOF DRUCK- UND VERLAGSGES. MBH 682153
Tizianplatz 35, 64546 MÖRFELDEN-WALLDORF
Tel: 6105 22001 **Fax:** 6105 25486
Email: info@freitags-anzeiger.de
Web site: http://www.freitags-anzeiger.de

Titles:
FREITAGS-ANZEIGER FÜR MÖRFELDEN-WALLDORF, KELSTERBACH UND ZEPPELINHEIM

ME2-VERLAG, RAIMOND AHLBORN UG 1763366
Papyrusweg 17, 22117 HAMBURG
Tel: 40 34924336
Email: 1stmail@ahlborn-friends.de
Web site: http://www.me2-verlag.de

Titles:
ZEIT FÜR DIE FRAU

MEBU VERLAG E. ECKSTEIN 1768420
Am Kurfürstenweg 2a, 85232 BERGKIRCHEN
Tel: 8131 354759 **Fax:** 8131 354760
Email: info@medienbulletin.de
Web site: http://www.mebucom.de

Titles:
MEDIEN BULLETIN

MECKLENBURGER BLITZ VERLAG UND WERBEAGENTUR GMBH & CO. KG 679548
Tribseer Damm 2, 18437 STRALSUND
Tel: 3831 2677400 **Fax:** 3831 2677402
Email: vpb@blitzverlag.de
Web site: http://www.blitzverlag.de

Titles:
BODDEN BLITZ AM SONNTAG
DEMMINER BLITZ AM SONNTAG
GREVESMÜHLENER BLITZ AM SONNTAG
LUDWIGSLUSTER BLITZ AM SONNTAG
MECKLENBURGER BLITZ AM SONNTAG
PARCHIMER BLITZ AM SONNTAG
PEENE BLITZ AM SONNTAG
ROSTOCKER BLITZ AM SONNTAG
RÜGEN BLITZ AM SONNTAG
SCHWERINER BLITZ AM SONNTAG
STRALSUNDER BLITZ AM SONNTAG
UECKER-RANDOW BLITZ AM SONNTAG
VIER TORE BLITZ AM SONNTAG
VORPOMMERN BLITZ AM SONNTAG
WISMARER BLITZ AM SONNTAG

MEDCOM INTERNATIONAL GMBH 677521
René-Schickele-Str. 10, 53123 BONN
Tel: 228 308210 **Fax:** 228 3082133
Email: info@medcominternational.de

Titles:
AKTIV
HAUT & ALLERGIE AKTUELL

MÉDECINS SANS FRONTIÈRES - ÄRZTE OHNE GRENZEN E.V. 677580
Am Köllnischen Park 1, 10179 BERLIN
Tel: 30 7001300 **Fax:** 30 700130340
Email: office@berlin.msf.org
Web site: http://www.aerzte-ohne-grenzen.de

Titles:
AKUT

MEDIA & SERVICE BÜRO BERND LOCHMÜLLER 700389
Crüwellstr. 11, 33615 BIELEFELD **Tel:** 521 124044
Fax: 521 124088
Email: info@fz-profiboerse.de
Web site: http://www.fz-profiboerse.de

Titles:
PROFIBÖRSE

MEDIABUNT GMBH 1713756
Am Luftschacht 20, 45307 ESSEN
Tel: 201 896260 **Fax:** 201 8962626
Email: info@mediabunt.de
Web site: http://www.mediabunt.de

Titles:
VIVERITO

MEDIACITY VERLAG & WERBEAGENTUR 680212
Alstädter Kirchenweg 43, 75175 PFORZHEIM
Tel: 7231 313102 **Fax:** 7231 314394
Email: city-stadtmagazin@regiomarkt.de
Web site: http://www.city-stadtmagazin.de

Titles:
CITY

MEDIA-DATEN VERLAG/ SPRINGER FACHMEDIEN WIESBADEN GMBH 677411
Abraham-Lincoln-Str. 46, 65189 WIESBADEN
Tel: 611 78780 **Fax:** 611 7878400
Web site: http://www.mediadaten.com

Titles:
MEDIA DATEN FACHZEITSCHRIFTEN
MEDIA DATEN RADIO/TV
MEDIA DATEN ZEITSCHRIFTEN
MEDIA DATEN ZEITUNGEN ANZEIGENBLÄTTER
MEDIA SPECTRUM
REDAKTIONS ADRESS

MEDIALOG GMBH & CO. KG 677248
Medienplatz 1, 76571 GAGGENAU
Tel: 7225 916230 **Fax:** 7225 916290
Email: medialog@medialog.de
Web site: http://www.medialog.de

Titles:
MARKANT HANDELSMAGAZIN
RUNDSCHAU FÜR DEN LEBENSMITTELHANDEL

MEDIA-MICRO-CENSUS GMBH 685427
Am Weingarten 25, 60487 FRANKFURT
Tel: 69 1568050 **Fax:** 69 15680540
Email: agma@agma-mmc.de
Web site: http://www.agma-mmc.de

Titles:
MA PRESSEMEDIEN
MA RADIO

MEDIAN-VERLAG VON KILLISCH-HORN GMBH 680350
Im Breitspiel 11a, 69126 HEIDELBERG
Tel: 6221 905090 **Fax:** 6221 9050920
Email: info@median-verlag.de
Web site: http://www.median-verlag.de

Titles:
HÖRAKUSTIK
ZEITSCHRIFT FÜR AUDIOLOGIE

MEDIAPRINT WEKA INFOVERLAG GMBH 1781867
Lechstr. 2, 86415 MERING **Tel:** 8233 3840
Fax: 8233 384106
Email: info@mp-infoverlag.de
Web site: http://www.mp-infoverlag.de

Titles:
MARKETING-CLUB DÜSSELDORF

MEDIASCRIPT-VERLAG UND SERVICE GMBH 678626
Pannesheider Str. 48, 52134 HERZOGENRATH
Tel: 2407 918297 **Fax:** 2407 918298
Email: info@mediascript-verlag.de
Web site: http://www.mediascript-verlag.de

Titles:
AV SIGNAGE
AV-VIEWS

MEDIAWELT PRODUKTIONS UND AGENTUR GMBH 1651450
Papiermühlenweg 74, 40882 RATINGEN
Tel: 2102 16780 **Fax:** 2102 167828
Email: info@mediawelt-services.de
Web site: http://www.mediawelt-services.de

Titles:
DER AUGENSPIEGEL
MAFO
OPHTHALMO-INDEX
OPTOINDEX

MEDICAL TRIBUNE VERLAGSGES. MBH 678031
Unter den Eichen 5, 65195 WIESBADEN
Tel: 611 97460 **Fax:** 611 9746112
Email: kontakt@medical-tribune.de
Web site: http://www.medical-tribune.de

Titles:
KOLLOQUIUM
MEDICAL TRIBUNE
MEDICAL TRIBUNE
MEDICAL TRIBUNE
MEDICAL TRIBUNE

MEDIEN 31 GMBH 1626678
Baustr. 44, 31785 HAMELN **Tel:** 5151 200157
Fax: 5151 200155
Email: kontakt@medien31.de
Web site: http://www.medien31.de

Titles:
DEWEZET.DE

MEDIEN VERLAGS GMBH 680913
Schweriner Str. 48, 01067 DRESDEN
Tel: 351 807210 **Fax:** 351 8072133
Email: redaktion@dresdner.nu
Web site: http://www.dresdner.nu

Titles:
DRESDNER

MEDIENAGENTUR FRANK KÜPPING 680219
Markt 1, 41460 NEUSS **Tel:** 2131 21293
Fax: 2131 275760
Email: info@kuepping.de
Web site: http://www.kuepping.de

Titles:
DER CITY-FÜHRER FÜR GASTRONOMIE UND FREIZEIT

MEDIENBÜRO ROBERT MÄCHTEL 688991
Ringstr. 58, 91080 UTTENREUTH **Tel:** 9131 50532
Fax: 9131 50544
Email: info@stoneplus.de
Web site: http://www.stoneplus.de

Titles:
STONEPLUS

MEDIENFABRIK GÜTERSLOH GMBH 1630302
Carl-Bertelsmann-Str. 33, 33311 GÜTERSLOH
Tel: 5241 2348010 **Fax:** 5241 2348022
Email: kontakt@medienfabrik.de
Web site: http://www.medienfabrik.de

Titles:
GARTEN EDEN

MEDIENGRUPPE MAIN-POST GMBH 1717722
Berner Str. 2, 97084 WÜRZBURG **Tel:** 931 60010
Fax: 931 6001252
Web site: http://www.mainpost.de

Titles:
BOTE VOM HASSGAU
DIEDERICH FACHKALENDER
SCHWEINFURTER TAGBLATT
VOLKSBLATT
VOLKSZEITUNG

MEDIENGRUPPE OBERFRANKEN-BUCH-UND-FACHVERLAGE GMBH & CO. KG 679435
E.-C.-Baumann-Str. 5, 95326 KULMBACH
Tel: 9221 949393 **Fax:** 9221 949377
Email: bfv@mg-oberfranken.de
Web site: http://www.ku-gesundheitsmanagement.de

Titles:
DBI DER BAYERISCHE INTERNIST
KU GESUNDHEITSMANAGEMENT
KU GESUNDHEITSMANAGEMENT
NATUR-HEILKUNDE JOURNAL

MEDIENGRUPPE OBERFRANKEN-ZEITUNGSVERLAGE GMBH & CO. KG 1768885
Gutenbergstr. 1, 96050 BAMBERG **Tel:** 951 1880
Fax: 951 188118
Web site: http://www.infranken.de

Titles:
FRÄNKISCHER TAG

MEDIENHANDBUCH PUBLIKATIONSGES. MBH 1690874
Mönckebergstr. 13, 20095 HAMBURG
Tel: 40 48090104 **Fax:** 40 462676
Email: service@medienhandbuch.de
Web site: http://www.medienhandbuch.de

Titles:
MEDIENHANDBUCH.DE

MEDIENHAUS VERLAG GMBH
680935
Bertram-Blank-Str. 8, 51427 BERGISCH GLADBACH **Tel:** 2204 92140 **Fax:** 2204 921430
Email: info@medienhaus-verlag.de
Web site: http://www.medienhaus-verlag.de

Titles:
DV-DIALOG
IT MITTELSTAND
IT-DIRECTOR
MOBILE BUSINESS

MEDIENREPORT VERLAGS-GMBH
680380
Hegnacher Str. 30, 71336 WAIBLINGEN
Tel: 7151 23331 **Fax:** 7151 23338
Email: medienreport@yahoo.de
Web site: http://www.medienreport.de

Titles:
CORPORATE AV

MEDIENVERBAND DER EVANGELISCHEN KIRCHE IM RHEINLAND GGMBH
1653866
Kaiserswerther Str. 450, 40474 DÜSSELDORF
Tel: 211 43690350 **Fax:** 211 43690300
Email: info@medienverband.de
Web site: http://www.medienverband.de

Titles:
CHRISMON PLUS RHEINLAND

MEDIENWERK DER EVANGELISCH-METHODISTISCHEN KIRCHE GMBH
682244
Ludolfusstr. 2, 60487 FRANKFURT
Tel: 69 242521150 **Fax:** 69 242521159
Email: medienwerk@emk.de
Web site: http://www.emk.de

Titles:
UNTERWEGS

MEDIKOM PUBLISHING JUNIOR-VERLAG GMBH & CO. KG
1784505
Raboisen 30, 20095 HAMBURG
Tel: 40 357291940 **Fax:** 40 357291949
Email: schoening@medikom.de
Web site: http://www.wireltern.de

Titles:
BABY & GESUNDHEIT

MEDIZINISCH LITERARISCHE VERLAGSGES. MBH
677375
Groß Liederner Str. 45, 29525 UELZEN
Tel: 581 80891813 **Fax:** 581 80891890
Email: vertrieb@mlverlag.de
Web site: http://www.mlverlag.de

Titles:
ORTHOPÄDISCHE PRAXIS

MEDIZINISCHE MEDIEN INFORMATIONS GMBH
682409
Am Forsthaus Gravenbruch 7, 63263 NEU-ISENBURG **Tel:** 6102 5020 **Fax:** 6102 53779
Email: info@mmi.de
Web site: http://www.mmi.de

Titles:
GELBE LISTE IDENTA
GELBE LISTE PHARMINDEX
GELBE LISTE PHARMINDEX
GELBE LISTE PHARMINDEX
GELBE LISTE PHARMINDEX
GELBE LISTE PHARMINDEX
GELBE LISTE PHARMINDEX
GELBE LISTE PHARMINDEX
GELBE LISTE PHARMINDEX
GELBE LISTE PHARMINDEX
GELBE LISTE PHARMINDEX
GELBE LISTE PHARMINDEX
HANDBUCH REHA- UND VORSORGE-EINRICHTUNGEN

MEGAZIN MEDIA VERLAG GMBH
685503
Bergbräustr. 2, 85049 INGOLSTADT
Tel: 841 1560 **Fax:** 841 1406
Email: redaktion@megazin.de
Web site: http://www.megazin.de

Titles:
MEGAZIN

MEHRING VERLAG GMBH
682626
Margaretenstr. 12, 45145 ESSEN
Tel: 201 6462106 **Fax:** 3222 3711097
Email: vertrieb@mehring-verlag.de
Web site: http://www.mehring-verlag.de

Titles:
GLEICHHEIT.

MEININGER MEDIENGES. MBH
682136
Neu-Ulmer Str. 8a, 98617 MEININGEN
Tel: 3693 44030 **Fax:** 3693 440335
Email: verlag@fw-mt.de

Titles:
FW MEININGER TAGEBLATT

MEININGER VERLAG GMBH
678885
Maximilianstr. 7, 67433 NEUSTADT
Tel: 6321 89080 **Fax:** 6321 890873
Email: contact@meininger.de
Web site: http://www.meininger.de

Titles:
DER DEUTSCHE WEINBAU
EURODECOR
FIZZZ
GETRÄNKE ZEITUNG
SOMMELIER MAGAZIN
WEINWELT
WEINWIRTSCHAFT

MEISENBACH GMBH
678653
Franz-Ludwig-Str. 7a, 96047 BAMBERG
Tel: 951 8610 **Fax:** 951 861158
Web site: http://www.meisenbach.de

Titles:
BABY & JUNIOR
BLECH ROHRE PROFILE
COFFEE & MORE
DRAHT
ELEKTROMARKT
MEDIASELLER
DAS SPIELZEUG
STIL & MARKT
TEXTILE NETWORK
UMFORMTECHNIK
WIRE

MEISSNER TAGEBLATT VERLAGS GMBH
685522
Am Sand 1c, 01665 DIERA-ZEHREN
Tel: 3525 71860 **Fax:** 3525 718612
Email: tageblatt@satztechnik-meissen.de

Titles:
MEISSNER TAGEBLATT

MEMO-MEDIA VERLAGS-GMBH
1676074
Rölefeld 31, 51545 WALDBRÖL **Tel:** 2296 900946
Fax: 2296 900947
Email: info@memo-media.de
Web site: http://www.memo-media.de

Titles:
HANDBUCH MEMO-MEDIA
SHOWCASES

MENSCH UND LEBEN VERLAGSGES. MBH
683278
Niederstedter Weg 5, 61348 BAD HOMBURG
Tel: 6172 95830 **Fax:** 6172 958321
Email: mlverlag@wsth.de

Titles:
HLZ

MENSCH & NATUR HEUTE VERLAGS GMBH
1765865
Wendenstr. 1a, 20097 HAMBURG
Tel: 40 5302405555 **Fax:** 40 5302402401
Email: info@mensch-natur-heute.de
Web site: http://www.mensch-natur-heute.de

Titles:
MENSCH & NATUR

M-E-P NETWORK UG
1709762
Mathildenstr. 20, 58507 LÜDENSCHEID
Tel: 2351 985990 **Fax:** 2351 9859922
Email: info@nachtflug-magazin.de
Web site: http://www.nachtflug-magazin.de

Titles:
NACHTFLUG - (AUSG. MK-SÜD/OE-GM)

MERCADO VERLAG GMBH
678655
Friedensallee 43, 22765 HAMBURG
Tel: 40 30685202 **Fax:** 40 30685210
Email: mercado-verlag@t-online.de

Titles:
BACKBUSINESS
COST & LOGIS

MERGES-VERLAG
1687253
Hauptstr. 25, 69117 HEIDELBERG
Tel: 6221 6594877 **Fax:** 6221 6594879
Email: merges@merges.com
Web site: http://www.merges.com

Titles:
HEIDELBERG

MERKUR VERLAG
679126
Siegfriedstr. 204, 10365 BERLIN **Tel:** 30 4725393
Fax: 30 4732251
Email: berliner-merkur@t-online.de
Web site: http://www.berliner-merkur.de

Titles:
BERLINER MERKUR

MESSE FRANKFURT MEDIEN UND SERVICE GMBH
682303
Ludwig-Erhard-Anlage 1, 60327 FRANKFURT
Tel: 69 75756919 **Fax:** 69 75756802
Email: publishing.services@messefrankfurt.com
Web site: http://www.publishingservices.messefrankfurt.com

Titles:
HOTELGUIDE FRANKFURT RHEIN MAIN

MESSE TREFF VERLAGS-GMBH
685460
Weyerstraßerweg 159, 50969 KÖLN
Tel: 221 376030 **Fax:** 221 374020
Email: info@messetreff.com
Web site: http://www.messetreff.com

Titles:
MEDIA GUIDE
MEDIA GUIDE
SALES GUIDE KÖLN COLOGNE

METAC MEDIEN VERLAGS GMBH
679615
Waldstr. 226, 63071 OFFENBACH **Tel:** 69 850080
Fax: 69 85008298
Email: service@op-online.de
Web site: http://www.op-online.de

Titles:
OFFENBACH-POST ONLINE

METH MEDIA DEUTSCHLAND GMBH
1791628
Mozartstr. 51, 70180 STUTTGART
Tel: 711 32067616 **Fax:** 711 32067611
Email: office@provocateur-magazin.de
Web site: http://www.provocateur-magazin.de

Titles:
PROVOCATEUR

METROPOLIS AG
1652209
Heinestr. 72, 72762 REUTLINGEN
Tel: 7121 348100 **Fax:** 7121 348111
Email: info@metropolis-ag.de
Web site: http://www.metropolis-ag.de

Titles:
MULTIMEDIA.DE

MEYER & MEYER FACHVERLAG UND BUCHHANDEL GMBH
678696
Von-Coels-Str. 390, 52080 AACHEN
Tel: 241 958100 **Fax:** 241 9581010
Email: verlag@m-m-sports.com
Web site: http://www.dersportverlag.de

Titles:
CONDITION
DEUTSCHES TURNEN
FECHTSPORT
JUDO MAGAZIN
Ü

MFI MEINE FAMILIE UND ICH VERLAG GMBH
683449
Arabellastr. 23, 81925 MÜNCHEN **Tel:** 89 92500
Fax: 89 92503030
Web site: http://www.lustaufgenuss.de

Titles:
LUST AUF GENUSS
MEINE FAMILIE & ICH

MG CAR CLUB DEUTSCHLAND E.V.
1653205
Habichtsweg 1, 64380 ROSSDORF
Tel: 6154 800155 **Fax:** 6154 6089909
Email: sekretaer@mgcc.de
Web site: http://www.mgcc.de

Titles:
MG KURIER

MGV - MEDIENGESTALTUNGS- UND VERMARKTUNGS GMBH & CO. KG
1768055
Frankfurter Str. 8, 36043 FULDA **Tel:** 661 2800
Fax: 661 280125

Titles:
MARKTKORB

MHP-VERLAG GMBH
1605431
Marktplatz 13, 65183 WIESBADEN
Tel: 611 5059331 **Fax:** 611 5059311
Email: info@mhp-verlag.de
Web site: http://www.mhp-verlag.de

Titles:
HYGIENE + MEDIZIN
WUND MANAGEMENT
ZENTRALSTERILISATION CENTRAL SERVICE

MIBA-VERLAG IN DER VGB VERLAGSGRUPPE BAHN GMBH
678067
Am Fohlenhof 9, 82256 FÜRSTENFELDBRUCK
Tel: 8141 534810 **Fax:** 8141 53481200
Email: service@miba.de
Web site: http://www.miba.de

Titles:
MIBA

MICE AG
1760626
Friedrichstr. 76, 10117 BERLIN **Tel:** 30 20625900
Fax: 30 206259400
Email: info@mice.ag
Web site: http://www.mice.ag

Titles:
TAGUNGSPLANER.DE

MICHAEL E. BRIEDEN VERLAG GMBH
679346
Gartroper Str. 42, 47138 DUISBURG
Tel: 203 42920 **Fax:** 203 4292149
Email: info@brieden.de
Web site: http://www.brieden.de

Titles:
CAR & HIFI
DIGITAL HOME
HEIMKINO
HIFI TEST
KLANG + TON

MICHAEL MÜLLER GMBH
678529
Homburger Landstr. 851, 60437 FRANKFURT
Tel: 69 5074214 **Fax:** 69 5073444
Email: redaktion@rhein-main-magazin.de
Web site: http://www.rhein-main-magazin.de

Titles:
MAGAZIN

MIELITZ VERLAG GMBH
1742530
Goldstr. 16, 33602 BIELEFELD **Tel:** 521 932560
Fax: 521 9325699
Email: info@mielitz-verlag.de
Web site: http://www.mielitz-verlag.de

Titles:
HARTMANNBUND VERBAND DER ÄRZTE DEUTSCHLANDS

MIETERVEREIN DORTMUND UND UMGEBUNG
685615
Kampstr. 4, 44137 DORTMUND **Tel:** 231 5576560
Fax: 231 55765616
Email: info@mieterverein-dortmund.de
Web site: http://www.mieterverein-dortmund.de

Titles:
MIETERFORUM

M.I.G. MEDIEN INNOVATION GMBH
685119
Hubert-Burda-Platz 1, 77652 OFFENBURG
Tel: 781 8401

Titles:
LISA
LISA BLUMEN & PFLANZEN
LISA KOCHEN & BACKEN
LISA WOHNEN & DEKORIEREN
MEINE LAND KÜCHE
NEUE WOCHE

VIEL SPASS
WOHNEN & GARTEN

MIKROVENT GMBH 1791466
Pittersdorf 5, 84104 RUDELZHAUSEN
Tel: 8752 869066
Email: deiter@mikroproduktion.com
Web site: http://www.mikroproduktion.com

Titles:
MIKROPRODUKTION

MIM VERLAGSGES. MBH 1771055
Im Geisbaum 1b, 63329 EGELSBACH
Tel: 6103 300240 **Fax:** 6103 3002429
Web site: http://www.mim-verlag.de

Titles:
NATURAMED

MINERVA-VERLAG GMBH 677413
Monschauer Str. 2, 41068
MÖNCHENGLADBACH **Tel:** 2161 9463820
Fax: 2161 9463840
Email: info@minervaverlag.de
Web site: http://www.minervaverlag.de

Titles:
HUNDEWELT
HUNDEWELT SPORT
OUR CATS

MINISTERIUM DES INNERN DES LANDES BRANDENBURG 1743608
Henning-von-Tresckow-Str. 9, 14467 POTSDAM
Tel: 331 8844123 **Fax:** 331 884416123
Email: vertrieb@geobasis-bb.de
Web site: http://www.vermessung.brandenburg.de

Titles:
VERMESSUNG BRANDENBURG

MINISTERIUM FÜR UMWELT UND FORSTEN RHEINLAND-PFALZ 689827
Kaiser-Friedrich-Str. 1, 55116 MAINZ
Tel: 6131 164433 **Fax:** 6131 164629
Email: ralph.plugge@mufv.rlp.de
Web site: http://www.mufv.de

Titles:
UMWELT JOURNAL RHEINLAND-PFALZ

MISSY MAGAZIN GBR 1757881
Eschelsweg 4, 22767 HAMBURG
Tel: 40 20933967 **Fax:** 40 31792103
Email: redaktion@missy-mag.de
Web site: http://www.missy-magazine.de

Titles:
MISSY MAGAZINE

MITTELBAYERISCHER VERLAG KG 677562
Margaretenstr. 4, 93047 REGENSBURG
Tel: 941 2070
Email: mittelbayerische@mittelbayerische.de
Web site: http://www.mittelbayerische.de

Titles:
BAYERWALD-ECHO
KÖTZTINGER UMSCHAU
MITTELBAYERISCHE ZEITUNG FÜR DEN NÖRDLICHEN LANDKREIS REGENSBURG
MITTELBAYERISCHE ZEITUNG FÜR DEN SÜDLICHEN LANDKREIS REGENSBURG
MITTELBAYERISCHE ZEITUNG FÜR HEMAU UND DEN WESTLICHEN LANDKREIS
MITTELBAYERISCHE ZEITUNG FÜR KELHEIM, ABENSBERG UND NEUSTADT
MITTELBAYERISCHE ZEITUNG FÜR NITTENAU UND BRUCK
MITTELBAYERISCHE ZEITUNG FÜR REGENSBURG
MITTELBAYERISCHE ZEITUNG FÜR SCHWANDORF, DAS STÄDTEDREIECK UND NEUNBURG
NEUMARKTER TAGBLATT
RUNDSCHAU
WÖRTHER ANZEIGER

MITTELDEUTSCHE DRUCK- UND VERLAGSHAUS GMBH & CO. KG 685877
Delitzscher Str. 65, 06112 HALLE **Tel:** 345 5650
Fax: 345 5652351
Email: service@mz-web.de
Web site: http://www.mz-web.de

Titles:
MITTELDEUTSCHE ZEITUNG

MITTELHESSISCHE DRUCK- UND VERLAGSGES. MBH 677620
Marburger Str. 18, 35390 GIESSEN
Tel: 641 30030 **Fax:** 641 3003300
Web site: http://www.giessener-allgemeine.de

Titles:
ALSFELDER ALLGEMEINE
GIESSENER ALLGEMEINE
WETTERAUER ZEITUNG

MITTELRHEIN-VERLAG GMBH 683487
August-Horch-Str. 28, 56070 KOBLENZ
Tel: 261 89200 **Fax:** 261 892770
Email: redaktion@rhein-zeitung.net
Web site: http://www.rhein-zeitung.de

Titles:
KIRNER ZEITUNG
NAHE-ZEITUNG
ÖFFENTLICHER ANZEIGER
RHEIN-HUNSRÜCK-ZEITUNG
RHEIN-LAHN-ZEITUNG
RHEIN-ZEITUNG
RHEIN-ZEITUNG.DE
WESTERWÄLDER ZEITUNG

MIX VERLAGS-GMBH 696930
Goebenstr. 14, 28209 BREMEN **Tel:** 421 6964340
Fax: 421 69643499
Email: verlag@mix-online.de
Web site: http://www.mix-online.de

Titles:
MIX

MK PUBLISHING GMBH 678842
Döllgaststr. 7, 86199 AUGSBURG
Tel: 821 344570 **Fax:** 821 3445719
Email: info@mkpublishing.de
Web site: http://www.mkpublishing.de

Titles:
ERHALTEN & GESTALTEN
HOLZ PLUS
PAPER MANAGER

MKV MEDIENKONTOR VERLAGSGES. MBH & CO. KG 695740
Rathausstr. 28, 22941 BARGTEHEIDE
Tel: 4532 28670 **Fax:** 4532 286750
Email: info@mkv-medienkontor.de
Web site: http://www.mkv-apotheken-kombi.de

Titles:
TV GESUND & LEBEN

MLP FINANZDIENSTLEISTUNGEN AG 682002
Alte Heerstr. 40, 69168 WIESLOCH
Tel: 6222 3081135 **Fax:** 6222 3081131
Email: christian.martin@mlp.de
Web site: http://www.mlp.de

Titles:
FORUM MLP - WIRTSCHAFTSAUSG.

MM-MUSIK-MEDIA-VERLAG GMBH 681548
Emil-Hoffmann-Str. 13, 50996 KÖLN
Tel: 2236 962170 **Fax:** 2236 962175
Email: info@musikmedia.de
Web site: http://www.musikmedia.de

Titles:
EVENT PARTNER
GITARRE & BASS
KEYBOARDS
PRODUCTION PARTNER
SOUND & RECORDING
STICKS

MMVG MÄRKISCHE MEDIENVERLAGSGES. MBH 1739734
Am Kanal, Geb. 59, 15749 MITTENWALDE
Tel: 33764 23000 **Fax:** 33764 23001
Email: info@annalisa.info
Web site: http://www.annalisa.info

Titles:
ANNALISA

MO MEDIEN VERLAG GMBH 679540
Schrempfstr. 8, 70597 STUTTGART
Tel: 711 24897600 **Fax:** 711 24897628
Web site: http://www.mo-web.de

Titles:
9ELF
BMW MOTORRÄDER
KLASSIK MOTORRAD
MOTORRAD JAHRBUCH
MOTORRAD MAGAZIN MO
MOTORRAD TESTBUCH

MOBIL + FREIZEIT UND AUTOBAHN-SERVICE VERLAGSGES. ASV MBH 678571
Schloßbergstr. 61a, 77876 KAPPELRODECK
Tel: 7842 948811
Email: fotopress-international@t-online.de

Titles:
AUTOBAHN SERVICE

MOBILE. INTERNATIONAL GMBH 1652214
Marktplatz 1, 14532 KLEINMACHNOW
Tel: 30 81097500 **Fax:** 30 81097132
Email: service@team.mobile.de
Web site: http://www.mobile.de

Titles:
MOBILE.DE

MODELLSPORT VERLAG GMBH 694853
Schulstr. 12, 76532 BADEN-BADEN
Tel: 7221 95210 **Fax:** 7221 952145
Email: modellsport@modellsport.de
Web site: http://www.modellsport.de

Titles:
MFI MODELLFLUG INTERNATIONAL
ROTOR

MODERNE ZEITEN MEDIEN GMBH & CO. SAX DRESDNER JOURNAL KG 688061
Bautzner Str. 22, 01099 DRESDEN
Tel: 351 829390 **Fax:** 351 8293949
Email: verlag@cybersax.de
Web site: http://www.cybersax.de

Titles:
SAX

MOHR SIEBECK VERLAG 678300
Wilhelmstr. 18, 72074 TÜBINGEN **Tel:** 7071 9230
Fax: 7071 51104
Email: info@mohr.de
Web site: http://www.mohr.de

Titles:
JOURNAL OF INSTITUTIONAL AND THEORETICAL ECONOMICS JITE

MÖLLER NEUE MEDIEN VERLAGS GMBH 1759518
Ehrig-Hahn-Str. 4, 16356 AHRENSFELDE
Tel: 30 419090 **Fax:** 30 41909299
Email: info@moellerdruck.de
Web site: http://www.moellerdruck.de

Titles:
REITEN UND ZUCHT IN BERLIN UND BRANDENBURG-ANHALT
RUTE & ROLLE

MÖNCH VERLAGSGES. MBH 685208
Heilsbachstr. 26, 53123 BONN **Tel:** 228 64830
Fax: 228 6483109
Email: info@mpgbonn.de
Web site: http://www.monch.com

Titles:
MILITARY TECHNOLOGY
TECNOLOGIA MILITAR
WT WEHRTECHNIK

MONTAN- UND WIRTSCHAFTSVERLAG GMBH 688863
Sohnstr. 65, 40237 DÜSSELDORF **Tel:** 211 67070
Fax: 211 6707629
Email: stahlmarkt@stahleisen.de
Web site: http://www.stahleisen.de

Titles:
STAHLMARKT

MOPO ONLINE GMBH 1626760
Griegstr. 75, 22763 HAMBURG **Tel:** 40 8090570
Web site: http://www.mopo.de

Titles:
HAMBURGER MORGENPOST
WWW.MOPO.DE

MORGENPOST VERLAG GMBH 682927
Griegstr. 75, 22763 HAMBURG **Tel:** 40 8090570
Fax: 40 809057640
Email: verlag@mopo.de
Web site: http://www.mopo.de

Titles:
HAMBURGER MORGENPOST

MORGENWELT KOMMUNIKATION & VERLAGS GMBH 679762
Treibgasse 19, 63739 ASCHAFFENBURG
Tel: 6021 444880 **Fax:** 6021 4448844
Email: anzeigen@morgen-welt.de
Web site: http://www.morgen-welt.de

Titles:
BROT & SPIELE
FRIZZ

MORGENWELT WÜRZBURG GMBH 1771049
Gerberstr. 7, 97070 WÜRZBURG **Tel:** 931 329990
Fax: 931 3299922
Email: info@morgen-welt.de
Web site: http://www.morgen-welt.de

Titles:
FRIZZ

MORITZ-VERLAGS-GMBH 685965
Kreuzenstr. 94, 74076 HEILBRONN
Tel: 7131 15300 **Fax:** 7131 1530111
Email: buero@moritz.de
Web site: http://www.moritz.de

Titles:
MORITZ
MORITZ
MORITZ
MORITZ
MORITZ

MOSAIK STEINCHEN FÜR STEINCHEN VERLAG + PROCOM WERBEAGENTUR GMBH 677256
Lindenallee 5, 14050 BERLIN **Tel:** 30 3069270
Fax: 30 30692729
Email: mosaik@abrafaxe.de
Web site: http://www.abrafaxe.com

Titles:
MOSAIK

MOSER VERLAG GMBH 1762987
Widenmayerstr. 16, 80538 MÜNCHEN
Tel: 89 2900150 **Fax:** 89 29001515
Email: info@moser-verlag.com
Web site: http://www.moser-verlag.com

Titles:
CUT

MOTOR PRESSE STUTTGART GMBH & CO. KG 677305
Leuschnerstr. 1, 70174 STUTTGART
Tel: 711 18201 **Fax:** 711 1821779
Web site: http://www.motorpresse.de

Titles:
AEROKURIER
AUTO KATALOG
AUTO MOTOR UND SPORT
AUTO MOTOR UND SPORT ECO DRIVE
AUTO STRASSENVERKEHR
AUTOKAUF
AUTO-MOTOR-UND-SPORT.DE
CARAVANING
CARAVANING
CROSS-ROAD AUTO MOTOR UND SPORT
DSV AKTIV SKI & SPORTMAGAZIN
DSV SKI-ATLAS
FLUG REVUE
GEBRAUCHTWAGEN AUTO MOTOR UND SPORT
KLASSIKER DER LUFTFAHRT
KLETTERN
MOTOR KLASSIK
MOTORRAD
MOTORRAD
MOTORRAD CLASSIC
MOTORRAD KATALOG
MOTORRAD ROLLER SPEZIAL
MOUNTAIN BIKE
MOUNTAIN BIKE ONLINE
OUTDOOR
PLANETSNOW
PRO MOBIL
PROMOBIL.DE
PS
SPORT AUTO
YOUNGTIMER

MOTORAVER MEDIEN GMBH
685978
Harkortstr. 162, 22765 HAMBURG
Tel: 40 226228710 Fax: 40 226228720
Email: info@motoraver.de
Web site: http://www.motoraver.de

Titles:
MOTORAVER MAGAZINE

MOTORETTA GMBH VERLAGS- U. MEDIENGRUPPE CO. KG
695638
Wickingstr. 1, 45657 RECKLINGHAUSEN
Tel: 2361 93580 **Fax:** 2361 16495
Email: info@motoretta.de
Web site: http://www.motoretta.de

Titles:
MOTOR BIKE
MOTORETTA
MOTORETTA SPEZIAL MOTORROLLER
MOTORETTA SPEZIAL MOTORROLLER
MOTORETTA SPEZIAL QUAD

MOTOROUTE THOMAS VINZELBERG
1640537
Ernststr. 6, 96476 RODACH **Tel:** 9564 8380
Fax: 9564 83855
Email: info@motoroute.de
Web site: http://www.motoroute.de

Titles:
MOTOROUTE MAGAZIN

MOTORSPORT-TOTAL.COM GMBH
1651790
Sendlinger-Tor-Platz 10, 80336 MÜNCHEN
Tel: 89 51555820 **Fax:** 89 51555821
Email: info@motorsport-total.com
Web site: http://www.motorsport-total.com

Titles:
MOTORSPORT-TOTAL.COM

MOTOURMEDIA E.K.
1621596
Hastener Str. 140, 42349 WUPPERTAL
Tel: 202 94600226 **Fax:** 202 94600229
Email: verlag@motourmedia.de
Web site: http://www.motourmedia.de

Titles:
ALPENADRIA

MS MEDIENTEAM GMBH
1748168
Ziegelkamp 9, 21635 JORK **Tel:** 7222 9311110
Email: redaktion@ms-medienteam.de

Titles:
AKTUELL FÜR DIE FRAU

MSC WINKELMESSER FRANKFURT E.V.
1622425
Gartenstr. 7, 61184 KARBEN **Tel:** 6039 46127
Email: andrea.haemmelmann@winkelmesser-frankfurt.de
Web site: http://www.winkelmesser-frankfurt.de

Titles:
DER WINKELMESSER

MTD-VERLAG GMBH
686006
Schomburger Str. 11, 88279 AMTZELL
Tel: 7520 9580 **Fax:** 7520 95899
Email: info@mtd.de
Web site: http://www.mtd.de

Titles:
MTD MEDIZIN-TECHNISCHER DIALOG

MTV NETWORKS GERMANY GMBH
1652237
Stralauer Allee 7, 10245 BERLIN **Tel:** 30 7001000
Fax: 30 700100599
Email: kontakt@mtv.de
Web site: http://www.mtv.de

Titles:
MTV

MÜLLER DITZEN DRUCKEREI AG
1679949
Hoebelstr. 19, 27572 BREMERHAVEN
Tel: 471 9798100 **Fax:** 471 9798918
Email: info@muellerditzen.de
Web site: http://www.muellerditzen.de

Titles:
IHK WIRTSCHAFT AN STROM UND MEER

MULTI MED VISION GBR R. BUBENZER & M. KADEN
1690736
Lützowstr. 47, 10785 BERLIN **Tel:** 30 80613679
Fax: 30 80613680
Email: info@heilpflanzen-welt.de

Titles:
HEILPFLANZEN-WELT

MULTIMEDIA WERBE- UND VERLAGS-GMBH
686247
Hamburger Str. 277, 38114 BRAUNSCHWEIG
Tel: 531 3900750 **Fax:** 531 3900753
Email: nb-anzeigen@nb-online.de
Web site: http://www.nb-online.de

Titles:
NEUE BRAUNSCHWEIGER

MÜNCHENER ZEITUNGS-VERLAG GMBH & CO. KG
686035
Paul-Heyse-Str. 2, 80336 MÜNCHEN
Tel: 89 53060 **Fax:** 89 53068651
Email: info@merkur-online.de
Web site: http://www.merkur-online.de

Titles:
MÜNCHNER MERKUR

MÜNCHNER KULTUR GMBH
695617
Giselastr. 4/Rgb., 80802 MÜNCHEN
Tel: 89 3061000 **Fax:** 89 30610012
Email: info@muenchner.de
Web site: http://www.muenchner.de

Titles:
DELIKATESSEN

MÜNCHNER STADTMEDIEN GMBH
682650
Arcisstr. 68, 80801 MÜNCHEN **Tel:** 89 5505660
Fax: 89 55056612
Email: go@gomuenchen.de
Web site: http://www.gomuenchen.de

Titles:
HABEN & SEIN
MÜNCHEN GEHT AUS

MUNDSCHENK DRUCK- UND VERLAGSGES. MBH
679481
Harburger Str. 63, 29614 SOLTAU **Tel:** 5191 8080
Fax: 5191 808165
Email: bz@soltau-online.de
Web site: http://www.boehme-zeitung.de

Titles:
BÖHME-ZEITUNG
MITTWOCH AKTUELL
SCHNEVERDINGER ZEITUNG

MUNICH ONLINE GMBH
1626822
Paul-Heyse-Str. 2, 80336 MÜNCHEN
Tel: 89 53060 **Fax:** 89 53068418
Email: info@merkur-online.de
Web site: http://www.merkur-online.de

Titles:
MERKUR-ONLINE.DE
TZ

MÜNSTERLAND-ECHO-VERLAGS GMBH & CO. KG
680243
Emsteker Str. 14, 49661 CLOPPENBURG
Tel: 4471 92250 **Fax:** 4471 922510
Email: info@mev-online.de
Web site: http://www.mev-online.de

Titles:
CLOPPENBURGER WOCHENBLATT

MUSIKHANDEL VERLAGSGES. MBH
686085
Friedrich-Wilhelm-Str. 31, 53113 BONN
Tel: 228 539700 **Fax:** 228 5397070
Email: info@musikverbaende.de

Titles:
MUSIKHANDEL

MUSIKMARKT GMBH & CO. KG
1643273
Fürstenrieder Str. 265, 81377 MÜNCHEN
Tel: 89 74126450 **Fax:** 89 74126451
Email: info@musikmarkt.de
Web site: http://www.musikmarkt.de

Titles:
MUSIKMARKT
POSITION

MVB MARKETING- UND VERLAGSSERVICE DES BUCHHANDELS GMBH
677341
Großer Hirschgraben 17, 60311 FRANKFURT
Tel: 69 13060 **Fax:** 69 1306201
Web site: http://www.mvb-online.de

Titles:
BÖRSENBLATT
BUCHJOURNAL

MVG MEDIEN VERLAGSGES. MBH & CO.
680386
Arabellastr. 33, 81925 MÜNCHEN **Tel:** 89 92340
Fax: 89 9234202
Web site: http://www.mvg.de

Titles:
COSMOPOLITAN
JOY
SHAPE

MWD UG
1717422
Brombeerweg 111, 25479 ELLERAU
Tel: 4106 6270023 **Fax:** 4106 804041
Email: w.trede@medizinische-wirtschaftsdienste.de
Web site: http://www.medizinische-wirtschaftsdienste.de

Titles:
BAO DEPESCHE

MZV MURRHARDTER ZEITUNGSVERLAG GMBH & CO.
686062
Grabenstr. 23, 71540 MURRHARDT
Tel: 7192 92900 **Fax:** 7192 929019
Email: info@murrhardter-zeitung.de
Web site: http://www.murrhardter-zeitung.de

Titles:
MURRHARDTER ZEITUNG

MZ-WEB GMBH
1626831
Delitzscher Str. 65, 06112 HALLE
Tel: 345 5655005 **Fax:** 345 5655010
Email: robby.braune@mz-web.de
Web site: http://www.mz-web.de

Titles:
MZ-WEB.DE

NABU SAARLAND E.V.
686195
Antoniusstr. 18, 66822 LEBACH **Tel:** 6881 936190
Fax: 6881 9361911
Email: lgs@nabu-saar.de
Web site: http://www.nabu-saar.de

Titles:
NATURSCHUTZ IM SAARLAND

NABU SCHLESWIG-HOLSTEIN
1739702
Färberstr. 51, 24534 NEUMÜNSTER
Tel: 4321 53734 **Fax:** 4321 5981
Email: redaktion.bn@nabu-sh.de
Web site: http://www.nabu-sh.de

Titles:
BETRIFFT: NATUR

NASSAUISCHER VEREIN FÜR NATURKUNDE
1616889
Rheinstr. 10, 65185 WIESBADEN **Tel:** 6127 61976
Fax: 6127 969527
Email: webmaster@naturkunde-online.de
Web site: http://www.naturkunde-online.de

Titles:
NASSAUISCHER VEREIN FÜR NATURKUNDE MITTEILUNGEN

NATUR & TEXT IN BRANDENBURG GMBH
679016
Friedensallee 21, 15834 RANGSDORF
Tel: 33708 20431 **Fax:** 33708 20433
Email: verlag@nut-online.de
Web site: http://www.naturmagazin.info

Titles:
NATURMAGAZIN

NATUR UND TIER-VERLAG GMBH
680887
An der Kleimannbrücke 39, 48157 MÜNSTER
Tel: 251 133390 **Fax:** 251 1333933
Email: verlag@ms-verlag.de
Web site: http://www.ms-verlag.de

Titles:
DATZ

NATUR & UMWELT SERVICE- UND VERLAGS GMBH
679938
Am Köllnischen Park 1, 10179 BERLIN
Tel: 30 2758640 **Fax:** 30 27586440
Email: bund@bund.net
Web site: http://www.bund.net

Titles:
BUNDMAGAZIN

NATURFREUNDE DEUTSCHLANDS, VERBAND FÜR UMWELTSCHUTZ, SPORT UND KULTUR, LANDESVERBAND HAMBURG E.V.
682928
Adenauerallee 48, 20097 HAMBURG
Tel: 40 247858 **Fax:** 40 243911
Email: naturfreunde-hh@gmx.de
Web site: http://www.naturfreunde-hh.de

Titles:
NATURFREUNDE HAMBURG

NATURFREUNDE-VERLAG FREIZEIT UND WANDERN GMBH
686182
Warschauer Str. 58a, 10243 BERLIN
Tel: 30 29773263 **Fax:** 30 29773280
Email: verlag@naturfreunde.de
Web site: http://www.naturfreunde-verlag.de

Titles:
NATURFREUNDIN

NATURPARK SCHWÄBISCH-FRÄNKISCHER WALD E.V.
1738867
Marktplatz 8, 71540 MURRHARDT
Tel: 7192 213888 **Fax:** 7192 213880
Email: info@naturpark-sfw.de
Web site: http://www.naturpark-sfw.de

Titles:
NATURPARKTELLER

NATURSCHUTZBUND DEUTSCHLAND E.V.
686194
Charitéstr. 3, 10117 BERLIN **Tel:** 30 2849840
Fax: 30 2849842000
Email: nabu@nabu.de
Web site: http://www.nabu.de

Titles:
NATURSCHUTZ HEUTE

NATURSCHUTZBUND DEUTSCHLAND (NABU), LANDESVERBAND HAMBURG E.V.
686196
Osterstr. 58, 20259 HAMBURG **Tel:** 40 69708912
Fax: 40 69708919
Email: nabu@nabu-hamburg.de
Web site: http://www.nabu-hamburg.de

Titles:
NATURSCHUTZ IN HAMBURG

NATURSCHUTZJUGEND HESSEN E.V.
1743859
Friedenstr. 26, 35578 WETZLAR **Tel:** 6441 946903
Email: info@naju-hessen.de
Web site: http://www.naju-hessen.de

Titles:
RUNDBRIEF DER NAJU HESSEN UND THÜRINGEN

NECKARTAL-PRINTMEDIEN GMBH & CO. KG
1768645
Neugasse 2, 69117 HEIDELBERG **Tel:** 6221 5191
Fax: 6221 217
Email: anzeigen@rnz.de
Web site: http://www.eberbacher-zeitung.de

Titles:
EBERBACHER ZEITUNG

NECKAR-VERLAG GMBH
678255
Klosterring 1, 78050 VILLINGEN-SCHWENNINGEN **Tel:** 7721 89870
Fax: 7721 898750
Email: info@neckar-verlag.de
Web site: http://www.neckar-verlag.de

Titles:
BRANDHILFE - AUSG. BADEN-WÜRTTEMBERG
ELEKTRO MODELL
KULTUS UND UNTERRICHT
MODELL
SCHIFFSMODELL
TU

NEON MAGAZIN GMBH 1691186
Am Baumwall 11, 20459 HAMBURG
Tel: 40 37030
Web site: http://www.neon.de

Titles:
NEON

NET VERLAGSSERVICE GMBH 686229
Baltzerstr. 30, 15569 WOLTERSDORF
Tel: 3362 75858 **Fax:** 3362 75857
Email: net@net-im-web.de
Web site: http://www.net-im-web.de

Titles:
NET

NETCOLOGNE GES. FÜR TELEKOMMUNIKATION MBH 1651559
Am Coloneum 9, 50829 KÖLN **Tel:** 221 22220
Fax: 221 2222390
Email: onlineredaktion@netcologne.de
Web site: http://www.netcologne.de

Titles:
INTERNETCOLOGNE
KOELN.DE

NETMEDIAEUROPE DEUTSCHLAND GMBH 1741857
Karl-Theodor-Str. 55, 80803 MÜNCHEN
Tel: 89 3090450 **Fax:** 89 309045555

Titles:
ITESPRESSO.DE

NETWORK PRESS GERMANY GMBH 1757736
Kemptener Str. 2f, 86163 AUGSBURG
Tel: 821 66109326 **Fax:** 821 66109327
Email: ulrich.abele@allaboutsourcing.de
Web site: http://www.allaboutsourcing.de

Titles:
ALL ABOUT SOURCING

NEU & GIERIG MEDIEN GMBH 682208
Katharinenstr. 21, 04109 LEIPZIG
Tel: 341 1494045 **Fax:** 341 1494047
Email: buero@leipzig-frizz.de
Web site: http://www.leipzig-frizz.de

Titles:
FRIZZ
FRIZZ
FRIZZ

NEUE ANZEIGENBLATT VERLAGS GMBH & CO. KG 682596
Woltorfer Str. 118, 31224 PEINE
Tel: 5171 5069811 **Fax:** 5171 5069812
Email: anzeigen@peiner-woche.de

Titles:
GIFHORNER RUNDBLICK AM SONNTAG
NEUE PEINER WOCHE AM SONNTAG
SALZGITTER WOCHE AM SONNTAG
WOLFSBURGER RUNDBLICK AM SONNTAG

NEUE BILDPOST GMBH & CO. KG 686243
Lange Str. 335, 59067 HAMM **Tel:** 2381 940400
Fax: 2381 9404040
Email: kontakt@bildpost.de
Web site: http://www.bildpost.de

Titles:
NEUE BILDPOST

NEUE BUXTEHUDER VERLAGSGES. MBH 684664
Bahnhofstr. 46, 21614 BUXTEHUDE
Tel: 4161 50630 **Fax:** 4161 506344
Email: anz-bux@kreiszeitung.net
Web site: http://www.kreiszeitung.net

Titles:
KREISZEITUNG NEUE BUXTEHUDER WOCHENBLATT
KREISZEITUNG NEUE STADER WOCHENBLATT

NEUE DEUTSCHE SCHULE VERLAGSGES. MBH 686249
Nünningstr. 11, 45141 ESSEN **Tel:** 201 2940306
Fax: 201 2940314
Email: info@nds-verlag.de
Web site: http://www.nds-verlag.de

Titles:
NDS

NEUE KREIS-RUNDSCHAU GMBH 687914
Grabenstr. 14, 74405 GAILDORF **Tel:** 7971 95880
Fax: 7971 958822
Email: rundschau.redaktion@swp.de
Web site: http://www.rundschau-gaildorf.de

Titles:
RUNDSCHAU FÜR DEN SCHWÄBISCHEN WALD

NEUE MEDIENGES. ULM MBH 680308
Bayerstr. 16a, 80335 MÜNCHEN **Tel:** 89 741170
Fax: 89 74117101
Email: info@nmg.de
Web site: http://www.nmg.de

Titles:
COM!
DOTNETPRO
INTERNET WORLD BUSINESS
INTERNET WORLD BUSINESS GUIDE ONLINE WERBEPLANUNG
TELECOM HANDEL

NEUE OSNABRÜCKER ZEITUNG GMBH & CO. KG 679167
Große Str. 17, 49074 OSNABRÜCK **Tel:** 541 3100
Fax: 541 310696
Web site: http://www.noz.de

Titles:
BERSENBRÜCKER KREISBLATT
BRAMSCHER NACHRICHTEN
EMS-ZEITUNG
LINGENER TAGESPOST
MELLER KREISBLATT
MEPPENER TAGESPOST
NEUE OZ OSNABRÜCKER ZEITUNG
WITTLAGER KREISBLATT

NEUE PRESSE VERLAGS-GMBH 677724
Medienstr. 5, 94036 PASSAU **Tel:** 851 8020
Fax: 851 802256
Email: npv@vgp.de
Web site: http://www.vgp.de

Titles:
ALT-NEUÖTTINGER ANZEIGER
DER BAYERWALD-BOTE
BURGHAUSER ANZEIGER
DEGGENDORFER ZEITUNG
GRAFENAUER ANZEIGER
LANDAUER NEUE PRESSE
OSTERHOFENER ZEITUNG
PASSAUER NEUE PRESSE
PLATTLINGER ZEITUNG
ROTTALER ANZEIGER
VIECHTACHER BAYERWALD-BOTE
VILSHOFENER ANZEIGER

NEUE PRESSEGES. MBH & CO. KG 686545
Rosenstr. 24, 73033 GÖPPINGEN **Tel:** 7161 2040
Fax: 7161 204152
Email: kaufm.anzeigen-team@nwz.de
Web site: http://www.nwz.de

Titles:
NWZ GÖPPINGER KREISNACHRICHTEN
SÜDWEST PRESSE
ULMER WOCHENBLATT
WOCHENBLATT

NEUE PRESSEGES. MBH & CO. KG, VERLAGSBEREICH TAUBER-ZEITUNG 689234
Ledermarkt 8, 97980 BAD MERGENTHEIM
Tel: 7931 5960 **Fax:** 7931 59644
Email: info@tauber-zeitung.de
Web site: http://www.tauber-zeitung.de

Titles:
TAUBER-ZEITUNG
WOCHENBLATT DER TAUBER-ZEITUNG

DER NEUE TAG OBERPFÄLZISCHER KURIER DRUCK- UND VERLAGSHAUS GMBH 679642
Weigelstr. 16, 92637 WEIDEN **Tel:** 961 850
Fax: 961 418336
Web site: http://www.oberpfalznetz.de

Titles:
DER NEUE TAG

NEUE TÖNE W. MENDE VERLAGS OHG 680856
Am Haag 10, 97234 REICHENBERG
Tel: 931 69469 **Fax:** 931 69470
Email: info@doppelpunkt.de
Web site: http://www.doppelpunkt.de

Titles:
DOPPELPUNKT

NEUES DEUTSCHLAND DRUCKEREI UND VERLAG GMBH 686304
Franz-Mehring-Platz 1, 10243 BERLIN
Tel: 30 29781111 **Fax:** 30 29781600
Email: verlag@nd-online.de
Web site: http://www.neues-deutschland.de

Titles:
NEUES DEUTSCHLAND

NEUSSER DRUCKEREI UND VERLAG GMBH 684207
Moselstr. 14, 41464 NEUSS **Tel:** 2131 404133
Fax: 2131 404424
Web site: http://www.ndv.de

Titles:
DÜSSELDORF GEHT AUS!
FLORIAN HESSEN
IHK MAGAZIN
RHEINISCHES ZAHNÄRZTEBLATT
RHEINLANDS REITER+PFERDE
ZAHNÄRZTEBLATT WESTFALEN-LIPPE

NEUSTÄDTER VERLAG 1718375
Friedensallee 26, 22765 HAMBURG
Tel: 40 39908181 **Fax:** 40 39903182
Email: info@neustaedter.de
Web site: http://www.neustaedter.de

Titles:
NEUSTÄDTER BERLIN
NEUSTÄDTER HAMBURG
NEUSTÄDTER KÖLN
NEUSTÄDTER MÜNCHEN

NEUTRALES GRAU AGENTUR FÜR KOMMUNIKATION & VERLAGSGESELLSCHAFT UG 1783424
Chausseestr. 104, 10115 BERLIN
Tel: 30 40005668
Email: info@neutralesgrau.de
Web site: http://www.bold-magazine.eu

Titles:
BOLD

NEW BUSINESS VERLAG GMBH & CO. KG 686362
Nebendahlstr. 16, 22041 HAMBURG
Tel: 40 6090090 **Fax:** 40 60900915
Email: info@new-business.de
Web site: http://www.new-business.de

Titles:
CP MONITOR
MARKENARTIKEL
MEDIENWIRTSCHAFT
NEW BUSINESS
PUBLIC MARKETING
RED BOX
TRANSFER

NEW LOOK ELECTRONIC PUBLISHING GMBH 1651463
Hans-Pinsel-Str. 10a, 85540 HAAR
Tel: 89 4623700 **Fax:** 89 466096
Email: mail@newlook.de
Web site: http://www.auto-news.de

Titles:
AUTO NEWS

NEW MEDIA MAGAZINE VERLAG GMBH 684944
Dietlindenstr. 18, 80802 MÜNCHEN
Tel: 89 36888180 **Fax:** 89 36888181
Email: mail@largeformat.de
Web site: http://www.largeformat.de

Titles:
LARGE FORMAT

NEWS AKTUELL GMBH 686160
Mittelweg 144, 20148 HAMBURG
Tel: 40 41132850 **Fax:** 40 41132876
Email: info@newsaktuell.de
Web site: http://www.newsaktuell.de

Titles:
NA NEWSLETTER

NEWS STADTMAGAZIN GMBH & CO. KG 686370
Ritterstr. 16, 32423 MINDEN **Tel:** 571 828550
Fax: 571 8285510
Email: redaktion@news-dasmagazin.de
Web site: http://www.news-dasmagazin.de

Titles:
NEWS

NFM-VERLAG 686404
Wilhelm-Giese-Str. 26, 27616 BEVERSTEDT
Tel: 4747 87410 **Fax:** 4747 8741222
Email: info@nfm-verlag.de
Web site: http://www.nfm-verlag.de

Titles:
NFM NUTZFAHRZEUGEMANAGEMENT

NICOLAISCHE VERLAGSBUCHHANDLUNG GMBH 1744426
Neue Grünstr. 17, 10179 BERLIN **Tel:** 30 2537380
Fax: 30 25373839
Email: info@nicolai-verlag.de
Web site: http://www.nicolai-verlag.de

Titles:
DER ARCHITEKT

NIEDERSÄCHSISCHER LANDESBETRIEB FÜR WASSERWIRTSCHAFT, KÜSTEN- UND NATURSCHUTZ 683696
Göttinger Chaussee 76a, 30453 HANNOVER
Tel: 511 30343305 **Fax:** 511 30343501
Email: naturschutzinformation@nlwkn-h.niedersachsen.de
Web site: http://www.nlwkn.niedersachsen.de

Titles:
INFORMATIONSDIENST NATURSCHUTZ NIEDERSACHSEN

NISSAN CENTER EUROPE GMBH 1606077
Renault-Nissan-Str. 6, 50321 BRÜHL
Tel: 2232 570 **Fax:** 2232 572801
Web site: http://www.nissan.de

Titles:
NISSAN LIVE

NNN NORDDEUTSCHE NEUESTE NACHRICHTEN GMBH 1777081
Bergstr. 10, 18057 ROSTOCK **Tel:** 381 491168706
Fax: 381 491168705
Email: nnn@nnn.de
Web site: http://www.nnn.de

Titles:
NORDDEUTSCHE NEUESTE NACHRICHTEN

NOMOS VERLAGSGES. MBH + CO. KG 678269
Waldseestr. 3, 76530 BADEN-BADEN
Tel: 7221 21040 **Fax:** 7221 210427
Email: nomos@nomos.de
Web site: http://www.nomos.de

Titles:
BLÄTTER DER WOHLFAHRTSPFLEGE
GESUNDHEITS- UND SOZIALPOLITIK
KOMMJUR
KRITISCHE JUSTIZ
M&K MEDIEN & KOMMUNIKATIONSWISSENSCHAFT
NJ NEUE JUSTIZ
NK NEUE KRIMINALPOLITIK
NORDÖR ZEITSCHRIFT FÜR ÖFFENTLICHES RECHT IN NORDDEUTSCHLAND
PVS POLITISCHE VIERTELJAHRESSCHRIFT
SOZIALWIRTSCHAFT
SOZIALWIRTSCHAFT AKTUELL
SOZW SOZIALE WELT
SVR STRASSENVERKEHRSRECHT
ZAR ZEITSCHRIFT FÜR AUSLÄNDERRECHT UND AUSLÄNDERPOLITIK
ZÖGU ZEITSCHRIFT FÜR ÖFFENTLICHE UND GEMEINWIRTSCHAFTLICHE UNTERNEHMEN
ZUM ZEITSCHRIFT FÜR URHEBER- UND MEDIENRECHT
ZUR ZEITSCHRIFT FÜR UMWELTRECHT

NORDBAYERISCHE ANZEIGENVERWALTUNG GMBH 688539
Marienstr. 11, 90402 NÜRNBERG **Tel:** 911 2160
Fax: 911 2162970
Email: blitzwerbung@pressenetz.de
Web site: http://www.nordbayern.de

Titles:
SONNTAGSBLITZ

NORDBAYERISCHE VERLAGSGES. MBH 686548
Marienstr. 9, 90402 NÜRNBERG **Tel:** 911 23510
Fax: 911 23512000
Email: nz-redaktion@pressenetz.de
Web site: http://www.nz-online.de

Titles:
NZ NORDBAYERISCHE ZEITUNG
NZ NÜRNBERGER ZEITUNG

NORDBAYERISCHER KURIER GMBH & CO. ZEITUNGSVERLAG KG
686469
Theodor-Schmidt-Str. 17, 95448 BAYREUTH
Tel: 921 2940 **Fax:** 921 294107
Email: verlag@kurier.tmt.de
Web site: http://www.nordbayerischer-kurier.de

Titles:
NORDBAYERISCHER KURIER

DER NORD-BERLINER ZEITUNG UND ZEITSCHRIFTEN VERLAG GMBH
1650206
Hermsdorfer Damm 149, 13467 BERLIN
Tel: 30 41909160 **Fax:** 30 41909156
Email: redaktion@nord-berliner.de
Web site: http://www.nord-berliner.de

Titles:
DER NORD-BERLINER

NORDDEUTSCHE VERLAGSGES. MBH
682298
Schaarsteinweg 14, 20459 HAMBURG
Tel: 40 37034363 **Fax:** 40 37034362
Web site: http://www.gala.de

Titles:
GALA
GALA MEN
GALA STYLE

NORDIS VERLAG GMBH
1738816
Maxstr. 64, 45127 ESSEN **Tel:** 201 872290
Fax: 201 8942511
Email: verlag@nordis.com
Web site: http://www.nordis.com

Titles:
NORDIS
REISEHANDBUCH SKANDINAVIEN

NORDMETALL VERBAND DER METALL- UND ELEKTROINDUSTRIE E.V.
688870
Kapstadtring 10, 22297 HAMBURG
Tel: 40 63784231 **Fax:** 40 63784234
Email: haas@nordmetall.de
Web site: http://www.nordmetall.de

Titles:
STANDPUNKTE

NORDSEE-TOURISMUS-SERVICE GMBH
1739743
Zingel 5, 25813 HUSUM **Tel:** 4841 897575
Fax: 4841 4843
Email: info@nordseetourismus.de
Web site: http://www.nordseetourismus.de

Titles:
NORDSEE* URLAUBSMAGAZIN

NORDSEE-ZEITUNG GMBH
686415
Hafenstr. 140, 27576 BREMERHAVEN
Tel: 471 5970 **Fax:** 471 597551
Email: nzbremerhaven@nordsee-zeitung.de
Web site: http://www.nordsee-zeitung.de

Titles:
NORDSEE-ZEITUNG

NORDWEST-ZEITUNG VERLAGSGES. MBH & CO. KG
683750
Peterstr. 28, 26121 OLDENBURG **Tel:** 441 998801
Fax: 441 99889966
Web site: http://www.nwzonline.de

Titles:
MEER & FLAIR
NORDWEST ZEITUNG
NWZ ONLINE

NÓVÉ-MEDIENVERLAG
690904
Mendelssohnstr. 3, 04109 LEIPZIG
Tel: 341 2122124 **Fax:** 341 2111118
Email: info@zeitpunkt-kulturmagazin.de
Web site: http://www.zeitpunkt-kulturmagazin.de

Titles:
ZEITPUNKT
ZEITPUNKT HOTEL- UND GASTRONOMIEFÜHRER

NRW.JETZT VERLAG GMBH
1770692
Max-Planck-Str. 6, 50858 KÖLN
Tel: 2234 91177662 **Fax:** 2234 91177667
Email: info@nrwjetzt.de
Web site: http://www.nrwjetzt.de

Titles:
NRW.JETZT

NUMOV NAH- UND MITTELOST-VEREIN E.V.
695190
Jägerstr. 63d, 10117 BERLIN **Tel:** 30 2064100
Fax: 30 20641010
Email: numov@numov.de
Web site: http://www.numov.de

Titles:
WIRTSCHAFTSFORUM NAH- UND MITTELOST

NÜRNBERGMESSE GMBH
1741720
Messezentrum, 90471 NÜRNBERG
Tel: 911 86068330 **Fax:** 911 86068580
Web site: http://www.mailingtage.de

Titles:
MAILINGTAGE [NEWS]

NWB VERLAG GMBH & CO. KG
678955
Eschstr. 22, 44629 HERNE **Tel:** 2323 141900
Fax: 2323 141123
Web site: http://www.nwb.de

Titles:
BETRIEBSWIRTSCHAFTLICHE FORSCHUNG UND PRAXIS BFUP
DIE BUCHFÜHRUNG
ERBEN + VERMÖGEN
DIE GROSSHANDELSKAUFLEUTE
DIE INDUSTRIEKAUFLEUTE
DIE MEDIZINISCHE FACHANGESTELLTE
NWB INTERNATIONALES STEUER- UND WIRTSCHAFTSRECHT IWB
NWB RECHNUNGSWESEN BBK
NWB STEUER- UND WIRTSCHAFTSRECHT
NWB UNTERNEHMENSTEUERN UND BILANZEN STUB
DIE RECHTSANWALTS- UND NOTARFACHANGESTELLTEN
STEUER + STUDIUM
DIE STEUERFACHANGESTELLTEN
DIE ZAHNMEDIZINISCHE FACHANGESTELLTE

NWN NEBENWERTE NACHRICHTEN AG
696932
Leibstr. 61, 85540 HAAR **Tel:** 89 43571171
Fax: 89 43571381
Email: info@nebenwerte-journal.de
Web site: http://www.nebenwerte-journal.de

Titles:
NEBENWERTE JOURNAL

OBERBADISCHES VERLAGSHAUS GEORG JAUMANN GMBH + CO. KG
679962
Am Alten Markt 2, 79539 LÖRRACH
Tel: 7621 40330 **Fax:** 7621 403383
Email: info@verlagshaus-jaumann.de
Web site: http://www.die-oberbadische.de

Titles:
MARKGRÄFLER TAGBLATT
DIE OBERBADISCHE
WEILER ZEITUNG

OBERBAYERISCHES VOLKSBLATT GMBH & CO. MEDIENHAUS KG
680147
Hafnerstr. 5, 83022 ROSENHEIM **Tel:** 8031 2130
Fax: 8031 213236
Email: chefsekretariat@ovb.net
Web site: http://www.ovb-online.de

Titles:
CHIEMGAU-ZEITUNG
MANGFALL BOTE
MÜHLDORFER ANZEIGER
NEUMARKTER ANZEIGER
OBERBAYERISCHES VOLKSBLATT
WALDKRAIBURGER NACHRICHTEN
WASSERBURGER ZEITUNG

OBERMAIN-TAGBLATT MEISTER DRUCK GOTTLOB MEISTER OHG
677986
Hirtenstr. 5, 96215 LICHTENFELS
Tel: 9571 95050 **Fax:** 9571 950561
Email: technik@obermain.de
Web site: http://www.obermain.de

Titles:
OBERMAIN-TAGBLATT

OBSTBAUVERSUCHSRING DES ALTEN LANDES E.V.
685769
Moorende 53, 21635 JORK **Tel:** 4162 6016154
Fax: 4162 6016600
Email: redaktion@esteburg-jork.de
Web site: http://www.esteburg-jork.de

Titles:
MITTEILUNGEN DES OBSTBAUVERSUCHSRINGES DES ALTEN LANDES E.V. AN DER ESTEBURG - OBSTBAUZENTRUM JORK

DER ODERLANDSPIEGEL VERLAGSGES. MBH
686604
Rosa-Luxemburg-Str. 42, 15230 FRANKFURT
Tel: 335 558990 **Fax:** 335 55899107
Email: kontakt@der-oderland-spiegel.de
Web site: http://www.der-oderland-spiegel.de

Titles:
DER ODERLANDSPIEGEL - REG.-AUSG. FRANKFURT (ODER)/LANDKREIS MÄRK.-ODERLAND

OEKOM VERLAG GES. FÜR ÖKOLOGISCHE KOMMUNIKATION MBH
1650922
Waltherstr. 29, 80337 MÜNCHEN **Tel:** 89 5441840
Fax: 89 54418449
Email: kontakt@oekom.de
Web site: http://www.oekom.de

Titles:
GAIA
NATIONALPARK
ÖKOLOGISCHES WIRTSCHAFTEN
POLITISCHE ÖKOLOGIE
UMWELT AKTUELL
DER UMWELT BEAUFTRAGTE

OEMUS MEDIA AG
678210
Holbeinstr. 29, 04229 LEIPZIG **Tel:** 341 484740
Fax: 341 48474290
Email: kontakt@oemus-media.de
Web site: http://www.oemus-media.de

Titles:
DENTALZEITUNG
ZWP ZAHNARZT WIRTSCHAFT PRAXIS

OFF ONE'S ROCKER PUBLISHING LTD.
1762928
Strelitzer Str. 2, 10115 BERLIN **Tel:** 30 28884043
Fax: 30 28884044
Email: info@off-ones-rocker.de
Web site: http://www.off-ones-rocker.de

Titles:
INTERSECTION

OFF ROAD VERLAG AG
686745
Alte Landstr. 21, 85521 OTTOBRUNN
Tel: 89 608210 **Fax:** 89 60821200
Email: zentrale@off-road.de
Web site: http://www.off-road.de

Titles:
OFF ROAD
OFF ROAD SPECIAL ALLRADKATALOG
OFF ROAD SPECIAL TESTJAHRBUCH

OK! VERLAG GMBH & CO. KG
1744666
Gänsemarkt 24, 20354 HAMBURG
Tel: 40 4118825101 **Fax:** 40 4118825102
Email: info@ok-magazin.de
Web site: http://www.ok-magazin.de

Titles:
OK!

ÖKO-INSTITUT E.V.
686632
Merzhauser Str. 173, 79100 FREIBURG
Tel: 761 452950 **Fax:** 761 4529588
Email: redaktion@oeko.de
Web site: http://www.oeko.de

Titles:
ECO@WORK

ÖKO-TEST VERLAG GMBH
686637
Kasseler Str. 1a, 60486 FRANKFURT
Tel: 69 977770 **Fax:** 69 97777139
Email: verlag@oekotest.de
Web site: http://www.oekotest.de

Titles:
ÖKO TEST
ÖKO TEST

ÖKOZENTRUM BONN E.V.
679594
Hatschiergasse 2, 53111 BONN **Tel:** 228 692220
Fax: 228 9768615
Email: umwelt@oez-bonn.de
Web site: http://www.oez-bonn.de

Titles:
BONNER UMWELT ZEITUNG

OLDENBOURG INDUSTRIEVERLAG GMBH
1759155
Rosenheimer Str. 145, 81671 MÜNCHEN
Tel: 89 450510 **Fax:** 89 45051207
Email: oiv-info@oldenbourg.de
Web site: http://www.oldenbourg-industrieverlag.de

Titles:
ATP EDITION
EB ELEKTRISCHE BAHNEN
GAS
GI GESUNDHEITS INGENIEUR
GWF GAS ERDGAS
GWF WASSER ABWASSER

OLDENBOURG SCHULBUCHVERLAG GMBH
681958
Rosenheimer Str. 145, 81671 MÜNCHEN
Tel: 89 450510 **Fax:** 89 45051310
Web site: http://www.oldenbourg-bsv.de

Titles:
FÖRDER MAGAZIN
GRUNDSCHULMAGAZIN
GRUNDSCHULUNTERRICHT
KLEIN & GROSS
PRAXIS FREMDSPRACHENUNTERRICHT
SCHULMAGAZIN 5 BIS 10
SCHUL-MANAGEMENT

OLDENBOURG WISSENSCHAFTSVERLAG GMBH
678036
Rosenheimer Str. 145, 81671 MÜNCHEN
Tel: 89 450510 **Fax:** 89 45051207
Email: vertrieb-zs@oldenbourg.de
Web site: http://www.oldenbourg-verlag.de

Titles:
IT INFORMATION TECHNOLOGY
TM TECHNISCHES MESSEN

OLDENBURGISCHE VOLKSZEITUNG DRUCKEREI UND VERLAG GMBH + CO. KG
684841
Neuer Markt 2, 49377 VECHTA **Tel:** 4441 95600
Fax: 4441 9560310
Email: info@ov-online.de
Web site: http://www.ov-online.de

Titles:
OLDENBURGISCHE VOLKSZEITUNG

OLYMPIA-VERLAG GMBH
677691
Badstr. 4, 90402 NÜRNBERG **Tel:** 911 2160
Fax: 911 2162204
Email: info@olympia-verlag.de
Web site: http://www.olympia-verlag.de

Titles:
ALPIN
KICKER ONLINE
KICKER SPORTMAGAZIN
UNTERWASSER
UNTERWASSER.DE

OLZOG VERLAG GMBH
679154
Welserstr. 1, 81373 MÜNCHEN **Tel:** 89 71046664
Fax: 89 71046661
Email: coachingbriefe@olzog.de
Web site: http://www.birkenbihlbrief.de

Titles:
DER VERA F. BIRKENBIHL-BRIEF

OMNIMED VERLAGSGES. MBH
680577
Borsteler Chaussee 85, Haus 16, 22453 HAMBURG **Tel:** 40 232334 **Fax:** 40 230292
Email: info@omnimedonline.de
Web site: http://www.omnimedonline.de

Titles:
DERM
FORUM
GYN
PÄD

OPERNGLAS VERLAGSGES. MBH 686791
Grelckstr. 36, 22529 HAMBURG **Tel:** 40 585501
Fax: 40 585505
Email: info@opernglas.de
Web site: http://www.opernglas.de

Titles:
DAS OPERNGLAS

OPS NETZWERK GMBH 1621055
Melscher Str. 1, 04299 LEIPZIG **Tel:** 341 2406100
Fax: 341 2406166
Email: info@op-pt.de
Web site: http://www.pt-magazin.de

Titles:
P.T. MAGAZIN FÜR WIRTSCHAFT UND POLITIK

ORA OSTRUHR ANZEIGENBLATTGES. MBH & CO. KG 680216
Bert-Brecht-Str. 29, 45128 ESSEN
Tel: 201 8042836 **Fax:** 201 8041857
Email: ora@ora-anzeigenblaetter.de
Web site: http://www.ora-anzeigenblaetter.de

Titles:
STADT ANZEIGER CITY-ANZEIGER
STADT ANZEIGER NORD-ANZEIGER
STADT ANZEIGER OST-ANZEIGER
STADT ANZEIGER SÜD-ANZEIGER
STADT ANZEIGER WEST-ANZEIGER

ORANGE-P GMBH 682881
Max-Planck-Ring 45, 65205 WIESBADEN
Tel: 6122 70740 **Fax:** 6122 707410
Email: info@hailights.de
Web site: http://www.hailights.de

Titles:
HAI-LIGHTS

ORNITHOLOGENVERBAND SACHSEN-ANHALT E.V. 678224
Postfach 730107, 06045 HALLE
Web site: http://www.osa-internet.de

Titles:
APUS

ORSCHEL VERLAG GMBH 680294
Malvenweg 4, 51061 KÖLN **Tel:** 221 9635640
Fax: 221 96356427
Email: orschel-verlag@orschel-verlag.de
Web site: http://www.orschel-verlag.de

Titles:
GERMANY PARTNER OF THE WORLD

OS TECHNOLOGY RESEARCH INSTITUT FÜR TECHNOLOGIETRANSFER UND INNOVATIONSENTWICKLUNG GMBH 1720402
Dillwächterstr. 4, 80686 MÜNCHEN
Tel: 89 76900352 **Fax:** 89 76900359
Email: redaktion@university-journal.de
Web site: http://www.university-journal.de

Titles:
UNIVERSITYJOURNAL

OSTFRIESISCHE NACHRICHTEN GMBH 686848
Kirchstr. 8, 26603 AURICH **Tel:** 4941 17080
Fax: 4941 170813
Email: on-info@on-online.de
Web site: http://www.on-online.de

Titles:
OSTFRIESISCHE NACHRICHTEN

OSTFRIESISCHER KURIER GMBH & CO. KG 1759094
Stellmacherstr. 14, 26506 NORDEN
Tel: 4931 9250 **Fax:** 4931 925360
Email: verlag@skn.info
Web site: http://www.skn.info

Titles:
OSTFRIESISCHER KURIER

OSTSEE-ZEITUNG GMBH & CO. KG 686857
Richard-Wagner-Str. 1a, 18055 ROSTOCK
Tel: 381 3650 **Fax:** 381 365302
Email: redaktion@ostsee-zeitung.de
Web site: http://www.ostsee-zeitung.de

Titles:
OSTSEE ZEITUNG

OTTO FUCHS KG 682231
Derschlager Str. 26, 58540 MEINERZHAGEN
Tel: 2354 73580 **Fax:** 2354 73201
Email: fuchsbau@otto-fuchs.com
Web site: http://www.otto-fuchs.com

Titles:
FUCHSBAU

OTTO HOFFMANNS VERLAG GMBH 677380
Arnulfstr. 10, 80335 MÜNCHEN **Tel:** 89 5458450
Fax: 89 54584530
Email: media@ohv-online.de
Web site: http://www.ohv-online.de

Titles:
ÄRZTLICHES JOURNAL REISE & MEDIZIN
ÄRZTLICHES JOURNAL REISE & MEDIZIN NEUROLOGIE/PSYCHIATRIE
ÄRZTLICHES JOURNAL REISE & MEDIZIN ONKOLOGIE
ÄRZTLICHES JOURNAL REISE & MEDIZIN ORTHOPÄDIE/RHEUMATOLOGIE

OTZ-OSTTHÜRINGER ZEITUNG VERLAG GMBH & CO. KG 686859
Alte Str. 3, 04626 LÖBICHAU **Tel:** 3447 525901
Fax: 3447 525904
Email: verlag@otz.de
Web site: http://www.otz.de

Titles:
OSTTHÜRINGER ZEITUNG OTZ
OTZ.DE OSTTHÜRINGER ZEITUNG
SCHMÖLLNER NACHRICHTEN

OUT+PUT AGENTUR & VERLAGS GMBH 1615894
Henkersgraben 42, 89073 ULM **Tel:** 731 800090
Fax: 731 8000920
Email: info@frizz-ulm.de
Web site: http://www.frizz-ulm.de

Titles:
FRIZZ - AUSG. ULM

OVB PUBLISHING GMBH 698057
Von-Boch-Str. 1, 66679 LOSHEIM **Tel:** 6836 8070
Web site: http://www.brigittevonbochliving.de

Titles:
LIVING BRIGITTE VON BOCH

OWC-VERLAG FÜR AUSSENWIRTSCHAFT GMBH 680153
Regenskamp 18, 48157 MÜNSTER
Tel: 251 9243090 **Fax:** 251 92430999
Email: info@owc.de
Web site: http://www.owc.de

Titles:
CHINA CONTACT
GERMANYCONTACT INDIA
INDIENCONTACT
JAPAN CONTACT
KOREA CONTACT
OSTIAUSSCHUSS INFORMATIONEN
OST-WEST CONTACT
TAIWAN CONTACT

OWZ OBERPFÄLZER WOCHENZEITUNGS-VERLAG GMBH 686578
Weigelstr. 16, 92637 WEIDEN **Tel:** 961 850
Fax: 961 42003

Titles:
OBERPFÄLZER WOCHENZEITUNG OWZ
WOCHENBLATT - AUSG. WEIDEN/ NEUSTADT

OXO-MEDIA, ECKERT-MEINOLD, FIEBIG, MEYER-ADLER GBR 1773052
Neuer Kamp 25, 20359 HAMBURG
Tel: 40 8797659 **Fax:** 40 879765920
Email: info@inshoes-online.de
Web site: http://www.inshoes-online.de

Titles:
IN SHOES

OZ-LOKALZEITUNGS-VERLAG GMBH 1644537
Markt 25, 18528 BERGEN **Tel:** 3838 2014811
Fax: 3838 2014812

Titles:
URLAUBS LOTSE

OZ-VERLAGS-GMBH 678099
Römerstr. 90, 79618 RHEINFELDEN
Tel: 7623 9640 **Fax:** 7623 964200
Email: info@oz-verlag.de
Web site: http://www.oz-verlag.de

Titles:
BACKEN LEICHT GEMACHT
BACKEN-AKTUELL
BASTEL-SPASS
CREATIV-IDEE
DEKORATIVES HÄKELN
DIANA MODEN
FILETHÄKELN LEICHT GEMACHT
DIE KLEINE DIANA
KOCHEN LEICHT GEMACHT
KOCHEN MIT LIEBE
LEA SPECIAL BASTELN
LECKERES AUS OMAS KÜCHE
LENA
SABRINA
SABRINA WOMAN
SANDRA
STRICKTRENDS

P3 PRINTMEDIEN VERLAGSGES. GBR 678338
Eulerweg 11, 64291 DARMSTADT
Tel: 6151 9515247 **Fax:** 6151 9515249
Email: info@printdesign24.de
Web site: http://www.arheilger-post.de

Titles:
ERZHÄUSER ANZEIGER

P. KEPPLER VERLAG GMBH & CO. KG 678219
Industriestr. 2, 63150 HEUSENSTAMM
Tel: 6104 6060 **Fax:** 6104 606336
Email: info@kepplermediengruppe.de
Web site: http://www.kepplermediengruppe.de

Titles:
APR AKTUELLE PAPIER-RUNDSCHAU
PHARMA RUNDSCHAU
VR. VERPACKUNGS-RUNDSCHAU

PABEL-MOEWIG VERLAG GMBH 678616
Karlsruher Str. 31, 76437 RASTATT **Tel:** 7222 130
Fax: 7222 13351
Email: mail@vpm.de
Web site: http://www.vpm.de

Titles:
AVANTI
LISSY.DE
MACH MAL PAUSE
MEIN LEBEN
MEINE MELODIE
MINI
MINI EXTRA
PERRY RHODAN HOMEPAGE
ROLF KAUKAS BUSSI BÄR
ROMANWOCHE
SCHÖNE WOCHE
WAHRE GESCHICHTEN
WOCHE HEUTE

PABST SCIENCE PUBLISHERS 680281
Eichengrund 28, 49525 LENGERICH
Tel: 5484 308 **Fax:** 5484 550
Email: pabst.publishers@t-online.de
Web site: http://www.pabst-publishers.de

Titles:
AKTUELLE NEPHROLOGIE
APPLIED CARDIOPULMONARY PATHOPHYSIOLOGY
ENTSPANNUNGSVERFAHREN
FORENSISCHE PSYCHIATRIE UND PSYCHOTHERAPIE
JOURNAL FÜR ANÄSTHESIE UND INTENSIVBEHANDLUNG
PRAXIS KLINISCHE VERHALTENSMEDIZIN UND REHABILITATION
TRANSPLANTATIONSMEDIZIN
WIRTSCHAFTSPSYCHOLOGIE

PACS GMBH VERLAG 679993
Gewerbestr. 9, 79219 STAUFEN **Tel:** 7633 933200
Fax: 7633 9332020
Email: pacs@pacs-online.com
Web site: http://www.pacs-online.com

Titles:
BUS TOURIST
GESUNDE MEDIZIN
JOURNAL FÜR DIE APOTHEKE
PRAXIS MAGAZIN

PÄDAGOGIK & HOCHSCHUL VERLAG DPHV-VERLAGSGES. MBH 679329
Graf-Adolf-Str. 84, 40210 DÜSSELDORF
Tel: 211 3558104 **Fax:** 211 3558095
Email: dassow@dphv-verlag.de
Web site: http://www.dphv-verlag.de

Titles:
PROFIL

PAGE VERLAG, EBNER VERLAG GMBH & CO. KG 1731972
Borselstr. 28/i, 22765 HAMBURG
Tel: 40 85183400 **Fax:** 40 85183449
Email: info@page-online.de
Web site: http://www.page-online.de

Titles:
PAGE

PALI DEUTSCHLAND GMBH 1687049
Im Mediapark 4d, 50670 KÖLN **Tel:** 221 420400
Fax: 221 42040444
Email: info@kontaktchance.de
Web site: http://www.kontaktchance.de

Titles:
KONTAKT CHANCE

PALSTEK VERLAG GMBH 686893
Eppendorfer Weg 57a, 20259 HAMBURG
Tel: 40 40196340 **Fax:** 40 40196341
Email: info@palstek.de
Web site: http://www.palstek.de

Titles:
PALSTEK

PANINI VERLAGS GMBH 678792
Rotebühlstr. 87, 70178 STUTTGART
Tel: 711 947680 **Fax:** 711 9476830
Email: info@panini.de
Web site: http://www.panini.de

Titles:
BOB DER BAUMEISTER
CARD MASTER
HEY!
JESSY
JUST KICK-IT!
MAD
MEGA HIRO
PETTERSSON UND FINDUS
PFERDE FREUNDE FÜRS LEBEN
PUMUCKL MAGAZIN
SESAMSTRASSE
SIMPSONS COMICS
TIERE FREUNDE FÜRS LEBEN

PANORAMA VERLAGS- UND WERBEGES. MBH 677681
Sudbrackstr. 14, 33611 BIELEFELD **Tel:** 521 5850
Fax: 521 585480
Email: wb@westfalen-blatt.de
Web site: http://www.westfalen-blatt.de

Titles:
BAD DRIBURG AKTUELL
BRAKEL ERLEBEN
HUXARIA EXTRA

PAPIERFABRIK AUGUST KOEHLER AG 684499
Hauptstr. 2, 77704 OBERKIRCH **Tel:** 7802 810
Fax: 7802 814330
Email: ruth.karcher@koehlerpaper.com
Web site: http://www.koehlerpaper.com

Titles:
KOEHLER RUNDSCHAU

PAPYROSSA VERLAG 682096
Luxemburger Str. 202, 50937 KÖLN
Tel: 221 448545 **Fax:** 221 444305
Email: mail@papyrossa.de
Web site: http://www.papyrossa.de

Titles:
WIR FRAUEN

PARADOKX VERLAG GMBH 1732264
Bayerstr. 38, 53332 BORNHEIM **Tel:** 2222 952213
Fax: 2222 952111
Email: info@paradokx.de
Web site: http://www.paradokx.de

Titles:
LA CUCINA ITALIANA

PARAGON VERLAGSGES. MBH & CO. KG 686427
Misburger Str. 119, 30625 HANNOVER
Tel: 511 56059930 **Fax:** 511 56059939
Email: info@paragon.de
Web site: http://www.reitsport-magazin.de

Titles:
REITSPORT MAGAZIN

PARTNER MEDIEN VERLAGS- UND BETEILIGUNGS GMBH
1651226
Julius-Hölder-Str. 47, 70597 STUTTGART
Tel: 711 7252229 **Fax:** 711 7252320
Email: info@partnermedienverlag.de
Web site: http://www.partnermedienverlag.de

Titles:
PATCHWORK MAGAZIN

PASSAUER BISTUMSBLATT GMBH
686951
Domplatz 3, 94032 PASSAU **Tel:** 851 3931323
Fax: 851 31893
Email: alois.poeschl@bistum-passau.de
Web site: http://www.passauer-bistumsblatt.de

Titles:
PASSAUER BISTUMSBLATT

PATRICK SCHAAB PR
689198
Luisenstr. 88, 53721 SIEGBURG **Tel:** 2241 66115
Fax: 2241 67862
Email: redaktion@take-online.de
Web site: http://www.take-online.de

Titles:
TAKE!

PATZER VERLAG GMBH & CO. KG
678867
Koenigsallee 65, 14193 BERLIN **Tel:** 30 8959030
Fax: 30 89590317
Email: info@patzerverlag.de
Web site: http://www.patzerverlag.de

Titles:
ABZ ALLGEMEINE BAUZEITUNG
GARTEN & FREIZEITMARKT
HANDELS MAGAZIN
JAHRBUCH GARTEN- UND LANDSCHAFTSBAU
NEUE LANDSCHAFT
STADT + GRÜN

PAUL PAREY ZEITSCHRIFTENVERLAG GMBH & CO. KG
680609
Erich-Kästner-Str. 2, 56379 SINGHOFEN
Tel: 2604 9780 **Fax:** 2604 978190
Email: online@paulparey.de
Web site: http://www.paulparey.de

Titles:
DEUTSCHE JAGD ZEITUNG
FISCH & FANG
JAGEN WELTWEIT
DER RAUBFISCH
REITER REVUE INTERNATIONAL
WEIDWERK IN MECKLENBURG VORPOMMERN
WILD UND HUND

PAULINUS VERLAG GMBH
685138
Maximineracht 11c, 54295 TRIER **Tel:** 651 46080
Fax: 651 4608221
Email: verlag@paulinus.de
Web site: http://www.paulinus.de

Titles:
PAULINUS

PBL MEDIA VERLAG
1746025
Meisenstr. 96, 33607 BIELEFELD
Tel: 521 2997390 **Fax:** 521 2997391
Email: info@mawi-westfalen.de
Web site: http://www.mawi-westfalen.de

Titles:
MARKT & WIRTSCHAFT WESTFALEN

PCL MEDIEN & VERLAGS GMBH
1675338
Adams-Lehmann-Str. 61, 80797 MÜNCHEN
Tel: 89 32729990 **Fax:** 89 327299928
Email: pcl-verlag@porsche-club-life.de
Web site: http://www.porsche-club-deutschland.de

Titles:
PORSCHE CLUB LIFE

PEINER ALLGEMEINE ZEITUNG VERLAGSGES. MBH & CO. KG
686980
Werderstr. 49, 31224 PEINE **Tel:** 5171 4060
Fax: 5171 406159
Email: anzeigen@paz-online.de
Web site: http://www.paz-online.de

Titles:
PEINER ALLGEMEINE ZEITUNG

PEREGRINUS GMBH
1769617
Brunckstr. 17, 67346 SPEYER **Tel:** 6232 31830
Fax: 6232 32599
Email: verlag@pilger-druckerei.de

Titles:
DER PILGER

PERFORMANCE VERLAG GMBH
699854
Dr.-Gessler-Str. 16a, 93051 REGENSBURG
Tel: 941 465270270 **Fax:** 941 465270279
Email: info@performance-online.de
Web site: http://www.performance-online.de

Titles:
PERFORMANCE

PERLENTAUCHER MEDIEN GMBH
1652333
Eichendorffstr. 21, 10115 BERLIN
Tel: 30 40055830 **Fax:** 30 400558399
Email: service@perlentaucher.de
Web site: http://www.perlentaucher.de

Titles:
PERLENTAUCHER.DE

PERRY PUBLICATIONS GMBH
679987
Schulstr. 34, 80634 MÜNCHEN **Tel:** 89 13014320
Fax: 89 130143222
Email: bt@businesstraveller.de
Web site: http://www.businesstraveller.de

Titles:
BUSINESS TRAVELLER

PETER DIESLER
1652059
Holzgasse 29, 91781 WEISSENBURG
Tel: 9141 873949 **Fax:** 9141 874067
Email: pdiesler@journalismus.com
Web site: http://www.journalismus.com

Titles:
JOURNALISMUS.COM

PETER SCHOPPE VERLAG
679701
Walderseestr. 48, 30177 HANNOVER
Tel: 511 6262663 **Fax:** 511 90925022
Email: verlag@schoppe.de
Web site: http://www.schoppe.de

Titles:
BREMER ÄRZTE JOURNAL

PFALZ.MARKETING E.V.
1709961
Martin-Luther-Str. 69, 67433 NEUSTADT
Tel: 6321 912322 **Fax:** 6321 12881
Email: info@pfalz-marketing.de
Web site: http://www.pfalz-marketing.de

Titles:
PFALZCLUB MAGAZIN

PFEIFFER VERLAG UND MEDIENSERVICE GMBH & CO. KG
683184
Nürnberger Str. 7, 91217 HERSBRUCK
Tel: 9151 73070 **Fax:** 9151 2000
Email: verlag@hersbrucker-zeitung.de
Web site: http://www.hersbrucker-zeitung.de

Titles:
HERSBRUCKER ZEITUNG

PFERDESPORT-VERLAG EHLERS GMBH
686565
Rockwinkeler Landstr. 20, 28355 BREMEN
Tel: 421 2575544 **Fax:** 421 2575543
Email: info@pferdesportverlag.de
Web site: http://www.pferdesportverlag.de

Titles:
QUARTER HORSE JOURNAL

PHARMA-AKTUELL VERLAGSGRUPPE GMBH
1644600
Lehmweg 11, 26316 VAREL **Tel:** 4451 950395
Fax: 4451 950390
Email: info@pharma-aktuell-online.de
Web site: http://www.pharma-aktuell-online.de

Titles:
PHARMA-AKTUELL

PHARMAZEUTISCHER VERLAG DR. HORST BENAD
682932
Zinnkrautweg 24, 22359 HAMBURG
Tel: 40 6004860 **Fax:** 40 60048686
Email: info@benad-verlag.de
Web site: http://www.benad-verlag.de

Titles:
HAMBURGER ZAHNÄRZTEBLATT

PHILAPRESS-ZEITSCHRIFTEN- UND MEDIEN GMBH & CO. KG
679739
Benzstr. 1c, 37083 GÖTTINGEN **Tel:** 551 499050
Fax: 551 4990530
Email: info@philapress.de
Web site: http://www.philapress.de

Titles:
BRIEFMARKEN SPIEGEL
BRIEFMARKENPOST MIT MÜNZENPOST

PHILIPP AUG. WEINAUG VERLAG UND NEUE MEDIEN GMBH
680547
Bahnhofstr. 5, 30890 BARSINGHAUSEN
Tel: 5105 77070 **Fax:** 5105 770733
Email: redaktion@deister-leine-zeitung.de
Web site: http://www.deister-leine-zeitung.de

Titles:
DEISTER-LEINE-ZEITUNG

PHILIPPKA-SPORTVERLAG
680626
Rektoratsweg 36, 48159 MÜNSTER
Tel: 251 230050 **Fax:** 251 2300599
Email: info@philippka.de
Web site: http://www.philippka.de

Titles:
FUSSBALL TRAINING
HANDBALL TRAINING
HM
LEICHTATHLETIK TRAINING
LEISTUNGSSPORT
TISCHTENNIS
VOLLEYBALL MAGAZIN

PHOENIX PHARMAHANDEL GMBH & CO KG
695736
Pfingstweidstr. 10, 68199 MANNHEIM
Tel: 621 8505440 **Fax:** 621 8505599
Email: o.christiansen@phoenixgroup.eu
Web site: http://www.phoenixgroup.eu

Titles:
PHOENIX SPEZIAL - MAGAZIN IHRES PHOENIX VERTRIEBSZENTRUMS, AUSG. AUGSBURG
PHOENIX SPEZIAL - MAGAZIN IHRES PHOENIX VERTRIEBSZENTRUMS, AUSG. BAD KREUZNACH
PHOENIX SPEZIAL - MAGAZIN IHRES PHOENIX VERTRIEBSZENTRUMS, AUSG. BERLIN
PHOENIX SPEZIAL - MAGAZIN IHRES PHOENIX VERTRIEBSZENTRUMS, AUSG. BIELEFELD
PHOENIX SPEZIAL - MAGAZIN IHRES PHOENIX VERTRIEBSZENTRUMS, AUSG. COTTBUS
PHOENIX SPEZIAL - MAGAZIN IHRES PHOENIX VERTRIEBSZENTRUMS, AUSG. FREIBURG
PHOENIX SPEZIAL - MAGAZIN IHRES PHOENIX VERTRIEBSZENTRUMS, AUSG. FÜRTH
PHOENIX SPEZIAL - MAGAZIN IHRES PHOENIX VERTRIEBSZENTRUMS, AUSG. GOTHA
PHOENIX SPEZIAL - MAGAZIN IHRES PHOENIX VERTRIEBSZENTRUMS, AUSG. GÖTTINGEN
PHOENIX SPEZIAL - MAGAZIN IHRES PHOENIX VERTRIEBSZENTRUMS, AUSG. HAMBURG
PHOENIX SPEZIAL - MAGAZIN IHRES PHOENIX VERTRIEBSZENTRUMS, AUSG. HANAU
PHOENIX SPEZIAL - MAGAZIN IHRES PHOENIX VERTRIEBSZENTRUMS, AUSG. HANNOVER
PHOENIX SPEZIAL - MAGAZIN IHRES PHOENIX VERTRIEBSZENTRUMS, AUSG. KÖLN
PHOENIX SPEZIAL - MAGAZIN IHRES PHOENIX VERTRIEBSZENTRUMS, AUSG. LEIPZIG
PHOENIX SPEZIAL - MAGAZIN IHRES PHOENIX VERTRIEBSZENTRUMS, AUSG. MANNHEIM
PHOENIX SPEZIAL - MAGAZIN IHRES PHOENIX VERTRIEBSZENTRUMS, AUSG. MÜNCHEN
PHOENIX SPEZIAL - MAGAZIN IHRES PHOENIX VERTRIEBSZENTRUMS, AUSG. NEUHAUSEN
PHOENIX SPEZIAL - MAGAZIN IHRES PHOENIX VERTRIEBSZENTRUMS, AUSG. RUHR
PHOENIX SPEZIAL - MAGAZIN IHRES PHOENIX VERTRIEBSZENTRUMS, AUSG. WESER-EMS
TOP PRISMA

PHOTON EUROPE GMBH
687114
Jülicher Str. 376, 52070 AACHEN **Tel:** 241 40030
Fax: 241 4003300
Email: verlag@photon.de
Web site: http://www.photon.de

Titles:
PHOTON
PHOTON INTERNATIONAL

PHYSICA-VERLAG
677663
Tiergartenstr. 17, 69121 HEIDELBERG
Tel: 6221 4878492 **Fax:** 6221 4878177
Email: subscriptions@springer.com
Web site: http://www.springeronline.com

Titles:
CENTRAL EUROPEAN JOURNAL OF OPERATIONS RESEARCH
JOURNAL OF PLANNING AND CONTROL
MATHEMATICAL METHODS OF OPERATIONS RESEARCH

PIAG PRESSE INFORMATIONS AG
687119
Lothar-von-Kübel-Str. 18, 76547 SINZHEIM
Tel: 7221 3017560 **Fax:** 7221 3017570
Email: office@piag.de
Web site: http://www.piag.de

Titles:
VISUELL

PIRANHA MEDIA GMBH
684111
Sandstr. 3, 80335 MÜNCHEN **Tel:** 89 3077420
Fax: 89 30774233
Email: verlag@piranha-media.de
Web site: http://www.piranha-media.de

Titles:
JUICE
KING MAGAZINE
PIRANHA
SPEX

PISTE SCHWERIN VERLAG GMBH
1709605
Mecklenburgstr. 67, 19053 SCHWERIN
Tel: 385 7788631 **Fax:** 385 7788629
Email: schwerin@piste.de
Web site: http://www.piste-schwerin.de

Titles:
PISTE

PIXEL PRODUKTION
685994
Nirmerstr. 7, 52080 AACHEN **Tel:** 241 9519600
Fax: 241 9519601
Email: gb@kulturzone.net
Web site: http://www.moviebeta.de

Titles:
MOVIEBETA

PLAKART GMBH & CO. KG
1742867
Hönnestr. 45, 58809 NEUENRADE
Tel: 2394 61690 **Fax:** 2394 61691
Email: info@plakart.de
Web site: http://www.plakart.de

Titles:
BLICK PUNKT BALVE

PLANIMED GMBH GES. FÜR KOMMUNIKATION
1788393
Kiefernweg 6, 55291 SAULHEIM
Tel: 6732 6002873 **Fax:** 6732 6002874
Email: info@planimed-online.de
Web site: http://www.planimed-online.de

Titles:
GYNE

PLANUNGSGEMEINSCHAFT WESTPFALZ
1755675
Bahnhofstr. 1, 67655 KAISERSLAUTERN
Tel: 631 2057740 **Fax:** 631 20577420
Email: pgw@westpfalz.de
Web site: http://www.westpfalz.de

Titles:
WESTPFALZ-INFORMATIONEN

PLÄRRER VERLAGS GMBH
684887
Singerstr. 26, 90443 NÜRNBERG **Tel:** 911 424780
Fax: 911 4247899
Email: info@plaerrer.de
Web site: http://www.plaerrer.de

Titles:
PLÄRRER

DER PLATOW BRIEF, SPRINGER FACHMEDIEN WIESBADEN GMBH
687163
Stuttgarter Str. 25, 60329 FRANKFURT
Tel: 69 2426390 **Fax:** 69 236909
Email: info@platow.de
Web site: http://www.platow.de

Titles:
DER PLATOW BRIEF

PLAYBOY DEUTSCHLAND PUBLISHING GMBH 1603365
Arabellastr. 21, 81925 MÜNCHEN **Tel:** 89 92500
Fax: 89 92501220
Email: team@playboy.de
Web site: http://www.playboy.de

Titles:
PLAYBOY
PLAYBOY

PLAZA PUBLISHING GROUP DEUTSCHLAND 1677245
Kastanienallee 71, 10435 BERLIN
Tel: 30 61628115 **Fax:** 30 61628111
Email: berlin@plazamagazine.com
Web site: http://www.plazamagazine.com

Titles:
PLAZA MAGAZINE

PLUGGED MEDIA GMBH 683028
Franz-Haniel-Str. 20, 47443 MOERS
Tel: 2841 887760 **Fax:** 2841 8877629
Email: info@pluggedmedia.de
Web site: http://www.pluggedmedia.de

Titles:
MOBILE ZEIT

PMI PUBLISHING VERLAG GMBH & CO. KG 1639941
Hanns-Seidel-Platz 5, 81737 MÜNCHEN
Tel: 89 6427970 **Fax:** 89 64279777
Email: info@journal-international.de
Web site: http://www.pmi-publishing.de

Titles:
DINERS CLUB MAGAZIN
GESUNDHEITS JOURNAL

PN VERLAG DR. WOLF ZIMMERMANN 1639902
Leitenberg 5, 86923 FINNING **Tel:** 8806 95770
Fax: 8806 957711
Email: ktm@pn-verlag.de
Web site: http://www.pn-verlag.de

Titles:
KTM KRANKENHAUS TECHNIK + MANAGEMENT

POHL-VERLAG CELLE GMBH 680024
Herzog-Ernst-Ring 1, 29221 CELLE
Tel: 5141 98890 **Fax:** 5141 988922
Email: verlag@pohl-verlag.com
Web site: http://www.pohl-verlag.com

Titles:
NIEDERSÄCHSISCHE RECHTSPFLEGE

POLYGO VERLAG GMBH 1776245
Prinzenstr. 12, 30159 HANNOVER
Tel: 511 1699690 **Fax:** 511 16996921
Email: hallo@regjo.de
Web site: http://www.hannover.regjo.de

Titles:
NIEDERSACHSEN GLOBAL

POLYMEDIA PUBLISHER GMBH 1773590
Dammer Str. 112, 41066 MÖNCHENGLADBACH
Tel: 2161 6884469 **Fax:** 2161 6884468
Email: info@bioplasticsmagazine.com
Web site: http://www.bioplasticsmagazine.com

Titles:
BIOPLASTICS MAGAZINE.COM

PONT 9 WERBEAGENTUR GMBH 1741568
Untermainkai 29, 60329 FRANKFURT
Tel: 69 83831214 **Fax:** 69 83831212
Email: fashion@pont9.de
Web site: http://www.p9mag.de

Titles:
P9MAG

PORT MEDIA GMBH 680423
Senefelderstr. 14, 80336 MÜNCHEN
Tel: 89 7415090 **Fax:** 89 74150911
Email: info@portmedia.de
Web site: http://www.portmedia.de

Titles:
CRESCENDO

PORTFOLIO VERLAGSGESELLSCHAFT MBH 698639
Kleine Hochstr. 9, 60313 FRANKFURT
Tel: 69 85708112 **Fax:** 69 85708149
Email: kontakt@portfolio-verlag.com
Web site: http://www.portfolio-international.de

Titles:
PORTFOLIO INSTITUTIONELL
PORTFOLIO INTERNATIONAL

POS.NEWS 1640343
Auf dem Dattel 17, 56332 HATZENPORT
Tel: 2605 8499722 **Fax:** 2605 8499727
Email: info@posnews.de
Web site: http://www.posnews.de

Titles:
POS.NEWS

POTSDAMER ZEITUNGSVERLAGSGES. MBH & CO. KG 687251
Platz der Einheit 14, 14467 POTSDAM
Tel: 331 23760 **Fax:** 331 2376200
Web site: http://www.pnn.de

Titles:
POTSDAM AM SONNTAG
POTSDAMER NEUESTE NACHRICHTEN

PPI AG 1630540
Moorfuhrtweg 13, 22301 HAMBURG
Tel: 40 2274330 **Fax:** 40 227433333
Web site: http://www.ppi.de

Titles:
PPI FORUM

PPVMEDIEN GMBH 681625
Dachauer Str. 37b, 85232 BERGKIRCHEN
Tel: 8131 56550 **Fax:** 8131 565510
Email: info@ppvmedien.de
Web site: http://www.ppvmedien.de

Titles:
FLIEGER REVUE
GUITAR
KEYS
LPI LIGHTING PRESS INTERNATIONAL
PMA PRODUCTION MANAGEMENT
SOUNDCHECK

PR-CONSULT BERLIN 694648
Dernburgstr. 47, 14057 BERLIN **Tel:** 30 3213615
Fax: 30 3216558
Email: info@bonnesvacances.de
Web site: http://www.bonnesvacances.de

Titles:
BONNES VACANCES

PREMEDIA-NEWSLETTER GMBH 1743220
Adalbert-Seifriz-Str. 53, 69151 NECKARGEMÜND **Tel:** 6223 74757
Fax: 6223 74139
Email: info@premedianewsletter.de
Web site: http://www.premedianewsletter.de

Titles:
PREMEDIA NEWSLETTER

PREMIUMPARK GMBH 1771892
Herzogparkstr. 1, 81679 MÜNCHEN
Tel: 89 80032070
Email: info@premiumpark.de
Web site: http://www.premiumpark.de

Titles:
PURE BY PREMIUMPARK

PREMIUS GMBH 1773671
Ölmühle 9, 20357 HAMBURG **Tel:** 40 18086753
Email: redaktion@premius-online.de
Web site: http://www.premius-online.de

Titles:
PREMIUS

PRESS MEDIEN GMBH & CO. KG 681189
Richthofenstr. 96, 32756 DETMOLD
Tel: 5231 981000 **Fax:** 5231 9810033

Titles:
WIRTSCHAFT REGIONAL

PRESSE DIENSTLEISTUNGSGES. MBH & CO. KG 1733088
Borsigstr. 5, 31061 ALFELD **Tel:** 5181 80090
Fax: 5181 800933
Email: info@p-d-ges.de

Titles:
ARCHIV FÜR LEBENSMITTELHYGIENE
RFL RUNDSCHAU FÜR FLEISCHHYGIENE UND LEBENSMITTELÜBERWACHUNG

PRESSE FACHVERLAG GMBH & CO. KG 680788
Nebendahlstr. 16, 22041 HAMBURG
Tel: 40 6090090 **Fax:** 40 60900915
Email: info@presse-fachverlag.de
Web site: http://www.presse-fachverlag.de

Titles:
DNV DER NEUE VERTRIEB
PRESSE REPORT
DER TITELSCHUTZ ANZEIGER
DER TITELSCHUTZ ANZEIGER MIT DER SOFTWARE TITEL

PRESSE VERLAGSGES. FÜR ZEITSCHRIFTEN UND NEUE MEDIEN MBH 678368
Ludwigstr. 37, 60327 FRANKFURT **Tel:** 69 974600
Fax: 69 97460400
Email: journal@mmg.de

Titles:
FRANKFURT KAUFT EIN!
GENUSS MAGAZIN
JOURNAL EDITION
JOURNAL FRANKFURT
JOURNAL FRANKFURT FÜHRER
KINO JOURNAL FRANKFURT
PUR
UNI JOURNAL FRANKFURT

PRESSE-DRUCK- UND VERLAGS-GMBH 677452
Curt-Frenzel-Str. 2, 86167 AUGSBURG
Tel: 821 7770 **Fax:** 821 7772408
Web site: http://www.augsburger-allgemeine.de

Titles:
AICHACHER NACHRICHTEN
AUGSBURGER ALLGEMEINE
AUGSBURGER ALLGEMEINE ONLINE
DILLINGER EXTRA
DONAU ZEITUNG
DONAUWÖRTHER ZEITUNG
EXTRA-RAN
FRIEDBERGER ALLGEMEINE
GÜNZBURGER EXTRA
GÜNZBURGER ZEITUNG
ILLERTISSER ZEITUNG
LANDSBERGER TAGBLATT
MINDELHEIMER ZEITUNG
MITTELSCHWÄBISCHE NACHRICHTEN
NEUBURGER EXTRA
NEUBURGER RUNDSCHAU
NEU-ULMER ZEITUNG
RIESER NACHRICHTEN
SCHWABMÜNCHNER ALLGEMEINE
UNTERALLGÄU RUNDSCHAU
WERTINGER ZEITUNG

PRESSEHAUS BINTZ-VERLAG GMBH & CO. KG 682944
Waldstr. 226, 63071 OFFENBACH **Tel:** 69 850080
Fax: 69 85008298
Email: service@op-online.de
Web site: http://www.op-online.de

Titles:
HEIMATBOTE
OFFENBACH-POST
RODGAUPOST
STADTPOST DREIEICH
STADTPOST LANGEN-EGELSBACH
STADTPOST OFFENBACH
STADTPOST RÖDERMARK

PRINT'N'PRESS VERLAG GMBH 684446
Oranienstr. 9, 52066 AACHEN **Tel:** 241 94500
Fax: 241 9450180
Email: info@p-n-p.de
Web site: http://www.p-n-p.de

Titles:
KLENKES

PRISMA-VERLAG GMBH & CO. KG 687302
Zülpicher Str. 10, 40549 DÜSSELDORF
Tel: 211 507028 **Fax:** 211 5051549
Email: info@prisma-verlag.de
Web site: http://www.prisma-verlag.de

Titles:
PRISMA

PRIVATE WEALTH GMBH & CO. KG 1655186
Südliche Auffahrtsallee 29, 80639 MÜNCHEN
Tel: 89 25543915 **Fax:** 89 25542971
Email: info@private-wealth.de
Web site: http://www.private-wealth.de

Titles:
PRIVATE WEALTH

PRO FAMILIA BUNDESVERBAND 1709573
Stresemannallee 3, 60596 FRANKFURT
Tel: 69 639002 **Fax:** 69 639852
Email: magazin@profamilia.de
Web site: http://www.profamilia.de

Titles:
PRO FAMILIA MAGAZIN

PRO RUHRGEBIET E.V. 687390
Semperstr. 51, 45138 ESSEN **Tel:** 201 894150
Fax: 201 8941510
Email: info@proruhrgebiet.de
Web site: http://www.proruhrgebiet.de

Titles:
PRO RUHRGEBIET

PROF. DR. HARTMUT LODE 690922
Eichenallee 36a, 14050 BERLIN **Tel:** 30 3125059
Fax: 30 3124742
Email: redaktion@zct-berlin.de
Web site: http://www.zct-berlin.de

Titles:
ZEITSCHRIFT FÜR CHEMOTHERAPIE

PROFIL VERLAG GMBH 686292
Harsefelder Str. 5, 21680 STADE **Tel:** 4141 53360
Fax: 4141 609900
Email: info@reifenpresse.de
Web site: http://www.neuereifenzeitung.de

Titles:
NEUE REIFENZEITUNG

PROFILEPUBLISHING GERMANY GMBH 1752857
Augustinusstr. 11d, 50226 FRECHEN
Tel: 2234 202581 **Fax:** 2234 659694
Email: info@profilepublishing.de
Web site: http://www.bi-magazine.net

Titles:
BUSINESS INTELLIGENCE MAGAZINE

PROJEKTBÜRO ARMIN MÜCK 1680264
Lossiusstr. 2, 21337 LÜNEBURG
Tel: 4131 268678 **Fax:** 721 151459750
Email: info@vegetarisch-einkaufen.de
Web site: http://www.vegetarisch-einkaufen.de

Titles:
VEGETARISCH-EINKAUFEN.DE

PROMEDIA VERLAG 689203
Poststr. 36, 20354 HAMBURG **Tel:** 40 288096710
Fax: 431 288096720
Email: redaktion.hamburg@tango-online.de
Web site: http://www.tango-online.de

Titles:
PRO MEDIA
TANGO

PROMO VERLAG GMBH 682118
Unterwerkstr. 5, 79115 FREIBURG
Tel: 761 45153400 **Fax:** 761 45153401
Email: info@promo-verlag.de
Web site: http://www.promo-verlag.de

Titles:
FREIBURGER UNI-MAGAZIN
HOTEL- UND GASTSTÄTTEN-KURIER

PROMOTOR VERLAGS- UND FÖRDERUNGSGES. MBH 680091
Borsigstr. 3, 76185 KARLSRUHE **Tel:** 721 565140
Fax: 721 5651450
Email: verlag@cci-promotor.de
Web site: http://www.cci-promotor.de

Titles:
CCI

PROPOS MEDIA VERLAG 1653240
Zum Letten 26, 66450 BEXBACH **Tel:** 6826 2348
Fax: 6826 510559
Email: info@eurosaar.info
Web site: http://www.eurosaar.info

Titles:
EURO SAAR

PROPRESS VERLAGSGES. MBH 1653136
Am Buschhof 8, 53227 BONN **Tel:** 228 970970
Fax: 228 9709775
Email: verlag@behoerdenspiegel.de
Web site: http://www.behoerdenspiegel.de

Titles:
BEHÖRDEN SPIEGEL
BERLINER BEHÖRDEN SPIEGEL
BESCHAFFUNG SPECIAL

PRÜFER MEDIENMARKETING ENDRISS & ROSENBERGER GMBH 678668
Lichtentaler Str. 35, 76530 BADEN-BADEN
Tel: 7221 21190 **Fax:** 7221 211915
Email: medienmarketing@pruefer.com
Web site: http://www.pruefer.com

Titles:
IHK MAGAZIN NORDSCHWARZWALD
IHK MAGAZIN RHEIN-NECKAR
IHK-REPORT DARMSTADT RHEIN MAIN NECKAR
WIRTSCHAFT IM SÜDWESTEN

PSBN VERLAGS GMBH 680602
Eisenhüttenstr. 4, 40882 RATINGEN
Tel: 2102 2046830 **Fax:** 2102 895825
Email: info@deutsche-briefmarken-revue.de
Web site: http://www.deutsche-briefmarken-revue.de

Titles:
DEUTSCHE BRIEFMARKEN-REVUE

PSCHORR VERLAG 1686578
Maximilianstr. 8, 82319 STARNBERG
Tel: 8151 5550563 **Fax:** 8151 666538
Email: info@pschorr.de

Titles:
SCHÖNER FÜHLEN

PSE REDAKTIONSSERVICE GMBH 677738
Kirchplatz 8, 82538 GERETSRIED
Tel: 8171 911870 **Fax:** 8171 60974
Email: info@pse-redaktion.de
Web site: http://www.pse-redaktion.de

Titles:
ALUMINIUM KURIER NEWS

PSI PROMOTIONAL PRODUCT SERVICE INSTITUTE, NIEDERLASSUNG DER REED EXHIBITIONS DEUTSCHLAND GMBH 687411
Völklinger Str. 4, 40219 DÜSSELDORF
Tel: 211 901910 **Fax:** 211 90191180
Web site: http://www.psi-network.de

Titles:
PSI JOURNAL

PSYCHIATRIE-VERLAG GMBH 687419
Thomas-Mann-Str. 49a, 53111 BONN
Tel: 228 7253414 **Fax:** 228 7253420
Email: verlag@psychiatrie.de
Web site: http://www.verlag.psychiatrie.de

Titles:
SOZIALPSYCHIATRISCHE INFORMATIONEN

PSYCHOSOZIAL-VERLAG 683948
Walltorstr. 10, 35390 GIESSEN **Tel:** 641 9699780
Fax: 641 96997819
Email: info@psychosozial-verlag.de
Web site: http://www.psychosozial-verlag.de

Titles:
PSYCHOANALYTISCHE FAMILIENTHERAPIE
PSYCHOTHERAPIE IM ALTER

PSYCHOTHERAPEUTEN-VERLAG, VERLAGSGRUPPE HÜTHIG JEHLE REHM GMBH 1690198
Im Weiher 10, 69121 HEIDELBERG
Tel: 6221 4890 **Fax:** 6221 489529
Email: info@hjr-verlag.de
Web site: http://www.hjr-verlag.de

Titles:
PSYCHOTHERAPEUTENJOURNAL

PTV PLANUNG TRANSPORT VERKEHR AG 1622165
Stumpfstr. 1, 76131 KARLSRUHE **Tel:** 721 96510
Fax: 721 9651699
Email: public.relations@ptv.de
Web site: http://www.ptv.de

Titles:
PTV COMPASS

PUBLICA VERLAG GMBH 685512
Plauener Str. 160, 13053 BERLIN **Tel:** 30 9830850
Fax: 30 98308510
Email: redaktion@publicaverlag.de
Web site: http://www.publicaverlag.de

Titles:
MEIN ERLEBNIS
MEINE GESCHICHTE

PUBLIK-FORUM VERLAGSGES. MBH 687403
Krebsmühle, 61440 OBERURSEL **Tel:** 6171 70030
Fax: 6171 700340
Email: verlag@publik-forum.de
Web site: http://www.publik-forum.de

Titles:
PUBLIK-FORUM

PUBLIKOM Z VERLAGSGES. FÜR ZIELGRUPPEN-PUBLIZISTIK UND KOMMUNIKATION MBH 677519
Frankfurter Str. 168, 34121 KASSEL
Tel: 561 60280450 **Fax:** 561 60280499
Email: info@publikom_z.de
Web site: http://www.publikom-z.de

Titles:
SOVD ZEITUNG

PUBLIMED MEDIZIN UND MEDIEN GMBH 694761
Paul-Heyse-Str. 28, 80336 MÜNCHEN
Tel: 89 51616171 **Fax:** 89 51616199
Email: schreiber@publimed.de
Web site: http://www.publimed.de

Titles:
FRAUENARZT

PUBLISH-INDUSTRY VERLAG GMBH 678504
Nymphenburger Str. 86, 80636 MÜNCHEN
Tel: 89 5003830 **Fax:** 89 50038310
Email: info@publish-industry.net
Web site: http://www.publish-industry.net

Titles:
A&D
E&E FASZINATION ELEKTRONIK
MOBILITY 2.0
P&A

PULSE PUBLISHING GMBH 1785598
Offakamp 9a, 22529 HAMBURG **Tel:** 40 57002670
Fax: 40 570026718

Titles:
BLONDE

PV PROJEKT VERLAG GMBH 685095
Falbenhennenstr. 17, 70180 STUTTGART
Tel: 711 60171717 **Fax:** 711 60171729
Email: info@lift-online.de
Web site: http://www.lift-online.de

Titles:
LIFT STUTTGART
SOMMERGASTRO
STUTTGART GEHT AUS

PWW GMBH 679990
Nägelsbachstr. 33, 91052 ERLANGEN
Tel: 9131 9192501 **Fax:** 9131 9192594
Email: publishing-magazines@publicis-erlangen.de
Web site: http://www.publicis-erlangen.de

Titles:
E-INSTALLATION

GO!
MOTION WORLD
MOVE UP

PZH VERLAG GMBH 1742921
An der Universität 2, 30823 GARBSEN
Tel: 511 76219434
Email: redaktion@phi-hannover.de
Web site: http://www.phi-hannover.de

Titles:
PHI PRODUKTIONSTECHNIK HANNOVER INFORMIERT

QONTUR: PUBLICATIONS-MEDIA LTD. 1760871
Uhlandring 18, 72829 ENGSTINGEN
Tel: 7129 930180 **Fax:** 7129 930184
Email: woerkshop@qontur.de
Web site: http://www.qontur.de

Titles:
WÖRKSHOP

QUALIMEDIC.COM AG 1652382
Brückenstr. 1, 50667 KÖLN **Tel:** 221 27050
Fax: 221 2705555
Email: info@qualimedic.de
Web site: http://www.qualimedic.de

Titles:
QUALIMEDIC

QUERFORMAT GMBH 1748475
Rothmundstr. 6, 80337 MÜNCHEN
Tel: 89 552971633 **Fax:** 89 552971625
Email: redaktion@leo-magazin.de
Web site: http://www.leo-live.de

Titles:
LEO

QUINTESSENZ VERLAGS-GMBH 680686
Komturstr. 18, 12099 BERLIN **Tel:** 30 761805
Fax: 30 76180692
Email: info@quintessenz.de
Web site: http://www.quintessenz.de

Titles:
SCHLESWIG-HOLSTEINISCHES ÄRZTEBLATT

QUOKA GMBH 677629
Chemiestr. 14, 68623 LAMPERTHEIM
Tel: 180 5511255 **Fax:** 180 5511256
Email: info@quoka.de
Web site: http://www.quoka.de

Titles:
BIKER SZENE

R & T VERLAGS- & VERTRIEBSGES. MBH 682980
Hallerstr. 27, 30161 HANNOVER **Tel:** 511 340240
Fax: 511 3402464
Web site: http://www.schaedelspalter.de

Titles:
HANNOVER GEHT AUS!
HANNOVER KAUFT EIN
SCHÄDELSPALTER

R. V. DECKER VERLAGSGRUPPE HÜTHIG JEHLE REHM GMBH 682688
Im Weiher 10, 69121 HEIDELBERG
Tel: 6221 4890 **Fax:** 6221 489529
Email: info@hjr-verlag.de
Web site: http://www.hjr-verlag.de

Titles:
UNTERRICHTSBLÄTTER

R.A.G.T SAATEN DEUTSCHLAND GMBH 685318
Lockhauser Str. 68, 32052 HERFORD
Tel: 5221 76520 **Fax:** 5221 71853
Email: info@ragt.de
Web site: http://www.ragt.de

Titles:
MAIS INFORMATION

RAINER HAMPP VERLAG 683591
Marktplatz 5, 86415 MERING **Tel:** 8233 4783
Fax: 8233 30755
Email: hampp@rhverlag.de
Web site: http://www.hampp-verlag.de

Titles:
MANAGEMENT REVUE
ZEITSCHRIFT FÜR PERSONALFORSCHUNG

RATHMANN VERLAG GMBH & CO. KG 687071
Schloßgarten 3, 24103 KIEL **Tel:** 431 8881230
Fax: 431 9828711
Email: info@rathmann-verlag.de
Web site: http://www.rathmann-verlag.de

Titles:
PFERD + SPORT IN SCHLESWIG-HOLSTEIN UND HAMBURG
DER TRAKEHNER

RAUTENBERG MEDIA & PRINT VERLAG KG 677606
Kasinostr. 28, 53840 TROISDORF **Tel:** 2241 2600
Fax: 2241 260259
Email: anzeigen@rmp.de
Web site: http://www.rmp.de

Titles:
DER POSTILLION

READER'S DIGEST DEUTSCHLAND: VERLAG DAS BESTE GMBH 687544
Vordernbergstr. 6, 70191 STUTTGART
Tel: 711 66020 **Fax:** 711 6602547
Email: verlag@readersdigest.de
Web site: http://www.readersdigest.de

Titles:
DAHEIM IN DEUTSCHLAND
READER'S DIGEST DEUTSCHLAND

REALIS VERLAGS-GMBH 1759297
Sämannstr. 14a, 82166 GRÄFELFING
Tel: 89 7415300 **Fax:** 89 74153019
Email: info@starting-up.de
Web site: http://www.realis.de

Titles:
STARTING UP

RED INDIANS PUBLISHING GMBH & CO. KG 1752872
Obere Wässere 5, 72764 REUTLINGEN
Tel: 7121 4330470 **Fax:** 7121 73304710
Email: info@ramp-magazin.de
Web site: http://www.ramp-magazin.de

Titles:
RAMP

REDAKTION MITTELDEUTSCHE MITTEILUNGEN DIPL.-ING. (FH) BARBARA SCHMIDT 1715194
Wolframstr. 25, 39116 MAGDEBURG
Tel: 391 6239286 **Fax:** 391 6239286
Email: redaktion@schmidt-tdp.de

Titles:
MITTELDEUTSCHE MITTEILUNGEN

REDAKTIONS- UND VERLAGSGES. BAUTZEN/ KAMENZ MBH 687961
Lauengraben 18, 02625 BAUTZEN
Tel: 3591 49505010 **Fax:** 3591 49505011

Titles:
SÄCHSISCHE ZEITUNG

REDAKTIONSWERFT GMBH 1638820
Schanzenstr. 70, 20357 HAMBURG
Tel: 40 18888581 **Fax:** 40 18888588
Email: fk@dvd-magazin.de
Web site: http://www.dvd-magazin.de

Titles:
SCREEN DVD MAGAZIN

REFA BUNDESVERBAND E.V. 681718
Wittichstr. 2, 64295 DARMSTADT **Tel:** 6151 88010
Fax: 6151 880127
Email: refa@refa.de
Web site: http://www.refa.de

Titles:
INDUSTRIAL ENGINEERING

REGIONALE 2010 AGENTUR STANDORTMARKETING REGION KÖLN/BONN GMBH 1720052
Ottoplatz 1, 50679 KÖLN **Tel:** 221 92547721
Fax: 221 92547799
Email: buero@regionale2010.de
Web site: http://www.regionale2010.de

Titles:
:ZEITPUNKT

REGIONALE INTERNET KONZEPTIONEN 1690733
Rossmarkt 6, 80331 MÜNCHEN **Tel:** 89 23077611
Fax: 89 24223508
Email: schmitz@ganz-muenchen.de
Web site: http://www.ganz-muenchen.de

Titles:
GANZ-MUENCHEN.DE

REGIO-VERLAG SCHWÄBISCH HALL E.K. 1739039
Am Kühnbach 27, 74523 SCHWÄBISCH HALL
Tel: 791 53864 **Fax:** 791 959243
Email: info@wheelies.de
Web site: http://www.wheelies.de

Titles:
WHEELIES

REHA-VERLAG GMBH 680600
Baumschulenweg 11, 53424 REMAGEN
Tel: 2642 992696 **Fax:** 2642 992652
Email: reha-verlag@online.de
Web site: http://www.reha-verlag.com

Titles:
DEUTSCHE BEHINDERTEN-ZEITSCHRIFT

REIFENWELT MEDIEN- UND VERLAGSGES. MBH 1771134
Stiftswaldstr. 60, 67657 KAISERSLAUTERN
Tel: 631 534872100 **Fax:** 631 534872007
Email: info@reifenwelt.de
Web site: http://www.reifenwelt.de

Titles:
REIFENWELT

REIFF VERLAG KG 677833
Marlener Str. 9, 77656 OFFENBURG
Tel: 781 5040 **Fax:** 781 5041409
Email: info@reiff.de
Web site: http://www.reiff.de

Titles:
BADEN ONLINE
INSIDE B
KEHLER ZEITUNG
MITTELBADISCHE PRESSE
OFFENBURGER TAGEBLATT

REINER H. NITSCHKE VERLAGS-GMBH 679320
Eifelring 28, 53879 EUSKIRCHEN
Tel: 2251 650460 **Fax:** 2251 6504699
Email: service@nitschke-verlag.de

Titles:
DRUMS & PERCUSSION
FONO FORUM
MOTORRAD ABENTEUER
MOTORRADFAHRER
STEREO
TOURENFAHRER

REINKEN GMBH 1643440
Auf dem Berge 26, 28844 WEYHE
Tel: 421 841330 **Fax:** 421 8092348
Web site: http://www.kradblatt.de

Titles:
KRADBLATT

REISE & PREISE VERLAGS GMBH 687620
Hauptstr. 14, 21614 BUXTEHUDE
Tel: 4161 71690 **Fax:** 4161 716915
Email: verlag@reise-preise.de
Web site: http://www.reise-preise.de

Titles:
REISE & PREISE
REISE-PREISE.DE

REISEN.DE SERVICE GMBH 1652420
Planegger Str. 16, 82110 GERMERING
Tel: 1805 618000 **Fax:** 1805 618099
Email: service@reisen.de
Web site: http://www.reisen.de

Titles:
REISEN.DE

REITMEIER INPUT MANAGEMENT SERVICES GMBH 1714675
Haldenbergerstr. 28, 80997 MÜNCHEN
Tel: 89 14902790 **Fax:** 89 149027929
Email: info@research-results.de
Web site: http://www.research-results.de

Titles:
RESEARCH & RESULTS

REMS-ZEITUNG IM VERLAG DER REMSDRUCKEREI SIGG, HÄRTEL U. CO. KG 1742927
Paradiesstr. 12, 73525 SCHWÄBISCH GMÜND
Tel: 7171 60060 **Fax:** 7171 600658
Email: info@rems-zeitung.de
Web site: http://www.rems-zeitung.de

Titles:
REMS-ZEITUNG

REPORT VERLAG GMBH 688514
Hochkreuzallee 1, 53175 BONN **Tel:** 228 3680403
Fax: 228 3680402
Email: info@report-verlag.de
Web site: http://www.report-verlag.de

Titles:
STRATEGIE & TECHNIK

REPORT VERLAGSGES. MBH 679545
Jägerstr. 1, 46395 BOCHOLT **Tel:** 2871 25980
Fax: 2871 6963
Email: zentrale@bocholter-report.de
Web site: http://www.bocholter-report.de

Titles:
BOCHOLTER REPORT

RESERVEOFFIZIERKAMERAD-SCHAFT "DIE ZIFKRAS" 1728175
Ahrweg 140, 53347 ALFTER
Email: sonneck@zifkras.de

Titles:
WIR ZIFKRAS

RETTET DEN REGENWALD E.V. 687582
Jupiterweg 15, 22391 HAMBURG **Tel:** 40 4103804
Fax: 40 4500144
Email: info@regenwald.org
Web site: http://www.regenwald.org

Titles:
REGENWALD REPORT

REUTLINGER GENERAL-ANZEIGER VERLAGS GMBH & CO. KG 681042
Burgstr. 1, 72764 REUTLINGEN **Tel:** 7121 3020
Fax: 7121 302677
Email: v.lehari.jr@gea.de
Web site: http://www.gea.de

Titles:
ECHAZ-BOTE
GEA.DE REUTLINGER GENERAL-ANZEIGER
METZINGER-URACHER GENERAL-ANZEIGER
REUTLINGER GENERAL-ANZEIGER

REUTLINGER WOCHENBLATT GMBH 681394
Marktplatz 16, 72764 REUTLINGEN
Tel: 7121 93810 **Fax:** 7121 938110
Email: reutlingerwochenblatt@rtw.zgs.de
Web site: http://www.reutlinger-wochenblatt.de

Titles:
REUTLINGER WOCHENBLATT
TÜBINGER WOCHENBLATT

REWE-VERLAG GMBH 681066
Domstr. 20, 50668 KÖLN **Tel:** 221 1491070
Fax: 221 1499108
Email: presse@rewe-group.com

Titles:
ECHO
LAVIVA

RHEIN MAIN WOCHENBLATTVERLAGSGES. MBH 677742
Erich-Dombrowski-Str. 2, 55127 MAINZ
Tel: 6131 485505 **Fax:** 6131 485533
Email: verlag@rhein-main-wochenblatt.de
Web site: http://www.rhein-main-wochenblatt.de

Titles:
ALZEYER WOCHENBLATT
BINGER WOCHENBLATT
INGELHEIMER WOCHENBLATT
MAINZER WOCHENBLATT
RHEINGAUER WOCHENBLATT
RHEINHESSISCHES WOCHENBLATT
RÜSSELSHEIMER WOCHENBLATT
UNTERTAUNUS WOCHENBLATT
WIESBADENER WOCHENBLATT
WORMSER WOCHENBLATT

RHEINER ANZEIGENBLATT VERLAGSGES. MBH 687687
Poststr. 1, 48431 RHEINE **Tel:** 5971 404661
Fax: 5971 404699
Email: info@rheiner-anzeiger.de
Web site: http://www.rheiner-anzeiger.de

Titles:
RHEINER ANZEIGER

RHEINGOLD, INSTITUT FÜR QUALITATIVE MARKT- UND MEDIENANALYSEN 687690
Kaiser-Wilhelm-Ring 46, 50672 KÖLN
Tel: 221 9127770 **Fax:** 221 91277755
Email: rheingold@rheingold-online.de
Web site: http://www.rheingold-online.de

Titles:
RHEINGOLD MOVE

RHEINISCH-BERGISCHE WIRTSCHAFTSFÖRDERUNGS-GES. MBH 1741865
Friedrich-Ebert-Str., 51429 BERGISCH GLADBACH **Tel:** 2204 97630 **Fax:** 2204 976399
Email: info@rbw.de
Web site: http://www.rbw.de

Titles:
PUNKT.RBW

RHEINISCHE NOTARKAMMER, KÖLN 687759
Burgmauer 53, 50667 KÖLN **Tel:** 221 2575292
Fax: 221 2575293
Email: rnotz@rhnotk.de
Web site: http://www.rnotz.de

Titles:
RNOTZ RHEINISCHE NOTAR-ZEITSCHRIFT

RHEINISCHE POST VERLAGSGES. MBH 679074
Zülpicher Str. 10, 40549 DÜSSELDORF
Tel: 211 5050 **Fax:** 211 5052575
Web site: http://www.rp-online.de

Titles:
BERGISCHE MORGENPOST
NEUSS=GREVENBROICHER ZEITUNG
RHEINISCHE POST
SOLINGER MORGENPOST

RHEINISCHER LANDWIRTSCHAFTS-VERLAG GMBH 685255
Rochusstr. 18, 53123 BONN **Tel:** 228 52006500
Fax: 228 52006543
Web site: http://www.rl-verlag.de

Titles:
LZ RHEINLAND
MONATSSCHRIFT
SPARGEL & ERDBEER PROFI

RHEINISCH-WESTFÄLISCHE TECHNISCHE HOCHSCHULE, FORSCHUNGSINSTITUT FÜR RATIONALISIERUNG E.V. 689943
Pontdriesch 14, 52062 AACHEN **Tel:** 241 477050
Fax: 241 47705199
Email: redaktion-udz@fir.rwth-aachen.de
Web site: http://www.fir.rwth-aachen.de

Titles:
UDZ UNTERNEHMEN DER ZUKUNFT

RHEIN-MAIN.NET GMBH 1626928
Frankenallee 71, 60327 FRANKFURT
Tel: 69 75014060 **Fax:** 69 75014069
Email: info@rhein-main.net
Web site: http://www.rhein-main.net

Titles:
RHEIN-MAIN.NET

RHEINMETALL AG 686393
Rheinmetall-Platz 1, 40476 DÜSSELDORF
Tel: 211 47304 **Fax:** 211 4734157
Email: rolf-dieter.schneider@rheinmetall.com
Web site: http://www.rheinmetall.com

Titles:
DAS PROFIL

RHEIN-NECKAR-ZEITUNG GMBH 687707
Neugasse 2, 69117 HEIDELBERG **Tel:** 6221 5191
Fax: 6221 22369
Email: rnz-kontakt@rnz.de
Web site: http://www.rnz.de

Titles:
RHEIN-NECKAR-ZEITUNG

RHEINPFALZ VERLAG UND DRUCKEREI GMBH & CO. KG 685025
Amtsstr. 5, 67059 LUDWIGSHAFEN
Tel: 621 590201 **Fax:** 621 5902313
Email: rheinpfalz@rheinpfalz.de
Web site: http://www.rheinpfalz.de

Titles:
DIE RHEINPFALZ

RHOMBOS-VERLAG 677240
Kurfürstenstr. 17, 10785 BERLIN **Tel:** 30 2616854
Fax: 30 2616300
Email: verlag@rhombos.de
Web site: http://www.rhombos.de

Titles:
ABFALLWIRTSCHAFTLICHER INFORMATIONSDIENST
RESOURCE

RIB SOFTWARE AG 1719604
Vaihinger Str. 151, 70567 STUTTGART
Tel: 711 7873369 **Fax:** 711 787388369
Email: transparent@rib-software.com
Web site: http://www.rib-software.com

Titles:
TRANSPARENT

RICHARD BOORBERG VERLAG GMBH & CO KG 680096
Scharrstr. 2, 70563 STUTTGART **Tel:** 711 73850
Fax: 711 7385100
Email: mail@boorberg.de
Web site: http://www.boorberg.de

Titles:
BEHINDERTENRECHT
DEUTSCHES POLIZEIBLATT FÜR DIE AUS- UND FORTBILDUNG DPOLBL
DIE GEMEINDEKASSE BAYERN
NDSVBL. NIEDERSÄCHSISCHE VERWALTUNGSBLÄTTER
POLIZEI-HEUTE
RDW KURZREPORT AUS STEUERN UND RECHT
SÄCHSVBL. SÄCHSISCHE VERWALTUNGSBLÄTTER
STEUERANWALTSMAGAZIN
THÜRVBL. THÜRINGER VERWALTUNGSBLÄTTER
VBLBW VERWALTUNGSBLÄTTER FÜR BADEN-WÜRTTEMBERG
ZEITSCHRIFT FÜR DAS FÜRSORGEWESEN ZFF

RICHARD PFLAUM VERLAG GMBH & CO. KG 678713
Lazarettstr. 4, 80636 MÜNCHEN **Tel:** 89 126070
Fax: 89 12607333
Email: kundenservice@pflaum.de
Web site: http://www.pflaum.de

Titles:
DER BÄCKERMEISTER
LICHT
DER METZGERMEISTER
NATURHEILPRAXIS MIT NATURMEDIZIN
PT ZEITSCHRIFT FÜR PHYSIOTHERAPEUTEN

RIGODON-VERLAG 688180
Nieberdingstr. 18, 45147 ESSEN **Tel:** 201 778111
Fax: 201 775174
Email: schreibheft@netcologne.de
Web site: http://www.schreibheft.de

Titles:
SCHREIBHEFT

RIMBACH VERLAG E.K. 679149
Karl-Hofer-Str. 11, 14163 BERLIN **Tel:** 30 8021071
Fax: 30 8029988
Email: info@berlin-programm.de
Web site: http://www.berlin-programm.de

Titles:
BERLIN PROGRAMM

RIMO VERLAGS GMBH 685990
Hauptstr. 31, 53797 LOHMAR **Tel:** 2246 9480000
Fax: 2246 9480004
Email: info@motorsport-xl.de
Web site: http://www.motorsport-xl.de

Titles:
MOTOR SPORT XL

RIND IM BILD
1745764
Rendsburger Str. 178, 24537 NEUMÜNSTER
Tel: 4321 905300 **Fax:** 4321 905396
Email: redaktion@rsheg.de
Web site: http://www.rsheg.de

Titles:
RIND IM BILD

RINGIER PUBLISHING GMBH
1641866
Lennéstr. 1, 10785 BERLIN **Tel:** 30 981941100
Fax: 30 981941199
Email: verlag@cicero.de
Web site: http://www.cicero.de

Titles:
CICERO

RITTERBACH VERLAG GMBH
677846
Rudolf-Diesel-Str. 5, 50226 FRECHEN
Tel: 2234 18660 **Fax:** 2234 186690
Email: zeitschriften@ritterbach.de
Web site: http://www.ritterbach.de

Titles:
JUNGE KUNST
KUNSTHANDWERK & DESIGN
NEUES GLAS NEW GLASS
SCHULE NRW

RIW GMBH & CO. WIR AGENTUR UND VERLAG KG
690667
Schloß Bergfeld, 54533 EISENSCHMITT
Tel: 6567 967000 **Fax:** 6567 967018

Titles:
ERFOLGREICH SELBSTÄNDIG

RKW RATIONALISIERUNGS- UND INNOVATIONSZENTRUM DER DEUTSCHEN WIRTSCHAFT E.V.
698028
Düsseldorfer Str. 40, 65760 ESCHBORN
Tel: 6196 4952813 **Fax:** 6196 4954801
Email: k.grossheim@rkw.de
Web site: http://www.rkw.de

Titles:
RKW MAGAZIN

RL-PRESS
690456
Ostlandstr. 1, 50858 KÖLN **Tel:** 2234 73488
Fax: 2234 73598
Email: redaktion@welt-der-farben.de
Web site: http://www.welt-der-farben.de

Titles:
WELT DER FARBEN

ROBIN WOOD E.V.
687762
Rosa-Luxemburg-Str. 24, 16303 SCHWEDT
Tel: 3332 252010 **Fax:** 3332 252011
Email: magazin@robinwood.de
Web site: http://www.robinwood.de

Titles:
ROBIN WOOD MAGAZIN

ROCK HARD VERLAGS- UND HANDELSGES. MBH
687767
Paderborner Str. 17, 44143 DORTMUND
Tel: 231 5620140 **Fax:** 231 56201433
Email: megazine@rockhard.de
Web site: http://www.rockhard.de

Titles:
ROCK HARD
ROCK HARD ONLINE

RODALE-MOTOR-PRESSE GMBH & CO. KG
687929
Leuschnerstr. 1, 70174 STUTTGART
Tel: 711 18201 **Fax:** 711 1822082

Titles:
RUNNER'S WORLD

RODALE-MOTOR-PRESSE GMBH & CO. KG VERLAGSGES.
685557
Leuschnerstr. 1, 70174 STUTTGART
Tel: 711 18201 **Fax:** 711 1821155
Web site: http://www.motorpresse.de

Titles:
COACH MEN'S HEALTH
MEN'S HEALTH
MEN'S HEALTH BEST FASHION
MENSHEALTH.DE

RODMANN & PARTNER GBR
690992
Woldsenweg 14, 20249 HAMBURG
Tel: 40 487576 **Fax:** 40 4804412

Titles:
JS MAGAZIN

RÖHM VERLAG & MEDIEN GMBH & CO. KG
689186
Böblinger Str. 76, 71065 SINDELFINGEN
Tel: 7031 8620 **Fax:** 7031 862201
Email: redaktion@szbz.de
Web site: http://www.szbz.de

Titles:
SZ SINDELFINGER ZEITUNG
SZ SINDELFINGER ZEITUNG BZ BÖBLINGER ZEITUNG

ROI MANAGEMENT CONSULTING AG
1622152
Nymphenburger Str. 86, 80636 MÜNCHEN
Tel: 89 1215900 **Fax:** 89 12159010
Email: dialog@roi.de
Web site: http://www.roi.de

Titles:
ROI DIALOG

ROLAND SCHERER VERLAGS- & WERBESERVICE GMBH
680368
Graf-Adolf-Str. 80, 40210 DÜSSELDORF
Tel: 211 384660 **Fax:** 211 3846616
Email: redaktion.duesseldorf@coolibri.de
Web site: http://www.coolibri.de

Titles:
COOLIBRI - AUSG. DÜSSELDORF, NEUSS U. KREIS ME
COOLIBRI - AUSG. RUHRSTADT

ROLF SOLL VERLAG GMBH
679188
Kahden 17b, 22393 HAMBURG **Tel:** 40 6068820
Fax: 40 60688288
Email: info@soll.de
Web site: http://www.soll.de

Titles:
BESCHAFFUNGSDIENST GALABAU
BULA

ROMBACH DRUCK UND VERLAGSHAUS GMBH & CO. KG
680807
Unterwerkstr. 5, 79115 FREIBURG **Tel:** 761 45000
Fax: 761 45002124
Email: info@dka.de
Web site: http://www.dka.de

Titles:
DKA DEUTSCHES KRANKENHAUS ADRESSBUCH MIT ÖSTERREICH UND SCHWEIZ MIT "EUROHOSPITAL" BEZUGSQUELLENNACHWEIS

ROSEBUD INC., RALF HERMS
687790
Pelzetleite 65, 90614 AMMERNDORF
Tel: 172 8942290 **Fax:** 9127 577581
Email: ask@rosebudmagazine.com
Web site: http://www.rosebudmagazine.com

Titles:
+ROSEBUD

RÖSER PRESSE GMBH
679640
Fritz-Erler-Str. 23, 76133 KARLSRUHE
Tel: 721 9338020 **Fax:** 721 93380220
Email: info@roeser-presse.de
Web site: http://www.roeser-presse.de

Titles:
TRAUMHAFTE HOCHZEIT REGIONAL

ROSTOCKER MEDIENVERLAG HELGE JOSWIG, STEFAN NORDEN GBR
1742388
Wollenweberstr. 59, 18055 ROSTOCK
Tel: 381 37706966 **Fax:** 381 37706961
Email: info@szenerostock.de
Web site: http://www.szenerostock.de

Titles:
SZENE ROSTOCK

ROTARY VERLAGS GMBH
687799
Raboisen 30, 20095 HAMBURG **Tel:** 40 3499970
Fax: 40 34999717
Web site: http://www.rotary.de

Titles:
ROTARY MAGAZIN

ROTENBERG VERLAG GMBH
680041
Wilhelmstr. 18, 70372 STUTTGART
Tel: 711 955680 **Fax:** 711 9556833
Web site: http://www.cannstatter-zeitung.de

Titles:
CANNSTATTER ZEITUNG
UNTERTÜRKHEIMER ZEITUNG

RÖTTER DRUCK UND VERLAG GMBH
687718
Industriestr. 8, 97616 BAD NEUSTADT
Tel: 9771 91930 **Fax:** 9771 919355
Email: service@rhoen-undsaalepost.de
Web site: http://www.rhoen-undsaalepost.de

Titles:
RHÖN- U. SAALEPOST

RR MEDIA GMBH
1762490
Friedrich-Lueg-Str. 10, 44867 BOCHUM
Tel: 2327 991490 **Fax:** 2327 9914911
Email: post@woman-itc.de
Web site: http://www.woman-itc.de

Titles:
WOMAN IN THE CITY
WOMAN IN THE CITY

RS MEDIA GMBH
684077
Watmarkt 1, 93047 REGENSBURG
Tel: 941 584030 **Fax:** 941 5840379
Email: info@rsmedia-verlag.de
Web site: http://www.rsmedia-verlag.de

Titles:
JOURNAL MED
JOURNAL ONKOLOGIE

RTA.DESIGN GMBH
1741068
Heisinger Str. 14, 87437 KEMPTEN
Tel: 831 206394 **Fax:** 831 2065117
Email: info@all-in.de
Web site: http://www.all-in.de

Titles:
ALL-IN.DE

RTV MEDIA GROUP GMBH
680241
Breslauer Str. 300, 90471 NÜRNBERG
Tel: 911 892010 **Fax:** 911 8920135
Email: info@rtv-mediagroup.de
Web site: http://www.rtvmediagroup.de

Titles:
CLIVIA
RTV

RUDOLF HAUFE VERLAG GMBH & CO. KG
1615900
Fraunhoferstr. 5, 82152 PLANEGG **Tel:** 89 895170
Fax: 89 89517250
Email: online@haufe.de
Web site: http://www.haufe.de

Titles:
DER KLEINE BUSINESS KOMPASS

RÜHLE-DIEBENER-VERLAG GMBH + CO. KG
682863
Friedrichstr. 167, 71638 LUDWIGSBURG
Tel: 7141 8744800 **Fax:** 7141 8744819
Email: rdv@rdv-online.com
Web site: http://www.rdv-online.com

Titles:
INNOVATION UND TECHNIK

RUNDSCHAU VERLAGSGES. MBH
679076
Otto-Hausmann-Ring 185, 42115 WUPPERTAL
Tel: 202 271440 **Fax:** 202 716292
Email: info@wuppertaler-rundschau.de
Web site: http://www.wuppertaler-rundschau.de

Titles:
TOP MAGAZIN WUPPERTAL
WÜLFRATHER RUNDSCHAU
WUPPERTALER RUNDSCHAU AM MITTWOCH

RUNDSCHAU-VERLAG OTTO KÖNIGER GMBH & CO.
687911
Karlstr. 41, 89073 ULM **Tel:** 731 1520193
Fax: 731 1520188
Web site: http://www.ebnerverlag.de

Titles:
RUNDSCHAU
RUNDSCHAU

RUNDSCHAU-VERLAGS GMBH & CO. ANZEIGENBLATT KG
680462
Konrad-Adenauer-Str. 27, 85221 DACHAU
Tel: 8131 51810 **Fax:** 8131 518130
Email: anzeigen@dachauer-rundschau.de
Web site: http://www.dachauer-rundschau.de

Titles:
DACHAUER RUNDSCHAU

RUNDY MEDIA GMBH
687928
Am Glockenturm 6, 63814 MAINASCHAFF
Tel: 6021 583880 **Fax:** 6021 5838822
Email: info@rundy.de
Web site: http://www.rundy.de

Titles:
RUNDY
RUNDY TITELSCHUTZ JOURNAL

RWS VERLAG KOMMUNIKATIONSFORUM GMBH
681330
Aachener Str. 222, 50931 KÖLN **Tel:** 221 400880
Fax: 221 4008879
Email: info@rws-verlag.de
Web site: http://www.rws-verlag.de

Titles:
ENTSCHEIDUNGEN ZUM WIRTSCHAFTSRECHT EWIR
ZEITSCHRIFT FÜR WIRTSCHAFTSRECHT ZIP

RZ-MAINZ GMBH
1685240
Große Bleiche 17, 55116 MAINZ **Tel:** 6131 28270
Fax: 6131 2827128
Email: mainz@rhein-zeitung.net
Web site: http://www.mainz-online.de

Titles:
MAINZER RHEIN ZEITUNG

S. HIRZEL VERLAG
677311
Birkenwaldstr. 44, 70191 STUTTGART
Tel: 711 2582240 **Fax:** 711 2582290
Email: service@hirzel.de
Web site: http://www.hirzel.de

Titles:
JAHRBUCH ÖKOLOGIE

S. KARGER VERLAG FÜR MEDIZIN UND NATURWISSENSCHAFTEN GMBH
680157
Wilhelmstr. 20a, 79098 FREIBURG
Tel: 761 452070 **Fax:** 761 4520714
Email: information@karger.de
Web site: http://www.karger.com

Titles:
FORSCHENDE KOMPLEMENTÄRMEDIZIN RESEARCH IN COMPLEMENTARY MEDICINE
ONKOLOGIE
SCHWEIZERISCHE ZEITSCHRIFT FÜR GANZHEITSMEDIZIN
TRANSFUSION MEDICINE AND HEMOTHERAPY
VERHALTENSTHERAPIE
VISZERALMEDIZIN

S. RODERER VERLAG
689095
In der Obern Au 12, 93055 REGENSBURG
Tel: 941 7992270 **Fax:** 941 795198
Email: info@roderer-verlag.de
Web site: http://www.roderer-verlag.de

Titles:
SUIZIDPROPHYLAXE

S & D VERLAG GMBH
684613
Otto-Hahn-Str. 16, 47608 GELDERN
Tel: 2831 13000 **Fax:** 2831 130020
Email: mail@sud-verlag.de
Web site: http://www.sud-verlag.de

Titles:
KOPF FIT
NATURHEILKUNDE & GESUNDHEIT
RÄTSEL-AKTUELL
UNSERE BESTEN FREUNDE

S & T SCAN REPRODUKTIONS GMBH
1630099
Flottenstr. 4a, 13407 BERLIN **Tel:** 30 4145081
Fax: 30 4145083
Email: js@st-berlin.de
Web site: http://www.berlin-visavis.de

Titles:
BERLIN VIS-À-VIS EXTRATOUR

SAALE VERLAGSGES. MBH 688547
Franckestr. 2, 06110 HALLE **Tel:** 345 204090
Fax: 345 2040990
Email: info@sonntagsnachrichten.de
Web site: http://www.saaleverlag.de

Titles:
SONNTAGSNACHRICHTEN HALLESCHER KURIER

SAARBRÜCKER ZEITUNG VERLAG UND DRUCKEREI GMBH 687940
Gutenbergstr. 11, 66117 SAARBRÜCKEN
Tel: 681 5020
Web site: http://www.saarbruecker-zeitung.de

Titles:
SAAR.AMATEUR
SAARBRÜCKER ZEITUNG

SAARLÄNDISCHE WOCHENBLATT VERLAGSGES. MBH 680750
Bleichstr. 21, 66111 SAARBRÜCKEN
Tel: 681 388020 **Fax:** 681 35333
Email: info@wochenspiegelonline.de
Web site: http://www.wochenspiegelonline.de

Titles:
WOCHENSPIEGEL BLIESTAL/ MANDELBACHTAL
WOCHENSPIEGEL DILLINGEN MIT DILLINGER STADTRUNDSCHAU
WOCHENSPIEGEL HOCHWALD MIT HOCHWALD RUNDSCHAU
WOCHENSPIEGEL HOMBURG
WOCHENSPIEGEL ILLTAL MIT ILLTAL RUNDSCHAU
WOCHENSPIEGEL MERZIG MIT MERZIGER STADTRUNDSCHAU
WOCHENSPIEGEL SAARBRÜCKEN
WOCHENSPIEGEL SAARLOUIS MIT SAARLOUISER STADTRUNDSCHAU
WOCHENSPIEGEL ST. INGBERT
WOCHENSPIEGEL SULZBACHTAL/ FISCHBACHTAL
WOCHENSPIEGEL VÖLKLINGEN MIT VÖLKLINGER STADTRUNDSCHAU

SAARLÄNDISCHER LEHRERINNEN- UND LEHRERVERBAND E.V. IM VERBAND BILDUNG UND ERZIEHUNG 685004
Lisdorfer Str. 21b, 66740 SAARLOUIS
Tel: 6831 49440 **Fax:** 6831 46601
Web site: http://www.sllv.de

Titles:
LEHRER UND SCHULE HEUTE

SÄCHSISCHER BOTE WOCHENBLATT VERLAG GMBH 687959
Devrientstr. 5, 01067 DRESDEN **Tel:** 351 8657100
Fax: 351 8657110
Email: info@saechsischer-bote.de
Web site: http://www.saechsischer-bote.de

Titles:
SÄCHSISCHER BOTE - WOCHENZTG. F. DRESDEN, AUSG. NORD

SANKT ULRICH VERLAG GMBH 684257
Hafnerberg 2, 86152 AUGSBURG
Tel: 821 502420 **Fax:** 821 5024280
Email: verlag@suv.de

Titles:
DER KATHOLISCHE MESNER
KATHOLISCHE SONNTAGSZEITUNG FÜR DAS BISTUM AUGSBURG

SATORI VERLAGSANSTALT 679833
Bergstr. 18, 47906 KEMPEN **Tel:** 2845 80593
Fax: 2845 80392
Email: satori@budoworld.net
Web site: http://www.budoworld.net

Titles:
BUDO KARATE BUDOWORLD

SATZTECHNIK MEISSEN GMBH 683426
Am Sand 1c, 01665 DIERA-ZEHREN
Tel: 3525 718600 **Fax:** 3525 718612
Email: info@satztechnik-meissen.de
Web site: http://www.satztechnik-meissen.de

Titles:
NEUE SÄCHSISCHE LEHRERZEITUNG
ZAHNÄRZTEBLATT

SAXACON DMC 687956
Karsdorfer Str. 1, 01768 GLASHÜTTE
Tel: 3504 6949500 **Fax:** 3504 6949529
Email: sachsenbummel@saxacon.de
Web site: http://www.sachsenbummel.de

Titles:
SACHSENBUMMEL

SAZ VERLAG GMBH 688062
Rumfordstr. 42, 80469 MÜNCHEN
Tel: 89 2121100 **Fax:** 89 21211039
Email: saz@saz.de
Web site: http://www.saz.de

Titles:
SAZ BIKE
SAZ SPORTSFASHION MAGAZIN

SB 67 VERLAGSGES. MBH 1621623
Asternweg 35, 50259 PULHEIM **Tel:** 2238 963322
Fax: 2238 963323
Email: cbarz@t-online.de

Titles:
SB

SBM VERLAG GMBH 678884
Hermann-von-Barth-Str. 2, 87435 KEMPTEN
Tel: 831 522040 **Fax:** 831 5220450
Email: info@sbm-verlag.de
Web site: http://www.sbm-verlag.de

Titles:
BAU MAGAZIN
BAUSTOFF PARTNER

SCHADINSKY-WERBUNG GMBH & CIE KG 689226
Bahnhofstr. 30, 29221 CELLE **Tel:** 5141 92920
Fax: 5141 929292
Email: info@celler-blickpunkt.de
Web site: http://www.celler-blickpunkt.de

Titles:
CELLER BLICKPUNKT

SCHÄFFER-POESCHEL VERLAG FÜR WIRTSCHAFT, STEUERN, RECHT GMBH 680520
Werastr. 21, 70182 STUTTGART **Tel:** 711 21940
Fax: 711 2194119
Email: info@schaeffer-poeschel.de
Web site: http://www.schaeffer-poeschel.de

Titles:
DBW DIE BETRIEBSWIRTSCHAFT
KLEINES TABELLENBUCH FÜR STEUERLICHE BERATER
ZFO ZEITSCHRIFT FÜHRUNG + ORGANISATION

SCHATTAUER GMBH, VERLAG FÜR MEDIZIN UND NATURWISSENSCHAFTEN 681809
Hölderlinstr. 3, 70174 STUTTGART
Tel: 711 229870 **Fax:** 711 2298750
Email: info@schattauer.de
Web site: http://www.schattauer.de

Titles:
ADIPOSITAS
ARTHRITIS + RHEUMA
ÄRZTLICHE PSYCHOTHERAPIE UND PSYCHOSOMATISCHE MEDIZIN
HÄMOSTASEOLOGIE
KINDER- UND JUGENDMEDIZIN
MEDWELT DIE MEDIZINISCHE WELT
METHODS
NERVENHEILKUNDE
ONKOLOGISCHE WELT
OSTEOLOGIE OSTEOLOGY
PDP PSYCHODYNAMISCHE PSYCHOTHERAPIE
PHLEBOLOGIE
DIE PSYCHIATRIE
PTT PERSÖNLICHKEITSSTÖRUNGEN THEORIE UND THERAPIE
THROMBOSIS AND HAEMOSTASIS
TIERÄRZTLICHE PRAXIS G
TIERÄRZTLICHE PRAXIS K
VCOT VETERINARY AND COMPARATIVE ORTHOPAEDICS AND TRAUMATOLOGY

SCHAUFENSTER GMBH & CO. 688088
Großer Zimmerhof 25, 38300 WOLFENBÜTTEL
Tel: 5331 98990 **Fax:** 5331 989956
Email: anzeigen@schaufenster-wf.de
Web site: http://www.schaufenster-wf.de

Titles:
WOLFENBÜTTELER SCHAUFENSTER

SCHAUMBURGER NACHRICHTEN VERLAGSGES. MBH & CO. KG 688499
Am Markt 12, 31665 STADTHAGEN
Tel: 5721 809230 **Fax:** 5721 2007
Email: sn@madsack.de
Web site: http://www.sn-online.de

Titles:
SCHAUMBURGER NACHRICHTEN

SCHEELEN AG, INSTITUT FÜR MANAGEMENTBERATUNG UND DIAGNOSTIK 681563
Klettgaustr. 21, 79761 WALDSHUT-TIENGEN
Tel: 7741 96940 **Fax:** 7741 969420
Email: info@scheelen-institut.de
Web site: http://www.scheelen-institut.de

Titles:
EXECUTIVE EXCELLENCE

SCHENKELBERG STIFTUNG & CO. KGAA 1744173
Am Hambuch 17, 53340 MECKENHEIM
Tel: 2225 88930 **Fax:** 2225 8893170
Email: info@schenkelberg-ag.de
Web site: http://www.schenkelberg-ag.de

Titles:
MARBURGER BUND ZEITUNG

SCHIFFAHRTS-VERLAG 679352
Georgsplatz 1, 20099 HAMBURG
Tel: 40 70708002 **Fax:** 40 707080214
Email: anzeigen@hansa-online.de
Web site: http://www.hansa-online.de

Titles:
BINNENSCHIFFFAHRT
HANSA

SCHIMMEL MEDIA VERLAG GMBH & CO. KG 1638838
Kantstr. 38, 97074 WÜRZBURG **Tel:** 931 359810
Fax: 931 3598111
Email: info@schimmel-media.de
Web site: http://www.schimmel-media.de

Titles:
ZENTRADA.MAGAZIN

SCHLANGENBRUT E.V. 688123
Postfach 200922, 53139 BONN **Tel:** 228 1802094
Fax: 228 1802092
Email: info@schlangenbrut.de
Web site: http://www.schlangenbrut.de

Titles:
SCHLANGENBRUT

SCHLÜTERSCHE VERLAGSGES. MBH & CO. KG 679349
Hans-Böckler-Allee 7, 30173 HANNOVER
Tel: 511 85500 **Fax:** 511 85501103
Email: info@schluetersche.de
Web site: http://www.schluetersche.de

Titles:
AMZ AUTO MOTOR ZUBEHÖR
BERLINER UND MÜNCHENER TIERÄRZTLICHE WOCHENSCHRIFT
BFP FUHRPARK + MANAGEMENT
BINDEREPORT
BLECH
DEUTSCHES TIERÄRZTEBLATT BTK
EURO LASER
GENAU
GO GLOBAL BIZ
KONSTRUKTION & ENTWICKLUNG
NCFERTIGUNG
NKW PARTNER FÜR ERSATZTEILE UND REPARATUR VON NUTZFAHRZEUGEN
NORDDEUTSCHES HANDWERK
DER PRAKTISCHE TIERARZT
STEINBRUCH UND SANDGRUBE
TIHO-ANZEIGER

SCHNÄPPCHENFÜHRER-VERLAG GMBH 1643369
Metzinger Str. 40, 70794 FILDERSTADT
Tel: 711 7799738 **Fax:** 711 777206
Email: info@schnaeppchenfuehrer.com
Web site: http://www.schnaeppchenfuehrer.com

Titles:
SCHNÄPPCHENFÜHRER DEUTSCHLAND

SCHNEIDER DRUCK GMBH 682065
Erlbacher Str. 102, 91541 ROTHENBURG
Tel: 9861 4000 **Fax:** 9861 40016
Email: info@rotabene.de
Web site: http://www.rotabene.de

Titles:
DER DEUTSCHE FALLSCHIRMJÄGER

SCHNEIDER VERLAG HOHENGEHREN GMBH 680293
Wilhelmstr. 13, 73666 BALTMANNSWEILER
Tel: 7153 41206 **Fax:** 7153 48761
Email: schneiderverlag@t-online.de
Web site: http://www.paedagogik.de

Titles:
...TEXTIL...

SCHOLTEN VERLAG GMBH 1764034
Leuschnerstr. 1, 70174 STUTTGART
Tel: 711 1822101 **Fax:** 711 1822102
Email: redaktion@cavallo.de
Web site: http://www.cavallo.de

Titles:
CAVALLO

SCHOLZ FILM FERNSEH ABC FACHVERLAG E. K. 688167
Dassauweg 4a, 22145 HAMBURG
Tel: 40 6781704 **Fax:** 40 6782833
Email: info@filmabc.de
Web site: http://www.filmabc.de

Titles:
SCHOLZ FILM FERNSEH ABC

SCHONGAUER NACHRICHTEN KARL MOTZ GMBH & CO. KG 688169
Münzstr. 14, 86956 SCHONGAU **Tel:** 8861 920
Fax: 8861 92136
Email: gs.sog-nachrichten@merkur-online.de
Web site: http://www.merkur-online.de

Titles:
SCHONGAUER NACHRICHTEN

SCHOTT MUSIC GMBH & CO. KG 686083
Weihergarten 5, 55116 MAINZ **Tel:** 6131 246857
Fax: 6131 246483
Email: zeitschriften.leserservice@schott-music.com
Web site: http://www.schott-music.com

Titles:
MUSIK IN DER GRUNDSCHULE
MUSIK & BILDUNG
NEUE ZEITSCHRIFT FÜR MUSIK
DAS ORCHESTER
ÜBEN & MUSIZIEREN

SCHUH VERLAG 1782619
Wolfgang-Stock-Str. 17, 72076 TÜBINGEN
Tel: 7071 369095 **Fax:** 7071 369093
Email: pass-wort@t-online.de
Web site: http://www.verlag-schuh.de

Titles:
IM BLICK

SCHULZ-KIRCHNER VERLAG GMBH 681380
Mollweg 2, 65510 IDSTEIN **Tel:** 6126 93200
Fax: 6126 932050
Email: info@schulz-kirchner.de
Web site: http://www.schulz-kirchner.de

Titles:
ERGOTHERAPIE UND REHABILITATION
FORUM LOGOPÄDIE
PFAD

SCHÜREN VERLAG GMBH 678490
Universitätsstr. 55, 35037 MARBURG
Tel: 6421 63084 **Fax:** 6421 681190
Email: info@schueren-verlag.de
Web site: http://www.schueren-verlag.de

Titles:
AUGENBLICK
MEDIENWISSENSCHAFT

SCHÜRMANN + KLAGGES GMBH & CO. KG 677483
Industriestr. 34, 44894 BOCHUM **Tel:** 234 92140
Fax: 234 9214102
Email: sk@skala.de
Web site: http://www.skala.de

Titles:
AKADEMIE
IHK WIRTSCHAFT IM REVIER
LION

SCHWABENVERLAG AG 680736
Senefelderstr. 12, 73760 OSTFILDERN
Tel: 711 44060 **Fax:** 711 4406138
Email: info@schwabenverlag.de
Web site: http://www.schwabenverlag.de

Titles:
KATHOLISCHES SONNTAGSBLATT
ZEITSCHRIFT FÜR MEDIZINISCHE ETHIK

SCHWÄBISCHE ZEITUNG LINDAU GMBH & CO. KG 685103
Inselgraben 6, 88131 LINDAU **Tel:** 8382 93740
Fax: 8382 937430
Web site: http://www.szon.de

Titles:
LINDAUER ZEITUNG

SCHWÄBISCHE ZEITUNG ONLINE GES. FÜR MULTIMEDIA MBH + CO. KG 1652460
Rudolf-Roth-Str. 18, 88299 LEUTKIRCH
Tel: 7561 80751 **Fax:** 7561 809789
Email: info@szon.de
Web site: http://www.schwaebische.de

Titles:
SCHWÄBISCHE.DE

SCHWÄBISCHER VERLAG GMBH & CO. KG, DREXLER, GESSLER 684006
Rudolf-Roth-Str. 18, 88299 LEUTKIRCH
Tel: 7561 800 **Fax:** 7561 80134
Web site: http://www.schwaebische.de

Titles:
AALENER NACHRICHTEN
IPF- UND JAGST-ZEITUNG
SCHWÄBISCHE ZEITUNG

SCHWÄBISCHES TAGBLATT GMBH 688234
Uhlandstr. 2, 72072 TÜBINGEN **Tel:** 7071 9340
Fax: 7071 934109
Email: verlagsleitung@tagblatt.de
Web site: http://www.tagblatt.de

Titles:
SCHWÄBISCHES TAGBLATT
SÜDWEST PRESSE

SCHWARZWÄLDER BOTE MEDIENGES. MBH 684657
Kirchtorstr. 14, 78727 OBERNDORF
Tel: 7423 780 **Fax:** 7423 78328
Email: service@schwarzwaelder-bote.de
Web site: http://www.schwarzwaelder-bote.de

Titles:
SCHWARZWALD GÄSTE-JOURNAL
SCHWARZWÄLDER BOTE

SCHWETZINGER ZEITUNGSVERLAG GMBH + CO. KG 1680995
Carl-Theodor-Str. 1, 68723 SCHWETZINGEN
Tel: 6202 2050 **Fax:** 6202 205392
Email: juergen.gruler@schwetzinger-zeitung.de

Titles:
HOCKENHEIMER TAGESZEITUNG
SCHWETZINGER ZEITUNG

SD MEDIA SERVICES 695061
Reuchlinstr. 10, 10553 BERLIN **Tel:** 30 36286430
Fax: 30 36286437
Email: office@sd-media.de
Web site: http://www.sd-media.de

Titles:
SEENLAND SEENPLATTE
SPREE

SDK SCHUTZGEMEINSCHAFT DER KAPITALANLEGER E.V. 1717441
Hackenstr. 7b, 80331 MÜNCHEN
Tel: 89 20208460 **Fax:** 89 202084610
Email: info@sdk.org
Web site: http://www.sdk.org

Titles:
AKTIONÄRSREPORT

SDZ DRUCK UND MEDIEN GMBH & CO. KG 682642
Vordere Schmiedgasse 18, 73525 SCHWÄBISCH GMÜND **Tel:** 7171 60010
Fax: 7171 6001763
Web site: http://www.gmuender-tagespost.de

Titles:
GMÜNDER TAGESPOST
SCHWÄBISCHE POST
WIRTSCHAFT REGIONAL

SECUMEDIA VERLAGS-GMBH 684284
Lise-Meitner-Str. 4, 55435 GAU-ALGESHEIM
Tel: 6725 93040 **Fax:** 6725 5994
Email: info@secumedia.de
Web site: http://www.secumedia.de

Titles:
<KES>
WIK ZEITSCHRIFT FÜR DIE SICHERHEIT DER WIRTSCHAFT

SEEREISENMAGAZIN VERLAG GMBH 1690948
Hofäckerweg 22, 63743 ASCHAFFENBURG
Tel: 6021 6253030 **Fax:** 6021 6253031
Email: verlag@seereisenmagazin.de
Web site: http://www.seereisenmagazin.de

Titles:
SEEREISENMAGAZIN

SEG STEGENWALLER ENTERTAINMENT GROUP GMBH & CO. KG 1686889
Ruhrtalstr. 67, 45239 ESSEN **Tel:** 201 246880
Fax: 201 24688100
Email: seg@stegenwaller.de
Web site: http://www.stegenwaller.de

Titles:
EINFACH GUT GRILLEN
EINFACH GUT KOCHEN
GUTE LAUNE
LECKER KOCHEN & BACKEN
MEINE PAUSE

SEIPT.MEDIA 694733
Friedrich-Ebert-Str. 29, 14467 POTSDAM
Tel: 331 2006060 **Fax:** 331 9678027
Email: info@seipt-media.de
Web site: http://www.seipt-media.de

Titles:
EVENTS

SEITENSATZ VERLAG UG 683203
Robert-Bosch-Str. 10, 63477 MAINTAL
Tel: 6181 94340 **Fax:** 6181 45719
Email: kontakt@seitensatz.de
Web site: http://www.muehlens-media.de

Titles:
HESSISCHE GASTRONOMIE
SKÅL INTERNATIONAL JOURNAL DEUTSCHLAND

SEITENSTRASSEN VERLAG GMBH 1606043
Tieckstr. 8, 10115 BERLIN **Tel:** 30 48496230
Fax: 30 48496236
Email: verlag@dasmagazin.de
Web site: http://www.dasmagazin.de

Titles:
DAS MAGAZIN

SELBSTHILFE-BUND BLASENKREBS E.V. 1772850
Siepmanns Hof 9, 45479 MÜLHEIM
Tel: 208 62196041 **Fax:** 32222 479547
Email: bockelbrink@selbsthilfe-bund-blasenkrebs.de
Web site: http://www.harnblasenkrebs.de

Titles:
DIE HARNBLASE

SELIGENSTÄDTER EINHARD-VERLAG SCHWARZKOPF GMBH 684840
Marktplatz 14, 63500 SELIGENSTADT
Tel: 6182 22821 **Fax:** 6182 28283
Web site: http://www.der-kurier.de

Titles:
DER KURIER

SELLIER. EUROPEAN LAW PUBLISHERS GMBH 1640251
Geibelstr. 8, 81679 MÜNCHEN **Tel:** 89 451084580
Fax: 89 451084589
Email: info@sellier.de
Web site: http://www.sellier.de

Titles:
IHR INTERNATIONALES HANDELSRECHT

SENDLINGER ANZEIGER FÜRST OHG 686051
Luise-Kiesselbach-Platz 31, 81377 MÜNCHEN
Tel: 89 4524360 **Fax:** 89 45243650
Email: info@sendlingeranzeiger.de
Web site: http://www.sendlingeranzeiger.de

Titles:
MÜNCHNER WOCHEN ANZEIGER SENDLINGER ANZEIGER

SENNER-DRUCK GMBH & CO. KG 686533
Carl-Benz-Str. 1, 72622 NÜRTINGEN
Tel: 7022 94640 **Fax:** 7022 9464112
Email: forum@ntz.de
Web site: http://www.ntz.de

Titles:
NÜRTINGER ZEITUNG
WENDLINGER ZEITUNG
WENDLINGER ZEITUNG NÜRTINGER ZEITUNG

SERC WILD WINGS 695671
Zum Mooswäldle 9, 78054 VILLINGEN-SCHWENNINGEN **Tel:** 7720 97790
Fax: 7720 977915
Email: info@serc-wildwings.de
Web site: http://www.serc-wildwings.de

Titles:
SERC 04

SERGEJ MEDIEN- UND VERLAGS-GMBH 688386
Sophienstr. 8, 10178 BERLIN **Tel:** 30 4431980
Fax: 30 44319877
Email: info@blu.fm
Web site: http://www.blu.fm

Titles:
MATE

SERVICE & VERLAG GMBH 1690385
Festplatzstr. 6, 84030 ERGOLDING
Tel: 871 760586 **Fax:** 871 760588
Email: sv@bosch-druck.de
Web site: http://www.service-vlg.de

Titles:
NIEDERBAYERISCHE WIRTSCHAFT

SERVICEGESELLSCHAFT DES BUNDES DER SELBSTÄNDIGEN/ GEWERBEVERBAND BAYERN E.V. MBH 1741606
Schwanthalerstr. 110, 80339 MÜNCHEN
Tel: 89 540560 **Fax:** 89 5026493
Email: redaktion@unus-online.de
Web site: http://www.unus-online.de

Titles:
UNUS

SERVICE-GMBH DER BAUWIRTSCHAFT SÜDBADEN 678847
Holbeinstr. 16, 79100 FREIBURG **Tel:** 761 703020
Fax: 761 7030230
Email: service@bausuedbaden.de
Web site: http://www.bausuedbaden.de

Titles:
BAUFACHBLATT

SERVICE-RING BERLIN E.V. 1784594
Spandauer Damm 46, 14059 BERLIN
Tel: 30 8594010 **Fax:** 30 8594023
Email: deutscher_service_ring@web.de
Web site: http://www.deutscher-service-ring.de

Titles:
SERVICE KURIER

SEVENONE INTERMEDIA GMBH 1734851
Medienallee 6, 85774 UNTERFÖHRING
Tel: 89 950710 **Fax:** 89 95078901
Email: kontakt@sevenoneintermedia.de
Web site: http://www.sevenoneintermedia.de

Titles:
ECHT KABELEINS
PROSIEBEN

SHELL DEUTSCHLAND OIL GMBH 689260
22284 HAMBURG **Tel:** 40 63240 **Fax:** 40 63246814
Web site: http://www.shell.de

Titles:
TEAM

SH:Z SCHLESWIG-HOLSTEINISCHER ZEITUNGSVERLAG GMBH & CO. KG 1766890
Schloßstr. 5, 23701 EUTIN **Tel:** 4521 7790
Fax: 4521 7792925
Email: anzeigen.eutin@shz.de
Web site: http://www.shz.de

Titles:
ECKERNFÖRDER ZEITUNG
ELMSHORNER NACHRICHTEN
FLENSBURGER TAGEBLATT
HOLSTEINISCHER COURIER
HUSUMER NACHRICHTEN
DER INSEL-BOTE
NORDDEUTSCHE RUNDSCHAU
NORDFRIESLAND TAGEBLATT
OSTHOLSTEINER ANZEIGER
SCHLEI BOTE
SCHLESWIGER NACHRICHTEN
SCHLESWIG-HOLSTEINISCHE LANDESZEITUNG
STORMARNER TAGEBLATT
SYLTER RUNDSCHAU
WILSTERSCHE ZEITUNG
DIE WOCHE IM BLICKPUNKT

SIEGENER ZEITUNG, VORLÄNDER & ROTHMALER GMBH & CO. KG 683524
Obergraben 39, 57072 SIEGEN **Tel:** 271 59400
Fax: 271 5940398
Email: sekretariat@siegener-zeitung.de
Web site: http://www.siegener-zeitung.de

Titles:
SIEGENER ZEITUNG
SIEGENER ZEITUNG ONLINE

SIEMENS AG, CORPORATE COMMUNICATIONS 1724174
Wittelsbacherplatz 2, 80333 MÜNCHEN
Tel: 89 63633246 **Fax:** 89 63635292
Email: ulrich.eberl@siemens.com
Web site: http://www.siemens.com/pof

Titles:
PICTURES OF THE FUTURE

SIG MEDIA GMBH & CO. KG 697951
Pasteurstr. 1a, 50735 KÖLN **Tel:** 221 92182550
Fax: 221 92182516
Email: info@sig-media.de
Web site: http://www.sig-media.de

Titles:
BUSINESS GEOMATICS
BUSINESS GEOMATICS FOKUS

SIGILLUM-VERLAG GMBH 690975
Neumarkter Str. 87, 81673 MÜNCHEN
Tel: 89 43198550 **Fax:** 89 4312211
Email: anzeigen@zfk.de
Web site: http://www.zfk.de

Titles:
ZFK ZEITUNG FÜR KOMMUNALE WIRTSCHAFT

SIGNAL IDUNA GRUPPE, UNTERNEHMENSKOMMUNI-KATION 1776341
Joseph-Scherer-Str. 3, 44139 DORTMUND
Tel: 231 1354245 **Fax:** 231 135134245
Email: claus.rehse@signal-iduna.de
Web site: http://www.signal-iduna.de

Titles:
KONTAKTE

SIGNUM[KOM AGENTUR FÜR KOMMUNIKATION 684921
Richard-Wagner-Str. 18, 50674 KÖLN
Tel: 221 9255512 **Fax:** 221 9255513
Email: kontakt@signum-kom.de
Web site: http://www.signum-kom.de

Titles:
GRÜN IST LEBEN
LANDSCHAFT BAUEN & GESTALTEN

SIGS DATACOM GMBH 683990
Lindlaustr. 2c, 53842 TROISDORF
Tel: 2241 2341100 **Fax:** 2241 2341199
Email: info@sigs-datacom.de
Web site: http://www.sigs-datacom.de

Titles:
JAVASPEKTRUM
OBJEKT SPEKTRUM

SINNARIO GMBH 698877
Komturhof 2, 08527 PLAUEN **Tel:** 3741 1232116
Fax: 3741 1232112
Email: mail@viadukt-online.de
Web site: http://www.viadukt-online.de

Titles:
VIADUKT

SISU STEINSCHULTE VERLAG 682357
Lyngsbergstr. 16, 53177 BONN
Tel: 2228 42951951 **Fax:** 2228 42951952
Email: steinschulte.bonn@freenet.de
Web site: http://www.sechzig-na-und.de

Titles:
SECHZIG NA UND?

SITECO BELEUCHTUNGSTECHNIK GMBH 680585
Ohmstr. 50, 83301 TRAUNREUT **Tel:** 8669 330
Fax: 8669 33397
Email: info@siteco.de
Web site: http://www.siteco.de

Titles:
DESIGN + LICHT

SITUATIONSPRESSE LOEVEN + GORNY 684199
Finkenstr. 56, 47057 DUISBURG
Email: situationspresse@gmx.de
Web site: http://www.buchhandlung-weltbuehne.de

Titles:
KALLIPYGOS-BRIEFE

SKN DRUCK UND VERLAG GMBH & CO. KG 686845
Stellmacherstr. 14, 26506 NORDEN
Tel: 4931 9250 **Fax:** 4931 925360
Email: info@skn.info
Web site: http://www.skn.info

Titles:
OSTFRIESLAND MAGAZIN

SKYLINE MEDIEN VERLAGS GMBH 682203
Varrentrappstr. 53, 60486 FRANKFURT
Tel: 69 97951720 **Fax:** 69 97951729

Titles:
FRIZZ
FRIZZ
UNI FRIZZ

SLOGAN WERBUNG, MARKETING, CONSULTING GMBH 688491
Mühlwiesenstr. 32, 70794 FILDERSTADT
Tel: 7158 939020 **Fax:** 7158 9390277
Email: info@slogan.de
Web site: http://www.slogan.de

Titles:
SLOGANS

SLOW FOOD DEUTSCHLAND E.V. 1736147
Luisenstr. 45, 10117 BERLIN **Tel:** 30 24625939
Fax: 3 24625941
Email: info@slowfood.de
Web site: http://www.slowfood.de

Titles:
SLOW FOOD MAGAZIN

SMT-VERLAG 694722
Oberer Schenkgarten 4, 55218 INGELHEIM
Tel: 6132 431647 **Fax:** 6132 431649
Email: info@smt-verlag.de
Web site: http://www.smt-verlag.de

Titles:
EMV-ESD ELEKTROMAGNETISCHE VERTRÄGLICHKEIT

SMV SÜDWEST MEDIEN VERLAG GMBH 1650919
Barbarossaplatz 6, 76137 KARLSRUHE
Tel: 721 937867 **Fax:** 721 9378696
Email: karlsruhe@smv-medien.de
Web site: http://www.smv-medien.de

Titles:
FRIZZ
FRIZZ
FRIZZ

SN-VERLAG MICHAEL STEINERT 682278
An der Alster 21, 20099 HAMBURG
Tel: 40 2484540 **Fax:** 40 2803788
Email: vertrieb@snfachpresse.de
Web site: http://www.snfachpresse.de

Titles:
BTH HEIMTEX
FUSSBODEN TECHNIK
HAUSTEX
PARKETT IM HOLZHANDEL
PARKETT MAGAZIN
PARQUET INTERNATIONAL
WRP WÄSCHEREI + REINIGUNGS/PRAXIS

SOCIAL PUBLISH VERLAG GMBH 1772936
Planckstr. 13, 22765 HAMBURG **Tel:** 40 88885775
Fax: 40 88885781
Email: kontakt@enorm-magazin.de
Web site: http://www.enorm-magazin.de

Titles:
ENORM

SOFTWARE & SUPPORT VERLAG GMBH 681332
Geleitsstr. 14, 60599 FRANKFURT
Tel: 69 6300890 **Fax:** 69 63008989
Email: info@software-support.biz
Web site: http://www.software-support.biz

Titles:
ENTWICKLER MAGAZIN
JAVAMAGAZIN

SOK VERLAGSGES. MBH 1646288
Obergplatz 14, 47804 KREFELD **Tel:** 2151 152560
Fax: 2151 1525628
Email: info@sok-verlag.de
Web site: http://www.schmidtoverlaender.de

Titles:
HI TEC ELEKTROFACH
HI TEC HANDEL
HI TEC HOME

SOLAR UND NET 688511
Reifenberg 85, 91365 WEILERSBACH
Tel: 9194 8985 **Fax:** 9194 4262
Email: zeitschrift@solarmobil.de
Web site: http://www.solarmobil.de/zeitschrift

Titles:
EMOBILE PLUS SOLAR

SOLARENERGIE-FÖRDERVEREIN DEUTSCHLAND E.V. 1622004
Frère-Roger-Str. 8, 52062 AACHEN
Tel: 241 511616 **Fax:** 241 535786
Email: zentrale@sfv.de
Web site: http://www.sfv.de

Titles:
SOLARBRIEF

SOLARPRAXIS AG 698875
Zinnowitzer Str. 1, 10115 BERLIN
Tel: 30 726296300 **Fax:** 30 726296309
Email: service@pv-magazine.com
Web site: http://www.pv-magazine.com

Titles:
PV MAGAZINE

SONNENVERLAG GMBH & CO. KG 682107
Rotweg 8, 76532 BADEN-BADEN **Tel:** 7221 35010
Fax: 7221 3501204
Email: kontakt@klambt.de
Web site: http://www.media.klambt.de

Titles:
BACKEN NACH GROSSMUTTERS ART
FRAU MIT HERZ
FRAU MIT HERZ EINMACHEN & EINKOCHEN
FRAU MIT HERZ MUFFINS & CUPCAKES
FRAU MIT HERZ OFENHITS
FRAU MIT HERZ SÜSSES AUS OMAS BACKBUCH
FRISUREN
FRISUREN WELT DER FRAU SPEZIAL
LEA
LEA EXTRA AUFLÄUFE & GRATINS
LEA FÜR GÄSTE KÜCHEN KLASSIKER
LEA SPECIAL FRISUREN
REZEPTE MIT PFIFF
DIE SCHÖNSTEN BACKREZEPTE
WELT DER FRAU

SONNTAG AKTUELL GMBH 688534
Plieninger Str. 150, 70567 STUTTGART
Tel: 711 72050 **Fax:** 711 72051509
Email: redaktion@soak.zgs.de
Web site: http://www.sonntag-aktuell.de

Titles:
SONNTAG AKTUELL

SONNTAG VERLAG IN MVS MEDIZINVERLAGE STUTTGART GMBH & CO. KG 690928
Oswald-Hesse-Str. 50, 70469 STUTTGART
Tel: 711 89310 **Fax:** 711 8931706
Web site: http://www.sonntag-verlag.com

Titles:
ZEITSCHRIFT FÜR GANZHEITLICHE TIERMEDIZIN

SONNTAGS-MEDIEN GMBH & CO. KG 682902
August-Madsack-Str. 1, 30559 HANNOVER
Tel: 511 5182021 **Fax:** 511 5182023
Email: info@hallo-sonntag.de
Web site: http://www.hallo-sonntag.de

Titles:
HALLO ANZEIGER
HALLO HANNOVERSCHES WOCHENBLATT - AUSG. NORD
HALLO LAATZENER WOCHE
HALLO RUNDBLICK GARBSEN/SEELZE

SOZIALVERBAND VDK DEUTSCHLAND E.V. 688572
Wurzerstr. 4a, 53175 BONN **Tel:** 228 820930
Fax: 228 8209343
Email: presse@vdk.de
Web site: http://www.vdk.de

Titles:
VDK ZEITUNG

SPANGEMACHER VERLAGS GMBH & CO. KG 681950
Papiermühlenweg 74, 40882 RATINGEN
Tel: 2102 16780 **Fax:** 2102 167828
Email: media@euro-focus.de
Web site: http://www.euro-focus.de

Titles:
FOCUS

SPECIAL MEDIA CONSULTING 685092
Steeler Bergstr. 96, 45276 ESSEN
Tel: 201 8508513 **Fax:** 201 8508514
Email: chrkolb@pressesprecher.de
Web site: http://www.life-at.de

Titles:
LIFE@MAGAZIN

SPEEDPOOL MULTIMEDIA-SERVICE GMBH 1652386
Bernhard-Nocht-Str. 99, 20359 HAMBURG
Tel: 40 3006820 **Fax:** 40 30068222
Email: info@speedpool.com
Web site: http://www.speedpool.com

Titles:
UP TREND

SPEKTRUM AKADEMISCHER VERLAG, IMPRINT DER SPRINGER-VERLAG GMBH 1769259
Tiergartenstr. 17, 69121 HEIDELBERG
Tel: 6221 4870 **Fax:** 6221 48768043
Web site: http://www.spektrum-verlag.de

Titles:
NEURO FORUM

SPEKTRUM AKADEMISCHER VERLAG, SPRINGER-VERLAG GMBH 679372
Tiergartenstr. 17, 69121 HEIDELBERG
Tel: 6221 4870 **Fax:** 6221 48768043
Email: biospektrum@springer.com
Web site: http://www.spektrum-verlag.de

Titles:
BIOSPEKTRUM

SPEKTRUM DER WISSENSCHAFT VERLAGSGES. MBH 688606
Slevogtstr. 3, 69126 HEIDELBERG
Tel: 6221 9126600 **Fax:** 6221 9126751
Email: verlag@spektrum.com
Web site: http://www.spektrum.de

Titles:
SPEKTRUM DER WISSENSCHAFT
STERNE UND WELTRAUM

SPIEGEL ONLINE GMBH 1792897
Brandstwiete 19, 20457 HAMBURG
Tel: 40 38080222 **Fax:** 40 38080223
Email: spiegel@spiegel.de
Web site: http://www.spiegel.de

Titles:
SPIEGEL ONLINE

SPIEGEL-VERLAG RUDOLF AUGSTEIN GMBH & CO. KG 684777
Brandstwiete 19, 20457 HAMBURG **Tel:** 40 30070
Fax: 40 30072247
Email: spiegel@spiegel.de
Web site: http://www.spiegel.de

Titles:
KULTURSPIEGEL
DER SPIEGEL
UNI SPIEGEL

SPIRIDON-VERLAGS GMBH 688684
Dorfstr. 18a, 40699 ERKRATH **Tel:** 211 726364
Fax: 211 786823
Email: spiridon@gmx.com
Web site: http://www.laufmagazin-spiridon.de

Titles:
SPIRIDON

SPITTA VERLAG GMBH & CO. KG 684552
Ammonitenstr. 1, 72336 BALINGEN
Tel: 7433 9520 **Fax:** 7433 952321
Web site: http://www.spitta.de

Titles:
KONGRESS KALENDER MEDIZIN INTERNATIONAL CONGRESS CALENDAR MEDICINE
ZMK
ZP ZAHNARZT & PRAXIS

SPITZENVERBAND DER LANDWIRTSCHAFTLICHEN SOZIALVERSICHERUNG 1766962
Weißensteinstr. 72, 34131 KASSEL
Tel: 561 9359241 **Fax:** 561 9359244
Email: presse1@spv.lsv.de
Web site: http://www.lsv.de

Titles:
LSV KOMPAKT

SPO SONNTAGS POST VERLAG GMBH & CO. KG 1606036
Europaallee 33b, 50226 FRECHEN
Tel: 2234 957440 **Fax:** 2234 95744499
Email: joachim.hesse@mds.de
Web site: http://www.rheinische-anzeigenblaetter.de

Titles:
SONNTAGS POST FRECHEN
SONNTAGS POST HÜRTH
SONNTAGS POST PULHEIM

SPORT1 ONLINE GMBH 1651882
Münchener Str. 101g, 85737 ISMANING
Tel: 89 960662700 **Fax:** 89 960662709
Email: info@sport1.de
Web site: http://www.sport1.de

Titles:
SPORT1

SPORTÄRZTEBUND NORDRHEIN E.V. 688724
Am Sportpark Müngersdorf 6, 50933 KÖLN
Tel: 221 493785 **Fax:** 221 493207
Email: sportaerztebundnr@t-online.de
Web site: http://www.sportaerztebund.de

Titles:
SPORTMEDIZIN IN NORDRHEIN

SPORTVERLAG SCHMIDT + DREISILKER GMBH 680656
Böblinger Str. 68/1, 71065 SINDELFINGEN
Tel: 7031 862800 **Fax:** 7031 862801

Titles:
DEUTSCHE TENNIS ZEITUNG
RUDERSPORT
TENNISSPORT

SPOTLIGHT VERLAG GMBH
677326
Fraunhoferstr. 22, 82152 PLANEGG
Tel: 89 856810 **Fax:** 89 85681105
Email: abo@spotlight-verlag.de
Web site: http://www.spotlight-verlag.de

Titles:
ADESSO
BUSINESS SPOTLIGHT
DEUTSCH PERFEKT
ÉCOUTE
SPOT ON
SPOTLIGHT

SPREE-PRESSE- UND PR-BÜRO GMBH
682285
Märkisches Ufer 34, 10179 BERLIN
Tel: 30 2474680 **Fax:** 30 2425104
Email: agentur@spree-pr.com
Web site: http://www.spree-pr.com

Titles:
WASSERZEITUNG ZVK

SPRINGER AUTOMOTIVE MEDIA/SPRINGER FACHMEDIEN MÜNCHEN GMBH
1784590
Aschauer Str. 30, 81549 MÜNCHEN
Tel: 89 2030430
Web site: http://www.springer-transport-media.de

Titles:
ASP AUTO SERVICE PRAXIS
ASP AUTOSERVICEPRAXIS.DE
AUTOFLOTTE
AUTOFLOTTE ONLINE
AUTOHAUS
AUTOHAUS ONLINE
GW-TRENDS
TANKSTELLEN MARKT
VKU VERKEHRSUNFALL UND FAHRZEUGTECHNIK

SPRINGER AUTOMOTIVE MEDIA/SPRINGER FACHMEDIEN WIESBADEN GMBH
1757838
Abraham-Lincoln-Str. 46, 65189 WIESBADEN
Tel: 611 78780 **Fax:** 611 7878400
Email: sam-service@springer.com
Web site: http://www.springerautomotivemedia.de

Titles:
ATZ AUTOMOBILTECHNISCHE ZEITSCHRIFT
MTZ MOTORTECHNISCHE ZEITSCHRIFT

SPRINGER FACHMEDIEN WIESBADEN GMBH
1788276
Abraham-Lincoln-Str. 46, 65189 WIESBADEN
Tel: 611 78780 **Fax:** 611 7878400
Web site: http://www.best-ad-media.de

Titles:
H & V JOURNAL

SPRINGER GESUNDHEITS- UND PHARMAZIEVERLAG GMBH
1731861
Am Forsthaus Gravenbruch 5, 63263 NEU-ISENBURG **Tel:** 6102 5060 **Fax:** 6102 506382
Email: kontakt@springer.com
Web site: http://www.springer-gup.de

Titles:
APOTHEKE + MARKETING

SPRINGER MEDIZIN, ÄRZTE ZEITUNG VERLAGSGES. MBH
1783412
Am Forsthaus Gravenbruch 5, 63263 NEU-ISENBURG **Tel:** 6102 5060 **Fax:** 6102 506123
Email: info@aerztezeitung.de
Web site: http://www.aerztezeitung.de

Titles:
APOTHEKERPLUS
ARZNEIMITTEL ZEITUNG
ÄRZTE ZEITUNG FÜR NEUROLOGEN UND PSYCHIATER
ÄRZTE ZEITUNG KLINIKREPORT
ARZTONLINE
ARZTRAUM
FORSCHUNG UND PRAXIS
MEDICA AKTUELL
PHARMA KOMMUNIKATION
PHARMA WOCHE

SPRINGER-VDI-VERLAG GMBH & CO. KG
678861
VDI-Platz 1, 40468 DÜSSELDORF **Tel:** 211 61030
Fax: 211 6103300
Email: info@technikwissen.de
Web site: http://www.technikwissen.de

Titles:
BAUINGENIEUR
BWK
GEFAHRSTOFFE REINHALTUNG DER LUFT
HLH LÜFTUNG/KLIMA HEIZUNG/SANITÄR GEBÄUDETECHNIK
KONSTRUKTION
LÄRMBEKÄMPFUNG
LOGISTIK FÜR UNTERNEHMEN
SPECIAL ANTRIEBSTECHNIK
TECHNISCHE SICHERHEIT
UMWELT MAGAZIN
VDI-Z INTEGRIERTE PRODUKTION

SPRINGER-VERLAG GMBH
678799
Tiergartenstr. 17, 69121 HEIDELBERG
Tel: 6221 4870 **Fax:** 6221 4878366
Email: subscriptions@springer.com
Web site: http://www.springer.com

Titles:
>>ÄSTHETISCHE DERMATOLOGIE & KOSMETOLOGIE
>>EXTRACTA GYNAECOLOGICA
>>EXTRACTA ORTHOPAEDICA
ACTA NEUROPATHOLOGICA
DER ANAESTHESIST
ANALYTICAL AND BIOANALYTICAL CHEMISTRY
ANNALS OF FINANCE
ANNALS OF HEMATOLOGY
ARCHIVE OF APPLIED MECHANICS
ARCHIVES OF DERMATOLOGICAL RESEARCH
ARCHIVES OF GYNECOLOGY AND OBSTETRICS
ARCHIVES OF ORTHOPAEDIC AND TRAUMA SURGERY
ARCHIVES OF TOXICOLOGY
ARTHROSKOPIE
BASIC RESEARCH IN CARDIOLOGY
BEST PRACTICE ONKOLOGIE
BIOPROCESS AND BIOSYSTEMS ENGINEERING
BRAIN STRUCTURE AND FUNCTION
BUNDESGESUNDHEITSBLATT GESUNDHEITSFORSCHUNG GESUNDHEITSSCHUTZ
CANCER CHEMOTHERAPY AND PHARMACOLOGY
CHILD'S NERVOUS SYSTEM CHNS
DER CHIRURG
DER CHIRURG BDC
CII CANCER IMMUNOLOGY IMMUNOTHERAPY
CLINICAL AUTONOMIC RESEARCH CAR
CLINICAL ORAL INVESTIGATIONS
CLINICAL RESEARCH IN CARDIOLOGY
CME
COLLOID AND POLYMER SCIENCE
COMPUTATIONAL MECHANICS
COMPUTER SCIENCE - RESEARCH AND DEVELOPMENT
DFZ DER FREIE ZAHNARZT
DER DIABETOLOGE
DIABETOLOGIA
EMERGENCY RADIOLOGY
ENVIRONMENTAL CHEMISTRY LETTERS
ENVIRONMENTAL SCIENCE AND POLLUTION RESEARCH
ERWERBS-OBSTBAU
EUROPEAN ARCHIVES OF OTO-RHINO-LARYNGOLOGY
EUROPEAN ARCHIVES OF PSYCHIATRY AND CLINICAL NEUROSCIENCE
EUROPEAN FOOD RESEARCH AND TECHNOLOGY
EUROPEAN JOURNAL OF APPLIED PHYSIOLOGY
EUROPEAN JOURNAL OF CLINICAL PHARMACOLOGY
EUROPEAN JOURNAL OF FOREST RESEARCH
EUROPEAN JOURNAL OF NUCLEAR MEDICINE AND MOLECULAR IMAGING
EUROPEAN JOURNAL OF NUTRITION
EUROPEAN JOURNAL OF PLASTIC SURGERY
EUROPEAN JOURNAL OF WILDLIFE RESEARCH
EUROPEAN RADIOLOGY
EUROPEAN SPINE JOURNAL
EXPERIMENTAL BRAIN RESEARCH
FORENSISCHE PSYCHIATRIE, PSYCHOLOGIE, KRIMINOLOGIE
FORSCHUNG IM INGENIEURWESEN
FORUM
FORUM DER PSYCHOANALYSE
DER GASTROENTEROLOGE
GEFÄSSCHIRURGIE
GESUNDE PFLANZEN
GPS SOLUTIONS
GRAEFE'S ARCHIVE FOR CLINICAL AND EXPERIMENTAL OPHTHALMOLOGY
DER GYNÄKOLOGE
GYNÄKOLOGISCHE ENDOKRINOLOGIE
GYNECOLOGICAL SURGERY
DER HAUTARZT
HEAT AND MASS TRANSFER
HERZSCHRITTMACHERTHERAPIE + ELEKTROPHYSIOLOGIE
HNO
INDEX FÜR DIE GESUNDHEITSWIRTSCHAFT
INFORMATIK SPEKTRUM
INTENSIVE CARE MEDICINE
INTENSIVMEDIZIN UND NOTFALLMEDIZIN
INTERNATIONAL ARCHIVES OF OCCUPATIONAL AND ENVIRONMENTAL HEALTH
INTERNATIONAL JOURNAL OF COLORECTAL DISEASE
INTERNATIONAL JOURNAL OF LEGAL MEDICINE
THE INTERNATIONAL JOURNAL OF LIFE CYCLE ASSESSMENT
INTERNATIONAL ORTHOPAEDICS
DER INTERNIST
JOURNAL FÜR ÄSTHETISCHE CHIRURGIE
JOURNAL OF CANCER RESEARCH AND CLINICAL ONCOLOGY
JOURNAL OF COMPARATIVE PHYSIOLOGY B
JOURNAL OF MOLECULAR MEDICINE
JOURNAL OF MOLECULAR MODELING
JOURNAL OF NEUROLOGY
JOURNAL OF ORNITHOLOGY
JOURNAL OF PEST SCIENCE
JOURNAL OF PUBLIC HEALTH
DER KARDIOLOGE
KNEE SURGERY SPORTS TRAUMATOLOGY ARTHROSCOPY
LANGENBECK'S ARCHIVES OF SURGERY
MANUELLE MEDIZIN
MEDICAL MICROBIOLOGY AND IMMUNOLOGY
MEDIZINISCHE GENETIK
MICROSYSTEM TECHNOLOGIES
MONATSSCHRIFT KINDERHEILKUNDE
NAUNYN-SCHMIEDEBERG'S ARCHIVES OF PHARMACOLOGY
DER NEPHROLOGE
DER NERVENARZT
NEURORADIOLOGY
NEUROSURGICAL REVIEW
NOTFALL + RETTUNGSMEDIZIN
OBERE EXTREMITÄT
DER ONKOLOGE
DER OPHTHALMOLOGE
OR SPECTRUM
ORAL AND MAXILLOFACIAL SURGERY
DER ORTHOPÄDE
PADDY AND WATER ENVIRONMENT
DER PATHOLOGE
PEDIATRIC NEPHROLOGY
PEDIATRIC RADIOLOGY
PEDIATRIC SURGERY INTERNATIONAL
DER PNEUMOLOGE
POLYMER BULLETIN
PORTUGUESE ECONOMIC JOURNAL
PRÄVENTION UND GESUNDHEITSFÖRDERUNG
PRODUCTION ENGINEERING
PSYCHOLOGICAL RESEARCH
PSYCHOPHARMACOLOGY
PSYCHOTHERAPEUT
DER RADIOLOGE
RAUMFORSCHUNG UND RAUMORDNUNG
RECHTSMEDIZIN
REGIONAL ENVIRONMENTAL CHANGE
RHEUMATOLOGY INTERNATIONAL
DER SCHMERZ
SEMINARS IN IMMUNOPATHOLOGY
SKELETAL RADIOLOGY
SLEEP AND BREATHING
SOMNOLOGIE
SUPPORTIVE CARE IN CANCER
TRAUMA UND BERUFSKRANKHEIT
UMWELTWISSENSCHAFTEN UND SCHADSTOFF-FORSCHUNG
DER UNFALLCHIRURG
DER UROLOGE
UWF UMWELT WIRTSCHAFTS FORUM
VIRCHOWS ARCHIV
WORLD JOURNAL OF UROLOGY
ZEITSCHRIFT FÜR DIE GESAMTE VERSICHERUNGSWISSENSCHAFT
ZEITSCHRIFT FÜR EPILEPTOLOGIE
ZEITSCHRIFT FÜR GERONTOLOGIE + GERIATRIE
ZEITSCHRIFT FÜR HERZ-, THORAX- UND GEFÄSSCHIRURGIE
ZEITSCHRIFT FÜR RHEUMATOLOGIE

SPV SÜDDEUTSCHER PÄDAGOGISCHER VERLAG GMBH
677713
Silcherstr. 7a, 70176 STUTTGART
Tel: 711 2103070 **Fax:** 711 21030799
Email: info@spv-s.de
Web site: http://www.spv-s.de

Titles:
AKTIVER RUHESTAND
B&W BILDUNG UND WISSENSCHAFT

ST. BENNO BUCH- UND ZEITSCHRIFTENVERLAGSGES. MBH
689191
Stammerstr. 11, 04159 LEIPZIG **Tel:** 341 467770
Fax: 341 4677740
Email: service@st-benno.de
Web site: http://www.st-benno.de

Titles:
TAG DES HERRN

ST. MICHAELSBUND, DIÖZESANVERBAND MÜNCHEN UND FREISING E.V.
686034
Herzog-Wilhelm-Str. 5, 80331 MÜNCHEN
Tel: 89 232250 **Fax:** 89 23225440
Email: info@st-michaelsbund.de
Web site: http://www.st-michaelsbund.de

Titles:
MÜNCHNER KIRCHENZEITUNG

STAATSANZEIGER FÜR BADEN-WÜRTTEMBERG GMBH
679025
Breitscheidstr. 69, 70176 STUTTGART
Tel: 711 666010 **Fax:** 711 6660119
Email: verlag@staatsanzeiger.de
Web site: http://www.staatsanzeiger-verlag.de

Titles:
AKTIV FRAUEN IN BADEN-WÜRTTEMBERG
SCHLÖSSER BADEN-WÜRTTEMBERG
STAATSANZEIGER

STAATSBAD BAD WILDUNGEN GMBH
1622218
Brunnenallee 1, 34537 BAD WILDUNGEN
Tel: 5621 9656724 **Fax:** 5621 9656737
Email: nahler@badwildungen.net
Web site: http://www.bad-wildungen.de

Titles:
BAD WILDUNGEN LIVE

STAATSBAD WILDBAD BÄDER- UND KURBETRIEBSGES. MBH
1621740
Baetznerstr. 85, 75323 BAD WILDBAD
Tel: 7081 3030 **Fax:** 7081 303100
Email: info@staatsbad-wildbad.de
Web site: http://www.bad-wildbad.de

Titles:
ENZTAL

STADT ARNSBERG, FACHSTELLE "ZUKUNFT ALTER"
1622292
Lange Wende 16a, 59755 ARNSBERG
Tel: 2932 2012207 **Fax:** 2932 529056
Email: m.gerwin@arnsberg.de
Web site: http://www.arnsberg.de/senioren

Titles:
SICHT

STADT, DEZERNAT FÜR SOZIALES, JUGEND UND SPORT
1605933
Hansaallee 150, 60320 FRANKFURT
Tel: 69 21233405 **Fax:** 69 21230741
Email: info.senioren-zeitschrift@stadt-frankfurt.de
Web site: http://www.senioren-zeitschrift-frankfurt.de

Titles:
SENIOREN ZEITSCHRIFT

STADT ESSEN, UMWELTAMT, R. 14.25
1745929
Porscheplatz, 45127 ESSEN **Tel:** 201 8859219
Fax: 201 8859009
Email: info@essen.de
Web site: http://www.essen.de

Titles:
OZON INFORMATIONEN

STADT ESSLINGEN AM NECKAR, BEAUFTRAGTE FÜR SENIOREN UND BÜRGERSCHAFTLICHES ENGAGEMENT
1622346
Ritterstr. 16, 73728 ESSLINGEN
Tel: 711 35123108 **Fax:** 711 3512552614
Email: renate.schaumburg@esslingen.de
Web site: http://www.forum-esslingen.de

Titles:
POSTMICHEL-BRIEF

STADT, FACHBEREICH NEUE MEDIEN, SENIORENBEIRAT
1622295
Langemarkstr. 19, 46042 OBERHAUSEN
Tel: 208 8252724 **Fax:** 208 2056264
Email: wfe@oberhausen.de
Web site: http://bibliothek.oberhausen.de/seniorenzeitung

Titles:
WIR FÜR EUCH

STADT HAMM, AMT FÜR SOZIALE INTEGRATION 681753
Sachsenweg 6, 59073 HAMM **Tel:** 2381 176761
Fax: 2381 176730
Email: pieper@stadt.hamm.de
Web site: http://www.hamm.de
Titles:
DAS FENSTER

STADT MÖNCHENGLADBACH, GLEICHSTELLUNGSSTELLE 1650007
Fliethstr. 86, 41061 MÖNCHENGLADBACH
Tel: 2161 253611 **Fax:** 2161 253619
Email: gleichstellungsstelle@moenchengladbach.de
Web site: http://www.moenchengladbach.de
Titles:
FRAUEN KALENDER

STADT RECKLINGHAUSEN, SENIORENBEIRAT 1622505
Rathausplatz 3, 45655 RECKLINGHAUSEN
Tel: 2361 501106 **Fax:** 2361 501112
Email: seniorenbeirat@recklinghausen.de
Web site: http://www.seniorenbeirat-recklinghausen.de
Titles:
RE-SOLUT

STADT SCHWERTE, AKTIVE SENIOREN 1616885
Konrad-Zuse-Str. 4, 58239 SCHWERTE
Tel: 2304 242726 **Fax:** 2304 242726
Email: info@as.citynetz.com
Web site: http://www.as.citynetz.com
Titles:
AS AKTIVE SENIOREN

STADT, SENIORENBEAUFTRAGTE 1621987
Hertinger Str. 12, 59423 UNNA **Tel:** 2303 256903
Fax: 2303 256905
Email: herbstblattredaktion@gmx.de
Web site: http://www.unna.de
Titles:
HERBST-BLATT

STADT SIEGBURG 682237
Nogenter Platz 10, 53721 SIEGBURG
Tel: 2241 102290 **Fax:** 2241 102284
Email: rathaus@siegburg.de
Web site: http://www.siegburg.de
Titles:
65ER NACHRICHTEN DER STADT SIEGBURG

STADT, SOZIALAMT, REFERAT FÜR ALTENARBEIT 688379
Obere Königsstr. 8, 34117 KASSEL
Tel: 561 7875071 **Fax:** 561 7875299
Email: uwe.wolk@stadt-kassel.de
Web site: http://www.stadt-kassel.de
Titles:
SENIORENPROGRAMM

STADT STUTTGART 677898
Marktplatz 1, 70173 STUTTGART
Tel: 711 2162453 **Fax:** 711 2167705
Email: info@stuttgart.de
Web site: http://www.stuttgart.de
Titles:
STUTTGARTER AMTSBLATT

STADT UND RAUM MESSE UND MEDIEN GMBH 688846
Alte Schule Bannetze, 29308 WINSEN
Tel: 5146 98860 **Fax:** 5146 988629
Email: info@stadtundraum.de
Web site: http://www.stadt-und-raum.de
Titles:
STADT UND RAUM

STADT, VOLKSHOCHSCHULE, ARBEITSKREIS WIR 690587
Bredenscheider Str. 19, 45525 HATTINGEN
Tel: 2324 2042336
Web site: http://www.hattingen.de
Titles:
WIR

STADT WIEHL, OFFENE ARBEIT FÜR SENIOREN 1723937
Homburger Str. 7, 51674 WIEHL **Tel:** 2262 797123
Fax: 22362 797121
Email: oase@wiehl.de
Web site: http://www.wiehl.de
Titles:
INFO OASE

STADTANZEIGER-VERLAGS GMBH & CO. KG 682829
Scheffelstr. 21, 77654 OFFENBURG
Tel: 781 93400 **Fax:** 781 9340153
Email: anzeigen.guller@staz-online.de
Web site: http://www.stadtanzeiger-ortenau.de
Titles:
DER GULLER - AUSG. ACHERN/OBERKIRCH

STADTENTWÄSSERUNGS-BETRIEBE KÖLN, AÖR 1600534
Ostmerheimer Str. 555, 51109 KÖLN
Tel: 221 22122407 **Fax:** 221 22124533
Email: info@steb-koeln.de
Web site: http://www.steb-koeln.de
Titles:
KOMPETENZ WASSER

STÄDTISCHE WERKE MAGDEBURG 684838
Am Alten Theater 1, 39104 MAGDEBURG
Tel: 391 5870 **Fax:** 391 5872828
Email: info@sw-magdeburg.de
Web site: http://www.sw-magdeburg.de
Titles:
:OTTO

STADTREVUE VERLAG GMBH 1638444
Maastrichter Str. 49, 50672 KÖLN
Tel: 221 9515410 **Fax:** 221 95154111
Email: geschaeftsfuehrung@stadtrevue.de
Web site: http://www.stadtrevue.de
Titles:
HEIMVORTEIL
IMMERGRÜN
STADTREVUE
STADTREVUE SPEZIAL WEITERBILDUNG
TAGNACHT

STADTSTREICHER GMBH 688838
Am Feldschlößchen 18, 09116 CHEMNITZ
Tel: 371 383800 **Fax:** 371 3838038
Email: info@stadtstreicher.de
Web site: http://www.stadtstreicher.de
Titles:
STADTSTREICHER

STADTWERKE GÜTERSLOH GMBH 681260
Berliner Str. 260, 33330 GÜTERSLOH
Tel: 5241 822521 **Fax:** 5241 8242521
Email: info@stadtwerke-gt.de
Web site: http://www.stadtwerke-gt.de
Titles:
E.NEWS

STADTWERKE HANNOVER AG 681289
Ihmeplatz 2, 30449 HANNOVER **Tel:** 511 4301753
Fax: 511 4302024
Email: kommunikation@enercity.de
Web site: http://www.enercity.de
Titles:
TOP5

STAHL-INFORMATIONS-ZENTRUM 1691167
Sohnstr. 65, 40237 DÜSSELDORF
Tel: 211 6707849 **Fax:** 211 6707344
Email: horst.woeckner@stahl-info.de
Web site: http://www.stahl-info.de
Titles:
FASZINATION STAHL

STAMM VERLAG GMBH 681422
Goldammerweg 16, 45134 ESSEN
Tel: 201 843000 **Fax:** 201 472590
Email: info@stamm.de
Web site: http://www.stamm.de
Titles:
E & W ERZIEHUNG UND WISSENSCHAFT
ERZIEHUNG UND WISSENSCHAFT - ZS. D. BILDUNGSGEWERKSCHAFT GEW (BUNDESAUSG.)
STAMM

STATION TO STATION VERLAGS-GMBH 688884
Exerzierplatz 14, 24103 KIEL **Tel:** 431 702100
Fax: 431 7021010
Email: station@station.de
Web site: http://www.station.de
Titles:
STATION TO STATION

STATISTISCHES AMT SAARLAND 682957
Virchowstr. 7, 66119 SAARBRÜCKEN
Tel: 681 5015925 **Fax:** 681 5015915
Email: statistik@lzd.saarland.de
Web site: http://www.statistik.saarland.de
Titles:
MÄRKTE IM SAARLAND MIT WOCHENKALENDER

STAUFENBIEL INSTITUT GMBH 679184
Maria-Hilf-Str. 15, 50677 KÖLN **Tel:** 221 9126630
Fax: 221 9126639
Email: info@staufenbiel.de
Web site: http://www.staufenbiel.de
Titles:
STAUFENBIEL WIRTSCHAFTSWISSENSCHAFTLER

STEIN-MEDIEN GMBH 689632
Rudolf-Wissell-Str. 18, 37075 GÖTTINGEN
Tel: 551 389000 **Fax:** 551 3890011
Email: info@trends-fun.de
Web site: http://www.trends-fun.de
Titles:
TRENDS&FUN

STEINTOR-VERLAG GMBH 679532
Grapengießerstr. 30, 23556 LÜBECK
Tel: 451 8798849 **Fax:** 451 8798837
Email: info@steintor-verlag.de
Titles:
BLUTALKOHOL

STEIN-VERLAG BADEN-BADEN GMBH 678883
Josef-Herrmann-Str. 1, 76473 IFFEZHEIM
Tel: 7229 6060 **Fax:** 7229 60610
Email: infostv@stein-verlaggmbh.de
Web site: http://www.stein-verlaggmbh.de
Titles:
GP GESTEINS-PERSPEKTIVEN

STEIN-WERBUNG GMBH 682930
Großmoorring 18, 21079 HAMBURG
Tel: 40 7901640 **Fax:** 40 79016422
Email: info@stein-werbung.de
Web site: http://www.stein-werbung.de
Titles:
TISCHLERMEISTER NORD

STELLENANZEIGEN.DE GMBH & CO. KG 1690880
Rablstr. 26, 81669 MÜNCHEN **Tel:** 89 651076100
Fax: 89 651076999
Email: info@stellenanzeigen.de
Web site: http://www.stellenanzeigen.de
Titles:
STELLENANZEIGEN.DE

STELLEN-ONLINE.DE AG 1652543
Reinhold-Frank-Str. 63, 76133 KARLSRUHE
Tel: 721 9205533 **Fax:** 721 9205544
Email: info@stellen-online.de
Web site: http://www.stellen-online.de
Titles:
STELLEN-ONLINE.DE

STERN-BUCH;VERLAG GRUNER + JAHR AG + CO KG 1630437
Am Baumwall 11, 20459 HAMBURG
Tel: 40 37030
Web site: http://www.guj.de
Titles:
DAS WAR . . .

STERN.DE GMBH 1626896
Am Baumwall 11, 20459 HAMBURG
Tel: 40 37030 **Fax:** 40 37036000
Web site: http://www.stern.de
Titles:
STERN.DE

STEUERBERATERKAMMER HESSEN 684212
Gutleutstr. 175, 60327 FRANKFURT
Tel: 69 1530020 **Fax:** 69 15300260
Email: geschaeftsstelle@stbk-hessen.de
Web site: http://www.stbk-hessen.de
Titles:
KAMMERRUNDSCHREIBEN

STEUERBERATERVERBAND SCHLESWIG-HOLSTEIN E.V. 690043
Willy-Brandt-Ufer 10, 24143 KIEL **Tel:** 431 997970
Fax: 431 9979717
Email: info@stbvsh.de
Web site: http://www.stbvsh.de
Titles:
VERBANDSNACHRICHTEN

STEUERBERATERVERBAND WESTFALEN-LIPPE E.V. 690044
Gasselstiege 33, 48159 MÜNSTER
Tel: 251 535860 **Fax:** 251 5358660
Email: info@stbv.de
Web site: http://www.stbv.de
Titles:
PROFILE

STEUER-GEWERKSCHAFTSVERLAG 688959
Friedrichstr. 169, 10117 BERLIN
Tel: 30 206256650 **Fax:** 30 206256601
Email: stgv@dstg-verlag.de
Web site: http://www.dstg-verlag.de
Titles:
BLICKPUNKT DSTG
DSTG MAGAZIN
DIE STEUER-WARTE

STIEBEL ELTRON GMBH & CO. KG 689472
Dr.-Stiebel-Str., 37603 HOLZMINDEN
Tel: 5531 70295684 **Fax:** 5531 70295584
Email: presse@stiebel-eltron.de
Web site: http://www.stiebel-eltron.de
Titles:
TIPP

STIEBNER VERLAG GMBH 686512
Nymphenburger Str. 86, 80636 MÜNCHEN
Tel: 89 1257378 **Fax:** 89 12162282
Email: verlag@stiebner.com
Web site: http://www.stiebner.com
Titles:
NOVUM

STIFTUNG FÜR DIE RECHTE ZUKÜNFTIGER GENERATIONEN 682482
Ludwig-Erhard-Str. 16a, 61440 OBERURSEL
Tel: 6171 982367 **Fax:** 6171 952566
Email: kontakt@srzg.de
Web site: http://www.srzg.de
Titles:
JOURNAL FÜR GENERATIONENGERECHTIGKEIT

STIFTUNG GESUNDHEIT 1627119
Behringstr. 28a, 22765 HAMBURG
Tel: 40 8090870 **Fax:** 40 809087555
Email: info@stiftung-gesundheit.de
Web site: http://www.stiftung-gesundheit.de
Titles:
STIFTUNGSBRIEF

STIFTUNG WARENTEST 681851
Lützowplatz 11, 10785 BERLIN **Tel:** 30 26310
Fax: 30 26312727
Email: email@stiftung-warentest.de
Web site: http://www.test.de
Titles:
FINANZ TEST JAHRBUCH
FINANZ TEST SPEZIAL
FINANZTEST
TEST

STOLLFUSS MEDIEN GMBH & CO. KG 677230
Dechenstr. 7, 53115 BONN **Tel:** 228 7240
Fax: 228 72491181
Email: info@stollfuss.de
Web site: http://www.stollfuss.de
Titles:
B+P. ZEITSCHRIFT FÜR BETRIEB UND PERSONAL

BFHE ENTSCHEIDUNGEN DES BUNDESFINANZHOFS
BUNDESSTEUERBLATT
DSTZ DEUTSCHE STEUER-ZEITUNG
EFG ENTSCHEIDUNGEN DER FINANZGERICHTE
STBG DIE STEUERBERATUNG
UVR UMSATZSTEUER- UND VERKEHRSSTEUER-RECHT
ZFZ ZEITSCHRIFT FÜR ZÖLLE UND VERBRAUCHSTEUERN

STORCK VERLAG HAMBURG
679697
Striepenweg 31, 21147 HAMBURG
Tel: 40 7971301 **Fax:** 40 79713101
Email: info@storck-verlag.de
Web site: http://www.storck-verlag.de

Titles:
DEUTSCHE SEESCHIFFAHRT
DER GEFAHRGUTBEAUFTRAGTE
GEFÄHRLICHE LADUNG

STRABAG AG
683637
Siegburger Str. 241, 50679 KÖLN
Tel: 221 8242472 **Fax:** 221 8242385
Web site: http://www.strabag.de

Titles:
INFORM

STRANDGUT VERLAGS GMBH
688996
Ederstr. 10, 60486 FRANKFURT **Tel:** 69 9791030
Fax: 69 7075125
Email: info@strandgut.de
Web site: http://www.strandgut.de

Titles:
STRANDGUT

STROBEL VERLAG GMBH & CO. KG
681925
Zur Feldmühle 9, 59821 ARNSBERG
Tel: 2931 89000 **Fax:** 2931 890038
Email: leserservice@strobel-verlag.de
Web site: http://www.strobel-verlag.de

Titles:
FLÜSSIGGAS
IKZ HAUSTECHNIK
IKZ PRAXIS
INWOHNEN
K & L-MAGAZIN
DER KÜCHENPLANER

STROEMFELD VERLAG BUCHVERSAND GMBH
681834
Holzhausenstr. 4, 60322 FRANKFURT
Tel: 69 9552260 **Fax:** 69 95522624
Email: info@stroemfeld.de
Web site: http://www.stroemfeld.com

Titles:
ZEITSCHRIFT FÜR PSYCHOANALYTISCHE THEORIE UND PRAXIS

STROETMANN VERLAG & AGENTUR GMBH
682983
Lange Laube 22, 30159 HANNOVER
Tel: 511 15551 **Fax:** 511 1316169
Web site: http://www.stroetmann-verlag.de

Titles:
HANNOVER LIVE
MAGASCENE
UNISCENE

STROH. DRUCK UND MEDIEN GMBH
678662
Postgasse 7, 71522 BACKNANG **Tel:** 7191 8080
Fax: 7191 808111
Email: w.stroh@bkz.de
Web site: http://www.bkz-online.de

Titles:
BACKNANGER KREISZEITUNG

STROOMER PR/CONCEPT GMBH
1742941
Rellinger Str. 64a, 20257 HAMBURG
Tel: 40 8531330 **Fax:** 40 85313322
Email: mail@stroomer-pr.de
Web site: http://www.stroomer-pr.de

Titles:
TRANSFER

STÜNINGS MEDIEN GMBH
679979
Dießemer Bruch 167, 47805 KREFELD
Tel: 2151 51000 **Fax:** 2151 5100105
Email: medien@stuenings.de
Web site: http://www.stuenings.de

Titles:
BUS FAHRT
BUS ZIELE
CLICK
KFZ ANZEIGER
KR KREFELD LIFE
LINKS + RECHTS DER AUTOBAHN
MOT-BAU
NFZ WERKSTATT
REISEDIENST
WIRTSCHAFTS NACHRICHTEN

STUTTGARTER NACHRICHTEN VERLAGSGES. MBH
1740412
Plieninger Str. 150, 70567 STUTTGART
Tel: 711 72050 **Fax:** 711 72057138
Web site: http://www.stuttgarter-nachrichten.de

Titles:
FELLBACHER WOCHENBLATT
FELLBACHER ZEITUNG
STUTTGARTER NACHRICHTEN

STUTTGARTER WOCHENBLATT GMBH
689046
Plieninger Str. 150, 70567 STUTTGART
Tel: 711 72080 **Fax:** 800 3202233
Email: anzeigen@stw.zgs.de
Web site: http://www.stuttgarter-wochenblatt.de

Titles:
STUTTGARTER WOCHENBLATT

STUTTGARTER ZEITUNG VERLAGSGES. MBH
1767310
Plieninger Str. 150, 70567 STUTTGART
Tel: 711 72050 **Fax:** 711 72056162
Email: vertrieb@stz.zgs.de
Web site: http://www.stuttgarter-zeitung.de

Titles:
STUTTGARTER ZEITUNG

STYLEPARK AG
1686466
Brönnerstr. 22, 60313 FRANKFURT
Tel: 69 29722222 **Fax:** 69 29722223
Email: magazin@stylepark.com
Web site: http://www.stylepark.com

Titles:
STYLEPARK

SUBDESIGN WERBEAGENTUR GMBH
680916
Görlitzer Str. 16, 01099 DRESDEN
Tel: 351 811840 **Fax:** 351 8029950
Email: info@subdesign.net
Web site: http://www.subdesign.net

Titles:
DRESDNER KINOKALENDER

SUBMISSIONS-ANZEIGER VERLAG GMBH
682926
Schopenstehl 15, 20095 HAMBURG
Tel: 40 4019400 **Fax:** 40 40194031
Email: info@submission.de
Web site: http://www.submission.de

Titles:
SUBMISSIONS-ANZEIGER

SUBWAY MEDIEN GMBH
683259
Kohlmarkt 2, 38100 BRAUNSCHWEIG
Tel: 531 243200 **Fax:** 531 2432020
Email: info@subway.de
Web site: http://www.subwaymedien.de

Titles:
INDIGO
SUBWAY

SUCH & FIND OFFERTENZEITUNG GMBH
689060
Rosa-Luxemburg-Str. 27, 04301 LEIPZIG
Tel: 341 913750 **Fax:** 341 9137555
Email: dtp@sufi-ost.de
Web site: http://www.sufi-ost.de

Titles:
SUCH & FIND

SÜDDEUTSCHE ZEITUNG GMBH
684011
Hultschiner Str. 8, 81677 MÜNCHEN
Tel: 89 21830 **Fax:** 89 21838315
Email: verlag@sueddeutsche.de
Web site: http://www.sueddeutsche.de

Titles:
SÜDDEUTSCHE ZEITUNG
SÜDDEUTSCHE ZEITUNG DAS MAGAZIN ZUM JAHRESWECHSEL

SÜDDEUTSCHE.DE GMBH
1640433
Hultschiner Str. 8, 81677 MÜNCHEN
Tel: 89 21830 **Fax:** 89 21839715
Email: wir@sueddeutsche.de
Web site: http://www.sueddeutsche.de

Titles:
SUEDDEUTSCHE.DE

SÜDDEUTSCHER VERLAG ONPACT GMBH
1744323
Hultschiner Str. 8, 81677 MÜNCHEN
Tel: 89 21837261 **Fax:** 89 21837212
Email: info@sv-onpact.de
Web site: http://www.sv-onpact.de

Titles:
DEUTSCHE ZEITSCHRIFT FÜR SPORTMEDIZIN
LUX
RAUMBRAND
WWF MAGAZIN

SÜDKURIER GMBH
679551
Max-Stromeyer-Str. 178, 78467 KONSTANZ
Tel: 7531 9990 **Fax:** 7531 9991485
Email: info@suedkurier.de
Web site: http://www.suedkurier-medienhaus.de

Titles:
ALB BOTE
SÜDKURIER
SÜDKURIER FRIEDRICHSHAFEN
SÜDKURIER SNOW&FUN

SÜDTHÜRINGER VERLAG GMBH
689051
Andreasstr. 11, 36433 BAD SALZUNGEN
Tel: 3695 555050 **Fax:** 3695 555051
Email: verlag@stz-online.de
Web site: http://www.stz-online.de

Titles:
SÜDTHÜRINGER ZEITUNG STZ

SUHLER VERLAGSGES. MBH & CO. KG
682137
Schützenstr. 2, 98527 SUHL **Tel:** 3681 8510
Fax: 3681 800271
Email: marketing@freies-wort.de
Web site: http://www.freies-wort.de

Titles:
FREIES WORT

SULZBACH-ROSENBERGER ZEITUNG DRUCK- UND VERLAGSHAUS GMBH, ZWEIGNIEDERLASSUNG VON DER NEUE TAG OBERPFÄLZISCHER KURIER DRUCK- UND VERLAGSHAUS GMBH
1741098
Luitpoldplatz 22, 92237 SULZBACH-ROSENBERG **Tel:** 9661 87290 **Fax:** 9661 872923

Titles:
SULZBACH-ROSENBERGER ZEITUNG

SUNMEDIA VERLAGSGES. MBH
1684755
Hans-Böckler-Allee 7, 30173 HANNOVER
Tel: 511 85502560 **Fax:** 511 85502500
Web site: http://www.erneuerbareenergien.de

Titles:
ERNEUERBARE ENERGIEN
WIND TURBINE MARKET

SUPER ILLU VERLAG GMBH & CO. KG
689107
Zimmerstr. 28, 10969 BERLIN **Tel:** 30 23876600
Fax: 30 23876395
Email: post@super-illu.de
Web site: http://www.super-illu.de

Titles:
GUTER RAT
GUTERRAT.DE
SUPER ILLU
SUPER ILLU.DE

SUPER SONNTAG VERLAG GMBH
686349
Dresdener Str. 3, 52068 AACHEN
Tel: 241 5101569 **Fax:** 241 5101550
Email: info@supersonntag.de
Web site: http://www.supersonntag.de

Titles:
SUPER MITTWOCH - AUSG. STOLBERG
SUPER SONNTAG - AUSG. ALSDORF - HERZOGENRATH
SUPER SONNTAG - AUSG. DÜREN-JÜLICH

SUT-SCHIFFAHRT UND TECHNIK VERLAGSGES. MBH
1638736
Siebengebirgsstr. 14, 53757 ST. AUGUSTIN
Tel: 2241 1482517 **Fax:** 2241 1482518
Email: info@schiffahrtundtechnik.de
Web site: http://www.schifffahrtundtechnik.de

Titles:
SCHIFFAHRT HAFEN BAHN UND TECHNIK

SÜWE VERTRIEBS- UND DIENSTLEISTUNGSGES. MBH & CO. KG
682078
Amtsstr. 5, 67059 LUDWIGSHAFEN
Tel: 621 5902493 **Fax:** 621 5902504
Email: suewe@wobla.de
Web site: http://www.wobla.de

Titles:
TRIFELS KURIER
WOCHENBLATT FRANKENTHAL
WOCHENBLATT GERMERSHEIM MIT LINGENFELD
WOCHENBLATT HASSLOCH
WOCHENBLATT KAISERSLAUTERN
WOCHENBLATT KIRCHHEIMBOLANDEN MIT GÖLLHEIM UND EISENBERG
WOCHENBLATT LANDAU
WOCHENBLATT LUDWIGSHAFEN
WOCHENBLATT PIRMASENS
WOCHENBLATT RÜLZHEIM, BELLHEIM, JOCKGRIM
WOCHENBLATT SPEYER

SV MAGAZIN-VERLAG GMBH & CO. KG
1785760
Rudolf-Roth-Str. 18, 88299 LEUTKIRCH
Tel: 7561 80706 **Fax:** 7561 80134
Web site: http://www.schwaebische.de

Titles:
SINNIOR

SVG HAMBURG EG
686492
Bullerdeich 36, 20537 HAMBURG **Tel:** 40 254500
Fax: 40 25450301
Email: info@svg-hamburg.de
Web site: http://www.svg-hamburg.de

Titles:
NORD VERKEHR

SVG SERVICE VERLAGS GMBH & CO. KG
679602
Schwertfegerstr. 1, 23556 LÜBECK
Tel: 451 898974 **Fax:** 451 898557
Web site: http://www.svg-verlag.de

Titles:
SEGLER-ZEITUNG
SPORTSCHIPPER
WASSERSPORT
WASSERSPORT-WIRTSCHAFT

SVG SÜDHESSISCHE VERLAGSGES. LAMPERTHEIM MBH
684897
Alte Viernheimer Str. 9, 68623 LAMPERTHEIM
Tel: 6206 95200 **Fax:** 6206 952020
Email: info@lampertheimer-zeitung.de

Titles:
LAMPERTHEIMER ZEITUNG

S-W VERLAG GMBH & CO. KG FÜR LOKALINFORMATIONEN
678688
Göbelstr. 23, 56727 MAYEN **Tel:** 2651 981870
Fax: 2651 981699
Email: info@sw-verlag.de
Web site: http://www.wochenspiegellive.de

Titles:
BAD KREUZNACHER WOCHENSPIEGEL
HUNSRÜCKER WOCHENSPIEGEL
IDAR-OBERSTEINER WOCHENSPIEGEL
NAHE-GLAN WOCHENSPIEGEL
RHEIN-MOSEL WOCHENSPIEGEL

SWOBODA-LEITNER VERLAG GDBR
1746229
Augustenstr. 19, 93049 REGENSBURG
Tel: 941 20009970 **Fax:** 941 20009980
Email: info@beste-jahre.com
Web site: http://www.beste-jahre.com

Titles:
BESTE JAHRE

SYBURGER VERLAG GMBH
684858
Hertinger Str. 60, 59423 UNNA **Tel:** 2303 98550
Fax: 2303 98559
Email: info@syburger.de
Web site: http://www.syburger.de

Titles:
KURVE
MOTORRAD KONTAKTE
MOTORRAD NEWS
MOTORRAD TREFF
MOTORRADSZENE BAYERN
MOTORRADTREFF SPINNER
DER NÜRBURGER
DER SYBURGER

SYLTER SPIEGEL VERLAG 689172
Bomhoffstr. 2, 25980 WESTERLAND
Tel: 4651 26166 **Fax:** 4651 24400
Email: info@sylterspiegel.de
Web site: http://www.sylterspiegel.de

Titles:
SYLTER SPIEGEL

SYMPRA GMBH (GPRA) 689175
Stafflenbergstr. 32, 70184 STUTTGART
Tel: 711 947670 **Fax:** 711 9476787
Email: pr@sympra.de
Web site: http://www.sympra.de

Titles:
SYMPRAXIS

SYSTEM-MANAGEMENT BRAUN, RASCHE + PARTNER GMBH 687516
Rheinlandstr. 5, 42579 HEILIGENHAUS
Tel: 2056 98290 **Fax:** 2056 982920
Email: info@system-management.com
Web site: http://www.system-management.com

Titles:
RASCHE NACHRICHTEN

SZENE KULTUR VERLAG 698899
Poststr. 11, 88239 WANGEN **Tel:** 7522 795030
Fax: 7522 795050
Email: redaktion@szene-kultur.de
Web site: http://www.szene-kultur.de

Titles:
SZENE KULTUR

T&M MEDIA GMBH & CO. KG 695599
Hilpertstr. 3, 64295 DARMSTADT **Tel:** 6151 39070
Fax: 6151 3907929
Email: info@cimunity.com
Web site: http://www.cimunity.com

Titles:
CIM CONFERENCE & INCENTIVE MANAGEMENT
CIM ONLINE
TRAVEL.ONE

TANDEM MEDIA GMBH 689202
117er Ehrenhof 3, 55118 MAINZ **Tel:** 6131 218080
Fax: 6131 2180890
Email: info@tandem-media.de
Web site: http://www.tandem-media.de

Titles:
TANDEM MAGAZIN

TANZWELT VERLAG GMBH 689217
Otto-Fleck-Schneise 12, 60528 FRANKFURT
Tel: 69 67736780 **Fax:** 69 67728530
Email: tanzspiegel@tanzsport.de
Web site: http://www.tanzsport.de

Titles:
TANZSPIEGEL

TAUNUS VERLAG WAGNER DRUCK GMBH & CO. 680019
Am Riedborn 20, 61250 USINGEN **Tel:** 6081 1050
Fax: 6081 105100
Email: redaktion@usinger-anzeiger.de
Web site: http://www.usinger-anzeiger.de

Titles:
USINGER ANZEIGENBLATT
USINGER ANZEIGER

TAUSENDFÜSSLER VERLAG GMBH 1709834
Gottlieb-Daimler-Str. 9, 24568 KALTENKIRCHEN
Tel: 4191 722770 **Fax:** 4191 7227711
Email: info@tausendfuessler.de
Web site: http://www.tausendfuessler.de

Titles:
TAUSENDFÜSSLER

TAXI-FACHVERLAG 682909
Jakobistr. 20, 28195 BREMEN **Tel:** 421 170470
Fax: 421 170473
Email: verlag@hallo-taxi.de
Web site: http://www.hallo-taxi.de

Titles:
HALLO TAXI

TAZ VERLAGS- UND VERTRIEBS GMBH 685945
Rudi-Dutschke-Str. 23, 10969 BERLIN
Tel: 30 2515028 **Fax:** 30 25902177
Email: redaktion@taz.de
Web site: http://www.taz.de

Titles:
LE MONDE DIPLOMATIQUE
TAZ.DE
TAZ.DIE TAGESZEITUNG

TEAM 2 GMBH & CO. KG 688830
Bahnhofstr. 66, 46145 OBERHAUSEN
Tel: 208 661655 **Fax:** 208 661659
Email: info@team2-werbeagentur.com
Web site: http://www.team2-werbeagentur.com

Titles:
STADTREPORT OBERHAUSEN

TEAMWORK MEDIA GMBH 689265
Hauptstr. 1, 86925 FUCHSTAL **Tel:** 8243 96920
Fax: 8243 969222
Email: service@teamwork-media.de
Web site: http://www.teamwork-media.de

Titles:
DENTAL DIALOGUE
TEAM WORK

TECH TEX-VERLAG GMBH & CO KG 1641574
Schäferstr. 2, 55257 BUDENHEIM
Tel: 6139 293443 **Fax:** 6139 960455
Email: info@techtex-verlag.com
Web site: http://www.techtex-verlag.com

Titles:
STAPLER WORLD

TECHNIK-DOKUMENTATIONS-VERLAG GMBH 683872
Zu den Sandbeeten 2, 35043 MARBURG
Tel: 6421 30860 **Fax:** 6421 308618
Web site: http://www.tedo-verlag.com

Titles:
IT & PRODUCTION
SPS MAGAZIN

TECHNIKER KRANKENKASSE 689503
Bramfelder Str. 140, 22305 HAMBURG
Tel: 40 69092187
Email: redaktion@tk-online.de
Web site: http://www.tk-online.de

Titles:
TK AKTUELL

TECKLENBORG VERLAG 686175
Siemensstr. 4, 48565 STEINFURT
Tel: 2552 92002 **Fax:** 2552 920150
Email: info@tecklenborg-verlag.de
Web site: http://www.tecklenborg-verlag.de

Titles:
MÜNSTERLAND
SCHWARZWEISS
WIRTSCHAFT MÜNSTERLAND FÜR DEN KREIS STEINFURT

TELEPUBLIC VERLAG GMBH & CO. MEDIEN KG 1603362
Podbielskistr. 325, 30659 HANNOVER
Tel: 511 3348400 **Fax:** 511 3348499
Email: info@teletalk.de
Web site: http://www.teletalk.de

Titles:
TELETALK

TELERAT GMBH 689296
Josef-Nawrocki-Str. 30, 12587 BERLIN
Tel: 30 7550090 **Fax:** 30 75500911
Email: info@telerat.de
Web site: http://www.telerat.de

Titles:
TELERAT-NACHRICHTEN

TEMEDIA VERLAGS GMBH 1632063
Alte Heerstr. 1, 53121 BONN **Tel:** 228 9629380
Fax: 228 9629390
Email: info@sicherheits-berater.de
Web site: http://www.sicherheits-berater.de

Titles:
SICHERHEITS-BERATER

TEMMING VERLAG KG 1776678
Europaplatz 26, 46399 BOCHOLT **Tel:** 2871 2840
Fax: 2871 284119
Email: info@bbv-net.de
Web site: http://www.bbv-net.de

Titles:
BBV-NET
BOCHOLTER BORKENER VOLKSBLATT

TENNISVERBAND NIEDERRHEIN E.V. 1783720
Kaiserstr. 22, 41061 MÖNCHENGLADBACH
Tel: 2161 948760 **Fax:** 2161 9487617
Email: info@tvn-tennis.de
Web site: http://www.tvn-tennis.de

Titles:
NIEDERRHEIN TENNIS

TERRA-VERLAG GMBH 682202
Neuhauser Str. 21, 78464 KONSTANZ
Tel: 7531 81220 **Fax:** 7531 812299
Email: info@terra-verlag.de
Web site: http://www.terra-verlag.de

Titles:
FRISEUR WELT
HOCHZEIT - DEUTSCHLAND AUSG.
KLEINTIERMEDIZIN
PROFI KOSMETIK
TU TIERÄRZTLICHE UMSCHAU

TEUBERT VERLAG 1653708
Im Krummen Ort 6, 28870 FISCHERHUDE
Tel: 4293 7894890 **Fax:** 4293 7894891
Email: info@teubert-kommunikation.de
Web site: http://www.teubert-kommunikation.de

Titles:
EXZELLENT

TEXT VERLAG GMBH 685363
Beim Schlump 13 a, 20144 HAMBURG
Tel: 40 229260 **Fax:** 40 2278676
Email: verlag@textintern.de
Web site: http://www.textintern.de

Titles:
TEXT INTERN

TEXTIL-FORUM-SERVICE 689329
Friedenstr. 5, 30175 HANNOVER **Tel:** 511 817006
Fax: 511 813108
Email: tfs@etn-net.org
Web site: http://www.tfs-etn.com

Titles:
TEXTILEFORUM

TFI-VERLAGSGES. MBH 1638783
Oberfeld 32, 82319 STARNBERG
Tel: 8151 277907 **Fax:** 8151 277909
Email: info@tfi-publications.com
Web site: http://www.tfi-publications.com

Titles:
TRADE FAIRS INTERNATIONAL

TFV TECHNISCHER FACHVERLAG GMBH 678870
Forststr. 131, 70193 STUTTGART **Tel:** 711 636720
Fax: 711 63672747
Email: info@baumetall.de
Web site: http://www.baumetall.de

Titles:
BAUMETALL

TH MEDIEN KG 1781389
Businesspark A96, 86842 TÜRKHEIM
Tel: 8245 967600 **Fax:** 8245 96760100
Email: info@th-medien.com
Web site: http://www.th-medien.com

Titles:
POS-MANAGER TECHNOLOGY

THOMAS DERSEE 688995
Waldstr. 49, 15566 SCHÖNEICHE
Tel: 30 4352840 **Fax:** 30 64329167
Email: strahlentelex@t-online.de
Web site: http://www.strahlentelex.de

Titles:
STRAHLENTELEX MIT ELEKTROSMOG-REPORT

THOMAS INDUSTRIAL MEDIA GMBH 1638445
Ruhrallee 185, 45136 ESSEN **Tel:** 201 8945210
Fax: 201 894558210
Email: info@technische-revue.eu
Web site: http://www.technische-revue.eu

Titles:
TR TECHNISCHE REVUE

THÜRINGER ALLGEMEINE VERLAG GMBH & CO. KG 689420
Gottstedter Landstr. 6, 99092 ERFURT
Tel: 361 2274 **Fax:** 361 2275023
Web site: http://www.thueringer-allgemeine.de

Titles:
THÜRINGER ALLGEMEINE
THÜRINGER ALLGEMEINE ONLINE

THÜRINGER LANDESANSTALT FÜR UMWELT UND GEOLOGIE 684922
Göschwitzer Str. 41, 07745 JENA **Tel:** 3641 6840
Fax: 3641 684222
Email: tlug.post@tlugjena.thueringen.de
Web site: http://www.tlug-jena.de

Titles:
LANDSCHAFTSPFLEGE UND NATURSCHUTZ IN THÜRINGEN

THÜRINGER TOURISMUS GMBH 679829
Willy-Brandt-Platz 1, 99084 ERFURT
Tel: 361 37420 **Fax:** 361 3742388
Email: service@thueringen-tourismus.de
Web site: http://www.thueringen-tourismus.de

Titles:
BUCHUNGSKATALOG THÜRINGEN

THÜRINGISCHE LANDESZEITUNG VERLAG GMBH U. CO. KG 689506
Marienstr. 14, 99423 WEIMAR **Tel:** 3643 206400
Fax: 3643 206402
Email: geschaeftsfuehrung@tlz.de
Web site: http://www.tlz.de

Titles:
TLZ EISENACH EISENACHER PRESSE
TLZ ERFURT THÜRINGISCHE LANDESZEITUNG
TLZ GERA THÜRINGISCHE LANDESZEITUNG
TLZ GOTHA GOTHAER TAGESPOST
TLZ JENA THÜRINGISCHE LANDESZEITUNG
TLZ.DE

THYSSENKRUPP STEEL EUROPE AG 680309
Kaiser-Wilhelm-Str. 100, 47166 DUISBURG
Tel: 203 5224515 **Fax:** 203 5225707
Email: christiane.hoch-baumann@thyssenkrupp.com
Web site: http://www.thyssenkrupp-steel-europe.com

Titles:
COMPACT

TIMES MEDIA GMBH 1736786
Tempelhofer Ufer 23, 10963 BERLIN
Tel: 30 21505400 **Fax:** 30 21505447
Email: info@times-media.de
Web site: http://www.times-media.de

Titles:
THE AFRICAN TIMES
THE ASIA PACIFIC TIMES
THE ATLANTIC TIMES
THE GERMAN TIMES FOR EUROPE

TIP VERLAG GMBH & CO. KG 679107
Karl-Liebknecht-Str. 29, 10178 BERLIN
Tel: 30 250030 **Fax:** 30 25003399
Email: redaktion@tip-berlin.de
Web site: http://www.tip-berlin.de

Titles:
TIP BERLIN

TIP WERBEVERLAG GMBH & CO. KG
689476
Karl-Wüst-Str. 15, 74076 HEILBRONN
Tel: 7131 15403 **Fax:** 7131 1548584
Email: tip-info@tip-werbeverlag.de
Web site: http://www.tip-werbeverlag.de

Titles:
TIP DER WOCHE - AUSG. AHLEN
TIP DER WOCHE - AUSG. DRESDEN-KOHLESTR.

TIPS-VERLAG GMBH
1759327
Königsstr. 46, 48143 MÜNSTER **Tel:** 251 899340
Fax: 251 8993420
Email: kontakt@tips-verlag.de
Web site: http://www.tips-verlag.de

Titles:
BIELEFELD GEHT AUS
BIELEFELD SPEZIAL SCHENKEN FEIERN LEBEN
BIELEFELDER
GÜTERSLOH GEHT AUS
MÜNSTER GEHT AUS
MÜNSTER KAUFT EIN
MÜNSTER SPEZIAL SCHENKEN FEIERN LEBEN
SPEZIAL SCHENKEN FEIERN LEBEN

TIRAGE LIMITÉ
689480
Postfach 4024, 40687 ERKRATH
Tel: 2104 1384968 **Fax:** 2104 1384969
Email: elite@tirage-limite.com
Web site: http://www.tirage-limite.com

Titles:
TIRAGE LIMITÉ

TITANIC-VERLAG GMBH & CO. KG
689501
Kopischstr. 10, 10965 BERLIN **Tel:** 30 74755000
Fax: 30 74755001
Email: verlag@titanic-magazin.de
Web site: http://www.titanic-magazin.de

Titles:
TITANIC

TITZE VERLAG
678707
Grüntenseestr. 26, 87466 OY-MITTELBERG
Tel: 8361 3330 **Fax:** 8361 3338
Email: info@titze-verlag.de

Titles:
BAD WÖRISHOFEN KNEIPP & THERMAL IM ALLGÄU
WEGWEISER OBERSTAUFEN MIT OFFIZIELLEM ORTSPLAN UND FREIZEITKARTE DER UMGEBUNG

TMB TOURISMUS-MARKETING BRANDENBURG GMBH
687613
Am Neuen Markt 1, 14467 POTSDAM
Tel: 331 298730 **Fax:** 331 2987373
Email: tmb@reiseland-brandenburg.de
Web site: http://www.reiseland-brandenburg.de

Titles:
GASTGEBERKATALOG BRANDENBURG

TMM MARKETING UND MEDIEN GMBH & CO. KG
689538
Kantstr. 151, 10623 BERLIN **Tel:** 30 2062673
Fax: 30 20626750
Email: mail@tmm.de
Web site: http://www.tmm.de

Titles:
BERLIN-BRANDENBURGISCHES HANDWERK
BERLINER ZUGPFERDE
TOP MAGAZIN HOCHZEITSTRÄUME

TOM CONSULTING LTD.
1650153
Birkenleiten 11, 81543 MÜNCHEN
Tel: 89 62439772 **Fax:** 89 62439771
Email: tb@tomontour.de
Web site: http://www.tomontour.de

Titles:
GAYFRIENDLY CANADA
GAYFRIENDLY FLANDERN
GAYFRIENDLY SPAIN
GAYFRIENDLY USA
TOMONTOUR SUMMER
TOMONTOUR WINTER

TOMORROW FOCUS MEDIA GMBH
1630124
Steinhauser Str. 1, 81677 MÜNCHEN
Tel: 89 92502404
Web site: http://www.tomorrow-focus.de

Titles:
AMICA
CINEMA ONLINE
FIT FOR FUN
FOCUS MONEY ONLINE
FOCUS ONLINE
FREUNDIN.DE
MAX
TV SPIELFILM ONLINE

TOP HAIR INTERNATIONAL GMBH
1638460
Medienplatz 1, 76571 GAGGENAU
Tel: 7225 916300 **Fax:** 7225 916320
Email: info@tophair.de
Web site: http://www.tophair.de

Titles:
TOP HAIR INTERNATIONAL FASHION

TOP MAGAZIN STUTTGART VERLAG & MARKETING GMBH
689546
Zettachring 2, 70567 STUTTGART
Tel: 711 9008001 **Fax:** 711 7227100
Email: stuttgart@top-magazin.de
Web site: http://www.top-magazin-stuttgart.de

Titles:
TOP MAGAZIN STUTTGART

TOP TIPPS GMBH
689550
Kemnader Str. 13a, 44797 BOCHUM
Tel: 234 8102297 **Fax:** 234 8102296
Email: info@top-tipps.org
Web site: http://www.top-tipps.org

Titles:
CITY GUIDE BOCHUM TOP TIPPS
CITY GUIDE DORTMUND TOP TIPPS
CITY GUIDE DÜSSELDORF TOP TIPPS
CITY GUIDE ESSEN TOP TIPPS
CITY GUIDE WUPPERTAL TOP TIPPS

TORGAU DRUCK SÄCHSISCHE LOKALPRESSE GMBH
688550
Elbstr. 3, 04860 TORGAU **Tel:** 3421 72100
Fax: 3421 721050
Email: torgau@sonntagswochenblatt.de
Web site: http://www.sonntagswochenblatt.de

Titles:
SONNTAGSWOCHENBLATT - AUSG. TORGAU

TORGAUER VERLAGSGES. MBH & CO. KG
689554
Elbstr. 1, 04860 TORGAU **Tel:** 3421 72100
Fax: 3421 721050
Email: web@torgauerzeitung.com
Web site: http://www.torgauerzeitung.com

Titles:
TORGAUER ZEITUNG

TOTAL DEUTSCHLAND GMBH
679588
Schützenstr. 25, 10117 BERLIN **Tel:** 30 20276237
Fax: 30 2027796237
Email: cornelia.schulze@total.de
Web site: http://www.total.de

Titles:
BONJOUR

TOURISMUS+CONGRESS GMBH FRANKFURT AM MAIN
1716001
Kaiserstr. 56, 60329 FRANKFURT
Tel: 69 21238800 **Fax:** 69 21237880
Email: info@infofrankfurt.de
Web site: http://www.frankfurt-tourismus.de

Titles:
MARKETINGAKTIONEN

TOURISMUSVERBAND ALLGÄU/BAYERISCH-SCHWABEN E.V.
1758193
Schießgrabenstr. 14, 86150 AUGSBURG
Tel: 821 4504010 **Fax:** 821 45040120
Email: info@tvabs.de
Web site: http://www.bayerisch-schwaben.de

Titles:
BAYERISCH SCHWABEN MAGAZIN

TOURISMUSVERBAND ELBE-ELSTER-LAND E.V.
1729825
Markt 20, 04924 BAD LIEBENWERDA
Tel: 35341 30652 **Fax:** 35341 12672
Email: info@elbe-elster-land.de
Web site: http://www.elbe-elster-land.de

Titles:
ELBE-ELSTER-LAND REISEJOURNAL

TOURISMUSVERBAND NIEDERLAUSITZ E.V.
1729071
Schlossbezirk 3, 03130 SPREMBERG
Tel: 3563 602340 **Fax:** 3563 602342
Email: info@niederlausitz.de
Web site: http://www.niederlausitz.de

Titles:
DIE NIEDERLAUSITZ URLAUBS- UND FREIZEITMAGAZIN

TOURISMUSVERBAND OSTBAYERN E.V.
686839
Luitpoldstr. 20, 93047 REGENSBURG
Tel: 941 585390 **Fax:** 941 5853939
Email: info@ostbayern-tourismus.de
Web site: http://www.ostbayern-tourismus.de

Titles:
OSTBAYERN WINTERJOURNAL

TOURISTIK PR UND MEDIEN GBR
1644502
Loisachufer 26, 82515 WOLFRATSHAUSEN
Tel: 8171 41866 **Fax:** 8171 16967
Email: fvp@srt-redaktion.de
Web site: http://www.srt-verlag.de

Titles:
TOURISTIK MEDIEN

TOURISTIK VERLAG GMBH
681481
Alsterdorfer Str. 262, 22297 HAMBURG
Tel: 40 4908043 **Fax:** 40 499034

Titles:
EUROGUIDE
INTERNATIONALES HOTELVERZEICHNIS INTERNATIONAL HOTEL GUIDE GUIDE INTERNATIONAL DES HÔTELS IHV

TPD MEDIEN GMBH
689508
Nymphenburger Str. 81, 80636 MÜNCHEN
Tel: 89 35759310 **Fax:** 89 35759359
Email: info@tpd.de
Web site: http://www.tpd.de

Titles:
TOYOTA MAGAZIN

TRADEMARK PUBLISHING
1724664
Westendstr. 87, 60325 FRANKFURT
Tel: 69 43057847
Email: info@trademark-publishing.de
Web site: http://www.trademark-publishing.de

Titles:
STYLEPARK

TRADERS' MEDIA GMBH
1643833
Barbarastr. 31, 97074 WÜRZBURG
Tel: 931 452260 **Fax:** 931 4522613
Email: info@traders-mag.com
Web site: http://www.traders-mag.com

Titles:
TRADERS'

TRAILER VERLAG JOACHIM BERNDT
695737
Dr.-C.-Otto-Str. 196, 44879 BOCHUM
Tel: 234 941910 **Fax:** 234 9419191
Email: info@trailer-kinokultur.de
Web site: http://www.trailer-ruhr.de

Titles:
TRAILER

TRANSMEDIA VERLAG GMBH & CO KG
1621207
Weyertal 59, 50937 KÖLN **Tel:** 221 4722300
Fax: 221 4722370
Email: info@karrierefuehrer.de
Web site: http://www.karrierefuehrer.de

Titles:
KARRIEREFÜHRER BAUINGENIEURE
KARRIEREFÜHRER FINANZDIENSTLEISTUNGEN

TRAVEL TRIBUNE
689609
Unterster Zwerchweg 8, 60599 FRANKFURT
Tel: 69 625025 **Fax:** 69 625026
Email: info@travel-tribune.de
Web site: http://www.travel-tribune.de

Titles:
TRAVEL TRIBUNE

TRE TORRI VERLAG GMBH
1750363
Sonnenberger Str. 43, 65191 WIESBADEN
Tel: 611 5055840 **Fax:** 611 5055842
Email: info@tretorri.de
Web site: http://www.tretorri.de

Titles:
FINE DAS WEINMAGAZIN

TRIBÜNE-VERLAG
689639
Habsburgerallee 72, 60385 FRANKFURT
Tel: 69 9433000 **Fax:** 69 94330023
Email: tribuene_verlag@t-online.de
Web site: http://www.tribuene-verlag.de

Titles:
TRIBÜNE

TROCHOS GMBH
1650973
Georg-Koch-Str. 4, 82223 EICHENAU
Tel: 171 8292939 **Fax:** 89 92185093
Email: verlag@it-free.info
Web site: http://www.it-free.info

Titles:
IT FREELANCER MAGAZIN

TROPICA VERDE E.V.
1622050
Siesmayerstr. 61, 60323 FRANKFURT
Tel: 69 751550 **Fax:** 69 752182
Email: mail@tropica-verde.de
Web site: http://www.tropica-verde.de

Titles:
TUKAN

TRURNIT & PARTNER VERLAG GMBH
679475
Putzbrunner Str. 38, 85521 OTTOBRUNN
Tel: 89 6080010 **Fax:** 89 60800130
Email: info@trurnit.de
Web site: http://www.trurnit.de

Titles:
GEWERBE & ENERGIE

L' TUR TOURISMUS AG
1652169
Augustaplatz 8, 76530 BADEN-BADEN
Tel: 1805 212121 **Fax:** 1805 212196
Email: impressum@ltur.de
Web site: http://www.ltur.de

Titles:
L' TUR NIX WIE WEG.

TUSH MAGAZINE
1724427
Barmbeker Str. 33, 22303 HAMBURG
Tel: 40 28004466 **Fax:** 40 28004488
Email: info@tushmagazine.com
Web site: http://www.tushmagazine.com

Titles:
TUSH

TÜV MEDIA GMBH
682388
Am Grauen Stein, 51105 KÖLN **Tel:** 221 8063535
Fax: 221 8063510
Email: tuev-media@de.tuv.com
Web site: http://www.tuev-media.de

Titles:
GEFAHRGUT PROFI
MT MEDIZINTECHNIK
PROJEKTMANAGEMENT AKTUELL
STRAHLENSCHUTZ PRAXIS
ZEITSCHRIFT FÜR VERKEHRSSICHERHEIT ZVS

TÜV SÜD AG
689702
Westendstr. 199, 80686 MÜNCHEN
Tel: 89 57912648 **Fax:** 89 57912224
Email: info@tuev-sued.de
Web site: http://www.tuev-sued.de

Titles:
TÜV SÜD JOURNAL

TV SPIELFILM VERLAG GMBH
689765
Christoph-Probst-Weg 1, 20251 HAMBURG
Tel: 40 41310 **Fax:** 40 41312002
Email: info@milchstrasse.de
Web site: http://www.milchstrasse.de

Titles:
TV SPIELFILM
TV TODAY
TV TODAY ONLINE

TW WOCHENSPIEGEL GMBH & CO. KG
679166
Max-Planck-Str. 10, 54296 TRIER **Tel:** 651 71650
Fax: 651 716530
Email: info@tw-verlag.de
Web site: http://www.wochenspiegellive.de

Titles:
HOCHWÄLDER WOCHENSPIEGEL
MOSEL-RUWERTALER WOCHENSPIEGEL
PRÜMER WOCHENSPIEGEL
TRIERER WOCHENSPIEGEL

TYPO DRUCK HORN UND KOHLER-BEAUVOIR GMBH 685313
117er Ehrenhof 5, 55118 MAINZ **Tel:** 6131 965330
Fax: 6131 9653399
Email: briefkasten@dermainzer.net
Web site: http://www.dermainzer.net
Titles:
DER MAINZER

ÜBERBLICK VERLAGS GMBH 680970
Höherweg 287, 40231 DÜSSELDORF
Tel: 211 7357681 **Fax:** 211 7357680
Email: info@ueberblick.de
Web site: http://www.ueberblick.de
Titles:
AUSGEHEN IN HAMBURG
BERGISCHES LAND GEHT AUS!
DORTMUND GEHT AUS!
DÜSSELDORF FÜR KINDER!
DÜSSELDORF IM ÜBERBLICK!
DÜSSELDORF KAUFT EIN!
EDITION ÜBERBLICK NIEDERRHEIN GEHT AUS!
ESSEN GEHT AUS!
MALLORCA GEHT AUS!
MÜNCHEN KAUFT EIN!
SO SCHMECKT MÜNCHEN!
SYLT GEHT AUS!

UETERSENER NACHRICHTEN GMBH 689795
Großer Sand 3, 25436 UETERSEN
Tel: 4122 92500 **Fax:** 4122 1858
Email: anzeigen@uena.de
Web site: http://www.uena.de
Titles:
UETERSENER NACHRICHTEN

UGB-BERATUNGS- UND VERLAGS-GMBH 689799
Sandusweg 3, 35435 WETTENBERG
Tel: 641 808960 **Fax:** 641 8089650
Email: info@ugb.de
Web site: http://www.ugb.de
Titles:
UGB-FORUM

UK SUPPORT COMMAND (GERMANY) 1687153
Industriestr. 20, 33689 BIELEFELD
Tel: 5205 998660 **Fax:** 5205 9986629
Email: news@sixth-sense-newspaper.de
Web site: http://www.sixthsense.bfgnet.de
Titles:
SIXTH SENSE

ULLSTEIN GMBH 1743179
Axel-Springer-Str. 65, 10969 BERLIN
Tel: 30 25910 **Fax:** 30 259173049
Email: redaktion@morgenpost.de
Web site: http://www.morgenpost.de
Titles:
BERLINER MORGENPOST

ULRICH SCHMITZ 690699
Rheinaustr. 37, 53225 BONN **Tel:** 228 972003
Email: schmitz@wwponline.de
Web site: http://www.wwponline.de
Titles:
WISSENSCHAFT WIRTSCHAFT POLITIK

ULTIMO VERLAG GMBH 689811
Herforder Str. 237, 33609 BIELEFELD
Tel: 521 3297384
Email: info@ultimo-bielefeld.de
Web site: http://www.ultimo-bielefeld.de
Titles:
ULTIMO

ULTIMO-VERLAG LENDER & MAHNOLI GBR 689810
Wahmstr. 39, 23552 LÜBECK **Tel:** 451 72031
Fax: 451 74850
Email: info@ultimo-luebeck.de
Web site: http://www.ultimo-luebeck.de
Titles:
ULTIMO

ULTIMO-VERLAG OHG 689809
Eichenweg 2, 24214 NOER **Tel:** 431 86757
Fax: 431 82330
Email: info@ultimo-kiel.de
Web site: http://www.ultimo-kiel.de
Titles:
ULTIMO

UMG VERLAGSGES. MBH 689829
Frielinger Str. 31, 28215 BREMEN
Tel: 421 4984251 **Fax:** 421 4984252
Email: info@umg-verlag.de
Web site: http://www.umg-verlag.de
Titles:
UMWELT-MEDIZIN GESELLSCHAFT

UMSCHAU ZEITSCHRIFTENVERLAG GMBH 1634363
Otto-Volger-Str. 15, 65843 SULZBACH
Tel: 6196 76670 **Fax:** 6196 7676269
Email: uzv@uzv.de
Web site: http://www.uzv.de
Titles:
DEUTSCHE SCHÜTZENZEITUNG
ERNÄHRUNGS UMSCHAU
PTA DIE PTA IN DER APOTHEKE

UMWELTBUNDESAMT 1719358
Corrensplatz 1, 14195 BERLIN **Tel:** 30 89035468
Fax: 30 89031830
Email: umid@uba.de
Web site: http://www.umweltbundesamt.de
Titles:
UMID UMWELT UND MENSCH - INFORMATIONSDIENST

UMWELTFORUM OSNABRÜCKER LAND E.V. 1740914
Am Schölerberg 8, 49082 OSNABRÜCK
Tel: 541 589184 **Fax:** 541 57528
Email: nabu-os@osnanet.de
Web site: http://www.nabu-os.de
Titles:
NATURSCHUTZ-INFORMATIONEN

UMWELTINSTITUT MÜNCHEN E.V. 1754580
Landwehrstr. 64a, 80336 MÜNCHEN
Tel: 89 3077490 **Fax:** 89 30774920
Email: a21@umweltinstitut.org
Web site: http://www.umweltinstitut.org
Titles:
MÜNCHNER STADTGESPRÄCHE
UMWELTINSTITUT MÜNCHEN E.V. INFOBRIEF

UMWELTZENTRUM DER BÜRGERAKTION UMWELTSCHUTZ ZENTRALES OBERRHEINGEBIET E.V. 1603073
Kronenstr. 9, 76133 KARLSRUHE **Tel:** 721 380575
Web site: http://www.umverka.de
Titles:
UMWELT & VERKEHR KARLSRUHE

UMWELT-ZENTRUM DÜSSELDORF E.V. 1603363
Merowingerstr. 88, 40225 DÜSSELDORF
Tel: 211 330737 **Fax:** 211 330738
Email: kontakt@umwelt-zentrum.de
Web site: http://www.umwelt-zentrum.de
Titles:
GRÜNSTIFT

UMWELTZENTRUM HEERSER MÜHLE E.V. 1641804
Heerser Mühle 1, 32107 BAD SALZUFLEN
Tel: 5222 797151 **Fax:** 5222 797990
Email: umweltzentrum@badsalzuflen.de
Web site: http://www.heerser-muehle.de
Titles:
MÜHLENMAGAZIN

UNCLESALLY*S GMBH & CO. KG 689842
Waldemarstr. 37, 10999 BERLIN **Tel:** 30 69409663
Fax: 30 6913137
Email: sallys@sallys.net
Web site: http://www.sallys.net
Titles:
UNCLESALLY*S

UNFALLKASSE RHEINLAND-PFALZ 1726789
Orensteinstr. 10, 56626 ANDERNACH
Tel: 2632 9600 **Fax:** 2632 960100
Email: info@ukrlp.de
Web site: http://www.ukrlp.de
Titles:
AMPEL

UNGEHEUER + ULMER KG GMBH + CO. 1741598
Körnerstr. 14, 71634 LUDWIGSBURG
Tel: 7141 1300 **Fax:** 7141 130347
Email: anzeigen@lkz.de
Web site: http://www.lkz.de
Titles:
LUDWIGSBURGER KREISZEITUNG
NECKAR- UND ENZBOTE

UNICUM VERLAG GMBH & CO. KG 689852
Ferdinandstr. 13, 44789 BOCHUM
Tel: 234 961510 **Fax:** 234 9615111
Email: info@unicum-verlag.de
Web site: http://www.unicum.de
Titles:
UNICUM
UNICUM ABI
UNICUM BERUF
UNICUM.DE

UNION BETRIEBS-GMBH 682111
Egermannstr. 2, 53359 RHEINBACH
Tel: 2226 8020 **Fax:** 2226 802222
Email: verlag@ubgnet.de
Web site: http://www.ubgnet.de
Titles:
FRAU & POLITIK
RATHAUSCONSULT
WIRTSCHAFTS BILD

UNITEC-MEDIENVERTRIEB E.K. 1641867
Ludwigstr. 11, 86669 STENGELHEIM
Tel: 8433 929476 **Fax:** 8433 1726
Email: unitec_medienvertrieb@web.de
Web site: http://www.unitec-medienvertrieb.de
Titles:
MOTORRAD PROFILE

UNITI BERATUNGSGESELLSCHAFT FÜR MINERALÖL-ANWENDUNGSTECHNIK MBH 685639
Jägerstr. 6, 10117 BERLIN **Tel:** 30 755414400
Fax: 30 755414474
Email: info@uniti.de
Web site: http://www.uniti.de
Titles:
MINERALÖLTECHNIK

UNIVERSITÄT HAMBURG, INSTITUT FÜR JOURNALISTIK UND KOMMUNIKATIONS-WISSENSCHAFT 1772274
Allende-Platz 1, 20146 HAMBURG
Tel: 40 41429881
Email: post@journalistik-hamburg.de
Web site: http://www.journalistik-hamburg.de
Titles:
HALBSTARK

UNIVERSITÄT OSNABRÜCK, PRESSE- UND ÖFFENTLICHKEITSARBEIT 689881
Schloss, Neuer Graben, 49074 OSNABRÜCK
Tel: 541 9694114 **Fax:** 541 9694570
Email: pressestelle@uni-osnabrueck.de
Web site: http://www.uni-osnabrueck.de
Titles:
UNIZEIT

UNIVERSITÄT ZU LÜBECK 1783426
Ratzeburger Allee 160, 23562 LÜBECK
Tel: 451 5003646 **Fax:** 451 5005718
Email: kube@zuv.uni-luebeck.de
Web site: http://www.uni-luebeck.de
Titles:
FOCUS UNI-LUEBECK

UNIVERSITÄTSVERLAG WINTER GMBH HEIDELBERG 677758
Dossenheimer Landstr. 13, 69121 HEIDELBERG
Tel: 6221 770260 **Fax:** 6221 770269
Email: info@winter-verlag-hd.de
Web site: http://www.winter-verlag-hd.de
Titles:
GYMNASIUM

UNIVERSUM VERLAG GMBH 678268
Taunusstr. 54, 65183 WIESBADEN **Tel:** 611 90300
Fax: 611 9030181
Email: kontakt@universum.de
Web site: http://www.universum.de
Titles:
DGUV ARBEIT & GESUNDHEIT
DGUV PLUSPUNKT
TASCHENBUCH FÜR ARBEITSSICHERHEIT
TASCHENBUCH FÜR SICHERHEITSBEAUFTRAGTE - AUSG. METALL

UNSER GARTEN VERLAG GMBH - KULTURZENTRUM BETTINGER MÜHLE 683206
Hüttersdorfer Str. 29, 66839 SCHMELZ
Tel: 6887 9032999 **Fax:** 6887 9032998
Email: info@unsergarten-verlag.de
Web site: http://www.unsergarten-verlag.de
Titles:
DER HESSISCHE OBST- U. GARTENBAU
LUXEMBURGER OBST- UND GARTENBAUFREUND
RATGEBER FÜR DEN GARTENLIEBHABER
UNSER GARTEN

UNTERNEHMER MEDIEN GMBH 689945
Schlossallee 10, 53179 BONN **Tel:** 228 9545985
Fax: 228 9545980
Email: verlag@unternehmermagazin.de
Web site: http://www.unternehmermagazin.de
Titles:
UNTERNEHMERMAGAZIN

UNTERNEHMERVERLAG 1752003
Im Wingert 13, 53424 REMAGEN
Tel: 2228 9129120 **Fax:** 2228 91991210
Email: info@unternehmerverlag.de
Web site: http://www.unternehmerverlag.de
Titles:
FRANCHISE €RFOLGE

UNTERWEGS-VERLAG MANFRED KLEMANN 698703
Dr.-Andler-Str. 28, 78224 SINGEN
Tel: 7731 63544 **Fax:** 7731 62401
Email: info@reisefuehrer.com
Web site: http://www.reisefuehrer.com
Titles:
DER NEUE GROSSE FREIZEITFÜHRER FÜR DEUTSCHLAND

UNTITLED VERLAG UND AGENTUR GMBH & CO. KG 1763365
Innocentiastr. 33, 20144 HAMBURG
Tel: 40 1898810 **Fax:** 40 189881111
Email: info@untitled-verlag.de
Web site: http://www.untitled-verlag.de
Titles:
GZ GOLDSCHMIEDE ZEITUNG
GZ LIVE
PHOTOGRAPHIE
ZEITLOS

UP2MEDIA AG 680011
Quellenstr. 32, 67433 NEUSTADT **Tel:** 6321 89980
Fax: 6321 899899
Email: info@up2media.de
Web site: http://www.up2media.de
Titles:
CAD NEWS

UPRESS 1784432
Soesttor 12, 59555 LIPPSTADT **Tel:** 2941 9589111
Email: hallo@upress.info
Web site: http://www.upress.info
Titles:
MAN IST WAS MAN ISST

URBAN MEDIA GMBH 1626906
Askanischer Platz 3, 10963 BERLIN
Tel: 30 290211860 **Fax:** 30 2902199918690
Web site: http://www.urban-media-daten.de

Titles:
MEINBERLIN.DE
ZITTY BERLIN

URBAN & VOGEL GMBH 677625
Aschauer Str. 30, 81549 MÜNCHEN
Tel: 89 2030431300 **Fax:** 89 2030431399
Email: info@urban-vogel.de
Web site: http://www.springermedizin.de

Titles:
ALLERGO JOURNAL
ANGEWANDTE SCHMERZTHERAPIE UND PALLIATIVMEDIZIN
CARDIO NEWS
CARDIOVASC
CHINESISCHE MEDIZIN
CLINICAL NEURORADIOLOGY
COLOPROCTOLOGY
DER DEUTSCHE DERMATOLOGE
DNP DER NEUROLOGE & PSYCHIATER
EUROPEAN JOURNAL OF TRAUMA AND EMERGENCY SURGERY
GASTRONEWS
GYNÄKOLOGIE + GEBURTSHILFE
DER HAUSARZT
HAUTNAH DERMATOLOGIE
HEILBERUFE
HERZ
HNO NACHRICHTEN
IM FOCUS ONKOLOGIE
INFECTION
INFO DIABETOLOGIE
INFO NEUROLOGIE & PSYCHIATRIE
INFO ONKOLOGIE
MEDIZINISCHE KLINIK
MMW FORTSCHRITTE DER MEDIZIN
NEUROTRANSMITTER
OPERATIVE ORTHOPÄDIE UND TRAUMATOLOGIE
ORTHOPÄDIE & RHEUMA
PÄDIATRIE
PNEUMONEWS
PRODIALOG
SCHMERZ & AKUPUNKTUR
STRAHLENTHERAPIE UND ONKOLOGIE
URO-NEWS

URBAN-VERLAG HAMBURG/WIEN GMBH 678054
Neumann-Reichardt-Str. 34, 22041 HAMBURG
Tel: 40 6569450 **Fax:** 40 6569450
Email: urban@oilgaspublisher.de
Web site: http://www.oilgaspublisher.de

Titles:
ERDÖL ERDGAS KOHLE
OIL GAS EUROPEAN MAGAZINE

USMEDIA 1652445
Hauptstr. 33, 83684 TEGERNSEE
Tel: 8022 706390 **Fax:** 8022 7063940
Email: redaktion@rund-ums-baby.de
Web site: http://www.rund-ums-baby.de

Titles:
RUND UMS BABY

UVK VERLAGSGES. MBH 680624
Schützenstr. 24, 78462 KONSTANZ
Tel: 7531 90530 **Fax:** 7531 905398
Email: presse@uvk.de
Web site: http://www.uvk.de

Titles:
DEUTSCHER PRESSERAT JAHRBUCH

UVP-GESELLSCHAFT E.V. 689983
Sachsenweg 9, 59073 HAMM **Tel:** 2381 52129
Fax: 2381 52195
Email: info@uvp.de
Web site: http://www.uvp.de

Titles:
UVP REPORT

VACATION VILLAS INTERNATIONAL GMBH 1690732
Ludwig-Erhard-Str. 4, 34131 KASSEL
Tel: 561 92095010 **Fax:** 561 920950150
Email: presse@fewo-direkt.de
Web site: http://www.fewo-direkt.de

Titles:
FEWO-DIREKT.DE

VAF BUNDESVERBAND TELEKOMMUNIKATION E.V. 1744042
Otto-Hahn-Str. 16, 40721 HILDEN
Tel: 2103 700250 **Fax:** 2103 700106
Email: info@vaf-ev.de
Web site: http://www.vaf-ev.de

Titles:
VAF REPORT

VAMOS ELTERN-KIND-REISEN GMBH 1630499
Hindenburgstr. 27, 30175 HANNOVER
Tel: 511 4007990 **Fax:** 511 40079999
Email: kontakt@vamos-reisen.de
Web site: http://www.vamos-reisen.de

Titles:
VAMOS ELTERN-KIND-REISEN

VANDENHOECK & RUPRECHT GMBH & CO. KG 677242
Theaterstr. 13, 37073 GÖTTINGEN
Tel: 551 508440 **Fax:** 551 5084422
Email: info@v-r.de
Web site: http://www.v-r.de

Titles:
GRUPPENPSYCHOTHERAPIE UND GRUPPENDYNAMIK
HOMILETISCHE MONATSHEFTE
PRAXIS DER KINDERPSYCHOLOGIE UND KINDERPSYCHIATRIE
ZEITSCHRIFT FÜR INDIVIDUALPSYCHOLOGIE
ZEITSCHRIFT FÜR PSYCHOSOMATISCHE MEDIZIN UND PSYCHOTHERAPIE

VDAV-VERBAND DEUTSCHER AUSKUNFTS- UND VERZEICHNISMEDIEN E.V. 690124
Heerdter Sandberg 30, 40549 DÜSSELDORF
Tel: 211 5779950 **Fax:** 211 57799544
Email: info@vdav.org
Web site: http://www.vdav.de

Titles:
AUSKUNFTS- UND VERZEICHNIS-MEDIEN

VDCA VERBAND DEUTSCHER CYTOLOGISCH TÄTIGER ASSISTENTEN E.V. 680449
Mittelfeldweg 20c, 27607 LANGEN
Tel: 4743 275646 **Fax:** 4743 912554
Email: h.hahn@vdca.de
Web site: http://www.vdca.de

Titles:
CYTO-INFO

VDE VERLAG GMBH 679881
Bismarckstr. 33, 10625 BERLIN **Tel:** 30 3480010
Fax: 30 3480019088
Email: vertrieb@vde-verlag.de
Web site: http://www.vde-verlag.de

Titles:
BUILDING & AUTOMATION
ETZ
NTZ
OPEN AUTOMATION

VDH SERVICE GMBH 689927
Westfalendamm 174, 44141 DORTMUND
Tel: 231 565000 **Fax:** 231 592440
Email: info@vdh.de
Web site: http://www.vdh.de

Titles:
UNSER RASSEHUND

VDI VERLAG GMBH 683646
VDI-Platz 1, 40468 DÜSSELDORF **Tel:** 211 61880
Fax: 211 6188112
Email: info@vdi-nachrichten.com
Web site: http://www.vdi-nachrichten.com

Titles:
VDI NACHRICHTEN
VDI-NACHRICHTEN.COM

VDL-VERLAG GMBH VERLAG & DIENSTLEISTUNGEN 682260
Heinrich-Heine-Str. 5, 63322 RÖDERMARK
Tel: 6074 920880 **Fax:** 6074 93334
Email: vdl-verlag@t-online.de
Web site: http://www.fs-journal.de

Titles:
F & S FILTRIEREN UND SEPARIEREN

VDMA VERLAG GMBH 688900
Lyoner Str. 18, 60528 FRANKFURT **Tel:** 69 66030
Fax: 69 66031611
Email: verlag@vdma-verlag.de
Web site: http://www.vdma-verlag.com

Titles:
STATISTISCHES HANDBUCH FÜR DEN MASCHINENBAU
VDMA NACHRICHTEN

VDP-VERLAG MATHE 680020
Postfach 1151, 30927 BURGWEDEL
Tel: 5139 894507 **Fax:** 5139 894508
Email: info@videomedia-online.de
Web site: http://www.videomedia-online.de

Titles:
VIDEOMEDIA

VDSTRA. FACHGEWERKSCHAFT IN DER DONAR VERLAG GMBH 1640584
Rösrather Str. 565, 51107 KÖLN
Tel: 2203 5031110 **Fax:** 2203 5031120
Email: info@vdstra.de
Web site: http://www.vdstra.de

Titles:
STRASSENWÄRTER

VEGETARIERBUND DEUTSCHLAND E.V. (VEBU) 686174
Blumenstr. 3, 30159 HANNOVER
Tel: 511 3632050 **Fax:** 511 3632007
Email: info@vebu.de
Web site: http://www.vebu.de

Titles:
NATÜRLICH VEGETARISCH

VEHICLES AND MORE GMBH 1773971
Wilhelm-Giese-Str. 26, 27616 BEVERSTEDT
Tel: 4747 87410 **Fax:** 4747 8741222
Email: info@kran-und-hebetechnik.de
Web site: http://www.kran-und-hebetechnik.de

Titles:
BKH BAUMASCHINEN | KRANE | HEBETECHNIK

VEITENSTEIN MEDIA GMBH 1684545
Hambacher Weg 12, 96450 COBURG
Tel: 9561 354270
Web site: http://www.mohr-stadtillu.de

Titles:
MAURITIUS
MOHR STADTILLU
MOHR STADTILLU

VERBAND ANGESTELLTER AKADEMIKER UND LEITENDER ANGESTELLTER DER CHEMISCHEN INDUSTRIE E.V. 1657431
Mohrenstr. 11, 50670 KÖLN **Tel:** 221 160010
Fax: 221 160016
Email: info@vaa.de
Web site: http://www.vaa.de

Titles:
VAA MAGAZIN

VERBAND BAYERISCHER BERUFSFISCHER E.V. 681865
Königstorgraben 11, 90402 NÜRNBERG
Tel: 911 223910 **Fax:** 911 241453
Email: post@fischer-teichwirt.de
Web site: http://www.berufsfischer.de

Titles:
FISCHER & TEICHWIRT

VERBAND DER HAUS-, WOHNUNGS- UND GRUNDEIGENTÜMER DES SAARLANDES E.V. 683031
Bismarckstr. 52, 66121 SAARBRÜCKEN
Tel: 681 668370 **Fax:** 681 68035
Email: info@haus-und-grund-saarland.de
Web site: http://www.haus-und-grund-saarland.de

Titles:
HAUS & GRUND SAARLAND

VERBAND DER HAUS-, WOHNUNGS- UND GRUNDEIGENTÜMER FREIBURG UND UMGEBUNG E.V. 682119
Erbprinzenstr. 7, 79098 FREIBURG
Tel: 761 380560 **Fax:** 761 3805660
Email: verband@haus-grund-freiburg.de
Web site: http://www.haus-grund-freiburg.de

Titles:
FREIBURGER HAUSBESITZER-ZEITUNG

VERBAND DER LANDWIRTE IM NEBENBERUF SAAR E.V. 683682
Saarlouiser Str. 54, 66346 PÜTTLINGEN
Tel: 171 2632635 **Fax:** 6806 920661
Email: info@vln-saar.de
Web site: http://www.vln-saar.de

Titles:
FACHBLATT DER NEBENBERUFLICHEN LANDWIRTSCHAFT

VERBAND DER VERWALTUNGSBEAMTEN IN BADEN-WÜRTTEMBERG E.V. 690122
Panoramastr. 27, 70174 STUTTGART
Tel: 711 2263262 **Fax:** 711 2263280
Email: info@vdv-bw.de
Web site: http://www.vdv-bw.de

Titles:
VERWALTUNGSZEITUNG BADEN-WÜRTTEMBERG

VERBAND DEUTSCHER LESEZIRKEL E.V. 685674
Grafenberger Allee 241, 40237 DÜSSELDORF
Tel: 211 6907320 **Fax:** 211 674947
Email: lzverband@aol.com

Titles:
MITGLIEDERVERZEICHNIS

VERBAND FÜR LANDWIRTSCHAFTLICHE FACHBILDUNG, AMT FÜR LANDWIRTSCHAFT UND FORSTEN 681121
94094 ROTTHALMÜNSTER **Tel:** 8533 960702
Fax: 8533 9607130

Titles:
EHEMALIGENBRIEF ROTTHALMÜNSTER

VERBAND SÜDDEUTSCHER ZUCKERRÜBENANBAUER E.V. 681022
Marktbreiter Str. 74, 97199 OCHSENFURT
Tel: 9331 91875 **Fax:** 9331 91874
Email: vsz@vsz.de
Web site: http://www.vsz.de

Titles:
DZZ DIE ZUCKER RÜBENZEITUNG
ZUCKERRÜBEN-MAGAZIN

VERBAND VERKEHRSWIRTSCHAFT UND LOGISTIK NORDRHEIN-WESTFALEN E.V. 1603048
Erkrather Str. 141, 40233 DÜSSELDORF
Tel: 211 734780 **Fax:** 211 7347831
Web site: http://www.vvwl-transport.de

Titles:
VERKEHRSWIRTSCHAFT UND LOGISTIK NRW

VERBRAUCHER INITIATIVE SERVICE GMBH 683596
Elsenstr. 106, 12435 BERLIN **Tel:** 30 5360733
Fax: 30 53607345
Email: mail@verbraucher.org
Web site: http://www.verbraucher.org

Titles:
VERBRAUCHER KONKRET

VER.DI, FACHBEREICH 8 BERLIN-BRANDENBURG 688757
Köpenicker Str. 30, 10179 BERLIN
Tel: 30 88664106 **Fax:** 30 88664902

Titles:
SPRACHROHR

VER.DI VEREINTE DIENSTLEISTUNGSGEWERKSCHAFT 1600636
Paula-Thiede-Ufer 10, 10179 BERLIN
Tel: 30 69560 **Fax:** 30 69563141
Email: info@verdi.de
Web site: http://www.verdi.de

Titles:
KUNST+KULTUR
M MENSCHEN MACHEN MEDIEN
VER.DI HANDEL

VER.DI VEREINTE DIENST-LEISTUNGSGEWERKSCHAFT E.V., FACHBEREICH TK/IT 1685590
Paula-Thiede-Ufer 10, 10179 BERLIN
Tel: 30 69560 **Fax:** 30 69563141
Web site: http://tk-it.verdi.de
Titles:
KOMM TK IT

VEREIN DER FREUNDE DES ERSTEN DEUTSCHEN NATIONALPARKS BAYERISCHER WALD E.V. 1621101
Bahnhofstr. 22, 94481 GRAFENAU
Tel: 8552 625060 **Fax:** 8552 920529
Email: redaktion@nationalparkzeitung.de
Web site: http://www.nationalparkfreunde.de
Titles:
SCHÖNER BAYERISCHER WALD

VEREIN DER PILZFREUNDE STUTTGART E.V. 1622049
Danziger Str. 27, 73262 REICHENBACH
Web site: http://www.pilzverein.de
Titles:
SÜDWESTDEUTSCHE PILZRUNDSCHAU

VEREIN DER SCHIFFSINGENIEURE IN BREMEN E.V. 678126
Senator-Bömers-Str. 4, 28197 BREMEN
Tel: 421 5288314 **Fax:** 421 544949
Titles:
ANTRIEB

VEREIN DER SCHIFFS-INGENIEURE ZU HAMBURG E.V. 688111
Gurlittstr. 32, 20099 HAMBURG **Tel:** 40 2803883
Fax: 40 2803565
Email: vsih-vdsi@t-online.de
Web site: http://www.schiffsingenieure.de
Titles:
SCHIFFS-INGENIEUR JOURNAL

VEREIN DER STUDIERENDEN DER DEUTSCHEN AUSSENHANDELS- UND VERKEHRS-AKADEMIE 681169
Universitätsallee 18, 28359 BREMEN
Tel: 421 94991020 **Fax:** 421 94991019
Email: einsteiger@bvl-campus.de
Web site: http://www.dav-einsteiger.de
Titles:
EINSTEIGER

VEREIN DEUTSCHER INGENIEURE, BEZIRKSVEREIN MÜNCHEN, OBERBAYERN UND NIEDERBAYERN E.V. 1771319
Westendstr. 199, 80686 MÜNCHEN
Tel: 89 57912200 **Fax:** 89 57912161
Email: tib@bv-muenchen.vdi.de
Web site: http://www.technik-in-bayern.de
Titles:
TECHNIK IN BAYERN

VEREIN FÜR DEUTSCHE SPITZE E.V. GEGR. 1899 680646
Angerstr. 5, 86179 AUGSBURG **Tel:** 821 812943
Fax: 821 812943
Email: peter.machetanz@freenet.de
Web site: http://www.deutsche-spitze.de
Titles:
DER DEUTSCHE SPITZ

VEREIN FÜR DEUTSCHE WACHTELHUNDE E.V. 680592
Dorfstr. 3, 74594 KRESSBERG
Email: info@wachtelhund.de
Web site: http://www.wachtelhund.de
Titles:
DEUTSCHE WACHTELHUND ZEITUNG

VEREIN MEPPENER SENIORENZEITUNG "KIEN TIED ... KIEN TIED" E.V. 1622422
Im Sack 12, 49716 MEPPEN **Tel:** 5931 929333
Email: seniorenzeitung.kientied@ewetel.net
Titles:
KIEN TIED ... KIEN TIED

VEREIN NATURSCHUTZPARK E.V. 686197
Niederhaverbeck 7, 29646 BISPINGEN
Tel: 5198 987030 **Fax:** 5198 987039
Email: vnp-info@t-online.de
Web site: http://www.verein-naturschutzpark.de
Titles:
NATURSCHUTZ UND NATURPARKE

VEREIN OSTFRIESISCHER STAMMVIEHZÜCHTER 1638853
Nessestr. 1, 26789 LEER **Tel:** 491 80040
Fax: 491 800422
Email: info@vost.de
Web site: http://www.vostov.de
Titles:
RINDERZUCHT & MILCHPRODUKTION

VEREIN SENIOREN HEUTE 688376
Häuserstr. 15a, 37154 NORTHEIM **Tel:** 5551 1589
Titles:
SENIOREN HEUTE

VEREIN ZUR FÖRDERUNG ALTERNATIVER MEDIEN E.V. 688157
Roonstr. 3a, 53175 BONN **Tel:** 228 604760
Fax: 228 6047620
Email: schnuess@schnuess.de
Web site: http://www.schnuess.de
Titles:
SCHNÜSS

VEREINIGTE FACHVERLAGE GMBH 678127
Lise-Meitner-Str. 2, 55129 MAINZ **Tel:** 6131 9920
Fax: 6131 992100
Email: info@vfmz.de
Web site: http://www.industrie-service.de
Titles:
ANTRIEBSTECHNIK
DER BETRIEBSLEITER
DRUCKLUFTTECHNIK
F+H FÖRDERN UND HEBEN
F+H PROJEKTGUIDE INTRALOGISTIK
F+H REPORT
INDUSTRIALVISION
DER KONSTRUKTEUR
MOBILE MASCHINEN
MSR MAGAZIN
O+P
O+P KONSTRUKTIONS JAHRBUCH
O+P REPORT
TERRATECH
VERFAHRENSTECHNIK
WLB WASSER, LUFT UND BODEN

VEREINIGUNG DER ANGEHÖRIGEN UND FREUNDE DES AUFKLÄRUNGSGE-SCHWADERS 51 IMMELMANN E.V. 1994 687551
Bennebeker Chaussee 100, 24848 KROPP
Tel: 4624 301440 **Fax:** 4624 301199
Email: mail@recce.de
Web site: http://www.recce.de
Titles:
RECCE

VERKEHRSBLATT-VERLAG 690092
Schleefstr. 14, 44287 DORTMUND
Tel: 231 128047 **Fax:** 231 128009
Email: info@verkehrsblatt.de
Web site: http://www.verkehrsblatt.de
Titles:
VERKEHRSBLATT

VERKEHRSGESCHICHTLICHE BLÄTTER E.V. 690005
Zingster Str. 30, 13051 BERLIN **Tel:** 30 68814184
Fax: 30 68814184
Email: wolf.machel@web.de
Web site: http://www.verkehrsgeschichtliche-blaetter.de
Titles:
VB VERKEHRSGESCHICHTLICHE BLÄTTER

VERKEHRS-VERLAG J. FISCHER GMBH & CO. KG 681864
Corneliusstr. 49, 40215 DÜSSELDORF
Tel: 211 991930 **Fax:** 211 6801544
Email: vvf@verkehrsverlag-fischer.de
Web site: http://www.verkehrsverlag-fischer.de
Titles:
ZEITSCHRIFT FÜR VERKEHRSWISSENSCHAFT

VERLAG 8. MAI GMBH 1741075
Torstr. 6, 10119 BERLIN **Tel:** 30 5363550
Fax: 30 53635544
Email: verlag@jungewelt.de
Web site: http://www.jungewelt.de
Titles:
JUNGE WELT

VERLAG AACHENER ANZEIGENBLATT GMBH & CO. KG 677210
Dresdener Str. 3, 52068 AACHEN
Tel: 241 5101569 **Fax:** 241 5101550
Email: info@supersonntag.de
Web site: http://www.supersonntag.de
Titles:
AACHENER WOCHE SUPER MITTWOCH

VERLAG AENNE BURDA GMBH & CO. KG 678073
Arabellastr. 23, 81925 MÜNCHEN **Tel:** 89 92500
Email: burdastyle@burda.com
Web site: http://www.burdastyle.de
Titles:
BURDA EASY FASHION
BURDA PLUS FASHION
BURDA STYLE

VERLAG ANDREAS LANGER 687612
Auf den Höhen 13, 93138 LAPPERSDORF
Tel: 941 2802402 **Fax:** 941 2802404
Email: magazin.reisefieber@gmx.de
Web site: http://www.reisefieber-magazin.de
Titles:
REISEFIEBER

VERLAG ANDREAS REIFFER 1767306
Hauptstr. 16b, 38527 MEINE **Tel:** 5304 501783
Fax: 5304 501796
Email: reiffer@verlag-reiffer.de
Web site: http://www.verlag-reiffer.de
Titles:
THE PUNCHLINER

VERLAG ANZEIGENBLÄTTER GMBH CHEMNITZ 680136
Brückenstr. 15, 09111 CHEMNITZ
Tel: 371 65620000 **Fax:** 371 65627000
Email: geschaeftsfuehrung@blick.de
Web site: http://www.blick.de
Titles:
BLICK
BLICK
BLICK
BLICK
BLICK
BLICK
BLICK
BLICK
BLICK
BLICK
BLICK AM SONNTAG
BLICK - LOKALANZEIGER F. D. VOGTLAND, AUSG. AUERBACH, REICHENBACH
BLICK - LOKALANZEIGER F. D. VOGTLAND, AUSG. PLAUEN
FREIBERG AKTUELL
WILLKOMMEN IM ERZGEBIRGE
WILLKOMMEN IM NATURTHEATER GREIFENSTEINE
WILLKOMMEN IM VOGTLAND

VERLAG ARBEIT UND WIRTSCHAFT OHG 684419
Stemmerstr. 91, 78266 BÜSINGEN
Tel: 7734 6061 **Fax:** 7734 7112
Titles:
VERTRAULICHE MITTEILUNGEN AUS POLITIK, WIRTSCHAFT UND GELDANLAGE

VERLAG AXEL STINSHOFF 684000
Sülzburgstr. 74, 50937 KÖLN **Tel:** 221 9414888
Fax: 221 413166
Email: redaktion@jazzthing.de
Titles:
JAZZ THING & BLUE RHYTHM

VERLAG B. KÄMMER 682047
Georgenstr. 19, 80799 MÜNCHEN
Tel: 89 34018900 **Fax:** 89 34018901
Email: bk@verlag-kaemmer.de
Web site: http://www.verlag-kaemmer.de
Titles:
FOTO DIGITAL
VIDEO KAMERA OBJEKTIV

VERLAG BAADER GMBH 677600
Gutenbergstr. 1, 72525 MÜNSINGEN
Tel: 7381 1870 **Fax:** 7381 3171
Email: i.zoldos-muhr@swp.de
Titles:
ALB BOTE
WOCHENANZEIGER FÜR DIE STÄDTE MÜNSINGEN, HAYINGEN UND TROCHTELFINGEN, DIE ORTE ENGSTINGEN, GOMADINGEN, HOHENSTEIN, HEROLDSTATT, MEHRSTETTEN, PFRONSTETTEN, RÖMERSTEIN, ZWIEFALTEN UND WEITERE 53 ORTSCHAFTEN AUF DER MITTLEREN ALB

VERLAG BAU + TECHNIK GMBH 678834
Steinhof 39, 40699 ERKRATH **Tel:** 211 924990
Fax: 211 9249955
Email: info@verlagbt.de
Web site: http://www.verlagbt.de
Titles:
BAUEN FÜR DIE LANDWIRTSCHAFT
BETON
CEMENT INTERNATIONAL

VERLAG BAYERISCHE ANZEIGENBLÄTTER GMBH 683885
Stauffenbergstr. 2a, 85051 INGOLSTADT
Tel: 841 9666640 **Fax:** 841 9666645
Email: info@iz-regional.de
Web site: http://www.iz-regional.de
Titles:
IZ REGIONAL PFAFFENHOFENER ANZEIGER

VERLAG BAYERISCHE KOMMUNALPRESSE GMBH 678902
Breslauer Weg 44, 82538 GERETSRIED
Tel: 8171 930711 **Fax:** 8171 80514
Email: info@gemeindezeitung.de
Web site: http://www.gemeindezeitung.de
Titles:
BAYERISCHE GEMEINDEZEITUNG

VERLAG BAYERISCHE STAATSZEITUNG GMBH 678927
Herzog-Rudolf-Str. 3, 80539 MÜNCHEN
Tel: 89 29014250 **Fax:** 89 29014270
Email: anzeigen@bsz.de
Web site: http://www.bsz.de
Titles:
BAYERISCHE STAATSZEITUNG UND BAYERISCHER STAATSANZEIGER

VERLAG BAYERNKURIER 678934
Nymphenburger Str. 64, 80335 MÜNCHEN
Tel: 89 120040 **Fax:** 89 12004133
Email: vertrieb@bayernkurier.de
Web site: http://www.bayernkurier.de
Titles:
BAYERNKURIER

VERLAG C. H. BECK OHG 678130
Wilhelmstr. 9, 80801 MÜNCHEN **Tel:** 89 381890
Fax: 89 38189398
Web site: http://www.beck.de
Titles:
BC ZEITSCHRIFT FÜR BILANZIERUNG, RECHNUNGSWESEN UND CONTROLLING
BKR ZEITSCHRIFT FÜR BANK- UND KAPITALMARKTRECHT
DEUTSCHE NOTAR-ZEITSCHRIFT
DEUTSCHES STEUERRECHT DSTR
JURISTISCHE ARBEITSBLÄTTER JA
JUS JURISTISCHE SCHULUNG
KAMMER FORUM
KULTUR & TECHNIK
MARKETING
MEDR MEDIZINRECHT
NJW NEUE JURISTISCHE WOCHENSCHRIFT
R+S RECHT UND SCHADEN
DER SACHVERSTÄNDIGE
SCHIEDSVZ ZEITSCHRIFT FÜR SCHIEDSVERFAHREN
WIRTSCHAFT UND RECHT IN OSTEUROPA WIRO
ZEV ZEITSCHRIFT FÜR ERBRECHT UND VERMÖGENSNACHFOLGE

VERLAG CHMIELORZ GMBH 678719
Marktplatz 13, 65183 WIESBADEN
Tel: 611 360980 **Fax:** 611 301303
Email: info@chmielorz.de
Web site: http://www.chmielorz.de
Titles:
BÄKO MAGAZIN
C.EBRA
DHZ DER HESSISCHE ZAHNARZT

FUB FLÄCHENMANAGEMENT UND BODENORDNUNG
SCHUHMARKT
U.J.S. UHREN JUWELEN SCHMUCK
VDV MAGAZIN

VERLAG CHRISTLICHE FAMILIE GMBH 680179
Komödienstr. 48, 50667 KÖLN **Tel:** 221 1300790
Fax: 201 1301857
Web site: http://www.katholische-sonntagszeitung.de
Titles:
KATHOLISCHE SONNTAGSZEITUNG FÜR DAS BISTUM REGENSBURG
KATHOLISCHE SONNTAGSZEITUNG FÜR DEUTSCHLAND

VERLAG DER ARZT 678375
Gorkistr. 142, 13509 BERLIN **Tel:** 30 40208060
Fax: 30 40208059
Email: der-arzt@inter.net
Web site: http://www.der-arzt.de
Titles:
DER ARZT

VERLAG DER BOTE HANNS BOLLMANN GMBH & CO. 679626
Nürnberger Str. 5, 90537 FEUCHT
Tel: 9128 70720 **Fax:** 9128 707225
Email: verlag@der-bote.de
Web site: http://www.der-bote.de
Titles:
DER BOTE FÜR NÜRNBERG-LAND

VERLAG DER FINANZBERATER GMBH 681842
Hauptstr. 8b, 82319 STARNBERG
Tel: 8151 65650 **Fax:** 8151 656529
Email: info@der-finanzberater.de
Web site: http://www.der-finanzberater.de
Titles:
DER FINANZBERATER

VERLAG DER INGENIEUR GMBH 1638680
Rheinstr. 129c, 76275 ETTLINGEN
Tel: 7243 39396 **Fax:** 7243 39395
Email: info@ingenieurverlag.de
Web site: http://www.ingenieurverlag.de
Titles:
ABI AKTUELLE BERICHTE UND INFORMATIONEN FÜR ARCHITEKTEN UND INGENIEURE

VERLAG DER MARKTSPIEGEL GMBH 685382
Burgschmietstr. 2, 90419 NÜRNBERG
Tel: 911 399080 **Fax:** 911 3990812
Email: media@marktspiegel.de
Web site: http://www.marktspiegel.de
Titles:
DER MARKTSPIEGEL
DER MARKTSPIEGEL

VERLAG DER SAAR-HANDWERKER 687942
Grülingsstr. 115, 66113 SAARBRÜCKEN
Tel: 681 948610 **Fax:** 681 9486199
Email: sh@agvh.de
Web site: http://www.saarhandwerker.de
Titles:
DER SAAR-HANDWERKER

VERLAG DER SIEBDRUCK 688435
Grapengießerstr. 30, 23556 LÜBECK
Tel: 451 8798887 **Fax:** 451 8798893
Email: verlag@draeger.de
Web site: http://www.der-siebdruck.de
Titles:
DER SIEBDRUCK & DIGITALDRUCK

VERLAG DER TAGESSPIEGEL GMBH 689195
Askanischer Platz 3, 10963 BERLIN
Tel: 30 290210 **Fax:** 30 2902112090
Email: infotsp@tagesspiegel.de
Web site: http://www.tagesspiegel.de
Titles:
DER TAGESSPIEGEL
DER TAGESSPIEGEL ONLINE

VERLAG DEUTSCHE POLIZEILITERATUR GMBH 680351
Forststr. 3a, 40721 HILDEN **Tel:** 211 71040
Fax: 211 7104174
Web site: http://www.vdpolizei.de
Titles:
DEUTSCHE POLIZEI

VERLAG DIE ABENDZEITUNG GMBH & CO. 8 UHR-BLATT KG 695518
Winklerstr. 15, 90403 NÜRNBERG **Tel:** 911 23310
Fax: 911 2331192
Email: info@abendzeitung-nuernberg.de
Web site: http://www.abendzeitung-nuernberg.de
Titles:
AZ NÜRNBERG

VERLAG DIE ABENDZEITUNG GMBH & CO. KG 677233
Rundfunkplatz 4, 80335 MÜNCHEN **Tel:** 89 23770
Fax: 89 2377478
Email: info@abendzeitung.de
Web site: http://www.abendzeitung.de
Titles:
ABENDZEITUNG
ABENDZEITUNG.DE

VERLAG DIE SCHWESTERN-REVUE GMBH 684071
Am Schwarzenberg 28, 97078 WÜRZBURG
Tel: 7303 910030 **Fax:** 7303 5299
Email: redaktion@krankenpflege-journal.de
Web site: http://www.krankenpflege-journal.com
Titles:
KRANKENPFLEGE JOURNAL

VERLAG DIETER A. KUBERSKI GMBH 680466
Reinsburgstr. 82, 70178 STUTTGART
Tel: 711 238860 **Fax:** 711 2388619
Email: info@verlagsmarketing.de
Web site: http://www.verlagsmarketing.de
Titles:
DACH + GRÜN
KBD KOMMUNALER BESCHAFFUNGS-DIENST

VERLAG DIETER HANKE 686776
Am Weitgarten 37, 53227 BONN **Tel:** 228 9442853
Fax: 228 445280
Email: info@omnibusspiegel.de
Web site: http://www.omnibusspiegel.de
Titles:
OMNIBUS NACHRICHTEN
OMNIBUS SPIEGEL

VERLAG DIETER NIEDECKEN GMBH 682284
Wandsbeker Allee 1, 22041 HAMBURG
Tel: 40 414480 **Fax:** 40 41448999
Web site: http://www.fvw-mediengruppe.de
Titles:
BIZTRAVEL
FVW
TRAVELTALK
URLAUB PERFEKT

VERLAG DINGES & FRICK GMBH 679388
Greifstr. 4, 65199 WIESBADEN **Tel:** 611 9310941
Fax: 611 9310943
Email: e.koenig@dinges-frick.de
Web site: http://www.dinges-frick.de
Titles:
B.I.T. ONLINE
INFORMATION WISSENSCHAFT & PRAXIS

VERLAG DIRK SCHNEEKLOTH 686946
Svendborger Str. 23, 24109 KIEL **Tel:** 431 687875
Fax: 431 687897
Email: partout-fl@t-online.de
Web site: http://www.partout-online.de
Titles:
PARTOUT

VERLAG DOKUMENTE GMBH 1768922
Dottendorfer Str. 86, 53129 BONN
Tel: 228 9239805 **Fax:** 228 690385
Email: redaktion@dokumente-documents.info
Web site: http://www.dokumente-documents.info
Titles:
DOKUMENTE DOCUMENTS

VERLAG DR. ALBERT BARTENS KG 691007
Lückhoffstr. 16, 14129 BERLIN **Tel:** 30 8035678
Fax: 30 8032049
Email: sugarindustry@bartens.com
Web site: http://www.bartens.com
Titles:
SUGAR INDUSTRY ZUCKER INDUSTRIE

VERLAG DR. FRIEDRICH PFEIL 1616832
Wolfratshauser Str. 27, 81379 MÜNCHEN
Tel: 89 7428270 **Fax:** 89 7242772
Email: info@pfeil-verlag.de
Web site: http://www.pfeil-verlag.de
Titles:
RUNDGESPRÄCHE DER KOMMISSION FÜR ÖKOLOGIE

VERLAG DR. OTTO SCHMIDT KG 677408
Gustav-Heinemann-Ufer 58, 50968 KÖLN
Tel: 221 9373801 **Fax:** 221 93738900
Email: verlag@otto-schmidt.de
Web site: http://www.otto-schmidt.de
Titles:
AG DIE AKTIENGESELLSCHAFT
DER AO STEUER-BERATER
DER ARBEITS-RECHTS-BERATER
BRAK-MITTEILUNGEN
COMPUTER UND RECHT
DER ERBSCHAFT-STEUER-BERATER
DER ERTRAG-STEUER-BERATER
FR FINANZ-RUNDSCHAU ERTRAGSTEUERRECHT
GESR GESUNDHEITSRECHT
GMBHRUNDSCHAU
DER GMBH-STEUER-BERATER
DER IT-RECHTS-BERATER
MONATSSCHRIFT FÜR DEUTSCHES RECHT MDR
NOTBZ
STEUER UND WIRTSCHAFT
STEUERBERATER WOCHE
DER UMSATZ STEUER-BERATER
UR UMSATZSTEUER-RUNDSCHAU
ZEITSCHRIFT FÜR KONFLIKT-MANAGEMENT

VERLAG DR. WALTHER THIEDE 686816
An der Ronne 184, 50859 KÖLN **Tel:** 2234 70584
Fax: 2234 79154
Titles:
ORNITHOLOGISCHE MITTEILUNGEN

VERLAG DREIEICH-ZEITUNG 680900
Dreieichstr. 4, 64546 MÖRFELDEN-WALLDORF
Tel: 6105 9802300 **Fax:** 6105 9802327
Email: info@dreieich-zeitung.de
Web site: http://www.dreieich-zeitung.de
Titles:
DREIEICH-ZEITUNG

VERLAG DRESDNER NACHRICHTEN GMBH & CO. KG 680919
Hauptstr. 21, 01097 DRESDEN **Tel:** 351 80750
Fax: 351 8075112
Email: info@dnn-online.de
Web site: http://www.dnn-online.de
Titles:
DRESDNER NEUESTE NACHRICHTEN

VERLAG E. HOLTERDORF GMBH & CO KG 1681253
Engelbert-Holterdorf-Str. 4, 59302 OELDE
Tel: 2522 730 **Fax:** 2522 73270
Email: postmaster@die-glocke.de
Web site: http://www.die-glocke.de
Titles:
AHLENER TAGEBLATT
DIE GLOCKE

VERLAG E. S. MITTLER & SOHN GMBH 681496
Georgsplatz 1, 20099 HAMBURG
Tel: 40 70708001 **Fax:** 40 707080324
Email: vertrieb@koehler-mittler.de
Web site: http://www.koehler-mittler.de
Titles:
EUROPÄISCHE SICHERHEIT
EUROPEAN SECURITY AND DEFENCE
MARINE FORUM

VERLAG EFFECTEN-SPIEGEL AG 681112
Tiergartenstr. 17, 40237 DÜSSELDORF
Tel: 211 683022
Web site: http://www.effecten-spiegel.de
Titles:
EFFECTEN SPIEGEL

VERLAG EMSDETTENER VOLKSZEITUNG GMBH & CO. KG 681265
Im Hagenkamp 4, 48282 EMSDETTEN
Tel: 2572 95600 **Fax:** 2572 956029
Web site: http://www.emsdettener-volkszeitung.de
Titles:
EMSDETTENER VOLKSZEITUNG

VERLAG ENERGIEBERATUNG GMBH 688886
Richard-Wagner-Str. 41, 45128 ESSEN
Tel: 201 810840 **Fax:** 201 8108430
Email: info@vik.de
Web site: http://www.vik.de
Titles:
STATISTIK DER ENERGIEWIRTSCHAFT

VERLAG ERNST UND WERNER GIESEKING GMBH 680620
Deckertstr. 30, 33617 BIELEFELD **Tel:** 521 14674
Fax: 521 143715
Email: kontakt@gieseking-verlag.de
Web site: http://www.gieseking-verlag.de
Titles:
DER DEUTSCHE RECHTSPFLEGER RPFLEGER
ZEITSCHRIFT FÜR DAS GESAMTE FAMILIENRECHT MIT BETREUUNGSRECHT ERBRECHT VERFAHRENSRECHT ÖFFENTLICHEM RECHT FAMRZ

VERLAG EUROBUS GMBH 681476
Kanzlerweg 3, 55291 SAULHEIM **Tel:** 6732 4588
Fax: 6732 4587
Email: info@eurobus.de
Web site: http://www.eurobus.de
Titles:
EUROBUS

VERLAG F. WOLFF & SOHN KG 681467
Junkernstr. 13, 31028 GRONAU **Tel:** 5182 92190
Fax: 5182 921925
Email: ldz-anzeigen@leinetal-online.de
Web site: http://www.leinetal-online.de
Titles:
LEINE DEISTER ZEITUNG
RUBS

VERLAG FELIX HASSELBRINK 685976
Raiffeisenstr. 16, 36275 KIRCHHEIM
Tel: 6628 8687 **Fax:** 6628 915397
Email: motalia@motalia.de
Web site: http://www.motalia.de
Titles:
MOTALIA

VERLAG FOCUS ROSTFREI GMBH 681952
Sonsbecker Str. 40, 46509 XANTEN
Tel: 2801 98260 **Fax:** 2801 982611
Email: info@focus-rostfrei.com
Web site: http://www.focus-rostfrei.de
Titles:
FOCUS NEREZ
FOCUS NIERDZEWNE
HÄNDLER-VERZEICHNIS FOCUS ROSTFREI

VERLAG FRACHT-DIENST 1743018
Jasperallee 82, 38102 BRAUNSCHWEIG
Tel: 531 2346197 **Fax:** 531 2347101
Email: info@frachtdienst-online.de
Web site: http://www.frachtdienst-online.de
Titles:
FRACHT DIENST

VERLAG FRANK NEHRING GMBH 679870
Zimmerstr. 56, 10117 BERLIN **Tel:** 30 4790710
Fax: 30 47907120
Email: info@officeabc.de
Web site: http://www.officeabc.de
Titles:
DAS BÜRO

OFFICE BRANDS
TEMPRA 365

VERLAG FRANZ VAHLEN GMBH
1769739
Wilhelmstr. 9, 80801 MÜNCHEN **Tel:** 89 381890
Fax: 89 38189398
Email: info@vahlen.de
Web site: http://www.vahlen.de

Titles:
ZFBR ZEITSCHRIFT FÜR DEUTSCHES UND INTERNATIONALES BAU- UND VERGABERECHT

VERLAG FRITZ KNAPP GMBH
678769
Aschaffenburger Str. 19, 60599 FRANKFURT
Tel: 69 9708330 **Fax:** 69 7078400
Email: info@kreditwesen.de
Web site: http://www.kreditwesen.de

Titles:
AUSGABE TECHNIK
BM BANK UND MARKT
CARDS KARTEN CARTES
ZEITSCHRIFT FÜR DAS GESAMTE KREDITWESEN

VERLAG FÜR ABSATZWIRTSCHAFT GMBH
681902
Littenstr. 10, 10179 BERLIN **Tel:** 30 246259613
Fax: 30 246259620
Email: info@flf.de
Web site: http://www.flf.de

Titles:
FLF FINANZIERUNG LEASING FACTORING

VERLAG FÜR ANZEIGENBLÄTTER GMBH
685189
Hinter der Jungenstr. 22, 56218 MÜLHEIM-KÄRLICH **Tel:** 261 92810 **Fax:** 261 928129
Email: lokalanzeiger@vfa-online.de
Web site: http://www.vfa-online.de

Titles:
LOKALANZEIGER ANDERNACHER KURIER
SUPER SONNTAG - AUSG. BENDORF

VERLAG FÜR ARZTRECHT
678378
Fiduciastr. 2, 76227 KARLSRUHE
Tel: 721 4538880 **Fax:** 721 4538888
Email: verlag@arztrecht.org
Web site: http://www.arztrecht.org

Titles:
ARZTRECHT

VERLAG FÜR CHEMISCHE INDUSTRIE, H. ZIOLKOWSKY GMBH
683938
Beethovenstr. 16, 86150 AUGSBURG
Tel: 821 325830 **Fax:** 821 3258323
Email: vci@sofw.com
Web site: http://www.sofw.com

Titles:
SÖFW JOURNAL

VERLAG FÜR CONTROLLINGWISSEN AG
680362
Munzinger Str. 9, 79111 FREIBURG **Tel:** 761 8980
Fax: 761 8983990
Email: online@haufe.de
Web site: http://www.controllermagazin.de

Titles:
CONTROLLER MAGAZIN

VERLAG FÜR DIE DEUTSCHE WIRTSCHAFT AG
677269
Theodor-Heuss-Str. 2, 53177 BONN
Tel: 228 82050 **Fax:** 228 359710
Email: info@vnr.de
Web site: http://www.vnr.de

Titles:
DER GROSSE KNIGGE

VERLAG FÜR FACHPUBLIZISTIK GMBH
678833
Mörikestr. 15, 70178 STUTTGART
Tel: 711 25855630 **Fax:** 711 6408972
Email: redaktion@bauelemente-bau.eu

Titles:
BAUELEMENTE BAU
BAUELEMENTE BAU INTERNATIONAL

VERLAG FÜR HAUSBESITZER
683012
Gerokstr. 3, 70188 STUTTGART **Tel:** 711 210480
Fax: 711 2104826
Email: verein@hausundgrund-stuttgart.de

Titles:
HAUS & GRUND WÜRTTEMBERG

VERLAG FÜR MEDIZINISCHE PUBLIKATIONEN
685494
Vogelsang 28, 21682 STADE **Tel:** 4141 801199
Fax: 4141 801197
Email: verlagbvhallern@t-online.de
Web site: http://www.medizinundpraxis.de

Titles:
MEDIZIN & PRAXIS SPEZIAL

VERLAG FÜR MOBILITÄT (VFM) GMBH & CO. KG
1713051
Buchbrunner Str. 21, 97318 KITZINGEN
Tel: 9321 388520 **Fax:** 9321 388510
Email: info@vfm.travel
Web site: http://dmm.travel

Titles:
DMM DER MOBILITÄTSMANAGER

VERLAG FÜR STANDESAMTSWESEN GMBH
688913
Hanauer Landstr. 197, 60314 FRANKFURT
Tel: 69 405894900 **Fax:** 69 405894550
Email: info@vfst.de
Web site: http://www.vfst.de

Titles:
STAZ DAS STANDESAMT

VERLAG G. KÖHLER
688927
Meerkamp 120, 41238 MÖNCHENGLADBACH
Tel: 2166 984183 **Fax:** 2166 984185
Email: info@stein-keramik-sanitaer.de
Web site: http://www.stein-keramik-sanitaer.de

Titles:
STEIN KERAMIK SANITÄR

VERLAG GEORG D. W. CALLWEY GMBH & CO. KG
678869
Streitfeldstr. 35, 81673 MÜNCHEN
Tel: 89 4360050 **Fax:** 89 436005113
Email: info@callwey.de
Web site: http://www.callwey.de

Titles:
BAUMEISTER
GARTEN + LANDSCHAFT
MALER TASCHENBUCH
MAPPE
RESTAURO
STEIN
TOPOS

VERLAG GODULLA GDBR
684416
Kreuzstr. 3, 76133 KARLSRUHE **Tel:** 721 380893
Fax: 721 380121
Email: info@klappeauf.de
Web site: http://www.klappeauf.de

Titles:
KLAPPE AUF

VERLAG GOSLARSCHE ZEITUNG KARL KRAUSE GMBH & CO. KG
681609
Bäckerstr. 31, 38640 GOSLAR **Tel:** 5321 3330
Fax: 5321 333399
Email: verlag@goslarsche-zeitung.de
Web site: http://www.goslarsche.de

Titles:
EXTRA AM MITTWOCH
GOSLARSCHE.DE

VERLAG GÜNTER HENDRISCH GMBH & CO. KG
679181
Klinkumer Str. 40, 41844 WEGBERG
Tel: 2434 80080 **Fax:** 2434 800810
Email: info@hendrisch.de
Web site: http://www.hendrisch.de

Titles:
BERUFS KRAFTFAHRER ZEITUNG

VERLAG GUSTAV KOPF GMBH
684162
Haldenweg 18, 71336 WAIBLINGEN
Tel: 7146 87650 **Fax:** 7146 876565
Email: info@kopfverlag.de

Titles:
KACHELOFEN & KAMIN

VERLAG HANS GRÖNER
688789
Stadtplatz 11, 94209 REGEN **Tel:** 9921 80334
Fax: 9921 6632
Email: verlag-groener@t-online.de
Web site: http://www.verlag-groener.de

Titles:
URLAUB UND FREIZEIT

VERLAG HANS SCHÖNER GMBH
682286
Walther-Rathenau-Str. 13, 75203 KÖNIGSBACH-STEIN **Tel:** 7232 40070
Fax: 7232 400799
Email: info@verlag-schoener.de
Web site: http://www.verlag-schoener.de

Titles:
FZ EUROPAS TREND-MAGAZIN FÜR UHREN, SCHMUCK & ACCESSOIRES

VERLAG HANS-JÜRGEN BÖCKEL GMBH
682629
Beim Zeugamt 4, 21509 GLINDE **Tel:** 40 7109080
Fax: 40 71090888
Email: info@glinder-zeitung.de

Titles:
GLINDER ZEITUNG

VERLAG HAUS UND GRUND
683034
Grüneburgweg 64, 60322 FRANKFURT
Tel: 69 729458 **Fax:** 69 172635
Email: hughessen@arcor.de
Web site: http://www.hausundgrundhessen.de

Titles:
HAUS & GRUND

VERLAG HAUS & GRUND ESSEN GMBH
694804
Huyssenallee 50, 45128 ESSEN **Tel:** 201 810660
Fax: 201 8106644
Email: gmbh@hug-essen.de
Web site: http://www.hug-essen.de

Titles:
HAUS & GRUND

VERLAG HAUS & MARKT MICHAEL KRAUSE
683046
Zschortauer Str. 71, 04129 LEIPZIG
Tel: 341 6010017 **Fax:** 341 6010023
Web site: http://www.hausundmarkt-mitteldeutschland.de

Titles:
HAUS & MARKT - AUSG. DRESDEN

VERLAG HEINRICH VOGEL/ SPRINGER FACHMEDIEN MÜNCHEN GMBH
679182
Aschauer Str. 30, 81549 MÜNCHEN
Tel: 89 2030430
Web site: http://www.springer-transport-media.de

Titles:
BERUFSKRAFTFAHRER UNTERWEGS
FAHRLEHRER-BRIEF
FAHRSCHULE
GEFAHR/GUT
KEP SPEZIAL
KRAFTVERKEHRSHANDBUCH
MERCEDES-BENZ OMNIBUS
MERCEDES-BENZ OMNIBUS
MERCEDES-BENZ OMNIBUS
MERCEDES-BENZ OMNIBUS
MERCEDES-BENZ OMNIBUS
MERCEDES-BENZ OMNIBUS
OMNIBUSREVUE
SICHERHEITS PROFI
TAXI
TRUCK, BUS + CO
TRUCKER
TRUCKMARKET
TRUCKMARKET
VERKEHRS RUNDSCHAU - SICHERHEITSPROFI D. BG VERKEHR, AUSG. B
VERKEHRS RUNDSCHAU - WOCHENMAGAZIN F. SPEDITION, TRANSPORT U. LOGISTIK, AUSG. A
VERKEHRS RUNDSCHAU - WOCHENMAGAZIN F. SPEDITION, TRANSPORT U. LOGISTIK, AUSG. C
VERKEHRSDIENST

VERLAG HELMUT RICHARDI GMBH
684940
Aschaffenburger Str. 19, 60599 FRANKFURT
Tel: 69 9708330 **Fax:** 69 7078400
Email: info@kreditwesen.de
Web site: http://www.kreditwesen.de

Titles:
IMMOBILIEN UND FINANZIERUNG
VERMÖGEN & STEUERN

VERLAG HEPHAISTOS
683163
Gnadenberger Weg 4, 87509 IMMENSTADT
Tel: 8379 728016 **Fax:** 8379 728018
Email: info@metall-aktiv.de
Web site: http://www.metall-aktiv.de

Titles:
HEPHAISTOS

VERLAG HERDER GMBH
678175
Hermann-Herder-Str. 4, 79104 FREIBURG
Tel: 761 27170 **Fax:** 761 2717426
Email: kundenservice@herder.de
Web site: http://www.herder.de

Titles:
ANZEIGER FÜR DIE SEELSORGE
CHRIST IN DER GEGENWART
HERDER KORRESPONDENZ
KINDERGARTEN HEUTE
MOBILE

VERLAG HORST AXTMANN GMBH
681825
Marktplatz 13, 65183 WIESBADEN
Tel: 611 360980 **Fax:** 611 372878
Email: info@filmecho.de
Web site: http://www.filmecho.de

Titles:
FILMECHO FILMWOCHE

VERLAG HORST BRÖSTLER GMBH
684237
Baumhofstr. 37, 97828 MARKTHEIDENFELD
Tel: 9391 98450 **Fax:** 9391 9845155
Email: broestler@anzeigenblatt-online.de
Web site: http://www.anzeigenblatt-online.de

Titles:
MARKTHEIDENFELDER ANZEIGENBLATT

VERLAG INDAT GMBH
1685876
Aachener Str. 222, 50931 KÖLN **Tel:** 221 8882110
Fax: 221 88821139
Web site: http://www.indat-report.de

Titles:
INDAT-REPORT

VERLAG INTERPUBLIC
679992
Friedrich-Wolf-Str. 16a, 12527 BERLIN
Tel: 30 6743977 **Fax:** 30 6744508
Email: info@bus-systeme.com
Web site: http://www.bussysteme.de

Titles:
BUS SYSTEME
BUS SYSTEMS

VERLAG J. BAUER KG
1742609
Kampstr. 84b, 45772 MARL **Tel:** 2365 1070
Fax: 2365 1071490
Email: info@medienhaus-bauer.de
Web site: http://www.medienhaus-bauer.de

Titles:
DATTELNER MORGENPOST
HERTENER ALLGEMEINE
MARLER ZEITUNG
RECKLINGHÄUSER ZEITUNG
STIMBERG ZEITUNG
WALTROPER ZEITUNG

VERLAG J. FLEISSIG GMBH & CO.
1680929
Rosenstr. 2, 48653 COESFELD **Tel:** 2541 9210
Fax: 2541 921129
Email: pressehaus@azonline.de
Web site: http://www.azonline.de

Titles:
ALLGEMEINE ZEITUNG
BILLERBECKER ANZEIGER
GESCHERER ZEITUNG

VERLAG J. HORSTMANNSCHE BUCHHANDLUNG GMBH & CO. KG
680961
Marktstr. 25, 48249 DÜLMEN **Tel:** 2594 9560
Fax: 2594 95649
Email: info@dzonline.de
Web site: http://www.dzonline.de

Titles:
DÜLMENER ZEITUNG

VERLAG J. P. PETER, GEBR. HOLSTEIN GMBH & CO. KG 681543
Erlbacher Str. 104, 91541 ROTHENBURG
Tel: 9861 400358 **Fax:** 9861 40079
Email: sonntagsblatt@rotabene.de
Web site: http://www.evangelisches-sonntagsblatt.de
Titles:
EVANGELISCHES SONNTAGSBLATT AUS BAYERN

VERLAG JÖRG STOECKICHT 677404
Marienstr. 3, 24534 NEUMÜNSTER
Tel: 4321 559590 **Fax:** 4321 5595914
Email: info@afterdark.de
Web site: http://www.afterdark.de
Titles:
AFTER DARK

VERLAG JUNGE SAMMLER 684126
Postfach 1353, 52503 GEILENKIRCHEN
Tel: 2452 187606 **Fax:** 2452 187607
Email: junge_sammler@t-online.de
Titles:
JUNGE SAMMLER

VERLAG JÜRGENS GMBH 682390
Gabriele-Münter-Str. 5, 82110 GERMERING
Tel: 89 894184300 **Fax:** 89 894184320
Email: office@gefluegel-boerse.de
Web site: http://www.gefluegel-boerse.de
Titles:
GEFLÜGEL-BÖRSE

VERLAG KARL GOERNER 680915
Gritznerstr. 3, 76227 KARLSRUHE
Tel: 721 5966990 **Fax:** 721 59669959
Email: info@karl-goerner.de
Web site: http://www.karl-goerner.de
Titles:
KARLSRUHER KIND

VERLAG KARL SASSE GMBH & CO. KG 684042
Große Str. 37, 27356 ROTENBURG **Tel:** 4261 720
Fax: 4261 72200
Email: redaktion.rotenburg@kreiszeitung.de
Web site: http://www.kreiszeitung.de
Titles:
JOURNAL AM MITTWOCH
JOURNAL AM SONNTAG
ROTENBURGER KREISZEITUNG
VISSELHÖVEDER NACHRICHTEN

VERLAG KAUFHOLD GMBH 678580
Philipp-Nicolai-Weg 3, 58313 HERDECKE
Tel: 2330 91830 **Fax:** 2330 13570
Email: info@verlag-kaufhold.de
Web site: http://www.verlag-kaufhold.de
Titles:
FREIE WERKSTATT
MAGAZIN FREIE WERKSTATT

VERLAG KIRCHHEIM + CO GMBH 677645
Kaiserstr. 41, 55116 MAINZ **Tel:** 6131 960700
Fax: 6131 9607070
Email: info@kirchheim-verlag.de
Web site: http://www.kirchheim-verlag.de
Titles:
DER ALLGEMEINARZT
DIABETES FORUM
DIABETES JOURNAL
DIABETES, STOFFWECHSEL UND HERZ
DIABETES-CONGRESS-REPORT
KINDERÄRZTLICHE PRAXIS
DER NIEREN PATIENT
SUBKUTAN
TANKSTELLE

VERLAG KWF E.V. 681989
Sprembergerstr. 1, 64823 GROSS-UMSTADT
Tel: 6078 78562 **Fax:** 6078 78550
Email: fti@kwf-online.de
Web site: http://www.kwf-online.de
Titles:
FORSTTECHNISCHE INFORMATIONEN

VERLAG LEBENDIGE ERDE IM DEMETER E.V. 684971
Brandschneise 1, 64295 DARMSTADT
Tel: 6155 841243 **Fax:** 6155 846911
Email: redaktion@lebendigeerde.de
Web site: http://www.lebendigeerde.de
Titles:
LEBENDIGE ERDE

VERLAG LENSING-WOLFF GMBH & CO. KG 680873
Westenhellweg 86, 44137 DORTMUND
Tel: 231 90590 **Fax:** 231 160053
Email: geschaeftsleitung@mdhl.de
Titles:
GREVENER ZEITUNG
MÜNSTERLAND ZEITUNG
MÜNSTERSCHE ZEITUNG
RUHR NACHRICHTEN

VERLAG LIBORIUSBLATT GMBH & CO. KG 685066
Lange Str. 335, 59067 HAMM **Tel:** 2381 940400
Fax: 2381 9404040
Email: verlag@liborius.de
Web site: http://www.liboriusblatt.de
Titles:
LIBORIUSBLATT

VERLAG LOKALPRESSE GMBH 679066
Kurze Str. 4, 38550 ISENBÜTTEL **Tel:** 5374 840
Fax: 5374 4428
Titles:
CELLER KURIER
HELMSTEDTER BLITZ
WOLFSBURGER KURIER

VERLAG MATTHIAS ESS 683718
Bleichstr. 25, 55543 BAD KREUZNACH
Tel: 671 839930 **Fax:** 671 8399339
Email: info@ess.de
Web site: http://www.ess.de
Titles:
INITIATIV - DAS WIRTSCHAFTSMAGAZIN
VORSICHT

VERLAG MATTHIAS RITTHAMMER GMBH 684705
Andernacher Str. 5a, 90411 NÜRNBERG
Tel: 911 955780 **Fax:** 911 9557811
Email: media@ritthammer-verlag.de
Web site: http://www.ritthammer-verlag.de
Titles:
KÜCHE & BAD FORUM
MÖBELMARKT
POLSTER FASHION

VERLAG MAX SCHMIDT-RÖMHILD KG 678309
Mengstr. 16, 23552 LÜBECK **Tel:** 451 703101
Fax: 451 7031253
Email: info@schmidt-roemhild.de
Web site: http://www.schmidt-roemhild.de
Titles:
JÄGER IN SCHLESWIG-HOLSTEIN
KINDER KRANKENSCHWESTER
MOBIL UND SICHER
RADIOLOGIE TECHNOLOGIE
TECHNISCHE KOMMUNIKATION
WIR
WIRTSCHAFT ZWISCHEN NORD- UND OSTSEE - AUSG. LÜBECK

VERLAG MEDIA & CONSULTING WEHRSTEDT 1783350
Hagenbreite 9, 06463 FALKENSTEIN
Tel: 34743 62090 **Fax:** 34743 62091
Email: info@wehrstedt.org
Web site: http://www.wehrstedt.org
Titles:
PVT POLIZEI VERKEHR + TECHNIK

VERLAG MICHAELA ROTHE 679970
Darmstädter Str. 121, 64625 BENSHEIM
Tel: 6251 93490 **Fax:** 6251 934949
Email: info@busblickpunkt.de
Web site: http://www.busnetz.de
Titles:
BUS BLICKPUNKT

VERLAG MODERNE INDUSTRIE GMBH 678383
Justus-von-Liebig-Str. 1, 86899 LANDSBERG
Tel: 8191 1250 **Fax:** 8191 125211
Email: fachmedien@mi-verlag.de
Web site: http://www.mi-verlag.de
Titles:
ANTRIEBS PRAXIS
ARZT & WIRTSCHAFT
AUTOMOBIL PRODUKTION
DAS BESTE - SONDERAUSG. D. KE FERTIGUNG
FLUID
FLUID MARKT
INSTANDHALTUNG
KE KONSTRUKTION & ENGINEERING
MATERIALFLUSS
PRODUKTION
TECHNIK+EINKAUF
WERKZEUG & FORMENBAU

VERLAG MODERNES LERNEN 687269
Schleefstr. 14, 44287 DORTMUND
Tel: 231 128008 **Fax:** 231 128009
Email: info@verlag-modernes-lernen.de
Web site: http://www.verlag-modernes-lernen.de
Titles:
PRAXIS DER PSYCHOMOTORIK
PRAXIS ERGOTHERAPIE
DIE SPRACHHEILARBEIT
ZEITSCHRIFT FÜR SYSTEMISCHE THERAPIE UND BERATUNG

VERLAG MONIKA ERDENBRINK 1729034
Ahornweg, 79804 DOGERN **Tel:** 7751 6186
Fax: 7751 700214
Email: erdenbrink@t-online.de
Web site: http://www.ohlala-freizeitmagazin.com
Titles:
OH LÀ LÀ FREIZEITMAGAZIN

VERLAG MORITZ SCHÄFER GMBH & CO. KG 682561
Paulinenstr. 43, 32756 DETMOLD **Tel:** 5231 92430
Fax: 5231 924343
Email: info@vms-detmold.de
Web site: http://www.vms-detmold.de
Titles:
MÜHLE + MISCHFUTTER
WASSERKRAFT & ENERGIE
WASSERTRIEBWERK

VERLAG MÜLLER + BUSMANN KG 693404
Hofaue 63, 42103 WUPPERTAL **Tel:** 202 248360
Fax: 202 2483610
Email: mb@mueller-busmann.com
Web site: http://www.mueller-busmann.com
Titles:
BUILD

VERLAG NATUR & HEILEN 686200
Nikolaistr. 5, 80802 MÜNCHEN **Tel:** 89 3801590
Fax: 89 38015916
Email: info@naturundheilen.de
Web site: http://www.naturundheilen.de
Titles:
NATUR & HEILEN

VERLAG NEUE SZENE GBR 686324
Am Katzenstadel 28, 86152 AUGSBURG
Tel: 821 153009 **Fax:** 821 158043
Email: redaktion@neue-szene.de
Web site: http://www.neue-szene.de
Titles:
NEUE SZENE AUGSBURG

VERLAG NEUER MERKUR GMBH 677250
Paul-Gerhardt-Allee 46, 81245 MÜNCHEN
Tel: 89 3189050 **Fax:** 89 31890538
Email: info@vnmonline.de
Web site: http://www.vnmonline.de
Titles:
ABI-TECHNIK
BIO MATERIALIEN
DAS DENTAL LABOR
PODOLOGIE
RHW MANAGEMENT
RHW PRAXIS

VERLAG NIBELUNGEN-KURIER GMBH 686406
Prinz-Carl-Anlage 20, 67547 WORMS
Tel: 6241 95780 **Fax:** 6241 957814
Email: info@nibelungen-kurier.de
Web site: http://www.nibelungen-kurier.de
Titles:
NIBELUNGEN KURIER

VERLAG NÜRNBERGER PRESSE DRUCKHAUS NÜRNBERG GMBH & CO. 677723
Marienstr. 9, 90402 NÜRNBERG **Tel:** 911 2160
Fax: 911 2162326
Titles:
ALTMÜHL-BOTE
ERLANGER NACHRICHTEN
FRÄNKISCHER ANZEIGER
FÜRTHER NACHRICHTEN
HILPOLTSTEINER ZEITUNG
NEUMARKTER NACHRICHTEN
NORDBAYERISCHE NACHRICHTEN
NORDBAYERN.DE
NÜRNBERGER NACHRICHTEN
NÜRNBERGER STADTANZEIGER
PEGNITZ-ZEITUNG
ROTH-HILPOLTSTEINER VOLKSZEITUNG
SCHWABACHER TAGBLATT
TREUCHTLINGER KURIER
WEISSENBURGER TAGBLATT
WINDSHEIMER ZEITUNG

VERLAG ORTHOPÄDIE-TECHNIK 686820
Reinoldistr. 7, 44135 DORTMUND
Tel: 231 55705050 **Fax:** 231 55705070
Email: info@ot-forum.de
Web site: http://www.ot-forum.de
Titles:
ORTHOPÄDIE TECHNIK

VERLAG PARZELLER GMBH & CO. KG 681632
Frankfurter Str. 8, 36043 FULDA **Tel:** 661 2800
Fax: 661 280125
Email: marketing@parzeller.de
Web site: http://www.parzeller.de
Titles:
FULDAER ZEITUNG
HÜNFELDER ZEITUNG
KINZIGTAL-NACHRICHTEN
SCHLITZER BOTE

VERLAG PERFUSION GMBH 687000
Storchenweg 20, 90617 PUSCHENDORF
Tel: 9101 9901110 **Fax:** 9101 9901119
Email: info@verlag-perfusion.de
Web site: http://www.verlag-perfusion.de
Titles:
PERFUSION

VERLAG PETER HOFFMANN 682205
Postfach 110570, 35350 GIESSEN
Tel: 641 932610 **Fax:** 641 9326161
Email: redaktion@frizz-mittelhessen.net
Web site: http://www.frizz-online.de
Titles:
FRIZZ

VERLAG PETER KITTEL 1744048
Margaretenstr. 8, 93047 REGENSBURG
Tel: 941 53836 **Fax:** 941 560242
Email: rsz@regensburger-stadtzeitung.de
Web site: http://www.regensburger-stadtzeitung.de
Titles:
DIE REGENSBURGER STADTZEITUNG

VERLAG PHÄNOMEN FARBE F. M. ALBERT 687090
Nördlinger Str. 15, 40597 DÜSSELDORF
Tel: 211 7182314 **Fax:** 211 7182366
Email: pf-verlag@t-online.de
Web site: http://www.phaenomen-farbe.de
Titles:
PHÄNOMEN FARBE

VERLAG PUPPEN & SPIELZEUG, GERT WOHLFARTH GMBH 687442
Stresemannstr. 20, 47051 DUISBURG
Tel: 203 305270 **Fax:** 203 30527820
Email: info@wohlfarth.de
Web site: http://www.puppen-und-spielzeug.de
Titles:
PUPPEN & SPIELZEUG

VERLAG R. S. SCHULZ GMBH, EIN UNTERNEHMEN VON WOLTERS KLUWER DEUTSCHLAND GMBH 685364
Freisinger Str. 3, 85716 UNTERSCHLEISSHEIM
Tel: 89 360070 **Fax:** 89 360073320
Web site: http://www.wolterskluwer.de

Titles:
ZFSH/SGB

VERLAG RECHT UND WIRTSCHAFT GMBH 679215
Mainzer Landstr. 251, 60326 FRANKFURT
Tel: 69 75952703 **Fax:** 69 75952780
Email: verlag@ruw.de
Web site: http://www.ruw.de

Titles:
BETRIEBS BERATER
KOMMUNIKATION & RECHT
N & R NETZWIRTSCHAFTEN & RECHT
RECHT DER FINANZINSTRUMENTE
RECHT DER INTERNATIONALEN WIRTSCHAFT
DER STEUERBERATER
ZHR ZEITSCHRIFT FÜR DAS GESAMTE HANDELSRECHT UND WIRTSCHAFTSRECHT

VERLAG REINHARD SEMMLER GMBH 1743447
Parzellenstr. 21, 03050 COTTBUS
Tel: 355 4838730 **Fax:** 355 4838739
Email: info@verlag-semmler.de
Web site: http://www.verlag-semmler.de

Titles:
LAUSITZER SEENLAND FERIENJOURNAL

VERLAG RIECK GMBH & CO. KG 680553
Lange Str. 122, 27749 DELMENHORST
Tel: 4221 156666 **Fax:** 4221 156999
Email: verlag@dk-online.de
Web site: http://www.dk-online.de

Titles:
DELMENHORSTER KREISBLATT
DELMENHORSTER KREISBLATT ONLINE

VERLAG ROMMERSKIRCHEN GMBH & CO. KG 700414
Mainzer Str. 16, 53424 REMAGEN **Tel:** 2228 9310
Fax: 2228 931149
Email: info@rommerskirchen.com
Web site: http://www.rommerskirchen.com

Titles:
JOURNALIST
PR MAGAZIN
THEMEN

VERLAG ROTTWINKEL-KRÖBER GMBH 687061
Brückenort 15, 49565 BRAMSCHE
Tel: 5461 940210 **Fax:** 5461 940220
Email: info@verlagkroeber.de
Web site: http://www.verlagkroeber.de

Titles:
WESER-EMS MANAGER

VERLAG RUPRECHT KERTSCHER 684145
Am Schlag 1, 82223 EICHENAU **Tel:** 8141 82458

Titles:
JUROPE

VERLAG SCHNELL & STEINER GMBH 684070
Leibnizstr. 13, 93055 REGENSBURG
Tel: 941 787850 **Fax:** 941 7878516
Email: post@schnell-und-steiner.de
Web site: http://www.schnell-und-steiner.de

Titles:
JOURNAL FÜR KUNSTGESCHICHTE
DAS MÜNSTER

VERLAG SCHÖNERE HEIMAT 678819
Ludwigstr. 23/Rgb., 80539 MÜNCHEN
Tel: 89 2866290 **Fax:** 89 282434
Email: info@heimat-bayern.de
Web site: http://www.heimat-bayern.de

Titles:
DER BAUBERATER

VERLAG SCHWÄBISCHER BAUER 680000
Gartenstr. 63, 88212 RAVENSBURG
Tel: 751 361590 **Fax:** 751 3615930
Email: sb@bwagrar.de
Web site: http://www.bwagrar.de

Titles:
BW AGRAR SCHWÄBISCHER BAUER

VERLAG SELBER TAGBLATT GMBH & CO. KG 1649334
Marienstr. 11, 95100 SELB **Tel:** 9287 99870
Fax: 9287 998770
Email: anzeigen@selber-tagblatt.de
Web site: http://www.selber-tagblatt.de

Titles:
SELBER TAGBLATT FRANKENPOST

VERLAG SIEGFRIED ROHN GMBH & CO. KG 678889
Stolberger Str. 84, 50933 KÖLN **Tel:** 221 54970
Fax: 221 5497278
Email: info@rohn.de
Web site: http://www.rohn.de

Titles:
BAU MARKT MANAGER
MARKT IN GRÜN
MOTORIST

VERLAG SILZER GMBH 1718268
Junkernstr. 3, 29320 HERMANNSBURG
Tel: 5052 912118 **Fax:** 5052 912119
Email: info@a-tavola.info
Web site: http://www.a-tavola.info

Titles:
A TAVOLA!

VERLAG STAHLEISEN GMBH 680283
Sohnstr. 65, 40237 DÜSSELDORF **Tel:** 211 67070
Fax: 211 6707517
Email: stahleisen@stahleisen.de
Web site: http://www.stahleisen.de

Titles:
JAHRBUCH STAHL
MPT INTERNATIONAL METALLURGICAL PLANT AND TECHNOLOGY
STAHL UND EISEN

VERLAG STERNEFELD GMBH & CO. KG 681099
Oberkasseler Str. 100, 40545 DÜSSELDORF
Tel: 211 577080 **Fax:** 211 5770812
Email: verlag@sternefeld.de
Web site: http://www.sternefeld.de

Titles:
GESUNDHEITS PROFI
LEDERWAREN REPORT
SCHUHKURIER
STEP

VERLAG SÜDDEUTSCHE BAUWIRTSCHAFT 689065
Wilhelm-Hertz-Str. 14, 70192 STUTTGART
Tel: 711 2573333 **Fax:** 711 2573422
Email: horst.kimmich@googlemail.com

Titles:
SÜDDEUTSCHE BAUWIRTSCHAFT UND ZEITSCHRIFT FÜR DENKMALSCHUTZ

VERLAG SÜDDEUTSCHER VERKEHRSKURIER 689066
Leonrodstr. 48, 80636 MÜNCHEN
Tel: 89 1266290 **Fax:** 89 12662925
Email: svk@lbt.de
Web site: http://www.lbt.de

Titles:
SVK SÜDDEUTSCHER VERKEHRSKURIER

VERLAG TH. MANN GMBH 680477
Maxstr. 64, 45127 ESSEN **Tel:** 201 89425574
Fax: 201 89425573
Email: vertrieb@th-mann.de
Web site: http://www.th-mann.de

Titles:
DMW DIE MILCHWIRTSCHAFT
EDM EUROPEAN DAIRY MAGAZINE

VERLAG THEODOR KÖRNER KG 677894
Horber Str. 42, 71083 HERRENBERG
Tel: 7032 95250 **Fax:** 7032 9525109
Email: anzeigen@gaeubote.de

Titles:
GÄUBOTE

VERLAG ULRICH RAVENS 1690193
Südl. Auffahrtsallee 73, 80639 MÜNCHEN
Tel: 89 10119151 **Fax:** 89 174230
Email: ulliravens@aol.com
Web site: http://www.onkologie-heute.org

Titles:
ONKOLOGIE HEUTE

VERLAG UND BUCHHANDLUNG DER EVANGELISCHEN GESELLSCHAFT STUTTGART GMBH 678454
Augustenstr. 124, 70197 STUTTGART
Tel: 711 601000 **Fax:** 711 6010076
Email: verlag@evanggemeindeblatt.de
Web site: http://www.evanggemeindeblatt.de

Titles:
KERBE

VERLAG + DRUCK LINUS WITTICH KG 1650048
Staudacher Str. 22, 83250 MARQUARTSTEIN
Tel: 8641 97810 **Fax:** 8641 978122
Email: anzeigen@wittich-chiemgau.de
Web site: http://www.wittich.de

Titles:
HEIMAT ECHO
MOTOR CHIEMGAU
MÜRITZ AKTUELL
WESTRICHER RUNDSCHAU

VERLAG UND DRUCKEREI MAIN-ECHO GMBH & CO. KG 1605927
Weichertstr. 20, 63741 ASCHAFFENBURG
Tel: 6021 3960 **Fax:** 6021 396367
Web site: http://www.main-netz.de

Titles:
BOTE VOM UNTER=MAIN
LOHRER ECHO
MAIN-ECHO
SPESSART
WERTHEIMER ZEITUNG
WIRTSCHAFT AM BAYERISCHEN UNTERMAIN

VERLAG VCP VIKANT CRAFTS PUBLISHING GMBH 1759391
Bahnhofstr. 50, 29556 SUDERBURG
Tel: 5826 958950 **Fax:** 5826 9589520

Titles:
VERENA STRICKEN

VERLAG VERSICHERUNGSWIRTSCHAFT GMBH 677538
Klosestr. 20, 76137 KARLSRUHE **Tel:** 721 35090
Fax: 721 3509201
Email: info@vvw.de
Web site: http://www.vvw.de

Titles:
DER AKTUAR
PKV PUBLIK
VERSICHERUNGSMEDIZIN
VERSICHERUNGSWIRTSCHAFT

VERLAG VERSORGUNGSWIRTSCHAFT GMBH 690118
Fraunhoferstr. 17, 80469 MÜNCHEN
Tel: 89 2023144 **Fax:** 89 2023055
Email: kundenservice@verlag-versorgungswirtschaft.de
Web site: http://www.verlag-versorgungswirtschaft.de

Titles:
VERSORGUNGSWIRTSCHAFT

VERLAG W. GIRARDET KG 690834
Königsallee 27, 40212 DÜSSELDORF
Tel: 211 83820 **Fax:** 211 83822392
Email: westdeutsche.zeitung@wz-newsline.de
Web site: http://www.wz-newsline.de

Titles:
WESTDEUTSCHE ZEITUNG
WZ BERGISCHER VOLKSBOTE
WZ NEWSLINE

VERLAG W. KOHLHAMMER GMBH 677714
Heßbrühlstr. 69, 70565 STUTTGART
Tel: 711 78630 **Fax:** 711 78638430
Web site: http://www.kohlhammer.de

Titles:
BERICHTE ÜBER LANDWIRTSCHAFT
BRANDSCHUTZ / DEUTSCHE FEUERWEHR-ZEITUNG
DER GEMEINDEHAUSHALT
DAS KRANKENHAUS
DER LANDKREIS
NATUR UND LANDSCHAFT
PFLEGEZEITSCHRIFT
VERWALTUNGSRUNDSCHAU VR
ZEITSCHRIFT FÜR BEAMTENRECHT

VERLAG W. KWIECINSKI 677268
Fichtestr. 18, 30625 HANNOVER **Tel:** 511 554048
Fax: 511 554040
Email: info@kwie.de
Web site: http://www.kwie.de

Titles:
NORDDEUTSCHE HOTEL- UND GASTSTÄTTEN NACHRICHTEN

VERLAG W. RECKINGER GMBH & CO. KG 684543
Luisenstr. 100, 53721 SIEGBURG
Tel: 2241 938340 **Fax:** 2241 9383433
Email: info@reckinger.de
Web site: http://www.reckinger.de

Titles:
KOMMUNALE STEUER-ZEITSCHRIFT
KOMMUNAL-KASSEN-ZEITSCHRIFT

VERLAG W. SACHON GMBH + CO. KG 677525
Schloss Mindelburg, 87719 MINDELHEIM
Tel: 8261 9990 **Fax:** 8261 999391
Email: info@sachon.de
Web site: http://www.sachon.de

Titles:
BRAUINDUSTRIE
BREWING AND BEVERAGE INDUSTRY INTERNATIONAL
DER DOEMENSIANER
GETRÄNKE FACHGROSSHANDEL
GETRÄNKEINDUSTRIE
INDUSTRIEBEDARF
DER MALER UND LACKIERERMEISTER

VERLAG W. WÄCHTER GMBH 681624
Elsasser Str. 41, 28211 BREMEN **Tel:** 421 348420
Fax: 421 3476766
Email: info@waechter.de
Web site: http://www.waechter.de

Titles:
BERLINER GARTENFREUND
DER FACHBERATER
GARTENFREUND
GARTENFREUND
GARTENFREUND
GARTENFREUND
SIEDLUNG UND EIGENHEIM

VERLAG WALTER DE GRUYTER GMBH & CO. KG 677346
Genthiner Str. 13, 10785 BERLIN **Tel:** 30 260050
Fax: 30 26005251
Email: wdg-info@degruyter.de
Web site: http://www.degruyter.de

Titles:
BIOLOGICAL CHEMISTRY
BIOMEDIZINISCHE TECHNIK / BIOMEDICAL ENGINEERING
CCLM CLINICAL CHEMISTRY AND LABORATORY MEDICINE
HOLZFORSCHUNG
JOURNAL OF PERINATAL MEDICINE
LABORATORIUMSMEDIZIN / JOURNAL OF LABORATORY MEDICINE

VERLAG WERBEN & VERKAUFEN GMBH 1764639
Hultschiner Str. 8, 81677 MÜNCHEN
Tel: 89 21837999 **Fax:** 89 21837868
Web site: http://verlag.wuv.de

Titles:
KONTAKTER
KONTAKTER.DE
W&V
W&V ANALYSE
W&V BOOKING
W&V DIGITAL
W&V EXTRA
W&V GUIDE
W&V MEDIA
W&V ONLINE
W&V SOCIETY
W&V SPOTS FERNSEHEN PLANUNGSDATEN
W&V SPOTS HÖRFUNK PLANUNGSDATEN

VERLAG WERDENER NACHRICHTEN WIMMER GMBH & CO. KG 690473
Grafenstr. 41, 45239 ESSEN **Tel:** 201 49977
Fax: 201 849422

Titles:
WERDENER NACHRICHTEN

VERLAG WETTERAU + VOGELSBERG GMBH 684650
Zeppelinstr. 11, 63667 NIDDA **Tel:** 6043 5020
Fax: 6043 50240
Email: vertrieb@kreis-anzeiger.de
Web site: http://www.kreis-anzeiger.de

Titles:
KREIS-ANZEIGER

VERLAG WILHELM BÖNING VERLAG DER KREISZEITUNG WESERMARSCH GMBH & CO. KG 684665
Bahnhofstr. 36, 26954 NORDENHAM
Tel: 4731 9430 **Fax:** 4731 943101
Email: nordenham.redaktion@kreiszeitung-wesermarsch.de
Web site: http://www.kreiszeitung-wesermarsch.de

Titles:
KREISZEITUNG WESERMARSCH

VERLAG WILHELM HESS & CO. GMBH 678646
Rodensteinstr. 6, 64625 BENSHEIM
Tel: 6251 10080 **Fax:** 6251 100841
Email: ba-bensheim@bergstraesser-anzeiger.de

Titles:
BA BERGSTRÄSSER ANZEIGER

VERLAG WIRTSCHAFTSVERBAND GARTENBAU E.V. 682330
Johann-Neudörffer-Str. 2, 28355 BREMEN
Tel: 421 536410 **Fax:** 421 552182
Email: foega@hdgbremen.de
Web site: http://www.hdgbremen.de

Titles:
GARTENBAU IN NIEDERSACHSEN UND BREMEN

VERLAG WÜRZBURGER KATHOLISCHES SONNTAGSBLATT 690810
Kardinal-Döpfner-Platz 5, 97070 WÜRZBURG
Tel: 931 38611200 **Fax:** 931 38611299
Email: info@sobla.de
Web site: http://www.sobla.de

Titles:
WÜRZBURGER KATHOLISCHES SONNTAGSBLATT

VERLAGSANSTALT ALEXANDER KOCH GMBH 677477
Fasanenweg 18, 70771 LEINFELDEN-ECHTERDINGEN **Tel:** 711 75910 **Fax:** 711 7591415
Email: info@ait-online.de
Web site: http://www.ait-online.de

Titles:
AIT ARCHITEKTUR INNENARCHITEKTUR TECHNISCHER AUSBAU
AIT ARCHITEKTUR INNENARCHITEKTUR TECHNISCHER AUSBAU ARCHITECTURE INTERIOR TECHNICAL SOLUTIONS
XIA INTELLIGENTE ARCHITEKTUR

VERLAGSANSTALT HANDWERK GMBH 680638
Auf'm Tetelberg 7, 40221 DÜSSELDORF
Tel: 211 390980 **Fax:** 211 3909829
Email: info@verlagsanstalt-handwerk.de
Web site: http://www.verlagsanstalt-handwerk.de

Titles:
BAUINFO
DEUTSCHES HANDWERKSBLATT
FRISEUR DIRECT
GLAS + RAHMEN
TACHO METER

VERLAGSBÜRO UETERSEN 679506
Großer Sand 3, 25436 UETERSEN **Tel:** 4103 6362
Fax: 4103 17678
Email: info@blickpunkt-wedel.de
Web site: http://www.blickpunkt-wedel.com

Titles:
BLICKPUNKT WEDEL

VERLAGSGES. BORGARDT GMBH & CO. KG 679710
Marktstr. 30, 27432 BREMERVÖRDE
Tel: 4761 9970 **Fax:** 4761 99759
Email: anzeigen@brv-zeitung.de
Web site: http://www.brv-zeitung.de

Titles:
BREMERVÖRDER ZEITUNG

VERLAGSGES. FÜR ACKERBAU MBH 687438
Bertha-von-Suttner-Str. 7, 34131 KASSEL
Tel: 561 93012400 **Fax:** 561 938545378
Email: info@verlag-ackerbau.de

Titles:
P & S PFLUG UND SPATEN

VERLAGSGES. HAUS UND MARKT MBH 683045
Hans-Böckler-Allee 7, 30173 HANNOVER
Tel: 511 85500 **Fax:** 511 85502420
Email: info@hausundmarkt.de
Web site: http://www.hausundmarkt.de

Titles:
HAUS & MARKT - AUSG. HANNOVER/ HILDESHEIM

VERLAGSGES. MADSACK GMBH & CO. KG 1603377
August-Madsack-Str. 1, 30559 HANNOVER
Tel: 511 5180 **Fax:** 180 1234457
Email: info@madsack.de
Web site: http://www.madsack.de

Titles:
HANNOVERSCHE ALLGEMEINE ZEITUNG
LEINE-ZEITUNG GARBSEN SEELZE
LEINE-ZEITUNG NEUSTADT WUNSTORF
NEUE PRESSE

VERLAGSGES. PISTE HAMBURG MBH 687139
Georgswerder Bogen 4, 21109 HAMBURG
Tel: 40 32093190 **Fax:** 40 32093198
Email: hamburg@piste.de
Web site: http://www.piste.de

Titles:
PISTE

VERLAGSGES. ROTENBURGER RUNDSCHAU GMBH & CO. KG 685381
Große Str. 79, 27356 ROTENBURG
Tel: 4261 92900 **Fax:** 4261 929019
Email: info@rotenburger-rundschau.de
Web site: http://www.rotenburger-rundschau.de

Titles:
ROTENBURGER RUNDSCHAU

VERLAGSGES. RUDOLF MÜLLER GMBH & CO. KG 678288
Stolberger Str. 84, 50933 KÖLN **Tel:** 221 5497100
Fax: 221 5497326
Email: info@rudolf-mueller.de
Web site: http://www.rudolf-mueller.de

Titles:
B+B BAUEN IM BESTAND
BAUGEWERBE
CARO
DDH DAS DACHDECKER-HANDWERK
DDH EDITION
FLIESEN & PLATTEN
TROCKENBAU AKUSTIK
WHO IS WHO IM TROCKENBAU

VERLAGSGES. STUMPF & KOSSENDEY MBH 687663
Rathausstr. 1, 26188 EDEWECHT **Tel:** 4405 91810
Fax: 4405 918130
Email: service@skverlag.de
Web site: http://www.skverlag.de

Titles:
RETTUNGSDIENST

VERLAGSGES. TISCHLER GMBH 699919
Kaunstr. 34, 14163 BERLIN **Tel:** 30 8011018
Fax: 30 8016661
Email: verlagsgesellschaft@firmengruppe-tischler.de
Web site: http://www.firmengruppe-tischler.de

Titles:
MEDIZINISCH-ORTHOPÄDISCHE TECHNIK
REPORT NATURHEILKUNDE

VERLAGSGES. UNSER WALD MBH 689933
Meckenheimer Allee 79, 53115 BONN
Tel: 228 9459830 **Fax:** 228 9459833
Email: unser-wald@sdw.de
Web site: http://www.sdw.de

Titles:
UNSER WALD

VERLAGSGES. VOGELSBERG GMBH & CO. KG 1740477
Am Kreuz 10, 36304 ALSFELD **Tel:** 6331 96690
Fax: 6331 966923

Titles:
LAUTERBACHER ANZEIGER
OBERHESSISCHE ZEITUNG

VERLAGSGESELLSCHAFT HARDTHÖHE MBH 1743185
Karthäuserstr. 38, 53332 BORNHEIM
Tel: 2222 9915404 **Fax:** 2222 9915405
Email: redaktion@hardthoehenkurier.de
Web site: http://www.hardthoehenkurier.de

Titles:
HARDTHÖHEN-KURIER

VERLAGSGRUPPE BAHN GMBH 681183
Am Fohlenhof 9a, 82256 FÜRSTENFELDBRUCK
Tel: 8141 534810 **Fax:** 8141 5348133
Email: bestellung@vgbahn.de
Web site: http://www.vgbahn.de

Titles:
EISENBAHN JOURNAL

VERLAGSGRUPPE HANDELSBLATT GMBH 682961
Kasernenstr. 67, 40213 DÜSSELDORF
Tel: 211 8870 **Fax:** 211 8872980
Email: handelsblatt@vhb.de
Web site: http://www.vhb.de

Titles:
HANDELSBLATT ONLINE

VERLAGSGRUPPE RHEIN MAIN GMBH & CO. KG 677666
Erich-Dombrowski-Str. 2, 55127 MAINZ
Tel: 6131 4830 **Fax:** 6131 485033
Web site: http://www.vrm.de

Titles:
AAR-BOTE
ALLGEMEINE ZEITUNG
BÜRSTÄDTER ZEITUNG
IDSTEINER ZEITUNG
MAIN-SPITZE
WIESBADENER TAGBLATT
WORMSER ZEITUNG

VERLAGSGRUPPE WIEDERSPAHN 678866
Biebricher Allee 11b, 65187 WIESBADEN
Tel: 611 846515 **Fax:** 611 801252
Email: kontakt@verlagsgruppewiederspahn.de
Web site: http://www.verlagsgruppewiederspahn.de

Titles:
STAHLBAU NACHRICHTEN
[UMRISSE]

VERLAGSHAUS GRUBER GMBH 685559
Max-Planck-Str. 2, 64859 EPPERTSHAUSEN
Tel: 6071 39410 **Fax:** 6071 344111
Email: info@verlagshaus-gruber.de
Web site: http://www.verlagshaus-gruber.de

Titles:
MEP MARKETING EVENT PRAXIS

VERLAGSHAUS KATJA MÜLLER 1675752
Vor dem Bardowicker Tore 6, 21339 LÜNEBURG
Tel: 4131 735715 **Fax:** 4131 760482
Email: redaktion@stadtlichter.com
Web site: http://www.stadtlichter.com

Titles:
STADTLICHTER

VERLAGSHAUS MEINCKE GMBH 683130
Rugenbarg 53a, 22848 NORDERSTEDT
Tel: 40 523080 **Fax:** 40 52308130
Email: info@verlagshaus-meincke.de
Web site: http://www.verlagshaus-meincke.de

Titles:
HEIMATSPIEGEL
HEIMATSPIEGEL EXTRA

VERLAGSHAUS SPEYER GMBH 681538
Beethovenstr. 4, 67346 SPEYER **Tel:** 6232 24926
Fax: 6232 132344
Email: info@verlagshaus-speyer.de
Web site: http://www.verlagshaus-speyer.de

Titles:
EVANGELISCHER KIRCHENBOTE

VERLAGS-MARKETING STUTTGART GMBH 683551
Reinsburgstr. 82, 70178 STUTTGART
Tel: 711 238860 **Fax:** 711 2388625
Email: info@verlagsmarketing.de
Web site: http://www.immoclick24.de

Titles:
DER IMMOBILIENVERWALTER
LIEGENSCHAFT AKTUELL
MODERNISIERUNGS MAGAZIN FÜR BAUGESELLSCHAFTEN - NEUBAU UND BESTAND -

DER VERMÖGENSBERATER VERLAGS- UND SERVICEGES. MBH 1759071
Münchener Str. 1, 60329 FRANKFURT
Tel: 69 23840 **Fax:** 69 2384185
Email: deutsche.vermoegensberatung@dvag.com
Web site: http://www.dvag.com

Titles:
VERMÖGENSBERATER

VERNISSAGE VERLAG GMBH & CO. KG 690100
Bergheimer Str. 104, 69115 HEIDELBERG
Tel: 6221 653060 **Fax:** 6221 6530630
Email: info@vernissageverlag.de
Web site: http://www.vernissageverlag.de

Titles:
BUSINESS & LAW
BUSINESS & LAW
BUSINESS & LAW
BUSINESS & LAW
BUSINESS & LAW
MEDIZIN FÜR MANAGER
MEDIZIN FÜR MANAGER
MEDIZIN FÜR MANAGER
MEDIZIN FÜR MANAGER

VERSICHERUNGSJOURNAL VERLAG GMBH 1652663
Rathausstr. 15, 22926 AHRENSBURG
Tel: 4102 7777880
Email: kontakt@versicherungsjournal.de
Web site: http://www.versicherungsjournal.de

Titles:
VERSICHERUNGSJOURNAL EXTRABLATT

VERTIKAL VERLAG 684642
Sundgauallee 15, 79114 FREIBURG
Tel: 761 8978660 **Fax:** 761 8866814
Email: info@vertikal.net
Web site: http://www.vertikal.net

Titles:
KRAN & BÜHNE

VESTISCHE MEDIENGRUPPE WELKE GMBH & CO. KG 1766471
Hertener Mark 7, 45699 HERTEN
Tel: 2366 808400 **Fax:** 2366 808409
Email: a.welke@vest-netz.de

Titles:
AUDI SCENE LIVE
CHROM & FLAMMEN
DRIVE
EASYRIDERS
FLASH
VW GOLF & CO. VW SCENE INTERNATIONAL

VETERINÄR VERLAGS GMBH 690129
Hindenburgstr. 71, 27442 GNARRENBURG
Tel: 4763 6280340 **Fax:** 4763 6280342
Email: vetimpulse@t-online.de
Web site: http://www.vetimpulse.de

Titles:
VET IMPULSE

VF VERLAGSGES. MBH 694757
Lise-Meitner-Str. 2, 55129 MAINZ **Tel:** 6131 9920
Fax: 6131 992100
Email: info@oldtimer-markt.de
Web site: http://www.oldtimer-markt.de

Titles:
BRITISH CLASSICS
LAST&KRAFT
OLDTIMER MARKT
OLDTIMER PRAXIS
OLDTIMER TRAKTOR

VFW VEREIN ZUR FÖRDERUNG DER RECHTSRHEINISCHEN GEWERBLICHEN WIRTSCHAFT KÖLN E.V. 1742928
Gottfried-Hagen-Str. 60, 51105 KÖLN
Tel: 221 839110
Email: heinz.bettmann@rheinzeiger.de
Titles:
RHEINZEIGER

VFZ-VERLAG FÜR ZIEL-GRUPPENINFORMATIONEN GMBH & CO. KG 685094
Hengsener Str. 14, 44309 DORTMUND
Tel: 231 92505550 **Fax:** 231 92505559
Email: abo@vfz-verlag.de
Web site: http://www.vfz-verlag.de
Titles:
TÜR-TOR-FENSTER REPORT

VGB POWERTECH SERVICE GMBH 690142
Klinkestr. 27, 45136 ESSEN **Tel:** 201 8128300
Fax: 201 8128302
Email: pr@vgb.org
Web site: http://www.vgb.org
Titles:
VGB POWERTECH

VGE VERLAG GMBH 678106
Montebruchstr. 2, 45219 ESSEN **Tel:** 2054 9240
Fax: 2054 924139
Email: info@vge.de
Web site: http://www.vge.de
Titles:
FELSBAU MAGAZIN
GEOTECHNIK
GLÜCKAUF
GLÜCKAUF MINING REPORTER
TUNNELBAU

VGS VERLAGSGRUPPE STEGENWALLER GMBH 682846
Ruhrtalstr. 67, 45239 ESSEN **Tel:** 201 246880
Fax: 201 24688100
Email: vgs@stegenwaller.de
Web site: http://www.stegenwaller.de
Titles:
FREIZEIT TOTAL
SCHÖNE WELT
SMAG

VHW-DIENSTLEISTUNG GMBH 690157
Hinter Hoben 149, 53129 BONN **Tel:** 228 7259930
Fax: 228 7259919
Email: verlag@vhw.de
Web site: http://www.vhw.de
Titles:
FORUM WOHNEN UND STADTENTWICKLUNG

VIA-VERLAG JOACHIM RITTER E.K. 698568
Marienfelder Str. 18, 33330 GÜTERSLOH
Tel: 5241 307260 **Fax:** 5241 3072640
Email: info@via-internet.com
Web site: http://via-verlag.com
Titles:
PROFESSIONAL LIGHTING DESIGN
PROFESSIONAL LIGHTING DESIGN

VIAVITAL VERLAG GMBH 681941
Otto-Hahn-Str. 7, 50997 KÖLN **Tel:** 2236 3760
Fax: 2236 376999
Email: post@viavital.net
Web site: http://www.viavital.net
Titles:
HAUT
LYMPHOLOGIE IN FORSCHUNG UND PRAXIS
VASOMED

VIEWEG + TEUBNER VERLAG/ SPRINGER FACHMEDIEN WIESBADEN GMBH 1627122
Abraham-Lincoln-Str. 46, 65189 WIESBADEN
Tel: 611 78780 **Fax:** 611 7878400
Email: springerfachmedien-wiesbaden@springer.com
Web site: http://www.viewegteubner.de
Titles:
ADHÄSION KLEBEN & DICHTEN
ALL4ENGINEERS
BRANCHEN INDEX GALVANOTECHNIK DÜNNE SCHICHTEN
CHROMATOGRAPHIA
JOT JOURNAL FÜR OBERFLÄCHENTECHNIK
WASSER UND ABFALL
WASSERWIRTSCHAFT
ZEITSCHRIFT FÜR ENERGIEWIRTSCHAFT

VIK VERBAND DER INDUSTRIELLEN ENERGIE- U. KRAFTWIRTSCHAFT E.V. 1649574
Richard-Wagner-Str. 41, 45128 ESSEN
Tel: 201 810840 **Fax:** 201 8108430
Email: info@vik.de
Web site: http://www.vik.de
Titles:
VIK MITTEILUNGEN

VINCENTZ NETWORK GMBH & CO. KG 1626804
Plathnerstr. 4c, 30175 HANNOVER
Tel: 511 9910000 **Fax:** 511 9910099
Email: info@vincentz.net
Web site: http://www.vincentz.net
Titles:
ALTENHEIM
ALTENPFLEGE
BESSER LACKIEREN!
CARE KONKRET
EC EUROPEAN COATINGS JOURNAL
FARBE UND LACK
HÄUSLICHE PFLEGE
PFLEGE PARTNER
TH ARBEITSSCHUTZ AKTUELL
TH TECHNISCHER HANDEL

VIOS MEDIEN GMBH 1627044
Waldstr. 26, 82194 GRÖBENZELL
Tel: 8142 667884 **Fax:** 8142 667885
Email: info@vios-medien.de
Web site: http://www.vios-medien.de
Titles:
TREFFPUNKT 55 PLUS

VISAVIS VERLAGSGES. MBH 693464
Auguststr. 19, 53229 BONN **Tel:** 228 307940
Fax: 228 3079410
Email: visavis@visavis.de
Web site: http://www.visavis.de
Titles:
VISAVIS WEB-BUSINESS

VISION MEDIA GMBH 1737583
Leonrodstr. 52, 80636 MÜNCHEN **Tel:** 89 697490
Fax: 89 69749430
Email: info@vision-media.de
Web site: http://www.vision-media.de
Titles:
JOLIE
MÄDCHEN
POPCORN
YAM.DE

VISIONS VERLAG GMBH 690204
Heiliger Weg 1, 44135 DORTMUND
Tel: 231 5571310 **Fax:** 231 55713131
Email: info@visions.de
Web site: http://www.visions.de
Titles:
FESTIVALPLANER
VISIONS

VITAPUBLIC GMBH 1677445
Ganghoferstr. 68, 80339 MÜNCHEN
Tel: 89 41856050 **Fax:** 89 418560519
Email: info@vitanet.de
Web site: http://www.vitanet.de
Titles:
VITANET.DE

VM VERLAG GMBH 687161
Gleueler Str. 373, 50935 KÖLN **Tel:** 221 439256
Fax: 221 438121
Email: f.vollmer@vm-verlag.com
Web site: http://www.extrusion-info.com
Titles:
EXTRUSION
PLASTCOURIER-RUSSIA
WORLD OF PLASTICS

VM VERLAGSGRUPPE MACKE GMBH 684539
Arnstädter Str. 28, 99096 ERFURT
Tel: 361 5662070 **Fax:** 361 5662072
Email: info@macke.net
Web site: http://www.macke.net
Titles:
KOMMUNAL DIREKT

VMM WIRTSCHAFTSVERLAG GMBH & CO. KG 690641
Sedanstr. 27, 97082 WÜRZBURG
Tel: 931 4194561 **Fax:** 931 4194588
Email: wuerzburg@vmm-wirtschaftsverlag.de
Web site: http://www.vmm-wirtschaftsverlag.de
Titles:
B4B MITTELSTAND
FAKTOR WIRTSCHAFT
FORUM
QUIP
TALBLICK TANNHEIMER TAL
WIRTSCHAFT IN MAINFRANKEN

VOGEL BUSINESS MEDIA GMBH & CO. KG 699968
Max-Planck-Str. 7, 97082 WÜRZBURG
Tel: 931 4180 **Fax:** 931 4182100
Web site: http://www.vogel.de
Titles:
AUTO FACHMANN
AUTOMOBIL INDUSTRIE
BIKE UND BUSINESS
BLECHNET
BULK SOLIDS HANDLING
CSR MAGAZIN
ELEKTRONIK PRAXIS
ELEKTRONIK PRAXIS
ELEKTROTECHNIK
ELEKTROTECHNIK
GEBRAUCHTWAGEN PRAXIS
KFZ-BETRIEB
KONSTRUKTIONS PRAXIS
KONSTRUKTIONSPRAXIS.DE
LABORPRAXIS
MM LOGISTIK
MM MASCHINENMARKT
MM ZULIEFERER
PHARMATEC
PROCESS
SCHÜTTGUT

VOGEL IT-MEDIEN GMBH 683874
August-Wessels-Str. 27, 86156 AUGSBURG
Tel: 821 21770 **Fax:** 821 2177150
Email: zentrale@vogel-it.de
Web site: http://www.vogel-it.de
Titles:
EGOVERNMENT COMPUTING
IT-BUSINESS

VOGTLAND-ANZEIGER GMBH 690248
Martin-Luther-Str. 50, 08525 PLAUEN
Tel: 3741 5970 **Fax:** 3741 597740
Email: verlag@vogtland-anzeiger.de
Web site: http://www.vogtland-anzeiger.de
Titles:
VOGTLAND-ANZEIGER

VOLKER GUNZENHEIMER DRUCKEREI 686849
Paulinenstr. 32, 97645 OSTHEIM **Tel:** 9777 518
Fax: 9777 1563
Titles:
OSTHEIMER ZEITUNG

VOLKSFREUND-DRUCKEREI NIKOLAUS KOCH GMBH 1741030
Hanns-Martin-Schleyer-Str. 8, 54294 TRIER
Tel: 651 71990 **Fax:** 651 7199990
Email: verlag@volksfreund.de
Web site: http://www.volksfreund.de
Titles:
MACHER
TRIERISCHER VOLKSFREUND

VOLKSHOCHSCHULE DER STADT MÜNSTER 1729782
Aegidiimarkt 3, 48143 MÜNSTER **Tel:** 251 315861
Email: hildegard.schulte@t-online.de
Web site: http://www.muenster.org/msz
Titles:
MSZ

VON BENTZEL UND PARTNER GMBH 682675
Konrad-Zuse-Platz 10, 81829 MÜNCHEN
Tel: 89 5468540 **Fax:** 89 5804439
Email: redaktion@golfaktuell.com
Web site: http://www.golfaktuell.com
Titles:
GOLF AKTUELL

VORLÄNDER GMBH & CO. KG BUCH- UND OFFSETDRUCKEREI 679480
Obergraben 39, 57072 SIEGEN **Tel:** 271 59400
Fax: 271 5940373
Email: buchverlag@vorlaender.de
Web site: http://www.vorlaender.de
Titles:
WIRTSCHAFTS REPORT

VPM YOUNG MEDIA KG 1686026
Karlsruher Str. 31, 76437 RASTATT **Tel:** 7222 130
Fax: 7222 13218
Web site: http://www.vpm.de
Titles:
CARD COLLECTOR

VS MEDIEN GMBH 1638718
Sachsenring 73, 50677 KÖLN **Tel:** 221 9128760
Fax: 221 9128766
Web site: http://www.vsmedien.de
Titles:
CALIBER

VS VERLAG FÜR SOZIALWISSENSCHAFTEN/ SPRINGER FACHMEDIEN WIESBADEN GMBH 679121
Abraham-Lincoln-Str. 46, 65189 WIESBADEN
Tel: 611 78780 **Fax:** 611 7878400
Email: springerfachmedien-wiesbaden@springer.com
Web site: http://www.vsverlag.de
Titles:
LEVIATHAN
ORGANISATIONSBERATUNG, SUPERVISION, COACHING (OSC)
PUBLIZISTIK

VSE AG 684573
Heinrich-Böcking-Str. 10, 66121 SAARBRÜCKEN **Tel:** 681 6071153
Fax: 681 6071155
Email: neidhardt-armin@vse.de
Web site: http://www.vse.de
Titles:
KONTAKT

VSP BUSINESS MEDIA GMBH 693457
Friedenstr. 41, 44139 DORTMUND
Tel: 231 9145463500 **Fax:** 231 9145463590
Email: info@vsp-business-media.de
Web site: http://www.vsp-business-media.de
Titles:
TW.DIREKT

VSRW-VERLAG DR. HAGEN PRÜHS GMBH 693312
Rolandstr. 48, 53179 BONN **Tel:** 228 951240
Fax: 228 9512490
Email: vsrw@vsrw.de
Web site: http://www.vsrw.de
Titles:
GMBH CHEF. GMBH CHEF. GMBH-STEUERPRAXIS

VULKAN-VERLAG GMBH 680728
Huyssenallee 52, 45128 ESSEN **Tel:** 201 820020
Fax: 201 8200240
Web site: http://www.vulkan-verlag.de
Titles:
3R
3R INTERNATIONAL
DICHTUNGSTECHNIK
GASWÄRME INTERNATIONAL
HEAT PROCESSING
INDUSTRIEARMATUREN
INDUSTRIEPUMPEN + KOMPRESSOREN

VVA INTERNATIONAL HEALTH PUBLICATIONS 1638835
Theodor-Althoff-Str. 39, 45133 ESSEN
Tel: 201 8712673 **Fax:** 201 87126940
Email: a.parr@vva.de
Web site: http://www.arab-medico.com
Titles:
ALL ARABIAN PRODUCT & BUYER'S GUIDE
ARAB MEDICO

VWB-VERLAG FÜR WISSENSCHAFT UND BILDUNG
1630418
Besselstr. 13, 10969 BERLIN **Tel:** 30 2510415
Fax: 30 2511136
Email: info@vwb-verlag.com
Web site: http://www.vwb-verlag.com

Titles:
CURARE

VWD NETSOLUTIONS GMBH
1763581
Krausenstr. 8, 10117 BERLIN **Tel:** 30 2005980
Web site: http://www.finanztreff.de

Titles:
FINANZTREFF.DE

VWP VERLAG FÜR WERBE-PUBLIKATIONEN GMBH & CO. KG
681591
Friedensplatz 2, 53721 SIEGBURG
Tel: 2241 96650 **Fax:** 2241 9665499
Email: joachim.hesse@mds.de
Web site: http://www.rheinische-anzeigenblaetter.de

Titles:
NIEDERKASSEL AKTUELL MIT AMTSBLATT DER STADT NIEDERKASSEL

W. BERTELSMANN VERLAG GMBH & CO. KG
678509
Auf dem Esch 4, 33619 BIELEFELD
Tel: 521 911010 **Fax:** 521 9110179
Email: service@wbv.de
Web site: http://www.wbv.de

Titles:
BWP BERUFSBILDUNG IN WISSENSCHAFT UND PRAXIS
DIE ZEITSCHRIFT FÜR ERWACHSENENBILDUNG

W. JAHN VERLAG GMBH & CO. KG
688507
Schloitweg 19, 59494 SOEST **Tel:** 2921 6880
Fax: 2921 688121
Web site: http://www.soester-anzeiger.de

Titles:
SOESTER ANZEIGER

W. NOSTHEIDE VERLAG GMBH
681774
Bahnhofstr. 22, 96117 MEMMELSDORF
Tel: 951 406660 **Fax:** 951 4066649
Email: nostheide@nostheide.de
Web site: http://www.nostheide.de

Titles:
BRANCHENBRIEF INTERNATIONAL
FESTIVAL CHRISTMAS
FESTIVAL GIFTS SOUVENIRS TROPHIES
FESTIVAL SEASONS
SPIELBOX
SPIELMITTEL

W & M VERLAGSGES. MBH
698625
Parkstrasse 2, 14469 POTSDAM **Tel:** 331 201660
Fax: 331 2016699
Email: potsdam@wirtschaftundmarkt.de
Web site: http://www.wirtschaftundmarkt.de

Titles:
WIRTSCHAFT & MARKT

W. ZUCKSCHWERDT VERLAG GMBH
686031
Industriestr. 1, 82110 GERMERING
Tel: 89 8943490 **Fax:** 89 89434950
Email: post@zuckschwerdtverlag.de
Web site: http://www.zuckschwerdtverlag.de

Titles:
MÜNCHNER ÄRZTLICHE ANZEIGEN
ZEITSCHRIFT FÜR REGENERATIVE MEDIZIN

WA VERLAG GMBH
681351
Waltherstr. 49, 51069 KÖLN **Tel:** 221 689110
Fax: 221 6891110
Email: info@waorg.com
Web site: http://www.waorg.com

Titles:
EPPI
PROMOTION PRODUCTS
WA WERBEARTIKEL NACHRICHTEN

WAFFENMARKT-INTERN / MESSERMARKT-INTERN INH. MAGGY SPINDLER
680017
Theodor-Heuss-Ring 62, 50668 KÖLN
Tel: 221 2005412 **Fax:** 221 2005423
Email: info@waffenmarkt.de
Web site: http://www.waffenmarkt.de

Titles:
WM WAFFENMARKT-INTERN/ MESSERMARKT INTERN

WAGER ! KOMMUNIKATION GMBH
1768072
In der Halde 20, 72657 ALTENRIET
Tel: 7127 9315807 **Fax:** 7127 9315808
Email: info@wager.de
Web site: http://www.wager.de

Titles:
WEIN-BOULEVARD

WAGNER & WIMME VERLAG GMBH
685297
Ziegelstr. 24, 91126 REDNITZHEMBACH
Tel: 9122 630290 **Fax:** 9122 6302999
Email: info@scooterundsport.de
Web site: http://www.scooterundsport.de

Titles:
SCOOTER & SPORT
SCOOTER & SPORT KATALOG

WAGO KONTAKTTECHNIK GMBH & CO. KG
697082
Hansastr. 27, 32423 MINDEN **Tel:** 571 8870
Fax: 571 887169
Email: info@wago.com
Web site: http://www.wago.com

Titles:
WAGO DIRECT
WAGO DIRECT INTERNATIONAL

WALDBESITZERVERBAND FÜR RHEINLAND-PFALZ E.V.
1652953
Burgenlandstr. 7, 55543 BAD KREUZNACH
Tel: 671 7931114 **Fax:** 671 7931199
Email: dr.schuh@waldbesitzerverband-rlp.de

Titles:
DER WALDBESITZER

WALDBESITZERVEREINIGUNG HOLZKIRCHEN W.V.
690333
Tegernseer Str. 8, 83607 HOLZKIRCHEN
Tel: 8024 48037 **Fax:** 8024 49429
Email: info@wbv-holzkirchen.de
Web site: http://www.wbv-holzkirchen.de

Titles:
DER WALDBAUER

WALDBESITZERVEREINIGUNG KELHEIM-THALDORF E.V.
1751069
Regensburger Str. 148, 93309 KELHEIM
Tel: 9441 175029 **Fax:** 9441 174916
Email: gs@wbv-kelheim-thaldorf.de
Web site: http://www.wbv-kelheim-thaldorf.de

Titles:
DER HOLZFUCHS

WALDBESITZERVEREINIGUNG WASSERBURG/INN-HAAG E.V.
1753041
Asham 9, 83123 AMERANG **Tel:** 8075 9390
Fax: 8075 9391
Email: wbv-wshaag@gmx.de
Web site: http://www.wbv-wasserburg.de

Titles:
INFORMATIONEN AUS ERSTER HAND

WALHALLA UND PRAETORIA VERLAG GMBH & CO. KG
677567
Haus an der Eisernen Brücke, 93059 REGENSBURG **Tel:** 941 5684100 **Fax:** 941 5684111
Email: walhalla@walhalla.de
Web site: http://www.walhalla.de

Titles:
DER AKTUELLE STEUERRATGEBER
DER AKTUELLE STEUERRATGEBER ÖFFENTLICHER DIENST
ANNUAL MULTIMEDIA
VDB MAGAZIN

WÄLISCHMILLER DRUCK UND VERLAGS GMBH
680754
Laaberstr. 2, 84130 DINGOLFING **Tel:** 8731 7030
Fax: 8731 70333
Email: redaktion@dingolfinger-anzeiger.de
Web site: http://www.waelischmiller-druck.de

Titles:
DINGOLFINGER ANZEIGER

WALLSTREET:ONLINE AG
1652679
Winsstr. 62, 10405 BERLIN **Tel:** 30 20456420
Fax: 30 20456350
Email: info@wallstreet-online.de
Web site: http://www.wallstreet-online.ag

Titles:
WALLSTREET:ONLINE

WALTER DE GRUYTER GMBH & CO. KG
678059
Genthiner Str. 13, 10785 BERLIN **Tel:** 30 260050
Fax: 30 26005251
Email: info@degruyter.com
Web site: http://www.degruyter.com

Titles:
JURA JURISTISCHE AUSBILDUNG
LEBENDE SPRACHEN

WARTBURG VERLAG GMBH
677876
Lisztstr. 2a, 99423 WEIMAR **Tel:** 3643 246144
Fax: 3643 246118
Email: abo@wartburgverlag.de
Web site: http://www.wartburgverlag.de

Titles:
GLAUBE+HEIMAT - MITTELDT. KIRCHENZTG., AUSG. SACHSEN-ANHALT PLUS
GLAUBE+HEIMAT - MITTELDT. KIRCHENZTG., AUSG. THÜRINGEN

WASSER-INFO-TEAM BAYERN E.V.
1743011
Hauptstr. 19, 84168 AHAM **Tel:** 8744 96120
Fax: 8744 961222
Email: info@wit-bayern.de
Web site: http://www.wit-bayern.de

Titles:
AQUA FORUM

WAXMANN VERLAG GMBH
683951
Steinfurter Str. 555, 48159 MÜNSTER
Tel: 251 265040 **Fax:** 251 2650426
Email: order@waxmann.com
Web site: http://www.waxmann.com

Titles:
DIE DEUTSCHE SCHULE

WAZ-WOMEN GROUP GMBH
681062
Münchener Str. 101/09, 85737 ISMANING
Tel: 89 272700

Titles:
ECHO DER FRAU
FRAU AKTUELL
FRAU IM SPIEGEL
FREIZEIT EXKLUSIV
DAS GOLDENE BLATT
NEUE WELT

WDV GES. FÜR MEDIEN & KOMMUNIKATION MBH & CO. OHG
677235
Siemensstr. 6, 61352 BAD HOMBURG
Tel: 6172 6700 **Fax:** 6172 670144
Email: info@wdv.de
Web site: http://www.wdv.de

Titles:
ABENTEUER UND REISEN
ABENTEUER UND REISEN
BLEIBGESUND
J:O EXTRA
MERCEDES-BENZ CLASSIC
MOBIL
SICHERHEITSREPORT
UNILIFE
VIGO
WELCOME! MAGAZIN
ZUKUNFT JETZT

WEBPOOL GMBH
1651525
Max-Planck-Str. 6, 50858 KÖLN **Tel:** 221 91116
Fax: 221 911169
Email: info@webpool.de
Web site: http://www.webpool.de

Titles:
BIKER.DE
JAGD.DE
MODEL.SZENE.DE
SINGLE.DE

WEFRA PUBLISHING GES. FÜR PRINT- UND ONLINE-MEDIEN MBH
685491
Mitteldicker Weg 1, 63263 NEU-ISENBURG
Tel: 69 69500852 **Fax:** 69 69500827
Email: info@medizinische-kongresse.de
Web site: http://www.medizinische-kongresse.de

Titles:
MEDIZINISCHE KONGRESSE

WEGWEISER GMBH BERLIN
680234
Novalisstr. 7, 10115 BERLIN **Tel:** 30 2848810
Fax: 30 28488111
Email: info@wegweiser.de
Web site: http://www.wegweiser.de

Titles:
JAHRBUCH VERWALTUNGSMODERNISIERUNG

WEIMANN PRESSE & VERLAG
684151
Böllerts Höfe 3, 45479 MÜLHEIM **Tel:** 208 426502
Fax: 208 428271
Email: verlag@weimannpresse.de
Web site: http://www.weimannpresse.de

Titles:
Z.F.R ZEITSCHRIFT FÜR REFERENDARE

WEISS-VERLAG GMBH & CO. KG
677324
Hans-Georg-Weiss-Str. 7, 52156 MONSCHAU
Tel: 2472 9820 **Fax:** 2472 982200
Email: info@weiss-verlag.de
Web site: http://www.weiss-verlag.de

Titles:
ADENAUER WOCHENSPIEGEL
AHRTALER WOCHENSPIEGEL
DAUN-GEROLSTEINER WOCHENSPIEGEL
DIE ENTSCHEIDUNG
EUSKIRCHENER WOCHENSPIEGEL
GLÜCK
SCHLEIDENER WOCHENSPIEGEL

WEKA FACHMEDIEN GMBH
681213
Hinterer Floßanger 10, 96450 COBURG
Tel: 9561 64910 **Fax:** 9561 6180
Email: elektroboerse@wekanet.de
Web site: http://www.elektroboerse-online.de

Titles:
COMPUTER & AUTOMATION
DESIGN&ELEKTRONIK
ELEKTROBÖRSE HANDEL
ELEKTROBÖRSE SMARTHOUSE
ELEKTRONIK
ELEKTRONIK AUTOMOTIVE
ENERGIE & TECHNIK
FUNKSCHAU
FUNKSCHAU
FUNKSCHAU HANDEL
MARKT&TECHNIK

WEKA MEDIA GMBH & CO. KG
685624
Römerstr. 4, 86438 KISSING **Tel:** 8233 230
Fax: 8233 237111
Email: info@weka.de
Web site: http://www.weka.de

Titles:
DACHBAU MAGAZIN
ELEKTROFACHKRAFT.DE
MIKADO
PRAXISCHECK

WEKA MEDIA PUBLISHING GMBH
678771
Richard-Reitzner-Allee 2, 85540 HAAR
Tel: 89 255561000 **Fax:** 89 255561199
Web site: http://www.weka-media-publishing.de

Titles:
AUDIO
AUTOHIFI
BUSINESS&IT
COFFEE
COLORFOTO
CONNECT
INTERNET MAGAZIN
MAGNUS.DE CONNECT
PC GO
PC MAGAZIN
STEREOPLAY
VIDEO HOMEVISION

WELCOME ABOARD VERLAGS-GMBH 690446
von-Tschirsky-Weg 12, 32602 VLOTHO
Tel: 5733 960458 **Fax:** 5733 960459
Email: info@welcome-aboard.de
Web site: http://www.welcome-aboard.de

Titles:
WELCOME ABOARD

WELTHER VERLAG GMBH 1605427
Uhlandstr. 1, 10623 BERLIN **Tel:** 30 4000680
Fax: 30 40006829
Email: mail@welther-verlag.de
Web site: http://www.fondszeitung.de

Titles:
FONDSZEITUNG
FONDSZEITUNG DAS MAGAZIN

WEMCARD MEDIEN 681128
Am Flugplatz 7, 31137 HILDESHEIM
Tel: 5121 9187030 **Fax:** 5121 9187059
Email: info@wemcard.de
Web site: http://www.wemcard.de

Titles:
EIER WILD GEFLÜGEL MARKT
MILCHWOCHE
DIE MOLKEREIZEITUNG WELT DER MILCH

WERBE- UND VERLAGS-GES. RUPPERT MBH 1653006
Emil-Hoffmann-Str. 13, 50996 KÖLN
Tel: 2236 3366114 **Fax:** 2236 3366118
Email: redaktion@events-magazine.de
Web site: http://www.events-magazine.com

Titles:
EVENTS

WERBEAGENTUR GIESDORF GMBH & CO. KG 677837
Ohmstr. 7, 32758 DETMOLD **Tel:** 5231 9110
Fax: 5231 911173
Email: info@wag-lippe.de
Web site: http://www.wag-lippe.de

Titles:
OSTWESTFÄLISCHE WIRTSCHAFT

WERBEAGENTUR KLEINE ARCHE GMBH 689778
Holbeinstr. 73, 99096 ERFURT **Tel:** 361 7467480
Fax: 361 7467485
Email: info@kleinearche.de
Web site: http://www.kleinearche.de

Titles:
TZB THÜRINGER ZAHNÄRZTE BLATT

WERBEAGENTUR MANDL 680045
Berliner Str. 7, 64409 MESSEL **Tel:** 6159 1292
Fax: 6159 913838
Email: info@capripost.de
Web site: http://www.capripost.de

Titles:
CAPRI POST

WERBEGESTALTUNG & DESIGN CRISTIAN DUMITRU 679716
Blumenstr. 271b, 86633 NEUBURG
Tel: 8431 42836 **Fax:** 8431 42853
Email: info@brennessel.com
Web site: http://www.brennessel.com

Titles:
BRENNESSEL MAGAZIN

WERBELIEBE E.V. 1741175
Tiefenbronner Str. 65, 75175 PFORZHEIM
Tel: 7231 286277 **Fax:** 7231 286666
Email: marketingdigest@werbeliebe.de
Web site: http://www.werbeliebe.de

Titles:
MD MARKETING DIGEST

WERK 2 WERBEAGENTUR 685955
Salzufler Str. 145, 33719 BIELEFELD
Tel: 521 2018812 **Fax:** 521 2018834
Email: info@werkzwei.info
Web site: http://www.werkzwei.info

Titles:
MONOKEL

WERNER MEDIA GROUP GMBH 1603361
Großbeerenstr. 186, 12277 BERLIN
Tel: 30 269470 **Fax:** 30 26947500
Email: info@wernermedia.de
Web site: http://www.wernermedia.de

Titles:
EUROPA EXPRESS
VSYA EVROPA

WERRA VERLAG KLUTHE KG 1680927
Vor dem Berge 2, 37269 ESCHWEGE
Tel: 5651 335955 **Fax:** 5651 335920
Email: vertrieb@werra-rundschau.de
Web site: http://www.werra-rundschau.de

Titles:
WERRA-RUNDSCHAU

WESER PRESSE VERLAG GMBH & CO. KG 678040
Contrescarpe 56, 28195 BREMEN
Tel: 421 330350 **Fax:** 421 3303529
Email: info@bremen-magazin.de
Web site: http://www.bremen-magazin.de

Titles:
BREMEN MAGAZIN

WESER-REGION WERBEVERLAG GMBH 678161
Baustr. 44, 31785 HAMELN **Tel:** 5151 57880
Fax: 5151 578822
Email: info@wrw-hameln.de
Web site: http://www.wrw-hameln.de

Titles:
HAMELNER MARKT
PYRMONTER RUNDBLICK

WESTDEUTSCHE ALLGEMEINE ZEITUNGSVERLAG GMBH 683077
Friedrichstr. 34, 45128 ESSEN **Tel:** 201 8040
Fax: 201 8046539
Email: zentralredaktion@waz.de
Web site: http://www.derwesten.de

Titles:
RUHR-ANZEIGER WAZ
VELBERTER ZEITUNG WAZ
WESTDEUTSCHE ALLGEMEINE WATTENSCHEIDER ZEITUNG WAZ
WESTDEUTSCHE ALLGEMEINE WAZ

WESTERMAYER VERLAGS-GMBH 686351
Fuchswinkel 2, 82349 PENTENRIED
Tel: 89 2722028 **Fax:** 89 2730058
Email: mail@westermayer-verlag.de
Web site: http://www.westermayer-verlag.de

Titles:
NEURO AKTUELL

WESTERWALD-VEREIN E.V. 690501
Koblenzer Str. 17, 56410 MONTABAUR
Tel: 2602 9496690 **Fax:** 2602 9496691
Email: info@westerwaldverein.de
Web site: http://www.westerwaldverein.de

Titles:
DER WESTERWALD

WESTFALEN AG 690507
Industrieweg 43, 48155 MÜNSTER **Tel:** 251 6950
Fax: 251 695194
Email: info@westfalen-ag.de
Web site: http://www.westfalen-ag.de

Titles:
WESTFALEN REPORTER

WESTFALEN-BLATT VEREINIGTE ZEITUNGSVERLAGE GMBH 681434
Sudbrackstr. 14, 33611 BIELEFELD **Tel:** 521 5850
Fax: 521 585370
Email: wb@westfalen-blatt.de
Web site: http://www.westfalen-blatt.de

Titles:
ESPELKAMPER ZEITUNG
LÜBBECKER KREISZEITUNG
SCHLÄNGER ZEITUNG
STEMWEDER ZEITUNG
VERLER ZEITUNG
WESTFALEN-BLATT

WESTFALENPOST GMBH 690799
Schürmannstr. 4, 58097 HAGEN **Tel:** 2331 9170
Fax: 2331 9174206
Email: westfalenpost@westfalenpost.de
Web site: http://www.westfalenpost.de

Titles:
WP WESTFALENPOST

WESTFALICA-VERLAG MICHAEL GERBER 1737062
Hauptstr. 28, 32457 PORTA WESTFALICA
Tel: 571 9752950 **Fax:** 571 9752915
Email: welcome@westfalica-verlag.de
Web site: http://www.westfalica-verlag.de

Titles:
HALLO TOURIST!
HALLO TOURIST!
HALLO TOURIST!
HALLO TOURIST!
HALLO TOURIST!

WESTFÄLISCHER ANZEIGER VERLAGSGES. MBH + CO. KG 1752539
Gutenbergstr. 1, 59065 HAMM **Tel:** 2381 1050
Fax: 2381 105426
Email: sekretariat@wa.de
Web site: http://www.wa.de

Titles:
WESTFÄLISCHER ANZEIGER

WESTFÄLISCH-LIPPISCHER LANDFRAUENVERBAND E.V. 1766086
Nevinghoff 40, 48147 MÜNSTER
Tel: 251 2376409 **Fax:** 251 2376408
Email: info@wllv.de
Web site: http://www.wllv.de

Titles:
DIE ZEITUNG

WESTKREUZ-VERLAG GMBH 678371
Töpchiner Weg 198, 12309 BERLIN
Tel: 30 7452047 **Fax:** 30 7453066
Email: vertrieb@westkreuz.de
Web site: http://www.westkreuz.de

Titles:
DER ARZNEIMITTELBRIEF

WESTONLINE GMBH & CO. KG 1768172
Westenhellweg 86, 44137 DORTMUND
Tel: 231 90590 **Fax:** 231 90598707
Email: redaktion@westline.de
Web site: http://www.westline.de

Titles:
WESTLINE

WETTBEWERBE AKTUELL VERLAGSGES. MBH 690517
Maximilianstr. 5, 79100 FREIBURG
Tel: 761 774550 **Fax:** 761 7745511
Email: verlag@wettbewerbe-aktuell.de
Web site: http://www.wettbewerbe-aktuell.de

Titles:
WA WETTBEWERBE AKTUELL

WETTER.COM AG 1652707
Werner-von-Siemens-Str. 22, 78224 SINGEN
Tel: 7731 8380 **Fax:** 7731 83819
Email: contact@wetter.com
Web site: http://www.wetter.com

Titles:
WETTER.COM

WETZLARDRUCK GMBH 1680934
Elsa-Brandström-Str. 18, 35578 WETZLAR
Tel: 6441 9590 **Fax:** 6441 959292
Email: redaktion.wnz@mittelhessen.de
Web site: http://www.mittelhessen.de

Titles:
DILL-POST
DILL-POST AM SONNTAG
HAIGERER ZEITUNG
HERBORNER TAGEBLATT
HINTERLÄNDER ANZEIGER
HINTERLÄNDER ANZEIGER AM SONNTAG
NASSAUER TAGEBLATT
NASSAUER TAGEBLATT AM SONNTAG
SOLMS-BRAUNFELSER
SOLMS-BRAUNFELSER AM SONNTAG
WEILBURGER TAGEBLATT
WETZLARER NEUE ZEITUNG
WETZLARER NEUE ZEITUNG AM SONNTAG

WFG - WIRTSCHAFTSFÖRDERUNGSGESELLSCHAFT DES LANDKREISES SCHWÄBISCH HALL MBH 1731741
Münzstr. 1, 74523 SCHWÄBISCH HALL
Tel: 791 7557214 **Fax:** 791 7557399
Email: info@wfgsha.de
Web site: http://www.wfgonline.de

Titles:
FRISCH VOM BAUERN

WHO'S WHO INTERNATIONAL MAGAZINE 690525
Postfach 1427, 61404 OBERURSEL
Tel: 6171 51055 **Fax:** 6171 53542
Email: europamagazin@who-magazine.com
Web site: http://www.who-magazine.com

Titles:
WHO'S WHO EUROPA MAGAZIN

WIADOK WIRTSCHAFTS-ARCHIV MIT DOKUMENTATION BECKER GMBH + CO. KG 677559
Portastr. 2, 32423 MINDEN **Tel:** 571 23729
Fax: 571 28768
Email: info@wiadok.de
Web site: http://www.wiadok.de

Titles:
DAS AKTUELLE FÜR ÄRZTE, HEIL- UND PFLEGEBERUFE
DAS AKTUELLE GMBH UND IHRE GESELLSCHAFTER
DAS AKTUELLE UMSATZSTEUER
KURZ-INFOS AUS STEUER UND WIRTSCHAFT FÜR DEN BERATER

WICHERN-VERLAG, ABT. CZV 679118
Georgenkirchstr. 69, 10249 BERLIN
Tel: 30 28874810 **Fax:** 30 28874812
Email: info@wichern.de
Web site: http://www.wichern.de

Titles:
DIE KIRCHE

WIESBADENER KURIER BESITZ- UND VERPACHTUNGSGES. MBH 683311
Langgasse 21, 65183 WIESBADEN **Tel:** 611 3550

Titles:
KREISSTADT ECHO

WIESBADENER KURIER GMBH & CO. VERLAG + DRUCKEREI KG 679487
Langgasse 21, 65183 WIESBADEN **Tel:** 611 3550
Fax: 611 3555255
Web site: http://www.main-rheiner.de

Titles:
WIESBADENER KURIER

WIF-WIRTSCHAFTSFÖRDERUNGS-GES. IM LANDKREIS GÖPPINGEN MBH 1739791
Robert-Bosch-Str. 6, 73037 GÖPPINGEN
Tel: 7161 5023585 **Fax:** 7161 5023581
Email: wif@wif-gp.de
Web site: http://www.wif-gp.de

Titles:
WIF PORTAL

WIKU VERLAGSGES. MBH 1744194
Kleine Grottenau, 86150 AUGSBURG
Tel: 821 44050 **Fax:** 821 4405409
Web site: http://www.wirtschaftskurier.de

Titles:
WIRTSCHAFTSKURIER

WILDESHAUSER ZEITUNG LUDWIG LÖSCHEN GMBH & CO. OHG 1718277
Bahnhofstr. 13, 27793 WILDESHAUSEN
Tel: 4431 98910 **Fax:** 4431 9891149

Titles:
WILDESHAUSER ZEITUNG

WILDWECHSEL VERLAG, REDAKTION & WERBEAGENTUR 690561
Sternstr. 40, 34414 WARBURG **Tel:** 5641 60094
Fax: 5641 60813
Email: redaktion@wildwechsel.de
Web site: http://www.wildwechsel.de

Titles:
WILDWECHSEL - AUSG. KASSEL/ PADERBORN
WILDWECHSEL - AUSG. MARBURG/ KASSEL/FULDA

WILEY-VCH VERLAG GMBH & CO. KGAA 677290
Rotherstr. 21, 10245 BERLIN **Tel:** 30 47031300
Fax: 30 47031399
Email: physics@wiley-vch.de
Web site: http://www.wiley-vch.de

Titles:
ADVANCED ENGINEERING MATERIALS
ADVANCED FUNCTIONAL MATERIALS
ADVANCED MATERIALS
ANGEWANDTE CHEMIE
ARCHIV DER PHARMAZIE
ASTRONOMISCHE NACHRICHTEN
BIOLOGIE IN UNSERER ZEIT
CHEMICAL ENGINEERING & TECHNOLOGY
CHEMIE IN UNSERER ZEIT
CHEMIE INGENIEUR TECHNIK
CHEMMEDCHEM
CHEMSUSCHEM
ELECTROANALYSIS
EUROPEAN JOURNAL OF IMMUNOLOGY
EUROPEAN JOURNAL OF INORGANIC CHEMISTRY
EUROPEAN JOURNAL OF LIPID SCIENCE AND TECHNOLOGY
JOURNAL OF SEPARATION SCIENCE
LEBENSMITTELCHEMIE
MATERIALS AND CORROSION WERKSTOFFE UND KORROSION
MATERIALWISSENSCHAFT UND WERKSTOFFTECHNIK
MOLECULAR NUTRITION & FOOD RESEARCH
PHARMAZIE IN UNSERER ZEIT
PHYSIK JOURNAL
PROPELLANTS, EXPLOSIVES, PYROTECHNICS
STARCH
STEEL RESEARCH
VAKUUM IN FORSCHUNG UND PRAXIS

WILHELM BING DRUCKEREI UND VERLAG GMBH 682072
Lengefelder Str. 6, 34497 KORBACH
Tel: 5631 56000 **Fax:** 5631 560159
Email: info@wlz-fz.de
Web site: http://www.wlz-fz.de

Titles:
FRANKENBERGER ZEITUNG
HAPPY INFO
WALDECKISCHE LANDESZEITUNG

WILLIBALDVERLAG GMBH 684380
Solnau 2, 85072 EICHSTÄTT **Tel:** 8421 97810
Fax: 8421 978120
Email: verlag@kirchenzeitung-eichstaett.de
Web site: http://www.kirchenzeitung-eichstaett.de

Titles:
KIRCHENZEITUNG FÜR DAS BISTUM EICHSTÄTT

WINKLER MEDIEN VERLAG GMBH 680535
Nymphenburger Str. 1, 80335 MÜNCHEN
Tel: 89 2900110 **Fax:** 89 29001199
Email: info@winkler-online.de
Web site: http://www.winkler-online.de

Titles:
DECO
RZ RAUM & AUSSTATTUNG

WINKLER & STENZEL GMBH 682985
Schulze-Delitzsch-Str. 35, 30938 BURGWEDEL
Tel: 5139 89990 **Fax:** 5139 899950
Email: info@winkler-stenzel.de
Web site: http://www.winkler-stenzel.de

Titles:
HAUS UND GRUND NIEDERSACHSEN
DIE NIEDERSÄCHSISCHE GEMEINDE
DER NORDDEUTSCHE SCHÜTZE
NSTN NACHRICHTEN
STADT UND GEMEINDE INTERAKTIV

WINNIE LIVE MEDIA S.L. & CO. KG 1652880
Lindemannstr. 81, 44137 DORTMUND
Tel: 231 22227700 **Fax:** 231 22227788
Email: dortmund@top-magazin.de
Web site: http://www.top-magazin.de

Titles:
TOP MAGAZIN RUHRSTADT DORTMUND

WINSENER ANZEIGER RAVENS & MAACK GMBH 690576
Schloßring 5, 21423 WINSEN **Tel:** 4171 6580
Fax: 4171 2953
Email: info@winsener-anzeiger.de
Web site: http://www.winsener-anzeiger.de

Titles:
WINSENER ANZEIGER
WOCHENBLATT MARSCH & HEIDE

WINTHERBURG-MEDIENAGENTUR 1734395
Bergsonstr. 29a, 81245 MÜNCHEN
Tel: 89 12768801 **Fax:** 89 12768803
Email: info@wintherburg.de
Web site: http://www.wintherburg.de

Titles:
DWZ

WIN-VERLAG GMBH & CO. KG 678576
Johann-Sebastian-Bach-Str. 5, 85591 VATERSTETTEN **Tel:** 8106 3500 **Fax:** 8106 350190
Email: info@win-verlag.de
Web site: http://www.win-verlag.de

Titles:
AUTOCAD & INVENTOR MAGAZIN
AUTODESK PARTNERLÖSUNGEN
DIGITALBUSINESS
E COMMERCE MAGAZIN

WIRTSCHAFTS GMBH DES DPVKOM 680884
Postfach 1431, 53004 BONN **Tel:** 228 9114090
Fax: 228 9114098
Email: manuel.kotte@dpvkom.de
Web site: http://www.dpvkom.de

Titles:
DPVKOM MAGAZIN

WIRTSCHAFTSBLATT VERLAGSGES. MBH 1773963
Graf-Adolf-Platz 1, 40213 DÜSSELDORF
Tel: 211 31120600 **Fax:** 211 311206010
Email: verlag@wirtschaftsblatt.de
Web site: http://www.wirtschaftsblatt.de

Titles:
WIRTSCHAFTSBLATT
WIRTSCHAFTSBLATT
WIRTSCHAFTSBLATT
WIRTSCHAFTSBLATT
WIRTSCHAFTSBLATT
WIRTSCHAFTSBLATT
WIRTSCHAFTSBLATT
WIRTSCHAFTSBLATT NIEDERRHEIN

WIRTSCHAFTSFÖRDERUNGSGES. FÜR DEN KREIS VIERSEN MBH 1748134
Willy-Brandt-Ring 13, 41747 VIERSEN
Tel: 2162 817901 **Fax:** 2162 8179180
Email: info@wfg-kreis-viersen.de
Web site: http://www.wfg-kreis-viersen.de

Titles:
VIEW

WIRTSCHAFTSFÖRDERUNGSGES. GARTENBAUVERBAND NORD MBH 686472
Brennerhof 121, 22113 HAMBURG
Tel: 40 73601590 **Fax:** 40 787687
Email: info@gartenbauverband-nord.de
Web site: http://www.wifoeg.de

Titles:
NORDDEUTSCHE GARTENBAU-MITTEILUNGEN

WIRTSCHAFTSFÖRDERUNGSGES. HAMM MBH 1768755
Münsterstr. 5, 59065 HAMM **Tel:** 2381 92930
Fax: 2381 9293222
Email: info@wf-hamm.de
Web site: http://www.wf-hamm.de

Titles:
WIRTSCHAFT INFORM

WIRTSCHAFTSFORUM VERLAG GMBH 690655
Sassestr. 14, 48431 RHEINE **Tel:** 5971 921640
Fax: 5971 9216438
Email: info@wirtschaftsforum-verlag.de
Web site: http://www.wirtschaftsforum.de

Titles:
WIRTSCHAFTSFORUM

WIRTSCHAFTSGES. DES FACHVERBANDES METALL BAYERN MBH 678936
Erhardtstr. 6, 80469 MÜNCHEN **Tel:** 89 2025623
Fax: 89 20256250
Email: info@fachverband-metall-bayern.de
Web site: http://www.fachverband-metall-bayern.de

Titles:
BAYERN METALL

WIRTSCHAFTSGES. MBH DES KFZ-GEWERBES SCHLESWIG-HOLSTEIN/MECKLENBURG-VORPOMMERN 1657424
Faluner Weg 28, 24109 KIEL **Tel:** 431 533310
Fax: 431 525067
Email: info@kfz-sh.de
Web site: http://www.kfz-sh.de

Titles:
KFZ-SH.DE

WIRTSCHAFTSHILFE DES BAYERISCHEN GROSS- UND AUSSENHANDELS GMBH 685056
Max-Joseph-Str. 5, 80333 MÜNCHEN
Tel: 89 5459370 **Fax:** 89 54593730
Email: info@lgad.de
Web site: http://www.lgad.de

Titles:
LGAD-NACHRICHTEN

WIRTSCHAFTS-MEDIEN-VERLAG LTD. & CO.KG 1764646
Koblenzer Str. 75, 57482 WENDEN
Tel: 2762 985228 **Fax:** 2762 985229
Email: info@wirtschaftsjournalsuedwest.de
Web site: http://www.wirtschaftsjournalsuedwest.de

Titles:
WIRTSCHAFTS JOURNAL SÜD-WEST

WIRTSCHAFTSPRÜFER-KAMMER 1640334
Rauchstr. 26, 10787 BERLIN **Tel:** 30 7261610
Fax: 30 726161228
Email: magazin@wpk.de
Web site: http://www.wpk.de

Titles:
WPK MAGAZIN

WIRTSCHAFTSVEREINIGUNG GROSS- UND AUSSENHANDEL HAMBURG E.V. 683692
Sonninstr. 28, 20097 HAMBURG **Tel:** 40 2360160
Fax: 40 23601610
Email: contact@wga-hh.de
Web site: http://www.wga-hh.de

Titles:
INFORMATIONSDIENST GROSS- UND AUSSENHANDEL

WIRTSCHAFTSVERLAG BACHEM GMBH 693224
Ursulaplatz 1, 50668 KÖLN **Tel:** 221 16190
Fax: 221 1619231
Email: info@bachem-verlag.de
Web site: http://www.bachem-verlag.de

Titles:
ANGEWANDTE ARBEITSWISSENSCHAFT

WISSENSCHAFTLICHE VERLAGSGES. MBH 677785
Birkenwaldstr. 44, 70191 STUTTGART
Tel: 711 25820 **Fax:** 711 2582290
Email: service@wissenschaftliche-verlagsgesellschaft.de
Web site: http://www.wissenschaftliche-verlagsgesellschaft.de

Titles:
ARZNEIMITTELTHERAPIE
CHEMOTHERAPIE JOURNAL
DEUTSCHE AKADEMIE DER NATURFORSCHER LEOPOLDINA JAHRBUCH
NATURWISSENSCHAFTLICHE RUNDSCHAU NR
PPT PSYCHOPHARMAKOTHERAPIE

WISSNER-VERLAG GMBH & CO. KG 687958
Im Tal 12, 86179 AUGSBURG **Tel:** 821 2598911
Fax: 821 2598999
Email: schalwig@wissner.com
Web site: http://www.wissner.com/zfv

Titles:
ZFV

WISTA-MANAGEMENT GMBH 1715982
Rudower Chaussee 17, 12489 BERLIN
Tel: 30 63922238 **Fax:** 30 63922236
Email: pr@wista.de
Web site: http://www.adlershof.de

Titles:
ADLERSHOF JOURNAL

WOCHENANZEIGER GMBH 686049
Moosacher Str. 56, 80809 MÜNCHEN
Tel: 89 5529460 **Fax:** 89 55294639
Email: info@wochenanzeiger.de
Web site: http://www.wochenanzeiger.de

Titles:
MÜNCHNER WOCHEN ANZEIGER MOOSACHER ANZEIGER

WOCHENBLATT ERDING VERLAGS GMBH 1600479
Landshuter Str. 47a, 85435 ERDING
Tel: 8122 97920 **Fax:** 8122 979225
Email: erding@wochenblatt.de
Web site: http://www.wochenblatt.de

Titles:
WOCHENBLATT

WOCHENBLATT VERLAG RAVENSBURG GMBH & CO. KG 690722
Olgastr. 8, 88214 RAVENSBURG **Tel:** 751 37090
Fax: 751 370960
Email: wochenblatt.gesamt@wbrv.de
Web site: http://www.wochenblatt-online.de

Titles:
WOCHENBLATT - AUSG. BIBERACH
WOCHENBLATT - AUSG. FRIEDRICHSHAFEN/ÜBERLINGEN
WOCHENBLATT - AUSG. RAVENSBURG
WOCHENBLATT - AUSG. RIEDLINGEN

WOCHENBLATT VERLAGSGRUPPE GMBH & CO. KG 677748
Maybachstr. 8, 84030 LANDSHUT **Tel:** 871 14190
Fax: 871 1419118
Email: verlag@wochenblatt.de
Web site: http://www.wochenblatt.de

Titles:
BAYERWALD WOCHENBLATT
DEGGENDORFER WOCHENBLATT
LANDSHUTER WOCHENBLATT
REGENSBURGER WOCHENBLATT - AUSG. LANDKREIS
ROTTAL-INN WOCHENBLATT
STRAUBINGER WOCHENBLATT
WOCHENBLATT PASSAUER WOCHE

WOCHENBLATT-VERLAG LIMBURG GMBH 1760679
Ste.-Foy-Str. 27, 65549 LIMBURG
Tel: 6431 91330 **Fax:** 6431 23458
Email: lokalanzeiger@vfa-online.de
Web site: http://www.vfa-online.de

Titles:
LOKALANZEIGER LAHN-POST

WOCHENBLATT-VERLAG SCHRADER GMBH & CO. KG 684663
Bendestorfer Str. 3, 21244 BUCHHOLZ
Tel: 4181 20030 **Fax:** 4181 200366
Email: anz-buch@kreiszeitung-wochenblatt.de
Web site: http://www.kreiszeitung-wochenblatt.de

Titles:
KREISZEITUNG ELBE GEEST WOCHENBLATT
KREISZEITUNG NORDHEIDE/ELBE&GEEST WOCHENBLATT ZUM WOCHENENDE

WOCHENSCHAU VERLAG DR. KURT DEBUS GMBH 683667
Adolf-Damaschke-Str. 10, 65824 SCHWALBACH
Tel: 6196 86065 **Fax:** 6196 86060
Email: info@wochenschau-verlag.de
Web site: http://www.wochenschau-verlag.de

Titles:
POLITISCHE BILDUNG

WOCHENSPIEGEL SACHSEN VERLAG GMBH CHEMNITZ 680138
Heinrich-Lorenz-Str. 2, 09120 CHEMNITZ
Tel: 371 5289232 **Fax:** 371 5289115
Email: info@wochenspiegel-sachsen.de
Web site: http://www.wochenspiegel-sachsen.de

Titles:
HEIRATEN - IHR HOCHZEITSPLANER FÜR CHEMNITZ UND UMGEBUNG
RECHT DEUTLICH
WIRTSCHAFT IN SÜDWESTSACHSEN

WOCHENSPIEGEL VERLAG MAYEN GMBH & CO. KG 1725029
Rosengasse, 56727 MAYEN **Tel:** 2651 901070
Fax: 2651 901072
Email: info@wvm-verlag.de
Web site: http://www.wochenspiegellive.de

Titles:
COCHEMER WOCHENSPIEGEL
MAYENER WOCHENSPIEGEL
ZELLER WOCHENSPIEGEL

WOCHENSPIEGEL VERLAGSGES. MBH POTSDAM & CO. KG
688799
Friedrich-Engels-Str. 24, 14473 POTSDAM
Tel: 331 2840891 **Fax:** 331 2840894
Email: anzeigen@wochenspiegel-brb.de
Web site: http://www.wochenspiegel-brb.de

Titles:
WOCHENSPIEGEL BAD BELZIG TREUENBRIETZEN

WOCHENZEITUNGEN AM OBERRHEIN VERLAGS-GMBH
681248
Denzlinger Str. 42, 79312 EMMENDINGEN
Tel: 7641 93800 **Fax:** 7641 938050
Email: office@wzo.de
Web site: http://www.wzo.de

Titles:
ETTENHEIMER STADTANZEIGER
KAISERSTÜHLER WOCHENBERICHT
VON HAUS ZU HAUS
WOCHENZEITUNG EMMENDINGER TOR

WOHN!DESIGN VERLAG AG
1634313
Mörikestr. 67, 70199 STUTTGART
Tel: 711 96666410 **Fax:** 711 96666415
Email: verlag@wohndesign.de
Web site: http://www.wohndesign.de

Titles:
WOHN!DESIGN

WOHNSTIFT AM TIERGARTEN E.V.
688971
Bingstr. 30, 90480 NÜRNBERG **Tel:** 911 40300
Fax: 911 4030241
Email: stiftsleitung@wohnstift-am-tiergarten.de
Web site: http://www.wohnstift-am-tiergarten.de

Titles:
DER STIFTSBOTE

WOHNVERLAG GMBH
1684551
Wilhelm-Sinsteden-Str. 6, 47533 KLEVE
Tel: 2821 997930 **Fax:** 2821 9979340
Email: info@wohnverlag.de
Web site: http://www.wohnverlag.de

Titles:
ROMANTISCH WOHNEN
WINING & DINING

WOLF VERLAG GMBH
686629
Hostackerweg 21, 69198 SCHRIESHEIM
Tel: 6220 6562 **Fax:** 6220 911023
Email: verlag@umweltdirekt.de
Web site: http://www.umweltdirekt.de

Titles:
UMWELTDIREKT

WOLFF PUBLISHING E.K., INH. ANDREAS WOLFF
1744191
Herrenstr. 3, 58119 HAGEN **Tel:** 2334 442111
Fax: 2334 442113
Email: info@wolff-publishing.de
Web site: http://www.b-und-i.de

Titles:
B&I BETRIEBSTECHNIK INSTANDHALTUNG

WOLTERS KLUWER DEUTSCHLAND GMBH
1630539
Luxemburger Str. 449, 50939 KÖLN
Tel: 221 943737000 **Fax:** 221 943737201
Email: info@wolterskluwer.de
Web site: http://www.wolterskluwer.de

Titles:
BAURECHT
FACHANWALT ARBEITSRECHT
FUR FAMILIE UND RECHT
GUG GRUNDSTÜCKSMARKT UND GRUNDSTÜCKSWERT
INFORMATIONSBRIEF AUSLÄNDERRECHT
JUGENDHILFE
DAS JURISTISCHE BÜRO
NEUE ZEITSCHRIFT FÜR WEHRRECHT
PERSONALWIRTSCHAFT
RIA RECHT IM AMT
STRAFVERTEIDIGER
WEITERBILDUNG
ZMR ZEITSCHRIFT FÜR MIET- UND RAUMRECHT

WOMAN IN THE CITY GMBH
1791499
Holzkoppelweg 15, 24118 KIEL **Fax:** 4349 919544
Email: info@witc-verlag.de
Web site: http://www.witc-verlag.de

Titles:
WOMAN IN THE CITY
WOMAN IN THE CITY

WORDART GMBH
687184
Mühlstr. 16, 86911 DIESSEN **Tel:** 8807 928911
Fax: 8807 928929
Email: verlag@pm-report.de
Web site: http://www.pm-report.de

Titles:
PM-REPORT
PM-REPORT SPECIAL: SELBSTMEDIKATION

WORT & BILD VERLAG KONRADSHÖHE GMBH & CO. KG
677379
Konradshöhe, 82065 BAIERBRUNN
Tel: 89 744330 **Fax:** 89 74433150
Email: kontakt@wortundbildverlag.de
Web site: http://www.wortundbild-media.de

Titles:
APOTHEKEN UMSCHAU - AUSG. A
ÄRZTLICHER RATGEBER FÜR WERDENDE UND JUNGE ELTERN
BABY UND FAMILIE
DIABETES RATGEBER
MEDIZINI MIT SUPER-POSTER
SENIOREN RATGEBER

WORTWEBER, KREATIVBÜRO FÜR TEXT & BILD
1653838
Borsigstr. 30, 73249 WERNAU **Tel:** 7153 923248
Email: info@wortweber.de
Web site: http://www.wortweber.de

Titles:
LUFTRETTUNG

W.P. EUROPRESSE VERLAGS GMBH
678607
Paffrather Str. 80, 51465 BERGISCH GLADBACH **Tel:** 2202 41857 **Fax:** 2202 41877
Email: info@eurotuner.de
Web site: http://www.tuning2go.de

Titles:
EURO TUNER
MAXIMUM TUNER
MERCEDES TUNER
VW&AUDI TUNER MAGAZIN

WPM-WERBEPARTNER GMBH
688310
Wismarsche Str. 146, 19053 SCHWERIN
Tel: 385 590580 **Fax:** 385 5905840
Email: redaktion@schwerinonline.de
Web site: http://www.schwerinonline.de

Titles:
SCHWERINER KURIER

WPV. WIRTSCHAFTS- UND PRAXISVERLAG GMBH
686416
Otto-Hahn-Str. 7, 50997 KÖLN **Tel:** 2236 376711
Fax: 2236 37692530
Email: post@wpv.de
Web site: http://www.wpv.de

Titles:
DER NIEDERGELASSENE ARZT
WIRTSCHAFTSMAGAZIN FÜR DEN FRAUENARZT
WIRTSCHAFTSMAGAZIN FÜR DEN HAUTARZT
WIRTSCHAFTSMAGAZIN FÜR DEN KINDERARZT
WIRTSCHAFTSMAGAZIN FÜR DEN NERVENARZT
WIRTSCHAFTSMAGAZIN FÜR DEN ORTHOPÄDEN
WIRTSCHAFTSMAGAZIN FÜR DEN UROLOGEN

WST WERBESTUDIO IN THÜRINGEN GMBH
687776
Legefelder Hauptstr. 14a, 99438 WEIMAR
Tel: 3643 903224 **Fax:** 3643 511933
Email: wstgmbh.weimar@t-online.de
Web site: http://www.wst-verlag.de

Titles:
NTI NEUE THÜRINGER ILLUSTRIERTE
OSTBAU
ROHRBAU JOURNAL

WÜRTTEMBERGISCHER NOTARVEREIN E.V.
1684597
Kronenstr. 34, 70174 STUTTGART
Tel: 711 2237951 **Fax:** 711 2237956
Email: wuertt.notv@t-online.de
Web site: http://www.notare-wuerttemberg.de

Titles:
BWNOTZ ZEITSCHRIFT FÜR DAS NOTARIAT IN BADEN-WÜRTTEMBERG

WÜRZBURGER VERSORGUNGS- UND VERKEHRS-GMBH
1775109
Haugerring 5, 97070 WÜRZBURG **Tel:** 931 3600
Email: info@wvv.de
Web site: http://www.wvv.de

Titles:
WVV ENERGIE PLUS

W.V.G. WERBE- UND VERLAGSGES. MBH & CO. KG
680823
Ferdinand-Clasen-Str. 21, 41812 ERKELENZ
Tel: 2431 96860 **Fax:** 2431 81651
Email: verlag@hs-woche.de
Web site: http://www.hs-woche.de

Titles:
DN-WOCHE
HS-WOCHE - AUSG. HEINSBERG
JÜLICHER WOCHE

WVGW WIRTSCHAFTS- UND VERLAGSGES. GAS UND WASSER MBH
681295
Josef-Wirmer-Str. 3, 53123 BONN
Tel: 228 919140 **Fax:** 228 9191499
Email: info@wvgw.de
Web site: http://www.wvgw.de

Titles:
BBR FACHMAGAZIN FÜR BRUNNEN- UND LEITUNGSBAU
DVGW ENERGIEIWASSER-PRAXIS

WVW WESTDEUTSCHE VERLAGS- UND WERBEGES. MBH & CO. KG
679605
Bert-Brecht-Str. 29, 45128 ESSEN
Tel: 201 8042836 **Fax:** 201 8041857
Email: wvw@wvw-anzeigenblaetter.de
Web site: http://www.wvw-anzeigenblaetter.de

Titles:
BORBECK KURIER
KETTWIG KURIER
NORD ANZEIGER
RUHR KURIER
STEELER KURIER
SÜD ANZEIGER
WERDEN KURIER
WEST ANZEIGER

WWF VERLAGSGES. MBH
680661
Am Eggenkamp 37, 48268 GREVEN
Tel: 2571 937630 **Fax:** 2571 937650
Email: verlag@wwf-medien.de
Web site: http://www.wwf-medien.de

Titles:
RHEINISCHES ÄRZTEBLATT

WWK UNTERNEHMENSGRUPPE
690825
Marsstr. 37, 80335 MÜNCHEN **Tel:** 89 51140
Fax: 89 51142765
Email: info@wwk.de
Web site: http://www.wwk.de

Titles:
WWK-FORUM

WWS VERLAG KLAUS-PETER PIONTKOWSKI
1740696
Neuenbaumer Str. 5, 41470 NEUSS
Tel: 2131 936970 **Fax:** 2131 9369720
Email: info@wws-verlag.de
Web site: http://www.wws-verlag.de

Titles:
GENUSS PUR PROFESSIONAL

X-MEDIEN AG
1687256
Schlossgut Weyhern, 82281 EGENHOFEN
Tel: 8134 55500 **Fax:** 8134 555066
Email: christian.marks@musix.de
Web site: http://www.musix.de

Titles:
MUSIX

YAEZ VERLAG GMBH
1649622
Kornbergstr. 44, 70176 STUTTGART
Tel: 711 9979830 **Fax:** 711 99798322
Email: info@yaez-verlag.de
Web site: http://www.yaez-verlag.de

Titles:
YAEZ

YOU+ME-VERLAG MARCUSS WESTPHAL
690853
Elberfelder Str. 44, 40822 METTMANN
Tel: 2104 341050
Email: marcuss.westphal@bewegungsmelder.de
Web site: http://www.youandme.de

Titles:
YOU + ME

ZAHNÄRZTLICHER FACH-VERLAG GMBH
678038
Mont-Cenis-Str. 5, 44623 HERNE
Tel: 2323 593137 **Fax:** 2323 593135
Email: anzeigen@dhug.de
Web site: http://www.dzw.de

Titles:
ARZT ZAHNARZT & NATURHEILVERFAHREN
DZW KOMPAKT
DZW ZAHNTECHNIK
PROPHYLAXE IMPULS
DIE ZAHNARZT WOCHE DZW

ZARBOCK MEDIA GMBH & CO. KG
1784490
Sontraer Str. 6, 60386 FRANKFURT
Tel: 69 42090372 **Fax:** 69 42090370
Email: verlag@zarbock.de
Web site: http://www.zarbock-media.de

Titles:
PBS REPORT

ZEIT KUNSTVERLAG GMBH & CO. KG
678500
Balanstr. 73/Geb.8, 81541 MÜNCHEN
Tel: 89 1269900 **Fax:** 89 12699040
Email: info@weltkunst.de
Web site: http://www.zeitkunstverlag.de

Titles:
WELTKUNST

ZEIT ONLINE GMBH
1626933
Speersort 1, 20095 HAMBURG **Tel:** 40 32800
Fax: 40 32805003
Email: kontakt@zeit.de
Web site: http://www.zeit.de

Titles:
ZEIT ONLINE

ZEITTECHNIK-VERLAG GMBH
690705
Friedhofstr. 13, 63263 NEU-ISENBURG
Tel: 6102 31910 **Fax:** 6102 31960
Email: info@zeittechnik-verlag.de
Web site: http://www.zeittechnik-verlag.de

Titles:
WKSB

ZEITUNGSVERLAG AACHEN GMBH
677209
Dresdener Str. 3, 52068 AACHEN **Tel:** 241 51010
Fax: 241 5101850
Email: info@zeitungsverlag-aachen.de
Web site: http://www.zeitungsverlag-aachen.de

Titles:
AACHENER NACHRICHTEN
AACHENER ZEITUNG
AN-ONLINE.DE
AZ-WEB.DE
DÜRENER NACHRICHTEN
DÜRENER ZEITUNG
EIFELER NACHRICHTEN
EIFELER ZEITUNG
ESCHWEILER NACHRICHTEN
ESCHWEILER ZEITUNG
JÜLICHER NACHRICHTEN
JÜLICHER ZEITUNG
STOLBERGER NACHRICHTEN
STOLBERGER ZEITUNG

ZEITUNGSVERLAG DER PATRIOT GMBH
682528
Hansastr. 2, 59557 LIPPSTADT **Tel:** 2941 20100
Fax: 2941 201285
Email: zeitungsverlag@derpatriot.de
Web site: http://www.derpatriot.de

Titles:
GESEKER ZEITUNG
DER PATRIOT

ZEITUNGSVERLAG FÜR DAS HOCHSTIFT PADERBORN GMBH 690505
Imadstr. 40, 33102 PADERBORN **Tel:** 5251 8960
Fax: 5251 896169

Titles:
WESTFÄLISCHES VOLKSBLATT

ZEITUNGSVERLAG GMBH & CO. WAIBLINGEN KG 677880
Albrecht-Villinger-Str. 10, 71332 WAIBLINGEN
Tel: 7151 5660 **Fax:** 7151 566400
Email: info@zvw.de
Web site: http://www.zvw.de

Titles:
SCHORNDORFER NACHRICHTEN
WAIBLINGER KREISZEITUNG
WELZHEIMER ZEITUNG
WINNENDER ZEITUNG

ZEITUNGSVERLAG ISERLOHN 683854
Theodor-Heuss-Ring 4, 58636 ISERLOHN
Tel: 2371 8220 **Fax:** 2371 822102
Email: ikz@ikz-online.de
Web site: http://www.ikz-online.de

Titles:
ISERLOHNER KREISANZEIGER UND ZEITUNG

ZEITUNGSVERLAG KORNWESTHEIM GMBH & CO. KG 1640180
Rechbergstr. 10, 70806 KORNWESTHEIM
Tel: 7154 13120 **Fax:** 7154 131221
Email: info@kornwestheimer-zeitung.zgs.de
Web site: http://www.kornwestheimer-zeitung.de

Titles:
KORNWESTHEIM & KREIS LUDWIGSBURG
KORNWESTHEIMER STADT ANZEIGER
KORNWESTHEIMER ZEITUNG

ZEITUNGSVERLAG KRAUSE GMBH & CO. KG 677719
Glückstädter Str. 10, 21682 STADE
Tel: 4141 9360 **Fax:** 4141 936294
Email: redaktion-std@tageblatt.de
Web site: http://www.tageblatt.de

Titles:
ALTLÄNDER TAGEBLATT
BUXTEHUDER TAGEBLATT
STADER TAGEBLATT

ZEITUNGSVERLAG LEONBERG GMBH 685027
Stuttgarter Str. 7, 71229 LEONBERG
Tel: 7152 9370 **Fax:** 7152 9372809
Web site: http://www.leonberger-kreiszeitung.de

Titles:
LEONBERGER KREISZEITUNG

ZEITUNGSVERLAG NAUMBURG NEBRA GMBH & CO. KG 686210
Salzstr. 8, 06618 NAUMBURG **Tel:** 3445 2307830
Fax: 3445 2307839
Email: naumburger.tageblatt@mz-web.de
Web site: http://www.naumburger-tageblatt.de

Titles:
NAUMBURGER TAGEBLATT
NAUMBURGER TAGEBLATT ONLINE

ZEITUNGSVERLAG NEUE WESTFÄLISCHE GMBH & CO. KG 681414
Niedernstr. 21, 33602 BIELEFELD **Tel:** 521 5550
Fax: 521 555515
Web site: http://www.nw-news.de

Titles:
NEUE WESTFÄLISCHE

ZEITUNGSVERLAG NIEDERRHEIN GMBH & CO. ESSEN KG 686517
Friedrichstr. 34, 45128 ESSEN **Tel:** 201 8040
Fax: 201 8042621
Web site: http://www.derwesten.de

Titles:
NRZ NEUE RHEIN ZEITUNG
NRZ NEUE RUHR ZEITUNG

ZEITUNGSVERLAG OBERBAYERN GMBH & CO. KG 1744178
Pfaffenrieder Str. 9, 82515 WOLFRATSHAUSEN
Tel: 8171 2690 **Fax:** 8171 269240
Email: gswol@merkur-online.de
Web site: http://www.merkur-online.de

Titles:
DACHAUER NACHRICHTEN
DORFENER ANZEIGER
EBERSBERGER ZEITUNG
ERDINGER ANZEIGER
FREISINGER TAGBLATT
FÜRSTENFELDBRUCKER TAGBLATT
GARMISCH-PARTENKIRCHNER TAGBLATT
GERETSRIEDER MERKUR
HOLZKIRCHNER MERKUR
ISAR-LOISACHBOTE
MIESBACHER MERKUR
MURNAUER TAGBLATT
PENZBERGER MERKUR
STARNBERGER MERKUR
TEGERNSEER ZEITUNG
TÖLZER KURIER
WEILHEIMER TAGBLATT

ZEITUNGSVERLAG SCHWÄBISCH HALL GMBH 1686503
Haalstr. 5, 74523 SCHWÄBISCH HALL
Tel: 791 4040 **Fax:** 791 404180
Email: info@hallertagblatt.de
Web site: http://www.hallertagblatt.de

Titles:
HALLER TAGBLATT

ZEITUNGSVERLAG SCHWERIN GMBH & CO. KG 1603390
Gutenbergstr. 1, 19061 SCHWERIN
Tel: 385 63780 **Fax:** 385 3975140
Email: redaktion@svz.de
Web site: http://www.svz.de

Titles:
ELDE EXPRESS
NORDWEST EXPRESS
PRIGNITZ EXPRESS
DER PRIGNITZER
SCHWERINER EXPRESS
SCHWERINER VOLKSZEITUNG

ZEITUNGSVERLAG TZ MÜNCHEN GMBH & CO. KG 1640096
Paul-Heyse-Str. 2, 80336 MÜNCHEN
Tel: 89 53060 **Fax:** 89 5306552

Titles:
TZ
WOCHENEND TZ

ZEITUNGSVERLAG WESTFALEN GMBH & CO. KG 1687271
Ostenhellweg 42, 44135 DORTMUND
Tel: 231 95730 **Fax:** 231 95731202
Web site: http://www.westfaelische-rundschau.de

Titles:
WR WESTFÄLISCHE RUNDSCHAU

ZEITVERLAG GERD BUCERIUS GMBH & CO. KG 690897
Speersort 1, 20095 HAMBURG **Tel:** 40 32800
Fax: 40 327111
Email: diezeit@zeit.de
Web site: http://www.zeit.de

Titles:
DIE ZEIT
ZEIT WISSEN

ZENTRAL- UND LANDESBIBLIOTHEK 679288
Breite Str. 36, 10178 BERLIN **Tel:** 30 90226456
Fax: 30 90226539
Email: redaktion.bibliotheksdienst@zlb.de
Web site: http://www.zlb.de/aktivitaeten/bd_neu

Titles:
BIBLIOTHEKSDIENST

ZENTRALRAT DER JUDEN IN DEUTSCHLAND 1793656
Hausvogteiplatz 12, 10117 BERLIN
Tel: 30 4998880 **Fax:** 30 49889899
Email: verlag@juedische-presse.de
Web site: http://www.juedische-allgemeine.de

Titles:
JÜDISCHE ALLGEMEINE

ZENTRALVERBAND DES DEUTSCHEN HANDWERKS E.V. 1641057
Mohrenstr. 20, 10117 BERLIN **Tel:** 30 206190
Fax: 30 20619460
Email: info@zdh.de
Web site: http://www.zdh.de

Titles:
HANDFEST

ZENTRALVERBAND DEUTSCHES BAUGEWERBE 697863
Kronenstr. 55, 10117 BERLIN **Tel:** 30 203140
Fax: 30 20314419
Email: bau@zdb.de
Web site: http://www.zdb.de

Titles:
DIREKT

ZEPPELIN BAUMASCHINEN GMBH 1653207
Graf-Zeppelin-Platz 1, 85748 GARCHING
Tel: 89 320000 **Fax:** 89 32000418
Email: zeppelin@zeppelin.com
Web site: http://www.fahrerclub.de

Titles:
DEUTSCHES BAUBLATT
PROFI CLUBSHOP

ZEPPELIN VERLAG GMBH 681619
Janningsstr. 5, 70563 STUTTGART
Tel: 711 733010 **Fax:** 711 733015
Email: info@zeppelin-verlag.de
Web site: http://www.zeppelin-verlag.de

Titles:
FABRIKVERKAUF IN DEUTSCHLAND

ZEUS ZENTRALE FÜR EINKAUF UND SERVICE GMBH & CO. KG 690974
Celler Str. 47, 29614 SOLTAU **Tel:** 5191 802833
Fax: 5191 98664833
Email: liane.biermann@zeus-online.de
Web site: http://www.zeus-online.de

Titles:
DIE ZEUS

ZGM ZEITUNGSGRUPPE MÜNSTERLAND 1727501
An der Hansalinie 1, 48163 MÜNSTER
Tel: 251 6900 **Fax:** 251 6904570
Email: anzeigen@zgm-muensterland.de
Web site: http://www.zgm-muensterland.de

Titles:
ZGM ZEITUNGSGRUPPE MÜNSTERLAND

ZGO ZEITUNGSGRUPPE OSTFRIESLAND GMBH 682479
Untenende 21, 26817 RHAUDERFEHN
Tel: 4952 9270 **Fax:** 4952 927555
Email: info@ga-online.de
Web site: http://www.ga-online.de

Titles:
GENERAL-ANZEIGER
NORDERNEYER BADEZEITUNG
OSTFRIESEN ZEITUNG

ZHH DIENSTLEISTUNG GMBH 1741685
Eichendorffstr. 3, 40474 DÜSSELDORF
Tel: 211 4705074 **Fax:** 211 4705085
Email: vertrieb@zhh-mv.de
Web site: http://www.zhh.de

Titles:
ZHH-INFORMATION

ZIEGLER VERLAGS GMBH 678739
Birkenweiherstr. 14, 63505 LANGENSELBOLD
Tel: 6184 923330 **Fax:** 6184 923355
Email: info@ziegler-verlag.de
Web site: http://www.ziegler-verlag.de

Titles:
BAHNSPORT AKTUELL
MOTOCROSS ENDURO

ZIEL GMBH 1744162
Zeuggasse 7, 86150 AUGSBURG
Tel: 821 4209977 **Fax:** 821 4209978
Email: wub@ziel.org
Web site: http://www.ziel-verlag.de

Titles:
W&B WIRTSCHAFT UND BERUFSERZIEHUNG

ZITTY VERLAG GMBH 690990
Askanischer Platz 3, 10963 BERLIN
Tel: 30 290210 **Fax:** 30 2902199941090
Email: kontakt@zitty.de
Web site: http://www.zitty.de

Titles:
[030]
ZITTY BERLIN

ZOSCHKE DATA GMBH 1651147
Blomenburg, 24238 SELENT **Tel:** 4384 593490
Fax: 4384 5934999
Email: info@zoschke.com
Web site: http://www.zoschke.com

Titles:
DEVDORADO.DE

ZWECKVERBAND FÜR ABFALLWIRTSCHAFT IN NORDWEST-OBERFRANKEN 1685015
von-Werthern-Str. 6, 96487 DÖRFLES-ESBACH
Tel: 9561 858013
Email: info@zaw-coburg.de
Web site: http://www.zaw-coburg.de

Titles:
UMWELT JOURNAL

ZWEIBRÜCKER DRUCKEREI UND VERLAGSGES. MBH 1743451
Hauptstr. 66, 66482 ZWEIBRÜCKEN
Tel: 6332 800050 **Fax:** 6332 800039
Email: merkur@pm-zw.de
Web site: http://www.pfaelzischer-merkur.de

Titles:
PFÄLZISCHER MERKUR

ZWEI:C WERBEAGENTUR GMBH 682931
Doormannsweg 22, 20259 HAMBURG
Tel: 40 41433380 **Fax:** 40 414333818
Email: henner.schulz.karstens@zwei-c.com
Web site: http://www.zwei-c.com

Titles:
HAMBURGER WIRTSCHAFT

ZWEIGNIEDERLASSUNG VON DER NEUE TAG OBERPFÄLZISCHER KURIER DRUCK- UND VERLAGSHAUS GMBH 1741084
Mühlgasse 2, 92224 AMBERG **Tel:** 9621 3060
Fax: 9621 306290

Titles:
AMBERGER ZEITUNG

ZWEIPLUS MEDIENAGENTUR 687501
Pallaswiesenstr. 109, 64293 DARMSTADT
Tel: 6151 81270 **Fax:** 6151 893098
Email: info@zweiplus.de
Web site: http://www.zweiplus.de

Titles:
RADWELT

ZWEIRAD-VERLAG 691055
Boxdorfer Str. 13, 90765 FÜRTH **Tel:** 911 3072970
Fax: 911 30709771
Email: info@zweirad-online.de
Web site: http://www.zweirad-online.de

Titles:
ZWEIRAD

ZWEITE HAND VERLAGS-GMBH 691057
Am Treptower Park 75, 12435 BERLIN
Tel: 30 534310 **Fax:** 30 53431112
Email: zweitehand@zweitehand.de
Web site: http://www.zweitehand.de

Titles:
AUTONET
BOOTSHANDEL
FAHRZEUGE

ZWEITES DEUTSCHES FERNSEHEN, HA KOMMUNIKATION 683905
ZDF-Str. 1, 55127 MAINZ **Tel:** 6131 701
Fax: 6131 702170
Email: info@zdf.de
Web site: http://www.zdf.de

Titles:
JAHRBUCH

[MAURITZ & GREWE] GMBH & CO. KG 1654021
Am Leinekanal 4, 37073 GÖTTINGEN
Tel: 551 5042818 **Fax:** 551 5042819
Email: info@mauritz-grewe.de
Web site: http://www.mauritz-grewe.de
Titles:
37

Gibraltar

GIBRALTAR CHRONICLE 21270
Watergate House, Casemates, PO Box 27
Tel: 71 627 **Fax:** 79 927
Email: gibchron@glbnet.gi
Titles:
GIBRALTAR CHRONICLE

GUIDE LINE PROMOTIONS LTD 698784
PO Box 561, Imossi House, Irish Town, Suite 6377 **Tel:** 77 748 **Fax:** 77 748
Titles:
THE GIBRALTAR MAGAZINE

INSIGHT PUBLICATIONS LTD 698795
Suite D, 1st Floor, Ellesmere House, City Mill Lane **Tel:** 40 913 **Fax:** 48 665
Titles:
INSIGHT MAGAZINE

PANORAMA PUBLISHING 1201338
75 Irish Town, PO Box 225 **Tel:** 200 79 797
Fax: 200 74 664
Email: gibnews@gibraltar.gi
Titles:
PANORAMA

ZENITH PROMOTIONS LTD 1600309
PO Box 306, Leon House, Suite 1 **Tel:** 77 414
Fax: 72 531
Titles:
VOX

Greece

DIM/KOS ORGANISMOS LAMBRAKIS A.E. 699502
Michalakopoulou 80, 115 28 ATHINA
Tel: 210 33 33 630 **Fax:** 210 32 38 740
Web site: http://www.dolnet.gr
Titles:
TA NEA
TO VIMA

IHT - KATHIMERINI S.A. 699592
Ethnarhou Makariou & 2 Falireos, 185 47 NEO FALIRO **Tel:** 210 48 08 000 **Fax:** 210 48 08 055
Titles:
KATHIMERINI

KERDOS EKDOTIKI A.E. 699499
Vasileos Georgiou 44 kai Kalvou, 152 33 HALANDRI **Tel:** 210 67 47 881 **Fax:** 210 67 47 893
Titles:
KERDOS

KOINONIA ASTIKOU DIKAIOU 1201438
Anthimou Gazi 9, 105 61 ATHINA
Tel: 210 32 20 631 **Fax:** 210 32 43 071
Titles:
ESTIA

LIBERIS PUBLICATIONS SA 1200896
Ioannou Metaxa 80, Karelas, 194 00 KOROPI - ATTICA **Tel:** 210 66 88 000 **Fax:** 210 66 88 300
Web site: http://www.liberis.gr
Titles:
2BOARD

MAKEDONIKI EKDOTIKI & EKTIPOTIKI A.E. 700179
Monastiriou 85, 546 27 THESSALONIKI
Tel: 31 56 00 00 **Fax:** 31 53 48 22
Titles:
MAKEDONIA

P. ATHANASSIADES & CO S.A 1792540
Lenorman 205, Kolonos, 104 42 ATHINA
Tel: 210 51 98 000 **Fax:** 2105139905
Titles:
NAFTEMPORIKI

PIGASOS EKDOTIKI A.E. 1680321
Mpenaki & Aggiou Nektariou 5, 152 38 METAMORFOSI HALANDRIOU
Titles:
ETHNOS
ETHNOS TIS KIRIAKIS

PROVOLI EKMETALLEVSI M.A. VOREIOU ELLADOSE.P.E. 700220
Tsimiski 45, 546 23 THESSALONIKI
Tel: 2310 77 91 11 **Fax:** 2310 24 38 52
Titles:
AGGELIOFOROS

RIZOSPASTIS SYNHRONI EPOHI EKDOTIKI A.E. 700215
Lefkis 134, 145 65 KRIONERI ATTIKIS
Tel: 210 62 97 000 **Fax:** 210 62 97 999
Titles:
RIZOSPASTIS

TEGOPOULOS EDITIONS 1201386
Minoos 10-16, 117 43 NEOS KOSMOS
Tel: 210 92 96 001 **Fax:** 210 90 28 312
Titles:
ELEFTHEROTYPIA
KIRIAKATIKI

Hungary

ABSURD KFT. 1742195
Irányi D. u. 6., 8000 SZÉKESFEHÉRVÁR **Tel:** 22/502-525 **Fax:** 22/502-526
Titles:
FEHÉRVÁRI START AUTÓS MAGAZIN

ACSI LOGISZTIKA ZRT. 1742199
Újszolok u. 9. III/1., 2120 DUNAKESZI **Tel:** 27/630-731 **Fax:** 333-8170
Titles:
ANYAGMOZGATÁS - CSOMAGOLÁS (A + CS)

ADL KIADÓ KFT. 1678666
Fogarasi út 5. 27. épület, 1148 BUDAPEST
Tel: 1/460-0289 **Fax:** 1/460-0289
Titles:
MAGYAR ELEKTRONIKA

ADOC-SEMIC KIADÓI KFT. 1677847
Fehér út 10., 1106 BUDAPEST **Tel:** 27/540-266
Fax: 27/540-266
Titles:
GARFIELD

AGROINFORM KIADÓ ÉS NYOMDA KFT 1678796
Páter K. u. 1., 2103 GÖDÖLLO **Tel:** 28/522-042
Fax: 28/522-042
Titles:
HUNGARIAN AGRICULTURAL RESEARCH

ALBION PRESS KFT. 1678558
Budafoki út 60., 1117 BUDAPEST **Tel:** 1/464-3880
Fax: 1/382-0211
Titles:
HÁZIMOZI

ALEXANDER-CAR BT. 1742305
Dózsa Gy. út 32., 1071 BUDAPEST **Tel:** 1/343-1816 **Fax:** 1/413-7131
Titles:
CSAJOK MAGAZIN

ALL NUTRITION KFT. 1742216
Telepes u. 51., 1147 BUDAPEST **Tel:** 1/222-6023
Fax: 1/363-3121
Titles:
FIT MUSCLE

ALMAMÉDIA KFT. 1748848
Kozma u. 9-11., 1108 BUDAPEST **Tel:** 1/210-0435
Fax: 1/210-0436
Titles:
DÉLPESTI KISHEKKI

ALWAYS MARKETING KFT. 1742239
Nagy Lajos király útja 191., 1149 BUDAPEST
Tel: 20/555-7998 **Fax:** 1/460-0795
Titles:
UTAZZ VELÜNK MAGAZIN

ARANYPÉNZ LAP- ÉS KÖNYVK. ZRT. 1742174
Október 6. u. 7., 1051 BUDAPEST **Tel:** 1/266-5372 **Fax:** 1/266-6391
Titles:
BANK & TOZSDE

ARTAMONDÓ KFT. 1730351
Andrássy út 124., 1062 BUDAPEST **Tel:** 1/354-2350 **Fax:** 1/354-2359
Titles:
MAGYAR DEMOKRATA

ATZO KIADÓ KFT. 1679040
Obsitos tér 1., 1155 BUDAPEST **Tel:** 1/415-0318
Fax: 1/415-0318
Titles:
MODERN HÁZAK, LAKÁSOK

AUTO NEWS KIADÓ KFT. 1678398
Rottenbiller u. 31., 1077 BUDAPEST **Tel:** 1/322-0421 **Fax:** 1/322-0421
Titles:
AZ AUTÓ

AXEL SPRINGER-BUDAPEST KFT 1677823
Városmajor u. 11., 1122 BUDAPEST **Tel:** 1/488-5700 **Fax:** 1/488-5775
Titles:
100XSZÉP
AUTO BILD MAGYARORSZÁG
AUTÓ MOTOR
FANNY
GLAMOUR
GYÖNGY
HÖLGYVILÁG
KISKEGYED
KISKEGYED KONYHÁJA
LAKÁSKULTÚRA
POPCORN

AXEL SPRINGER-MAGYARORSZÁG KFT 1677798
Városmajor u. 11., 1122 BUDAPEST **Tel:** 1/488-5726 **Fax:** 1/488-5719
Titles:
24 ÓRA
BÉKÉS MEGYEI HÍRLAP
HEVES MEGYEI HÍRLAP
PETOFI NÉPE
SOMOGYI HÍRLAP
TOLNAI NÉPÚJSÁG
ÚJ DUNÁNTÚLI NAPLÓ
ÚJ NÉPLAP

AXEL SPRINGER-MO. KFT.-TOLNA M 1678519
Fo u. 34-36., 1011 BUDAPEST **Tel:** 1/202-1092
Fax: 1/202-1534
Titles:
FORRÓ DRÓT

AZ EZREDVÉG ALAPÍTVÁNY 1678508
Kupeczky u. 8., 1025 BUDAPEST **Tel:** 1/326-5759
Titles:
EZREDVÉG

BABA MAGAZIN KIADÓI KFT. 1678390
Váci út 168/B, 1138 BUDAPEST **Tel:** 1/238-0386
Fax: 1/450-1069
Titles:
ANYÁK LAPJA
BABA MAGAZIN
BABA PATIKA

BABAINFO BT. 1742264
Bolygó u. 1/B, 2000 SZENTENDRE **Tel:** 26/309-126 **Fax:** 26/500-291
Titles:
BABAINFO MAGAZIN

BALATON MASTERS BT. 1748908
Véghely D. u. 1., 8220 BALATONALMÁDI **Tel:** 70/383-6770
Titles:
FITTTIPP 2009

BALATONPRESS KIADÓ KFT. 1730689
Mikszáth u. 19/B, 8600 SIÓFOK **Tel:** 84/313-656
Fax: 84/313-656
Titles:
BALATONI TIPP NYÁRI MAGAZIN

BANACH KIADÓ KFT. 1679163
Palotás u. 1., 1152 BUDAPEST **Tel:** 1/271-1118
Fax: 1/271-1119
Titles:
VIDEOPRAKTIKA

BELÜGYI ÉS RENDV. DOLG. SZAKSZ 1679141
Nádor u. 4., 1051 BUDAPEST **Tel:** 1/237-4347
Fax: 1/237-4349
Titles:
T-MA

BÉTA PRESS STÚDIÓ KFT. 1679422
Kápolna u. 9., 6000 KECSKEMÉT **Tel:** 76/509-424
Fax: 76/509-426
Titles:
3 DIMENZIÓ
ZÖLD DIMENZIÓ

BIKEMAG LAPKIADÓ KFT. 1765523
Varrógépgyár 8-10., 1211 BUDAPEST **Tel:** 70/336-9896 **Fax:** 22/596-069
Titles:
BIKEMAG

BIO-COM KFT. 1742265
Folyondár u. 15/A fszt. 5., 1037 BUDAPEST
Tel: 1/240-9549 **Fax:** 1/240-9549
Titles:
BIO INFO

BORBARÁT-LAP KFT. 1730641
Horvát u. 14-24. V.em, 1027 BUDAPEST **Tel:** 24/460-833 **Fax:** 24/460-833
Titles:
BORBARÁT

BTBW KFT. 1678434
Gyarmat u. 53/B, 1145 BUDAPEST **Tel:** 1/250-5469 **Fax:** 1/250-5469
Titles:
BORN TO BE WILD

BTH BUDAPESTI TURISZT. KHT. 1679482
Március 15 tér. 7, 1056 BUDAPEST **Tel:** 1/266-5853 **Fax:** 1/338-4293
Titles:
BUDAPEST GUIDE

BUDAPEST MENÜ BT. 1679221
Lechner Ödön fasor 1-2. A/818., 1095 BUDAPEST **Tel:** 1/555-2746
Titles:
BUDAPEST MENÜ

Hungary

BURDA MAGYARORSZÁG KFT. 1730917
Naphegy tér 8., 1016 BUDAPEST **Tel:** 1/267-0584 **Fax:** 1/267-0584
Titles:
BURDA

BUSINESS MEDIA MAGYARORSZÁG 1742080
Neumann János u. 1., 2040 BUDAÖRS **Tel:** 23/422-455 **Fax:** 23/422-383
Titles:
ALAPRAJZ
CSALÁDI HÁZ MAGAZIN
ÖTLETTÁR

BZT MEDIA KFT. 1742133
Kunigunda útja 18., 1037 BUDAPEST **Tel:** 1/453-0752 **Fax:** 1/240-7583
Titles:
BUDAPESTER ZEITUNG

CADVILÁG LAPKIADÓ KFT. 1678974
Koszeg u. 4., 1141 BUDAPEST **Tel:** 20/466-2014 **Fax:** 1/273-3411
Titles:
CADVILÁG

CE ÜZLETI MÉDIA KFT. 1730955
Felsoerdosor u. 12-14., 1068 BUDAPEST **Tel:** 1/769-1446 **Fax:** 1/785-6968
Titles:
ENTREPRENEUR - AZ ÜZLETTÁRS

CELSUS KFT. 1678583
Margit krt. 56. I/4., 1027 BUDAPEST **Tel:** 1/225-2012
Titles:
IDEÁL

CENTRALPRESS HUNGARY KFT. 1742198
József u. 26-28., 1084 BUDAPEST **Tel:** 1/327-0188 **Fax:** 1/266-8190
Titles:
CAFÉ & BAR
VENDÉGLÁTÁS

CHASECAR KFT. 1742170
Angyali sziget 127., 2300 RÁCKEVE **Tel:** 70/314-5544 **Fax:** 70/903-1611
Titles:
AMS

COMPLEX KIADÓ KFT. 1730448
Prielle Kornélia u. 21-35., 1117 BUDAPEST **Tel:** 40/464-565 **Fax:** 1/464-5637
Titles:
ADÓ SZAKLAP
ADÓ TB-KALAUZ
ADÓ-KÓDEX

CRIER MÉDIA MAGYARORSZÁG KFT. 1678842
Rákospatak u. 70-72., 1142 BUDAPEST **Tel:** 1/467-0618 **Fax:** 1/384-5307
Titles:
PROGRESSZÍV MAGAZIN

DEBRECEN ÖNK.LAPKIADÓ KFT 1742158
Simonffy u. 2/A, 4025 DEBRECEN **Tel:** 52/581-818 **Fax:** 52/581-803
Titles:
DEBRECEN

DEIS LAP- ÉS KÖNYVKIADÓ 1678643
Pf. 40, 2730 ALBERTIRSA **Tel:** 30/307-8439
Titles:
PIHENJ ITTHON

DINGÓ LAPKIADÓ KFT. 1730533
Budafoki út 93/C I/4., 1117 BUDAPEST **Tel:** 1/386-0223 **Fax:** 1/386-0223
Titles:
NEMZETKÖZI KUTYA MAGAZIN

DIREX MÉDIA KFT. 1678474
Fehér út 10. (FMV) 8-as épület, 1106 BUDAPEST **Tel:** 1/260-1148 **Fax:** 1/260-4869
Titles:
ÉKSZER MAGAZIN
ÓRA MAGAZIN

DÓM BT. 1677881
Rákóczi út 9., 1088 BUDAPEST **Tel:** 1/266-0025 **Fax:** 1/266-0025
Titles:
KÖNYVES EXTRA

DUAX KFT. 1677663
Bécsi út 60., 1034 BUDAPEST **Tel:** 70/320-3051
Titles:
DIPLOMACY & TRADE

ECOVIT VÁLLALKOZÁSSZERV. KFT. 1678630
Homokos dulo 1., 1031 BUDAPEST **Tel:** 1/430-0571 **Fax:** 1/240-5670
Titles:
A CONTROLLER

EFFEKT HUNGARY SZ. KIADÓ KFT. 1758693
Tamási Áron u. 18/B., 1124 BUDAPEST **Tel:** 20/663-4814
Titles:
NATURE KÖRNYEZETVÉDELMI MAGAZIN
SAFETY & SECURITY

ENERGETIKAI KIADÓ KHT. 1679244
Köztársaság tér 7., 1081 BUDAPEST **Tel:** 1/299-0267 **Fax:** 1/299-0268
Titles:
ENERGIAFOGYASZTÓK LAPJA

ENERGIAGAZD. TUD. EGYESÜLET 1679010
Fo u. 68. V/525., 1027 BUDAPEST **Tel:** 1/353-2751 **Fax:** 1/353-3894
Titles:
ENERGIAGAZDÁLKODÁS

ÉPÍTÉSÜGYI TÁJÉKOZTATÁSI KP. 1679017
Hársfa u. 21., 1074 BUDAPEST **Tel:** 1/342-7734 **Fax:** 1/342-7337
Titles:
ÉPÍTŐVILÁG

E-PRESS REKLÁMIRODA 1678983
Czobor u. 82., 1147 BUDAPEST **Tel:** 1/363-1122
Titles:
DRINFO EGÉSZSÉGMAGAZIN

ÉPÜLETGÉPÉSZET KIADÓ KFT. 1678668
Fo u. 68. I/133., 1027 BUDAPEST **Tel:** 1/201-2562 **Fax:** 1/201-2562
Titles:
MAGYAR ÉPÜLETGÉPÉSZET

ES EXKLUZÍV SZOLGÁLTATÓ KFT. 1758673
Pannónia u. 19., 1136 BUDAPEST **Tel:** 1/359-1826 **Fax:** 1/359-1826
Titles:
HOTELEPROGRAM

ESOTERA KFT. 1678897
Kapás u. 26-44. D. lph. IV/11., 1027 BUDAPEST **Tel:** 1/315-1725 **Fax:** 1/315-1725
Titles:
TERMÉSZETGYÓGYÁSZ MAGAZIN

EST MÉDIA GROUP 1765500
Lajos u. 74-76., 1036 BUDAPEST **Tel:** 1/436-5000 **Fax:** 1/436-5001
Titles:
FIDELIO EST
PESTI EST

ESTON INTERNATIONAL ING. ZRT. 1730639
Lövoház u. 39., 1024 BUDAPEST **Tel:** 1/877-1000 **Fax:** 1/877-1001
Titles:
PROPERTY WATCH

ESZENCIA-PRESS KFT. 1765593
Kupeczky u. 9., 1025 BUDAPEST **Tel:** 1/346-0159 **Fax:** 1/346-0160
Titles:
ESZENCIA

ÉTEK PRESS KFT. 1678675
Szentkirályi u. 1/B, 1088 BUDAPEST **Tel:** 1/267-0505 **Fax:** 1/267-0303
Titles:
MAGYAR KONYHA

EUROMÉDIA BT. 1677981
Szugló u. 81-85., 1141 BUDAPEST **Tel:** 1/460-4880 **Fax:** 1/460-4882
Titles:
BLIKK NOK
BRAVO
BRAVO GIRL!
HOT! MAGAZIN
TINA

EUROMÉDIA KIADÓ KFT. 1730550
Diósárok 26/B, 1125 BUDAPEST **Tel:** 20/915-7099 **Fax:** 1/209-2303
Titles:
SIKERES SPORTHORGÁSZ

EX-BB KIADÓI KFT. 1679565
Teréz krt. 38., 1066 BUDAPEST **Tel:** 1/428-2250 **Fax:** 1/428-2250
Titles:
BASTEI ROMANTIK REGÉNYFÜZETEK

THE EXPLORER GROUP KFT. 1742234
Kelenhegyi út 29/A, 1118 BUDAPEST **Tel:** 1/319-1539 **Fax:** 1/279-0253
Titles:
THE EXPLORER MAGAZIN

EXPRESSZ MAGYARORSZÁG ZRT. 1730328
Babér u. 7., 1131 BUDAPEST **Tel:** 1/479-7919 **Fax:** 1/479-7916
Titles:
EXPRESSZ AUTÓ-MOTOR

EXTRA DÉL-INFÓ SZERKESZTOSÉGE 1742244
Játék u. 8., 1221 BUDAPEST **Tel:** 1/229-0438 **Fax:** 1/229-0438
Titles:
ESKÜVO ELOTT-ESKÜVO UTÁN
OKTATÁSI MELLÉKLET

EZO TÉR KFT. 1748917
Ritsmann Pál u. 25., 2051 BIATORBÁGY **Tel:** 70/210-9833
Titles:
EZO TÉR MAGAZIN

FEJÉR MEGYEI KIK 1678530
Hosszúsétatér 4-6., 8000 SZÉKESFEHÉRVÁR **Tel:** 22/510-310 **Fax:** 22/510-312
Titles:
GAZDASÁGI KALAUZ

GABREX KFT. 1742167
Donáti u. 69., 1015 BUDAPEST **Tel:** 30/294-0063 **Fax:** 1/325-7414
Titles:
A CIPO

GALENUS GYÓGYSZERÉSZETI KFT. 1678536
Dózsa György út 19., 1146 BUDAPEST **Tel:** 1/467-8060 **Fax:** 1/363-9223
Titles:
GYÓGYSZERÉSZI HÍRLAP
PATIKA MAGAZIN

GENERÁLMED-PRESS KFT. 1748886
Görgey u. 40., 1041 BUDAPEST **Tel:** 1/389-2595 **Fax:** 1/389-2595
Titles:
MEDICUS UNIVERSALIS

GEOMÉDIA KIADÓI ZRT. 1730196
Lajos u. 48-66. B lph. II. em., 1036 BUDAPEST **Tel:** 1/489-8846 **Fax:** 1/430-1536
Titles:
AMELIE
EXTRA FRIZURA
HORIZON
SZABAD FÖLD
VIDÉK ÍZE

GEOPRESS ZRT. 1742138
Egyetem tér 5., 1053 BUDAPEST **Tel:** 1/318-5001 **Fax:** 1/318-5001
Titles:
PESTI MUSOR

GÉPIPARI TUDOMÁNYOS EGYESÜLET 1678535
Fo u. 68., 1027 BUDAPEST **Tel:** 1/202-0656 **Fax:** 1/202-0252
Titles:
GÉPGYÁRTÁS
GÉPIPAR
MUANYAG ÉS GUMI

G-MENTOR KIADÓ KFT. 1679160
Szobránc köz 6., 1143 BUDAPEST **Tel:** 1/210-8345 **Fax:** 1/210-8356
Titles:
ITTHON OTTHON VAN

GONZO MÉDIA SZOLGÁLTATÓ KFT. 1730508
Kapisztrán u. 8., 1192 BUDAPEST **Tel:** 1/260-2449 **Fax:** 1/260-2449
Titles:
KISPESTI MAGAZIN

G-PUBLISHING KFT. 1679563
Falk Miksa u. 3., 1055 BUDAPEST **Tel:** 1/783-4486 **Fax:** 1/783-4486
Titles:
NAPI ÁSZ

G.T. & Z.A. V.E.R.L.A.G. BT. 1678754
Pf. 23, 2473 VÁL **Tel:** 30/962-6310 **Fax:** 22/353-406
Titles:
MOTORSPORT MAGYARORSZÁGON

GUSTO PRODUCTION MO. KFT. 1730486
Kapy u. 44., 1025 BUDAPEST **Tel:** 1/200-4545 **Fax:** 1/200-4971
Titles:
GUSTO

HAMILTON PROJECT KFT. 1765521
Budapesti út 87/A, 2040 BUDAÖRS **Tel:** 30/302-0545
Titles:
AUTÓTESZT
ROLLING TONS

HAMU ÉS GYÉMÁNT KFT. 1678747
Pálya u. 9., 1012 BUDAPEST **Tel:** 1/487-5200 **Fax:** 1/487-5203
Titles:
DECANTER MAGAZIN
HAMU ÉS GYÉMÁNT
INTERCITY MAGAZIN
STÍLUS & LENDÜLET MAGAZIN
VOLKSWAGEN MAGAZIN
WAN2 MAGAZIN

HASZON LAPKIADÓ KFT. 1678553
Bécsi út 57-59., 1036 BUDAPEST **Tel:** 1/353-0575 **Fax:** 1/269-2051
Titles:
HASZON MAGAZIN

HEALTH AND BEAUTY MEDIA KFT. 1678420
Naphegy tér 8., 1016 BUDAPEST **Tel:** 1/457-0067 **Fax:** 1/201-3248
Titles:
BEAUTY FORUM
HAJ ÉS STÍLUS

HEARST SANOMA BUDAPEST 1792570
Montevideo u. 9, 1037 BUDAPEST **Tel:** 1 4373947 **Fax:** 1 4371180
Titles:
ELLE

HEILING MÉDIA KFT. 1678480
Erzsébet királyné útja 125., 1142 BUDAPEST **Tel:** 1/231-4040
Titles:
ELEKTRONET

HEIM PÁL GYERMEKKÓRHÁZ 1678541
Üllői út 86., 1089 BUDAPEST **Tel:** 1/459-9142 **Fax:** 1/459-9143
Titles:
GYÓGYHÍREK

HEINEKEN HUNGÁRIA SÖRGY.ZRT. 1758690
Vörösmarty tér 1., 1051 BUDAPEST **Tel:** 1/429-9094 **Fax:** 99/516-111
Titles:
SÖRLEVÉL

HEKUS RENDORSÉGI KIADÓ KFT. 1765510
József nádor tér 9., 1051 BUDAPEST **Tel:** 1/266-7572 **Fax:** 1/266-7574
Titles:
HEKUS BUNÜGYI MAGAZIN

HÍRKÖZLÉSI ÉS INFORM. TUD. EGY 1678564
Kossuth tér 6-8., 1055 BUDAPEST **Tel:** 1/353-1027
Titles:
HÍRADÁSTECHNIKA

HITELEZÉS-KOCKÁZATK. ÚJSÁG KFT 1730958
Tel: 70/595-0123
Titles:
HITELEZÉS-KOCKÁZATKEZELÉS ÚJSÁG

HORIZONT MÉDIA KFT. 1678372
Katona J. u. 6., 6400 KISKUNHALAS **Tel:** 77/529-593 **Fax:** 77/529-593
Titles:
AGRÁRÁGAZAT

HOTELINFO KFT. 1679503
Váci u. 78-80., 1056 BUDAPEST **Tel:** 1/266-3741 **Fax:** 1/267-0896
Titles:
HUNGARY INFO

HVG KIADÓI ZRT. 1730347
Montevideo u. 14., 1037 BUDAPEST **Tel:** 1/436-2020 **Fax:** 1/436-2089
Titles:
HVG

HVG PRESS KFT. 1730580
Montevideo u. 14., 1037 BUDAPEST **Tel:** 1/336-2472 **Fax:** 1/436-2087
Titles:
MAI PIAC

HYDROCONSULT KFT. 1758686
Sas u. 25., 1051 BUDAPEST **Tel:** 1/353-3241 **Fax:** 1/473-0055
Titles:
VÍZMU PANORÁMA

IDG HUNGARY KFT. 1730485
Madách út 13-14. A/4, 1075 BUDAPEST **Tel:** 1/577-4300 **Fax:** 1/266-4343
Titles:
COMPUTERWORLD
GAMESTAR
PC WORLD

II. KERÜLETI ÖNKORMÁNYZAT 1678076
Bimbó út 1., 1022 BUDAPEST **Tel:** 1/316-3410 **Fax:** 1/316-3410
Titles:
BUDAI POLGÁR

IMMOPRESS KIADÓ KFT. 1678024
Károly krt. 9., 1075 BUDAPEST **Tel:** 1/342-8971 **Fax:** 1/352-7143
Titles:
INGATLAN ÉS BEFEKTETÉS

IMN HUNGARY KFT. 1748869
Bécsi út 57-61. I/11., 1136 BUDAPEST **Tel:** 1/453-3310 **Fax:** 1/453-3313
Titles:
SPORT AUTO

IMPRESS-REGIO LAPKIADÓ KFT. 1678077
Szentendrei út 32., 1035 BUDAPEST **Tel:** 1/235-0417 **Fax:** 1/430-1250
Titles:
ÓBUDA

INFO-PROD KFT. 1679499
Nyugati tér. 8, 1056 BUDAPEST **Tel:** 1/349-3347 **Fax:** 1/339-8638
Titles:
MUANYAG- ÉS GUMIIPARI ÉVKÖNYV

INFORM MÉDIA KFT. 1677751
Zsolcai kapu 3., 3526 MISKOLC **Tel:** 46/502-900 **Fax:** 46/501-260
Titles:
ÉSZAK-MAGYARORSZÁG
FUTÁR
HAJDÚ-BIHARI NAPLÓ
KELET-MAGYARORSZÁG
TV PLUSZ MAGAZIN

INFORMATIKA KIADÓI BT. 1677742
Péterfai út 1/H Pf. 504, 8800 NAGYKANIZSA **Tel:** 30/969-3115 **Fax:** 93/326-905
Titles:
KANIZSA MAGAZIN

INTERCOM 1730472
Perc u. 8., 1036 BUDAPEST **Tel:** 1/467-1400 **Fax:** 1/467-4242
Titles:
DVD ÚJDONSÁGOK

IRODALOM KFT. 1677840
Rezso tér 15., 1089 BUDAPEST **Tel:** 1/210-5149 **Fax:** 1/303-9241
Titles:
ÉLET ÉS IRODALOM

IT-BUSINESS PUBLISHING KFT. 1748839
Rákóczi út 28., 1072 BUDAPEST **Tel:** 1/577-7970 **Fax:** 1/577-7995
Titles:
ITBUSINESS

JUPITER KIADÓ ÉS TERJESZTO KFT 1742178
Lehel u. 5. II/25., 1062 BUDAPEST **Tel:** 1/349-5933 **Fax:** 1/349-5933
Titles:
ELIXÍR MAGAZIN

KAFI PRESS BT. 1678061
Csokonai u. 3. fszt. 1., 7100 SZEKSZÁRD **Tel:** 74/511-709 **Fax:** 74/414-853
Titles:
TOLNA MEGYEI KRÓNIKA

KALANGYA KKT. 1678363
Róna u. 120-122., 1149 BUDAPEST **Tel:** 1/469-6480 **Fax:** 1/469-6476
Titles:
A MI OTTHONUNK

KÉPMÁS 2002 KFT. 1730505
Villányi út 5-7., 1114 BUDAPEST **Tel:** 1/365-1414 **Fax:** 1/365-1415
Titles:
KÉPMÁS CSALÁDMAGAZIN

KÉT ZSIRÁF KFT. 1742166
Lajos u. 42., 1036 BUDAPEST **Tel:** 1/318-4246 **Fax:** 1/318-4246
Titles:
ZSIRÁF DIÁKMAGAZIN

KON-NEXT KIADÓ 1679440
Ágoston u. 18., 1032 BUDAPEST **Tel:** 70/317-4380 **Fax:** 1/437-0166
Titles:
ÉPÍTOGÉPEK, ÉPÍTÉSGÉPESÍTÉS

KÖRNYEZETKULTÚRA KIADÓI KFT. 1678869
Ferenc tér 13. II/8., 1094 BUDAPEST **Tel:** 1/456-8050 **Fax:** 1/218-0254
Titles:
SZÉPLAK

KRÓNIKÁS KIADÓ 1730511
Nagybányai út 74., 1025 BUDAPEST **Tel:** 30/992-6032 **Fax:** 1/394-2891
Titles:
KÖZÉLETI GAZDASÁGI KRÓNIKA

KULT MÉDIA 2000 BT. 1730962
Fekete u. 3., 5100 JÁSZBERÉNY **Tel:** 20/913-4079
Titles:
KIS-VÁROS-KÉP MAGAZIN

LAPCOM KFT. 1677786
Szabadkai út 20., 6729 SZEGED **Tel:** 62/567-888 **Fax:** 62/567-881
Titles:
DÉLMAGYARORSZÁG
KISALFÖLD

LAPCOM KFT. DÉLMAGYARORSZÁG 1678153
Szabadkai út 20., 6720 SZEGED **Tel:** 62/567-888 **Fax:** 62/567-881
Titles:
SZEGEDI TÜKÖR

M-12/B KFT. 1678942
Róbert Károly krt. 90., 1134 BUDAPEST **Tel:** 1/450-0868 **Fax:** 1/236-0899
Titles:
VILLANYSZERELOK LAPJA

MAGAZIN MÉDIA PRESS KFT. 1748857
Diós árok 5., 1125 BUDAPEST **Tel:** 1/488-6060 **Fax:** 1/488-6061
Titles:
B.O.S.S. MAGAZIN
LABINFÓ

MAGYAR ÁLLATORVOSI KAMARA 1679206
István u. 2., 1078 BUDAPEST **Tel:** 1/478-4272 **Fax:** 1/478-4272
Titles:
KAMARAI ÁLLATORVOS

MAGYAR ÁPOLÁSI EGYESÜLET 1679210
Pf. 190, 1431 BUDAPEST **Tel:** 1/266-5935 **Fax:** 1/266-5935
Titles:
ÁPOLÁSÜGY

MAGYAR AUTÓKLUB 1678402
Keveháza u. 1-3., 1119 BUDAPEST **Tel:** 1/357-6110 **Fax:** 1/357-6120
Titles:
AUTÓSÉLET

MAGYAR EBTENYÉSZTOK ORSZ. EGY. 1730445
Tétényi út 128/B-130., 1116 BUDAPEST **Tel:** 70/457-2761 **Fax:** 1/208-2305
Titles:
A KUTYA

MAGYAR EGÉSZSÉGÜGYI SZAK. K. 1731038
Üllői út 82., 1082 BUDAPEST **Tel:** 1/323-2070 **Fax:** 1/323-2079
Titles:
HIVATÁSUNK

MAGYAR ELEKTROTECHNIKAI EGYES. 1678483
Kossuth Lajos tér 6-8., 1055 BUDAPEST **Tel:** 1/353-1108 **Fax:** 1/353-4069
Titles:
ELEKTROTECHNIKA

MAGYAR ÉPÍTOIPARI KIADÓ KFT. 1730521
Fo u. 68., 1027 BUDAPEST **Tel:** 1/201-8416 **Fax:** 1/201-8416
Titles:
MAGYAR ÉPÍTOIPAR

MAGYAR HÍRLAP KIADÓI KFT. 1730330
Thököly út 105-107., 1145 BUDAPEST **Tel:** 1/260-8404 **Fax:** 1/260-8404
Titles:
MAGYAR HÍRLAP

MAGYAR KÉMIKUSOK EGYESÜLETE 1678676
Fo u. 68. I/105., 1027 BUDAPEST **Tel:** 1/201-6883 **Fax:** 1/201-8056
Titles:
MAGYAR KÉMIKUSOK LAPJA

MAGYAR KÖZLEKEDÉSI KIADÓ KFT. 1677900
Klapka u. 6., 1134 BUDAPEST **Tel:** 1/349-2574 **Fax:** 1/210-5862
Titles:
NAVIGÁTOR

MAGYAR MEDIPRINT SZAKKIADÓ KFT 1678677
Balassi Bálint u. 7., 1055 BUDAPEST **Tel:** 1/301-3864 **Fax:** 1/301-3814
Titles:
ELEKTROINSTALLATEUR
KÓRHÁZ
KÖRNYEZETVÉDELEM
LG PHX
MAGYAR ÉPÍTÉSTECHNIKA
MAGYAR FOGORVOS
MAGYAR INSTALLATEUR
MAGYAR ORVOS

MAGYAR MEZOGAZDASÁG KFT. 1730349
Tel: 30/231-6169
Titles:
BORÁSZATI FÜZETEK
ERDOGAZDASÁG ÉS FAIPAR
KERTBARÁT MAGAZIN
KERTÉSZET ÉS SZOLÉSZET
KERTI KALENDÁRIUM
KISTERMELOK LAPJA
MAGYAR ÁLLATORVOSOK LAPJA
MAGYAR ÁLLATTENYÉSZTOK LAPJA
MAGYAR MEZOGAZDASÁG
MÉHÉSZET

MAGYAR NOORVOS TÁRSASÁG 1730605
Podmaniczky u. 111., 1062 BUDAPEST **Tel:** 1/475-2568 **Fax:** 1/475-2568
Titles:
MAGYAR NOORVOSOK LAPJA

MAGYAR ORVOSTÁRS. ÉS EGYES. SZ 1679349
Nádor u. 36., 1051 BUDAPEST **Tel:** 1/312-3807 **Fax:** 1/383-7918
Titles:
MOTESZ MAGAZIN

MAGYAR TEJIPARI EGYESÜLÉS 1679144
Bartók Béla út 152/C I. em., 1115 BUDAPEST **Tel:** 1/204-5278 **Fax:** 1/204-5278
Titles:
TEJIPARI HÍRLAP

MAGYARNARANCS.HU KFT. 1677898
Naphegy tér 8., 1016 BUDAPEST **Tel:** 1/441-9000/2400 **Fax:** 1/356-9691
Titles:
MAGYAR NARANCS

MAMMUT ZRT. 1730665
Ribáry u. 1/B, 1022 BUDAPEST **Tel:** 1/275-5051 **Fax:** 1/275-5051
Titles:
MAMMUT MAGAZIN

MAP MAGAZINE KIADÓ KFT. 1678829
Hajógyári sziget 213., 1033 BUDAPEST **Tel:** 1/505-0872 **Fax:** 1/505-0806
Titles:
PLAYBOY

MARATON LAPCSOPORT KFT. 1677901
Házgyári út 12., 8200 VESZPRÉM **Tel:** 88/541-763 **Fax:** 88/541-688
Titles:
DUNAÚJVÁROSI MARATON
FEHÉRVÁRI 7 NAP
FEHÉRVÁRI 7 NAP PLUSSZ
VESZPRÉMI 7 NAP PLUSSZ

MARECO INGATLAN ZRT. 1765592
Bajcsy-Zsilinszky út 12., 1051 BUDAPEST **Tel:** 1/267-0161 **Fax:** 1/267-0253
Titles:
INGATLANRIPORT

MARQUARD MEDIA MO. KFT. 1678453
Hajógyári sziget 213., 1033 BUDAPEST **Tel:** 1/505-0800 **Fax:** 1/505-0806
Titles:
CKM
FITT MAMA
JOY
JOY CELEBRITY
SHAPE

MARYON BT. 1730471
Boróka u. 7., 2094 NAGYKOVÁCSI **Tel:** 26/355-106 **Fax:** 26/355-106
Titles:
BELVÁROSI TIMES DOWNTOWN

MÁV ZRT. 1730390
Andrássy út 73-75., 1062 BUDAPEST **Tel:** 1/511-3801 **Fax:** 1/511-4931
Titles:
VASUTAS MAGAZIN

MÉDIA CREDIT BT. 1748937
Miklós tér 1., 1033 BUDAPEST **Tel:** 20/661-1252 **Fax:** 1/242-4339
Titles:
ITTHON

MÉDIAHUB KFT. 1748855
Lehel út 61., 1135 BUDAPEST **Fax:** 1/577-2018
Titles:
4X4 - QUAD FUN MAGAZIN

MÉTE KIADÓ 1678741
Fo u. 68., 1027 BUDAPEST **Tel:** 1/214-6691 **Fax:** 1/214-6692
Titles:
ÁSVÁNYVÍZ, ÜDÍTOITAL, GYÜMÖLCSLÉ
CUKORIPAR
ÉDESIPAR
ÉLELMEZÉSI IPAR
A HÚS
KONZERVÚJSÁG
OLAJ, SZAPPAN, KOZMETIKA
SÜTOIPAROSOK, PÉKEK
TEJGAZDASÁG

MEZOHÍR MÉDIA KFT. 1730527
Gyenes tér 1., 6000 KECSKEMÉT **Tel:** 30/943-9158
Titles:
MEZOHÍR

MGL KIADÓI KFT. 1679617
Hársfa u. 21., 1074 BUDAPEST **Tel:** 1/413-6646 **Fax:** 1/413-6647
Titles:
MAGYAR GAZDASÁGI MAGAZIN

MOHOSZ 1678674
Ó utca 3., 1066 BUDAPEST **Tel:** 1/311-3232 **Fax:** 1/311-3232
Titles:
MAGYAR HORGÁSZ

MOON AND SHARK HUNGARY KFT. 1765572
Csantavér u. 9. I/4., 1146 BUDAPEST **Tel:** 23/444-070 **Fax:** 23/444-069
Titles:
CÉGAUTÓ MAGAZIN

MOTOR-PRESSE BUDAPEST KFT. 1677822
Nagyszolos u. 11-15., 1113 BUDAPEST **Tel:** 1/577-2600 **Fax:** 1/577-2690
Titles:
AUTÓMAGAZIN
AUTÓPIAC
CHIP
MM MUSZAKI MAGAZIN
MOTORREVÜ
PC GURU

MTG METRO GRATIS KFT. 1677805
Tüzér u. 39-41., 1134 BUDAPEST **Tel:** 1/431-6400 **Fax:** 1/431-6465
Titles:
METROPOL

MYNYDD GYNIDR KFT. 1730453
Lehel út 61., 1135 BUDAPEST **Tel:** 1/452-7830 **Fax:** 1/452-7830
Titles:
ALMALAP

NAGY-KÁR BT. 1679441
Kismartoni u. 55., 2040 BUDAÖRS-KAMARAERDO **Tel:** 23/444-438 **Fax:** 23/444-437
Titles:
ESKÜVOI DIVAT

NAPI GAZDASÁG KIADÓ KFT. 1677806
Csata u. 32., 1135 BUDAPEST **Tel:** 1/450-9600 **Fax:** 1/450-9601
Titles:
NAPI GAZDASÁG

NEMZET LAP- ÉS KÖNYVKIADÓ KFT. 1730329
Wesselényi u. 8., 1075 BUDAPEST **Tel:** 1/342-6164 **Fax:** 1/342-6132
Titles:
MAGYAR NEMZET

NEMZETKÖZI TÜKÖR KFT. 1748867
Nádor u. 29/B, 4400 NYÍREGYHÁZA **Tel:** 42/950-142 **Fax:** 42/406-913
Titles:
ÜZLETI KALAUZ

NÉPSZAVA LAPKIADÓ KFT. 1765446
Könyvek K. krt. 76., 1087 BUDAPEST **Tel:** 1/477-9030 **Fax:** 1/477-9033
Titles:
NÉPSZAVA

NYOMDÁSZSZAKSZERVEZET 1730795
Benczúr u. 37. fszt. 1., 1068 BUDAPEST **Tel:** 1/266-0064 **Fax:** 1/266-0028
Titles:
TYPOGRAPHIA

OFFICINA '96 KIADÓ 1678742
Medve u. 34-40., 1027 BUDAPEST **Tel:** 1/225-0748 **Fax:** 1/212-0340
Titles:
NIMRÓD VADÁSZÚJSÁG

OFFLINE ACTION SPORT KFT. 1678801
Kassai u. 84., 1142 BUDAPEST **Tel:** 1/363-8099 **Fax:** 1/363-8099
Titles:
OFFLINE MAGAZIN

OTTHON TUDÓS KFT. 1730715
Dózsa Gy. út 32., 1071 BUDAPEST **Tel:** 1/343-1816 **Fax:** 1/413-7131
Titles:
OTTHON TUDÓS MAGAZIN

PANNON LAPOK TÁRSASÁGA 1677813
Vasmu u. 41. fszt. 6., 2400 DUNAÚJVÁROS **Tel:** 25/402-985 **Fax:** 25/402-986
Titles:
DUNAÚJVÁROSI HÍRLAP
FEJÉR MEGYEI HÍRLAP
NAPLÓ
VAS NÉPE
ZALAI HÍRLAP

PANNON LAPOK TÁRSASÁGA KFT. 1765502
Almádi u. 3., 8200 VESZPRÉM **Tel:** 88/579-443 **Fax:** 88/583-267
Titles:
RTV TIPP

PANORÁMA KFT. 1678547
Nagybátonyi u. 4., 1037 BUDAPEST **Tel:** 1/439-1319 **Fax:** 1/240-4386
Titles:
POLGÁRI OTTHON

PANORÁMA STÚDIÓ KFT. 1730490
Bartók Béla út 152. H. III. em, 1115 BUDAPEST **Tel:** 1/275-4187 **Fax:** 1/275-4187
Titles:
HAJÓ MAGAZIN

PAPÍR- ÉS NYOMDAIP. MUSZ. EGY. 1730603
Fo u. 68. IV/416., 1027 BUDAPEST **Tel:** 1/457-0633 **Fax:** 1/202-0256
Titles:
MAGYAR GRAFIKA
PAPÍRIPAR

PATIKA TÜKÖR LAPKIADÓ KFT. 1678818
Francia út 5. I/1., 1143 BUDAPEST **Tel:** 1/479-8020 **Fax:** 1/479-8029
Titles:
PATIKA TÜKÖR

PENTASYS KFT. 1679928
Eörsy Péter u. 25/A, 9024 GYOR **Tel:** 96/525-014 **Fax:** 96/525-015
Titles:
ÉLELMEZÉS

PIAC ÉS PROFIT KIADÓ KFT. 1677739
Dózsa György út 144., 1134 BUDAPEST **Tel:** 1/239-8400 **Fax:** 1/239-9595
Titles:
PIAC ÉS PROFIT

PLANET KFT. 1742197
Zichy Jeno u. 4., 1066 BUDAPEST **Tel:** 1/321-1939 **Fax:** 1/301-7049
Titles:
TTG HUNGARY

PMC CONSULTING KFT. 1742169
Böszörményi út 3/A, 1126 BUDAPEST **Tel:** 1/212-8182 **Fax:** 1/212-7951
Titles:
AQUA VÍZISPORT ÉS ÉLETMÓD MAGAZIN

POLGÁRMESTERI HIVATAL 1677654
Batthyány u. 1., 3525 MISKOLC **Tel:** 46/503-020 **Fax:** 46/344-657
Titles:
MISKOLC INFO

PRESS GT KFT. 1731020
Üteg u. 49., 1139 BUDAPEST **Tel:** 1/349-6135 **Fax:** 1/452-0270
Titles:
GYÓGYHÍR MAGAZIN

PRESSCOMP EGYÉNI VÁLLALKOZÁS 1758691
Buday László u. 5/B., 1024 BUDAPEST **Tel:** 20/950-4601 **Fax:** 70/908-5075
Titles:
MAGYARORSZÁGI BEDEKKER

PRÍMA KONYHA KFT. 1678835
József krt. 31/B, 1085 BUDAPEST **Tel:** 1/230-3051 **Fax:** 1/220-3760
Titles:
PRÍMA KONYHA MAGAZIN

PRIMUS NÉPSZABADSÁG MÉDIA-KÉPV 1677807
Bécsi út 122-124., 1034 BUDAPEST **Tel:** 1/436-4441 **Fax:** 1/250-1118
Titles:
NÉPSZABADSÁG

PRINTXBUDAVÁR ZRT. 1730304
Király u. 16., 1061 BUDAPEST **Tel:** 1/887-4848 **Fax:** 1/887-4849
Titles:
BUSINESS HUNGARY
DINING GUIDE
WHERE MAGAZIN

PRO ARTE ALAPÍTVÁNY 1730779
Borbástó u. 2., 4150 PÜSPÖKLADÁNY **Tel:** 54/451-214 **Fax:** 54/451-214
Titles:
MAGYAR TANTUSZ

PROFESSIONAL PUBLISHING KFT. 1742081
Montevideo u. 3/B, 1037 BUDAPEST **Tel:** 1/430-4544 **Fax:** 1/430-4549
Titles:
ÉLELMISZER
TURIZMUS TREND

PROMENADE PUBLISHING HOUSE KFT 1742202
Istenhegyi út 29., 1125 BUDAPEST **Tel:** 1/224-5450 **Fax:** 1/224-5457
Titles:
ORVOSOK LAPJA

QUALITY TRAINING STUDIO KFT. 1678979
Haller u. 40., 1096 BUDAPEST **Tel:** 1/476-1080 **Fax:** 1/476-1085
Titles:
CEO MAGAZIN

RÁDIÓVILÁG KFT. 1678571
Dagály u. 11/A I. emelet, 1138 BUDAPEST **Tel:** 1/239-4933 **Fax:** 1/239-4933/34
Titles:
RÁDIÓTECHNIKA

READER'S DIGEST KIADÓ KFT. 1742194
Népfürdo u. 22., 1138 BUDAPEST **Tel:** 1/66-61-730 **Fax:** 1/66-61-801
Titles:
READER'S DIGEST

REGIMENT MILITARIA KFT. 1730982
Kerepesi út 29/B, 1087 BUDAPEST **Tel:** 1/323-1359 **Fax:** 1/323-1360
Titles:
ARANYSAS

RINGIER KIADÓ KFT. 1677800
Szugló u. 81-85., 1141 BUDAPEST **Tel:** 1/460-2541 **Fax:** 1/460-2579
Titles:
BLIKK
NEMZETI SPORT

SALDO ZRT. 1730554
Mór u. 2-4., 1135 BUDAPEST **Tel:** 1/237-9843 **Fax:** 1/237-9841
Titles:
ADÓ ÉS ELLENORZÉSI ÉRTESÍTO

SPEKTRUM LAP- ÉS KÖNYVK. KFT. 1679123
Tel: 465-0248 **Fax:** 788-0379
Titles:
LAKÁSFELÚJÍTÁS

SPRINT KFT. 1678079
Újpesti rkp. 7. Fszt. 2., 1137 BUDAPEST **Tel:** 1/237-5060 **Fax:** 1/237-5069
Titles:
XIII. KERÜLETI HÍRNÖK

STARFISH MÉDIA CSOPORT 1748826
Teve u. 41., 1139 BUDAPEST **Tel:** 1/288-7070 **Fax:** 1/237-1209
Titles:
FÉSZEKRAKÓ MAGAZIN

STAR-JOURNAL KFT. 1678486
Lehel út 61., 1135 BUDAPEST **Tel:** 1/288-8560 **Fax:** 1/288-8570
Titles:
ELITE MAGAZIN

STENCIL KULTURÁLIS ALAPÍTVÁNY 1678423
Akadémia u. 1. fszt. 48-50., 1054 BUDAPEST **Tel:** 1/302-2912 **Fax:** 1/302-1271
Titles:
BESZÉLO

ST.PLUSZ KÖNYV- ÉS LAPK. KFT. 1677920
Angol u. 65-69., 1149 BUDAPEST **Tel:** 1/251-0000 **Fax:** 1/383-1773
Titles:
SPORT PLUSSZ

SYCAMORE MÉDIA KFT. 1748963
Karinthy Frigyes u. 17., 1117 BUDAPEST **Tel:** 1/789-4933 **Fax:** 1/788-0920
Titles:
SUPPLY CHAIN MONITOR

SYNERGON INFORMATIKA NYRT. 1730659
Baross u. 91-95., 1047 BUDAPEST **Tel:** 1/399-5500 **Fax:** 1/399-5599
Titles:
SZINERGIA

SZAKILAP MÉDIA KFT. 1748860
Péterfia u. 4., 4026 DEBRECEN **Tel:** 20/419-0016
Titles:
ÉPÍTOIPARI SZAKILAP

SZÉP HÁZAK KFT. 1679133
Dísz tér 16., 1014 BUDAPEST **Tel:** 1/202-0185 **Fax:** 1/375-0462
Titles:
SZÉP HÁZAK

SZERENCSEJÁTÉK ZRT. KOM. IG. 1748842
Csalogány u. 30-32., 1015 BUDAPEST **Tel:** 1/224-3424 **Fax:** 1/224-3403
Titles:
SZERENCSE MIX

SZILIKÁTIPARI TUD. EGYESÜLET 1742269
Fo u. 68., 1027 BUDAPEST **Tel:** 1/201-9360 **Fax:** 1/201-9360
Titles:
ÉPÍTOANYAG

SZUKITS KÖNYVKIADÓ KFT. 1742285
Szövo u. 31., 6726 SZEGED **Tel:** 62/425-787 **Fax:** 62/555-632
Titles:
EURÓPAI HÁZAK

TBW MEDIA KFT. 1679400
Ady E. út 147/D fszt. 2., 1221 BUDAPEST **Tel:** 30/645-0390 **Fax:** 26/371-399
Titles:
THEBUSINESSWOMAN

TELECOM PRESS BT. 1678892
Pacsirtamezo u. 32. II/29., 1036 BUDAPEST **Tel:** 1/237-0855 **Fax:** 1/237-0856
Titles:
TELECOM MAGAZIN

TELEGRÁF KIADÓ KFT. 1677815
Bécsi út 3-5., 1023 BUDAPEST **Tel:** 1/438-5570 **Fax:** 1/438-5575
Titles:
168 ÓRA

TERMÉKMIX MARKETING KFT. 1678896
Mogyoródi út 32., 1149 BUDAPEST **Tel:** 1/210-1830 **Fax:** 1/210-4150
Titles:
TERMÉKMIX

TERMÉSZETBÚVÁR ALAPÍTVÁNY 1679148
Október 6. u. 7., 1051 BUDAPEST **Tel:** 1/266-3036 **Fax:** 1/266-3343
Titles:
TERMÉSZETBÚVÁR

TERRA MÉDIA KFT. 1679457
Medve u. 24. V/1., 1027 BUDAPEST **Tel:** 1/355-0550 **Fax:** 1/225-0650
Titles:
MAGYAR ESKÜVO

THÉMA LAPKIADÓ KFT. 1730765
Fehérvári út 87., 1119 BUDAPEST **Tel:** 1/814-4755 **Fax:** 1/814-4756
Titles:
HELYI TÉMA - AGGLOMERÁCIÓ

TISZASZOLOS ÖNKORMÁNYZATA 1758703
Fo út 21., 5244 TISZASZOLOS **Tel:** 59/511-408 **Fax:** 59/511-408
Titles:
SZOLOSI HÍREK

TUDOMÁNY KIADÓ KFT. 1748880
Hermina út 57-59., 1146 BUDAPEST **Tel:** 1/273-2840 **Fax:** 1/384-5399
Titles:
DIABETES
DIABETOLOGIA HUNGARICA

TURIZMUS KFT. 1677811
Munkás u. 9., 1074 BUDAPEST **Tel:** 1/266-5853 **Fax:** 1/338-4293
Titles:
BUDAPEST PANORÁMA
NEXUS
TURIZMUS PANORÁMA

TYPON INTERNATIONAL 1678445
Pf. 327, 1437 BUDAPEST **Tel:** 1/390-4474 **Fax:** 1/390-4474
Titles:
CAMION TRUCK & BUS MAGAZIN
DETEKTOR PLUSZ

ÚJ MÉDIA KFT. 1742303
Csengery út 22., 8800 NAGYKANIZSA **Tel:** 20/423-0042 **Fax:** 93/516-984
Titles:
ÉPÍTO ÉLET
FUVARLEVÉL

ÚJ MUVÉSZET KIADÓ 1730566
Nagymezo u. 49., 1065 BUDAPEST **Tel:** 1/341-5598 **Fax:** 1/479-0232
Titles:
ÚJ MUVÉSZET

ÚJ PRAXIS KFT. 1678834
Krúdy Gyula u. 12. III/17., 1088 BUDAPEST **Tel:** 1/266-1540 **Fax:** 1/266-1540
Titles:
PRAXIS

VÁROS-KÉP KHT. 1730127
Szabadság tér 9., 4400 NYÍREGYHÁZA **Tel:** 42/411-826 **Fax:** 42/411-826
Titles:
MEGYEI NAPLÓ
NYÍREGYHÁZI NAPLÓ

VASÁRNAPI PLUSZ KFT. 1678406
Hajóállomás u. 1., 1095 BUDAPEST **Tel:** 1/323-3125 **Fax:** 1/323-3127
Titles:
AZ UTAZÓ

VH KIADÓ KFT. 1677993
Avar u. 8., 1016 BUDAPEST **Tel:** 1/319-2333 **Fax:** 1/319-2333
Titles:
VASÁRNAPI HÍREK

VIA PANNÓNIA REKLÁMÜGYN. KFT. 1679477
Tisza u. 6. V. em. 26., 1133 BUDAPEST **Tel:** 1/359-3103 **Fax:** 1/359-3103
Titles:
BABA-MAMA KALAUZ
GYERMEKVILÁG KALAUZ
GYÓGYVÍZ KALAUZ
SZÍNHÁZI KALAUZ

VIDEO-PART KFT. 1730814
Ferenc krt. 26., 1092 BUDAPEST **Tel:** 1/456-3006 **Fax:** 1/217-1288
Titles:
VIDEO-PART MAGAZIN

VIVA MÉDIA HOLDING 1677986
Szegedi út 37-39., 1135 BUDAPEST **Tel:** 1/288-7702 **Fax:** 1/288-7703
Titles:
PROGRAMME MAGAZINE
VÁM-ZOLL

V-TREND KFT. 1730748
Hajógyári sziget 132., 1033 BUDAPEST **Tel:** 1/392-7964 **Fax:** 1/392-7963
Titles:
BUDAPEST LIFE INGATLAN EXTRA
BUDAPEST LIFE MAGAZIN

V.U.M. KIADÓ ÉS SZOLG. KFT. 1730572
Nagy Lajos király útja 210/A, 1149 BUDAPEST **Tel:** 1/300-1251 **Fax:** 1/300-1254
Titles:
VILÁGJÁRÓ UTAZÁSI MAGAZIN

XI. KERÜLETI ÖNKORMÁNYZAT 1678084
Szent Gellért tér 1-3., 1111 BUDAPEST **Tel:** 1/372-0960 **Fax:** 1/372-0961
Titles:
ÚJBUDA

XIV. KERÜLETI ÖNKORMÁNYZAT 1678086
Pétervárad u. 7/B, 1145 BUDAPEST **Tel:** 1/467-2337 **Fax:** 1/467-2337
Titles:
ZUGLÓI LAPOK

X-MEDITOR LAPKIADÓ KFT. 1678404
Csaba u. 21., 9023 GYOR **Tel:** 96/618-074 **Fax:** 96/618-063
Titles:
AUTÓTECHNIKA JAVÍTÁS ÉS KERESKEDELEM
MAGYAR ASZTALOS ÉS FAIPAR

ZEMAK HUNGÁRIA KFT. 1748840
Falk Miksa u. 3., 1055 BUDAPEST **Tel:** 1/783-4486 **Fax:** 1/783-4486
Titles:
CINEMA MAGAZIN

ZÖLD ÚJSÁG ZRT. 1742129
Maros u. 19-21., 1122 BUDAPEST **Tel:** 1/489-1165 **Fax:** 1/489-1159
Titles:
PÉNZÜGYI ÉVKÖNYV
VILÁGGAZDASÁG

Iceland

ÀRVAKUR NF 621528
Hádegismóum 2, 110 REYKJAVÍK **Tel:** 569 11 00 **Fax:** 569 11 10
Email: netfrett@mbl.is
Web site: www.mbl.is
Titles:
MBL.IS
MORGUNBLADID

ATHYGLI 1745169
Sídumuli 1, 108 REYKJAVIK **Tel:** 515 52 00 **Fax:** 515 52 01
Web site: www.athygli.is
Titles:
AEGIR

BIRTINGUR 1200539
Lynghháls 5, IS-110 REYKJAVÍK **Tel:** 515 5500 **Fax:** 515 5599
Email: birtingur@birtingur.is
Web site: www.birtingur.is
Titles:
BLEIKT OG BLATT
GESTGJAFINN
NYTT LIF
SED OG HEYRT
VIKAN

DAGBLADID-VISIR UTGAFUFELAG 1744845
Krokhalsi 6, 110 REYKJAVÍK **Tel:** 512 70 00 **Fax:** 515 55 99
Email: ritstjorn@dv.is
Web site: www.dv.is
Titles:
DAGBLADID VISIR

FARMERS' ASSOCIATION OF ICELAND 1200533
Farmers House, PO Box 7080, IS-127 REYKJAVIK **Tel:** 563 0300 **Fax:** 562 3068
Email: bbl@bi.bondi.is
Web site: http://www.bondi.is
Titles:
THE FARMERS MAGAZINE
FREYR

Iceland

HEIMUR HF 694507
Borgartún 23, 105 REYKJAVÍK **Tel:** 512 75 75
Fax: 561 86 46
Email: heimur@heimur.is
Web site: www.heimur.is

Titles:
ATLANTICA
ICELAND REVIEW
TÖLVUHEIMUR
VEIDIMADURINN
WHAT'S ON IN REYKJAVÍK

Irish Republic

21ST CENTURY MEDIA LTD 1778540
19 Nassau Street, DUBLIN 2 **Tel:** 1 63 33 993
Fax: 16334353

Titles:
SOCIAL & PERSONAL
SOCIAL & PERSONAL LIVING
SOCIAL & PERSONAL WEDDINGS

ADVANCE PUBLICATIONS LTD 1778985
Acorn House, 38 St. Peter's Road, Phibsborough, DUBLIN 7 **Tel:** 1 86 86 640
Fax: 18686651

Titles:
PROJECT MANAGEMENT

ADVENTURE PUBLISHING LTD 1779151
20 Fitzwilliam Street Upper, DUBLIN 2 **Tel:** 1 643-2308

Titles:
OUTSIDER - IRELAND'S OUTDOOR MAGAZINE

AGE ACTION IRELAND 1781994
30-31 Lower Camden Street, DUBLIN 2
Tel: 1 4756989 **Fax:** 14756011

Titles:
AGEING MATTERS IN IRELAND

THE AGRICULTURAL TRUST 1781285
The Irish Farm Centre, Bluebell, DUBLIN 12
Tel: 1 42 76 400 **Fax:** 14276450

Titles:
THE IRISH CATHOLIC
IRISH FARMERS JOURNAL
THE IRISH FIELD

ALIVE GROUP 1781995
St. Mary's Priory, Tallaght, DUBLIN 24
Tel: 1 40 48 187 **Fax:** 14596784

Titles:
ALIVE!

ALL ABOUT PUBLISHING 1781926
Cunningham House, 130 Francis Street, DUBLIN 8 **Tel:** 1 41 67 900 **Fax:** 14167901

Titles:
PRUDENCE

ARCHAEOLOGY IRELAND 698388
Media House, South County Business Park, Leopardstown, DUBLIN 18 **Tel:** 1 27 65 221
Fax: 1 27 65 201

Titles:
ARCHAEOLOGY IRELAND

ARD OILEAN PRESS LTD 1680463
28 Ardilaun Road, Newcastle, Galway
Tel: 91 52 72 32 **Fax:** 91 52 72 32

Titles:
PRIMARY TIMES IN THE WEST OF IRELAND

ARGYLL COMMUNICATIONS 1777659
29 Charlemont Lane, Clontarf, DUBLIN 3
Tel: 1 83 30 560 **Fax:** 18330826

Titles:
MOVING IN MAGAZINE

ASHVILLE MEDIA GROUP 1778073
Longboat Quay, 57-59 Sir John Rogerson Quay, DUBLIN 2 **Tel:** 1 43 22 200 **Fax:** 1 67 27 100

Titles:
ASHFORD & DROMOLAND CASTLE GUEST RELATIONS MAGAZINE
MATERNITY
MATERNITY & INFANT
YOU & YOUR MONEY

ASSOCIATED NEWSPAPERS (IRELAND) LTD 1779251
3rd Floor Embassy House, Herbert Park Lane, Ballsbridge, DUBLIN 4 **Tel:** 1 63 75 800
Fax: 16375920

Titles:
IRISH DAILY MAIL
IRISH MAIL ON SUNDAY
METRO HERALD

ASTI PUBLICATIONS 1780960
Winetavern Street, DUBLIN 8 **Tel:** 1 60 40 160
Fax: 16719280

Titles:
ASTIR

ASTRONOMY IRELAND 1780901
PO Box 2888, DUBLIN 5 **Tel:** 1 84 70 777
Fax: 18470771

Titles:
ASTRONOMY & SPACE

ATHLETIC PROMOTIONS LTD 1779629
Edelweiss, Cushina, Portarlington, CO. LAOIS
Tel: 57 86 45 343

Titles:
WALKING WORLD IRELAND

ATHLETICS IRELAND PROPERTY HOLDINGS 1788533
Unit 19, Northwood Court, Northwood Business Campus, Santry, DUBLIN 9 **Tel:** 1 88 69 962
Fax: 18421334

Titles:
IRISH RUNNER

ATHLONE TOPIC 1780351
Arcade Buildings, Barrack Street, Athlone, CO. WESTMEATH **Tel:** 90 64 94 433 **Fax:** 906494964

Titles:
ATHLONE TOPIC

AUTOBIZ LTD 1781003
Shangort, Knocknacarra, GALWAY XXX XXX
Tel: 91 523 292 **Fax:** 91 584 411

Titles:
AUTOBIZ

AUTOMOTIVE PUBLICATIONS LTD 625091
Glencree House, Lanesborough Road, ROSCOMMON TOWN **Tel:** 90 66 25 676
Fax: 90 66 37 410
Email: info@autopub.ie
Web site: http://www.autopub.ie

Titles:
AUTO TRADE JOURNAL
IRISH BODYSHOP JOURNAL
MOTORSHOW CAR BUYERS' GUIDE
TYRE TRADE JOURNAL

THE AVONDHU PRESS LTD 1781098
18 Lower Cork Street, Mitchelstown, CO. CORK
Tel: 25 24 451 **Fax:** 2584463

Titles:
THE AVONDHU

BALLINCOLLIG NEWSLETTER LTD 1781988
Parknamore Lodge, West Village, Ballincollig, CO. CORK **Tel:** 21 48 77 665 **Fax:** 214871404

Titles:
THE BALLINCOLLIG NEWSLETTER

BANDON 698551
76 South Main Street, Bandon, CO. CORK
Fax: 2 34 22 77

Titles:
THE OPINION

BEEHIVE MEDIA LTD 1731957
7 Cranford Centre, Montrose, DUBLIN 4
Tel: 1 26 01 114 **Fax:** 1 26 00 911
Email: gspl@eircom.net

Titles:
INTERMEZZO

BELGRAVE GROUP LTD 1778977
A12 Calmount Park, Ballymount, DUBLIN 12
Tel: 1 45 02 422 **Fax:** 14502954

Titles:
BUSINESS TRAVEL
IRISH TRAVEL TRADE NEWS

BES AND R MEDIA LTD 1640412
51 Allen Park Road, Stillorgan, CO DUBLIN
Tel: 1 20 56 895 **Fax:** 1 28 88 179

Titles:
GOING PLACES MAGAZINE
PREGNANCY AND PARENTING

BOOKS IRELAND 1782579
11 Newgrove Avenue, DUBLIN 4 **Tel:** 1 26 92 185

Titles:
BOOKS IRELAND

BRADÁN GROUP 1782311
5 Eglington Road, Bray, CO WICKLOW
Tel: 1 28 69 111 **Fax:** 12869074

Titles:
WICKLOW TIMES SERIES

BRADÁN PUBLISHING LIMITED 1778305
5 Eglinton Road, Bray, CO. WICKLOW
Tel: 1 28 69 111 **Fax:** 12869074

Titles:
PUBLIC SECTOR TIMES

BUSINESS & FINANCE MEDIA GROUP 1791380
Unit 1a, Waters Edge, Charlotte Quay, DUBLIN 4
Tel: 1 41 67 800 **Fax:** 1 416 7898

Titles:
BUSINESS & FINANCE

BUSINESS AND LEADERSHIP LTD. 1780914
Top Floor, Block 43B, Yeats Way, Park West Business Park, Nangor Road, DUBLIN 12
Tel: 1 625 1480 **Fax:** 16251402

Titles:
IRISH DIRECTOR

BUSINESS LIMERICK PUBLICATIONS 1778133
48 O'Connell Street, Limerick, CO. LIMERICK
Tel: 61 46 75 18 **Fax:** 61 40 49 40

Titles:
BUSINESS LIMERICK MAGAZINE

C & L PUBLICATIONS 1780855
78 O'Connell Street, Dungarvan, CO. WATERFORD **Tel:** 58 41 203 **Fax:** 5845301

Titles:
DUNGARVAN LEADER

C. J. FALLON, EDUCATIONAL PUBLISHERS 698640
Ground Floor, Block B, Liffey Valley Office Campus, DUBLIN 22 **Tel:** 1 61 66 400
Fax: 1 61 66 499
Email: editorial@cjfallon.ie

Titles:
SCIENCE PLUS

CAR BUYERS GUIDE 1778035
3rd Floor, Arena House, Arena Road, Sandyford Industrial Estate, DUBLIN 18 **Tel:** 1 240 5555
Fax: 1 240 5550

Titles:
BIKE BUYERS GUIDE
CAR BUYERS GUIDE - IRISH NEW CAR GUIDE
MODIFIED MOTORS

CARNBEG LTD 1779430
97 Henry Street, Rutland Street, LIMERICK
Tel: 61 41 33 22 **Fax:** 61417684

Titles:
LIMERICK POST

CARRIGLUSKY 1788559
Wylie House, Main Street, Carrigaline, CO. CORK **Tel:** 21 43 73 557 **Fax:** 214373559

Titles:
THE CARRIGDHOUN NEWSPAPER

CELTIC MEDIA GROUP 2373
Market Square, Navan, CO. MEATH
Tel: 46 90 79 600 **Fax:** 46 90 23 565
Web site: http://www.anglocelt.ie

Titles:
THE ANGLO-CELT
INSPIRE
THE MEATH CHRONICLE

CHECKOUT PUBLICATIONS LTD 1781189
Adelaide Hall, 3 Adelaide Street, Dun Laoghaire, CO. DUBLIN **Tel:** 1 23 00 322 **Fax:** 12365900

Titles:
CHECKOUT

THE CHILDCARE DIRECTORY LTD 1715126
Burnaby Buildings, Church Road, Greystones, CO. WICKLOW **Tel:** 1 20 16 000 **Fax:** 1 20 16 002
Email: editor@childcare.ie
Web site: http://www.childcare.ie

Titles:
CHILDCARE.IE MAGAZINE

CHILDREN'S BOOKS IRELAND 1780201
17 North Great George St., DUBLIN 1
Tel: 1 87 27 475 **Fax:** 18727476

Titles:
INIS

CIRCA ART MAGAZINE 1791448
Tel: 1 6401585

Titles:
CIRCA ART MAGAZINE

CITY WIDE PUBLICATIONS 1779026
42 Northwood, Business Campus, DUBLIN 9
Tel: 1 86 23 939 **Fax:** 18306833

Titles:
CITY WIDE NEWS
LIFETIMES

CKN PUBLISHING 1791099
167 Bluebell Woods, Oranmore, CO GALWAY
Tel: 91 776472 **Fax:** 91 788526

Titles:
SLAINTE MAGAZINE

CLARE COLLEGE NEWS LTD 1778402
Mill Road, ENNIS, CO.CLARE **Tel:** 65 68 95 500
Fax: 656895501

Titles:
THE CLARE PEOPLE SERIES

CLARE COUNTY EXPRESS 1782647
Clonakilla, Ballynacally, Ennis, CO. CLARE 0
Tel: 65 68 26 464 **Fax:** 656826465

Titles:
CLARE COUNTY EXPRESS

COMHAR TEO 1788444
5 Merrion Row, DUBLIN 2 **Tel:** 1 67 85 443
Fax: 16785443

Titles:
COMHAR

COMMERCIAL MEDIA GROUP 1779017
Quantum House, Temple Road, Blackrock, CO. DUBLIN **Tel:** 1 28 33 233 **Fax:** 12833254
Titles:
IRISH CONSTRUCTION INDUSTRY MAGAZINE

THE CONNACHT TRIBUNE LTD 1777360
15 Market Street, GALWAY **Tel:** 91 53 62 22 **Fax:** 91567242
Titles:
CONNACHT SENTINEL
CONNACHT TRIBUNE
THE GALWAY CITY TRIBUNE

CONNAUGHT TELEGRAPH 1781278
Cavendish Lane, Castlebar, CO. MAYO
Tel: 94 90 21 711 **Fax:** 949024007
Titles:
THE CONNAUGHT TELEGRAPH

CONSUMERS' ASSOCIATION OF IRELAND 1781906
43-44 Chelmsford Road, DUBLIN 6
Tel: 1 49 78 600 **Fax:** 1 4978601
Titles:
CONSUMER CHOICE

CORK & COUNTY ADVERTISER 1788646
Shannon House, Connolly Street, Bandon, CO. CORK **Tel:** 23 88 29 048 **Fax:** 238829049
Titles:
CORK & COUNTY ADVERTISER INCORPORATING WEST CORK ADVERTISER

CORK INDEPENDENT NEWSPAPERS LTD 1779337
North Point House, North Point Business Park, New Mallow Road, CORK **Tel:** 21 42 88 566 **Fax:** 214288567
Titles:
CORK INDEPENDENT

CORPORATE COMMUNICATIONS 1728283
Iarnrd Ireann, Connolly Station, Amiens Street, DUBLIN 1 **Tel:** 1 70 32 627 **Fax:** 1 70 32 515
Web site: http://www.irishrail.ie
Titles:
RAIL BRIEF

AN COSANTOIR MAGAZINE 2431
Defence Forces Headquarters, Parkgate, Infirmary Road, DUBLIN 7 **Tel:** 1 80 42 691 **Fax:** 1 67 79 018
Email: ancosantoir@defenceforces.iol.ie
Web site: http://www.military.ie
Titles:
AN COSANTÓIR MAGAZINE

COURIER PUBLICATIONS LTD. 1779915
Ballycasey Design Centre, Shannon, CO. CLARE
Tel: 61 36 16 43 **Fax:** 61361178
Titles:
CLARE COURIER

D & B LTD 1780381
23 South Frederick Street, DUBLIN 2
Tel: 1 67 25 939 **Fax:** 16725948
Titles:
STUBBS GAZETTE

DANSTONE GROUP 2324
Taney Hall, Eglinton Terrace, Dundrum, DUBLIN 14 **Tel:** 1 29 60 000 **Fax:** 1 29 60 383
Email: info@maccom.ie
Web site: http://www.imn.ie
Titles:
IRISH MEDICAL NEWS
OLD MOORE'S ALMANAC
VISITOR

DBA PUBLICATIONS LTD 1692798
56 Carysfort Avenue, Blackrock, CO.DUBLIN
Tel: 1 28 87 247 **Fax:** 1 28 83 583
Web site: http://www.dbapublishing.ie
Titles:
OUR GAMES - OFFICIAL GAA ANNUAL

DERRY JOURNAL LTD 1778667
Larkin House, Oldtown Road, Letterkenny, DONEGAL **Tel:** 74 91 88 204 **Fax:** 749128001
Titles:
DONEGAL ON SUNDAY
DONEGAL PEOPLE'S PRESS

DERRYSHALAGH PUBLISHING LTD 1721897
19 Irishtown Road, DUBLIN 4 **Tel:** 1 23 13 593 **Fax:** 1 66 77 742
Titles:
INSIDE GOVERNMENT

THE DESIGN ROOM 1779702
129 Lower Baggot Street, DUBLIN 2
Tel: 1 67 90 380 **Fax:** 16761940
Titles:
THE PROPERTY PROFESSIONAL

DILLON PUBLICATIONS 1778726
PO Box 7130, DUBLIN 18 **Tel:** 1 27 80 841
Titles:
DECISION

DINING IN DUBLIN 1777216
35 Ferndale Court, Rathmichael, CO DUBLIN
Tel: 1 2721188 **Fax:** 1 2721970
Titles:
DINING IN DUBLIN

DISABLED DRIVERS ASSOCIATION OF IRELAND 622514
Ballindine, Claremorris, CO. MAYO
Tel: 94 93 64 054 **Fax:** 94 93 64 336
Email: info@ddai.ie
Web site: http://www.ddai.ie
Titles:
STEERING WHEEL

DKS LTD 1788643
5 Serpentine Road, DUBLIN 4 **Tel:** 1 66 83 066
Titles:
SCIENCE SPIN

DOMINICAN PUBLICATIONS 622516
42 Parnell Square, DUBLIN 1 **Tel:** 1 87 21 611 **Fax:** 1 87 31 760
Email: info@dominicanpublications.com
Web site: http://www.dominicanpublications.com
Titles:
DOCTRINE & LIFE
RELIGIOUS LIFE REVIEW
SPIRITUALITY

DONEGAL DEMOCRAT LTD 1777263
Larkin House, Oldtown road, DONEGAL PE27DS
Tel: 7491 28000
Titles:
DONEGAL DEMOCRAT

DROGHEDA INDEPENDENT NEWS & MEDIA LTD 1777367
Partnership Court, Park Street, Dundalk, CO. LOUTH **Tel:** 42 93 34 632 **Fax:** 429331643
Titles:
THE ARGUS
DROGHEDA INDEPENDENT SERIES
FINGAL INDEPENDENT SERIES

DROGHEDA LEADER 1779636
35 Laurence Street, Drogheda, CO. LOUTH
Tel: 41 98 36 100 **Fax:** 419841517
Titles:
DROGHEDA LEADER

DU PUBLICATIONS 1779074
6 Trinity College, DUBLIN 2 **Tel:** 1 89 62 335
Titles:
TRINITY NEWS

DUBLIN AIRPORT AUTHORITY PLC 1780590
Level 5, Terminal Building, Dublin Airport, CO. DUBLIN **Tel:** 1 81 44 273
Titles:
CONNECTIONS

DUBLIN CITY COUNCIL 1783319
Corporate Services, Communications Unit, 3 Palace Street, DUBLIN 2 **Tel:** 1 222 2266 **Fax:** 1 22223776
Titles:
CLASSMATE

DUBLIN PEOPLE GROUP 1777942
80-83 Omni Park, Santry, DUBLIN 9
Tel: 1 86 21 611 **Fax:** 18621626
Titles:
NORTHSIDE PEOPLE EAST EDITION
NORTHSIDE PEOPLE WEST EDITION
SOUTHSIDE PEOPLE

DUBLINER MEDIA LTD 1780277
3 Ely Place, DUBLIN 2 **Tel:** 1 48 04 700
Titles:
THE DUBLINER

THE DUNDALK DEMOCRAT 1779353
11 Crowe Street, Dundalk, CO. LOUTH 0
Tel: 42 93 34 058 **Fax:** 429331399
Titles:
THE DUNDALK DEMOCRAT SERIES

DUNGARVAN OBSERVER LTD 1781147
Shandon, Dungarvan, CO. WATERFORD
Tel: 58 41 205 **Fax:** 5841559
Titles:
DUNGARVAN OBSERVER

DYFLIN PUBLICATIONS 1778583
1st Floor, Cunningham House, 130 Francis Street, DUBLIN 8 **Tel:** 1 41 67 900 **Fax:** 14167901
Titles:
CONFETTI
CONSTRUCTION
HOUSE AND HOME
KITCHENS AND BATHROOMS
RENOVATE YOUR HOUSE AND HOME
SPOKEOUT

THE ECHO GROUP 1779126
Village Green, Tallaght, DUBLIN 24
Tel: 1 46 64 500 **Fax:** 1 46 64 555
Titles:
THE ECHO SERIES

ECONOMIC & SOCIAL STUDIES ESRI 1781064
Department of Economics, University College Dublin, Belfield, DUBLIN 4 **Tel:** 1 71 68 239
Titles:
THE ECONOMIC & SOCIAL REVIEW

EDMUND HOURICAN 1782537
Clownings, Straffan, KILDARE **Tel:** 87 29 36 015 **Fax:** 16270126
Titles:
TRAVEL EXTRA

ELECTRONICWORLD PUBLISHING 1777691
3 Inishkeen, Kilcoole, CO.WICKLOW
Tel: 86 24 85 842
Titles:
ELECTRONICS COMPONENTS WORLD
ELECTRONICS PRODUCTION WORLD

EMERALD GROUP PUBLISHING LTD 1778717
Jones Lang LaSalle, 10-11 Molesworth Street, DUBLIN 2
Titles:
JOURNAL OF CORPORATE REAL ESTATE

ENTERPRISE IRELAND 1782790
The Plaza, Eastpoint Business Park, DUBLIN 3
Tel: 1 72 72 954
Titles:
THE MARKET

ENTERPRISING IRELAND 1780577
The Plaza, East Point Business Park, DUBLIN 3
Tel: 1 727 2954 **Fax:** 17272086
Titles:
TECHNOLOGY IRELAND

ENVIRO-SOLUTIONS 1780346
28 Venetian Hall, Howth Road, DUBLIN 5
Tel: 86 81 59 243
Titles:
ENVIRO-SOLUTIONS - NEWS UPDATE

EU PUBLISHING 1777500
24 South Frederick Street, DUBLIN 2
Tel: 1 70 71 931 **Fax:** 17079941
Titles:
SIGNAL

EUROPEAN SOCIETY OF CATARACT & REFRACTIVE SURGEONS 1780982
Temple House, Temple Road, Blackrock, CO. DUBLIN **Tel:** 1 20 91 100 **Fax:** 12091112
Titles:
EUROTIMES

EXAMINER PUBLICATIONS (CORK) LTD 1777674
City Quarter, Lapps Quay, CORK
Tel: 21 48 02 142 **Fax:** 21 48 02 135
Titles:
EVENING ECHO
HOLLY BOUGH
THE IRISH EXAMINER

EXPO EVENTS 1778037
Unit 17, Building 2, The Courtyard, Carmenhall Road, Sandyford, DUBLIN 18 **Tel:** 1 29 58 181
Titles:
SALON IRELAND

FDI WORLD DENTAL PRESS LTD 1777231
Oral Health Services Research Centre, University Dental School and Hospital, Wilton, CORK
Tel: 21 49 01 210 **Fax:** 214545391
Titles:
COMMUNITY DENTAL HEALTH

FEASTA 1782397
43 Na Cluainter, Trá Lí, CO CHIARRAÍ 2
Tel: 1 47 83 814
Titles:
FEASTA

THE FEDERATION OF IRISH BEEKEEPERS 1777308
Innisfail, Kickham Street, Thurles, CO. TIPPERARY **Tel:** 504 22 228
Titles:
THE IRISH BEEKEEPER (AN BEACHAIRE)

THE FEDERATION OF WOMENS CLUBS 1710718
Tel: 1 86 80 080
11 St. Peter's Road, Phibsboro, DUBLIN 7
Tel: 1 86 80 080
Titles:
WOMEN'S CLUB MAGAZINE

FILMBASE 1780733
Curved Street, DUBLIN 2 **Tel:** 1 67 96 716 **Fax:** 16796717
Titles:
FILM IRELAND

FINTEL PUBLICATIONS LTD
1777170
6 The Mall, Beacon Court, Sandyford, DUBLIN 18 **Tel:** 1 29 30 566 **Fax:** 12930560
Titles:
FINANCE MAGAZINE

FIRSTHAND PUBLISHING
622565
24 Terenure Road East, Rathgar, DUBLIN 6
Tel: 1 49 02 244 **Fax:** 1 49 20 578
Titles:
RUNNING YOUR BUSINESS

FOILSEACHAN NA MARA
1777518
Annagry, Letterkenny, CO DONEGAL
Tel: 74 95 62 843 **Fax:** 749548940
Titles:
THE IRISH SKIPPER

FOINSE
1788553
An Cheathru Rua, CO. NA GAILLIMHE
Tel: 9 15 95 520 **Fax:** 91595524
Titles:
FOINSE

FORAS NA GAEILGE
698477
7 Cearnóg Mhuirfean, Baile Átha Cliath 2, DUBLIN 2 **Tel:** 1 67 63 222 **Fax:** 1 63 98 400
Email: saol@eircom.net
Web site: http://www.gaeilge.ie
Titles:
SAOL

FRANK QUINN
694193
PO Box 7992, Dun Laoghaire, CO. DUBLIN
Tel: 1 28 40 137 **Fax:** 1 28 40 137
Web site: http://www.irishrugbyreview.com
Titles:
IRISH CYCLING REVIEW
IRISH RUGBY REVIEW

THE FURROW TRUST
1780862
St. Patrick's College, Maynooth, CO. KILDARE
Tel: 1 70 83 741 **Fax:** 17083908
Titles:
THE FURROW

GALWAY ADVERTISER
1778362
41-42 Eyre Square, GALWAY 0 **Tel:** 91 53 09 00
Fax: 91565627
Titles:
GALWAY ADVERTISER

GENIE COMMUNICATIONS LTD
1777410
5th Floor, Phibsboro Tower, DUBLIN 7
Tel: 1 83 03 533 **Fax:** 18303331
Titles:
GARDA REVIEW

GLOSS PUBLICATIONS LTD
1781072
The Courtyard, 40 Main Street, Blackrock, CO. DUBLIN **Tel:** 1 27 55 130 **Fax:** 12755131
Titles:
THE GLOSS

GOLD STAR MEDIA LTD
621654
7 Cranford Centre, Montrose, DUBLIN 4
Tel: 1 26 00 899 **Fax:** 1 26 00 911
Email: gspl@eircom.net
Titles:
SNAFFLE

GOLDEN EGG PRODUCTIONS LTD
1778582
Harris House, Tuam Road, CO. GALWAY
Tel: 91 38 43 50
Titles:
GALWAYNOW
LIMERICK NOW

THE GOLF BUSINESS
625098
Birkdale, 4 Rathmichael Manor, Loughlinstown, CO. DUBLIN **Tel:** 1 28 27 269 **Fax:** 1 28 27 483
Titles:
BACKSPIN GOLF MAGAZINE

GOLF IRELAND
1788374
PO Box 8111, Swords, CO. DUBLIN
Tel: 1 80 78 122 **Fax:** 18078203
Titles:
GOLF IRELAND-IRELANDS NATIONAL GOLF MAGAZINE

GREEN CROSS PUBLISHING
1779770
7 Adelaide Court, Adelaide Road, DUBLIN 2
Tel: 1 4189799 **Fax:** 1 4789449
Titles:
IRISH PHARMACIST

HARMONIA
1779188
Rosemount House, Dundrum Road, Dundrum, DUBLIN 14 **Tel:** 1 24 05 300 **Fax:** 16619757
Titles:
FOOD & WINE MAGAZINE
IRELAND OF THE WELCOMES
IRISH TATLER
U MAGAZINE
WOMAN'S WAY
YOUR NEW BABY

HARMONIA LTD.
1783614
Rosemount House, Dundrum Road, Dundrum, DUBLIN 14 **Tel:** 1 240 5300 **Fax:** 1 661 9486
Titles:
AUTO IRELAND

HERALD PRINTING & PUBLISHING COMPANY LTD
1777254
Dublin Road, Tuam, CO. GALWAY **Tel:** 93 24 183
Fax: 9324478
Titles:
THE TUAM HERALD

HISTORY PUBLICATIONS LTD
1780797
6 Palmerston Place, DUBLIN 7 **Tel:** 87 68 89 412
Titles:
HISTORY IRELAND

HKM PUBLISHING IRELAND
1778718
7 Camden House, Camden Street, DUBLIN 2
Tel: 1 47 91 111 **Fax:** 14791116
Titles:
TOTALLY DUBLIN

HOMEBOND THE NATIONAL HOUSE BUILDING GUARANTEE CO
1783733
Construction House, Canal Road, DUBLIN 6
Tel: 1491 5000 **Fax:** 1496 6548
Titles:
HOUSING TIMES

IBOA THE FINANCE UNION
1780907
IBOA House, Upper Stephen Street, DUBLIN 8
Tel: 1 47 55 908 **Fax:** 14780567
Titles:
SPECTRUM

IFP MEDIA
1777487
31 Deansgrange Road, Blackrock, CO. DUBLIN
Tel: 1 28 93 305 **Fax:** 12896406
Titles:
THE ENGINEERS JOURNAL
IRISH FARMERS MONTHLY
IRISH FOOD
IRISH MOTOR MANAGEMENT
IRISH VETERINARY JOURNAL

IMAGE PUBLICATIONS LTD
1779068
Crofton Hall, 22 Crofton Road, Dun Laoghaire, CO. DUBLIN **Tel:** 1 28 08 415 **Fax:** 12808309
Titles:
IMAGE
IMAGE INTERIORS

IMPACT TRADE UNION
1788452
Nerneys Court, Off Temple Street, DUBLIN 1
Tel: 1 81 71 538 **Fax:** 18171503
Titles:
WORK & LIFE

INDEPENDENT NEWSPAPERS LTD
1777137
Independent House, 27-32 Talbot Street, DUBLIN 1 **Tel:** 1 70 55 722 **Fax:** 1 70 55 784
Titles:
EVENING HERALD
IRISH INDEPENDENT
THE KERRYMAN SERIES
LIFE MAGAZINE
MOTHERS & BABIES
SUNDAY INDEPENDENT

INDEPENDENT STAR LTD
1779325
Star House, 62A Terenure Road North, DUBLIN 6 **Tel:** 1 49 01 228 **Fax:** 14902193
Titles:
THE IRISH DAILY STAR

THE INISH TIMES
1777951
33 Upper Main Street, Buncrana, Inishowen, CO. DONEGAL **Tel:** 74 93 41 055 **Fax:** 749341059
Titles:
THE INISH TIMES

INSIDE IRELAND
1777628
PO Box 1886, DUBLIN 16 **Tel:** 1 49 31 359
Fax: 14934538
Titles:
INSIDE IRELAND INFORMATION SERVICE AND BI-MONTHLY E-NEWSLETTER

INST. OF CERTIFIED PUBLIC ACCOUNTANTS IN IRELAND
1781307
17 Harcourt Street, DUBLIN 2 **Tel:** 1 42 51 000
Fax: 14251001
Titles:
ACCOUNTANCY PLUS

INSTITUTE OF BANKERS IN IRELAND
621651
1 North Wall Quay, DUBLIN 1 **Tel:** 1 61 16 500
Fax: 1 61 16 565
Email: info@bankers.ie
Web site: http://www.bankers.ie
Titles:
BANKING IRELAND

INSTITUTE OF CHARTERED ACCOUNTANTS IN IRELAND
1792154
Chartered Accountants House, 47-49 Pearse Street, DUBLIN 2 **Tel:** 1 637 7392 **Fax:** 1 523 3995
Titles:
ACCOUNTANCY IRELAND

INSTITUTE OF GUIDANCE COUNSELLORS
1778307
Heywood Community School, Ballinakill, CO. LAOIS **Tel:** 57 87 3333 **Fax:** 578733314
Titles:
GUIDELINE

INSTITUTE OF PUBLIC ADMINISTRATION
1778303
Vergemount Hall, Clonskeagh, DUBLIN 6
Tel: 1 24 03 600 **Fax:** 12698644
Titles:
ADMINISTRATION JOURNAL

INTENT MEDIA LTD
1793998
1st Floor, Suncourt House, 18-26 Essex Road, DUBLIN 18 **Tel:** 1 29 47 783 **Fax:** 020 7354 6049
Titles:
TVB EUROPE

INTERART MEDIA LTD
1788308
Regus House, Harcourt Road, DUBLIN 2
Tel: 1 47 73 933 **Fax:** 14029590
Titles:
THE EVENT GUIDE

INTERNATIONAL LIVING PUBLISHING LTD
1692317
Elysium House, Ballytruckle Road, WATERFORD
Tel: 51 30 45 57 **Fax:** 51 30 45 61
Email: customerservice@internationalliving.com
Web site: http://www.internationalliving.com
Titles:
INTERNATIONAL LIVING

IRELANDS HORSE REVIEW
622536
Garden Street, Ballina, CO. MAYO **Tel:** 96 73 500
Fax: 96 72 077
Titles:
IRELAND'S HORSE REVIEW

IRISH ANGLER PUBLICATIONS
1792464
IPI Centre, Breaffy Road, Castlebar, CO. MAYO
Tel: 94 90 27 656 **Fax:** 949027861
Titles:
IRISH ANGLER

IRISH AQUACULTURAL ASSOCIATION BIM
1788483
Crofton Road, Dun Laoghaire, CO. DUBLIN
Tel: 1 66 80 043
Titles:
AQUACULTURE IRELAND

IRISH ARTS REVIEW LTD
625085
State Apartments, Dublin Castle, DUBLIN 2
Tel: 1 67 93 525 **Fax:** 1 67 34 417
Web site: http://www.irishartsreview.com
Titles:
IRISH ARTS REVIEW

IRISH AUCTIONEERS' AND VALUERS' INSTITUTE
2293
38 Merrion Square, DUBLIN 2 **Tel:** 1 66 11 794
Fax: 1 66 11 797
Email: info@iavi.ie
Web site: http://www.iavi.ie
Titles:
THE PROPERTY VALUER

IRISH BRIDES & HOMES LTD
1780354
Crannagh House, 198 Rathfarnham Road, DUBLIN 14 **Tel:** 1 49 00 550 **Fax:** 14906763
Titles:
IRISH BRIDES MAGAZINE

IRISH BROKER
1778022
136 Baldoyle Industrial Estate, DUBLIN 13
Tel: 1 83 95 060 **Fax:** 18395062
Titles:
IRISH BROKER

THE IRISH BUSINESS & EMPLOYERS' CONFEDERATION
1778775
Confederation House, 84-86 Lower Baggot Street, DUBLIN 2 **Tel:** 1 60 51 500 **Fax:** 16381508
Titles:
IBEC AGENDA

IRISH EMIGRANT PUBLICATIONS
1777725
Unit 4, Campus Innovation Centre, Upper Newcastle Road, GALWAY **Tel:** 9 15 69 158
Titles:
BOOKVIEW IRELAND
IRISH EMIGRANT

IRISH HOTELS FEDERATION
1784384
13 Northbrook Road, Ranelagh, DUBLIN 6
Tel: 1 49 76 459 **Fax:** 1 49 74 613
Titles:
IRELANDHOTELS.COM

IRISH INSTITUTE OF CREDIT MANAGEMENT
1782245
17 Kildare Street, DUBLIN 2 **Tel:** 1 6099444
Fax: 1 6099445
Titles:
CREDIT FOCUS

IRISH INSTITUTE OF TRAINING AND DEVELOPMENT
1780815
38 Chestnut Meadows, Glanmire, CORK
Tel: 21 48 23 346
Titles:
HRD IRELAND

IRISH JESUITS 700099
36 Lower Leeson Street, DUBLIN 2
Tel: 1 67 66 785 **Fax:** 1 67 62 984
Titles:
STUDIES AND IRISH QUARTERLY REVIEW

IRISH JOURNAL OF EDUCATION 1783192
Educational Research Centre, St. Patrick's College, DUBLIN 9 **Tel:** 1 83 73 789 **Fax:** 18378997
Titles:
IRISH JOURNAL OF EDUCATION

IRISH LEAGUE OF CREDIT UNIONS 1782441
33-41 Lower Mount Street, CO. DUBLIN
Tel: 1 61 46 914 **Fax:** 16146708
Titles:
CU FOCUS

IRISH MARINE PRESS PUBLICATIONS LTD 1788510
2 Lower Glenageary Road, Dun Laoghaire, CO. DUBLIN **Tel:** 1 28 46 161 **Fax:** 12846192
Titles:
IRELAND AFLOAT MAGAZINE

IRISH MEDICAL DIRECTORY 1777957
PO Box 5049, DUBLIN 6 **Tel:** 1 49 26 040
Fax: 14926040
Titles:
IRISH MEDICAL DIRECTORY

IRISH MEDICAL ORGANISATION 1780597
IMO House, 10 Fitzwilliam Place, DUBLIN 2
Tel: 1 67 67 273 **Fax:** 16612758
Titles:
IRISH MEDICAL JOURNAL

IRISH NATIONAL TEACHERS' ORGANISATION 1791512
35 Parnell Square, DUBLIN 1 **Tel:** 1 80 47 700
Fax: 18722462
Titles:
IN TOUCH

IRISH ORGANIC FARMERS AND GROWERS ASSOCIATION LTD 1779128
Main Street, Newtown Forbes, CO. LONGFORD
Tel: 43 3342495 **Fax:** 433342496
Titles:
ORGANIC MATTERS

IRISH PEATLAND CONSERVATION COUNCIL 625512
Irish Peatland Conservation Council, Lullymore, Rathangan, CO. KILDARE **Tel:** 45 86 01 33
Fax: 45 86 04 81
Email: bogs@ipcc.ie
Web site: http://www.ipcc.ie
Titles:
PEATLAND NEWS

IRISH PHARMACY UNION 1779034
Butterfield House, Butterfield Avenue, Rathfarnham, DUBLIN 14 **Tel:** 1 49 36 401
Fax: 14936626
Titles:
IPU REVIEW

IRISH RED CROSS 1780253
16 Merrion Square, DUBLIN 2 **Tel:** 1 64 24 600
Fax: 16614461
Titles:
IRISH RED CROSS REVIEW

IRISH SHOOTER'S DIGEST 698463
Shannon Oughter, SLIGO **Tel:** 71 91 47 841
Fax: 71 91 47 841
Web site: http://www.irishshootersdigest.ie
Titles:
IRISH SHOOTER'S DIGEST

IRISH TAXATION INSTITUTE 1780530
South Block, Longboat Quay, Grand Canal Harbour, DUBLIN 2 **Tel:** 1 66 31 700 **Fax:** 16688387
Titles:
IRISH TAX REVIEW

THE IRISH TIMES LTD 1777252
Unit 15-3rd Floor, Kilmartin N6 Centre, Athlone, CO. WESTMEATH **Tel:** 90 64 70 920
Fax: 90 64 79 646
Titles:
ATHLONE ADVERTISER SERIES
THE IRISH TIMES
IRISHTIMES.COM

IRISH VILLAGE PAPERS 1781881
Ratoath, CO. MEATH **Tel:** 1 82 54 434
Titles:
MEATH ECHO

IRISH WEDDING DIARY.IE 1780997
10 Rathgar Road, Rathmines, DUBLIN 6
Tel: 1 49 83 242 **Fax:** 14983217
Titles:
IRISH WEDDING DIARY

IRISH YOUTHWORK CENTRE 628807
Youth Work Ireland, 20 Lower Dominick Street, DUBLIN 1 **Tel:** 1 87 29 933 **Fax:** 1 87 24 183
Web site: http://www.iywc.com
Titles:
IRISH YOUTH WORK SCENE

IRN PUBLISHING 1777494
121-123 Ranelagh, DUBLIN 6 **Tel:** 1 66 71 152
Fax: 14972779
Titles:
HEALTH & SAFETY REVIEW
INDUSTRIAL RELATIONS NEWS
PENSIONS IRELAND
PEOPLE FOCUS

JEMMA PUBLICATIONS LTD 1778724
Grattan House, Temple Road, Blackrock, CO. DUBLIN **Tel:** 1 76 42 700 **Fax:** 17642750
Titles:
CONSTRUCTION AND PROPERTY NEWS
IRISH HARDWARE
IRISH PRINTER
LICENSING WORLD

JETWOOD LTD 1782638
1 Albert Park, Sandycove, CO. DUBLIN
Tel: 1 28 44 456 **Fax:** 12807735
Titles:
MARKETING

JJDS PUBLICATIONS LTD 1779907
D'Alton Street, Claremorris, CO. MAYO
Tel: 94 93 72 819 **Fax:** 949373571
Titles:
FLEET TRANSPORT

JOHNSTON PRESS PLC 1777362
Leader House, Dublin Road, LONGFORD
Tel: 43 45 241 **Fax:** 4341489
Titles:
LONGFORD LEADER
THE NATIONALIST & MUNSTER ADVERTISER SERIES
TIPPERARY STAR

KEELAUN LTD 2406
9 Maypark, Malahide Road, DUBLIN 5
Tel: 1 83 29 243 **Fax:** 1 83 29 246
Email: education@keelaun.ie
Titles:
EDUCATION

KENNO LTD 1780296
22 Ashe Street, Tralee, CO. KERRY
Tel: 66 71 49 200 **Fax:** 667123163
Titles:
KERRY'S EYE

THE KERRYMAN LTD 1780400
The Spa, Mallow, CO. CORK **Tel:** 22 31 443
Fax: 2243183
Titles:
THE CORKMAN SERIES

KILDARE TIMES 1780581
Unit 1, Eurospar, Fairgreen, Naas, CO. KILDARE
Tel: 4 58 95 111 **Fax:** 45895099
Titles:
KILDARE TIMES

KILKENNY PEOPLE 1777724
34 High Street, KILKENNY **Tel:** 56 77 21 015
Fax: 56 77 21 414
Titles:
KILKENNY PEOPLE

KILLARNEY ADVERTISER 1778122
Unit 1, Ballycasheen, Killarney, CO. KERRY 0
Tel: 64 66 32 215 **Fax:** 64 66 327 22
Titles:
KILLARNEY ADVERTISER

THE KINGDOM NEWSPAPER 1777944
65 New Street, Killarney, CO. KERRY
Tel: 64 66 31 392 **Fax:** 646634609
Titles:
THE KINGDOM NEWSPAPER

KINSALE & DISTRICT NEWSLETTER 1777365
Emmet Place, Kinsale, CO. CORK
Tel: 21 47 74 313 **Fax:** 214774339
Titles:
KINSALE ADVERTISER
KINSALE & DISTRICT NEWSLETTER

KWIKPRINT LTD 1778972
ICSA, 9 Lyster, Port Laose, CO LOIS
Tel: 57 86 62 120 **Fax:** 578662121
Titles:
DRYSTOCK FARMER

LAW SOCIETY OF IRELAND 1791550
Blackhall Place, DUBLIN 7 **Tel:** 1 67 24 828
Fax: 16724877
Titles:
LAW SOCIETY GAZETTE

LEINSTER EXPRESS LTD 1777361
Dublin Road, Portaloise, CO. LAOIS
Tel: 57 86 21 666 **Fax:** 578620491
Titles:
LEINSTER EXPRESS (LAOIS AND DISTRICTS)
OFFALY EXPRESS

LEINSTER LEADER LTD 1779258
19 South Main Street, Naas, CO. KILDARE
Tel: 45 89 73 02 **Fax:** 45871168
Titles:
LEINSTER LEADER

LEITRIM OBSERVER 1777653
Unit 3, Hartley Business Park, Carrick-on-Shannon, CO. LEITRIM **Tel:** 71 96 20 025
Fax: 719620039
Titles:
LEITRIM OBSERVER SERIES

LIFFEY CHAMPION 1778970
The Cornmill, Mill Lane, Leixlip, CO. KILDARE
Tel: 1 62 45 533 **Fax:** 16243013
Titles:
LIFFEY CHAMPION

LIMERICK LEADER LTD 1779232
54 O'Connell Street, LIMERICK **Tel:** 61 21 45 00
Fax: 61401424
Titles:
LIMERICK LEADER & CHRONICLE SERIES
SOUTH TIPP TODAY

THE LOCAL NEWS GROUP 1780350
Bank House Centre, 331 South Circular Road, DUBLIN 8 **Tel:** 1 45 34 011 **Fax:** 14549024
Titles:
THE LOCAL NEWS SERIES

LOUISVILLE PUBLISHING LTD. 1782264
Louisville, Enniskerry, CO. WICKLOW NA
Tel: 1 20 46 230
Titles:
DRINKS INDUSTRY IRELAND

LYNN PUBLICATIONS LTD 625477
Kells Business Park, Kells, CO. MEATH
Tel: 46 92 41 923 **Fax:** 46 92 41 926
Web site: http://www.hoganstand.com
Titles:
HOGAN STAND
IRISH TRUCKER

MADISON PUBLICATIONS LTD 1781171
Adelaide Hall, 3 Adelaide Street, Dun Laoghaire, CO DUBLIN **Tel:** 1 23 65 880 **Fax:** 12300325
Titles:
HOSPITALITY IRELAND

MANDATE TRADE UNION 1779875
9 Cavendish Row, DUBLIN 1 **Tel:** 1 87 46 321
Fax: 18729581
Titles:
MANDATE NEWS

MANGO DESIGN LTD 1654247
72 South Mall, CORK **Tel:** 21 42 22 404
Fax: 21 42 22 403
Email: info@corklife.ie
Web site: http://www.corklife.ie
Titles:
CORKLIFE

MARINE MEDIA LTD 1777517
Ballymoon Industrial Estate, Kilcar, CO. DONEGAL **Tel:** 74 97 38 836 **Fax:** 749738841
Titles:
MARINE TIMES NEWSPAPER

MAXMEDIA COMMUNICATIONS LIMITED 1782473
The Courtyard, 20E Castle Street, Dalkey, CO. DUBLIN 0 **Tel:** 1 66 38 949 **Fax:** 1 6638006
Titles:
CARA MAGAZINE

MAYO NEWS 1779434
The Fairgreen, Westport, CO. MAYO
Tel: 98 25 311 **Fax:** 98 26 108
Titles:
MAYO NEWS

THE MCGLINN GROUP 1780582
Agher, Summerhill, CO. MEATH **Tel:** 46 95 58 666
Fax: 469558667
Titles:
IRELAND'S HORSE & PONY MAGAZINE

MD ASSOCIATES 1780278
16 South Terrace, CORK **Tel:** 21 431 6776
Titles:
COIN-OP NEWS EUROPE

MEATH CHRONICLE GROUP OF PUBLICATIONS 1779814
Unit 4, Galway Retail Park, Headford Road, GALWAY **Tel:** 91 56 90 00 **Fax:** 91569333
Titles:
GALWAY INDEPENDENT

MEDIA PEOPLE IRELAND LTD 1782175
Abbey Street, Roscommon Town, ROSCOMMON **Tel:** 90 66 34 633 **Fax:** 906634303
Titles:
ROSCOMMON PEOPLE

MEDIATEAM 1778256
Media House, South County Business Park, Leopardstown, DUBLIN 18 **Tel:** 1 29 47 777 **Fax:** 12947799
Titles:
COMPUTERSCOPE
IRISH COMPUTER
THE IRISH GARDEN
PC LIVE
SHELFLIFE
SMART COMPANY

MEDICAL PUBLICATIONS (IRELAND) LTD 1777933
24-26 Upper Ormond Quay, DUBLIN 7
Tel: 1 81 76 300
Titles:
IRISH MEDICAL TIMES
MIMS (IRELAND)

MEDIEVAL DUBLIN 1782874
PO Box 3430, Tallaght, DUBLIN 24
Tel: 1 45 19 000 **Fax:** 1 4519805
Titles:
THE TALLAGHT NEWS

MEDMEDIA LTD 1777525
25 Adelaide Street, Dun Loaghaire, CO DUBLIN
Tel: 1 28 03 967
Titles:
DIABETES IRELAND FORUM
MODERN MEDICINE OF IRELAND
NURSING IN THE COMMUNITY
WIN - WORLD OF IRISH NURSING & MIDWIFERY

MESSENGER PUBLICATIONS 1779025
37 Lower Leeson Street, DUBLIN 2
Tel: 1 676 7491 **Fax:** 16767493
Titles:
THE SACRED HEART MESSENGER

METRO PUBLISHING CONSULTANCY LTD 1780642
46 Upper Dorset Street, DUBLIN 1
Tel: 1 87 83 223 **Fax:** 18783917
Titles:
METRO EIREANN

MGN 1780113
Floor 4, Park House, 191-197 North Circular Road, DUBLIN 7 **Tel:** 1 86 88 600 **Fax:** 18688626
Titles:
THE IRISH DAILY MIRROR
THE IRISH SUNDAY MIRROR

MIDLAND TRIBUNE 1781706
Barrack Street, Ennis, CO. CLARE
Tel: 65 68 28 105 **Fax:** 656820374
Titles:
THE CLARE CHAMPION
MIDLAND TRIBUNE

MINJARA LTD 1784056
2-4 Ely Place, DUBLIN 2 **Tel:** 1 48 04 700
Fax: 14807799
Titles:
KISS

MISSIONARY SOCIETY OF ST. COLUMBAN 1780210
St. Columbans, Navan, CO. MEATH
Tel: 46 90 21 525 **Fax:** 469071297
Titles:
THE FAR EAST

MJM PUBLICATIONS LTD 2317
7 Ballingarrane, Cahir Road, Clonmel, CO TIPPERRARY **Tel:** 52 70 767 **Fax:** 52 23 999
Titles:
DAIRY & FOOD INDUSTRIES MAGAZINE

MMG MEDIA LTD 1734388
324 Clontarf Road, Clontarf, DUBLIN 3
Tel: 1 85 33 620
Titles:
INSIDE MAGAZINE

MMM COMMUNICATIONS 1780211
Rosemount, Rosemount Terrace, Booterstown, CO.DUBLIN **Tel:** 1 28 87 180 **Fax:** 12834626
Titles:
HEALING & DEVELOPMENT

MOHH PUBLISHING LTD 1781127
PO Box 28, An Post Mail Centre, Dublin Road, ATHLONE **Tel:** 87 98 89 771 **Fax:** 906476300
Titles:
IRISH HAIRDRESSER INTERNATIONAL MAGAZINE

MONWICK PUBLISHING 1781914
H and R House, Carton Court, Maynooth, CO. KILDARE **Tel:** 1 62 85 447 **Fax:** 16285447
Titles:
HOTEL & RESTAURANT TIMES

MOUNT MEDIA LTD 1777234
45 Upper Mount Street, DUBLIN 2
Tel: 1 66 11 660 **Fax:** 16611632
Titles:
IRISH MARKETING JOURNAL

MOUNTAINEERING COUNCIL OF IRELAND 1777935
Sport HQ, 13 Joyce Way, Parkwest Business Park, DUBLIN 12 **Tel:** 1 62 51 115 **Fax:** 16251116
Titles:
IRISH MOUNTAIN LOG

THE MUNSTER EXPRESS 1781191
37 The Quay, WATERFORD **Tel:** 51 87 21 41
Fax: 51873452
Titles:
THE MUNSTER EXPRESS

NALAC LTD 1784034
30 Morehampton Road, DUBLIN 4
Tel: 1 660 8400 **Fax:** 1 660 4540
Titles:
BUSINESS PLUS

NATIONAL & INTERNATIONAL PUBLICATIONS LTD 1780163
1 Windsor Mews, Summerhill Parade, Sandycove, CO. DUBLIN **Tel:** 1 44 29 264
Fax: 12846328
Titles:
IRISH BUILDING MAGAZINE

THE NATIONALIST 1777355
Coliseum Lane, PORTLAOISE **Tel:** 57 86 70 216
Fax: 578661399
Titles:
LAOIS NATIONALIST
THE NATIONALIST (CARLOW)

NCBI 1777991
Whitworth Road, Drumcondra, DUBLIN 9
Tel: 1 83 07 033 **Fax:** 18307787
Titles:
FOCUS

NENAGH GUARDIAN 1781113
13 Summerhill, Nenagh, CO. TIPPERARY
Tel: 67 31 214 **Fax:** 6733401
Titles:
NENAGH GUARDIAN

NETWORK MAGAZINES 1783684
63 Granitefield, Dun Laoghaire, CO. DUBLIN
Tel: 1 285 4004 **Fax:** 12854784
Titles:
HANDLING NETWORK

NEWS INTERNATIONAL (IRELAND) 1778997
4th Floor, Bishop's Square, Redmond's Hill, DUBLIN 2 **Tel:** 1 47 92 579 **Fax:** 14792590
Titles:
THE IRISH SUN

NLGF LTD 1779699
Unit 2 Scarlet Row, West Essex Street, DUBLIN 8 **Tel:** 1 67 19 076 **Fax:** 16713549
Titles:
GAY COMMUNITY NEWS

NORTHERN STANDARD 1781923
The Diamond, MONAGHAN 0 **Tel:** 47 82 188
Fax: 4772257
Titles:
NORTHERN STANDARD

NORTH-WEST OF IRELAND PTG. & PUB. CO. LTD 1785078
St. Annes Court, High Road, Letterkenny, CO. DONEGAL **Tel:** 74 91 21 491 **Fax:** 74 91 22 881
Titles:
DONEGAL NEWS (DERRY PEOPLE)

NOVA PUBLISHING 1778734
19 Upper Fitz William Street, DUBLIN 2
Tel: 1 29 58 115 **Fax:** 1 29 59 350
Titles:
ARCHITECTURE IRELAND HOUSE

OCEAN PUBLISHING 1781195
14 Upper Fitzwilliam Street, DUBLIN 2
Tel: 1 67 85 165 **Fax:** 16785191
Titles:
EMERGENCY SERVICES IRELAND

OMEGA PUBLISHING 1778117
NCBI (National Council for the Blind of Ireland), Head Office, Whitworth Road, Drumcondra, DUBLIN 9 **Tel:** 1 85 03 34 353 **Fax:** 18307787
Titles:
NCBI NEWS

OPW 1780247
51 St. Stephen's Green, DUBLIN 2
Tel: 1 64 76 000 **Fax:** 16476491
Titles:
OBAIR

OSNOVINA LTD 1780081
13 Trinity Street, DUBLIN 2 **Tel:** 1 24 11 500
Fax: 12411538
Titles:
HOT PRESS
MQ - MUSIC QUARTERLY - IMRO MAGAZINE

PAGE 7 MEDIA LTD 1780934
3rd Floor, Arena House, Arena Road, Sandyford Industrial Estate, DUBLIN 18 **Tel:** 1 24 05 555
Fax: 1 29 45 261
Titles:
CAR BUYER'S GUIDE
DOUGLAS NEWMAN GOOD CITY & TOWN MAGAZINE
IN DUBLIN
MUSGRAVE MAGAZINE

PEMBROKE PUBLISHING LTD 1782926
Unit F5, Bymac Centre, North West Business Park, DUBLIN 15 **Tel:** 1 82 24 477 **Fax:** 18224485
Titles:
COMMERCIAL INTERIORS OF IRELAND
IRISH INTERIORS
MUNSTER INTERIORS

PENFIELD ENTERPRISES LTD 1784042
44 Lower Baggot Street, DUBLIN 2
Tel: 1 66 11 062 **Fax:** 16624532
Titles:
THE PHOENIX

PEOPLE NEWSPAPERS LTD 1778156
Channing House, Rowe Street, Wexford, CO. WEXFORD 0
Titles:
BRAY PEOPLE
CARLOW PEOPLE
ENNISCORTHY AND GOREY GUARDIAN
IRELAND'S OWN
WEXFORD PEOPLE SERIES

PHARMACEUTICAL SOCIETY OF IRELAND 2424
18 Shrewsbury Road, Ballsbridge, DUBLIN 4
Tel: 1 21 84 000 **Fax:** 1 28 37 678
Web site: http://www.pharmaceuticalsociety.ie
Titles:
IRISH PHARMACY JOURNAL

PIONEER TOTAL ABSTINANCE ASSOCIATION 1792308
27 Upper Sherrard Street, DUBLIN 1
Tel: 1 87 49 464 **Fax:** 18748485
Titles:
PIONEER

PLAN MAGAZINES LTD 1780378
Quantum House, Temple Road, Blackrock, CO DUBLIN **Tel:** 1 28 33 233 **Fax:** 12833045
Titles:
PLAN

POETRY IRELAND 1640042
2 Proud's Lane, Off St. Stephens Green, DUBLIN 2 **Tel:** 1 47 89 974
Titles:
POETRY IRELAND REVIEW

PORTFOLIO 1788641
Unit 8, Docklands Innovation Park, East Wall Road, DUBLIN 3 **Tel:** 1 67 25 831
Titles:
PORTFOLIO

PREMIER PUBLISHING LTD 1778945
51 Archville, Magheramappien, Comvoy, CO. DONEGAL **Tel:** 74 91 34 242 **Fax:** 749134958
Titles:
ENVIRONMENT & ENERGY MANAGEMENT
FOOD & DRINK BUSINESS EUROPE

PRESSLINE LTD 2295
Carraig Court, Georges Avenue, Blackrock, CO. DUBLIN **Tel:** 1 28 85 001 **Fax:** 1 28 86 966
Web site: http://www.pressline.ie
Titles:
BS NEWS (BUILDING SERVICES NEWS)

PRIVATE RESEARCH 2446
Coliemore House, Coliemore Road, Dalkey, CO. DUBLIN **Tel:** 1 28 48 911 **Fax:** 1 20 48 177
Titles:
PRIVATE RESEARCH

PROACTIVE PUBLICATIONS 1727398
88 Lower Baggot Street, DUBLIN 2
Tel: 1 61 10 932
Web site: http://www.glowmagazine.ie
Titles:
GLOW*

PSYCHOLOGICAL SOCIETY OF IRELAND 1777537
CX House, 2A Corn Exchange Place, Poolbeg Street, DUBLIN 2 **Tel:** 1 47 49 160 **Fax:** 11614749
Titles:
THE IRISH PSYCHOLOGIST

PWDI (PEOPLE WITH DISABILITIES IN IRELAND) 1654245
Jervis House, Jervis Street, DUBLIN 1
Tel: 1 87 21 744
Email: info@pwdi.ie
Web site: http://www.pwdi.ie
Titles:
CUMHACHT

RADIO TELEFIS EIREANN 1779276
TV Building, Donnybrook, DUBLIN 4
Tel: 1 20 82 920 **Fax:** 1 20 83 085
Titles:
RTE GUIDE

READOUT PUBLICATIONS 1777484
Caoran, Baile na Habhnan, CO GALWAY
Tel: 87 26 63 282 **Fax:** 91506872

Titles:
READ-OUT

REDEMPTORIST COMMUNICATIONS 698340
75 Orwell Road, Rathgar, DUBLIN 6
Tel: 1 49 22 488 **Fax:** 1 49 27 999
Email: info@faceup.ie
Web site: http://www.faceup.ie

Titles:
FACE UP
REALITY

RELEVANCE PUBLISHING COMPANY 1778385
Block 3A, Mill Bank Industrial Estate, Lower Road, Lucan, CO. DUBLIN 0 **Tel:** 1 60 10 240
Fax: 16010251

Titles:
BLANCH GAZETTE
GAZETTE SERIES

RIVER MEDIA 1780290
Unit W5D, Toughers Business Park, Newbridge, CO. KILDARE **Tel:** 45 40 93 50 **Fax:** 45409351

Titles:
KILDARE POST
LETTERKENNY POST

ROSEBANK MEDIA 1788505
72 Tyrconnell Road, Inchicore, DUBLIN 8
Tel: 1 41 63 678 **Fax:** 14545119

Titles:
RISK MANAGER

ROYAL ACADEMY OF MEDICINE IN IRELAND 2421
Frederick House, 19 South Frederick Street, DUBLIN 2 **Tel:** 1 63 34 820 **Fax:** 1 63 34 918
Email: secretary@rami.ie
Web site: http://www.rami.ie

Titles:
IRISH JOURNAL OF MEDICAL SCIENCE

S AND L PROMOTIONS 1790524
Unit 1, 15 Oxford Lane, DUBLIN 6
Tel: 1 67 61 811 **Fax:** 16761944

Titles:
SENIOR TIMES

SALESIAN BULLETIN 628787
Salesian College, Celbridge, COUNTY KILDARE
Tel: 1 62 75 060 **Fax:** 1 63 03 601
Email: sdbmedia@eircom.net
Web site: http://www.homepage.eircom.net/~sdbmedia

Titles:
SALESIAN BULLETIN

SAOIRSE IRISH FREEDOM 698488
223 Parnell Street, DUBLIN 1 **Tel:** 1 87 29 747
Fax: 1 87 29 757
Web site: http://www.saoirse.rr.nu

Titles:
SAOIRSE IRISH FREEDOM

SEEL PUBLISHING LTD 1779086
Leader House, North Street, Swords, CO. DUBLIN **Tel:** 1 84 00 200 **Fax:** 18400550

Titles:
NORTH COUNTY LEADER

SELECT FURNITURE AND INTERIORS OF IRELAND LTD 1780355
51 Southern Cross Business Park, Boghall Road, Bay, CO. WICKLOW **Tel:** 1 20 21 598

Titles:
SELECT INTERIORS
SELECT KITCHENS AND BATHROOMS

SELECT MEDIA 699429
19 Clare Street, DUBLIN 2 **Tel:** 1 66 22 266

Titles:
THE COLLEGE TIMES
IRISH GOLF REVIEW
IRISH GOLF WORLD
IRISH MUSIC MAGAZINE
TODAY'S PARENTS

SLIGO CHAMPION LTD 1779346
Connacht House, Markievicz Road, CO. SLIGO
Tel: 71 91 69 222 **Fax:** 719169833

Titles:
SLIGO CHAMPION

SLIGO WEEKENDER 1777250
Waterfront House, Bridge Street, SLIGO
Tel: 71 91 74 900 **Fax:** 719174911

Titles:
SLIGO WEEKENDER

SOUTHERN STAR 1777357
Ilen Street, Skibbereen, CO. CORK
Tel: 28 21 200 **Fax:** 2821212

Titles:
SOUTHERN STAR

SPIDERS WEB PUBLISHING LTD 1781133
3 Inishkeen, Kilcool, CO WICKLOW
Tel: 86 24 85 842

Titles:
WORLD TRAVEL TRADE NEWS

SPORTSWORLD PUBLISHING GROUP 1780376
48 North Great Georges Street, DUBLIN 1
Tel: 1 87 80 444 **Fax:** 18787740

Titles:
MOTORING LIFE

ST. PATRICK'S COLLEGE 1778969
St. Patrick's College, Maynooth, CO. KILDARE
Tel: 1 70 83 496 **Fax:** 17083441

Titles:
IRISH THEOLOGICAL QUARTERLY

SUNDAY NEWSPAPERS LTD 1781252
Independent House, 27-32 Talbot Street, DUBLIN 1 **Tel:** 1 88 49 000 **Fax:** 1 88 49 001

Titles:
SUNDAY WORLD
SUNDAY WORLD MAGAZINE

TARA PUBLISHING CO. LTD 2318
Poolbeg House, 1-2 Poolbeg Street, DUBLIN 2
Tel: 1 24 13 000 **Fax:** 1 24 13 020
Email: retailnews@tarapublishingco.com
Web site: http://www.tarapublishingco.com

Titles:
FOOD IRELAND
IRISH PHARMACHEM INDUSTRY BUYERS GUIDE
RETAIL NEWS

TEAGASC 1777888
Oak Park, CARLOW **Tel:** 59 91 70 200
Fax: 599183498

Titles:
TODAY'S FARM

TEMPLE MEDIA LTD 1784058
PO Box 9688, Blackrock, CO DUBLIN
Tel: 1 21 07 513 **Fax:** 12107512

Titles:
CONSTRUCT IRELAND (FOR A SUSTAINABLE FUTURE)

THINK MEDIA 1784039
The Malthouse, 537 NCR, DUBLIN 1
Tel: 1 85 61 166 **Fax:** 18561169

Titles:
JOURNAL OF THE IRISH DENTAL ASSOCIATION

THOMAS CROSBIE HOLDINGS LTD 1777351
Slaney Place, Enniscorthy, CO. WEXFORD
Tel: 53 92 33 231 **Fax:** 53 92 33 506

Titles:
THE ECHO SERIES (ENNISCORTHY)
KILDARE NATIONALIST
ROSCOMMON HERALD SERIES
THE SUNDAY BUSINESS POST
WATERFORD NEWS & STAR

THOMSON REUTERS ROUND HALL 1778757
43 Fitzwilliam Place, DUBLIN 2 **Tel:** 1 66 25 301
Fax: 16625302

Titles:
COMMERCIAL LAW PRACTITIONER
EMPLOYMENT LAW REPORTS
IRISH CURRENT LAW MONTHLY DIGEST
IRISH JOURNAL OF FAMILY LAW
IRISH JURIST
IRISH LAW TIMES
IRISH PLANNING & ENVIRONMENTAL LAW JOURNAL
MEDICO - LEGAL JOURNAL OF IRELAND

TIMES NEWSPAPERS LTD 1778983
Bishop's Square, 4th Floor, Redmond's Hill, DUBLIN 2 **Tel:** 1 47 92 424 **Fax:** 14792421

Titles:
THE SUNDAY TIMES (IRELAND)

TIRCONAILL TRIBUNE LTD 1782666
Main Street, Milford, CO. DONEGAL
Tel: 74 91 53 600 **Fax:** 749153607

Titles:
TIRCONAILL TRIBUNE

TODAYS GROCERY MAGAZINE 2332
The Mews, Eden Road Upper, Dun Laoghaire, Co. Dublin **Tel:** 1 28 09 466
Email: info@todaysgrocery.com
Web site: http://www.todaysgrocery.com

Titles:
TODAY'S GROCERY MAGAZINE

TOPIC NEWSPAPERS LTD 1782325
6 Dominick Street, Mullingar, CO. WESTMEATH
Tel: 44 93 48 868 **Fax:** 449343777

Titles:
IRELAND'S EYE
TOPIC SERIES

TRINITY COLLEGE DUBLIN PUBLICATIONS 1779873
House 6, Trinity College, DUBLIN 2
Tel: 1 89 62 335

Titles:
ICARUS

TULLAMORE TRIBUNE LTD 1777265
William Street, Tullamore, CO. OFFALY
Tel: 57 93 21 152 **Fax:** 579321927

Titles:
TULLAMORE TRIBUNE

UNIVERSITY COLLEGE CORK 1780115
Forum, University College Cork, CORK
Tel: 21 49 03 133 **Fax:** 214903219

Titles:
THE UCC EXPRESS

UPSTAIRS DOWNSTAIRS 1788479
U9 Killkerrin Business Park, Liosban, Tuam Road, CO. GALWAY **Tel:** 91 76 27 50
Fax: 91762753

Titles:
UPSTAIRS DOWNSTAIRS

UR PUBLISHING LTD 1789778
Unit 12, Glenrock Business Park, Bothar na Minne, Ballybane, GALWAY **Tel:** 91 76 27 03
Fax: 91762843

Titles:
UR DREAM HOME

VERITAS COMPANY LTD 1777952
Catholic Communications Office, Columba Centre, Maynooth, CO KILDARE **Tel:** 1 50 53 000
Fax: 16016413

Titles:
INTERCOM

VIP MAGAZINE 1778070
2-4 Ely Place, DUBLIN 2 **Tel:** 1 48 07 700
Fax: 14804799

Titles:
TV NOW!
VIP MAGAZINE

WALTON MEDIA LTD 1788378
E7 Calmount Office Park, Ballymount, DUBLIN 12 **Tel:** 1 41 99 604 **Fax:** 14293910

Titles:
GOLF DIGEST IRELAND

WATERFORD TODAY 1781243
36 Mayor's Walk, WATERFORD **Tel:** 5 18 54 135
Fax: 51854140

Titles:
WATERFORD TODAY

WEEKLY OBSERVER 1788560
19 Bridge Street, Mallow, CO. CORK
Tel: 22 22 910 **Fax:** 2222959

Titles:
OBSERVER & STAR SERIES

WESTERN PEOPLE 1777246
Tone Street, Ballina, CO. MAYO **Tel:** 96 60999
Fax: 96 73458

Titles:
WESTERN PEOPLE

WESTMEATH EXAMINER LTD 1779439
Blackhall Place, Mullingar, CO. WESTMEATH
Tel: 44 93 46 700 **Fax:** 449330765

Titles:
WESTMEATH EXAMINER

WESTMEATH-OFFALY INDEPENDENT 1779358
The Mall, Tullamore, CO. OFFALY
Tel: 57 93 21 403 **Fax:** 579325184

Titles:
OFFALY INDEPENDENT
WESTMEATH INDEPENDENT

WHELAN BYRNE ASSOCIATES 1777428
2 Sunbury, Kilcullen, CO. KILDARE
Tel: 45 48 10 90

Titles:
IRISH CAR AND TRAVEL
IRISH VAN & TRUCK

WHITESPACE PUBLISHING GROUP 1780040
Top Floor, 43B Yeats Way, Park West Business Park, Nangor Road, DUBLIN 12 **Tel:** 1 62 51 444
Fax: 16251402

Titles:
KNOWLEDGE IRELAND
MARKETING AGE

WILEY-BLACKWELL PUBLISHING 1780945
47 Eccles Street, DUBLIN 7 **Tel:** 1 80 32 098
Fax: 18034389

Titles:
BJUI

WMB PUBLISHING 1781258
47 Harrington Street, DUBLIN 8 **Tel:** 1 41 55 056

Titles:
WMB WOMEN MEAN BUSINESS

WOODFIELD PUBLISHING LTD 1778587
Top Floor, 75-76 Camden Street, DUBLIN 2
Tel: 87 647 84 87 **Fax:** 14757301

Titles:
BACKPACKER EUROPE

XL TECHNOLOGY 1778189
Beech Park, Ennis, CO. CLARE **Tel:** 65 68 24 751

Titles:
GLOBAL COMPANY NEWS

ZAHRA PUBLISHING 1778586
1st Floor, 19 Railway Road, Dalkey, CO. DUBLIN
Tel: 1 23 51 408 **Fax:** 12354434

Irish Republic

Titles:
EASY FOOD MAGAZINE
EASY HEALTH
EM

Italy

3NTINI EDITORESRL 1723123
Via Pier Luigi Nervi, 1/B, 44011 ARGENTA (FE)
Tel: 0532 852085 **Fax:** 0532 852692
Titles:
IDEA TATTOO

ABC COMUNICAZIONE 1750212
Piazza Privata Caltagirone 75, 20099 SESTO SAN GIOVANNI **Tel:** 022440579 **Fax:** 0226263674
Titles:
IL DIARIO DEL NORD MILANO

ACACIA EDIZIONI S.R.L. 1722876
Via Saliceto 22 E, 40013 CASTEL MAGGIORE (BO) **Tel:** 051 0933850 **Fax:** 051 0933869
Titles:
AC - AUTOCARAVAN NOTIZIE
COMPUTER IDEA
LEGEND BIKE
PC MAGAZINE
WINDSURF ITALIA

ACE2 1722516
Viale Europa 4/A, 23870 CERNUSCO LOMBARDONE LC **Tel:** 0399900545
Fax: 0399718912
Titles:
FLORTECNICA

ACI/MONDADORI 1771060
Via Cassanese, 224 - Pal. Tiepolo, Milano Oltre, 20090 SEGRATE MI **Tel:** 02 26937550
Fax: 02 26937560
Titles:
PANORAMAUTO

ACINNOVA SRL 1722855
Corso Venezia 43, 20121 MILANO
Tel: 02 7745239 **Fax:** 02 7745201
Titles:
VIA!

ADVENTURES SRL 1722408
Via Comelico 3, 20135 MILANO **Tel:** 02 55188494
Fax: 02 5464407
Titles:
SUB

AG&P S.N.C. IMMAGINE & C 1722943
Via Monte Rosa, 18/A, 20030 SENAGO MI
Tel: 02 99055532 **Fax:** 02 99055532
Titles:
IMMOBILI & CO.

AGRA EDITRICE 1723272
Via Nomentana, 257, 00199 ROMA
Tel: 06 44254205 **Fax:** 06 44254239
Titles:
LEGGERE: TUTTI

ALBA EDITING SRL 1788416
Via San Giacomo, 8, 26030 MALAGNINO
Tel: 0372 444180 **Fax:** 0372 444180
Titles:
AUTOCAPITAL

ALTROCONSUMO NUOVE EDIZIONI SRL 1722673
Via Valassina, 22, 20159 MILANO MI
Tel: 02 668901 **Fax:** 02 66890288
Titles:
ALTROCONSUMO
SOLDI & DIRITTI (ALTROCONSUMO)
TEST SALUTE (ALTROCONSUMO)

AMB ADVERTISING SRL 1784941
Via XXIX Maggio, 18, 20025 LEGNANO MI
Tel: 0323 30122 **Fax:** 032330558
Titles:
SNOWBOARDER MAGAZINE

ARBE EDIT. PUBBLICITARIA 1722883
Via privata Maria Teresa, 11, 20123 MILANO
Tel: 02 89015334 **Fax:** 02 86990124
Titles:
MM MAGAZINE

ARCADATA SRL 1722421
Via Raimondi, 10, 20156 MILANO
Tel: 02 36517220 **Fax:** 02 36517229
Titles:
L' ARCA

ARES ASS.RICERCHE E STUDI 1722640
Via A. Stradivari 7, 20131 MILANO
Tel: 0229526156 **Fax:** 02 29520163
Titles:
STUDI CATTOLICI

ARIETE SERVIZI EDITORIALI SRL 1722565
Corso Venezia, 6, 20121 MILANO MI
Tel: 02 76003516 **Fax:** 02 76003678
Titles:
CORRIERE MEDICO

ARNOLDO MONDADORI EDITORE 1722334
Via Cassanese, 224 - Pal. Tiepolo, Milano Oltre, 20090 SEGRATE MI **Tel:** 02 26937500
Fax: 02 26937525
Titles:
AUTOMOBILE CLUB
CASA FACILE
CASABELLA
CASAVIVA
CHI
CHI RM
CIAK
CIAK RM
CONFIDENZE
CUCINA MODERNA
DONNA IN FORMA (DONNA MODERNA)
DONNA MODERNA
ECONOMY
FLAIR
GRAZIA
GRAZIA CASA
GUIDA TV
HP TRASPORTI CLUB
INTERNI
PANORAMA
PANORAMA - RM
PANORAMA TRAVEL
PC PROFESSIONALE
PROMETEO
SALE & PEPE
TU STYLE
TV SORRISI & CANZONI
TV SORRISI E CANZONI RM
VILLEGIARDINI

ARS ARPEL GROUP 1722353
Via Ippolito Nievo 33, 20145 MILANO
Tel: 02 319121 **Fax:** 02 33611619
Titles:
ARPEL
ARPEL FUR
ARS SUTORIA

ARTI GRAFICHE BOCCIA 1763484
Via Tevere 44, 00198 ROMA **Tel:** 0685356494
Fax: 0668892416
Titles:
TIR - LA RIVISTA DELL'AUTOTRASPORTO

ARUM SRL 1723119
Via Larga, 31, 20122 MILANO **Tel:** 0258376237
Fax: 02 58307557
Titles:
DIRIGENTI INDUSTRIA

ASA AZIENDA SERVIZI ANIMA SRL 1723115
Via Scarsellini, 13, 20161 MILANO
Tel: 02 45418500 **Fax:** 02 45418545
Titles:
L' INDUSTRIA MECCANICA

ASS. ANTIQUARI ITALIA 1722952
Via del Parione, 11, 50123 FIRENZE
Tel: 055 282635 **Fax:** 055 214831
Titles:
GAZZETTA ANTIQUARIA

ASS. ITALIANA EDITORI 1722397
Corso di Porta Romana 108, 20122 MILANO
Tel: 02 89280802 **Fax:** 0289280862
Titles:
GIORNALE DELLA LIBRERIA

ASS. LOMBARDA GIORNALISTI 1722635
Viale Montesanto 7, 20124 MILANO **Tel:** 02 63751
Fax: 02 6595842
Titles:
IL GIORNALISMO

ASSIMPREDIL 1722729
Via San Maurilio, 21, 20123 MILANO MI
Tel: 02 8812951 **Fax:** 02 8056802
Titles:
DEDALO

ASSINFORM SRL 1723255
Viale Dante 12, 33170 PORDENONE
Tel: 0434 26136 **Fax:** 0434 20645
Titles:
ASSINEWS

ASSOCIAZIONE CULTURALE ARTE GIOVANI 1749910
Piazza Zara 3, 10133 TORINO **Tel:** 0116312666
Fax: 0116317243
Titles:
CORRIERE DELL'ARTE

ASSOCIAZIONE ENOLOGI ENOTECNICI ITALIANI 1722641
Via Privata Vasto 3, 20121 MILANO
Tel: 02 99785721 **Fax:** 0299785724
Titles:
L' ENOLOGO

ASSOCIAZIONE GULLIVER 1722771
Via Prati alla Farnesina, 43, 00194 ROMA
Tel: 06 3331718 **Fax:** 06 3331716
Titles:
GULLIVER

ASSTRA SERVICE SRL 1722743
Piazza Cola Di Rienzo, 80/A, 00192 ROMA
Tel: 06 68603548 **Fax:** 06 3226301
Titles:
TRASPORTI PUBBLICI TP

AUTO & DESIGN SRL 1722586
Corso Francia, 54, 10143 TORINO
Tel: 011 488225 **Fax:** 011 488120
Titles:
AUTO & DESIGN

AUTOMOBILE CLUB D'ITALIA 1722555
ACI Sede Centrale - Via Marsala, 8, 00185 ROMA **Tel:** 06 49982277 **Fax:** 06 49982513
Titles:
ONDA VERDE

AVVENIRE NUOVA ED.IT. SPA 1722383
Piazza Carbonari, 3, 20125 MILANO MI
Tel: 02 67801 **Fax:** 02 6780208
Titles:
AVVENIRE
LUOGHI DELL'INFINITO (AVVENIRE)
NOI GENITORI E FIGLI (AVVENIRE)

DI BAIO EDITORE 1722342
Via Settembrini, 11, 20124 MILANO
Tel: 02 67495250 **Fax:** 02 67495333
Titles:
99 IDEE IL BAGNO
L' ARREDAMENTO IN CUCINA
IL CAMINO
CASA GREEN - CASA 99 IDEE
CASE DI CAMPAGNA
CASE DI MONTAGNA
CHIESA OGGI - ARCHITETTURA E COMUNICAZIONE
MILANO CASA OGGI MODI DI VIVERE
LA PISCINA

BANCARIA EDITRICE 1722479
Via delle Botteghe Oscure, 54, 00186 ROMA
Tel: 06 6767465 **Fax:** 06 6767649
Titles:
BANCARIA

BARBERO EDITORI GROUP S.P.A. 1722563
Via Galileo Galilei, 3, 10023 CHIERI TO
Tel: 011 9470400 **Fax:** 011 9470577
Titles:
LA MIA 4X4
LA MIA AUTO
TUTTORALLY

BCI ITALIA SRL 1722945
Via V. Monti 23, 27100 PAVIA **Tel:** 0382 304985
Fax: 0382 303290
Titles:
TOOL NEWS

BEAT PRESS SRL 1723165
Via Newton, 4, 20090 ASSAGO MI
Tel: 02 47791858 **Fax:** 02 45713259
Titles:
BEAT MAGAZINE

BE-MA EDITRICE SRL 1722344
Via Teocrito, 47, 20128 MILANO **Tel:** 02 252071
Fax: 02 27000692
Titles:
ACQUA & ARIA
CONTATTO ELETTRICO
FINITURE&COLORE
MICE - MEETINGS INCENTIVES CONFERENCES EVENTS
MODULO
PELLICCE MODA
PROGETTARE PER LA SANITA'
RI RASSEGNA DELL'IMBALLAGGIO
SPECIALIZZATA EDILIZIA
SUITE
TURISMO D'ITALIA

BLU PRESS 1723110
Via Cavour 65/67, 05100 TERNI **Tel:** 0744 441339
Fax: 0744 432018
Titles:
FEDELTA' DEL SUONO

BMM SRL 1749847
Via Magazzini Anteriori, 51, 48100 RAVENNA
Tel: 0544 590490 **Fax:** 0544 590480
Titles:
BMM

BONELLI CONSULTING SRL 1722705
Viale Parioli, 50, 00197 ROMA RM
Tel: 06 8082643 **Fax:** 06 8072844
Titles:
ITP EVENTS INTERNATIONAL TOURIST PRESS

BRIO SRL 1723188
Via degli Scipioni, 132, 00192 ROMA RM
Tel: 06 32609760 **Fax:** 06 32609768
Titles:
GOSSIP

CAIRO EDITORE 1722423
Corso Magenta 55, 20123 MILANO **Tel:** 02433131
Fax: 02 43313574
Titles:
AIRONE
ANTIQUARIATO
ARTE
BELL'EUROPA
BELL'ITALIA
DI PIU'
DI PIU' - RM
DI PIU' TV
FOR MEN MAGAZINE
GARDENIA
IN VIAGGIO
NATURAL STYLE

C.A.M.A. SAS 1722644
Via Rosales 3, 20124 MILANO **Tel:** 02653270
Fax: 02 29060005
Titles:
SIPARIO

CAMERA COM. SVIZZ. ITALIA 1722623
Via Palestro 2, 20121 MILANO **Tel:** 02 7632031 **Fax:** 02 781084
Titles:
LA SVIZZERA

CAMPUS EDITORI SPA - GRUPPO CLASS EDITORI 1722510
Via Burigozzo, 5, 20122 MILANO MI **Tel:** 02582191 **Fax:** 02 58317438
Titles:
CAMPUS

CARDI EDITORE 1773379
Via Pier Luigi da Palestrina 13, 20124 MILANO **Tel:** 02 67101088 **Fax:** 02 67101041
Titles:
ASSICURA
AZIENDABANCA

CASA ED. UNIVERSO SPA 1722619
Corso di Porta Nuova 3/a, 20121 MILANO **Tel:** 02 63675300 **Fax:** 02 63675519
Titles:
BIMBISANI & BELLI

CASA EDITRICE LA FIACCOLA SRL 1722368
Via Conca Del Naviglio, 37, 20123 MILANO **Tel:** 0289421350 **Fax:** 02 89421484
Titles:
COSTRUZIONI
ITALIAN BUILDING CONSTRUCTION
LE STRADE
VIE & TRASPORTI

CASA EDITRICE SCODE SPA 1722356
Corso Monforte, 36, 20122 MILANO MI **Tel:** 02 7788501 **Fax:** 02 76004905
Titles:
IL MONDO DEL GOLF
SCI
SCIFONDO

C.E.I. SRL 1722607
Piazza San Camillo De Lellis 1, 20124 MILANO **Tel:** 02 66984880 **Fax:** 02 6705538
Titles:
GARDEN & GRILL

CENTRO ITALIANO PUBBLICITÀ SRL 1722466
Via C. Pisacane 26, 20129 MILANO **Tel:** 0229419135 **Fax:** 02 29419056
Titles:
CONGRESS TODAY & INCENTIVE TRAVEL

CENTRO STUDI L'UOMO E L'AMBIENTE 1722476
Via Uguccio De Boso 11, 35124 PADOVA **Tel:** 0498806109 **Fax:** 0498806109
Titles:
AMBIENTE RISORSE SALUTE

CHIRIOTTI EDITORI SRL 1722646
Viale Rimembranza 60, 10064 PINEROLO TO **Tel:** 0121 393127 **Fax:** 0121 794480
Titles:
INDUSTRIE DELLE BEVANDE
INGREDIENTI ALIMENTARI
PASTICCERIA INTERNAZIONALE

CHRONOMEDIA SRL 1722656
Via Giovanni Penta 51, 00157 ROMA **Tel:** 06 41735432 **Fax:** 06 62276256
Titles:
OROLOGI - LE MISURE DEL TEMPO

C.I.P.A. SRL 1722604
Via Andrea Palladio 26, 20135 MILANO **Tel:** 02 58301528 **Fax:** 02 58434326
Titles:
IA INGEGNERIA AMBIENTALE
RS RIFIUTI SOLIDI

CISL 1722415
Via Po, 22, 00198 ROMA **Tel:** 06 8473430 **Fax:** 06 8541233
Titles:
CONQUISTE DEL LAVORO

CITY ITALIA SPA 1751198
Via Rizzoli 8, 20132 MILANO MI **Tel:** 02 50951 **Fax:** 0250952120
Titles:
URBAN

CIUFFA EDITORE SRL 1722517
Via Rasella, 139, 00187 ROMA RM **Tel:** 06 4821150 **Fax:** 06 485964
Titles:
SPECCHIO ECONOMICO

LA CIVILTA' CATTOLICA 1722747
Via di Porta Pinciana 1, 00187 ROMA **Tel:** 06 6979201 **Fax:** 06 69792022
Titles:
LA CIVILTA' CATTOLICA

CLASS EDITORI SPA 1722333
Via Burigozzo, 5, 20122 MILANO MI **Tel:** 02 58219281 **Fax:** 02 58219920
Titles:
CAPITAL
CASE & COUNTRY
CLASS
MFF - MAGAZINE FOR FASHION (MF)
MILANO FINANZA
MILANO FINANZA RM

CLUB ALPINO ITALIANO 1722614
Via Petrella 19, 20124 MILANO **Tel:** 02 2057231 **Fax:** 02 205723201
Titles:
RIVISTA DEL CLUB ALPINO IT. LO SCARPONE - CAI
RIVISTA DEL CLUB ALPINO ITALIANO - CAI

COMMUNICATION AGENCY INT. SRL 1722878
Via San Simpliciano 4, 20121 MILANO **Tel:** 02 862327 **Fax:** 02 863856
Titles:
MASTER MEETING

COMPAGNIA EDITORIALE SRL 1722438
Via Capogrossi, 50, 00155 ROMA RM **Tel:** 06 2285728 **Fax:** 06 2285915
Titles:
CICLOTURISMO GRAN FONDO TECNICHE E RAID

LA CONCERIA SRL 1722919
Via Brisa, 3, 20123 MILANO MI **Tel:** 028807711 **Fax:** 02 865732
Titles:
MDP - LA CONCERIA E LE MANIFATTURE DELLE PELLI

CONDE' NAST SPA 1749900
Piazza Castello, 27, 20121 MILANO MI **Tel:** 0285611 **Fax:** 0285612377
Titles:
WIRED

CONQUISTE DEL LAVORO SRL 1722585
Via Castelfidardo 47, 00185 ROMA **Tel:** 06 44881302 **Fax:** 06 4463878
Titles:
PENSIONATI

CONSORZIO TECNOIMPRESE 1722714
Via Console Flaminio, 19, 20134 MILANO **Tel:** 02 210111250 **Fax:** 02 210111222
Titles:
A&V ELETTRONICA
LED-IN

CONSULENZA EDITORIALE CASA EDITRICE 1723070
Via Lago Gerundo, 26, 26100 CREMONA CR **Tel:** 348 0561675 0372 25591 **Fax:** 0372 450926
Titles:
IL BATTELLIERE

CONTESTI CREATIVI SRL 1771063
Via Tirone, 11, 00146 ROMA **Tel:** 0645213395 **Fax:** 0645213301
Titles:
FASHION FILES
LUXURY FILES

CONTI EDITORE SPA 1722329
Via Del Lavoro, 7, 40068 SAN LAZZARO DI SAVENA BO **Tel:** 051 6227111 **Fax:** 051 6258310
Titles:
AM AUTOMESE
AUTO
AUTOSPRINT
GUERIN SPORTIVO
IN MOTO
MOTOSPRINT

CONVEGNI SRL 1722545
Via Ezio Biondi, 1, 20154 MILANO MI **Tel:** 02 349921 **Fax:** 02 34992290
Titles:
CONVEGNI INCENTIVE & COMUNICAZIONE

COOP EDITRICE CONSUMATORI 1722634
Viale Aldo Moro, 16, 40127 BOLOGNA **Tel:** 051 6316911 **Fax:** 051 6316908
Titles:
CONSUMATORI

COOP. GIORNALISTI SEVEN ARTS SRL 1722779
Via F.lli Cervi-Residenza Archi, 20090 SEGRATE MI **Tel:** 02 26410457 **Fax:** 0278627501
Titles:
JAM VIAGGIO NELLA MUSICA

COOP. GIORNALISTICA MONDO NUOVO 1722560
Casella Postale 18340, 00164 ROMA - BRAVETTA **Tel:** 06 44702611 **Fax:** 06 44702612
Titles:
ANNUARIO DEL SUONO
SUONO

CORRIERE DELLO SPORT SRL 1722414
Piazza Indipendenza, 11/B, 00185 ROMA RM **Tel:** 06 49921 **Fax:** 06 4992690
Titles:
CORRIERE DELLO SPORT-STADIO

CRESPI EDITORI SRL 1722543
C.so Sempione 35, 20015 PARABIAGO MI **Tel:** 0331491440 **Fax:** 0331559410
Titles:
BONSAI & NEWS

D'ANNUNZIO SPA 1774257
c/o Edit. Nord - Piazza De Angeli 9, 20149 MILANO **Tel:** 0287245150 **Fax:** 0287245164
Titles:
TOP GIRL

DAVIDE SRL 1723185
Via IV Novembre 12/A, 21052 BUSTO ARSIZIO MI **Tel:** 0331 327220 **Fax:** 0331 327221
Titles:
LOMBARDIA OGGI (LA PREALPINA)

DBC EDIZIONI SRL 1792226
Via Ferri, 6, 20092 CINISELLO BALSAMO MI **Tel:** 02 66018238 **Fax:** 02 66595846
Titles:
LIGHTING DESIGN COLLECTION

DEL DUCA EDITORE SPA 1722537
Corso di Porta Nuova 3/A, 20121 MILANO MI **Tel:** 02 63675403 **Fax:** 02 63675515
Titles:
CUCINARE BENE
GRAND HOTEL
TELESETTE

DELETTERA EDITORE SRL 1723199
Via A. Tadino, 25, 20124 MILANO **Tel:** 02 36584135
Titles:
CITY PROJECT
RECUPERO E CONSERVAZIONE
STRUCTURAL

DESIGN DIFFUSION WORLD SRL 1722709
Via Lucano, 3, 20135 MILANO **Tel:** 02 5516109 **Fax:** 02 5450120
Titles:
ACTIVA FASHION DESIGN MANAGEMENT
BLU & ROSSO
CASA DI
DDN - DESIGN DIFFUSION NEWS

DEUS EDITORE SRL 1723034
Via Spallanzani 10, 20129 MILANO **Tel:** 02 7422221 **Fax:** 02 74222223
Titles:
DM & COMUNICAZIONE

DG EDIZIONI SRL 1722428
Circonvallazione Nomentana, 212/214, 00162 ROMA **Tel:** 06 8606129 **Fax:** 06 8606324
Titles:
CHRONO WORLD
L' OROLOGIO

DUKE ITALIA SRL 1722720
Via F. Confalonieri 36, 20124 MILANO **Tel:** 0256609300 **Fax:** 0257419081
Titles:
SYSTEM I NEWS EDIZIONE ITALIANA

ED. ABITARE SEGESTA SPA - RCS MEDIA GROUP 1722345
Via Ventura, 5, 20134 MILANO **Tel:** 02 210581 **Fax:** 02 21058316
Titles:
ABITARE
CASE DA ABITARE
COSTRUIRE

ED. ADV ENTE PATRIM.UICCA 1722628
Via Chiantigiana 30 - Falciani, 50023 IMPRUNETA FI **Tel:** 055 2326291 **Fax:** 055 2326241
Titles:
VITA E SALUTE

ED. CENTRO STUDI D'ARTE CULINARIA 1723060
Via Zanella 44/7, 20133 MILANO **Tel:** 0276115315 **Fax:** 02 76115316
Titles:
L' ARTE IN CUCINA

ED. CINQUANTA & PIU' 1722753
L.go Arenula, 34, 00186 ROMA RM **Tel:** 06 68134552 **Fax:** 0668139323
Titles:
50 & PIU'

ED. CITTA' NUOVA 1722750
Via degli Scipioni 265, 00192 ROMA **Tel:** 06 3203620 **Fax:** 06 3219909
Titles:
CITTA' NUOVA

ED. ECOMOTORI 1722765
Piazza A. Moro 33/A, 70122 BARI **Tel:** 080 5242204 **Fax:** 080 5214073
Titles:
ECO MOTORI

ED. FEDERAZIONE ITALIANA CINEFORUM 1722610
Via Pignolo 123, 24121 BERGAMO
Tel: 035361361 Fax: 035341255
Titles:
CINEFORUM

ED. INCONTRI NAUTICI SRL 1722611
Largo Angelicum 6, 00184 ROMA Tel: 06 6990100
Fax: 06 6990137
Titles:
BOLINA MAGAZINE

ED. MUSICA E DISCHI SRL 1722420
Via De Amicis 47, 20123 MILANO
Tel: 02 89402837 Fax: 02 8323843
Titles:
M & D - MUSICA E DISCHI

EDI. CER SPA 1722631
Viale Monte Santo, 40, 41049 SASSUOLO MO
Tel: 0536 804585 Fax: 0536 806510
Titles:
CER - IL GIORNALE DELLA CERAMICA

EDI. ERMES SRL 1722608
Viale Forlanini, 65, 20134 MILANO
Tel: 02 7021121 Fax: 02 70211283
Titles:
SPORT & MEDICINA

EDI TEAM SNC 1722514
Via XXV Aprile 15, 20020 ARESE MI
Tel: 02 93588188 Fax: 02 93588298
Titles:
CASA TESSIL REPORTER
CORTINA AUTO - IL PIACERE DI GUIDARE

EDIBRICO SRL 1722389
Via Vallemme 21, 20135 MILANO MI
Tel: 0143645037 Fax: 0143 645049
Titles:
FAI DA TE FACILE
FAR DA SE'

EDIDOSS SRL 1723037
Via Smareglia 7, 20133 MILANO Tel: 02714298
Fax: 02 7382852
Titles:
GRAN FONDO
RIVISTA TECNO MTB

EDIEMME SRL GRUPPO EDITORIALE 1722920
Zona Artigianale - Contrada Piano Mulino - Stab. 9, 94010 CATENANUOVA EN Tel: 0935 75399
Fax: 0935 545151
Titles:
BOMBONIERA ITALIANA

EDIFIS SPA 1771954
Viale Coni Zugna 71, 20144 MILANO
Tel: 023451230 Fax: 023451231
Titles:
ARTICOLI CASALINGHI E DA REGALO
ARTICOLI CASALINGHI ED ELETTROCASALINGHI
CANTIERI STRADE COSTRUZIONI
L' INDUSTRIA DELLA GOMMA/ELASTICA
L' ORAFO ITALIANO

EDIFORUM SRL 1722450
Via Pietrasanta 14, 20141 MILANO Tel: 02535981
Fax: 0253598247
Titles:
MEDIAFORUM

EDILSTAMPA SRL 1722572
Via Guattani, 24, 00161 ROMA Tel: 0684567403
Fax: 0644232981
Titles:
L' INDUSTRIA DELLE COSTRUZIONI

EDIMAN SRL 1722440
Via Ripamonti 89, 20141 MILANO
Tel: 0257311532 Fax: 02 55231486
Titles:
MC MEETING E CONGRESSI
TURISMO D'AFFARI

EDIMET SPA 1722668
Via Brescia, 117, 25018 MONTICHIARI (BS)
Tel: 030 9981045 Fax: 030 9981055
Titles:
AL - ALLUMINIO E LEGHE

EDINTERNI SRL 1722358
Viale Andrea Doria, 35, 20124 MILANO
Tel: 02 66988188 Fax: 02 66988190
Titles:
BIO CASA
RIFINITURE D'INTERNI
TEX HOME

EDIPUBBLICITÀ SRL 1722751
Viale Romagna 71, 20161 MILANO
Tel: 02 36524496 Fax: 02 70602845
Titles:
COLORE & HOBBY

EDIS EDIZIONI SPECIALIZZATE SRL 1722784
Via Pietro Miliani 7, 40132 BOLOGNA
Tel: 051 6419611 Fax: 051 6419620
Titles:
ESSECOME

EDISERVICE S.R.L. 1722550
Via XX Settembre 60, 50129 FIRENZE
Tel: 055 4633439 Fax: 0554626720
Titles:
JP4 MENSILE DI AERONAUTICA E SPAZIO
PANORAMA DIFESA
PESCA IN MARE

EDISPORT EDITORIALE SPA 1722352
Via Don Luigi Sturzo 7, 20016 PERO (MI)
Tel: 02 38085262 Fax: 02 38010393
Titles:
ARMI E TIRO
AUTOMOBILISMO
CICLISMO
MOTOCICLISMO
MOTOCICLISMO D'EPOCA
MOTOCICLISMO FUORI STRADA
SPECIALI DI MOTOCICLISMO
SUPER WHEELS
IL TENNIS ITALIANO
VELA E MOTORE

EDIT PROM SRL 1723162
Via A.G. Ragazzi 9, 40011 ANZOLA DELL'EMILIA BO Tel: 051 6424004 Fax: 051 733008
Titles:
PNEURAMA

EDITORE GIANFRANCO FINI 1722413
Via Della Scrofa, 43, 00186 ROMA RM
Tel: 06 68899221 Fax: 06 6861598
Titles:
SECOLO D'ITALIA

EDITORE MINISTERO DELLA DIFESA 1770040
Via di San Marco, 8, 00186 ROMA RM
Tel: 06 47357373 Fax: 0647358139
Titles:
RIVISTA MILITARE

EDITORE PANINI SPA 1762088
c/o Emmei - Via Guido Reni 33, 00196 ROMA RM Tel: 0645615060
Titles:
CIOE'
CIOE' GIRL
CLEO'
DEBBY PIU'
PUPA
TWEENS

EDITORE SIPI SRL 1722447
Viale Dell'Astronomia 30 - c/o Confindustria, 00144 ROMA Tel: 0632507379 Fax: 0697656829
Titles:
QUALEIMPRESA

EDITORI PER LA FINANZA 1723160
Via Tristano Calco, 2, 20123 MILANO
Tel: 02 303026 1 Fax: 02 303026240
Titles:
BORSA & FINANZA
FINANZA & MERCATI

EDITORIALE AERONAUTICA 1722727
Via del Corso, 504, 00186 ROMA RM
Tel: 063217922 Fax: 06 3612368
Titles:
AIR PRESS

EDITORIALE C&C SRL 1746073
Via Molise, 3, 20085 LOCATE TRIULZI MI
Tel: 02 9048111 Fax: 02 904811210
Titles:
AUTO TECNICA
MOTO STORICHE & D' EPOCA
SUPER MOTOTECNICA

EDITORIALE DELFINO SRL 1722717
Via Lomellina, 33, 20133 MILANO
Tel: 02 70004542 Fax: 02 70005054
Titles:
ELETTRIFICAZIONE

EDITORIALE DI FOTOSHOE SRL 1722441
Via Leonardo Da Vinci, 43, 20090 TREZZANO SUL NAVIGLIO MI Tel: 02 4459091
Fax: 02 48402959
Titles:
FOTO SHOE 15
FOTO SHOE 30

EDITORIALE DOMUS SPA 1722426
Via Gianni Mazzocchi 1/3, 20089 ROZZANO MI
Tel: 02824721 Fax: 02 82472386
Titles:
DOMUS
MERIDIANI
QUATTRORUOTE
QUATTRORUOTE AUTOPRO
QUATTRORUOTINE
RUOTECLASSICHE
TUTTOTRASPORTI
VOLARE

EDITORIALE DUESSE SPA 1722745
Via Donatello, 5/B, 20131 MILANO MI
Tel: 02 277961 Fax: 02 27796300
Titles:
BEST MOVIE
SELL OUT
TIM-TRADE INTERACTIVE MULTIMEDIA
TRADE CONSUMER ELECTRONICS
TRADE HOME ENTERTAINMENT

EDITORIALE GENESIS SRL 1722460
Via Vincenzo Monti 15, 20123 MILANO
Tel: 02 48194401 Fax: 02 4818658
Titles:
PRIMA COMUNICAZIONE

EDITORIALE GIORNALIDEA S.R.L. 1722542
Piazza della Repubblica 19, 20124 MILANO
Tel: 02 6888775 Fax: 02 6888780
Titles:
FARMA MESE
SAPERE & SALUTE

EDITORIALE IN PIU' 1722394
Via Tacito, 74, 00193 ROMA Tel: 06 32600149
Fax: 06 32600168
Titles:
L' AGENZIA DI VIAGGI

EDITORIALE LA NUOVA ECOLOGIA SOC. COOP. 1722461
Via Salaria, 403, 00199 ROMA Tel: 06 86203691
Fax: 06 86218474
Titles:
LA NUOVA ECOLOGIA

EDITORIALE LARGO CONSUMO 1722506
Via Bodoni 2, 20155 MILANO Tel: 023271646
Fax: 02 325190
Titles:
LARGO CONSUMO

EDITORIALE LARIANA 1791822
Via Ciro Menotti 11/D, 20129 MILANO MI
Tel: 02 76110303 Fax: 02 7496183
Titles:
CIVILTA' DEL BERE

EDITORIALE LAUDENSE SRL 1722416
Via Gorini, 34, 26900 LODI Tel: 0371 544200
Fax: 0371 544201
Titles:
IL CITTADINO LODI

EDITORIALE LIBERTÀ 1723018
Via Benedettine 68, 29100 PIACENZA
Tel: 0523 393939 Fax: 0523 343976
Titles:
LIBERTA'

EDITORIALE MODA SRL 1722651
Via Giardini 476/N, 41124 MODENA
Tel: 059342001 Fax: 059351290
Titles:
INTIMO PIU' MARE
MAGLIERIA ITALIANA
MENU'

EDITORIALE OLIMPIA SPA 1722427
Via Zante, 14, 20138 MILANO Tel: 0236633301
Fax: 0236633339
Titles:
ARMI E MUNIZIONI
CANI
CRONACA FILATELICA
CRONACA NUMISMATICA
DIANA
HOBBY ZOO
MIGRAZIONE E CACCIA
MONDO SOMMERSO - INTERNATIONAL OCEAN MAGAZINE
PESCARE MARE
IL PESCATORE D'ACQUA DOLCE

EDITORIALE SPORT ITALIA 1722497
Via Masaccio, 12, 20149 MILANO MI
Tel: 02 4815396 Fax: 02 4690907
Titles:
CORRERE
IL NUOVO CALCIO

EDITORIALE TRASPORTI SRL 1722606
Piazza S. Silvestro 13 - Sala stampa italiana, 00141 ROMA RM Tel: 06 99330133
Fax: 0699330134
Titles:
CORRIERE DEI TRASPORTI

EDITRICE BIBLIOGRAFICA 1722398
Via G. Bergonzoli, 1/5, 20127 MILANO
Tel: 02 28315998 Fax: 02 28315906
Titles:
BIBLIOTECHE OGGI

EDITRICE CUSTOM S.A.S. 1722879
Via Ciro Di Pers 38, 33030 MAJANO UD
Tel: 0432 948570 Fax: 0432 948606
Titles:
BIKERS LIFE

EDITRICE DIAMANTE 1722658
Via Cusani, 10, 20121 MILANO MI Tel: 02809606
Fax: 02809609
Titles:
MOTOCROSS

EDITRICE KREA 1722702
Piazzatta Scannaserpe 3, 90146 PALERMO
Tel: 091543506 Fax: 0916373378
Titles:
SIKANIA

EDITRICE KURTIS SRL 1722597
Via Luigi Zoja 30, 20153 MILANO
Tel: 02 48202740 **Fax:** 02 48201219
Titles:
AGGIORNAMENTO MEDICO
AGING

EDITRICE LA SCUOLA 1722601
Via Cadorna, 11, 25124 BRESCIA **Tel:** 030 29931
Fax: 030 2993299
Titles:
DIDATTICA DELLE SCIENZE E INFORM.SCUOLA
SCUOLA ITALIANA MODERNA

EDITRICE L'AMMONITORE 1722626
Via Crispi, 19, 21100 VARESE **Tel:** 0332 283039
Fax: 0332 234666
Titles:
L' AMMONITORE

EDITRICE LEADER INTERSERVICE SRL 1723114
Corso Vercelli 53, 20145 MILANO MI
Tel: 02463334 **Fax:** 02 4980526
Titles:
PLUS MAGAZINE

EDITRICE LECCHESE SRL 1722499
Corso XXV Aprile, 74/b, 22036 ERBA CO
Tel: 031 646300 **Fax:** 031 646222
Titles:
GIORNALE DI ERBA
IL GIORNALE DI LECCO

EDITRICE MAESTRI S.R.L. 1723036
Piazza Sant'Agostino, 22, 20123 MILANO
Tel: 0229412353 **Fax:** 02 29416826
Titles:
AE-ATTUALITA' ELETTROTECNICA NEWS

EDITRICE MODERNE INTERNAZIONALE SRL 1722430
Via Gadames, 123, 20151 MILANO MI
Tel: 02 36588435 **Fax:** 0236588222
Titles:
CHERIE BIMBI
PRIMA CASA

EDITRICE MRC SPA 1722887
Viale del Policlinico, 131, 00161 ROMA RM
Tel: 06 441831 **Fax:** 06 44183254
Titles:
LIBERAZIONE - QUOT. PARTITO RIFOND. COMUN.

EDITRICE PROGRESSO SRL 1722474
Viale Piceno, 14, 20129 MILANO MI
Tel: 02 70002222 **Fax:** 02 713030
Titles:
TUTTI FOTOGRAFI
ZOOM - LA RIVISTA DELL'IMMAGINE

EDITRICE QUADRATUM SPA 1722513
Piazza Aspromonte, 13, 20131 MILANO MI
Tel: 02 706421 **Fax:** 0270638544
Titles:
LA CUCINA ITALIANA
INTIMITA'
ROLLING STONE

L' EDITRICE SAS 1723112
Via Lomellina 33, 20133 MILANO
Tel: 02 55181842 **Fax:** 02 55184161
Titles:
LA TERMOTECNICA

EDITRICE SKIPPER SRL 1722512
Viale Papiniano 10, 20123 MILANO
Tel: 02 58323055 **Fax:** 02 58318001
Titles:
INVESTIRE

EDITRICE TEMI SRL 1722459
Via Italia 39, 20052 MONZA **Tel:** 0392302398
Fax: 0392302383
Titles:
LOGISTICA MANAGEMENT

EDITRICE TRASPORTI SAS DI BOIDI ANNA MARIA & C. 1722581
Via B. Eustachi, 47, 20129 MILANO
Tel: 02 6690427 **Fax:** 02 6694185
Titles:
TRASPORTI NEWS

EDITRICE VIMERCATESE SRL 1722942
Via Cavour 59, 20059 VIMERCATE MI
Tel: 039 625151 **Fax:** 039 6853349
Titles:
IL GIORNALE DI VIMERCATE

EDITRICE ZEUS SAS 1722434
V.le Lunigiana, 14, 20125 MILANO MI
Tel: 02 67100605 **Fax:** 02 67100621
Titles:
ITALIAN FOOD MACHINES
ITALIAN MAGAZINE FOOD PROCESSING
RASSEGNA ALIMENTARE

EDIWEB 1722433
Via Ferri 6, 20092 CINISELLO BALSAMO MI
Tel: 02 61294990 **Fax:** 02 66594914
Titles:
IL VORTICE

EDIZIONI ARIMINUM SRL 1723029
Via Negroli, 51, 20133 MILANO MI **Tel:** 02 730091
Fax: 02 717346
Titles:
VEDERE ITALIA

EDIZIONI BAIAMONTI SRL 1723215
Piazzale Baiamonti, 2, 20154 MILANO MI
Tel: 02 653272 **Fax:** 02 87393845
Titles:
OLGA E OLIVER

EDIZIONI C&C SRL 1722857
Via Naviglio 37/2, 48018 FAENZA RA
Tel: 0546 22112 **Fax:** 0546662046
Titles:
RADIO KIT ELETTRONICA

EDIZIONI CARRARA 1723122
Via Calepio, 4, 24125 BERGAMO **Tel:** 035 243618
Fax: 035 270298
Titles:
CELEBRIAMO

EDIZIONI CESIL SRL 1722407
Via Olmetto 5, 20123 MILANO **Tel:** 02 878397
Fax: 02 866576
Titles:
LEADER FOR CHEMIST HEALTH STRATEGY
LEADERSHIP MEDICA

EDIZIONI CONDE' NAST SPA 1722406
P.zza Castello 27, 20121 MILANO
Tel: 02 85612401 **Fax:** 02 8692363
Titles:
AD ARCHITECTURAL DIGEST
GLAMOUR
GQ
SPOSABELLA
TRAVELLER
L' UOMO VOGUE
VANITY FAIR
VOGUE BAMBINI
VOGUE GIOIELLO
VOGUE ITALIA
VOGUE PELLE
VOGUE SPOSA

EDIZIONI D'ARGENZIO SRL 1722349
Via L. B. Alberti, 12, 20149 MILANO
Tel: 02 33600952 **Fax:** 02 3314397
Titles:
TREND AVANTGARDE WAVE

EDIZIONI DATIVO SRL 1722967
Via B. Crespi, 30/2, 20159 MILANO
Tel: 0269007733 **Fax:** 02 69007664
Titles:
ITALIAIMBALLAGGIO

EDIZIONI DEDALO 1722522
Via Farfa 22-24, 00142 ROMA **Tel:** 06 54602121
Fax: 06 54602129
Titles:
SAPERE

EDIZIONI ECOMARKET SPA 1722486
Piazza Pio XI, 1, 20123 MILANO MI **Tel:** 02806201
Fax: 02 80620444
Titles:
FASHION

EDIZIONI ESAV SRL 1722593
Via Cavour 50, 10123 TORINO **Tel:** 01183921111
Fax: 0118125661
Titles:
ALLURE
ESTETICA

EDIZIONI GOLD SRL 1722525
Via Angelo della Pergola, 9, 20159 MILANO
Tel: 02 680189 **Fax:** 02 606298
Titles:
18 KARATI - GOLD & FASHION

EDIZIONI IENS SRL 1722666
Via Taramelli 19, 20124 MILANO **Tel:** 0269007179
Fax: 02 6072078
Titles:
SISTEMI DI TELECOMUNICAZIONI

EDIZIONI INFORMATORE AGRARIO SPA 1722596
Via Bencivenga-Biondani, 16, 37133 VERONA
Tel: 045 8057547 **Fax:** 045 597510
Titles:
L' INFORMATORE AGRARIO
VITA IN CAMPAGNA

EDIZIONI LA CUBA SRL 1722409
Via Della Maratone 66, 00194 ROMA
Tel: 063629021 **Fax:** 06 36309950
Titles:
BICI DA MONTAGNA - MOUNTAIN BIKE WORLD
LA BICICLETTA
IL SUBACQUEO

EDIZIONI LA STAMPA SPA 1722382
Via Carlo Marenco, 32, 10126 TORINO TO
Tel: 011 6568111 **Fax:** 011 6568924
Titles:
LA STAMPA
TUTTOSCIENZE (LA STAMPA)

EDIZIONI L'INCONTRO 1722621
Via Consolata 11, 10122 TORINO
Tel: 011 5212000 **Fax:** 011 5212000
Titles:
L' INCONTRO

EDIZIONI MADRE SRL 1722652
Via Callegari 6, 25121 BRESCIA **Tel:** 030 42132
Fax: 030 290521
Titles:
MADRE

EDIZIONI MASTER 1766190
Contrada Lecco, 64 Z.I., 87036 RENDE CS
Tel: 0984 8319200 **Fax:** 0984 8319225
Titles:
GO! ONLINE INTERNET MAGAZINE
IDEA WEB
LINUX MAGAZINE
OFFICE MAGAZINE
QUALE COMPUTER
WEEKEND & VIAGGI
WIN MAGAZINE

EDIZIONI MIGLIO SRL 1722916
Via Emilia Ponente 26, 40133 BOLOGNA
Tel: 051 385700 **Fax:** 051 384793
Titles:
TOP SPORT

EDIZIONI MIMOSA S.R.L. 1722351
Piazza De Angeli 9, 20146 MILANO
Tel: 0236505607 **Fax:** 02 48110494
Titles:
RAKAM

EDIZIONI MINERVA MEDICA 1722707
C.so Bramante 83, 10126 TORINO
Tel: 011 678282 **Fax:** 011 674502
Titles:
GAZZETTA MEDICA ITALIANA
MEDICINA DELLO SPORT
MINERVA ANESTESIOLOGICA
MINERVA CARDIOANGIOLOGICA
MINERVA CHIRURGICA
MINERVA GINECOLOGICA
MINERVA MEDICA
MINERVA PEDIATRICA
MINERVA STOMATOLOGICA

EDIZIONI PEGASO INTERNATIONAL SRL 1722524
Villa Torzo - Via Prato Fiera 19, 31100 TREVISO
Tel: 0422 412727 **Fax:** 0422 541875
Titles:
AUTO D'EPOCA

EDIZIONI PEI SRL 1722791
Strada Naviglio Alto 46/1, 43100 PARMA
Tel: 0521771818 **Fax:** 0521 773572
Titles:
PRESENZA TECNICA IN EDILIZIA
QUARRY AND CONSTRUCTION

EDIZIONI PLEIN AIR 1722632
P.zza Irnerio, 11, 00165 ROMA RM
Tel: 06 6632628 **Fax:** 06 6637266
Titles:
PLEINAIR

EDIZIONI RIZA SPA 1722454
Via L. Anelli 1, 20122 MILANO **Tel:** 02 5845961
Fax: 02 58318162
Titles:
DIMAGRIRE
RIZA PSICOSOMATICA
RIZA SCIENZE
SALUTE NATURALE

EDIZIONIZERO SRL 1723253
Via Orti, 14, 20122 MILANO MI **Tel:** 02 5403141
Fax: 0254031450
Titles:
ZERO

E.G.E.A. 1722500
Via Roentgen, 1, 20136 MILANO **Tel:** 02 58363706
Fax: 02 58363791
Titles:
FINANZA MARKETING E PRODUZIONE

ELI ED. LIVING SRL 1722536
Via Anton Giulio Bragaglia 33, 00123 ROMA RM
Tel: 06 96521600 **Fax:** 06 96521622
Titles:
VILLE & CASALI

ELLEDICI 1722570
P.zza Ateneo Salesiano 1 c/o Univ. Pontificia, 00139 SALESIANA - ROMA **Tel:** 06 87290505
Fax: 06 87290505
Titles:
ARMONIA DI VOCI
MONDO ERRE

ELSEVIER SRL 1722367
Via Paleocapa, 7, 20121 MILANO **Tel:** 02 88184 1
Fax: 02 881841302
Titles:
CORTEX
DENTAL CADMOS
IL GIORNALE DELL'ODONTOIATRA
MONDO ORTODONTICO

EMMEK SRL - MOTORESEARCH SRL
1735195
Via Ponte Gardena, 46, 00124 ROMA RM
Tel: 06 50910640 **Fax:** 0645227207

Titles:
SCOOTER MAGAZINE

ENTE EDITORIALE PER L'ARMA DEI CARABINIERI
1723097
Piazza San Bernardo 109, 00187 ROMA
Tel: 06483780 **Fax:** 06 48904053

Titles:
IL CARABINIERE

EPC PERIODICI SRL
1722443
Via Dell'Acqua Traversa 187/189, 00135 ROMA
Tel: 06 33245 1 **Fax:** 06 3313212

Titles:
AMBIENTE & SICUREZZA SUL LAVORO
ANTINCENDIO

EPE SRL
1722757
Via La Spezia, 33, 20142 MILANO MI
Tel: 02 89501830 **Fax:** 0289501604

Titles:
LINEAVERDE

EPH (ZAGABRIA)
1753114
Via Sarnano, 36, 00156 ROMA **Tel:** 335 395537
Fax: 06 62276298

Titles:
JUTARNJI LIST

ERIS PROGRAM SRL
1722966
Va E. Tellini 19, 20155 MILANO **Tel:** 02 3108121
Fax: 02 33611129

Titles:
PLAST DESIGN

E.S.I. SRL
1722562
Via Della Balduina 88, 00136 ROMA
Tel: 06 35344859 **Fax:** 06 35454503

Titles:
TENNIS OGGI

E.S.T.E. SRL
1722393
Via A. Vassallo, 31, 20125 MILANO MI
Tel: 02 91434400 **Fax:** 02 91434424

Titles:
SISTEMI & IMPRESA
SVILUPPO & ORGANIZZAZIONE

EUROFORUM SRL
1723016
Via Gaggia 1/A, 20124 MILANO **Tel:** 02 6774101
Fax: 0267741050

Titles:
BUSINESS

EUROSPORT EDITORIALE SRL
1722908
Via della Bufalotta, 378, 00139 ROMA RM
Tel: 06 45231502 **Fax:** 06 45231598

Titles:
ELABORARE

EV SRL
1722580
Palazzo Trecchi, 26100 CREMONA
Tel: 0372 403507 **Fax:** 0372 457091

Titles:
VETERINARIA - RIVISTA UFFICIALE DELLA SCIVAC

FED. IT. GIOCO BRIDGE
1722744
Via Ciro Menotti 11/C, 20129 MILANO MI
Tel: 02 70000333 **Fax:** 02 70001398

Titles:
BRIDGE D'ITALIA

FEDERAZIONE AEIT
1722616
Via Mauro Macchi, 32, 20124 MILANO MI
Tel: 0287389967 **Fax:** 0266989023

Titles:
AEIT
L' ENERGIA ELETTRICA

FIERA MILANO EDITORE S.P.A
1742985
SS Sempione 28, 20017 RHO MI **Tel:** 0249971
Fax: 0249976573

Titles:
AO - AUTOMAZIONE OGGI
AUTOMAZIONE E STRUMENTAZIONE
EO NEWS
INQUINAMENTO - TECNOLOGIE AMBIENTE UOMO
MIXER
PROGETTARE
RMO - RIVISTA DI MECCANICA OGGI

FIERA MILANO EDITORE S.P.A - DIVISIONE TECHNOLOGY
1749809
S.S. del Sempione, 28, 20017 RHO - MI
Tel: 02 49976516 **Fax:** 02 49976570

Titles:
ELETTRONICA OGGI

FINANZA E FISCO SNC
1722731
Via Cristoforo Colombo, 436, 00145 ROMA RM
Tel: 06 5416320 **Fax:** 06 5415822

Titles:
FINANZA & FISCO

FIORATTI EDITORE SRL
1722742
Via Alessandro Tadino 5, 20124 MILANO
Tel: 02 6570414 **Fax:** 02 6555791

Titles:
ITINERARI E LUOGHI

F.LLI PINI EDITORI SRL
1722449
Via L.B. Alberti, 10, 20149 MILANO
Tel: 02 33101836 **Fax:** 02 3450749

Titles:
DATA MANAGER

FLOR MEDIA SRL
1722534
Via Torino 64, 20123 MILANO **Tel:** 02 72000035
Fax: 02 89013013

Titles:
PUBBLICO

FONDAZIONE APOSTOLICAM ACTUOSITATEM
1722852
Via Aurelia, 481, 00165 ROMA RM **Tel:** 06 661321
Fax: 06 66132360

Titles:
SEGNO NEL MONDO

FONDAZIONE COLOGNI
1777097
Via Statuto, 10, 20121 MILANO MI
Tel: 02 6572444 **Fax:** 02 6592695

Titles:
ARTIGIANATO TRA ARTE E DESIGN

FONDAZIONE D'ARS OSCAR SIGNORINI ONLUS
1722520
Giardino Aristide Calderini 3 - Via S.Agnese 3, 20123 MILANO **Tel:** 02 860290 **Fax:** 02 865909

Titles:
D'ARS

FOTOGRAFARE SRL
1722677
Via Camerata Picena, 385, 00138 ROMA RM
Tel: 068818752 **Fax:** 068803658

Titles:
FOTOGRAFARE

FREE WHEELS SRL
1722904
Via XXV Aprile, 99, 20068 PESCHIERA BORROMEO MI **Tel:** 02 55300839
Fax: 02 55300837

Titles:
TUTTO FUORISTRADA

GAMBERO ROSSO EDITORE
1722448
Via Enrico Fermi, 161, 00146 ROMA RM
Tel: 06 551121 **Fax:** 06 55112260

Titles:
GAMBERO ROSSO

GESTO EDITORE SRL
1722531
Viale Coni Zugna 71, 20144 MILANO
Tel: 023451230 **Fax:** 023451231

Titles:
MODA E INDUSTRIA

GGF EDITORE SRL
1788415
Via Angelo Maj, 12, 20135 MILANO MI
Tel: 02 55196076 **Fax:** 02 54108521

Titles:
PENELOPE

GIA DI GIORGIO ARIU
1722754
Via Sardegna 132, 09124 CAGLIARI
Tel: 070728356 **Fax:** 070728356

Titles:
IL CAGLIARITANO

GIANCARLO POLITI EDITORE
1722528
Via Carlo Farini, 68, 20159 MILANO MI
Tel: 02 6887341 **Fax:** 02 66801290

Titles:
FLASH ART ITALIA

GIDIEMME
1722364
Via Fieramosca, 31, 20052 MONZA MI
Tel: 039 2620010 **Fax:** 039 834190

Titles:
ITALY EXPORT

GIENNE EDITORE SRL
1794253
c/o Arbe - Via Emilia Ovest 1014, 41123 MODENA **Tel:** 059896957 **Fax:** 059896951

Titles:
BIANCO & BRUNO

GIORGIO NADA EDITORE
1722994
Via Claudio Treves, 15/17, 20090 VIMODRONE MI **Tel:** 02 27301126 27301462 **Fax:** 02 27301454

Titles:
LA LIBRERIA DELL'AUTOMOBILE MAGAZINE

GIUFFRE' EDITORE
1722470
Via Lanzone, 4 - c/o Studio Portale, 20123 MILANO **Tel:** 02 720881 **Fax:** 02 72088300

Titles:
BANCA BORSA E TITOLI DI CREDITO
DIRITTO DEL COMMERCIO INTERNAZIONALE
IL DIRITTO DELL'INFORMAZ. E INFORMATICA
DIRITTO ED ECONOMIA DELL'ASSICURAZIONE
GIUSTIZIA CIVILE
RIVISTA GIURIDICA DELL'AMBIENTE

GIUNTI EDITORE
1722431
Via Bolognese 165, 50139 FIRENZE
Tel: 055 5062303 **Fax:** 055 5062298

Titles:
ARCHEOLOGIA VIVA
ART E DOSSIER
LA VITA SCOLASTICA

GIVI SRL
1722591
Via San Gregorio, 6, 20124 MILANO MI
Tel: 02 2020431 **Fax:** 02 20204343

Titles:
GUIDA VIAGGI

GO.TU SRL
1722437
Via Winckelmann 2, 20146 MILANO
Tel: 0242419 1 **Fax:** 02 48953252

Titles:
LA CORSA
GOLF & TURISMO
ONBOARD

GRAFILL EDITORIA TECNICA SRL
1723201
Via Principe di Palagonia, 87, 90145 PALERMO PA **Tel:** 091 6823069 **Fax:** 091 6823313

Titles:
LAVORI PUBBLICI

GREENTIME S.P.A.
1723041
Via Ugo Bassi, 7, 40121 BOLOGNA BO
Tel: 051 223327 **Fax:** 051222946

Titles:
ARCO
CACCIA & TIRO

GRIONI EDITORE SRL
1735186
Via G. Verga 4, 26831 CASALMAIOCCO LO
Tel: 02 4239446 **Fax:** 02 98175029

Titles:
GIORNALE DEL RIVENDITORE EDILE
IL GIORNALE DELL'EDILIZIA ITALIANA

GRUNER+JAHR-MONDADORI
1722773
Via Battistotti Sassi 11/a, 20133 MILANO MI
Tel: 02 762101 **Fax:** 02 76013379

Titles:
FOCUS
JACK

GRUPPO B EDITORE SRL
1722801
Via T. Tasso, 7, 20123 MILANO **Tel:** 02 43990124
Fax: 02 43910204

Titles:
NUOVO ORIONE

GRUPPO ED. L'ESPRESSO SPA
1722332
Via Cristoforo Colombo, 90, 00147 ROMA
Tel: 0649821 **Fax:** 06 49822303

Titles:
AFFARI & FINANZA (LA REPUBBLICA)
D LA REPUBBLICA DELLE DONNE (LA REPUBBLICA)
L' ESPRESSO
L' ESPRESSO MI
LA REPUBBLICA
IL VENERDI' DI REPUBBLICA (LA REPUBBLICA)
XL MAGAZINE (LA REPUBBLICA)

GRUPPO EDITORIALE COLLINS SRL
1722755
Via G. Pezzotti 4, 20141 MILANO **Tel:** 028372897
Fax: 028373458

Titles:
FERRAMENTA & CASALINGHI
NOTIZIARIO MOTORISTICO

GRUPPO IL SOLE 24 ORE S.P.A.
1722335
Via C. Pisacane 1, 20016 PERO MI
Tel: 0230223002 **Fax:** 0230226025

Titles:
COSTRUIRE IN LATERIZIO
FRAMES ARCHITETTURA DEI SERRAMENTI
LAVORO SICURO - IL SOLE 24 ORE
MARK UP
SICUREZZA
IL SOLE 24 ORE
IL SOLE 24 ORE CENTRONORD - FI
IL SOLE 24 ORE EDILIZIA E TERRITORIO
IL SOLE 24 ORE GUIDA AGLI ENTI LOCALI
IL SOLE 24 ORE SANITA'
IL SOLE 24 ORE SCUOLA
IL SOLE 24 ORE TRASPORTI
TERZO SETTORE

GRUPPO POCKET SRL
1735218
Via A. Bertoloni 49, 00197 ROMA RM
Tel: 0680692327 **Fax:** 0680693415

Titles:
POCKET

GUIDO TALARICO EDITORE SPA
1743985
Via Archimede, 201, 00197 ROMA RM
Tel: 06 8080099 **Fax:** 06 99700312

Titles:
INSIDE ART

GUIDO VENEZIANI EDITORE FOOD
1735193
Viale Tunisi 21, 20124 MILANO MI
Tel: 0289656612

Titles:
STOP
VERO
VERO SALUTE (VERO)

HACHETTE RUSCONI SPA
1762261
Viale Sarca, 235, 20126 MILANO MI **Tel:** 02 66191
Fax: 02 66192717

Titles:
GIOIA CUCINA (GIOIA)
GIOIA SALUTE (GIOIA)

HEALTH COMMUNICATION SRL
1735192
Via Vittore Carpaccio, 18, 00147 ROMA
Tel: 06 594461 **Fax:** 06 59446228
Titles:
IL FARMACISTA

HEARST LIFESTYLE MEDIA
1792096
Viale Sarca, 235, 20126 MILANO MI
Tel: 02 36609611 **Fax:** 0236609631
Titles:
YACHT DIGEST

HEARST MAGAZINES ITALIA
1723017
Viale Sarca 235, 20126 MILANO MI
Tel: 02 66192866 **Fax:** 02 66192651
Titles:
AUTO & FUORISTRADA
COSMOPOLITAN
ELLE
ELLE DECOR
GENTE
GENTE MOTORI
GENTE - RM
GIOIA
GIOIA BAMBINI (GIOIA)
HOME HACHETTE
YACHT CAPITAL

H.M.C ITALIA SRL
1763485
Viale Sarca, 235, 20126 MILANO
Tel: 02 66193795 **Fax:** 02 66192483
Titles:
MARIE CLAIRE

IDM SRL
1722575
Piazza Agrippa, 1, 20141 MILANO MI
Tel: 02 89546696 **Fax:** 02 89515438
Titles:
AREALEGNO
L' INDUSTRIA DEL MOBILE
IL LEGNO

Il CORRIERE.NET SRL
1722533
Via Duccio Galimberti, 7, 12051 ALBA CN
Tel: 0173045250 **Fax:** 0173281280
Titles:
OASIS

INFLY ADM EDITORI
1791316
MILANO
Titles:
IN TRAVEL

INTERLINEA EDITRICE SCRL
1722710
Via del Corso 303, 00186 ROMA **Tel:** 0669921143
Fax: 0669921143
Titles:
FARE VELA

INTERNATIONAL SEA PRESS
1723066
Via Giuseppe Tartini, 13/c, 20158 MILANO
Tel: 02 39359111 **Fax:** 02 39359122
Titles:
BARCHE

INTERNAZIONALE
1723230
Viale Regina Margherita, 294, 00198 ROMA
Tel: 06 4417301 **Fax:** 06 44252718
Titles:
INTERNAZIONALE

IPSOA WOLTERS KLUWER ITALIA S.R.L.
1722410
Strada 1 Palazzo F. 6, 20090 MILANOFIORI ASSAGO MI **Tel:** 02 82476085 **Fax:** 02 82476800
Titles:
AMMINISTRAZIONE & FINANZA
AZIENDA & FISCO
COMMERCIO INTERNAZIONALE
CORRIERE TRIBUTARIO
LE SOCIETA'

L' ISOLA
1722504
Piazza Roma, 1, 22070 LURAGO MARINONE CO **Tel:** 031937736 **Fax:** 031937362
Titles:
MOTOTURISMO

L' ISOLA SRL
1723175
Via Sempione, 25, 20016 PERO MI
Tel: 02 3581586
Titles:
L' ISOLA

ISTITUTO PIME
1735184
Via Guerrazzi, 11, 00152 ROMA **Tel:** 06 58320223
Fax: 06 58157756
Titles:
ASIA NEWS

ITALIA OGGI ED. ERINNE
1722341
Via Marco Burigozzo, 5, 20122 MILANO
Tel: 02 582191 **Fax:** 02 58317598
Titles:
ITALIA OGGI
ITALIA OGGI SETTE

ITER SRL
1722924
Via Rovetta, 18, 20127 MILANO **Tel:** 02 2831161
Fax: 02 28311666
Titles:
VOICECOM NEWS

JRP SRL
1749817
Via Quarnero, 1, 20146 MILANO **Tel:** 02 467781
Fax: 02 46778111
Titles:
AZ FRANCHISING

JUST BE SRL
1783131
Via Messina, 47, 20154 MILANO MI
Titles:
COMPUTERWORLD ITALIA
PC WORLD ITALIA

K IDEA EDITORE SRL
1722715
Via Don Romano Grosso, 45/11, 10060 AIRASCA TO **Tel:** 011 9908841 **Fax:** 011 9908841
Titles:
MOTORINEWS

KOSTER PUBLISHING SPA
1722484
Via della Liberazione, 1, 20068 PESCHIERA BORROMEO MI **Tel:** 02 55305067
Fax: 02 55305068
Titles:
BELLAUTO
IL GIORNALE DELLA LOGISTICA
IL GOMMONE E LA NAUTICA PER TUTTI

LEDITORE SRL
1722961
Via Gadames, 123, 20151 MILANO MI
Tel: 02 365881 **Fax:** 02 36588222
Titles:
AF DIGITALE
MONTEBIANCO

LIBERETA' SPA
1722445
Via Dei Frentani 4/A, 00185 ROMA
Tel: 06 44481291 **Fax:** 06 4469012
Titles:
LIBERETA'

LIFEGATE SPA
1735212
Via Manzoni, 18, 22046 MERONE CO
Tel: 031 61803 **Fax:** 031 6180310
Titles:
LIFEGATE.IT

LINEA COMMERCIALE EP &C.
1723168
Via della Stradella 14, 20900 MONZA MB
Tel: 039 737312 **Fax:** 039 736547
Titles:
LA CARTOLERIA

LOGOS PUBLISHING SRL
1722348
Strada Curtatona 5/2, 41125 MODENA
Tel: 059412432 **Fax:** 059412623
Titles:
COLLEZIONI TRENDS
DOLCI
GIARDINI & AMBIENTE

LOMBARD EDITORI
1774739
Via Burigozzo 5, 20122 MILANO **Tel:** 02 582191
Fax: 02 58317518
Titles:
LOMBARD

LOTUS PUBLISHING
1743080
Via Calcare, 15, 00048 NETTUNO RM
Tel: 06452216742 **Fax:** 06 23328541
Titles:
CASA CHIC

LUXOS ITALIA SRL
1750348
Via Pietrasanta 12, 20141 MILANO MI
Tel: 0287387400 **Fax:** 0287387719
Titles:
LUXOS

MADE IN ITALY S.R.L.
1722759
C.so Vittorio Emanuele 15, 20122 MILANO
Tel: 0236560315 **Fax:** 02 561727
Titles:
MADE IN ITALY

MAG EDITORI SRL
1723214
Via Eustachi, 31, 20129 MILANO **Tel:** 02 20241592
Fax: 02 20249336
Titles:
CARAVAN E CAMPER GRANTURISMO

MAGGIOLI EDITORE SPA
1722728
Via F. Albani, 21, 20149 MILANO
Tel: 02 48545811 **Fax:** 0248517108
Titles:
ILLUMINOTECNICA

MAGGIOLI SPA
1722671
c/o CPO Rimini - via Coriano, 58, 47900 RIMINI
Tel: 0541 628111 **Fax:** 0541 622100
Titles:
COMUNI D'ITALIA
CROCEVIA
DISCIPLINA DEL COMMERCIO & DEI SERVIZI
PAESAGGIO URBANO - DOSSIER DI CULTURA E PROGETTO
RU - RISORSE UMANE NELLA P.A. SANITA' PUBBLICA E PRIVATA
I SERVIZI DEMOGRAFICI
L' UFFICIO TECNICO

MANI DI FATA SRL
1722569
Via Vettabbia, 7, 20122 MILANO **Tel:** 02 58310413
Fax: 0258310536
Titles:
MANI DI FATA

IL MANIFESTO COOP. ED.
1722380
Via Bargoni, 8, 00153 ROMA RM **Tel:** 06 687191
Fax: 06 68719573
Titles:
IL MANIFESTO

MAT EDIZIONI
1771953
Via Confalonieri, 36, 20124 MILANO MI
Tel: 025660931 02 56609380 **Fax:** 0256609344
Titles:
COMPUTER DEALER & VAR
LINEA EDP
TOP TRADE INFORMATICA
WINDOWS & .NET MAGAZINE - ED. ITALIANA

MATTEL ITALY S.R.L.
1722796
Centro Direzionale Maciachini, Via B. Crespi 19/C, 20159 MILANO MI **Tel:** 02 699631
Fax: 02 69963699
Titles:
BARBIE MAGAZINE

MAX BUNKER PRESS
1722509
Via Fatebenefratelli, 15, 20121 MILANO
Tel: 02 6592969 **Fax:** 02 6570226
Titles:
ALAN FORD

MAXIM ITALIA SPA
1722950
V.le Sondrio, 7, 20124 MILANO **Tel:** 02 89051800
Fax: 02 89051814
Titles:
MAXIM MAGAZINE

MEDIA AGE SRL
1722633
Via San Michele del Carso, 13, 20144 MILANO MI **Tel:** 02 43910135 **Fax:** 02 43999112
Titles:
MONITOR RADIO TELEVISIONE

MEDIA ERIS SRL
1750314
Via Enrico Tellini, 19, 20155 MILANO
Tel: 02 3108121 **Fax:** 02 33611129
Titles:
NT NATURE TRADE

MEDIA KEY SRL
1722439
Via Arcivescovo Romilli, 20/8, 20139 MILANO
Tel: 02 5220371 **Fax:** 02 55213037
Titles:
MEDIA KEY
TV KEY

MEDIA PLUS SRL
1722655
Via Capecelatro, 53/2, 20148 MILANO MI
Tel: 02 4039949
Titles:
MEDIAPLUSNEWS

MEDIASPAZIO SRL
1722615
Via M. Melloni, 17, 20129 MILANO **Tel:** 02 718341
Fax: 02 714067
Titles:
FOTONOTIZIARIO VIDEO NOTIZIARIO

MEGA REVIEW SRL
1743344
Via Vasco De Gama, 65, 50127 FIRENZE
Tel: 055 412199 **Fax:** 055 4360111
Titles:
FLORENCE CONCIERGE

MESSAGGERO DI S.ANTONIO EDITRICE
1722659
Via Orto Botanico, 11, 35123 PADOVA
Tel: 049 8225909 **Fax:** 049 8225650
Titles:
MESSAGGERO DEI RAGAZZI
MESSAGGERO DI S. ANTONIO

MILANO FINANZA ED. SPA
1722979
Via Burigozzo, 5, 20122 MILANO MI
Tel: 0258219375 **Fax:** 02 58317429
Titles:
GENTLEMAN

IL MIO CASTELLO SPA
1722388
Via Feltre, 28/6, 20132 MILANO **Tel:** 02 270861
Fax: 02 87365819
Titles:
IL MIO VINO

MIRATA SRL
1750324
Via Pietrasanta, 14 Edificio 2, 20141 MILANO (MI) **Tel:** 02 55015253 **Fax:** 0255195851
Titles:
ENJOY

MONDADORI RODALE SRL
1722561
Via Mondadori, 1, 20090 SEGRATE MI
Tel: 02 75423190 **Fax:** 02 75423193
Titles:
MEN'S HEALTH
STARBENE

MONEYPENNY SRL
1749840
Via delle Lame, 113 a, 40122 BOLOGNA
Tel: 051 5870750 **Fax:** 051 5870752
Titles:
ETIQUETTE

MORALES SRL 1722718
Piazza San Giovanni, 6, 23017 MORBEGNO SO **Tel:** 0342 611979 **Fax:** 0342 611717

Titles:
NUOVA ELETTRAUTO

MOTONAUTICA EDITRICE SRL 1722403
Via IV Novembre, 54, 20019 SETTIMO MILANESE (MI) **Tel:** 02 33553234 **Fax:** 02 33513441

Titles:
MOTONAUTICA

MTE EDIZIONI SRL 1722711
Via Romolo Gessi, 28, 20146 MILANO **Tel:** 02 4239443 **Fax:** 02 4123405

Titles:
EXPORT MAGAZINE

MULTIVISION SRL 1722736
Via Fabio Massimo 107, 00192 ROMA **Tel:** 06 45437670 **Fax:** 06 45437670

Titles:
PRIMISSIMA

IL MUSICHIERE 1722748
Via Monte Tomatico, 1, 00141 ROMA **Tel:** 06 86219922 **Fax:** 06 86219788

Titles:
CHITARRE

MY WAY MEDIA SRL 1723321
Viale Sarca, 235, 20126 MILANO MI **Tel:** 02 217681 **Fax:** 0266192622

Titles:
SERIES

NAUTICA EDITRICE SRL 1722554
Via Tevere, 44, 00198 ROMA **Tel:** 06 8413060 **Fax:** 06 8543653

Titles:
NAUTICA

NETWEEK - MEDIA LOCALI 1722902
Strada Statale 31, Km 22, 15030 VILLANOVA MONFERRATO AL **Tel:** 0142 338249 **Fax:** 0142 483907

Titles:
SPENDIBENE

NEW EXPLORER S.A.S. 1758545
Piazza Bonghi, 16, 10147 TORINO **Tel:** 0112629577 **Fax:** 0112203441

Titles:
A4 AUTORUOTE 4X4

NEWBAY MEDIA ITALY SRL 1722982
S.Felice Strada Prima, 12, 20090 SEGRATE MI **Tel:** 02 92884940 **Fax:** 02 70300211

Titles:
BROADCAST & PRODUCTION ITALIA

NEWMEDIAPRO SRL 1722391
Via Monte Nero, 101, 00012 GUIDONIA MONTECELIO (RM) **Tel:** 06 8720331 **Fax:** 06 87139141

Titles:
ACS - AUDIOCARSTEREO
AUDIO REVIEW
DIGITAL VIDEO HOME THEATER

NEWSPAPER MILANO SRL 1722549
Via Gaetano Negri, 4, 20123 MILANO **Tel:** 02 7218701 **Fax:** 02 7218708

Titles:
BANCAFINANZA
ESPANSIONE
GIORNALE DELLE ASSICURAZIONI

NOVA CHARTA SAS 1722790
Via Giudecca, 671, 30133 VENEZIA **Tel:** 041 5211204 **Fax:** 041 5208538

Titles:
CHARTA - COLLEZIONISMO ANTIQUARIATO MERCATI

NUOV@ PERIODICI ITALIA SRL 1722369
Via Zante, 16/2, 20138 MILANO MI **Tel:** 02 580381 **Fax:** 02 58013422

Titles:
MACWORLD ITALIA
NETWORK WORLD ITALIA (COMPUTERWORLD)

NUOVA EDITORIALE SPORTIVA 1722384
Corso Svizzera, 185, 10149 TORINO TO **Tel:** 011 77731 **Fax:** 011 7773483

Titles:
TUTTOSPORT

NUOVA INIZIATIVA EDITORIALE SPA 1723045
Via Ostiense 131/L, 00153 ROMA RM **Tel:** 06 585571 **Fax:** 06 58557219

Titles:
L' UNITA'

OPINIONI SCGRL 1743124
Piazzale De Agostini, 3, 20146 MILANO MI **Tel:** 02 42297513 **Fax:** 02 99981609

Titles:
SUPERPARTES IN THE WORLD

O.P.S. SRL 1722664
P.le Accursio, 14, 20156 MILANO **Tel:** 02 3920621 **Fax:** 02 39257050

Titles:
PROMOTION MAGAZINE

OPTOSERVICE SRL 1723030
Via Cenisio, 32, 20154 MILANO MI **Tel:** 02 33611052 **Fax:** 02 3491374

Titles:
OTTICA ITALIANA

OTTIS SURL 1722419
Via Winckelmann, 2, 20146 MILANO MI **Tel:** 02 424191 **Fax:** 0248953252

Titles:
SCIARE MAGAZINE

PANAMA EDITORE 1722706
Via Quaranta, 52, 20139 MILANO MI **Tel:** 02 5358111 **Fax:** 0256802965

Titles:
IL GIORNALE DELLA VELA
IL GIORNALE DELLE BARCHE A MOTORE
TREND

PANINI SPA 1722548
Via Eugenio Villoresi, 15, 20143 MILANO MI **Tel:** 02 89404021 **Fax:** 028361182

Titles:
FORZA MILAN!

PARAGON SRL 1742984
Via Alberto Mario 20 c/o Paragon Srl, 20149 MILANO **Tel:** 02 4816353 **Fax:** 02 4818968

Titles:
AMADEUS

PASSONI EDITORE 1723013
Piazza Duca d'Aosta, 12, 20124 MILANO MI **Tel:** 02 6760681 **Fax:** 02 6702680

Titles:
M.D. MEDICINAE DOCTOR

PATRIZIA ROGNONI 1723134
Via Fornari, 8, 20146 MILANO MI **Tel:** 02 4073270 **Fax:** 02 4073270

Titles:
COLLANA CREAIDEE

PERIODICI SAN PAOLO SRL 1722327
Via Giotto 36, 20145 MILANO MI **Tel:** 02 48071 **Fax:** 02 48072778

Titles:
FAMIGLIA CRISTIANA
JESUS

IL PERIODICO EDITORE SRL 1743343
Via Pisacane, 16, 20129 MILANO **Tel:** 02 70100135 **Fax:** 02 70102517

Titles:
CIOCCOLATA & C.

PIMEDIT ONLUS 1722595
Via Mose' Bianchi, 94, 20149 MILANO **Tel:** 02 43822317 **Fax:** 02 43822397

Titles:
E VAI
MONDO E MISSIONE

PISANI EDITORE S.R.L. 1722417
Via C. Colombo, 1, 20094 CORSICO MI **Tel:** 02 89159373 **Fax:** 02 89159349

Titles:
LINEA INTIMA ITALIA

PISCOPO EDITORE SRL 1735182
Viale Platone, 24, 00136 ROMA **Tel:** 0639746755 **Fax:** 063231847

Titles:
ASTRELLA
EVA 3000
VIP

PLAY MEDIA COMPANY SRL 1722378
Viale Forlanini, 23, 20134 MILANO **Tel:** 02 45472867 **Fax:** 02 45472869

Titles:
CHIP
GIRLFRIEND

LE POINT VETERINAIRE ITALIE 1723068
Via Medardo Rosso, 11, 20159 MILANO **Tel:** 02 6085231 **Fax:** 06 6682866

Titles:
LA SETTIMANA VETERINARIA

POLIGRAFICI ED. SPA 1722339
Via Stradivari, 4, 20131 MILANO **Tel:** 02 277991 **Fax:** 02 27799537

Titles:
IL GIORNO
LA NAZIONE
QN MODA
IL RESTO DEL CARLINO

PRESS & IMAGE 2001 SPA 1722590
Via Leopoldo Serra, 32, 00153 ROMA **Tel:** 06 585501 **Fax:** 06 5809826

Titles:
VOCE DEL TABACCAIO

PRIMA PAGINA EDIZIONI 1722953
Via Inama, 7, 20133 MILANO MI **Tel:** 02 89500028 **Fax:** 02 89512140

Titles:
TUTTOBICI

PRINCIPEMEDIA S.R.L. 1723169
Via Volturno, 31, 25126 BRESCIA BS **Tel:** 030 3730487 **Fax:** 030 3730368

Titles:
DENTRO CASA

PRO.COM 1735227
Via delle Alpi, 13, 00198 ROMA RM **Tel:** 06 44202596 **Fax:** 06 44254426

Titles:
TECHNOSHOPPING

PROGEDIT EDITORIALE SRL 1722498
Via Rovereto, 6, 00198 ROMA **Tel:** 06 8552649 **Fax:** 06 8558885

Titles:
CAR AUDIO & FM
CAR STEREO & FM

PROMAPLAST SRL 1722636
Milanofiori Palazzo F3, 20090 ASSAGO MI **Tel:** 02 82283775 **Fax:** 02 57512490

Titles:
MACPLAS

PROMEDIA SRL 1771827
Via B. De Rolandi, 15, 20156 MILANO MI **Tel:** 02 324434 **Fax:** 02 39257668

Titles:
LA CHIMICA E L'INDUSTRIA

PROMODIS ITALIA EDITRICE 1722797
Via Corfù,50, 25125 BRESCIA **Tel:** 030 220261 **Fax:** 030 225868

Titles:
NUOVA DISTRIBUZION&

PROMOS EDIZIONI SRL 1722493
Via G.Watt, 37, 20143 MILANO MI **Tel:** 02 89151814 **Fax:** 02 89151830

Titles:
QUALITYTRAVEL DIRECTORY

PROSCEGNIO SRL 1722762
Via Carlo Botta, 4, 20135 MILANO **Tel:** 02 55193793 **Fax:** 02 5460154

Titles:
L' OPERA

PROSCENIUM S.A.S 1722473
Piazza Statuto, 1, 10122 TORINO **Tel:** 011 19703356 **Fax:** 011 19703356

Titles:
BALLETTO OGGI

PUBBLINDUSTRIA SRL 1723007
Via Giuseppe Mazzini, 132, 56125 PISA **Tel:** 050 49490 **Fax:** 050 49451

Titles:
FOOD INDUSTRIA
HI-TECH AMBIENTE
SURGELATI MAGAZINE

PUBLIBRANDS ITALIA S.R.L. 1723210
Via Milazzo 6, 20121 MILANO **Tel:** 02 36 63 6738 **Fax:** 02 4983358

Titles:
INTOWN MAGAZINE

PUBLICATIONS&PROMOTION SRL 1722465
Via Mauro Macchi, 28, 20124 MILANO **Tel:** 02 66714341 **Fax:** 02 66713975

Titles:
SPORTIVO

LA PUBLIEDIM SRL 1722738
Via Matteo Civitali, 51, 20148 MILANO **Tel:** 02 48703201 **Fax:** 02 48703614

Titles:
EI-TECH
ON DOMESTIC HI-TECH

PUBLIFASHION S.R.L. 1722970
Via Offienze, 156, 00154 ROMA RM **Tel:** 06 83394637 **Fax:** 06 5743052

Titles:
BOOK MODA
BOOK MODA UOMO

PUNTO EFFE SRL 1723309
Via Boscovich, 61, 20124 MILANO **Tel:** 02 2022941 **Fax:** 02 29513121

Titles:
PUNTO EFFE

QUOTIDIANO IL TEMPO SRL 1722340
Piazza Colonna, 366, 00187 ROMA RM **Tel:** 06 675881 **Fax:** 06 67588232

Titles:
IL TEMPO

RCS LIBRI SPA 1722638
Via Mecenate, 91, 20138 MILANO **Tel:** 02 50951 **Fax:** 02 50952309

Titles:
ECONOMIA & MANAGEMENT
L' EDUCATORE

RCS PUBLISHING ITALIA SRL 1723307
Via Rizzoli 8, 20132 MILANO **Tel:** 02 50956836 **Fax:** 02 50956878
Titles:
DOVE

RCS QUOTIDIANI S.P.A. 1722385
Via Solferino 28, 20121 MILANO **Tel:** 02 6339 **Fax:** 02 62059668
Titles:
CORRIERE DELLA SERA
CORRIERE ECONOMIA (CORRIERE DELLA SERA)
CORRIERE SALUTE (CORRIERE DELLA SERA)
LA GAZZETTA DELLO SPORT
SETTE (CORRIERE DELLA SERA)
VIVIMILANO (CORRIERE DELLA SERA)

RCS RIZZOLI PERIODICI SPA 1722331
Via A. Rizzoli 8, 20132 MILANO **Tel:** 02 25841 **Fax:** 02 25843905
Titles:
A ANNA
AMICA
ASTRA
BRAVA CASA
CASAMICA (CORRIERE DELLA SERA)
DOMENICA QUIZ
IO DONNA (IL CORRIERE DELLA SERA)
MAX
IL MONDO
NOVELLA 2000
OGGI
OGGI - RM
OK LA SALUTE PRIMA DI TUTTO
VISTO

REED BUSINESS INFORMATION SPA 1777095
Viale G. Richard, 1, 20143 MILANO MI **Tel:** 02 81830648 **Fax:** 0281830414
Titles:
ATELIER BAGNO
IL BAGNO OGGI E DOMANI
IL GELATIERE ITALIANO
IL GIORNALE DELL'INSTALLATORE ELETTRICO
NUOVA FINESTRA
IL PANIFICATORE ITALIANO
PARTS
IL PASTICCIERE ITALIANO
PLAST - RIVISTA DELLE MATERIE PLASTICHE
TIS - IL CORRIERE TERMOIDROSANITARIO

REGIONE EMILIA ROMAGNA 1723077
V.le A. Moro, 52, 40127 BOLOGNA **Tel:** 051 5275926 **Fax:** 051 6395596
Titles:
LE ISTITUZIONI DEL FEDERALISMO

RENOGRAFICA 1722701
Via Seragnoli, 13, 40138 BOLOGNA **Tel:** 051 6026111 **Fax:** 051 6026150
Titles:
CORTINA MAGAZINE

RIMA EDITRICE SRL 1722401
Viale Sarca, 243, 20126 MILANO **Tel:** 02 66103539 **Fax:** 02 66103558
Titles:
CASARREDO & DESIGN
IL GDA GIORNALE DELL'ARREDAMENTO
RIABITA

RIZZOLI PUBLISHING ITALIA SRL 1792227
Via Rizzoli 8, 20132 MILANO **Tel:** 02 50952713 **Fax:** 0250952720
Titles:
Y&S YACHT&SAIL (CORRIERE DELLA SERA)

ROCCHI EDITORE SRL 1723081
Via dei Gracchi 318, 00192 ROMA **Tel:** 0632120148 **Fax:** 067232256
Titles:
A TAVOLA

S3 STUDIUM SRL 1722956
Corso Vittorio Emanuele II, 209, 00186 ROMA **Tel:** 06 68210415 **Fax:** 06 68213114
Titles:
NEXT - STRUMENTI PER L'INNOVAZIONE

LE SCIENZE S.P.A. 1722490
Via Cristoforo Colombo, 149, 00147 ROMA RM **Tel:** 06 49823181 **Fax:** 06 49823184
Titles:
LE SCIENZE

SCUOLA BEATO ANGELICO - FONDAZIONE DI CULTO 1722719
Via S. Gimignano, 19, 20146 MILANO MI **Tel:** 02 48302854 **Fax:** 02 48301954
Titles:
ARTE CRISTIANA RIVISTA INTERNAZIONALE

SEDIT SRL SERVIZI EDITORIALI 1722906
Via Delle Orchidee, 1 - A.S.I. BARI, 70026 MODUGNO BA **Tel:** 080 5857444 **Fax:** 080 5857428
Titles:
GAZZETTA DELL'ECONOMIA

S.E.G.E. SRL 1722435
Via Di Porta Maggiore, 95, 00185 ROMA **Tel:** 06 70300005 **Fax:** 06 70300007
Titles:
PORTA PORTESE

SEPE 1722758
Corso Vittorio Emanuele, 101, 00186 ROMA **Tel:** 06 6852397 **Fax:** 06 6861726
Titles:
AGRICOLTURA NUOVA
MONDO AGRICOLO

SET SRL 1722494
Piazza A. Mancini, 4/G, 00196 ROMA **Tel:** 06 3233195 **Fax:** 06 3233309
Titles:
MOTOR

SFERA EDITORE SPA 1722424
Via Rizzoli, 8, 20132 MILANO **Tel:** 02 50366687 **Fax:** 02 50366688
Titles:
DONNA & MAMMA
IL GIORNALE DELL'INFANZIA
IMAGINE
INSIEME
IO E IL MIO BAMBINO

SHINDA EDIZIONI SRL 1722355
Vial Olgiati, 26, 20143 MILANO MI **Tel:** 02 89151200 **Fax:** 02889151237
Titles:
CDA - CONDIZIONAMENTO DELL'ARIA
GIORNALE DELLA SUBFORNITURA
ICP-RIVISTA DELL'INDUSTRIA CHIMICA

SOC. ED. IL MULINO SPA 1722582
Strada Maggiore, 37, 40125 BOLOGNA **Tel:** 051 222419 **Fax:** 051 6486014
Titles:
IL MULINO
NUOVA INFORMAZIONE BIBLIOGRAFICA
LE REGIONI

SOC. EUROPEA DI EDIZIONI 1722374
Via Gaetano Negri, 4, 20123 MILANO MI **Tel:** 02 85661 **Fax:** 02 72023880
Titles:
IL GIORNALE

SOCCER SAS DI BRAND MANAGEMENT SRL 1722390
Via di Trigoria Km 3,600 c/o Centro Sportivo F. B, 00128 ROMA **Tel:** 06 5062163 **Fax:** 06 50651013
Titles:
LA ROMA

SOCIETÀ COOPERATIVA EDITORIALE ETICA 1723238
Via Copernico, 1, 20125 MILANO **Tel:** 02 67199099 **Fax:** 02 67491691
Titles:
VALORI

SOCIETA' ED.IL MESSAGGERO 1722422
Via Del Tritone 152, 00187 ROMA **Tel:** 06 47201 **Fax:** 06 4720665
Titles:
IL MESSAGGERO

SOCIETÀ EDITORIALE PERRONE SPA 1722566
Piazza Piccapietra, 21, 16121 GENOVA GE **Tel:** 010 53881 **Fax:** 010 5388426
Titles:
IL SECOLO XIX

SOCIETÀ EDITRICE UMBERTO ALLEMANDI & C. SPA 1722467
Via Mancini, 8, 10131 TORINO TO **Tel:** 011 8199111 **Fax:** 011 8393771
Titles:
IL GIORNALE DELL'ARTE

SOIEL INTERNATIONAL SRL 1722895
Via Martiri Oscuri, 3, 20125 MILANO **Tel:** 02 26148855 **Fax:** 02 26149333
Titles:
EXECUTIVE.IT
OFFICE AUTOMATION
OFFICELAYOUT

IL SOLE 24 ORE - EDITORIA SPECIALIZZATA SRL 1722475
Via Goito, 13, 40126 BOLOGNA **Tel:** 051 6575857 **Fax:** 051 6575856
Titles:
COLTURE PROTETTE
INFORMATORE ZOOTECNICO
TERRA E VITA
VIGNEVINI

IL SOLE 24 ORE SPA 1722376
Via Pisacane 1, 20016 PERO MI **Tel:** 02 30221 **Fax:** 0230226244
Titles:
AMBIENTE CUCINA
APPLICANDO
AUTOMAZIONE INDUSTRIALE
BAGNO E ACCESSORI
BARGIORNALE
CERAMICA INFORMAZIONE
LA CERAMICA MODERNA & ANTICA
COME RISTRUTTURARE LA CASA
EUROSAT
GDOWEEK
GDOWEEK BLU
GDS IL GIORNALE DEL SERRAMENTO
MILLECANALI
PCB MAGAZINE
PIANETA HOTEL
RISTORAZIONE COLLETTIVA - CATERING
SELEZIONE DI ELETTRONICA
US

SOTHIS EDITRICE SRL 1723091
Via Pietro Maestri, 3, 00191 ROMA **Tel:** 06 3295642 **Fax:** 06 3295624
Titles:
LA CLESSIDRA

SPORTSWEAR INTERNATIONAL 1722990
Piazza Pio XI, 1, 20123 MILANO **Tel:** 02 806 20 1 **Fax:** 02 806 20 333
Titles:
SPORTSWEAR INTERNATIONAL

SPREA EDITORI S.P.A. 1722539
Via Torino, 51, 20063 CERNUSCO S.N. **Tel:** 02 924321 **Fax:** 02 92432236
Titles:
AMICI DI CASA
ARGOS
COMPUTER ARTS
COMPUTER MAGAZINE
CUCINA LIGHT
DIGITAL CAMERA MAGAZINE
IL FOTOGRAFO
THE GAMES MACHINE
GIOCHI PER IL MIO COMPUTER
IL MIO COMPUTER

ST. PAULS INTERNATIONAL 1722630
Via Giotto, 36, 20145 MILANO **Tel:** 02 48010498 **Fax:** 02 48021801
Titles:
CLUB 3 - VIVERE IN ARMONIA

STAFF EDITORIALE SNC 1723191
Via G. Rossetti, 9, 20145 MILANO **Tel:** 02 48007449 **Fax:** 02 48007493
Titles:
COMPOARREDO
COMPOLUX
ITALIAN LIGHTING

STEMAX COOP. 1722756
Via Antonio Silvani, 8 (scala D int. 4), 00139 ROMA **Tel:** 068121374 **Fax:** 06 8108317
Titles:
MUCCHIO SELVAGGIO

STUDIO ZETA SRL 1722480
Via San Fruttuoso 10, 20052 MONZA MI **Tel:** 039 736451 **Fax:** 039 736500
Titles:
MONOVOLUME & STATION WAGON RADAR
OROLOGI DA POLSO

SUNNYCOM PUBLISHING SRL 1722377
Via Stromboli, 18, 20144 MILANO **Tel:** 02 48516207 **Fax:** 02 43400509
Titles:
COMUNICANDO
ITALIA PUBLISHERS MAGAZINE

SUPERPRINT EDITORIALE SRL 1722526
Via Mattei, 106, 40138 BOLOGNA **Tel:** 051 6006068 **Fax:** 051 6006657
Titles:
CAVALLO MAGAZINE & LO SPERONE

TECNICHE NUOVE SPA 1722347
Via Eritrea 21, 20157 MILANO **Tel:** 02390901 **Fax:** 0239090331
Titles:
AE - APPARECCHI ELETTRODOMESTICI
AUTOMAZIONE INTEGRATA
BAGNO DESIGN
BEAUTYLINE
COMMERCIO IDROTERMOSANITARIO
CONFEZIONE
CUCINA NATURALE
IL DENTISTA MODERNO
L' ERBORISTA
FARMACIA NEWS
FLUID - TRASMISSIONI DI POTENZA
GEC - IL GIORNALE DEL CARTOLAIO
IL GIORNALE DELL'ALBERGATORE
GT IL GIORNALE DEL TERMOIDRAULICO
HOTEL DOMANI
IMBOTTIGLIAMENTO
L' IMPIANTO ELETTRICO & DOMOTICO
IMPRESE EDILI
INTERNET.PRO
ITALIA GRAFICA
KOSMETICA
LABORATORIO 2000
LAMIERA
LOGISTICA
LUCE E DESIGN
MACCHINE UTENSILI
MEDICINA NATURALE
NOLEGGIO
IL NUOVO CANTIERE
ORGANI DI TRASMISSIONE
PROGETTARE ARCHITETTURA CITTÀ TERRITORIO
IL PROGETTISTA INDUSTRIALE
RCI - RISCALDAMENTO CLIMATIZZAZ. IDRONICA
SERRAMENTI + DESIGN
TECNICA CALZATURIERA
TEMA FARMACIA
ZERO SOTTO ZERO

TECNOEDIZIONI S.R.L. 1773562
Via Garbiera, 1, 20021 BOLLATE **Tel:** 0292865345 **Fax:** 0292865340
Titles:
TECNOPLAST

Italy

TEKNOSCIENZE SRL
1722469
Viale Brianza, 22, 20127 MILANO
Tel: 02 26809375 **Fax:** 02 2847226
Titles:
CHIMICA OGGI

TICHE ITALIA SRL
1743093
Via Settala, 2, 20124 MILANO **Tel:** 02 36537800
Fax: 02 36537814
Titles:
FILM TV

TOURING CLUB ITALIANO
1722456
Corso Italia, 10, 20122 MILANO **Tel:** 02 8526529
Fax: 02 8526299
Titles:
QUI TOURING

TRAVEL AGENT BOOK SRL
1722735
Via Merlo, 1, 20122 MILANO MI **Tel:** 02 76316846
Fax: 02 76013193
Titles:
TRAVEL QUOTIDIANO

TRAVEL FACTORY SRL
1722704
Via di Sant'Agata De Goti, 2, 00184 ROMA
Tel: 06 6789984 **Fax:** 06 6991260
Titles:
MASTER VIAGGI

LE TRE ARANCE SRL
1723002
Via Tortona, 14, 20144 MILANO MI
Tel: 0258106415 **Fax:** 0258106428
Titles:
FUTURA MAGAZINE

TRE D EDITORIALE SRL
1722859
Corso di Porta Nuova, 3/a, 20121 MILANO
Tel: 02 636751 **Fax:** 02 63675522
Titles:
SILHOUETTE DONNA

TTG ITALIA SPA
1722404
Via Alberto Nota, 6, 10122 TORINO
Tel: 011 4366300 **Fax:** 011 4366500
Titles:
TTG ITALIA

TURISMO E ATTUALITA' SRL
1722700
Via S. Prisca 16, 00153 ROMA **Tel:** 06 5747450
Fax: 06 5744154
Titles:
TURISMO E ATTUALITA'

TUTTOPRESS EDITRICE SRL
1722452
Via Ercole Oldofredi, 41, 20124 MILANO
Tel: 02 6691692 **Fax:** 02 66711461
Titles:
LOCALI TOP

TVN MEDIA GROUP SRL
1773942
Via Gian Battista Vico, 42, 20123 MILANO MI
Tel: 02 81830313
Titles:
ADV
PUBBLICITA' ITALIA

TWISTER SRL
1769909
Via Palermo, 13, 00184 ROMA RM
Tel: 06 48906778 **Fax:** 0648907058
Titles:
RAGAZZA MODERNA

UNIBETA SRL
1723082
Corso di Porta Nuova, 3/a, 20121 MILANO
Tel: 02 63675455 **Fax:** 02 63675523
Titles:
IN SELLA

UNIDELTA SRL
1762605
Corso di Porta Nuova, 3/a, 20121 MILANO MI
Tel: 02 63675403 **Fax:** 02 63675515
Titles:
CASA IN FIORE

UNIMEDIA SRL
1723006
Corso di Porta Nuova, 3/a, 20121 MILANO
Tel: 02 63675455 **Fax:** 02 63675523
Titles:
AL VOLANTE

UNIONE ITALIANA VINI SOC COOP
1722453
Via S.Vittore al Teatro, 3, 20123 MILANO MI
Tel: 02 7222281 **Fax:** 02 866226
Titles:
IL CORRIERE VINICOLO

UNIQUE MEDIA
1791703
Via Cadolini 34, 20137 MILANO MI
Tel: 02 89075700 **Fax:** 0236642899
Titles:
KULT MAGAZINE

UNITOP SRL
1784368
Corso di Porta Nuova, 3/a, 20121 MILANO
Tel: 0263675300 **Fax:** 02 63675519
Titles:
COME STAI

VADO E TORNO EDIZIONI
1723021
Via Cassano d'Adda, 20, 20139 MILANO
Tel: 02 55230950 **Fax:** 02 55230592
Titles:
AUTOBUS
DIESEL
TRATTORI
VADO E TORNO

VEGA EDITRICE SRL
1722663
Via Ramazzotti, 20, 20052 MONZA PARCO MI
Tel: 039 493101 **Fax:** 039 493102
Titles:
AUTORAMA (IL MONDO DEI TRASPORTI)
IL MONDO DEI TRASPORTI

VIAGGI NEL MONDO
1722451
Largo Grigioni, 7, 00152 ROMA **Tel:** 06 53293401
Fax: 06 53293446
Titles:
AVVENTURE NEL MONDO

VIGNALE COMUNICAZIONI SRL
1722931
SS 1 Via Aurelia km 237, 57020 VIGNALE RIOTORTO LI **Tel:** 0565 24720 **Fax:** 0565 24210
Titles:
NUOVO CONSUMO

VIRGILIO DEGIOVANNI ED.
1722552
Vai Farnese, 3, 20146 MILANO **Tel:** 02 83303433
Fax: 02 83303426
Titles:
MILLIONAIRE

THE WALT DISNEY COMPANY ITALIA S.R.L.
1722432
Via Sandro Sandri, 1, 20121 MILANO
Tel: 02 290851 **Fax:** 02 29085345
Titles:
BAMBI
TOPOLINO

WOLTERS KLUWER ITALIA PROFESSIONALE SPA
1722411
Strada 1 Palazzo F. 6, 20090 MILANOFIORI ASSAGO MI **Tel:** 02 824761 **Fax:** 02 82476436
Titles:
DIRITTO & PRATICA DEL LAVORO

WORLD SERVIZI EDITORIALI SRL
1772833
Corso di Porta Nuova, 3/a, 20121 MILANO MI
Tel: 02 63675403 **Fax:** 02 63675515
Titles:
COSE DI CASA

WWF ITALIA ONG
1722661
Via Po, 25/c, 00198 ROMA **Tel:** 06 84497455
Fax: 06 85300612
Titles:
PANDA

ZECCHINI EDITORE
1723094
Via Tonale, 60, 21100 VARESE **Tel:** 0332 335606
Fax: 0332 331013
Titles:
MUSICA

Latvia

A/S LAUKU AVIZE
697635
SIA Lauku Avize, Dzirnavu iela 21, RIGA LV-1010
Tel: 70 96 600 **Fax:** 70 96 645
Email: redakcija@la.lv
Web site: http://www2.la.lv
Titles:
LATVIJAS AVIZE

FENSTER SIA
697695
Mukusalas Street 41, RIGA LV-1004
Tel: 70 63 230 **Fax:** 70 63 232
Email: svetar@fenster.lv
Web site: http://www.fenster.lv
Titles:
7 SEKRETOV
DELOVYE VESTI
LATVIJAS SANTIMS
TV PROGRAMMA
VESTI
VESTI SEGODNJA

LATVIJAS VESTNESIS VU
697696
Bruninieku 36 - 2, RIGA LV-1011 **Tel:** 73 10 675
Fax: 73 12 190
Titles:
LATVIJAS VESTNESIS

PETITS LTD
1500164
Peldu 15, RIGA LV-1050 **Tel:** 70 88 712
Fax: 72 11 067
Email: www@petits.lv
Web site: http://www.petits.lv
Titles:
CHAS
REKLAMA.LV
SUBBOTA
TELEPROGRAMMA S DJADEJ MISHEJ

SIA B&B REDAKCIJA
1743641
Kr.Valdemāra 149, RĪGA LV-1013
Titles:
BIZNESS & BALTIJA
BIZNESS PLIUS
NEDVIZIMOSTJ & DOM
NEDVIZIMOSTJ & VYSTAVKA

SIA DIENAS BIZNESS
697595
Terbatas 30, RIGA LV-1011 **Tel:** 70 84 480
Fax: 70 84 433
Email: editor@db.lv
Web site: http://www.db.lv
Titles:
DIENAS BIZNESS

SIA LAIKRAKSTS DIENA
1743374
Mūkusalas iela 15, RĪGA LV - 1004 **Tel:** 70 63 243
Fax: 70 63 291
Web site: http://www.diena.lv
Titles:
DIENA

SIA MEDIJU NAMS
697632
Cēsu iela 31- 2, RIGA **Tel:** 78 86 700
Fax: 78 86 788
Email: office@medijunams.lv
Titles:
NEATKARIGA RITA AVIZE

SIA ZURNALS SANTA
1500177
Stabu iela 34, RĪGA LV-1880 **Tel:** 6 70 06 100
Fax: 6 70 06 111
Email: info@santa.lv
Web site: http://www.santa.lv
Titles:
CEMODANS
IEVA
PRIVATA DZIVE

Liechtenstein

GEMEINDE TRIESENBERG
680865
Rathaus, 9497 TRIESENBERG **Tel:** 3 2655024
Fax: 3 2655011
Email: info@triesenberg.li
Web site: http://www.triesenberg.li
Titles:
DORFSPIEGEL TRIESENBERG

HILTI AG
1774363
Feldkircher Str. 100, 9494 SCHAAN
Tel: 3 2342630 **Fax:** 3 2346630
Email: anja.buechel@hilti.com
Web site: http://www.hilti.com
Titles:
HILTI TEAM

INSERTAS ANNONCEN AG
679267
Städtle 11, 9490 VADUZ **Tel:** 3 2301740
Fax: 3 2375601
Email: bhz@markt.li
Web site: http://www.bhz.li
Titles:
BHZ LIECHTENSTEINER BAU- & HAUSZEITUNG

LIECHTENSTEINER VOLKSBLATT AG
685087
Im alten Riet 103, 9494 SCHAAN **Tel:** 3 2375151
Fax: 3 2375166
Email: verlag@volksblatt.li
Web site: http://www.volksblatt.li
Titles:
LIECHTENSTEINER VOLKSBLATT
LIECHTENSTEINER VOLKSBLATT

LIECHTENSTEINISCHE TRACHTENVEREINIGUNG
681172
Heiligkreuz 19, 9490 VADUZ **Tel:** 3 2323439
Web site: http://www.trachten.li
Titles:
EINTRACHT

NEUE VERLAGSANSTALT
1714911
In der Fina 18, 9494 SCHAAN **Tel:** 3 2334381
Fax: 3 2334382
Email: info@neue-verlagsanstalt.li
Web site: http://www.neue-verlagsanstalt.li
Titles:
STYLE

OSCARS VERLAG AG
1752025
Industriestr. 753, 9492 ESCHEN **Tel:** 3 3750075
Fax: 3 3750074
Email: office@oscars.li
Web site: http://www.oscars.li
Titles:
OSCAR'S HOTEL & GOURMET MAGAZIN INTERNATIONAL

VADUZER MEDIENHAUS AG
1643365
Austr. 81, 9490 VADUZ **Tel:** 3 2361616
Fax: 3 2361617
Email: info@medienhaus.li
Web site: http://www.medienhaus.li
Titles:
ABC-SCHÜTZEN
AUTO FRÜHLING
BAUEN WOHNEN
LIECHTENSTEINER VATERLAND
LIECHTENSTEINER VATERLAND
LIECHTENSTEINS FUSSBALL
LIFESTYLE
NEUE LIEWO
PE CE
WEIHNACHTEN
WIRTSCHAFT REGIONAL

VERWALTUNGS- UND PRIVAT-BANK AG
1712590
Aeulestr. 6, 9490 VADUZ **Tel:** 3 2356969
Fax: 3 2356513
Email: info@vpbank.com
Web site: http://www.vpbank.com
Titles:
ASSET MANAGEMENT

WIRTSCHAFTSKAMMER LIECHTENSTEIN FÜR GEWERBE, HANDEL UND DIENSTLEISTUNG 1725041
Zollstr. 23, 9494 SCHAAN **Tel:** 3 2377788
Fax: 3 2377789
Email: info@wirtschaftskammer.li
Web site: http://www.wirtschaftskammer.li

Titles:
UNTERNEHMER.

Lithuania

JOINT STOCK COMPANY LIETUVOS RYTAS 1201213
Gedimino pr 12 A, Floor 3, LT- 01103 VILNIUS
Tel: 2 22 63 89 **Fax:** 2 22 76 56

Titles:
LIETUVOS RYTAS

LITOVSKIJ KURJER 1621951
Ul. Sodu 4, LT- 03211 VILNIUS **Tel:** 5 21 20 320
Fax: 5 21 20 320
Email: info@kurier.lt
Web site: http://www.kurier.lt

Titles:
LITOVSKIJ KURJER

NAUJASIS AITVARAS 1641633
Jogailos g. 11/2 -11, LT- 2600 VILNIUS
Tel: 2 61 15 44 **Fax:** 2 61 15 44

Titles:
VAKARO ZINIOS

RESPUBLIKOS LEIDINIAI 697627
A. Smetonos g. 2, LT-01115 VILNIUS
Tel: 5 21 23 112 **Fax:** 5 21 23 538

Titles:
RESPUBLIKA

UAB EKSPRESS LEIDYBA 1741477
Ozo g. 10A, 08200 VILNIUS **Tel:** 5 276 17 67
Email: info@ekspress.lt
Web site: http://www.ekspress.lt

Titles:
PANELE

UAB FLOBIS 1741847
Konstitucijos pr. 12, LT-VILNIUS **Tel:** 5 27 31 773
Email: obzor@mail.com

Titles:
OBZOR

UAB JUNGTINIAI LEIDINIAI 697643
A.Goštauto g. 12A, LT-01108 VILNIUS
Tel: 5 24 28 781 **Fax:** 5 24 27 127
Email: info@cosmopolitan.lt

Titles:
COSMOPOLITAN

UAB KRIMINALISTIKA 1621881
Žemalės g. 16, LT-48280 KAUNAS
Tel: 3 73 60 422 **Fax:** 3 73 60 426

Titles:
AKISTATA

UAB LIETUVOS ZINIOS 1621971
Kęstučio g. 4/14, LT- 08117 VILNIUS
Tel: 5 24 92 152 **Fax:** 5 27 51 292

Titles:
LIETUVOS ZINIOS

UAB NEW WORLD BALTIC 1742548
Savanorių pr. 287-241, LT-50127 KAUNAS
Tel: 37 31 15 39 **Fax:** 37 31 15 39
Email: jums@dokeda.lt
Web site: http://www.jumsinfo.lt

Titles:
JUMS

UAB SAVAITĖ 697890
Laisvės pr. 60-917, LT-2056 VILNIUS
Tel: 5 24 00 816 **Fax:** 5 24 60 622

Titles:
SAVAITE

UAB SAVAITĖS EKSPRESAS 1759454
Laisvės pr. 60-917, LT-2056 VILNIUS
Email: biuras@savaite.lt

Titles:
EKSPRESS NEDELIA

UAB VEIDO PERIODIKOS LEIDYKLA 1621970
A. Gostauto g. 8 (la.), LT-2000 VILNIUS
Tel: 5 26 49 439 **Fax:** 5 26 22 407
Email: mail@veidas.lt
Web site: http://www.veidas.lt

Titles:
COMPUTER BILD LIETUVA
COMPUTER BILD PATARAJAS

UAB VERSLO ŽINIOS 1742746
J. Jasinskio g. 16A, LT-01112 VILNIUS
Tel: 5 25 26 400 **Fax:** 5 25 26 313
Email: info@verslozinios.lt
Web site: http://www.verslozinios.lt

Titles:
VERSLO KLASE

UAB ZURNALU LEIDYBOS GRUPE 697642
J. Jasinskio g. 16, LT-01112 VILNIUS
Tel: 5 25 26 530 **Fax:** 5 25 26 531
Email: office@redakcija.lt
Web site: http://www.redakcija.lt

Titles:
JI
ZMONES

Luxembourg

ALIALI 1320
L-1330, LUXEMBOURG

Titles:
REVUE TECHNIQUE LUXEMBOURGOISE

ASSOCIATION DES MÉDECINS ET MÉDECINS-DENTISTES 1489
L-2680, LUXEMBOURG

Titles:
LE CORPS MEDICAL

EDITIONS D' LETZEBURGER LAND SARL 1785075
BP 2083, L-1020 LUXEMBOURG **Tel:** 48 57 57 1
Fax: 49 63 09

Titles:
D'LETZEBUERGER LAND

EDITIONS LËTZEBURGER JOURNAL SA 1785074
BP 2101, L-1021 LUXEMBOURG **Tel:** 49 30 331
Fax: 49 20 65

Titles:
LËTZEBUERGER JOURNAL

EDITIONS REVUES 1784817
PO Box 2755, L-1027 LUXEMBOURG
Tel: 49 81 81 **Fax:** 487722

Titles:
AUTO REVUE
GRAFFITI
REVUE

EDITOP SARL 1788149
BP 48, L-7201 WALFERDANGE, LUXEMBOURG
Tel: 4213 5 51 **Fax:** 421352299

Titles:
GASTROTOUR

EDITPRESS SA 1784833
44, rue du Canal, L-4050 ESCH SUR ALZETTE
Tel: 22 05 50 **Fax:** 220544

Titles:
LE JEUDI
LE QUOTIDIEN
TAGEBLATT - ZEITUNG FIR LETZEBUERG

EXCELLENTIA 1785172
14, rue Lentz, 3509 DUDELANGE,
LUXEMBOURG **Tel:** 26 52 29 22 **Fax:** 26 52 29 23

Titles:
EXCELLENTIA MAGAZINE

GROUPE SAINT-PAUL SA 1784814
2, Rue Christophe Plantin, L-2988
LUXEMBOURG **Tel:** 49 93 337 **Fax:** 49 93 448

Titles:
CONTACTO

IMPRIMERIE SAINT-PAUL LUXEMBOURG 1784821
63 rue de Luxembourg, L-8140 BRIDEL,
LUXEMBOURG **Tel:** 33 99 69 **Fax:** 26 330 781

Titles:
BULLETIN DE LA SOCIÉTÉ DES SCIENCES MÉDICALES DU GRAND DUCHÉ DE LUXEMBOURG

LIGUE LUXEMBOURGEOISE DU COIN DE TERRE ET DU FOYER CTF 1784808
97, rue de Bonnevoie, L-1260 LUXEMBOURG
Tel: 48 01 99 **Fax:** 409798

Titles:
GAART AN HEEM

LPPD 1176
L-1014, LUXEMBOURG

Titles:
RAPPEL

MIKE KOEDINGER EDITIONS 1784771
BP 728, L-2017 BONNEVOIE **Tel:** 29 66 181
Fax: 296619

Titles:
CITY MAGAZINE
DESIRS
FLYDOSCOPE
NICO
PAPERJAM

MMM BUSINESS MEDIA 1785873
Tel: 269 5 85 **Fax:** 26810282, LUXEMBOURG

Titles:
FLEET EUROPE

NEW MEDIA LUX 1774198
21st Century Building, 19, rue de Bitbourg, L-1273 LUXEMBOURG **Tel:** 26 29991 **Fax:** 26299984

Titles:
352 LUXEMBOURG NEWS

SAINT-PAUL LUXEMBOURG SA 1784796
2, rue Christophe Plantin, L-2988
LUXEMBOURG **Tel:** 49 93 231 **Fax:** 4993757

Titles:
AUTO MOTO
D'WORT (LUXEMBOURG)
MAGAZINE HORESCA
TELECRAN
LA TOQUE BLANCHE
LA VOIX DU LUXEMBOURG

SYNDICAT NATIONAL DES ENSEIGNANTS 1784799
PO Box 2437, BONNEVOIE, LUXEMBOURG
Tel: 48 11 18 1 **Fax:** 407356

Titles:
ECOLE & VIE

WOXX 1785774
BP 684, L-2016 LUXEMBOURG **Tel:** 29 79 990
Fax: 29 79 79

Titles:
WOXX

ZEITUNG 1785096
PO Box 403, L-4005 ESCH-SUR-ALZETTE,
LUXEMBOURG **Tel:** 44 60 66 1 **Fax:** 44 60 66 66

Titles:
ZLV - ZEITUNG VUM LËTZEBUERGER VOLLEK

Macedonia

CENTER FOR PEACE AND DEMOCRACY 1622268
Orce Nikolov 155, 1000 SKOPJE **Tel:** 2 36 19 51
Fax: 2 30 61 282
Email: maleska@sonet.com.mk
Web site: http://www.newbalkanpolitics.org.mk

Titles:
NEW BALKAN POLITICS

DNID MAKEDONSKO SONCE 699670
Leninova No.79, 1000 SKOPJE **Tel:** 2 31 30 137
Fax: 2 31 30 377
Email: redakcija@makedonskosonce.com
Web site: http://www.makedonskosonce.com

Titles:
MAKEDONSKO SONCE

KRUG 1500191
Teodosij Gologanov 28, 1000 SKOPJE
Tel: 2 32 36 800 **Fax:** 2 32 36 801
Email: dnevnik@dnevnik.com.mk
Web site: http://www.dnevnik.com.mk

Titles:
DNEVNIK

MAKEDONSKI SPORT DOO 1744437
3/6 Lermontova street, 1000 SKOPJE
Tel: 2 321 20 19 **Fax:** 2 321 20 19
Email: sport@on.net.mk
Web site: http://www.sport.com.mk

Titles:
MAKEDONSKI SPORT

MOST LTD 699035
Dimitrie Cupovski 11/5, 1000 SKOPJE
Tel: 2 32 36 900 **Fax:** 2 32 36 901
Email: vesnik@utrinski.com.mk
Web site: http://www.utrinskivesnik.com.mk

Titles:
UTRINSKI VESNIK

VECER PRESS 1653104
Bul. Nikola Vapcarov 2, 1000 SKOPJE

Titles:
VECER

ZONIK DOOEL-SKOPJE 1642256
Naum Ohridski 47, 1000 SKOPJE **Tel:** 2 27 36 120
Fax: 2 27 36 121
Email: zonik47@mt.net.mk

Titles:
NOVA MAKEDONIJA

Malta

ALLIED NEWSPAPERS LTD 1600244
Allied Newspapers Limited, Strickland House, 341 St Paul Street, VALLETTA VLT 1211
Tel: 25 59 45 00 **Fax:** 25 59 45 10
Web site: www.timesofmalta.com

Titles:
THE SUNDAY TIMES
THE TIMES

MALTA CATHOLIC ACTIONS 1711631
The Catholic Institute, FLORIANA FRN 1441
Tel: 21 22 58 47 **Fax:** 21 22 58 47

Titles:
LEHEN IS-SEWWA

MEDIA LINK 625816
Dar Centrali, Herbert Ganado Street, PIETA HMR 08 **Tel:** 21 24 36 41 **Fax:** 21 22 66 39
Web site: http://www.media.link.com.mt

Titles:
IL- MUMENT
IN- NAZZJON

SOUND VISION PRINT 1650232
Centru Nazzjonali Laburista, Triq Milend, HAMRUN HMR 1717 **Tel:** 21 23 53 12
Fax: 21 23 82 52
Email: felix@kullhadd.com
Web site: www.kullhadd.com

Titles:
KULLHADD

Malta

STANDARD PUBLICATIONS LTD 1200972
Standard House, Birkikara Hill, ST JULIANS STJ 1149 **Tel:** 21 34 58 88 **Fax:** 21 34 34 60
Email: tmid@independent.com.mt
Web site: www.independent.com.mt
Titles:
THE MALTA INDEPENDENT
THE MALTA INDEPENDENT ON SUNDAY

UNION PRESS CO. LTD. 1600325
A41 Marsa Industrial Estate, MARSA LQA 06
Tel: 2124 7687 **Fax:** 2123 8484
Email: info@unionprint.com.mt
Web site: http://www.unionprint.com.mt
Titles:
L- ORIZZONT
IT- TORCA

Moldova

COMERSANT PLUS LTD. 1622183
str. Puskin 22, 2012 CHISINAU **Tel:** 2 23 36 94 **Fax:** 2 23 33 13
Titles:
COMERSANT PLUS

CONTRAFORT S.R.L. 699623
Bd. Stefan cel Mare 134, 2012 CHISINAU
Tel: 2 21 06 08 **Fax:** 2 21 06 08
Titles:
CONTRAFORT

KISINEVSKY OBOZREVATEL S.R.L 699591
Vlaiku Pyrkelab 45, office 405, 2012 CHISINAU
Tel: 2 21 02 64 **Fax:** 2 21 02 64
Email: obozrevateli@mail.ru
Web site: http://www.ko.md
Titles:
KISINEVSKY OBOZREVATEL

LOGOS PRESS S.A. 699671
Stefan cel Mare 180, 2004 CHISINAU
Tel: 2 24 06 98 **Fax:** 2 24 69 50
Titles:
ECONOMICESKOJE OBOZRENIJE

MOLDAVSKIE VEDOMOSTI 699481
Banulescu-Bodoni st. 21, 2012 KISHINEV
Tel: 2 23 86 18 **Fax:** 2 23 86 18
Titles:
MOLDAVSKIE VEDOMOSTI

PRAVIDELSTVO RESPUBLIKI MOLDOVA 699627
str. Puskin 22, 11052 CHISINAU **Tel:** 2 23 31 41 **Fax:** 2 23 31 41
Titles:
NEZAVISIMAYA MOLDOVA

SRL "JURNAL DE CHICHINEL" 1634306
str. Puskin 22, Casa Presei, 4 etazh, of. 446, 2012 CHISINAU **Tel:** 2 23 40 97 **Fax:** 2 23 40 97
Titles:
JURNAL DE CHIŞINĂU

TIMPUL DE DIMINATEA 699681
str. M. Eminescu, 55, 2004 CHISINAU
Tel: 2 23 30 49 **Fax:** 2 23 30 36
Titles:
TIMPUL DE DIMINEAŢA

WELCOME MOLDOVA 699625
PO Box 256, 2012 CHISINAU **Tel:** 22 23 42 34 **Fax:** 22 22 51 35
Titles:
WELCOME MOLDOVA

Monaco

EDITIONS MINERVE 1745192
27 boulevard d'Italie, 98000 MONACO
Tel: 9 79 75 95 9 **Fax:** 9 79 75 95 0
Titles:
L' OBSERVATEUR DE MONACO

GAZETTE DE MONACO 1626090
57 rue Grimaldi, Le Panorama - Bloc A-B, 98000 MONACO **Tel:** 9 32 52 03 6 **Fax:** 9 79 80 14 1
Titles:
LA GAZETTE DE MONACO

MONACO HEBDO 1626145
27 boulevard d'Italie, 98000 MONACO
Tel: 9 35 05 65 2 **Fax:** 9 35 01 92 2
Titles:
MONACO HEBDO

NICE MATIN 1793978
41 rue Grimaldi, 98000 MONACO
Tel: 9 31 04 39 0 **Fax:** 9 31 04 39 9
Titles:
MONACO-MATIN EDITION MONEGASQUE DE NICE-MATIN

PASSION PALACES 1753151
'Le Victoria', 13 boulevard Princesse Charlotte, 98000 MONACO **Tel:** 97 70 24 10 **Fax:** 93 25 54 13
Titles:
PASSION PALACES

SAM EDICOM 1781832
Sam Edicom - Le Roqueville, Bât C -20 bd Princesse-Charlotte, 98000 MONACO
Tel: 9 79 70 62 7 **Fax:** 9 79 70 62 8
Titles:
PNEUMATIQUE MAGAZINE

S.A.M GEDIP 1679922
Le Soleil d'Or, 20 Boulevard Rainier III, 98000 MONACO **Tel:** 9 21 61 80 2 **Fax:** 9 21 61 80 3
Titles:
MONACO ECONOMIE

Netherlands

100% NL MAGAZINE B.V. 1764366
Morseweg 2, 1131 PK VOLENDAM
Tel: 592 379571 **Fax:** 10 7044752
Email: info@100pmagazine.nl
Web site: http://www.100pmagazine.nl
Titles:
100% NL MAGAZINE

2XPLAIN V.O.F. 1636205
Postbus 1519, 5602 BM EINDHOVEN
Tel: 88 7518160 **Fax:** 342 494299
Email: administratie@2xplain.nl
Web site: http://www.2xplain.nl
Titles:
PAYROLL

A EN C MEDIA B.V. 1635123
Postbus 528, 6040 AM ROERMOND
Tel: 73 6271777 **Fax:** 73 6220570
Email: info@aencmedia.nl
Web site: http://www.aencmedia.nl.nl
Titles:
TROMPETTER ROERMOND WEEKEND

A.A. IDEMA B.V. 1636092
Postbus 18, 1670 AA MEDEMBLIK
Tel: 73 6271777 **Fax:** 73 6220570
Email: drukkerij@idemadruk.nl
Web site: http://www.idemagrafimedia.nl
Titles:
DE KOGGENLANDER
MEDEMBLIKKER COURANT

AARDAPPELWERELD B.V. 1636431
Postbus 84102, 2508 AC DEN HAAG
Tel: 88 2697183 **Fax:** 314 343839
Web site: http://www.aardappelwereld.nl
Titles:
AARDAPPELWERELD MAGAZINE

AARDSCHOK B.V. 1637930
Postbus 7, 5690 AA SON
Web site: http://www.aardschok.com
Titles:
AARDSCHOK

ABP CONCERN COMMUNICATIE 1754230
Postbus 4911, 6401 JS HEERLEN
Tel: 88 2697049 **Fax:** 20 5159700
Email: concern.communicatie@abp.nl
Web site: http://www.abp.nl
Titles:
ABP WERELD

ABVAKABO FNV 1707326
Postbus 3010, 2700 KT ZOETERMEER
Tel: 88 2697062 **Fax:** 314 343839
Web site: http://www.abvakabofnv.nl
Titles:
PLATFORM A

ACADEMIC JOURNALS 1685128
Postbus 101, 6980 AC DOESBURG
Tel: 58 2845745 **Fax:** 88 2697490
Email: info@academicjournals.nl
Web site: http://www.academicjournals.nl
Titles:
VOEDING & VISIE

ACADEMISCH MEDISCH CENTRUM 1636297
Postbus 22660, 1100 DD AMSTERDAM
Tel: 58 2845745 **Fax:** 88 2697490
Email: voorlichting@amc.nl
Web site: http://www.amc.nl
Titles:
AMC MAGAZINE

ACCO.BURO 1637587
Postbus 4, 2400 MA ALPHEN A/D RIJN
Tel: 88 2697112 **Fax:** 88 2696983
Email: support@acco.nl
Web site: http://www.acco.nl
Titles:
ACCO.WIJZER

AD NIEUWSMEDIA B.V. 1636492
Postbus 8759, 3009 AT ROTTERDAM
Tel: 88 0139945 **Fax:** 570 647803
Email: ad@ad.nl
Titles:
AD GROENE HART
AD ROTTERDAMS DAGBLAD
AD UTRECHTS NIEUWSBLAD

ADFORMATIE GROEP 1634404
Postbus 75462, 1070 AL AMSTERDAM
Tel: 76 5250906 **Fax:** 342 494299
Web site: http://www.adformatiegroep.nl
Titles:
COMMUNICATIE
CREATIE
INTERNE COMMUNICATIE
MARKETINGRSLT
TIJDSCHRIFT VOOR MARKETING

AENEAS B.V. 1636140
Postbus 101, 5280 AC BOXTEL **Tel:** 88 3263334 **Fax:** 88 3263335
Email: mail@aeneas.nl
Web site: http://www.aeneas.nl
Titles:
BOUW IQ
ENERGIE+
TOETS

AGRIMEDIA B.V. 1635063
Postbus 42, 6700 AA WAGENINGEN
Tel: 76 5250906 **Fax:** 342 494299
Email: mail@agrimedia.info
Web site: http://www.agrimedia.nl
Titles:
VEEHOUDER & DIERENARTS, ED. RUNDVEEHOUDERIJ
VEEHOUDERIJ TECHNIEK
DE ZELFKAZER

AGRIO UITGEVERIJ B.V. 1634560
Postbus 168, 7040 AD 'S-HEERENBERG
Tel: 88 7518000 **Fax:** 35 6474569
Email: info@agrio.nl
Web site: http://www.agrio.nl
Titles:
AGRAAF
STAL & AKKER
VELDPOST
VVA MAGAZINE

AHV, AMSTERDAMSE HENGELSPORT VERENIGING 1754189
Beethovenstraat 178, 1077 JX AMSTERDAM
Tel: 88 7518650 **Fax:** 88 7518652
Email: ahv@ahv.nl
Web site: http://www.ahv.nl
Titles:
VISSEN

AIDS FONDS 1753616
Keizersgracht 390-394, 1016 GB AMSTERDAM
Tel: 70 3147856 **Fax:** 314 361456
Email: aidsfonds@aidsfonds.nl
Web site: http://www.aidsfonds.nl
Titles:
INFO AIDS FONDS

ALAN ROGERS CAMPINGGIDSEN 1757063
Van Boetzelaerlaan 20, 3828 NS HOOGLAND
Tel: 71 5161527 **Fax:** 88 7518481
Email: info@alanrogers.nl
Web site: http://www.alanrogers.nl
Titles:
ALAN ROGERS CAMPINGGIDSEN

ALBRON CATERING 1636326
Postbus 70, 3454 ZH DE MEERN **Tel:** 88 2696557 **Fax:** 88 2696946
Email: info@albron.nl
Web site: http://www.albron.nl
Titles:
FOODNOTE NIEUWS

ALIVRA B.V. 1636468
Postbus 160, 4100 AD CULEMBORG
Tel: 20 5249842 **Fax:** 88 2696946
Email: info@alivra.nl
Web site: http://www.alivra.nl
Titles:
' THUIS MAGAZINE

ALZHEIMER NEDERLAND 1754437
Postbus 183, 3980 CD BUNNIK **Tel:** 10 4066646 **Fax:** 10 4066979
Email: info@alzheimer-nederland.nl
Web site: http://www.alzheimer-nederland.nl
Titles:
ALZHEIMER MAGAZINE

AM MEDIA B.V. 1638284
J.J. Viottastraat 50, 1071 JT AMSTERDAM
Tel: 88 2696665 **Fax:** 88 2696946
Email: info@am-magazine.nl
Web site: http://www.am-media.nl
Titles:
AM MAGAZINE

AMNESTY INTERNATIONAL 1636031
Postbus 1968, 1000 BZ AMSTERDAM
Tel: 10 2894075 **Fax:** 88 7518652
Email: amnesty@amnesty.nl
Web site: http://www.amnesty.nl
Titles:
AMNESTY IN ACTIE
AMNESTYNL

AMSTERDAM AIRPORT SCHIPHOL, AFD. CORPORATE 1753886
Postbus 7501, 1118 ZG SCHIPHOL
Tel: 570 673344 **Fax:** 70 7999840
Email: schipholland@schiphol.nl
Web site: http://www.schiphol.nl
Titles:
SCHIPHOLLAND

AMSTERDAM TOERISME & CONGRES BUREAU 1710097
Postbus 3901, 1001 AS AMSTERDAM
Tel: 58 2845745 **Fax:** 20 5159700
Email: info@atcb.nl
Web site: http://www.atcb.nl
Titles:
CONTOUR AMSTERDAM

AMSTERDAM UNIVERSITY PRESS 1635748
Herengracht 221, 1016 BG AMSTERDAM
Tel: 79 3628628 **Fax:** 20 5159145
Email: info@aup.nl
Web site: http://www.aup.nl
Titles:
ACADEMISCHE BOEKENGIDS

ANBO 1636586
Postbus 18003, 3501 CA UTRECHT
Tel: 570 673344 **Fax:** 70 7999840
Email: info@anbo.nl
Web site: http://www.anbo.nl
Titles:
ANBO MAGAZINE

ANDO, ALG. NED. DRANKBESTRIJDERS ORGANISATIE 1753847
Paviljoenstraat 32, 9001 BR GROUW
Tel: 88 2697183
Email: margalitti.dolfijn@hetnet.nl
Titles:
ANDO NUCHTER BEKEKEN

ANGO, ALGEMENE NEDERLANDSE GEHANDICAPTEN 1636650
Postbus 850, 3800 AW AMERSFOORT
Tel: 70 3146665
Email: info@ango.nl
Web site: http://www.ango.nl
Titles:
COLLECTEKRANT

ANWB B.V. 1636566
Postbus 93200, 2509 BA DEN HAAG
Tel: 70 3789880 **Fax:** 314 343839
Email: verkeerskunde@anwb.nl
Titles:
GLAMPING MAGAZINE
VERKEERSKUNDE

ANWB MEDIA 1634433
Postbus 93200, 2509 BA DEN HAAG
Tel: 88 2697062 **Fax:** 88 2697660
Web site: http://www.anwb-media.nl
Titles:
ANWB LEDENWIJZER: HANDBOEK FIETSEN
ANWB LEDENWIJZER: HANDBOEK KAMPEREN
ANWB LEDENWIJZER: OP STAP IN NEDERLAND
ANWB SPECIAL WINTERSPORT
BUITENLEVEN
CAMPINGGIDSEN EUROPA
OP PAD
REIZEN MAGAZINE
TOERACTIEF
WATERKAMPIOEN

APG MCD 1756475
Postbus 4818, 6401 JL HEERLEN **Tel:** 45 5792379
Fax: 88 2697660
Email: concern.communicatie@apg.nl
Web site: http://www.apg.nl
Titles:
ABP MAGAZINE

APPR B.V. 1636658
Postbus 5135, 1410 AC NAARDEN
Tel: 570 673344 **Fax:** 70 7999840
Email: info@appr.nl
Web site: http://www.appr.nl
Titles:
FACILITY MANAGEMENT INFORMATIE
PROFESSIONEEL SCHOONMAKEN

APPRENTICE UITGEVERS 1634853
Velperweg 89, 6824 HH ARNHEM
Email: info@apprenticeuitgevers.nl
Web site: http://www.apprenticeuitgevers.nl
Titles:
SCHOOLMAGAZINE

APR GROEP B.V. 1634543
Postbus 2696, 3800 GE AMERSFOORT
Tel: 88 2697062 **Fax:** 314 343839
Email: info@aprgroep.nl
Web site: http://www.aprgroep.nl
Titles:
TVB ZORG

ARGO SPECIAL MEDIA B.V. 1634428
Postbus 531, 2150 AM NIEUW-VENNEP
Tel: 70 3789880 **Fax:** 20 5159577
Web site: http://www.argomediagroep.nl
Titles:
THE HOLLAND TIMES
OOR
VILLA D'ARTE

ARIËS GRAFISCHE VORMGEVING 1753751
Torenberglaan 42, 5682 EP EINDHOVEN
Tel: 88 7518160 **Fax:** 342 494299
Titles:
NEVAC BLAD

ARKO SPORTS MEDIA B.V. 1634784
Postbus 393, 3430 AJ NIEUWEGEIN
Tel: 10 7044008 **Fax:** 10 7044752
Email: info@sportsmedia.nl
Web site: http://www.sportsmedia.nl
Titles:
RECREATIE & TOERISME
SPORTACCOM

ARKO UITGEVERIJ B.V. 1635908
Postbus 616, 3430 AP NIEUWEGEIN
Tel: 172 466400 **Fax:** 172 493270
Email: info@arko.nl
Web site: http://www.arko.nl
Titles:
PARKEER

ARRAY PUBLICATIONS B.V. 1635170
Postbus 2211, 2400 CE ALPHEN A/D RIJN
Tel: 23 5565509 **Fax:** 342 494299
Email: array@array.nl
Web site: http://www.array.nl
Titles:
DATABASE MAGAZINE
LAN MAGAZINE
OPTIMIZE
RELEASE
TELECOMMAGAZINE

ARTNED B.V. 1636167
Postbus 16, 7160 AA NEEDE **Tel:** 73 6271777
Fax: 73 6220570
Email: info@artned.com
Web site: http://www.artned.com
Titles:
DE FOTOGRAAF

ARTSEN ZONDER GRENZEN 1753938
Postbus 10014, 1001 EA AMSTERDAM
Tel: 88 3233333 **Fax:** 314 343839
Email: info@artsenzondergrenzen.nl
Web site: http://www.artsenzondergrenzen.nl
Titles:
HULPPOST

ASN BANK 1756460
Postbus 30502, 2500 GM DEN HAAG
Tel: 70 3789639 **Fax:** 70 3855505
Email: informatie@asnbank.nl
Web site: http://www.asnbank.nl/spaarmotief
Titles:
SPAARMOTIEF

A.S.W.S. 1637776
Noordenseweg 1, 2421 XW NIEUWKOOP
Tel: 88 7518000 **Fax:** 35 6474569
Email: vaknieuws@asws.nl
Web site: http://www.asws.nl
Titles:
KREAVAK

AUDAX PUBLISHING B.V. 1635399
Postbus 94300, 1090 GH AMSTERDAM
Tel: 88 7518000 **Fax:** 35 6474569
Email: info@publishing.audax.nl
Web site: http://www.audax.nl
Titles:
AVANTGARDE
GIRLZ!
SCIENTIFIC AMERICAN
STARS

AUTOGIDS NEDERLAND B.V. 1634638
Postbus 8648, 3009 AP ROTTERDAM
Tel: 20 5218938 **Fax:** 70 7999840
Email: ag.mailbox@autogids.nl
Titles:
AUTOGIDS VOOR ROTTERDAM

AUTOPED 1634745
Schiehavenkade 166, 3024 EZ ROTTERDAM
Tel: 314 349888
Email: post@boekie-boekie.nl
Titles:
BOEKIEBOEKIE

AVRO KUNST 1645225
Postbus 2, 1200 JA HILVERSUM **Tel:** 314 349562
Fax: 527 620984
Web site: http://www.avrokunst.nl
Titles:
KUNST EN KLASSIEK MAGAZINE

AXIOMA COMMUNICATIE & RELATIEMEDIA 1635105
Postbus 176, 3740 AD BAARN **Tel:** 88 3263320
Fax: 20 5159577
Email: informatie@axioma.nl
Web site: http://www.axioma.nl
Titles:
GEZOND THUIS
LIJF & LEVEN
VITRAS/CMD BIJ U THUIS

AZIË MAGAZINE PRODUCTIONS 1636393
Striensestraat 100, 5241 AZ ROSMALEN
Email: boazie@wxs.nl
Titles:
AZIË

B. BURUMA 1636597
Jipperdastraat 17, 9074 CW HALLUM
Tel: 570 673344 **Fax:** 70 7999840
Titles:
SAWN STJERREN NIJS

B & D V.O.F. 1636671
De Mossel 9, 1723 HZ NOORD-SCHARWOUDE
Tel: 570 673344 **Fax:** 70 7999840
Email: info@slijtersvakblad.nl
Titles:
DRINKS SLIJTERSVAKBLAD

BABY WERELD B.V. 1768472
Postbus 151, 1270 AD HUIZEN **Tel:** 70 3789880
Fax: 20 5159143
Email: ruiters@baby-wereld.nl
Titles:
BABY WERELD

BABYSTUF B.V. 1635478
Postbus 151, 1270 AD HUIZEN **Tel:** 70 3789880
Fax: 70 3789783
Email: info@babystuf.nl
Titles:
BABYSTUF

BAR UITGEVERIJ B.V. 1636531
Postbus 2, 2990 AA BARENDRECHT
Tel: 70 3378124 **Fax:** 172 422856
Email: info@baruitgeverij.nl
Titles:
DE OVERSCHIESE KRANT

BARENBRUG HOLLAND B.V. 1754226
Postbus 1338, 6501 BH NIJMEGEN
Tel: 88 2697049 **Fax:** 20 5159700
Email: info@barenbrug.nl
Web site: http://www.barenbrug.nl
Titles:
ZAAD & VOER MAGAZINE

BASISMEDIA B.V. 1635488
Postbus 2620, 1000 CP AMSTERDAM
Tel: 70 3147856 **Fax:** 20 5159700
Web site: http://www.basismedia.nl
Titles:
SPITS

BBP B.V. 1635595
Postbus 276, 3440 AG WOERDEN
Tel: 23 5565509 **Fax:** 342 494299
Email: klantenservice@bbp.nl
Web site: http://www.bbp.net
Titles:
HOLLAND MANAGEMENT REVIEW
SPONSORTRIBUNE
TELECOMMERCE
VIP/DOC

BC BIOS 1754058
Tolhoren 55, 2201 VK NOORDWIJK
Tel: 20 5218938
Web site: http://www.bcbios.nl
Titles:
BIOS SKALA

BCM PUBLISHING B.V. 1634485
Postbus 1392, 5602 BJ EINDHOVEN
Tel: 76 5312311 **Fax:** 70 7999840
Email: bcm@bcm.nl
Web site: http://www.bcm.nl
Titles:
DIER & VRIEND
DRAF & RENSPORT
HORSE INTERNATIONAL
OFF THE RECORD
ONZE HOND
SINT
VOETBAL MAGAZINE

BELANGENGROEP RECHTEN VOOR AL WAT LEEFT 1754335
Leonard Bramerstraat 18, 1816 TR ALKMAAR
Tel: 88 3263300 **Fax:** 88 3263339
Email: boerveenrvawl@chello.nl
Titles:
RELATIE MENS EN DIER

BEM PUBLISHERS B.V. 1773497
Koopmanslaan 3, 7005 BK DOETINCHEM
Tel: 10 4518007
Titles:
BEM! MAGAZINE

BENECKE 1635802
Arena Boulevard 61-75, 1101 DL AMSTERDAM
Tel: 88 7518000 **Fax:** 35 6474569
Web site: http://www.benecke.nl
Titles:
MEDISCHE ONCOLOGIE
DE PSYCHIATER

BÈTA PUBLISHERS B.V. 1640201
Postbus 19949, 2500 CX DEN HAAG
Tel: 20 5218939
Email: info@betapublishers.nl
Web site: http://www.betapublishers.nl
Titles:
MARITIEM NEDERLAND
MENS & MOLECULE

BETER HOREN 1757019
Postbus 140, 6980 AC DOESBURG
Tel: 88 3263334 **Fax:** 88 3263335
Email: hoor@amplifon.com
Web site: http://www.beterhoren.nl
Titles:
HOOR!

BETONVERENIGING 1637564
Postbus 411, 2800 AK GOUDA **Tel:** 79 3628628
Fax: 10 4066979
Email: info@betonvereniging.nl
Web site: http://www.betonvereniging.nl
Titles:
BETONVERENIGINGSNIEUWS

BIBLION UITGEVERIJ 1634486
Postbus 437, 2260 AK LEIDSCHENDAM
Tel: 70 3378124 **Fax:** 172 422856
Email: boek-delen@nbdbiblion.nl
Web site: http://www.nbdbiblion.nl
Titles:
BIBLIOTHEEKBLAD
JEUGDLITERATUUR IN PRAKTIJK

BINDINC 1634550
Postbus 580, 1200 AN HILVERSUM
Tel: 23 5565509 **Fax:** 342 494299
Web site: http://www.tvmagazines.nl
Titles:
KRO MAGAZINE
NCRV-GIDS

BIONEXT 1637507
Postbus 12048, 3501 AA UTRECHT
Tel: 10 4066646 **Fax:** 10 4066979
Email: info@bionext.nl
Web site: http://www.biologica.nl

Titles:
SMAAKMAKEND

BKK B.V. 1634876
Schoolsteeg 4, 1621 CE HOORN **Tel:** 314 349888
Email: info@beroepskeuzekrant.nl

Titles:
BKK BEROEPSKEUZEKRANT, EDITIE HAVO/ VWO EN MBO NIVEAU 3 EN 4
BKK BEROEPSKEUZEKRANT, EDITIE VMBO

BLAUW MEDIA UITGEVERIJ B.V. 1635166
Postbus 1043, 3600 BA MAARSSEN
Tel: 20 5218938 **Fax:** 70 7999840
Email: mannenmode@blauwmedia.com
Web site: http://www.blauwmedia.com

Titles:
FOTOGRAFIE
FOTOVISIE
MANNENMODE
TRED
TREND BOUTIQUE

BLINK UITGEVERS 1767886
Postbus 380, 5201 AJ 'S-HERTOGENBOSCH
Tel: 88 2697364 **Fax:** 58 2130930
Web site: http://www.blinkuitgevers.nl

Titles:
OKKI

BNO, BEROEPSORGANISATIE NEDERLANDSE ONTWERPERS 1753758
Postbus 20698, 1001 NR AMSTERDAM
Tel: 20 7581000 **Fax:** 20 7581030
Email: bno@bno.nl
Web site: http://www.bno.nl

Titles:
VORMBERICHTEN

BODY BIZ INTERNATIONAL B.V. 1637338
Postbus 178, 6590 AD GENNEP **Tel:** 88 7518480
Fax: 88 7518481
Email: info@bodybiz.nl

Titles:
BODY BIZ

BODYMIND OPLEIDINGEN 1755356
Eerste Pijnackerstraat 135a, 3035 GS ROTTERDAM
Email: info@bodymindopleidingen.nl
Web site: http://www.bodymindopleidingen.nl

Titles:
BODYMIND OPLEIDINGEN

BOEKENCENTRUM UITGEVERS 1634474
Postbus 29, 2700 AA ZOETERMEER
Tel: 70 3789880 **Fax:** 70 3789783
Email: info@boekencentrum.nl
Web site: http://www.boekencentrum.nl

Titles:
EREDIENSTVAARDIG
DE ORGELVRIEND
PREDIKANT EN SAMENLEVING

BOEKENPOST 1636162
Jupiterstraat 101, 9742 EV GRONINGEN
Tel: 73 6271777 **Fax:** 73 6220570
Email: boekenpost@wxs.nl

Titles:
BOEKENPOST

BOHIL MEDIA B.V. 1640279
Postbus 93097, 1090 BB AMSTERDAM
Tel: 172 466471 **Fax:** 172 422886
Email: info@bohilmedia.nl

Titles:
BOTEN
CAMPERS & CARAVANS

BOHN STAFLEU VAN LOGHUM B.V. 1634588
Postbus 246, 3990 GA HOUTEN
Web site: http://www.bsl.nl

Titles:
AD-VISIE
HET CARDIOVASCULAIR FORMULARIUM
CRITICAL CARE
EADV-MAGAZINE
ERGOTHERAPIE
HART BULLETIN
HUISARTS EN WETENSCHAP (H&W)
JGZ, TIJDSCHRIFT VOOR JEUGDGEZONDHEIDSZORG
MAATWERK
MEDNET MAGAZINE
NEDERLANDS TIJDSCHRIFT VOOR TRAUMATOLOGIE
NETHERLANDS HEART JOURNAL
NEUROPRAXIS
ONDERWIJS EN GEZONDHEIDSZORG
PALLIUM
PODOSOPHIA
PSYCHOLOGIE & GEZONDHEID
REVALIDATIE MAGAZINE
STANDBY
SYNTHESHIS
TANDARTSPRAKTIJK (TP)
TIJDSCHRIFT VOOR BEDRIJFS- EN VERZEKERINGSGENEESKUNDE
TIJDSCHRIFT VOOR GERONTOLOGIE EN GERIATRIE
TIJDSCHRIFT VOOR KINDERGENEESKUNDE
TIJDSCHRIFT VOOR OUDERENGENEESKUNDE
TIJDSCHRIFT VOOR UROLOGIE
VADEMECUM MONDHYGIËNISTEN

BOLDPUBLISHING 1636155
Postbus 69654, 1060 CS AMSTERDAM
Tel: 73 6271777 **Fax:** 73 6220570

Titles:
RELOAD

BOND VAN LANDPACHTERS 1635837
Hoofdweg 68, 7782 PV DE KRIM **Tel:** 88 2697856

Titles:
DE LANDPACHTER

BOND VOOR MATERIALENKENNIS 1754429
Postbus 359, 5600 AJ EINDHOVEN
Tel: 79 3628628 **Fax:** 172 466577
Email: info@materialenkennis.nl
Web site: http://www.materialenkennis.nl

Titles:
NIEUWSBRIEF BOND VOOR MATERIALENKENNIS

BONSAI EUROPE 1638236
Postbus 17, 4040 DA KESTEREN **Tel:** 30 6383736
Fax: 30 6383999
Email: info@bonsaifocus.com

Titles:
BONSAI FOCUS

BOOM JURIDISCHE UITGEVERS 1681809
Postbus 85576, 2508 CG DEN HAAG
Email: info@bju.nl
Web site: http://www.bju.nl

Titles:
MARKT & MEDEDINGING
ONDERNEMING & FINANCIERING (O&F)

BOOMERANG B.V. 1791280
Postbus 37398, 1030 AJ AMSTERDAM
Tel: 10 4066646 **Fax:** 10 4066979
Email: info@boomerang.nl
Web site: http://www.boomerang.nl

Titles:
PREVIEW

BORSTKANKERVERENIGING NEDERLAND 1754216
Postbus 8065, 3503 RB UTRECHT
Tel: 317 484020 **Fax:** 317 424060
Email: info@borstkankervereniging.nl
Web site: http://www.borstkanker.nl

Titles:
MAMMAZONE

BOSS & WIJNHOVEN 1636118
Postbus 85293, 3508 AG UTRECHT
Tel: 172 466400 **Fax:** 172 493270
Email: info@boss-wijnhoven.nl
Web site: http://www.boss-wijnhoven.nl

Titles:
TON

BOSTON TERRIER CLUB NEDERLAND 1753852
Hoogte Kadijk 176, 1018 BW AMSTERDAM
Tel: 88 2697183
Web site: http://www.bostonterrierclubnederland.nl

Titles:
ONZE BOSTONS

BRANDING MEDIA GROEP 1638206
Postbus 6030, 2001 HA HAARLEM
Tel: 88 3263334 **Fax:** 88 3263335
Email: info@brandingmedia.nl
Web site: http://www.brandingmedia.nl

Titles:
AMSTELRING PLUS

BRITISH WOMEN'S CLUB, THE HAGUE 1754144
Plein 24, 2511 CS DEN HAAG **Tel:** 71 5271111
Web site: http://www.bwclubthehague.demon.nl

Titles:
THE BRITISH WOMEN'S CLUB MAGAZINE

BRONKHORST PUBLISHING COMPANY V.O.F. 1637991
Het Var 41, 8939 BJ LEEUWARDEN
Tel: 10 2894018 **Fax:** 35 6563174

Titles:
BOUWSKALA

BRUGMEDIA 1634944
Postbus 179, 8260 AD KAMPEN **Tel:** 88 7518000
Fax: 88 3263324
Email: info@brugmedia.nl
Web site: http://www.brugmedia.nl

Titles:
BRUGMEDIA REGIONAAL

BRUIDMEDIA B.V. 1635002
Postbus 230, 3800 AE AMERSFOORT
Tel: 70 3789880 **Fax:** 20 5159577
Email: info@bruidmedia.nl

Titles:
BRUID & BRUIDEGOM MAGAZINE

BUIJZE PERS B.V. 1634455
Postbus 8, 2200 AA NOORDWIJK
Tel: 36 5398208 **Fax:** 342 494250
Email: info@buijzepers.nl
Web site: http://www.buijzepers.nl

Titles:
DE HAARLEMMER
LEIDS NIEUWSBLAD WEEKEND
DE ZEEKANT

BUREAU KATHOLIEK ONDERWIJS 1636627
Postbus 481, 3440 AL WOERDEN
Tel: 570 673344 **Fax:** 70 7999840
Email: info@bkonet.nl
Web site: http://www.bondkbo.nl

Titles:
SCHOOLBESTUUR

BURO MENNO HELING 1635101
Planciusstraat 13b, 1013 MD AMSTERDAM
Tel: 79 3628628
Email: info@mmnieuws.nl

Titles:
MMNIEUWS

BUSINESS COMMUNICATIONS UITGEVERS B.V. 1634489
Postbus 416, 8600 AK SNEEK **Tel:** 172 466471
Fax: 172 422886
Email: bcuitgevers@planet.nl
Web site: http://www.bcuitgevers.nl

Titles:
HOFPOORT INFO
IKAZIA MAGAZINE
OOSTERSCHELDE MAGAZINE
OP KOERS
RUWAARD VAN PUTTEN INFO
VIECURI
VLIETLAND MAGAZINE
ZEEUWS VLAANDEREN MAGAZINE

THE BUSINESS COMPANY 1635967
Postbus 257, 8530 AG LEMMER **Tel:** 79 3628628
Fax: 20 5159145
Email: info@businesscompany.nl
Web site: http://www.businesscompany.nl

Titles:
FLEVOLAND BUSINESS
GOOI- EN EEMLAND BUSINESS

BUSINESS DESIGN 1636947
Postbus 1004, 3380 AA GIESSENBURG
Tel: 70 3789880 **Fax:** 314 343839
Email: busy@ll.nl
Web site: http://www.ll.nl

Titles:
BUSY

BUSINESS PUBLISHERS RIJNMOND B.V. 1634749
Postbus 4137, 2980 GC RIDDERKERK
Tel: 20 5218938 **Fax:** 70 7999840
Email: info@rijnmondbusiness.nl
Web site: http://www.rijnmondbusiness.nl

Titles:
RIJNMOND BUSINESS

BUUR MULTIMEDIA B.V. 1635979
Postbus 1050, 2340 BB OEGSTGEEST
Tel: 88 2696557 **Fax:** 88 2696946
Email: info@buurmultimedia.nl
Web site: http://www.buurmultimedia.nl

Titles:
DITJES & DATJES
ORANJE BOVEN

CAMPINA B.V. 1753786
Postbus 2100, 5300 CC ZALTBOMMEL
Tel: 79 3628628 **Fax:** 20 5159145
Web site: http://www.campina.nl

Titles:
MYCAMPINA MAGAZINE

CENE BANKIERS 1755785
Postbus 85100, 3508 AC UTRECHT
Tel: 70 3378124 **Fax:** 172 422856
Email: contact@cenebankiers.nl
Web site: http://www.cenebankiers.nl

Titles:
ZORGALERT

CHANNEL B.V. 1699257
Mgr. Dr. H. Poelslaan 140, 1187 BE AMSTELVEEN
Email: info@connexie.nl

Titles:
CHANNELCONNECT
CONNEXIE

CHELLOMEDIA PROGRAMMING B.V. 1637013
Kon. Wilhelminaplein 2-4, 1062 HK AMSTERDAM **Tel:** 10 2894075
Web site: http://www.chellomedia.com

Titles:
FILM1 SPORT1 MAGAZINE

CHRISTENUNIE 1636270
Postbus 439, 3800 AK AMERSFOORT
Tel: 88 2697183 **Fax:** 88 2697490
Email: handschrift@christenunie.nl
Web site: http://www.christenunie.nl

Titles:
HANDSCHRIFT

CHRISTIAAN VROLIJK 1754561
Joke Smitlaan 20, 2104 TG HEEMSTEDE
Tel: 20 5218938

Titles:
THE OFFICIAL DUTCH BAYWATCH AND DAVID HASSELHOFF FANCLUB

C.I.V. SUPERUNIE B.A. 1636408
Postbus 80, 4153 ZH BEESD **Tel:** 88 2696670
Fax: 88 2696331
Email: info@superunie.nl
Web site: http://www.superunie.nl

Titles:
BOODSCHAPPEN
TSJAKKA!

CJP 1634630
Postbus 3572, 1001 AJ AMSTERDAM
Email: cjp@cjp.nl
Web site: http://www.cjp.nl

Titles:
CJP MAGAZINE

CLIPBOARD PUBLICATIONS B.V. 1635629
Delftweg 147, 2289 BD RIJSWIJK
Tel: 70 3789880 **Fax:** 70 3789783
Email: info@clipboard-publishing.nl
Web site: http://www.clipboard-publishing.nl

Titles:
BAAZ
DIGIFOTO PRO MAGAZINE
WINMAG PRO MAGAZINE

CLSK/STG. VKAM, STAFGROEP VLIEGVEILIGHEID, KWALITEIT, 1754185
Postbus 8762, 4820 BB BREDA **Tel:** 70 3789880
Fax: 314 343839
Email: avkam@mindef.nl

Titles:
VEILIG VLIEGEN

CMEDIA PRODUCTIONS B.V. 1637502
Postbus 231, 8300 AE EMMELOORD
Tel: 314 349562 **Fax:** 527 620984
Email: mailbox@geoinformatics.com

Titles:
CAD-MAGAZINE
GEOINFORMATICS
GIS-MAGAZINE

CNV ONDERWIJS 1635587
Postbus 2510, 3500 GM UTRECHT
Tel: 20 5159666 **Fax:** 342 494299
Email: algemeen@cnvo.nl
Web site: http://www.cnvo.nl

Titles:
SCHOOLJOURNAAL

CNV PUBLIEKE ZAAK 1753763
Postbus 84500, 2508 AM DEN HAAG
Tel: 79 3628628 **Fax:** 70 7999840
Email: publiciteit@cnvpubliekezaak.nl
Web site: http://www.cnvpubliekezaak.nl

Titles:
MIJN VAKBOND.NL

CNV VAKMENSEN 1774280
Postbus 2525, 3500 GM UTRECHT
Tel: 10 4518007 **Fax:** 36 7501771
Web site: http://www.cnvvakmensen.nl

Titles:
VAK M

COC NIJMEGEN 1754184
In de Betouwstraat 9, 6511 GA NIJMEGEN
Tel: 70 3789880 **Fax:** 314 343839
Email: info@cocnijmegen.nl
Web site: http://www.cocnijmegen.nl

Titles:
PINK

COC ZWOLLE 1754139
Kamperstraat 17, 8011 LJ ZWOLLE
Tel: 20 5218938 **Fax:** 20 5159700
Email: info@coczwolle.nl
Web site: http://www.coczwolle.nl

Titles:
COC ZWOLLE MAGAZINE

COLLECTOR'S PERIODIEK 1637686
Postbus 154, 7240 AD LOCHEM
Email: info@mensportbooks.nl

Titles:
MODELAUTO

COLLEGE VOOR ZORGVERZEKERINGEN, AFD. STRATEGIE, 1754031
Postbus 320, 1110 AH DIEMEN **Tel:** 20 5159429
Fax: 20 5159036
Email: info@cvz.nl
Web site: http://www.cvz.nl

Titles:
FARMACOTHERAPEUTISCH KOMPAS

COMITÉ TER VOORBEREIDING VAN OUDERLINGEN- 1754288
Verwoldsebeek 64, 8033 DC ZWOLLE
Tel: 58 2845745

Titles:
AMBTELIJK CONTACT

COMPASSO MEDIA B.V. 1635086
Postbus 111, 5750 AC DEURNE **Tel:** 88 3233333
Fax: 314 343839
Email: administratie@compassomedia.nl
Web site: http://www.compassomedia.nl

Titles:
KATTENMANIEREN

CONFESSIONEEL GEREFORMEERD BERAAD 1754172
Oostvoornelaan 9, 2554 BE DEN HAAG
Tel: 20 3446050
Web site: http://www.cgb.nu

Titles:
CREDO

CONSUMENTENBOND 1634736
Postbus 1000, 2500 BA DEN HAAG
Tel: 314 349888 **Fax:** 314 343839
Web site: http://www.consumentenbond.nl

Titles:
CONSUMENTENGIDS
DIGITAALGIDS
GELDGIDS
GEZONDGIDS

CONTEKST PUBLISHERS B.V. 1637650
Postbus 757, 4116 ZK BUREN **Tel:** 88 2697112
Fax: 88 2696983
Web site: http://www.contekst.nl

Titles:
PROAUDIOVIDEO

CONTINENTAL SOUND 1634872
Postbus 81065, 3009 GB ROTTERDAM
Tel: 570 673344 **Fax:** 70 7999840
Email: info@continentalart.org
Web site: http://www.continentalart.org

Titles:
SIGNS

CONVERSION MEDIA INTERNATIONAL B.V. 1770571
Markerkant 1382, 1314 AN ALMERE
Tel: 10 4518007 **Fax:** 36 7501771
Email: info@vakantiekrant.nl

Titles:
DE VAKANTIEKRANT

CORDAID/MEMISA 1753787
Postbus 16438, 2500 BK DEN HAAG
Tel: 79 3628628 **Fax:** 20 5159145
Email: info@cordaidmemisa.nl
Web site: http://www.cordaidmemisa.nl

Titles:
GEZONDHEID! SAMEN DELEN

CORDAID/MENSEN IN NOOD 1753439
Postbus 16436, 2500 BK DEN HAAG
Tel: 314 349888 **Fax:** 314 343839
Email: info@cordaidmenseninnood.nl
Web site: http://www.cordaidmenseninnood.nl

Titles:
MENSEN IN NOOD NIEUWS

CORDARES 1634808
Postbus 637, 1000 EE AMSTERDAM
Tel: 20 5218938 **Fax:** 20 5159145
Email: info@cordares.nl
Web site: http://www.cordares.nl

Titles:
CORDARES-POST

CREDITS MEDIA B.V. 1634834
Vijzelgracht 21-25, 1017 HN AMSTERDAM
Tel: 88 2696557 **Fax:** 88 2696946
Email: creditsmedia@creditsmedia.nl
Web site: http://www.creditsmedia.nl

Titles:
BLVD MAN
JOIE DE VIVRE

CROW 1637055
Postbus 37, 6710 BA EDE **Tel:** 88 2697049
Fax: 88 2697356
Email: crow@crow.nl
Web site: http://www.crow.nl

Titles:
CROW ET CETERA

CRV HOLDING B.V. 1636217
Postbus 454, 6800 AL ARNHEM **Tel:** 88 2696557
Fax: 88 2696946
Email: veeteelt@crv4all.com

Titles:
VEETEELT
VEETEELTVLEES

CUBIC*MEDIA B.V. 1638329
Lijnbaan 17a, 3231 AE BRIELLE **Tel:** 10 4518007
Fax: 36 7501771
Email: info@cubicmedia.nl
Web site: http://www.cubicmedia.nl

Titles:
WONEN-DOE-JE-ZO.NL

CXO MEDIA B.V. 1638330
Burgemeester Haspelslaan 63, 1181 NB AMSTELVEEN **Tel:** 70 3789880 **Fax:** 70 3789783
Email: info@cxomedia.nl
Web site: http://www.cxomedia.nl

Titles:
F & O

CYCLETOURS FIETSVAKANTIES 1754006
Buiksloterweg 7a, 1031 CC AMSTERDAM
Tel: 570 673344 **Fax:** 70 7999840
Email: info@cycletours.nl
Web site: http://www.cycletours.nl

Titles:
EERST LEZEN DAN FIETSEN

DA RETAILGROEP B.V. 1634927
Postbus 82, 8000 AB ZWOLLE **Tel:** 70 3789880
Fax: 70 3789783
Email: info@da.nl
Web site: http://www.da.nl

Titles:
DA BEAUTÉ
LEVE JE LIJF-BLAD

DAGBLAD DE PERS 1731683
Anthony Fokkerweg 61, 1059 CP AMSTERDAM
Tel: 20 5852688 **Fax:** 297 541072
Email: info@depers.nl

Titles:
DAGBLAD DE PERS

DAMENROMIJN 1657598
Van der Does de Willeboissingel 2, 5211 CA 'S-HERTOGENBOSCH **Tel:** 71 5161527
Fax: 88 7518481
Email: info@damenromijn.nl
Web site: http://www.damenromijn.nl

Titles:
MONUMENTEN MAGAZINE
WEL THUIS

DATA SCRIPTA B.V. 1754124
Postbus 6, 8408 ZH LIPPENHUIZEN
Tel: 10 2894075 **Fax:** 88 7518652
Email: editors@media-update.nl
Web site: http://www.media-update.nl

Titles:
MEDIA UPDATE

DCHG 1654735
Hendrik Figeeweg 3g-20, 2031 BJ HAARLEM
Tel: 20 5218939 **Fax:** 342 494299
Email: info@dchg.nl
Web site: http://www.dchg.nl

Titles:
NEDERLANDS TIJDSCHRIFT VOOR DERMATOLOGIE & VENEREOLOGIE

DCMP 1636474
Keurenplein 53, 1069 CD AMSTERDAM
Tel: 172 466471 **Fax:** 172 422886
Email: office@dcmp.nl
Web site: http://www.dcmp.nl

Titles:
247 WONEN

DE GELDERLANDER 1635207
Postbus 36, 6500 DA NIJMEGEN **Tel:** 342 494889
Fax: 342 494299
Web site: http://www.gelderlander.nl

Titles:
DE GELDERLANDER

DE HOOP GGZ 1636410
Provincialeweg 70, 3329 KP DORDRECHT
Email: info@dehoop.org
Web site: http://www.dehoop.org

Titles:
CONNECT

DE HYPOTHEEKSHOP C.O. B.V. 1737732
Postbus 333, 1270 AH HUIZEN **Tel:** 45 5792379
Email: info@hypotheekshop.nl
Web site: http://www.hypotheekshop.nl

Titles:
HYPOTHEEKSHOP MAGAZINE

DE LEVENSSTROOM GEMEENTE 1753591
Postbus 222, 2350 AE LEIDERDORP
Tel: 20 5159666 **Fax:** 20 5159700
Email: info@levensstroom.nl
Web site: http://www.levensstroom.nl

Titles:
LEVENSSTROOM

DE PERSGROEP NEDERLAND B.V. 1634947
Postbus 2730, 1000 CS AMSTERDAM
Tel: 10 2894075
Web site: http://www.persgroep.nl

Titles:
TROUW
DE VOLKSKRANT

DE TOREN, COÖPERATIEVE VERENIGING U.A. 1636818
Postbus 210, 7770 AE HARDENBERG
Tel: 88 2696670 **Fax:** 88 2696331
Email: info@detoren.net
Web site: http://www.detoren.net

Titles:
DE TOREN

DE WINTER MEDIAMAKERS 1638241
Postbus 26, 5400 AA UDEN **Tel:** 88 2697183
Fax: 88 2697490
Email: contact@dewinter.nl
Web site: http://www.dewinter.nl

Titles:
BEDRIJVIG BOXTEL/SCHIJNDEL
IDEE MAGAZINE

DE ZORGGEVERIJ BV 1634579
Florijn 1j, 9251 MP BERGUM **Tel:** 58 2845745
Web site: http://www.zorggeverij.nl

Titles:
DR. YEP

DELA, COÖP. VOOR HET VERZEKEREN EN VERZORGEN 1753486
Postbus 522, 5600 AM EINDHOVEN
Tel: 342 494259 **Fax:** 342 494250
Email: info@dela.nl
Web site: http://www.dela.nl

Titles:
DELA KRONIEK

DEO JUVANTE 1754889
Eikenlaan 19, 3474 HB ZEGVELD **Tel:** 88 3263320
Email: studiogg@hetnet.nl

Titles:
DE BERICHTGEVER

DIACONAAL CENTRUM PAULUSKERK 1755563
Hang 7, 3011 GG ROTTERDAM **Tel:** 70 3789880
Fax: 70 3789783
Email: ksa@xs4all.nl

Titles:
PAULUSWERK

DIAGNED 1755739
Postbus 85612, 2508 CH DEN HAAG
Tel: 70 3378124 **Fax:** 172 422856
Email: info@diagned.nl
Web site: http://www.diagned.nl

Titles:
DIAGNED MAGAZINE

DIENST WERK EN INKOMEN
1753707
Weesperstraat 113, 1018 VN AMSTERDAM
Tel: 88 2697856 **Fax:** 88 2697943
Email: info@dwi.amsterdam.nl
Web site: http://www.dwi.amsterdam.nl

Titles:
WERKWOORD

DIGISCRIPT
1634569
Postbus 120, 6500 AC NIJMEGEN
Tel: 70 3789880
Email: info@digiscript.nl

Titles:
VAKANTIEJOURNAAL

DOE EEN WENS STICHTING NEDERLAND
1755780
Postbus 2016, 3440 DA WOERDEN
Tel: 70 3378124 **Fax:** 172 422856
Email: info@doe-een-wens.org
Web site: http://www.doeeenwens.nl

Titles:
DOE EEN WENSKRANT

DORIZON MEDIA
1636435
Postbus 135, 1900 AC CASTRICUM
Tel: 70 3146665
Email: info@dorizon.nl
Web site: http://www.dorizon.nl

Titles:
MERIDIAN TRAVEL!

DRUKKERIJ, BOEK- EN KANTOORBOEKHANDEL HAAN
1636179
Stationsweg 29, 9781 CG BEDUM
Tel: 73 6271777 **Fax:** 73 6220570
Email: info@haan-bedum.nl
Web site: http://www.haan-bedum.nl

Titles:
BEDUMER NIEUWS EN ADVERTENTIEBLAD

DRUKKERIJ EN UITGEVERIJ SONO B.V.
1635364
Postbus 10, 8140 AA HEINO **Tel:** 570 673344
Fax: 20 5159700
Email: info@sonodruk.nl
Web site: http://www.sonodruk.nl

Titles:
RAALTE KOERIER

DRUKKERIJ HENO
1636517
Postbus 8, 3420 DA OUDEWATER
Tel: 570 673344 **Fax:** 475 551033
Email: heno@ijsselbode.nl

Titles:
DE IJSSELBODE

DRUKKERIJ HERSELMAN B.V.
1635682
Postbus 8, 4420 AA KAPELLE **Tel:** 570 673344
Fax: 70 7999840
Email: info@scheldepost.nl
Web site: http://www.herselman.nl

Titles:
DE SCHELDEPOST

DRUKKERIJ KUIPER
1636780
Westeinde 17, 8064 AJ ZWARTSLUIS
Tel: 88 2697049 **Fax:** 20 5159700
Email: info@drukkerijkuiper.nl
Web site: http://www.drukkerijkuiper.nl

Titles:
ZWARTSLUIZER REKLAMEBLAD

DRUKKERIJ VAN LEER & DE JONG
1634644
Postbus 31, 9076 ZN ST. ANNAPAROCHIE
Tel: 20 5208657 **Fax:** 314 343839
Email: info@bildtsepost.nl

Titles:
DE BILDTSE POST

DRUKKERIJ WEEVERS
1634615
Postbus 22, 7250 AA VORDEN **Tel:** 20 5218939
Fax: 342 494299
Email: avk@weevers.nl
Web site: http://www.weevers.nl

Titles:
ELNA

DSV MEDIA B.V.
1640303
Postbus 14651, 1001 LD AMSTERDAM
Tel: 88 0139945 **Fax:** 172 494044
Email: info@dsvmedia.nl

Titles:
DE SMAAK VAN ITALIË

DUINWATERBEDRIJF ZUID-HOLLAND
1753606
Postbus 34, 2270 AA VOORBURG
Tel: 71 5273596 **Fax:** 35 6474569
Web site: http://www.duinwaterbedrijf.nl

Titles:
DE WATERKRANT

DUTCH FOUNDATION OF WOMEN AND HEALTH RESEARCH,
1754166
Meibergdreef 15, 1105 AZ AMSTERDAM
Tel: 20 3446050

Titles:
MAGAZINE VROUWEN EN GEZONDHEID

EBERSON & NIJHOF UITGEVERS
1636701
Postbus 31179, 6503 CD NIJMEGEN
Tel: 88 7518480 **Fax:** 88 7518481
Email: info@eberson-nijhof.nl
Web site: http://www.eberson-nijhof.nl

Titles:
NIJMEGEN BUSINESS

ECONOMISCHE FACULTEITSVERENIGING ROTTERDAM
1636461
Burg. Oudlaan 50, Kamer CB-03, 3062 PA ROTTERDAM
Email: secretaris@efr.nl
Web site: http://www.efr.nl

Titles:
ECLAIRE

EDG DISTRIBUTIE & MEDIA
1638123
Postbus 40266, 3504 AB UTRECHT
Tel: 70 3789880 **Fax:** 70 3789783
Email: info@edg.nl
Web site: http://www.edg.nl

Titles:
DOCENTENAGENDA
PRIMAONDERWIJS.NL
PRIMAOUDERS.NL

DE EEMSLANDER
1637475
Postbus 46, 9930 AA DELFZIJL **Tel:** 79 3628628
Fax: 172 466577
Email: eemslander@noordpers.nl

Titles:
DE EEMSLANDER

EENDRACHTBODE
1635038
Postbus 5, 4697 ZG ST. ANNALAND
Tel: 88 2697049 **Fax:** 20 5159700
Email: westbrabander@eendrachtbode.nl
Web site: http://www.eendrachtbode.nl

Titles:
EENDRACHTBODE, DE THOOLSE COURANT

EENVOUDIG COMMUNICEREN B.V.
1635442
Postbus 10208, 1001 EE AMSTERDAM
Tel: 88 2697183 **Fax:** 88 2697490
Email: info@eenvoudigcommuniceren.nl
Web site: http://www.eenvoudigcommuniceren.nl

Titles:
OKEE-KRANT

EIKELENBOOM B.V.
1756892
Keienbergweg 54, 1101 GC AMSTERDAM
Tel: 23 5565509 **Fax:** 342 494299
Email: info@eikelenboom.nl
Web site: http://www.eikelenboom.nl

Titles:
OAK

EISMA BOUWMEDIA B.V.
1782341
Postbus 361, 7007 CP DOETINCHEM
Tel: 88 7518000
Web site: http://www.eismamediagroep.nl

Titles:
AANNEMER
GEBOUWBEHEER
GLAS IN BEELD
SCHILDERSVAKKRANT

EISMA BUSINESSMEDIA B.V.
1636059
Postbus 340, 8901 BC LEEUWARDEN
Email: businessmedia@eisma.nl
Web site: http://www.eismabusinessmedia.nl

Titles:
BIT
EISMA VOEDINGSMIDDELENINDUSTRIE
PLATTELANDSPOST
HET SCHAAP
SIGN+ MAGAZINE
STITCH & PRINT INTERNATIONAL
DE VOETBALTRAINER

EISMA INDUSTRIAL MEDIA B.V.
1770796
Postbus 361, 7000 AJ DOETINCHEM
Tel: 88 2697183
Email: industrialmedia@eisma.nl
Web site: http://www.eisma.nl

Titles:
AANDRIJFTECHNIEK
BULK
METAAL MAGAZINE
RECYCLING MAGAZINE BENELUX
TTM (TRUCK & TRANSPORT MANAGEMENT)

EISMA TRADE MEDIA V.O.F.
1773079
Postbus 340, 8901 BC LEEUWARDEN
Tel: 88 2697112 **Fax:** 88 2696983
Web site: http://www.eisma.nl

Titles:
VIS MAGAZINE

ELBA MEDIA
1635277
Postbus 2160, 3800 CD AMERSFOORT
Email: info@elbamedia.nl
Web site: http://www.elbamedia.nl

Titles:
VITALE STAD

ELEKTOR INTERNATIONAL MEDIA B.V.
1635059
Postbus 11, 6114 ZG SUSTEREN **Tel:** 70 3789880
Fax: 314 343839
Web site: http://www.elektor.nl

Titles:
ELEKTOR

ELF B.V.
1637831
Postbus 97843, 2509 GE DEN HAAG
Tel: 76 5301713 **Fax:** 20 5159577
Email: info@elfvoetbal.nl
Web site: http://www.elfvoetbal.nl

Titles:
ELF VOETBAL

EMD, EUROPEAN MANAGEMENT DEVELOPMENT CENTRE
1754086
Naarderstraat 296, 1272 NT HUIZEN
Tel: 76 5312311 **Fax:** 70 7999840
Email: tvmd@emdcentre.com
Web site: http://www.emdcentre.com

Titles:
TIJDSCHRIFT VOOR MANAGEMENT DEVELOPMENT

ERASMUS UNIVERSITEIT ROTTERDAM
1636481
Postbus 1738, 3000 DR ROTTERDAM
Tel: 570 673344 **Fax:** 20 5159700
Email: erasmusmagazine@gmail.com
Web site: http://www.eur.nl

Titles:
ERASMUS MAGAZINE

ERFGOED BRABANT
1636636
Postbus 1325, 5200 BJ 'S-HERTOGENBOSCH
Tel: 88 7518000 **Fax:** 35 6474569
Email: info@erfgoedbrabant.nl
Web site: http://www.erfgoedbrabant.nl

Titles:
MUSEUMGIDS NOORD-BRABANT

ESS MEDIA B.V.
1635820
Postbus 40266, 3542 CA URECHT
Tel: 88 2697112 **Fax:** 88 2696983
Email: ess@ess.nl
Web site: http://www.ess.nl

Titles:
COS (COMPUTERS OP SCHOOL)

ETOS B.V.
1754496
Postbus 3101, 1500 HE ZAANDAM
Tel: 88 2697112 **Fax:** 88 2696983
Web site: http://www.etos.nl

Titles:
MOOI

EUROFORUM UITGEVERIJ B.V.
1635149
Postbus 125, 5600 AC EINDHOVEN
Tel: 10 2894075 **Fax:** 88 7518652
Email: info@euroforum-uitgeverij.nl
Web site: http://www.euroforum-uitgeverij.nl

Titles:
BELONING EN BELASTING
CONTROLLERS JOURNAAL
FISCOLOOG

EUROPEAN PIANO TEACHERS ASSOCIATION, AFD.
1640208
Postbus 4288, 3102 GE SCHIEDAM
Tel: 20 5218938
Web site: http://www.eptanederland.nl

Titles:
PIANO BULLETIN

EVANGELISCHE OMROEP
1635279
Postbus 21000, 1200 BA HILVERSUM
Email: eo@eo.nl
Web site: http://www.eo.nl

Titles:
EVA
INSITE

EVO
1638109
Postbus 350, 2700 AJ ZOETERMEER
Tel: 30 6383736 **Fax:** 30 6383999
Email: evo@evo.nl
Web site: http://www.evo.nl

Titles:
EVO LOGISTIEK
EVO MAGAZINE

F & L BUSINESS PUBLICATIONS B.V.
1767090
Postbus 31331, 6503 CH NIJMEGEN
Tel: 70 3789880 **Fax:** 70 3789783
Email: fnl@fnl.nl
Web site: http://www.fnl.nl

Titles:
LA CUCINA ITALIANA

F & L PUBLISHING GROUP B.V.
1637051
Postbus 31331, 6503 CH NIJMEGEN
Tel: 88 5567205 **Fax:** 88 5567355
Email: info@fnl.nl
Web site: http://www.fnl.nl

Titles:
CHIP
CHIP FOTO-VIDEO DIGITAAL
COMPUTER EASY
C'T MAGAZINE VOOR COMPUTER TECHNIEK

FACULTATIEVE VERZEKERINGEN N.V.
1753453
Postbus 80532, 2508 GM DEN HAAG
Tel: 314 349888 **Fax:** 314 343839
Email: info@facultatieve-verzekeringen.nl
Web site: http://www.facultatieve-verzekeringen.nl

Titles:
OOIT

FC KLAP
1769778
Postbus 1062, 1200 BB HILVERSUM
Tel: 88 2696670 **Fax:** 88 2696331
Email: info@fcklap.nl
Web site: http://www.fcklap.nl

Titles:
BROADCAST MAGAZINE
Z@PPMAGAZINE

FCOE, VERENIGING FILATELISTISCHE CONTACTGROEP 1754296
p/a Boomstede 424, 3608 BE MAARSSEN
Tel: 58 2845745 **Fax:** 20 5159700
Email: secr-fcoe@ziggo.nl
Web site: http://www.fcoe.nl

Titles:
OOST EUROPA FILATELIE

FD PERIODIEKEN 1634812
Postbus 690, 8901 BL LEEUWARDEN
Tel: 79 3628282 **Fax:** 88 2696983

Titles:
CHRISTELIJK WEEKBLAD

FEDERATIE NEDERLANDSE RUBBER- EN KUNSTSTOFINDUSTRIE 1753836
Postbus 420, 2260 AK LEIDSCHENDAM
Tel: 73 6271777 **Fax:** 73 6220570
Email: info@nrk.nl
Web site: http://www.nrk.nl

Titles:
NRK NETWERK

FÉDÉRATION INTERNATIONALE PHARMACEUTIQUE 1637377
Postbus 84200, 2508 AE DEN HAAG
Tel: 523 285330 **Fax:** 20 5159145
Email: publications@fip.org
Web site: http://www.fip.org

Titles:
INTERNATIONAL PHARMACY JOURNAL

FELIKAT 1637838
Zwaluwstraat 60, 3121 XX SCHIEDAM
Tel: 76 5301713
Email: info@felikat.com
Web site: http://www.felikat.org

Titles:
FELIKAT MAGAZINE

FIAT AUTO NEDERLAND B.V. 1753937
Postbus 203, 1170 AE BADHOEVEDORP
Tel: 88 3233333 **Fax:** 314 343839
Web site: http://www.fiat.nl

Titles:
FIAT MAGAZINE

FIBONACCI PRESS 1754420
Postbus 27, 7670 AA VRIEZENVEEN
Tel: 10 4066646 **Fax:** 10 4066979
Email: fibonacci-press@xs4all.nl

Titles:
ELLIOTT

FIETSERSBOND 1636972
Postbus 2828, 3500 GV UTRECHT
Tel: 10 2894075 **Fax:** 88 7518652
Email: info@fietsersbond.nl
Web site: http://www.fietsersbond.nl

Titles:
VOGELVRIJE FIETSER

FILATELISTISCHE MOTIEFGROEP PAPIER EN DRUK-NEDERLAND 1753618
p/a Florastraat 34a, 1695 BK BLOKKER
Tel: 70 3147856

Titles:
DRUK DOENDE

FINANCIAL MARKETING CONSULTANTS B.V. 1765557
Postbus 5017, 1380 GA WEESP **Tel:** 71 5273596
Fax: 88 2696983
Email: dfp@3xi.nl
Web site: http://www.3xi.nl

Titles:
RICHE

HET FINANCIEELE DAGBLAD B.V. 1635148
Postbus 216, 1000 AE AMSTERDAM
Tel: 71 5273596 **Fax:** 20 5928600
Email: info@fd.nl

Titles:
FD OUTLOOK
FD PERSOONLIJK

FIRST ROYAL TELECOM B.V. 1763080
Postbus 26046, 2502 GA DEN HAAG
Tel: 73 6157171

Titles:
DE OUD-HAGENAAR

FISCAAL UP TO DATE 1754118
Postbus 125, 5600 AC EINDHOVEN
Tel: 88 7518000 **Fax:** 88 3263324
Web site: http://www.futd.nl

Titles:
DOUANE UPDATE

FISCALERT 1640104
Postbus 3695, 1001 AL AMSTERDAM
Tel: 70 3378124 **Fax:** 172 422856
Email: info@fiscalert.nl
Web site: http://www.fiscalert.nl

Titles:
FISCALERT

FK MEDIA B.V. 1634476
Postbus 155, 6000 AD WEERT **Tel:** 88 3263334
Fax: 88 3263335
Email: info@fkmedia.nl
Web site: http://www.fkmedia.nl

Titles:
TYREZONE
ZAKENBLAD REGIO WEERT

FLEVOMEDIA B.V. 1635348
Postbus 8, 8860 AA HARLINGEN **Tel:** 58 2845745
Fax: 20 5159700
Email: info@fh.nl
Web site: http://www.fh.nl

Titles:
EXTRA

FM MEDIA B.V. 1638153
Postbus 925, 1000 AX AMSTERDAM
Tel: 70 3378124
Email: info@foxymagazine.nl

Titles:
FOXY

FNV BONDGENOTEN 1753952
Postbus 9208, 3506 GE UTRECHT
Tel: 570 673344 **Fax:** 20 5159700
Web site: http://www.fnvbondgenoten.nl

Titles:
RECHTSPOOR

FORCE LINK PUBLICATIES EN PROMOTIE B.V. 1638025
Haarlemmermeerstraat 26, 1058 KA AMSTERDAM

Titles:
LINK MODEVAKBLAD

FORMULA ONCE PUBLISHING 1757024
Postbus 154, 1940 AD BEVERWIJK
Tel: 88 3263334 **Fax:** 88 3263335
Email: info@formula-once.nl
Web site: http://www.formula-once.nl

Titles:
RTL GP

FOTOMARKT B.V. 1637113
Postbus 905, 2003 RX HAARLEM **Tel:** 20 5218938
Fax: 20 5159700
Email: fotomarkt@focusmedia.nl
Web site: http://www.focusmedia.nl

Titles:
FM FOTOMARKT

FRAME PUBLISHERS B.V. 1638019
Laan der Hesperiden 68, 1076 DX AMSTERDAM

Titles:
FRAME

FRANCHISEPLUS B.V. 1636420
Postbus 199, 3740 AD BAARN **Tel:** 88 2697183
Fax: 314 343839
Email: info@franchiseplus.nl
Web site: http://www.franchiseplus.nl

Titles:
FRANCHISE PLUS

FREE MEDIA GROUP B.V. 1637094
H.J.E. Wenckebachweg 200, 1096 AS AMSTERDAM **Tel:** 88 7518000 **Fax:** 35 6474569
Email: info@freemediagroup.nl
Web site: http://www.freemediagroup.nl

Titles:
ESQUIRE
FHM (FOR HIM MAGAZINE)

FRIESLAND HOLLAND TOURIST INFORMATION TRAVEL 1637681
Postbus 163, 8470 AD WOLVEGA
Tel: 70 3378125 **Fax:** 20 5159145
Email: info@frieslandholland.nl
Web site: http://www.frieslandholland.nl

Titles:
FRIESLAND HOLLAND VAKANTIEMAGAZINE
HOLLAND HIGHLIGHTS

FUNDEON 1753401
Postbus 440, 3840 AK HARDERWIJK
Tel: 76 5312311 **Fax:** 76 5144531
Email: info@fundeon.nl
Web site: http://www.fundeon.nl

Titles:
BOUWEN
FUNDAMENT

G + J PUBLISHING C.V. 1640276
Dalsteindreef 82-92, 1112 XC DIEMEN
Email: info@jan-magazine.nl
Web site: http://www.genj.nl

Titles:
GLAMOUR
JAN
NATIONAL GEOGRAPHIC
NATIONAL GEOGRAPHIC TRAVELER
QUEST
QUEST HISTORIE
QUEST PSYCHOLOGIE

GALL & GALL 1757073
Postbus 3130, 1500 HH ZAANDAM
Tel: 71 5161527
Email: info@gall.nl
Web site: http://www.gall.nl

Titles:
PROEF&

GAY INTERNATIONAL PRESS 1638052
Postbus 76609, 1070 HE AMSTERDAM
Tel: 70 3789880 **Fax:** 70 3789783

Titles:
GAY NEWS

GEHRELS MUZIEKEDUCATIE 1636478
De Meerkoet 1, 2761 SM ZEVENHUIZEN
Tel: 570 673344
Email: informatie@gehrelsmuziekeducatie.nl
Web site: http://www.gehrelsmuziekeducatie.nl

Titles:
DE PYRAMIDE

DE GELDERBLOM 1754043
Arij Koplaan 65, 3123 CA SCHIEDAM
Tel: 570 673344
Email: degelderblom@planet.nl

Titles:
DE GELDERBLOM

GEMEENTE KRIMPEN A/D IJSSEL 1638029
Postbus 200, 2920 AE KRIMPEN A/D IJSSEL
Email: gemeente@krimpenaandenijssel.nl
Web site: http://www.krimpenaandenijssel.nl

Titles:
DE KLINKER

GEMEENTE OLDAMBT 1636825
Postbus 175, 9670 AD WINSCHOTEN
Tel: 88 2696670 **Fax:** 88 2696331
Email: info@gemeente-oldambt.nl
Web site: http://www.gemeente-oldambt.nl

Titles:
DE OLDAMBTSTER

GENOOTSCHAP VAN DE GODDELIJKE GENADE 1753971
Hereweg 46, 6373 VJ LANDGRAAF
Tel: 342 494889 **Fax:** 172 466577

Titles:
KINDSCHAP GODS

GEOMARES PUBLISHING 1636284
Postbus 112, 8530 AC LEMMER **Tel:** 58 2845745
Fax: 88 2697490
Email: info@geomares.nl

Titles:
HI, HYDRO INTERNATIONAL

GEPEA RETAILSERVICE B.V. 1635993
Postbus 145, 6930 AC WESTERVOORT
Tel: 79 3628628 **Fax:** 20 5159145
Email: info@gepea.nl
Web site: http://www.gepea.nl

Titles:
ENTOURAGE

GLOBAL ROEL MEDIA 1776041
Looierslaan 107, 2272 BJ VOORBURG

Titles:
PADDESTOELEN

GLOBAL VILLAGE MEDIA 1642254
Spuistraat 239d, 1012 VP AMSTERDAM
Tel: 70 3789880 **Fax:** 70 7999840
Email: administratie@globalvillagemedia.nl
Web site: http://www.globalvillagemedia.nl

Titles:
ONZEWERELD

GLOBE ADVERTISING 1637939
Kronkelbaan 11, 1157 LH ABBEKERK
Tel: 88 7518000 **Fax:** 35 6474569
Email: info@globe-advertising.nl
Web site: http://www.globe-advertising.nl

Titles:
WINTERVAKANTIEMAGAZINE
ZOMERVAKANTIEMAGAZINE

GMG B.V. 1635530
Postbus 267, 1000 AG AMSTERDAM
Tel: 342 494889 **Fax:** 342 494299
Email: info@gmg.nl
Web site: http://www.gmg.nl

Titles:
JACKIE
JACKIE BUSINESS

GODDIJN & GODDIJN 1646272
Postbus 78, 1400 AB BUSSUM **Tel:** 20 5218938
Fax: 20 5159145

Titles:
PIANOWERELD

GOODWILL MEDIA B.V. 1638359
Postbus 10040, 7301 GA APELDOORN
Tel: 70 3789880 **Fax:** 70 3789783
Email: info@goodwill.nl
Web site: http://www.goodwill.nl

Titles:
KINDER PUZZEL & KLEURBOEK

GOOI EN STICHT 1635047
Postbus 5018, 8260 GA KAMPEN **Tel:** 88 7518000
Fax: 35 6474569
Email: gens@kok.nl
Web site: http://www.kok.nl

Titles:
BRON VAN CHRISTELIJKE GEEST

GOV, VERENIGING VAN KERKMUSICI 1754773
Hoogkamp 65, 7152 GL EIBERGEN
Tel: 88 7518000

Titles:
MUZIEK&LITURGIE

GRAFICO DE POOST 1754259
Postbus 6118, 5600 HC EINDHOVEN
Tel: 88 3263300 **Fax:** 88 3263339
Email: info@poost.nl
Web site: http://www.poost.nl

Titles:
MAL & MASKER

GREEN INTERACTIVE MEDIA B.V. 1764008
Baarsjesweg 311, 1058 AH AMSTERDAM
Tel: 73 6157171 **Fax:** 10 7044752
Email: info@clubgreen.nl
Web site: http://www.clubgreen.nl

Titles:
CLUBGREEN JAARMAGAZINE

GROOT HELLEVOET UITGEVERIJ B.V. 1636080
Postbus 51, 3220 AB HELLEVOETSLUIS
Tel: 10 2894075 **Fax:** 88 7518652

Titles:
BRIELS NIEUWSLAND
GROOT HELLEVOET
GROOT WESTLAND
WEEKBLAD SPIJKENISSE

DEN HAAG MARKETING 1637961
Postbus 85456, 2508 CD DEN HAAG
Tel: 88 7518000 **Fax:** 35 6474569
Email: info@denhaag.com
Web site: http://www.denhaag.com

Titles:
DEN HAAG INFORMATIEGIDS

HAILAIT MEDIA PRODUCTIONS 1732421
Jacob Marisstraat 34-2, 1058 JA AMSTERDAM
Email: hmpbusiness@gmail.com
Web site: http://www.hmpbusiness.com

Titles:
ARKE MAGAZINE
WERELDS

HANZEHOGESCHOOL GRONINGEN 1638044
Postbus 30030, 9700 RM GRONINGEN
Tel: 10 2894018
Email: hanzemag@org.hanze.nl
Web site: http://www.hanze.nl

Titles:
HANZEMAG

HARTPATIËNTEN NEDERLAND 1753479
Postbus 1002, 6040 KA ROERMOND
Tel: 20 5159429 **Fax:** 20 5159036
Email: roermond@hartpatienten.nl
Web site: http://www.hartpatienten.nl

Titles:
HARTBRUG MAGAZINE

HB MEDIA B.V. 1635566
Postbus 28, 1960 AA HEEMSKERK
Tel: 20 5159666 **Fax:** 20 5159700
Email: info@passie.nl

Titles:
PASSIE

HDC MEDIA B.V. 1634452
Postbus 2, 1800 AA ALKMAAR **Tel:** 88 2697856
Fax: 88 2697943
Web site: http://www.hdcmedia.nl

Titles:
ALMERE VANDAAG
ALPHEN.CC
IJMUIDER COURANT

HEARST MAGAZINES NEDERLAND 1634831
Postbus 10209, 1001 EE AMSTERDAM
Tel: 70 3789880 **Fax:** 70 3789783
Email: singel@hearstmagazines.nl
Web site: http://www.hearstmagazines.nl

Titles:
COLOR STUDIO
ELLE
ELLE ETEN
PRIVIUM UPDATE
QUOTE
RED
SANTÉ

HEM, HOME ENTERTAINMENT MEDIA B.V. 1636747
Postbus 155, 6500 AD NIJMEGEN
Tel: 76 5250906 **Fax:** 342 494299
Email: info@bp-m.nl

Titles:
HVT

HEMELS PUBLISHERS 1636340
Postbus 369, 1200 AJ HILVERSUM
Tel: 88 7518000 **Fax:** 35 6474569
Email: mail@hemels.com
Web site: http://www.hemels.com

Titles:
FLYING DUTCHMAN
MERCEDES MAGAZINE
MY TOYOTA

HHS UITGEVERIJ 1637232
Postbus 150, 5360 AD GRAVE **Tel:** 58 2845745
Fax: 20 5159700
Email: info@hhsuitgeverij.nl
Web site: http://www.hhsuitgeverij.nl

Titles:
EÉN-EÉN-TWEE

HIGH PROFILE B.V. 1638016
Postbus 7209, 3430 JE NIEUWEGEIN
Email: info@highprofile.nl
Web site: http://www.highprofile.nl

Titles:
EVENTS

HISWA MULTIMEDIA B.V. 1634870
Postbus 102, 3970 AC DRIEBERGEN
Tel: 20 5218939 **Fax:** 342 494299
Email: multimedia@hiswa.nl
Web site: http://www.hiswa.nl

Titles:
HISWA-MAGAZINE

HMS EUROCOM B.V. 1756955
Postbus 82, 7710 AB NIEUWLEUSEN
Tel: 88 7518480 **Fax:** 88 7518481
Email: info@hmseuro.com
Web site: http://www.hmseuro.com

Titles:
WELLNESS LIFE

HOFFMANN BEDRIJFSRECHERCHE B.V. 1754072
Postbus 60090, 1320 AB ALMERE
Tel: 36 5398208 **Fax:** 342 494250
Email: info@hoffmannbv.nl
Web site: http://www.hoffmannbv.nl

Titles:
HOFFMANN STATISTIEK
RECHERCHETIPS VOOR HET BEDRIJFSLEVEN

HOGESCHOOL INHOLLAND 1638247
Postbus 558, 2003 RN HAARLEM **Tel:** 88 5567205
Email: inzine@inholland.nl
Web site: http://www.inholland.nl

Titles:
INZINE

HOLAPRESS COMMUNICATIE B.V. 1637897
Postbus 130, 5550 AC VALKENSWAARD
Email: info@holapress.com
Web site: http://www.holapress.com

Titles:
RIOLERING

HOLBOX MEDIA B.V. 1651335
Kraanpoort 10, 6041 EG ROERMOND
Tel: 76 5250906 **Fax:** 342 494299
Email: info@navenant.nl
Web site: http://www.holbox.nl

Titles:
NAVENANT

HOLCO PUBLICATIONS B.V. 1757034
Postbus 267, 1800 AG ALKMAAR **Tel:** 88 3263300
Fax: 88 3263304

Titles:
PENNY

HOLCUS 1753874
Postbus 94005, 1090 GA AMSTERDAM
Tel: 88 5567205 **Fax:** 88 5567355
Email: tijdschrift@wereldfietser.nl

Titles:
DE WERELDFIETSER

HOLLAND COMBINATIE, TELEGRAAF LOKALE MEDIA 1653904
Postbus 20619, 1001 NP AMSTERDAM
Tel: 88 7518000 **Fax:** 35 6474569
Email: info@hollandcombinatie.nl
Web site: http://www.hollandcombinatie.nl

Titles:
CTR/DE POLDERBODE
HEEMSTEEDSE COURANT
NIEUWSBLAD VOOR CASTRICUM
HET OP ZONDAG
DE POSTILJON, EDITIE ALEXANDERPOLDER
E.O. DE POSTILJON, EDITIE ZOETERMEER
HET SCHAGER WEEKBLAD
WESTFRIES WEEKBLAD
WIERINGER COURANT
WITTE WEEKBLAD EDITIE BADHOEVEDORP
E.O. WITTE WEEKBLAD EDITIE HILLEGOM
E.O. WITTE WEEKBLAD EDITIE TEYLINGEN & NOORDWIJKERHOUT
WITTE WEEKBLAD EDITIE ZWANENBURG
E.O. DE WOONBODE 'T GOOI
ZONDAGOCHTENDBLAD BEVERWIJK/ HEEMSKERK
ZONDAGOCHTENDBLAD HEILOO/ CASTRICUM

HOOFDLIJNEN 1754338
Verl. Bonedijkestraat 287, 4383 BC VLISSINGEN
Tel: 88 3263300
Email: hoofdlijnen@nvlknf.nl
Web site: http://www.nvlknf.nl

Titles:
HOOFDLIJNEN

HOOGTE 80 1756898
Postbus 30095, 6803 AB ARNHEM
Tel: 88 3263300 **Fax:** 88 3263304
Email: info@hoogte80.com
Web site: http://www.hoogte80.com

Titles:
FLORE MAGAZINE

HUB UITGEVERS 1634718
Postbus 3389, 2001 DJ HAARLEM
Tel: 76 5250906 **Fax:** 342 494299
Email: info@hub.nl
Web site: http://www.hub.nl

Titles:
COMPUTER IDEE
PC-ACTIVE

HUISMUZIEK, VERENIGING VOOR MUZIEK EN INSTRUMENTENBOUW 1636097
Postbus 9, 6800 AA ARNHEM **Tel:** 88 3263320
Fax: 20 5159577
Email: info@huismuziek.nl
Web site: http://www.huismuziek.nl

Titles:
DE BOUWBRIEF
HUISMUZIEK NIEUWSBRIEF

DE HUWELIJKSDATA GIDS 1753312
Postbus 277, 1520 AG WORMERVEER
Tel: 20 5208657 **Fax:** 314 343839
Email: info@huwelijksdatagids.nl
Web site: http://www.huwelijksdatagids.nl

Titles:
DE HUWELIJKSDATA GIDS

IBFD, INTERNATIONAL BUREAU OF FISCAL DOCUMENTATION 1755636
Postbus 20237, 1000 HE AMSTERDAM
Tel: 70 3789880 **Fax:** 70 3789783
Email: info@ibfd.org
Web site: http://www.ibfd.org

Titles:
DERIVATIVES AND FINANCIAL INSTRUMENTS

IDG NEDERLAND 1637383
Postbus 20646, 1001 NP AMSTERDAM
Tel: 70 3789880
Email: marketing@idg.nl
Web site: http://www.idg.nl

Titles:
COMPUTERITOTAAL
TIPS & TRUCS
ZOOM.NL

IHC MERWEDE 1753926
Postbus 204, 3360 AE SLIEDRECHT
Tel: 88 5567205 **Fax:** 88 5567355
Email: info@ihcmerwede.com
Web site: http://www.ihcmerwede.com

Titles:
PORTS AND DREDGING

INCH, INTERNATIONAL NETWORK CONNECTING HOSPITALITY 1636974
Postbus 2192, 3500 GD UTRECHT
Tel: 10 2894075
Email: secretariaat@inch.nl
Web site: http://www.inch.nl

Titles:
HOTELLO

INDUSTRIËLE PERS AMERSFOORT B.V. 1635034
Postbus 1297, 3800 BG AMERSFOORT
Tel: 570 673344 **Fax:** 70 7999840
Email: info@indpers.com
Web site: http://www.indpers.com

Titles:
NPT PROCESTECHNOLOGIE

INDUSTRIELINQS PERS EN PLATFORM B.V. 1709738
Postbus 12936, 1100 AX AMSTERDAM
Tel: 88 7518000 **Fax:** 35 6474569
Email: info@petrochem.nl
Web site: http://www.industrielinqs.nl

Titles:
IMAINTAIN
PETROCHEM
UTILITIES

ING CAR LEASE NEDERLAND 1643404
Postbus 6890, 4802 HW BREDA **Tel:** 592 379571
Fax: 10 7044752
Web site: http://www.ingcarlease.nl

Titles:
CROSSOVER

INK PUBLISHING UK 1784628
Tel: 36 5398208 **Fax:** 342 494250
Stroombaan 4, 1181 VX AMSTELVEEN
Tel: 20 5979409 **Fax:** 20 5979505
Email: info@ink-publishing.com

Titles:
HOLLAND HERALD

INSPIRIT MEDIA 1635060
Emmastraat 18, 8011 AG ZWOLLE
Tel: 88 3263334 **Fax:** 88 3263335
Email: info@inspiritmedia.nl
Web site: http://www.inspiritmedia.nl

Titles:
AAN DE HAND
UITDAGING
XIST IN CHRIST

INSURANCE PUBLISHERS B.V. 1635741
Postbus 5017, 1380 GA WEESP **Tel:** 88 7518160
Fax: 342 494299
Email: infinance@3xi.nl
Web site: http://www.3xi.nl

Titles:
INFINANCE

INT. PERSCENTRUM NIEUWSPOORT 1634815
Lange Poten 10, 2511 CL DEN HAAG
Tel: 73 6271777 **Fax:** 73 6220570
Web site: http://www.nieuwspoort.nl

Titles:
NIEUWSPOORT NIEUWS

INTERGAMMA B.V. 1757080
Postbus 100, 3830 AC LEUSDEN **Tel:** 71 5161527
Fax: 88 7518481
Web site: http://www.intergamma.nl

Titles:
ZIEZO

INTERMEDIUM PUBLISHERS B.V. 1636841
Postbus 2008, 3800 CA AMERSFOORT
Tel: 172 466639 **Fax:** 172 466577
Email: info@pets.nl

Titles:
PETS INTERNATIONAL MAGAZINE

INTERSAFE GROENEVELD B.V. 1754426
Postbus 86, 3300 AB DORDRECHT
Tel: 79 3628628 **Fax:** 172 466577
Email: info@intersafe-groeneveld.nl
Web site: http://www.intersafe.nl

Titles:
VEILIGHEIDSNIEUWS

INVESTMENT PUBLISHERS B.V. 1765559
Postbus 5017, 1380 GA WEESP **Tel:** 58 2845745
Fax: 88 2697490
Email: cash@3xi.nl
Web site: http://www.3xi.nl

Titles:
CASH

IOS PRESS 1635037
Nieuwe Hemweg 6b, 1013 BG AMSTERDAM
Tel: 88 2697856 **Fax:** 88 2697943
Email: info@iospress.nl
Web site: http://www.iospress.nl

Titles:
INFORMATION SERVICES & USE

IPMS - NEDERLAND 1754178
Eefsebeek 35, 1509 ER ZAANDAM
Tel: 20 3446050
Email: bestuur@imps.nl
Web site: http://www.ipms.nl

Titles:
MODELBOUW IN PLASTIC

IPO, INTERPROVINCIAAL OVERLEG 1755273
Postbus 16107, 2500 BC DEN HAAG
Tel: 88 7518000 **Fax:** 35 6474569
Email: ipo-info@wb.ipo.nl
Web site: http://www.ipo.nl

Titles:
IPO MILIEUWERK

IS TEKST & PRODUCTIE 1753481
Meyhorst 91-21, 6537 KJ NIJMEGEN
Tel: 36 5398208 **Fax:** 36 5398167
Email: info@bloedsuiker.nl

Titles:
BLOEDSUIKER

I.S.I.S., INTERNATIONAL STUDYCENTRE FOR 1754163
De Ruijterstraat 74, 2518 AV DEN HAAG
Tel: 20 3446050 **Fax:** 20 5159145
Email: luciferred@stichtingisis.org
Web site: http://www.stichtingisis.org

Titles:
LUCIFER

IT'S AMAZING BUSINESS COMMUNICATION B.V. 1634855
Postbus 122, 3100 AC SCHIEDAM
Tel: 71 5273596 **Fax:** 20 5928600
Email: itsabc@itsamazing.nl
Web site: http://www.itsamazing.nl

Titles:
COIFFURE GENERATION

IUCN NEDERLANDS COMITÉ 1754348
Plantage Middenlaan 2k, 1018 DD AMSTERDAM
Tel: 523 285330 **Fax:** 88 3263339
Email: mail@iucn.nl
Web site: http://www.iucn.nl

Titles:
ECOLOGIE EN ONTWIKKELING

JANSZ MEDIA B.V. 1636163
Postbus 2117, 3700 CC ZEIST **Tel:** 73 6271777
Fax: 73 6220570
Email: info@cameranet.nl

Titles:
CAMERA MAGAZINE

JD COMMUNICATIE B.V. 1638136
Postbus 1067, 2001 BB HAARLEM
Tel: 314 349969 **Fax:** 314 349323
Email: info@jdcomm.nl
Web site: http://www.jdcomm.nl

Titles:
APOTHEEK & GEZONDHEID
NATURAL BODY

JETTY VAN DER HULST SPECIALS 1637964
Booldersdijk 29, 6031 PK NEDERWEERT
Tel: 88 7518000 **Fax:** 35 6474569
Email: jetty@worldonline.nl
Web site: http://www.jetty.nl

Titles:
GROOMERS EUROPE

JEUGD EN WERK B.V. 1764597
Postbus 50073, 1305 AB ALMERE
Tel: 592 379571 **Fax:** 10 7044752
Email: info@jeugdenwerk.nl
Web site: http://www.jeugdenwerk.nl

Titles:
IKGAWERKEN.NL

JEUNES RESTAURATEURS D'EUROPE 1699354
Pastoor van der Voortlaan 16, 5591 JB HEEZE
Tel: 88 3263310 **Fax:** 342 494299
Email: info@jre.eu
Web site: http://www.jre.eu

Titles:
TALENT & PASSION

JJ PRODUCTIONS B.V. 1636862
Postbus 49, 2250 AA VOORSCHOTEN
Tel: 20 3446050 **Fax:** 20 5159145
Email: jjproductions@familyproductions.nl
Web site: http://www.familyproductions.nl

Titles:
U EN UW BABY

JOHN BENJAMINS B.V. 1634563
Postbus 36224, 1020 ME AMSTERDAM
Tel: 88 7518000 **Fax:** 35 6474569
Email: customer.services@benjamins.nl
Web site: http://www.benjamins.com

Titles:
PRAGMATICS & COGNITION
WRITTEN LANGUAGE AND LITERACY

JUDO BOND NEDERLAND 1634746
Postbus 7012, 3430 JA NIEUWEGEIN
Tel: 314 349888 **Fax:** 314 343839
Email: judobond@jbn.nl
Web site: http://www.jbn.nl

Titles:
JUDO VISIE

JUMBO SUPERMARKTEN B.V. 1756875
Postbus 8, 5460 AA VEGHEL **Tel:** 172 466471
Fax: 172 422886
Email: jumbomagazine@jumbosupermarkten.nl
Web site: http://www.jumbosupermarkten.nl

Titles:
JUMBO MAGAZINE

KAMER VAN KOOPHANDEL NEDERLAND 1634979
Postbus 191, 3440 AD WOERDEN
Tel: 88 5567205 **Fax:** 88 5567355
Web site: http://www.kvk.nl

Titles:
EIGEN BEDRIJF
EIGEN BEDRIJF, REGIO AMSTERDAM
EIGEN BEDRIJF, REGIO BRABANT
EIGEN BEDRIJF, REGIO CENTRAAL GELDERLAND
EIGEN BEDRIJF, REGIO DEN HAAG
EIGEN BEDRIJF, REGIO FRIESLAND
EIGEN BEDRIJF, REGIO GOOI-, EEM- EN FLEVOLAND
EIGEN BEDRIJF, REGIO MIDDEN-NEDERLAND
EIGEN BEDRIJF, REGIO NOORD EN MIDDEN LIMBURG
EIGEN BEDRIJF, REGIO OOST-NEDERLAND
EIGEN BEDRIJF, REGIO ROTTERDAM
STARTERSMAGAZINE

KANSPLUS, BELANGENNETWERK VERSTANDELIJK 1753943
Postbus 85274, 3508 AG UTRECHT
Tel: 570 673344 **Fax:** 20 5159700
Email: info@kansplus.nl
Web site: http://www.kansplus.nl

Titles:
PLUSPUNT

KARATE-DO BOND NEDERLAND 1636470
Eisenhowerlaan 198-202, 3527 HK UTRECHT
Tel: 570 673344 **Fax:** 20 5159700
Email: info@kbn.nl
Web site: http://www.kbn.nl

Titles:
TAIKO

KATH. ST. VOOR BLINDEN EN SLECHTZIENDEN 1754081
St. Elisabethstraat 4, 5361 HK GRAVE
Tel: 76 5312311 **Fax:** 70 7999840
Email: info@ksbs.nl

Titles:
DE STEM VAN GRAVE

KBO BRABANT 1757008
Postbus 3240, 5203 DE 'S-HERTOGENBOSCH
Tel: 20 5852688 **Fax:** 297 541072
Email: info@kbo-brabant.nl
Web site: http://www.kbo-brabant.nl

Titles:
ONS

KEESING NEDERLAND B.V. 1635371
Postbus 1118, 1000 BC AMSTERDAM
Tel: 570 673344 **Fax:** 70 7999840
Email: info@keesing.com
Web site: http://www.keesing.nl

Titles:
BINGO!
DENKSPORT PUZZELBLADEN

KEIJSER 18 MEDIAPRODUCTIES B.V. 1637631
Postbus 11497, 1001 GL AMSTERDAM
Tel: 88 2697112 **Fax:** 88 2696983
Email: office@k18.nl
Web site: http://www.k18.nl

Titles:
SLAGWERKKRANT

KENNISCENTRUM DIERPLAGEN (KAD) 1636918
Postbus 350, 6700 AJ WAGENINGEN
Tel: 70 3789880 **Fax:** 70 3789783
Email: info@kad.nl
Web site: http://www.kad.nl

Titles:
DIERPLAGEN INFORMATIE

KERK IN ACTIE, PROTESTANTSE KERK IN NEDERLAND 1753393
Postbus 456, 3500 AL UTRECHT **Tel:** 20 5208657
Fax: 314 343839
Email: servicedesk@kerkinactie.nl
Web site: http://www.kerkinactie.nl

Titles:
VANDAAR

KERKGENOOTSCHAP LEGER DES HEILS 1753930
Postbus 3006, 1300 EH ALMERE **Tel:** 76 5312311
Fax: 70 7999840
Web site: http://www.legerdesheils.nl

Titles:
HEILS- EN STRIJDZANGEN
INTERCOM

K.F.F.B., KRISTLIK FRYSKE FOLKSBIBLETEEK 1753945
Tjalling H. Haismastraat 26, 9251 AV BERGUM
Tel: 20 5612070
Web site: http://www.kffb.nl

Titles:
DE FLEANENDE KRIE

KIDSCOM B.V. 1638265
Postbus 75757, 1070 AT AMSTERDAM
Tel: 88 5567205 **Fax:** 88 5567355
Web site: http://www.kidscom.nl

Titles:
NATIONALE KIDSKRANT

KLM, AFD. INTERNE COMMUNICATIE, AMS/DR 1754233
Postbus 7700, 1117 ZL SCHIPHOL
Tel: 88 2697062

Titles:
WOLKENRIDDER MAGAZINE

KLOCK'S MEDIA GROEP B.V. 1756880
Hunzebos 2a, 1447 TX PURMEREND
Tel: 88 7518750 **Fax:** 88 7518751
Email: info@klocks.nl
Web site: http://www.klocks.nl

Titles:
DE STATUS

KLOOSTERHOF ACQUISITIE SERVICES - UITGEVERIJ B.V. 1638338
Napoleonsweg 128a, 6086 AJ NEER
Email: info@kloosterhof.nl
Web site: http://www.kloosterhof.nl

Titles:
TIJDSCHRIFT VOOR NUCLEAIRE GENEESKUNDE

KLUWER 1634575
Postbus 4, 2400 MA ALPHEN A/D RIJN
Tel: 172 466848 **Fax:** 172 422856
Email: info@kluwer.nl
Web site: http://www.kluwer.nl

Titles:
ARBEIDSRECHT
ARBO
BASISSCHOOLMANAGEMENT
BB BINNENLANDS BESTUUR
BB DIGITAAL BESTUUR
BODEM
FACTO MAGAZINE
FINANCE & CONTROL
DE HYPOTHEEKADVISEUR
MANAGEMENT CONTROL & ACCOUNTING (MCA)
MESO MAGAZINE
MILIEUMAGAZINE
OPENBAAR BESTUUR
OR INFORMATIE
PENSIOEN MAGAZINE
PRAKTIJKBLAD SALARISADMINISTRATIE
SECURITY MANAGEMENT
SIGMA
TIJDSCHRIFT ADMINISTRATIE
TIJDSCHRIFT CONTROLLING
VAKBLAD FINANCIËLE PLANNING

KLUWER LAW INTERNATIONAL 1634432
Postbus 316, 2400 AH ALPHEN A/D RIJN
Tel: 88 7518000 **Fax:** 35 6474569
Web site: http://www.kluwerlaw.com

Titles:
COMMON MARKET LAW REVIEW
EUROPEAN FOREIGN AFFAIRS REVIEW
EUROPEAN REVIEW OF PRIVATE LAW
INTERTAX
JOURNAL OF WORLD TRADE

K.N.A.G., KON. NED. AARDRIJKSKUNDIG GENOOTSCHAP 1636391
Postbus 805, 3500 AV UTRECHT
Email: info@knag.nl
Web site: http://www.knag.nl

Titles:
GEOGRAFIE

KNB, KON. VERBOND VAN NED. BAKSTEENFABRIKANTEN 1754893
Postbus 153, 6880 AD VELP **Tel:** 88 3263320
Fax: 20 5159577
Email: knb@knb-baksteen.nl
Web site: http://www.knb-baksteen.nl

Titles:
BAKSTEEN

KNBLO-WANDELSPORTORGANISATIE NEDERLAND 1636320
Postbus 1020, 6501 BA NIJMEGEN
Email: info@wandel.nl
Web site: http://www.wandel.nl

Titles:
LANDELIJK WANDEL PROGRAMMA
HET WANDELSPORTMAGAZINE

KNGF 1753820
Postbus 248, 3800 AE AMERSFOORT
Tel: 20 5218938 **Fax:** 70 7999840
Email: hoofdkantoor@kngf.nl
Web site: http://www.kngf.nl

Titles:
FYSIOPRAXIS
NEDERLANDS TIJDSCHRIFT VOOR FYSIOTHERAPIE

KNMP, KON. NED. MIJ. TER BEVORDERING DER 1636398
Postbus 30460, 2500 GL DEN HAAG
Tel: 88 2697183 **Fax:** 88 2697490

Titles:
PHARMACEUTISCH WEEKBLAD

KNPV, KON. NED. POLITIEHOND VERENIGING 1636423
Liendertseweg 108, 3815 BJ AMERSFOORT
Tel: 88 2697183 **Fax:** 314 343839
Email: bureau-knpv@planet.nl
Web site: http://www.knpv.nl

Titles:
DE POLITIEHOND

K.N.R.B., KON. NED. ROEIBOND 1636540
Bosbaan 6, 1182 AG AMSTELVEEN
Tel: 570 673344 **Fax:** 475 551033
Email: info@knrb.nl
Web site: http://www.knrb.nl

Titles:
ROEIEN

KNRM, KONINKLIJKE NEDERLANDSE REDDING MAATSCHAPPIJ 1753955
Postbus 434, 1970 AK IJMUIDEN **Tel:** 570 673344
Fax: 475 551033
Email: info@knrm.nl
Web site: http://www.knrm.nl

Titles:
DE REDDINGBOOT

K.N.S.A., KON. NED. SCHUTTERS ASSOCIATIE 1636615
Postbus 303, 3830 AJ LEUSDEN **Tel:** 570 673344
Fax: 70 7999840
Email: info@knsa.nl
Web site: http://www.knsa.nl

Titles:
SCHIETSPORT

KNTV 1637465
Grote Bickersstraat 50a, 1013 KS AMSTERDAM
Tel: 79 3628628 **Fax:** 172 466577
Email: office@kntv.nl
Web site: http://www.kntv.nl

Titles:
KNTV-MAGAZINE

KNV, KON.NED.VERVOER 1636117
Postbus 19365, 2500 CJ DEN HAAG
Tel: 79 3628628 **Fax:** 35 6726847
Email: knvmedia@knv.nl
Web site: http://www.knv.nl

Titles:
NEDERLANDS VERVOER

K.N.V.V.L. AFD. BALLONVAREN 1754221
Spechtstraat 16, 1223 NZ HILVERSUM
Tel: 88 2697049
Email: secretariaat@knvvlballonvaren.info
Web site: http://www.knvvlballonvaren.info

Titles:
BALLONSTOF

KOGGESCHIP VAKBLADEN B.V. 1634539
Postbus 1198, 1000 BD AMSTERDAM
Tel: 88 2696557 **Fax:** 88 2696946
Email: info@koggeschip-vakbladen.nl
Web site: http://www.koggeschip-vakbladen.nl

Titles:
KUNSTSTOF MAGAZINE
PROF NAIL
LE SALON
VISAGIE
VOETVAK+

KOLK & GEENSE VOF 1763001
Buiten Molenstraat 7, 4101 CJ CULEMBORG
Tel: 73 6157171
Email: redactie@kolkengeense.nl
Web site: http://www.kolkengeense.nl

Titles:
LIEF!

KON. BDU UITGEVERS B.V. 1634571
Postbus 67, 3770 AB BARNEVELD
Tel: 342 494268 **Fax:** 342 494299
Email: tijdschriften@bdu.nl
Web site: http://www.bdu.nl

Titles:
LAND + WATER
MOBILIA INTERIEURTEXTIEL
MOTORBOOT
NATUURSTEEN
PLAFOND EN WAND.INFO
TEGELTOTAAL
TIMMERFABRIKANT
TRANSPORTVISIE

KON. BRILL N.V. 1634510
Postbus 9000, 2300 PA LEIDEN **Tel:** 88 2697139
Fax: 88 2697175
Email: cs@brill.nl
Web site: http://www.brill.nl

Titles:
EUROPEAN JOURNAL OF HEALTH LAW
HELSINKI MONITOR
JOURNAL OF EMPIRICAL THEOLOGY
QUAERENDO

KON. LUCHTMACHT 1651329
Postbus 20703, 2500 ES DEN HAAG
Tel: 20 5159700 **Fax:** 342 494299
Web site: http://www.luchtmacht.nl

Titles:
PROGRAMMABOEK OPEN DAGEN KONINKLIJKE LUCHTMACHT

KON. NED. MIJ. VOOR DIERGENEESKUNDE 1636849
Postbus 421, 3990 GE HOUTEN **Tel:** 88 3263300
Fax: 88 3263339
Email: info@knmvd.nl
Web site: http://www.knmvd.nl

Titles:
TIJDSCHRIFT VOOR DIERGENEESKUNDE

KON. NED. SCHAAKBOND 1636604
Frans Halsplein 5, 2021 DL HAARLEM
Tel: 570 673344 **Fax:** 70 7999840
Email: bondsbureau@schaakbond.nl
Web site: http://www.schaakbond.nl

Titles:
SCHAAK MAGAZINE

KON. NED. VERENIGING ONS LEGER 1636287
Vogelzand 2311, 1788 GE DEN HELDER
Tel: 58 2845745 **Fax:** 88 2697490
Email: armex@onsleger.nl
Web site: http://www.onsleger.nl

Titles:
ARMEX DEFENSIE MAGAZINE

KON. NED. VERENIGING VAN LUCHTVAART, AFD. 1636805
Postbus 618, 6800 AP ARNHEM **Tel:** 222 362620
Fax: 20 5159700
Email: knvvlth@xs4all.nl
Web site: http://www.zweefportaal.nl

Titles:
THERMIEK

KON. VERENIGING VAN ARCHIVARISSEN IN NEDERLAND 1636112
Markt 1, 6811 CG ARNHEM **Tel:** 76 5301713
Fax: 20 5159577
Email: bureau@kvan.nl
Web site: http://www.kvan.nl

Titles:
ARCHIEVENBLAD

KONINKLIJKE KVGO 1753749
Postbus 220, 1180 AE AMSTELVEEN
Tel: 79 3628628 **Fax:** 20 5159145
Email: info@kvgo.nl
Web site: http://www.kvgo.nl

Titles:
KVGO-KERNNIEUWS

KONINKLIJKE LANDMACHT 1753712
Postbus 90004, 3509 AA UTRECHT
Tel: 88 2697856 **Fax:** 88 2697943
Web site: http://www.landmacht.nl

Titles:
LANDMACHT

KONINKLIJKE NEDERLANDSE MUNT 1755110
Postbus 2407, 3500 GK UTRECHT
Tel: 76 5301713 **Fax:** 73 6210512
Email: info@coins.nl
Web site: http://www.knm.nl

Titles:
MUNTPERS

KONINKLIJKE VERMANDE 1634716
Postbus 20025, 2500 EA DEN HAAG
Tel: 88 5567205 **Fax:** 88 5567355
Email: sdu@sdu.nl
Web site: http://www.sdu.nl

Titles:
NOTARIAAT MAGAZINE
WPNR

KUNST EN ANTIEK INITIATIEVEN B.V. 1637045
Postbus 5220, 2000 GE HAARLEM
Tel: 88 2697049

Titles:
ORIGINE

KUNST EN CULTUUR NOORD-HOLLAND 1636415
Postbus 3043, 1801 GA ALKMAAR
Tel: 88 3263300
Email: info@kcnh.nl
Web site: http://www.kcnh.nl

Titles:
UITWAAIER

KUNST EN SCHRIJVEN B.V. 1638560
Postbus 10859, 1001 EW AMSTERDAM
Tel: 20 3446050 **Fax:** 26 7501802

Titles:
KUNSTSCHRIFT

KUSTVERENIGING EUCC 1635154
Postbus 11232, 2301 EE LEIDEN
Email: info@kustenzee.nl
Web site: http://www.eucc.nl

Titles:
KUST & ZEEGIDS

KVNRO, KON. VERENIGING VAN NED. RESERVE 1636524
Postbus 95395, 2509 CJ DEN HAAG
Tel: 570 673344 **Fax:** 475 551033
Email: pr-werving@kvnro.nl
Web site: http://www.kvnro.nl

Titles:
DE RESERVE OFFICIER

KVOK, KON. VER. VAN ORGANISTEN EN KERKMUSICI 1635342
Klipper 49, 9801 MT ZUIDHORN **Tel:** 79 3628628
Email: secretaris@kvok.nl
Web site: http://www.kvok.nl

Titles:
HET ORGEL

KVZ PUBLICATIONS B.V. 1637640
Postbus 19, 3737 ZJ GROENEKAN
Tel: 88 2697112 **Fax:** 88 2696983
Email: 4wd@4wdautomagazine.nl

Titles:
4 WD AUTO-MAGAZINE

KWF KANKERBESTRIJDING 1757082
Postbus 75508, 1070 AM AMSTERDAM
Tel: 71 5161527 **Fax:** 88 7518481
Email: info@kwfkankerbestrijding.nl
Web site: http://www.kwfkankerbestrijding.nl

Titles:
KRACHT

KYNOTRAIN 1643696
Dahliastraat 36, 4702 CJ ROOSENDAAL
Tel: 88 5567205
Email: info@kynotrain.nl
Web site: http://www.kynotrain.nl

Titles:
HA DIE PUP!

L & T MEDIA B.V. 1635321
Stieltjesweg 4, 6827 BV ARNHEM
Tel: 20 5159429 **Fax:** 20 5159036

Titles:
EYELINE

LABEL STRATEGISCHE MEDIA B.V. 1756877
Postbus 123, 6800 AC ARNHEM **Tel:** 10 7044008
Fax: 10 7044752
Email: info@lbl.nl
Web site: http://www.lbl.nl

Titles:
HUISSTIJL

LANDELIJKE BEROEPSVERENIGING REMEDIAL TEACHERS 1636961
Kosterijland 7a, 3981 AJ BUNNIK **Tel:** 88 7518650
Fax: 88 7518652
Email: bureau@lbrt.nl
Web site: http://www.lbrt.nl

Titles:
TIJDSCHRIFT VOOR REMEDIAL TEACHING

LANDELIJKE VVD 1637247
Postbus 30836, 2500 GV DEN HAAG
Tel: 58 2845745 **Fax:** 20 5159700
Email: bestuurders@vvd.nl
Web site: http://www.vvdbv.nl

Titles:
PROVINCIE EN GEMEENTE

LANDELIJKE WOONBOTEN ORGANISATIE 1637799
Postbus 8192, 3503 RD UTRECHT
Tel: 88 3263320 **Fax:** 20 5159577
Email: lwo@lwoorg.nl
Web site: http://www.lwoorg.nl

Titles:
WOONBOOT MAGAZINE

LANGFORDS PUBLICATIONS 1638277
Postbus 10099, 1001 EB AMSTERDAM
Tel: 70 3789880 **Fax:** 58 2987505
Email: info@railangfords.nl
Web site: http://www.railangfords.nl

Titles:
FLEETMOTIVE

LAVA-LITERAIR TIJDSCHRIFT 1754265
Lange Leidsedwarsstraat 22a, 1017 NL AMSTERDAM
Email: info@lavaliterair.nl
Web site: http://www.lavaliterair.nl

Titles:
LAVA LITERAIR TIJDSCHRIFT

LECTURIS MEDIASERVICE 1636073
Postbus 43, 5600 AA EINDHOVEN
Tel: 79 3628628 **Fax:** 35 6726847
Email: mail@lecturis.nl
Web site: http://www.lecturis.nl

Titles:
NEDERLANDS TIJDSCHRIFT VOOR VOEDING & DIËTETIEK

LEIDS UNIVERSITAIR MEDISCH CENTRUM 1753428
Postbus 9600, 2300 RC LEIDEN **Tel:** 314 349888
Fax: 314 343839
Email: cicero@lumc.nl
Web site: http://www.lumc.nl

Titles:
CICERO

LEPRASTICHTING 1753722
Postbus 95005, 1090 HA AMSTERDAM
Tel: 88 2697856 **Fax:** 88 2697943
Email: info@leprastichting.nl
Web site: http://www.leprastichting.nl

Titles:
DE KLEPPER

LHV, LANDELIJKE HUISARTSEN VERENIGING 1776439
Postbus 20056, 3502 LB UTRECHT
Tel: 88 7518000 **Fax:** 35 6474569

Titles:
DE DOKTER

LIFESTYLE MEDIA B.V. 1635322
Postbus 50, 7650 AB TUBBERGEN
Tel: 20 5159429 **Fax:** 20 5159036

Titles:
LIFESTYLE MAGAZINE
MANAGEMENT INFO

LIFTINSTITUUT B.V. 1754298
Postbus 36027, 1020 MA AMSTERDAM
Tel: 58 2845745 **Fax:** 20 5159700
Email: info@liftinstituut.nl
Web site: http://www.liftinstituut.nl

Titles:
LIFTINSTITUUT-MAGAZINE

LINDEMAN UITGEVERS B.V. 1636077
Salomonstraat 24, 1812 PA ALKMAAR
Tel: 71 5273596 **Fax:** 20 5928600
Email: info@lumail.nl
Web site: http://www.lindemanuitgevers.nl

Titles:
ROOFS
ROOFS HANDBOEK VOOR DE DAKBRANCHE

LIVE XS POPMAGAZINE/ALLXS B.V. 1636666
Nachtwachtlaan 155, 1058 EE AMSTERDAM
Tel: 570 673344 **Fax:** 70 7999840
Email: info@livexs.nl

Titles:
LIVEXS

LOUWERS UITGEVERSORGANISATIE B.V. 1634740
Postbus 249, 6000 AE WEERT **Tel:** 20 5218938
Fax: 70 7999840
Email: info@louwersuitgevers.nl
Web site: http://www.louwersuitgevers.nl

Titles:
BOUWEN AAN DE ZORG
GEVELBOUW
INSTORE
LIVECOMM
STEDENBOUW
Z & R

LSEM, LANDELIJK STEUNPUNT EDUCATIE MOLUKKERS 1754231
Postbus 13375, 3507 LJ UTRECHT
Tel: 88 2697049 **Fax:** 20 5159700
Email: info@lsem.nl
Web site: http://www.lsem.nl

Titles:
STEUNPUNTSGEWIJS

LVAG 1755195
Postbus 20058, 3502 LB UTRECHT
Tel: 88 7518000 **Fax:** 88 3263324
Email: secretariaat@lvag.nl
Web site: http://www.lvag.nl

Titles:
AIOS

M&P MEDIA 1637766
Postbus 10, 4060 GA OPHEMERT
Tel: 342 494889 **Fax:** 342 494299
Email: menp@menp.nl
Web site: http://www.menp.nl

Titles:
TEXTIELBEHEER

MAASLAND UITGEVERIJ B.V. 1636013
Postbus 348, 5340 AH OSS **Tel:** 88 3263334
Fax: 88 3263335
Email: info@maasland.com
Web site: http://www.maasland.com

Titles:
DIERENPRAKTIJKEN
NORDIC MAGAZINE

MAASSLUISE COURANT B.V. 1635937
Postbus 24, 3140 AA MAASSLUIS
Tel: 79 3628628 **Fax:** 20 5159145
Email: info@thuisbladen.nl
Web site: http://www.thuisbladen.nl

Titles:
DE HOEKSE KRANT
MONSTERSE COURANT
ROZENBURGSE COURANT DE SCHAKEL
WESTVOORNSE COURANT

MAF NEDERLAND 1754490
Postbus 65, 3840 AB HARDERWIJK
Tel: 88 2697112 **Fax:** 88 2696983
Email: info@maf.nl
Web site: http://www.maf.nl

Titles:
MAF LUCHTPOST

MAGAZIJN DE BIJENKORF B.V. 1634405
Postbus 12870, 1100 AW AMSTERDAM
Tel: 88 3263300 **Fax:** 486 476448
Web site: http://www.bijenkorf.nl

Titles:
DE BIJENKORF MAGAZINE

MAGENTA PUBLISHING 1635621
Bijsterhuizen 31-47, 6604 LV WIJCHEN
Tel: 20 5218939 **Fax:** 342 494299
Email: magenta@kantoornet.nl

Titles:
CBM (COMPUTER BUSINESS MAGAZINE)
KBM (KANTOOR BUSINESSMAGAZINE)

MAINPRESS B.V. 1635947
Postbus 231, 3100 AE SCHIEDAM
Tel: 79 3628628 **Fax:** 20 5159145
Web site: http://www.mainpress.nl

Titles:
MANAGEMENT EN LITERATUUR

MANAGEMENTMEDIA B.V. 1635045
Postbus 1932, 1200 BX HILVERSUM
Tel: 88 7518000 **Fax:** 35 6563174
Email: info@managementmedia.nl
Web site: http://www.managementmedia.nl

Titles:
PUBLISH
VERPAKKEN
VERPAKKINGSMANAGEMENT

MARKETING ASSOCIATIE RUG (MARUG) 1638047
Postbus 800, 9700 AV GRONINGEN
Tel: 10 2894018
Email: info@marug.nl
Web site: http://www.marug.nl

Titles:
MARKANT

MARKETING ASSOCIATIE TILBURG (MA-TILBURG) 1754160
Postbus 90153, 5000 LE TILBURG
Tel: 20 3446050 **Fax:** 20 5159145
Email: info@ma-tilburg.nl
Web site: http://www.ma-tilburg.nl

Titles:
MARKETHINGS

MARKETONS B.V. 1754267
Postbus 1310, 6501 BH NIJMEGEN
Tel: 172 466639 **Fax:** 172 466577
Email: info@marketons.nl
Web site: http://www.marketons.nl

Titles:
BUSINESS TECHNOLOGY ISSUES

MARUBA B.V. SPORTS PUBLISHERS 1636197
Winthontlaan 200, 3526 KV UTRECHT
Tel: 58 2845745 **Fax:** 20 5159700
Email: maruba@maruba.com
Web site: http://www.maruba.com

Titles:
BUYER'S GUIDE
LIFT MAGAZINE
SNOWBOARDER MAGAZINE
SPORT PARTNER

MATERIEEL BENELUX B.V. 1637253
Postbus 794, 5700 AT HELMOND
Tel: 58 2845745 **Fax:** 20 5159700
Email: service@bouwmaterieel-benelux.nl

Titles:
BMB BOUWMATERIEELBENELUX

MATUE DE MARKETEER 1754113
Postbus 4032, 5604 EA EINDHOVEN
Tel: 70 3490165
Email: info@matue.nl
Web site: http://www.matue.nl

Titles:
MARKTVISIE

MAYPRESS 1635428
Postbus 53, 1700 AB HEERHUGOWAARD
Tel: 88 7518000 **Fax:** 35 6474569
Email: maypress@maypress.nl
Web site: http://www.maypress.nl

Titles:
INFORMATIEGIDS STAD AMSTERDAM
KIJKKEZ
KIJKKEZ GEZONDHEIDSZORG

MBO COURANT B.V. 1638028
Postbus 9250, 1800 GG ALKMAAR
Email: mailbox@mbo-hbo.nl

Titles:
MBO&HBO COURANT

M.C. PUBLISHERS B.V. 1635981
Postbus 24, 2460 AA TER AAR
Email: info@jobinderegio.nl

Titles:
JOB IN DE REGIO, ED. REGIO HAAGLANDEN

ME@D MEDIA B.V. 1765378
Postbus 3864, 4800 DW BREDA **Tel:** 10 7044008
Fax: 10 7044752
Email: info@regiojournaal.nl
Web site: http://www.me-ad.nl

Titles:
REGIOJOURNAAL, EDITIE BERGEN OP ZOOM/ROOSENDAAL
REGIOJOURNAAL, EDITIE BREDA/ OOSTERHOUT

MEDIA COLLECTIEF B.V. 1634425
Postbus 157, 8600 AD SNEEK
Email: info@mediacollectief.com
Web site: http://www.mediacollectief.com

Titles:
SCHAATSMARATHON

MEDIA GROEP LIMBURG B.V. 1635877
Postbus 5100, 6130 PC SITTARD **Tel:** 88 2697856
Fax: 88 2697943
Web site: http://www.mgl.nl

Titles:
DAGBLAD DE LIMBURGER
LIMBURGS DAGBLAD

MEDIA MEDICA 1637590
Tweede Jacob van Campenstraat 101, 1073 XP AMSTERDAM **Tel:** 88 2697112 **Fax:** 88 2696983
Email: info@mediamedica.nl
Web site: http://www.mediamedica.nl

Titles:
ARTS EN APOTHEKER

MEDIA MIJ. B.V. 1634377
Postbus 36302, 1020 MH AMSTERDAM
Tel: 172 466639 **Fax:** 172 466577
Email: info@mediamij.nl
Web site: http://www.mediamij.nl

Titles:
WELKE WONEN

MEDIA PARTNERS 1635439
Postbus 2215, 1180 EE AMSTELVEEN
Tel: 58 2845745 **Fax:** 88 2697490
Email: info@mediapartners.nl
Web site: http://www.mediapartners.nl

Titles:
FAVORITES
NL

MEDIA PRIMAIR B.V. 1681264
Anthonie Fokkerstraat 2, 3772 MR BARNEVELD
Tel: 23 5565509 **Fax:** 342 494299
Email: info@mediaprimair.nl
Web site: http://www.mediaprimair.nl

Titles:
MENSPORT

MEDIA SLIM B.V. 1776670
Postbus 3389, 2001 DJ HAARLEM
Tel: 88 2697112 **Fax:** 88 2696983

Titles:
JANSEN

MEDIADAM 1638289
Postbus 56810, 1040 AV AMSTERDAM
Tel: 45 5795877 **Fax:** 88 2696946
Email: info@mediadam.nl
Web site: http://www.mediadam.nl

Titles:
SI GIDS

MEDIAMIKX B.V. 1653359
Postbus 424, 4200 AK GORINCHEM
Tel: 88 0139945
Email: info@mediamikx.nl

Titles:
WOONSTIJL

MEDIAVENTURA B.V. 1637743
Postbus 59267, 1040 KG AMSTERDAM
Tel: 20 5218938 **Fax:** 20 5159145
Email: info@mediaventura.nl

Titles:
PENTHOUSE

MEESTERS MEDIA B.V. 1636293
Posthoornstraat 69, 6219 NV MAASTRICHT
Tel: 58 2845745 **Fax:** 88 2697490
Email: info@meestersmedia.com
Web site: http://www.meestersmedia.com

Titles:
ONS WEEKBLAD

MEMO PUBLICITEIT 1644515
Postbus 262, 1860 AG BERGEN **Tel:** 10 4066646
Fax: 10 4066979
Email: info@technishow.nl

Titles:
TECHNI-SHOW MAGAZINE

MEMORY PUBLICATIONS B.V. 1634417
Keizersgracht 424, 1016 GC AMSTERDAM
Tel: 172 466639 **Fax:** 172 466577
Email: info@memory.nl

Titles:
HET CARRIÈRE JAARBOEK
MEMORY MAGAZINE

MENZ EN MEDIA B.V. 1776647
Nijbracht 120, 7821 CE EMMEN **Tel:** 30 6383736
Fax: 30 6383999
Email: info@menzenmedia.nl
Web site: http://www.menzenmedia.nl

Titles:
VVV UITKRANT GRONINGEN, FRIESLAND, DRENTHE

METRO CASH & CARRY NEDERLAND B.V. 1756869
Postbus 22579, 1100 DB AMSTERDAM
Tel: 314 349562 **Fax:** 314 340515

Titles:
MAKRO GASTVRIJ

MEZZO 1731794
Postbus 179, 3980 CD BUNNIK **Tel:** 20 5852688
Email: info@mezzo.nl
Web site: http://www.mezzo.nl

Titles:
DE MANTELZORGER

MIDDENSTANDSRECLAMEVE-RENIGING NIEUWLEUSEN 1637954
Postbus 61, 7710 AB NIEUWLEUSEN
Tel: 88 7518000 **Fax:** 35 6474569

Titles:
DE DALFSER MARSKRAMER

MIMICRY UITGEVERIJ 1635114
Postbus 345, 8600 AH SNEEK **Tel:** 88 7518000
Fax: 35 6474569
Email: info@mimicry.nl
Web site: http://www.mimicry.nl

Titles:
ANTONIUS MAGAZINE
MCL JOURNAAL
NY SMELLINGHE NIEUWS
ONDER DOKTERS
SIONSBERG MAGAZINE

MIN. VAN DEFENSIE 1636116
Postbus 20703, 2500 ES DEN HAAG
Tel: 35 6726842 **Fax:** 35 6726847
Email: nmgt@mindef.nl

Titles:
NEDERLANDS MILITAIR GENEESKUNDIG TIJDSCHRIFT

MINISTERIE VAN DEFENSIE 1753365
Postbus 20701, 2500 ES DEN HAAG
Tel: 88 2697062 **Fax:** 314 343839
Email: defensiekrant@mindef.nl
Web site: http://www.mindef.nl

Titles:
DEFENSIEKRANT

MINISTERIE VAN LANDBOUW, NATUUR EN VOEDSELKWALITEIT, 1754313
Postbus 20401, 2500 EK DEN HAAG
Tel: 58 2845745 **Fax:** 20 5159700
Email: pbih@minlnv.nl
Web site: http://www.minlnv.nl

Titles:
BERICHTEN BUITENLAND

MIXPRESS B.V. 1634652
Postbus 55, 5240 AB ROSMALEN
Tel: 20 3446050 **Fax:** 20 5159145
Web site: http://www.mixonline.nl

Titles:
MIX

MOA, CENTER FOR MARKETING INTELLIGENCE AND RESEARCH 1637625
Arlandaweg 92, 1043 EX AMSTERDAM
Tel: 88 2697112 **Fax:** 88 2696983
Email: info@moaweb.nl
Web site: http://www.moaweb.nl

Titles:
CLOU

MOCO MEDIA B.V. 1755526
Het Bat 8, 6211 EX MAASTRICHT
Tel: 70 3789880 **Fax:** 70 3789783
Email: info@chapeaumagazine.com

Titles:
CHAPEAU! MAGAZINE

MOJO CONCERTS 1757007
Noordeinde 19-21, 2611 KE DELFT
Tel: 20 5852688
Web site: http://www.mojo.nl

Titles:
BROCHURE NORTH SEA JAZZ FESTIVAL

MOOD FOR MAGAZINES 1643309
Adriaan Dortsmanplein 3, 1411 RC NAARDEN
Tel: 88 5567205 **Fax:** 88 5567355
Email: info@moodformagazines.nl

Titles:
LINDA
LINDA.MAN
LINDA.WONEN.

MOTIVE MEDIA B.V. 1634847
Postbus 256, 4100 AG CULEMBORG
Tel: 314 349888 **Fax:** 314 343839
Email: info@bigtwin.nl
Web site: http://www.motivemedia.nl

Titles:
BIGTWIN BIKERLIFESTYLE

MT MEDIA GROEP 1762291
Paul van Vlissingenstraat 10e, 1096 BK AMSTERDAM **Tel:** 23 5565509 **Fax:** 342 494299
Email: info@mtmediagroep.nl

Titles:
SPROUT

MULTIPLE SCLEROSE VERENIGING NEDERLAND 1636324
Postbus 30470, 2500 GL DEN HAAG
Tel: 70 3789880 **Fax:** 70 7999840
Email: info@msvn.nl
Web site: http://www.msvereniging.nl

Titles:
MENSEN

MUSIC MAKER MEDIA GROUP 1636072
Postbus 720, 6800 AS ARNHEM

Titles:
MUSICMAKER

MUSIC POST PRODUCTIONS INTERNATIONAL AND 1754425
Joke Smitlaan 20, 2104 TG HEEMSTEDE
Tel: 10 4066646
Email: music-master@zonnet.nl

Titles:
MUSIC POST JUST FOR YOU

MUZIEK CENTRUM NEDERLAND 1636835
Rokin 111, 1012 KN AMSTERDAM
Tel: 20 3446080 **Fax:** 88 7518652
Email: info@mcn.nl
Web site: http://www.mcn.nl

Titles:
FRET MAGAZINE

MVM PRODUCTIES B.V. 1637845
Postbus 6684, 6503 GD NIJMEGEN
Email: info@vanmunstermedia.nl
Web site: http://www.vanmunstermedia.nl

Titles:
AV&ENTERTAINMENT MAGAZINE
MEETING MAGAZINE.NL
OFFICE MAGAZINE.NL
RIVIERENLAND BUSINESS

MYBUSINESSMEDIA B.V. 1766384
Postbus 94545, 1090 GM AMSTERDAM
Tel: 222 362620 **Fax:** 20 5159700

Titles:
EIGENWIJS
ELEKTRO-DATA
ELEKTRONICA
HET HOUTBLAD
ISOLATIE MAGAZINE
KUNSTSTOF EN RUBBER
MEDIAFACTS
METAAL & TECHNIEK
NIEUWSBRIEF VOEDSELVEILIGHEID
PRODUCT
SALES MANAGEMENT
SCHOENVISIE
SPORTCULT
SWZ MARITIME
TEXTILIA
VOEDING NU
WEST
ZM - MAGAZINE

NAI UITGEVERS 1753750
Mauritsweg 23, 3012 JR ROTTERDAM
Tel: 10 7044008 **Fax:** 10 7044752
Email: info@naipublishers.nl
Web site: http://www.naipublishers.nl/open

Titles:
OASE

NAMAC, NED. ALG. MINIATUUR AUTO CLUB 1636575
Postbus 16004, 2301 GA LEIDEN **Tel:** 570 673344
Email: voorzitter@namac.nl
Web site: http://www.namac.nl

Titles:
AUTO IN MINIATUUR

NATIONAAL PARK DUINEN VAN TEXEL 1763625
Ruijslaan 90, 1796 AZ DE KOOG **Tel:** 73 6157171
Web site: http://www.npduinenvantexel.nl

Titles:
NATUUREILAND TEXEL

NATIONALE VERENIGING DE ZONNEBLOEM 1637132
Postbus 2100, 4800 CC BREDA **Tel:** 20 5218938
Fax: 20 5159700
Email: info@zonnebloem.nl
Web site: http://www.zonnebloem.nl

Titles:
ZONNEBLOEM

NATUURHISTORISCH GENOOTSCHAP IN LIMBURG 1753813
Godsweerderstraat 2, 6041 GH ROERMOND
Tel: 88 7518160
Email: kantoor@nhgl.nl
Web site: http://www.nhgl.nl

Titles:
NATUURHISTORISCH MAANDBLAD

NBP, NED. BOND VOOR PENSIOENBELANGEN 1637028
Scheveningseweg 7, 2517 KS DEN HAAG
Tel: 20 3446080 **Fax:** 342 494250
Email: info@pensioenbelangen.nl
Web site: http://www.pensioenbelangen.nl

Titles:
PENSIOENBELANGEN

NBVP, VROUWEN VAN NU 1636413
Jan van Nassaustraat 63, 2596 BP DEN HAAG
Tel: 88 2697183 **Fax:** 88 2697490
Email: bureau@nbvp.nl
Web site: http://www.nbvp.nl

Titles:
VROUWEN VAN NU

NCDO, NATIONALE COMISSIE VOOR INTERNATIONALE 1753593
Postbus 94020, 1090 GA AMSTERDAM
Tel: 20 5159666 **Fax:** 20 5159700
Email: info@ncdo.nl
Web site: http://www.ncdo.nl

Titles:
INTERNATIONALE SAMENWERKING-IS
SAMSAM

NCF, NEDERLANDSE CATEGORIALE VAKVERENIGING 1753826
Strevelsweg 700/305, 3083 AS ROTTERDAM
Tel: 73 6271777 **Fax:** 73 6220570
Email: info@ncfned.nl
Web site: http://www.ncfned.nl

Titles:
FINANZIEN

NDA, NEDERLANDSE DAKDEKKERS ASSOCIATIE B.V. 1636206
Postbus 1010, 1300 BA ALMERE **Tel:** 73 6271777
Fax: 73 6220570
Email: info@dakinfo.nl
Web site: http://www.nda.nl

Titles:
DAK+BOUW

NDC MEDIAGROEP 1635036
Postbus 60, 9700 MC GRONINGEN
Tel: 88 3233333 **Fax:** 314 343839
Email: info@ndcmediagroep.nl
Web site: http://www.ndcmediagroep.nl

Titles:
DAGBLAD VAN HET NOORDEN
NIEUWSBLAD VAN NOORD-OOST FRIESLAND
DE NOORDOOSTPOLDER
SNEEKER NIEUWSBLAD

NED. AGRARISCH JONGEREN KONTAKT 1754087
Postbus 816, 3500 AV UTRECHT **Tel:** 76 5312311
Fax: 70 7999840
Email: post@najk.nl
Web site: http://www.najk.nl

Titles:
BNDR

NED. BOND VAN HANDELAREN IN VEE 1636920
Postbus 251, 2700 AG ZOETERMEER
Tel: 70 3789880 **Fax:** 70 3789783
Email: info@nbhv.nl
Web site: http://www.nbhv.nl

Titles:
VEE EN VLEES

NED. BOND VAN VOGELLIEFHEBBERS 1636307
Postbus 74, 4600 AB BERGEN OP ZOOM
Tel: 70 3789880 **Fax:** 70 7999840
Email: info@nbvv.nl
Web site: http://www.nbvv.nl

Titles:
ONZE VOGELS

NED. BRANCHEVERENIGING AANGEPASTE VAKANTIES 1637957
Postbus 12, 3740 AA BAARN **Tel:** 88 7518000
Fax: 35 6474569
Email: info@deblauwegids.nl
Web site: http://www.nbav.nl

Titles:
DE BLAUWE GIDS.NL

NED. FILATELISTEN VER. SKANDINAVIË 1755279
Urkwal 74, 1324 HR ALMERE **Tel:** 88 7518000
Fax: 35 6474569
Web site: http://www.nfvskandinavie.nl

Titles:
HET NOORDERLICHT

NED. INST. VOOR MILITAIRE HISTORIE 1636044
Postbus 90701, 2509 LS DEN HAAG
Tel: 79 3628628 **Fax:** 20 5159145
Email: info@kvbk.nl
Web site: http://www.kvbk.nl

Titles:
MILITAIRE SPECTATOR

NED. MUSEUMVERENIGING 1636071
Postbus 2975, 1000 CZ AMSTERDAM
Tel: 88 7518160 **Fax:** 88 7518161
Email: info@museumvereniging.nl
Web site: http://www.museumvereniging.nl

Titles:
MUSEUMVISIE

NED. ONDERWATERSPORT BOND 1640101
Postbus 326, 3900 AH VEENENDAAL
Tel: 88 2697183 **Fax:** 88 2697490
Email: info@onderwatersport.org
Web site: http://www.onderwatersport.org

Titles:
ONDERWATERSPORT

NED. ORCHIDEEËN VERENIGING 1636343
Veenwijksweg 10, 8427 RS RAVENSWOUD
Tel: 79 3628628
Email: secretaris@nov-orchidee.nl
Web site: http://www.nov-orchidee.nl

Titles:
ORCHIDEEËN

NED. ORDE VAN BELASTINGADVISEURS 1636076
Postbus 2977, 1000 CZ AMSTERDAM
Tel: 88 7518160 **Fax:** 88 7518161
Email: nob@nob.net
Web site: http://www.nob.net

Titles:
EXPOSÉ

NED. ORNITHOLOGISCHE UNIE 1753356
Ir. van Stuivenbergweg 4, 6644 AB EWIJK
Tel: 88 2697856
Web site: http://www.nou.nu

Titles:
LIMOSA

NED. POLITIEBOND 1636421
Postbus 68, 3440 AB WOERDEN **Tel:** 88 2697183
Fax: 314 343839
Email: info@politiebond.nl
Web site: http://www.politiebond.nl

Titles:
DE POLITIE

NED. SHETLAND PONY STAMBOEK 1637718
Nieuwstad 89, 7201 NM ZUTPHEN
Tel: 20 5218938 **Fax:** 20 5159145
Email: info@shetlandponystamboek.nl
Web site: http://www.shetlandponystamboek.nl

Titles:
DE SHETLAND PONY

NED. TRIATHLON BOND 1637825
Postbus 1267, 3430 BG NIEUWEGEIN
Tel: 76 5301713 **Fax:** 20 5159577
Email: info@nedtriathlonbond.org
Web site: http://www.nedtriathlonbond.org

Titles:
TRIATHLON SPORT

NED. VERENIGING TOT BESCHERMING VAN DIEREN 1634962
Postbus 85980, 2508 CR DEN HAAG
Tel: 70 3789880 **Fax:** 70 3789783
Email: info@dierenbescherming.nl
Web site: http://www.dierenbescherming.nl

Titles:
DIER
KIDS FOR ANIMALS

NED. VERENIGING VAN DOKTERS-ASSISTENTEN 1637937
Othellodreef 91-93, 3561 GT UTRECHT
Tel: 88 7518000 **Fax:** 35 6474569
Web site: http://www.nvda.nl

Titles:
DE DOKTERSASSISTENT

NED. VERENIGING VAN KALFSVLEESPRODUCENTEN 1636991
Postweg 8, 7963 PD RUINEN **Tel:** 10 2894075
Fax: 88 7518652
Email: info@dekalverhouder.nl

Titles:
DE KALVERHOUDER

NED. VERENIGING VAN MODELBOUWERS 1636052
Veenweg 95, 1493 ZC DEN HAAG
Tel: 79 3628628
Email: info@modelbouwers.nl
Web site: http://www.modelbouwers.nl

Titles:
DE MODELBOUWER

NED. VERENIGING VAN POSTSTUKKEN- EN POSTSTEMPEL- 1753928
Oude Hoflaan 11, 9751 BK HAREN
Tel: 88 5567205
Web site: http://www.po-en-po.nl

Titles:
DE POSTZAK

NED. VERENIGING VOOR ERGONOMIE 1637042
Postbus 1145, 5602 BC EINDHOVEN
Tel: 88 2697049 **Fax:** 88 2697356
Email: nvve@planet.nl
Web site: http://www.ergonoom.nl

Titles:
TIJDSCHRIFT VOOR ERGONOMIE

NED. VERENIGING VOOR HART- EN VAAT-VERPLEEGKUNDIGEN 1731555
Postbus 2087, 3440 DB WOERDEN
Tel: 523 285330
Email: secretariaat@nvhvv.nl
Web site: http://www.nvhvv.nl

Titles:
CORDIAAL

NED. VERENIGING VOOR PLEEGGEZINNEN 1753942
Postbus 1139, 3500 BC UTRECHT
Tel: 570 673344 **Fax:** 20 5159700
Email: info@denvp.nl
Web site: http://www.denvp.nl

Titles:
PLEEGCONTACT

NED. VERENIGING VOOR SLECHTHORENDEN 1650891
Postbus 129, 3990 DC HOUTEN **Tel:** 70 3378125
Fax: 20 5159145
Email: info@nvvs.nl
Web site: http://www.nvvs.nl

Titles:
HOREN

NEDEM BUSINESS PUBLICATIONS B.V. 1638006
Postbus 7839, 1008 AA AMSTERDAM
Tel: 222 362620 **Fax:** 20 5159700

Titles:
GAAF GOED
TEXPRESS

NEDERLANDS DAGBLAD B.V. 1636113
Postbus 111, 3770 AC BARNEVELD
Tel: 35 6726842 **Fax:** 35 6726847
Email: info@nd.nl

Titles:
NEDERLANDS DAGBLAD

HET NEDERLANDSE BOEK 1753822
De Lairessestraat 108, 1071 PK AMSTERDAM
Tel: 79 3628628

Titles:
HET NEDERLANDSE BOEK

NEDERLANDSE HARTSTICHTING 1754142
Postbus 300, 2501 CH DEN HAAG
Tel: 35 5482416 **Fax:** 20 5159700
Email: info@hartstichting.nl
Web site: http://www.hartstichting.nl

Titles:
HARTSLAG

HET NEDERLANDSE RODE KRUIS 1637862
Postbus 28120, 2502 KC DEN HAAG
Tel: 76 5301713 **Fax:** 73 6210512
Email: info@redcross.nl
Web site: http://www.rodekruis.nl

Titles:
HELPEN

NEDERLANDSE RODE KRUIS/ UTRECHT MIDDEN 1754343
Koningsweg 2, 3582 GE UTRECHT
Tel: 88 3263300 **Fax:** 88 3263339
Email: info@rodekruisutrechtmidden.nl
Web site: http://www.rodekruis.nl/utrecht

Titles:
NIEUWSBLAD RODE KRUIS UTRECHT MIDDEN

NEDERLANDSE VERENIGING VOOR ANESTHESIOLOGIE 1732309
Postbus 5800, 6202 AZ MAASTRICHT
Tel: 20 3446050 **Fax:** 88 2696331
Email: ntva@sane.azm.nl

Titles:
NEDERLANDS TIJDSCHRIFT VOOR ANESTHESIOLOGIE

NEN-BOUW 1643208
Postbus 5059, 2600 GB DELFT **Tel:** 20 7581000
Fax: 20 7581030
Email: info@nen.nl
Web site: http://www.nen.nl

Titles:
NORMALISATIENIEUWS

N.F.E., NEDERLANDSE FEDERATIE VAN EDELPELSDIEREN- 1754220
Postbus 488, 6600 AL WIJCHEN **Tel:** 88 2697049
Fax: 88 2697356
Email: info@nfe.nl
Web site: http://www.nfe.nl

Titles:
DE PELSDIERENHOUDER

NIJGH PERIODIEKEN B.V. 1634737
Postbus 122, 3100 AC SCHIEDAM
Tel: 70 3789880 **Fax:** 70 3789783
Email: waterbranche@nijgh.nl
Web site: http://www.nijgh.nl

Titles:
BANKING REVIEW

NIP-BUREAU 1770815
Postbus 2085, 3500 GB UTRECHT
Tel: 570 673344 **Fax:** 20 5159700
Email: info@psynip.nl
Web site: http://www.psynip.nl

Titles:
DE PSYCHOLOOG

NIROV, NED. INSTITUUT VOOR RUIMTELIJKE ORDENING 1636467
Postbus 30833, 2500 GV DEN HAAG
Tel: 20 5218938 **Fax:** 70 7999840
Email: info@nirov.nl
Web site: http://www.nirov.nl

Titles:
S+RO
TIJDSCHRIFT VOOR DE VOLKSHUISVESTING

NKB, NED. KANOBOND 1754337
Postbus 2656, 3430 GB NIEUWEGEIN
Tel: 88 3263300 **Fax:** 88 3263339
Email: info@nkb.nl
Web site: http://www.nkb.nl

Titles:
KANOSPORT

N.K.B., NED. KERMIS BOND 1754477
Oudegracht 186, 1811 CP ALKMAAR
Tel: 79 3628628 **Fax:** 10 4066979
Email: nkbalkmaar@hetnet.nl
Web site: http://www.denederlandsekermisbond.nl

Titles:
DE KOMEET

NKC (NEDERLANDSE KAMPEERAUTO CLUB) 1637078
Postbus 424, 3760 AK SOEST **Tel:** 88 2697049
Fax: 20 5159700
Email: secretariaat@kampeerauto.nl
Web site: http://www.nkc.nl

Titles:
KAMPEERAUTO

NOAB 1637887
Postbus 2478, 5202 CL 'S-HERTOGENBOSCH
Tel: 88 3263320 **Fax:** 88 3263324
Email: noab@noab.nl
Web site: http://www.noab.nl

Titles:
ACTIVA

NOBILES MEDIA EXPLOITATIE B.V. 1636464
Postbus 17616, 1001 JM AMSTERDAM
Tel: 88 3263334 **Fax:** 88 3263335
Email: info@nobiles.nl

Titles:
NOBILES JURISTENGIDS
NOBILES MAGAZINE
NOBILES MASTERGIDS

NOJG, NED. ORGANISATIE VOOR JACHT & GRONDBEHEER 1638055
Postbus 72, 7480 AB HAAKSBERGEN
Tel: 70 3789880 **Fax:** 70 3789783
Email: nojg@planet.nl
Web site: http://www.nojg.nl

Titles:
JACHT & BEHEER

NOTA BENE B.V. 1637820
Postbus 44, 1620 AA HOORN **Tel:** 88 3263320
Fax: 20 5159577
Email: info@weekbladzondag.nl

Titles:
ZONDAG, WEEKBLAD VOOR WEST-FRIESLAND

NOVEMA UITGEVERS B.V. 1790043
Tussendiepen 21, 9206 AA DRACHTEN
Tel: 172 466639 **Fax:** 172 466577
Email: drachten@novema.nl
Web site: http://www.novema.nl

Titles:
OF
HET ONDERNEMERSBELANG

NRC MEDIA 1634442
Postbus 8812, 3009 AV ROTTERDAM
Tel: 10 7044008 **Fax:** 10 7044752
Web site: http://www.nrcmedia.nl

Titles:
NRC HANDELSBLAD
NRC WEEKBLAD

NS REIZIGERS, AFD. MARKETING COMMUNICATIE 1637416
Postbus 2025, 3500 HA UTRECHT
Tel: 172 466639 **Fax:** 172 466577
Web site: http://www.ns.nl

Titles:
SPOOR

NTB, VAKBOND VOOR MUSICI EN ACTEURS 1636083
Postbus 10947, 1001 EX AMSTERDAM
Tel: 88 7518160 **Fax:** 88 7518161
Email: info@ntb.nl
Web site: http://www.ntb.nl

Titles:
MUZIEKWERELD

NTI 1755460
Postbus 2222, 2301 CE LEIDEN **Tel:** 10 2894018
Fax: 35 6563174
Email: info@nti.nl
Web site: http://www.nti.nl

Titles:
NTI-STUDIEGIDS

NU'91 1637351
Postbus 6001, 3503 PA UTRECHT
Tel: 88 3263300 **Fax:** 88 3263339
Email: nu91@nu91.nl
Web site: http://www.nu91.nl

Titles:
ZORG ANNO NU

NUFFIC, NED. ORG. VOOR INT. SAMENWERKING 1637112
Postbus 29777, 2502 LT DEN HAAG
Tel: 20 5218938 **Fax:** 20 5159145
Email: nuffic@nuffic.nl
Web site: http://www.nuffic.nl

Titles:
LIFE AND STUDY IN HOLLAND

NUMMER 1 B.V. 1637621
Postbus 26, 6120 AA BORN **Tel:** 88 2697112
Fax: 88 2696983
Email: info@nummer1.nl

Titles:
NUMMER 1

NUVO, NED. UNIE VAN OPTIEKBEDRIJVEN 1636239
Postbus 643, 3440 AP HAARLEM
Email: info@nuvo.nl
Web site: http://www.nuvo.nl

Titles:
OCULUS

N.V. NUON 1690127
Postbus 41920, 1009 DC AMSTERDAM
Tel: 88 2696665 **Fax:** 88 2696946
Email: nuongids@nuon.com
Web site: http://www.nuon.nl

Titles:
NUON SEIZOENGIDS

NVBM, NEDERLANDSE VERENIGING VAN BEROEPSMETEOROLOGEN 1754197
Postbus 464, 6700 AL WAGENINGEN
Tel: 10 2894075
Web site: http://www.nvbm.nl

Titles:
METEOROLOGICA

N.V.B.S., NED. VERENIGING VAN BELANGSTELLENDEN
1636318
De Savornin Lohmanplantsoen 34, 2253 VP VOORSCHOTEN
Email: secretariaat@nvbs.com
Web site: http://www.nvbs.com

Titles:
OP DE RAILS

NVD, NED. VERENIGING VAN DANSLERAREN
1634955
Marathonlaan 71, 1183 VC AMSTELVEEN
Tel: 79 3628628 **Fax:** 20 5159145

Titles:
DE DANSMEESTER

NVTF, NEDERLANDSE VERENIGING VOOR THEMATISCHE
1753373
Taxushaag 3, 7207 MB ZUTPHEN
Tel: 88 2697062
Web site: http://www.nvtf.nl

Titles:
THEMA - NVTF

NVVE, NED. VERENIGING VOOR EEN VRIJWILLIG
1653188
Postbus 75331, 1070 AH AMSTERDAM
Tel: 71 5273596 **Fax:** 35 6474569
Email: euthanasie@nvve.nl
Web site: http://www.nvve.nl

Titles:
RELEVANT

NVVS, NEDERLANDSE VERENIGING VAN SKI- EN
1755280
St. Annastraat 4, 1381 XR WEESP
Tel: 88 7518000 **Fax:** 35 6474569
Email: nvvski@xs4all.nl
Web site: http://www.nvvski.org

Titles:
SKIKANTEN

NZO, NEDERLANDSE ZUIVELORGANISATIE
1754134
Postbus 165, 2700 AD ZOETERMEER
Tel: 58 2845745 **Fax:** 20 5159700
Email: info@nzo.nl
Web site: http://www.nzo.nl

Titles:
VOEDINGSMAGAZINE

ODE NEDERLAND B.V.
1634482
Postbus 2402, 3000 CK ROTTERDAM
Tel: 570 673344
Email: ode@ode.nl
Web site: http://www.ode.nl

Titles:
ODE

ODE, ORGANISATIE VOOR DUURZAME ENERGIE
1672833
Postbus 750, 3500 AT UTRECHT **Tel:** 70 3378125
Fax: 20 5159145
Email: info@duurzameenergie.org
Web site: http://www.duurzameenergie.org

Titles:
WINDNIEUWS

OLTHOF/M&MP B.V.
1635316
Postbus 13, 7064 ZG SILVOLDE **Tel:** 70 3378124
Fax: 172 422856
Email: info@gezondheidplus.nl

Titles:
GEZONDHEIDPLUS
REKREAVAKKRANT
TUINIDEEKRANT

OMNI-TRADING B.V.
1636070
Postbus 1044, 7301 BG APELDOORN
Tel: 88 7518160 **Fax:** 88 7518161
Email: info@muntkoerier.com

Titles:
MUNTKOERIER

OMROEP MAX
1757013
Postbus 518, 1200 AM HILVERSUM
Email: info@omroepmax.nl
Web site: http://www.omroepmax.nl

Titles:
MAX MAGAZINE

ONDERNEMERS PERS NEDERLAND B.V.
1636103
Postbus 16, 2460 AA TER AAR **Tel:** 88 7518000
Fax: 35 6474569

Titles:
LEVENSMIDDELENKRANT
OUT.OF.HOME-SHOPS

ONS HUIS/TAURUS B.V.
1637138
Postbus 13060, 3507 LB UTRECHT
Tel: 20 5218938 **Fax:** 20 5159700
Email: info@onshuis.nl
Web site: http://www.onshuis.nl

Titles:
ONS HUIS

ORGANISATIE VOOR DE ERKENDE VERHUIZERS
1636930
Laan van Ypenburg 122, 2497 GC DEN HAAG
Tel: 70 3789880 **Fax:** 314 343839
Email: info@erkendeverhuizers.nl
Web site: http://www.erkende-verhuizers.nl

Titles:
VERHUIZEN

ORTHO COMMUNICATIONS & SCIENCE B.V.
1637429
Postbus 82, 7080 AB GENDRINGEN
Tel: 172 466639 **Fax:** 172 466577
Email: ortho@orthoeurope.com
Web site: http://www.ortho.nl

Titles:
FIT MET VOEDING
ORTHO

OSTEOPOROSE VERENIGING
1636202
Postbus 445, 5240 AK ROSMALEN
Tel: 73 6271777 **Fax:** 73 6220570
Email: info@osteoporosevereniging.nl
Web site: http://www.osteoporosevereniging.nl

Titles:
BROS/OSTEOPOROSE NIEUWS

OTTO CRAMWINCKEL UITGEVER
1634536
Herengracht 416, 1017 BZ AMSTERDAM
Tel: 88 7518000 **Fax:** 35 6474569
Email: info@cram.nl
Web site: http://www.cram.nl

Titles:
INFORMATIE PROFESSIONAL
MEDIAFORUM

OUDERS & COO
1754423
Postbus 125, 3970 AC DRIEBERGEN
Tel: 10 4066646 **Fax:** 10 4066979
Email: info@ouders.net
Web site: http://www.ouders.net

Titles:
OUDERS & COO MAGAZINE

OVERTOOM INTERNATIONAL B.V., AFD. RECLAME
1753867
Postbus 2, 3734 ZG DEN DOLDER
Tel: 70 3789880 **Fax:** 314 343839
Email: info@overtoom.nl
Web site: http://www.overtoom.nl

Titles:
OVERTOOM, ZO GEREGELD

OVN, OPTOMETRISTEN VERENINGING NEDERLAND
1691137
Postbus 10417, 6000 GK WEERT **Tel:** 76 5301713
Fax: 20 5159577
Email: info@optometrie.nl
Web site: http://www.optometrie.nl

Titles:
VISUS

OXFAM NOVIB
1754431
Postbus 30919, 2500 GX DEN HAAG
Tel: 79 3628628 **Fax:** 172 466577
Email: info@oxfamnovib.nl
Web site: http://www.oxfamnovib.nl

Titles:
OXFAM NOVIB NIEUWS

PARAVISIE B.V.
1636982
Postbus 1876, 1200 BW HILVERSUM
Tel: 10 2894075 **Fax:** 88 7518652
Web site: http://www.paravisie.nl

Titles:
PARAVISIE

HET PAROOL B.V.
1635295
Postbus 433, 1000 AK AMSTERDAM
Tel: 79 3628628 **Fax:** 20 5159145

Titles:
HET PAROOL

PAUZE
1791320
Haarlemmerdijk 159, 1013 KH AMSTERDAM
Tel: 88 2697856

Titles:
PAUZE MAGAZINE

PCOB
1635027
Postbus 1238, 8001 BE ZWOLLE **Tel:** 88 3233333
Fax: 314 343839
Email: info@pcob.nl
Web site: http://www.pcob.nl

Titles:
PERSPECTIEF

PELICAN MAGAZINES HEARST
1756694
Postbus 69530, 1060 CN AMSTERDAM
Tel: 70 3789880 **Fax:** 70 3789783
Email: info@pelicanmags.nl
Web site: http://www.pelicanmags.nl

Titles:
THE BIG BLACK BOOK
CARROS MAGAZINE
COSMOGIRL!
EN FRANCE
NAUTIQUE MAGAZINE
RESIDENCE

PENSIOENFONDS METAAL EN TECHNIEK
1756874
Postbus 1965, 2280 DE RIJSWIJK
Tel: 88 3263334 **Fax:** 88 3263335
Email: info@bpmt.nl
Web site: http://www.bpmt.nl

Titles:
BINK!
PENSIOEN JOURNAAL

PENSIOENFONDS PGGM
1640209
Postbus 2014, 3700 CA ZEIST **Tel:** 70 3789880
Fax: 70 3789783
Email: info@pggm.nl
Web site: http://www.pggm.nl

Titles:
EIGEN TIJD

PERFORMA UITGEVERIJ B.V.
1790440
Torenstraat 144b, 2513 BW DEN HAAG
Tel: 70 3789880 **Fax:** 70 3789783
Email: info@performa.nl
Web site: http://www.performa.nl

Titles:
AAN DE SLAG

PERIODIEK EN PARTNERS
1640204
Postbus 20, 7770 AA HARDENBERG
Tel: 71 5273596 **Fax:** 35 6474569
Email: kn@periodiekenpartners.nl
Web site: http://www.periodiekenpartners.nl

Titles:
KIJK OP OOST-NEDERLAND

PERSONELE ZAKEN B.V.
1636291
Postbus 9250, 1800 GG ALKMAAR
Email: info@werk-in.nl
Web site: http://www.werk-in.nl

Titles:
WERKINAMSTERDAM.NL

PET
1635473
Postbus 88, 7900 AB HOOGEVEEN
Tel: 70 3147856 **Fax:** 20 5159143
Email: hoogeveenschecourant@petonline.nl
Web site: http://www.petonline.nl

Titles:
HOOGEVEENSCHE COURANT

PIER K
1753773
Postbus 110, 2130 AC HOOFDDORP
Tel: 73 6271777 **Fax:** 73 6220570
Email: info@pier-k.nl
Web site: http://www.pier-k.nl

Titles:
CURSUSGIDS

PIJPER MEDIA B.V.
1635605
Postbus 5070, 9700 GB GRONINGEN
Tel: 88 5567205 **Fax:** 88 5567355
Email: info@surfmagazine.nl
Web site: http://www.pijpermedia.nl

Titles:
SURF MAGAZINE

PINPOINT PARENTS B.V.
1729654
Postbus 20689, 1001 NR AMSTERDAM
Tel: 76 5250906 **Fax:** 342 494299
Web site: http://www.pinpointparents.nl

Titles:
REKELS

LA PLACE
1757020
Postbus 8226, 3503 RE UTRECHT
Tel: 88 3263334
Web site: http://www.laplace.nl

Titles:
LE MAGAZINE

PLUS UITGEVERS
1761946
Akeleiweg 200, 9731 JD GRONINGEN
Tel: 70 3146665
Email: info@autoplusonline.nl

Titles:
AUTO-PLUS

DE POEZENKRANT
1753873
Postbus 70053, 1007 KB AMSTERDAM
Email: info@poezenkrant.com
Web site: http://www.poezenkrant.com

Titles:
DE POEZENKRANT

POLITIE DIEREN- EN MILIEUBESCHERMING
1636422
Sparrenlaan 26, 7642 VC WIERDEN
Tel: 88 2697183 **Fax:** 314 343839
Email: secr@politiedierenenmilieu.nl
Web site: http://www.politiedierenenmilieu.nl

Titles:
DIER EN MILIEU

POLSSLAG
1775894
Postbus 109, 3769 ZJ SOESTERBERG
Tel: 88 2697183 **Fax:** 314 343839

Titles:
POLSSLAG

PORTAAL
1756861
Postbus 375, 3900 AJ VEENENDAAL
Tel: 88 2696557 **Fax:** 88 2696946
Email: info@portaal.nl
Web site: http://www.portaal.nl

Titles:
POST VAN PORTAAL

HET PORTAAL UITGEVERS B.V.
1638244
Postbus 125, 1520 AC WORMERVEER
Tel: 88 3233333 **Fax:** 314 343839
Email: info@hetportaal.com
Web site: http://www.hetportaal.com

Titles:
QM, QUALITY IN MEETINGS

POSITIVE RESULT
1732316
Dorpsstraat 608, 1723 HJ NOORD-SCHARWOUDE **Tel:** 20 3446050
Email: info@positiveresult.nl
Web site: http://www.positiveresult.nl

Titles:
BABY'S EERSTE JAREN

POUR VOUS PARFUMERIE B.V.
1634850
Postbus 299, 3740 AG BAARN **Tel:** 314 349888
Fax: 314 343839
Email: info@pourvous.nl
Web site: http://www.pourvous.nl

Titles:
POUR VOUS

PPG COATINGS NEDERLAND B.V. 1636054
Postbus 42, 1420 AA UITHOORN **Tel:** 79 3628628
Fax: 20 5159145
Email: info@sigma.nl
Web site: http://www.sigma.nl

Titles:
BRANDER AFBOUW
SIGMAFOON

PRELUM UITGEVERS 1635721
Postbus 545, 3990 GH HOUTEN **Tel:** 35 7999333
Fax: 15 2690253
Email: info@prelum.nl
Web site: http://www.prelum.nl

Titles:
NEDERLANDS TIJDSCHRIFT VOOR TANDHEELKUNDE (NTVT)

PRÉNATAL MOEDER & KIND B.V. 1637448
Postbus 30004, 1303 AA ALMERE
Tel: 172 466639 **Fax:** 172 466577
Email: info@prenatal.nl
Web site: http://www.prenatal.nl

Titles:
PRÉNATAL MAGAZINE

PRESSURE HOLDING B.V. 1635882
Postbus 8648, 3009 AP ROTTERDAM
Tel: 88 2697364 **Fax:** 88 2696116

Titles:
AUTO BUSINESS AMSTERDAM
AUTO BUSINESS DEN HAAG
AUTO BUSINESS DRECHTSTEDEN E.O.
AUTO BUSINESS HOEKSCHE WAARD
AUTO BUSINESS ROTTERDAM
AUTO BUSINESS 'T GOOI
AUTO BUSINESS UTRECHT
AUTO BUSINESS VOORNE PUTTEN

PRIMAMEDIA B.V. 1634982
Postbus 6194, 4000 HD TIEL **Tel:** 76 5301713
Email: info@primamedia.nl
Web site: http://www.primamedia.nl

Titles:
RIVIERENLAND VISIE

PROCA-MPP UITGEVERIJ 1635366
Postbus 50, 6880 AB VELP **Tel:** 36 5398208
Fax: 36 5398167
Email: info@proca-mpp.com
Web site: http://www.proca-mpp.com

Titles:
VOEDINGSINDUSTRIE

PROEFDIERVRIJ 1754111
Groot Hertoginnelaan 201, 2517 ES DEN HAAG
Tel: 20 3446050 **Fax:** 20 5159145
Email: info@proefdiervrij.nl

Titles:
PROEFDIERVRIJ MAGAZINE

PSH MEDIA SALES 1637888
Postbus 30095, 6803 AB ARNHEM
Tel: 20 3446050 **Fax:** 314 343839
Email: info@pshmediasales.nl
Web site: http://www.pshmediasales.nl

Titles:
VASTGOED

PSV MEDIA 1770841
Postbus 886, 5600 AW EINDHOVEN
Tel: 70 3789880 **Fax:** 70 3789783
Email: media@psv.nl
Web site: http://www.psv.nl

Titles:
PSV INSIDE

PTMD COLLECTION 1769269
Braziliëlaan 22, 1432 DG AALSMEER
Email: info@ptmd.nl
Web site: http://www.ptmd.nl

Titles:
THE STYLE MAGAZINE

PUBLICITEITSBUREAU LEEUWENBERGH B.V. 1634871
Postbus 139, 2170 AC SASSENHEIM
Tel: 20 5218938 **Fax:** 20 5159700
Email: leeuwenbergh@planet.nl
Web site: http://www.leeuwenbergh.net

Titles:
ZAKENNIEUWS VOOR HAAGLANDEN & RIJNLAND

PUBLIKATIEBURO/ UITGEVERIJ DE TOLBOOM B.V. 1637680
Postbus 96, 3890 AB ZEEWOLDE
Tel: 88 3263320 **Fax:** 20 5159577
Email: info@tolboom.nl
Web site: http://www.tolboom.nl

Titles:
BRANDWEER ONTSPANNINGS MAGAZINE

PUBLIMORE MEDIA 1638159
Weegschaalstraat 3, 5632 CW EINDHOVEN
Tel: 70 3378124 **Fax:** 172 422856
Email: info@signpro.nl

Titles:
SIGNPRO BENELUX

PUBLISHING HOUSE & FACILITIES B.V. 1634922
Postbus 119, 7000 AC DOETINCHEM
Email: info@publishinghouse.nl
Web site: http://www.publishinghouse.nl

Titles:
DE KARPERWERELD
DE ROOFVIS
HET VISBLAD
WITVIS TOTAAL

PUNT UIT MEDIA B.V. 1637746
Postbus 1980, 3000 BZ ROTTERDAM
Tel: 88 2697112 **Fax:** 88 2696983
Email: digidesk@puntuitmedia.nl
Web site: http://www.puntuitmedia.nl

Titles:
FRIENDS IN BUSINESS
ROTTERDAM PUNT UIT

PVCF, PERSONEELSVERENIGING VOOR COMPUTERGEBRUIKERS 1755148
Postbus 832, 7301 BB APELDOORN
Tel: 88 2697364 **Fax:** 88 2697490
Email: secretariaat@pvcf.nl
Web site: http://www.pvcf.nl

Titles:
COMPUTER EXPRESS

PVDA 1753771
Postbus 1310, 1000 BH AMSTERDAM
Tel: 79 3628628 **Fax:** 20 5159145
Email: rood@pvda.nl
Web site: http://www.pvda.nl

Titles:
ROOD

QCREATORS B.V. 1757502
Postbus 166, 3880 AD PUTTEN **Tel:** 10 7044008
Fax: 10 7044752
Email: info@qcreators.nl
Web site: http://www.qcreators.nl

Titles:
HOTSPOTS
MIDDEN NEDERLAND MAGAZINE

QU MEDIA 1634786
Postbus 123, 7200 AC ZUTPHEN **Tel:** 20 3446050
Fax: 88 2696331
Email: info@qumedia.nl
Web site: http://www.qumedia.nl

Titles:
KEUKEN STUDIO
ZONVAK MAGAZINE

QUE MEDIA 1791706
Brielselaan 14d, 3081 LB ROTTERDAM
Tel: 10 4518007
Email: info@qaviaar.nl

Titles:
QAVIAAR

RAI LANGFORDS B.V. 1634648
Postbus 10099, 1001 EB AMSTERDAM
Tel: 88 5567205 **Fax:** 88 5567355
Email: info@railangfords.nl
Web site: http://www.railangfords.nl

Titles:
AUTOKOMPAS
AUTOMOTIVE
PROOST!

RAI, NEDERLANDSE VERENIGING DE RIJWIEL- 1753948
Postbus 74800, 1070 DM AMSTERDAM
Tel: 570 673344 **Fax:** 20 5159700
Web site: http://www.raivereniging.nl

Titles:
RAI VOORRANG

RANDSTAD NEDERLAND 1753954
Postbus 12600, 1100 AP AMSTERDAM
Tel: 342 494889 **Fax:** 342 494299
Email: contentmanagement@nl.randstad.com
Web site: http://www.randstad.nl

Titles:
DE WERKPOCKET

THE READER'S DIGEST N.V. 1634626
Postbus 23330, 1100 DV AMSTERDAM
Tel: 88 2697062 **Fax:** 314 343839
Web site: http://www.rdmediaplanning.nl

Titles:
READER'S DIGEST, HET BESTE

READERSHOUSE BRAND MEDIA 1634945
Postbus 9090, 1006 AB AMSTERDAM
Tel: 317 484020 **Fax:** 317 424060
Email: info@rhbm.nl
Web site: http://www.rhbm.nl

Titles:
AUDI MAGAZINE
AUTO IN BEDRIJF
BMW MAGAZINE
LEASEPLAN DRIVE
VOLKSWAGEN MAGAZINE
WINTERSPORT MAGAZINE
ZIE

RECLAMIJ B.V. 1636211
Barentzplein 6b, 1013 NJ AMSTERDAM
Tel: 76 5312311
Email: info@reclamij.nl
Web site: http://www.reclamij.nl

Titles:
KRAAMZORG
WHY'S IN DE KRAAMTIJD
WHY'S IN VERWACHTING
WHY'S MET KLEINTJES

REED BUSINESS B.V. 1634378
Postbus 4, 7000 BA DOETINCHEM
Email: klantenservice@reedbusiness.nl
Web site: http://www.reedbusiness.nl

Titles:
ARBO MAGAZINE
AS, MAANDBLAD VOOR DE ACTIVITEITENSECTOR
AUTO & MOTOR TECHNIEK
BIKE EUROPE
BOUWMARKT
CONTROLLERS MAGAZINE
ELSEVIER BELASTING ALMANAK
ELSEVIER SALARISMAGAZINE
FISCAAL ADVIES
ICT ZORG
DE IT-AUDITOR
MANAGEMENT KINDEROPVANG
NEDERLANDS TIJDSCHRIFT VOOR HEELKUNDE
NURSING
OPLEIDING & ONTWIKKELING
P&OACTUEEL
PENSIOEN & PRAKTIJK
PLUIMVEEHOUDERIJ
RUNDVEEHOUDERIJ - VAKDEEL VAN BOERDERIJ
SNACKKOERIER
TIJDSCHRIFT VOOR DE POLITIE
TREKKER
TVV, TIJDSCHRIFT VOOR VERZORGENDEN
TVZ, TIJDSCHRIFT VOOR VERPLEEGKUNDIGEN
TWEEWIELER
VARKENSHOUDERIJ - VAKDEEL VAN BOERDERIJ
ZORG + WELZIJN
ZORGVISIE

REFLEX REKLAME V.O.F. 1637093
Startvenseweg 69, 6601 EL WIJCHEN
Tel: 88 2697049 **Fax:** 20 5159700
Email: reflex-nieuws@online.nl

Titles:
WIJ IN WIJCHEN, DUKENBURG EN LINDENHOLT

REFORMATORISCH DAGBLAD B.V. 1636512
Postbus 613, 7300 AP APELDOORN
Tel: 570 673344 **Fax:** 475 551033
Email: directie@refdag.nl

Titles:
REFORMATORISCH DAGBLAD

REISREVUE GROEP B.V. 1753590
Stationsplein 3, 1211 EX HILVERSUM
Tel: 88 7518000 **Fax:** 35 6474569
Email: info@reisrevue.nl
Web site: http://www.reisrevue.nl

Titles:
VAKANTIEDELUXE
VAKANTIEMAGAZINE

REMEIJ B.V. 1637197
Postbus 1010, 6436 ZG AMSTENRADE
Tel: 58 2845745 **Fax:** 20 5159700

Titles:
DE PENSIOENSPECIAL

RENDEMENT UITGEVERIJ B.V. 1636160
Postbus 27020, 3003 LA ROTTERDAM
Email: info@rendement.nl
Web site: http://www.rendement.nl

Titles:
ARBO RENDEMENT
FA RENDEMENT
FISCAAL RENDEMENT

RETAILTRENDS B.V. 1654729
Postbus 196, 6710 BD EDE **Tel:** 20 5218939
Fax: 342 494299
Email: info@retailtrends.nl
Web site: http://www.retailtrends.nl

Titles:
RETAILTRENDS

REUMAFONDS 1636527
Postbus 59091, 1040 KB AMSTERDAM
Tel: 570 673344 **Fax:** 475 551033
Email: info@reumafonds.nl
Web site: http://www.reumafonds.nl

Titles:
ROND REUMA

DE REUS MEDIA 1636705
Postbus 74, 2230 AB RIJNSBURG
Tel: 20 5218938 **Fax:** 70 7999840
Email: info@rijnstreekbusiness.nl

Titles:
RIJNSTREEK BUSINESS

RIJKSUNIVERSITEIT GRONINGEN 1634940
Postbus 72, 9700 AB GRONINGEN
Tel: 342 494259 **Fax:** 342 494250
Email: alumni@rug.nl
Web site: http://www.rug.nl/alumni

Titles:
BROERSTRAAT 5

RMU, REFORMATORISCH MAATSCHAPPELIJKE UNIE 1753650
Postbus 900, 3900 AX VEENENDAAL
Tel: 88 2696285 **Fax:** 88 2696983
Email: info@rmu.org
Web site: http://www.rmu.org

Titles:
HET RICHTSNOER

RODI ADD'VICE UITGEVERIJ 1634880
Postbus 4152, 1620 HD HOORN **Tel:** 71 5273596
Fax: 20 5928600
Email: rodiaddvice@rodi.nl

Titles:
STREEKPOST AMSTELVEEN

RODI MEDIA B.V. 1635639
Postbus 150, 1723 ZK NOORD-SCHARWOUDE
Email: rodimedia@rodi.nl
Web site: http://www.rodimedia.nl

Titles:
SCHAGEN OP ZONDAG
ZAANSTREEK OP ZONDAG

ROSIER COMMUNICATIE 1636834
Postbus 78, 1610 AB GROOTEBROEK
Tel: 88 2696670 **Fax:** 88 2696331
Email: info@rosier.nl
Web site: http://www.rosier.nl

Titles:
DE MIDDENSTANDER

ROTTERDAM FESTIVALS 1714616
Postbus 21362, 3001 AJ ROTTERDAM
Email: stuitr@rotterdamfestivals.nl
Web site: http://www.rotterdamfestivals.nl

Titles:
UIT AGENDA

ROTTERDAMPAS 1635052
Postbus 1024, 3000 BA ROTTERDAM
Tel: 20 5249842 **Fax:** 88 2696946
Email: info@rotterdampas.nl
Web site: http://www.rotterdampas.nl

Titles:
JAARBOEKJE ROTTERDAMPAS
ROTTERDAMPAS

RUSH PUBLICATIONS B.V. 1775395
De Opgang 2, 9203 GD DRACHTEN
Tel: 88 7518000 **Fax:** 35 6474569
Email: info@rush.nl
Web site: http://www.rush.nl

Titles:
RUSH ON AMSTERDAM

SALA COMMUNICATIONS HOLDING B.V. 1637208
Postbus 1067, 5900 BB VENLO
Email: sales@dealerinfo.nl

Titles:
DEALER INFO

SAM WAPENMAGAZINE B.V. 1637226
Postbus 446, 6800 AK ARNHEM **Tel:** 58 2845745
Fax: 20 5159700
Email: info@samwapenmagazine.nl
Web site: http://www.samwapenmagazine.nl

Titles:
SAM-WAPENMAGAZINE

SANOMA MEDIA B.V. 1634517
Postbus 1900, 2130 JH HOOFDDORP
Web site: http://www.sanomamedia.nl

Titles:
BABYGIDS
COSMOPOLITAN
DONALD
DONALD DUCK EXTRA
ESTA
FANCY
FIETS
FIETS ACTIEF
FLAIR
FLOW
FORMULE1.NL
GAMES GUIDE
GOLFERS MAGAZINE
GOLFJOURNAAL
GROTER GROEIEN
HELDEN
JAMES
KATRIEN
KEK MAMA
KIJK
LEKKER
MARIE CLAIRE
MORE THAN CLASSIC
MOTO 73
MOTOR
NOUVEAU
OOK
OUDERS VAN NU
PLAYBOY
ROOTS
STORY
TINA
TRUCKSTAR
VIVA
VORSTEN ROYALE
VT WONEN
ZEILEN
ZIN
ZOZITDAT
ZWANGER
ZWANGER & ZO

SBB, ST. BISSCHOP BEKKERS 1753968
Postbus 77, 3410 CB LOPIK **Tel:** 570 673344
Fax: 475 551033
Email: sbb-bureau@planet.nl
Web site: http://www.sbb-info.nl

Titles:
ZORG, CARE IN DEVELOPMENT

SCAPINO BALLET ROTTERDAM 1757732
Eendrachtsstraat 8, 3012 XL ROTTERDAM
Tel: 88 0139945 **Fax:** 172 494044
Email: info@scapinoballet.nl
Web site: http://www.scapinoballet.nl

Titles:
SPITZ

DE SCHAAPSKOOI 1685130
Postbus 90, 8180 AB HEERDE **Tel:** 70 3789880
Fax: 70 3789783
Email: villamedia@online.nl

Titles:
SCHAAPSKOOI

SCHOUWBURG HET PARK 1753693
Westerdijk 4, 1621 LE HOORN **Tel:** 71 5273596
Fax: 20 5928600
Email: info@parkhoorn.nl
Web site: http://www.hetpark.nl

Titles:
SEIZOENSBROCHURE SCHOUWBURG HET PARK

SCOPE BUSINESS MEDIA B.V. 1636784
Postbus 23, 1190 AA OUDERKERK A/D AMSTEL
Tel: 20 5218938 **Fax:** 20 5159700
Email: info@scopebusinessmedia.nl
Web site: http://www.scopebusinessmedia.nl

Titles:
MANAGEMENT SCOPE
ONDERNEMEN!

SCOUTING NEDERLAND 1634413
Postbus 210, 3830 AE LEUSDEN **Tel:** 570 673344
Fax: 70 7999840
Email: info@scouting.nl
Web site: http://www.scouting.nl

Titles:
BEVERPOST
SCOUTING NIEUWSBRIEF

SDU UITGEVERS 1634535
Postbus 20025, 2500 EA DEN HAAG
Email: sdu@sdu.nl
Web site: http://www.sdu.nl

Titles:
BURGEMEESTERSBLAD
FINANCIËLE & MONETAIRE STUDIES
GAWALO
GEVAARLIJKE LADING
INSTALLATIE JOURNAAL
OD (OVERHEIDSDOCUMENTATIE)
PERSONEELBELEID
REGELINGEN ONDERWIJS
RIJ-INSTRUCTIE
TREMA
VNG MAGAZINE
HET WATERSCHAP

SDU UITGEVERS, AFD. BOUW 1776131
Postbus 16262, 2500 BG DEN HAAG
Email: sdu@sdu.nl
Web site: http://www.sdu.nl

Titles:
IT-INFRA
PT INDUSTRIEEL MANAGEMENT
VASTGOEDMARKT

SEAL PRODUCTIONS 1732308
Postbus 44, 9974 ZG ZOUTKAMP
Tel: 10 4066646 **Fax:** 10 4066979
Email: seal.productions@planet.nl

Titles:
LAUWERSMEER KOERIER
MARNE-INFO

SENIOR PUBLICATIONS NEDERLAND B.V. 1637882
Postbus 44, 3740 AA BAARN **Tel:** 88 2697364
Fax: 88 2697490
Email: info@spn.nl
Web site: http://www.spn.nl

Titles:
PLUS MAGAZINE

SERVICEPASPOORT 1757029
Postbus 6166, 2001 HD HAARLEM
Tel: 88 3263334 **Fax:** 88 3263335
Email: info@servicepaspoort.nl
Web site: http://www.servicepaspoort.nl

Titles:
SENZ

SGJ CHRISTELIJKE JEUGDZORG 1755866
Postbus 1564, 3800 BN AMERSFOORT
Tel: 70 3378124 **Fax:** 172 422856
Email: info@sgj.nl
Web site: http://www.sgj.nl

Titles:
SGJ NIEUWS

SHELFLIFE PUBLISHING B.V. 1635019
Molenveldlaan 104, 6523 RN NIJMEGEN
Tel: 70 3378125 **Fax:** 20 5159145
Email: vakblad@foodpersonality.nl

Titles:
FOODPERSONALITY

S.I. PUBLICATIES B.V. 1754495
Postbus 188, 6800 AD OOSTERBEEK
Tel: 79 3628628 **Fax:** 314 343839
Email: si@sipublicaties.nl
Web site: http://www.sipublicaties.nl

Titles:
TOEN & NU '40-'45

S.I.B.S., STICHTING INFORMATIE BEROEPEN 1634689
Postbus 4461, 3006 AL ROTTERDAM
Tel: 20 5208657 **Fax:** 314 343839

Titles:
BEROEPENKRANT VMBO/MBO

SINTE BARBARA 1636661
Tra 26, 8084 CX 'T HARDE **Tel:** 570 673344

Titles:
SINTE BARBARA

SKN, STICHTING KINDERPOSTZEGELS NEDERLAND 1753727
Schipholweg 73-75, 2316 ZL LEIDEN
Tel: 88 2697856 **Fax:** 88 2697943
Email: info@kinderpostzegels.nl
Web site: http://www.kinderpostzegels.nl

Titles:
DE KINDERPOSTZEGEL KRANT

SOA~AIDS NEDERLAND 1636336
Keizersgracht 390-394, 1016 GB AMSTERDAM
Tel: 79 3628628 **Fax:** 70 7999840
Email: info@soaaids.nl
Web site: http://www.soaaids.nl

Titles:
SEKSOA

SOS-KINDERDORPEN 1753668
Postbus 9104, 1006 AC AMSTERDAM
Tel: 71 5273596 **Fax:** 88 2696983
Email: info@soskinderdorpen.nl
Web site: http://www.soskinderdorpen.nl

Titles:
SOS-BULLETIN

S.P. 1754400
Vijverhofstraat 65, 3032 SC ROTTERDAM
Tel: 342 494889 **Fax:** 342 494299
Email: sp@sp.nl
Web site: http://www.sp.nl

Titles:
TRIBUNE

SPECIALBITE B.V. 1638309
Postbus 256, 1110 AG DIEMEN **Tel:** 10 4518007
Fax: 36 7501771
Email: info@specialbite.com
Web site: http://www.specialbite.com

Titles:
SPECIALBITE JAARGIDS

SPOOR & PARTNERS UITGEEFDIENSTEN B.V. 1776657
Postbus 20, 2040 AA ZANDVOORT
Tel: 88 7518000 **Fax:** 35 6563174
Email: info@spoorenpartners.nl
Web site: http://www.spoorenpartners.nl

Titles:
TOP HAIR BENELUX

SPOTLIGHT PRODUCTIONS 1634458
Ekselerbrink 84, 7812 VM EMMEN
Tel: 314 349888

Titles:
COUNTRY LIFE MAGAZINE

SPRINGER MEDIA B.V. 1636129
Postbus 340, 3990 GC HOUTEN **Tel:** 76 5301713
Fax: 73 6210512
Email: info@springermedia.nl
Web site: http://www.springermedia.nl

Titles:
JEUGDBELEID
KIND EN ADOLESCENT
REFLEXZONE
SPORTMASSAGE
TENNIS MAGAZINE

ST. AMSTERDAMS UITBURO 1635805
Kleine-Gartmanplantsoen 21, 1017 RP AMSTERDAM **Tel:** 20 3446050 **Fax:** 20 5159145
Email: receptie@aub.nl
Web site: http://www.uitburo.nl/amsterdam

Titles:
UITGIDS
UITKRANT
UITMARKT

ST. ARBOUW 1636338
Postbus 213, 3840 AE HARDERWIJK
Tel: 20 3446050 **Fax:** 20 5159145
Email: info@arbouw.nl
Web site: http://www.arbouw.nl

Titles:
ARBOUW MAGAZINE

ST. ARCHIS 1644677
Postbus 14702, 1001 LE AMSTERDAM
Tel: 88 5567205 **Fax:** 88 5567355
Email: info@archis.org
Web site: http://www.archis.org

Titles:
VOLUME

ST. B.A.S.M. 1754778
Postbus 190, 1520 AD WORMERVEER
Email: basmbehoud@xs4all.nl
Web site: http://www.basm.nl

Titles:
SLEEP & DUWVAART

ST. BEHOUD EN BEVORDERING FRUITCULTUUR 1637952
Postbus 83, 6980 AB DOESBURG
Email: fructus@scarlet.nl

Titles:
FRUCTUS

ST. BUS 1638038
Postbus 19365, 2500 CJ DEN HAAG

Titles:
TOUR MAGAZINE

ST. CHEMIE AKTUEEL 1644671
De Moeshof 9, 5258 ER BERLICUM
Tel: 222 362620
Email: info@chemieaktueel.nl

Titles:
CHEMIE AKTUEEL

ST. CHRISTENEN VOOR ISRAËL 1635484
Postbus 1100, 3860 BC NIJKERK **Tel:** 70 3147856
Fax: 20 5159700
Email: info@christenenvoorisrael.nl
Web site: http://www.christenenvoorisrael.nl

Titles:
ISRAËL AKTUEEL

ST. DAG VAN DE AARDE 1756959
Gerestein 1, 4158 GB DEIL **Tel:** 88 7518480
Email: info@dagvandeaarde.nl
Web site: http://www.dagvandeaarde.nl

Titles:
KRANT VAN DE AARDE

ST. DE BEELDENAAR 1636715
Postbus 11, 3500 AA UTRECHT **Tel:** 58 2845745
Fax: 342 494250
Email: info@debeeldenaar.nl
Web site: http://www.debeeldenaar.nl
Titles:
DE BEELDENAAR

ST. DE BETERE WERELD 1756988
Prinsengracht 675, 1017 JT AMSTERDAM
Tel: 561 616577 **Fax:** 88 7518751
Email: info@debeterewereld.nl
Web site: http://www.debeterewereld.nl
Titles:
DE BETERE WERELD

ST. DE KOEPEL 1636332
Zonnenburg 2, 3512 NL UTRECHT
Tel: 20 5218938 **Fax:** 20 5159700
Email: info@dekoepel.nl
Web site: http://www.dekoepel.nl
Titles:
ZENIT

ST. DE LEVENDE NATUUR 1637658
Lekkumerweg 87, 9081 AK LEKKUM
Tel: 70 3147112
Email: bestuur@delevendenatuur.nl
Titles:
DE LEVENDE NATUUR

ST. DE NATUURGIDS 1636099
Pergamijndonk 16, 6218 GV MAASTRICHT
Tel: 88 7518160 **Fax:** 88 7518161
Titles:
DE NATUURGIDS

ST. DE NIEUWE SCHAKEL 1637599
Torenhoekstraat 15, 5056 AM BERKEL-ENSCHOT **Tel:** 88 2697112
Email: info@denieuweschakel.nl
Titles:
DE NIEUWE SCHAKEL

ST. DE REGENBOOG GROEP 1754387
Postbus 10887, 1001 EW AMSTERDAM
Tel: 172 466639 **Fax:** 172 466577
Email: meeleven@deregenboog.org
Web site: http://www.deregenboog.org
Titles:
MEELEVEN

ST. DE SPORTFISKER 1755571
Fugelsang 8, 8403 BA JONKERSLAN
Email: info@sportfisker.nl
Web site: http://www.sportfisker.nl
Titles:
DE SPORTFISKER

ST. DUTCH BIRDING ASSOCIATION 1753293
Postbus 75611, 1070 AP AMSTERDAM
Tel: 314 349969
Web site: http://www.dutchbirding.nl
Titles:
DUTCH BIRDING

ST. EDUKANS 1754017
Postbus 1492, 3800 BL AMERSFOORT
Tel: 570 673344 **Fax:** 70 7999840
Email: info@edukans.nl
Web site: http://www.edukans.nl
Titles:
SCHOOLSCHRIFT

ST. EELDER DORPSGEMEENSCHAP 1635099
Postbus 38, 9765 ZG EELDE **Tel:** 88 3233333
Fax: 314 343839
Titles:
DORPSKLANKEN

ST. FNV-PERS 1635217
Postbus 8456, 1005 AL AMSTERDAM
Tel: 70 3789880
Titles:
CASCO
FNVB MAGAZINE

ST. FRIEDENSSTIMME NEDERLAND 1754430
Postbus 15, 2800 AA GOUDA **Tel:** 10 4066646
Fax: 10 4066979
Email: info@friedensstimme.nl
Web site: http://www.friedensstimme.nl
Titles:
FRIEDENSSTIMME CONTACT

ST. FUURLAND 1634862
Prinsengracht 770/4e etage, 1017 LE AMSTERDAM **Tel:** 314 349888
Email: info@filmkrant.nl
Titles:
DE FILMKRANT

ST. GREENPEACE NEDERLAND 1754110
Postbus 3946, 1001 AS AMSTERDAM
Tel: 20 3446050 **Fax:** 20 5159145
Email: info@greenpeace.nl
Web site: http://www.greenpeace.nl
Titles:
GREENPEACE

ST. GROENLINKS 1636442
Postbus 8008, 3503 RA UTRECHT
Tel: 88 5567205 **Fax:** 88 5567355
Email: magazine@groenlinks.nl
Web site: http://www.groenlinks.nl
Titles:
GROEN LINKS MAGAZINE

ST. GRONINGER STUDENTENKRANT 1637936
Sint Walburgstraat 22c, 9712 HX GRONINGEN
Email: bestuur@studentenkrant.org
Titles:
GRONINGER STUDENTENKRANT

ST. GRONINGER UNIVERSITEITSBLAD 1636886
Postbus 80, 9700 AB GRONINGEN
Tel: 20 3446050 **Fax:** 20 5159145
Email: uk@rug.nl
Titles:
UNIVERSITEITSKRANT GRONINGEN

ST. HANDBOEKBINDEN 1754781
Postbus 50076, 1305 AB ALMERE
Tel: 88 7518000
Email: secretariaat@stichting-handboekbinden.nl
Web site: http://www.stichting-handboekbinden.nl
Titles:
HANDBOEKBINDEN

ST. HET VOGELJAAR 1636970
Boterbloemstraat 20, 5321 RR HEDEL
Tel: 10 2894075
Web site: http://www.vogeljaar.nl
Titles:
HET VOGELJAAR

ST. HET ZUID-HOLLANDS LANDSCHAP 1637371
Nesserdijk 368, 3063 NE ROTTERDAM
Tel: 523 285330 **Fax:** 88 3263339
Email: zhl@zuidhollandslandschap.nl
Web site: http://www.zuidhollandslandschap.nl
Titles:
ZUID-HOLLANDS LANDSCHAP

ST. HISTORISCHE MOTOR DOCUMENTATIE 1636843
Postbus 61141, 2506 AC DEN HAAG
Tel: 20 3446050 **Fax:** 88 2696331
Email: info@motorrijwiel.nu
Titles:
HET MOTORRIJWIEL

ST. JANVIOOL 1687536
Postbus 1022, 4388 ZG OOST-SOUBURG
Tel: 20 5159666 **Fax:** 20 5159700
Email: info@newfolksounds.nl
Titles:
NEW FOLKSOUNDS

ST. KENNISNET 1638335
Postbus 778, 2700 AT ZOETERMEER
Tel: 70 3789880 **Fax:** 58 2987505
Email: info@kennisnet.nl
Web site: http://www.kennisnet.nl
Titles:
KENNISNETINDRUK PO

ST. KRITIEK 1637649
Postbus 13141, 3507 LC UTRECHT
Tel: 88 2697112 **Fax:** 88 2696983
Email: info@kritiek.org
Web site: http://www.kritiek.org
Titles:
KRITIEK

ST. LES ROUTIERS EUROPÉENS 1636568
Pieter Zeemanstraat 3, 6603 AV WIJCHEN
Tel: 222 362620 **Fax:** 20 5159700
Email: routiers@routiers.nl
Titles:
ROUTIERS

ST. MAINLINE, GEZONDHEIDS- EN PREVENTIEWERK 1754316
Postbus 58303, 1040 HH AMSTERDAM
Tel: 58 2845745 **Fax:** 20 5159700
Email: info@mainline.nl
Web site: http://www.mainline.nl
Titles:
MAINLINE

ST. METROPOLIS M 1635082
Postbus 19263, 3501 DG UTRECHT
Tel: 88 3233333 **Fax:** 314 343839
Email: info@metropol.nl
Web site: http://www.metropolism.com
Titles:
METROPOLIS M

ST. NED. MAANDBLAD VOOR PHILATELIE 1636121
Roelofsstraat 31, 2596 VK DEN HAAG
Tel: 79 3628628
Web site: http://www.defilatelie.nl
Titles:
FILATELIE

ST. NIJMEEGSE STADSKRANT 1637579
Postbus 265, 6500 AG NIJMEGEN
Tel: 88 2697112
Email: nsk@antenna.nl
Titles:
DE NIJMEEGSE STADSKRANT

ST. NOORDERBREEDTE 1636207
Westerkade 2, 9718 AN GRONINGEN
Tel: 73 6271777 **Fax:** 73 6220570
Email: stichting@noorderbreedte.nl
Web site: http://www.noorderbreedte.nl
Titles:
NOORDERBREEDTE

ST. NVRD 1637098
Postbus 1218, 6801 BE ARNHEM **Tel:** 58 2845745
Fax: 20 5159700
Email: post@nvrd.nl
Web site: http://www.nvrd.nl
Titles:
GEMEENTEREINIGING & AFVALMANAGEMENT

ST. OOM, OPLEIDINGS- EN ONTWIKKELINGSFONDS VOOR DE 1764040
Postbus 15, 2390 AA HAZERSWOUDE-DORP
Tel: 592 379571 **Fax:** 10 7044752
Email: info@oom.nl
Web site: http://www.oom.nl
Titles:
METAALJOURNAAL

ST. OOSTEUROPA ZENDING 1634936
Postbus 81127, 3009 GC ROTTERDAM
Tel: 58 2845745 **Fax:** 342 494250
Email: oeznl@oosteuropazending.com
Web site: http://www.oosteuropazending.com
Titles:
NIEUWS OOSTEUROPA ZENDING

ST. OP LEMEN VOETEN 1636229
Postbus 10695, 1001 ER AMSTERDAM
Tel: 88 2697183 **Fax:** 88 2697490
Web site: http://www.oplemenvoeten.nl
Titles:
OP LEMEN VOETEN

ST. OPTIMA FARMA 1636855
Postbus 393, 5340 AJ OSS **Tel:** 20 3446050
Fax: 20 5159145
Email: secretariaat@optimafarma.nl
Web site: http://www.optimafarma.nl
Titles:
OPTIMA FARMA

ST. ORGANISATIE OUDE MUZIEK 1637757
Postbus 19267, 3501 DG UTRECHT
Tel: 342 494889 **Fax:** 342 494299
Email: info@oudemuziek.nl
Web site: http://www.oudemuziek.nl
Titles:
TIJDSCHRIFT OUDE MUZIEK

ST. ORTHOMOLECULAIRE EDUCATIE 1637846
Postbus 1237, 1300 BE ALMERE **Tel:** 76 5301713
Fax: 20 5159577
Email: secretariaat@soe.nl
Web site: http://www.soe.nl
Titles:
TIJDSCHRIFT VOOR ORTHOMOLECULAIRE GENEESKUNDE

ST. PROPRIA CURES 1636463
Vendelstraat 2, 1012 XX AMSTERDAM
Tel: 79 3628628 **Fax:** 88 5567355
Email: propriacures@knoware.nl
Titles:
PROPRIA CURES

ST. PUBLIC AFFAIRS 1637765
Postbus 658, 3700 AR ZEIST **Tel:** 342 494889
Fax: 342 494299
Email: info@stpublicaffairs.nl
Web site: http://www.stpublicaffairs.nl
Titles:
TANDTECHNISCH MAGAZINE

ST. RONALD MCDONALD KINDERFONDS 1754533
Postbus 25, 3730 AA DE BILT **Tel:** 70 3378125
Fax: 20 5159145
Email: info@kinderfonds.nl
Web site: http://www.kinderfonds.nl
Titles:
HAND IN HAND

ST. SANQUIN BLOEDVOORZIENING 1756867
Plesmanlaan 125, 1066 CX AMSTERDAM
Tel: 70 3789880 **Fax:** 70 3789783
Email: bloedverwant@sanquin.nl
Web site: http://www.sanquin.nl
Titles:
BLOEDVERWANT

ST. SCHOKKEND NIEUWS 1638566
Trompenburgstraat 20-3, 1079 TX AMSTERDAM
Tel: 88 7518000 **Fax:** 35 6563174
Email: info@schokkendnieuws.nl
Titles:
SCHOKKEND NIEUWS

ST. STRAATKRANT 1638004
Mauritsplaats 24, 3012 CD ROTTERDAM
Email: straatkrant@hotmail.com
Titles:
STRAAT MAGAZINE

ST. TONG TONG 1637672
Bezuidenhoutseweg 331, 2594 AR DEN HAAG
Tel: 88 3263334 **Fax:** 88 3263335
Email: info@tongtong.nl
Web site: http://www.tongtong.nl
Titles:
INDISCH ANDERS
PASARKRANT

ST. VAKBLAD GROEN 1635313
Achtergracht 71, 1381 BL WEESP
Tel: 20 5159700
Titles:
GROEN

ST. VAKBLADEN GEMENGDE BRANCHES 1635131
Postbus 7105, 2701 AC ZOETERMEER
Tel: 342 494889 **Fax:** 172 466577
Email: stiva@gebra.nl
Web site: http://www.gemengdebranche.nl
Titles:
SPEELGOED EN HOBBY

ST. VETERANENINSTITUUT 1636898
Postbus 125, 3940 AC DOORN **Tel:** 88 2697364
Fax: 58 2130930
Email: info@veteraneninstituut.nl
Web site: http://www.veteraneninstituut.nl
Titles:
CHECKPOINT

ST. VOOR ACADEMISCHE REIZEN 1636725
Prinsengracht 783-785, 1017 JZ AMSTERDAM
Tel: 76 5301717 **Fax:** 76 5144531
Email: info@academischereizen.nl
Web site: http://www.academischereizen.nl
Titles:
CULTOURA

ST. VOOR KERK EN GELOOF 1753321
Dorpsstraat 90, 5735 EG AARLE RIXTEL
Tel: 314 349888
Titles:
CATHOLICA MAGAZINE

ST. VOOR NED. KUNSTHISTORISCHE PUBLIKATIES 1691136
p/a Drift 10, 3512 BS UTRECHT **Tel:** 570 673344
Fax: 70 7999840
Email: simiolus@let.uu.nl
Titles:
SIMIOLUS

ST. VRIJE ACADEMIE VOOR KUNSTHISTORISCH 1637263
Keizersgracht 258, 1016 EV AMSTERDAM
Tel: 58 2845745 **Fax:** 20 5159700
Email: post@vrijeacademie.nl
Web site: http://www.kunstgeschiedenis.nl
Titles:
TAFERELEN

ST. WADDENFEDERATIE 1753983
Postbus 20, 8880 AA TERSCHELLING WEST
Tel: 88 3263310 **Fax:** 342 494299
Email: info@vvvterschelling.nl
Web site: http://www.wadden.nl
Titles:
WADDENREISGIDS

ST. WERKGROEP KATHOLIEKE JONGEREN 1637948
Postbus 19005, 3501 DA UTRECHT
Tel: 88 7518000
Email: administratie@omega-magazine.nl
Web site: http://www.wkj.nl
Titles:
OMEGA

ST. ZELDZAME HUISDIERRASSEN 1637863
Runderweg 6, 8219 PK LELYSTAD
Email: szh@planet.nl
Web site: http://www.szh.nl
Titles:
ZELDZAAM HUISDIER

STAATSBOSBEHEER 1753432
Postbus 1300, 3970 BH DRIEBERGEN
Tel: 314 349888 **Fax:** 314 343839
Email: info@staatsbosbeheer.nl
Web site: http://www.staatsbosbeheer.nl
Titles:
ONVERWACHT NEDERLAND

DE STADSKRANT 1637866
Grote Kerkstraat 24b, 1135 BD EDAM
Tel: 76 5301713 **Fax:** 73 6210512
Email: stadskrant@wxs.nl
Web site: http://www.stadskrant.net
Titles:
DE STADSKRANT

STATIONERY TEAM EUROPE B.V. 1634800
Reaal 2b, 2353 TL LEIDERDORP **Tel:** 20 5159666
Fax: 20 5159700
Email: info@stationeryteam.nl
Web site: http://www.stationeryteam.nl
Titles:
CONVERSE AGENDA
GSUS AGENDA
LOONEY TUNES AGENDA
O'NEILL AGENDA
STUDIE AGENDA

STAYOKAY 1636812
Postbus 92076, 1090 AB AMSTERDAM
Tel: 342 494268 **Fax:** 20 5159700
Web site: http://www.stayokay.com
Titles:
DAARBUITEN

STEM LEKTUURZENDING 1754080
Postbus 3605, 6019 ZG WESSEM
Tel: 76 5312311 **Fax:** 70 7999840
Email: heroldverlag@t-online.de
Web site: http://www.herold-schriftenmission.de
Titles:
DE STEM IN DE WOESTIJN

DE STENTOR 1636159
Postbus 99, 7300 AB APELDOORN
Tel: 10 4067211
Web site: http://www.destentor.nl
Titles:
DE STENTOR

STERKIN 1753839
Postbus 20127, 7302 HC APELDOORN
Tel: 73 6271777 **Fax:** 73 6220570
Email: info@sterkin.nl
Web site: http://www.sterkin.nl
Titles:
GASWIJS

STIBANS, ST. TOT BEHOUD VAN AF TE VOEREN 1753951
Landweg 7, 7041 VS 'S-HEERENBERG
Tel: 570 673344
Email: secretariaat@stibans.nl
Web site: http://www.stibans.nl
Titles:
STIBANS BULLETIN

STICHTING BEHOUD WATERLAND 1754277
Dijkwater 177, 1025 CW AMSTERDAM
Tel: 58 2845745
Titles:
WATER & LAND

STICHTING BOUWGARANT 1681859
Postbus 340, 2700 AH ZOETERMEER
Tel: 23 5565509 **Fax:** 342 494299
Email: info@bouwgarant.nl
Web site: http://www.bouwgarant.nl
Titles:
VERBOUWBLAD

STICHTING CHILDREN'S RELIEF 1776339
Postbus 2026, 2930 AA KRIMPEN A/D LEK
Tel: 58 2845745 **Fax:** 342 494250
Email: info@childrensrelief.nl
Web site: http://www.childrensrelief.nl
Titles:
CHILDREN'S RELIEF MAGAZINE

STICHTING DE REVISOR 1753880
Postbus 3879, 1001 AR AMSTERDAM
Tel: 570 673344 **Fax:** 475 551033
Email: info@revisor.nl
Titles:
DE REVISOR

STICHTING DE TONEELSCHUUR 1754374
Lange Begijnestraat 9, 2011 HH HAARLEM
Tel: 70 3147112
Email: informatie@toneelschuur.nl
Web site: http://www.toneelschuur.nl
Titles:
TONEELSCHUUR/FILMSCHUUR

STICHTING GENEESMIDDELENBULLETIN 1754261
Postbus 2190, 3500 GD UTRECHT
Tel: 88 3263300 **Fax:** 88 3263339
Email: gebu@fed.knmg.nl
Web site: http://www.geneesmiddelenbulletin.nl
Titles:
GENEESMIDDELENBULLETIN

STICHTING GEOLOGISCHE AKTIVITEITEN 1753472
Rietspinner 15, 3831 DP LEUSDEN
Tel: 342 494889
Web site: http://www.gea-geologie.nl
Titles:
GEA

STICHTING HET ZEILEND ZEESCHIP 1754136
Postbus 63140, 3002 JC ROTTERDAM
Tel: 20 5218938 **Fax:** 20 5159700
Email: info@eendracht.nl
Web site: http://www.eendracht.nl
Titles:
EENDRACHT MAGAZINE

STICHTING INSPIRATIE 1637473
Postbus 1557, 5200 BP 'S-HERTOGENBOSCH
Tel: 79 3628628 **Fax:** 172 466577
Email: info@inspiratiemagazine.nl
Titles:
INSPIRATIE MAGAZINE

STICHTING JOHAN MAASBACH WERELDZENDING 1753827
Postbus 44, 2501 CA DEN HAAG **Tel:** 73 6271777
Fax: 73 6220570
Email: info@maasbach.com
Web site: http://www.maasbach.com
Titles:
NIEUW LEVEN

STICHTING KRÖDDE 1753883
Walta 34, 9202 JN DRACHTEN **Tel:** 570 673344
Email: info@krodde.nl
Web site: http://www.krodde.nl
Titles:
KRÖDDE

STICHTING KUNST EN WETENSCHAP 1690898
Smidstraat 12, 8746 NG SCHRAARD
Tel: 570 673344 **Fax:** 475 551033
Email: kunstenwetenschap@planet.nl
Titles:
KUNST EN WETENSCHAP

STICHTING LANDGRAAF KOERIER 1636385
Kerkplein 39, 6372 EZ LANDGRAAF
Email: stichting@landgraagkoerier.nl
Titles:
LANDGRAAF KOERIER

STICHTING LANDSCHAP NOORD-HOLLAND 1635219
Postbus 257, 1900 AG CASTRICUM
Tel: 342 494889 **Fax:** 342 494299
Email: info@landschapnoordholland.nl
Web site: http://www.landschapnoordholland.nl
Titles:
LANDSCHAP NOORD-HOLLAND

STICHTING LAWINE 1754152
Postbus 56690, 1040 AR AMSTERDAM
Tel: 88 2696670
Email: st.lawine@worldonline.nl
Web site: http://www.stichtinglawine.org
Titles:
LAWINE NIEUWSBRIEF

STICHTING NIF 1636078
Bosboom Toussaintlaan 78b, 2103 SN HEEMSTEDE **Tel:** 88 7518160 **Fax:** 88 7518161
Web site: http://www.stichtingnif.nl
Titles:
FONDSENWERVING

STICHTING OUT MEDIA 1636176
Postbus 10482, 1001 EL AMSTERDAM
Tel: 73 6271777 **Fax:** 73 6220570
Email: info@outmedia.nl
Titles:
GAY & NIGHT

STICHTING PARMENTIER 1754120
Postbus 1084, 6501 BB NIJMEGEN
Email: info@literairtijdschriftparmentier.nl
Web site: http://www.literairtijdschriftparmentier.nl
Titles:
PARMENTIER

STICHTING PEDDELPRAAT 1754255
Peperstraat 35, 5311 CS GAMEREN
Email: info@peddelpraat.nl
Web site: http://www.peddelpraat.nl
Titles:
PEDDELPRAAT

STICHTING PLINT 1754309
Postbus 164, 5600 AD EINDHOVEN
Tel: 58 2845745 **Fax:** 20 5159700
Email: informatie@plint.nl
Web site: http://www.plint.nl
Titles:
DADA

STICHTING TOT HEIL DES VOLKS 1753863
Oudezijds Voorburgwal 241, 1012 EZ AMSTERDAM **Tel:** 70 3789880 **Fax:** 70 7999840
Email: info@deoogst.nl
Web site: http://www.totheildesvolks.nl
Titles:
DE OOGST

STICHTING VAKBLAD NATUUR BOS EN LANDSCHAP 1686368
Postbus 618, 6700 AP WAGENINGEN
Tel: 570 673344 **Fax:** 70 7999840
Email: vakblad@vakbladnbl.nl
Web site: http://www.vakbladnbl.nl
Titles:
VAKBLAD NATUUR BOS LANDSCHAP

STICHTING VERVOERADRES 1754918
Postbus 24023, 2490 AA DEN HAAG
Tel: 88 3263320 **Fax:** 20 5159577
Email: info@beurtvaartadres.nl
Web site: http://www.sva.nl
Titles:
WEG EN WAGEN

STICHTING ZINKINFO BENELUX 1754116
Postbus 3196, 4800 DD BREDA **Tel:** 70 3789880
Fax: 314 343839
Web site: http://www.zinkinfobenelux.com
Titles:
THERMISCH VERZINKEN

STIPTO MEDIA 1759516
Postbus 32, 3500 AA UTRECHT **Tel:** 10 2894018
Fax: 35 6563174
Email: info@stiptomedia.nl
Web site: http://www.stiptomedia.nl
Titles:
SUM
SUM HOGESCHOOL AGENDA
SUM UNIVERSITEITS AGENDA

STUDIOPRESS B.V. 1638267
Molensingel 73, 6229 PC MAASTRICHT
Tel: 88 5567205 **Fax:** 88 5567355
Email: info@niveaumagazine.nl
Web site: http://www.studiopress.nl
Titles:
NIVEAU EUREGIOMAGAZINE

SUCCULENTA 1753892
Geuldersedijk 2, 5944 NH ARCEN
Tel: 76 5312311
Email: info@succulenta.nl
Titles:
SUCCULENTA

SUPERTROOPERS 1768480
Postbus 69654, 1060 CS AMSTERDAM
Tel: 10 4518007 **Fax:** 10 4421023
Web site: http://www.supertroopers.tv
Titles:
RUN2DAY MAGAZINE

T&S PRODUCTIONS 1761773
Postbus 120, 6500 AC NIJMEGEN
Tel: 88 2697112
Email: reisburo@t-en-s-productions.nl
Web site: http://www.t-en-s-productions.nl
Titles:
SUPERMARKT ACTUEEL

TALKIES B.V. 1635750
Postbus 174, 2600 AD DELFT **Tel:** 71 5273596
Fax: 20 5928600
Email: info@talkiesmagazine.nl
Web site: http://www.talkiestv.nl
Titles:
TALKIES MAGAZINE

TARGET PRESS 1636495
Ambachtweg 2, 2841 LZ MOORDRECHT
Tel: 570 673344 **Fax:** 20 5159700
Email: studio@targetpress.nl
Web site: http://www.targetpress.nl
Titles:
BROMFIETS

TCM MEDIA B.V. 1634980
De Laat de Kanterstraat 27a, 2313 JS LEIDEN
Tel: 58 2845745 **Fax:** 20 5159700
Titles:
ROESTVAST STAAL

TECHNISCHE UNIVERSITEIT EINDHOVEN 1636800
Postbus 513, 5600 MB EINDHOVEN
Tel: 40 2473330 **Fax:** 35 6563174
Web site: http://www.tue.nl
Titles:
CURSOR
MATRIX

TECHWATCH B.V. 1638111
Snelliusstraat 6, 6533 NV NIJMEGEN
Tel: 70 3789880 **Fax:** 70 3789783
Email: info@techwatch.nl
Web site: http://www.techwatch.nl
Titles:
BITS&CHIPS

DE TELEFOONGIDS B.V. 1754130
Postbus 77863, 1070 LL AMSTERDAM
Tel: 88 2697049 **Fax:** 88 2697356
Titles:
DE TELEFOONGIDS

TELEGRAAF MEDIA NEDERLAND 1634546
Postbus 376, 1000 EB AMSTERDAM
Tel: 88 3263334 **Fax:** 88 3263335
Email: tijdschriften@telegraafmedia.nl
Titles:
PRIVÉ

TERDEGE B.V. 1637176
Postbus 75, 7300 AB APELDOORN
Tel: 58 2845745 **Fax:** 342 494250
Email: info@terburg.nl
Titles:
TERDEGE

TERRE DES HOMMES NEDERLAND 1754146
Zoutmanstraat 42-44, 2518 GS DEN HAAG
Tel: 71 5271111 **Fax:** 20 5159700
Email: info@tdh.nl
Web site: http://www.terredeshommes.nl
Titles:
TERRE MAGAZINE

THE ADCOMPANY 1792482
Marconistraat 14e, 2181 AK HILLEGOM
Tel: 10 7044008 **Fax:** 10 7044752
Titles:
STOER!

DE TIJDSTROOM UITGEVERIJ B.V. 1636857
Postbus 775, 3500 AT UTRECHT **Tel:** 20 3446050
Fax: 20 5159145
Email: info@tijdstroom.nl
Web site: http://www.tijdstroom.nl
Titles:
TIJDSCHRIFT VOOR PSYCHIATRIE

TNT POST B.V. AFD. COMMUNICATIE 1754174
Postbus 30250, 2500 GG DEN HAAG
Tel: 20 3446050 **Fax:** 20 5159145
Web site: http://www.tntpost.nl/zakelijk
Titles:
ZAKENPOST

TNT POST B.V., CONSUMENTENMARKT 1635957
Postbus 30250, 2500 GG DEN HAAG
Tel: 79 3628628 **Fax:** 20 5159145
Web site: http://www.tntpost.nl
Titles:
COLLECT

TNT POST B.V., CORPORATE COMMUNICATIE 1755378
Postbus 30250, 2500 GG DEN HAAG
Tel: 88 7518000 **Fax:** 35 6474569
Email: mail@tntpost.nl
Web site: http://www.tntpost.nl
Titles:
MAIL!

TOBE PUBLISHING B.V. 1757078
Doetinchemseweg 59, 7007 CB DOETINCHEM
Tel: 561 616577
Email: info@tobemagazine.nl
Titles:
TOBE

TOPPERS MEDIA B.V. 1635176
Driezeeg 4, 5258 LE BERLICUM **Tel:** 88 2697183
Fax: 88 2697490
Email: info@toppers.nl
Web site: http://www.toppers.nl
Titles:
ZAKELIJK

TORTUCA 1753625
Postbus 23267, 3001 KG ROTTERDAM
Tel: 70 3147856
Web site: http://www.tortuca.com
Titles:
TORTUCA

TPK MEDIA PARTNERS 1636430
Postbus 322, 6130 AH SITTARD **Tel:** 10 4518007
Fax: 36 7501771
Email: info@tpk-media.nl
Web site: http://www.tpk-media.nl
Titles:
DE POOK
TUINZAKEN

TRAMWEG-STICHTING 1753865
Erfvoort 32, 2211 DE NOORDWIJKERHOUT
Tel: 70 3789880
Email: post@tramwegstichting.nl
Web site: http://www.tramwegstichting.nl
Titles:
OP OUDE RAILS

TREND CROSS MEDIA B.V. 1636828
Van Hogendorplaan 51, 7003 CM DOETINCHEM
Tel: 88 2696670 **Fax:** 88 2696331
Email: trend@trendcrossmedia.nl
Web site: http://www.trendcrossmedia.nl
Titles:
TREND

TROUWEN B.V. 1637910
Postbus 84081, 3009 CB ROTTERDAM
Tel: 88 7518000 **Fax:** 35 6474569
Email: info@trouwen.nl
Titles:
TROUWEN

TT CIRCUIT ASSEN 1653218
Postbus 150, 9400 AD ASSEN **Tel:** 76 5250906
Fax: 342 494299
Email: info@tt-assen.com
Web site: http://www.tt-assen.com
Titles:
TT CIRCUIT ASSEN

TVA! SPECIAL PROJECTS 1637100
Postbus 663, 7000 AR DOETINCHEM
Tel: 58 2845745 **Fax:** 20 5159700
Titles:
ACHTERHOEK MAGAZINE

U GAAT BOUWEN B.V. 1635282
Postbus 10242, 6000 GE WEERT **Tel:** 88 7518480
Fax: 88 7518481
Email: info@ugaatbouwen.nl
Web site: http://www.ugaatbouwen.nl
Titles:
STALLENBOUW

UITG. ST. DE TWAALF AMBACHTEN 1754133
Mezenlaan 2, 5282 HB BOXTEL **Tel:** 88 2697049
Fax: 20 5159700
Email: info@de12ambachten.nl
Web site: http://www.de12ambachten.nl
Titles:
DE TWAALF AMBACHTEN/NIEUWSBRIEF

UITGEVERIJ ABDIJ VAN BERNE B.V. 1753382
Postbus 60, 5473 ZH HEESWIJK-DINTHER
Tel: 570 673344 **Fax:** 475 551033
Email: vieren@wlh.nl
Titles:
DE ZONDAG VIEREN

UITGEVERIJ ARIMPEX B.V. 1736784
Postbus 94279, 1090 GG AMSTERDAM
Tel: 70 3789639 **Fax:** 70 3855505
Email: info@boten.nl
Titles:
BOTEN.NL

UITGEVERIJ BAS LUBBERHUIZEN 1637483
Singel 389, 1012 WN AMSTERDAM
Tel: 58 2845745 **Fax:** 342 494250
Email: info@lubberhuizen.nl
Web site: http://www.lubberhuizen.nl
Titles:
OVER MULTATULI

UITGEVERIJ BN DESTEM PZC B.V. 1636737
Postbus 3229, 4800 MB BREDA **Tel:** 76 5312311
Fax: 70 7999840
Titles:
BN DESTEM
PROVINCIALE ZEEUWSE COURANT

UITGEVERIJ CCM 1773952
Europark 24, 4904 SX OOSTERHOUT
Tel: 570 673344 **Fax:** 475 551033
Email: info@ccmonline.nl
Web site: http://www.ccmonline.nl
Titles:
CCM

UITGEVERIJ COMPRES B.V. 1634570
Postbus 55, 2300 AB LEIDEN **Tel:** 70 3789880
Fax: 70 7999840
Email: info@uitgeverijcompres.nl
Web site: http://www.uitgeverijcompres.nl
Titles:
PRINT BUYER

UITGEVERIJ DAKENRAAD V.O.F. 1636895
Postbus 427, 4940 AK RAAMSDONKSVEER
Tel: 20 3446050 **Fax:** 20 5159145
Email: info@dakenraad.nl
Web site: http://www.dakenraad.nl
Titles:
DAKENRAAD

UITGEVERIJ DE ATLAS 1636504
Postbus 4155, 1620 HD HOORN **Tel:** 570 673344
Fax: 20 5159700
Email: deatlas@cs.com
Web site: http://www.lokalepost.nl
Titles:
LOKALE POST

UITGEVERIJ DE BUNSCHOTER B.V. 1634762
Postbus 10, 3750 GA BUNSCHOTEN-SPAKENBURG
Email: info@de.bunschoter.nl
Web site: http://www.debunschoter.nl
Titles:
DE BUNSCHOTER (H.A.H.)

UITGEVERIJ DE INZET B.V. 1635489
Postbus 11497, 1001 GL AMSTERDAM
Tel: 70 3789880 **Fax:** 70 3789783
Email: info@zingmagazine.nl
Titles:
GITARIST
ZING MAGAZINE

UITGEVERIJ DE ROSKAM B.V. 1636138
Postbus 810, 7600 AV ALMELO **Tel:** 73 6271777
Fax: 73 6220570
Email: info@roskam.nl
Web site: http://www.roskam.nl
Titles:
DE ROSKAM

UITGEVERIJ DE RUYGT 1640291
Postbus 2108, 7302 EM APELDOORN
Tel: 172 466471 **Fax:** 172 422886
Email: info@metaalnieuws.nl
Web site: http://www.udr-media.nl
Titles:
METAALNIEUWS

UITGEVERIJ DE SCHOUW B.V. 1635715
De Trompet 2148b, 1967 DC HEEMSKERK
Tel: 58 2845745
Titles:
HUISHOUD ELECTRO
KEUKEN EN BAD TECHNIEK

UITGEVERIJ DE VRIJBUITER B.V. 1637685
Postbus 100, 5126 ZJ GILZE **Tel:** 88 7518000
Fax: 35 6474569
Titles:
INTIEM

UITGEVERIJ DEN HOLLANDER 1754098
Postbus 325, 7400 AH DEVENTER
Tel: 88 3263334 **Fax:** 88 3263335
Email: info@denhollander.info
Web site: http://www.denhollander.info
Titles:
TIJDSCHRIFT VOOR AGRARISCH RECHT

UITGEVERIJ DISQUE '67 B.V. 1635903
Minervaplein 22-3, 1077 TR AMSTERDAM
Tel: 20 5218938 **Fax:** 20 5159700
Titles:
LUCHTVRACHT
ZAKENREIS

UITGEVERIJ DIVO 1637469
Cyclaamrood 2, 2718 SE ZOETERMEER
Tel: 79 3628628 **Fax:** 172 466577
Email: info@macfan.nl
Web site: http://www.divo.nl
Titles:
MACFAN

UITGEVERIJ ED/BD 1763093
Postbus 534, 5600 AM EINDHOVEN
Tel: 88 0139945 **Fax:** 570 647803

Titles:
BD MAGAZINE
BRABANTS DAGBLAD
ED

UITGEVERIJ & MEDIA-ADVIESBURO TOPAAZ 1634519
Kamplaan 2, 9462 TS GASSELTE **Tel:** 88 3263300
Fax: 88 3263304
Email: topaaz@wxs.nl

Titles:
HONDENSPORT EN SPORTHONDEN

UITGEVERIJ GENOEG 1637795
Ridderstraat 56, 5342 AL OSS **Tel:** 88 3263320
Fax: 20 5159577
Email: info@genoeg.nl
Web site: http://www.genoeg.nl

Titles:
GENOEG

UITGEVERIJ GROEN 1754202
Postbus 484, 8440 AL HEERENVEEN
Tel: 10 2894075 **Fax:** 88 7518652

Titles:
DE VRIEND VAN OUD EN JONG

UITGEVERIJ HAPPINEZ 1640287
Postbus 5040, 1410 AA NAARDEN
Tel: 172 466471 **Fax:** 172 422886
Email: info@happinez.nl

Titles:
HAPPINEZ

UITGEVERIJ HERAUT 1637401
Postbus 43, 2650 AA BERKEL EN RODENRIJS
Tel: 172 466639 **Fax:** 172 466577
Email: info@de-heraut.nl
Web site: http://www.de-heraut.nl

Titles:
DE HERAUT

UITGEVERIJ HET HUIS VAN LINNAEUS B.V. 1636299
Amstel 157, 1018 ER AMSTERDAM
Tel: 58 2845745 **Fax:** 88 2697490

Titles:
ONZEEIGENTUIN

UITGEVERIJ HET NOORDEN 1637167
Zuidergrachtswal 25, 8933 AE LEEUWARDEN
Tel: 58 2845745 **Fax:** 342 494250
Email: uhn@planet.nl
Web site: http://www.uhn.nl

Titles:
ARCHITECTUUR EN BOUWEN

UITGEVERIJ INTERDIJK B.V. 1635205
Postbus 10, 1420 AA UITHOORN **Tel:** 10 2894018
Fax: 35 6563174
Email: info@interdijk.nl
Web site: http://www.interdijk.nl

Titles:
CARAVANNEN!
HET TWEEDE HUIS

UITGEVERIJ KATERN 1635015
Postbus 10, 7437 ZG BATHMEN **Tel:** 70 3378124
Fax: 172 422856
Email: katern@katern.nl
Web site: http://www.katern.nl

Titles:
ZUIDKRANT

UITGEVERIJ LAKERVELD B.V. 1635477
Postbus 160, 2290 AD WATERINGEN
Tel: 76 5301713 **Fax:** 20 5159577
Email: uitgeverij@lakerveld.nl
Web site: http://www.lakerveld.nl

Titles:
HOME & LIVING
POMPSHOP
SUPPORT MAGAZINE

UITGEVERIJ LUNA 1637968
Postbus 14, 2000 AA HAARLEM **Tel:** 88 7518000
Fax: 35 6474569
Email: mars@xs4all.nl
Web site: http://www.uitgeverijluna.nl

Titles:
UITKRANT HAARLEM

UITGEVERIJ MARKEN B.V. 1635895
Postbus 355, 5900 AJ VENLO **Tel:** 20 5218938
Fax: 20 5159145
Email: info@uitgeverijmarken.nl
Web site: http://www.uitgeverijmarken.nl

Titles:
WEIGHTWATCHERS MAGAZINE

UITGEVERIJ MOBILIA B.V. 1636051
Postbus 15341, 1001 MH AMSTERDAM
Tel: 76 5301713 **Fax:** 20 5159577
Email: mobilia@interieur.net

Titles:
MOBILIA VLOEREN

UITGEVERIJ ONS AMSTERDAM B.V. 1644670
Hillegomstraat 12-14, 1058 LS AMSTERDAM
Tel: 88 2697183 **Fax:** 88 2697490
Web site: http://www.onsamsterdam.nl

Titles:
ONS AMSTERDAM

UITGEVERIJ PION 1636680
Postbus 1193, 5602 BD EINDHOVEN
Tel: 20 5218939 **Fax:** 342 494299
Email: info@uitgeverijpion.nl
Web site: http://www.pionline.nl

Titles:
EINDHOVEN BUSINESS

UITGEVERIJ PRODUCT PROMOTIONS B.V. 1637950
Postbus 233, 2870 AE SCHOONHOVEN
Tel: 88 7518000 **Fax:** 35 6474569

Titles:
INTERNATIONAL JEANS CULT

UITGEVERIJ PS: B.V. 1634669
Postbus 14165, 3508 SG UTRECHT
Tel: 10 4518007 **Fax:** 10 4421023
Email: info@uitgeverijps.nl
Web site: http://www.uitgeverijps.nl

Titles:
HOSPITALITY MANAGEMENT

UITGEVERIJ RAMPRESS 1635598
De Zarken 20, 1141 BL MONNICKENDAM
Email: prettigweekend@xs4all.nl

Titles:
PRETTIG WEEKEND

UITGEVERIJ ROODUIJN 1636038
Prinsegracht 166a, 2512 GE DEN HAAG
Tel: 79 3628628 **Fax:** 20 5159145
Email: uitgeverij@rooduijn.com

Titles:
DEN HAAG AGENDA

UITGEVERIJ SCHOOL B.V. 1636358
Stationsweg 44a, 7941 HE MEPPEL
Tel: 88 7518000 **Fax:** 35 6563174

Titles:
DIDAKTIEF

UITGEVERIJ SPIEGEL DER ZEILVAART 1636707
Postbus 653, 2003 RR HAARLEM **Tel:** 20 5218938
Fax: 70 7999840
Email: spiegelderzeilvaart@gmail.com
Web site: http://www.spiegelderzeilvaart.nl

Titles:
SPIEGEL DER ZEILVAART

UITGEVERIJ THIEMEMEULENHOFF 1770506
Postbus 400, 3800 AK AMERSFOORT
Tel: 88 2697049 **Fax:** 20 5159700
Web site: http://www.thiememeulenhoff.nl

Titles:
DE WERELD VAN HET JONGE KIND (HJK)

UITGEVERIJ THUREDRECHT PROMOTIONS B.V. 1729767
Postbus 3049, 3301 DA DORDRECHT
Tel: 88 3263300 **Fax:** 486 476448
Email: info@thuredrecht.nl

Titles:
WEGWIJS

UITGEVERIJ TRIADE BENELUX B.V. 1637847
Postbus 15341, 1001 MH AMSTERDAM
Tel: 76 5301713 **Fax:** 20 5159577
Email: pi@interieur.net

Titles:
PI, PROJEKT & INTERIEUR

UITGEVERIJ TRIDENS V.O.F. 1637623
Postbus 526, 1970 AM IJMUIDEN
Tel: 88 2697112 **Fax:** 88 2696983
Email: tridens@practica.nl

Titles:
OFFSHORE VISIE

UITGEVERIJ UIT DE KUNST B.V. 1635892
Postbus 1839, 8901 CC LEEUWARDEN
Tel: 88 2697856 **Fax:** 20 5159700

Titles:
NIGHTLIFE MAGAZINE

UITGEVERIJ UQUILAIR 1634526
Postbus 153, 5201 AD 'S-HERTOGENBOSCH
Tel: 88 2697062 **Fax:** 314 343839
Email: info@railmagazine.nl

Titles:
RAIL MAGAZINE

UITGEVERIJ VAN VLAARDINGEN B.V. 1636774
Postbus 115, 3738 ZN MAARTENSDIJK
Tel: 35 5482416 **Fax:** 20 5159700
Email: info@vanvlaardingen.nl

Titles:
TABAK & GEMAK

UITGEVERIJ VAN WESTERING B.V. 1636880
Postbus 16, 3740 AA BAARN **Tel:** 88 3263320
Fax: 20 5159577
Email: uitgever@gezondbouwenenwonen.nl
Web site: http://www.vwg.net

Titles:
EKOLAND
GEZOND BOUWEN & WONEN
WATCHING

UITGEVERIJ VANTILT 1634884
Postbus 1411, 6501 BK NIJMEGEN
Tel: 20 3446050 **Fax:** 20 5159145
Email: info@vantilt.nl
Web site: http://www.vantilt.nl

Titles:
DE BOEKENWERELD

UITGEVERIJ VERHAGEN B.V. 1634814
Postbus 3066, 2220 CB KATWIJK
Tel: 20 5218939 **Fax:** 342 494299
Web site: http://www.uitgeverijverhagen.nl

Titles:
KATWIJK SPECIAAL
DE KATWIJKSCHE POST
LEIDERDORPS WEEKBLAD
NOORDWIJKERHOUTS WEEKBLAD
DE WASSENAARDER

UITGEVERIJ VERLOREN 1634738
Postbus 1741, 1200 BS HILVERSUM
Tel: 88 2697856 **Fax:** 88 2697943
Email: info@verloren.nl
Web site: http://www.verloren.nl

Titles:
HOLLAND
DE NEDERLANDSCHE LEEUW

UITGEVERIJ VITA LEVEN 1637007
Wg-Plein 380, 1054 SG AMSTERDAM
Tel: 10 2894075 **Fax:** 88 7518652
Email: va@xs4all.nl

Titles:
VA MAGAZINE (VRUCHTBARE AARDE)

UITGEVERIJ VORSSELMANS B.V. 1635597
Postbus 22, 4880 AA ZUNDERT
Email: zetterij@vorsselmans.nl

Titles:
DE BERGEN OP ZOOMSE BODE
DE BERGEN OP ZOOMSE BODE, ED. ZONDAG
DE BREDASE BODE
DE ETTEN-LEURSE BODE
DE HALDERBERGSE BODE
DE ROOSENDAALSE BODE
DE ROOSENDAALSE BODE, ED. ZONDAG
DE RUCPHENSE BODE
DE WOENSDRECHTSE BODE
DE ZUNDERTSE BODE

UITGEVERIJ WERELDBEELD 1636588
Van Breestraat 57, 1071 ZG AMSTERDAM
Tel: 570 673344

Titles:
DRINKS ONLY!
SAMEN OP VAKANTIE MET BABY'S, PEUTERS EN KLEUTERS

UITGEVERSMAATSCHAPPIJ DE TELEGRAAF B.V. 1635175
Postbus 376, 1000 EB AMSTERDAM
Tel: 35 5482416 **Fax:** 20 5159700

Titles:
DE TELEGRAAF

UITVAART MEDIA 1637663
Postbus 80532, 2508 GM DEN HAAG
Tel: 70 3378125 **Fax:** 20 5159145
Email: uitgever@uitvaartmedia.com
Web site: http://www.uitvaartmedia.com

Titles:
HET UITVAARTWEZEN

UNETO-VNI 1634874
Postbus 188, 2700 AD ZOETERMEER
Tel: 88 2696557 **Fax:** 88 2696946
Email: info@uneto-vni.nl
Web site: http://www.uneto-vni.nl

Titles:
SANITAIR REGISTER
VERWARMING VENTILATIE +

UNICEF NEDERLAND 1754168
Postbus 67, 2270 AB VOORBURG
Tel: 20 3446050 **Fax:** 20 5159145
Email: info@unicef.nl
Web site: http://www.unicef.nl

Titles:
UNICEF MAGAZINE

DE UNIE 1636004
Postbus 400, 4100 AK CULEMBORG
Tel: 79 3628628 **Fax:** 20 5159145
Email: info@unie.nl
Web site: http://www.unie.nl

Titles:
UWMAGAZINE

UNIE KBO 1635870
Postbus 325, 5201 AH 'S-HERTOGENBOSCH
Tel: 88 2697856 **Fax:** 88 2697943
Email: info@uniekbo.nl
Web site: http://www.uniekbo.nl

Titles:
KBO-WEGWIJZER

UNIE NFTO 1637665
Postbus 295, 4100 AG CULEMBORG
Tel: 70 3378125 **Fax:** 20 5159145
Email: info@unienfto.nl
Web site: http://www.unienfto.nl

Titles:
UNIENFTO-TIJDSCHRIFT

UNIVERSITEIT LEIDEN, STRATEGISCHE COMMUNICATIE EN 1753366
Postbus 9500, 2300 RA LEIDEN **Tel:** 71 5271111
Email: leidskwartier@bb.leidenuniv.nl
Web site: http://www.alumni.leidenuniv.nl

Titles:
LEIDRAAD
LEIDS KWARTIER

UNIVERSITEIT TWENTE, BUREAU COMMUNICATIE 1636892
Postbus 217, 7500 AE ENSCHEDE
Tel: 222 362620 **Fax:** 20 5159700

Titles:
UT-NIEUWS

UNIVERSITEIT UTRECHT, COMMUNICATIE SERVICE 1754463
Postbus 80125, 3508 TC UTRECHT
Tel: 79 3628628 **Fax:** 10 4066979
Email: illuster@uu.nl
Web site: http://www.uu.nl

Titles:
ILLUSTER

UNIVERSITEIT VAN AMSTERDAM, BUREAU ALUMNIRELATIES 1754014
Postbus 94325, 1090 GH AMSTERDAM
Tel: 570 673344 **Fax:** 70 7999840
Email: alumni@uva.nl
Web site: http://www.uva.alumni.nl

Titles:
SPUI

UTRECHT BUSINESS 1636497
Postbus 14101, 3508 SE UTRECHT
Tel: 570 673344 **Fax:** 20 5159700
Email: ub@wxs.nl

Titles:
UTRECHT BUSINESS

UWV, AFD. DIRECTORAAT CLIËNTENSERVICE & 1634702
Postbus 58285, 1040 HG AMSTERDAM
Tel: 88 7518000
Web site: http://www.uwv.nl

Titles:
UWV PERSPECTIEF

UWV WERKBEDRIJF 1756908
Postbus 58285, 1040 HG AMSTERDAM
Web site: http://www.werk.nl

Titles:
WERKBLAD

V&VN-SPV 1753906
Hosingenhof 5, 5625 NJ EINDHOVEN
Tel: 88 3233333 **Fax:** 314 343839
Web site: http://www.venvn-spv.nl

Titles:
SOCIALE PSYCHIATRIE

DE VAKBOND VOOR DEFENSIEPERSONEEL, VBM/NOV, 1653906
Postbus 93037, 2509 AA DEN HAAG
Tel: 88 7518000 **Fax:** 35 6474569
Email: vbmnov@vbmnov.nl
Web site: http://www.vbmnov.nl

Titles:
TRIVIZIER

VAN DEN MUNCKHOF B.V. 1636378
Postbus 1, 5800 AA VENRAY **Tel:** 76 5312311
Fax: 76 5144531
Email: info@vandenmunckhof.nl
Web site: http://www.vandenmunckhof.nl

Titles:
PEEL EN MAAS

VAN DER GELD SALES & SUPPORT B.V. 1635841
Postbus 6808, 6503 GH NIJMEGEN
Tel: 88 2697364 **Fax:** 88 2696116
Email: info@vdgeld.nl
Web site: http://www.vdgeld.nl

Titles:
MUSIC EMOTION

VAN DER VALK PUBLICATIES B.V. 1637470
Postbus 121, 5580 AC WAALRE **Tel:** 73 6157171
Fax: 10 7044752
Email: info@publicaties.valk.com
Web site: http://www.valk.com

Titles:
VALK MAGAZINE

VAN HELVOORT UITGEVERIJ B.V. 1634739
Postbus 22, 5420 AA GEMERT **Tel:** 10 4518007
Fax: 36 7501771
Email: gemertsnieuwsblad@vanhelvoortgroep.nl
Web site: http://www.vanhelvoortgroep.nl

Titles:
START

VAN ZESSEN KLAAR 1767674
Maresingel 6, 2316 HA LEIDEN **Tel:** 73 6157171
Fax: 10 7044752
Email: contact@v6k.eu
Web site: http://www.vanzessenklaar.eu

Titles:
LOS MAGAZINE

VAN ZUIDEN COMMUNICATIONS B.V. 1634439
Postbus 2122, 2400 CC ALPHEN A/D RIJN
Tel: 88 7518000 **Fax:** 35 6474569
Email: zuiden@zuidencom.nl
Web site: http://www.vanzuidencommunications.nl

Titles:
MODERN MEDICINE
THE NETHERLANDS JOURNAL OF MEDICINE

VARLN, VERENIGING ALFA ROMEO LIEFHEBBERS 1754578
Dorpstraat 4a, 5504 HH VELDHOVEN
Tel: 342 494889 **Fax:** 342 494299
Email: info@varln.nl
Web site: http://www.varln.nl

Titles:
DUEMILA

VASTGOEDPERSONALITY 1651336
Thomas R. Malthusstraat 3c, 1066 JR AMSTERDAM **Tel:** 76 5250906
Email: info@vastgoedpersonality.nl
Web site: http://www.vastgoedpersonality.nl

Titles:
VASTGOEDPERSONALITY

VBOK 1753657
Postbus 559, 3800 AN AMERSFOORT
Tel: 88 2696285
Email: info@vbok.nl
Web site: http://www.vbok.nl

Titles:
LAAT LEVEN

VEEN MAGAZINES 1788221
Postbus 13288, 3507 LG UTRECHT
Tel: 20 5159666 **Fax:** 342 494299
Web site: http://www.veenmagazines.nl

Titles:
BRIGHT
FILOSOFIE MAGAZINE
GALERIE GIDS
HISTORISCH NIEUWSBLAD
DE INGENIEUR
KUNSTBEELD
MAARTEN!
NWT NATUURWETENSCHAP & TECHNIEK
VOLGENS

VEILIG VERKEER NEDERLAND 1635588
Postbus 66, 3800 AB AMERSFOORT
Tel: 70 3789880
Email: info@vvn.nl
Web site: http://www.veiligverkeernederland.nl

Titles:
JEUGDVERKEERSKRANT
OP VOETEN EN FIETSEN
VEILIGHEID VOOROP

VERDRU 1753473
Postbus 434, 8000 AK ZWOLLE **Tel:** 342 494889

Titles:
THE COINHUNTER MAGAZINE

VERENIGDE GIPSVERBANDMEESTERS NEDERLAND 1636752
Bas Paauwestraat 116, 3077 MP ROTTERDAM
Tel: 76 5312311
Web site: http://www.vgned.nl

Titles:
IN DIT VERBAND

VERENIGING ACTUARIEEL GENOOTSCHAP 1637163
Postbus 2433, 3500 GK UTRECHT
Tel: 58 2845745 **Fax:** 342 494250
Email: info@ag-ai.nl
Web site: http://www.ag-ai.nl

Titles:
DE ACTUARIS

VERENIGING AFVALBEDRIJVEN 1636724
Postbus 2184, 5202 CD 'S-HERTOGENBOSCH
Tel: 20 5218938 **Fax:** 70 7999840
Email: info@verenigingafvalbedrijven.nl
Web site: http://www.verenigingafvalbedrijven.nl

Titles:
AFVALFORUM

VERENIGING DIT KONINGSKIND 1754384
Postbus 85275, 3508 AG UTRECHT
Tel: 172 466639 **Fax:** 172 466577
Email: info@ditkoningskind.nl
Web site: http://www.ditkoningskind.nl

Titles:
KLEUR

VERENIGING EIGEN HUIS 1638239
Postbus 735, 3800 AS AMERSFOORT
Tel: 30 6383736 **Fax:** 30 6383999
Email: magazine@veh.nl
Web site: http://www.eigenhuis.nl

Titles:
EIGEN HUIS MAGAZINE

VERENIGING GEHANDICAPTENZORG NEDERLAND 1636590
Postbus 413, 3500 AK UTRECHT **Tel:** 570 673344
Fax: 70 7999840
Email: markant@vgn.org
Web site: http://www.vgn.org

Titles:
MARKANT

VERENIGING KATTENZORG 1754342
Postbus 85686, 2508 CJ DEN HAAG
Tel: 88 3263300
Email: secretariaat@kattenzorg-denhaag.nl
Web site: http://www.kattenzorg-denhaag.nl

Titles:
KATTEN KATERN

VERENIGING KLASSIEKE ZAKEN 1638066
Postbus 226, 1200 AE HILVERSUM
Tel: 70 3789880 **Fax:** 70 3789783
Email: info@klassiekezaken.nl

Titles:
KLASSIEKE ZAKEN

VERENIGING MILIEUDEFENSIE 1636042
Postbus 19199, 1000 GD AMSTERDAM
Tel: 79 3628628 **Fax:** 20 5159145
Email: service@milieudefensie.nl
Web site: http://www.milieudefensie.nl

Titles:
DOWN TO EARTH

VERENIGING NATUURMONUMENTEN 1753812
Postbus 9955, 1243 ZS 'S-GRAVELAND
Tel: 88 7518000 **Fax:** 35 6563174
Web site: http://www.natuurmonumenten.nl

Titles:
NATUURBEHOUD

VERENIGING NED. VLIEGVISSERS 1637216
Dunantstraat 1041, 2713 TL ZOETERMEER
Tel: 58 2845745
Email: webteam@vnv.nu
Web site: http://www.vnv.nu

Titles:
DE NEDERLANDSE VLIEGVISSER

VERENIGING NEDERLANDS FOTOGENOOTSCHAP 1754377
Postbus 90701, 2509 LS DEN HAAG
Tel: 172 466639 **Fax:** 172 466577
Email: secretaris@fotogenootschap.nl
Web site: http://www.fotogenootschap.nl

Titles:
FOTOGRAFISCH GEHEUGEN

VERENIGING OUD-UTRECHT P/A MUSEUM CATHARIJNECONVENT 1636350
Postbus 8518, 3503 RM UTRECHT
Tel: 79 3628628 **Fax:** 70 7999840
Email: secretariaat@oud-utrecht.nl
Web site: http://www.oud-utrecht.nl

Titles:
OUD-UTRECHT

VERENIGING SPIERZIEKTEN NEDERLAND 1636847
Lt. Generaal van Heutszlaan 6, 3743 JN BAARN
Tel: 20 3446050 **Fax:** 88 2696331
Email: vsn@vsn.nl
Web site: http://www.vsn.nl

Titles:
CONTACT VSN

VERENIGING VAN BEDRIJF-STAKPENSIOENFONDSEN 1754215
Postbus 93158, 2509 AD DEN HAAG
Tel: 20 3446080
Email: info@pensioenfederatie.nl
Web site: http://www.vb.nl

Titles:
VB CONTACT

VERENIGING VAN DE NED. CHEMISCHE INDUSTRIE 1637667
Postbus 443, 2260 AK LEIDSCHENDAM
Tel: 70 3378125 **Fax:** 20 5159145
Email: info@vnci.nl
Web site: http://www.vnci.nl

Titles:
CHEMIE MAGAZINE

VERENIGING VAN ERKENDE PANNEKOEKENRESTAURANTS 1638208
Postbus 566, 3440 AN WOERDEN
Tel: 70 3378124 **Fax:** 172 422856
Email: vep@horeca.org
Web site: http://www.pannenkoekenrestaurants.nl

Titles:
WAAR PANNENKOEKEN ETEN?

VERENIGING VAN KEURSLAGERS 1637302
Postbus 185, 3830 AD LEUSDEN **Tel:** 58 2845745
Fax: 20 5159700
Email: info@keurslager.nl
Web site: http://www.keurslager.nl

Titles:
PROEF...

VERENIGING VAN MILIEUPROFESSIONALS (VVM) 1638080
Postbus 2195, 5202 CD 'S-HERTOGENBOSCH
Tel: 70 3789880 **Fax:** 70 3789783
Email: bureau@vvm.info
Web site: http://www.vvm.info

Titles:
MILIEU

VERENIGING VAN NEDERLANDSE VERKEERSVLIEGERS 1636314
Postbus 192, 1170 AD BADHOEVEDORP
Tel: 70 3789880 **Fax:** 70 7999840
Web site: http://www.vnv-dalpa.nl

Titles:
OP DE BOK

VERENIGING VAN ORGANISTEN DER GEREFORMEERDE 1754108
Welhorst 25, 3332 RP ZWIJNDRECHT
Tel: 20 3446050

Titles:
KERK EN MUZIEK

VERENIGING VOOR BIOLOGISCH-DYNAMISCHE LANDBOUW 1637547
Wisentweg 12, 8251 PC DRONTEN
Tel: 10 4066646 **Fax:** 10 4066979
Email: info@bdvereniging.nl
Web site: http://www.bdvereniging.nl

Titles:
DYNAMISCH PERSPECTIEF

VERENIGING VRIENDEN VAN HET HISTORISCH MUSEUM 1753844
J. Matthijssenlaan 10, 3232 ED BRIELLE
Tel: 20 7581000
Email: fteggens@wanadoo.nl
Web site: http://www.historischmuseumdenbriel.nl

Titles:
BRIELSE MARE

VERENIGING WERELDKINDEREN 1754263
Riouwstraat 191, 2585 HT DEN HAAG
Tel: 88 3263300 **Fax:** 88 3263339
Email: info@wereldkinderen.nl
Web site: http://www.wereldkinderen.nl

Titles:
WERELDKINDEREN

VERENIGING YPSILON 1753756
Prins Bernhardlaan 177, 2273 DP VOORBURG
Tel: 88 7518160 **Fax:** 342 494299
Email: ypsilon@ypsilon.org
Web site: http://www.ypsilon.org

Titles:
YPSILON NIEUWS

VERKEERSRECHT/ANWB 1636931
Postbus 93200, 2509 BA DEN HAAG
Tel: 70 3789880 **Fax:** 314 343839
Email: verkeersrecht@anwb.nl

Titles:
VERKEERSRECHT

VIDEO EMOTION B.V. 1638032
Postbus 6808, 6503 GH NIJMEGEN
Web site: http://www.video-emotion.nl

Titles:
VIDEO EMOTION

VIPMEDIA PUBLISHING & SERVICES 1636651
Postbus 7272, 4800 GG BREDA **Tel:** 88 3263300
Fax: 88 3263304
Email: info@vipmedia.nl
Web site: http://www.vipmedia.nl

Titles:
BEET SPORTVISSERS-MAGAZINE
BLOEMEN & PLANTEN
DUIKEN
HART VOOR DIEREN
TUINONTWERP
TUINPLUS

VIRTÙMEDIA 1638107
Postbus 595, 3700 AN ZEIST **Tel:** 76 5301713
Fax: 20 5159577
Email: info@virtumedia.nl
Web site: http://www.virtumedia.nl

Titles:
ARCHEOLOGIE MAGAZINE
SCHRIJVEN MAGAZINE

VIVACE MEDIA B.V. 1637829
Postbus 8648, 3009 AP ROTTERDAM
Tel: 88 2696557 **Fax:** 88 2696946
Email: info@vivacemedia.nl

Titles:
VIVACE MAGAZINE

VIVES MEDIA B.V. 1635727
Postbus 3389, 2001 DJ HAARLEM
Tel: 342 494268 **Fax:** 342 494299
Email: info@vives.nl
Web site: http://www.vives.nl

Titles:
VIVES WEBBOEKJE

DE VLINDERSTICHTING 1637826
Postbus 506, 6700 AM WAGENINGEN
Tel: 76 5301713
Email: info@vlinderstichting.nl
Web site: http://www.vlinderstichting.nl

Titles:
VLINDERS

VMN, VEREENIGING VAN MUZIEKHANDELAREN EN 1753810
Stationslaan 117-5, 3844 GC HARDERWIJK
Tel: 88 7518160 **Fax:** 88 7518161
Email: info@vmn.nl
Web site: http://www.vmn.nl

Titles:
DE MUZIEKHANDEL

VNU MEDIA B.V. 1634869
Postbus 37040, 1030 AA AMSTERDAM
Tel: 20 5159666 **Fax:** 20 5159700
Email: info@vnumedia.nl
Web site: http://www.vnumedia.nl

Titles:
ICT CONSULTANCY GUIDE
INTERMEDIAIRPW

VOB DE AMELANDER B.V. 1644674
Strandweg 1, 9162 EV BALLUM AMELAND
Tel: 88 7518000 **Fax:** 35 6474569
Email: info@deamelander.nl

Titles:
DE AMELANDER

VOGELBESCHERMING NEDERLAND 1753721
Postbus 925, 3700 AX ZEIST **Tel:** 88 2697856
Fax: 88 2697943
Email: info@vogelbescherming.nl
Web site: http://www.vogelbescherming.nl

Titles:
VOGELS

VOLVO CARS NEDERLAND B.V. 1636978
Postbus 16, 4153 ZG BEESD **Tel:** 10 2894075
Fax: 88 7518652
Web site: http://www.volvocars.nl

Titles:
LIV

VONDEL PUBLICATIONS B.V. 1690142
Postbus 75202, 1070 AE AMSTERDAM
Tel: 172 466400 **Fax:** 172 493270
Email: info@vondelpublications.nl
Web site: http://www.vondelpublications.nl

Titles:
INCOMPANY

VONK & SCHOOT NEDERLAND 1753348
Varikstraat 77, 1106 CT AMSTERDAM
Tel: 88 2697062

Titles:
D' AMSTERDAMSE TRAM

VOOR JOU UITGEVERIJ 1769912
Postbus 2644, 3800 GD AMERSFOORT
Tel: 10 4518007

Titles:
AMERSFOORT VOOR JOU

VOORSTER NIEUWS V.O.F. 1637761
Postbus 205, 7390 AE TWELLO **Tel:** 342 494889
Fax: 342 494299
Email: info@voorsternieuws.nl

Titles:
VOORSTER NIEUWS

VORMEN UIT VUUR 1653189
Lampongstraat 6 II, 1094 AT AMSTERDAM

Titles:
VORMEN UIT VUUR

VOS & PARTNERS WIJNKOPERS 1767148
Postbus 4031, 4900 CA OOSTERHOUT
Tel: 73 6271777

Titles:
WIJN AAN TAFEL

VPT, VERENIGING VOOR PODIUMTECHNOLOGIE 1637783
Postbus 15172, 1001 MD AMSTERDAM
Tel: 88 7518000 **Fax:** 35 6474569
Email: secretariaat@vpt.nl
Web site: http://www.vpt.nl

Titles:
ZICHTLIJNEN

VRIENDEN VAN DE OLIFANT 1636268
Postbus 44, 1430 AA AALSMEER **Tel:** 88 5567205
Email: info@olifanten.org
Web site: http://www.elephantfriends.org

Titles:
DE OLIFANT

VRIJE UNIVERSITEIT AMSTERDAM, DIENST COMMUNICATIE 1634403
De Boelelaan 1091, kamer OE-60, 1081 HV AMSTERDAM **Tel:** 88 3263334
Web site: http://www.vu.nl

Titles:
VU MAGAZINE

VSG MEDIA & EVENTS 1637695
Postbus 103, 6860 AC OOSTERBEEK
Tel: 20 5218938 **Fax:** 20 5159145
Email: info@sportengemeenten.nl
Web site: http://www.sportengemeenten.nl

Titles:
SPORTLOKAAL

VSSD, VERENIGING VOOR STUDIE- EN STUDENTENBELANGEN 1636236
Leeghwaterstraat 42, 2628 CA DELFT
Tel: 79 3628628 **Fax:** 70 7999840
Email: bestuur@vssd.nl
Web site: http://www.vssd.nl

Titles:
HET ORAKEL

VU MEDISCH CENTRUM, DIENST COMMUNICATIE 1754654
Postbus 7057, 1007 MB AMSTERDAM
Tel: 10 4066646 **Fax:** 10 4066979
Email: communicatie@vumc.nl
Web site: http://www.vumc.nl

Titles:
SYNAPS

VVP VERENIGDE PERIODIEKEN B.V. 1634956
Postbus 433, 2040 AK ZANDVOORT
Tel: 70 3789880 **Fax:** 70 3789783
Email: info@vvpbv.nl
Web site: http://www.vvpbv.nl

Titles:
DHZ MARKT

VVV MAASTRICHT 1634514
Kleine Staat 1, 6211 ED MAASTRICHT
Tel: 88 2697364 **Fax:** 88 2696116
Email: info@vvvmaastricht.nl
Web site: http://www.vvvmaastricht.nl

Titles:
MAASTRICHT: STADSGIDS

WADDENVERENIGING 1636466
Postbus 90, 8860 AB HARLINGEN
Tel: 20 3446080 **Fax:** 342 494250
Email: magazine@waddenvereniging.nl
Web site: http://www.waddenvereniging.nl

Titles:
WADDENMAGAZINE

WAGENINGEN UR 1759157
Postbus 409, 6700 AK WAGENINGEN
Tel: 317 484020 **Fax:** 317 424060
Email: resource@wur.nl
Web site: http://www.wur.nl

Titles:
RESOURCE

WANTIJ, ZEEUWSE MILIEUFEDERATIE 1636321
Postbus 334, 4460 AS GOES **Tel:** 70 3789880
Fax: 70 7999840
Email: info@zmf.nl
Web site: http://www.zmf.nl

Titles:
WANTIJ

WARD MEDIA 1754361
Tijnjedijk 89, 8936 AC LEEUWARDEN
Tel: 70 3789880 **Fax:** 70 3789783
Email: info@wardmedia.nl
Web site: http://www.wardmedia.nl

Titles:
HUWELIJK IN...

WATERNET 1754149
Postbus 94370, 1090 GJ AMSTERDAM
Tel: 222 362620 **Fax:** 20 5159700
Email: info@waternet.nl
Web site: http://www.waternet.nl

Titles:
STRUINEN

WAVIN NEDERLAND B.V. 1753979
Postbus 5, 7770 AA HARDENBERG
Tel: 570 673344 **Fax:** 475 551033
Email: info@wavin.nl
Web site: http://www.wavin.nl

Titles:
WAVIN INFO

WEBREGIO MEDIA 1699366
Postbus 187, 1440 AD PURMEREND
Tel: 88 7518000 **Fax:** 35 6474569
Email: info@webregiomedia.nl
Web site: http://www.webregiomedia.nl

Titles:
WATERLAND WELZIJN

HET WEEKBLAD B.V. 1637071
Pieter Calandlaan 323, 1068 NH AMSTERDAM
Tel: 76 5312311 **Fax:** 570 647803
Email: info@westerpost.nl

Titles:
WOONWEST

WEEKBLAD HUIS AAN HUIS 1636594
Postbus 14, 1970 AA IJMUIDEN **Tel:** 570 673344
Fax: 70 7999840
Email: info@weekbladhuisaanhuis.nl

Titles:
HUIS AAN HUIS

WEEKBLADCOMBINATIE GELDERLAND OVERIJSSEL B.V. 1634397
Postbus 149, 7000 AC DOETINCHEM
Tel: 88 0139945 **Fax:** 570 647803
Email: info@wcgo.nl
Web site: http://www.wcgo.nl

Titles:
MONTFERLAND NIEUWS
RIJSSENS NIEUWSBLAD

WEEKBLADPERS TIJDSCHRIFTEN 1635090
Postbus 764, 1000 AT AMSTERDAM
Tel: 88 3263334 **Fax:** 88 3263335
Web site: http://www.weekbladpers.nl

Titles:
J/M
MEN'S HEALTH
OPZIJ
PSYCHOLOGIE MAGAZINE
RUNNER'S WORLD
VRIJ NEDERLAND

WEGENER MEDIA B.V. REGIO 1634373
Postbus 692, 7500 AR ENSCHEDE
Email: info@wegenermedia.nl
Web site: http://www.wegenermedia.nl

Titles:
RECREATIEKRANT VELUWE
STADSNIEUWS

WEGENER MEDIA B.V. REGIO MIDDEN-NEDERLAND 1753309
Postbus 472, 3990 GG HOUTEN **Tel:** 88 7518160
Fax: 342 494299
Email: info@wegenermedia.nl
Web site: http://www.wegenermedia.nl

Titles:
DE MAKELAAR

WEIJMANS PUBLISHERS B.V. 1634498
Postbus 464, 5700 AL HELMOND **Tel:** 88 7518480
Fax: 88 7518481
Email: publishers@weijmans.com
Web site: http://www.weijmans.com

Titles:
BRABANT BUSINESS MAGAZINE
'T CONTACT
YINX MAGAZINE

WEKA UITGEVERIJ B.V. 1634888
Postbus 61196, 1005 HD AMSTERDAM
Tel: 88 3263334 **Fax:** 88 3263335
Email: info@weka.nl
Web site: http://www.weka.nl

Titles:
REAL ESTATE MAGAZINE
STEDEBOUW & ARCHITECTUUR

WELEDA NEDERLAND N.V. 1754224
Postbus 733, 2700 AS ZOETERMEER
Tel: 88 2697049 **Fax:** 88 2697356
Email: info@weleda.nl
Web site: http://www.weleda.nl

Titles:
WELEDA BERICHTEN

WELSH SPRINGER SPANIEL CLUB IN NEDERLAND 1753832
Aarweg 3. 01, 8071 WV NUNSPEET
Tel: 73 6271777
Web site: http://www.wssc.nl

Titles:
DE WELSH SPRINGER

WELZO MEDIA PRODUCTIONS B.V. 1636814
Postbus 26, 9989 ZG WARFFUM **Tel:** 88 2696670
Fax: 88 2696331
Email: welzo.media@worldonline.nl

Titles:
OVER DIEREN

WERELD NATUUR FONDS 1636361
Postbus 7, 3700 AA ZEIST **Tel:** 70 3789880
Fax: 70 3789783
Email: info@wnf.nl
Web site: http://www.wwf.nl

Titles:
PANDA
TAMTAM

WERELDWIJDE KERK VAN GOD 1754137
Postbus 1505, 1300 BM ALMERE **Tel:** 20 5218938
Email: info@lifeblad.nl
Web site: http://www.wkg-lifeline.nl

Titles:
LIFELINE

WERKGROEP R. TEN BERGE 1754244
De Vallei 42, 9405 KK ASSEN **Tel:** 20 5218938
Fax: 20 5159700
Email: ebijma@planet.nl

Titles:
SCHOON SCHIP 93

WESTZAANSE GEMEENSCHAP 1638045
Middel 165, 1551 SV WESTZAAN **Tel:** 10 2894018
Email: wessaner@gmail.com

Titles:
DE WESSANER

WIJ SPECIAL MEDIA B.V. 1637092
Postbus 2584, 1620 EN HOORN **Tel:** 70 3378124
Fax: 172 422856
Email: info@wij.nl
Web site: http://www.wijspecialmedia.nl

Titles:
EÉN JAAR!
GEBOORTE
WIJ JONGE OUDERS
ZWANGER!

WIJS & VAN OOSTVEEN 1636061
Herengracht 493, 1017 BT AMSTERDAM
Tel: 79 3628628 **Fax:** 20 5159145
Email: info@wijs.nl
Web site: http://www.wijs.nl

Titles:
GELD & BELEGGEN

WILBERS PUBLISHING B.V. 1635701
Postbus 10, 7070 AA ULFT **Tel:** 58 2845745
Fax: 20 5159700
Email: info@hetautomobiel.nl
Web site: http://www.wilberspublishing.nl

Titles:
AUTO MOTOR KLASSIEK
HET AUTOMOBIEL KLASSIEKER MAGAZINE

THE WINE & FOOD ASSOCIATION 1638050
Winkeldijk 12a, 1391 HL ABCOUDE
Tel: 88 3263334 **Fax:** 88 3263335
Email: info@thewinesite.nl
Web site: http://www.thewinesite.nl

Titles:
PROEFSCHRIFT-WINE & FOOD PROFESSIONAL

DE WINTER DRUKKERS & UITGEVERS 1636273
Postbus 26, 5400 AA UDEN **Tel:** 58 2845745
Fax: 20 5159700
Email: contact@dewinter.nl
Web site: http://www.dewinter.nl

Titles:
STADSKRANT VEGHEL
UDENS WEEKBLAD
WEEKBLAD REGIO OSS

WLO, WERKGEMEENSCHAP LANDSCHAPSECOLOGISCH 1637713
Postbus 80123, 3508 TC UTRECHT
Tel: 20 5218938 **Fax:** 20 5159145
Email: wlo@knag.nl

Titles:
LANDSCHAP

WOLTERS UITGEVERIJ B.V. 1753761
Postbus 32, 7220 AA STEENDEREN
Tel: 58 2845745 **Fax:** 88 2697490
Email: info@schoolfacilities.nl

Titles:
SCHOOLFACILITIES

WOMEN'S GLOBAL NETWORK FOR REPRODUCTIVE 1754085
Vrolikstraat 453d, 1092 TJ AMSTERDAM
Tel: 76 5312311 **Fax:** 70 7999840
Email: office@wgnrr.nl
Web site: http://www.wgnrr.org

Titles:
WOMEN'S GLOBAL NETWORK FOR REPRODUCTIVE RIGHTS NEWSLETTER

WONENWONEN.NL B.V. 1706526
Postbus 173, 5100 AD DONGEN **Tel:** 23 5565509
Fax: 342 494299
Email: info@wonenwonen.nl

Titles:
WONENWONEN.NL

Y & W 1635187
Binnenpad 28, 8355 BR GIETHOORN
Tel: 79 3628628 **Fax:** 88 5567355
Email: info@wiedenenweerribben.nl

Titles:
IJSSELHAMMER

Y-PUBLICATIES 1636550
Postbus 10208, 1001 EE AMSTERDAM
Tel: 20 5218938 **Fax:** 20 5159700
Email: info@y-publicaties.nl
Web site: http://www.y-publicaties.nl

Titles:
KRAAMSUPPORT
OK OPERATIONEEL
VERPLEEGKUNDE
WMO MAGAZINE

ZACCO NETHERLANDS B.V. 1753828
Postbus 75683, 1070 AR AMSTERDAM
Tel: 73 6271777 **Fax:** 73 6220570
Email: info.amsterdam@zacco.com
Web site: http://www.zacco.nl

Titles:
NIEUWSBRIEF ZACCO (VOORHEEN SCHIELDMARK)

ZAMI, PLATFORM VOOR ZWARTE MIGRANTEN EN 1755349
VEC, Bijlmerdreef 1301, 1103 TV AMSTERDAM
Tel: 88 7518000
Email: info@zami.nl
Web site: http://www.zami.nl

Titles:
ZAMIKRANT

ZEEUWS VLAAMS MEDIABEDRIJF B.V. 1638226
Postbus 51, 4530 AB TERNEUZEN
Tel: 70 3378124
Email: zvm@zvm.eu
Web site: http://www.zvm.eu

Titles:
STYLE CITY MAGAZINE ZEEUWS-VLAANDEREN

DE ZEEUWSE MOLEN 1753903
Singel 68, 4382 LB VLISSINGEN **Tel:** 88 3233333
Email: info@zeeuwsemolens.nl
Web site: http://www.zeeuwsemolens.nl

Titles:
DE WINDMOLEN

ZILTE ZAKEN V.O.F. 1763550
Burgwal 37, 1791 AH DEN BURG **Tel:** 73 6157171
Fax: 10 7044752
Email: info@ziltezaken.nl
Web site: http://www.ziltezaken.nl

Titles:
TEXELNU

ZITY PUBLISHERS B.V. 1637786
Postbus 8013, 8903 KA LEEUWARDEN
Tel: 58 2845745 **Fax:** 20 5159700
Email: redactie@lourens.nl
Web site: http://www.zity.com

Titles:
LOURENS J.C.

ZORG EN ZEKERHEID 1755899
Postbus 400, 2300 AK LEIDEN **Tel:** 88 2696665
Fax: 88 2696946
Web site: http://www.zorgenzekerheid.nl

Titles:
GEZZOND

ZORGSAAM 1754131
Zwolseweg 290, 7315 GZ APELDOORN
Tel: 88 2697049 **Fax:** 88 2697356
Email: info@zorgsaam.nl
Web site: http://www.zorgsaam.nl

Titles:
ZORGSAAM

ZORGVERZEKERAAR VGZ 1753633
Postbus 30374, 6503 HZ NIJMEGEN
Tel: 20 5159666 **Fax:** 20 5159700
Web site: http://www.vgz.nl

Titles:
GEZOND VGZ MAGAZINE

ZORN UITGEVERIJ B.V. 1754253
Postbus 4001, 2302 RA LEIDEN **Tel:** 58 2845745
Fax: 342 494250
Email: info@zorn.nl
Web site: http://www.zorn.nl

Titles:
KENMERK

Z-PRESS JUNIOR MEDIA 1643205
Postbus 1015, 3300 BA DORDRECHT
Tel: 45 5792379 **Fax:** 88 2697660
Email: info@zpress-magazines.nl
Web site: http://www.zpress-magazines.nl

Titles:
AJAX LIFE
GOAL! MAGAZINE
KR@SH MAGAZINE
MEIDENMAGAZINE
SESAMSTRAAT MAGAZINE

Norway

ABM-MEDIA 1735645
Pb. 4, St. Olavsplass, 0130 OSLO **Tel:** 41 33 77 86

Titles:
BOK OG BIBLIOTEK
MUSEUMSNYTT

AD FONTES MEDIER AS 1772009
Postboks 1180, Sentrum, 0330 OSLO
Tel: 23 31 02 39

Titles:
KULTMAG

ADD MEDIA 1768025
Postboks 9178, Grønland, 0134 OSLO
Tel: 69308830 **Fax:** 22 17 25 08

Titles:
UTEMILJØ

ADD MEDIA AS 1794180
Rådhusgata 4 A, 1051 OSLO **Tel:** 23100470
Fax: 23100480

Titles:
HOLD PUSTEN

ADD MEDIA PUBLISHING 1643929
Pb 9178 Grønland, 0134 OSLO **Tel:** 69308830
Fax: 22172508

Titles:
HMT - HELSE MEDISIN TEKNIKK

ADRESSEAVISEN ASA 1643945
Industriveien 13, 7003 TRONDHEIM **Tel:** 07 20 0
Fax: 72 50 15 00

Titles:
ADRESSEAVISEN
TRØNDELAGSPAKKEN

ADVOKATFORENINGEN 1793412
kr. Augustsgate 9, 0164 OSLO **Tel:** 22035132
Fax: 22115325

Titles:
ADVOKATBLADET; ADVOKATBLADET.NO

AFGHANISTANKOMITEEN I NORGE 1628211
Osterhausgate 27, 0183 OSLO **Tel:** 22989315
Fax: 22989301

Titles:
AFGHANISTAN-NYTT

AFTENPOSTEN 1650371
Pb. 1, 0051 OSLO **Tel:** 22 86 39 42 **Fax:** 22428967

Titles:
AFTENPOSTEN; UTENRIKSREDAKSJONEN
GOLF.NO

AFTENPOSTEN AS 1649819
Pb. 1 Sentrum, 0051 OSLO **Tel:** 22 86 40 40

Titles:
AFTENPOSTEN A-MAGASINET
AFTENPOSTEN; DEBATTREDAKSJONEN
AFTENPOSTEN INNSIKT
AFTENPOSTEN; LEVE
AFTENPOSTEN; SPORTSREDAKSJONEN

AFTENPOSTEN FORLAG 1732485
Pb. 1, 0185 OSLO **Tel:** 22863000

Titles:
AFTENPOSTEN; HYTTE MAGASINET

AFTENPOSTEN MULTIMEDIA AS 1627761
Pb. 1 Sentrum, 0051 OSLO **Tel:** 22 86 30 00
Fax: 22 86 41 30

Titles:
FORBRUKER.NO

AFTENSPOSTEN FORLAG AS 1789347
Pb. 1, 0051 OSLO **Tel:** 23 36 19 70

Titles:
AFTENPOSTEN; MAMMA

AGDER MOTORHISTORISKE KLUBB 1628212
Bernt Erik Olsen, Astrids vei 2, 4633 KRISTIANSAND **Tel:** 38097489 **Fax:** 38090964
Titles:
FJÆRBLADET

AGDERPOSTEN AS 1792489
Pb. 8, 4801 ARENDAL **Tel:** 37 00 37 00
Fax: 37 00 37 17
Titles:
AGDERPOSTEN

AKERSHUS AMTSTIDENDE AS 1627765
Pb. 12, 1440 DRØBAK **Tel:** 64 90 54 00
Titles:
AKERSHUS AMTSTIDENDE

AKRSHUS AMTSTIDENDE AS 1745009
Postboks 12, 1440 DRØBAK **Tel:** 64 90 54 00
Titles:
AKERSHUS AMTSTIDENDE-AVD. NESODDEN

AKSJONÆRFORENINGEN I NORGE 1628768
Pb. 1963 Vika, 0125 OSLO **Tel:** 24 11 78 62
Fax: 24 11 78 61
Titles:
AKSJONÆREN

AKTIVITØRENES LANDSFORBUND (ALF) 1794082
Aktivitørenes Landsforbund v/ Karina Sandnes, Krakelivegen 237, 6490 EIDE **Tel:** 48251202
Titles:
AKTIVITØREN

ALLER INTERNET MEDIA AS 1793964
Stenersgt 2-8, 0184 OSLO **Tel:** 40 60 20 80
Titles:
DINGZ.NO

ALLER INTERNETT 1680689
Stenersgata 8, 0184 OSLO **Tel:** 40 60 10 30
Titles:
DIGI.NO
DINSIDE; BOLIG
ITAVISEN.NO
TOPP.NO

ALLER MEDIA AS 1794120
2743 HARESTUA **Tel:** 33390220 **Fax:** 33390221
Titles:
VAKRE HJEM OG INTERIØR

ALLERS FAMILIE-JOURNAL AS 1628216
Pb. 1169 Sentrum, 0107 OSLO **Tel:** 21301000
Fax: 21301204
Titles:
ALLERS
AUTOFIL
BÅTMAGASINET
COSMOPOLITAN
HENNE
HENNE.NO
KK

ALTERNATIVT NETTVERK AS 1628674
Øvre Slottsgt. 7, 0157 OSLO **Tel:** 22 33 84 04
Fax: 22 33 84 09
Titles:
VISJON

AMBULANSEFORUM AS 1628221
Nardoveien 4b, 7430 TRONDHEIM **Tel:** 73964434
Titles:
AMBULANSEFORUM
AMBULANSEFORUM; AMBULANSEFORUM.NO

AMCAR MAGAZINE AS 1643948
Pb. 6006, 7434 TRONDHEIM **Tel:** 72896000
Fax: 72896020
Titles:
AMCAR

ANIMALIA 1793687
Pb 396 Økern, 0513 OSLO **Tel:** 22 09 23 00
Fax: 22 22 00 16
Titles:
GO'MØRNING

ANLEGGSMASKINEN 1643914
Fred Olsens gate 3, 0152 OSLO **Tel:** 22404190
Titles:
ANLEGGSMASKINEN

APERITIF AS 1794230
Furuveien 39c, 0678 OSLO **Tel:** 2219 0075
Fax: 22671477
Titles:
APÉRITIF
BAR APÉRITIF

APPETITT SKANDINAVIA AS 1692229
Tømmerbakkeveien 19, 1453 BJØRNEMYR
Tel: 66918163
Titles:
APPETITT

ARBEIDERNES KOMMUNISTPARTI AKP 1643947
Pb 124 Sentrum, 3251 LARVIK
Titles:
RØDT!

ARBEIDSMILJØSENTERET AVD. OSLO 1712916
Pb. 9326 Grønland, 0135 OSLO **Tel:** 81 55 97 50
Fax: 22 05 78 39
Titles:
ARBEIDSMILJØ

AS DAGBLADET 1649820
Pb. 1184 Sentrum, 0150 OSLO **Tel:** 24 00 10 00
Fax: 22 42 95 48
Titles:
DAGBLADET; NYHETSREDAKSJONEN
DAGBLADET; SØNDAGSMAGASIN

AS HELGELAND ARBEIDERBLAD 1792563
8654 MOSJØEN **Tel:** 75 11 36 00 **Fax:** 75113630
Titles:
HELGELAND ARBEIDERBLAD

AS KOBO 1793982
Pb 14 Røa, 0701 OSLO **Tel:** 23 25 32 32
Fax: 22 52 24 80
Titles:
HYTTE INFORMASJON

ASK MEDIA AS 1752768
Pb. 130, 2261 KIRKENAER **Tel:** 91123330
Titles:
AKTUELL SIKKERHET
BEDRE GARDSDRIFT
FASTFOOD
HMS MAGASINET
HORECA
INDUSTRIEN
MAGASINET TREINDUSTRIEN
PERSONAL OG LEDELSE
PERSONAL OG LEDELSE; LEDERNETT.NO
PLASTFORUM
RENHOLDSNYTT

ASKER OG BÆRUM BOLIGBYGGELAG BA 1644124
P.B 385, 1301 SANDVIKA **Tel:** 67574000
Titles:
ABBL NYTT

ASKER OG BÆRUMS BUDSTIKKE ASA 1792901
Pb 133, 1376 BILLINGSTAD **Tel:** 66 77 00 00
Fax: 66 77 00 60
Titles:
BUDSTIKKA

ATLANTIC COMMUNICATIONS 1644017
Lisbeth Lødner, Media Call A/S, 1358 JAR
Tel: 67156290 **Fax:** 67156291
Titles:
OFFSHORE ENGINEER

ATLANTIC FORLAG AS 1628716
Skuteviksboder 11, 5035 BERGEN
Tel: 55 30 48 60
Titles:
KYSTMAGASINET

ATTAC NORGE V/STEINAR ALSOS 1793947
Solidaritetshuset, Osterhausgate 27, 0183 OSLO
Tel: 22 98 93 04
Titles:
UTVEIER

AUTORISERTE TRAFIKKSKOLERS LANDSFORBUND 1628636
Autoriserte Trafikkskolers Landsforbund, Pb. 144 Manglerud, 0612 OSLO **Tel:** 22 62 60 80
Fax: 22 62 60 81
Titles:
TRAFIKKSKOLEN

AVIS HOLDING AS 1793713
Postboks 79, Bryn, 0345 OSLO **Tel:** 23 20 56 00
Titles:
LOKALAVISEN FROGNER - ST.HANSHAUGEN

AVISEN AGDER AS 1644081
Pb 40, 4401 FLEKKEFJORD **Tel:** 38 32 03 00
Fax: 38 32 45 60
Titles:
AGDER; AVISENAGDER.NO

AVISEN SKOLEMAGASINET 1652917
Avisen SkoleMagasinet, co Redaktør Per Rune Eknes, Postboks 301, 1379 NESBRU
Tel: 92 23 48 47 **Fax:** 62 53 53 94
Titles:
SKOLEMAGASINET

AVISEN VÅRT LAND AS 1792595
Pb. 1180 Sentrum, 0107 OSLO **Tel:** 22310310
Fax: 22310 05
Titles:
VÅRT LAND

AVISHUSET FIRDA AS 1644095
Firda Media AS, Pb. 160, 6801 FØRDE
Tel: 57 83 33 00 **Fax:** 57 20 53 11
Titles:
FIRDA

B2B PUBLISHING 1793695
Prinsensgate 46, 7011 TRONDHEIM
Tel: 992 89 500 **Fax:** 73 51 65 50
Titles:
CONPOT

BABYMEDIA AS 1793957
Gullhaugveien 1, 0441 OSLO **Tel:** 22 58 50 00
Titles:
BARNIMAGEN.COM

BABYMEDIA AS OG HJEMMET MORTENSEN INTERAKTIV 1687102
NO-0277 OSLO **Tel:** 45 25 25 48
Titles:
DINBABY.COM

BARNEMAGASINET 1791665
C/O Barnemagasinet, 0441 OSLO
Tel: 23 00 81 83 **Fax:** 22 58 05 85
Titles:
GLADE BARN I BARNEHAGEN

BEFALETS FELLESORGANISASJON 1628141
Pb 501, Sentrum, 0105 OSLO **Tel:** 23 10 02 42
Fax: 23 10 02 25
Titles:
OFFISERSBLADET

BELLONA MILJØSTIFTELSEN 1644035
Pb 2141 Grünerløkka, 0505 OSLO
Tel: 23 23 46 00 **Fax:** 22 38 38 62
Titles:
BELLONA.NO

BENJAMIN PUBLICATIONS AS 1747464
Pb. 1010 Sentrum, 0104 OSLO **Tel:** 22 40 12 40
Fax: 22 40 12 41
Titles:
FHM.NO

BERGEN HUSEIERFORENING 1793984
Øvregaten 21, 5003 BERGEN **Tel:** 55 31 69 16
Fax: 55234154
Titles:
HUSEIER

BERGEN TURLAG 1628239
Tverrgaten 4-6, 5017 BERGEN **Tel:** 55 33 58 10
Fax: 55 33 58 29
Titles:
STI OG VARDE

BERGENS TIDENDE AS 1792780
Krinkelkroken 1, Postboks 7240, 5020 BERGEN
Tel: 05 50 0
Titles:
BERGENS TIDENDE

BERGENSAVISEN AS 1793026
Pb. 824, Sentrum, 5807 BERGEN **Tel:** 55 23 50 00
Fax: 55310030
Titles:
BERGENSAVISEN; DEBATT
BERGENSAVISEN; MEG & DEG-REDAKSJONEN

BIBELLESERINGEN 1692266
Pb. 9285 Grønland, 0134 OSLO **Tel:** 22 99 29 69
Fax: 22 99 29 60
Titles:
1LOGOS

BIBLIOTEKARFORBUNDET 1629078
Runnen 4, 6800 FØRDE **Tel:** 91 31 80 01
Fax: 94 76 22 12
Titles:
BIBLIOTEKAREN

BILFORLAGET AS 1628325
Postboks 63 Skøyen, 0134 OSLO **Tel:** 23036600
Fax: 23036640
Titles:
BIL
BILNORGE.NO
MOTORBRANSJEN
YRKESBIL

BILMAGASINET AS 1644179
Vækerøveien 203, 0751 BILLINGSTAD
Tel: 22500737
Titles:
BILMAGASINET

BILNYTT AS 1793889
Postboks 63 Skøyen, 0212 OSLO **Tel:** 23 03 66 00
Fax: 23 03 66 40
Titles:
BILNYTT.NO

BIOINGENIØRFAGLIG INSTITUTT, NITO 1732488
NITO - Norges Ingeniør- og Teknologorganisasjon, Postboks 9100 Grønland, 0133 OSLO **Tel:** 22 05 35 00 **Fax:** 22 17 24 80
Titles:
BIOINGENIØREN

BIOLOGISK DYNAMISK FORENING 1629107
Biologisk-dynamisk forening, Skonhovedveien 149, 2318 HAMAR **Tel:** 61 18 44 50 **Fax:** 61 18 44 51
Titles:
HERBA

BIOMED CENTRAL 1753262
Idse, 4102 IDSE **Tel:** 51 74 14 80 **Fax:** 51 74 14 81
Titles:
SCANDINAVIAN JOURNAL OF TRAUMA, RESUSCIATION AND EMERGENCY MEDICINE (SJTREM)

BIOTEKNOLOGINEMNDA 1651297
Pb. 522 Sentrum, 0105 OSLO **Tel:** 24 15 60 20 **Fax:** 24 15 60 29
Titles:
GEN-I-ALT

BIVIRKNINGSGRUPPEN FOR ODONTOLOGISKE BIOMATERIALER 1794192
Bivirkningsgruppen, Årstadveien 17, 5009 BERGEN **Tel:** 55586271 **Fax:** 55589862
Titles:
BIVIRKNINGSBLADET

BJØRGU AS 1628110
Pb 11, 1411 KOLBOTN **Tel:** 66822121 **Fax:** 66822120
Titles:
ANLEGG & TRANSPORT
MODERNE TRANSPORT
TRANSPORT INSIDE

BLÅ KORS NORGE 1654100
Pb 4793 Sofienberg, 0506 OSLO **Tel:** 22 03 27 40 **Fax:** 22 03 27 41
Titles:
RUSFRI

BLADET LEDERNE 1712902
Pb. 2523 Solli, 0202 OSLO **Tel:** 22 54 51 50 **Fax:** 22 55 65 48
Titles:
LEDERNE

BLADET NORDLYS AS 1792908
Pb. 2515, 9272 TROMSØ **Fax:** 77 62 35 01
Titles:
NORDLYS

BLADET VESTERÅLEN AS 1793816
Pb. 33, 8401 SORTLAND **Tel:** 76 11 09 00 **Fax:** 76110891
Titles:
BLADET VESTERÅLEN; BLV.NO

BLIKK AS 1735652
Pb 8875 Youngstorget, 0028 OSLO **Tel:** 22 33 44 55 **Fax:** 22 33 66 37
Titles:
BLIKK

BO BYGG OG BOLIG AS 1791548
HM Fagmedia AS, avd. Markedskontakt, Redaksjonen Bo Bygg og Bolig, Postboks 24, 1485 HAKADAL **Tel:** 67 06 46 02 **Fax:** 67064611
Titles:
BO BYGG OG BOLIG

BOARDING.NO 1651267
Pb. 557, 4055 STAVANGER LUFTHAVN SOLA **Tel:** 40 85 41 37 **Fax:** 51 65 25 11
Titles:
BOARDING.NO

BOKAVISEN ANS 1732645
Christiesgate 28, 0557 OSLO **Tel:** 40001957
Titles:
BOKAVISEN.NO

BOKVENNEN FORLAG AS 1629055
Postboks 6794 St. Olavs plass, 0130 OSLO **Tel:** 22 19 14 25 **Fax:** 22 19 14 26
Titles:
BOKVENNEN

BONDEUNGDOMSLAGET I STAVANGER 1649860
Pb 451 Madla, 4090 HAFRSFJORD **Tel:** 51 55 95 15 **Fax:** 51 55 95 16
Titles:
HOLMGANG

BONNIER MEDIA AS 1649855
Pb. 1010, Sentrum, 0104 OSLO **Tel:** 22401200 **Fax:** 22401241
Titles:
COSTUME
COSTUME.NO
FHM
TARA
WOMAN
WOMAN.NO

BONNIER MEDIA II AS 1791361
Bonnier Media AS, Postboks 1010 Sentrum, 0104 OSLO **Tel:** 22407000
Titles:
BOLIGPLUSS

BONNIER PUBLICATIONS A/S 1710245
Bonnier Media A/S, 0158 OSLO **Tel:** 22 04 70 00
Titles:
NATIONAL GEOGRAPHIC
SPIS BEDRE

BONNIER PUBLICATIONS INTERNATIONAL AS 1644157
Torvgt. 15 B, 2000 LILLESTRØM **Tel:** 63883807
Titles:
DIGITAL FOTO
GJØR DET SELV
I FORM
ILLUSTRERT VITENSKAP

BONNIER RESPONSEMEDIER AS 1644196
Pb. 797 Sentrum, 0106 OSLO **Tel:** 22047400 **Fax:** 23310301
Titles:
VI I VILLA

BRIDGE I NORGE AS 1628259
Nesgaten 25, 4400 FLEKKEFJORD **Tel:** 38 32 10 60 **Fax:** 38 32 10 61
Titles:
BRIDGE I NORGE

BRYLLUPSMAGASINET NORGE A/S 1649843
Trykkeriveien 6, 1653 SELLEBAKK **Tel:** 69351800 **Fax:** 69351809
Titles:
BRYLLUPSMAGASINET

BS MEDIA AS 1793993
Pb. 473, 6414 MOLDE **Tel:** 71 20 12 00 **Fax:** 71 20 12 01
Titles:
BOMAGASINET

BULL MEDIA CONSULTING AS 1650161
Box 4335 Nydalen, 0402 OSLO **Tel:** 920 22 199 **Fax:** 2155 55 62
Titles:
LEDERNYTT

BYGG OG ANLEGG MEDIA AS 1628032
Pb. 6831 St. Olavs plass, 0130 OSLO **Tel:** 23 70 95 00 **Fax:** 23 70 95 01
Titles:
BYGGEINDUSTRIEN
BYGGEINDUSTRIEN; BYGG.NO

BYGGFAKTA DOCU AS 1769463
Pb. 1024, 1510 MOSS **Tel:** 69 91 24 00 **Fax:** 69 91 24 04
Titles:
BYGGAKTUELT
BYGGAKTUELT; BYGGAKTUELT.NO
OFFENTLIG DRIFT
RYKOGREIS.NO

BYGGFORLAGET AS 1794218
Pb. 5475 Majorstuen, 0305 OSLO **Tel:** 23087500 **Fax:** 23087550
Titles:
BYGGMESTEREN

CANIS NORGE 1651253
Canis AS, Mediahuset Vestre Rosten 78, 7075 TILLER **Tel:** 72 87 86 50 **Fax:** 72 87 86 55
Titles:
CANIS

CARE NORGE 1794385
Universitetsgata 12, 0164 OSLO **Tel:** 22992600 **Fax:** 22992601
Titles:
I CARE

CASTRA AS 1794084
Fred Olsens gate 1, 0303 OSLO **Tel:** 22416077 **Fax:** 22416011
Titles:
MILITÆRTEKNIKK

CEREBRAL PARESE-FORENINGEN 1794202
Bergsalleen 21, 0854 OSLO **Tel:** 22599900 **Fax:** 22599901
Titles:
CP-BLADET

CHILI PUBLICATIONS AS 1745740
Henrik Ibsensgt 28, 0175 OSLO **Tel:** 21 56 90 00 **Fax:** 21569001
Titles:
SPIRIT

CICERO- SENTER FOR KLIMAFORSKNING 1739526
CICERO Senter for klimaforskning, Pb. 1129 Blindern, 0318 OSLO **Tel:** 22858750 **Fax:** 22858751
Titles:
KLIMA

CIVITAN INTERNATIONAL NORGES 1753079
Pb. 18, 4701 VENNESLA **Tel:** 38 15 50 80
Titles:
CIVINORD

C/O BONNIER PUBLICATIONS INTERNATIONAL AS, PB. 433 SENTRUM 1793990
C/O Bonnier Publications International AS, Pb. 433 sentrum, 0103 OSLO **Tel:** 22 40 12 00
Titles:
HAGEN FOR ALLE

COX AS 1739595
Ask Media, Pb 130, 2261 KIRKENAER **Tel:** 92258431
Titles:
GAVE OG INTERIØR

CREDITINFORM AS 1628274
Pb. 5275 Majorstuen, 0303 OSLO **Tel:** 81 55 54 54 **Fax:** 22 93 20 80
Titles:
FAGBLADET CREDITINFORM

CROSS MEDIA AS 1757162
Maridalsv. 87, 0461 OSLO **Tel:** 22 04 06 00
Titles:
SKIER

CUBAFORENINGEN I NORGE 1793681
Pb. 8708 Youngstorget, 0028 OSLO **Tel:** 2217 2900 **Fax:** 2217 2902
Titles:
CUBA-NYTT

DAG OG TID AS 1627882
Pb. 7044 St. Olavs plass, 0130 OSLO **Tel:** 21 50 47 47 **Fax:** 21 50 47 49
Titles:
DAG OG TID

DAGBLADET DAGEN AS 1792629
Pb. 2394, Solheimsviken, 5824 BERGEN **Tel:** 55 55 97 25 **Fax:** 55 55 97 20
Titles:
DAGEN

DAGBLADET FINNMARKEN AS 1627788
Pb. 616, 9811 VADSØ **Tel:** 78 95 55 00 **Fax:** 78 95 55 60
Titles:
FINNMARKEN

DAGENS NÆRINGSLIV AS 1792900
Pb. 1182 Sentrum, 0107 OSLO **Tel:** 22001190
Titles:
D2
DAGENS NÆRINGSLIV

DALANE TIDENDE OG EGERSUNDS AVIS AS 1627782
Pb. 68, 4379 EGERSUND **Tel:** 51 46 11 00 **Fax:** 51 46 11 01
Titles:
DALANE TIDENDE

DARKLANDS 1765381
c/o Darklands, Henrik Wergelandsgt. 47, 4612 KRISTIANSAND **Tel:** 47 29 85 20
Titles:
RIMFROST MAGAZINE

DATABASE VEST AS 1628277
Pb 9 Kokstad, 5863 BERGEN **Tel:** 51 82 02 00 **Fax:** 51 82 02 05
Titles:
BILLISTEN.NO

DB MEDIALAB AS 1692237
Postboks 1184, Sentrum, 0150 OSLO **Tel:** 24 00 10 00
Titles:
DAGBLADET.NO- KJENDIS.NO

DE NASJONALE FORSKNINGSETISKE KOMITEER 1628811
Pb 522 Sentrum, 0105 OSLO **Tel:** 23 31 83 00 **Fax:** 23 31 83 01
Titles:
FORSKNINGSETIKK

DEMOKRATEN AS 1793729
Pb. 82, 1601 FREDRIKSTAD **Tel:** 69 36 80 00
Titles:
DEMOKRATEN; KULTURREDAKSJONEN
DEMOKRATEN; SPORTSREDAKSJONEN

DEN KONSERVATIVE STUDENTFORENING (DKSF) 1794383
Akersgaten 20, 0158 OSLO **Tel:** 92898571 **Fax:** 22829092
Titles:
MINERVA

DEN NORSKE ADVOKATFORENING 1793392
Advokatforeningen, Kristian Augustsgate 9, 0164 OSLO **Tel:** 22035050 **Fax:** 22115325
Titles:
ADVOKATBLADET

Norway

DEN NORSKE BOKHANDLERFORENING 1628022
Øvre Vollgt 15, 0158 OSLO **Tel:** 22 40 45 40
Titles:
BOK OG SAMFUNN
BOK OG SAMFUNN; BOKOGSAMFUNN.NO

DEN NORSKE HELSINGFORSKOMITÉ 1794393
Kirkegata 5, 0153 OSLO **Tel:** 22479202
Fax: 22416076
Titles:
MENNESKERETTIGHETSMAGASINET MR

DEN NORSKE JORDMORFORENING 1794182
Den norske jordmorforening, Tollbugata 35, 0157 OSLO **Tel:** 21023372 **Fax:** 21023377
Titles:
TIDSSKRIFT FOR JORDMØDRE

DEN NORSKE LÆGEFORENING 1794170
Pb 1152 Sentrum, 0107 OSLO **Tel:** 23109050
Fax: 23109090
Titles:
TIDSSKRIFT FOR DEN NORSKE LEGEFORENING

DET FRIVILLIGE SKYTTERVESEN 1732489
Pb. 298, Økern, 0511 OSLO **Tel:** 911 77 680
Fax: 23 17 21 01
Titles:
NORSK SKYTTERTIDENDE

DET GODE LIV AS 1794313
Postboks 123 Bogstadveien, 0323 OSLO
Tel: 23204450
Titles:
MAGASINET DET GODE LIV

DET HVITE BÅND 1628942
Torggt. 1, 0181 OSLO **Tel:** 23 21 45 37
Fax: 23 21 45 01
Titles:
DET HVITE BÅND

DET NORSKE HAGESELSKAP 1794072
Pb 53 Manglerud, 0612 OSLO **Tel:** 23031600
Fax: 23031601
Titles:
NORSK HAGETIDEND

DET NORSKE SHAKESPEARESELSKAP 1692278
Litteraturhuset, Wergelandsveien 29, 0167 OSLO
Tel: 22 44 69 28
Titles:
NORSK SHAKESPEARE OG TEATER-TIDSSKRIFT

DET NORSKE SKOGSELSKAP 1628138
Wergelandsveien 23 B, 0167 OSLO
Tel: 23 36 58 60 **Fax:** 22 60 41 89
Titles:
NORSK SKOGBRUK

DET NORSKE TOTALAVHOLDSSELSKAP 1628301
Det Norske Totalavholdsselskap, Pb 8885 Youngstorget, 0028 OSLO **Tel:** 23 21 45 70
Fax: 23 21 45 51
Titles:
MENNESKEVENNEN

DEVELOPMENT TODAY AS 1776885
Box 140, 1371 ASKER **Tel:** 66902660
Titles:
DEVELOPMENT TODAY

DINE PENGER AS 1791574
Postboks 1185 sentrum, 0277 OSLO
Tel: 22 00 00 50 **Fax:** 22 00 00 60
Titles:
DINE PENGER

DINE PENGER, SCHIBSTED FORLAGENE AS 1692239
Postboks 1185 sentrum, 0107 OSLO
Tel: 22 00 00 50 **Fax:** 22000060
Titles:
DINEPENGER.NO

DINSIDE AS - ALLER INTERNETT 1692240
Postboks 1169, 0107 OSLO **Tel:** 4060 1000
Fax: 2103 2052
Titles:
DINSIDE
DINSIDE; DATA
DINSIDE; MOTOR
DINSIDE; ØKONOMI
DINSIDE; REISE

DIREKTORATET FOR ARBEIDSTILSYNET 1643944
Direktoratet for Arbeidstilsynet, Statens Hus, 7468 TRONDHEIM **Tel:** 97 40 70 73
Fax: 73 19 97 01
Titles:
ARBEIDERVERN

DIREKTORATET FOR UTVIKLINGSSAMARBEID (NORAD) 1794356
Pb 8034 Dep, 0030 OSLO **Tel:** 22242040
Fax: 22242066
Titles:
BISTANDSAKTUELT

DITT HUS AS 1794031
Pb. 1266 Majorstuveien 17, 0367 OSLO
Tel: 22 43 80 10
Titles:
DITT HUS

DNT FJELLSPORT OSLO 1768691
DNT Fjellsport Oslo, Pb 7 Sentrum, 0101 OSLO
Tel: 22 82 28 42 **Fax:** 22 82 29 00
Titles:
BREPOSTEN

DNT UNG 1761004
Den Norske Turistforening, Youngsgt. 1, 0181 OSLO **Tel:** 400 01 868
Titles:
UT

DØVEPROSTEN I NORGE 1754103
Døveprosten i Norge, Fagerborggaten 12, 0360 OSLO **Tel:** 70 11 45 66 **Fax:** 70 11 45 68
Titles:
DØVES BLAD

DRAMMENS SPORTSFISKERE 1628307
Drammens Sportsfiskere, Pb. 335, 3001 DRAMMEN **Tel:** 32 82 09 31
Titles:
SPORTSFISKER'N

DYSLEKSIFORBUNDET I NORGE 1793699
Pb. 8731 Youngstorget, 0028 OSLO
Tel: 22 47 44 50 **Fax:** 22 42 95 54
Titles:
DYSLEKTIKEREN

E24 A/S V/VG OG AFTENPOSTEN 1791838
Postboks 1185, 0051 0107 OSLO OSLO OSLO OSLO OSLO **Tel:** 22 86 40 25 **Fax:** 22 86 43 77
Titles:
E24 NÆRINGSLIV

EBL KOMPETANSE 1794097
Pb 7184 Majorstua, 0307 OSLO **Tel:** 23088900
Fax: 23088901
Titles:
EBL FORUM

EDDA DIGITAL AS 1770288
Tek.no c/o Edda Digital, Postboks 428 Sentrum, 0103 OSLO **Tel:** 920 53683 **Fax:** 21 56 97 01
Titles:
SPILLVERKET.NO

EDDA MEDIA 1770287
Tek.no, c/o Edda Digital. Postboks 428 Sentrum, 0103 OSLO **Tel:** 920 53683 **Fax:** 21 56 97 01
Titles:
AKAM.NO
AUDIOVISUELT.NO

EDDA VESTFOLD AS 1743038
Pb. 85, 3191 HORTEN **Tel:** 33 02 00 00
Fax: 33 02 00 30
Titles:
GJENGANGEREN

EDDA VESTFOLD DIGITAL 1745814
Edda Vestfold, Postboks 2003, 3103 TØNSBERG **Tel:** 33 37 30 00 **Fax:** 33 37 30 32
Titles:
HYTTEAVISEN.NO

EGEDE INSTITUTTET/TAPIR AKADEMISKE FORLAG 1692279
Egede Instituttet, Postboks 5144 Majorstua, 0302 OSLO **Tel:** 22 59 06 91 **Fax:** 22 59 05 30
Titles:
NORSK TIDSSKRIFT FOR MISJONSVITENSKAP

EGMONT HJEMMET MORTENSEN AS 1788351
Gullhaugveien 1, 0441 OSLO **Tel:** 22 58 50 00
Titles:
KLIKK.NO
MANN
VILLMARKSLIV

EGMONT SERIEFORLAGET AS 1628230
Fridtjof Nansensvei 14, 0369 OSLO
Tel: 24 05 13 00
Titles:
HJEMMETS HOBBY KRYSS

EIKER AVIS AS 1644232
Pb. 55, 3301 HOKKSUND **Tel:** 32 25 39 50
Fax: 32 25 36 51
Titles:
EIKER AVIS

EKSPORTUTVALGET FOR FISK 1687132
Pb. 6176, 9291 TROMSØ **Tel:** 77 60 33 33
Fax: 77 68 00 12
Titles:
EKSPORTUTVALGET FOR FISK - GODFISK

ELEKTROMEDIA AS 1651273
Energiteknikk, Postboks 4, 1371 ASKER
Tel: 66787535 **Fax:** 66 78 14 45
Titles:
ENERGITEKNIKK
ENERGITEKNIKK; ELEKTRONETT.NO

ELEKTRONIKKFORLAGET AS 1628040
Elektronikkforlaget AS, Pb 570, 1337 SANDVIKA
Tel: 67804280 **Fax:** 67804290
Titles:
ELEKTRONIKK
ELEKTRONIKK; ELEKTRONIKKNETT.NO

ENERGI FORLAG AS 1791979
Pb. 1182, Sentrum, 0107 OSLO **Tel:** 22001150
Fax: 22001083
Titles:
VÅR ENERGI

ENERGIFORSYNINGENS LEDERFORENING 1794098
Oksenøyvn. 14, 1366 LYSAKER **Tel:** 67512333
Fax: 67512335
Titles:
ENERGI & LEDELSE

ENKELT AS 1754532
Pb. 784, 7651 VERDAL **Tel:** 924 43 987
Titles:
ENKELT

ERLIKMAGASINET 1686364
Skippergata 14, 0152 OSLO **Tel:** 22 42 16 70
Titles:
=OSLO

ESPEN SLETNER 1757588
Innovation Media avd Oslo, PB 266 Sentrum, 0103 OSLO **Tel:** 22419441
Titles:
NATT&DAG
NATT&DAG; NATTOGDAG.NO

ESTATE MEDIA 1794026
Estate Media AS.Holbergsgate 21, 0166 OSLO
Tel: 21951000 **Fax:** 21951001
Titles:
ESTATE MAGASIN

ESTHETIQUE 3118 1794331
Pb 6137 Etterstad, 0602 OSLO **Tel:** 22576900
Fax: 22576901
Titles:
ESTHETIQUE

EUROPOWER AS 1649848
Pb. 1182, Sentrum, 0107 OSLO
Titles:
ENERGI
ENERGI; ENERGI-NETT.NO
EUROPOWER

EXACT MEDIA AS 1794292
Postboks 454, 2305 HAMAR **Tel:** 62519630
Fax: 62519631
Titles:
EXACT

FÆDRELANDSVENNEN AS 1792912
Pb 369, 4664 KRISTIANSAND S **Tel:** 38113000
Fax: 38113001
Titles:
FÆDRELANDSVENNEN

FAGAKTUELT AS 1650307
Fagaktuelt AS - Pb. 1, 7701 STEINKJER
Tel: 90 74 67 52
Titles:
HUSBYGGEREN; HUSBYGGEREN.NO

FAGBOKFORLAGET AS 1644031
Institutt for matematiske realfag og teknologi, Pb 5003, 1432 ÅS **Tel:** 64 96 54 72 **Fax:** 64 96 54 01
Titles:
KART OG PLAN

FAGBOKFORLAGET VIGMOSTAD & BJØRKE AS 1628236
Kirurgisk Serviceklinikk Etg 3, Haukeland Universite, 5021 BERGEN **Tel:** 55976894
Fax: 55976898
Titles:
OMSORG
TIDSSKRIFT FOR VELFERDSFORSKNING

FAGBOKFORLAGET VIGMOSTAD & BJØRKE AS/ STATSKONSULT 1692296
Universitetsforlaget, Postboks 508 Sentrum, 0105 OSLO **Tel:** 24 14 75 00 **Fax:** 24 14 75 01
Titles:
STAT & STYRING

FAGFORBUNDET 1791584
Pb. 7003 St. Olavs plass, 0130 OSLO
Tel: 23 06 40 00 **Fax:** 23 06 44 07
Titles:
FAGBLADET

FALLSKJERMSEKSJONEN/ NORGES LUFTSPORTSFORBUND 1649788
C/O Kitt Grønningsæter, Furuvegen 15, 3560 HEMSEDAL **Tel:** 90 12 71 54
Titles:
FRITT FALL

FAMILIE & MEDIER - KRISTENT MEDIEFORUM 1791673
Skjenet 2, 5353 STRAUME **Tel:** 56 31 40 50
Fax: 56314051
Titles:
PÅ BØLGELENGDE

FARMASIFORBUNDET 1794156
Farmasiforbundet, Hegdehaugsveien 8, 0167 OSLO **Tel:** 22992660 **Fax:** 22201301
Titles:
FARMASILIV

FARSUNDS AVIS 1627929
Pb. 23, 4551 FARSUND **Tel:** 38 39 50 00
Fax: 38 39 20 86
Titles:
FARSUNDS AVIS

FELLESFORBUNDET 1794033
Pb. 231 Sentrum, 0103 OSLO **Tel:** 23063391
Fax: 23063394
Titles:
MAGASINET FOR FAGORGANISERTE

FELLESKJØPET AGRI 1769279
Felleskjøpet Agri, Postboks 469 Sentrum, 0105 OSLO **Tel:** 22 86 10 04 **Fax:** 22 86 10 01
Titles:
SAMVIRKE

FELLESORGANISASJONEN FOR BARNEVERNPEDAGOGER, SOSIO 1794355
Pb. 231, Sentrum, 0103 OSLO **Tel:** 23061170
Fax: 23061111
Titles:
FONTENE

FELLESRÅDET FOR AFRIKA 1628562
Osterhausgata 27, 0183 OSLO **Tel:** 22 98 93 11
Fax: 22 98 93 01
Titles:
AFRICA NEWS UPDATE

FELLESRÅDET FOR AFRIKA, SAIH, LAG, UTVIKLINGSFONDET 1794373
Osterhausgata 27, 0183 OSLO **Tel:** 22989332
Titles:
VERDENSMAGASINET X

FILM & KINO 1686784
Pb 446 Sentrum, 0104 OSLO **Tel:** 22 47 46 28
Fax: 22 47 46 98
Titles:
FILM & KINO

FILMMAGASINET AS 1692245
Gjerdrumsvei 19, 0484 OSLO **Tel:** 21 50 80 00
Fax: 21 50 80 84
Titles:
FILMMAGASINET

FILOLOGISK FORENING 1776886
P.B. 106 Blindern, 0314 OSLO
Titles:
FILOLOGEN

FINANSFORBUNDET 1794354
Pb 9234 Grønland, 0134 OSLO **Tel:** 22056300
Fax: 22170690
Titles:
FINANSFOKUS

FINDEXA FORLAG 1794330
Findexa Forlag, Pb. 457 Sentrum, 0104 OSLO
Tel: 21508020
Titles:
MILJØSTRATEGI

FINDEXA FORLAG AS 1747915
Findexa Forlag AS, Pb 457 sentrum, 0609 OSLO
Tel: 21 50 80 00 **Fax:** 21 50 80 01
Titles:
NORTRADE.COM
NORWAY EXPORTS
REIS
TRAVEL NEWS

FINNMARK DAGBLAD AS 1680679
Pb. 293, 9615 HAMMERFEST **Tel:** 78 42 86 00
Fax: 78 42 86 39
Titles:
FINNMARK DAGBLAD
FINNMARK DAGBLAD; KULTUR

FISKEBÅTREDERNES FORBUND 1628334
Pb 67, 6001 ÅLESUND **Tel:** 70 10 14 60
Fax: 70 10 14 80
Titles:
FISKEBÅT-MAGASINET

FISKERIBLADET FISKAREN AS 1745680
Bontelabo 2, 5003 BERGEN **Tel:** 55 21 33 00
Titles:
FISKERIBLADETFISKAREN.NO

FISKERIBLADETFISKAREN AS 1747840
Bontelabo 2, 5003 BERGEN **Tel:** 55 21 33 00
Titles:
FISKERIBLADETFISKAREN~ AVD. BERGEN

FJORD 1 NORDVESTLANDSKE 1735666
Pb. 354, 6901 FLORØ **Tel:** 957 51 992
Titles:
FJORD 1 MAGASINET

FJORDABALDET AS 1745378
Pb. 74, 6771 NORDFJORD **Tel:** 57 88 53 10
Fax: 57885111
Titles:
FJORDABALDET; SPORTSREDAKSJONEN

FLAVUS DATA AS 1653652
Grønvoldvegen 7, 3830 ULEFOSS **Tel:** 90192708
Titles:
ESTRATEGI.NO

FN-SAMBANDET I NORGE 1628753
Storgata 33a, 0184 OSLO **Tel:** 22 86 84 00
Fax: 22 86 84 01
Titles:
ARBEIDSLIV
FN-SAMBANDET - FN.NO

FN-VETERANENES LANDSFORBUND 1681007
Pb 1635 Vika, 0119 OSLO **Tel:** 23 09 35 49
Titles:
SJEKKPOSTEN

FOKUS 1793625
Storg. 11, 0155 OSLO **Tel:** 23 01 03 00
Fax: 23010301
Titles:
KVINNER SAMMEN

FOLK OG FORSVAR 1628338
Arbeidersamfunnets Pl. 1 C, 0181 OSLO
Tel: 22 98 83 60 **Fax:** 22 98 83 61
Titles:
FOLK OG FORSVAR

FOLKEAKADEMIENES LANDSFORBUND 1628198
Tøyengata 26, 0190 OSLO **Tel:** 22 68 22 06
Fax: 22 68 78 31
Titles:
NØKKELEN

FORBRUKERRÅDET 1628342
Pb 4594 Nydalen, 0404 OSLO **Tel:** 23 40 05 00
Fax: 23 42 39 61
Titles:
FORBRUKERRAPPORTEN

FORBUNDET FOR LEDELSE OG TEKNIKK HOLDING AS 1794062
Pb 8906 Youngstorget, 0028 OSLO **Tel:** 23061029
Fax: 23061017
Titles:
LEDELSE OG TEKNIKK

FORBUNDET KYSTEN 1794336
v/Bente Foldvik, Djupvikveien 27, 9519 KVIBY
Tel: 78440833
Titles:
KYSTEN

FORBUNDET MOT RUSGIFT 1629432
Forbundet Mot Rusgift, Torggata 1, 0181 OSLO
Tel: 23 21 45 26 **Fax:** 23 21 45 01
Titles:
MOT RUSGIFT

FORBUNDET TENNER OG HELSE 1628666
Forbundet Tenner og Helse, Postboks 6416, Etterstad, 0605 OSLO **Tel:** 23054565
Titles:
TENNER & HELSE

FORENINGEN 1793953
Foreningen "Vi som har et barn for lite", Pb. 4730 Nydalen, 0421 OSLO **Tel:** 81 54 85 01
Titles:
ET BARN FOR LITE

FORENINGEN 2 FORELDRE 1629114
Postboks 9924, 7079 TRONDHEIM
Tel: 88 00 88 45 **Fax:** 6487 3954
Titles:
TIDSSKRIFTET 2 FORELDRE

FORENINGEN FOR HJERTESYKE BARN 1732490
Postboks 4535 Nydalen, 0103 OSLO
Tel: 22799450 **Fax:** 22799451
Titles:
HJERTEBARNET

FORENINGEN FOR MUSKELSYKE 1794160
Foreningen for Muskelsyke, Brynsveien 96, 1352 KOLSÅS **Tel:** 51113938
Titles:
MUSKELNYTT

FORENINGEN FRIKANALEN 1770424
FORENINGEN FRIKANALEN, Pb 4743 NYDALEN, 0421 OSLO
Titles:
FRIKANALEN

FORENINGEN NORGE-KINA 1794365
Pb 320, 1301 SANDVIKA **Tel:** 22382243
Fax: 22382243
Titles:
KINA OG VI

FORENINGEN NORGES DØVBLINDE 1627880
Pb 354, 4803 ARENDAL **Tel:** 37 02 11 47
Titles:
DØVBLINDES UKEBLAD

FORLAGET FIDELITY AS 1654622
Halvdan Svartes Gt. 8, 0268 OSLO
Tel: 905 40 974
Titles:
FIDELITY

FORLAGET FOTOGRAFI AS 1628599
Postboks 703, Skøyen, 0214 OSLO **Tel:** 67120610
Titles:
FOTOGRAFI
FOTOGRAFI; FOTOGRAFI.NO

FORLAGET NYE MEDIER AS 1794100
Postb. 33, 3209 SANDEFJORD **Tel:** 22 11 24 55
Fax: 94770442
Titles:
MONITOR

FORLAGET SKOLEPSYKOLOGI 1628808
Pb. 165, 2711 GRAN **Tel:** 61 33 16 16
Fax: 61 33 01 07
Titles:
SKOLEPSYKOLOGI

FORSKERFORBUNDET 1757230
Pb. 1025 Sentrum, 0104 OSLO **Tel:** 21 02 34 00
Fax: 21 02 34 01
Titles:
FORSKERFORUM.NO

FORSØKSRINGENE I ØKOLOGISK LANDBRUK 1793887
Reddalsveien 215, 4886 GRIMSTAD
Tel: 91 87 08 93 **Fax:** 37257739
Titles:
ØKOLOGISK LANDBRUK

FORSVARSSTABEN 1747443
Forsvarsforum Oslo Mil/ Akershus, 0015 OSLO
Tel: 23 09 20 40
Titles:
F - FORSVARETS FORUM
F - FORSVARETS FORUM; FOFO.NO
F- FORSVARETS FORUM~BARDUFOSS

FORTIDSMINNEFORENINGEN 1628355
Dronningens gt. 11, 0152 OSLO **Tel:** 23 31 70 71
Fax: 23 31 70 50
Titles:
FORTIDSVERN

FORUM FOR MILJØ OG HELSE 1794188
Forum for miljø og helse c/o Svein Kvakland, Molde kommune, Rådhusplassen 1, 6413 MOLDE **Tel:** 71111245
Titles:
MILJØ & HELSE

FORUT, SOLIDARITETSAKSJON FOR UTVIKLING 1794363
Pb 300, 2803 GJØVIK **Tel:** 61187400
Fax: 61187401
Titles:
FORUT-NYTT

FOSNA-FOLKET AS 1627797
Pb. 205, 7129 BREKSTAD **Tel:** 72 51 57 00
Fax: 72 51 57 01
Titles:
FOSNA-FOLKET

Norway

FOTO-, PRESSE- & PR-SERVICE 1793999
Pb 153, 2302 HAMAR **Tel:** 950 68 540
Fax: 62519971
Titles:
BADETEKNISK FORUM

FRAKTEFARTØYENES REDERIFORENING 1628359
Pb 2020 Nordnes, 5817 BERGEN **Tel:** 55 55 16 20
Fax: 55 55 16 21
Titles:
FRAKTEMANN

FRAMTIDEN I VÅRE HENDER (FIVH) 1692246
Fredensborgveien 24g, 0177 OSLO **Tel:** 22033150
Fax: 22033151
Titles:
FOLKEVETT

FREDRIKSSTAD BLAD AS 1680645
Postboks 143, 1601 FREDRIKSTAD
Tel: 46 80 77 77
Titles:
FREDRIKSSTAD BLAD

FREDRIKSTAD BLAD 1773965
Postboks 143, 1601 FREDRIKSTAD
Tel: 69388000
Titles:
FREDRIKSSTAD BLAD; SPORTEN

FREMOVER AS 1793043
Pb. 324, 8504 NARVIK **Tel:** 76 95 00 00
Fax: 76 95 00 30
Titles:
FREMOVER

FREMSKRITTPARTIET HOVEDORGANISASJON 1794368
0159 OSLO **Tel:** 23135450 **Fax:** 23135451
Titles:
MEDLEMSAVISEN FREMSKRITT

FREMTIDEN I VÅRE HENDER 1793882
Fredensborgveien 24 G, 0177 OSLO
Tel: 222 03 31 62
Titles:
NORWATCH.NO

FRI FLYT AS 1654121
Mølleparken 6, 0459 OSLO **Tel:** 22 04 46 00
Fax: 22 04 46 09
Titles:
FRI FLYT
FRILUFTSMAGASINET UTE
TERRENGSYKKEL

FRILUFTSLIV MULTIMEDIA AS 1629068
Postboks 3, 7221 MELHUS **Tel:** 92 44 76 45
Titles:
FRILUFTSLIV MULTIMEDIA

FRIMURERORDEN DEN NORSKE 1628286
Nedre Vollgate 19, 0158 OSLO **Tel:** 92 05 05 05
Titles:
FRIMURERBLADET

FUTURUM FORLAG AS 1794361
Hjelmsgate 3, 0355 OSLO **Tel:** 22466896
Titles:
GATEAVISA

GAMEZ PUBLISHING A/S 1770151
Gamez Publishing Nuf, Postboks 479 Sentrum, 0105 OSLO **Tel:** 47026909
Titles:
GAMEREACTOR
GAMEREACTOR; GAMEREACTOR.NO

GAUSDAL INFORMASJON 1793715
2653 VESTRE GAUSDAL **Tel:** 61 22 34 23
Fax: 61 22 35 30
Titles:
GAUSDØL'N - LOKALAVISA FOR GAUSDAL

GENERALINSPEKTØREN FOR HEIMEVERNET 1628607
Oslo mil/Akershus festning, 0015 OSLO
Tel: 23 09 81 23 **Fax:** 23 09 81 24
Titles:
HV-BLADET

GENO - AVL OG SEMIN 1732653
Holsetgata 22, 2326 HAMAR **Tel:** 62 52 06 00
Titles:
BUSKAP

GEOFORUM 1629026
GeoForum, Kvernberggata 5, 3510 HØNEFOSS
Tel: 32 12 31 66 **Fax:** 32 12 06 16
Titles:
POSISJON

GEOPUBLISHING AS 1794235
GeoPublishing co/NGU, Postboks 6315 Sluppen, 7491 TRONDHEIM **Tel:** 73904090 **Fax:** 73921620
Titles:
GEO

GLÅMDALEN AS 1627803
PB 757, 2204 KONGSVINGER **Tel:** 62 88 25 00
Fax: 62 88 25 70
Titles:
GLÅMDALEN

GLASS OG FASADEFORENINGEN 1783574
Glass og Fasadeforeningen, Fridtjof Nansens vei 19, 0369 OSLO **Tel:** 47 47 47 05
Titles:
GLASS & FASADE

GRAFILL - NORSK ORGANISASJON FOR VILSUELL KOMMUNIKASJON 1736816
Skovveien 20, 0505 OSLO **Tel:** 22 12 82 00
Titles:
SNITT

GRIEG MEDIA AS 1792046
Pb 287 Sentrum, 5012 BERGEN **Tel:** 55 21 31 00
Fax: 55213140
Titles:
VI OVER 60

GRØNN HVERDAG 1757623
Grensen 9B, 0159 OSLO **Tel:** 23 10 95 50
Fax: 23 10 95 51
Titles:
GRONNHVERDAG.NO
KLIMAKLUBBEN.NO

GRØNN HVERDAG V/ EIRIN FREMSTAD 1794335
Grensen 9B, 0159 OSLO **Tel:** 23109550
Fax: 23109551
Titles:
GRØNN HVERDAG MAGASIN

GRY BJØRHOVDE 1747179
Kirkegaten 20, 0153 OSLO **Tel:** 22 40 12 00
Fax: 22401201
Titles:
BO BEDRE
BO BEDRE; BOBEDRENORGE.NO

GUDBRANDSDØLEN DAGNINGEN AS 1680651
Pb. 954, 2604 LILLEHAMMER **Tel:** 61 22 10 00
Fax: 61 25 09 20
Titles:
GUDBRANDSDØLEN DAGNINGEN

GYLDENDAL NORSK FORLAG AS 1628370
Gyldendal Akademisk, Pb. 6860 St. Olavs Plass, 0130 OSLO **Tel:** 22 03 42 71 **Fax:** 22 03 41 05
Titles:
VINDUET

H. ASCHEHOUG & CO 1793950
H. Aschehoug & Co, Pb. 363 Sentrum, 0102 OSLO **Tel:** 22 40 04 00
Titles:
AGORA

H. ASCHEHOUG & CO. W. NYGAARD AS 1794367
Pb 363, Sentrum, 0102 OSLO **Tel:** 22400406
Fax: 22206395
Titles:
SAMTIDEN

HADELAND AS 1792902
Pb. 227, 2711 GRAN **Tel:** 61 31 31 32
Fax: 61 31 31 01
Titles:
HADELAND

HALDEN ARBEIDERBLAD AS 1680646
Pb. 113, 1751 HALDEN **Tel:** 69 21 56 00
Fax: 69 21 56 01
Titles:
HALDEN ARBEIDERBLAD

HAMAR MEDIA AS 1793042
Pb. 262, 2302 HAMAR **Fax:** 62 51 95 55
Titles:
HAMAR ARBEIDERBLAD

HANDEL OG KONTOR I NORGE 1628374
Pb. 231, Sentrum, 0103 OSLO **Tel:** 23 06 33 80
Fax: 23 06 11 11
Titles:
HK-NYTT

HARALD A. MØLLER AS 1628800
Pb. 46 Kjelsås, 0411 OSLO **Tel:** 22 95 33 00
Fax: 22 95 33 90
Titles:
VOLKSWAGEN MAGASINET

HARDANGER FOLKEBLAD AS 1627812
Pb. 374, 5750 ODDA **Tel:** 53 65 06 00
Fax: 53 65 06 21
Titles:
HARDANGER-FOLKEBLAD.NO

HARDWARE ONLINE AS 1791418
C/O Mediehuset Tek, Postboks 1314 Vika, 0110 OSLO **Tel:** 22 82 32 36 **Fax:** 22 82 32 33
Titles:
GAMER.NO
HARDWARE.NO

HARSTAD TIDENDE AS 1627813
Pb. 85, 9481 HARSTAD **Tel:** 77 01 80 00
Fax: 77 01 80 05
Titles:
HARSTAD TIDENDE
HARSTAD TIDENDE; KULTURREDAKSJONEN
HARSTAD TIDENDE; SPORTREDAKSJONEN

HAUGESUNDS AVIS AS 1793013
Pb. 2024 Postterminalen, 5504 HAUGESUND
Tel: 52 72 00 00 **Fax:** 52 72 04 44
Titles:
HAUGESUNDS AVIS

HEGNAR MEDIA AS 1791450
Pb 724 Skøyen, 0214 OSLO **Tel:** 2329 63 00
Fax: 2329 63 01
Titles:
FINANSAVISEN
HEGNAR ONLINE
INTERIØR MAGASINET
KAPITAL

HELSENETT AS 1692250
Helsenett AS, P.T. Mallingsvei 40d, 0286 OSLO
Titles:
HELSENETT.NO

HELSETILSYNET 1692251
Pb. 8128 Dep, 0032 OSLO **Tel:** 21 52 99 00
Fax: 21 52 99 99
Titles:
HELSETILSYNET

HENNING JACOBSEN 1747539
Pb. 524, 1401 SKI **Tel:** 22 20 80 90
Titles:
IN-PUBLISH

HERØYNYTT 1651299
Pb. 187, 6099 FOSNAVÅG **Tel:** 9910 6090
Titles:
HERØYNYTT

HESTEGUIDEN.COM AS 1650402
Pb. 386 Økern, NO-0513 OSLO
Titles:
HESTEGUIDEN.COM

HESTEPORTALEN AS 1650311
Klebervn 3, 1540 VETSBY **Tel:** 64 98 51 40
Fax: 64 98 51 49
Titles:
HEST.NO

HJEMMET MORTENSEN ANNONSEBLADER AS 1629053
Hjemmet Mortensen Fagmedia AS/BruktNytt, Postboks 67, Bryn, 0611 OSLO **Tel:** 22757520
Fax: 22757521
Titles:
BRUKTNYTT
MASKINREGISTERET
MC-BØRSEN

HJEMMET MORTENSEN AS 1628091
Sandakerveien 116, 0441 OSLO **Tel:** 22585000
Fax: 22585239
Titles:
ALT OM FISKE
BEDRE HELSE
BONYTT
BONYTT; BONYTT.NO
C!
DOKTORONLINE.NO
FAMILIEN
FORELDRE & BARN
GRAVID
HJEMME-PC
HJEMME-PC; HJEMMEPC.NO
HJEMMET
HYTTELIV
KAMILLE
KAMILLE.NO
KAMPANJE
NORSK UKEBLAD
DET NYE
ROM123
SHAPE-UP
VI MENN
VI MENN BÅT
VI MENN BIL
VI MENN FOTBALL
VIMENN.NO

HJEMMET MORTENSEN FAGMEDIA AS 1747916
Pb. 67 Bryn, 0611 OSLO **Tel:** 22 75 75 00
Titles:
TRANSPORTMAGASINET

HJEMMET MORTENSEN FAGMEDIAAS 1743006
Pb. 67, Bryn, 0611 OSLO **Tel:** 22757500
Fax: 22757521
Titles:
ANLEGGSMAGASINET

HL MEDIA AS 1794122
Østre Akervei 22, 0581 OSLO **Tel:** 22659555
Titles:
STUFF

HØRSELSHEMMEDES LANDSFORBUND (HLF) 1794164
Pb 6652 Etterstad, 0609 OSLO **Tel:** 22639900
Titles:
DIN HØRSEL

HUMAN RIGHTS SERVICE 1743976
Møllergata 9, 0179 OSLO **Tel:** 22 33 80 00
Titles:
RIGHTS.NO

HUMAN-ETISK FORBUND 1643973
Pb 6744 St. Olavs Plass, 0130 OSLO
Tel: 23 15 60 00 **Fax:** 23 15 60 21
Titles:
FRI TANKE

HUMAN-ETISK FORBUNDS 1774281
Pb 6744, St. Olavs plass, 0130 OSLO
Tel: 23156020 **Fax:** 23156021
Titles:
FRITANKE.NO

HUSEIERNES LANDSFORBUND 1791788
Fred Olsens Gt. 5, 0152 OSLO **Tel:** 22 47 75 00
Fax: 22 41 19 90
Titles:
HUS & BOLIG

HYTTA VÅR AS 1794025
Sundrev. 81, 3570 ÅL **Tel:** 32 08 21 33
Fax: 32 08 12 65
Titles:
HYTTA VÅR

ICA 1794312
Kristian Augusts gate 14, 0164 OSLO
Tel: 23358330
Titles:
GLAD I MAT

IDEFORLAGET MALKA METTE 1643987
Idéforlaget Nydalen Allé 23, 0484 OSLO
Tel: 92 23 95 96 **Fax:** 22 22 02 22
Titles:
KUNDEFOKUS
SALGSIMPULS
SALGSLEDELSE

IDÉHISTORISK TIDSSKRIFT ARR 1793954
Huitfeldts Gate 15, 0253 OSLO **Tel:** 22 44 87 76
Titles:
ARR - IDEHISTORISK TIDSSKRIFT

IDG AS 1747864
Pb. 9090 Grønland, 0133 OSLO **Tel:** 22 05 30 00
Fax: 22 05 30 21
Titles:
PC WORLD ONLINE

IDG MAGAZINES NORGE 1653793
Pb. 9090 Grønland, 0133 OSLO **Tel:** 22 05 30 00
Titles:
COMPUTERWORLD.NO
IDG.NO

IDG MAGAZINES NORGE AS 1649857
IDG Magazines Norge, Postboks 9090, Grønland, 0133 OSLO **Tel:** 22053000
Fax: 22053051
Titles:
COMPUTERWORLD
IT-BRANSJEN
IT-BRANSJEN - NETT
IT-KARRIERE

IKO-FORLAGET AS 1649797
IKO - Kirkelig pedagogisk senter, Pb. 2623, St. Hanshaugen, 0103 OSLO **Tel:** 22 59 53 00
Fax: 22 59 53 01
Titles:
PRISMET

IN MEDIA MARKEDSKOMMUNIKASJON AS 1644023
Pb 88 Sentrum, 4001 STAVANGER **Tel:** 51849500
Fax: 51849505
Titles:
BOINFORM

INDRE AKERSHUS BLAD AS 1792562
Pb. 68, 1941 BJØRKELANGEN **Tel:** 63 85 48 00
Fax: 63855590
Titles:
INDRE AKERSHUS BLAD

DEN INDRE SJØMANNSMISJON 1643956
Postboks 1904 Damsgård, 5828 BERGEN
Tel: 55349310 **Fax:** 55349311
Titles:
TRYGG HAVN

INFO FORLAG AS 1794369
Info Forlag AS, Postboks 1113, 1705 SARPSBORG **Tel:** 69971790 **Fax:** 69971717
Titles:
RETT OG PLIKT I ARBEIDSLIVET

INFO-COMPAGNIET AS 1644268
Pb 183, 1377 BILLINGSTAD **Tel:** 66983860
Fax: 66983869
Titles:
BENSINFORHANDLEREN

INFORMASJONSKONTORET FOR FARGE OG INTERIØR 1791787
IFI - Informasjonskontoret for farge og interiør, Hamang terrasse 63, 1336 SANDVIKA
Tel: 67 55 46 80 **Fax:** 67554681
Titles:
FARGEMAGASINET
INSPIRASJON

INFOTEK AS 1793716
2580 FOLLDAL **Tel:** 62 49 05 55 **Fax:** 62 49 05 63
Titles:
FOLLDALS MARKED

INGENIØRFORLAGET AS 1628162
Pb 5844 Majorstua, 0308 OSLO **Tel:** 23 19 93 00
Fax: 23 19 93 01
Titles:
TEKNISK UKEBLAD
VÅRE VEGER

INGENIØRFORØLAGET AS 1747893
Pb 5844 Majorstua, 0308 OSLO **Tel:** 23 19 93 00
Fax: 23 19 93 01
Titles:
TU.NO

INGENIØRNYTT AS 1793994
Pb. 164, 1332 ØSTERÅS **Tel:** 67 16 34 99
Fax: 67 16 34 55
Titles:
INGENIØRNYTT

INGRID M. GJERDE 1757438
HM Kongens Garde, Pb 7 Røa, 0701 OSLO
Tel: 23 09 80 00 **Fax:** 23 09 72 78
Titles:
GARDISTEN

INSIDE PUBLISH AS 1794228
Pb. 524, 1401 SKI **Tel:** 22208090
Titles:
IN-PUBLISH.NO

INSIDE STUDENTAVIS 1628601
Nydalsveien 15, 0484 OSLO **Tel:** 464 10 931
Titles:
INSIDE 24 - STUDENTAVISEN PÅ BI

INSITUTT FOR KULTURSTUDIER OG ORIENTALSKE SPRÅK 1794381
Institutt for kulturstudier og orientalske språk, Pb 1010 Blindern, 0315 OSLO **Tel:** 22854549
Titles:
BABYLON

INSTITUTT FOR LINGVISTIKK OG LITTERATURVITENSKAP, UIB 1793946
Sydnesplass 7, 5007
Titles:
PROSOPOPEIA

INSTITUTT FOR SAMFUNNSFORSKNING 1794384
Pb. 3233 Elisenberg, 0208 OSLO **Tel:** 23086100
Fax: 23086101
Titles:
ISF SAMMENDRAG

INTER MEDIA RESEARCH 1654437
Pb 1118, 1787 BERG I ØSTFOLD
Titles:
SAMFUNNSMAGASINET

INTERFLORA NORGE AL 1793693
Billingstadsletta 13, 1396 BILLINGSTAD
Tel: 66857500 **Fax:** 66857575
Titles:
BLOMSTER

INTERNASJONAL KVINNELIGA FOR FRED OG FRIHET (IKFF) 1794364
Pb 8810 Youngstorget, 0028 OSLO **Tel:** 23010340
Fax: 23010301
Titles:
FRED OG FRIHET

INTERNATIONAL DATA GROUP MAGAZINES NORGE AS 1794067
Pb 9090 Grønland, 0133 OSLO **Tel:** 22053000
Titles:
NETTVERK & KOMMUNIKASJON

INTERNATIONAL DATA GROUP NORGE AS 1791880
PB 9090 Grønland, 0133 OSLO **Tel:** 22 05 30 00
Fax: 22053021
Titles:
PC WORLD NORGE

INTRAFISH MEDIA AS 1629168
Bontelabo 2, 5003 BERGEN **Tel:** 55 21 33 00
Fax: 55 21 33 40
Titles:
INTRAFISH.NO

IO, IB, IV 1654012
Militærhospitalet, Grev Wedels Plass 1, 0151 OSLO **Tel:** 22 40 50 90 **Fax:** 22 40 50 91
Titles:
ST. HALLVARD

ITPRO ENK 1791451
Tormods gate 3b, 7030 TRONDHEIM
Tel: 46446624
Titles:
ITPRO.NO

JAN EIRIK SCHØITZ 1748458
Pb. 2352 Strømsø, 3003 DRAMMEN
Tel: 99798302
Titles:
AMNYTT MAGAZINE

JENS CHR BRYNILDSEN 1686589
Grønland 18, 0188 OSLO **Tel:** 906 91 786
Titles:
FLASHMAGAZINE

JENS HENNEBERG 1794068
Komputer for alle, Kirkegaten 20, 0153 OSLO
Tel: 23068705 **Fax:** 23068730
Titles:
KOMPUTER FOR ALLE

JENTER I SKOGBRUKET 1794024
Serviceboks 606, 4809 ARENDAL **Tel:** 37 01 75 17
Titles:
JENTER I SKOGBRUKET

JURISTFORENINGEN 1628722
Karl Johansgt. 47, 0162 OSLO **Tel:** 22 85 98 25
Fax: 22 85 98 02
Titles:
STUD.JUR

KABB - KRISTENT ARBEID BLANT BLINDE OG SVAKSYNTE 1793692
Pb 333, 1802 ASKIM **Tel:** 69 81 69 81
Fax: 69 88 57 66
Titles:
KABB-NYTT

KAMPANJE FORLAG AS 1791477
Prinsens gate 22, 0157 OSLO **Tel:** 22 33 31 00
Titles:
KAMPANJE.COM

KFO 1643934
Postboks 9202 Grønland, 0134 OSLO
Tel: 21 01 36 00 **Fax:** 21 01 36 50
Titles:
KOMMUNIKÉ
KOMMUNIKÉ; KOMMUNIKE.NO

KILDEN SENTER FOR KVINNE- OG KJØNNSFORSKNING 1644016
Grensen 5, 0159 OSLO **Tel:** 24 05 59 95
Fax: 24 05 59 60
Titles:
TIDSSKRIFT FOR KJØNNSFORSKNING

KIRKENS INFORMASJONSTJENESTE, KIRKERÅDET 1649866
Pb. 799 Sentrum, 0106 OSLO **Tel:** 23 08 12 00
Fax: 23 08 12 01
Titles:
KIRKEAKTUELT

KIRKENS NØDHJELP/ NORWEGIAN 1794370
Pb 7100, St.Olavs Plass, 0130 OSLO
Tel: 22092700 **Fax:** 22092720
Titles:
KIRKENS NØDHJELP MAGASINET

KJETIL FAYE LUND 1735633
Pb. 51, 4854 NEDENES **Tel:** 909 23 795
Titles:
BUSINESS Q4 SØRLANDET

KJØTTBRANSJENS LANDSFORBUND 1692259
Fred Olsens gate 5, 0152 OSLO **Tel:** 23244470
Fax: 23244480
Titles:
KJØTTBRANSJEN

KLOKKERGÅRDEN MEDIA AS 1773149
Postboks 10, 1851 0164 OSLO MYSEN
Tel: 922 58 954
Titles:
GAMLE HUS & HAGER

KOMMUNAL RAPPORT AS 1628100
Pb. 1940 Vika, 0125 OSLO **Tel:** 24 13 64 50
Fax: 22 83 23 72
Titles:
KOMMUNAL RAPPORT

KOMMUNALØKONOMISK FORLAG 1628452
NKK Kommunaløkonomisk forlag, Henrik Ibsensgt. 20, 0255 OSLO **Tel:** 22 94 76 93
Titles:
KOMMUNAL ØKONOMI

KONDIS 1643958
Dovregata 2, 0170 OSLO **Tel:** 22 60 94 70 **Fax:** 22 60 90 67
Titles:
KONDIS

KONTURMEDIA 1651138
Titles:
KONTURTIDSSKRIFT

KREATIVT FORUM 1628778
Fredensborgvn. 24 M, 0177 OSLO **Tel:** 22 03 30 00 **Fax:** 22 03 30 01
Titles:
KF UKESLUTT
KREATIVT FORUM

KREFTFORENINGEN 1794158
Pb. 4 Sentrum, 0101 OSLO **Tel:** 07877 **Fax:** 22866610
Titles:
SAMMEN MOT KREFT

KRETSLØPET AS 1794329
Boks 541 Sentrum, 015 OSLO **Tel:** 92433582
Titles:
KRETSLØPET

KRIGSINVALIDEFORBUNDET 1628416
Pb 749 Sentrum, 0106 OSLO **Tel:** 23 09 50 12 **Fax:** 23 09 50 11
Titles:
KRIGSINVALIDEN

KRIMINALTEKNISK FORUM 1651265
Pb. 240, 4001 STAVANGER **Tel:** 51 89 92 98
Titles:
BEVIS - KRIMINALTEKNISK FORUM

KRISTELIG FOLKEPARTI 1732585
KrF v/Idéredaksjonen, Pb. 478 Sentrum, 0105 OSLO **Tel:** 23102800 **Fax:** 23102810
Titles:
MAGASINET IDÉ

KRISTEN MEDIAALLIANSE DRIFT AS 1649851
Fjøsangerveien 28, 5054 BERGEN **Tel:** 55 92 29 00 **Fax:** 55 29 55 00
Titles:
NORGE I DAG

KRISTENT ARBEID BLANT BLINDE OG SVAKSYNTE 1793690
Pb 333, 1802 ASKIM **Tel:** 69 81 69 81 **Fax:** 69885766
Titles:
LIVET

KRISTENT PEDAGOGISK FORBUND 1628420
Kristent Pedagogisk Forum, Collets gt 43, 01456 OSLO **Tel:** 954 564 22
Titles:
FAVN (EX. KPF-KONTAKTEN)

KS 1686949
Haakon VIIs gate 9, 0161 OSLO **Tel:** 24 13 28 33
Titles:
KS.NO

KULDEFORLAGET AS 1793997
Marielundsveien 5, 1358 JAR **Tel:** 67 12 06 59 **Fax:** 67121790
Titles:
KULDE SKANDINAVIA

KUNST OG DESIGN I SKOLEN 1643982
Kunst og Design i skolen, Postboks 4703, 0506 OSLO **Tel:** 24 14 11 90
Titles:
TIDSSKRIFTET FORM

KUNSTKLUBBEN A/S 1680725
Postboks 2644 St.Hanshaugen, 0175 OSLO **Tel:** 22 99 54 18
Titles:
MAGASINET KUNST

KVINNEFRONTEN 1794382
Osterhausgata 27, 0183 OSLO **Tel:** 95139006
Titles:
FETT - FEMINISTISK TIDSSKRIFT

KVINNEFRONTEN I NORGE 1628423
Osterhausgt 27, 0183 OSLO **Tel:** 22 20 64 00
Titles:
VI ER MANGE

KVINNERS FRIVILLIGE BEREDSKAP 1628424
Pb. 796 Sentrum, 0106 OSLO **Tel:** 22 42 49 12 **Fax:** 22 42 85 52
Titles:
TRYGGE SAMFUNN

KVINNFORSK 1654122
KVINNEFORSK-Senter For Kvinne- og kjønnsforsk - UiT, 9037 TROMSØ **Tel:** 77 64 52 40 **Fax:** 77 64 64 20
Titles:
KVINNFORSKS SKRIFTSERIE

LAAGENDALSPOSTEN AS 1680656
Pb. 480, 3605 KONGSBERG **Tel:** 32 77 10 00
Titles:
LAAGENDALSPOSTEN

LANDBRUKSSAMVIRKETS INFORMASJONSKONTOR; MIDT-NORGE 1680729
Landbrukstidende, 7500 STJØRDAL **Tel:** 90 12 69 63
Titles:
LANDBRUKSTIDENDE

LANDSFORBUNDET DISSIMILIS 1732584
Emma Hjorths vei 50, 1336 SANDVIKA **Tel:** 67 17 48 80 **Fax:** 67 13 16 10
Titles:
CRESCENDO

LANDSFORBUNDET MOT STOFFMISBRUK 1629042
Grønland 12, 0188 OSLO **Tel:** 23 08 05 50 **Fax:** 23 08 05 51
Titles:
MOT STOFF

LANDSFORENINGEN FOR HJERTE OG LUNGESYKE 1644120
Pb 4375 Nydalen, 0402 OSLO **Tel:** 22799300 **Fax:** 22223833
Titles:
DET NYTTER

LANDSFORENINGEN FOR NYREPASIENTER 1628429
Pb 6727 Etterstad, 0609 OSLO **Tel:** 23 05 45 50 **Fax:** 23 05 45 51
Titles:
LNT-NYTT

LANDSFORENINGEN UVENTET BARNEDØD 1767859
Landsforeningen uventet barnedød, Ole Fladagers gt. 1 A, 0353 OSLO **Tel:** 22 54 52 00 **Fax:** 22 54 52 01
Titles:
OSS FORELDRE I MELLOM

LANDSLAGET DRAMA I SKOLEN 1628431
co. Hedda Fredly, Kongensgate 16, 0153 OSLO **Tel:** 97 66 63 61
Titles:
DRAMA-NORDISK DRAMAPEDAGOGISK TIDSSKRIFT

LANDSLAGET FOR NORSKUNDERVISNING LNU 1628437
Astrid Elisabeth Kleiveland, Kastellhagen 6a, 1176 OSLO **Tel:** 92 68 37 21
Titles:
NORSKLÆRAREN/NORSKLÆREREN

LANDSLAGET FOR SPELEMENN 1628436
Tyinvegen 27, 2900 FAGERNES **Tel:** 907 68 797 **Fax:** 61 35 99 01
Titles:
BLADET FOLKEMUSIKK

LANDSLAGET FYSISK FOSTRING I SKOLEN 1649869
Landslaget Fysisk Fostring i Skolen, Møllegaten 10, 3111 TØNSBERG **Tel:** 33 31 53 00 **Fax:** 33 31 52 66
Titles:
KROPPSØVING

LANDSORGANISASJONEN I NORGE 1644009
Postboks 231 Sentrum, 0103 OSLO **Tel:** 23063359
Titles:
LO-AKTUELT

LATIN-AMERIKA GRUPPENE I NORGE 1628845
LAG Norge, Osterhausgate 27, 0183 OSLO **Tel:** 22 98 93 20 **Fax:** 55 58 99 11
Titles:
LATINAMERIKA

LINC MEDIA AS 1649863
Tørkoppveien 10, 1570 DILLING **Tel:** 69700570 **Fax:** 69700550
Titles:
VVS AKTUELT
VVS AKTUELT; VVSAKTUELT.NO

LINDESNES AS 1627826
Pb. 41, 4501 MANDAL **Tel:** 38 27 10 00 **Fax:** 38 27 10 01
Titles:
LINDESNES AVIS

LINHART & RINGHOF 1753208
Vakåsveien 9, 1395 HVALSTAD **Tel:** 66 98 11 56
Titles:
DET BESTE

LIZACOM.COM 1744110
Lizacom DA, Pb. 123, 2150 ÅRNES **Tel:** 63 90 37 10
Titles:
LINUXMAGASINET

LO STAT OSLO 1643932
Møllergata 10, 0179 OSLO **Tel:** 23 06 15 61 **Fax:** 23062271
Titles:
MAGASINET AKTUELL

LOFOTPOSTEN AS 1680676
Avisgata 15, 8305 SVOLVÆR **Tel:** 76 06 78 00 **Fax:** 76 07 00 09
Titles:
LOFOTPOSTEN

MAN. UNITED SUPPORTERS CLUB SCANDINAVIAN BRANCH 1793617
Pb 1992, Nordnes, 5817 BERGEN **Tel:** 69 16 63 94 **Fax:** 55962033
Titles:
UNITED SUPPORTEREN

MANDAG MORGEN NORGE AS 1644264
Postboks 1180 Sentrum, 0181 OSLO **Tel:** 22 99 18 18 **Fax:** 22 99 18 10
Titles:
MANDAG MORGEN

MANGSETH AS 1692238
Høilundhagen 4, 1440 DRØBAK **Tel:** 64 98 89 10
Titles:
DE DANSEGLADE

MARGMEDIA DA 1794391
Strandveien 95, 9006 TROMSØ **Tel:** 77600423
Titles:
MARG - NOTATER FRA RANDSONEN

MARITIMT MAGASIN AS 1644262
Postboks 44, 6282 BRATTVÅG **Tel:** 70 20 78 65
Titles:
MARITIMT MAGASIN

MAT&HELSE AS 1686786
Tun Media AS, Postboks 9309 Grønland, 0135 OSLO **Tel:** 21314408
Titles:
MAT & HELSE

MATAVISEN.NO / MICROENTA MEDIA GROUP AS 1773148
Microenta Media Group AS, Kingos gate 15, 0457 OSLO **Tel:** 92 89 93 05
Titles:
MATAVISEN.NO

MATFORSK AS 1654560
Postboks 6122, 9291 TROMSÆ **Tel:** 77 62 90 00 **Fax:** 77 62 91 00
Titles:
NOFIMA.NO

MATTILSYNET 1654185
Pb. 383, 2381 BRUMUNDDAL **Tel:** 23 21 66 32 **Fax:** 23 21 70 01
Titles:
MATPORTALEN
MATTILSYNET

MED ISRAEL FOR FRED 1794360
Pb 9101, 3006 DRAMMEN **Tel:** 41176780
Titles:
MIDTØSTEN I FOKUS

MEDIA OSLO AS 1643933
Media Oslo AS, Boks 119 Manglerud, 0612 OSLO **Tel:** 23 15 85 00
Titles:
KJEMI
SKOGINDUSTRI
SKOGINDUSTRI; SKOGINDUSTRI.NO

MEDIA ØST TRYKK AS 1627766
Pb 235, 2001 LILLESTRØM **Tel:** 63 80 50 50 **Fax:** 63 80 48 70
Titles:
ROMERIKES BLAD

MEDIA-FON AS 1793682
Pb. 2385, 3003 DRAMMEN STRØMSØ **Tel:** 32 20 56 00
Titles:
STALLSKRIKET

MEDIAHUSET AS 1628862
Niels Juels gate 5, 0242 OSLO **Tel:** 975 17 980
Titles:
MUSIKKPRAKSIS

MEDIAHUSET NETTAVISEN AS 1791524
Pb. 9386 Grønland, 0135 OSLO **Tel:** 21 00 60 00 **Fax:** 22570942
Titles:
NETTAVISEN; SIDE2.NO

MEDIANAVIGERING AS 1794317
Gartnerveien 1, 1394 NESBRU **Tel:** 21377790 **Fax:** 66774061
Titles:
SEILMAGASINET

MEDIEFABRIKKEN AS 1649823
Fri Flyt AS, Mølleparken 6, 0459 OSLO **Tel:** 22 04 06 00 **Fax:** 22 04 06 09
Titles:
KLATRING

MEDIEHUSET DIGITAL AS 1747704
PB 9025 Grønland, 0133 OSLO **Tel:** 21 00 60 00 **Fax:** 22 20 21 11
Titles:
DIGIT.NO
MOBILEN.NO
TEKNOFIL
TEKNOFIL.NO

MEDIEHUSET MOSS AVIS AS 1793065
Pb. 248/250, 1501 MOSS **Tel:** 69 20 50 00
Titles:
MOSS AVIS
MOSS AVIS; KULTURREDAKSJONEN

MEDIEHUSET NÆRINGSEIENDOM AS 1794103
Pb 2374 Solli, 0201 OSLO **Tel:** 23115600 **Fax:** 23115601
Titles:
NÆRINGSEIENDOM

MEDIEHUSET NETTAVISEN AS 1791478
Pb. 9386 Grønland, 0135 OSLO **Tel:** 21 00 60 00 **Fax:** 22570942
Titles:
NETTAVISEN
NETTAVISEN; SPORTREDAKSJONEN

MEDIEHUSET OPP AS 1649850
Inge Krokanns vei 11, 7340 OPPDAL **Tel:** 72 42 40 04 **Fax:** 72 42 25 25
Titles:
OPP

MEDIEHUSET ØSTLANDS-POSTEN AS 1745364
Postboks 5, 3285 LARVIK **Tel:** 33 16 30 00 **Fax:** 33 16 30 01
Titles:
ØSTLANDS-POSTEN

MEDLEX NORSK HELSEINFORMASJON DA 1794171
MEDLEX Norsk Helseinformasjon, Pb 6611 St.Olavsplass, 0129 OSLO **Tel:** 23354700 **Fax:** 23354701
Titles:
MEDISINSK INFORMASJON

MEIDASTUD AS 1746070
Elgesetergt. 1, 7030 TRONDHEIM **Tel:** 73 53 18 13
Titles:
UNDER DUSKEN; UNDERDUSKEN.NO

MENTOR MEDIER 1794387
Pb. 1180 Sentrum, 0170 OSLO **Tel:** 22310224 **Fax:** 22310305
Titles:
LE MONDE DIPLOMATIQUE

MENTOR MEDIER AS 1735641
Pb. 1180 Sentrum, 0107 OSLO **Tel:** 22 31 02 20 **Fax:** 22 31 02 25
Titles:
GRÜNDER ØKONOMISK RAPPORT
PROGRAMBLADET
UKEAVISENLEDELSE.NO

MIC 1675612
Pb. 2674 Solli, 0203 OSLO **Tel:** 23 27 63 00 **Fax:** 23 27 63 01
Titles:
BALLADE.NO

MICROSOFT NORGE AS 1794020
Pb. 43, Lilleaker, 0216 OSLO **Tel:** 22022500 **Fax:** 22950664
Titles:
MICROSOFT MAGAZINE

MODELLJERNBANEFOREN-INGEN I NORGE 1628867
Modelljernbaneforeningen i Norge, Pb. 467 Skøyen, 0213 OSLO **Tel:** 994 18 736
Titles:
MJ-BLADET

MODERNE PRODUKSJON AS 1792478
Pb. 163, 1332 ØSTERÅS **Tel:** 671634 00 **Fax:** 67163410
Titles:
MODERNE PRODUKSJON

MOMA PUBLISHING AS 1791581
Pb. 5134 Majorstua, 0302 OSLO **Tel:** 23 36 98 00 **Fax:** 23 36 98 01
Titles:
ELLE

MORGENBLADET AS 1792905
Karl Johansgt 25, 0159 OSLO **Tel:** 21006300 **Fax:** 21006301
Titles:
MORGENBLADET

MOTOMEDIA AS 1791519
Postboks 2123, 9507 ALTA **Tel:** 78 44 06 70 **Fax:** 78442508
Titles:
SCOOTERNORGE.NO

MOTOPRESS AS 1629122
Smalvollveien 63 Etg 2, 0667 OSLO **Tel:** 23401030 **Fax:** 23401034
Titles:
BIKE
BIKE.NO

MOTOR CYCLE AVISA AS 1628856
Box 3009, 4392 SANDNES **Tel:** 51675300 **Fax:** 51672326
Titles:
MC-AVISA
MC-AVISA; MC-AVISA.NO

MOTORFLYSEKSJONEN, NORSK LUFTSPORTFORBUND 1747463
Flynytt, NLF, Pb. 383 Sentrum, 0102 OSLO **Tel:** 23 01 04 50 **Fax:** 23 01 04 51
Titles:
FLYNYTT

MOTORFØRERNES AVHOLDSFORBUND 1794297
Pb 80 Alnabru, 0614 OSLO **Tel:** 22956969 **Fax:** 22956968
Titles:
MOTORFØREREN

MULTIPPEL SKLEROSE FORBUNDET I NORGE 1794155
Tollbugata 35, 0157 OSLO **Tel:** 22477992 **Fax:** 22477991
Titles:
MS-BLADET

MUR+BETONG AS 1794059
Pb. 102 Lilleaker, 0216 OSLO **Tel:** 22 87 84 21 **Fax:** 22 87 84 01
Titles:
MUR+BETONG

MUSIKK-KULTUR AS 1653764
Postboks 9246 Grønland, 0134 OSLO **Tel:** 22 05 28 20 **Fax:** 22 05 28 21
Titles:
MUSIKK-KULTUR

MUSIQ.NO 1629166
Co / Geir Atle Ellingsen, Tøane 11, 4760 BIRKELAND
Titles:
MUSIQ

NÆRINGSFORENINGEN I STAVANGER-REGIONEN 1794380
Pb. 182, 4001 STAVANGER **Tel:** 51510880 **Fax:** 51510881
Titles:
ROSENKILDEN - NÆRINGSLIVSMAGASINET

NÆRINGSLIVET MEDIA V/KENT STEINHAUG 1710181
Luksefjellveien 186, 3721 SKIEN **Tel:** 35 59 49 00 **Fax:** 35 59 00 80
Titles:
NÆRINGSLIVET I TELEMARK

NÆRINGSLIVETS FORLAG AS 1793712
Pb. 1180 Sentrum, 0107 OSLO **Tel:** 22310210 **Fax:** 22310215
Titles:
UKEAVISEN LEDELSE

NÆRINGSLIVSAVISEN NA24.NO AS 1743572
Postboks 9386 Grønland, 0135 OSLO **Tel:** 400 13 500
Titles:
NA24.NO
NA24.NO; PROPAGANDA

NÆRINGSLIVSAVISENNA24 AS 1743289
Postboks 9386 Grønland, 0135 OSLO **Tel:** 400 13 500
Titles:
NA24.NO; FINANS

NÆRINGSRAPPORT AS 1794223
Pb 1166, 9262 TROMSØ **Tel:** 40052883 **Fax:** 77639051
Titles:
NÆRINGSRAPPORT

NAF / HJEMMET MORTENSEN AS 1791855
Østensjøveien 14 på Helsfyr, 0441 OSLO **Tel:** 22 58 50 00 **Fax:** 22 58 59 59
Titles:
MOTOR

NASJONALFORENINGEN FOR FOLKEHELSEN 1628192
Pb 7139 Majorstuen, 0307 OSLO **Tel:** 23120000 **Fax:** 23120001
Titles:
AKTUELT FRA NASJONALFORENINGEN

NATIONEN AS 1793126
Pb. 9390 Grønland, 0135 OSLO **Tel:** 21310000
Titles:
NATIONEN

NATUR OG UNGDOM 1794327
Pb 4783 Sofienberg, 0506 OSLO **Tel:** 23327400 **Fax:** 23327429
Titles:
PUTSJ

NATURFAGSENTERET 1692275
Pb. 1099 Blindern, 0317 OSLO **Fax:** 22 85 44 09
Titles:
NORDINA

NATURVERNFORBUNDET I OSLO OG AKERSHUS 1794328
Naturvernforbundet i Oslo og Akershus, Maridalsveien 120, 0461 OSLO **Tel:** 22383520
Titles:
GREVLINGEN

NATURVITERFORBUNDET 1794308
Keysers Gt. 5, 0165 OSLO **Tel:** 22033400 **Fax:** 22033401
Titles:
NATURVITEREN

NELFOS ELINFORM 1692243
Pb. 5467 Majorstua, 0305 OSLO **Tel:** 23087700
Titles:
ELMAGASINET

NETTAVISEN 1768069
Postboks 9386 Grønland, 0323 OSLO **Tel:** 2100 6000 **Fax:** 2257 0942
Titles:
DITT DYR

NETTMEDIEHUSET AS 1735653
V/Roger Evensen, Riskestien 7, 1529 MOSS **Tel:** 90033545
Titles:
GAMERSWEB.NO

NHST 1753163
Pb. 1182, Sentrum, 0107 OSLO **Tel:** 22 00 10 00
Titles:
DAGENSIT.NO

NHST MEDIA GROUP 1763188
PO Box 1182 Sentrum, NO-0107 OSLO **Tel:** 24101700 **Fax:** 24101710
Titles:
RECHARGE AS
RECHARGE AS ~ HOUSTON
RECHARGE AS~ LONDON
RECHARGE AS~ STAVANGER
RECHARGE AS~RIO DE JANEIRO
RECHARGE AS~SINGAPORE
UPSTREAM
UPSTREAM ONLINE

NIFUSTEP STUDIER AV INNOVSJON FORSKNING OG UTDANNING 1653769
Wergelandsveien 7, 0167 OSLO **Tel:** 22 59 51 00 **Fax:** 22 59 51 01
Titles:
FORSKNINGSPOLITIKK

NINA FURU 1741725
Postboks 41 Sentrum, Pb. 41 Sentrum, 0101 OSLO **Tel:** 454 75 000
Titles:
WEB MAGASIN

NOFIMA AS 1794310
Muninbakken 9-13, Breivika, 9291 TROMSØ **Tel:** 77629000 **Fax:** 77629100
Titles:
MATNYTTIG

NOFU-KOMMUNIKASJONS-FORBUNDET 1653763
Pb 9187 Grønland, 0134 OSLO **Tel:** 21 01 36 00 **Fax:** 21 01 37 50
Titles:
NEGOTIA MAGASIN

NOPA - NORSK FORENING FOR KOMPONISTER OG TEKSTFORFAT 1692274
Kongensgt. 4, 0153 OSLO **Tel:** 22 47 30 00 **Fax:** 22 17 25 60
Titles:
NOPA-NYTT

NORAD 1628761
Pb 8034 Dep, 0030 OSLO **Tel:** 22 24 20 40
Fax: 22 24 05 72
Titles:
BISTANDSAKTUELT.NO

NORDAVIS AS 1627767
Labyrinten 5, 9510 ALTA **Tel:** 78 45 67 00
Fax: 78 45 67 40
Titles:
ALTAPOSTEN

NORDENS NYHETER AS 1794058
Postboks 76 Smestad, 0309 OSLO **Tel:** 22741498
Titles:
NORDENS NYHETER

NORDISK KJÆLEDYRFORLAG AS 1629069
Godtfredsensvei 4, 1617 FREDRIKSTAD
Tel: 92 09 51 22 **Fax:** 69 39 70 11
Titles:
HUND & FRITID

NORDMANNS-FORBUNDET 1628610
Nordmanns-Forbundet, Rådhusgata 23 B, 0158 OSLO **Tel:** 23 35 71 70 **Fax:** 23 35 71 75
Titles:
THE NORSEMAN

NORDNORSK KOMPETANSESENTER - RUS 1794194
KoRus-Nord, Pb. 385, 8505 NARVIK
Tel: 76966500 **Fax:** 76966879
Titles:
SPOR

NORDNORSK MAGASIN AS 1793890
Bankbygget, 9392 STONGLANDSEIDET
Tel: 77 85 46 10
Titles:
NORDNORSK MAGASIN

NORDRE AKER BUDSTIKKE AS 1793714
Postboks 79, Bryn, 0611 OSLO **Tel:** 23 20 56 60
Fax: 22 13 30 29
Titles:
NORDRE AKER BUDSTIKKE

NORDSTRANDS BLAD AS 1792132
Postboks 79, Bryn, 0611 OSLO **Tel:** 23 20 56 30
Fax: 23205601
Titles:
ØSTKANTAVISA

NOREGS KRISTELEGE FOLKEHØGSKOLELAG 1643992
Noregs Kristelege Folkehøgskolelag, Postboks 420 Sentrum, 0103 OSLO **Tel:** 22 47 43 00
Titles:
KRISTEN FOLKEHØGSKOLE

NOREGS MÅLLAG 1628884
Pb 474 Sentrum, 0105 OSLO **Tel:** 23 00 29 30
Fax: 23 00 29 31
Titles:
NORSK TIDEND

NORESKE MEDIA AS 1746010
Norske Media AS, c/o Olsvold & co AS, Postboks 34, 1483 SKYTTA **Tel:** 90882518
Titles:
AGI NORSK GRAFISK TIDSSKRIFT

NORGES ASTMA- OG ALLERGIFORBUND 1643916
Pb. 2603 St. Hanshaugen, 0131 OSLO
Tel: 23353535 **Fax:** 23353530
Titles:
ALLERGI I PRAKSIS
ASTMA ALLERGI

NORGES AUTORISERTE REGNSKAPSFØRERES FORENING 1769248
Pb. 99 Sentrum, 0101 OSLO **Tel:** 23 35 69 00
Fax: 23 35 69 20
Titles:
REGNSKAP & ØKONOMI

NORGES BEDRIFTSIDRETTSFORBUND 1769648
Norges Bedriftsidrettsforbund, Ullevål Stadion, Sognsveien 75, 0840 OSLO **Tel:** 21 02 94 68
Fax: 21 02 94 51
Titles:
AKTIV LIVSSTIL - AKTIVLIVSSTIL.NO

NORGES BILBRANSJEFORBUNDS SERVICEKONTOR 1628015
Norges Bilbransjeforbunds servicekontor, Pb. 2804 Solli, 0204 OSLO **Tel:** 22 54 21 00
Fax: 22 44 10 56
Titles:
BILBRANSJEN

NORGES BIRØKTERLAG 1628249
Dyrskuevegen 20, 2040 KLØFTA **Tel:** 63 94 20 80
Titles:
BIRØKTEREN

NORGES BLINDEFORBUND 1629396
Pb 5900 Majorstuen, 0308 OSLO **Tel:** 23 21 50 00
Fax: 23 21 50 72
Titles:
BLINDESAKEN
NORGES BLINDE

NORGES BOKSEFORBUND 1628889
Serviceboks 1, 0840 OSLO **Tel:** 926 63 633
Titles:
BOKSING.NO

NORGES BORDTENNISFORBUND 1628890
Serviceboks, Ullevål Stadion, 0840 OSLO
Tel: 21 02 97 82
Titles:
NORSK BORDTENNIS

NORGES BRYTERFORBUND 1752877
Norges Bryteforbund, Serviceboks 1, 0840 OSLO **Tel:** 922 41 690
Titles:
BRYTING.NO

NORGES BUESKYTTERFORBUND 1628893
Serviceboks 1, 0840 OSLO **Tel:** 21 02 97 85
Fax: 21 02 90 03
Titles:
BUESTIKKA

NORGES COLONIALGROSSISTERS FORBUND 1794073
Pb. 793, Sentrum, 0106 OSLO **Tel:** 22348760
Fax: 22348761
Titles:
HANDELSBLADET FK

NORGES DIABETESFORBUND 1794169
Pb 6442 Etterstad, 0605 OSLO **Tel:** 23051800
Fax: 23051801
Titles:
DIABETES
DIABETESFORUM

NORGES DØVEFORBUND 1754104
Grensen 9, 0159 OSLO **Tel:** 23 31 06 30
Fax: 23 31 06 40
Titles:
DØVES TIDSSKRIFT

NORGES FARMACEUTISKE FORENING 1794157
Tollbugata 35, 0157 OSLO **Tel:** 21023352
Fax: 21023350
Titles:
NORSK FARMACEUTISK TIDSSKRIFT

NORGES FJORDHESTLAG 1793943
Løken, 6770 NORDFJORDEID **Tel:** 952 16 161
Fax: 57864801
Titles:
FJORDHESTEN

NORGES FOLKESPORTS FORBUND 1628897
Norges Folkesportforbund, Pb. 147, 1471 LØRENSKOG **Tel:** 67 90 55 36 **Fax:** 67 90 91 44
Titles:
TURMARSJNYTT

NORGES FORSKNINGSRÅD 1629025
Norges Forskningsråd, Pb 2700 St.Hanshaugen, 0131 OSLO **Tel:** 22 03 70 82 **Fax:** 22 03 71 66
Titles:
BLADET FORSKNING
FORSKNING.NO
KILDEN - INFORMASJONSSENTER FOR KJØNNSFORSKNING

NORGES FORSVARSFORENING 1628898
Nordengveien 39, 0755 OSLO **Tel:** 22 52 59 96
Titles:
NORGES FORSVAR

NORGES GULLSMEDFORBUND 1628187
Storgt. 14, 0184 OSLO **Tel:** 22348900
Fax: 22348919
Titles:
GULL & UR

NORGES GYMNASTIKK- OG TURNFORBUND 1628442
Norges Gymnastikk- og Turnforbund, 0840 OSLO **Tel:** 21 02 96 16 **Fax:** 21 02 96 11
Titles:
GYM & TURN

NORGES HÅNDBALLFORBUND 1628445
Norges Håndballforbund, 0840 OSLO
Tel: 21 02 90 00 **Fax:** 21 02 99 51
Titles:
HÅNDBALLMAGASINET

NORGES HANDELS OG SJØFARTSTIDENDE AS 1791573
Pb 1182 Sentrum, 0107 OSLO **Tel:** 22001000
Fax: 22 00 12 33
Titles:
DN.NO

NORGES HANDELSHØYSKOLE 1652856
NHH, Helleveien 30, 5045 BERGEN
Tel: 55 95 97 02
Titles:
NHH - BULETTIN

NORGES HANDIKAPFORBUND 1644153
Pb 9217 Grønland, 0134 OSLO **Tel:** 24 10 24 00
Fax: 24 10 24 99
Titles:
HANDIKAPNYTT

NORGES HUNDER LANDSFORBUND 1628444
Norges Hunder Landsforbund, Postboks 880, 3007 DRAMMEN
Titles:
HUNDEN VÅR

NORGES HUSEIERFORBUND 1643950
Norges Huseierforbund, Universitetsgaten 20, 0162 OSLO **Tel:** 22 42 17 90 **Fax:** 22 42 76 51
Titles:
HUSEIERINFO

NORGES HUSFLIDSLAG 1628132
Øvre Slottsgate 2B, 0157 OSLO **Tel:** 22 00 87 00
Fax: 22 00 87 50
Titles:
NORSK HUSFLID

NORGES HYTTEFORBUND 1644261
Arbinsgt. 1, 0253 OSLO **Tel:** 23 27 37 60
Fax: 23 27 37 61
Titles:
HYTTE & FRITID

NORGES INGENIØRORG. NITO 1793627
Pb. 9100 Grønland, 0133 OSLO **Tel:** 22 05 35 25
Fax: 22 17 24 80
Titles:
NITO REFLEKS

NORGES JEGER- OG FISKERFORBUND 1791791
Hvalstadåsen 5, Postboks 94, 1378 OSLO
Tel: 66 79 22 00 **Fax:** 66 90 15 87
Titles:
JAKT & FISKE

NORGES JURISTFORBUND 1628087
Juristenes Hus, K. Augustsgate 9, 0164 OSLO
Tel: 22 03 50 50 **Fax:** 22 03 50 30
Titles:
JURISTKONTAKT

NORGES KANINAVLSFORBUND 1628449
Bjørn Egeland, Frøyerv. 46, 4328 SANDNES
Tel: 51 67 19 00
Titles:
TIDSSKRIFT FOR KANINAVL

NORGES KFUK-KFUM-SPEIDERE 1649838
Pb 6810 St.Olavspl., 0130 OSLO **Tel:** 22 99 15 50
Fax: 22 99 15 51
Titles:
SPEIDERBLADET

NORGES KOKKEMESTERES LANDSFORENING 1629030
Norges Kokkemesteres Landsforening, Pb 8034, 4068 STAVANGER **Tel:** 51 83 37 95
Titles:
KJØKKENSJEFEN

NORGES KOMMUNEREVISORFORBUND 1628453
Trondheim Kommunerevisjon, 7004 TRONDHEIM
Titles:
KOMMUNEREVISOREN

NORGES KORFORBUND 1628454
Nedre Vollgate 3, 0158 OSLO **Tel:** 22 39 68 50
Fax: 22 39 68 51
Titles:
KORBLADET

NORGES KVINNE- OG FAMILIEFORBUND (K&F) 1692262
Øvre Slottsgate 6, 0157 OSLO **Tel:** 22 47 83 80
Fax: 22478399
Titles:
KVINNER & FAMILIE

NORGES LASTEBILEIER-FORBUND 1643935
Pb 7134, St.Olavs plass, 0130 OSLO
Tel: 22 03 32 00 Fax: 22 20 56 15
Titles:
NORSK TRANSPORT

NORGES LOTTEFORBUND 1628458
Pb 908 Sentrum, 0104 OSLO Tel: 22 47 82 52
Fax: 22 33 27 23
Titles:
LOTTEBLADET

NORGES LUFTSPORTSFORBUND/ NORSK AERO KLUBB 1643925
Pb 383 Sentrum, 0102 OSLO Tel: 23 01 04 50
Fax: 23 01 04 51
Titles:
SEILFLYSPORT

NORGES MILJØVERNFORBUND 1628705
Pb.593, 5806 BERGEN Tel: 55 30 67 00
Fax: 55 30 67 01
Titles:
MILJØMAGASINET

NORGES MUSIKKORPS FORBUND 1644195
Pb. 674 Sentrum, 5807 BERGEN Tel: 815 56 777
Fax: 40 00 17 07
Titles:
AMBIS

NORGES NATURVERNFORBUND 1628639
Grensen 9b, 0101 OSLO Tel: 23 10 96 10
Fax: 23 10 96 11
Titles:
NATUR & MILJØ

NORGES OFFISERSFORBUND 1628460
Møllergata 10, 0179 OSLO Tel: 98 28 33 10
Fax: 23 06 15 77
Titles:
BEFALSBLADET

NORGES OPTIKERFORBUND 1628191
Norges Optikerforbund, Øvre Slottsgt. 18/20, 0157 OSLO Tel: 23 35 54 50 Fax: 23 35 54 40
Titles:
OPTIKEREN

NORGES PELSDYRALSLAG 1628462
Pb 175 Økern, 0509 OSLO Tel: 23 25 81 00
Fax: 22 64 35 91
Titles:
NORSK PELSDYRBLAD

NORGES RØDE KORS 1791946
Pb 1 Grønland, 0133 OSLO Tel: 22 05 40 00
Fax: 22 05 40 40
Titles:
RØDE KORS MAGASINET

NORGES RYTTERFORBUND 1628465
Norges Rytterforbund, Serviceboks 1 Ullevål Stadion, 0840 OSLO Tel: 21 02 96 50
Fax: 21 02 96 51
Titles:
HESTESPORT

NORGES SAMEMISJON 1794389
Norges Samemisjon, Vestre Kanalkai 20, 7010 TRONDHEIM Tel: 47476161 Fax: 73512505
Titles:
SAMENES VENN

NORGES SJAKKFORBUND 1628467
Sandakerveien 24 D, 0473 OSLO Tel: 21 01 98 11
Titles:
NORSK SJAKKBLAD

NORGES SKIFORBUND OG NORGES SKISKYTTERFORBUND 1768220
Pb. 6, 0855 OSLO Tel: 67 13 46 46
Fax: 67 13 46 47
Titles:
SKIGUIDEN
SKISPORT

NORGES SKOGEIERFORBUND 1628152
Pb. 1438 Vika, 0115 OSLO Tel: 23 00 07 50
Fax: 22 42 16 90
Titles:
SKOGEIEREN

NORGES SNOWBOARDFORBUND 1629136
Bentsebrugt. 13 B, 0476 OSLO Tel: 22 09 88 40
Fax: 22 09 88 46
Titles:
PULP NEWS

NORGES SPEIDERFORBUND 1628471
Postboks 6910, 0130 OSLO Tel: 22 99 22 30
Fax: 22 86 20 50
Titles:
SPEIDEREN

NORGES TANNTEKNIKERFORBUND 1794153
Pb. 244, 2901 FAGERNES Tel: 61366900
Fax: 61366901
Titles:
TENNER I FOKUS

NORGES TAXIFORBUND 1643998
Pb. 6754 Rodeløkka, 0503 OSLO Tel: 22 38 95 00
Fax: 22 38 95 01
Titles:
TAXI

NORGES VEKTLØFTERFORBUND 1628473
Serviceboks 1, 0840 OSLO Tel: 21 02 98 65
Fax: 21 02 90 03
Titles:
NYTT FRA NORGES VEKTLØFTERFORBUND

NORILCO 1794172
NORILCO. Pb. 4, Sentrum, 0102 OSLO
Tel: 93420838
Titles:
NORILCO-NYTT

NORSK ALLER AS 1741726
Pb. 1169 Sentrum, 0107 OSLO Tel: 21 30 10 00
Titles:
PÅ TV

NORSK ARBEIDSMANDFORBUND 1748457
Pb 231 Sentrum, 0103 OSLO Tel: 23063371
Fax: 23061111
Titles:
ARBEIDSMANDEN

NORSK ASTROLOGISK FORENING 1628481
Pb 1432 Vika, 0115 OSLO Tel: 93 43 31 35
Titles:
ASTROLOGISK FORUM

NORSK AUDIOGRAFFORBUND (NAF) 1628711
Monica Rolandsen, Krystallveien 2, 8410 9481 HARSTAD LØDINGEN Tel: 951 62 367
Titles:
AUDIOGRAFEN

NORSK AVISDRIFT AS 1627946
Norsk Avisdrift AS, 7032 TRONDHEIM
Tel: 73 95 49 00
Titles:
BYENS NÆRINGSLIV

NORSK BARNEVERNSAMBAND 1644001
Storgata 10 A, 1055 OSLO Tel: 22 41 74 46
Titles:
NORGES BARNEVERN

NORSK BASSETKLUBB 1644002
Bjørn Sønsteby, Sandbakken Veldresagvegen 370, 2380 BRUMUNDDAL Tel: 62 35 64 13
Titles:
BASSETPOSTEN

NORSK BIBLIOTEKFORENING 1629020
Postboks 6540, 0606 OSLO Tel: 23 24 34 30
Fax: 22 67 23 68
Titles:
BIBLIOTEKFORUM

NORSK BIOKJEMISK SELSKAP 1790523
Tel: 64965257 Fax: 41337230
Titles:
NBS-NYTT

NORSK BOKFORLAG AS 1794159
Norsk Bokforlag, Pb. 103, 3529 RØYSE
Tel: 32161550 Fax: 32161551
Titles:
SUNNHETSBLADET

NORSK BONDE- OG SMÅBRUKARLAG 1791547
Solfjellsjøen, 8820 DØNNA Tel: 48 25 37 00
Titles:
BONDE OG SMÅBRUKER

NORSK BOTANISK FORENING 1628984
NHM, Pb. 1172 Blindern, 0318 OSLO
Tel: 22 85 17 01 Fax: 22 85 18 35
Titles:
BLYTTIA

NORSK BRANNVERNFORENING 1649780
Stiftelsen Norsk brannvernforening, Pb. 6754, Etterstad, 0609 OSLO Tel: 23 15 71 00
Fax: 23 15 71 01
Titles:
BRANN & SIKKERHET

NORSK BRIDGEFORBUND 1628663
Serviceboks 1 Ullevaal Stadion, 0840 OSLO
Tel: 21 02 90 00 Fax: 21 02 91 45
Titles:
NORSK BRIDGE

NORSK CARAVAN CLUB SERVICE AS 1794323
Pb 104, 1921 SØRUMSAND Tel: 63829990
Fax: 63829999
Titles:
CARAVAN

NORSK CØLIAKIFORENING 1794204
Boks 4725 Nydalen, 0421 OSLO Tel: 22799170
Fax: 22799395
Titles:
CØLIAKI-NYTT

NORSK ENTOMOLOGISK FORENING 1628490
Pb 386, 4002 STAVANGER Tel: 994 50 917
Titles:
INSEKT-NYTT

NORSK EPILEPSIFORBUND 1628698
Karl Johansgt. 7, 0154 OSLO Tel: 22 47 66 00
Fax: 23 35 31 01
Titles:
EPILEPSI NYTT

NORSK ERGOTERAPEUT FORBUND 1794151
Lakkegata 21, 0187 OSLO Tel: 22059900
Fax: 22059901
Titles:
ERGOTERAPEUTEN

NORSK FAGLITTERÆR FORFATTER- OG OVERSETTERFORENING 1793626
Norsk faglitterær forfatter- og oversetterforening, Uranienborgveien 2, 0258 OSLO Tel: 22 12 11 40
Fax: 22 12 11 50
Titles:
NFF-BULLETIN

NORSK FAGLITTERÆR FORFATTER-OVERSETTERFORENING 1692288
PROSA, Uranienborgveien 2, 0258 OSLO
Tel: 22 12 11 40 Fax: 22 12 11 50
Titles:
PROSA, FAGLITTERÆRT TIDSSKRIFT

NORSK FAMILIEFORLAG 1686064
Pb 184, 4349 BRYNE Fax: 51 77 50 01
Titles:
NORSK FAMILIEØKONOMI

NORSK FENGSELS- OG FRIOMSORGSFORBUND 1791860
Møllergata 10, 0179 OSLO Tel: 23 06 15 92
Fax: 23 06 22 71
Titles:
MAGASINET AKTUELL FOR NORSK FENGSELS- OG FRIOMSORGSF

NORSK FILMKLUBBFORBUND 1628495
Filmens Hus, Dronningens Gate 16, 0157 OSLO
Tel: 22 47 46 80 Fax: 22 47 46 92
Titles:
Z FILMTIDSSKRIFT

NORSK FISKEOPPDRETT AS 1628125
Pb 4084 Dreggen, 5835 BERGEN Tel: 55 54 13 00
Fax: 55 54 13 01
Titles:
NORSK FISKEOPPDRETT

NORSK FISKERINÆRING AS 1628496
Pb. 244, 2071 RÅHOLT Tel: 63 95 90 90
Titles:
NORSK FISKERINÆRING

NORSK FISKESENTER AS 1686854
Jølstramuseet, 6847 VASSENDEN
Titles:
FISKEGUIDEN.NO

NORSK FJØRFELAG 1794237
Lørenveien 38, 0585 OSLO Tel: 22090712
Fax: 22090710
Titles:
FJØRFE

NORSK FOLKEHJELP 1794372
Pb 8844 Youngstorget, 0028 OSLO Tel: 22037700
Fax: 22200870
Titles:
APPELL

NORSK FOLKEHØGSKOLELAG 1644004
Pb. 420 Sentrum, 0103 OSLO **Tel:** 22 47 43 00
Titles:
FOLKEHØGSKOLEN

NORSK FORBUND FOR SVAKSYNTE 1629119
Enebakkveien 457, 1290 OSLO **Tel:** 22 61 60 60
Fax: 22 61 60 68
Titles:
VÅRT SYN

NORSK FORBUND FOR UTVIKLINGSHEMMEDE 1628505
Norsk forbund for utiklingshemmede, Pb. 8953, Youngstorget, 0028 OSLO **Tel:** 22 39 60 50
Fax: 22 39 60 60
Titles:
SAMFUNN FOR ALLE

NORSK FORENING FOR ERNÆRING OG DIETETIKK (NFED) 1794229
Kost- og ernæringsforbundet, Pb 9202 Grønland, 0134 OSLO **Tel:** 21013600
Titles:
KJØKKENSKRIVEREN

NORSK FORENING FOR KIRKEGÅRDSKULTUR 1644204
Neslandsvatn, 3750 DRANGEDAL
Tel: 35 99 45 74 **Fax:** 35 99 45 73
Titles:
KIRKEGÅRDEN

NORSK FORENING FOR MUSIKKTERAPI 1692270
Pb 4727 Sofienberg, 0103 OSLO **Tel:** 22 00 56 45
Titles:
MUSIKKTERAPI

NORSK FORSKERFORBUND 1628195
Pb. 1025 Sentrum, 0104 OSLO **Tel:** 21 02 34 00
Fax: 21 02 34 01
Titles:
FORSKERFORUM

NORSK FOSTERHJEMSFORENING 1628506
Storgata 10a, 0155 OSLO **Tel:** 23 31 54 00
Fax: 23 31 54 01
Titles:
FOSTERHJEMSKONTAKT

NORSK FYSIOTERAPEUTFORBUND 1643926
Pb 2704 St.Hanshaugen, 0131 OSLO
Tel: 22933050 **Fax:** 22565825
Titles:
FYSIOTERAPEUTEN

NORSK GARTNERFORBUND 1628064
Schweigaardsgate 34 F, 0191 OSLO
Tel: 23 15 93 50 **Fax:** 23 15 93 51
Titles:
GARTNERYRKET
PARK & ANLEGG

NORSK HELSESEKRETÆRFORBUND 1791881
Norsk Helsesekretærforbund, Pb 9202 Grønland, 0134 OSLO **Tel:** 21 01 36 00 **Fax:** 21 01 36 60
Titles:
HELSESEKRETÆREN

NORSK HOMØOPATISK PASIENTFORENING 1793955
Kjøpmannsgt. 51, 7404 TRONDHEIM
Tel: 235223 07 **Fax:** 73522307
Titles:
HOMØOPATISK TIDSSKRIFT

NORSK INTERESSEFORENING FOR STAMME (NIFS) 1692294
Postboks 31, 2860 HOV **Tel:** 61129611
Titles:
STAMPOSTEN

NORSK JERNBANEFORBUND 1791854
Postboks 231 Sentrum, 0179 OSLO
Tel: 23 06 33 59 **Fax:** 23062271
Titles:
MAGASINET AKTUELL FOR NORSK JERNBANEFORBUND

NORSK JOURNALISTLAG 1628085
Pb 8793 Youngstorget, 0028 OSLO
Tel: 4000 4888
Titles:
JOURNALISTEN

NORSK KENNEL KLUB 1628900
Pb 163 Bryn, 0611 OSLO **Tel:** 21 60 09 00
Fax: 21 60 09 01
Titles:
HUNDESPORT

NORSK KOLONIHAGEFORBUND 1628410
Møllerveien 2, 0182 OSLO **Tel:** 22 11 00 90
Titles:
KOLONIHAGEN

NORSK KOMMUNALTEKNISK FORENING 1628101
Norsk Kommunalteknisk Forening, Pb. 1905 Vika, 0124 OSLO **Tel:** 22 04 81 40 **Fax:** 22 04 81 49
Titles:
KOMMUNALTEKNIKK

NORSK KOMMUNIKASJONSFORENING 1794353
Norsk kommunikasjonsforening, Postboks 333 Sentrum, 0153 OSLO **Tel:** 23315900
Fax: 23315909
Titles:
KOMMUNIKASJON

NORSK KULTURARV 1692260
Vågåvegen 35, 2680 VÅGÅ **Tel:** 61 21 77 20
Fax: 61 21 77 01
Titles:
KULTURARVEN

NORSK LOKALRADIOFORBUND 1628912
Skippergata 14, 6413 MOLDE **Tel:** 22 40 27 20
Fax: 22 40 27 30
Titles:
LOKALRADIOPOSTEN

NORSK LUTHERSK MISJONSSAMBAND 1649791
Sinsenveien 25, 0572 OSLO **Tel:** 22 00 72 00
Fax: 22 00 72 03
Titles:
ITRO.NO
UTSYN

NORSK MÅLUNGDOM 1629035
Pb 285 Sentrum, 0103 OSLO **Tel:** 23 00 29 40
Fax: 23 00 29 31
Titles:
MOTMÆLE

NORSK MARINTEKNISK FORSKNINGSINSTITUTT AS 1794227
Pb 4125 Valentinlyst, 7450 TRONDHEIM
Tel: 73595500 **Fax:** 73595776
Titles:
MARINTEK REVIEW

NORSK MARITIMT FORLAG AS 1794316
Leangbukta 40, 1392 VETTRE **Tel:** 66764950
Fax: 66764951
Titles:
BÅTGUIDEN
SEILAS

NORSK MARKEDSANALYSE FORENING 1628908
Pb. 5077 Majorstuen, 0301 OSLO **Tel:** 22 60 16 77
Titles:
ANALYSEN

NORSK MEDISINSTUDENTFORENING 1794081
Nye Studentpaviljongen, Ullevål Sykehus, 0407 OSLO **Tel:** 22117854 **Fax:** 22117854
Titles:
ÆSCULAP

NORSK MOTORCYKKEL UNION 1793491
Pb 351, 1502 MOSS **Tel:** 90837374 **Fax:** 69240809
Titles:
MC-BLADET

NORSK MOTORVETERAN AS 1794296
Pb. 67 Bryn Senter, 0667 OSLO **Tel:** 22757500
Fax: 22757501
Titles:
NORSK MOTORVETERAN

NORSK MUSIKKRÅD 1628834
Pstboks 4651, Sofienberg, 0506 OSLO
Tel: 22 00 56 00 **Fax:** 22 00 56 01
Titles:
MUSIKK.NO

NORSK ORNITOLOGISK FORENING 1628915
Norsk Ornitologisk Forening, Avdeling Hordaland, Boks 280, 5751 ODDA
Tel: 53 64 29 37
Titles:
FUGLAR I HORDALAND
ORNIS NORVEGICA
VÅR FUGLEFAUNA

NORSK PENSJONISTFORBUND 1791883
Lilletorget 1, 0184 OSLO **Tel:** 22 98 17 70
Fax: 22348783
Titles:
PENSJONISTEN

NORSK PLAN NYNETT AS 1793944
Næringsbedet i Vatlandsvåg, 4235 HEBNES
Tel: 52 79 04 89 **Fax:** 52790481
Titles:
MAGASINETT.NO

NORSK POLARINSTITUTT 1793623
Polarmiljøsenteret, 9296 TROMSØ
Tel: 77 75 05 00 **Fax:** 77 75 05 01
Titles:
NORSK POLARINSTITUTTS RAPPORTSERIE
POLAR RESEARCH

NORSK POST- OG KOMMUNIKASJONSFORBUND 1794371
Møllergata 10, 0179 OSLO **Tel:** 23061561
Fax: 23062271
Titles:
POSTHORNET

NORSK PSYKOLOGFORENING 1794178
Postboks 419 Sentrum, 0103 OSLO
Tel: 23103130 **Fax:** 22424292
Titles:
TIDSSKRIFT FOR NORSK PSYKOLOGFORENING

NORSK PUDDELKLUBB 1628918
Norsk Puddelklubb, Pb. 932, 0104 OSLO
Titles:
PUDDELPOSTEN

NORSK RADIO RELÆ LIGA 1794101
Pb 20 Haugenstua, 0915 OSLO **Tel:** 22213790
Fax: 22213791
Titles:
AMATØRRADIO

NORSK RADIOLOGISK FORENING 1794173
P.B. 1045 Sentrum, 0104 OSLO **Tel:** 23034513
Fax: 24101221
Titles:
NORAFORUM

NORSK REVMATIKERFORBUND 1794166
Pb 2653 Solli, 0203 OSLO **Tel:** 22547600
Fax: 22431251
Titles:
REVMATIKEREN

NORSK SANGERFORBUND 1692303
Norsk Sangerforbund, Samfunnshuset, 0181 OSLO **Tel:** 22 20 51 42
Titles:
TONENS MAKT

NORSK SAU OG GEIT 1685807
Postboks 104, 1431 Ås, 0201 OSLO
Tel: 23 08 47 70 **Fax:** 22 43 16 60
Titles:
SAU OG GEIT

NORSK SKIPSMEGLERFORBUND 1628150
Postboks 1895 Vika, 0124 OSLO **Tel:** 22 20 14 85
Titles:
SKIPSMEGLEREN.NO

NORSK SKOLELEDERFORBUND 1628923
Lakkegata 21, 0187 OSLO **Tel:** 24 10 19 16
Fax: 24 10 19 10
Titles:
SKOLELEDEREN

NORSK SLEKTSHISTORISK FORENING 1628924
Norsk Slektshistorisk Forening, Lakkegata 21, 0187 OSLO
Titles:
GENEALOGEN
GENEALOGI.NO

NORSK SPRÅKRÅD 1628926
Språkrådet, Pb 8107 Dep, 0032 OSLO
Tel: 22 54 19 50
Titles:
STATSSPRÅK

NORSK SYKEPLEIERFORBUND FINNMARK 1643940
Postboks 456 Sentrum, 0104 OSLO
Tel: 22043304
Titles:
SYKEPLEIEN

NORSK TANNPLEIERFORENING 1794154
Pb. 9202 Grønland, 0134 OSLO **Tel:** 21013600
Titles:
TANNSTIKKA

NORSK TANNVERN 1793504
Norsk Tannvern, Pb 9341 Grønland, 0135 OSLO
Tel: 22113440 **Fax:** 22113441
Titles:
MUNNPLEIEN

NORSK TEATER- OG ORKESTERFORENING 1782059
Storgt. 10B, 0155 OSLO **Tel:** 23 29 29 00
Titles:
SCENEKUNST.NO

NORSK TERRIER KLUB 1628589
Norsk Terrier Klubb, Postboks 90 Økern, 0580 OSLO **Tel:** 974 74 944
Titles:
TERRIER-BLADET

NORSK TJENESTEMANNSLAG 1791978
Møllergata 10, 0179 OSLO **Tel:** 23061561 **Fax:** 23062271
Titles:
TJENESTEMANNSBLADET

NORSK TJENESTEMANNSLAG (NTL) 1692224
NTL Forsvaret, Pb 8788 Youngstorget, 0028 OSLO **Tel:** 22 41 04 00
Titles:
101 BLADET

NORSK TOLLERFORBUND 1628931
Pb 8122 Dep., 0032 OSLO **Tel:** 22 86 03 00
Titles:
NORSK TOLLBLAD

NORSK TRANSPORT-ARBEIDERFORBUND 1732627
Hammersborg Torg 3, 0179 OSLO **Tel:** 40 64 64 64 **Fax:** 22 20 50 89
Titles:
TRANSPORTARBEIDEREN

NORSK UTENRIKSPOLITISK INSTITUTT 1628937
Pb 8159 Dep, 0033 OSLO **Tel:** 22 99 40 00 **Fax:** 22 36 21 82
Titles:
FORUM FOR DEVELOPMENT STUDIES
HVOR HENDER DET?
INTERNASJONAL POLITIKK
NORDISK ØSTFORUM

NORSK VANNFORENING 1692308
Norsk Vannforening, Postboks 2312 Solli, 0201 OSLO **Tel:** 22 94 75 75
Titles:
VANN

NORSK VISEFORUM 1644007
Norsk Viseforum, Postb. 4647, 0506 OSLO **Tel:** 22 00 56 30 **Fax:** 22 00 56 01
Titles:
VISER.NO

NORSK ZOOLOGISK FORENING 1794318
Norsk Zoologisk Forening, Postboks 102 Blindern, 0314 OSLO **Tel:** 22261131
Titles:
FAUNA

NORSKE 4H 1628764
4H Norge, Pb 113, 2026 SKJETTEN **Tel:** 64 83 21 00 **Fax:** 64 83 21 19
Titles:
AKTIVITET

NORSKE ARKITEKTERS LANDSFORBUND 1628010
Josefinesgate 34, 0351 OSLO **Tel:** 23 33 25 45 **Fax:** 23 33 25 50
Titles:
ARKITEKTNYTT
ARKITEKTUR N

DEN NORSKE FAGPRESSES FORENING 1628659
Akersgata 43, 0158 OSLO **Tel:** 24 14 61 00 **Fax:** 24 14 61 10
Titles:
FAGPRESSENYTT.NO

NORSKE FOTTERAPEUTERS FORBUND 1794174
Pb 9202 Grønland, 0134 OSLO **Tel:** 99450090
Titles:
FOTTERAPEUTEN

NORSKE FRISØR- OG VELVÆREBEDRIFTER 1776884
Pb 7017 Majorstua, 0306 OSLO **Tel:** 23 08 79 60 **Fax:** 23 08 79 70
Titles:
FRISØR

DEN NORSKE HISTORISKE FORENING (HIFO) 1692253
HIFO, AHKR, Postboks 7805, 5020 BERGEN **Tel:** 55 58 32 60 **Fax:** 55 58 96 54
Titles:
HIFO-NYTT

NORSKE KOSMETOLOGERS OG HUDTERAPEUTERS FORBUND 1794333
Brekkelia 57, 3153 TOLVSRØD **Tel:** 91556068 **Fax:** 33019954
Titles:
KOSMETIKA

NORSKE KUNSTHÅNDVERKERE 1628941
Rådhusgt. 20, 0151 OSLO **Tel:** 22 91 02 60 **Fax:** 22 91 02 61
Titles:
KUNSTHÅNDVERK

NORSKE KVINNERS SANITETSFORENING 1628054
Munthes gate 33, 0260 OSLO **Tel:** 24 11 56 20 **Fax:** 22 44 76 21
Titles:
FREDRIKKE

DEN NORSKE LEGEFORENING 1747907
Pb 1152 Sentrum, 0107 OSLO **Tel:** 23 10 90 50 **Fax:** 23 10 90 40
Titles:
TIDSSKRIFTET.NO

NORSKE MEDIA AS 1794241
Boks 9231 Grønland, 0134 OSLO **Tel:** 92201214 **Fax:** 22172508
Titles:
PRINT & PUBLISERING

NORSKE MEIERIFOLKS LANDSFORENING 1794219
Postboks 9370, Grønland, 0135 OSLO **Tel:** 23002710
Titles:
MEIERIPOSTEN

NORSKE MURMESTRES LANDSFORENING 1793390
Per Christian Berg, Bjerkelundsveien 5, 1358 JAR **Tel:** 92043200
Titles:
MURMESTEREN

NORSKE NATURTERAPEUTERS HOVEDORGANISASJON 1794185
Postboks 9397 Grønland, 0136 OSLO **Tel:** 21013700 **Fax:** 21013705
Titles:
NATURTERAPEUTEN

DEN NORSKE REVISORFORENINGS SERVICEKONTOR 1628144
Den norske Revisorforening, Postboks 2914 Solli, 0230 OSLO **Tel:** 23 36 52 00 **Fax:** 23 36 52 02
Titles:
REVISJON OG REGNSKAP

NORSKE SJØMATBEDRIFTERS LANDSFORENING (NSL) 1649821
Norske Sjømatbedrifters Landsforening, Pb 639 Sentrum, 7406 TRONDHEIM **Tel:** 73 84 14 00 **Fax:** 73 84 14 01
Titles:
NORSK SJØMAT

DEN NORSKE TANNLEGEFORENING 1644034
Pb 3063 Elisenberg, 0207 OSLO **Tel:** 22547400
Titles:
DEN NORSKE TANNLEGEFOR. TIDENDE

NORSKE TREKKSPILLERES LANDSFORBUND 1790936
co Per J. Grøthe, Einerveien 11, 3092 SUNDBYFOSS **Tel:** 906 44 927
Titles:
TREKKSPILLNYTT

DEN NORSKE TURISTFORENING 1628049
Den Norske Turistforening, DNT Youngstorget 1, 0181 OSLO **Tel:** 4000 1868 **Fax:** 22 82 28 01
Titles:
FJELL OG VIDDE

DEN NORSKE VETERINÆRFORENING 1628139
Pb 6781 St. Olavs plass, 0130 OSLO **Tel:** 22 99 46 00 **Fax:** 22 99 46 01
Titles:
NORSK VETERINÆRTIDSSKRIFT

NORSPO AS 1629090
SPORTSBRANSJEN AS, Sjølyst Plass 3, 0278 OSLO **Tel:** 23 00 15 33 **Fax:** 23 00 15 32
Titles:
SPORT

NORSVIN 1649867
Pb 504, Norsvinsenteret, Hamar, 2304 HAMAR **Tel:** 62 51 01 00 **Fax:** 62 51 01 01
Titles:
SVIN

THE NORWAY POST AS 1628840
P.O.Box 25, Ringeriksveien 243, 1340 BÆRUM **Tel:** 67176850 **Fax:** 67176851
Titles:
THE NORWAY POST

NORWEGIAN AIR SHUTTLE ASA 1735668
Pb. 115, NO-1330 FORNEBU **Tel:** 67 59 30 43 **Fax:** 67 59 30 01
Titles:
NORWEGIAN

NRK 1742978
Bj. Bjørnsons Plass 1, 0340 OSLO **Tel:** 23 04 70 00
Titles:
NRK GULL (KANAL)

NROF OG KOL 1652900
Postboks 908 Sentrum, 0104 OSLO **Tel:** 22 47 82 50 **Fax:** 22 33 27 23
Titles:
PROPATRIA/VÅRT VERN

NRR 1710236
NRR - Østre Strandvei 70, 3482 TOFTE **Tel:** 924 47 217
Titles:
ARISTOKATT

NSO/NSR 1654098
Pb 5468 Majorstua, 0305 OSLO **Tel:** 23 08 85 30 **Fax:** 23 08 85 50
Titles:
SIKKERHET

NTNU 1628727
NTNU - Informasjonsavdelingen, 7491 TRONDHEIM **Tel:** 73 59 55 40 **Fax:** 73 59 54 37
Titles:
UNIVERSITETSAVISA.NO

NTNU, VITENSKAPSMUSEET, SEKSJON FOR NATURHISTORIE, 1794002
NTNU, Vitenskapsmuseet, Seksjon for naturhistorie, 2, 7491 TRONDHEIM **Tel:** 73592382 **Fax:** 73592295
Titles:
FAUNA NORVEGICA

NVHF FORLAG 1649786
JB Forlag, Drammensveien 70 C, 0271 OSLO **Tel:** 22 43 10 07 **Fax:** 22 44 99 11
Titles:
RELEASE

NY TID AS 1791131
Pb 50 Økern, 0107 OSLO **Tel:** 22 31 04 70 **Fax:** 22 31 02 25
Titles:
NY TID

NYE TROMS AS 1644106
Boks 44, 9329 MOEN **Tel:** 778 37 913
Titles:
NYE TROMS; SPORTSREDAKSJONEN

NYTT OM BIL NORGE AS 1686788
Pb 183, 1377 BILLINGSTAD **Tel:** 66854460 **Fax:** 66981408
Titles:
NYTT OM BIL

OAK INVESTMENTS, JP MORGAN, J-POWER, MIZUHO, SCHIBSTED OG DE ANSATTE 1752912
Pb. 7120 St.Olavs plass, 0130 OSLO **Tel:** 22 40 53 40 **Fax:** 22 40 53 41
Titles:
POINTCARBON.COM
TRAIDING CARBON MAGAZINE

OBOS 1794104
Pb. 6666 St. Olavs Plass, 0129 OSLO **Tel:** 22865785 **Fax:** 22868210
Titles:
OBOS BLADET

OFFSHORE MEDIA GROUP AS 1654429
Trollhaugsmyra 15, 5353 STRAUME **Tel:** 56314020 **Fax:** 56314030
Titles:
OFFSHORE & ENERGY
OFFSHORE & ENERGY; OFFSHORE.NO

OG REDAKSJON: ALFHEIM BLADFORLAG 1794094
Breivikskjenet 29, 5179 GODVIK **Tel:** 55509760 **Fax:** 55509768
Titles:
VARMENYTT

OIKOS - ØKOLOGISK LANDSLAG 1649835
Ren Mat c/o OIKOS, Grensen 9b, 0159 OSLO **Tel:** 38095278 **Fax:** 23109641
Titles:
REN MAT

OIL INFORMATION AS 1793956
Lagårdsveien 77-81, co Vaalandsbakken7, 4010 STAVANGER **Tel:** 51 91 76 50 **Fax:** 51 91 76 51
Titles:
PETRONEWS

ØKOKRIM 1793951
Økokrim, Pb. 8193 Dep., 0034 OSLO **Tel:** 23291000 **Fax:** 23291001
Titles:
MILJØKRIM

OLJEDIREKTORATET 1732483
Oljedirektoratet, Pb. 600, 4003 STAVANGER
Tel: 51876000 **Fax:** 51551571
Titles:
NORSK SOKKEL

OPPLAND ARBEIDERBLAD AS 1627840
Pb 24, 2801 GJØVIK **Tel:** 61 18 93 00
Fax: 61 17 07 25
Titles:
OPPLAND ARBEIDERBLAD

OPPLYSNINGSKONTORENE I LANDBRUKET 1792647
P. b. 395 Økern, 0513 OSLO **Tel:** 22 09 25 60
Titles:
MAT.NO

ORGANISASJONEN VOKSNE FOR BARN 1628202
Organisasjonen voksne for barn, Stortorvet 10, 0155 OSLO **Tel:** 23 10 06 10 **Fax:** 23 10 06 11
Titles:
MAGASINET VFB

ØSFOLDPRESSEN AS 1745301
Pb. B, 1801 ASKIM **Tel:** 69 81 61 56
Fax: 69 88 95 84
Titles:
SMAALENENES AVIS;
SPORTSREDAKSJONEN

OSLO BEDRIFTSIDRETTSKRETS 1628950
Ekebergveien 101, 1178 OSLO **Tel:** 22 57 97 73
Titles:
BEDRIFTSIDRETT I OSLO

OSLO BEKHTEREVFORENING 1644140
Pb 2653 Solli, 0203 OSLO **Tel:** 482 53 810
Titles:
BEKHTEREVER'N

OSLO BRANNKORPSFORENING 1628954
Arne Garborgs Plass 1, 0179 OSLO
Tel: 928 00 378
Titles:
BRANNMANNEN

OSLO FYLKESLAG AV HLF 1793691
Inkognitogt. 12, 0258 OSLO **Tel:** 22 55 73 58
Titles:
HØRELUREN

OSLO IDRETTSKRETS 1628955
Oslo Idrettskrets, Ekebergveien 101, 1178 OSLO
Tel: 22 57 97 00 **Fax:** 22 57 97 01
Titles:
OSLOIDRETT

OSLO MILITÆRE SAMFUND 1628137
Tollbugata 10, 0152 OSLO **Tel:** 22 33 62 33
Fax: 22 42 87 87
Titles:
NORSK MILITÆRT TIDSSKRIFT

OSLO RØDE KORS HJELPEKORPS 1794184
Pb 3 Grønland, 0133 OSLO **Tel:** 22992330
Titles:
DISTRIKTSINFO (RØDE KORS)

ØSTLENDINGEN AS 1793041
Pb 231, 2402 ELVERUM **Tel:** 62 43 25 00
Titles:
ØSTLENDINGEN

PANDORAMA MEDIA / XIO MEDIA 1644240
Henning Poulsen, øvrefoss 4b, 0555 OSLO
Tel: 22 60 69 30
Titles:
PANORAMA.NO

PAPAYA DESIGN & MARKETING AS 1769968
Postboks 2814 Solli, 0204 OSLO **Tel:** 400 02 254
Titles:
GOLFEREN.NO

PARAT 1794386
Pb 9029 Grønland, 0133 OSLO **Tel:** 21013600
Fax: 21013800
Titles:
MEDLEMSBLADET PARAT

PEAK MAGAZINE/ INSIGHTELECTRONICS 1794071
Pb. 122, 1300 SANDVIKA **Tel:** 67559555
Fax: 67559556
Titles:
PEAK MAGAZINE

PEDICEL A/S 1794311
Pedicel AS, Postboks 3130 Elisenberg, 0207 OSLO **Tel:** 23086846
Titles:
VINFORUM

PEDLEX NORSK SKOLEINFORMASJON 1692254
PEDLEX Norsk Skoleinformasjon, Postboks 6611, St. Olavs plas, 0129 OSLO **Tel:** 23 35 47 00
Fax: 23 35 47 01
Titles:
HJEM & SKOLE
NORSK BARNEHAGENYTT

PER-KR. AASEN OG KJELL ARNE NORDLI DA 1794022
Stenholtsvei 15a, 1738 BORGENHAUGEN
Tel: 69 35 40 90 **Fax:** 69 35 40 98
Titles:
OFFENTLIG HANDEL

PLAYBOARD MAGAZINE A/S 1692285
Nesflåtveien 18, 4018 STAVANGER
Tel: 51 58 03 03
Titles:
PLAYBOARD MAGAZINE

PLUSS - LANDSFORENINGEN MOT AIDS 1794191
Christian Krohgs gate 34, 0186 OSLO
Tel: 21314580 **Fax:** 21314581
Titles:
POSITIV

POLAR REPORTER AS 1628657
Postboks 2050 Vika, 0125 OSLO **Tel:** 23 38 82 50
Titles:
REISELIV

POLITIETS FELLESFORBUND 1628848
Møllergata 39, 0184 OSLO **Tel:** 23 16 31 00
Fax: 23 16 31 40
Titles:
POLITIFORUM

POSTEN NORGE AS 1651271
Posten Norge AS, 0001 OSLO **Tel:** 23 14 84 10
Fax: 23 14 80 25
Titles:
POST & BRINGAVISEN

PRESS TELEGRAPH AS 1628074
c/o Press Telegraph A/S, Postboks 3004 Elisenberg, 0207 OSLO **Tel:** 22 44 05 06
Fax: 22 56 08 61
Titles:
BABY, HOBBY & LEKETØY
PARFYMERIET

PRICEWATERHOUSECOOPERS AS AVD OSLO 1653786
Tel: 95 26 00 00
Titles:
MENTOR

PRIVATE BARNEHAGERS LANDSFORBUND 1793628
Private Barnehagers Landsforbund, Pb. 23 Stormyra, 8088 BODØ **Tel:** 75 54 16 90
Fax: 75 54 16 91
Titles:
BARNEHAGE

PRIVATPRAKTISERENDE FYSIOTERAPEUTERS FORBUND 1794165
Schwartzgt. 2, 3043 DRAMMEN **Tel:** 32893719
Titles:
FYSIOTERAPI I PRIVAT PRAKSIS

PSYKOLOGISK INSTITUTT 1794163
Psykologisk Institutt, Svt-fakultetet, Ntnu, 7491 TRONDHEIM **Tel:** 73550737 **Fax:** 73591920
Titles:
PSYKOLOGISK TIDSSKRIFT

PSYKOLOGISK INSTITUTT, UNIVERSITETET I OSLO 1794175
Pb 1094 Blindern, 0317 OSLO **Tel:** 22845030
Titles:
IMPULS-TIDSSKRIFT FOR PSYKOLOGI

PUBLICATIO AS 1643955
Pb 5023 Majorstua, 0301 OSLO **Tel:** 22 87 12 00
Fax: 22 87 12 01
Titles:
BYGGENYTT

PUBLISH AS 1628996
Billingstadsletta 19 B, 1396 BILLINGSTAD
Tel: 81573510 **Fax:** 81573511
Titles:
LYD & BILDE
LYDOGBILDE.NO

PUBLITECH AS 1732477
Postboks A - Bygdøy, 0211 OSLO **Tel:** 24115707
Titles:
VOLT

QUILTEFORLAGET AS 1794000
Quilteforlaget AS, Mulvadsgate 14, 1610 FREDRIKSTAD **Tel:** 69 31 59 26
Titles:
QUILTEMAGASINET

RÅDET FOR PSYKISK HELSE 1794177
Postboks 817 Sentrum, 0104 OSLO
Tel: 23103880 **Fax:** 23103881
Titles:
PSYKISK HELSE

REDD BARNA 1794374
Postboks 6902 St.Olavsplass, 0130 OSLO
Tel: 22990900 **Fax:** 22990850
Titles:
MAGASINET REDD BARNA

REDNINGSSELSKAPET 1794346
Redningsselskapet, Postboks 500, 1323 HØVIK
Tel: 67577777
Titles:
TRYGG PÅ SJØEN

REED BUSINESS INFORMATION NORWAY AS 1643923
Byggfakta Docu AS, postboks 1024, 1510 MOSS
Tel: 69 91 24 00
Titles:
HOTELLMAGASINET;
HOTELLMAGASINET.NO

REISELIV PUBLISHING AS 1629021
Øvre Slottsgate 12, 0157 OSLO **Tel:** 22 41 71 18
Fax: 22 41 71 99
Titles:
HOTELL, RESTAURANT & REISELIV

REISER & FERIE AS 1629045
Postboks 1110, 0104 OSLO **Tel:** 22 40 30 20
Fax: 22 40 30 21
Titles:
REISER & FERIE

REKLAMEAVISER AS 1793717
Pb 73, 1720 GREÅKER **Tel:** 69 12 75 00
Fax: 69127501
Titles:
ØSTFOLDAVISEN

RICA EIENDOM AS 1644131
Tel: 21608190
Titles:
RICA MAGASIN

RIKSMÅLSFORBUNDET 1628529
Rosenborggaten 3, 0256 OSLO **Tel:** 22 60 88 59
Fax: 22 60 03 74
Titles:
ORDET

RØDT & HVITT AS 1774012
Hausmannsgate 6, 0186 OSLO **Tel:** 97494427
Titles:
RØDT & HVITT VINMAGASIN

ROGALANDS AVIS AS 1793014
Pb 233, 4001 STAVANGER **Tel:** 51 82 20 00
Fax: 51822140
Titles:
ROGALANDS AVIS
ROGALANDS AVIS; PULSREDAKSJONEN

ROMSDALS BUDSTIKKE AS 1627847
Pb. 2100, 6402 MOLDE **Tel:** 71 25 00 00
Fax: 71 25 00 14
Titles:
ROMSDALS BUDSTIKKE

RØROS MEDIA AS 1793708
Kjerkgata 48, 7374 0130 OSLO RØROS
Tel: 72 41 27 86 **Fax:** 850 37 701
Titles:
KULTURAVISA - BREIDABLIKK

RØYKFRITT MILJØ NORGE 1644013
Pb. 8701 Youngstorget, 0028 OSLO
Tel: 22 65 35 79
Titles:
RØYKFRITT.NO

RUSH PRINT AS 1628533
Dronningensgate 16, 0152 OSLO **Tel:** 22 47 46 43
Fax: 22 82 24 22
Titles:
RUSH PRINT

SAFE 1794225
Postboks 145 Sentrum, 4001 STAVANGER
Tel: 51843900 **Fax:** 51843940
Titles:
SAFEMAGASINET

SAMFUNNSØKONOMENES FORENING 1628565
Pb 8872 Youngstorget, 0028 OSLO
Tel: 22 31 79 90 **Fax:** 22 31 79 91
Titles:
SAMFUNNSØKONOMEN

SAMFUNSSØKONOMENES FORENING 1692280
Pb. 8872 Youngstorget, 0028 OSLO
Tel: 22317990 **Fax:** 22317991
Titles:
NORSK ØKONOMISK TIDSSKRIFT

SANDEFJORDS BLAD AS 1792564
Pb. 143, 3201 SANDEFJORD **Tel:** 33422000
Fax: 33422011
Titles:
SANDEFJORDS BLAD

SANDNES BOLIGBYGGELAG 1644239
Pb. 630, 4305 SANDNES **Tel:** 51 68 31 00
Fax: 51 68 31 40
Titles:
BOLIGAKTØREN

SANDVIKEN INNOVATIVE AS 1680723
Markveien 55, 1337 SANDVIKA **Tel:** 67 57 53 00
Titles:
KARRIEREMAGASINET KALEIDOSKOPET

SAPRBORG ARBEIDERBLAD AS 1793728
Pb. 83, 1701 SARPSBORG **Tel:** 69 11 11 11
Fax: 69 11 11 00
Titles:
SARPSBORG ARBEIDERBLAD;
SPORTSREDAKSJONEN

SARPSBORG ARBEIDERBLAD AS 1627850
Pb. 83, 1701 SARPSBORG **Tel:** 69 11 11 11
Fax: 69 11 10 74
Titles:
SARPSBORG ARBEIDERBLAD

SCANDINAVIAN OIL-GAS MAGAZINE AS 1654431
Pb 6865 St.Olavs Plass, 0130 OSLO
Tel: 22447270 **Fax:** 22447287
Titles:
SCANDINAVIAN OIL-GAS MAGAZINE
SCANDINAVIAN OIL-GAS MAGAZINE;
SCANDOIL.COM

SCHENKER AS 1767844
Schenker AS, Erling Sæther, Pb 223 Økern, 0510 OSLO **Tel:** 22 72 74 44 **Fax:** 22 72 74 60
Titles:
LOGISTIKK NETTVERK

SCHIBSTED ASA 1747236
Pb 6970, St. Olav's Plass, 0130 OSLO
Tel: 934 30 200 **Fax:** 24 14 68 81
Titles:
DAGENS MEDISIN; DAGENSMEDISIN.NO

SCHIBSTED FORLAGENE AS 1649814
Pb. 6974, St.Olavs plass, 0130 OSLO
Tel: 24 14 69 40
Titles:
DESIGN:INTERIØR
INTERIØRMAGASINET MAISON

SE OG HØR FORLAGET 1692234
Pb. 1169 Sentrum, 0107 OSLO **Tel:** 22912222
Titles:
BOLIG I UTLANDET

SE OG HØR FORLAGET AS 1628440
Pb. 1164 Sentrum, 0107 OSLO **Tel:** 22 91 22 00
Titles:
D!
GATEBIL MAGAZINE
JEGER, HUND & VÅPEN
MAG
NORSK GOLF
SE OG HØR
SEHER.NO
TOPP

SENTER FOR ARBEIDSLIVSFORBEREDELSE AS 1776889
Sverres gate 3, 5057 BERGEN **Tel:** 55 54 66 55
Titles:
MEGAFON

SENTER FOR INTERNASJONALISERING AV HØYERE UTDANNING 1651277
Pb 1093, 5811 BERGEN **Tel:** 55 30 38 00
Fax: 55 30 88 01
Titles:
EUROPAVEGEN

SENTERUNGDOMMEN 1686671
Senterungdommen, Postboks 1191 Sentrum, 0107 OSLO **Tel:** 23690100 **Fax:** 23690101
Titles:
DESENTRALIST

SIGNY FARDAL; FORLAGSREDKATØR MOMA PUBLISHING 1747279
Pb. 5134 Majorstua, 0302 OSLO **Tel:** 23 36 98 00
Fax: 23 36 98 01
Titles:
ELLE.NO

SIGNY FARDAL; FORLAGSSJEF MOMA PUBLISHING AS 1793992
Pb. 5134 Majorstua, 0302 OSLO **Tel:** 23369800
Fax: 22369801
Titles:
ELLE INTERIØR

SINTEF OG NTNU 1794114
7465 TRONDHEIM **Tel:** 73592476
Titles:
GEMINI

SJØFARTSDIREKTORATET 1644129
Postboks 2222, N-5509 HAUGESUND
Tel: 52745000 **Fax:** 52745001
Titles:
NAVIGARE

SJØMANNSKIRKEN - NORSK KIRKE I UTLANDET 1793498
Sjømannskirken, Pb 2007, 5817 BERGEN
Tel: 55 55 22 55
Titles:
BUD OG HILSEN

SJØMILITÆRE SAMFUND 1629153
Sjømilitære Samfund, Jens Jørgen Jensen, Harald Sæverudsv 103, 5239 RÅDAL
Tel: 92691877
Titles:
NORSK TIDSSKRIFT FOR SJØVESEN

SKARLAND PRESS AS 1628045
Skarland Press AS, Postboks 2843, Tøyen, 0608 OSLO **Tel:** 22 70 83 00 **Fax:** 22 70 83 01
Titles:
FDV - FORVALTNING, DRIFT OG VEDLIKEHOLD
FISK - INDUSTRI & MARKED
FISK - INDUSTRI OG MARKED; NETFISK.NO
GASSMAGASINET
MALEREN
MATINDUSTRIEN
MØBEL & INTERIØR
NORSK ENERGI
NORSK VVS
PACKNEWS
RØRFAG

SKATTEBETALERFOR-ENINGEN 1643938
Pb. 213 Sentrum, 0103 OSLO **Tel:** 22 97 97 04
Titles:
SKATTEBETALEREN

SKIFORENINGEN 1628559
Kongeveien 5, 0787 OSLO **Tel:** 22 92 32 00
Fax: 22 92 32 50
Titles:
SNØ & SKI

SKIPSREVYEN AS 1628560
Pb 224 Nyborg, 5871 BERGEN **Tel:** 55 19 77 70
Fax: 55 19 77 80
Titles:
NORSK SKIPSFART OG FISKERI AKTUELT
SKIPSREVYEN
SKIPSREVYEN; SKIPSREVYEN.NO

SKOFORLAGET AS 1794337
Fredrik Selmers vei 2, 0663 OSLO **Tel:** 22653941
Fax: 22657353
Titles:
SKO

SKOLENES LANDSFORBUND 1628561
Keysersgt 15, 0130 OSLO **Tel:** 23 06 40 00
Fax: 23 06 40 07
Titles:
I SKOLEN

SKOLERÅDGIVERLAGET 1643983
Pb. 574, 3412 LIERSTRANDA **Tel:** 32 22 06 12
Fax: 32 22 06 00
Titles:
RÅDGIVERNYTT

SNORRE NÆSS 1654101
v/Monica Celius, Skimten Søndre, 2090 Hurdal, 2090 HURDAL **Tel:** 90 98 32 16
Titles:
HUNDEKJØRING

SOGNDAL TRIVSEL A/S 1650310
Titles:
TRIVSEL.NET

SOLAR MEDIA AS 1794197
Solar Media AS, Postboks 217, 2381 BRUMUNDDAL **Tel:** 41177953
Titles:
ERGOSTART

SOS RASISME 1794359
Pb. 7073 St. Olavsplass, 0166 OSLO
Tel: 23353200 **Fax:** 23353201
Titles:
ANTIRASISTEN

SOSIALANTROPOLOGISK FORE. & UNIVERSITETSFORLAGET AS 1692277
Att: Mari D. Bergseth, Sosialantropologisk institutt, Pb 1091 Blindern, 0317 OSLO
Fax: 22854502
Titles:
NORSK ANTROPOLOGISK TIDSSKRIFT

SOSIALISTISK UNGDOM 1794366
Sosialistisk Ungdom, Akersgt. 35, 0158 OSLO
Tel: 21933350 **Fax:** 21933301
Titles:
RØDT PRESS

SOSIALISTISK VENSTREPARTI 1793696
Akersgata 35, 0158 OSLO **Tel:** 21933300
Fax: 21933301
Titles:
VENSTRE OM

SOSIALØKONOMENES FAGUTVALG 1628579
Pb 1095 Blindern, 0317 OSLO **Tel:** 22 85 59 42
Fax: 22 85 50 35
Titles:
OBSERVATOR

SPAREBANKFORENINGEN I NORGE 1628153
Pb 6772 St. Olavs Plass, 0130 OSLO
Tel: 22 11 00 75 **Fax:** 22 36 25 33
Titles:
SPAREBANKBLADET

SPORTMEDIA AS 1628018
Rakkestadveien 1, 1814 ASKIM **Tel:** 69 81 97 00
Fax: 69 88 94 33
Titles:
BIRKEBEINER'N
BOBIL & CARAVAN
FRIIDRETT
HESTELIV
IDRETT & ANLEGG
MOTORSPORT.NO
MOTORSPORT.NO
RACING
SPORTMEDIA
VEIVALG

SPRÅKRÅDET 1732596
Pb. 8107, Dep., 0032 OSLO **Tel:** 22 54 19 50
Titles:
SPRÅKNYTT

SSP 1651260
Senter for seniorpolitikk, St. Olavs plass 3, 0165 OSLO **Tel:** 23 15 65 50
Titles:
SENIORPOLITIKK.NO

STABENFELDT AS 1644020
Pb 8054, 4068 STAVANGER **Tel:** 51 84 54 54
Fax: 51 84 54 90
Titles:
BOING

STATENS FORVALTNINGSTJENESTE 1793888
Norsk lysingsblad, Skrivarvegen 2, 6863 LEIKANGER **Tel:** 800 30 301 **Fax:** 57 65 50 55
Titles:
NORSK LYSINGSBLAD PÅ NETT

STATENS RÅD FOR FUNKSJONSHEMMEDE 1644014
Statens råd for likestilling av, Postboks 7075 St. Olavs plass, 0130 OSLO **Tel:** 81 02 00 50
Fax: 24 16 30 04
Titles:
NOTABENE

STATENS VEGVESEN VEGDIREKTORATET 1628585
Pb 8142 Dep, 0033 OSLO **Tel:** 22 07 36 92
Fax: 22 07 35 11
Titles:
VEGEN OG VI

STATISTISK SENTRALBYRÅ AVD OSLO 1644022
Statistisk sentralbyrå, Forskningsavdelingen, Pb 8131 Dep, 0033 OSLO **Tel:** 21090000
Fax: 21090040
Titles:
ØKONOMISKE ANALYSER
SAMFUNNSSPEILET
STATISTISK SENTRALBYRÅ - SSB.NO

STAVANGER AFTENBLAD ASA 1792877
Pb. 229, 4001 STAVANGER **Tel:** 0515 0
Fax: 51893005
Titles:
STAVANGER AFTENBLAD

STIFTELSEN ADBUSTERS 1794388
Adbusters v/ Hausmania, Hausmannsgate 34, 0187 OSLO
Titles:
VRENG

STIFTELSEN BYGGFAG 1686587
Grønland 12, 0188 OSLO **Tel:** 22 99 28 70
Fax: 22992871
Titles:
BYGGFAGBLADET

STIFTELSEN DAGSAVISEN 1793011
Pb. 1183 Sentrum, 0107 OSLO **Tel:** 22998000
Fax: 22998252
Titles:
DAGSAVISEN

STIFTELSEN ELEKTRONIKK-BRANSJEN 1732486
Pb. 6640 Etterstad, 0607 OSLO **Tel:** 23060707 **Fax:** 23060700
Titles:
ELEKTRONIKKBRANSJEN

STIFTELSEN FRI FAGBEVEGELSE - LO MEDIA 1692273
Pb. 231 Sentrum, 0103 OSLO **Tel:** 23063381
Titles:
NETTVERK

STIFTELSEN LOVDATA 1794069
Postboks 2016 Vika, 0125 OSLO **Tel:** 23 11 83 00 **Fax:** 23118301
Titles:
LOV & DATA

STIFTELSEN MATMERK - NORSKE MATMERKER 1794220
KSL Matmerk, Postboks 487 - Sentrum, 0158 OSLO **Tel:** 24148300 **Fax:** 24148313
Titles:
MERKBART

STIFTELSEN NORSK LUFTAMBULANSE 1794161
Pb 94, 1441 DRØBAK **Tel:** 64904444 **Fax:** 64904445
Titles:
NORSK LUFTAMBULANSE MAGASIN

STIFTELSEN OBOS-INNSKYTERNES 1793980
Pb 6666 St. Olavs Pl., 0129 OSLO **Tel:** 22 86 82 19
Titles:
BOLIG & MILJØ

STIFTELSEN ODIN 1710154
Pb. 440, Sentrum, 0103 OSLO **Tel:** 22 00 56 66
Titles:
JAZZNYTT

STIFTELSEN PULS 1644184
Eilert Sundts gt. 41, 0355 OSLO **Tel:** 91 55 11 11
Titles:
PULS
PULS.NO

STIFTELSEN SAMORA 1794376
Pløens gt. 4, 0182 OSLO **Tel:** 22209690 **Fax:** 22209691
Titles:
SAMORA MAGASIN

STIFTELSEN SOS-BARNEBYER NORGE 1794375
Pb 733 Sentrum, 0105 OSLO **Tel:** 23353900 **Fax:** 23353901
Titles:
SOS-BARNEBYER

STIFTELSEN SOSIAL TRYGD 1794224
Hegdehaugsveien 36 A, 0352 OSLO **Tel:** 22850770 **Fax:** 22850771
Titles:
VELFERD

STIFTELSEN UTPOSTEN 1628578
RMR/UTPOSTEN v/Tove Rutle, Sjøbergveien 32, 2050 JESSHEIM **Tel:** 63 97 32 22 **Fax:** 63 97 16 25
Titles:
UTPOSTEN/FOR ALLMENN- OG SAMFUNNSMEDISIN

STIFTELSEN WWF - VERDENS NATURFOND 1794321
Pb. 6784 St. Olavs Plass, 0130 OSLO **Tel:** 22036500 **Fax:** 22200666
Titles:
VERDENS NATUR (WWF)

STIFTINGA DET NORSKE SAMLAGET 1643960
Pb 4672 Sofienberg, 0506 OSLO **Tel:** 22 70 78 00 **Fax:** 22 68 75 02
Titles:
MAAL OG MINNE
SYN OG SEGN

STØTTEFORENINGEN FOR KREFTSYKE BARN 1649836
Pb. 4 Sentrum, 0101 OSLO **Tel:** 02099
Titles:
VÅRE BARN

STREK MEDIA AS 1739527
Strek Media AS, St. Olavsgt. 24, 0166 OSLO **Tel:** 22 310 335
Titles:
STREK

STREZLEZ MEDIA AS 1644267
PB 6064 Etterstad, 6064 ETTERSTAD **Tel:** 23 24 78 00 **Fax:** 23 24 78 01
Titles:
VÅL'ENGA MAGASIN

STUDENTAVISEN UNIKUM 1644227
Serviceboks 422, 4604 KRISTIANSAND S **Tel:** 38 14 21 95
Titles:
UNIKUM

STUDENTSAMFUNNET I ÅS 1628724
Pb 1211, 1432 ÅS **Tel:** 64 96 63 63 **Fax:** 64 94 73 73
Titles:
TUNTREET

STUDENTSAMFUNNET I SOGNDAL 1628725
Studentsamfunnet i Sogndal, Pb. 230, 6856 SOGNDAL **Tel:** 57 67 69 30 **Fax:** 57 67 69 31
Titles:
RØYNDA

STUDENTTORGET 1774013
Youngstorget 4 / Pløensgate 4, 0181 OSLO **Tel:** 24 20 04 12 **Fax:** 24 20 15 94
Titles:
STUDENTTORGET.NO

SUNNMØRE MUSEUM 1628960
Sunnmøre Museum, Borgundgavlen, 6015 ÅLESUND **Tel:** 70 17 40 00 **Fax:** 70 17 40 01
Titles:
GAVLEN

SUNNMØRSPOSTEN AS 1627857
Pb. 123, 6001 ÅLESUND **Tel:** 70 12 00 00 **Fax:** 70 12 46 42
Titles:
SUNNMØRSPOSTEN

SYKKELMAGASINET OFFROAD AS 1628604
Postboks 20, Grefsen, 0409 OSLO **Tel:** 23058100 **Fax:** 23058101
Titles:
SYKKELMAGASINET

SYKLISTENES LANDSFORENING (SLF) 1692289
Pb 8883 Youngstorget, 0028 OSLO **Tel:** 22 47 30 30 **Fax:** 22 47 30 31
Titles:
PÅ SYKKEL

TAPIR AKADEMISK FORLAG 1651257
v. Thor Indset, NAKMI, Søsterhjemmet, Ullevål Universitetssykehus, 0407 OSLO **Tel:** 23 01 60 64
Titles:
NORSK TIDSSKRIFT FOR MIGRASJONSFORSKNING (NTM)

TAYLOR & FRANCIS AS 1628982
Pb. 12 Posthuset, 0051 OSLO **Tel:** 23 10 34 60 **Fax:** 23 10 34 61
Titles:
MARINE BIOLOGY RESEARCH
NORDIC JOURNAL OF PSYCHIATRY

TEGNERFORBUNDET 1776888
Tegnerforbundet, Rådhusgata 17, 0158 OSLO **Tel:** 22 42 38 06
Titles:
NUMER

TEKNA - TEKNISK-NATURVITENSKAPELIG FORENING 1794057
Pb 2312 Solli, 0201 OSLO **Tel:** 22947500 **Fax:** 22947501
Titles:
MAGASINET TEKNA

TEKSTILFORUM AS 1643942
Sjølyst Plass 3, 0278 OSLO **Tel:** 46941000 **Fax:** 62948705
Titles:
TEKSTILFORUM
TEKSTILFORUM.NO

TELEPENSJONISTENES LANDSFORBUND 1794105
Telepensjonistenes Landsforbund, Kirkegata 9, 1331 FORNEBU **Tel:** 22776952 **Fax:** 22776955
Titles:
TELEPENSJONISTEN

TEMA FORLAG A/S 1794042
Bygdøy allé 64 a, 0265 OSLO **Tel:** 94872363 **Fax:** 22443552
Titles:
DECOR-MAGASINET

TIDENS KRAV AS 1790342
Pb. 8, 6501 KRISTIANSUND N **Tel:** 71 57 00 00 **Fax:** 71570002
Titles:
TIDENS KRAV
TIDENS KRAV; SPORTSREDAKSJONEN

TIDSSKRIFTET MATERIALISTEN 1651134
Sagveien 10, 0459 OSLO
Titles:
MATERIALISTEN

TJA MARKETING AS 1794063
Hausmannsgt. 6, 0186 OSLO **Tel:** 22997620 **Fax:** 22116151
Titles:
NY TEKNIKK

TONO 1692304
Pb. 9171, Grønland, 0134 OSLO **Tel:** 22 05 72 00 **Fax:** 22 05 72 50
Titles:
TONO-NYTT

TRADE PRESS AS 1794074
Rosenholmveien 20, 1252 OSLO **Tel:** 22629190 **Fax:** 22629199
Titles:
DAGLIGVAREHANDELEN

TRADEWINDS AS 14340
Christian Krohgs gate 16, 0186 OSLO **Tel:** 22001200 **Fax:** 22001210
Titles:
TRADEWINDS

TRANSPORTBEDRIFTENES LANDSFORENING (TL) 1692306
Pb. 5477 Majorstua, 0305 OSLO **Tel:** 23 08 86 00 **Fax:** 23 08 86 01
Titles:
TRANSPORTFORUM

TRANSPORTØKONOMISK FORUM AS 1628627
Pb. 130, 1306 BÆRUM POSTTERMINAL **Tel:** 67 55 54 30 **Fax:** 67 55 54 31
Titles:
LOGISTIKK & LEDELSE

TRANSPORTØKONOMISK INSTITUTT 1732602
Gaustadalléen 21, 0349 OSLO **Tel:** 22 57 38 00 **Fax:** 22609200
Titles:
SAMFERDSEL

TRAV OG GALOPP-NYTT AS 1628975
Pb 10, Årvoll, 0515 OSLO **Tel:** 22 88 30 00 **Fax:** 22 88 30 10
Titles:
TRAV OG GALOPP-NYTT

TRELAST- OG BYGGEVAREHANDELENS FELLESORGANISASJON 1692236
Trelast- og byggevarehandelens Fellesorganisasjon, Vollsveien 13H, 1366 LYSAKER **Tel:** 67 20 41 40 **Fax:** 67204141
Titles:
BYGG & HANDEL

TRENINGFORUM 1650401
Grønlivegen 9, 3922 PORSGRUNN **Tel:** 47 37 51 27
Titles:
TRENINGSFORUM.NO

TRIM.NO 1650400
Trim.no AS, 6789 LOEN **Tel:** 913 85 926
Titles:
IFORM.NO

TRIM.NO AS 1794023
Trim.no AS, 6789 LOEN **Tel:** 913 85 926
Titles:
TRIM.NO

TROMS FOLKEBLAD AS 1793730
Pb. 308, 9305 FINNSNES **Tel:** 77 85 20 60 **Fax:** 77 85 20 30
Titles:
TROMS FOLKEBLAD; SPORTSREDAKSJONEN

TROPEGRUPPEN AS 1654169
Klæbuveien 196 B, 2etg, 7037 TRONDHEIM **Tel:** 98 29 71 00 **Fax:** 73 95 17 55
Titles:
KJÆLEDYRBLADET

TRYGG TRAFIKK 1629091
Pb 2610 St.Hanshaugen, 0131 OSLO **Tel:** 22 40 40 40 **Fax:** 22 40 40 70
Titles:
TRYGGTRAFIKK.NO

TU INDUSTRI AS 1765353
TU Industri AS, Pb. 5844 Majorstuen, 0308 OSLO **Tel:** 23199300
Titles:
AUTOMATISERING
INDUSTRIEN

TUN MEDIA AS 1643921
Tun Media, Pb. 9303 Grønland, 0135 OSLO **Tel:** 21 31 44 00 **Fax:** 21 31 44 01
Titles:
BONDEBLADET
LEVLANDLIG
NORSK LANDBRUK
TRAKTOR

TV 2 INTERAKTIV AS 1628680
Pb. 2 Sentrum, NO-0101 OSLO **Tel:** 02 25 5 **Fax:** 21 00 60 03
Titles:
TV2 INTERAKTIV

TVILLINGFORELDREFOREN-INGEN 1644255
Stortorvet 10, 0155 OSLO **Tel:** 22 33 14 22 **Fax:** 22 33 14 24
Titles:
TVILLINGNYTT

UIO, INSTITUTT FOR ARKEOLOGI, KONSERVERING OG HISTORIE 1776887
Universitetet i Oslo, IAKH, Fortid, Pb. 1008 Blindern, 0315 OSLO
Titles:
FORTID

UNGDOMMENS SJAKKFORBUND 1794001
Ungdommens Sjakkforbund, Sandakerveien 24D, 0473 OSLO **Tel:** 924 09 376
Titles:
FØRSTERADEN

UNGDOMSGRUPPEN DNT OSLO OG OMENG 1644030
Pb. 7 Sentrum, 0101 OSLO **Tel:** 22822841
Titles:
UNGFOTEN

UNICOM-GRUPPEN AS 1628863
Color Line AS - Color Club, Postboks 2090, 3202 SANDEFJORD **Tel:** 24 11 71 00 **Fax:** 24 11 71 01
Titles:
COLOR CLUB MAGASIN

UNINETT 1650317
UNINETT - Abels gate 5 - Teknobyen, 7465 TRONDHEIM **Tel:** 73 55 79 00 **Fax:** 73 55 79 01
Titles:
UNINYTT

UNIVERSITETET I BERGEN FORMIDLINGSAVDELINGEN 1654428
Pb. 7800, 5020 BERGEN **Tel:** 55 58 69 00
Titles:
HUBRO

UNIVERSITETI TROMSØ 1743973
Labyrint, Avdeling for kommunikasjon og samfunnskontakt, Universitetet i Tromsø, 9037 TROMSØ **Tel:** 77 64 40 00
Titles:
LABYRINT

UNIVERSITETSFORLAGET 1710185
Universitetsforlaget, Postboks 508 Sentrum, 0105 OSLO **Tel:** 22 85 02 20
Titles:
RUS & SAMFUNN

UNIVERSITETSFORLAGET AS 1628395
NHH, Helleveien 30, 5045 BERGEN **Tel:** 55 95 94 89
Titles:
BETA - TIDSSKRIFT FOR BEDRIFTSØKONOMI
EDDA
FOKUS PÅ FAMILIEN
KUNST OG KULTUR
LOV OG RETT
NORDISK DOMSSAMLING
NORSK FILOSOFISK TIDSSKRIFT
NORSK LITTERATURVITENSKAPELIG TIDSSKRIFT
NORSK MEDIETIDSSKRIFT
NORSK PEDAGOGISK TIDSSKRIFT
NORSK STATSVITENSKAPELIG TIDSSKRIFT
NORSK TEOLOGISK TIDSSKRIFT
NYTT NORSK TIDSSKRIFT
PLAN
PRAKTISK ØKONOMI & FINANS
SKATTERETT
STUDIA MUSICOLOGICA NORVEGICA
TIDSSKRIFT FOR PSYKISK HELSEARBEID
TIDSSKRIFT FOR RETTSVITENSKAP
TIDSSKRIFT FOR SAMFUNNSFORSKNING

USBL 1794060
Pb 4764 Sofienberg, 0506 OSLO **Tel:** 22983800 **Fax:** 22983893
Titles:
USBL-NYTT

UTDANNINGSAKADEMIET 1644206
Pb. 9191 Grønland, 0134 OSLO **Tel:** 24 14 20 00 **Fax:** 22 00 21 50
Titles:
BEDRE SKOLE

UTDANNINGSFORBUNDET 1649783
Pb. 9191, Grønland, 0134 OSLO **Tel:** 24 14 20 00 **Fax:** 24 14 21 57
Titles:
SPESIALPEDAGOGIKK
UTDANNING
UTDANNING.NO

UTFLUKT 1793949
Pb. 4757 Sofienberg, 0506 OSLO
Titles:
UTFLUKT

UTROPIA 1629125
Hovedgården - Universitetet i Tromsø, 9037 TROMSØ **Tel:** 776 45 901
Titles:
UTROPIA - STUDENTAVISA I TROMSØ

VAGABOND FORLAG AS 1768221
Sagveien 21 A, 0459 OSLO **Tel:** 23 23 05 50
Titles:
VAGABOND

VALDRES AS 1792903
Pb. 54, 2901 FAGERNES **Tel:** 61 36 42 00
Titles:
VALDRES

VANEBO PUBLISHING AS 1768301
Vestre Rosten 78, 7075 TILLER **Tel:** 72450095
Titles:
KJEDEMAGASINET
KNUTEPUNKT

VARDEN AS 1793039
Pb. 2873, Kjørbekk, 3702 SKIEN **Tel:** 35 54 30 00 **Fax:** 35 54 30 85
Titles:
VARDEN

VELFERDSTINGET I BERGEN 1628957
Parkveien 1, 5007 BERGEN **Tel:** 55 54 52 06 **Fax:** 55 32 84 05
Titles:
STUDVEST

VENTUS, STUDENTMEDIEHUSET I BODØ 1752688
Høgskolen i Bodø, 8049 BODØ **Tel:** 900 67 019
Titles:
VENTUS NETT

VERDENS GANG AS 1790378
Pb 1185 Sentrum, 0107 OSLO **Tel:** 22 00 00 00 **Fax:** 22 42 75 04
Titles:
VG
VG - HELG

VEST VIND MEDIA AS 1794301
Vest Vind Media AS, Bruhagen, Sentrumsbygg, 6530 AVERØY **Tel:** 71513470 **Fax:** 71513473
Titles:
BAKER OG KONDITOR

VESTFOLD NETTAVIS AS 1793675
Løvenskioldsgate 10, 3916 PORSGRUNN **Tel:** 915 74 756
Titles:
NÆRINGSAVISEN

VESTLANDSKE BOLIGBYGGELAG 1628175
Pb 1947 Nordnes, 5817 BERGEN **Tel:** 55 30 96 00
Titles:
VESTBO-INFO

VETERAN AS 1794298
Ryensvingen 15, 0680 OSLO **Tel:** 90623492 **Fax:** 22682965
Titles:
VETERAN & SPORTSBIL

VG MULTIMEDIA AS 1649832
VG Multimedia, Pb. 1185 Sentrum, 0107 OSLO **Tel:** 22 00 00 00
Titles:
VG; VEKTKLUBB.NO

VI I VILLA.NO AS 1792012
Pb. 797 Sentrum, 0106 OSLO **Tel:** 22 04 74 00 **Fax:** 23 31 03 01
Titles:
VIIVILLA.NO

VOLVAT MEDISINSKE SENTER 1644012
Pb. 5280 Majorstua, 0303 OSLO **Tel:** 22957500 **Fax:** 22957635
Titles:
VOLVAT DOKTOR

WEB INFOTECH AS-KULTURKANALEN PLUTO OG DA KULTURSPEI 1650319
K. Moe Schweigaardsgt. 94 D, 0656 OSLO **Tel:** 2268 8516
Titles:
KULTURSPEILET

WIDERØES FLYVESELSKAP ASA 1768209
Universitetsgaten 14, 0164 OSLO **Tel:** 21 60 81 90
Titles:
PERSPEKTIV - WIDERØES FLYMAGASIN

YGGDRASIL - STUDENTAVISA I MOLDE 1692311
Pb. 2110, 6402 MOLDE **Tel:** 71 19 59 73
Titles:
YGGDRASIL

YNGRE LEGERS FORENING FORUM 1794222
Yngre legers forening, postboks 1152 Sentrum, 0107 OSLO **Tel:** 23109000 **Fax:** 23109150
Titles:
YLF-FORUM

YRKESTRAFIKKFORBUNDET 1628029
Pb. 9175 Grønland, 0134 OSLO **Tel:** 932 40011 **Fax:** 21 01 38 51
Titles:
YRKESTRAFIKK

ZINE TRAVEL AS 1732472
Bispegata 16, 0191 OSLO **Tel:** 901 22 242
Titles:
ZINE TRAVEL

Poland

"A4 MAGAZINE" IWONA CZEMPIŃSKA 1768784
ul. Wiktorska, 14, 17, 02-587 WARSZAWA **Tel:** 22 848 02 82 **Fax:** 22 848 02 82
Titles:
A4 MAGAZYN

"INSTALATOR POLSKI" 1768737
al. Komisji Edukacji Narodowej, 95, 02-777 WARSZAWA **Tel:** 22 678 64 90 **Fax:** 22 679 71 01
Titles:
AUTO MOTO SERWIS

4S MEDIA 1736035
al. KEN, 21, 86, 02-722 WARSZAWA **Tel:** 22 855 62 72 **Fax:** 22 641 70 15
Titles:
TENISKLUB

ABRYS 1736005
ul. Daleka, 33, 60-124 POZNAŃ **Tel:** 61 655 81 50 **Fax:** 61 655 81 01
Titles:
CZYSTA ENERGIA
PRZEGLĄD KOMUNALNY
RECYKLING
WODOCIĄGI-KANALIZACJA
ZIELEŃ MIEJSKA

ADPRESS WYDAWNICTWO REKLAMOWE 1692624
ul. Zdrojowa, 38, 02-927 WARSZAWA **Tel:** 22 424 04 45-48 **Fax:** 22 642 86 86
Titles:
BRIEF

AGENCJA PROMOCJI TURYSTYKI 1692773
ul. Robotnicza, 20, 05-850 OŻARÓW MAZ. **Tel:** 22 721 10 15 **Fax:** 22 721 10 15
Titles:
RYNEK PODRÓŻY

AGENCJA REKLAMOWA MEDIUM SC 1768799
ul. Karczewska, 18, 04-112 WARSZAWA **Tel:** 22 810 23 18 **Fax:** 22 810 27 42
Titles:
EKSPERT BUDOWLANY
ELEKTRO.INFO

AGENCJA SUKURS 1692655
skr. poczt. 109, 00-950 WARSZAWA **Tel:** 22 832 36 12 **Fax:** 22 832 36 12
Titles:
BIBLIOTEKA W SZKOLE

AGENCJA WYDAWNICZO-REKLAMOWA "MADIN" 1768743
ul. Przemysłowa, 3, 40-020 KATOWICE **Tel:** 32 757 24 01 **Fax:** 32 757 24 02
Titles:
RAPORT BRANŻOWY

AGENCJA WYDAWNICZO-REKLAMOWA WPROST 1692758
ul. Postępu 18 B, 02-676 WARSZAWA
Titles:
MÓJ PIES
WIK
WPROST

AGORA SA 1692572
ul. Czerska 8/10, 00-732 WARSZAWA
Titles:
AVANTI
BUKIETY
CZTERY KĄTY
DZIECKO
GAZETA WYBORCZA
KUCHNIA
KWIETNIK
ŁADNY DOM
LOGO
LUBIĘ GOTOWAĆ
METRO
MOTOCYKLE ŚWIATA
OGRODY, OGRÓDKI, ZIELEŃCE
PORADNIK DOMOWY
ŚLUB JAK Z BAJKI
ŚWIAT MOTOCYKLI

AHE W ŁODZI 1768806
ul. Rewolucji 1905 r., 52, 90-213 ŁÓDŹ **Tel:** 42 631 59 40 **Fax:** 42 631 59 77
Titles:
MAGAZYN MŁODEJ KULTURY SLAJD

Poland

AKW TUNING PRESS 1692767
ul. Heroldów, 6, 01-991 WARSZAWA
Tel: 22 569 98 99 **Fax:** 22 569 98 96
Titles:
GT

ALFA-PRINT 1730008
Ul. Świętokrzyska 14A, 00-050 WARSZAWA
Tel: 22 828 14 00 **Fax:** 22 828 14 00
Titles:
POLIGRAFIKA

ALPIN MEDIA 1692757
ul. Głowackiego, 10b, 26, 30-085 KRAKÓW
Tel: 12 638 25 93 **Fax:** 12 638 25 93
Titles:
MAGAZYN GÓRSKI
SKI MAGAZYN

ANDERSEN PRESS SP. Z.O.O. 1768804
Dobrego Pasterza, 31a, 31-416 KRAKÓW
Tel: 12 442 48 01 **Fax:** 12 442 48 02
Titles:
GRACZ
PRACA I ŻYCIE ZA GRANICĄ

ARDO-STUDIO 1730049
ul. Łucka, 15, 1907, 00-842 WARSZAWA
Tel: 515 251 052
Titles:
DEKARZ I CIEŚLA
FACHOWY ELEKTRYK
FACHOWY INSTALATOR

AROMEDIA POLSKA 1729994
ul. Bruna, 16, 11, 02-781 WARSZAWA
Tel: 22 875 29 05 **Fax:** 22 825 28 78
Titles:
STUDIOWAĆ

ARW FOTO-KURIER 1730031
ul. Rzędzińska, 23, 01-368 WARSZAWA
Tel: 22 665 24 33 **Fax:** 22 665 41 79
Titles:
FOTO KURIER

AUDE 1757987
ul. Puławska, 118a, 02-620 WARSZAWA
Tel: 22 843 49 83 **Fax:** 22 353 94 38
Titles:
PESO PERFECTO

AVT - KORPORACJA 1758016
ul. Leszczynowa 11, 03-197 WARSZAWA
Titles:
AUDIO
AUTOMATYKA, PODZESPOŁY, APLIKACJE
DOM POLSKI
ELEKTRONIKA DLA WSZYSTKICH
ELEKTRONIKA PRAKTYCZNA
ESTRADA I STUDIO
ŚWIAT RADIO
T3
WNĘTRZA

AVT KORPORACJA SP Z O.O 1768787
ul. Leszczynowa, 11, 03-197 WARSZAWA
Tel: 22 257 84 99 **Fax:** 22 257 84 32
Titles:
PERKUSISTA

AVT-KORPORACJA 1730059
ul. Leszczynowa, 11, 03-197 WARSZAWA
Tel: 22 257 84 72 **Fax:** 22 257 84 77
Titles:
BUDUJEMY DOM
ELEKTRONIK
INTERNET MAKER
MAGAZYN INTERNET
MŁODY TECHNIK

AWR TDM 1692709
ul. Giżycka, 4, 60-348 POZNAŃ
Tel: 61 8656 38 60 **Fax:** 61 656 38 88
Titles:
KUP AUTO

AXEL SPRINGER POLSKA 1692663
ul. Suwak, 3, 02-676 WARSZAWA
Tel: 22 232 08 00 **Fax:** 22 232 55 02
Titles:
AUTO ŚWIAT
FAKT
FORBES
KOMPUTER ŚWIAT
KOMPUTER ŚWIAT BIBLIOTECZKA
KOMPUTER ŚWIAT EKSPERT
KOMPUTER ŚWIAT TWÓJ NIEZBĘDNIK
NEWSWEEK POLSKA
PRZEGLĄD SPORTOWY

BDB MEDIA 1757972
ul. Krakowskie Przedmieście, 24, 203, 00-927 WARSZAWA **Tel:** 22 552 02 29 **Fax:** 22 552 02 29
Titles:
GAZETA STUDENCKA

BESTSELLER GROUP 1768775
ul. Toruńska, 6/8, 95-200 PABIANICE
Tel: 42 214 91 16 **Fax:** 42 214 91 18
Titles:
MODA & STYL

BIEGANIE 1736015
ul. Grochowska, 316/320, 03-839 WARSZAWA
Tel: 22 353 85 32 **Fax:** 22 353 85 33
Titles:
BIEGANIE

BIURO PROMOCJI I REKLAMY GENERALCZYK 1692621
ul. Garbary, 106/108, 61-757 POZNAŃ
Tel: 61 852 08 94 **Fax:** 61 851 92 41
Titles:
HANDLOWIEC
PORADNIK HANDLOWCA
PORADNIK RESTAURATORA

BIZNES PRESS SP. Z O.O. 1768761
ul. Świętokrzyska, 20, p. 302,322, 00-002 WARSZAWA **Tel:** 22 827 24 01 **Fax:** 22 827 24 01
Titles:
AGRO SERWIS

BIZNESPOLSKA MEDIA SP. Z O.O. 1769276
ul. Św. Bonifacego 92 lok. 13, 02-920 WARSZAWA
Titles:
BIZPOLAND

BONNIER BUSINESS (POLSKA) 1729956
ul. Kijowska, 1, 03-738 WARSZAWA
Tel: 22 333 99 99 **Fax:** 22 333 99 98
Titles:
PULS BIZNESU

BRITISH POLISH CHAMBER OF COMMERCE 1745315
Al. Jana Pawla II 23, 4th Floor, 00-854 WARSZAWA **Tel:** 22 320 01 00 **Fax:** 22 621 19 37
Email: info@bpcc.org.pl
Web site: http://bpcc.org.pl
Titles:
CONTACT INTERNATIONAL BUSINESS VOICE

BROG MEDIA BIZNESU 1692684
ul. Krzywickiego, 34, 02-078 WARSZAWA
Tel: 22 521 20 00 **Fax:** 22 521 20 20
Titles:
MED INFO
NOWOŚCI GASTRONOMICZNE
RYNEK GAZOWY
SHOPPING CENTER POLAND
STACJA BENZYNOWA
SUPERMARKET POLSKA
ŚWIAT HOTELI

BURDA COMMUNICATIONS 1757971
ul. Topiel, 23, 00-342 WARSZAWA
Tel: 22 320 19 00 **Fax:** 22 320 19 01
Titles:
CHIP
CRN COMPUTER RESELLER NEWS POLSKA

BURDA POLSKA 1692593
ul. Ostrowskiego, 7, 53-238 WROCŁAW
Tel: 71 376 28 42 **Fax:** 71 376 28 02
Titles:
MÓJ PIĘKNY OGRÓD - EKSTRA

BURDA PUBLISHING POLSKA 1757975
ul. Ostrowskiego, 7, 53-238 WROCŁAW
Tel: 71 376 28 46-47 **Fax:** 71 376 28 47
Titles:
BURDA
ELLE
ELLE DECORATION
MÓJ PIĘKNY OGRÓD
SAMO ZDROWIE
SÓL I PIEPRZ

BURDA PUBLISHING POLSKA SP. Z O.O. 1768770
ul. Warecka, 11a, 00-034 WARSZAWA
Tel: 22 448 83 15 **Fax:** 22 448 80 01
Titles:
MÓJ PIĘKNY DOM

BURDA PUBLISHING POLSKA SP. ZO.O. 1768749
ul. Warecka, 11a, 00-034 WARSZAWA
Tel: 22 448 83 35 **Fax:** 22 448 80 01
Titles:
DOBRE RADY

BUSINESS CENTRE 1692700
pl. Żelaznej Bramy, 10, 01-318 WARSZAWA
Tel: 22 625 30 37 **Fax:** 22 582 61 67
Titles:
INFORMATOR BCC - FIRMY DORADCZE I KANCELARIE PRAWNICZE
MAGAZYN BCC (W MIESIĘCZNIKU BUSINESSMAN.PL)

BUSINESS MEDIA GROUP 1729993
ul. Kochanowskiego, 10, 5, 40-035 KATOWICE
Tel: 32 206 76 77 **Fax:** 32 253 99 96
Titles:
BUSINESS MEDIA

CEE MEDIA 1730060
ul. Łucka, 15, 313, 00-842 WARSZAWA
Tel: 22 586 30 14 **Fax:** 22 586 30 11
Titles:
CENTRAL EASTERN EUROPEAN REAL ESTATE GUIDE

CENTRUM PRAWA BANKOWEGO I INFORMACJI 1736011
ul. Solec, 101, 5, 00-382 WARSZAWA
Tel: 22 629 18 77 **Fax:** 22 629 18 72
Titles:
BANK
EUROPEJSKI DORADCA SAMORZĄDOWY
FINANSOWANIE NIERUCHOMOŚCI
KURIER FINANSOWY
NOWOCZESNY BANK SPÓŁDZIELCZY

CHARAKTERY 1692739
ul. Warszawska, 6, 25-512 KIELCE
Tel: 41 343 28 40 **Fax:** 41 343 28 40
Titles:
CHARAKTERY

CICHA LIPA 1692698
ul. Pilchowicka, 16a, 02-185 WARSZAWA
Tel: 22 886 85 60 **Fax:** 22 886 85 60
Titles:
FLUID

COLORFUL MEDIA 1768750
ul. Lednicka, 23, 60-413 POZNAŃ
Tel: 61 833 63 28 **Fax:** 61 833 63 28
Titles:
BUSINESS ENGLISH MAGAZINE

CONTACT POLAND 1768781
al. Solidarności, 104, 01-016 WARSZAWA
Tel: 22 632 29 29 **Fax:** 22 862 91 32
Titles:
ŚWIAT ELIT

CUSTOM MEDIA GROUP 1768798
ul. Grażyny 13, 02-548 WARSZAWA
Tel: 22 46 599 46 **Fax:** 22 46 593 30
Email: redakcja@chicmagazine.pl
Titles:
CHIC LUXURY LIFESTYLE MAGAZINE

DAZ PRESS 1692601
ul. ks. J. Popiełuszki, 19/21, 01-595 WARSZAWA
Tel: 22 833 14 07 **Fax:** 22 833 14 07
Titles:
DECISION MAKER
DECYDENT

DESA UNICUM 1739650
ul. Okrzei, 1a, 03-715 WARSZAWA
Tel: 22 333 80 00 **Fax:** 22 333 88 99
Titles:
ANTYKI

DOM WYDAWNICZY KRUSZONA 1692695
ul. Grunwaldzka, 104, 60-307 POZNAŃ
Tel: 61 869 91 77 **Fax:** 61 865 99 09
Titles:
ARTEON

DOM WYDAWNICZY KUSZONA 1692694
ul. Grunwaldzka, 104, 60-307 POZNAŃ
Tel: 61 869 91 77 **Fax:** 61 865 99 09
Titles:
N.P.M.

DOROTA STARZYŃSKA 1692780
ul. Łotewska, 9a, 03-918 WARSZAWA
Tel: 22 429 41 30 **Fax:** 22 617 60 10
Titles:
RACHUNKOWOŚĆ BUDŻETOWA. PORADNIK KSIĘGOWEGO, PERSONEL OD A DO Z

DVC 1692761
ul. Marconich 3, 02-954 WARSZAWA
Tel: 22 858 20 40 **Fax:** 22 858 28 98
Titles:
ARSENAŁ

EDIPRESSE POLSKA 1692724
ul. Wiejska, 19, 00-480 WARSZAWA
Tel: 22 584 23 35 **Fax:** 22 584 23 36
Titles:
MAMO, TO JA
PARTY
PRZYJACIÓŁKA
TWOJE DZIECKO
VITA
VIVA!

EDIPRESSE POLSKA SA 1692725
ul. Wiejska 19, 00-480 WARSZAWA
Titles:
CIENIE I BLASKI
DOM & WNĘTRZE
PANI DOMU
PANI DOMU POLECA
URODA

EDYTOR 1692554
ul. Tracka, 5, 10-364 OLSZTYN **Tel:** 89 539 77 00
Fax: 89 539 75 11
Titles:
GAZETA OLSZTYŃSKA/DZIENNIK ELBLĄSKI
NASZA MIERZEJA
ROLNICZE ABC

EGMONT POLSKA 1692735
ul. Dzielna, 60, 01-029 WARSZAWA
Tel: 22 838 41 00 **Fax:** 22 838 42 00
Titles:
HOT WHEELS

EUROBUILD PUBLISHING HOUSE 1745480
Al. Jerozolimskie 53, 00-697 WARSZAWA
Tel: 22 356 25 00 **Fax:** 22 356 25 01
Email: eurobuild@eurobuildcee.com
Web site: http://www.eurobuild.pl
Titles:
EUROBUILD

EUROCONTACT POLSKA 1739648
ul. Kubickiego, 7, 13, 02-954 WARSZAWA
Tel: 22 550 61 23 **Fax:** 22 550 61 25
Titles:
KURIER MEDYCYNY

EURO-MEDIA 1729961
al. Komisji Edukacji Narodowej, 95, 02-777 WARSZAWA **Tel:** 22 678 66 09 **Fax:** 22 678 54 21
Titles:
CHŁODNICTWO & KLIMATYZACJA
OCHRONA MIENIA I INFORMACJI
ŚWIAT SZKŁA

EUROPEJSKIE CENTRUM JAKOŚCI 1739632
ul. Ciołka 13, WARSZAWA 01-445
Titles:
QUALITY NEWS

EUROSYSTEM 1692716
ul. Wawelska, 78, 30, 02-034 WARSZAWA
Titles:
PRAKTYKA LEKARSKA
WIADOMOŚCI TURYSTYCZNE

FABAS POLSKA 1692775
ul. 10 Lutego, 5, 7, 81-366 GDYNIA
Tel: 58 612 15 51 **Fax:** 58 620 47 51
Titles:
STREET XTREME
TRAILER MAGAZINE

FASHION GROUP SP. Z O.O. 1768772
ul. Słupska, 6a, 02-495 WARSZAWA
Tel: 22 867 04 64/65 **Fax:** 22 867 04 64
Titles:
FASHION MAGAZINE

FORMACJA TWORZYWO 1692703
ul. Felińskiego, 44, 01-563 WARSZAWA
Tel: 22 839 32 44 **Fax:** 22 839 32 44
Titles:
GAZETA SZKOLNA

FUNDACJA EDUKACJA W POŁOŻNICTWIE I GINEKOLOGII WE WSPÓŁPRACY Z TERMEDIĄ 1692677
ul. Wenedów, 9/1, 61-614 POZNAŃ
Tel: 61 822 77 81 **Fax:** 61 822 77 81
Titles:
GINEKOLOGIA PRAKTYCZNA

FUNDACJA GREEN PARK 1758001
ul. Trylogii 2/16, 01-982 WARSZAWA
Titles:
PRZEMYSŁ I ŚRODOWISKO

FUNDACJA KINO 1692747
ul. Chełmska, 21 bud. 4, 28, 00-724 WARSZAWA
Tel: 22 841 68 43 **Fax:** 22 841 90 57
Titles:
KINO

FUN-SPORT 1692762
ul. Wolności, 179, 58-560 JELENIA GÓRA
Tel: 75 755 98 88 **Fax:** 75 755 98 89
Titles:
BIKE ACTION

FWR ARCHIVOLTA MICHAŁ STĘPIEŃ 1692630
C12, 23, 32-086 WĘGRZCE **Tel:** 12 285 73 25
Fax: 12 285 73 25
Titles:
ARCHIVOLTA

G+J MEDIA 1729986
ul. Wynalazek, 4, 02-677 WARSZAWA
Tel: 22 640 07 21/22 **Fax:** 22 640 07 23
Titles:
GLAMOUR

G+J RBA 1692628
ul. Wynalazek, 4, 02-677 WARSZAWA
Tel: 22 607 02 56/57 **Fax:** 22 607 02 61
Titles:
NATIONAL GEOGRAPHIC POLSKA
NATIONAL GEOGRAPHIC TRAVELER

GAZETA FINANSOWA 1692581
Al. Jerozolimskie, 123a, 02-017 WARSZAWA
Tel: 22 438 87 76 **Fax:** 22 438 87 64
Titles:
GAZETA FINANSOWA

GEODETA SP. Z O.O. 1745470
ul. Narbutta 40/20, 02-541 WARSZAWA
Email: redakcja@geoforum.pl
Titles:
GEODETA

GJC INTER MEDIA 1729997
ul. Podbiałowa, 11, 61-680 POZNAŃ
Tel: 61 825 73 22 **Fax:** 61 825 84 85
Titles:
GIFTS JOURNAL

GOLDMAN 1692645
ul. Armii Krajowej, 86, 83-110 TCZEW
Tel: 58 777 01 25 **Fax:** 58 777 01 25
Titles:
LAKIERNICTWO PRZEMYSŁOWE

GOLDMAN - GOLDMAN MEDIA GROUP 1730013
ul. Armii Krajowej, 86, 83-110 TCZEW
Tel: 58 777 01 25 **Fax:** 58 777 01 25
Titles:
POLSKI CARAVANING

GRUNER + JAHR POLSKA 1729975
Ul. Wynalazek 4, 02-677 WARSZAWA
Titles:
CLAUDIA
FOCUS
GALA
MOJE GOTOWANIE
NAJ
RODZICE

GRUPA C2 1736000
ul. Krakowskie Przedmieście, 58, 14, 20-076 LUBLIN **Tel:** 81 534 44 29 **Fax:** 81 534 44 29
Titles:
AUTO TUNING ŚWIAT

GRUPA WYDAWNICZA INFOR SA 1692567
ul. Okopowa, 58/72, 01-042 WARSZAWA
Tel: 22 530 41 75 **Fax:** 22 530 42 22
Titles:
BIULETYN PODATKÓW DOCHODOWYCH

HEARST - MARQUARD PUBLISHING - BEATA MILEWSKA 1692616
ul. Wilcza, 50/52, 00-679 WARSZAWA
Tel: 22 421 10 00 **Fax:** 22 421 11 11
Titles:
COSMOPOLITAN

HEARST-MARQUARD PUBLISHING - BEATA MILEWSKA 1692615
ul. Wilcza, 50/52, 00-679 WARSZAWA
Tel: 22 421 10 00 **Fax:** 22 421 11 11
Titles:
SHAPE

HI-FI I MUZYKA 1735971
ul. Blokowa, 24, 03-641 WARSZAWA
Tel: 22 679 56 42 **Fax:** 22 679 52 17
Titles:
HI-FI

ICAN SPÓŁKA Z OGRANICZONĄ ODPOWIEDZIALNOŚCIĄ SP.K. (DAWNIEJ: CANADIAN INTERNATIONAL MANAGEMENT INSTITUTE SP. Z O.O.) 1768788
Al. Jerozolimskie, 65/79, 00-697 WARSZAWA
Tel: 22 630 66 87 **Fax:** 22 630 66 85
Titles:
HARVARD BUSINESS REVIEW POLSKA

INFOMARKET 1768807
ul. Trylogii, 2/16, 50, 01-982 WARSZAWA
Tel: 22 835 19 17 **Fax:** 22 835 19 17
Titles:
INFOMARKET - MAGAZYN AGD I RTV

INFOMAX KATOWICE 1736008
ul. Porcelanowa, 11c, 40-246 KATOWICE
Tel: 32 730 32 32 **Fax:** 32 258 16 45
Titles:
EKOLOGIA

INFOR BIZNES SP. Z O.O. 1768820
ul. Okopowa, 58/72, 01-042 WARSZAWA
Titles:
DZIENNIK GAZETA PRAWNA
GAZETA PRAWNA
GAZETA PRAWNA

INFOR EKSPERT SP. Z O.O. 1768727
ul. Okopowa, 58/72, 01-042 WARSZAWA
Tel: 22 530 41 75 **Fax:** 22 530 42 22
Titles:
BIULETYN RACHUNKOWOŚCI
BIULETYN VAT
CONTROLLING I RACHUNKOWOŚĆ ZARZĄDCZA
MONITOR KSIĘGOWEGO
MONITOR PRAWA PRACY I UBEZPIECZEŃ
PERSONEL I ZARZĄDZANIE
PORADNIK GAZETY PRAWNEJ
PORADNIK ORGANIZACJI NON-PROFIT
PRAWO SPÓŁEK
RACHUNKOWOŚĆ BUDŻETOWA
SEKRETARIAT
SERWIS PRAWNO-PRACOWNICZY
TWÓJ BIZNES

INFOR SA 1757968
ul. Okopowa 58/72, 01-042 WARSZAWA
Tel: 22 530 42 75 **Fax:** 22 530 41 30
Titles:
PRAWO PRZEDSIĘBIORCY

INFORMATOR HANDLOWY ZAOPATRZENIOWIEC 1730045
ul. Roztocze, 5, 5, 20-722 LUBLIN
Tel: 81 743 65 91 **Fax:** 81 535 09 69
Titles:
ŚWIAT KOMINKÓW

INSTALATOR POLSKI 1692731
al. Komisji Edukacji Narodowej, 95, 02-777 WARSZAWA **Tel:** 22 678 35 92 **Fax:** 22 678 32 52
Titles:
DORADCA ENERGETYCZNY
POLSKI INSTALATOR

INSTALATOR POLSKI SP. Z O.O. 1757977
al. Komisji Edukacji Narodowej, 95, 02-777 WARSZAWA **Tel:** 22 678 37 47 **Fax:** 22 678 61 38
Titles:
ELEKTROINSTALATOR

INSTYTUT BADAŃ NAD STOSUNKAMI MIĘDZYNARODOWYMI 1730046
ul. Ordynacka, 11, 5, 00-364 WARSZAWA
Tel: 22 498 15 37 **Fax:** 22 644 63 70
Titles:
STOSUNKI MIĘDZYNARODOWE

INSTYTUT MECHANIZACJI BUDOWNICTWA I GÓRNICTWA SKALNEGO 1745508
IMBiGS, ul. Racjonalizacji 6/8, 02-673 WARSZAWA **Tel:** 22 853 81 13 **Fax:** 22 853 81 13
Email: wydawnictwo@imbigs.org.pl
Titles:
PRZEGLĄD MECHANICZNY

INTERIORS 1735970
ul. Bora-Komorowskiego, 35, 161, 03-982 WARSZAWA **Tel:** 22 406 39 14 **Fax:** 22 406 39 15
Titles:
REZYDENCJE

INTERNATIONAL CONNECTIONS COMPANY 1692741
al. 3 Maja, 12, 411, 00-391 WARSZAWA
Tel: 22 625 78 79 **Fax:** 22 625 78 79
Titles:
WHAT'S UP IN WARSAW

INTERNATIONAL DATA GROUP POLAND SA 1692579
ul. Jordanowska 12, 04-204 WARSZAWA
Tel: 22 321 78 00 **Fax:** 22 321 78 88
Email: idg@idg.com.pl
Web site: http://www.idg.com.pl/informacje.html
Titles:
CEO
CEO MOTO
CFO
CIO
COMPUTERWORLD
CSO
IDG.PL
KINO DOMOWE
NETWORLD
PC WORLD KOMPUTER

INTERTEAM SC 1748997
Aleja W. Korfantego 195, 40-153 KATOWICE
Tel: 32 730 23 65
Email: poczta@mojdom.pub.pl
Titles:
MÓJ DOM

IPM 1692744
ul. Racławicka, 15/19, 53-149 WROCŁAW
Tel: 71 783 51 16 **Fax:** 71 783 51 00
Titles:
MOTORYZACYJNY RAPORT SPECJALNY
OUTSOURCING MAGAZINE

IPM INTERNET PRASA MEDIA 1729998
ul. Racławicka, 15/19, 53-149 WROCŁAW
Tel: 71 783 51 00 **Fax:** 71 783 51 01
Titles:
AUTO FIRMOWE

ITER 1745479
ul. Pilicka 22, 02-613 WARSZAWA
Email: wydawnictwo@iter.com.pl
Titles:
PROJEKTOWANIE I KONSTRUKCJE INŻYNIERSKIE

KARTEL PRESS SA 1692643
ul. Szosa Bydgoska, 56, 87-100 TORUŃ
Tel: 56 660 31 60 **Fax:** 56 660 31 61
Titles:
RYNKI ALKOHOLOWE

KOMENDA GŁÓWNA PAŃSTWOWEJ STRAŻY POŻARNEJ WE WSPÓŁPRACY Z FUNDACJĄ EDUKACJA I TECHNIKA RATOWNICTWA 1692759
ul. Podchorążych, 38, 00-463 WARSZAWA
Tel: 22 523 33 06/08 **Fax:** 22 523 33 05
Titles:
PRZEGLĄD POŻARNICZY

KOŃ POLSKI 1692594
ul. Wał Miedzeszyński, 872, 4, 03-917 WARSZAWA **Tel:** 22 869 93 18
Titles:
KOŃ POLSKI

KONCEPT 1729965
ul. Bacciarellego, 54 bud. C, 51-649 WROCLAW
Tel: 71 347 83 88 **Fax:** 71 347 83 87
Email: koncept@koncept-wydawnictwo.pl
Web site: http://www.koncept-wydawnictwo.pl
Titles:
MAGAZYN ROWEROWY
ŚWIAT REZYDENCJI WNĘTRZ I OGRODÓW
WŁASNY DOM Z KONCEPTEM

KREATIV SP. Z O. O. 1771897
Kłopotowskiego 22, 03-717 WARSZAWA
Tel: 40 670 26 40 **Fax:** 40 244 26 90
Email: kontakt@kreativ.pl
Titles:
MEDIA2.PL

KURIER SZCZECIŃSKI SP. Z O.O. 1768826
pl. Hołdu Pruskiego, 8, 70-550 SZCZECIN
Tel: 91 442 91 00/01 **Fax:** 91 442 91 05
Titles:
KURIER SZCZECIŃSKI DZIENNIK POMORZA ZACHODNIEGO

LAMPA I ISKRA BOŻA, PAWEŁ DUNIN-WĄSOWICZ 1692749
ul. Hoża, 42, 8, 00-516 WARSZAWA
Tel: 22 622 10 09
Titles:
LAMPA

LESZEK KRYNIEWSKI PRESS & MEDIA 1730000
ul. Powstańców Śl., 32a, 1, 45-087 OPOLE
Tel: 77 402 52 52 **Fax:** 77 423 14 27
Titles:
CABINES

LINUX NEW MEDIA POLSKA 1735969
ul. Mangalia, 4, 02-758 WARSZAWA
Tel: 22 742 14 55 **Fax:** 22 642 70 05
Titles:
DARMOWE PROGRAMY
EASYLINUX
LINUX MAGAZINE

ŁÓDŹ-SAT 1692712
ul. Traugutta, 25, 90-113 ŁÓDŹ **Tel:** 42 632 99 12
Fax: 42 639 78 83
Titles:
TV-SAT MAGAZYN

ŁOWIEC POLSKI 1692607
ul. Nowy Świat, 35, 00-029 WARSZAWA
Tel: 22 556 82 80 **Fax:** 22 556 82 99
Titles:
ŁOWIEC POLSKI

LUPO MEDIA MAJA I SŁAWOMIR WILK 1729990
ul. Henryka Sienkiewicza 4 lok. 6, 90-113 ŁÓDŹ
Titles:
PRZEWODNIK ŚLUBNY

MARKA: PUBLIKACJE 1692611
ul. Piotrkowska, 94, 90-103 ŁÓDŹ
Tel: 42 632 61 79 **Fax:** 42 632 07 59
Titles:
F1 RACING

MARQUARD MEDIA POLSKA 1692617
ul. Wilcza 50/52, 00-679 WARSZAWA
Titles:
CKM
OLIVIA
PLAYBOY
VOYAGE

MAXICON 1692632
ul. Zgoda, 9, 81-361 GDYNIA **Tel:** 58 622 63 00
Fax: 58 622 63 00
Titles:
CITY MAX
MAXMAGAZINE

MAXMEDIA MARIUSZ GRYŻEWSKI 1730030
ul. Estrady 67, 01-932 WARSZAWA
Email: wydawnictwo@maxmedia.org.pl
Titles:
FAKTY
VIP POLITYKA PRAWO GOSPODARKA

MECICAL TRIBUNE POLSKA 1729967
ul. 29 Listopada, 10, 00-465 WARSZAWA
Tel: 22 444 24 00 **Fax:** 22 832 10 77
Titles:
MAGAZYN WETERYNARYJNY

MEDI PRESS 1692769
ul. Niedźwiedzia, 12a, 02-737 WARSZAWA
Tel: 22 853 73 72 **Fax:** 22 853 73 72
Titles:
PORADNIK STOMATOLOGICZNY
PORADNIK ZDROWIA Z KALENDARZEM
SERIA INFO
SUPER LINIA
SUPER LINIA - WYDANIE SPECJALNE

MEDI PRESS SP. Z O.O. 1768818
ul. Niedźwiedzia, 12a, 02-737 WARSZAWA
Tel: 22 853 73 72 **Fax:** 22 853 73 72
Titles:
MEDYCYNA WIEKU ROZWOJOWEGO

MEDIA4MAT 1739664
ul. Dietla, 50/6, 31-039 KRAKÓW
Tel: 12 428 76 03 **Fax:** 12 376 45 81
Titles:
ECHO MIASTA KRAKÓW

MEDIA 500 1730003
ul. Górnośląska, 14, 00-432 WARSZAWA
Tel: 22 628 25 58 **Fax:** 22 628 76 69
Titles:
CHŁOPSKA DROGA

MEDIA ADVERTISING SP. Z O.O. 1768736
ul. Locci, 30, 02-928 WARSZAWA
Tel: 22 852 17 31 **Fax:** 22 899 29 45
Titles:
LAIF
LAIFSTYLE

MEDIA DIRECT 1730029
ul. Śmiała, 26, 01-523 WARSZAWA
Tel: 22 327 16 82 **Fax:** 22 327 16 87
Titles:
KOSMETYKI
ŻYCIE HANDLOWE

MEDIA ONE 1692633
ul. Chmielna, 7, 14, 00-021 WARSZAWA
Tel: 22 826 29 92 **Fax:** 22 890 98 55
Titles:
HIRO

MEDIA POINT GROUP 1729970
Al. Jerozolimskie, 146c, 02-305 WARSZAWA
Tel: 22 347 50 00 **Fax:** 22 347 50 01
Titles:
DLACZEGO
DLATEGO
FILM
MACHINA

MEDIA PRESS 1768769
ul. Niedźwiedzia, 12a, 02-737 WARSZAWA
Tel: 22 853 73 72 **Fax:** 22 853 73 72
Titles:
ŻYJMY DŁUŻEJ

MEDIA REGIONALNE SP. Z O.O. 1768824
ul. Prosta 51, 00-838 WARSZAWA
Titles:
GAZETA LUBUSKA
GŁOS POMORZA

MEDIA REGIONALNE SP. Z O.O. II O. W BYDGOSZCZY 1768822
ul. Zamoyskiego, 2, 85-063 BYDGOSZCZ
Tel: 52 326 31 64/00 **Fax:** 52 322 10 31
Titles:
GAZETA POMORSKA (GAZETA KUJAWSKA)

MEDIA REGIONALNE SP. Z O.O., O. W BIAŁYMSTOKU 1768828
ul. św. Mikołaja, 1, 15-419 BIAŁYSTOK
Tel: 85 748 74 00 **Fax:** 85 748 74 01
Titles:
GAZETA WSPÓŁCZESNA
KURIER PORANNY

MEDIA SKOK 1729992
ul. Pilotów 21, 80-460 GDAŃSK
Titles:
GAZETA BANKOWA

MEDIA TOUCH GROUP 1692733
ul. Miączyńska, 57a, 02-637 WARSZAWA
Tel: 22 898 04 15 **Fax:** 22 898 04 21
Titles:
BRAIN DAMAGE

MEDIA TV PLUS 1692743
ul. Jaracza, 2, 00-378 WARSZAWA
Tel: 22 622 98 34 **Fax:** 22 622 98 34
Titles:
NA ZDROWIE. DOSTĘPNE BEZ RECEPTY
NA ZDROWIE. MANAGER APTEKI

MEDIAPRINT POLSKA SP. Z O.O. 1744695
Noakowskiego 4, 05-820 PIASTÓW
Tel: 22 424 47 57 **Fax:** 22 723 41 25
Email: janusz@swiatpoligrafii.pl
Titles:
ŚWIAT POLIGRAFII

MEDIATEKA/FUNDACJA REGIONALIS 1735972
ul. Zbożowa, 4, 25-416 KIELCE **Tel:** 41 344 38 77
Fax: 41 344 38 77
Titles:
DEDAL

MEDICAL TRIBUNE POLSKA 1739636
ul. 29 Listopada, 10, 00-465 WARSZAWA
Tel: 22 444 24 00 **Fax:** 22 832 10 77
Titles:
MEDICAL TRIBUNE
MEDYCYNA PO DYPLOMIE

MEDYCYNA PRAKTYCZNA 1692619
ul. Skawińska, 8, 31-066 KRAKÓW
Tel: 12 293 40 20 **Fax:** 12 293 40 30
Titles:
MEDYCYNA PRAKTYCZNA
MEDYCYNA PRAKTYCZNA - CHIRURGIA
MEDYCYNA PRAKTYCZNA - GINEKOLOGIA I POŁOŻNICTWO
MEDYCYNA PRAKTYCZNA - PEDIATRIA
NEUROLOGY

MIGUT MEDIA 1729995
ul. Tytoniowa, 20, 04-228 WARSZAWA
Tel: 22 515 01 87 **Fax:** 22 613 25 84
Titles:
APARTAMENTY I MIESZKANIA
DIGITAL FOTO VIDEO
PRAWO TELEINFORMATYCZNE

MIGUT MEDIA SA 1692719
ul. Tytoniowa, 20, 04-228 WARSZAWA
Tel: 22 515 00 17 **Fax:** 22 613 25 84
Titles:
AUDIO VIDEO
BUSINESSMAN.PL
ENERGIA & PRZEMYSŁ
IT RESELLER
OFFICE WORLD
RAPORT TELEINFO
ŚWIAT MOTORYZACJI
TELEINFO
VIDEO MIX
VILLA

MIT MEDIA 1729969
ul. Rakietników, 27/29, 10, 02-495 WARSZAWA
Tel: 22 882 37 33 **Fax:** 22 882 37 66
Titles:
CONFERENCE & BUSINESS
LAPTOP MAGAZYN
MOBILITY

MJ MEDIA 1739633
os. Na Murawie, 7, 4, 61-655 POZNAŃ
Tel: 61 825 30 47 **Fax:** 61 825 30 47
Titles:
FUNDUSZE EUROPEJSKIE

MKM 1735992
ul. Chopina, 24, 68-200 ŻARY **Tel:** 68 470 07 00
Fax: 68 470 07 17
Titles:
GAZETA REGIONALNA

MOTOR-PRESSE POLSKA 1692686
ul. Ostrowskiego, 7, 53-238 WROCŁAW
Tel: 71 780 66 11 **Fax:** 71 780 66 12
Titles:
AUTO MOTOR I SPORT
CIĘŻARÓWKI I AUTOBUSY
MAXI TUNING
MEN'S HEALTH
MOTOCYKL

MURATOR SA 1768728
ul. Kamionkowska 45, 03-812 WARSZAWA
Titles:
ARCHITEKTURA - MURATOR
DOBRE WNĘTRZE
DOBRE WNĘTRZE NUMER SPECJALNY
M JAK MAMA
M JAK MIESZKANIE
M JAK MIESZKANIE POLECA
MOJE MIESZKANIE
MURATOR
MURATOR NUMER SPECJALNY
PODRÓŻE
SUPER EXPRESS
WYKAŃCZAMY DOM
ŻAGLE
ZBUDUJ DOM
ZDROWIE

MURATOR SA (DAWNIEJ WYDAWNICTWO MURATOR) 1757973
ul. Kamionkowska, 45, 03-812 WARSZAWA
Tel: 22 590 52 96 **Fax:** 22 590 54 22
Titles:
MURATOR - WYDANIE SPECJALNE

NATHUSIUS INVESTMENTS 1730004
św. Bonifacego, 92, 13/18, 02-940 WARSZAWA
Tel: 22 642 43 12 **Fax:** 22 642 36 25
Titles:
FORUM MLECZARSKIE
FORUM SŁODKO-SŁONE

NEWMAN 1730027
Al. Jerozolimskie 123A, lok. 308, 02-017 WARSZAWA
Titles:
PILOT CLUB MAGAZINE
PROJEKTORY I EKRANY

NUMEDIA 1692580
Aleje Jerozolimskie 101/14, 02-011 WARSZAWA
Titles:
GENTLEMAN
HOME & MARKET

OBERON POLSKA 1735973
ul. Świeradowska, 44a, 02-662 WARSZAWA
Tel: 22 898 04 15 **Fax:** 22 898 04 21
Titles:
SNOW IT!
SURF IT!

OFF-ROAD PL GRZEGORZ SUROWIEC, TOMASZ KONIK SJ 1768764
ul. Konecznego, 6, 9u, 31-216 KRAKÓW
Tel: 12 412 26 57 **Fax:** 12 412 26 57
Titles:
OFF-ROAD PL MAGAZYN 4 X 4

OFICYNA WYDAWNICZA MEDIUM SC 1768792
ul. Karczewska, 18, 04-112 WARSZAWA
Tel: 022 810 58 09 **Fax:** 22 810 27 42
Titles:
IZOLACJE

OFICYNA WYDAWNICZA OIKOS 1692590
ul. Kaliska, 1, 8, 02-316 WARSZAWA
Tel: 22 883 39 52 **Fax:** 22 822 66 49
Titles:
AGROMECHANIKA
BRAĆ ŁOWIECKA
DRWAL
LAS POLSKI

OFICYNA WYDAWNICZA RYNEK POLSKI 1729966
ul. Elektoralna, 13, 4, 00-137 WARSZAWA
Tel: 22 620 31 42 **Fax:** 22 620 31 37
Titles:
POLISH MARKET

OFICYNA WYDAWNICZA VEGA 1692591
ul. Bruna, 34, 02-594 WARSZAWA
Tel: 22 825 25 00 **Fax:** 22 849 86 00
Titles:
WEGETARIAŃSKI ŚWIAT

OFICYNA WYDAWNICZA WIELKOPOLSKI 1692558
ul. Grunwaldzka, 19, 60-782 POZNAŃ
Tel: 61 860 60 00 **Fax:** 61 860 60 69
Titles:
GAZETA POZNAŃSKA

OKRĘGOWA IZBA LEKARSKA W WARSZAWIE 1692763
ul. Kozia, 3/5, 31, 00-070 WARSZAWA
Tel: 22 828 36 39 **Fax:** 22 828 36 39
Titles:
PULS

OOH MAGAZINE MONIKA OPAŁKA 1768802
ul. Kochanowskiego, 10, 5, 40-035 KATOWICE
Tel: 32 206 76 77 **Fax:** 32 253 99 96
Titles:
OOH MAGAZINE

OP & EC 1768773
ul. Bohomolca, 17, 1, 01-613 WARSZAWA
Tel: 22 865 67 41 **Fax:** 22 865 67 41
Titles:
ART & LIFE

OP&EC POLSKA 1757997
ul. Bohomolca, 17, 1, 01-613 WARSZAWA
Tel: 22 865 67 41 **Fax:** 22 834 74 85
Titles:
BUSINESS & LIFE

ORANGE MEDIA 1692751
ul. Cedrowa, 34, 04-533 WARSZAWA
Tel: 22 517 13 60 **Fax:** 22 517 13 61
Titles:
TERAZ ROCK
TOPSPEED

ORBI PLUS & EUROPEAN CENTER 1692582
ul. Bohomolca, 17, 01-613 WARSZAWA
Tel: 22 865 67 41 **Fax:** 22 865 67 41
Titles:
GOLF & LIFE
GOLF VADEMECUM

OŚRODEK WDROŻEŃ EKONOMICZNO-ORGANIZACYJNYCH BUDOWNICTWA PROMOCJA SP. Z O.O. 1768740
ul. Migdałowa, 4, 02-796 WARSZAWA
Tel: 22 242 54 39 **Fax:** 22 242 54 45
Titles:
LICZ I BUDUJ

PHOENIX PRESS 1692680
ul. św. Antoniego, 7, 50-073 WROCŁAW
Tel: 71 344 77 75 **Fax:** 71 346 01 74
Titles:
KALEJDOSKOP LOSÓW
NA ŚCIEŻKACH ŻYCIA
SEKRETY I NAMIĘTNOŚCI
SUKCESY I PORAŻKI. WYDANIE SPECJALNE
TO LUBIĘ!
Z ŻYCIA WZIĘTE. WYDANIE SPECJALNE

PMR LTD. SP. Z O.O. 1745457
ul. Supniewskiego 9, 31-527, 31-527, KRAKÓW
Tel: 12 618 90 00 **Fax:** 12 618 90 08
Titles:
POLISH CONSTRUCTION REVIEW
POLISH MARKET REVIEW

PODWYSOCKA, J. KUJAŁOWICZ, M. SŁODOWNIK SJ 1768789
ul. Krakowskie Przedmieście, 79, 401, 00-079 WARSZAWA **Tel:** 22 394 84 66 **Fax:** 22 829 21 90
Titles:
H2O

POLAND BUSINESS PUBLISHING 1730043
ul. Łucka, 15, 3 p., 00-842 WARSZAWA
Tel: 22 586 30 00 **Fax:** 22 586 30 01
Titles:
POLAND MONTHLY

POLAND MARKETING BARAŃSKI SP. Z O. O. 1748065
Tel: 22 859 19 65 **Fax:** 22 859 19 67
ul. Pasaż Ursynowski 1/45, 02-784 WARSZAWA
Tel: 22 859 19 65 **Fax:** 22 859 19 67
Email: www.posbud.com.pl
Web site: http://posbud.com.pl
Titles:
MASZYNY BUDOWLANE
POŚREDNIK BUDOWLANY

POLANDBUSINESSNETWORK 1757979
ul. Roosevelta, 18, 60-829 POZNAŃ
Tel: 61 845 10 13 **Fax:** 61 845 10 14
Titles:
BIZNES POZNAŃSKI

POLITYKA SPÓŁDZIELNIA PRACY 1692604
ul. Słupecka, 6, 02-309 WARSZAWA
Tel: 22 451 60 96 **Fax:** 22 451 61 64
Titles:
FORUM
POLITYKA

POLSKAPRESSE 1735984
ul. 3 Maja 14, 20-078 LUBLIN **Tel:** 81 532 66 34 **Fax:** 81 532 68 35
Titles:
KURIER LUBELSKI
NASZEMIASTO.PL
POLSKA (METROPOLIA WARSZAWSKA)
SUPER TELE
TELE MAGAZYN

POLSKAPRESSE O. PRASA BAŁTYCKA 1729897
ul. Targ Drzewny, 9/11, 80-894 GDAŃSK
Tel: 58 300 33 00 **Fax:** 58 300 33 03
Titles:
POLSKA DZIENNIK BAŁTYCKI

POLSKAPRESSE O. PRASA KRAKOWSKA 1692565
al. Pokoju, 3, 31-548 KRAKÓW **Tel:** 12 688 80 00 **Fax:** 12 688 81 09
Titles:
POLSKA GAZETA KRAKOWSKA

POLSKAPRESSE, O. PRASA ŁÓDZKA 1692573
ul. ks. I. Skorupki, 17/19, 90-532 ŁÓDŹ
Tel: 42 665 92 03 **Fax:** 42 665 92 06
Titles:
EXPRESS ILUSTROWANY

POLSKAPRESSE O. PRASA ŚLĄSKA 1692557
ul. Młyńska, 1, 40-954 KATOWICE
Tel: 32 358 21 04 **Fax:** 32 358 31 04
Titles:
POLSKA DZIENNIK ZACHODNI

POLSKAPRESSE O. PRASA WROCŁAWSKA 1692566
ul. Strzegomska, 42a, 53-611 WROCŁAW
Tel: 71 374 81 00 **Fax:** 71 374 81 75
Titles:
POLSKA GAZETA WROCŁAWSKA

POLSKAPRESSE SP. Z O.O. 1768779
ul. Domaniewska, 41, 02-672 WARSZAWA
Tel: 22 201 40 27 **Fax:** 22 201 40 30
Titles:
MOTO EXPRESS

POLSKAPRESSE SP. Z O.O. O. BIURO REKLAMY 1768823
ul. ks. I. Skorupki, 17/19, 90-532 ŁÓDŹ
Tel: 42 665 91 04 **Fax:** 42 665 91 01
Titles:
DZIENNIK ŁÓDZKI - WIADOMOŚCI DNIA

POLSKAPRESSE SP. Z O.O. O. PRASA POZNAŃSKA 1768821
ul. Grunwaldzka, 19, 60-782 POZNAŃ
Tel: 61 869 41 00 **Fax:** 61 860 61 15
Titles:
POLSKA GŁOS WIELKOPOLSKI

POLSKI DRUKARZ 1729985
ul. Obywatelska, 115, 94-104 ŁÓDŹ
Tel: 42 687 12 92 **Fax:** 42 687 12 99
Titles:
ŚWIAT DRUKU

POLSKIE WYDAWNICTWA SPECJALISTYCZNE PROMEDIA 1692750
ul. Okrzei, 1a, 03-715 WARSZAWA
Tel: 22 333 80 00 **Fax:** 22 333 88 82
Titles:
HOTELARZ
POLSKI JUBILER
RYNEK TURYSTYCZNY

POLSKIE WYDAWNICTWO EKONOMICZNE SA 1692578
ul. Canaletta, 4, 00-099 WARSZAWA
Tel: 22 827 80 01 **Fax:** 22 827 55 67
Titles:
GOSPODARKA MATERIAŁOWA I LOGISTYKA
MARKETING I RYNEK
PRACA I ZABEZPIECZENIE SPOŁECZNE
PRZEGLĄD USTAWODAWSTWA GOSPODARCZEGO

POLSKIE WYDAWNICTWO FACHOWE 1729978
ul. Wał Miedzeszyński 630, 03-994 WARSZAWA
Titles:
FOOD SERVICE
HANDEL

POLSKIE WYDAWNICTWO TRANSPORTOWE 1692732
ul. Miedziana, 3a, 21, 00-814 WARSZAWA
Tel: 22 620 92 23 **Fax:** 22 890 98 32
Titles:
POLSKA GAZETA TRANSPORTOWA

PPH NESTOR TOMASZ KAWECKI 1769447
ul. Łąkowa 27, 32-082 BOLECHOWICE
Titles:
GLOBTROTER

PPWP 1729973
ul. Dzika, 4, 00-194 WARSZAWA
Tel: 22 635 73 70 **Fax:** 22 635 74 62
Titles:
AGD-RTV
FORUM PRZEMYSŁU DRZEWNEGO
LEKI WSPÓŁCZESNEJ TERAPII
NARZĘDZIA I ELEKTRONARZĘDZIA
SPEDYCJA TRANSPORT LOGISTYKA
ŚWIAT FRYZJERSTWA
TECHNIKA W DOMU

PRELITE 1730002
ul. Zeylanda, 4, 6, 60-808 POZNAŃ
Titles:
PIAR.PL

PRESS & MEDIA 1769789
ul. Powstańców Śl., 32a, 1, 45-087 OPOLE
Titles:
SOLARIUM

PRESS ART PROMOTION SP. Z O.O. 1768811
ul. Wichrowa, 20, 30-438 KRAKÓW
Tel: 12 262 22 44 **Fax:** 12 262 22 44
Titles:
PRESTIGE MAGAZINE

PRESS SP. Z O.O. 1768738
ul. Płocka, 5a, 01-231WARSZAWA
Titles:
PRESS

PRESSCOM 1730064
ul. Tadeusza Kościuszki, 29, 2, 50-011 WROCŁAW **Tel:** 71 797 28 46 **Fax:** 71 797 28 16
Titles:
FINANSE PUBLICZNE
PRZETARGI PUBLICZNE

PRESSKONTAKT 1730023
ul. Kochanowskiego, 25, 31-127 KRAKÓW
Tel: 12 633 99 01 **Fax:** 12 633 90 01
Titles:
HIP HOP RGB

PRESSPUBLICA 1692553
ul. Prosta, 51, 00-838 WARSZAWA
Tel: 22 463 06 00 **Fax:** 22 463 05 10
Titles:
PARKIET - GAZETA GIEŁDY
RZECZPOSPOLITA
ŻYCIE WARSZAWY

PRO MEDIA 1692568
ul. Powstańców Śląskich, 9, 45-086 OPOLE
Tel: 77 443 25 00 **Fax:** 77 443 25 15
Titles:
NOWA TRYBUNA OPOLSKA

PROFIT SYSTEM 1730024
ul. Brązownicza, 16, 01-929 WARSZAWA
Tel: 22 560 80 20 **Fax:** 22 560 80 21
Titles:
WŁASNY BIZNES FRANCHISING

PROFUS MANAGEMENT 1692603
ul. Stawki, 2, 00-193 WARSZAWA
Tel: 22 536 92 81/82 **Fax:** 22 536 92 83
Titles:
PIŁKA NOŻNA
PIŁKA NOŻNA PLUS

PROMEDIA 1730021
ul. Stępińska, 22/30, 00-739 WARSZAWA
Tel: 22 559 39 61 **Fax:** 22 559 39 62
Titles:
AMBIENTE
JEANS & SPORTSWEAR
MODA DAMSKA
MODA MĘSKA
OBUWIE I GALANTERIA
TEKSTYLIA W DOMU

PRÓSZYŃSKI MEDIA 1692754
ul. Garażowa, 7, 02-651 WARSZAWA
Tel: 22 607 77 71 **Fax:** 22 848 22 66
Titles:
AKADEMIA KURTA SCHELLERA
MAJSTER
NOWA FANTASTYKA
ŚWIAT NAUKI
TAK MIESZKAM
WIEDZA I ŻYCIE

PRÓSZYŃSKI MEDIA SP. Z O.O.
1768760
ul. Garażowa 7, 02-651 WARSZAWA
Tel: 22 60 777 71 **Fax:** 22 84 822 66
Email: proszynskimedia@proszynskimedia.pl

Titles:
INNE OBLICZA HISTORII

PRZEDSIĘBIORSTWO WYDAWNICZE RZECZPOSPOLITA SA
1729968
Al. Jerozolimskie, 107, 02-011 WARSZAWA
Tel: 22 429 24 36 **Fax:** 22 429 25 90

Titles:
PRZEGLĄD PSZCZELARSKI
ZABYTKI

PRZEGLĄD LOTNICZY AVIATION REVUE
1729999
ul. Zamoyskiego, 4, 03-801 WARSZAWA
Tel: 22 670 06 08 **Fax:** 22 670 06 08

Titles:
PRZEGLĄD LOTNICZY AVIATION REVUE

PTWP SA
1768729
ul. Jana Matejki, 3, 40-077 KATOWICE
Tel: 32 209 10 42 **Fax:** 32 782 13 10

Titles:
NOWY PRZEMYSŁ
RYNEK ZDROWIA

PUBLIKATOR
1692721
ul. Andersa, 38, 15-113 BIAŁYSTOK
Tel: 85 653 90 00 **Fax:** 85 653 98 56

Titles:
100% WNĘTRZA
DOM DLA POCZĄTKUJĄCYCH
ŁAZIENKA
MEBLE PLUS
MEBLE.COM.PL
PODŁOGI I ŚCIANY
POLSKIE DOMY - PRZEWODNIK PO PROJEKTACH
PRODUKCJA MEBLI
RESTAURATOR
SALON I SYPIALNIA
SPA BUSINESS
ŚWIAT ALKOHOLI
ŚWIAT ŁAZIENEK I KUCHNI

PUBLISHING AND DESIGN GROUP SP. Z O.O.
1768774
ul. Odolańska, 60, 02 - 562 WARSZAWA
Tel: 22 880 04 65 **Fax:** 22 880 04 66

Titles:
FUTU MAGAZINE

PWB MEDIA
1768786
ul. Rolna, 155, 1, 02-729 WARSZAWA
Tel: 22 853 06 87 **Fax:** 22 853 06 86

Titles:
BUILDER (D. KALEJDOSKOP BUDOWLANY)
SPORTPLUS

PWB MEDIA ZDZIEBŁOWSKI
1739646
ul. Rolna, 155, 1, 02-729 WARSZAWA
Tel: 22 853 06 87 **Fax:** 22 853 06 86

Titles:
MAX - PRZEWODNIK DLA INWESTORA

RAM SP. Z O.O
1745469
ul. Świętokrzyska 12, p. 513, 30-015 KRAKÓW
Tel: 12 630 23 61 **Fax:** 12 632 34 02
Email: RAM.biuro@architekturaibiznes.com.pl
Web site: http://www.architekturaibiznes.com.pl

Titles:
ARCHITEKTURA I BIZNES

READER'S DIGEST PRZEGLĄD
1729960
ul. Taśmowa, 7, 02-677 WARSZAWA
Tel: 22 319 32 00 **Fax:** 22 319 32 99

Titles:
READER'S DIGEST EDYCJA POLSKA

REJTAN SP Z O.O.
1769719
Al. Jerozolimskie, 125/127, 02-017 WARSZAWA
Tel: 22 699 72 22 **Fax:** 22 628 76 73

Titles:
NOWE PAŃSTWO

RHEMA PRESS
1739634
ul. Wąwozowa 7B, 75-339 KOSZALIN

Titles:
IMPULS

RZECZ PIĘKNA - FUNDACJA ROZWOJU WYDZIAŁU FORM PRZEMYSŁOWYCH ASP W KRAKOWIE
1768751
ul. Smoleńsk 9, 31-108 KRAKÓW
Tel: 12 292 62 12 **Fax:** 12 422 34 44

Titles:
2+3D GRAFIKA PLUS PRODUKT

SANITAS SP. Z O.O.
1750257
ul. Jana Brożka 4, 01-442 WARSZAWA
Tel: 22 836 77 77 **Fax:** 22 836 83 33
Email: sekretariat@sluzbazdrowia.com.pl

Titles:
SŁUŻBA ZDROWIA

SEMPRES
1736025
ul. Straży Ludowej, 9, 60-465 POZNAŃ
Tel: 61 842 29 89 **Fax:** 61 842 25 59

Titles:
TERAZ DOM

SILK MEDIA
1730035
ul. św. Antoniego, 15, 50-049 WROCŁAW
Tel: 71 335 21 60 **Fax:** 71 335 21 61

Titles:
TWÓJ WEEKEND

SOFTWARE WYDAWNICTWO
1730025
ul. Bokserska 1, 02-682 WARSZAWA

Titles:
.PSD
BOSTON IT SECURITY REVIEW
BUSINES APPLICATIONS REVIEW
HAKIN9
LINUX+
PHP SOLUTIONS
SOFTWARE DEVELOPERS JOURNAL

SOFTWARE-WYDAWNICTWO
1730020
ul. Bokserska, 1, 02-682 WARSZAWA
Tel: 22 887 13 45 **Fax:** 22 887 10 11

Titles:
LINUX+EXTRA

SPES
1692561
ul. Żeligowskiego, 16/20, 04-476 WARSZAWA
Tel: 22 515 77 77 **Fax:** 22 515 77 78

Titles:
NASZ DZIENNIK

SPOŁECZNY INSTYTUT WYDAWNICZY ZNAK
1692602
ul. Kościuszki, 37, 30-105 KRAKÓW
Tel: 12 619 95 30 **Fax:** 12 619 95 02

Titles:
ZNAK

STOW. EWANGELIZACJI PRZEZ MEDIA - LIST
1692692
ul. Dominikańska, 3, 12, 31-043 KRAKÓW
Tel: 12 429 54 79 **Fax:** 12 429 54 79

Titles:
LIST

STOWARZYSZENIE AKADEMICKIE MAGPRESS, AL. NIEPODLEGŁOŚCI 162, LOK. 66A, 02-554 WARSZAWA
1730040
al. Niepodległości, 162, 66a, 02-554 WARSZAWA **Tel:** 22 564 97 57 **Fax:** 22 849 53 12

Titles:
MAGIEL

STOWARZYSZENIE PRZYJACIÓŁ INTEGRACJI
1692687
ul. Sapieżyńska, 10a, 00-215 WARSZAWA
Tel: 22 635 13 30 **Fax:** 22 635 11 82

Titles:
INTEGRACJA

STUDENT NEWS - MEDIA I MARKETING
1729989
ul. Laurowa, 37, 10, 03-197 WARSZAWA
Tel: 22 747 07 00 **Fax:** 22 747 07 01

Titles:
STUDENT NEWS

TARGET PRESS
1768782
ul. Łucka, 15, 1907, 00-842 WARSZAWA
Tel: 22 635 41 08

Titles:
BUDOWLANIEC

TATRZAŃSKI PARK NARODOWY
1736032
ul. Chałubińskiego, 42a, 34-500 ZAKOPANE
Tel: 18 202 32 26 **Fax:** 18 202 32 50

Titles:
TATRY

TDM - AGENCJA WYDAWNICZO-REKLAMOWA
1692708
ul. Giżycka, 4, POZNAŃ **Tel:** 61 656 38 60 **Fax:** 61 656 38 88

Titles:
KUP DOM

TELEPROGRAM
1692704
ul. Okrężna, 9, 02-916 WARSZAWA
Tel: 22 671 50 00 **Fax:** 22 671 48 88

Titles:
TELEPROGRAM

TERMEDIA
1692676
ul. Żeromskiego, 113, 90-549 ŁÓDŹ
Tel: 42 639 34 65 **Fax:** 42 639 34 65

Titles:
ARCHIVES OF MEDICAL SCIENCE
CENTRAL EUROPEAN JOURNAL OF IMMUNOLOGY
FOLIA NEUROPATHOLOGICA
HEREDITARY CANCER IN CLINICAL PRACTICE
KARDIOCHIRURGIA I TORAKOCHIRURGIA POLSKA
KARDIOLOGIA POLSKA
MENEDŻER ZDROWIA
NEUROLOGIA I NEUROCHIRURGIA POLSKA
POSTĘPY DERMATOLOGII I ALERGOLOGII
POSTĘPY W CHIRURGII GŁOWY I SZYI
POSTĘPY W KARDIOLOGII INTERWENCYJNEJ
PRZEGLĄD GASTROENTEROLOGICZNY
PRZEGLĄD MENOPAUZALNY
PRZEWODNIK LEKARZA
REUMATOLOGIA
WIDEOCHIRURGIA I INNE TECHNIKI MAŁOINWAZYJNE
WOKÓŁ ENERGETYKI
WSPÓŁCZESNA ONKOLOGIA

TOP MEDIA SP. Z O.O.
1768805
ul. Gilarska, 58, 03-589 WARSZAWA
Tel: 22 394 54 32 **Fax:** 22 435 70 49

Titles:
PERSONEL PLUS
RYNEK KONFERENCJI I SZKOLEŃ

TOP MULTIMEDIA
1692610
ul. Tużycka, 16, 03-683 WARSZAWA
Tel: 22 678 79 83 **Fax:** 22 678 01 67

Titles:
GAZETA MAŁYCH I ŚREDNICH PRZEDSIĘBIORSTW

TOWARZYSTWO WIĘŹ
1692737
ul. Trębacka, 3, 00-074 WARSZAWA
Tel: 22 827 29 17 **Fax:** 22 827 29 17

Titles:
WIĘŹ

TOWARZYSTWO WYDAWNICZE I LITERACKIE
1735991
ul. Szara, 10a, 00-420 WARSZAWA
Tel: 22 635 84 10 **Fax:** 22 635 62 85

Titles:
PRZEGLĄD

TRADE MARKETING INVESTMENTS SP. Z O.O.
1793179
ul. Puławska 405, 16, 02-801 WARSZAWA
Tel: 22 257 06 00 **Fax:** 22 257 06 01

Titles:
DETAL DZISIAJ

TRADE MEDIA INTERNATIONAL SP. Z O.O.
1745509
ul. Wita Stwosza 59a, 02-661 WARSZAWA
Tel: 22 852 44 15 **Fax:** 22 899 30 23
Email: mike_majchrzak@trademedia.us
Web site: http://www.trademedia.us

Titles:
DESIGN NEWS POLSKA
INŻYNIERIA I UTRZYMANIE RUCHU ZAKŁADÓW PRZEMYSŁOWYCH
MSI POLSKA

TRADER.COM (POLSKA)
1692635
al. Pokoju, 3, 31-548 KRAKÓW **Tel:** 12 430 41 31 **Fax:** 12 412 80 06

Titles:
AUTO-BIT
AUTOBIZNES OGŁOSZENIA
BUSINESS TRUCK
NIERUCHOMOŚCI WARSZAWA I OKOLICE

TWOJA KOMÓRKA SP. Z O.O.
1747248
Al. Reymonta 50, 01-842 WARSZAWA
Tel: 22 864 16 83 **Fax:** 22 864 27 17

Titles:
TWOJA KOMÓRKA

TWOJE MEDIA
1692768
ul. Saska, 9a, 03-968 WARSZAWA
Tel: 22 616 16 04 **Fax:** 22 616 15 24

Titles:
JACHTING
WĘDKARSTWO MOJE HOBBY

TYGODNIK POWSZECHNY
1692764
ul. Wiślna, 12, 31-007 KRAKÓW **Tel:** 12 422 25 18 **Fax:** 12 421 67 31

Titles:
TYGODNIK POWSZECHNY

ULTRAMARYNA
1692629
pl. Sejmu Śląskiego, 2, 40-032 KATOWICE
Tel: 32 785 77 77 **Fax:** 32 785 77 88

Titles:
ULTRAMARYNA

UNIT - WYDAWNICTWO INFORMACJE BRANŻOWE
1692693
ul. Kierbedzia, 4, 00-728 WARSZAWA
Tel: 22 320 15 00 **Fax:** 22 320 15 50

Titles:
CHRONOS
FILM & TV KAMERA
PAPIERNICZY ŚWIAT
ŚWIAT BUTÓW
ŚWIAT SKÓR
TEXTILWIRTSCHAFT MODA FORUM
TOP CLASS
ZEGARKI & BIŻUTERIA

US PHARMACIA
1692778
ul. Ziębicka 40, 50-507 WROCŁAW

Titles:
FARMACJA I JA

VALKEA MEDIA SA
1757970
ul. Elbląska, 15/17, 01-747 WARSZAWA
Tel: 22 639 85 67 **Fax:** 22 639 85 69

Titles:
AKTIVIST
EXKLUSIV XMAGAZYN
PRESTIGE HOUSE
WARSAW BUSINESS JOURNAL
WARSAW INSIDER

VFP COMMUNICATIONS
1692727
ul. Wał Miedzeszyński, 630, 03-994 WARSZAWA
Tel: 22 514 65 00 **Fax:** 22 740 50 55

Titles:
MEDIA & MARKETING POLSKA

VIA MEDICA SP. Z O.O. 1749658
ul. Świętokrzyska 73, 80-180 GDAŃSK
Email: viamedica@viamedica.pl
Web site: http://www.viamedica.pl

Titles:
DIABETOLOGIA DOŚWIADCZALNA I KLINICZNA
DIABETOLOGIA PRAKTYCZNA

VIDART ARTUR DZIEDZIC 1730052
ul. Sokratesa, 15, 01-909 WARSZAWA
Tel: 22 834 80 35 **Fax:** 22 834 80 34

Titles:
PRINT PARTNER

VIMEDIA 1692661
ul. Marii Konopnickiej, 6, 00-491 WARSZAWA
Tel: 22 625 59 24 **Fax:** 22 625 49 95

Titles:
HIP HOP ARCHIWUM

VOGEL BURDA COMMUNICATIONS 1692597

Titles:
CHIP FOTO-VIDEO DIGITAL
CHIP KOMPUTER TEST

VOGEL BUSINESS MEDIA 1729964
ul. Grabiszyńska, 163, 53-439 WROCŁAW
Tel: 71 782 31 80 **Fax:** 71 782 31 84

Titles:
AUTOEXPERT
MM MAGAZYN PRZEMYSŁOWY

WARSAW VOICE SA 1692711
ul. Księcia Janusza, 64, 01-452 WARSZAWA
Tel: 22 335 97 00/41 **Fax:** 22 335 97 10

Titles:
SALON I ELEGANCJA
TERAPIA
THE WARSAW VOICE

WDP BERNARDINUM 1692765
ul. Walecznych 40 lok. 5, 03-916 WARSZAWA
Tel: 696 492 170 **Fax:** 22 616 40 08

Titles:
POZNAJ ŚWIAT

WĘDKARZ POLSKI 1692631
ul. Łódzka, 19, 50-521 WROCŁAW
Tel: 71 791 30 14 **Fax:** 71 791 30 15

Titles:
WĘDKARZ POLSKI

WESTA-DRUK, MIROSŁAW KULIŚ 1692586
ul. Piotrkowska, 94, 90-103 ŁÓDŹ
Tel: 42 632 61 79 **Fax:** 42 632 07 59

Titles:
ANGORA

WOLTERS KLUWER POLSKA 1730015
Płocka, 5a, 01-231 WARSZAWA **Tel:** 22 535 80 00
Fax: 22 535 80 01

Titles:
WWW.ABC.COM.PL

WORLD TRADE CENTER POZNAŃ 1692641
ul. Bukowska 12, 60-810 POZNAŃ
Tel: 61 865 38 90 **Fax:** 61 866 61 34

Titles:
POZNAŃ PO GODZIANCH

WRC MEDIA 1757982
ul. Kochanowskiego, 16, 11, 40-035 KATOWICE
Tel: 32 251 70 86 **Fax:** 32 251 70 86

Titles:
WRC MAGAZYN RAJDOWY

WSCHODNIA FUNDACJA KULTURY "AKCENT" PRZY WSPÓŁUDZIALE BIBLIOTEKI NARODOWEJ 1768766
ul. Grodzka, 3, 20-112 LUBLIN **Tel:** 81 532 74 69
Fax: 81 532 74 69

Titles:
AKCENT

WYD. JAGIELLONIA SA 1768827
ul. Wielopole, 1, 31-072 KRAKÓW
Tel: 12 619 92 00 **Fax:** 12 619 92 75

Titles:
DZIENNIK POLSKI

WYDAWCA OLSZTYN 1739665
ul. Tracka, 7, 10-364 OLSZTYN **Tel:** 89 539 77 30
Fax: 89 539 77 34

Titles:
NASZ OLSZTYNIAK

WYDAWNICTWO BAUER 1692650
al. Stanów Zjednoczonych, 61a, 04-028 WARSZAWA **Tel:** 22 516 34 81 **Fax:** 22 516 34 80

Titles:
AUTO MOTO
BELLA RELAKS
BRAVO SPORT
CD ACTION
CHWILA DLA CIEBIE
CLICK
IMPERIUM TV
KOBIETA I ŻYCIE
KURIER TV
MAM DZIECKO
MOTOR
PANI
PC FORMAT
REWIA
SHOW
SUPER TV
ŚWIAT & LUDZIE
ŚWIAT KOBIETY
ŚWIAT SERIALI
TAKIE JEST ŻYCIE
TELE MAX
TELE ŚWIAT
TELE TYDZIEŃ
TINA
TO & OWO
TWÓJ STYL
TWOJE IMPERIUM
ŻYCIE NA GORĄCO

WYDAWNICTWO CH BECK 1692691
ul. Bonifraterska, 17, 00-203 WARSZAWA
Tel: 22 337 76 00 **Fax:** 22 337 74 91

Titles:
EDUKACJA PRAWNICZA
MONITOR PODATKOWY
MONITOR PRAWA PRACY
MONITOR PRAWNICZY
MONITOR RACHUNKOWOŚCI I FINANSÓW
NIERUCHOMOŚCI CH BECK

WYDAWNICTWO CHARAKTERY 1735968
ul. Warszawska, 6, 25-512 KIELCE
Tel: 41 343 28 64 **Fax:** 41 343 28 49

Titles:
PSYCHOLOGIA W SZKOLE
STYLE I CHARAKTERY

WYDAWNICTWO CHFŻIM KOINONIA 1692642
ul. 3 Maja, 14, 43-450 USTROŃ **Tel:** 33 854 45 22
Fax: 33 854 18 14

Titles:
NASZE INSPIRACJE

WYDAWNICTWO CICHA LIPA 1692699
ul. Pilchowicka, 16a, 02-175 WARSZAWA
Tel: 22 886 85 60 **Fax:** 22 886 85 60

Titles:
BUNNY HOP

WYDAWNICTWO CZELEJ 1769601
Al. Racławickie 1, 20-059 LUBLIN

Titles:
PIELĘGNIARSTWO XXI WIEKU

WYDAWNICTWO ELAMED 1735999
al. Rożdzieńskiego, 188, 40-203 KATOWICE
Tel: 32 788 51 69 **Fax:** 32 788 51 64

Titles:
CUKIERNICTWO I PIEKARSTWO
LABORATORIUM - PRZEGLĄD OGÓLNOPOLSKI
LEKARZ
MAGAZYN AUTOSTRADY
MAGAZYN PRZEMYSŁU MIĘSNEGO
MOSTY
NOWOCZESNE HALE
NOWOCZESNY TECHNIK DENTYSTYCZNY
OPM - OGÓLNOPOLSKI PRZEGLĄD MEDYCZNY
PROMOTOR
STAL METALE & NOWE TECHNOLOGIE
TPS - TWÓJ PRZEGLĄD STOMATOLOGICZNY
W AKCJI
WETERYNARIA W PRAKTYCE

WYDAWNICTWO FORUM 1736009
ul. Polska 13, 60-595 POZNAŃ

Titles:
FLOTA
SAMOCHODY UŻYTKOWE

WYDAWNICTWO GÓRY 1692598
ul. Bajana, 4, 11, 31-465 KRAKÓW
Tel: 12 421 14 82 **Fax:** 12 421 14 82

Titles:
GÓRY

WYDAWNICTWO GOSPODARCZE 1730001
ul. Wałbrzyska, 11, 254, 02-793 WARSZAWA
Tel: 22 549 94 60 **Fax:** 22 549 94 50

Titles:
WIADOMOŚCI KOSMETYCZNE

WYDAWNICTWO GOSPODARCZE SP. Z O.O. 1768763
ul. Wałbrzyska, 11, 254, 02-739 WARSZAWA
Tel: 22 549 94 50 **Fax:** 22 549 94 50

Titles:
WIADOMOŚCI HANDLOWE

WYDAWNICTWO KIF SYLWERIUSZ ŁYSIAK 1692784
ul. Ostrzycka, 2/4, 04-035 WARSZAWA
Tel: 22 673 77 95 **Fax:** 22 870 78 08

Titles:
KULTURYSTYKA I FITNESS

WYDAWNICTWO KWIECIŃSKI 1692626
ul. Stokrotek, 51, 43-384 JAWORZE
Tel: 33 817 38 79 **Fax:** 33 817 36 31

Titles:
DOMY JEDNORODZINNE

WYDAWNICTWO MANTA 1736036
ul. Ogrodowa, 28/30, 00-896 WARSZAWA
Tel: 22 620 01 68 **Fax:** 22 620 01 68

Titles:
WIELKI BŁĘKIT

WYDAWNICTWO MARKETING W PRAKTYCE 1793164
Sady Żoliborskie 13/16, 01-772 WARSZAWA
Tel: 22 353 25 11 **Fax:** 22 435 51 21

Titles:
MARKETING W PRAKTYCE

WYDAWNICTWO NRG 1692637
ul. Praska, 4, 30-328 KRAKÓW **Tel:** 12 431 22 80
Fax: 12 259 00 22

Titles:
BIKEBOARD

WYDAWNICTWO OKTO 1730055
ul. Kolumba, 86, 70-035 SZCZECIN
Tel: 91 489 22 83 **Fax:** 91 482 68 08

Titles:
NURKOWANIE

WYDAWNICTWO PODATKOWE GOFIN SP. Z O.O. 1768813
ul. Owocowa, 8, 66-400 GORZÓW WLKP.
Tel: 95 720 85 40 **Fax:** 95 720 85 60

Titles:
GAZETA PODATKOWA
PORADNIK VAT
PRZEGLĄD PODATKU DOCHODOWEGO
UBEZPIECZENIA I PRAWO PRACY
ZESZYTY METODYCZNE RACHUNKOWOŚCI

WYDAWNICTWO POLSKIEJ PROWINCJI DOMINIKANÓW - W DRODZE 1692577
ul. Kościuszki, 99, 60-920 POZNAŃ
Tel: 61 850 47 22 **Fax:** 61 850 17 82

Titles:
W DRODZE

WYDAWNICTWO PROMOCYJNE MIĘDZY NAMI 1692689
ul. Bagno, 3, 165, 00-112 WARSZAWA
Tel: 601 203 411 **Fax:** 22 828 54 17

Titles:
MIĘDZY NAMI CAFE

WYDAWNICTWO PRZEKRÓJ SP. Z O.O. 1769622
ul. Nowogrodzka 47a, IV p., 00-695 WARSZAWA
Tel: 22 525 99 33 **Fax:** 22 525 99 88

Titles:
PRZEKRÓJ

WYDAWNICTWO PRZEWODNIK BUDOWLANY 1692595
ul. Katowicka, 19, 03-932 WARSZAWA
Tel: 22 616 10 88 **Fax:** 22 616 10 89

Titles:
PRZEWODNIK BUDOWLANY

WYDAWNICTWO SIGMA-NOT 1736037
ul. Ratuszowa, 11, 743a, 03-450 WARSZAWA
Tel: 22 818 65 21 **Fax:** 22 818 65 21

Titles:
CHŁODNICTWO
CIEPŁOWNICTWO, OGRZEWNICTWO, WENTYLACJA
DOZÓR TECHNICZNY
ELEKTRONIKA - KONSTRUKCJE, TECHNOLOGIE, ZASTOSOWANIA
GAZ, WODA I TECHNIKA SANITARNA
GAZETA CUKROWNICZA
GOSPODARKA MIĘSNA
GOSPODARKA WODNA
HUTNIK - WIADOMOŚCI HUTNICZE
INŻYNIERIA MATERIAŁOWA
MASZYNY, TECHNOLOGIE, MATERIAŁY - TECHNIKA ZAGRANICZNA
MATERIAŁY BUDOWLANE
OCHRONA PRZED KOROZJĄ
OPAKOWANIE
PROBLEMY JAKOŚCI
PRZEGLĄD ELEKTROTECHNICZNY
PRZEGLĄD GASTRONOMICZNY
PRZEGLĄD GEODEZYJNY
PRZEGLĄD PAPIERNICZY
PRZEGLĄD PIEKARSKI I CUKIERNICZY
PRZEGLĄD TECHNICZNY. GAZETA INŻYNIERSKA
PRZEGLĄD TELEKOMUNIKACYJNY - WIADOMOŚCI TELEKOMUNIKACYJNE
PRZEGLĄD WŁÓKIENNICZY - WŁÓKNO, ODZIEŻ, SKÓRA
PRZEGLĄD ZBOŻOWO-MŁYNARSKI
PRZEMYSŁ CHEMICZNY
PRZEMYSŁ FERMENTACYJNY I OWOCOWO-WARZYWNY
PRZEMYSŁ SPOŻYWCZY
RUDY I METALE NIEŻELAZNE
SZKŁO I CERAMIKA
WIADOMOŚCI ELEKTROTECHNICZNE
WOKÓŁ PŁYTEK CERAMICZNYCH

WYDAWNICTWO TECHNIKA BUDOWLANA 1692600
ul. marsz. F. Focha, 7, 4, 80-156 GDAŃSK
Tel: 58 306 29 27 **Fax:** 58 306 29 27

Titles:
MAGAZYN INSTALATORA

WYDAWNICTWO TE-JOT 1692659
ul. Malczewskiego, 19, 02-612 WARSZAWA
Tel: 22 854 14 14 **Fax:** 22 854 14 49

Titles:
WERANDA
WRÓŻKA

WYDAWNICTWO TRENDY 1692697
ul. Okrzei, 1a, 03-715 WARSZAWA
Tel: 22 333 80 00 **Fax:** 22 333 88 99

Titles:
DORADCA PODATNIKA
FISKUS

Poland

WYDAWNICTWO VIMEDIA 1692782
ul. Marii Konopnickiej, 6, 00-491 WARSZAWA
Tel: 22 628 97 65 **Fax:** 22 625 59 24
Titles:
BOUTIQUE
EDEN

WYDAWNICTWO WĘDKARSKI ŚWIAT 1692654
ul. Miedziana, 11, 00-835 WARSZAWA
Tel: 22 652 19 21 **Fax:** 22 652 15 15
Titles:
WĘDKARSKI ŚWIAT

WYDAWNICTWO WIEDZA I PRAKTYKA 1692722
ul. Łotewska, 9a, 03-918 WARSZAWA
Tel: 22 518 29 29 **Fax:** 22 617 60 10
Titles:
DOKUMENTACJA KADROWA
PODATKI DOCHODOWE W PRAKTYCE
PORADNIK PRZEDSIĘBIORCY BUDOWLANEGO
PRAWO I PODATKI
RACHUNKOWOŚĆ DLA PRAKTYKÓW
ZARZĄDZANIE JAKOŚCIĄ W PRAKTYCE. NORMY ISO SERII 9000
ZARZĄDZANIE PRODUKCJĄ W PRAKTYCE

WYDAWNICTWO ZAGRODA 1736030
ul. Zastawie, 12, 05-074 HALINÓW
Tel: 22 760 41 67 **Fax:** 22 783 66 82
Titles:
WOLIERA

WYDAWNICTWO ZWIERCIADŁO 1692618
ul. Karowa, 31a, 00-324 WARSZAWA
Tel: 22 312 37 12 **Fax:** 22 312 37 21
Titles:
ZWIERCIADŁO

XXL MEDIA 1692718
ul. Krakowiaków, 16, 02-255 WARSZAWA
Tel: 22 356 85 00/01 **Fax:** 22 356 85 02
Titles:
MODA NA FARMACJĘ
MODA NA ZDROWIE

ZAKOPIAŃSKIE TOWARZYSTWO GOSPODARCZE SP. Z O.O. 1768812
ul. Kościuszki, 3, 34-500 ZAKOPANE
Tel: 18 200 00 00 **Fax:** 18 200 00 01
Titles:
TYGODNIK PODHALAŃSKI

ZARZĄD GŁÓWNY ZWIĄZKU POLSKICH ARTYSTÓW PLASTYKÓW 1736834
ul. Nowy Świat, 7, 6, 00-496 WARSZAWA
Tel: 692 439 567 **Fax:** 22 621 01 37
Titles:
ARTLUK

Portugal

ABOUTMEDIA - COMUNICAÇÃO, LDA. 1721438
R. da Madalena, 191 - 4°, 1100-319 LISBOA
Tel: 218 806 123 **Fax:** 218 111 300
Titles:
ÁGUA & AMBIENTE
ANIVERSÁRIO

ABPG - ASSOCIAÇÃO DE BENEFICIÊNCIA POPULAR DE GOUVEIA 1642828
R. Dr. António Mendes, 6290-311 GOUVEIA
Tel: 238 491 626 **Fax:** 238 491 616
Titles:
NOTÍCIAS DE GOUVEIA

AÇORMÉDIA - COMUNICAÇÃO MULTIMÉDIA E EDIÇÃO DE PUBLICAÇÕES, S.A. 1721425
R. Dr. Bruno Tavares Carreiro, 34/36, 9500-055 PONTA DELGADA **Tel:** 296 202 800
Fax: 296 202 825
Titles:
AÇORIANO ORIENTAL

ADRIANO LUCAS - GESTÃO E COMUNICAÇÃO SOCIAL, LDA. 1642514
R. Adriano Lucas, 3020 COIMBRA
Tel: 239 499 900 **Fax:** 239 499 912
Titles:
DIÁRIO DE AVEIRO
DIÁRIO DE COIMBRA
DIÁRIO DE LEIRIA
DIÁRIO DE VISEU

AECOPS - ASSOCIAÇÃO DAS EMPRESAS DE CONSTRUÇÃO E OBRAS PÚBLICAS 1642483
Praça de Alvalade, 6 - 6° Fte., 1700-036 LISBOA
Tel: 213 110 200 **Fax:** 213 554 810
Titles:
JORNAL DA CONSTRUÇÃO

AICEP PORTUGAL GLOBAL 1757899
O'Porto Bessa Leite Complex, R. António Bessa Leite, 1430 - 2°, 4150-074 PORTO
Tel: 226 055 300 **Fax:** 226 055 399
Titles:
AICEP PORTUGAL GLOBAL

AJE - SOCIEDADE EDITORIAL, LDA. 1642498
R. Barão de Sabrosa, 165 - A, 1900-088 LISBOA
Tel: 218 110 130
Titles:
FARMÁCIA DISTRIBUIÇÃO

ALGARVE MAIS - COMUNICAÇÃO E IMAGEM, UNIPESSOAL, LDA. 1721449
R. José Prudêncio Vieira, Lote 3 - 1° R/C, Apartado 28, 8365-909 ARMAÇÃO DE PÊRA
Tel: 282 310 720 **Fax:** 282 310 729
Titles:
ALGARVE MAIS

ANA MARIA SOUSA SANTOS DE JESUS LINHA 1642684
Largo Alves Roçadas, 8 - A, 8400-313 LAGOA
Tel: 282 341 512 **Fax:** 282 341 512
Titles:
GAZETA DE LAGOA

ANTERO DOS SANTOS 1722100
Estrada Nacional 249/4, Lote 7 - 1° Andar, 2785-599 SÃO DOMINGOS DE RANA **Tel:** 214 452 899
Fax: 214 673 061
Titles:
NOTÍCIAS DO MAR

ANTÓNIO MANUEL DE SOUSA GUEDES 1722300
R. António da Costa, 3, Apartado 39, 3441-999 SANTA COMBA DÃO **Tel:** 232 888 358
Fax: 232 881 135
Titles:
VOZ DO DÃO

ANTÓNIO SOUSA (HERDEIROS), LDA. 1721684
R. Pedro Rocha, 27-31, 3000-330 COIMBRA
Tel: 239 852 710 **Fax:** 239 497 759
Titles:
O DESPERTAR

APDC - ASSOCIAÇÃO PORTUGUESA PARA O DESENVOLVIMENTO DAS COMUNICAÇÕES 1721638
R. Tomás Ribeiro, 41 - 8°, 1050-225 LISBOA
Tel: 213 129 670 **Fax:** 213 129 688
Titles:
COMUNICAÇÕES

APTP - ASSOCIAÇÃO DE PROFISSIONAIS DE TURISMO DE PORTUGAL 1772807
R. do Janes, 15 - 1°, 4700-318 BRAGA
Tel: 253 693 733 **Fax:** 253 693 733
Titles:
PROFISSIONAIS DE TURISMO

ARCADA NOVA - COMUNICAÇÃO, MARKETING E PUBLICIDADE, S.A. 1721664
Praceta do Magistério, 34, Maximinos, 4700-236 BRAGA **Tel:** 253 309 500 **Fax:** 253 309 525
Titles:
CORREIO DO MINHO

ARTNEWS - SOCIEDADE DE COMUNICAÇÕES E ARTE, LDA. 1758396
Largo do Valverde, 27, 2070-040 CARTAXO
Tel: 243 702 154 **Fax:** 243 779 000
Titles:
O POVO DO CARTAXO

ASSOCIAÇÃO CRECOR - CULTURA RECREIO E DESPORTO DE CORTEGAÇA 1722149
Praceta Centro d'Villa, 15, Apartado 29, 3886-908 CORTEGAÇA **Tel:** 256 754 413
Fax: 256 752 437
Titles:
O POVO DE CORTEGAÇA

ASSOCIAÇÃO DE MUNICÍPIOS DO BAIXO ALENTEJO E ALENTEJO LITORAL 1721436
Praça da República, 12, 7800-427 BEJA
Tel: 284 310 165 **Fax:** 284 240 881
Titles:
DIÁRIO DO ALENTEJO

ASSOCIAÇÃO DINAMIZADORA DOS INTERESSES DE BASTO - ADIB 1642633
R. Antunes Basto, Refojos, 4860-000 CABECEIRAS DE BASTO **Tel:** 253 661 601
Fax: 253 666 156
Titles:
ECOS DE BASTO

ASSOCIAÇÃO IGREJANOVENSE DE MELHORAMENTOS 1642759
R. Pé da Costa Baixo, 26 - A, 2300-000 TOMAR
Tel: 249 312 615 **Fax:** 249 312 615
Titles:
DESPERTAR DO ZÊZERE

ASSOCIAÇÃO NACIONAL DAS EMPRESAS DO COMÉRCIO E REPARAÇÃO AUTOMÓVEL 1642476
R. Luís de Camões, 118-A, 1300-362 LISBOA
Tel: 213 929 030 **Fax:** 213 978 504
Titles:
ANECRA REVISTA

ASSOCIAÇÃO PORTUGUESA DE BARBEARIAS CABELEIREIROS E INSTITUTOS DE BELEZA, LDA. 1721524
R. dos Fanqueiros, 135 - 2°, 1100-227 LISBOA
Tel: 218 820 840 **Fax:** 218 877 264
Titles:
BARBEIROS & CABELEIREIROS

ATL - ASSOCIAÇÃO DE TURISMO DE LISBOA 1642674
R. do Arsenal, N° 15, 1100-038 LISBOA
Tel: 210 312 717 **Fax:** 210 312 899
Titles:
FOLLOW ME

ATM - EDIÇÕES E PUBLICIDADE, LDA. 1642470
Av. Infante Santo, 343 R/C Esq., 1350-177 LISBOA
Titles:
AMBIENTE MAGAZINE
AMBITUR

AUTOMÓVEL CLUB DE PORTUGAL 1643081
R. Rosa Araújo, 24 - 26, 1250-195 LISBOA
Tel: 213 180 184 **Fax:** 213 159 121
Titles:
REVISTA ACP

BAIÃO REPÓRTER - SOCIEDADE EDITORIAL, LDA. 1722186
R. Dr. Francisco Sá Carneiro, 230, Apartado 200, 4630-279 MARCO DE CANAVESES
Tel: 255 521 307 **Fax:** 255 437 000
Titles:
REPÓRTER DO MARÃO

BALESKAPRESS - PUBLICAÇÕES E MARKETING, LDA. 1721906
Av. António Augusto Aguiar, 11 - 1° Esq., 1050-010 LISBOA **Tel:** 213 103 370 **Fax:** 213 153 115
Titles:
HAPPY WOMAN

BE PROFIT - MARKETING, LOGÍSTICA, DISTRIBUIÇÃO E PUBLICAÇÕES, LDA. 1762327
Av. das Robíneas, 10, Rinchoa, 2635-545 RIO DE MOURO **Tel:** 219 198 228 **Fax:** 219 171 053
Titles:
ARQUITECTURA 21
MUNDO DO DVD ROM

BIO RUMO - PROMOÇÃO E EDUCAÇÃO AMBIENTAL, LDA. 1721468
Edifício Capitólio, Av. de França, 256 - E, Sala 3.1, 4050-276 PORTO **Tel:** 228 349 580
Fax: 228 349 589
Titles:
ANUÁRIO DE SUSTENTABILIDADE

BLEED - SOCIEDADE EDITORIAL E ORGANIZAÇÃO DE EVENTOS, LDA. 1752054
Campo Grande 30, 9° C, 1700-093 LISBOA
Tel: 217 957 045 **Fax:** 217 957 047
Titles:
INDÚSTRIA

BOM SENSO - EDIÇÕES E ACONSELHAMENTOS DE MERCADO, LDA. 1721948
R. Infante D. Fernando, Lote 2, Porta 2 B, Apartado 81, 2440-901 BATALHA
Tel: 244 767 583 **Fax:** 244 767 739
Titles:
JORNAL DA BATALHA

CADEIA METROPOLITANA DE RÁDIOS 1792756
Av. Visconde Barreiros, 89 - 5° Andar, 4470-151 MAIA **Tel:** 229 439 380 **Fax:** 229 439 381
Titles:
PRIMEIRA MÃO

CADERNOS DO SOM PUBLICAÇÕES, LDA. 1721492
R. D.João V, 6 - R/C Esq., 1250-090 LISBOA
Tel: 213 190 650 **Fax:** 213 190 659
Titles:
ÁUDIO & CINEMA EM CASA

CÂMARA DE COMÉRCIO E INDÚSTRIA LUSO-ESPANHOLA 1721429
Av. Marquês de Tomar, N° 2 - 7°, 1050-155 LISBOA **Tel:** 213 509 310 **Fax:** 213 526 333
Titles:
ACTUALIDAD€ - ECONOMIA IBÉRICA

CANAL DE NEGÓCIOS - EDIÇÃO DE PUBLICAÇÕES, LDA. 1721522
Av. João Crisóstomo, 72 - 1°, 1069-043 LISBOA
Tel: 213 180 900 **Fax:** 213 540 361
Titles:
FÓRUM EMPRESARIAL
JOGO DA BOLSA
JORNAL DE NEGÓCIOS
MBA
SAÚDE
WEEKEND

CAPITAL DA ESCRITA 1743620
Av. da Liberdade 13, 1250-139 LISBOA
Tel: 213 593 100 **Fax:** 213 593 131
Titles:
TIME OUT ALGARVE

CARGO EDIÇÕES, LDA. 1642486
Edifício Rocha Conde d'Óbidos, 1° A, Cais de Alcântara, 1350-352 LISBOA **Tel:** 213 973 968
Fax: 213 973 984
Titles:
CARGO

CASA VÉRITAS - EDITORA, LDA. 1642424
R. Marquês de Pombal, 55/61, 6300-728 GUARDA **Tel:** 271 222 105 **Fax:** 271 208 387
Titles:
A GUARDA

CCS - CULTURA E COMUNICAÇÃO SOCIAL, S.A. 1721464
R. dos Bombeiros, 44, 2600-116 VILA FRANCA DE XIRA **Tel:** 263 200 550 **Fax:** 263 200 560
Titles:
VIDA RIBATEJANA

CEMPALAVRAS - COMUNICAÇÃO EMPRESARIAL, LDA 1740124
Av. Almirante Reis, 114 - 2° C, 1150-023 LISBOA
Tel: 218 141 574 **Fax:** 218 142 664
Titles:
GUIA DE EMPRESAS CERTIFICADAS

CENESTAP - CENTRO DE ESTUDOS TÊXTEIS APLICADOS 1721997
R. Fernando Mesquita, Edifício do Citeve, N° 2785 - Antas, Apartado 265, 4760-034 VILA NOVA DE FAMALICÃO **Tel:** 252 302 020
Titles:
MODTISSIMO

CENTRO EDITOR LIVREIRO DA ORDEM DOS ARQUITECTOS 1721946
Travessa do Carvalho, 23, 1249-003 LISBOA
Tel: 213 241 100 **Fax:** 213 241 101
Titles:
ARQUITECTOS INFORMAÇÃO
JORNAL ARQUITECTOS

CENTRO - PRODUÇÃO E EDIÇÃO DE CONTEÚDOS, LDA. 1721385
Bairro S. João da Carreira, R. D. Maria Gracinda Torres Vasconcelos, Lote 10 - R/C, 3500-187 VISEU **Tel:** 232 437 461 **Fax:** 232 431 225
Titles:
JORNAL DO CENTRO

CÍRCULO DE CULTURA FAMALICENSE 1721615
R. 5 de Outubro, Edifício Vilarminda - Loja 204, Apartado 218, 4764-976 VILA NOVA DE FAMALICÃO **Tel:** 252 301 780 **Fax:** 252 301 789
Titles:
CIDADE HOJE

CITÉCNICA - PUBLICAÇÕES TÉCNICAS E CIENTÍFICAS, LDA. 1642840
R. Tristão Vaz, 15 - 2° Dto., 1449-023 LISBOA
Tel: 213 011 989 **Fax:** 213 015 539
Titles:
NOTÍCIAS MÉDICAS

CITYMAP - EDITORA E PUBLICIDADE, LDA. 1721863
Av. de Ceuta, Urbanização A Nora, Bloco 6 - Loja Carteia, 8125-116 QUARTEIRA
Tel: 289 315 560 **Fax:** 289 389 756
Titles:
CARTEIA

COFINA SGPS, S.A. 1724210
Av. João Crisóstomo, 72, 1069-043 LISBOA
Tel: 213 307 741 **Fax:** 213 540 643
Titles:
CASAMENTO & LUA DE MEL

COMÉRCIO DA PÓVOA DE VARZIM - EMPRESA EDITORA, LDA. 1642856
R. Caverneira, 18, 1°, 4490-500 PÓVOA DE VARZIM **Tel:** 252 626 921
Titles:
O COMÉRCIO DA PÓVOA DE VARZIM

COMPANHIA DAS CORES - DESIGN E COMUNICAÇÃO EMPRESARIAL, LDA. 1721578
R. Sampaio Pina, 58 - 2° Dto., 1070-250 LISBOA
Tel: 213 825 610 **Fax:** 213 825 619
Titles:
CÂMARAS VERDES
TOM SOBRE TOM

COMPANY ONE PUBLICAÇÕES, LDA. 1721612
Av. Almirante Reis, 39, 1169-039 LISBOA
Tel: 218 110 896
Titles:
ESPIRAL DO TEMPO

CONFERÊNCIAS DE S. VICENTE DE PAULO DE VILA REAL 1722299
R. D. António Valente da Fonseca, 22, Apartado 212, 5001-911 VILA REAL **Tel:** 259 340 290
Fax: 259 340 299
Titles:
A VOZ DE TRÁS-OS-MONTES

CONVIDA, LDA. 1743584
R. do Loreto, 16 - 2° Dto., 1200-242 LISBOA
Tel: 213 408 090 **Fax:** 213 256 809
Titles:
BAIRRO ALTO & PRÍNCIPE REAL
BAIXA & CHIADO
CONVIDA
ROMA & ALVALADE
SANTOS

COOPERATIVA JORNALÍSTICA DE MANTEIGAS, C.R.L. 1724251
R. General Póvoas, N° 7, 6260-173 MANTEIGAS
Tel: 275 982 476 **Fax:** 275 982 481
Titles:
NOTÍCIAS DE MANTEIGAS

CTCS - COMPOSIÇÃO DE TEXTO PARA COMUNICAÇÃO SOCIAL E AFINS, LDA. 1721761
R. Alfredo Mirante, 10 B, 7350-154 ELVAS
Tel: 268 622 697 **Fax:** 268 620 192
Titles:
LINHAS DE ELVAS

DECO PROTESTE, EDITORES, LDA. 1721744
Av. Engenheiro Arantes e Oliveira, 13 - 1° B, Olaias, 1900-221 LISBOA **Tel:** 218 410 800
Fax: 218 410 802
Titles:
DINHEIRO & DIREITOS
PRO TESTE
TESTE SAÚDE

DICAS & PISTAS - EDIÇÕES E PROMOÇÕES, LDA. 1721755
Av. Fontes Pereira de Melo, 35, 14° D, 1050-118 LISBOA **Tel:** 213 559 015 **Fax:** 213 559 020
Titles:
TRANSPORTES EM REVISTA

DIFERENTE & MELHOR - EDIÇÕES E PUBLICAÇÕES UNIPESSOAL, LDA. 1767923
R. Santo António, 41 - 1° Andar, Apartado 66, 5400-909 CHAVES **Tel:** 276 334 447
Fax: 276 334 447
Titles:
NOTÍCIAS DE CHAVES

DIOCESE DA GUARDA 1642823
R. Jornal Notícias da Covilhã, 65 R/C, 6201-015 COVILHÃ **Tel:** 275 330 700 **Fax:** 275 330 709
Titles:
NOTÍCIAS DA COVILHÃ

DIOCESE DO ALGARVE 1721707
R. do Município, 14 - 1° Dto., 8000-398 FARO
Tel: 289 822 319 **Fax:** 289 821 529
Titles:
FOLHA DO DOMINGO

DISTRIFA, SOLUÇÕES DE SAÚDE 1740115
R. dos Bem-Lembrados, 141, Manique, 2645-471 ALCABIDECHE **Tel:** 214 449 660
Fax: 214 449 651
Titles:
FITO+SAÚDE

EDIÇÕES DO GOSTO 1759245
Calçada do Cardeal, 16 B, 1100-116 LISBOA
Tel: 218 822 992 **Fax:** 218 884 504
Titles:
INTER MAGAZINE

EDIÇÕES JPM - PUBLICAÇÕES, PUBLICIDADE E PROMOÇÕES, LDA. 1743587
Ed. Vale do Ave, Bl. A - 1° Esq - Portela, 4765-110 DELÃES **Tel:** 252 905 511 **Fax:** 252 905 696
Titles:
MOTO GUIA

EDIÇÕES LAMPARINA, LDA. 1721457
Parque Industrial de Sobreposta, R. da Piscina, 70, 4715-553 BRAGA **Tel:** 253 689 040
Fax: 253 689 049
Titles:
AMBIENTE PISCINAS

EDIÇÕES PÉ DA SERRA - SOCIEDADE EDITORIAL, LDA. 1722232
R. dos Carvalhais, 17, Vila Verde, 2705-879 TERRUGEM SNT **Tel:** 219 613 205
Fax: 219 613 206
Titles:
SUPER CICLISMO

EDIÇÕES PLURAL ESPECIALIZADAS, UNIPESSOAL, LDA. 1721575
Av. Duque d'Ávila, 69 - R/C Esq., 1000-139 LISBOA **Tel:** 213 568 250 **Fax:** 213 524 050
Titles:
TELECULINÁRIA

EDIÇÕES PRÓ-HOMEM, LDA. 1721812
R. da Misericórdia, 17 - 2°, 1249-041 LISBOA
Tel: 213 421 242 **Fax:** 213 460 013
Titles:
INTERNACIONAL CANETAS

EDIÇÕES ROMANO, LDA. 1721530
Av. das Forças Armadas, 4 S/L ou 4 B, 1600-082 LISBOA **Tel:** 217 614 500 **Fax:** 217 614 520
Titles:
ESTÉTICA PORTUGAL

EDIESTA - EDITORIAL ESTARREJENSE, LDA. 1721971
R. dos Bombeiros Voluntários de Estarreja, 65 - 2° Esq., Apartado 65, 3860-001 ESTARREJA
Tel: 234 849 713 **Fax:** 234 849 713
Titles:
JORNAL DE ESTARREJA

EDIGARBE - SOCIEDADE EDITORA DO ALGARVE, LDA. 1721513
R. Miguel Bombarda, 67/69, 8200-855 PADERNE/ALBUFEIRA **Tel:** 289 367 288
Fax: 289 367 488
Titles:
A AVEZINHA

EDIMOTO - SOCIEDADE DE PUBLICAÇÕES PERIÓDICAS, LDA. 1721646
R. Prof. Alfredo Sousa, 1 - Lj D, 1600-188 LISBOA **Tel:** 217 543 190 **Fax:** 217 543 199
Titles:
MOTO JORNAL
MOTO JORNAL - CATÁLOGO

EDIREVISTAS - SOCIEDADE EDITORIAL, S.A. 1721485
Av. João Crisóstomo, 72 - 5°, 1069-043 LISBOA
Tel: 213 185 200 **Fax:** 213 156 146
Titles:
AUTO MOTOR
COZINHA PORTUGUESA
FLASH
GQ
MÁXIMA
MÁXIMA INTERIORES
RECORDAR
ROTAS & DESTINOS
SEMANA INFORMÁTICA
TV GUIA
VOGUE

EDISPORT - SOCIEDADE DE PUBLICAÇÕES DESPORTIVAS, S.A. 1721717
Estrada Regional Estádio - Feteiras, 9500-559 PONTA DELGADA **Tel:** 296 385 115
Fax: 296 385 115
Titles:
AGENDA
GUIA DE FUTEBOL
JORNAL DO TÉNIS
RECORD
UM ANO EM REVISTA

EDITAVE MULTIMÉDIA, LDA. 1740939
Editave Multimédia, Lda., R. 8 de Dezembro, Antas S. Tiago, 214, Apartado 410, 4760-016 VILA NOVA DE FAMALICÃO **Tel:** 252 308 145
Fax: 252 308 149
Titles:
OPINIÃO PÚBLICA

EDITORA ANTONINO DIAS, LDA. 1642829
R. de Santo António, 125 A - 1°, Apartado 43, 4800-162 GUIMARÃES **Tel:** 253 512 674
Fax: 253 517 909
Titles:
NOTÍCIAS DE GUIMARÃES

EDITORA PORTA DA ESTRELA, LDA. 1642919
Av. Luís Vaz de Camões, Edifício Jardim III, 6270-484 SEIA **Tel:** 238 315 240 **Fax:** 238 314 501
Titles:
PORTA DA ESTRELA

EDITORA RH 1643073
R. do Mercado, N°7, 1800-271 LISBOA
Tel: 218 551 203 **Fax:** 218 551 204
Titles:
RECURSOS HUMANOS MAGAZINE

EDITORIAL GRUPO V - PORTUGAL, LDA. 1721880
Av. Infante D. Henrique, 306, 1900-717 LISBOA
Tel: 218 310 920 **Fax:** 218 310 939
Titles:
CAÇA & CÃES DE CAÇA
CÃES & COMPANHIA
MUNDO DA PESCA
SUPER FOTO DIGITAL

EDITORIAL O POVO DE GUIMARÃES, C.R.L. 1724224
R. Gil Vicente, 123 - 1°, Apartado 157, 4801-910 GUIMARÃES **Tel:** 253 412 767 **Fax:** 253 412 767
Titles:
O POVO DE GUIMARÃES

EDITORIAL VÉNUS, LDA. 1642807
R. Braamcamp, 12 - R/C Esq., 1250-050 LISBOA
Tel: 213 862 019 Fax: 213 862 426
Titles:
MODA & MODA

EDUARDO PINTO SOARES 1721383
Av. Joaquim Neves dos Santos, (Traseiras do Cemitério de Sendim), Apartado 2201, 4451-901 MATOSINHOS Tel: 229 516 880 Fax: 229 516 719
Titles:
JORNAL DE MATOSINHOS

EMPES - EMPRESA DE PUBLICIDADE DE ESPINHO, LDA. 1721680
Av. 8, 456 - 1°, Sala R, Centro Comercial Solverde 1, Apartado 39, 4501-853 ESPINHO
Tel: 227 341 525 Fax: 227 319 911
Titles:
DEFESA DE ESPINHO

EMPRESA DE EXPOSIÇÕES SUCESSO, S.A. 1721865
Av. 5 de Outubro, 17 - 2°, 1050-047 LISBOA
Tel: 210 300 970 Fax: 210 300 977
Titles:
FOLHA DE PORTUGAL

EMPRESA DIÁRIO DE NOTÍCIAS, LDA. 1642609
R. Dr. Fernão de Ornelas, 56 - 3°, 9054-514 FUNCHAL Tel: 291 202 300 Fax: 291 202 305
Titles:
DIÁRIO DE NOTÍCIAS DA MADEIRA

EMPRESA DIÁRIO DO MINHO, LDA. 1721737
R. de Santa Margarida, 4 A, 4710-306 BRAGA
Tel: 253 609 460 Fax: 253 609 465
Titles:
DIÁRIO DO MINHO

EMPRESA DO DIÁRIO DOS AÇORES, LDA. 1721713
R. Dr. João Francisco de Sousa, 16, 9500-187 PONTA DELGADA Tel: 296 284 355
Fax: 296 284 840
Titles:
DIÁRIO DOS AÇORES

EMPRESA DO JORNAL CORREIO DE FAFE, LDA. 1642968
Largo de Portugal, 17, Apartado 41, 4824-909 FAFE Tel: 253 490 820 Fax: 253 490 829
Titles:
CORREIO DE FAFE

EMPRESA DO JORNAL DA MADEIRA, LDA. 1721465
R. Dr. Fernão de Ornelas, 35, 9001-905 FUNCHAL Tel: 291 210 400 Fax: 291 210 401
Titles:
JORNAL DA MADEIRA

EMPRESA EDITORA CIDADE DE TOMAR, LDA. 1721607
Praça da República, N° 27, 1°, Apartado 62, 2304-909 TOMAR Tel: 249 324 041
Fax: 249 323 898
Titles:
CIDADE DE TOMAR

EMPRESA JORNALÍSTICA GAZETA DA BEIRA, LDA. 1642682
R. dos Bombeiros Voluntários, 37, Apartado 40, São Pedro do Sul, 3660-502 VISEU
Tel: 232 723 408 Fax: 232 712 150
Titles:
GAZETA DA BEIRA

EMPRESA JORNALÍSTICA RENASCIMENTO, LDA. 1722183
Av. General Humberto Delgado, 37 - R/C Esq., 3534-005 MANGUALDE Tel: 232 623 232
Fax: 232 622 295
Titles:
RENASCIMENTO

ENZIMA AMARELA EDIÇÕES, LDA. 1767914
Av. Infante Dom Henrique, 333H - 44, Edifício Oriente, 1800-282 LISBOA
Titles:
BRIEFING
FIBRA

EULOGIA, LDA. 1740160
R. Dr. Francisco Peres, Edifício Jardins do Caniço, Loja 18, 9125-014 CANIÇO/MADEIRA
Tel: 291 934 930 Fax: 291 934 930
Titles:
MADEIRA MOTOR SPORT

EUROMÉDICE, EDIÇÕES MÉDICAS, LDA. 1762673
Alameda António Sérgio, 22 - 4° B, Edifício Amadeo de Souza-Cardoso, Miraflores, 1495-132 ALGÉS Tel: 214 121 144 Fax: 214 121 145
Titles:
POSTGRADUATE MEDICINE

EVASÃO - EDIÇÕES E PUBLICAÇÕES, LDA. 1722261
R. Bartolomeu Dias, 170 - 1° A, 1400-031 LISBOA Tel: 213 021 148 Fax: 213 020 431
Titles:
TODO TERRENO

FÁBRICA DA IGREJA PAROQUIAL DA FREGUESIA DE SÃO PEDRO DE TORRES NOVAS 1721453
Travessa da Cerca, N° 35, 2354-909 TORRES NOVAS Tel: 249 812 499 Fax: 249 812 446
Titles:
O ALMONDA

FÁBRICA DA IGREJA PAROQUIAL DA FREGUESIA DE SÃO PEDRO E SANTIAGO DE TORRES VEDRAS 1721517
Praça 25 Abril, 6 - 1° Esq., 2561-311 TORRES VEDRAS Tel: 261 335 476 Fax: 261 315 170
Titles:
BADALADAS

FÁBRICA DA IGREJA PAROQUIAL DE NOSSA SENHORA DA ANUNCIAÇÃO DA LOURINHÃ 1721455
Centro Pastoral de Santo António, 2530-120 LOURINHÃ Tel: 261 416 171 Fax: 261 416 174
Titles:
ALVORADA

FÁBRICA DA IGREJA PAROQUIAL DE OVAR 1721942
Av. do Bom Reitor, 3880-110 OVAR
Tel: 256 574 173 Fax: 256 588 545
Titles:
JOÃO SEMANA

FÁBRICA DA IGREJA PAROQUIAL DE SANTA MARIA 1722006
Bairro Azul, Colectiva B1, Apartado 6, 7500-999 VILA NOVA DE SANTO ANDRÉ Tel: 269 752 205
Fax: 269 084 307
Titles:
O LEME

FÁBRICA DO SANTUÁRIO DE NOSSA SENHORA DE FÁTIMA 1722286
Santuário de Fátima - Apartado 31, 2496-908 FÁTIMA Tel: 249 539 600 Fax: 249 539 605
Titles:
VOZ DA FÁTIMA

FÁBRICA IGREJA PAROQUIAL NOSSA SENHORA DA OLIVEIRA 1721647
R. Santa Maria, 6, 4810-248 GUIMARÃES
Tel: 253 416 144 Fax: 253 416 113
Titles:
O CONQUISTADOR

FAIXA EXCLUSIVA, LDA. 1792684
Av. dos Maristas, 82 A, 2775-241 PAREDE
Tel: 211 545 910 Fax: 211 545 919
Titles:
BIT

FIDEMO - SOCIEDADE DE MEDIA, LDA. 1792749
R. Marcelino Mesquita, 15 - Loja 1, 2795-134 LINDA-A-VELHA Tel: 214 209 400
Titles:
PC GUIA

FOLHA CULTURAL, C.R.L. 1724214
Parque das Nações, Edifício Centro de Comunicação, ALAMEDA DOS OCEANOS, LOTE 2.08.01 1990-075 LISBOA Tel: 218 931 620
Fax: 218 931 629
Titles:
CORREIO DE AZEMÉIS

FÓLIO - COMUNICAÇÃO GLOBAL, LDA. 1721628
R. Santa Catarina, 722 - 1 Sala 104, 4000-000 PORTO Tel: 220 103 900 Fax: 220 103 971
Titles:
O PRIMEIRO DE JANEIRO

FORMALPRESS - PUBLICAÇÕES E MARKETING, LDA. 1722042
R. Dr. Egas Moniz, 11 - Loja A, 2675-341 ODIVELAS Tel: 217 573 459 Fax: 217 576 316
Titles:
MEDIA XXI

FOZCOM - PRODUÇÃO E COMUNICAÇÃO MULTIMÉDIA, S.A. 1721606
R. de O Figueirense N°14, 3080-059 FIGUEIRA DA FOZ Tel: 233 402 930 Fax: 233 402 931
Titles:
O FIGUEIRENSE

FRANCISCO CASTANHEIRA CARVALHO E FILHOS, LDA. 1721965
R. Dr. Veiga Simões, 1 e 3, Apartado 48, 3300-048 ARGANIL Tel: 235 202 432 Fax: 235 204 364
Titles:
JORNAL DE ARGANIL

FUNDAÇÃO AMI 1740046
Pátio Manuel Guerreiro, R. José do Patrocínio, 49 - Marvila, 1949-008 LISBOA Tel: 218 362 100
Fax: 218 362 199
Titles:
AMI NOTÍCIAS

FUNDAÇÃO FREI PEDRO 1643140
R. Soeiro Viegas, 2 B, Apartado 201, 6300-758 GUARDA Tel: 271 223 110 Fax: 271 223 112
Titles:
TERRAS DA BEIRA

FUNDAÇÃO MENSAGEIRO DE BRAGANÇA 1721715
R. Dr. Herculano da Conceição, Apartado 77, 5301-901 BRAGANÇA Tel: 273 323 367
Fax: 273 329 176
Titles:
MENSAGEIRO DE BRAGANÇA

G + J PORTUGAL - EDIÇÕES, PUBLICIDADE E DISTRIBUIÇÃO, LDA. 1792683
R. Policarpo Anjos, 4, 1495-742 CRUZ QUEBRADA/DAFUNDO Tel: 214 154 500
Fax: 214 154 504
Titles:
BEBÉ D'HOJE
COSMOPOLITAN
SUPER INTERESSANTE

GABINETE 1 - IMPRENSA, PROMOÇÃO E RELAÇÕES PÚBLICAS, LDA. 1642642
Praça Luis de Camões, 36 - 2° Dto., 1200-243 LISBOA Tel: 213 224 660 Fax: 213 224 679
Titles:
ELES & ELAS

GIRA SOL - ASSOCIAÇÃO DE DESENVOLVIMENTO DE FEBRES 1721495
Praça Florindo José Frota, 17, Apartado 79, 3061-906 FEBRES Tel: 231 469 090
Fax: 231 469 092
Titles:
AURI NEGRA

GLOBAL NOTÍCIAS, PUBLICAÇÕES, S.A. 1721388
R. Gonçalo Cristóvão, 195/219, 4049-011 PORTO Tel: 213 187 500 Fax: 213 187 866
Titles:
1000 MAIORES EMPRESAS (DN + JN)
ÁGORA
AMBIENTE (DN + JN)
AUTO
CLASSIFICADOS TUTI
CLASSIFICADOS TUTI
DESPORTO
DIÁRIO DE NOTÍCIAS
DN EMPREGO
DOSSIER SAÚDE
DOSSIER SAÚDE
EDIÇÃO NORTE
EVASÕES
FRANCHISING (DN + JN)
JN NEGÓCIOS
JORNAL DE NOTÍCIAS
JORNAL DE NOTÍCIAS - NORTE
MARCAS HISTÓRICAS
MEDICINA VETERINÁRIA
NOTÍCIAS MAGAZINE
NOTÍCIAS SÁBADO
PORTO
REGIÕES (DN + JN)
REVISTA DA QUEIMA DAS FITAS
ROTEIROS GASTRONÓMICOS
SEGURANÇA INFANTIL (DN + JN)
TERRA DO NUNCA
VIDA SAUDÁVEL (DN + JN)
VOLTA AO MUNDO

GOLF PRESS - EDIÇÃO DE PUBLICAÇÕES, LDA. 1721890
Alameda das Linhas de Torres, 179, 1750-142 LISBOA Tel: 217 541 450 Fax: 217 541 458
Titles:
GOLF DIGEST

GOODY - CONSULTORIA, S.A. 1721533
Av. Infante D. Henrique, 306 - Lote 6, R/C, 1950-421 LISBOA Tel: 218 621 530 Fax: 218 621 540
Titles:
BGAMER
T3

GRÁFICA AÇORIANA, LDA. 1721424
R. Dr. João Francisco de Sousa, 14, 9500-187 PONTA DELGADA Tel: 296 201 060
Titles:
AÇORIANÍSSIMA
ATLÂNTICO EXPRESSO
CORREIO DOS AÇORES

GRÁFICA GONDOMARENSE - EDIÇÃO DE PUBLICAÇÕES GRÁFICA, LDA. 1642858
R. da Guiné, 18, Apartado 72, 4420-159 PORTO
Tel: 224 644 902 Fax: 224 644 902
Titles:
COMÉRCIO DE GONDOMAR

GRITO DE FORÇA - COMUNICAÇÃO E PUBLICIDADE UNIPESSOAL, LDA. 1763892
R. Camilo Castelo Branco, 45, Apartado 474, 4760-127 VILA NOVA DE FAMALICÃO
Tel: 252 378 165 Fax: 252 378 167
Titles:
O POVO FAMALICENSE

GRUPO EDITORIAL BOLINA - BENTO, LEMOS & BURNAY - ED. PROD. E COMERCIALIZAÇÃO DE PUB PER E N/PER LDA. 1724216
Edifício Central Park, R. Alexandre Herculano, 3 - 3° B, 2795-240 LINDA-A-VELHA
Tel: 214 131 600 **Fax:** 214 131 601
Titles:
ELEKTOR ELECTRÓNICA
PRODUÇÃO ÁUDIO
PRODUÇÃO PROFISSIONAL

GRUPO MEDIA CENTRO 1721583
R. Cidade Halle, Bloco 7/9 R/C, 3000-107 COIMBRA **Tel:** 239 497 750 **Fax:** 239 497 759
Titles:
CAMPEÃO DAS PROVÍNCIAS
INDEPENDENTE DE CANTANHEDE
NOTÍCIAS DE VOUZELA

GRUPO OESTE CAPITAL 1773348
R. Heróis da Grande Guerra, 84 - 1°, Apartado 122, 2501-216 CALDAS DA RAINHA
Tel: 262 844 443 **Fax:** 262 844 022
Titles:
JORNAL DAS CALDAS

GRUPO SANTIAGO - GUIMAPRESS, S.A. 1744338
R. Dr. José Sampaio, 264 - Apartado 485, 4801-850 GUIMARÃES **Tel:** 253 421 700
Fax: 253 421 709
Titles:
O COMÉRCIO DE GUIMARÃES
DESPORTIVO DE GUIMARÃES

HEINRICH BAUER EDICIONES S.L.S. EN C. 1721741
R. Joaquim A. Aguiar, 35 - 3°, 1070-149 LISBOA
Tel: 213 839 580 **Fax:** 213 839 581
Titles:
BRAVO
HORÓSCOPO

HERDEIROS DE ANTÓNIO JOSÉ GUERREIRO CEPA 1721580
R. da Corredoura, 117, 4910-133 CAMINHA
Tel: 258 921 754 **Fax:** 258 721 041
Titles:
O CAMINHENSE

HERDEIROS DE JAIME BARBOSA DE MACEDO 1642730
Estrada da Falagueira, 8-B, 2700-362 AMADORA **Tel:** 214 989 780 **Fax:** 214 989 788
Titles:
JORNAL DA AMADORA

HIWAY S.F.D. AUDIOVISUAL, LDA. 1792769
R. Carlos Pereira, 4 C/V Dta., 1500-139 LISBOA
Titles:
TELE CABO

HORIZONTE DE PALAVRAS - EDIÇÕES UNIPESSOAL, LDA. 1792754
R. Rei Ramiro, 870 - 6° B, 4400-281 VILA NOVA DE GAIA **Tel:** 220 993 250 **Fax:** 220 993 250
Titles:
PONTOS DE VISTA.COM.PT

IFE - INTERNATIONAL FACULTY FOR EXECUTIVES, S.A. 1740076
R. Basílio Teles, 35 - 1° Dto., 1070-020 LISBOA
Tel: 210 033 800 **Fax:** 210 033 888
Titles:
DISTRIBUIÇÃO HOJE
LOGÍSTICA & TRANSPORTES HOJE
NEGÓCIOS & FRANCHISING
VIDA RURAL

IMOEDIÇÕES - EDIÇÕES PERIÓDICAS E MULTIMÉDIA, LDA. 1722071
R. Gonçalo Cristóvão, 111 - 6°, 4049-037 PORTO **Tel:** 223 399 400 **Fax:** 222 058 098
Titles:
VIDA IMOBILIÁRIA

IMPALA - EDITORES, S.A. 1721386
Edifício Grupo Impala, Ranholas, 2710-460 SINTRA **Tel:** 219 238 463
Titles:
100% JOVEM
ANA
CINEMA
DIABETES
ESTAÇÕES
FOCUS
MARIA
MULHER MODERNA NA COZINHA
NOVA GENTE
NOVA GENTE DECORAÇÃO
RECEITAS PRÁTICAS
SEGREDOS DE COZINHA
SOPAS
SUSHI
TV 7 DIAS
VIP
VIP SAÚDE E BELEZA

IMPREMÉDICA - IMPRENSA MÉDICA, LDA. 1721430
R. Abranches Ferrão, N° 23, 3° Andar, 1600-296 LISBOA **Tel:** 214 788 620 **Fax:** 214 788 621
Titles:
TEMPO MEDICINA

INATEL - INSTITUTO NACIONAL PARA O APROVEITAMENTO DOS TEMPOS LIVRES DOS TRABALHADORES 1722246
Calçada de Sant' Ana, 180, 1169-062 LISBOA
Tel: 210 027 000 **Fax:** 210 027 061
Titles:
TEMPO LIVRE
TURISMO SOCIAL

INFOMÚSICA, EDIÇÃO DE PUBLICAÇÕES, LDA 1740092
Av. David Mourão Ferreira, Lote 15.5C, Esc. B, 1750-067 LISBOA
Titles:
DANCE CLUB

INFORMARTE - INFORMAÇÃO REGIONAL, S.A. 1642765
Av. 1° de Maio, 39 - 1° Dto., 6000-086 CASTELO BRANCO **Tel:** 272 320 090 **Fax:** 272 320 091
Titles:
GAZETA DO INTERIOR

INGENIUM - EDIÇÕES, LDA. 1721935
Av. António Augusto de Aguiar, N° 3 Dto., 1069-030 LISBOA **Tel:** 213 132 600 **Fax:** 213 524 632
Titles:
INGENIUM

INSAT - CONSULTORIA E SERVIÇOS, LDA. 1721758
R. Cidade de Bolama, Lote 17 - 7° B, 1800-079 LISBOA **Tel:** 218 537 812 **Fax:** 218 537 807
Titles:
MARKET REPORT

INSTALADOR PUBLICAÇÕES, LDA. 1642876
R. do Alecrim, 53 - R/C Ftr., 1200-014 LISBOA
Tel: 218 820 160 **Fax:** 218 820 169
Titles:
O INSTALADOR

INSTITUTO DO EMPREGO E FORMAÇÃO PROFISSIONAL 1642622
R. de Xabregas, 52, 1949-003 LISBOA
Tel: 218 614 100 **Fax:** 218 614 621
Titles:
DIRIGIR

JAS FARMA COMUNICAÇÃO, LDA. 1721702
Edifício Lisboa Oriente Office, Av. Infante D.Henrique, 333 H - 5°, 1800-282 LISBOA
Tel: 218 504 000 **Fax:** 218 504 009
Titles:
MUNDO MÉDICO
SAÚDE (DN + JN)

JM - JORNAL DA MEALHADA, LDA. 1721708
R. das Escolas Novas, 36, Apartado 30, 3050-901 MEALHADA **Tel:** 231 203 167 **Fax:** 231 203 167
Titles:
JORNAL DA MEALHADA

JOÃO ARRUDA SUCESSORES, LDA. 1642591
R. Serpa Pinto, 98/104, Apartado 323, 2000-046 SANTARÉM **Tel:** 243 333 116 **Fax:** 243 333 258
Titles:
CORREIO DO RIBATEJO

JOAQUIM ANTÓNIO ANTUNES EMÍDIO E MARIA DE FÁTIMA FRANCO SALGADO EMÍDIO 1721390
R. 31 de Janeiro, 22, Apartado 389, 2005-188 SANTARÉM **Tel:** 243 305 080 **Fax:** 243 305 081
Titles:
LEZÍRIA TEJO

JORLIS - EDIÇÕES E PUBLICAÇÕES, LDA. 1642746
R. Comandante João Belo, 31, 2400-159 LEIRIA
Tel: 244 800 400 **Fax:** 244 800 400
Titles:
250 MAIORES EMPRESAS (JL + P)
JORNAL DE LEIRIA
LEIRIA GLOBAL

JORNAL 1X2, LDA. 1721943
Apartado 148, 2801-997 ALMADA
Tel: 212 760 511 **Fax:** 212 743 421
Titles:
JORNAL 1X2

JORNAL DA MARINHA GRANDE, LDA. 1642735
Travessa Vieira de Leiria, 9, Apartado 102, 2430-902 MARINHA GRANDE **Tel:** 244 502 628
Fax: 244 569 093
Titles:
JORNAL DA MARINHA GRANDE

JORNAL DE CHAVES, LDA. 1643110
Praça Camões, 12 A - 2°, Apartado 91, 5400-150 CHAVES **Tel:** 276 333 333 **Fax:** 276 333 034
Titles:
SEMANÁRIO TRANSMONTANO

JORNAL DO FUNDÃO EDITORA, LDA. 1642761
R. Jornal do Fundão, 4/6, 6231-406 FUNDÃO
Tel: 275 779 350 **Fax:** 275 779 369
Titles:
JORNAL DO FUNDÃO

JORNAL GRAFE EDIÇÕES, LDA. 1721591
Largo da Misericórdia, 65, 4974-009 ARCOS DE VALDEVEZ **Tel:** 258 514 440 **Fax:** 258 514 441
Titles:
NOTÍCIAS DOS ARCOS

JORNAL MIRADOURO EDIÇÕES, LDA. 1642770
Casa Azenha, Boassas, Apartado 71, 4690-405 CINFÃES **Tel:** 255 561 337 **Fax:** 255 561 337
Titles:
MIRADOURO

JORNAL TRIBUNA PACENSE, LDA. 1722235
Av. dos Templários, 318, 4590-509 PAÇOS DE FERREIRA **Tel:** 255 863 987 **Fax:** 255 862 456
Titles:
TRIBUNA PACENSE

JORNALINVESTE COMUNICAÇÃO, S.A. 1642877
R. Gonçalo Cristóvão, 195, 4000-269 PORTO
Tel: 222 096 147 **Fax:** 222 096 127
Titles:
O JOGO

JORTEJO JORNAIS, RÁDIO E TELEVISÃO, LDA. 1762032
Quinta das Cegonhas, Apartado 355, 2002-000 SANTARÉM **Tel:** 243 309 600
Titles:
O RIBATEJO

JOSÉ MARIA DA PIEDADE BARROS 1642721
R. Major Olival, Centro Comercial Charlot, Loja 12, 8100-000 LOULÉ **Tel:** 289 410 640
Fax: 289 410 649
Titles:
A VOZ DE LOULÉ

JOSÉ MARIA DE SOUSA FERREIRA ALVES SOCIEDADE UNIPESSOAL, LDA. 1722164
Praça Capitão Torres Meireles, 30 - 2°, sala H, 4580-211 PAREDES **Tel:** 255 781 520
Fax: 255 777 030
Titles:
O PROGRESSO DE PAREDES

JOSÉ SOARES DA SILVA, LDA. 1642886
R. 11 de Outubro, 178, Apartado 135, 3700-210 SÃO JOÃO DA MADEIRA **Tel:** 256 822 783
Fax: 256 822 654
Titles:
O REGIONAL

JPJ - EDITORA DE EDIÇÕES PERIÓDICAS, LDA. 1721594
R. Luís Soares Barbosa, 42, 4710-403 BRAGA
Tel: 253 215 466 **Fax:** 253 215 468
Titles:
ARQ & DESIGN

KGB - CONSULTORIA GLOBAL 1722178
R. de Penafiel, 100, 4100-402 PORTO
Tel: 226 106 970 **Fax:** 226 106 971
Titles:
REFLEXOS MODA

LABORPRESS - EDIÇÕES E COMUNICAÇÃO SOCIAL, LDA. 1721826
R. Camilo Castelo Branco, 200 A, Apartado 104, 3701-910 S. JOÃO DA MADEIRA **Tel:** 256 202 600
Fax: 256 202 609
Titles:
LABOR.PT

LAMARTINE SOARES & RODRIGUES, S.A. 1722052
Av. da Igreja, 37 - E, 1700-233 LISBOA
Tel: 217 939 775 **Fax:** 217 972 574
Titles:
MID / DIMENSÃO

LAMEGRÁFICA - SOCIEDADE COMERCIAL E EDITORIAL, LDA. 1721393
R. de S. João, Urbanização da Ortigosa, Bloco 21 - Sub-Cave Dto., Apartado 40, 5100-909 LAMEGO **Tel:** 254 613 930 **Fax:** 254 655 508
Titles:
DOURO HOJE

LETRA DE FORMA 1762181
R. Alexandre Herculano, N° 1 - 2° Dto., 1150-005 LISBOA **Tel:** 210 962 060 **Fax:** 213 553 235
Titles:
O CRIME
O DIABO

LOSANGO MÁGICO, PUBLICAÇÕES E PUBLICIDADE, LDA. 1721854
Av. Luísa Todi, 408 - 1°, 2900 SETÚBAL
Tel: 265 520 716 **Fax:** 265 520 717
Titles:
JORNAL DE SETÚBAL

Portugal

LPM COMUNICAÇÃO 1746940
Edifício Lisboa Oriente, Av. Infante D. Henrique, 333 H, Esc. 49, 1800-282 LISBOA
Tel: 218 508 110 **Fax:** 218 530 426
Titles:
FARMÁCIA SAÚDE
PLANO DE ACTIVIDADES
TURISMO DE LISBOA

LUCIDUS PUBLICAÇÕES, LDA. 1642457
R. Joaquim António de Aguiar, 45 - 5° Esq., 1099-058 LISBOA **Fax:** 213 862 746
Titles:
PORTUGAL BRASIL

LUDGERO DE FIGUEIREDO DE MATOS 1721678
R. Pinheiro de Ázere, 7, 3440-000 SANTA COMBA DÃO **Tel:** 231 922 667 **Fax:** 231 922 667
Titles:
DEFESA DA BEIRA

LUSOSINAL - EDIÇÃO E COMUNICAÇÃO, S.A. 1719955
Edifício Atrium Saldanha, Praça Duque de Saldanha, 1 - 11° A, 1069-970 LISBOA
Tel: 213 170 850 **Fax:** 213 160 297
Titles:
IMOBILIÁRIA

MANUEL SÉRGIO MACHADO LOPES VINAGRE 1721688
R. Dr. Abílio Torres, 520, 4815-552 VIZELA
Tel: 253 584 010 **Fax:** 253 587 653
Titles:
NOTÍCIAS DE VIZELA

MARÇO - EDITORA, LDA. 1721568
R. Alexandre Herculano, 2 - 2° Dto., 1150-006 LISBOA **Tel:** 218 823 300 **Fax:** 211 204 349
Titles:
INTER.FACE - ADMINISTRAÇÃO PÚBLICA
INTER.FACE - BANCA & SEGUROS
INTER.FACE - SAÚDE

MARIA ELVIRA PIRES TEIXEIRA 1642419
R. Dr. António José de Almeida, 41, 3260-420 FGUEIRÓ DOS VINHOS **Tel:** 236 553 669
Fax: 236 553 692
Titles:
A COMARCA

MARKETING FOR YOU, LDA. 1740145
Beloura Office Park, Edifício 4, Escritório1.2, 2710-693 SINTRA **Tel:** 219 247 670
Fax: 219 247 679
Titles:
JORNAL DO CENTRO DE SAÚDE

MATCH SCORE, LDA. 1762946
Av. Columbano Bordalo Pinheiro, 87 - 5°, 1070-042 LISBOA
Titles:
NEW GOLF
URBAN MAN

MEDFARMA - EDIÇÕES MÉDICAS, LDA. 1792721
Al. António Sérgio, 22 - 4° B, Edifício Amadeo de Souza-Cardoso, 1495-132 ALGÉS
Tel: 214 121 142 **Fax:** 214 121 146
Titles:
JADA

MEDIA CAPITAL EDIÇÕES, LDA. 1740073
R. Mário Castelhano, 40 - Queluz de Baixo, 2734-502 BARCARENA **Tel:** 214 345 902
Fax: 214 345 901
Titles:
LUX
LUX DECORAÇÃO
LUX WOMAN
REVISTA DE VINHOS

MEDIA LINE - COMUNICAÇÃO E IMAGEM LDA. 1751926
Rua da Piedade, 15 C, 1495- 104 ALGÉS
Titles:
CLIMATIZAÇÃO

MEDIPRESS - SOCIEDADE JORNALÍSTICA E EDITORIAL, LDA. 1721415
R. Calvet de Magalhães, 242 - Laveiras, 2770-022 PAÇO DE ARCOS **Tel:** 214 698 000
Fax: 214 698 500
Titles:
1000 MAIORES EMPRESAS (E)
ACTIVA
ACTIVA - NOIVAS
AUTO SPORT
BLITZ
BOA MESA
CABELOS
CARAS
CARAS DECORAÇÃO
CASA CLÁUDIA
CERTA
COSMOBELEZA
CULINÁRIA
ENSINO SUPERIOR
EXAME INFORMÁTICA
PÓS GRADUAÇÕES, MESTRADOS, MBA
REVISTA UNIBANCO
ROTEIRO
SAÚDE & BELEZA
TELE NOVELAS
TV MAIS
VISÃO
VISÃO 7 GUIA
VISÃO 7 LISBOA E SUL
VISÃO 7 PORTO E NORTE
VISÃO GOURMET

MEDIREGIÃO - EDIÇÃO DE DISTRIBUIÇÃO DE PUBLICAÇÕES, LDA. 1740064
Edifício Pátio da Rocha, Loja 46 - Piso 0 BA, Praia da Rocha, Apartado 168, 8501-911 PORTIMÃO **Tel:** 282 480 220 **Fax:** 282 480 221
Titles:
BARLAVENTO

METRO NEWS PUBLICAÇÕES, S.A. 1721716
Estrada da Outurela, 118, Parque Holanda - Edifício Holanda, 2790-114 CARNAXIDE
Tel: 214 169 210 **Fax:** 214 169 228
Titles:
DESTAK
DESTAK LISBOA

MILHO REI - COOPERATIVA POPULAR DE INFORMAÇÃO E CULTURA DE BARCELOS, C.R.L. 1724213
Av. João Paulo II, 355, 4750-304 BARCELOS
Tel: 253 813 585 **Fax:** 253 823 362
Titles:
BARCELOS POPULAR

MOON LIFE, LDA. 1773934
Largo Alberto Sampaio 3-A, 2795-007 LINDA-A-VELHA **Tel:** 214 146 217 **Fax:** 214 146 218
Titles:
SAÚDE NOTÍCIAS

MOON MEDIA COMUNICAÇÃO, LDA. 1765708
R. General Firmino Miguel, 3 - Torre 2, 3°, 1600-100 LISBOA **Tel:** 210 410 324 **Fax:** 210 410 306
Titles:
CASAS DE PORTUGAL
PESSOAL

MOTORPRESS LISBOA - EDIÇÃO E DISTRIBUIÇÃO, S.A. 1642509
R. Policarpo Anjos, 4, 1495-742 CRUZ QUEBRADA/DAFUNDO **Tel:** 214 154 500
Fax: 214 154 504
Titles:
AUTO HOJE
BIKE MAGAZINE
CATÁLOGO
GESTÃO DE FROTAS (AH + VC)
GUIA DE ESTILO
GUIA DO AUTOMÓVEL
MEN'S HEALTH
MOTOCICLISMO
NAVEGAR
PAIS & FILHOS
RELÓGIOS & JÓIAS
SPORT LIFE
VEÍCULOS COMERCIAIS
ZOOM I.T.

MTG - EDIÇÃO E PUBLICIDADE, LDA. 1743576
Praceta do Esteval, 51, 2870-421 MONTIJO
Tel: 212 431 592 **Fax:** 212 312 909
Titles:
ARTE & CONSTRUÇÃO

MULTIBASE - SERVIÇOS DE INFORMÁTICA, LDA. 1722060
R. Campolide, 31 - 1° Dto., 1070-026 LISBOA
Tel: 213 841 460 **Fax:** 213 841 461
Titles:
MULHER PORTUGUESA.COM

MULTIPUBLICAÇÕES - EDIÇÃO PUBLICAÇÃO DE INFORMAÇÃO E PRESTAÇÃO DE SERVIÇOS DE COMUNICAÇÃO, LDA. 1721893
R. Basílio Teles, 36 - 6° Dto., 1070-020 LISBOA
Tel: 210 123 400 **Fax:** 210 123 444
Titles:
EXECUTIVE DIGEST
MARKETEER

NATURAL MEDIA - COMUNICAÇÕES, LDA. 1721843
R. dos Bem Lembrados, 141, Manique, 2645-471 ALCABIDECHE **Tel:** 214 449 690
Fax: 214 449 691
Titles:
100% NATURAL
PERFORMANCE

NERIBI - EDIÇÃO E PUBLICIDADE, LDA. 1642658
Av. Miguel Bombarda, 42 - 3° D, 1050-166 LISBOA **Tel:** 217 971 683 **Fax:** 217 820 295
Titles:
ESTÉTICA VIVA

NERLEI - NÚCLEO EMPRESARIAL DA REGIÃO DE LEIRIA 1721682
Av. bernardo Pimenta, Ed. NERLEI, 2403-010 LEIRIA **Tel:** 244 890 200 **Fax:** 244 890 210
Titles:
DESAFIOS

NODIGRÁFICA - INFORMAÇÃO E ARTES GRÁFICAS, LDA. 1721567
Complexo Conventurispress, Av. do Convento, N° 1, 3511-907 VISEU **Tel:** 232 410 410
Fax: 232 410 418
Titles:
NOTÍCIAS DE VISEU

NOTÍCIAS DO BOMBARRAL - EMPRESA JORNALÍSTICA REGIONAL, LDA. 1722067
R. da Fonte Velha, 11 - B, 2540-909 BOMBARRAL **Tel:** 262 603 054 **Fax:** 262 603 054
Titles:
NOTÍCIAS DO BOMBARRAL

NOVA GUARDA - AGÊNCIA DE INFORMAÇÃO, LDA. 1773931
R. António Sérgio, Edifício Liberal, Loja Q, 6300-665 GUARDA **Tel:** 271 210 105 **Fax:** 271 210 106
Titles:
NOVA GUARDA

NUGON - PUBLICAÇÕES E REPRESENTAÇÕES PUBLICITÁRIAS, LDA. 1721557
R. Nelson Pereira Neves, Lojas 1 e 2, 2670-338 LOURES **Tel:** 219 830 130 **Fax:** 219 833 359
Titles:
A BOLSA M.I.A.

OCASIÃO EDIÇÕES PERIÓDICAS, LDA. 1642896
R. Capitão Leitão, 66 N, 2800-133 ALMADA
Tel: 707 260 260 **Fax:** 707 270 270
Titles:
OCASIÃO

OPEN MEDIA - DESIGN E PUBLICAÇÕES, S.A. 1721838
Parque Empresarial do Algarve, 7, Apartado 59, 8401-901 LAGOA **Tel:** 282 341 333
Fax: 282 341 360
Titles:
HEALTH & BEAUTY

ORDEM DOS ECONOMISTAS 1740103
R. Francisco Rodrigues Lobo, 2 - R/C Dto., 1070-134 LISBOA **Tel:** 213 859 950
Fax: 213 851 430
Titles:
O ECONOMISTA

PÁGINA EXCLUSIVA - PUBLICAÇÕES PERIÓDICAS, LDA. 1771938
R Augusto Lessa, 251 Esq. - 13, 4200-100 PORTO **Tel:** 225 023 907 **Fax:** 225 023 908
Titles:
PORTUGAL INOVADOR

PARQUE BIOLÓGICO DE BRAGA, E.E.M. 1792747
R. da Cunha, 4430-681 AVINTES **Tel:** 227 878 120
Fax: 227 833 583
Titles:
PARQUES E VIDA SELVAGEM

PAULUS EDITORA - SOCIEDADE UNIPESSOAL, LDA. 1771025
R. Dom Pedro de Cristo, 10-12, 1749-092 LISBOA **Tel:** 218 437 620 **Fax:** 218 437 629
Titles:
FAMÍLIA CRISTÃ

PBLUE - EDIÇÃO DE PUBLICAÇÕES, LDA. 1721537
BLUE MEDIA
Titles:
BLUE COOKING
BLUE TRAVEL

PETRICA EDITORES, LDA. 1722198
R. Sousa Viterbo, 48 - C, 1900-427 LISBOA
Tel: 218 131 944 **Fax:** 218 131 816
Titles:
REVISTA SEGURANÇA

PI - PRODUÇÃO DE IDEIAS, LDA. 1721866
Largo da Portagem, 18 - 2° Dto., 3000-337 COIMBRA **Tel:** 239 832 264
Titles:
FOLHA DE SANTA CLARA

PIÇARRA & COMPANHIA, LDA. 1642612
Travessa de Santo André, 6 - 8, Apartado 2037, 7000-951 ÉVORA **Tel:** 266 744 444
Fax: 266 741 252
Titles:
DIÁRIO DO SUL

PLOT CONTENT AGENCY 1792722
R. Joaquim António de Aguiar, 45 - 2° Dto., 1050-150 LISBOA **Tel:** 213 804 010
Fax: 213 804 011
Titles:
JARDINS

PLURIJORNAL - SOCIEDADE EDITORA, LDA. 1721813
R. Arronches Junqueiro, 82, Apartado 182, 2902-000 SETÚBAL **Tel:** 265 528 132 **Fax:** 265 528 131
Titles:
SAÚDE
O SETUBALENSE

PM MEDIA - COMUNICAÇÃO, S.A. 1721917
Centro Empresarial Lionesa, R. da Lionesa, 446 - Fracção G19, 4465-671 LEÇA DO BALIO
Tel: 229 069 530 **Fax:** 229 069 539
Titles:
VILLAS & GOLFE

POSTAL DO ALGARVE - PUBLICAÇÕES E EDITORES, LDA. 1721815
R. Dr. Silvestre Falcão, 13 C, 8800-412 TAVIRA
Tel: 281 320 900 **Fax:** 281 320 915
Titles:
POSTAL DO ALGARVE

PRAIA OCEÂNICA - INVESTIMENTOS TURÍSTICOS E IMOBILIÁRIOS, S.A. 1642589
R. de Ansião, 33, Apartado 111, 3100-474 POMBAL **Tel:** 236 207 460 **Fax:** 236 219 542
Titles:
O CORREIO DE POMBAL

PRESÉPIO DE PORTUGAL - COMUNICAÇÃO SOCIAL, UNIPESSOAL, LDA. 1722107
R. Renato Leitão Lourenço, 11, 2580-335 ALENQUER **Tel:** 263 711 130
Titles:
NOVA VERDADE

PRESS COAST 1769974
R. Bernardo Lima, 47 - 2° Esq., 1150-078 LISBOA **Tel:** 213 149 025
Titles:
GENTLEMEN MAGAZINE

PRESS FÓRUM - COMUNICAÇÃO SOCIAL, S.A. 1721873
Travessa das Pedras Negras, 1 - 4° Andar, 1100-404 LISBOA **Tel:** 218 854 730 **Fax:** 218 877 666
Titles:
FÓRUM ESTUDANTE

PRESSELIVRE - IMPRENSA LIVRE, S.A. 1721421
Av. João Crisóstomo, 72, 1069-043 LISBOA
Tel: 213 185 200 **Fax:** 213 185 200
Titles:
AÇORES
ALGARVE
CLASSIFICADOS
CORREIO DA MANHÃ
DOMINGO
EDIÇÃO DE NATAL
ENSINO SUPERIOR
FESTAS
FUTEBOL
GUIA DE GESTÃO DO CONDOMÍNIO
NATAL
NORTE
PRIMEIRA ESCOLHA
PRIMEIRO EMPREGO
SÁBADO
SANTARÉM
SPORT
TV

PRESSPEOPLE - EDIÇÃO DE PUBLICAÇÕES, LDA. 1721532
Cascais Office, Rotunda das Tojas, 2° E, 2645-091 ALCABIDECHE **Tel:** 214 606 100
Fax: 214 606 119
Titles:
BACALHAU
BACALHAU
BOLOS E TORTAS
CLÁSSICOS DA TV
MARIANA
MARIANA CULINÁRIA

PROGRESSO - EDIÇÕES E PUBLICIDADE, LDA. 1721466
Alameda do Mosteiro, Loja 2, N° 52, 4590-909 PAÇOS DE FERREIRA **Tel:** 255 860 960
Fax: 255 860 969
Titles:
IMEDIATO

PROMERCADO - MARKETING, PROMOÇÃO E SERVIÇOS, LDA. 1642522
R. General Ferreira Martins, N° 10 - 6° B, Miraflores, 1495-137 ALGÉS **Tel:** 219 959 510
Fax: 219 959 515
Titles:
BEBÉ SAÚDE
MÃE IDEAL

PRONÚPCIAS - EDIÇÕES, REPRESENTAÇÕES E EVENTOS, LDA. 1724207
R. Alexandre Herculano, 341 - 4°, Sala14, 4000-055 PORTO **Tel:** 222 073 040 **Fax:** 222 073 044
Titles:
AMBIENTES DE FESTA

PROPRIEDADE ADHP - ASSOCIAÇÃO DOS DIRECTORES DE HOTÉIS DE PORTUGAL 1745072
Pr. de Alvalade, 6 - 10° Esq., 1700-036 LISBOA
Tel: 217 986 759 **Fax:** 217 986 764
Titles:
DIRHOTEL

PUBLICAÇÕES DACOSTA, LDA. 1721500
Largo do Cruzeiro, Nogueira, Apartado 2157, 4715-177 BRAGA **Tel:** 253 204 180
Fax: 253 204 185
Titles:
AUTO COMPRA & VENDA

PÚBLICO - COMUNICAÇÃO SOCIAL, S.A. 1721437
R. Viriato, 13, 1069-315 LISBOA **Tel:** 210 111 000
Fax: 210 111 006
Titles:
PÚBLICO

PUBLIÇOR - PUBLICAÇÕES E PUBLICIDADE, LDA. 1721514
Rua Praia dos Santos, 10, 9500-706 PONTA DELGADA **Tel:** 296 630 080 **Fax:** 296 630 089
Titles:
TERRA NOSTRA

PUBLINDÚSTRIA - PRODUÇÃO DE COMUNICAÇÃO, LDA. 1721650
Praça da Corujeira, 38, Apartado 3825, 4300-144 PORTO **Tel:** 225 899 620 **Fax:** 225 899 629
Titles:
O ELECTRICISTA
FUNDIÇÃO
RENOVÁVEIS MAGAZINE
TECNOHOSPITAL

PUBLIREGIÕES - SOCIEDADE JORNALÍSTICA E EDITORIAL, LDA. 1764622
Alameda António Sérgio, 7 - 1° Dto., 2799-531 LINDA-A-VELHA **Tel:** 214 157 200 **Fax:** 214 150 781
Titles:
JORNAL DA REGIÃO

PUBLITÂMEGA - PUBLICAÇÕES DO TÂMEGA, LDA. 1721964
Largo de S. Pedro, 2° C, Apartado 75, 4600-036 AMARANTE **Tel:** 255 432 914
Titles:
JORNAL DE AMARANTE

RBA - REVISTAS PORTUGAL, S.A. 1740937
R. Filipe Folque, 40 - 4°, 1079-124 LISBOA
Tel: 213 164 200 **Fax:** 213 104 201
Titles:
ELLE
ESPIRAL DO TEMPO
MODA
NATIONAL GEOGRAPHIC

RCO - PRODUÇÕES GRÁFICAS, LDA. 1721611
Global Chick, Publicações, Lda., R. dos Cafés, 24 Sobreloja, 4490-595 PÓVOA DE VARZIM
Tel: 252 637 570 **Fax:** 252 637 570
Titles:
CHICK - INTIMATE CULT

REGIÃO DE TURISMO DO ALGARVE 1740125
Av. 5 de Outubro, 18, 8000-076 FARO
Tel: 289 800 400 **Fax:** 289 800 489
Titles:
GUIA DO ALGARVE

REPRESSE - EDIÇÕES ESPECIALIZADAS, LDA. 1721655
R. Prof. Alfredo de Sousa, 1, 1600-188 LISBOA
Tel: 217 543 140 **Fax:** 217 543 188
Titles:
SAÚDE E BEM ESTAR
SUPER BEBÉS
VIAJAR

SANTA CASA DA MISERICÓRDIA DE ALMEIRIM 1642849
Santa Casa da Misericórdia, R. Almirante Reis, N° 32, 2080-060 ALMEIRIM **Tel:** 243 594 360
Fax: 243 594 368
Titles:
O ALMEIRINENSE

SEDITON - SOCIEDADE EDITORA TONDELENSE, LDA. 1642756
R. Dr. Marques da Costa, Apartado 97, 3460-000 TONDELA **Tel:** 232 822 137 **Fax:** 232 821 118
Titles:
JORNAL DE TONDELA

SELECÇÕES DO READER'S DIGEST (PORTUGAL), S.A. 1721870
Lagoas Park, Edifício 11, 1°, 2740-270 PORTO SALVO **Tel:** 213 810 000 **Fax:** 213 859 203
Titles:
SELECÇÕES DO READERS DIGEST

SERRA PINTO HEALTH SOLUTIONS 1740185
R. Padre Luís Aparício, 11 - 3° A, 1150-248 LISBOA **Tel:** 213 584 301 **Fax:** 213 584 309
Titles:
NURSING
SEMANA MÉDICA

SÍLVIO JOAQUIM FRANCISCO FERREIRA TEIXEIRA 1642762
R. Dr. Roque da Silveira, 57 - 1°, Apartado 156, 5000-630 VILA REAL **Tel:** 259 321 772
Fax: 259 322 079
Titles:
JORNAL DO NORTE

SOBERANIA DO POVO EDITORA, S.A. 1643119
Av. Dr. Eugénio Ribeiro, 89, 3°, Apartado 145, 3754-909 ÁGUEDA **Tel:** 234 622 626
Fax: 234 601 836
Titles:
SOBERANIA DO POVO

SOCIEDADE INSTRUTIVA REGIONAL EBORENSE, S.A. 1721475
R. da Misericórdia, 9-13, Apartado 28, 7002-501 ÉVORA **Tel:** 266 750 550 **Fax:** 266 750 559
Titles:
A DEFESA

SOCIEDADE TERCEIRENSE DE PUBLICIDADE, LDA. 1721740
Av. Infante D. Henrique, I, 9700-098 ANGRA DO HEROÍSMO **Tel:** 295 401 050 **Fax:** 295 214 246
Titles:
DIÁRIO INSULAR

SOCIEDADE VICRA DESPORTIVA, S.A. 1721416
Travessa da Queimada, 23 - R/C, 1° e 2°, 1249-113 LISBOA **Tel:** 213 463 981 **Fax:** 213 464 503
Titles:
ANIVERSÁRIO
AUTO FOCO
A BOLA
CADERNOS DE FUTEBOL
MODALIDADES

SOCIJOR - SOC.JORNALÍSTICA, LDA. 1643166
Av. Manuel Alpedrinha, 16 - D, 2720-354 AMADORA **Tel:** 214 998 600 **Fax:** 214 998 609
Titles:
URBANISMO & CONSTRUÇÃO

SOGAE EDITORA, LDA. 1643159
R. da Cova da Moura, 2 - 2° Esq., 1350-177 LISBOA **Tel:** 213 929 640 **Fax:** 213 929 650
Titles:
TURISVER

SOJOPOR - SOCIEDADE JORNALÍSTICA PORTUGUESA, LDA. 1721711
Av. Elias Garcia, 57 7°, 1049-017 LISBOA
Tel: 217 957 668 **Fax:** 217 957 665
Titles:
O EMIGRANTE - MUNDO PORTUGUÊS

SOJORMEDIA BEIRAS, S.A. 1750271
R. Abel Dias Urbano, 4, 2°, 3000-001 COIMBRA
Tel: 239 980 280 **Fax:** 239 980 281
Titles:
DIÁRIO AS BEIRAS

SOJORMEDIA - COMUNICAÇÃO SOCIAL, S.A. 1721936
R. D. Carlos I, 2 - Apartado 288, 2415-405 LEIRIA **Tel:** 244 819 950 **Fax:** 244 822 047
Titles:
O AVEIRO
JORNAL DA BAIRRADA

SOJORNAL - SOCIEDADE JORNALÍSTICA E EDITORIAL, S.A. 1642663
Edifício S. Francisco de Sales, R. Calvet de Magalhães, 242, 2770-022 PAÇO DE ARCOS
Tel: 214 544 000 **Fax:** 214 435 310
Titles:
ATUAL
ECONOMIA
EMPREGO
ESPAÇOS & CASAS
EXAME
EXPRESSO
FÉRIAS E VIAGENS
INOVAÇÃO & TECNOLOGIA
MAMÃS & BEBÉS
NAUTICAMPO
REVISTA ÚNICA
SAÚDE PÚBLICA

SOL É ESSENCIAL, S.A. 1724271
R. de S. Nicolau, 120, 1100-550 LISBOA
Tel: 213 246 500 **Fax:** 213 246 540
Titles:
FOREIGN POLICY

ST & SF - SOCIEDADE DE PUBLICAÇÕES, LDA. 1721389
R. Vieira da Silva, 45, 1350-342 LISBOA
Tel: 213 236 700 **Fax:** 213 236 701
Titles:
1000 MAIORES EMPRESAS (DE)
BANCA ON-LINE
CONFERÊNCIAS
DIÁRIO ECONÓMICO
FORA DE SÉRIE
INOVAÇÃO BES
PME LÍDER
SISTEMAS DE INFORMAÇÃO GEOGRÁFICA

TALKMEDIA - EDIÇÃO DE PUBLICAÇÕES, LDA. 1722012
Alameda do Grupo Desportivo Alcochetense, 133 - 137, 2890-110 ALCOCHETE
Tel: 212 348 450 **Fax:** 214 043 506
Titles:
LOGÍSTICA MODERNA

Portugal

TARGETOCEAN, LDA. 1792768
Edifício S. Francisco de Sales, R. Calvet de Magalhães, 242, 2770-022 PAÇO DE ARCOS
Tel: 214 544 000 **Fax:** 214 435 310

Titles:
SURF PORTUGAL

TELE SATÉLITE - PUBLICAÇÕES PORTUGAL, S.A. 1724209
R. Bernardo Lima, 35 - 4° A/B, 1150-075 LISBOA
Tel: 213 570 418 **Fax:** 213 142 767

Titles:
AUTO
TELE SATÉLITE

TEMA CENTRAL, LDA. 1792752
R. Latino Coelho, 87, Sala 33, 1050-133 LISBOA

Titles:
PESSOAL - GREAT PLACE TO WORK (JN + S)

TEMPLÁRIO - SOCIEDADE EDITORA DE PUBLICAÇÕES, LDA. 1722245
R. José Raimundo Ribeiro, 28, Apartado 152, 2304-909 TOMAR **Tel:** 249 322 733
Fax: 249 322 734

Titles:
O TEMPLÁRIO

TERRA DE LETRAS, COMUNICAÇÃO UNIPESSOAL, LDA. 1762033
Av. Tomás Ribeiro, 129, Edifício Quinta do Jamor, Sala 11, 2790-466 QUEIJAS
Tel: 211 918 875 **Fax:** 211 919 874

Titles:
TURBO

TIPOGRAFIA MEDINA, S.A. 1642755
Av. Heliodoro Salgado, 6, 2710-572 SINTRA
Tel: 219 106 831 **Fax:** 219 106 837

Titles:
JORNAL DE SINTRA

TRANSJORNAL EDIÇÃO DE PUBLICAÇÕES, S.A. 1740170
R. Tenente Valadim, 181, 4100-479 PORTO
Tel: 226 062 806

Titles:
METRO CASA
METRO LISBOA
METRO PORTUGAL

TREVIM - COOPERATIVA EDITORA E DE PROMOÇÃO CULTURAL, S.C.A.R.L. 1721452
Praça Cândido dos Reis, 15, 3200-901 LOUSÃ
Tel: 239 992 266 **Fax:** 239 991 117

Titles:
TREVIM

TURIPRESS PUBLICAÇÕES, LDA. 1642630
R. da Atalaia, 67 - 3° Esq., 1200-037 LISBOA
Tel: 213 430 236 **Fax:** 213 476 770

Titles:
ECO REGIONAL

UNIÃO GRÁFICA ANGRENSE UNIPESSOAL, LDA. 1721406
R. da Rosa, 19, 9700-171 ANGRA HEROÍSMO
Tel: 295 214 275 **Fax:** 295 214 030

Titles:
A UNIÃO

VAGA LITORAL - PUBLICAÇÕES E EDIÇÕES, LDA. 1721441
R. Prof. Mota Pinto, Loja 4, Bairro do Pombal, 2780-275 OEIRAS **Tel:** 214 430 095
Fax: 214 422 531

Titles:
O CORREIO DA LINHA

VENTURE MEDIA, LDA. 1745074
R. Vasco da Gama, Loja 60 E, 2775-297 PAREDE **Tel:** 214 589 100 **Fax:** 214 589 109

Titles:
ELITE NEGÓCIOS & LIFESTYLE

VÉRTICE ESCOLHIDO - PUBLICAÇÕES PERIÓDICAS, LDA. 1792753
R. Augusto Lessa, 251, 12, 4200-100 PORTO
Tel: 225 091 181

Titles:
PESSOAS & NEGÓCIOS

VERTIMAG - A VERTIGEM DAS IMAGENS DOS SONS E DAS PALAVRAS, UNIPESSOAL LDA. 1761073
R. Vitorino Nemésio, 12, 3° Esq., 1750-307 LISBOA

Titles:
EPICUR

VFBM COMUNICAÇÃO, LDA. 1642800
Ed. Lisboa Oriente Office, Av. Infante D. Henrique, 333 - H, 4°, Sala 45, 1800-282 LISBOA
Tel: 218 532 916 **Fax:** 218 532 918

Titles:
MÉDICO DE FAMÍLIA

VIDA ECONÓMICA EDITORIAL, S.A. 1743579
R. Gonçalo Cristóvão, 111 - 6°, 4049-037 PORTO **Tel:** 223 399 404 **Fax:** 222 058 098

Titles:
BOLSA DE TURISMO DE LISBOA
INDÚSTRIA FARMACÊUTICA
INOVAÇÃO
SAÚDE E BEM ESTAR
VIDA ECONÓMICA

VIPRENSA - SOCIEDADE EDITORA DO ALGARVE, LDA. 1721410
R. Jornal do Algarve, 46, Apartado 23, 8900-000 VILA REAL DE SANTO ANTÓNIO **Tel:** 281 511 955
Fax: 281 511 958

Titles:
JORNAL DO ALGARVE

VIRTUAL POVOENSE - EDITORA, LDA. 1721620
Praça do Almada, 10 1°, 4490-438 PÓVOA DE VARZIM **Tel:** 252 615 198 **Fax:** 252 627 636

Titles:
CONSTRUÇÃO E IMOBILIÁRIA
PÓVOA SEMANÁRIO

VITINVEST - PUBLICAÇÕES, LDA. 1721939
Largo Rainha Santa Isabel, 1 - 1° Esq., 2410-165 LEIRIA **Tel:** 244 811 205 **Fax:** 244 838 549

Titles:
INVEST

VOZ DA FIGUEIRA - EDIÇÃO DE PUBLICAÇÕES PERIÓDICAS, LDA. 1721703
R. do Paço, 8, Apartado 2224, 3081-903 FIGUEIRA DA FOZ **Tel:** 233 422 272

Titles:
A VOZ DA FIGUEIRA

VOZ DA PÓVOA - COMUNICAÇÃO SOCIAL, S.A. 1722289
Av. Vasco da Gama - Galerias Recife, N° 523 - Loja 13, 4490-410 PÓVOA DE VARZIM
Tel: 252 614 038 **Fax:** 252 614 038

Titles:
A VOZ DA PÓVOA

WORKMEDIA - COMUNICAÇÃO, S.A. 1751920
R. General Firmino Miguel, 3 - Torre 2, 3°, 1600-100 LISBOA **Tel:** 210 410 300 **Fax:** 210 410 306

Titles:
MEIOS & PUBLICIDADE
PUBLITURIS

ZOOTMEDIA, LDA. 1722307
R. Rodrigues Faria, 103, Edifício 1, Espaço 1.15, 1300-501 LISBOA **Tel:** 213 142 800
Fax: 213 142 800

Titles:
ZOOT MAGAZINE

Romania

3 D MEDIA COMMUNICATIONS SRL 1768013
Str. N.D. Cocea, Nr.12, BRASOV 500010
Tel: 268 41 51 58

Titles:
CHIP COMPUTER & COMMUNICATIONS

BUSINESS MEDIA GROUP 697738
Str. Alexandru Moruzzi Voievod nr. 9C, Sector 4, BUCURESTI **Tel:** 21 33 53 473 **Fax:** 21 33 53 474

Titles:
BIZ

CICERO SA 1600168
Calea Victoriei 39 A, O.P. 49, C.P. 45, Sector 1, 70101 BUCURESTI **Tel:** 21 31 38 296
Fax: 21 31 20 128

Titles:
AZI

CMG ROMANIA 1759298
Bd. Iuliu Maniu nr.7, Corp A, et.2, Sector 6, BUCURESTI **Tel:** 21 315 90 31 **Fax:** 21 315 90 29
Email: office@cmgromania.ro
Web site: http://www2.cmgromania.ro

Titles:
MAGAZINUL PROGRESIV

CRUCIŞĂTORUL S.A 1747204
Piata Presei Libere nr.1, Corp A3-A4, Sector 1, BUCURESTI

Titles:
GANDUL

PUBLIMEDIA INTERNATIONAL SA 697718
Strada Baratiei, nr. 31, Sector 3, BUCURESTI
Tel: 31 82 56 282 **Fax:** 31 82 56 285

Titles:
PROTV MAGAZIN
ZIARUL FINANCIAR

RINGIER ROMANIA 697658
Bulevardul Dimitrie Pompeiu nr. 6, Sector 2, 020337 BUCURESTI **Tel:** 21 20 30 800
Fax: 21 20 30 801
Web site: http://www.ringier.ro

Titles:
CAPITAL
DIVA
LIBERTATEA
TV MANIA

ROMAS COMERCIAL SRL 1621802
Splaiul Unirii 74, Sector 4, BUCURESTI
Tel: 21 33 11 133 **Fax:** 21 33 01 055

Titles:
XTREMPC MAGAZINE

S. C. POLIGRAF S. R. L. 672088
Casa Presei Libere corp A3, etaj 4, Sector 1, BUCURESTI **Tel:** 21 31 73 193 **Fax:** 21 31 73 203

Titles:
COTIDIANUL

SANOMA HEARST ROMANIA SRL 1769910
Str. Buzeşti nr. 85, et. 4-8, Sector 1, 011013 BUCURESTI **Tel:** 31 22 58 700 **Fax:** 31 22 58 715
Email: office@sanomahearst.ro
Web site: http://www.sanomahearst.ro

Titles:
BUCATARIA DE AZI
FEMEIA DE AZI

SC ADEVARUL SA 697634
Şos. Fabrica de Glucoză, nr 21, Sector 2, BUCURESTI **Tel:** 21 22 42 832 **Fax:** 21 22 43 612

Titles:
ADEVARUL

SC. CURIERUL NATIONAL SA 1500077
Str. Ministerului 2-4, Sector 1, 70107 BUCURESTI **Tel:** 21 31 53 802 **Fax:** 21 31 21 300
Email: curierul@pitesti.ro

Titles:
CURIERUL NATIONAL

SC RING PRESS SRL 697717
Popa Tatu Str. Nr. 71, Sector 1, 010804 BUCURESTI **Tel:** 21 31 54 356 **Fax:** 21 31 24 556

Titles:
BURSA

SC ZIUA SRL 625840
Strada C-tin Mille numarul 17, Sector 1, BUCURESTI **Tel:** 21 31 13 155 **Fax:** 21 31 59 160

Titles:
ZIUA

SOCIETATEA "R" SA 621533
Str. Nerva Traian nr. 3, bl. M 101, etaj 4, Sector 3, CP 031041, BUCURESTI **Tel:** 21 20 28 100
Fax: 21 22 32 071

Titles:
ROMANIA LIBERA

Russian Federation

A FOND PUBLISHER 1622435
Bolshoy Karetny per. 17, str.2, 127051 MOSKVA
Tel: 495 699 41 54 **Fax:** 495 251 80 47
Email: info@prorus.ru
Web site: http://www.prorus.ru

Titles:
PROYEKT INTERNATIONAL
PROYEKT KLASSIKA
PROYEKT ROSSIYA

A.B.E. MEDIA PUBLISHING HOUSE 1746210
P.O. box 127, 119048 MOSKVA
Tel: 495 626 53 56 **Fax:** 495 933 02 97
Email: e_semenov@ato.ru
Web site: http://www.ato.ru

Titles:
AVIATRANSPORTNOYE OBOZRENIYE
RUSSIA/CIS OBSERVER

ADRESA PETERBURGA 1717244
P.O. Box 12, 192007 SANKT PETERBURG
Tel: 12 962 42 41 **Fax:** 12 962 42 47
Email: chief@adresaspb.ru
Web site: http://www.adresaspb.ru

Titles:
ADRESA PETERBURGA

AEROMEDIA 1751996
ul. Baltiyskaya 15, office 527, MOSKVA
Tel: 495 798 81 19 **Fax:** 495 644 17 33
Email: info@take-off.ru
Web site: http://www.take-off.ru

Titles:
VZLIOT

AGENTSTVO EXPRESS SERVICE 1717236
P.O. Box 137, 191002 SANKT PETERBURG
Tel: 12 325 35 95 **Fax:** 12 575 63 86
Email: media@es.ru
Web site: http://www.es.ru

Titles:
FREE TIME
NA NEVSKOM
POD KLYLUCH

AKTION MEDIA 1752183
ul. Novodmitrovskaya 5a, str. 8, 127015 MOSKVA **Tel:** 495 785 01 13 **Fax:** 495 788 53 17

Titles:
FINANS
GLAVBUKH
KADROVOYE DELO
UCHET. NALOGI. PRAVO
YURIST KOMPANII

ALMAZ MEDIA PUBLISHING HOUSE 1747475
Leningradsky prospekt 80, 125190 MOSKVA
Tel: 495 788 91 90 **Fax:** 495 788 91 90
Email: info@almaz-media.ru
Web site: http://www.almaz-media.ru

Titles:
VOYENNO-PROMYSHLENNY KURIER
VOZDUSHNO-KOSMICHESKAYA OBORONA

AMERICAN CHAMBER OF COMMERCE IN RUSSIA 694213
ul. Dolgorukovskaya 7, 14 Etage, Sadovaya Plaza, 127006 MOSKVA **Tel:** 495 961 21 41
Fax: 495 961 21 42

Titles:
AMCHAM NEWS

ARGUMENTY I FAKTY PUBLISHING HOUSE 697940
2 Tverskaya-Yamskaya ul. 10, 125047 MOSKVA
Tel: 495 221 74 20
Email: letters@aif.ru
Web site: http://gazeta.aif.ru/info/structure

Titles:
AIF MOSKVA
ARGUMENTY I FAKTY

ARNOLD PRIZE GROUP 1741352
ul. Lizy Chaykinoy 1, 6 floor, 125190 MOSKVA
Tel: 495 93 30 290
Web site: www.arnold-prize.ru

Titles:
HOMES & GARDENS
VOTRE BEAUTÉ

ASSET 1717263
ul. Chernyshevskogo 153, office 307, 410028 SARATOV

Titles:
AGRONOVOSTI

AUDIT I NALOGOOBLOZHENIYE 1717062
ul. Prechistenka 10, str. 1, office 49, 119034 MOSKVA
Email: ain@complat.ru
Web site: http://www.auditpress.ru

Titles:
AUDIT I NALOGOOBLOZHENIYE

AXEL SPRINGER RUSSIA 1745795
16 Dokukina str., building 1, floor 6, 129226 MOSKVA **Tel:** 495 980 52 52
Email: info@axelspringer.ru
Web site: http://www.axelspringer.ru

Titles:
FORBES

B2B MEDIA 1746211
M. Tolmachevski pereulok 1, 3 floor, 119017 MOSKVA **Tel:** 495 933 55 19 **Fax:** 495 933 54 46
Email: info@b2bmedia.ru
Web site: http://www.b2bmedia.ru

Titles:
FINANSOVY DIREKTOR
HR-MANAGEMENT
KOMMERCHESKIY DIREKTOR
MSFO
RISK MANAGEMENT

BANZAI 1745186
ul. Uralskaya 3, office 8, YEKATERINBURG
Tel: 343 216 37 37 **Fax:** 343 216 37 35
Web site: http://www.banzay.ru

Titles:
BANZAI
NATIONAL BUSINESS
PRO DIGITAL
VTORAYA POLOVINA

BELY KEDR 1717057
ul. Staraya Basmannaya 38/2, korp. 1, office 210, 105066 MOSKVA **Tel:** 495 933 85 64
Email: info@nicotiana.ru
Web site: http://www.belkedr.ru

Titles:
NICOTIANA ARISTOCRATICA

BIONIKA GROUP 1745366
ul. Profsoyuznaya 57, MOSKVA
Fax: 495 786 25 57
Email: info@bionika.ru
Web site: http://bionika.ru

Titles:
MEDITSINSKI VESTNIK

BIZNES ZHURNAL 1745181
2 Roschinsky proyezd 8, 115419 MOSKVA
Tel: 495 633 11 07 **Fax:** 495 956 23 85
Email: info@b-mag.ru
Web site: http://www.business-magazine.ru

Titles:
BIZNES ZHURNAL

BONNIER BUSINESS PRESS 1717242
ul. Akademika Pavlova, River House, 5 floor, 197022 SANKT PETERBURG **Tel:** 12 326 97 30
Fax: 12 326 97 31
Email: Nira.Vinnik@dp.ru
Web site: http://www.bonnierrussia.ru

Titles:
DELOVOY PETERBURG

BRIDGE MAGAZINES 1749018
ul. Mira 25, 350000 KRASNODAR
Tel: 61 262 71 45 **Fax:** 61 262 71 46
Web site: http://www.bmpress.ru

Titles:
MUZHSKOY KLUB
OBUSTROYSTVO

BRITISH STYLE 1745182
bld. 5/1, proezd Solomennoi, Storozhki, 125206 MOSKVA **Tel:** 495 772 20 44 **Fax:** 495 979 69 21
Email: info@british-style.ru
Web site: http://www.british-style.ru

Titles:
BRITISH STYLE

BUSINESS COMMUNICATIONS AGENCY 1621732
ul. 1-ya Tverskaya-Yamskaya, d. 2, 127006 MOSKVA **Tel:** 495 251 08 62 **Fax:** 495 251 08 62
Email: adk27@adkbca.ru
Web site: http://www.ifvremya.ru

Titles:
INTERFAX VREMYA

BUSINESS WORLD 1757966
Khoroshevskoye shosse 32a, 123007 MOSKVA
Tel: 495 981 10 50 **Fax:** 495 240 64 49
Email: reklama@d-mir.ru
Web site: http://d-mir.ru

Titles:
AVTOMOBILI I TSENY
KRASOTA I ZDOROVIYE

BUSINESSTIME 1751063
Shenkursky proyezd 3b, office 207, 127349 MOSKVA **Tel:** 495 406 48 65 **Fax:** 495 406 48 65
Email: info@worldenergy.ru

Titles:
MIROVAYA ENERGETIKA

CHASTNAYA SOBSTEVENNOST 1716869
ul. Oktyabrskoy Revolutsii 73, 450057 UFA

Titles:
EVRAZIA UFA

CIA CENTER 1759556
ul. B. Semenovskaya 49, office 331, 107023 MOSKVA **Tel:** 499 369 79 20
Email: publisher@cia-center.ru
Web site: http://www.cia-center.ru

Titles:
SOVREMENNY SKLAD

C-MEDIA 1758224
ul. Malaya Pochtovaya 12, korp. 1, office 307-310, 105082 MOSKVA **Tel:** 495 229 62 00
Fax: 495 229 62 01
Web site: http://cmedia-online.ru

Titles:
BILLBOARD (RUSSIAN EDITION)
IVAN
NEON

COLLINS&BARTONS PUBLISHING HOUSE 1750409
ul. Mezdunarodnaya 28, korpus 1, office 123, 125009 MOSKVA **Tel:** 495 671 37 41
Fax: 812 325 75 18

Titles:
MOBILNYE NOVOSTI

COMPUTERPRESS 698040
Gorokhovskiy Per. 7, 105064 MOSKVA
Tel: 495 234 65 82 **Fax:** 495 234 65 82
Email: ad@compress.ru
Web site: http://www.cpress.ru

Titles:
COMPUART
COMPUTERPRESS
DIRECTORINFO
MIR ETIKETKI
SAPR AND GRAFIKA

CONDE NAST 1731854
Bolshaya Dmitrovka 11, str. 7, 125009 MOSKVA
Tel: 495 74 55 565 **Fax:** 495 77 70 024

Titles:
AD/ARCHITECTURAL DIGEST
GLAMOUR
GQ
VOGUE

CONNECT PUBLISHING HOUSE 1750410
ul. Selskokhozhyastvennaya 19, korpus 2, 129226 MOSKVA **Tel:** 495 925 11 18
Fax: 495 925 11 18
Email: post@connect.ru
Web site: http://www.connect.ru

Titles:
CONNECT! MIR SVYAZI
FOTODELO

EDIPRESSE KONLIGA 1758094
ul. Bakuninskaya 71, str. 10, 105082 MOSKVA

Titles:
RUSSKOYE ISKUSSTVO
STILNYIE PRICHESKY

FINE STREET PRINT & PUBLISH 697878
Leningradskoye shosse 18, korp. 1, office 342, 125171 MOSKVA **Tel:** 12 438 15 38

Titles:
4ROOM:
IT EXPERT
IT MANAGER
IT NEWS
KOMPONENTY I TEKHNOLOGII
SILOVAYA ELEKTRONIKA
ZHILAYA SREDA

FINPRESS PUBLISHING 1756523
ul. Bolshaya Spasskaya 10/1, 129010 MOSKVA
Tel: 495 148 95 62
Email: info@dis.ru
Web site: http://www.finpress.ru

Titles:
MARKETING V ROSSII I ZA RUBEZHOM

FOLIUM PUBLISHING COMPANY 1759511
ul. Dmitorvskoye shosse 58, P. O. Box 42, 127238 MOSKVA
Email: info@folium.ru
Web site: http://folium.ru

Titles:
RUSSIAN JOURNAL OF HERPETOLOGY

FORUM ART GOROD 1717237
P.O. Box 531, 190000 SANKT PETERBURG
Tel: 12 320 29 98 **Fax:** 12 702 77 35
Email: office@artcitiez.com

Titles:
ART GOROD

FORWARD MEDIA GROUP 1762985
Debrenevskaya naberezhnaya 7, str.9, 115114 MOSKVA

Titles:
INTERIER + DIZAIN
MEDVED

GAMELAND 1746304
ul. Timura Frunze 11, str. 44-45, 4 floor, 119992 MOSKVA **Tel:** 495 935 70 34 **Fax:** 495 780 88 24
Email: Dmitri@GameLand.ru
Web site: http://www.glc.ru

Titles:
DVDXPERT
FOOTBALL
HOOLIGAN
LUTSHIYE TSIFROVYE KAMERY
MAXI TUNING
MC (MOBILE COMPUTERS)
MOUNTAIN BIKE
ONBOARD
SKIPASS
SMOKE
SVOY BIZNES
SYNC
T3
TOTAL FOOTBALL

GAZETA 1716861
pl. Lenina 4, office 505, 163061 ARCHANGELSK

Titles:
NASH SEVERNIY KRAI

GRISHINEL 1717265
PO box 217, 410005 SARATOV

Titles:
PROMYSHLENNOST' POVOLZHYA

GROTECK 1760996
P. O. Box 82, 123007 MOSKVA **Tel:** 495 609 32 31
Web site: http://www.tssonline.ru

Titles:
BROADCASTING

GRUNER + JAHR RUSSIA 1770833
Shmitovsky proyezd 3, str. 3, 123100 MOSKVA
Email: contact@gjrussia.com
Web site: http://www.guj.ru

Titles:
GEO

GRUPPA EKSPERT 1745165
ul. Pravdy 24, 6 floor, 125866 MOSKVA
Tel: 495 510 56 43 **Fax:** 495 510 56 39
Web site: http://www.expert.ru

Titles:
EXPERT
EXPERT SEVERO-ZAPAD
EXPERT VOLGA

GRUPPA KOMPANII VOKRUG SVETA 1747721
ul. Meshcheryakova 5, korpus 1, 125362 MOSKVA
Email: office@vokrugsveta.ru

Titles:
VOKRUG SVETA

GSC PUBLISHING HOUSE READER'S DIGEST 1200997
PO box 8, 117218 MOSKVA **Tel:** 495 258 55 58
Fax: 495 258 55 59

Titles:
READER'S DIGEST (RUSSIA)

HACHETTE FILIPACCHI SHKULEV 691271
ul. Shabolovka 31b, MOSKVA **Tel:** 495 204 17 77
Fax: 495 795 08 15
Email: hfs@hfm.ru
Web site: http://www.hfs.ru

Titles:
ELLE
ELLE DECORATION
MARIE CLAIRE

HR MEDIA 1750702
Elektrichesky per. 3/10, office 314, 123557 MOSKVA **Tel:** 495 255 95 79
Email: hello@hrmedia.ru
Web site: http://www.hrmedia.ru

Titles:
SHTAT

IMAGE MEDIA 1747321
ul. Usacheva 11, office 529, 119992 MOSKVA
Email: mail@marketelectro.ru

Titles:
PROMYSHLENNY MARKETING
REALTOR

IMPRESSMEDIA 1750704
4 Roschinsky proyezd 20, str. 5, 115191 MOSKVA
Email: info@cre.ru
Web site: http://www.cre.ru

Titles:
COMMERCIAL REAL ESTATE
FLOORING PROFESSIONAL MAGAZINE
KOMMERCHESKAYA NEDVIZHIMOST ROSSII
OFFISNIY INTERIER
TVOYA IPOTEKA
UPRAVLENIYE NEDVIZHIMOSTYU

INDEPENDENT MEDIA SANOMA MAGAZINES 1742740
ul.Polkovaya 3, stroyeniye 1, 127018 MOSKVA
Tel: 495 23 23 200
Email: j.tokaier@imedia.ru
Web site: http://www.imedia.ru

Titles:
COSMOPOLITAN
DOMASHNII OCHAG
GRAZIA
HARPER'S BAZAAR
HERMITAGE MAGAZINE
MEN'S HEALTH
THE MOSCOW TIMES
NATIONAL GEOGRAPHIC RUSSIA
NATIONAL GEOGRAPHIC TRAVELER
ROBB REPORT ROSSIYA
SMARTMONEY
VEDOMOSTI

INDUSTRIYA 1748370
ul. Profsouyznaya 57, 117420 MOSKVA
Tel: 495 933 66 93 **Fax:** 495 933 66 94
Email: info@indpg.ru
Web site: http://www.indpg.ru

Titles:
NEFT' I KAPITAL
NEFTESERVIS
NEFTYANAYA TORGOVLYA
TRANSPORT

IRTS GAZPROM LTD 1751062
ul. Obrucheva 27, korp. 2, 117630 MOSKVA

Titles:
SCIENCE & TECHNOLOGY IN GAS INDUSTRY

IZDATELSKIY DOM BURDA 697916
ul. Polkovaya 3, str. 4, 127018 MOSKVA
Tel: 495 787 33 92 **Fax:** 495 797 45 99
Email: press@burda.ru
Web site: http://burda.ru

Titles:
AVTOMIR
BURDA
CHIP
LISA
LISA. MOY UYUTNY DOM
LISA. PRIYATNOGO APPETITA!
MINI
MOY PREKRASNY SAD
OTDOKHNI!
PLAYBOY

IZDATELSKIY DOM EKONOMICHESKAYA GAZETA 1200994
ul. Chernyakhovskogo 16, 125319 MOSKVA
Tel: 495 250 57 93 **Fax:** 495 257 34 13
Web site: http://www.ideg.ru

Titles:
EKONOMIKA I ZHIZN
EKONOMIKO - PRAVOVOY BULLETEN
EZH-JURIST
VOZDUSHNY TRANSPORT

IZDATELSKIY DOM KOMMERSANT 698033
ul. Vrubelya dom 4, str. 1, 125080 MOSKVA
Tel: 495 943 97 00 **Fax:** 495 943 97 05

Titles:
AVTOPILOT
DENGI
KOMMERSANT
VLAST

IZDATELSKIY DOM RODIONOVA 697813
ul. Boshaya Andronevskaya 17, 109544 MOSKVA **Tel:** 495 788 53 70 **Fax:** 495 745 84 02
Email: aklimenko@idr.ru
Web site: http://www.idr.ru

Titles:
BUSINESSWEEK ROSSIYA
FHM
KARIERA
KOMPANIYA
XXL

IZDATELSKY DOM GREBENNIKOVA 1744997
2 Hutorskaya 38a, str.15, 127287 MOSKVA
Tel: 495 787 51 73 **Fax:** 495 787 51 74
Email: mail@grebennikov.ru
Web site: http://www.grebennikov.ru

Titles:
BRAND MANAGEMENT

IZDATELSKY DOM SOTSIUM 1745306
ul. Srednemoskovskaya 7/192, 394030 VORONEZH **Tel:** 4732 61 07 71 **Fax:** 4732 29 25 30
Email: rdw@rdw.vrn.ru
Web site: http://www.idsocium.vrn.ru

Titles:
SHEF

IZDATELSTVO 625 1621015
Malaya Nikiskaya 4, P.O. Box 143, MOSKVA, 121069 **Tel:** 495 291 77 24 **Fax:** 495 202 95 88
Email: magazine625@mtu-net.ru
Web site: http://www.625-net.ru

Titles:
625-NET

JOURNALIST 1717064
ul. Chernyakhovskogo 16, 125319 MOSKVA

Titles:
JOURNALIST

KOPEYECHKA 1717330
ul. Gorkogo 153, IZHEVSK **Tel:** 3412 43 83 48
Fax: 3412 43 85 88
Email: udmck@mail.ru
Web site: http://www.soverkon.ru

Titles:
CK

KURSIV 1762149
ul. Elektrozavodskaya 37/4, str. 7, 107140 MOSKVA **Tel:** 495 725 60 01 **Fax:** 495 725 60 01
Email: kursiv@kursiv.ru
Web site: http://www.kursiv.ru/kursivnew/index.php

Titles:
PACKAGING INTERNATIONAL/PACKET

LENINGRAD 1717239
ul. Aleksandra Nevskogo 12, 191167 SANKT PETERBURG

Titles:
BIRZHA TRUDA

LUKOIL 1717079
P.O. Box 230, 10100 MOSKVA **Tel:** 495 627 16 91
Email: nr@oilru.com
Web site: http://www.oilru.com

Titles:
NEFT' ROSSII

LUKOIL OVERSEAS SERVICE LTD. 1650462
ul. Bolshaya Ordynka 1, 115035 MOSKVA
Tel: 495 92 71 677 **Fax:** 495 92 71 653
Email: pr@lukoil.com
Web site: http://www.lukoil-overseas.com

Titles:
NEFTYANYE VEDOMOSTI

MAIK "NAUKA/ INTERPERIODICA" 600729
Profsoyuznaia 90, 117997 MOSKVA
Tel: 495 336 16 00 **Fax:** 495 336 06 66
Email: compmg@maik.ru
Web site: http://www.maik.rssi.ru

Titles:
GLASS PHYSICS AND CHEMISTRY
PRIKLADNAYA BIOKHIMIYA I MIKROBIOLOGIYA

MART MEDIA 1717066
Tverskoy bul. 22, 125009 MOSKVA
Tel: 495 629 05 35 **Fax:** 495 629 92 59

Titles:
GASTRONOMIYA. BAKALEYA
KONDITERSKIYE IZDELIYA. CHAI, KOFE, KAKAO
SPIRTNIYE NAPITKI I PIVO

MEDIA HOLDING EXPERT 1717291
ul. Pravdy 24, office 623, 125866 MOSKVA
Tel: 495 510 56 43 **Fax:** 495 510 56 39
Email: info@expert.ru
Web site: http://www.expert.ru

Titles:
D'

MEDIA HOLDING URALSKI RABOCHIY 1717276
ul. Malysheva 44, 620014 YEKATERINBURG
Email: secr@urn.ru
Web site: http://ur-ra.ru

Titles:
VECHERNY YEKATERINBURG

MEDIASIGN 1746305
ul. 4-aya Magistralnaya 11, MOSKVA
Tel: 495 510 15 25 **Fax:** 495 510 15 24
Web site: http://mediasign.ru

Titles:
PC+MOBILE

MOSCOVIA 1757607
ul. 1905 goda 7, 123022 MOSKVA
Tel: 495 707 28 83
Email: direct@oblnews.ru
Web site: http://oblnews.ru

Titles:
PODMOSKOVIYE

MOSKOVSKY KOMSOMOLETS 1619196
ul. 1905 goda 7, 123995 MOSKVA
Tel: 495 253 20 94 **Fax:** 495 259 46 39
Email: inet@mk.ru
Web site: http://www.mk.ru

Titles:
DELOVIE LYUDI
MK MOSKOVSKY KOMSOMOLETS
MK SUBBOTA + VOSKRESENYE

NEVSKAYA STORONA 1717256
ul. Karavaevskaya 30, 92177 SANKT PETERBURG

Titles:
SLAVYANKA SEGODNYA

NEXION PUBLISHING 1746213
Zvezdny bulvar 21, str.3, office 406, 129085 MOSKVA **Tel:** 495 616 25 75

Titles:
BOLSHOY BUSINESS

NOVYE IZVESTIYA 1745180
ul. Elektrozavodskaya 33, MOSKVA
Email: info@newnews.ru
Web site: http://www.newizv.ru

Titles:
NOVYE IZVESTIYA

OAO REDAKTSIA GAZETY IZVESTIA 1200995
ul. Tverskaja 18, Korpus 1, 127994 MOSKVA
Fax: 495 209 53 94

Titles:
IZVESTIA

OBYEDINENNYE MEDIA 1745791
ul. 2-aya Khutorskaya 38A, str.23, 127994 MOSKVA **Tel:** 495 660 88 75 **Fax:** 495 221 22 32
Email: reclama@businessfm.ru

Titles:
BUSINESS & FINANCIAL MARKETS
POPULARNYE FINANSY

O.O.O. "FIRMA BETA" 698754
Abaneneskiy Vyeshik 7, 127521 MOSKVA
Tel: 495 689 97 99 **Fax:** 495 689 54 12

Titles:
SAKHARNAYA SVEKLA

OOO IZDATELSTVO PISHCHEVAYA PROMYSHLENNOST 1619218
Sadovaya-Spasskaya 18, komn. 601, 607, 107996 MOSKVA **Tel:** 495 207 20 87
Fax: 495 207 28 61
Email: foodprom@ropnet.ru
Web site: http://www.foodprom.ru

Titles:
KHLEBOPECHENIYE ROSSII
KHRANENIJE I PERERABOTKA SEL'KHOZSYRYA
KONDITERSKOYE PROIZVODSTVO
MASLOZHIROVAYA PROMYSHLENNOST
PISHCHEVAYA PROMYSHLENNOST
PISHCHEVYE INGREDIENTY: SYRIO I DOBAVKI
PIVO I NAPITKI
PROIZVODSTVO SPIRTA I LIKERO-VODOCHNYH IZDELIY
VINODELIYE I VINOGRADARSTVO

OPEN SYSTEMS PUBLICATIONS 697851
Elektricheskiy Pereulok 8, Korp. 3, 123O56 MOSKVA **Tel:** 495 253 90 20 **Fax:** 495 253 92 04

Titles:
COMPUTERWORLD RUSSIA
LAN
MIR PK
OIL & GAS JOURNAL RUSSIA

ORE AND METALS PUBLISHING HOUSE 698181
PO Box 71, 119049 MOSKVA **Tel:** 495 230 45 18
Fax: 495 230 45 18
Email: rim@rudmet.ru
Web site: http://www.rudmet.ru

Titles:
GORNYI ZHURNAL
MATERIALY ELEKTRONNOI TEKHNIKI
OBOGASHCHENIE RUD

OSTANOVNOYA NEKOMMERCHESKAYA ORGANIZACIA REDAKCIA NAUKA I ZHIZN 698039
ul. Myasnitskaya 24, 101990 MOSKVA
Tel: 495 924 18 35 **Fax:** 495 200 22 59

Titles:
NAUKA I ZHIZN

PANORAMA 1758793
P. O. Box 49, 107031 MOSKVA **Tel:** 495 211 54 18
Fax: 495 625 96 11
Email: aps@panor.ru

Titles:
ELEKTROOBORUDOVANIYE: EKSPLUATATSIYA I REMONT
GLAVNY ENERGETIK
KHLEBOPEKARNOYE PROIZVODSTVO

PARK MEDIA 1757181
Leninskiye gory, str. 75G, korp. 6, office 626, 119991 MOSKVA **Tel:** 495 930 88 50
Fax: 495 930 87 07
Email: magataev@strf.ru
Web site: http://www.nanorf.ru

Titles:
ROSSISKIYE NANOTEKHNOLOGII

PETROTSENTR 1745184
ul. Chapayeva 11/4, litera A, 197046 SANKT PETERBURG **Tel:** 12 346 46 92 **Fax:** 12 230 94 07
Email: iic@ipc.spb.ru
Web site: http://www.ipc.spb.ru

Titles:
PETERBURGSKY DNEVNIK

PLASTICS MEDIA OOO 1712486
1 Entuziastov 3, str. 1, 111024 MOSCOW
Tel: 495 23 12 115 **Fax:** 46 27 64 045

Titles:
PLASTIKS: INDUSTRIYA PERERABOTKI PLASTMASS

POSTER GROUP 1747540
ul. Mozhayskaya 15, 190013 SANKT PETERBURG **Tel:** 12 317 80 05 **Fax:** 12 317 80 02
Email: dmitrieva@poster-group.ru
Web site: http://www.ibmagazine.ru

Titles:
INTERBIZNES

PRAVITELSTVO ROSSIISKOY FEDERACII 1686181
ul. Pravdy 24, 125993 MOSKVA

Titles:
ROSSIISKAYA GAZETA
RUSSIA BEYOND THE HEADLINES

PRINT EXPO 1717249
ul. Blagodatnaya 6, lit. b, office 205, 196128 SAINT PETERSBURG **Tel:** 12 336 31 30
Fax: 12 336 31 32
Email: info@printexpo.ru
Web site: http://www.printexpo.ru

Titles:
MORSKAYA BIRZHA

PROFI-PRESS 1745796
ul. Admirala Makarova 23, korpus 2, 125212 MOSKVA **Tel:** 495 601 92 08 **Fax:** 495 741 09 06
Web site: http://www.profi-press.ru
Titles:
BANKOVSKIYE TEKHNOLOGII
BLIKI
MOBILNYE TELEKOMMUNIKATSII

PUBLISHER PERIODIKA 676889
ul. Titova 3, 185610 PETROZAVODSK
Tel: 142 78 36 29 **Fax:** 142 78 36 29
Email: periodika@sampo.ru
Titles:
KARJALAN SANOMAT

PUBLISHING HOUSE FINANCE AND CREDIT 1717063
P.O. Box, ul. Mashkova 3, str. 1, 111401 MOSKVA **Tel:** 495 621 69 49 **Fax:** 495 621 91 90
Email: post@financepress.ru
Web site: http://www.fin-izdat.ru
Titles:
BUHGALTER I ZAKON
BUHGALTERSKY UCHET W BUDZHETNYKH I NEKOMMERCHESKIKH ORGANIZATSIYAKH
BUHGALTERSKY UCHET W IZDATELSTVE I POLIGRAFII
DIGEST FINANSY
EKONOMICHESKI ANALIZ: TEORIA I PRAKTIKA
FINANSY I KREDIT
MEZHDUNARODNY BUHGALTERSKY UCHIOT
NATSIONALNYE INTERESY: PRIORITETY I BEZOPASTNOST'
REGIONALNAYA EKONOMIKA: TEORIYA I PRAKTIKA
VSYE DLYA BUHGALTERA

PUBLISHING HOUSE KRESTIANIN 1717209
ul. Goroda Volos 6, 8 floor, 344000 ROSTOV-NA-DONU
Email: fomin@krestianin.ru
Web site: http://www.krestianin.ru
Titles:
DELOVOY KRESTIANIN

PUBLISHING HOUSE SOBESEDNIK 1717091
ul. Novoslobodskaya 73, str 1, 127055 MOSKVA
Tel: 495 685 56 65
Email: info@sobesednik.ru
Web site: http://www.sobesednik.ru
Titles:
SOBESEDNIK

PUBLISHING HOUSE VENETO 1744963
ul. Gilyarovskogo 10, bld. 1, 129090 MOSKVA
Tel: 495 745 68 98 **Fax:** 495 681 73 59
Web site: http://www.veneto.ru
Titles:
NATURAL
REMONT I STROITELSTVO
SHAPE
UPGRADE
UPGRADE SPECIAL

PUBLISHING HOUSE VREMYA 1745166
ul. Pyatnitskaya 25, 115326 MOSKVA
Email: barbolina@vremya.ru
Web site: http://www.vremya.ru
Titles:
VREMYA NOVOSTEY

RBK MEDIA 1745179
ul. Profsouyuznaya 78, 117393 MOSKVA
Tel: 495 363 11 11 **Fax:** 495 363 11 27
Email: daily@rbc.ru
Web site: http://www.rbkdaily.ru
Titles:
RBC MAGAZINE

RDW MEDIA 1770835
Maly Drovyanoy per. 3, str.1, 109004 MOSKVA
Tel: 495 956 76 26 **Fax:** 495 956 76 26
Web site: http://www.rdwmedia.ru
Titles:
VASH DOSUG

REDAKCIA ZHURNALA VOPROSY EKONOMIKI 1622009
Pr. Nakhimovsky 32, 117218 MOSKVA
Tel: 495 129 04 44 **Fax:** 495 124 52 28
Titles:
VOPROSY EKONOMIKI

REGION INFO 1748369
ul. Sibirsky trakt 34, korpus 4, office 403-404, KAZAN'
Email: post@g9e.ru
Titles:
GDE DEN'GI

REMEDIUM 1752196
ul. Bakuninskaya 71, str. 10, 105082 MOSKVA
Tel: 495 780 34 25 **Fax:** 495 780 34 26
Email: kosareva@remedium.ru
Web site: http://www.remedium.ru
Titles:
REMEDIUM
ROSSISKIYE APTEKI

REN MEDIA GROUP 1686594
Tverskoy bulvar 14, str. 1, 125009 MOSKVA
Tel: 495 980 97 20 **Fax:** 495 980 97 20
Titles:
THE NEW TIMES

RIA NOVOSTI 1621974
Zubovskiy Bulvar, d. 4, 119021 MOSKVA
Tel: 495 645 64 05 **Fax:** 495 637 27 46
Email: sales@rian.ru
Web site: http://www.rian.ru
Titles:
RUSSIA PROFILE

ROSAERO 1717059
Sheremetevo, P.O. Box Aviaglobus, 141426 KHIMKI **Tel:** 495 518 63 81 **Fax:** 495 578 43 20
Email: pr@aviaglobus.ru
Web site: http://www.aviaglobus.ru
Titles:
AVIAGLOBUS

ROSSIYSKAYA TORGOVLYA 1752198
ul. Myasnitskaya 47, 107084 MOSKVA
Tel: 495 607 73 28
Email: rt@ropnet.ru
Web site: http://ros-torg.net
Titles:
ROSSIISKAYA TORGOVLYA

RUSSIAN ASSOCIATION ABOK 1622180
ul. Rozhdestvenka 11, 107031 MOSKVA
Tel: 495 621 80 48 **Fax:** 495 621 80 48
Email: abok@abok.ru
Web site: http://www.abok.ru
Titles:
ABOK JOURNAL (VENTILATION, HEATING, AIR-CONDITIONING)
ENERGOSBEREZHENIYE
SANTECHNIKA

RUSSKIYE VERTOLIOTNIYE SISTEMY 1751994
Tretya Tverskaya-Yamskaya 21/23, 125047 MOSKVA **Tel:** 495 785 85 47 **Fax:** 495 778 60 85
Email: mail@helisystems.ru
Web site: http://www.helisystems.ru
Titles:
VERTOLIOTNAYA INDUSTRIYA

RUSSKY KURIER 1745014
Luzhnetskaya nab.2.4, 119270 MOSKVA
Email: ruscourier@ruscourier.ru
Web site: http://www.ruscourier.ru
Titles:
RUSSKY KURIER

SALON-PRESS PUBLISHING HOUSE 1758475
ul. Nagatinskaya 1, str. 29, 117105 MOSKVA
Tel: 495 933 43 43 **Fax:** 495 937 52 15
Titles:
IDEI VASHEGO DOMA
SALON INTERIOR

SCHIBSTED ASA 1747235
ul. Odoevskogo 27, lit. A, 4 floor, 199155 SANKT PETERBURG
Titles:
MOY RAION - MOSKVA
MOY RAION - SANKT PETERBURG

SIBIRPRESS 1717115
ul. Nemirovicha-Danchenko 104, 11 gloor, 630048 NOVOSIBIRSK **Tel:** 3832 21 18 29
Email: post@sibpress.ru
Web site: http://www.com.sibpress.ru
Titles:
KONTINENT SIBIR
STRATEGII USPEKHA

SK PRESS 675203
ul. Marksistkaya 34, Korp. 10, office 338, 109147 MOSKVA **Tel:** 495 974 22 60 **Fax:** 495 974 22 63
Email: info@skpress.ru
Web site: http://www.skpress.ru
Titles:
BYTE
COMPUTER RESELLER NEWS RUSSIA
DOMODEDOVO
INSTYLE
INTELLIGENT ENTERPRISE
PC MAGAZINE
PC WEEK

SPN PUBLISHING 622910
Novodanilovskaya Nab. 4a, 117105 MOSKVA
Tel: 495 510 22 11 **Fax:** 495 510 49 69
Email: o.sivohin@spn.ru
Web site: http://spn.ru
Titles:
AIRUNION MAGAZINE
AVTOPARK
DIGITAL MAGAZINE
INFLIGHT REVIEW
MOBILE
PYATOYE KOLESO
ROLLING STONE
WHERE MOSCOW

STARAYA KREPOST 1759317
1 Volokolamsky proyezd 10, str. 1, Science & Technology Park, 123060 MOSKVA
Tel: 495 981 94 91
Email: info@cosmopress.ru
Web site: http://cosmopress.ru
Titles:
COSMETICS IN RUSSIA
ESTETICHESKAYA MEDITSINA
KOSMETICHESKY RYNOK SEGODNYA
NOGTEVOY SERVIS
LES NOUVELLES ESTHETIQUES (RUSSIAN EDITION)

STRANA OZ 1717082
ul. Pyatnitskaya 25, office 518, 115326 MOSKVA
Tel: 495 231 18 75 **Fax:** 495 974 39 47
Email: oz@vremya.ru
Web site: http://www.strana-oz.ru
Titles:
OTECHESTVENNYE ZAPISKI

TELESPUTNIK 675731
PO Box 505, 190000 ST. PETERSBURG
Tel: 12 230 04 62 **Fax:** 12 230 93 51
Email: telesputnik@telesputnik.ru
Web site: http://www.telesputnik.ru
Titles:
TELE-SPUTNIK

TOMSKY VESTNIK 1717304
pr. Lenina 91, 634050 TOMSK
Titles:
TOMSKY VESTNIK

TOURBUSINESS LTD 692394
ul. Seleznevskaya 11 A, str. 2, ofis 611, 101485 MOSKVA **Tel:** 495 972 26 19 **Fax:** 495 972 26 58
Titles:
TOURBUSINESS

TRADE MEDIA INTERNATIONAL OOO 1757184
ul. Krasnoprudnaya 12/1, str. 1, office 15, 107140 MOSKVA **Tel:** 495 784 71 16
Fax: 495 784 71 16
Email: info@russia.trademedia.us
Web site: http://www.trademedia.us
Titles:
CONTROL ENGINEERING RUSSIA

TRUD PUBLISHING 625770
ul. Elektrozavodskaya 27, str. 4, Business Centre LeFort, MOSKVA **Tel:** 495 299 75 05
Titles:
TRUD

TURINFO LTD 1201225
Aviatsionny Pereulok 4, P.O. Boc 54, 125319 MOSKVA **Tel:** 495 234 08 30 **Fax:** 495 234 33 72
Email: tourinfo@online.comstar.ru
Web site: http://www.tourinfo.ru
Titles:
TOURINFO

VITRINA PUBLISHING HOUSE 1621654
2, Electrodnaya str., 111141 MOSKVA
Tel: 495 933 02 29 **Fax:** 495 250 75 72
Email: taz@vitrina.com.ru
Web site: http://www.vitrinapress.ru
Titles:
VINNAYA KARTA
VITRINA. MIR SUPERMARKETA

VLADIVOSTOK NOVOSTI 1717192
Narodny pr. 13, 690600 VLADIVOSTOK
Titles:
VLADIVOSTOK

VORONEZH PUBLISHING HOUSE 1745013
ul. Plekhanovskaya 53, office 510, VORONEZH
Tel: 4732 51 93 70 **Fax:** 4732 51 93 70
Email: vrn@vmail.ru
Web site: http://ru.voronezh.ru
Titles:
VORONEZH

VOYENNY PARAD 1717056
2-aya Entuziasov 5, korp. 36, 119330 MOSKVA
Tel: 495 123 45 67 **Fax:** 495 123 45 69
Email: info@milparade.ru
Web site: http://www.milparade.com
Titles:
MILITARY PARADE

VYATSKY KRAI 1716967
ul. Stepana Khalturina 2A, 610000 KIROV
Tel: 332 64 32 54
Email: kray@kray.kirov.ru
Web site: http://www.vk-smi.ru
Titles:
VYATSKY KRAI

ZA RULIOM 1717069
Narshkinskaya alleya 5, str. 2, 127167 MOSKVA
Tel: 495 978 03 89
Email: gazeta@zr.ru
Web site: http://gzr.zr.ru
Titles:
ZA RULIOM - REGION

ZAO ID KOMSOMOLSKAYA PRAVDA 1621690
Petrovsko-Razumovsky stary proyezd, 1/23, stroyeniye 1, 127287 MOSKVA
Titles:
KOMSOMOLSKAYA PRAVDA

ZAO IZDATELSTVO SEM DNEY 697942
Leningradskoye Shosse 5 A, 125080 MOSKVA
Tel: 495 753 41 45 **Fax:** 495 943 47 90
Titles:
ITOGI

ZAO KALININGRADSKAYA PRAVDA 1716959
ul. Karla Marksa 18, 236000 KALININGRAD
Titles:
KALININGRADSKAYA PRAVDA

ZAO KONCERN VECHERNAYA MOSKVA 1621688
ul. 1905 goda, d. 7, 123995 MOSKVA
Tel: 495 259 52 52 **Fax:** 495 259 81 87
Titles:
VECHERNAYA MOSKVA

Russian Federation

ZAO MAPT-MEDIA 1621684
Smolenskaya pl. 13/21, 121099 MOSKVA
Tel: 495 291 23 76 **Fax:** 495 291 23 76
Titles:
NASHA VERSIA

ZAO PUBLISHER HOUSE KHLEBOPRODUCTY 694037
1-y Shipkovsky Pereulok 20, 115093 MOSKVA
Tel: 495 959 66 49 **Fax:** 495 959 66 49
Titles:
KHLEBOPRODUCTY

ZAO REDAKCIA NEZAVISIMAYA GAZETA 1621993
ul. Myasnitskaya, d. 13, 101000 MOSKVA
Tel: 495 925 94 63 **Fax:** 495 925 55 43
Titles:
NEZAVISIMAYA GAZETA

ZHIVOTNOVODSTVO ROSSII 698082
Orlikov per., 3, build. 1, 107139 MOSKVA
Tel: 495 207 83 37 **Fax:** 495 208 76 04
Titles:
ZHIVOTNOVODSTVO ROSSII

ZOLOTOY ROG 1717190
pr. Krasnogo Znameni 10, 690950 VLADIVOSTOK **Tel:** 4232 45 04 85
Fax: 4232 45 04 85
Email: zr@zrpress.ru
Web site: http://www.zrpress.ru
Titles:
DALNEVOSTOCHNY KAPITAL

ZOND REKLAMA COMPANY GROUP 1717303
ul. Frunze 115, 634021 TOMSK
Titles:
TOMSK MAGAZINE

San Marino

TURISMO ITINERANTE SRL 697887
Strada Cardio, 10, GALAZZANO SM-47899
Tel: 71 2901272 **Fax:** 71 2907170
Titles:
ITINERARI GUSTOSI
TURIT

Serbia

DAN GRAF D O O 671999
Alekse Nenadovica 19-23 / V, BEOGRAD 11000
Tel: 11 34 41 186 **Fax:** 11 34 41 186
Titles:
DANAS

GLAS D O O 1622431
Vlajkovićeva 8, BEOGRAD 11000
Tel: 11 32 29 944 **Fax:** 11 32 49 244
Titles:
GLAS JAVNOSTI

IZDAVAČKO PREDUZEĆE NOVINE BORBA 1734633
Trg Nikole Pašića 7/II, BEOGRAD 11000
Tel: 11 339 81 37
Email: office@borba.rs
Web site: http://www.borba.rs
Titles:
BORBA

NOVOSTI D O O 699456
Trg Nikole Pašića 7, BEOGRAD 11000
Tel: 11 30 28 000 **Fax:** 11 32 98 337
Titles:
VECERNJE NOVOSTI

POLITIKA NOVINE I MAGAZINI D.O.O 1745971
Makedonska 29, 11000 BEOGRAD
Tel: 11 33 01 152 **Fax:** 11 33 73 022
Email: kabinetgen.dir@politika.rs
Web site: http://www.politika.rs
Titles:
POLITIKA

Slovakia

DIGITAL VISIONS S R O 699079
Kladnianska 60, 821 05 BRATISLAVA
Tel: 2 43 42 09 56 **Fax:** 2 43 42 09 58
Titles:
PC REVUE

ECOPRESS A.S. 671667
Seberíniho ul. č. 1, P.O. Box 35, 820 07 BRATISLAVA **Tel:** 2 48 23 81 02 **Fax:** 2 48 23 81 01
Titles:
HOSPODÁRSKE NOVINY

EXPA GROUP S.R.O. 1677396
Jelsova 3, 831 01 BRATISLAVA **Tel:** 2 54 79 20 44
Fax: 2 54 79 20 45
Email: info@modarevue.sk
Web site: http://www.modarevue.sk
Titles:
MÓDA REVUE

INFODOM S.R.O. 1718331
Lubovnianska 5, 851 07 BRATISLAVA
Tel: 2 63 53 31 41
Titles:
ALARM SECURITY

PEREX A.S. 671740
Trnavská cesta 39/A, 831 04 BRATISLAVA 3
Tel: 2 50 63 41 14 **Fax:** 2 50 63 47 59
Titles:
PRAVDA

PETIT PRESS A S 698990
Lazaretska 12, 811 08 BRATISLAVA
Tel: 2 59 23 32 71 **Fax:** 2 59 23 32 79
Web site: http://www.petitpress.sk
Titles:
KOSICKY DENNIK KORZAR
PRESOVKY DENNIK KORZAR
SME
SPISSKY DENNIK KORZAR
TATRANSKY DENNIK KORZAR
ÚJ SZÓ
ZEMPLINSKY DENNIK KORZAR

PORADCA PODNIKATELA SPOL S R O 699082
Martina Rázusa 23A, 010 01 ZILINA
Tel: 41 70 53 310 **Fax:** 41 70 53 613
Titles:
EPI - EKONOMICKÝ A PRÁVNY PORADCA PODNIKATELA

RINGIER SLOVAKIA A.S. 671776
Prievozská 14, 821 09 BRATISLAVA
Tel: 2 58 22 71 11 **Fax:** 2 58 22 74 50
Titles:
NOVÝ CAS
NOVY CAS VÍKEND
ZIVOT

THE ROCK SPOL. S.R.O. 671771
Namestie SNP 30, PO Box 260, 811 00 BRATISLAVA **Tel:** 2 59 23 33 11 **Fax:** 2 59 23 33 19
Email: spectator@spectator.sk
Web site: http://www.slovakspectator.sk
Titles:
THE SLOVAK SPECTATOR

SPOLOCNOST 7 PLUS S.R.O. 671900
Panónska cesta 9, 852 93 BRATISLAVA
Tel: 2 68 26 01 01 **Fax:** 2 68 26 01 41
Email: bilicka@7plus.sk
Titles:
PLUS 7 DNI

TREND HOLDING SPOL. S.R.O. 671725
Tomášikova 23, 821 01 BRATISLAVA 2
Tel: 2 48 23 92 39 **Fax:** 2 48 23 92 40
Email: redakcia@trend.sk
Web site: http://www.etrend.sk
Titles:
TREND

TV TIP A.S. 699056
Jasikova 2, 821 03 BRATISLAVA
Tel: 2 43 41 40 85 **Fax:** 2 43 41 40 87
Titles:
MARKÍZA

Slovenia

ADELITA D.O.O. 1687488
Dimičeva 16, 1000 LJUBLJANA **Tel:** 1 4364-700
Fax: 1 4364-701
Titles:
MOBIL

ČZP VEČER, D.D. 1686770
Svetozarevska 14, 2000 MARIBOR **Tel:** 2 2353-500 **Fax:** 2 2353-369
Titles:
PREMOŽENJE

DELO D.D. 1687436
Dunajska 5, 1509 LJUBLJANA **Tel:** 1 4737-400
Fax: 1 4737-406
Titles:
DELO
DELO IN DOM
DRUŽINSKI DELNIČAR

DNEVNIK, ČASOPISNA DRUŽBA, D.D. 1687423
Kopitarjeva 2 in 4, 1510 LJUBLJANA **Tel:** 1 3082-100 **Fax:** 1 3082-369
Titles:
DENAR & SVET NEPREMIČNIN
DIREKT
DNEVNIK
MOJ DOM
NEDELJSKI DNEVNIK

DNEVNIK D.D. 1687496
Kopitarjeva 2 in 4, 1510 LJUBLJANA **Tel:** 1 3082-100 **Fax:** 1 3082-369
Titles:
NIKA

DOMUS, ZALOŽBA IN TRGOVINA D.O.O. 1687521
Šmartinska 106, 1000 LJUBLJANA **Tel:** 1 5205-084
Titles:
SLOVENIA TIMES

DRUŽINA D.O.O. 1687449
Krekov trg 1, p.p. 95, 1000 LJUBLJANA
Tel: 1 3602-800 **Fax:** 1 3602-848
Titles:
DRUŽINA

GOSPODARSKA ZBORNICA SLOVENIJE 1687457
Dimičeva 13, 1000 LJUBLJANA **Tel:** 1 5898-414
Fax: 1 5898-100
Titles:
GLAS GOSPODARSTVA

MLADINA, ČASOPISNO PODJETJE D.D. 1687454
Dunajska 51, 1000 LJUBLJANA **Tel:** 1 2306-500
Fax: 1 2306-510
Titles:
MLADINA

NOVA OBZORJA, D.O.O. 1687439
Komenskega 11, p.p. 4315, 1000 LJUBLJANA
Tel: 1 4345-448 **Fax:** 1 4345-462
Titles:
DEMOKRACIJA

PALEGRA D.O.O. 1687420
Podjunska ulica 13, 1000 LJUBLJANA
Tel: 1 5838-400 **Fax:** 1 5838-409
Titles:
ADUT

REGIONALNI MEDIJI D.O.O. 1687445
Volkmerjev prehod, 2000 MARIBOR **Tel:** 2 2346-630 **Fax:** 2 2346-637
Titles:
DOBRO JUTRO

TEHNIŠKA ZALOŽBA SLOVENIJE D.D. 1687465
Lepi pot 6, 1000 LJUBLJANA **Tel:** 1 4790-211
Fax: 1 4790-230
Titles:
IDEJA

Spain

014 MEDIA SL 1686765
Londres 38, E-28028 MADRID **Tel:** 91 42 63 880
Fax: 91 72 57 735
Email: info@014media.com
Web site: http://www.014media.com
Titles:
CINERAMA

EL ADELANTADO DE SEGOVIA 20718
Peñalara 3, Polígono Industrial el Cerro, E-40006 SEGOVIA **Tel:** 921 43 72 61 **Fax:** 921 44 24 32
Titles:
EL ADELANTADO DE SEGOVIA

ALESPORT SA 20463
Gran Vía 8-10, 6ª planta, E-08908 HOSPITALET DE LLOBREGAT (BARCELONA) **Tel:** 93 43 15 533
Fax: 93 42 20 693
Titles:
SÓLO CAMIÓN
SÓLO MOTO ACTUAL

AN SCOOP 20397
Campo de Tajonar s/n, E-31192 TAJONAR (NAVARRA) **Tel:** 94 82 99 400 **Fax:** 94 82 99 420
Email: f.beroiz@anscoop.es
Titles:
ACCIÓN COOPERATIVA

ANPE - SINDICATO INDEPENDIENTE GRAFINAT 698694
Carretas 14, 5° A, E-28012 MADRID
Tel: 91 52 29 056 **Fax:** 91 52 21 237
Titles:
ANPE

ARLANZA EDICIONES SA 21356
Calle Javier Ferrero 9, E-28002 MADRID
Tel: 91 58 64 363 **Fax:** 91 58 64 314
Titles:
LA AVENTURA DE LA HISTORIA

ASOCIACIÓN DE LA PRENSA HISPANOAMERICANA 20751
Alonso Cano 66, 1° Local 6, E-28003 MADRID
Tel: 91 55 47 354 **Fax:** 91 55 39 395
Titles:
GACETA INTERNACIONAL

ASOC. DE USUARIOS DE SERVICIOS BANCARIOS 20223
Calle Altamirano 33, local izquierda, E-28008 MADRID **Tel:** 91 54 16 161 **Fax:** 91 54 17 260
Titles:
AUSBANC
MERCADO DE DINERO

ASOCIACIÓN EL MUNDO DIPLOMÁTICO 21334
Calle San Bernardo 107, E-28015 MADRID
Tel: 91 44 62 000 **Fax:** 91 44 74 666
Titles:
EL MUNDO DIPLOMÁTICO

AUDIOVISUAL ESPAÑOLA 2000 SA 21329
Calle Josefa Valcarcel 42, E-28027 MADRID
Tel: 91 32 47 000 **Fax:** 91 32 08 952
Titles:
LA RAZÓN

AUTO MAX EDICIONES SL 623404
Calle Duende 4, E-18214 NIVAR-GRANADA
Tel: 902 10 36 63 **Fax:** 958 42 91 02
Email: gtmax@auto-max.net
Web site: http://www.auto-max.net
Titles:
AUTO MAX

AXEL SPRINGER ESPAÑA SA 20290
Los Vascos 17, E-28040 MADRID
Tel: 91 51 40 600 **Fax:** 91 39 96 930
Web site: http://www.axelspringer.es
Titles:
COMPUTER HOY
PLAY2MANÍA

AYUDA DEL AUTOMOVILISTA SA 21205
Avenida de América 37, Edif. Torres Blancas, planta 22, E-28002 MADRID **Tel:** 91 41 31 044
Fax: 91 41 33 330
Email: publicidad@ada.es
Web site: http://www.ada.es
Titles:
REVISTA ADA

BGO EDITORES SL 20558
Calle López de Hoyos 141-4 planta Izda, E-28002 MADRID **Tel:** 91 74 40 395 **Fax:** 91-51 94 992
Titles:
TRANSPORTE PROFESIONAL

BORRMART SA 20453
Don Ramón de la Cruz 68, 6° derecha, E-28001 MADRID **Tel:** 91 40 29 607 **Fax:** 91 40 18 874
Web site: http://www.borrmart.es
Titles:
SEGURITECNÍA

BURGOS PUBLICACIONES SA 698076
Plaza de Aragón, 5 bajo, E-09001 BURGOS
Tel: 947 10 10 00 **Fax:** 947 25 78 51
Titles:
EL CORREO DE BURGOS

CÁMARA OFICIAL DE COMERCIO IND. Y NAV. DE BARCELONA 20632
Avda. Diagonal 452, E-08006 BARCELONA
Tel: 902 44 84 48 **Fax:** 93 41 69 396
Titles:
BUTLLETI DE LA CAMBRA

CANAVISA SA 20963
Calle Salamanca 5, E-38006 SANTA CRUZ DE TENERIFE **Tel:** 922 27 23 50
Titles:
DIARIO DE AVISOS

CANTÁBRICO DE PRENSA SA 20715
Calle Primero de Mayo s/n, B° San Martín - Peñacastillo, E-39011 SANTANDER (CANTABRIA) **Tel:** 942 32 00 33 **Fax:** 942 32 11 46
Titles:
ALERTA-EL DIARIO DE CANTABRIA

CESVIMAP SA 20454
Ctra. Ávila a Valladolid, Km. 1, E-05004 ÁVILA
Tel: 91 20 63 00 **Fax:** 91 20 63 19
Titles:
CESVIMAP

CIALIT SA 20491
Calle Francia 15-25, Poligon Industrial Rosanes, E-08769 CASTELLVI DE ROSANES BARCELONA **Tel:** 93 77 68 800 **Fax:** 93 77 68 801
Titles:
FOTO SISTEMA

EL COLEGIO OFICIAL DE DIPLOMADOS Y ENFERMERIA DE MADRID 21446
Avenida Menéndez Pelayo 93, E-28007 MADRID
Tel: 91 55 26 604 **Fax:** 91 50 11 281
Web site: http://www.cge.enfermundi.com
Titles:
TRIBUNA SANITARIA

EL COMERCIO SA 20683
Calle del Diario El Comercio 1, E-33207 GIJÓN (ASTURIAS) **Tel:** 98 51 79 800 **Fax:** 98 53 40 955
Titles:
EL COMERCIO

COMISARIADO EUROPEO DEL AUTOMÓVIL 21379
Calle Almagro 31, E-28010 MADRID
Tel: 91 55 76 800 **Fax:** 91 55 76 835
Titles:
AUTOCEA

COMPRARCASA SERVICIOS INMOBILIARIOS SA 694116
Retama 3, Edif. Ejesur, E-28045 MADRID
Tel: 90 24 04 151 **Fax:** 91 14 10 181
Email: comprarcasa@comprarcasa.com
Web site: http://www.comprarcasa.com
Titles:
COMPRARCASA

CONSEJO GENERAL DE COL. OF. DE FARMACÉUTICOS 21238
Calle Villanueva 11, 7ª, E-28001 MADRID
Tel: 91 43 12 560 **Fax:** 91 43 28 100
Titles:
FARMACÉUTICOS

CONSEJO GENERAL DE LA ABOGACÍA ESPAÑOLA 698832
Paseo Recoletos 13, E-28004 MADRID
Tel: 91 52 32 593 **Fax:** 91 53 27 836
Titles:
ABOGACIA ESPAÑOLA

CONSEJO SUPERIOR COLEGIOS ARQUITECTOS ESPAÑA 20258
Paseo de la Castellana 12, E-28046 MADRID
Tel: 91 43 52 200 **Fax:** 91 57 53 839
Email: revista@arquinex.es
Titles:
ARQUITECTOS

CONTENIDOS E INFORMATION DE SALUD SL 674583
Calle Hermanos Garcia Noblejas 37A, 2ª planta, E-28037 MADRID **Tel:** 91 38 34 324
Fax: 91 38 32 796
Titles:
EL GLOBAL

CORPORACIÓN DE MEDIOS DE ANDALUCÍA SA 20686
Poligono Asegra, Calle Huelva 2, E-18210 PELIGROS (GRANADA) **Tel:** 95 84 05 161
Fax: 95 84 05 072
Titles:
IDEAL

CORPORACIÓN DE MEDIOS DE EXTREMADURA SA 20661
Carretera Madrid-Lisboa 22, E-06008 BADAJOZ
Tel: 924 21 43 00 **Fax:** 924 21 43 01
Titles:
HOY - DIARIO DE EXTREMADURA

CORPORACIÓN DE MEDIOS DE MURCIA SA 20656
Camino Viejo de Monteagudo s/n, Edif. La Verdad, E-30160 MURCIA **Tel:** 968 36 91 00
Fax: 968 36 91 47
Titles:
LA VERDAD
LA VERDAD (ALBACETE)
LA VERDAD (ALICANTE)

EL CORREO DE ANDALUCIA SL 692539
Americo Vespucio 39, E-41092 ISLA DE LA CARTUCA (SEVILLA) **Tel:** 954 48 85 00
Fax: 954 46 28 81
Titles:
EL CORREO DE ANDALUCÍA
ODIEL INFORMACION

EL CROQUIS EDITORIAL SL 21046
Avda. de los Reyes Católicos 9, E-28280 EL ESCORIAL (MADRID) **Tel:** 91 89 69 410
Fax: 91 89 69 411
Titles:
EL CROQUIS

CRUZ ROJA ESPAÑOLA 20475
Rafael Villa s/n, E-28023 EL PLANTIO (MADRID)
Tel: 91 33 54 444 **Fax:** 91 33 54 455
Titles:
CRUZ ROJA

CURT EDICIONES SA 20576
Pau Claris 99-101, bajos, E-08009 BARCELONA
Tel: 93 31 80 101 **Fax:** 93 31 83 505
Email: curtediciones@curtediciones.com
Web site: http://www.curtediciones.com
Titles:
HOGARES
PISCINAS

D.E.S.O.E. COMISIÓN EJECUTIVA FEDERAL 20888
Gobelas 31, E-28023 MADRID **Tel:** 91 58 20 044
Fax: 91 58 20 045
Titles:
EL SOCIALISTA

EL DÍA DE CUENCA 21265
Polígono La Carreja, Parcela 77-78, 16004 CUENCA **Tel:** 969 21 22 91 **Fax:** 969-22 32 00
Titles:
EL DÍA DE CUENCA

EL DÍA DE TOLEDO SA 20723
Poligono La Carreja, Parcela 77-78, 16004 CUENCA **Tel:** 925 22 11 71 **Fax:** 925 21 40 65
Titles:
EL DÍA DE TOLEDO

DIARI DE GIRONA SA 21106
Paseo General Mendosa 2, E-17002 GIRONA
Tel: 97 22 02 066 **Fax:** 97 22 02 005
Titles:
DIARI DE GIRONA

DIARI DE PONENT SA 698106
Polígono industrial El Segre 118, Apdo. de Correus 11, E-25080 LLEIDA **Tel:** 973 20 46 00
Fax: 973 20 58 10
Titles:
LA MAÑANA

DIARIO AS SL 21105
Calle Albasanz 14, 4ª planta, E-28037 MADRID
Tel: 91 37 52 500 **Fax:** 91 37 52 558
Titles:
AS

DIARIO CÓRDOBA SA 20680
Ingeniero Juan de la Cierva 18, Polígono Industrial La Torrecilla, E-14013 CÓRDOBA
Tel: 957 42 03 02 **Fax:** 957 29 55 31
Titles:
CÓRDOBA

DIARIO DE BURGOS SA 21267
Avenida Castilla y Leon, 62 -64, E-09007 BURGOS **Tel:** 947 26 83 75 **Fax:** 947 26 80 03
Titles:
DIARIO DE BURGOS

DIARIO DE IBIZA SA 20735
Avda. de la Paz (esquina C/ Aubarca), E-07800 IBIZA **Tel:** 971 19 03 22 **Fax:** 971 19 03 22
Titles:
DIARIO DE IBIZA

DIARIO DE LEÓN SA 21447
Carretera León-Astorga, Km. 4,5, E-24010 TROBAJO DEL CAMINO (LEÓN) **Tel:** 987 84 03 00
Fax: 987 84 03 14
Titles:
DIARIO DE LEÓN

DIARIO DE NAVARRA SA 20708
Zapatería 49, Apdo. 5, E-31001 PAMPLONA
Tel: 948 24 12 50 **Fax:** 948 15 04 84
Titles:
DIARIO DE NAVARRA

DIARIO EL CORREO SA 20668
Pintor Losada 7, E-48004 BILBAO (VIZCAYA)
Tel: 94 48 70 100 **Fax:** 94 48 70 111
Titles:
EL CORREO

DIARIO EL PAÍS SL 20650
Calle Miguel Yuste 40, E-28037 MADRID
Tel: 91 33 78 200 **Fax:** 91 30 48 766
Titles:
EL PAÍS

DIARIO JAÉN SA 20692
Calle Torredonjimeno 1, Polígono los Olivares, Apdo. de Correos 81, E-23009 JAEN
Tel: 953 28 18 10 **Fax:** 953 28 02 77
Email: diariojaen@diariojaen.es
Titles:
JAÉN

EL DIARIO PALENTINO SAU 20707
Mayor 52, E-34001 PALENCIA **Tel:** 97 97 06 308
Fax: 97 97 06 651
Titles:
EL DIARIO PALENTINO

DIFUSIÓN Y COMUNICACIÓN 2000 SL 21316
Ctra de Cádiz km 177.8, E-29600 MARBELLA (MÁLAGA) **Tel:** 95 28 67 484 **Fax:** 95 28 67 775
Titles:
LA TRIBUNA DE LA COSTA DEL SOL

DINERO Y SALUD SL 21375
Calle Altamirano 33 bajo izquierda, E-28008 MADRID **Tel:** 91 54 72 662 **Fax:** 91 54 17 132
Titles:
DINERO Y SALUD

EDICIONES CONDÉ NAST SA 20768
P° de la Castellana, 9-11, 2ª Plata, E-28046 MADRID **Tel:** 91 70 04 170 **Fax:** 91 31 99 325
Titles:
VOGUE BELLEZA
VOGUE COLECCIONES
VOGUE ESPAÑA

EDICIONES DE AUTOMOCIÓN SL 21085
General Pardiñas 29, E-28001 MADRID
Tel: 91 43 11 725 **Fax:** 91 57 60 090
Titles:
FLOTAS DE LEASE PLAN

EDICIONES DE FRANQUICIA SL 21209
Alcala 128 1°, E-28009 MADRID **Tel:** 91 30 96 513
Fax: 91 30 92 848
Titles:
EN FRANQUICIA

EDICIONES DEL NORTE SL 20208
Avenida de los Castros 36, 1ª, E-39012 SANTANDER **Tel:** 942 29 12 00 **Fax:** 942 29 12 02
Titles:
VALDECILLA NOTICIAS

EDICIONES DEPORTIVAS CATALANES SA 694508
Valencia 49-51bajos, E-08015 BARCELONA
Tel: 93 22 79 400 **Fax:** 93 22 79 435
Titles:
SPORT

EDICIONES DOYMA SL 20589
Travesera de Gracia 17-21, E-08021 BARCELONA **Tel:** 93 20 00 711 **Fax:** 93 24 06 163
Web site: http://www.doyma.es

Titles:
JANO MEDICINA Y HUMANIDADES
NURSING

EDICIONES EL JUEVES, SA 21158
Calle Viladomat 135, 3ª planta, E-08015 BARCELONA **Tel:** 932 92 22 17 **Fax:** 932 37 58 24

Titles:
EL JUEVES

EDICIONES INTERCOMARCALES SA 20667
Sant Antoni Mª Claret 32, E-08240 MANRESA (BARCELONA) **Tel:** 93 87 72 233 **Fax:** 93 87 73 633

Titles:
REGIÓ 7

EDICIONES JARDÍN SL 20638
Pintores, 2 desp 102-7, E-28923 ALCORCÓN (MADRID) **Tel:** 91 54 01 880 **Fax:** 91 54 15 055
Email: grupocasa@edijardin.com
Web site: http://www.edijardin.com

Titles:
CASA Y JARDÍN

EDICIONES MAYO SA 20340
Aribau 185-187, 2ª planta, E-08021 BARCELONA **Tel:** 93 20 90 255 **Fax:** 93 20 20 643
Email: sietedm@edicionesmayo.es
Web site: http://www.edicionesmayo.es

Titles:
SIETE DÍAS MÉDICOS

EDICIONES MUNDO NATURA SL 20995
Islas Marquesas 28 B, E-28035 MADRID **Tel:** 91 38 65 152 **Fax:** 91 38 60 265

Titles:
VINOS DE ESPAÑA

EDICIONES PRENSA Y VIDEO SL 623772
Pza. de las Navas 11, E-08004 BARCELONA
Tel: 93 29 25 840 **Fax:** 93 29 25 841
Email: info@hair-styles.com
Web site: http://www.hair-styles.com

Titles:
PELUQUERIAS

EDICIONES PRIMERA PLANA SA 20651
Consell de Cent 425-427, E-08009 BARCELONA
Tel: 93 26 55 353 **Fax:** 93 48 46 512

Titles:
CIUDAD DE ALCOY
EQUIPO
EL PERIÓDICO DE CATALUNYA

EDICIONES REUNIDAS SA 20259
Calle O'Donnell 12, E-28009 MADRID
Tel: 91 58 63 300 **Fax:** 91 58 69 780

Titles:
RONDA IBÉRIA

EDICIONES REUNIDAS SA (GRUPO ZETA) 671828
O'Donnel, 12, E-28009 BARCELONA
Tel: 93 48 46 600

Titles:
PLAYSTATION 2
WOMAN

EDICIONES SOCIALES SL 20313
Rosellón 186, 4° 1ª, E-08036 BARCELONA
Tel: 93 32 31 491 **Fax:** 93 45 48 565
Email: edissa@telefonica.net
Web site: http://www.edicionessociales.com

Titles:
EL SOMMELIER

EDICIONES TOCADO SCP 20377
Muntaner, 401, Entlo 1ª, E-08021 BARCELONA
Tel: 93 24 14 690 **Fax:** 93 20 01 544
Email: tocado@cosmobelleza.com
Web site: www.cosmobelleza.com

Titles:
TOCADO

EDICIONES VALMAYOR SL 623187
Los Nardos 2, San Lorenzo, E-28200 DEL EL ESCORIAL (MADRID) **Tel:** 91 89 02 290
Fax: 91 89 07 762

Titles:
ARMAS Y MUNICIONES

EDICIONES ZETA SA (GRUPO ZETA) 20752
Calle O'Donnell 12, E-28009 MADRID
Tel: 91 58 63 300 **Fax:** 91 58 63 555

Titles:
INTERVIU
TIEMPO DE HOY

EDICIONS DEL GARRAF SL 698216
Carrer Jardí 37, Apartad de Correus 33, E-08800 VILANOVA I LA GELTRÚ (BARCELONA)
Tel: 93 81 49 191 **Fax:** 93 89 34 565

Titles:
DIARI DE VILANOVA

EDICIONS EL BASSEGODA SL 698228
Plaça del Mig 2, local 406, E-17800 OLOT
Tel: 972 27 47 97 **Fax:** 972 26 36 05

Titles:
LA COMARCA D'OLOT

EDICOSMA SA 20702
c/ Isla Gomera, Local 3, Fuengirola, 29640 MÁLAGA **Tel:** 902 88 61 52 **Fax:** 902 88 61 53
Email: soporte@edicosma.com

Titles:
DIARIO MÁLAGA COSTA DEL SOL

EDIMEDIA SL. 699028
Calle De los Alejos 13, Apartado de correos 4233, E-30080 MURCIA **Tel:** 968 85 80 53
Fax: 968 30 51 78

Titles:
LA ECONOMIA

EDIPREM COMUNICACIÓN, SL 698506
Perez 36, 2ª, E-08012 BARCELONA
Tel: 93 41 61 788 **Fax:** 93 23 70 659

Titles:
MUY SALUDABLE

EDIPRESSE-HYMSA 20763
Paseo San Gervasio, 16 - 20, E-08022 BARCELONA **Tel:** 93 50 87 000 **Fax:** 93 45 48 071
Email: hymsa@hymsa.com
Web site: http://www.hymsa.com

Titles:
CLARA
COCINA FÁCIL
COMER BIEN
HABITANIA
LABORES DEL HOGAR
LECTURAS
LECTURAS ESPECIAL COCINA
LECTURAS MODA
PATRONES

EDITORA BALEAR SA 20736
Calle Puerto Rico 15, Polígono de Levante, E-07007 PALMA DE MALLORCA **Tel:** 971 17 03 00
Fax: 971 17 03 01

Titles:
DIARIO DE MALLORCA

EDITORA DE MEDIO DE VALENCIA ALICANTE Y CASTELLÓN SA 698629
Eduardo Boscá 33 - 1° dcha, E-46023 VALENCIA **Tel:** 96 33 79 320 **Fax:** 96 33 71 683
Email: valencia@el-mundo.es

Titles:
EL MUNDO VALENCIA

EDITORA DE MEDIOS DE CASTILLA Y LEÓN SA 20727
Avda. de Burgos 33, E-47009 VALLADOLID
Tel: 983 42 17 00 **Fax:** 983 42 17 15

Titles:
EL MUNDO DE CASTILLA Y LEÓN
EL MUNDO DIARIO DE VALLADOLID

EDITORES MÉDICOS SA 20599
Calle Alsasua 16, E-28023 MADRID
Tel: 91 38 60 033 **Fax:** 91 37 39 907

Titles:
NOTICIAS MÉDICAS - EL SEMANARIO DE LA MEDICINA

EDITORIAL AMÉRICA IBÉRICA SA 20284
Calle Miguel Yuste 33 bis, E-28037 MADRID
Tel: 91 32 77 950 **Fax:** 91 30 44 746
Web site: http://www.eai.es

Titles:
AÑO CERO

EDITORIAL ANDALUZA DE PERIODICOS INDEPENDIENTES SA 698080
Rioja 13, 1°, E- 41001 SEVILLA **Tel:** 954 50 62 00
Fax: 954 50 62 22

Titles:
DIARIO DE SEVILLA

EDITORIAL CANTÁBRIA SA 20716
Calle la Prensa s/n, La Albericia, E-39012 SANTANDER **Tel:** 942 35 40 00 **Fax:** 942 34 18 06

Titles:
EL DIARIO MONTAÑES

EDITORIAL COMPOSTELA SA 20717
Preguntoiro 29, E-15704 SANTIAGO DE COMPOSTELA (LA CORUÑA) **Tel:** 981 54 37 00
Fax: 981 56 23 06

Titles:
EL CORREO GALLEGO

EDITORIAL DEL PUEBLO VASCO SA 20670
Camino Capucino de Vasurto 2, E-48013 BILBAO **Tel:** 94 47 39 110 **Fax:** 94 47 30 208

Titles:
EL MUNDO DEL PAÍS VASCO

EDITORIAL ECOPRENSA 1710735
Condesa de Venadito 1 3ª planta, E-28027 MADRID **Tel:** 91 32 46 700 **Fax:** 91 32 46 727

Titles:
EL ECONOMISTA

EDITORIAL EXTREMADURA SA 20672
Dr. Marañón 2, local 7, E-10002 CÁCERES
Tel: 927 62 06 00 **Fax:** 927 62 06 26

Titles:
EL PERIÓDICO DE EXTREMADURA

EDITORIAL GRUPO V SLU 20810
Calle Calportillo Primera No 11, E-28108 ALCOBENDAS (MADRID) **Tel:** 91 66 22 137
Fax: 91 66 22 654
Web site: http://www.grupov.es

Titles:
COMPUTER MUSIC
PC PRO

EDITORIAL IPARRAGUIRRE SA 20669
Carretera Bilbao-Galdakao 8, Bolueta, E-48004 BILBAO **Tel:** 94 45 99 100 **Fax:** 94 45 99 120

Titles:
DEIA

EDITORIAL LA CAPITAL SL 20681
Poligono de Pocomaco, Parcela C 12, E-15190 MESOIRO LA CORUÑA **Tel:** 981 17 30 40
Fax: 981 29 93 27

Titles:
EL IDEAL GALLEGO

EDITORIAL L'EMPORDÁ SL 698236
Ronda Barcelona 22, Apdo 21, E-17600 FIGUERES **Tel:** 972 51 07 15 **Fax:** 972 67 36 61

Titles:
SETMANARI DE L'ALT EMPORDA

EDITORIAL LEONCIO RODRÍGUEZ SA 20742
Avenida Buenos Aires 71, E-38005 SANTA CRUZ DE TENERIFE **Tel:** 92 22 38 325
Fax: 92 22 13 834

Titles:
EL DÍA

EDITORIAL MENORCA SA 20737
Cap de Cavallería 5, E-07714 MAHÓN
Tel: 97 13 51 600 **Fax:** 97 13 51 983

Titles:
MENORCA DIARIO INSULAR

EDITORIAL NUEVA ALCARRIA, SA 698213
Francisco Aripio 76, E-19003 GUADALAJARA
Tel: 949 24 74 72 **Fax:** 949 22 50 99

Titles:
NUEVA ALCARRIA

EDITORIAL PRENSA ALICANTINA SA 20658
Avenida del Doctor Rico, 17, Apdo. 214, E-03005 ALICANTE **Tel:** 965 98 91 00
Fax: 965 98 91 65

Titles:
INFORMACIÓN

EDITORIAL PRENSA ASTURIANA SA 20706
Calvo Sotelo 7, E-33007 OVIEDO
Tel: 98 52 79 700 **Fax:** 98 52 79 711

Titles:
LA NUEVA ESPAÑA

EDITORIAL PRENSA CANARIA SA 20739
Avda. Alcalde Ramírez Bethencourt, 8, E-35003 LAS PALMAS DE GRAN CANARIA
Tel: 928 47 94 00 **Fax:** 928 47 94 13

Titles:
LA PROVINCIA

EDITORIAL PRENSA IBÉRICA 698150
Av. Diagonal 463 Bis 8ª planta, E-08036 BARCELONA **Tel:** 922 47 18 00 **Fax:** 922 47 18 01

Titles:
LA OPINIÓN A CORUÑA
LA OPINIÓN DE MÁLAGA
LA OPINIÓN DE TENERIFE
LA OPINIÓN - EL CORREO DE ZAMORA

EDITORIAL PRENSA VALENCIANA SA 20726
Traginers 7, E-46014 VALENCIA **Tel:** 96 39 92 200
Fax: 96 39 92 308

Titles:
LEVANTE DE CASTELLÓN
LEVANTE (EL MERCANTIL VALENCIANO)

E.E.S.L 698225
Méndez Nuñez 43-45, E-17600 FIGUERAS
Tel: 972 50 59 58 **Fax:** 972 67 85 37

Titles:
HORA NOVA

ESTRENOS 21 SL 674841
José Abascal 55, entreplanta Izquierda, E-28003 MADRID **Tel:** 91 78 18 980 **Fax:** 91 57 79 109

Titles:
ESTRENOS DE VÍDEO

ESTRUCTURA GRUPO DE ESTUDIOS ECONÓMICOS SA 20645
Gran Vía 32, 2ª planta, E-28013 MADRID **Tel:** 91-53 86 163 **Fax:** 91-52 31 068

Titles:
CINCO DÍAS

EUMEDIA SA 20414
Calle Claudio Coello 16, 1° derecha., E-28001 MADRID **Tel:** 91 42 64 430 **Fax:** 91 57 53 297
Email: redaccion@eumedia.es
Web site: http://www.eumedia.es

Titles:
AGRONEGOCIOS
VIDA RURAL

EUROPEAN SPORT PRESS S.L. 698656
Segovia 19, ES-28005 MADRID **Tel:** 91 354 03 97 **Fax:** 91 354 03 14

Titles:
DXT

FARO DE VIGO SA 20730
Avenida de Redondela Chapela s/n, E-36320 VIGO (PONTEVEDRA) **Tel:** 986 81 46 00 **Fax:** 986 81 46 14

Titles:
FARO DE VIGO

FEDERACIÓN DE ENSEÑANZA DE CCOO 20940
Pza. Cristino Martos, 4ª planta, E-28015 MADRID **Tel:** 91 54 72 953 **Fax:** 91 54 80 320

Titles:
TRABAJADORES DE LA ENSEÑANZA

FEDERICO DOMENECH SA 676884
C. Gremis 4, E-46014 VALENCIA **Tel:** 96 35 02 211 **Fax:** 96 35 98 288

Titles:
LAS PROVINCIAS

JOAQUÍN FERRER Y CÍA SL 20675
Sargento Mena 8, E-51001 CEUTA (CÁDIZ) **Tel:** 95 65 24 148 **Fax:** 95 65 24 147

Titles:
EL FARO DE CEUTA

FIN EDICIONES SL 20553
Calle Aragon 466 E ntresuelo, E-08013 BARCELONA **Tel:** 93 20 75 052 **Fax:** 93 20 76 133

Titles:
PRIMERAS NOTICIAS DE COMUNICACIÓN Y PEDAGOGÍA
PRIMERAS NOTICIAS DE LITERATURA INFANTIL Y JUVENIL

FRANCHISE DEVELOPMENT SERVICES ESPAÑA SL 694126
Joaquin Molins 5, 5° 4ª, E-08028 BARCELONA **Tel:** 93-49 06 465 **Fax:** 93-49 01 962

Titles:
FRANQUICIAS Y NEGOCIOS

FUNDACIÓN ESPRIU 20785
Avda. Josep Tarradellas 123-127, 4° planta, E-08029 BARCELONA **Tel:** 93-49 54 490 **Fax:** 93-49 54 492

Titles:
COMPARTIR

FUNDACIÓN INTERVIDA 674563
Pujades 77-79, E-08005 BARCELONA **Tel:** 93 30 01 101 **Fax:** 93 30 96 868

Titles:
CONTIGO

FUNDACIÓN PARA LA INFORMACIÓN DE TERUEL 623810
Avenida Sagunto 27, E-44002 TERUEL **Tel:** 978 61 70 86 **Fax:** 978 60 06 82

Titles:
DIARIO DE TERUEL

FUNDACIÓN TÉCNICA INDUSTRIAL 21234
Avenida Pablo Iglesias 2, 2°, E-28003 MADRID **Tel:** 91 55 41 806 **Fax:** 91 55 37 566

Titles:
TÉCNICA INDUSTRIAL

G3 COMERCIO ESTERIOR SL 20606
General Alvare de Castro 41, Entresuelo izquierda, E-28010 MADRID **Tel:** 91 59 38 326 **Fax:** 91 59 32 027

Titles:
GACETA DENTAL

G & J ESPAÑA EDICIONES SL S EN C 20291
Calle Consuegra, 7 - 2da Planta, E-28036 MADRID **Tel:** 91 43 69 800 **Fax:** 91 57 51 280
Web site: http://www.gyj.es

Titles:
CAPITAL
COSMOPOLITAN
MARIE CLAIRE
MÍA
MUY INTERESANTE

GLOBUS COMUNICACIÓN SA 20267
Calle Covarrubias 1, 1° Planta, E-28010 MADRID **Tel:** 91 44 71 202 **Fax:** 91 44 71 043
Email: amanon@globuscom.es
Web site: http://www.globuscom.es

Titles:
VIVE

GRUPO ARTHAX 20817
Paseo Marqués de Monistrol 7, 2° izquierda., E-28011 MADRID **Tel:** 91 52 68 080 **Fax:** 91 52 61 012

Titles:
AIRELIBRE

GRUPO AXEL SPRINGER SL 20772
Los Vascos 17, E-28040 MADRID **Tel:** 91-51 40 600 **Fax:** 91 51 40 630

Titles:
NUEVO ESTILO

GRUPO CORREO "VOSENTO" SL 21443
Pza. de la Catedral 6, E-02001 ALBACETE **Tel:** 967 21 93 11 **Fax:** 967 21 07 81

Titles:
LA VOZ DE AVILÉS - EL COMERCIO

GRUPO FINANCIAL COMUNICACIÓN SL 20300
Calle Santo Angel 21, E-28043 MADRID **Tel:** 91 38 84 200 **Fax:** 91 30 00 610

Titles:
FINANCIAL FOOD

GRUPO NEGOCIOS DE EDICIONES Y PUBLICACIONES SL 20647
Calle Pantoja 14, E-28002 MADRID **Tel:** 91 43 27 612 **Fax:** 91 43 27 769

Titles:
DINERO
LA GACETA DE LOS NEGOCIOS

GRUPO PROMOTOR SALMANTINO SA 20712
Avda. de los Cipreses 81, Apdo. 52, E-37004 SALAMANCA **Tel:** 923 25 20 20 **Fax:** 923 25 61 55

Titles:
LA GACETA REGIONAL DE SALAMANCA

GRUPO YÉBENES EDITORES SL 21056
Calle Gral. Moscardó 33, 1°E, E-280020 MADRID **Tel:** 91 53 42 801 **Fax:** 91 55 32 468
Web site: http://www.grupoyebenes.com

Titles:
LABOREO

GRUPPO CODICE SL 21129
Plaza de España 18, 9 planta, E-28008 MADRID **Tel:** 91 54 81 808 **Fax:** 91 54 81 886

Titles:
NEGOCIO INMOBILIARIO

GUÍA DEL TRANSPORTE MARÍTIMO 21255
Santa Maria de la Cabeza, 11 Tpd., 2ª A., E-11007 CÁDIZ **Tel:** 956 26 45 25 **Fax:** 956 26 45 25

Titles:
GUÍA DEL TRANSPORTE MARÍTIMO

HACHETTE FILIPACCHI SA 20764
santa Engracia 23, E-28010 MADRID **Tel:** 91 72 87 000 **Fax:** 91 72 89 279
Web site: http://www.hachette.es

Titles:
AR LA REVISTA DE ANA ROSA
DIEZ MINUTOS
ELLE
EMPRENDEDORES
FOTOGRAMAS & DVD
MICASA
QUÉ ME DICES
QUO
RAGAZZA
REVISTA TELEPROGRAMA
SUPERTELE
TELENOVELA

HEARST MAGAZINES 1793015
C/Santa Engracia, 23, 28010 MADRID **Tel:** 91 7287000 **Fax:** 91 7289308

Titles:
CASA DIEZ
ELLE DECO

HEINRICH BAUER EDICIONES SLS EN C 20841
Jacometrezo 15, 3ª planta, E-28013 MADRID **Tel:** 91 54 76 800 **Fax:** 91 55 90 818
Email: tpc@bauer.es
Web site: http://www.bauer.es

Titles:
BRAVO

HERALDO DE ARAGÓN SA 20691
Paseo de la Independencia 29, Apdo. 175, E-50001 ZARAGOZA **Tel:** 976 76 50 00 **Fax:** 976 76 50 01

Titles:
HERALDO DE ARAGÓN
HERALDO DE HUESCA

HERMES COMUNICACIONS SA 20684
Carrer Santa Eugènia, 42, E-17005 GIRONA **Tel:** 972-18 64 00 **Fax:** 972-18 64 20

Titles:
EL PUNT
EL PUNT (VALENCIA)

HI TECH EDICIONES SL 20525
Carrer Roca i Batlle 5, entlo. 1ª, E-08023 BARCELONA **Tel:** 93 41 84 724 **Fax:** 93 41 84 312
Email: dvd@musicspain.com
Web site: http://www.dvdactualidad.com

Titles:
DVD ACTUALIDAD

HOLA MAGAZINE SA 21444
Miguel Angel 1, 4ª planta, E-28010 MADRID **Tel:** 91 70 21 300 **Fax:** 91 31 96 444

Titles:
HOLA

HORA NOVA SA 20733
Palacio de la Prensa, Paseo Mallorca 9A, E-07011 PALMA DE MALLORCA **Tel:** 971 78 83 22 **Fax:** 971 45 57 40

Titles:
DIARI DE BALEARES
MAJORCA DAILY BULLETIN
ULTIMA HORA

HUELVA INFORMACIÓN SA 20689
Avenida Francisco Montenegro, 2° Transversal, s/n, E-21004 HUELVA **Tel:** 959 54 11 80 **Fax:** 959 25 94 67

Titles:
HUELVA INFORMACIÓN

ICEX 21214
P° de la Castellana 14, E-28046 MADRID **Tel:** 91 34 96 243 **Fax:** 91 43 58 876

Titles:
SPAIN GOURMETOUR

IDEA EUROPEAS PUBLICITARIAS SL 1627020
Calle Belmonte del Tajo 19, E-28019 MADRID **Tel:** 91 56 01 233 **Fax:** 91 56 51 569

Titles:
DIRIGENTES
NUESTROS NEGOCIOS

IMPRESIONES DE CATALUNYA SA 20666
Diputación 119, E-08015 BARCELONA **Tel:** 93 49 62 415 **Fax:** 93 49 62 408

Titles:
EL MUNDO DE CATALUNYA

INFORMACION ESTADIO DEPORTIVO SA 21314
Avda. San Francisco, Javier 2, Edif. Sevilla, Planta 11, Modelo 25, E-41001 SEVILLA **Tel:** 95 42 21 920 **Fax:** 95 42 18 099

Titles:
ESTADIO DEPORTIVO

INFORMACIONES CANARIAS SA 20738
Urbanización El Sebadal, Calle Profesor Lozano 7, E-35008 LAS PALMAS DE GRAN CANARIA **Tel:** 928 30 13 00 **Fax:** 928 30 13 33

Titles:
CANARIAS 7

INICIATIVA JOVEN SL 21427
Timón 18 Pozuelo, Somosaguas Centro, E-28223 MADRID **Tel:** 91 35 22 800 **Fax:** 91 35 26 642

Titles:
PERIÓDICO ESTUDIANTES UNIVERSITARIOS

INVERSOR EDICIONES SL 20232
Juan Ignacio Luca de Tena 6, 3ª planta, E-28003 MADRID **Tel:** 91 45 63 320 **Fax:** 91 45 63 328
Web site: http://www.inverca.com

Titles:
INVERSIÓN Y CAPITAL
MI CARTERA DE INVERSIÓN

ITEL 20449
C. Cadi, 3, Polígono industrial Riu d'Or, E-08272 SANT FRUITÓS DE BAGES (BARCELONA) **Tel:** 93 87 74 101 **Fax:** 93 87 74 078
Email: revitec@itelspain.com
Web site: http://www.itelspain.com

Titles:
LIMPIEZA INFORM
REVITEC

JOLY DIGITAL 20674
Calle Muro, 3, E-11201 ALGECIRAS (CÁDIZ) **Tel:** 95 68 04 660 **Fax:** 95 68 36 717
Email: redaccion@diariodecadiz.com
Web site: http://www.diariodecadiz.es

Titles:
EL DÍA DE CORDOBA
DIARIO DE CÁDIZ
DIARIO DE JEREZ
EUROPA SUR

JULIÁN SANZ SORIA SL 20664
Vinyals 61, E-08221 TERRASSA (BARCELONA) **Tel:** 937 28 37 00 **Fax:** 937 28 37 18

Titles:
DIARI DE TERRASSA

KUNZER INTERNATIONAL SL 20286
Calle Marques de Lema 13, local bajo, E-28003 MADRID **Tel:** 91 45 62 660 **Fax:** 91 53 51 221

Titles:
QUIÉN ES QUIÉN EN INFORMÁTICA Y TELECOMUNICACIONES

LUIKE IBEROAMERICANA DE REVISTAS S. L. 623446
Cardenal Herrera Oria, 296, E-28035 MADRID **Tel:** 91 35 46 000 **Fax:** 91 35 40 155
Web site: http://www.luike.com

Titles:
FORMULA AUTOFACIL

LURKOI SL 20419
Pza. Simón Bolivar 14, 1°, E-01003 VITORIA **Tel:** 94 52 75 477 **Fax:** 94 52 75 731

Titles:
ARDATZA

LUZÁN 5 SA 20485
Pasaje Virgen de la Alegría 14, E-28027 MADRID **Tel:** 93 40 51 595 **Fax:** 91 40 34 907

Titles:
PORCI

MC EDICIONES SA 20523
Paseo San Gervasio 16-20, E-08022 BARCELONA **Tel:** 93 25 41 250 **Fax:** 93 25 41 263
Web site: http://www.mcediciones.es

Titles:
ALTA FIDELIDAD

MEDIA EUROPA SL 21344
Sardenya 544, 1°, 4 ª, E-08024 BARCELONA
Tel: 93 28 48 911 **Fax:** 93 28 48 192

Titles:
INFORMATIU COMERÇ

MEDIAPUBLI SOCIEDAD DE PUBLICACIONES Y EDICIONES S. L. 1743318
Virgilio, 13, Ciudad de la Imagen, Pozuelo de Alarcón, 28223 MADRID **Tel:** 93 476 15 51
Fax: 93 476 15 52
Email: dndamin@mediapro.es
Web site: www.mediapro.es

Titles:
PÚBLICO

MEDIGRUP DIGITAL SA 20890
Carrer Jordi Girona 16, E-08034 BARCELONA
Tel: 93 28 00 008 **Fax:** 93 20 43 940

Titles:
MON EMPRESARIAL

MEDIOS DE AZAHAR 698726
Calle Enmedio 81, E-12001 CASTELLÓN
Tel: 964 34 08 00 **Fax:** 964 21 75 06

Titles:
EL MUNDO CASTELLÓN AL DÍA

MEDIOS DEL NOROESTE SL 20455
Avda. Transversal 16, urb. El Monte, E-28250 TORRELODONES (MADRID) **Tel:** 91 85 99 353
Fax: 91 85 99 361

Titles:
HORAS PUNTA DEL MOTOR

MEDIOS INFORMATIVOS DE CANARIAS SA 20740
Avda. el Paso, Edificio multiuso Los Majuelos, E-38108 LA LAGUNA (TENERIFE) **Tel:** 922 82 15 55
Fax: 922 82 14 60

Titles:
EL MUNDO Y LA GACETA DE CANARIAS

MEGAMULTIMEDIA SL 698657
Avenida Meridiana 350, Planta 12 C, E-08027 BARCELONA **Tel:** 95 23 63 143 **Fax:** 95 23 64 101

Titles:
ARROBA

EL MERCADO TÉCNICO SL 20358
Puente de Deusto 7, 6°, E-48014 BILBAO
Tel: 94-47 53 813 **Fax:** 94-47 62 790

Titles:
REVISTA TOPE
SELECCIONES TO P.E.

LA MODA EN LAS CALLES 20440
Calle Abtao 11, 2° C, E-28007 MADRID
Tel: 91 55 19 197 **Fax:** 91 50 12 388

Titles:
CASA MODA
JOYA MODA

MOTORPRESS IBÉRICA SA 21425
Calle Ancora 40, E-28045 MADRID
Tel: 91 34 70 100 **Fax:** 91 34 70 152
Email: motoroess-iberica@mpib.es
Web site: http://www.motoroess-iberica.es

Titles:
AUTO VÍA
AVIÓN REVUE
CONNECT
TRANSPORTE MUNDIAL

MOTORPRESS RODALE SL 698425
Ancora 40, E-28045 MADRID **Tel:** 91 34 70 100
Fax: 91 34 70 152
Email: motorpress-iberica@mpib.es
Web site: http://www.motorpress-iberica.es

Titles:
MEN'S HEALTH

MUFACE 21237
Paso de Juan XXIII, 26, E-28071 MADRID
Tel: 91 27 39 867 **Fax:** 91 27 39 876

Titles:
MUFACE

MULTIPRENSA Y MÁS S.L. 1714812
Plaza Callao 4, 2ª planta, Palacio de la Prensa, E-28013 MADRID **Tel:** 91 70 15 600
Fax: 91 70 15 660

Titles:
CALLE 20

EL MUNDO DEPORTIVO SA 20648
Avda. Diagonal 477 - 5° planta, E-08036 BARCELONA **Tel:** 93 34 44 100 **Fax:** 93 34 44 250

Titles:
EL MUNDO DEPORTIVO

MUNDO NEGRO 21305
Calle Arturo Soria 101, E-28043 MADRID
Tel: 91 41 58 000 **Fax:** 91 51 92 550

Titles:
MUNDO NEGRO

MUNDO REVISTAS SL 20292
Avda. Diagonal 477, 2° planta, E-08036 BARCELONA **Tel:** 93 27 04 570 **Fax:** 93 27 04 582

Titles:
PLAYBOY

NORMA EDITORIAL SA 623418
Calle Fluviá 89, E-08019 BARCELONA **Tel:** 93-30 36 820 **Fax:** 93-30 36 831

Titles:
DIBUS

EL NORTE DE CASTILLA 21300
Vázquez de Menchaca 8-10, Polígono Industrial Argales, E-47008 VALLADOLID **Tel:** 983 41 21 10
Fax: 983 41 21 10

Titles:
EL NORTE DE CASTILLA

NOTICIAS DE BURGOS SL 674600
Calle Victoria, 9, 1ª izquierda, E-09004 BURGOS
Tel: 94 72 57 600 **Fax:** 94 72 57 453
Email: publicidad@genteenburgos.com
Web site: http://www.genteenburgos.com

Titles:
GENTE EN BURGOS

NOVOTÉCNICA SA 20660
Avda. del Mediterraneo 159°, Edif. Laura 1° Planta, E-04007 ALMERÍA **Tel:** 950 28 00 36
Fax: 950 25 64 58

Titles:
LA VOZ DE ALMERÍA

NUEVA RIOJA SA 20697
Vara del Rey 74, E-26002 LOGROÑO
Tel: 941 27 91 10 **Fax:** 941 27 91 09

Titles:
LA RIOJA

LA OPINIÓN DE MURCIA SA 20704
Pza. de Castilla 3, E-30009 MURCIA
Tel: 96 82 81 888 **Fax:** 96 82 81 861

Titles:
LA OPINIÓN DE MURCIA

POOL DE MEDIOS SA 20937
Paseo de la Castellana 66, E-28046 MADRID
Tel: 91 33 70 005 **Fax:** 91 33 70 006

Titles:
GACETA UNIVERSITARIA

PREMSA D'OSONA SA 20662
Pza. de la Catedral 2, E-08500 BARCELONA
Tel: 93 72 09 990 **Fax:** 93 71 21 025

Titles:
EL 9 NOU D'OSONA I DEL RIPOLLÈS
EL 9 NOU-VALLES ORIENTAL

PRENSA CATALANA SA 20663
Enric Granados, 84, entresòl, E-08008 BARCELONA **Tel:** 93 31 63 900 **Fax:** 93 31 63 945

Titles:
AVUI+

PRENSA DIARIA ARAGONESA SA 20732
Calle Hernán Cortés 37, E-50005 ZARAGOZA
Tel: 976-70 04 00 **Fax:** 976-70 04 60

Titles:
EL PERIÓDICO DE ARAGÓN

PRENSA LERIDANA SAL 20695
Calle del Río 6, Apdo. 543, E-25007 LÉRIDA
Tel: 973 24 80 00 **Fax:** 973 24 60 31

Titles:
SEGRE

PRENSA MALAGUEÑA SA 21318
Avda. Dr Marañón 48, Apdo. 98, E-29009 MÁLAGA **Tel:** 95 26 49 600 **Fax:** 95 22 79 508

Titles:
SUR

PRENSA UNIVERSAL 692543
Pza. de Navarra 3, 1° esc. izda 1° B, E-28804 ALCALÁ DE HENARES (MADRID)
Tel: 91 88 94 235 **Fax:** 91 88 95 115
Email: diarioalcala@tsai.es
Web site: http://www.diarioalcala.es

Titles:
DIARIO DE ALCALÁ

PRISMA PUBLICACIONES SA 698262
Avda. Diagonal 477, 2ª planta, E-08036 BARCELONA **Tel:** 932 70 45 55 **Fax:** 932 70 45 82

Titles:
INTERIORES, IDEAS Y TENDENCIAS

PRIVILEGE SA 21385
Ctra. de Alboraya s/n, Pol. Lladró, Tavernes Blanques, E-46016 VALENCIA **Tel:** 96 31 87 000
Fax: 96 18 55 128

Titles:
LLADRÓ PRIVILEGE

PROGRESA 698664
Julián Camarillo, 29-B, 1ª planta, 28037 MADRID
Tel: 91 53 86 104 **Fax:** 91 52 22 291
Email: correo@progresa.es
Web site: http://www.progresa.es

Titles:
CINEMANÍA

EL PROGRESO DE LUGO SL 20699
Calle Rivadeo 5, E-27002 LUGO **Tel:** 982 29 81 00
Fax: 982 29 81 02

Titles:
DIARIO DE PONTEVEDRA
EL PROGRESO

PROMECAM 20679
Calle Juan II 7, 1ª planta, E-13001 CIUDAD REAL
Tel: 926 21 53 01 **Fax:** 926 21 53 06

Titles:
LA TRIBUNA DE CIUDAD REAL

PROMICSA SA 20721
Domènech Guansé 2, E-43005 TARRAGONA
Tel: 977 29 97 20 **Fax:** 977 22 30 13

Titles:
DIARI DE TARRAGONA

PROMOCENTRO HISPÁNICA SL 20834
Londres 38, E-28028 MADRID **Tel:** 91 42 63 880
Fax: 91 57 51 296

Titles:
FREESTYLE

PROMOCIONES PERIODISTICAS LEONESAS 20693
Calle Moises León 49, E-24006 LEÓN
Tel: 987 21 25 12 **Fax:** 987 21 31 52

Titles:
LA CRÓNICA DE LEÓN

PROMOCIONES Y EDICIONES CULTURALES SA 20677
Carretera Almassora s/n, E-12005 CASTELLÓN DE LA PLANA **Tel:** 964 34 95 00 **Fax:** 964 34 95 05

Titles:
EL PERIODICO MEDITERRÁNEO

PROYECTOS EDITORIALES SALAMANCA SA 20713
Cañón de Río-Lobos, Parcela 14, Polígono el Montalvo 2, E-37188 Salamanca **Tel:** 923 19 11 11
Fax: 923 19 11 52

Titles:
LA TRIBUNA DE SALAMANCA

PUBALSA 20655
Paseo de la Cuba 14, E-02005 ALBACETE
Tel: 967 19 10 00 **Fax:** 967 24 03 86

Titles:
LA TRIBUNA DE ALBACETE

PUBLICACIONES EKDOSIS SA 20782
Gran Vía Carlos III 124, 5° Planta, E-08034 BARCELONA **Tel:** 93 20 61 540 **Fax:** 93 28 05 555

Titles:
NUEVO VALE
SUPER POP

PUBLICACIONES HERES SA 20766
Gran Vía de Carlos III 124, 5ª planta, E-08034 BARCELONA **Tel:** 932 06 15 40 **Fax:** 932 80 55 55

Titles:
PRONTO

PUBLICACIONES JOYERAS SA 20573
Vía Layetana 71, pral., E-08003 BARCELONA
Tel: 93 31 83 738 **Fax:** 93 31 85 984

Titles:
DUPLEX PRESS

PUBLICACIONES MEN-CAR SA 20555
Passeig de Colom 24 2° floor, E-08002 BARCELONA **Tel:** 93 30 15 516 **Fax:** 93 31 86 645
Email: men-car@men-car.com
Web site: http://www.men-car.com

Titles:
PORTNEWSPAPER

PUBLICACIONES REGIONALES SA 20711
Gran Vía 56, E-37001 SALAMANCA
Tel: 92 32 80 228 **Fax:** 92 32 80 261

Titles:
EL ADELANTO DE SALAMANCA

PUBLICACIONES TECNOLÓGICAS MKM 693749
Avda. Generalisimo 14, 2° B, E-28660 BOADILLA DEL MONTE (MADRID) **Tel:** 91 63 23 827
Fax: 91 63 32 564

Titles:
BYTE
DR DOBB'S ESPAÑA
MONOGRAFICOS BYTE

PUBLICACIONES Y EDICIONES DEL ALTO ARAGÓN SA 20690
La Palma 9, Apdo. 21, E-22001 HUESCA
Tel: 97 42 23 993 **Fax:** 97 42 45 444

Titles:
DIARIO DEL ALTO ARAGÓN

PUBLICACIONS ANOIA SL 698234
Retir 40, E-08700 IGUALADA **Tel:** 93 80 42 451
Fax: 93 80 54 171

Titles:
LA VEU DE L'ANOIA

PUBLICACIONS PENEDÈS SA 698219
Papiol 1, E-08720 VILAFRANCA DEL PENEDÈS (BARCELONA) **Tel:** 93 89 21 035 **Fax:** 93 81 80 236

Titles:
EL 3 DE VUIT

PUBLICITARIO FARMACÉUTICO SL 21321
Beatriz de Suabia 57, E-41005 SEVILLA
Tel: 95 45 70 149 **Fax:** 95 49 80 185
Titles:
CONSEJOS DE TU FARMACÉUTICO

PUNTO Y SEGUIDO SA 20220
Plaza de España 18, Torre de Madrid 3-11, E-28008 MADRID **Tel:** 91 51 60 806 **Fax:** 91 51 60 824
Titles:
EL NUEVO LUNES DE LA ECONOMÍA Y LA SOCIEDAD

RACC AUTOMOVIL CLUB 698914
Avenida Diagonal 687, E-08028 BARCELONA
Tel: 93 49 55 029 **Fax:** 93 44 82 490
Titles:
RACC CLUB - REIAL AUTOMOBIL CLUB DE CATALUNYA

RBA REVISTAS SA 20371
Pérez Galdós 36 bis, E-08012 BARCELONA
Tel: 93 41 57 374 **Fax:** 93 21 77 378
Web site: http://www.rba.es
Titles:
CASA AL DIA
COSAS DE CASA
COSAS DE COCINA
HISTORIA NATIONAL GEOGRAPHIC
EL MUEBLE
NATIONAL GEOGRAPHIC MAGAZINE ESPAÑA

READER'S DIGEST SELECCIONES SA 698214
Azalea 1 (mini parc) Edif. B 1ª Planta, El soto de la moraleja, E-28109 ALCOBENDAS (MADRID)
Tel: 91 76 88 611 **Fax:** 91 30 20 223
Titles:
READER'S DIGEST SELECCIONES

REAL AUTOMÓVIL CLUB DE ESPAÑA 20868
Calle Isaac Newton 4, E-28760 TRES CANTOS (MADRID) **Tel:** 91 59 47 379 **Fax:** 91 59 47 514
Titles:
AUTOCLUB

REAL FEDERACIÓN ESPAÑOLA DE ATLETISMO 20816
Avenida de Valladolid 81, 1°, E-28008 MADRID
Tel: 91 54 82 423 **Fax:** 91 54 76 113
Titles:
ATLETISMO ESPAÑOL

RECOLETOS GRUPO DE COMUNICACIÓN SA 20203
Avenida de San Luis 25-27, E-28033 MADRID
Tel: 91 33 73 220 **Fax:** 91 56 28 415
Titles:
ACTUALIDAD ECONÓMICA
EXPANSIÓN
GACETA UNIVERSITARIA DE BARCELONA
TELVA

RECOLETOS GRUPO DE COMUNICACIONES SA 698882
Avenida de San Luis, 25-27, E-28033 MADRID
Tel: 91 33 73 220 **Fax:** 91 33 73 245
Web site: http://www.recoletos.es
Titles:
MARCA
MARCA MOTOR

REED BUSINESS INFORMATION SA 20355
C/ Albarracín, 34, 28037 MADRID
Tel: 94 42 85 600 **Fax:** 94 44 25 116
Email: rbi@rbi.es
Web site: http://www.rbi.es
Titles:
EQUIPOS PRODUCTOS INDUSTRIALES (EPI)

REED BUSINESS INFORMATION SA (BILBAO) 1626594
Zancoeta 9, 5ª planta, E-48013 BILBAO (VIZCAYA) **Tel:** 94 42 85 600 **Fax:** 94 44 25 116
Email: rbi@rbi.es
Web site: http://www.rbi.es
Titles:
PRODUCTOS EQUIPOS CONSTRUCCIÓN PEC

LA REGIÓN SA 20705
Polígono San Ciprián de Viñas, Calle Cuatro 19, E-32901 OURENSE **Tel:** 988 22 22 11
Fax: 988 25 66 33
Titles:
LA REGIÓN

RENFE 699048
P° del Rey 30 - 1ª planta, E-28008 MADRID
Tel: 91 54 03 062 **Fax:** 91 54 03 472
Titles:
LINEAS DEL TREN

REPORTER SA 694504
Paseo Recoletos 16, E-28001 MADRID
Tel: 91 43 60 138 **Fax:** 91 43 14 215
Titles:
IMAGINATE

REY SOL SA 20734
Avda. 16 de Julio 75, (Polígono Son Castelló), E-07009 PALMA DE MALLORCA **Tel:** 971 76 76 50
Fax: 971 76 76 33
Titles:
EL MUNDO / EL DIA DE BALEARES

RÍAS BAIXAS COMUNICACIÓN SA 20728
Avenida Camelias 102-104 bajo, E-36211 VIGO (PONTEVEDRA) **Tel:** 986 20 86 86
Fax: 986 20 12 69
Titles:
ATLÁNTICO DIARIO

SANED SL 20591
Capitán Haya 60, E-28020 MADRID
Tel: 91 74 99 500 **Fax:** 91 74 99 507
Email: com.saned@medynet.com
Titles:
EL MEDICO

SATSE 20603
Edificio SATSE, Cuesta de Santo Domingo 6, E-28013 MADRID **Tel:** 91 54 29 393 **Fax:** 91 54 22 068
Titles:
CRÓNICA SANITARIA
MUNDO SANITARIO (PERIÓDICO DE ENFERMERÍA)

SEMANA SL 20644
Cuesta de San Vicente 28, 3°, E-28008 MADRID
Tel: 91 55 90 202 **Fax:** 91 55 90 506
Titles:
SEMANA

SFERA EDITORES (ESPAÑA) SL 20774
Parque de Negocios Mas Blau, Edificio Prima Muntadas Solsonès B-2, E-08820 EL PRAT DE LLOBREGAT (BARCELONA) **Tel:** 93 37 08 585
Fax: 93 37 05 060
Titles:
LA GUÍA DEL EMBARAZO Y PARTO
MI BEBÉ Y YO
SU PRIMER AÑO

SOCIEDAD VASCONGADA DE PUBLICACIONES SA 20714
Camino de Portuetxe 2, E-20018 SAN SEBASTIÁN **Tel:** 943 41 07 00 **Fax:** 943 41 08 14
Titles:
EL DIARIO VASCO

SOGECABLE 21102
Avda. de los Artesanos 6, E-28760 TRES CANTOS (MADRID) **Tel:** 91 73 67 000
Email: prensa@sogecable.com
Titles:
DIGITAL PLUS

SORIA IMPRESIÓN SA 21315
El Collado 17, E-42002 SORIA **Tel:** 975 23 36 07
Fax: 975 22 92 11
Titles:
HERALDO DE SORIA 7 DÍAS

SUGERENCIA EDITORIAL SL 21003
Carranza 13, 2° A, E-28004 MADRID
Tel: 91 44 63 845 **Fax:** 91 44 73 034
Titles:
GENERACIÓN XXI

SYNERGIAS DE PRENSA, SL 21066
Calle Francisco Perez Cabrero 11 B, entresuelo 8ª, E-08021 BARCELONA **Tel:** 93 36 20 580
Fax: 93 36 20 581
Email: vipclub@lugaresdivinos.com
Web site: www.lugaresdivinos.com
Titles:
BARCELONA DIVINA
LUGARES DIVINOS

TAI EDITORIAL SA 21199
Catra. Fuencarral-Alcobendas, Km. 14500, E-28108 ALCOBENDA (MADRID) **Tel:** 902 30 40 33
Fax: 902 38 78 95
Web site: http://www.pymes.tai.es
Titles:
PYMES

TALLER DE EDICIONES CORPORATIVAS SL (TE CORP) 699268
José Abascal, 56, 7ª plta., E-28003 MADRID
Tel: 91 45 64 711 **Fax:** 91 45 64 696
Titles:
CANAL OCIO

TALLER DE EDITORES SA 1603383
Juan Ignacio Luca de Tena, 6, E-28027 MADRID
Tel: 91 456 46 00 **Fax:** 91 456 47 03
Titles:
MUJER HOY
EL SEMANAL

TRADER SEGUNDAMANO SL 623237
Rambla Samá 39, 2ª planta, local 8, E-08800 VILANOVA Y LA GELTRU **Tel:** 93 81 41 017
Fax: 93 81 40 892
Titles:
CLAXON GARRAF PENEDES
CLAXON MANRESA
CLAXON TARRAGONA

UNIDAD EDITORIAL SA 20649
Avenida San Luís 25-27, E-28003 MADRID
Tel: 91 443 50 00
Titles:
DIARIO MÉDICO
EL MUNDO DE ALICANTE
EL MUNDO DE ANDALUCIA
EL MUNDO DEL SIGLO VEINTIUNO

LA UNIÓ DE LLAURADORS I RAMADERS 20421
Calle Marques de 2 aguas, E-46002 VALENCIA
Tel: 96 35 30 036 **Fax:** 96 35 30 018
Titles:
CAMP VALENCIA

UNIÓN DE PEQUEÑOS AGRICULTORES Y GANADEROS 20409
Agustín de Bethancourt 17, E-28003 MADRID
Tel: 91 53 39 781 **Fax:** 91 53 50 827
Titles:
LA TIERRA DEL AGRICULTOR Y EL GANADERO

UNIÓN PROFESIONAL DE ENFERMERÍA 20993
Calle Fuente del Rey 2, E-28023 MADRID
Tel: 91 33 45 513 **Fax:** 91 33 45 523
Titles:
ENFERMERÍA FACULTATIVA

VALLESANA PUBLICACIONES SA 20710
Sant Quirze 37-41, E-08201 SABADELL (BARCELONA) **Tel:** 937 26 11 00 **Fax:** 937 27 08 65
Email: redaccio@diarisabadell.com
Titles:
DIARI DE SABADELL

LA VANGUARDIA EDICIONES SL 20652
Diagonal 477, 2°, E-08036 BARCELONA
Tel: 93 481 2200 **Fax:** 93 318 5587
Titles:
LA VANGUARDIA

VINO Y GASTRONOMÍA COMUNICACIÓN SL 20315
Calle Amador y Fernando 6, E-28040 MADRID
Tel: 91 31 10 500 **Fax:** 91 45 95 700
Email: vyg@vinoygastronomia.net
Titles:
VINO Y GASTRONOMÍA

VIVIPRESS SL 693806
Calle Marquez Pico de Velazco 46 A, E-28027 MADRID **Tel:** 91 47 20 998
Email: info@redejecutivos.com
Titles:
EJECUTIVOS

VNU BUSINESS PUBLICATIONS ESPAÑA SA 600737
C/ Julián Camarillo 29, Edificio Diapasón 1 - 3ª planta Este, E-28037 MADRID **Tel:** 91 31 37 900
Fax: 91 32 73 704
Titles:
PC ACTUAL

VOCENTO SA 20642
Juan Ignacio Luca de Tena 7, E-28027 MADRID
Tel: 91 33 99 000 **Fax:** 91 32 03 620
Titles:
ABC

LA VOZ DE ASTURIAS SA (GRUPO ZETA) 20700
C\ La Lila 6, E-33002 OVIEDO (ASTURIAS)
Tel: 985 10 15 00 **Fax:** 985 10 15 12
Titles:
EL PERIÓDICO LA VOZ DE ASTURIAS

LA VOZ DE GALICIA SA 20682
Avda. de la Prensa 84-85, Polígono de Sabón, E-15142 ARTEIXO LA CORUÑA **Tel:** 981 18 01 80
Fax: 981 18 04 10
Titles:
LA VOZ DE GALICIA

ZEROA MULTIMEDIA SA 20688
Altzutzate 8, Poligono Industrial Areta, E-31620 HUARTE (PAMPLONA) **Tel:** 948 33 25 33
Fax: 948 33 25 18
Titles:
DIARIO DE NOTICIAS DE NAVARRA

Sweden

1974 SWEDEN HB 1686590
Box 2002, 403 11 GÖTEBORG **Tel:** 706 88 63 11
Titles:
ZERO MUSIC MAGAZINE

ABB 1748038
Communication Center, 721 83 VÄSTERÅS
Tel: 21 32 45 01
Titles:
INBLICK ABB

ABF, ARBETARNAS BILDNINGSFÖRBUND 1790296
Box 522, 101 30 STOCKHOLM **Tel:** 8 613 50 00
Fax: 8 24 69 56
Titles:
FÖNSTRET

ACTIVE MEDIA FÖRLAG AB 1793576
Sandvägen 2, 352 45 VÄXJO **Tel:** 470 702 770
Fax: 470 702 771
Titles:
BLICKPUNKT: BYGG & FASTIGHET

ADAPTION MEDIA AB
1748453
Box 7438, 103 91 STOCKHOLM **Tel:** 8 500 084 90
Titles:
POPULÄR HÄLSA

ÄDLA DRYCKER TIDNINGS AB
1793677
Box 26162, 100 41 STOCKHOLM **Tel:** 8 662 90 50
Titles:
DINA VINER

ADOPTIONSCENTRUM
1793874
Adoptionscentrum, Box 30073, 104 25 STOCKHOLM **Tel:** 8 587 499 00 **Fax:** 858749999
Titles:
ATT ADOPTERA

AFASIFÖRBUNDET I SVERIGE
1790464
Kampementgatan 14, 115 38 STOCKHOLM
Tel: 8 545 663 60 **Fax:** 854566379
Titles:
AFASI-NYTT

AFFÄRS- & KAPITALNYTT AB
1628082
Båtbyggaregatan 198, 216 42 LIMHAMN
Tel: 40 15 30 50 **Fax:** 40153070
Titles:
AFFÄRS- & KAPITALNYTT
AFFÄRS- & KAPITALNYTT; AFFKAPNYTT.SE

AFTONBLADET ALLT OM AB
1791279
c/o Aftonbladet, 105 18 STOCKHOLM
Tel: 872526 00
Titles:
ALLT OM STOCKHOLM

AFTONBLADET HIERTA AB
1789309
Besöksadress: Västra Järnvägsgatan 21, 105 18 STOCKHOLM **Tel:** 8 725 20 00 **Fax:** 8 600 01 77
Titles:
AFTONBLADET
AFTONBLADET; AFTONBLADET.SE

AFTONBLADET KVÄLLSTIDNINGAR AB
1789376
Budadress: Blekholmsgatan 18, 111 64 Stockholm, 105 18 STOCKHOLM **Tel:** 8 725 20 00
Fax: 8 562 528 18
Titles:
AFTONBLADET; RÄTTSREDAKTIONEN
AFTONBLADET; SPORTMAGASINET

AGRIFACK (SACO)
1630275
Box 2062, 131 24 NACKA **Tel:** 8 562 920 00
Fax: 8 20 20 81
Titles:
NATURVETARE

AIP MEDIA PRODUKTION AB
1790070
105 60 STOCKHOLM **Tel:** 8 700 26 00
Fax: 8 411 65 42
Titles:
AKTUELLT I POLITIKEN
AKTUELLT I POLITIKEN; AIP.NU
NY TID
TIDEN
TIDEN;
ARBETARRORELSENSTANKESMEDJA.SE

AKADEMIKERFÖRBUNDET SSR
1653346
Box 12800, 112 96 STOCKHOLM **Tel:** 8 617 44 37
Fax: 8 617 44 40
Titles:
SOCIONOMEN

AKADEMISKA SJUKHUSET, LANDSTINGET I UPPSALA LÄN
1732753
Akademiska sjukhuset, 751 85 UPPSALA
Tel: 18 611 96 11
Titles:
RONDEN, PERSONALTIDNING FÖR AKADEMISKA SJUKHUSET

AKTUELL GRAFISK INFORMATION AB
1628676
Jörgen Kocksgatan 9, 211 20 MALMÖ
Tel: 40 12 78 40 **Fax:** 40 12 58 20
Titles:
AGI

ALBA
1792024
Andra Långgatan 20, 413 28 GOTEBORG
Tel: 31 12 76 40 **Fax:** 31 14 37 77
Titles:
ALBA

ALBINSSON & SJÖBERG, FÖRLAGS AB
1793570
Box 529, 371 23 KARLSKRONA **Tel:** 455 33 53 75
Fax: 455311715
Titles:
4 WHEEL DRIVE

ÄLDREFORSKNINGENS HUS
1732686
Gävlegatan 16, 113 30 STOCKHOLM
Tel: 8 690 58 00 **Fax:** 86906889
Titles:
TIDSKRIFTEN ÄLDRE I CENTRUM

ALEKURIREN
1628019
Göteborgsvägen 94, 446 33 ÄLVÄNGEN
Tel: 303 74 99 40 **Fax:** 303 74 99 45
Titles:
ALEKURIREN
ALEKURIREN; ALEKURIREN.SE

ALLEGO AB
1640054
Box 406, 791 28 FALUN **Tel:** 23 70 57 00
Fax: 23 70 57 05
Titles:
ANBUDSJOURNALEN
ANBUDSJOURNALEN; ALLEGO.SE

ALLER BUSINESS AB
1639783
Tel: 8 564 886 44
Titles:
FOGNINGSTEKNIK
LEVERANSTIDNINGEN ENTREPRENAD
MOTOR-MAGASINET;
MOTORMAGASINET.NET

ALLER CUSTOM PUBLISHING
1790092
Box 27712, Aller Custom Publishing, 115 91 STOCKHOLM **Tel:** 8 578 010 14
Titles:
VILLAÄGAREN

ALLER MAGAZINE AB
1746007
BOX 27708, 115 91 Stockholm, 114 46 STOCKHOLM **Tel:** 8 57 80 10 00 **Fax:** 8 457 80 80
Titles:
CAFÉ
CAFÉ; CAFE.SE
CAFÉ COLLECTIONS
ELLE
ELLE; ELLE.SE
ELLE MAT & VIN

ALLER MAGAZINEAB
1746009
Postadress: Box 27 706, 115 91 STOCKHOLM
Tel: 8 457 80 00 **Fax:** 8 457 80 80
Titles:
ELLE INTERIÖR

ALLERS FÖRLAG
1732752
Allers Förlag, 251 85 HELSINGBORG
Tel: 42 17 35 00 **Fax:** 42 17 35 68
Titles:
ALLERS
ALLERS JULMAGASIN
SE & HÖR

ALLERS FÖRLAG AB
1789270
205 35 MALMO **Tel:** 40 38 59 00 **Fax:** 40 38 59 64
Titles:
ALLAS VECKOTIDNING
ALLERS TRÄDGÅRD
ANTIK & AUKTION
ÅRET RUNT
FEMINA
FISKEJOURNALEN
FOTO
HÄNT BILD
HÄNT EXTRA
HEMMETS VECKOTIDNING
JAKTJOURNALEN
MÅ BRA
MÅ BRA; MABRA.COM
MAGASINET SKÅNE
MATMAGASINET

ALLERS FÖRLAG AB, HELSINGBORG
1789271
Budadress: Humlegårdsgatan 6, Box 27710, 115 91 STOCKHOLM **Tel:** 8 679 46 00
Titles:
SVENSK DAMTIDNING

ALLMÄNNA FÖRSVARSFÖRENINGEN
1628844
Teatergatan 3, 111 48 STOCKHOLM
Tel: 8 678 15 10 **Fax:** 8 667 22 53
Titles:
VÅRT FÖRSVAR

ALLT OM HOBBY AB
1791580
Box 90133, 120 21 STOCKHOLM **Tel:** 8 99 93 33
Fax: 8 99 88 66
Titles:
ALLT OM HOBBY

ALLT OM VETENSKAP FÖRLAGS AB
1643412
Industrigatan 2A, 112 85 STOCKHOLM
Tel: 8 758 52 60
Titles:
ALLT OM VETENSKAP

ALMA MEDIA
1774092
Box: 3640, 103 59 STOCKHOLM
Titles:
GODOME

ALMEGA
1790451
Box 55545, 102 04 STOCKHOLM **Tel:** 8 762 69 00
Fax: 87626957
Titles:
ALMEGATIDNINGEN

ALTERNATIV MEDIA STOCKHOLM AB
1791554
Alternativ Media Stockholm AB, Löjtnantsgatan 17, 115 50 STOCKHOLM **Tel:** 8 545 871 30
Fax: 8 664 63 30
Titles:
REALTID.SE

ALZHEIMERFÖRENINGEN I SVERIGE
1732694
Box 197, 221 00 LUND **Tel:** 46 14 73 66
Fax: 46188976
Titles:
ALZHEIMERTIDNINGEN

AMATÖRTEATERNS RIKSFÖRBUND
1743653
Box 1194, 721 29 VÄSTERÅS **Tel:** 21 470 41 64
Fax: 21 470 41 69
Titles:
TEATERFORUM

AMELIA PUBLISHING GROUP
1789492
Budadress: Malmskillnadsgatan 39, 105 44 STOCKHOLM **Tel:** 8 736 52 00 **Fax:** 8 24 02 13
Titles:
AMELIA

AMNESTY INTERNATIONAL/SV. SEKTIONEN
1793586
Box 4719, 116 92 STOCKHOLM **Tel:** 8 729 02 00
Fax: 8 729 02 01
Titles:
AMNESTY PRESS

AMNINGSHJÄLPEN
1655124
Ludvigslätt, 231 99 KLAGSTORP **Tel:** 410 294 42
Titles:
AMNINGSNYTT

ANDERS NORDIN
1657599
Box 100, 231 22 TRELLEBORG **Tel:** 410 460 55
Fax: 410 460 45
Titles:
VILLAFORUM

ANNA LISA ENEROTH
1790266
Norrtullsgatan 45, 1 tr, 113 46 STOCKHOLM
Tel: 8 702 98 10
Titles:
FRED OCH FRIHET

ANNONSMARKNAN
1639835
Kulla 11, 517 91 BOLLEBYGD **Tel:** 33 28 41 20
Fax: 33 28 52 52
Titles:
ANNONS-MARKNA'N

ANSV. UTGIVARE ANNA-KARIN JANSSON
1793394
Box 627, 441 17 ALINGSÅS **Tel:** 322 66 83 00
Fax: 322 66 83 01
Titles:
ALINGSÅS KURIREN

ANTIKBÖRSENS FÖRLAG AB
1790943
Lilla Nygatan 20, 111 28 STOCKHOLM
Tel: 8 545 470 40 **Fax:** 86948510
Titles:
ANTIKVÄRLDEN
ANTIKVÄRLDEN; ANTIKVARLDEN.SE
GÅRD & TORP

APOTEKARSOCIETETEN
1791285
Box 1136, 111 81 STOCKHOLM **Tel:** 8 723 50 00
Fax: 8149580
Titles:
LÄKEMEDELSVÄRLDEN
LÄKEMEDELSVÄRLDEN;
LAKEMEDELSVARLDEN.SE

APOTEKET AB
1629574
Apoteket AB, 118 81 STOCKHOLM
Tel: 10447 50 00 **Fax:** 8 466 15 90
Titles:
APOTEKET - TIDNING FÖR APOTEKETS KUNDER

APPELBERG MAGASIN FÖRLAG AB OCH MÅLAREMÄSTARNA
1732658
Box 73 44, 103 90 STOCKHOLM **Tel:** 8 406 54 00
Fax: 8 406 54 99
Titles:
ROOMSERVICE PRO

AR MEDIA INTERNATIONAL AB
1790167
Västberga Allé 32, 126 30 HAGERSTEN
Tel: 8 556 306 80
Titles:
DETEKTOR SCANDINAVIA

ARBETARBLADET AB
1789483
Box 287, 801 04 GÄVLE **Tel:** 26 15 93 00
Fax: 26 18 52 70
Titles:
ARBETARBLADET

ARBETSFÖRMEDLINGEN
1790398
Arbetsförmedlingen, 113 99 STOCKHOLM
Tel: 8508 801 00 **Fax:** 8 508 801 78
Titles:
ARBETSMARKNADEN

ARBETSMARKNADS-STYRELSEN, AMS
1790496
Arbetsmarknadsstyrelsen, 113 99 STOCKHOLM
Tel: 8 586 060 00 **Fax:** 858606485
Titles:
ARBETSMARKNADEN;
ARBETSMARKNADEN.SE

ARBETSMILJÖFORUM I SVERIGE AB
1735349
Box 17550, 118 91 STOCKHOLM **Tel:** 8 442 46 00
Fax: 84424607

Titles:
DU & JOBBET
DU & JOBBET; DUOCHJOBBET.SE

ARBIO AB 1639822
Box 55525, 102 04 STOCKHOLM **Tel:** 8 762 72 77
Fax: 87627990
Titles:
TRÄINFORMATION-EN TIDNING FRÅN SKOGSINDUSTRIERNA

ARENA MEDIER 1790424
Drottninggatan 83, 111 60 STOCKHOLM
Tel: 8 789 11 70 **Fax:** 84114242
Titles:
CHEFSTIDNINGEN, HR- OCH LEDARSKAPSMAGASIN FÖR AKADEMIKER

ARENA UPPHANDLING AB 1743571
IDG, 106 78 STOCKHOLM **Tel:** 8 453 63 12
Titles:
UPPHANDLING24

ARKITEKTUR FÖRLAG AB 1791257
Box 4296, 102 66 STOCKHOLM **Tel:** 8 702 78 50
Fax: 8 611 52 70
Titles:
ARKITEKTUR

ARTDATABANKEN, SLU 1640057
Box 7007, 750 07 UPPSALA **Tel:** 18 67 25 77
Titles:
FAUNA OCH FLORA

ASSYRISKA RIKSFÖRBUNDET I SVERIGE 1732685
Assyriska riksförbundet, Box 6019, 151 06 SÖDERTÄLJE **Tel:** 8 550 166 83 **Fax:** 36140661
Titles:
HUJÅDÅ

ASTMA- OCH ALLERGIFÖRBUNDET 1793602
Box 17069, 104 62 STOCKHOLM
Tel: 8 506 282 15 **Fax:** 8 506 282 49
Titles:
ALLERGIA

AUTO MOTOR & SPORT SVERIGE AB 1793571
Gårdsvägen 4, 169 70 SOLNA **Tel:** 8 470 92 60
Titles:
SPORTBILEN

AUTOMOBIL / OK FÖRLAGET AB 1791112
Box 23800, 104 35 STOCKHOLM **Tel:** 8 736 12 42
Fax: 8 736 12 49
Titles:
AUTOMOBIL
AUTOMOBIL; AUTOMOBIL.SE

AVELSFÖRENINGEN FÖR SVENSKA VARMBLODIGA TRAVHÄSTAR 1640060
ASVT, 161 89 STOCKHOLM **Tel:** 8 445 23 00
Fax: 8 445 23 09
Titles:
TRAVHÄSTEN

AVFALL SVERIGE AB 1735412
Prostgatan 2, 211 25 MALMO **Tel:** 40 35 66 00
Fax: 40 35 66 26
Titles:
AVFALL OCH MILJÖ

AXESS PUBLISHING 1793802
Jakobsbergsgatan 2, 6tr., 111 44 STOCKHOLM
Tel: 8 788 50 50
Titles:
AXESS MAGASIN

B & J INVEST 1627310
Box 6040, 200 11 MALMÖ **Tel:** 40 611 06 90
Fax: 40 797 37
Titles:
ELBRANSCHEN

B & J:S FÖRLAG 1793517
Box 6040, 200 11 MALMO **Tel:** 40 611 06 90
Fax: 4079737
Titles:
SVENSK BERGS- OCH BRUKSTIDNING

BÅNGMAN & ÖRNBORG FÖRLAG AB 1640608
Box 22 559, 104 22 STOCKHOLM
Tel: 7 704 571 16 **Fax:** 86520300
Titles:
GLID MAGAZINE

BANVERKET 1735368
Göran Fält, Banverket, 781 85 BORLÄNGE
Tel: 243 44 55 73 **Fax:** 243 44 55 56
Titles:
RALLAREN

BANVERKET PRODUKTION 1793537
Banverket Produktion, 781 85 BORLÄNGE
Tel: 243 44 62 45 **Fax:** 243446250
Titles:
UPPSPÅRAT

BARN I STAN AB 1790608
Gröndalsvägen 38, 117 66 STOCKHOLM
Tel: 8 558 012 50
Titles:
BARN I STAN

BARNCANCERFONDEN 1627987
Box 5408, 114 84 STOCKHOLM **Tel:** 8 584 209 00
Fax: 8 584 109 00
Titles:
BARN & CANCER

BÅTBRANSCHENS RIKSFÖRBUND 1629528
Ö. Vittusgatan 36, 371 33 KARLSKRONA
Tel: 455 297 80 **Fax:** 455 36 97 99
Titles:
BÅTBRANSCHEN

BAUER MEDIA 1732721
Nybohallen, 820 40 JÄRVSÖ **Tel:** 651 150 50
Titles:
MEDICINSK ACCESS

BCF AMAZONA I STOCKHOLMS LÄN. 1790947
BCF (bröstcancerföreningen) amazona i Stockholms län, 113 26 STOCKHOLM
Tel: 8 32 55 90
Titles:
AMAZONABLADET

BENEFIT MEDIA AB 1790450
Benefit Media, Nybrogatan 35, 114 39 STOCKHOLM **Tel:** 8 66159 99 **Fax:** 8 660 07 70
Titles:
PERSONALAKTUELLT

BERGLUND & SÖNER (PUBLISHING) AB 1735386
Box 2001, 191 02 SOLLENTUNA
Tel: 708 80 04 07 **Fax:** 8 35 80 25
Titles:
MEDTECH MAGAZINE

BERGSLAGARNAS TIDNINGS AB 1789768
711 81 LINDESBERG **Tel:** 581 844 00
Fax: 581 844 41
Titles:
NA BERGSLAGSPOSTEN

BERGSMANNEN FÖRLAGS AB 1630008
Skeppargatan 27, 114 52 STOCKHOLM
Tel: 8 442 86 30 **Fax:** 86622950
Titles:
BERGSMANNEN MED JERNKONTORETS ANNALER
BERGSMANNEN MED JERNKONTORETS ANNALER; BERGSMANNEN.SE

BERGSTRÖM PUBLIC RELATIONS 1732684
Box 624, 114 56 STOCKHOLM **Tel:** 733 16 00 37
Titles:
AFFÄRSLIV

BIBLIOTEK I SAMHÄLLE 1629186
Rosenbadsgatan 9, 652 26 KARLSTAD
Tel: 54 10 18 13
Titles:
BIS

BILDA IDÉ, BOX 42053, 126 13 STOCKHOLM 1790281
Box 70458, 107 26 STOCKHOLM **Tel:** 8 700 26 00
Fax: 8 411 65 42
Titles:
MORGONBRIS, S-KVINNORS TIDNING

BIODYNAMISKA FÖRENINGEN 1627405
Biodynamiska Föreningen, Box 97, 161 26 BROMMA **Tel:** 70 216 33 90 **Fax:** 8 730 13 46
Titles:
BIODYNAMISK ODLING

BJÖRN SMITTERBERG 1653075
Lidköpingsnytt.nu, Särnarksgatan 24, 531 31 LIDKÖPING **Tel:** 510 212 90 **Fax:** 31 313 13 03
Titles:
LIDKÖPINGSNYTT.NU

BLACK ARMY 1639848
Box 21166, 100 31 STOCKHOLM
Tel: 737 24 01 86
Titles:
GNAGAREN

BLEKINGE LÄNS TIDNING AB 1789667
371 89 KARLSKRONA **Tel:** 455 770 00
Fax: 455 821 70
Titles:
BLEKINGE LÄNS TIDNING
BLEKINGE LÄNS TIDNING; BLT.SE

BLENDOW GROUP 1735691
Nybrogatan 57 A, 114 40 STOCKHOLM
Tel: 8 579 366 00 **Fax:** 8 667 97 60
Titles:
DAGENS JURIDIK

BLENDOW GROUP AB 1743423
Banérgatan 16, 115 23 STOCKHOLM
Tel: 8 579 366 00 **Fax:** 8 667 97 60
Titles:
LEGALLY YOURS

BLODCANCERFÖRBUNDET 1743031
Tel: 703 47 47 63 **Fax:** 8 546 405 49
Titles:
HÆMA

BLOMSTER-BRANSCHEN I BROMMA AB 1628958
Box 808, 161 24 BROMMA **Tel:** 8 25 97 31
Fax: 8 26 96 06
Titles:
BLOMSTER-BRANSCHEN

BLONDINBELLA AB 1792199
114 34 STOCKHOLM
Titles:
BLONDINBELLA

BMW GROUP SVERIGE 1628943
c/o Chiffer AB, 118 20 STOCKHOLM
Tel: 8 410 321 00 **Fax:** 8 611 60 21
Titles:
BMW MAGASIN

BOHUSLÄNINGENS AB 1789649
451 83 UDDEVALLA **Tel:** 522 990 00
Titles:
BOHUSLÄNINGEN
BOHUSLÄNINGEN; BOHUSLANINGEN.SE

BOKBODEN 1629696
Nedre Tjärna 2, 780 41 GAGNEF **Tel:** 241 618 09
Titles:
BOKBODEN

BONNIER ALANDIA AB 1630022
Krusegränd 42 C, 212 25 MALMÖ
Tel: 40 601 88 00
Titles:
DIGITALFOTO FÖR ALLA
DIGITALFOTO FÖR ALLA; DIGITALFOTOFORALLA.SE

BONNIER NOVA FÖRLAG 1789880
Budadress: Malmskillnadsgatan 39, 111 38 Stockholm, 105 44 STOCKHOLM **Tel:** 8 736 52 00
Fax: 8 24 16 02
Titles:
VECKO-REVYN

BONNIER & SPOON 1776839
Bonnier Tidskrifter AB, 105 44 STOCKHOLM
Tel: 8442 96 20
Titles:
FIXA SJÄLV

BONNIER PUBLICATION INTERNATIONAL AS 1790171
Gör Det Själv, 205 50 MALMO **Tel:** 8 555 454 02
Fax: 8 555 454 50
Titles:
GÖR DET SJÄLV

BONNIER PUBLICATIONS A/S 1793817
205 50 MALMO **Tel:** 8 555 454 05
Titles:
ILLUSTRERAD VETENSKAP; WEBB

BONNIER PUBLICATIONS INTERNATIONAL AS 1649759
Kundtjänst, 205 50 MALMÖ **Tel:** 8 555 454 53
Fax: 8 555 454 50
Titles:
NATIONAL GEOGRAPHIC
PC-TIDNINGEN
PC-TIDNINGEN; PCTIDNINGEN.SE

BONNIER RESPONSMEDIER AB 1639872
Box 4040, 181 04 LIDINGÖ **Tel:** 8 731 29 00
Fax: 8 731 00 22
Titles:
VI I VILLA
VI I VILLA; WEBB

BONNIER SPECIALTIDNINGAR 1790112
Sveavägen 53, 105 44 STOCKHOLM
Tel: 8 736 53 00 **Fax:** 8312560
Titles:
PRIVATA AFFÄRER
PRIVATA AFFÄRER; PRIVATAAFFARER.SE

BONNIER TIDSKRIFTER 1789390
BONNIER TIDSKRIFTER, Sveavägen 53, 105 44 STOCKHOLM **Tel:** 8 736 53 00
Titles:
101 NYA IDÉER
TARA

BONNIER TIDSKRIFTER AB 1627316
Bonnier Tidskrifter AB, 105 44 STOCKHOLM
Tel: 8 736 53 00 **Fax:** 8 736 54 41

Titles:
ALLT I HEMMET
ALLT OM FRITIDSHUS
ALLT OM MAT
ALLT OM MAT; ALLTOMMAT.SE
ALLT OM RESOR
ALLT OM TRÄDGÅRD
AMELIA - BABY
AMELIA - BRUD & BRÖLLOP
AMELIA - HÅR & SKÖNHET
AMELIA - JUL
AMELIA - KROPP & SKÖNHET
AMELIA - SOMMAR
AMELIA - VÄNTA BARN
AMELIA - VIKT & HÄLSA
DAMERNAS VÄRLD
DAMERNAS VÄRLD; DAMERNAS.SE
DAMERNAS VÄRLD - DV MODE
FAMILY LIVING
HEM & ANTIK
KAMRATPOSTEN
KAMRATPOSTEN; KPWEBBEN.SE
MAMA MAGASIN
M-MAGASIN
PRIVATA AFFÄRER PLACERINGSGUIDEN
SKÖNA HEM
SKÖNA HEM; SKONAHEM.COM
TEKNIKENS VÄRLD
TEKNIKENS VÄRLD; TEKNIKENSVARLD.COM
TOPPHÄLSA
VECKO-REVYN; VECKOREVYN.COM
VI FÖRÄLDRAR
VI FÖRÄLDRAR; VIFORALDRAR.SE

BONNIER TIDSKRIFTER & TV4 1791274
105 44 STOCKHOLM **Tel:** 8 736 53 00
Titles:
VECKANS AFFÄRER; VA.SE

BONNIERS PUBLICATIONS INTERNATIONAL AS 1789555
Pipersgatan 7, 112 24 STOCKHOLM
Tel: 8 441 07 90
Titles:
I FORM

BORÅSARN 1628090
Björkhemsgatan 38, 506 46 BORÅS
Tel: 33 10 10 03 **Fax:** 33 10 32 13
Titles:
BORÅS.BIZ

BÖRJE DAHL 1628255
Box 34, 171 11 SOLNA **Tel:** 8 545 453 30
Titles:
TIDNINGEN FAMILJEDAGHEM

BÖRSVECKAN AB 1732715
Box 1399, 111 93 STOCKHOLM **Tel:** 8 10 33 50
Fax: 8 20 14 00
Titles:
BÖRSVECKAN

BOSPA FÖRLAG 1792011
Åsbovägen 68, 152 52 SÖDERTÄLJE
Tel: 8 550 628 73
Titles:
DIASPORA / DIJASPORA

BOTKYRKA KOMMUN 1629938
Botkyrka kommun, Munkhättevägen 45, 147 85 TUMBA **Tel:** 8 530 618 05 **Fax:** 8 530 616 36
Titles:
PEJL PÅ BOTKYRKA

BOVERKET 1790346
Boverket, Box 534, 371 23 KARLSKRONA
Tel: 455 35 30 00 **Fax:** 455 35 32 15
Titles:
PLANERA BYGGA BO

BRA MEDIA FÖRLAG I SVERIGE AB 1629367
Box 4173, 102 64 STOCKHOLM **Tel:** 8 556 933 70
Fax: 8910907
Titles:
INCITAMENT

BRAND EYE AB 1630049
Box 3457, 103 69 STOCKHOLM **Tel:** 8 406 09 00
Fax: 8 20 38 10
Titles:
BRAND NEWS
PATENT EYE

BR-FÖRLAGET AB 1627460
Box 1236, 181 24 LIDINGÖ **Tel:** 8 767 88 31
Fax: 8 765 71 74
Titles:
BORÄTT,
BOSTADSRÄTTSFÖRENINGSTIDNINGEN

BRIGHT VERKSAMHETSUTVECKLING AB 1741917
Pipersgatan 1, 112 24 STOCKHOLM
Tel: 702 66 28 15
Titles:
LINK MAGAZINE

BRIS (BARNENS RÄTT I SAMHÄLLET) 1790576
Box 3415, Sveavägen 38, 103 68 STOCKHOLM
Tel: 8 598 888 00 **Fax:** 859888801
Titles:
BRIS-TIDNINGEN BARN OCH UNGDOM

BRODERSKAPSRÖRELSENS NÄTVERK FÖR MUSLIMSKA SOCIALDEMOKRATER 1776842
Titles:
ISLAM & POLITIK

BRÖLLOPSGUIDEN NORDEN AB 1793457
BröllopsGuiden Norden AB, Högbergsgatan 99, 118 54 STOCKHOLM **Tel:** 8 545 245 55
Fax: 8 442 39 70
Titles:
BRÖLLOPSGUIDEN

BRÖLLOPSMAGASINET AB 1639768
Björkbäcksvägen 9, 451 55 UDDEVALLA
Tel: 522 68 11 90 **Fax:** 522681199
Titles:
BRÖLLOPSMAGASINET

BROTTSFÖREBYGGANDE RÅDET 1793601
Box 1386, 111 93 STOCKHOLM **Tel:** 8 401 87 00
Fax: 84119075
Titles:
APROPÅ

BROTTSOFFERJOURERNAS RIKSFÖRBUND 1627475
Box 11014, 100 61 STOCKHOLM **Tel:** 8 644 88 00
Fax: 8 644 88 28
Titles:
TIDNINGEN BROTTSOFFER

BUSINESS REGION GÖTEBORG AB 1747913
Box 111 19, 404 23 GOTEBORG **Tel:** 31 61 24 02
Fax: 31612401
Titles:
BUSINESS

BUSSBRANSCHEN BW AB 1793489
Daldocksvägen 11, 34395 VINGÅKER
Tel: 221 175 00 **Fax:** 221 175 08
Titles:
BUSSBRANSCHEN

BWW POPULÄRKULTUR AB 1743899
114 59 STOCKHOLM **Tel:** 8 555 880 50
Fax: 8 545 682 41
Titles:
RODEO
RODEO; RODEO.NET

BYAHORNET 1792026
Hägnaden 923, 247 96 SK. FAGERHULT
Tel: 433 500 80 **Fax:** 43350086
Titles:
BYAHORNET

BYGDEGÅRDARNAS RIKSFÖRBUND 1746008
Bygdegårdarnas Riksförbund, Box 26017, 100 41 STOCKHOLM **Tel:** 8 440 51 90 **Fax:** 86115590
Titles:
BYGDEGÅRDEN

BYGGCHEFERNA - EN FÖRENING INOM LEDARNA 1790390
Burson Marsteller, Box 5266, 102 46 STOCKHOLM **Tel:** 8 440 12 20
Titles:
BYGGCHEFEN

BYGGFÖRLAGET AB 1639818
Box 55 669, 102 15 STOCKHOLM
Tel: 8 665 36 50 **Fax:** 8 667 72 78
Titles:
BYGGINDUSTRIN
BYGGINDUSTRIN; BYGGINDUSTRIN.COM

CAN- CENTRALFÖRB. FÖR ALKOHOL- & NARKOTIKAUPPLYSNING 1630052
Box 70412, 107 25 STOCKHOLM **Tel:** 8 412 46 00
Fax: 8 10 46 41
Titles:
ALKOHOL & NARKOTIKA

CANCERFONDEN 1793510
David Bagares Gata 5, 101 55 STOCKHOLM
Tel: 8 677 10 00 **Fax:** 86771001
Titles:
RÄDDA LIVET

CARAVAN CLUB OF SWEDEN 1793616
Kyrkvägen 25, 703 75 OREBRO **Tel:** 19 23 46 10
Fax: 19 23 44 25
Titles:
CARAVANBLADET

CARLSHAMNS COMMERSEN AB 1789680
Lotsgatan 5, 374 35 KARLSHAMN **Tel:** 454 341 30
Fax: 454 341 39
Titles:
COMMERSEN

CAROLINE ALVESSON 1743880
Stridsvagnsvägen 8A, 291 39 KRISTIANSTAD
Tel: 44 20 75 74 **Fax:** 44 12 58 25
Titles:
KÅRIREN

CBM 1629060
CBM, Box 7007, 750 07 UPPSALA
Tel: 18 67 13 94 **Fax:** 18 67 34 80
Titles:
BIODIVERSE

CE KONSUMENTELEKTRONIK-BRANSCHEN AB 1744713
Box 22307, 104 22 STOCKHOLM
Tel: 8 508 938 57 **Fax:** 8 508 938 01
Titles:
ELEKTRONIKBRANSCHEN

CENTERPARTIETS RIKSORGANISATION 1793582
Centerpartiet, Box 2200, 103 15 STOCKHOLM
Tel: 8 617 38 18 **Fax:** 8 617 38 10
Titles:
TIDNINGEN C.

CENTERPARTIETS UNGDOMSFÖRBUND 1793592
Box 2200, 103 15 STOCKHOLM **Tel:** 8 617 38 54
Fax: 86173854
Titles:
UNG CENTER

CENTRUM FÖR INTERNATIONELLT UNGDOMSUTBYTE 1628649
CIU, Ludvigsbergsgatan 22, 118 23 STOCKHOLM **Tel:** 8 440 87 80 **Fax:** 8 20 35 30
Titles:
MY TELLUS.POCKET

CENTRUM FÖR LÄTTLÄST 1629945
Box 9145, 102 72 STOCKHOLM **Tel:** 8 640 70 90
Fax: 8 642 76 00
Titles:
8 SIDOR
8 SIDOR; 8SIDOR.SE

CENTUM AB 1629943
Wallingatan 18, 111 24 STOCKHOLM
Tel: 8 10 81 81 **Fax:** 8104140
Titles:
NYHETSBREVET DAGENS FASTIGHETSAKTIE
TIDNINGEN FASTIGHETSAKTIEN
TIDNINGEN FASTIGHETSAKTIEN; WEBB

CHALMERS STUDENTKÅR 1629946
Teknologgården 2, 412 58 GÖTEBORG
Tel: 31 772 39 23 **Fax:** 31 772 39 67
Titles:
TOFSEN CHALMERS KÅRTIDNING

CHECK-IN FÖRLAG AB 1629110
181 44 LIDINGÖ **Tel:** 660 37 09 79
Fax: 660 37 09 31
Titles:
CHECK-IN

CHEF STOCKHOLM HB 1735425
Sveavägen 92, 113 50 STOCKHOLM
Tel: 8 555 245 00 **Fax:** 8 555 245 50
Titles:
TIDNINGEN CHEF

CHRISTIAN BORG 1791045
Box 31036, 400 32 GOTEBORG **Tel:** 31 13 44 10
Titles:
LIRA MUSIKMAGASIN

CHRISTIAN CARLSSON 1793544
Roslagstullsbacken 11, Albanova Universitetscentrum, 106 91 STOCKHOLM
Tel: 8 30 99 05 **Fax:** 8 30 99 12
Titles:
IDROTT & KUNSKAP

CITY MEDIA I VÄXJÖ AB 1628464
Prästgatan 12, 252 24 HELSINGBORG
Tel: 42 21 20 80 **Fax:** 42 21 51 54
Titles:
NÖJESNYTT; HELSINGBORG
NÖJESNYTT; JÖNKÖPING
NÖJESNYTT; KALMAR
NÖJESNYTT; VÄXJÖ

CIVILEKONOMERNA 1790055
Box 4720, 116 92 STOCKHOLM **Tel:** 8 783 27 50
Fax: 8 783 27 52
Titles:
CIVILEKONOMEN
CIVILEKONOMEN; CIVILEKONOMEN.SE

CIVILFÖRSVARSFÖRBUNDET 1790263
Box 2034, 169 02 SOLNA **Tel:** 8 629 63 72
Fax: 8 629 63 83
Titles:
CIVIL

COBRA FÖRLAG AB 1790343
Box 82, 533 04 HÄLLEKIS **Tel:** 510 862 00
Fax: 51086220
Titles:
LÄTTA LASTBILAR

COLLEGIUM PALYNOLOGICUM SCANDINAVICUM 1793604
Taylor & Francis AB, Box 3255, 103 65 STOCKHOLM **Tel:** 8 440 80 40 **Fax:** 8 440 80 50
Titles:
GRANA

COMPRO MEDIA AB 1627417
Box 6910, 102 39 STOCKHOLM **Tel:** 8 459 24 00 **Fax:** 8 660 75 22
Titles:
EVENT & EXPO
KONFERENSVÄRLDEN
PRODUKTAKTUELLT

COMPUTER SWEDEN OCH DAGENS MEDICIN 1735378
Computer Sweden, 106 78 STOCKHOLM **Tel:** 8 453 60 50 **Fax:** 8 453 60 55
Titles:
IT I VÅRDEN
IT I VÅRDEN; WEBB

CONNOISSEUR INTERNATIONAL AB 1790059
Smedjegatan 8, 131 54 NACKA **Tel:** 8 718 29 00 **Fax:** 8 716 23 00
Titles:
CONNOISSEUR

CONSTRUEDO AB 1790391
Box 3437, 103 68 STOCKHOLM **Tel:** 70 630 22 17 **Fax:** 8 24 54 64
Titles:
SAMHÄLLSBYGGAREN

CONVENTUS COMMUNICATION AB 1736179
Box 24053, 104 50 STOCKHOLM **Tel:** 8 506 244 00
Titles:
AKTUELLA BYGGEN
MODERN INTERIÖR
NORDISK INDUSTRI
NORDISK INFRASTRUKTUR

CONVENTUS INDUSTRY AB 1746036
Convenus Industry, Box 240 53, 104 50 STOCKHOLM **Tel:** 8 506 244 95 **Fax:** 850624499
Titles:
NORDISK ENERGI

CSIDE AB 1710350
JE Mediaproduktion, PL 2178, 760 15 GRÄDDÖ **Tel:** 176 181 90
Titles:
MAGASINSKÄRGÅRD

CU TIDNINGS AB 1629552
Box 4411, 102 69 STOCKHOLM **Tel:** 8 462 02 14 **Fax:** 8 462 02 15
Titles:
CLOSE-UP MAGAZINE

CYKELFRÄMJANDET - CYKLISTERNAS 1793553
Box 47, 250 53 HELSINGBORG **Tel:** 8 545 910 30
Titles:
CYKLING

DÄCKSPECIALISTERNAS SERVICE AB 1773192
c/o Stormen kommunikation, 432 44 VARBERG **Tel:** 340 67 3000
Titles:
DÄCK DEBATT

DAGBLADET SUNDSVALL AB 1789721
Box 466, 851 06 SUNDSVALL **Tel:** 60 66 35 82 **Fax:** 60 61 11 50
Titles:
DAGBLADET, NYA SAMHÄLLET; DAGBLADET.SE
DAGBLADET, NYA SAMHÄLLET; HUVUDREDAKTION

DAGEN 1649903
105 36 STOCKHOLM **Tel:** 8 619 24 00 **Fax:** 86566051
Titles:
DAGEN; DAGEN.SE
IKON1931

DAGENS ARBETE AB 1629926
Dagens Arbete, 105 52 Stockholm, 105 52 STOCKHOLM **Tel:** 8 786 03 00 **Fax:** 8 796 81 59
Titles:
DAGENS ARBETE
DAGENS ARBETE; DAGENSARBETE.SE

DAGENS INDUSTRI 1790235
Torsgatan 21, 113 90 STOCKHOLM **Tel:** 8 573 650 50
Titles:
DAGENS INDUSTRI; DI.SE

DAGENS INDUSTRI AB 1789278
Torsgatan 21, 113 90 STOCKHOLM **Tel:** 8 573 650 00 **Fax:** 8 57365031
Titles:
DAGENS INDUSTRI

DAGENS MEDIA SVERIGE AB 1628493
Postadress: Dagens Media, 106 12 STOCKHOLM **Tel:** 8 545 222 00
Titles:
DAGENS MEDIA
DAGENS MEDIA; WEBB

DAGENS MEDICIN SVERIGE AB 1790061
Box 4612, 116 91 STOCKHOLM **Tel:** 8 545 123 00 **Fax:** 8 411 01 02
Titles:
DAGENS MEDICIN
DAGENS MEDICIN; DAGENSMEDICIN.SE

DAGENS NYHETER AB 1789276
Gjörwellsgatan 30, 105 15 STOCKHOLM **Tel:** 8 738 10 00 **Fax:** 8 738 21 90
Titles:
DAGENS NYHETER
DAGENS NYHETER; DN.SE
DAGENS NYHETER; FAMILJEREDAKTIONEN

DALA DEMOKRATEN 1789715
Box 825, 791 29 FALUN **Tel:** 23 475 00
Titles:
DALA-DEMOKRATEN

DALARNAS TIDNINGAR 1745376
Box 29, 781 21 BORLÄNGE **Tel:** 243 644 08 **Fax:** 243 644 61
Titles:
BORLÄNGE TIDNING
FALU KURIREN
NYA LUDVIKA TIDNING
SÖDRA DALARNES TIDNING

DALARNAS TIDNINGAR AB 1789719
Strandgatan 28, 792 30 MORA **Tel:** 250 59 24 20 **Fax:** 250 59 24 45
Titles:
MORA TIDNING

DALSLANDSKURIREN 1628822
Storgatan 20, 460 65 BRÅLANDA **Tel:** 521 310 75 **Fax:** 521 310 75
Titles:
DALSLANDSKURIREN

DANSTIDNINGEN I STOCKHOLM EKONOMISK FÖRENING 1643383
Box 2133, 103 14 STOCKHOLM **Tel:** 703 34 69 98
Titles:
DANSTIDNINGEN
DANSTIDNINGEN; DANSTIDNINGEN.SE

DATAINSPEKTIONEN 1747910
Box 8114, 104 20 STOCKHOLM **Tel:** 8 657 61 00 **Fax:** 8 652 86 52
Titles:
INTEGRITET I FOKUS

DAUS TRYCK & MEDIA 1793530
Svenska Bordtennisförbundet, 171 41 SOLNA **Tel:** 8 627 46 54 **Fax:** 8932733
Titles:
PINGIS

DAUS TRYCK & MEDIA AB 1653583
Svenska Skidförbundet Riksskidstadion, 791 19 FALUN **Tel:** 23 874 40 **Fax:** 23 874 41
Titles:
SKI & BOARD MAGAZINE
TIDNINGEN HOCKEY

DE HANDIKAPPADES RIKSFÖRBUND 1790459
Box 47305, 100 74 STOCKHOLM **Tel:** 8 685 80 70 **Fax:** 86456541
Titles:
SVENSK HANDIKAPPTIDSKRIFT, SHT

DELS TIDSKRIFTER AB 1752910
c/o Söderbergh, Lädersättravägen 15, 176 70 JÄRFÄLLA **Tel:** 8 584 904 32
Titles:
PARNASS

DEMENSFÖRBUNDET 1790470
Lundagatan 42A, 5tr., 117 27 STOCKHOLM **Tel:** 8 658 99 20 **Fax:** 86586068
Titles:
DEMENSFORUM

DG COMMUNICATIONS 1792087
DG Communications, 111 57 STOCKHOLM **Tel:** 8 797 03 00 **Fax:** 87975315
Titles:
SCANORAMA

DIAKONIA. 1628184
172 99 SUNDBYBERG **Tel:** 8 453 69 00 **Fax:** 8 453 69 29
Titles:
DELA MED

DIK-FÖRBUNDET 1629371
Box 760, 131 24 NACKA **Tel:** 8 466 24 00
Titles:
DIK-FORUM

DIREKTPRESS 1789679
421 31 VÄSTRA FRÖLUNDA **Tel:** 317 205 516 **Fax:** 314 954 00
Titles:
ÖRGRYTE-HÄRLANDA TIDNING

DIVER GROUP SCANDINAVIA APS 1629081
Fjordvägen 4, 439 31 ONSALA **Tel:** 300 600 77 **Fax:** 0 7026 9015
Titles:
TIDNINGEN DYK
TIDNINGEN DYK; DYK.NET

DJURSKYDDET SVERIGE 1649775
Rökerigatan 19, 12162 JOHANNESHOV **Tel:** 8 673 35 11 **Fax:** 8 673 36 66
Titles:
DJURSKYDDET

DORIAN FÖRLAG AB 1758892
Box 75 92, 103 93 STOCKHOLM **Tel:** 8 715 06 80
Titles:
DORIAN MAGAZINE

DRIVA EGET AB 1745673
Poppelvägen 55, 135 52 TYRESÖ **Tel:** 8 798 81 26
Titles:
DRIVA EGET

DYSLEXIFÖRBUNDET FMLS 1743543
c/o FMLS, Solnavägen 100, 169 51 SOLNA **Tel:** 8 665 17 00 **Fax:** 86607977
Titles:
LÄS OCH SKRIV

E-BUTIK I NORDEN AB 1773193
Erstagatan 26, 116 36 STOCKHOLM **Tel:** 8 410 097 50 **Fax:** 86475174
Titles:
NÄTSMART

EFS - EVANGELISKA FOSTERLANDS-STIFTELSEN 1732732
EFS, Kyrkans hus, 751 70 UPPSALA **Tel:** 18 16 98 00 **Fax:** 18 16 98 01
Titles:
EFS.NU

EGMONT KÄRNAN AB 1627643
Box 702 72, 107 22 STOCKHOLM **Tel:** 8 519 384 00 **Fax:** 8 519 384 40
Titles:
DJURTIDNINGEN PETS
GO GIRL
GOAL
JULIA
JULIA SPECIAL
OKEJ
PRO HOCKEY

EGMONT TIDSKRIFTER 1793401
Box 200, 141 38 STOCKHOLM **Tel:** 701 77 21 69
Titles:
MANOLO
MODETTE.SE

EGMONT TIDSKRIFTER AB 1789610
Egmont Tidskrifter AB, 205 07 MALMO **Tel:** 40 38 52 00
Titles:
FÅR JAG LOV
HEMMETS JOURNAL
HEMMETS JOURNAL; WWW.HEMMETSJOURNAL.SE
KING MAGAZINE

EIO:S MEDLEMSSERVICE AB 1629096
Box 17537, 118 91 STOCKHOLM **Tel:** 8 762 75 00 **Fax:** 86684014
Titles:
ELINSTALLATÖREN
ELINSTALLATÖREN; ELINSTALLATOREN.SE

EK. FÖR. NYA TEATERTIDNINGEN 1789965
Box 4066, 102 62 STOCKHOLM **Tel:** 8 84 92 87
Titles:
TEATERTIDNINGEN

EKOLOGISKA LANTBRUKARNA 1793704
Sågargatan 10A, 753 18 UPPSALA **Tel:** 18 10 10 06 **Fax:** 18101066
Titles:
EKOLOGISKT LANTBRUK

EKON - HANDELSHÖGSKOLAN I GÖTEBORG STUDENTKÅR 1630045
Box 680, 405 30 GÖTEBORG **Tel:** 31 711 13 83
Titles:
EKON

EKONOMEDIA AFFÄRSPRESS AB 1639843
Sjögatan 23, 852 34 SUNDSVALL **Tel:** 60 16 21 45 **Fax:** 60 17 54 36
Titles:
NÄRINGSLIV AFFÄRSTIDNINGEN I DITT LÄN

EKSJÖ PUBLIKATION AB 1744850
Box 101, 575 21 EKSJÖ **Tel:** 381 130 81
Fax: 381 130 84
Titles:
RACE MC-SPORT

ELECTRONIC PRESS I HUDDINGE AB 1629990
Box 178, 444 22 STENUNGSUND
Tel: 303 77 04 90
Titles:
ELEKTOR

ELEKTRONIK I NORDEN AB 1627439
Box 91, 182 11 DANDERYD **Tel:** 8 445 20 70
Fax: 8 445 20 77
Titles:
ELEKTRONIK I NORDEN
ELEKTRONIK I NORDEN; ELEKTRONIKINORDEN.COM

ELEKTRONIKTIDNINGEN SVERIGE AB 1710642
Katarinavägen 19, 1tr, 116 45 STOCKHOLM
Tel: 8 644 51 20 **Fax:** 8 644 51 21
Titles:
ELEKTRONIKTIDNINGEN
ELEKTRONIKTIDNINGEN; ETN.SE

ELEKTRONIKVÄRLDEN FÖRLAG AB 1791262
Box 529, 371 23 KARLSKRONA **Tel:** 455 30 80 40
Titles:
LJUD & BILD/ELEKTRONIKVÄRLDEN

ELLESTRÖMS FÖRLAG 1756194
Fredsgatan 6, 222 20 LUND **Tel:** 46 32 32 95
Titles:
LYRIKVÄNNEN

EMMA PUBLISHING AB 1639871
Repslagargatan 17 B, 11846 STOCKHOLM
Tel: 8 545 064 00 **Fax:** 8 6795710
Titles:
GRIP MAGASIN (MALMÖ AVIATION'S MAGAZINE)
RES
TRAVEL NEWS; TRAVELNEWS.SE

EMMABODA TIDNING AB 1789673
392 33 KALMAR **Tel:** 471 339 84
Titles:
EMMABODA TIDNING

ENABYGDENS REKLAM AB 1791269
Box 8, 746 21 BÅLSTA **Tel:** 171 46 81 50
Fax: 171 46 70 17
Titles:
BÅLSTA-UPPLANDS-BRO-BLADET

ENERGICA FÖRLAG AB 1629714
Turistvägen 504, 794 93 ORSA **Tel:** 250 55 20 05
Fax: 250 431 91
Titles:
FREE

ENERGIMYNDIGHETEN 1790114
Energimyndigheten, Box 310, 631 04 ESKILSTUNA **Tel:** 16 544 20 00 **Fax:** 165442099
Titles:
ENERGIVÄRLDEN

ENKÖPINGS-POSTENS AB 1629520
Box 918, 745 25 ENKÖPING **Tel:** 171 41 46 55
Fax: 171 44 04 01
Titles:
ENKÖPINGS-POSTEN
ENKÖPINGS-POSTEN; EPOSTEN.SE

ENS 2000 1627724
ENS 2000, Box 9003, 700 09 ÖREBRO
Tel: 19 27 10 10 **Fax:** 19 27 05 12
Titles:
RESPONS FÖRETAGSTIDNING
RESPONS UNGDOMSTIDNING

ENZYM KOMMUNIKATION EK FÖR. 1627540
Andra Långgatan 53, 413 27 GÖTEBORG
Tel: 31 42 12 46
Titles:
NÄRINGSMEDICINSK TIDSKRIFT

EPOK MEDIA AB 1790394
Box 5575, 114 85 STOCKHOLM **Tel:** 8 545 684 00
Fax: 86627350
Titles:
PERSONAL & LEDARSKAP

ERIK OCH ASTA SUNDINS STIFTELSE 1629919
601 83 NORRKÖPING **Tel:** 11 20 00 00
Fax: 11 20 01 40
Titles:
NORRKÖPINGS TIDNINGAR
NORRKÖPINGS TIDNINGAR; NT.SE

ERLANDSSON & BLOOM AB 1791043
c/o Erlandsson & Bloom, 113 27 STOCKHOLM
Tel: 8 648 49 00
Titles:
DOKTORN

ESBRI 1792053
ESBRI, Saltmätargatan 9, 113 59 STOCKHOLM
Tel: 8 458 78 00
Titles:
ENTRÉ - FORSKNING OM ENTREPRENÖRSKAP OCH SMÅFÖRETAG

ESKILSTUNA-KURIREN AB 1629953
Box 120, 631 02 ESKILSTUNA **Tel:** 16 15 60 00
Titles:
ESKILSTUNA-KURIREN / STRENGNÄS TIDNING
ESKILSTUNA-KURIREN / STRENGNÄS TIDNING; WEBB

ESTLANDSSVENSKARNAS KULTURFÖRENING (SOV) 1628621
Roslagsgatan 57, 113 54 STOCKHOLM
Tel: 8 612 75 99 **Fax:** 8 612 77 85
Titles:
KUSTBON

ETC FÖRLAG 1746035
Box 4403, 102 68 STOCKHOLM **Tel:** 8 410 357 00
Fax: 8 410 357 01
Titles:
KLOKA HEM

ETC FÖRLAG AB 1735343
Box 4403, 102 68 STOCKHOLM **Tel:** 8 410 357 00
Fax: 8 410 357 01
Titles:
DAGENS ETC
ETC.NU
ETC.SE

EVA ABRAHAMSSON 1790420
Bonnier Tidskrifter AB, 105 44 STOCKHOLM
Tel: 8 736 52 00 **Fax:** 8 34 11 38
Titles:
SKÖNA HEM - SKAPA STILEN

EVANGELIIPRESS FÖRLAGS AB 1790598
Box 220 10, 702 02 OREBRO **Tel:** 19 16 54 20
Fax: 19124160
Titles:
HEMMETS VÄN

EVANGELISKA FOSTERLANDS STIFTELSEN 1629699
751 70 UPPSALA **Tel:** 18 16 98 28 **Fax:** 18 16 98 02
Titles:
BUDBÄRAREN - EFS MISSIONSTIDNING

EXAKT MEDIA AB 1791394
Box 4034, 102 61 STOCKHOLM **Tel:** 8 455 67 70
Titles:
NYHETSBREVET TELEKOMNYHETERNA

EXPRESSEN 1789516
Gjörwellsgatan 30, 105 16 STOCKHOLM
Tel: 8 738 30 00
Titles:
EXPRESSEN; GI&HÄLSA

FABAS 1775503
Förlags AB Albinsson & Sjöberg, Box 529, 371 29 KARLSKRONA
Titles:
SOLDAT & TEKNIK

FACILITIES NORDEN AB 1790135
Box 2076, 403 12 GOTEBORG **Tel:** 31 704 45 80
Fax: 31136618
Titles:
FACILITIES

FACKFÖRBUNDET ST 1640061
Box 5044, 102 41 STOCKHOLM **Tel:** 8 790 51 00
Fax: 8 790 52 86
Titles:
ST PRESS
ST PRESS; STPRESS.SE

FAIRWAY GOLF MAGAZINE AB 1732701
Skonertgränd 9, 260 93 TOREKOV
Tel: 431 152 50
Titles:
GOLFBLADET

FAKTAPRESS AB 1790581
Backebogatan 3, 129 40 HAGERSTEN
Tel: 8 410 056 36
Titles:
FÖRÄLDRAKRAFT

FÄLTBIOLOGERNA RIKSFÖRENINGEN 1628430
Brunnsg. 62, 802 52 Gävle, 802 52 GÄVLE
Tel: 26 61 06 70 **Fax:** 26 22 22 073
Titles:
FÄLTBIOLOGEN

FALU OCH BORLÄNGE STUDENTKÅRER 1747344
Åsögatan 37, 791 71 FALUN **Tel:** 23 77 71 60
Fax: 23 77 71 67
Titles:
KELEN

FAMILJELIV MEDIA AB 1790612
Familjeliv Media AB, Valhallavägen 117, 115 31 STOCKHOLM **Tel:** 8 473 33 60
Titles:
FAMILJELIV

FAMILJEMEDIA AB 1789608
c/o Lindberg, Bastugatan 27 3 tr, 118 25 STOCKHOLM **Tel:** 705 72 97 17
Titles:
MEDBARN

FAR SRS 1737251
Box 6417, 113 82 STOCKHOLM **Tel:** 8 506 112 40
Fax: 8 506 112 44
Titles:
BALANS
BALANS; TIDSKRIFTENBALANS.SE

FAR SRS FÖRLAG AB 1793867
Box 6497, 113 82 STOCKHOLM **Tel:** 8 506 112 60
Fax: 850611258
Titles:
NYTT FRÅN REVISORN

FARMACIFÖRBUNDET 1790454
Västmannagatan 66, 113 25 STOCKHOLM
Tel: 8 31 64 10 **Fax:** 8340808
Titles:
FARMACIFACKET

FASTIGHETSÄGARNA SVERIGE 1790345
Intellecta Corporate, Box 19063, 104 32 STOCKHOLM **Tel:** 8 506 286 00 **Fax:** 8 506 287 00
Titles:
FASTIGHETSTIDNINGEN
FASTIGHETSTIDNINGEN; FASTIGHETSTIDNINGEN.SE

FASTIGHETSANSTÄLLDAS FÖRBUND 1790122
Box 70446, 107 25 STOCKHOLM **Tel:** 8 696 11 50
Fax: 8 20 59 89
Titles:
FASTIGHETSFOLKET
FASTIGHETSFOLKET; FASTIGHETSFOLKET.SE

FASTIGO AB 1790478
Box 70397, 107 24 STOCKHOLM **Tel:** 8 676 69 00
Fax: 8207575
Titles:
FASTIGO

FIGHTER MAGAZINE AB 1790986
Karl Gustavsgatan 49, 411 31 GOTEBORG
Tel: 31 711 86 00
Titles:
FIGHTER MAGAZINE

FILMBRANSCHENS SAMARBETSKOMMITTÉ 1713009
Dorian Mabb AB, Box 20115, 104 60 STOCKHOLM **Tel:** 8 578 665 00 **Fax:** 8 578 665 19
Titles:
BIOGUIDEN.SE

FINANSFÖRBUNDET 1629986
Box 720, 101 34 STOCKHOLM **Tel:** 8 614 03 00
Fax: 8 614 03 98
Titles:
FINANSVÄRLDEN
FINANSVÄRLDEN; WEBB

FINNVEDEN NU TIDNINGS AB 1738650
Box 111, 331 32 VÄRNAMO **Tel:** 370 69 16 40
Fax: 370 129 86
Titles:
FINNVEDEN NU; WEBB

FINSKA FÖRSAMLINGEN I STOCKHOLM 1628628
Box 2281, 103 17 STOCKHOLM **Tel:** 8 440 82 03
Fax: 8 440 82 01
Titles:
LEVANDE STENAR - ELÄVÄT KIVET

FIRST PUBLISHING AB 1790351
Box 3187, 350 43 VÄXJO **Tel:** 470 76 24 00
Fax: 470 76 24 25
Titles:
DIGITAL FOTO
DIGITAL FOTO; WEBB

FIRST PUBLISHING GROUP 1639855
Box 3187, 350 43 VÄXJÖ **Tel:** 470 76 24 00
Fax: 470 76 24 25
Titles:
ALLT OM PC & TEKNIK

FIRST PUBLISHING GROUP AB 1639827
Box 3187, 350 43 VÄXJÖ **Tel:** 470 76 24 00
Fax: 470762425
Titles:
FIRST POKER
IN TOUCH

FISKE FÖR ALLA AB (ETT FÖRLAG INOM LRF MEDIA AB) 1710381
Bergendorffsgatan 5 B, 652 24 KARLSTAD
Tel: 8 588 366 00
Titles:
ALLT OM FLUGFISKE

FISKE-FEBER AB 1654095
Box 22100, 250 23 HELSINGBORG
Tel: 42 211 22 **Fax:** 42 211 37
Titles:
FISKE-FEBER

FIT MEDIA 1793525
Karlagatan 21, 416 61 GOTEBORG
Tel: 31 40 52 33
Titles:
INNEBANDYMAGAZINET

FITNESS MEDIA I SVERIGE AB 1629653
c/o Forma Publishing Group AB, Box 6151, 102 33 STOCKHOLM **Tel:** 8 30 10 70 **Fax:** 8 30 16 70
Titles:
FITNESS MAGAZINE
FITNESS MAGAZINE; WEBB

FLM MEDIA AB 1744431
Tomtebogatan 3, 1 tr, 113 39 STOCKHOLM
Tel: 705 26 53 45
Titles:
FLM

FL-NET AB 1791267
VILL EJ HA PRESSMEDD. VIA BREV
Tel: 480 42 18 40
Titles:
IT-NYTT.NU

FLYGREVYN FÖRLAGS AB 1628563
Övre Välsta gård, 137 92 TUNGELSTA
Tel: 8 500 379 00 **Fax:** 8 500 379 01
Titles:
FLYGREVYN

FLYGTORGET AB 1650396
Box 3389, 103 68 STOCKHOLM **Tel:** 8 791 94 94
Fax: 8 791 97 99
Titles:
FLYGTORGET AIRMAIL

FMK 1735462
Box 6019, 175 06 Järfälla, 114 37 STOCKHOLM
Tel: 8 761 82 82 **Fax:** 7 046 182 82
Titles:
TRAFIK & MOTOR

FOLKKAMPANJEN MOT KÄRNKRAFT-KÄRNVAPEN 1790121
c/o Folkkampanjen mot Kärnkraft och Kärnvapen, Tegelviksgatan 40, 118 20 STOCKHOLM **Tel:** 8 84 14 90 **Fax:** 8 84 51 81
Titles:
MEDSOLS

FOLKRÖRELSEN NEJ TILL EU 1629677
c/o Torstensson, Rondovägen 312, 142 41 SKOGÅS **Tel:** 8 771 43 79
Titles:
KRITISKA EU-FAKTA

FOLKUNIVERSITETET 1627677
Folkuniversitetet, Box 26152, 100 41 STOCKHOLM **Tel:** 8 679 29 50 **Fax:** 8 678 15 44
Titles:
TIDSKRIFTEN FOLKUNIVERSITETET

FOODWIRE AB 1629821
Box 1011, 444 26 STENUNGSUND
Tel: 303 678 20 **Fax:** 708 10 44 31
Titles:
FOODWIRE.SE

FÖRÄLDRAR OCH BARN AB 1744936
Box 4403, 102 68 STOCKHOLM **Tel:** 8 588 33 848
Fax: 8 428 90 13
Titles:
FÖRÄLDRAR & BARN ATT VARA GRAVID
FÖRÄLDRAR & BARN JUNIOR

FÖRBUNDET BLÖDARSJUKA I SVERIGE 1791732
Box 1386, Sturegatan 4, 5 tr., 172 27 SUNDBYBERG **Tel:** 8 546 405 10 **Fax:** 8 546 405 14
Titles:
GENSVAR

FÖRBUNDET DJURENS RÄTT 1627495
Box 2005, 125 02 ÄLVSJÖ **Tel:** 8 555 914 00
Fax: 8 555 914 50
Titles:
DJURENS RÄTT!

FÖRBUNDET SVERIGES ARBETSTERAPEUTER (SACO) 1630274
Box 760, 131 24 NACKA **Tel:** 8 466 24 40
Fax: 8 466 24 24
Titles:
ARBETSTERAPEUTEN

FORDONS KOMPONENT GRUPPEN AB 1627428
Box 126, 793 23 LEKSAND **Tel:** 247 137 25
Titles:
THE VEHICLE COMPONENT

FÖRENADE ISRAELINSAMLINGEN 1789969
Förenade Israelinsamlingen, Box 5053, 102 42 STOCKHOLM **Tel:** 8 667 67 70 **Fax:** 86637676
Titles:
MENORAH

FÖRENINGEN ARENA 1627718
Drottninggatan 83, 111 60 STOCKHOLM
Tel: 8 789 11 62 **Fax:** 8 411 42 42
Titles:
ARENA
ARENA; WEBB
DAGENS ARENA

FÖRENINGEN BANG 1790060
Bang, Bergsundsgatan 25, 117 37 STOCKHOLM
Tel: 8 15 71 75 **Fax:** 8 15 94 72
Titles:
BANG

FÖRENINGEN BEBYGGELSEHISTORISK TIDSKRIFT 1629643
Konstvetenskapliga institutionen, Stockholms Univ., 106 91 STOCKHOLM **Tel:** 8 16 33 88
Fax: 8 16 14 07
Titles:
BEBYGGELSEHISTORISK TIDSKRIFT

FÖRENINGEN CORAS VÄNNER 1653106
Bengt Ekehjelmsgatan 2B, 118 54 STOCKHOLM
Tel: 8 668 74 92
Titles:
CORA, EN TIDNING MED HJÄRTA

FÖRENINGEN DIALOGER 1792010
c/o Santerus Förlag, Sturbrunnsgatan 56, 6 tr, 113 49 STOCKHOLM **Tel:** 8 30 34 62
Titles:
DIALOGER

FÖRENINGEN FJÄRDE VÄRLDEN 1792025
Box 16320, 103 26 STOCKHOLM **Tel:** 8 84 49 15
Fax: 8201252
Titles:
FJÄRDE VÄRLDEN

FÖRENINGEN FLOTTANS MÄN 1686946
Teatergatan 3 tr, 111 48 STOCKHOLM
Tel: 8 678 09 08 **Fax:** 8 678 09 08
Titles:
FLOTTANS MÄN

FÖRENINGEN FOLKET I BILD / KULTURFRONT 1629870
Bondegatan 69, 116 34 STOCKHOLM
Tel: 8 644 50 32 **Fax:** 855695035
Titles:
FOLKET I BILD / KULTURFRONT
FOLKET I BILD / KULTURFRONT; FIB.SE

FÖRENINGEN FÖR ORIENTALISKA STUDIER 1628978
Orientaliska Studier, Stockholms Universitet, Kräftriket 4B, 106 91 STOCKHOLM
Tel: 8 16 17 75 **Fax:** 8 15 54 64
Titles:
ORIENTALISKA STUDIER

FÖRENINGEN FÖR SAMHÄLLSPLANERING, FFS 1627616
Mats Johan Lundström, AQ Arkitekter, Box 235, 631 03 ESKILSTUNA **Fax:** 16 14 01 55
Titles:
TIDSKRIFTEN PLAN

FÖRENINGEN FÖR STUDIA NEOPHIOLOGICA 1629352
Taylor & Francis AB, Box 3255, 103 65 STOCKHOLM **Tel:** 8 440 80 40 **Fax:** 8 440 80 50
Titles:
STUDIA NEOPHILOLOGICA

FÖRENINGEN FÖR SVENSK KULTURHISTORIA 1792015
Finngatan 8, 223 62 LUND **Tel:** 46 29 13 14
Fax: 462229849
Titles:
RIG, KULTURHISTORISK TIDSKRIFT

FÖRENINGEN FÖR SVENSKAR I VÄRLDEN 1790374
Box 5501, 114 85 STOCKHOLM **Tel:** 8 783 81 81
Fax: 86605264
Titles:
SVENSKAR I VÄRLDEN

FÖRENINGEN FÖR TIDIG MUSIK 1629899
Box 16344, 103 26 STOCKHOLM **Tel:** 8 407 17 23
Fax: 8 407 17 27
Titles:
TIDIG MUSIK

FÖRENINGEN FÖR UTGIVANDE AV TIDSKRIFT FÖR LITT.VET. 1654960
Box 200, 405 30 GÖTEBORG **Tel:** 31 786 45 59
Fax: 31 786 44 60
Titles:
TIDSKRIFT FÖR LITTERATURVETENSKAP

FÖRENINGEN GRÄVANDE JOURNALISTER 1790054
Grävande Journalister, c/o JMK, Box 27861, 115 93 STOCKHOLM **Tel:** 8 16 44 25 **Fax:** 8 31 44 25
Titles:
SCOOP

FÖRENINGEN HÄFTEN FÖR KRITISKA STUDIER 1792041
c/o Fredriksson, Tulegatan 25 2 tr ög, 113 53 STOCKHOLM **Tel:** 8 673 22 07 **Fax:** 8 673 22 07
Titles:
HÄFTEN FÖR KRITISKA STUDIER

FÖRENINGEN KARAVAN 1627561
Box 17131, 104 62 STOCKHOLM **Tel:** 8 442 02 13
Titles:
KARAVAN - LITTERÄR TIDSKRIFT PÅ RESA MELLAN KULTURER

FÖRENINGEN KRITISK UTBILDNINGSTIDSKRIFT 1627323
Andra Långgatan 20, 413 28 GÖTEBORG
Tel: 31 12 76 40 **Fax:** 31 14 37 77
Titles:
KRUT - KRITISK UTBILDNINGSTIDSKRIFT

FÖRENINGEN LAMBDA NORDICA 1629385
c/o Göran Söderström, 115 21 STOCKHOLM
Tel: 704 63 17 40
Titles:
LAMBDA NORDICA

FÖRENINGEN LÄRARE I RELIGIONKUNSKAP, FLR 1652898
C/o Christina Osbeck, Ängskogsvägen 35, 656 71 SKATTÄRR **Tel:** 5 486 41 76
Titles:
RELIGION & LIVSFRÅGOR

FÖRENINGEN MUNSKÄNKARNA 1793676
Box 92184, 120 09 STOCKHOLM **Tel:** 8 30 10 43
Fax: 8301152
Titles:
MUNSKÄNKEN MED VINJOURNALEN

FÖRENINGEN NORDEN 1792785
Box 12707, 112 94 STOCKHOLM
Tel: 8 506 113 00 **Fax:** 850611320
Titles:
NORDENS TIDNING

FÖRENINGEN ORDFRONT 1793574
Box 17506, 118 91 STOCKHOLM **Tel:** 8 462 44 00
Fax: 8 462 44 90
Titles:
ORDFRONT MAGASIN

FÖRENINGEN POMONA 1627372
Box 19074, 104 32 STOCKHOLM **Tel:** 8 612 10 49
Fax: 8 612 10 77
Titles:
TIDSKRIFTEN 10TAL

FÖRENINGEN REKRYTERINGSGRUPPEN 1790458
Vanadisvägen 21, 113 46 STOCKHOLM
Tel: 8 545 472 00 **Fax:** 8 545 472 10
Titles:
KICK

FÖRENINGEN SARA 1793791
Gångbrogatan 2, 372 37 RONNEBY
Tel: 457 267 49
Titles:
2000-TALETS VETENSKAP

FÖRENINGEN SKOGEN 1628745
Box 1159, 111 81 STOCKHOLM **Tel:** 8 412 15 00
Fax: 8 412 15 10
Titles:
SKOGEN

FÖRENINGEN SOCIALMEDICINSK TIDSKRIFT 1627689
Box 7245, 402 35 GÖTEBORG **Tel:** 31 16 09 80
Titles:
SOCIALMEDICINSK TIDSKRIFT

FÖRENINGEN STIFTELSEN SKÄRGÅRDSBÅTEN 1629132
Nybrogatan 76, 114 41 STOCKHOLM
Tel: 8 662 89 02
Titles:
SKÄRGÅRDSBÅTEN

FÖRENINGEN SVENSK FORM 1793581
Arvinius Förlag AB, Box 6040, 102 31 STOCKHOLM **Tel:** 8 32 00 15 **Fax:** 8320095
Titles:
FORM

FÖRENINGEN SVENSKA KOMMUNALEKONOMER (KEF). 1791290
Odinsgatan 20 A, 411 03 GOTEBORG
Tel: 31 13 02 56
Titles:
KOMMUNAL EKONOMI

FÖRENINGEN SVENSKA TECKNARE 1790452
Svenska Tecknare, Götgatan 48, 118 26 STOCKHOLM **Tel:** 8 556 029 18 **Fax:** 855602919
Titles:
TECKNAREN

FÖRENINGEN SVERIGES SÄNDAREAMATÖRER 1628707
FSS, Box 45, 191 21 SOLLENTUNA
Tel: 8 585 702 73 **Fax:** 8 585 702 74
Titles:
QTC AMATÖRRADIO

FÖRENINGEN SVERIGES VÄGINGENJÖRER 1628368
Roxx Media Sverige, Box 164, 598 23 VIMMERBY **Tel:** 793 15 **Fax:** 793 49
Titles:
VÄGMÄSTAREN

FÖRENINGEN TIDSKRIFT FÖR GENUSVETENSKAP 1752899
Linköpings Universitet, Linköpings Universitet, 581 83 LINKÖPING **Tel:** 1 328 2239
Titles:
TIDSKRIFT FÖR GENUSVETENSKAP

FÖRENINGEN VALÖR 1793805
c/o Konstvetenskapliga institutionen, Box 630, 751 26 UPPSALA **Tel:** 18 471 58 35
Fax: 184712892
Titles:
VALÖR, KONSTVETENSKAPLIGA STUDIER

FÖRENINGEN VÄRMLÄNDSK KULTUR 1740174
Verkstadsgatan 1, 652 19 KARLSTAD
Tel: 54 10 06 19 **Fax:** 54100619
Titles:
VÄRMLÄNDSK KULTUR

FÖRENINGEN VERDANDI 1790480
Slakthusgatan 9, 121 62 STOCKHOLM
Tel: 8 642 28 80 **Fax:** 86422820
Titles:
VERDANDISTEN

FÖRETAGARFÖRBUNDET 1732737
Gamla Vägen 3, 262 43 ÄNGELHOLM
Tel: 20 760 761 **Fax:** 43183185
Titles:
FRIA FÖRETAGARE

FÖRETAGARNA 1653158
Spoon Publishing AB, Kungstensgatan 21 B, 113 57 STOCKHOLM **Tel:** 8 406 17 00 **Fax:** 8 442 96 39
Titles:
FÖRETAGAREN
FÖRETAGAREN; FORETAGARNA.SE

FÖRLAG AB ALBINSSON OCH SJÖBERG 1627621
Box 529, 371 23 KARLSKRONA **Tel:** 455 33 53 25
Fax: 455 31 17 15
Titles:
NOSTALGIA

FÖRLAG AB FRI TID 1752907
142 43 SKOGÅS **Tel:** 8 771 56 00 **Fax:** 8 771 56 00
Titles:
HUSBILEN TEST

FÖRLAGET AKTUELL SÄKERHET CFSI AB 1649897
Skeppargatan 27, 114 52 STOCKHOLM
Tel: 8 442 86 30 **Fax:** 86621180
Titles:
AKTUELL SÄKERHET
AKTUELL SÄKERHET; AKTUELLSAKERHET.SE

FÖRLAGET APÉRITIF AB 1790344
Skeppargatan 27, 114 52 STOCKHOLM
Tel: 8 442 86 30 **Fax:** 86621180
Titles:
APÉRITIF
APÉRITIF; APERITIFMAG.SE

FÖRLAGET DAGENS SEKRETERARE AB 1649772
Skeppargatan 27, 114 52 STOCKHOLM
Tel: 8 442 86 30 **Fax:** 8 662 11 80
Titles:
DAGENS SEKRETERARE

FÖRLAGET I KAMPAVALL 1744660
Kampavall, 540 17 LERDALA **Tel:** 511 822 30
Fax: 511 822 38
Titles:
HUNDLIV

FÖRLAGET TAXI IDAG AB 1649898
Skeppargatan 27, 114 52 STOCKHOLM
Tel: 708 88 96 07 **Fax:** 8 662 11 80
Titles:
TAXI IDAG

FÖRLAGET VIN & BAR JOURNALEN AB 1793363
Skeppargatan 27, 114 52 STOCKHOLM
Tel: 8 442 86 30 **Fax:** 86621180
Titles:
VIN&BARJOURNALEN
VIN&BARJOURNALEN; VINOCHBAR.SE

FÖRLAGS AB ALBINSSON & SJÖBERG 1628218
Box 529, 371 23 KARLSKRONA **Tel:** 455 33 53 30
Fax: 455 31 17 15
Titles:
ALLT OM MC
BILSPORT
BILSPORT BÖRSEN
BILSPORT GATBILAR.SE
BILSPORT JUNIOR
LJUD & BILD/ELEKTRONIKVÄRLDEN; EV.SE
TRAILER
TRAILER; TRAILER.SE
TRUCKING SCANDINAVIA

FÖRLAGS AB BYGG & TEKNIK 1627473
Box 19099, 104 32 STOCKHOLM **Tel:** 8 612 17 50
Fax: 8 612 54 81
Titles:
BYGG & TEKNIK

FÖRLAGS AB FLUGFISKE I NORDEN 1791178
Box 22032, Thommy Gustavsson / Flugfiske i Norden, 702 02 ÖREBRO **Tel:** 19 22 33 03
Titles:
FLUGFISKE I NORDEN

FÖRLAGS AB VERKSTADSTIDNINGEN 1627399
Box 2082, 169 02 SOLNA **Tel:** 8 514 934 10
Fax: 851493419
Titles:
AUTOMATION
BYGGAREN
JÄRN-BYGG-FÄRG, TIDSKRIFT FÖR FACKHANDELN
VERKSTADSTIDNINGEN

FÖRLAGS AB VVS 1790120
Box 104, 301 04 HALMSTAD **Tel:** 35 10 41 50
Fax: 35 18 65 09
Titles:
ENERGIMAGASINET
ENERGIMAGASINET; ENERGIMAGASINET.COM

FORMA PUBLISHING GROUP 1789262
Budadress: Hälsingegatan 49, Forma Publishing Group, Box 6630, 113 82 STOCKHOLM
Tel: 8 728 24 66 **Fax:** 8 545 703 49
Titles:
HÄLSA - FÖR KROPP OCH SJÄL I BALANS
HUS & HEM
ICA-KURIREN
ICA-KURIREN; ICAKURIREN.SE
ICANYHETER
MARKET
RESTAURANGVÄRLDEN

FORMAS 1793679
Box 1206, 111 82 STOCKHOLM **Tel:** 8 775 40 11
Titles:
MILJÖFORSKNING

FORSA, FÖRBUNDET FÖR FORSKNING I SOCIALT ARBE 1793798
Institutionen för socialt arbete, Box 720, 405 30 GÖTEBORG **Tel:** 31 773 1614
Titles:
SOCIALVETENSKAPLIG TIDSKRIFT

FORSKNINGSFÖRLAGET I GÖTEBORG AB 1793793
Drottninggatan 9, 411 14 GÖTEBORG
Tel: 31 701 07 30 **Fax:** 31 701 07 74
Titles:
FORSKNING

FÖRSVARETS CIVILA TJÄNSTEMANNAFÖRBUND 1627577
Box 5328, 102 47 STOCKHOLM **Tel:** 8 402 40 00
Fax: 8 20 56 92
Titles:
OM FÖRSVARSFÖRBUNDET

FORTBILDNING AB 1790937
Box 34, 171 11 SOLNA **Tel:** 8 545 453 30
Titles:
FÖRSKOLETIDNINGEN

FORTBILDNINGS FÖRLAGET 1628922
Fortbildning AB Box 34, 171 11 SOLNA
Tel: 8 545 453 30 **Fax:** 8 545 453 49
Titles:
ÄLDREOMSORG

FORTBILDNINGSFÖRLAGET AB 1790938
Box 34, 171 11 SOLNA **Tel:** 8 545 453 30
Titles:
GRUNDSKOLETIDNINGEN

FORUM AID FÖRLAG AB 1743614
Strandvägen 19, 114 56 STOCKHOLM
Tel: 8 555 400 00 **Fax:** 855540074
Titles:
FORUM AID

FPG MEDIA AB 1791058
FPG Media AB, Wallingatan 12, 111 60 STOCKHOLM **Tel:** 8 456 34 60 **Fax:** 8 456 34 72
Titles:
FOKUS
FOKUS; FOKUS.SE

FRÄLSNINGSARMÉNS FÖRLAGS AB 1627590
Box 5090, 102 42 STOCKHOLM **Tel:** 8 562 282 00
Fax: 8 562 283 97
Titles:
STRIDSROPET

FRAMTIDSUTVECKLING 1790605
Box 1207, 131 27 NACKA STRAND
Tel: 8 545 424 50 **Fax:** 8 729 00 75
Titles:
YH-GUIDEN

FRAMTIDSUTVECKLING AB 1790409
Box 1207, 131 52 NACKA STRAND
Tel: 8 545 424 50 **Fax:** 8 729 00 75
Titles:
GYMNASIEGUIDEN

FRIA MODERATA STUDENTFÖRBUNDET 1793614
c/o FMSF, Box 2294, 103 17 STOCKHOLM
Tel: 8 791 50 05
Titles:
SVENSK LINJE

FRIDA FÖRLAG 1793637
Frida Förlag, Hammarby kajväg 18, 120 30 STOCKHOLM **Tel:** 8 587 481 00
Titles:
GLITTER

FRIDA FÖRLAG AB 1789272
Frida Förlag AB, Hammarby Kajväg 18, 120 30 STOCKHOLM **Tel:** 8 587 481 00
Titles:
FRIDA
FRIDA SPECIAL
FRIDA; WEBB
GLAZE
SOLO
VECKANS NU

FRIHET MEDIA EKONOMISK FÖRENING 1762618
Box 115 44, 100 61 STOCKHOLM
Tel: 8 714 48 00 **Fax:** 8 714 95 08
Titles:
FRIHET

FRILANSRIKS INOM SVENSKA JOURNALISTFÖRBUNDET 1629550
c/o Garbo Reportage, Katarina Bangata 48, 116 39 STOCKHOLM
Titles:
FRILANSJOURNALISTEN

FRILUFTSFRÄMJANDET 1627538
Instrumentsvägen 14, 126 53 HÄGERSTEN
Tel: 8 447 44 40 **Fax:** 8 447 44 44
Titles:
FRILUFTSLIV - I ALLA VÄDER

FRIVILLIGA SKYTTERÖRELSEN 1628709
Harvens väg 11, 820 77 GNARP **Tel:** 652 240 60
Fax: 652 240 60
Titles:
SVENSK SKYTTESPORT

FUZZ MEDIA AB 1628518
414 63 GÖTEBORG **Tel:** 31 711 68 06
Fax: 31 711 68 07
Titles:
FUZZ

FWT PUBLISHING AB 1791173
Box 302 10, 104 25 STOCKHOLM
Tel: 8 505 301 00 **Fax:** 8 505 301 01
Titles:
GOURMET

G EKSTRÖMS FÖRLAG AB 1749707
Box 462, 581 05 LINKÖPING **Tel:** 13 31 41 75
Fax: 13143849
Titles:
YTFORUM
YTFORUM; WEBB

GALAGO FÖRLAG 1792013
Box 17506, 118 91 STOCKHOLM **Tel:** 8 462 44 00
Fax: 8 462 44 90
Titles:
GALAGO

GAMEZ 1630025
Hamngatan 10, 831 31 ÖSTERSUND
Tel: 63 10 11 23
Titles:
GAMEREACTOR MAGAZINE
GAMEREACTOR MAGAZINE; WEBB

GATE REPORT MEDIA AB 1793899
Mediafabriken, 111 27 STOCKHOLM
Tel: 8 508 807 78 **Fax:** 8 587 075 01
Titles:
GATE REPORT

GÄVLE TIDNINGAR AB 1745212
Box 367, 801 05 GÄVLE **Tel:** 26 15 96 78
Fax: 26661443
Titles:
NÖJESMIX

GEFLE DAGBLAD 1789548
Box 367, 801 05 GÄVLE **Tel:** 26 15 96 00
Titles:
GEFLE DAGBLAD; GD.SE

GEFLE DAGBLADS AB 1789716
Box 367, 801 05 GÄVLE **Tel:** 26 15 96 00
Titles:
GEFLE DAGBLAD

GENBERG & CO AB 1737565
Örnaberga Gård, 272 94 SIMRISHAMN
Tel: 414 235 80 **Fax:** 41423125
Titles:
GALOPPMAGASINET

GENERAL MOTORS SVERIGE 1757768
Box 101, 371 22 KARLSKRONA **Tel:** 455 36 25 18
Fax: 455 36 25 01
Titles:
SAAB MAGAZINE

GEOLOGISKA FÖRENINGEN 1748450
c/o Qi-Media AB, Gjuterigatan 9, 553 18
JÖNKÖPING **Tel:** 708 20 50 10
Titles:
GEOLOGISKT FORUM

GETAWARE EKONOMISK FÖRENING 1791110
House of Win-Win, Tredje Låggatan 13B, 413 03
GOTEBORG **Tel:** 31242426
Titles:
CAMINO

GISAB 1790067
Tunprint AB, Box 457, 633 42 ESKILSTUNA
Tel: 16 200 30 20 **Fax:** 510 087
Titles:
SMÉJOURNALEN

GISAB (GRATIS TIDNINGAR I SVERIGE AB) 1790940
Östra Bangatan 26, 703 61 OREBRO
Tel: 19 17 07 80 **Fax:** 19 12 83 20
Titles:
ÖREBROAR'N

AB GJUTERIINFORMATION I JÖNKÖPING 1793507
Box 2033, 550 02 JÖNKÖPING **Tel:** 36 301 217
Fax: 36 16 68 66
Titles:
GJUTERIET

GKSS 1629545
GKSS Box 5039, 426 05 VÄSTRA FRÖLUNDA
Tel: 31 29 90 40
Titles:
SEGLARBLADET

GLASBRANSCHFÖRENINGEN 1793575
Box 16286, 103 25 STOCKHOLM **Tel:** 8 453 90 70
Fax: 84539071
Titles:
GLAS

GO OUTSIDE MEDIA SWEDEN AB 1793552
Smålandsgatan 6, 352 35 VÄXJO **Tel:** 470 264 30
Titles:
OUTSIDE

GOLDCUP AB U N Ä 1791526
Box 13028, 103 01 STOCKHOLM
Tel: 8 587 898 60
Titles:
NEO

GOLFRESAN MEDIA AB 1790984
Alströmergatan 20 A, 112 47 STOCKHOLM
Tel: 8 410 191 90 **Fax:** 86543819
Titles:
GOLFRESAN

GOLVBRANSCHENS RIKSORGANISATION GBR 1627469
Box 12250, 102 26 STOCKHOLM **Tel:** 8 651 56 20
Titles:
GOLV TILL TAK

GOTA MEDIA AB 1789738
Allégatan 67, 501 85 BORÅS **Tel:** 33 700 07 00
Fax: 33 10 14 36
Titles:
BORÅS TIDNING
BORÅS TIDNING; BT.SE

GÖTEBORG FILM FESTIVAL 1629991
Olof Palmes plats, 413 04 GÖTEBORG
Tel: 31 339 30 14 **Fax:** 31 41 00 63
Titles:
FILMKONST

GÖTEBORGS UNIVERSITET, EXTERNA RELATIONER 1710427
Göteborgs universitet, Box 100, 405 30
GÖTEBORG **Tel:** 31 786 10 21 **Fax:** 31 786 43 54
Titles:
GU-JOURNALEN

GÖTEBORGSREGIONENS KOMMUNALFÖRBUND 1653684
Box 31019, 400 32 GÖTEBORG **Tel:** 31 775 03 83
Titles:
ETT23

GOTHIA FÖRLAG AB 1743654
Box 22543, 104 22 STOCKHOLM **Tel:** 8 462 26 70
Fax: 84620322
Titles:
SKOLHÄLSOVÅRD

GOTLANDSGUIDEN AB 1629934
Norra Hansegatan 18, 621 41 VISBY
Tel: 498 21 00 00 **Fax:** 498 27 15 48
Titles:
GOTLANDSGUIDEN

GOTLANDSPRESS AB 1789722
Box 1284, 621 23 VISBY **Tel:** 498 20 25 50
Fax: 498 20 25 97
Titles:
GOTLANDS ALLEHANDA
GOTLANDS TIDNINGAR

GP 1789237
Polhemsplatsen 5, 405 02 GOTEBORG
Tel: 31 62 40 00
Titles:
GÖTEBORGS-POSTEN; GP.SE

GRAFISKA SÄLLSKAPET 1628086
Hornsgatan 6, 118 20 STOCKHOLM
Tel: 33 41 98 60 **Fax:** 33 13 27 58
Titles:
GRAFIKNYTT

GRAND PUBLISHING AB 1732689
Grand Publishing AB, 115 56 STOCKHOLM
Tel: 8 535 280 50 **Fax:** 86639349
Titles:
GRAND

GREKISKA RIKSFÖRBUNDET 1628988
c/o Grekiska Riksförbundet, Box 1900, 104 32
STOCKHOLM **Tel:** 8 627 00 27 **Fax:** 8 627 00 26
Titles:
GREKER I NORDEN

GRÖN UNGDOM 1791152
Grön Ungdom, Pustegränd 1-3, 118 20
STOCKHOLM **Tel:** 46 16 22 55
Titles:
AVTRYCK

GRÖNA NÄRINGENS RIKSORGANISATION, GRO 1627478
105 33 STOCKHOLM **Tel:** 8 787 53 80
Fax: 8 787 53 81
Titles:
VIOLA

GT/EXPRESSEN 1789726
Kungstorget 2, 401 26 GOTEBORG
Tel: 31 725 90 00
Titles:
GT
GT; GT.SE

GUIDENFÖRLAGET AB 1791795
113 78 STOCKHOLM **Tel:** 8 692 66 80
Fax: 86920155
Titles:
V75-GUIDEN

GUNNAR LOXDAL 1793883
Box 17518, 118 91 STOCKHOLM **Tel:** 8 442 44 90
Fax: 87204491
Titles:
NYHETSBREVET FOND & BANK

HÅKAN LARSSON 1790058
Allt om Vin, Box 1198, 181 23 LIDINGÖ
Titles:
ALLT OM VIN

HALLANDSPOSTEN 1627713
Fiskaregatan 21, 302 38 HALMSTAD
Tel: 730 29 81 48
Titles:
ENTRÉ HALMSTAD
HALLANDS AFFÄRER
HALLANDSPOSTEN
HALLANDSPOSTEN; WEBB

HALLBYRÅN AB I SAMARBETE MED DIV. FÖRETAGSGRUPPER 1629883
Säterivägen 7, 651 03 KARLSTAD **Tel:** 5417 56 00
Fax: 54 20 35 15
Titles:
VÄRMLANDS AFFÄRER

HALLPRESSEN AB 1789984
331 84 VÄRNAMO **Tel:** 370 30 06 00
Fax: 37049090
Titles:
VÄRNAMO NYHETER

HALMSTAD STUDENTKÅR 1732723
Halmstads Studentkår, Box 847, 301 18
HALMSTAD **Tel:** 35 16 92 61
Titles:
BREEZE MAGAZINE

HÄLSINGETIDNINGAR AB 1627499
Box 1201, 824 15 HUDIKSVALL **Tel:** 650 355 00
Fax: 65035560
Titles:
HUDIKSVALLS TIDNING
HUDIKSVALLS TIDNING; HT.SE
LJUSDALS-POSTEN
LJUSDALS-POSTEN; LJP.SE
LJUSNAN
LJUSNAN; LJUSNAN.SE

HÅLTAGNINGSENTREPRENÖRERNA INOM SV. BYGGINDUSTRIER 1685023
Box 5054, 102 42 STOCKHOLM **Tel:** 8 698 58 73
Fax: 8 698 59 00
Titles:
HIB-INFO

HANDELSANSTÄLLDAS FÖRBUND 1627397
Box 1146, 111 81 STOCKHOLM **Tel:** 8 412 68 00
Fax: 8 21 43 33
Titles:
HANDELSNYTT
HANDELSNYTT; WEBB

HANS LANDBERG 1684652
Box 2263, 103 16 STOCKHOLM **Tel:** 8 696 70 00
Fax: 8 696 70 01
Titles:
KULTURVÄRDEN

HANS MÅNSON 1789560
205 05 MALMO **Tel:** 40 28 12 00
Titles:
SYDSVENSKAN; SYDSVENSKAN.SE

HANSEN MEDIA AB 1627679
Prästgatan 2, 416 66 GOTEBORG
Tel: 31 775 65 50 **Fax:** 317756549
Titles:
MONITOR
MUSIKERMAGASINET - MM

HAPARANDABLADET AB 1789569
Box 144, 953 23 HAPARANDA **Tel:** 922 280 00
Fax: 922 280 10
Titles:
HAPARANDABLADET/HAAPARANNANLEHTI

HÄSTENS FÖRLAG 1629596
Hästens förlag, Kampavall, 540 17 LERDALA
Tel: 511 822 30
Titles:
HÄSTEN

HEDEMORA GRAFISKA AB 1628438
Box 176, 811 23 SANDVIKEN **Tel:** 26 24 84 84
Fax: 26 24 84 85
Titles:
ANNONSBLADET I SANDVIKEN

HELENA RÖNNBERG 1789753
Bonnier Tidskrifter AB, Budadress:
Rådmansgatan 49, 105 44 STOCKHOLM
Tel: 8 736 53 00 **Fax:** 8 34 00 43
Titles:
VI FÖRÄLDRAR GRAVID

HELSINGBORGS DAGBLAD 1789438
251 83 HELSINGBORG **Tel:** 42 489 90 00
Fax: 42 489 90 01
Titles:
HELSINGBORGS DAGBLAD
HELSINGBORGS DAGBLAD; HD.SE

HERENCO AB 1789646
551 80 JÖNKÖPING **Tel:** 36 30 40 50
Fax: 36 12 27 15
Titles:
JÖNKÖPINGS-POSTEN
SMÅLÄNNINGEN
VETLANDA-POSTEN
VETLANDA-POSTEN - ÅSEDA

HEXANOVA MEDIA GROUP AB 1627654
Drakenbergsgatan 2, 117 41 STOCKHOLM
Tel: 31 775 15 80
Titles:
FASTIGHETSFÖRVALTAREN
LOOK AT SCANDINAVIA
OFFENTLIGA AFFÄRER
SVENSK LEVERANTÖRSTIDNING

HISTORISKA MEDIA AB 1791111
Box 1206, 221 05 LUND **Tel:** 4 633 34 60
Titles:
ALLT OM HISTORIA
POPULÄR HISTORIA

HJÄLPMEDELSINSTITUTET 1790465
Box 510, 162 15 VÄLLINGBY **Tel:** 8 620 17 00
Fax: 87392152
Titles:
ALLT OM HJÄLPMEDEL
ALLT OM HJÄLPMEDEL; WEBB

HJÄRNKRAFT 1790463
Nybohovsgränd 12, 117 63 STOCKHOLM
Tel: 8 447 45 30 **Fax:** 8 447 45 39
Titles:
HJÄRNKRAFT

HJÄRT- OCH LUNGSJUKAS RIKSFÖRBUND 1793511
Box 9090, 102 72 STOCKHOLM **Tel:** 8 556 062 00
Fax: 86682385
Titles:
STATUS

HJÄRTEBARNSFÖRENINGEN 1713016
Box 9087, 102 72 STOCKHOLM **Tel:** 8 442 46 50
Fax: 8 442 46 59
Titles:
HJÄRTEBARNET

HJÄRT-LUNGFONDEN 1793794
Hjärt-Lungfonden, Box 5413, 114 84
STOCKHOLM **Tel:** 8 566 242 00 **Fax:** 8 566 242 29
Titles:
FORSKNING FÖR HÄLSA

HJEMMET MORTENSEN AB 1652963
Box 164, 830 13 ÅRE **Tel:** 647 514 40
Fax: 64751444
Titles:
ÅKA SKIDOR
ALLT OM HUSVAGN & CAMPING
AUTO MOTOR & SPORT
AUTO MOTOR & SPORT; AUTOMOTORSPORT.SE
BODY MAGAZINE; BODY.SE
CLASSIC MOTOR
CLASSIC MOTOR; CLASSICMOTOR.SE
DATORMAGAZIN
DATORMAGAZIN; DATORMAGAZIN.SE
PC GAMER
PC GAMER; PCGAMER.SE
POWER MAGAZINE
PRAKTISKT BÅTÄGANDE
SPORTFACK
SPORTFACK; SPORTFACK.SE
UPPSNAPPAT
UTEMAGASINET
UTEMAGASINET; WEBB
WHEELS MAGAZINE

HKM PUBLISHING AB 1732722
Box 395, 701 47 OREBRO **Tel:** 19 10 84 90
Fax: 19108430
Titles:
NOLLNITTON
ÖREBRO MARKNAD

HOOM AB 1743544
Gyllenstiernsgatan 10, 115 26 STOCKHOLM
Tel: 8 717 06 00
Titles:
HOOM
HOOM; WEBB

HÖRSELSKADADES RIKSFÖRBUND 1790466
Box 6605, 113 84 STOCKHOLM **Tel:** 8 457 55 00
Fax: 84575503
Titles:
AURIS

HOTELL- OCH RESTAURANGFACKET 1793611
Box 1143, 111 81 STOCKHOLM **Tel:** 771 57 58 59
Fax: 8 20 47 28
Titles:
HOTELLREVYN
HOTELLREVYN; WEBB

HSB RIKSFÖRBUND 1790933
Box 8310, 104 20 STOCKHOLM **Tel:** 8 785 30 00
Titles:
HEMMA I HSB
HSB UPPDRAGET

HUMANISTISKA FÖRENINGEN PÅ STOCKHOLMS UNIVERSITET 1710462
Box 50096, 104 05 STOCKHOLM **Tel:** 8 16 76 63
Titles:
TIDSKRIFTEN KÄNGURU

HUSHÅLLNINGSSÄLLSKAPEN I MALMÖHUS OCH KRISTIANSTAD 1793697
Hushållningssällskapet Kristianstad, 291 09
KRISTIANSTAD **Tel:** 44 22 99 01 **Fax:** 44229310
Titles:
SKÅNSKA LANTBRUK

HUSHÅLLNINGSSÄLLSKAPET I NORRBOTTEN 1747911
Köpmangatan 2, 972 38 LULEÅ
Titles:
LANDSBYGD I NORR

HYRESGÄSTFÖRENINGEN 1789314
Postadress: Box 7514, 103 92 STOCKHOLM
Tel: 8 519 103 00 **Fax:** 8 519 103 10
Titles:
HEM & HYRA

IDEELLA FÖRENINGEN SOCIALPOLITISK DEBATT 1793929
Eriksberg 137, 451 96 UDDEVALLA
Tel: 31 14 48 08
Titles:
SOCIALPOLITIK

IDÉGRUPPEN VI RESENÄRER KB 1735408
Box 70 387, 107 24 STOCKHOLM
Tel: 8 776 39 50
Titles:
VI RESENÄRER

IDG 1628998
IDG AB, Karlbergsvägen 77, 106 78
STOCKHOLM **Tel:** 8 453 64 00
Titles:
CIO SWEDEN
CIO SWEDEN; WEBB
COMPUTER SWEDEN; CS HEMMA
IT24
MILJÖAKTUELLT
MILJÖAKTUELLT; MILJOAKTUELLT.SE
M-PLUS

IDG AB 1627497
106 78 STOCKHOLM **Tel:** 8 453 61 00
Titles:
BIGTWIN
BIOTECH SWEDEN
BIOTECH SWEDEN; HTTP://BIOTECH.IDG.SE
CAP & DESIGN
CAP & DESIGN; CAPDESIGN.SE
COMPUTER SWEDEN
COMPUTER SWEDEN; COMPUTERSWEDEN.SE
CSO CHIEF SECURITY OFFICER
INTERNETWORLD
IT.BRANSCHEN
IT.BRANSCHEN; WEBB
M3 DIGITAL WORLD
M3 HEMMABIO
M3; WEBB
MACWORLD
MACWORLD;MACWORLD.SE
PC FÖR ALLA
PC FÖR ALLA; WWW.PCFORALLA.IDG.SE
TECHWORLD
TECHWORLD MIKRODATORN
TECHWORLD; WEBB

IDG INTERNATIONAL DATA GROUP AB 1735422
Att: Redaktionen, 106 78 STOCKHOLM
Tel: 8 453 64 70
Titles:
STUDIO
STUDIO; STUDIO.SE

IF FRISKIS&SVETTIS STOCKHOLM 1735379
Kungsholms Strand 127, 112 33 STOCKHOLM
Tel: 8 20 19 25 **Fax:** 8 20 16 35
Titles:
FRISKISPRESSEN

IM, INDIVIDUELL MÄNNISKOHJÄLP 1791287
Box 45, 221 00 LUND **Tel:** 46 32 99 30
Fax: 46158309
Titles:
MEDMÄNSKLIGHET

IMIT, INSTITUTE FOR MGNT OF INNOVATION AND TECH. 1793785
Vera Sandbergs allé 8, 412 96 GOTEBORG
Tel: 31 772 12 29
Titles:
MANAGEMENT OF TECHNOLOGY

INDIKAT AB 1793569
Box 510, 192 05 SOLLENTUNA **Tel:** 8 594 950 75
Titles:
INDIKAT

INFO TEAM AB 1629628
Box 2079, 433 02 SÄVEDALEN **Tel:** 31 340 98 00
Fax: 313409801
Titles:
AFFÄRSTIDNINGEN NÄRINGSLIV
AFFÄRSTIDNINGEN NÄRINGSLIV; NARINGSLIV.SE

INFO.AVDELNINGEN VID CHALMERS 1627365
Informationsavdelningen, 412 96 GÖTEBORG
Tel: 31 772 25 10 **Fax:** 31 772 25 61
Titles:
CHALMERS MAGASIN

INFOKOMM DP 1686282
Videum Science Park, 351 96 VÄXJO
Tel: 470 72 47 17
Titles:
DIGITAL LIFE
DIGITAL LIFE; DIGITALLIFE.SE

INFORMA HEALTHCARE 1742595
c/o Informa Healthcare, Box 3255, 103 65
STOCKHOLM **Tel:** 8 440 80 40 **Fax:** 8 440 80 50
Titles:
ADVANCES IN PHYSIOTHERAPY
I VÅRDEN
SCAND. CARDIOVASCULAR JOURNAL
SCAND. JOURNAL OF INFECTIOUS DISEASES

INFORMA HEALTHCARE AB 1793607
Informa Healthcare, Box 3255, 103 65
STOCKHOLM **Tel:** 8 440 80 43 **Fax:** 8 440 80 50
Titles:
I VÅRDEN

INFORMATION & DESIGN REKLAMBYRÅ 1789674
Box 158, 681 23 KRISTINEHAMN **Tel:** 550 199 00
Fax: 550 199 01
Titles:
KRISTINEHAMN-STORFORS AKTUELLT

INFORMATIONSENHETEN 1628088
Inf.enheten, Lunds universitet, Box 117, 221 00
LUND **Tel:** 46 222 95 24
Titles:
LUM, LUNDS UNIVERSITETS MAGASIN

INFOTORG AB 1791053
InfoTorg AB, 105 99 STOCKHOLM
Tel: 8 738 48 00 **Fax:** 8 738 48 01
Titles:
INFOTORG JURIDIKS

INFO@TTG.SE 1750318
Box 26206, 113 92 STOCKHOLM
Tel: 8588 366 70 **Fax:** 850667809
Titles:
VI BÅTÄGARE; WEBB

INGEMAR THULIN 1628558
St. Hellevigsgatan 2, 451 55 UDDEVALLA
Tel: 522 384 80
Titles:
UDDEVALLAREN

INGRESS MEDIA AB 1789494
Storgatan 28 B, 732 46 ARBOGA **Tel:** 589 857 00
Titles:
ARBOGA TIDNING
AVESTA TIDNING
BÄRGSLAGSBLADET / ARBOGA TIDNING
SALA ALLEHANDA

INNERSTADSPRESS AB 1628001
Box 5290, 102 46 STOCKHOLM **Tel:** 8 545 870 70
Fax: 8 545 870 89
Titles:
ÖSTERMALMSNYTT
VÅRT KUNGSHOLMEN
VI I VASASTAN

INSTITUTET FÖR BIOMEDICINSK LABORATORIEVETENSKAP 1793801
Röntgenv. 3, 141 52 HUDDINGE **Tel:** 8 24 01 31
Titles:
TIDSKRIFTEN LABORATORIET

INSTITUTET FÖR FRAMTIDSSTUDIER 1684653
Box 591, 101 31 STOCKHOLM **Tel:** 8 402 12 00
Fax: 8245014
Titles:
FRAMTIDER

INSTITUTIONEN FÖR BARN- OCH UNGDOMSVETENSKAP 1790935
Stockholms universitet, 106 91 STOCKHOLM
Tel: 8 737 55 85
Titles:
LOCUS - TIDSKRIFT FÖR FORSKNING OM BARN OCH UNGDOMAR

INSTITUTIONEN FÖR HUMANIORA VID VÄXJÖ UNIVERSITET 1791103
Institutionen för humaniora, Växjö universitet,
351 95 VÄXJO **Tel:** 470 70 86 61 **Fax:** 470751888
Titles:
HUMANETTEN

INTELLECTA COMMUNICATION AB 1793577
Box 19063, 104 32 STOCKHOLM
Tel: 8 506 286 00 **Fax:** 850628720
Titles:
CORPORATE INTELLIGENCE

INTELLIBRA FÖRLAGSLABEL 1654423
c/o Intellibra, Ortvik, Garvargatan 5, 112 21
STOCKHOLM **Tel:** 8 652 95 95
Titles:
FRONTFACE MAGAZINE

INTELLIGENT LOGISTIK HB 1735366
Bastugatan 6, 118 20 STOCKHOLM
Tel: 8 641 54 08 **Fax:** 8 641 54 08
Titles:
INTELLIGENT LOGISTIK

INTERDO AB 1738606
Tel: 35 21 28 30
Titles:
MAGASIN ZOONEN

INTERFLORA AB 1744335
Box 808, 161 24 BROMMA **Tel:** 8 634 44 00
Fax: 8 26 96 06
Titles:
INSPIRERA BY INTERFLORA

INTERNATIONAL BUSINESS MEDIA AB 1790609
International Business Media AB, Stora Åvägen
21, 436 34 ASKIM **Tel:** 431 156 12 **Fax:** 317238499
Titles:
DINA BARNS UTVECKLING

INTRUM JUSTITIA AB 1651251
c/o Intrum Justitia AB, 105 24 STOCKHOLM
Tel: 8 546 102 00 **Fax:** 8 546 102 11
Titles:
INTRUM MAGAZINE

IOGT-NTO-FÖRBUNDET 1629715
Box 12825, 112 97 STOCKHOLM **Tel:** 8 672 60 50
Fax: 8 672 60 01
Titles:
ACCENT
ACCENT; WEBB

IOGT-NTOS JUNIORFÖRBUND 1629683
Box 12825, 112 97 STOCKHOLM **Tel:** 8 672 60 52
Fax: 8 672 60 01
Titles:
STRUTEN

IPG AB 1793711
Box 6320, 102 35 STOCKHOLM **Tel:** 8 555 911 55
Fax: 855591130
Titles:
ALLT OM BRÖLLOP

IPG PUBLISHING GROUP 1655300
Box 6320, 102 35 STOCKHOLM **Tel:** 8 555 911 55
Fax: 855591150
Titles:
ESCAPE 360°

IPG-SWEDEN 1676005
IPG-sweden, Box 6320, 102 35 STOCKHOLM
Tel: 8 555 911 00 **Fax:** 8 555 911 50
Titles:
KONSTVÄRLDEN & DISAJN

IQ STUDENT AB 1628488
Box 3101, 103 62 STOCKHOLM **Tel:** 8 587 075 00
Fax: 8 587 075 01
Titles:
STUDENTMAGASINET

IRANSK-SVENSKA SOLIDARITETSFÖRENINGEN (ISS) 1791661
Box 4514, 203 20 MALMO **Tel:** 40 18 70 05
Fax: 40 689 13 68
Titles:
MANA

IRIS INTERMEDIA 1629823
122 88 ENSKEDE **Tel:** 8 39 91 40 **Fax:** 8 659 26 25
Titles:
PÅ TAL OM STOCKHOLM

ISPI OCH SMFF 1755577
Box 34 245, 100 26 STOCKHOLM
Titles:
MUSIKINDUSTRIN, MI

IT IS MEDIA AB 1649992
Birger Jarlsgatan 20, 114 34 STOCKHOLM
Tel: 8 667 92 10 **Fax:** 8 667 92 11
Titles:
RUM

IUSTUS FÖRLAG AB 1629707
Box 1994, 751 49 UPPSALA **Tel:** 18 65 03 30
Fax: 18 69 30 99
Titles:
SKATTENYTT
SVENSK JURISTTIDNING

JA TILL LIVET 1790930
Fyrisborgsgatan 4, 754 50 UPPSALA
Tel: 18 12 71 09 **Fax:** 18 12 55 34
Titles:
ENIM

JÄGARNAS RIKSFÖRBUND 1627447
Slottsgatan 21, 722 11 VÄSTERÅS
Tel: 21 14 78 50 **Fax:** 21 14 73 50
Titles:
JAKT & JÄGARE

JÄMTLANDS LÄNS LANDSTING 1710377
Jämtlands Läns Landsting, Landstingshuset, Box 654, 831 27 ÖSTERSUND **Tel:** 63 14 76 29
Titles:
FRI SIKT

JAN ARVIDSON PROMOTION 1640632
Vasagatan 20, 682 30 FILIPSTAD **Tel:** 590 102 60
Fax: 590 102 60
Titles:
GRÖNYTELEVERANTÖRERNA

JAN GILLBERG 1793573
Box 99, 563 22 GRÄNNA **Tel:** 390 107 50
Fax: 39010750
Titles:
DSM

JENNY CAHIER 1710435
LinTek, Tekniska högskolan, 581 83 LINKÖPING
Tel: 13 25 45 81
Titles:
LITHANIAN

JG COMMUNICATION 1774397
Box 1042, 164 21 KISTA **Tel:** 8 610 20 00
Titles:
KONTAKTEN/CONTACT

JOACHIM SVÄRDH 1628913
Ilanda Gård 120, 653 50 KARLSTAD
Tel: 54 18 77 18 **Fax:** 54 53 45 80
Titles:
FASTIGHETSMARKNADEN

JOBS AND SOCIETY NYFÖRETAGARCENTRUM 1654961
c/o Jobs and Society NyföretagarCentrum, 111 30 STOCKHOLM **Tel:** 8 14 44 00 **Fax:** 8 21 14 54
Titles:
ALLT OM EGET FÖRETAG I SVERIGE

JOHAN LINDSTEDT 1793857
Box 7137, 103 87 STOCKHOLM **Tel:** 8 31 90 85
Fax: 317760601
Titles:
OTC - PLACERAREN

JOHAN STRID 1794028
Svenska Scoutrådet, Box 12 280, 102 27 STOCKHOLM **Tel:** 8 672 66 04
Titles:
SCOUTEN

JOHAN ZETTERSTEDT 1639837
Wallingatan 37, 111 24 STOCKHOLM
Tel: 8 652 89 80 **Fax:** 8 652 89 81
Titles:
FASTIGHETSNYTT

JÖNKÖPING NU TIDNINGS AB 1710358
Box 264, 551 14 JÖNKÖPING **Tel:** 36 30 94 90
Fax: 36 16 04 90
Titles:
JÖNKÖPING NU; WEBB

JÖNKÖPINGS NYTT MEDIA GROUP HB 1712984
Gjuterigatan 9, 553 18 JÖNKÖPING
Tel: 36 340 300
Titles:
JNYTT.SE

JÖNKÖPINGS SPÅRVAGNS- OCH BUSSHISTORISKA SÄLLSKAP 1655195
c/o Hans Fredriksson, Gullvivebacken 12, 554 56 JÖNKÖPING **Tel:** 36 17 67 15
Titles:
LÅDAN

JÖNKÖPINGS STUDENTKÅR 1791014
Jönköpings Studentkår, Gjuterigatan 3 C, 553 18 JÖNKÖPING **Tel:** 36 15 75 86 **Fax:** 36 16 62 61
Titles:
KÅRSORDET

JORDBRUKSAKTUELLT SVERIGE 1757284
Boställsvägen 4, 702 27 ÖREBRO
Tel: 19 16 61 30 **Fax:** 19 16 61 45
Titles:
SKOGSAKTUELLT

JUNIA MISSION 1790276
Rallarvägen 37, 184 40 ÅKERSBERGA
Tel: 8 540 203 28 **Fax:** 854020328
Titles:
JUNIA

JUSEK 1629159
Box 5167, 102 44 STOCKHOLM **Tel:** 8 665 29 20
Fax: 8 662 79 23
Titles:
JUSEKTIDNINGEN
JUSEKTIDNINGEN; WEBB

JUST MEDIA SVERIGE AB 1732756
Box 310 19, 400 32 GOTEBORG **Tel:** 31 775 03 90
Titles:
ASSISTANS
ELECTRONIC ENVIRONMENT

KANAL 12 I KARLSTAD AB 1629692
Tage Erlanderg. 4, 652 20 KARLSTAD
Tel: 54 17 59 00
Titles:
KANAL 12

KARL-HEINZ FORSBERG 1789675
Järnvägsgatan 74, 216 16 LIMHAMN
Tel: 40 15 74 77 **Fax:** 40158680
Titles:
LIMHAMNS-TIDNINGEN
MALMÖTIDNINGEN

KARLSKOGA KURIREN AB 1628817
Kungsvägen 34, 691 24 KARLSKOGA
Tel: 586 784 300 **Fax:** 586 357 57
Titles:
KARLSKOGA-KURIREN
KARLSKOGA-KURIREN; INSÄNDARAVDELNINGEN
KARLSKOGA-KURIREN; WEBB

KAROLINSKA INSTITUTET 1789750
Karolinska Institutet, 171 77 STOCKHOLM
Tel: 8 524 800 00 **Fax:** 8 33 88 33
Titles:
MEDICINSK VETENSKAP

KATRINEHOLMS-KURIREN AB 1789717
Box 111, 641 22 KATRINEHOLM **Tel:** 150 728 00
Fax: 150 539 00
Titles:
KATRINEHOLMS-KURIREN
KATRINEHOLMS-KURIREN; WEBB

KATTLIV FÖRLAGS HB 1791292
Borgås gårdsväg 1, 434 39 KUNGSBACKA
Tel: 300 334 44 **Fax:** 30033749
Titles:
KATTLIV

KCF SERVICE AB 1639816
Box 55680, 102 15 STOCKHOLM **Tel:** 8 762 65 25
Titles:
KÖTTBRANSCHEN

KEKA KONSULT AB 1630039
Berga, Stenåsen 311, 692 93 KUMLA
Tel: 19 57 60 90 **Fax:** 19 58 00 50
Titles:
GRIS

KELAM RELATION & PUBLISHING 1644370
Box 1201, 751 42 UPPSALA **Tel:** 18 60 44 80
Fax: 18 10 70 40
Titles:
RELATION

KING PUBLISHING AB 1732682
King Publishing AB, Erik Dahlbergsgatan 30, 115 32 STOCKHOLM **Tel:** 8 528 000 55
Fax: 8 528 000 51
Titles:
KINGSIZE MAGAZINE

KLARKULLEN AB 1710602
Gränsö Slott, 593 92 VÄSTERVIK **Tel:** 490 824 20
Fax: 490 354 46
Titles:
RESMÅL

KLAS KIHLBERG 1793759
Klubbacken 15, 129 39 HAGERSTEN
Tel: 707 53 33 83
Titles:
TIDNINGEN TRÄDGÅRDSLIV SVERIGE

KLIMATMAGASINET EFFEKT EKONOMISK FÖRENING 1793906
Box 17506, 118 91 STOCKHOLM
Tel: 708 88 17 23
Titles:
KLIMATMAGASINET EFFEKT

KLT TRYCK AB 1628892
Box 23, 386 21 FÄRJESTADEN **Tel:** 485 307 19
Titles:
KALMAR LÄNS TIDNING / NYBRO TIDNING; WEBB

KOALA PUBLISHING AB 1735362
Box 1223, 164 28 KISTA **Tel:** 8 612 42 20
Fax: 86124280
Titles:
MEETINGS INTERNATIONAL
MEETINGS INTERNATIONAL; WEBB

KOLONITRÄDGÅRDSFÖRBUNDET 1627407
Åsögatan 149, 116 32 STOCKHOLM
Tel: 8 556 930 82 **Fax:** 8 640 38 98
Titles:
KOLONITRÄDGÅRDEN

KOMMUNALARBETAREN I SVERIGE AB 1789433
Box 19034, 104 32 STOCKHOLM
Tel: 10442 73 00 **Fax:** 8 30 61 42
Titles:
KOMMUNALARBETAREN
KOMMUNALARBETAREN; WEBB

KOMMUNISTISKA PARTIET 1790497
Box 31187, 400 32 GOTEBORG **Tel:** 31 24 45 44
Fax: 31244464
Titles:
PROLETÄREN
PROLETÄREN; PROLETAREN.SE

KOMPETENSGRUPPEN 1790413
World Trade center D8, 111 64 STOCKHOLM
Tel: 8 20 21 10
Titles:
IT-CHEFEN
IT-CHEFEN; WEBB

KOMPETENSGRUPPEN I SVERIGE AB 1743639
World Trade Center D8, 111 64 STOCKHOLM
Tel: 8 20 21 10 **Fax:** 8 20 78 10
Titles:
HR-TIDNINGEN PERSONALCHEFEN

KONCIS AFFÄRSINFORMATION AB 1628166
Box 204, 541 25 SKÖVDE **Tel:** 500 43 55 10 **Fax:** 500 43 55 01
Titles:
JOURNAL CHOCOLAT

KOST OCH NÄRING - EN BRANSCHFÖRENING INOM LEDARNA 1710641
Kost och Näring, c/o Ledarna, Box 12069, 102 22 STOCKHOLM **Tel:** 8 598 990 00
Titles:
NÄRINGSVÄRT - OM KOST OCH NÄRING

KOUNTRY KORRAL FÖRENINGEN 1628615
Box 6031, 791 06 FALUN **Tel:** 243 22 86 30 **Fax:** 243 673 23
Titles:
KOUNTRY KORRAL MAGAZINE

KRAV 1793371
c/o Redaktörerna, Box 92170, 120 08 STOCKHOLM **Tel:** 8 56 20 86 90
Titles:
REKO

KRISTDEMOKRATISKA UNGDOMSFÖRBUNDET 1793591
Box 2373, 103 18 STOCKHOLM **Tel:** 8 723 25 30 **Fax:** 8 723 25 10
Titles:
NY FRAMTID

KRONOBERGS LÄNS HEMBYGDSFÖRBUND 1792042
c/o Johansson, Hantverkaregatan 3, 341 36 LJUNGBY **Tel:** 372 624 61
Titles:
I VÄREND OCH SUNNERBO

KULTURENS VÄRLD 1792020
S:t Paulsgatan 31, 118 48 STOCKHOLM **Tel:** 8 640 15 01 **Fax:** 86401110
Titles:
KULTURENS VÄRLD

KULTURFÖRENINGEN HJÄRNSTORM 1791102
Box 4172, 102 64 STOCKHOLM **Tel:** 18 782 94 58 **Fax:** 84474539
Titles:
KULTURTIDSKRIFTEN HJÄRNSTORM

KULTURFÖRENINGEN SHERIFFI 1792031
Snoilskygatan 2b, 416 57 GOTEBORG **Tel:** 708 58 82 35
Titles:
SHERIFFI

KUNGL. KRIGSVETENSKAPS-AKADEMIEN 1791289
Teatergatan 3, 5 tr, 111 48 STOCKHOLM **Tel:** 8 611 14 00 **Fax:** 8 667 22 53
Titles:
KUNGL KRIGSVETENSKAPSAKADEMIENS HANDLINGAR OCH TIDSKRIFT

KUNGL. VETENSKAPSAKADEMIEN 1793703
Ambio, Kungl. Vetenskapsakademien, Box 50005, 104 05 STOCKHOLM **Tel:** 8 673 95 51 **Fax:** 8166251
Titles:
AMBIO - A JOURNAL OF THE HUMAN ENVIRONMENT

KUNGL. VITTERHETSAKADEMIEN 1654998
Box 5622 Vitterhetsakademien, 114 86 STOCKHOLM **Tel:** 8 440 42 80 **Fax:** 8 440 42 90
Titles:
FORNVÄNNEN

KUNGLIGA INGENJÖR-SVETENSKAPSAKADEMIEN 1790404
Box 5073, 102 42 STOCKHOLM **Tel:** 8 791 29 79 **Fax:** 8 791 30 18
Titles:
IVA-AKTUELLT

KUNGLIGA ÖRLOGSMANNASÄLLSKAPET 1629356
VÄXJÖ **Tel:** 470 212 45
Titles:
TIDSKRIFT I SJÖVÄSENDET

KURDISKA RIKSFÖRBUNDET 1628272
Box 5013, 131 05 NACKA **Tel:** 8 644 66 22 **Fax:** 8 650 21 20
Titles:
BERBANG

KUSTFÖRLAGET AB 1630038
Virkesvägen 2 B, 4 tr, 120 30 STOCKHOLM **Tel:** 854 54 27 00 **Fax:** 8 545 427 27
Titles:
SKÄRGÅRDEN; SKARGARDEN.SE
SKÄRGÅRDSLIV

KVÄLLSPOSTEN 1627732
AB kvällstidningen Expressen Kvällsposten, 205 26 MALMÖ **Tel:** 40 602 01 00 **Fax:** 40 93 92 24
Titles:
KVÄLLSPOSTEN; KVP.SE

AB KVÄLLSTIDNINGEN EXPRESSEN 1789277
Gjörwellsgatan 30, 105 16 STOCKHOLM **Tel:** 8 738 30 00 **Fax:** 8 619 04 50
Titles:
EXPRESSEN
EXPRESSEN; EXPRESSEN.SE

KVILTFÖRENINGEN RIKSTÄCKET 1628435
Box 27, 191 21 SOLLENTUNA **Tel:** 8 32 49 30
Titles:
RIKSTÄCKET

KYLENTREPRENÖRERNAS FÖRENING 1629532
Box 47122, 100 74 STOCKHOLM **Tel:** 8 762 75 00 **Fax:** 8 669 78 37
Titles:
KYLA+VÄRMEPUMPAR

KYRKANS AKADEMIKERFÖRBUND 1627565
Box 300 78, 104 25 STOCKHOLM **Tel:** 8 441 85 60 **Fax:** 8 441 85 77
Titles:
KYRKFACK

KYRKLIGA FÖRBUNDET F.E.L.T. 1790402
Träringen 52 1/2, 416 79 GOTEBORG **Tel:** 31 707 42 94 **Fax:** 317074295
Titles:
KYRKA OCH FOLK

KYRKOMUSIKERNAS RIKSFÖRBUND 1629094
c/o Henrik Tobin, Giggvägen 6, 443 42 GRÅBO **Tel:** 302 412 37 **Fax:** 302 412 37
Titles:
KYRKOMUSIKERNAS TIDNING

LA PRENSA 1789373
Karlavägen 21, 172 76 SUNDBYBERG **Tel:** 70 833 40 32
Titles:
LJUVA LIVET

LÄKARTIDNINGEN FÖRLAG AB 1774218
Tel: 8 790 33 00
Titles:
HÄLSA & VETENSKAP

LANDSTINGET DALARNA 1792085
Box 712, 791 29 FALUN **Tel:** 23 49 04 92 **Fax:** 23490169
Titles:
INBLICK

LANDSTINGET FÖREBYGGER AIDS, SLL 1629775
Box 175 33, 118 91 STOCKHOLM **Tel:** 8 737 35 46
Titles:
INSIKT OM HIV, SEX & SÅNT

LANDSTINGET HALLAND 1793610
Box 517, Landstinget Halland, 301 80 HALMSTAD **Tel:** 35 13 48 00
Titles:
GINSTEN

LANDSTINGET I JÖNKÖPINGS LÄN 1630026
Box 1024, Informationsavdelningen, Landstingets kansli, 551 11 JÖNKÖPING **Tel:** 36 32 40 45
Titles:
LANDSTINGSNYTT
PULSEN

LANDSTINGET I ÖSTERGÖTLAND 1790995
Landstinget i Östergötland, 581 91 LINKÖPING **Tel:** 13 22 20 00
Titles:
HÄLSOTECKEN

LANDSTINGET KRONOBERG 1793608
Landstinget Kronoberg, 351 88 VÄXJO **Tel:** 470 58 85 61 **Fax:** 470 58 87 70
Titles:
BLADET

LANDSTINGET VÄSTMANLAND 1793516
Landstingshuset, 721 51 VÄSTERÅS **Tel:** 21 17 46 47 **Fax:** 21174509
Titles:
VÄSTMANNAKONTAKT

LÄNKARNAS RIKSFÖRBUND 1793358
Box 9069, 126 09 HAGERSTEN **Tel:** 8 18 96 88 **Fax:** 8182989
Titles:
VI LÄNKAR

AB LÄNSTIDNINGEN 1789766
Kyrkgatan 52, 831 89 ÖSTERSUND **Tel:** 63 15 55 00
Titles:
LÄNSTIDNINGEN ÖSTERSUND

LÄNSTIDNINGEN, SÖDERTÄLJE AB 1789771
151 82 SÖDERTÄLJE **Tel:** 8 550 921 00 **Fax:** 8 550 877 72
Titles:
LÄNSTIDNINGEN SÖDERTÄLJE; LT.SE

LÄRARFÖRBUNDET 1627518
Box 12 239, 102 26 STOCKHOLM **Tel:** 8 540 866 41
Titles:
BILD I SKOLAN
CHEF & LEDARSKAP
CHEF & LEDARSKAP; CHEFOCHLEDARSKAP.SE
FÖRSKOLAN
FOTNOTEN
FRITIDSPEDAGOGEN
HUSHÅLLSVETAREN
IDROTTSLÄRAREN
LÄRARNAS TIDNING
LÄRARNAS TIDNING; LARARNASTIDNING.NET
PEDAGOGISKA MAGASINET
PEDAGOGISKA MAGASINET; WEBB
SLÖJDFORUM
SPECIALPEDAGOGIK
YRKESLÄRAREN
YRKESLÄRAREN; WEBB

LÄRARNAS RIKSFÖRBUND 1790064
Box 3265, 103 65 STOCKHOLM **Tel:** 8 50 55 62 00 **Fax:** 8 55 62 90
Titles:
SKOLVÄRLDEN

LARS ANDERSSON FÖRLAG 1792009
Norra Parkv. 18, 730 91 RIDDARHYTTAN **Tel:** 222 132 13
Titles:
GRUFVAN

LEDGE MEDIA PRODUKTION AB 1732663
Nygatan 11, 722 14 VÄSTERÅS **Tel:** 8 410 417 00
Titles:
EDGE MAGAZINE

LENA THUNBERG 1710395
c/o Afrikagrupperna, Linnégatan 21A, 413 04 GÖTEBORG **Tel:** 31 24 72 30
Titles:
VÄSTSAHARA

LENNART HÅKANSSON 1649732
971 83 LULEÅ **Tel:** 920 360 00 **Fax:** 920 892 10
Titles:
NORRLÄNDSKA SOCIALDEMOKRATEN; NSD.SE

LETTERHEAD AB 1792539
Repslagargatan 17 B, 118 46 STOCKHOLM **Tel:** 8 449 46 90
Titles:
BON MAGAZINE

LETTERSTEDTSKA FÖRENINGEN 1792021
Box 22333, 104 22 STOCKHOLM **Tel:** 8 654 75 70 **Fax:** 8 654 75 72
Titles:
NORDISK TIDSKRIFT FÖR VETENSKAP, KONST, INDUSTRI

LIAB LIBERAL INFORMAION AB 1749754
Box 6508, 111 27 STOCKHOLM **Tel:** 8 410 242 00 **Fax:** 8 509 116 83
Titles:
NU - DET LIBERALA NYHETSMAGASINET; WEBB

LIAB LIBERAL INFORMATION AB 1792904
Box 2045, 103 11 STOCKHOLM **Tel:** 8 410 242 00
Titles:
NU - DET LIBERALA NYHETSMAGASINET

LIBERALA TIDNINGAR AB 1789767
701 92 OREBRO **Tel:** 19 15 50 00 **Fax:** 19 10 52 90
Titles:
NERIKES ALLEHANDA

LIBERALA UNGDOMSFÖRBUNDET 1793590
Box 6508, 113 83 STOCKHOLM **Tel:** 8 410 242 00
Titles:
LIEBLING

LIC AUDIO 1793600
LIC Audio AB, Box 603, 194 26 UPPLANDS VÄSBY **Tel:** 8 590 00 450 **Fax:** 8 590 00 490
Titles:
AUDIONYTT

LIDINGÖ TIDNING AB 1629850
Box 1274, 181 24 LIDINGÖ **Tel:** 8 55055210
Fax: 8 731 90 80
Titles:
LIDINGÖ TIDNING
LIDINGÖ TIDNING; LT.NU

LINDSTRÖM & EDSTRÖM MEDIA GROUP AB 1639849
Klutmark 136, 931 97 SKELLEFTEÅ
Tel: 910 72 66 70 **Fax:** 910 72 66 80
Titles:
SNOWMOBILE

LINKÖPINGS UNIVERSITET 1793808
Externa relationer, Linköpings universitet, 581 83 LINKÖPING **Tel:** 13 28 16 93 **Fax:** 13 28 25 50
Titles:
LIU MAGASIN

LIV & FREDINSTITUTET 1649904
Sysslomansgatan 7, 753 11 UPPSALA
Tel: 18 16 95 00 **Fax:** 18 69 30 59
Titles:
NEW ROUTES

LIVSHÄLSA - RÅD OM VÅRD 1628635
Box 3010, 630 03 ESKILSTUNA **Tel:** 16 13 58 03
Titles:
LIVSHÄLSAN

LIVSMEDELSSTIFTELSEN 1735380
Tavastgatan 22, 118 24 STOCKHOLM
Tel: 8 714 50 46 **Fax:** 8.640 80 45
Titles:
LIVSMEDEL I FOKUS
LIVSMEDEL I FOKUS; LIVSMEDELIFOKUS.SE

LIVSMEDELSVERKET 1791171
Box 622, 751 26 UPPSALA **Tel:** 18 17 55 00
Fax: 18 17 53 50
Titles:
NYHETER FRÅN LIVSMEDELSVERKET

LIWALL FÖRLAGS AB 1629054
Box 3163, 903 04 UMEÅ **Tel:** 90 14 93 70
Fax: 90 18 81 18
Titles:
TIDNINGEN SNÖSKOTER

LJUSKULTUR AB 1629982
Box 12653, 112 93 STOCKHOLM
Tel: 8 566 367 00
Titles:
LJUSKULTUR

LOKALFÖRLAGET I GÖTEBORG AB 1745738
Lokalförlaget i Göteborg AB, Trädgårdsgatan 1, 411 08 GÖTEBORG **Tel:** 31 68 39 20
Fax: 31 68 39 60
Titles:
LOKALNYTT

LOKALGUIDEN SVERIGE AB 1732730
Torsgatan 5, 411 04 GOTEBORG **Tel:** 31 23 71 00
Fax: 31 23 71 15
Titles:
LOKALGUIDEN

LOKALTIDNINGEN MITT I STOCKHOLM AB 1789642
Bellevuegatan 6, 151 73 SÖDERTÄLJE
Tel: 8 550 641 14
Titles:
SÖDERTÄLJE POSTEN

LO-TIDNINGEN AB 1790400
Box 1372, 111 93 STOCKHOLM **Tel:** 8 796 25 00
Fax: 8 411 52 08
Titles:
LO-TIDNINGEN
LO-TIDNINGEN; WEBB

LRF COSMOMAG AB 1789491
113 92 STOCKHOLM **Tel:** 8 588 366 00
Fax: 8 588 369 59
Titles:
COSMOPOLITAN

LRF MEDIA 1653685
ATL/Boggi, Box 6044, 200 11 MALMÖ
Tel: 40 601 64 78 **Fax:** 40 601 64 99
Titles:
BOGGI
SEGLING

LRF MEDIA AB 1627493
Box 26206, 113 92 STOCKHOLM
Tel: 8 588 366 00 **Fax:** 8 506 678 09
Titles:
ALLT OM KÖK OCH BAD
ATL LANTBRUKETS AFFÄRSTIDNING
BÅTNYTT
DRÖMHEM & TRÄDGÅRD
DRÖMHEM & TRÄDGÅRD - BYGGA NYTT & RENOVERA
DRÖMHEM & TRÄDGÅRD - TRÄDGÅRD & BLOMMOR
FISKE FÖR ALLA
FÖRÄLDRAR & BARN
GODS & GÅRDAR
HÄRLIGA HUND
HÄSTMAGAZINET
JAKTMARKER & FISKEVATTEN
LAND LANTBRUK; WEBB
LAND SKOGSLAND
LAND SKOGSLAND; WEBB
LANTLIV
LANTMANNEN
RESIDENCE
TOIVEKOTI & PUUTARHA
TRAKTOR POWER
VI BÅTÄGARE
VI SKOGSÄGARE

LUCKYRIDER 1685670
Box 16, 686 20 SUNNE **Tel:** 565 108 02
Fax: 565 108 02
Titles:
LUCKYRIDER MAGAZINE

LUNDS MISSIONSSÄLLSKAP (LMS) 1627658
Västergatan 22, 211 21 MALMÖ **Tel:** 40 17 11 64
Titles:
UPPDRAG MISSION

LYSEKILS NYA TRYCKERI AB 1789718
Box 93, 453 22 LYSEKIL **Tel:** 523 66 70 81
Fax: 523 66 70 98
Titles:
LYSEKILSPOSTEN

MAAX NORDISKA MEDIA AB 1739893
Box 655, 135 26 TYRESÖ **Tel:** 8 410 053 40
Fax: 8 643 60 50
Titles:
AKTIVA

MADELENE AXELSSON 1713015
Såggatan 46, 414 67 GÖTEBORG
Tel: 31 704 80 80 **Fax:** 31 704 80 89
Titles:
GÖTEBORGS FRIA TIDNING; WEBB

MAGASINET FASTIGHETSSVERIGE 1686094
Trädgårdsgatan 1, 411 08 GÖTEBORG
Tel: 31 13 91 16 **Fax:** 31 68 39 60
Titles:
MAGASINET FASTIGHETSSVERIGE

MAGNUS KARLSSON 1639828
Box 529, 371 23 KARLSKRONA **Tel:** 455 33 53 25
Fax: 455 31 17 15
Titles:
BILSPORT CLASSIC

MAGNUS SÖDERLUND 1629519
Box 1059, Stationsgatan 8, 821 12 BOLLNÄS
Tel: 278275 50 **Fax:** 278 132 18
Titles:
BOLLNÄSNYTT
SÖDERHAMNSNYTT

MÄKLARSAMFUNDET SERVICE I SVERIGE AB 1629786
Box 1487, 171 28 SOLNA **Tel:** 8 555 00 900
Fax: 8 555 00 999
Titles:
FASTIGHETSMÄKLAREN

MÄLARDALEN - BERGSLAGENS AFFÄRER AB 1627317
Storgatan 53, 703 63 ÖREBRO **Tel:** 19 17 07 60
Fax: 19 12 56 42
Titles:
MÄLARDALEN - BERGSLAGENS AFFÄRER

MÄLARDALENS STUDENTKÅR 1652897
Mälardalens studentkår, Smedjegatan 32 B, 632 20 ESKILSTUNA **Tel:** 16 15 37 11 **Fax:** 16 15 36 19
Titles:
KÅRANEN

MÄLARÖ MEDIA AB 1789676
Box 100, 178 22 EKERÖ **Tel:** 8560 358 00
Fax: 8 560 358 00
Titles:
MÄLARÖARNAS NYHETER

MALMÖ STAD 1789650
Malmö stad, Stadskontoret, 205 80 MALMO
Tel: 40 34 10 00 **Fax:** 40 34 20 92
Titles:
VÅRT MALMÖ

MÅNSKARA FÖRLAG 1685669
Månskara Förlag, Skoghem, 179 96 SVARTSJÖ
Tel: 8 545 510 61 **Fax:** 8 653 31 20
Titles:
EQUIPAGE

MARIETORP FÖRLAG AB 1627536
Box 30, 432 03 TRÄSLÖVSLÄGE **Tel:** 340 415 25
Fax: 340 417 95
Titles:
UTEMILJÖ

MARKBLADET AB 1628461
Box 113, 511 21 KINNA **Tel:** 320 20 91 40
Fax: 320 20 91 57
Titles:
MARKBLADET

MASKINENTREPRENÖRERNA 1790393
Box 1609, 114 79 STOCKHOLM **Tel:** 8 762 70 65
Titles:
MASKINENTREPRENÖREN / ME-TIDNINGEN
MASKINENTREPRENÖREN / ME-TIDNINGEN; WEBB

MASSAGE & KROPPSVÅRD I SVERIGE AB 1646296
Villa Ekeberga, 614 97 SÖDERKÖPING
Tel: 121 411 33 **Fax:** 121 411 33
Titles:
MASSAGE & KROPPSVÅRD

MAT & VÄNNER FÖRLAG AB 1791184
Box 22100, 250 23 HELSINGBORG
Tel: 42 21 11 22 **Fax:** 42 21 11 37
Titles:
MAT & VÄNNER
MAT & VÄNNER; MATOCHVANNER.SE

MAXXIUM SWEDEN FINE WINE & SPIRITS AB 1639794
Box 5314, 102 47 STOCKHOLM **Tel:** 8 440 83 00
Fax: 8208780
Titles:
LIQUID INSPIRATION

MCM FÖRLAG AB/PERSSON-CARLESON 1649687
Torsgatan 65, 113 37 STOCKHOLM
Tel: 8 34 04 07 **Fax:** 8 34 04 22
Titles:
MCM - MOTORCYKELMAGASINET

MEDIA SPJUTH AB 1793529
c/o Media Spjuth AB, Box 3288, 550 03 JÖNKÖPING **Tel:** 36 30 36 30 **Fax:** 36 19 02 60
Titles:
HANDBOLLSMAGASINET

MEDIA SUPPORT AB 1793928
Pålsjögatan 21 f, 252 40 HELSINGBORG
Tel: 42 12 43 00
Titles:
DESTINATION HELSINGBORG

MEDIABOLAGET 1732734
Swedenborgsgatan 7, 118 48 STOCKHOLM
Tel: 8 556 963 10 **Fax:** 8 641 95 44
Titles:
BO BÄTTRE

MEDIAGRUPPEN I MALMÖ AB 1735367
Box 30057, 200 61 LIMHAMN **Tel:** 40 16 25 22
Fax: 40 16 25 23
Titles:
MEKANIK- INFORMATION MED INDUSTRINYTT

MEDIAHUSET I GÖTEBORG AB 1793640
Mediahuset i Göteborg AB, Marieholmsgatan 10, 415 02 GOTEBORG **Tel:** 31 707 19 30
Fax: 31848682
Titles:
GASTROKURIREN

MEDIAKONTAKT I UMEÅ AB 1791295
Box 303, 901 07 UMEÅ **Tel:** 90 13 31 77
Fax: 90130986
Titles:
UPP I NORR

MEDIAPRODUCENTERNA I DALARNA AB 1793827
Kupolen 112, 781 70 BORLÄNGE **Tel:** 243 160 80
Fax: 24316039
Titles:
NOLLTVÅ

MEDIAPROVIDER SCANDINAVIA AB 1736197
Birger Jarlsgatan 20, 114 34 STOCKHOLM
Tel: 8 667 92 10 **Fax:** 8 667 92 11
Titles:
CINEMA
CINEMA; CINEMA.SE
KAMERA OCH BILD
KAMERA OCH BILD; WEBB
MOBIL
MOBIL; MOBIL.SE
PRYLPORTALEN.SE

MEDIAPULS 1747551
Box 22541, 104 22 STOCKHOLM **Tel:** 8 650 88 80
Titles:
SPORTGUIDEN

AB MEDIATRENDER 1747227
Allégatan 5 B, 777 31 SMEDJEBACKEN
Tel: 240 706 66 **Fax:** 240 755 09
Titles:
MEDIATRENDER; MEDIAFAX

MEDIAWAY SCANDINAVIA AB 1745211
Nöjesmagasinet City c/o VK, 901 10 UMEÅ
Tel: 90 15 10 30 **Fax:** 90 10 05 15
Titles:
NÖJESMAGASINET CITY; UMEÅ

MEDICINSKA FÖRENINGEN I STOCKHOLM 1791288
Medicinska Föreningen i Stockholm, Box 250, 171 77 STOCKHOLM **Tel:** 8 524 830 70
Titles:
MEDICOR MAGASIN

MEDIEHUSET ST 1735416
Mediehuset ST, 851 72 SUNDSVALL
Tel: 60 19 70 00 Fax: 60 12 22 12
Titles:
VÅNING & VILLA

MEDMERA AB 1789341
Budadress: Svetsarvägen 4B, 171 88 SOLNA
Tel: 8 743 10 00
Titles:
MERSMAK

MELLANRUMETS VÄNFÖRENING 1732774
c/o May Nilsson, Högalidsgatan 48, 117 30 STOCKHOLM Tel: 8 716 07 44 Fax: 8 716 07 44
Titles:
MELLANRUMMET TIDSKR. OM BARN & UNGDOMSPSYKO.

MENTOR COMMUNICATION AB 1790348
Box 72001, 181 72 LIDINGÖ Tel: 8 545 513 33
Fax: 86502491
Titles:
FRI KÖPENSKAP
FRI KÖPENSKAP; WEBB

MENTOR COMMUNICATIONS AB 1627312
Budadress: Tryffelslingan 10, Box 72001, 181 72 LIDINGÖ Tel: 8 6704158
Titles:
BRANSCHTIDNINGEN FAST FOOD
DAGENS HANDEL
DAGENS HANDEL; DAGENS HANDEL.SE
GRAFISKT FORUM
GRAFISKT FORUM; WEBB
KEMIVÄRLDEN BIOTECH MED KEMISK TIDSKRIFT
KOSMETIK
MOTOR-MAGASINET
NTT SÅG & TRÄ, NORDISK TRÄTEKNIK
PACKMARKNADEN
PLASTFORUM
PROCESS NORDIC
PROCESS NORDIC; PROCESSNET.SE
RECYCLING & MILJÖTEKNIK
RENT
RESTAURANGER & STORKÖK
TRANSPORT IDAG/ LOGISTIK IDAG
TRANSPORT IDAG; TRANSPORTNET.SE
UNDERHÅLL OCH DRIFTSÄKERHET
VERKSTÄDERNA
VERKSTÄDERNA; VERKSTADERNA.SE

MENTOR GRUPPEN AB 1790356
Box 72001, 181 72 STOCKHOLM Tel: 8 670 41 00
Fax: 8 661 64 55
Titles:
HABIT SKO & MODE

MENTOR ONLINE 1639780
Box 72001, 181 72 LIDINGÖ Tel: 8 670 41 00
Fax: 86616455
Titles:
NORDISK PAPPERSTIDNING/NORDIC PAPER JOURNAL

MENTOR ONLINE AB 1749694
Box 601, 251 06 HELSINGBORG
Tel: 42 490 19 00
Titles:
MENTORONLINE.SE

METODISTKYRKAN FÖRLAGET SANCTUS 1627436
Metodistkyrkan i Sverige, Danska Vägen 20, 412 66 GÖTEBORG Tel: 31 733 78 40
Fax: 31 733 78 49
Titles:
SVENSKA SÄNDEBUDET

MHF CAMPING CLUB 1627539
c/o Hellgren, Kilby Vasängen 319, 748 91 ÖSTERBYBRUK Tel: 174 361 75
Titles:
KULTRYCKET

MIDÄLVA INFORMATION AB 1793495
Thulegatan 10A, 852 32 SUNDSVALL
Tel: 60 12 33 30 Fax: 60123339
Titles:
TIDNINGEN SKOGSTEKNIK

MIKAEL BECKER PUBLISHING 1793829
Box 6067, 102 31 STOCKHOLM Tel: 8 500 091 00
Fax: 850009119
Titles:
LOFTBOOKAZINE

MILJÖFÖRBUNDET JORDENS VÄNNER 1791684
Box 7048, 402 31 GOTEBORG Tel: 31 12 18 08
Fax: 31 12 18 17
Titles:
MILJÖTIDNINGEN

MILJÖMAGASINET ALTERNATIVET AB 1791306
Box 11203, 100 61 STOCKHOLM Tel: 8 640 82 80
Titles:
MILJÖMAGASINET

MILJÖPARTIET DE GRÖNA 1793589
Pustegränd 1-3, 281 37 STOCKHOLM
Titles:
GRÖNT

MISSING LINK CONSULTANTS AB 1793788
Järneksvägen 10, 131 40 NACKA Tel: 8 718 51 30
Fax: 87164330
Titles:
AJOURODONT

MITTMEDIA 1789822
Box 514, 826 27 SÖDERHAMN Tel: 270 740 00
Fax: 270 740 70
Titles:
SÖDERHAMNS KURIREN
SÖDERHAMNS KURIREN; SODERHAMNSKURIREN.SE

MITTMEDIA FÖRVALTNINGS AB 1789985
871 81 HÄRNÖSAND Tel: 611 55 48 00
Fax: 611 156 60
Titles:
TIDNINGEN ÅNGERMANLAND

MODERATA SAMLINGSPARTIET 1793584
Box 2080, 103 12 STOCKHOLM Tel: 8 676 80 00
Fax: 8204171
Titles:
MEDBORGAREN

MODERATA UNGDOMSFÖRBUNDET 1793587
Box 2080, 103 12 STOCKHOLM Tel: 8 676 81 52
Fax: 8 20 34 49
Titles:
BLÅTT

MODERN TEKNIK I STOCKHOLM AB 1793837
Box 216, 162 13 VÄLLINGBY Tel: 705 90 09 02
Titles:
MODERN TEKNIK
MODERN TEKNIK; MODERNTEKNIK.NU

MOTALA AIF 1A - VÄTTERNRUNDAN 1630033
Box 48, 591 21 MOTALA Tel: 141 22 32 90
Fax: 141 21 12 88
Titles:
CYKLA

MOTALA TIDNING AB 1629473
Industrigatan 9, 591 35 MOTALA
Tel: 141 22 36 00 Fax: 141 588 68
Titles:
MOTALA & VADSTENA TIDNING
MOTALA & VADSTENA TIDNING; MOTALATIDNING.SE

MOTOPRESS AB 1650196
Box 23800, 104 35 SOLNA Tel: 8 736 12 00
Fax: 8 736 12 49
Titles:
BIKE
BIKE; BIKE.SE

MOTORBRANSCHENS RIKSFÖRBUND MRF 1747462
Box 5611, 114 86 STOCKHOLM Tel: 8 701 63 19
Fax: 8 20 67 47
Titles:
MOTORBRANSCHEN

MOTORFÖRARNAS HELNYKTERHETSFÖRBUND 1789966
Heliosgatan 11, 120 30 STOCKHOLM
Tel: 8 555 765 55
Titles:
MOTORFÖRAREN
MOTORFÖRAREN; WEBB

MOTORMÄNNENS RIKSFÖRBUND 1789255
Box 3265, Kungsgatan 48, 103 65 STOCKHOLM
Tel: 8 50 55 62 21
Titles:
MOTOR

MTG 1758916
Box 171 04, 104 62 STOCKHOLM
Tel: 8 562 023 00
Titles:
TV3 ;TEXT-TV

NACKA FÖRLAGS AB 1627580
Paviljongvägen 5, 132 40 SALTSJÖ-BOO
Tel: 8 642 68 05
Titles:
AKTUELL PRODUKTION

NACKAPOSTEN AB 1628318
Box 735, 131 24 NACKA Tel: 8 555 266 20
Fax: 8 555 266 41
Titles:
NACKA VÄRMDÖ POSTEN
NACKA VÄRMDÖ POSTEN; NVP.SE

NÄMNDEMÄNNENS RIKSFÖRBUND 1627579
Helsingborgsvägen 44, 262 72 ÄNGELHOLM
Tel: 431 168 00 Fax: 431162 32
Titles:
NÄMNDEMANNEN

NATIONALEKONOMISKA FÖRENINGEN 1793045
Lunds universitet, Box 7082, 200 07 LUND
Tel: 4 622 286 76
Titles:
EKONOMISK DEBATT
EKONOMISK DEBATT; EKONOMISKDEBATT.SE

NATIONELLA SEKRETARIATET FÖR GENUSFORSKNING 1793803
Box 200, Nationella sekretariatet för genusforskning, 405 30 GOTEBORG
Tel: 31 786 56 02 Fax: 317865604
Titles:
GENUS

NÄTTIDNINGEN GOTLÄNDSKA NYHETERNA 1639865
Box 1087, 621 21 VISBY Tel: 49827 13 00
Fax: 498 21 17 46
Titles:
GOTLÄNDSKA.SE

NCSC, NORDIC COUNCIL OF SHOPPING CENTERS 1735346
Nordic Council of Shopping Centers, Slöjdgatan 9, 111 57 STOCKHOLM Tel: 8 611 11 42
Fax: 86111299
Titles:
CENTERNYTT

NEBEL & SÖDERSTRÖM FÖRLAG AB 1732744
Betaniaplan 3 B, 211 55 MALMÖ Tel: 40 12 55 90
Fax: 40 12 55 90
Titles:
OPUS

NEUROLOGISKT HANDIKAPPADES RIKSFÖRBUND 1790474
Box 49084, 100 28 STOCKHOLM Tel: 8 677 70 10
Fax: 8241315
Titles:
REFLEX

NEWMANINSTITUTET AB 1710454
Slottsgränd 6, 753 09 UPPSALA Tel: 1858007 10
Fax: 1858007 20
Titles:
SIGNUM
SIGNUM; SIGNUM.SE

NEXT WORLD MEDIA 1789493
Storgatan 45, 171 52 SOLNA Tel: 8 670 95 00
Titles:
ALLT OM VILLOR & HUS
LIFESTYLE MAGAZINE

NEXT WORLD MEDIA AB 1789489
Storgatan 45, 171 52 SOLNA Tel: 8 670 95 00
Titles:
AKTUELL FORSKNING & UTVECKLING
ENERGITEKNIK

NEXT WORLD SVERIGE AB 1732693
Storgatan 45, 171 52 SOLNA Tel: 8670 95 00
Titles:
ALLT OM HOTELL & RESOR
ALLT OM KLOCKOR OCH SMYCKEN
ALLT OM MÖBLER
BAD&KÖKGUIDEN

NJS, FORUM FÖR NORDISKT JÄRNVÄGSSAMARBETE 1735358
c/o Prenler, Kittåkers väg 16, 784 55 BORLÄNGE
Tel: 705 24 24 61
Titles:
NORDISK JÄRNBANETIDSKRIFT

NJURFÖRBUNDET 1743460
Njurförbundet, Box 1386, 172 27 SUNDBYBERG
Tel: 8 546 405 00 Fax: 8 546 405 04
Titles:
NJURFUNK

NÖJESGUIDENS FÖRLAG MSG AB 1747225
Viktoriagatan 3, 411 25 GOTEBORG
Tel: 31 20 36 66
Titles:
NÖJESGUIDEN; GÖTEBORG
NÖJESGUIDEN; MALMÖ/LUND
NÖJESGUIDEN; NOJESGUIDEN.SE
NÖJESGUIDEN; STOCKHOLM

NOLLELVA MEDIA AB 1791256
Drottninggatan 55, 602 32 NORRKÖPING
Tel: 11 10 21 01
Titles:
NOLLELVA

NOLLTRETTON MEDIA AB 1791268
Box 320, 581 02 LINKÖPING Tel: 13 12 26 16
Fax: 13239251
Titles:
NOLLTRETTON

NORDISK FILATELI AB 1627342
Box 90, 277 21 KIVIK **Tel:** 414 702 30
Titles:
NORDISK FILATELI

AB NORDISKA KOMPANIET 1793638
NK 100, 111 77 STOCKHOLM **Tel:** 8 762 90 00
Fax: 8 792 90 89
Titles:
NK STIL

NORDISKA R3-FÖRENINGEN 1628348
Box 65, 240 13 GENARP **Tel:** 40 50 01 18
Fax: 40 50 01 48
Titles:
RENHETSTEKNIK / NORDISK JOURNAL FÖR RENHETSTEKNIK

NORDISKA TIDNINGSBOLAGET 1790096
Nordiska Tidningsbolaget, 111 40 STOCKHOLM
Tel: 8 20 39 40
Titles:
KUPÉ

NORDMARKSBYGDEN AB 1789677
Elovsbyn, Hage, 670 10 TÖCKSFORS
Tel: 573 260 28 **Fax:** 57326062
Titles:
NORDMARKSBYGDEN

AB NORDREPORTERN 1628851
Box 104, 901 03 UMEÅ **Tel:** 90 70 09 00
Titles:
KVALITETSMAGASINET
KVALITETSMAGASINET; WEBB
MILJÖ & UTVECKLING
MILJÖ & UTVECKLING; WEBB
TELEKOM IDAG
TELEKOM IDAG; TELEKOMIDAG.COM

NORGE OCH SVERIGES ASTMA- OCH ALLERGIFÖRBUND 1655299
Box 17069, 104 62 STOCKHOLM
Tel: 8 506 282 16 **Fax:** 850628249
Titles:
ALLERGI I PRAXIS

NORRBOTTENS LÄNS LANDSTING 1639868
Norrbottens läns landsting, 971 89 LULEÅ
Tel: 920 28 43 64
Titles:
LANDSTINGSTIDNINGEN

NORRBOTTENS ORNITOLOGISKA FÖRENING 1732759
c/o Stefan Holmberg Piteåvägen 19, 930 82 ARVIDSJAUR **Tel:** 960 50085
Titles:
FÅGLAR I NORRBOTTEN

NORRBOTTENS-KURIREN AB 1789926
971 81 LULEÅ **Tel:** 920 26 29 03 **Fax:** 920 26 29 53
Titles:
NORRBOTTENS-KURIREN

NORRTELJE TIDNING AB 1789928
761 84 NORRTÄLJE **Tel:** 176 795 00
Fax: 176 100 08
Titles:
NORRTELJE TIDNING

NORTUNA HERRGÅRD AB 1639801
Romfartuna, Nortuna, 725 94 VÄSTERÅS
Tel: 21 270 40 **Fax:** 21 270 45
Titles:
ALUMINIUM SCANDINAVIA

NOTA BENE AB 1793858
Nota Bene AB, Prästgården Lönashult, 340 30 VISLANDA **Tel:** 470 72 66 30 **Fax:** 470726635
Titles:
LEXAFFÄR
LEXSKATT

NYA FOLKBLADET I ÖSTERGÖTLAND AB 1789765
Folkbladet, 601 84 NORRKÖPING
Tel: 11 20 04 00 **Fax:** 11 20 04 65
Titles:
FOLKBLADET
FOLKBLADET; FOLKBLADET.SE

NYA LIDKÖPINGS-TIDNINGEN AB 1789932
531 81 LIDKÖPING **Tel:** 510 897 00 **Fax:** 51089730
Titles:
NYA LIDKÖPINGS-TIDNINGEN; NLT.SE

NYA MEDIAPLAN 1627741
Box 6903, 102 39 STOCKHOLM **Tel:** 8 31 00 07
Titles:
DITT & DATT

NYA MEDIAPLAN AB 1628337
Box 6903, 102 39 STOCKHOLM **Tel:** 8 31 00 07
Titles:
MUSIKTIDNINGEN MUSIKOMANEN

NYA VÄSTERBOTTENS FOLKBLAD AB 1789956
Box 3164, 903 04 UMEÅ **Tel:** 90 17 00 00
Fax: 90 17 02 50
Titles:
VÄSTERBOTTENS FOLKBLAD
VÄSTERBOTTENS FOLKBLAD; WEBB

NYA VÄSTERBYGDENS TIDNINGS AB 1629492
Junogatan 3, 451 41 UDDEVALLA **Tel:** 522 350 50
Fax: 522 66 51 50
Titles:
UDDEVALLA-POSTEN; WEBB

NYA WERMLANDS-TIDNINGEN AB 1628679
Box 925, 671 29 ARVIKA **Tel:** 570 71 44 00
Fax: 570 149 30
Titles:
ARVIKA NYHETER
ARVIKA NYHETER; ARVIKANYHETER.SE
DALSLÄNNINGEN / BENGTSFORS-TIDNINGEN
FILIPSTADS TIDNING
FILIPSTADS TIDNING; WEBB
FRYKSDALS-BYGDEN
FRYKSDALS-BYGDEN; FBYGDEN.SE
KARLSKOGA TIDNING
MARIESTADS-TIDNINGEN
NYA KRISTINEHAMNS-POSTEN
NYA KRISTINEHAMNS-POSTEN; NKP.SE
NYA WERMLANDS-TIDNINGEN
NYA WERMLANDS-TIDNINGEN; NWT.SE
SÄFFLE-TIDNINGEN; SAFFLETIDNING.SE

NYLIBERALEN 1793583
BreviaBox 620, 114 79 STOCKHOLM
Tel: 8 34 56 47
Titles:
NYLIBERALEN

NYNÄSHAMNS POSTEN AB 1629878
Box 24, 149 21 NYNÄSHAMN **Tel:** 8587 122 00
Titles:
NYNÄSHAMNS POSTEN; NHP.SE

OFFICERSFÖRBUNDET 1790472
Förbundskansliet, Box 5338, 102 47 STOCKHOLM **Tel:** 8 440 83 30 **Fax:** 84408340
Titles:
OFFICERSTIDNINGEN

OFFSIDE PRESS AB 1629037
Östra Hamngatan 45, 411 10 GÖTEBORG
Tel: 31 711 98 82 **Fax:** 31 774 22 10
Titles:
FILTER
OFFSIDE FOTBOLLSMAGASINET

OGSAW FÖRLAGS AB 1627353
OGSAW Förlags AB, Wallingatan 25, 784 34 BORLÄNGE **Tel:** 243 832 80
Titles:
FRITID OCH PARK I SVERIGE

OHLSON & WINNFORS AB 1790357
Box 508, 701 50 OREBRO **Tel:** 19 10 80 50
Fax: 19108055
Titles:
CIRKULATION, VA-TIDSKRIFTEN

OK FÖRLAGET AB 1652946
Box 23800, 10435 STOCKHOLM **Tel:** 8 736 12 00
Fax: 8 736 12 49
Titles:
KLASSIKER
MC-NYTT
RIKSETTAN
VI BILÄGARE
VI BILÄGARE; WEBB

OLOV NORBRINK 1791234
Box 2036, 103 11 STOCKHOLM **Tel:** 8 643 38 46
Fax: 86433898
Titles:
GRÖNKÖPINGS VECKOBLAD

ONLINE MEDIA PUBLISHING AB 1732728
Nystades Företagscentrum, Idrottsvägen 5, 952 61 KALIX **Tel:** 923 789 40 **Fax:** 92310018
Titles:
NÄRINGSLIV I NORR

OPSIS KALOPSIS AB 1790578
St. Paulsgatan 13, 118 46 STOCKHOLM
Tel: 8 641 66 68 **Fax:** 86411668
Titles:
OPSIS BARNKULTUR

OPTIKERFÖRBUNDET 1790407
Karlbergsvägen 22, 113 27 STOCKHOLM
Tel: 8 612 89 60 **Fax:** 8 612 56 90
Titles:
OPTIK

ÖREBRO STUDENTKÅR 1629730
Fakultetsgatan 3, 702 18 ÖREBRO
Tel: 19 676 23 53
Titles:
LÖSNUMMER

ÖRNSKÖLDSVIKS ALLEHANDA 1789823
Box 110, 891 23 ÖRNSKÖLDSVIK
Tel: 660 29 55 00 **Fax:** 660 145 85
Titles:
ÖRNSKÖLDSVIKS ALLEHANDA

ORTSTIDNINGAR I VÄST AB 1629481
Box 523, 442 15 KUNGÄLV **Tel:** 303 20 68 00
Fax: 303 155 41
Titles:
KUNGÄLVS-POSTEN
MÖLNDALS-POSTEN; MOLNDALSPOSTEN.SE

ORTSTIDNINGEN NORRA HALLAND 1791733
Box 10244, 434 24 KUNGSBACKA
Tel: 300 107 95 **Fax:** 300 167 44
Titles:
NORRA HALLAND

ÖSTERSUNDS-POSTENS TRYCKERI AB 1789824
Box 720, 831 28 ÖSTERSUND **Tel:** 63 16 16 00
Fax: 63 16 16 55
Titles:
ÖSTERSUNDS-POSTEN

AB ÖSTGÖTA CORRESPONDENTEN 1789236
581 89 LINKÖPING **Tel:** 13 28 00 00
Fax: 13 28 03 24
Titles:
ÖSTGÖTA CORRESPONDENTEN

ÖSTRA SMÅLAND AB 1789819
Box 4, 572 21 OSKARSHAMN **Tel:** 491 772 22
Fax: 49184349
Titles:
ÖSTRAN / NYHETERNA - OSKARSHAMN; NYHETERNA.NET
ÖSTRAN / NYHETERNA; OSTRAN.SE

OTLAS AB 1628750
Sågbacksvägen 8, 792 91 MORA **Tel:** 250 228 85
Fax: 250 228 83
Titles:
SNOW RIDER

OTW PUBLISHING 1742593
Budadress: Hälsingegatan 49, 113 31, Box 6630, 113 84 STOCKHOLM **Tel:** 8 728 23 00
Titles:
BUFFÉ
TIDNINGEN ULLA

P&K PRINT 1652895
Box 119, 643 22 VINGÅKER **Tel:** 151 303 10
Fax: 151 303 10
Titles:
SCREEN&MARKNADEN

PAPERWORKS MEDIA IN SWEDEN AB 1793528
Box 2161, 403 13 GOTEBORG **Tel:** 31 711 02 10
Fax: 31 700 81 89
Titles:
MATCH

PÄR LINNERTZ, DISTR. NÄTVERKSTAN 1791255
Sunnanväg 6N, 222 26 LUND **Tel:** 211 99 82
Titles:
FILM INTERNATIONAL

PARKINSONFÖRBUNDET 1732671
Box 1386, 172 27 SUNDBYBERG
Tel: 8 546 405 27 **Fax:** 854640439
Titles:
PARKINSONJOURNALEN

PARTISEKRETERARE PERNILLA ZETHRÆÉUS BLOCH 1793585
Box 12660, 112 93 STOCKHOLM **Tel:** 8 654 08 20
Fax: 86532385
Titles:
VÄNSTERPRESS

PASSION PUBLISHING 1748163
c/o Network 21, Stureplan 4A, 114 35 STOCKHOLM **Tel:** 735206600
Titles:
PASSION FOR BUSINESS

PASTORERNAS RIKSFÖRBUND 1627619
C/O Teologiska Högskolan Stockholm, Åkeshovsg 29, 168 39 BROMMA
Tel: 8 564 357 16
Titles:
TIDSKRIFTEN TRO & LIV

PEAB 1747851
Peab, Information, 260 92 FÖRSLÖV
Tel: 431 890 00 **Fax:** 431 45 00 83
Titles:
PEABJOURNALEN

PERFECT MEDIA GROUP 1735350
Skeppargatan 55, 114 59 STOCKHOLM
Tel: 8 702 22 8
Titles:
MOORE MAGAZINE; MOORE.SE

PETER FORSMAN 1790932
Box 7514, 103 92 STOCKHOLM **Tel:** 8 791 02 00
Fax: 8 20 56 97
Titles:
HYRESGÄSTFÖRENINGEN AKTUELLT

PETIT STOCKHOLM AB 1793642
Box 191 74, 104 32 STOCKHOLM **Tel:** 8 33 34 65
Titles:
PETIT MAGAZINE

PETTER BERGSTRÖM 1743792
521 94 GUDHEM **Tel:** 515 72 05 72
Titles:
TIDNINGEN ÅTER

PHARMA INDUSTRY PUBLISHING AB 1793521
Tyra Lundgrens Väg 6, 134 40 GUSTAVSBERG
Tel: 8 570 105 20
Titles:
ONKOLOGI I SVERIGE
PHARMA INDUSTRY

PHILIPSON & SÖDERBERG AB 1790944
Box 29163, 100 52 STOCKHOLM
Tel: 8 598 112 00 **Fax:** 859811241
Titles:
PHILIPSON SÖDERBERG MAGAZINE

PIA LUNDSTRÖM 1793609
Getabocksvägen 4, 187 54 TABY
Tel: 8 510 515 00
Titles:
DIALÄSEN

PIG POULTRY PRESS AB 1793686
Näset, 741 91 KNIVSTA **Tel:** 18 34 62 52
Fax: 18346253
Titles:
FJÄDERFÄ
SVENSK GRIS MED KNORR

PITEÅ-TIDNINGENS AB 1789825
Box 193, 941 24 PITEÅ **Tel:** 911 645 00
Titles:
PITEÅ-TIDNINGEN
PITEÅ-TIDNINGEN; PITEA-TIDNINGEN.SE

PLAN SVERIGE PRODUKTION&FÖRSÄLJNING AB 1761971
Plan Sverige, Box 92150, 120 08 STOCKHOLM
Tel: 8 587 755 00 **Fax:** 8 587 755 10
Titles:
BARNENS FRAMTID

PLÅTSLAGERIERNAS SERVICE AB 1793869
Box 17536, 118 91 STOCKHOLM **Tel:** 8 762 75 85
Fax: 86160072
Titles:
PLÅT & VENT MAGASINET

PLAZA PUBLISHING GROUP AB 1627459
Box 302 10, 104 25 Stockholm, 112 51 STOCKHOLM **Tel:** 8 501 188 00
Titles:
PLAZA INTERIÖR
PLAZA KVINNA
PLAZA MAGAZINE
PLAZA STORA; HUS, KÖK & BADGUIDEN
PLAZA WATCH

PM-PRESS MEDIA 1773119
ÖSTERBYBRUK **Tel:** 295 205 60
Titles:
DÄCK NYTT

PM-PRESS MEDIA I SAMARBETE MED DRF 1755560
Vasavägen 33, 352 61 VÄXJÖ **Tel:** 470 637 63
Fax: 470 620 08
Titles:
DÄCK-DEBATT

POKER MAGAZINE I STOCKHOLM AB 1672754
Birger Jarlsgatan 20, 114 34 STOCKHOLM
Tel: 8 653 59 00 **Fax:** 8 440 40 77
Titles:
POKER MAGAZINE

POLISFÖRBUNDET 1790475
Box 5583, 114 85 STOCKHOLM **Tel:** 8 676 97 00
Fax: 8 23 24 10
Titles:
POLISTIDNINGEN

POLITIKENS LOKALAVISER 1639748
Storgatan 40, 262 43 ÄNGELHOLM
Tel: 431 881 22
Titles:
LOKALTIDNINGEN ÄNGELHOLM; WEBB
LOKALTIDNINGEN AVENYN; WEBB
LOKALTIDNINGEN BÅSTAD; WEBB
LOKALTIDNINGEN HELSINGBORG; WEBB
LOKALTIDNINGEN HÖGANÄS; WEBB
LOKALTIDNINGEN KÄVLINGE NYA
LOKALTIDNINGEN KÄVLINGE NYA; WEBB
LOKALTIDNINGEN KLIPPAN/PERSTORP/BJUV/ÅSTORP/ÖRKELLJUNGA: WEBB
LOKALTIDNINGEN KRISTIANSTAD; WEBB
LOKALTIDNINGEN LAHOLM; WEBB
LOKALTIDNINGEN LANDSKRONA; WEBB
LOKALTIDNINGEN LOMMABLADET
LOKALTIDNINGEN LOMMABLADET; WEBB
LOKALTIDNINGEN LUND; WEBB
LOKALTIDNINGEN MELLANSKÅNE; WEBB
LOKALTIDNINGEN SKURUP; WEBB
LOKALTIDNINGEN SVEDALA; WEBB
LOKALTIDNINGEN TRELLEBORG; WEBB

POLITIKENS LOKALAVISER AS 1744662
Lilla Strandgatan 5b, 261 31 LANDSKRONA
Tel: 418 44 66 66 **Fax:** 418 44 66 51
Titles:
LOKALTIDNINGEN SVALÖV; WEBB

POLYINFO AB 1629593
Box 2136, 250 02 HELSINGBORG
Tel: 42 13 85 00 **Fax:** 42 12 20 75
Titles:
POLYMERVÄRLDEN

POSTEN AB 1742771
Spoon Publishing, Kungstensg. 21 B, 113 57 STOCKHOLM **Tel:** 8 442 96 20 **Fax:** 8 442 96 39
Titles:
DU & CO

PRAKTIKERTJÄNST AB 1627729
Praktikertjänst AB, 103 55 STOCKHOLM
Tel: 8 789 40 00
Titles:
PRAKTIKAN

LA PRENSA AB 1735363
Box 145, 125 23 ÄLVSJÖ **Tel:** 8 568 790 30
Fax: 856879031
Titles:
AFFÄRSRESENÄREN
KICK OFF

PRESENCE INFORMATION 1644332
Box 5191, 200 75 MALMÖ **Tel:** 40 26 77 09
Titles:
MILJÖLEDAREN

PRESSINFO MEDIA AB 1713008
Mässans Gata 10, 412 51 GÖTEBORG
Tel: 31 708 66 86
Titles:
BIBLIOTEKET I FOKUS

PREVENT 1790397
Box 20133, 104 60 STOCKHOLM **Tel:** 8 402 02 00
Fax: 8 402 02 50
Titles:
ARBETSLIV
ARBETSLIV; WEBB

AB PREVIA 1793707
AB Previa, Box 4080, 171 04 SOLNA
Tel: 8 627 43 00 **Fax:** 8 627 43 99
Titles:
PRIMA

PRO - PENSIONÄRERNAS RIKSORGANISATION 1790228
Box 3274, 103 65 STOCKHOLM **Tel:** 8 701 67 00
Fax: 8 20 33 58
Titles:
PROPENSIONÄREN

PRODUKTIONSGRUPPEN AB 1791291
Box 4152, 131 04 NACKA **Tel:** 8 448 25 50
Fax: 84482577
Titles:
BYGGKONTAKT
LIVETS GODA
LIVETS GODA; LIVETSGODA.SE

PROFFICE SVERIGE AB 1790072
Box 70368, 107 24 STOCKHOLM
Tel: 20 170 70 70 **Fax:** 855341915
Titles:
DAGENS MÖJLIGHETER

PROFORMIA AB 1790124
Box 15128, 167 15 BROMMA **Tel:** 8 517 008 72
Titles:
PROFORMIA HÄLSA

PROJEKTMEDIA AB 1767665
Smidesvägen 10-12, 171 41 SOLNA
Tel: 8 510 608 90
Titles:
DMH, DEN MODERNA HANTVERKAREN

PSO, PSORIASISFÖRBUNDET 1793509
Box 5173, 121 18 JOHANNESHOV
Tel: 8 600 36 36 **Fax:** 855610919
Titles:
PSORIASISTIDNINGEN

PSYKOANALYTISKT FORUM 1792044
Psykoanalytiskt Forum, 141 38 HUDDINGE
Tel: 8 462 01 10
Titles:
DIVAN-TIDSKRIFT FÖR PSYKOANALYS OCH KULTUR

PUBLISH AS 1652855
Box 5240, 102 45 STOCKHOLM **Tel:** 8 13 78 60
Titles:
BILD & LJUD HEMMA

QX FÖRLAG AB 1629500
Box 17218, 104 62 STOCKHOLM **Tel:** 8 720 30 01
Titles:
QX
QX; QX.SE

R&D FÖRLAG 1685661
Voltavägen 2-4, 168 69 BROMMA
Tel: 8 704 22 30 **Fax:** 87042234
Titles:
SVENSKA BRANSCHMAGASINET

RÅD & RÖN AB 1746279
Box 38001, 100 64 STOCKHOLM **Tel:** 8 674 43 10
Fax: 8 6744325
Titles:
RÅD & RÖN
RÅD & RÖN; RADRON.SE

RÄDDA BARNEN 1790574
Rädda Barnen, 107 88 STOCKHOLM
Tel: 8 698 90 00 **Fax:** 8 698 90 14
Titles:
BARN
BARN; TIDNINGENBARN.SE

RBI SWEDEN AB / BYGGFAKTA 1639790
Reed Business Information Sweden AB / Byggfakta, 827 81 LJUSDAL **Tel:** 651 55 25 00
Fax: 6 515 525 85
Titles:
BYGGFAKTA PROJEKTNYTT

READER'S DIGEST AB 1640439
117 34 STOCKHOLM **Tel:** 8 587 108 87
Fax: 8 587 108 89
Titles:
READER'S DIGEST

REDAKTÖRSFÖRENINGEN INTERNA MEDIER 1627375
Rim, Kniva 129, 791 96 FALUN **Tel:** 31 40 56 98
Titles:
REDAKTÖREN

REED BUSINESS INFORMATION SWEDEN AB 1744712
Reed Business Sweden AB, 827 81 LJUSDAL
Tel: 651 55 25 00 **Fax:** 651 55 25 90
Titles:
VILLAFAKTA

REGIONBIBLIOTEK I STOCKHOLMS LÄN 1735414
Punkt Medis, Box 17 604, 118 92 STOCKHOLM
Tel: 8 508 308 23
Titles:
PONTON

REIDAR HANSSON ANNONS AB 1790389
Box 21105, 100 31 STOCKHOLM **Tel:** 8 34 76 90
Fax: 8 31 86 70
Titles:
BREAD & CAKES

REKORD MEDIA & PRODUKTION AB 1790138
Box 2132, 103 14 STOCKHOLM **Tel:** 812207402
Titles:
NORDISKA PROJEKT

RES & TRAFIK MEDIA I STOCKHOLM AB 1629721
Box 72001, 181 72 LIDINGÖ **Tel:** 8670 41 00
Fax: 8661 64 55
Titles:
RES & TRAFIKFORUM; WEBB
RESFORUM
TRAFIKFORUM

RESET MEDIA AB 1655301
Reset Media AB, Kungsgatan 55, 111 22 STOCKHOLM **Tel:** 8 24 41 14 **Fax:** 8 24 41 20
Titles:
LEVEL

RESTAURATÖRENS FÖRLAGS AB 1793826
Box3546, 103 69 STOCKHOLM **Tel:** 8 762 74 00
Fax: 8 411 38 16
Titles:
RESTAURATÖREN

RESUMÉ FÖRLAG 1789611
Birgerjarlsgatan 6B, 113 90 STOCKHOLM
Tel: 8 736 30 00 **Fax:** 8 736 05 25
Titles:
RESUMÉ
RESUMÉ; RESUME.SE

RETORIKFORLAGET AB 1735410
Retorikförlaget AB, Box 10, 254 03 ÖDÅKRA
Tel: 42 679 59 **Fax:** 42 679 54
Titles:
RETORIKMAGASINET

REVOLUTIONÄR KOMMUNISTISK UNGDOM 1793594
Box 31187, 400 32 GOTEBORG **Tel:** 31 24 44 17 **Fax:** 31 24 51 72
Titles:
REBELL

RFHL 1793506
c/o RFHL Lagerlöfsgatan 8, 112 60 STOCKHOLM **Tel:** 8 545 560 60 **Fax:** 8 33 58 66
Titles:
OBEROENDE

RFSL MEDIA OCH INFO AB 1735370
Box 350, 101 26 STOCKHOLM **Tel:** 8 501 629 13 **Fax:** 850162999
Titles:
KOM UT

RFSU 1740274
RFSU, Box 4331, 102 67 STOCKHOLM **Tel:** 8 692 07 28
Titles:
TIDSKRIFTEN OTTAR

RICKARD ÅSTRÖM 1639745
GIH:s studentkår, Box 5626, 114 86 STOCKHOLM **Tel:** 8 20 06 18 **Fax:** 8 20 96 80
Titles:
PHLINGAN

RIFFI 1628606
Norrtullsgatan 45, 113 45 STOCKHOLM **Tel:** 8 30 21 89 **Fax:** 8 33 53 23
Titles:
INVANDRARKVINNAN

RIKSBYGGEN 1790392
Riksbyggen, 106 18 STOCKHOLM **Tel:** 771 860 860 **Fax:** 8 698 41 10
Titles:
TIDNINGEN ÖPPET HUS

RIKSDAGENS FÖRVALTNINGSKONTOR 1629729
100 12 STOCKHOLM **Tel:** 8 786 40 00 **Fax:** 8 786 61 95
Titles:
RIKSDAG & DEPARTEMENT
RIKSDAG & DEPARTEMENT; ROD.SE

RIKSFÖRBUNDET CYSTISK FIBROS 1790468
Kålsängsgränd 10 D, 753 19 UPPSALA **Tel:** 18 15 16 22 **Fax:** 18127074
Titles:
CF-BLADET

RIKSFÖRBUNDET DHB 1790520
Kungsgatan 19, 703 61 OREBRO **Tel:** 19 17 08 30
Titles:
DHB-DIALOG

RIKSFÖRBUNDET ENSKILDA VÄGAR 1793542
Riddargatan 35-37, 114 57 STOCKHOLM **Tel:** 8 20 27 50 **Fax:** 8 20 74 78
Titles:
REV BULLETINEN

RIKSFÖRBUNDET FÖR RÖRELSEHINDRADE BARN OCH UNGDOMAR 1790521
Box 8026, 104 20 STOCKHOLM **Tel:** 8 677 73 00 **Fax:** 8 677 73 09
Titles:
RÖRELSE

RIKSFÖRBUNDET FÖR TRAFIK-, OLYCKSFALLS- OCH POLIOSKADADE, RTP 1793580
Box 2031, 169 02 SOLNA **Tel:** 8 629 27 80 **Fax:** 8 28 15 60
Titles:
LIV

RIKSFÖRBUNDET FÖRÄLDRAFÖRENINGEN MOT NARKOTIKA 1640051
Friluftsvägen 29, 172 40 SUNDBYBERG **Tel:** 8 642 06 50 **Fax:** 8 640 00 65
Titles:
ANHÖRIG, FMN

RIKSFÖRBUNDET FUB 1790525
Box 6436, 113 82 STOCKHOLM **Tel:** 8 508 866 00 **Fax:** 850886666
Titles:
UNIK

RIKSFÖRBUNDET HEM OCH SAMHÄLLE 1629818
C/O BiCo PR, Strandvägen 50, 193 30 SIGTUNA **Tel:** 8 592 565 90
Titles:
HEM OCH SAMHÄLLE

RIKSFÖRBUNDET KRISTEN FOSTRAN 1629155
Gullbergsvägen 42, 511 59 KINNA **Tel:** 320 134 49 **Fax:** 320 134 49
Titles:
KRISTEN FOSTRAN

RIKSFÖRBUNDET LÄRARE I SVENSKA SOM ANDRASPRÅK 1629680
c/o Annika Bergström, Virvelvindsgatan 12 A, 417 14 GÖTEBORG
Titles:
LISETTEN

RIKSFÖRBUNDET LOKALREVYER I SVERIGE 1629423
Landbogatan 4, 521 42 FALKÖPING **Tel:** 21 30 38 55 **Fax:** 21 30 38 56
Titles:
LIS-AKTUELLT

RIKSFÖRBUNDET NARKOTIKAFRITT SAMHÄLLE 1629924
Ragvaldsgatan 14, 118 46 STOCKHOLM **Tel:** 8 643 04 67 **Fax:** 8 643 04 98
Titles:
NARKOTIKAFRÅGAN

RIKSFÖRBUNDET SVENSK TRÄDGÅRD 1793746
Högåsvägen 6, 741 41 KNIVSTA **Tel:** 18 34 29 72 **Fax:** 18341107
Titles:
HEMTRÄDGÅRDEN

RIKSFÖRBUNDET SVERIGES LOTTAKÅRER 1627595
Box 2240, 103 16 STOCKHOLM **Tel:** 8 666 10 80 **Fax:** 8 666 10 99
Titles:
LOTTANYTT

RIKSFÖRBUNDET VISIR 1628128
Hälsans Hus, Fjällgatan 23 A, 116 28 STOCKHOLM **Tel:** 8 591 282 11 **Fax:** 8 556 988 88
Titles:
FRISKARE LIV, VISIR-AKTUELLT

RIKSFÖRENINGEN FÖR BARNSJUKSKÖTERSKOR 1640369
Stensjöberg 15, 431 36 MÖLNDAL **Tel:** 31 27 39 27
Titles:
BARNBLADET

RIKSFÖRENINGEN FÖR FÖRETAGSSKÖTERSKOR 1639839
Att: Kristina Andersson, Alviva AB, 374 38 KARLSHAMN **Tel:** 454 75 16 81
Titles:
FÖRETAGSSKÖTERSKAN

RIKSFÖRENINGEN FÖR LÄRARNA I MODERNA SPRÅK 1628332
VÄXJÖ UNIVERSITET, 351 95 VÄXJÖ **Tel:** 470 70 82 69 **Fax:** 470 75 18 88
Titles:
MODERNA SPRÅK

RIKSFÖRENINGEN FÖR SJUKSKÖTERSKOR I CANCERVÅRD 1793639
c/o Diana lindén, Imatragatan 122, 164 78 KISTA **Tel:** 8 517 745 15
Titles:
CANCERVÅRDEN

RIKSFÖRENINGEN OSTEOPOROTIKER 1640056
Riksföreningen Osteoporotiker, 414 51 GÖTEBORG **Tel:** 31 12 35 98
Titles:
OSTEOPOROSNYTT

RIKSHEMVÄRNSRÅDET 1627983
107 85 STOCKHOLM **Tel:** 8 788 75 00 **Fax:** 8 664 57 90
Titles:
TIDNINGEN HEMVÄRNET

RIKSORGANISATIONEN FOLKETS HUS OCH PARKER 1628203
AiP Media, 105 60 STOCKHOLM **Tel:** 8 700 26 46 **Fax:** 8 411 65 42
Titles:
SCEN OCH SALONG

RIKSORGANISATIONEN FÖR KVINNOJOURER O TJEJJOURER 1790277
Hornsgatan 66, 1 tr, 118 21 STOCKHOLM **Tel:** 8 442 99 30 **Fax:** 86127325
Titles:
KVINNOTRYCK

RIKSORGANISATIONEN MAKALÖSA FÖRÄLDRAR 1790601
Götgatan 100, 118 62 STOCKHOLM **Tel:** 8 720 14 13
Titles:
MAKALÖSA FÖRÄLDRAR

RIKSORGANISATIONEN UFO-SVERIGE 1629358
Box 175, 733 23 SALA **Tel:** 18 55 50 00
Titles:
UFO-AKTUELLT

RIKSPOLISSTYRELSEN 1629608
Box 12256, 102 26 STOCKHOLM **Tel:** 8 401 90 00 **Fax:** 8 401 90 65
Titles:
SVENSK POLIS
SVENSK POLIS; WEBB

RIKSUTSTÄLLNINGAR 1793927
Box 1033, 621 21 VISBY **Tel:** 498 79 90 00 **Fax:** 498 27 21 20
Titles:
RIKSUTSTÄLLNINGAR

AB RIVSTART 1713014
Box 65, 736 22 KUNGSÖR **Tel:** 227 121 40
Titles:
GASOLINE MAGAZINE

ROMANTISKA FÖRBUNDET 1627750
c/o Katarina Wallin, Katarina Skolgata 38 A, 118 53 STOCKHOLM **Tel:** 8 592 505 27
Titles:
AURORA

ROSÉN & DACKEVALL MEDIA AB 1653109
R&D Media AB, Gårdsvägen 4, 169 70 SOLNA **Tel:** 8 470 92 60
Titles:
CLASSIC BIKE

RSMH, RIKSFÖRBUNDET FÖR SOCIAL OCH MENTAL HÄLSA 1640053
Instrumentvägen 10, 2tr, 126 53 HAGERSTEN **Tel:** 8 772 33 60 **Fax:** 8 772 33 61
Titles:
REVANSCH!

RUBRIK AB 1680299
Rubrik AB; Vallgatan 27, 411 16 GÖTEBORG **Tel:** 31 719 06 00 **Fax:** 31 15 34 46
Titles:
HONDA VISION

RUBRIK MEDIA 1753186
Box 24, 149 21 NYNÄSHAMN **Tel:** 8 524 404 00 **Fax:** 852440437
Titles:
NYNÄSHAMNS POSTEN

RVUX 1630068
c/o Akademikerservice Box 3215, 103 64 STOCKHOLM **Tel:** 8 567 060 00 **Fax:** 8 567 060 99
Titles:
KOM

SÅ ÅKERIFÖRLAGET AB 1789485
Box 508, 182 15 DANDERYD **Tel:** 8 753 54 40 **Fax:** 8 755 88 95
Titles:
SVENSK ÅKERITIDNING

SABO FÖRLAGS AB 1790962
Box 474, 101 29 STOCKHOLM **Tel:** 8 441 53 73
Titles:
BOFAST

SAC 1793787
Box 6507, 113 83 STOCKHOLM **Tel:** 8 673 35 59 **Fax:** 86733580
Titles:
SYNDIKALISTEN

SAC - SYNDIKALISTERNA 1790423
Box 6507, 113 83 STOCKHOLM **Tel:** 8 16 08 90
Titles:
ARBETAREN
ARBETAREN; ARBETAREN.SE

SÅGVERKSFÖRENINGEN SÅG I SYD, SÅSY AB 1793995
Box 37, 551 12 JÖNKÖPING **Tel:** 36 34 30 00 **Fax:** 36 12 86 10
Titles:
SKOG & SÅG

SÄLJARNAS RIKSFÖRBUND 1790395
Box 12668, 112 93 STOCKHOLM **Tel:** 8 617 02 21 **Fax:** 86521515
Titles:
SÄLJAREN

SAMHALL AB 1790453
Box 27705, 115 91 STOCKHOLM **Tel:** 8 553 411 20 **Fax:** 855341101
Titles:
I FOKUS - EN TIDNING FRÅN SAMHALL

SAMHÄLLSGEMENSKAPS FÖRLAGS AB 1629509
Box 2356, 103 18 STOCKHOLM **Tel:** 8 723 25 81 **Fax:** 86127953
Titles:
KRISTDEMOKRATEN
KRISTDEMOKRATEN; WEBB

SÁMINUORRA - SVENSKA SAMERNAS RIKSUNGDOMSFÖRBUND 1710429
Adolf Hedinsvägen 36, 981 33 KIRUNA
Tel: 980 821 47 **Fax:** 980 270 77
Titles:
NUORAT

SAMPLER MEDIA AB 1641698
Box 9142, 102 72 STOCKHOLM **Tel:** 8 702 15 50
Titles:
SONIC

SAS MEDIA 1794029
Sergels Torg 12, 111 57 STOCKHOLM
Tel: 8 797 03 10 **Fax:** 8 21 31 71
Titles:
SEASONS

SBI 1790418
Stålbyggnadsinstitutet, Box 27751, SE-115 92 STOCKHOLM **Tel:** 70 630 22 17 **Fax:** 84119226
Titles:
TIDNINGEN STÅLBYGGNAD

SC AUTO SWEDEN AB 1743425
Box 8144, 163 08 SPÅNGA **Tel:** 8 474 54 00
Fax: 8 621 18 61
Titles:
MITSUBISHI MOTORS MAGAZINE

SCANTYPE FÖRLAG & MEDIA AB 1793689
c/o Scantype Förlag & Media AB, 114 75 STOCKHOLM **Tel:** 8 663 55 30 **Fax:** 8 663 55 32
Titles:
NATURLIGT OM HÄLSA

SCHIBSTED CLASSIFIED MEDIA 1793419
Tel: 8 732 2800 **Fax:** 87322829
Titles:
BYTBIL.COM

SCHIZOFRENIFÖRBUNDET 1686237
Hantverkarg. 3G, 112 21 STOCKHOLM
Tel: 8 545 559 80
Titles:
PHRENICUS

SCIENTOLOGI-KYRKAN I STOCKHOLM 1629984
Månskärsvägen 10 A, 141 75 KUNGENS KURVA
Tel: 8 615 21 81 **Fax:** 8 615 21 81
Titles:
FREEDOM

SCOP AB 1793872
Box 786, 191 27 SOLLENTUNA **Tel:** 8 631 90 70
Fax: 8 585 700 47
Titles:
PROFESSIONELL DEMOLERING
SVENSK RENTAL TIDNING

SEKO, FACKET FÖR SERVICE OCH KOMMUNIKATION 1790406
Box 1102, 111 81 STOCKHOLM **Tel:** 8 791 41 00
Fax: 8 21 16 94
Titles:
SEKOTIDNINGEN
SEKOTIDNINGEN; SEKOTIDNINGEN.SE

SEKO SJÖFOLK 1793533
Box 31176, 413 27 GOTEBORG **Tel:** 31 42 94 20
Fax: 31429501
Titles:
SJÖMANNEN

SEKO VÄG & BAN 1793786
Fjärde Långgatan 48, 413 27 GOTEBORG
Tel: 31 42 94 30 **Fax:** 31429440
Titles:
VÄGBANAREN - TIDNINGEN SOM BANAR VÄG

SFAM-SVENSK FÖRENING FÖR ALLMÄNMEDICIN 1793603
SFAMs kansli, Box 503, 114 11 STOCKHOLM
Tel: 8 23 24 05 **Fax:** 8200335
Titles:
ALLMÄN MEDICIN

SFF 1628258
Box 626, Vasagatan 12, 101 32 STOCKHOLM
Tel: 8 87 04 30 **Fax:** 8 445 88 00
Titles:
SVENSKA FRISÖRTIDNINGEN

SFIS SERVICE AB 1735373
Osquars Backe 25, c/o KTH, 100 44 STOCKHOLM **Tel:** 8 678 23 20
Titles:
INFOTREND - NORDISK TIDSKRIFT FÖR INFORMATIONSSPEC.

SGU, HYDROGEOLOGISKA ENHETEN 1629929
SGU, Box 670, 751 28 UPPSALA **Tel:** 18 17 90 00
Fax: 18 17 92 10
Titles:
GRUNDVATTEN

SHIPPAX INFORMATION 1640607
ShipPax Information, Box 7067, 300 07 HALMSTAD **Tel:** 35 21 83 70 **Fax:** 35130129
Titles:
CRUISE & FERRY INFO

SHR 1628404
Dalagatan 76, 113 24 STOCKHOLM
Tel: 8 30 94 40
Titles:
SHR-JOURNALEN

SIDA 1627752
105 25 STOCKHOLM **Tel:** 8 698 50 00
Fax: 8 698 5606
Titles:
DISA
OMVÄRLDEN

SILF MEDIA AB 1745737
Box 1278, 164 29 KISTA **Tel:** 8 752 16 90
Fax: 8 750 64 10
Titles:
INKÖP+LOGISTIK

SIS, SWEDISH STANDARDS INSTITUTE 1710365
118 80 STOCKHOLM **Tel:** 8 555 520 00
Fax: 8 555 521 09
Titles:
STANDARD MAGAZINE

SITUATION GBG EK FÖR 1639785
Stampgatan 50, 411 01 GOTEBORG
Tel: 31 63 22 90 **Fax:** 31159545
Titles:
FAKTUM

SITUATION STHLM AB 1649776
Box 19026, 104 32 STOCKHOLM **Tel:** 8 545 95 38
Fax: 8 16 73 30
Titles:
SITUATION STHLM

SJ 1745527
Centralplan 19, 105 50 STOCKHOLM
Tel: 10 751 51 85
Titles:
SJ NYTT

SJÖBEFÄLSFÖRBUNDET 1790482
Box 12100, 102 23 STOCKHOLM
Tel: 8 598 991 21 **Fax:** 86510848
Titles:
SJÖBEFÄL

SJUKGYMNASTEN TIDNING OCH FÖRLAG AB 1745506
LSR/Fysioterapi, Box 3196, 103 63 STOCKHOLM **Tel:** 8 567 061 00
Titles:
FYSIOTERAPI
FYSIOTERAPI; WEBB

SJUKHUSLÄKARFÖRENINGEN 1791020
Box 5610, 114 86 STOCKHOLM **Tel:** 8 790 33 00
Titles:
SJUKHUSLÄKAREN
SJUKHUSLÄKAREN; SJUKHUSLAKAREN.SE

SKANDINAVISKA CAD-MAGASINET, FÖRLAG 1649902
Bagersgatan 2, 211 25 MALMÖ **Tel:** 40 23 22 37
Fax: 40 23 70 87
Titles:
CAD & RITNYTT

SKÅNEMEDIA AB 1789545
Storgatan 36A, 272 31 SIMRISHAMN
Tel: 414 179 80 **Fax:** 41428999
Titles:
ÖSTERLENMAGASINET
TRELLEBORGS ALLEHANDA
TRELLEBORGS ALLEHANDA; WEBB
YSTADS ALLEHANDA
YSTADS ALLEHANDA; WEBB

SKÅNSKA DAGBLADET, AB 1789918
281 81 HÄSSLEHOLM **Tel:** 451 74 50 00
Fax: 451 74 50 32
Titles:
NORRA SKÅNE
NORRA SKÅNE; NSK.SE
SKÅNSKA DAGBLADET

SKARABORG ALLEHANDA 1789821
Box 407, 541 28 SKÖVDE **Tel:** 500 46 75 00
Fax: 500 48 05 82
Titles:
SKARABORGS ALLEHANDA

SKARABORGSBYGDENS TIDNINGSFÖRENING UPA 1629489
Box 204, 532 23 SKARA **Tel:** 511 302 50
Fax: 51112620
Titles:
SKARABORGSBYGDEN
SKARABORGSBYGDEN; SKARABORGSBYGDEN.SE

SKÄRGÅRDSSTIFTELSEN 1643700
Skärgårdsstiftelsen, Box 7669, 103 94 STOCKHOLM **Tel:** 8 440 56 00 **Fax:** 84405619
Titles:
STÅNGMÄRKET

SKATTEBETALARNAS FÖRENING 1793885
Box 3319, 103 66 STOCKHOLM **Tel:** 8 613 17 00
Fax: 86131760
Titles:
SUNT FÖRNUFT

AB SKF 1791132
AB SKF, 415 50 GOTEBORG **Tel:** 31 337 10 00
Fax: 31 337 17 22
Titles:
EVOLUTION

SKODA AUTO SVERIGE AB 1628065
Skoda Auto Sverige, 151 88 SÖDERTÄLJE
Tel: 8 553 865 17
Titles:
SKODAWORLD

SKOGEN I SKOLAN 1639788
Kansliet för lärarutbildning, Umeå universitet, 901 87 UMEÅ **Tel:** 90 786 68 58
Titles:
SKOGEN I SKOLAN

SKOGSINDUSTRIERNA 1793700
Box 55525, 102 04 STOCKHOLM **Tel:** 8 762 72 02
Fax: 86117122
Titles:
SKOG & INDUSTRI

SKOGSSTYRELSEN 1790934
Skogsstyrelsen, 551 83 JÖNKÖPING
Tel: 36 35 39 00 **Fax:** 36166170
Titles:
SKOGSEKO

SKOLMATENSVÄNNER 1793710
105 33 STOCKHOLM **Tel:** 70 237 99 29
Titles:
SKOLMATENS VÄNNER

SKOMAGAZINET FÖRLAG AB 1790410
Bergvägen 12 A, 182 46 ENEBYBERG
Tel: 8 768 85 03 **Fax:** 87688523
Titles:
SKOMAGAZINET

SKRIVARHUSET TID & SMYCKEN 1641010
Gustaf Kjellbergsväg 2, 756 43 UPPSALA
Tel: 18 12 04 68 **Fax:** 417 312 61
Titles:
TID & SMYCKEN

SKRIVARKLUBBEN I BLEKINGE 1629665
c/o Johansson, Trastvägen 8, 374 50 ASARUM
Tel: 454 874 75
Titles:
GROBLAD

SKTF MEDIA AB 1790062
Box 7825, 103 97 STOCKHOLM **Tel:** 8 789 63 00
Fax: 8 789 64 79
Titles:
SKTF-TIDNINGEN

SKTF (PRODUCERAS AV SKTF MEDIA AB) 1790491
Box 7825, 103 97 STOCKHOLM **Tel:** 8 789 64 61
Fax: 8 789 64 79
Titles:
CHEFEN I FOKUS

SLITZ MEDIAPRODUKTION AB 1629642
MDM Media AB, 120 30 STOCKHOLM
Tel: 8 506 122 00 **Fax:** 850612201
Titles:
SLITZ
SLITZ; SLITZ.SE

SMÅLANDSPOSTEN 1789559
351 70 VÄXJO **Tel:** 470 77 05 00 **Fax:** 47048425
Titles:
SMÅLANDSPOSTEN; SMP.SE

SMÅLANDSPOSTEN AB 1789925
351 70 VÄXJO **Tel:** 470 77 05 00 **Fax:** 470 484 25
Titles:
SMÅLANDSPOSTEN

SMÅLANDSTIDNINGENS TRYCKERI AB 1789653
Missionsgatan 2, 573 23 TRANAS **Tel:** 140 674 40
Titles:
TRANÅS TIDNING

SMHI 1628787
SMHI, Väder & Vatten, 601 76 NORRKÖPING
Tel: 11 495 80 00 **Fax:** 11 495 80 01
Titles:
VÄDER OCH VATTEN

SMITTSKYDDSINSTITUTET 1630257
Nobels väg 18, 171 82 SOLNA **Tel:** 8 457 23 00
Titles:
SMITTSKYDD

SMKF 1629158
SMKF, Östhammarsgatan 70, 115 28 STOCKHOLM **Tel:** 8 51439972 **Fax:** 851439970

Titles:
SVENSK MÅNGKAMP

SOCIALISTISKA PARTIET 1627425
Box 5073, 121 16 JOHANNESHOV **Tel:** 8 31 70 70

Titles:
INTERNATIONALEN
INTERNATIONALEN; WEBB
RÖDA RUMMET

SÖDERMANLANDS NYHETER AB 1629620
611 79 NYKÖPING **Tel:** 155 767 00

Titles:
SÖDERMANLANDS NYHETER
SÖDERMANLANDS NYHETER; SN.SE

SÖDERTÖRNS HÖGSKOLAS STUDENTKÅR 1629359
SöderS, Södertörns Högskola, 141 89 HUDDINGE **Tel:** 8 608 40 35 **Fax:** 8 608 40 81

Titles:
SODA - SÖDERTÖRNS HÖGSKOLAS KÅRTIDNING

SOLLENTUNA KOMMUN 1732772
Sollentuna kommun, 191 86 SOLLENTUNA **Tel:** 8 579 211 61

Titles:
SOLLENTUNAJOURNALEN

SOLRESOR I SVERIGE AB 1735355
Identitet c/o Community, Gustav Adolfs Torg 10B, 211 39 MALMÖ **Tel:** 40 66 55 792 **Fax:** 40 66 55 799

Titles:
PRIME TIME MAGAZINE

SOS-BARNBYAR SVERIGE 1629675
Box 24165, 104 51 STOCKHOLM **Tel:** 8 545 832 00 **Fax:** 8 545 832 22

Titles:
BARNBYAR

SP SVERIGES TEKNISKA FORSKNINGSINSTITUT. BRANDTEKN 1743953
Box 857, 501 15 BORÅS **Tel:** 10 516 50 00 **Fax:** 33417759

Titles:
BRANDPOSTEN

SPEARHEAD PRODUCTION AB 1790973
Skeppargatan 27, 114 52 STOCKHOLM **Tel:** 8 442 86 30 **Fax:** 86621180

Titles:
MÄKLARVÄRLDEN

SPEL & SERVICEHANDLARNAS RIKSFÖRBUND 1790353
Servicehandlarn i Sverige AB, 716 31 FJUGESTA **Tel:** 585 317 01

Titles:
SERVICEHANDLAREN

SPF SKÅNEDISTRIKTET 1628934
SPFs Distrikskansli i Höör, 243 31 HÖÖR **Tel:** 413 291 14 **Fax:** 413 291 17

Titles:
SKÅNEVETERANEN

SPOON PUBLISHING 1789222
Spoon Publishing, Kungstensgatan 21 B, 113 57 STOCKHOLM **Tel:** 8 442 96 20

Titles:
SALT & PEPPAR

SPOON PUBLISHING AB 1793535
Spoon Publishing, Kungstensgatan 21B, 113 57 STOCKHOLM **Tel:** 8 442 96 20 **Fax:** 8 442 96 39

Titles:
SATS MAGASIN

SPORRE MEDIA AB 1735421
Vitsand, 152 95 SÖDERTÄLJE **Tel:** 8 541 38 420

Titles:
STUDENTGUIDEN

SPRÅKTIDNINGEN I SVERIGE AB 1740715
Folkungagatan 122, 116 30 302 43 HALMSTAD STOCKHOLM **Tel:** 8 551 109 50

Titles:
SPRÅKTIDNINGEN

SPRINGTIME PUBLISHING AB 1627686
Box 22559, 112 21 STOCKHOLM **Tel:** 8 545 535 38 **Fax:** 8 545 535 49

Titles:
CYKELTIDNINGEN KADENS
GLID- SVENSK LÄNGDÅKNING

SRF, FÖRENINGEN FÖR SYNREHABILITERING 1752908
SRF, 122 88 ENSKEDE **Tel:** 8 39 92 98

Titles:
NYA SYNVÄRLDEN

SRF STOCKHOLMS OCH GOTLANDS LÄN 1790526
Box 20074, 104 60 STOCKHOLM **Tel:** 8 462 45 27 **Fax:** 84624502

Titles:
VÅR SYNPUNKT

STAMPEN 1789773
Polhemsplatsen 5, 405 02 GOTEBORG **Tel:** 31 62 40 00 **Fax:** 31 80 27 69

Titles:
GÖTEBORGS-POSTEN
HALLANDS NYHETER
HALLANDS NYHETER; WWW.HN.SE

STAND BY PUBLISHING APS 1793620
Eriksbergsgatan 46 4 tr, 114 30 STOCKHOLM **Tel:** 8 694 70 55 **Fax:** 86947075

Titles:
STAND BY - SCANDINAVIAN TRAVEL TRADE JOURNAL

STATENS VÄG- OCH TRANS-PORTFORSKNINGSINSTITUT 1744935
Olaus Magnus väg 35, 581 95 LINKÖPING **Tel:** 13 20 40 00 **Fax:** 13 14 14 36

Titles:
VTI AKTUELLT

STATION 5 AB 1639861
Box 30210, 104 25 STOCKHOLM **Tel:** 8 501 188 50

Titles:
HEM LJUVA HEM
HEM LJUVA HEM TRÄDGÅRD
TOVE HEM & TRÄDGÅRD

STATISTISKA CENTRALBYRÅN 1790262
Statistiska centralbyrån, Box 24300, 104 51 STOCKHOLM **Tel:** 8 506 940 00 **Fax:** 850694772

Titles:
VÄLFÄRD

STEFAN LJUNGDAHL 1790379
Tel: 19 166 130 **Fax:** 19166145

Titles:
ENTREPRENADAKTUELLT

STEFAN & CO TIDNINGSPRODUKTION 1789659
Box 830, 245 18 STAFFANSTORP **Tel:** 46 25 02 02

Titles:
SPEGELN SVEDALABLADET

STIFTELSEN CEREALIA FOU 1628287
Box 30192, 104 25 STOCKHOLM **Tel:** 8 657 42 20

Titles:
C, IDÉTIDSKRIFT OM CEREALIER

STIFTELSEN CONTRA 1627406
Box 8052, 104 20 STOCKHOLM **Tel:** 8 720 01 45

Titles:
CONTRA

STIFTELSEN DATORN I UTBILDNING 1629742
c/o Peter Becker, Förridargränd 16, 165 57 HÄSSELBY **Tel:** 8 32 57 76 **Fax:** 8 32 57 76

Titles:
DATORN I UTBILDNINGEN

STIFTELSEN EXPO 1791355
Box 8165, 104 20 STOCKHOLM **Tel:** 8 652 60 04 **Fax:** 86526204

Titles:
EXPO

STIFTELSEN FÄRGFABRIKEN 1793644
Färgfabriken, Lövholmsbrinken 1, 117 43 STOCKHOLM **Tel:** 8 645 07 07 **Fax:** 86455030

Titles:
FÄRGFABRIKEN MAGAZINE

STIFTELSEN INVANDRARE & MINORITETER 1628072
Fittja gård, Värdshusvägen 46, 145 50 NORSBORG **Tel:** 8 531 757 60 **Fax:** 8 531 734 30

Titles:
I&M, INVANDRARE & MINORITETER

STIFTELSEN JABBOK 1629736
Skarpnäcks Allé 58, 128 33 SKARPNÄCK **Tel:** 8 604 25 89

Titles:
JABBOK

STIFTELSEN JUDISK KRÖNIKA 1629673
Box 5053, 102 42 STOCKHOLM **Tel:** 8 660 70 62 **Fax:** 8 660 38 72

Titles:
JUDISK KRÖNIKA

STIFTELSEN KATOLSK KYRKOTIDNING 1629985
Box 2038, 750 02 UPPSALA **Tel:** 18 13 61 40 **Fax:** 18136145

Titles:
KATOLSKT MAGASIN
KATOLSKT MAGASIN; WEBB

STIFTELSEN KONSTPERSPEKTIV 1793825
Box 600 65, 216 10 MALMO **Tel:** 40 36 26 60 **Fax:** 40162607

Titles:
KONSTPERSPEKTIV

STIFTELSEN KYRKLIGT FORUM 1639838
Box 2085, 750 02 UPPSALA **Tel:** 18 51 09 86 **Fax:** 18 55 09 86

Titles:
SVENSK PASTORALTIDSKRIFT

STIFTELSEN NOAKS ARK I SAMARBETE MED LÄKARE MOT AIDS 1732761
Stiftelsen Noaks Ark-Röda korset, Eriksbergsgatan 46, 114 30 STOCKHOLM **Tel:** 8 700 46 00 **Fax:** 8 700 46 10

Titles:
PERSPEKTIV PÅ HIV

STIFTELSEN ORD & BILD 1627670
Box 31120, 400 32 GÖTEBORG **Tel:** 31 743 99 10 **Fax:** 31 743 99 06

Titles:
ORD & BILD

STIFTELSEN ORKESTER JOURNALEN 1743288
Box 16344, 103 26 STOCKHOLM **Tel:** 8 407 17 45 **Fax:** 8 407 17 49

Titles:
ORKESTER JOURNALEN - OM JAZZ

STIFTELSEN PALETTEN 1629505
Heurlins Plats 1, 413 01 GÖTEBORG **Tel:** 31 743 99 15 **Fax:** 31 743 99 16

Titles:
PALETTEN

STIFTELSEN SAMEFOLKET 1639775
Box 86, 933 22 ARVIDSJAUR **Tel:** 960 134 30

Titles:
SAMEFOLKET

STIFTELSEN SKANDINAVISK YOGA OCH MEDITATIONSSKOLA 1744661
Västmannagatan 62, 113 25 STOCKHOLM **Tel:** 8 32 12 18 **Fax:** 8 31 44 06

Titles:
BINDU

STIFTELSEN SKELLEFTEÅPRESS 1790597
Box 58, 931 21 SKELLEFTEÅ **Tel:** 910 577 00 **Fax:** 910 578 75

Titles:
NORRAN

STIFTELSEN SKOGSSÄLLSKAPET 1732717
Skogssällskapet, Box 5083, 402 22 GÖTEBORG **Tel:** 771 22 00 44 **Fax:** 31 335 89 07

Titles:
SKOGSVÄRDEN

STIFTELSEN STOCKHOLMS JURIDISKA FAKULTETS TID 1629697
Artillerigatan 67, 114 45 STOCKHOLM **Tel:** 8 662 00 80 **Fax:** 8 662 00 86

Titles:
JURIDISK TIDSKRIFT

STIL, STOCKHOLMSKOOPERATIVET FÖR INDEPENDENT LIVING 1662497
Arenavägen 63 7tr., 121 77 JOHANNESHOV **Tel:** 8 506 221 50 **Fax:** 850622170

Titles:
STILETTEN

STOCKHOLMS FRIA EKONOMISKA FÖRENING 1627318
Fraktflygargatan 18, 128 30 SKARPNÄCK **Tel:** 8 600 80 80

Titles:
NYHETSTIDNINGEN SESAM
NYHETSTIDNINGEN SESAM; SESAM.NU
STOCKHOLMS FRIA TIDNING; STOCKHOLMSFRIA.NU

STOCKHOLMS HAMN AB 1793546
Box 27314, 102 54 STOCKHOLM **Tel:** 8 670 26 00 **Fax:** 8 670 26 55

Titles:
VIA STOCKHOLMS HAMNAR

STOCKHOLMS HANDELSKAMMARE 1793879
Box 16050, 103 21 STOCKHOLM **Tel:** 8 555 100 00 **Fax:** 856631600

Titles:
HANDELSKAMMARTIDNINGEN

STOCKHOLMS LÄNS LANDSTING 1790600
Hälso- och sjukvårdsnämndens förvaltning Box 690, Hantverkargatan 11 B, 102 39 STOCKHOLM **Tel:** 8123 132 70

Titles:
VÅRDGUIDEN

Sweden

STOCKHOLMS UNIVERSITETS STUDENTKÅR 1627387
Box 500 06, 104 05 STOCKHOLM
Tel: 8 674 62 49 **Fax:** 8 16 71 68
Titles:
GAUDEAMUS

STODAB 1743462
Box 23, 261 07 ASMUNDTORP **Tel:** 418 43 28 00
Fax: 418 43 28 00
Titles:
DIETISTAKTUELLT

STÖDKOMMITTÉN FÖR KVINNOR I IRAN - SKI 1790282
Box 7069, 402 32 GOTEBORG **Tel:** 707 22 80 83
Titles:
KVINNOR MOT FUNDAMENTALISM

STORSTOCKHOLMS DIABETESFÖRENING 1639797
Torsgatan 8, 111 23 STOCKHOLM
Tel: 8 654 00 40 **Fax:** 8 654 80 20
Titles:
LEVA MED DIABETES

STR SERVICE AB 1639796
Järvgatan 4, 261 44 LANDSKRONA
Tel: 418 40 10 00 **Fax:** 418 132 50
Titles:
MITT I TRAFIKEN-EN KUNSKAPSTIDNING OM TRAFIKSÄKERHET

STUDENTKÅREN HÖGSKOLAN GÄVLE 1628538
Box 6018, 800 06 GÄVLE **Tel:** 26 64 86 23
Fax: 26 60 96 51
Titles:
GEFLA HÖGTRYCK

STUDENTKÅREN I ÖSTERSUND 1630023
Studentkåren i Östersund, Mittuniversitetet, 831 25 ÖSTERSUND **Tel:** 63 16 54 80
Titles:
DEKÅR

STUDENTKÅREN I VÄXJÖ 1628546
Box 5015, 350 05 VÄXJÖ **Tel:** 470 75 54 62
Fax: 470 75 54 50
Titles:
SISTA BREFVET

STUDENTMEDIA AB 1790489
Studentmedia AB, Box 3101, 103 62 STOCKHOLM **Tel:** 8 587 075 00 **Fax:** 8 587 075 01
Titles:
PIRAJA

STUDIEFÖRBUNDET VUXENSKOLAN 1627552
Box 1109, 111 81 STOCKHOLM **Tel:** 8 587 686 00
Fax: 8 587 686 03
Titles:
IMPULS

STUDIEFRÄMJANDETS RIKSFÖRBUND 1710449
Studiefrämjandet Riksförbundet, Box 49013, 100 28 STOCKHOLM **Tel:** 8 545 707 00
Fax: 8 545 707 39
Titles:
CIRKELN

SUNDSVALL TIDNING AB 1789924
851 72 SUNDSVALL **Tel:** 60 19 70 00
Titles:
SUNDSVALLS TIDNING

SUNE HELLSTRÖMER 1790985
Box 1216, 171 23 SOLNA **Tel:** 8 735 09 00
Titles:
MAGASINET FOTBOLL

SVEAGRUPPEN TIDNINGS AB 1789723
Box 280, 781 23 BORLÄNGE **Tel:** 243 21 30 80
Fax: 243213085
Titles:
DALABYGDEN; DALABYGDEN.SE
GÄSTRIKLANDS TIDNING; WEBB
LÄNS-POSTEN; LANSPOSTEN.SE
UPPLANDS NYHETER; WEBB
VÄSTMANLANDS NYHETER; WEBB

SVEN JANBRINK 1735353
Högbyvägen 155, 175 54 JÄRFÄLLA
Tel: 8 58 01 68 02 **Fax:** 8 58 08 24 24
Titles:
BÄTTRE PRODUKTIVITET

SVENLJUNGA & TRANEMO TIDNING AB 1640055
Box 33, 514 23 TRANEMO **Tel:** 325 400 00
Fax: 325 406 58
Titles:
SVENLJUNGA & TRANEMO TIDNING
SVENLJUNGA & TRANEMO TIDNING; WEBB

SVENSK AMATÖRASTRONOMISK FÖRENING, SAAF 1629734
c/o D. Söderström, Götgatan 4, 753 15 UPPSALA **Tel:** 18 26 19 93
Titles:
TELESCOPIUM

SVENSK BENSINHANDEL 1790408
Box 1763, 111 87 STOCKHOLM **Tel:** 8 700 63 36
Fax: 87006349
Titles:
BENSIN & BUTIK

SVENSK BIBLIOTEKSFÖRENING 1627483
Box 70380, 107 24 STOCKHOLM
Tel: 8 545 132 40 **Fax:** 8 545 132 31
Titles:
BIBLIOTEKSBLADET, BBL

SVENSK ENERGI-SWEDENENERGY - AB 1710643
101 53 STOCKHOLM **Tel:** 8 677 26 20
Titles:
ERA
ERA; ERA.SE

SVENSK FJÄRRVÄRME 1640372
Mitt ordval, Miraallén 21, 417 58 GOTEBORG
Tel: 31 22 78 11
Titles:
FJÄRRVÄRMETIDNINGEN

SVENSK FÖRENING FÖR DIABETOLOGI 1793597
SU Sahlgrenska, 413 45 GOTEBORG
Tel: 31 342 10 00 **Fax:** 31270087
Titles:
DIABETOLOGNYTT

SVENSK FÖRENING FÖR RÖNTGENSJUKSKÖTERSKOR 1793515
Frostgränd 48, 931 51 SKELLEFTEÅ
Tel: 910 193 63 **Fax:** 91019363
Titles:
RÖRET

SVENSK FÖRENING FÖR SJUKSKÖTERSKOR I DIABETESVÅRD 1793641
c/o Britt-Marie Carlsson, Ljungås, 519 91 ISTORP **Tel:** 320 77 90 16
Titles:
DIABETESVÅRD

SVENSK GALOPP 1649611
161 89 STOCKHOLM **Tel:** 8 627 20 00
Fax: 8 764 50 28
Titles:
SKANDINAVISK GALOPP

AB SVENSK HANDELSTIDNING JUSTITIA 1790396
105 99 STOCKHOLM **Tel:** 8 519 012 00
Fax: 8169932
Titles:
SVENSK HANDELSTIDNING JUSTITIA

SVENSK IDROTTSMEDICINSK FÖRENING 1793512
Tuna Industriväg 4, 153 30 JÄRNA
Tel: 8 550 102 00 **Fax:** 855010409
Titles:
SVENSK IDROTTSMEDICIN

AB SVENSK KONSTNÄRSSERVICE 1763547
Norrtullsgatan 45, 117 43 STOCKHOLM
Tel: 8 545 420 83 **Fax:** 8 545 420 89
Titles:
KONSTNÄREN

SVENSK KYRKOTIDNINGS FÖRLAG AB 1629354
c/o Göran Lundstedth, Tryffelvägen 72, 756 46 UPPSALA **Tel:** 18 32 44 20
Titles:
SVENSK KYRKOTIDNING

SVENSK MJÖLK 1793685
Box 1146, 631 81 ESKILSTUNA **Tel:** 16 16 34 42
Fax: 16212 16
Titles:
NÖTKÖTT

SVENSK MJÖLK AB 1627446
Svensk Mjölk, Box 1146, 631 80 ESKILSTUNA
Tel: 16 16 35 56 **Fax:** 1621125
Titles:
HUSDJUR
KÄRNFULLT
MJÖLKSPEGELN
PEJLING FRÅN SVENSK MJÖLK

SVENSK ORTOPEDISK FÖRENING 1793513
Everöd 19, 273 93 TOMELILLA **Tel:** 417 310 26
Fax: 41731261
Titles:
ORTOPEDISKT MAGASIN

AB SVENSK PAPPERSTIDNING 1793536
Box 5515, 114 85 STOCKHOLM **Tel:** 8 783 84 00
Fax: 8 661 73 44
Titles:
NORDIC PULP AND PAPER RESEARCH JOURNAL

SVENSK RAPS AB 1628190
Box 96, 230 53 ALNARP **Tel:** 40 46 20 80
Fax: 40 46 20 85
Titles:
SVENSK FRÖTIDNING

SVENSK SJÖFARTS TIDNINGS FÖRLAG AB 1627414
Box 370, 401 25 GÖTEBORG **Tel:** 31 62 95 70
Fax: 31 80 27 50
Titles:
SVENSK SJÖFARTS TIDNING

SVENSK SJUKSKÖTERSKEFÖRENING 1643776
Baldersgatan 1, 114 27 STOCKHOLM
Tel: 8 412 24 00 **Fax:** 8 412 24 24
Titles:
OMVÅRDNADSMAGASINET

SVENSKA AFGHANISTANKOMMITTÉN 1629077
Trekantsvägen 1, 6tr., 117 43 STOCKHOLM
Tel: 8 545 818 40 **Fax:** 8 545 818 55
Titles:
AFGHANISTAN-NYTT

SVENSKA BADMINTONFÖRBUNDET 1627699
Blekingegatan 8, 118 56 STOCKHOLM
Tel: 70 574 82 34
Titles:
SPELA BADMINTON

SVENSKA BARNBOKSINSTITUTET 1629937
Odengatan 61, 113 22 STOCKHOLM
Tel: 8 545 420 50 **Fax:** 8 545 420 54
Titles:
BARNBOKEN - TIDSKRIFT FÖR BARNLITTERATURFORSKNING

SVENSKA BARNMORSKEFÖRBUNDET 1793606
Baldersgatan 1, 114 27 STOCKHOLM
Tel: 8 10 70 88 **Fax:** 8244946
Titles:
JORDEMODERN

SVENSKA BÅTUNIONEN FÖRLAG AB 1629555
Ö. Vittusgatan 36, 371 38 KARLSKRONA
Tel: 455 297 80 **Fax:** 455 36 97 99
Titles:
BÅTLIV
BÅTLIV; BATLIV.SE

SVENSKA BETONGFÖRENINGEN 1791258
Svenska Betongföreningen, 100 44 STOCKHOLM **Tel:** 8 564 102 14 **Fax:** 8 564 102 39
Titles:
TIDSKRIFTEN BETONG

SVENSKA BIOENERGIFÖRENINGEN 1735405
Torsgatan 12, 111 23 STOCKHOLM
Tel: 8 441 70 95 **Fax:** 8 441 70 89
Titles:
BIOENERGI

SVENSKA BLÅ STJÄRNAN 1793357
Box 2034, 169 02 SOLNA **Tel:** 8 629 63 60
Fax: 86296383
Titles:
BLÅ STJÄRNAN

SVENSKA BMW MC KLUBBEN 1630064
c/o Hagen Hopp, Grindtorpsvägen 35, 183 49 TÄBY **Tel:** 8 758 64 66
Titles:
BUMSEN

SVENSKA BOKHANDLARFÖRENINGEN/ KPR 1640064
Blå Kontoret, Drottninggatan 83, 111 60 STOCKHOLM **Tel:** 8 32 38 92
Titles:
PAPPER & KONTOR

SVENSKA BOKSTAVSBOLAGET 1773652
c/o Workshop, 11438 STOCKHOLM
Tel: 73 5000 600
Titles:
EN LAGOM DOS GRÖNT.SE

SVENSKA BOSTÄDER 1657601
Box 95, 162 12 VÄLLINGBY **Tel:** 8 508 370 33
Fax: 8 508 611 68
Titles:
GODA GRANNAR

SVENSKA BOTANISKA FÖRENINGEN 1627486
c/o Växtekologiska avd. Villavägen 14, 752 36 UPPSALA **Tel:** 18 471 28 91 **Fax:** 18 55 34 19
Titles:
SVENSK BOTANISK TIDSKRIFT

SVENSKA BRANDSKYDDSFÖRENINGENS SERVICE AB 1790188
Luntmakargatan 90, 113 51 STOCKHOLM
Tel: 8 23 43 10
Titles:
BRANDSÄKERT

SVENSKA BRUKSHUNDKLUBBEN 1793932
Nordenskiöldsg 13, 211 19 MALMO
Tel: 4 061 190 11
Titles:
BRUKSHUNDEN

SVENSKA BYGGINGENJÖRERS RIKSFÖRBUND, SBR 1629629
Box 4415, 102 69 STOCKHOLM **Tel:** 8 462 17 90
Titles:
HUSBYGGAREN

SVENSKA BYGGNADSARBETA-REFÖRBUNDET 1790414
106 32 STOCKHOLM **Tel:** 8 728 48 00
Fax: 8 728 49 80
Titles:
BYGGNADSARBETAREN
BYGGNADSARBETAREN; BYGGNADSARBETAREN.SE

SVENSKA BYGGNADSARBETA-REFÖRBUNDET AVD. 1 1790422
Box 1288, 171 25 SOLNA **Tel:** 8 734 65 00
Fax: 87346660
Titles:
BYGGETTAN

SVENSKA BYGGNADSVÅRDS-FÖRENINGEN 1649716
Svenska byggnadsvårdsföreningen, Box 6442, 113 82 STOCKHOLM **Tel:** 23 278 78
Fax: 23 278 77
Titles:
BYGGNADSKULTUR

SVENSKA CARDIOLOGFÖRENINGEN 1790239
Sveavägen 17, 8 tr, 111 57 STOCKHOLM
Tel: 8 546 910 00 **Fax:** 854691001
Titles:
SVENSK CARDIOLOGI

SVENSKA CELIAKIFÖRBUNDET 1790469
Västra Vägen 5B, 171 23 SOLNA **Tel:** 8 730 05 72
Fax: 87300502
Titles:
BULLETINEN

SVENSKA CURLINGFÖRBUNDET 1628483
Idrottshuset, 123 43 FARSTA **Tel:** 8 683 30 16
Fax: 8 604 70 78
Titles:
SVENSK CURLING

SVENSKA CYKELSÄLLSKAPET 1627529
Torneågatan 10, 164 79 KISTA **Tel:** 8 751 62 04
Titles:
NYA CYKELTIDNINGEN

SVENSKA DAGBLADET AB 1789383
Besöksadress: Västra Järnvägsgatan 21, 105 17 STOCKHOLM **Tel:** 8 13 50 00 **Fax:** 8 13 50 01
Titles:
SVENSKA DAGBLADET
SVENSKA DAGBLADET; K
SVENSKA DAGBLADET;SVD.SE

SVENSKA DIABETESFÖRBUNDET 1639819
Box 1107, 172 22 SUNDBYBERG
Tel: 8 564 821 00 **Fax:** 8 564 821 39
Titles:
DIABETES

SVENSKA DISTRIKTSLÄKAR-FÖRENINGEN (DLF) 1629581
Svenska Distriktsläkarföreningen, Box 5610, 114 86 STOCKHOLM **Tel:** 8 790 33 91 **Fax:** 8 790 33 95
Titles:
DISTRIKTSLÄKAREN

SVENSKA ELEKTRIKERFÖRBUNDET 1629588
Modern Teknik i Stockholm AB, Box 216, 162 13 VÄLLINGBY **Tel:** 70 590 09 02
Titles:
ELEKTRIKERN
ELEKTRIKERN; ELEKTRIKERN.NU

SVENSKA EPILEPSIFÖRBUNDET 1629928
Box 1386, 172 27 SUNDBYBERG **Tel:** 8 669 41 06
Fax: 8 669 15 88
Titles:
SVENSKA EPILEPSIA

SVENSKA FALLSKÄRMSFÖRBUNDET 1628723
Himmelsdyk, Box 110, 438 23 LANDVETTER
Tel: 31 91 88 01
Titles:
SVENSK FALLSKÄRMSSPORT

SVENSKA FÅRAVELSFÖRBUNDET 1793683
Lillegården Brismene, 521 93 FALKÖPING
Tel: 515 530 45
Titles:
FÅRSKÖTSEL

SVENSKA FISKHANDELSFÖRBUNDET 1628762
Pirhus 1 Fiskhamnspiren, 414 58 GÖTEBORG
Tel: 31 14 40 12 **Fax:** 31 14 40 12
Titles:
SVENSK FISKHANDEL

SVENSKA FN-FÖRBUNDET 1629997
Box 15115, 104 65 STOCKHOLM **Tel:** 8 462 25 58
Fax: 8 641 88 76
Titles:
VÄRLDSHORISONT

SVENSKA FOLKDANSRINGEN 1792055
Box 34056, 100 26 STOCKHOLM **Tel:** 8 695 00 15
Fax: 86950022
Titles:
HEMBYGDEN

SVENSKA FOLKHÖGSKOLANS LÄRARFÖRBUND 1627389
SFHL, Box 1057, 172 22 SUNDBYBERG
Tel: 8 564 835 35
Titles:
FOLKHÖGSKOLAN

SVENSKA FÖRBUNDET FÖR SPECIALPEDAGOGIK 1790456
Jakobsbergsgatan 29, 271 39 YSTAD
Tel: 411 122 43 **Fax:** 41112243
Titles:
ATT UNDERVISA

SVENSKA FÖRENINGEN FÖR PSYKISK HÄLSA 1793514
Box 3445, 103 69 STOCKHOLM **Tel:** 8 34 70 65
Titles:
PSYKISK HÄLSA

SVENSKA FÖRSVARSUTBILD-NINGSFÖRBUNDET 1735426
Box 5034, 102 41 STOCKHOLM **Tel:** 8 587 742 00
Fax: 8 587 742 90
Titles:
FÖRSVARSUTBILDAREN

SVENSKA FOTOGRAFERS FÖRBUND 1627710
Årstaängsvägen 5 B, S-117 43 STOCKHOLM
Tel: 8 702 03 71 **Fax:** 8 641 22 10
Titles:
FOTOGRAFISK TIDSKRIFT
FOTOGRAFISK TIDSKRIFT; WEBB

SVENSKA FREDS- OCH SKILJEDOMSFÖRENINGEN 1629887
Box 4134, 102 63 STOCKHOLM
Tel: 8 55 80 31 88 **Fax:** 8 702 18 46
Titles:
FREDSTIDNINGEN PAX

SVENSKA FRISKSPORTFÖRBUNDET 1793522
Brahegatan 32A, 553 34 JÖNKÖPING
Tel: 36 71 17 46
Titles:
FRISKSPORT

SVENSKA GASFÖRENINGEN SERVICE AB 1790119
Box 49134, 100 29 STOCKHOLM **Tel:** 8 692 18 47
Fax: 86544615
Titles:
ENERGIGAS

SVENSKA GITARR OCH LUTA SÄLLSKAPET 1629663
c/o Mårten Falk, Järnvägsgatan 9, 640 34 SPARREHOLM **Tel:** 702 08 60 60
Titles:
GITARR OCH LUTA

SVENSKA GOLFFÖRBUNDET AFFÄRSUTVECKLING AB 1790170
Box 84, 182 11 DANDERYD **Tel:** 8 622 15 00
Fax: 8 755 84 39
Titles:
GOLF.SE
SVENSK GOLF

SVENSKA HAMNARBETARFÖRBUNDET 1793532
c/o Ödesjö, Runmarö Söderby 610, 130 38 RUNMARÖ **Tel:** 70 527 09 19 **Fax:** 86678447
Titles:
TIDNINGEN HAMNARBETAREN

SVENSKA HANDIKAPPID-ROTTSFÖRBUNDET 1790457
Sigma, Havregatan 7, 118 59 STOCKHOLM
Tel: 8 640 90 21 **Fax:** 8 640 29 69
Titles:
HANDIKAPPIDROTT

SVENSKA HEMSLÖJDSFÖRENINGARNAS RIKSFÖRBUND 1629892
Celia B. Dackenberg, Västra Kyrkogatan 3, 903 29 UMEÅ **Tel:** 90 71 83 02 **Fax:** 90 71 83 05
Titles:
HEMSLÖJDEN

SVENSKA IDROTTSLÄRARFÖRENINGEN 1760863
Tegelbruksgatan 17, 853 56 SUNDSVALL
Tel: 60 17 48 62
Titles:
TIDSKRIFTEN I IDROTT OCH HÄLSA

SVENSKA INSTITUTET FÖR MISSIONSFORSKNING 1628765
Box 1526, 751 45 UPPSALA **Tel:** 18 13 00 60
Fax: 18 13 00 60
Titles:
SVENSK MISSIONSTIDSKRIFT

SVENSKA JÄGAREFÖRBUNDET 1789521
Öster Malma, 611 91 NYKÖPING
Tel: 155 24 62 90 **Fax:** 155 24 62 95
Titles:
SVENSK JAKT
SVENSK JAKT NYHETER

SVENSKA JÄRN- & METALLGJUTERIERS FÖRENING 1630009
Box 116, 671 23 ARVIKA **Tel:** 570 100 90
Fax: 570 151 50
Titles:
LÄTTSMÄLT

SVENSKA JÄRNVÄGSKLUBBEN, SJK 1793520
Tingsvägen 17 4tr, 191 61 SOLLENTUNA
Tel: 8 84 04 01 **Fax:** 8 84 04 06
Titles:
TÅG

SVENSKA JOURNALISTFÖRBUNDET 1629619
Box 1116, 111 81 STOCKHOLM **Tel:** 8 613 75 00
Titles:
JOURNALISTEN
JOURNALISTEN; JOURNALISTEN.SE

SVENSKA KENNELKLUBBEN 1627444
Box 20136, 161 02 BROMMA **Tel:** 8 80 85 65
Fax: 8 80 85 95
Titles:
HUNDSPORT
HUNDSPORT SPECIAL
HUNDSPORT; WEBB

SVENSKA KLÄTTERFÖRBUNDET 1793526
Lagerlöfsgatan 8, 112 60 STOCKHOLM
Tel: 8 618 82 70
Titles:
BERGSPORT

SVENSKA KOMMUNALPENSIONÄRERS FÖRBUND (SKPF) 1732679
Box 310 19, 413 21 GOTEBORG **Tel:** 31 775 03 90
Titles:
HÄR&NU KOMMUNALPENSIONÄREN

SVENSKA KOMMUNAL-TEKNISKA FÖRENINGEN (KT) 1793824
Hamngatan 6 B, 652 24 KARLSTAD
Tel: 54 15 32 92 **Fax:** 54153414
Titles:
STADSBYGGNAD

SVENSKA KONSTNÄRSFÖRBUNDET 1627989
Karl Johans gata 2, 414 59 GÖTEBORG
Tel: 31 42 47 31 **Fax:** 31 14 36 55
Titles:
BILDKONSTNÄREN

SVENSKA KRYSSARKLUBBEN 1627451
Box 1189, 131 27 NACKA STRAND
Tel: 8 448 28 80
Titles:
PÅ KRYSS

SVENSKA KVINNORS VÄNSTERFÖRBUND 1629361
Linnégatan 21 B, 1 tr, 413 04 GÖTEBORG
Tel: 31 14 40 28 **Fax:** 31 14 40 28
Titles:
VI MÄNSKOR

SVENSKA KYRKAN 1630006
Svenska kyrkan, Informationsavdelningen, 751 70 UPPSALA **Tel:** 18 18 24 40 **Fax:** 18 16 99 31
Titles:
VÄRLDENS TIDNING

Sweden

SVENSKA KYRKANS FÖRSAMLINGSFÖRBUND 1628009
Box 4312, 102 67 STOCKHOLM **Tel:** 8 737 70 00
Fax: 8 737 71 45
Titles:
FÖR

SVENSKA KYRKANS LEKMANNAFÖRBUND. SKL 1627719
Tel: 63 12 30 30
Titles:
LEKMAN I KYRKAN

SVENSKA KYRKANS PRESS AB 1629951
Box 22 543, 112 21 STOCKHOLM
Tel: 8 462 28 00 **Fax:** 8 644 76 86
Titles:
AMOS
KYRKANS TIDNING
KYRKANS TIDNING; WEBB

SVENSKA LIVRÄDDNINGSSÄLLSKAPET 1627990
SLS, Spångavägen 47, 168 75 BROMMA
Tel: 31 744 16 52
Titles:
SIMFRÄMJAREN LIVRÄDDAREN

SVENSKA LIVSMEDELS-ARBETAREFÖRBUNDET 1790460
Box 1156, 111 81 STOCKHOLM **Tel:** 8 796 29 00
Fax: 8208490
Titles:
MÅL & MEDEL
MÅL & MEDEL; MALMEDEL.NU

SVENSKA LOGOPEDFÖRBUNDET 1793598
Box 760, 131 24 NACKA **Tel:** 8 466 24 00
Fax: 84662413
Titles:
LOGOPEDNYTT

SVENSKA MÅLAREFÖRBUNDET 1790449
Box 1113, 111 81 STOCKHOLM **Tel:** 8 587 274 00
Titles:
MÅLARNAS FACKTIDNING

SVENSKA MEDIA DOCU AB 1735377
Tingsgatan 2, 827 32 LJUSDAL **Tel:** 651 150 50
Fax: 651 133 33
Titles:
ÅKERI & ENTREPRENAD
HOTELL & RESTAURANG
LANTBRUKSMAGASINET

SVENSKA MEKANISTERS RIKSFÖRENING, SMR 1629894
Box 2045, 135 02 TYRESÖ **Tel:** 8 667 93 20
Fax: 8 712 43 56
Titles:
MEKANISTEN

SVENSKA MOBILKRAN FÖRENINGEN 1639759
Box 22307, 111 22 STOCKHOLM
Tel: 8 508 938 00 **Fax:** 8 508 938 01
Titles:
LYFTET

SVENSKA MONTESSORIFÖRBUDET 1790577
c/o Box Information, Drottninggatan 31, 411 14 GOTEBORG **Tel:** 31 17 11 10 **Fax:** 317112144
Titles:
MONTESSORITIDNINGEN

SVENSKA MUSIKERFÖRBUNDET 1629606
Box 49144, 100 29 STOCKHOLM
Tel: 8 587 060 00 **Fax:** 8 16 80 20
Titles:
MUSIKERN

SVENSKA NATURSKYDDSFÖRENINGEN 1793705
Box 4625, 116 91 STOCKHOLM **Tel:** 8 702 65 00
Titles:
SVERIGES NATUR

SVENSKA NYHETSBREV AB 1627663
Svenska Nyhetsbrev AB, 113 46 STOCKHOLM
Tel: 8 54 600 509 **Fax:** 8 54 600 599
Titles:
NYHETSBREVET FOND & BANK ONLINE
NYHETSBREVET PENSIONER & FÖRMÅNER
NYHETSBREVET PHARMA ONLINE
NYHETSBREVET RISK & FÖRSÄKRING
NYHETSBREVET TELEKOM ONLINE
NYHETSBREVET TELEKOM ONLINE SPECIAL
PHARMA REPORT

SVENSKA ORGELSÄLLSKAPET 1629967
Västra Storgatan 7B, 694 30 HALLSBERG
Tel: 582 158 16
Titles:
ORGELFORUM

SVENSKA ORIENTERINGSFÖRBUNDET 1793523
Box 22, 171 18 SOLNA **Tel:** 8 587 720 00
Fax: 858772088
Titles:
SKOGSSPORT

SVENSKA ÖSTERBOTTENS LITTERATURFÖRENING 1628548
Österskogsvägen 23, 590 12 BOXHOLM
Tel: 14 31 28 32
Titles:
HORISONT

SVENSKA PAPPERS- OCH CELLULOSAINGENIÖRSFÖR-ENINGEN 1793518
SPCI, Box 5515, 114 85 STOCKHOLM
Tel: 8 783 84 00 **Fax:** 86617344
Titles:
SPCI/SVENSK PAPPERSTIDNING

SVENSKA PISTOLSKYTTEFÖRBUNDET 1628339
Box 5435, 114 84 STOCKHOLM **Tel:** 8 553 401 60
Fax: 8 553 401 69
Titles:
NATIONELLT PISTOLSKYTTE

SVENSKA RIDSPORTFÖRBUNDET 1789562
Ridsportens Hus, 734 94 STRÖMSHOLM
Tel: 220 456 00
Titles:
HÄST & RYTTARE

SVENSKA RÖDA KORSET 1789996
Box 17563, 118 91 STOCKHOLM **Tel:** 8 452 46 00
Fax: 8 452 48 01
Titles:
HENRY - RÖDA KORSETS TIDNING

SVENSKA RODDFÖRBUNDET 1628126
Box 131, 275 23 SJÖBO **Tel:** 415 410 95
Fax: 415 410 95
Titles:
SVENSK RODD

SVENSKA RYGGFÖRENINGEN (PATIENTFÖRENING) 1732749
Svenska Ryggföreningen, Box 244, 17724 STOCKHOLM **Tel:** 8 621 07 35
Titles:
RYGGTIDNINGEN

SVENSKA SIMFÖRBUNDET 1793527
Svenska Simförbundet, 171 41 SOLNA
Tel: 8 627 46 43 **Fax:** 87246861
Titles:
AQUA

SVENSKA SKIDLÄRARFÖRENINGEN 1649612
Torreby 38, 455 93 MUNKEDAL **Tel:** 524 213 00
Fax: 524 211 22
Titles:
SKIDLÄRAREN

SVENSKA SKOLIDROTTSFÖRBUNDET 1791552
Idrottens hus, 114 73 STOCKHOLM
Tel: 8 699 60 00
Titles:
SVENSK SKOLIDROTT

SVENSKA SMÄRTFÖRENINGEN 1732692
Smärtföreningens kansli, Sabbatsbers sjukhus, 113 24 STOCKHOLM **Tel:** 8 690 60 64
Titles:
LEVA MED SMÄRTA

SVENSKA SPORTDYKARFÖRBUNDET 1629941
Idrottshuset, 123 43 FARSTA **Tel:** 8 605 88 05
Fax: 8 605 88 32
Titles:
SPORTDYKAREN

SVENSKA SPORTSKYTTEFÖRBUNDET 1628061
Box 5435, 114 84 STOCKHOLM **Tel:** 8 449 95 90
Fax: 8 449 95 99
Titles:
SVENSK SKYTTESPORT

SVENSKA TANDSKÖTERSKEFÖRBUNDET (STF) 1793810
Svenska tandsköterskeförbundet, Söder Mälarstrand 21, 118 20 STOCKHOLM
Tel: 8 411 19 12
Titles:
TANDSKÖTERSKETIDNINGEN

SVENSKA TEATERFÖRBUNDET 1793355
Teaterförbundet, Box 12710, 112 94 STOCKHOLM **Tel:** 8 28 01 48 **Fax:** 8280148
Titles:
AKT - TEATERFÖRBUNDETS TIDSKRIFT

SVENSKA TEKNIK&DESIGNFÖRETAGEN, CLINTON AGENCY, REDAKTÖRERNA 1776840
Svenska Teknik&Designföretagen, Box 555 45, 102 04 STOCKHOLM **Tel:** 8 762 67 00
Fax: 8 762 67 10
Titles:
INFLUENS

SVENSKA TIDNINGSUTGIVA-REFÖRENINGEN 1627558
Box 22500, 104 22 STOCKHOLM **Tel:** 8 692 46 00
Fax: 8 692 46 13
Titles:
MEDIEVÄRLDEN
MEDIEVÄRLDEN; MEDIEVARLDEN.SE

SVENSKA TONSÄTTARES INTERNATIONELLA MUSIKBYRÅ 1627434
Box 27327, 102 54 STOCKHOLM **Tel:** 8 783 88 00
Fax: 8 783 95 95
Titles:
STIM-MAGASINET

SVENSKA TORNEDALINGARS RIKSFÖRBUND 1792090
Box 118, 980 63 KANGOS **Tel:** 978 304 50
Titles:
MET-AVIISI-TIDSKR. FÖR TORNEDALEN/ MALMFÄLTEN

SVENSKA TRANSPORT-ARBETAREFÖRBUNDET 1790514
Box 714, Bud: Östra Järnvägsgatan 24 111 20 Stockholm, 101 33 STOCKHOLM
Tel: 10480 30 00 **Fax:** 8 723 00 76
Titles:
TRANSPORTARBETAREN

SVENSKA TURISTFÖRENINGEN, STF 1790095
Box 17251, 104 62 STOCKHOLM **Tel:** 8 463 21 00
Fax: 8 678 19 58
Titles:
TURIST

SVENSKA TYNGDLYFTNINGS-FÖRBUNDET 1629706
Svenska Tyngdlyftningsförbundet, Box 15023, 700 15 ÖREBRO **Tel:** 19 17 55 80 **Fax:** 19 10 20 70
Titles:
TYNGDLYFTAREN

SVENSKA VEGETARISKA FÖRENINGEN 1793694
Fjällgatan 23 B, 1 tr, 116 28 STOCKHOLM
Tel: 8 702 11 16
Titles:
VEGETAR

SVENSKA VOLLEYBOLLFÖRBUNDET 1639850
Smidesvägen 5, 171 41 SOLNA **Tel:** 8 627 40 85
Titles:
VOLLEYBOLL

SVENSK-KOREANSKA FÖRENINGEN 1628399
Titles:
KOREA-INFORMATION

SVENSKT KULTURARV 1792052
Västergatan 11, 222 29 LUND **Tel:** 46 39 99 40
Fax: 46399941
Titles:
TIDSKRIFTEN KULT

SVENSKT NÄRINGSLIV 1793958
114 82 STOCKHOLM **Tel:** 8 762 61 90
Titles:
ENTREPRENÖR

SVENSKT VATTEN AB 1791153
Box 47607, 117 94 STOCKHOLM
Tel: 8 506 002 00 **Fax:** 850600210
Titles:
TIDNINGEN SVENSKT VATTEN

SVERIGES ADVOKATSAMFUND 1629787
Box 27321, 102 54 STOCKHOLM **Tel:** 8 459 03 25
Fax: 8 662 30 19
Titles:
ADVOKATEN
ADVOKATEN; WEBB

SVERIGES ÅKERIFÖRETAG 1750265
Box 508, 182 15 DANDERYD **Tel:** 8753 54 00
Fax: 87556001
Titles:
SVENSK ÅKERITIDNING; AKERITIDNING.COM

SVERIGES AKTIESPARARES RIKSFÖRBUND 1790129
113 89 STOCKHOLM **Tel:** 8 506 515 00
Fax: 8 32 61 22

Titles:
AKTIESPARAREN
AKTIESPARAREN; AKTIESPARARNA.SE

SVERIGES ANNONSÖRER 1793629
Box 1327, 111 83 STOCKHOLM **Tel:** 8 545 252 30
Fax: 8235510
Titles:
ANNONSÖREN

SVERIGES ARKITEKTER 1627468
Box 5027, 102 41 STOCKHOLM **Tel:** 8 505 577 00
Fax: 8 505 577 05
Titles:
ARKITEKTEN

SVERIGES BAGERIFÖRBUND 1790447
Budadress: Storgatan 19, Box 556 80, 102 15 STOCKHOLM **Tel:** 8 762 60 00 **Fax:** 8 678 66 64
Titles:
BRÖD

SVERIGES BEGRAVNINGSBYRÅERS FÖRBUND 1790113
SBF, Upplagsvägen 1, 117 43 STOCKHOLM
Tel: 8 556 811 80 **Fax:** 855681188
Titles:
MEMENTO

SVERIGES BLÅBANDSFÖRBUND 1792926
Box 1233, 701 12 OREBRO **Tel:** 19 13 05 75
Fax: 19121136
Titles:
BLÅ BANDET

SVERIGES CAMPING- OCH STUGÄGARES RIKSORGANISATION 1789505
SCR, Box 5079, 402 22 GOTEBORG
Tel: 31 355 60 00 **Fax:** 313556003
Titles:
SVEA

SVERIGES DÖVAS RIKSFÖRBUND, SDR 1790492
SDR, Förmansv. 2, plan 6, 117 43 STOCKHOLM
Tel: 70 342 60 68 **Fax:** 86499046
Titles:
DÖVAS TIDNING

SVERIGES DRAGSPELARES RIKSFÖRBUND 1628296
c/o R. Häggqvist, Lasarettsgatan 23, 891 32 ÖRNSKÖLDSVIK **Tel:** 660 21 16 43
Fax: 660 21 16 43
Titles:
DRAGSPELSNYTT

SVERIGES DRAMATIKERFÖRBUND 1629702
c/o Sveriges Dramatikerförbund, Drottningg 85, 1 tr., 111 60 STOCKHOLM **Tel:** 8 21 33 10
Fax: 8 613 39 79
Titles:
JOURNAL

SVERIGES EXPORTRÅD 1732681
Exportrådet, Box 240, 101 24 STOCKHOLM
Tel: 8 588 660 00 **Fax:** 8 588 661 90
Titles:
SVENSK EXPORT

SVERIGES FARMACEVTFÖRBUND 1627373
Box 3215, 103 64 STOCKHOLM **Tel:** 8 507 999 14
Fax: 8 507 999 99
Titles:
SVENSK FARMACI

SVERIGES FILATELIST FÖRBUND - SFF 1627676
Box 15074, 750 15 UPPSALA **Tel:** 18 50 20 21
Titles:
SFF-FILATELISTEN/SVENSK FILATELISTISK TIDSKRIFT

SVERIGES FILM- OCH VIDEOFÖRBUND 1629989
Gröna Gatan 14 A, kv, 151 32 SÖDERTÄLJE
Tel: 705 62 94 10
Titles:
FILMKRETS

SVERIGES FISKARES RIKSFÖRBUND 1628670
Fiskets Hus, Fiskhamnsgatan 33, 414 58 GÖTEBORG **Tel:** 31 12 45 93 **Fax:** 31 24 86 35
Titles:
YRKESFISKAREN

SVERIGES FISKEVATTEN-ÄGAREFÖRBUND 1628710
105 33 STOCKHOLM **Tel:** 8 787 50 00
Fax: 8 787 53 10
Titles:
VÅRA FISKEVATTEN

SVERIGES FÖRENADE FILMSTUDIOS 1629743
Box 27126, 102 52 STOCKHOLM **Tel:** 8 665 11 00
Titles:
FILMRUTAN

SVERIGES FÖRFATTARFÖRBUND 1629646
C/O Sveriges Författarförbund, Box 3157, 103 63 STOCKHOLM **Tel:** 8 545 132 00 **Fax:** 8 545 132 10
Titles:
FÖRFATTAREN

SVERIGES GLAS- OCH PORSLINSHANDLARFÖRBUND 1639853
Haneson Förlag, Stationsvägen 2, 430 30 FRILLESÅS **Tel:** 340 65 77 20 **Fax:** 340 65 77 45
Titles:
GLAS OCH PORSLIN

SVERIGES HAMNAR 1793534
Box 5384, 102 49 STOCKHOLM **Tel:** 8 762 71 51
Fax: 86111218
Titles:
SVENSK HAMNTIDNING

SVERIGES HEMBYGDSFÖRBUND 1628719
Box 6167, 102 33 STOCKHOLM **Tel:** 8 441 54 83
Fax: 8 34 74 74
Titles:
BYGD OCH NATUR

SVERIGES INGENJÖRER 1789430
Box 1419, 111 84 STOCKHOLM **Tel:** 8 613 80 00
Titles:
INGENJÖREN
INGENJÖREN; INGENJOREN.SE

SVERIGES JÄRNVÄGARS TJÄNSTEMANNAFÖRBUND 1793519
Box 2131, 103 14 STOCKHOLM **Tel:** 8 14 29 65
Fax: 8108067
Titles:
SVENSK TRAFIKTIDNING

SVERIGES KATTKLUBBARS RIKSFÖRBUND, SVERAK 1627995
Säby Nyckelbacken, 732 94 ARBOGA
Tel: 33 10 15 65 **Fax:** 33 10 08 99
Titles:
VÅRA KATTER

SVERIGES KOMMUNER OCH LANDSTING 1735344
118 82 STOCKHOLM **Tel:** 8 452 73 00
Fax: 86423013
Titles:
DAGENS SAMHÄLLE
DAGENS SAMHÄLLE; DAGENSSAMHALLE.SE

SVERIGES KÖRFÖRBUND 1710430
Box 163 44, 103 26 STOCKHOLM
Tel: 31 84 42 02
Titles:
TIDNINGEN KÖRSÅNG

SVERIGES KVINNLIGA BILKÅRERS RIKSFÖRBUND 1628136
Box 5435, 114 84 STOCKHOLM **Tel:** 8 579 388 90
Fax: 8 579 388 95
Titles:
BILKÅRISTEN

SVERIGES KYRKOGÅRDS- OCH KREMATORIEFÖRBUND 1627551
Box 19071, 104 32 STOCKHOLM **Tel:** 8 643 10 35
Fax: 8 612 80 36
Titles:
KYRKOGÅRDEN

SVERIGES LÄKARFÖRBUND 1791062
Box 5603, 114 86 STOCKHOLM **Tel:** 8 790 33 00
Fax: 8 20 76 19
Titles:
LÄKARTIDNINGEN
LÄKARTIDNINGEN; WWW.LAKARTIDNINGEN.SE

SVERIGES LÄKARSEKRETERARFÖRBUND 1629833
114 21 STOCKHOLM **Tel:** 8 411 31 00
Fax: 8 21 03 26
Titles:
LSF-MAGAZINET

SVERIGES LANTMÄSTARFÖRBUND 1639805
Tejarps gård, 230 41 KLÅGERUP **Tel:** 40 40 86 80
Titles:
LANTMÄSTAREN

SVERIGES LANTMÄTAREFÖRENING 1629717
Sveriges Lantmätareförening, Box 3437, 103 68 STOCKHOLM **Tel:** 8 667 95 90 **Fax:** 8 24 54 64
Titles:
ASPECT

SVERIGES LÅSSMEDSMÄSTARES RIKSFÖRBUND 1790168
Transportvägen 9, 117 43 STOCKHOLM
Tel: 8 721 40 55 **Fax:** 87214056
Titles:
LÅSMÄSTAREN

SVERIGES MOTORCYKLISTER 1735387
Forskargatan 3, 781 70 BORLÄNGE
Tel: 243 822 80
Titles:
MC-FOLKET

SVERIGES ORKESTERFÖRBUND 1629557
Sveriges Orkesterförbund, Box 163 44, 103 26 STOCKHOLM **Tel:** 8 470 24 42 **Fax:** 8 470 24 24
Titles:
MUSIKANT

SVERIGES ORNITOLOGISKA FÖRENING 1627697
c/o Sören Svensson, Ekologiska inst., Ekologihuset, 223 62 LUND **Tel:** 46 222 38 21
Fax: 46 222 47 16
Titles:
ORNIS SVECICA
VÅR FÅGELVÄRLD

SVERIGES PENSIONÄRERS RIKSFÖRBUND 1789758
Bjurholmsgatan 16, 116 38 STOCKHOLM
Tel: 8 702 28 80 **Fax:** 87022640
Titles:
SPRF-TIDNINGEN

SVERIGES PENSIONÄRSFÖRBUND, SPF 1789520
Box 22574, 104 22 STOCKHOLM **Tel:** 8 692 32 50
Fax: 8 651 15 53
Titles:
VETERANEN

SVERIGES PSYKOLOG FÖRBUND 1629796
Box 3287, 103 65 STOCKHOLM **Tel:** 8 567 064 50
Fax: 8 567 064 90
Titles:
PSYKOLOGTIDNINGEN

SVERIGES RADIO AB 1627380
Verkstadsgatan 20, 651 03 KARLSTAD
Tel: 54 22 11 00 **Fax:** 54 18 26 21
Titles:
SR P4; EFTER TOLV
SR P4 STOCKHOLM; NYHETSREDAKTIONEN SR.SE

SVERIGES REDOVISNINGSKONSULTERS FÖRBUND SRF 1746037
Box 143, 791 23 FALUN **Tel:** 23 79 49 50
Fax: 23 637 88
Titles:
KONSULTEN

SVERIGES RIKSIDROTTSFÖRBUND 1629484
Idrottens hus, 114 73 STOCKHOLM
Tel: 8 699 61 04 **Fax:** 8 94 81 84
Titles:
SVENSK IDROTT
SVENSK IDROTT; WEBB

SVERIGES SCHACKFÖRBUND 1627754
Slottsg 155, 602 20 NORRKÖPING
Tel: 11 10 74 20 **Fax:** 11 18 23 41
Titles:
TIDSKRIFT FÖR SCHACK

SVERIGES SKRÄDDERIFÖRBUND 1629836
Sv Skrädderiförbund, Box 10111, 100 55 STOCKHOLM **Tel:** 8 662 07 45
Titles:
SKRÄDDERI

SVERIGES SOCIALDEMOKRATISKA STUDENTFÖRBUND 1793613
Box 11544, 100 61 STOCKHOLM **Tel:** 8 714 48 00
Titles:
LIBERTAS

SVERIGES SOCIALDEMOKRATISKA UNGDOMSFÖRBUND 1792961
Box 11544, 100 61 STOCKHOLM **Tel:** 8 714 48 06
Fax: 87149508
Titles:
TVÄRDRAG

SVERIGES SPELMÄNS RIKSFÖRBUND 1627678
c/o Ahlbom, Bultvägen 5, 126 38 HÄGERSTEN
Tel: 8 18 34 11 **Fax:** 8 407 16 50
Titles:
SPELMANNEN

SVERIGES STENINDUSTRIFÖRBUND (I SAMARBETE M STEN) 1793454
Stenutveckling Nordiska AB, Värmdövägen 738-740, 132 35 SALTSJÖ-BOO **Tel:** 8 747 76 71 **Fax:** 87477641
Titles:
STEN

SVERIGES TANDHYGIENISTFÖRENING 1793502
Box 1419, 111 84 STOCKHOLM **Tel:** 8 442 44 60
Titles:
TANDHYGIENIST TIDNINGEN

SVERIGES TANDLÄKARFÖRBUND 1791061
Box 1217, 111 82 STOCKHOLM **Tel:** 8 666 15 00 **Fax:** 8 666 15 95
Titles:
TANDLÄKARTIDNINGEN
TANDLÄKARTIDNINGEN; TANDLAKARTIDNINGEN.SE

SVERIGES TELEVISION 1685157
Agenda, Sveriges Television, 105 10 STOCKHOLM **Tel:** 8 784 00 00
Titles:
SVT NYHETER OCH SAMHÄLLE; AGENDA
VIPÅTV

SVERIGES UNIVERSITETS-LÄRARFORBUND 1793800
Box 1227, 111 82 STOCKHOLM **Tel:** 8 505 836 00 **Fax:** 8208305
Titles:
UNIVERSITETSLÄRAREN

SVERIGES VÄGLEDARFÖRENING 1629362
c/o A.Söderlund, Vävstuguvägen 12, 862 41 NJURUNDA **Tel:** 60 310 89
Titles:
VÄGLEDAREN I UTBILDNING OCH ARBETSLIV

SVERIGES VETERINÄRFÖRBUND 1793797
Box 12709, 112 94 STOCKHOLM **Tel:** 8 545 558 30 **Fax:** 854555829
Titles:
SVENSK VETERINÄRTIDNING

SVERIGES YNGRE LÄKARES FÖRENING (SYLF) 1627333
Box 5610, 114 86 STOCKHOLM **Tel:** 8 790 33 66 **Fax:** 8 21 18 68
Titles:
MODERNA LÄKARE

SVEROF, FÖRBUNDET SVERIGES RESERVOFFICERARE 1790473
Box 5417, 114 84 STOCKHOLM **Tel:** 8 661 86 42
Titles:
RESERVOFFICEREN

SVETSTEKNISKA FÖRENINGEN / SVETSKOMMISSIONEN 1627476
Svetskommissionen, Box 5073, 102 42 STOCKHOLM **Tel:** 8 791 29 00 **Fax:** 8 679 94 04
Titles:
SVETSEN

SWARTLING & WRANDING MEDIA AB 1791266
Swartling & Wranding Media AB, Sveavägen 62, 111 34 STOCKHOLM **Tel:** 8 545 160 64 **Fax:** 8 545 160 69
Titles:
TRANSITION

SWEDEN ROCK MAGAZINE 1639779
Norjebokevägen 10, 294 76 SÖLVESBORG **Tel:** 456 317 17 **Fax:** 456 310 50
Titles:
SWEDEN ROCK MAGAZINE

SWEDISH-ENGLISH LITERARY TRANSLATORS' ASSOCIATION 1649729
Mossgatan 5, 413 21 GÖTEBORG **Tel:** 31 16 62 20 **Fax:** 31 16 62 20
Titles:
SWEDISH BOOK REVIEW

SWEET WILLIAMS 1640448
Strandvägen 19, 114 56 STOCKHOLM **Tel:** 8 661 18 90
Titles:
SHOWROOM

SYDOSTPRESS AB 1789666
391 88 KALMAR **Tel:** 480 591 00 **Fax:** 480 864 06
Titles:
BAROMETERN - OT
BAROMETERN-OT; BAROMETERN.SE

SYDÖSTRA SVERIGES DAGBLAD 1629380
371 88 KARLSKRONA **Tel:** 455 33 46 00 **Fax:** 455 124 03
Titles:
SYDÖSTRAN; SYDOSTRAN.SE

SYDÖSTRAN AB 1789927
371 88 KARLSKRONA **Tel:** 455 33 46 00 **Fax:** 455 124 03
Titles:
SYDÖSTRAN

SYDSVENSKA DAGBLADET AB 1745965
Krusegatan 19, 205 05 MALMO **Tel:** 40 28 12 00
Titles:
SYDSVENSKAN
SYDSVENSKAN; FEATUREREDAKTIONEN

SYDSVENSKA DAGBLADETS AB 1789280
Krusegatan 19, 205 05 MALMO **Tel:** 40 28 12 44
Titles:
SYDSVENSKAN; TV

SYDSVENSKA INDUSTRI- OCH HANDELSKAMMARENS SERVICE AB 1793884
Sydsvenska Industri- och Handelskammaren, Skeppsbron 2, 211 20 MALMO **Tel:** 40 690 24 00 **Fax:** 406902490
Titles:
SYDSVENSKT NÄRINGSLIV

SYDVED AB 1793724
Box 626, 551 18 JÖNKÖPING **Tel:** 36 30 17 50 **Fax:** 36308840
Titles:
AKTIVT SKOGSBRUK

SYMF SVERIGES YRKESMUSIKERFÖRBUND 1793799
Box 49144, 100 29 STOCKHOLM **Tel:** 8 693 03 35 **Fax:** 84060555
Titles:
SYMFONI

SYNSKADADES RIKSFÖRBUND 1629932
SRF, 122 88 ENSKEDE **Tel:** 8 39 92 98 **Fax:** 8 39 93 22
Titles:
FÖRÄLDRAKONTAKTEN
SRF-PERSPEKTIV

SYSTEMBOLAGET 1793678
Systembolaget AB, 103 84 STOCKHOLM **Tel:** 8 503 300 00
Titles:
BOLAGET

TALENTUM SWEDEN AB 1789281
Mäster Samuelsgatan 56, 106 12 STOCKHOLM **Tel:** 8 796 65 00
Titles:
AFFÄRSVÄRLDEN
AFFÄRSVÄRLDEN; AFFÄRSVÄRLDEN24
ARBETARSKYDD
BYGGVÄRLDEN
NY TEKNIK
NY TEKNIK; NY TEKNIK.SE

TANDTEKNIKERFÖRBUNDET / DENTALLAB. RIKSFÖRB. 1793503
Skidvägen 10, 812 30 STORVIK **Tel:** 707 60 22 28 **Fax:** 29012181
Titles:
TANDTEKNIKERN

TANDVÅRDSSKADEFÖR-BUNDET 1793501
Bergsunds Strand 9, 117 38 STOCKHOLM **Tel:** 8 428 92 42 **Fax:** 8 641 90 81
Titles:
TF-BLADET

TASTY NEWS PUBLISHING CO 1793723
Nyvägen 55, 138 34 ÄLTA **Tel:** 8 39 27 72 **Fax:** 8396444
Titles:
ALLT OM WHISKY
VÄRLDENS VINER

TAYLOR & FRANCIS AB 1628164
Box 3255, 103 65 STOCKHOLM **Tel:** 8 440 80 40 **Fax:** 8 440 80 50
Titles:
ACTA OTO-LARYNGOLOGICA
BLOOD PRESSURE
INTERNATIONAL FORUM OF PSYCHOANALYSIS
KONSTHISTORISK TIDSKRIFT
MICROBIAL ECOLOGY IN HEALTH AND DISEASE
SCAND. ACTUARIAL JOURNAL
SCAND. JOURNAL OF PLASTIC AND RECONSTR. SURG. SCAND. JOURNAL OF UROLOGY AND NEPHROLOGY
SVENSK KIRURGI

TEAM CATH PRODUCTION AB 1628027
Rubanksgatan 6, 741 71 KNIVSTA **Tel:** 18 34 90 85
Titles:
INKÖPSJOURNALEN

TEJARPS FÖRLAG AB 1790403
Tejarps Gård, 230 41 KLÅGERUP **Tel:** 40 40 86 80
Titles:
LANTBRUKETS AFFÄRER
SVENSKA LIVSMEDEL

TEKNIKFÖRETAGENS FÖRLAG AB 1791271
Box 5510, 114 85 STOCKHOLM **Tel:** 8 782 08 00 **Fax:** 8 782 09 00
Titles:
TEKNIKFÖRETAGEN DIREKT

TEKNIKFÖRLAGET TF AB 1629912
Box 104, 301 04 HALMSTAD **Tel:** 35 10 41 50 **Fax:** 35 18 65 09
Titles:
UPPFINNAREN/KONSTRUKTÖREN
UPPFINNAREN/KONSTRUKTÖREN; WEBB

TEKNISKA HÖGSKOLANS STUDENTKÅR 1627388
THS, 100 44 STOCKHOLM **Tel:** 8 790 98 70 **Fax:** 8 20 62 03
Titles:
OSQLEDAREN

THE SOCIETY FOR PUBL. OF ACTA DERMATO-VENEREOLOGICA 1793795
Trädgårdsgatan 14, 753 09 UPPSALA **Tel:** 18 580 50 91 **Fax:** 18557332
Titles:
ACTA DERMATO-VENEROLOGICA

TIDNINGEN FOLKET AB 1789714
Box 368, Besöksadress: J.A Selanders gata 1, 632 20 ESKILSTUNA **Tel:** 161775 50 **Fax:** 16 17 75 55
Titles:
FOLKET
FOLKET; FOLKET.SE

TIDNINGEN HIFI MUSIK AB 1627351
Box 230 84, 104 35 STOCKHOLM **Tel:** 8 34 29 70 **Fax:** 8 34 29 71
Titles:
HEMMABIO
HIFI & MUSIK
VAPENTIDNINGEN

TIDNINGEN LUNDAGÅRD 1791021
Sandgatan 2, 223 50 LUND **Tel:** 46 14 40 20
Titles:
TIDNINGEN LUNDAGÅRD

TIDNINGEN SPRINGTIME HB 1790094
Box 22559, 104 22 STOCKHOLM **Tel:** 8 545 535 30 **Fax:** 8 545 535 39
Titles:
RUNNERS WORLD

AB TIDNINGEN VI, INGÅR I KF MEDIA AB 1789652
Box 2052, 103 12 STOCKHOLM **Tel:** 8 769 86 00 **Fax:** 8 769 86 22
Titles:
VI

TIDNINGS AB METRO 1640116
Drottninggatan 36, Box 11275, 404 26 GOTEBORG **Tel:** 31 743 81 00 **Fax:** 31 743 81 19
Titles:
METRO GÖTEBORG
METRO SKÅNE
METRO STOCKHOLM
METRO.SE

TIDNINGS AB RIDSPORT 1629651
Box 14, 619 21 TROSA **Tel:** 156 132 40 **Fax:** 15634878
Titles:
RIDSPORT
RIDSPORT SPECIAL

TIDNINGS AB SÄNDAREN 1735423
Box 22543, 104 22 STOCKHOLM **Tel:** 8 545 784 50 **Fax:** 8 23 45 67
Titles:
SÄNDAREN
SÄNDAREN; SANDAREN.SE

TIDNINGS AB SVENSK BOKHANDEL 1791170
Box 6888, 113 86 STOCKHOLM **Tel:** 8 545 417 70 **Fax:** 8 545 417 75
Titles:
SVENSK BOKHANDEL
SVENSK BOKHANDEL; SVB.SE

TIDNINGSBYRÅN I JÖNKÖPINGS LÄN AB 1793698
Tidningsbyrån, Brunnsgatan 16, 553 16 JÖNKÖPING **Tel:** 36 340 600 **Fax:** 36340601
Titles:
VI PÅ LANDET

TIDNINGSFÖRENINGEN DEN GÖTHEBORGSKE SPIONEN 1629769
Studenternas Hus, Götabergsgatan 17, 411 34 GÖTEBORG **Tel:** 31 773 53 70 **Fax:** 31 773 53 71
Titles:
GÖTHEBORGSKE SPIONEN

TIDNINGSFÖRENINGEN I KIRUNA 1791692
Adolfs Hedinsvägen 58, 981 33 KIRUNA
Tel: 980 805 81 Fax: 98080191
Titles:
KIRUNA TIDNINGEN

TIDNINGSFÖRENINGEN NORRSKENSFLAMMAN U.P.A. 1629516
Kungsgatan 84, 112 27 STOCKHOLM
Tel: 8 650 80 10 Fax: 8 650 83 15
Titles:
FLAMMAN; FLAMMAN.SE

TIDNINGSHUSET KVÄLLSSTUNDEN AB 1793930
Box 1080, 721 27 VÄSTERÅS Tel: 21 19 04 15
Fax: 21 13 62 62
Titles:
KVÄLLSSTUNDEN

TIDNINGSSTATISTIK AB 1628779
114 78 STOCKHOLM Tel: 8 507 424 00
Fax: 8 507 424 01
Titles:
TS-TIDNINGEN

TIDSKRIFTEN OPERA EKONOMISK FÖRENING 1710398
Väringatan 27, 113 33 STOCKHOLM
Tel: 8 643 95 44
Titles:
TIDSKRIFTEN OPERA

TIDSKRIFTSFÖRENINGEN FILM & TV 1627693
Box 2068, Stora Nygatan 21, Gamla Stan, 103 12 STOCKHOLM Tel: 8 545 275 22
Fax: 8 545 275 09
Titles:
FILM & TV

TIDSKRIFTSFÖRENINGEN OFFENSIV 1790444
Box 73, 123 22 FARSTA Tel: 8 605 94 03
Fax: 8 556 252 52
Titles:
OFFENSIV; WEBB

TIDSKRIFTSFÖRENINGEN SYDASIEN 1629524
Råbygatan 5 A, 223 61 LUND Tel: 46 13 35 68
Titles:
SYDASIEN

TJÄNSTEMÄNNENS CENTRALORGANISATION (TCO) 1639757
TCO, 114 94 STOCKHOLM Tel: 8 782 91 00
Fax: 8 662 36 79
Titles:
STUDENTLIV
STUDENTLIV; STUDENTLIV.SE
TCO-TIDNINGEN
TCO-TIDNINGEN; TCOTIDNINGEN.SE

TMF, TRÄ- OCH MÖBELINDUSTRIFÖRBUNDET 1653277
Box 55525, 102 04 STOCKHOLM Tel: 8 762 72 50
Fax: 8 762 72 24
Titles:
TRÄ & MÖBEL FORUM

TOM SVENSSON 1650167
Stensundsvägen 23 B, 619 30 TROSA
Tel: 8 559 216 75
Titles:
PILOTMAGAZINET.SE

TOMMY GARDEBRING 1793531
Sjöfartsverket, Huvudkontoret, 601 78 NORRKÖPING Tel: 11 19 14 35
Titles:
SJÖRAPPORTEN

TOMORROW MEDIA AB 1791296
Box 10177, 100 55 STOCKHOLM Tel: 78 23 47 10
Titles:
MILJÖRAPPORTEN

TORSLANDA TIDNINGEN 1629685
Flygmotorvägen 3, 423 37 TORSLANDA
Tel: 31 92 45 80 Fax: 31 92 25 87
Titles:
TORSLANDA TIDNINGEN

TRADE PROMOTION FÖRLAG AB 1629804
Box 944, 251 09 HELSINGBORG Tel: 42 20 71 66
Fax: 42 20 71 96
Titles:
NORD-EMBALLAGE

TRAFIKMAGASINET 1 AB 1791300
Trädgårdsgatan 35, 590 31 BORENSBERG
Tel: 42 23 64 48
Titles:
TIDNINGEN TRAFIKMAGASINET

TRAFIKVERKET 1773807
781 87 BORLÄNGE Tel: 771 921 921
Fax: 243 789 00
Titles:
TRAFIKVERKETS PERSONALTIDNING

TRANÅS-POSTEN AB 1629618
Box 1020, 573 28 TRANÅS Tel: 140 38 55 70
Fax: 140 121 11
Titles:
TRANÅS-POSTEN; TRANASPOSTEN.SE

TRANSNEWS COMMUNICATIONS 1687130
Box 3414, 165 23 HASSELBY Tel: 8 89 29 19
Titles:
PÅHUGGET

TRANSPORT NYTT FÖRLAG AB 1793490
Box 2082, 169 02 SOLNA Tel: 8 514 934 70
Titles:
TRANSPORTNYTT

TRAV OCH GALOPPRONDEN, AB 1790999
Box 20046, 161 02 BROMMA Tel: 8 564 820 00
Fax: 8283613
Titles:
TRAVRONDEN

TRAVEL MEDIA SCANDINAVIA AB 1686203
Travel Media Scandinavia, Grev Magnigatan 6, 114 55 STOCKHOLM Tel: 8 545 660 00
Titles:
AFFÄRSRESEMAGASINET
XPRESS, OMBORDMAGASIN PÅ ARLANDA EXPRESS

TRE INSPIRATÖRER AB 1743459
Box 403, 401 26 GOTEBORG Tel: 739 05 53 11
Titles:
UNIQUE GENERATION

TRELLEBORG AB 1627738
Trelleborg AB, Box 153, 231 22 TRELLEBORG
Tel: 410 670 00
Titles:
T-TIME

TRYCKERI AB DALSLAND 1789826
Box 29, 662 21 ÅMÅL Tel: 532 123 90
Fax: 532 165 15
Titles:
PROVINSTIDNINGEN DALSLAND

TRYCKERI AB ÖLAND 1629886
Västra Kyrkogatan 18, 387 22 BORGHOLM
Tel: 485 56 09 00 Fax: 485 56 09 19
Titles:
ÖLANDSBLADET
ÖLANDSBLADET; WEBB

TTG SVERIGE AB 1791275
Egmont tidskrifter, Pyramidvägen 7, 169 91 SOLNA Tel: 8 506 678 31 Fax: 8 506 678 09
Titles:
GOLF DIGEST
RESIDENCE HEM & TREND

TUIFLY NORDIC AB 1743461
Mediabolaget, Swedenborgsgatan 7, 118 48 STOCKHOLM Tel: 8 556 963 10 Fax: 8 641 95 44
Titles:
TUIFLY MAGAZINE

TULL-KUST (TCO) 1790401
Box 1220, 111 82 STOCKHOLM Tel: 8 405 05 40
Fax: 8247146
Titles:
PÅ GRÄNSEN

TUNDELL OCH SALMSON 1752909
Tobaksspinnargatan 2, 117 36 STOCKHOLM
Tel: 8 720 20 80
Titles:
NUET

TURIST I VÄRMLAND AB 1639821
Gjutaregatan 2 E, 681 50 KRISTINEHAMN
Tel: 550 10988 Fax: 550 10988
Titles:
TURIST I VÄRMLAND

TURLÅDAN AB 1793622
Prästgården Kårstaby, 186 96 VALLENTUNA
Tel: 8 512 36 20
Titles:
HIT & DIT, TURISM & RESOR

TV4 1628911
115 79 STOCKHOLM Tel: 8 459 40 00
Titles:
TV4; NYHETSKANALEN.SE
TV4; TEXT-TV

TVÅSTADS TIDNINGS AB 1789959
Box 111, 462 22 VÄNERSBORG Tel: 521 26 46 00
Fax: 521 57 59 18
Titles:
TTELA
TTELA ~ TROLLHÄTTAN
TTELA; TTELA.SE

TYRESÖ NYHETER EKONOMISK FÖRENING 1789678
Björkbacksvägen 37, 135 40 TYRESÖ
Tel: 8 798 91 01
Titles:
TYRESÖ NYHETER

UGGLA & FORSSTRÖM AB 1639832
Nybrogatan 18, 114 39 STOCKHOLM
Tel: 8 5280 08 99
Titles:
DAGENS PS

ULF JOHANSSON 1710415
Box 19, 182 05 DJURSHOLM Tel: 8 753 00 21
Titles:
FRONYTT

ULRICEHAMNS TIDNING AB 1789955
Box 310, 523 26 ULRICEHAMN Tel: 321 262 00
Fax: 321 262 39
Titles:
ULRICEHAMNS TIDNING
ULRICEHAMNS TIDNING; UT.SE

ULTIMEDIA AB 1629656
Holländargatan 23, 111 60 STOCKHOLM
Tel: 8 791 96 75 Fax: 8 406 04 44
Titles:
FÖRETAGSVÄRLDEN

ULVEN FÖRLAG AB 1685660
Box 7, 342 06 MOHEDA Tel: 472 705 25
Fax: 472 716 00
Titles:
HÄSTFOCUS

UMEÅ KYRKLIGA SAMFÄLLIGHET 1735411
Box 521, 901 10 UMEÅ Tel: 90 200 25 00
Titles:
TIDNINGEN SPIRA

UNG VÄNSTER 1793593
Box 12660, 112 93 STOCKHOLM Tel: 8 654 31 00
Fax: 8 650 85 57
Titles:
RÖD PRESS

UNGDOMENS NYKTERHETSFÖRBUND, UNF 1639798
Box 128 25, 112 97 STOCKHOLM
Tel: 8 672 60 60 Fax: 86726001
Titles:
MOTDRAG

UNIONEN 1744292
Attention Kollega, Olof Palmes Gata 17, 105 32 STOCKHOLM Tel: 8 504 150 00 Fax: 8 618 67 22
Titles:
KOLLEGA

UNIVERSEUM COMMUNICATIONS 1790412
Box 7691, 103 95 STOCKHOLM Tel: 8 562 930 90
Titles:
SHORTCUT

UNIVERSITETSSJUKHUSET I LUND, UNIVERSITETSSJUKHUSET MAS, MEDICINSKA FAKULTETEN V 1740714
Medicinska fakulteten, Lunds universitet, Box 117, 221 00 LUND Tel: 46 222 00 00
Titles:
AKTUELLT OM VETENSKAP & HÄLSA

UNIVERSUM COMMUNICATIONS AB 1732739
Box 7053, 103 86 STOCKHOLM Tel: 8 562 027 00
Fax: 8 562 930 50
Titles:
CAMPUS EKONOMI
CAMPUS JURIST
CAMPUS TEKNIK

UNIVERSUM COMMUNICATIONS SWEDEN AB 1750437
Box 7053, 103 86 STOCKHOLM
Tel: 8 56 20 27 00 Fax: 8 56 29 30 50
Titles:
CAMPUS.SE

UPPLANDS ORNITOLOGISKA FÖRENING 1628809
Upplands Ornitologiska Förening, Box 59, 751 03 UPPSALA Tel: 730 48 34 49
Titles:
FÅGLAR I UPPLAND

UPPSALA STUDENTKÅR 1629613
Övre Slottsgatan 7, 753 10 UPPSALA
Tel: 18 480 31 30 Fax: 18 480 31 29
Titles:
ERGO
ERGO; ERGO.NU

UPSALA NYA TIDNING 1628799
Nymärstagatan 2, 195 30 MÄRSTA
Tel: 8 594 405 70 Fax: 8 594 405 99
Titles:
SIGTUNABYGDEN MÄRSTA TIDNING
UPSALA NYA TIDNING

UTRIKESDEPARTEMENTET 1629747
103 39 STOCKHOLM **Tel:** 8 405 59 35
Fax: 8 723 11 76
Titles:
UD-KURIREN

UTRIKESPOLITISKA INSTITUTET, UI 1627642
Box 27035, 102 51 STOCKHOLM
Tel: 8 511 768 00 **Fax:** 851176899
Titles:
INTERNATIONELLA STUDIER
VÄRLDSPOLITIKENS DAGSFRÅGOR

VAGABOND MEDIA AB 1791180
Repslagargatan 17B, 1tr, 118 46 STOCKHOLM
Tel: 8 545 064 20 **Fax:** 86795710
Titles:
TRAVEL NEWS
VAGABOND
VAGABOND; VAGABOND.SE

VÄGPRESS AB 1790446
Kornhultsvägen 19, 310 21 HISHULT
Tel: 430 422 50 **Fax:** 43042232
Titles:
TIDNINGEN PROFFS

VÄGVERKET PRODUKTION 1732675
Svevia, Box 4018, 171 04 SOLNA **Tel:** 8 404 10 00
Fax: 8 404 10 50
Titles:
PÅ VÄG

VÄNNERNAS SAMFUND I SVERIGE, KVÄKARNA 1629952
Box 9166, 102 72 STOCKHOLM **Tel:** 175 604 25
Fax: 175 604 25
Titles:
KVÄKARTIDSKRIFT

VÄNSKAPSFÖRBUNDET SVERIGE-NICARAGUA 1792043
VFSN, Tegelviksgatan 40, 118 46 STOCKHOLM
Tel: 8 642 08 81 **Fax:** 8 641 11 35
Titles:
NYHETER FRÅN NICARAGUA

VÅR SKOLA FÖRLAG AB 1627598
Skarpövägen 2, 185 91 VAXHOLM
Tel: 8 541 30160 **Fax:** 8 541 306 90
Titles:
VÅR SKOLA SKOLÅR 1-3
VÅR SKOLA SKOLÅR 4-7
VÅR SKOLA - SPECIALUNDERVISNING

VÅRDFÖRBUNDET 1790471
Box 3207, 103 64 STOCKHOLM **Tel:** 8 14 77 00
Fax: 8 14 77 00
Titles:
VÅRDFOKUS

VÄRLDEN IDAG AB 1639863
Box 6420, 751 36 UPPSALA **Tel:** 18 430 40 00
Fax: 18 430 40 01
Titles:
VÄRLDEN IDAG
VÄRLDEN IDAG; WEBB

VÄRLDSNATURFONDEN WWF 1793701
Världsnaturfonden WWF, Ulriksdals Slott, 170 81 SOLNA **Tel:** 8 624 74 00
Titles:
WWF EKO

VÄRMLANDS FOLKBLAD AB 1789549
Box 67, 651 03 KARLSTAD **Tel:** 54 17 55 00
Fax: 54 17 55 99
Titles:
VÄRMLANDS FOLKBLAD
VÄRMLANDS FOLKBLAD; NÄRINGSLIV
VÄRMLANDS FOLKBLAD; VF.SE

VÅRT NYA FÖRLAG AB 1749666
Tel: 8 517 880 00 **Fax:** 851788001
Titles:
VÅRT NYA HEM

VÄSTBO ANDAN AB 1627692
Fabriksgatan 21, 342 32 ALVESTA
Tel: 472 440 31 **Fax:** 47230091
Titles:
JORD & SKOG
LOKALTIDNINGEN VÄSTBO ANDAN

VÄSTERÅS TIDNING 1627564
Norra Källgatan 17, 722 11 VÄSTERÅS
Tel: 21 30 46 00 **Fax:** 21 30 46 09
Titles:
VÄSTERÅS TIDNING
VÄSTERÅS TIDNING; WEBB

VÄSTERBOTTENS KURIREN AB 1789983
901 70 UMEÅ **Tel:** 90 15 10 00 **Fax:** 90 77 46 47
Titles:
VÄSTERBOTTENS-KURIREN

VÄSTERBOTTENS LÄNS HEMBYGDSFÖRBUND 1792014
Box 3183, 903 04 UMEÅ **Tel:** 90 17 18 02
Fax: 90779000
Titles:
TIDSKRIFTEN VÄSTERBOTTEN

VÄSTERVIKS-TIDNINGEN 1789964
Stora Torget 2, 593 82 VÄSTERVIK
Tel: 490 666 00 **Fax:** 490 666 99
Titles:
VÄSTERVIKS-TIDNINGEN
VÄSTERVIKS-TIDNINGEN; VT.SE

VÄSTGÖTA-TIDNINGAR AB 1789772
521 42 FALKÖPING **Tel:** 515 67 04 00
Titles:
FALKÖPINGS TIDNING
SKARABORGS LÄNS TIDNING
VÄSTGÖTA-BLADET

VÄSTKUSTTIDNINGAR AB 1790931
Box 344, 431 44 MÖLNDAL **Tel:** 31 27 51 20
Fax: 31 27 68 61
Titles:
VILLA & FRITID

VÄSTRA GÖTALANDSREGIONEN 1640162
Regionens Hus, Residenset, 462 80 VÄNERSBORG **Tel:** 521 27 58 19
Titles:
REGIONMAGASINET

VÄSTSVENSKA INDUSTRI- OCH HANDELSKAMMAREN 1629913
Box 5253, 402 25 GÖTEBORG **Tel:** 31 83 59 00
Titles:
NYHETSBREVET NOTERAT

VÄSTSVENSKA LOKALTIDNINGAR AB, ROGER IVARSSON 9 % 1640523
Box 93, 432 22 VARBERG **Tel:** 340 177 71
Fax: 340 144 70
Titles:
VARBERGS POSTEN
VARBERGS POSTEN; VARBERGSPOSTEN.SE

VEGANFÖRENINGEN 1627358
Klövervägen 6, 647 30 MARIEFRED
Tel: 159 344 04
Titles:
VEGAN

VERKO AB 1654112
Datavägen 12 A, 436 32 ASKIM **Tel:** 31 68 00 00
Fax: 31 68 00 09
Titles:
VERKO

VERKSTADSFORUM FÖRLAGS AB 1739929
Box 200 39, 104 60 STOCKHOLM **Tel:** 8 30 79 90
Titles:
VERKSTADSFORUM

VERKSTADSKONTAKT I LIDKÖPING AB 1790349
Box 82, 533 04 HÄLLEKIS **Tel:** 510 862 00
Fax: 51086220
Titles:
DIREKTKONTAKT - ENTREPENAD
DIREKTKONTAKT - SKOG
DIREKTKONTAKT - TRANSPORT
VERKSTADSKONTAKT

VERTEX/KÅRMEDIA UMEÅ HB 1710639
Box 7652, 907 13 UMEÅ **Tel:** 90 786 90 20
Fax: 90 13 09 28
Titles:
VERTEX
VERTEX; VERTEX.NU

VESTMANLANDS LÄNS TIDNING AB 1789957
Box 3, 721 03 VÄSTERÅS **Tel:** 21 19 90 00
Fax: 21 19 90 60
Titles:
VESTMANLANDS LÄNS TIDNING
VESTMANLANDS LÄNS TIDNING; VLT.SE

VETENSKAPSRÅDET 1630036
Vetenskapsrådet, 103 78 STOCKHOLM
Tel: 8 546 440 00 **Fax:** 8 546 441 80
Titles:
FORSKA
FORSKNING & MEDICIN
TENTAKEL

VIA MEDIA I LANDSKRONA AB 1627624
c/o Ewa Rensfelt, Okvägen 33, 281 51 HÄSSLEHOLM **Tel:** 45110781
Titles:
SKOLHÄLSAN
VENTILEN

VICE SCANDINAVIA HQ 1767079
Rosenlundsgatan 36 B, 118 53 STOCKHOLM
Tel: 8 675 00 58 **Fax:** 8 692 62 74
Titles:
VICE

VILLA AKTUELLT AB 1793748
Årstaängsvägen 1 A, 11tr, 117 43 STOCKHOLM
Tel: 8 555 930 00 **Fax:** 8 555 930 30
Titles:
VILLA AKTUELLT

VILLALIV AB 1790380
Villaliv AB, Köpmansgatan 12, 302 42 HALMSTAD **Tel:** 35 27 11 90 **Fax:** 35 22 72 80
Titles:
VILLALIV

VIMMERBY TIDNING OCH TRYCKERI EKONOMISK FÖREN 1789730
598 80 VIMMERBY **Tel:** 492 160 00
Fax: 492 141 02
Titles:
LÄNSTIDNINGEN NORR/VIMMERBY TIDNING

VIMMERBY TIDNING OCH TRYCKERI EKONOMISK FÖRENG 1732668
598 80 VIMMERBY **Tel:** 492 160 00
Fax: 492 101 02
Titles:
ÅKERI & TRANSPORT; WEBB

VIMMERBY TIDNING OCH TRYCKERI EKONOMISK FÖRENING 1630040
Smålands näringsliv, Stångågatan 46, 598 80 VIMMERBY **Tel:** 492 160 00 **Fax:** 492 101 02
Titles:
SMÅLANDS NÄRINGSLIV

VIMMERBY TIDNING OCH TRYCKERIFÖRENING 1750266
Västergatan 7, 352 31 VÄXJÖ **Tel:** 470 71 99 50
Fax: 470 209 30
Titles:
VÄXJÖBLADET/KRONOBERGAREN; WEBB

VINDELD AB 1627706
Ehrensvärdsgatan 3, nb, 112 35 STOCKHOLM
Tel: 736 91 48 07
Titles:
KONSTTIDNINGEN

VINNOVA 1745736
101 58 STOCKHOLM **Tel:** 8 473 30 00
Fax: 84733005
Titles:
VINNOVA-NYTT

VOLKSWAGEN GROUP SVERIGE AB/AUDI 1743615
Volkswagen Group Sverige AB/Audi, 151 88 SÖDERTÄLJE **Tel:** 8 553 865 00 **Fax:** 8 550 881 33
Titles:
AUDI MAGASIN

VOLKSWAGEN PERSONBILAR 1628122
Volkswagen Personbilar, 151 88 SÖDERTÄLJE
Tel: 8 553 865 00 **Fax:** 8 550 162 81
Titles:
VOLKSWAGEN MAGASIN

AB VOLVO 1639874
AB Volvo VHK, 405 08 GÖTEBORG
Tel: 31 66 11 77
Titles:
GLOBAL MAGAZINE

VOLVO AERO CORPORATION 1629614
Volvo Aero Corporation, avd. 1500, 461 81 TROLLHÄTTAN **Tel:** 520 944 01 **Fax:** 520 985 00
Titles:
AERO-MAGAZINET

VOLVO LASTVAGNAR AB 1710453
Volvo Lastvagnar AB, LVA6, 405 08 GÖTEBORG
Tel: 31 322 61 77 **Fax:** 31 330 20 42
Titles:
VOLVO PÅ VÄG

VOLVO PERSONBILAR SVERIGE AB 1628971
VCI-2, 405 31 GÖTEBORG **Tel:** 31 352 25 06
Fax: 31 325 27 70
Titles:
VOLVO LIFE

V-TAB, NORRTÄLJE 2006 1735381
Jenny Nyströms gränd 2, 392 33 KALMAR
Tel: 480 72 02 00 **Fax:** 48 072 02 00
Titles:
KALMARPOSTEN

VVS TEKNISKA FÖRENINGEN 1793455
Vasagatan 52, 3 tr, 111 20 STOCKHOLM
Tel: 8 791 66 80 **Fax:** 8 660 39 44
Titles:
ENERGI & MILJÖ
ENERGI & MILJÖ; SIKI.SE

VVS-INSTALLATÖRERNA 1790352
Box 47014, 100 74 STOCKHOLM **Tel:** 8 762 75 00
Fax: 8 669 12 04
Titles:
VVS-FORUM
VVS-FORUM; WEBB

WALDORFSKOLEFEDERATIONEN 1628706
Box 120, 161 26 BROMMA **Tel:** 8 653 20 16
Fax: 8 650 80 11
Titles:
PÅ VÄG

WALLIN & WIKLUND FÖRLAGS AB 1628818
Björkudden Lits Prästbord 126, 836 92 LIT
Tel: 63 13 45 65 **Fax:** 63 13 45 71
Titles:
ALLT OM JAKT & VAPEN

WENDELAS VÄNNER 1629832
c/o Mattsson, Badhusgatan 8, 151 73
SÖDERTÄLJE **Tel:** 8 550 305 84
Titles:
WENDELAVISAN

AB WILLIAM MICHELSENS BOKTRYCKERI 1789668
Södra Ringgatan 14, 441 85 ALINGSÅS
Tel: 322 67 00 00 **Fax:** 322 67 00 66
Titles:
ALINGSÅS TIDNING
ALINGSÅS TIDNING; ALINGSASTIDNING.SE

WWW.SVERIGESKULTURNÄT.SE, WWW.KULTUR1.SE 1685570
Box 2009, 103 11 STOCKHOLM **Tel:** 8 411 47 70
Titles:
MAGASIN1

YOUTH SKILLS SWEDEN 1732691
c/o Appelberg, Box 7344, 103 90 STOCKHOLM
Tel: 8 406 54 00 **Fax:** 8 406 54 99
Titles:
YRKESLANDSLAGET MAGASIN

YRKESFÖRENINGEN MILJÖ OCH HÄLSA 1650019
c/o Cicci Wik, Lingonstigen 5, 667 31
FORSHAGA **Tel:** 54 87 07 54
Titles:
MILJÖ & HÄLSA

ZETTERQVIST FÖRLAG 1639753
Amalia Jönssons gata 16, 421 31 VÄSTRA
FRÖLUNDA **Tel:** 31 743 21 75 **Fax:** 31 743 20 90
Titles:
BRANT

ZOO PEOPLE 1793630
Zoo, Grindsg 33 (vill ej ha pressmedd. via brev),
118 57 STOCKHOLM
Titles:
SAMHÄLLSTIDNINGEN RE:PUBLIC SERVICE

Switzerland

20 MINUTEN AG 1757227
Brühlgasse 15, 9004 ST. GALLEN **Tel:** 71 2268820
Fax: 71 2268821
Email: verlag.sg@20minuten.ch
Web site: http://www.20minuten.ch
Titles:
20 MINUTEN

7SKY PUBLISHING 688396
6, Mont-de-Faux, 1023 CRISSIER
Tel: 21 6374070 **Fax:** 21 6374110
Email: admin@7skymagazine.ch
Web site: http://www.7skymagazine.ch
Titles:
7SKY MAG
7SKY PEOPLE

A. BÜRLI AG DRUCKEREI 679637
Hauptstr. 19, 5312 DÖTTINGEN **Tel:** 56 2692525
Fax: 56 2692520
Email: buerli@botschaft.ch
Web site: http://www.botschaft.ch
Titles:
DIE BOTSCHAFT

A + M VERLAGS AG 699573
Riedmühlestr. 1, 8306 BRÜTTISELLEN
Tel: 41 3101985 **Fax:** 41 3101985
Email: acs-aktuell@gmx.net
Web site: http://www.acs-luzern.ch
Titles:
ACS AKTUELL

A & W VERLAG AG 1649878
Riedstr. 10, 8953 DIETIKON **Tel:** 43 4991860
Fax: 43 4991861
Email: verlag@auto-wirtschaft.ch
Web site: http://www.auto-wirtschaft.ch
Titles:
AUTO & ÉCONOMIE
AUTO & TECHNIK
AUTO & WIRTSCHAFT

AARE DRUCK AG 678163
Rütifeldstr. 17, 3294 BÜREN **Tel:** 32 3520430
Fax: 32 3520435
Email: anzeiger.bueren@aare-druck.ch
Titles:
ANZEIGER BÜREN UND UMGEBUNG

AARGAUER ZEITUNG AG 1722662
Neumattstr. 1, 5001 AARAU **Tel:** 58 2005555
Fax: 58 2005556
Email: azverlag@azag.ch
Web site: http://www.azag.ch
Titles:
AARGAUER ZEITUNG AZ

AARGAUISCHER LEHRERINNEN- UND LEHRER-VERBAND 688206
Entfelder Str. 61, 5001 AARAU **Tel:** 62 8247760
Fax: 62 8240260
Email: alv@alv-ag.ch
Web site: http://www.alv-ag.ch
Titles:
SCHULBLATT

ABB SCHWEIZ AG 1644616
Brown-Boveri-Str. 6, 5400 BADEN
Web site: http://www.abb.ch
Titles:
CONNECT
CONNECT

ADV PUBLISHING HOUSE SA 682300
via Besso, 42, 6903 LUGANO **Tel:** 91 9663810
Fax: 91 9661447
Email: adv@adv-publishing.ch
Web site: http://www.adv-publishing.ch
Titles:
GALATEA

AERO-CLUB OSTSCHWEIZ 698434
Postfach 279, 9320 ARBON **Tel:** 79 4467066
Email: info@aeroclub-ostschweiz.ch
Web site: http://www.aeroclub-ostschweiz.ch
Titles:
NACHRICHTEN AERO-CLUB OSTSCHWEIZ

AG BUCHDRUCKEREI SCHIERS 687261
Bahnhofstr. 120, 7220 SCHIERS **Tel:** 81 3281566
Fax: 81 3281955
Email: info@drucki.ch
Web site: http://www.drucki.ch
Titles:
PRÄTTIGAUER UND HERRSCHÄFTLER

AG FÜR RADIOPUBLIKATIONEN 1640995
Brunnenhofstr. 22, 8024 ZÜRICH **Tel:** 43 3005200
Fax: 43 3005201
Email: redaktion@radiomagazin.ch
Web site: http://www.radiomagazin.ch
Titles:
RADIO MAGAZIN

AG VERLAG HOCH- UND TIEFBAU 688266
Weinbergstr. 49, 8006 ZÜRICH **Tel:** 44 2588333
Fax: 44 2610324
Email: verlag@baumeister.ch
Titles:
SCHWEIZER BAUWIRTSCHAFT
SCHWEIZER HOLZBAU

AG WINTERTHURER STADTANZEIGER 1643199
Garnmarkt 10, 8401 WINTERTHUR
Tel: 52 2669900 **Fax:** 52 2669913
Email: mwenger@zieglerdruck.ch
Web site: http://www.stadi-online.ch
Titles:
WINTERTHURER STADTANZEIGER

AGEDIP SA 699400
33, av. de la Gare, 1001 LAUSANNE
Tel: 21 3494822 **Fax:** 21 3494830
Titles:
BILAN

AGRI 698344
1 av. de Jordils, 1000 LAUSANNE 6
Tel: 21 6130646 **Fax:** 21 6130640
Email: journal@agrihebdo.ch
Web site: http://www.agrihebdo.ch
Titles:
AGRI

AGROPRESS AG 699090
Baselstr. 48, 4125 RIEHEN **Tel:** 61 3869090
Fax: 61 3869099
Email: ghb@agropress.com
Web site: http://www.agropress.com
Titles:
THE CLIPPER

AIDS-HILFE SCHWEIZ 1717450
Postfach 1118, 8031 ZÜRICH **Tel:** 44 4471111
Fax: 44 4471112
Email: med.info@aids.ch
Web site: http://www.aids.ch
Titles:
SWISS AIDS NEWS

AKI REGION BASEL 1681451
Klybeckstr. 64, 4057 BASEL **Tel:** 61 2052929
Fax: 61 2052928
Email: info@behindertenforum.ch
Web site: http://www.behindertenforum.ch
Titles:
HANDICAPFORUM

ALA, SCHWEIZERISCHE GESELLSCHAFT FÜR VOGELKUNDE UND VOGELSCHUTZ 686814
6204 SEMPACH **Tel:** 26 4963537
Email: sekretariat@ala-schweiz.ch
Web site: http://www.ala-schweiz.ch
Titles:
DER ORNITHOLOGISCHE BEOBACHTER

ALFONS WIRTH 1640574
Waldacker 1, 9000 ST. GALLEN **Tel:** 71 2776067
Fax: 71 2776079
Email: info@agora-agenda.ch
Web site: http://www.agora-agenda.ch
Titles:
AGORA

ALLGEMEINE ANTHROPOSOPHISCHE GESELLSCHAFT 682655
Postfach, 4143 DORNACH 1 **Tel:** 61 7064464
Fax: 61 7064465
Email: info@dasgoetheanum.ch
Web site: http://www.dasgoetheanum.ch
Titles:
DAS GOETHEANUM

ALPENROSEN VERLAG GMBH 1649393
Lehnfelstr. 13, 4702 OENSINGEN **Tel:** 62 3964029
Fax: 32 3964028
Email: hanspeter.balsiger@alpenrosen.ch
Web site: http://www.alpenrosen.ch
Titles:
ALPENROSEN

ALPMEDIA AG 698949
Saltinaplatz 1, 3900 BRIG-GLIS **Tel:** 27 9222911
Fax: 27 9222910
Email: info@rz-online.ch
Web site: http://www.rz-online.ch
Titles:
RZ RHONE ZEITUNG

ALTERSWOHNHEIM BRUNNEN 1742534
Heideweg 10, 6440 BRUNNEN **Tel:** 41 8250825
Fax: 41 8250826
Email: alterswohnheim@brunnen.ch
Web site: http://www.brunnen.ch/alterswohnheim
Titles:
MITENAND

ALTERSZENTRUM STAFFELNHOF 1690752
Staffelnhofstr. 60, 6015 REUSSBÜHL
Tel: 41 2593030 **Fax:** 41 2593039
Email: staffelnhof@littau.ch
Web site: http://www.littau.ch
Titles:
STAFFLE-BLITZ

ANDERMATT BIOCONTROL AG 678049
Stahlermatten 6, 6146 GROSSDIETWIL
Tel: 62 9175005 **Fax:** 62 9175006
Email: sales@biocontrol.ch
Web site: http://www.biocontrol.ch
Titles:
ANDERMATT GRUPPE JOURNAL

ANIMAN PUBLICATIONS SA 678063
Quai des Sirènes, 66, rte. de Lausanne, 1110
MORGES **Tel:** 21 6015250 **Fax:** 21 6015259
Email: laura.carro@animan.ch
Web site: http://www.animan.ch
Titles:
ANIMAN

ANZEIGER DES AMTES WANGEN AG 1749712
Bahnhofstr. 39, 4900 LANGENTHAL
Tel: 62 9235555 **Fax:** 62 9235566
Email: inserate@aawangen.ch
Web site: http://www.aawangen.ch
Titles:
ANZEIGER DES AMTES WANGEN

ANZEIGER LANGENTHAL 678151
Bahnhofstr. 39, 4900 LANGENTHAL
Tel: 62 9226555 **Fax:** 62 9229327
Email: inserate@anzeigerlangenthal.ch
Web site: http://www.anzeigerlangenthal.ch/news.aspx
Titles:
ANZEIGER LANGENTHAL UND UMGEBUNG

ANZEIGER VON WALLISELLEN 678187
Kirchstr. 2, 8304 WALLISELLEN **Tel:** 44 8302309
Fax: 44 8310297
Email: info@avwa.ch
Web site: http://www.avwa.ch
Titles:
ANZEIGER VON WALLISELLEN
ANZEIGER VON WALLISELLEN

ANZEIGERVERBAND KIRCHBERG 678147
Eystr. 1, 3422 KIRCHBERG **Tel:** 34 4452946
Fax: 34 4454537
Email: inserate@anzeiger-kirchberg.ch
Web site: http://www.anzeiger-kirchberg.ch
Titles:
ANZEIGER

APHASIE SUISSE 678195
Zähringerstr. 19, 6003 LUZERN **Tel:** 41 2400583
Fax: 41 2400754
Email: info@aphasie.org
Web site: http://www.aphasie.org
Titles:
APHASIE UND VERWANDTE GEBIETE/ET DOMAINES ASSOCIÉS

APPENZELLER MEDIENHAUS AG 677847
Kasernenstr. 64, 9101 HERISAU **Tel:** 71 3546464
Fax: 71 3546465
Email: info@appon.ch
Web site: http://www.appon.ch
Titles:
AMTSBLATT
APPENZELLER ZEITUNG

ARCHITHEMA VERLAG AG 678444
Rieterstr. 35, 8002 ZÜRICH **Tel:** 44 2041818
Fax: 44 2041820
Email: verlag@archithema.com
Web site: http://www.archithema.com
Titles:
ATRIUM
EINFAMILIENHÄUSER

ÄRZTINNEN UND ÄRZTE FÜR UMWELTSCHUTZ 686635
Postfach 111, 4013 BASEL **Tel:** 61 3224949
Fax: 61 3224851
Email: info@aefu.ch
Web site: http://www.aefu.ch
Titles:
OEKOSKOP

ASSOCIATION DE LA REVUE MILITAIRE SUISSE 698094
3, av. de Florimont, 1006 LAUSANNE
Tel: 21 3114817 **Fax:** 21 3119709
Email: administration@revuemilitairesuisse.ch
Web site: http://www.revuemilitairesuisse.ch
Titles:
REVUE MILITAIRE SUISSE

ASSOCIATION DES ANCIENS ÉLÈVES DE L'ECOLE D'INGÉNIEURS DE GENÈVE 1644612
c.p. 1120, 1211 GENF 1
Titles:
ATG BULLETIN TECHNIQUE DE L'ASSOCIATION DES ANCIENS ÉLÈVES DE L'ECOLE D'INGÉNIEURS DE GENÈVE

ASSOCIATION PIERRE FAVRE 1714953
18, rue Jacques-Dalphin, 1227 CAROUGE
Tel: 22 8274676 **Fax:** 22 8274670
Email: administration@choisir.ch
Web site: http://www.choisir.ch
Titles:
CHOISIR

ASSOCIAZIONE CONSUMATRICI E CONSUMATORI DELLA SVIZZERA ITALIANA 679616
c.p. 165, 6932 BREGANZONA **Tel:** 91 9229755
Fax: 91 9220471
Email: acsi@acsi.ch
Web site: http://www.acsi.ch
Titles:
LA BORSA DELLA SPESA

ASTAG SCHWEIZERISCHER NUTZFAHRZEUGVERBAND 698608
Weissenbühlweg 3, 3007 BERN **Tel:** 31 3708585
Fax: 31 3708589
Email: astag@astag.ch
Web site: http://www.astag.ch
Titles:
STRASSEN TRANSPORT
TRANSPORT ROUTIER

ASTRODATA AG 1641523
Albisrieder Str. 232, 8047 ZÜRICH
Tel: 43 3433300 **Fax:** 43 3433301
Email: redaktion@astrologieheute.ch
Web site: http://www.astrologieheute.ch
Titles:
ASTROLOGIE HEUTE

AVIATION MEDIA AG 1652829
Oberteufenerstr. 58, 8428 TEUFEN
Tel: 44 8817261 **Fax:** 44 8817263
Email: info@skynews.ch
Web site: http://www.skynews.ch
Titles:
SKYNEWS.CH

AXEL SPRINGER SCHWEIZ AG 1748083
Förrlibuckstr. 70, 8005 ZÜRICH **Tel:** 43 4445540
Fax: 43 4445541
Web site: http://www.tvzeitschriften.ch
Titles:
BEOBACHTER
BILANZ
TELE
TVSTAR

AXEL SPRINGER SCHWEIZ AG HANDELSZEITUNG 1750677
Förrlibuckstr. 70, 8021 ZÜRICH **Tel:** 43 4445870
Fax: 43 4445936
Email: verlag@handelszeitung.ch
Web site: http://www.handelszeitung.ch
Titles:
HANDELSZEITUNG & THE WALL STREET JOURNAL

AXEL SPRINGER SCHWEIZ HANDELSZEITUNG FACHVERLAG AG 687183
Förrlibuckstr. 70, 8021 ZÜRICH **Tel:** 43 4445111
Fax: 43 4445091
Email: jpage@handelszeitung.ch
Web site: http://www.handelszeitung.ch
Titles:
IO NEW MANAGEMENT
PME MAGAZINE
PRIVATE BANKING
SCHWEIZER BANK
SCHWEIZER VERSICHERUNG

AXEL SPRINGER SCHWEIZ HANDELSZEITUNG UND FINANZRUNDSCHAU AG 682964
Förrlibuckstr. 70, 8021 ZÜRICH **Tel:** 43 4445900
Fax: 43 4445932
Email: verlag@handelszeitung.ch
Web site: http://www.handelszeitung.ch
Titles:
STOCKS
TOP

AYER-AMS SÀRL 683988
190, rte. de Cossonay, 1020 RENENS
Tel: 21 7031306 **Fax:** 21 7031305
Email: info@ayer-ams.ch
Web site: http://www.jardin.ch
Titles:
JARDIN ROMAND

AZ ANZEIGER AG 688788
Ziegelfeldstr. 60, 4601 OLTEN **Tel:** 62 2057596
Fax: 62 2057586
Email: info@stadtanzeiger-olten.ch
Web site: http://www.stadtanzeiger-olten.ch
Titles:
STADTANZEIGER

AZ FACHVERLAGE AG 678816
Neumattstr. 1, 5001 AARAU **Tel:** 58 2005658
Fax: 58 2006867
Web site: http://www.az-verlag.ch
Titles:
ANNEMARIE WILDEISEN'S KOCHEN
BÄTITECH
CR CHEMISCHE RUNDSCHAU
ET ELEKTROTECHNIK
FIT FOR LIFE
HK GEBÄUDETECHNIK
MEGALINK
NATÜRLICH LEBEN
SWISSPLASTICS
TECHNICA
WIR ELTERN

AZ WOCHENZEITUNGEN 1750718
Kronenplatz 12, 5600 LENZBURG
Tel: 58 2005772 **Fax:** 58 2005821
Email: oscar.meier@azag.ch
Web site: http://www.aargauerzeitung.ch
Titles:
LENZBURGER BEZIRKS-ANZEIGER
DER SEETALER-DER LINDENBERG

AZ WOCHENZEITUNGEN AG 677218
Kronenplatz 12, 5600 LENZBURG
Tel: 58 2005820 **Fax:** 58 2005821
Email: verlag@azag.ch
Web site: http://www.azag.ch
Titles:
STADT-ANZEIGER AARAU
STADT-ANZEIGER BADEN

B + L VERLAGS AG 677569
Steinwiesenstr. 3, 8952 SCHLIEREN
Tel: 44 7333999 **Fax:** 44 7333989
Email: info@blverlag.ch
Web site: http://www.blverlag.ch
Titles:
AKTUELLE TECHNIK
ARCHITEKTUR TECHNIK
IDEA

BACHMANN MEDIEN AG 1763785
Thiersteinerallee 17, 4053 BASEL **Tel:** 61 5341084
Fax: 61 5354184
Email: verlag@edito-online.ch
Web site: http://www.bachmannmedien.ch
Titles:
EDITO + KLARTEXT
EDITO + KLARTEXT

BASELLANDSCHAFTLICHE ZEITUNG AG 1714852
Rheinstr. 3, 4410 LIESTAL **Tel:** 61 9272600
Fax: 61 9212604
Email: verlag@bz-ag.ch
Web site: http://www.bz-ag.ch
Titles:
BASELLANDSCHAFTLICHE ZEITUNG BZ
BASELLANDSCHAFTLICHE ZEITUNG BZ

BASLER ZEITUNG AG 678811
Hochberger Str. 15, 4002 BASEL **Tel:** 61 6391111
Fax: 61 6311959
Email: verlag@baz.ch
Web site: http://www.baz.ch
Titles:
BASLER ZEITUNG

BDO VISURA 690209
Biberiststr. 16, 4501 SOLOTHURN
Tel: 32 6246205 **Fax:** 32 6246208
Web site: http://www.bdo.ch
Titles:
ZOOM

BERNER KMU 699065
Technikumstr. 14, 3401 BURGDORF
Tel: 34 4206565 **Fax:** 34 4230732
Email: info@bernerkmu.ch
Web site: http://www.bernerkmu.ch
Titles:
BERNER KMU AKTUELL

BERNER LANDBOTE AG 679159
Schulhausgasse 16, 3110 MÜNSINGEN
Tel: 31 7206000 **Fax:** 31 7215333
Email: redaktion@berner-landbote.ch
Web site: http://www.berner-landbote.ch
Titles:
BERNER LANDBOTE

BERNER ZEITUNG AG 679165
Dammweg 9, 3013 BERN **Tel:** 31 3303111
Fax: 31 3316087
Email: verlag@bernerzeitung.ch
Web site: http://www.espace.ch
Titles:
BERNER ZEITUNG BZ

BERNISCHER ANWALTSVERBAND 1714775
Platanenstr. 2, 3401 BURGDORF **Tel:** 34 4231189
Fax: 34 4231192
Web site: http://www.bav-aab.ch
Titles:
IN DUBIO

BERNISCHER STAATSPERSONALVERBAND 679807
Postgasse 60, 3000 BERN 8 **Tel:** 31 3111166
Fax: 31 3111118
Email: sekretariat@bspv.ch
Web site: http://www.bspv.ch
Titles:
DIAGONAL

BFU - BERATUNGSSTELLE FÜR UNFALLVERHÜTUNG 678449
Hodlerstr. 5a, 3011 BERN **Tel:** 31 3902222
Fax: 31 3902230
Email: info@bfu.ch
Web site: http://www.bfu.ch
Titles:
AREA SICUREZZA
OBJECTIF SÉCURITÉ
SICHER LEBEN

BIEL-BIENNE VERLAG 679298
Burggasse 14, 2501 BIEL **Tel:** 32 3293939
Fax: 32 3293938
Email: news@bielbienne.com
Web site: http://www.bielbienne.com
Titles:
BIEL BIENNE

BILDUNGSDEPARTEMENT DES KANTONS ST. GALLEN 677835
Davidstr. 31, 9001 ST. GALLEN **Tel:** 71 2294383
Fax: 71 2294479
Email: info.schulblatt@sg.ch
Web site: http://www.schule.sg.ch
Titles:
SCHULBLATT DES KANTONS ST. GALLEN

BINKERT MEDIEN AG 1643418
Basler Str. 15, 5080 LAUFENBURG
Tel: 62 8697900 **Fax:** 62 8697901
Email: binkertmedien@binkert.ch
Web site: http://www.binkert-medien.ch
Titles:
L-T LEBENSMITTEL-TECHNOLOGIE
SCHWEIZER LOGISTIK KATALOG
SCHWEIZER VERPACKUNGS KATALOG
TECHNISCHE RUNDSCHAU

BIRKHÄUSER VERLAG AG 678234
Viaduktstr. 42, 4051 BASEL **Tel:** 61 2050707
Fax: 61 2050799
Email: contact@birkhauser.ch
Web site: http://www.springer.com/birkhauser
Titles:
FORM
INTERNATIONAL JOURNAL OF PUBLIC HEALTH

BOLERO ZEITSCHRIFTENVERLAG AG 679579
Giesshübelstr. 62i, 8045 ZÜRICH **Tel:** 44 4548282
Fax: 44 4548272
Email: service@boleroweb.ch
Web site: http://www.boleroweb.ch
Titles:
BOLERO

BOLL VERLAG AG 1724753
Stationsstr. 49, 8902 URDORF **Tel:** 44 7358000
Fax: 44 7358001
Email: info@bollverlag.ch
Web site: http://www.bollverlag.ch
Titles:
WOHNREVUE

BORGWARD INTERESSENGEMEINSCHAFT SCHWEIZ 1653492
Hinterer Engelstein 11, 8344 BÄRETSWIL
Tel: 44 9392521 **Fax:** 44 9392521
Email: sekretariat@borgward-ig.ch
Web site: http://www.borgward-ig.ch
Titles:
CLUBZEITUNG

BRUNNER AG, DRUCK UND MEDIEN 684677
Arsenalstr. 24, 6010 KRIENS **Tel:** 41 3183434
Fax: 41 3183470
Email: verlag@bag.ch
Web site: http://www.bag.ch
Titles:
FOOD AKTUELL
GASTROFÜHRER

BUAG GRAFISCHES UNTERNEHMEN AG 1714862
Täfernstr. 14, 5405 BADEN **Tel:** 56 4845454
Fax: 56 4930525
Web site: http://www.buag.ch
Titles:
WOHNIWIRTSCHAFT

BUCHDRUCKEREI DAVOS AG 680511
Promenade 60, 7270 DAVOS PLATZ
Tel: 81 4158181 **Fax:** 81 4158182
Email: verkauf@budag.ch
Web site: http://www.budag.ch
Titles:
KLOSTERSER ZEITUNG

BUCHDRUCKEREI LÜDIN AG 679353
Kirchweg 10, 4102 BINNINGEN **Tel:** 61 4212580
Fax: 61 4215636
Email: redaktion@binningeranzeiger.ch
Web site: http://www.binningeranzeiger.ch
Titles:
BINNINGER ANZEIGER

BUCHDRUCKEREI TURBENTHAL AG 689515
Tösstalstr. 74, 8488 TURBENTHAL
Tel: 52 3851119 **Fax:** 52 3852901
Email: info@toessthaler.ch
Web site: http://www.toessthaler.ch

Titles:
DER TÖSSTHALER

BUCHER DRUCKMEDIEN AG 690753
Dorfplatz, 6354 VITZNAU **Tel:** 41 3970303
Fax: 41 3971747
Email: wochenzeitung@bucherdruck.ch
Web site: http://www.bucherdruck.ch

Titles:
WOCHEN-ZEITUNG

BÜCHLER GRAFINO AG 697614
Dammweg 9, 3001 BERN **Tel:** 31 3303939
Fax: 31 3303930
Email: verlag@buechler-grafino.ch
Web site: http://www.buechler-grafino.ch

Titles:
DER GEMÜSEBAU LE MARAÎCHER

BUCHSMEDIEN AG 690815
Bahnhofstr. 14, 9471 BUCHS **Tel:** 81 7500202
Fax: 81 7500209
Email: info@buchsmedien.ch
Web site: http://www.w-und-o.ch

Titles:
WERDENBERGER & OBERTOGGENBURGER
WERDENBERGER & OBERTOGGENBURGER

BÜLACHER INDUSTRIEN 1748879
Steinackerstr. 7, 8180 BÜLACH **Tel:** 44 8727474
Fax: 44 8727475
Email: kundendienst@wiegand.ch
Web site: http://www.buelacher-industrien.ch

Titles:
BÜLACHER INDUSTRIEN NACHRICHTEN

BUNDESAMT FÜR LANDWIRTSCHAFT 1714892
Mattenhofstr. 5, 3003 BERN **Tel:** 31 3222534
Fax: 31 3222634
Email: info@blw.admin.ch
Web site: http://www.blw.admin.ch

Titles:
AGRARFORSCHUNG

BUNDESAMT FÜR RAUMENTWICKLUNG 699127
Kochergasse 10, 3003 BERN **Tel:** 31 3224060
Fax: 31 3224716
Email: info@are.admin.ch
Web site: http://www.are.ch

Titles:
FORUM RAUMENTWICKLUNG DU DÉVELOPPEMENT TERRITORIAL SVILUPPO TERRITORIALE

BUNDESAMT FÜR UMWELT 683425
Postfach, 3003 BERN **Tel:** 31 3229311
Fax: 31 3227054
Email: info@bafu.admin.ch
Web site: http://www.bafu.admin.ch

Titles:
UMWELT

BÜNDNER GEWERBEVERBAND 679854
Hinterm Bach 40, 7002 CHUR **Tel:** 81 2570323
Fax: 81 2570324
Email: info@kgv-gr.ch
Web site: http://www.kgv-gr.ch

Titles:
BÜNDNER GEWERBE

BVMEDIA CHRISTLICHE MEDIEN GMBH 689277
Witzbergstr. 7, 8330 PFÄFFIKON **Tel:** 43 2888010
Fax: 43 2888011
Email: info@bvmedia.ch
Web site: http://www.bvmedia.ch

Titles:
FAMILY
JOYCE
LEBENSLAUF >>
TEENSMAG

CAMERA DI COMMERCIO, DELL'INDUSTRIA, DELL'ARTIGIANATO E DEI SERVIZI DEL CANTONE TICINO 1714839
Corso Elvezia, 16, 6900 LUGANO **Tel:** 91 9115132
Fax: 91 9115112
Email: pantini@cci.ch
Web site: http://www.cciati.ch

Titles:
TICINO BUSINESS

CASANOVA DRUCK + VERLAG GMBH 1773859
Rossbodenstr. 33, 7004 CHUR **Tel:** 81 2583346
Fax: 81 2583343
Email: info@casanova.ch
Web site: http://www.casanova.ch

Titles:
TRUMPF-AS

CAT MEDIEN AG 684997
Neuenhoferstr. 101, 5401 BADEN **Tel:** 56 2032200
Fax: 56 2032299
Email: info@catmedien.ch
Web site: http://www.catmedien.ch

Titles:
LEBEN & GLAUBEN
SONNTAG

CENTRALE SUISSE DES ENTREPRISES D'ENTRAÎNEMENT 1715912
69, rue Jardinière, 2300 LA-CHAUX-DE-FONDS
Tel: 32 9109404 **Fax:** 32 9109401
Email: info@practicefirms.ch
Web site: http://www.practicefirms.ch

Titles:
ECHO
ECHO

CFD CHRISTLICHER FRIEDENSDIENST 680110
Falkenhöheweg 8, 3001 BERN **Tel:** 31 3005060
Fax: 31 3005069
Email: info@cfd-ch.org
Web site: http://www.cfd-ch.org

Titles:
CFD ZEITUNG

LA COLOMBE GOURMANDE 1752342
4, rue de l'Etang, 2013 COLOMBIER
Tel: 32 8417250 **Fax:** 32 8411521

Titles:
GUIDE PLAISIRS GASTRONOMIE MAGAZINE

COMEDIA ZENTRALSEKRETARIAT 685256
Monbijoustr. 33, 3001 BERN **Tel:** 31 3906611
Fax: 31 3906691
Email: info@comedia.ch
Web site: http://www.comedia.ch

Titles:
FACHHEFTE GRAFISCHE INDUSTRIE BULLETIN TECHNIQUE

COOP PRESSE 680370
St.-Jakobs-Str. 175, 4053 BASEL **Tel:** 61 3367140
Fax: 61 3367072
Web site: http://www.coop.ch

Titles:
COOP COOPZEITUNG

COSMOS VERLAG AG 698292
Kräyigenweg 2, 3074 MURI **Tel:** 31 9506464
Fax: 31 9506460
Email: info@steuerrevue.ch
Web site: http://www.steuerrevue.ch

Titles:
STEUER REVUE REVUE FISCALE

COTE MAGAZIN 1791465
37, rue Eugène Marziano, 1227 GENF
Tel: 22 7365656 **Fax:** 22 7363738
Web site: http://www.cotemagazine.com

Titles:
COTE MAGAZINE

CRB SCHWEIZERISCHE ZENTRALSTELLE FÜR BAURATIONALISIERUNG/ CENTRE SUISSE D'ÉTUDES POUR LA RATIONALISATION DE LA CONSTRUCTION 1725072
Steinstr. 21, 8036 ZÜRICH **Tel:** 44 4564545
Fax: 44 4564566
Email: info@crb.ch
Web site: http://www.crb.ch

Titles:
CRB BULLETIN.

CREATIVE CONSULTING GMBH 1640979
Grubenstr. 11, 8045 ZÜRICH **Tel:** 44 4504410
Email: wolfram.meister@schweizerische-weinzeitung.ch
Web site: http://www.schweizerische-weinzeitung.ch

Titles:
SCHWEIZERISCHE WEINZEITUNG

CRUISING CLUB DER SCHWEIZ 1642202
Marktgasse 9, 3000 BERN 7 **Tel:** 31 3101100
Fax: 31 3101109
Email: info@cruisingclub.ch
Web site: http://www.cruisingclub.ch

Titles:
CCS CRUISING

CRYPTO AG 1676061
Postfach 460, 6301 ZUG **Tel:** 41 7497781
Fax: 41 7412272
Email: gabriela.hofmann@crypto.ch
Web site: http://www.crypto.ch

Titles:
CRYPTO MAGAZINE
CRYPTO MAGAZINE
CRYPTO MAGAZINE
CRYPTO MAGAZINE
CRYPTO MAGAZINE

CVA-VERLAG 685332
Tulpenweg 12, 4528 ZUCHWIL **Tel:** 32 6853578
Email: praesident@circusfreunde.ch
Web site: http://www.circusfreunde.ch

Titles:
MANEGE

D + D VERLAG GMBH 678835
Werriker Str. 7, 8606 NÄNIKON **Tel:** 44 9409953
Fax: 44 9420522
Email: info@bauenheute.ch
Web site: http://www.bauenheute.ch

Titles:
BAUEN HEUTE

DEK-VERLAGS AG 1642201
Im Lutereich 44, 4411 SELTISBERG
Tel: 61 3381638 **Fax:** 61 3381600
Email: dek@laupper.ch
Web site: http://www.laupper.ch

Titles:
BAU FLASH
EML EINKAUF MATERIALWIRTSCHAFT LOGISTIK
NEUE PRODUKTE
SHR SCHWEIZER HOLZ-REVUE
UMWELTTECHNIK SCHWEIZ

DFMEDIA 679381
Zürcher Str. 238, 8501 FRAUENFELD
Tel: 58 3449494 **Fax:** 58 3449481
Email: anzeigen.frauenfeld@dfmedia.ch
Web site: http://www.dfmedia.ch

Titles:
ALLGEMEINER ANZEIGER
CARROSSIER
ELECTRO REVUE
MODELL FLUGSPORT
ST. GALLER BAUER
THURGAUER BAUER

DIETSCHI AG 686768
Ziegelfeldstr. 60, 4601 OLTEN **Tel:** 62 2057575
Fax: 62 2057500
Email: verlag@oltnertagblatt.ch
Web site: http://www.oltnertagblatt.ch

Titles:
OLTNER TAGBLATT OT

DOCU MEDIA SCHWEIZ GMBH 1714950
Bahnhofstr. 24, 8803 RÜSCHLIKON
Tel: 44 7247770 **Fax:** 44 7247877
Email: info@docu.ch
Web site: http://www.docu.ch

Titles:
BAUHERREN MAGAZIN

DR. ROLF TH. STIEFEL & PARTNER AG 685324
Felsentr. 88, 9000 ST. GALLEN **Tel:** 71 7800955
Fax: 71 7800956
Email: info@stiefel-rolf-th.ch
Web site: http://www.stiefel-rolf-th.ch

Titles:
MANAGEMENT-ANDRAGOGIK UND ORGANISATIONSENTWICKLUNG (MAO)

DRUCKEREI AKERET AG 678043
Landstr. 70, 8450 ANDELFINGEN **Tel:** 52 3052909
Fax: 52 3171243
Email: info@andelfinger.ch
Web site: http://www.andelfinger.ch

Titles:
ANDELFINGER ZEITUNG

DRUCKEREI CRATANDER AG 679295
Missionsstr. 36, 4012 BASEL **Tel:** 61 2646434
Fax: 61 2646433
Web site: http://www.bibo.ch

Titles:
BIBO BIRSIGTAL-BOTE

DRUCKEREI GRAF AG 686300
Bahnhofstr. 44, 8180 BÜLACH **Tel:** 44 8641515
Fax: 44 8461555
Email: nbt@nbt.ch
Web site: http://www.nbt.ch

Titles:
NEUES BÜLACHER TAGBLATT
NEUES BÜLACHER TAGBLATT

DRUCKEREI K. AUGUSTIN AG 698053
Im Merzenbrunnen, 8240 THAYNGEN
Tel: 52 6454111 **Fax:** 52 6454199
Email: heimatblatt.redaktion@augustin.ch

Titles:
HEIMATBLATT FÜR DIE GEMEINDEN THAYNGEN (MIT ALTDORF, BARZHEIM, BIBERN, HOFEN UND OPFERTSHOFEN), BÜTTENHARDT, DÖRFLINGEN, LOHN UND STETTEN

DRUCKEREI SCHÜRCH AG 678153
Bahnhofstr. 9, 4950 HUTTWIL **Tel:** 62 9598070
Fax: 62 9598074
Email: info@schuerch-druck.ch
Web site: http://www.schuerch-druck.ch

Titles:
ANZEIGER TRACHSELWALD

DRUCKEREI STECKBORN LOUIS KELLER AG 679631
Seestr. 118, 8266 STECKBORN **Tel:** 52 7620222
Fax: 52 7620223
Email: info@druckerei-steckborn.ch
Web site: http://www.druckerei-steckborn.ch

Titles:
BOTE VOM UNTERSEE UND RHEIN

DRUCKEREI SUTER AG 679751
Schönenwerderstr. 13, 5036 OBERENTFELDEN
Tel: 62 7379000 **Fax:** 62 7379005
Web site: http://www.suterdruck.ch

Titles:
DER LANDANZEIGER

DU KULTURMEDIEN AG 1743241
Stadelhoferstr. 25, 8001 ZÜRICH **Tel:** 44 2668555
Fax: 44 2668558
Email: info@du-magazin.com
Web site: http://www.du-magazin.com

Titles:
DU

DZ-VERLAG 678858
Linsebühlstr. 89, 9004 ST. GALLEN
Tel: 71 2980006 **Fax:** 71 2985480
Email: dzverlag@bluewin.ch
Web site: http://www.dz-verlag.ch

Titles:
BAU INFO

E. KALBERER AG BUCH- UND OFFSETDRUCK 677733
Bahnhofstr. 10, 9602 KIRCHBERG
Tel: 71 9311011 **Fax:** 71 9313331
Email: milo.kalberer@druckereikalberer.ch
Web site: http://www.druckereikalberer.ch

Titles:
ALTTOGGENBURGER

EA DRUCK + VERLAG AG 681168
Zürichstr. 57, 8840 EINSIEDELN **Tel:** 55 4188282
Fax: 55 4188284
Email: info@eadruck.ch
Web site: http://www.einsiedleranzeiger.ch

Titles:
EINSIEDLER ANZEIGER
EINSIEDLER ANZEIGER

ECJ PUBLISHING LTD. ADMINISTRATIONSBÜRO 1714959
Oberneuhofstr. 5, 6341 BAAR **Tel:** 41 7667779
Fax: 41 7667780
Email: info@cigar-cult.com
Web site: http://www.cigar-cult.com

Titles:
EUROPEAN CIGAR JOURNAL

ECONOMIE FORESTIÈRE SUISSE 681973
Rosenweg 14, 4501 SOLOTHURN
Tel: 32 6258800 **Fax:** 32 6258899
Email: info@wvs.ch
Web site: http://www.wvs.ch

Titles:
LA FORET

EDIPRESSE PUBLICATIONS SA 681748
33, av. de la Gare, 1001 LAUSANNE
Tel: 21 3494545 **Fax:** 21 3494319
Web site: http://www.edipresse.ch

Titles:
LA BROYE

EDITION RENTERIA SA 1641573
Hopfenstr. 10, 8045 ZÜRICH **Tel:** 44 4514647
Fax: 44 4513638
Email: contact@renteria.ch
Web site: http://www.renteria.ch

Titles:
SCHWEIZER PR- & MEDIEN-VERZEICHNIS RÉPERTOIRE RP & MÉDIAS SUISSES

EDITION SALZ & PFEFFER AG 680192
Stampfenbachstr. 117, 8042 ZÜRICH
Tel: 44 3602080 **Fax:** 44 3602089
Email: info@salz-pfeffer.ch
Web site: http://www.salz-pfeffer.ch

Titles:
CIGAR

EDITIONS MÉDECINE ET HYGIÈNE 1649587
46, ch. de la Mousse, 1225 CHÊNE-BOURG
Tel: 22 7029311 **Fax:** 22 7029355
Email: administration@medhyg.ch
Web site: http://www.medecinehygiene.ch

Titles:
GENETIC COUNSELING
PHARMA-FLASH
PSYCHOTHÉRAPIES
REVUE MÉDICALE SUISSE
THERAPIE FAMILIALE

EDITIONS PLUS SÀRL 1640475
2, av. de la Rasude, 1001 LAUSANNE
Tel: 21 3100131 **Fax:** 21 3100139
Email: bas@bonasavoir.ch
Web site: http://www.bonasavoir.ch

Titles:
BON À SAVOIR

EDITIONS RINGIER ROMANDIE 680752
3, pont Bessières, 1005 LAUSANNE
Tel: 21 3317000 **Fax:** 21 3317001
Email: ringier.romandie@ringier.ch
Web site: http://www.ringier.ch

Titles:
EDELWEISS
EDELWEISS MEN
L' HEBDO
L' ILLUSTRÉ

EFFINGERHOF AG 679797
Storchengasse 15, 5201 BRUGG **Tel:** 56 4607712
Fax: 56 4607780
Email: r.aeschlimann@effingerhof.ch
Web site: http://www.effingerhof.ch

Titles:
GENERAL-ANZEIGER GA RUNDSCHAU RS

EINWOHNERGEMEINDE WORBEN 1691026
Hauptstr. 19, 3252 WORBEN **Tel:** 32 3872050
Fax: 32 3872056
Email: info@worben.ch
Web site: http://www.worben.ch

Titles:
INFO-BLATT

ELECTROSUISSE 688395
Luppmenstr. 1, 8320 FEHRALTORF
Tel: 44 9561111 **Fax:** 44 9561511
Email: bulletin@electrosuisse.ch
Web site: http://www.electrosuisse.ch

Titles:
BULLETIN

EMH SCHWEIZERISCHER ÄRZTEVERLAG AG 685495
Farnsburger Str. 8, 4132 MUTTENZ
Tel: 61 4678555 **Fax:** 61 4678556
Email: verlag@emh.ch
Web site: http://www.emh.ch

Titles:
KARDIOVASKULÄRE MEDIZIN MÉDECINE CARDIOVASCULAIRE
MEDKALENDER
PIPETTE
PRIMARY CARE
SÄZ SCHWEIZERISCHE ÄRZTEZEITUNG BMS BOLLETTINO DEI MEDICI SVIZZERI BULLETIN DES MÉDECINS SUISSES
SCHWEIZERISCHES MEDIZINISCHES JAHRBUCH ANNUAIRE MÉDICAL SUISSE
SMF SCHWEIZERISCHES MEDIZIN-FORUM SWISS MEDICAL FORUM FMS FORUM MÉDICAL SUISSE
SWISS MEDICAL WEEKLY
SYNAPSE

ENGELI & PARTNER VERLAG 686216
Bahnhofstr. 17, 9326 HORN **Tel:** 71 8468874
Fax: 71 8468879
Email: verlag@kmu-magazin.ch

Titles:
NEBELSPALTER

ESPACE MEDIA AG 1765849
Dammweg 9, 3001 BERN **Tel:** 31 3303111
Fax: 31 3303686
Email: verlag@bernerzeitung.ch
Web site: http://www.ebund.ch

Titles:
BERNER BÄR
DER BUND

ETERNIT (SCHWEIZ) AG 698109
Postfach, 8867 NIEDERURNEN **Tel:** 55 6171111
Fax: 55 6171502
Email: arch@eternit.ch
Web site: http://www.eternit.ch

Titles:
ARCH

ETH EIDGENÖSSISCHE TECHNISCHE HOCHSCHULE ZÜRICH 679898
Rämistr. 101, 8092 ZÜRICH **Tel:** 44 6324252
Fax: 44 6323525
Email: ethglobe@hk.ethz.ch
Web site: http://www.ethz.ch

Titles:
ETH GLOBE

ETZEL-VERLAG AG 681157
Knonauer Str. 56, 6330 CHAM **Tel:** 41 7855085
Fax: 41 7855088
Email: info@etzel-verlag.ch
Web site: http://www.etzel-verlag.ch

Titles:
ATMOSPHÈRE
ATMOSPHÈRE

EUROTAXGLASS'S INTERNATIONAL AG 1714814
Wolleraustr. 11a, 8807 FREIENBACH
Tel: 848 333100 **Fax:** 55 4158200
Web site: http://www.eurotaxglass.ch

Titles:
AM WERKSTATTDATEN LEICHTE NUTZFAHRZEUGE BIS 3,5 T GESAMTGEWICHT
INTERCLASSIC
KLEINBUSSE UND LIEFERWAGEN MINIBUS ET VÉHICULES DE LIVRAISON MINIBUS E FURGONI
LASTWAGEN CAMIONS
MOTOCLASSIC
PERSONENWAGEN VOITURES DE TOURISME AUTOVETTURE
WOHNWAGEN CARAVANES
ZWEIRAD DEUX ROUES DUE RUOTE

EVANGELISCHES GEMEINSCHAFTSWERK 690824
Postfach 101, 3048 WORBLAUFEN
Tel: 31 3304643 **Fax:** 31 3304640
Email: info@egw.ch
Web site: http://www.egw.ch

Titles:
WORT+WÄRCH

EXOTIS SCHWEIZ 1750715
Gässlimattweg 8, 5703 SEON **Tel:** 62 7774258
Fax: 62 7774259
Email: schriftleitung@exotis.ch
Web site: http://www.exotis.ch

Titles:
GEFIEDERTER FREUND

FACHPRESSE.COM GMBH 1752361
Schützenmattstr. 39a, 4051 BASEL
Tel: 61 2050380 **Fax:** 61 2050381
Email: info@fachpresse.com
Web site: http://www.fachpresse.com

Titles:
SKR DIE SCHWEIZERISCHE KOMMUNAL-REVUE

FAKTOR VERLAG AG 1651003
Hardstr. 322a, 8005 ZÜRICH **Tel:** 44 3161060
Fax: 44 3161061
Email: info@faktor.ch
Web site: http://www.faktor.ch

Titles:
FAKTOR

FÉDERATION DES ENTERPRISES ROMANDES GENÈVE 681327
98, rue de Saint-Jean, 1211 GENF 11
Tel: 22 7153244 **Fax:** 22 7153214
Email: er@fer-ge.ch
Web site: http://www.fer-ge.ch

Titles:
ENTREPRISE ROMANDE
FER INFORMATIONS

FÉDÉRATION ROMANDE IMMOBILIÈRE 687389
15, rue du Midi, 1003 LAUSANNE **Tel:** 21 3414142
Fax: 21 3414146
Email: mail@fri.ch
Web site: http://www.fri.ch

Titles:
PROPRIÉTÉ

FIBL FORSCHUNGSINSTITUT FÜR BIOLOGISCHEN LANDBAU 697786
Ackerstr., 5070 FRICK **Tel:** 62 8657272
Fax: 62 8657273
Web site: http://www.fibl.org

Titles:
BIO ACTUALITÉS
BIO AKTUELL

FINANCIALMEDIA AG 1748618
Pfingstweidstr. 6, 8005 ZÜRICH
Email: info@punktmagazin.com
Web site: http://www.punktmagazin.com

Titles:
PUNKT

FINESOLUTIONS AG 1690244
Culmannstr. 37, 8006 ZÜRICH **Tel:** 44 2458585
Fax: 44 2458595
Email: info@finesolutions.ch
Web site: http://www.finesolutions.ch

Titles:
SOLUTIONS

FISCHER AG FÜR DATA UND PRINT 688270
Bahnhofplatz 1, 3110 MÜNSINGEN
Tel: 31 7205352 **Fax:** 31 7205112
Email: abo@fischerprint.ch
Web site: http://www.fischerprint.ch

Titles:
ANTHOS

FISCHER MEDIA AG 1749703
Bahnhofplatz 1, 3110 MÜNSINGEN
Tel: 31 7205367 **Fax:** 31 7205377
Web site: http://www.fischermedia.ch

Titles:
SCHWEIZER GARTEN

FIZ FRAUENINFORMATIONS-ZENTRUM FÜR FRAUEN AUS AFRIKA, ASIEN, LATEINAMERIKA UND OSTEUROPA 1711082
Badener Str. 134, 8004 ZÜRICH **Tel:** 44 2404422
Fax: 4144 2404423
Email: contact@fiz-info.ch
Web site: http://www.fiz-info.ch

Titles:
RUNDBRIEF

FJF INTERMEDIA AG 682176
Am Falter 11, 8966 OBERWIL **Tel:** 56 6317717
Fax: 56 6317624
Email: info@fjf-intermedia.ch
Web site: http://www.fjf-intermedia.ch

Titles:
FREUNDIN

FMM FACHMEDIEN MOBIL AG 1737847
Dammweg 9, 3001 BERN **Tel:** 31 3303030
Fax: 31 3303033

Titles:
AUTOMOBIL REVUE
KATALOG DER AUTOMOBIL REVUE CATALOGUE DE LA REVUE AUTOMOBILE
REVUE AUTOMOBILE

FÖDERATION SCHWEIZER PSYCHOLOGINNEN UND PSYCHOLOGEN (FSP) 687418
Choisystr. 11, 3000 BERN 14 **Tel:** 31 3888800
Fax: 31 3888801
Email: fsp@psychologie.ch
Web site: http://www.psychologie.ch

Titles:
PSYCHOSCOPE

FONDATION FRANZ WEBER 684064
case postale, 1820 MONTREUX 1
Tel: 21 9643737 **Fax:** 21 9645736
Email: ffw@ffw.ch
Web site: http://www.ffw.ch

Titles:
JOURNAL FRANZ WEBER

FÖRDERVEREIN FÜR UMWELTVERTRÄGLICHE PAPIERE UND BÜROÖKOLOGIE SCHWEIZ 686919
Postfach 705, 9501 WIL **Tel:** 71 9111630
Fax: 71 9111630
Email: sekretariat@fups.ch
Web site: http://www.papier.info

Titles:
PAPIER & UMWELT

FRACTAL VERLAG GMBH 698619
Postfach 29, 4124 SCHÖNENBUCH
Tel: 61 6838876 **Fax:** 61 6838877
Email: admin@itbusiness.ch
Web site: http://www.itbusiness.ch

Titles:
IT BUSINESS

FREIBURGER NACHRICHTEN AG
682121
Bahnhofplatz 5, 1701 FREIBURG **Tel:** 26 3473002
Fax: 26 3473019
Email: fn.verlag@freiburger-nachrichten.ch
Web site: http://www.freiburger-nachrichten.ch

Titles:
ANZEIGER VON KERZERS
FREIBURGER NACHRICHTEN
DER MURTENBIETER
DER MURTENBIETER

FREUNDE ALTER MOTORRÄDER
1714681
Scalettastr. 128, 7000 CHUR
Web site: http://www.fam-amv.ch

Titles:
S'MOTO

FRIEDRICH REINHARDT AG
698126
Missionsstr. 36, 4012 BASEL **Tel:** 61 2646450
Fax: 61 2646488
Email: verlag@reinhardt.ch
Web site: http://www.reinhardt.ch

Titles:
50 PLUS - AUSG. BERN
50 PLUS - AUSG. NORDWESTSCHWEIZ
50 PLUS - AUSG. OSTSCHWEIZ
50 PLUS - AUSG. ZÜRICH
ALLSCHWILER WOCHENBLATT
BIRSFELDER ANZEIGER
MUTTENZER ANZEIGER
PRATTLER ANZEIGER

FSU VERLAG
680284
Vadianstr. 37, 9001 ST. GALLEN **Tel:** 71 2225252
Fax: 71 2222609
Email: redaktion-collage@f-s-u.ch
Web site: http://www.f-s-u.ch

Titles:
COLLAGE

GASTRO SUISSE
698350
Blumenfeldstr. 20, 8046 ZÜRICH **Tel:** 44 3775111
Fax: 44 3775590
Email: info@gastrosuisse.ch
Web site: http://www.gastrosuisse.ch

Titles:
GASTRO JOURNAL

GEBRÜDER HUNZIKER AG
1657247
Pflanzschulstr. 17, 8411 WINTERTHUR
Tel: 52 2345050 **Fax:** 52 2345099
Email: info@hunzikerwater.ch
Web site: http://www.hunzikerwater.ch

Titles:
MESSPUNKT

GEMEINDEVERBAND ANZEIGER REGION BERN
1776433
Postfach 5113, 3001 BERN **Tel:** 32 3820000
Fax: 32 3821090
Web site: http://www.anzeigerbern.ch

Titles:
ANZEIGER REGION BERN - REGIONALAUSG. ANZEIGER REGION BERN - STADTAUSG.

GENOSSENSCHAFT ANZEIGER FÜR GÄU UND THAL
678176
Pf 707, 4710 BALSTHAL **Tel:** 62 3878000
Fax: 62 3878005
Email: amin@gaeuanzeiger.ch
Web site: http://www.gaeuanzeiger.ch

Titles:
ANZEIGER THAL GÄU OLTEN

GENOSSENSCHAFT INFOLINK
690798
Hardturmstr. 66, 8031 ZÜRICH **Tel:** 44 4481414
Fax: 44 4481415
Email: woz@woz.ch
Web site: http://www.woz.ch

Titles:
WOZ DIE WOCHENZEITUNG

GEROLD AREGGER
698404
Burgunderstr. 132, 3018 BERN **Tel:** 31 9914823
Fax: 31 9914823

Titles:
GEGENWART

GESELLSCHAFT FÜR MILITÄRISCHE BAUTECHNIK UND RETTUNG
689510
Postfach, 5620 BREMGARTEN
Web site: http://www.bauenretten.ch

Titles:
BAUEN & RETTEN

GESELLSCHAFT SCHWEIZERISCHER ROSENFREUNDE
699944
Buebeseggstr. 25, 9650 NESSLAU
Tel: 71 9941969
Email: info@rosenfreunde.ch
Web site: http://www.rosenfreunde.ch

Titles:
ROSENBLATT

GEWERBEVERBAND DES KANTONS LUZERN
1755514
Eichwaldstr. 15, 6002 LUZERN **Tel:** 41 3180318
Fax: 41 3181319
Email: info@gewerbeverband-lu.ch
Web site: http://www.gewerbeverband-lu.ch

Titles:
GEWERBE LUZERN

GEWERKSCHAFT KOMMUNIKATION
680331
Looslistr. 15, 3027 BERN **Tel:** 31 9395211
Fax: 31 9395262
Email: member@syndicom.ch
Web site: http://www.gewerkschaftkom.ch

Titles:
COMTEXTE

GISLER DRUCK AG
689963
Gitschenstr. 9, 6460 ALTDORF **Tel:** 41 8741616
Fax: 41 8741632
Email: mail@gislerdruck.ch
Web site: http://www.gislerdruck.ch

Titles:
URNER WOCHENBLATT

GOTTLIEB DUTTWEILER INSTITUTE
682375
Landhaldenstr. 21, 8803 RÜSCHLIKON
Tel: 44 7246111 **Fax:** 44 7246262
Email: impuls@gdi.ch
Web site: http://www.gdi-impuls.ch

Titles:
GDI IMPULS

GRAUE PANTHER BASEL
686910
Im Ettingerhof 2, 4055 BASEL **Tel:** 61 3010667
Email: info@grauepanther.ch
Web site: http://www.grauepanther.ch

Titles:
PANTHER POST

GRUNER + JAHR (SCHWEIZ) AG
1640476
Zeltweg 15, 8032 ZÜRICH **Tel:** 44 2697070
Fax: 44 2697071
Email: guj.schweiz@guj.de
Web site: http://www.guj.de

Titles:
BRIGITTE

GYR EDELMETALLE AG
1640637
Postfach 1034, 6341 BAAR **Tel:** 41 7660044
Fax: 41 7660055
Email: info@goldor.ch
Web site: http://www.goldor.ch

Titles:
GOLD'OR

HANDEL HEUTE-VERLAGS AG
697999
Industriestr. 37, 3178 BÖSINGEN **Tel:** 31 7409730
Fax: 31 7409739
Email: info@handel-heute.ch
Web site: http://www.handel-heute.ch

Titles:
HANDEL HEUTE

HANDELSKAMMER DEUTSCHLAND-SCHWEIZ
680128
Tödistr. 60, 8002 ZÜRICH **Tel:** 44 2836161
Fax: 44 2836100
Email: redaktion@handelskammer-d-ch.ch
Web site: http://www.handelskammer-d-ch.ch

Titles:
CH-D WIRTSCHAFT

HANDELVERLAGS AG
682965
Klosterstr. 32, 9403 GOLDACH **Tel:** 71 8416262
Fax: 71 8452606
Email: info@handelverlag.ch
Web site: http://www.handelverlag.ch

Titles:
HANDEL + FREIZEIT

HAUPT VERLAG AG
677414
Falkenplatz 14, 3012 BERN **Tel:** 31 3090900
Fax: 31 3090990
Email: info@haupt.ch
Web site: http://www.haupt.ch

Titles:
AGOGIK

HAUSEIGENTÜMERVERBAND SCHWEIZ
688280
Seefeldstr. 60, 8032 ZÜRICH **Tel:** 44 2549020
Fax: 44 2549021
Email: info@hev-schweiz.ch
Web site: http://www.hev-schweiz.ch

Titles:
DER SCHWEIZERISCHE HAUSEIGENTÜMER

HAUSEIGENTÜMERVERBAND ZÜRICH
691018
Albisstr. 28, 8038 ZÜRICH **Tel:** 44 4871700
Fax: 44 4871777
Email: hev@hev-zuerich.ch
Web site: http://www.hev-zuerich.ch

Titles:
DER ZÜRCHER HAUSEIGENTÜMER

HEILSARMEE VERLAG VIVACE
683081
Laupenstr. 5, 3001 BERN **Tel:** 31 3880591
Fax: 31 3880595

Titles:
DIALOGUE
ESPOIR

HELBING & LICHTENHAHN VERLAG AG
678131
Elisabethenstr. 8, 4051 BASEL **Tel:** 61 2289070
Fax: 61 2989071
Email: zeitschriften@helbing.ch
Web site: http://www.helbing.ch

Titles:
ANWALTS REVUE DE L'AVOCAT
DIE PRAXIS
DER STEUERENTSCHEID STE

HELLER MEDIA AG
682147
Seetalstr. 7, 5630 MURI **Tel:** 56 6751050
Fax: 56 6751055
Email: info@hellermedia.ch
Web site: http://www.hellermedia.ch

Titles:
DER FREISCHÜTZ

HERAUSGEBERVEREIN JUMI
697971
Postfach 25, 4628 WOLFWIL **Tel:** 62 9264522
Fax: 62 9264521
Email: info@jumi.ch
Web site: http://www.jumi.ch

Titles:
JUMI

HILFSWERK DER EVANGELISCHEN KIRCHEN SCHWEIZ
682959
Seminarstrasse 28, 8042 ZÜRICH **Tel:** 44 3608800
Fax: 44 3608801
Email: info@heks.ch
Web site: http://www.heks.ch

Titles:
HANDELN >>>>>>

HISTORIC RHB
1653834
Postfach 662, 7002 CHUR **Tel:** 79 6098858
Email: info@historic-rhb.ch
Web site: http://www.historic-rhb.ch

Titles:
DIE BÜNDNER KULTURBAHN

HK HANDELSKUNDE VERLAG AG
683714
Talstr. 15, 8620 WETZIKON **Tel:** 44 9307858
Fax: 44 9304931
Email: infos@hkverlag.ch
Web site: http://www.hkverlag.ch

Titles:
INFOS, FÜR JUNGE KAUFLEUTE

HOCHPARTERRE AG
683284
Ausstellungsstr. 25, 8005 ZÜRICH
Tel: 44 4442888 **Fax:** 44 4442889
Email: verlag@hochparterre.ch
Web site: http://www.hochparterre.ch

Titles:
HOCHPARTERRE
HOCHPARTERRE.WETTBEWERBE
ORNATIP

HUG VERLAG AG
684220
Hohenrainweg 1, 8802 KILCHBERG
Tel: 44 7161616 **Fax:** 44 7161617
Email: info@junior.ch
Web site: http://www.junior.de

Titles:
JUNIOR - AUSG. DEUTSCHLAND U. ÖSTERREICH

IDG COMMUNICATIONS AG
698855
Witikoner Str. 15, 8032 ZÜRICH **Tel:** 44 3874444
Fax: 44 3874583
Web site: http://www.idg.ch

Titles:
COMPUTERWORLD
PCTIPP

IDPURE MAGAZINE
1750422
4a, chemin du Pré, 1110 MORGES 1
Tel: 848 437873
Email: info@idpure.com
Web site: http://www.idpure.ch

Titles:
IDPURE

IMMOBILIEN & BUSINESS VERLAGS AG
683539
Grubenstr. 56, 8045 ZÜRICH **Tel:** 43 3333949
Fax: 43 3333950
Email: immobilienbusiness@ibverlag.ch
Web site: http://www.immobilienbusiness.ch

Titles:
IMMOBILIEN BUSINESS

IMPRIMERIE BERNARD BORCARD S.A.R.L.
687653
116, av. de la Gare, 1470 ESTAVAYER-LE-LAC
Tel: 26 6631267 **Fax:** 26 6632521
Email: journal@lerepublicain.ch
Web site: http://www.lerepublicain.ch

Titles:
LE REPUBLICAIN

IMPRIMERIE MODERNE DE SION
686509
13, rue de l'Industrie, 1950 SION **Tel:** 27 3297511
Fax: 27 3297578
Email: marketing@nouvelliste.ch
Web site: http://www.lenouvelliste.ch

Titles:
LE NOUVELLISTE

IMPULS-SERVICE GENOSSENSCHAFT
1690323
Lagerplatz 10, 8400 WINTERTHUR
Tel: 52 2692770 **Fax:** 52 2692777
Email: werbung@impuls-service.ch
Web site: http://www.impulsdrogerie.ch

Titles:
D IMPULS MAGAZIN

INFEL AG 1656198
Militärstr. 36, 8021 ZÜRICH **Tel:** 44 2994141
Fax: 44 2994140
Email: info@infel.ch
Web site: http://www.infel.ch

Titles:
VIA

INFOMED-VERLAGS-AG 697862
Bergliweg 17, 9500 WIL **Tel:** 71 9100866
Fax: 71 9100877
Email: infomed@infomed.ch
Web site: http://www.infomed.org

Titles:
PHARMA-KRITIK

INNOVATIO VERLAGS AG 685481
Rothstr. 54, 8057 ZÜRICH **Tel:** 43 2551925
Fax: 4143 2551929
Email: mailbox@innovatio.de
Web site: http://www.innovatio.de

Titles:
MEDIA TENOR
MEDIA TENOR

INSERATENUNION AG 678808
Hochbergerstr. 15, 4002 BASEL **Tel:** 61 6391050
Fax: 61 6391020
Email: verlag@baslerstab.ch
Web site: http://www.baslerstab.ch

Titles:
BASLERSTAB

INSPIRATION PRESS GMBH 1649433
Zürichstrasse 98, 8600 DÜBENDORF 1
Tel: 44 9103230 **Fax:** 44 9105260
Email: info@inspiration-press.com
Web site: http://www.inspiration-press.com

Titles:
INSPIRATION

INSTITUT G2W 682864
Birmensdorferstr. 52, 8036 ZÜRICH
Tel: 43 3222244 **Fax:** 43 3222240
Email: g2w.sui@bluewin.ch
Web site: http://www.g2w.eu

Titles:
G2W

INSTITUT SUISSE DE PRÉVENTION DE L' ALCOOLISME ET AUTRES TOXICOMANIES 677241
14, av. Ruchonnet, 1001 LAUSANNE
Tel: 21 3212976 **Fax:** 21 3212940
Email: info@sfa-ispa.ch
Web site: http://www.sfa-ispa.ch

Titles:
SFA/ISPA CONTACT

INTERESSENGEMEINSCHAFT BINATIONAL 699880
Postfach 3063, 8021 ZÜRICH **Tel:** 79 4166722
Email: info@ig-binational.ch
Web site: http://www.ig-binational.ch

Titles:
BULLETIN BINATIONAL

INTERNAT. TRADE CENTRE PALAIS DES NATIONS 1718287
Palais des Nations, 1211 GENF 10
Tel: 22 7300111 **Fax:** 22 7337176
Email: itcreg@intracen.org
Web site: http://www.intracen.org

Titles:
INTERNATIONAL TRADE FORUM

INTERNATIONALE GEWÄSSER-SCHUTZKOMMISSION FÜR DEN BODENSEE 1677018
Bahnhofsstr. 55, 8510 FRAUENFELD
Tel: 52 7242432 **Fax:** 52 7242848

Titles:
SEESPIEGEL

INTERNATIONALE VEREINIGUNG CHRISTLICHER GESCHÄFTSLEUTE 682518
Postfach, 8034 ZÜRICH **Tel:** 44 2567012
Fax: 44 2567014
Web site: http://www.ivcg.org

Titles:
REFLEXIONEN

INTERPHARMA 682555
Petersgraben 35, 4003 BASEL **Tel:** 61 2643434
Fax: 61 2643435
Email: info@interpharma.ch
Web site: http://www.interpharma.ch

Titles:
DAS GESUNDHEITSWESEN IN DER SCHWEIZ LEISTUNGEN, KOSTEN, PREISE
PHARMA-MARKT SCHWEIZ

INTERVINUM AG 690189
Thurgauer Str. 66, 8050 ZÜRICH **Tel:** 44 2685240
Fax: 44 2685205
Email: info@vinum.ch
Web site: http://www.vinum.ch

Titles:
VINUM

JARDIN SUISSE, UNTERNEHMERVERBAND GÄRTNER SCHWEIZ 682704
Forchstr. 287, 8008 ZÜRICH **Tel:** 44 3885353
Fax: 44 3885340
Email: redaktion@jardinsuisse.ch
Web site: http://www.jardinsuisse.ch

Titles:
G'PLUS

JAZZTIME-VERLAG AG 698055
Täfernstr. 37, 5405 BADEN **Tel:** 56 4833737
Fax: 56 4833739
Email: verlag@jazztime.com
Web site: http://www.jazztime.com

Titles:
JAZZ TIME

JORDI AG DAS MEDIENHAUS 678172
Belpbergstr. 15, 3123 BELP **Tel:** 31 8180111
Fax: 31 8198871
Email: info@jordibelp.ch
Web site: http://www.jordibelp.ch

Titles:
COCKPIT

JÜDISCHE MEDIEN AG 689189
Tödistr. 42, 8027 ZÜRICH **Tel:** 44 2064200
Fax: 44 2064210
Email: verlag@tachles.ch
Web site: http://www.tachles.ch

Titles:
REVUE JUIVE

K. KAELIN AG DRUCK UND VERLAG 687732
Gutenbergweg 3, 6410 ARTH **Tel:** 41 8551241
Fax: 41 8551247
Email: rp@kaelindruck.ch
Web site: http://www.rigipost.ch

Titles:
RIGI-POST

KAMBERMEDIA GMBH 1755524
Stüsslingerstr. 1, 4654 LOSTORF **Tel:** 62 2980155
Fax: 62 2980156
Email: kamber@kambermedia.ch
Web site: http://www.sicherheitspolitik.ch

Titles:
SICHERHEITSPOLITIK

KANTON BASEL-LANDSCHAFT, BAU- UND UMWELTSCHUTZ-DIREKTION 1719579
Rheinstr. 29, 4410 LIESTAL **Tel:** 61 9255404
Fax: 61 9256948
Email: catia.allemann@bl.ch

Titles:
BAU- UND UMWELT-ZEITUNG

KANTON ZÜRICH, BAUDIREKTION, GS/BAKU, KOORDINATIONSSTELLE FÜR UMWELTSCHUTZ 691020
Stampfenbachstr. 14, 8006 ZÜRICH
Tel: 43 2592417 **Fax:** 43 2595126
Email: kofu@bd.zh.ch
Web site: http://www.umweltschutz.zh.ch

Titles:
ZÜRCHER UMWELT PRAXIS

KANTONAL SCHWYZERISCHER GEWERBEVERBAND 1714676
Seestr. 205, 8806 FREIENBACH **Tel:** 44 6874547
Fax: 44 6874540
Email: sekretariat@ksgv.ch
Web site: http://www.ksgv.ch

Titles:
SCHWYZER GEWERBE

KANTONALER GEWERBEVERBAND ZÜRICH 699261
Badener Str. 21, 8050 ZÜRICH **Tel:** 43 2883366
Fax: 43 2883360
Email: info@kgv.ch
Web site: http://www.kgv.ch

Titles:
ZÜRCHER WIRTSCHAFT

KANTONAL-SOLOTHURNISCHER GEWERBEVERBAND, SOLOTHURNER HANDELSKAMMER 684471
Hans-Huber-Str. 38, 4500 SOLOTHURN
Tel: 32 6244624 **Fax:** 32 6244625
Email: info@kgv-so.ch
Web site: http://www.kgv-so.ch

Titles:
WIRTSCHAFTS FLASH

KAPI-MEDIA 1769732
Hinterbergstr. 2, 8604 VOLKETSWIL
Tel: 44 9451333 **Fax:** 44 3813443
Email: office@kapi-media.ch
Web site: http://www.kapi-media.ch

Titles:
ICT KOMMUNIKATION

KAUFMÄNNISCHER VERBAND AARGAU OST 1755656
Postfach 2114, 5430 WETTINGEN
Tel: 56 4371916 **Fax:** 56 4371910
Email: info@kvagost.ch
Web site: http://www.kvschweiz.ch/aargau-ost

Titles:
TOP INFORMATIONEN

KAUFMÄNNISCHER VERBAND BASEL 1755506
Aeschengraben 13, 4002 BASEL **Tel:** 61 2715470
Fax: 61 2722441
Email: info@kvbasel.ch
Web site: http://www.kvbasel.ch

Titles:
KV. NACHRICHTEN

KAUFMÄNNISCHER VERBAND BERN UND UMGEBUNG 1755307
Zieglerstr. 20, 3007 BERN **Tel:** 31 3906030
Fax: 31 3906020
Email: info@kvbern.ch
Web site: http://www.kvbern.ch

Titles:
AKTIV

KAUFMÄNNISCHER VERBAND SCHWEIZ 680357
Hans-Huber-Str. 4, 8002 ZÜRICH
Tel: 44 28345433
Email: context@kvschweiz.ch
Web site: http://www.kvschweiz.ch

Titles:
CONTEXT

KAUFMÄNNISCHER VERBAND ZUG 1755511
Postfach 235, 6312 STEINHAUSEN
Tel: 41 7114660 **Fax:** 41 7402778
Email: kv.verein.zug@datazug.ch
Web site: http://www.kvschweiz.ch

Titles:
KV ZUG AKTUELL

KI KONSUMENTENINFO AG 1649434
Wolfbachstr. 15, 8024 ZÜRICH **Tel:** 44 2661707
Fax: 44 2661700
Web site: http://www.konsuminfo.ch

Titles:
K GELD

KOENIG VERBINDUNGSTECHNIK AG 684867
Lagerstr. 8, 8953 DIETIKON **Tel:** 44 7433333
Fax: 44 7406566
Email: info@kvt.ch
Web site: http://www.kvt.ch

Titles:
KVT AKTUELL

KONSUMENTENFORUM KF 1641638
Grossmannstr. 29, 8049 ZÜRICH **Tel:** 44 3445060
Fax: 44 3445066
Email: forum@konsum.ch
Web site: http://www.konsum.ch

Titles:
KF INFO

KOORDINIERTER SANITÄTSDIENST 1654909
Worblentalstr. 36, 3063 ITTIGEN **Tel:** 31 3242842
Fax: 31 3242744
Email: info-ksd@vtg.admin.ch
Web site: http://www.ksd-ssc.ch

Titles:
KOORDINIERTER SANITÄTSDIENST SERVICE SANITAIRE COORDONNÉ SERVIZIO SANITARIO COORDINATO

KOPRINT AG 686342
Untere Gründlistr. 3, 6055 ALPNACH DORF
Tel: 41 6729010 **Fax:** 41 6729019
Email: gk@koprint.ch
Web site: http://www.koprint.ch

Titles:
VIERTELJAHRSSCHRIFT DER NATURFORSCHENDEN GESELLSCHAFT IN ZÜRICH

KREIENBÜHL DRUCK AG 682133
Bahnhofstr. 39, 6403 KÜSSNACHT
Tel: 41 8542525 **Fax:** 41 8542520
Email: verlag@freierschweizer.ch
Web site: http://www.freierschweizer.ch

Titles:
FS FREIER SCHWEIZER

K-TIPP VERLAG 684698
Wolfbachstr. 15, 8024 ZÜRICH **Tel:** 44 2661717
Fax: 44 2661700
Web site: http://www.konsuminfo.ch

Titles:
K TIPP

KÜNZLERBACHMANN MEDIEN AG 678447
Geltenwilenstr. 8a, 9001 ST. GALLEN
Tel: 71 2269292 **Fax:** 71 2269293
Email: info@kbmedien.ch
Web site: http://www.kbmedien.ch

Titles:
BAU & ARCHITEKTUR
FASSADE
INTERIEUR
JAHRBUCH MARKETING KOMMUNIKATION
KÖ. PRINTMEDIEN SCHWEIZ ZEITSCHRIFTEN
SCHWEIZER ENERGIEFACHBUCH
SWISS ENGINEERING RTS
SWISS ENGINEERING STZ

KÜNZLERBACHMANN VERLAG AG 1713917
Zürcher Str. 601, 9015 ST. GALLEN
Tel: 71 3140444 **Fax:** 70 3140445
Email: kbverlag@kueba.ch
Web site: http://www.kueba.ch

Titles:
KIDY SWISS FAMILY

LABMED 698587
Postgasse 17, 3011 BERN **Tel:** 31 3138822
Fax: 31 3138899
Web site: http://www.labmed.ch

Titles:
LABMED SCHWEIZ SUISSE SVIZZERA

LANDI-MEDIEN 1644377
Schaffhauser Str. 6, 8401 WINTERTHUR
Tel: 52 2642724 **Fax:** 52 2132161
Email: info@landi.ch
Web site: http://www.landi.ch

Titles:
UFA REVUE
UFA REVUE

LA LECHE LIGA SCHWEIZ 679921
Postfach 197, 8053 ZÜRICH **Tel:** 81 9433300
Fax: 81 9433300
Email: info@stillberatung.ch
Web site: http://www.elternzeitschrift.org

Titles:
WIRBELWIND

LIFE MEDIEN GMBH 1748415
Leimgrubenweg 4, 4053 BASEL **Tel:** 61 3382000
Fax: 61 3382022
Email: info@lifemedien.ch
Web site: http://www.lifemedien.ch

Titles:
BAU LIFE

LIMMATDRUCK AG 680435
Limmatplatz 6, 8005 ZÜRICH **Tel:** 44 4473606
Fax: 44 4473679
Email: verlag@saison.ch
Web site: http://www.saison.ch

Titles:
SAISON-KÜCHE

LZ FACHVERLAG AG 1770553
Sihlbruggstr. 105a, 6341 BAAR **Tel:** 41 7677676
Fax: 41 7677911
Email: info@lzfachverlag.ch
Web site: http://www.lzfachverlag.ch

Titles:
CAMPING REVUE
EL FORUM
HOCHZEITSFÜHRER
PACK AKTUELL
PERSORAMA
PROBLEM
ST SCHWEIZER TOURISTIK

MARMITE VERLAGS AG 1774831
Grubenstr.56, 8045 ZÜRICH **Tel:** 43 3333949
Fax: 43 3333950
Email: info@marmite.ch
Web site: http://www.marmite.ch

Titles:
MARMITE

MARQUARD MEDIA AG 1713536
Baarer Str. 22, 6300 ZUG **Tel:** 41 7252020
Fax: 41 7252025
Email: groupsecretary@jmg.ch
Web site: http://www.mvg.de

Titles:
COSMOPOLITAN
JOY
SHAPE

MEDIACITY VERLAGS AG 1788913
17, rue de Genève, 1002 LAUSANNE
Tel: 21 3314141 **Fax:** 21 3314110
Email: e.valette@mediacity.ch
Web site: http://www.mediacity.ch

Titles:
PROFIL
WORK
WORK

MEDIASEC AG 687967
Tägernstr. 1, 8127 FORCH **Tel:** 43 3662020
Fax: 43 3662030
Email: info@mediasec.ch
Web site: http://www.mediasec.ch

Titles:
SAFETY-PLUS
SICHERHEIT SFORUM

MEDICOM SCHWEIZ VERLAGS GMBH 1649643
Baarer Str. 86a, 6300 ZUG **Tel:** 41 7123131
Fax: 41 7123130
Email: office@medicom.ch
Web site: http://www.medicom.cc

Titles:
INTENSIV-NEWS
NEPHRO-NEWS

MED-ICT VERLAGS AG 1752360
Steinenvorstadt 33, 4001 BASEL **Tel:** 61 5350911
Fax: 4161 5356820
Email: wacker@med-ict.ch
Web site: http://www.med-ict.ch

Titles:
SIR MEDICAL

MEDIENBOTSCHAFT VERLAG & EVENTS GMBH 1654002
Oberstr. 2, 8274 TÄGERWILEN **Tel:** 71 6666570
Fax: 71 6666574
Email: info@medienbotschaft.com
Web site: http://www.medienbotschaft.com

Titles:
DISCO MAGAZIN

MEIER + CIE. AG, VERLAG SCHAFFHAUSER NACHRICHTEN 688074
Vordergasse 58, 8201 SCHAFFHAUSEN
Tel: 52 6333111 **Fax:** 52 6333401
Email: verlag@shn.ch
Web site: http://www.shn.ch

Titles:
SCHAFFHAUSER NACHRICHTEN
SCHAFFHAUSER NACHRICHTEN

MENGIS DRUCK + VERLAG AG 1719321
Terbinerstr. 2, 3930 VISP **Tel:** 27 9483030
Fax: 27 9483031
Email: mdv@mengis-visp.ch
Web site: http://www.mengis-visp.ch

Titles:
WALLISER BOTE

METROCOMM AG 1754565
Zürcher Str. 170, 9014 ST. GALLEN
Tel: 71 2728050 **Fax:** 71 2728051
Email: info@metrocomm.ch
Web site: http://www.metrocomm.ch

Titles:
LEADER

MHD SA 1640478
1, Ch. du Bugnon, 1803 CHARDONNE
Tel: 21 9221690 **Fax:** 21 9221691
Email: info@marieclaire-suisse.ch
Web site: http://www.marieclaire-suisse.ch

Titles:
MARIE CLAIRE

MOTORMEDIA GMBH 1755402
Europastr. 15, 8152 GLATTBRUGG
Tel: 58 3449000 **Fax:** 58 3449001
Email: info@motormedia.ch
Web site: http://www.tir.ch

Titles:
BUS TRANSNEWS
TIR TRANSNEWS

MOTOR-PRESSE (SCHWEIZ) AG 1635459
Industriestr. 28, 8604 VOLKETSWIL
Tel: 44 8065555 **Fax:** 44 8065500
Email: verlag@motorpresse.ch
Web site: http://www.motorsport-aktuell.com

Titles:
AUTO ILLUSTRIERTE
MOTOR SPORT AKTUELL

MÜLLER MARKETING & DRUCK AG 678185
Kirchstr., 3780 GSTAAD **Tel:** 33 7488874
Fax: 33 7488884
Email: redaktion@anzeigervonsaanen.ch
Web site: http://www.mdruck.ch

Titles:
ANZEIGER VON SAANEN

NAGRA NATIONALE GENOSSENSCHAFT FÜR DIE LAGERUNG RADIOAKTIVER ABFÄLLE 686155
Hardstr. 73, 5430 WETTINGEN **Tel:** 56 4371111
Fax: 56 4371207
Email: info@nagra.ch
Web site: http://www.nagra.ch

Titles:
INFO.

NATÜRLICH GESUND VERLAGS GMBH 1771120
Grosspeterstr. 23, 4052 BASEL **Tel:** 69 6656320
Fax: 69 66563222
Email: info@asiavision.de

Titles:
BODY & MIND

NEUE FRICKTALER ZEITUNG AG 682183
Albrechtsplatz 3, 4310 RHEINFELDEN
Tel: 61 8350000 **Fax:** 61 8350099

Titles:
NEUE FRICKTALER ZEITUNG
NEUE FRICKTALER ZEITUNG

NEUE LUZERNER ZEITUNG AG 685245
Maihofstr. 76, 6002 LUZERN **Tel:** 41 4295252
Fax: 41 4295378
Email: verlag@neue-lz.ch
Web site: http://www.zisch.ch

Titles:
NEUE LUZERNER ZEITUNG
NEUE NIDWALDNER ZEITUNG
NEUE OBWALDNER ZEITUNG
NEUE SCHWYZER ZEITUNG
NEUE URNER ZEITUNG
NEUE ZUGER ZEITUNG

NEUE ZÜRCHER ZEITUNG AG 686339
Falkenstr. 11, 8021 ZÜRICH **Tel:** 44 2581111
Fax: 44 2581323
Email: verlag@nzz.ch
Web site: http://www.nzz.ch

Titles:
NEUE ZÜRCHER ZEITUNG

NOCH ERFOLGREICHER! AG 697622
Augustin-Keller-Str. 31, 5600 LENZBURG
Tel: 62 8884054 **Fax:** 62 8884055
Email: info@noch-erfolgreicher.com
Web site: http://www.noch-erfolgreicher.com

Titles:
NOCH ERFOLGREICHER!

OBERSEE NACHRICHTEN AG 686581
Hauptplatz 5, 8640 RAPPERSWIL-JONA
Tel: 55 2208181 **Fax:** 55 2208191
Email: info@obersee-nachrichten.ch
Web site: http://www.obersee-nachrichten.ch

Titles:
OBERSEE NACHRICHTEN

OBT AG 684472
Rorschacher Str. 63, 9004 ST. GALLEN
Tel: 71 2433434 **Fax:** 71 2433400
Email: info@obt.ch
Web site: http://www.obt.ch

Titles:
KMU-PRAXIS

ÖKK KRANKEN- UND UNFALLVERSICHERUNGEN AG 698169
Bahnhofstr. 9, 7302 LANDQUART **Tel:** 58 4561010
Fax: 58 4561011
Email: magazin@oekk.ch
Web site: http://www.oekk.ch

Titles:
ÖKK DOSSIER FÜR UNTERNEHMEN
ÖKK MAGAZIN
ÖKK MAGAZINE

OSKAR BALDINGER 680324
Aarestr. 83, 5222 UMIKEN **Tel:** 56 4410043
Fax: 56 4414854
Email: editor@dplanet.ch

Titles:
COMPUTER SPECTRUM
INDUSTRIEARCHÄOLOGIE

P.A. MEDIA AG 683340
Zypressenstr. 60, 8040 ZÜRICH **Tel:** 44 2454510
Fax: 44 2454500
Email: verlag@home-electronics.ch
Web site: http://www.home-electronics.ch

Titles:
HOME ELECTRONICS

PALLOTTINER-VERLAG 681765
Friedbergstr. 16, 9200 GOSSAU **Tel:** 71 3885330
Fax: 71 3885339
Web site: http://www.ferment.ch

Titles:
FERMENT

PARTNER PUBLICATION GMBH 686942
via del Tiglio, 24B, 6605 LOCARNO
Tel: 91 7600888 **Fax:** 91 7600889
Email: redaktion@eis.ch
Web site: http://www.eis.ch

Titles:
NETCOM MAGAZIN

PAUL SCHERRER INSTITUT 1741830
5232 VILLIGEN **Tel:** 56 3102956 **Fax:** 56 3104411
Email: energiespiegel@psi.ch
Web site: http://www.psi.ch

Titles:
ENERGIE-SPIEGEL

PERSENS AG 697970
Felsenstr. 88, 9000 ST. GALLEN **Tel:** 71 2284580
Fax: 71 2284540
Email: info@persens.ch
Web site: http://www.indexonline.ch

Titles:
INDEX

PERSÖNLICH VERLAGS AG 687012
Hauptplatz 5, 8640 RAPPERSWIL **Tel:** 55 2208171
Fax: 55 2208177
Email: info@persoenlich.com
Web site: http://www.persoenlich.com

Titles:
PERSÖNLICH

PFARRBLATTGEMEINSCHAFT NORDWESTSCHWEIZ 687055
Innere Margarethenstr. 26, 4051 BASEL
Tel: 61 3630170 **Fax:** 61 3630171
Email: sekretariat@kirche-heute.ch
Web site: http://www.kirche-heute.ch

Titles:
KIRCHE HEUTE

PILGERMISSION ST. CHRISCHONA 680168
Chrischonarain 200, 4126 BETTINGEN
Tel: 61 6464557 **Fax:** 61 6464277
Email: medienstelle@chrischona.ch
Web site: http://www.chrischona.org

Titles:
CHRISCHONA PANORAMA

PLURALITY PRESSE S.A. 1734661
8, rue Jacques Grosselin, 1227 CAROUGE
Tel: 22 3070220 **Fax:** 22 3070222
Email: info@toutimmobilier.ch
Web site: http://www.toutimmobilier.ch

Titles:
TOUT L'IMMOBILIER

POPOLO E LIBERTÀ EDIZIONI SA 687222
via Ghiringhelli, 7, 6500 BELLINZONA
Tel: 91 8251245 **Fax:** 91 8258551
Email: info@ppd-ti.ch
Web site: http://www.ppd-ti.ch

Titles:
POPOLO E LIBERTÀ

PRESTIGE MEDIA AG 1768949
Leimgrubenweg 4, 4053 BASEL **Tel:** 61 3382007
Fax: 61 3382029
Email: info@prestigemedia.ch
Web site: http://www.prestigemedia.ch

Titles:
GF GESCHÄFTSFÜHRER

PRICEWATERHOUSECOOPERS AG 678443
Birchstr. 160, 8050 ZÜRICH **Tel:** 58 7924400
Fax: 58 7924410
Web site: http://www.pwc.ch

Titles:
CEO*

PRIMUS VERLAG AG 685611
Hammerstr. 81, 8032 ZÜRICH **Tel:** 44 3875757
Fax: 44 3875707
Email: info@primusverlag.ch
Web site: http://www.primusverlag.ch

Titles:
TRAVEL INSIDE
TRAVEL INSIDE
TRAVELMANAGER
TRAVELTIP

PRO NATURA ZENTRALSEKRETARIAT 1649564
Dornacherstr. 192, 4053 BASEL **Tel:** 61 3179191
Fax: 61 3179266
Email: mailbox@pronatura.ch
Web site: http://www.pronatura.ch

Titles:
PRO NATURA MAGAZIN

PRO SENECTUTE, KANTON ZUG 677361
Baarerstr. 131, 6300 ZUG **Tel:** 41 7275050
Fax: 41 7275060
Email: info@zg.pro-senectute.ch
Web site: http://www.zg.pro-senectute.ch

Titles:
HORIZONTE

PROFILEPUBLISHING GMBH 1752861
Pfadacher 5, 8623 WETZIKON **Tel:** 43 4881844
Fax: 43 4881843
Email: info@profilepublishing.ch
Web site: http://www.profilepublishing.ch

Titles:
BUSINESS INTELLIGENCE MAGAZINE
ECO LIFE
ICT IN FINANCE

PROMOEDITION SA 681231
35, rue des Bains, 1205 GENF **Tel:** 22 8099460
Fax: 22 7811414
Web site: http://www.promoedition.ch

Titles:
ELLE
SWISS BANKING YEARBOOK

PUBBLICITÀ SACCHI 1649678
via Cantonale, 34a, 6928 MANNO **Tel:** 91 6002070
Fax: 91 6002074
Email: info@pubblicitasacchi.ch
Web site: http://www.pubblicitasacchi.ch

Titles:
ANNUARIO IMPRESARI COSTRUTTORI TICINESI
CANTIERI & ABITARE

PUBLIBRANDS SA 1643227
49, route des Jeunes, 1227 CAROUGE
Tel: 22 3015918 **Fax:** 22 3015914
Email: info@market.ch
Web site: http://www.market.ch

Titles:
MARKET.CH
MARKET.CH

PUBLICA-PRESS HEIDEN AG 685393
Carl-Böckli-Weg 1, 9410 HEIDEN **Tel:** 71 8988010
Fax: 71 8988020
Email: direct@pph.ch

Titles:
MASCHINENBAU

PUBLICONTEXT AG 679629
Wengistr. 7, 8026 ZÜRICH **Tel:** 44 2654010
Fax: 44 2654011
Email: info@publicontext.com
Web site: http://www.publicontext.com

Titles:
ANLAGETRENDS FONDS
FIRSTCLASS
VORSORGE

PUBLISUISSE SA 677458
Giacomettistr. 15, 3000 BERN 31 **Tel:** 31 3583111
Fax: 31 3583100
Email: webteam@publisuisse.ch
Web site: http://www.publisuisse.ch

Titles:
IMPACT

READER'S DIGEST SCHWEIZ: VERLAG DAS BESTE AUS READER'S DIGEST AG 679200
Räffelstr. 11, 8045 ZÜRICH **Tel:** 44 4557250
Fax: 44 4557119
Web site: http://www.readersdigest.ch

Titles:
READER'S DIGEST SCHWEIZ
READER'S DIGEST SUISSE
SÉLECTION

REDAKTION 699490
c.p. 125, 1018 LAUSANNE 18
Email: redaction@distinction.ch
Web site: http://www.distinction.ch

Titles:
LA DISTINCTION

REFORMIERTE KIRCHGEMEINDE NEUENEGG 699464
Postfach 94, 3176 NEUENEGG **Tel:** 31 7478392
Email: info@neuenegg.org
Web site: http://www.kirchenbezirk-laupen.ch/neuenegg

Titles:
AM WÄGRAND

REGIO NACHRICHTEN AG 1773130
Seewenweg 5, 4153 REINACH **Tel:** 61 6907777
Fax: 61 6907788
Email: info@swissbusiness-society.ch
Web site: http://www.swissbusiness-society.ch

Titles:
SOCIETY

REGION OBERAARGAU 679890
Jurastr. 29, 4901 LANGENTHAL **Tel:** 62 9227721
Fax: 62 9230658
Email: tourismus@oberaargau.ch
Web site: http://www.oberaargau.ch

Titles:
EMPFEHLUNGEN
ESSEN & SCHLAFEN
VELO

REK & THOMAS MEDIEN AG 696943
Schmiedgasse 1, 9001 ST. GALLEN
Tel: 71 2282011 **Fax:** 71 2282014

Titles:
SENSOR REPORT

REZZONICO EDITORE SA 1737796
via Luini, 19, 6601 LOCARNO **Tel:** 91 7562400
Fax: 91 7562409
Email: info@rezzonico.ch
Web site: http://www.rezzonico.ch

Titles:
TESSINER ZEITUNG MIT AGENDA
LA VOCE DELLE VALLI/IL SAN BERNARDINO

RHEINAUBUND SCHWEIZERISCHE ARGE FÜR NATUR UND HEIMAT 686205
Weinsteig 192, 8201 SCHAFFHAUSEN
Tel: 52 6252658 **Fax:** 52 6252651
Email: redaktion@rheinaubund.ch
Web site: http://www.rheinaubund.ch

Titles:
NATUR UND MENSCH

RHEINTAL VERLAG AG 1785092
Hafnerwisenstr. 1, 9442 BERNECK
Tel: 71 7472222 **Fax:** 71 7472220
Email: wuffli@rheintalverlag.ch
Web site: http://www.rheintalverlag.ch

Titles:
DER RHEINTALER
RHEINTALISCHE VOLKSZEITUNG
RHEINTALISCHE VOLKSZEITUNG

RHEINTALER DRUCKEREI UND VERLAG AG 681390
Hafnerwisenstr. 1, 9442 BERNECK
Tel: 71 7472222 **Fax:** 71 7472254
Email: rdv@rdv.ch
Web site: http://www.rdv.ch

Titles:
MK MARKETING & KOMMUNIKATION
MQ MANAGEMENT UND QUALITÄT

RIEHENER ZEITUNG AG 687730
Schopfgässchen 8, 4125 RIEHEN 1
Tel: 61 6451000 **Fax:** 61 6451010
Email: inserate@riehener-zeitung.ch
Web site: http://www.riehener-zeitung.ch

Titles:
RIEHENER ZEITUNG

RIGI ANZEIGER GMBH 687731
Luzernerstr. 2c, 6037 ROOT **Tel:** 41 2289000
Fax: 41 2289009
Email: verlag@rigianzeiger.ch
Web site: http://www.rigianzeiger.ch

Titles:
RIGI ANZEIGER

RINGIER AG 698163
Dufourstr. 49, 8008 ZÜRICH **Tel:** 44 2596507
Fax: 44 2596930
Email: ruj@ringier.ch
Web site: http://www.glueckspost.ch

Titles:
AL DENTE
BLICK
GAULT MILLAU GUIDE SCHWEIZ
GLÜCKS POST
SCHWEIZER ILLUSTRIERTE
SCHWEIZER LANDLIEBE
SONNTAGS BLICK

ROBE VERLAG AG 698503
Bollackerweg 2, 5024 KÜTTIGEN **Tel:** 62 8274500
Fax: 62 8274501
Email: info@robe-verlag.ch
Web site: http://www.robe-verlag.ch

Titles:
SPEKTRUM GEBÄUDETECHNIK

ROSENFLUH PUBLIKATIONEN AG 678382
Schaffhauser Str. 13, 8212 NEUHAUSEN
Tel: 52 6755060 **Fax:** 52 6755061
Email: info@rosenfluh.ch
Web site: http://www.rosenfluh.ch

Titles:
ARS MEDICI
ARS MEDICI DOSSIER
ARS MEDICI THEMA PHYTOTHERAPIE
GYNÄKOLOGIE
[MEDICOS]
PÄ PÄDIATRIE
PSYCHIATRIE & NEUROLOGIE
SCHWEIZER ZEITSCHRIFT FÜR ERNÄHRUNGSMEDIZIN
SCHWEIZER ZEITSCHRIFT FÜR ONKOLOGIE

ROTHUS AG, GRAFIK UND VERLAG 688308
Rathausgasse 20a, 4501 SOLOTHURN
Tel: 32 6231633 **Fax:** 32 6235036
Email: rothus@rothus.ch
Web site: http://www.rothus.ch

Titles:
SCHWEIZ

RUB GRAF-LEHMANN AG 1640956
Murtenstr. 40, 3001 BERN **Tel:** 31 3801490
Fax: 31 3801491
Email: presseverlag@rubmedia.ch
Web site: http://www.rubmedia.ch

Titles:
HUNDE
DIE NEUE STEUERPRAXIS
SCHWEIZERISCHE ZEITSCHRIFT FÜR SPORTMEDIZIN UND SPORTTRAUMATOLOGIE REVUE SUISSE DE MÉDECINE ET DE TRAUMATOLOGIE DU SPORT RIVISTA SVIZZERA DI MEDICINA E TRAUMATOLOGIA DELLO SPORT
TOUR

S. KARGER AG 677292
Allschwiler Str. 10, 4055 BASEL **Tel:** 61 3061111
Fax: 61 3061234
Email: karger@karger.ch
Web site: http://www.karger.com

Titles:
ACTA HÆMATOLOGICA
GYNÄKOLOGISCH-GEBURTSHILFLICHE RUNDSCHAU
KARGER GAZETTE
NEONATOLOGY
NEPHRON
NEURODEGENERATIVE DISEASES
NEUROIMMUNOMODULATION
NEUROPSYCHOBIOLOGY
OPHTHALMOLOGICA
ORL
PANCREATOLOGY
UROLOGIA INTERNATIONALIS

S + MS DIENSTLEISTUNGEN 688303
Oergelackerstr. 4, 8707 UETIKON **Tel:** 44 9207940
Fax: 44 9207941
Email: info@sportbiz.ch
Web site: http://www.sportbiz.ch

Titles:
SCHWEIZER SPORT & MODE SPORT & MODE SUISSE

SA DE LA TRIBUNE DE GENEVE 689643
11, rue des Rois, 1204 GENF **Tel:** 22 3224000
Fax: 22 7810107
Web site: http://www.tribune.ch

Titles:
LA TRIBUNE DE GENÈVE

SALDO REDAKTION & VERLAG 1728844
Schifflände 22, 8001 ZÜRICH **Tel:** 44 2543232
Fax: 44 2543230
Email: redaktion@saldo.ch

Titles:
SALDO

SA-NA VERLAG AG 690240
Riehentorstr. 15, 3005 BERN **Tel:** 61 6910666
Fax: 61 6913635
Email: verlag@vogelgryff.ch
Web site: http://www.vogelgryff.ch

Titles:
VOGEL GRYFF

SANATREND AG 1641514
Zürcher Str. 17, 8173 NEERACH **Tel:** 44 8591000
Fax: 44 8591009
Email: contact@sanatrend.ch
Web site: http://www.sanatrend.ch

Titles:
OTX WORLD
OTX WORLD

SARGANSERLÄNDER DRUCK AG 688036
Zeughausstr. 50, 8887 MELS **Tel:** 81 7253232
Fax: 81 7253230
Email: druckerei@sarganserlaender.ch

Titles:
SARGANSERLÄNDER

SCHAUB MEDIEN AG 690268
Hauptstr. 33, 4450 SISSACH **Tel:** 61 9761010
Fax: 61 9761011
Email: redaktion@volksstimme.ch
Web site: http://www.volksstimme.ch

Titles:
VOLKSSTIMME
VOLKSSTIMME

SCHINDLER AUFZÜGE AG 688115
Zuger Str. 13, 6030 EBIKON **Tel:** 41 4454356
Fax: 41 4454435
Email: marketing@ch.schindler.com
Web site: http://www.schindler.ch

Titles:
NEXT FLOOR

SCHLAEFLI + MAURER AG 678165
Bahnhofstr. 15, 3800 INTERLAKEN
Tel: 33 8288080 **Fax:** 33 8288035
Email: anzeiger@schlaefli.ch

Titles:
ANZEIGER AMT INTERLAKEN

SCHULE UND WEITERBILDUNG SCHWEIZ 681083
Bennwilerstr. 6, 4434 HÖLSTEIN **Tel:** 61 9569070
Fax: 61 9569079
Email: info@swch.ch
Web site: http://www.swch.ch

Titles:
ECOLE ROMANDE
SCHULE KONKRET

SCHULTHESS JURISTISCHE MEDIEN AG 1640525
Zwinglipatz 2, 8022 ZÜRICH **Tel:** 44 2002999
Fax: 44 2002908
Email: zs.verlag@schulthess.com
Web site: http://www.schulthess.com

Titles:
BLÄTTER FÜR ZÜRCHERISCHE RECHTSPRECHUNG

SCHWEIZERISCHES ZENTRALBLATT FÜR STAATS- UND VERWALTUNGSRECHT
SJZ SCHWEIZERISCHE JURISTEN-ZEITUNG REVUE SUISSE DE JURISPRUDENCE
SZIER SCHWEIZERISCHE ZEITSCHRIFT FÜR INTERNATIONALES UND EUROPÄISCHES RECHT RSDIE REVUE SUISSE DE DROIT INTERNATIONAL ET EUROPÉEN
ZEITSCHRIFT FÜR KINDES- UND ERWACHSENENSCHUTZ REVUE DELA PROTECTION DES MINEURS ET DES ADULTES RIVISTA DELLA PROTIZIONE DEL MINORI E DEGLI ADULTI

SCHWABE AG 682536
Steinentorstr. 13, 4010 BASEL **Tel:** 61 2789565
Fax: 61 2789566
Email: verlag@schwabe.ch
Web site: http://www.schwabe.ch

Titles:
SWISS MEDICAL INFORMATICS

SCHWEIZER AGRAR- UND LEBENMITTELINGENIEURE 683568
Schwarztorstr. 26, 3001 BERN **Tel:** 31 3903336
Fax: 31 3903335
Email: info@alis.ch
Web site: http://www.alis.ch

Titles:
IMPULS

SCHWEIZER AGRARMEDIEN GMBH 678846
Thunstr. 78, 3000 BERN 15 **Tel:** 31 9583333
Fax: 31 9583334

Titles:
BAUERNZEITUNG
BAUERNZEITUNG NORDWESTSCHWEIZ, BERN UND FREIBURG
FRAUENLAND
DIE GRÜNE

SCHWEIZER ALPEN-CLUB 677683
Monbijoustr. 61, 3000 BERN 23 **Tel:** 31 3701818
Fax: 31 3701890
Email: alpen@sac-cas.ch
Web site: http://www.sac-cas.ch

Titles:
DIE ALPEN

SCHWEIZER ALPEN-CLUB, SEKTION BERN 1776869
Postfach, 3000 BERN 7
Email: redaktion-cn@sac-bern.ch
Web site: http://www.sac-bern.ch

Titles:
CLUBNACHRICHTEN SAC SEKTION BERN

SCHWEIZER BAUER BETRIEBSGESELLSCHAFT 1748121
Dammweg 9, 3001 BERN **Tel:** 31 3303024
Fax: 31 3303732
Email: verlag@schweizerbauer.ch
Web site: http://www.schweizerbauer.ch

Titles:
SCHWEIZER BAUER
SCHWEIZER LAND + LEBEN

SCHWEIZER BERGHILFE 679070
Soodstr. 55, 8134 ADLISWIL **Tel:** 44 7126060
Fax: 44 7126050
Email: info@berghilfe.ch
Web site: http://www.berghilfe.ch

Titles:
BERGHILF-ZIITIG

SCHWEIZER BERUFSVERBAND DER PFLEGEFACHFRAUEN UND -MÄNNER 684641
Choisystr. 1, 3001 BERN **Tel:** 31 3883636
Fax: 31 3883635
Email: info@sbk-asi.ch
Web site: http://www.sbk-asi.ch

Titles:
KRANKENPFLEGE SOINS INFIRMIERS CURE INFERMIERISTICHE

SCHWEIZER FAMILIENGÄRTNER-VERBAND 1640972
Sturzeneggstr. 23, 9015 ST. GALLEN
Tel: 71 3112719 **Fax:** 71 2744078
Email: waschaffner@bluewin.ch
Web site: http://www.familiengaertner.ch

Titles:
DER GARTENFREUND LE JARDIN FAMILIAL

SCHWEIZER FLEISCH-FACHVERBAND 1713191
Steinwiesstr. 59, 8032 ZÜRICH **Tel:** 44 2507060
Fax: 44 2507061
Email: info@carnasuisse.ch
Web site: http://www.metzgerei.ch

Titles:
FLEISCH UND FEINKOST VIANDE ET TRAITEURS CARNE E COMMESTIBILI

SCHWEIZER HAGEL 682878
Seilergraben 61, 8021 ZÜRICH **Tel:** 44 2572211
Fax: 44 2572212
Email: info@hagel.ch
Web site: http://www.hagel.ch

Titles:
HAGEL KURIER

SCHWEIZER HEIMATSCHUTZ 683129
Seefeldstr. 5a, 8008 ZÜRICH **Tel:** 44 2545700
Fax: 44 2522870
Email: info@heimatschutz.ch
Web site: http://www.heimatschutz.ch

Titles:
HEIMATSCHUTZ PATRIMOINE

SCHWEIZER KADER ORGANISATION SKO 1715998
Schaffhauser Str. 2, 8006 ZÜRICH
Tel: 43 3005050 **Fax:** 43 3005061
Email: info@sko.ch
Web site: http://www.sko.ch

Titles:
SKO ASC ASQ LEADER
SKO ASC ASQ LEADER SPEZIAL

SCHWEIZER KUNSTVEREIN 684800
Zeughausstr. 55, 8026 ZÜRICH **Tel:** 44 2983030
Fax: 44 2983038
Email: info@kunstbulletin.ch
Web site: http://www.kunstbulletin.ch

Titles:
KUNST BULLETIN

SCHWEIZER MILCHPRODUZENTEN SMP 688059
Weststr. 10, 3000 BERN 6 **Tel:** 31 3595770
Fax: 31 3595855

Titles:
LE MENU

SCHWEIZER WANDERWEGE 687679
Monbijoustr. 61, 3000 BERN 23 **Tel:** 31 3701020
Fax: 31 3701021
Email: info@wandern.ch
Web site: http://www.wandern.ch

Titles:
WANDERLAND

SCHWEIZERISCHE AKADEMIE DER MEDIZINISCHEN WISSENSCHAFTEN 1643732
Petersplatz 13, 4051 BASEL **Tel:** 61 2699030
Fax: 61 2699039
Email: mail@samw.ch
Web site: http://www.samw.ch

Titles:
BULLETIN ASSM
BULLETIN SAMW

SCHWEIZERISCHE AKADEMIE DER TECHNISCHEN WISSENSCHAFTEN 1655212
Seidengasse 16, 8001 ZÜRICH **Tel:** 44 2265011
Fax: 44 2265020
Email: info@satw.ch
Web site: http://www.satw.ch

Titles:
TECHNO SCOPE

SCHWEIZERISCHE ARBEITSGEMEINSCHAFT FÜR DIE BERGGEBIETE 685957
Sellerstr. 4, 3001 BERN **Tel:** 31 3821010
Fax: 31 3821016
Email: info@sab.ch
Web site: http://www.sab.ch

Titles:
MONTAGNA

SCHWEIZERISCHE CHEMISCHE GESELLSCHAFT (SCG) 680150
Schwarztorstr. 9, 3007 BERN **Tel:** 31 3104090
Fax: 31 3121678
Email: info@swiss-chem-soc.ch
Web site: http://www.swiss-chem-soc.ch

Titles:
CHIMIA

SCHWEIZERISCHE DIABETES-GESELLSCHAFT 680804
Rütistr. 3a, 5400 BADEN **Tel:** 56 2001790
Fax: 56 2001795
Email: sekretariat@diabetesgesellschaft.ch
Web site: http://www.diabetesgesellschaft.ch

Titles:
D-JOURNAL
D-JOURNAL

SCHWEIZERISCHE ENERGIE-STIFTUNG 681293
Sihlquai 67, 8005 ZÜRICH **Tel:** 44 2752121
Fax: 44 2752120
Email: info@energiestiftung.ch
Web site: http://www.energiestiftung.ch

Titles:
ENERGIE & UMWELT

SCHWEIZERISCHE GESELLSCHAFT FÜR GESUNDHEITSPOLITIK 1643828
Postfach 686, 3000 BERN 8 **Tel:** 31 3138866
Fax: 31 3138899
Email: info@sggp.ch
Web site: http://www.sggp.ch

Titles:
GESUNDHEITSPOLITISCHE INFORMATIONEN GPI POLITIQUE DE SANTÉ: INFORMATIONS PSI

SCHWEIZERISCHE GESELLSCHAFT FÜR PALLIATIVE MEDIZIN, PFLEGE UND BEGLEITUNG 1724420
Seebahnstr. 231, 8004 ZÜRICH **Tel:** 44 2401621
Fax: 44 2429535
Email: admin@palliative.ch

Titles:
PALLIATIVE-CH

SCHWEIZERISCHE GESELLSCHAFT FÜR VOLKSKUNDE 688285
Spalenvorstadt 2, 4001 BASEL **Tel:** 61 2671163
Fax: 61 2671163
Email: sgv-sstp@volkskunde.ch
Web site: http://www.volkskunde.ch

Titles:
SCHWEIZERISCHES ARCHIV FÜR VOLKSKUNDE

SCHWEIZERISCHE LIGA GEGEN EPILEPSIE 1644617
Seefeldstr. 84, 8042 ZÜRICH **Tel:** 43 4886777
Fax: 43 4886778
Email: becker@epi.ch
Web site: http://www.epi.ch

Titles:
EPILEPTOLOGIE

SCHWEIZERISCHE METALL-UNION 685585
Seestr. 105, 8027 ZÜRICH **Tel:** 44 2857777
Fax: 44 2857778
Email: info@smu.ch
Web site: http://www.metallunion.ch

Titles:
METALL

SCHWEIZERISCHE METALL-UNION, FACHVERBAND LANDTECHNIK 1783118
Chräjeninsel 2, 3270 AARBERG **Tel:** 32 3917028
Fax: 32 3917029
Email: bildungszentrum@smu.ch
Web site: http://www.metallunion.ch

Titles:
FORUM LANDTECHNIK

SCHWEIZERISCHE STIFTUNG PRO MENTE SANA 687382
Hardturmstr. 261, 8031 ZÜRICH **Tel:** 44 3618272
Fax: 44 3618216
Email: kontakt@promentesana.ch
Web site: http://www.promentesana.ch

Titles:
PRO MENTE SANA AKTUELL

SCHWEIZERISCHE VEREINIGUNG FÜR SCHIFFFAHRT UND HAFENWIRTSCHAFT (SVS) 689135
Südquaistr. 14, 4019 BASEL **Tel:** 61 6312727
Fax: 61 6311483
Email: svs@swissonline.ch
Web site: http://www.svs-online.ch

Titles:
SVS AKTUELL

SCHWEIZERISCHE VEREINIGUNG FÜR SONNENENERGIE 1641552
Aarbergergasse 21, 3011 BERN **Tel:** 31 3718000
Fax: 31 3718000
Email: redaktion@sses.ch
Web site: http://www.sses.ch

Titles:
ENERGIES RENOUVELABLES
ERNEUERBARE ENERGIEN

SCHWEIZERISCHE ZENTRALSTELLE FÜR FENSTER UND FASSADEN SZFF 681706
Riedstr. 14, 8953 DIETIKON **Tel:** 44 7422434
Fax: 44 7415553
Email: info@szff.ch
Web site: http://www.szff.ch

Titles:
FASSADE FAÇADE

SCHWEIZERISCHER BURGENVEREIN 685874
Blochmonterstr. 22, 4054 BASEL **Tel:** 61 3612444
Fax: 61 3639405
Email: info@burgenverein.ch
Web site: http://www.burgenverein.ch

Titles:
MITTELALTER MOYEN AGE MEDIOEVO TEMP MEDIEVAL

SCHWEIZERISCHER DROGISTENVERBAND, MARKETINGZENTRALE 680931
Nidaugasse 15, 2502 BIEL **Tel:** 32 3285030
Fax: 32 3285031
Email: info@drogistenverband.ch
Web site: http://www.drogistenverband.ch

Titles:
DROGISTENSTERN

SCHWEIZERISCHER FEUERWEHRVERBAND 1640491
Morgenstr. 1, 3073 GÜMLIGEN **Tel:** 31 9588118
Fax: 31 9588111
Email: admin@swissfire.ch
Web site: http://www.swissfire.ch

Titles:
118 SWISSFIRE.CH

SCHWEIZERISCHER FORSTVEREIN 698327
Postfach 13, 8808 PFÄFFIKON **Tel:** 55 4202293
Fax: 55 4202290
Email: admin@forstverein.ch
Web site: http://www.forstverein.ch

Titles:
SCHWEIZERISCHE ZEITSCHRIFT FÜR FORSTWESEN

SCHWEIZERISCHER FOURIERVERBAND 678347
Aufdorfstr. 193, 8708 MÄNNEDORF
Tel: 79 3467670 **Fax:** 44 2584030
Email: swalder@bluewin.ch
Web site: http://www.armee-logistik.ch
Titles:
ARMEE-LOGISTIK

SCHWEIZERISCHER FRIEDENSRAT 682213
Gartenhofstr. 7, 8004 ZÜRICH **Tel:** 44 2429321
Fax: 44 2412926
Email: info@friedensrat.ch
Web site: http://www.friedensrat.ch
Titles:
FRIZ

SCHWEIZERISCHER GEMEINDEVERBAND 1644635
Solothurnstr. 22, 3322 URTENEN **Tel:** 31 8583116
Fax: 31 8583115
Email: info@chgemeinden.ch
Web site: http://www.chgemeinden.ch
Titles:
SCHWEIZER GEMEINDE COMMUNE SUISSE COMUNE SVIZZERO VISCHNANCA SVIZRA

SCHWEIZERISCHER GEMEINNÜTZIGER FRAUENVEREIN 1725043
Bleicherain 7, 5600 LENZBURG **Tel:** 62 8880110
Fax: 62 8880101
Email: info@sgf.ch
Web site: http://www.sgf.ch
Titles:
IDEELLE

SCHWEIZERISCHER SIGRISTEN-VERBAND 688454
Trislerstr. 15, 8952 SCHLIEREN **Tel:** 44 7344012
Fax: 44 7344007
Email: red.sigrist@hispeed.ch
Web site: http://www.sigristen.ch
Titles:
SIGRISTEN-VERBAND AKTUELL

SCHWEIZERISCHER TONKÜNSTLERVEREIN 1643267
11bis, av. du Grammont, 1007 LAUSANNE
Tel: 21 6143290 **Fax:** 21 6143299
Email: info@dissonance.ch
Web site: http://www.dissonance.ch
Titles:
DISSONANCE

SCHWEIZERISCHER TURNVERBAND 1718387
Bahnhofstr. 38, 5001 AARAU **Tel:** 62 8378200
Fax: 62 8241401
Email: stv@stv-fsg.ch
Web site: http://www.stv-fsg.ch
Titles:
GYM LIVE

SCHWEIZERISCHER VERBAND DER STRASSEN- UND VERKEHRSFACHLEUTE 689000
Sihlquai 255, 8005 ZÜRICH **Tel:** 44 2694020
Fax: 44 2523130
Email: info@vss.ch
Web site: http://www.vss.ch
Titles:
STRASSE UND VERKEHR ROUTE ET TRAFIC

SCHWEIZERISCHER VERBAND FÜR LANDTECHNIK 1724697
Ausserdorfstr. 31, 5223 RINIKEN **Tel:** 56 4412022
Fax: 56 4416731
Email: zs@agrartechnik.ch
Web site: http://www.agrartechnik.ch
Titles:
SCHWEIZER LANDTECHNIK TECHNIQUE AGRICOLE

SCHWEIZERISCHER VERBAND FÜR MATERIALWIRTSCHAFT UND EINKAUF 699442
Laurenzenvorstadt 90, 5001 AARAU
Tel: 62 8375700 **Fax:** 62 8375710
Email: svme@svme.ch
Web site: http://www.svme.ch
Titles:
BESCHAFFUNGSMANAGEMENT

SCHWEIZERISCHER VERBAND FÜR WOHNUNGSWESEN 1641798
Bucheggstr. 109, 8057 ZÜRICH **Tel:** 44 3602660
Fax: 44 3626971
Email: svw@svw.ch
Web site: http://www.svw.ch
Titles:
WOHNEN

SCHWEIZERISCHER VEREIN DES GAS- UND WASSERFACHES 1643847
Grütlistr. 44, 8027 ZÜRICH **Tel:** 44 2883333
Fax: 44 2883326
Email: e.pintimalli@svgw.ch
Web site: http://www.gwa.ch
Titles:
GWA

SCHWEIZERISCHER WERKLEHRERINNEN- UND WERKLEHRERVEREIN 690479
Loretohöhe 46b, 6300 ZUG **Tel:** 41 7101085
Fax: 41 7201088
Email: info@werkspuren.ch
Web site: http://www.werkspuren.ch
Titles:
WERKSPUREN

SCHWEIZERISCHES HANDELSAMTSBLATT 1643445
Effingerstr. 1, 3001 BERN **Tel:** 31 3240992
Fax: 31 3240961
Email: info@shab.ch
Web site: http://www.shab.ch
Titles:
SHAB.CH SCHWEIZERISCHES HANDELSAMTSBLATT FOSC.CH FEUILLE OFFICIELLE SUISSE DU COMMERCE FUSC.CH FOGLIO UFFICIALE SVIZZERO DI COMMERCIO

SCHWEIZERISCHES INSTITUT ZUR FÖRDERUNG DER SICHERHEIT 1640492
Nüschelerstr. 45, 8001 ZÜRICH **Tel:** 44 2174333
Fax: 44 2117030
Email: safety@swissi.ch
Web site: http://www.swissi.ch
Titles:
SICHERHEIT SÉCURITÉ SICUREZZA

SCHWENGELER VERLAG AG 681461
Hinterburgstr. 8, 9442 BERNECK **Tel:** 71 7272120
Fax: 71 7272123
Email: info@schwengeler.ch
Web site: http://www.schwengeler.ch
Titles:
ETHOS

SIX MULTIPAY AG 697651
Hardturmstrasse 201, 8021 ZÜRICH
Tel: 44 8329111 **Fax:** 44 8329115
Email: info@six-multipay.com
Web site: http://www.six-multipay.com
Titles:
ACCEPT
ACCEPT

SOCIETÀ EDITRICE RIVISTA DI LUGANO SA 687750
via Canonica, 6, 6900 LUGANO **Tel:** 91 9235631
Fax: 91 9213043
Email: publirdl@ticino.com
Titles:
RIVISTA DI LUGANO

SOCIÉTÉ DE PUBLICATIONS NOUVELLES SA 682588
22, av. du Mail, 1211 GENF 4 **Tel:** 22 8072211
Fax: 22 8072233
Email: info@ghi.ch
Web site: http://www.ghi.ch
Titles:
GHI GENÈVE HOME INFORMATIONS

SOCIÉTÉ VAUDOISE DE MÉDECINE 699295
1, ch.de Mornex, 1002 LAUSANNE
Tel: 21 6510505 **Fax:** 21 6510500
Email: info@svmed.ch
Web site: http://www.svmed.ch
Titles:
COURRIER DU MÉDECIN VAUDOIS

SOLOTHURNER ZEITUNG AG 677368
Zuchwiler Str. 21, 4501 SOLOTHURN
Tel: 32 6247111 **Fax:** 32 6247444
Email: info@szonline.ch
Web site: http://www.szonline.ch
Titles:
AZEIGER
GRENCHNER TAGBLATT GT
SOLOTHURNER ZEITUNG SZ

SPRINGER BUSINESS MEDIA SCHWEIZ AG 685458
Neugasse 10, 8031 ZÜRICH **Tel:** 44 2502830
Fax: 44 2502851
Email: info@media-daten.ch
Titles:
MEDIA TREND JOURNAL
WERBEWOCHE

SPROSS AG VERLAG 678155
Gerbegasse 2, 8302 KLOTEN **Tel:** 44 8001111
Fax: 44 8001133
Email: mail@kloteneranzeiger.ch
Web site: http://www.kloteneranzeiger.ch
Titles:
KLOTENER ANZEIGER
KLOTENER ANZEIGER

SRG SSR IDÉE SUISSE, UNTERNEHMENSKOMMUNIKATION 1775560
Giacomettistr. 1, 3000 BERN 31 **Tel:** 31 3509111
Email: publishing@srg-ssr.ch
Web site: http://www.srg-ssr.ch
Titles:
CHIFFRES, DONNÉES, FAITS SRG SSR IDÉE SUISSE
FACTS AND FIGURES SRG SSR IDÉE SUISSE
FATTI E CIFRE SRG SSR IDÉE SUISSE
SERVICE PUBLIC
SERVICE PUBLIC
LE SERVICE PUBLIC
SERVIZIO PUBBLICO
ZAHLEN, DATEN, FAKTEN SRG SSR IDÉE SUISSE

ST. GALLER TAGBLATT AG 686856
Fürstenlandstr. 122, 9014 ST. GALLEN
Tel: 71 2727888 **Fax:** 71 2727475
Email: verlag@tagblatt.ch
Web site: http://www.tagblatt.ch
Titles:
DIE NEUE SCHULPRAXIS
ST. GALLER TAGBLATT
TAGBLATT

STAATSKANZLEI 698346
Regierungsgebäude, 9001 ST. GALLEN
Tel: 71 2293259 **Fax:** 71 2293955
Email: amtsblatt.sk@sg.ch
Web site: http://www.amtsblatt-sg.ch
Titles:
AMTSBLATT DES KANTONS ST. GALLEN

STAATSKANZLEI DES KANTONS SOLOTHURN 677942
Postfach, 4509 SOLOTHURN **Tel:** 32 6272026
Fax: 32 6272994
Titles:
AMTSBLATT DES KANTONS SOLOTHURN

STAATSKANZLEI DES KANTONS ZÜRICH 677943
Neumühlequai 10, 8090 ZÜRICH **Tel:** 43 2592020
Fax: 43 2595939
Email: info@sk.zh.ch
Web site: http://www.amtsblatt.zh.ch
Titles:
AMTSBLATT DES KANTONS ZÜRICH

STADT 1644609
Rathaus, 7000 CHUR **Tel:** 81 2544113
Fax: 81 2544120
Email: stadtkanzlei@chur.ch
Titles:
AMTSBLATT DER STADT CHUR UND DER GEMEINDEN CHURWALDEN, FELSBERG, HALDENSTEIN, MALADERS, TRIMMIS, TSCHIERTSCHEN-PRADEN

STÄMPFLI AG 678272
Wölflistr. 1, 3001 BERN **Tel:** 31 3006666
Fax: 31 3006699
Email: info@staempfli.com
Web site: http://www.staempfli.com
Titles:
MEDIA LEX
DIE PRAXIS DES FAMILIENRECHTS LA PRATIQUE DU DROIT DE LA FAMILLE LA PRASSI DEL DIRETTO DI FAMIGLIA FAMPRA.CH
RECHT
RECHTSPRECHUNG IN STRAFSACHEN BULLETIN DE JURISPRUDENCE PÉNALE
SAV SCHWEIZERISCHE AKTUARVEREINIGUNG ASA ASSOCIATIONSUISSE DES ACTUAIRES SAA SWISS ASSOCIATION OF ACTUARIES MITTEILUNGEN - BULLETIN
ZEITSCHRIFT DES BERNISCHEN JURISTENVEREINS REVUE DE LA SOCIÉTÉ DES JURISTES BERNOIS ZBJV

STANDESKANZLEI URI 684223
Rathausplatz 1, 6460 ALTDORF **Tel:** 41 8752017
Fax: 41 8706651
Email: amtsblatt@ur.ch
Web site: http://www.ur.ch
Titles:
KANTON URI AMTSBLATT

STIFTUNG FORUM 682014
Hirschengraben 72, 8023 ZÜRICH
Tel: 44 2661272 **Fax:** 44 2661273
Email: forum@zh.kath.ch
Web site: http://www.kath.ch/zh/forum
Titles:
FORUM

STIFTUNG PRAKTISCHER UMWELTSCHUTZ SCHWEIZ 689401
Hottingerstr. 4, 8024 ZÜRICH **Tel:** 44 2674411
Fax: 44 2674414
Email: mail@umweltschutz.ch
Web site: http://www.umweltschutz.ch
Titles:
THEMA UMWELT

STIFTUNG SCHWEIZERISCHER NATIONALPARK 680416
Chastè Planta-Wildenberg, 7530 ZERNEZ
Tel: 81 8514111 **Fax:** 81 8514112
Email: info@nationalpark.ch
Web site: http://www.nationalpark.ch
Titles:
CRATSCHLA

STRAWBERRY-VERLAG 1681382
Werdstr. 34, 8004 ZÜRICH **Tel:** 44 2418050
Fax: 44 2417585
Email: bruno-thomas@bluewin.ch
Web site: http://www.evergreens.ch
Titles:
SUNNIGI NACHRICHTE

SUCHT INFO SCHWEIZ 1747845
14, av. Ruchonnet, 1001 LAUSANNE
Tel: 21 3212911 **Fax:** 21 3212940
Email: info@sucht-info.ch
Web site: http://www.sucht-info.ch
Titles:
ABHÄNGIGKEITEN

SÜDOSTSCHWEIZ PRESSE AG 1711097
Zwinglistr. 6, 8750 GLARUS **Tel:** 55 6452828
Fax: 55 6406440
Web site: http://www.suedostschweiz.ch
Titles:
ARENA ALVA
AROSER ZEITUNG
BÜWO BÜNDNER WOCHE
GLARISSIMO BUSINESS
NOVITATS
PÖSCHTLI
DIE SÜDOSTSCHWEIZ

SÜDOSTSCHWEIZ PRINT AG 1719348
Kasernenstr. 1, 7007 CHUR **Tel:** 81 2555418
Fax: 81 2555105
Web site: http://www.suedostschweiz.ch
Titles:
BÜNDNER WALD

SULZER MANAGEMENT AG
689268
Zürcher Str. 14, 8401 WINTERTHUR
Tel: 52 2626554 **Fax:** 52 2620025
Email: sulzertechnicalreview@sulzer.com
Web site: http://www.sulzer.com

Titles:
SULZER TECHNICAL REVIEW

SURSEER WOCHE AG
689116
Unterstadt 22, 6210 SURSEE **Tel:** 41 9218521
Fax: 41 9217533
Email: info@surseerwoche.ch
Web site: http://www.surseerwoche.ch

Titles:
SURSEER WOCHE

SVG-VERLAG S. BRUDERER
682554
Blumenbergstr. 47, 8633 WOLFHAUSEN
Tel: 55 2433614 **Fax:** 55 2433648
Email: susbruderer@bluewin.ch
Web site: http://www.gesundheitstechnik.ch

Titles:
GESUNDHEITSSCHUTZ UND UMWELTTECHNIK

SWISS BUSINESSPRESS SA
689155
Köschenrütistr. 109, 8052 ZÜRICH
Tel: 44 3064700 **Fax:** 44 3064711
Email: info@swissbusinesspress.ch
Web site: http://www.swissbusinesspress.ch

Titles:
UNTERNEHMER-ZEITUNG
ZÜRCHER UNTERNEHMER

SWISS DENTAL HYGIENISTS
680569
Bahnhofstr. 7b, 6210 SURSEE **Tel:** 41 9260790
Fax: 41 9260799
Email: info@dentalhygienists.ch
Web site: http://www.dentalhygienists.ch

Titles:
DIMENSIONS

SWISS EQUITY MEDIEN AG
1643421
Freigutstr. 26, 8002 ZÜRICH **Tel:** 43 3005380
Fax: 43 3005388
Email: info@se-medien.ch
Web site: http://www.se-medien.ch

Titles:
SWISS EQUITY MAGAZIN

SWISS IT MEDIA AG
683876
Seestr. 95, 8800 THALWIL **Tel:** 44 7227700
Fax: 44 7227701
Email: info@vogel-media.ch

Titles:
SWISS IT RESELLER

SWISSAVANT - WIRTSCHAFTSVERBAND HANDWERK UND HAUSHALT
687028
Neugutstr. 12, 8304 WALLISELLEN
Tel: 44 8787060 **Fax:** 44 8787055
Email: perspective@swissavant.ch
Web site: http://www.swissavant.ch

Titles:
PERSPECTIVE

SWISSBOAT YACHTING AG
1773649
Ekkehardstr. 16, 8006 ZÜRICH **Tel:** 44 35005885
Fax: 32 3848634
Email: info@yachting.ch
Web site: http://www.yachting.ch

Titles:
YACHTING SWISS BOAT

SWISSCLASSICS PUBLISHING AG
1653235
Schlyffistr. 21, 8806 FREIENBACH
Tel: 43 8880005 **Fax:** 43 8880946
Email: info@swissclassics.com
Web site: http://www.swissclassics.com

Titles:
SWISSCLASSICS REVUE

SWISSMECHANIC
1720596
Felsenstr. 6, 8570 WEINFELDEN **Tel:** 71 6262800
Fax: 71 6262809
Email: redaktion@swissmechanic.ch
Web site: http://www.swissmechanic.ch

Titles:
SWISSMECHANIC

SWISSMEDIC SCHWEIZERISCHES HEILMITTELINSTITUT
698321
Hallerstr. 7, 3000 BERN 9 **Tel:** 31 3220211
Fax: 31 3220212
Email: media@swissmedic.ch
Web site: http://www.swissmedic.ch

Titles:
JOURNAL SWISSMEDIC

SWISSPACK INTERNATIONAL GMBH
688685
Herrligstr. 35, 8048 ZÜRICH **Tel:** 44 4316445
Fax: 44 4316497
Email: info@swisspack.ch
Web site: http://www.swisspack.ch

Titles:
SPI SWISSPACK INTERNATIONAL

SWISSPRINTERS ST. GALLEN AG
686813
Fürstenlandstr. 122, 9014 ST. GALLEN
Tel: 58 7875757
Web site: http://www.swissprinters.ch

Titles:
AERO REVUE
GYM LIVE
GYM LIVE
DIE VOLKSWIRTSCHAFT

SWISSPROFESSIONALMEDIA AG
683772
Grosspeterstr. 23, 4002 BASEL **Tel:** 58 9589600
Fax: 58 9589660
Email: info@medical-tribune.ch
Web site: http://www.medical-tribune.ch

Titles:
INTERNATIONAL REGISTER OF FORWARDING AND LOGISTICS COMPANIES
ITJ INTERNATIONAL TRANSPORT JOURNAL - (ENGL. AUSG.)
LOGISTIK & FÖRDERTECHNIK
MEDICAL TRIBUNE
MEDICAL TRIBUNE KOLLOQUIUM
PSYCHE UND SOMA
SELECTA
SELECTA

SWISSQUOTE BANK SA
1771713
33, Chemin de la Crétaux, 1196 GLAND
Tel: 22 8258888 **Fax:** 22 8258889
Email: magazine@swissquote.ch
Web site: http://www.swissquote.ch

Titles:
SWISSQUOTE

SWS MEDIEN AG VERLAG
690256
Am Viehmarkt 1, 6130 WILLISAU **Tel:** 41 9726030
Fax: 41 9726021
Email: verlag@swsmedien.ch
Web site: http://www.swsmedien.ch

Titles:
SEETALER BOTE
WILLISAUER BOTE

TAMEDIA AG
678074
Werdstr. 21, 8021 ZÜRICH **Tel:** 44 2486333
Fax: 44 2486328
Email: unternehmenskommunikation@tamedia.ch
Web site: http://www.tamedia.ch

Titles:
ANNABELLE
DAS MAGAZIN
SCHWEIZER FAMILIE
SONNTAGS ZEITUNG
TAGES ANZEIGER

TCS TOURING CLUB SCHWEIZ
689560
4, chemin de Blandonnet, 1214 VERNIER
Tel: 22 4172727 **Fax:** 22 4172020
Email: tcs@tcs.ch
Web site: http://www.tcs.ch

Titles:
CAMPCAR

TCS TOURING CLUB SUISSE, CAMPING TCS
680031
4, chemin de Blandonnet, 1214 VERNIER
Tel: 22 4172030 **Fax:** 22 4172042
Email: cpg@tcs.ch
Web site: http://www.campingtcs.ch

Titles:
GUIDE CAMPING CAMPING FÜHRER GUIDA DEI CAMPEGGI

TECHNOPARK IMMOBILIEN AG
1721025
Technoparkstr. 1, 8005 ZÜRICH **Tel:** 44 4451000
Fax: 44 4451001
Email: info@technopark.ch
Web site: http://www.technopark.ch

Titles:
TP LEADER

TELCOM AG
1691402
Rotzbergstr. 15, 6362 STANSSTAD
Tel: 41 6180808 **Fax:** 41 6180818
Email: info@telcom-ag.ch
Web site: http://www.telcom-ag.ch

Titles:
NEWS

LE TEMPS SA
689310
3, pl. de Cornavin, 1211 GENF 2 **Tel:** 22 7995858
Fax: 22 7995859
Email: info@letemps.ch
Web site: http://www.letemps.ch

Titles:
LE TEMPS

TERTIANUM STIFTUNG
698595
Seminarstr. 28, 8057 ZÜRICH **Tel:** 43 5441515
Fax: 43 5441500
Email: tertianum@tertianum.ch
Web site: http://www.tertianum.ch

Titles:
TERTIANUM

THEILER DRUCK AG
683298
Verenastr. 2, 8832 WOLLERAU **Tel:** 44 7870300
Fax: 44 7870301
Email: info@theilerdruck.ch
Web site: http://www.theilerdruck.ch

Titles:
HÖFNER VOLKSBLATT
MARCH-ANZEIGER

THURGAUER MEDIEN AG
1649702
Promenadenstr. 16, 8500 FRAUENFELD
Tel: 52 7235511 **Fax:** 52 7235404
Email: verlag.zeitschriften@huber.ch
Web site: http://www.thurgauerzeitung.ch

Titles:
THURGAUER ZEITUNG

TICINO MANAGEMENT SA
1773996
via Vergiò, 8, 6932 BREGANZONA
Tel: 91 6102929 **Fax:** 91 6102910
Email: info@ticinomanagement.ch
Web site: http://www.ticinomanagement.ch

Titles:
TICINO MANAGEMENT

TIPOGRAFIA MENGHINI SA
682757
strada S. Bartolomeo, 7742 POSCHIAVO
Tel: 81 8440163 **Fax:** 81 8441323

Titles:
IL GRIGIONE ITALIANO

TOGGENBURG MEDIEN AG
1749693
Sonneggstr. 28, 9642 EBNAT-KAPPEL
Tel: 71 9926020 **Fax:** 71 9926021
Email: info@toggenburgernachrichten.ch
Web site: http://www.toggenburgernachrichten.ch

Titles:
TOGGENBURGER NACHRICHTEN UND "OBERTOGGENBURGER WOCHENBLATT"

TOURBILLON MAGAZIN
1792995
Heinestr. 17, 9008 ST. GALLEN **Tel:** 71 2456362
Fax: 71 2454127
Email: info@tourbillon-magazin.ch
Web site: http://www.tourbillon-magazin.ch

Titles:
TOURBILLON

TREDICOM SA
1640477
via Massagno, 10, 6908 LUGANO **Tel:** 91 9732010
Fax: 91 9724565
Email: tredicom@illustrazione.ch
Web site: http://www.illustrazione.ch

Titles:
ILLUSTRAZIONE TICINESE

TREUHAND-KAMMER
688305
Limmatquai 120, 8023 ZÜRICH **Tel:** 44 2677575
Fax: 44 2677555
Email: publikationen@treuhand-kammer.ch
Web site: http://www.treuhand-kammer.ch

Titles:
DER SCHWEIZER TREUHÄNDER L'EXPERT-COMPTABLE SUISSE

TRINER DRUCK AG
679625
Schmiedgasse 7, 6431 SCHWYZ **Tel:** 41 8190810
Fax: 41 8190853
Email: verlag@triner.ch
Web site: http://www.bote.ch

Titles:
BOTE DER URSCHWEIZ

UMDASCH SHOP-CONCEPT
1720046
Suhrer Str. 57, 5036 OBERENTFELDEN
Tel: 62 7372525 **Fax:** 62 7372550
Email: usco@umdasch.com
Web site: http://www.umdasch-shop-concept.com

Titles:
SHOP AKTUELL

UMWELTSEKRETARIAT OBERWALLIS
1740450
Postfach 669, 3900 BRIG-GLIS **Tel:** 27 9236162
Email: umweltsekretariat@rhone.ch
Web site: http://www.umwelt-oberwallis.ch

Titles:
UMWELT

UNION SUISSE DES ARTS ET MÉTIERS
684056
Schwarztorstr. 26, 3007 BERN **Tel:** 31 3801414
Fax: 31 3801415
Email: info@sgv-usam.ch
Web site: http://www.sgv-usam.ch

Titles:
JOURNAL DES ARTS ET MÉTIERS

UNIUN RUMANTSCHA DA SURMEIR
700132
Stradung 23, 7460 SAVOGNIN **Tel:** 81 6842838
Fax: 81 6843262
Email: pagina@bluewin.ch
Web site: http://www.u-r-s.ch

Titles:
LA PAGINA DA SURMEIR

UNIVERSITÄT ST. GALLEN, INSTITUT FÜR ÖFFENTLICHE DIENSTLEISTUNGEN UND TOURISMUS
1755495
Dufourstr. 40a, 9000 ST. GALLEN **Tel:** 71 2242525
Fax: 71 2242536
Email: idthsg@unisg.ch
Web site: http://www.idt.unisg.ch

Titles:
JAHRESBERICHT

UNIVERSITÄT ZÜRICH KOMMUNIKATION
689857
Rämistr. 42, 8001 ZÜRICH **Tel:** 44 6344430
Fax: 44 6342346
Web site: http://www.unizh.ch

Titles:
UNIJOURNAL

UNIVERSITÄTSBIBLIOTHEK BERN
679164
Münstergasse 61, 3000 BERN 8 **Tel:** 31 6319211
Fax: 31 6319299
Email: info@ub.unibe.ch
Web site: http://www.ub.unibe.ch

Titles:
BERNER ZEITSCHRIFT FÜR GESCHICHTE

URANG GMBH 1714624
Kempttalstr. 56, 8308 ILLNAU **Tel:** 52 3552111
Fax: 52 3552110
Email: info@umweltperspektiven.ch
Web site: http://www.umweltperspektiven.ch

Titles:
UMWELT PERSPEKTIVEN

USIC, GESCHÄFTSSTELLE 1646245
Aarberger Gasse 16, 3011 BERN **Tel:** 31 9700881
Fax: 31 9700882
Email: usic@usic.ch
Web site: http://www.usic.ch

Titles:
USIC NEWS

UTK MEDIA GMBH 687329
Frauenfelder Str. 49, 8370 SIRNACH
Tel: 71 9666080 **Fax:** 71 9666081
Email: info@utk.ch
Web site: http://www.utk.ch

Titles:
PROFESSIONAL COMPUTING

VELOJOURNAL REDAKTION & VERLAG 1641604
Cramerstr. 17, 8004 ZÜRICH **Tel:** 44 2426035
Fax: 44 2416032
Email: info@velojournal.ch
Web site: http://www.velojournal.ch

Titles:
VELOJOURNAL

VERBAND HEIME UND INSTITUTIONEN SCHWEIZ 1621268
Zieglerstr. 53, 3000 BERN 14 **Tel:** 31 3853333
Fax: 31 3853334
Email: info@curaviva.ch
Web site: http://www.curaviva.ch

Titles:
CURAVIVA

VERBAND LES ROUTIERS SUISSES 689147
26, rue de la Chocolatière, 1026 ECHANDENS
Tel: 21 7062000 **Fax:** 21 7062009
Web site: http://www.routiers.ch

Titles:
SWISS CAMION

VERBAND SCHWEIZER BILDHAUER- UND STEINMETZMEISTER 1645442
Aarberger Gasse 16, 3011 BERN **Tel:** 31 9700881
Fax: 31 9700882
Email: vsbs@vsbs.ch
Web site: http://www.vsbs.ch

Titles:
KUNST + STEIN

VERBAND SCHWEIZER GEBÄUDEHÜLLEN-UNTERNEHMUNGEN 680467
Lindenstr. 4, 9240 UZWIL **Tel:** 71 9557030
Fax: 71 9557040
Email: info@gh-schweiz.ch
Web site: http://www.gh-schweiz.ch

Titles:
GEBÄUDEHÜLLE SCHWEIZ

VERBAND SCHWEIZER PRESSE 681889
Konradstr. 14, 8021 ZÜRICH **Tel:** 44 3186464
Fax: 44 3186462
Email: contact@schweizerpresse.ch
Web site: http://www.schweizerpresse.ch

Titles:
FLASH

VERBAND SCHWEIZERISCHER ASSISTENZ- UND OBERÄRZTE/INNEN 1645374
Bahnhofplatz 10a, 3001 BERN **Tel:** 31 3504488
Fax: 31 3504489
Email: journal@vsao.ch
Web site: http://www.vsao.ch

Titles:
VSAO JOURNAL

VERBAND SCHWEIZERISCHER POLIZEIBEAMTER 698567
Villenstr. 2, 6005 LUZERN **Tel:** 41 3672121
Fax: 41 3672122
Email: mail@vspb.org
Web site: http://www.vspb.org

Titles:
POLICE

VERBAND SWISS EXPORT 1649438
Staffelstr. 8, 8045 ZÜRICH **Tel:** 44 2043484
Fax: 44 2043480
Email: info@swiss-export.com
Web site: http://www.swissexport.com

Titles:
SWISS EXPORT JOURNAL

VERBAND VERKAUFSORIENTIERTER FACHLEUTE UND FIRMEN 698526
Grünaustr. 10, 3084 WABERN **Tel:** 31 9615481
Fax: 31 9615130
Email: info@verkaufschweiz.ch
Web site: http://www.verkaufschweiz.ch

Titles:
PITCH

VERBANDSMANAGEMENT INSTITUT 1646285
90, bd. de Pérolles, 1701 FREIBURG
Tel: 26 3008400 **Fax:** 26 3009755
Email: info@vmi.ch
Web site: http://www.vmi.ch

Titles:
VERBANDS MANAGEMENT

VEREIN FEMINISTISCHE WISSENSCHAFT SCHWEIZ, GESCHÄFTSSTELLE 1643890
Blaumatt 3, 3250 LYSS **Tel:** 32 3853725
Email: info@femwiss.ch
Web site: http://www.femwiss.ch

Titles:
FEMINFO

VEREIN MÄNNERZEITUNG 1711346
Mühlegasse 14, 3400 BURGDORF
Tel: 34 4225008
Email: ivo.knill@maennerzeitung.ch
Web site: http://www.maennerzeitung.ch

Titles:
MÄNNERZEITUNG

VEREIN PUBLIKATIONEN SPEZIALKULTUREN VPS 698135
Schloss, 8820 WÄDENSWIL **Tel:** 44 7836325
Fax: 44 7836379
Email: uta.gafner@acw.admin.ch
Web site: http://www.szow.ch

Titles:
SCHWEIZISCHE ZEITSCHRIFT FÜR OBST- UND WEINBAU

VEREINIGTE SCHAUSTELLER-VERBÄNDE DER SCHWEIZ 1755616
Bändlistr. 100, 8064 ZÜRICH **Tel:** 79 6479080
Email: info@vsvs.ch
Web site: http://www.vsvs.ch

Titles:
SCHAUSTELLER

VEREINIGUNG DER URNER MINERALIENFREUNDE 685636
Postfach 161, 6472 ERSTFELD **Tel:** 79 3535965
Email: info@mineralienfreund.ch
Web site: http://www.mineralienfreund.ch

Titles:
MINERALIENFREUND

VEREINIGUNG FÜR UMWELTRECHT 1643400
Postfach 2430, 8026 ZÜRICH **Tel:** 44 2417691
Fax: 44 2417905
Email: info@vur-ade.ch
Web site: http://www.vur-ade.ch

Titles:
UMWELTRECHT IN DER PRAXIS DROIT DE L'ENVIRONNEMENT DANS LA PRATIQUE

VEREINIGUNG SCHWEIZERISCHER SPITZENMACHERINNEN 699066
Hohliebi, 3150 SCHWARZENBURG
Tel: 31 7310843 **Fax:** 31 7310360
Email: madeleine.raetz@dplanet.ch

Titles:
BULLETIN VSS/FDS

VERKEHRS-CLUB DER SCHWEIZ VCS 689796
Postfach 1613, 8201 SCHAFFHAUSEN
Tel: 52 6722819
Email: hugo.mahler@bluewin.ch
Web site: http://www.vcs-sh.ch

Titles:
ÜSI MEINIG

VERLAG ANZEIGER LUZERN AG 678179
Reusseggstr. 9, 6002 LUZERN **Tel:** 41 4919494
Fax: 41 4919495
Email: verlag@anzeiger-luzern.ch
Web site: http://www.anzeiger-luzern.ch

Titles:
ANZEIGER LUZERN

VERLAG BAUERNZEITUNG ZENTRALSCHWEIZ/AARGAU 1763647
Schellenrain 6, 6210 SURSEE **Tel:** 41 9258040
Fax: 41 9217337
Email: bauernzeitung.sursee@luzernerbauern.ch
Web site: http://www.bauernzeitung.ch

Titles:
BAUERNZEITUNG ZENTRALSCHWEIZ/AARGAU

VERLAG BEZIRKS-AMTSBLATT DER BEZIRKE LANDQUART UND PRÄTTIGAU/DAVOS 679241
Schulstr. 19, 7302 LANDQUART **Tel:** 81 3000360
Fax: 81 3000361
Email: info@bezirksamtsblatt.ch
Web site: http://www.bezirksamtsblatt.ch

Titles:
BEZIRKS-AMTSBLATT

VERLAG DER GARTENBAU 682326
Gärtnerstr. 12, 4501 SOLOTHURN
Tel: 32 6226622 **Fax:** 32 6228162
Email: info@gartenbau-verlag.ch
Web site: http://www.gartenbau-online.ch

Titles:
DER GARTENBAU L'HORTICULTURE

VERLAG DIE REGION 687588
Maihofstr. 76, 6002 LUZERN **Tel:** 41 4295454
Fax: 41 4295439
Email: mail@dieregion.ch
Web site: http://www.dieregion.ch

Titles:
REGION
REGION

VERLAG DIETSCHI AG 682417
Hauptstr. 22, 4437 WALDENBURG
Tel: 61 9659765 **Fax:** 61 9659769
Web site: http://www.dietschi.ch

Titles:
OBZ OBERBASELBIETER ZEITUNG

VERLAG EQUI-MEDIA AG 1755332
Brunnenstr. 7, 8604 VOLKETSWIL
Tel: 44 9084560 **Fax:** 44 9084540
Email: redaktion@asmz.ch

Titles:
ASMZ SICHERHEIT SCHWEIZ

VERLAG EXCLUSIV 1643788
Rancho, 7031 LAAX **Tel:** 79 6813181
Email: rchatelain@exclusiv.ch
Web site: http://www.exclusiv.ch

Titles:
TOP KÖCHE GRAUBÜNDEN

VERLAG FINANZ UND WIRTSCHAFT AG 698676
Hallwylstr. 71, 8004 ZÜRICH **Tel:** 44 2983535
Fax: 44 2983500
Email: verlag@fuw.ch
Web site: http://www.fuw.ch

Titles:
FINANZ UND WIRTSCHAFT

VERLAG HANS HUBER AG 679916
Länggassstr. 76, 3000 BERN 9 **Tel:** 31 3004500
Fax: 31 3004590
Email: verlag@hanshuber.com
Web site: http://www.verlag.hanshuber.com

Titles:
PHARMAJOURNAL
PRAXIS
THERAPEUTISCHE UMSCHAU
ZEITSCHRIFT FÜR KINDER- UND JUGENDPSYCHIATRIE UND PSYCHOTHERAPIE
ZEITSCHRIFT FÜR PSYCHIATRIE, PSYCHOLOGIE UND PSYCHOTHERAPIE

VERLAG HELVETICA CHIMICA ACTA AG 1641869
Hofwiesenstr. 26, 8042 ZÜRICH **Tel:** 44 3602434
Fax: 44 3602435
Email: vhca@vhca.ch

Titles:
HELVETICA CHIMICA ACTA

VERLAG HUBER 1775214
Zürcher Str. 180, 8501 FRAUENFELD
Tel: 52 7236050 **Fax:** 52 7236059
Email: info@verlaghuber.ch
Web site: http://www.ofv.ch

Titles:
SCHWEIZERISCHER FORSTKALENDER

VERLAG MIETRECHTSPRAXIS/MP 697837
Postfach, 8026 ZÜRICH **Tel:** 43 2434050
Fax: 43 2434051
Email: info@mietrecht.ch
Web site: http://www.mietrecht.ch

Titles:
MP MIETRECHTSPRAXIS

VERLAG MOBILITÄT GROB ORGANISATION 700147
Obergasse 34, 8402 WINTERTHUR
Tel: 52 2132317 **Fax:** 52 2132319
Email: groborg@mobilitaet-verlag.ch
Web site: http://www.mobilitaet-verlag.ch

Titles:
MOBILITÄT

VERLAG NIGGLI AG 678115
Steinackerstr. 8, 8583 SULGEN **Tel:** 71 6449111
Fax: 71 6449190
Email: info@niggli.ch
Web site: http://www.niggli.ch

Titles:
ARCHITHESE

VERLAG ORGANISATOR AG 1640976
Hafnerwisenstr. 1, 9442 BERNECK
Tel: 71 7472222 **Fax:** 71 7472220
Email: verlag@organisator.ch
Web site: http://www.rdv.ch

Titles:
ORGANISATOR

VERLAG RÜEGGER 678536
Albisrieder Str. 80a, 8003 ZÜRICH
Tel: 44 4912130 **Fax:** 44 4931176
Email: info@rueggerverlag.ch
Web site: http://www.rueggerverlag.ch

Titles:
AUSSENWIRTSCHAFT

VERLAG SCHAFFHAUSER BOCK AG 1718347
Wiesengasse 20, 8222 BERINGEN
Tel: 52 6323030 **Fax:** 52 6323090
Email: info@bockonline.ch
Web site: http://www.bockonline.ch

Titles:
SCHAFFHAUSER BOCK

VERLAG WERK AG 699706
Talstr. 29, 8001 ZÜRICH **Tel:** 44 2181430
Fax: 44 2181434
Email: redaktion@wbw.ch
Web site: http://www.werkbauenundwohnen.ch

Titles:
WERK, BAUEN + WOHNEN

VERLAG ZEITLUPE 1729086
Schulhausstr. 55, 8027 ZÜRICH **Tel:** 44 2838913
Fax: 44 2838910
Email: info@zeitlupe.ch
Web site: http://www.zeitlupe.ch

Titles:
ZEITLUPE

VERLAGS-AG DER AKADEMISCHEN-TECHNISCHEN VEREINE 697983
Staffelstr. 12, 8045 ZÜRICH **Tel:** 44 3802155
Fax: 44 3802157
Email: h.knoepfel@seatu.ch

Titles:
ARCHI
TEC 21
TRACÉS

VERLAGSGENOSSENSCHAFT SCHWEIZER SOLDAT 1755623
Weinbergstr. 11, 8268 SALENSTEIN
Tel: 71 6632644
Email: redaktion@schweizer-soldat.ch
Web site: http://www.schweizer-soldat.ch

Titles:
SCHWEIZER SOLDAT

VERLAGSGES. NIDWALDNER BLITZ AG 686412
Dorfplatz 2, 6383 DALLENWIL **Tel:** 41 6297979
Fax: 41 6297997
Email: inserate@blitz-info.ch
Web site: http://www.nw-blitz.ch

Titles:
NIDWALDNER BLITZ

VERSUS VERLAG AG 1755666
Merkurstr. 45, 8032 ZÜRICH **Tel:** 44 2510892
Fax: 44 2626738
Email: info@versus.ch
Web site: http://www.versus.ch

Titles:
DIE UNTERNEHMUNG

VIASTORIA AG 698688
Kapellenstr. 5, 3011 BERN **Tel:** 31 3007050
Fax: 31 3007069
Email: info@viastoria.ch
Web site: http://www.viastoria.ch

Titles:
WEGE UND GESCHICHTE LES CHEMINS ET L'HISTOIRE STRADE E STORIA

VKMB SCHWEIZERISCHE VEREINIGUNG ZUM SCHUTZ DER KLEINEN UND MITTLEREN BAUERN 1651181
Schützengässchen 5, 3001 BERN **Tel:** 31 3126400
Fax: 31 3126403
Email: vkmb@bluewin.ch
Web site: http://www.kleinbauern.ch

Titles:
ÖKOLOGO

VNU BUSINESS MEDIA SA 699008
25, rte. des Acacias, 1211 GENF 26
Tel: 22 3077837 **Fax:** 22 3003748
Web site: http://www.europastar.com

Titles:
EUROTEC

VOGEL BUSINESS MEDIA AG 1748476
Seestr. 95, 8800 THALWIL **Tel:** 44 7227700
Fax: 44 7201078
Email: info@vogel-media.ch
Web site: http://www.vogel-media.ch

Titles:
MSM LE MENSUEL DE L'INDUSTRIE
SMM GUIDE MSM GUIDE
SMM SCHWEIZER MASCHINENMARKT

VPS VERLAG AG 688299
Taubenhausstr. 38, 6002 LUZERN
Tel: 41 3170707 **Fax:** 41 3170700
Email: vps@vps.ch
Web site: http://www.vps.ch

Titles:
SCHWEIZER PERSONALVORSORGE PREVOYANCE PROFESSIONNELLE SUISSE

VRK VERLAG REISE UND KULTUR AG 698309
Steinenbachgässlein 49, 4051 BASEL
Tel: 61 2817177 **Fax:** 61 2818118
Email: medipress@hin.ch

Titles:
AERZTE/MEDICO JOURNAL

W. GASSMANN AG 679306
Längfeldweg 135, 2501 BIEL **Tel:** 32 3448111
Fax: 32 3448353
Email: anzeigen@gassmann.ch
Web site: http://www.gassmann.ch

Titles:
BIELER TAGBLATT
LE JOURNAL DU JURA

WALDWIRTSCHAFT SCHWEIZ 690338
Rosenweg 14, 4501 SOLOTHURN
Tel: 32 6258800 **Fax:** 32 6258899
Email: info@wvs.ch
Web site: http://www.wvs.ch

Titles:
WALD UND HOLZ

WALLIMANN DRUCK UND VERLAG AG 1751066
Aargauer Str. 12, 6215 BEROMÜNSTER
Tel: 41 9324050 **Fax:** 41 9324055
Web site: http://www.anzeiger-michelsamt.ch

Titles:
ANZEIGER FÜR DAS MICHELSAMT

WALTER GAMMETER GRAPHISCHE UNTERNEHMUNG AG 681299
via Surpunt, 54, 7500 ST. MORITZ
Tel: 81 8379090 **Fax:** 81 8379091
Email: verlag@engadinerpost.ch
Web site: http://www.engadinerpost.ch

Titles:
ENGADINER POST

WEINWISSER AG 698177
Lavaterstr. 40, 8002 ZÜRICH **Tel:** 55 2445244
Fax: 55 2445245
Email: info@weinwisser.com
Web site: http://www.weinwisser.com

Titles:
WEINWISSER

WELTWOCHE VERLAGS AG 1752063
Förrlibuckstr. 70, 8005 ZÜRICH **Tel:** 43 4445111
Fax: 43 4445607
Email: verlag@weltwoche.ch
Web site: http://www.weltwoche.ch

Titles:
DIE WELTWOCHE

WETTBEWERBSKOMMISSION 1644633
Monbijoustr. 43, 3003 BERN **Tel:** 31 3222040
Fax: 31 3222053
Email: weko@weko.admin.ch
Web site: http://www.wettbewerbskommission.ch

Titles:
RPW RECHT UND POLITIK DES WETTBEWERBS DPC DROIT ET POLITIQUE DE LA CONCURRENCE DPC DIRITTO E POLITICA DELLA CONCORRENZA

WG VERLAG & LIZENZEN AG 1748624
Bahnhofstr. 111, 9240 UZWIL **Tel:** 71 9557711
Fax: 71 9557717
Email: info@wg-verlag.ch
Web site: http://www.wg-verlag.com

Titles:
STAR PLUS

WINTERTHUR VERSICHERUNGEN 687291
Paulstr. 9, 8401 WINTERTHUR **Tel:** 52 2612121
Fax: 52 2136620
Email: info.ch@axa-winterthur.ch
Web site: http://www.winterthur-leben.ch

Titles:
[VORSORGE

WIRTSCHAFTSFÖRDERUNG KANTON BERN 1717172
Münsterplatz 3, 3011 BERN **Tel:** 31 6334120
Fax: 31 6334088
Email: info@berneinvest.com
Web site: http://www.berneinvest.com

Titles:
BERNE CAPITAL AREA
BERNE CAPITAL AREA
NEWSLETTER
NEWSLETTER

WIRTSCHAFTSFÖRDERUNG KANTON SCHAFFHAUSEN 1655108
Herrenacker 15, 8200 SCHAFFHAUSEN
Tel: 52 6740615 **Fax:** 52 6740609
Email: economic.promotion@generis.ch
Web site: http://www.economy.sh

Titles:
NEWSLETTER

WIRTSCHAFTSKAMMER BASELLAND 1748678
Altmarktstr. 96, 4410 LIESTAL **Tel:** 61 9276464
Fax: 61 9276550
Email: info@kmu.org
Web site: http://www.kmu.org

Titles:
STANDPUNKT DER WIRTSCHAFT

WM-DRUCK SEMPACHER ZEITUNG AG 688371
Sempachstr. 7, 6203 SEMPACH-STATION
Tel: 41 4671919 **Fax:** 41 4672355
Email: verlag@sempacherwoche.ch
Web site: http://www.sempacherwoche.ch

Titles:
SEMPACHER WOCHE

WWF SCHWEIZ 686895
Hohlstr. 110, 8004 ZÜRICH **Tel:** 44 2972121
Fax: 44 2972100
Email: info@wwf.ch
Web site: http://www.wwf.ch

Titles:
WWF MAGAZIN
WWF RIVISTA

WWF SCHWYZ 688318
Bahnhofstr. 1, 8852 ALTENDORF **Tel:** 55 4107061
Fax: 55 4107062
Email: wwf.schwyz@mythen.ch
Web site: http://www.wwf-sz.ch

Titles:
SCHWYZER PANDA

ZEHNDER MEDIEN AG 1713056
Am Marktplatz 4, 9400 RORSCHACH
Tel: 71 8442350 **Fax:** 71 8442351
Email: verlagshaus@zehnder.ch
Web site: http://www.zehnder.ch

Titles:
BODENSEE NACHRICHTEN

ZEHNDER PRINT AG 1713058
Hubstr. 60, 9500 WIL **Tel:** 71 9134711
Fax: 71 9134799
Email: info@zehnder.ch
Web site: http://www.zehnder.ch

Titles:
BÜNDNER NACHRICHTEN
NEUE OLTNER ZEITUNG NOZ
ZUGER WOCHE

ZEITPUNKT VERLAG 690905
Werkhofstr. 19, 4500 SOLOTHURN
Tel: 32 6218111 **Fax:** 32 6218110
Email: verlag@zeitpunkt.ch
Web site: http://www.zeitpunkt.ch

Titles:
ZEITPUNKT

ZIEGLER DRUCK- UND VERLAGS-AG 697900
Rudolf-Diesel-Str. 22, 8401 WINTERTHUR
Tel: 52 2669900 **Fax:** 52 2669910
Email: verlag@zieglerdruck.ch
Web site: http://www.zieglerdruck.ch

Titles:
DER LANDBOTE
DER LANDBOTE

ZOFINGER TAGBLATT AG 690997
Henzmannstr. 20, 4800 ZOFINGEN
Tel: 62 7459393 **Fax:** 62 7459349
Email: zt@ztonline.ch
Web site: http://www.ztonline.ch

Titles:
AMTSBLATT DES KANTONS AARGAU
ZOFINGER TAGBLATT ZT

ZÜRCHER BAUERNVERBAND 700134
Nüschelerstr. 35, 8001 ZÜRICH **Tel:** 44 2177733
Fax: 44 2177732
Email: bauernverband@zbv.ch
Web site: http://www.zbv.ch

Titles:
ZÜRCHER BAUER

ZÜRCHER FRAUENZENTRALE 1716436
Am Schanzengraben 29, 8002 ZÜRICH
Tel: 44 2063020 **Fax:** 44 2063021
Email: zh@frauenzentrale.ch
Web site: http://www.frauenzentrale-zh.ch

Titles:
BULLETIN

ZÜRCHER KANTONALBANK 691022
Postfach, 8010 ZÜRICH **Tel:** 44 2922075
Fax: 44 2922068
Web site: http://www.zkb.ch

Titles:
ZÜRCHER WIRTSCHAFTS MAGAZIN

ZÜRCHER NOTARIATSVEREIN 698574
Sunnebüelstr. 34, 8604 VOLKETSWIL
Tel: 43 5344596
Email: info@zbgr.ch
Web site: http://www.zbgr.ch

Titles:
ZBGR SCHWEIZERISCHE ZEITSCHRIFT FÜR BEURKUNDUNGS- UND GRUNDBUCHRECHT RNRF REVUE SUISSE DU NOTARIAT ET DU REGISTRE FONCIER

ZÜRCHER STADTVERBAND FÜR SPORT 698364
Postfach, 8027 ZÜRICH **Tel:** 44 3962555
Fax: 44 3962552
Email: info@zss.ch
Web site: http://www.zss.ch

Titles:
ZÜRISPORT

ZÜRCHER UNTERLAND MEDIEN AG 682271
Schulstr. 12, 8157 DIELSDORF **Tel:** 44 8548282
Fax: 44 8530690

Titles:
ZÜRCHER UNTERLÄNDER

ZÜRICHSEE PRESSE AG 685111
Seestr. 86, 8712 STÄFA **Tel:** 44 9285111
Fax: 44 9285520
Email: abo@zsz.ch
Web site: http://www.zsz.ch

Titles:
ZÜRICHSEE-ZEITUNG
ZÜRICHSEE-ZEITUNG
ZÜRICHSEE-ZEITUNG
ZÜRICHSEE-ZEITUNG

Turkey

BOYUT YAYINCILIK 1732510
Tekstilkent, Koza Plaza A Blok Kat:26, Tem Otoyolu Üzeri Atışalanı Mevkii, Esenler, 34235 İSTANBUL **Tel:** 212 413 33 33 **Fax:** 212 413 33 34
Web site: http://www.boyut.com.tr

Titles:
BANYO MUTFAK
GASTRONOMI

Turkey

MOBILYA TEKSTIL
OFIS İLETIŞIM

CEBA BASIN YAYIN TANITIM LTD. STI. ADINA 699525
1391 Sok. No 4/201, Alsancak, IZMIR
Tel: 232 46 36 300 **Fax:** 232 46 35 300
Web site: http://www.kazete.com.tr

Titles:
KAZETE

ÇUKUROVA GRUBU 1732506
Davutpaşa C. No.34 34020, Zeytinburnu, İSTANBUL **Tel:** 212 4493000 **Fax:** 212 4819561

Titles:
AKŞAM
GÜNEŞ

CUMHURIYET GRUBU 1732521
Türkocağı Cd. No:39/41 34334 (P.K.246 34435 Sirkeci-İst.), Cağaloğlu, İSTANBUL
Tel: 212 343 72 74 **Fax:** 212 291 49 76

Titles:
CUMHURIYET

DIĞER 1732526
Yayıncılar S. 10/A Kat:2, Seyrantepe, 34418 İSTANBUL

Titles:
AYDIN TICARET ODASI DERGISI
BUSINESS TRAVEL IN TURKEY
CD OYUN
CHAT
CORNUCOPIA
CYPRUS TODAY
EGE LIFE
ELEGANS
THE GUIDE ANKARA
THE GUIDE ANTALYA
THE GUIDE BODRUM
THE GUIDE İSTANBUL
POPÜLER BILIM
ROTARY
STAR
TELEPATI TELEKOM
TERMODINAMIK
TESISAT MARKET
TICARET GAZETESI
VIP
YELKEN DÜNYASI
YENI ŞAFAK

DOGAN BURDA RIZZOLI YAYINCILIK VE PAZARLAMA AS 692578
Hürriyet Medya Towers, Güneşli, 34212 İSTANBUL **Tel:** 212 41 03 421 **Fax:** 212 41 03 528

Titles:
CAPITAL
CHIP
ELLE
PC NET

DOĞAN GRUBU 1732504
Hürriyet Medya Towers 34212, Güneşli, 34212 İSTANBUL

Titles:
AUTO SHOW
EKONOMIST
FANATIK
FANATIK BASKET
HÜRRIYET
MILLIYET
POSTA
RADIKAL
TURKISH DAILY NEWS

DOĞAN BURDA DERGI YAYINCILIK VE PAZARLAMA A.Ş. 1768725
Hürriyet Medya Towers, 34212 Güneşli, İSTANBUL **Tel:** 212 2179371 **Fax:** 212 2179532

Titles:
LEVEL

ELEMENT İLETIŞIM 1732528
CemiBağdat Caddesi, Esen Apt. No.175 Daire:7, Kadıköy, İSTANBUL

Titles:
HUMAN RESOURCES

FEZA GAZETECILIK A.Ş 1762133
Ahmet Taner Kislali Cad. No: 6, 34194 Yenibosna, ISTANBUL

Titles:
ZAMAN

IHLAS FUAR HIZMETLERI A.S. 1640561
29 Ekim Mah., İhlas Holding Medya Blok Kat:1, 34530 YENIBOSNA - ISTANBUL
Tel: 212 45 42 503 **Fax:** 212 45 42 506
Email: info@ihlasfuar.com
Web site: http://www.ihlasfuar.com

Titles:
MEDIKAL & TEKNIK

İHLAS GRUBU 1732509
29 Ekim Mah. İhlas Holding Medya Blok Kat:1, Yenibosna, 34197 ISTANBUL

Titles:
MATBAA TEKNIK
TEKSTIL TEKNIK
TÜRKIYE

MERKEZ DERGI GRUBU 1732513
Tel: 212 274 10 90 **Fax:** 212 273 03 39
Barbaros Bulvarı Cam Han No:125, Beşiktaş, İSTANBUL **Tel:** 212 4112000 **Fax:** 212 3544745

Titles:
COSMO GIRL!

ROTA YAYIN YAPIM TANITIM TICARET LTD 1768010
Prof. N. Mazhar Ökten Sok. No. 1, Şişli, 80240 İSTANBUL **Tel:** 212 224 01 44 **Fax:** 212 233 72 43
Email: rota@rotayayin.com.tr
Web site: http://www.rotaline.com

Titles:
MARKETING TÜRKIYE

SABAH GRUBU 1732507
Gaziosmanpasa Bulvari 5, 35210 ÇANKAYA
Tel: 232 4415000 **Fax:** 232 4464222
Email: yasir@yeniasir.com.tr
Web site: http://www.yeniasir.com.tr

Titles:
SABAH
YENI ASIR

VOGEL GRUBU 1732514
Vefa Bayırı Sok. Gayrettepe İş Merkezi B.Blok 34349, Gayrettepe, İSTANBUL **Tel:** 212 217 93 71
Fax: 212 217 95 32

Titles:
WINDOWS NET MAGAZINE

ZAMAN GRUBU 1732505
Fevzi Çakmak Mah. A. Taner Kışlalı Cad. No:6 34194, Yenibosna, İSTANBUL **Tel:** 212 4541454
Fax: 212 4548625

Titles:
AKSIYON
TODAY S ZAMAN

Ukraine

AD-WORLD 1752530
ul. Gaidara 27, office 10, KIEV **Tel:** 44 200 45 45
Fax: 44 200 45 45

Titles:
SMS

APK-INFORM 1740029
ul. Chicherina 21, 49006 DNEPROPETROVSK
Email: info@apk-inform.com
Web site: http://www.apk-inform.com

Titles:
APK-INFORM RUSSIA

COMUNALNE PREDPRIYEMSTVO REDAKTSYA GAZETY VECHIRNY KYIV 1621702
ul. Marshala Grechka 13, 04136 KYIV
Tel: 44 43 46 109 **Fax:** 44 44 39 609

Titles:
VECHIRNIY KYIV 100

DONBASS 1793488
Kievsky Avenue 48, 83118 DONETSK
Tel: 62 3116 610 **Fax:** 62 3112101

Titles:
DONBASS

DP BURDA-UKRAINA 1619209
ul. Vladimirskaya 101, Korpus 2, 4th Floor, 01033 KYIV **Tel:** 44 49 08 361 **Fax:** 44 49 08 360
Web site: http://www.burda.com.ua

Titles:
BURDA-UKRAINA
CHIP

FAKTY I KOMMENTARII 699461
ul. Vandy Vasilevskoy 27/29, 04116 KYIV
Tel: 44 24 45 781 **Fax:** 44 21 68 580

Titles:
FAKTY I KOMMENTARII

I.A. AUTOCENTRE 1621065
ul. Degtyarevskaya 52, 04112 KYIV
Tel: 44 45 96 001 **Fax:** 44 44 18 591

Titles:
AUTOCENTRE

ITC PUBLISHING 699472
51 Krasnozvezdny ave, 03110 KYIV
Tel: 44 270 3891

Titles:
DOMASHNIY PC
MOBILITY

IZDATELSKIY DOM ORMOS 699571
ul. Tverskaya 6, 03150 KYIV **Tel:** 44 26 97 822
Fax: 44 26 97 452

Titles:
ZERKALO NEDELI

JED SUNDEN, KP MEDIA 677141
Lesya Ukrainka Blvd. 34, Room 501, 01133 KYIV
Tel: 44 49 61 111 **Fax:** 44 28 66 465
Email: jed@kpmedia.ua

Titles:
KYIV POST

PP UKRAINA MOLODA 699462
pr. Peremogi 50, 5 floor, 03047 KYIV
Tel: 44 44 18 392

Titles:
UKRAINA MOLODA

SEGODNYA MULTIMEDIA 1619211
Ul. Borshagovskaya 152-B, 03056 KYIV 56
Tel: 44 45 72 401 **Fax:** 44 45 72 387
Web site: http://www.segodnya.ua

Titles:
SEGODNYA

THE UKRAINIAN PRESS GROUP 691120
ul. Marshala Tymoshenka 2L, 04212 KYIV
Tel: 44 41 44 066 **Fax:** 44 41 44 920

Titles:
DEN

VAVILON 1619215
ul. Melnikova 12A, Office 8, 04050 KYIV
Tel: 44 56 85 798 **Fax:** 44 56 85 896

Titles:
XXL MAGAZINE

Vatican City

EDIZIONI TIPOGRAFIA VATICANA - EDITRICE L' OSSERVATORE ROMANO 7519
Via Del Pellegrino, 00120 CITTÀ DEL VATICANO
Tel: 06 69 88 34 61 **Fax:** 06 69 88 36 75

Titles:
L' OSSERVATORE ROMANO

Willings Volume 2
Section 7

Broadcasting

This section lists Broadcast media within Europe in alphabetical order by country and then by broadcast organisation.

Andorra

REGIONAL TV STATIONS

ANDORRA TELEVISIÓ 53298
Baixada del Molí 24, ANDORRA LA VELLA, AD500 **Tel:** 87 37 77. **Fax:** 86 49 99.
Email: info@rtva.ad
Web site: www.informatius.ad
Director: Enric Castellet

Austria

NATIONAL TV STATIONS

ORF ÖSTERREICHISCHER RUNDFUNK 753381
Würzburggasse 30, 1136 WIEN
Tel: 1 878780. **Fax:** 1 8787812738.
Web site: http://orf.at
News Editor: Karl Amon; *Editor:* Wolfgang Lorenz

REGIONAL TV STATIONS

SERVUSTV 740999
Ludwig-Bieringer-Platz 1, 5073 WALS
Tel: 662 842244. **Fax:** 662 84224428181.
Email: office@servustv.at
Web site: http://www.servustv.at
News Editor: Jörg Harzem; *Editor:* Wolfgang Pütz

NATIONAL RADIO STATIONS

ORF ÖSTERREICHISCHER RUNDFUNK 738292
Argentinierstr. 30a, 1040 WIEN
Tel: 1 5010118213. **Fax:** 1 5010118410.
Web site: http://www.orf.at
News Editor: Uschi Theiretzbacher; *Editor:* Wilhelm Mitsche

REGIONAL RADIO STATIONS

ANTENNE STEIERMARK 753262
Am Sendergrund 1, 8143 DOBL
Tel: 3136 5050. **Fax:** 3136 505333.
Email: info@antenne.net
Web site: http://www.antenne.net
Editor: Christiane Stöckler

Belarus

NATIONAL TV STATIONS

1 KANAL TV 763144
9 Makayonka Street, MINSK 220807
Tel: 17 26 48 182. **Fax:** 17 26 48 182.
Email: pr@tvr.by
Web site: http://www.tvr.by
Director: Alexander Viktorovich Kapionkin

NATIONAL RADIO STATIONS

KANAL KULTURA 1615416
ul. Krasnaya 4, 220807 MINSK
Tel: 17 28 44 620. **Fax:** 17 29 06 242.
Email: kultura_br@tvr.by
Web site: http://www.tvr.by
News Editor: Svetlana Kolmak; *Editor:* Elena Letun

PERVIY NACIONALNIY KANAL BELARUSSKOGO RADIO 763143
ul. Krasnaya 4, 220807 MINSK
Tel: 17 28 43 922. **Fax:** 17 29 06 242.
Email: radio1@tvr.by
Web site: http://www.tvr.by/rus
News Editor: Pyotr Fyedorovich Romanchuk; *Director:* Anton Vasukevich

PILOT FM 1804094
ul. K. Marksa 40, office 9, 220030 MINSK
Tel: 17 29 06 863. **Fax:** 17 29 06 841.
Email: pilot-fm@mail.ru
Web site: www.pilotfm.com

RADIO ROKS 763142
vul. Storozhevskaya 8A, MINSK 220002
Tel: 17 28 60 807. **Fax:** 17 28 60 927.
Email: news@roks.com
Web site: http://www.roks.com
News Editor: Tatiana Sulimova; *Director:* Valentina Pismak

RADIOSTANTSIYA BELARUS 1615421
ul. Krasnaya 4, 220807 MINSK
Tel: 17 28 45 758. **Fax:** 17 28 48 574.
Email: radiostation-belarus@tvr.by
Web site: http://www.radiobelarus.tvr.by/eng/default.asp
News Editor: Grigoriy Mitjushnikov; *Director:* Naum Galpyerovich

UNISTAR 99.5 1800686
pr. Nezavisimosti 7, office 701-705, 220050 MINSK **Tel:** 17 20 95 376. **Fax:** 17 20 95 375.
Email: radio@unistar.by
Web site: http://www.unistar.by
Director: Anastasya Shatilo

Belgium

NATIONAL TV STATIONS

CLUB RTL 1858
Avenue Jacques-Georgin, 2, B-1030 BRUXELLES **Tel:** 2 337 68 11.
Fax: 2 337 68 12.
Email: redaction@rtl.be
Web site: http://www.clubrtl.be

KANAAL Z 1647730
Medialaan 1, 1800 VILVOORDE
Tel: 2255 37 08.
Email: info@z-nieuws.be
Web site: http://kanaalz.rnews.be
Producer: Lies Rottiers

RTL - TVI 1861
Avenue Jacques-Georgin 2, 1030 BRUXELLES **Tel:** 2 337 68 11.
Fax: 2 337 68 12.
Email: redaccharleroi@rtl.be
Web site: http://www.rtltvi.be
Producer: Charlotte Baut

REGIONAL TV STATIONS

ATV - ANTWERPSE TELEVISIE 2115
Hangar 26-27 - Rijnkaai 104, 2000 ANTWERP **Tel:** 3212 13 60. **Fax:** 32121361.
Email: redactie@atv.be
Web site: http://www.atv.be
Editor: Hans Hellemans; *Director:* Frank Bell

AVS-OOST-VLAAMSE TELEVISIE 2116
Adolphe Pégoud, 20, 9051 SINT-DENIJS-WESTREM **Tel:** 9378 07 78. **Fax:** 93783077.
Email: redactie@avs.be
Web site: http://www.avs.be
Director: Lucie de Zutter

CANAL ZOOM 2118
Paasage des déportés, 2, 5030 GEMBLOUX
Tel: 8161 30 09. **Fax:** 81612999.
Email: redaction@canalzoom.com
Web site: http://www.canalzoom.com
Director: André Baijot; *Producer:* Roland Vandenheuvel

FOCUS TELEVISIE 2119
Kwadestraat, 151 b, 8800 ROESELARE
Tel: 5125 95 11. **Fax:** 51259552.
Email: redactie@focustv.be
Web site: http://www.rmm.be
Editor: Bart Coopman

MATELE 2137
Rue Joseph Wauters, 22, 5580 JEMELLE
Tel: 8422 21 79. **Fax:** 84221102.
Email: redaction@matele.be
Web site: http://www.matele.be
Director: Philippe Halloy

NOTÉLÉ 2121
Rue du Follet 4 C, 7540 KAINTOURNAI
Tel: 6989 19 19. **Fax:** 69891919.
Email: redaction@notele.be
Web site: http://www.notele.be

RING-TV 2122
Luchthavenlaan,22, 1800 VILVOORDE
Tel: 2255 95 95. **Fax:** 22530505.
Email: nieuws@ringtv.be
Web site: http://www.ringtv.be
Editor: Dirk de Weert

RTC LIEGE 2126
Rue du Laveu, 58, 4000 LIEGE
Tel: 425 49 999. **Fax:** 42549998.
Email: info@rtc.be
Web site: http://www.rtc.be

RTV KEMPEN-MECHELEN 1647775
Lossing, 16, 2260 WESTERLO
Tel: 1459 15 25. **Fax:** 14585966.
Email: redactie@rtv.be
Web site: http://www.rtv.be
Editor: Jan Peeters

TELE MB 2131
Carré des Arts, Rue des Soeurs Noires, 4 A, 7000 MONS **Tel:** 6540 00 40.
Fax: 65400033.
Email: redaction@telemb.be
Web site: http://www.telemb.be
Director: Jean-Claude Marechal

TELESAMBRE 2133
Espace Sud, Esplanade René-Magritte, 10, 6010 COUILLET **Tel:** 7147 37 37.
Fax: 71475775.
Web site: http://www.telesambre.be
Director: Tom Galand

TELEVESDRE 2132
Rue Neufmoulin, 3, 4820 DISON
Tel: 8733 76 25. **Fax:** 87338263.
Email: televesdre@televesdre.be
Web site: http://www.televesdre.be
Director: Urbain Ortmans

TLB - TELE BRUXELLES 2130
Rue Gabrielle Petit, 32, 1080 BRUXELLES
Tel: 2421 21 21. **Fax:** 24212122.
Email: info@telebruxelles.be
Web site: http//:www.telebruxelles.be

TV COM 2135
Rue de la Station, 10, 1341 CEREUX - MOUSTY **Tel:** 1041 01 96. **Fax:** 10414168.
Email: info@tvcom.be
Web site: http://www.tvcom.be

TV OOST (KANAAL 3) 2120
IZ Hoogveld Zone D, Vosmeer, 16, 9200 DENDERMONDE **Tel:** 3 778 73 00.
Fax: 37787301.
Email: info@tvoost.be
Web site: http://www.tvoost.be
Editor: Michiel Ameloot; *Presenter:* Sylvie Verleye

TV-BRUSSEL 2134
Belvédèrestraat 27 A, 1050 ELSENE
Tel: 2702 87 30. **Fax:** 2702 87 41.
Email: nieuws@tvbrussel.be
Web site: http://www.tvbrussel.be

TV-LIMBURG 1647799
Via Media, 4, 3500 HASSELT
Tel: 1171 22 11. **Fax:** 11712212.
Email: info@tvl.be
Web site: http://www.tvl.be
Editor: Miranda Gijsen

WTV-ZUID 2139
Accent Business Park, Kwadestraat, 151 b, 8800 ROESELARE **Tel:** 5125 95 25.
Fax: 51259522.
Email: redactie@focus-wtv.be
Web site: http://www.focus-wtv.be
Editor: Bart Coopman

SATELLITE TV

C'EST LA CHAINE! 1790979
AVS - Mediagebouw, A. Pegoudlaan 20, 9051 SINT - DENIJS - WESTREM
Tel: 933 000 00.
Email: info@stelevisie.be
Web site: http://www.stelevisie.be

MTV BELGIUM 1648264
MTV Networks Belgium, Fabriekstraat, 38, B-2547 LINT **Tel:** 3 400 38 20.
Fax: 3 400 38 63.
Email: info@tmf.com
Web site: http://www.mtvnetworks.be
Editor: Stijn Smets

NATIONAL RADIO STATIONS

BEL RTL 1832
Avenue Jacques Georgin, 2, 1030 BRUXELLES **Tel:** 2337 69 11.
Fax: 2337 69 12.
Email: belrtl@belrtl.be
Web site: http://www.belrtl.be

BFM TODAY 1915
Avenue des Croix de Guerre 94, 1120 BRUXELLES **Tel:** 2 244 27 13.
Fax: 2 244 27 03.
Email: mabfm@bfm.be
Web site: http://www.bfm.be
Director: Christian Miroir

FUN RADIO 1836
Avenue Télémaque, 33, 1190 FOREST
Tel: 2345 08 35. **Fax:** 23467199.
Web site: http://www.funradio.be

NRJ + CHERIE FM 1839
Chaussée de Louvain, 467, 1030 BRUXELLES **Tel:** 2513 28 08.
Fax: 2511 07 81.
Email: redaction@nrj.be
Web site: http://www.nrj.be

RADIO NOSTALGIE 1891
Chaussée de Louvain, 775, 1140 BRUXELLES **Tel:** 2227 04 50.
Fax: 22231455.
Email: redaction@nostalgie.be
Web site: http://www.nostalgie.be
Editor: Michel Geyer

Bosnia-Herzegovina

NATIONAL TV STATIONS

BH TV1 766119
Bulevar Meše Selimovića 12, SARAJEVO 71000 **Tel:** 33 65 04 52. **Fax:** 33 45 07 17.
Email: milenko.vockic@bhrt.ba
Web site: http://www.bhrt.ba
News Editor: Fadil Smajić; *Director:* Milenko Vočkić

NATIONAL RADIO STATIONS

BH RADIO 1 766126
Bulevar Meše Selimovića 12, 71000 SARAJEVO **Tel:** 33 46 11 01.
Fax: 33 45 51 13.
Email: kontakt@bhrt.ba
Web site: http://www.bhrt.ba
News Editor: Emir Habul; *Director:* Senada Ćumurović

Cyprus

NATIONAL RADIO STATIONS

ENERGY 107.6 1810553
23 Ayias Paraskevis str., Strovolos, Karantokis Bld - 4th Floor, P.O.BOX 22108, NICOSIA 22108 **Tel:** 22 46 69 66.
Fax: 22 37 99 44.
Email: info@energy1076.com
Web site: http://www.energy1076.com

Denmark

NATIONAL TV STATIONS

TV 2 / DANMARK 630365
Rugaardsvej 25, DK-5100 ODENSE C
Tel: 65 91 91 91. **Fax:** 65 91 33 22.
Email: tv2@tv2.dk
Web site: http://www.tv2.dk

REGIONAL TV STATIONS

SBS-NET - FYN/ SØNDERJYLLAND 3573
Unsbjergvej 2A, 5220 ODENSE SØ
Tel: 66 11 21 12. **Fax:** 66 15 46 39.
Email: redaktion@sbssyd.dk
Web site: http://www.sbssyd.dk/

SBS-NET -ØSTJYLLAND 634880
Gunnar Clausensvej 66, 8260 VIBY J.
Tel: 70 10 00 98. **Fax:** 70 10 00 08.
Email: redaktionen@tvdanmark.dk
Web site: http://www.tvdanmark.dk

SBS-NET -VESTSJÆLLAND 634881
Dania 38, 4700 NÆSTVED **Tel:** 72 45 11 00.
Fax: 72 45 11 17.
Email: stst@sj-medier.dk
Web site: http://www.sj-medier.dk

TV 2 / MIDT-VEST 630364
Søvej 2, 7500 HOLSTEBRO **Tel:** 96 12 12 12.
Fax: 96121213.
Email: redaktionen@tvmidtvest.dk
Web site: http://www.tvmidtvest.dk

VESTERBRO LOKAL TV 3577
Lyrskovgade 4, DK-1758 KØBENHAVN V
Tel: 33 88 89 94.
Email: vltv@hotmail.com
Web site: http://www.vesterbrolokaltv.dk/
Editor: Kai Mikkelsen

CABLE TV

TV3 / TV3+ 3399
Wildersgade 8, 1408 KØBENHAVN K
Tel: 77 30 55 00. **Fax:** 77 30 55 10.
Email: tv3@viasat.dk
Web site: http://www.tv3.dk

NATIONAL RADIO STATIONS

DR P1 759100
Emil Holms Kanal 20, DK-0999 KØBENHAVN C **Tel:** 35 20 30 40.
Fax: 35 20 62 17.
Email: p1online@dr.dk
Web site: http://www.dr.dk/p1

REGIONAL RADIO STATIONS

AMAGER LANDS LOKALRADIO 3436
Amager Boulevard 126, 2300 KØBENHAVN S **Tel:** 32 54 35 20. **Fax:** 32 59 58 76.
Email: post@amagerlandslokalradio.dk
Web site: http://www.amagerlandslokalradio.dk

FRELSENS HÆRS NÆRRADIO 3447
Frederiksberg Allé 9, DK-1621 KØBENHAVN V **Tel:** 33 31 41 25. **Fax:** 33 25 30 80.
Email: frelsens@den.salvationarmy.org
Web site: http://www.frelsens-haer.dk

LOKALRADIOERNE I BRØNDERSLEV 3465
Algade 32, 1., DK-9700 BRØNDERSLEV
Tel: 98 80 15 55. **Fax:** 98 80 15 66.
Email: bjarne@9700.dk
Web site: http://www.9700.dk
Editor: Bjarne Axelsen

LØKKEN-VRÅ NÆRRADIO 3466
Stadionvej 11, DK-9760 VRÅ
Tel: 98 98 19 99. **Fax:** 98 98 22 23.
Email: lvn@radiolvn.dk
Web site: http://www.radiolvn.dk
Editor: Jeppe Larsen-Ledet

MIDTFJORD RADIO 3467
Købmagergade 14, DK-9670 LØGSTØR
Tel: 98 67 41 00. **Fax:** 98 67 38 16.
Email: mail@midtfjordradio.dk

NORDSJÆLLANDS LOKALRADIO-RADIO KATTEGAT 3471
Stationsvej 6, DK-3210 VEJBY
Tel: 48 70 57 87. **Fax:** 48 70 58 27.
Email: kattegat@post5.tele.dk
Web site: http://www.radiokattegat.dk
Editor: Belinda Nielsen

RADIO 1 3518
Fredensgade 1, 8600 SILKEBORG
Tel: 86 81 65 66. **Fax:** 86 81 05 59.
Email: redaktion@radio1.nu
Web site: http://www.radio1.nu

RADIO AKTIV 3478
Postbox 267, 5700 SVENDBORG
Tel: 62 22 28 28. **Fax:** 62 22 33 79.
Email: kontor@radioaktiv.dk
Web site: http://www.radioaktiv.dk
Editor: Max Rask

RADIO ALS+ØNR 3480
Peblingestien 1, DK-6430 NORDBORG
Tel: 74 45 10 10. **Fax:** 74 45 07 00.
Email: radioals@radioals.dk
Web site: http://www.radioals.dk
Editor: Hardy Antonsen

RADIO CHARLIE 3483
Sct. Nikolaj Kirke Plads, DK-6800 VARDE
Tel: 75 22 54 22. **Fax:** 75 22 53 30.
Email: charlie@radiocharlie.dk
Web site: http://www.radiocharlie.dk

RADIO HALSNÆS 3491
Nørregade 7, DK-3390 HUNDESTED
Tel: 47 98 02 03.
Email: radio@1045fm.dk
Web site: http://www.1045fm.dk
Presenter: Martin Jørgensen

RADIO HORSENS 3499
Nørregade 42, DK-8700 HORSENS
Tel: 76 27 20 70. **Fax:** 75 61 83 22.
Email: radiohorsens@radiohorsens.dk
Web site: http://www.radiohorsens.dk
Presenter: Flemming Jensen

RADIO HUMLEBORG 3500
Nørredamsvej 18, DK-3480 FREDENSBORG
Tel: 48 47 59 00. **Fax:** 48 48 33 50.
Email: radio@humleborg.dk
Web site: http://www.humleborg.dk/
Editor: Kurt Kammersgaard

RADIO KLITHOLM 3502
Nørregade 4, DK-6960 HVIDE SANDE
Tel: 97 31 23 44. **Fax:** 97 31 24 83.
Email: post@radioklitholm.dk
Web site: http://www.radioklitholm.dk

RADIO KØGE 3503
P.O. Box 222, Astersvej 23 B, 4600 KØGE
Tel: 56 65 52 22. **Fax:** 56 66 29 27.
Email: radio@radio-koege.dk
Web site: http://www.radio-koege.dk

RADIO LANGELAND 3504
Ahlefeldtsgade 13-15, DK-5900 RUDKØBING **Tel:** 62 51 45 46.
Fax: 62 51 45 43.
Email: post@radio-langeland.dk
Web site: http://www.radio-langeland.dk
Editor: Kurt Karlsson

RADIO MOJN 3509
P.O. Box 44, DK-6200 AABENRAA
Tel: 74 62 63 49. **Fax:** 74 62 57 76.
Email: redaktion@mojn.dk
Web site: http://www.mojn.dk

RADIO ØST SMBA 3514
Kongensgade 30 A, DK-9293 KONGERSLEV
Tel: 98 33 21 99. **Fax:** 98 33 21 97.
Email: info@radiooest.dk
Web site: http://www.radiooest.dk/
Editor: Ronny Jensen

RADIO SKIVE 3521
Nordbanevej 1, 7800 SKIVE
Tel: 97 52 77 22. **Fax:** 97 52 01 19.
Email: radioskive@radioskive.dk
Web site: http://www.radioskive.dk/

RADIO SLR 3522
Dania 28, DK-4700 NÆSTVED
Tel: 72 45 11 00. **Fax:** 72 45 11 08.
Email: radioredaktion@sj-medier.dk
Web site: http://www.radioslr.dk

RADIO SYDHAVSØERNE 3525
Tværgade 16, DK-4800 NYKØBING F
Tel: 54 88 03 45. **Fax:** 54 82 22 28.
Email: redaktion@sydhavsradio.dk
Web site: http://www.sydhavsradio.dk

RADIO VALDE 3530
Rådhustorvet 5-7, DK-4760 VORDINGBORG
Tel: 55 34 00 01. **Fax:** 55 34 00 05.
Email: radiovalde@radiovalde.dk
Web site: http://www.radiovalde.dk
Editor: John Nielsen

RADIO VIBORG HIT FM 3533
Vesterbrogade 9, DK-8800 VIBORG
Tel: 86 61 02 00. **Fax:** 86 61 02 11.
Email: kontakt@radioviborg.dk
Web site: http://radioviborg.dk/

RADIONET 3437
Rhikimäkivej 6, DK-9200 AALBORG
Tel: 94 34 99 34. **Fax:** 99 34 99 01.
Email: kontakt@guld.fm
Web site: http://www.radionet.dk

RINGKØBING LOKALRADIO 3538
Reberbanen 51, DK-6950 RINGKØBING
Tel: 97 32 24 44. **Fax:** 97 32 37 59.
Email: kontakt@radioringkobing.dk
Web site: www.radioringkobing.dk
Editor: Peter Haue

RØDOVRE KANALEN 3541
Højnæsvej 63, DK-2610 RØDOVRE
Tel: 36 72 11 22. **Fax:** 36 72 32 12.
Email: radio@foreningshuset.dk
Web site: http://www.foreningshuset.dk
Editor: Flemming Riedel

SKALA FM 3520
Dalbygade 40, DK-6000 KOLDING
Tel: 79 12 45 00. **Fax:** 75 53 21 44.
Email: nyheder@skala.fm
Web site: http://www.skalafm.dk

STEVNS LOKALRADIO 3547
Rengegade 7, DK-4660 STORE HEDDINGE
Tel: 56 50 42 40. **Fax:** 56 50 42 52.
Email: slr@stevnslokalradio.dk
Web site: http://www.stevnslokalradio.dk/

VLR 3558
Nyboesgade 35, 7100 VEJLE
Tel: 76 40 04 00. **Fax:** 76 40 04 01.
Email: nyhed@vlr.dk
Web site: http://www.vlr.dk/

Estonia

NATIONAL TV STATIONS

CITV 1644209
Jõe 5, 10151 TALLINN **Tel:** 6 99 96 03.
Fax: 6 99 96 01.
Email: citv@citv.ee
Web site: http://www.citv.ee/index.htm

EESTI TELEVISIOON 1644212
Gonsiori 27, 15029 TALLINN **Tel:** 6 28 41 00.
Fax: 6 28 41 55.
Email: err@err.ee
Web site: http://etv.err.ee/
Editor: Ainar Ruusaar

KANAL 2 1600476
Maakri 23 A, 10145 TALLINN
Tel: 6 66 24 50. **Fax:** 6 66 24 51.
Email: info@kanal2.ee
Web site: http://www.kanal2.ee
Editor: Olle Mirme

Estonia

PERVÕI BALTIISKI KANAL
1644377
Pärnu mnt 139 C, 11317 TALLINN
Tel: 6 78 87 92. **Fax:** 6 78 87 01.
Email: mmerima@sky.ee
Web site: http://www.1tv.lv/1tv.nsf/(main1)?OpenAgent&lang=4
Editor: Margus Merima

TV3
1600477
Peterburi Str. 81, 11415 TALLINN
Tel: 6 22 02 20. **Fax:** 6 22 02 21.
Email: tv3@tv3.ee
Web site: http://www.tv3.ee
Editor: Sven Soiver

NATIONAL RADIO STATIONS

ENERGY FM
1644215
Pärnu mnt 139 C, 11317 TALLINN
Tel: 6 788700. **Fax:** 6 78 87 01.
Email: info@energyfm.ee
Web site: http://www.energyfm.ee/
Editor: Margus Müürsepp

KLASSIKARAADIO
763007
Kreutzwaldi 14, 10124 TALLINN
Tel: 611 4121. **Fax:** 6 11 44 28.
Email: klassika@err.ee
Web site: http://klassikaraadio.err.ee

KUKU
1644262
Veerenni 58A, 11314 TALLINN
Tel: 6 30 70 31. **Fax:** 6 30 70 88.
Email: kuku@kuku.ee
Web site: www.kuku.ee
Editor: Ave Marleen

RAADIO 2
1600457
Gonsiori 21, 15020 TALLINN **Tel:** 6 11 42 00.
Fax: 6 114441.
Email: r2@er.ee
Web site: http://www.r2.ee

RAADIO 4
1600458
Gonsiori 21, 15020 TALLINN **Tel:** 6 11 41 26.
Fax: 6 11 41 46.
Email: raadio4@err.ee
Web site: http://r4.err.ee
Editor: Andrey Sozinov

RAADIO 7
1615354
PK 3396, 10506 TALLINN **Tel:** 6 60 78 30.
Fax: 6 60 78 28.
Email: raadio7@raadio7.ee
Web site: http://www.raadio7.ee
Editor: Anti Tiik; *Producer:* Alice Tiik

RAADIO ELMAR
763074
Õpetajate 9 A, 51005 TARTU **Tel:** 7 42 75 20.
Fax: 6 30 70 88.
Email: elmar@elmar.ee
Web site: http://www.elmar.ee
Editor: Taivo Nigol

RAADIO UUNO
765703
Narva mnt. 63, 10152 TALLINN
Tel: 6 30 70 80. **Fax:** 6 30 70 85.
Email: uuno@uuno.ee
Web site: http://www.uuno.ee
Editor: Doris Vija

RAADIO VIRU
1644417
Ragavere tee 35, 45312 RAKVERE
Tel: 3 223905.
Email: info@raadioviru.ee
Web site: http://www.raadioviru.ee
Editor: Tanel Raudla

VIKERRAADIO
763003
Gonsiori 21, 15020 TALLINN **Tel:** 6 11 43 18.
Fax: 6 11 41 24.
Email: viker@er.ee
Web site: http://www.er.ee/viker/
Editor: Riina Roomus; *Director:* Riina Roomus

Finland

NATIONAL TV STATIONS

FST5 NYHETSVERKSAMHETEN
705592
PB 10, 00024 RUNDRADION
Tel: 9 14 80 47 52. **Fax:** 9 14 80 40 82.
Email: tv-nytt@yle.fi
Web site: http://svenska.yle.fi/nyheter
Director: Gunilla Ohls

MTV3 FINLAND
15174
Ilmalantori 2, 00033 MTV **Tel:** 10 30 03 00.
Email: uutissuunnittelu@mtv3.fi
Web site: http://www.mtv3.fi
Producer: Onerva Österberg

MTV3 UUTISTOIMINTA
705689
Ilmalantori 2, 00033 MTV3 **Tel:** 10 30 03 00.
Fax: 9 14 01 60.
Email: uutiset@mtv3.fi
Web site: http://www.mtv3.fi/tieto
Presenter: Tanja Huutonen; *Producer:* Jukka Vuori

RUUTUNELONEN AB
713065
PL 350/ Tehtaankatu 27-29 C, 00151 HELSINKI **Tel:** 9 45 451.
Email: uutiset@nelonen.fi
Web site: http://www.ruutu.fi
Director: Kristiina Werner-Autio

YLE AJANKOHTAISOHJELMAT
705601
PL 79, 00024 YLEISRADIO **Tel:** 9 14 801.
Email: yle.uutiset@yle.fi
Web site: http://www.yle.fi/a2
Presenter: Baba Lybeck

YLE TV-UUTISET SUUNNITTELU
705687
PL 10/Radiokatu 5, 00024 YLEISRADIO
Tel: 9 14 801.
Email: yle.uutiset@yle.fi
Web site: http://www.yle.fi/uutiset
Producer: Riitta Jäälinoja

YLEISRADIO OY AB
15175
Radiokatu 5, 00240 HELSINKI **Tel:** 9 14 801.
Web site: http://www.yle.fi
Director: Riitta Pihlajamäki; *Producer:* Seppo Rokka

REGIONAL TV STATIONS

DIGGARI
705685
PL 1506/ Kiveläntie 4, 70461 KUOPIO
Tel: 44 22 020.
Web site: http://www.diggari.fi

K5
705561
PL 99/ Kosti Aaltosen tie 9, 80141 JOENSUU
Tel: 13 25 51. **Fax:** 132552363.
Email: toimitus@k5mediat.fi
Web site: http://www.karjalainen.fi

MTV3 ALUETOIMITUS JOENSUU
705578
Länsikatu 15, 80110 JOENSUU
Tel: 13 26 37 300.
Web site: http://www.mtv3.fi

MTV3 ALUETOIMITUS OULU
705582
Kirkkokatu 19 A 11, 90100 OULU
Tel: 40 82 26 688.
Email: hannu.alsta@mtv3.fi
Web site: http://www.mtv3.fi/toimitus/alueet.html

MTV3 ALUETOIMITUS TAMPERE
705584
Hallituskatu 16, 33200 TAMPERE
Tel: 10 30 95 300. **Fax:** 32166222.
Email: tuula.malin@mtv3.fi
Web site: http://www.mtv3.fi

SUB
706632
Ilmalantori 2, 00033 MTV **Tel:** 10 30 03 00.
Fax: 10 30 05 487.
Web site: http://www.sub.fi

TURKU TV
705686
PL 95/ Kauppiaskatu 5, 20101 TURKU
Tel: 2 26 93 311.
Email: turkutv@turunsanomat.fi
Web site: http://www.turkutv.fi

TV-UUTISET ALUETOIMITUS KUOPIO
705997
PL 99/ Kotkankallionkatu 12, 70101 KUOPIO
Tel: 17 24 71 11. **Fax:** 172478990.
Email: pekka.niiranen@yle.fi
Web site: http://yle.fi/uutiset

TV-UUTISET ALUETOIMITUS OULU
705998
PL 277/ Sepänkatu 20, 90101 OULU
Tel: 8 53 73 800. **Fax:** 85371100.
Email: leena.rimpilainen@yle.fi
Web site: http://yle.fi/uutiset

TV-UUTISET ALUETOIMITUS ROVANIEMI
705999
PL 8113/ Jorma Eton tie 8, 96101 ROVANIEMI **Tel:** 16 30 06 073.
Fax: 16 33 06 005.
Email: matti.torvinen@yle.fi
Web site: http://www.yle.fi/uutiset

TV-UUTISET ALUETOIMITUS TAMPERE
706000
PL 110/ Vuolteenkatu 20, 33101 TAMPERE
Tel: 3 34 56 822. **Fax:** 3 34 56 910.
Email: heli.mansikka@yle.fi
Web site: http://www.yle.fi/uutiset

TV-UUTISET ALUETOIMITUS TURKU
706001
PL 400/ Aurakatu 8, 20101 TURKU
Tel: 2 27 09 00. **Fax:** 22717997.
Email: pirjo.peltoniemi@yle.fi
Web site: http://www.yle.fi/uutiset

TV-UUTISET ALUETOIMITUS VAASA
706002
PL 1000/ Ahventie 20, 65101 VAASA
Tel: 6 22 98 604. **Fax:** 62298606.
Email: hannu.puikkonen@yle.fi
Web site: http://www.yle.fi/tvuutiset

NATIONAL DIGITAL TV

FST5
717752
PB 83, 00024 RUNDRADION
Tel: 9 14 80 33 01. **Fax:** 9 14 80 40 82.
Email: fst@yle.fi
Web site: http://svenska.yle.fi/fst5
Producer: Robert Tamm

NELONEN PRO
717756
Tehtaankatu 27-29 D, 00151 HELSINKI
Tel: 9 45 451. **Fax:** 9 87 77 467.
Email: info@urheilukanava.fi
Web site: http://www.nelonenpro.fi

YLE TEEMA
717755
PL 97, 00024 YLEISRADIO **Tel:** 9 14 801.
Fax: 9 14 80 24 21.
Web site: http://www.yle.fi/teema

YLE.FI
705638
PL 24, 00024 YLEISRADIO **Tel:** 9 14 801.
Email: yle.uutiset@yle.fi
Web site: http://www.yle.fi/uutiset
Producer: Elina Yli-Ojanperä

NATIONAL RADIO STATIONS

ÅLANDS RADIO OCH TV AB
705568
PB 140/Ålandsvägen 24, 22101 MARIEHAMN **Tel:** 18 26 060.
Fax: 18 26 520.
Email: redaktion@radiotv.ax
Web site: http://www.radiotv.aland.fi
Producer: Tom Wiklund

ISKELMÄRADIO
749745
PL 957/ Kehräsaari B 5, 33101 TAMPERE
Tel: 20 74 74 100. **Fax:** 20 74 74 129.
Web site: http://www.iskelma.fi

NRJ (RADIO ENERGY) HELSINKI
705915
Kiviaidankatu 2 I, 00210 HELSINKI
Tel: 9 68 19 00. **Fax:** 9 68 19 01 02.
Web site: http://www.nrj.fi
Presenter: Renne Korppila; *Producer:* Annika Takaniemi

RADIO GROOVE FM & SUOMIPOP & METRO FM
706401
Pursimiehenkatu 29-31 C, 00150 HELSINKI
Tel: 20 77 68 360.
Web site: http://www.metroradio.fi
Presenter: Minni Salminen

RADIO NOVA
15415
PL 123/ Ilmalankatu 2 C, 00241 HELSINKI
Tel: 10 30 01 00. **Fax:** 10 30 05 637.
Email: toimitus@radionova.fi
Web site: http://www.radionova.fi
Presenter: Ile Jokinen

RADIO ROCK & RADIO AALTO
705802
PL 350/ Tehtaankatu 27-29 A, 00151 HELSINKI **Tel:** 9 45 45 250.
Email: uutiset@radioaalto.fi
Web site: http://www.radiorock.fi
Presenter: Jussi Heikelä; *Producer:* Paula Niska

RADIOMEDIA RY
15173
PL 312/ Lönnrotinkatu 11 A, 00121 HELSINKI **Tel:** 9 22 87 73 40.
Fax: 9 64 82 21.
Email: info@radiomedia.fi
Web site: http://www.radiomedia.fi

YLE NYHETER
705575
PB 62, 00024 RUNDRADION **Tel:** 9 14 801.
Email: nyheter@yle.fi
Web site: http://www.yle.fi/fsr
Producer: Stefan Brunow

YLE RADIO 1
705832
PL 6/ Radiokatu 5, 00024 YLEISRADIO
Tel: 9 14 801. **Fax:** 9 14 80 44 06.
Email: yle.radio1@yle.fi
Web site: http://www.yleradio1.fi
Presenter: Timo Tersävuori

YLE RADIO PUHE
706406
PL 57, 00024 YLEISRADIO **Tel:** 9 14 801.
Fax: 9 14 80 83 30.
Email: radiouutiset@yle.fi
Web site: http://www.yle.fi/puhe
Producer: Tapio Kaartinen

YLE RADIO SUOMI AJANTASA
706357
PL 57/ Radiokatu 5, 00024 YLEISRADIO
Tel: 9 14 801. **Fax:** 9 14 80 51 80.
Email: radio.suomi@yle.fi
Web site: http://yle.fi/radiosuomi

YLE RADIO VEGA
706251
PB 62, 00024 RUNDRADION **Tel:** 9 14 801.
Fax: 9 14 80 24 98.
Email: aktuellt@yle.fi
Web site: http://www.yle.fi/vega

YLE VENÄJÄNKIELINEN TOIMITUS 752890
PL 3, 00024 YLEISRADIO **Tel:** 9 14 80 48 91.
Fax: 9 14 80 51 48.
Email: radio.finland@yle.fi
Web site: http://www.yle.fi/rfinland
Producer: Heidi Zidan

YLEN RADIOIDEN UUTISTOIMINTA 705565
PL 3/ Radiokatu 5, 00024 YLEISRADIO
Tel: 9 14 801. **Fax:** 9 14 80 24 65.
Email: radiouutiset@yle.fi
Web site: http://yle.fi/uutiset
Producer: Inkeri Kuisma

YLEX 705569
PL 17/ Radiokatu 5 D, 00024 YLEISRADIO
Tel: 9 14 801. **Fax:** 9 14 82 650.
Email: ylex.toimitus@yle.fi
Web site: http://www.yle.fi/ylex

REGIONAL RADIO STATIONS

ISKELMÄ JANNE 705806
Vanajantie 7, 13110 HÄMEENLINNA
Tel: 3 61 51 371. **Fax:** 3 65 37 033.
Email: radiojanne@hameensanomat.fi
Web site: http://www.radiojanne.fi

ISKELMÄ OIKEA ASEMA 706624
Sammonkatu 16 A, 70500 KUOPIO
Tel: 17 28 96 700. **Fax:** 17 28 26 760.
Email: toimitus@oikeaasema.fi
Web site: http://www.oikeaasema.fi

ISKELMÄ POHJANMAA 705817
Puistotie 2, 62100 LAPUA **Tel:** 6 42 32 900.
Email: hannu.harju@nic.fi
Web site: http://www.radiopaitapiiska.fi

ISKELMÄ SATAKUNTA 705815
Kappelikuja 3, 32700 HUITTINEN
Tel: 2 56 01 000. **Fax:** 2 56 62 20.
Email: toimitus@iskelmasatakunta.fi
Web site: http://www.iskelmasatakunta.fi

JÄRVIRADIO 15231
Kiertotie 5, 62900 ALAJÄRVI
Tel: 6 55 72 345. **Fax:** 6 55 72 899.
Email: jr@jarviradio.fi
Web site: http://www.jarviradio.fi
Presenter: Hannu Matintupa

KANSAN RADIO 705496
Hämeentie 32, 00530 HELSINKI
Tel: 9 70 13 300. **Fax:** 9 70 11 033.
Email: lahi.radio@kara.inet.fi
Web site: http://www.kansanradioliitto.fi

LÄHIRADIO KSL 705502
Hämeentie 36, 00530 HELSINKI
Tel: 9 22 94 21.
Web site: http://www.lahiradio.fi
Producer: Olli Sydänmaa

OIKEA ASEMA IISALMI 705820
Pohjolankatu 5, 74100 IISALMI
Tel: 17 82 19 111. **Fax:** 17 81 47 75.
Email: toimitus@oikeaasema.fi
Web site: http://www.oikeaasema.fi

RADIO 957 705808
PL 957/ Kehräsaari B porras, 5 krs, 33101 TAMPERE **Tel:** 20 74 74 100.
Fax: 20 74 74 129.
Email: tero.kainulainen@radio957.fi
Web site: http://www.radio957.fi
Presenter: Antti Granlund; *Producer:* Joni Hartikainen

RADIO AURAN AALLOT 15232
Yliopistonkatu 14, 20100 TURKU
Tel: 2 26 93 905. **Fax:** 2 47 82 658.
Email: auran.aallot@auranaallot.fi
Web site: http://www.auranaallot.fi

RADIO EXTREM (X3M) 706009
PB 13/ Radiogatan 5, 00024 RUNDRADION
Tel: 9 14 80 23 04. **Fax:** 9 14 80 46 66.
Email: hotline@yle.fi
Web site: http://www.yle.fi/extrem
Producer: Kristian Martikainen

RADIO EXTREM (X3M) VASA 706010
PB 1000, 65101 VASA **Tel:** 6 22 981.
Web site: http://www.yle.fi/extrem

RADIO HELSINKI 749635
PL 80/ Töölönlahdenkatu 2, 00085 SANOMA
Tel: 9 12 22 794.
Email: palaute@radiohelsinki.fi
Web site: http://www.radiohelsinki.fi
Producer: Jyrki Jantunen

RADIO JYVÄSKYLÄ 718494
PL 480/ Väinönkatu 26 A, 40101 JYVÄSKYLÄ **Tel:** 20 74 74 150.
Fax: 20 74 74 159.
Email: toimitus@radiojkl.fi
Web site: http://www.radiojkl.fi
Producer: Jari Lindström

RADIO KAJAUS 705823
PL 230/ Kauppakatu 21, 87101 KAJAANI
Tel: 8 62 99 57. **Fax:** 8624114.
Email: kajaus.toimitus@radiokajaus.fi
Web site: http://www.radiokajaus.fi

RADIO MANTA 705809
PL 101/Hopunkatu 1, 38201 SASTAMALA
Tel: 3 51 41 416.
Email: toimitus@radiomanta.fi
Web site: http://www.radiomanta.fi

RADIO MELODIA 706575
Yliopistonkatu 14, 20100 TURKU
Tel: 2 26 93 890. **Fax:** 24782658.
Email: info@radiomelodia.fi
Web site: http://www.radiomelodia.fi
Presenter: Eero Karisalmi; *Producer:* Ilona Puttonen

RADIO POOKI 705822
Niittykatu 5 C 3, 92100 RAAHE
Tel: 8 21 18 200. **Fax:** 8 21 18 210.
Email: toimitus.raahe@radiopooki.fi
Web site: http://www.radiopooki.fi

RADIO PORI 705814
Itäpuisto 3, 28100 PORI **Tel:** 2 62 02 550.
Fax: 2 62 02 575.
Email: toimitus@radiopori.fi
Web site: http://www.radiopori.fi
Presenter: Satu Saarivuori

RADIO PRO 705498
Urheilukatu 6, 95400 TORNIO
Tel: 16 45 13 42.
Email: info@radiopro.fi
Web site: http://www.radiopro.fi

RADIO RAMONA 705816
PL 5/ Eteläkatu 31, 26101 RAUMA
Tel: 10 83 36 551. **Fax:** 108336293.
Email: ramona@radioramona.fi
Web site: http://www.radioramona.fi
Presenter: Risto Leino

RADIO REX 15236
PL 928/ Malmikatu 5 B II krs, 80101 JOENSUU **Tel:** 13 24 89 281.
Fax: 13 24 89 290.
Email: toimitus@radiorex.fi
Web site: http://www.radiorex.fi

RADIO ROBIN HOOD 705824
Itäinen Rantakatu 64 b, 20810 TURKU
Tel: 2 27 73 666. **Fax:** 2 25 00 905.
Email: info@radiorobinhood.fi
Web site: http://www.radiorobinhood.fi

RADIO SATA 705813
Läntinen Rantakatu 53, 2 krs, 20100 TURKU
Tel: 20 74 74 170. **Fax:** 20 74 74 179.
Email: toimitus@sata.fi
Web site: http://www.sata.fi
Presenter: Anne Ylitalo

RADIO SPUTNIK 749740
Kauppakartanonkatu 7 A 2, 00930 HELSINKI
Tel: 9 34 36 300. **Fax:** 9 34 36 30 30.
Email: info@radiosputnik.fi
Web site: http://www.radiosputnik.fi
News Editor: Irina Kuzmina; *Presenter:* Natalia Erchova

RADIO VAASA 15237
PL 371/ Hovioikeudenpuistikko 16, 65101 VAASA **Tel:** 6 32 03 910. **Fax:** 6 31 26 410.
Email: toimitus@radiovaasa.fi
Web site: http://www.radiovaasa.fi

RADIO VOIMA 705835
PL 80/ Aleksanterinkatu 10, 15101 LAHTI
Tel: 3 75 75 986. **Fax:** 3 75 75 486.
Email: toimitus@radiovoima.fi
Web site: http://www.radiovoima.fi

SUN FM 705811
PL 67/ Pilvilinnankatu 1, 39501 IKAALINEN
Tel: 3 45 87 787. **Fax:** 34586226.
Email: toimitus@radiosun.fi
Web site: http://www.radiosun.fi
Producer: Beni Siltala

YLE ETELÄ-KARJALAN RADIO LAPPEENRANTA 705533
PL 100/ Kristiinankatu 11 A, 53101 LAPPEENRANTA **Tel:** 5 63 031.
Fax: 5 45 30 577.
Email: ekradio.toimitus@yle.fi
Web site: http://yle.fi/alueet/etela-karjala
Producer: Vesa Winberg

YLE ETELÄ-SAVON RADIO MIKKELI 705532
PL 361/ Vilhonkatu 11, 50101 MIKKELI
Tel: 15 41 57 70. **Fax:** 15 41 57 745.
Email: toimitus.esradio@yle.fi
Web site: http://www.etelasavonradio.fi
Producer: Satu Haapanen

YLE ETELÄ-SAVON RADIO SAVONLINNA 705530
Olavinkatu 24, 57130 SAVONLINNA
Tel: 15 41 57 70. **Fax:** 154157745.
Email: toimitus.esradio@yle.fi
Web site: http://www.etelasavonradio.fi

YLE KAINUUN RADIO KAJAANI 705545
PL 111/ Lönnrotinkatu 14 B, 87101 KAJAANI
Tel: 8 61 98 80 60. **Fax:** 8624190.
Email: kainuunradio@yle.fi
Web site: http://yle.fi/alueet/kainuu
Presenter: Jari Sirviö; *Producer:* Kari Repo

YLE KYMENLAAKSON RADIO KOTKA 705535
PL 229/ Ruotsinsalmenkatu 12, 48101 KOTKA **Tel:** 5 81 37 300. **Fax:** 206011031.
Email: kymenlaaksonradio@yle.fi
Web site: http://yle.fi/alueet/kymenlaakso
Producer: Maija Tuunila

YLE KYMENLAAKSON RADIO KOUVOLA 705534
PL 192/ Salpausselänkatu 40, 45101 KOUVOLA **Tel:** 5 81 37 300.
Fax: 206011031.
Email: kymenlaaksonradio@yle.fi
Web site: http://yle.fi/alueet/kymenlaakso

YLE LAHDEN RADIO 705524
PL 120/ Aleksanterinkatu 8, 15111 LAHTI
Tel: 3 46 86 900. **Fax:** 37825127.
Email: lahden.radio@yle.fi
Web site: http://yle.fi/alueet/lahti
Producer: Suvi Turunen

YLE LAPIN RADIO INARI 706526
PL 38/ Menesjärventie 2, 99871 INARI
Tel: 16 67 57 500. **Fax:** 166757501.
Email: lapinradio@yle.fi
Web site: http://yle.fi/alueet/lappi

YLE LAPIN RADIO KEMIJÄRVI 705541
PL 64/ Kuumaniemenkatu 2, 98101 KEMIJÄRVI **Tel:** 16 81 34 24.
Fax: 16813401.
Email: lapinradio@yle.fi
Web site: http://yle.fi/alueet/lappi

YLE LAPIN RADIO ROVANIEMI 705539
PL 8113/ Jorma Etontie 8, 96101 ROVANIEMI **Tel:** 16 33 06 000.
Fax: 16 33 06 005.
Email: lapinradio@yle.fi
Web site: http://yle.fi/alueet/lappi
Producer: Juha Mäntykenttä

YLE OULU RADIO KUUSAMO 705547
Kuusamotalo, Kitkantie 4, 93600 KUUSAMO
Tel: 8 85 11 833. **Fax:** 88521822.
Email: ouluradio@yle.fi
Web site: http://www.ouluradio.fi

YLE OULU RADIO OULU 706528
PL 277/ Sepänkatu 20, 90101 OULU
Tel: 8 53 73 800. **Fax:** 85371100.
Email: ouluradio@yle.fi
Web site: http://www.ouluradio.fi
Presenter: Anna Keränen; *Producer:* Arto Veräjänkorva

YLE OULU RADIO YLIVIESKA 705549
Torikatu 3 A 25, 84100 YLIVIESKA
Tel: 8 42 07 33.
Email: ouluradio@yle.fi
Web site: http://www.ouluradio.fi

YLE POHJANMAAN RADIO SEINÄJOKI 705552
PL 1000/ Marttilantie 24, 60101 SEINÄJOKI
Tel: 6 21 18 400. **Fax:** 64142892.
Email: pora@yle.fi
Web site: http://yle.fi/alueet/pohjanmaa
Director: Anssi Leppänen; *Presenter:* Terttu Karhumaa

YLE POHJANMAAN RADIO VAASA 705550
PL 1000/ Ahventie 20, 65101 VAASA
Tel: 6 22 981. **Fax:** 63179141.
Email: pora@yle.fi
Web site: http://yle.fi/alueet/pohjanmaa
Director: Anssi Leppänen; *Presenter:* Antti Haavisto

YLE POHJOIS-KARJALAN RADIO 705529
PL 206/ Kirkkokatu 20, 80101 JOENSUU
Tel: 13 51 07 450. **Fax:** 13 51 07 451.
Email: pohjoiskarjalan.radio@yle.fi
Web site: http://yle.fi/alueet/pohjois-karjala
Producer: Tapio Laakkonen

YLE RADIO HÄME 705525
Viipurintie 4 E, 13200 HÄMEENLINNA
Tel: 3 54 46 969. **Fax:** 35446968.
Email: radiohame@yle.fi
Web site: http://yle.fi/alueet/hame
Producer: Maarit Piri-Lahti

YLE RADIO HÄME FORSSA 705526
Hämeentie 7 II krs, 30100 FORSSA
Tel: 3 42 21 521. **Fax:** 34356168.
Email: radiohame@yle.fi
Web site: http://yle.fi/alueet/hame

YLE RADIO ITÄ-UUSIMAA 705560
PL 903/ Rihkamakatu 2, 06101 PORVOO
Tel: 9 14 80 88 35. **Fax:** 195245230.
Web site: http://yle.fi/alueet/helsinki/radio-ita-uusimaa
Producer: Marja Karjalainen

Finland

YLE RADIO KESKI-POHJANMAA 705551
PL 1000/ Rantakatu 16, 67101 KOKKOLA
Tel: 6 21 98 100. **Fax:** 68220733.
Email: radiokeskipohjanmaa@yle.fi
Web site: http://yle.fi/alueet/keski-pohjanmaa
Presenter: Kati Latva-Teikari

YLE RADIO KESKI-SUOMI 705537
PL 3/ Kauppakatu 33, 40101 JYVÄSKYLÄ
Tel: 14 44 58 211. **Fax:** 144458215.
Email: rks@yle.fi
Web site: http://yle.fi/alueet/keski-suomi
Producer: Arvo Vuorela

YLE RADIO PERÄMERI KEMI 705540
PL 202/ Torikatu 4, 94101 KEMI
Tel: 16 33 57 400. **Fax:** 163357405.
Email: radioperameri@yle.fi
Web site: http://yle.fi/alueet/perameri
Producer: Jari Peltoperä

YLE RADIO SAVO KUOPIO 705730
PL 99/ Kotkankallionkatu 12, 70101 KUOPIO
Tel: 17 24 78 900. **Fax:** 172478990.
Email: radiosavo@yle.fi
Web site: http://yle.fi/alueet/savo
Presenter: Petri Julkunen; *Producer:* Varpu Mäntymäki

YLE RADIO VEGA ÅBOLAND 705706
PB 400/ Auragatan 8, 20101 ÅBO
Tel: 2 27 17 855. **Fax:** 2 27 17 850.
Email: radiovega.aboland@yle.fi
Web site: http://www.yle.fi/vega
Presenter: Nilla Hansson

YLE RADIO VEGA ÅBOLAND I KIMITO 705544
Arkadiavägen 3, 25700 KIMITO
Tel: 2 42 17 77. **Fax:** 2423524.
Email: monica.forssell@yle.fi
Web site: http://www.yle.fi/vega

YLE RADIO VEGA HUVUDSTADSREGIONEN 705559
PB 87/ Radiogatan 5 A, 00024 RUNDRADION **Tel:** 9 14 801.
Fax: 914803421.
Email: vega.huvudstadsregionen@yle.fi
Web site: http://www.yle.fi/vega

YLE RADIO VEGA ÖSTERBOTTEN JAKOBSTAD 706422
Box 1000/ Rådhusgatan 11, 68601 JAKOBSTAD **Tel:** 6 22 98 444.
Fax: 67232466.
Email: radiovega.osterbotten@yle.fi
Web site: http://svenska.yle.fi//osterbotten

YLE RADIO VEGA ÖSTERBOTTEN VASA 706427
Box 1000/ Aborrvägen 20, 65101 VASA
Tel: 6 22 98 547. **Fax:** 63122807.
Email: radiovega.osterbotten@yle.fi
Web site: http://svenska.yle.fi//osterbotten
Producer: Malin Hulkki

YLE RADIO VEGA ÖSTNYLAND 705733
Krämaregatan 2, 06100 BORGÅ
Tel: 19 66 18 810. **Fax:** 195245230.
Email: radiovega.ostnyland@yle.fi
Web site: http://www.yle.fi/vega

YLE RADIO VEGA VÄSTNYLAND 705708
PB 33/ Långgatan 13, 10601 EKENÄS
Tel: 19 26 48 840. **Fax:** 192648854.
Email: radiovega.vastnyland@yle.fi
Web site: http://www.yle.fi/vega

YLE RADIO YLEN LÄNTINEN 705564
PL 86/ Laurinkatu 57 A, 08101 LOHJA
Tel: 9 14 80 88 80. **Fax:** 19318811.
Email: ylenlantinen@yle.fi
Web site: http://yle.fi/alueet/helsinki
Producer: Kirsi Väänänen

YLE SAAMEN RADIO UTSJOKI 705557
99980 UTSJOKI **Tel:** 16 67 73 55.
Fax: 16677480.
Email: sami.radio@yle.fi
Web site: http://www.yle.fi/samiradio

YLE SÁMI RADIO 705555
PL 38/ Tammukkatie, 99871 INARI
Tel: 16 67 57 500. **Fax:** 166757501.
Email: sami.radio@yle.fi
Web site: http://www.yle.fi/samiradio
Producer: Veikko Aikio

YLE SATAKUNNAN RADIO 705542
PL 113/ Mikonkatu 4 D, 28101 PORI
Tel: 2 55 57 950. **Fax:** 2 63 34 773.
Email: satakunta@yle.fi
Web site: http://yle.fi/sataradio
Producer: Mika Viljanen

YLE TAMPEREEN RADIO 705523
PL 110 /Vuolteenkatu 20, 33101 TAMPERE
Tel: 3 34 56 111. **Fax:** 32140900.
Email: tampereen.radio@yle.fi
Web site: http://yle.fi/alueet/tampere
Presenter: Mari Vesanummi; *Producer:* Kai Kostamo

YLE TURUN RADIO 705704
PL 400/ Aurakatu 8, 7 krs, 20101 TURKU
Tel: 2 27 09 00. **Fax:** 2 27 17 800.
Email: turku@yle.fi
Web site: http://www.turunradio.fi
Presenter: Kalle Talonen; *Producer:* Päivi Leppänen

YLE YLEN AIKAINEN HELSINKI 705558
PL 88/ Radiokatu 5, 00024 YLEISRADIO
Tel: 9 14 80 32 29. **Fax:** 914803271.
Email: ylen.aikainen@yle.fi
Web site: http://www.ylenaikainen.fi
Producer: Anne Achté

HOSPITAL RADIO

RADIO FOLKHÄLSAN 706219
Topeliusgatan 20, 00250 HELSINGFORS
Tel: 9 31 50 00. **Fax:** 9 31 55 102.
Email: radio@folkhalsan.fi
Web site: http://www.folkhalsan.fi

STUDENT RADIO

RADIO MOREENI 705501
Kalevantie 4, 33014 TAMPEREEN YLIOPISTO **Tel:** 3 35 51 69 46.
Fax: 3 35 51 72 50.
Email: moreeni@uta.fi
Web site: http://moreeni.uta.fi

France

NATIONAL TV STATIONS

ARTE 6127
ARTE GEIE, 4 quai du Chanoine Winterer, CS 20035 CEDEX, 67080 STRASBOURG
Tel: 3 88 14 22 22. **Fax:** 3 88 14 22 00.
Email: claude.savin@arte.tv
Web site: http://www.arte.tv

FRANCE 2 6133
France Télévisions, 7 esplanade Henri de France, CEDEX 15, 75907 PARIS
Tel: 1 56 22 42 42.
Email: contact@francetv.fr
Web site: http://www.france2.fr

FRANCE 3 7385
France Télévisions, 7 esplanade Henri de France, CEDEX 15, 75907 PARIS
Tel: 1 56 22 30 30.
Web site: http://www.france3.fr

FRANCE 5 6131
10 rue Horace Vernet, CEDEX 9, 92785 ISSY LES MOULINEAUX **Tel:** 1 56 22 91 91.
Fax: 1 56 22 95 95.
Web site: http://www.france5.fr

M6 6134
89 avenue Charles de Gaulle, CEDEX, 92575 NEUILLY SUR SEINE **Tel:** 1 41 92 66 66.
Fax: 1 41 92 66 10.
Email: pnom@m6.fr
Web site: http://www.m6.fr

TF1 6137
1 quai du Point du Jour, CEDEX, 92656 BOULOGNE BILLANCOURT
Tel: 1 41 41 12 34. **Fax:** 1 41 41 28 40.
Web site: http://www.tf1.fr

REGIONAL TV STATIONS

ATV 766174
Ruelle Saint Nicolas, 57360 AMNEVILLE-LES-THERMES **Tel:** 3 87 70 26 26.
Fax: 3 87 70 83 95.
Email: eatv@esathd.net
Web site: http://www.espace-atv.com

CANAL C 2117
Parvis des Esserts, 36 rue du Marcelly, 74300 CLUSES **Tel:** 4 50 96 20 10.
Fax: 4 50 96 29 58.
Web site: http://www.canalctv.fr

FRANCE 3 AQUITAINE 6348
136 rue Ernest Renan, CEDEX, 33075 BORDEAUX **Tel:** 5 56 01 39 00.
Fax: 5 56 51 02 87.
Email: redaction-bordeaux@francetv.fr
Web site: http://www.aquitaine.france3.fr

FRANCE 3 PARIS IDF CENTRE 6347
66 rue Jean Bleuzen, BP 42, CEDEX, 92170 VANVES **Tel:** 1 41 09 33 33.
Fax: 1 41 09 33 00.
Web site: http://www.france3.fr

SATELLITE TV

L' EQUIPE TV 6144
145 rue Jean Jacques Rousseau, CEDEX, 92138 ISSY LES MOULINEAUX
Tel: 1 41 23 30 00. **Fax:** 1 41 23 30 07.
Email: redaction@lequipe.fr
Web site: http://www.lequipetv.fr

EURONEWS 6145
60 chemin des Mouilles, BP 161, CEDEX, 69131 LYON ECULLY **Tel:** 4 72 18 80 00.
Fax: 4 78 33 27 17.
Web site: http://www.euronews.net

EUROSPORT FRANCE 6146
3 rue Gaston et René Caudron, CEDEX 9, 92798 ISSY LES MOULINEAUX
Tel: 1 40 93 80 00. **Fax:** 1 40 93 80 01.
Email: redaction.fr@eurosport.com
Web site: http://www.eurosport.fr

GAME ONE 6150
22 rue Jacques Dulud, CEDEX, 92521 NEUILLY SUR SEINE **Tel:** 1 70 94 94 94.
Fax: 1 70 94 94 95.
Web site: http://www.gameone.net

LCI - LA CHAINE INFO 622612
1 quai du Point du Jour, CEDEX, 92656 BOULOGNE BILLANCOURT
Tel: 1 41 41 23 45. **Fax:** 1 41 41 38 50.
Web site: http://www.tf1news.fr

NATIONAL RADIO STATIONS

BEUR FM PARIS 106.7 6107
Beur FM, BP 249, Cedex 11, 75524 PARIS
Tel: 8 9268 1067.
Email: redaction@beurfm.net
Web site: http://www.beurfm.net

CHERIE FM 6108
GROUPE NRJ, 22 rue Boileau, 75016 PARIS
Tel: 1 40 71 40 00. **Fax:** 1 40 71 41 32.
Web site: http://www.cheriefm.fr

EUROPE 1 6109
26 bis rue François 1er, 75008 PARIS
Tel: 820 31 90 00. **Fax:** 1 47 23 17 10.
Email: courrier@europe1.fr
Web site: http://www.europe1.fr

FRANCE INFO PARIS 105.5 6111
116 avenue du Président-Kennedy, 75220 CEDEX 16 PARIS **Tel:** 1 56 40 22 22.
Fax: 1 56 40 42 20.
Web site: http://www.france-info.com

FUN RADIO 6113
20 rue Bayard, 75008 PARIS
Tel: 1 40 70 48 48. **Fax:** 1 40 70 48 00.
Web site: http://www.funradio.fr

LE MOUV' 707073
116, avenue du président Kennedy, cedex 16, 75220 PARIS **Tel:** 1 56 40 22 22.
Web site: http://www.lemouv.com
Director: Hervé Riesen

RADIO CLASSIQUE 6122
12 bis place Henri Bergson, 75008 PARIS
Tel: 1 40 08 50 00. **Fax:** 1 40 08 50 80.
Web site: http://www.radioclassique.com

RFI RADIO FRANCE INTERNATIONALE 622744
116 avenue du Président-Kennedy, BP 9516, 75762 CEDEX 16 PARIS **Tel:** 1 56 40 12 12.
Fax: 1 56 40 30 71.
Email: service.culture@rfi.fr
Web site: http://www.rfi.fr
Director: Noëlle Velly; *Presenter:* Ziad Maalouf

RTL 6119
22 rue Bayard, 75008 PARIS
Tel: 141 86 2149.
Web site: http://www.rtl.fr
Director: Julien Cardon; *Presenter:* Caroline Alexy

REGIONAL RADIO STATIONS

RADIO ALFA 3479
1 rue Vasco de Gama, CEDEX, 94046 CRETEIL **Tel:** 1 45 10 98 60.
Fax: 1 43 89 43 90.
Email: redac@radioalfa.net
Web site: http://www.radioalfa.net

RADIO LATINA 2045
167 rue du Chevaleret, 75013 PARIS
Tel: 2 38 70 80 00. **Fax:** 8 25 84 68 44.
Email: bloppin@adofm.fr
Web site: http://www.latina.fr

RADIO MEGA 705821
35 rue Prompsault, 26000 VALENCE
Tel: 4 75 44 16 15.
Email: contact@radio-mega.com
Web site: http://www.radio-mega.com

RADIO NOVA 31983
127 avenue Ledru Rollin, 75011 PARIS
Tel: 1 53 33 33 15. **Fax:** 1 43 47 33 39.
Email: radionova@radionova.com
Web site: http://www.novaplanet.com

Germany

NATIONAL TV STATIONS

3SAT 753292
Otto-Schott-Str. 13, 55127 MAINZ
Tel: 6131 706200. **Fax:** 6131 706806.
Email: info@3sat.de
Web site: http://www.3sat.de
Editor: Daniel Fiedler

DEUTSCHE WELLE TV 753288
Voltastr. 6, 13355 BERLIN **Tel:** 30 46460.
Fax: 30 4631998.
Email: dw-tv@dw-world.de
Web site: http://www.dw-world.de
News Editor: Dagmar Engel; *Editor:* Christoph Lanz

KABEL EINS 732271
Medienallee 7, 85774 UNTERFÖHRING
Tel: 89 95072100. **Fax:** 89 95072158.
Email: info@kabeleins.de
Web site: http://www.kabeleins.de
News Editor: Hendrik Niederhoff; *Editor:* Katja Hofem-Best

PRO SIEBEN 739655
Medienallee 7, 85774 UNTERFÖHRING
Tel: 89 95077700. **Fax:** 89 95077710.
Email: zuschauerservice@prosieben.de
Web site: http://www.prosieben.de
News Editor: Michael Marx; *Editor:* Andreas Bartl

SAT.1 741095
Jägerstr. 32, 10117 BERLIN **Tel:** 30 20900.
Fax: 30 20902090.
Email: info@sat1.de
Web site: http://www.sat1.de
Editor: Katja Hofem-Best

SAT.1 1662606
Oberwallstr. 6, 10117 BERLIN
Tel: 1805 114111. **Fax:** 1805 114112.
Email: info@sat1.de
Web site: http://www.sat1.de
Editor: Ruslan Krohn

VOX 746754
Picassoplatz 1, 50679 KÖLN **Tel:** 221 45680.
Fax: 221 45681509.
Email: mail@vox.de
Web site: http://www.vox.de
News Editor: Uwe Fohrmann; *Editor:* Ladya van Eeden

REGIONAL TV STATIONS

17.30 SAT.1 BAYERN 741103
Hollerithstr. 3, 81829 MÜNCHEN
Tel: 89 2040070. **Fax:** 89 204007103.
Email: info@sat1bayern.de
Web site: http://www.sat1bayern.de
News Editor: Harry Klein; *Editor:* Alexander Stöckl

17.30 SAT.1 LIVE RHEINLAND-PFALZ UND HESSEN 741102
Otto-Schott-Str. 9, 55127 MAINZ
Tel: 6131 6002501. **Fax:** 6131 6002503.
Email: redaktion@1730live.de
Web site: http://www.1730live.de
Editor: Richard Kremershof

17:30 SAT.1 REGIONAL 741101
Goseriede 9, 30159 HANNOVER
Tel: 511 12123456. **Fax:** 511 12123470.
Email: hannover.sat1@sat1.de
Web site: http://www.sat1regional.de
Editor: Matthias Janott

ABM ARBEITSGEMEINSCHAFT BEHINDERUNG UND MEDIEN 721052
Bonner Platz 1, 80803 MÜNCHEN
Tel: 89 3079920. **Fax:** 89 30799222.
Email: info@abm-medien.de
Web site: http://www.abm-medien.de
News Editor: Christof Stolle; *Editor:* Christof Stolle

AUGSBURG.TV 745551
Curt-Frenzel-Str. 4, 86167 AUGSBURG
Tel: 821 700100. **Fax:** 821 7001029.
Email: info@augsburg.tv
Web site: http://www.augsburg.tv
Editor: Andrea Horn

DRESDEN FERNSEHEN 725638
Schandauer Str. 64, 01277 DRESDEN
Tel: 351 3154070. **Fax:** 351 31540799.
Email: fernsehen@dresden-fernsehen.de
Web site: http://www.dresden-fernsehen.de
Editor: Monika Großmann

HR-FERNSEHEN 753328
Bertramstr. 8, 60320 FRANKFURT
Tel: 69 1551. **Fax:** 69 1552900.
Email: fernsehen@hr-online.de
Web site: http://www.hr-online.de
News Editor: Alois Theisen; *Editor:* Alois Theisen

INTV 731557
Donaustr. 11, 85049 INGOLSTADT
Tel: 841 935650. **Fax:** 841 9356519.
Email: info@intv.de
Web site: http://www.intv.de
News Editor: Siegfried Andree; *Editor:* Gustl Vogl

MDR FERNSEHEN 753359
Kantstr. 71, 04275 LEIPZIG **Tel:** 341 3000.
Fax: 341 3006789.
Web site: http://www.mdr.de
News Editor: Bettina Ruprecht; *Editor:* Wolfgang Kenntemich

NDR FERNSEHEN 753367
Hugh-Greene-Weg 1, 22529 HAMBURG
Tel: 40 41560. **Fax:** 40 447602.
Email: fernsehen@ndr.de
Web site: http://www.ndr.de
News Editor: Stefan Niemann; *Editor:* Frank Beckmann

N-TV 737710
Richard-Byrd-Str. 4, 50829 KÖLN
Tel: 221 91520. **Fax:** 221 91522090.
Email: planung@n-tv.de
Web site: http://www.n-tv.de
News Editor: Volker Wasmuth; *Editor:* Volker Wasmuth

OBERPFALZ TV 737836
Fleurystr. 9, 92224 AMBERG
Tel: 9621 48550. **Fax:** 9621 485555.
Email: info@otv.de
Web site: http://www.otv.de
News Editor: Christoph Rolf; *Editor:* Lothar Höher

RADIOBREMEN 753414
Diepenau 10, 28195 BREMEN **Tel:** 421 2460.
Fax: 421 24642899.
Email: rbonline@radiobremen.de
Web site: http://www.radiobremen.de
News Editor: Guido Schulenberg; *Editor:* Martin Reckweg

RBB FERNSEHEN 753616
Masurenallee 8, 14057 BERLIN
Tel: 30 979930. **Fax:** 30 9799319.
Email: info@rbb-online.de
Web site: http://www.rbb-online.de
News Editor: Peter Laubenthal; *Editor:* Claudia Nothelle

REGIONAL FERNSEHEN LANDSHUT 740154
Fischergasse 660, 84028 LANDSHUT
Tel: 871 922000. **Fax:** 871 9220050.
Email: redaktion@rfltv.de
Web site: http://www.rfltv.de
News Editor: Robert May; *Editor:* Norbert Haimerl

REGIOTV REGIONAL-FERNSEHEN 740695
Naststr. 23, 70376 STUTTGART
Tel: 711 25257220. **Fax:** 711 25257219.
Email: redaktion-stuttgart@regio-tv.de
Web site: http://www.regio-tv.de
News Editor: Chris Fleischhauer; *Editor:* Chris Fleischhauer

RTL HESSEN 740682
Solmsstr. 4, 60486 FRANKFURT
Tel: 69 716780. **Fax:** 69 71678191.
Email: hessen@rtl.de
Web site: http://www.rtlhessen.de
Editor: Eberhard Volk

RTL NORD 740684
Straßenbahnring 18, 20251 HAMBURG
Tel: 40 521030. **Fax:** 40 52103190.
Email: gutenabend@rtl.de
Web site: http://www.rtlregional.de
News Editor: Jens Gaiser; *Editor:* Michael Pohl

RTL WEST 740685
Picassoplatz 1, 50679 KÖLN
Tel: 221 45676230. **Fax:** 221 45676249.
Email: info@rtl-west.de
Web site: http://www.rtl-west.de
News Editor: Sabine Jasper; *Editor:* Jörg Zajonc

SAT.1 LIVE FÜR HAMBURG UND SCHLESWIG-HOLSTEIN 741100
Jenfelder Allee 80, 22039 HAMBURG
Tel: 40 66886002. **Fax:** 40 66886020.
Email: hamburg.sat1@sat1.de
Web site: http://www.sat1hamburg.de
Editor: Sascha Pforten

SR FERNSEHEN 753612
Franz-Mai-Str., 66121 SAARBRÜCKEN
Tel: 681 6020. **Fax:** 681 6023874.
Email: info@sr-online.de
Web site: http://www.sr-online.de
News Editor: Roman Bonnaire; *Editor:* Hans-Günther Brüske

SWR FERNSEHEN BADEN-WÜRTTEMBERG 753623
Neckarstr. 230, 70190 STUTTGART
Tel: 711 9290. **Fax:** 711 9292600.
Email: info@swr.de
Web site: http://www.swr.de
News Editor: Uschi Strautmann; *Editor:* Michael Zeiß

TRP 1 744439
Dr.-Emil-Brichta-Str. 5, 94036 PASSAU
Tel: 851 988840. **Fax:** 851 9888440.
Email: info@trp1.de
Web site: http://www.trp1.de
Editor: Christian Repa

TV TOURING WÜRZBURG 745593
Mergentheimer Str. 7, 97082 WÜRZBURG
Tel: 931 796220. **Fax:** 931 7962299.
Email: redaktion@tvtouring.de
Web site: http://www.tvtouring.de
News Editor: Maria Saemann; *Editor:* Olivier Luksch

TV.BERLIN 745553
Rudi-Dutschke-Str. 4, 10969 BERLIN
Tel: 30 2090974900. **Fax:** 30 2090974908.
Email: cvd@tvb.de
Web site: http://www.tvb.de
News Editor: Agnes Fischer; *Editor:* Wolfram Schweizer

WDR FERNSEHEN 753645
Appellhofplatz 1, 50667 KÖLN
Tel: 221 2200. **Fax:** 221 2204800.
Email: fernsehen@wdr.de
Web site: http://www.wdr.de
News Editor: Markus Nievelstein; *Editor:* Verena Kulenkampff

SATELLITE TV

ARTE DEUTSCHLAND TV 721240
Schützenstr. 1, 76530 BADEN-BADEN
Tel: 7221 93690. **Fax:** 7221 936950.
Email: info@arte-tv.de
Web site: http://www.arte.tv
Editor: Klaus Wenger

SUPER RTL 744000
Picassoplatz 1, 50679 KÖLN
Tel: 221 45651100. **Fax:** 221 45651109.
Email: info@superrtl.de
Web site: http://www.superrtl.de
Editor: Carsten Göttel

VIVA 746587
Stralauer Allee 7, 10245 BERLIN
Tel: 30 7001000. **Fax:** 30 700100599.
Email: info@viva.tv
Web site: http://www.viva.tv

CABLE TV

JOY-MUSIC-VIDEO 732156
Blumenthalstr. 18, 10783 BERLIN
Tel: 30 2614544.
Email: office@joyvideo.de
Web site: http://www.joytvchannel.com
Editor: Gertraud L. Mayer

K 3 KULTURKANAL 732479
Wallstr. 11, 55122 MAINZ
Tel: 6131 2264740. **Fax:** 6131 22647428.
Email: verwaltung@k3-fernsehen.de
Web site: http://www.k3-fernsehen.de
Editor: Claus-Peter Liebhold

NATIONAL RADIO STATIONS

89.0 RTL 1704312
Große Ulrichstr. 60d, 06108 HALLE
Tel: 345 52580. **Fax:** 345 5258450.
Email: service@89.0rtl.de
Web site: http://www.89.0rtl.de
Editor: Tim Grunert

BERLINER RUNDFUNK 91!4 1704520
Grunewaldstr. 3, 12165 BERLIN
Tel: 30 20191400. **Fax:** 30 20191200.
Email: info@berliner-rundfunk.de
Web site: http://www.berliner-rundfunk.de
Editor: Nadine Seeger

DEUTSCHE WELLE 725117
Kurt-Schumacher-Str. 3, 53113 BONN
Tel: 228 4290. **Fax:** 228 4293000.
Email: info@dw-world.de
Web site: http://www.dw-world.de
Editor: Christian Gramsch

DEUTSCHLANDRADIO KULTUR 725153
Hans-Rosenthal-Platz 1, 10825 BERLIN
Tel: 30 85030. **Fax:** 30 85036168.
Email: presse@dradio.de
Web site: http://www.dradio.de
News Editor: Thomas Wiecha; *Editor:* Peter Lange

FFN 1662505
Stiftstr. 8, 30159 HANNOVER
Tel: 511 16660. **Fax:** 511 1666110.
Email: webmasterin@ffn.de
Web site: http://www.ffn.de
Editor: Katrin Wulfert

KLASSIK RADIO 753351
Planckstr. 15, 22765 HAMBURG
Tel: 40 3005050. **Fax:** 40 30050544.
Email: info@klassikradio.de
Web site: http://www.klassikradio.de
News Editor: Thilo Winnefeld; *Editor:* Holger Wemhoff

REGIONAL RADIO STATIONS

102.2 RADIO ESSEN 753443
Lindenallee 6, 45127 ESSEN
Tel: 201 245850. **Fax:** 201 2458522.
Email: info@radioessen.de
Web site: http://www.radioessen.de
Editor: Christian Pflug

104.6 RTL RADIO 753343
Kurfürstendamm 207, 10719 BERLIN
Tel: 30 884840. **Fax:** 30 88484121.
Email: zentrale@104.6rtl.com
Web site: http://www.104.6rtl.com
News Editor: Stephan Krüger; *Editor:* Arno Müller

106.4 TOP FM 753434
Schöngeisinger Str. 11, 82256 FÜRSTENFELDBRUCK **Tel:** 8141 32320.
Fax: 8141 323260.
Email: redaktion@top-fm.de
Web site: http://www.top-fm.de
News Editor: Martin Schelauske; *Editor:* Martin Schelauske

107.7 RADIO HAGEN 753470
Rathausstr. 23, 58095 HAGEN
Tel: 2331 20050. **Fax:** 2331 200520.
Email: redaktion@107.7radiohagen.de
Web site: http://www.107.7radiohagen.de
News Editor: Cordula Aßmann; *Editor:* Cordula Aßmann

90.8 RADIO HERNE 753475
Berliner Platz 9, 44623 HERNE
Tel: 2323 14900. **Fax:** 2323 149010.
Email: wolfgang.tatzel@radioherne.de
Web site: http://www.radioherne.de
Editor: Wolfgang Tatzel

90ACHT RADIO HERNE 1662508
Berliner Platz 9, 44623 HERNE
Tel: 2323 14900. **Fax:** 2323 149010.
Email: info@90.8radioherne.de
Web site: http://www.90.8radioherne.de
Editor: Wolfgang Tatzel

92.9 RADIO MÜLHEIM 753260
Essener Str. 99, 46047 OBERHAUSEN
Tel: 208 450070. **Fax:** 208 4500733.
Email: redaktion@radiomuelheim.de
Web site: http://www.radiomuelheim.de
Editor: Olaf Sandhöfer-Daniel

94.9 RADIO HERFORD 753474
Goebenstr. 3, 32052 HERFORD
Tel: 5221 18000. **Fax:** 5221 180065.
Email: info@radioherford.de
Web site: http://www.radioherford.de
Editor: Jörg Brökel

98.5 RADIO BOCHUM 753389
Huestr. 25, 44787 BOCHUM
Tel: 234 689990. **Fax:** 234 6899910.
Email: info@98.5radiobochum.de
Web site: http://www.98.5radiobochum.de
Editor: Andrea Donat

98.7 RADIO EMSCHER LIPPE 753439
Hochstr. 68, 45894 GELSENKIRCHEN
Tel: 209 360880. **Fax:** 209 3608844.
Email: post@radioemscherlippe.de
Web site: http://www.radioemscherlippe.de
Editor: Ralf Laskowski

98.8 KISS FM 753250
Grunewaldstr. 3, 12165 BERLIN
Tel: 30 20191700. **Fax:** 30 20191715.
Email: kissfm@kissfm.de
Web site: http://www.kissfm.de
Editor: Sebastian Voigt

ALSTER RADIO 106!8 ROCK 'N POP 753253
Messberg 4, 20095 HAMBURG
Tel: 40 3709070. **Fax:** 40 37090720.
Email: info@106acht.de
Web site: http://www.106acht.de
News Editor: Michael Rosebrock; *Editor:* Ulrich Bunsmann

ANTENNE BAYERN 753254
Münchener Str. 101c, 85737 ISMANING
Tel: 89 992770. **Fax:** 89 99277119.
Email: redaktion@antenne.de
Web site: http://www.antenne.de
News Editor: Detlef Kuschka; *Editor:* Detlef Kuschka

ANTENNE BAYERN 1660844
Münchener Str. 101c, 85737 ISMANING
Tel: 89 992770. **Fax:** 89 9927788.
Email: redaktion@antenne.de
Web site: http://www.antenne.de
Editor: Detlef Kuschka

ANTENNE DÜSSELDORF 753255
Kaistr. 7, 40221 DÜSSELDORF
Tel: 211 9301010. **Fax:** 211 9301099.
Email: redaktion@antenneduesseldorf.de
Web site: http://www.antenneduesseldorf.de
News Editor: Joachim Bonn; *Editor:* Michael Mennicken

ANTENNE MV 753258
Funkhaus Plate, 19086 PLATE
Tel: 3861 55000. **Fax:** 3861 550051.
Email: info@antennemv.de
Web site: http://www.antennemv.de
News Editor: Sandra Luner; *Editor:* Peer Wellendorf

ANTENNE NIEDERRHEIN 753259
Stechbahn 2, 47533 KLEVE
Tel: 2821 722710. **Fax:** 2821 722799.
Email: redaktion@antenneniederrhein.de
Web site: http://www.antenneniederrhein.de
News Editor: Wolfgang Notten; *Editor:* Thomas Bollmann

ANTENNE THÜRINGEN 753263
Belvederer Allee 25, 99425 WEIMAR
Tel: 3643 552552. **Fax:** 3643 552444.
Email: redaktion@antennethueringen.de
Web site: http://www.antennethueringen.de
News Editor: Petra Kühling; *Editor:* Carsten Hoyer

ANTENNE UNNA 753265
Mozartstr. 1, 59423 UNNA **Tel:** 2303 20020.
Fax: 2303 200259.
Email: redaktion@antenneunna.de
Web site: http://www.antenneunna.de
Editor: Tim Schmutzler

BADEN.FM 753460
Munzinger Str. 1, 79111 FREIBURG
Tel: 761 456660. **Fax:** 761 4566620.
Email: redaktion@funkhaus-freiburg.de
Web site: http://www.baden.fm
News Editor: Rainer Gauglitz; *Editor:* Stefanie Werntgen

BAYERISCHER RUNDFUNK 722136
Rundfunkplatz 1, 80335 MÜNCHEN
Tel: 89 590001. **Fax:** 89 59002375.
Email: info@br-online.de
Web site: http://www.br-online.de
News Editor: Klaus Greiner; *Editor:* Johannes Grotzky

BAYERNWELLE SÜDOST 753587
Fürstenweg 1, 83395 FREILASSING
Tel: 8654 777343. **Fax:** 8654 777340.
Email: redaktion@bayernwelle.de
Web site: http://www.bayernwelle.de
News Editor: Markus Gollinger; *Editor:* Dietmar Nagelmüller

BB RADIO 753274
Großbeerenstr. 185, 14482 POTSDAM
Tel: 331 74400. **Fax:** 331 7440212.
Email: info@bbradio.de
Web site: http://www.bbradio.de
News Editor: Oleg Grünert; *Editor:* Torsten Birenheide

BB RADIO NIEDERLAUSITZ 107,2 753275
Karl-Liebknecht-Str. 136, 03046 COTTBUS
Tel: 355 4936570. **Fax:** 355 4936571.
Email: cvd@bbradio.de
Web site: http://www.bbradio.de
Editor: Robert Förster

BB RADIO NORD-OST 753276
Steinstr. 2, 16225 EBERSWALDE
Tel: 3334 3899683. **Fax:** 3334 3899682.
Web site: http://www.bbradio.de
Editor: Ulrike Dinse

BERLINER RUNDFUNK 91.4 753277
Grunewaldstr. 3, 12165 BERLIN
Tel: 30 20191400. **Fax:** 30 20191200.
Email: info@berliner-rundfunk.de
Web site: http://www.berliner-rundfunk.de
News Editor: Mark Schubert; *Editor:* Detlef Noormann

DELTA RADIO 753287
Wittland 3, 24109 KIEL **Tel:** 180 5155000.
Fax: 180 5165000.
Email: delta@deltaradio.de
Web site: http://www.deltaradio.de
Editor: Inga Schmaser

DONAU3FM 753429
Basteistr. 37, 89073 ULM **Tel:** 731 800130.
Fax: 731 8001313.
Email: info@donau3fm.de
Web site: http://www.donau3fm.de
News Editor: Sven Stevens; *Editor:* Kristof Wachsmuth

ENERGY BERLIN 103,4 753304
Hardenbergstr. 5, 10623 BERLIN
Tel: 30 254350. **Fax:** 30 25435350.
Email: energy-berlin@energy.de
Web site: http://www.energy.de
News Editor: Thomas Kutz; *Editor:* Alexander Urban

ENERGY BREMEN 753594
Erste Schlachtpforte 1, 28195 BREMEN
Tel: 421 335660. **Fax:** 421 3356677.
Email: radio@energy-bremen.de
Web site: http://www.energy-bremen.de
News Editor: Lars Brokate; *Editor:* Mathias Bartels

ENERGY MÜNCHEN 753302
Liebherrstr. 5, 80538 MÜNCHEN
Tel: 89 23190746. **Fax:** 89 23190730.
Email: infomuenchen@energy.de
Web site: http://www.energy.de
News Editor: Stefan Ibelshäuser; *Editor:* Stefan Ibelshäuser

ENERGY REGION STUTTGART 753606
Naststr. 31, 70376 STUTTGART
Tel: 711 9330350. **Fax:** 711 93303519.
Email: redaktionstuttgart@energy.de
Web site: http://www.energy.de
Editor: Mike Wagner

ERF RADIO 753311
Berliner Ring 62, 35576 WETZLAR
Tel: 6441 9570. **Fax:** 6441 957120.
Email: info@erf.de
Web site: http://www.erf.de
News Editor: Horst Kretschi; *Editor:* Udo Vach

EXTRA-RADIO 753313
Kreuzsteinstr. 2, 95028 HOF
Tel: 9281 83000. **Fax:** 9281 830052.
Email: redaktion@extra-radio.de
Web site: http://www.extra-radio.de
News Editor: Gerhard Prokscha; *Editor:* Gerhard Prokscha

GONG FM 753323
Lilienthalstr. 3c, 93049 REGENSBURG
Tel: 941 502070. **Fax:** 941 560390.
Email: gongfm@gongfm.de
Web site: http://www.gongfm.de
News Editor: Michael Hegele; *Editor:* Harry Landauer

HELLWEG RADIO 753326
Jakobistr. 46a, 59494 SOEST
Tel: 2921 37770. **Fax:** 2921 37710.
Email: redaktion@hellwegradio.de
Web site: http://www.hellwegradio.de
Editor: Ruth Heinemann

HESSISCHER RUNDFUNK 730205
Bertramstr. 8, 60320 FRANKFURT
Tel: 69 1551. **Fax:** 69 1552900.
Web site: http://www.hr-online.de
News Editor: Anke Knafla-Heynold; *Editor:* Katja Marx

HIT RADIO FFH 753335
FFH-Platz 1, 61118 BAD VILBEL
Tel: 6101 9880. **Fax:** 6101 988500.
Email: hitradio@ffh.de
Web site: http://www.ffh.de
News Editor: Roger Hofmann; *Editor:* Roel Oosthout

HIT-RADIO ANTENNE 1 753331
Plieninger Str. 150, 70567 STUTTGART
Tel: 711 72727380. **Fax:** 711 72727385.
Email: redaktion@antenne1.de
Web site: http://www.meinantenne1.de
News Editor: Klaus Michler; *Editor:* Alexander Heine

HIT-RADIO ANTENNE NIEDERSACHSEN 753330
Goseriede 9, 30159 HANNOVER
Tel: 511 91180. **Fax:** 511 9118209.
Email: zentrale.hannover@antenne.com
Web site: http://www.antenne.com
News Editor: Torben Hildebrandt; *Editor:* Oliver Schnabel

HIT-RADIO ANTENNE NIEDERSACHSEN 1661855
Goseriede 9, 30159 HANNOVER
Tel: 511 9118135. **Fax:** 511 9118137.
Email: stephan.scholte@antenne.com
Web site: http://www.antenne.com
Editor: Stephan Scholte

HIT-RADIO N1 753336
Senefelderstr. 7, 90409 NÜRNBERG
Tel: 911 51910. **Fax:** 911 5191121.
Email: studio@hitradion1.de
Web site: http://www.hitradion1.de
News Editor: Sandra Bardenbacher; *Editor:* Marco König

HITRADIO OHR 753523
Hauptstr. 83a, 77652 OFFENBURG
Tel: 781 5043000. **Fax:** 781 5043109.
Email: info@hitradio-ohr.de
Web site: http://www.hitradio-ohr.de
Editor: Markus Knoll

HITRADIO.RT1 753552
Curt-Frenzel-Str. 4, 86167 AUGSBURG
Tel: 821 7774000. **Fax:** 821 7774029.
Email: radio@rt1.de
Web site: http://www.rt1.de
News Editor: Philipp Kleininger; *Editor:* Philipp Kleininger

HITRADIO.RT1 1704666
Curt-Frenzel-Str. 4, 86167 AUGSBURG
Tel: 821 7774500. **Fax:** 821 7774509.
Email: hitradio@rt1.de
Web site: http://www.rt1.de
Editor: Felix Kovac

HITRADIO.RT1 NORDSCHWABEN 753553
Artur-Proeller-Str. 1, 86609 DONAUWÖRTH
Tel: 906 706010. **Fax:** 906 3949.
Email: info@rt1-nordschwaben.de
Web site: http://www.rt1-nordschwaben.de
News Editor: Alexander Kunz; *Editor:* Mirko Zeitler

HITRADIO.RT 1 SÜDSCHWABEN 753536
Donaustr. 14, 87700 MEMMINGEN
Tel: 8331 952421. **Fax:** 8331 952419.
Email: redaktion@rt1-suedschwaben.de
Web site: http://www.rt1-suedschwaben.de
Editor: Andreas Schales

JAM FM 753346
Am Kleinen Wannsee 5, 14109 BERLIN
Tel: 30 8069200. **Fax:** 30 80692035.
Email: redaktion@jamfm.de
Web site: http://www.jamfm.de
Editor: Kai Paulsen

JAZZTIME NÜRNBERG 753348
Vestnertormauer 24, 90403 NÜRNBERG
Tel: 911 364297. **Fax:** 911 361690.
Email: jazztime@jazzstudio.de
Web site: http://www.jazzstudio.de
Editor: Alfred Mangold

LANDESWELLE THÜRINGEN 753352
Mehringstr. 5, 99086 ERFURT
Tel: 361 2222222. **Fax:** 361 2222182.
Email: kontakt@landeswelle.de
Web site: http://www.landeswelle.de
News Editor: Marco Kamphaus; *Editor:* Lars Gerdau

LORA 92.4 RADIO 753357
Gravelottestr. 6, 81667 MÜNCHEN
Tel: 89 4802851. **Fax:** 89 4802852.
Email: info@lora924.de
Web site: http://www.lora924.de

MITTELDEUTSCHER RUNDFUNK 736246
Gerberstr. 2, 06108 HALLE **Tel:** 345 3000.
Fax: 391 3005271.
Web site: http://www.mdr.de
Editor: Johann Michael Möller

DIE NEUE 107,7 753621
Königstr. 2, 70173 STUTTGART
Tel: 711 163550. **Fax:** 711 1635555.
Email: info@dieneue1077.de
Web site: http://www.dieneue1077.de
News Editor: Stephanie Heusslein; *Editor:* Bert Helbig

NE-WS 89.4 753366
Moselstr. 16, 41464 NEUSS
Tel: 2131 40000. **Fax:** 2131 400011.
Email: redaktion@news894.de
Web site: http://www.news894.de
News Editor: Sascha Kruchen; *Editor:* Stefan Kruchen

NORDDEUTSCHER RUNDFUNK 737603
Rothenbaumchaussee 132, 20149 HAMBURG **Tel:** 40 41560. **Fax:** 40 447602.
Web site: http://www.ndr.de
Editor: Joachim Knuth

OLDIE 95 753322
Spitalerstr. 10, 20095 HAMBURG
Tel: 40 237330. **Fax:** 40 23733101.
Email: nachrichten@oldie95.de
Web site: http://www.oldie95.de
News Editor: Gabriele Hoberg; *Editor:* Florian Wittmann

OSTSEEWELLE HIT-RADIO MECKLENBURG-VORPOMMERN 753383
Warnowufer 59a, 18057 ROSTOCK
Tel: 381 44077110. **Fax:** 381 44077120.
Email: redaktion@ostseewelle.de
Web site: http://www.ostseewelle.de
Editor: Tino Sperke

RADIO 2DAY 753584
Schneemannstr. 25, 81369 MÜNCHEN
Tel: 89 7237750.
Email: info@radio2day.de
Web site: http://www.radio2day.com
News Editor: Barbara Bertelshofer; *Editor:* Peter Bertelshofer

RADIO 7 753566
Gaisenbergstr. 29, 89073 ULM
Tel: 731 1477201. **Fax:** 731 1477202.
Email: redaktion@radio7.de
Web site: http://www.radio7.de
News Editor: Andreas Panthöfer; *Editor:* Michael Merx

RADIO 8 753388
Schalkhäuser Landstr. 5, 91522 ANSBACH
Tel: 981 6300. **Fax:** 981 63089.
Email: redaktion@radio8.de
Web site: http://www.radio8.de
News Editor: Heike Geißler; *Editor:* Klaus Seeger

RADIO 90,1 753516
Lüpertzender Str. 6, 41061 MÖNCHENGLADBACH **Tel:** 2161 9019010.
Fax: 2161 9019099.
Email: redaktion@radio901.de
Web site: http://www.radio901.de
News Editor: Petra Koch; *Editor:* Gudrun Gehl

RADIO 91.2 753436
Karl-Zahn-Str. 11, 44141 DORTMUND
Tel: 231 95770. **Fax:** 231 957750.
Email: redaktion@radio912.de
Web site: http://www.radio912.de
Editor: Martin Busch

RADIO ARABELLA 753401
Paul-Heyse-Str. 2, 80336 MÜNCHEN
Tel: 89 5447000. **Fax:** 89 54470055.
Email: redaktion@radioarabella.de
Web site: http://www.radioarabella.de
News Editor: Franziska Eggert; *Editor:* Roland Schindzielorz

RADIO BAMBERG 753406
Gutenbergstr. 5, 96050 BAMBERG
Tel: 951 982900. **Fax:** 951 9829090.
Email: redaktion@radio-bamberg.de
Web site: http://www.radio-bamberg.de
News Editor: Claudia Bachmann; *Editor:* Mischa Salzmann

RADIO BIELEFELD 753412
Niedernstr. 21, 33602 BIELEFELD
Tel: 521 555111. **Fax:** 521 555112.
Email: info@radiobielefeld.de
Web site: http://www.radiobielefeld.de
News Editor: Claudia Knoppke; *Editor:* Martin Knabenreich

RADIO BONN/RHEIN-SIEG 753413
Kennedybrücke 4, 53225 BONN
Tel: 228 400710. **Fax:** 228 4007136.
Email: redaktion@radiobonn.de
Web site: http://www.radiobonn.de
Editor: Jörg Bertram

RADIO BONN/RHEIN-SIEG 1704566
Kennedybrücke 4, 53225 BONN
Tel: 228 400710. **Fax:** 228 4007136.
Web site: http://www.radio-bonn.de

RADIO BROCKEN 1662500
Große Ulrichstr. 60d, 06108 HALLE
Tel: 345 52580. **Fax:** 345 5258450.
Email: mail@radiobrocken.de
Web site: http://www.radiobrocken.de
Editor: André Rüprich

RADIO CHARIVARI 753421
Lilienthalstr. 3c, 93049 REGENSBURG
Tel: 941 502070. **Fax:** 941 50207770.
Email: charivari@charivari.com
Web site: http://www.charivari.com
News Editor: Harry Landauer; *Editor:* Harry Landauer

RADIO CHARIVARI 753422
Hafnerstr. 5, 83022 ROSENHEIM
Tel: 8031 30080. **Fax:** 8031 300838.
Email: info@radio-charivari.de
Web site: http://www.radio-charivari.de
Editor: Andreas Nickl

RADIO CHARIVARI 753423
Semmelstr. 15, 97070 WÜRZBURG
Tel: 931 308090. **Fax:** 931 3080917.
Email: info@charivari.fm
Web site: http://www.charivari.fm
News Editor: Christoph Schmid; *Editor:* Stefan Drollmann

RADIO DUISBURG 753432
Harry-Epstein-Platz 2, 47051 DUISBURG
Tel: 203 800890. **Fax:** 203 8008970.
Email: redaktion@radioduisburg.de
Web site: http://www.radioduisburg.de
Editor: Markus Augustiniak

RADIO ENNEPE RUHR 753440
Rathausstr. 23, 58095 HAGEN
Tel: 2331 200590. **Fax:** 2331 200525.
Email: info@radioenneperuhr.de
Web site: http://www.radioenneperuhr.de
Editor: Tom Hoppe

RADIO ERFT 753442
Kölner Str. 44, 50389 WESSELING
Tel: 2236 888990. **Fax:** 2236 888999.
Email: redaktion@radioerft.de
Web site: http://www.radioerft.de
Editor: Andreas Houska

RADIO EUROHERZ 753444
Pfarr 1, 95028 HOF **Tel:** 9281 880880.
Fax: 9281 880140.
Email: redaktion@funkhaus-hof.de
Web site: http://www.euroherz.de
News Editor: Anke Rieß; *Editor:* Anke Rieß

RADIO F 753450
Senefelderstr. 7, 90409 NÜRNBERG
Tel: 911 51910. **Fax:** 911 5191100.
Email: radiof@funkhaus.de
Web site: http://www.funkhaus.de
News Editor: Christian Fein; *Editor:* Michael Lein

RADIO FANTASY 753451
Ludwigstr. 1, 86150 AUGSBURG
Tel: 821 5077600. **Fax:** 821 5077666.
Email: radio@fantasy.de
Web site: http://www.fantasy.de
News Editor: Joa Bradke; *Editor:* Joa Bradke

RADIO FFN 753452
Stiftstr. 8, 30159 HANNOVER
Tel: 511 16660. **Fax:** 511 1666110.
Email: radio@ffn.de
Web site: http://www.ffn.de
News Editor: Ina Tenz; *Editor:* Ina Tenz

RADIO GONG 96,3 753464
Franz-Joseph-Str. 14, 80801 MÜNCHEN
Tel: 89 38166266. **Fax:** 89 38166288.
Email: redaktion@radiogong.de
Web site: http://www.radiogong.de
News Editor: Andreas Werner; *Editor:* Georg Dingler

RADIO GONG 97,1 753465
Senefelderstr. 7, 90409 NÜRNBERG
Tel: 911 51910. **Fax:** 911 5191100.
Email: gong@funkhaus.de
Web site: http://www.gong971.de
News Editor: Marc Wirtz; *Editor:* Marc Wirtz

RADIO GONG WÜRZBURG 753466
Semmelstr. 15, 97070 WÜRZBURG
Tel: 931 308090. **Fax:** 931 3080917.
Email: info@radiogong.com
Web site: http://radiogong.com
News Editor: Christoph Schmid; *Editor:* Frank Beyhl

RADIO GÜTERSLOH 753469
Kahlertstr. 4, 33330 GÜTERSLOH
Tel: 5241 92000. **Fax:** 5241 920065.
Email: info@radioguetersloh.de
Web site: http://www.radioguetersloh.de
Editor: Carsten Schoßmeier

RADIO HAMBURG 753471
Spitalerstr. 10, 20095 HAMBURG
Tel: 40 3397140. **Fax:** 40 339714628.
Email: aktuell@radiohamburg.de
Web site: http://www.radiohamburg.de
News Editor: Gabriele Hoberg; *Editor:* Marzel Becker

RADIO HAMBURG 1662507
Spitalerstr. 10, 20095 HAMBURG
Tel: 40 8222278476. **Fax:** 40 339714627.
Email: service@radiohamburg.de
Web site: http://www.radiohamburg.de
Editor: Florian Wittmann

RADIO HOCHSTIFT 753476
Frankfurter Weg 22, 33106 PADERBORN
Tel: 5251 17370. **Fax:** 5251 173765.
Email: info@radiohochstift.de
Web site: http://www.radiohochstift.de
News Editor: Norbert Janowski; *Editor:* Martin Lausen

RADIO IN 753479
Schillerstr. 2, 85055 INGOLSTADT
Tel: 841 30090. **Fax:** 841 30097.
Email: service@radio-in.de
Web site: http://www.radio-in.de
Editor: Kerstin Schulz

RADIO KIEPENKERL 753486
Coesfelder Str. 36, 48249 DÜLMEN
Tel: 2594 782230. **Fax:** 2594 7822310.
Email: redaktion@radio-kiepenkerl.de
Web site: http://www.radio-kiepenkerl.de
News Editor: Marc Weiss; *Editor:* Andreas Kramer

RADIO KÖLN 753488
Im Mediapark 5, 50670 KÖLN
Tel: 221 951990. **Fax:** 221 9519921.
Email: redaktion@radiokoeln.de
Web site: http://www.radiokoeln.de
Editor: Claudia Schall

RADIO K.W. 753490
Poppelbaumstr. 1, 46483 WESEL
Tel: 281 1649390. **Fax:** 281 16493912.
Email: info@radiokw.de
Web site: http://www.radiokw.de

RADIO LAUSITZ 753353
Untermarkt 19, 02826 GÖRLITZ
Tel: 3581 309600. **Fax:** 3581 309666.
Email: mail@radiolausitz.de
Web site: http://www.radiolausitz.de
Editor: Matthias Montag

RADIO LEVERKUSEN 753494
Breidenbachstr. 19, 51373 LEVERKUSEN
Tel: 214 868330. **Fax:** 214 8683366.
Email: redaktion@radioleverkusen.de
Web site: http://www.radioleverkusen.de

RADIO LIPPE 753496
Lagesche Str. 17, 32756 DETMOLD
Tel: 5231 616160. **Fax:** 5231 6161699.
Email: info@radiolippe.de
Web site: http://www.radiolippe.de
News Editor: Markus Knoblich; *Editor:* Thorsten Wagner

RADIO LIPPE WELLE HAMM 753497
Königstr. 39, 59065 HAMM
Tel: 2381 105105. **Fax:** 2381 105450.
Email: redaktion@lippewelle.de
Web site: http://www.lippewelle.de
Editor: Gerd Heistermann

RADIO MAINWELLE 753500
Richard-Wagner-Str. 33, 95444 BAYREUTH
Tel: 921 757500. **Fax:** 921 7575012.
Email: redaktion@mainwelle.fm
Web site: http://www.mainwelle.fm
News Editor: Martin Sollik; *Editor:* Horst Mayer

RADIO MK 753508
Vinckestr. 9, 58636 ISERLOHN
Tel: 2371 79030. **Fax:** 2371 790355.
Email: info@radio-mk.de
Web site: http://www.radio-mk.de
Editor: Andreas Heine

RADIO ND 1 753512
Schillerstr. 2, 85055 INGOLSTADT
Tel: 841 30090. **Fax:** 841 30097.
Email: service@radio-in.de
Web site: http://www.radio-in.de
Editor: Kerstin Schulz

RADIO NEANDERTAL 753513
Elberfelder Str. 81, 40822 METTMANN
Tel: 2104 919010. **Fax:** 2104 919099.
Email: redaktion@radioneandertal.de
Web site: http://www.radioneandertal.de
Editor: Tatjana Pioschyk

RADIO NECKARBURG 753514
August-Schuhmacher-Str. 10, 78664 ESCHBRONN **Tel:** 7403 8000.
Fax: 7403 8002.
Email: info@radio-neckarburg.de
Web site: http://www.radio-neckarburg.de
News Editor: Christoph Grenzer; *Editor:* Christoph Grenzer

Germany

RADIO NORA
1662512
Wittland 3, 24109 KIEL **Tel:** 431 9906635.
Fax: 431 9906666.
Email: info@radionora.de
Web site: http://www.radionora.de
Editor: Jan-Henrik Schmelter

RADIO NRW
753520
Essener Str. 55, 46047 OBERHAUSEN
Tel: 208 85870. **Fax:** 208 853099.
Email: info@radionrw.de
Web site: http://www.radionrw.de
News Editor: Marc Weiß; *Editor:* Udo Becker

RADIO OBERLAND
753522
Marienplatz 17, 82467 GARMISCH-PARTENKIRCHEN **Tel:** 8821 93020.
Fax: 8821 930230.
Email: redaktion@radio-oberland.de
Web site: http://www.radio-oberland.de
Editor: Lars-Peter Schwarz

RADIO PLASSENBURG
753531
E.-C.-Baumann-Str. 5, 95326 KULMBACH
Tel: 9221 8272200. **Fax:** 9221 8272150.
Email: redaktion@radio-plassenburg.de
Web site: http://www.radio-plassenburg.de
News Editor: Marlen Vohwinkel; *Editor:* Anke Rieß

RADIO PRIMATON
753537
Carl-Zeiss-Str. 10, 97424 SCHWEINFURT
Tel: 9721 20900. **Fax:** 9721 209066.
Email: info@primatononline.de
Web site: http://www.primatononline.de
Editor: Christine Kleinz

RADIO PRIMAVERA
753538
Am Funkhaus 1, 63743 ASCHAFFENBURG
Tel: 6021 38830. **Fax:** 6021 388388.
Email: redaktion@primanet.de
Web site: http://www.primavera24.de
Editor: Dirk Kronewald

RADIO PSR
753539
Thomasgasse 2, 04109 LEIPZIG
Tel: 341 355355700. **Fax:** 341 355355750.
Email: info@radiopsr.de
Web site: http://www.radiopsr.de
Editor: Erwin Linnenbach

RADIO RAMASURI
753542
Unterer Markt 35, 92637 WEIDEN
Tel: 961 482482. **Fax:** 961 44773.
Email: radio@ramasuri.de
Web site: http://www.ramasuri.de
News Editor: Dieter Bleisteiner; *Editor:* Thomas Conrad

RADIO REGENBOGEN
753543
Dudenstr. 12, 68167 MANNHEIM
Tel: 621 33750. **Fax:** 621 3375222.
Email: info@regenbogen.de
Web site: http://www.regenbogen.de
News Editor: Manuela Bleifuß; *Editor:* Klaus Schunk

RADIO RST
753551
Poststr. 3, 48431 RHEINE **Tel:** 5971 92090.
Fax: 5971 920955.
Email: redaktion@radiorst.de
Web site: http://www.radiorst.de
News Editor: Marc Weiß; *Editor:* Andrea Stullich

RADIO RUR
753555
August-Klotz-Str. 21, 52349 DÜREN
Tel: 2421 12080. **Fax:** 2421 120819.
Email: redaktion@radiorur.de
Web site: http://www.radiorur.de
Editor: Dietrich Meier

RADIO SALÜ 107,7
753557
Richard-Wagner-Str. 58, 66111 SAARBRÜCKEN **Tel:** 681 93770.
Fax: 681 372522.
Email: redaktion@salue.de
Web site: http://www.salue.de
News Editor: Hans Werner Heinzer; *Editor:* Sascha Thiel

RADIO SAUERLAND
753559
Steinstr. 30, 59872 MESCHEDE
Tel: 291 29010. **Fax:** 291 290130.
Email: redaktion@radiosauerland.de
Web site: http://www.radiosauerland.de
News Editor: Anke Gebhardt; *Editor:* Paul Senske

RADIO SAW
753560
Hansapark 1, 39116 MAGDEBURG
Tel: 391 6300. **Fax:** 391 630449.
Email: info@radiosaw.de
Web site: http://www.radiosaw.de
News Editor: Tilo Vogelsang; *Editor:* Mario A. Liese

RADIO SAW
1662516
Hansapark 1, 39116 MAGDEBURG
Tel: 391 6300. **Fax:** 391 630409.
Email: info@radiosaw.de
Web site: http://www.radiosaw.de
Editor: Jens Kerner

RADIO SEEFUNK
753564
Konzilstr. 1, 78462 KONSTANZ
Tel: 7531 28650. **Fax:** 7531 286522.
Email: redaktion@radio-seefunk.de
Web site: http://www.radio-seefunk.de
News Editor: Janine Konopka; *Editor:* Stefan Steigerwald

RADIO SIEGEN
753572
Obergraben 33, 57072 SIEGEN
Tel: 271 2322230. **Fax:** 271 2322240.
Email: redaktion@radio-siegen.de
Web site: http://www.radio-siegen.de
News Editor: Bernd Müller; *Editor:* Rüdiger Schlund

RADIO TON
753578
Allee 2, 74072 HEILBRONN
Tel: 7131 650117. **Fax:** 7131 650100.
Email: redaktion@radioton.de
Web site: http://www.radioton.de
Editor: Klaus Höflinger

RADIO TRAUSNITZ
753583
Porschestr. 21, 84030 LANDSHUT
Tel: 871 923090. **Fax:** 871 9230999.
Email: redaktion@radio-trausnitz.de
Web site: http://www.radio-trausnitz.de
News Editor: Norbert Bauer; *Editor:* Thomas von Seckendorff

RADIO VEST
753453
Schaumburgstr. 14, 45657 RECKLINGHAUSEN **Tel:** 2361 9460.
Fax: 2361 946127.
Email: redaktion@radiovest.de
Web site: http://www.radiovest.de
Editor: Markus Schwab

RADIO WAF
753590
Schweinemarkt 3, 48231 WARENDORF
Tel: 2581 63780. **Fax:** 2581 637865.
Email: info@radiowaf.de
Web site: http://www.radiowaf.de
Editor: Frank Haberstroh

RADIO WESTFALICA
753593
Johanniskirchhof 2, 32423 MINDEN
Tel: 571 837830. **Fax:** 571 8378365.
Email: info@radiowestfalica.de
Web site: http://www.radiowestfalica.de
News Editor: Ingo Tölle; *Editor:* Ingo Tölle

RADIO WMW
753646
Heinrich-Hertz-Str. 6, 46325 BORKEN
Tel: 2861 9010. **Fax:** 2861 901300.
Email: redaktion@radiowmw.de
Web site: http://www.radiowmw.de
Editor: Reiner Mannheims

RADIO WUPPERTAL
753597
Otto-Hausmann-Ring 185, 42115 WUPPERTAL **Tel:** 202 257702.
Fax: 202 2577099.
Email: redaktion@radiowuppertal.de
Web site: http://www.radiowuppertal.de
News Editor: Marc Weiß; *Editor:* Georg Rose

RADIO Z
753599
Kopernikusplatz 12/Rgb., 90459 NÜRNBERG **Tel:** 911 450060.
Fax: 911 4500677.
Email: info@radio-z.net
Web site: http://www.radio-z.net
News Editor: Marco Schrage; *Editor:* Heike Demmel

RADIOBREMEN
739866
Diepenau 10, 28195 BREMEN
Tel: 421 24640. **Fax:** 421 2461010.
Web site: http://www.radiobremen.de
Editor: Dirk Hansen

RPR1.
753550
Turmstr. 10, 67059 LUDWIGSHAFEN
Tel: 621 590000. **Fax:** 621 628000.
Email: info@rpr1.de
Web site: http://www.rpr1.de
News Editor: Armin Mack; *Editor:* Dirk Alexander Lude

RS2
1704665
Grunewaldstr. 3, 12165 BERLIN
Tel: 30 20191900. **Fax:** 30 20191200.
Email: rs2@rs2.de
Web site: http://www.rs2.de

R.SA
753379
Thomasgasse 2, 04109 LEIPZIG
Tel: 341 355355800. **Fax:** 341 355355850.
Email: service@rsa-sachsen.de
Web site: http://www.rsa-sachsen.de
Editor: Erwin Linnenbach

R.SH RADIO SCHLESWIG-HOLSTEIN
753562
Wittland 3, 24109 KIEL **Tel:** 1805 051555.
Fax: 1805 051777.
Email: redaktion@rsh.de
Web site: http://www.rsh.de
News Editor: Christiane Hampe; *Editor:* Bill de Lisle

R.SH RADIO SCHLESWIG-HOLSTEIN
1662579
Wittland 3, 24109 KIEL **Tel:** 180 5051555.
Fax: 180 5051777.
Email: redaktion@rsh.de
Web site: http://www.rsh.de
Editor: Alice Blohmann

SAARLÄNDISCHER RUNDFUNK
740901
Funkhaus Halberg, 66121 SAARBRÜCKEN
Tel: 681 6020. **Fax:** 681 6023874.
Email: info@sr-online.de
Web site: http://www.sr-online.de
News Editor: Michael Conrad; *Editor:* Hans-Günther Brüske

SÜDWESTRUNDFUNK SWR4 RHEINLAND-PFALZ
743955
Am Fort Gonsenheim 139, 55122 MAINZ
Tel: 6131 9290. **Fax:** 6131 9292050.
Web site: http://www.swr-online.de
News Editor: Olaf Kapp; *Editor:* Wolfhard Klein

SUNSHINE LIVE
753624
Hafenstr. 68, 68159 MANNHEIM
Tel: 621 181910. **Fax:** 621 18191100.
Email: radio@sunshine-live.de
Web site: http://www.sunshine-live.de
News Editor: Susa Triebskorn; *Editor:* Jürgen Wiesbeck

UNSERRADIO
753631
Medienstr. 5, 94036 PASSAU
Tel: 851 802702. **Fax:** 851 802722.
Email: info@funkhaus-passau.de
Web site: http://www.unserradio.de
News Editor: Thomas Wensauer; *Editor:* Walter Berndl

WDR RADIO
747269
Appellhofplatz 1, 50667 KÖLN
Tel: 221 2200. **Fax:** 221 2204800.
Email: redaktion@wdr.de
Web site: http://www.wdr.de
News Editor: Klaus Bochenek; *Editor:* Wolfgang Schmitz

Gibraltar

NATIONAL TV STATIONS

GBC TELEVISION
765020
Broadcasting House, 18 South Barrack Road **Tel:** 200 79 760. **Fax:** 200 76 414.
Email: news@gbc.gi
Web site: http://www.gbc.gi
Editor: Stephen Neish

NATIONAL RADIO STATIONS

RADIO GIBRALTAR
765039
Broadcasting House, 18 South Barrack Road **Tel:** 200 79 760. **Fax:** 200 78 673.
Email: news@gbc.gi
Web site: http://www.gbc.gi
Editor: Gerard Teuma

Hungary

NATIONAL TV STATIONS

ATV TELEVÍZIÓ
708110
Korösi Csoma Sándor u. 19, 1102 BUDAPEST **Tel:** 1/877-0800. **Fax:** 1/877-0870.
Email: info@atv.hu
Web site: http://www.atv.hu

MINIMAX
708088
Lomb u. 23-27., 1139 BUDAPEST **Tel:** 1/236-9100. **Fax:** 1/236-9147.
Email: minimax@minimax.hu
Web site: http://www.minimax.hu

RTL KLUB
708111
Nagytétényi út 29., 1222 BUDAPEST **Tel:** 1/382-8501. **Fax:** 1/382-8519.
Email: info@rtlklub.hu
Web site: http://www.rtlklub.hu

SATELLITE TV

DUNA TELEVÍZIÓ
708097
Mészáros u. 48., 1016 BUDAPEST **Tel:** 1/489-1200. **Fax:** 1/489-1366.
Email: info@dunatv.hu
Web site: http://www.dunatv.hu

NATIONAL RADIO STATIONS

DANUBIUS RÁDIÓ
707063
Váci út 141., 1138 BUDAPEST **Tel:** 1/452-6100. **Fax:** 1/452-6181.
Email: info@danubius.hu
Web site: http://www.danubius.hu

MR1 - KOSSUTH RÁDIÓ
707054
Bródy S. u. 5-7., 1800 BUDAPEST **Tel:** 1/328-7588.
Email: reklamig@radio.hu
Web site: http://www.radio.hu

MR2 - PETOFI RÁDIÓ
708109
Bródy S. u. 5-7., 1800 BUDAPEST **Tel:** 1/328-7588.
Email: reklamig@radio.hu
Web site: http://www.radio.hu

MR3 - BARTÓK RÁDIÓ
708107
Bródy S. u. 5-7., 1800 BUDAPEST **Tel:** 1/328-7588.
Email: reklamig@radio.hu
Web site: http://www.radio.hu

SLÁGER RÁDIÓ 708080
Fo u. 14-18., 1011 BUDAPEST **Tel:** 1/888-3030. **Fax:** 1/888-3099.
Email: jootunde@slagerradio.hu
Web site: http://www.slagerradio.hu

REGIONAL RADIO STATIONS

96.4 ROXY RÁDIÓ 707057
Naphegy tér 8., 1016 BUDAPEST **Tel:** 1/212-5029. **Fax:** 1/317-7247.
Email: roxy@roxy.hu
Web site: http://www.roxy.hu

Irish Republic

NATIONAL TV STATIONS

3E 1762681
TV 3 Network Limited, Westgate Business Park, Ballymount, DUBLIN 24
Tel: 1 65 06 666. **Fax:** 16506655.
Email: info@tv3.ie
Web site: http://3e.tv3.ie

FARM TV 1667075
8 William Street, Tullamore, CO. OFFALY
Tel: 57 93 22 906. **Fax:** 57 93 22 908.
Email: info@farmtv.ie
Web site: http://www.farmtv.ie
News Editor: Malachy Mangan

RTÉ RADIO TELEFÍS ÉIREANN (TV) 4270
Donnybrook, DUBLIN 4 **Tel:** 1 20 83 111.
Fax: 12083080.
Email: newsdesk@rte.ie
Web site: http://www.rte.ie
News Editor: Newsroom

TG4 628731
Baile na hAbhann, CO. GALWAY
Tel: 91 50 50 50. **Fax:** 91505021.
Email: nuacht@tg4.ie
Web site: http://www.tg4.ie

TV 3 4271
Unit 5, Westgate Business Park, Ballymount Industrial Estate, DUBLIN 24
Tel: 1 41 93 333. **Fax:** 14193322.
Email: news@tv3.ie
Web site: http://www.tv3.ie
News Editor: Joe Walsh

SATELLITE TV

SETANTA GOLF 1794293
Setanta Sports, George's Quay House, 43 Townsend Radio, DUBLIN 2
Tel: 1 47 48 000.
Email: setanta.irl@setanta.com
Web site: http://www.setanta.com
News Editor: Leonard Ryan

SETANTA SPORT 41952
George's Quay House, 43 Townsend Street, DUBLIN 2 **Tel:** 1 47 48 000.
Email: setanta.irl@setanta.com
Web site: http://www.setanta.com
News Editor: Leonard Ryan

NATIONAL RADIO STATIONS

100-102 TODAY FM 4267
Marconi House, Digges Lane, DUBLIN 2
Tel: 1 80 49 000. **Fax:** 18049069.
Email: news@todayfm.com
Web site: http://www.todayfm.com
News Editor: Cathy Farrell

2FM 764408
RTE, Donnybrook, DUBLIN 4
Tel: 1 20 82 193. **Fax:** 12083086.
Email: newsdesk@rte.ie
Web site: http://www.2fm.ie
News Editor: News Editor

NEWSTALK 764487
Marconi House, Digges Lane, DUBLIN 2
Tel: 1 64 45 100. **Fax:** 16445199.
Email: newsroom@newstalk.ie
Web site: http://www.newstalk.ie
News Editor: John Keogh

RADIO 1 (RTÉ) 767225
Donnybrook, DUBLIN 4 **Tel:** 1 20 83 111.
Fax: 12083086.
Email: newsdesk@rte.ie
Web site: http://www.radio1.ie
News Editor: Ray Burke

RTÉ LYRIC FM 628759
Cornmarket Square, LIMERICK
Tel: 61 20 73 00. **Fax:** 61207390.
Email: lyric@rte.ie
Web site: http://www.rte.ie/lyricfm

RTE RADIO TELEFIS EIREANN (RADIO NEWS) 4269
Donnybrook, DUBLIN 4 **Tel:** 1 20 83 111.
Fax: 12083086.
Email: newsdesk@rte.ie
Web site: http://www.rte.ie
News Editor: Donal Byrne

RTÉ RAIDIÓ NA GAELTACHTA 764494
Casla, Conamara, CO. NA GAILLIMHE
Tel: 91 50 66 77. **Fax:** 91 50 66 88.
Email: rnag@rte.ie
Web site: http://www.rte.ie/rnag
News Editor: Aine Ni Dhiorai

REGIONAL RADIO STATIONS

103.2 DUBLIN CITY FM 4276
Unit 6, Docklands Innovation Park, East Wall Road, DUBLIN 3 **Tel:** 1 86 58 020.
Email: info@dublincityfm.ie
Web site: http://www.dublincityfm.ie
News Editor: Mick Hanley

4FM 1894745
Latin Hall, Golden Lane, DUBLIN 8
Tel: 1 42 55 400. **Fax:** 14255444.
Email: news@4fm.ie
Web site: http://www.4fm.ie

92.5 PHOENIX FM 754503
Unit 333, Services Centre, The Blanchardstown Centre, DUBLIN 15
Tel: 1 82 27 222.
Email: info@phoenixfm.ie
Web site: http://www.phoenixfm.ie
News Editor: Alan Connolly

C103 (NORTH) 4280
Gouldshill, Mallow, CO. CORK
Tel: 22 42 430. **Fax:** 2242488.
Email: sara@c103.ie
Web site: http://www.c103.ie
News Editor: Sara McMahon; *Producer:* John-Paul McNamara

C103 (WEST) 4281
Weir Street, Bandon, CO. CORK
Tel: 23 43 103. **Fax:** 2344294.
Email: westcorknews@c103.ie
Web site: http://www.c103.ie
News Editor: Catherine Foley; *Producer:* John-Paul McNamara

CLARE FM 4278
Abbey Field Centre, Francis Street, Ennis, CO. CLARE 0 **Tel:** 65 68 46 712.
Fax: 656840787.
Email: news@clarefm.ie
Web site: http://www.clarefm.ie
News Editor: John Cooke

COMMUNITY RADIO CASTLEBAR 629804
Mosaic Centre Harlequin Plaza, Castlebar, Garvey Rd., CO. MAYO - **Tel:** 94 902 5555.
Email: info@crcfm.ie
Web site: http://www.crcfm.ie

COMMUNITY RADIO YOUGHAL 629833
Cumann Na Daoine, 4 Catherine Street, Youghal, CO. CORK - **Tel:** 24 91 199.
Fax: 2491199.
Email: info@youghalradio.com
Web site: http://www.youghalradio.com
News Editor: Noel Cronan

CONNEMARA COMMUNITY RADIO 629806
Letterfrack, CO. GALWAY - **Tel:** 95 41 616.
Fax: 9541112.
Email: info@connemarafm.com
Web site: http://www.connemarafm.com
News Editor: Bridie Cashin

CORK 96FM AND 103FM 4279
Broadcasting House, Patrick's Place, CORK
Tel: 21 43 92 317. **Fax:** 21 45 51 500.
Email: news@96fm.ie
Web site: http://www.96fm.ie
News Editor: Barry O'Mahony

CORK CAMPUS RADIO 98.3FM 629829
Aras na Mac Leinn, University College Cork, CORK **Tel:** 21 49 02 170. **Fax:** 214903108.
Email: radio@ucc.ie
Web site: http://www.ucc.ie/ccr
News Editor: Kieran Hurley

DUBLIN SOUTH 93.9 FM 754505
Date Complex Level 5, Dundrum Town Centre, Sandyford Road, DUBLIN 16
Tel: 1 29 60 939.
Email: tinadffm939@gmail.com
Web site: http://dublinsouthfm.ie
Producer: Brendan Hickey

DUBLIN'S 98 FM 4282
South Block, The Malt House, Grand Canal Quay, DUBLIN 2 **Tel:** 1 67 08 989.
Fax: 16708968.
Email: news@98fm.com
Web site: http://www.98fm.com
News Editor: Teena Gates

DUBLIN'S COUNTRY MIX 106.8FM 714585
Radio Centre, Killarney Road, Bray, CO. WICKLOW **Tel:** 1 27 24 770. **Fax:** 12724753.
Email: mail@countrymix.ie
Web site: http://www.countrymix.ie
News Editor: Karen Lawless

DUBLIN'S Q 102 754488
Macken House, 39-40 Upper Mayor Street, DUBLIN 1 **Tel:** 1 850 6512.
Email: news@q102.ie
Web site: http://www.q102.ie
News Editor: Newsroom

EAST COAST FM 4283
Radio Centre, Killarney Road, Bray, CO. WICKLOW **Tel:** 1 27 24 700. **Fax:** 12724701.
Email: news@eastcoast.fm
Web site: http://www.eastcoast.fm
News Editor: Garreth Farrell

FLIRT FM 101.3 629813
c/o Áras na MacLéinn, NUI, GALWAY
Tel: 91 49 3470. **Fax:** 91525700.
Email: info@flirtfm.ie
Web site: http://flirtfm.ie
News Editor: Paula Healy

FM 104 DUBLIN 4284
Macken House, Mayor Street Upper, DUBLIN 1 **Tel:** 1 50 06 600. **Fax:** 16689414.
Email: news@fm104.ie
Web site: http://www.fm104.ie
News Editor: Trish Laverty

GALWAY BAY FM 4285
Sandy Road, GALWAY **Tel:** 91 77 00 77.
Fax: 91735168.
Email: news@galwaybayfm.ie
Web site: http://www.galwaybayfm.ie
News Editor: Bernadette Prendergast

HIGHLAND RADIO 4286
Pine Hill, Letterkenny, CO. DONEGAL
Tel: 74 91 25 000. **Fax:** 74 91 25 344.
Email: news@highlandradio.com
Web site: http://www.highlandradio.com
News Editor: Newsroom

INISHOWEN COMMUNITY RADIO 754529
Pound Street Business Park, Carndonagh, Inishowen, CO. DONEGAL
Tel: 74 93 29 105. **Fax:** 749329107.
Email: studio@icrfm.ie
Web site: http://www.icrfm.ie
News Editor: Brian McGowan

KCLR 96FM 1667070
Carlow Studios, Exchequer House, Potato Market, CARLOW 0 **Tel:** 56 77 96 296.
Fax: 567796299.
Email: news@kclr96fm.com
Web site: http://www.kclr96fm.com
News Editor: Sue Nunn

KFM 1667580
KFM Broadcast Centre, Newhall, NAAS 0
Tel: 45 89 89 99. **Fax:** 45898993.
Email: info@kfmradio.com
Web site: http://www.kfmradio.com
News Editor: Ciara Plunkett

LIMERICK'S LIVE 95 FM 4275
PO Box 295, Radio House, Richmond Court, Dock Road, LIMERICK **Tel:** 61 46 19 00.
Fax: 61419595.
Email: news@live95fm.ie
Web site: http://www.live95fm.ie
News Editor: Gillian Devlin

LM FM 4287
Rathmullen Road, Drogheda, CO. LOUTH
Tel: 41 98 32 000. **Fax:** 419832957.
Email: info@lmfm.ie
Web site: http://www.lmfm.ie
News Editor: Michael Carolan

MID WEST RADIO FM 629783
Clare Street, Ballyhaunis, CO. MAYO
Tel: 94 96 30 553. **Fax:** 949630285.
Email: teresa@midwestradio.ie
Web site: http://www.midwestradio.ie
News Editor: Teresa O'Malley

MIDLANDS 103 628760
Tindall House, Axis Business Park, Tullamore, CO. OFFALY **Tel:** 57 93 51 333.
Fax: 57 93 52 546.
Email: newsroom@midlandsradio.fm
Web site: http://www.midlandsradio.fm
News Editor: Clara Walshe

NEAR 90 FM 764485
Northside Civic Centre, Bunratty Road, DUBLIN 17 **Tel:** 1 86 71 190. **Fax:** 18486111.
Email: access@nearfm.ie
Web site: http://www.nearfm.ie
News Editor: Zandra Ball; *Producer:* Michael Fitzgerald

NORTHERN SOUND 4289
Milltown Business Park, Milltown, MONAGHAN **Tel:** 47 72 666. **Fax:** 47 84 447.
Email: news@northernsound.ie
Web site: http://www.northernsound.ie
News Editor: Mary-Claire Grealy

OCEAN FM 629790
North West Business Park, Coolooney, SLIGO **Tel:** 71 91 18 100. **Fax:** 719118101.
Email: niall.delaney@oceanfm.ie
Web site: http://www.oceanfm.ie
News Editor: Niall Delaney

Irish Republic

PHANTOM 105.2 767249
73 North Wall Quay, DUBLIN 1
Tel: 1 88 85 151. **Fax:** 18885171.
Email: info@phantom.ie
Web site: http://www.phantom.ie
News Editor: News Team

RADIO KERRY 4291
Maine Street, Tralee, CO. KERRY 0
Tel: 66 71 23 666. **Fax:** 66 71 22 282.
Email: news@radiokerry.ie
Web site: http://www.radiokerry.ie
News Editor: Treasa Murphy

RAIDIO CORCA BAISCINN 754525
Community Centre, Circular Road, Kilkee, CO. CLARE **Tel:** 65 90 83 022.
Fax: 659056602.
Email: info@raidiocorcabaiscinn.ie
Web site: http://www.raidiocorcabaiscinn.ie
News Editor: Ciaran Ryan

RAIDIÓ NA LIFE 106.4 FM 628762
7 Merrion Square, DUBLIN 2
Tel: 1 66 16 333. **Fax:** 16398401.
Email: eolas@raidionalife.ie
Web site: http://www.raidionalife.ie
News Editor: Dónal Ó Donnabháin

RED FM 104 - 106 767229
1 University Technology Centre, Bishoptown, CORK **Tel:** 21 48 65 566. **Fax:** 214865501.
Email: news@redfm.ie
Web site: http://www.redfm.ie
News Editor: Lana O'Connor

SHANNONSIDE FM 4294
Unit 1E, Master Tech Business Park, Athlone Road, LONGFORD **Tel:** 43 3347777.
Fax: 43 3349384.
Email: news@shannonside.ie
Web site: http://www.shannonside.ie
Presenter: Joe Finnegan

SOUTH EAST RADIO 4295
Custom Quay, WEXFORD -
Tel: 53 91 45 200. **Fax:** 539145295.
Email: news@southeastradio.ie
Web site: http://www.southeastradio.ie
News Editor: Michael Sinnott

SPIN 103.8 767231
3rd Floor, The Malthouse, Grand Canal Quay, DUBLIN 2 **Tel:** 1 65 64 600.
Fax: 1 65 64 690.
Email: info@spin1038.com
Web site: http://www.spin1038.com
News Editor: Rory Nugent; *Director:* Chris Doyle

SPIN SOUTH WEST 1814052
2nd Floor, Landmark Buildings, Raheen, LIMERICK - **Tel:** 61 218 800. **Fax:** 61218899.
Email: news@spinsouthwest.com
Web site: http://www.spinsouthwest.com
News Editor: Ciara Revins

TIPP FM 4296
Gortnafleur Business Park, Powerstown, Clonmel, CO. TIPPERARY 0
Tel: 52 6125 456. **Fax:** 52 615225447.
Email: news@tippfm.com
Web site: http://www.tippfm.com
News Editor: Seamus Martin

TIPPERARY MID-WEST COMMUNITY RADIO 4297
St. Michael Street, TIPPERARY
Tel: 62 52 555. **Fax:** 6252671.
Email: tippmidwest@eircom.net
Web site: http://www.tippmidwestradio.com
News Editor: Joe Pryce

WEST DUBLIN ACCESS RADIO 1665380
Ballyfermot Community Civic Centre, Ballyfermot Road, DUBLIN 10
Tel: 1 62 07 139.
Email: wdar@eircom.net
Web site: http://www.wdar.ie
News Editor: Marian Butler

WIRED FM (LIMERICK) 629832
Mary Immaculate College, South Circular Road, LIMERICK 0 **Tel:** 61 31 57 73.
Email: studio@wiredfm.ie
Web site: http://www.wiredfm.ie
News Editor: Martina O'Brien

WLR FM 4298
The Broadcast Centre, Ardkeen, WATERFORD 0 **Tel:** 51 87 74 71.
Fax: 51846148.
Email: news@wlrfm.com
Web site: http://www.wlrfm.com
News Editor: Liz Reddy

HOSPITAL RADIO

CORK HOSPITAL RADIO 102 FM 764416
Cork University Hospital, Wilton, CORK 4
Tel: 21 43 42 117.
Email: noelwelchcork@yahoo.ie
News Editor: Noel Welch

REGIONAL HOSPITAL RADIO 94.2FM 1665391
Mid-Western Regional Hospital 94.2 FM, H.S.E West, Dooradoyle, LIMERICK
Tel: 61 48 24 23. **Fax:** 61 48 26 80.
Email: tom.osullivan@hse.ie
News Editor: Tom O'Sullivan

ST. ITA'S HOSPITAL RADIO 767226
St. Ita's Hospital, Portrane, Donabate, CO DUBLIN **Tel:** 1 84 36 633.
Email: info@hospitalradio.ie
News Editor: Tom Noctor

Italy

NATIONAL TV STATIONS

MTV ITALIA 14014
Corso Europa, 5, 20122 MILANO
Tel: 02 762171171. **Fax:** 02 762117227.
Email: comunicazioni@mtvne.com
Web site: http://www.mtv.it

REGIONAL TV STATIONS

CANALE ITALIA 764666
Via Pacinotti, 18, 35030 RUBANO PD
Tel: 049 8733111. **Fax:** 049 8733137.
Email: telegiornale@canaleitalia.it
Web site: http://www.canaleitalia.it
Director: Angelo Cimarosti

NATIONAL RADIO STATIONS

RADIO 105 NETWORK 13998
Via Moscova, 14/A, 20121 MILANO
Tel: 02 62537480. **Fax:** 02 6551801.
Web site: http://www.105.net
Editor: Daniela Ducoli; *Director:* Paolo Del Forno

RADIO CUORE SARDEGNA 764373
Via Carpaccio Vittore, 26, 09170 ORISTANO OR **Tel:** 0783 310221. **Fax:** 0783 310427.
Email: redazione@radiocuore.net
Web site: http://www.radiocuore.net

RADIO ITALIA SOLO MUSICA IT. - NOTIZIE 13993
Viale Europa, 49, 20093 COLOGNO MONZESE MI **Tel:** 02 254441.
Fax: 02 25444220.
Email: redazione@radioitalia.it
Web site: http://www.radioitalia.it

RADIO MONTECARLO - NEWS 13995
Via Moscova, 14/a, 20121 MILANO MI
Tel: 02 231521. **Fax:** 02 6551801.
Web site: http://www.radiomontecarlo.net
Editor: Daniela Ducoli; *Director:* Paolo Del Forno

RADIO RADICALE 13996
Via Principe Amedeo, 2, 00185 ROMA
Tel: 06 488781. **Fax:** 06 4880196.
Email: redazione@radioradicale.it
Web site: http://www.radioradicale.it

REGIONAL RADIO STATIONS

MALVISI NETWORK 764890
Str. Piacentine, 105, 43011 LOCALITÀ RONCOLE VERDI PR **Tel:** 0524 930188.
Fax: 0524 931519.
Email: musica@malvisi.it
Web site: http://www.malvisi.it

RADIO BELLAVITA SASSARI 766004
Piazza Castello, 11, 07100 SASSARI
Tel: 079 231851. **Fax:** 079 231851.
Email: redazione@stereoquattro.it
Web site: http://www.stereoquattro.it

RADIO CENTRO SUONO 766100
Via S. Talamo, 47/49, 00177 ROMA RM
Tel: 06 2588830. **Fax:** 062588830.
Email: centrosuono@radiocentrosuono.it
Web site: http://www.radiocentrosuono.it

RADIO DIMENSIONE SUONO 766107
Via Pier Ruggiero Piccio, 55, 00136 ROMA
Tel: 06 377041. **Fax:** 0637704350.
Email: segr.redazione@rds.it
Web site: http://www.rds.it

Liechtenstein

NATIONAL RADIO STATIONS

RADIO LIECHTENSTEIN 1841048
Dorfstr. 24, 9495 TRIESEN **Tel:** 3 3991313.
Fax: 3 3991399.
Email: redaktion@radio.li
Web site: http://www.radio.li
News Editor: Martin Frommelt; *Editor:* Alois Ospelt

Luxembourg

NATIONAL TV STATIONS

RTL TÉLÉ LËTZEBUERG 1867
45, bd. Pierre Frieden, L-1543 LUXEMBOURG **Tel:** 42 14 28 10.
Fax: 421427431.
Email: telenews@rtl.lu
Web site: http://www.rtl.lu

NATIONAL RADIO STATIONS

RADIO 100.7 (RSC) 1856
PO box 1833, L-1018 LUXEMBOURG
Tel: 44 00 44 1. **Fax:** 440044940.
Email: redaction@100komma7.lu
Web site: http://www.100komma7.lu
Director: Fernand Weides

RTL RADIO LËTZEBUERG 1855
45, bd. Pierre Frieden, L-1543 LUXEMBOURG **Tel:** 42 14 28 00.
Fax: 421423753.
Email: news@rtl.lu
Web site: http://www.rtl.lu

REGIONAL RADIO STATIONS

DNR 1942
2, Rue Christophe Plantin, L-2339 LUXEMBOURG **Tel:** 40 24 01. **Fax:** 407998.
Email: redaktioun@dnr.lu
Web site: http://www.dnr.lu

ELDORADIO 1944
45, boulevard Pierre Frieden, L-1543 LUXEMBOURG **Tel:** 40 95 091.
Fax: 409509509.
Email: redaction@eldoradio.lu
Web site: http://www.eldoradio.lu
Director: Christophe Gossens; *Producer:* Ivano Andresini

RADIO ARA 2029
2, rue de la Boucherie, L-1247 LUXEMBOURG **Tel:** 22 22 89. **Fax:** 222266.
Email: radioara@pt.lu
Web site: http://www.ara.lu

Monaco

REGIONAL RADIO STATIONS

RADIO MONACO 1835190
7 rue du Gabian, 98000 MONACO
Tel: 9 77 00 62 1. **Fax:** 9 77 73 50 1.
Email: redaction@radio-monaco.com
Web site: http://www.radio-monaco.com
Presenter: Benjamin Duconge

RADIO RIVIERA MONACO 106.3 1620317
10-12 quai Antoine-1er, 98000 MONACO
Tel: 979 794 75. **Fax:** 979 794 95.
Email: info@rivieraradio.mc
Web site: http://www.rivieraradio.mc
Director: Dominique Denry

Norway

NATIONAL TV STATIONS

CANAL+ FILM 1 1810341
Pb. 80 Bryn, 0611 OSLO **Tel:** 22 93 93 33.
Fax: 22 65 72 52.
Email: dialog@canalplus.no
Web site: http://www.canalplus.no

CANAL+ FILM 2 1810340
Pb. 80 Bryn, 0611 OSLO **Tel:** 22 93 93 33.
Fax: 22 65 72 52.
Email: dialog@canalplus.no
Web site: http://www.canalplus.no

CANAL+ FILM 3 1810344
Pb. 80 Bryn, 0611 OSLO **Tel:** 22 93 93 33.
Fax: 22 65 72 52.
Email: dialog@canalplus.no
Web site: http://www.canalplus.no

CANAL+ MIX FILM 1810342
Pb. 80 Bryn, 0611 OSLO **Tel:** 22 93 93 33.
Fax: 22 65 72 52.
Email: dialog@canalplus.no
Web site: http://www.canalplus.no

CANAL+ SPORT 1 1810345
Pb. 80 Bryn, 0611 OSLO **Tel:** 22 65 72 52.
Fax: 22 65 72 52.
Email: dialog@canalplus.no
Web site: http://www.canalplus.no

CANAL+ SPORT 2 1810347
Pb. 80 Bryn, 0611 OSLO **Tel:** 22 93 93 33.
Fax: 22 65 72 52.
Email: dialog@canalplus.no
Web site: http://www.canalplus.no

CANAL+ SPORT HD 1810348
Pb. 80 Bryn, 0611 OSLO **Tel:** 22 93 93 33.
Fax: 22 65 72 52.
Email: dialog@canalplus.no
Web site: http://www.canalplus.no

FEM 1827754
TVNorge, Pb. 11 Sentrum, NO-0101 OSLO
Tel: 21 02 20 00.
Email: info@femtv.no
Web site: http://www.femtv.no

NRK 1; AMIGO 1740896
Email: amigo@nrk.no

NRK 1; BEAT FOR BEAT 1740899
Email: beatforbeat@nrk.no
Web site: http://www.nrk.no/beatforbeat
Presenter: Ivar Dyrhaug

NRK 1; GUDSTJENESTEN 1740904
Email: gudstjenesten@nrk.no

NRK 1; KAOSKONTROLL 1740905
Email: kaoskontroll@nrk.no

NRK 1; NORGE I DAG 1863336
Marienlyst, 0340 OSLO **Tel:** 23 04 80 00.
Email: nyheter@nrk.no

NRK 1; NYTT PÅ NYTT 1740908
Email: nyttpanytt@nrk.no
Web site: http://www.nrk.no/nyttpanytt

NRK 1; SPORTSREVYEN 1740910
Email: sporten@nrk.no

NRK 2; NATTØNSKET 1740916
Email: natt@nrk.no

NRK 2; URIX 1740914
NRK URIX, 0340 OSLO **Tel:** 23048210.
Email: urix@nrk.no
Web site: http://www.nrk.no/programmer/sider/urix
Editor: Stein Bjøntegård; *Presenter:* Gunnar Myklebust

NRK DAGSNYTT 1863941
Marienlyst, 0340 OSLO **Tel:** 23 04 70 00.
Email: nyheter@nrk.no
Web site: http://www.nrk.no/nyheter

NRK DAGSREVYEN 1625465
0340 OSLO **Tel:** 23 04 82 10.
Fax: 23047178.
Email: dagsrevyen@nrk.no
Web site: http://www.nrk.no/nyheter

NRK SPORT (AVDELING) 1740911
NRK Sport, FF13, 0340 OSLO
Tel: 23 04 95 05. **Fax:** 23047450.
Email: sporten@nrk.no
Web site: http://www.nrk.no/sport

NRK SUPER 1830171
0340 OSLO **Tel:** 23 04 70 00.
Fax: 23 04 75 75.
Email: NRKSuper@nrk.no
Web site: http://www.nrksuper.no

SPORTN 1740740
SportN Pb. Viasat Youngstorget, 0028 OSLO
Tel: 22 99 00 33. **Fax:** 22 99 00 19.
Email: info@sportn.tv
Web site: http://www.sportn.tv

TV1000 NORGE 32106
Pb 8864 Youngstorget, 0028 OSLO
Tel: 22 99 01 30. **Fax:** 22 99 01 35.
Email: redaksjonen@tv1000.no
Web site: http://www.tv1000.no

TV2 FILMKANALEN 1810355
Pb. 2, Sentrum, NO-0101 OSLO
Email: info@tv2filmkanalen.no
Web site: http://pub.tv2.no/TV2/tv2filmkanalen

TV2 ZEBRA 1740759
Pb. 7222, NO-5020 BERGEN **Tel:** 02 25 5.
Email: info@tv2zebra.no
Web site: http://pub.tv2.no/TV2/zebra

TV3 1625460
Pb TV3 Youngstorget, 0028 OSLO
Tel: 22 99 00 33. **Fax:** 22990018.
Email: info@tv3.no
Web site: http://www.tv3.no

TV3; SPORT 1697385
Email: sport@tv3.no

TVNORGE 1625463
Nydalen Allé 37, 0484 OSLO
Tel: 21 02 20 00. **Fax:** 22051000.
Email: tvnorge@tvnorge.no
Web site: http://www.tvnorge.no

TVNORGE; SPORTEN 1740765
Email: sporten@tvnorge.no

VIASAT4 ; NYHETER FRA P4 1828652
Pb. 8864 Youngstorget, 0028 OSLO
Tel: 61 24 84 44.
Email: nyhetene@p4.no
Web site: http://www.viasat4.no

VIASAT SPORT 1740741
Akersgaten 73, 0028 OSLO **Tel:** 22 99 00 33.
Fax: 22990019.
Email: sport@viasatsport.no
Web site: http://www.viasat.no

THE VOICE 1693023
Pb. 1102 Sentrum, 0104 OSLO
Tel: 22 02 33 00.
Email: redaksjonen@thevoice.no
Web site: http://www.thevoicetv.no

REGIONAL TV STATIONS

NRK MØRE OG ROMSDAL (DISTRIKTSKONTOR) 32065
NRK Møre og Romsdal, 6025 ÅLESUND
Tel: 70 11 52 00.
Email: mr@nrk.no
Web site: http://www.nrk.no/mr
Presenter: Ivar Eidheim

NRK ØSTAFJELLS (DISTRIKTSKONTOR) 32061
NRK Østafjells, Postboks 284, 3901 PORSGRUNN **Tel:** 02 34 5. **Fax:** 35560254.
Email: 02345@nrk.no
Web site: http://www.nrk.no/buskerud

NRK ØSTFOLD (DISTRIKTSKONTOR) 32069
Pb 33, 1629 GAMLE FREDRIKSTAD
Tel: 69 38 48 00. **Fax:** 69 38 48 07.
Email: ostfold@nrk.no
Web site: http://www.nrk.no/ostfold

NRK SOGN OG FJORDANE (DISTRIKTSKONTOR) 32072
Pb 100, 6801 FØRDE **Tel:** 57 72 42 42.
Email: sfj@nrk.no
Web site: http://www.nrk.no/sfj
Presenter: Kjellrun Lavik

NRK SØRLANDET (DISTRIKTSKONTOR) 32074
Pb. 413, 4668 KRISTIANSAND S
Tel: 38 12 12 12. **Fax:** 38121799.
Email: sorlandet@nrk.no
Web site: http://www.nrk.no/sorlandet

TV2 32108
Nøstegaten 72, Pb 7222, 5020 BERGEN
Tel: 02255. **Fax:** 55908105.
Email: pressemelding@tv2.no
Web site: http://www.tv2.no

TV2~ AVD. HAMAR 32079
2317 HAMAR **Tel:** 62 52 22 69.
Fax: 62 53 41 68.
Web site: http://www.tv2.no

TV2~ AVD. KRISTIANSAND 32080
Tordenskjoldsgate 9, 4612 KRISTIANSAND S **Tel:** 38 02 38 08. **Fax:** 38 02 38 53.
Email: pressemelding@tv2.no
Web site: http://www.tv2.no

TV2~ AVD. STAVANGER 32082
Lagerveien 19, 4033 STAVANGER
Tel: 51 57 08 80. **Fax:** 51 57 08 81.
Email: pressemelding@tv2.no
Web site: http://www.tv2.no

TV2~ AVD. TROMSØ 32083
Pb 3, 9251 TROMSØ **Tel:** 77 61 11 11.
Fax: 77 61 11 10.
Email: pressemelding@tv2.no
Web site: http://www.tv2.no

TV2~ AVD. TRONDHEIM 32084
Kjøpmannsgata 23, 7013 TRONDHEIM
Tel: 73 50 73 10. **Fax:** 73 50 73 20.
Email: terje.dalen@tv2.no
Web site: http://www.tv2.no

TV TELEMARK 32086
Pb. 2833, 3702 SKIEN **Tel:** 35 50 40 00.
Fax: 35 50 40 01.
Email: red@tvtelemark.no
Web site: http://www.ta.no/tvtelemark
Presenter: Tone Lensebakken

CABLE TV

BTV 32114
Pb 7240, 5020 BERGEN **Tel:** 05 50 0.
Fax: 55 31 92 31.
Email: tips@bt.no
Web site: http://www.bt.no/btv

NÆRSYNET 32097
Pb 500, 6101 VOLDA **Tel:** 70 07 51 89.
Fax: 70 07 51 55.
Email: nett@hivolda.no
Web site: http://www.hivolda.no

STUDENT-TV / STV 32104
Elgsetergt. 1, 7030 TRONDHEIM
Tel: 73 59 80 94.
Email: tips@stv.no
Web site: http://www.stv.no

TV BUDSTIKKA 32088
Pb. 133, 1376 BILLINGSTAD
Tel: 66 77 00 00. **Fax:** 66 77 00 60.
Email: nettredaksjonen@budstikka.no
Web site: http://www.tvbudstikka.no
Presenter: Kim van der Linden

TV GRORUDDALEN 32091
Pb 100 Grorud, NO-0905 OSLO
Tel: 22 91 88 20. **Fax:** 22 16 01 05.
Email: redaksjonen@groruddalen.no
Web site: http://www.groruddalen.no

TV HAUGALAND 32112
Pb 408, 5501 HAUGESUND
Tel: 52 80 88 00. **Fax:** 52 80 88 01.
Email: frode.nygaard@tvhaugaland.no
Web site: http://www.tvhaugaland.no
Presenter: Mona Terjesen

TV ISLAM AHMADIYYA 32115
Pb 3002 Elisenberg, 0207 OSLO
Tel: 22 44 71 88. **Fax:** 22 43 78 17.
Email: ahmadiyya@online.no

TV NORDVEST 32116
Pb 471, 6501 KRISTIANSUND N
Tel: 71 57 01 00. **Fax:** 71 57 01 01.
Email: tvn@tvn.no
Web site: http://www.tvnordvest.no

TV SUNNMØRE 32119
Moaveien 11, 6018 ÅLESUND
Tel: 70 15 84 50. **Fax:** 70 15 84 51.
Email: tips@tvs.no
Web site: http://www.tvs.no
Editor: Per Magne Thalberg

NATIONAL RADIO STATIONS

NRK BARN 1810300
Bjørnstjerne Bjørnsons Plass 1, NO-0340 OSLO **Tel:** 23 04 70 00. **Fax:** 23 04 71 78.

NRK MP3 (KANAL) 1740893
NRK mPetre, 7005 TRONDHEIM
Tel: 73 88 14 00. **Fax:** 73 88 18 09.
Email: helge@nrk.no
Web site: http://www.nrk.no/mpetre

NRK P1 (KANAL) 1645204
NRK P1, 7005 TRONDHEIM
Tel: 73 88 14 00. **Fax:** 73881400.
Email: p1@nrk.no
Web site: http://www.nrk.no/p1

NRK P1; KVELDSMAT 1740831
Email: kveldsmat@nrk.no

NRK P1; NOSTALGIA 1740835
Nostalgia i nrk P1, Marienlyst RB 22, 0342 OSLO
Email: nostalgia@nrk.no
Web site: http://www.nrk.no/programmer/sider/nostalgia

NRK P1; ØNSKEKONSERTEN 1740848
Ønskekonserten NRK, 7005 TRONDHEIM
Tel: 73 88 14 00.
Email: onskekonserten@nrk.no
Web site: http://www.nrk.no/programmer/sider/oenskekonserten

NRK P1; PÅ DANSEFOT 1740839
På dansefot, NRK P1, 7005 TRONDHEIM
Tel: 73 88 18 20.
Email: dansefot@nrk.no
Web site: http://www.nrk.no/dansefot
Presenter: Erik Forfod

NRK P1; PEPPER & PASJON 1740838
Pepper & pasjon, NRK underholdning, RB 22, 0340 OSLO **Tel:** 23042822.
Email: pepper@nrk.no
Web site: http://www.nrk.no/pepper
Presenter: Ragnhild Silkebækken

NRK P1; P.I.L.S. 1740836
Email: pils@nrk.no
Web site: http://www.nrk.no/programmer/sider/pils

NRK P1; RADIOSPORTEN 1740840
NRK. Radiosporten, 0340 OSLO
Tel: 23 04 79 87. **Fax:** 23 04 78 45.
Email: radiosporten@nrk.no
Web site: http://www.nrk.no/radiosporten

NRK P1; RUNDT MIDNATT 1740841
Email: midnatt@nrk.no
Web site: http://www.nrk.no/programmer/sider/rundt_midnatt

NRK P1; RYK OG REIS 1740842
Ryk og reis, NRK P1, 7005 TRONDHEIM
Email: rykogreis@nrk.no
Web site: http://www.nrk.no/rykogreis

NRK P1; SALMER TIL ALLE TIDER 1740843
Salmer til alle tider, NRK P1, 7005 TRONDHEIM **Tel:** 73 88 18 15.
Email: salmer@nrk.no
Web site: http://www.nrk.no/programmer/sider/salmer_til_alle_tider

NRK P1; SANGTIMEN 1740844
NRK Sangtimen, 5400 STORD
Tel: 53 41 36 00.
Email: nils.abrahamsen@nrk.no
Web site: http://www.nrk.no/programmer/sider/sangtimen
Presenter: Nils Abrahamsen

NRK P1; SØLVSUPER 1740845
Sølvsuper, NRK Tyholt, 7005 TRONDHEIM
Email: solvsuper@nrk.no
Web site: http://www.nrk.no/solvsuper

NRK P1; TOPP 40 1740846
Email: topp40@nrk.no
Web site: http://www.nrk.no/programmer/sider/topp_40

NRK P1; TRAFIKKRADIO 1740847
NRK NYHETER **Tel:** 23048000.
Email: nyheter@nrk.no
Web site: http://www.nrk.no/trafikk

NRK P2; BLINDEBUKK 1740849
Email: blindebukk@nrk.no

NRK P2; BLUESASYLET 1740850
Tel: 23 04 72 74.
Email: bluesasylet@nrk.no
Web site: http://www.nrk.no/programmer/sider/bluesasylet

NRK P2; FOLKEMUSIKKTIMEN 1740852
Tel: 23 04 73 88.
Email: folkemusikk@nrk.no
Web site: http://www.nrk.no/programmer/sider/folkemusikktimen
Presenter: Leiv Solberg

NRK P2; JAZZKLUBBEN 1740855
NRK Jazz, RT 32, NRK, 0340 OSLO
Tel: 23 04 85 51.
Email: jazz@nrk.no
Web site: http://www.nrk.no/programmer/sider/jazzklubben

NRK P2; JUNGELTELEGRAFEN 1740856
Jungeltelegrafen, RT 32, NRK, 0340 OSLO
Tel: 23 04 26 58.
Email: jungeltelegrafen@nrk.no
Web site: http://www.nrk.no/programmer/sider/jungeltelegrafen
Presenter: Arne Berg

NRK P2 (KANAL) 1625396
Bjønstjerne Bjørnsons Plass 1, 0340 OSLO
Tel: 23 04 84 06. **Fax:** 23047480.
Email: p2desken@nrk.no
Web site: http://www.nrk.no/p2

NRK P2; MORGENKÅSERI 1740858
Morgenkåseriet v/Harald Overå, NRK, RM 21, 0340 OSLO **Tel:** 41409120.
Web site: http://www.nrk.no/programmer/sider/morgenkaaseri
Editor: Harald Overå

NRK P2; MUSEUM 1740860
MUSEUM c/O NRK Østfold Pb. 33, 1629 GAMLE FREDRIKSTAD **Tel:** 69 38 48 00.
Email: museum@nrk.no
Web site: http://www.nrk.no/programmer/sider/museum

NRK P2; MUSIKK I BRENNPUNKTET 1740861
Email: musikkibrennpunktet@nrk.no
Web site: http://www.nrk.no/programmer/sider/musikk_i_brennpunktet

NRK P2; MUSIKKANTIKK 1740862
Tel: 23 04 88 93.
Email: musikkantikk@nrk.no
Web site: http://www.nrk.no/programmer/sider/musikkantikk
Presenter: Halfdan Bleken

NRK P2; MUSIKKMANESJEN 1740863
Email: musikkmanesjen@nrk.no
Web site: http://www.nrk.no/programmer/sider/musikkmanesjen

NRK P2; PÅ LIVET LAUS 1740867
På livet laus, NRK P2, FG22, 0340 OSLO
Email: livet@nrk.no
Web site: http://www.nrk.no/programmer/sider/paa_livet_laus
Editor: Jan Erlend Leine; *Presenter:* Astrid Brekken

NRK P2; PÅ SPORET - NYTT PÅ CD 1740868
Email: pa.sporet@nrk.no
Web site: http://www.nrk.no/programmer/sider/paa_sporet

NRK P2; RADIODOKUMENTAREN 1740869
OFRD, FG 22, NRK, 0340 OSLO
Tel: 23 04 75 01. **Fax:** 23 04 94 63.
Email: radiodokumentar@nrk.no
Web site: http://www.nrk.no/radiodokumentaren

NRK P2; RADIOFRONT 1740872
Tel: 23049309.
Email: radiofront@nrk.no
Web site: http://www.nrk.no/programmer/sider/radiofront

NRK P2; RADIOSELSKAPET 1740873
Tel: 23 04 94 69.
Email: radioselskapet@nrk.no
Web site: http://www.nrk.no/programmer/sider/radioselskapet

NRK P2; RING INN MUSIKKEN 1740874
Email: ring.inn.musikken@nrk.no
Web site: http://www.nrk.no/programmer/sider/ring_inn_musikken

NRK P2; SÅNN ER LIVET 1740876
Tel: 23 04 95 02.
Email: sannerlivet@nrk.no
Web site: http://www.nrk.no/programmer/sider/saann_er_livet

NRK P2; SPRÅKTEIGEN 1740875
Språkteigen, NRK P2, 7005 TRONDHEIM
Tel: 55 27 52 69.
Email: teigen@nrk.no
Web site: http://www.nrk.no/programmer/sider/spraakteigen

NRK P2; TRANSIT 1740877
Bjørnstjerne Bjørnsons plass 1, 0340 OSLO
Tel: 23 04 88 54.
Email: kjetil.bjorgan@nrk.no
Web site: http://www.nrk.no/programmer/sider/transit
Presenter: Kjetil Bjørgan

NRK P2; UKAS P2-ARTIST 1740878
NRK, 0340 OSLO **Tel:** 23 04 72 74.
Email: anne.sofie.stang@nrk.no
Web site: http://www.nrk.no/programmer/sider/ukas_p2-artist

NRK P2; VERDIBØRSEN 1740879
Tel: 2304401.
Email: verdiborsen@nrk.no
Web site: http://www.nrk.no/programmer/sider/verdiboersen

NRK P2; VERDT Å VITE 1740880
Verdt å Vite, FG22, 0340 OSLO
Tel: 23042785.
Email: vite@nrk.no
Web site: http://www.nrk.no/programmer/sider/verdt_aa_vite
Presenter: Espen Eggen

NRK P3; P3MORGEN 1740885
Bjørnstjerne Bjørnsons Plass 1, Marienlyst, OSLO
Email: p3morgen@nrk.no
Web site: http://nrkp3.no/p3morgen
Presenter: Yngve Reite

NRK P3; PIA 1740887
Pia Skevik, NRK P3, 0340 OSLO
Email: pia.skevik@nrk.no
Web site: http://nrk.no/p3/program/pia
Presenter: Pia Skevik

NRK P3; PYRO 1740888
Email: pyro@nrk.no
Web site: http://nrk.no/p3/program/pyro

P4 RADIO~ AVD. BERGEN 1740680
5012 BERGEN **Tel:** 55 90 36 03.
Email: p4@p4.no

P4 RADIO~ AVD. KRISTIANSAND 1740681
4612 KRISTIANSAND **Tel:** 38 02 36 46.
Email: p4@p4.no

P4 RADIO~ AVD. OSLO 1740679
0159 OSLO **Tel:** 23 00 00 44.
Email: p4@p4.no

P4 RADIO~ AVD. TROMSØ 1740682
Pb. 754, 9001 TROMSØ **Tel:** 77 64 33 09.
Email: p4@p4.no

P4 RADIO; MISJONEN MED ANTONSEN OG GOLDEN 1985626
Email: misjonen@p4.no
Web site: http://www.p4.no/programmer/homepage.aspx?id=751

P4 RADIO; OPP OG HOPP MED NISSA OG ELISABETH 1985627
Serviceboks, 2626 2626 LILLEHAMMER LILLEHAMMER
Email: oppoghopp@p4.no
Web site: http://www.p4.no/programmer/homepage.aspx?id=422

P4 RADIO; VI OG VERDEN - INNENRIKS 1985727
Serviceboks, 2626 LILLEHAMMER
Email: viogverden@p4.no
Web site: http://www.p4.no/programmer/homepage.aspx?id=393

RADIO NORGE 1645200
Jernbanetorget 4 A, 3 etg, PB 1102 Sentrum, 0104 OSLO **Tel:** 07270.
Email: redaksjon@radionorge.com
Web site: http://www.radionorge.com
Editor: Kristoffer Vangen; *Presenter:* Hege Tepstad

RADIO NORGE; NORGESNYHETENE 1840345
Pb. 144, 1601 FREDRISKTAD
Tel: 815 110 24. **Fax:** 69 70 76 01.
Email: nyheter@radionorge.com
Web site: http://www.radionorge.fm

RADIO PRIME HALDEN 1740768
Postboks 233, 1752 HALDEN
Tel: 69 17 50 00.
Email: halden@radioprime.com
Web site: http://www2.radioprime.com/halden
Presenter: John Erik Strøm

REGIONAL RADIO STATIONS

ACEM RADIO 31807
Pb 2559 Solli, 0202 OSLO **Tel:** 23 11 87 00.
Email: acem@acem.no
Web site: http://www.acem.no
Editor: Geir Wærnes

BUDSTIKKA RADIO TRØNDELAG 31812
Pb 391, 7501 STJØRDAL **Tel:** 74 83 95 95.
Fax: 74 83 95 90.
Email: budstikka.radio@ktv.no
Web site: http://www.budstikkaradio.no
Editor: Jostein Mork

BYGDERADIO VEST 32031
Pb 216, 6101 VOLDA **Tel:** 70 07 85 00.
Email: post@bygderadiovest.no
Web site: http://bygderadiovest.no

CREATIVE RADIO - ØSTLANDSRADIOEN 31815
Pb. 113, 1417 SOFIEMYR **Tel:** 66 80 11 05.
Fax: 66 80 16 45.
Email: post@radio.no
Web site: http://www.radio.no/ostlandsradioen/index.htm

DRANGEDAL NÆRRADIO 31816
Kjørkeveien 1, 3750 DRANGEDAL
Tel: 35 99 63 00. **Fax:** 35 99 67 67.

EXACT MEDIA 31942
Pb 454, 2304 HAMAR **Tel:** 62 51 96 30.
Fax: 62 51 96 31.
Email: red@exact24.no
Web site: http://www.exact24.no
Presenter: Thomas Mølstad

GIMLEKOLLEN RADIO 31820
Serviceboks 410, 4604 KRISTIANSAND S
Tel: 38 14 50 35.
Email: ksv@gimra.no
Web site: http://www.gimra.no
Editor: Kai-Steinar Vangen

HALLO KRAGERØ 31825
Frydenborgveien 4, 3770 KRAGERØ
Tel: 35 98 00 00.
Email: post@hallokragero.no
Web site: http://www.hallokragero.no

HÅPETS RØST 31833
Restaurationsveien 1, 4085 HUNDVÅG
Tel: 51 86 12 26.
Email: movaag@online.no
Web site: http://www.haapetsrost.no
Editor: Morten Vågshaug

HAVØYSUND NÆRRADIO 31827
Pb 123, 9691 HAVØYSUND
Tel: 78 42 34 44. **Fax:** 78 42 37 44.

HJALARHORNET RADIO 31828
Pb. 3, 3840 SELJORD **Tel:** 35 05 20 05.
Email: post@hjalar.no
Web site: http://www.hjalar.no

INNLANDET NÆRRADIO 31834
Pb. 211, 9365 BARDU **Tel:** 975 975 13.
Fax: 77 19 00 20.
Email: post@inr.no
Web site: http://www.inr.no
Editor: Mirsad Kekic

JÆREN MISJONSRADIO 31835
Tryggheimvegen 13, 4365 NÆRBØ
Tel: 51 79 80 00. **Fax:** 51 79 80 81.
Email: bvoll@tryggheim.no
Web site: http://www.norea.no

JÆRRADIOEN (JRG) 31836
Pb 10, 4301 SANDNES **Tel:** 51 97 92 00.
Fax: 51 97 92 56.
Email: post@jaerradioen.no
Web site: http://www.jaerradioen.no

KONTAKT RADIO 31842
Florsgate 1 B, 3211 SANDEFJORD
Tel: 33 48 22 22.
Web site: http://salemsandefjord.no

KYSTRADIOEN 31844
Skjenet 2, 5353 STRAUME **Tel:** 56 32 17 01.
Email: post@kystradioen.no
Web site: http://www.kystradioen.no
Editor: Johnn R. Hardang

MJØSRADIOEN (FILADELFIA) 31850
Grønnegata 33, 2317 HAMAR
Tel: 62 53 45 50.
Email: post@mjosradioen.no
Web site: http://www.mjosradioen.no

MØTET MED JESUS NÆRRADIO 31853
Møtet med Jesus Tro og Misjonsenter, Farmoveien 9, 4520 SØR-AUDNEDAL
Tel: 38 25 70 55. **Fax:** 38 25 80 51.
Email: mmjesus@online.no
Presenter: Jan Frode Johansen

NEA RADIO 31854
Postboks 60, 7581 SELBU **Tel:** 73 81 74 00.
Fax: 73 81 74 99.
Email: nr-selbu@nearadio.no
Web site: http://www.nearadio.no

NESNA RADIO 31856
Moveien 25, 8700 NESNA **Tel:** 75 05 65 00.
Email: postmottak@nesnaradio.no
Web site: http://nesnaradio.no

NORDFJORD NÆRRADIO 31858
Teina 7, 6823 SANDANE **Tel:** 57 86 67 50.

NORRØNA RADIO, ÅLESUND 31861
Pb. 7503 Spjelkavik, 6022 ÅLESUND
Tel: 70 17 44 00. **Fax:** 70 17 44 10.
Email: post@norronaradio.no
Web site: http://www.norronaradio.no

NORRØNA RADIO, MOLDE 31860
co/ Hans Bergane, Solemdal, 6456 SKÅLA
Tel: 71 25 18 55.
Email: hberga@online.no
Web site: http://www.nlm.no

NRK ROGALAND (DISTRIKTSKONTOR) 31875
Pb 614 Madla, 4090 HAFRSFJORD
Tel: 51 72 72 72. **Fax:** 51 72 72 55.
Email: rogaland@nrk.no
Web site: http://www.nrk.no/rogaland
Presenter: Øystein Ellingsen

NRK TROMS & FINNMARK-TROMS (DISTRIKTSKONTOR) 31879
Nrk Troms, 9291 TROMSØ **Tel:** 77 66 12 00.
Fax: 77 66 12 84.
Email: troms@nrk.no
Web site: http://www.nrk.no/nordnytt

OTTADALSRADIOEN 31882
Brennveien 3, 2680 VÅGÅ **Tel:** 61 23 95 00.
Fax: 61 23 95 01.
Email: ottadals@online.no

P5 BERGEN 1985631
Kløverhuset, Strandgaten 15, 5013 BERGEN
Web site: http://bergen.p5.no
Presenter: Sigrid Haaland

RADIO 102 31903
Pb 102, 5506 HAUGESUND **Tel:** 52 720 102.
Fax: 52 84 61 03.
Email: post@radio102.no
Web site: http://www.radio102.no
Editor: Thor-Magnar Thorsen; *Presenter:* Per Ivar Reine

RADIO 1 BERGEN 31891
Christian Michelsensgt. 2a, 5012 BERGEN
Tel: 55 94 84 00.
Email: kontakt@radio1.no
Web site: http://www.radio1.no

RADIO 1 OSLO 31898
Pb 1102, Sentrum, 0104 OSLO
Tel: 22 02 33 00. **Fax:** 22 02 33 14.
Email: kontakt@radio1.no
Web site: http://www.radio1.no

RADIO 1 STAVANGER 31900
Skagen 27, 4006 STAVANGER
Tel: 51 53 75 75. **Fax:** 51 53 765 55.
Email: kontakt@radio1.no
Web site: http://www.radio1.no

RADIO 1 TRONDHEIM 31902
Bassengbakken 1, 7042 TRONDHEIM
Tel: 73 50 05 00. **Fax:** 73 50 00 00.
Email: lars.petter.berg@radio1.no
Web site: http://www.radio1.no

RADIO 3 BODØ 31905
Storgata 38, 8002 BODØ **Tel:** 75 52 50 00.
Email: epost@radio3.no
Web site: http://www.radio3.no
Presenter: Anders Hammer

RADIO ÅLESUND (JRG) 32041
Lorkenesgaten 1, 6002 ÅLESUND
Tel: 70 11 10 50. **Fax:** 70 11 10 55.
Email: post@radioaalesund.no
Web site: http://www.radioaalesund.no
Presenter: Egil Farstad

RADIO ALTA 31909
Pb 1193, 9504 ALTA **Tel:** 78 45 67 00.
Fax: 78 45 67 41.
Email: redaksjonen@radioalta.no
Web site: http://www.altaposten.no
Presenter: Arne Hauge

RADIO BØLGEN 32022
Pinsekirken Tabernaklet, Postboks 404 Marken, 5828 BERGEN **Tel:** 55 55 36 80.
Fax: 55 55 36 81.
Email: radio@ptb.no
Web site: http://www.radiobolgen.no

RADIO DSF 31921
Finnlandsveien 14, 9730 KARASJOK
Tel: 78 46 72 05. **Fax:** 78 46 71 64.
Email: radio.dsf@samemisjonen.no
Web site: http://www.samemisjonen.no/media/radioarbeidet
Presenter: Alf Kr. Tellefsen

RADIO E6 31922
Inge Krokansvei 11, 7340 OPPDAL
Tel: 72 42 20 80. **Fax:** 72 42 25 25.
Email: perroar@opp.no
Web site: http://www.opp.nu

RADIO EVJE 31923
Pb 257, 4734 EVJE **Tel:** 37 93 13 50.
Fax: 37 93 07 07.

RADIO FANA 31924
postboks 364 Nesttun, 5853 BERGEN
Tel: 55 52 75 30.
Email: radiofana@nesttunbedehus.no
Web site: http://nesttunbedehus.no

RADIO FILADELFIA, DRAMMEN 31818
Tomtegt. 2, 3015 DRAMMEN
Tel: 32 83 15 50.
Email: post@radiofiladelfia.no
Web site: http://www.radiofiladelfia.no

RADIO FOLGEFONN 31931
Røldalsveien 2, 5750 ODDA
Tel: 53 64 44 44. **Fax:** 53 64 34 89.
Email: post@radiofolgefonn.no
Web site: http://www.radiofolgefonn.no

RADIO FOLLO 31932
Pb. 201, 1431 ÅS **Tel:** 64 94 10 02.
Fax: 64 94 10 88.
Email: post@radiofollo.no
Web site: http://www.radiofollo.no
Editor: Rodny Kaastad

RADIO GNISTEN 31936
Sigurdsgate 6, 5015 BERGEN
Tel: 55 90 48 00. **Fax:** 55 90 48 10.
Email: radiognisten@nlm.no
Web site: http://www.radiognisten.no

RADIO GRIMSTAD 31939
Pb 300, 4892 GRIMSTAD **Tel:** 37 04 30 99.
Fax: 37 04 39 10.
Email: post@radiogrimstad.no
Web site: http://www.radiogrimstad.no

RADIO HALLINGDAL 31941
Pb 54, 3575 HOL **Tel:** 32 08 91 11.
Fax: 32 08 92 76.
Email: post@radiohallingdal.no
Web site: http://www.radiohallingdal.no

RADIO HARSTAD 31944
Pb. 251, 9483 HARSTAD **Tel:** 77 06 14 30.
Email: post@radioharstad.no
Web site: http://www.radioharstad.no

RADIO HAUGALAND 31945
Haraldsgaten 110, 5501 HAUGESUND
Tel: 52 71 72 73. **Fax:** 52 71 72 72.
Email: post@radiohaugaland.no
Web site: http://www.radiohaugaland.no
Presenter: Arnstein Jensen

RADIO HELGELAND 31946
Postboks 174, 8801 SANDNESSJØEN
Tel: 75 04 30 00. **Fax:** 75 04 30 01.
Email: radio@hblad.no

RADIO ISLAM AHMADIYYA 31951
Pb 3002 Elisenberg, 0207 OSLO
Tel: 22 44 71 88.
Email: kontakt@radioislam.no
Web site: http://www.radioislamahmadiyya.com

RADIO KARLSØY 31953
Bilrevyen, Pb. 105, 9130 3061 SVELVIK HANSNES **Tel:** 77 74 74 66.
Fax: 77 74 75 99.
Email: radio@online.no
Web site: http://home.online.no/~radio

RADIO KONGSVINGER 31955
Glåmdalen, postboks 757, 2204 KONGSVINGER **Tel:** 62 88 24 00.
Email: studio@radiokongsvinger.no
Web site: http://www.radiokongsvinger.no

RADIO LINDESNES 31845
Pb. 162, 4524 SØR-AUDNEDAL
Tel: 918 57 550.
Email: post@radiolindesnes.no
Web site: http://www.lnr.no

RADIO LØDINGEN 31962
Postboks 205, 8411 LØDINGEN
Tel: 76 93 23 00. **Fax:** 76 93 22 10.
Email: radio@lodingen.com
Web site: http://www.lodingen.com

RADIO LOLAND 31964
Loland, 4715 ØVREBØ **Tel:** 38 13 96 00.
Fax: 38 13 96 53.
Email: post@radiololand.no
Web site: http://www.radiololand.no
Editor: Tor Stray; *Presenter:* Tormod Ulleberg

RADIO LYNGDAL 31967
Pb. 318, 4577 LYNGDAL **Tel:** 38 34 31 90.
Fax: 38 34 36 36.
Email: post@radio-lyngdal.no
Web site: http://www.radio-lyngdal.no
Editor: Jan Birger Galdal

RADIO MEHAMN 31969
Pb 353, 9770 MEHAMN **Tel:** 78 49 65 50.
Email: radiomehamn@nsn.no

RADIO MIDT-TELEMARK 31973
Pb 163, 3833 BØ I TELEMARK
Tel: 35 95 43 43.
Email: radio@rmt.no
Web site: http://www.rmt.no
Presenter: Siv Tone Innleggen

RADIO NORDKAPP 31980
Radio Nordkapp AL, Storgata 9, 9750 HONNINGSVÅG **Tel:** 78 47 70 90.
Fax: 78 47 70 81.
Email: kontakt@radionordkapp.no
Web site: http://www.radionordkapp.no

RADIO NORD-SALTEN 31982
Pb. 50, 8283 LEINESFJORD
Tel: 75 77 83 11.
Email: radio.nordsalten@c2i.net
Web site: http://www.radionordsalten.no

RADIO + GJØVIK & LILLEHAMMER 31904
Pb. 1144, 2806 GJØVIK **Tel:** 61 17 93 03.
Fax: 61 17 05 20.
Email: post@radiopluss.no
Web site: http://www.radiopluss.no

RADIO ØST 31987
Pb 14, 1641 RÅDE **Tel:** 69 29 42 42.
Fax: 69 29 42 50.
Email: redaksjonen@radio-ost.no
Web site: http://www.radio-ost.no

RADIO ØSTLENDINGEN 31888
Radio Østlendingen Solør, Postboks C, 2271 FLISA **Tel:** 46 900 800. **Fax:** 62 95 40 41.
Email: studio@radio-ostlendingen.no
Web site: http://www.radio-ostlendingen.no
Presenter: Per Bjørkli

RADIO PR 31991
Pb. 86, 5902 ISDALSTØ **Tel:** 56 35 10 80.

Norway

RADIO RANDSFJORD 31994
Pb 55, 2714 JAREN **Tel:** 61 33 88 33.
Fax: 61 33 88 32.
Email: redaksjon@radiorandsfjord.no
Web site: http://www.radiorandsfjord.no

RADIO RAUMA 31996
Pb 141, 6301 ÅNDALSNES **Tel:** 71 22 60 00.
Web site: http://www.radiorauma.no

RADIO RJUKAN 31998
Pb 4, 3661 RJUKAN **Tel:** 35 08 24 20.
Fax: 35 08 24 21.
Email: post@radiorjukan.no
Web site: http://www.radiorjukan.no

RADIO RØST 32000
Meland, 8064 RØST **Tel:** 76 09 64 25.
Email: tor.andreassen@rost.kommune.no

RADIO SANDEFJORD (JRG) 32024
Andebuveien 74, 3171 SEM **Tel:** 333 19 555.
Fax: 333 19 555.
Email: post@radiosandefjord.no
Web site: http://www.radiosandefjord.no
Editor: Kjetil Aasheim; *Presenter:* Kjetil Aasheim

RADIO SANDNES 32002
Pb 10, 4301 SANDNES **Tel:** 51 97 92 00.
Fax: 51 97 92 56.
Email: post@radiosandnes.no
Web site: http://www.radiosandnes.no

RADIO SENTRUM, ÅLESUND 32008
Pb 171 Sentrum, 6001 ÅLESUND
Tel: 70 12 99 80. **Fax:** 70 12 01 24.
Email: post@radiosentrum.no
Web site: http://www.radiosentrum.no

RADIO SENTRUM, TRONDHEIM 32004
Odins Veg 9, 7033 TRONDHEIM
Tel: 73 94 00 15. **Fax:** 73 94 00 17.
Email: post@radiosentrum.org
Web site: http://www.radiosentrum.org
Presenter: Jon Amundal

RADIO SKJEBERG 32012
SKJEBERG FOLKEHØYSKOLE, Oldtidsveien 35, 1747 SKJEBERG **Tel:** 69 16 81 04.
Fax: 69 16 87 82.
Email: skjeberg.fhs@ostfoldfk.no
Web site: http://www.skjeberg.fhs.no
Editor: Willy-André Martinsen

RADIO SOTRA 32018
Pb 128, 5341 STRAUME **Tel:** 56 31 36 60.
Fax: 56 31 36 61.
Email: redaksjon@radiosotra.no
Web site: http://www.radiosotra.no

RADIO STORFJORD 32020
Pb 14, 6201 STRANDA **Tel:** 70 26 26 26.
Fax: 70 26 12 81.
Email: redaksjon@radio-storfjord.no
Web site: http://www.radiostorfjord.no
Presenter: Jan Michael Langlo

RADIO TANGO 32023
Radio Tango, Middelthunsgate 25b, Postboks 48, 0368 OSLO **Tel:** 21 37 90 89.
Email: strand@radiotango.no
Web site: http://www.radiotango.no
Editor: Hans Jørgen Strand

RADIO TØNSBERG (JRG) 32025
Andebuveien 74, 3170 SEM
Tel: 33 37 85 55. **Fax:** 333 19 555.
Email: post@radiotonsberg.no
Web site: http://www.radiotonsberg.no
Editor: Kenneth Berg

RADIO TOTEN 32026
Pb. 102, 2830 RAUFOSS **Tel:** 61 19 48 00.
Fax: 61 19 48 11.
Email: radtoten@online.no
Web site: http://www.radiototen.no
Presenter: Akexander Bryntesen

RADIO VIKA 32034
Postboks 83, 7551 HOMMELVIK
Web site: http://www.radiovika.no

RADIORAKEL 32038
Pb. 6826 St.Olavspl., 0130 OSLO
Tel: 23 32 69 60. **Fax:** 22 11 20 65.
Email: redaktor@radiorakel.no
Web site: http://www.radiorakel.no
Editor: Dana Wanounou

RADIOS 32039
Pb 234, 5202 OS **Tel:** 56 30 14 30.
Fax: 56 30 21 01.
Email: redaksjonen@radios.no
Web site: http://www.radios.no

STAVANGER STUDENTRADIO 32045
Univeristetet i Stavanger, 4068 STAVANGER
Tel: 99746019.
Email: hugin@smis.no
Web site: http://smis.no
Editor: Kristoffer Møllevik

STUDENTRADIOEN, BERGEN 32048
Parkveien 1, 5007 BERGEN **Tel:** 55 45 51 58.
Email: kontakt@srib.no
Web site: http://www.srib.no

STUDENTRADIOEN, KRISTIANSAND 32047
Serviceboks 422, 4604 KRISTIANSAND S
Tel: 38 14 20 98.
Email: post@studentradioen.no
Web site: http://www.studentradioen.no

VALDRES RADIO 32054
Pb 223, 2901 FAGERNES **Tel:** 61 35 99 70.
Fax: 61 35 99 80.
Email: post@valdresradio.no
Web site: http://www.valdresradio.no/frame2.htm
Editor: Magnar Øyen

VÅLER NÆRRADIO 32055
2436 VÅLER I SOLØR **Tel:** 62 42 08 20.
Fax: 62 42 30 78.
Email: studio@vaalerradio.net
Web site: http://vaalerradio.net

VOLDA STUDENTRADIO 32035
Høgskulen i Volda, 6100 VOLDA
Tel: 986 59 517.
Email: studentradioen@gmail.com
Web site: http://www.voldastudentradio.no

Poland

NATIONAL TV STATIONS

TV 4 1798732
al. Stanów Zjednoczonych, 53, 04-028 WARSZAWA **Tel:** 22 715 92 50.
Fax: 22 715 92 40.
Email: sekretariat@tv4.pl
Web site: http://www.tv4.pl

TVN 1798727
ul. Wiertnicza, 166, 02-952 WARSZAWA
Tel: 22 856 64 00. **Fax:** 22 856 64 95/96.
Email: reklama@tvn.pl
Web site: http://www.tvn.pl

TVP 1 1819806
ul. J.P. Woronicza, 17, 00-999 WARSZAWA
Tel: 22 547 63 20. **Fax:** 22 547 43 22.
Email: tvp@tvp.pl
Web site: http://www.tvp.pl/tvp1
Editor: Izabela Papuga

TVP 2 1819807
ul. J.P. Woronicza, 17, 00-999 WARSZAWA
Tel: 22 547 62 10. **Fax:** 22 547 42 23.
Email: tvp@tvp.pl
Web site: http://www.tvp.pl/tvp2

REGIONAL TV STATIONS

TVL 1932915
ul. Tysiąclecia, 2, 59-300 LUBIN
Tel: 76 847 86 78. **Fax:** 76 847 86 75.
Email: sekretariat@tvl.pl
Web site: http://www.tvl.pl

TVP SA O. KATOWICE 1819810
ul. Telewizyjna, 1, 40-953 KATOWICE
Tel: 32 259 52 00. **Fax:** 32 259 52 06.
Email: sekretariat@kat.tvp.pl
Web site: http://www.kat.tvp.pl

SATELLITE TV

4FUN.TV 1798927
ul. Bobrowiecka, 1a, 00-728 WARSZAWA
Tel: 22 488 42 00. **Fax:** 22 488 42 50.
Email: 4fun@4fun.tv
Web site: http://www.4fun.tv

AXN 1798928
ul. Puławska, 17, 02-515 WARSZAWA
Tel: 22 852 88 00. **Fax:** 22 852 88 02.
Email: biuroprasoweaxn@hbo.pl
Web site: http://www.axn.pl

BBC ENTERTAINMENT 1798919
Wood Lane, 201, W127TQ LONDYN
Web site: http://poland.bbcentertainment.com

CLUB 1798932
Stępińska, 13, 00-739 WARSZAWA
Tel: 22 841 73 53. **Fax:** 22 841 00 63.
Email: karasek@zonevision.com.pl
Web site: http://www.club-channel.pl

COMEDY CENTRAL POLSKA 1821083
ul. Targowa, 24, 03-728 WARSZAWA
Tel: 22 334 23 00. **Fax:** 22 334 23 01.
Email: comedycentral@comedycentral.pl
Web site: http://www.comedycentral.pl

CYFRA+ 1798730
Canal+ Cyfrowy, ul. Kawalerii, 5, 00-468 WARSZAWA **Tel:** 22 657 07 01.
Fax: 22 657 07 50.
Web site: http://www.cyfraplus.pl

CYFROWY POLSAT SA 1798731
ul. Łubinowa, 4a, 03-878 WARSZAWA
Tel: 22 356 00 00/01. **Fax:** 22 356 00 03.
Email: cyfrowypolsat@cyfrowypolsat.pl
Web site: http://cyfrowypolsat.pl

JIMJAM 1933476
ul. Chocimska, 6, 00-791 WARSZAWA
Tel: 22 547 02 40. **Fax:** 22 547 02 50.
Email: krzysztof.lindner@chellocentraleurope.com
Web site: http://www.jimjam.tv

MTV POLSKA 1798930
ul. Targowa, 24, 03-728 WARSZAWA
Tel: 22 334 23 00. **Fax:** 22 334 23 01.
Email: mtv@mtv.pl
Web site: http://www.mtv.pl

NATIONAL GEOGRAPHIC CHANNEL 1798910
ul. Puławska, 12, 10, 02-515 WARSZAWA
Tel: 22 856 72 51. **Fax:** 22 849 42 82.
Email: foxlifepl@fox.com
Web site: http://www.ngc.pl

NICKELODEON POLSKA 1933481
ul. Targowa, 24, 03-728 WARSZAWA
Tel: 22 334 23 00. **Fax:** 22 334 23 01.
Web site: http://www.nick.com.pl

POLONIA1/POLCAST TELEVISION 1798908
ul. Domaniewska, 50, 02-672 WARSZAWA
Tel: 22 337 87 70. **Fax:** 22 337 87 71.
Email: info@polcast.tv
Web site: http://www.polonia1.pl

SPORTKLUB+ 1933495
Media Production sp. z o.o., ul. Domaniewska 41, 02-672 WARSZAWA
Tel: 22 874 38 10. **Fax:** 22 874 38 11.
Email: kontakt@sportklubplus.pl
Web site: http://www.sportklubplus.pl

SUPERSTACJA 1821101
ul. Inżynierska, 4, 03-422 WARSZAWA
Tel: 22 618 00 65. **Fax:** 22 618 03 25.
Email: redakcja@superstacja.tv
Web site: http://www.superstacja.tv

TV BIZNES 1821093
ul. Heliodora Święcickiego, 1, 60-781 POZNAŃ **Tel:** 61 869 20 10.
Fax: 61 869 20 36.
Email: sekretariat@tvbiznes.pl
Web site: http://www.tvbiznes.pl

TV POLONIA 1821092
ul. J.P. Woronicza, 17, 00-999 WARSZAWA
Tel: 22 547 62 11. **Fax:** 22 547 88 78.
Email: tvpolonia@tvp.pl
Web site: http://www.tvp.pl/polonia

TV RELIGIA 1933490
ul. Kłobucka, 23, 02-699 WARSZAWA
Tel: 22 358 23 00. **Fax:** 22 358 23 01.
Email: beata.marzec@n.pl
Web site: http://n.pl/oferta/kanaly/pakiety/informacja_i_rozrywka/religiatv.html

TVN24 1798925
ul. Wiertnicza, 166, 02-952 WARSZAWA
Tel: 22 856 64 00. **Fax:** 22 856 64 95/96.
Email: reklama@tvn.pl
Web site: http://www.tvn24.pl

TVN7 1798911
ul. Wiertnicza, 166, 02-952 WARSZAWA
Tel: 22 856 64 00. **Fax:** 22 856 64 95/96.
Email: reklama@tvn.pl
Web site: http://www.tvnsiedem.pl

TVP HISTORIA 1821079
ul. Woronicza, 17, 00-999 WARSZAWA
Tel: 22 547 62 55. **Fax:** 22 547 62 55.
Email: historia@tvp.pl
Web site: http://www.tvp.pl/historia

TVP KULTURA 1821090
ul. J.P. Woronicza, 17, 00-999 WARSZAWA
Tel: 22 547 57 56. **Fax:** 22 547 57 54.
Email: tvpkultura@tvp.pl
Web site: http://www.tvp.pl/kultura

TVP SPORT 1821094
ul. J.P. Woronicza, 17, 00-999 WARSZAWA
Tel: 22 547 66 51. **Fax:** 22 547 62 52.
Web site: http://www.tvp.pl/sport

VH1 POLSKA 1821074
ul. Targowa, 24, 03-728 WARSZAWA
Tel: 22 334 23 00. **Fax:** 22 334 23 01.
Email: vh1@vh1.pl
Web site: http://www.vh1.pl

VIVA POLSKA 1821059
ul. Targowa, 24, 03-728 WARSZAWA
Tel: 22 334 23 00. **Fax:** 22 334 23 01.
Email: viva@viva-tv.pl
Web site: http://www.viva-tv.pl

ZONE CLUB 1821076
ul. Chocimska, 6, 00-791 WARSZAWA
Tel: 22 547 02 40. **Fax:** 22 547 02 50.
Email: katarzyna.sady@chellocentraleurope.com
Web site: http://www.zoneclub.tv

ZONE EUROPA 1821068
ul. Chocimska, 6, 00-791 WARSZAWA
Tel: 22 547 02 40. **Fax:** 22 547 02 50.
Email: Krzysztof.Lindner@chellocentraleurope.com
Web site: http://www.zoneeuropa.tv

ZONE REALITY 1821067
ul. Chocimska, 6, 00-791 WARSZAWA
Tel: 22 547 02 40. **Fax:** 22 547 02 50.
Email: katarzyna.sady@chellocentraleurope.com
Web site: http://www.zonereality.tv

CABLE TV

MULTIMEDIA POLSKA 1798939
ul. Tadeusza Wendy, 7/9, 81-341 GDYNIA
Tel: 58 666 03 00. **Fax:** 58 666 03 39.
Email: sekretariat.zarzadu@multimedia.pl
Web site: http://multimedia.pl

NATIONAL RADIO STATIONS

DWÓJKA (POLSKIE RADIO PROGRAM 2) 1819735
al. Niepodległości, 77/85, 00-977 WARSZAWA **Tel:** 22 645 98 04.
Fax: 22 645 39 37.
Email: dwojka@polskieradio.pl
Web site: http://www.polskieradio.pl/dwojka

JEDYNKA (POLSKIE RADIO PROGRAM I) 1819734
al. Niepodległości, 77/85, 00-977 WARSZAWA **Tel:** 22 645 35 15.
Fax: 22 645 59 15.
Email: jedynka@polskieradio.pl
Web site: http://www.polskieradio.pl/jedynka

POLSKIE RADIO EURO 1798738
al. Niepodległości, 77/85, 00-977 WARSZAWA **Tel:** 22 645 99 44.
Fax: 22 645 59 08.
Email: euro@polskieradio.pl
Web site: http://www.polskieradioeuro.pl

RADIO ZET 1819737
ul. Żurawia, 8, 00-503 WARSZAWA
Tel: 22 583 33 82. **Fax:** 22 622 79 00.
Email: radiozet@radiozet.com.pl
Web site: http://www.radiozet.pl

TRÓJKA (POLSKIE RADIO PROGRAM III) 1819736
ul. Myśliwiecka, 3/5/7, 00-977 WARSZAWA
Tel: 22 645 55 47. **Fax:** 22 645 59 47.
Email: trojka@polskieradio.pl
Web site: http://www.polskieradio.pl/trojka

REGIONAL RADIO STATIONS

BON TON RADIO SA 1798839
ul. Wojsławicka, 7, 22-100 CHEŁM
Tel: 563 22 22. **Fax:** 82 563 91 50.
Email: radio@bonton.chelm.pl
Web site: http://www.bonton.chelm.pl

NASZE RADIO 104,7 FM 1798793
Rynek 14, 98-200 SIERADZ
Tel: 43 822 23 11. **Fax:** 43 822 11 11.
Email: redakcja@nasze.fm
Web site: reklama@nasze.fm

RADIO LELIWA 1932910
ul. Wyspiańskiego, 12, 5, 39-400 TARNOBRZEG **Tel:** 15 823 66 55.
Fax: 15 823 01 78.
Email: reklama@leliwa.pl
Web site: http://leliwa.pl

RADIO MERKURY SA 1798845
ul. Berwińskiego, 5, 60-765 POZNAŃ
Tel: 61 664 49 00. **Fax:** 61 866 03 10.
Email: office@radiomerkury.pl
Web site: http://www.radiomerkury.pl

RADIO PLUS GDAŃSK 1819767
ul. Suwalska, 46, 80-215 GDAŃSK
Tel: 58 347 63 95. **Fax:** 58 347 62 19.
Email: radio@plusgdansk.pl
Web site: http://www.plusgdansk.pl

RADIO PLUS GLIWICE 1932901
ul. Głowackiego, 3, 44-100 GLIWICE
Tel: 32 232 68 86. **Fax:** 32 232 68 85.
Email: plus@plus.gliwice.pl
Web site: http://www.plus.gliwice.pl

RADIO PLUS RADOM 1798825
ul. Młyńska, 23/25, 26-612 RADOM
Tel: 48 381 15 45. **Fax:** 48 381 15 45.
Email: radio@plus.radom.pl
Web site: http://www.radioplus.com.pl

RADIO STREFA FM PIOTRKÓW (D. RADIO PIOTRKÓW) 1819744
ul. Jagiellońska, 7, 97-300 PIOTRKÓW TRYBUNALSKI **Tel:** 44 732 37 03.
Fax: 44 732 37 02.
Email: radio@strefa.fm
Web site: http://www.strefa.fm

RADIO VANESSA 1798838
ul. Batorego, 5, 47-400 RACIBÓRZ
Tel: 32 755 14 00. **Fax:** 32 755 13 00.
Email: vanessa@vanessa.com.pl
Web site: http://vanessa.com.pl

RADIO WAWA - ZAWSZE POLSKA MUZYKA 1798757
ul. Senatorska, 12, 00-082 WARSZAWA
Tel: 22 448 92 01. **Fax:** 22 448 92 03.
Email: radio@wawa.com.pl
Web site: http://www.wawa.com.pl

RADIO ZŁOTE PRZEBOJE TREFL 103 I 99,2 FM 1798819
ul. Tkacka 7/8, 80-836 GDAŃSK
Tel: 58 551 52 29. **Fax:** 58 551 57 59.
Email: trojmiasto@zloteprzeboje.pl
Web site: http://www.zloteprzeboje.pl

NEWS INFORMATION SERVICES

ONET.PL 1835874
ul. Gabrieli Zapolskiej, 44, 30-126 KRAKÓW
Tel: 12 277 40 00. **Fax:** 12 277 40 02.
Email: onet@onet.pl
Web site: http://www.onet.pl

WPROST24.PL 1929258
ul. Domaniewska, 39a, 02-672 WARSZAWA
Tel: 22 529 11 00. **Fax:** 22 852 90 16.
Email: m.zdunczyk@wprost.pl
Web site: http://wprost24.pl
Editor: Elżbieta Majewska

STUDENT RADIO

RADIOFONIA 100.5 1819753
ul. Rostafińskiego 8, 30-072 KRAKÓW
Tel: 12 617 37 38. **Fax:** 12 636 74 26.
Email: newsroom@radioakademickie.pl
Web site: http://www.radioakademickie.pl

Portugal

NATIONAL TV STATIONS

RTP 1 1643258
Av. Marechal Gomes da Costa, 37, 1849-030 LISBOA **Tel:** 217 947 000.
Fax: 217 947 570.
Email: rpublicas@rtp.pt
Web site: http://www.rtp.pt
Editor: Adília Godinho; *Presenter:* Catarina Furtado

SIC 622815
Estrada da Outurela, 119, 2794-052 CARNAXIDE **Tel:** 214 179 400.
Fax: 214 173 119.
Email: atendimento@sic.pt
Web site: http://sic.pt
Editor: Paula Santos; *Presenter:* Rita Ferro Rodrigues

TVI 1643344
R. Mário Castelhano, 40, Queluz de Baixo, 2734-502 BARCARENA **Tel:** 214 347 500.
Fax: 214 347 654.
Email: relacoes.publicas@tvi.pt
Web site: http://www.tvi.iol.pt
Editor: Paulo Almoster; *Presenter:* Leonor Poeiras

CABLE TV

SIC NOTÍCIAS 1643278
Estrada da Outurela, 119, 2794-052 CARNAXIDE **Tel:** 214 179 400.
Fax: 214 173 119.
Email: atendimento@sic.pt
Web site: http://sicnoticias.pt
Editor: António Cancela

SPORT TV1 1643285
Parque das Nações - Edifício Sport TV, Alameda dos Oceanos - Lote 2.08.01 - 2°, 1998-014 LISBOA **Tel:** 218 917 800.
Fax: 218 917 900.
Email: agenda@sporttv.pt
Web site: http://www.sporttv.pt
Presenter: Catarina Faustino

NATIONAL RADIO STATIONS

RÁDIO COMERCIAL 622977
R. Sampaio e Pina, 24, 1099-044 LISBOA
Tel: 213 821 500. **Fax:** 213 821 589.
Email: info@radiocomercial.clix.pt
Web site: http://radiocomercial.clix.pt
Presenter: Pedro Ribeiro; *Producer:* Mafalda Escudero

RECONQUISTA 1643220
R. de S. Miguel, 3 - 5, 6000-181 CASTELO BRANCO **Tel:** 272 321 357.
Fax: 272 328 919.
Email: reconquista@reconquista.pt
Web site: http://www.reconquista.pt

RENASCENÇA 19480
R. Ivens, 14, 1249-108 LISBOA
Tel: 213 239 200. **Fax:** 213 239 299.
Email: mail@rr.pt
Web site: http://rr.sapo.pt
Editor: Raquel Abecasis; *Presenter:* Luís Loureiro

RFM 1643252
R. Ivens, 14, 1249-108 LISBOA
Tel: 213 239 200. **Fax:** 213 239 314.
Email: mail@rfm.pt
Web site: http://rfm.sapo.pt
Presenter: Joaquim Cannas

TSF 1643341
Edifício Altejo, R. 3 da Matinha, 3° Piso - Sala 301, 1900-823 LISBOA
Tel: 218 612 500. **Fax:** 218 612 510.
Email: tsf@tsf.pt
Web site: http://www.tsf.pt
Editor: Mário Fernando

REGIONAL RADIO STATIONS

A PLANÍCIE 19511
R. Santana e Costa, 18 - R/C Esq., 7860 MOURA **Tel:** 285 251 730. **Fax:** 285 252 440.
Email: jplanicie@radioplanicie.com
Web site: http://www.radioplanicie.com/jornal.php

REGIÃO BAIRRADINA 1643222
R. dos Olivais, 22, 3780-909 ANADIA
Tel: 231 504 321. **Fax:** 231 504 322.
Email: geral@regiaobairradina.com
Web site: http://www.regiaobairradina.com

REGIÃO DE LEIRIA 1643225
R. D. Carlos I, 2 - 4, Apartado 102, 2415-405 LEIRIA **Tel:** 244 819 950. **Fax:** 244 828 905.
Email: redaccao@regiaodeleiria.pt
Web site: http://www.regiaodeleiria.pt
Editor: João Paulo Silva

REGIÃO SUL 1643226
Betunes, 8100-254 LOULÉ **Tel:** 289 463 890.
Fax: 289 463 955.
Email: jornal@regiao-sul.pt
Web site: http://www.regiao-sul.pt

NEWS INFORMATION SERVICES

PÚBLICO ONLINE 1643088
R. do Viriato, 17 - 3°, 1069-315 LISBOA
Tel: 210 111 000. **Fax:** 210 111 006.
Email: publico@publico.pt
Web site: http://www.publico.pt
Editor: Alexandre Martins

Russian Federation

NATIONAL TV STATIONS

DOMASHNIY 1862592
ul. Pravdy 15a, 125124 MOSKVA
Tel: 495 785 63 33. **Fax:** 495 642 94 51.
Email: info@domashny.ru
Web site: http:domashny.ru
Presenter: Yana Laputina

NTV 1774184
ul. Akademika Koroleva 12, 127427 MOSKVA **Tel:** 495 725 53 83.
Fax: 495 725 54 01.
Email: info@ntv.ru
Web site: http://www.ntv.ru

PERVIY KANAL 763354
ul. Akademika Korolyova 12, 127427 MOSKVA **Tel:** 495 217 82 88.
Fax: 495 215 11 39.
Email: pr@1tv.ru
Web site: http://www.1tv.ru

PIYATY KANAL 1774576
ul. Chapygina 6, 197376 SANKT PETERBURG **Tel:** 12 335 15 60.
Fax: 12 234 38 46.
Email: trk@spbtv.ru
Web site: http://www.5-tv.ru

REN TV 763403
Zubovskiy Bulvar 17, str. 1, 119847 MOSKVA **Tel:** 495 246 59 33.
Fax: 495 246 06 55.
Email: press@ren-tv.com
Web site: http://www.ren-tv.com
Producer: Dmitri Velikanov

ROSSIYA (RTR) 1774057
5 ul. Yamskogo Polya 22, MOSKVA
Tel: 495 232 63 33. **Fax:** 495 234 87 7.
Email: pr@rfn.ru
Web site: http://www.rutv.ru

TELEKANAL KULTURA 1774031
ul. Malaya Nikitinskaya 24, 123995 MOSKVA
Tel: 495 780 56 01.
Email: pr@tv-culture.ru
Web site: http://www.tvkultura.ru

REGIONAL TV STATIONS

3 KANAL 1937488
ul. Akademika Koroleva 12, 127427 MOSKVA **Tel:** 495 617 81 13.
Fax: 495 615 19 45.
Email: sec@3channel.ru
Web site: http://www.3channel.ru

7 KANAL 1936902
ul. Baumana 22, 660028 KRASNOYARSK
Tel: 391 258 11 30. **Fax:** 391 258 11 31.
Email: trk7@trk7.ru
Web site: http://www.trk7.ru

AIST 1936850
ul. Rossiiskaya 13a, 662040 IRKUTSK
Tel: 3952 334 402. **Fax:** 3952 334 358.
Email: aist@aisttv.ru
Web site: http://aisttv.ru

MIR TV NOVOSIBIRSK 1936865
ul. Gorskaya 16, 630032 NOVOSIBIRSK
Tel: 383 355 55 53. **Fax:** 383 346 25 10.
Email: vmeste@tcm10.ru
Web site: http://www.tcm10.ru

NIKA TV 1936809
ul. Moskovskaya 189, 248021 KALUGA
Tel: 4842 55 53 66. **Fax:** 4842 55 37 16.
Email: news@nikatv.ru
Web site: http://www.nikatv.ru

NTM YAROSLAVL 1936697
ul. Sovetskaya 69, 150003 YAROSLAVL
Tel: 4852 74 48 74. **Fax:** 4852 74 48 74.
Email: news@ntm-tv.ru
Web site: http://www.ntm-tv.ru
Editor: Alexander Leukhin

PODMOSKOVIE TV 1936813
ul. 1 Magistralnaya 11/9, 123007 MOSKVA
Tel: 499 259 42 76. **Fax:** 499 259 54 81.
Email: news@mosobltv.ru
Web site: http://www.mosobltv.ru

PRIMA TV 1936814
pr. Mira 27, 660049 KRASNOYARSK
Tel: 391 298 38 00. **Fax:** 391 298 38 98.
Email: prima@prima-tv.ru
Web site: http://www.prima-tv.ru

RIFEY TV 1937292
ul. Ordzhonikidze 14, 614045 PERM
Tel: 342 235 00 90. **Fax:** 342 235 02 44.
Email: promo@rifey.ru
Web site: http://www.rifey.ru

ROSSIYA NOVOSIBIRSK 1936693
ul. Rimskogo-Korsakova 7, 630048 NOVOSIBIRSK **Tel:** 383 314 60 00.
Fax: 383 314 70 89.
Email: panorama@nsktv.ru
Web site: http://novosibirsk.rfn.ru
Director: Svetlana Voitovich

TNT SANKT PETERBURG 1774342
ul. Prof. Popova 23b, 197376 SANKT PETERGURG **Tel:** 12 702 16 34.
Email: tnt@tnt-spb.ru
Web site: http://www.tnt-spb.ru

TNV 1936798
ul. Shamila Usmanova 9, 420095 KAZAN'
Tel: 43 570 51 02. **Fax:** 43 554 30 40.
Email: pr@tnvtv.ru
Web site: http://www.tnv.ru

TRTR TV 1937295
ul. Permyakova 3A, 625013 TYUMEN
Tel: 3452 33 10 13. **Fax:** 3452 41 81 65.
Email: primary@trtr.ru
Web site: http://www.trtr.ru

TV 2 TOMSK 766529
ul. Elizarovykh 51a, 634012 TOMSK
Tel: 3822 54 18 00. **Fax:** 3822 54 07 17.
Email: tv2@tv2.tomsk.ru
Web site: http://www.tv2.tomsk.ru
Director: Svetlana Sereda

TV 6 VLADIMIR 1936806
ul. Ofitserskaya 9a, 600001 VLADIMIR
Tel: 4922 320808. **Fax:** 4922 320808.
Email: news@6tv.ru
Web site: http://www.6tv.ru

TV 7 VOLOGDA 1936867
ul. Pugacheva 79, 160011 VOLOGDA
Tel: 172 28 00 00. **Fax:** 172 27 49 19.
Email: info@tv7-vologda.ru
Web site: http://www.tv7vologda.ru
News Editor: Irina Barysheva

TV TOMSK 1936845
ul. Yakovleva 5, 634050 TOMSK
Tel: 3822 65 24 88. **Fax:** 3822 65 22 30.
Email: atf@tvtomsk.ru
Web site: http://www.tvtomsk.ru
Director: Elena Ulyana

TVK 6 1936848
ul Kopylova 50, 660001 KRASNOYARSK
Tel: 391 202 70 01. **Fax:** 391 244 14 30.
Email: tvk6@tvk6.ru
Web site: http://www.tvk6.ru
News Editor: Sergey Dostovalov

URAL-INFORM TV 1936801
ul. Krupskei 2, 614000 PERM'
Tel: 342 290 20 91.
Email: new@uitv.ru
Web site: http://www.uitv.ru
Editor: Nataliya Tenkovskaya

VOLGA TV 1936907
ul. Belinskogo 9a, 603600 NIZHNIY NOVGOROD **Tel:** 31 433 34 00.
Fax: 31 430 32 91.
Email: volga@volga-tv.ru
Web site: http://www.volga-tv.ru

SATELLITE TV

KOSMOS TV 763367
ul. Botanicheskaya 10d, str. 1, 127276 MOSKVA **Tel:** 495 231 19 25.
Fax: 495 231 19 29.
Email: info@kosmostv.ru
Web site: http://www.kosmostv.ru

RUSSIA TODAY 1774487
Zubovsky Blvd. 4, korp. 1, 119021 MOSKVA
Tel: 495 649 89 89. **Fax:** 495 649 89 79.
Email: info@rttv.ru
Web site: http://rt.com
Presenter: George Watts

SGU TV 1937524
ul. Nizhnegorodskaya 32, str. 4, 109029 MOSKVA **Tel:** 495 727 12 49.
Fax: 495 727 12 49.
Email: sgutv@sgutv.ru
Web site: http://www.sgutv.ru
Director: Irina Yurtaeva

TV CENTRE 1937525
ul. Bolshaya Tatarskaya 33, str. 1, 115184 MOSKVA **Tel:** 495 959 39 00.
Fax: 495 959 39 66.
Email: web@tvc.ru
Web site: http://www.tvc.ru
Presenter: Konstantin Zatulin

NATIONAL RADIO STATIONS

BUSINESS FM 1774302
ul. 2 Khutorskaya 38a, str. 23, 127287 MOSKVA **Tel:** 495 660 88 75.
Fax: 495 660 88 75.
Email: reclama@businessfm.ru
Web site: http://radio.businessfm.ru

ECHO MOSKVY 1774082
Novy Arbat 11, 119992 MOSKVA
Tel: 495 202 92 29. **Fax:** 495 202 91 02.
Email: echo@echo.msk.ru
Web site: http://www.echo.msk.ru

GOLOS ROSSII 1774237
ul. Pyatnitskaya 25, 115326 MOSKVA
Fax: 495 951 95 52.
Email: russng@ruvr.ru
Web site: http://www.ruvr.ru

HIT FM 1774681
3 Khoroshevskaya 12, 123298 MOSKVA
Tel: 495 995 10 36.
Email: hitfm@hitfm.ru
Web site: http://www.hitfm.ru

RADIO MAYAK 1615818
ul. Pyatnitskaya, d.25, 115326 MOSKVA
Tel: 495 950 61 81. **Fax:** 495 777 42 84.
Email: inform@radiomayak.ru
Web site: http://www.radiomayak.ru
Director: Sergey Kurokhtin

RADIO ROSSII 763344
5 ulica Yamskogo Polya 19/21, 125010 MOSKVA **Tel:** 495 950 69 89.
Fax: 495 217 97 89.
Email: PR@radiorus.ru
Web site: http://www.radiorus.ru
Director: Vyacheslav Umanovsky

RUSSKAYA SLUZHBA NOVOSTEY 1774589
3 Khoroshevskaya 12, 123298 MOSKVA
Tel: 495 925 35 08.
Email: rusnovosti@rr.ru
Web site: http://www.rusnovosti.ru

REGIONAL RADIO STATIONS

BEST FM 1774490
ul. Baumanovskaya 15, korp.6, MOSKVA
Tel: 495 995 10 05.
Email: info@bestfm.ru
Web site: http://www.best-fm.ru
Director: Mikhail Zotov

CITY FM 87.9 763338
ul. Trifonovskaya 57, str.3, 129272 MOSKVA
Tel: 495 221 99 09. **Fax:** 495 221 99 09.
Email: mail@city-fm.ru
Web site: http://city-fm.ru

FINAM FM 1774541
Potapovsky pereulok 4, str. 1, 101000 MOSKVA **Fax:** 495 628 45 68.
Email: Radio@finam.fm
Web site: http://www.finam.fm
Director: Oleg Medvedev

GOVORIT MOSKVA 763346
ul. B. Tatarskaya 35, str. 5, 3 floor, 113184 MOSKVA **Tel:** 495 729 33 56.
Fax: 495 729 33 55.
Email: gm@krc.ru
Web site: http://www.govoritmoskva.ru
Editor: Tatiana Taratynova

RADIO BALTIKA 763395
Kamennoostrovskiy Prospekt 67, 197022 SANKT PETERBURG **Tel:** 12 327 51 51.
Fax: 12 234 98 48.
Email: rbia@rbalt.ru
Web site: http://baltika.fm

RADIO EUROPA+ 763358
ul. Professora Popova 47, 197376 ST. PETERBURG **Tel:** 12 325 94 94.
Fax: 12 234 97 12.
Email: office@europaplus.spb.ru
Web site: http://www.europaplus.spb.ru

RELAX FM 1774203
ul. Trofimovskaya 57, str. 3, 129272 MOSKVA **Tel:** 495 221 99 09.
Fax: 495 221 99 09.
Email: Svetlana@relax-fm.ru
Web site: http://relax-fm.ru

San Marino

NATIONAL TV STATIONS

SAN MARINO RTV 764895
San Marino RTV Spa., Viale J.F. Kennedy 13, SM-47890 **Tel:** 549 88 20 17.
Fax: 549 88 28 55.
Email: redazione@sanmarinortv.sm
Web site: http://www.sanmarinortv.sm
Editor: Sergio Barducci; *Director:* Michèle Mangiafico

Spain

NATIONAL TV STATIONS

ANTENA 3 TELEVISIÓN 1697619
Avda. Isla Graciosa 13, E-28700 SAN SEBASTIAN DE LOS REYES (MADRID)
Tel: 91 62 30 500. **Fax:** 91 62 30 769.
Email: noticias@antena3tv.es
Web site: http://www.antena3.com
Editor: Indira García

ETB TV VASCA-EUSKAL TELEBISTA 52957
Iurreta, E-48215 VIZCAYA **Tel:** 94 60 31 000.
Fax: 94 60 31 095.
Email: info@eitb.com
Web site: http://www.eitb.com
Editor: Rosa Sofia Zufia; *Director:* Andoni Ortúzar

EUROPOCKET TV 1799034
Felix R. de la Fuenta 3, E- 46185, LA POBLA DE VALLBONA **Tel:** 96 166 17 74.
Fax: 96 166 27 17.
Email: meabh@europocket.tv
Web site: http://www.europocket.tv
News Editor: Meabh Mc Mahon

TELEMADRID 52963
Ciudad de la Imagen, Paseo del Príncipe 3, E-28223 POZUELO DE ALARCÓN (MADRID)
Tel: 91 51 28 200. **Fax:** 91 51 23 799.
Email: correo@telemadrid.es
Web site: http://www.telemadrid.com
News Editor: Agustin Grado; *Editor:* Agustin Grado

TV3 TELEVISIO DE CATALUNYA 52959
Carrer de la TV 3, s/n, E-08970 SANT JOAN DESPÍ (BARCELONA) **Tel:** 93 49 99 333.
Fax: 93 47 30 671.
Email: tvccom.b@tvcatalunya.com
Web site: http://www.tvcatalunya.com
News Editor: Jaume Masdeu; *Director:* Francesca Escribano

TVE 52960
Calle Avenida Radio Televisión 4, E-28223 MADRID **Tel:** 91 34 64 000.
Fax: 91 58 17 547.
Email: consultas@rtve.es
Web site: http://www.rtve.es/comercial.htmail
Director: Manuel Perez Estemera

REGIONAL TV STATIONS

BARCELONA TELEVISIÓN 53300
Pl. Tísner 1, E-08001 BARCELONA
Tel: 93 506 42 00. **Fax:** 93 506 42 01.
Email: comunicacio@barcelonatv.cat
Web site: http://www.barcelonatv.cat
Editor: Francesc Centelles

CANAL 28 ALMERÍA 53303
Calle Jerez 24, E-04007 ALMERIA
Tel: 950 62 00 62. **Fax:** 950 27 55 22.
Email: informativos@canal28tv.com
Editor: Maria José Vilaplana Saez; *Director:* Magdalena Saez

CANAL 4 53305
Ctra. de Valldemossa, Km. 7,4, Parcela 9A - Edif. Lleret, E-07121 PALMA DE MALLORCA
Tel: 971 75 25 99. **Fax:** 971 75 30 76.
Email: informatius@canal-4.tv
Web site: http://www.canal-4.tv
News Editor: Joana Dols; *Director:* Juan Segui

CANAL 54 TV 53306
Eduardo Martínez del Campo 12, 2°, E-09003 BURGOS (MADRID)
Tel: 947 25 70 70. **Fax:** 947 25 72 15.
Email: redaccion@canal54.e.telefonica.net
Editor: Laura Garcia Juez; *Director:* Juan Antonio Gallego

CANAL 6 53331
Calle Agustin Millares Sal Ed. Mapfre, 1ª Pl. Locale E, E-35008 LAS PALMAS DE GRAN CANARIA **Tel:** 928 46 46 40.
Fax: 928 46 12 82.
Email: canal6_tv@hotmail.com
Editor: Pepe Carvallo; *Director:* Pepe Carvallo

CANAL 7 TELEVISIÓN 53307
Agastia 5, E-28027 MADRID
Tel: 91 36 83 037. **Fax:** 91 36 78 609.
Email: canal7tv@canal7tv.com
Web site: www.canal7tv.com
Editor: José Garijo; *Director:* José Garijo

CANAL 9 1696247
RTVV, Polígono de Acceso a Ademuz s/n, E-46100 BURJJASSOT (VALENCIA)
Tel: 96 31 83 000. **Fax:** 96 31 83 001.
Email: informatius@rtvv.es
Web site: http://www.rtvv.es
Editor: Lluís Motes; *Director:* José Llorca

CANAL BLAU TELEVISIÓN 53309
Rambla de l'Exposició, 61-69, Edifici Neàpolis, E-08800 VILANOVA I LA GELTRU (BARCELONA) **Tel:** 93 81 41 245.
Fax: 93 81 43 727.
Email: noticies@canalblau.cat
Web site: www.canalblau.cat
Editor: Xavier Abello; *Director:* Xavier Abello

9 CANAL CULTURAL BADAJOZ 53311
Martin Cansado 3A, E-06001 BADAJOZ
Tel: 924 20 04 50. **Fax:** 924 20 04 53.
Email: icordoba@telefronterabadajoz.com
Web site: http://www.telefronterabadajoz.com
Editor: Inez Gonzalez Martinez; *Director:* Ignacio Cordoba Perez

CANAL SI-ALMERÍA 53314
Puerto Deportivo Aguadulce, Muelle de Rivera Local 6 B, E-04720 AGUADULCE (ALMERÍA) **Tel:** 950 34 57 88.
Fax: 950 34 59 08.
Email: drinformativos@canalsitv.com
Editor: David Banios; *Director:* Juan Ortega

CANAL TERRASSA TV 53352
Calle Colon 90, E-08222 TERRASSA (BARCELONA) **Tel:** 93 73 97 000.
Fax: 93 73 64 004.
Email: joan.rovira@terrassa.org
Web site: http://www.canalterrassatv.com
Editor: Pere Gibert; *Director:* Montse Prat

CANAL V GUADALAJARA 53315
Christofer Colomb parcelas 230-231, Poligono del Henares, E-19004 GUADALAJARA **Tel:** 949 25 42 07.
Fax: 949 25 42 06.
Email: informativos@guadalajara.tv
Web site: http://www.guadalajara.tv
Editor: José Luis Carabias; *Director:* Jesús Saboya

EUSKAL TELEBISTA 53320
ETB Euskal Telebista, E-48215 IURRETA (BIZKAIA) **Tel:** 94 60 31 000.
Fax: 94 60 31 095.
Email: info@eitb.com
Web site: http://www.eitb.com
Editor: Juan Luis Diego; *Director:* Bingen Zupiria

LOCALIA TV (ALICANTE) 53302
Gran Vía, Tramo Santa, Pola 19 - B, E-03009 ALICANTE **Tel:** 96 525 52 16.
Fax: 96 51 85 128.
Email: localiatv@televisionalicante.com
Editor: Jose Luis Perez-Aranda; *Director:* Benjamin Llorens

MÁLAGA TV 53323
Calle Strachan 1, 1°, E-29015 MÁLAGA
Tel: 95 20 61 490. **Fax:** 95 26 09 679.
Email: produccion@tvmalaga.com
Web site: http://www.tvmalaga.com
Editor: Mariano Díaz; *Director:* José Maria de Loma

ONDA JEREZ TV 53324
Caballeros, 35, E-11403 JEREZ DE LA FRONTERA (CÁDIZ) **Tel:** 956 35 98 00.
Fax: 956 35 98 11.
Email: ondajerez@ondajerez.com
Web site: http://www.ondajerez.com
Editor: Adolfo Alvaro; *Director:* Pedro Rollan Rollan

OVIEDO TELEVISION 53356
Tenderina Baja 200, E-33010 OVIEDO (ASTURIAS) **Tel:** 98 51 12 639.
Fax: 98 52 97 653.
Email: redaccion@oviedotv.com
Web site: http://www.oviedotelevision.com/
Editor: Juan Ignacio Rodriguez; *Director:* Adolfo Casaprima

PUNT DOS 1696249
RTVV, Polígono de Acceso a Ademuz s/n, E-46100 BURJJASSOT (VALENCIA)
Tel: 96 31 83 000. **Fax:** 96 31 83 001.
Email: informatius@rtvv.es
Web site: http://www.rtvv.es
Editor: Lluís Motes; *Director:* Lola Johnson

RTV 3.40 COSTA DEL SOL 53328
Urbanización Polarsol s/n, E-29649 MIJAS COSTA (MALAGA) **Tel:** 95 25 83 030.
Fax: 95 25 82 161.
Email: redaccion@mijate.com
Web site: http://www.mijate.com
News Editor: Juan Diego Sanchez; *Editor:* Juan Diego Sanchez

TELE 7 53329
Errotabarria, 1, E-48903 LUTXANA BARAKALDO **Tel:** 94 49 70 067.
Fax: 94 49 93 377.
Email: tele7@tele7.com
Web site: http://www.tele7.tv
Editor: Yolanda Alicia González

TELE BILBAO 53330
Aita Larramendi 3, 1°, E-48012 BILBAO
Tel: 94 41 05 254. **Fax:** 94 41 04 977.
Email: gestion@telebilbao.es
Editor: Irene Diaz; *Director:* Enrique Campos

TELE UTRERA 53332
Zorrilla 4, E-41710 UTRERA (SEVILLA)
Tel: 95 58 65 086. **Fax:** 95 58 61 464.
Email: uvitel@uvitel.com
Web site: http://www.teleutrera.com
News Editor: Felix Marchena Roldan; *Director:* Juan Miguel Rivas

TELECABARGA 53335
Polígono de Raos s/n, E-39600 CAMARGO (CANTABRIA) **Tel:** 942 36 92 22.
Fax: 942 36 91 31.
Email: info@telecabarga.es
Web site: http://www.telecabarga.es
Editor: Marcos Diez

TELEDONOSTI 53337
Parque Empresarial Zuatzu, Zuatzu Kalea 1, Edificio Ulía, Oficina 8, E-20018 DONOSTIA SAN SEBASTIAN **Tel:** 943 31 64 44.
Fax: 943 31 64 43.
Email: teledonosti@teledonosti.tv
Web site: http://www.teledonosti.tv
Editor: Pedro José Castillo Arteta; *Director:* Tito Irazusta

TELENIEVE 53339
Crtr Gójar - La Zubia 4, E-18150 GÓJAR (GRANADA) **Tel:** 958 50 86 01.
Fax: 958 50 86 19.
Email: admo@telenieve.tv
Web site: http://www.telenieve.tv
Editor: Fernando Arguelles Castillo

TELESIERRA 53340
Calle Isaac Newton 5 ptm, E-28760 TRES CANTOS (MADRID) **Tel:** 91 80 49 180.
Fax: 91 80 37 158.
Email: tvl@cestel.es
Web site: http://www.telesierra.com
Editor: Charro de Campo; *Director:* Charro de Campo

TELETOLEDO 53341
Agen 3, E-45005 TOLEDO **Tel:** 925 49 11 13.
Fax: 925 22 06 51.
Email: teletoledo@telefonica.net
Editor: Javier Busnadiego

TELEVIGO 53336
Conde de Torrecedeira 17 bajo, E-36202 VIGO (PONTEVEDRA) **Tel:** 986 44 71 05.
Fax: 986 43 10 77.
Email: televigo@televigo.com
Web site: http://www.televigo.com
Editor: Ana Lago Rodriguez

TELEVISIÓ DE MATARÓ (TVM) 53357
Colón 69, E-08301 MATARÓ (BARCELONA)
Tel: 93 79 04 071. **Fax:** 93 79 06 070.
Email: redaccio@tvmataro.com
Editor: Anna Palà; *Director:* Luís Lligonya

TELEVISIÓN BURGOS 53351
Calle Los Titos 1 bajo, E-09007 BURGOS
Tel: 947 04 20 42. **Fax:** 947 22 15 20.
Email: tvburgos@retecal.es
Web site: http://www.tvcyl.es
Editor: Silvia de Diego; *Director:* Alejandro Almarcha Ruíz

TELEVISIÓN DE CUENCA 53344
Polígono Los Palançares, Calle F, E-16004 CUENCA **Tel:** 969 22 75 88.
Fax: 969 23 09 40.
Email: canalcnc@terra.es
News Editor: Isabel González; *Director:* Carlos Iserte

TELEVISIÓN DE ELCHE 53345
Doctor Caro 43, E-03201 ELCHE (ALICANTE) **Tel:** 96 54 43 111.
Fax: 96 66 64 535.
Email: rtvelche@mail.rtvelche.com
Web site: http://www.rtvelche.com
Editor: Juan Garrigos

TELEVISION DE GALICIA 766470
Compañía de Radio Televisión de Galicia, San Marcos s/n, E-15780 SANTIAGO DE COMPOSTELA (A CORUÑA)
Tel: 981 54 06 40. **Fax:** 981 54 06 19.
Email: crtvg@crtvg.es
Web site: http://www.crtvg.es
News Editor: Anxo Pérez; *Director:* Anxo Quintanilla

TELEVISIÓN LOCAL GIJÓN - TLG 53346
Puerto de Palo 4, E-33207 GIJÓN
Tel: 98 50 93 433. **Fax:** 98 50 93 460.
Email: informativos@tlg.es
Web site: http://www.tlg.es
Editor: Nelli Diaz; *Director:* Jesús Rodríguez Lanza

TELEVISIÓN LOCAL SANT CUGAT 53342
San Marti 32 entlos., E-08172 SANT CUGAT DEL VALLES (BARCELONA)
Tel: 93 58 95 366. **Fax:** 93 58 98 360.
Email: informatius@tvsantacogat.com
Web site: http://www.tvsantcugat.com
Editor: Silvia Viñas; *Director:* Román Ventura Sala

TELEVISIÓN MURCIANA 53347
Avda. Juan Carlos I, Zona Industrial 1, Nave 6, E-30100 ESPINARDO (MURCIA)
Tel: 968 30 83 09. **Fax:** 968 85 94 53.
Email: tvm@tvm.es
Web site: http://www.tvm.es
Editor: Alejandro Garcia; *Director:* Juan Fran Zambudio

TELEVISIÓN PALENCIA 53348
C/ Gil de Fuentes, 2, E-34001 PALENCIA
Tel: 979 10 04 00. **Fax:** 979 10 03 00.
Email: tvpalencia@tvcyl.es
Web site: http://www.tvcyl.es
Editor: Daniel Pascual; *Director:* Alfonso Rodriguez

TELEVISIÓN SEGOVIA 53349
Calle Miraflores 14, E-40005 SEGOVIA
Tel: 921 44 15 19. **Fax:** 921 44 33 10.
Email: tvsegovia@tvcyl.es
Web site: http://www.tvcyl.es
Editor: Yolanda Fernández Barrio; *Director:* Luis Martín

TELEVITORIA 53350
Polvorin Viejo 4, E-01003 VITORIA
Tel: 94 51 20 738. **Fax:** 94 52 51 758.
Email: gestion@televitoria.es
Editor: Juan Bravo Martinez; *Director:* Juan Bravo Martínez

TV BENAVENTE 765511
Aguadores, 10 bajo, E-49600 BENAVENTE (ZAMORA) **Tel:** 980 16 23 61.
Fax: 980 16 23 62.
Email: tvb@tvcyl.es
Web site: http://www.tvcyl.es
Editor: Eva Crespo; *Director:* Juan Francisco Martín

SATELLITE TV

DIGITAL PLUS 52966
Avda. Artesanos 6, E-28760 TRES CANTOS (MADRID) **Tel:** 91 73 67 000.
Fax: 91 73 68 914.
Email: clientes@sogecable.com
Web site: http://www.plus.es
Director: Carlos Abad

EUROSPORT 52967
Eurosport España, cue Alcala 516, E-28027 MADRID **Tel:** 91 75 48 259.
Fax: 91 32 71 781.
Email: fruiz@eurosport.com
Web site: http://www.eurosport.es
Editor: Fernando Ruiz

TVE CANAL CLÁSICO 52969
Casa de la Radio Prado del Rey, Pozuelo de Alarcon, E-28223 MADRID
Tel: 91 24 61 632. **Fax:** 91 58 17 547.
Email: radio_clasica.rne@rtve.es
Web site: http://www.rtve.es/comercial.html

TVE INTERNACIONAL AMÉRICA 52971
Torre España, Calle Alcalde Saenz de Baranda 92, 7°, E-28007 MADRID
Tel: 91 34 68 519. **Fax:** 91 34 69 751.
Email: dir_internacional.tve@rtve.es
Web site: http://www.rtve.es/comercial.html

TVE INTERNACIONAL EUROPA 52972
Torre España, Calle Alcalde Saenz de Baranda No. 92, E-28007 MADRID
Tel: 91 34 68 519. **Fax:** 91 34 69 751.
Email: dir_internacional.tve@rtve.es
Web site: http://www.rtve.es/comercial.html
Director: José Luis Rodríguez Puertolas

TVE INTERNACIONAL HISPAVISIÓN 52973
Torre España, Calle Alcalde Saenz de Baranda No. 92, E-28007 MADRID
Tel: 91 34 68 519. **Fax:** 91 34 69 751.
Email: dir_internacional.tve@rtve.es
Web site: http://www.rtve.es/comercial.html
Director: José Luis Rodríguez Puertolas

TVE TELEDEPORTE 52970
Merce Vilaret s/n, 08190 San Cugat de Valles, E-08190 BARCELONA
Tel: 93 58 23 909. **Fax:** 91 58 23 610.
Email: teledeporte.b.tve@rtve.es
Web site: http://www.rtve.es/comercial.html
Director: Jorge Antonio Sanchez Dominguez

TVVI 1696250
RTVV, Polígono de Acceso a Ademuz s/n, E-46100 BURJJASSOT (VALENCIA)
Tel: 96 31 83 000. **Fax:** 96 31 83 001.
Email: informatius@rtvv.es
Web site: http://www.rtvv.es
Editor: Lluís Motes; *Director:* Tomás Lezcano

CABLE TV

PROCONO TV MÁLAGA 53367
Alderete 22, E-29013 MÁLAGA
Tel: 95 26 51 199. **Fax:** 95 26 51 870.
Email: ptvmalaga@ptvtelecom.com
Web site: http://www.ptvtelecom.com
Editor: Francisco Cuenca; *Director:* Quintin Cruz

PROCONO TV VALENCIA 53369
Calle Ciudad de Mula 16, bajo, E-46021 VALENCIA **Tel:** 96 36 11 162.
Fax: 96 39 30 068.
Email: ptvvalencia@ptvtelecom.com
Web site: http://www.ptvtelecom.com
Editor: Carlos Bonastre; *Director:* Susana Ibañez

NATIONAL RADIO STATIONS

CADENA DIAL 52942
Gran Vía 32, 7ª planta, E-28013 MADRID
Tel: 91 34 70 740. **Fax:** 91 52 11 753.
Email: jmgarciam@unionradio.es
Web site: http://www.cadenadial.com
Editor: Juan Manuel García; *Director:* Juan Carlo Chavez

M 80 RADIO 52944
Gran Vía 32, 7ª planta, E-28013 MADRID
Tel: 913 47 08 07. **Fax:** 915 22 86 93.
Email: programas@m80radio.com
Web site: http://www.m80radio.com
Director: Manuel Davila Moreno

OCR ONDA CERO RADIO 52945
Jose Ortega y Gasset 22-24, E-28006 MADRID **Tel:** 914 36 64 00.
Fax: 914 36 61 13.
Email: programas@ondacero.es
Web site: http://www.ondacero.es

RADIO CADENA TOP 52943
Calle Manuel Silvela 9, E-28010 MADRID
Tel: 91 44 75 300. **Fax:** 91 44 77 026.
Email: info@topradio.es
Web site: http://www.topradio.es
Editor: Tirso Esteve; *Director:* Tirso Esteve

RADIO NACIONAL DE ESPAÑA 52949
Casa de la Radio, Prado del Rey, E-28223 POZUELO DE ALARCÓN (MADRID)
Tel: 913 46 10 00. **Fax:** 913 46 17 86.
Email: secretario_general.rne@rtve.es
Web site: http://www.rtve.es/rne
News Editor: Javier Arenas; *Editor:* Pedro Piqueras

RADIO POPULAR 52950
Alfonso 11, 4 Edificio Cope, E-28014 MADRID **Tel:** 91 59 51 200.
Fax: 91 401 07 81.
Email: programas.madrid@cadenacope.net
Web site: http://www.cope.es
Editor: Ignacio Villa; *Director:* Jenaro Jorge Yerro

REGIONAL RADIO STATIONS

97 PUNTO 7 LA RADIO 53082
Pasaje Dr. Serra 2, 10ª planta 2°, E-46004 VALENCIA **Tel:** 96 35 20 776.
Fax: 96 39 44 743.
Email: informa@la977.com
Web site: http://www.la977.com
Editor: José Vicente Miralles

CADENA SER ADRA 53175
Calle Guadix 8, E-04770 ADRA (ALMERÍA)
Tel: 950 40 12 65. **Fax:** 950 40 16 65.
Email: radiogaviota@larural.es
Web site: http://www.radiogaviota.es.vg
Director: Francisco Garcia Villegas

LA CALA RADIO 53085
Sant Joan 55, 2° 1ª, E-43860 L'AMETLLA DE MAR (TARRAGONA) **Tel:** 977 49 30 37.
Fax: 977 49 30 07.
Email: lacalaradio@ametllamar.com
Web site: http://baixebre.net/lacalaradio
Editor: Francesc Callau i González

CANAL BLAU RADIO 53086
Carrer Escolapis, 6, E-08800 VILANOVA I LA GELTRU (BARCELONA) **Tel:** 93 81 42 526.
Fax: 93 89 36 972.
Email: cbfm@canalblau.net
Web site: http://www.canalblau.net

CATALUNYA RADIO 53088
Avda. Diagonal 614-616, E-08021 BARCELONA **Tel:** 93 30 69 200.
Fax: 93 30 69 201.
Email: correo@catradio.com
Web site: http://www.catradio.com

COPE PIRINEOS 53089
Calle San Sebastián, 6 Local, E-22440 BENASQUE (HUESCA) **Tel:** 97 45 51 290.
Fax: 97 45 51 583.
Email: antenadelpirineo@telefonica.net
Director: Aurelio Mora Barrabés

FLAIX FM BARCELONA 53092
Paseo de Gracia 54, 1°, E-08007 BARCELONA **Tel:** 93 50 55 555.
Fax: 93 48 80 775.
Email: flaixfm@grupflaix.net
Web site: http://www.flaixfm.net

FLAIX FM TARRAGONA 53093
Plaça Pati 2, E-43800 VALLS (TARRAGONA)
Tel: 977 61 28 88. **Fax:** 977 60 57 06.
Email: toni@flaixtgn.net
Web site: http://www.flaixtgn.net
News Editor: Antonio Vargas Spinosa; *Director:* Antonio Vargas Spinosa

HERRI IRRATIA POPULAR LOIOLA 53095
Santuario de Loiola, E-20730 AZPEITIA (GUIPÚZCOA) **Tel:** 943 81 44 58.
Fax: 943 81 39 44.
Email: info@herri-irratia.com
Web site: http://www.herri-irratia.com
News Editor: Urko Odriozola; *Editor:* Iñaki Mujika

HERRI IRRATIA POPULAR SAN SEBASTIÁN 53096
Garibay 19, E-20004 SAN SEBASTIÁN (GUIPÚZCOA) **Tel:** 943 42 36 44.
Fax: 943 42 95 67.
Email: info@herri-irratia.com
Web site: http://www.herri-irratia.com
News Editor: Urko Odriozola; *Editor:* Iñaki Mujika

HERRI IRRATIA RADIO POPULAR BILBAO 53094
Alameda de Mazarredo 47, 7°, E-48009 BILBAO **Tel:** 94 42 39 200.
Fax: 94 42 34 703.
Email: programacion@radiopopular.com
Web site: http://www.radiopopular.com
News Editor: Coldo Campo; *Editor:* Coldo Campo

INTERECONOMÍA 53097
Paseo de la Castellana 36-38, 10ª planta, E-28046 MADRID **Tel:** 91 42 37 600.
Fax: 91 57 78 591.
Email: radio@intereconomia.com
Web site: http://www.intereconomia.com
Editor: Natalia Obregón

KOSTA LATINA 107.7FM 764738
Calle San Vicente Martín, 213 bajo, E-46007 VALENCIA **Tel:** 96 31 86 084.
Fax: 96 38 04 027.
Email: kostalatina@kostalatina.com
Web site: http://www.kostalatina.com
News Editor: Salva Riera; *Editor:* Salva Riera

ONDA ARANJUEZ 53100
Calle Infantas 55, E-28300 ARANJUEZ (MADRID) **Tel:** 91 89 10 072.
Fax: 91 89 25 747.
Email: onda@aranjuez-realsitio.com
Editor: Paco Martin; *Director:* Francisco Martín Martín

ONDA CERO LUGO 53282
Plaza Santo Domingo No.3 3ª C, E-27001 LUGO **Tel:** 982 28 45 90. **Fax:** 982 28 45 35.
Email: labuide@ondacero.es
Web site: http://www.ondacero.es
News Editor: Lourdes Abuide; *Editor:* Monica Santos

ONDA FUENLABRADA 53101
Calle Honda 29, E-28994 FUENLABRADA (MADRID) **Tel:** 91 69 77 095.
Fax: 91 69 77 602.
Email: luisangel@ondafuenlabrada.com
Web site: http://www.ondafuenlabrada.com
News Editor: Luis Angel Culebras; *Director:* Francisco de Gregorio

ONDA NARANJA COPE 53104
Avda. Valencia 18 Apdo. 27, E-46780 OLIVA (VALENCIA) **Tel:** 96 28 39 818.
Fax: 96 28 39 845.
Email: logistica@ondanaranjacope.com
Web site: http://www.ondanaranjacope.com
Editor: Maricarmen Merzosa; *Director:* Cesar Jouquén García Aparisi

ONDA REGIONAL DE MURCIA 53105
Avda. de la Libertad 6, bajo, E-30009 MURCIA **Tel:** 968 20 00 00.
Fax: 968 24 33 27.
Email: informativos.or@carm.es
Web site: http://www.ondaregionalmurcia.es
Editor: Joaquin Aztarren; *Director:* Juan Marquez

2 ONDA SIERRA 53106
Calle Jeronimo Sastene 2, E-28790 MIRAFLORES **Tel:** 91 84 63 223.
Fax: 91 84 49 022.
Email: ondasierra@ondasierra.com
Editor: Alejandro de la Morena

RADIO 90 (MOTILLA DEL PALANCAR) 53110
Ctra. de La Roda 39, E-16200 MOTILLA DEL PALANCAR (CUENCA) **Tel:** 969 33 21 30.
Fax: 969 33 18 10.
Email: radio90.net@radio90.net
Web site: http://www.radio90.net
Editor: Javier Ruiz; *Director:* Gabriel Montero Tornero

RADIO AGUILAS 53111
Calle Ramon y Cajal 27, E-30880 AGUILAS (MURCIA) **Tel:** 968 44 76 62.
Fax: 968 44 76 62.
Email: radioaguilas@mixmail.com
Editor: Antonio Carabajal Carrasco

RADIO ALBACETE 53113
Avenida de la Estacion 5, E-02001 ALBACETE **Tel:** 967 52 11 30.
Fax: 967 21 45 48.
Web site: http://www.cadenaser.com
News Editor: Imaculada Ruiz; *Editor:* Imaculada Ruiz

RADIO ALCOY 53114
Doctor Sempere 16 B-C, E-03803 ALCOY (ALICANTE) **Tel:** 96 53 34 443.
Fax: 96 53 34 389.
Email: radioalcoy@radioalcoy.com
Editor: Enrique Luis; *Director:* Juan Jorda Raduan

RADIO ALICANTE 53116
Calderón de la Barca 26, E-03004 ALICANTE
Tel: 96 52 03 511. **Fax:** 96 52 19 143.
Email: ralicante.cial@unionradio.com
Editor: Carlos Arcaya; *Director:* Benjamin Llorens

RADIO ALMANZORA 53117
Pza. Nueva 1, Edificio Avenida Pio II, E-04800 ALBOX (ALMERÍA) **Tel:** 950 12 08 21.
Fax: 950 43 14 45.
Email: radioalmanzora@seralmeria.com
Web site: http://www.seralmeria.com
Editor: Paqui Martinez Sanchez; *Director:* Modesto Rubio

RADIO ANDUJAR 53119
Calle Ollerías 51 1°, E-23740 ANDUJAR (JAÉN) **Tel:** 953 50 21 00. **Fax:** 953 51 20 24.
Email: radioandujar@radioandujar.com
Web site: http://www.radioandujar.com
Editor: Francesca de Esteban Pedrajas; *Director:* Juan Parras Garcia

RADIO ANTENA NORTE 53120
Mercaderes 6, E-33500 LLANES (ASTURIAS)
Tel: 98 54 01 234. **Fax:** 98 54 03 728.
Email: prp@llanesnet.com
Editor: Jose Antonio Anca Gomez; *Director:* Anselmo Julio Carrera de Caso

RADIO ARANDA 53121
Isilla 2, 1°, E-09400 ARANDA DE DUERO (BURGOS) **Tel:** 947 50 63 90.
Fax: 947 50 88 98.
Email: redactor@radioaranda.com
Web site: http://www.radioaranda.com
News Editor: Vicente Herrero Carreter; *Editor:* Juan Luis Iglesias

RADIO ARANJUEZ 53122
Carerra de Andalucia 112, E-28300 ARANJUEZ (MADRID) **Tel:** 91 89 17 440.
Fax: 91 89 22 996.
Email: radioaranjuez@terra.es
Editor: Beatriz Fernandez; *Director:* Ignacio Sánchez Pérez Moneo

RADIO ARNEDO 53123
Santo Domingo 5, 3°, E-26580 ARNEDO (LA RIOJA) **Tel:** 941 38 33 50. **Fax:** 941 38 33 83.
Email: ondarioja@ondarioja.com
Web site: http://www.ondarioja.com
Editor: Pedro Vega Hernández

RADIO ARRATE 53125
Apdo. 212, E-20600 EIBAR (GUIPÚZCOA)
Tel: 943 12 01 61. **Fax:** 943 12 01 73.
Email: arrateirratia@euskalnet.net
Editor: Bernardo Ibarra

RADIO ASTURIAS 53126
Calle Asturias 19 bajo, E-33004 OVIEDO
Tel: 98 52 36 823. **Fax:** 98 52 72 924.
Email: ser@radioasturias.com
Web site: http://www.radioasturias.com
Editor: Pablo Canga; *Director:* Luis Toyos

RADIO AXARQUIA (VELEZ) 53127
Calle Jon de Bozancon 1ª planta, E-29700 VELEZ (MÁLAGA) **Tel:** 95 25 06 170.
Fax: 95 25 06 393.
Email: radioaxarquia@unionradio.es
Web site: http://www.cadenaser.com
Editor: Antoni Zapata; *Director:* Juan Francisco Urendez Sánchez

RADIO AZUL PEDROÑERAS SER 53128
Avda. Juan Carlos I, 18, E-16660 LAS PEDROÑERAS (CUENCA) **Tel:** 967 16 05 56.
Fax: 967 16 11 11.
Email: radioazul@radioazul.com
Web site: http://www.radioazul.es
News Editor: M. Carmen Izquierdo; *Editor:* M. Carmen Izquierdo

RADIO BARBASTRO 53129
Pablo Sahún 2, E-22300 BARBASTRO (HUESCA) **Tel:** 974 31 39 31.
Fax: 974 31 38 31.
Email: radiobarbastro@radiohuesca.com
Web site: http://www.cadenaser.es
Editor: José Sánchez Martín

RADIO BARCELONA 53130
Caspe 6, E-08010 BARCELONA
Tel: 93 34 41 400. **Fax:** 93 31 79 579.
Email: rb.ser@bcn.servicom.es
Web site: http://www.cadenaser.es
News Editor: Jordi Marti; *Director:* Josep Maria Girona

RADIO BAZA 53131
Calle San Francisco 3 4° A, E-18800 BAZA (GRANADA) **Tel:** 958 86 14 15.
Fax: 958 86 14 86.
Email: radiobaza@radiobaza.com
Web site: http://www.cadenaser.com
Editor: Manuel Sánjez Peréz; *Director:* Adolfo Machado de la Quintana

RADIO BENAVENTE 53132
Calle Erreros 13, 1°, E-49600 BENAVENTE (ZAMORA) **Tel:** 980 63 37 11.
Fax: 980 63 32 94.
Email: benaventeser@telefonica.net
Web site: http://www.cadenaser.com
Editor: María Luisa Gallego; *Director:* Miguel Angel González

RADIO BENIDORM 53133
Avda. Mediterráneo 53, E-03503 BENIDORM
Tel: 96 58 58 162. **Fax:** 96 58 57 320.
Email: serbenidor@terra.es
News Editor: Julio Marín; *Editor:* Javier Jiménez García

RADIO BIERZO 53135
Avda. de España 12, 4d, E-24400 PONFERRADA (LEÓN) **Tel:** 987 40 21 11.
Fax: 987 42 42 23.
Email: informativos@radiobierzo.com
Web site: http://www.radiobierzo.com
News Editor: Fernando Tascón; *Director:* Enrique García Astigarraga

RADIO BILBAO 53136
Calle Epalza 8, 5°, E-48007 BILBAO
Tel: 94 48 72 100. **Fax:** 94 48 72 118.
Email: radiobilbao@unionradio.es
Web site: http://www.cadenaser.com
News Editor: Javier Hoyos; *Director:* Rámon Gabilondo

RADIO BURGADO 53137
Sabino Berthelot 49, 4°, E-38002 SANTA CRUZ DE TENERIFE **Tel:** 922 27 38 12.
Fax: 922 27 38 16.
Email: burgado2002@hotmail.com
Editor: Andrés Chaves

RADIO CÁDIZ 53155
Paseo Maritimo 1, E-11010 CÁDIZ
Tel: 956 28 54 05. **Fax:** 956 27 42 80.
Email: radiocadiz@unionradio.es
Web site: http://www.cadenaser.com
Editor: Blanca Juste Pérez

RÁDIO CALELLA 53139
Fabrica Llobet i Gury s/n, Calle San Jaime 339 2° piso, E-08370 CALELLA (BARCELONA) **Tel:** 93 76 60 333.
Fax: 93 76 97 487.
Email: radio@calella.com
Web site: http://www.radiocalella.com
Editor: Giordi Bota; *Director:* Giordi Bota

RADIO CANFALI-ONDA-MANCHA 53141
Doctor Bon Ardell 1, 1ª Edificio Mercado de Abasto, Mercado de Abastos, 1ª, E-13600 ALCAZAR DE SAN JUAN (CIUDAD REAL)
Tel: 926 55 09 41. **Fax:** 926 55 09 44.
Email: canfaliradio@hotmail.com
Editor: Rosalinda Tejera; *Director:* Manuel Esquembre Bañuls

RADIO CASTILLA (BURGOS) 53144
Venerables 8, E-09005 BURGOS
Tel: 947 20 66 66. **Fax:** 947 27 59 59.
Email: radiocastilla.redaccion@unionradio.es
Web site: http://www.cadenaser.com
Editor: Pedro Sedano; *Director:* Enrique de la Viuda

RADIO CAZORLA 53145
Hilario Marco 13 bajo, E-23470 CAZORLA (JAÉN) **Tel:** 953 72 16 17. **Fax:** 953 72 16 18.
Email: dialcazorla@terra.es
Editor: María José Bayona Ruiz

RADIO CEUTA 53146
Poblado marinero, local 32, E-51001 CEUTA
Tel: 956 51 18 20. **Fax:** 956 51 68 20.
Email: radiocuenta@unionradio.es
Web site: http://www.cadenaser.com
Editor: Miguel Angel Mendoza; *Director:* Antonio Rosa

RADIO CLUB 25 53147
Muntaner 305 principal 2ª, E-08021 BARCELONA **Tel:** 93 20 98 488.
Fax: 93 20 98 898.
Email: radioclub25@radioclub25.com
Web site: http://www.radioclub25.com
Editor: Xavi Salillas; *Director:* Xavi Salillas

RADIO CLUB NORTE 53148
Pza. Reyes Católicos 6, E-38400 PUERTO DE LA CRUZ (TENERIFE) **Tel:** 922 38 00 08.
Fax: 922 38 42 26.
Email: tenerifenor@inicia.es
Editor: Maribel Diez Taular; *Director:* Mª José Pérez

RADIO CLUB TENERIFE 53149
Avda. de Anaga 35, 2°, E-38001 SANTA CRUZ DE TENERIFE **Tel:** 922 27 04 00.
Fax: 922 28 10 43.
Email: radioclubtenerife@unionradio.es
Web site: http://www.cadenaser.com
Editor: Juan Carlos Mateo

RADIO CÓRDOBA 53151
García Lovera 3, E-14002 CÓRDOBA
Tel: 957 48 40 80. **Fax:** 957 47 68 21.
Email: redacion.radiocordoba@unionradio.es
Web site: http://www.radiocordoba.es
Editor: María Eugenia Vilchez; *Director:* Javier Hernando

RADIO CORUÑA 53152
Pza. de Orense 3, 1°, E-15004 LA CORUÑA
Tel: 981 22 07 19. **Fax:** 981 20 37 22.
Email: ra.cadenaser@radiocoruna.es
Web site: http://www.radiocoruna.es
News Editor: Consuelo Bautista; *Editor:* Consuelo Bautista

RADIO COSTA BRAVA 53153
Didac Garell 10, E-17230 PALAMOS (GIRONA) **Tel:** 972 31 83 50.
Fax: 972 31 62 58.
Email: rcbrava@onacatalana.com
Web site: http://www.onacatalana.com
Editor: Dolores Rivera; *Director:* Carmen Galerias

RADIO CUELLAR 53154
Padre Balbino Velasco 2, E-40200 CUELLAR (SEGOVIA) **Tel:** 921 14 11 11.
Fax: 921 14 17 23.
Email: radiocuellar@radiosegovia.com
Editor: Ignacio Montavillo; *Director:* Luis Antonio Hernández

RADIO DENIA COSTABLANCA 53157
Marqués de Campo 39, E-03700 DENIA (ALICANTE) **Tel:** 96 57 84 242.
Fax: 96 64 21 828.
Email: radiodenia@terra.es
Web site: http://www.radiodenia.com
Editor: Ángel Albi; *Director:* Vicente Miralles Ferrer

RADIO DUNAS 53158
Avda. de Tejeda, 72, Centro Cultural de Maspalomas, E-35100 SAN BARTOLOMÉ DE TIRAJANA (GRAN CANARIA)
Tel: 928 76 52 28. **Fax:** 928 76 61 70.
Email: radiodunas@hotmail.com
Director: Hijinio Rayo

RADIO EIBAR 53167
Calle Zezen-bide 7, E-20600 EIBAR (GUIPÚZCOA) **Tel:** 943 20 41 41.
Fax: 943 20 40 48.
Email: radioeibar@unionradio.es
Web site: http://www.radioestudio.com
News Editor: Javier Rodríguez; *Editor:* Juan Manuel Cano

RADIO ELCHE 53160
Doctor Caro 43, E-03201 ELCHE (ALICANTE) **Tel:** 96 54 43 111.
Fax: 96 66 64 535.
Email: javiermu@rtvelche.com
Web site: http://www.rtvelche.com
Editor: Javier Muñoz

RADIO ELDA 53161
Avda. de Chapi 41 entlo 3, Entre Suelo, E-03600 ELDA (ALICANTE) **Tel:** 96 53 82 845.
Fax: 96 53 94 861.
Email: reldaser@terra.es
Director: Maria Dolores Gil Martinez

RADIO ENCUENTRO (UTIEL) 53162
Calle Alamos, 3°, E-46300 UTIEL (VALENCIA) **Tel:** 96 21 73 249.
Fax: 96 21 73 063.
Email: radio-encuentro@telefonica.net
Web site: http://www.radioencuentro.es
News Editor: Luis Agüe Parra; *Editor:* Luís Agüe Parra

RADIO ESTEL 53164
Carrer Comtes de Bell Lloc 67-69, E-08014 BARCELONA **Tel:** 93 40 92 810.
Fax: 93 40 92 815.
Email: radioestel@radioestel.com
Web site: http://www.radioestel.com
Editor: Aure Serán

RADIO ESTUDIO - LA RADIO DE CACERES 53166
Luis Alvárez Lencero 8, Urb. Los Castellanos, E-10005 CACERES
Tel: 927 23 13 13. **Fax:** 927 23 02 51.
Email: andresmcampos@terra.es
Web site: http://www.radioestudio.com
News Editor: Jesús Marin; *Director:* Andrés Campos

RADIO ESTUDIO - LA RADIO NORTE DE MADRID 53168
Pasaje de la Radio 1, E-28100 ALCOBENDAS (MADRID) **Tel:** 91 65 31 199.
Fax: 91 65 33 072.
Email: redaccion@radioestudio.com
Editor: Sonia Picon; *Director:* Pilar García

RADIO ESTUDIO - LA RADIO SUR DE MADRID 53169
Calle Pinto 52, E-28980 PARLA (MADRID)
Tel: 91 65 31 199. **Fax:** 91 69 83 080.
Email: redacionsur@radioestudio.com
Web site: http://www.radioestudio.com
Editor: Pilar García

RADIO EUSKADI 53170
Gran Vía 85, 1°, E-48011 BILBAO
Tel: 94 40 12 400. **Fax:** 94 40 12 195.
Email: radio_euskadi@eitb.com
Web site: http://www.eitb.com
News Editor: Miguel Reparas; *Editor:* Thema Mora

RADIO EXTREMADURA 53171
Ramón Albarrán 2, 3ª, E-06002 BADAJOZ
Tel: 924 22 22 60. **Fax:** 924 22 14 24.
Email: radioextremadura@unionradio.es
Web site: http://www.cadenaser.com
Editor: Lucio Poves Verde; *Director:* Angel Luis Lopez De Bejarano

RADIO FARO (CHANTADA) 53172
Avda. de Orense 17, Edificio Almaco, E-27500 CHANTADA (LUGO)
Tel: 982 44 18 24. **Fax:** 982 44 00 19.
Email: radiofaro@hispavista.com
Editor: Marise Matia Rodriguez; *Director:* Julio Beberide

RADIO GALICIA 53173
San Pedro de Mezonzo 3, 1°, E-15701 SANTIAGO DE COMPOSTELA
Tel: 981 59 46 00. **Fax:** 981 57 35 35.
Email: radiogalicia@unionradio.es
News Editor: Aida Pena; *Editor:* Gonzalo Cortizo

RADIO GANDIA 53174
Calle Loreto 32, E-46701 GANDIA (VALENCIA) **Tel:** 96 28 71 648.
Fax: 96 28 71 848.
Email: informativos@radiogandia.net
Web site: http://www.radiogandia.net/
Editor: Modesto Ferrer; *Director:* Francisco Sanz Sevilla

RADIO GIRONA 53176
Plaça Josep Pla 2, ent., E-17001 GIRONA
Tel: 972 22 11 00. **Fax:** 972 22 36 22.
Email: radiogirona@unionradio.es
Web site: http://www.cadenaser.com
Director: Jaume Serra

RADIO GORBEA 53178
Polvorin Viejo 4, E-01003 VITORIA-GASTEIZ (ALAVA) **Tel:** 94 525 16 61.
Fax: 94 525 17 58.
Email: informativos@radiogorbea.com
Web site: http://www.radiogorbea.com
Director: Juan Bravo Martínez

RADIO GRANADA 53179
Calle Santa Paula 2, E-18001 GRANADA
Tel: 958 28 13 00. **Fax:** 958 20 98 04.
Email: radiogranada@radiogranada.es
Web site: http://www.radiogranada.es
Editor: Agustin Martínez; *Director:* José Luis Ramirez Domenich

RADIO GUADAÍRA 53180
Pza. del Duque 5, Apdo. de Correos 117, E-41500 ALCALÁ DE GUADAIRA (SEVILLA)
Tel: 95 49 79 234. **Fax:** 95 497 92 29.
Email: gc@ciudadalcala.com
Web site: http://www.ciudadalcala.com
Editor: Francisco Javier Maestre Caballero; *Director:* Jose Luis Diaz

RADIO GUADIX 53181
Avda. Medina Olmos 22, Edificio Las Palmeras, E-18500 GUADIX (GRANADA)
Tel: 958 66 21 61. **Fax:** 958 66 25 00.
Email: radioguadix@radiogranada.es
Web site: http://www.cadenaser.com
Editor: Manuel Sanchéz Peréz; *Director:* Adolfo Machado de la Quintana

RADIO HARO 53182
C/ La Vega, 30 Bajos, E-26200 HARO (LA RIOJA) **Tel:** 941 31 07 33. **Fax:** 941 30 33 02.
Email: emisora@radioharo.com
Web site: http://www.radioharo.com
Editor: José Genacio Capellán; *Director:* Rafael Martínez García

RADIO HUELVA 53183
Calle Méndez Nuñez 15, E-21001 HUELVA
Tel: 959 25 22 90. **Fax:** 959 28 15 57.
Email: radiohuelva@unionradio.es
Web site: www.cadenaser.com
Director: Pedro Neble Hasta

RADIO HUESCA 53184
Calle Alcalde Carderera, 1, E-22002 HUESCA **Tel:** 974 21 40 50.
Fax: 974 22 12 59.
Email: rahusa@radiohuesca.es
Web site: http://www.radiohuesca.com
Editor: Felix Fernández Vizarra Altarés

RADIO IRÚN 53189
Calle Iglesia 2, 1°, E-20302 IRÚN (GUIPUZCOA) **Tel:** 943 63 24 23.
Fax: 943 63 18 80.
Email: radioirun@unionradio.es
Web site: www.cadenaser.com
Editor: Rafael Miguel; *Director:* Rafael Miguel

RADIO ISLA TENERIFE 53190
Plaza José Arozena Paredes 1, Edf. Parque Recreativo, 1 - 6° A-B, E-38003 SANTA CRUZ DE TENERIFE **Tel:** 922 29 13 00.
Fax: 922 29 12 47.
Email: informativos@radioislatenerife.com
Web site: http://www.radioislatenerife.info
Editor: José Antonio Pardellas Casas

RADIO JACA 53191
Mayor 22, E-22700 JACA (HUESCA)
Tel: 974 36 24 24. **Fax:** 974 36 25 11.
Email: rahusa@ctv.es
Web site: http://www.radiohuesca.com
Editor: Antonio Lecuona Pérez; *Director:* Antonio Lecuona Pérez

RADIO JAÉN 53192
Obispo Aguilar 1, E-23001 JAÉN
Tel: 953 19 00 00. **Fax:** 953 19 00 04.
Email: radiojaen@radiojaen.es
Web site: http://www.radiojaen.es
Director: Antonio Gómez Lendinez

RADIO JEREZ 53193
Guadalete 12, E-11403 JEREZ DE LA FRONTERA (CADIZ) **Tel:** 856 05 05 05.
Fax: 856 05 05 04.
Email: tecnica@radiojerez.com
Web site: http://www.radiojerez.com
Editor: Ana Huguet; *Director:* José García Ganaza

RADIO LA PALMA 53199
Avda. Díaz Pimienta 10, Edificio Marbell 4°, E-38760 LOS LLANOS DE ARIDANE (TENERIFE) **Tel:** 922 40 13 13.
Fax: 922 46 31 69.
Email: lapalma@cadenaser.com
Web site: http://www.cadenaser.com
Editor: Álvaro Javier Pages Cárdenas

RADIO LAS PALMAS CADENA RADIO VOZ 53201
Profesor Lozano 5, 2ª planta, E-35008 LAS PALMAS DE GRAN CANARIA
Tel: 928 46 20 52. **Fax:** 928 46 20 57.
Email: informacion@radiolaspalmas.com
Web site: http://www.radiolaspalmas.com
Editor: Carmelo Perez; *Director:* Pilar Roda Márquez

RADIO LEÓN 53202
Villafranca 6, E-24001 LEÓN
Tel: 987 25 29 05. **Fax:** 987 25 23 58.
Email: radioleon@radioleon.com
Web site: http://www.radioleon.com
Editor: Javier García Beberide

RADIO L'HORTA 93.1 FM 53197
Avda. Real de Madrid 138, E-46017 VALENCIA **Tel:** 656 97 48 45.
Fax: 96 38 04 27.
Email: 931fm@931fm.com
Web site: http://www.931fm.com
Editor: Manuel García

RADIO LIMIA (XINZO) 53203
Avda. de Orense 82, 1° B, E-32630 XINZO DE LIMIA (OURENSE) **Tel:** 988 46 24 85.
Fax: 988 46 24 85.
Email: radiolimia@radioorense.com
Web site: http://www.radioorense.com
Editor: Elisa Agullo Diaz; *Director:* Julio Aragón Valencia

RADIO LINARES 53204
Plaza Ramón y Cajal 8, ático, E-23700 LINARES (JAÉN) **Tel:** 953 69 31 51.
Fax: 953 65 10 04.
Email: radiolinares@unionradio.es
Web site: http://www.cadenaser.com
News Editor: Juan Luis Sotes; *Editor:* Miguel Ortega

RADIO LLEIDA 53206
Vila Antonia 5, E-25007 LERIDA
Tel: 973 24 50 00. **Fax:** 973 24 19 33.
Email: lleida@cadenaser.com
Web site: http://www.cadenaser.com
Editor: Mercé March i Cuberes; *Director:* José Luis Cadena

RADIO LORCA 53207
Calle Pío XII 31, 2ª planta, E-30800 LORCA
Tel: 968 44 40 68. **Fax:** 968 46 22 79.
Email: radiolorca@unionradio.es
Web site: http://www.cadenaser.com
Editor: Isabel Maria Sanchez; *Director:* Ventura Garcia Estruch

RADIO LUGO 53208
Plaza Santo Domingo 3, E-27001 LUGO
Tel: 982 284 020. **Fax:** 982 227 512.
Email: radiolugo@radiolugo.info
Web site: http://www.lugonet.com/radiolugo
Editor: Juan Carlos Rodríguez; *Director:* Olga Beberide

RADIO LUNA 53209
San Gregorio 29, E-14440 VILLANUEVA DE CÓRDOBA **Tel:** 957 12 00 02.
Fax: 957 12 31 33.
Email: radioluna@telefonoca.net
Web site: http://www.radiolunaser.com
Editor: Vicente Barrera; *Director:* Juan Mohedano Torralbo

RADIO MADRID 53210
Gran Vía 32, 8ª planta, E-28013 MADRID
Tel: 913 47 77 00. **Fax:** 915 32 12 41.
Email: redaccion@cadenaser.com
Web site: http://www.cadenaser.com
News Editor: Rodolfo Irago

RADIO MANLLEU 53212
Plaça de Dalt Vila, Edificio Can Puget, E-08560 MANLLEU BARCELONA
Tel: 93 85 11 500. **Fax:** 93 85 14 107.
Email: radiomanlleu@infonegocio.com
Web site: http://www.osona.com/radiomanlleu.htm
Editor: Marc Riera

RÀDIO MARINA 53214
Calle La Guidó 1, Apdo. 234, E-17300 BLANES (GIRONA) **Tel:** 972 33 45 00.
Fax: 972 33 64 84.
Email: informatius@radiomarina.com
Web site: http://www.radiomarina.com
Editor: Joan Ferrer

RADIO MARIÑA (VIVERO) 53215
Nicolás Cora Montenegro 50 Entresuelo, E-27850 VIVERO (LUGO) **Tel:** 982 56 15 05.
Fax: 982 56 14 51.
Email: radiomarina@radiolugo.com
Web site: http://www.cadenaser.com
Editor: Cristina López; *Director:* Julio Beberide Martinez

RADIO MELILLA 53217
Muelle Puerto Ribera 18 B, E-52005 MELILLA **Tel:** 952 68 17 08.
Fax: 952 68 15 73.
Email: radiomelilla@unionradio.es
Web site: http://www.cadenaser.com
Editor: José Manuel Guival; *Director:* Antonia Ramos Peláez

RADIO MENORCA 53218
Obispo Goñalons 27, E-07703 MAHON (MENORCA) **Tel:** 971 35 47 00.
Fax: 971 35 18 42.
Email: radiomenorca@radiomenorca.com
Web site: http://www.radiomenorca.com
Editor: Sergi Ribera

RADIO MONZON 53221
San Isidro 2, E-22400 MONZON (HUESCA)
Tel: 974 40 39 63. **Fax:** 974 40 37 61.
Email: rahusa@ctv.es
Web site: http://www.radiohuesca.com
Editor: José Luis Barrio

RADIO MORA D'EBRE 53222
Antonio Asens 7 - 2°, E-43740 MORA DE EBRE (TARRAGONA) **Tel:** 977 40 28 18.
Fax: 977 24 42 72.
Email: mora@cadenaser.com
Web site: http://www.cadenaser.com
Editor: Encarna Fernández; *Director:* Gabriel Sanz

RADIO MORÓN 53223
Pozo Nuevo 60 Planta 2, E-41530 MORÓN DE LA FRONTERA (SEVILLA)
Tel: 95 485 25 35. **Fax:** 95 485 25 01.
Email: radiomoron@zoom.es
Web site: http://www.cadenaser.com
Director: Carlos Camacho García

RADIO MOTRIL 53224
Avenida de Salobreña 19, E-18600 MOTRIL (GRANADA) **Tel:** 958 60 26 25.
Fax: 958 60 10 10.
Email: radiomotril@radiogranada.es
Web site: http://www.radiogranada.es
Editor: José Manuel Gonzalez Arquero; *Director:* José Manuel Gonzalez Arquero

RADIO MULA 53225
Pintor Villacis s/n bajo, E-30170 MULA (MURCIA) **Tel:** 968 66 16 61.
Fax: 968 66 21 13.
Email: radiomulaser@eresmas.com
Web site: www.cadenaser.com
Editor: Juana Dolores Valera Moreno; *Director:* Damian Gonzalez Jimenez

RADIO MURCIA 53226
Calle Radio Murcia 4, E-30001 MURCIA
Tel: 968 22 00 05. **Fax:** 968 22 16 15.
Email: radiomurcia@unionradio.es
Web site: www.cadenaser.com
Editor: Ismael Galliana Alonso; *Director:* Ventura García

RADIO NAVALMORAL CADENA COPE 53228
Alberto Montero 4, E-10300 NAVALMORAL DE LA MATA **Tel:** 927 53 17 53.
Fax: 927 53 21 68.
Email: radionavalmoral@terra.es
Web site: http://www.cope.es
News Editor: Jesús Rubio Fernández; *Director:* Jesús Rubio Fernández

RADIO NERVIÓN 53229
Hurtado de Amézaga 27, 17 ª, E-48008 BILBAO **Tel:** 944 43 33 17.
Fax: 944 44 83 02.
Email: radionervion@radionervion.com
Web site: http://www.radionervion.com
Editor: Eva Argote; *Director:* Enrique Campos

RADIO NOU 53109
Avda. Blasco Ibáñez 136, Bajo, E-46022 VALENCIA **Tel:** 96 31 83 600.
Fax: 96 31 83 602.
Email: radionou@radionou.com
Web site: http://www.radionou.com
News Editor: Marta Ramada; *Editor:* Juan Jose Braulio

RADIO NUEVA 53230
Plaça de l'Hort dels Escribano, 2 bajos, E-12500 VINAROS (CASTELLÓN)
Tel: 964 40 22 34. **Fax:** 964 40 22 33.
Email: noticias@radio-nueva.com
Web site: http://www.radionueva.es/
News Editor: Julio Vidal; *Editor:* Juan José Benito

RADIO OLOT 53232
Plaça del Mig, Edificio Can Trinxeria, E-17800 OLOT (GIRONA) **Tel:** 972 26 17 50.
Fax: 972 26 13 57.
Email: direccio@radio-olot.com
Web site: http://www.radio-olot.com
Editor: Francesc Rubio Puig; *Director:* Francesc Rubio Puig

RADIO ORENSE 53234
Rua do Paseo 30 entresuelo, E-32003 ORENSE **Tel:** 988 22 12 63.
Fax: 988 25 03 00.
Email: cadenaser@radioorense.com
Web site: http://www.radioorense.com
Editor: José Domínguez González; *Director:* Julio Aragón Valencia

RADIO ORIHUELA 53235
Avenida Teodomiro 21, E-03300 ORIHUELA (ALICANTE) **Tel:** 965 30 20 45.
Fax: 966 74 06 28.
Editor: Alfonso Herrero

RADIO PALENCIA 53236
Calle de los Soldados 1, 2° planta, E-34001 PALENCIA **Tel:** 979 70 08 88.
Fax: 979 75 22 43.
Email: palencia@cadenaser.com
Web site: www.cadenaser.com
Editor: Angel López Bejarano

RADIO PAMPLONA 53237
Poligono Plazaola, Manzana F2° A, E-31195 AIZOAIN **Tel:** 948 24 65 50.
Fax: 948 23 36 01.
Email: informativosnavarra@cadenaser.com
Web site: www.cadenaser.com
Editor: Javier Martínez de Zuñiga; *Director:* José Maria Tejerina

RADIO PINEDA 53239
Calle Justicia 23-25, Apto. 195, E-08397 PINEDA DE MAR (BARCELONA)
Tel: 937 67 19 19. **Fax:** 937 67 10 50.
Email: inimitable@radiopineda.com
Web site: http://www.radiopineda.com
Editor: Manuel Colas; *Director:* Manuel Colas

RADIO REALEJOS NORTE FM 105.1 53241
Calle San Isidro s/n, Centro Comercial Realejos, E-38410 LOS REALEJOS (TENERIFE) **Tel:** 922 34 41 63.
Fax: 922 35 47 25.
Email: radiorealejos@telefonica.net
Editor: Isidro Perez Brito; *Director:* José Manuel Martín

RADIO REQUENA 53243
Plaza Albornoz 14, Apartado de Correos 41, E-46340 REQUENA (VALENCIA)
Tel: 962 30 01 58. **Fax:** 962 30 24 59.
Email: oyentes@radiorequena.com
Web site: http://www.radiorequena.com/
Editor: Maria José Arroyo; *Director:* Antonio Soriano

RADIO REUS 53244
Tomás Bergada, 3 - Piso 1, E-43204 REUS (TARRAGONA) **Tel:** 977 77 21 21.
Fax: 977 75 52 57.
Email: radioreus@unionradio.es
Web site: http://www.cadenaser.com
Editor: Gema Torrens; *Director:* Josep Roquer Zaragoza

RADIO RIBEIRO 53245
Rua Carballiño 40, 1°, E-32400 RIBADAVIA (ORENSE) **Tel:** 988 47 22 32.
Fax: 988 47 22 32.
Email: radioribeiro@radioourense.com
Editor: Javier Gomez; *Director:* Julio Aragón Valencia

RADIO RIOJA 53246
Avda. de Portugal 12 Piso 1, E-26001 LOGROÑO (LA RIOJA) **Tel:** 941 22 26 12.
Fax: 941 25 93 66.
Email: radio@radiorioja.es
Web site: http://www.radiorioja.es
News Editor: Alonso Hojas; *Editor:* Jorge Gomez Del Casal

RADIO RIOJA CALAHORRA 53138
Bebricio 38, E-26500 CALAHORRA (LA RIOJA) **Tel:** 941 13 27 08. **Fax:** 941 14 65 62.
Email: radiocalahorra_mig@telefonica.net
Web site: http://www.cadenaser.com
News Editor: Sara Orradre; *Director:* Javier Cermeño

RADIO SALAMANCA 53248
Calle Veracruz 2, E-37008 SALAMANCA
Tel: 923 21 82 00. **Fax:** 923 27 03 26.
Email: ser@radiosalamanca.com
Web site: http://www.radiosalamanca.com
Editor: Jesús García; *Director:* Maria Victoria Prieto

RADIO SALUT 53249
Avda. Diagonal 460, 3°, E-08006 BARCELONA **Tel:** 93 41 53 006.
Fax: 93 41 59 158.
Email: radiosalut@radiosalut.com
Web site: http://www.radiosalut.com
Editor: Pepe Nieves; *Director:* Juan Carlos Ballve

RADIO SANTANDER 53251
Pasaje de Peña 2 Int., 7ª planta, E-39008 SANTANDER **Tel:** 942 31 95 95.
Fax: 942 36 42 79.
Email: informativos@radiosantander.com
Web site: http://www.radiosantander.com
News Editor: Luis Angel Portugal; *Editor:* Julián de Arriba Crego

RADIO SENSACIÓN 53253
Calle Camino Hondo, 69 - 3 B, 30010 MURCIA **Tel:** 968 345 931.
Fax: 968 259 974.
Email: sensacion@radiosensacionfm.com
Web site: http://www.radiosensacionfm.com/
Editor: Juan Delgado; *Director:* Fernando González Contreras

RADIO SEVILLA 53255
Rafael González Abreu 6, E-41001 SEVILLA
Tel: 95 44 80 300. **Fax:** 95 44 80 334.
Email: radiosevilla@cadenaser.com
Web site: http://www.cadenaser.com
News Editor: Antonio Yelamo; *Director:* Jose Gutierrez

RADIO SIERRA DE ARACENA 53256
Juan del Cid López s/n, E-21200 ARACENA (HUELVA) **Tel:** 959 12 63 15.
Fax: 959 12 74 53.
Email: rsaracena@terra.com
Web site: www.cadenaser.com
Editor: Carmen Borrero; *Director:* María Dolores Gómez Sarabia

RADIO SINTONÍA 53257
Pza. San Pedro 1, 3ª planta, E-30820 ALCANTARILLA (MURCIA)
Tel: 968 89 00 10. **Fax:** 968 89 85 03.
Email: rsintonia1078@terra.es
Editor: José Navarro García

RADIO SURCO - CADENA COPE MANZANARES 53259
Virgen del Carmen 2, E-13200 MANZANARES (CIUDAD REAL)
Tel: 926 62 03 00. **Fax:** 926 62 03 03.
Email: manzanares@radiosurco.es
Web site: http://www.radiosurco.es
Editor: Montserrat Castellanos Cañones; *Director:* María José Serrano

RADIO SURCO - CASTILLA LA MANCHA 53258
Concordia 14, E-13700 TOMELLOSO (CIUDAD REAL) **Tel:** 926 50 59 59.
Fax: 926 50 59 61.
Email: direccion@radiosurco.es
Web site: http://www.radiosurco.es/
News Editor: Carlos. Montañes-Lomas; *Editor:* Francisco Castellanos Cuellar

RADIO SURCO - COPE LA MANCHA 53260
Rondilla de la Cruz Verde 102, E-13600 ALCAZAR DE SAN JUAN (CIUDAD REAL)
Tel: 926 54 72 50. **Fax:** 926 54 72 62.
Email: alcazar@radiosurco.es
Web site: http://www.surcortv.com
Editor: Enrique Castellanos; *Director:* Francisco Castellanos Cuellar

RADIO TARANCON 53261
Avda. Pablo Picasso 2, 5 ª planta, E-16400 TARANCON (CUENCA) **Tel:** 969 32 19 14.
Fax: 969 32 19 15.
Email: radiotarancon@cadenaser.com
Web site: www.cadenaser.com
Editor: Julio Clemente; *Director:* Francisco Cremades

RADIO TELETAXI 53293
Calle Sant Carles, 40, Santa Coloma de Gramenet, E-08922 BARCELONA
Tel: 934 66 56 56. **Fax:** 934 66 15 34.
Email: radioteletaxi@radioteletaxi.com
Web site: http://www.radioteletaxi.com
Director: Justo Molinero

RADIO TERRASSA 53262
Gutenberg, 3 - 6ª, E-08224 TERRASSA (BARCELONA) **Tel:** 93 78 06 166.
Fax: 93 78 03 358.
Email: info@radioterrassa.com
Web site: http://www.radioterrassa.com/
Editor: José Manuel Salillas García; *Director:* José Manuel Salillas García

RADIO TUDELA 53264
Díaz Bravo 1, 9 H, E-31500 TUDELA (NAVARRA) **Tel:** 948 82 76 00.
Fax: 948 82 75 61.
Email: radiotudela@unionradio.es
Web site: www.cadenaser.com
Editor: Ana Laura De Diego

RADIO UBEDA 53265
Córdoba, 11 - 1°, E-23400 UBEDA (JAÉN)
Tel: 953 75 49 41. **Fax:** 953 75 49 40.
Email: radioubeda@inicia.es
Web site: http://www.radioubeda.com
Editor: Victoria Jiménez Hibalgo; *Director:* Manuel Expósito Moreno

RADIO UTRERA 53266
Pza. de la Constitución, 12 D, Local 6, Apdo. 62, E-41710 UTRERA (SEVILLA)
Tel: 95 58 60 513. **Fax:** 95 58 61 517.
Email: radioutrera@radioutrera.com
Web site: http://www.radioutrera.com
News Editor: Antonia Vargas; *Editor:* Antonia Vargas

RADIO VALENCIA 53267
Don Juan de Austria 3, E-46002 VALENCIA
Tel: 96 31 87 600. **Fax:** 96 35 28 886.
Email: valencia@cadenaser.com
Web site: http://www.cadenaser.com
News Editor: Eva Márquez; *Editor:* Bernardo Guzmán

RADIO VALL D'UXO 53269
Plaza Silvestre Segarra 5 - 2ª, E-12600 VALL D'UXO (CASTELLON) **Tel:** 964 69 11 33.
Fax: 964 69 12 54.
Email: radiovallduxo@unionradio.es
Web site: www.cadenaser.com
Editor: Luis Segarra; *Director:* Fransisco Andújar Gallego

RADIO VALLADOLID 53270
Montero Calvo 7, Planta 2, E-47001 VALLADOLID **Tel:** 983 21 75 00.
Fax: 983 29 11 82.
Email: radiovalladolid@cadenaser.com
Web site: http://www.radiovalladolid.com
News Editor: Pilar Herrero Prieto; *Director:* José Castrillo Bernal

RADIO VALLS 53271
El Pati, 2 entresol, E-43800 VALLS (TARRAGONA) **Tel:** 977 61 28 88.
Fax: 977 60 57 06.
Email: informacion@radiovalls.net
Web site: http://www.radiovalls.net
Editor: Antonio Vargas Espinosa

RADIO VIGO 53272
Calle Arenal, 6 - 8. 6ª planta, E-36201 VIGO (PONTEVEDRA) **Tel:** 986 43 87 00.
Fax: 986 43 05 06.
Email: ser@radiovigo.com
Web site: http://www.radiovigo.com
Editor: Salvador García

RADIO VILA REAL 53273
Ausias March, 1, bajo, E-12540 VILLARREAL (CASTELLÓN) **Tel:** 964 53 53 11.
Fax: 964 50 50 12.
Email: direccio@radiovila-real.info
Web site: http://www.radiovila-real.info
Editor: Gema Font; *Director:* Carmen Lourdes Costa Llorens

RADIO VILLENA 53274
Paseo Chapí 17, E-03400 VILLENA (ALICANTE) **Tel:** 96 58 00 204.
Fax: 96 58 08 061.
Email: radiovillenal@unionradio.es
Web site: http://www.cadenaser.es
Editor: Isidro Hernández Más; *Director:* Isidro Hernández Más

RADIO VITORIA 53276
Calle Domingo Martinez de Aragon 5 - 7, E-01006 VITORIA **Tel:** 94 50 12 500.
Fax: 94 50 12 695.
Email: barredo@eitb.com
Web site: http://www.eitb24.com
News Editor: Jesús Barredo; *Editor:* José Ramón Diez Unzueta

RADIO VOZ 53296
Ronda de Outeiro 1-3, E-15006 LA CORUÑA
Tel: 981 18 01 80. **Fax:** 981 18 03 43.
Email: redac@radiovoz.com
Web site: http://www.radiovoz.com
News Editor: Manuel Mantilla Fernández; *Editor:* Carlos Carballo Varela

RADIO VOZ BERGANTIÑOS 53278
Gran Vía, 84 - 1°, E-15100 CARBALLO (LA CORUÑA) **Tel:** 981 70 22 00.
Fax: 981 70 21 51.
Email: redac.carballo@lavoz.es
Web site: http://www.radiovoz.com
Editor: Antonio Dias Dourado

RADIO VOZ COMPOSTELA 53279
Salgueiriños de Arriba 44, bajo, E-15703 SANTIAGO DE COMPOSTELA
Tel: 981 55 91 00. **Fax:** 981 55 91 09.
Email: vocesdecompostela@radiovoz.com
Web site: www.radiovoz.com
Editor: Eva Millan

RADIO VOZ VIGO 53289
Avda. García Barbón 104, bajo, E-36201 VIGO (PONTEVEDRA) **Tel:** 986 26 86 00.
Fax: 986 26 86 34.
Email: radiovoz.vigo@lavoz.com
Web site: http://www.radiovoz.com
Editor: Concha Gómez; *Director:* Manuel Rodriguez Carballo

RADIO XÀTIVA 53196
Pasaje Moncada 3, 3°, E-46800 XÀTIVA (VALENCIA) **Tel:** 96 22 72 213.
Fax: 96 22 82 258.
Email: serjativa@unionradio.es
Web site: http://www.cadenaser.com
Director: José Manuel Vicente Perales

RADIO ZARAGOZA 53291
Paseo de la Constitución 21, E-5001 ZARAGOZA **Tel:** 976 71 16 00.
Fax: 976 22 81 18.
Email: radiozaragoza@unionradio.es
Web site: http://www.cadenaser.com
News Editor: Placido Diéz; *Editor:* Placido Diéz

SER LANZAROTE 53277
José Antonio 114, E-35500 ARRECIFE (LANZAROTE) **Tel:** 928 80 16 98.
Fax: 928 80 24 56.
Email: serlanzarote@inicia.es
Web site: http://www.cadenaser.com
News Editor: Sergio Calleja; *Director:* Victoria Higuera

SOLO RADIO HELLIN 53187
Plaza Santa Ana 11 - 1°, Apto. Correos 45, E-02400 HELLIN (ALBACETE)
Tel: 967 30 53 21. **Fax:** 967 30 53 74.
Email: participahellin@soloradio.es
Web site: http://www.hellinsoloradio.com
Editor: Francisca Pinar; *Director:* José Aurelio Martinez Medina

TELEMADRID RADIO 53102
Paseo del Príncipe 3, E-28223 POZUELO DE ALARCÓN (MADRID) **Tel:** 91 51 28 200.
Fax: 91 51 28 300.
Email: telenoticias@telemadrid.es
Web site: http://www.telemadrid.com
Editor: Miguel Perez Pla; *Director:* Miguel Perez Pla

ULTIMA HORA RADIO 53294
Gremi Selleters i Basters, 14, Polígon Son Castelló, E-07009 PALMA DE MALLORCA
Tel: 971 43 48 48. **Fax:** 971 43 16 69.
Email: mc.uhradio@bitel.es
Web site: http://www.gruposerra.com
Director: Paula Serra Magraner

LA UNIÓN RADIO 8 53295
Pza. del Mercado Antiguo s/n, E-30360 LA UNION (MURCIA) **Tel:** 968 54 00 00.
Fax: 968 54 00 00.
Email: launionradio8@lamangadelmarmenor.com
Editor: Maria José Martínez Garcerán; *Director:* Antonio de la Concha Rex

Sweden

NATIONAL TV STATIONS

TV3 SVERIGE AB 51622
Box 171 04, 104 62 STOCKHOLM
Tel: 8 562 023 00. **Fax:** 8 562 023 30.
Email: press@tv3.se
Web site: http://www.tv3.se

TV4 AB 50763
Tegeluddsvägen 3, 115 79 STOCKHOLM
Tel: 8 459 40 00. **Fax:** 8 459 44 44.
Email: nyheterna@tv4.se
Web site: http://www.tv4.se

TV8 622971
Box 17119, 104 62 STOCKHOLM
Email: info@tv8.se
Web site: http://www.tv8.se
Presenter: Iréne Lindblad; *Producer:* Bo Wadman

REGIONAL TV STATIONS

TV4 SVERIGE AB ~TV4 STOCKHOLM 622970
Tegeluddsvägen 3, 115 79 STOCKHOLM
Tel: 8 459 41 00.
Email: nyheterna.stockholm@tv4.se
Web site: http://nyhetskanalen.se/lokalt/stockholm
Editor: Cjell Fransson; *Presenter:* Soraya Lavasani

CABLE TV

CANAL+ 51625
115 84 STOCKHOLM **Tel:** 202 400 24.
Fax: 8 459 28 60.
Email: info@canalplus.se
Web site: http://www.canalplus.se

REGIONAL RADIO STATIONS

106,7 ROCKKLASSIKER 50929
Box 34108, 100 26 STOCKHOLM
Tel: 8 450 33 00. **Fax:** 8 450 33 93.
Email: cloffe@rockklassiker.se
Web site: http://www.rockklassiker.se
Presenter: Ian Haugland

LUGNA FAVORITER 104,7 50877
MTG Radio, Södermälarstrand 43, 118 25 STOCKHOLM **Tel:** 8 562 720 00.
Fax: 8 562 720 88.
Web site: http://www.lugnafavoriter.com
Presenter: Peter Borossy

Sweden

MIX MEGAPOL - 104,2 BOHUSLÄN 50878
Kungsgatan 17, 453 33 LYSEKIL
Tel: 5 231 21 60. **Fax:** 523 135 96.
Email: info@mixmegapol.se
Web site: http://www.mixmegapol.se/?loc=bohuslan

MIX MEGAPOL - 104,3 & 92,0 STOCKHOLM/SÖDERTÄLJE 50879
Gjörwellsgatan 30, BOX 34108, 100 26 STOCKHOLM **Tel:** 8 450 33 00.
Fax: 8 450 33 60.
Email: info@mixmegapol.com
Web site: http://www.mixmegapol.se/?loc=sodertalje

MIX MEGAPOL - 104,7 ÖREBRO 50880
Box 245, 702 22 ÖREBRO **Tel:** 19 17 01 04.
Fax: 19 17 01 05.
Email: info@mixmegapol.com
Web site: http://www.mixmegapol.se/?loc=orebro

MIX MEGAPOL - 105,5 FALUN/BORLÄNGE 50881
Box 265, 791 26 FALUN **Tel:** 239 35 78.
Email: info@mixmegapol.com
Web site: http://www.mixmegapol.se/?loc=falun

MIX MEGAPOL - 106,1 VÄSTMANLAND 50886
c/o Radiobokningen, 722 12 VÄSTERÅS
Tel: 21 19 90 10.
Email: info@mixmegapol.com
Web site: http://www.mixmegapol.com

MIX MEGAPOL - 106,7 GÄVLE/SANDVIKEN 50884
Box 1028, 801 34 GÄVLE **Tel:** 26 14 17 30.
Fax: 26 14 17 40.
Email: gavle@mixmegapol.com
Web site: http://www.mixmegapol.com

MIX MEGAPOL - 106,8 MORA/SÄLEN 707026
Box 265, 791 26 FALUN **Tel:** 243 22 81 05.
Fax: 243 22 81 06.
Email: info@mixmegapol.com
Web site: http://www.mixmegapol.se/?loc=mora

MIX MEGAPOL - 106,9 & 99,2 ÖSTERGÖTLAND/MOTALA 50885
Box 655, 582 23 LINKÖPING
Tel: 13 14 14 53. **Fax:** 13 14 20 50.
Email: linkoping@mixmegapol.com
Web site: http://www.mixmegapol.se/?loc=ostergotland

MIX MEGAPOL - 107,3 & 93,1 SÖRMLAND 50887
Rinmansgatan 18, 633 46 ESKILSTUNA
Tel: 16 12 10 73. **Fax:** 16 51 02 90.
Email: eskilstuna@mixmegapol.com
Web site: http://www.mixmegapol.se/?loc=sormland

MIX MEGAPOL - 107,3 SKARABORG 50883
Mariestadsvägen 86, 541 45 SKÖVDE
Tel: 500 42 75 00. **Fax:** 500 42 75 01.
Email: skovde@mixmegapol.com
Web site: http://www.mixmegapol.se/?loc=skovde

MIX MEGAPOL RADIO CITY 107,0 - SKÅNE 50892
Box 4417, 203 15 MALMÖ **Tel:** 40 35 27 00.
Fax: 40 35 27 11.
Email: redaktion.mlm@radiocity.se
Web site: http://www.mixmegapol.se/?loc=malmo
Editor: Susanna Dzamic; *Presenter:* Henrik Wiberg

MIX MEGAPOL RADIO CITY 107,3 - GÖTEBORG 50893
Kajskjul 107, Frihamnen, 417 07 GÖTEBORG
Tel: 31 726 10 00. **Fax:** 31 726 10 07.
Email: info.gbg@radiocity.se
Web site: http://www.mixcity.se/gbg
Presenter: Linda Maria Strömberg; *Producer:* Mats Lillienberg

VINYL 107 50931
Box 34108, 100 26 STOCKHOLM
Tel: 8 450 33 00. **Fax:** 8 22 21 07.
Email: info@vinyl107.se
Web site: http://www.vinyl107.se
Director: Johan Forssell; *Presenter:* Jonas Nilsson

Switzerland

REGIONAL TV STATIONS

TELE 1 744444
Maihofstr. 76, 6002 LUZERN
Tel: 41 4295804. **Fax:** 41 4295801.
Email: redaktion@tele1.ch
Web site: http://www.teletell.ch
News Editor: Daniel Wyrsch; *Editor:* Oliver Kuhn

TELE M1 744436
Neumattstr. 1, 5001 AARAU
Tel: 58 2004610. **Fax:** 58 2004601.
Email: redaktion@telem1.ch
Web site: http://www.telem1.ch
News Editor: Corinne Trachsel; *Editor:* Stephan Gassner

TELE OSTSCHWEIZ 744440
Bionstr. 4, 9001 ST. GALLEN
Tel: 71 3130013. **Fax:** 71 3130010.
Email: redaktion@teleostschweiz.ch
Web site: http://www.teleostschweiz.ch
News Editor: Mario Bächle; *Editor:* Mario Aldrovandi

TELE TOP 744447
Bürglistr. 31a, 8401 WINTERTHUR
Tel: 52 2648000. **Fax:** 52 2648001.
Email: top@teletop.ch
Web site: http://www.toponline.ch
Editor: Marcel Fischer

REGIONAL RADIO STATIONS

CAPITAL FM 753449
Dammweg 9, 3001 BERN **Tel:** 31 3271127.
Fax: 31 3271161.
Email: redaktion@capitalfm.ch
Web site: http://www.capitalfm.ch
Editor: Peter Scheurer

DRS 1 741648
Brunnenhofstr. 22, 8042 ZÜRICH
Tel: 44 3661111. **Fax:** 44 3661112.
Web site: http://www.drs1.ch
News Editor: Roman Mezzasalma; *Editor:* Heidi Ungerer

FM1 753394
Bionstr. 4, 9001 ST. GALLEN
Tel: 71 2722272. **Fax:** 71 2722273.
Email: kontakt@radiofm1.ch
Web site: http://www.radiofm1.ch
Editor: Ralph Weibel

NRJ ENERGY BERN 753455
Optingenstr. 56, 3001 BERN
Tel: 31 3405040. **Fax:** 31 3405044.
Email: redaktion@energybern.ch
Web site: http://www.energybern.ch
News Editor: Mark Siegenthaler; *Editor:* Nik Eugster

NRJ ENERGY ZÜRICH 753600
Kreuzstr. 26, 8032 ZÜRICH **Tel:** 44 2509000.
Fax: 44 2529026.
Email: redaktion@energyzueri.ch
Web site: http://www.energyzueri.ch
Editor: Reto Suter

RADIO 24 753589
Limmatstr. 183, 8005 ZÜRICH
Tel: 44 4482424. **Fax:** 44 4482490.
Email: info@radio24.ch
Web site: http://www.radio24.ch
Editor: Helen Hürlimann

RADIO 32 753603
Niklaus-Konrad-Str. 26, 4500 SOLOTHURN
Tel: 32 6258230. **Fax:** 32 6258235.
Email: redaktion@radio32.ch
Web site: http://www.radio32.ch
Editor: Thomas Denzel

RADIO CANAL 3 753416
Robert-Walser-Platz 7, 2501 BIEL
Tel: 32 3276060. **Fax:** 32 3276090.
Email: redaktion@canal3.ch
Web site: http://www.canal3.ch
Editor: Reto Hofmann

RADIO JURA BERNOIS 753483
9, L'Orgerie, 2710 TAVANNES
Tel: 32 4826010. **Fax:** 32 4826017.
Email: redaction@rjb.ch
Web site: http://www.rjb.ch
News Editor: François Comte; *Editor:* Lise Bailat

RADIO MUNOT 753511
Bachstr. 29a, 8201 SCHAFFHAUSEN
Tel: 52 6334411. **Fax:** 52 6334412.
Email: redaktion@radiomunot.ch
Web site: http://www.radiomunot.ch
News Editor: Philipp Inauen; *Editor:* Philipp Inauen

RADIO R3III 753554
via Carona, 6, 6815 MELIDE
Tel: 91 6401515. **Fax:** 91 6401559.
Email: info@r3i.ch
Web site: http://www.r3i.ch
Editor: Marco Bazzi

RFJ RADIO FRÉQUENCE JURA 753320
20, rue du 23-Juin, 2800 DELÉMONT
Tel: 32 4217040. **Fax:** 32 4217027.
Email: redaction@rfj.ch
Web site: http://www.rfj.ch
Editor: Pierre Steulet

RTN 753610
16a, Champs-Montants, 2074 MARIN
Tel: 32 7560140. **Fax:** 32 7560127.
Email: redaction@rtn.ch
Web site: http://www.rtn.ch
Editor: Fabio Payot

Willings Volume 2
Section 8

Master Index
Main Master Index

Numbers in **BOLD TYPEFACE** take you to the MAIN LISTING for any periodical in Section 4, or to Section 7, Broadcasting

Numbers in MEDIUM TYPEFACE take you to Section 6 - Publishers by Country;

Numbers in *ITALICS* take you to Section 2 - Periodicals Index or Section 3 - Newspaper Index

Aktualitätslexikon Umweltschutz

Section 8 Master Index

B

Bewusster Leben

Section 8 Master Index

Bremer Blatt Verlags Gmbh

Section 8 Master Index

D

Der Doemensianer

E

Euro

F

G

Section 8 Master Index

H

I

J

Section 8 Master Index

K

Section 8 Master Index

M

Les Messages du Secours Catholique

Motorboot

N

Section 8 Master Index

Section 8 Master Index

P

Q

Section 8 Master Index

S

Seilas

Section 8 Master Index

Section 8 Master Index

U

V

W

X

Y

Z

ZP Zahnarzt & Praxis

Section 8 Master Index